Volume 2: Index
141st Edition

Commercial
Atlas & Marketing Guide
2010

The First Place to Look for Up-to-Date Business Planning Data!

Population, Economic, and Geographic Data for more than 120,000 U.S. places — complete with large-scale, detailed maps.

Rand McNally 2010 Commercial Atlas & Marketing Guide

Published in the USA. Printed in the USA.

If you have questions, concerns, or even a compliment, contact us by visiting our website at **go.randmcnally.com/contact** or e-mail us at **consumeraffairs@randmcnally.com** or write to:
Rand McNally Consumer Affairs
P.O. Box 7600
Chicago, IL 60680-9915

How to order the *Commercial Atlas & Marketing Guide*

To order the Rand McNally 2010 *Commercial Atlas & Marketing Guide*, please contact Rand McNally at 1-800-275-RAND (-7263).

The information in this atlas was collected directly from the sources cited or from other sources considered reliable. The atlas is published for general reference and not as a substitute for independent verification by users of this information when circumstances warrant. While care and diligence have been used in its preparation, the publisher does not guarantee the accuracy of the information.

1 WA 09

Contents

Volume 1

Volume 2 Contents on next page

Contents | Volume 2

Index and State Statistics

Volume 2 of the *Commercial Atlas* is organized by state. Each state section includes summary statistics, followed by an index that includes references to the state maps in Volume 1.

State Statistics

This section includes general summary statistics for the state, a listing of Ranally Metro Areas (RMAs) with their abbreviations, a list of Principal Places and a table showing Business Data statistics by county.

General summary statistics include land area, inland water area, total area, the name of the state capital, and the date of admission to the United States.

The **Principal Places** table lists, in descending order by city population size, all cities, towns, Minor Civil Divisions, and other localities with a population of 5,000 or more. Population figures are July 1, 2008 estimates by Devonshire Associates Ltd. and Scan/US, Inc., 2000 Census figures, or recent estimates by Rand McNally.

A table called **County Business Data** provides information for each county in the state, as well as the state as a whole. The County FIPS Code and county seat are also provided. Land area figures are from the 2000 Census. Census populations for 1990 and 2000, and the resulting percentage change, are also given for each county.

The County Business Data tables also provide data on wholesale trade from the 2002 Economic Census. Wholesale Trade is the sale of merchandise to retailers and business users, farmers, governments, and other wholesalers. It also includes agents and brokers who buy for or sell to such clients or customers. Data on manufacturing from the 2002 Census of Manufactures are also shown in these tables. The number of establishments, total employees and value added by manufacture for each county and the number of Ranally Manufacturing Units based on the value added data is shown for each county.

Index

The *Commercial Atlas* index lists more than 120,000 places, including counties, townships (towns), incorporated places, and unincorporated places. Definitions and more detailed descriptions of the various types of places and information that appear in the index may be found in the **Glossary of Terms** in Volume 1.

Each index record includes the following data:

Place name. Most places have only one name, but some places are known by more than one name. It is not uncommon for a place to have a post office name that differs from its corporate name, or from the name used by a railroad serving the place. All such known instances are mentioned in the index.

When a place has more than one name, the main index entry is typically under the name recognized by the U.S. Board on Geographic Names. This main entry also contains all other index information about the place. For example, consider the hypothetical case of a village officially recognized as Bridgeport with a post office named Bridgeport, but locally known as Bridgeville and served by the railroad under the name of Bridgeport Junction. The main entry for this place will be found under its official name of Bridgeport, where its alternative names of Bridgeville and Bridgeport Junction will be listed between parentheses. The index would also provide cross references as follows: Bridgeville, see Bridgeport; Bridgeport Junction, see Bridgeport.

Place type. Following the place name the index indicates whether the place is an incoporated place, a Census Designated Place, a Minor Civil Division, an Independent City, or a Rand McNally Designated Place. See the Glossary of Terms in Volume 1 for definitions of these terms.

County seat. A symbol ⊡ designates places that are county seats.

County name. The index always lists the county in which a place is located. If a place is located in more than one county, the index lists first the county in which most of the place is located, followed by all other counties in order of relative importance.

Minor Civil Division name. A ▲ symbol indicates the Minor Civil Divisions (MCDs) in which a place is located, for the following states: CT, ME, MA, MI, NH, NJ, NY, OH, PA, RI, VT, and WI.

Map key. Most places have a page number and a letter and number key following the county or MCD name. This map key refers to the location of the place on the map based on the letters and numbers along the map border. For example, a place with a key of **212** D-9 would be located at the intersection of row D and column 9, on the map on page 212 in volume 1.

The state maps do not contain all of the places in the index, as this would cause excessive crowding of map symbols and text. Even if the place is not on the map, the map key can still be used to determine its general location. A * symbol before the map key is used to designate such places.

Elevation. The elevation for selected places is given in feet and meters.

Post office. The index entry will indicate by the symbol **P** if a place has its own post office.

Hospitals. Places with one or more hospitals carry an **H** notation.

Colleges. Places with at least one accredited four-year university or college that had an enrollment of at least 600 in 2007 carry a **C** notation. The combined student population for all universities and colleges is also shown. The source of this data Higher Education Publications, Inc.

Principal Business Center. Principal Business Centers (PBCs) are indicated with a ■. A table listing all Principal Business Centers appears in Volume 1.

Ranally Metropolitan Area. Ranally Metropolitan Area (RMA) abbreviations follow a ★ for places that are located within an RMA. A list of all RMAs and their abbreviations is given in the State Statistics section.

ZIP Codes. ZIP Codes or ZIP Code ranges are given for all places that are recognized by the U.S. Postal Service, and for many other places that are not recognized. For places where the name of the town is not recognized by the U.S. Postal Service as an acceptable "last line" on an envelope, the place name that should instead be shown is given immediately before the ZIP code. For example, an index entry for Tinyplace, AL shows "mail Someplace **Z** 12345". In this example, Someplace is an acceptable last line on an envelope, while Tinyplace is not.

USPS definitions of city boundaries do not necessarily correspond to legal corporate boundaries. The ZIP Codes listed in this atlas for a given city include ZIPs for which the USPS considers that city name to be an acceptable last line.

Populations. In each index entry, the most current population figure is the one that comes at the very end of the entry. Other significant population figures, such as a comparative figure for an earlier date, may also appear within the body of the indexed entry. The symbols for populations used in an index entry follow:

- © **Final Census Population:** 2000 Census population.
- Ⓟ **Previous Census Population:** 1990 Census population.
- Ⓢ **Special Census Population:** Census population figure taken at a time other than the normal Census.
- Ⓐ **Annexation Population:** Population following an annexation since the last Census.
- Ⓡ **Revised Census Population:** Revision of final 2000 Census figure.
- ◆ **Estimated Population:** Population estimates as of 7/1/08 for counties, Principal Business Centers, and other large cities. Source: Devonshire Associates Ltd. and Scan/US, Inc. 2008.
- ● **Rand McNally Estimated Population:** Populations estimated by Rand McNally.

Index and State Statistics, *Continued*

Sample Index Entry

The sample of an index entry below indicates how detailed, specific and factual information is concisely presented about each place. If written out in full, this sample entry would read: The place known as Rand City, and also known as Randtown, is an incorporated place located in McNally County, and is the county seat of McNally County. Rand City is also located in a Minor Civil Division called Randway.

Rand City is located at map key F-13 on the map on page 170. The presence of the * symbol means that, due to space limitations, Rand City does not actually appear on the map.

Rand City has an elevation of 601 feet or 183 meters. It has one or more of the following: a post office, a hospital, and a college. The total college student population of Rand City is 8,000.

Rand City is a Principal Business Center. It is located within the Ranally Metro Area with the abbreviation CHI (Chicago).

The ZIP Code range for Rand City is 76001 plus zones up to and including 76009.

The population of Rand City according to the 1990 Census is 232,427. According to the 2000 Census the population is 278,937. The Devonshire Associates Ltd. and Scan/US Inc. population estimate for 2008 is 273,841.

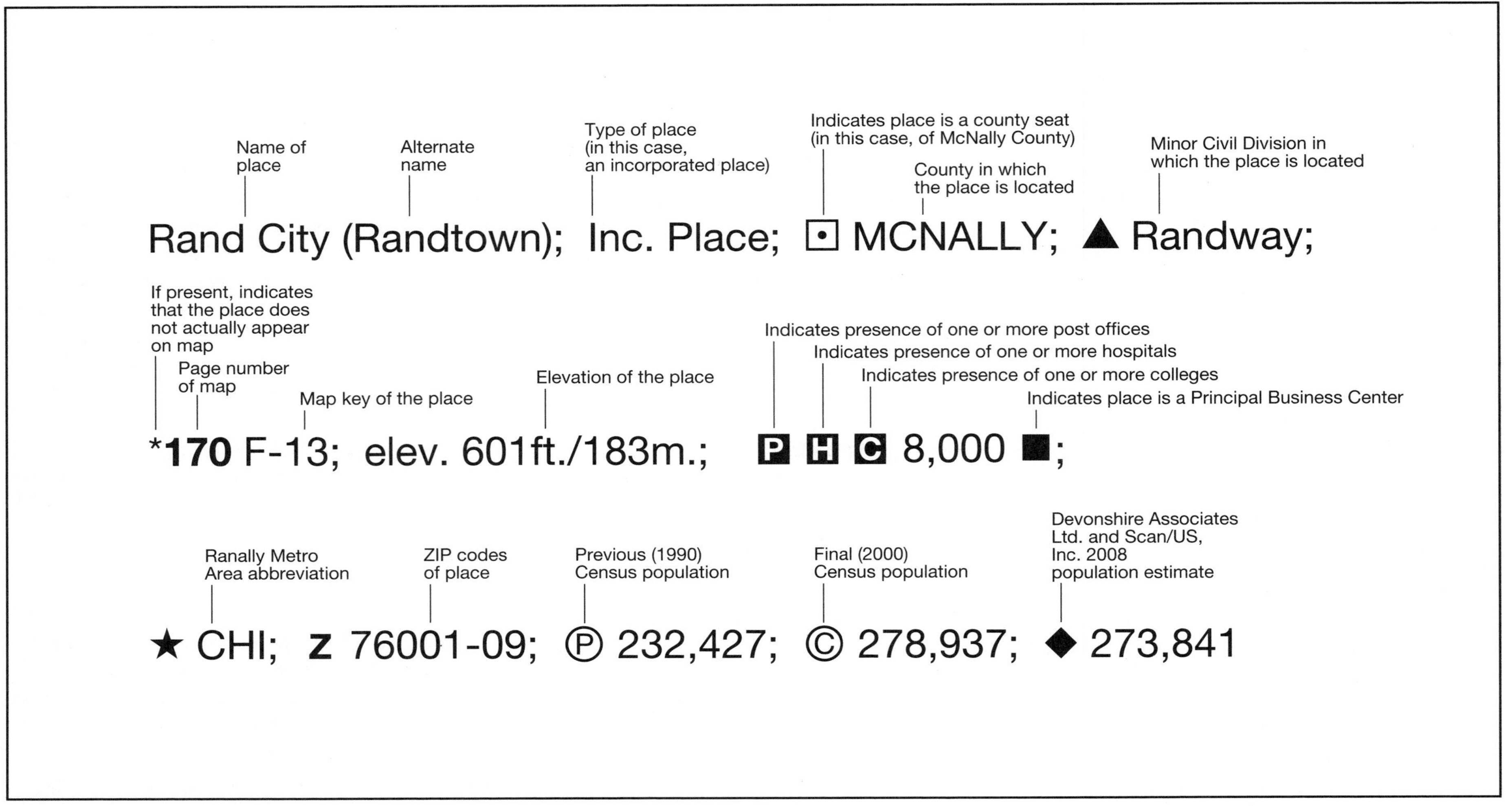

NUMBER OF PLACES, COUNTY SUBDIVISIONS, AND COUNTIES IN INDEX, BY STATE

The table below shows the number of places in the United States in population-size groups by state. This table also provides a count of the total number of places listed in the index, including many that are not credited with any population (Parts of other places, rural communities, etc.); specifies the number of counties or county equivalents in each state; and provides the number of county subdivisions in selected states. Only cross-references are not counted in the table.

States	Number of Places Over 100,000 Population	Number of Places Over 50,000 Population	Number of Places Over 25,000 Population	Number of Places Over 10,000 Population	Number of Places Over 5,000 Population	Number of Places Over 2,500 Population	Number of Places Over 1,000 Population	Number of Places Over 700 Population	Number of Places Over 500 Population	Number of Places Over 300 Population	Number of Places Over 200 Population	Number of Places Over 100 Population	Total Number of Places with Population Given	Number of Places with No Population Given††	Number of County Subdivisions	Number of Counties*	Grand Total
Alabama	4	9	21	58	107	171	302	365	429	543	682	910	1,687	1,588		67	3,342
Alaska†	1	1	3	4	14	31	56	79	110	158	198	264	428	171		27	626
Arizona	9	18	31	52	78	127	195	225	270	315	355	422	521	386		15	922
Arkansas	1	8	17	35	61	113	201	261	311	398	488	680	1,165	1,155		75	2,395
California	69	176	285	459	626	803	1,084	1,222	1,342	1,535	1,706	1,951	2,175	1,633		58	3,866
Colorado	12	18	30	49	91	133	238	283	326	395	484	631	794	471		64	1,329
Connecticut	5	18	32	48	82	120	219	260	302	372	425	482	531	436	169	8	1,144
Delaware	0	1	3	8	17	24	89	127	155	216	265	334	419	174		3	596
District of Columbia	1	1	1	1	1	1	1	1	1	1	1	1	1	85		1	87
Florida	15	57	123	279	444	632	902	1,032	1,136	1,324	1,474	1,724	1,905	868		67	2,840
Georgia	7	14	39	89	144	239	391	479	553	692	815	1,058	1,359	1,347		159	2,865
Hawaii	1	1	8	21	43	72	136	156	177	211	229	256	301	58		5	364
Idaho	1	5	11	16	29	51	77	99	127	163	190	241	330	382		44	756
Illinois	8	26	92	206	324	468	734	883	1,039	1,279	1,524	1,915	2,690	1,517	1,431	102	5,740
Indiana	4	14	35	72	123	185	347	427	510	658	847	1,224	2,028	795	1,008	92	3,923
Iowa	2	10	19	34	77	129	279	383	476	609	745	926	1,332	273		99	1,704
Kansas	5	8	16	32	56	105	207	257	307	395	481	630	947	333		105	1,385
Kentucky	2	4	14	39	84	142	238	312	383	524	700	1,116	1,970	2,038		120	4,128
Louisiana†	5	9	14	53	106	165	290	343	403	518	622	819	1,087	968		64	2,119
Maine	0	1	3	12	30	61	121	152	185	265	346	558	894	595	466	16	1,971
Maryland	2	15	48	119	206	343	627	763	870	1,078	1,263	1,540	1,919	1,524		24	3,467
Massachusetts	5	23	61	109	154	242	393	465	516	587	637	734	823	766	305	14	1,908
Michigan	7	28	53	115	186	286	492	571	657	850	1,008	1,270	1,710	575	1,242	83	3,610
Minnesota	3	18	36	83	127	211	343	423	496	615	714	873	1,325	510		87	1,922
Mississippi	1	3	9	37	68	103	192	226	278	363	454	611	896	928		82	1,906
Missouri	5	11	26	73	130	214	371	441	523	667	849	1,203	1,722	1,181		115	3,018
Montana	0	3	6	7	20	37	86	119	137	174	214	295	507	221		56	784
Nebraska	2	3	6	17	34	51	117	165	211	298	373	475	662	127		93	882
Nevada	7	9	11	19	32	49	68	79	86	103	131	153	212	136		17	365
New Hampshire	1	2	5	15	26	38	80	106	140	215	281	386	508	218	221	10	957
New Jersey	5	20	55	186	311	452	686	777	851	958	1,058	1,224	1,381	749	242	21	2,393
New Mexico	1	4	11	22	48	72	137	165	191	262	317	423	626	331		33	990
New York	5	18	61	195	364	581	1,007	1,230	1,489	1,935	2,199	2,687	3,276	1,925	929	62	6,192
North Carolina	9	17	34	67	123	240	434	535	643	861	1,045	1,361	2,058	1,655		100	3,813
North Dakota	1	3	4	9	13	17	55	82	105	139	186	271	645	153		53	851
Ohio	6	17	59	178	283	438	681	807	948	1,224	1,529	2,024	2,825	1,247	1,307	88	5,467
Oklahoma	4	9	14	38	69	126	232	293	354	455	550	732	1,015	484		77	1,576
Oregon	4	10	20	50	91	128	202	240	274	340	418	503	720	528		36	1,284
Pennsylvania	4	9	32	112	297	589	1,157	1,495	1,811	2,366	2,905	3,822	5,436	2,544	1,546	67	9,593
Rhode Island	1	4	9	17	23	36	57	67	85	107	123	154	171	193	31	5	400
South Carolina	2	6	16	44	85	160	309	362	404	497	589	765	1,079	611		46	1,736
South Dakota	1	2	2	10	15	29	70	105	137	182	220	283	520	129		66	715
Tennessee	6	9	25	52	96	159	286	334	396	541	681	1,017	1,925	2,340		95	4,360
Texas	31	62	112	209	351	566	978	1,153	1,309	1,585	1,841	2,271	3,077	2,568		254	5,899
Utah	5	11	33	47	74	108	156	182	211	257	288	341	425	154		29	608
Vermont	0	0	1	3	13	21	44	59	78	141	203	339	519	259	237	14	1,029
Virginia	9	18	39	80	138	204	409	515	608	804	1,032	1,438	2,300	2,228		134	4,662
Washington	6	16	47	99	171	263	400	471	527	639	736	905	1,237	563		39	1,839
West Virginia	0	0	5	15	30	65	174	234	309	490	673	1,054	1,625	1,175		55	2,855
Wisconsin	3	13	30	78	131	208	385	464	541	671	790	1,002	1,613	433	1,260	72	3,378
Wyoming	0	2	4	9	17	27	56	68	80	103	130	169	307	93		23	423
United States	**288**	**764**	**1671**	**3681**	**6263**	**9835**	**16,791**	**20,342**	**23,807**	**30,078**	**36,014**	**46,467**	**65,628**	**41,821**	**10,394**	**3,141**	**120,984**

† The divisions of Louisiana are known as parishes; those shown for Alaska are boroughs and census areas.
†† Includes rural areas and places that are parts of other places for which population is given.

* Includes four classes of areas: (a) 3.071 counties and parishes; (b) the District of Columbia; (c) 42 cities independent of any county: Baltimore, MD; St. Louis, MO; Carson City, NV; and 39 independent cities in Virginia; (d) and the 27 boroughs and census areas in Alaska at the time of the 2000 census.

ALABAMA

Statistics

Total area (2000) — 52,419 square miles
Land area (2000) — 50,744 square miles
Water area (2000) — 1,675 square miles
Capital — Montgomery
Admitted as state — December, 1819

Maps

State maps can be found on pages 142-254 in Vol. 1

Ranally Metro Areas (RMAs) and Abbreviations

Anniston, AL — ANNI
Auburn-Opelika, AL — AU-OP
Birmingham, AL — BIR
Columbus, GA-AL — COL
Decatur, AL — DEC
Dothan, AL — DOTH
Florence, AL — FLO
Gadsden, AL — GAD
Huntsville, AL — HNTS
Mobile, AL — MOB
Montgomery, AL — MTGY
Tuscaloosa, AL — TUSC

Principal Places

Place Name	Place Type	County	Population
Birmingham	Inc. Place	JEFFERSON	◆ 229,700
Montgomery	Inc. Place	MONTGOMERY	◆ 209,348
Mobile	Inc. Place	MOBILE	◆ 192,460
Huntsville	Inc. Place	MADISON	◆ 180,258
Tuscaloosa	Inc. Place	TUSCALOOSA	◆ 87,391
Dothan	Inc. Place	HOUSTON	◆ 65,972
Hoover	Inc. Place	JEFFERSON	◆ 65,313
Decatur	Inc. Place	MORGAN	◆ 52,644
Auburn	Inc. Place	LEE	◆ 51,682
Madison	Inc. Place	MADISON	◆ 39,104
Gadsden	Inc. Place	ETOWAH	◆ 36,455
Florence	Inc. Place	LAUDERDALE	◆ 33,869
Phenix City	Inc. Place	RUSSELL	◆ 31,128
Vestavia Hills	Inc. Place	JEFFERSON	◆ 30,830
Prattville	Inc. Place	AUTAUGA	◆ 30,088
Bessemer	Inc. Place	JEFFERSON	◆ 28,027
Prichard	Inc. Place	MOBILE	◆ 26,779
Opelika	Inc. Place	LEE	◆ 26,290
Smiths	CDP-Census Area Only	LEE	◆ 26,237
Alabaster	Inc. Place	SHELBY	◆ 26,011
Homewood	Inc. Place	JEFFERSON	◆ 25,045
Enterprise	Inc. Place	COFFEE	◆ 24,482
Anniston	Inc. Place	CALHOUN	◆ 23,663
Athens	Inc. Place	LIMESTONE	◆ 23,121
Northport	Inc. Place	TUSCALOOSA	◆ 21,340
Mountain Brook	Inc. Place	JEFFERSON	◆ 21,042
Oxford	Inc. Place	CALHOUN	◆ 20,406
Pelham	Inc. Place	SHELBY	◆ 19,566
Selma	Inc. Place	DALLAS	◆ 18,160
Albertville	Inc. Place	MARSHALL	© 17,247
Talladega	Inc. Place	TALLADEGA	◆ 16,963
Daphne	Inc. Place	BALDWIN	© 16,581
Tillmans Corner	CDP	MOBILE	© 15,685
Hueytown	Inc. Place	JEFFERSON	© 15,364
Alexander City	Inc. Place	TALLAPOOSA	® 15,325
Center Point	Inc. Place	JEFFERSON	● 15,200
Center Point	CDP-Census Area Only	JEFFERSON	◆ 15,159
Ozark	Inc. Place	DALE	© 15,119
Scottsboro	Inc. Place	JACKSON	© 14,762
Cullman	Inc. Place	CULLMAN	◆ 14,301
Troy	Inc. Place	PIKE	© 13,935
Eufaula	Inc. Place	BARBOUR	© 13,908
Jasper	Inc. Place	WALKER	◆ 12,969
Fort Payne	Inc. Place	DEKALB	© 12,938
Trussville	Inc. Place	JEFFERSON	© 12,924
Sylacauga	Inc. Place	TALLADEGA	® 12,819
Fairhope	Inc. Place	BALDWIN	© 12,480
Fairfield	Inc. Place	JEFFERSON	© 12,381
Saraland	Inc. Place	MOBILE	© 12,288
Hartselle	Inc. Place	MORGAN	© 12,019
Muscle Shoals	Inc. Place	COLBERT	© 11,924
Tuskegee	Inc. Place	MACON	© 11,846
Gardendale	Inc. Place	JEFFERSON	© 11,626
Saks	CDP	CALHOUN	© 10,698
Forestdale	CDP	JEFFERSON	© 10,509
Leeds	Inc. Place	JEFFERSON	© 10,455
Millbrook	Inc. Place	ELMORE	© 10,386
Helena	Inc. Place	SHELBY	© 10,296
Pleasant Grove	Inc. Place	JEFFERSON	© 9,983
Irondale	Inc. Place	JEFFERSON	© 9,813
Sheffield	Inc. Place	COLBERT	© 9,652
Pell City	Inc. Place	ST. CLAIR	© 9,565
Valley	Inc. Place	CHAMBERS	© 9,198
Russellville	Inc. Place	FRANKLIN	© 8,971
Andalusia	Inc. Place	COVINGTON	© 8,794
Clay	Inc. Place	JEFFERSON	● 8,600
Rainbow City	Inc. Place	ETOWAH	© 8,428
Jacksonville	Inc. Place	CALHOUN	© 8,404
Moody	Inc. Place	ST. CLAIR	© 8,053
Lanett	Inc. Place	CHAMBERS	© 7,897
Tuscumbia	Inc. Place	COLBERT	© 7,856
Bay Minette	Inc. Place	BALDWIN	© 7,820
Clanton	Inc. Place	CHILTON	© 7,800
Atmore	Inc. Place	ESCAMBIA	© 7,676
Foley	Inc. Place	BALDWIN	© 7,590
Demopolis	Inc. Place	MARENGO	© 7,540
Boaz	Inc. Place	MARSHALL	© 7,411
Guntersville	Inc. Place	MARSHALL	© 7,395
Greenville	Inc. Place	BUTLER	© 7,228
Arab	Inc. Place	MARSHALL	© 7,174
Southside	Inc. Place	ETOWAH	© 7,036
Tarrant City	Inc. Place	JEFFERSON	© 7,022
Pinson	Inc. Place	JEFFERSON	● 7,000
Monroeville	Inc. Place	MONROE	© 6,862
Theodore	CDP	MOBILE	© 6,811
Hamilton	Inc. Place	MARION	© 6,786
Opp	Inc. Place	COVINGTON	© 6,607
Fultondale	Inc. Place	JEFFERSON	© 6,595
Attalla	Inc. Place	ETOWAH	© 6,592
Roanoke	Inc. Place	RANDOLPH	© 6,563
Chickasaw	Inc. Place	MOBILE	© 6,364
Fort Rucker	CDP-Census Area Only	DALE	© 6,052
Lake Purdy	CDP-Census Area Only	SHELBY	© 5,799
Wetumpka	Inc. Place	ELMORE	© 5,726
Satsuma	Inc. Place	MOBILE	© 5,687
Midfield	Inc. Place	JEFFERSON	© 5,626
Oneonta	Inc. Place	BLOUNT	© 5,576
Brewton	Inc. Place	ESCAMBIA	© 5,498
Grayson Valley	CDP-Census Area Only	JEFFERSON	© 5,447
Spanish Fort	Inc. Place	BALDWIN	© 5,423
Jackson	Inc. Place	CLARKE	© 5,419
Cahaba Heights	CDP	JEFFERSON	© 5,203
Moores Mill	CDP	MADISON	© 5,178
Glencoe	Inc. Place	ETOWAH	© 5,152
Piedmont	Inc. Place	CALHOUN	© 5,120
Gulf Shores	Inc. Place	BALDWIN	© 5,044
Pinson	CDP-Census Area Only	JEFFERSON	© 5,033

County Business Data

County	FIPS Code	County Seat	Land Area (Sq. Mi.)	Census Population			Wholesale Trade		Manufacturing, 2002			
				4/1/2000	4/1/1990	% Change 1990-2000	Sales, 2002 ($1,000)	% Change 1997-2002	Establish-ments	Total Employees	Value Added ($1,000)	Ranally Mfg. Units
Autauga	001	Prattville	596	43,671	34,222	27.6	(d)	(d)	29	(d)	(d)	...
Baldwin	003	Bay Minette	1,596	140,415	98,280	42.9	979,646	98.5	145	4,957	525,997	278
Barbour	005	Clayton	885	29,038	25,417	14.2	(d)	(d)	40	4,495	311,384	165
Bibb	007	Centreville	623	20,826	16,576	25.6	37,335	-29.8	...	(d)	(d)	...
Blount	009	Oneonta	646	51,024	39,248	30.0	(d)	(d)	49	1,563	71,297	38
Bullock	011	Union Springs	625	11,714	11,042	6.1	(d)	(d)	5	(d)	(d)	...
Butler	013	Greenville	777	21,399	21,892	-2.3	(d)	(d)	26	1,493	85,964	45
Calhoun	015	Anniston	608	112,249	116,034	-3.3	1,058,280	18.8	150	9,368	995,122	526
Chambers	017	Lafayette	597	36,583	36,876	-0.8	15,514	-82.6	37	4,515	334,859	177
Cherokee	019	Centre	553	23,988	19,543	22.7	35,935	-44.9	26	867	81,427	43
Chilton	021	Clanton	694	39,593	32,458	22.0	(d)	(d)	51	1,186	110,116	58
Choctaw	023	Butler	914	15,922	16,018	-0.6	41,769	-61.3	6	(d)	(d)	...
Clarke	025	Grove Hill	1,238	27,867	27,240	2.3	33,341	-2.8	30	2,095	224,625	119
Clay	027	Ashland	605	14,254	13,252	7.6	(d)	(d)	12	2,299	161,746	86
Cleburne	029	Heflin	560	14,123	12,730	10.9	(d)	(d)	12	947	60,310	32
Coffee	031	Elba	679	43,615	40,240	8.4	(d)	(d)	40	2,702	157,892	84
Colbert	033	Tuscumbia	595	54,984	51,666	6.4	332,462	-17.8	110	3,736	456,999	242
Conecuh	035	Evergreen	851	14,089	14,054	0.2	48,196	-16.0	15	717	53,539	28
Coosa	037	Rockford	652	12,202	11,063	10.3	(d)	(d)	10	674	31,399	17
Covington	039	Andalusia	1,034	37,631	36,478	3.2	338,798	51.9	31	3,008	231,834	123
Crenshaw	041	Luverne	610	13,665	13,635	0.2	(d)	(d)	9	523	32,303	17
Cullman	043	Cullman	738	77,483	67,613	14.6	(d)	(d)	109	4,724	336,224	178
Dale	045	Ozark	561	49,129	49,633	-1.0	(d)	(d)	32	1,086	51,726	27
Dallas	047	Selma	981	46,365	48,130	-3.7	126,491	-40.7	57	4,731	490,879	260
DeKalb	049	Fort Payne	778	64,452	54,651	17.9	323,282	4.4	191	11,684	705,619	373
Elmore	051	Wetumpka	621	65,874	49,210	33.9	(d)	(d)	66	3,660	311,681	165
Escambia	053	Brewton	947	38,440	35,518	8.2	205,495	74.4	47	2,032	311,179	165
Etowah	055	Gadsden	535	103,459	99,840	3.6	413,895	(d)	138	6,504	440,326	233
Fayette	057	Fayette	628	18,495	17,962	3.0	(d)	(d)	25	1,201	77,533	41
Franklin	059	Russellville	636	31,223	27,814	12.3	83,100	-16.7	51	3,643	414,326	219
Geneva	061	Geneva	576	25,764	23,647	9.0	(d)	(d)	23	805	47,252	25
Greene	063	Eutaw	646	9,974	10,153	-1.8	2,647	(d)	...	(d)	(d)	...
Hale	065	Greensboro	644	17,185	15,498	10.9	(d)	(d)	17	(d)	(d)	...
Henry	067	Abbeville	562	16,310	15,374	6.1	(d)	(d)	20	1,402	106,061	56
Houston	069	Dothan	580	88,787	81,331	9.2	1,233,450	75.0	118	7,184	626,169	331
Jackson	071	Scottsboro	1,079	53,926	47,796	12.8	199,145	-2.0	79	5,598	509,862	270
Jefferson	073	Birmingham	1,113	662,047	651,525	1.6	15,660,455	8.2	727	31,151	3,076,948	1,628
Lamar	075	Vernon	605	15,904	15,715	1.2	(d)	(d)	21	2,272	141,797	75
Lauderdale	077	Florence	669	87,966	79,661	10.4	493,804	33.9	103	3,964	273,965	145
Lawrence	079	Moulton	693	34,803	31,513	10.4	14,505	(d)	23	(d)	(d)	...
Lee	081	Opelika	609	115,092	87,146	32.1	(d)	(d)	100	6,275	890,988	471
Limestone	083	Athens	568	65,676	54,135	21.3	194,463	(d)	72	5,919	755,417	400
Lowndes	085	Hayneville	718	13,473	12,658	6.4	120,799	353.3	12	(d)	(d)	...
Macon	087	Tuskegee	611	24,105	24,928	-3.3	(d)	(d)	...	(d)	(d)	...
Madison	089	Huntsville	805	276,700	238,912	15.8	2,857,662	(d)	337	21,589	2,391,726	1,265
Marengo	091	Linden	977	22,539	23,084	-2.4	(d)	(d)	25	2,170	220,760	117
Marion	093	Hamilton	741	31,214	29,830	4.6	130,692	-46.4	45	2,955	333,015	176
Marshall	095	Guntersville	567	82,231	70,832	16.1	866,500	0.9	134	11,446	816,576	432
Mobile	097	Mobile	1,233	399,843	378,643	5.6	3,144,855	-5.6	403	17,752	2,345,352	1,241
Monroe	099	Monroeville	1,026	24,324	23,968	1.5	61,572	-27.5	20	2,450	354,898	188
Montgomery	101	Montgomery	790	223,510	209,085	6.9	3,472,457	18.2	215	10,218	1,256,940	665
Morgan	103	Decatur	582	111,064	100,043	11.0	787,204	(d)	211	(d)	(d)	...
Perry	105	Marion	719	11,861	12,759	-7.0	(d)	(d)	9	560	27,767	15
Pickens	107	Carrollton	881	20,949	20,699	1.2	(d)	(d)	20	626	39,569	21
Pike	109	Troy	671	29,605	27,595	7.3	159,379	-10.2	29	1,740	121,732	64
Randolph	111	Wedowee	581	22,380	19,881	12.6	(d)	(d)	25	1,690	74,644	39
Russell	113	Phenix City	641	49,756	46,860	6.2	181,043	(d)	35	1,443	140,830	75
St. Clair	115	Ashville	634	64,742	50,009	29.5	1,107,587	(d)	70	2,489	340,579	180
Shelby	117	Columbiana	795	143,293	99,358	44.2	4,218,550	19.5	160	6,107	593,995	314
Sumter	119	Livingston	905	14,798	16,174	-8.5	50,441	7.4	...	(d)	(d)	...
Talladega	121	Talladega	740	80,321	74,107	8.4	226,719	23.9	101	7,407	473,209	250
Tallapoosa	123	Dadeville	718	41,475	38,826	6.8	(d)	(d)	46	3,222	246,417	130
Tuscaloosa	125	Tuscaloosa	1,324	164,875	150,522	9.5	(d)	(d)	162	11,530	1,359,420	719
Walker	127	Jasper	794	70,713	67,670	4.5	214,262	1.7	60	1,286	70,389	37
Washington	129	Chatom	1,081	18,097	16,694	8.4	(d)	(d)	12	(d)	(d)	...
Wilcox	131	Camden	889	13,183	13,568	-2.8	(d)	(d)	12	(d)	(d)	...
Winston	133	Double Springs	614	24,843	22,053	12.7	144,065	13.3	79	4,732	288,316	153
The State			**50,744**	**4,447,100**	**4,040,587**	**10.1**	**43,641,369**	**6.5**	**5,119**	**284,127**	**28,641,670**	**15,153**

(d) Data not available. Corresponding percentages or Ranally Manufacturing Units are estimates.
... Represents 0 or amount too minimal to be reported.

Entries in **UPPERCASE** are counties.
Entries in **bold** have populations of 2,500 or more.
Names in parentheses are alternate names.
Inc. Place — Incorporated Place
RMC Place — Rand McNally Designated Place
CDP — Census Designated Place
MCD — Minor Civil Division

⊡ County Seat
▲ Minor Civil Division
elev. Elevation
🅿 Post Office

H Hospital
C College
■ Principal Business Center
★ Ranally Metro Area (RMA) Abbreviation
z Zip Code(s)

Ⓟ Previous Census Population
® Revised Census Population
Ⓐ Annexation Population
● Rand McNally Population Estimate
© Final Census Population
Ⓢ Special Census Population
◆ Estimated Population

For additional definitions see Glossary, Volume 1, and Introduction, Volume 2.

Index of Places and Counties

A

Abanda; RMC Place; CHAMBERS; **142** G-10; mail Wadley z 36276; ● 150
Abbeville; Inc. Place; ⊡ HENRY, CLEBURNE; **143** M-11; elev. 450ft./137m.; 🅿; z 36310; Ⓟ 3,173; Ⓒ 2,987
Abel; RMC Place; CLEBURNE; **142** F-10; mail Delta z 36258; ● 100
Abercrombie; RMC Place; BIBB; ***142** H-5; elev. 333ft./101m.; mail Centreville z 35042; rural
Aberfoil; RMC Place; BULLOCK; **143** K-10; elev. 586ft./179m.; mail Union Springs z 36089; ● 70
Abernant; RMC Place; TUSCALOOSA; **142** G-5; elev. 500ft./152m.; 🅿; z 35440; ● 500
Abernathy; RMC Place; CLEBURNE; ***142** E-11; elev. 1,036ft./316m.; mail Heflin z 36264; rural
Acipcoville; RMC Place; JEFFERSON; ***142** F-6; ★ **BIR**; mail Birmingham z 35207; pop. incl. with Birmingham (Inc. Place)
Ackerville; RMC Place; WILCOX; **143** K-6; elev. 286ft./87m.; mail Pine Apple z 36768; rural
Acmar; RMC Place; ST. CLAIR; ***142** F-7; elev. 700ft./213m.; 🅿; ★ **BIR**; z 35004; pop. incl. with Moody (Inc. Place)
Active; RMC Place; BIBB; **142** H-6; elev. 442ft./135m.; mail Lawley z 36793
Ada; RMC Place; MONTGOMERY; **143** K-8; elev. 328ft./100m.; mail Ramer z 36069; ● 30
Adamsburg; RMC Place; DEKALB; ***142** C-10; mail Fort Payne z 35967; ● 50
Adams Crossroads; RMC Place; CHEROKEE; ***142** D-10; elev. 728ft./222m.; mail Centre z 35960; rural
Adamsville; Inc. Place; JEFFERSON; **142** F-6; elev. 578ft./176m.; 🅿; ★ **BIR**; z 35005; Ⓟ 4,532; Ⓒ 4,965
Addison; Inc. Place; WINSTON; **142** C-5; elev. 779ft./237m.; 🅿; z 35540; Ⓟ 626; Ⓒ 723
Adger; RMC Place; JEFFERSON; ***142** F-5; elev. 550ft./168m.; 🅿; ★ **BIR**; z 35006; ● 530
Adler; RMC Place; PERRY; ***142** I-5; elev. 400ft./122m.; rural
Aimwell; RMC Place; MARENGO; ***143** K-3; elev. 276ft./84m.; mail Sweet Water z 36782
Airport Highlands; RMC Place; JEFFERSON; ***142** F-7; ★ **BIR**; mail Birmingham z 35206; pop. incl. with Birmingham (Inc. Place)
Akron; Inc. Place; HALE; **142** H-4; elev. 130ft./40m.; 🅿; z 35441; Ⓟ 468; Ⓒ 521
Alabama City; RMC Place; ETOWAH; ***142** D-9; elev. 544ft./166m.; ★ **GAD**; mail Gadsden z 35904; pop. incl. with Gadsden (Inc. Place)
Alabama Fork; RMC Place; LIMESTONE; ***142** A-6; elev. 775ft./236m.; mail Athens z 35614; rural
Alabama Port; RMC Place; MOBILE; **143** Q-2; elev. 10ft./3m.; mail Coden z 36523; ● 200
Alabama Shores; RMC Place; COLBERT; ***142** A-4; ★ **FLO**; mail Sheffield z 35660; ● 100
Alabaster; Inc. Place; SHELBY; **142** G-6; elev. 500ft./152m.; 🅿 🅷; ★ **BIR**; z 35007, z 35144; Ⓟ 14,732; Ⓒ 22,619; Ⓡ 23,667; ◆ 26,011
Alaga; RMC Place; HOUSTON; ***143** O-12; elev. 130ft./40m.; mail Gordon z 36343; rural
Alberta; RMC Place; WILCOX; **143** K-4; elev. 205ft./62m.; 🅿; z 36720; ● 200
Alberta City; RMC Place; TUSCALOOSA; ★ **TUSC**; mail Tuscaloosa z 35401; pop. incl. with Tuscaloosa (Inc. Place)
Alberton; RMC Place; COFFEE; ***143** N-9; elev. 172ft./52m.; mail Kinston z 36453; rural
Albertville; Inc. Place; MARSHALL; **142** C-8; elev. 1,063ft./324m.; 🅿; z 35950-51; Ⓟ 14,507; Ⓒ 17,247
Alder Springs; RMC Place; MARSHALL; ***142** C-8; mail Albertville z 35951; ● 50
Aldrich; RMC Place; SHELBY; **142** G-6; mail Montevallo z 35115; pop. incl. with Montevallo (Inc. Place)
Aldridge; RMC Place; WALKER; ***142** E-5; mail Parrish z 35580; ● 80
Aldridge Grove; RMC Place; LAWRENCE; ***142** C-5; mail Moulton z 35650; ● 50
Alexander City; Inc. Place; TALLAPOOSA; **142** H-9; elev. 707ft./215m.; 🅿 🅷; z 35010-11; Ⓟ 14,917; Ⓒ 15,008; Ⓡ 15,325
Alexander Heights; RMC Place; LAUDERDALE; ***142** A-4; ★ **FLO**; pop. incl. with Florence (Inc. Place)
Alexandria; CDP; CALHOUN; **142** E-9; elev. 569ft./173m.; 🅿; ★ **ANNI**; z 36250; Ⓒ 3,692
Alexis; RMC Place; CHEROKEE; ***142** C-10; mail Centre z 35960; ● 90
Aliceville; Inc. Place; PICKENS; **142** G-2; elev. 212ft./65m.; 🅿; z 35442; Ⓟ 3,009; Ⓒ 2,567
Allen (Suggsville); RMC Place; CLARKE; **143** M-4; elev. 250ft./76m.; 🅿; z 36451 & mail Whatley z 36482; ● 70
Allens Crossroads; RMC Place; MARSHALL; ***142** C-7; mail Union Grove z 35175; rural
Allenton; RMC Place; WILCOX; **143** L-6; mail Pine Apple z 36768; ● 50
Allenton Station; RMC Place; WILCOX; ***143** L-6; elev. 194ft./59m.; mail Pine Apple z 36768; rural
Allenville; RMC Place; HALE; ***142** J-4; elev. 212ft./65m.; mail Faunsdale z 36738; rural
Allgood (Chepultepec); Inc. Place; BLOUNT; **142** E-7; elev. 788ft./240m.; 🅿; z 35013; Ⓟ 464; Ⓒ 629
Allsboro; RMC Place; COLBERT; **142** B-2; mail Cherokee z 35616; ● 80
Allsop; RMC Place; CALHOUN; ***142** D-10; elev. 670ft./204m.; mail Piedmont z 36272; rural
Alma (Perrys Chapel); RMC Place; CLARKE; **143** M-3; elev. 390ft./119m.; 🅿; z 36501; ● 40
Almeria; RMC Place; BULLOCK; ***143** K-9; elev. 540ft./165m.; mail Union Springs z 36089; ● 30
Almond; RMC Place; RANDOLPH; **142** G-10; elev. 843ft./257m.; mail Wadley z 36276, Wedowee z 36278; ● 50
Almont; RMC Place; SHELBY; ***142** G-6; elev. 400ft./122m.; mail Montevallo z 35115; ● 200
Alpha Springs; RMC Place; AUTAUGA; ***142** I-8; elev. 329ft./100m.; mail Deatsville z 36022; rural
Alpine (Lake Howard, River Park); RMC Place; DEKALB; ***142** B-10; mail Mentone z 35984; ● 80
Alpine; RMC Place; TALLADEGA; **142** G-8; elev. 466ft./142m.; 🅿; z 35014; ● 300
Alston; BARBOUR; see Texasville (RMC Place)
Alta; RMC Place; FAYETTE; ***142** E-4; elev. 525ft./160m.; mail Berry z 35546; rural
Altadena Valley; RMC Place; JEFFERSON; ***142** F-7; ★ **BIR**; mail Birmingham z 35243; ● 1,000
Alton; RMC Place; JEFFERSON; ***142** F-7; elev. 778ft./237m.; 🅿; ★ **BIR**; z 35015; ● 300
Altoona; Inc. Place; ETOWAH; **142** D-8; elev. 925ft./282m.; 🅿; z 35952; Ⓟ 960; Ⓒ 984
America; RMC Place; WALKER; **142** E-5; elev. 451ft./137m.; mail Parrish z 35580; ● 250
Andalusia; Inc. Place; ⊡ COVINGTON; **143** N-7; elev. 300ft./91m.; 🅿 🅷; z 36420-21; Ⓟ 9,269; Ⓒ 8,794
Anderson; RMC Place; ETOWAH; ***142** D-9; ★ **GAD**; mail Gadsden z 35901; rural
Anderson; Inc. Place; LAUDERDALE; **142** A-5; elev. 665ft./203m.; 🅿; z 35610; Ⓟ 339; Ⓒ 354
Andrews Chapel; RMC Place; MORGAN; ***142** C-6; elev. 640ft./195m.; mail Danville z 35619; ● 30
Angel; RMC Place; CALHOUN; ***142** E-9; ★ **ANNI**; mail Jacksonville z 36265; rural
Anne Manie (Arlington); RMC Place; WILCOX; **143** K-4; elev. 150ft./46m.; 🅿; z 36721 & mail Arlington z 36722; ● 60
Anniston; Inc. Place; ⊡ CALHOUN; **142** E-9; elev. 710ft./216m.; 🅿 🅷 ■; ★ **ANNI**; z 36201-07, z 36210; includes Blue Mountain annexed December 15, 2000; Ⓟ 26,623; Ⓒ 24,276; Ⓐ 24,509; ◆ 23,663
Ansley; RMC Place; PIKE; **143** L-8; mail Troy z 36079; ● 50
Antioch; RMC Place; CALHOUN; ★ **ANNI**; mail Bynum z 36253
Antioch; RMC Place; COVINGTON; **143** N-8; mail Andalusia z 36420; ● 100
Antioch; RMC Place; PIKE; ***143** L-9; elev. 515ft./157m.; mail Troy z 36079; rural
Appleton; RMC Place; ESCAMBIA; ***143** N-5; elev. 234ft./71m.; mail Brewton z 36426; ● 30
Aqua Vista; RMC Place; LAUDERDALE; ***142** A-4; ★ **FLO**; mail Killen z 35645; ● 200
Aquilla; RMC Place; CHOCTAW; ***143** L-1; elev. 393ft./120m.; mail Millry z 36558; rural
Arab; Inc. Place; MARSHALL, CULLMAN; **142** C-7; elev. 1,124ft./343m.; 🅿; z 35016; Ⓟ 6,321; Ⓒ 7,174
Ararat; RMC Place; CHOCTAW; ***143** L-2; mail Toxey z 36921; ● 50
Arbor Acres; RMC Place; MADISON; ★ **HNTS**; mail Huntsville z 35810; pop. incl. with Huntsville (Inc. Place)
Arcola; RMC Place; HALE; ***142** I-3; elev. 113ft./34m.; mail Gallion z 36742; rural
Ardell; RMC Place; CULLMAN; ***142** D-5; mail Crane Hill z 35053; rural
Ardilla; RMC Place; HOUSTON; ***143** N-12; mail Dothan z 36301; pop. incl. with Dothan (Inc. Place)
Ardmore; Inc. Place; LIMESTONE; **142** A-6; elev. 900ft./274m.; 🅿; z 35739; Ⓟ 1,090; Ⓒ 1,034
Argo; Inc. Place; JEFFERSON, ST. CLAIR; **142** E-7; elev. 801ft./244m.; ★ **BIR**; mail Trussville z 35173; Ⓟ 930; Ⓒ 1,780
Argo (Argo Heights); RMC Place; WALKER; ***142** E-5; ★ **BIR**; mail Cordova z 35550; ● 480
Argo Heights; WALKER; see Argo (RMC Place)
Arguta; RMC Place; DALE; ***143** M-10; elev. 450ft./137m.; mail Ozark z 36360; ● 30
Ariton; Inc. Place; DALE; **143** M-10; elev. 450ft./137m.; 🅿; z 36311; Ⓟ 743; Ⓒ 772
Arkadelphia; RMC Place; CULLMAN; **142** E-6; elev. 370ft./113m.; mail Bremen z 35033
Arkdell; RMC Place; LAUDERDALE; ***142** A-4; elev. 700ft./213m.; ★ **FLO**; mail Lexington z 35648; rural
Arkwright; RMC Place; SHELBY; ***142** F-8; mail Vincent z 35178; pop. incl. with Vincent (Inc. Place)
Arley; Inc. Place; WINSTON; **142** D-5; elev. 787ft./240m.; 🅿; z 35540-41; Ⓟ 338; Ⓒ 290
Arlington; RMC Place; WILCOX; ***143** K-4; elev. 194ft./59m.; 🅿; z 36722; ● 170
Arlington; WILCOX; see Anne Manie (RMC Place)
Armstead; RMC Place; BLOUNT; ***142** E-7; elev. 683ft./208m.; mail Oneonta z 35121; ● 30
Armstrong; RMC Place; MACON; **143** K-10; elev. 330ft./101m.; mail Union Springs z 36089; ● 60
Arona (Aroney); RMC Place; DEKALB; ***142** C-9; mail Boaz z 35957; ● 100
Aroney; DEKALB; see Arona (RMC Place)
Arrowhead; RMC Place; MONTGOMERY; ★ **MTGY**; mail Montgomery z 36109; pop. incl. with Montgomery (Inc. Place)
Arrowwood; RMC Place; TUSCALOOSA; ★ **TUSC**; mail Tuscaloosa z 35405; pop. incl. with Tuscaloosa (Inc. Place)
Asberry; RMC Place; CALHOUN; ***142** E-10; elev. 690ft./210m.; ★ **ANNI**; mail Piedmont z 36272; rural
Asbury; RMC Place; DALE; ***143** M-10; elev. 418ft./127m.; mail Ozark z 36360; rural
Asbury; RMC Place; MARSHALL; ***142** C-8; elev. 1,100ft./335m.; mail Albertville z 35951; ● 80
Ashbank; RMC Place; WINSTON; ***142** D-4; elev. 622ft./190m.; mail Nauvoo z 35578; rural
Ashby; RMC Place; BIBB; **142** H-6; mail Brierfield z 35035; ● 100
Ashford; Inc. Place; HOUSTON; **143** N-11; elev. 241ft./73m.; 🅿; ★ **DOTH**; z 36312; Ⓟ 1,926; Ⓒ 1,853
Ashland; Inc. Place; ⊡ CLAY; **142** G-9; elev. 1,130ft./344m.; 🅿 🅷; z 36251; Ⓟ 2,034; Ⓒ 1,965
Ashland; RMC Place; MADISON; ***142** A-7; elev. 750ft./229m.; ★ **HNTS**; mail Huntsville z 35811; ● 350
Ashridge; RMC Place; WINSTON; **142** C-4; mail Haleyville z 35565; ● 100
Ashville; Inc. Place; ⊡ ST. CLAIR; **142** E-8; elev. 570ft./174m.; 🅿; z 35953; Ⓟ 1,494; Ⓒ 2,260
Askea Grove; RMC Place; MARSHALL; ***142** C-7; elev. 1,000ft./305m.; mail Arab z 35016; rural
Aspel; RMC Place; JACKSON; ***142** B-8; mail Scottsboro z 35768; rural
Athens; Inc. Place; ⊡ LIMESTONE; **142** A-6; elev. 720ft./219m.; 🅿 🅷 🅲 2,777; z 35611-14; Ⓟ 16,901; Ⓒ 18,967; ◆ 23,121
Atkeison (Atkinson); RMC Place; CLARKE; **143** L-4; mail Thomasville z 36784; ● 100
Atkinson; CLARKE; see Atkeison (RMC Place)
Atmore; Inc. Place; ESCAMBIA; **143** O-4; elev. 287ft./87m.; 🅿 🅷; z 36502-04; Ⓟ 8,046; Ⓒ 7,676
Attalla; Inc. Place; ETOWAH; **142** D-8; elev. 550ft./168m.; 🅿; ★ **GAD**; z 35954; Ⓟ 6,859; Ⓒ 6,592
Atwood; RMC Place; FRANKLIN; **142** C-3; elev. 736ft./224m.; mail Hodges z 35571, Vina z 35593; ● 30
Auburn; Inc. Place; LEE; **142** I-10; elev. 709ft./216m.; 🅿 🅲 23,547 ■; ★ **AU-OP**; z 36830-32, z 36849; Ⓟ 33,830; Ⓒ 42,987; ◆ 51,682
Auburn University; RMC Place; LEE; ***142** I-10; 🅿; z 36849; pop. incl. with Auburn (Inc. Place)
Augustin; RMC Place; PERRY; ***142** J-5; elev. 159ft./48m.; mail Selma z 36701; rural
Aurora; RMC Place; ETOWAH; **142** D-8; elev. 888ft./271m.; mail Boaz z 35956; ● 50
Aurora Springs; RMC Place; COLBERT; mail Cherokee z 35616
Austinville; RMC Place; MORGAN; ***142** B-6; ★ **DEC**; mail Decatur z 35601; pop. incl. with Decatur (Inc. Place)
AUTAUGA; **142** J-7; Ⓟ 34,222; Ⓒ 43,671; ◆ 50,833
Autaugaville; Inc. Place; AUTAUGA; **142** J-7; elev. 165ft./50m.; 🅿; z 36003; Ⓟ 681; Ⓒ 820
Avalon Park; RMC Place; JEFFERSON; ***142** F-6; ★ **BIR**; mail Bessemer z 35020; pop. incl. with Hueytown (Inc. Place)
Avant; RMC Place; BUTLER; ***143** M-7; mail Georgiana z 36033; ● 30
Avery; RMC Place; JACKSON; mail Stevenson z 35772; pop. incl. with Stevenson (Inc. Place)
Avon; Inc. Place; HOUSTON; **143** N-11; elev. 239ft./73m.; ★ **DOTH**; mail Ashford z 36312; Ⓟ 462; Ⓒ 466
Avondale; RMC Place; JEFFERSON; ***142** F-6; ★ **BIR**; mail Birmingham z 35222; pop. incl. with Birmingham (Inc. Place)
Avondale Mill; RMC Place; TALLAPOOSA; mail Alexander City z 35010; pop. incl. with Alexander City (Inc. Place)
Avondale Village; RMC Place; ST. CLAIR; ***142** F-8; mail Pell City z 35125; pop. incl. with Pell City (Inc. Place)
Avon Park; RMC Place; JEFFERSON; ***142** F-6; ★ **BIR**; mail Birmingham z 35234; pop. incl. with Birmingham (Inc. Place)
Awin; RMC Place; WILCOX; **143** L-6; mail Pine Apple z 36768
Axis; RMC Place; MOBILE; **143** O-3; elev. 36ft./11m.; 🅿; z 36505; ● 950
Ayres; RMC Place; JEFFERSON; ***142** E-7; elev. 999ft./304m.; ★ **BIR**; mail Pinson z 35126; rural

B

Babbie; Inc. Place; COVINGTON; **143** N-8; elev. 259ft./79m.; mail Andalusia z 36420; Ⓟ 576; Ⓒ 627
Baccus; MARION; see Rock City (RMC Place)
Bacon Level; RMC Place; RANDOLPH; ***142** G-11; elev. 745ft./227m.; mail Roanoke z 36274; rural
Bagley; RMC Place; JEFFERSON; ***142** E-6; ★ **BIR**; mail Dora z 35062; rural
Bailey Cove; RMC Place; MADISON; ★ **HNTS**; mail Huntsville z 35802; pop. incl. with Huntsville (Inc. Place)
Baileys' Mill; CULLMAN; see Baileytown (RMC Place)
Bailey Springs; RMC Place; LAUDERDALE; ***142** A-4; ★ **FLO**; mail Florence z 35634; ● 100
Baileyton; Inc. Place; CULLMAN; **142** C-7; elev. 973ft./297m.; 🅿; z 35019; Ⓟ 352; Ⓒ 684
Baileytown (Baileys' Mill); RMC Place; CULLMAN; ***142** D-7; mail Baileyton z 35019; rural
Baker Hill; Inc. Place; BARBOUR; **143** L-11; elev. 529ft./161m.; 🅿; z 36027; incorporated July 2, 1997; not reported in 2000 Census; Ⓡ 327
Bald Hill; RMC Place; GENEVA; ***143** N-10; elev. 295ft./90m.; mail Slocomb z 36375; rural
BALDWIN; **143** P-4; Ⓟ 98,280; Ⓒ 140,415; ◆ 175,086
Balkum; RMC Place; HENRY; ***143** M-11; mail Headland z 36345; rural
Ballplay; RMC Place; ETOWAH; **142** D-9; ★ **GAD**; mail Gadsden z 35903; ● 30
Bangor; RMC Place; BLOUNT; **142** D-7; elev. 523ft./159m.; mail Hayden z 35079; ● 130
Bankhead; RMC Place; DEKALB; ***142** B-10; mail Mentone z 35984; ● 40
Bankhead; RMC Place; WALKER; **142** E-5; elev. 391ft./119m.; mail Parrish z 35580; ● 90
Banks; Inc. Place; PIKE; **143** L-9; elev. 553ft./169m.; 🅿; z 36005, z 36061; Ⓟ 195; Ⓒ 224
Bankston; RMC Place; FAYETTE; **142** E-4; elev. 358ft./109m.; 🅿; z 35542; ● 150
Barachias; RMC Place; MONTGOMERY; ★ **MTGY**; mail Pike Road z 36064; pop. incl. with Montgomery (Inc. Place)
Barber; RMC Place; HOUSTON; ***143** N-11; ★ **DOTH**; mail Ashford z 36312; rural
BARBOUR; **143** L-11; Ⓟ 25,417; Ⓒ 29,038; ◆ 29,511
Barfield; RMC Place; CLAY; **142** F-10; mail Lineville z 36266; ● 300
Barlow; RMC Place; WASHINGTON; ***143** M-2; elev. 192ft./59m.; mail Millry z 36558; rural
Barlow Bend; RMC Place; CLARKE; **143** M-4; elev. 254ft./77m.; mail Jackson z 36545; rural
Barnes; RMC Place; DALE; ***143** M-10; elev. 499ft./152m.; mail Ariton z 36311; rural
Barnesville; RMC Place; MARION; ***142** D-3; elev. 500ft./152m.; mail Hamilton z 35570; ● 60
Barnett Chapel; RMC Place; WINSTON; ***142** D-5; elev. 761ft./232m.; mail Houston z 35572; rural
Barnett Crossroads; RMC Place; ESCAMBIA; **143** N-5; elev. 355ft./108m.; mail Brewton z 36426; ● 30
Barney (Barney Mines); RMC Place; WALKER; ***142** E-5; elev. 464ft./141m.; mail Cordova z 35550; ● 200
Barney Mines; WALKER; see Barney (RMC Place)
Barnisdale Forest; RMC Place; JEFFERSON; ***142** F-7; ★ **BIR**; mail Birmingham z 35215; pop. incl. with Birmingham (Inc. Place)
Barnwell; RMC Place; BALDWIN; ***143** Q-3; ★ **MOB**; mail Fairhope z 36532; rural
Barrett; RMC Place; HOUSTON; ***143** N-11; ★ **DOTH**; pop. incl. with Dothan (Inc. Place)
Barrytown; RMC Place; CHOCTAW; **143** L-2; mail Gilbertown z 36908; ● 100
Barton; RMC Place; COLBERT; **142** A-3; mail Cherokee z 35616; ● 150
Basham; RMC Place; MORGAN; **142** B-6; elev. 752ft./229m.; ★ **DEC**; mail Decatur z 35601
Bashi; RMC Place; CLARKE; **143** L-3; mail Thomasville z 36784; ● 200
Basin; RMC Place; COFFEE; ***143** N-8; mail Elba z 36323; rural
Bass; RMC Place; JACKSON; **142** A-9; mail Stevenson z 35772; rural
Bassetts Creek; RMC Place; WASHINGTON; ***143** M-3; mail Wagarville z 36585; ● 50
Batesville; RMC Place; BARBOUR; **143** K-11; elev. 264ft./80m.; mail Midway z 36053; rural
Battelle; RMC Place; DEKALB; ***142** B-10; elev. 889ft./271m.; mail Valley Head z 35989; rural
Battens Crossroads; RMC Place; COFFEE; ***143** N-9; mail Chancellor z 36316, Enterprise z 36330; rural
Battleground; RMC Place; CULLMAN; ***142** C-6; elev. 1,079ft./329m.; mail Vinemont z 35179; ● 120
Battles Wharf; RMC Place; BALDWIN; ***143** Q-3; ★ **MOB**; mail Fairhope z 36532
Bauxite; RMC Place; CHEROKEE; ***142** D-10; elev. 875ft./267m.; mail Centre z 35960; rural
Bay Minette; Inc. Place; ⊡ BALDWIN; **143** O-3; elev. 280ft./85m.; 🅿 🅷; z 36507; Ⓟ 7,168; Ⓒ 7,820
Bayou La Batre; Inc. Place; MOBILE; **143** Q-2; elev. 7ft./2m.; 🅿; ★ **MOB**; z 36509; Ⓟ 2,456; Ⓒ 2,313
Bay Shore Junction; RMC Place; MOBILE; ★ **MOB**; mail Mobile z 36610; pop. incl. with Prichard (Inc. Place)
Bayside; RMC Place; MOBILE; ★ **MOB**; mail Mobile z 36605; pop. incl. with Mobile (Inc. Place)
Bayside; RMC Place; MORGAN; ***142** B-6; elev. 570ft./174m.; ★ **DEC**; mail Decatur z 35603; pop. incl. with Decatur (Inc. Place)
Bay Springs; RMC Place; CHEROKEE; ***142** C-10; mail Centre z 35960; ● 100
Bay View; RMC Place; JEFFERSON; **142** F-6; ★ **BIR**; mail Adamsville z 35005, Mulga z 35118
Bazemore; RMC Place; FAYETTE; **142** E-4; mail Glen Allen z 35559; pop. incl. with Glen Allen (Inc. Place)
Beachwood Park; RMC Place; JEFFERSON; ★ **BIR**; mail Birmingham z 35212; pop. incl. with Birmingham (Inc. Place)
Beamon; RMC Place; DALE; ***143** M-10; elev. 314ft./96m.; mail Ozark z 36360; rural
Bean Rock; RMC Place; MARSHALL; ***142** B-7; mail Union Grove z 35175; rural
Bear Creek; Inc. Place; MARION; **142** C-4; elev. 804ft./245m.; 🅿; z 35543; Ⓟ 913; Ⓒ 1,053
Bear Point; RMC Place; BALDWIN; ***143** R-4; elev. 2ft./1m.; mail Orange Beach z 36561; pop. incl. with Orange Beach (Inc. Place)
Beason Mill; CLEBURNE; see Beasons Mill (RMC Place)
Beasons Mill (Beason Mill); RMC Place; CLEBURNE; ***142** F-10; mail Heflin z 36264; rural
Beatrice; Inc. Place; MONROE; **143** L-5; elev. 273ft./83m.; 🅿; z 36425; Ⓟ 454; Ⓒ 412
Beaty Crossroads; RMC Place; DEKALB; ***142** B-10; mail Ider z 35981; pop. incl. with Ider (Inc. Place)
Beauregard; RMC Place; LEE; ***142** I-11; elev. 610ft./186m.; mail Opelika z 36804; rural
Beaverton; Inc. Place; LAMAR; **142** D-3; elev. 359ft./109m.; 🅿; z 35544; Ⓟ 319; Ⓒ 226
Beaver Town; RMC Place; PICKENS; **142** G-2; mail Aliceville z 35442; ● 80
Beck; RMC Place; COVINGTON; ***143** N-7; mail Andalusia z 36420; rural
Beda; RMC Place; COVINGTON; ***143** O-7; elev. 232ft./71m.; mail Wing z 36483; rural
Beehive; RMC Place; LEE; ***142** I-10; elev. 490ft./149m.; mail Loachapoka z 36865; ● 100
Bel Air; RMC Place; JEFFERSON; ***142** F-7; ★ **BIR**; mail Birmingham z 35210; pop. incl. with Birmingham (Inc. Place)
Bel Air; RMC Place; MOBILE; ***143** P-2; ★ **MOB**; mail Mobile z 36616; pop. incl. with Mobile (Inc. Place)
Belchers; RMC Place; BIBB; ***142** G-5; elev. 377ft./115m.; mail West Blocton z 35184; rural
Belforest; RMC Place; BALDWIN; ***143** P-3; elev. 152ft./46m.; mail Daphne z 36526; ● 200
Belgreen; RMC Place; FRANKLIN; **142** B-3; mail Russellville z 35653; ● 250
Belk; Inc. Place; FAYETTE; **142** E-3; elev. 310ft./94m.; 🅿; z 35545; Ⓟ 255; Ⓒ 214
Bellamy; RMC Place; SUMTER; **142** J-2; elev. 109ft./33m.; 🅿; z 36901; ● 750
Bellefontaine; RMC Place; BALDWIN; ***143** P-4; mail Robertsdale z 36567; rural
Bellefonte; RMC Place; JACKSON; ***142** B-9; elev. 650ft./198m.; mail Hollywood z 35752; rural
Bellemeade; RMC Place; LAUDERDALE; ***142** A-4; elev. 600ft./183m.; ★ **FLO**; mail Florence z 35634; ● 550
Belle Mina; RMC Place; LIMESTONE; **142** B-6; elev. 600ft./183m.; 🅿; z 35615; ● 400
Belleville; RMC Place; CONECUH; **143** N-5; elev. 446ft./136m.; mail Evergreen z 36401, Repton z 36475; ● 170
Bellevue; RMC Place; ETOWAH; ***142** D-9; ★ **GAD**; mail Gadsden z 35904; pop. incl. with Gadsden (Inc. Place)
Bell Springs; RMC Place; MORGAN; ***142** C-6; mail Falkville z 35622; rural
Bellview; RMC Place; WILCOX; **143** L-5; elev. 165ft./50m.; mail Camden z 36726; rural
Bellwood; RMC Place; GENEVA; **143** N-10; elev. 150ft./46m.; 🅿; z 36313; ● 300
Bellwood; RMC Place; JEFFERSON; ★ **BIR**; mail Fairfield z 35064; pop. incl. with Fairfield (Inc. Place)
Belmont; RMC Place; SUMTER; **142** I-3; mail Livingston z 35470
Beloit; RMC Place; DALLAS; **142** J-5; mail Marion Junction z 36759, Orrville z 36767; ● 160
Belt Junction; RMC Place; MOBILE; ★ **MOB**; pop. incl. with Mobile (Inc. Place)
Beltline; RMC Place; MORGAN; ***142** B-6; ★ **DEC**; mail Decatur z 35601; pop. incl. with Decatur (Inc. Place)
Belview Heights; RMC Place; COLBERT; ***142** B-4; ★ **FLO**; mail Tuscumbia z 35674; pop. incl. with Tuscumbia (Inc. Place)
Bemiston; RMC Place; TALLADEGA; ***142** F-8; mail Talladega z 35160; pop. incl. with Talladega (Inc. Place)
Bendale; RMC Place; JEFFERSON; ***142** F-6; ★ **BIR**; mail Birmingham z 35217; pop. incl. with Birmingham (Inc. Place)
Benevola; RMC Place; PICKENS; **142** G-3; elev. 207ft./63m.; mail Gordo z 35466; rural
Benoit; RMC Place; WALKER; ***142** E-5; ★ **BIR**; mail Cordova z 35550; ● 50
Benson; CHILTON; see Isabella (RMC Place)
Bentley Hills; RMC Place; JEFFERSON; ***142** F-7; ★ **BIR**; mail Birmingham z 35216; pop. incl. with Mountain Brook (Inc. Place)
Benton; Inc. Place; LOWNDES; **142** J-6; elev. 137ft./42m.; 🅿; z 36785; Ⓟ 48; Ⓒ 47
Ben Vines Gap; RMC Place; JEFFERSON; ★ **BIR**; mail Mulga z 35118; pop. incl. with Maytown (Inc. Place)
Berkley; RMC Place; MADISON; ***142** B-7; ★ **HNTS**; mail Gurley z 35748; ● 250
Berkley Hills; RMC Place; JEFFERSON; ***142** F-7; ★ **BIR**; mail Birmingham z 35215; pop. incl. with Birmingham (Inc. Place)
Berlin; RMC Place; CULLMAN; **142** D-7; mail Cullman z 35055, z 35058; ● 60
Bermuda; RMC Place; CONECUH, MONROE; **143** M-5; elev. 339ft./103m.; mail Evergreen z 36401, Monroeville z 36460, Repton z 36475; ● 90
Berney Points; RMC Place; JEFFERSON; ***142** F-6; elev. 571ft./174m.; ★ **BIR**; mail Birmingham z 35211; pop. incl. with Birmingham (Inc. Place)
Berry; Inc. Place; FAYETTE; **142** E-4; elev. 451ft./137m.; 🅿; z 35546; Ⓟ 1,218; Ⓒ 1,238
Bertha; RMC Place; DALE; **143** M-11; elev. 465ft./142m.; mail Newville z 36353, Skipperville z 36374; ● 50
Bessemer; Inc. Place; JEFFERSON; **142** F-6; elev. 513ft./156m.; 🅿 🅷 ■; ★ **BIR**; z 35020-23; Ⓟ 33,497; Ⓒ 29,672; ◆ 28,027
Bessemer Gardens; RMC Place; JEFFERSON; ***142** F-6; ★ **BIR**; mail Bessemer z 35020; pop. incl. with Hueytown (Inc. Place)
Bessemer Homestead; RMC Place; JEFFERSON; ***142** F-6; ★ **BIR**; mail Bessemer z 35020; pop. incl. with Bessemer (Inc. Place)
Bessie; RMC Place; JEFFERSON; ***142** E-6; elev. 320ft./98m.; ★ **BIR**; mail Adamsville z 35005; rural
Bessie Junction; RMC Place; JEFFERSON; ***142** E-6; elev. 350ft./107m.; ★ **BIR**; mail Adamsville z 35005; rural
Bethel; RMC Place; BARBOUR; ***143** M-10; elev. 440ft./134m.; mail Ariton z 36311; rural
Bethel; RMC Place; CULLMAN; ***142** C-6; elev. 905ft./276m.; mail Cullman z 35057; rural
Bethel; RMC Place; LIMESTONE; ***142** A-6; mail Elkmont z 35620, Toney z 35773; rural
Bethlehem; RMC Place; MONTGOMERY; ***143** K-8; elev. 416ft./127m.; mail Lapine z 36046; ● 50
Bethsaida; RMC Place; FRANKLIN; ***142** B-4; elev. 600ft./183m.; mail Russellville z 35654; rural
Beulah; RMC Place; COVINGTON; ***143** N-8; elev. 296ft./90m.; mail Opp z 36467; rural
Beulah; RMC Place; LEE; **142** I-11; elev. 717ft./219m.; mail Valley z 36854; ● 400
Beverly Station; RMC Place; JEFFERSON; ***142** F-6; ★ **BIR**; mail Birmingham z 35211; pop. incl. with Birmingham (Inc. Place)
Bexar; RMC Place; MARION; **142** C-2; mail Hamilton z 35570; ● 50
BIBB; **142** H-6; Ⓟ 16,576; Ⓒ 20,826; Ⓡ 19,889; ◆ 21,709
Bibbville; RMC Place; BIBB; ***142** G-5; mail Woodstock z 35188; rural
Biddle Crossroads; RMC Place; DEKALB; ***142** B-10; mail Henagar z 35978; pop. incl. with Henagar (Inc. Place)
Bigbee; RMC Place; WASHINGTON; **143** M-2; elev. 104ft./32m.; 🅿; z 36558; ● 40
Big Creek; RMC Place; HOUSTON; ***143** O-11; elev. 199ft./61m.; mail Cottonwood z 36320, Dothan z 36301; ● 50
Big Oak; RMC Place; LAUDERDALE; ***142** A-4; elev. 650ft./198m.; ★ **FLO**; mail Killen z 35645; ● 410
Billingsley (Billingsly); Inc. Place; AUTAUGA; **142** I-7; elev. 368ft./112m.; 🅿; z 36006; Ⓟ 150; Ⓒ 116
Billingsly; AUTAUGA; see Billingsley (Inc. Place)
Billy Goat Hill; RMC Place; CHEROKEE; ***142** C-10; elev. 610ft./186m.; mail Centre z 35960; ● 50
Bingham; ELMORE; see Old Bingham (RMC Place)
Birdeye (Birdine); RMC Place; GREENE; ***142** I-3; elev. 100ft./30m.; mail Forkland z 36740; rural
Birdine; GREENE; see Birdeye (RMC Place)
Birdsong; RMC Place; CULLMAN; ***142** C-7; mail Cullman z 35058; rural
Birmingham; Inc. Place; ⊡ JEFFERSON, SHELBY; **142** F-6; elev. 601ft./183m.; 🅿 🅷 🅲 26,347 ■; ★ **BIR**; z 35201-24, z 35226, z 35228-29, z 35231-38, z 35242-44, z 35246, z 35249, z 35253-55, z 35259-61, z 35266, z 35282-83, z 35285, z 35287-88, z 35290-98; Ⓟ 265,968; Ⓒ 242,820; ◆ 229,700
Birmingham Green; RMC Place; JEFFERSON; ***142** F-6; ★ **BIR**; mail Birmingham z 35237; pop. incl. with Birmingham (Inc. Place)
Birminghamport; JEFFERSON; see Port Birmingham (RMC Place)
Birwat; RMC Place; JEFFERSON; ★ **BIR**; mail Birmingham z 35217; pop. incl. with Tarrant City (Inc. Place)
Bishop; RMC Place; COLBERT; ***142** B-2; elev. 507ft./155m.; mail Cherokee z 35616; rural
Biven; RMC Place; JEFFERSON; ***142** F-6; ★ **BIR**; mail Birmingham z 35214; pop. incl. with Brookside (Inc. Place)
Black; Inc. Place; GENEVA; **143** O-10; elev. 220ft./67m.; 🅿; z 36314; Ⓟ 174; Ⓒ 202
Blackankle; RMC Place; JACKSON; ***142** A-9; elev. 630ft./192m.; mail Scottsboro z 35768; rural
Black Bottom; RMC Place; CULLMAN; ***142** D-6; elev. 324ft./99m.; mail Hanceville z 35077; ● 50
Black Diamond; RMC Place; JEFFERSON; ***142** G-6; ★ **BIR**; mail Bessemer z 35023; ● 200
Black Pond; RMC Place; WINSTON; ***142** D-5; elev. 800ft./244m.; mail Double Springs z 35553; rural
Black Rock; RMC Place; CRENSHAW; **143** L-8; elev. 416ft./127m.; mail Honoraville z 36042, Rutledge z 36071; rural
Blacksher; RMC Place; BALDWIN; **143** N-3; mail Bay Minette z 36507, Little River z 36550
Blackwood; RMC Place; HENRY; ***143** N-11; mail Headland z 36345; ● 50
Bladon Springs; RMC Place; CHOCTAW; **143** L-2; elev. 96ft./29m.; mail Silas z 36919; ● 150
Blakely; RMC Place; MOBILE; ★ **MOB**; pop. incl. with Mobile (Inc. Place)
Blanche; RMC Place; CHEROKEE; **142** C-10; elev. 717ft./219m.; mail Gaylesville z 35973; ● 60
Blanton; RMC Place; LEE; ***142** I-12; elev. 649ft./198m.; mail Valley z 36854; rural
Bleecker; RMC Place; LEE; **142** I-11; mail Salem z 36874; ● 100
Blocton; RMC Place; BIBB; pop. incl. with West Blocton (Inc. Place)
Blossburg; RMC Place; JEFFERSON; **143** P-10; elev. 356ft./109m.; ★ **BIR**; mail Graysville z 35073; ● 190
BLOUNT; **142** D-8; Ⓟ 39,248; Ⓒ 51,024; ◆ 57,468
Blount Springs; RMC Place; BLOUNT; **142** D-6; ★ **BIR**; mail Hayden z 35079; ● 80
Blountsville; Inc. Place; BLOUNT; **142** D-7; elev. 714ft./218m.; 🅿; z 35031; Ⓟ 1,527; Ⓒ 1,768
Blow Gourd; RMC Place; BLOUNT; ***142** D-7; elev. 603ft./184m.; mail Cleveland z 35049; rural
Blue Creek; RMC Place; JEFFERSON; ***142** F-6; ★ **BIR**; mail Bessemer z 35023; ● 200
Blue Creek Junction; RMC Place; JEFFERSON; ***142** F-6; ★ **BIR**; mail Bessemer z 35020; pop. incl. with Bessemer (Inc. Place)
Blue Mountain; RMC Place; CALHOUN; **142** E-9; elev. 800ft./244m.; 🅿; ★ **ANNI**; z 36204 & mail Anniston z 36201; former incorporated place; became part of Anniston December 15, 2000; pop. incl. with Anniston (Inc. Place); Ⓟ 221; Ⓒ 233
Blue Pond; RMC Place; CHEROKEE; ***142** C-10; elev. 549ft./167m.; mail Cedar Bluff z 35959; ● 50
Blue Ridge; CDP-Census Area Only; ELMORE; ***142** J-8; ★ **MTGY**; mail Wetumpka z 36093; Ⓟ 1,151; Ⓒ 1,331
Blue Ridge Estates; RMC Place; JEFFERSON; ★ **BIR**; mail Birmingham z 35226; pop. incl. with Hoover (Inc. Place)
Blues Old Stand; RMC Place; BULLOCK; ***143** K-10; elev. 479ft./146m.; mail Perote z 36061; rural
Blue Spring; RMC Place; MADISON; ***142** A-7; ★ **HNTS**; mail Huntsville z 35810; pop. incl. with Huntsville (Inc. Place)
Blue Spring Garden; RMC Place; MADISON; ***142** A-7; elev. 750ft./229m.; ★ **HNTS**; mail Huntsville z 35811; ● 900
Blue Springs; Inc. Place; BARBOUR; **143** M-10; elev. 304ft./93m.; mail Clio z 36017; Ⓟ 108; Ⓒ 121
Blue Springs; RMC Place; BLOUNT; ***142** D-7; mail Blountsville z 35031; rural
Blue Springs; RMC Place; COVINGTON; ***143** N-8; elev. 296ft./90m.; mail Opp z 36467; rural
Bluff; RMC Place; FAYETTE; **142** E-3; mail Fayette z 35555; ● 60
Bluff City; MORGAN; see Echols Crossroads (RMC Place)
Bluff Park; RMC Place; JEFFERSON; ***142** F-6; elev. 1,000ft./305m.; 🅿; ★ **BIR**; z 35226, z 35244 & mail Birmingham z 35260; pop. incl. with Hoover (Inc. Place)
Bluff Springs; RMC Place; CLAY; **142** G-9; mail Ashland z 36251; ● 301
Bluff Springs; RMC Place; COFFEE; ***143** M-9; elev. 386ft./118m.; mail Elba z 36323; rural
Bluffton; RMC Place; CHEROKEE; **142** D-10; mail Esom Hill z 30138; ● 30
Boar Tush; RMC Place; WINSTON; ***142** C-4; elev. 893ft./272m.; mail Haleyville z 35565; rural
Boaz; Inc. Place; MARSHALL, ETOWAH; **142** C-8; elev. 1,080ft./329m.; 🅿 🅷; z 35956-57; Ⓟ 6,928; Ⓒ 7,411
Bobo; RMC Place; FAYETTE; ***142** E-3; mail Winfield z 35594; pop. incl. with Winfield (Inc. Place)
Bobo; RMC Place; MADISON; ***142** A-7; elev. 868ft./265m.; ★ **HNTS**; mail Toney z 35773; ● 50
Boiling Springs; RMC Place; CALHOUN; ***142** E-9; mail Ohatchee z 36271; rural
Boiling Springs; RMC Place; WILCOX; ***143** K-4; elev. 250ft./76m.; mail Catherine z 36728; rural
Boldo; RMC Place; WALKER; ***142** E-5; mail Jasper z 35504; ● 80
Boley Springs; RMC Place; FAYETTE; ***142** E-4; elev. 720ft./219m.; mail Berry z 35546; ● 60
Boligee; Inc. Place; GREENE; **142** I-3; elev. 124ft./38m.; 🅿; z 35443; Ⓟ 268; Ⓒ 369
Bolinger; RMC Place; CHOCTAW; **143** L-2; elev. 150ft./46m.; 🅿; z 36919; pop. incl. with Silas (Inc. Place)
Bolivar; RMC Place; JACKSON; ***142** A-9; mail Bridgeport z 35740; rural
Bolling; RMC Place; BUTLER; **143** L-7; elev. 301ft./92m.; mail Georgiana z 36033, Greenville z 36037; ● 80
Bomar; RMC Place; CHEROKEE; **142** D-10; mail Centre z 35960; ● 30
Bon Air; Inc. Place; TALLADEGA; **142** G-8; elev. 439ft./134m.; 🅿; z 35032; Ⓟ 91; Ⓒ 96
Bonita; RMC Place; AUTAUGA; ***142** I-6; elev. 345ft./105m.; mail Jones z 36749; rural
Bonnie Doone; RMC Place; LIMESTONE; ***142** A-6; elev. 800ft./244m.; mail Athens z 35611; pop. incl. with Athens (Inc. Place)
Bonny Brook; RMC Place; CALHOUN; ***142** E-10; elev. 700ft./213m.; ★ **ANNI**; mail Jacksonville z 36265; ● 100
Bon Secour; RMC Place; BALDWIN; **143** R-3; elev. 13ft./4m.; 🅿; z 36511; ● 900
Booth; RMC Place; AUTAUGA; **142** J-7; elev. 285ft./87m.; 🅿; z 36008; ● 220
Boot Hill; RMC Place; BARBOUR; ***143** L-10; elev. 472ft./144m.; mail Louisville z 36048; rural
Boozer Heights; RMC Place; CALHOUN; ★ **ANNI**; mail Oxford z 36203; pop. incl. with Oxford (Inc. Place)
Borden Springs; RMC Place; CLEBURNE; **142** D-10; 🅿; z 36272 & mail Fruithurst z 36262; ● 90
Borden Wheeler Springs; RMC Place; CLEBURNE; ***142** D-10; mail Fruithurst z 36262; ● 50
Boromville; RMC Place; MACON; ***142** J-11; elev. 450ft./137m.; mail Hurtsboro z 36860; rural
Boston; RMC Place; MARION; mail Brilliant z 35548; pop. incl. with Brilliant (Inc. Place)
Boswell; BULLOCK; see Omega (RMC Place)
Bowden Grove; RMC Place; CLAY; ***142** G-9; elev. 1,444ft./440m.; mail Lineville z 36266; rural
Bowles; RMC Place; CONECUH; ***143** M-6; mail Evergreen z 36401; rural
Bowman Crossroads (Bowmans Crossroads); RMC Place; JACKSON; ***142** B-9; elev. 1,420ft./433m.; mail Dutton z 35744, Henagar z 35978; rural
Bowmans Crossroads; JACKSON; see Bowman Crossroads (RMC Place)
Boyd; RMC Place; SUMTER; ***142** I-2; mail Livingston z 35470
Boykin; RMC Place; ESCAMBIA; ***143** O-6; elev. 156ft./48m.; mail Brewton z 36426; ● 30
Boykin (Gees Bend); RMC Place; WILCOX; **143** K-5; elev. 112ft./34m.; 🅿; z 36723; ● 100
Boyles; RMC Place; JEFFERSON; ★ **BIR**; mail Birmingham z 35217; pop. incl. with Birmingham (Inc. Place)
Boylston; RMC Place; MONTGOMERY; ***142** J-8; elev. 209ft./64m.; ★ **MTGY**; mail Montgomery z 36110; pop. incl. with Montgomery (Inc. Place)
Boys Ranch; RMC Place; DALLAS; ***143** K-6; mail Minter z 36761; ● 140
Bradford; RMC Place; COOSA; ***142** H-9; mail Kellyton z 35089; ● 60
Bradford (Dixiana); RMC Place; JEFFERSON; ***142** E-7; elev. 516ft./157m.; ★ **BIR**; mail Pinson z 35126; ● 250
Bradley; RMC Place; ESCAMBIA; **143** O-7; mail Wing z 36483; ● 50
Bradleyton; RMC Place; CRENSHAW; **143** L-8; mail Grady z 36036, Highland Home z 36041; ● 50
Braggs; RMC Place; LOWNDES; **143** K-6; elev. 296ft./90m.; mail Minter z 36761
Branchville; Inc. Place; ST. CLAIR; **142** E-8; elev. 765ft./233m.; 🅿; ★ **BIR**; z 35120; Ⓟ 370; Ⓒ 825
Brandontown; RMC Place; MADISON; ***142** A-7; ★ **HNTS**; mail Huntsville z 35805; pop. incl. with Huntsville (Inc. Place)
Brannon Stand; RMC Place; HOUSTON; ***143** N-11; elev. 297ft./91m.; ★ **DOTH**; mail Dothan z 36305; pop. incl. with Dothan (Inc. Place)
Brantley; Inc. Place; CRENSHAW; **143** M-8; elev. 295ft./90m.; 🅿; z 36009; Ⓟ 1,015; Ⓒ 920
Brantley; RMC Place; DALLAS; **142** J-6; elev. 137ft./42m.; mail Selma z 36703; ● 60
Brantleyville; RMC Place; SHELBY; **142** G-6; ★ **BIR**; mail Maylene z 35114; ● 300
Bread Tray Hill; RMC Place; BULLOCK; ***143** K-10; elev. 539ft./164m.; mail Union Springs z 36089; rural
Bremen; RMC Place; CULLMAN; **142** D-6; elev. 547ft./167m.; 🅿; z 35033; ● 80
Brent; Inc. Place; BIBB; **142** H-5; elev. 240ft./73m.; 🅿; z 35034; Ⓟ 2,776; Ⓒ 4,024; Ⓡ 3,087
Brewersville; RMC Place; SUMTER; ***142** J-2; elev. 179ft./55m.; mail Livingston z 35470; rural
Brewton; Inc. Place; ⊡ ESCAMBIA; **143** O-6; elev. 82ft./25m.; 🅿 🅷; z 36426-27; Ⓟ 5,885; Ⓒ 5,498
Briar Hill; RMC Place; PIKE; **143** L-8; elev. 412ft./126m.; mail Goshen z 36035; rural
Bridgeport; Inc. Place; JACKSON; **142** A-10; elev. 664ft./202m.; 🅿 🅷; z 35740; Ⓟ 2,936; Ⓒ 2,728
Bridgeville; RMC Place; PICKENS; ***142** G-2; elev. 150ft./46m.; mail Aliceville z 35442; rural
Bridlewood Forest Estates; RMC Place; JEFFERSON; ***142** E-7; ★ **BIR**; mail Birmingham z 35215
Brierfield; RMC Place; BIBB; **142** H-6; elev. 500ft./152m.; 🅿; z 35035; ● 17
Brighton; Inc. Place; JEFFERSON; **143** S-10; elev. 500ft./152m.; 🅿; ★ **BIR**; z 35020; Ⓟ 4,518; Ⓒ 3,640
Bright Star; RMC Place; BLOUNT; ***142** D-7; elev. 900ft./274m.; mail Horton z 35980; rural
Brilliant; Inc. Place; MARION; **142** D-3; elev. 628ft./191m.; 🅿; z 35548; Ⓟ 751; Ⓒ 762
Brisco Store; RMC Place; JACKSON; ***142** A-9; mail Stevenson z 35772; rural
Broadmoor; RMC Place; JEFFERSON; ★ **BIR**; mail Bessemer z 35020; pop. incl. with Bessemer (Inc. Place)
Bromley; RMC Place; BALDWIN; ***143** P-3; elev. 101ft./31m.; mail Bay Minette z 36507; ● 50
Brompton; RMC Place; ST. CLAIR; ***142** F-7; elev. 702ft./214m.; ★ **BIR**; mail Moody z 35004; pop. incl. with Moody (Inc. Place)
Brookhurst; RMC Place; JEFFERSON; ***142** F-7; ★ **BIR**; mail Birmingham z 35215; pop. incl. with Birmingham (Inc. Place)
Brookhurst; RMC Place; MADISON; ***142** A-7; ★ **HNTS**; mail Huntsville z 35810; pop. incl. with Huntsville (Inc. Place)
Brookley; RMC Place; MOBILE; ★ **MOB**; mail Mobile z 36605; pop. incl. with Mobile (Inc. Place)
Brooklyn; RMC Place; COFFEE; ***143** N-8; elev. 316ft./96m.; mail Kinston z 36453; rural
Brooklyn; RMC Place; CONECUH; **143** N-6; elev. 250ft./76m.; 🅿; z 36429; ● 120
Brooklyn; RMC Place; CULLMAN; **142** C-7; mail Holly Pond z 35083; ● 60
Brooks; RMC Place; COVINGTON; ***143** M-7; mail Mc Kenzie z 36456
Brookside; Inc. Place; JEFFERSON; **143** P-10; elev. 364ft./111m.; 🅿; ★ **BIR**; z 35036; Ⓟ 1,365; Ⓒ 1,393
Brooksville; RMC Place; BLOUNT; **142** D-7; mail Blountsville z 35031; ● 210
Brooksville; RMC Place; MORGAN; ***142** B-6; ★ **DEC**; mail Somerville z 35670; pop. incl. with Priceville (Inc. Place)
Brookwood; Inc. Place; TUSCALOOSA; **142** G-5; elev. 531ft./162m.; 🅿; z 35444; Ⓟ 658; Ⓒ 1,483
Brookwood Forest; RMC Place; LIMESTONE; ***142** A-6; mail Athens z 35613; pop. incl. with Athens (Inc. Place)
Broomtown; RMC Place; CHEROKEE; ***142** C-10; elev. 679ft./207m.; mail Gaylesville z 35973; rural
Broughton (Ocre); RMC Place; RANDOLPH; ***142** G-11; elev. 1,044ft./318m.; mail Roanoke z 36274; rural
Browns; RMC Place; DALLAS; **142** J-5; elev. 178ft./54m.; mail Marion Junction z 36759; ● 100
Brownsboro; RMC Place; MADISON; **142** A-7; elev. 633ft./193m.; 🅿; ★ **HNTS**; z 35741; ● 400
Browns Corner; RMC Place; MADISON; ***142** A-7; ★ **HNTS**; mail Toney z 35773; ● 50
Browns Crossroad; RMC Place; DALE; ***143** N-10; mail Ozark z 36360; rural
Browns Crossroad; RMC Place; HENRY; ***143** M-11; mail Abbeville z 36310, Columbia z 36319, Headland z 36345; rural
Brownsville; RMC Place; CLAY; ***142** G-9; mail Goodwater z 35072; rural
Browntown; RMC Place; JACKSON; ***142** B-9; mail Henagar z 35978; ● 80
Brown Town; RMC Place; MOBILE; ***143** O-1; elev. 269ft./82m.; mail Leakesville z 39451; rural
Brownville; RMC Place; CONECUH; ***143** M-6; mail Evergreen z 36401; rural
Brownville; RMC Place; JEFFERSON; ★ **BIR**; mail Birmingham z 35211; pop. incl. with Birmingham (Inc. Place)
Brownville; RMC Place; TUSCALOOSA; **142** F-3; elev. 249ft./76m.; mail Northport z 35475; ● 250
Bruceville; RMC Place; BULLOCK; ***143** K-9; mail Union Springs z 36089; rural
Brundidge; Inc. Place; PIKE; **143** L-9; elev. 474ft./144m.; 🅿; z 36010; Ⓟ 2,472; Ⓒ 2,341
Brunnet Heights; RMC Place; JEFFERSON; ***142** F-7; ★ **BIR**; mail Birmingham z 35217; pop. incl. with Tarrant City (Inc. Place)
Brushy Creek; RMC Place; BUTLER; ***143** M-7; mail Georgiana z 36033, Greenville z 36037; ● 50
Brushy Pond; RMC Place; CULLMAN; ***142** D-6; elev. 783ft./239m.; mail Bremen z 35033; ● 30
Bryant; RMC Place; JACKSON; **142** A-10; elev. 1,559ft./475m.; 🅿; z 35958; ● 150
Bryant's Lower Landing; RMC Place; BALDWIN; ***143** O-3; mail Stockton z 36579; ● 50
Buchanan Peninsula; RMC Place; COLBERT; mail Cherokee z 35616; summer pop. 100
Buckhorn; RMC Place; MADISON; ***142** A-7; elev. 790ft./241m.; ★ **HNTS**; mail New Market z 35761; rural
Buckhorn; RMC Place; PIKE; ***143** L-10; elev. 487ft./148m.; mail Banks z 36005; rural
Buck Island Shores; RMC Place; MARSHALL; ***142** C-8; elev. 620ft./189m.; mail Guntersville z 35976; ● 100
Bucks; RMC Place; MOBILE; **143** O-3; elev. 43ft./13m.; 🅿; z 36512; ● 190
Bucksnort; RMC Place; MARSHALL; ***142** B-8; mail Grant z 35747; ● 30
Bucksville; RMC Place; TUSCALOOSA; ***142** G-6; elev. 500ft./152m.; mail Mc Calla z 35111; rural
Buckville (Wallstreet); RMC Place; TALLAPOOSA; ***142** J-9; elev. 300ft./91m.; mail Tallassee z 36078; ● 150
Buena Vista; RMC Place; MONROE; **143** L-5; mail Beatrice z 36425; ● 30
Buena Vista Highlands; RMC Place; JEFFERSON; ***142** F-6; ★ **BIR**; mail Birmingham z 35209; pop. incl. with Homewood (Inc. Place)
Buffalo; RMC Place; CHAMBERS; **142** H-11; mail Lafayette z 36862; ● 60
Buggs Chapel; RMC Place; MADISON; ***142** B-7; ★ **HNTS**; mail Owens Cross Roads z 35763; pop. incl. with New Hope (Inc. Place)
Bug Tussle; CULLMAN; see Wilburn (RMC Place)
Buhl; RMC Place; TUSCALOOSA; **142** G-3; elev. 248ft./76m.; 🅿; ★ **TUSC**; z 35446; ● 350
Bull City; RMC Place; TUSCALOOSA; ***142** F-5; elev. 578ft./176m.; mail Adger z 35006, Kellerman z 35468; rural
Bull Gap; RMC Place; CLAY; ***142** G-9; elev. 1,180ft./360m.; mail Millerville z 36267; rural
Bullock; RMC Place; CRENSHAW; **143** M-8; elev. 497ft./151m.; mail Brantley z 36009; ● 70
BULLOCK; **143** K-10; Ⓟ 11,042; Ⓒ 11,714; ◆ 11,333
Burchfield; RMC Place; TUSCALOOSA; **142** G-5; mail Brookwood z 35444; ● 30
Burgreen Gin; RMC Place; LIMESTONE; ***142** B-6; elev. 700ft./213m.; ★ **HNTS**; mail Madison z 35756; rural
Burkeville; LOWNDES; see Burkville (RMC Place)
Burks Gardens; RMC Place; TUSCALOOSA; ***142** G-4; ★ **TUSC**; mail Tuscaloosa z 35401; pop. incl. with Tuscaloosa (Inc. Place)
Burkville (Burkeville); RMC Place; LOWNDES; **142** J-7; elev. 151ft./46m.; 🅿; z 36752; ● 150
Burl; RMC Place; WILCOX; mail Mc Williams z 36753
Burlington; RMC Place; ELMORE; ***142** I-9; mail Tallassee z 36078; rural
Burningtree Estates; RMC Place; MORGAN; ***142** B-6; elev. 570ft./174m.; ★ **DEC**; mail Decatur z 35603; pop. incl. with Decatur (Inc. Place)
Burningtree Mountain; RMC Place; MORGAN; ***142** B-6; elev. 900ft./274m.; ★ **DEC**; mail Decatur z 35603; pop. incl. with Decatur (Inc. Place)
Burns; RMC Place; CALHOUN; ***142** E-10; mail Piedmont z 36272; rural
Burnsville; RMC Place; DALLAS; **142** J-6; elev. 181ft./55m.; mail Selma z 36703; ● 100
Burnt Corn; RMC Place; MONROE; **143** M-5; elev. 500ft./152m.; 🅿; z 36401; ● 150
Burntout; RMC Place; FRANKLIN; ***142** C-3; elev. 748ft./228m.; mail Vina z 35593; ● 60
Burnwell; RMC Place; WALKER; **142** E-6; elev. 404ft./123m.; 🅿; ★ **BIR**; z 35038; pop. incl. with Dora (Inc. Place)
Burstall; RMC Place; JEFFERSON; ★ **BIR**; mail Bessemer z 35020; pop. incl. with Bessemer (Inc. Place)
Butler; Inc. Place; ⊡ CHOCTAW; **143** K-2; elev. 172ft./52m.; 🅿; z 36904; Ⓟ 1,872; Ⓒ 1,952
BUTLER; **143** L-7; Ⓟ 21,892; Ⓒ 21,399; ◆ 19,925
Butler Springs; RMC Place; BUTLER; **143** L-6; mail Forest Home z 36030; rural
Buttston; RMC Place; TALLAPOOSA; ***142** H-10; elev. 737ft./225m.; mail Dadeville z 36853; ● 50
Buyck; RMC Place; ELMORE; ***142** I-8; elev. 457ft./139m.; mail Titus z 36080; rural
Bynum; CDP; CALHOUN; **142** F-9; elev. 700ft./213m.; 🅿; ★ **ANNI**; z 36253; Ⓟ 1,917; Ⓒ 1,863

C

Caddo; RMC Place; LAWRENCE; ***142** B-5; ★ **DEC**; mail Trinity z 35673; ● 80
Caffee Junction (Coffee Junction); RMC Place; TUSCALOOSA; ***142** G-5; elev. 671ft./205m.; mail Mc Calla z 35111; ● 300
Cahaba; RMC Place; DALLAS; **142** J-5; elev. 107ft./33m.; mail Orrville z 36767; ● 30
Cahaba Heights; CDP; JEFFERSON; **143** S-13; elev. 649ft./198m.; 🅿; ★ **BIR**; z 35243; Ⓟ 4,778; Ⓒ 5,203
Cahaba Hills; RMC Place; JEFFERSON; ***142** F-7; ★ **BIR**; mail Leeds z 35094; pop. incl. with Leeds (Inc. Place)
Cahaba River Estates; RMC Place; SHELBY; ***142** F-6; ★ **BIR**; mail Birmingham z 35244; pop. incl. with Hoover (Inc. Place)
Calcis; RMC Place; SHELBY; **142** F-7; mail Vincent z 35178; ● 230
Caldwell (Pleasant Hill); RMC Place; ST. CLAIR; ***142** E-8; elev. 633ft./193m.; ★ **BIR**; mail Springville z 35146; rural
Caledonia; RMC Place; WILCOX; ***143** L-6; mail Mc Williams z 36753, Pine Apple z 36768; rural
Calera; Inc. Place; SHELBY, CHILTON; **142** G-7; elev. 497ft./151m.; 🅿; z 35040; Ⓟ 2,136; Ⓒ 3,158
Calhoun; RMC Place; LOWNDES; **143** K-7; mail Letohatchee z 36047; ● 250
CALHOUN; **142** E-10; Ⓟ 116,034; Ⓒ 112,249; ◆ 112,472
Calumet; RMC Place; WALKER; ***142** E-5; elev. 400ft./122m.; mail Parrish z 35580; ● 100
Calvert; RMC Place; WASHINGTON, WASHINGTON; **143** N-3; elev. 55ft./17m.; 🅿; z 36513; ● 540
Camden; Inc. Place; ⊡ WILCOX; **143** K-5; elev. 207ft./63m.; 🅿 🅷; z 36726; Ⓟ 2,414; Ⓒ 2,257
Camelot; RMC Place; MADISON; ★ **HNTS**; mail Huntsville z 35803; pop. incl. with Huntsville (Inc. Place)
Cameronsville; RMC Place; JACKSON; ***142** A-10; mail Stevenson z 35772; rural
Campbell; RMC Place; CHILTON; ***142** H-6; elev. 585ft./178m.; mail Jemison z 35085; ● 50
Campbell; RMC Place; CLARKE; **143** L-3; elev. 97ft./30m.; 🅿; z 36727; ● 100
Campbells Crossroads; RMC Place; CLAY; ***142** F-9; elev. 1,027ft./313m.; mail Lineville z 36266; rural
Campbell Springs; RMC Place; CLAY; ***142** F-9; elev. 994ft./303m.; mail Lineville z 36266; rural
Campbellville; RMC Place; WALKER; ***142** E-6; mail Empire z 35063; rural
Camp Branch; RMC Place; SHELBY; ***142** G-7; elev. 595ft./181m.; mail Alabaster z 35007; ● 50
Camp Hill; Inc. Place; TALLAPOOSA; **142** H-10; elev. 684ft./208m.; 🅿; z 36850; Ⓟ 1,415; Ⓒ 1,273
Camp Oliver; RMC Place; JEFFERSON; ***142** F-5; mail Quinton z 35130; ● 30
Canaan; MONTGOMERY; see Ridgecrest (RMC Place)
Canoe; RMC Place; ESCAMBIA; **143** O-4; elev. 281ft./86m.; mail Atmore z 36502; ● 170
Cantebury Heights; RMC Place; MOBILE; ★ **MOB**; mail Mobile z 36609; pop. incl. with Mobile (Inc. Place)
Cantelous (Cantelous Spur); RMC Place; MONTGOMERY; ***142** J-7; elev. 200ft./61m.; ★ **MTGY**; mail Montgomery z 36113; ● 50
Cantelous Spur; MONTGOMERY; see Cantelous (RMC Place)
Canton Bend; RMC Place; WILCOX; ***143** K-5; elev. 220ft./67m.; mail Camden z 36726; ● 60
Capitol Heights; RMC Place; MONTGOMERY; ***142** J-8; ★ **MTGY**; mail Montgomery z 36107; pop. incl. with Montgomery (Inc. Place)
Capps; RMC Place; HENRY; **143** M-11; elev. 429ft./131m.; mail Newville z 36353; ● 30
Capshaw; RMC Place; LIMESTONE; **142** A-6; elev. 680ft./207m.; 🅿; ★ **HNTS**; z 35742; ● 300
Carbon Hill; Inc. Place; WALKER; **142** E-4; elev. 423ft./129m.; 🅿; z 35549; Ⓟ 2,115; Ⓒ 2,071
Cardiff; Inc. Place; JEFFERSON; **143** P-10; elev. 357ft./109m.; 🅿; ★ **BIR**; z 35041; Ⓟ 72; Ⓒ 82
Carlisle; RMC Place; ETOWAH; ***142** D-8; mail Boaz z 35956; ● 50
Carlowville; RMC Place; DALLAS; **143** K-6; elev. 383ft./117m.; mail Minter z 36761; ● 80
Carlton; RMC Place; CLARKE; **143** N-3; elev. 182ft./55m.; 🅿; z 36515; ● 50
Carns; RMC Place; JACKSON; **142** A-9; mail Fackler z 35746; ● 80
Carolina; Inc. Place; COVINGTON; **143** N-7; elev. 326ft./99m.; mail Andalusia z 36420; Ⓟ 201; Ⓒ 248
Carolyn; RMC Place; MONTGOMERY; ***142** J-8; ★ **MTGY**; mail Montgomery z 36106; pop. incl. with Montgomery (Inc. Place)
Carpenter; RMC Place; BALDWIN; ***143** P-3; mail Bay Minette z 36507; rural
Carriger; RMC Place; LIMESTONE; ***142** A-5; elev. 700ft./213m.; mail Athens z 35611; rural
Carr Mill; RMC Place; CLAY; ***142** G-9; elev. 814ft./248m.; mail Ashland z 36251; ● 30
Carrollton; Inc. Place; ⊡ PICKENS; **142** G-2; elev. 256ft./78m.; 🅿 🅷; z 35447; Ⓟ 1,170; Ⓒ 987
Carrville; RMC Place; TALLAPOOSA; ***142** I-9; elev. 396ft./121m.; mail Tallassee z 36078; pop. incl. with Tallassee (Inc. Place)
Carson; RMC Place; WASHINGTON; ***143** M-3; elev. 53ft./16m.; mail Leroy z 36548; ● 30
Carter Grove; RMC Place; MADISON; ***142** A-7; ★ **HNTS**; mail Hazel Green z 35750; rural
Cartersville; RMC Place; DEKALB; ***142** A-10; elev. 1,640ft./500m.; mail Fort Payne z 35967; rural
Cartwright; RMC Place; LIMESTONE; **142** A-6; mail Elkmont z 35620; ● 100
Carver Court; RMC Place; MACON; mail Tuskegee Institute z 36088; pop. incl. with Tuskegee (Inc. Place)
Casemore; RMC Place; HALE; ***142** I-4; mail Gallion z 36742
Casey; RMC Place; DALLAS; **142** J-6; mail Selma z 36701; ● 80
Castleberry; Inc. Place; CONECUH; **143** N-6; elev. 164ft./50m.; 🅿; z 36432; Ⓟ 669; Ⓒ 590
Catalpa (Ebenezer); RMC Place; PIKE; **143** L-9; mail Troy z 36081; rural
Catherine; RMC Place; WILCOX; **143** K-4; elev. 179ft./55m.; 🅿; z 36728; ● 300
Cavalry Hill; RMC Place; MADISON; ***142** A-7; ★ **HNTS**; mail Huntsville z 35805; pop. incl. with Huntsville (Inc. Place)
Cave Spring; RMC Place; COLBERT; ***142** B-4; ★ **FLO**; mail Tuscumbia z 35674; rural
Cave Spring; RMC Place; MADISON; ***142** B-8; ★ **HNTS**; mail Owens Cross Roads z 35763; ● 300
Cave Springs; RMC Place; ETOWAH; ***142** D-9; ★ **GAD**; mail Attalla z 35954; rural
Cecil; RMC Place; MONTGOMERY; **142** J-9; elev. 246ft./75m.; 🅿; ★ **MTGY**; z 36013; ● 150
Cedar Bluff; Inc. Place; CHEROKEE; **142** C-10; elev. 602ft./183m.; 🅿; z 35959; Ⓟ 1,174; Ⓒ 1,467
Cedar Cove; RMC Place; TUSCALOOSA; ***142** G-5; mail Cottondale z 35453; rural
Cedar Fork; RMC Place; CLARKE; ***143** M-4; mail Whatley z 36482; rural
Cedar Grove; RMC Place; BALDWIN; ***143** R-3; elev. 13ft./4m.; mail Gulf Shores z 36542; rural
Cedar Grove; RMC Place; COVINGTON; ***143** N-8; elev. 350ft./107m.; mail Andalusia z 36420; ● 50
Cedar Grove; RMC Place; JACKSON; **142** A-9; mail Stevenson z 35772; ● 60
Cedar Hill; RMC Place; FAYETTE; ***142** E-3; elev. 408ft./124m.; mail Fayette z 35555; ● 30
Cedar Hill; RMC Place; LIMESTONE; ***142** A-6; mail Ardmore z 35739; rural
Cedar Hills Estates; RMC Place; COLBERT; ***142** B-4; ★ **FLO**; mail Tuscumbia z 35674; ● 90
Cedar Lake; RMC Place; MORGAN; ***142** B-6; ★ **DEC**; pop. incl. with Decatur (Inc. Place)
Cedar Plains; RMC Place; MORGAN; ***142** C-6; mail Falkville z 35622; rural
Cedar Point; RMC Place; MADISON; ***142** B-8; ★ **HNTS**; mail New Hope z 35760; rural
Cedar Springs (Center Springs); RMC Place; BLOUNT; ***142** E-7; mail Trafford z 35172; ● 150
Cedar Springs; RMC Place; CALHOUN; ***142** E-9; ★ **ANNI**; mail Jacksonville z 36265; rural
Cedrum; RMC Place; WALKER; ***142** E-4; elev. 365ft./111m.; mail Carbon Hill z 35549; rural
Center; RMC Place; WINSTON; ***142** C-4; elev. 974ft./297m.; mail Haleyville z 35565; rural
Centercrest; RMC Place; JEFFERSON; ***142** E-7; ★ **BIR**; mail Birmingham z 35215
Center Grove; RMC Place; MORGAN; ***142** C-7; mail Somerville z 35670; rural
Center Hill; RMC Place; CHILTON; ***142** H-6; elev. 674ft./205m.; mail Jemison z 35085; ● 30
Center Hill; RMC Place; CULLMAN; **142** D-7; elev. 606ft./185m.; mail Hanceville z 35077; ● 250
Center Hill; RMC Place; LAUDERDALE; ***142** A-4; ★ **FLO**; mail Killen z 35645, Lexington z 35648; ● 120
Center Hill; RMC Place; LIMESTONE; ***142** A-6; ★ **HNTS**; mail Toney z 35773; rural
Center Point; RMC Place; CLARKE; ***143** L-3; elev. 268ft./82m.; mail Coffeeville z 36524; ● 30

Entries in **UPPERCASE** are counties.
Entries in **bold** have populations of 2,500 or more.
Names in parentheses are alternate names.

Inc. Place	Incorporated Place
RMC Place	Rand McNally Designated Place
CDP	Census Designated Place
MCD	Minor Civil Division
⊡	County Seat
▲	Minor Civil Division
elev.	Elevation
🅿	Post Office
🅷	Hospital
🅲	College
■	Principal Business Center
★	Ranally Metro Area (RMA) Abbreviation
z	Zip Code(s)
Ⓟ	Previous Census Population
Ⓡ	Revised Census Population
Ⓐ	Annexation Population
●	Rand McNally Population Estimate
Ⓒ	Final Census Population
Ⓢ	Special Census Population
◆	Estimated Population

For additional definitions see Glossary, Volume 1, and Introduction, Volume 2.

Center Point; Inc. Place; JEFFERSON; 142 E-7; elev. 832ft./254m.; 🄿; ★ BIR; z 35215, z 35220, z 35235; incorporated March 18, 2002; not reported in 2000 Census; ● 15,200
Center Point; CDP-Census Area Only; JEFFERSON; 142 E-7; elev. 860ft./262m.; 🄿; ★ BIR; z 35215, z 35220, z 35235; Ⓟ 22,658; © 22,784; ◆ 15,159
Center Point Gardens; RMC Place; JEFFERSON; *142 E-7; ★ BIR; mail Birmingham z 35215
Center Springs; BLOUNT; see Cedar Springs (RMC Place)
Center Star; RMC Place; LAUDERDALE; 142 A-4; ★ FLO; mail Killen z 35645; ● 250
Centerville; BIBB; see Centreville (Inc. Place)
Centerville; RMC Place; CONECUH; 143 N-6; mail Evergreen z 36401; rural
Centerwood Estates; RMC Place; JEFFERSON; *142 E-7; ★ BIR; mail Birmingham z 35215
Central; RMC Place; CULLMAN; *142 C-6; mail Cullman z 35057; rural
Central; RMC Place; ELMORE; 142 I-9; elev. 638ft./194m.; mail Eclectic z 36024, Wetumpka z 36092; ● 100
Central; RMC Place; JACKSON; *142 B-9; elev. 1,340ft./408m.; mail Henagar z 35978, Pisgah z 35765; ● 30
Central City; RMC Place; COFFEE; 143 N-9; mail Enterprise z 36330
Central Heights; RMC Place; LAUDERDALE; 142 A-3; elev. 616ft./188m.; ★ FLO; mail Florence z 35633; ● 280
Central Highlands; RMC Place; JEFFERSON; *142 F-7; ★ BIR; mail Birmingham z 35206; pop. incl. with Birmingham (Inc. Place)
Central Mills; RMC Place; DALLAS; *142 J-4; elev. 242ft./74m.; mail Safford z 36773; rural
Centre; Inc. Place; ⊡ CHEROKEE; 142 D-10; elev. 658ft./201m.; 🄿 🄷; z 35960; Ⓟ 2,893; © 3,216
Centreville (Centerville); Inc. Place; ⊡ BIBB; 142 H-5; elev. 224ft./68m.; 🄿 🄷; z 35042; Ⓟ 2,508; © 2,466
Ceramic; RMC Place; RUSSELL; ★ COL; mail Phenix City z 36867; pop. incl. with Phenix City (Inc. Place)
Chalkville; CDP; JEFFERSON; 142 E-7; ★ BIR; mail Birmingham z 35215, Pinson z 35126; © 3,829
Chalybeate Springs; RMC Place; LAWRENCE; *142 B-5; ★ DEC; mail Hillsboro z 35643; ● 50
CHAMBERS; 142 H-11; Ⓟ 36,876; © 36,583; ◆ 34,250
Champion; RMC Place; BLOUNT; *142 D-7; mail Oneonta z 35121; rural
Chance; RMC Place; CLARKE; *143 L-4; elev. 81ft./25m.; mail Lower Peach Tree z 36751; ● 50
Chancellor; RMC Place; GENEVA; 143 N-9; elev. 300ft./91m.; 🄿; z 36316; ● 250
Chandler Mountain; RMC Place; ST. CLAIR; *142 D-8; elev. 1,277ft./389m.; mail Steele z 35987; ● 50
Chandler Springs; RMC Place; TALLADEGA; 142 G-9; elev. 867ft./264m.; mail Talladega z 35160; ● 120
Chapel Hill; RMC Place; CHAMBERS; *142 H-11; elev. 846ft./258m.; mail Lafayette z 36862; rural
Chapel Hill; RMC Place; JEFFERSON; *142 F-6; ★ BIR; mail Birmingham z 35216; pop. incl. with Hoover (Inc. Place)
Chapman; RMC Place; BUTLER; 143 M-7; elev. 270ft./82m.; 🄿; z 36015; ● 380
Chapman Heights; RMC Place; MADISON; *142 A-7; ★ HNTS; mail Huntsville z 35810; pop. incl. with Huntsville (Inc. Place)
Chase; RMC Place; MADISON; 142 A-14; elev. 793ft./242m.; ★ HNTS; mail Huntsville z 35811; ● 30
Chastang; RMC Place; MOBILE; *143 O-3; mail Mount Vernon z 36560
Chatom; Inc. Place; ⊡ WASHINGTON; 143 M-2; elev. 150ft./46m.; 🄿 🄷; z 36518; Ⓟ 1,094; © 1,193
Chelsea; RMC Place; MADISON; *142 B-7; ★ HNTS; mail Huntsville z 35801; pop. incl. with Huntsville (Inc. Place)
Chelsea; Inc. Place; SHELBY; 142 G-7; elev. 500ft./152m.; 🄿; ★ BIR; z 35043; Ⓟ 1,329; © 2,949
Chepultepec; BLOUNT; see Allgood (Inc. Place)
Cherokee; Inc. Place; COLBERT; 142 A-3; elev. 541ft./165m.; 🄿; z 35616; Ⓟ 1,479; © 1,237
CHEROKEE; 142 C-10; Ⓟ 19,543; © 23,988; ◆ 24,319
Cherokee Bluffs; RMC Place; TALLAPOOSA; *142 I-9; elev. 579ft./176m.; mail Tallassee z 36078; ● 50
Cherokee Forest; RMC Place; JEFFERSON; *142 F-6; ★ BIR; mail Birmingham z 35223; pop. incl. with Mountain Brook (Inc. Place)
Cherry Grove; RMC Place; LIMESTONE; *142 A-5; mail Athens z 35611; rural
Chesson; RMC Place; MACON; 142 J-9; mail Fitzpatrick z 36029; rural
Chesterfield; RMC Place; CHEROKEE; *142 C-10; mail Menlo z 30731; rural
Chestnut; RMC Place; MONROE; 143 L-5; mail Beatrice z 36425; rural
Chestnut Grove; RMC Place; COFFEE; *143 M-9; mail Brundidge z 36010, Jack z 36346; rural
Chetopa; RMC Place; JEFFERSON; *142 E-6; ★ BIR; mail Graysville z 35073; rural
Chickasaw; Inc. Place; MOBILE; 143 P-2; elev. 25ft./8m.; 🄿; ★ MOB; z 36611 & mail Mobile z 36671; Ⓟ 6,649; © 6,364
Chigger Hill; RMC Place; DEKALB; *142 C-9; mail Fyffe z 35971, Groveoak z 35975; ● 50
Childersburg; Inc. Place; TALLADEGA, SHELBY; 142 G-8; elev. 419ft./128m.; 🄿; z 35044; Ⓟ 4,579; © 4,927
Chilton; RMC Place; CLARKE; *143 L-3; elev. 158ft./48m.; mail Grove Hill z 36451; rural
CHILTON; 142 H-7; Ⓟ 32,458; © 39,593; ◆ 42,770
China; RMC Place; CONECUH; *143 M-6; elev. 376ft./115m.; mail Evergreen z 36401; rural
China Grove; RMC Place; PIKE; 143 K-9; mail Troy z 36081
Chinnabee (Chinneby); RMC Place; TALLADEGA; *142 F-9; ★ ANNI; mail Munford z 36268; rural
Chinneby; TALLADEGA; see Chinnabee (RMC Place)
Chisholm; RMC Place; MONTGOMERY; *142 J-8; elev. 206ft./63m.; ★ MTGY; mail Montgomery z 36110; pop. incl. with Montgomery (Inc. Place)
Choccolocco; RMC Place; CALHOUN; *142 E-10; elev. 671ft./205m.; 🄿; z 36254; ● 280
Choctaw; CHOCTAW; see Choctaw City (RMC Place)
CHOCTAW; 143 K-2; Ⓟ 16,018; © 15,922; ◆ 13,661
Choctaw Bluff; RMC Place; CLARKE; *143 N-3; mail Jackson z 36545; rural
Choctaw City (Choctaw); RMC Place; CHOCTAW; *143 K-2; elev. 104ft./32m.; mail Butler z 36904, Pennington z 36916; ● 30
Choctow Corner; RMC Place; CLARKE; mail Thomasville z 36784; pop. incl. with Thomasville (Inc. Place)
Christiana; RMC Place; RANDOLPH; *142 F-10; elev. 995ft./303m.; mail Delta z 36258; rural
Chrysler; RMC Place; MONROE; 143 N-4; elev. 107ft./33m.; mail Little River z 36550, Uriah z 36480; ● 50
Chulafinnee; RMC Place; CLEBURNE; *142 F-10; mail Heflin z 36264; rural
Chulavista; RMC Place; ST. CLAIR; *142 F-8; elev. 760ft./232m.; mail Pell City z 35125; ● 100
Chunchula; RMC Place; MOBILE; 143 O-2; elev. 112ft./34m.; 🄿; ★ MOB; z 36521; ● 750
Circlewood; RMC Place; TUSCALOOSA; ★ TUSC; mail Tuscaloosa z 35405; pop. incl. with Tuscaloosa (Inc. Place)
Citronelle; Inc. Place; MOBILE; 143 O-2; elev. 326ft./99m.; 🄿; z 36522; Ⓟ 3,671; © 3,659
Claiborne; RMC Place; MONROE; 143 M-4; elev. 500ft./152m.; mail Perdue Hill z 36470; ● 150
Clairmont Springs; RMC Place; CLAY; *142 F-9; elev. 921ft./281m.; mail Talladega z 35160; rural
Clanton; Inc. Place; ⊡ CHILTON; 142 H-7; elev. 599ft./183m.; 🄿 🄷; z 35045-46; Ⓟ 7,669; © 7,800
Clarence; BLOUNT; see Susan Moore (Inc. Place)
CLARKE; 143 M-3; Ⓟ 27,240; © 27,867; ◆ 25,691
Clarksville; RMC Place; CLARKE; *143 L-3; mail Coffeeville z 36524; rural
Claud; RMC Place; ELMORE; 142 I-9; elev. 316ft./96m.; mail Eclectic z 36024; ● 50
Clay; Inc. Place; JEFFERSON; 142 E-7; incorporated June 6, 2000; not reported in 2000 Census; ● 8,600
Clay; CDP; JEFFERSON; 142 E-7; elev. 936ft./285m.; 🄿; ★ BIR; z 35048; © 4,947
CLAY; 142 G-10; Ⓟ 13,252; © 14,254; ◆ 13,702
Clay City; RMC Place; BALDWIN; *143 Q-3; ★ MOB; mail Fairhope z 36532; ● 60
Clayhatchee; Inc. Place; DALE; 143 N-10; elev. 191ft./58m.; mail Daleville z 36322; Ⓟ 411; © 501
Clayhill; RMC Place; MARENGO; *143 K-3; mail Thomasville z 36784; rural
Claysville; RMC Place; MARSHALL; 142 C-8; mail Guntersville z 35976; ● 650
Clayton; Inc. Place; ⊡ BARBOUR; 143 L-11; elev. 596ft./182m.; 🄿; z 36016; Ⓟ 1,564; © 1,475
Clearview; RMC Place; COVINGTON; *143 M-8; mail Dozier z 36028; rural
Clearview; RMC Place; CRENSHAW; *143 K-8; mail Highland Home z 36041; ● 70
CLEBURNE; 142 F-11; Ⓟ 12,730; © 14,123; ◆ 15,005
Cleveland; Inc. Place; BLOUNT; 142 D-7; elev. 535ft./163m.; 🄿; z 35049; Ⓟ 739; © 1,241
Cleveland; RMC Place; FAYETTE; *142 E-4; mail Bankston z 35542; ● 50
Cleveland Crossroads (Elias); RMC Place; CLAY; 142 G-9; mail Goodwater z 35072; ● 50
Cliff Haven; RMC Place; COLBERT; *142 A-4; ★ FLO; mail Sheffield z 35660; pop. incl. with Sheffield (Inc. Place)
Clift Acres; RMC Place; MADISON; ★ HNTS; mail Madison z 35758; pop. incl. with Madison (Inc. Place)
Clifty; CULLMAN; see Corinth (RMC Place)
Clinton; RMC Place; GREENE; 142 H-3; elev. 188ft./57m.; 🄿; z 35448; ● 180
Clintonville; RMC Place; COFFEE; 143 N-9; elev. 439ft./134m.; mail New Brockton z 36351; ● 50
Clio; Inc. Place; BARBOUR; 143 L-10; elev. 511ft./156m.; 🄿; z 36017; Ⓟ 1,365; © 2,206
Clisby Park; RMC Place; MONTGOMERY; ★ MTGY; mail Montgomery z 36104; pop. incl. with Montgomery (Inc. Place)
Clopton; RMC Place; DALE; 143 M-11; elev. 510ft./155m.; 🄿; z 36317; ● 120
Cloverdale; RMC Place; JEFFERSON; *142 F-7; ★ BIR; mail Birmingham z 35215; pop. incl. with Birmingham (Inc. Place)
Cloverdale; RMC Place; LAUDERDALE; 142 A-3; elev. 584ft./178m.; 🄿; z 35617; ● 700
Cloverdale; RMC Place; MOBILE; *143 Q-1; elev. 50ft./15m.; ★ MOB; mail Grand Bay z 36541; rural
Cloverdale; RMC Place; TUSCALOOSA; *142 G-4; ★ TUSC; mail Tuscaloosa z 35401; pop. incl. with Tuscaloosa (Inc. Place)
Cloverdale Heights; RMC Place; LAUDERDALE; *142 A-4; ★ FLO; mail Florence z 35633
Clowers Crossroads; RMC Place; COFFEE; *143 M-9; elev. 410ft./125m.; mail Brundidge z 36010, Jack z 36346; rural
Clubview Heights; RMC Place; ETOWAH; *142 D-9; elev. 600ft./183m.; ★ GAD; mail Gadsden z 35901; pop. incl. with Gadsden (Inc. Place)
Coal Bluff; RMC Place; WILCOX; *143 L-4; mail Pine Hill z 36769; rural
Coalburg; RMC Place; JEFFERSON; *142 F-6; elev. 449ft./137m.; 🄿; ★ BIR; z 35068
Coal City; RMC Place; ST. CLAIR; *142 E-8; elev. 509ft./155m.; mail Ragland z 35131, Wattsville z 35182; rural
Coal Fire; RMC Place; PICKENS; 142 F-2; mail Reform z 35481; ● 60
Coaling; Inc. Place; TUSCALOOSA; 142 G-5; elev. 390ft./119m.; 🄿; z 35449, z 35453; © 1,115
Coalmont; RMC Place; SHELBY; *142 G-6; ★ BIR; mail Maylene z 35114; rural
Coal Valley; RMC Place; WALKER; *142 E-5; elev. 365ft./111m.; mail Oakman z 35579; rural
Coatopa; RMC Place; SUMTER; 142 J-2; elev. 152ft./46m.; 🄿; z 35470; ● 80
Cobb City; RMC Place; ETOWAH; ★ GAD; mail Gadsden z 35905; pop. incl. with Glencoe (Inc. Place)
Cobbs Ford; RMC Place; ELMORE; 142 J-8; ★ MTGY; mail Elmore z 36025; pop. incl. with Millbrook (Inc. Place)
Cochrane; RMC Place; PICKENS; 142 H-2; mail Aliceville z 35442; ● 30
Coden; RMC Place; MOBILE; 143 Q-2; elev. 14ft./4m.; 🄿; ★ MOB; z 36523; ● 1,050
Cody; RMC Place; LAMAR; *142 E-3; elev. 523ft./159m.; mail Fayette z 35555, Kennedy z 35574; rural
COFFEE; 143 M-9; Ⓟ 40,240; © 43,615; ◆ 48,584
Coffee Junction; TUSCALOOSA; see Caffee Junction (RMC Place)
Coffee Springs; Inc. Place; GENEVA; 143 N-9; elev. 238ft./73m.; 🄿; z 36318; Ⓟ 294; © 251
Coffeeville; Inc. Place; CLARKE; 143 L-2; elev. 150ft./46m.; 🄿; z 36524; Ⓟ 431; © 360
Cohasset; CONECUH; see Cohassett (RMC Place)
Cohassett (Cohasset); RMC Place; CONECUH; *143 N-7; mail Red Level z 36474; rural
Coker; Inc. Place; TUSCALOOSA; 142 G-4; elev. 450ft./137m.; 🄿; ★ TUSC; z 35452; © 808
COLBERT; 142 B-3; Ⓟ 51,666; © 54,984; ◆ 54,109
Colbert Heights; RMC Place; COLBERT; 142 B-4; mail Tuscumbia z 35674; ● 600
Cold Spring; RMC Place; ELMORE; *142 I-8; ★ MTGY; mail Deatsville z 36022; ● 60
Cold Springs; RMC Place; CULLMAN; 142 D-6; mail Bremen z 35033; ● 100
Coldwater; RMC Place; CALHOUN; 142 F-9; ★ ANNI; mail Anniston z 36201-02, Eastaboga z 36260, Oxford z 36203; pop. incl. with Oxford (Inc. Place)
Coldwater; RMC Place; COVINGTON; *143 M-8; elev. 350ft./107m.; mail Andalusia z 36420; ● 50
Cole Spring; RMC Place; MORGAN; 142 C-6; elev. 800ft./244m.; mail Falkville z 35622; ● 60
Coleta; RMC Place; CLAY; *142 G-9; elev. 886ft./270m.; mail Millerville z 36267; rural
Collbran; RMC Place; DEKALB; 142 C-9; mail Fort Payne z 35967; ● 50
Collins Chapel; RMC Place; CHILTON; *142 H-7; mail Clanton z 35045; ● 50
Collinsville; Inc. Place; DEKALB, CHEROKEE; 142 C-9; elev. 718ft./219m.; 🄿; z 35961; Ⓟ 1,429; © 1,644
Collirene; RMC Place; LOWNDES; 143 K-6; mail Tyler z 36785; ● 40
Coloma; CHEROKEE; see Ellisville (RMC Place)
Colonial Gardens; RMC Place; MADISON; *142 A-7; elev. 780ft./238m.; ★ HNTS; mail Meridianville z 35759
Colonial Heights; RMC Place; COLBERT; *142 B-4; ★ FLO; mail Tuscumbia z 35674; pop. incl. with Tuscumbia (Inc. Place)
Colony; CULLMAN; see The Colony (Inc. Place)
Colony; RMC Place; TUSCALOOSA; ★ TUSC; pop. incl. with Tuscaloosa (Inc. Place)
Columbia; Inc. Place; HOUSTON; 143 N-12; elev. 211ft./64m.; 🄿; z 36319; Ⓟ 922; © 804
Columbiana; Inc. Place; ⊡ SHELBY; 142 G-7; elev. 524ft./160m.; 🄿; z 35051; Ⓟ 2,968; © 3,316
Columbus City; RMC Place; MARSHALL; 142 B-8; mail Guntersville z 35976; ● 90
Colwell; RMC Place; CALHOUN; *142 E-9; ★ ANNI; mail Gadsden z 35905; rural
Comer; RMC Place; BARBOUR; 143 K-11; mail Midway z 36053; ● 60
Concord; RMC Place; FAYETTE; *142 F-4; elev. 500ft./152m.; mail Fayette z 35555; rural
Concord; CDP; JEFFERSON; 142 F-6; elev. 589ft./180m.; ★ BIR; mail Bessemer z 35023; © 1,809
CONECUH; 143 N-6; Ⓟ 14,054; © 14,089; ◆ 12,695
Congo; RMC Place; CHEROKEE; *142 C-10; elev. 673ft./205m.; mail Cedar Bluff z 35959; rural
Consul; RMC Place; MARENGO; 142 J-4; mail Catherine z 36728, Thomaston z 36783; rural
Cook Springs; ST. CLAIR; see Cooks Springs (RMC Place)
Cooks Springs (Cook Springs); RMC Place; ST. CLAIR; 142 F-8; elev. 553ft./169m.; ★ BIR; mail Cook Springs z 35052; ● 200
Cool Springs; RMC Place; ST. CLAIR; *142 E-8; elev. 581ft./177m.; mail Ashville z 35953; ● 70
Coon Creek (Owens Chapel); RMC Place; WALKER; *142 E-6; elev. 523ft./159m.; mail Empire z 35063; ● 200
Cooper; RMC Place; CHILTON; 142 I-7; mail Clanton z 35046; ● 200
COOSA; 142 H-8; Ⓟ 11,063; © 12,202; Ⓡ 11,885; ◆ 10,635
Coosa Court; RMC Place; TALLADEGA; *142 G-8; mail Childersburg z 35044; pop. incl. with Childersburg (Inc. Place)
Coosada; Inc. Place; ELMORE; 142 J-8; elev. 350ft./107m.; 🄿; ★ MTGY; z 36020; Ⓟ 912; © 1,382
Coosa River; RMC Place; ELMORE; *142 I-8; elev. 409ft./125m.; ★ MTGY; mail Deatsville z 36022; rural
Copeland; RMC Place; WASHINGTON; 143 M-1; mail Millry z 36558; rural
Copeland Bridge; RMC Place; DEKALB; *142 C-9; mail Collinsville z 35961; ● 30
Copeland Ferry; RMC Place; WALKER; *142 E-5; elev. 300ft./91m.; mail Quinton z 35130; ● 80
Copper Springs; RMC Place; ST. CLAIR; *142 E-7; ★ BIR; mail Odenville z 35120; ● 30
Coppinville; RMC Place; COFFEE; *143 N-9; mail Enterprise z 36330; pop. incl. with Enterprise (Inc. Place)
Corcoran; RMC Place; PIKE; *143 L-9; elev. 532ft./162m.; mail Troy z 36081; pop. incl. with Troy (Inc. Place)
Cordova; Inc. Place; WALKER; 142 E-5; elev. 311ft./95m.; 🄿; z 35550; Ⓟ 2,623; © 2,423
Corinth; RMC Place; BULLOCK; *143 L-10; elev. 525ft./160m.; mail Troy z 36081; rural
Corinth (Clifty); RMC Place; CULLMAN; *142 C-6; mail Vinemont z 35179; ● 60
Corinth; RMC Place; RANDOLPH; *142 G-10; elev. 886ft./270m.; mail Wadley z 36276, Wedowee z 36278; ● 50
Corinth; RMC Place; RANDOLPH; *142 F-10; elev. 1,014ft./309m.; mail Wedowee z 36278; rural
Corner; RMC Place; JEFFERSON; *142 E-6; elev. 744ft./227m.; ★ BIR; mail Warrior z 35180; ● 400
Cornerstone; RMC Place; BULLOCK; *143 K-9; elev. 289ft./88m.; mail Union Springs z 36089; rural
Cornhouse; RMC Place; RANDOLPH; *142 G-10; elev. 851ft./259m.; mail Roanoke z 36274; rural
Cornwall Furnace; RMC Place; CHEROKEE; *142 C-10; mail Cedar Bluff z 35959; ● 50
Corona; RMC Place; WALKER; 142 E-4; mail Oakman z 35579; ● 100
Cortelyou; RMC Place; WASHINGTON; *143 N-3; mail Wagarville z 36585; rural
Cotaco; RMC Place; MORGAN; 142 B-7; mail Somerville z 35670; ● 120
Cottage Grove; RMC Place; COOSA; 142 H-8; elev. 708ft./216m.; mail Kellyton z 35089
Cottage Hill; RMC Place; JEFFERSON; *142 F-6; ★ BIR; mail Pleasant Grove z 35127; pop. incl. with Pleasant Grove (Inc. Place)
Cottage Hill; RMC Place; MOBILE; *143 P-2; elev. 183ft./56m.; ★ MOB; mail Mobile z 36609, z 36691; pop. incl. with Mobile (Inc. Place)
Cotton; RMC Place; ELMORE; *142 I-9; elev. 638ft./194m.; mail Eclectic z 36024; rural
Cottondale; RMC Place; TUSCALOOSA; 142 G-4; elev. 319ft./97m.; 🄿; z 35453; pop. incl. with Tuscaloosa (Inc. Place)
Cottonton; RMC Place; RUSSELL; 143 K-12; elev. 217ft./66m.; 🄿; z 36851, z 36859; ● 100
Cottontown; RMC Place; COLBERT; 142 B-4; mail Leighton z 35646; ● 150
Cotton Valley; RMC Place; MACON; *142 J-10; mail Tuskegee z 36083; ● 60
Cottonville; RMC Place; MARSHALL; *142 C-8; mail Grant z 35747; ● 30
Cottonwood; Inc. Place; HOUSTON; 143 O-11; elev. 170ft./52m.; 🄿; z 36320; Ⓟ 1,385; © 1,170
Country Club Acres; RMC Place; LIMESTONE; *142 A-6; mail Athens z 35611; pop. incl. with Athens (Inc. Place)
Country Club Estates; RMC Place; MADISON; ★ HNTS; mail Birmingham z 35201, Huntsville z 35810; pop. incl. with Huntsville (Inc. Place)
Country Club Estates; RMC Place; MOBILE; *143 P-2; ★ MOB; mail Mobile z 36608; pop. incl. with Mobile (Inc. Place)
Country Club Village; RMC Place; MOBILE; *143 P-2; ★ MOB; mail Mobile z 36608; pop. incl. with Mobile (Inc. Place)
Country Estates; RMC Place; JEFFERSON; ★ BIR; mail Birmingham z 35215
Country Estates; RMC Place; MONTGOMERY; *142 J-8; elev. 171ft./52m.; ★ MTGY; mail Montgomery z 36108; pop. incl. with Montgomery (Inc. Place)
County Line; Inc. Place; BLOUNT, JEFFERSON; 142 E-7; elev. 569ft./173m.; ★ BIR; mail Trafford z 35172; Ⓟ 189; © 257
County Line; RMC Place; COVINGTON; *143 N-8; mail Kinston z 36453; ● 100
County Line; RMC Place; CULLMAN; *142 C-7; elev. 1,000ft./305m.; mail Baileyton z 35019; ● 30
County Line; RMC Place; PIKE; *143 M-9; mail Glenwood z 36034; rural
Courtland; Inc. Place; LAWRENCE; 142 B-5; elev. 564ft./172m.; 🄿; z 35618; Ⓟ 803; © 769
Covin; RMC Place; FAYETTE; 142 E-3; mail Fayette z 35555; ● 60
COVINGTON; 143 N-8; Ⓟ 36,478; © 37,631; ◆ 36,878
Cowarts; Inc. Place; HOUSTON; 143 N-11; elev. 327ft./100m.; 🄿; ★ DOTH; z 36321; Ⓟ 1,400; © 1,546
Cox Beach; RMC Place; MOBILE; ★ MOB; mail Satsuma z 36572; pop. incl. with Satsuma (Inc. Place)
Coxey; RMC Place; LIMESTONE; 142 A-5; mail Athens z 35611; ● 50
Coy; RMC Place; WILCOX; 143 L-4; elev. 99ft./30m.; 🄿; z 36435; ● 300
Cragford; RMC Place; CLAY; 142 G-10; elev. 860ft./262m.; 🄿; z 36255; ● 150
Crane Hill; RMC Place; CULLMAN; 142 D-6; elev. 828ft./252m.; 🄿; z 35053; ● 250
Crawford; RMC Place; MOBILE; ★ MOB; mail Mobile z 36608
Crawford; RMC Place; RUSSELL; 142 J-11; elev. 452ft./138m.; mail Phenix City z 36869-70
Creek Stand; RMC Place; MACON; 142 J-10; elev. 456ft./139m.; mail Union Springs z 36089; rural
Creel (Creeltown); RMC Place; WALKER; 142 E-6; elev. 501ft./153m.; mail Empire z 35063; ● 180
Creeltown; WALKER; see Creel (RMC Place)
CRENSHAW; 143 M-8; Ⓟ 13,635; © 13,665; ◆ 13,774
Creola; Inc. Place; MOBILE; 143 O-2; elev. 24ft./7m.; 🄿; ★ MOB; z 36525; Ⓟ 1,896; © 2,002
Crescent Heights; RMC Place; JEFFERSON; *142 F-6; ★ BIR; mail Bessemer z 35020; pop. incl. with Lipscomb (Inc. Place)
Crestline; RMC Place; JEFFERSON; ★ BIR; mail Birmingham z 35213; pop. incl. with Mountain Brook (Inc. Place)
Crestline Gardens; RMC Place; JEFFERSON; *142 F-7; ★ BIR; mail Birmingham z 35210; pop. incl. with Birmingham (Inc. Place)
Crestline Heights; RMC Place; JEFFERSON; *142 F-7; elev. 800ft./244m.; 🄿; ★ BIR; z 35213; pop. incl. with Mountain Brook (Inc. Place)
Crestline Park; RMC Place; JEFFERSON; *142 F-7; ★ BIR; mail Birmingham z 35213; pop. incl. with Birmingham (Inc. Place)
Crestview; RMC Place; MOBILE; ★ MOB; mail Mobile z 36609; pop. incl. with Mobile (Inc. Place)
Crestview Gardens; RMC Place; ST. CLAIR; *142 F-8; mail Pell City z 35125; pop. incl. with Pell City (Inc. Place)
Crestwood; RMC Place; MADISON; ★ HNTS; mail Huntsville z 35807; pop. incl. with Huntsville (Inc. Place)
Creswell; RMC Place; SHELBY; *142 G-8; mail Harpersville z 35078; ● 30
Crews; RMC Place; LAMAR; 142 D-3; elev. 344ft./105m.; mail Sulligent z 35586; ● 50
Crichton; RMC Place; MOBILE; *143 P-2; ★ MOB; mail Mobile z 36607, z 36670; pop. incl. with Mobile (Inc. Place)
Crocker Junction; RMC Place; JEFFERSON; *142 E-6; elev. 552ft./168m.; ★ BIR; mail Mount Olive z 35117; ● 50
Cromwell; RMC Place; CHOCTAW; 143 K-2; elev. 169ft./52m.; ● 230
Crooked Oak; RMC Place; COLBERT; 142 B-3; mail Tuscumbia z 35674; ● 30
Cropwell; RMC Place; ST. CLAIR; *142 F-8; elev. 478ft./146m.; 🄿; z 35054; pop. incl. with Pell City (Inc. Place)
Crosby; RMC Place; HOUSTON; *143 O-12; elev. 145ft./44m.; mail Gordon z 36343; rural
Cross Key; RMC Place; LIMESTONE; *142 A-6; mail Elkmont z 35620; rural
Crossroads; RMC Place; BALDWIN; 143 P-3; mail Bay Minette z 36507; ● 100
Crossroads; RMC Place; MARSHALL; *142 C-8; elev. 646ft./197m.; mail Guntersville z 35976; pop. incl. with Guntersville (Inc. Place)
Crosston; RMC Place; JEFFERSON; *142 E-7; elev. 470ft./143m.; ★ BIR; mail Pinson z 35126; ● 100
Crossville; Inc. Place; DEKALB; 142 C-9; elev. 1,141ft./348m.; 🄿; z 35962; Ⓟ 1,350; © 1,431
Crossville; RMC Place; LAMAR; 142 E-3; elev. 480ft./146m.; mail Vernon z 35592; ● 60
Crudup; RMC Place; ETOWAH; *142 D-9; ★ GAD; mail Attalla z 35954; pop. incl. with Reece City (Inc. Place)
Crumley Chapel; RMC Place; JEFFERSON; 143 Q-10; ★ BIR; mail Birmingham z 35214; ● 1,630
Cuba; Inc. Place; SUMTER; 142 J-2; elev. 234ft./71m.; 🄿; z 36907; Ⓟ 390; © 363
Culebra (Sandy Creek); RMC Place; CHAMBERS; *142 H-10; mail Camp Hill z 36850; rural
Cullman; Inc. Place; ⊡ CULLMAN; 142 D-6; elev. 799ft./244m.; 🄿 🄷 ■; z 35055-58; Ⓟ 13,367; © 13,995; ◆ 14,301
CULLMAN; 142 D-7; Ⓟ 67,613; © 77,483; ◆ 80,376
Cullomburg; RMC Place; CHOCTAW; 143 L-2; elev. 237ft./72m.; mail Silas z 36919; ● 150
Cunningham; RMC Place; CLARKE; *143 L-2; elev. 313ft./95m.; mail Campbell z 36727; rural
Cunningham; RMC Place; PICKENS; *142 G-2; mail Aliceville z 35442; rural
Curry; RMC Place; TALLADEGA; *142 F-9; elev. 537ft./164m.; mail Munford z 36268
Curry; RMC Place; WALKER; *142 D-5; elev. 631ft./192m.; mail Jasper z 35504; ● 150
Currytown; RMC Place; DALE; *143 N-10; ★ DOTH; mail Midland City z 36350; pop. incl. with Dothan (Inc. Place)
Curtis; RMC Place; COFFEE; *143 N-8; mail Elba z 36323; ● 30
Curtiston; RMC Place; ETOWAH; *142 D-8; ★ GAD; mail Attalla z 35954; pop. incl. with Attalla (Inc. Place)
Cusseta; Inc. Place; CHAMBERS; 142 I-11; elev. 724ft./221m.; 🄿; z 36852; incorporated April 26, 2007; not reported in 2000 Census; ● 100
Cypress; RMC Place; HALE; 142 H-4; elev. 131ft./40m.; 🄿; z 35474; ● 100
Cypress Heights; RMC Place; LAUDERDALE; *142 A-4; ★ FLO; pop. incl. with Florence (Inc. Place)
Cyril; RMC Place; CHOCTAW; *143 K-1; elev. 235ft./72m.; mail Lisman z 36912; rural

D

Dadeville; Inc. Place; ⊡ TALLAPOOSA; 142 H-10; elev. 717ft./219m.; 🄿 🄷; z 36853; Ⓟ 3,276; © 3,212
Daisey City; RMC Place; JEFFERSON; *142 F-6; ★ BIR; mail Birmingham z 35214; pop. incl. with Graysville (Inc. Place)
DALE; 143 M-10; Ⓟ 49,633; © 49,129; ◆ 48,050
Daleville; Inc. Place; DALE; 143 N-10; elev. 333ft./101m.; 🄿; z 36322; Ⓟ 5,117; © 4,653
Dallas; RMC Place; BLOUNT; 142 E-7; elev. 555ft./169m.; mail Trafford z 35172; ● 300
Dallas; RMC Place; MADISON; *142 A-7; ★ HNTS; mail Huntsville z 35801; pop. incl. with Huntsville (Inc. Place)
DALLAS; 142 J-5; Ⓟ 48,130; © 46,365; ◆ 42,110
Damascus; RMC Place; COFFEE; *143 N-9; elev. 357ft./109m.; mail Elba z 36323; ● 30
Damascus; RMC Place; ESCAMBIA; 143 N-6; mail Brewton z 36426; ● 30
Dancy; RMC Place; PICKENS; 142 H-2; elev. 189ft./58m.; mail Aliceville z 35442; ● 30
Dancy Quarter; RMC Place; MORGAN; *142 B-6; elev. 590ft./180m.; ★ DEC; mail Decatur z 35603
Danley Crossroads; COFFEE; see Danleys Crossroads (RMC Place)
Danleys Crossroads (Danley Crossroads); RMC Place; COFFEE; 143 N-8; mail Elba z 36323; rural
Danville; RMC Place; MORGAN; 142 C-5; elev. 600ft./183m.; 🄿; z 35619; ● 300
Danway; RMC Place; CHAMBERS; *142 I-11; elev. 715ft./218m.; mail Cusseta z 36852; rural
Daphne; Inc. Place; BALDWIN; 143 P-3; elev. 157ft./48m.; 🄿 🄷 🄲 650; ★ MOB; z 36526; Ⓟ 11,291; © 16,581
Dargin; RMC Place; SHELBY; *142 G-7; mail Calera z 35040; pop. incl. with Calera (Inc. Place)
Darlington; RMC Place; WILCOX; 143 L-5; elev. 217ft./66m.; mail Camden z 36726; ● 100
Darwin Downs; RMC Place; MADISON; *142 A-7; ★ HNTS; mail Huntsville z 35801; pop. incl. with Huntsville (Inc. Place)
Dauphin Island; Inc. Place; MOBILE; 143 R-2; elev. 10ft./3m.; 🄿; z 36528; Ⓟ 824; summer pop. 3,500; © 1,371
Davenport (Devenport); RMC Place; LOWNDES, MONTGOMERY; 143 K-8; mail Letohatchee z 36047; ● 80
Davis Hills; RMC Place; MADISON; *142 A-7; ★ HNTS; mail Huntsville z 35805; pop. incl. with Huntsville (Inc. Place)
Daviston; Inc. Place; TALLAPOOSA; 142 H-10; elev. 767ft./234m.; 🄿; z 36256; Ⓟ 261; © 267
Davisville; RMC Place; MACON; 142 J-10; elev. 301ft./92m.; mail Tuskegee z 36083; ● 60
Dawes; RMC Place; MOBILE; *143 P-2; elev. 168ft./51m.; ★ MOB; mail Mobile z 36601; rural
Dawson; RMC Place; DEKALB; 142 C-9; elev. 1,157ft./353m.; 🄿; z 35963; ● 150
Dawsons Mill; RMC Place; AUTAUGA; *142 I-6; mail Jones z 36749; rural
Dayton; Inc. Place; MARENGO; 142 J-4; elev. 249ft./76m.; 🄿; z 36738; Ⓟ 77; © 60
DeArmanville; RMC Place; CALHOUN; 142 F-10; elev. 679ft./207m.; 🄿; ★ ANNI; z 36257; ● 580
Deason Hill; RMC Place; WALKER; *142 E-5; elev. 400ft./122m.; mail Cordova z 35550; ● 50
Deatsville; Inc. Place; ELMORE; 142 I-8; elev. 304ft./93m.; 🄿; ★ MTGY; z 36022; © 340
Deavers Town (Deavertown); RMC Place; BLOUNT; *142 D-7; mail Cleveland z 35049; rural
Deavertown; BLOUNT; see Deavers Town (RMC Place)
Decatur; Inc. Place; ⊡ MORGAN, LIMESTONE; 142 B-6; elev. 590ft./180m.; 🄿 🄷 ■; ★ DEC; z 35601-03, z 35609, z 35699; Ⓟ 48,778; © 53,929; ◆ 52,644
Deerhurst; RMC Place; SHELBY; *142 G-6; elev. 522ft./159m.; mail Pelham z 35124; rural
Deer Park; RMC Place; WASHINGTON; 143 N-2; elev. 154ft./47m.; 🄿; z 36529; ● 330
Deer Range; CONECUH; see Range (RMC Place)
DeFoor; RMC Place; WINSTON; *142 C-4; elev. 851ft./259m.; mail Haleyville z 35565; rural
DEKALB; 142 B-10; Ⓟ 54,651; © 64,452; ◆ 67,283
Delchamps; RMC Place; MOBILE; *143 Q-2; elev. 18ft./5m.; ★ MOB; mail Coden z 36523; rural
Delmar; RMC Place; WINSTON; 142 D-4; elev. 900ft./274m.; 🄿; z 35551; ● 300
Delta; RMC Place; CLAY; 142 F-10; elev. 1,066ft./325m.; 🄿; z 36258; ● 200
Demopolis; Inc. Place; MARENGO; 142 J-3; elev. 125ft./38m.; 🄿 🄷; z 36732; Ⓟ 7,512; © 7,540
Dempsey; RMC Place; FRANKLIN; *142 B-3; elev. 831ft./253m.; mail Russellville z 35653; ● 30
Deposit; RMC Place; MADISON; 142 A-7; mail New Market z 35761; ● 30
Detroit; Inc. Place; LAMAR; 142 D-2; elev. 360ft./110m.; 🄿; z 35552; Ⓟ 291; © 247
Devenport; LOWNDES, MONTGOMERY; see Davenport (RMC Place)
Dexter; RMC Place; ELMORE; *142 I-8; ★ MTGY; mail Wetumpka z 36092; ● 70
Diamond; RMC Place; MARSHALL; *142 C-8; elev. 609ft./186m.; mail Guntersville z 35976; ● 50
Dickenson; CLARKE; see Dickinson (RMC Place)
Dickert; RMC Place; RANDOLPH; *142 G-10; elev. 690ft./210m.; mail Wadley z 36276; ● 70
Dickinson (Dickenson); RMC Place; CLARKE; 143 L-4; elev. 215ft./66m.; 🄿; z 36436; ● 300
Dillard; RMC Place; DALE; *143 M-10; elev. 112ft./34m.; mail Ozark z 36360; rural
Dilworth; RMC Place; WALKER; *142 E-6; elev. 426ft./130m.; ★ BIR; mail Empire z 35063; ● 80
Dime; RMC Place; FRANKLIN; *142 C-4; elev. 950ft./290m.; mail Phil Campbell z 35581; rural
Dixiana; JEFFERSON; see Bradford (RMC Place)
Dixie; RMC Place; ESCAMBIA; 143 O-7; mail Andalusia z 36420; ● 60
Dixie Springs; RMC Place; WALKER; *142 E-5; elev. 377ft./115m.; mail Oakman z 35579; rural
Dixon Corner; RMC Place; MOBILE; 143 Q-2; ★ MOB; mail Irvington z 36544; ● 300
Dixon Shop; RMC Place; CHEROKEE; *142 D-10; elev. 547ft./167m.; mail Leesburg z 35983; ● 50
Dixons Mills; RMC Place; MARENGO; 143 K-3; elev. 250ft./76m.; 🄿; z 36736; ● 290
Dixonville; RMC Place; ESCAMBIA; 143 O-6; mail Brewton z 36426
Docena; RMC Place; JEFFERSON; 143 Q-10; elev. 600ft./183m.; 🄿; ★ BIR; z 35060; ● 1,000
Dock; RMC Place; BUTLER; *143 L-7; elev. 335ft./102m.; mail Greenville z 36037; rural
Dodge City; Inc. Place; CULLMAN; *142 D-6; mail Cullman z 35057, Hanceville z 35077; Ⓟ 467; © 612
Dog Town; RMC Place; DEKALB; *142 C-10; elev. 1,357ft./414m.; mail Fort Payne z 35967; ● 80
Dogtown; RMC Place; WALKER; *142 D-4; elev. 591ft./180m.; mail Carbon Hill z 35549; rural
Dogwood; RMC Place; SHELBY; *142 G-6; mail Montevallo z 35115; ● 100
Dolcito; RMC Place; JEFFERSON; ★ BIR; mail Birmingham z 35217; pop. incl. with Tarrant City (Inc. Place)
Doliska; RMC Place; WALKER; *142 E-5; ★ BIR; mail Quinton z 35130; pop. incl. with Dora (Inc. Place)
Dolomite; RMC Place; JEFFERSON; *142 F-6; elev. 581ft./177m.; 🄿; ★ BIR; z 35061; pop. incl. with Birmingham (Inc. Place)
Dolonah; RMC Place; JEFFERSON; *142 F-6; ★ BIR; mail Bessemer z 35022; pop. incl. with Bessemer (Inc. Place)
Dora; Inc. Place; WALKER; 142 E-6; elev. 387ft./118m.; 🄿; ★ BIR; z 35062; Ⓟ 2,214; © 2,413
Doster; RMC Place; BARBOUR; 143 M-10; mail Ariton z 36311; ● 100
Dothan; Inc. Place; ⊡ HOUSTON, DALE, HENRY; 143 N-11; elev. 326ft./99m.; 🄿 🄷 ■; ★ DOTH; z 36301-05; Ⓟ 53,721; © 57,737; ◆ 65,972
Double Bridges; RMC Place; CLAY; *142 G-9; elev. 1,000ft./305m.; mail Ashland z 36251
Double Bridges; RMC Place; HENRY; *143 L-12; mail Abbeville z 36310; rural
Double Bridges; RMC Place; MARSHALL; *142 C-8; mail Boaz z 35957; ● 100
Double Bridges; RMC Place; MARSHALL; *142 C-8; elev. 900ft./274m.; mail Albertville z 35951; ● 30
Doublehead; RMC Place; CHAMBERS; *142 G-11; mail Lafayette z 36862; rural
Double Springs; Inc. Place; ⊡ WINSTON; 142 D-5; elev. 827ft./252m.; 🄿; z 35553; Ⓟ 1,138; © 1,003
Douglas; RMC Place; DEKALB; *142 C-10; mail Fort Payne z 35967; pop. incl. with Fort Payne (Inc. Place)
Douglas; Inc. Place; MARSHALL; 142 D-8; elev. 940ft./287m.; 🄿; z 35964; Ⓟ 474; © 530
Douglasville; RMC Place; JEFFERSON; *142 F-6; ★ BIR; mail Birmingham z 35207; pop. incl. with Birmingham (Inc. Place)
Downing; RMC Place; MONTGOMERY; 143 K-9; mail Mathews z 36052
Downs (Edwards); RMC Place; MACON; *142 J-10; mail Hardaway z 36039; ● 50
Downtown; RMC Place; MADISON; *142 B-7; ★ HNTS; mail Huntsville z 35801, z 35804; pop. incl. with Huntsville (Inc. Place)
Downtown; RMC Place; MONTGOMERY; *142 J-8; ★ MTGY; mail Montgomery z 36101-04; pop. incl. with Montgomery (Inc. Place)
Downtown; RMC Place; TUSCALOOSA; *142 G-4; ★ TUSC; mail Tuscaloosa z 35401; pop. incl. with Tuscaloosa (Inc. Place)
Dozier; Inc. Place; CRENSHAW; 143 M-8; elev. 230ft./70m.; 🄿; z 36028; Ⓟ 483; © 391
Drewry; RMC Place; MONROE; *143 M-5; mail Monroeville z 36460; rural
Drummond; RMC Place; WALKER; *142 E-6; ★ BIR; mail Empire z 35063; ● 50
Dry Forks; RMC Place; WILCOX; 143 L-5; mail Camden z 36726; rural
Dry Valley; RMC Place; SHELBY; *142 H-6; elev. 553ft./169m.; mail Montevallo z 35115; ● 300
Dry Valley; RMC Place; TALLADEGA; *142 F-9; mail Lincoln z 35096
Dublin; RMC Place; MONTGOMERY; 143 K-8; elev. 539ft./164m.; mail Grady z 36036; ● 160
Duck Nest Springs; RMC Place; TALLADEGA; *142 F-9; elev. 920ft./280m.; ★ ANNI; mail Munford z 36268; rural
Duck Springs; RMC Place; ETOWAH; *142 D-9; mail Attalla z 35954; ● 50
Dudley; RMC Place; TUSCALOOSA; *142 G-5; mail Vance z 35490; rural
Dudleyville; RMC Place; TALLAPOOSA; *142 H-10; mail Camp Hill z 36850; ● 30
Duke; RMC Place; CALHOUN; 142 E-9; elev. 575ft./175m.; ★ ANNI; mail Wellington z 36279; ● 160
Dunavant; SHELBY; see Winburn (RMC Place)
Duncan; RMC Place; TALLAPOOSA; *142 H-9; elev. 707ft./215m.; mail Alexander City z 35010; pop. incl. with Alexander City (Inc. Place)
Duncan Crossroads; RMC Place; JACKSON; *142 B-9; elev. 1,299ft./396m.; mail Section z 35771; ● 100
Duncanville; RMC Place; TUSCALOOSA; 142 H-4; elev. 240ft./73m.; 🄿; z 35456; ● 150
Dundee; RMC Place; GENEVA; *143 O-10; elev. 254ft./77m.; mail Hartford z 36344; pop. incl. with Hartford (Inc. Place)
Dunn; RMC Place; PIKE; *143 L-9; elev. 549ft./167m.; mail Troy z 36081; rural
Dunns; RMC Place; COVINGTON; *143 M-7; elev. 264ft./80m.; mail Andalusia z 36420
Dupree; RMC Place; HOUSTON; *143 O-11; elev. 203ft./62m.; mail Ashford z 36312; rural
Dutton; Inc. Place; JACKSON; 142 B-9; elev. 1,360ft./415m.; 🄿; z 35744; Ⓟ 243; © 310
Duval; RMC Place; COVINGTON; mail Opp z 36467; pop. incl. with Opp (Inc. Place)
Dyas; RMC Place; BALDWIN; *143 O-4; elev. 152ft./46m.; mail Bay Minette z 36507; rural
Dyers Crossroads; RMC Place; CULLMAN; *142 C-6; mail Cullman z 35058, Vinemont z 35179; rural

E

Eady City; RMC Place; CHAMBERS; *142 H-11; mail Valley z 36854; pop. incl. with Valley (Inc. Place)
Eagle; RMC Place; WINSTON; *142 D-5; elev. 818ft./249m.; mail Addison z 35540; ● 100
Earlytown; RMC Place; GENEVA; *143 O-9; elev. 226ft./69m.; mail Kinston z 36453; ● 30
Eastaboga; RMC Place; CALHOUN, TALLADEGA; 142 F-9; elev. 600ft./183m.; 🄿; z 36260; ● 330
East Birmingham; RMC Place; JEFFERSON; *142 F-6; ★ BIR; mail Birmingham z 35204; pop. incl. with Birmingham (Inc. Place)
East Boyles; RMC Place; JEFFERSON; ★ BIR; mail Birmingham z 35217; pop. incl. with Birmingham (Inc. Place)
East Brewton; Inc. Place; ESCAMBIA; 143 O-6; elev. 125ft./38m.; 🄿; z 36426 & mail Brewton z 36427; Ⓟ 2,579; © 2,496
East Brookwood; RMC Place; TUSCALOOSA; *142 G-5; mail Brookwood z 35444; ● 210
Eastern Hills; RMC Place; TUSCALOOSA; *142 G-4; elev. 277ft./84m.; ★ TUSC; mail Cottondale z 35453; ● 100
Eastern Valley; RMC Place; JEFFERSON; 143 T-10; elev. 567ft./173m.; ★ BIR; mail Bessemer z 35020, z 35023; ● 2,000
East Florence; RMC Place; LAUDERDALE; *142 A-4; ★ FLO; pop. incl. with Florence (Inc. Place)
East Gadsden; RMC Place; ETOWAH; *142 D-9; elev. 565ft./172m.; ★ GAD; mail Gadsden z 35903; pop. incl. with Gadsden (Inc. Place)
East Hampton; RMC Place; LIMESTONE; *142 A-6; mail Athens z 35611; pop. incl. with Athens (Inc. Place)
East Haven; RMC Place; JEFFERSON; *142 F-7; ★ BIR; mail Birmingham z 35215
East Irondale; RMC Place; JEFFERSON; *142 F-7; ★ BIR; mail Birmingham z 35210; pop. incl. with Irondale (Inc. Place)
East Killen; RMC Place; LAUDERDALE; *142 A-4; ★ FLO; mail Killen z 35645; pop. incl. with Killen (Inc. Place)
East Lake; JEFFERSON; see East Lake Roebuck (RMC Place)
East Lake Roebuck (East Lake); RMC Place; JEFFERSON; *142 F-7; elev. 648ft./198m.; ★ BIR; mail Birmingham z 35206; pop. incl. with Birmingham (Inc. Place)
East Point; RMC Place; CULLMAN; *142 C-6; mail Cullman z 35055, z 35058; ● 80
Eastside; RMC Place; TUSCALOOSA; *142 G-4; ★ TUSC; mail Tuscaloosa z 35404; pop. incl. with Tuscaloosa (Inc. Place)
East Tallassee; RMC Place; TALLAPOOSA; *142 I-9; 🄿; z 36023; pop. incl. with Tallassee (Inc. Place)
East Thomas; RMC Place; JEFFERSON; *142 F-6; ★ BIR; mail Birmingham z 35204; pop. incl. with Birmingham (Inc. Place)
Eastwood; RMC Place; BLOUNT; *142 D-7; elev. 904ft./276m.; mail Oneonta z 35121; pop. incl. with Oneonta (Inc. Place)
Eastwood; RMC Place; JEFFERSON; *142 F-7; ★ BIR; mail Birmingham z 35224; pop. incl. with Birmingham (Inc. Place)
Ebenezer; RMC Place; CULLMAN; *142 C-6; mail Vinemont z 35179; ● 60
Ebenezer; PIKE; see Catalpa (RMC Place)
Echo; RMC Place; DALE; 143 M-11; mail Midland City z 36350, Newville z 36353, Ozark z 36360; ● 140
Echola; RMC Place; TUSCALOOSA; 142 G-3; elev. 290ft./88m.; 🄿; z 35457; ● 150
Echols Crossroads (Bluff City); RMC Place; MORGAN; *142 B-6; mail Somerville z 35670; rural
Echols Hills; RMC Place; MADISON; ★ HNTS; mail Huntsville z 35801; pop. incl. with Huntsville (Inc. Place)
Eclectic; Inc. Place; ELMORE; 142 I-9; elev. 577ft./176m.; 🄿; z 36024; Ⓟ 1,087; © 1,037
Eddings Town; RMC Place; BIBB; *142 G-6; elev. 500ft./152m.; mail Montevallo z 35115; ● 30
Eddy; RMC Place; MARSHALL; *142 C-7; mail Arab z 35016; pop. incl. with Arab (Inc. Place)
Eden; RMC Place; ST. CLAIR; *142 F-8; mail Pell City z 35125; pop. incl. with Pell City (Inc. Place)
Edgefield; RMC Place; BARBOUR; *143 L-11; mail Clayton z 36016; ● 30
Edgefield; RMC Place; JACKSON; *142 A-9; mail Stevenson z 35772; rural
Edgemont; RMC Place; JEFFERSON; *142 F-6; ★ BIR; mail Birmingham z 35209; pop. incl. with Homewood (Inc. Place)
Edgemont Park; RMC Place; JEFFERSON; *142 F-6; ★ BIR; mail Birmingham z 35209; pop. incl. with Homewood (Inc. Place)
Edgewater; CDP; JEFFERSON; 143 R-10; ★ BIR; mail Birmingham z 35224; © 730
Edmonton Heights; RMC Place; MADISON; *142 A-7; ★ HNTS; mail Huntsville z 35810; pop. incl. with Huntsville (Inc. Place)
Edna; RMC Place; CHOCTAW; 142 J-2; mail Ward z 36922; ● 50
Edwards; MACON; see Downs (RMC Place)
Edwardsville; Inc. Place; CLEBURNE; 142 E-10; elev. 940ft./287m.; 🄿; z 36261; Ⓟ 118; © 186
Edwin; RMC Place; HENRY; 143 M-11; elev. 391ft./119m.; mail Clopton z 36317; ● 150
Egypt; RMC Place; ETOWAH; *142 D-8; mail Altoona z 35952; rural
Egypt; RMC Place; MARSHALL; *142 C-7; elev. 1,000ft./305m.; mail Arab z 35016; rural
Eight Mile; RMC Place; MOBILE; *143 P-2; elev. 40ft./12m.; 🄿; ★ MOB; z 36613 & mail Mobile z 36663; pop. incl. with Prichard (Inc. Place)
Elamville; RMC Place; BARBOUR; 143 M-10; elev. 524ft./160m.; mail Ariton z 36311; ● 100
Elba; Inc. Place; ⊡ COFFEE; 143 N-9; elev. 193ft./59m.; 🄿 🄷; z 36323; Ⓟ 4,011; © 4,185
Elberta; Inc. Place; BALDWIN; 143 Q-4; elev. 48ft./15m.; 🄿; z 36530; Ⓟ 458; © 552
Eldridge; Inc. Place; WALKER; 142 D-4; elev. 593ft./181m.; 🄿; z 35554; Ⓟ 225; © 184
Elgin; RMC Place; LAUDERDALE; 142 A-5; elev. 643ft./196m.; ★ FLO; mail Rogersville z 35652; ● 400
Elias; CLAY; see Cleveland Crossroads (RMC Place)
Eliska; RMC Place; MONROE; 143 N-4; elev. 143ft./44m.; mail Uriah z 36480; ● 50
Elkmont; Inc. Place; LIMESTONE; 142 A-6; elev. 800ft./244m.; 🄿; z 35620; Ⓟ 389; © 470
Elkwood; RMC Place; MADISON; 142 A-7; ★ HNTS; mail Toney z 35773
Ellards; RMC Place; PERRY; *142 H-5; mail Brent z 35034; rural
Elliotsville; RMC Place; SHELBY; *142 G-6; elev. 500ft./152m.; ★ BIR; mail Alabaster z 35007, Siluria z 35144; pop. incl. with Alabaster (Inc. Place)
Ellisville; RMC Place; BALDWIN; *143 P-3; mail Loxley z 36551; rural
Ellisville (Coloma); RMC Place; CHEROKEE; 142 D-10; elev. 577ft./176m.; mail Centre z 35960; ● 90
Elm Bluff (Shepardville); RMC Place; DALLAS; *143 K-6; elev. 350ft./107m.; mail Minter z 36761; rural
Elmore; Inc. Place; ELMORE; 142 I-8; elev. 184ft./56m.; 🄿; ★ MTGY; z 36025; © 199; Ⓡ 261
ELMORE; 142 I-9; Ⓟ 49,210; © 65,874; ◆ 80,805
Elrath (Pollards Bend); RMC Place; CHEROKEE; *142 D-10; mail Leesburg z 35983; ● 70
Elrod; RMC Place; TUSCALOOSA; 142 G-3; elev. 252ft./77m.; 🄿; z 35458; ● 450
Elsanor; RMC Place; BALDWIN; 143 Q-4; mail Robertsdale z 36567; ● 60
Elsmeade; RMC Place; MONTGOMERY; *142 J-8; ★ MTGY; mail Montgomery z 36116; pop. incl. with Montgomery (Inc. Place)
Elting; RMC Place; LAUDERDALE; *142 A-4; ★ FLO; mail Florence z 35630; pop. incl. with Florence (Inc. Place)
Elyton; RMC Place; JEFFERSON; *142 F-6; ★ BIR; mail Birmingham z 35204; pop. incl. with Birmingham (Inc. Place)
Emelle; Inc. Place; SUMTER; 142 I-2; elev. 254ft./77m.; 🄿; z 35459; Ⓟ 44; © 31
Emerald Shores; RMC Place; LAUDERDALE; *142 A-4; ★ FLO; mail Florence z 35634; ● 430
Empire; RMC Place; WALKER; 142 E-6; elev. 513ft./156m.; 🄿; z 35063; ● 370
Englewood; RMC Place; TUSCALOOSA; *142 G-4; elev. 185ft./56m.; ★ TUSC; mail Tuscaloosa z 35405; ● 350
English Village; RMC Place; JEFFERSON; *142 F-6; ★ BIR; mail Birmingham z 35223; pop. incl. with Mountain Brook (Inc. Place)
English Village; RMC Place; MADISON; ★ HNTS; mail Huntsville z 35802; pop. incl. with Huntsville (Inc. Place)
Enon; RMC Place; BULLOCK; 143 K-10; elev. 541ft./165m.; mail Midway z 36053; ● 50
Enon; RMC Place; CULLMAN; *142 C-6; mail Vinemont z 35179; rural
Enon; RMC Place; HOUSTON; *143 N-11; ★ DOTH; mail Webb z 36376; ● 150
Enon; RMC Place; PIKE; *143 L-10; mail Banks z 36005; rural
Ensley; RMC Place; JEFFERSON; *142 F-6; elev. 519ft./158m.; 🄿; ★ BIR; z 35218; pop. incl. with Birmingham (Inc. Place)
Ensley Heights; JEFFERSON; see West Ensley (RMC Place)
Enterprise; RMC Place; CHILTON; *142 I-7; elev. 671ft./205m.; mail Verbena z 36091; ● 50
Enterprise; Inc. Place; COFFEE, DALE; 143 N-9; elev. 349ft./106m.; 🄿 🄷 ■; z 36330-31; Ⓟ 20,123; © 21,178; ◆ 24,482
Eoda; RMC Place; COVINGTON; 143 N-8; elev. 393ft./120m.; mail Andalusia z 36420; rural
Eoline; RMC Place; BIBB; 142 H-5; elev. 270ft./82m.; mail Centreville z 35042; ● 100
Epes; Inc. Place; SUMTER; 142 I-2; elev. 159ft./48m.; 🄿; z 35460; Ⓟ 267; © 206
Equality; RMC Place; COOSA; 142 I-8; elev. 713ft./217m.; 🄿; z 36026; ● 150
Erin; RMC Place; CLAY; *142 F-9; mail Lineville z 36266; rural
ESCAMBIA; 143 O-5; Ⓟ 35,518; © 38,440; ◆ 37,493
Escatawpa; RMC Place; WASHINGTON; *143 N-1; mail Vinegar Bend z 36584; ● 40
Estelle; RMC Place; WILCOX; *143 L-5; mail Camden z 36726; rural
Estes Crossroads; RMC Place; CHEROKEE; *142 D-10; elev. 618ft./188m.; mail Piedmont z 36272; rural
Estillfork; RMC Place; JACKSON; 142 A-8; elev. 700ft./213m.; 🄿; z 35745; ● 180
Ethelsville (Ethelville); Inc. Place; PICKENS; 142 F-2; elev. 345ft./105m.; 🄿; z 35461; Ⓟ 52; © 81
Ethelville; PICKENS; see Ethelsville (Inc. Place)
ETOWAH; 142 D-9; Ⓟ 99,840; © 103,459; ◆ 101,911
Euclid Estates; RMC Place; JEFFERSON; *142 F-7; ★ BIR; mail Birmingham z 35217; pop. incl. with Mountain Brook (Inc. Place)
Eufaula; Inc. Place; BARBOUR; 143 L-12; elev. 257ft./78m.; 🄿 🄷; z 36027, z 36072; Ⓟ 13,220; © 13,908
Eulaton; RMC Place; CALHOUN; *142 E-9; ★ ANNI; mail Anniston z 36201; ● 1,450
Eunola; RMC Place; GENEVA; 143 O-9; elev. 145ft./44m.; mail Geneva z 36340; disincorporated April 29, 2007; Ⓟ 199; © 182
Eureka; RMC Place; JACKSON; *142 A-9; mail Stevenson z 35772; rural
Eutaw; Inc. Place; ⊡ GREENE; 142 H-3; elev. 220ft./67m.; 🄿 🄷; z 35462; Ⓟ 2,281; © 1,878
Eva; Inc. Place; MORGAN; 142 C-6; elev. 1,080ft./329m.; 🄿; z 35621; Ⓟ 438; © 491
Evansville; RMC Place; HALE; *142 H-3; elev. 135ft./41m.; mail Akron z 35441; rural
Evergreen; RMC Place; AUTAUGA; *142 I-7; mail Billingsley z 36006; ● 30
Evergreen; Inc. Place; ⊡ CONECUH; 143 M-6; elev. 367ft./112m.; 🄿; z 36401; Ⓟ 3,911; © 3,630
Ewell; RMC Place; DALE; 143 M-10; elev. 406ft./124m.; mail Ozark z 36360; ● 130
Excel; Inc. Place; MONROE; 143 N-5; elev. 409ft./125m.; 🄿; z 36439; Ⓟ 571; © 582
Exie; RMC Place; CHEROKEE; *142 D-10; elev. 700ft./213m.; mail Piedmont z 36272; rural
Exmoor; RMC Place; MARENGO; *143 K-3; elev. 124ft./38m.; mail Sweet Water z 36782; rural

F

Fabius; RMC Place; JACKSON; 142 A-9; elev. 474ft./144m.; mail Flat Rock z 35966; ● 50
Fackler; RMC Place; JACKSON; 142 A-9; elev. 610ft./186m.; 🄿; z 35746; ● 400
Fadette; RMC Place; GENEVA; 143 O-10; mail Graceville z 32440, Slocomb z 36375; ● 100
Fairdale; RMC Place; BIBB; *142 H-5; mail Centreville z 35042; pop. incl. with Centreville (Inc. Place)
Fairfax; RMC Place; CHAMBERS; *142 H-11; elev. 657ft./200m.; mail Valley z 36854; pop. incl. with Valley (Inc. Place)
Fairfield; RMC Place; COVINGTON; *143 N-7; elev. 190ft./58m.; mail Andalusia z 36420; ● 30
Fairfield; Inc. Place; JEFFERSON; 142 F-6; elev. 560ft./171m.; 🄿 🄷; ★ BIR; z 35064; Ⓟ 12,200; © 12,381
Fairfield; RMC Place; LAWRENCE; *142 B-5; ★ DEC; mail Moulton z 35650; ● 50
Fairfield Highlands; RMC Place; JEFFERSON; *142 F-6; ★ BIR; mail Birmingham z 35228, Fairfield z 35064; pop. incl. with Midfield (Inc. Place)
Fairford; RMC Place; WASHINGTON; 143 N-2; mail Mc Intosh z 36553; ● 50
Fairhope; Inc. Place; BALDWIN; 143 Q-3; elev. 122ft./37m.; 🄿 🄷; ★ MOB; z 36532-33; Ⓟ 8,490; © 12,480
Fair Meadows; RMC Place; MONTGOMERY; ★ MTGY; pop. incl. with Montgomery (Inc. Place)
Fairmont; LIMESTONE; see Fairmount (RMC Place)
Fairmount (Fairmont); RMC Place; LIMESTONE; *142 A-6; elev. 700ft./213m.; mail Athens z 35611; ● 30
Fairnelson; RMC Place; CONECUH; *143 M-6; elev. 363ft./111m.; mail Evergreen z 36401; rural
Fair Oaks; RMC Place; SUMTER; *142 H-2; mail Panola z 35477; rural
Fairview; RMC Place; CHILTON; 142 I-7; elev. 669ft./204m.; mail Clanton z 35045; ● 30
Fairview; RMC Place; COFFEE; *143 N-9; elev. 318ft./97m.; mail Elba z 36323, Enterprise z 36330, Samson z 36477; ● 30
Fairview; RMC Place; CONECUH; *143 N-6; elev. 262ft./80m.; mail Evergreen z 36401; ● 100
Fairview; Inc. Place; CULLMAN; 142 C-7; elev. 926ft./282m.; mail Cullman z 35058; Ⓟ 383; © 522
Fairview; RMC Place; DEKALB; *142 C-9; mail Dawson z 35963; rural
Fairview (Five Points West Shopping City); RMC Place; JEFFERSON; *142 F-6; ★ BIR; mail Birmingham z 35208
Fairview; RMC Place; LIMESTONE; *142 A-6; ★ HNTS; mail Athens z 35611; ● 50
Fairview; RMC Place; MARION; *142 C-3; mail Hackleburg z 35564; pop. incl. with Hackleburg (Inc. Place)
Fairview; RMC Place; MOBILE; *143 P-2; elev. 210ft./64m.; ★ MOB; mail Wilmer z 36587; ● 1,800
Fairview; RMC Place; MORGAN; *142 B-6; ★ DEC; mail Decatur z 35601; pop. incl. with Decatur (Inc. Place)
Fairview; RMC Place; PICKENS; *142 F-3; elev. 395ft./120m.; mail Gordo z 35466; ● 30
Fairview; RMC Place; ST. CLAIR; *142 E-8; mail Ragland z 35131; rural
Fairview; RMC Place; WINSTON; *142 D-5; mail Addison z 35540; rural
Fairview West; RMC Place; CULLMAN; *142 D-6; mail Hanceville z 35077; rural
Falco; RMC Place; COVINGTON; *143 O-7; elev. 264ft./80m.; mail Wing z 36483; rural
Falkville; Inc. Place; MORGAN; 142 C-6; elev. 611ft./186m.; 🄿; ★ DEC; z 35622; Ⓟ 1,337; © 1,202
Falls City; RMC Place; WINSTON; *142 D-5; elev. 552ft./168m.; mail Double Springs z 35553; ● 30
Fannie; RMC Place; ESCAMBIA; *143 O-5; elev. 90ft./27m.; mail Flomaton z 36441; rural
Farill; RMC Place; CHEROKEE; *142 C-10; elev. 664ft./202m.; mail Cedar Bluff z 35959; ● 50
Farley; RMC Place; MADISON; ★ HNTS; mail Huntsville z 35802; pop. incl. with Huntsville (Inc. Place)
Farmersville; RMC Place; LOWNDES; 143 K-6; elev. 287ft./87m.; mail Minter z 36761; ● 60
Farmville (The Bottle); RMC Place; LEE; *142 I-10; mail Opelika z 36801; ● 80
Fatama; RMC Place; WILCOX; 143 L-5; mail Camden z 36726; rural
Faunsdale; Inc. Place; MARENGO; 142 J-4; elev. 208ft./63m.; 🄿; z 36738; Ⓟ 96; © 87
Fayette; Inc. Place; ⊡ FAYETTE; 142 E-3; elev. 360ft./110m.; 🄿 🄷; z 35555; Ⓟ 4,909; © 4,922
FAYETTE; 142 E-4; Ⓟ 17,962; © 18,495; ◆ 17,137
Fayetteville; RMC Place; TALLADEGA; 142 G-8; mail Sylacauga z 35151; ● 500
Ferguson Crossroad (Fergusons Cross Roads); RMC Place; ST. CLAIR; *142 D-8; elev. 836ft./255m.; mail Gallant z 35972; ● 30
Fergusons Cross Roads; ST. CLAIR; see Ferguson Crossroad (RMC Place)
Fernbank; RMC Place; LAMAR; 142 F-2; elev. 260ft./79m.; mail Millport z 35576; ● 30
Fernland; RMC Place; MOBILE; *143 Q-2; elev. 113ft./34m.; ★ MOB; mail Grand Bay z 36541
Fernwood Estates; RMC Place; JEFFERSON; *142 F-7; ★ BIR; mail Birmingham z 35215; pop. incl. with Center Point (CDP-Census Area Only)
Fieldstown; RMC Place; JEFFERSON; *143 P-11; ★ BIR; mail Gardendale z 35071
Fig Tree; RMC Place; AUTAUGA; *142 J-6; elev. 397ft./121m.; mail Jones z 36749; ● 80
Finchburg; RMC Place; MONROE; *143 M-4; mail Franklin z 36444; ● 60
Finley Crossing; RMC Place; CLARKE; *143 L-4; mail Thomasville z 36784; rural
Fisher Crossroads; RMC Place; DEKALB; *142 B-10; mail Fort Payne z 35967; pop. incl. with Fort Payne (Inc. Place)
Fish Pond; RMC Place; LAWRENCE; *142 B-5; mail Hillsboro z 35643; ● 50
Fish River; RMC Place; BALDWIN; *143 Q-3; ★ MOB; mail Magnolia Springs z 36555; ● 250
Fisk; RMC Place; MADISON; 142 A-7; ★ HNTS; mail Hazel Green z 35750; rural
Fitzpatrick; RMC Place; BULLOCK; 143 K-9; elev. 266ft./81m.; 🄿; z 36029; ● 60
Five Points; RMC Place; BLOUNT; *142 D-7; mail Cleveland z 35049; rural
Five Points; Inc. Place; CHAMBERS; 142 H-11; elev. 870ft./265m.; 🄿; z 36855; Ⓟ 200; © 146
Five Points; RMC Place; CLEBURNE; *142 F-10; mail Heflin z 36264; rural
Five Points; RMC Place; DALE; *143 N-10; ★ DOTH; mail Newton z 36352; rural
Five Points; RMC Place; DALLAS; *143 K-5; elev. 202ft./62m.; mail Orrville z 36767; ● 50
Five Points; RMC Place; ELMORE; *142 J-8; ★ MTGY; mail Elmore z 36025; ● 60
Five Points; RMC Place; HOUSTON; *143 O-11; elev. 183ft./56m.; mail Cottonwood z 36320; pop. incl. with Madrid (Inc. Place)

Entries in **UPPERCASE** are counties.
Entries in **bold** have populations of 2,500 or more.
Names in parentheses are alternate names.

Inc. Place	Incorporated Place
RMC Place	Rand McNally Designated Place
CDP	Census Designated Place
MCD	Minor Civil Division
⊡	County Seat
▲	Minor Civil Division
elev.	Elevation
🄿	Post Office
🄷	Hospital
🄲	College
■	Principal Business Center
★	Ranally Metro Area (RMA) Abbreviation
z	Zip Code(s)
Ⓟ	Previous Census Population
Ⓡ	Revised Census Population
Ⓐ	Annexation Population
●	Rand McNally Population Estimate
©	Final Census Population
Ⓢ	Special Census Population
◆	Estimated Population

For additional definitions see Glossary, Volume 1, and Introduction, Volume 2.

Five Points; RMC Place; LAWRENCE; 142 B-5; ★ DEC; mail Danville z 35619, Little River z 36550; ● 60
Five Points; RMC Place; MADISON; *142 A-7; ★ HNTS; mail Huntsville z 35801; ● 50
Five Points; RMC Place; MARSHALL; *142 C-8; mail Langston z 35755; ● 30
Five Points; RMC Place; WALKER; *142 E-5; elev. 531ft./162m.; mail Jasper z 35503-04; pop. incl. with Jasper (Inc. Place)
Five Points East; RMC Place; JEFFERSON; *142 F-7; elev. 715ft./218m.; ★ BIR; mail Birmingham z 35210; pop. incl. with Irondale (Inc. Place)
Five Points West Shopping City; JEFFERSON; see Fairview (RMC Place)
Flat Creek; RMC Place; JEFFERSON, WALKER; 142 E-5; ★ BIR; mail Quinton z 35130; rural
Flat Rock; RMC Place; CLAY; mail Lineville z 36266; pop. incl. with Lineville (Inc. Place)
Flat Rock; RMC Place; CONECUH; *143 M-6; elev. 375ft./114m.; mail Evergreen z 36401; rural
Flat Rock; RMC Place; JACKSON; 142 A-10; elev. 1,357ft./414m.; 🅿; z 35966; ● 150
Flat Top; RMC Place; JEFFERSON; *142 E-6; elev. 360ft./110m.; ★ BIR; mail Dora z 35062; rural
Flatwood; RMC Place; MONTGOMERY; *142 J-8; ★ MTGY; mail Montgomery z 36110; rural
Flatwood; RMC Place; WALKER; *142 D-4; mail Carbon Hill z 35549, Nauvoo z 35578; rural
Flatwood; RMC Place; WILCOX; 143 K-4; mail Catherine z 36728; ● 150
Flatwoods; RMC Place; LOWNDES; *143 K-8; elev. 435ft./133m.; mail Fort Deposit z 36032; ● 30
Fleetwood; RMC Place; TUSCALOOSA; *142 G-5; mail Cottondale z 35453; ● 270
Fleming Meadows; RMC Place; MADISON; *142 B-7; ★ HNTS; mail Huntsville z 35802; pop. incl. with Huntsville (Inc. Place)
Flemington Heights; RMC Place; MADISON; *142 B-7; ★ HNTS; mail Huntsville z 35802; pop. incl. with Huntsville (Inc. Place)
Fleta; RMC Place; MONTGOMERY; *143 K-8; elev. 305ft./93m.; mail Hope Hull z 36043; rural
Flint; MORGAN; see Flint City (RMC Place)
Flint City (Flint); RMC Place; MORGAN; *142 B-6; elev. 620ft./189m.; ★ DEC; mail Decatur z 35601; pop. incl. with Decatur (Inc. Place)
Flomaton; Inc. Place; ESCAMBIA; 143 O-5; elev. 72ft./22m.; 🅿; z 36441; ℗ 1,811; © 1,588
Florala; Inc. Place; COVINGTON; 143 O-8; elev. 330ft./101m.; 🅿 🅷; z 36442; ℗ 2,075; © 1,964
Floral Crest; RMC Place; JACKSON; *142 A-10; mail Bryant z 35958, Trenton z 35774; ● 50
Florence; Inc. Place; ⊡ LAUDERDALE; 142 E-13; elev. 541ft./165m.; 🅿 🅷 🅲 6,950 ■; ★ FLO; z 35630-34; ℗ 36,426; © 36,264; ◆ 33,869
Florette; RMC Place; MORGAN; 142 C-7; mail Somerville z 35670
Flower Hill; RMC Place; LAWRENCE; *142 B-5; elev. 613ft./187m.; mail Hillsboro z 35643; rural
Floyd; RMC Place; ELMORE; 142 I-9; elev. 460ft./140m.; mail Tallassee z 36078; ● 30
Foley; Inc. Place; BALDWIN; 143 Q-4; elev. 74ft./23m.; 🅿 🅷; z 36535-36; ℗ 4,937; © 7,590
Ford City; RMC Place; COLBERT; *142 A-4; ★ FLO; mail Sheffield z 35660; ● 100
Forest; RMC Place; PICKENS; *142 F-2; mail Ethelsville z 35461; ● 150
Forest Brook Estates; RMC Place; JEFFERSON; ★ BIR; mail Birmingham z 35226; pop. incl. with Hoover (Inc. Place)
Forestdale; CDP; JEFFERSON; 143 Q-11; 🅿; ★ BIR; z 35214 & mail Adamsville z 35005; ℗ 10,395; © 10,509
Forester Chapel; RMC Place; RANDOLPH; *142 G-10; elev. 952ft./290m.; mail Wadley z 36276; rural
Forest Hill; RMC Place; MOBILE; *143 P-2; elev. 188ft./57m.; ★ MOB; mail Mobile z 36608; pop. incl. with Mobile (Inc. Place)
Forest Hills; RMC Place; CALHOUN; *142 F-9; ★ ANNI; mail Oxford z 36203; pop. incl. with Oxford (Inc. Place)
Forest Hills; RMC Place; JEFFERSON; *142 F-6; ★ BIR; mail Fairfield z 35064; pop. incl. with Fairfield (Inc. Place)
Forest Hills; RMC Place; LAUDERDALE; *142 A-4; ★ FLO; mail Florence z 35630; pop. incl. with Florence (Inc. Place)
Forest Hills; RMC Place; TALLADEGA; *142 G-8; mail Childersburg z 35044; pop. incl. with Childersburg (Inc. Place)
Forest Home; RMC Place; BUTLER; 143 L-6; elev. 550ft./168m.; 🅿; z 36030; ● 150
Forest Park; RMC Place; JEFFERSON; *142 F-6; ★ BIR; mail Birmingham z 35222; pop. incl. with Birmingham (Inc. Place)
Forest Park; RMC Place; MOBILE; *143 P-2; ★ MOB; mail Mobile z 36608; pop. incl. with Mobile (Inc. Place)
Forkland; Inc. Place; GREENE; 142 I-3; elev. 152ft./46m.; 🅿; z 36740; ℗ 667; © 629
Forkville; RMC Place; WINSTON; 142 C-4; mail Haleyville z 35565; ● 30
Forney; RMC Place; CHEROKEE; 142 D-10; mail Centre z 35960; ● 100
Fort Dale; RMC Place; BUTLER; *143 L-7; elev. 515ft./157m.; mail Greenville z 36037; rural
Fort Davis; RMC Place; MACON; 143 K-10; elev. 317ft./97m.; 🅿; z 36031; ● 310
Fort Deposit; Inc. Place; LOWNDES; 143 K-7; elev. 445ft./136m.; 🅿; z 36032; ℗ 1,240; © 1,270
Fort Mitchell; RMC Place; RUSSELL; 142 J-12; elev. 317ft./97m.; 🅿; z 36856 & mail Holy Trinity z 36859; ● 750
Fort Morgan; RMC Place; BALDWIN; 143 R-3; mail Gulf Shores z 36542; ● 50
Fort Payne; Inc. Place; ⊡ DEKALB; 142 C-10; elev. 899ft./274m.; 🅿 🅷; z 35967-68; ℗ 11,838; © 12,938
Fort Rucker; CDP-Census Area Only; DALE; *143 N-10; 🅿; z 36362; ℗ 7,593; © 6,052
Fosheeton; RMC Place; TALLAPOOSA; *142 H-9; elev. 758ft./231m.; mail Alexander City z 35010; rural
Fosters (Sylvan); RMC Place; TUSCALOOSA; 142 H-4; elev. 150ft./46m.; 🅿; z 35463; ● 300
Fostoria; RMC Place; LOWNDES; 143 K-6; elev. 229ft./70m.; mail Minter z 36761; ● 50
Fountain; RMC Place; MONROE; 143 M-5; elev. 396ft./121m.; mail Monroeville z 36460-61; ● 120
Fountain Heights; RMC Place; JEFFERSON; *142 F-6; ★ BIR; mail Birmingham z 35204; pop. incl. with Birmingham (Inc. Place)
Fourmile; RMC Place; SHELBY; *142 G-7; mail Wilsonville z 35186; rural
Four Roads; RMC Place; DEKALB; *142 B-10; elev. 458ft./140m.; mail Mentone z 35984; ● 30
Four Wing Lake; RMC Place; SHELBY; *142 G-7; elev. 600ft./183m.; mail Alabaster z 35007; rural
Fowlers Crossroads; RMC Place; FAYETTE; *142 E-4; elev. 658ft./201m.; mail Bankston z 35542; rural
Fowl River; RMC Place; MOBILE; *143 Q-2; elev. 26ft./8m.; ★ MOB; mail Theodore z 36582; ● 100
Fox; RMC Place; TUSCALOOSA; ★ TUSC; mail Tuscaloosa z 35401
Foxwood; RMC Place; MONTGOMERY; *142 J-8; elev. 261ft./80m.; mail Pike Road z 36064; ● 30
Frances Heights; RMC Place; JEFFERSON; *142 F-6; ★ BIR; mail Fultondale z 35068; pop. incl. with Fultondale (Inc. Place)
Francisco; RMC Place; JACKSON; 142 A-8; elev. 770ft./235m.; mail Huntland z 37345; rural
Francis Mill; RMC Place; CALHOUN; *142 E-9; mail Ohatchee z 36271; rural
Frankfort; RMC Place; FRANKLIN; 142 B-3; elev. 741ft./226m.; mail Russellville z 35653; ● 70
Franklin; Inc. Place; MACON; *142 J-9; elev. 220ft./67m.; mail Tuskegee z 36083; ℗ 152; © 149
Franklin; RMC Place; MONROE; 143 L-4; elev. 335ft./102m.; 🅿; z 36444; ● 120
FRANKLIN; 142 B-3; ℗ 27,814; © 31,223; ◆ 29,689
Frankville; RMC Place; WASHINGTON; 143 M-2; elev. 149ft./45m.; 🅿; z 36538; ● 300
Fredonia; RMC Place; CHAMBERS; 142 H-11; elev. 789ft./240m.; mail Five Points z 36855; ● 70
Freemanville; RMC Place; ESCAMBIA; 143 O-4; mail Atmore z 36502; ● 350
Fremont; RMC Place; AUTAUGA; *142 I-6; elev. 180ft./55m.; mail Jones z 36749; rural
French Mill; RMC Place; LIMESTONE; *142 A-6; mail Athens z 35613; ● 80
Fresco; COFFEE; see Frisco (RMC Place)
Fridays Crossing; RMC Place; BLOUNT; *142 D-7; elev. 819ft./250m.; mail Oneonta z 35121; pop. incl. with Susan Moore (Inc. Place)
Friendship; RMC Place; BUTLER; *143 M-7; elev. 348ft./106m.; mail Georgiana z 36033; rural
Friendship; RMC Place; COVINGTON; *143 N-8; elev. 408ft./124m.; mail Opp z 36467; ● 30
Friendship; RMC Place; ELMORE; 142 I-9; elev. 479ft./146m.; mail Tallassee z 36078; ● 110
Friendship; RMC Place; MARSHALL; *142 C-7; elev. 1,019ft./311m.; mail Arab z 35016; rural
Friendship; RMC Place; MONTGOMERY; *143 K-8; elev. 500ft./152m.; mail Grady z 36036; rural
Frisco (Fresco); RMC Place; COFFEE; *143 M-9; elev. 400ft./122m.; mail Brundidge z 36010, Jack z 36346; ● 60
Frisco City; Inc. Place; MONROE; 143 M-5; elev. 401ft./122m.; 🅿; z 36445; ℗ 1,581; © 1,460
Frisco Quarters; RMC Place; WALKER; *142 E-5; elev. 320ft./98m.; mail Jasper z 35501; pop. incl. with Jasper (Inc. Place)
Frog Mountain (Frog Mountains); RMC Place; CHEROKEE; *142 D-10; elev. 666ft./203m.; mail Piedmont z 36272; rural
Frog Mountains; CHEROKEE; see Frog Mountain (RMC Place)
Frog Pond; LAUDERDALE; see Houstontown (RMC Place)
Frost; RMC Place; BIBB; mail Centreville z 35042; pop. incl. with Centreville (Inc. Place)
Fruitdale; RMC Place; WASHINGTON; 143 N-1; elev. 200ft./61m.; 🅿; z 36539; ● 520
Fruithurst; Inc. Place; CLEBURNE; 142 E-11; elev. 1,082ft./330m.; 🅿; z 36262; ℗ 177; © 270
Fry; RMC Place; MARSHALL; *142 C-7; elev. 1,000ft./305m.; mail Arab z 35016; rural
Fullers Crossroads; RMC Place; CRENSHAW; *143 L-8; mail Luverne z 36049; ● 30
Fullerton; RMC Place; CHEROKEE; *142 C-10; mail Gaylesville z 35973; rural
Fulton; Inc. Place; CLARKE; 143 L-3; elev. 234ft./71m.; 🅿; z 36446; ℗ 384; © 308
Fulton Bridge; RMC Place; MARION; *142 D-3; mail Hamilton z 35570
Fultondale; Inc. Place; JEFFERSON; 142 F-6; elev. 614ft./187m.; 🅿; ★ BIR; z 35068; ℗ 6,400; © 6,595
Fulton Springs; RMC Place; JEFFERSON; *142 F-6; ★ BIR; mail Fultondale z 35068; pop. incl. with Fultondale (Inc. Place)
Furman; RMC Place; WILCOX; 143 K-6; elev. 293ft./89m.; 🅿; z 36741; ● 200
Fyffe; Inc. Place; DEKALB; 142 C-9; elev. 1,276ft./389m.; 🅿; z 35971; ℗ 1,094; © 971

G

Gadsden; Inc. Place; ⊡ ETOWAH; 142 D-9; elev. 554ft./169m.; 🅿 🅷 ■; ★ GAD; z 35901-07; ℗ 42,523; © 38,978; ◆ 36,455
Gainer; GENEVA; see Ganer (RMC Place)
Gainestown; RMC Place; CLARKE; 143 M-4; elev. 267ft./81m.; 🅿; z 36540 & mail Alma z 36501; ● 90
Gainesville; Inc. Place; SUMTER; 142 H-2; elev. 131ft./40m.; 🅿; z 35464; ℗ 449; © 220
Gallant; RMC Place; ETOWAH; 142 D-8; elev. 800ft./244m.; 🅿; ★ GAD; z 35972; ● 720
Galleria; RMC Place; JEFFERSON; *142 F-6; ★ BIR; mail Birmingham z 35244; pop. incl. with Hoover (Inc. Place)
Gallion; RMC Place; HALE; 142 J-4; elev. 200ft./61m.; 🅿; z 36742; ● 220
Gamble; RMC Place; WALKER; *142 E-5; elev. 503ft./153m.; mail Jasper z 35503; ● 30
Gandys Cove; RMC Place; MORGAN; *142 C-6; elev. 800ft./244m.; mail Falkville z 35622; rural
Ganer (Gainer); RMC Place; GENEVA; 143 O-9; mail Samson z 36477; ● 100
Gann Crossroad; RMC Place; DEKALB; *142 A-10; elev. 1,683ft./513m.; mail Ider z 35981; ● 30
Gantt; Inc. Place; COVINGTON; 143 N-7; elev. 230ft./70m.; 🅿; z 36038; ℗ 265; © 241
Gantts Junction; RMC Place; TALLADEGA; *142 G-8; elev. 559ft./170m.; mail Sylacauga z 35151
Gantts Quarry; RMC Place; TALLADEGA; 142 G-8; mail Sylacauga z 35151; disincorporated December 31, 2001; ℗ 7
Garden; RMC Place; PICKENS; *142 G-2; mail Aliceville z 35442; rural
Garden City; Inc. Place; CULLMAN, BLOUNT; 142 D-7; elev. 496ft./151m.; 🅿; z 35070; ℗ 578; © 564
Gardendale; Inc. Place; JEFFERSON; 142 E-6; elev. 663ft./202m.; 🅿; ★ BIR; z 35071; ℗ 9,251; © 11,626
Garden Highlands; RMC Place; JEFFERSON; *142 F-6; ★ BIR; mail Birmingham z 35211; pop. incl. with Birmingham (Inc. Place)
Gardiners Gin; RMC Place; WALKER; 142 E-5; mail Cordova z 35550; ● 400
Garland; RMC Place; BUTLER; 143 M-6; mail Mc Kenzie z 36456; ● 70
Garth; RMC Place; JACKSON; 142 B-8; elev. 654ft./199m.; mail Paint Rock z 35764; ● 120
Gary Springs; RMC Place; BIBB; *142 H-6; mail Centreville z 35042; ● 30
Garywood; RMC Place; JEFFERSON; *142 F-6; ★ BIR; mail Bessemer z 35023; pop. incl. with Birmingham (Inc. Place)
Gasque; RMC Place; BALDWIN; 143 R-3; mail Gulf Shores z 36542
Gastonburg; RMC Place; WILCOX; 143 K-4; mail Catherine z 36728; ● 80
Gate City; RMC Place; JEFFERSON; *142 F-7; ★ BIR; mail Birmingham z 35212; pop. incl. with Birmingham (Inc. Place)
Gaylesville; Inc. Place; CHEROKEE; 142 C-10; elev. 586ft./179m.; 🅿; z 35973; ℗ 149; © 140
Gay Meadows; RMC Place; MONTGOMERY; ★ MTGY; mail Montgomery z 36111; pop. incl. with Montgomery (Inc. Place)
Gees Bend; WILCOX; see Boykin (RMC Place)
Geiger; Inc. Place; SUMTER; 142 H-2; mail Emelle z 35459; ℗ 270; © 161
Genery; RMC Place; JEFFERSON; *142 G-6; ★ BIR; mail Bessemer z 35020; ● 100
Geneva; Inc. Place; ⊡ GENEVA; 143 O-9; elev. 105ft./32m.; 🅿 🅷; z 36340; ℗ 4,681; © 4,388
GENEVA; 143 O-10; ℗ 23,647; © 25,764; ◆ 25,311
Gentilly Forest; RMC Place; JEFFERSON; ★ BIR; mail Birmingham z 35216; pop. incl. with Vestavia Hills (Inc. Place)
Georgetown; RMC Place; MOBILE; *143 O-2; ★ MOB; mail Chunchula z 36521; ● 120
Georgia; RMC Place; MORGAN; *142 C-6; ★ DEC; mail Hartselle z 35640; pop. incl. with Hartselle (Inc. Place)
Georgiana; Inc. Place; BUTLER; 143 M-7; elev. 293ft./89m.; 🅿 🅷; z 36033; ℗ 1,933; © 1,737
Gerald; RMC Place; DALE; *143 N-10; elev. 182ft./55m.; mail Daleville z 36322
Geraldine; Inc. Place; DEKALB; 142 C-9; elev. 1,148ft./350m.; 🅿; z 35974; ℗ 801; © 786
Germania; RMC Place; JEFFERSON; *142 F-6; ★ BIR; mail Birmingham z 35211; pop. incl. with Birmingham (Inc. Place)
Gibson Crossroads; RMC Place; DEKALB; *142 B-9; elev. 1,260ft./384m.; mail Fyffe z 35971; rural
Gibsonville; RMC Place; CLAY; *142 G-9; elev. 832ft./254m.; mail Ashland z 36251; ● 30
Gilbert Crossroads; RMC Place; DEKALB; *142 C-9; mail Dawson z 35963; rural
Gilbertown; Inc. Place; CHOCTAW; 143 L-2; elev. 150ft./46m.; 🅿; z 36908; ℗ 235; © 187
Gilbertsboro; RMC Place; LIMESTONE; *142 A-6; elev. 600ft./183m.; mail Lester z 35647; rural
Giles; RMC Place; BIBB; *142 G-5; mail Woodstock z 35188; rural
Gilliam Springs; RMC Place; MARSHALL; mail Arab z 35016; pop. incl. with Arab (Inc. Place)
Gilmore; RMC Place; JEFFERSON; mail Bessemer z 35023; ● 30
Gipsy; RMC Place; LIMESTONE; *142 A-6; mail Elkmont z 35620; rural
Girard; RMC Place; RUSSELL; 167 R-2; ★ COL; mail Phenix City z 36869; pop. incl. with Phenix City (Inc. Place)
Glades; RMC Place; CLAY; *142 G-9; elev. 1,023ft./312m.; mail Millerville z 36267; rural
Gladstone; RMC Place; MADISON; *142 A-7; ★ HNTS; mail Huntsville z 35806; rural
Glascow Hill; JEFFERSON; see Glasgow (RMC Place)
Glasgow (Glascow Hill); RMC Place; JEFFERSON; *142 F-6; elev. 412ft./126m.; ★ BIR; mail Adamsville z 35005; ● 100
Glass; RMC Place; CHAMBERS; *142 I-11; mail Valley z 36854
Gleandean; RMC Place; LEE; *142 I-10; ★ AU-OP; mail Auburn z 36830; pop. incl. with Auburn (Inc. Place)
Glen Acres (Glenn Acres); RMC Place; MOBILE; *143 P-2; elev. 223ft./68m.; ★ MOB; mail Mobile z 36608; ● 500
Glen Allen; Inc. Place; MARION, FAYETTE; 142 D-4; elev. 553ft./169m.; 🅿; z 35559; ℗ 350; © 442
Glen City; RMC Place; ST. CLAIR; *142 F-8; mail Pell City z 35125, z 35128; pop. incl. with Pell City (Inc. Place)
Glencoe; Inc. Place; ETOWAH, CALHOUN; 142 D-9; elev. 600ft./183m.; 🅿; ★ GAD; z 35905; ℗ 4,670; © 5,152
Glencoe; RMC Place; JEFFERSON; *142 F-7; ★ BIR; mail Birmingham z 35213; pop. incl. with Mountain Brook (Inc. Place)
Glen Hills; RMC Place; JEFFERSON; *142 F-6; ★ BIR; mail Bessemer z 35020; pop. incl. with Bessemer (Inc. Place)
Glen Mary; RMC Place; WINSTON; *142 D-4; elev. 701ft./214m.; mail Natural Bridge z 35577; ● 50
Glenn Acres; MOBILE; see Glen Acres (RMC Place)
Glen Oaks; RMC Place; JEFFERSON; *142 F-6; ★ BIR; mail Fairfield z 35064; pop. incl. with Fairfield (Inc. Place)
Glenville; RMC Place; RUSSELL; 143 K-11; elev. 461ft./141m.; mail Pittsview z 36871
Glenwood; Inc. Place; CRENSHAW; 143 M-8; elev. 285ft./87m.; 🅿; z 36034; ℗ 208; © 191
Gnatville; RMC Place; CHEROKEE; *142 D-10; elev. 679ft./207m.; mail Piedmont z 36272; ● 30
Godwin Estates; RMC Place; JEFFERSON; *142 E-7; ★ BIR; mail Birmingham z 35215
Gold Branch; RMC Place; COOSA; *142 H-8; mail Weogufka z 35183; rural
Golden Springs; RMC Place; CALHOUN; *142 E-9; ★ ANNI; mail Anniston z 36207; pop. incl. with Anniston (Inc. Place)
Gold Hill (Gold Ridge); RMC Place; LEE; 142 I-10; mail Waverly z 36879; ● 90
Gold Mine; RMC Place; MARION; *142 D-4; elev. 596ft./182m.; mail Brilliant z 35548; rural
Gold Ridge; RMC Place; CULLMAN; *142 C-7; mail Cullman z 35058; rural
Gold Ridge; LEE; see Gold Hill (RMC Place)
Gold Ridge; RMC Place; RANDOLPH; *142 F-11; elev. 1,116ft./340m.; mail Graham z 36263; ● 30
Goldville; Inc. Place; TALLAPOOSA; 142 G-9; elev. 1,018ft./310m.; mail Cragford z 36255, Wadley z 36276; ℗ 61; © 37
Gonce; RMC Place; JACKSON; *142 A-9; mail Stevenson z 35772; rural
Good Hope; Inc. Place; CULLMAN; 142 D-6; elev. 601ft./183m.; mail Cullman z 35055, z 35057; ℗ 1,700; © 1,966
Good Hope; RMC Place; ELMORE; *142 I-9; mail Eclectic z 36024; rural
Goodman; RMC Place; COFFEE; *143 N-9; mail Enterprise z 36330, New Brockton z 36351; ● 30
Good Spring; FRANKLIN; see Good Springs (RMC Place)
Good Springs (Good Spring); RMC Place; FRANKLIN; *142 B-4; elev. 591ft./180m.; mail Vina z 35593; rural
Good Springs; RMC Place; LIMESTONE; 142 A-5; mail Anderson z 35610; ● 100
Goodsprings; RMC Place; WALKER; 142 E-5; 🅿; z 35560; ● 450
Goodwater; Inc. Place; COOSA; 142 H-9; elev. 870ft./265m.; 🅿; z 35072; ℗ 1,840; © 1,633
Goodway; RMC Place; MONROE; 143 N-4; elev. 383ft./117m.; 🅿; z 36449; ● 200
Goodyear; RMC Place; ETOWAH; ★ GAD; mail Gadsden z 35903; pop. incl. with Gadsden (Inc. Place)
Goose Pond Crossroads; RMC Place; JACKSON; *142 B-9; mail Scottsboro z 35769; pop. incl. with Scottsboro (Inc. Place)
Gordo; Inc. Place; PICKENS; 142 G-3; elev. 274ft./84m.; 🅿; z 35466; ℗ 1,918; © 1,677
Gordon; Inc. Place; HOUSTON; 143 N-12; elev. 166ft./51m.; 🅿; z 36343; ℗ 493; © 408
Gordon Heights; RMC Place; JEFFERSON; *142 F-6; ★ BIR; mail Bessemer z 35020; pop. incl. with Lipscomb (Inc. Place)
Gordonsville (Gordonville); Inc. Place; LOWNDES; 143 K-7; mail Tyler z 36785; © 318
Gordonville; LOWNDES; see Gordonsville (Inc. Place)
Gorgas; RMC Place; WALKER; 142 E-5; mail Parrish z 35580; ● 110
Goshen; Inc. Place; PIKE; 143 L-9; elev. 317ft./97m.; 🅿; z 36035; ℗ 302; © 300
Gosport; RMC Place; CLARKE; 143 M-4; elev. 110ft./34m.; mail Whatley z 36482; ● 80
Gourdsville; RMC Place; LIMESTONE; *142 A-6; elev. 600ft./183m.; mail Lester z 35647; rural
Graball; RMC Place; HENRY; *143 M-11; elev. 485ft./148m.; mail Abbeville z 36310; pop. incl. with Abbeville (Inc. Place)
Grace; RMC Place; BUTLER; *143 M-6; elev. 294ft./90m.; mail Mc Kenzie z 36456; rural
Grady; RMC Place; MONTGOMERY; 143 K-8; elev. 462ft./141m.; 🅿; z 36036; ● 250
Graham; RMC Place; RANDOLPH; 142 F-11; elev. 1,103ft./336m.; 🅿; z 36263; ● 100
Grand Bay; CDP; MOBILE; 143 Q-2; elev. 87ft./27m.; 🅿; ★ MOB; z 36541; ℗ 3,383; © 3,918
Grangeburg; RMC Place; HOUSTON; 143 O-11; mail Gordon z 36343; ● 60
Grant; Inc. Place; MARSHALL; 142 B-8; elev. 1,207ft./368m.; 🅿; z 35747; ℗ 638; © 665
Grantley; RMC Place; CLEBURNE; *142 E-10; elev. 1,012ft./308m.; mail Piedmont z 36272; rural
Grant Town; RMC Place; TALLADEGA; *142 F-9; ★ ANNI; mail Munford z 36268; ● 100
Grasmere; RMC Place; TALLADEGA; *142 F-8; elev. 465ft./142m.; mail Alpine z 35014; rural
Grasselli (Grasselli Heights); RMC Place; JEFFERSON; *142 F-6; ★ BIR; mail Birmingham z 35211; pop. incl. with Birmingham (Inc. Place)
Grasselli Heights; JEFFERSON; see Grasselli (RMC Place)
Grassy; RMC Place; LAUDERDALE; *142 A-5; elev. 780ft./238m.; mail Lexington z 35648; ● 80
Grassy; RMC Place; MARSHALL; *142 C-7; mail Arab z 35016; ● 200
Gravel Hill; RMC Place; FRANKLIN; *142 B-4; mail Green Pond z 35074, Russellville z 35653; pop. incl. with Russellville (Inc. Place)
Gravelly Springs; RMC Place; LAUDERDALE; *142 A-3; mail Florence z 35633; rural
Gray Hill; RMC Place; BIBB; *142 G-6; elev. 465ft./142m.; mail Green Pond z 35074, West Blocton z 35184; ● 30
Graymont; RMC Place; JEFFERSON; *142 F-6; ★ BIR; mail Birmingham z 35204; pop. incl. with Birmingham (Inc. Place)
Grays Chapel; RMC Place; JACKSON; 142 A-8; elev. 700ft./213m.; mail Estillfork z 35745; rural
Grayson; RMC Place; WINSTON; 142 C-5; elev. 900ft./274m.; mail Houston z 35572; ● 300
Grayson Valley; CDP-Census Area Only; JEFFERSON; *142 E-7; ★ BIR; mail Birmingham z 35235; © 5,447
Graystone; RMC Place; BLOUNT; *142 D-7; mail Allgood z 35013; ● 120
Graysville; Inc. Place; JEFFERSON; 142 F-6; elev. 572ft./174m.; 🅿 🅷; ★ BIR; z 35073; ℗ 2,241; © 2,344
Grayton; RMC Place; CALHOUN; *142 E-9; ★ ANNI; mail Ohatchee z 36271; rural
Green Acres; RMC Place; JEFFERSON; *142 F-6; ★ BIR; mail Birmingham z 35228; pop. incl. with Birmingham (Inc. Place)
Greenbrier; RMC Place; LAUDERDALE; *142 A-4; ★ FLO; mail Florence z 35630; pop. incl. with Florence (Inc. Place)
Greenbrier; RMC Place; LIMESTONE; 142 B-6; mail Madison z 35756; ● 100
Green Chapel; RMC Place; DEKALB; *142 B-9; mail Fyffe z 35971; ● 50
GREENE; 142 H-3; ℗ 10,153; © 9,974; ◆ 9,204
Green Hill; RMC Place; LAUDERDALE; 142 A-4; ★ FLO; mail Florence z 35634; ● 600
Green Lantern; RMC Place; MONTGOMERY; *142 J-8; ★ MTGY; mail Montgomery z 36111; pop. incl. with Montgomery (Inc. Place)
Greenleas Heights (North Smithfield Estates); RMC Place; JEFFERSON; *142 F-6; ★ BIR; mail Birmingham z 35214; ● 350
Green Pond; RMC Place; BIBB; 142 G-5; elev. 581ft./177m.; 🅿; z 35074; ● 650
Greensboro; Inc. Place; ⊡ HALE; 142 I-4; elev. 290ft./88m.; 🅿 🅷; z 36744; ℗ 3,047; © 2,731
Greens Chapel; RMC Place; BLOUNT; *142 D-7; mail Cleveland z 35049; rural
Greensport; RMC Place; ST. CLAIR; *142 E-9; ★ GAD; mail Ashville z 35953; rural
Green Springs; RMC Place; JEFFERSON; ★ BIR; mail Birmingham z 35219; pop. incl. with Homewood (Inc. Place)
Green Street; RMC Place; CONECUH; *143 M-5; elev. 400ft./122m.; mail Evergreen z 36401; ● 40
Green Valley; RMC Place; ETOWAH; ★ GAD; mail Gadsden z 35903; pop. incl. with Southside (Inc. Place)
Green Valley; RMC Place; JEFFERSON; ★ BIR; mail Birmingham z 35216
Greenville; Inc. Place; ⊡ BUTLER; 143 L-7; elev. 422ft./129m.; 🅿 🅷; z 36037; ℗ 7,492; © 7,228
Greenwood; RMC Place; CLARKE; *143 L-3; elev. 350ft./107m.; mail Grove Hill z 36451; ● 120
Greenwood; RMC Place; JEFFERSON; *142 G-6; ★ BIR; mail Bessemer z 35020; pop. incl. with Bessemer (Inc. Place)
Greenwood; RMC Place; MACON; mail Tuskegee Institute z 36088
Greenwycke Village; RMC Place; MADISON; *142 B-7; ★ HNTS; mail Huntsville z 35802; pop. incl. with Huntsville (Inc. Place)
Griffith Bend; RMC Place; TALLADEGA; *142 F-8; elev. 500ft./152m.; mail Talladega z 35160; rural
Grimes; Inc. Place; DALE; 143 N-11; elev. 350ft./107m.; ★ DOTH; mail Dothan z 36303; ℗ 443; © 459
Grove Hill; Inc. Place; ⊡ CLARKE; 143 L-3; elev. 478ft./146m.; 🅿 🅷; z 36451; ℗ 1,551; © 1,438
Grove Oak; RMC Place; DEKALB; 142 C-9; elev. 1,200ft./366m.; 🅿; z 35975; ● 200
Grove Park; RMC Place; JEFFERSON; *142 F-6; ★ BIR; mail Birmingham z 35209; pop. incl. with Homewood (Inc. Place)
Grove Park; RMC Place; TALLADEGA; *142 G-8; mail Childersburg z 35044; pop. incl. with Childersburg (Inc. Place)
Grovewood (Grovewood Estates); RMC Place; MONTGOMERY; *142 J-8; ★ MTGY; mail Montgomery z 36108; pop. incl. with Montgomery (Inc. Place)
Grovewood Estates; MONTGOMERY; see Grovewood (RMC Place)
Guerryton; RMC Place; BULLOCK; *143 K-10; mail Hurtsboro z 36860; rural
Guest; RMC Place; DEKALB; *142 C-9; elev. 1,160ft./354m.; mail Fyffe z 35971
Guin; Inc. Place; MARION; 142 D-3; elev. 434ft./132m.; 🅿; z 35563; ℗ 2,464; © 2,389
Guinea; RMC Place; HALE; *142 H-4; elev. 152ft./46m.; mail Moundville z 35474; ● 30
Gulfcrest; RMC Place; MOBILE; *143 O-2; elev. 148ft./45m.; mail Chunchula z 36521; ● 50
Gulf Shores; Inc. Place; BALDWIN; 143 R-4; elev. 6ft./2m.; 🅿; z 36542, z 36547; ℗ 3,261; © 5,044
Gum Pond; RMC Place; MORGAN; *142 C-7; mail Baileyton z 35019, Eva z 35621; rural
Gum Spring; RMC Place; MORGAN; *142 C-6; mail Hartselle z 35640; rural
Gum Springs; RMC Place; BLOUNT; *142 D-7; mail Blountsville z 35031; rural
Guntersville; Inc. Place; ⊡ MARSHALL; 142 C-8; elev. 800ft./244m.; 🅿 🅷; z 35976; ℗ 7,038; © 7,395
Gurley; Inc. Place; MADISON; 142 B-8; elev. 644ft./196m.; 🅿; ★ HNTS; z 35748; ℗ 1,007; © 876
Guthery Crossroads; RMC Place; CULLMAN; *142 D-6; elev. 852ft./260m.; mail Crane Hill z 35053; rural
Gu-Win; Inc. Place; MARION, FAYETTE; 142 D-3; elev. 571ft./174m.; mail Guin z 35563; ℗ 243; © 204

H

Hackleburg; Inc. Place; MARION; 142 C-3; elev. 934ft./285m.; 🅿; z 35564; ℗ 1,161; © 1,527
Hackneyville; RMC Place; TALLAPOOSA; 142 H-9; mail Alexander City z 35010; ● 180
Hacoda; RMC Place; GENEVA; 143 O-8; elev. 151ft./46m.; mail Florala z 36442, Kinston z 36453, Samson z 36477; ● 70
Hagler; RMC Place; TUSCALOOSA; *142 H-5; elev. 264ft./80m.; mail Duncanville z 35456
Haig; JEFFERSON; see Majestic (RMC Place)
HALE; 142 I-4; ℗ 15,498; © 17,185; ® 18,285; ◆ 18,402
Haleburg; Inc. Place; HENRY; 143 N-12; elev. 337ft./103m.; mail Columbia z 36319; ℗ 97; © 108
Haleyville; Inc. Place; WINSTON, MARION; 142 C-4; elev. 931ft./284m.; 🅿 🅷; z 35565; ℗ 4,452; © 4,182
Half Acre; RMC Place; MARENGO; 143 K-3; elev. 116ft./35m.; mail Myrtlewood z 36763; rural
Halls Crossroads; BULLOCK; see Jenkins Crossroads (RMC Place)
Halls Crossroads; RMC Place; MONROE; *143 N-5; elev. 405ft./123m.; mail Frisco City z 36445; rural
Halltown; RMC Place; FRANKLIN; 142 C-3; mail Red Bay z 35582; ● 150
Halsell; RMC Place; CHOCTAW; 142 J-2; elev. 251ft./77m.; mail Lisman z 36912; ● 80
Halso Mill; RMC Place; BUTLER; *143 L-7; elev. 300ft./91m.; mail Greenville z 36037; rural
Hamburg; RMC Place; PERRY; *142 J-5; elev. 223ft./68m.; mail Marion Junction z 36759; rural
Hamburg; RMC Place; WILCOX; *143 L-6; elev. 252ft./77m.; mail Pine Apple z 36768; rural
Hamilton; Inc. Place; ⊡ MARION; 142 D-3; elev. 498ft./152m.; 🅿 🅷; z 35570; ℗ 5,787; © 6,786
Hamilton Crossroads; RMC Place; PIKE; *143 M-9; mail Brundidge z 36010; ● 50
Hammondville; Inc. Place; DEKALB; 142 B-10; elev. 1,000ft./305m.; 🅿; z 35989; ℗ 420; © 486
Hamner; RMC Place; SUMTER; *142 I-2; mail Epes z 35460; rural
Hampden; RMC Place; MARENGO; *143 K-4; mail Arlington z 36722; ● 60
Hanceville; Inc. Place; CULLMAN; 142 D-6; elev. 544ft./166m.; 🅿; z 35077; ℗ 2,246; © 2,951
Hancock Crossroads; RMC Place; JACKSON; *142 B-9; mail Section z 35771; ● 50
Hannah; RMC Place; LIMESTONE; *142 A-6; mail Athens z 35611; pop. incl. with Athens (Inc. Place)
Hannon; RMC Place; MACON; *143 K-10; mail Hurtsboro z 36860; rural
Hanover; RMC Place; COOSA; 142 H-8; mail Rockford z 35136
Hardaway; RMC Place; MACON; 142 J-9; elev. 250ft./76m.; 🅿; z 36039; ● 110
Hardwick; RMC Place; ST. CLAIR; *142 E-8; elev. 739ft./225m.; ★ BIR; mail Odenville z 35120; rural
Harkins Crossroads; RMC Place; CLAY; *142 G-9; mail Ashland z 36251; ● 70
Harlem Heights; RMC Place; JEFFERSON; *142 F-6; ★ BIR; mail Bessemer z 35023; pop. incl. with Hueytown (Inc. Place)
Harmon; RMC Place; BIBB; *142 H-5; elev. 318ft./97m.; mail Centreville z 35042; rural
Harmony; RMC Place; COVINGTON; *143 N-8; elev. 375ft./114m.; mail Andalusia z 36420; ● 50
Harmony; RMC Place; LAWRENCE; *142 B-5; elev. 702ft./214m.; ★ DEC; mail Moulton z 35650; rural
Harper Hill; RMC Place; HALE; *142 H-4; elev. 300ft./91m.; mail Moundville z 35474; rural
Harpersville; Inc. Place; SHELBY; 142 G-7; 🅿; z 35078; ℗ 772; © 1,620
Harrell; RMC Place; DALLAS; *142 J-5; elev. 210ft./64m.; mail Marion Junction z 36759
Harriman Park; RMC Place; JEFFERSON; *142 F-6; ★ BIR; mail Birmingham z 35207; pop. incl. with Birmingham (Inc. Place)
Harrisburg; RMC Place; BIBB; 142 H-5; mail Brent z 35034; ● 160
Harrisburg; RMC Place; ST. CLAIR; *142 F-8; mail Pell City z 35125; pop. incl. with Pell City (Inc. Place)
Harrisville; RMC Place; ETOWAH; *142 D-8; mail Altoona z 35952; rural
Hartford; Inc. Place; GENEVA; 143 O-10; elev. 278ft./85m.; 🅿; z 36344; ℗ 2,448; © 2,369
Hartselle; Inc. Place; MORGAN; 142 C-6; elev. 669ft./204m.; 🅿 🅷; ★ DEC; z 35640; ℗ 10,867; © 12,019
Harvest; CDP; MADISON; 142 A-7; 🅿; ★ HNTS; z 35749; ℗ 1,922; © 3,054
Hassell Gap; RMC Place; CLAY; *142 G-9; elev. 1,300ft./396m.; mail Lineville z 36266; rural
Hatchechubbee; RMC Place; RUSSELL; 142 J-11; elev. 319ft./97m.; 🅿; z 36858; ● 250
Hatton; RMC Place; COLBERT; *142 A-4; elev. 650ft./198m.; ★ FLO; mail Leighton z 35646; ● 100
Hatton; RMC Place; LAWRENCE; 142 B-5; mail Town Creek z 35672; ● 210
Havana; RMC Place; HALE; 142 H-4; elev. 250ft./76m.; 🅿; z 35474; ● 50
Hawk; RMC Place; RANDOLPH; 142 F-11; elev. 970ft./296m.; mail Woodland z 36280
Hawthorn; RMC Place; WASHINGTON; *143 N-2; elev. 72ft./22m.; mail Deer Park z 36529, Wagarville z 36585; rural
Hayden; Inc. Place; BLOUNT; 142 E-7; elev. 570ft./174m.; 🅿; ★ BIR; z 35079; ℗ 385; © 470
Haynes; RMC Place; AUTAUGA; *142 I-7; mail Prattville z 36067; rural
Haynes Crossing; RMC Place; JACKSON; *142 A-9; mail Stevenson z 35772; pop. incl. with Stevenson (Inc. Place)
Haynes Crossroad; RMC Place; CLAY; *142 F-10; elev. 978ft./298m.; mail Delta z 36258; rural
Hayneville; Inc. Place; ⊡ LOWNDES; 143 K-7; elev. 200ft./61m.; 🅿; z 36040; ℗ 969; © 1,177
Haysland; RMC Place; MADISON; *142 B-7; ★ HNTS; mail Huntsville z 35802-03, z 35815; pop. incl. with Huntsville (Inc. Place)
Haysland Estates; RMC Place; MADISON; *142 B-7; ★ HNTS; mail Huntsville z 35802; pop. incl. with Huntsville (Inc. Place)
Hays Mill; RMC Place; LIMESTONE; *142 A-6; elev. 766ft./233m.; mail Elkmont z 35620; rural
Haywood; RMC Place; RANDOLPH; *142 G-11; elev. 1,049ft./320m.; mail Wedowee z 36278, Woodland z 36280; rural
Hazel Green; CDP; MADISON; 142 A-7; elev. 786ft./240m.; 🅿; ★ HNTS; z 35750; ℗ 2,208; © 3,805
Hazen; RMC Place; DALLAS; 142 J-5; elev. 171ft./52m.; mail Orrville z 36767; rural
Headland; Inc. Place; HENRY; 143 N-11; elev. 385ft./117m.; 🅿; ★ DOTH; z 36345; ℗ 3,266; © 3,523
Healing Springs; RMC Place; WASHINGTON; *143 M-2; mail Millry z 36558; pop. incl. with Millry (Inc. Place)
Heath; Inc. Place; COVINGTON; 143 N-7; elev. 354ft./108m.; mail Andalusia z 36420; ℗ 182; © 249
Hebron; RMC Place; BIBB; *142 G-6; elev. 438ft./134m.; mail West Blocton z 35184; ● 30
Hebron; RMC Place; MARSHALL; *142 B-8; mail Grant z 35747; ● 30
Hector; RMC Place; BULLOCK; 143 K-9; elev. 367ft./112m.; mail Fitzpatrick z 36029; rural
Heflin; Inc. Place; ⊡ CLEBURNE; 142 E-10; elev. 977ft./298m.; 🅿; z 36264; ℗ 2,906; © 3,002
Heiberger; RMC Place; PERRY; 142 I-5; mail Marion z 36756
Helena; Inc. Place; SHELBY, JEFFERSON; 142 G-6; elev. 446ft./136m.; 🅿; ★ BIR; z 35022, z 35080; ℗ 3,918; © 10,296
Helicon; RMC Place; CRENSHAW; *143 L-8; mail Grady z 36036; ● 180
Helicon; RMC Place; WINSTON; 142 D-5; elev. 835ft./255m.; mail Arley z 35541; ● 150
Henagar; Inc. Place; DEKALB; 142 B-9; elev. 1,440ft./439m.; 🅿; z 35978; ℗ 1,934; © 2,400
Henderson; RMC Place; PIKE; 143 M-9; mail Glenwood z 36034, Goshen z 36035; ● 80
Hendrick Mill; RMC Place; BLOUNT; *142 E-7; mail Oneonta z 35121; rural
Hendrix; RMC Place; BLOUNT; *142 D-7; mail Blountsville z 35031, Oneonta z 35121
Hendrixville; RMC Place; DEKALB; *142 C-9; mail Collinsville z 35961; ● 30
HENRY; 143 M-12; ℗ 15,374; © 16,310; ◆ 16,548
Henryville; RMC Place; MARSHALL; *142 C-8; mail Guntersville z 35976; ● 30
Henson Springs; RMC Place; LAMAR; 142 D-3; mail Beaverton z 35544, Sulligent z 35586; ● 30
Herbert; RMC Place; CONECUH; 143 N-6; mail Evergreen z 36401; rural
Heron Bay; RMC Place; MOBILE; 143 Q-2; elev. 11ft./3m.; mail Coden z 36523; ● 330
Hester Heights; RMC Place; FRANKLIN; *142 B-4; mail Russellville z 35653; pop. incl. with Russellville (Inc. Place)
Hickory; RMC Place; PICKENS; *142 G-3; elev. 224ft./68m.; mail Aliceville z 35442; rural
Hickory Flat; RMC Place; CHAMBERS; 142 G-11; mail Roanoke z 36274; ● 50
Hickory Grove; RMC Place; LAWRENCE; *142 C-4; mail Mount Hope z 35651; rural
Hickory Hills; RMC Place; LAUDERDALE; *142 A-4; ★ FLO; mail Florence z 35630; pop. incl. with Florence (Inc. Place)
Hickory Hills; RMC Place; MORGAN; *142 B-6; elev. 600ft./183m.; ★ DEC; mail Decatur z 35603; pop. incl. with Decatur (Inc. Place)
Hidden Forest; RMC Place; ELMORE; *142 J-9; elev. 285ft./87m.; mail Wetumpka z 36093; rural
Hidden Valley; RMC Place; COOSA; *142 H-7; elev. 574ft./175m.; mail Sylacauga z 35151; ● 40
Hideaway Hills; RMC Place; LAUDERDALE; *142 A-4; ★ FLO; mail Killen z 35645; ● 80
Higdon; RMC Place; JACKSON; 142 A-10; elev. 1,400ft./427m.; 🅿; z 35979; ● 500
High Bluff; RMC Place; GENEVA; *143 N-10; mail Hartford z 36344; rural
Highfalls; RMC Place; GENEVA; *143 O-10; elev. 250ft./76m.; mail Hartford z 36344; rural
Highland; RMC Place; CHILTON; *142 I-7; elev. 744ft./227m.; mail Clanton z 35045; ● 50
Highland; RMC Place; CLAY; *142 F-9; elev. 1,198ft./365m.; mail Lineville z 36266
Highland Home; RMC Place; CRENSHAW; 143 L-8; elev. 594ft./181m.; 🅿; z 36041; ● 300
Highland Lake; Inc. Place; BLOUNT; 142 D-7; elev. 895ft./273m.; 🅿; z 35121; ℗ 304; © 408
Highland Park; RMC Place; MONTGOMERY; ★ MTGY; mail Montgomery z 36107; pop. incl. with Montgomery (Inc. Place)
Highmound; RMC Place; BLOUNT; *142 D-8; mail Horton z 35980; ● 30
Highnote; RMC Place; GENEVA; *143 O-10; elev. 173ft./53m.; mail Black z 36314; rural
High Pine; RMC Place; CLAY; *142 G-9; elev. 1,153ft./351m.; mail Millerville z 36267; rural
High Point; RMC Place; DEKALB; *142 B-10; mail Valley Head z 35989; rural
High Point; RMC Place; MARSHALL; 142 C-8; mail Albertville z 35950; ● 80
High Ridge; RMC Place; BULLOCK; *143 K-9; mail Union Springs z 36089; ● 30
Hightogy; RMC Place; LAMAR; 142 E-2; elev. 485ft./148m.; mail Vernon z 35592; ● 70
Hightower; RMC Place; CLEBURNE; 142 F-11; mail Graham z 36263, Ranburne z 36273; ● 80
Hillandale; RMC Place; MADISON; *142 B-7; ★ HNTS; mail Huntsville z 35805; pop. incl. with Huntsville (Inc. Place)
Hillard; WALKER; see Hilliard (RMC Place)
Hilliard (Hillard); RMC Place; WALKER; *142 E-5; elev. 366ft./112m.; mail Townley z 35587; rural
Hillman; RMC Place; JEFFERSON; *142 F-6; ★ BIR; mail Bessemer z 35020; pop. incl. with Birmingham (Inc. Place)
Hillman Gardens; RMC Place; JEFFERSON; *142 F-6; ★ BIR; mail Bessemer z 35020; pop. incl. with Birmingham (Inc. Place)
Hillman Park; RMC Place; JEFFERSON; *142 F-6; ★ BIR; mail Bessemer z 35020; pop. incl. with Birmingham (Inc. Place)
Hillsboro; Inc. Place; LAWRENCE; 142 B-5; elev. 598ft./182m.; 🅿; z 35643; ℗ 587; © 608
Hillsboro; RMC Place; MADISON; *142 A-7; ★ HNTS; mail New Market z 35761; rural
Hillsdale; RMC Place; WALKER; *142 E-5; elev. 490ft./149m.; mail Jasper z 35504; pop. incl. with Jasper (Inc. Place)
Hilltop; RMC Place; JEFFERSON; ★ BIR; mail Bessemer z 35020; pop. incl. with Bessemer (Inc. Place)
Hillview; RMC Place; JEFFERSON; 143 Q-11; ★ BIR; mail Birmingham z 35214; ● 3,080
Hinton; RMC Place; CHOCTAW; *143 K-1; mail Quitman z 39355; rural
Hirsch; RMC Place; RUSSELL; *143 K-12; mail Pittsview z 36871; rural
Hissop; RMC Place; COOSA; 142 H-8; elev. 792ft./241m.; mail Kellyton z 35089; ● 80
Hobbs Island (Taylorsville); RMC Place; MADISON; *142 B-7; elev. 582ft./177m.; mail Huntsville z 35803; ● 180
Hobgood; RMC Place; COLBERT; *142 B-4; elev. 514ft./157m.; ★ FLO; mail Tuscumbia z 35674; rural
Hoboken; RMC Place; BARBOUR; *143 L-12; mail Eufaula z 36027; pop. incl. with Eufaula (Inc. Place)
Hoboken; RMC Place; MARENGO; 143 K-3; mail Sweet Water z 36782
Hobson; RMC Place; WASHINGTON; *143 M-2; elev. 150ft./46m.; mail Chatom z 36518; ● 110
Hobson City; Inc. Place; CALHOUN; 142 F-9; elev. 700ft./213m.; ★ ANNI; mail Anniston z 36201; ℗ 794; © 878
Hodge; RMC Place; JACKSON; *142 B-9; elev. 1,401ft./427m.; mail Dutton z 35744; rural
Hodges; Inc. Place; FRANKLIN; 142 C-3; elev. 842ft./257m.; 🅿; z 35571; ℗ 272; © 261
Hodges Store; LAWRENCE; see Speake (RMC Place)
Hodgesville; RMC Place; HOUSTON; *143 O-11; mail Dothan z 36301; ● 50
Hodgewood; RMC Place; CHOCTAW; *143 L-2; mail Toxey z 36921; ● 30
Hogglesville; RMC Place; HALE; *142 H-4; mail Moundville z 35474; rural
Hog Jaw; RMC Place; MARSHALL; *142 C-7; mail Arab z 35016; ● 50
Hokes Bluff; Inc. Place; ETOWAH; 142 D-9; elev. 609ft./186m.; 🅿; ★ GAD; z 35903; ℗ 3,739; © 4,149
Holiday Homes; RMC Place; MADISON; ★ HNTS; mail Huntsville z 35807; pop. incl. with Huntsville (Inc. Place)
Holiday Park Estates; RMC Place; JEFFERSON; *142 E-7; ★ BIR; mail Birmingham z 35215
Holland Gin; RMC Place; LIMESTONE; *142 A-6; mail Elkmont z 35620; ● 50
Holley Crossroads; RMC Place; CALHOUN; *142 E-10; elev. 853ft./260m.; mail Piedmont z 36272; ● 30
Hollins; RMC Place; CLAY; 142 G-8; elev. 832ft./254m.; 🅿; z 35082; ● 300
Hollis Crossroads; RMC Place; CLEBURNE; 142 F-10; elev. 890ft./271m.; mail Heflin z 36264
Holly Grove; RMC Place; WALKER; *142 E-4; elev. 360ft./110m.; mail Townley z 35587; rural
Holly Pond; Inc. Place; CULLMAN; 142 D-7; elev. 849ft./259m.; 🅿; z 35083; ℗ 602; © 645
Holly Springs; RMC Place; BLOUNT; *142 E-7; mail Springville z 35146; rural
Hollytree; RMC Place; JACKSON; 142 A-8; elev. 663ft./202m.; 🅿; z 35751; ● 150
Hollywood; Inc. Place; JACKSON; 142 A-9; elev. 630ft./192m.; 🅿; z 35752; ℗ 916; © 950
Hollywood; RMC Place; JEFFERSON; *142 F-6; ★ BIR; mail Birmingham z 35209; pop. incl. with Homewood (Inc. Place)
Holman; RMC Place; ESCAMBIA; *143 O-4; elev. 280ft./85m.; mail Atmore z 36503; ● 20
Holman; RMC Place; TUSCALOOSA; *142 G-3; elev. 353ft./108m.; mail Gordo z 35466; rural
Holmes Gap; RMC Place; CULLMAN; *142 C-6; elev. 909ft./277m.; mail Vinemont z 35179; rural
Holt; CDP; TUSCALOOSA; 142 G-4; elev. 361ft./110m.; 🅿; ★ TUSC; z 35404; ℗ 4,125; © 4,103; ® 4,020
Holt Junction; RMC Place; TUSCALOOSA; ★ TUSC; mail Tuscaloosa z 35401; pop. incl. with Tuscaloosa (Inc. Place)
Holtville; RMC Place; ELMORE; 142 I-8; ★ MTGY; mail Deatsville z 36022; ● 300
Holy Trinity; RMC Place; RUSSELL; 143 K-12; elev. 300ft./91m.; 🅿; z 36859; ● 90
Homewood; Inc. Place; JEFFERSON; 142 F-6; elev. 720ft./219m.; 🅿 ■; ★ BIR; z 35209, z 35259 & mail Birmingham z 35219; ℗ 22,922; © 25,043; ◆ 25,045
Honoraville; RMC Place; CRENSHAW; 143 L-8; elev. 511ft./156m.; 🅿; z 36042; ● 100
Hoods Crossroads (Murphree Valley); RMC Place; BLOUNT; *142 D-8; elev. 790ft./241m.; mail Oneonta z 35121; rural
Hooks; RMC Place; RUSSELL; *143 K-11; elev. 323ft./98m.; mail Pittsview z 36871; rural
Hooks Crossroads; RMC Place; BULLOCK; *143 K-9; elev. 608ft./185m.; mail Union Springs z 36089; rural
Hoover; Inc. Place; JEFFERSON, SHELBY; 142 F-6; elev. 600ft./183m.; 🅿; ★ BIR; z 35216, z 35226, z 35236, z 35244; ℗ 39,788; © 62,742; ◆ 65,313
Hoover; RMC Place; MADISON; *142 A-7; elev. 870ft./265m.; ★ HNTS; mail Harvest z 35749; ● 200
Hope Hull (McGehees); RMC Place; MONTGOMERY; *142 J-8; elev. 197ft./60m.; 🅿; ★ MTGY; z 36043; pop. incl. with Montgomery (Inc. Place)
Hopewell; RMC Place; BLOUNT; *142 C-7; mail Arab z 35016; ● 80
Hopewell (Richardson); RMC Place; CHEROKEE; *142 C-10; elev. 586ft./179m.; mail Cedar Bluff z 35959, Leesburg z 35983; ● 60
Hopewell (New Hopewell); RMC Place; CLEBURNE; *142 E-11; mail Heflin z 36264; rural
Hopewell; RMC Place; DEKALB; *142 C-9; mail Geraldine z 35974; rural
Hopewell; RMC Place; JEFFERSON; *142 F-6; ★ BIR; mail Bessemer z 35020, z 35023; pop. incl. with Bessemer (Inc. Place)
Hoppes; RMC Place; BALDWIN; *143 Q-3; elev. 20ft./6m.; mail Foley z 36535; ● 250
Hornady; RMC Place; MACON; *142 J-9; elev. 218ft./66m.; mail Tuskegee z 36083; rural
Horn Hill; Inc. Place; COVINGTON; *143 N-8; elev. 300ft./91m.; mail Opp z 36467; ℗ 255; © 235
Horton; RMC Place; MARSHALL; 142 C-8; elev. 982ft./299m.; 🅿; z 35980; ● 250
Hortons Mill; RMC Place; BLOUNT; *142 D-7; mail Oneonta z 35121; rural
Houston; RMC Place; WINSTON; 142 D-5; elev. 761ft./232m.; 🅿; z 35572; ● 190
HOUSTON; 143 O-12; ℗ 81,331; © 88,787; ◆ 99,183
Houstontown (Frog Pond); RMC Place; LAUDERDALE; *142 A-4; elev. 600ft./183m.; ★ FLO; mail Killen z 35645; ● 50
Howard; RMC Place; FAYETTE; 142 E-4; elev. 646ft./197m.; mail Carbon Hill z 35549; ● 40
Howells Crossroads; RMC Place; CHEROKEE; *142 C-10; elev. 580ft./177m.; mail Centre z 35960; rural
Howelton; RMC Place; ETOWAH; *142 D-8; mail Altoona z 35952; rural
Howton; RMC Place; TUSCALOOSA; *142 G-5; elev. 561ft./171m.; mail Cottondale z 35453; pop. incl. with Brookwood (Inc. Place)
Hubbard; RMC Place; CHILTON; *142 H-6; elev. 616ft./188m.; mail Jemison z 35085; rural
Hubbertville; RMC Place; FAYETTE; mail Fayette z 35555
Hudson Gardens; RMC Place; JEFFERSON; *142 F-6; ★ BIR; mail Bessemer z 35020; pop. incl. with Lipscomb (Inc. Place)
Hudson Settlement; RMC Place; WALKER; *142 E-5; elev. 500ft./152m.; mail Jasper z 35503; pop. incl. with Jasper (Inc. Place)
Hueytown; Inc. Place; JEFFERSON; 142 F-6; elev. 600ft./183m.; 🅿; ★ BIR; z 35023 & mail Bessemer z 35022; ℗ 15,280; © 15,364
Hueytown Crest; RMC Place; JEFFERSON; *142 F-6; elev. 571ft./174m.; ★ BIR; mail Bessemer z 35020; pop. incl. with Hueytown (Inc. Place)
Huffman; RMC Place; JEFFERSON; *142 F-7; elev. 731ft./223m.; ★ BIR; mail Birmingham z 35215, z 35235; pop. incl. with Birmingham (Inc. Place)
Huffman Gardens; RMC Place; JEFFERSON; *142 F-7; ★ BIR; mail Birmingham z 35215; pop. incl. with Birmingham (Inc. Place)
Hugo; RMC Place; MARENGO; *142 J-4; elev. 159ft./48m.; mail Thomaston z 36783; rural
Huguley; CDP; CHAMBERS; *142 H-11; mail Lanett z 36863, Valley z 36854; ℗ 3,161; © 2,953
Hulaco; RMC Place; MORGAN; 142 C-7; mail Joppa z 35087; ● 200
Hull; RMC Place; WALKER; *142 E-6; elev. 484ft./148m.; ★ BIR; mail Empire z 35063, Sumiton z 35148; pop. incl. with Sumiton (Inc. Place)
Humpton; RMC Place; MARSHALL; *142 B-8; mail Grant z 35747; rural
Hunters Crossroads; RMC Place; HOUSTON; *143 N-12; elev. 301ft./92m.; mail Columbia z 36319; rural
Huntsville; Inc. Place; ⊡ MADISON, LIMESTONE; 142 A-13; elev. 641ft./195m.; 🅿 🅷 🅲 15,669 ■; ★ HNTS; z 35801-16, z 35824, z 35893-99; ℗ 159,789; © 158,216; ® 158,635; ◆ 180,258
Huntsville Park; RMC Place; MADISON; *142 B-7; ★ HNTS; mail Huntsville z 35807; pop. incl. with Huntsville (Inc. Place)
Hurricane; RMC Place; BALDWIN; *143 P-3; mail Bay Minette z 36507; ● 50
Hurtsboro; Inc. Place; RUSSELL; 142 J-11; elev. 345ft./105m.; 🅿; z 36860; ℗ 707; © 592
Hustleville; RMC Place; MARSHALL; 142 C-8; mail Albertville z 35951; ● 100
Huxford; RMC Place; ESCAMBIA; 143 N-4; elev. 330ft./101m.; 🅿; z 36543; ● 200
Hyatt; RMC Place; MARSHALL; *142 C-8; mail Horton z 35980; ● 30
Hybart; RMC Place; MONROE; 143 L-5; elev. 186ft./57m.; mail Vredenburgh z 36481; ● 100
Hyde Park; RMC Place; JEFFERSON; *142 F-6; ★ BIR; mail Birmingham z 35211; pop. incl. with Birmingham (Inc. Place)
Hytop; Inc. Place; JACKSON; 142 A-9; elev. 1,699ft./518m.; 🅿; z 35768; ℗ 300; © 315

I

Idaho; RMC Place; CLAY; *142 G-9; mail Ashland z 36251; ● 40
Ider; Inc. Place; DEKALB; 142 B-10; elev. 1,500ft./457m.; 🅿; z 35981; ℗ 671; © 664
Independence; RMC Place; AUTAUGA; 142 J-7; elev. 254ft./77m.; mail Autaugaville z 36003, Prattville z 36067; ● 60
Indian Creek; RMC Place; BULLOCK; *143 K-10; mail Perote z 36061; rural
Indian Forest; RMC Place; SHELBY; ★ BIR; mail Pelham z 35124; pop. incl. with Indian Springs Village (Inc. Place)
Indian Hill; RMC Place; TALLADEGA; *142 G-8; mail Childersburg z 35044; pop. incl. with Childersburg (Inc. Place)
Indian Springs; RMC Place; LAUDERDALE; *142 A-4; ★ FLO; mail Florence z 35634; pop. incl. with Florence (Inc. Place)
Indian Springs; RMC Place; MOBILE; *143 P-2; elev. 200ft./61m.; ★ MOB; mail Eight Mile z 36613; rural
Indian Springs; SHELBY; see Indian Springs Village (Inc. Place)
Indian Springs Village (Indian Springs); Inc. Place; SHELBY; 143 T-12; 🅿; ★ BIR; z 35124; ℗ 1,234; © 2,225
Indian Valley; RMC Place; SHELBY; *142 F-7; elev. 500ft./152m.; ★ BIR; mail Birmingham z 35244
Industrial City; RMC Place; JEFFERSON; *142 F-6; ★ BIR; mail Bessemer z 35023; pop. incl. with Hueytown (Inc. Place)
Industry; RMC Place; BUTLER; 143 M-7; elev. 308ft./94m.; mail Georgiana z 36033; ● 50
Ingate; RMC Place; BIBB; *142 H-5; elev. 275ft./84m.; mail Centreville z 35042; rural
Inglenook; RMC Place; JEFFERSON; *142 F-6; ★ BIR; mail Birmingham z 35217; pop. incl. with Birmingham (Inc. Place)
Ingram; RMC Place; HALE; *142 H-4; elev. 228ft./69m.; mail Moundville z 35474; rural
Inland; BLOUNT; see Inland Junction (RMC Place)
Inland Junction (Inland); RMC Place; BLOUNT; *142 E-7; mail Oneonta z 35121; rural
Inmanfield; RMC Place; WINSTON; *142 C-5; mail Addison z 35540; rural
Ino; RMC Place; COFFEE; 143 N-9; elev. 309ft./94m.; mail Kinston z 36453; ● 30
Interburan Heights; RMC Place; JEFFERSON; *142 F-6; ★ BIR; mail Fairfield z 35064; pop. incl. with Fairfield (Inc. Place)
Inverness; RMC Place; BULLOCK; 143 K-10; elev. 417ft./127m.; mail Union Springs z 36089; ● 50
Inverness; RMC Place; SHELBY; 143 T-13; ★ BIR; mail Birmingham z 35242; ℗ 2,528
Ironaton; RMC Place; TALLADEGA; *142 F-9; elev. 656ft./200m.; mail Munford z 36268; rural
Iron City; RMC Place; CALHOUN; *142 E-10; elev. 756ft./230m.; mail Anniston z 36207; ● 50
Irondale; Inc. Place; JEFFERSON; 143 R-13; elev. 747ft./228m.; 🅿; ★ BIR; z 35210; ℗ 9,454; © 9,813
Irvington; RMC Place; MOBILE; 143 Q-2; elev. 134ft./41m.; 🅿; ★ MOB; z 36544; ● 1,000
Isabella (Benson); RMC Place; CHILTON; *142 H-6; elev. 456ft./139m.; mail Maplesville z 36750; ● 100
Isbell; RMC Place; FRANKLIN; 142 B-4; mail Russellville z 35653; ● 130
Ishkooda; RMC Place; JEFFERSON; *142 F-6; ★ BIR; mail Birmingham z 35211; pop. incl. with Birmingham (Inc. Place)
Isney; RMC Place; CHOCTAW; 143 L-1; elev. 27ft./8m.; mail Silas z 36919; ● 30
Ivalee; RMC Place; ETOWAH; *142 D-8; ★ GAD; mail Attalla z 35954; ● 80
Ivanhoe; RMC Place; JEFFERSON; *142 F-6; ★ BIR; mail Birmingham z 35222; pop. incl. with Birmingham (Inc. Place)

J

Jachin; RMC Place; CHOCTAW; 143 K-2; elev. 109ft./33m.; 🅿; z 36910; ● 200
Jack; RMC Place; COFFEE; 143 M-9; elev. 398ft./121m.; 🅿; z 36346; ● 100
Jackson; Inc. Place; CLARKE; 143 M-3; elev. 227ft./69m.; 🅿 🅷; z 36501, z 36515, z 36545; ℗ 5,819; © 5,419
JACKSON; 142 A-9; ℗ 47,796; © 53,926; ◆ 52,257
Jackson Heights; RMC Place; MOBILE; *143 P-2; ★ MOB; mail Mobile z 36609; pop. incl. with Mobile (Inc. Place)
Jackson Oak; RMC Place; BALDWIN; *143 P-3; ★ MOB; mail Daphne z 36526; pop. incl. with Daphne (Inc. Place)
Jacksons Gap; Inc. Place; TALLAPOOSA; 142 H-9; elev. 600ft./183m.; 🅿; z 36861; ℗ 789; © 761
Jacksonville; Inc. Place; CALHOUN; 142 E-10; elev. 672ft./205m.; 🅿 🅷 🅲 8,957; ★ ANNI; z 36265; ℗ 10,283; © 8,404
Jack Springs; RMC Place; ESCAMBIA; *143 N-4; mail Atmore z 36502; rural
Jagger; WALKER; see New Jagger (RMC Place)
Jamback; RMC Place; BULLOCK; *143 L-10; elev. 450ft./137m.; mail Banks z 36005; ● 30
Jamestown; RMC Place; CHEROKEE; 142 C-10; mail Gaylesville z 35973; ● 50
Jamesville; RMC Place; LEE; *142 I-10; elev. 758ft./231m.; mail Waverly z 36879; rural
Jarrett; RMC Place; CHAMBERS; mail Valley z 36854; pop. incl. with Valley (Inc. Place)
Jasper; Inc. Place; ⊡ WALKER; 142 E-5; elev. 339ft./103m.; 🅿 🅷 ■; z 35501-04; ℗ 13,553; © 14,052; ◆ 12,969
Java; RMC Place; COFFEE; *143 M-9; mail Brundidge z 36010; rural
Jeddo; RMC Place; MONROE; *143 N-4; elev. 354ft./108m.; mail Uriah z 36480; ● 30
Jeff; RMC Place; MADISON; *142 A-7; ★ HNTS; mail Huntsville z 35806; ● 80
Jefferson; RMC Place; MARENGO; 142 J-3; elev. 233ft./71m.; 🅿; z 36745; ● 250
JEFFERSON; 142 E-7; ℗ 651,525; © 662,047; ◆ 656,897
Jefferson Hills; RMC Place; JEFFERSON; *142 F-6; ★ BIR; mail Birmingham z 35217; pop. incl. with Birmingham (Inc. Place)
Jefferson Park; RMC Place; JEFFERSON; *142 F-7; ★ BIR; mail Birmingham z 35210; pop. incl. with Irondale (Inc. Place)
Jefferson Station; RMC Place; MARENGO; *142 J-3; elev. 96ft./29m.; mail Jefferson z 36745; rural
Jemison; Inc. Place; CHILTON; 142 H-7; elev. 710ft./216m.; 🅿; z 35085; ℗ 1,898; © 2,248

Entries in **UPPERCASE** are counties.
Entries in **bold** have populations of 2,500 or more.
Names in parentheses are alternate names.

Inc. Place	Incorporated Place
RMC Place	Rand McNally Designated Place
CDP	Census Designated Place
MCD	Minor Civil Division
⊡	County Seat
▲	Minor Civil Division
elev.	Elevation
🅿	Post Office
🅷	Hospital
🅲	College
■	Principal Business Center
★	Ranally Metro Area (RMA) Abbreviation
z	Zip Code(s)
℗	Previous Census Population
®	Revised Census Population
Ⓐ	Annexation Population
●	Rand McNally Population Estimate
©	Final Census Population
Ⓢ	Special Census Population
◆	Estimated Population

For additional definitions see Glossary, Volume 1, and Introduction, Volume 2.

Jena; RMC Place; GREENE; ***142** G-3; elev. 204ft./62m.; mail Ralph z 35480; rural
Jenifer; RMC Place; TALLADEGA; **142** F-9; elev. 583ft./178m.; ★ **ANNI**; mail Munford z 36268; ● 180
Jenkins Crossroads (Halls Crossroads); RMC Place; BULLOCK; ***143** K-10; elev. 541ft./165m.; mail Union Springs z 36089; rural
Jericho; RMC Place; PERRY; ***142** I-5; mail Marion z 36756; rural
Jernigan; RMC Place; RUSSELL; ***143** K-12; elev. 304ft./93m.; mail Cottonton z 36851; rural
Jerusalem Heights; RMC Place; TUSCALOOSA; ***142** G-4; ★ **TUSC**; mail Tuscaloosa z 35405; ● 300
Joe Wheeler Dam; LAWRENCE; see Wheeler Dam Village (RMC Place)
Johns; JEFFERSON; see North Johns (Inc. Place)
Johnsons Crossing; RMC Place; CULLMAN; ***142** D-6; elev. 643ft./196m.; mail Hanceville z 35077; ● 230
Johnsonville (Johnstonville); RMC Place; CONECUH; ***143** N-6; mail Evergreen z 36401; ● 100
Johnstonville; CONECUH; see Johnsonville (RMC Place)
Jones; RMC Place; AUTAUGA; **142** I-6; elev. 444ft./135m.; 🅿; z 36749; ● 130
Jonesboro; RMC Place; BALDWIN; ***143** P-3; mail Daphne z 36526; ● 30
Jonesboro; RMC Place; FRANKLIN; ***142** B-3; elev. 968ft./295m.; mail Russellville z 35653; ● 30
Jonesboro; RMC Place; JEFFERSON; ***142** F-6; ★ **BIR**; mail Bessemer z 35020; pop. incl. with Bessemer (Inc. Place)
Jones Chapel; RMC Place; CULLMAN; **142** C-6; elev. 978ft./298m.; mail Cullman z 35057; ● 170
Jones Crossroads; RMC Place; LIMESTONE; ***142** B-6; mail Athens z 35611; ● 80
Jones Valley; RMC Place; JEFFERSON; ***142** F-6; ★ **BIR**; mail Birmingham z 35211; pop. incl. with Birmingham (Inc. Place)
Jones Valley Estates; RMC Place; MADISON; ***142** B-7; ★ **HNTS**; mail Huntsville z 35802; pop. incl. with Huntsville (Inc. Place)
Joppa; RMC Place; CULLMAN; **142** C-7; elev. 1,000ft./305m.; 🅿; z 35087; ● 230
Joquin; RMC Place; PIKE, CRENSHAW; ***143** L-8; elev. 476ft./145m.; mail Goshen z 36035, Luverne z 36049; rural
Jordan; RMC Place; ELMORE; **142** I-9; elev. 615ft./187m.; mail Wetumpka z 36092; ● 30
Jordan; RMC Place; WASHINGTON; **143** M-2; mail Chatom z 36518; ● 160
Jordans Mill; RMC Place; FRANKLIN; ***142** B-3; mail Vina z 35593; rural
Josephine; RMC Place; BALDWIN; **143** R-4; mail Elberta z 36530; ● 100
Joseph Springs; RMC Place; CALHOUN; ***142** E-10; mail Anniston z 36207; ● 50
Josie; RMC Place; PIKE; ***143** L-10; elev. 585ft./178m.; mail Banks z 36005; rural

K

Kahatchee; RMC Place; TALLADEGA; ***142** G-8; elev. 509ft./155m.; mail Childersburg z 35044; ● 100
Kansas; Inc. Place; WALKER; **142** E-4; elev. 460ft./140m.; 🅿; z 35573; Ⓟ 230; Ⓒ 260
Kaolin; RMC Place; RUSSELL; **167** R-3; ★ **COL**; mail Phenix City z 36869; pop. incl. with Phenix City (Inc. Place)
Kaulton; RMC Place; TUSCALOOSA; ★ **TUSC**; mail Tuscaloosa z 35401; pop. incl. with Tuscaloosa (Inc. Place)
Keego; RMC Place; ESCAMBIA; ***143** O-5; mail Brewton z 36426; ● 30
Keener; RMC Place; ETOWAH; **142** D-9; elev. 669ft./204m.; mail Attalla z 35954; ● 80
Kellerman; RMC Place; TUSCALOOSA; **142** G-5; elev. 500ft./152m.; 🅿; z 35468; ● 130
Kelly; RMC Place; DALE; ***143** N-10; ★ **DOTH**; mail Daleville z 36322; ● 40
Kelly Chapel; RMC Place; MARSHALL; ***142** B-8; elev. 1,300ft./396m.; mail Scottsboro z 35769; rural
Kellys Crossroads; RMC Place; COOSA; ***142** H-8; elev. 545ft./166m.; mail Rockford z 35136; rural
Kelly Springs; RMC Place; HOUSTON; ***143** N-11; elev. 340ft./104m.; ★ **DOTH**; mail Dothan z 36301, z 36303; pop. incl. with Dothan (Inc. Place)
Kellyton; Inc. Place; COOSA; **142** H-9; elev. 777ft./237m.; 🅿; z 35089; Ⓒ 226
Kendale Gardens; RMC Place; LAUDERDALE; ***142** A-4; ★ **FLO**; mail Florence z 35630; ● 300
Kennedy; Inc. Place; LAMAR; **142** F-3; elev. 334ft./102m.; 🅿; z 35574; Ⓟ 523; Ⓒ 541
Kent; RMC Place; ELMORE; **142** I-9; elev. 592ft./180m.; 🅿; z 36045; ● 500
Kent; RMC Place; PIKE; ***143** L-8; elev. 398ft./121m.; mail Goshen z 36035; ● 30
Kenwood; RMC Place; JEFFERSON; ★ **BIR**; mail Birmingham z 35226; pop. incl. with Hoover (Inc. Place)
Ketona; RMC Place; JEFFERSON; ***142** F-6; ★ **BIR**; mail Birmingham z 35217; pop. incl. with Tarrant City (Inc. Place)
Key; RMC Place; CHEROKEE; ***142** D-10; elev. 647ft./197m.; mail Centre z 35960; ● 40
Keyno; RMC Place; COOSA; ***142** H-9; elev. 757ft./231m.; mail Kellyton z 35089; rural
Keys Mill; RMC Place; MADISON; ***142** A-7; elev. 724ft./221m.; ★ **HNTS**; mail New Market z 35761; rural
Keystone; RMC Place; SHELBY; ***142** G-6; ★ **BIR**; mail Alabaster z 35007, Pelham z 35124; pop. incl. with Pelham (Inc. Place)
Keyton; RMC Place; COFFEE; ***143** N-9; mail Enterprise z 36330; pop. incl. with Enterprise (Inc. Place)
Kilby; RMC Place; MONTGOMERY; ***142** J-8; ★ **MTGY**; mail Montgomery z 36114; pop. incl. with Montgomery (Inc. Place)
Kilgore; RMC Place; JEFFERSON; ***142** E-6; elev. 400ft./122m.; ★ **BIR**; mail Dora z 35062; rural
Killen; Inc. Place; LAUDERDALE; **142** A-4; elev. 614ft./187m.; 🅿; ★ **FLO**; z 35645; Ⓟ 1,047; Ⓒ 1,119
Killough Springs; RMC Place; JEFFERSON; ***142** F-7; ★ **BIR**; mail Birmingham z 35235; pop. incl. with Birmingham (Inc. Place)
Kilpatrick; RMC Place; DEKALB; **142** C-9; mail Albertville z 35951; ● 150
Kimberly; Inc. Place; JEFFERSON; **142** E-6; elev. 457ft./139m.; 🅿; ★ **BIR**; z 35091; Ⓟ 1,096; Ⓒ 1,801
Kimbrel; JEFFERSON; see Kimbrell (RMC Place)
Kimbrell (Kimbrel); RMC Place; JEFFERSON; ***142** G-6; ★ **BIR**; mail Mc Calla z 35111; ● 70
Kimbrough; RMC Place; WILCOX; **143** K-4; elev. 91ft./28m.; mail Pine Hill z 36769; ● 150
Kincheon; RMC Place; CHILTON; ***142** I-7; mail Clanton z 35045; ● 50
Kings Landing; RMC Place; BALDWIN; ***143** Q-4; mail Seminole z 36574; ● 60
Kings Landing; RMC Place; DALLAS; ***142** J-6; elev. 110ft./34m.; mail Sardis z 36775; rural
Kingston; RMC Place; JEFFERSON; ***142** F-6; ★ **BIR**; mail Birmingham z 35234; pop. incl. with Birmingham (Inc. Place)
Kingsway Terrace; RMC Place; JEFFERSON; ***142** F-7; ★ **BIR**; mail Birmingham z 35206; pop. incl. with Birmingham (Inc. Place)
Kingtown; RMC Place; LAUDERDALE; ***142** A-5; ★ **FLO**; mail Rogersville z 35652; ● 50
Kingville; RMC Place; LAMAR; **142** E-3; mail Kennedy z 35574, Millport z 35576; rural
Kinsey; Inc. Place; HOUSTON; **143** N-11; elev. 297ft./91m.; 🅿; ★ **DOTH**; z 36303; Ⓟ 1,679; Ⓒ 1,796
Kinston; Inc. Place; COFFEE; **143** N-8; elev. 275ft./84m.; 🅿; z 36453; Ⓟ 595; Ⓒ 602
Kinterbish; RMC Place; SUMTER; ***142** J-2; elev. 266ft./81m.; mail Cuba z 36907; ● 30
Kirbytown; RMC Place; MARSHALL; ***142** B-8; mail Langston z 35755; rural
Kirk; RMC Place; PICKENS; ***142** G-3; mail Gordo z 35466; rural
Kirkland; RMC Place; ESCAMBIA; **143** N-6; mail Brewton z 36426; ● 100
Kirklands Crossroads; RMC Place; HENRY; ***143** N-11; elev. 362ft./110m.; mail Headland z 36345; ● 80
Kirks Grove; RMC Place; CHEROKEE; ***142** C-10; elev. 582ft./177m.; mail Centre z 35960; ● 70
Klein; RMC Place; SHELBY; ***142** G-7; elev. 421ft./128m.; mail Harpersville z 35078; rural
Knightens Crossroads; RMC Place; CALHOUN; ***142** D-10; elev. 622ft./190m.; mail Piedmont z 36272; ● 30
Knoxville; RMC Place; GREENE; **142** H-3; elev. 282ft./86m.; 🅿; z 35469; ● 80
Koenton; RMC Place; WASHINGTON; **143** M-2; mail Millry z 36558; ● 30
Kowaliga (Kowaliga Beach); RMC Place; ELMORE; ***142** I-9; mail Alexander City z 35010, Eclectic z 36024; summer pop. 300; ● 80
Kowaliga Beach; ELMORE; see Kowaliga (RMC Place)
Krafton; RMC Place; MOBILE; ★ **MOB**; mail Mobile z 36610; pop. incl. with Prichard (Inc. Place)
Kyles; RMC Place; JACKSON; ***142** A-9; mail Fackler z 35746; rural
Kymulga; RMC Place; TALLADEGA; **142** G-8; elev. 469ft./143m.; mail Alpine z 35014, Childersburg z 35044; ● 100

L

Laceys Chapel; RMC Place; JEFFERSON; **143** T-10; ★ **BIR**; mail Bessemer z 35020; pop. incl. with Bessemer (Inc. Place)
Laceys Spring; RMC Place; MORGAN; **142** B-7; elev. 600ft./183m.; 🅿; z 35754; ● 600
Lacon; RMC Place; MORGAN; **142** C-6; mail Falkville z 35622; ● 70
Ladiga; RMC Place; CALHOUN; ***142** D-10; mail Piedmont z 36272; ● 30
Ladonia; CDP; RUSSELL; **142** J-12; ★ **COL**; mail Phenix City z 36869-70; Ⓟ 2,905; Ⓒ 3,229
Lafayette; Inc. Place; ⊡ CHAMBERS; **142** H-11; elev. 849ft./259m.; 🅿; z 36862; Ⓟ 3,151; Ⓒ 3,234
Lake Coves; RMC Place; LAUDERDALE; ***142** A-4; ★ **FLO**; mail Florence z 35634; ● 230
Lake Drive Estates; RMC Place; JEFFERSON; ***142** F-6; ★ **BIR**; mail Birmingham z 35209; pop. incl. with Homewood (Inc. Place)
Lake Forest; RMC Place; BALDWIN; ***143** P-3; ★ **MOB**; mail Daphne z 36526; pop. incl. with Daphne (Inc. Place)
Lake Highlands; RMC Place; JEFFERSON; ***142** F-7; ★ **BIR**; mail Birmingham z 35206; pop. incl. with Birmingham (Inc. Place)
Lake Howard; DEKALB; see Alpine (RMC Place)
Lake Purdy; CDP-Census Area Only; SHELBY; ***142** F-7; ★ **BIR**; mail Birmingham z 35242; Ⓟ 1,840; Ⓒ 5,799
Lakeside Acres; RMC Place; LAUDERDALE; ***142** A-4; ★ **FLO**; mail Killen z 35645; ● 80
Lakeside Highlands; RMC Place; LAUDERDALE; ***142** A-4; ★ **FLO**; mail Florence z 35630; pop. incl. with Florence (Inc. Place)
Lakeview; Inc. Place; DEKALB; **142** C-9; elev. 1,182ft./360m.; mail Fyffe z 35971; Ⓟ 166; Ⓒ 163
Lakeview; RMC Place; MARSHALL; ***142** C-8; mail Guntersville z 35976; pop. incl. with Guntersville (Inc. Place)
Lake View; Inc. Place; TUSCALOOSA; ***142** G-5; 🅿; z 35111; Ⓒ 1,357
Lakeview Highlands; RMC Place; COLBERT; ***142** A-4; ★ **FLO**; mail Sheffield z 35660; pop. incl. with Muscle Shoals (Inc. Place)
Lakewood; RMC Place; JEFFERSON; ***142** F-7; ★ **BIR**; mail Birmingham z 35234; pop. incl. with Birmingham (Inc. Place)
Lakewood; RMC Place; LIMESTONE; ***142** A-6; mail Athens z 35611; pop. incl. with Athens (Inc. Place)
Lakewood; RMC Place; MADISON; ***142** A-7; ★ **HNTS**; mail Huntsville z 35810; pop. incl. with Huntsville (Inc. Place)
Lakewood Estates; RMC Place; JEFFERSON; ★ **BIR**; mail Bessemer z 35020; pop. incl. with Bessemer (Inc. Place)
Lamar; RANDOLPH; see Woodland (Inc. Place)
LAMAR; **142** E-3; Ⓟ 15,715; Ⓒ 15,904; ◆ 14,330
Lamison; RMC Place; WILCOX; **143** K-4; elev. 150ft./46m.; mail Catherine z 36728, Thomaston z 36783; ● 200
Land; RMC Place; CHOCTAW; **143** K-2; elev. 207ft./63m.; mail Butler z 36904; ● 50
Landersville; RMC Place; LAWRENCE; **142** B-5; mail Moulton z 35650, Town Creek z 35672; ● 150
Lands Crossroads; RMC Place; DEKALB; ***142** B-9; mail Rainsville z 35986; pop. incl. with Rainsville (Inc. Place)
Lane Springs; RMC Place; COLBERT; ***142** A-3; mail Cherokee z 35616; rural
Lanett; Inc. Place; CHAMBERS; **142** H-11; elev. 600ft./183m.; 🅿; z 36863; Ⓟ 8,985; Ⓒ 7,897
Langdale; RMC Place; CHAMBERS; ***142** H-11; elev. 586ft./179m.; mail Valley z 36854; pop. incl. with Valley (Inc. Place)
Langston; Inc. Place; JACKSON; **142** B-9; elev. 613ft./187m.; 🅿; z 35755; Ⓟ 207; Ⓒ 254
Langtown; LAWRENCE; see Longtown (RMC Place)
Laniers; RMC Place; TALLADEGA; ***142** F-8; mail Alpine z 35014; rural
Lapine; RMC Place; MONTGOMERY, CRENSHAW; **143** L-8; elev. 430ft./131m.; 🅿; z 36046; ● 200
La Place; RMC Place; MACON; **142** J-9; elev. 313ft./95m.; mail Shorter z 36075; rural
Larkinsville; RMC Place; JACKSON; **142** B-8; mail Scottsboro z 35768; pop. incl. with Scottsboro (Inc. Place)
Larkwood; RMC Place; JEFFERSON; ***142** E-7; ★ **BIR**; mail Birmingham z 35215
Lasca; RMC Place; MARENGO; ***143** K-3; elev. 222ft./68m.; mail Thomasville z 36784; rural
Latham; RMC Place; BALDWIN; ***143** O-3; mail Stockton z 36579; ● 30
Lathamville; RMC Place; DEKALB; ***142** C-9; elev. 1,129ft./344m.; mail Crossville z 35962; ● 80
Lattiwood; RMC Place; MARSHALL; ***142** C-8; mail Albertville z 35950; ● 30
LAUDERDALE; **142** A-4; Ⓟ 79,661; Ⓒ 87,966; ◆ 88,964
Lauderdale Beach; RMC Place; LAUDERDALE; ***142** A-4; ★ **FLO**; mail Florence z 35634; ● 50
Laurendine; RMC Place; MOBILE; ***143** Q-2; elev. 44ft./13m.; ★ **MOB**; mail Theodore z 36582; rural
Lavaca; RMC Place; CHOCTAW; **143** K-2; elev. 105ft./32m.; 🅿; z 36904; ● 160
Lawley; RMC Place; BIBB; **142** H-6; elev. 450ft./137m.; 🅿; z 36793; ● 100
Lawrence; RMC Place; CHEROKEE; ***142** C-10; elev. 596ft./182m.; mail Cedar Bluff z 35959; rural
LAWRENCE; **142** B-5; Ⓟ 31,513; Ⓒ 34,803; ◆ 34,410
Lawrence Cove; RMC Place; MORGAN; ***142** C-7; elev. 840ft./256m.; mail Eva z 35621; rural
Lawrence Mill; RMC Place; FAYETTE; ***142** E-3; mail Fayette z 35555; ● 60
Lawrenceville; RMC Place; HENRY; **143** M-11; elev. 529ft./161m.; mail Abbeville z 36310; ● 50
Leatherwood; RMC Place; CALHOUN; ***142** E-9; elev. 629ft./192m.; ★ **ANNI**; mail Anniston z 36201; rural
Lebanon; RMC Place; CLEBURNE; **142** E-11; mail Muscadine z 36269; ● 50
Lebanon; RMC Place; DEKALB; **142** C-9; mail Collinsville z 35961; ● 60
Lebanon; RMC Place; MORGAN; ***142** C-6; elev. 600ft./183m.; ★ **DEC**; mail Hartselle z 35640; ● 30
Lecta; RMC Place; CLEBURNE; ***142** F-11; elev. 1,022ft./312m.; mail Heflin z 36264; rural
LEE; **142** I-11; Ⓟ 87,146; Ⓒ 115,092; ◆ 138,822
Leeds; Inc. Place; JEFFERSON, SHELBY, ST. CLAIR; **142** F-7; elev. 622ft./190m.; 🅿; ★ **BIR**; z 35094; Ⓟ 9,946; Ⓒ 10,455
Leeds Mineral Well; RMC Place; JEFFERSON; ***142** F-7; ★ **BIR**; mail Leeds z 35094; pop. incl. with Leeds (Inc. Place)
Leesburg; Inc. Place; CHEROKEE; **142** C-9; elev. 584ft./178m.; 🅿; z 35983; Ⓟ 218; Ⓒ 799
Leesdale; RMC Place; MORGAN; ***142** C-6; elev. 602ft./183m.; ★ **DEC**; mail Falkville z 35622; pop. incl. with Falkville (Inc. Place)
Legg; LIMESTONE; see Leggtown (RMC Place)
Leggtown (Legg); RMC Place; LIMESTONE; **142** A-6; mail Elkmont z 35620; ● 50
Le Grand; RMC Place; MONTGOMERY; ***143** K-8; elev. 269ft./82m.; mail Montgomery z 36105; ● 30
Leighton; Inc. Place; COLBERT; **142** B-4; elev. 574ft./175m.; 🅿; ★ **FLO**; z 35646; Ⓟ 988; Ⓒ 849
Lenlock; RMC Place; CALHOUN; elev. 800ft./244m.; ★ **ANNI**; mail Anniston z 36201; pop. incl. with Anniston (Inc. Place)
Lenox; RMC Place; CONECUH; **143** N-5; elev. 450ft./137m.; 🅿; z 36454; ● 80
Leon; RMC Place; CRENSHAW; ***143** M-8; elev. 473ft./144m.; mail Dozier z 36028; rural
Leroy; RMC Place; WASHINGTON; **143** M-3; elev. 158ft./48m.; 🅿; z 36548; ● 250
Leslie; CHILTON; see Riderville (RMC Place)
Lester; Inc. Place; LIMESTONE; **142** A-5; elev. 820ft./250m.; 🅿; z 35647; Ⓟ 89; Ⓒ 107
Letcher; RMC Place; JACKSON; ***142** A-8; mail Woodville z 35776; pop. incl. with Skyline (Inc. Place)
Letchers; RMC Place; CALHOUN; ***142** E-9; ★ **ANNI**; mail Anniston z 36201
Letohatchee (Letohatchie); RMC Place; LOWNDES; **143** K-7; elev. 293ft./89m.; 🅿; z 36047; ● 250
Letohatchie; LOWNDES; see Letohatchee (RMC Place)
Level Plains; Inc. Place; DALE; **143** N-10; elev. 320ft./98m.; 🅿; z 36322 & mail Enterprise z 36330; Ⓟ 1,473; Ⓒ 1,544
Levelroad; RMC Place; RANDOLPH; ***142** G-10; mail Wadley z 36276, Wedowee z 36278; rural
Levert; RMC Place; PERRY; ***142** I-5; rural
Lewis; RMC Place; DALE; ***143** N-11; mail Midland City z 36350; rural
Lewisburg; RMC Place; JEFFERSON; ***142** F-6; ★ **BIR**; mail Birmingham z 35207
Lewiston; RMC Place; GREENE; ***142** H-3; mail Eutaw z 35462
Lexington; Inc. Place; LAUDERDALE; **142** A-5; elev. 780ft./238m.; 🅿; ★ **FLO**; z 35648; Ⓟ 821; Ⓒ 840
Liberty; RMC Place; BLOUNT; **142** D-7; elev. 845ft./258m.; mail Blountsville z 35031; rural
Liberty; RMC Place; BUTLER; ***143** L-7; mail Greenville z 36037; ● 160
Liberty; RMC Place; DEKALB; ***142** C-9; mail Boaz z 35957; ● 30
Liberty; RMC Place; PICKENS; ***142** F-2; elev. 331ft./101m.; mail Ethelsville z 35461; ● 30
Liberty City; RMC Place; MACON, TALLAPOOSA; **142** I-10; mail Notasulga z 36866; ● 120
Liberty Highlands; RMC Place; JEFFERSON; ***142** F-7; ★ **BIR**; mail Birmingham z 35210; pop. incl. with Birmingham (Inc. Place)
Liberty Hill; RMC Place; FRANKLIN; **142** C-3; elev. 983ft./300m.; mail Phil Campbell z 35581; ● 100
Liberty Hill; RMC Place; JACKSON; ***142** A-10; elev. 1,520ft./463m.; mail Flat Rock z 35966; rural
Libertyville; Inc. Place; COVINGTON; **143** N-7; elev. 260ft./79m.; mail Andalusia z 36420; Ⓟ 133; Ⓒ 106
Lickskillet; RMC Place; DEKALB; ***142** C-10; elev. 1,227ft./374m.; mail Fort Payne z 35967; ● 30
Lightwood; RMC Place; ELMORE; ***142** I-8; mail Deatsville z 36022; ● 100
Ligon Springs; RMC Place; COLBERT; ***142** B-4; mail Russellville z 35654; rural
Lillian; RMC Place; BALDWIN; **143** Q-4; elev. 8ft./2m.; 🅿; z 36549; summer pop. 3,000; ● 900
Lily Flag; RMC Place; MADISON; ★ **HNTS**; mail Huntsville z 35802; pop. incl. with Huntsville (Inc. Place)
Lime; RMC Place; RANDOLPH; ***142** G-11; mail Roanoke z 36274; rural
Lime Kiln; RMC Place; COLBERT; ***142** A-3; mail Cherokee z 35616; ● 50
Limestone; RMC Place; MONROE; ***143** M-5; elev. 300ft./91m.; mail Monroeville z 36460; rural
LIMESTONE; **142** A-6; Ⓟ 54,135; Ⓒ 65,676; ◆ 76,143
Lim Rock; RMC Place; JACKSON; **142** B-8; elev. 616ft./188m.; mail Woodville z 35776
Lincoln; RMC Place; MADISON; ***142** A-7; ★ **HNTS**; mail Huntsville z 35810; pop. incl. with Huntsville (Inc. Place)
Lincoln; Inc. Place; TALLADEGA; **142** F-8; elev. 505ft./154m.; 🅿; z 35096; Ⓟ 2,937; Ⓒ 4,577; Ⓡ 4,585
Lincoya Estates; RMC Place; JEFFERSON; ★ **BIR**; mail Birmingham z 35216; pop. incl. with Vestavia Hills (Inc. Place)
Lindbergh; RMC Place; JEFFERSON; ***142** F-6; ★ **BIR**; mail Graysville z 35073; rural
Linden; Inc. Place; ⊡ MARENGO; **142** J-3; elev. 134ft./41m.; 🅿; z 36748; Ⓟ 2,548; Ⓒ 2,424
Lineville; Inc. Place; CLAY; **142** G-10; elev. 1,057ft./322m.; 🅿; z 36266; Ⓟ 2,394; Ⓒ 2,401
Linn Crossing (Lynn Crossing); RMC Place; JEFFERSON; ***142** E-6; elev. 390ft./119m.; ★ **BIR**; mail Graysville z 35073; rural
Linwood; RMC Place; PIKE; ***143** L-9; elev. 368ft./112m.; mail Troy z 36081
Lipscomb; Inc. Place; JEFFERSON; **143** T-10; elev. 526ft./160m.; ★ **BIR**; mail Bessemer z 35020; Ⓟ 2,892; Ⓒ 2,458
Lisman; Inc. Place; CHOCTAW; **143** K-2; elev. 158ft./48m.; 🅿; z 36912 & mail Jachin z 36910; Ⓟ 481; Ⓒ 653
Little Oak; RMC Place; PIKE; ***143** L-9; elev. 441ft./134m.; mail Troy z 36079; rural
Little River; RMC Place; BALDWIN; **143** N-4; elev. 40ft./12m.; 🅿; z 36550; ● 40
Little River; RMC Place; CHEROKEE; ***142** C-10; elev. 593ft./181m.; mail Cedar Bluff z 35959; rural
Little Rock; RMC Place; ESCAMBIA; ***143** O-5; mail Atmore z 36502; rural
Little Shawmut; RMC Place; CHAMBERS; ***142** H-11; mail Lanett z 36863; pop. incl. with Lanett (Inc. Place)
Little Texas; RMC Place; MACON; ***142** J-10; mail Auburn z 36830, Tuskegee z 36083; ● 100
Littleton; RMC Place; ETOWAH; ***142** D-8; mail Attalla z 35954; rural
Littleton; RMC Place; JEFFERSON; ***142** E-6; ★ **BIR**; mail Graysville z 35073; rural
Littleville; Inc. Place; COLBERT; **142** B-4; elev. 692ft./211m.; mail Russellville z 35654, Tuscumbia z 35674; Ⓟ 925; Ⓒ 978
Littleville; RMC Place; WINSTON; ***142** C-4; mail Haleyville z 35565; rural
Live Oak Landing; RMC Place; BALDWIN; ***143** P-3; elev. 5ft./2m.; mail Bay Minette z 36507; ● 100
Livingston; Inc. Place; ⊡ SUMTER; **142** I-2; elev. 149ft./45m.; 🅿 🄲 3,633; z 35470; Ⓟ 3,530; Ⓒ 3,297
Loachapoka; Inc. Place; LEE; **142** I-10; elev. 687ft./209m.; 🅿; z 36865; Ⓟ 259; Ⓒ 165
Loango; RMC Place; COVINGTON; **143** N-7; elev. 314ft./96m.; mail Red Level z 36474; ● 50
Locke Crossroads; RMC Place; LIMESTONE; ***142** A-6; mail Elkmont z 35620; rural
Lockhart; Inc. Place; COVINGTON; **143** O-8; elev. 292ft./89m.; 🅿; z 36455; Ⓟ 484; Ⓒ 548
Lock Six; RMC Place; LAUDERDALE; ***142** A-4; ★ **FLO**; mail Killen z 35645; ● 100
Lock Three; RMC Place; LAUDERDALE; ***142** A-5; ★ **FLO**; mail Rogersville z 35652; rural
Locust Fork; Inc. Place; BLOUNT; **142** D-7; elev. 594ft./181m.; 🅿; z 35097; Ⓟ 342; Ⓒ 1,016
Loflin; RMC Place; RUSSELL; ***143** K-12; elev. 320ft./98m.; mail Holy Trinity z 36859; rural
Logan; RMC Place; CULLMAN; **142** D-6; elev. 709ft./216m.; 🅿; z 35098; ● 170
Logton; RMC Place; PIKE; ***143** L-9; elev. 472ft./144m.; mail Troy z 36081; rural
Lola City; RMC Place; JEFFERSON; ***142** F-7; elev. 597ft./182m.; ★ **BIR**; mail Trussville z 35173; ● 200
Lomax; RMC Place; CHILTON; ***142** H-7; mail Clanton z 35045; pop. incl. with Clanton (Inc. Place)
London; RMC Place; CONECUH; **143** N-5; mail Castleberry z 36432; ● 50
London; RMC Place; MONTGOMERY; ***142** J-9; mail Mathews z 36052; rural
Long Island; RMC Place; JACKSON; ***142** A-10; mail Bryant z 35958
Longleaf Estates; RMC Place; MORGAN; ***142** B-6; elev. 610ft./186m.; ★ **DEC**; mail Decatur z 35603; pop. incl. with Decatur (Inc. Place)
Longtown (Langtown); RMC Place; LAWRENCE; ***142** B-5; ★ **DEC**; mail Moulton z 35650; ● 350
Longview; RMC Place; CULLMAN; ***142** C-6; mail Vinemont z 35179; ● 60
Longview; RMC Place; SHELBY; ***142** G-6; mail Saginaw z 35137; pop. incl. with Alabaster (Inc. Place)
Longwood; RMC Place; MADISON; ***142** B-7; ★ **HNTS**; mail Huntsville z 35801; pop. incl. with Huntsville (Inc. Place)
Loop; RMC Place; CHEROKEE; ***142** C-10; elev. 669ft./204m.; mail Cedar Bluff z 35959; rural
Loop; RMC Place; MOBILE; ***143** P-2; ★ **MOB**; mail Mobile z 36606, z 36660; pop. incl. with Mobile (Inc. Place)
Loree; RMC Place; CONECUH; **143** M-5; mail Evergreen z 36401; rural
Lott; RMC Place; MOBILE; ***143** P-2; elev. 208ft./63m.; ★ **MOB**; mail Eight Mile z 36613; rural
Lottie; RMC Place; BALDWIN; **143** O-4; mail Atmore z 36502; ● 100
Louisville; Inc. Place; BARBOUR; **143** L-10; elev. 543ft./166m.; 🅿; z 36048; Ⓟ 728; Ⓒ 612
Love Hill; RMC Place; HOUSTON; ***143** O-11; elev. 230ft./70m.; mail Ashford z 36312; ● 100
Lovelace Crossroads; RMC Place; LAUDERDALE; ***142** A-4; ★ **FLO**; mail Florence z 35630; ● 50
Loveless; RMC Place; DEKALB; ***142** C-10; mail Fort Payne z 35967; rural
Loveless Park; RMC Place; JEFFERSON; ***142** G-6; ★ **BIR**; mail Bessemer z 35020; ● 100
Lovick; RMC Place; JEFFERSON; ***142** F-7; ★ **BIR**; mail Trussville z 35173; pop. incl. with Birmingham (Inc. Place)
Lower Peach Tree; RMC Place; WILCOX; **143** L-4; elev. 525ft./160m.; 🅿; z 36751; ● 400
Lowery; RMC Place; GENEVA; ***143** N-8; mail Kinston z 36453; ● 30
Lowerytown; RMC Place; BIBB; **142** G-5; mail West Blocton z 35184; ● 110
Low Gap; RMC Place; ST. CLAIR; ***142** E-7; elev. 860ft./262m.; ★ **BIR**; mail Odenville z 35120; ● 30
LOWNDES; **143** K-7; Ⓟ 12,658; Ⓒ 13,473; ◆ 12,473
Lowndesboro; LOWNDES; see Saint Clair (RMC Place)
Lowndesboro; Inc. Place; LOWNDES; **142** J-7; elev. 416ft./127m.; 🅿; z 36752; Ⓟ 139; Ⓒ 140
Lowry Mill; RMC Place; COFFEE; ***143** M-9; mail Jack z 36346; rural
Loxley; Inc. Place; BALDWIN; **143** P-3; elev. 171ft./52m.; 🅿; z 36551; Ⓟ 1,161; Ⓒ 1,348
Loxley Heights; RMC Place; BALDWIN; ***143** P-3; elev. 157ft./48m.; mail Loxley z 36551; ● 90
Lucille; RMC Place; BIBB; **142** G-5; mail West Blocton z 35184; ● 100
Lugo; RMC Place; BARBOUR; **143** L-11; mail Eufaula z 36027, Midway z 36053
Lumbull; RMC Place; MARION; ***142** C-4; elev. 921ft./281m.; mail Bear Creek z 35543; pop. incl. with Bear Creek (Inc. Place)
Lupton; RMC Place; WALKER; ***142** D-5; elev. 544ft./166m.; mail Nauvoo z 35578; ● 60
Luttrell; RMC Place; DEKALB; ***142** C-9; mail Fyffe z 35971; ● 30
Luverne; Inc. Place; ⊡ CRENSHAW; **143** L-8; elev. 366ft./112m.; 🅿 🄷; z 36049; Ⓟ 2,555; Ⓒ 2,635
Lydia; RMC Place; DEKALB; **142** C-9; elev. 1,226ft./374m.; mail Fort Payne z 35968; ● 60
Lyeffion; RMC Place; CONECUH; **143** M-6; mail Evergreen z 36401; ● 30
Lynn; Inc. Place; WINSTON; **142** D-4; elev. 722ft./220m.; 🅿; z 35575; Ⓟ 611; Ⓒ 597; Ⓡ 723
Lynn Acres; RMC Place; JEFFERSON; ***142** F-7; ★ **BIR**; mail Birmingham z 35215; pop. incl. with Birmingham (Inc. Place)
Lynn Crossing; JEFFERSON; see Linn Crossing (RMC Place)
Lynndale; RMC Place; MONTGOMERY; ***142** J-8; elev. 210ft./64m.; ★ **MTGY**; mail Montgomery z 36105; pop. incl. with Montgomery (Inc. Place)
Lynn Haven; RMC Place; TUSCALOOSA; ★ **TUSC**; mail Tuscaloosa z 35404; pop. incl. with Tuscaloosa (Inc. Place)
Lynns Park; RMC Place; WALKER; ***142** E-5; mail Cordova z 35550; ● 70
Lytle; RMC Place; GENEVA; ***143** O-9; mail Samson z 36477; rural

M

Mabson; RMC Place; DALE; ***143** M-10; mail Ozark z 36360; ● 80
Macedonia; RMC Place; CLEBURNE; ***142** F-11; elev. 1,279ft./390m.; mail Ranburne z 36273; ● 100
Macedonia; RMC Place; JACKSON; ***142** B-9; mail Section z 35771; ● 50
Macedonia; RMC Place; MONTGOMERY; ***142** J-8; ★ **MTGY**; mail Grady z 36036
Macedonia; RMC Place; PICKENS; ***142** F-2; mail Ethelsville z 35461; disincorporated December 15, 2000; Ⓟ 290; Ⓒ 291
Macedonia; RMC Place; WALKER; **142** D-5; mail Jasper z 35503; ● 110
Mackey; RMC Place; CHEROKEE; ***142** D-9; elev. 571ft./174m.; mail Leesburg z 35983; pop. incl. with Leesburg (Inc. Place)
Macon; RMC Place; CALHOUN; ***142** E-9; mail Ohatchee z 36271; rural
MACON; **142** J-10; Ⓟ 24,928; Ⓒ 24,105; ◆ 21,823
Madison; Inc. Place; MADISON, LIMESTONE; **142** B-11; elev. 675ft./206m.; 🅿 🄷; ★ **HNTS**; z 35756-58; Ⓟ 14,904; Ⓒ 29,329; ◆ 39,104
MADISON; **142** A-7; Ⓟ 238,912; Ⓒ 276,700; Ⓡ 276,951; ◆ 326,633
Madison Crossroads; RMC Place; MADISON; ***142** A-7; ★ **HNTS**; mail Stevenson z 35772; rural
Madison Heights; RMC Place; MADISON; ★ **HNTS**; pop. incl. with Huntsville (Inc. Place)
Madrid; Inc. Place; HOUSTON; **143** O-11; elev. 166ft./51m.; mail Cottonwood z 36320; Ⓟ 211; Ⓒ 303
Magazine; RMC Place; MOBILE; ***143** P-2; elev. 30ft./9m.; 🅿; ★ **MOB**; z 36610; pop. incl. with Mobile (Inc. Place)
Magnolia; RMC Place; MARENGO; **143** K-4; elev. 272ft./83m.; 🅿; z 36754; ● 100
Magnolia Beach; RMC Place; BALDWIN; ***143** Q-3; ★ **MOB**; mail Fairhope z 36532
Magnolia Courts; RMC Place; JEFFERSON; ***142** F-7; ★ **BIR**; mail Birmingham z 35215; pop. incl. with Birmingham (Inc. Place)
Magnolia Shores; RMC Place; CRENSHAW; ***143** L-8; elev. 450ft./137m.; mail Highland Home z 36041; ● 60
Magnolia Springs; Inc. Place; BALDWIN; **143** Q-3; elev. 21ft./6m.; 🅿; z 36535, z 36555; incorporated June 29, 2006; not reported in 2000 Census; ● 700
Magnolia Terminal; RMC Place; MARENGO; ***143** K-4; mail Arlington z 36722; ● 50
Mahrt; RMC Place; RUSSELL; ***143** K-12; elev. 253ft./77m.; mail Cottonton z 36851; rural
Majestic (Haig); RMC Place; JEFFERSON; **142** E-6; ★ **BIR**; mail Morris z 35116; ● 300
Malbis; RMC Place; BALDWIN; **143** P-3; elev. 196ft./60m.; ★ **MOB**; mail Daphne z 36526; ● 200
Malcolm; RMC Place; WASHINGTON; **143** N-3; elev. 49ft./15m.; 🅿; z 36556; ● 250
Malone; RMC Place; RANDOLPH; ***142** G-10; mail Wadley z 36276, Wedowee z 36278
Malta; RMC Place; ESCAMBIA; ***143** O-4; elev. 289ft./88m.; mail Atmore z 36502; rural
Malvern; Inc. Place; GENEVA; **143** O-10; elev. 281ft./86m.; 🅿; z 36349; Ⓟ 570; Ⓒ 1,215
Mamie; RMC Place; MONTGOMERY; ***143** K-9; elev. 321ft./98m.; mail Mathews z 36052; rural
Manack; RMC Place; LOWNDES; ***142** J-7; elev. 202ft./62m.; mail Lowndesboro z 36752; ● 30
Manchester; RMC Place; MARSHALL; ***142** C-8; elev. 700ft./213m.; mail Guntersville z 35976; rural
Manchester; RMC Place; WALKER; **142** E-5; mail Jasper z 35503; ● 180
Manila; RMC Place; CLARKE; ***143** M-4; elev. 353ft./108m.; mail Jackson z 36545; rural
Manningham; RMC Place; BUTLER; ***143** L-7; elev. 482ft./147m.; mail Greenville z 36037; ● 30
Mansion View; RMC Place; LAUDERDALE; ***142** A-4; ★ **FLO**; mail Florence z 35633; ● 450
Mantua; RMC Place; GREENE; **142** H-3; elev. 274ft./84m.; mail Eutaw z 35462; ● 40
Maple Hill; RMC Place; MADISON; ***142** A-6; ★ **HNTS**; mail Toney z 35773; ● 80
Maplesville; Inc. Place; CHILTON; **142** I-6; elev. 350ft./107m.; 🅿; z 36750; Ⓟ 725; Ⓒ 672
Maplewood; RMC Place; JEFFERSON; ***142** F-7; ★ **BIR**; mail Leeds z 35094; pop. incl. with Leeds (Inc. Place)
Maplewood; RMC Place; MADISON; ★ **HNTS**; mail Madison z 35758; pop. incl. with Madison (Inc. Place)
Marble City Heights; RMC Place; TALLADEGA; mail Sylacauga z 35150; pop. incl. with Sylacauga (Inc. Place)
Marble Valley; RMC Place; COOSA; **142** H-7; elev. 524ft./160m.; mail Sylacauga z 35151; rural
Marbury; RMC Place; AUTAUGA; **142** I-7; elev. 485ft./148m.; 🅿; z 36051; ● 380
Marcoot; RMC Place; CHAMBERS; ***142** H-10; elev. 777ft./237m.; mail Lafayette z 36862; ● 60
MARENGO; **143** K-4; Ⓟ 23,084; Ⓒ 22,539; ◆ 20,962
Margaret; Inc. Place; ST. CLAIR; **142** E-7; elev. 700ft./213m.; 🅿; ★ **BIR**; z 35112; Ⓟ 616; Ⓒ 1,169
Margerum; RMC Place; COLBERT; **142** A-3; mail Cherokee z 35616; ● 50
Marietta; RMC Place; WALKER; ***142** E-5; elev. 374ft./114m.; mail Oakman z 35579; pop. incl. with Oakman (Inc. Place)
Marion; Inc. Place; ⊡ PERRY; **142** I-5; elev. 376ft./115m.; 🅿 🄷 🄲 326; z 36756; Ⓟ 4,211; Ⓒ 3,511
MARION; **142** D-4; Ⓟ 29,830; Ⓒ 31,214; ◆ 29,135
Marion Junction; RMC Place; DALLAS; **142** J-5; elev. 213ft./65m.; 🅿; z 36759; ● 300
Markeeta; RMC Place; ST. CLAIR; ***142** F-7; ★ **BIR**; mail Leeds z 35094; pop. incl. with Moody (Inc. Place)
Marks Village; RMC Place; JEFFERSON; ***142** F-7; ★ **BIR**; mail Birmingham z 35222; pop. incl. with Birmingham (Inc. Place)
Marl; RMC Place; GENEVA; ***143** O-9; mail Samson z 36477; ● 30
Marley Mill; RMC Place; DALE; ***143** M-10; mail Ozark z 36360; pop. incl. with Ozark (Inc. Place)
Marlow; RMC Place; BALDWIN; **143** Q-3; ★ **MOB**; mail Summerdale z 36580; ● 160
Marshall; RMC Place; MARSHALL; ***142** C-8; elev. 1,100ft./335m.; mail Boaz z 35957; ● 50
MARSHALL; **142** B-8; Ⓟ 70,832; Ⓒ 82,231; ◆ 87,563
Mars Hill; RMC Place; CHILTON; ***142** H-6; elev. 570ft./174m.; mail Jemison z 35085; ● 30
Mars Hill; RMC Place; LAUDERDALE; ***142** A-4; ★ **FLO**; mail Florence z 35630; pop. incl. with Florence (Inc. Place)
Martins; RMC Place; JEFFERSON; ***142** F-6; ★ **BIR**; mail Birmingham z 35208; pop. incl. with Birmingham (Inc. Place)
Martintown; RMC Place; JACKSON; **142** A-9; mail Hollywood z 35752; ● 100
Martinville; RMC Place; ESCAMBIA; ***143** O-4; elev. 268ft./82m.; mail Atmore z 36502; ● 50
Martling; RMC Place; MARSHALL; **142** C-8; mail Albertville z 35950; ● 80
Marvel; RMC Place; BIBB; **142** G-6; mail Montevallo z 35115; ● 140
Marvyn; RMC Place; LEE; **142** J-11; elev. 500ft./152m.; mail Opelika z 36804; ● 100
Marylee; RMC Place; WALKER; ***142** D-5; elev. 637ft./194m.; mail Jasper z 35504; ● 30
Maryville; RMC Place; ETOWAH; ***142** D-9; ★ **GAD**; mail Attalla z 35954; ● 30
Mason City; RMC Place; JEFFERSON; ***142** F-6; ★ **BIR**; mail Birmingham z 35211; pop. incl. with Birmingham (Inc. Place)
Massey; RMC Place; MORGAN; ***142** C-6; elev. 614ft./187m.; mail Danville z 35619, Hartselle z 35640; ● 80
Masterson Mill; RMC Place; LAWRENCE; ***142** B-5; mail Moulton z 35650; ● 110
Mastin Lake; RMC Place; MADISON; ★ **HNTS**; mail Huntsville z 35810-11; pop. incl. with Huntsville (Inc. Place)
Mathews; MONTGOMERY; see Matthews (RMC Place)
Mattawana; RMC Place; BLOUNT; ***142** D-7; mail Oneonta z 35121; rural
Matthews (Mathews); RMC Place; MONTGOMERY; **142** J-9; elev. 251ft./77m.; mail Cecil z 36013, Mathews z 36052; ● 150
Maud; RMC Place; COLBERT; ***142** B-2; elev. 551ft./168m.; mail Cherokee z 35616; rural
Mauvilla (Mauville); RMC Place; MOBILE; ***143** P-2; elev. 150ft./46m.; ★ **MOB**; mail Eight Mile z 36613; ● 50
Mauville; MOBILE; see Mauvilla (RMC Place)
Maxine; RMC Place; JEFFERSON; ***142** F-5; elev. 286ft./87m.; mail Quinton z 35130; rural
Maxwell; RMC Place; TUSCALOOSA; ***142** G-4; elev. 277ft./84m.; mail Tuscaloosa z 35401; rural
Maxwellborn; RMC Place; CALHOUN; ***142** E-10; ★ **ANNI**; mail Piedmont z 36272; ● 30
Maxwell Heights; RMC Place; MONTGOMERY; ★ **MTGY**; mail Montgomery z 36113; pop. incl. with Montgomery (Inc. Place)
Mayes Crossroad (Mays Crossroads); RMC Place; ETOWAH; ***142** D-9; ★ **GAD**; mail Gadsden z 35903; rural
Mayfair; RMC Place; JEFFERSON; ***142** F-6; ★ **BIR**; mail Birmingham z 35209; pop. incl. with Homewood (Inc. Place)
Mayfair; RMC Place; MADISON; ***142** B-7; ★ **HNTS**; mail Huntsville z 35801; pop. incl. with Huntsville (Inc. Place)
Maylene; RMC Place; SHELBY; ***142** G-6; elev. 500ft./152m.; 🅿; ★ **BIR**; z 35114; pop. incl. with Alabaster (Inc. Place)
Maynard Cove (Maynards Cove); RMC Place; JACKSON; ***142** A-9; mail Scottsboro z 35768; rural
Maynards Cove; JACKSON; see Maynard Cove (RMC Place)
Mays Crossroads; RMC Place; CLARKE; ***143** M-3; rural
Mays Crossroads; ETOWAH; see Mayes Crossroad (RMC Place)
Maysville; RMC Place; MADISON; **142** A-7; mail Brownsboro z 35741, Huntsville z 35811; ● 350
Maytown; Inc. Place; JEFFERSON; **143** R-9; elev. 500ft./152m.; ★ **BIR**; mail Mulga z 35118; Ⓟ 651; Ⓒ 435
McCall; RMC Place; ESCAMBIA; ***143** O-5; elev. 187ft./57m.; mail Brewton z 36426; ● 30
McCalla; RMC Place; JEFFERSON; **142** G-6; elev. 550ft./168m.; 🅿; ★ **BIR**; z 35111; ● 1,000
McClure Town; RMC Place; PIKE; ***143** L-9; elev. 401ft./122m.; mail Troy z 36081; rural
McCollum (McCullum); RMC Place; WALKER; **142** E-5; mail Jasper z 35501; ● 300
McCord Crossroads; RMC Place; CHEROKEE; ***142** D-10; elev. 636ft./194m.; mail Centre z 35960; ● 30
McCulley (McCulley Hill); RMC Place; BIBB; ***142** G-6; mail West Blocton z 35184; ● 70
McCulley Hill; BIBB; see McCulley (RMC Place)
McCullough; RMC Place; ESCAMBIA; **143** N-4; elev. 301ft./92m.; 🅿; z 36502; ● 250
McCullum; WALKER; see McCollum (RMC Place)
McDonald Chapel; CDP; JEFFERSON; **143** R-10; elev. 578ft./176m.; ★ **BIR**; mail Birmingham z 35224; Ⓒ 1,054
McDowell; RMC Place; SUMTER; ***142** J-3; elev. 98ft./30m.; mail Livingston z 35470; rural
McElderry; RMC Place; TALLADEGA; ***142** F-9; elev. 565ft./172m.; ★ **ANNI**; mail Munford z 36268; ● 50
McGehees; MONTGOMERY; see Hope Hull (RMC Place)
McGhee (McGhees Bend); RMC Place; CHEROKEE; ***142** D-10; mail Centre z 35960; rural
McGhees Bend; CHEROKEE; see McGhee (RMC Place)
McGinty; RMC Place; CHAMBERS; ***142** I-11; elev. 676ft./206m.; mail Valley z 36854; pop. incl. with Valley (Inc. Place)
McIntosh; Inc. Place; WASHINGTON; **143** N-3; elev. 48ft./15m.; 🅿; z 36553; Ⓟ 250; Ⓒ 244
McKenzie; Inc. Place; BUTLER; **143** M-7; elev. 350ft./107m.; 🅿; z 36456; Ⓟ 464; Ⓒ 644
McKestes; RMC Place; DEKALB; ***142** C-9; mail Dawson z 35963; rural
McKinley; RMC Place; MARENGO; ***142** J-4; elev. 337ft./103m.; mail Catherine z 36728; ● 50
McLarty; RMC Place; BLOUNT; ***142** D-8; elev. 836ft./255m.; mail Horton z 35980; ● 100
McLendon; RMC Place; RUSSELL; ***143** K-12; mail Cottonton z 36851; rural
McMullen; Inc. Place; PICKENS; ***142** G-2; elev. 200ft./61m.; mail Aliceville z 35442; Ⓟ 112; Ⓒ 66
McQueen; RMC Place; AUTAUGA; ***142** J-8; elev. 150ft./46m.; ★ **MTGY**; mail Prattville z 36066; rural
McShan; RMC Place; PICKENS; **142** F-2; elev. 282ft./86m.; 🅿; z 35471; ● 150
McVay; RMC Place; CLARKE; **143** M-3; elev. 422ft./129m.; mail Grove Hill z 36451; ● 30
McVille; RMC Place; MARSHALL; ***142** C-8; mail Albertville z 35951; ● 30
McWilliams; RMC Place; WILCOX; **143** L-5; 🅿; z 36753; ● 280
Meadowbrook; CDP-Census Area Only; SHELBY; **143** T-14; 🅿; ★ **BIR**; z 35242; Ⓟ 4,621; Ⓒ 4,697
Meadow Hills; RMC Place; MADISON; ***142** A-7; ★ **HNTS**; mail Huntsville z 35810; pop. incl. with Huntsville (Inc. Place)
Meadows Crossroads; RMC Place; LEE; ***142** I-11; elev. 471ft./144m.; mail Salem z 36874; ● 30
Meadwood Heights; RMC Place; JEFFERSON; ***142** F-7; ★ **BIR**; mail Birmingham z 35217; pop. incl. with Birmingham (Inc. Place)
Mechanicsville; RMC Place; LEE; ***142** I-11; elev. 642ft./196m.; mail Salem z 36874; rural
Meeksville; RMC Place; PIKE; ***143** L-9; elev. 480ft./146m.; mail Troy z 36081; ● 30
Megargel; RMC Place; MONROE; **143** N-4; elev. 350ft./107m.; 🅿; z 36457; ● 200
Mellow Valley; RMC Place; CLAY; **142** G-10; elev. 916ft./279m.; mail Cragford z 36255; ● 100
Melrose; RMC Place; CONECUH; ***143** N-7; elev. 243ft./74m.; mail Evergreen z 36401; rural
Melrose; RMC Place; PICKENS; ***142** F-2; mail Mc Shan z 35471; rural
Melton; RMC Place; HALE; ***142** I-4; mail Sawyerville z 36776; rural
Meltonsville; RMC Place; MARSHALL; ***142** C-8; mail Langston z 35755; rural
Melvin; RMC Place; CHOCTAW; **143** L-1; elev. 333ft./101m.; 🅿; z 36913; ● 250
Memphis; Inc. Place; PICKENS; ***142** G-2; mail Macon z 39341; Ⓟ 54; Ⓒ 33
Mentone; Inc. Place; DEKALB; **142** B-10; elev. 1,708ft./521m.; 🅿; z 35984; Ⓟ 474; Ⓒ 451
Mercury; RMC Place; MADISON; ***142** A-7; elev. 767ft./234m.; ★ **HNTS**; mail Huntsville z 35811; pop. incl. with Huntsville (Inc. Place)
Meridianville; CDP; MADISON; **142** A-7; elev. 750ft./229m.; 🅿; ★ **HNTS**; z 35759; Ⓟ 2,852; Ⓒ 4,117
Merrell Beach; RMC Place; SHELBY; ***142** G-7; elev. 400ft./122m.; mail Shelby z 35143; ● 30
Merry; RMC Place; MONTGOMERY; ***142** J-9; ★ **MTGY**; mail Pike Road z 36064; rural
Mertz; RMC Place; MOBILE; ***143** P-2; ★ **MOB**; mail Mobile z 36606; pop. incl. with Mobile (Inc. Place)
Mexboro; RMC Place; MONROE; ***143** M-5; mail Frisco City z 36445, Mexia z 36458; rural
Mexia; RMC Place; MONROE; **143** M-5; elev. 418ft./127m.; 🅿; z 36458; ● 200
Mexia Crossing; RMC Place; MONROE; ***143** M-5; elev. 421ft./128m.; mail Mexia z 36458; rural
Micaville; RMC Place; CLEBURNE; ***142** F-10; mail Heflin z 36264; rural
Middle Brooks Crossroads; RMC Place; LEE; ***142** I-10; elev. 700ft./213m.; mail Waverly z 36879; rural
Middleton; RMC Place; CALHOUN; **142** E-9; ★ **ANNI**; mail Ohatchee z 36271; ● 170
Midfield; Inc. Place; JEFFERSON; **142** F-6; elev. 512ft./156m.; 🅿; ★ **BIR**; z 35228; Ⓟ 5,559; Ⓒ 5,626
Midland City; Inc. Place; DALE; **143** N-10; elev. 376ft./115m.; 🅿; ★ **DOTH**; z 36350; Ⓟ 1,819; Ⓒ 1,703
Midtown; RMC Place; MOBILE; ★ **MOB**; mail Mobile z 36604, z 36640-41; pop. incl. with Mobile (Inc. Place)
Midway; Inc. Place; BULLOCK; **143** K-10; elev. 542ft./165m.; 🅿; z 36053; Ⓟ 455; Ⓒ 457
Midway; RMC Place; BUTLER; **143** L-7; mail Honoraville z 36042; ● 100
Midway; RMC Place; CHILTON; ***142** I-7; mail Marbury z 36051; rural
Midway; RMC Place; CLAY; ***142** G-9; mail Goodwater z 35072; pop. incl. with Lineville (Inc. Place)
Midway; RMC Place; LAWRENCE; ***142** B-5; ★ **DEC**; mail Moulton z 35650, Trinity z 35673; ● 240
Midway; RMC Place; MONROE; ***143** L-6; mail Pine Apple z 36768; rural
Midway; RMC Place; TALLAPOOSA; ***142** H-9; elev. 610ft./186m.; mail Jacksons Gap z 36861; ● 30
Miflin; RMC Place; BALDWIN; **143** Q-4; mail Elberta z 36530; ● 100
Mignon; CDP; TALLADEGA; ***142** G-8; elev. 510ft./155m.; mail Sylacauga z 35150; Ⓟ 1,548; Ⓒ 1,348; Ⓡ 1,342
Miles; RMC Place; JEFFERSON; ★ **BIR**; mail Fairfield z 35064; pop. incl. with Fairfield (Inc. Place)
Millbrook; Inc. Place; ELMORE; **142** J-8; elev. 199ft./61m.; 🅿; ★ **MTGY**; z 36054; Ⓟ 6,050; Ⓒ 10,386
Miller; RMC Place; MARENGO; ***143** K-3; elev. 271ft./83m.; mail Linden z 36748; ● 30
Millers Ferry; RMC Place; WILCOX; **143** K-5; elev. 130ft./40m.; mail Camden z 36726; ● 120
Millertown; RMC Place; MOBILE; ***143** P-2; elev. 220ft./67m.; ★ **MOB**; mail Eight Mile z 36613, Semmes z 36575, Wilmer z 36587; ● 1,700
Millerville; RMC Place; CLAY; **142** G-9; elev. 833ft./254m.; 🅿; z 36267; ● 180
Millport; Inc. Place; LAMAR; **142** F-2; elev. 300ft./91m.; 🅿; z 35576; Ⓟ 1,203; Ⓒ 1,160
Millry; Inc. Place; WASHINGTON; **143** M-2; elev. 150ft./46m.; 🅿; z 36558; Ⓟ 781; Ⓒ 615
Mills Quarter's; RMC Place; BALDWIN; ***143** Q-3; elev. 23ft./7m.; mail Foley z 36535; pop. incl. with Foley (Inc. Place)
Milltown; RMC Place; CHAMBERS; **142** H-10; elev. 655ft./200m.; mail Lafayette z 36862; ● 60
Mill Village; RMC Place; MARSHALL; ***142** C-8; mail Guntersville z 35976; pop. incl. with Guntersville (Inc. Place)
Milstead; RMC Place; MACON; **142** J-9; elev. 206ft./63m.; mail Shorter z 36075; ● 120
Milton; RMC Place; AUTAUGA; ***142** I-6; elev. 263ft./80m.; mail Jones z 36749; ● 30
Mineral Springs; RMC Place; CHILTON; ***142** H-7; elev. 627ft./191m.; mail Jemison z 35085; ● 100
Minooka; RMC Place; CHILTON; ***142** H-7; mail Calera z 35040; rural
Minor; CDP; JEFFERSON; **143** R-10; ★ **BIR**; mail Birmingham z 35224; Ⓟ 3,313; Ⓒ 1,116
Minor Terrace; RMC Place; TALLADEGA; ***142** G-8; mail Childersburg z 35044; pop. incl. with Childersburg (Inc. Place)
Minter; RMC Place; DALLAS; **143** K-6; elev. 194ft./59m.; 🅿; z 36761; ● 80
Minvale; RMC Place; DEKALB; ***142** B-10; mail Fort Payne z 35967; pop. incl. with Fort Payne (Inc. Place)
Mitchell; RMC Place; BULLOCK; **143** K-9; elev. 240ft./73m.; mail Fitzpatrick z 36029; rural
Mitchell Crossroads; RMC Place; LEE; ***142** I-11; elev. 581ft./177m.; ★ **AU-OP**; mail Opelika z 36804; ● 60
Mitchelltown; RMC Place; LAUDERDALE; ***142** A-4; ★ **FLO**; mail Killen z 35645; rural
Mitylene; RMC Place; MONTGOMERY; ***142** J-8; ★ **MTGY**; pop. incl. with Montgomery (Inc. Place)
Mobile; Inc. Place; ⊡ MOBILE; **143** P-2; elev. 7ft./2m.; 🅿 🄷 🄲 16,606 ■; ★ **MOB**; z 36601-13, z 36615-19, z 36625, z 36628, z 36630, z 36633, z 36640-41, z 36644, z 36652, z 36660, z 36663, z 36670-71, z 36675, z 36685, z 36688-89, z 36691, z 36693, z 36695; Ⓟ 196,263; Ⓒ 198,915; Ⓡ 199,191; ◆ 192,460
MOBILE; **143** P-2; Ⓟ 378,643; Ⓒ 399,843; ◆ 401,171
Mobile Junction; RMC Place; JEFFERSON; ***142** F-6; elev. 580ft./177m.; ★ **BIR**; mail Bessemer z 35022; pop. incl. with Bessemer (Inc. Place)
Moffet (Moffett); RMC Place; MOBILE; ***143** P-1; elev. 105ft./32m.; mail Wilmer z 36587; rural
Moffett; MOBILE; see Moffet (RMC Place)
Mollie; RMC Place; CHOCTAW; ***143** K-2; elev. 208ft./63m.
Molloy; RMC Place; LAMAR; **142** E-2; elev. 314ft./96m.; mail Sulligent z 35586
Mon Louis; RMC Place; MOBILE; **143** Q-2; ★ **MOB**; mail Coden z 36523; ● 420
MONROE; **143** M-5; Ⓟ 23,968; Ⓒ 24,324; ◆ 21,943
Monroeville; Inc. Place; ⊡ MONROE; **143** M-5; elev. 418ft./127m.; 🅿 🄷; z 36460-62; Ⓟ 6,993; Ⓒ 6,862
Monrovia; RMC Place; MADISON; **142** A-11; ★ **HNTS**; mail Huntsville z 35806; ● 50
Montague; RMC Place; JACKSON; ***142** A-9; mail Bridgeport z 35740; rural
Monterey; RMC Place; BUTLER; **143** L-6; mail Forest Home z 36030
Monterey Heights; RMC Place; LEE; ***142** I-12; elev. 420ft./128m.; ★ **COL**; mail Smiths Station z 36877; ● 200
Monte-Sano; RMC Place; JEFFERSON; ***142** F-6; ★ **BIR**; mail Birmingham z 35228; pop. incl. with Birmingham (Inc. Place)
Montevallo; Inc. Place; SHELBY; **142** G-6; elev. 500ft./152m.; 🅿 🄲 2,931; z 35115; Ⓟ 4,239; Ⓒ 4,825
Monte Vista; RMC Place; ETOWAH; ***142** D-9; ★ **GAD**; mail Gadsden z 35904; pop. incl. with Gadsden (Inc. Place)
Montgomery; Inc. Place; **STATE CAPITAL**; ⊡ MONTGOMERY; **142** J-8; elev. 287ft./87m.; 🅿 🄷 🄲 15,292 ■; ★ **MTGY**; z 36101-21, z 36123-25, z 36130-35, z 36140-42, z 36177, z 36191 & mail Uriah z 36480; Ⓟ 187,543; Ⓒ 201,568; ◆ 209,348
MONTGOMERY; **143** K-9; Ⓟ 209,085; Ⓒ 223,510; ◆ 228,587
Monticello; RMC Place; PIKE; **143** L-10; mail Banks z 36005; rural
Montrose; RMC Place; BALDWIN; **143** Q-3; elev. 117ft./36m.; 🅿; ★ **MOB**; z 36559; pop. incl. with Fairhope (Inc. Place)
Moody; Inc. Place; ST. CLAIR; **142** F-7; elev. 683ft./208m.; 🅿; ★ **BIR**; z 35004; Ⓟ 4,921; Ⓒ 8,053
Moontown; RMC Place; MADISON; ***142** A-7; elev. 640ft./195m.; ★ **HNTS**; mail Brownsboro z 35741; ● 100
Moorefield; RMC Place; CHAMBERS; ***142** H-11; elev. 859ft./262m.; mail Lafayette z 36862; rural
Moores Bridge; RMC Place; TUSCALOOSA; **142** F-3; elev. 286ft./87m.; mail Northport z 35475; ● 50
Moores Crossroads; RMC Place; DEKALB; ***142** C-9; mail Fyffe z 35971; ● 100
Moores Crossroads; RMC Place; RANDOLPH; ***142** G-11; elev. 876ft./267m.; mail Roanoke z 36274; rural
Moores Crossroads; RMC Place; SHELBY; ***142** G-6; elev. 496ft./151m.; ★ **BIR**; mail Montevallo z 35115; ● 10
Moores Mill; CDP; MADISON; ***142** A-7; ★ **HNTS**; mail Huntsville z 35811; Ⓟ 3,362; Ⓒ 5,178
Moores Valley; RMC Place; MARENGO; ***143** K-4; elev. 137ft./42m.; mail Pine Hill z 36769; rural
Mooresville; Inc. Place; LIMESTONE; **142** B-6; elev. 570ft./174m.; 🅿; ★ **HNTS**; z 35649; Ⓟ 54; Ⓒ 59
Moreland; RMC Place; WINSTON; **142** C-5; elev. 877ft./267m.; mail Houston z 35572; ● 50
Morgan; RMC Place; JEFFERSON; ***142** G-6; elev. 540ft./165m.; ★ **BIR**; mail Bessemer z 35020; pop. incl. with Bessemer (Inc. Place)
MORGAN; **142** C-7; Ⓟ 100,043; Ⓒ 111,064; ◆ 113,402
Morgan City; RMC Place; MORGAN; **142** B-7; mail Laceys Spring z 35754, Union Grove z 35175; ● 300
Morganville; LOWNDES; see Tyson (RMC Place)
Moriah; RMC Place; COOSA; ***142** H-8; mail Rockford z 35136; rural
Morningside; RMC Place; JEFFERSON; ***142** F-7; ★ **BIR**; mail Birmingham z 35215
Morris; Inc. Place; JEFFERSON; **142** E-6; elev. 414ft./126m.; 🅿; ★ **BIR**; z 35116; Ⓟ 1,136; Ⓒ 1,827
Morrows Grove; RMC Place; GREENE; ***142** H-3; elev. 169ft./52m.; mail Eutaw z 35462; ● 100
Morvin; RMC Place; CLARKE; **143** K-3; elev. 237ft./72m.; 🅿; z 36762; ● 80
Moshat; RMC Place; CHEROKEE; ***142** D-10; elev. 675ft./206m.; mail Centre z 35960; rural
Moss (Mosses); Inc. Place; LOWNDES; ***143** K-7; mail Hayneville z 36040; Ⓟ 1,072; Ⓒ 1,101
Mosses; LOWNDES; see Moss (Inc. Place)
Mossy Grove; RMC Place; PIKE; ***143** L-9; mail Troy z 36079; ● 30
Mostellers; RMC Place; SHELBY; ***142** G-7; mail Shelby z 35143; rural
Motley; RMC Place; CLAY; ***142** G-10; elev. 927ft./283m.; mail Wadley z 36276; rural
Moulton; Inc. Place; ⊡ LAWRENCE; **142** B-5; elev. 650ft./198m.; 🅿 🄷; z 35650; Ⓟ 3,248; Ⓒ 3,260
Moulton Heights; RMC Place; MORGAN; ***142** B-6; ★ **DEC**; mail Decatur z 35601; pop. incl. with Decatur (Inc. Place)
Moundville; Inc. Place; HALE, TUSCALOOSA; **142** H-4; elev. 168ft./51m.; 🅿; z 35474; Ⓟ 1,348; Ⓒ 1,809; Ⓡ 1,794
Mountainboro; Inc. Place; ETOWAH; **142** D-8; elev. 1,075ft./328m.; mail Boaz z 35957; Ⓟ 261; Ⓒ 338
Mountain Brook; Inc. Place; JEFFERSON; **142** F-7; elev. 773ft./236m.; 🅿; ★ **BIR**; z 35223, z 35253 & mail Birmingham z 35243; Ⓟ 19,810; Ⓒ 20,604; ◆ 21,042
Mountain Brook; RMC Place; MADISON; ***142** B-7; ★ **HNTS**; mail Huntsville z 35801; pop. incl. with Huntsville (Inc. Place)
Mountain Brook Village; RMC Place; JEFFERSON; ***142** F-6; ★ **BIR**; mail Birmingham z 35223; pop. incl. with Mountain Brook (Inc. Place)
Mountain Chest; RMC Place; MARSHALL; mail Guntersville z 35976; pop. incl. with Guntersville (Inc. Place)
Mountain Creek; RMC Place; CHILTON; **142** I-7; elev. 533ft./162m.; mail Marbury z 36051; rural
Mountaindale; RMC Place; JEFFERSON; ***142** F-7; ★ **BIR**; mail Birmingham z 35213; pop. incl. with Birmingham (Inc. Place)
Mountain Gap; RMC Place; MARSHALL; ***142** C-8; elev. 1,000ft./305m.; mail Guntersville z 35976; rural
Mountain Grove; RMC Place; BLOUNT; ***142** D-7; elev. 812ft./247m.; mail Blountsville z 35031; rural
Mountain Home; RMC Place; LAWRENCE; ***142** B-5; elev. 750ft./229m.; ★ **DEC**; mail Trinity z 35673; ● 30
Mountain Park; RMC Place; JEFFERSON; ***142** F-6; ★ **BIR**; mail Birmingham z 35217; pop. incl. with Birmingham (Inc. Place)
Mountain Star; RMC Place; FRANKLIN; ***142** B-4; elev. 700ft./213m.; mail Russellville z 35654; ● 80
Mountain View; RMC Place; MARSHALL; ***142** C-8; mail Guntersville z 35976; pop. incl. with Guntersville (Inc. Place)
Mountain Woods; RMC Place; JEFFERSON; ★ **BIR**; mail Birmingham z 35216; pop. incl. with Vestavia Hills (Inc. Place)
Mountain Woods Park; RMC Place; JEFFERSON; ★ **BIR**; mail Birmingham z 35216; pop. incl. with Vestavia Hills (Inc. Place)
Mount Andrew; RMC Place; BARBOUR; **143** K-10; elev. 547ft./167m.; mail Midway z 36053; rural
Mount Carmel; RMC Place; JACKSON; **142** A-9; elev. 650ft./198m.; mail Bridgeport z 35740
Mount Carmel; RMC Place; MARSHALL; **142** C-8; mail Guntersville z 35976; ● 250
Mount Carmel; RMC Place; MONTGOMERY; **143** K-8; elev. 411ft./125m.; mail Lapine z 36046; ● 150
Mount Hebron; RMC Place; GREENE; **142** H-2; mail Boligee z 35443; rural
Mount Hebron; RMC Place; MARSHALL; **142** D-8; mail Boaz z 35957, Douglas z 35964; ● 150
Mount Hester; RMC Place; COLBERT; ***142** A-3; elev. 518ft./158m.; mail Cherokee z 35616
Mount Hillard (Mount Hilliard); RMC Place; BULLOCK; ***143** K-9; elev. 550ft./168m.; mail Union Springs z 36089; rural
Mount Hilliard; BULLOCK; see Mount Hillard (RMC Place)
Mount Hope; RMC Place; LAWRENCE; **142** C-4; elev. 677ft./206m.; 🅿; z 35651; ● 150
Mount Ida; RMC Place; CRENSHAW; ***143** M-8; mail Brantley z 36009, Luverne z 36049; ● 30
Mount Jefferson; RMC Place; LEE; ***142** I-11; ★ **AU-OP**; mail Opelika z 36801; rural
Mount Lebanon; RMC Place; MADISON; ***142** A-7; elev. 760ft./232m.; ★ **HNTS**; mail Meridianville z 35759; ● 30
Mount Meigs; RMC Place; MONTGOMERY; **142** J-9; elev. 232ft./71m.; 🅿; ★ **MTGY**; z 36057; ● 700
Mount Nebo; RMC Place; DALLAS; ***142** J-6; mail Tyler z 36785; rural
Mount Olive; RMC Place; COOSA; **142** H-8; elev. 826ft./252m.; mail Goodwater z 35072
Mount Olive; CDP; JEFFERSON; **142** E-6; elev. 616ft./188m.; 🅿; ★ **BIR**; z 35117; Ⓒ 3,957
Mount Olive; RMC Place; TUSCALOOSA; ***142** G-4; elev. 300ft./91m.; ★ **TUSC**; mail Coker z 35452; ● 100

Entries in **UPPERCASE** are counties.
Entries in **bold** have populations of 2,500 or more.
Names in parentheses are alternate names.

Inc. Place	Incorporated Place
RMC Place	Rand McNally Designated Place
CDP	Census Designated Place
MCD	Minor Civil Division
⊡	County Seat
▲	Minor Civil Division
elev.	Elevation
🅿	Post Office
🄷	Hospital
🄲	College
■	Principal Business Center
★	Ranally Metro Area (RMA) Abbreviation
z	Zip Code(s)
Ⓟ	Previous Census Population
Ⓡ	Revised Census Population
Ⓐ	Annexation Population
●	Rand McNally Population Estimate
Ⓒ	Final Census Population
Ⓢ	Special Census Population
◆	Estimated Population

For additional definitions see Glossary, Volume 1, and Introduction, Volume 2.

Mount Pinson; JEFFERSON; see Pinson (Inc. Place)
Mount Pleasant; RMC Place; COFFEE; *143 N-9; mail Enterprise z 36330; rural
Mount Pleasant; RMC Place; COLBERT; *142 A-4; elev. 550ft./168m.; ★ FLO; mail Muscle Shoals z 35661; ● 30
Mount Pleasant; RMC Place; MONROE; *143 N-4; mail Uriah z 36480; ● 50
Mount Rozell; RMC Place; LIMESTONE; 142 A-5; mail Lester z 35647
Mount Sinai; RMC Place; MONTGOMERY; *142 J-7; elev. 190ft./58m.; ★ MTGY; mail Montgomery z 36113; ● 150
Mount Sterling; RMC Place; CHOCTAW; 143 K-2; mail Butler z 36904; ● 100
Mount Tabor; RMC Place; MORGAN; *142 C-6; elev. 660ft./201m.; ★ DEC; mail Hartselle z 35640; rural
Mount Union; RMC Place; CONECUH; *143 N-6; mail Evergreen z 36401; rural
Mount Vernon; RMC Place; CULLMAN; *142 C-5; elev. 900ft./274m.; mail Vinemont z 35179; rural
Mount Vernon; RMC Place; DEKALB; *142 C-9; elev. 1,297ft./395m.; mail Fort Payne z 35967; rural
Mount Vernon; RMC Place; FAYETTE; *142 E-3; mail Fayette z 35555; rural
Mount Vernon; Inc. Place; MOBILE; 143 O-3; elev. 48ft./15m.; [P] [H]; z 36560; ℗ 902; © 844
Mount Willing; RMC Place; LOWNDES; 143 K-7; mail Fort Deposit z 36032; ● 100
Mount Zion; RMC Place; MONTGOMERY; mail Ramer z 36069; rural
Movico; RMC Place; MOBILE; *143 O-3; elev. 50ft./15m.; mail Mount Vernon z 36560; ● 200
MOWA Choctaw Reservation; Indian Reservation; WASHINGTON, MOBILE; State Reservation; © 124
Muck City; RMC Place; LAWRENCE; *142 B-5; mail Moulton z 35650; ● 110
Mud Creek; RMC Place; JEFFERSON; *142 F-5; elev. 388ft./118m.; mail Adger z 35006; rural
Mulberry; RMC Place; AUTAUGA; *142 J-6; elev. 315ft./96m.; mail Autaugaville z 36003; rural
Mulga; Inc. Place; JEFFERSON; 143 Q-9; elev. 584ft./178m.; [P]; ★ BIR; z 35118; ℗ 261; © 973
Mulga Mine; RMC Place; JEFFERSON; *142 F-6; ★ BIR; mail Mulga z 35118; ● 380
Mullins; RMC Place; HOUSTON; ★ DOTH; pop. incl. with Dothan (Inc. Place)
Munford; Inc. Place; TALLADEGA, TALLADEGA; 142 F-9; elev. 660ft./201m.; ★ ANNI; incorporated September 1, 2002; not reported in 2000 Census; ● 1,400
Munford; CDP-Census Area Only; TALLADEGA; 142 F-9; elev. 660ft./201m.; [P]; ★ ANNI; z 36268; © 2,446
Murphree Crossroads; RMC Place; ETOWAH; *142 D-8; elev. 943ft./287m.; mail Boaz z 35957; rural
Murphree Valley; BLOUNT; see Hoods Crossroads (RMC Place)
Murphy Cross Roads; RMC Place; LAUDERDALE; *142 A-3; elev. 850ft./259m.; mail Waterloo z 35677; ● 30
Murrays Chapel; RMC Place; ST. CLAIR; *142 E-8; elev. 645ft./197m.; mail Springville z 35146; rural
Muscadine; RMC Place; CLEBURNE; 142 E-11; elev. 1,036ft./316m.; [P]; z 36269; ● 200
Muscadine Junction; RMC Place; CLEBURNE; mail Muscadine z 36269
Muscle Shoals; Inc. Place; COLBERT; 142 F-13; elev. 516ft./157m.; [P] [H]; ★ FLO; z 35661-62; ℗ 9,611; © 11,924
Muscoda; RMC Place; JEFFERSON; 143 T-10; ★ BIR; mail Bessemer z 35020; ● 550
Mynot; RMC Place; COLBERT; *142 B-3; mail Cherokee z 35616; rural
Myrick Chapel; RMC Place; AUTAUGA; *142 I-7; elev. 400ft./122m.; mail Deatsville z 36022; rural
Myrtlewood; Inc. Place; MARENGO; 143 K-3; elev. 221ft./67m.; [P]; z 36763; ℗ 197; © 139

N

Nadawah; RMC Place; MONROE; *143 L-5; mail Camden z 36726; rural
Naftel; RMC Place; MONTGOMERY; *143 K-8; elev. 512ft./156m.; mail Lapine z 36046; rural
Nanafalia; RMC Place; MARENGO; 143 K-3; elev. 219ft./67m.; [P]; z 36764; ● 180
Nances Creek; RMC Place; CALHOUN; *142 E-10; mail Piedmont z 36272; ● 60
Napier Field; Inc. Place; DALE; *143 N-11; elev. 364ft./111m.; ★ DOTH; mail Dothan z 36303; ℗ 462; © 404
Napoleon; RMC Place; RANDOLPH; *142 G-11; elev. 1,176ft./358m.; mail Wedowee z 36278, Woodland z 36280; rural
Nat; RMC Place; JACKSON; mail Woodville z 35776; pop. incl. with Woodville (Inc. Place)
Natchez; RMC Place; MONROE; 143 L-5; mail Beatrice z 36425; rural
Nathan; RMC Place; WINSTON; mail Arley z 35541; pop. incl. with Arley (Inc. Place)
Natural Bridge; Inc. Place; WINSTON; 142 D-4; elev. 800ft./244m.; [P]; z 35577; © 28
Nauvoo; Inc. Place; WALKER, WINSTON; 142 D-4; elev. 562ft./171m.; [P]; z 35578; ℗ 240; © 284
Navco; RMC Place; MOBILE; *143 P-2; ★ MOB; mail Mobile z 36605; pop. incl. with Mobile (Inc. Place)
Nebo; RMC Place; MADISON; *142 B-8; elev. 600ft./183m.; ★ HNTS; mail New Hope z 35760; rural
Nectar; Inc. Place; BLOUNT; 142 D-7; elev. 500ft./152m.; mail Cleveland z 35049, Hayden z 35079; ℗ 238; © 372
Needham; Inc. Place; CHOCTAW; 143 K-2; elev. 200ft./61m.; [P]; z 36915; ℗ 99; © 97
Needmore; RMC Place; MARSHALL; *142 C-8; mail Boaz z 35957; rural
Needmore; RMC Place; PIKE; 143 L-9; elev. 458ft./140m.; mail Troy z 36081
Needmore; RMC Place; WINSTON; *142 C-4; mail Haleyville z 35565; ● 200
Neel; RMC Place; MORGAN; 142 C-6; mail Hartselle z 35640; ● 150
Neely; RMC Place; MOBILE; ★ MOB; pop. incl. with Mobile (Inc. Place)
Neenah; RMC Place; WILCOX; *143 L-5; mail Camden z 36726; rural
Nellie; RMC Place; WILCOX; *143 L-5; mail Camden z 36726; rural
Nelson Heights; RMC Place; JEFFERSON; *142 F-7; ★ BIR; mail Birmingham z 35215; pop. incl. with Birmingham (Inc. Place)
Neman; RMC Place; ELMORE; *142 I-9; elev. 357ft./109m.; mail Tallassee z 36078; rural
Neshota; RMC Place; MOBILE; *143 P-2; ★ MOB; mail Mobile z 36605; pop. incl. with Mobile (Inc. Place)
Nesmith; RMC Place; CULLMAN; *142 D-5; elev. 910ft./277m.; mail Cullman z 35057; rural
Ne Smith; RMC Place; LAWRENCE; *142 B-4; mail Town Creek z 35672; rural
Nettleboro; RMC Place; CLARKE; *143 L-4; mail Dickinson z 36436; rural
Newbern; Inc. Place; HALE; 142 I-4; elev. 188ft./57m.; [P]; z 36765; ℗ 222; © 231
Newberry Crossroads; RMC Place; CHEROKEE; *142 D-10; elev. 585ft./178m.; mail Centre z 35960; ● 30
New Brockton; Inc. Place; COFFEE; 143 N-9; elev. 468ft./143m.; [P]; z 36351; ℗ 1,184; © 1,250
Newburg; RMC Place; FRANKLIN; 142 B-4; elev. 664ft./202m.; mail Russellville z 35654; ● 100
New Castle; RMC Place; JEFFERSON; *142 E-6; elev. 530ft./162m.; [P]; ★ BIR; z 35119; pop. incl. with Gardendale (Inc. Place)
New Center; RMC Place; MORGAN; *142 B-6; elev. 760ft./232m.; ★ DEC; mail Hartselle z 35640; rural
New Dora; RMC Place; WALKER; *142 E-6; ★ BIR; mail Dora z 35062; pop. incl. with Dora (Inc. Place)
Newell; RMC Place; RANDOLPH; 142 F-11; elev. 852ft./260m.; [P]; z 36280; ● 80
New Georgia; RMC Place; WINSTON; *142 C-5; elev. 810ft./247m.; mail Addison z 35540; rural
New Haven; RMC Place; MADISON; *142 B-6; ★ HNTS; mail Madison z 35758; rural
New Hill; RMC Place; JEFFERSON; *142 F-6; ★ BIR; mail Bessemer z 35020; pop. incl. with Lipscomb (Inc. Place)
New Home; RMC Place; DEKALB; *142 B-10; mail Henagar z 35978; ● 60
New Hope; RMC Place; COFFEE; *143 M-9; elev. 369ft./112m.; mail Brundidge z 36010; ● 30
New Hope; RMC Place; CULLMAN; *142 C-7; mail Holly Pond z 35083; rural
New Hope; RMC Place; JACKSON; *142 B-8; mail Scottsboro z 35768; pop. incl. with Scottsboro (Inc. Place)
New Hope; Inc. Place; MADISON; 142 B-8; elev. 596ft./182m.; [P]; ★ HNTS; z 35760; ℗ 2,248; © 2,539
New Hope; RMC Place; MARION; *142 D-3; elev. 568ft./173m.; mail Winfield z 35594; rural
New Hope; RMC Place; SHELBY; *142 F-7; ★ BIR; mail Birmingham z 35243; pop. incl. with Indian Springs Village (Inc. Place)
New Hopewell; CLEBURNE; see Hopewell (RMC Place)
New Jagger (Jagger); RMC Place; WALKER; *142 E-5; elev. 377ft./115m.; mail Townley z 35587; rural
New Lexington; RMC Place; TUSCALOOSA; *142 F-4; mail Berry z 35546; ● 100
New London; RMC Place; ST. CLAIR; 142 F-8; elev. 461ft./141m.; mail Cropwell z 35054; ● 80
New Market; CDP; MADISON; 142 A-7; elev. 750ft./229m.; [P]; ★ HNTS; z 35761; ℗ 1,094; © 1,864
New Moon; RMC Place; CHEROKEE; *142 C-10; elev. 667ft./203m.; mail Gaylesville z 35973; rural
New Mount Hebron; RMC Place; GREENE; *142 H-2; elev. 140ft./43m.; mail Boligee z 35443; rural
New Prospect; RMC Place; AUTAUGA; *142 I-7; mail Marbury z 36051; ● 50
New Prospect; RMC Place; HALE; *142 H-4; elev. 152ft./46m.; mail Akron z 35441; rural
New Sharon; RMC Place; MADISON; *142 A-7; ★ HNTS; mail Hazel Green z 35750; rural
New Site; Inc. Place; TALLAPOOSA; 142 H-10; elev. 883ft./269m.; [P]; z 36256 & mail Alexander City z 35010; ℗ 669; © 848
Newsome; RMC Place; DEKALB; mail Rainsville z 35986; pop. incl. with Rainsville (Inc. Place)
Newton; Inc. Place; DALE; 143 N-10; elev. 300ft./91m.; [P]; ★ DOTH; z 36352; ℗ 1,580; © 1,708
Newton; RMC Place; HOUSTON; ★ DOTH; mail Dothan z 36301; pop. incl. with Dothan (Inc. Place)
Newtonville; RMC Place; FAYETTE; 142 F-3; mail Fayette z 35555
Newtown; RMC Place; FRANKLIN; mail Russellville z 35653; pop. incl. with Russellville (Inc. Place)
New Town; RMC Place; JACKSON; *142 A-9; mail Stevenson z 35772; pop. incl. with Stevenson (Inc. Place)
Newville; Inc. Place; HENRY; 143 N-11; elev. 398ft./121m.; [P]; z 36353; ℗ 531; © 553
New West Greene; RMC Place; GREENE; *142 H-2; elev. 148ft./45m.; mail Eutaw z 35462; rural
Nichburg; RMC Place; CONECUH; *143 M-5; elev. 330ft./101m.; mail Repton z 36475; rural
Nicholsville; RMC Place; MARENGO; *143 K-3; elev. 181ft./55m.; mail Thomasville z 36784; ● 50
Nitrate City; RMC Place; COLBERT; 142 A-4; ★ FLO; mail Sheffield z 35660; ● 250
Nixburg; RMC Place; COOSA; 142 H-8; elev. 734ft./224m.; mail Equality z 36026; ● 90
Nix Mill; RMC Place; FRANKLIN; *142 C-3; mail Phil Campbell z 35581; rural
Nixon Chapel (Nixons Chapel); RMC Place; MARSHALL; 142 C-8; mail Horton z 35980; ● 180
Nixons Chapel; MARSHALL; see Nixon Chapel (RMC Place)
Noah; RMC Place; CHEROKEE; *142 D-10; mail Centre z 35960; ● 40
Nokomis; RMC Place; ESCAMBIA; *143 O-4; mail Atmore z 36502; ● 70
Nolan Hills; RMC Place; MADISON; ★ HNTS; mail Madison z 35758; pop. incl. with Madison (Inc. Place)
Normal; RMC Place; MADISON; 142 A-14; elev. 750ft./229m.; [P]; ★ HNTS; z 35762; pop. incl. with Huntsville (Inc. Place)
North Arab; RMC Place; MARSHALL; *142 C-7; mail Arab z 35016; pop. incl. with Arab (Inc. Place)
North Athens; RMC Place; LIMESTONE; mail Athens z 35611; pop. incl. with Athens (Inc. Place)
North Bibb; BIBB, TUSCALOOSA; see Woodstock (Inc. Place)
North Birmingham; RMC Place; JEFFERSON; *142 F-6; ★ BIR; mail Birmingham z 35207; pop. incl. with Birmingham (Inc. Place)
North Courtland; Inc. Place; LAWRENCE; *142 B-5; mail Courtland z 35618; ℗ 973; © 799
North Daye Hill; RMC Place; MADISON; *142 A-7; elev. 850ft./259m.; ★ HNTS; mail Harvest z 35749; ● 70
North Elmore; RMC Place; ELMORE; *142 I-8; ★ MTGY; mail Elmore z 36025; ● 420
North Florence; RMC Place; LAUDERDALE; *142 A-4; ★ FLO; mail Florence z 35630; pop. incl. with Florence (Inc. Place)
North Highlands; RMC Place; JEFFERSON; *142 F-6; ★ BIR; mail Bessemer z 35020; pop. incl. with Hueytown (Inc. Place)
North Johns (Johns); Inc. Place; JEFFERSON; 142 F-5; ★ BIR; mail Adger z 35006; ℗ 177; © 142
North Mobile; RMC Place; MOBILE; *143 P-2; ★ MOB; mail Mobile z 36611; pop. incl. with Chickasaw (Inc. Place)
Northport; Inc. Place; TUSCALOOSA; 142 G-4; elev. 161ft./49m.; [P] [H]; ★ TUSC; z 35473, z 35475-76; ℗ 17,366; © 19,435; ® 19,610; ◆ 21,340
Northside; RMC Place; HOUSTON; *143 N-11; ★ DOTH; mail Dothan z 36304; pop. incl. with Dothan (Inc. Place)
Northside Acres; RMC Place; MADISON; *142 A-7; elev. 780ft./238m.; ★ HNTS; mail Huntsville z 35806; ● 100
North Smithfield Estates; JEFFERSON; see Greenleas Heights (RMC Place)
North Vinemont; RMC Place; CULLMAN; *142 C-6; mail Vinemont z 35179; rural
North Walter; RMC Place; CULLMAN; *142 D-7; mail Cullman z 35055; rural
Northwood Hills; RMC Place; LAUDERDALE; *142 A-4; ★ FLO; mail Florence z 35630; pop. incl. with Florence (Inc. Place)
Norton; RMC Place; ETOWAH; *142 D-8; elev. 554ft./169m.; ★ GAD; mail Attalla z 35954; rural
Norton; RMC Place; MADISON; *142 B-7; mail Huntsville z 35803; pop. incl. with Huntsville (Inc. Place)
Norwood; RMC Place; JEFFERSON; *142 F-6; ★ BIR; mail Birmingham z 35234; pop. incl. with Birmingham (Inc. Place)
Notasulga; Inc. Place; MACON, LEE; 142 I-10; elev. 521ft./159m.; [P]; z 36866; ℗ 979; © 916
Nottingham; RMC Place; TALLADEGA; *142 F-8; mail Alpine z 35014; rural
Nuckols; RMC Place; RUSSELL; *142 J-12; elev. 243ft./74m.; mail Fort Mitchell z 36856; rural
Nymph; RMC Place; CONECUH; *143 N-6; mail Evergreen z 36401

O

Oak; RMC Place; BALDWIN; *143 R-4; elev. 2ft./1m.; mail Gulf Shores z 36542; ● 50
Oak Bowery; RMC Place; CHAMBERS; 142 I-11; elev. 839ft./256m.; mail Lafayette z 36862; rural
Oak Crossing; RMC Place; JEFFERSON; *142 F-7; ★ BIR; mail Leeds z 35094; pop. incl. with Leeds (Inc. Place)
Oakdale; RMC Place; LIMESTONE; *142 A-6; mail Athens z 35613; rural
Oakdale Acres; RMC Place; LIMESTONE; *142 A-6; elev. 750ft./229m.; mail Athens z 35613; ● 150
Oakey Grove (Oakley Grove); RMC Place; HENRY; *143 M-11; elev. 400ft./122m.; mail Newville z 36353; rural
Oak Grove; RMC Place; AUTAUGA; *142 I-7; elev. 557ft./170m.; mail Prattville z 36067; ● 40
Oak Grove; RMC Place; CHILTON; *142 H-7; elev. 731ft./223m.; mail Jemison z 35085; ● 100
Oak Grove; RMC Place; FRANKLIN; 142 C-4; mail Russellville z 35654; rural
Oak Grove; RMC Place; GENEVA; *143 O-10; elev. 236ft./72m.; mail Black z 36314; ● 30
Oak Grove; RMC Place; HALE; *142 I-4; elev. 128ft./39m.; mail Gallion z 36742; ● 30
Oak Grove; RMC Place; JEFFERSON; 142 F-5; elev. 431ft./131m.; mail Adger z 35006, Bessemer z 35023; ● 230
Oak Grove; RMC Place; LIMESTONE; *142 A-6; mail Ardmore z 35739; rural
Oak Grove; RMC Place; MADISON; *142 B-7; elev. 600ft./183m.; ★ HNTS; mail New Hope z 35760; ● 80
Oak Grove; RMC Place; MARSHALL; *142 B-8; elev. 1,300ft./396m.; mail Scottsboro z 35769; ● 60
Oak Grove; RMC Place; MOBILE; *143 P-2; elev. 46ft./14m.; ★ MOB; mail Eight Mile z 36613; rural
Oak Grove; Inc. Place; TALLADEGA; 142 G-8; [P]; z 35150-51; ℗ 436; © 457
Oak Grove Estates; RMC Place; JEFFERSON; *142 F-6; ★ BIR; mail Birmingham z 35209; pop. incl. with Homewood (Inc. Place)
Oak Hill; RMC Place; DEKALB; *142 C-9; mail Crossville z 35962; rural
Oak Hill; Inc. Place; WILCOX; 143 L-6; elev. 500ft./152m.; [P]; z 36766; ℗ 28; © 37
Oak Hills; RMC Place; JEFFERSON; *142 F-6; ★ BIR; mail Birmingham z 35208; pop. incl. with Birmingham (Inc. Place)
Oakhurst; RMC Place; JEFFERSON; *142 F-6; ★ BIR; mail Birmingham z 35207; pop. incl. with Birmingham (Inc. Place)
Oakland; RMC Place; LAUDERDALE; 142 A-3; ★ FLO; mail Florence z 35633; ● 160
Oakleigh Estates; RMC Place; ETOWAH; ★ GAD; mail Gadsden z 35901; pop. incl. with Gadsden (Inc. Place)
Oak Level; RMC Place; CLEBURNE; 142 E-10; elev. 1,010ft./308m.; mail Fruithurst z 36262; ● 100
Oakley; RMC Place; BIBB; *142 H-6; elev. 500ft./152m.; mail Randolph z 36792; rural
Oakley Grove; HENRY; see Oakey Grove (RMC Place)
Oakman; Inc. Place; WALKER; 142 E-5; elev. 327ft./100m.; [P]; z 35579; ℗ 846; © 944
Oakmulgee; RMC Place; PERRY; *142 I-6; elev. 328ft./100m.; mail Lawley z 36793; rural
Oak Ridge; RMC Place; MORGAN; *142 B-6; mail Hartselle z 35640; ● 150
Oak Ridge; RMC Place; ST. CLAIR; *142 F-8; mail Pell City z 35125; pop. incl. with Pell City (Inc. Place)
Oak Ridge Park; RMC Place; JEFFERSON; *142 F-7; ★ BIR; mail Birmingham z 35212; pop. incl. with Birmingham (Inc. Place)
Oakville; RMC Place; JEFFERSON; *142 F-7; ★ BIR; mail Birmingham z 35206; pop. incl. with Birmingham (Inc. Place)
Oakville; RMC Place; LAWRENCE; 142 C-5; mail Danville z 35619; ● 150
Oakwood; RMC Place; JEFFERSON; ★ BIR; mail Bessemer z 35020; pop. incl. with Bessemer (Inc. Place)
Oakwood College; RMC Place; MADISON; *142 A-7; elev. 800ft./244m.; ★ HNTS; mail Huntsville z 35896; pop. incl. with Huntsville (Inc. Place)
Oakworth; RMC Place; MORGAN; *142 B-6; ★ DEC; mail Decatur z 35601; pop. incl. with Decatur (Inc. Place)
Oaky Streak; RMC Place; BUTLER; *143 M-7; elev. 398ft./121m.; mail Greenville z 36037; rural
Ocampo; RMC Place; CHILTON; *142 H-6; elev. 540ft./165m.; mail Calera z 35040; rural
Ocre; RANDOLPH; see Broughton (RMC Place)
Octagon; RMC Place; MARENGO; 143 K-3; elev. 285ft./87m.; mail Linden z 36748; ● 30
Odena; RMC Place; TALLADEGA; *142 G-8; mail Sylacauga z 35150; rural
Oden Ridge; RMC Place; MORGAN; *142 C-6; mail Eva z 35621, Falkville z 35622; ● 50
Odenville; Inc. Place; ST. CLAIR; 142 E-8; elev. 731ft./223m.; [P]; ★ BIR; z 35120; ℗ 796; © 1,131
Odom; BUTLER; see Odom Crossroads (RMC Place)
Odom Crossroads (Odom); RMC Place; BUTLER; *143 M-6; mail Mc Kenzie z 36456; rural
Ofelia; RMC Place; RANDOLPH; *142 G-10; mail Lineville z 36266; rural
Ohatchee (Ohatchie); Inc. Place; CALHOUN; 142 E-9; elev. 510ft./155m.; [P]; z 36271; ℗ 1,042; © 1,215
Ohatchie; CALHOUN; see Ohatchee (Inc. Place)
Okomo; RMC Place; SHELBY; *142 G-7; elev. 411ft./125m.; mail Shelby z 35143; ● 30
Old Bethel; RMC Place; COLBERT; *142 B-4; mail Leighton z 35646, Sheffield z 35660; rural
Old Bingham (Bingham); RMC Place; ELMORE; *142 J-8; elev. 194ft./59m.; mail Wetumpka z 36093; ● 80
Old Burleson; RMC Place; FRANKLIN; *142 C-3; mail Vina z 35593; rural
Old Davistown; CALHOUN; see Old Davisville (RMC Place)
Old Davisville (Old Davistown); RMC Place; CALHOUN; *142 E-10; mail Anniston z 36201; ● 50
Old Fabius; RMC Place; JACKSON; *142 A-9; elev. 760ft./232m.; mail Flat Rock z 35966; ● 100
Oldfield; RMC Place; TALLADEGA; *142 G-8; mail Sylacauga z 35150
Old Jonesboro; RMC Place; JEFFERSON; *142 F-6; ★ BIR; mail Birmingham z 35215; pop. incl. with Bessemer (Inc. Place)
Old Kingston; RMC Place; AUTAUGA; *142 I-7; elev. 413ft./126m.; mail Prattville z 36067; rural
Old Maylene; RMC Place; SHELBY; *142 G-6; ★ BIR; mail Maylene z 35114; pop. incl. with Alabaster (Inc. Place)
Old Mill Trace; RMC Place; TUSCALOOSA; *142 G-4; elev. 260ft./79m.; ★ TUSC; mail Cottondale z 35453; ● 150
Old Monrovia; RMC Place; MADISON; *142 A-7; ★ HNTS; mail Huntsville z 35806; rural
Old Nauvoo; RMC Place; FRANKLIN; *142 C-3; elev. 773ft./236m.; mail Russellville z 35653; rural
Old Samuel; RMC Place; CHOCTAW; *143 L-2; mail Gilbertown z 36908; rural
Old Sparta; RMC Place; CONECUH; *143 N-6; elev. 250ft./76m.; mail Evergreen z 36401; rural
Old Spring Hill; RMC Place; MARENGO; 142 J-3; mail Gallion z 36742; ● 30
Old Texas; RMC Place; MONROE; 143 L-6; elev. 438ft./134m.; mail Pine Apple z 36768; rural
Old Town; RMC Place; CONECUH; *143 N-6; mail Evergreen z 36401; rural
Old Town; RMC Place; DALLAS; *143 K-6; mail Tyler z 36785; rural
Oleander; RMC Place; MARSHALL; 142 C-7; mail Union Grove z 35175
Oliver; RMC Place; LAUDERDALE; 142 A-5; mail Rogersville z 35652; ● 100
Ollie; RMC Place; MONROE; *143 M-5; elev. 425ft./130m.; mail Monroeville z 36460; ● 300
Olney; RMC Place; PICKENS; *142 G-3; elev. 297ft./91m.; mail Aliceville z 35442; rural
Omaha; RMC Place; RANDOLPH; 142 G-11; elev. 1,307ft./398m.; mail Roanoke z 36274; rural
Omega (Boswell); RMC Place; BULLOCK; 143 K-10; mail Troy z 36081; rural
O'Neal; RMC Place; LIMESTONE; *142 A-6; mail Athens z 35614; ● 50
Oneonta; Inc. Place; ⊡ BLOUNT; 142 D-7; elev. 885ft./270m.; [P] [H]; z 35121; ℗ 4,844; © 5,576
Onycha; Inc. Place; COVINGTON; 143 N-8; elev. 324ft./99m.; mail Opp z 36467; ℗ 150; © 208
Opelika; Inc. Place; ⊡ LEE; 142 I-11; elev. 822ft./251m.; [P] [H] ■; ★ AU-OP; z 36801-04; ℗ 22,122; © 23,498; ◆ 26,290
Opine; RMC Place; CLARKE; 143 L-3; mail Thomasville z 36784
Opine; RMC Place; COVINGTON; *143 N-8; elev. 330ft./101m.; mail Opp z 36467; rural
Opp; Inc. Place; COVINGTON; 143 N-8; elev. 335ft./102m.; [P] [H]; z 36467; ℗ 6,985; © 6,607
Orange Beach; Inc. Place; BALDWIN; 143 R-4; elev. 8ft./2m.; [P] [C] 10,208; z 36561; ℗ 2,253; © 3,784
Orchard; RMC Place; MOBILE; *143 P-2; ★ MOB; mail Mobile z 36618; pop. incl. with Mobile (Inc. Place)
Ord; ETOWAH; see Owens (RMC Place)
Orion; RMC Place; PIKE; 143 L-9; elev. 565ft./172m.; mail Troy z 36081; ● 30
Orrville; Inc. Place; DALLAS; 142 J-5; elev. 189ft./58m.; [P]; z 36767; ℗ 234; © 230
Orrville (Orville); RMC Place; LIMESTONE; *142 B-6; mail Tanner z 35671; rural
Orville; LIMESTONE; see Orrville (RMC Place)
Osanippa; RMC Place; CHAMBERS; *142 I-11; elev. 666ft./203m.; mail Valley z 36854; pop. incl. with Valley (Inc. Place)
Osborn; RMC Place; PERRY; *142 I-5; rural
Oswichee; RMC Place; RUSSELL; *142 J-12; elev. 330ft./101m.; mail Fort Mitchell z 36856, Seale z 36875
Our Town; RMC Place; TALLAPOOSA; *142 H-9; elev. 647ft./197m.; mail Alexander City z 35010; ● 30
Overbrook; RMC Place; TALLADEGA; 142 G-8; mail Sylacauga z 35150; rural
Overton; RMC Place; JEFFERSON; 143 R-13; elev. 612ft./187m.; ★ BIR; mail Birmingham z 35210; pop. incl. with Irondale (Inc. Place)
Owassa; RMC Place; CONECUH; 143 M-6; mail Evergreen z 36401; ● 50
Owens (Ord); RMC Place; ETOWAH; *142 D-9; ★ GAD; mail Gadsden z 35901
Owens Chapel; WALKER; see Coon Creek (RMC Place)
Owens Cross Roads; Inc. Place; MADISON; 142 B-7; elev. 581ft./177m.; [P]; ★ HNTS; z 35763; ℗ 695; © 1,124
Owenton; RMC Place; JEFFERSON; ★ BIR; mail Birmingham z 35204; pop. incl. with Birmingham (Inc. Place)
Oxanna; RMC Place; CALHOUN; *142 E-9; ★ ANNI; pop. incl. with Anniston (Inc. Place)
Oxford; Inc. Place; CALHOUN, TALLADEGA; 142 F-9; elev. 658ft./201m.; [P]; ★ ANNI; z 36203; ℗ 9,362; © 14,592; ◆ 20,406
Oxford Lake; RMC Place; CALHOUN; ★ ANNI; mail Oxford z 36203; pop. incl. with Oxford (Inc. Place)
Oxmoor; RMC Place; JEFFERSON; 143 T-11; ★ BIR; mail Birmingham z 35211; pop. incl. with Birmingham (Inc. Place)
Oyster Bay; RMC Place; BALDWIN; *143 R-3; elev. 2ft./1m.; mail Foley z 36535, Gulf Shores z 36542; ● 100
Ozark; Inc. Place; ⊡ DALE; 143 M-10; elev. 409ft./125m.; [P] [H]; z 36360-61; ℗ 12,922; © 15,119

P

Painter; RMC Place; DEKALB; 142 C-9; elev. 1,115ft./340m.; mail Crossville z 35962; ● 70
Paint Rock; Inc. Place; JACKSON; 142 B-8; elev. 600ft./183m.; [P]; z 35764; ℗ 214; © 185
Palestine; RMC Place; CLEBURNE; 142 D-10; mail Fruithurst z 36262; ● 80
Palmerdale (Palmers); RMC Place; JEFFERSON; 142 E-7; elev. 688ft./210m.; [P]; ★ BIR; z 35123; ● 570
Palmers; JEFFERSON; see Palmerdale (RMC Place)
Palmers Crossroads; RMC Place; MONROE; *143 N-4; elev. 342ft./104m.; mail Uriah z 36480; rural
Palmetto; RMC Place; PICKENS; 142 F-3; mail Reform z 35481; ● 30
Palmetto Beach; RMC Place; BALDWIN; 143 R-3; mail Gulf Shores z 36542; ● 60
Palos; RMC Place; JEFFERSON; *142 E-6; elev. 337ft./103m.; ★ BIR; mail Quinton z 35130; rural
Panola; RMC Place; CRENSHAW; 143 L-8; elev. 605ft./184m.; mail Lapine z 36046; ● 30
Panola; RMC Place; SUMTER; 142 H-2; elev. 175ft./53m.; [P]; z 35477; ● 270
Pansey; RMC Place; HOUSTON; 143 N-11; elev. 209ft./64m.; [P]; z 36370; ● 250
Paran; RMC Place; RANDOLPH; *142 G-11; elev. 935ft./285m.; mail Roanoke z 36274; rural
Park City; RMC Place; BALDWIN; *143 P-3; ★ MOB; mail Daphne z 36526; pop. incl. with Daphne (Inc. Place)
Parkdale; RMC Place; COOSA; 142 G-8; elev. 861ft./262m.; mail Goodwater z 35072; ● 50
Parker Springs; RMC Place; ESCAMBIA; *143 O-6; elev. 284ft./87m.; mail Wing z 36483; rural
Park Hill; RMC Place; ST. CLAIR; *142 F-8; mail Pell City z 35125; pop. incl. with Pell City (Inc. Place)
Parkland; RMC Place; WALKER; mail Jasper z 35501; pop. incl. with Jasper (Inc. Place)
Park Place; RMC Place; JEFFERSON; *142 F-6; ★ BIR; mail Birmingham z 35221; pop. incl. with Birmingham (Inc. Place)
Parkway; RMC Place; MADISON; pop. incl. with Huntsville (Inc. Place)
Parkway Estates; RMC Place; MADISON; *142 B-7; ★ HNTS; mail Huntsville z 35802; pop. incl. with Huntsville (Inc. Place)
Parkwood; RMC Place; JEFFERSON; 143 T-11; elev. 605ft./184m.; ★ BIR; mail Bessemer z 35020; pop. incl. with Bessemer (Inc. Place)
Parrish; Inc. Place; WALKER; 142 E-5; elev. 333ft./101m.; [P]; z 35580; ℗ 1,433; © 1,268
Partridge Crossroads; RMC Place; JEFFERSON; 142 E-6; elev. 404ft./123m.; ★ BIR; mail Warrior z 35180; ● 30
Patsburg; RMC Place; CRENSHAW; 143 L-8; elev. 338ft./103m.; mail Luverne z 36049; ● 60
Patton (Patton Junction); RMC Place; WALKER; *142 E-4; mail Oakman z 35579; rural
Patton Chapel; RMC Place; JEFFERSON; *142 F-6; elev. 629ft./192m.; ★ BIR; mail Birmingham z 35216; pop. incl. with Hoover (Inc. Place)
Patton Junction; WALKER; see Patton (RMC Place)
Paul; RMC Place; CONECUH; 143 N-7; elev. 214ft./65m.; mail Evergreen z 36401; ● 100
Pauls Hill; RMC Place; JEFFERSON; *142 F-6; ★ BIR; mail Bessemer z 35020; pop. incl. with Bessemer (Inc. Place)
Pawnee; JEFFERSON; see Pawnee Heights (RMC Place)
Pawnee Heights (Pawnee); RMC Place; JEFFERSON; 143 P-13; ★ BIR; mail Birmingham z 35217; ● 300
Peachburg; RMC Place; BULLOCK; *143 K-10; elev. 536ft./163m.; mail Union Springs z 36089; rural
Peacock; RMC Place; CLARKE; *143 L-3; elev. 400ft./122m.; mail Grove Hill z 36451; rural
Pearces Mills; RMC Place; MARION; *142 D-3; elev. 505ft./154m.; mail Hamilton z 35570; rural
Pea Ridge; RMC Place; ESCAMBIA; *143 O-5; mail Brewton z 36426; ● 60
Pea Ridge; RMC Place; FAYETTE; *142 E-4; elev. 600ft./183m.; mail Berry z 35546; rural
Pea Ridge; RMC Place; MADISON; ★ HNTS; mail Huntsville z 35801; pop. incl. with Huntsville (Inc. Place)
Pea Ridge; RMC Place; MARION; *142 D-3; elev. 798ft./243m.; mail Guin z 35563; rural
Pea Ridge; RMC Place; SHELBY; 142 G-6; mail Montevallo z 35115; ● 800
Pearson; RMC Place; TUSCALOOSA; 142 H-5; mail Duncanville z 35456
Pearson Subdivision (Unity); RMC Place; TUSCALOOSA; *142 G-4; ★ TUSC; mail Tuscaloosa z 35401; ● 1,000
Pebble; RMC Place; WINSTON; *142 C-4; elev. 937ft./286m.; mail Haleyville z 35565; rural
Peckerwood; RMC Place; TALLAPOOSA; *142 H-9; elev. 618ft./188m.; mail Jacksons Gap z 36861; pop. incl. with Jacksons Gap (Inc. Place)
Peeks Corner; RMC Place; DEKALB; *142 C-9; elev. 1,286ft./392m.; mail Collinsville z 35961; ● 30
Peets Corner; RMC Place; LIMESTONE; 142 B-6; elev. 627ft./191m.; mail Athens z 35611; ● 30
Pelham; Inc. Place; SHELBY; 142 G-6; elev. 438ft./134m.; [P] [H]; ★ BIR; z 35124; ℗ 9,765; © 14,369; ® 14,307; ◆ 19,566
Pelham Heights; RMC Place; CALHOUN; *142 E-9; ★ ANNI; mail Anniston z 36201; pop. incl. with Anniston (Inc. Place)
Pell City; Inc. Place; ST. CLAIR; 142 F-8; elev. 600ft./183m.; [P] [H]; z 35125, z 35128; ℗ 8,118; © 9,565
Penfield Heights; RMC Place; JEFFERSON; *142 F-7; ★ BIR; mail Birmingham z 35217; pop. incl. with Birmingham (Inc. Place)
Penn; RMC Place; MORGAN; 142 C-6; mail Danville z 35619; ● 60
Pennington; Inc. Place; CHOCTAW; 143 K-3; elev. 106ft./32m.; [P]; z 36916; ℗ 302; © 353
Pennsylvania; RMC Place; MOBILE; *143 P-2; ★ MOB; mail Satsuma z 36572; pop. incl. with Satsuma (Inc. Place)
Penton; RMC Place; CHAMBERS; 142 H-10; elev. 798ft./243m.; mail Lafayette z 36862; ● 100
Pentonville; RMC Place; COOSA; *142 H-8; elev. 608ft./185m.; mail Rockford z 35136; rural
Pepperell; RMC Place; LEE; *142 I-11; elev. 702ft./214m.; ★ AU-OP; mail Opelika z 36801; pop. incl. with Opelika (Inc. Place)
Perdido; RMC Place; BALDWIN; 143 O-4; elev. 205ft./62m.; [P]; z 36562; ● 1,200
Perdido Beach; RMC Place; BALDWIN; 143 Q-4; elev. 9ft./3m.; mail Elberta z 36530
Perdue Hill; RMC Place; MONROE; 143 M-4; elev. 387ft./118m.; [P]; z 36470; ● 250
Perote; RMC Place; BULLOCK; 143 L-10; elev. 483ft./147m.; [P]; z 36061; ● 60
PERRY; 142 I-5; ℗ 12,759; © 11,861; ◆ 10,982
Perrys Chapel; CLARKE; see Alma (RMC Place)
Perry Store; RMC Place; COFFEE; *143 N-8; elev. 310ft./94m.; mail Kinston z 36453; ● 30
Perryville; RMC Place; PERRY; 142 I-5; mail Selma z 36701; rural
Peterman; RMC Place; MONROE; 143 M-5; elev. 178ft./54m.; [P]; z 36471; ● 300
Peterson; RMC Place; TUSCALOOSA; 142 G-4; elev. 386ft./118m.; [P]; ★ TUSC; z 35478; ● 950
Petersville; RMC Place; LAUDERDALE; 142 D-13; ★ FLO; mail Florence z 35633; ● 1,400
Petrey; Inc. Place; CRENSHAW; 143 L-8; elev. 364ft./111m.; [P]; z 36062; ℗ 80; © 63
Petronia; RMC Place; LOWNDES; *142 J-6; elev. 438ft./134m.; mail Tyler z 36785; rural
Pettusville; RMC Place; LIMESTONE; 142 A-6; mail Elkmont z 35620; ● 80
Peytona Points (Peytonia Points); RMC Place; COLBERT; *142 A-4; ★ FLO; mail Sheffield z 35660; ● 50
Peytonia Points; COLBERT; see Peytona Points (RMC Place)
Phelan; RMC Place; CULLMAN; *142 D-6; mail Cullman z 35055; rural
Phenix City; Inc. Place; ⊡ RUSSELL, LEE; 167 R-2; elev. 302ft./92m.; [P] [H]; ★ COL; z 36867-70; ℗ 25,312; © 28,265; ◆ 31,128
Phil Campbell; Inc. Place; FRANKLIN; 142 C-4; elev. 1,025ft./312m.; [P]; z 35581; ℗ 1,317; © 1,091
Phillips Crossroads; SHELBY; see Westover (Inc. Place)
Phillips Estates; RMC Place; JEFFERSON; ★ BIR; mail Bessemer z 35020; pop. incl. with Bessemer (Inc. Place)
Phillipsville; RMC Place; BALDWIN; *143 O-4; mail Bay Minette z 36507; rural
Phoenixville; RMC Place; JEFFERSON; *142 F-6; ★ BIR; mail Birmingham z 35221; pop. incl. with Birmingham (Inc. Place)
PICKENS; 142 G-3; ℗ 20,699; © 20,949; ◆ 19,206
Pickensville; Inc. Place; PICKENS; 142 G-2; elev. 200ft./61m.; [P]; z 35447; ℗ 169; © 662
Piedmont; Inc. Place; CALHOUN, CHEROKEE; 142 D-10; elev. 701ft./214m.; [P]; z 36272; ℗ 5,288; © 5,120
Piedmont; RMC Place; MADISON; *142 B-7; ★ HNTS; mail Huntsville z 35801; pop. incl. with Huntsville (Inc. Place)
Piedmont Springs; RMC Place; CALHOUN; 142 D-10; elev. 808ft./246m.; ★ ANNI; mail Piedmont z 36272; ● 60
Pigeon Creek; RMC Place; BUTLER; 143 M-7; mail Greenville z 36037; ● 30
PIKE; 143 L-10; ℗ 27,595; © 29,605; ◆ 30,467
Pike Road; Inc. Place; MONTGOMERY; 142 J-9; elev. 312ft./95m.; [P]; z 36064; © 310
Pikeville; RMC Place; JACKSON; 142 A-9; mail Scottsboro z 35768; rural
Pilgrims Rest; RMC Place; ETOWAH; *142 D-9; ★ GAD; mail Gadsden z 35907; pop. incl. with Southside (Inc. Place)
Pinckard; Inc. Place; DALE; 143 N-10; elev. 381ft./116m.; [P]; ★ DOTH; z 36371; ℗ 618; © 667
Pinder Hill; RMC Place; JACKSON; *142 A-9; mail Stevenson z 35772; pop. incl. with Stevenson (Inc. Place)
Pine Apple; Inc. Place; WILCOX; 143 L-6; elev. 329ft./100m.; [P]; z 36768; ℗ 365; © 145; ® 172
Pine Beach; RMC Place; BALDWIN; *143 R-3; mail Gulf Shores z 36542; rural
Pinebelt; RMC Place; DALLAS; *143 K-5; elev. 115ft./35m.; mail Orrville z 36767; rural
Pinecrest; RMC Place; MOBILE; *143 Q-1; elev. 73ft./22m.; ★ MOB; mail Grand Bay z 36541
Pine Dale; RMC Place; LIMESTONE; *142 A-6; elev. 227ft./69m.; mail Ardmore z 35739; rural
Pinedale; RMC Place; MONTGOMERY; *142 J-8; elev. 238ft./73m.; ★ MTGY; mail Montgomery z 36116; pop. incl. with Montgomery (Inc. Place)
Pinedale Acres; RMC Place; LAUDERDALE; *142 A-4; ★ FLO; mail Killen z 35645; ● 130
Pinedale Acres; RMC Place; LIMESTONE; *142 A-6; mail Athens z 35611; pop. incl. with Athens (Inc. Place)
Pinedale Shores; RMC Place; ST. CLAIR; 142 E-8; mail Ashville z 35953; ● 800
Pine Flat; RMC Place; AUTAUGA; *142 I-8; mail Deatsville z 36022; rural
Pine Grove; RMC Place; BALDWIN; *143 P-3; elev. 254ft./77m.; mail Bay Minette z 36507; ● 50
Pine Grove; RMC Place; BULLOCK; *143 K-10; elev. 506ft./154m.; mail Midway z 36053; rural
Pine Grove; RMC Place; CHEROKEE; 142 D-10; elev. 625ft./191m.; mail Centre z 35960; ● 80
Pine Grove; RMC Place; LEE; *142 I-11; elev. 750ft./229m.; mail Opelika z 36804
Pine Grove; RMC Place; PICKENS; *142 G-2; elev. 320ft./98m.; mail Carrollton z 35447, Ethelsville z 35461; ● 30
Pine Grove; RMC Place; TALLAPOOSA; *142 I-10; elev. 694ft./212m.; mail Camp Hill z 36850; ● 30
Pine Grove Village; RMC Place; SHELBY; *142 H-7; elev. 400ft./122m.; mail Shelby z 35143; ● 50
Pine Hill; RMC Place; RANDOLPH; *142 F-11; mail Graham z 36263; ● 30
Pine Hill; Inc. Place; WILCOX; 143 K-4; elev. 250ft./76m.; [P]; z 36769; ℗ 481; © 966
Pine Level; RMC Place; AUTAUGA; *142 I-7; mail Deatsville z 36022; ● 50
Pine Level; RMC Place; COFFEE; *143 M-8; elev. 467ft./142m.; mail Elba z 36323; rural
Pine Level; RMC Place; MONTGOMERY; 143 K-9; elev. 500ft./152m.; [P]; z 36065; ● 300
Pine Mountain; RMC Place; BLOUNT; *142 E-7; mail Remlap z 35133; rural
Pine Orchard; RMC Place; MONROE; 143 M-5; elev. 440ft./134m.; mail Peterman z 36471; ● 30
Pine Ridge; Inc. Place; DEKALB; *142 C-9; mail Fort Payne z 35968; ℗ 227; © 243
Pineview; RMC Place; ESCAMBIA; *143 O-5; elev. 304ft./93m.; mail Brewton z 36426; rural
Pineview; RMC Place; JEFFERSON; *142 F-7; ★ BIR; mail Birmingham z 35210; pop. incl. with Irondale (Inc. Place)
Pinewood Terrace; RMC Place; TALLADEGA; *142 G-8; mail Childersburg z 35044; pop. incl. with Childersburg (Inc. Place)
Piney; RMC Place; CHEROKEE; *142 D-10; mail Centre z 35960; ● 30
Piney Bend; RMC Place; FRANKLIN; *142 B-3; mail Vina z 35593; rural
Piney Chapel; RMC Place; LIMESTONE; *142 A-6; mail Athens z 35614; ● 80
Piney Grove; RMC Place; GENEVA; *143 N-9; elev. 250ft./76m.; mail Samson z 36477; rural
Piney Grove; RMC Place; LAWRENCE; 142 C-5; mail Danville z 35619; ● 30
Piney Grove; RMC Place; MARION; *142 D-4; elev. 682ft./208m.; mail Brilliant z 35548; rural
Piney Woods; RMC Place; CLEBURNE; *142 E-11; mail Fruithurst z 36262; ● 80
Pinkeyville; CLAY; see Pinkneyville (RMC Place)
Pinkney City; RMC Place; JEFFERSON; 143 P-10; ★ BIR; mail Birmingham z 35214; pop. incl. with Graysville (Inc. Place)
Pinkneyville (Pinkeyville); RMC Place; CLAY; *142 G-9; mail Goodwater z 35072; rural
Pinnell; RMC Place; TALLAPOOSA; *142 I-10; elev. 723ft./220m.; mail Camp Hill z 36850; rural
Pinson (Mount Pinson); Inc. Place; JEFFERSON; 142 E-7; elev. 604ft./184m.; ★ BIR; incorporated April 2, 2004; not reported in 2000 Census; ● 7,000
Pinson; CDP-Census Area Only; JEFFERSON; 142 E-7; elev. 604ft./184m.; [P]; ★ BIR; z 35126; © 5,033
Pintlala; RMC Place; MONTGOMERY; 143 K-8; elev. 258ft./79m.; mail Hope Hull z 36043; ● 80
Pisgah; Inc. Place; JACKSON; 142 B-9; elev. 1,374ft./419m.; [P]; z 35765; ℗ 652; © 706
Pisgah; RMC Place; LIMESTONE; *142 A-6; elev. 850ft./259m.; ★ HNTS; mail Toney z 35773; ● 50
Pisgah; RMC Place; MONTGOMERY; *143 K-9; elev. 490ft./149m.; mail Grady z 36036; rural
Pittman; RANDOLPH; see Springfield (RMC Place)
Pittsview; RMC Place; RUSSELL; 143 K-11; elev. 241ft./73m.; [P]; z 36871; ● 300
Plainview; RMC Place; CLEBURNE; *142 E-11; elev. 1,007ft./307m.; mail Heflin z 36264; rural
Plainview; RMC Place; DEKALB; *142 B-9; elev. 1,268ft./386m.; mail Rainsville z 35986; pop. incl. with Rainsville (Inc. Place)
Plantation Hills; RMC Place; BALDWIN; *143 P-3; elev. 150ft./46m.; mail Daphne z 36526; ● 100
Plant City; RMC Place; CHAMBERS; *142 H-11; mail Lanett z 36863; pop. incl. with Lanett (Inc. Place)
Plantersville; RMC Place; DALLAS; 142 I-6; elev. 238ft./73m.; [P]; z 36758; ● 750
Plantersville; RMC Place; TALLADEGA; 142 F-8; elev. 483ft./147m.; mail Alpine z 35014; ● 120
Plateau; RMC Place; MOBILE; *143 P-2; elev. 37ft./11m.; ★ MOB; mail Mobile z 36610; pop. incl. with Mobile (Inc. Place)
Plaza De Malaga; RMC Place; MOBILE; ★ MOB; mail Mobile z 36685; pop. incl. with Mobile (Inc. Place)
Pleasant Acres; RMC Place; MADISON; *142 A-7; elev. 750ft./229m.; ★ HNTS; mail Huntsville z 35811; ● 400
Pleasant Gap; RMC Place; CHEROKEE; *142 D-10; elev. 688ft./210m.; mail Piedmont z 36272; ● 30
Pleasant Grove; RMC Place; CHILTON; *142 H-6; elev. 621ft./189m.; mail Jemison z 35085; ● 50
Pleasant Grove (Pleasant Groves); Inc. Place; JACKSON; *142 A-8; mail Stevenson z 35772; ℗ 454; © 447
Pleasant Grove; Inc. Place; JEFFERSON; 142 F-6; elev. 726ft./221m.; [P]; ★ BIR; z 35127; ℗ 8,458; © 9,983
Pleasant Grove; RMC Place; MARSHALL; *142 C-8; elev. 1,000ft./305m.; mail Albertville z 35950; ● 100
Pleasant Grove Estates; RMC Place; JEFFERSON; *142 F-6; elev. 726ft./221m.; ★ BIR; mail Pleasant Grove z 35127; pop. incl. with Pleasant Grove (Inc. Place)
Pleasant Groves; JACKSON; see Pleasant Grove (Inc. Place)
Pleasant Hill; RMC Place; BARBOUR; *143 L-11; elev. 350ft./107m.; mail Eufaula z 36027; ● 30
Pleasant Hill; RMC Place; CHOCTAW; *143 L-2; elev. 297ft./91m.; mail Gilbertown z 36908; ● 30
Pleasant Hill; RMC Place; DALLAS; 143 K-6; mail Sardis z 36775, Selma z 36701; ● 70
Pleasant Hill; RMC Place; ESCAMBIA; *143 O-4; mail Atmore z 36502; rural
Pleasant Hill; RMC Place; FRANKLIN; *142 C-3; elev. 991ft./302m.; mail Spruce Pine z 35585; ● 30
Pleasant Hill; RMC Place; JEFFERSON; 143 T-10; ★ BIR; mail Bessemer z 35020; ● 100
Pleasant Hill; ST. CLAIR; see Caldwell (RMC Place)
Pleasant Hill; RMC Place; WINSTON; *142 C-4; elev. 828ft./252m.; mail Double Springs z 35553; ● 50
Pleasant Home; RMC Place; COVINGTON; *143 N-7; elev. 219ft./67m.; mail Andalusia z 36420; rural
Pleasant Plains; RMC Place; HOUSTON; *143 N-11; elev. 282ft./86m.; ★ DOTH; mail Ashford z 36312; rural
Pleasant Ridge; RMC Place; FRANKLIN; *142 B-4; mail Russellville z 35654; ● 150
Pleasant Ridge; RMC Place; GREENE; 142 H-2; mail Eutaw z 35462; rural
Pleasant Ridge; RMC Place; MARION; *142 D-3; elev. 661ft./201m.; mail Hamilton z 35570; pop. incl. with Hamilton (Inc. Place)
Pleasant Ridge; RMC Place; PIKE; *143 M-9; elev. 338ft./103m.; mail Glenwood z 36034; rural
Pleasant Site; RMC Place; FRANKLIN; 142 B-3; mail Red Bay z 35582; ● 120
Pletcher; RMC Place; CHILTON; *142 I-6; elev. 453ft./138m.; mail Maplesville z 36750; ● 50
Plevna; RMC Place; MADISON; 142 A-7; elev. 852ft./260m.; ★ HNTS; mail New Market z 35761; ● 150
Poarch; RMC Place; ESCAMBIA; 143 O-4; mail Atmore z 36502; ● 100
Poarch Creek Reservation; Indian Reservation; ESCAMBRIA, ELMORE; mail Atmore z 36502; © 156
Pocahontas; RMC Place; WALKER; *142 E-4; elev. 456ft./139m.; mail Carbon Hill z 35549; rural
Pogo; RMC Place; FRANKLIN; *142 B-2; mail Red Bay z 35582; rural
Point Clear; CDP; BALDWIN; 143 Q-3; elev. 11ft./3m.; [P]; ★ MOB; z 36564; ℗ 2,125; © 1,876
Polk; RMC Place; DALLAS; 142 J-6; elev. 248ft./76m.; mail Tyler z 36785; rural
Pollard; Inc. Place; ESCAMBIA; 143 O-5; elev. 64ft./20m.; mail Flomaton z 36441; ℗ 100; © 120
Pollards Bend; CHEROKEE; see Elrath (RMC Place)
Ponderosa (Ponderosa Estates); RMC Place; MOBILE; *143 P-2; elev. 224ft./68m.; ★ MOB; mail Semmes z 36575; ● 400
Ponderosa Estates; MOBILE; see Ponderosa (RMC Place)
Ponders; RMC Place; TALLAPOOSA; *142 I-10; mail Dadeville z 36853; rural
Pondville; RMC Place; BIBB; 142 H-5; elev. 387ft./118m.; mail Brent z 35034; ● 120
Pooles Crossroad; RMC Place; RANDOLPH; *142 G-10; elev. 836ft./255m.; mail Roanoke z 36274; rural
Pools Crossroads; RMC Place; CHILTON; *142 I-7; elev. 612ft./187m.; mail Clanton z 35045; ● 30
Pope; RMC Place; MARENGO; *143 K-4; mail Pine Hill z 36769; rural
Poplar Ridge; RMC Place; MADISON; *142 B-8; elev. 600ft./183m.; ★ HNTS; mail New Hope z 35760; rural
Poplar Springs; RMC Place; MARSHALL; *142 C-8; elev. 1,145ft./349m.; mail Albertville z 35951; ● 30
Poplar Springs; RMC Place; WINSTON; 142 D-5; elev. 746ft./227m.; mail Nauvoo z 35578; ● 70
Port Birmingham (Birminghamport); RMC Place; JEFFERSON; 142 F-5; ★ BIR; mail Mulga z 35118; ● 480
Porter; RMC Place; JEFFERSON; *142 F-6; ★ BIR; mail Adamsville z 35005; ● 160
Portersville (Porterville); RMC Place; DEKALB; 142 C-9; elev. 761ft./232m.; mail Collinsville z 35961
Porterville; DEKALB; see Portersville (RMC Place)
Posey Mill; RMC Place; FRANKLIN; *142 C-4; mail Haleyville z 35565; rural
Poseys Crossroads; RMC Place; AUTAUGA; *142 I-7; elev. 555ft./169m.; mail Prattville z 36067; rural
Poseys Crossroads; RMC Place; CHILTON; *142 H-6; elev. 615ft./187m.; mail Jemison z 35085; ● 30
Postoak; RMC Place; BULLOCK; *143 K-9; elev. 485ft./148m.; mail Troy z 36081, Union Springs z 36089; rural
Potash; RMC Place; RANDOLPH; *142 G-11; mail Roanoke z 36274; ● 30
Potter; RMC Place; DALLAS; *142 J-5; mail Selma z 36701; rural
Powderly; RMC Place; JEFFERSON; *142 F-6; ★ BIR; mail Birmingham z 35211; pop. incl. with Birmingham (Inc. Place)
Powderly Hills; RMC Place; JEFFERSON; *142 F-6; ★ BIR; mail Birmingham z 35211; pop. incl. with Birmingham (Inc. Place)
Powell (Powell's Crossroads); Inc. Place; DEKALB; 142 B-9; elev. 1,275ft./389m.; mail Fyffe z 35971; ℗ 762; © 926
Powell's Crossroads; DEKALB; see Powell (Inc. Place)
Powers; RMC Place; HALE; *142 H-4; mail Moundville z 35474; rural
Powhatan; RMC Place; JEFFERSON; *142 F-5; elev. 276ft./84m.; mail Mulga z 35118; ● 30
Powledge; RMC Place; LEE; *142 I-11; elev. 584ft./178m.; mail Salem z 36874; rural
Praco; RMC Place; JEFFERSON; 142 F-5; elev. 500ft./152m.; mail Quinton z 35130; ● 200
Prairie; RMC Place; WILCOX; 143 K-4; elev. 200ft./61m.; [P]; z 36728; ● 50
Prairieville; RMC Place; HALE; 142 J-4; elev. 191ft./58m.; mail Gallion z 36742; rural
Pratt City; RMC Place; JEFFERSON; *142 F-6; elev. 625ft./191m.; ★ BIR; mail Birmingham z 35214; pop. incl. with Birmingham (Inc. Place)
Pratts; RMC Place; BARBOUR; *143 L-10; mail Clayton z 36016; rural
Prattville; Inc. Place; ⊡ AUTAUGA, ELMORE; 142 J-7; elev. 193ft./59m.; [P] [H]; ★ MTGY; z 36066-68; ℗ 19,587; © 24,303; ◆ 30,088
Prescott; RMC Place; ST. CLAIR; *142 F-7; ★ BIR; mail Pell City z 35125; ● 60
Preston; RMC Place; MARSHALL; *142 B-8; mail Scottsboro z 35769; rural
Prestwick; RMC Place; WASHINGTON; 143 M-3; elev. 37ft./11m.; mail Leroy z 36548; ● 40
Priceville; Inc. Place; MORGAN; 142 B-6; ★ DEC; mail Decatur z 35603; ℗ 1,323; © 1,631
Prichard; Inc. Place; MOBILE; 143 P-2; elev. 30ft./9m.; [P]; ★ MOB; z 36610, z 36613, z 36617; ℗ 34,311; © 28,633; ◆ 26,779
Pride; RMC Place; COLBERT; *142 B-3; mail Tuscumbia z 35674; ● 50
Primitive Ridge; RMC Place; BIBB; *142 G-5; mail West Blocton z 35184; ● 150
Princeton; RMC Place; JACKSON; 142 A-8; elev. 638ft./194m.; [P]; z 35766; ● 250
Pronto; RMC Place; PIKE; *143 L-9; elev. 486ft./148m.; mail Brundidge z 36010, Troy z 36081; rural
Prospect; RMC Place; WALKER; 142 D-4; elev. 627ft./191m.; mail Nauvoo z 35578; ● 50
Providence; RMC Place; BUTLER; *143 L-6; mail Georgiana z 36033; ● 50
Providence; RMC Place; CULLMAN; *142 C-6; mail Vinemont z 35179; ● 30
Providence; Inc. Place; MARENGO; 142 J-3; mail Gallion z 36742; ℗ 307; © 311
Providence; RMC Place; WALKER; *142 E-5; elev. 310ft./94m.; mail Oakman z 35579; rural
Pruitton; RMC Place; LAUDERDALE; *142 A-4; ★ FLO; mail Florence z 35634; rural
Pulaski Pike; RMC Place; MADISON; *142 A-7; ★ HNTS; mail Huntsville z 35810; pop. incl. with Huntsville (Inc. Place)
Pull Tight; RMC Place; MARION; 142 D-3; elev. 612ft./187m.; mail Brilliant z 35548; ● 60
Pumpkin Center; RMC Place; DEKALB; *142 C-10; mail Fort Payne z 35967
Pumpkin Center (Stroups Crossroads); RMC Place; MORGAN; *142 B-6; elev. 628ft./191m.; mail Danville z 35619; ● 80
Pumpkin Center; RMC Place; WALKER; *142 E-5; mail Quinton z 35130; ● 50
Pushmataha; RMC Place; CHOCTAW; 143 K-2; elev. 239ft./73m.; mail Lisman z 36912; ● 120
Putnam; RMC Place; MARENGO; 143 K-3; elev. 210ft./64m.; mail Thomasville z 36784; ● 200
Pyriton; RMC Place; CLAY; *142 F-9; elev. 1,076ft./328m.; mail Lineville z 36266; rural

Q

Queenstown; RMC Place; JEFFERSON; *142 F-7; ★ BIR; mail Trussville z 35173; ● 500
Quicks Mill; MADISON; see Sulphur Springs (RMC Place)
Quinton; RMC Place; WALKER; 142 E-6; elev. 413ft./126m.; [P]; z 35130; ● 250
Quintown; RMC Place; JEFFERSON; *142 E-5; ★ BIR; mail Quinton z 35130; ● 150

R

Rabb; RMC Place; CONECUH; *143 M-6; mail Evergreen z 36401; rural
Rabbittown; RMC Place; CALHOUN; *142 E-10; mail Oxford z 36203, Piedmont z 36272; ● 30
Rabbit Town; RMC Place; MARSHALL; *142 C-8; mail Albertville z 35950; ● 50
Rabbittown; RMC Place; WINSTON; *142 C-4; elev. 961ft./293m.; mail Haleyville z 35565; rural
Rabun; RMC Place; BALDWIN; 143 O-4; elev. 260ft./79m.; mail Bay Minette z 36507; ● 200
Ragland; Inc. Place; ST. CLAIR; 142 E-8; elev. 500ft./152m.; [P]; z 35131; ℗ 1,807; © 1,918
Raimund; RMC Place; JEFFERSON; 143 T-10; ★ BIR; mail Bessemer z 35020; ● 400
Rainbow; RMC Place; MADISON; *142 A-7; elev. 790ft./241m.; ★ HNTS; mail Madison z 35758
Rainbow City; Inc. Place; ETOWAH; 142 D-9; elev. 560ft./171m.; [P]; ★ GAD; z 35906 & mail Gadsden z 35901; ℗ 7,673; © 8,428
Rainbow Mountain Heights; RMC Place; MADISON; *142 A-7; elev. 750ft./229m.; ★ HNTS; mail Madison z 35758; pop. incl. with Madison (Inc. Place)
Rainsville; Inc. Place; DEKALB; 142 B-9; elev. 1,255ft./383m.; [P]; z 35986; ℗ 3,875; © 4,499
Ralph; RMC Place; TUSCALOOSA; 142 H-3; elev. 159ft./48m.; [P]; z 35480; ● 280
Ramer; RMC Place; MONTGOMERY; 143 K-8; elev. 476ft./145m.; [P]; z 36069; ● 500
Ranburne; Inc. Place; CLEBURNE; 142 F-11; elev. 1,050ft./320m.; [P]; z 36273; ℗ 447; © 459
Randolph; RMC Place; BIBB; 142 H-6; elev. 450ft./137m.; [P]; z 36792; ● 220
RANDOLPH; 142 G-11; ℗ 19,881; © 22,380; ◆ 22,055
Range (Deer Range); RMC Place; CONECUH; 143 N-5; elev. 400ft./122m.; [P]; z 36473; ● 60
Rash; RMC Place; JACKSON; *142 A-9; mail Stevenson z 35772; rural
Rayburn; RMC Place; MARSHALL; *142 C-8; mail Guntersville z 35976; pop. incl. with Guntersville (Inc. Place)
Reads Mill; RMC Place; CALHOUN; *142 E-9; ★ ANNI; mail Wellington z 36279; ● 50
Red Bank; RMC Place; LAWRENCE; 142 A-5; elev. 561ft./171m.; mail Town Creek z 35672; ● 30
Red Bay; Inc. Place; FRANKLIN; 142 C-2; elev. 623ft./190m.; [P] [H]; z 35582; ℗ 3,451; © 3,374
Reddock Springs; RMC Place; BUTLER; *143 L-7; mail Greenville z 36037
Red Hill; RMC Place; BLOUNT; *142 E-6; ★ BIR; mail Empire z 35063; rural
Red Hill; RMC Place; ELMORE; 142 I-9; mail Tallassee z 36078; ● 100
Red Hill; RMC Place; MARSHALL; *142 C-8; mail Guntersville z 35976; ● 30
Redland Heights; RMC Place; CHAMBERS; mail Valley z 36854; pop. incl. with Valley (Inc. Place)
Red Level; Inc. Place; COVINGTON; 143 N-7; elev. 357ft./109m.; [P]; z 36474; ℗ 588; © 556
Redmont Park; RMC Place; JEFFERSON; *142 F-6; ★ BIR; mail Birmingham z 35213; pop. incl. with Mountain Brook (Inc. Place)
Red Ore; RMC Place; JEFFERSON; ★ BIR; mail Bessemer z 35020
Red Rock; RMC Place; COLBERT; *142 B-3; mail Tuscumbia z 35674; ● 30
Red Rock Junction; RMC Place; COLBERT; 142 B-3; mail Cherokee z 35616, Tuscumbia z 35674; ● 150
Redstone Arsenal; CDP-Census Area Only; MADISON; *142 B-7; ★ HNTS; mail Huntsville z 35808-09; ℗ 4,909; © 2,365
Redtown; RMC Place; BALDWIN; *143 O-4; elev. 313ft./95m.; mail Atmore z 36502; ● 30
Reece City (Reeseville); Inc. Place; ETOWAH; 142 D-9; elev. 580ft./177m.; ★ GAD; mail Attalla z 35954; ℗ 657; © 634
Reeds Ferry; RMC Place; WALKER; *142 E-5; elev. 300ft./91m.; ★ BIR; mail Quinton z 35130; ● 40
Reedtown; RMC Place; FRANKLIN; *142 B-4; mail Russellville z 35653; pop. incl. with Russellville (Inc. Place)

Entries in **UPPERCASE** are counties.
Entries in **bold** have populations of 2,500 or more.
Names in parentheses are alternate names.

Inc. Place	Incorporated Place
RMC Place	Rand McNally Designated Place
CDP	Census Designated Place
MCD	Minor Civil Division
⊡	County Seat
▲	Minor Civil Division
elev.	Elevation
[P]	Post Office
[H]	Hospital
[C]	College
■	Principal Business Center
★	Ranally Metro Area (RMA) Abbreviation
z	Zip Code(s)
℗	Previous Census Population
®	Revised Census Population
Ⓐ	Annexation Population
●	Rand McNally Population Estimate
©	Final Census Population
Ⓢ	Special Census Population
◆	Estimated Population

For additional definitions see Glossary, Volume 1, and Introduction, Volume 2.

Reeltown; RMC Place; TALLAPOOSA; ***142** I-9; elev. 628ft./191m.; mail Tallassee **z** 36078; ● 60
Reeseville; ETOWAH; see Reece City (Inc. Place)
Reform; Inc. Place; PICKENS; **142** F-3; elev. 249ft./76m.; 🄿; **z** 35481; Ⓟ 2,105; Ⓒ 1,978
Regency; RMC Place; LAUDERDALE; ***142** A-4; ★ **FLO**; mail Florence **z** 35630; pop. incl. with Florence (Inc. Place)
Regent Forest; RMC Place; JEFFERSON; ★ **BIR**; mail Birmingham **z** 35226; pop. incl. with Hoover (Inc. Place)
Rehobeth; Inc. Place; HOUSTON; **143** O-11; elev. 246ft./75m.; 🄿; ★ **DOTH**; **z** 36301 & mail Dothan **z** 36303, **z** 36305; Ⓒ 993
Rehoboth; RMC Place; WILCOX; ***143** K-5; mail Alberta **z** 36720; ● 30
Reid; RMC Place; LIMESTONE; ***142** A-6; mail Athens **z** 35611; ● 80
Remlap; RMC Place; BLOUNT; **142** E-7; elev. 74ft./23m.; 🄿; **z** 35133; ● 270
Renfroe; RMC Place; TALLADEGA; **142** F-8; mail Talladega **z** 35160; ● 120
Repton; Inc. Place; CONECUH; **143** N-5; elev. 352ft./107m.; 🄿; **z** 36475 & mail Lenox **z** 36454; Ⓟ 293; Ⓒ 280
Republic; RMC Place; JEFFERSON; **143** Q-11; elev. 414ft./126m.; ★ **BIR**; mail Birmingham **z** 35214; ● 400
Reynolds Mill; RMC Place; TALLADEGA; ***142** F-8; elev. 499ft./152m.; mail Alpine **z** 35014; rural
Rhoades; RMC Place; COFFEE; ***143** N-8; elev. 286ft./87m.; mail Kinston **z** 36453; rural
Rhodesville; RMC Place; LAUDERDALE; **142** A-3; mail Florence **z** 35633; ● 50
Rice; RMC Place; JEFFERSON; ***142** F-6; ★ **BIR**; mail Birmingham **z** 35201; ● 300
Richardson; CHEROKEE; see Hopewell (RMC Place)
Richmond; RMC Place; DALLAS; **143** K-6; elev. 393ft./120m.; mail Minter **z** 36761; rural
Richmond Hills; RMC Place; COLBERT; ***142** B-4; ★ **FLO**; mail Tuscumbia **z** 35674; pop. incl. with Tuscumbia (Inc. Place)
Richville; RMC Place; COOSA; ***142** H-8; elev. 500ft./152m.; mail Rockford **z** 35136; rural
Rideout Village; RMC Place; MADISON; ***142** A-7; ★ **HNTS**; mail Huntsville **z** 35806; pop. incl. with Huntsville (Inc. Place)
Riderville (Leslie); RMC Place; CHILTON; ***142** I-6; elev. 310ft./94m.; mail Stanton **z** 36790; rural
Riderwood; RMC Place; CHOCTAW; **143** K-2; elev. 238ft./73m.; mail Butler **z** 36904, Lisman **z** 36912; ● 150
Ridgecrest (Canaan); RMC Place; MONTGOMERY; ***142** J-8; elev. 200ft./61m.; ★ **MTGY**; mail Montgomery **z** 36105; pop. incl. with Montgomery (Inc. Place)
Ridgeville; RMC Place; BUTLER; **143** L-6; mail Forest Home **z** 36030; rural
Ridgeville; Inc. Place; ETOWAH; ***142** D-8; elev. 700ft./213m.; ★ **GAD**; mail Attalla **z** 35954; Ⓟ 178; Ⓒ 158
Ringgold; RMC Place; CHEROKEE; **142** C-10; elev. 676ft./206m.; mail Gaylesville **z** 35973
Ripley; RMC Place; LIMESTONE; **142** A-5; elev. 655ft./200m.; mail Athens **z** 35611; ● 40
Riverbend; RMC Place; BIBB; ***142** H-6; elev. 300ft./91m.; mail West Blocton **z** 35184; rural
Riverdale; RMC Place; DEKALB; ***142** B-10; mail Mentone **z** 35984; pop. incl. with Mentone (Inc. Place)
River Falls; Inc. Place; COVINGTON; **143** N-7; elev. 212ft./65m.; 🄿; **z** 36476; Ⓟ 710; Ⓒ 616
Rivermont; RMC Place; COLBERT; ***142** A-4; ★ **FLO**; mail Sheffield **z** 35660; pop. incl. with Sheffield (Inc. Place)
Rivermont; RMC Place; LAUDERDALE; ***142** A-4; ★ **FLO**; mail Florence **z** 35634; ● 300
River Park; RMC Place; BALDWIN; ***143** Q-3; ★ **MOB**; mail Fairhope **z** 36532; ● 30
River Park; DEKALB; see Alpine (RMC Place)
Riverside; RMC Place; BLOUNT; ***142** D-7; mail Blountsville **z** 35031; ● 40
Riverside; RMC Place; CULLMAN; ***142** D-7; elev. 668ft./204m.; mail Hanceville **z** 35077; ● 50
Riverside; Inc. Place; ST. CLAIR; **142** F-8; elev. 529ft./161m.; 🄿; **z** 35135; Ⓟ 1,004; Ⓒ 1,564
Riverton; RMC Place; COLBERT; **142** A-3; mail Cherokee **z** 35616
River View; RMC Place; CHAMBERS; ***142** H-11; mail Valley **z** 36854, **z** 36872
Riverview; Inc. Place; ESCAMBIA; **143** O-6; elev. 75ft./23m.; mail Brewton **z** 36426; Ⓟ 90; Ⓒ 99
Riverview; RMC Place; TUSCALOOSA; ★ **TUSC**; mail Tuscaloosa **z** 35401; pop. incl. with Tuscaloosa (Inc. Place)
Riverwood; RMC Place; TUSCALOOSA; ★ **TUSC**; mail Tuscaloosa **z** 35406; pop. incl. with Tuscaloosa (Inc. Place)
Roanoke; Inc. Place; RANDOLPH; **142** G-11; elev. 795ft./242m.; 🄿 🄷; **z** 36274; Ⓟ 6,362; Ⓒ 6,563
Roanoke Junction; RMC Place; LEE; ***142** I-11; ★ **AU-OP**; mail Opelika **z** 36801; pop. incl. with Opelika (Inc. Place)
Roba; RMC Place; MACON; **142** J-10; elev. 350ft./107m.; mail Union Springs **z** 36089; ● 30
Robbins Crossroads; RMC Place; JEFFERSON; ***142** E-6; elev. 349ft./106m.; ★ **BIR**; mail Dora **z** 35062; ● 300
Roberta; RMC Place; SHELBY; ***142** G-6; elev. 500ft./152m.; mail Calera **z** 35040; ● 60
Roberts; RMC Place; ESCAMBIA; ***143** O-6; mail Andalusia **z** 36420, Brewton **z** 36426; rural
Robertsdale; Inc. Place; BALDWIN; **143** Q-4; elev. 144ft./44m.; 🄿; **z** 36567, **z** 36574; Ⓟ 2,401; Ⓒ 3,782
Robinsons; RMC Place; LOWNDES; ***142** J-7; elev. 165ft./50m.; mail Lowndesboro **z** 36752; rural
Robinson Springs; RMC Place; ELMORE; ***142** J-8; elev. 329ft./100m.; ★ **MTGY**; mail Elmore **z** 36025; pop. incl. with Millbrook (Inc. Place)
Robinsonville; RMC Place; ESCAMBIA; **143** O-4; elev. 298ft./91m.; mail Atmore **z** 36502; rural
Robinwood; RMC Place; JEFFERSON; **143** Q-13; elev. 600ft./183m.; ★ **BIR**; mail Birmingham **z** 35217; pop. incl. with Tarrant City (Inc. Place)
Rock City; RMC Place; JACKSON; ***142** B-9; mail Section **z** 35771; rural
Rock City (Baccus); RMC Place; MARION; **142** D-4; mail Winfield **z** 35594; ● 80
Rock Creek; RMC Place; ESCAMBIA; ***143** O-6; elev. 238ft./73m.; mail Wing **z** 36483; rural
Rock Creek; CDP-Census Area Only; JEFFERSON; ***142** F-6; ★ **BIR**; Ⓒ 1,495
Rock Creek; RMC Place; WINSTON; ***142** C-5; elev. 795ft./242m.; mail Double Springs **z** 35553; ● 50
Rockdale; RMC Place; JEFFERSON; ***142** G-6; ★ **BIR**; mail Bessemer **z** 35020; ● 300
Rockford; Inc. Place; ⊡ COOSA; **142** H-8; elev. 720ft./219m.; 🄿; **z** 35136; Ⓟ 461; Ⓒ 428
Rock Hill; RMC Place; ESCAMBIA; ***143** O-6; mail Brewton **z** 36426; ● 60
Rockledge; RMC Place; ETOWAH; **142** D-8; mail Attalla **z** 35954; ● 250
Rock Mills; CDP; RANDOLPH; **142** G-11; elev. 749ft./228m.; mail Roanoke **z** 36274; Ⓒ 676
Rock Run; RMC Place; CHEROKEE; **142** D-10; mail Piedmont **z** 36272; ● 150
Rock Spring; RMC Place; ETOWAH; ***142** D-9; ★ **GAD**; mail Gadsden **z** 35905; pop. incl. with Glencoe (Inc. Place)
Rock Spring Quarry; RMC Place; ETOWAH; ★ **GAD**; mail Gadsden **z** 35905; pop. incl. with Glencoe (Inc. Place)
Rock Springs; RMC Place; BLOUNT; ***142** D-7; mail Blountsville **z** 35031; rural
Rock Springs; RMC Place; CHOCTAW; ***143** K-2; elev. 516ft./157m.; mail Butler **z** 36904; ● 40
Rock Stand; RMC Place; RANDOLPH; ***142** G-11; mail Roanoke **z** 36274; ● 30
Rockville; RMC Place; CLARKE; ***143** N-3; elev. 310ft./94m.; mail Jackson **z** 36545; rural
Rockwest; RMC Place; WILCOX; ***143** K-5; mail Camden **z** 36726; ● 60
Rockwood; RMC Place; FRANKLIN; **142** C-3; elev. 697ft./212m.; mail Russellville **z** 35653; ● 80
Rocky Head; RMC Place; DALE; **143** M-10; mail Ariton **z** 36311; ● 50
Rocky Hill; RMC Place; LAWRENCE; ***142** B-5; mail Town Creek **z** 35672; pop. incl. with Courtland (Inc. Place)
Rocky Hollow; RMC Place; WALKER; ***142** E-6; elev. 313ft./95m.; ★ **BIR**; mail Cordova **z** 35550; rural
Rocky Ridge; RMC Place; JEFFERSON; ***142** F-6; ★ **BIR**; mail Birmingham **z** 35243
Rodentown; RMC Place; DEKALB; **142** C-9; mail Boaz **z** 35957, Crossville **z** 35962; ● 150
Roebuck; RMC Place; JEFFERSON; ***142** F-7; ★ **BIR**; mail Birmingham **z** 35206; pop. incl. with Birmingham (Inc. Place)
Roebuck Crest Estates; RMC Place; JEFFERSON; ***142** F-7; ★ **BIR**; mail Birmingham **z** 35215; pop. incl. with Birmingham (Inc. Place)
Roebuck Forest; RMC Place; JEFFERSON; ***142** F-7; ★ **BIR**; mail Birmingham **z** 35235; pop. incl. with Birmingham (Inc. Place)
Roebuck Gardens; RMC Place; JEFFERSON; ***142** F-7; elev. 712ft./217m.; ★ **BIR**; mail Birmingham **z** 35235; pop. incl. with Birmingham (Inc. Place)
Roebuck Park; RMC Place; JEFFERSON; ***142** F-7; ★ **BIR**; mail Birmingham **z** 35215; pop. incl. with Birmingham (Inc. Place)
Roebuck Springs; RMC Place; JEFFERSON; ***142** F-7; ★ **BIR**; mail Birmingham **z** 35206; pop. incl. with Birmingham (Inc. Place)
Roebuck Terrace; RMC Place; JEFFERSON; ***142** F-7; ★ **BIR**; mail Birmingham **z** 35206; pop. incl. with Birmingham (Inc. Place)
Roeton; RMC Place; COFFEE; ***143** M-9; mail Brundidge **z** 36010; ● 30
Rogersville; Inc. Place; LAUDERDALE; **142** A-5; elev. 635ft./194m.; 🄿; **z** 35652; Ⓟ 1,125; Ⓒ 1,199
Rolling Hills; RMC Place; MORGAN; ***142** B-6; elev. 650ft./198m.; ★ **DEC**; mail Decatur **z** 35603; pop. incl. with Decatur (Inc. Place)
Rollins; RMC Place; AUTAUGA; ***142** I-7; elev. 369ft./112m.; mail Deatsville **z** 36022; rural
Romar Beach; RMC Place; BALDWIN; ***143** R-4; mail Orange Beach **z** 36561; pop. incl. with Orange Beach (Inc. Place) summer pop. 200
Rome; RMC Place; COVINGTON; **143** O-7; elev. 315ft./96m.; mail Andalusia **z** 36420; rural
Romulus; RMC Place; TUSCALOOSA; ***142** G-3; mail Buhl **z** 35446; ● 50
Roosevelt City; RMC Place; JEFFERSON; ***142** F-6; elev. 500ft./152m.; ★ **BIR**; mail Bessemer **z** 35020; pop. incl. with Birmingham (Inc. Place)
Roper; RMC Place; JEFFERSON; ***142** F-7; ★ **BIR**; mail Trussville **z** 35173; rural
Rosa; Inc. Place; BLOUNT; **142** D-7; elev. 633ft./193m.; 🄿; **z** 35121; Ⓟ 139; Ⓒ 313
Rosalie; RMC Place; JACKSON; **142** B-9; elev. 1,486ft./453m.; mail Pisgah **z** 35765; ● 380
Roseboro; RMC Place; MADISON; ***142** A-8; elev. 885ft./270m.; ★ **HNTS**; mail Elora **z** 37328; rural
Rosebud; RMC Place; WILCOX; **143** L-5; mail Oak Hill **z** 36766; ● 30
Rosedale; RMC Place; JEFFERSON; ***142** F-6; ★ **BIR**; mail Birmingham **z** 35209; pop. incl. with Homewood (Inc. Place)
Rose Hill; RMC Place; COVINGTON; **143** M-8; mail Dozier **z** 36028; ● 60
Rose Hill; RMC Place; JEFFERSON; **143** Q-14; ★ **BIR**; mail Birmingham **z** 35210; pop. incl. with Irondale (Inc. Place)
Rosehill; RMC Place; WALKER; ***142** D-5; elev. 642ft./196m.; mail Nauvoo **z** 35578; ● 30
Rosemont; RMC Place; JEFFERSON; ***142** F-6; ★ **BIR**; mail Birmingham **z** 35221; pop. incl. with Birmingham (Inc. Place)
Rose Park; RMC Place; LAUDERDALE; ***142** A-4; ★ **FLO**; mail Florence **z** 35630; pop. incl. with Florence (Inc. Place)
Rosinton; RMC Place; BALDWIN; ***143** P-4; elev. 50ft./15m.; mail Robertsdale **z** 36567; ● 100
Rossland City (Sipsey); RMC Place; FAYETTE; ***142** E-3; elev. 335ft./102m.; mail Fayette **z** 35555; ● 30
Roundhill; RMC Place; CLARKE; ***143** L-4; elev. 459ft./140m.; mail Thomasville **z** 36784; rural
Rowells Crossroad; LEE; see Rowells Crossroads (RMC Place)
Rowells Crossroads (Rowells Crossroad); RMC Place; LEE; ***142** I-10; elev. 600ft./183m.; mail Waverly **z** 36879; rural
Roxana; RMC Place; LEE; ***142** I-10; elev. 700ft./213m.; mail Camp Hill **z** 36850, Waverly **z** 36879; rural
Royal; RMC Place; BLOUNT; **142** D-7; elev. 750ft./229m.; mail Blountsville **z** 35031
Ruffner; RMC Place; JEFFERSON; ***142** F-7; ★ **BIR**; mail Birmingham **z** 35210
Russell; RMC Place; MOBILE; pop. incl. with Citronelle (Inc. Place)
RUSSELL; **142** J-12; Ⓟ 46,860; Ⓒ 49,756; ◆ 50,743
Russell Heights; RMC Place; JEFFERSON; ***142** F-7; ★ **BIR**; mail Leeds **z** 35094; pop. incl. with Leeds (Inc. Place)
Russell Mill; RMC Place; TALLAPOOSA; mail Alexander City **z** 35010; pop. incl. with Alexander City (Inc. Place)
Russell Village; RMC Place; MORGAN; ***142** B-6; elev. 600ft./183m.; ★ **DEC**; mail Decatur **z** 35603; pop. incl. with Decatur (Inc. Place)
Russellville; Inc. Place; ⊡ FRANKLIN; **142** B-4; elev. 764ft./233m.; 🄿 🄷; **z** 35653-54; Ⓟ 7,812; Ⓒ 8,971
Rutan; RMC Place; WASHINGTON; ***143** M-2; mail Chatom **z** 36518; rural
Ruth; RMC Place; MARSHALL; ***142** C-7; mail Arab **z** 35016; ● 50
Rutherford; RMC Place; RUSSELL; **143** K-11; mail Hurtsboro **z** 36860; rural
Rutledge; Inc. Place; CRENSHAW; **143** L-8; elev. 350ft./107m.; 🄿; **z** 36071; Ⓟ 473; Ⓒ 476
Rutledge Heights; RMC Place; JEFFERSON; ★ **BIR**; mail Birmingham **z** 35228, Fairfield **z** 35064; pop. incl. with Midfield (Inc. Place)
Rutledge Heights; RMC Place; MADISON; ***142** A-7; elev. 750ft./229m.; ★ **HNTS**; mail Huntsville **z** 35816; pop. incl. with Huntsville (Inc. Place)
Ryan; RMC Place; SHELBY; ***142** G-6; ★ **BIR**; mail Montevallo **z** 35115; rural
Ryan Crossroads; RMC Place; MORGAN; **142** C-7; mail Joppa **z** 35087; ● 70
Ryland; RMC Place; MADISON; **142** A-7; elev. 750ft./229m.; 🄿; ★ **HNTS**; **z** 35767; ● 180

S

Saco; RMC Place; PIKE; **143** L-9; mail Troy **z** 36081; ● 60
Safford; RMC Place; DALLAS; **142** J-5; elev. 228ft./69m.; 🄿; **z** 36773; ● 160
Saginaw; RMC Place; SHELBY; **142** G-6; elev. 500ft./152m.; 🄿; ★ **BIR**; **z** 35137; ● 700
Sahama Village; RMC Place; TUSCALOOSA; ***142** G-3; mail Tuscaloosa **z** 35401; pop. incl. with Tuscaloosa (Inc. Place)
Saint Bernard; RMC Place; CULLMAN; ***142** D-6; elev. 700ft./213m.; mail Cullman **z** 35055; pop. incl. with Cullman (Inc. Place)
Saint Clair (Lowndesboro); RMC Place; LOWNDES; **142** J-7; elev. 205ft./62m.; mail Lowndesboro **z** 36752; pop. incl. with Lowndesboro (Inc. Place); rural
ST. CLAIR; **142** E-8; Ⓟ 50,009; Ⓒ 64,742; ◆ 98,662
Saint Clair Springs; RMC Place; ST. CLAIR; **142** E-8; elev. 658ft./201m.; ★ **BIR**; mail Springville **z** 35146; ● 100
Saint Elmo; RMC Place; MOBILE; **143** Q-2; elev. 136ft./41m.; 🄿; ★ **MOB**; **z** 36568; ● 1,050
Saint Florian; Inc. Place; LAUDERDALE; **142** A-4; elev. 650ft./198m.; ★ **FLO**; mail Florence **z** 35634; Ⓟ 388; Ⓒ 335
Saints Crossroads; RMC Place; FRANKLIN; **142** B-4; elev. 623ft./190m.; mail Russellville **z** 35654; rural
Saint Stephens; RMC Place; WASHINGTON; **143** M-2; elev. 250ft./76m.; 🄿; **z** 36569; ● 240
Saks; CDP; CALHOUN; ***142** E-9; ★ **ANNI**; mail Anniston **z** 36201; Ⓟ 11,138; Ⓒ 10,698
Salem; RMC Place; DALLAS; ***142** J-5; elev. 156ft./48m.; mail Orrville **z** 36767; rural
Salem; RMC Place; FAYETTE; ***142** E-4; elev. 632ft./193m.; mail Berry **z** 35546; rural
Salem; RMC Place; LEE; **142** I-11; elev. 689ft./210m.; 🄿; **z** 36874; ● 480
Salem (Westmoreland); RMC Place; LIMESTONE; **142** A-5; mail Elkmont **z** 35620; ● 150
Salitpa; RMC Place; CLARKE; **143** M-3; elev. 184ft./56m.; mail Jackson **z** 36545; ● 350
Samantha; RMC Place; TUSCALOOSA; **142** F-4; elev. 367ft./112m.; 🄿; **z** 35482; ● 200
Samson; Inc. Place; GENEVA; **143** O-9; elev. 205ft./62m.; 🄿; **z** 36477; Ⓟ 2,190; Ⓒ 2,071
Samuels Chapel; RMC Place; ETOWAH; ***142** D-8; elev. 885ft./270m.; mail Altoona **z** 35952; rural
Sand Cut; RMC Place; CONECUH; ***143** N-5; elev. 380ft./116m.; mail Castleberry **z** 36432; rural
Sandfield; RMC Place; PIKE; ***143** L-9; elev. 644ft./196m.; mail Troy **z** 36081; rural
Sandfort; RMC Place; RUSSELL; ***142** J-11; elev. 506ft./154m.; mail Seale **z** 36875; rural
Sandhurst Park; RMC Place; MADISON; ★ **HNTS**; mail Huntsville **z** 35802; pop. incl. with Huntsville (Inc. Place)
Sand Rock; Inc. Place; CHEROKEE, DEKALB; **142** C-10; 🄿; **z** 35983 & mail Collinsville **z** 35961; Ⓟ 438; Ⓒ 509
Sandtown; RMC Place; TUSCALOOSA; ***142** F-4; elev. 660ft./201m.; mail Berry **z** 35546; rural
Sandusky; RMC Place; JEFFERSON; ***142** F-6; ★ **BIR**; mail Birmingham **z** 35214; pop. incl. with Birmingham (Inc. Place)
Sandy Creek; CHAMBERS; see Culebra (RMC Place)
Sandy Ridge; RMC Place; LOWNDES; **143** K-7; mail Letohatchee **z** 36047; ● 250
Sanford; Inc. Place; COVINGTON; **143** N-8; elev. 287ft./87m.; mail Andalusia **z** 36420; Ⓟ 282; Ⓒ 269
Sanie; RMC Place; ST. CLAIR; ***142** E-7; ★ **BIR**; mail Odenville **z** 35120; ● 30
San Souci Beach; RMC Place; MOBILE; ***143** Q-2; ★ **MOB**; mail Bayou La Batre **z** 36509
Santuck; RMC Place; ELMORE; **142** I-8; ★ **MTGY**; mail Wetumpka **z** 36092; ● 80
Sapps; RMC Place; PICKENS; ***142** G-2; elev. 314ft./96m.; mail Aliceville **z** 35442, Carrollton **z** 35447; ● 30
Saragossa; RMC Place; WALKER; **142** E-5; elev. 547ft./167m.; mail Nauvoo **z** 35578; ● 180
Saraland; Inc. Place; MOBILE; **143** P-2; elev. 12ft./4m.; 🄿; ★ **MOB**; **z** 36571; Ⓟ 11,760; Ⓒ 12,288
Saratoga; RMC Place; MARSHALL; ***142** C-8; mail Albertville **z** 35950; pop. incl. with Albertville (Inc. Place)
Sardine; RMC Place; ESCAMBIA; ***143** O-5; mail Flomaton **z** 36441; rural
Sardis; RMC Place; BULLOCK; ***143** K-10; mail Union Springs **z** 36089; ● 50
Sardis; RMC Place; CRENSHAW; ***143** L-8; elev. 584ft./178m.; mail Highland Home **z** 36041; ● 30
Sardis; RMC Place; DALLAS; **142** J-6; elev. 250ft./76m.; 🄿; **z** 36775; ● 300
Sardis; RMC Place; WALKER; ***142** E-5; mail Cordova **z** 35550; rural
Sardis City; Inc. Place; ETOWAH, DEKALB, MARSHALL; **142** D-8; elev. 1,060ft./323m.; 🄿; **z** 35956-57; Ⓟ 1,301; Ⓒ 1,438
Sardis Springs; RMC Place; LIMESTONE; ***142** A-6; mail Athens **z** 35613; ● 50
Satsuma; Inc. Place; MOBILE; **143** P-2; elev. 18ft./5m.; 🄿; ★ **MOB**; **z** 36572; Ⓟ 5,194; Ⓒ 5,687
Saucer; RMC Place; BUTLER; ***143** L-6; mail Forest Home **z** 36030; rural
Saville; RMC Place; CRENSHAW; ***143** L-8; elev. 484ft./148m.; mail Highland Home **z** 36041
Sawyerville; RMC Place; HALE; ***142** I-4; elev. 300ft./91m.; 🄿; **z** 36776; ● 150
Sayre; RMC Place; JEFFERSON; **142** E-6; elev. 420ft./128m.; 🄿; ★ **BIR**; **z** 35139; ● 600
Scant City; RMC Place; MARSHALL; **142** C-7; mail Arab **z** 35016; ● 200
Scarce Grease; RMC Place; LIMESTONE; ***142** A-5; mail Lester **z** 35647; rural
Scenic Heights; RMC Place; ETOWAH; ***142** D-9; ★ **GAD**; mail Gadsden **z** 35904; pop. incl. with Gadsden (Inc. Place)
Schmidts Mill; TALLADEGA; see Smiths Mill (RMC Place)
Schuster (Shuster Springs); RMC Place; WILCOX; ***143** L-6; elev. 308ft./94m.; mail Pine Apple **z** 36768; rural
Scotland; RMC Place; MONROE; ***143** M-5; mail Peterman **z** 36471; rural
Scotrock; RMC Place; SHELBY; ★ **BIR**; mail Alabaster **z** 35007; pop. incl. with Alabaster (Inc. Place)
Scott City; RMC Place; JEFFERSON; ***142** F-7; ★ **BIR**; mail Leeds **z** 35094; pop. incl. with Leeds (Inc. Place)
Scottland; RMC Place; BULLOCK; ***143** K-10; elev. 550ft./168m.; mail Union Springs **z** 36089; rural
Scottsboro; Inc. Place; ⊡ JACKSON; **142** B-9; elev. 653ft./199m.; 🄿 🄷; **z** 35768-69; Ⓟ 13,786; Ⓒ 14,762
Scranage; BALDWIN; see Serange (RMC Place)
Scranton; RMC Place; GENEVA; ***143** N-9; elev. 280ft./85m.; mail Bellwood **z** 36313; rural
Screamer; RMC Place; HENRY; ***143** M-11; elev. 450ft./137m.; mail Abbeville **z** 36310; rural
Scyrene; RMC Place; CLARKE; **143** L-4; elev. 509ft./155m.; mail Dickinson **z** 36436; ● 50
Seaboard; RMC Place; WASHINGTON; ***143** N-2; mail Deer Park **z** 36529, Tibbie **z** 36583; rural
Seacliff; RMC Place; BALDWIN; ***143** Q-3; ★ **MOB**; mail Fairhope **z** 36532; pop. incl. with Fairhope (Inc. Place)
Seale; RMC Place; RUSSELL; **142** J-11; elev. 350ft./107m.; 🄿; **z** 36875; ● 350
Sealy Springs; RMC Place; HOUSTON; ***143** O-11; mail Cottonwood **z** 36320; pop. incl. with Cottonwood (Inc. Place)
Searight; RMC Place; CRENSHAW; **143** M-8; mail Dozier **z** 36028; ● 80
Searles; RMC Place; TUSCALOOSA; ***142** G-5; mail Brookwood **z** 35444, Kellerman **z** 35468; ● 80
Section; Inc. Place; JACKSON; **142** B-9; elev. 1,320ft./402m.; 🄿; **z** 35771; Ⓟ 777; Ⓒ 769
Sedgefield; RMC Place; BULLOCK; ***143** K-10; elev. 366ft./112m.; mail Union Springs **z** 36089; ● 50
Segco; RMC Place; WALKER; ***142** E-5; elev. 341ft./104m.; mail Parrish **z** 35580; rural
Selbrook; RMC Place; MONTGOMERY; ***142** J-8; elev. 152ft./46m.; ★ **MTGY**; mail Montgomery **z** 36108; ● 1,000
Selfville; RMC Place; BLOUNT; **142** E-7; ★ **BIR**; mail Remlap **z** 35133, Trafford **z** 35172; ● 230
Sellers; RMC Place; MONTGOMERY; **143** K-8; elev. 290ft./88m.; mail Lapine **z** 36046; ● 50
Sellersville; RMC Place; GENEVA; **143** O-9; mail Coffee Springs **z** 36318, Samson **z** 36477; ● 130
Selma; Inc. Place; ⊡ DALLAS; **142** J-6; elev. 139ft./42m.; 🄿 🄷 🄲 930 ■; **z** 36701-03; Ⓟ 23,755; Ⓒ 20,512; ◆ 18,160
Selmont; RMC Place; DALLAS; ***142** J-6; elev. 118ft./36m.; mail Selma **z** 36703; ● 1,800
Selmont-West Selmont; CDP-Census Area Only; DALLAS; ***142** J-6; mail Selma **z** 36703; Ⓟ 3,823; Ⓒ 3,502
Seman; RMC Place; ELMORE; **142** I-9; elev. 747ft./228m.; mail Eclectic **z** 36024, Equality **z** 36026; ● 50
Seminole; RMC Place; BALDWIN; **143** Q-4; elev. 100ft./30m.; 🄿; **z** 36574; ● 320
Semmes; RMC Place; MOBILE; **143** P-2; elev. 235ft./72m.; 🄿; ★ **MOB**; **z** 36575; ● 2,350
Serange (Scranage); RMC Place; BALDWIN; ***143** N-4; mail Atmore **z** 36502; rural
Service; RMC Place; CHOCTAW; ***143** L-2; mail Silas **z** 36919; rural
Seven Hills; RMC Place; MOBILE; **143** P-2; ★ **MOB**; mail Mobile **z** 36601; rural
Seymour Bluff; RMC Place; BALDWIN; ***143** R-3; mail Gulf Shores **z** 36542; rural
Shacklesville; RMC Place; BUTLER; ***143** L-6; mail Georgiana **z** 36033, Greenville **z** 36037; ● 50
Shades Crest Estates; RMC Place; JEFFERSON; ★ **BIR**; mail Birmingham **z** 35226; pop. incl. with Hoover (Inc. Place)
Shady Grove; RMC Place; CLAY; ***142** G-9; mail Goodwater **z** 35072; rural
Shady Grove; RMC Place; COFFEE; ***143** M-9; elev. 333ft./101m.; mail Elba **z** 36323
Shady Grove; RMC Place; FRANKLIN; **142** C-4; mail Phil Campbell **z** 35581; ● 80
Shady Grove; RMC Place; JEFFERSON; ***142** F-6; elev. 578ft./176m.; ★ **BIR**; mail Adamsville **z** 35005; ● 250
Shady Grove; RMC Place; PIKE; **143** L-8; mail Goshen **z** 36035; ● 100
Shady Lane; RMC Place; MADISON; ***142** A-7; ★ **HNTS**; mail Huntsville **z** 35810; pop. incl. with Huntsville (Inc. Place)
Shakespeare; RMC Place; MONTGOMERY; ★ **MTGY**; mail Montgomery **z** 36117, **z** 36123; pop. incl. with Montgomery (Inc. Place)
Shanghai; RMC Place; LIMESTONE; ***142** A-6; mail Athens **z** 35614; ● 30
Shannon; RMC Place; JEFFERSON; **143** T-11; elev. 660ft./201m.; 🄿; ★ **BIR**; **z** 35142; ● 1,000
Shawmut; RMC Place; CHAMBERS; ***142** H-11; elev. 600ft./183m.; mail Valley **z** 36854; pop. incl. with Valley (Inc. Place)
Shawnee; RMC Place; WILCOX; ***143** K-5; elev. 312ft./95m.; mail Camden **z** 36726; ● 30
Sheffield; Inc. Place; COLBERT; **142** F-13; elev. 502ft./153m.; 🄿 🄷; ★ **FLO**; **z** 35660; Ⓟ 10,380; Ⓒ 9,652
Shelby; RMC Place; SHELBY; **142** G-7; elev. 489ft./149m.; 🄿; **z** 35143; ● 1,000
SHELBY; **142** G-7; Ⓟ 99,358; Ⓒ 143,293; ◆ 187,950
Shelby Shores; RMC Place; SHELBY; ***142** G-7; elev. 400ft./122m.; mail Shelby **z** 35143; rural
Shellhorn; RMC Place; PIKE; **143** L-9; elev. 430ft./131m.; mail Troy **z** 36079; ● 30
Shepardville; DALLAS; see Elm Bluff (RMC Place)
Sherman Heights; RMC Place; CALHOUN; ***142** E-9; ★ **ANNI**; mail Anniston **z** 36201; pop. incl. with Anniston (Inc. Place)
Sherwood Forest; RMC Place; LAUDERDALE; ***142** A-4; ★ **FLO**; mail Florence **z** 35630; pop. incl. with Florence (Inc. Place)
Sherwood Park; RMC Place; MADISON; ***142** B-7; ★ **HNTS**; mail Birmingham **z** 35206; pop. incl. with Huntsville (Inc. Place)
Shiloh; Inc. Place; DEKALB; **142** B-9; elev. 1,260ft./384m.; mail Fort Payne **z** 35968; Ⓟ 252; Ⓒ 289
Shiloh; RMC Place; MARENGO; **143** K-3; elev. 402ft./123m.; mail Magnolia **z** 36754; rural
Shiloh; RMC Place; PIKE; ***143** L-10; elev. 490ft./149m.; mail Banks **z** 36005; rural
Shinebone; RMC Place; CLAY; ***142** F-10; elev. 1,020ft./311m.; mail Lineville **z** 36266; rural
Shoals Acres; RMC Place; LAUDERDALE; ***142** A-4; ★ **FLO**; mail Killen **z** 35645; ● 200
Shopton; RMC Place; BULLOCK; ***143** K-9; mail Fitzpatrick **z** 36029; ● 40
Short Creek; RMC Place; JEFFERSON; ***142** F-5; elev. 321ft./98m.; ★ **BIR**; mail Mulga **z** 35118; ● 430
Shorter (Shorters); Inc. Place; MACON; **142** J-9; elev. 350ft./107m.; 🄿; **z** 36075; Ⓟ 461; Ⓒ 355
Shorters; MACON; see Shorter (Inc. Place)
Shorterville; RMC Place; HENRY; **143** M-12; elev. 417ft./127m.; 🄿; **z** 36373; ● 350
Shortleaf; RMC Place; MARENGO; ***142** J-3; elev. 100ft./30m.; mail Demopolis **z** 36732; pop. incl. with Demopolis (Inc. Place)
Shottsville; RMC Place; MARION; **142** C-2; mail Hamilton **z** 35570
Shreve; RMC Place; CONECUH; ***143** M-7; elev. 373ft./114m.; mail Mc Kenzie **z** 36456; rural
Shuster Springs; WILCOX; see Schuster (RMC Place)
Sico; RMC Place; TALLADEGA; ***142** G-8; elev. 513ft./156m.; mail Sylacauga **z** 35150; rural
Siddonsville; RMC Place; MARENGO; ***142** J-4; elev. 263ft./80m.; mail Faunsdale **z** 36738; rural
Sidney; RMC Place; MARSHALL; ***142** C-8; elev. 615ft./187m.; mail Guntersville **z** 35976; ● 30
Sigma; RMC Place; HOUSTON; ***143** N-11; elev. 231ft./70m.; mail Columbia **z** 36319, Webb **z** 36376; ● 30
Sigsbee; RMC Place; DEKALB; ***142** C-10; elev. 1,250ft./381m.; mail Fort Payne **z** 35967; rural
Sikesville; RMC Place; CLAY; ***142** G-10; elev. 976ft./297m.; mail Wadley **z** 36276; rural
Silas; Inc. Place; CHOCTAW; **143** L-2; elev. 250ft./76m.; 🄿; **z** 36919; Ⓟ 245; Ⓒ 529
Siloam; RMC Place; SUMTER; ***142** J-2; elev. 337ft./103m.; mail Cuba **z** 36907; ● 30
Siluria; RMC Place; SHELBY; ***142** G-6; 🄿; ★ **BIR**; **z** 35144; pop. incl. with Alabaster (Inc. Place)
Silver Cross; RMC Place; WASHINGTON; ***143** M-2; mail Frankville **z** 36538; rural
Silverhill; Inc. Place; BALDWIN; **143** Q-3; elev. 144ft./44m.; 🄿; **z** 36576; Ⓟ 556; Ⓒ 616
Silver Run; RMC Place; TALLADEGA; ***142** F-9; ★ **ANNI**; mail Munford **z** 36268; rural
Simcoe; RMC Place; CULLMAN; **142** C-7; mail Cullman **z** 35058; ● 50
Simmons Crossroads; RMC Place; TALLAPOOSA; ***142** I-10; elev. 733ft./223m.; mail Camp Hill **z** 36850; rural
Simmsville; RMC Place; SHELBY; **142** G-7; ★ **BIR**; mail Chelsea **z** 35043; pop. incl. with Chelsea (Inc. Place)
Sims Chapel; RMC Place; WASHINGTON; **143** N-2; mail Mc Intosh **z** 36553; ● 50
Simsville; RMC Place; BULLOCK; ***143** K-9; elev. 380ft./116m.; mail Union Springs **z** 36089; ● 30
Single Spring; RMC Place; FRANKLIN; ***142** C-3; elev. 685ft./209m.; mail Vina **z** 35593; rural
Sipsey; FAYETTE; see Rossland City (RMC Place)
Sipsey; Inc. Place; WALKER; **142** E-5; elev. 437ft./133m.; 🄿; **z** 35584; Ⓟ 568; Ⓒ 552
Sixmile; RMC Place; BIBB; **142** H-6; elev. 348ft./106m.; mail Brierfield **z** 35035, Centreville **z** 35042; ● 100
Six Way; RMC Place; MORGAN; ***142** B-6; elev. 600ft./183m.; ★ **DEC**; mail Decatur **z** 35603; pop. incl. with Priceville (Inc. Place)
Skaggs Corner; RMC Place; DEKALB; ***142** B-10; mail Henagar **z** 35978
Skeggs Crossroads; RMC Place; CLAY; ***142** G-8; mail Goodwater **z** 35072; rural
Skinem; RMC Place; MADISON; ***142** A-7; ★ **HNTS**; mail Hazel Green **z** 35750; rural
Skinnerton (Skinnertown); RMC Place; CONECUH; ***143** M-6; elev. 532ft./162m.; mail Evergreen **z** 36401; rural
Skinnertown; CONECUH; see Skinnerton (RMC Place)
Skipperville; RMC Place; DALE; **143** M-10; elev. 454ft./138m.; 🄿; **z** 36374; ● 80
Skirum; RMC Place; DEKALB; **142** C-9; mail Dawson **z** 35963; ● 130
Skyland; RMC Place; TUSCALOOSA; ★ **TUSC**; mail Tuscaloosa **z** 35405, **z** 35407; pop. incl. with Tuscaloosa (Inc. Place)
Skyline; Inc. Place; JACKSON; **142** A-8; mail Scottsboro **z** 35768; Ⓟ 740; Ⓒ 843
Skyline Acres; RMC Place; MADISON; ***142** B-7; ★ **HNTS**; mail Madison **z** 35758; ● 630
Skyline Estates; RMC Place; JEFFERSON; ★ **BIR**; mail Birmingham **z** 35226; pop. incl. with Hoover (Inc. Place)
Sky Ranch; RMC Place; JEFFERSON; ***142** F-6; ★ **BIR**; mail Birmingham **z** 35226; pop. incl. with Hoover (Inc. Place)
Skyview; RMC Place; JEFFERSON; ***142** F-6; ★ **BIR**; mail Bessemer **z** 35020; pop. incl. with Bessemer (Inc. Place)
Slackland; RMC Place; CHEROKEE; ***142** D-9; elev. 584ft./178m.; mail Gadsden **z** 35901; rural
Slicklizzard; RMC Place; WALKER; ***142** D-4; elev. 640ft./195m.; mail Nauvoo **z** 35578; ● 30
Slocomb; Inc. Place; GENEVA; **143** O-10; elev. 268ft./82m.; 🄿; **z** 36375; Ⓟ 1,906; Ⓒ 2,052
Smithfield; RMC Place; JEFFERSON; ***142** F-6; ★ **BIR**; mail Birmingham **z** 35204; pop. incl. with Birmingham (Inc. Place)
Smith Hill; RMC Place; BIBB; **142** G-5; mail West Blocton **z** 35184; ● 150
Smith Institute; RMC Place; ETOWAH; ***142** C-9; mail Boaz **z** 35956; ● 50
Smiths; CDP-Census Area Only; LEE; ***142** I-12; 🄿; ★ **COL**; **z** 36877; Ⓟ 3,456; Ⓒ 21,756; ◆ 26,237
Smiths Crossroads; RMC Place; ETOWAH; ★ **GAD**; mail Gadsden **z** 35905
Smiths Mill (Schmidts Mill); RMC Place; TALLADEGA; ***142** F-8; elev. 498ft./152m.; mail Lincoln **z** 35096; rural
Smithson; RMC Place; JEFFERSON; ***142** G-6; ★ **BIR**; mail Bessemer **z** 35020; rural
Smithsonia; RMC Place; LAUDERDALE; ***142** A-3; ★ **COL**; mail Florence **z** 35633; ● 80
Smiths Station; Inc. Place; LEE; **142** I-12; 🄿; ★ **COL**; **z** 36877; incorporated June 22, 2001; not reported in 2000 Census; ● 4,500
Smithtown; RMC Place; MOBILE; ***143** P-2; elev. 100ft./30m.; ★ **MOB**; mail Eight Mile **z** 36613; ● 70
Smoke Rise; CDP; BLOUNT; ***142** E-6; ★ **BIR**; mail Remlap **z** 35133; Ⓟ 1,367; Ⓒ 1,750
Smuteye; RMC Place; BULLOCK; **143** K-10; elev. 471ft./144m.; mail Perote **z** 36061; ● 40
Smyer; RMC Place; CLARKE; ***143** L-3; elev. 358ft./109m.; mail Campbell **z** 36727; rural
Smyrna; RMC Place; HOUSTON; ***143** N-11; elev. 253ft./77m.; ★ **DOTH**; mail Dothan **z** 36303; pop. incl. with Dothan (Inc. Place)
Snead; Inc. Place; BLOUNT; **142** D-8; elev. 800ft./244m.; 🄿; **z** 35952; Ⓟ 632; Ⓒ 748
Snoddy; RMC Place; GREENE; ***142** H-3; elev. 269ft./82m.; mail Eutaw **z** 35462; rural
Snowdoun; RMC Place; MONTGOMERY; **143** K-8; elev. 294ft./90m.; mail Montgomery **z** 36105; ● 100
Snow Hill; RMC Place; DALE; ***143** M-11; elev. 418ft./127m.; mail Ozark **z** 36360; ● 30
Snow Hill; RMC Place; WILCOX; **143** K-6; elev. 226ft./69m.; 🄿; **z** 36768; ● 120
Snowtown; RMC Place; JEFFERSON; ***142** E-6; ★ **BIR**; mail Dora **z** 35062; ● 300
Socapatoy; RMC Place; COOSA; ***142** H-9; elev. 725ft./221m.; mail Kellyton **z** 35089; ● 50
Society Hill; RMC Place; MACON; **142** J-11; mail Opelika **z** 36804; ● 130
Soleco; COOSA; see Soleo (RMC Place)
Soleo (Soleco); RMC Place; COOSA; ***142** H-9; mail Goodwater **z** 35072; ● 100
Somerville; Inc. Place; MORGAN; **142** C-6; elev. 755ft./230m.; 🄿; **z** 35670; Ⓟ 211; Ⓒ 347
South; RMC Place; COVINGTON; ***143** M-7; elev. 386ft./118m.; mail Red Level **z** 36474; rural
South; RMC Place; MONTGOMERY; ***142** J-8; ★ **MTGY**; mail Montgomery **z** 36116, **z** 36120; pop. incl. with Montgomery (Inc. Place)
South Calera; RMC Place; SHELBY; ***142** H-7; mail Calera **z** 35040; pop. incl. with Calera (Inc. Place)
South Gadsden; RMC Place; ETOWAH; ***142** D-9; ★ **GAD**; mail Gadsden **z** 35904; pop. incl. with Gadsden (Inc. Place)
South Guntersville; RMC Place; MARSHALL; mail Guntersville **z** 35976; pop. incl. with Guntersville (Inc. Place)
South Haleyville; RMC Place; WINSTON; mail Haleyville **z** 35565; pop. incl. with Haleyville (Inc. Place)
South Highland; RMC Place; JEFFERSON; ***142** F-7; ★ **BIR**; mail Birmingham **z** 35205; pop. incl. with Birmingham (Inc. Place)
South Lowell; RMC Place; WALKER; ***142** D-5; elev. 511ft./156m.; mail Jasper **z** 35503; ● 80
Southmont; RMC Place; MONTGOMERY; ***142** J-8; ★ **MTGY**; mail Montgomery **z** 36105; pop. incl. with Montgomery (Inc. Place)
South Park Estates; RMC Place; MADISON; ★ **HNTS**; mail Huntsville **z** 35802; pop. incl. with Huntsville (Inc. Place)
South Sheffield; RMC Place; COLBERT; ***142** A-4; ★ **FLO**; mail Tuscumbia **z** 35674; pop. incl. with Tuscumbia (Inc. Place)
Southside; Inc. Place; ETOWAH, CALHOUN; **142** D-9; elev. 550ft./168m.; 🄿; ★ **GAD**; **z** 35907; Ⓟ 5,580; Ⓒ 7,036
Southtown; RMC Place; MARSHALL; ***142** C-8; mail Guntersville **z** 35976; pop. incl. with Guntersville (Inc. Place)
South Vinemont; Inc. Place; CULLMAN; **142** C-6; elev. 909ft./277m.; mail Vinemont **z** 35179; Ⓟ 543; Ⓒ 425; Ⓡ 443
Southwood; RMC Place; JEFFERSON; ***142** F-6; ★ **BIR**; mail Birmingham **z** 35209; pop. incl. with Homewood (Inc. Place)
Souwilpa; RMC Place; CHOCTAW; ***143** L-2; elev. 128ft./39m.; mail Silas **z** 36919; rural
Spanish Fort; Inc. Place; BALDWIN; **143** P-3; elev. 150ft./46m.; 🄿; ★ **MOB**; **z** 36527, **z** 36577; Ⓟ 3,327; Ⓒ 5,423
Speake (Hodges Store); RMC Place; LAWRENCE; **142** C-5; mail Danville **z** 35619; ● 190
Speed; RMC Place; COOSA; ***142** I-8; elev. 507ft./155m.; mail Equality **z** 36026; rural
Speeds Water Mill; RMC Place; PICKENS; ***142** G-3; mail Gordo **z** 35466; rural
Speigener; ELMORE; see Speigner (RMC Place)
Speigner (Speigener); RMC Place; ELMORE; **142** I-8; ★ **MTGY**; mail Deatsville **z** 36022; ● 200
Spivey's; RMC Place; BALDWIN; ***143** Q-3; elev. 20ft./6m.; mail Foley **z** 36535
Sprague; RMC Place; MONTGOMERY; **143** K-8; elev. 277ft./84m.; mail Ramer **z** 36069; ● 200
Springbrook; RMC Place; TUSCALOOSA; ★ **TUSC**; mail Tuscaloosa **z** 35405; pop. incl. with Tuscaloosa (Inc. Place)
Spring Creek; RMC Place; SHELBY; ***142** G-7; elev. 431ft./131m.; mail Shelby **z** 35143; ● 50
Springdale; RMC Place; JEFFERSON; ***142** F-6; ★ **BIR**; mail Birmingham **z** 35217; pop. incl. with Tarrant City (Inc. Place)
Springfield; RMC Place; CLARKE; ***143** L-3; mail Thomasville **z** 36784; ● 30
Springfield; RMC Place; LAUDERDALE; ***142** A-5; ★ **FLO**; mail Rogersville **z** 35652; ● 30
Springfield (Pittman); RMC Place; RANDOLPH; ***142** G-11; mail Roanoke **z** 36274; rural
Spring Garden; RMC Place; CHEROKEE; **142** D-10; elev. 699ft./213m.; 🄿; **z** 36275; ● 140
Spring Hill; RMC Place; BARBOUR; **143** K-11; elev. 387ft./118m.; mail Midway **z** 36053; ● 60
Springhill; RMC Place; CLAY; ***142** G-9; elev. 1,142ft./348m.; mail Ashland **z** 36251; rural
Spring Hill; RMC Place; CONECUH; ***143** N-6; elev. 292ft./89m.; mail Evergreen **z** 36401; ● 30
Spring Hill; RMC Place; ESCAMBIA; ***143** O-6; elev. 203ft./62m.; mail Brewton **z** 36426; ● 80
Spring Hill; RMC Place; MOBILE; ***143** P-2; ★ **MOB**; mail Mobile **z** 36608; pop. incl. with Mobile (Inc. Place)
Spring Hill; RMC Place; PIKE; **143** M-9; mail Troy **z** 36079; ● 80
Spring Hill; RMC Place; WALKER; ***142** D-4; elev. 664ft./202m.; mail Carbon Hill **z** 35549; rural
Spring Valley; RMC Place; COLBERT; **142** B-4; elev. 512ft./156m.; ★ **FLO**; mail Tuscumbia **z** 35674; ● 170
Spring Valley; RMC Place; MONTGOMERY; ★ **MTGY**; mail Montgomery **z** 36116; pop. incl. with Montgomery (Inc. Place)
Springville; Inc. Place; ST. CLAIR; **142** E-7; elev. 726ft./221m.; 🄿; ★ **BIR**; **z** 35146; Ⓟ 1,910; Ⓒ 2,521
Springville Lake Estates; RMC Place; ST. CLAIR; ***142** E-7; ★ **BIR**; mail Springville **z** 35146; rural
Sprott; RMC Place; PERRY; **142** I-5; elev. 176ft./54m.; 🄿; **z** 36756; ● 30
Spruce Pine; RMC Place; FRANKLIN; **142** C-4; elev. 1,027ft./313m.; 🄿; **z** 35585; ● 600
Stafford; RMC Place; PICKENS; ***142** F-2; elev. 369ft./112m.; mail Ethelsville **z** 35461; ● 30
Standard; RMC Place; WALKER; ***142** E-5; elev. 420ft./128m.; mail Parrish **z** 35580; pop. incl. with Parrish (Inc. Place)
Standing Rock; RMC Place; CHAMBERS; **142** G-11; elev. 767ft./234m.; mail Five Points **z** 36855; ● 100
Stanley; RMC Place; COVINGTON; ***143** N-8; mail Andalusia **z** 36420; rural
Stansel; RMC Place; PICKENS; ***142** G-3; mail Reform **z** 35481; ● 50
Stanton; RMC Place; CHILTON; **142** I-6; elev. 500ft./152m.; 🄿; **z** 36790; ● 400
Stapleton; RMC Place; BALDWIN; **143** P-3; elev. 223ft./68m.; 🄿; **z** 36578; ● 1,300
Star; RMC Place; LAMAR; ***142** E-2; elev. 286ft./87m.; mail Millport **z** 35576; rural
Starlington; RMC Place; BUTLER; ***143** M-6; elev. 345ft./105m.; mail Georgiana **z** 36033; rural
State Line; RMC Place; HOUSTON; ***143** O-11; mail Cottonwood **z** 36320, Slocomb **z** 36375; rural
Statesville; RMC Place; AUTAUGA; ***142** J-6; mail Selma **z** 36703; rural
Steele; Inc. Place; ST. CLAIR; **142** D-8; elev. 582ft./177m.; 🄿; ★ **GAD**; **z** 35987; Ⓟ 1,046; Ⓒ 1,093
Steele Crossing; RMC Place; MADISON; ***142** A-8; ★ **HNTS**; mail Elora **z** 37328; rural
Steelwood; RMC Place; BALDWIN; **143** P-3; mail Loxley **z** 36551; ● 50
Steenson Hollow; RMC Place; COLBERT; ***142** A-4; ★ **FLO**; mail Sheffield **z** 35660; pop. incl. with Muscle Shoals (Inc. Place)
Steiner; RMC Place; MONTGOMERY; ***142** J-8; ★ **MTGY**; mail Montgomery **z** 36111; pop. incl. with Montgomery (Inc. Place)
Sterrett; RMC Place; SHELBY; **142** F-7; elev. 503ft./153m.; 🄿; ★ **BIR**; **z** 35147; ● 600
Stevenson; Inc. Place; JACKSON; **142** A-9; elev. 628ft./191m.; 🄿; **z** 35772; Ⓟ 2,046; Ⓒ 1,770
Stewards Store; LIMESTONE; see Tanner Crossroads (RMC Place)
Stewart; RMC Place; HALE; **142** H-4; elev. 131ft./40m.; 🄿; **z** 35441; ● 50
Stewarts; RMC Place; ST. CLAIR; ***142** F-8; elev. 520ft./158m.; ★ **BIR**; mail Pell City **z** 35125; ● 80
Stewartsville; COOSA; see Stewartville (RMC Place)
Stewartville (Stewartsville); RMC Place; COOSA; **142** H-8; mail Sylacauga **z** 35151; ● 150
Stills Crossroads; RMC Place; BULLOCK; ***143** K-9; mail Troy **z** 36081; rural
Stockdale; RMC Place; TALLADEGA; ***142** F-9; mail Munford **z** 36268; rural
Stockton; RMC Place; BALDWIN; **143** O-3; elev. 100ft./30m.; 🄿; **z** 36579; ● 200
Stokeley; RMC Place; COVINGTON; mail Andalusia **z** 36420; pop. incl. with Andalusia (Inc. Place)
Stokes; RMC Place; TUSCALOOSA; ***142** G-4; ★ **TUSC**; mail Duncanville **z** 35456; rural
Stoney Point; RMC Place; AUTAUGA; ***142** I-8; mail Deatsville **z** 36022; rural
Stotesville; RMC Place; BIBB; mail West Blocton **z** 35184
Stough; RMC Place; FAYETTE; ***142** E-4; mail Fayette **z** 35555; ● 30
Straight Mountain; RMC Place; BLOUNT; ***142** E-8; mail Oneonta **z** 35121; rural
Strata; RMC Place; MONTGOMERY; **143** K-8; mail Lapine **z** 36046; ● 40
Straughn; RMC Place; COVINGTON; ***143** N-8; elev. 371ft./113m.; mail Andalusia **z** 36420; ● 80
Strawberry; RMC Place; BLOUNT; ***142** C-7; elev. 892ft./272m.; mail Arab **z** 35016; ● 50
Stroud; RMC Place; CHAMBERS; **142** H-11; mail Five Points **z** 36855; ● 50
Stroups Crossroads; MORGAN; see Pumpkin Center (RMC Place)
Studdards Crossroads; RMC Place; FAYETTE; **142** E-4; mail Carbon Hill **z** 35549
Sturkie; RMC Place; CHAMBERS; ***142** H-10; elev. 856ft./261m.; mail Lafayette **z** 36862; rural
Sugar Creek; RMC Place; BLOUNT; ***142** D-7; elev. 419ft./128m.; mail Hayden **z** 35079; ● 80
Suggsville; RMC Place; CLARKE; **143** M-4; mail Whatley **z** 36482; ● 150
Suggsville; CLARKE; see Allen (RMC Place)
Sulligent; Inc. Place; LAMAR; **142** E-2; elev. 321ft./98m.; 🄿; **z** 35586; Ⓟ 1,886; Ⓒ 2,151
Sulpher Springs (Sulphur Springs); RMC Place; BLOUNT; ***142** D-6; ★ **BIR**; mail Hayden **z** 35079; rural
Sulphur Springs; BLOUNT; see Sulpher Springs (RMC Place)
Sulphur Springs; RMC Place; CALHOUN; ***142** E-9; mail Ohatchee **z** 36271; rural
Sulphur Springs; RMC Place; CULLMAN; ***142** D-6; elev. 700ft./213m.; mail Crane Hill **z** 35053; rural
Sulphur Springs; RMC Place; DEKALB; **142** B-10; mail Rising Fawn **z** 30738
Sulphur Springs; RMC Place; JACKSON; ***142** A-10; elev. 1,500ft./457m.; mail Flat Rock **z** 35966; rural
Sulphur Springs (Quicks Mill); RMC Place; MADISON; **142** A-7; ★ **HNTS**; mail New Market **z** 35761; ● 30
Sumiton; Inc. Place; WALKER, JEFFERSON; **142** E-6; elev. 522ft./159m.; 🄿; ★ **BIR**; **z** 35148; Ⓟ 2,604; Ⓒ 2,665
Summerdale; Inc. Place; BALDWIN; **143** Q-4; elev. 112ft./34m.; 🄿; **z** 36580; Ⓟ 559; Ⓒ 655
Summerfield; RMC Place; DALLAS; **142** J-6; elev. 340ft./104m.; mail Selma **z** 36701; ● 50
Summit; RMC Place; BLOUNT; **142** C-7; elev. 938ft./286m.; mail Blountsville **z** 35031
Summit Farm; RMC Place; JEFFERSON; ***142** G-6; elev. 600ft./183m.; ★ **BIR**; mail Bessemer **z** 35022; ● 100
SUMTER; **142** J-2; Ⓟ 16,174; Ⓒ 14,798; ◆ 12,885
Sumterville; RMC Place; SUMTER; **142** I-2; elev. 293ft./89m.; mail Epes **z** 35460; ● 80
Sunflower; RMC Place; WASHINGTON; **143** N-3; elev. 30ft./9m.; 🄿; **z** 36581; ● 110
Sunny Cove; RMC Place; MOBILE; ***143** Q-2; elev. 15ft./5m.; ★ **MOB**; mail Theodore **z** 36582; ● 60
Sunny South; RMC Place; WILCOX; **143** L-4; elev. 250ft./76m.; mail Pine Hill **z** 36769; ● 200
Sunset Cove; RMC Place; MADISON; ***142** B-7; ★ **HNTS**; mail Huntsville **z** 35802; pop. incl. with Huntsville (Inc. Place)
Sunset Mill Village; RMC Place; DALLAS; mail Selma **z** 36701; pop. incl. with Selma (Inc. Place)
Sunset Shores; RMC Place; BALDWIN; ***143** Q-3; mail Foley **z** 36535; ● 100
Sun Valley; RMC Place; JEFFERSON; ***142** E-7; ★ **BIR**; mail Birmingham **z** 35215
Surginer; RMC Place; MARENGO; **143** K-4; mail Magnolia **z** 36754; ● 100
Susan Moore (Clarence); Inc. Place; BLOUNT; **142** D-8; mail Altoona **z** 35952; Ⓟ 658; Ⓒ 721
Suspension; RMC Place; BULLOCK; ***143** K-10; elev. 431ft./131m.; mail Union Springs **z** 36089; rural
Suttle; RMC Place; PERRY; **142** J-5; elev. 153ft./47m.; mail Selma **z** 36701; ● 70
Swaim; RMC Place; JACKSON; **142** A-8; mail Paint Rock **z** 35764; rural
Swancott; RMC Place; LIMESTONE; ***142** B-6; elev. 600ft./183m.; ★ **HNTS**; mail Madison **z** 35756; pop. incl. with Huntsville (Inc. Place)
Swearengin; RMC Place; MARSHALL; ***142** B-8; mail Scottsboro **z** 35769; rural
Sweet Water; Inc. Place; MARENGO; **143** K-3; elev. 202ft./62m.; 🄿; **z** 36782; Ⓟ 243; Ⓒ 234
Sycamore; RMC Place; TALLADEGA; **142** G-8; elev. 548ft./167m.; 🄿; **z** 35149; ● 1,000
Sylacauga; Inc. Place; TALLADEGA; **142** G-8; elev. 548ft./167m.; 🄿 🄷; **z** 35150-51; Ⓟ 12,520; Ⓒ 12,616; Ⓡ 12,819
Sylvan; TUSCALOOSA; see Fosters (RMC Place)
Sylvan Grove; RMC Place; DALE; ***143** N-11; elev. 360ft./110m.; ★ **DOTH**; mail Midland City **z** 36350; rural
Sylvania; Inc. Place; DEKALB; **142** B-9; elev. 1,392ft./424m.; 🄿; **z** 35988; Ⓟ 932; Ⓒ 1,186
Sylvan Springs; Inc. Place; JEFFERSON; **143** R-9; elev. 659ft./201m.; 🄿; ★ **BIR**; **z** 35118; Ⓟ 1,470; Ⓒ 1,465

T

Tabernacle; RMC Place; COFFEE; ***143** M-9; mail New Brockton **z** 36351; ● 30
Tabernacle; RMC Place; HOUSTON; ***143** N-11; elev. 322ft./98m.; ★ **DOTH**; mail Dothan **z** 36301; pop. incl. with Taylor (Inc. Place)
Tabor; RMC Place; ETOWAH; ***142** D-9; mail Gadsden **z** 35904; ● 30
Taft; RMC Place; CHEROKEE; ***142** C-10; mail Gaylesville **z** 35973; rural
Taits Gap; RMC Place; BLOUNT; **142** D-8; mail Oneonta **z** 35121; ● 90
Talladega; Inc. Place; ⊡ TALLADEGA; **142** F-8; elev. 555ft./169m.; 🄿 🄷 🄲 425 ■; **z** 35160-61; Ⓟ 18,175; Ⓒ 15,143; Ⓡ 17,344; ◆ 16,963
TALLADEGA; **142** F-9; Ⓟ 74,107; Ⓒ 80,321; ◆ 79,559
Talladega Springs; Inc. Place; TALLADEGA; **142** G-7; elev. 432ft./132m.; mail Sylacauga **z** 35151; Ⓟ 148; Ⓒ 124
Tallahatta Springs; RMC Place; CLARKE; **143** L-3; elev. 200ft./61m.; mail Thomasville **z** 36784; ● 30
TALLAPOOSA; **142** H-10; Ⓟ 38,826; Ⓒ 41,475; Ⓡ 41,792; ◆ 40,492
Tallapoosa City; RMC Place; TALLAPOOSA; mail Tallassee **z** 36078; pop. incl. with Tallassee (Inc. Place)
Tallassee; Inc. Place; ELMORE, TALLAPOOSA; **142** I-9; elev. 395ft./120m.; 🄿 🄷; **z** 36023, **z** 36045, **z** 36078; Ⓟ 5,112; Ⓒ 4,934
Tallaweka; RMC Place; ELMORE; mail Tallassee **z** 36078; pop. incl. with Tallassee (Inc. Place)
Talucah; RMC Place; MORGAN; ***142** B-7; elev. 600ft./183m.; mail Valhermoso Springs **z** 35775; ● 50
Tannehill; RMC Place; TUSCALOOSA; ***142** G-6; elev. 465ft./142m.; mail Mc Calla **z** 35111; rural
Tanner; RMC Place; LIMESTONE; **142** B-6; elev. 670ft./204m.; 🄿; **z** 35671; ● 750
Tanner Crossroads (Stewards Store); RMC Place; LIMESTONE; ***142** B-6; mail Tanner **z** 35671; ● 180
Tanner Heights; RMC Place; MORGAN; ***142** C-6; ★ **DEC**; mail Hartselle **z** 35640; pop. incl. with Hartselle (Inc. Place)
Tanner Williams; RMC Place; MOBILE; **143** P-1; elev. 180ft./55m.; ★ **MOB**; mail Wilmer **z** 36587; ● 50
Tanyard; RMC Place; BULLOCK; ***143** L-10; elev. 496ft./151m.; mail Perote **z** 36061; rural
Tanyard; RMC Place; ST. CLAIR; ***142** E-8; elev. 565ft./172m.; ★ **BIR**; mail Pell City **z** 35125; rural
Tarentum; RMC Place; PIKE; **143** M-9; mail Brundidge **z** 36010; ● 30
Tarpley; RMC Place; JEFFERSON; ***142** F-6; ★ **BIR**; mail Birmingham **z** 35211; pop. incl. with Birmingham (Inc. Place)
Tarrant; JEFFERSON; see Tarrant City (Inc. Place)
Tarrant City (Tarrant); Inc. Place; JEFFERSON; **142** F-6; elev. 548ft./167m.; ★ **BIR**; mail Birmingham **z** 35217; Ⓟ 8,046; Ⓒ 7,022
Tarrant Heights; RMC Place; JEFFERSON; ***142** F-7; ★ **BIR**; mail Birmingham **z** 35217; pop. incl. with Tarrant City (Inc. Place)
Tasso; RMC Place; DALLAS; ***143** K-5; mail Orrville **z** 36767; rural
Tattlersville; RMC Place; CLARKE; ***143** L-2; elev. 182ft./55m.; mail Coffeeville **z** 36524; rural
Taylor; Inc. Place; HOUSTON, GENEVA; **143** N-11; elev. 332ft./101m.; 🄿; ★ **DOTH**; **z** 36301, **z** 36305; Ⓟ 1,352; Ⓒ 1,898
Taylors Crossroads; RMC Place; RANDOLPH; ***142** G-11; elev. 1,087ft./331m.; mail Roanoke **z** 36274; rural
Taylorsville; MADISON; see Hobbs Island (RMC Place)
Taylorville; RMC Place; TUSCALOOSA; **143** T-2; elev. 271ft./83m.; ★ **TUSC**; mail Tuscaloosa **z** 35405; ● 400
Teals Crossroads; RMC Place; BARBOUR; ***143** M-10; elev. 477ft./145m.; mail Ariton **z** 36311; rural
Teasleys Mill; RMC Place; MONTGOMERY; ***143** K-9; elev. 276ft./84m.; mail Mathews **z** 36052; ● 130
Tecumseh; RMC Place; CHEROKEE; **142** D-11; elev. 862ft./263m.; mail Esom Hill **z** 30138; ● 80
Teddy; RMC Place; ESCAMBIA; ***143** N-6; mail Brewton **z** 36426; rural
Ten Broeck; RMC Place; DEKALB; ***142** C-9; mail Fyffe **z** 35971
Tennala; RMC Place; CHEROKEE; ***142** D-10; elev. 565ft./172m.; mail Centre **z** 35960, Piedmont **z** 36272; ● 30
Tennant; RMC Place; RANDOLPH; ***142** G-10; elev. 1,061ft./323m.; mail Roanoke **z** 36274; rural
Tennille; RMC Place; PIKE; ***143** M-10; elev. 303ft./92m.; mail Brundidge **z** 36010; rural
Tensaw; RMC Place; BALDWIN; **143** O-3; mail Stockton **z** 36579; ● 60
Terese; RMC Place; BARBOUR; ***143** L-11; mail Eufaula **z** 36027; pop. incl. with Eufaula (Inc. Place)
Terminal Junction; RMC Place; MOBILE; ★ **MOB**; pop. incl. with Mobile (Inc. Place)
Terry Heights; RMC Place; MADISON; ***142** A-7; ★ **HNTS**; mail Huntsville **z** 35805; pop. incl. with Huntsville (Inc. Place)
Texasville (Alston); RMC Place; BARBOUR; **143** L-11; elev. 504ft./154m.; mail Clayton **z** 36016; ● 60
Thach (Thatch); RMC Place; LIMESTONE; ***142** A-6; mail Elkmont **z** 35620; ● 80
Thach; RMC Place; WALKER; ***142** D-5; mail Jasper **z** 35503; ● 100
Thames; RMC Place; MONTGOMERY; ★ **MTGY**; pop. incl. with Montgomery (Inc. Place)
Tharptown; RMC Place; FRANKLIN; **142** B-4; mail Russellville **z** 35654; ● 100
Thatch; LIMESTONE; see Thach (RMC Place)
The Bottle; LEE; see Farmville (RMC Place)
The Cedars; RMC Place; LAUDERDALE; ***142** A-4; ★ **FLO**; mail Florence **z** 35630; pop. incl. with Florence (Inc. Place)
The Colony (Colony); Inc. Place; CULLMAN; ***142** D-6; mail Hanceville **z** 35077; Ⓟ 298; Ⓒ 385
The Highlands; RMC Place; ETOWAH; ***142** D-9; ★ **GAD**; mail Gadsden **z** 35901; pop. incl. with Gadsden (Inc. Place)
The Highlands; RMC Place; MADISON; ***142** A-7; ★ **HNTS**; mail Huntsville **z** 35810; pop. incl. with Huntsville (Inc. Place)
Theodore; CDP; MOBILE; **143** Q-2; elev. 67ft./20m.; 🄿; ★ **MOB**; **z** 36582, **z** 36590, **z** 36619; Ⓟ 6,509; Ⓒ 6,811
The Ridge; RMC Place; MONROE; ***143** M-5; mail Monroeville **z** 36460; rural
Thomas; RMC Place; AUTAUGA; ***142** J-7; mail Prattville **z** 36067; ● 80
Thomas; RMC Place; JEFFERSON; ***142** F-6; ★ **BIR**; mail Birmingham **z** 35214; pop. incl. with Birmingham (Inc. Place)
Thomas Acres; RMC Place; JEFFERSON; ***142** F-6; ★ **BIR**; mail Bessemer **z** 35020; pop. incl. with Bessemer (Inc. Place)
Thomas Hill; RMC Place; TALLADEGA; mail Sylacauga **z** 35150
Thomas Junction; RMC Place; JEFFERSON; ★ **BIR**; pop. incl. with Birmingham (Inc. Place)
Thomaston; Inc. Place; MARENGO; **142** J-4; elev. 189ft./58m.; 🄿; **z** 36783; Ⓟ 497; Ⓒ 383
Thomasville; Inc. Place; CLARKE; **143** L-4; elev. 389ft./119m.; 🄿 🄷; **z** 36762, **z** 36784; Ⓟ 4,301; Ⓒ 4,649
Thompson; RMC Place; BULLOCK; ***143** K-9; elev. 283ft./86m.; mail Union Springs **z** 36089; rural
Thornhill; RMC Place; MARION; ***142** D-4; elev. 831ft./253m.; mail Haleyville **z** 35565; rural
Thornton; RMC Place; TALLAPOOSA; **142** I-10; mail Dadeville **z** 36853; rural
Thorntontown; RMC Place; LAUDERDALE; ***142** A-5; mail Rogersville **z** 35652; rural
Thorsby; Inc. Place; CHILTON; **142** H-7; elev. 700ft./213m.; 🄿; **z** 35171; Ⓟ 1,465; Ⓒ 1,820
Three Notch; RMC Place; BULLOCK; **143** K-10; elev. 479ft./146m.; mail Midway **z** 36053; ● 30
Threet; RMC Place; LAUDERDALE; ***142** A-3; elev. 643ft./196m.; mail Cloverdale **z** 35617, Florence **z** 35633; ● 30
Thurston; RMC Place; GENEVA; ***143** O-10; mail Geneva **z** 36340; rural
Tibbie; RMC Place; WASHINGTON; **143** N-2; elev. 250ft./76m.; 🄿; **z** 36583; ● 350
Tilden; RMC Place; DALLAS; ***143** K-5; elev. 299ft./91m.; mail Minter **z** 36761; rural
Tiller Crossroads; RMC Place; CHAMBERS; ***142** H-10; elev. 695ft./212m.; mail Camp Hill **z** 36850, Roanoke **z** 36274; rural
Tillery Crossroad; RMC Place; LEE; ***142** I-11; elev. 600ft./183m.; mail Valley **z** 36854; rural
Tillmans Corner; CDP; MOBILE; **143** P-2; ★ **MOB**; mail Mobile **z** 36619; Ⓟ 17,988; Ⓒ 15,685
Tinela; RMC Place; MONROE; ***143** L-5; elev. 213ft./65m.; mail Vredenburgh **z** 36481; rural
Tishabee; RMC Place; GREENE; ***142** I-3; elev. 142ft./43m.; mail Boligee **z** 35443; rural
Titus; RMC Place; ELMORE; **142** I-8; elev. 460ft./140m.; 🄿; **z** 36080; ● 150
Toadvine; RMC Place; JEFFERSON; ***142** F-5; elev. 330ft./101m.; ★ **BIR**; mail Bessemer **z** 35020; rural
Toddtown; RMC Place; CLARKE; ***143** M-3; mail Grove Hill **z** 36451; ● 50
Tompkinsville; RMC Place; CHOCTAW; ***143** K-3; mail Pennington **z** 36916; rural
Toney; RMC Place; MADISON; **142** A-7; elev. 830ft./253m.; 🄿; ★ **HNTS**; **z** 35773; ● 500
Toonersville; RMC Place; LAUDERDALE; ***142** A-5; mail Rogersville **z** 35652; rural
Toulminville; RMC Place; MOBILE; ***143** P-2; ★ **MOB**; mail Mobile **z** 36610; pop. incl. with Mobile (Inc. Place)
Town Creek; Inc. Place; LAWRENCE; **142** B-5; elev. 563ft./172m.; 🄿; **z** 35672; Ⓟ 1,379; Ⓒ 1,216
Towne West; RMC Place; MOBILE; ★ **MOB**; mail Mobile **z** 36618; pop. incl. with Mobile (Inc. Place)
Townley; RMC Place; WALKER; **142** E-4; elev. 352ft./107m.; 🄿; **z** 35587; ● 550
Toxey; Inc. Place; CHOCTAW; **143** L-2; elev. 100ft./30m.; 🄿; **z** 36921; Ⓟ 211; Ⓒ 152
Trade; RMC Place; CULLMAN; ***142** D-6; elev. 818ft./249m.; mail Crane Hill **z** 35053; ● 80
Trafford; Inc. Place; JEFFERSON; ***142** E-7; elev. 486ft./148m.; 🄿; ★ **BIR**; **z** 35172; Ⓟ 739; Ⓒ 523
Travis Bridge; RMC Place; CONECUH; ***143** M-6; mail Evergreen **z** 36401; rural
Tredegar; RMC Place; CALHOUN; ***142** E-9; ★ **ANNI**; mail Jacksonville **z** 36265; rural
Trenton; RMC Place; JACKSON; **142** A-8; elev. 700ft./213m.; 🄿; **z** 35774; ● 200
Triana; Inc. Place; MADISON; **142** B-7; elev. 620ft./189m.; 🄿; ★ **HNTS**; **z** 35758 & mail Madison **z** 35756; Ⓟ 499; Ⓒ 458
Trickem; RMC Place; LOWNDES; ***142** J-7; elev. 210ft./64m.; mail Tyler **z** 36785; pop. incl. with White Hall (Inc. Place)
Trimble; RMC Place; CULLMAN; **142** D-6; elev. 527ft./161m.; mail Cullman **z** 35057; ● 100

Entries in **UPPERCASE** are counties.
Entries in **bold** have populations of 2,500 or more.
Names in parentheses are alternate names.

Inc. Place	Incorporated Place
RMC Place	Rand McNally Designated Place
CDP	Census Designated Place
MCD	Minor Civil Division

⊡ County Seat
▲ Minor Civil Division
elev. Elevation
🄿 Post Office
🄷 Hospital
🄲 College
■ Principal Business Center
★ Ranally Metro Area (RMA) Abbreviation
z Zip Code(s)
Ⓟ Previous Census Population
Ⓡ Revised Census Population
Ⓐ Annexation Population
● Rand McNally Population Estimate
Ⓒ Final Census Population
Ⓢ Special Census Population
◆ Estimated Population

For additional definitions see Glossary, Volume 1, and Introduction, Volume 2.

Trinity; Inc. Place; MORGAN; **142** B-6; elev. 634ft./193m.; 🅿; ★ **DEC**; **z** 35673; Ⓟ 1,380; Ⓒ 1,841
Trotwood Park; RMC Place; JEFFERSON; ***142** F-7; ★ **BIR**; mail Birmingham **z** 35206; pop. incl. with Birmingham (Inc. Place)
Troy; Inc. Place; ⊡ PIKE; **143** L-9; elev. 543ft./166m.; 🅿 🅷 🅲 28,255; **z** 36079, **z** 36081-82; Ⓟ 13,051; Ⓒ 13,935
Trussville; Inc. Place; JEFFERSON; **142** F-7; elev. 708ft./216m.; 🅿; ★ **BIR**; **z** 35173; Ⓟ 8,266; Ⓒ 12,924
Tuckabatchie; RMC Place; ELMORE; ***142** J-9; mail Tallassee **z** 36078; pop. incl. with Tallassee (Inc. Place)
Tuckahoe Heights; RMC Place; ETOWAH; ***142** D-9; ★ **GAD**; mail Gadsden **z** 35904; pop. incl. with Gadsden (Inc. Place)
Tucker; RMC Place; MARION; ***142** D-3; elev. 565ft./172m.; mail Winfield **z** 35594; rural
Tucker Crossroads; RMC Place; CHEROKEE; ***142** D-10; elev. 577ft./176m.; mail Cedar Bluff **z** 35959; ● 50
Tumbleton; RMC Place; HENRY; **143** N-11; elev. 361ft./110m.; mail Headland **z** 36345; ● 250
Tunnel Springs; RMC Place; MONROE; **143** M-5; mail Peterman **z** 36471; ● 100
Tupelo; RMC Place; JACKSON; ***142** A-9; mail Scottsboro **z** 35768; rural
Turkey Branch; RMC Place; BALDWIN; ***143** Q-3; ★ **MOB**; mail Magnolia Springs **z** 36555; rural
Turkeytown; RMC Place; ETOWAH; ***142** D-9; elev. 547ft./167m.; ★ **GAD**; mail Gadsden **z** 35901; ● 30
Turner Crossroads; RMC Place; COFFEE; ***143** N-9; mail New Brockton **z** 36351; rural
Tuscaloosa; Inc. Place; ⊡ TUSCALOOSA; **142** G-4; elev. 227ft./69m.; 🅿 🅷 🅲 24,681 ■; ★ **TUSC**; **z** 35401-07, **z** 35485-87; Ⓟ 77,759; Ⓒ 77,906; Ⓡ 77,820; ◆ 87,391
TUSCALOOSA; **142** F-4; Ⓟ 150,522; Ⓒ 164,875; ◆ 189,928
Tuscumbia; Inc. Place; ⊡ COLBERT; **142** F-13; elev. 470ft./143m.; 🅿; ★ **FLO**; **z** 35674; Ⓟ 8,413; Ⓒ 7,856
Tuskegee; Inc. Place; ⊡ MACON; **142** J-10; elev. 468ft./143m.; 🅿 🅷 🅲 2,842; **z** 36083; Ⓟ 12,257; Ⓒ 11,846
Tuskegee Institute; RMC Place; MACON; ***142** J-10; 🅿; **z** 36087-88 & mail Tuskegee **z** 36083; pop. incl. with Tuskegee (Inc. Place)
Twilley Town; RMC Place; WALKER; ***142** E-6; elev. 380ft./116m.; mail Quinton **z** 35130; ● 70
Twin (Yampertown); Inc. Place; MARION; **142** D-3; mail Guin **z** 35563; incorporated August 6, 2002; not reported in 2000 Census; ● 150
Twin Oaks; RMC Place; MONTGOMERY; ★ **MTGY**; mail Montgomery **z** 36123; pop. incl. with Montgomery (Inc. Place)
Twinsprings; RMC Place; BARBOUR; ***143** K-12; mail Eufaula **z** 36027; rural
Tyler; RMC Place; DALLAS; **142** J-6; elev. 171ft./52m.; 🅿; **z** 36785; ● 200
Tyler Crossroads; RMC Place; BARBOUR; ***143** L-10; elev. 465ft./142m.; mail Louisville **z** 36048; rural
Tyson (Morganville); RMC Place; LOWNDES; ***143** K-8; elev. 238ft./73m.; mail Hope Hull **z** 36043; ● 30
Tysonville; RMC Place; MACON; ***142** J-9; elev. 204ft./62m.; mail Shorter **z** 36075; ● 30

U

Uchee; RMC Place; RUSSELL; **142** J-11; elev. 541ft./165m.; mail Hatchechubbee **z** 36858; rural
Underwood; RMC Place; LAUDERDALE; ***142** A-4; ★ **FLO**; mail Florence **z** 35633; ● 1,600
Underwood; RMC Place; SHELBY; ***142** G-6; mail Montevallo **z** 35115; ● 200
Underwood Crossroads; RMC Place; COLBERT; ***142** A-4; ★ **FLO**; mail Leighton **z** 35646, Sheffield **z** 35660; ● 30
Underwood-Petersville; CDP-Census Area Only; LAUDERDALE; ***142** A-4; ★ **FLO**; mail Florence **z** 35633; Ⓟ 3,092; Ⓒ 3,137
Union; RMC Place; CLAY; ***142** F-10; elev. 981ft./299m.; mail Delta **z** 36258; ● 30
Union; RMC Place; ETOWAH; ***142** D-8; mail Boaz **z** 35957; ● 50
Union; Inc. Place; GREENE; **142** H-3; mail Eutaw **z** 35462; Ⓟ 321; Ⓒ 227
Union; RMC Place; HENRY; ***143** M-11; elev. 414ft./126m.; mail Abbeville **z** 36310; rural
Union; RMC Place; MORGAN; ***142** C-7; mail Somerville **z** 35670; rural
Union; RMC Place; TALLAPOOSA; ***142** I-9; mail Dadeville **z** 36853; rural
Union Grove; RMC Place; CHILTON; **142** H-7; mail Jemison **z** 35085; ● 120
Union Grove; RMC Place; CULLMAN; ***142** C-7; mail Holly Pond **z** 35083; rural
Union Grove; RMC Place; JEFFERSON; ***142** F-6; ★ **BIR**; mail Adamsville **z** 35005; pop. incl. with Adamsville (Inc. Place)
Union Grove; Inc. Place; MARSHALL; **142** C-7; elev. 1,040ft./317m.; 🅿; **z** 35175; Ⓟ 119; Ⓒ 94
Union Hill; RMC Place; CLEBURNE; ***142** F-11; mail Ranburne **z** 36273; rural
Union Hill; RMC Place; LIMESTONE; ***142** A-5; mail Anderson **z** 35610; ● 30
Union Hill; RMC Place; MORGAN; **142** B-7; mail Laceys Spring **z** 35754
Union Springs; Inc. Place; ⊡ BULLOCK; **143** K-10; elev. 528ft./161m.; 🅿 🅷; **z** 36089; Ⓟ 3,975; Ⓒ 3,670
Uniontown; Inc. Place; PERRY; **142** J-4; elev. 287ft./87m.; 🅿; **z** 36786; Ⓟ 1,730; Ⓒ 1,636
Unity; RMC Place; AUTAUGA; ***142** I-6; elev. 400ft./122m.; mail Billingsley **z** 36006; ● 30
Unity; RMC Place; COOSA; **142** H-8; elev. 662ft./202m.; mail Weogufka **z** 35183
Unity; TUSCALOOSA; see Pearson Subdivision (RMC Place)
Universal Heights; RMC Place; TUSCALOOSA; ★ **TUSC**; mail Tuscaloosa **z** 35404
University of Montevallo; RMC Place; SHELBY; ***142** G-6; mail Montevallo **z** 35115; pop. incl. with Montevallo (Inc. Place)
University of South Alabama; RMC Place; MOBILE; ***143** P-2; ★ **MOB**; mail Mobile **z** 36608, **z** 36688; pop. incl. with Mobile (Inc. Place)
Upper Coalburg; RMC Place; JEFFERSON; ***142** F-6; ★ **BIR**; mail Fultondale **z** 35068
Upper Green Hill; RMC Place; LAUDERDALE; ***142** A-4; elev. 767ft./234m.; ★ **FLO**; mail Florence **z** 35634
Upshaw; RMC Place; WINSTON; ***142** C-5; elev. 915ft./279m.; mail Addison **z** 35540; rural
Uriah; RMC Place; MONROE; **143** N-4; elev. 354ft./108m.; 🅿; **z** 36480; ● 500

V

Valdosta; RMC Place; COLBERT; ***142** B-4; ★ **FLO**; mail Tuscumbia **z** 35674; pop. incl. with Tuscumbia (Inc. Place)
Valhermoso Springs; RMC Place; MORGAN; **142** B-7; elev. 600ft./183m.; 🅿; **z** 35775; ● 500
Valley; Inc. Place; CHAMBERS; **142** H-11; 🅿 🅷; **z** 36854, **z** 36872; Ⓟ 8,215; Ⓒ 9,198
Valley Creek; RMC Place; JEFFERSON; **142** F-6; ★ **BIR**; mail Bessemer **z** 35020; ● 250
Valley Creek Junction; RMC Place; DALLAS; ***142** I-6; elev. 469ft./143m.; mail Plantersville **z** 36758; rural
Valley Grande; Inc. Place; DALLAS; ***142** J-6; elev. 367ft./112m.; 🅿; **z** 36701, **z** 36703; incorporated February 3, 2003; not reported in 2000 Census
Valley Head; Inc. Place; DEKALB; **142** B-10; elev. 1,029ft./314m.; 🅿; **z** 35989; Ⓟ 577; Ⓒ 611
Valley Junction; RMC Place; SHELBY; ***142** H-6; elev. 560ft./171m.; mail Montevallo **z** 35115
Valley View; RMC Place; MORGAN; ***142** B-6; elev. 740ft./226m.; ★ **DEC**; mail Hartselle **z** 35640; pop. incl. with Hartselle (Inc. Place)
Vance; Inc. Place; TUSCALOOSA, BIBB; **142** G-5; elev. 516ft./157m.; 🅿; **z** 35490; Ⓟ 248; Ⓒ 500
Vanderbilt; RMC Place; JEFFERSON; ***142** F-6; ★ **BIR**; mail Birmingham **z** 35204; pop. incl. with Birmingham (Inc. Place)
Vandiver; RMC Place; SHELBY; ***142** F-7; elev. 500ft./152m.; 🅿; ★ **BIR**; **z** 35176; ● 500
Vangale; RMC Place; MARENGO; ***143** K-3; mail Sweet Water **z** 36782; rural
Vaughn; RMC Place; BALDWIN; **143** O-3; mail Stockton **z** 36579; ● 300
Vaughn Corners; RMC Place; MADISON; ***142** A-7; elev. 740ft./226m.; ★ **HNTS**; mail Madison **z** 35757; ● 100
Verbena; RMC Place; CHILTON; **142** I-7; elev. 457ft./139m.; 🅿; **z** 36091; ● 550
Verlie; RMC Place; SHELBY; ★ **BIR**; mail Alabaster **z** 35007; pop. incl. with Alabaster (Inc. Place)
Vernledge; RMC Place; CRENSHAW; ***143** L-8; mail Luverne **z** 36049; rural
Vernon; Inc. Place; ⊡ LAMAR; **142** E-2; elev. 304ft./93m.; 🅿; **z** 35592; Ⓟ 2,247; Ⓒ 2,143
Vernontown; RMC Place; BIBB; ***142** H-5; elev. 410ft./125m.; mail West Blocton **z** 35184; ● 60
Vestavia Hills; Inc. Place; JEFFERSON, SHELBY; **142** F-6; elev. 940ft./287m.; 🅿; ★ **BIR**; **z** 35216, **z** 35226, **z** 35242, **z** 35266; Ⓟ 19,749; Ⓒ 24,476; ◆ 30,830
Vesthaven; RMC Place; JEFFERSON; ★ **BIR**; mail Birmingham **z** 35216; pop. incl. with Vestavia Hills (Inc. Place)
Veto; RMC Place; LIMESTONE; **142** A-6; mail Elkmont **z** 35620; total pop., including Veto, TN, 60; ● 30
Vick; RMC Place; BIBB; ***142** H-6; mail Centreville **z** 35042; pop. incl. with Centreville (Inc. Place)
Victoria; RMC Place; COFFEE; **143** M-9; elev. 497ft./151m.; mail Elba **z** 36323, Jack **z** 36346; ● 30
Vida; RMC Place; AUTAUGA; **142** I-7; elev. 293ft./89m.; mail Prattville **z** 36067; ● 100
Vidette; RMC Place; CRENSHAW; **143** L-8; mail Luverne **z** 36049; rural
Vienna; RMC Place; PICKENS; ***142** H-2; elev. 139ft./42m.; mail Aliceville **z** 35442; rural
Viewpoint; RMC Place; DEKALB; ***142** C-9; mail Geraldine **z** 35974; rural
Vigo; RMC Place; CALHOUN; ***142** D-10; elev. 710ft./216m.; mail Piedmont **z** 36272; ● 50
Village Creek; RMC Place; JEFFERSON; ***142** F-6; ★ **BIR**; mail Birmingham **z** 35207; pop. incl. with Birmingham (Inc. Place)
Village Springs; RMC Place; BLOUNT, JEFFERSON; **142** E-7; ★ **BIR**; mail Pinson **z** 35126; ● 150
Villula; RMC Place; RUSSELL; ***142** J-11; mail Pittsview **z** 36871; rural
Vina; Inc. Place; FRANKLIN; **142** C-3; elev. 723ft./220m.; 🅿; **z** 35593; Ⓟ 356; Ⓒ 400
Vincent; Inc. Place; SHELBY, ST. CLAIR, TALLADEGA; **142** F-8; elev. 446ft./136m.; 🅿; **z** 35178; Ⓟ 1,767; Ⓒ 1,853
Vinegar Bend; RMC Place; WASHINGTON; **143** N-2; elev. 150ft./46m.; 🅿; **z** 36584; ● 200
Vine Hill; RMC Place; AUTAUGA; ***142** I-6; elev. 216ft./66m.; mail Plantersville **z** 36758; ● 50
Vineland; RMC Place; MARENGO; **143** K-4; elev. 150ft./46m.; mail Thomasville **z** 36784; rural
Vineland Park; RMC Place; JEFFERSON; ***142** F-6; ★ **BIR**; mail Bessemer **z** 35020; pop. incl. with Hueytown (Inc. Place)
Vinesville; RMC Place; JEFFERSON; ★ **BIR**; mail Birmingham **z** 35208; pop. incl. with Birmingham (Inc. Place)
Virginia; RMC Place; JEFFERSON; ***142** F-6; ★ **BIR**; mail Bessemer **z** 35020; pop. incl. with Hueytown (Inc. Place)
Virginia Shores; RMC Place; COLBERT; ***142** A-4; ★ **FLO**; mail Sheffield **z** 35660; ● 70
Vocation; RMC Place; MONROE; ***143** N-4; elev. 366ft./112m.; mail Huxford **z** 36543; rural
Volanta; RMC Place; BALDWIN; ***143** Q-3; elev. 100ft./30m.; ★ **MOB**; mail Fairhope **z** 36532; pop. incl. with Fairhope (Inc. Place)
Vredenburgh; Inc. Place; MONROE; **143** L-5; elev. 300ft./91m.; 🅿; **z** 36481; Ⓟ 313; Ⓒ 327
Vulcan City; RMC Place; JEFFERSON; ***142** F-6; ★ **BIR**; mail Birmingham **z** 35207; pop. incl. with Birmingham (Inc. Place)

W

Waco; RMC Place; FRANKLIN; **142** B-4; elev. 741ft./226m.; mail Russellville **z** 35654; ● 70
Wacoochee Valley; RMC Place; LEE; ***142** I-12; elev. 510ft./155m.; mail Salem **z** 36874; rural
Wadley; Inc. Place; RANDOLPH; **142** G-10; elev. 690ft./210m.; 🅿; **z** 36276; Ⓟ 517; Ⓒ 640
Wadsworth; RMC Place; AUTAUGA; ***142** I-7; elev. 423ft./129m.; mail Deatsville **z** 36022; ● 40
Wagar; RMC Place; WASHINGTON; ***143** M-3; elev. 33ft./10m.; mail Wagarville **z** 36585; rural
Wagarville; RMC Place; WASHINGTON; **143** M-3; elev. 60ft./18m.; 🅿; **z** 36585; ● 450
Wahouma; RMC Place; JEFFERSON; ***142** F-7; ★ **BIR**; mail Birmingham **z** 35206; pop. incl. with Birmingham (Inc. Place)
Walco; RMC Place; TALLADEGA; mail Sylacauga **z** 35150
Waldo; Inc. Place; TALLADEGA; **142** F-9; elev. 550ft./168m.; mail Talladega **z** 35160; Ⓟ 309; Ⓒ 281
WALKER; **142** E-5; Ⓟ 67,670; Ⓒ 70,713; ◆ 65,697
Walker Chapel; RMC Place; JEFFERSON; ***142** F-6; ★ **BIR**; mail Fultondale **z** 35068; pop. incl. with Fultondale (Inc. Place)
Walkers Corner; RMC Place; CULLMAN; ***142** D-7; elev. 807ft./246m.; mail Cullman **z** 35055, **z** 35058; rural
Walker Springs; RMC Place; CLARKE; **143** M-3; elev. 450ft./137m.; 🅿; **z** 36545; ● 200
Walkerton; RMC Place; ST. CLAIR; ***142** F-8; mail Pell City **z** 35125; pop. incl. with Pell City (Inc. Place)
Wallace; RMC Place; ESCAMBIA; ***143** N-5; elev. 167ft./51m.; mail Brewton **z** 36426
Walley; RMC Place; WASHINGTON; ***143** N-1; mail Vinegar Bend **z** 36584; rural
Wallsboro; RMC Place; ELMORE; ***142** I-8; ★ **MTGY**; mail Wetumpka **z** 36092; ● 200
Wall Street; RMC Place; LIMESTONE; ***142** B-6; ★ **HNTS**; mail Madison **z** 35756; rural
Wallstreet; TALLAPOOSA; see Buckville (RMC Place)
Walnut Grove; Inc. Place; ETOWAH; **142** D-8; elev. 858ft./262m.; 🅿; **z** 35990; Ⓟ 717; Ⓒ 710
Walnut Hill; RMC Place; TALLAPOOSA; **142** I-9; elev. 694ft./212m.; mail Dadeville **z** 36853; rural
Walnut Park; RMC Place; ETOWAH; ***142** D-9; ★ **GAD**; mail Gadsden **z** 35904; pop. incl. with Gadsden (Inc. Place)
Walter; RMC Place; CULLMAN; ***142** D-7; elev. 726ft./221m.; mail Hanceville **z** 35077; ● 200
Wannville; RMC Place; JACKSON; ***142** A-9; mail Hollywood **z** 35752; ● 50
Ward; RMC Place; BIBB; ***142** H-5; elev. 340ft./104m.; mail Centreville **z** 35042; rural
Ward; RMC Place; SUMTER; **142** J-2; elev. 209ft./64m.; 🅿; **z** 36922; ● 170
Ware; RMC Place; ELMORE; ***142** J-9; mail Tallassee **z** 36078; rural
Warrenton; RMC Place; MARSHALL; ***142** C-8; mail Guntersville **z** 35976; ● 170
Warrior; Inc. Place; JEFFERSON; **142** E-6; elev. 552ft./168m.; 🅿; ★ **BIR**; **z** 35180; Ⓟ 3,280; Ⓒ 3,169
Warriorstand; RMC Place; MACON; ***142** J-10; elev. 491ft./150m.; mail Union Springs **z** 36089; rural
Warsaw; RMC Place; SUMTER; **142** H-2; elev. 120ft./37m.; mail Panola **z** 35477; ● 20
WASHINGTON; **143** N-2; Ⓟ 16,694; Ⓒ 18,097; ◆ 16,666
Washington Heights; RMC Place; JEFFERSON; ***142** F-6; ★ **BIR**; mail Birmingham **z** 35207
Waterford; RMC Place; DALE; ***143** N-10; ★ **DOTH**; mail Newton **z** 36352; pop. incl. with Newton (Inc. Place)
Waterloo; Inc. Place; LAUDERDALE; **142** A-3; elev. 480ft./146m.; 🅿; **z** 35677; Ⓟ 250; Ⓒ 208
Water Valley; RMC Place; CHOCTAW; ***143** L-1; elev. 112ft./34m.; mail Gilbertown **z** 36908, Silas **z** 36919; ● 70
Watson; RMC Place; CHEROKEE; ***142** C-10; mail Gaylesville **z** 35973; ● 30
Watson; RMC Place; JEFFERSON; **143** P-11; elev. 524ft./160m.; 🅿; ★ **BIR**; **z** 35181; ● 360
Watsonville; RMC Place; WILCOX; ***143** L-5; mail Mc Williams **z** 36753, Pine Apple **z** 36768; rural
Watts Crossroads; RMC Place; CLAY; ***142** F-10; elev. 1,122ft./342m.; mail Lineville **z** 36266; rural
Wattsville; RMC Place; ST. CLAIR; **142** E-8; elev. 567ft./173m.; 🅿; **z** 35182; ● 350
Waugh; RMC Place; MONTGOMERY; **142** J-9; ★ **MTGY**; mail Montgomery **z** 36109; ● 70
Waverly; Inc. Place; CHAMBERS, LEE; **142** I-10; elev. 760ft./232m.; 🅿; **z** 36830, **z** 36879; Ⓟ 152; Ⓒ 184
Wawbeek; RMC Place; ESCAMBIA; ***143** O-5; mail Atmore **z** 36502; rural
Waxahatchee; RMC Place; SHELBY; ***142** H-7; elev. 420ft./128m.; mail Shelby **z** 35143; ● 30
Wayne; RMC Place; MARENGO; ***143** K-3; mail Sweet Water **z** 36782; rural
Wayside; RMC Place; FAYETTE; ***142** E-3; elev. 472ft./144m.; mail Winfield **z** 35594; rural
Weatherly Heights; RMC Place; MADISON; ***142** B-7; ★ **HNTS**; mail Huntsville **z** 35802; pop. incl. with Huntsville (Inc. Place)
Weaver; Inc. Place; CALHOUN; **142** E-9; elev. 892ft./272m.; 🅿; ★ **ANNI**; **z** 36277; Ⓟ 2,715; Ⓒ 2,619
Webb; Inc. Place; HOUSTON; **143** N-11; elev. 300ft./91m.; 🅿; ★ **DOTH**; **z** 36376; Ⓟ 1,039; Ⓒ 1,298
Webster Chapel; RMC Place; CALHOUN; ***142** D-9; ★ **ANNI**; mail Wellington **z** 36279; rural
Wedgewood; RMC Place; MONTGOMERY; ***142** J-7; elev. 169ft./52m.; ★ **MTGY**; mail Montgomery **z** 36108; ● 200
Wedgeworth; RMC Place; HALE; **142** H-3; mail Sawyerville **z** 36776; ● 50
Wedowee; Inc. Place; ⊡ RANDOLPH; **142** G-10; elev. 855ft./261m.; 🅿 🅷; **z** 36278; Ⓟ 796; Ⓒ 818
Weed; CRENSHAW; see Weed Crossroad (RMC Place)
Weed Crossroad (Weed); RMC Place; CRENSHAW; ***143** M-8; elev. 452ft./138m.; mail Brantley **z** 36009; ● 40
Weeden Heights; RMC Place; LAUDERDALE; ***142** A-4; ★ **FLO**; mail Florence **z** 35630; pop. incl. with Florence (Inc. Place)
Weeks; RMC Place; GENEVA; ***143** O-9; elev. 190ft./58m.; mail Kinston **z** 36453; rural
Wegra; RMC Place; JEFFERSON, WALKER; ***142** E-5; ★ **BIR**; mail Quinton **z** 35130; rural
Wehadkee; RMC Place; RANDOLPH; ***142** G-11; elev. 977ft./298m.; mail Roanoke **z** 36274; rural
Wellington; RMC Place; CALHOUN; **142** E-9; elev. 548ft./167m.; 🅿; ★ **ANNI**; **z** 36279; ● 250
Welti; RMC Place; CULLMAN; ***142** D-7; mail Cullman **z** 35055; rural
Wende; RMC Place; RUSSELL; ***142** J-11; mail Hurtsboro **z** 36860; rural
Wenonah; RMC Place; JEFFERSON; ***142** F-6; ★ **BIR**; mail Bessemer **z** 35020, Birmingham **z** 35211; pop. incl. with Birmingham (Inc. Place)
Weogufka; RMC Place; COOSA; **142** H-8; elev. 654ft./199m.; 🅿; **z** 35183; ● 230
Weoka; RMC Place; ELMORE; **142** I-8; elev. 591ft./180m.; mail Wetumpka **z** 36092; ● 30
Wessington; RMC Place; CHILTON; ***142** H-6; mail Calera **z** 35040; ● 50
West; RMC Place; MADISON; ***142** B-7; ★ **HNTS**; mail Huntsville **z** 35805-08, **z** 35812, **z** 35824; pop. incl. with Huntsville (Inc. Place)
West Alexandria; RMC Place; CALHOUN; ★ **ANNI**; mail Alexandria **z** 36250
West Anniston; RMC Place; CALHOUN; ★ **ANNI**; pop. incl. with Anniston (Inc. Place)
West Bend; RMC Place; CLARKE; **143** L-2; elev. 129ft./39m.; mail Coffeeville **z** 36524; ● 100
West Blocton; Inc. Place; BIBB; **142** G-5; elev. 458ft./140m.; 🅿; **z** 35184; Ⓟ 1,468; Ⓒ 1,372
West Decatur; RMC Place; MORGAN; ***142** B-6; ★ **DEC**; pop. incl. with Decatur (Inc. Place)
West End; CALHOUN; see West End Anniston (RMC Place)
West End; RMC Place; JEFFERSON; ***142** F-6; ★ **BIR**; mail Birmingham **z** 35211; pop. incl. with Birmingham (Inc. Place)
West End; RMC Place; MONTGOMERY; ★ **MTGY**; mail Montgomery **z** 36104, **z** 36108; pop. incl. with Montgomery (Inc. Place)
West End Anniston (West End); RMC Place; CALHOUN; **142** E-9; ★ **ANNI**; mail Anniston **z** 36201; ● 2,760
West End-Cobbtown; CDP-Census Area Only; CALHOUN; ***142** E-9; ★ **ANNI**; mail Anniston **z** 36201; Ⓟ 4,034; Ⓒ 3,924
West Ensley (Ensley Heights); RMC Place; JEFFERSON; ***142** F-6; ★ **BIR**; mail Birmingham **z** 35224; pop. incl. with Birmingham (Inc. Place)
Western Hills; RMC Place; MOBILE; ★ **MOB**; mail Mobile **z** 36618; pop. incl. with Mobile (Inc. Place)
Western Hills Estates; RMC Place; MADISON; ***142** A-7; elev. 900ft./274m.; ★ **HNTS**; mail Harvest **z** 35749; ● 220
West Fairfield; RMC Place; JEFFERSON; ***142** F-6; ★ **BIR**; mail Birmingham **z** 35228; pop. incl. with Midfield (Inc. Place)
West Greene; RMC Place; GREENE; **142** H-2; elev. 163ft./50m.; 🅿; **z** 35491; ● 80
West Highlands; RMC Place; JEFFERSON; ***142** F-6; ★ **BIR**; mail Bessemer **z** 35023
West Huntsville; RMC Place; MADISON; ***142** B-7; ★ **HNTS**; mail Huntsville **z** 35807; pop. incl. with Huntsville (Inc. Place)
West Jefferson; Inc. Place; JEFFERSON; ***142** E-6; elev. 416ft./127m.; ★ **BIR**; mail Quinton **z** 35130; Ⓟ 388; Ⓒ 344
West Lake Highlands; RMC Place; JEFFERSON; ***142** F-6; ★ **BIR**; mail Bessemer **z** 35020; pop. incl. with Bessemer (Inc. Place)
Westlawn; RMC Place; MADISON; **142** B-13; ★ **HNTS**; mail Huntsville **z** 35807; pop. incl. with Huntsville (Inc. Place)
West Monroeville; RMC Place; MONROE; ***143** M-5; mail Monroeville **z** 36460
Westmoreland; LIMESTONE; see Salem (RMC Place)
Weston; RMC Place; MARION; ***142** D-3; elev. 692ft./211m.; mail Hamilton **z** 35570; pop. incl. with Hamilton (Inc. Place)
Westover (Phillips Crossroads); Inc. Place; SHELBY; **142** G-7; elev. 457ft./139m.; 🅿; **z** 35147, **z** 35185; incorporated January 31, 2001; not reported in 2000 Census; ● 450
West Point; Inc. Place; CULLMAN; **142** C-6; mail Cullman **z** 35057; Ⓟ 257; Ⓒ 295
West Pratt; RMC Place; WALKER; mail Dora **z** 35062; pop. incl. with Dora (Inc. Place)
West Sayre; RMC Place; JEFFERSON; ***142** E-6; elev. 453ft./138m.; ★ **BIR**; mail Dora **z** 35062, Sayre **z** 35139; ● 450
West Selmont; RMC Place; DALLAS; ***142** J-6; elev. 116ft./35m.; mail Selma **z** 36703
West Side; RMC Place; JEFFERSON; ★ **BIR**; mail Bessemer **z** 35020; pop. incl. with Bessemer (Inc. Place)
West Side; RMC Place; MONTGOMERY; ***142** J-8; ★ **MTGY**; mail Montgomery **z** 36108; pop. incl. with Montgomery (Inc. Place)
West Wellington; RMC Place; CALHOUN; ***142** E-9; ★ **ANNI**; mail Wellington **z** 36279
Westwood; RMC Place; JEFFERSON; **143** Q-10; ★ **BIR**; mail Adamsville **z** 35005, Birmingham **z** 35214; ● 1,630
Wetumpka; Inc. Place; ⊡ ELMORE; **142** I-8; elev. 177ft./54m.; 🅿 🅷; ★ **MTGY**; **z** 36092-93; Ⓟ 4,670; Ⓒ 5,726
Wharton; CHEROKEE; see Whorton (RMC Place)
Whatley; RMC Place; CLARKE; **143** M-4; elev. 145ft./44m.; 🅿; **z** 36482; ● 400
Wheat; RMC Place; CULLMAN; ***142** D-6; mail Crane Hill **z** 35053; ● 50
Wheeler; RMC Place; LAWRENCE; **142** B-5; elev. 597ft./182m.; mail Courtland **z** 35618; ● 60
Wheeler Dam Village (Joe Wheeler Dam); RMC Place; LAWRENCE; ***142** A-5; elev. 578ft./176m.; mail Town Creek **z** 35672; summer pop. 1,000; ● 50
Wheelerville; RMC Place; MOBILE; ***143** P-2; ★ **MOB**; mail Mobile **z** 36608; pop. incl. with Mobile (Inc. Place)
Whistler; RMC Place; MOBILE; ***143** P-2; 🅿; ★ **MOB**; **z** 36612; pop. incl. with Prichard (Inc. Place)
White City; RMC Place; AUTAUGA; **142** I-7; elev. 554ft./169m.; mail Marbury **z** 36051; ● 60
White City; RMC Place; CULLMAN; ***142** D-6; elev. 617ft./188m.; mail Hanceville **z** 35077; ● 80
White Hall; Inc. Place; LOWNDES; **142** J-7; mail Hayneville **z** 36040; Ⓟ 814; Ⓒ 1,014
Whitehead; RMC Place; LAUDERDALE; ***142** A-5; mail Rogersville **z** 35652; rural
Whitehouse; RMC Place; MARION; ***142** D-4; elev. 645ft./197m.; mail Haleyville **z** 35565; rural
Whitehouse Forks; RMC Place; BALDWIN; ***143** P-3; elev. 242ft./74m.; mail Bay Minette **z** 36507; ● 100
Whiteoak; RMC Place; COLBERT; ***142** B-4; ★ **FLO**; mail Leighton **z** 35646; ● 30
White Oak; RMC Place; HENRY; ***143** L-12; elev. 269ft./82m.; mail Abbeville **z** 36310; ● 80
Whiteoak; RMC Place; MARSHALL; ***142** C-8; mail Albertville **z** 35950; pop. incl. with Albertville (Inc. Place)
White Plains; RMC Place; CALHOUN; **142** E-10; mail Anniston **z** 36207; ● 180
White Plains; RMC Place; CHAMBERS; **142** H-11; mail Lafayette **z** 36862; ● 70
Whites Bluff; RMC Place; DALLAS; ***142** J-5; mail Orrville **z** 36767; rural
Whitesboro; RMC Place; ETOWAH; ***142** D-9; mail Boaz **z** 35956; ● 100
Whitesburg; RMC Place; MADISON; ***142** B-7; ★ **HNTS**; mail Huntsville **z** 35802; pop. incl. with Huntsville (Inc. Place)
Whites Chapel; RMC Place; ST. CLAIR; ***142** F-7; elev. 700ft./213m.; ★ **BIR**; mail Trussville **z** 35173; pop. incl. with Moody (Inc. Place)
Whites Gap; RMC Place; CALHOUN; ***142** E-10; elev. 828ft./252m.; ★ **ANNI**; mail Jacksonville **z** 36265; rural
Whitesville; RMC Place; MARSHALL; ***142** D-8; mail Boaz **z** 35957; ● 30
Whitfield; RMC Place; SUMTER; **142** J-2; elev. 174ft./53m.; mail York **z** 36925; ● 60
Whitney; RMC Place; ST. CLAIR; ***142** E-8; elev. 617ft./188m.; mail Ashville **z** 35953; pop. incl. with Ashville (Inc. Place)
Whiton; RMC Place; DEKALB; **142** C-9; mail Crossville **z** 35962; ● 80
Whorton (Wharton); RMC Place; CHEROKEE; ***142** D-10; elev. 607ft./185m.; mail Centre **z** 35960; ● 40
Wicksburg; RMC Place; HOUSTON; **143** N-10; elev. 307ft./94m.; mail Newton **z** 36352; ● 50
Wiggins; RMC Place; COVINGTON; ***143** N-8; elev. 327ft./100m.; mail Andalusia **z** 36420; pop. incl. with Babbie (Inc. Place)
Wigginsville; RMC Place; LIMESTONE; ***142** A-6; mail Athens **z** 35611; pop. incl. with Athens (Inc. Place)
Wiginton; RMC Place; MARION; ***142** C-3; elev. 870ft./265m.; mail Hackleburg **z** 35564; pop. incl. with Hackleburg (Inc. Place)
Wilburn (Bug Tussle); RMC Place; CULLMAN; **142** D-6; elev. 514ft./157m.; mail Bremen **z** 35033; rural
WILCOX; **143** L-5; Ⓟ 13,568; Ⓒ 13,183; Ⓡ 13,020; ◆ 12,904
Wiley; RMC Place; MONTGOMERY; ***142** J-8; elev. 180ft./55m.; ★ **MTGY**; mail Montgomery **z** 36105; pop. incl. with Montgomery (Inc. Place)
Wiley; RMC Place; TUSCALOOSA; ***142** F-4; elev. 526ft./160m.; mail Jasper **z** 35501; rural
Wilkes; RMC Place; JEFFERSON; ***142** F-6; ★ **BIR**; mail Fairfield **z** 35064; pop. incl. with Midfield (Inc. Place)
Wilkinstown; RMC Place; COFFEE; ***143** M-9; mail Jack **z** 36346; rural
Williams; RMC Place; CALHOUN; ***142** E-9; elev. 702ft./214m.; ★ **ANNI**; mail Jacksonville **z** 36265; ● 200
Williams; RMC Place; HOUSTON; ***143** N-12; elev. 152ft./46m.; mail Columbia **z** 36319; rural
Williamsburg; RMC Place; JEFFERSON; ***142** F-6; elev. 402ft./123m.; ★ **BIR**; mail Adamsville **z** 35005; pop. incl. with Hoover (Inc. Place)
Williamstown; RMC Place; WALKER; ***142** E-5; elev. 342ft./104m.; mail Parrish **z** 35580; rural
Willowbrook; RMC Place; MADISON; ***142** B-7; ★ **HNTS**; mail Huntsville **z** 35802; pop. incl. with Huntsville (Inc. Place)
Willow Point Country Club; RMC Place; TALLAPOOSA; ***142** I-9; elev. 517ft./158m.; mail Alexander City **z** 35010; ● 100
Willow Springs; RMC Place; ELMORE; ***142** J-8; ★ **MTGY**; mail Wetumpka **z** 36093; ● 50
Wills Crossroads; RMC Place; HENRY; ***143** M-11; mail Abbeville **z** 36310; ● 120
Wills Valley; RMC Place; DEKALB; ***142** B-10; elev. 880ft./268m.; mail Fort Payne **z** 35968; pop. incl. with Fort Payne (Inc. Place)
Wilmer; RMC Place; MOBILE; **143** P-1; elev. 259ft./79m.; 🅿; ★ **MOB**; **z** 36587; ● 400
Wilson Bend; RMC Place; WINSTON; ***142** D-5; elev. 613ft./187m.; mail Arley **z** 35541; rural
Wilson Lake Shores; RMC Place; COLBERT; ***142** A-4; ★ **FLO**; mail Sheffield **z** 35660; ● 160
Wilson Quarters; RMC Place; HOUSTON; ***143** N-11; elev. 304ft./93m.; ★ **DOTH**; mail Dothan **z** 36303; pop. incl. with Dothan (Inc. Place)
Wilsonville; Inc. Place; SHELBY; **142** G-7; elev. 433ft./132m.; 🅿; **z** 35186; Ⓟ 1,185; Ⓒ 1,551
Wilton; Inc. Place; SHELBY; **142** H-6; elev. 500ft./152m.; 🅿; **z** 35187; Ⓟ 602; Ⓒ 580
Wimberly; CHOCTAW; see Wimbly (RMC Place)
Wimbly (Wimberly); RMC Place; CHOCTAW; **143** L-2; mail Toxey **z** 36921; ● 80
Winburn (Dunavant); RMC Place; SHELBY; ***142** F-7; ★ **BIR**; mail Vandiver **z** 35176; rural
Wind Creek Farms; RMC Place; TALLAPOOSA; ***142** H-9; elev. 542ft./165m.; mail Alexander City **z** 35010; ● 50
Windham Springs; RMC Place; TUSCALOOSA; ***142** F-4; mail Berry **z** 35546; ● 50
Windsor Highlands; RMC Place; JEFFERSON; ***142** F-6; ★ **BIR**; mail Birmingham **z** 35209; pop. incl. with Homewood (Inc. Place)
Winfield; Inc. Place; MARION, FAYETTE; **142** D-3; elev. 468ft./143m.; 🅿 🅷; **z** 35594; Ⓟ 3,689; Ⓒ 4,540
Wing; RMC Place; COVINGTON; **143** O-7; elev. 286ft./87m.; 🅿; **z** 36483; ● 150
Wingard; RMC Place; PIKE; **143** L-8; mail Goshen **z** 36035; rural
Wininger; RMC Place; JACKSON; ***142** A-8; elev. 1,567ft./478m.; mail Woodville **z** 35776; rural
Winn; RMC Place; CLARKE; ***143** M-3; elev. 167ft./51m.; mail Jackson **z** 36545; rural
Winslow; RMC Place; AUTAUGA; **142** J-6; mail Autaugaville **z** 36003; ● 70
WINSTON; **142** C-5; Ⓟ 22,053; Ⓒ 24,843; ◆ 23,870
Winterboro; RMC Place; TALLADEGA; **142** G-8; elev. 504ft./154m.; mail Alpine **z** 35014, Talladega **z** 35160; ● 350
Winton; RMC Place; MORGAN; ***142** B-7; elev. 591ft./180m.; mail Somerville **z** 35670; rural
Wolf Creek; RMC Place; ST. CLAIR; **142** F-8; mail Pell City **z** 35128; ● 60
Wolf Springs; RMC Place; LAWRENCE; ***142** B-4; elev. 683ft./208m.; mail Town Creek **z** 35672; rural
Womack Hill; RMC Place; CHOCTAW; **143** L-2; mail Gilbertown **z** 36908, Toxey **z** 36921; ● 90
Woodaire Estates; RMC Place; JEFFERSON; ***142** E-7; ★ **BIR**; mail Birmingham **z** 35215
Woodbluff; CLARKE; see Woods Bluff (RMC Place)
Woodcrest; RMC Place; JEFFERSON; ***142** F-7; ★ **BIR**; mail Birmingham **z** 35215; pop. incl. with Birmingham (Inc. Place)
Wooddale; RMC Place; SHELBY; ★ **BIR**; mail Pelham **z** 35124; pop. incl. with Pelham (Inc. Place)
Woodland; RMC Place; MACON; ***142** I-10; mail Notasulga **z** 36866; ● 100
Woodland (Lamar); Inc. Place; RANDOLPH; **142** F-11; elev. 1,000ft./305m.; 🅿; **z** 36280; Ⓟ 189; Ⓒ 192
Woodland Forest; RMC Place; TUSCALOOSA; ***142** G-4; elev. 350ft./107m.; ★ **TUSC**; mail Tuscaloosa **z** 35405; pop. incl. with Tuscaloosa (Inc. Place)
Woodland Lake; RMC Place; TUSCALOOSA; ***142** G-5; elev. 577ft./176m.; mail Mc Calla **z** 35111; ● 250
Woodlawn; RMC Place; JEFFERSON; ***142** F-7; elev. 640ft./195m.; ★ **BIR**; mail Birmingham **z** 35212; pop. incl. with Birmingham (Inc. Place)
Woodlawn Heights; RMC Place; FRANKLIN; ***142** B-4; mail Russellville **z** 35653; pop. incl. with Russellville (Inc. Place)
Woodlawn Heights; RMC Place; JEFFERSON; ***142** F-7; ★ **BIR**; mail Birmingham **z** 35212; pop. incl. with Birmingham (Inc. Place)
Woodley Park; RMC Place; MONTGOMERY; ★ **MTGY**; mail Montgomery **z** 36116; pop. incl. with Montgomery (Inc. Place)
Woodmeadow; RMC Place; JEFFERSON; ***142** F-6; ★ **BIR**; mail Birmingham **z** 35226; pop. incl. with Hoover (Inc. Place)
Woodmont; RMC Place; JEFFERSON; ***142** F-6; ★ **BIR**; mail Bessemer **z** 35020; pop. incl. with Hueytown (Inc. Place)
Woods Bluff (Woodbluff); RMC Place; CLARKE; ***143** L-2; mail Campbell **z** 36727; rural
Woodstock (North Bibb); Inc. Place; BIBB, TUSCALOOSA; **142** G-5; elev. 520ft./158m.; 🅿; **z** 35188; Ⓒ 986
Woodstock Junction; RMC Place; TUSCALOOSA; ***142** G-5; elev. 622ft./190m.; mail Woodstock **z** 35188; pop. incl. with Woodstock (Inc. Place)
Woodville; Inc. Place; JACKSON; **142** B-8; elev. 615ft./187m.; 🅿; **z** 35776; Ⓟ 687; Ⓒ 761
Woodward; RMC Place; JEFFERSON; **143** S-10; ★ **BIR**; mail Bessemer **z** 35020; pop. incl. with Bessemer (Inc. Place)
Woolfolk; RMC Place; TALLADEGA; ***142** F-9; mail Munford **z** 36268; rural
Wren; RMC Place; LAWRENCE; **142** C-5; mail Moulton **z** 35650; ● 280
Wright; RMC Place; LAUDERDALE; **142** A-3; mail Waterloo **z** 35677; ● 120
Wright Crossroads; RMC Place; LEE; ***142** I-10; elev. 500ft./152m.; mail Auburn **z** 36830; rural
Wyatt; RMC Place; WALKER; ***142** E-6; ★ **BIR**; mail Quinton **z** 35130; ● 200
Wylam; RMC Place; JEFFERSON; ***142** F-6; ★ **BIR**; mail Birmingham **z** 35224; pop. incl. with Birmingham (Inc. Place)
Wynn Drive; RMC Place; MADISON; ***142** A-7; ★ **HNTS**; mail Huntsville **z** 35806, **z** 35814, **z** 35816; pop. incl. with Huntsville (Inc. Place)
Wynnville; RMC Place; BLOUNT; ***142** D-8; mail Altoona **z** 35952; pop. incl. with Susan Moore (Inc. Place)

Y

Yampertown; MARION; see Twin (Inc. Place)
Yantley; RMC Place; CHOCTAW; **143** K-2; elev. 250ft./76m.; mail Lisman **z** 36912; ● 200
Yarbo; RMC Place; WASHINGTON; **143** M-2; mail Millry **z** 36558
Yelling Settlement; RMC Place; BALDWIN; ***143** P-3; mail Daphne **z** 36526; ● 30
Yellow Bluff; Inc. Place; WILCOX; ***143** L-4; elev. 101ft./31m.; mail Pine Hill **z** 36769; Ⓟ 245; Ⓒ 181
Yellow Creek Falls; RMC Place; CHEROKEE; ***142** C-10; mail Cedar Bluff **z** 35959; ● 50
Yellow Pine; RMC Place; WASHINGTON; **143** N-1; elev. 200ft./61m.; mail Fruitdale **z** 36539; ● 150
Yerkwood; RMC Place; WALKER; ***142** E-6; elev. 340ft./104m.; ★ **BIR**; mail Quinton **z** 35130; rural
York; Inc. Place; SUMTER; **142** J-2; elev. 152ft./46m.; 🅿; **z** 36925; Ⓟ 3,160; Ⓒ 2,854
Youngblood; RMC Place; PIKE; ***143** L-9; mail Troy **z** 36079; rural
Yucca; RMC Place; JACKSON; ***142** A-9; elev. 620ft./189m.; mail Flat Rock **z** 35966; rural
Yupon; RMC Place; BALDWIN; ***143** Q-3; mail Magnolia Springs **z** 36555; ● 30

Z

Zimco; RMC Place; CLARKE; ***143** L-3; mail Grove Hill **z** 36451; ● 50
Zion; RMC Place; MONTGOMERY; ***143** K-8; elev. 300ft./91m.; mail Letohatchee **z** 36047; rural
Zion; RMC Place; PICKENS; ***142** F-3; mail Gordo **z** 35466; ● 60
Zion City; RMC Place; JEFFERSON; ***142** F-7; ★ **BIR**; mail Birmingham **z** 35207; pop. incl. with Birmingham (Inc. Place)
Zion Heights; RMC Place; JEFFERSON; ***142** F-6; ★ **BIR**; mail Birmingham **z** 35207; pop. incl. with Birmingham (Inc. Place)
Zip City; RMC Place; LAUDERDALE; ***142** A-4; ★ **FLO**; mail Florence **z** 35634; ● 50
Zoar; RMC Place; COFFEE; ***143** M-9; elev. 448ft./137m.; mail Elba **z** 36323; rural

ALASKA

RUSSIA
CANADA
Juneau

Statistics

Total area (2000) — 663,267 square miles
Land area (2000) — 571,951 square miles
Water area (2000) — 91,316 square miles
Capital — Juneau
Admitted as state — January, 1959

Maps

State maps can be found on pages 142-254 in Vol. 1

Ranally Metro Areas (RMAs) and Abbreviations

Anchorage, AK — ANCH
Fairbanks, AK — FRBK

Principal Places

Place Name	Place Type	Borough/Census Area	Population
Anchorage	Inc. Place	ANCHORAGE	◆ 280,940
Fairbanks	Inc. Place	FAIRBANKS NORTH STAR	◆ 44,276
Juneau	Inc. Place	JUNEAU	◆ 31,193
College	CDP	FAIRBANKS NORTH STAR	© 11,402
Sitka	Inc. Place	SITKA	© 8,835
Ketchikan	Inc. Place	KETCHIKAN GATEWAY	◆ 7,355
Knik-Fairview	CDP-Census Area Only	MATANUSKA-SUSITNA	© 7,049
Kenai	Inc. Place	KENAI PENINSULA	© 6,942
Lakes	CDP-Census Area Only	MATANUSKA-SUSITNA	© 6,706
Kodiak	Inc. Place	KODIAK ISLAND	© 6,334
Kalifornsky	CDP	KENAI PENINSULA	© 5,846
Bethel	Inc. Place	BETHEL	© 5,471
Wasilla	Inc. Place	MATANUSKA-SUSITNA	© 5,469
Eielson AFB	CDP-Census Area Only	FAIRBANKS NORTH STAR	© 5,400

Borough or Census Area Business Data

Borough or Census Area	FIPS Code	Borough or Census Area Seat †	Land Area (Sq. Mi.)	Census Population 4/1/2000	Census Population 4/1/1990	Census Population % Change 1990-2000	Wholesale Trade Sales, 2002 ($1,000)	Wholesale Trade % Change 1997-2002	Manufacturing, 2002 Establish-ments	Manufacturing, 2002 Total Employees	Manufacturing, 2002 Value Added ($1,000)	Manufacturing, 2002 Ranally Mfg. Units
Aleutians East	013		6,988	2,697	2,464	9.5	(d)	(d)	4	(d)	(d)	...
Aleutians West	016		4,397	5,465	9,478	-42.3	39,926	-35.0	6	1,341	132,132	70
Anchorage	020		1,697	260,283	226,338	15.0	2,629,595	32.2	203	2,279	209,364	111
Bethel	050		40,633	16,006	13,656	17.2	9,991	810.8	...	(d)	(d)	...
Bristol Bay	060		505	1,258	1,410	-10.8	(d)	(d)	...	(d)	(d)	...
Denali	068		12,750	1,893	1,764	7.3	(d)	(d)	...	(d)	(d)	...
Dillingham	070		18,675	4,922	4,012	22.7	(d)	(d)	...	(d)	(d)	...
Fairbanks North Star	090		7,366	82,840	77,720	6.6	298,322	12.2	...	(d)	(d)	...
Haines	100		2,344	2,392	2,117	13.0	(d)	(d)	...	(d)	(d)	...
Juneau	110		2,717	30,711	26,751	14.8	(d)	(d)	...	(d)	(d)	...
Kenai Peninsula	122		16,013	49,691	40,802	21.8	193,826	-19.9	62	1,087	139,540	74
Ketchikan Gateway	130		1,233	14,070	13,828	1.8	63,226	-19.8	17	(d)	(d)	
Kodiak Island	150		6,560	13,913	13,309	4.5	(d)	(d)	17	1,266	90,002	48
Lake and Peninsula	164		23,782	1,823	1,668	9.3	(d)	(d)	...	(d)	(d)	...
Matanuska-Susitna	170		24,682	59,322	39,683	49.5	64,164	(d)	...	(d)	(d)	...
Nome	180		23,001	9,196	8,288	11.0	9,106	(d)	...	(d)	(d)	...
North Slope	185		88,817	7,385	5,979	23.5	70,463	65.6	...	(d)	(d)	...
Northwest Arctic	188		35,898	7,208	6,113	17.9	(d)	(d)	...	(d)	(d)	...
Prince of Wales-Outer Ketchikan	201		7,411	6,146	6,278	-2.1	17,323	-19.8	...	(d)	(d)	...
Sitka	220		2,874	8,835	8,588	2.9	23,292	(d)	...	(d)	(d)	...
Skagway-Hoonah-Angoon	232		7,896	3,436	3,851	-10.8	(d)	(d)	...	(d)	(d)	...
Southeast Fairbanks	240		24,815	6,174	5,913	4.4	(d)	(d)	...	(d)	(d)	...
Valdez-Cordova	261		34,319	10,195	9,952	2.4	(d)	(d)	...	(d)	(d)	...
Wade Hampton	270		17,193	7,028	5,791	21.4	(d)	(d)	...	(d)	(d)	...
Wrangell-Petersburg	280		5,835	6,684	7,042	-5.1	16,344	(d)	...	(d)	(d)	...
Yakutat	282		7,650	808	534	51.3	(d)	(d)	...	(d)	(d)	...
Yukon-Koyukuk	290		145,900	6,551	6,714	-2.4	(d)	(d)	...	(d)	(d)	...
The State			**571,951**	**626,932**	**550,043**	**14.0**	**3,616,674**	**21.0**	**514**	**10,933**	**1,283,586**	**679**

(d) Data not available. Corresponding percentages or Ranally Manufacturing Units are estimates.
... Represents 0 or amount too minimal to be reported.
† Not applicable

Administrative Divisions

Although Alaska has no counties, the State of Alaska and the U.S. Bureau of the Census have delineated 27 "boroughs" and "census areas" for use in presenting statistical information.

Boroughs: Boroughs cover much of the settled areas of Alaska. The governmental powers and activities of boroughs are somewhat similar to those of counties in other states. There are four consolidated city-borough governments. When Indian or military reservations lie within the boundaries of a borough, they are not part of the borough, unless so designated by law.

The 16 boroughs are Aleutians East, Anchorage, Bristol Bay, Denali, Fairbanks North Star, Haines, Juneau, Kenai Peninsula, Ketchikan Gateway, Kodiak Island, Lake and Peninsula, Matanuska-Susitna, North Slope, Northwest Arctic, Sitka, and Yakutat.

Census Areas: The Census Areas occupy the less settled portions of the state, and have no administrative or governmental significance. The 11 census areas are Aleutians West, Bethel, Dillingham, Nome, Prince of Wales-Outer Ketchikan, Skagway-Hoonah-Angoon, Southeast Fairbanks, Valdez-Cordova, Wade Hampton, Wrangell-Petersburg, and Yukon-Koyukuk.

Incorporated Places: The four consolidated city-borough governments are Anchorage, Juneau, Sitka, and Yakutat.

Index of Places, Boroughs and Census Areas

A

Adak; Inc. Place; ALEUTIANS WEST; ***144** J-9; 🅿; Z 99546, Z 99571; incorporated April 20, 2001; not reported in 2000 Census
Adak; CDP-Census Area Only; ALEUTIANS WEST; ***144** J-9; 🅿; Z 99546, Z 99571; © 316
Adak Island; ALEUTIANS WEST; see Adak Station (RMC Place)
Adak Station (Adak Island); RMC Place; ALEUTIANS WEST; **144** J-9; mail Adak Z 99546; Ⓟ 4,633; ● 600
Akhiok; Inc. Place; KODIAK ISLAND; **144** I-7; 🅿; Z 99615; Ⓟ 77; © 80
Akiachak; CDP; BETHEL; **144** G-5; 🅿; Z 99551; © 585
Akiak; Inc. Place; BETHEL; ***144** G-5; 🅿; Z 99552; Ⓟ 285; © 309
Akutan; Inc. Place; ALEUTIANS EAST; **144** I-11; 🅿; Z 99553; Ⓟ 589; © 713
Alakanuk; Inc. Place; WADE HAMPTON; **144** E-4; 🅿; Z 99554; Ⓟ 544; © 652
Alatna; CDP-Census Area Only; YUKON-KOYUKUK; ***144** D-7; mail Allakaket Z 99720; © 35
Alcan Border; CDP-Census Area Only; SOUTHEAST FAIRBANKS; ***144** F-10; © 21
Aleknagik; Inc. Place; DILLINGHAM; **144** H-5; 🅿; Z 99555; Ⓟ 185; © 221
Aleneva; CDP-Census Area Only; KODIAK ISLAND; ***144** H-7; © 68
ALEUTIANS EAST; ***144** J-4; Ⓟ 2,464; © 2,697; ◆ 3,307
ALEUTIANS WEST; ***144** J-3; Ⓟ 9,478; © 5,465; ◆ 4,311
Alexander; RMC Place; MATANUSKA-SUSITNA; ***144** F-8; elev. 30ft./9m.; ★ **ANCH**; mail Anchorage Z 99695; ● 20
Alitak; RMC Place; KODIAK ISLAND; ***144** I-7; mail Kodiak Z 99697; summer pop. 250; ● 30
Allakaket; Inc. Place; YUKON-KOYUKUK; **144** D-7; 🅿; Z 99720; Ⓟ 170; © 97
Alpine; CDP-Census Area Only; NORTH SLOPE; ***144** A-8; © 0
Ambler; Inc. Place; NORTHWEST ARCTIC; **144** C-6; 🅿; Z 99786; Ⓟ 311; © 309
Amchitka; RMC Place; ALEUTIANS WEST; ***144** J-8; mail Anchorage Z 99501; Ⓟ 25; ● 30
Amook; RMC Place; KODIAK ISLAND; ***144** I-7; mail Kodiak Z 99697; rural
Anaktuvuk Pass; Inc. Place; NORTH SLOPE; **144** C-8; 🅿; Z 99721; Ⓟ 259; © 282
Anchorage; Inc. Place; ANCHORAGE; **144** G-8; elev. 118ft./36m.; 🅿 🅷 🅲 19,001 ■; ★ **ANCH**; Z 99501-11, Z 99513-24, Z 99529-30, Z 99540, Z 99599, Z 99695; location of Indian Agency; Ⓟ 226,338; © 260,283; ◆ 280,940
ANCHORAGE; ***144** G-8; Ⓟ 226,338; © 260,283; ◆ 280,940
Anchor Point; CDP; KENAI PENINSULA; **144** G-7; 🅿; Z 99556; Ⓟ 866; © 1,845
Anderson; Inc. Place; DENALI; **144** E-8; elev. 533ft./162m.; 🅿; Z 99744; Ⓟ 628; © 367
Andreafsky; RMC Place; WADE HAMPTON; ***144** F-4; pop. incl. with Saint Marys (Inc. Place)
Angoon; Inc. Place; SKAGWAY-HOONAH-ANGOON; **144** H-12; 🅿; Z 99820; Ⓟ 638; © 572
Aniak; Inc. Place; BETHEL; **144** F-5; 🅿; Z 99557; Ⓟ 540; © 572
Annette (Annette Island); RMC Place; PRINCE OF WALES-OUTER KETCHIKAN; ***144** I-14; mail Metlakatla Z 99926; Ⓟ 43; ● 40
Annette Island; PRINCE OF WALES-OUTER KETCHIKAN; see Annette (RMC Place)
Annette Island Reserve; Indian Reservation; PRINCE OF WALES-OUTER KETCHIKAN, KETCHIKAN GATEWAY; © 1,447
Anvik; Inc. Place; YUKON-KOYUKUK; **144** F-5; 🅿; Z 99558; Ⓟ 82; © 104
Arctic Village; CDP; YUKON-KOYUKUK; **144** C-9; 🅿; Z 99722; Ⓟ 96; © 152
Atka; Inc. Place; ALEUTIANS WEST; **144** J-9; 🅿; Z 99547; Ⓟ 73; © 92
Atkasook; NORTH SLOPE; see Atqasuk (Inc. Place)
Atmautluak; CDP; BETHEL; **144** G-4; 🅿; Z 99559; © 294
Atqasuk (Atkasook); Inc. Place; NORTH SLOPE; **144** A-6; 🅿; Z 99791; Ⓟ 216; © 228
Attu (Attu Island); RMC Place; ALEUTIANS WEST; **144** J-7; mail Kodiak Z 99619; ● 30
Attu Island; ALEUTIANS WEST; see Attu (RMC Place)
Attu Station; CDP-Census Area Only; ALEUTIANS WEST; ***144** J-7; © 20
Auke Bay; RMC Place; JUNEAU; ***144** H-12; 🅿; Z 99821; pop. incl. with Juneau (Inc. Place)
Aurora; RMC Place; FAIRBANKS NORTH STAR; ***144** E-8; ★ **FRBK**; mail Fairbanks Z 99701; pop. incl. with Fairbanks (Inc. Place)
Aurora Lodge (Salchaket); RMC Place; FAIRBANKS NORTH STAR; ***144** E-9; elev. 750ft./229m.; mail Fairbanks Z 99701; ● 20

B

Baranof; RMC Place; SITKA; ***144** H-12; mail Sitka Z 99835; pop. incl. with Sitka (Inc. Place)
Barrow; Inc. Place; NORTH SLOPE; **144** A-7; 🅿 🅷; Z 99723, Z 99759, Z 99789, Z 99791 & mail Prudhoe Bay Z 99734; Ⓟ 3,469; © 4,581
Bartlett Cove; RMC Place; SKAGWAY-HOONAH-ANGOON; ***144** H-12; elev. 100ft./30m.; mail Gustavus Z 99826; summer pop. 150; ● 20
Bear Creek; CDP-Census Area Only; KENAI PENINSULA; ***144** G-8; © 1,748
Beaver; CDP-Census Area Only; YUKON-KOYUKUK; **144** D-9; 🅿; Z 99724; Ⓟ 103; © 84
Bell Island; PRINCE OF WALES-OUTER KETCHIKAN; see Bell Island Hot Springs (RMC Place)
Bell Island Hot Springs (Bell Island); RMC Place; PRINCE OF WALES-OUTER KETCHIKAN; ***144** I-13; mail Ketchikan Z 99901
Beluga; CDP-Census Area Only; KENAI PENINSULA; ***144** G-8; mail Anchorage Z 99695; © 32
Bethel; Inc. Place; BETHEL; **144** G-5; 🅿 🅷; Z 99559, Z 99637, Z 99679-80, Z 99690; location of Indian Agency; Ⓟ 4,674; © 5,471
BETHEL; ***144** G-5; Ⓟ 13,656; © 16,006; Ⓡ 16,046; ◆ 17,157
Bettles (Bettles Field); Inc. Place; YUKON-KOYUKUK; **144** C-8; mail Bettles Field Z 99726; Ⓟ 36; © 43
Bettles Field; YUKON-KOYUKUK; see Bettles (Inc. Place)
Big Delta; CDP; SOUTHEAST FAIRBANKS; **144** E-9; mail Delta Junction Z 99737; Ⓟ 400; © 749
Big Horn; RMC Place; FAIRBANKS NORTH STAR; ***144** E-9; elev. 500ft./152m.; mail Fairbanks Z 99701; ● 320
Big Lake; CDP-Census Area Only; MATANUSKA-SUSITNA; **144** F-8; 🅿; Z 99652; Ⓟ 1,477; © 2,635
Birch Creek; CDP; YUKON-KOYUKUK; **144** D-9; elev. 450ft./137m.; mail Fort Yukon Z 99740; Ⓟ 42; © 28
Birchwood; RMC Place; ANCHORAGE; ★ **ANCH**; mail Chugiak Z 99567; pop. incl. with Anchorage (Inc. Place)
Bird; RMC Place; ANCHORAGE; ★ **ANCH**; mail Indian Z 99540; pop. incl. with Anchorage (Inc. Place)
Bjerremark; RMC Place; FAIRBANKS NORTH STAR; ★ **FRBK**; mail Fairbanks Z 99701; pop. incl. with Fairbanks (Inc. Place)
Black Sand; RMC Place; YAKUTAT; mail Yakutat Z 99689
Bluff; RMC Place; FAIRBANKS NORTH STAR; ***144** E-9; mail Nome Z 99762; ● 10
Border (Border City); RMC Place; SOUTHEAST FAIRBANKS; ***144** E-10; 🅿; Z 99764 & mail Tok Z 99780; ● 10
Border City; SOUTHEAST FAIRBANKS; see Border (RMC Place)
Boswell Bay; RMC Place; VALDEZ-CORDOVA; ***144** G-9; elev. 100ft./30m.; mail Cordova Z 99574; rural
Boundary; RMC Place; SOUTHEAST FAIRBANKS; ***144** E-10; elev. 2,565ft./782m.; mail Tok Z 99780; ● 25
Brevig Mission (Teller Mission); Inc. Place; NOME; **144** D-4; 🅿; Z 99785; Ⓟ 198; © 276
BRISTOL BAY; ***144** H-6; Ⓟ 1,410; © 1,258; ◆ 906
Broadmoor; FAIRBANKS NORTH STAR; see Broadmoor Acres (RMC Place)
Broadmoor Acres (Broadmoor); RMC Place; FAIRBANKS NORTH STAR; mail Fairbanks Z 99701
Brooks Lodge; RMC Place; LAKE AND PENINSULA; ***144** H-6; mail King Salmon Z 99613; ● 20
Browerville; RMC Place; NORTH SLOPE; mail Barrow Z 99723; pop. incl. with Barrow (Inc. Place)
Buckland (Elephant Point); Inc. Place; NORTHWEST ARCTIC; **144** D-5; 🅿; Z 99727; Ⓟ 318; © 406
Buffalo Soapstone; CDP-Census Area Only; MATANUSKA-SUSITNA; ***144** F-8; © 699
Butte; CDP; MATANUSKA-SUSITNA; ***144** F-8; ★ **ANCH**; mail Palmer Z 99645; Ⓟ 2,039; © 2,561

C

Campbell; RMC Place; ANCHORAGE; ★ **ANCH**; mail Anchorage Z 99517; pop. incl. with Anchorage (Inc. Place)
Candle; RMC Place; NORTHWEST ARCTIC; **144** D-5; mail Kotzebue Z 99752; rural
Cantwell; CDP; DENALI; **144** E-8; elev. 2,212ft./674m.; 🅿; Z 99729; Ⓟ 147; © 222
Cape Newenham; RMC Place; BETHEL; ***144** H-4; mail Dillingham Z 99576; rural
Cape Pole; RMC Place; PRINCE OF WALES-OUTER KETCHIKAN; ***144** I-13; mail Ketchikan Z 99901; ● 20
Cape Yakataga; RMC Place; VALDEZ-CORDOVA; **144** G-10; mail Anchorage Z 99695; ● 20
Carlanna; RMC Place; KETCHIKAN GATEWAY; mail Ketchikan Z 99901; pop. incl. with Ketchikan (Inc. Place)
Central; CDP; YUKON-KOYUKUK; **144** D-9; elev. 1,220ft./372m.; 🅿; Z 99730; Ⓟ 52; © 134
Chalkyitsik (Fishhook); CDP; YUKON-KOYUKUK; **144** C-9; 🅿; Z 99788; Ⓟ 90; © 83
Chandalar; RMC Place; YUKON-KOYUKUK; ***144** C-8; mail Fairbanks Z 99701; rural
Charcoal Point; RMC Place; KETCHIKAN GATEWAY; mail Ketchikan Z 99901; pop. incl. with Ketchikan (Inc. Place)
Chase; CDP-Census Area Only; MATANUSKA-SUSITNA; ***144** F-8; elev. 500ft./152m.; mail Talkeetna Z 99676; Ⓟ 38; © 41
Chatanika (Old Chatanika); RMC Place; FAIRBANKS NORTH STAR; **144** D-9; mail Fairbanks Z 99712; rural
Chatham; RMC Place; SITKA; mail Juneau Z 99803; pop. incl. with Sitka (Inc. Place)
Chefornak; Inc. Place; BETHEL; **144** G-4; 🅿; Z 99561; Ⓟ 320; © 394
Chena Hot Springs; RMC Place; FAIRBANKS NORTH STAR; ***144** D-9; mail Fairbanks Z 99701; summer pop. 100
Chenega; CDP-Census Area Only; VALDEZ-CORDOVA; ***144** G-8; mail Cordova Z 99574, Whittier Z 99693; Ⓟ 94; © 86
Chenega Bay; RMC Place; VALDEZ-CORDOVA; ● 50
Chernofski; RMC Place; ALEUTIANS WEST; ***144** J-2; mail Unalaska Z 99685; rural
Chestochina; VALDEZ-CORDOVA; see Chistochina (CDP)
Chevak; Inc. Place; WADE HAMPTON; **144** F-4; 🅿; Z 99563; Ⓟ 598; © 765
Chickaloon; CDP; MATANUSKA-SUSITNA; **144** F-8; 🅿; Z 99674; Ⓟ 145; © 213
Chicken; CDP; SOUTHEAST FAIRBANKS; **144** E-10; 🅿; Z 99732; © 17
Chignik (Chignik Lagoon); Inc. Place; LAKE AND PENINSULA; **144** I-5; 🅿; Z 99548, Z 99564 & mail Chignik Lagoon Z 99565; Ⓟ 188; © 79
Chignik Lagoon; LAKE AND PENINSULA; see Chignik (Inc. Place)
Chignik Lagoon; CDP-Census Area Only; LAKE AND PENINSULA; ***144** I-5; 🅿; Z 99565; Ⓟ 53; © 103
Chignik Lake; CDP-Census Area Only; LAKE AND PENINSULA; ***144** I-5; 🅿; Z 99548; Ⓟ 133; © 145
Chiniak; CDP-Census Area Only; KODIAK ISLAND; ***144** I-7; 🅿; Z 99615; Ⓟ 69; © 50
Chisana; CDP; VALDEZ-CORDOVA; ***144** F-10; elev. 3,318ft./1,011m.; mail Tok Z 99780; © 0
Chistochina (Chestochina); CDP; VALDEZ-CORDOVA; **144** F-9; elev. 1,857ft./566m.; mail Gakona Z 99586; Ⓟ 60; © 93
Chitina; CDP; VALDEZ-CORDOVA; **144** F-9; elev. 545ft./166m.; 🅿; Z 99566; Ⓟ 49; © 123
Chuathbaluk; Inc. Place; BETHEL; **144** F-5; 🅿; Z 99557; Ⓟ 97; © 119
Chugiak; RMC Place; ANCHORAGE; ***144** F-8; 🅿; ★ **ANCH**; Z 99567; pop. incl. with Anchorage (Inc. Place)
Circle; CDP; YUKON-KOYUKUK; **144** D-9; elev. 900ft./274m.; 🅿; Z 99733; Ⓟ 73; © 100
Circle Hot Springs (Circle Hot Springs Station); RMC Place; YUKON-KOYUKUK; **144** D-9; elev. 1,000ft./305m.; mail Central Z 99730
Circle Hot Springs Station; YUKON-KOYUKUK; see Circle Hot Springs (RMC Place)
Clam Gulch; CDP; KENAI PENINSULA; ***144** G-8; 🅿; Z 99568; Ⓟ 79; © 173
Clarks Point; Inc. Place; DILLINGHAM; **144** H-6; 🅿; Z 99569; Ⓟ 60; © 75
Clear; RMC Place; DENALI; ***144** E-8; 🅿; Z 99704; ● 20
Clearwater Ranch; RMC Place; SOUTHEAST FAIRBANKS; ***144** E-9; elev. 1,050ft./320m.; mail Delta Junction Z 99737; rural
Clover Pass; RMC Place; KETCHIKAN GATEWAY; ***144** I-13; elev. 100ft./30m.; mail Ketchikan Z 99901; ● 450
Coffman Cove; Inc. Place; PRINCE OF WALES-OUTER KETCHIKAN; **144** I-13; 🅿; Z 99918; Ⓟ 186; © 199
Cohoe; CDP; KENAI PENINSULA; ***144** G-8; mail Kasilof Z 99610, Soldotna Z 99669; Ⓟ 508; © 1,168
Cold Bay; Inc. Place; ALEUTIANS EAST; **144** J-4; 🅿; Z 99571 & mail Adak Z 99546; Ⓟ 148; © 88
Coldfoot; CDP; YUKON-KOYUKUK; **144** C-8; 🅿; Z 99701; © 13
College; CDP; FAIRBANKS NORTH STAR; **144** A-1; ★ **FRBK**; mail Fairbanks Z 99701, Z 99708, Z 99775; Ⓟ 11,249; © 11,402
College Village; RMC Place; ANCHORAGE; ★ **ANCH**; mail Anchorage Z 99504; pop. incl. with Anchorage (Inc. Place)
Collegiate Park; RMC Place; FAIRBANKS NORTH STAR; ***144** E-8; elev. 427ft./130m.; ★ **FRBK**; mail Fairbanks Z 99701; ● 100
Colorado; RMC Place; MATANUSKA-SUSITNA; ***144** E-8; elev. 1,954ft./596m.; mail Anchorage Z 99695; ● 10
Cooper Landing; CDP; KENAI PENINSULA; ***144** G-8; 🅿; Z 99572; Ⓟ 243; © 369
Copper Center; CDP; VALDEZ-CORDOVA; **144** F-9; elev. 1,020ft./311m.; 🅿; Z 99573; Ⓟ 449; © 362
Copperville; CDP-Census Area Only; VALDEZ-CORDOVA; ***144** F-9; mail Copper Center Z 99573, Glennallen Z 99588; Ⓟ 163; © 179
Cordova; Inc. Place; VALDEZ-CORDOVA; **144** G-9; elev. 100ft./30m.; 🅿 🅷; Z 99574, Z 99677; Ⓟ 2,110; © 2,454
Corner Bay; RMC Place; SITKA; ***144** H-12; pop. incl. with Sitka (Inc. Place)
Cosna; RMC Place; YUKON-KOYUKUK; ***144** D-8; elev. 230ft./70m.; mail Manley Hot Springs Z 99756; ● 10
Cottonwood; RMC Place; MATANUSKA-SUSITNA; ***144** F-8; mail Wasilla Z 99654; ● 10
Council; RMC Place; NOME; **144** D-5; mail Nome Z 99762; rural
Covenant Life; CDP-Census Area Only; HAINES; ***144** G-12; mail Haines Z 99827; Ⓟ 47; © 102
Craig; Inc. Place; PRINCE OF WALES-OUTER KETCHIKAN; **144** I-13; 🅿; Z 99921; Ⓟ 1,260; © 1,397
Crooked Creek; CDP; BETHEL; **144** F-6; 🅿; Z 99575; Ⓟ 106; © 137
Crown Point; CDP-Census Area Only; KENAI PENINSULA; ***144** G-8; mail Seward Z 99664; Ⓟ 62; © 75
Cube Cove; CDP-Census Area Only; SKAGWAY-HOONAH-ANGOON; ***144** H-12; mail Juneau Z 99850; Ⓟ 156; © 72
Curry's Corner; FAIRBANKS NORTH STAR; see Steese (RMC Place)

D

Deadhorse; RMC Place; NORTH SLOPE; **144** A-8; mail Prudhoe Bay Z 99734; Ⓟ 26
Deering; Inc. Place; NORTHWEST ARCTIC; **144** D-5; 🅿; Z 99736; Ⓟ 157; © 136
Delta Junction; Inc. Place; SOUTHEAST FAIRBANKS; **144** E-9; 🅿; Z 99731, Z 99737; Ⓟ 652; © 840
Deltana; CDP-Census Area Only; SOUTHEAST FAIRBANKS; ***144** E-9; © 1,570
DENALI; ***144** E-8; Ⓟ 1,764; © 1,893; ◆ 1,789
Denali National Park; DENALI; see McKinley Park (CDP)
Denali Park; DENALI; see McKinley Park (CDP)
Derby Tract; RMC Place; FAIRBANKS NORTH STAR; ★ **FRBK**; mail Fairbanks Z 99701; pop. incl. with Fairbanks (Inc. Place)
Diamond Ridge; CDP-Census Area Only; KENAI PENINSULA; ***144** G-7; © 1,802
Dillingham; Inc. Place; DILLINGHAM; **144** H-6; 🅿 🅷; Z 99576; Ⓟ 2,017; © 2,466
DILLINGHAM; ***144** G-6; Ⓟ 4,012; © 4,922; ◆ 4,993
Diomede (Inalik, Little Diomede); Inc. Place; NOME; ***144** D-3; 🅿; Z 99762; Ⓟ 178; © 146
Dora Bay; RMC Place; PRINCE OF WALES-OUTER KETCHIKAN; ***144** I-13; mail Ketchikan Z 99901; Ⓟ 57; ● 60
Dot Lake; CDP; SOUTHEAST FAIRBANKS; **144** E-9; 🅿; Z 99737; Ⓟ 70; © 19
Dot Lake Village; CDP-Census Area Only; SOUTHEAST FAIRBANKS; ***144** E-9; © 38
Douglas; RMC Place; JUNEAU; **144** H-12; 🅿; Z 99824; pop. incl. with Juneau (Inc. Place)
Downtown; RMC Place; ANCHORAGE; ***144** G-8; ★ **ANCH**; mail Anchorage Z 99501, Z 99510; pop. incl. with Anchorage (Inc. Place)
Downtown; RMC Place; FAIRBANKS NORTH STAR; ***144** E-8; ★ **FRBK**; mail Fairbanks Z 99707; pop. incl. with Fairbanks (Inc. Place)
Driftwood Bay; RMC Place; ALEUTIANS WEST; ***144** J-3; mail Anchorage Z 99695; rural
Dry Creek; CDP-Census Area Only; SOUTHEAST FAIRBANKS; ***144** E-9; mail Delta Junction Z 99737; Ⓟ 106; © 128
Duncan Canal; RMC Place; WRANGELL-PETERSBURG; ***144** I-13; elev. 50ft./15m.; mail Petersburg Z 99833; rural
Dutch Harbor; RMC Place; ALEUTIANS WEST; **144** I-11; 🅿; Z 99692; ● 50

E

Eagle; Inc. Place; SOUTHEAST FAIRBANKS; **144** D-10; 🅿; Z 99738; Ⓟ 168; © 129
Eagle River; RMC Place; ANCHORAGE; **144** G-8; 🅿; ★ **ANCH**; Z 99577; pop. incl. with Anchorage (Inc. Place)
Eagle Village (Indian Village); CDP; SOUTHEAST FAIRBANKS; ***144** D-10; elev. 913ft./278m.; mail Eagle Z 99738; Ⓟ 35; © 68
Eastchester; RMC Place; ANCHORAGE; ***144** G-8; ★ **ANCH**; mail Anchorage Z 99501, Z 99520; pop. incl. with Anchorage (Inc. Place)
Edna Bay; CDP; PRINCE OF WALES-OUTER KETCHIKAN; ***144** I-13; 🅿; Z 99901, Z 99950; Ⓟ 86; © 49
Eek; Inc. Place; BETHEL; **144** G-5; 🅿; Z 99578; Ⓟ 254; © 280
Egegik; Inc. Place; LAKE AND PENINSULA; **144** H-6; 🅿; Z 99579; Ⓟ 122; © 116
Eielson AFB; CDP-Census Area Only; FAIRBANKS NORTH STAR; ***144** E-9; elev. 537ft./164m.; 🅿; Z 99702; Ⓟ 5,251; © 5,400
Eklutna; RMC Place; ANCHORAGE; ★ **ANCH**; mail Chugiak Z 99567; pop. incl. with Anchorage (Inc. Place)
Eklutna Housing Project; RMC Place; ANCHORAGE; ★ **ANCH**; mail Palmer Z 99645; pop. incl. with Anchorage (Inc. Place)
Ekuk; RMC Place; DILLINGHAM; **144** H-6; elev. 16ft./5m.; mail Anchorage Z 99695; summer pop. 800; ● 30
Ekwok; Inc. Place; DILLINGHAM; **144** H-6; 🅿; Z 99580; Ⓟ 77; © 130
Elephant Point; NORTHWEST ARCTIC; see Buckland (Inc. Place)
Elfin Cove; CDP; SKAGWAY-HOONAH-ANGOON; **144** H-12; 🅿; Z 99825; Ⓟ 57; © 32
Elim; Inc. Place; NOME; **144** D-5; 🅿; Z 99739; Ⓟ 264; © 313
Ellamar; RMC Place; VALDEZ-CORDOVA; ***144** G-9; mail Anchorage Z 99695; ● 10
Emanguk; WADE HAMPTON; see Emmonak (Inc. Place)
Emmonak (Emanguk); Inc. Place; WADE HAMPTON; **144** E-4; 🅿; Z 99581 & mail Nunam Iqua Z 99666; Ⓟ 642; © 767
English Bay; KENAI PENINSULA; see Nanwalek (CDP-Census Area Only)
Eska; RMC Place; MATANUSKA-SUSITNA; ***144** F-8; mail Sutton Z 99674; rural
Ester; CDP; FAIRBANKS NORTH STAR; ***144** E-8; 🅿; ★ **FRBK**; Z 99725; Ⓟ 147; © 1,680
Eureka; RMC Place; MATANUSKA-SUSITNA; ***144** F-9; elev. 3,289ft./1,002m.; mail Palmer Z 99645; ● 30
Eureka; RMC Place; YUKON-KOYUKUK; **144** D-8; elev. 775ft./236m.; mail Manley Hot Springs Z 99756; ● 20
Evansville; CDP; YUKON-KOYUKUK; ***144** C-8; elev. 643ft./196m.; mail Bettles Field Z 99726; Ⓟ 33; © 28
Excursion Inlet; CDP-Census Area Only; HAINES; **144** H-12; mail Juneau Z 99850; © 10

F

Fairbanks; Inc. Place; FAIRBANKS NORTH STAR; **144** E-9; 🅿 🅷 🅲 9,681 ■; ★ **FRBK**; Z 99701-02, Z 99705-12, Z 99714, Z 99716, Z 99767, Z 99775, Z 99790; location of Indian Agency; Ⓟ 30,843; © 30,224; ◆ 44,276
FAIRBANKS NORTH STAR; ***144** E-9; Ⓟ 77,720; © 82,840; ◆ 119,042
Fairview; RMC Place; ANCHORAGE; ★ **ANCH**; pop. incl. with Anchorage (Inc. Place)
False Pass; Inc. Place; ALEUTIANS EAST; **144** J-4; 🅿; Z 99583; Ⓟ 69; © 64
Farm Loop; CDP-Census Area Only; MATANUSKA-SUSITNA; ***144** F-8; © 1,067
Ferry; CDP-Census Area Only; DENALI; **144** E-8; mail Healy Z 99743; Ⓟ 56; © 29
Fire Lake; RMC Place; ANCHORAGE; ★ **ANCH**; mail Eagle River Z 99577; pop. incl. with Anchorage (Inc. Place)
Fishhook; CDP-Census Area Only; MATANUSKA-SUSITNA; ***144** F-8; © 2,030
Fishhook; YUKON-KOYUKUK; see Chalkyitsik (CDP)
Fishhook Junction; RMC Place; MATANUSKA-SUSITNA; ***144** F-8; ★ **ANCH**; mail Palmer Z 99645; ● 50
Flat; CDP; YUKON-KOYUKUK; **144** F-6; © 4
Fort Greely; CDP-Census Area Only; SOUTHEAST FAIRBANKS; ***144** E-9; elev. 1,314ft./401m.; 🅿; Z 99731; Ⓟ 1,147; © 461
Fort Yukon; Inc. Place; YUKON-KOYUKUK; **144** C-9; 🅿; Z 99740, Z 99788; Ⓟ 580; © 595
Four Corners; RMC Place; MATANUSKA-SUSITNA; ***144** F-8; ★ **ANCH**; mail Palmer Z 99645; ● 50
Four Mile Road; CDP-Census Area Only; YUKON-KOYUKUK; ***144** E-8; © 38
Fox; CDP; FAIRBANKS NORTH STAR; ***144** D-9; ★ **FRBK**; mail Fairbanks Z 99712; Ⓟ 275; © 300
Fox River; CDP-Census Area Only; KENAI PENINSULA; ***144** G-8; mail Homer Z 99603; Ⓟ 382; © 616
Freshwater Bay; RMC Place; SITKA; ***144** H-12; mail Juneau Z 99803; pop. incl. with Sitka (Inc. Place)
Fritz Cove; RMC Place; JUNEAU; mail Juneau Z 99801; pop. incl. with Juneau (Inc. Place)
Fritz Creek; CDP-Census Area Only; KENAI PENINSULA; ***144** G-8; elev. 460ft./140m.; 🅿; Z 99603; Ⓟ 1,426; © 1,603
Funny River; CDP-Census Area Only; KENAI PENINSULA; ***144** G-8; © 636
Funter; SKAGWAY-HOONAH-ANGOON; see Funter Bay (RMC Place)
Funter Bay (Funter); RMC Place; SKAGWAY-HOONAH-ANGOON; ***144** H-12; mail Juneau Z 99850; ● 20

G

Gakona; CDP; VALDEZ-CORDOVA; **144** F-9; 🅿; Z 99586; Ⓟ 25; © 215
Galena; Inc. Place; YUKON-KOYUKUK; **144** E-6; 🅿; Z 99741; Ⓟ 833; © 675
Gambell; Inc. Place; NOME; **144** D-2; 🅿; Z 99742; Ⓟ 525; © 649
Game Creek; CDP-Census Area Only; SKAGWAY-HOONAH-ANGOON; ***144** H-12; mail Hoonah Z 99829; Ⓟ 61; © 35
Ganes Creek; RMC Place; YUKON-KOYUKUK; ***144** E-6; mail Takotna Z 99675
Gateway; CDP-Census Area Only; MATANUSKA-SUSITNA; ***144** F-8; ★ **ANCH**; © 2,952
Girdwood; RMC Place; ANCHORAGE; ***144** G-8; 🅿; ★ **ANCH**; Z 99587, Z 99693; pop. incl. with Anchorage (Inc. Place)
Glacier View; CDP-Census Area Only; MATANUSKA-SUSITNA; ***144** F-9; © 249
Glennallen; CDP; VALDEZ-CORDOVA; **144** F-9; 🅿; Z 99588; Ⓟ 451; © 554
Gold Creek; RMC Place; MATANUSKA-SUSITNA; ***144** F-8; elev. 715ft./218m.; mail Anchorage Z 99695; rural
Golovin; Inc. Place; NOME; **144** D-5; 🅿; Z 99762; Ⓟ 127; © 144
Goodnews Bay; Inc. Place; BETHEL; **144** H-5; 🅿; Z 99589; Ⓟ 241; © 230

Entries in **UPPERCASE** are boroughs or Census Areas.
Entries in **bold** have populations of 2,500 or more.
Names in parentheses are alternate names.
Inc. Place — Incorporated Place
RMC Place — Rand McNally Designated Place
CDP — Census Designated Place
MCD — Minor Civil Division

⊡ Borough or Census Area Seat
▲ Minor Civil Division
elev. Elevation
🅿 Post Office

🅷 Hospital
🅲 College
■ Principal Business Center
★ Ranally Metro Area (RMA) Abbreviation
Z Zip Code(s)

Ⓟ Previous Census Population
Ⓡ Revised Census Population
Ⓐ Annexation Population
● Rand McNally Population Estimate
© Final Census Population
Ⓢ Special Census Population
◆ Estimated Population

For additional definitions see Glossary, Volume 1, and Introduction, Volume 2.

Goodnews Mining Camp; RMC Place; BETHEL; ***144** H-5; mail Platinum **z** 99651
Graehl; RMC Place; FAIRBANKS NORTH STAR; ★ **FRBK**; mail Fairbanks **z** 99701; pop. incl. with Fairbanks (Inc. Place)
Granite Mountain; RMC Place; NORTHWEST ARCTIC; mail Nome **z** 99762
Grayling; Inc. Place; YUKON-KOYUKUK; **144** F-5; 🅿; **z** 99590; Ⓟ 208; © 194
Gulkana; CDP; VALDEZ-CORDOVA; **144** F-9; elev. 1,378ft./420m.; mail Anchorage **z** 99695, Gakona **z** 99586; Ⓟ 103; © 88
Gustavus (Strawberry Point); Inc. Place; SKAGWAY-HOONAH-ANGOON; **144** H-12; 🅿; **z** 99826; incorporated April 1, 2004; not reported in 2000 Census
Gustavus; CDP-Census Area Only; SKAGWAY-HOONAH-ANGOON; **144** H-12; 🅿; **z** 99826; Ⓟ 258; © 429

H

Haines; RMC Place; HAINES; **144** G-12; 🅿; **z** 99827; disincorporated October 17, 2002; Ⓟ 1,238; © 1,811
HAINES; ***144** G-12; Ⓟ 2,117; © 2,392; ◆ 2,380
Halibut Cove; CDP; KENAI PENINSULA; ***144** G-8; 🅿; **z** 99603; Ⓟ 78; © 35
Hamilton Acres; RMC Place; FAIRBANKS NORTH STAR; ***144** E-9; ★ **FRBK**; mail Fairbanks **z** 99701; pop. incl. with Fairbanks (Inc. Place)
Hanus Bay; RMC Place; SITKA; rural
Happy Valley; CDP-Census Area Only; KENAI PENINSULA; ***144** G-7; mail Anchor Point **z** 99556; Ⓟ 309; © 489
Harding-Birch Lakes; CDP-Census Area Only; FAIRBANKS NORTH STAR; ***144** E-9; © 216
Hawk Inlet; RMC Place; SKAGWAY-HOONAH-ANGOON; **144** H-12; elev. 100ft./30m.; mail Juneau **z** 99850; ● 20
Haycock; RMC Place; NOME; ***144** D-5; mail Koyuk **z** 99753
Healy (Healy Fork); CDP; DENALI; **144** E-8; elev. 1,368ft./417m.; 🅿; **z** 99743 & mail Denali National Park **z** 99755; Ⓟ 487; © 1,000
Healy Fork; DENALI; see Healy (CDP)
Healy Lake; CDP-Census Area Only; SOUTHEAST FAIRBANKS; ***144** E-9; elev. 1,200ft./366m.; mail Delta Junction **z** 99737; Ⓟ 47; © 37
Herring Cove; RMC Place; KETCHIKAN GATEWAY; ***144** I-14; elev. 100ft./30m.; mail Ketchikan **z** 99901; ● 90
Hobart Bay; CDP-Census Area Only; SKAGWAY-HOONAH-ANGOON; ***144** H-13; mail Juneau **z** 99850; Ⓟ 187; © 3
Hogatza; RMC Place; YUKON-KOYUKUK; ***144** D-7; mail Fairbanks **z** 99701
Hollis; CDP-Census Area Only; PRINCE OF WALES-OUTER KETCHIKAN; ***144** I-13; mail Ketchikan **z** 99901; Ⓟ 111; © 139
Holy Cross; Inc. Place; YUKON-KOYUKUK; **144** F-5; 🅿; **z** 99602; Ⓟ 277; © 227
Homer; Inc. Place; KENAI PENINSULA; **144** G-7; 🅿 🅷; **z** 99603; Ⓟ 3,660; © 3,946
Hoonah; Inc. Place; SKAGWAY-HOONAH-ANGOON; **144** H-12; 🅿; **z** 99829; Ⓟ 795; © 860
Hooper Bay; Inc. Place; WADE HAMPTON; **144** F-4; 🅿; **z** 99604; Ⓟ 845; © 1,014
Hope; CDP; KENAI PENINSULA; **144** G-8; 🅿; **z** 99605; Ⓟ 161; © 137
Hot Springs; YUKON-KOYUKUK; see Manley Hot Springs (CDP)
Houston; Inc. Place; MATANUSKA-SUSITNA; **144** F-8; 🅿; **z** 99694; Ⓟ 697; © 1,202
Huffman; RMC Place; ANCHORAGE; mail Anchorage **z** 99511, **z** 99515-16; pop. incl. with Anchorage (Inc. Place)
Hughes; Inc. Place; YUKON-KOYUKUK; **144** D-7; 🅿; **z** 99745; Ⓟ 54; © 78
Huslia; Inc. Place; YUKON-KOYUKUK; **144** D-6; 🅿; **z** 99746; Ⓟ 207; © 293
Hydaburg; Inc. Place; PRINCE OF WALES-OUTER KETCHIKAN; **144** I-13; 🅿; **z** 99922; Ⓟ 384; © 382
Hyder; CDP; PRINCE OF WALES-OUTER KETCHIKAN; **144** I-14; 🅿; **z** 99923; Ⓟ 99; © 97

I

Icy Bay; RMC Place; VALDEZ-CORDOVA; ***144** G-10; mail Anchorage **z** 99695; ● 10
Iditarod; RMC Place; YUKON-KOYUKUK; **144** F-6; rural
Igiugig (Iguigig); CDP; LAKE AND PENINSULA; **144** H-6; 🅿; **z** 99613; Ⓟ 33; © 53
Iguigig; LAKE AND PENINSULA; see Igiugig (CDP)
Iliamna (New Iliamna); CDP; LAKE AND PENINSULA; **144** G-7; 🅿; **z** 99606, **z** 99647; Ⓟ 94; © 102
Inalik; NOME; see Diomede (Inc. Place)
Indian; RMC Place; ANCHORAGE; 🅿; ★ **ANCH**; **z** 99540; pop. incl. with Anchorage (Inc. Place)
Indian River; RMC Place; YUKON-KOYUKUK; mail Allakaket **z** 99720
Indian Village; SOUTHEAST FAIRBANKS; see Eagle Village (CDP)
Island Homes; RMC Place; FAIRBANKS NORTH STAR; ★ **FRBK**; mail Fairbanks **z** 99701; pop. incl. with Fairbanks (Inc. Place)
Ivanof Bay; CDP-Census Area Only; LAKE AND PENINSULA; **144** I-5; mail Anchorage **z** 99695; Ⓟ 35; © 22

J

Jakolof Bay; RMC Place; KENAI PENINSULA; ***144** H-8; elev. 584ft./178m.; mail Anchorage **z** 99695; Ⓟ 28; ● 30
Johnston; RMC Place; FAIRBANKS NORTH STAR; ★ **FRBK**; mail Fairbanks **z** 99701; pop. incl. with Fairbanks (Inc. Place)
Juneau; Inc. Place; **STATE CAPITAL**; JUNEAU; **144** H-12; 🅿 🅷 🅲 3,012 ■; **z** 99801-03, **z** 99811-12, **z** 99821, **z** 99824, **z** 99850; Ⓟ 26,751; © 30,711; ◆ 31,193
JUNEAU; ***144** H-12; Ⓟ 26,751; © 30,711; ◆ 30,180

K

Kachemak; KENAI PENINSULA; see Kachemak City (Inc. Place)
Kachemak City (Kachemak); Inc. Place; KENAI PENINSULA; ***144** G-8; mail Homer **z** 99603; Ⓟ 365; © 431
Kake; Inc. Place; WRANGELL-PETERSBURG; **144** H-13; 🅿; **z** 99830; Ⓟ 700; © 710
Kako; RMC Place; WADE HAMPTON; ***144** F-5; elev. 50ft./15m.; mail Russian Mission **z** 99657; ● 10
Kaktovik; Inc. Place; NORTH SLOPE; **144** A-9; 🅿; **z** 99747; Ⓟ 224; © 293
Kalifonski; KENAI PENINSULA; see Kalifornsky (CDP)
Kalifonsky; KENAI PENINSULA; see Kalifornsky (CDP)
Kalifornsky (Kalifonski, Kalifonsky); CDP; KENAI PENINSULA; ***144** G-8; elev. 50ft./15m.; mail Kasilof **z** 99610; Ⓟ 285; © 5,846
Kalskag (Upper Kalskag); Inc. Place; BETHEL; **144** F-5; 🅿; **z** 99607; Ⓟ 172; © 230
Kaltag; Inc. Place; YUKON-KOYUKUK; **144** E-6; 🅿; **z** 99748; Ⓟ 240; © 230
Kanakanak; RMC Place; DILLINGHAM; ***144** H-6; elev. 50ft./15m.; mail Dillingham **z** 99576; ● 30
Kantishna; RMC Place; DENALI; **144** B-12; elev. 1,690ft./515m.; mail Denali National Park **z** 99755
Karluk; CDP; KODIAK ISLAND; **144** I-7; 🅿; **z** 99608; Ⓟ 71; © 27
Kasaan; Inc. Place; PRINCE OF WALES-OUTER KETCHIKAN; **144** I-13; 🅿; **z** 99901, **z** 99950; Ⓟ 54; © 39
Kashegelok (Kashegeluk); RMC Place; BETHEL; ***144** G-6; elev. 500ft./152m.; mail Sleetmute **z** 99668; rural
Kashegeluk; BETHEL; see Kashegelok (RMC Place)
Kasigluk; CDP; BETHEL; **144** F-4; 🅿; **z** 99609; Ⓟ 425; © 543
Kasilof; CDP; KENAI PENINSULA; **144** G-8; 🅿; **z** 99610; Ⓟ 383; © 471
Kenai; Inc. Place; KENAI PENINSULA; **144** G-8; 🅿; **z** 99611, **z** 99635; Ⓟ 6,327; © 6,942
Kenai Lake; RMC Place; KENAI PENINSULA; mail Cooper Landing **z** 99572; summer pop. 400
Kenai Packers Cannery; RMC Place; KENAI PENINSULA; mail Kenai **z** 99611; pop. incl. with Kenai (Inc. Place)
KENAI PENINSULA; ***144** G-8; Ⓟ 40,802; © 49,691; ◆ 54,934
Kennicott; RMC Place; VALDEZ-CORDOVA; ***144** F-10; elev. 1,680ft./512m.; mail Glennallen **z** 99588; summer pop. 100; ● 10
Kenny Cove; RMC Place; VALDEZ-CORDOVA; ***144** G-9; mail Anchorage **z** 99695; ● 30
Kenny Lake; CDP-Census Area Only; VALDEZ-CORDOVA; ***144** F-9; mail Copper Center **z** 99573; Ⓟ 423; © 410
Ketchikan; Inc. Place; KETCHIKAN GATEWAY; **144** I-14; 🅿 🅷 ■; **z** 99901, **z** 99903, **z** 99918-19, **z** 99950; Ⓟ 8,263; © 7,922; Ⓡ 7,951; ◆ 7,355
KETCHIKAN GATEWAY; ***144** I-14; Ⓟ 13,828; © 14,070; Ⓡ 14,059; ◆ 12,834
Kiana; Inc. Place; NORTHWEST ARCTIC; **144** C-6; 🅿; **z** 99749; Ⓟ 385; © 388
King Cove; Inc. Place; ALEUTIANS EAST; **144** J-4; 🅿; **z** 99612; Ⓟ 451; © 792
King Salmon; CDP; BRISTOL BAY; **144** H-6; 🅿; **z** 99549, **z** 99613; Ⓟ 696; © 442
Kipnuk; CDP; BETHEL; **144** G-4; 🅿; **z** 99614; Ⓟ 470; © 644
Kitoi Bay; RMC Place; KODIAK ISLAND; ***144** H-7; mail Kodiak **z** 99697; rural
Kivalina; Inc. Place; NORTHWEST ARCTIC; **144** C-5; 🅿; **z** 99750; Ⓟ 317; © 377
Klawak; PRINCE OF WALES-OUTER KETCHIKAN; see Klawock (Inc. Place)
Klawock (Klawak); Inc. Place; PRINCE OF WALES-OUTER KETCHIKAN; **144** I-13; 🅿; **z** 99925; Ⓟ 722; © 854
Klukwan; CDP; SKAGWAY-HOONAH-ANGOON; **144** G-12; elev. 121ft./37m.; mail Haines **z** 99827; Ⓟ 129; © 139
Knik; RMC Place; MATANUSKA-SUSITNA; ***144** F-8; mail Wasilla **z** 99654; ● 30
Knik-Fairview; CDP-Census Area Only; MATANUSKA-SUSITNA; ***144** F-8; © 7,049
Knik River; CDP-Census Area Only; MATANUSKA-SUSITNA; ***144** F-8; ★ **ANCH**; © 582
Knudson Cove; RMC Place; KETCHIKAN GATEWAY; mail Ketchikan **z** 99901
Kobuk; Inc. Place; NORTHWEST ARCTIC; **144** C-6; 🅿; **z** 99751; Ⓟ 69; © 109
Kodiak; Inc. Place; KODIAK ISLAND; **144** H-7; 🅿 🅷; **z** 99615, **z** 99619, **z** 99697; Ⓟ 6,365; © 6,334
KODIAK ISLAND; ***144** I-7; Ⓟ 13,309; © 13,913; ◆ 12,931
Kodiak Station; CDP-Census Area Only; KODIAK ISLAND; ***144** H-7; elev. 50ft./15m.; mail Kodiak **z** 99615; Ⓟ 2,025; © 1,840
Kokhanok; CDP-Census Area Only; LAKE AND PENINSULA; **144** H-6; 🅿; **z** 99606; Ⓟ 152; © 174
Kokrines; RMC Place; YUKON-KOYUKUK; **144** D-7; mail Ruby **z** 99768; rural
Koliganek; CDP; DILLINGHAM; **144** G-6; 🅿; **z** 99576; Ⓟ 181; © 182
Kongiganak; CDP; BETHEL; **144** G-4; 🅿; **z** 99545, **z** 99559; Ⓟ 294; © 359
Kotlik; Inc. Place; WADE HAMPTON; **144** E-4; 🅿; **z** 99620; Ⓟ 461; © 591
Kotzebue; Inc. Place; NORTHWEST ARCTIC; **144** C-5; 🅿 🅷; **z** 99752; Ⓟ 2,751; © 3,082
Koyuk; Inc. Place; NOME; **144** D-5; 🅿; **z** 99753; Ⓟ 231; © 297
Koyukuk; Inc. Place; YUKON-KOYUKUK; **144** D-6; 🅿; **z** 99754; Ⓟ 126; © 101
Kupreanof (West Petersburg); Inc. Place; WRANGELL-PETERSBURG; ***144** I-13; elev. 50ft./15m.; mail Petersburg **z** 99833; Ⓟ 23; © 23
Kustatan; RMC Place; KENAI PENINSULA; ***144** G-7; mail Tyonek **z** 99682
Kwethluk; Inc. Place; BETHEL; **144** G-5; 🅿; **z** 99621; Ⓟ 558; © 713
Kwigillingok; CDP; BETHEL; **144** G-4; 🅿; **z** 99622; Ⓟ 278; © 338

L

LAKE AND PENINSULA; ***144** H-6; Ⓟ 1,668; © 1,823; ◆ 1,498
Lake Louise; CDP-Census Area Only; MATANUSKA-SUSITNA; ***144** F-9; © 88
Lake Minchumina; CDP; YUKON-KOYUKUK; **144** E-7; 🅿; **z** 99757; Ⓟ 32; © 32
Lake Otis; RMC Place; ANCHORAGE; ***144** G-8; ★ **ANCH**; mail Anchorage **z** 99507, **z** 99511; pop. incl. with Anchorage (Inc. Place)
Lakes; CDP-Census Area Only; MATANUSKA-SUSITNA; ***144** F-8; © 6,706
Lakloey Hill; RMC Place; FAIRBANKS NORTH STAR; ***144** E-9; ★ **FRBK**; mail North Pole **z** 99705; ● 160
Larsen Bay; Inc. Place; KODIAK ISLAND; **144** I-7; 🅿; **z** 99624; Ⓟ 147; © 115
Lawing; RMC Place; KENAI PENINSULA; ***144** G-8; elev. 139ft./42m.; mail Seward **z** 99664; rural
Lazy Mountain; CDP-Census Area Only; MATANUSKA-SUSITNA; ***144** F-8; mail Palmer **z** 99645; Ⓟ 838; © 1,158
Lemeta; RMC Place; FAIRBANKS NORTH STAR; ***144** E-8; ★ **FRBK**; mail Fairbanks **z** 99701; pop. incl. with Fairbanks (Inc. Place)
Lemon Creek; RMC Place; JUNEAU; mail Juneau **z** 99801; pop. incl. with Juneau (Inc. Place)
Lena Cove; RMC Place; JUNEAU; mail Juneau **z** 99801; pop. incl. with Juneau (Inc. Place)
Levelock (Old Kvichak); CDP; LAKE AND PENINSULA; **144** H-6; 🅿; **z** 99625; Ⓟ 105; © 122
Liberty; RMC Place; SOUTHEAST FAIRBANKS; ***144** E-10; elev. 2,000ft./610m.; mail Eagle **z** 99738; rural
Lime Village; CDP; BETHEL; **144** F-6; mail Mc Grath **z** 99627; Ⓟ 42; © 6; Ⓡ 46
Little Diomede; NOME; see Diomede (Inc. Place)
Little Port Walter; RMC Place; SITKA; ***144** I-13; elev. 200ft./61m.; mail Sitka **z** 99835; ● 10
Livengood; CDP; YUKON-KOYUKUK; **144** D-8; elev. 870ft./265m.; mail Fairbanks **z** 99701; © 29
Long; RMC Place; YUKON-KOYUKUK; **144** E-7; mail Ruby **z** 99768
Long Island; RMC Place; MATANUSKA-SUSITNA; ***144** F-8; mail Wasilla **z** 99654; ● 30
Lost River; RMC Place; NOME; mail Nome **z** 99762
Lost River; RMC Place; YAKUTAT; mail Yakutat **z** 99689
Lowell Point; CDP-Census Area Only; KENAI PENINSULA; ***144** G-8; © 92
Lower Kalskag; Inc. Place; BETHEL; **144** F-5; 🅿; **z** 99626; Ⓟ 291; © 267
Lower Mendenhall Valley; RMC Place; JUNEAU; mail Juneau **z** 99801; pop. incl. with Juneau (Inc. Place)
Lutak; CDP-Census Area Only; HAINES; ***144** G-12; mail Haines **z** 99827; Ⓟ 45; © 39

M

Mack; RMC Place; FAIRBANKS NORTH STAR; mail Fairbanks **z** 99701
Manley Hot Springs (Hot Springs); CDP; YUKON-KOYUKUK; **144** D-8; 🅿; **z** 99756; Ⓟ 96; © 72
Manokotak; Inc. Place; DILLINGHAM; **144** H-5; 🅿; **z** 99628; Ⓟ 385; © 399
Mansfield Village; RMC Place; SOUTHEAST FAIRBANKS; ***144** E-10; elev. 1,700ft./518m.; mail Nenana **z** 99760; rural
Marshall; Inc. Place; WADE HAMPTON; **144** F-5; 🅿; **z** 99585; Ⓟ 273; © 349
Marvel Creek; RMC Place; BETHEL; mail Aniak **z** 99557; ● 10
Mary's Igloo; RMC Place; NOME; ***144** D-4; mail Teller **z** 99778; rural
Matanuska; RMC Place; MATANUSKA-SUSITNA; ***144** F-8; ★ **ANCH**; mail Palmer **z** 99645; rural
MATANUSKA-SUSITNA; ***144** F-8; Ⓟ 39,683; © 59,322; ◆ 86,787
May Creek; RMC Place; VALDEZ-CORDOVA; ***144** F-10; elev. 1,614ft./492m.; mail Anchorage **z** 99695; rural
McCarthy; CDP; VALDEZ-CORDOVA; **144** F-10; mail Willow **z** 99688; Ⓟ 25; © 42
McGrath; Inc. Place; YUKON-KOYUKUK; **144** F-6; 🅿; **z** 99627, **z** 99675, **z** 99691; Ⓟ 528; © 401
McKinley Park (Denali National Park, Denali Park); CDP; DENALI; **144** E-8; mail Denali National Park **z** 99755; Ⓟ 171; summer pop. 800; © 142
Meade River; RMC Place; NORTH SLOPE; ***144** A-6; elev. 50ft./15m.; mail Atqasuk **z** 99791, Barrow **z** 99723; rural
Meadow Lakes; CDP-Census Area Only; MATANUSKA-SUSITNA; ***144** F-8; mail Wasilla **z** 99654; Ⓟ 2,374; © 4,819
Medfra; RMC Place; YUKON-KOYUKUK; **144** E-7; mail Mc Grath **z** 99627; rural
Meekins Roadhouse; RMC Place; MATANUSKA-SUSITNA; ***144** F-9; mail Palmer **z** 99645; rural
Meier; RMC Place; VALDEZ-CORDOVA; ***144** F-9; elev. 2,717ft./828m.; mail Delta Junction **z** 99737; rural
Mekoryuk; Inc. Place; BETHEL; **144** F-3; 🅿; **z** 99630; Ⓟ 177; © 210
Mendeltna; CDP-Census Area Only; VALDEZ-CORDOVA; ***144** F-9; elev. 1,420ft./433m.; mail Glennallen **z** 99588; Ⓟ 37; © 63
Mendeltna Lodge; RMC Place; MATANUSKA-SUSITNA; ***144** F-9; elev. 2,186ft./666m.; mail Palmer **z** 99645; rural
Mendenhall; RMC Place; JUNEAU; ***144** H-12; mail Juneau **z** 99803; pop. incl. with Juneau (Inc. Place)
Mendenhall Flats; RMC Place; JUNEAU; mail Juneau **z** 99801; pop. incl. with Juneau (Inc. Place)
Mentasta; VALDEZ-CORDOVA; see Mentasta Lake (CDP)
Mentasta Lake (Mentasta); CDP; VALDEZ-CORDOVA; **144** F-10; elev. 2,235ft./681m.; 🅿; **z** 99780; Ⓟ 96; © 142
Meshik; LAKE AND PENINSULA; see Port Heiden (Inc. Place)
Metlakahtla; PRINCE OF WALES-OUTER KETCHIKAN; see Metlakatla (CDP)
Metlakatla (Metlakahtla); CDP; PRINCE OF WALES-OUTER KETCHIKAN; **144** I-14; 🅿; **z** 99926; Ⓟ 1,407; © 1,375
Meyers Chuck; CDP; PRINCE OF WALES-OUTER KETCHIKAN; ***144** I-13; 🅿; **z** 99903; Ⓟ 37; © 21
Midtown; RMC Place; ANCHORAGE; ***144** G-8; ★ **ANCH**; mail Anchorage **z** 99503, **z** 99524; pop. incl. with Anchorage (Inc. Place)
Miller Landing; CDP-Census Area Only; KENAI PENINSULA; ***144** G-8; © 74
Minto (New Minto); CDP; YUKON-KOYUKUK; **144** D-8; 🅿; **z** 99758; Ⓟ 218; © 258
Montana (Montana Creek); RMC Place; MATANUSKA-SUSITNA; ***144** F-8; elev. 277ft./84m.; mail Willow **z** 99688; rural
Montana Creek; MATANUSKA-SUSITNA; see Montana (RMC Place)
Moose Creek; CDP; FAIRBANKS NORTH STAR; ***144** E-9; mail North Pole **z** 99705; Ⓟ 610; © 542
Moose Pass; CDP; KENAI PENINSULA; **144** G-8; 🅿; **z** 99631; Ⓟ 81; © 206
Moser Bay; RMC Place; KODIAK ISLAND; ***144** I-7; mail Kodiak **z** 99697; rural
Mosquito Lake; CDP-Census Area Only; HAINES; ***144** G-12; mail Haines **z** 99827; Ⓟ 80; © 221
Mountain Point; RMC Place; KETCHIKAN GATEWAY; ***144** I-14; mail Ketchikan **z** 99901; ● 300
Mountain View; RMC Place; ANCHORAGE; ***144** G-8; ★ **ANCH**; mail Anchorage **z** 99508; pop. incl. with Anchorage (Inc. Place)
Mountain Village; Inc. Place; WADE HAMPTON; **144** F-4; 🅿; **z** 99632; Ⓟ 674; © 755
Mount Edgecumbe; RMC Place; SITKA; ***144** I-12; mail Sitka **z** 99835; pop. incl. with Sitka (Inc. Place)
Mud Bay; CDP-Census Area Only; HAINES; ***144** G-12; © 137
Mud Bay; RMC Place; KETCHIKAN GATEWAY; ***144** I-13; elev. 100ft./30m.; mail Ketchikan **z** 99901; ● 100
Muldoon; RMC Place; ANCHORAGE; ***144** G-8; ★ **ANCH**; mail Anchorage **z** 99504, **z** 99521; pop. incl. with Anchorage (Inc. Place)

N

Nabesna; RMC Place; VALDEZ-CORDOVA; **144** F-10; elev. 3,000ft./914m.; mail Gakona **z** 99586; rural
Naknek; CDP; BRISTOL BAY; **144** H-6; 🅿; **z** 99633; Ⓟ 575; © 678
Nancy; RMC Place; MATANUSKA-SUSITNA; ***144** F-8; mail Willow **z** 99688; ● 200
Nanwalek (English Bay); CDP-Census Area Only; KENAI PENINSULA; **144** G-7; elev. 500ft./152m.; 🅿; **z** 99603; Ⓟ 158; © 177
Napaimute (Napamute); RMC Place; BETHEL; ***144** F-6; mail Aniak **z** 99557; rural
Napakiak (Napakiakamute); Inc. Place; BETHEL; **144** G-5; 🅿; **z** 99634; Ⓟ 318; © 353
Napakiakamute; BETHEL; see Napakiak (Inc. Place)
Napamute; BETHEL; see Napaimute (RMC Place)
Napaskiak; Inc. Place; BETHEL; **144** G-5; 🅿; **z** 99559; Ⓟ 328; © 390
Naukati Bay; CDP-Census Area Only; PRINCE OF WALES-OUTER KETCHIKAN; ***144** I-13; 🅿; **z** 99901; Ⓟ 93; © 135
Nelchina; CDP-Census Area Only; VALDEZ-CORDOVA; ***144** F-9; © 71
Nelson Lagoon; CDP; ALEUTIANS EAST; **144** I-5; 🅿; **z** 99571; Ⓟ 83; © 83
Nenana; Inc. Place; YUKON-KOYUKUK; **144** E-8; elev. 362ft./110m.; 🅿; **z** 99704, **z** 99744, **z** 99760; Ⓟ 393; © 402
Nenana Native Village; RMC Place; YUKON-KOYUKUK; mail Nenana **z** 99760; pop. incl. with Nenana (Inc. Place)
New Allakaket; CDP-Census Area Only; YUKON-KOYUKUK; ***144** D-7; © 36
Newhalen; Inc. Place; LAKE AND PENINSULA; **144** G-7; mail Iliamna **z** 99606; Ⓟ 160; © 160
New Iliamna; LAKE AND PENINSULA; see Iliamna (CDP)
Newktok; BETHEL; see Newtok (CDP)
New Minto; YUKON-KOYUKUK; see Minto (CDP)
New Stuyahok; Inc. Place; DILLINGHAM; **144** G-6; 🅿; **z** 99636; Ⓟ 391; © 471
Newtok (Newktok); CDP; BETHEL; **144** F-4; 🅿; **z** 99559; Ⓟ 207; © 321
New Tokeen; RMC Place; PRINCE OF WALES-OUTER KETCHIKAN; ***144** I-13; mail Ketchikan **z** 99901; ● 20
Nightmute; Inc. Place; BETHEL; **144** G-4; 🅿; **z** 99690; Ⓟ 153; © 208
Nikiski; CDP; KENAI PENINSULA; **144** G-8; 🅿; **z** 99635; Ⓟ 2,743; © 4,327
Nikolaevsk; CDP; KENAI PENINSULA; ***144** G-7; 🅿; **z** 99556; Ⓟ 371; © 345
Nikolai; Inc. Place; YUKON-KOYUKUK; **144** F-7; 🅿; **z** 99691; Ⓟ 109; © 100
Nikolski; CDP; ALEUTIANS WEST; **144** J-10; 🅿; **z** 99638; Ⓟ 35; © 39
Ninilchik; CDP; KENAI PENINSULA; **144** G-7; 🅿; **z** 99639; Ⓟ 456; © 772
Noatak; CDP; NORTHWEST ARCTIC; **144** C-5; 🅿; **z** 99761; Ⓟ 333; © 428
Nolan; YUKON-KOYUKUK; see Wiseman (CDP)
Nome; Inc. Place; NOME; **144** D-4; elev. 20ft./6m.; 🅿 🅷; **z** 99762; location of Indian Agency; Ⓟ 3,500; © 3,505
NOME; ***144** D-5; Ⓟ 8,288; © 9,196; ◆ 9,316
Nondalton; Inc. Place; LAKE AND PENINSULA; **144** G-7; 🅿; **z** 99640; Ⓟ 178; © 221
Nooiksut; NORTH SLOPE; see Nuiqsut (Inc. Place)
Noorvik; Inc. Place; NORTHWEST ARCTIC; **144** C-5; 🅿; **z** 99763; Ⓟ 531; © 634
North Douglas; RMC Place; JUNEAU; mail Juneau **z** 99801; pop. incl. with Juneau (Inc. Place)
North Pole; Inc. Place; FAIRBANKS NORTH STAR; **144** E-9; 🅿; ★ **FRBK**; **z** 99705; Ⓟ 1,456; © 1,570
NORTH SLOPE; ***144** B-7; Ⓟ 5,979; © 7,385; ◆ 6,394
Northway; CDP; SOUTHEAST FAIRBANKS; ***144** F-10; 🅿; **z** 99764; Ⓟ 123; © 95
Northway Junction; CDP-Census Area Only; SOUTHEAST FAIRBANKS; **144** E-10; elev. 1,808ft./551m.; mail Northway **z** 99764; Ⓟ 88; © 72
Northway Village; CDP; SOUTHEAST FAIRBANKS; ***144** E-10; elev. 1,713ft./522m.; mail Northway **z** 99764; Ⓟ 113; © 107
NORTHWEST ARCTIC; ***144** C-6; Ⓟ 6,113; © 7,208; ◆ 7,500
Nuiqsut (Nooiksut); Inc. Place; NORTH SLOPE; **144** A-8; 🅿; **z** 99789; Ⓟ 354; © 433
Nulato; Inc. Place; YUKON-KOYUKUK; **144** D-6; 🅿; **z** 99765; Ⓟ 359; © 336
Nunaka Valley; RMC Place; ANCHORAGE; ★ **ANCH**; mail Anchorage **z** 99504; pop. incl. with Anchorage (Inc. Place)
Nunam Iqua (Sheldon Point); Inc. Place; WADE HAMPTON; **144** F-4; 🅿; **z** 99666; Ⓟ 109; © 164
Nunapitchuk; Inc. Place; BETHEL; **144** G-4; 🅿; **z** 99641; Ⓟ 378; © 466
Nyac; RMC Place; BETHEL; ***144** G-5; mail Aniak **z** 99557; ● 20

O

Okagamute; RMC Place; BETHEL; mail Kalskag **z** 99607
Old Andreafski; RMC Place; WADE HAMPTON; mail Saint Marys **z** 99658
Old Chatanika; FAIRBANKS NORTH STAR; see Chatanika (RMC Place)
Old Harbor; Inc. Place; KODIAK ISLAND; **144** I-7; 🅿; **z** 99643; Ⓟ 284; © 237
Old Kvichak; LAKE AND PENINSULA; see Levelock (CDP)
Olnes; RMC Place; FAIRBANKS NORTH STAR; ***144** D-9; elev. 1,000ft./305m.; mail Fairbanks **z** 99701; rural
Olsonville; RMC Place; DILLINGHAM; ***144** H-6; elev. 50ft./15m.; mail Dillingham **z** 99576; ● 80
Oscarville; CDP; BETHEL; ***144** G-5; mail Bethel **z** 99559; Ⓟ 57; © 61
Ouzinkie (Uzinki); Inc. Place; KODIAK ISLAND; **144** H-7; 🅿; **z** 99644; Ⓟ 209; © 225

P

Palmer; Inc. Place; MATANUSKA-SUSITNA; **144** F-8; 🅿 🅷; ★ **ANCH**; **z** 99645; Ⓟ 2,866; © 4,533
Paradise Hill; RMC Place; YUKON-KOYUKUK; ***144** F-5; elev. 73ft./22m.; mail Holy Cross **z** 99602; pop. incl. with Holy Cross (Inc. Place)
Parks; KODIAK ISLAND; see Uyak (RMC Place)
Paxson; CDP-Census Area Only; VALDEZ-CORDOVA; **144** F-9; mail Delta Junction **z** 99737; Ⓟ 30; © 43
Pederson Point; RMC Place; DILLINGHAM; mail Naknek **z** 99633
Pedro Bay; CDP; LAKE AND PENINSULA; **144** G-7; 🅿; **z** 99647; Ⓟ 42; © 50
Pelican; Inc. Place; SKAGWAY-HOONAH-ANGOON; **144** H-12; 🅿; **z** 99832; Ⓟ 222; © 163
Peninsula Point; RMC Place; KETCHIKAN GATEWAY; ***144** I-13; elev. 100ft./30m.; mail Ketchikan **z** 99901; ● 130
Pennock Island; RMC Place; KETCHIKAN GATEWAY; ***144** I-14; elev. 100ft./30m.; mail Ketchikan **z** 99901; ● 100
Perryville; CDP; LAKE AND PENINSULA; **144** I-5; 🅿; **z** 99648; Ⓟ 108; © 107
Petersburg; Inc. Place; WRANGELL-PETERSBURG; **144** I-13; 🅿 🅷; **z** 99833; Ⓟ 3,207; © 3,224
Peters Creek; RMC Place; ANCHORAGE; ★ **ANCH**; mail Chugiak **z** 99567; pop. incl. with Anchorage (Inc. Place)
Petersville; CDP; MATANUSKA-SUSITNA; **144** F-8; © 27
Pilot Point; Inc. Place; LAKE AND PENINSULA; **144** H-6; 🅿; **z** 99649; Ⓟ 53; © 100
Pilot Station; Inc. Place; WADE HAMPTON; **144** F-5; 🅿; **z** 99650; Ⓟ 463; © 550
Pitkas Point; CDP; WADE HAMPTON; **144** F-4; mail Saint Marys **z** 99658; Ⓟ 135; © 125
Pittman; RMC Place; MATANUSKA-SUSITNA; ***144** F-8; mail Wasilla **z** 99654; ● 10
Platinum; Inc. Place; BETHEL; **144** H-5; 🅿; **z** 99651; Ⓟ 64; © 41
Pleasant Valley; CDP-Census Area Only; FAIRBANKS NORTH STAR; ***144** D-9; mail Fairbanks **z** 99712; Ⓟ 401; © 623
Point Baker; CDP; PRINCE OF WALES-OUTER KETCHIKAN; **144** I-13; 🅿; **z** 99927; Ⓟ 39; © 35
Point Higgins; RMC Place; KETCHIKAN GATEWAY; ***144** I-13; elev. 100ft./30m.; mail Ketchikan **z** 99901; ● 30
Point Hope (Tigara); Inc. Place; NORTH SLOPE; **144** B-4; 🅿; **z** 99766; Ⓟ 639; © 757
Point Lay; CDP; NORTH SLOPE; **144** A-5; 🅿; **z** 99759; Ⓟ 139; © 247
Point MacKenzie; CDP-Census Area Only; MATANUSKA-SUSITNA; ***144** G-8; © 111
Point Whiteshed; RMC Place; VALDEZ-CORDOVA; ***144** G-9; elev. 400ft./122m.; mail Cordova **z** 99574; rural
Poorman; RMC Place; YUKON-KOYUKUK; **144** E-7; mail Ruby **z** 99768; rural
Pope-Vannoy Landing; CDP-Census Area Only; LAKE AND PENINSULA; ***144** G-7; © 8
Portage; RMC Place; ANCHORAGE; ★ **ANCH**; mail Girdwood **z** 99587; pop. incl. with Anchorage (Inc. Place)
Portage Creek; CDP-Census Area Only; DILLINGHAM; ***144** H-6; mail Anchorage **z** 99695; © 36
Port Alexander; Inc. Place; WRANGELL-PETERSBURG; **144** I-13; 🅿; **z** 99836; Ⓟ 119; © 81
Port Alice; RMC Place; PRINCE OF WALES-OUTER KETCHIKAN; ***144** I-13; mail Ketchikan **z** 99901; Ⓟ 30; ● 30
Port Alsworth; CDP; LAKE AND PENINSULA; **144** G-7; 🅿; **z** 99653; Ⓟ 55; © 104
Port Armstrong; RMC Place; SITKA; ***144** I-13; mail Port Alexander **z** 99836; ● 10
Port Ashton; RMC Place; VALDEZ-CORDOVA; ***144** G-8; mail Anchorage **z** 99695; rural
Port Bailey; RMC Place; KODIAK ISLAND; ***144** H-7; mail Kodiak **z** 99697; summer pop. 60
Port Chilkoot; RMC Place; HAINES; pop. incl. with Haines (RMC Place)
Port Clarence; CDP; NOME; ***144** D-4; mail Fairbanks **z** 99790; Ⓟ 26; © 21
Port Graham; CDP; KENAI PENINSULA; **144** H-7; 🅿; **z** 99603; Ⓟ 166; © 171
Port Heiden (Meshik); Inc. Place; LAKE AND PENINSULA; **144** I-5; 🅿; **z** 99549; Ⓟ 119; © 119
Port Lions; Inc. Place; KODIAK ISLAND; **144** H-7; 🅿; **z** 99550; Ⓟ 222; © 256
Portlock; RMC Place; KENAI PENINSULA; ***144** H-7; mail Seldovia **z** 99663; ● 30
Port Moller; RMC Place; ALEUTIANS EAST; **144** I-5; mail Cold Bay **z** 99571; ● 30
Port Protection; CDP-Census Area Only; PRINCE OF WALES-OUTER KETCHIKAN; ***144** I-13; mail Ketchikan **z** 99901; Ⓟ 62; © 63
Port Williams; RMC Place; KODIAK ISLAND; ***144** H-7; mail Kodiak **z** 99697; rural
Potter; RMC Place; ANCHORAGE; ★ **ANCH**; mail Anchorage **z** 99501; pop. incl. with Anchorage (Inc. Place)
Primrose; CDP-Census Area Only; KENAI PENINSULA; ***144** G-8; mail Seward **z** 99664; Ⓟ 63; © 93
PRINCE OF WALES-OUTER KETCHIKAN; ***144** I-14; Ⓟ 6,278; © 6,146; Ⓡ 6,157; ◆ 5,294
Prudhoe Bay; CDP-Census Area Only; NORTH SLOPE; **144** A-8; 🅿; **z** 99734; Ⓟ 47; © 5

Q

Quartz Creek; RMC Place; KENAI PENINSULA; mail Cooper Landing **z** 99572, Moose Pass **z** 99631; summer pop. 200
Queen; RMC Place; BRISTOL BAY; mail Dillingham **z** 99576
Quinhagak; Inc. Place; BETHEL; **144** G-5; 🅿; **z** 99655; Ⓟ 501; © 555

R

Rainbow; RMC Place; ANCHORAGE; ★ **ANCH**; mail Anchorage **z** 99501; pop. incl. with Anchorage (Inc. Place)
Rampart; CDP; YUKON-KOYUKUK; **144** D-8; 🅿; **z** 99767; Ⓟ 68; © 45
Red Devil; CDP; BETHEL; **144** F-6; 🅿; **z** 99656; Ⓟ 53; © 48
Red Dog Mine; CDP-Census Area Only; NORTHWEST ARCTIC; ***144** B-5; © 32
Red Mountain; RMC Place; KENAI PENINSULA; mail Homer **z** 99603; ● 60
Red Salmon; RMC Place; DILLINGHAM; mail Naknek **z** 99633
Ridgeway; CDP-Census Area Only; KENAI PENINSULA; ***144** G-8; mail Soldotna **z** 99669; Ⓟ 201; © 1,932
Rodman; RMC Place; SITKA; mail Sitka **z** 99835; pop. incl. with Sitka (Inc. Place)
Rogers Park; RMC Place; ANCHORAGE; ★ **ANCH**; mail Anchorage **z** 99508; pop. incl. with Anchorage (Inc. Place)
Ruby; Inc. Place; YUKON-KOYUKUK; **144** E-7; 🅿; **z** 99768; Ⓟ 170; © 188
Russian Jack; RMC Place; ANCHORAGE; mail Anchorage **z** 99514; pop. incl. with Anchorage (Inc. Place)
Russian Mission; Inc. Place; WADE HAMPTON; **144** F-5; 🅿; **z** 99657; Ⓟ 246; © 296

S

Sagwon; RMC Place; NORTH SLOPE; **144** B-8
Saint George (Saint George Island); Inc. Place; ALEUTIANS WEST; **144** I-10; mail Saint George Island **z** 99591; Ⓟ 138; © 152
Saint George Island; ALEUTIANS WEST; see Saint George (Inc. Place)
Saint Marys; Inc. Place; WADE HAMPTON; **144** F-4; 🅿; **z** 99658; Ⓟ 441; © 500
Saint Marys Mission; RMC Place; WADE HAMPTON; mail Saint Marys **z** 99658; pop. incl. with Saint Marys (Inc. Place)
Saint Michael; Inc. Place; NOME; **144** E-5; 🅿; **z** 99659; Ⓟ 295; © 368
Saint Paul (Saint Paul Island); Inc. Place; ALEUTIANS WEST; **144** I-10; mail Saint George Island **z** 99591, Saint Paul Island **z** 99660; Ⓟ 763; © 532
Saint Paul Island; ALEUTIANS WEST; see Saint Paul (Inc. Place)
Salamatof; CDP; KENAI PENINSULA; ***144** G-8; elev. 32ft./10m.; mail Kenai **z** 99611; Ⓟ 999; © 954
Salcha; CDP-Census Area Only; FAIRBANKS NORTH STAR; ***144** E-9; 🅿; **z** 99714; Ⓟ 354; © 854
Salchaket; FAIRBANKS NORTH STAR; see Aurora Lodge (RMC Place)
Salmon Creek; RMC Place; JUNEAU; mail Juneau **z** 99801; pop. incl. with Juneau (Inc. Place)
Sand Lake; RMC Place; ANCHORAGE; ★ **ANCH**; mail Anchorage **z** 99502, **z** 99517-18, **z** 99522; pop. incl. with Anchorage (Inc. Place)
Sand Point; Inc. Place; ALEUTIANS EAST; **144** J-5; 🅿; **z** 99661; Ⓟ 878; © 952
San Juan; KODIAK ISLAND; see Uganik (RMC Place)
Savoonga; Inc. Place; NOME; **144** E-3; 🅿; **z** 99769; Ⓟ 519; © 643
Saxman; Inc. Place; KETCHIKAN GATEWAY; ***144** I-14; mail Ketchikan **z** 99901; Ⓟ 369; © 431; Ⓡ 402
Saxman East; RMC Place; KETCHIKAN GATEWAY; mail Ketchikan **z** 99901; pop. incl. with Saxman (Inc. Place)
Scammon Bay; Inc. Place; WADE HAMPTON; **144** F-4; 🅿; **z** 99662; Ⓟ 343; © 465
Scow Bay; RMC Place; WRANGELL-PETERSBURG; ***144** I-13; elev. 50ft./15m.; mail Petersburg **z** 99833; ● 100
Seal Bay; RMC Place; KODIAK ISLAND; ***144** H-7; elev. 300ft./91m.; mail Kodiak **z** 99697; rural
Selawik; Inc. Place; NORTHWEST ARCTIC; **144** C-6; 🅿; **z** 99770; Ⓟ 596; © 772
Seldovia; Inc. Place; KENAI PENINSULA; **144** H-7; 🅿; **z** 99663; Ⓟ 316; © 286
Seldovia Village; CDP-Census Area Only; KENAI PENINSULA; ***144** H-7; © 144
Seward; Inc. Place; KENAI PENINSULA; **144** G-8; 🅿 🅷; **z** 99664; Ⓟ 2,699; © 2,830
Shageluk; Inc. Place; YUKON-KOYUKUK; **144** F-5; 🅿; **z** 99665; Ⓟ 139; © 129
Shaktolik; NOME; see Shaktoolik (Inc. Place)
Shaktoolik (Shaktolik); Inc. Place; NOME; **144** E-5; 🅿; **z** 99771; Ⓟ 178; © 230
Shanley; RMC Place; FAIRBANKS NORTH STAR; ★ **FRBK**; mail Fairbanks **z** 99701; pop. incl. with Fairbanks (Inc. Place)
Sheldon Point; WADE HAMPTON; see Nunam Iqua (Inc. Place)
Shemya Station; RMC Place; ALEUTIANS WEST; ***144** J-7; mail Anchorage **z** 99501; ● 30
Shishmaref; Inc. Place; NOME; **144** C-4; 🅿; **z** 99772; Ⓟ 456; © 562
Shungnak; Inc. Place; NORTHWEST ARCTIC; **144** C-6; 🅿; **z** 99773; Ⓟ 223; © 256
Silver Springs; CDP-Census Area Only; VALDEZ-CORDOVA; ***144** F-9; © 130
Sitka; Inc. Place; SITKA; **144** I-12; 🅿 🅷; **z** 99835-36; Ⓟ 8,588; © 8,835
SITKA; ***144** I-12; Ⓟ 8,588; © 8,835; ◆ 8,543
Situk; RMC Place; YAKUTAT; mail Yakutat **z** 99689
Skagway; Inc. Place; SKAGWAY-HOONAH-ANGOON; **144** G-12; 🅿; **z** 99840; Ⓟ 692; © 862
SKAGWAY-HOONAH-ANGOON; ***144** H-12; split into Skagway municipality and Hoonah-Angoon census area on June 20, 2007; Ⓟ 3,851; © 3,436; ◆ 3,117
Skwentna; CDP-Census Area Only; MATANUSKA-SUSITNA; **144** F-8; 🅿; **z** 99667; Ⓟ 85; © 111
Slana; CDP; VALDEZ-CORDOVA; **144** F-10; 🅿; **z** 99586; Ⓟ 63; © 124
Slaterville; RMC Place; FAIRBANKS NORTH STAR; ***144** E-8; ★ **FRBK**; mail Fairbanks **z** 99701; pop. incl. with Fairbanks (Inc. Place)
Sleetmute; CDP; BETHEL; **144** F-6; 🅿; **z** 99668; Ⓟ 106; © 100
Smith Ranch; FAIRBANKS NORTH STAR; see South Bjerremark (RMC Place)
Snowball; RMC Place; FAIRBANKS NORTH STAR; mail Fairbanks **z** 99701
Snug Harbor; RMC Place; KENAI PENINSULA; ***144** G-8; mail Cooper Landing **z** 99572; summer pop. 100
Soldatna; KENAI PENINSULA; see Soldotna (Inc. Place)
Soldotna (Soldatna); Inc. Place; KENAI PENINSULA; **144** G-8; 🅿 🅷; **z** 99669; Ⓟ 3,482; © 3,759
Solomon; RMC Place; NOME; ***144** D-4; mail Fairbanks **z** 99790; rural
Sourdough; RMC Place; VALDEZ-CORDOVA; **144** F-9; elev. 1,949ft./594m.; mail Gakona **z** 99586; ● 30
South; RMC Place; ANCHORAGE; ★ **ANCH**; mail Anchorage **z** 99511; pop. incl. with Anchorage (Inc. Place)
South Bjerremark (Smith Ranch); RMC Place; FAIRBANKS NORTH STAR; ***144** E-8; elev. 425ft./130m.; ★ **FRBK**; mail Fairbanks **z** 99701; ● 500
SOUTHEAST FAIRBANKS; ***144** E-10; Ⓟ 5,913; © 6,174; ◆ 6,972
South Naknek; CDP; BRISTOL BAY; ***144** H-6; 🅿; **z** 99670; Ⓟ 136; © 137
Spenard; RMC Place; ANCHORAGE; ***144** G-8; ★ **ANCH**; mail Anchorage **z** 99509; pop. incl. with Anchorage (Inc. Place)
Squaw Harbor; RMC Place; ALEUTIANS EAST; **144** J-5; elev. 21ft./6m.; mail Sand Point **z** 99661; rural
Starr Hill; RMC Place; JUNEAU; ***144** H-12; mail Juneau **z** 99801; pop. incl. with Juneau (Inc. Place)
Stebbins; Inc. Place; NOME; **144** E-5; 🅿; **z** 99671; Ⓟ 400; © 547
Steele Creek; RMC Place; SOUTHEAST FAIRBANKS; ***144** E-10; elev. 1,788ft./545m.; mail Eagle **z** 99738; rural
Steese (Curry's Corner); RMC Place; FAIRBANKS NORTH STAR; ***144** D-9; 🅿; ★ **FRBK**; **z** 99710; ● 100
Sterling; CDP; KENAI PENINSULA; ***144** G-8; 🅿; **z** 99672; Ⓟ 3,802; © 4,705
Stevens Village; CDP; YUKON-KOYUKUK; **144** D-8; 🅿; **z** 99774 & mail Saint George Island **z** 99591, Saint Paul Island **z** 99660; Ⓟ 102; © 87
Stony River; CDP; BETHEL; **144** F-6; 🅿; **z** 99557; Ⓟ 51; © 61
Strawberry Point; SKAGWAY-HOONAH-ANGOON; see Gustavus (Inc. Place)
Strelna; RMC Place; VALDEZ-CORDOVA; ***144** F-10; mail Chitina **z** 99566; ● 30
Summit; RMC Place; DENALI; ***144** E-8; elev. 2,332ft./711m.; mail Cantwell **z** 99729; ● 30
Summit Lodge; RMC Place; VALDEZ-CORDOVA; mail Gakona **z** 99586
Sunnyside; RMC Place; SKAGWAY-HOONAH-ANGOON; ***144** H-12; mail Pelican **z** 99832; ● 20
Sunrise; CDP-Census Area Only; KENAI PENINSULA; ***144** G-8; © 18
Sunshine; RMC Place; MATANUSKA-SUSITNA; ***144** F-8; elev. 350ft./107m.; mail Anchorage **z** 99695; ● 100
Suntrana; RMC Place; DENALI; **144** E-8; elev. 1,500ft./457m.; mail Healy **z** 99743; rural
Susitna; CDP; MATANUSKA-SUSITNA; ***144** F-8; © 37
Sutton; RMC Place; MATANUSKA-SUSITNA; **144** F-8; 🅿; **z** 99674; Ⓟ 308; ● 310
Sutton-Alpine; CDP-Census Area Only; MATANUSKA-SUSITNA; ***144** F-8; © 1,080

T

Takotna; CDP; YUKON-KOYUKUK; **144** F-6; 🅿; **z** 99675; Ⓟ 38; © 50
Talkeetna; CDP; MATANUSKA-SUSITNA; **144** F-8; 🅿; **z** 99676; Ⓟ 250; © 772
Tanacross; CDP; SOUTHEAST FAIRBANKS; **144** E-10; 🅿; **z** 99776; Ⓟ 106; © 140
Tanaina; CDP-Census Area Only; MATANUSKA-SUSITNA; ***144** F-8; © 4,993
Tanana; Inc. Place; YUKON-KOYUKUK; **144** D-7; 🅿; **z** 99777; Ⓟ 345; © 308
Tatalina; RMC Place; YUKON-KOYUKUK; ***144** F-6; elev. 1,253ft./382m.; mail Mc Grath **z** 99627; rural
Tatitlek; CDP; VALDEZ-CORDOVA; **144** G-9; 🅿; **z** 99677; Ⓟ 119; © 107
Taylor; RMC Place; NOME; **144** D-4; mail Nome **z** 99762
Tazlina; CDP; VALDEZ-CORDOVA; ***144** F-9; © 149
Tee Harbor; RMC Place; JUNEAU; mail Juneau **z** 99801; pop. incl. with Juneau (Inc. Place)
Telida; RMC Place; YUKON-KOYUKUK; ***144** E-7; mail Anchorage **z** 99695; ● 10
Teller; Inc. Place; NOME; **144** D-4; 🅿; **z** 99778; Ⓟ 151; © 268
Teller Mission; NOME; see Brevig Mission (Inc. Place)
Tenakee Springs; Inc. Place; SKAGWAY-HOONAH-ANGOON; **144** H-12; 🅿; **z** 99841 & mail Stevens Village **z** 99774; Ⓟ 94; © 104
Terror Bay; RMC Place; KODIAK ISLAND; ***144** H-7; mail Kodiak **z** 99697; ● 10
Tetlin; CDP; SOUTHEAST FAIRBANKS; **144** E-10; Ⓟ 87; © 117
Tetlin Junction; RMC Place; SOUTHEAST FAIRBANKS; **144** E-10; mail Tok **z** 99780; ● 30
Thane; RMC Place; JUNEAU; mail Juneau **z** 99801; pop. incl. with Juneau (Inc. Place)
Thoms Place; CDP-Census Area Only; WRANGELL-PETERSBURG; ***144** I-13; © 22
Thorne Bay; Inc. Place; PRINCE OF WALES-OUTER KETCHIKAN; **144** I-13; 🅿; **z** 99919; Ⓟ 569; © 557
Tiekel; RMC Place; VALDEZ-CORDOVA; ***144** F-9; elev. 1,500ft./457m.; mail Valdez **z** 99686; rural
Tigara; NORTH SLOPE; see Point Hope (Inc. Place)
Tin City; RMC Place; NOME; mail Nome **z** 99762, Wales **z** 99783
Togiak; Inc. Place; DILLINGHAM; **144** H-5; 🅿; **z** 99678; Ⓟ 613; © 809
Tok (Tok Junction); CDP; SOUTHEAST FAIRBANKS; **144** E-10; 🅿; **z** 99776, **z** 99780; Ⓟ 935; © 1,393
Tokeen; RMC Place; PRINCE OF WALES-OUTER KETCHIKAN; ***144** I-13; mail Ketchikan **z** 99901
Tok Junction; SOUTHEAST FAIRBANKS; see Tok (CDP)
Toksook; BETHEL; see Toksook Bay (Inc. Place)
Toksook Bay (Toksook); Inc. Place; BETHEL; **144** G-4; 🅿; **z** 99637; Ⓟ 420; © 532
Tolsona; CDP-Census Area Only; VALDEZ-CORDOVA; ***144** F-9; © 27
Tonsina; CDP; VALDEZ-CORDOVA; **144** F-9; elev. 1,878ft./572m.; mail Copper Center **z** 99573; Ⓟ 38; © 92
Totem Bight; RMC Place; KETCHIKAN GATEWAY; mail Ketchikan **z** 99901
Totem Park; RMC Place; FAIRBANKS NORTH STAR; ***144** E-8; ★ **FRBK**; mail Fairbanks **z** 99709; ● 1,070
Trapper Creek; CDP; MATANUSKA-SUSITNA; **144** F-8; 🅿; **z** 99683; Ⓟ 296; © 423
Tuluksak; CDP; BETHEL; **144** F-5; 🅿; **z** 99679; © 428
Tuntutuliak; CDP; BETHEL; **144** G-4; 🅿; **z** 99680; Ⓟ 300; © 370
Tununak; CDP; BETHEL; **144** G-4; 🅿; **z** 99681; © 325
Turnagain; RMC Place; ANCHORAGE; ★ **ANCH**; mail Anchorage **z** 99517; pop. incl. with Anchorage (Inc. Place)
Turnagain by-the-Sea; RMC Place; ANCHORAGE; ★ **ANCH**; mail Anchorage **z** 99517; pop. incl. with Anchorage (Inc. Place)
Turnagain Heights; RMC Place; ANCHORAGE; ★ **ANCH**; mail Anchorage **z** 99517; pop. incl. with Anchorage (Inc. Place)
Twin Hills; CDP; DILLINGHAM; **144** H-5; 🅿; **z** 99576; Ⓟ 66; © 69
Two Rivers; CDP; FAIRBANKS NORTH STAR; ***144** D-9; 🅿; **z** 99716; Ⓟ 453; © 482
Tyonek; CDP; KENAI PENINSULA; **144** G-8; 🅿; **z** 99682; Ⓟ 154; © 193

U

Uganik (San Juan); RMC Place; KODIAK ISLAND; **144** H-7; mail Kodiak **z** 99697; rural
Ugashik; CDP; LAKE AND PENINSULA; **144** I-6; mail King Salmon **z** 99613; © 11
Umiat; RMC Place; NORTH SLOPE; **144** B-7; elev. 275ft./84m.; mail Fairbanks **z** 99701; ● 30
Unalakleet; Inc. Place; NOME; **144** E-5; 🅿; **z** 99684; Ⓟ 714; © 747
Unalaska; Inc. Place; ALEUTIANS WEST; **144** I-11; 🅿; **z** 99685, **z** 99692 & mail Atka **z** 99547; Ⓟ 3,089; © 4,283
Ungalik; RMC Place; NOME; ***144** E-5; mail Unalakleet **z** 99684
Upper Kalskag; BETHEL; see Kalskag (Inc. Place)
Upper Mendenhall Valley; RMC Place; JUNEAU; mail Juneau **z** 99801; pop. incl. with Juneau (Inc. Place)
Upper Nickeyville; RMC Place; KETCHIKAN GATEWAY; mail Ketchikan **z** 99901; pop. incl. with Ketchikan (Inc. Place)
Usibelli; RMC Place; DENALI; ***144** E-8; mail Healy **z** 99743; rural
Uyak (Parks); RMC Place; KODIAK ISLAND; ***144** I-7; mail Kodiak **z** 99697; ● 10
Uzinki; KODIAK ISLAND; see Ouzinkie (Inc. Place)

V

Valdez; Inc. Place; VALDEZ-CORDOVA; **144** G-9; 🅿 🅷; **z** 99686; Ⓟ 4,068; © 4,036; Ⓡ 4,043
VALDEZ-CORDOVA; ***144** F-9; Ⓟ 9,952; © 10,195; ◆ 9,022
Vank Island; RMC Place; WRANGELL-PETERSBURG; ***144** I-13; elev. 100ft./30m.; mail Wrangell **z** 99929; ● 3
Venetie; CDP; YUKON-KOYUKUK; **144** C-9; 🅿; **z** 99781; Ⓟ 182; © 202
View Cove; RMC Place; PRINCE OF WALES-OUTER KETCHIKAN; ***144** I-13; mail Ketchikan **z** 99901; ● 20
Village Island; KODIAK ISLAND; see West Point (RMC Place)

W

Wacker; KETCHIKAN GATEWAY; see Ward Cove (RMC Place)
WADE HAMPTON; ***144** F-4; Ⓟ 5,791; © 7,028; ◆ 7,791
Wainwright; Inc. Place; NORTH SLOPE; **144** A-6; 🅿; **z** 99782; Ⓟ 492; © 546
Wales; Inc. Place; NOME; **144** D-4; 🅿; **z** 99783; Ⓟ 161; © 152
Ward Cove (Wacker); RMC Place; KETCHIKAN GATEWAY; ***144** I-13; 🅿; **z** 99928; ● 150
Wasilla; Inc. Place; MATANUSKA-SUSITNA; **144** F-8; 🅿; **z** 99629, **z** 99652, **z** 99654, **z** 99687 & mail Houston **z** 99694; Ⓟ 4,028; © 5,469
Waterfall; RMC Place; PRINCE OF WALES-OUTER KETCHIKAN; ***144** I-13; mail Ketchikan **z** 99901; summer pop. 100
West Fairwest; RMC Place; FAIRBANKS NORTH STAR; ***144** E-8; elev. 430ft./131m.; ★ **FRBK**; mail Fairbanks **z** 99701; ● 250
Westgate; RMC Place; FAIRBANKS NORTH STAR; ***144** E-8; ★ **FRBK**; mail Fairbanks **z** 99701; pop. incl. with Fairbanks (Inc. Place)
West Juneau; RMC Place; JUNEAU; mail Juneau **z** 99801; pop. incl. with Juneau (Inc. Place)
West Petersburg; WRANGELL-PETERSBURG; see Kupreanof (Inc. Place)
West Point (Village Island); RMC Place; KODIAK ISLAND; ***144** H-7; mail Kodiak **z** 99697; ● 10
Westwood; RMC Place; FAIRBANKS NORTH STAR; mail Fairbanks **z** 99701
Whale Pass; CDP; PRINCE OF WALES-OUTER KETCHIKAN; ***144** I-13; mail Ketchikan **z** 99901; Ⓟ 75; © 58
White Mountain; Inc. Place; NOME; **144** D-5; 🅿; **z** 99784; Ⓟ 180; © 203
Whitestone Logging Camp; CDP-Census Area Only; SKAGWAY-HOONAH-ANGOON; ***144** H-12; mail Hoonah **z** 99829; Ⓟ 164; © 116
Whitney; RMC Place; ANCHORAGE; ★ **ANCH**; mail Anchorage **z** 99501; pop. incl. with Anchorage (Inc. Place)
Whittier; Inc. Place; VALDEZ-CORDOVA; **144** G-8; 🅿; **z** 99693; Ⓟ 243; © 182
Wild Lake; RMC Place; YUKON-KOYUKUK; ***144** C-8; elev. 1,500ft./457m.; mail Bettles Field **z** 99726; rural
Willow; CDP; MATANUSKA-SUSITNA; **144** F-8; 🅿; **z** 99683, **z** 99688; Ⓟ 285; © 1,658
Willow Creek; CDP-Census Area Only; VALDEZ-CORDOVA; ***144** F-9; © 201
Wiseman (Nolan); CDP; YUKON-KOYUKUK; **144** C-8; mail Fairbanks **z** 99790; © 21
Womens Bay; CDP-Census Area Only; KODIAK ISLAND; ***144** I-7; mail Kodiak **z** 99615; Ⓟ 620; © 690
Woodland Park; RMC Place; ANCHORAGE; ★ **ANCH**; mail Anchorage **z** 99517; pop. incl. with Anchorage (Inc. Place)
Wood River; RMC Place; DILLINGHAM; ***144** H-6; elev. 25ft./8m.; mail Dillingham **z** 99576; rural
Wrangell; Inc. Place; WRANGELL-PETERSBURG; **144** I-13; 🅿 🅷; **z** 99929; Ⓟ 2,479; © 2,308
WRANGELL-PETERSBURG; ***144** I-13; Ⓟ 7,042; © 6,684; ◆ 5,949

Y

Y; CDP-Census Area Only; MATANUSKA-SUSITNA; ***144** F-8; © 956
Yakutat; CDP; YAKUTAT; **144** G-11; 🅿; **z** 99689; Ⓟ 534; © 680
YAKUTAT; ***144** G-11; Ⓟ 534; © 808; ◆ 718
Yankee Creek; RMC Place; BETHEL; mail Takotna **z** 99675; seasonal pop. 60; rural
YUKON-KOYUKUK; ***144** D-8; Ⓟ 6,714; © 6,551; Ⓡ 6,510; ◆ 5,803

Z

Zachar Bay; RMC Place; KODIAK ISLAND; ***144** I-7; mail Kodiak **z** 99697; summer pop. 100

Entries in **UPPERCASE** are boroughs or Census Areas.
Entries in **bold** have populations of 2,500 or more.
Names in parentheses are alternate names.

Inc. Place	Incorporated Place
RMC Place	Rand McNally Designated Place
CDP	Census Designated Place
MCD	Minor Civil Division

⊡	Borough or Census Area Seat
▲	Minor Civil Division
elev.	Elevation
🅿	Post Office
🅷	Hospital
🅲	College
■	Principal Business Center
★	Ranally Metro Area (RMA) Abbreviation
z	Zip Code(s)
Ⓟ	Previous Census Population
Ⓡ	Revised Census Population
Ⓐ	Annexation Population
●	Rand McNally Population Estimate
©	Final Census Population
Ⓢ	Special Census Population
◆	Estimated Population

For additional definitions see Glossary, Volume 1, and Introduction, Volume 2.

ARIZONA

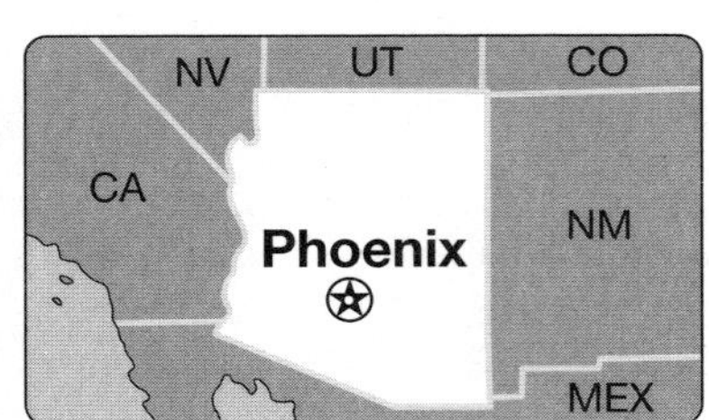

Statistics

Total area (2000) — 113,998 square miles
Land area (2000) — 113,635 square miles
Water area (2000) — 363 square miles
Capital — Phoenix
Admitted as state — February, 1912

Maps

State maps can be found on pages 142-254 in Vol. 1

Ranally Metro Areas (RMAs) and Abbreviations

Nogales, AZ-MEX. — NOGLS
Phoenix, AZ — PHOE
Tucson, AZ — TUC
Yuma, AZ-CA — YUMA

Principal Places

Place Name	Place Type	County	Population
Phoenix	Inc. Place	MARICOPA	◆ 1,675,791
Tucson	Inc. Place	PIMA	◆ 543,984
Mesa	Inc. Place	MARICOPA	◆ 475,847
Glendale	Inc. Place	MARICOPA	◆ 268,629
Chandler	Inc. Place	MARICOPA	◆ 250,632
Scottsdale	Inc. Place	MARICOPA	◆ 239,766
Gilbert	Inc. Place	MARICOPA	◆ 192,464
Peoria	Inc. Place	MARICOPA	◆ 176,537
Tempe	Inc. Place	MARICOPA	◆ 174,157
Yuma	Inc. Place	YUMA	◆ 93,000
Casas Adobes	CDP	PIMA	◆ 64,500
Catalina Foothills	CDP	PIMA	◆ 64,247
Avondale	Inc. Place	MARICOPA	◆ 63,757
Flagstaff	Inc. Place	COCONINO	◆ 63,307
Surprise	Inc. Place	MARICOPA	◆ 54,953
Maricopa	Inc. Place	PINAL	◆ 53,473
Lake Havasu City	Inc. Place	MOHAVE	◆ 52,465
Sun City	CDP	MARICOPA	◆ 51,147
Apache Junction	Inc. Place	PINAL	◆ 48,125
Casa Grande	Inc. Place	PINAL	◆ 43,290
Sierra Vista	Inc. Place	COCHISE	◆ 42,469
Bullhead City	Inc. Place	MOHAVE	◆ 41,823
Prescott	Inc. Place	YAVAPAI	◆ 40,148
Prescott Valley	Inc. Place	YAVAPAI	◆ 39,286
Oro Valley	Inc. Place	PIMA	◆ 39,145
Sun City West	CDP	MARICOPA	◆ 35,183

Place Name	Place Type	County	Population
Goodyear	Inc. Place	MARICOPA	◆ 32,566
Drexel Heights	CDP	PIMA	◆ 28,488
Fountain Hills	Inc. Place	MARICOPA	◆ 26,892
Florence	Inc. Place	PINAL	◆ 26,610
Kingman	Inc. Place	MOHAVE	◆ 26,489
Fortuna Foothills	CDP-Census Area Only	YUMA	◆ 23,692
San Luis	Inc. Place	YUMA	◆ 22,126
Nogales	Inc. Place	SANTA CRUZ	◆ 20,723
Marana	Inc. Place	PIMA	◆ 19,537
Sahuarita	Inc. Place	PIMA	◆ 19,454
Green Valley	CDP	PIMA	© 17,283
Douglas	Inc. Place	COCHISE	◆ 17,057
Tanque Verde	CDP	PIMA	© 16,195
Flowing Wells	CDP-Census Area Only	PIMA	© 15,050
New Kingman-Butler	CDP-Census Area Only	MOHAVE	© 14,810
Sierra Vista Southeast	CDP-Census Area Only	COCHISE	© 14,348
Mohave Valley	CDP-Census Area Only	MOHAVE	© 13,694
Paradise Valley	Inc. Place	MARICOPA	© 13,664
Payson	Inc. Place	GILA	© 13,620
Sun Lakes	CDP	MARICOPA	© 11,936
El Mirage	Inc. Place	MARICOPA	◆ 11,645
Buckeye	Inc. Place	MARICOPA	◆ 11,018
New River	CDP	MARICOPA	© 10,740
Cottonwood-Verde Village	CDP-Census Area Only	YAVAPAI	© 10,610
Eloy	Inc. Place	PINAL	© 10,375
Sedona	Inc. Place	COCONINO	© 10,192

Place Name	Place Type	County	Population
Tucson Estates	CDP	PIMA	© 9,755
Winslow	Inc. Place	NAVAJO	© 9,520
Camp Verde	Inc. Place	YAVAPAI	© 9,451
Safford	Inc. Place	GRAHAM	© 9,232
Cottonwood	Inc. Place	YAVAPAI	© 9,179
Tuba City	CDP	COCONINO	© 8,225
Picture Rocks	CDP-Census Area Only	PIMA	© 8,139
Chino Valley	Inc. Place	YAVAPAI	© 7,835
Coolidge	Inc. Place	PINAL	© 7,786
Queen Creek	Inc. Place	MARICOPA	◆ 7,695
Show Low	Inc. Place	NAVAJO	© 7,695
Globe	Inc. Place	GILA	© 7,486
Somerton	Inc. Place	YUMA	© 7,266
Catalina	CDP	PIMA	© 7,025
Page	Inc. Place	COCONINO	© 6,809
Dewey-Humboldt	CDP-Census Area Only	YAVAPAI	© 6,295
Bisbee	Inc. Place	COCHISE	© 6,090
Gold Camp	CDP-Census Area Only	PINAL	© 6,029
South Tucson	Inc. Place	PIMA	© 5,490
Chinle	CDP	APACHE	© 5,366
Three Points	CDP	PIMA	© 5,273
Big Park	CDP-Census Area Only	YAVAPAI	© 5,245
Guadalupe	Inc. Place	MARICOPA	© 5,228
Whiteriver	CDP	NAVAJO	© 5,220
Wickenburg	Inc. Place	MARICOPA	© 5,082
Avra Valley	CDP-Census Area Only	PIMA	© 5,038

County Business Data

County	FIPS Code	County Seat	Land Area (Sq. Mi.)	Census Population			Wholesale Trade		Manufacturing, 2002			
				4/1/2000	4/1/1990	% Change 1990-2000	Sales, 2002 ($1,000)	% Change 1997-2002	Establish-ments	Total Employees	Value Added ($1,000)	Ranally Mfg. Units
Apache	001	Saint Johns	11,205	69,423	61,591	12.7	(d)	(d)	...	(d)	(d)	...
Cochise	003	Bisbee	6,169	117,755	97,624	20.6	238,057	80.0	...	(d)	(d)	...
Coconino	005	Flagstaff	18,617	116,320	96,591	20.4	659,291	(d)	100	3,596	597,513	316
Gila	007	Globe	4,768	51,335	40,216	27.6	(d)	(d)	21	(d)	(d)	...
Graham	009	Safford	4,629	33,489	26,554	26.1	(d)	(d)	...	(d)	(d)	...
Greenlee	011	Clifton	1,847	8,547	8,008	6.7	(d)	(d)	...	(d)	(d)	...
La Paz	012	Parker	4,500	19,715	13,844	42.4	(d)	(d)	...	(d)	(d)	...
Maricopa	013	Phoenix	9,203	3,072,149	2,122,101	44.8	53,315,080	34.9	3,353	118,504	19,303,904	10,213
Mohave	015	Kingman	13,312	155,032	93,497	65.8	361,661	(d)	164	3,385	353,329	187
Navajo	017	Holbrook	9,953	97,470	77,658	25.5	134,427	36.3	47	(d)	(d)	
Pima	019	Tucson	9,186	843,746	666,880	26.5	2,842,167	3.0	748	29,393	3,937,005	2,083
Pinal	021	Florence	5,370	179,727	116,379	54.4	256,852	24.4	93	2,820	893,841	473
Santa Cruz	023	Nogales	1,238	38,381	29,676	29.3	1,180,807	5.0	41	(d)	(d)	...
Yavapai	025	Prescott	8,123	167,517	107,714	55.5	637,409	32.6	200	3,622	246,821	131
Yuma	027	Yuma	5,514	160,026	106,895	49.7	1,135,515	121.4	80	2,850	206,649	109
The State			**113,635**	**5,130,632**	**3,665,228**	**40.0**	**60,976,999**	**32.9**	**4,935**	**168,155**	**25,976,992**	**13,744**

(d) Data not available. Corresponding percentages or Ranally Manufacturing Units are estimates.
... Represents 0 or amount too minimal to be reported.

Index of Places and Counties

A

Adamana; RMC Place; APACHE; ***146** F-12; mail Holbrook **z** 86025; rural
Adamsville; RMC Place; PINAL; ***147** K-9; mail Florence **z** 85232; rural
Agua Caliente; RMC Place; MARICOPA; ***147** K-5; elev. 453ft./138m.; mail Dateland **z** 85333; rural
Agua Fria; YAVAPAI; see Prescott Valley (Inc. Place)
Agua Linda; RMC Place; SANTA CRUZ; ***147** N-10; mail Tumacacori **z** 85640; ● 120
Aguila; RMC Place; MARICOPA; **146** I-5; elev. 2,163ft./659m.; [P]; **z** 85320; ● 140
Ahwatukee; RMC Place; MARICOPA; ***146** J-8; ★ **PHOE**; mail Phoenix **z** 85044-45, **z** 85048, **z** 85076; pop. incl. with Phoenix (Inc. Place)
Airpark; RMC Place; MARICOPA; ★ **PHOE**; mail Scottsdale **z** 85260; pop. incl. with Scottsdale (Inc. Place)
Ajo; CDP; PIMA; **147** M-6; elev. 1,800ft./549m.; [P]; **z** 85321; Ⓟ 2,919; © 3,705
Ak Chin (San Serafin); RMC Place; PIMA; ***147** M-8; located on Papago Ind. Res.; mail Sells **z** 85634; ● 100
Akchin; PINAL; see Ak-Chin Village (CDP-Census Area Only)
Ak-Chin Village (Akchin); CDP-Census Area Only; PINAL; **147** K-7; located on Maricopa (Ak Chin) Ind. Res.; mail Maricopa **z** 85239; Ⓟ 353; © 669
Ak Chut Vaya; RMC Place; PIMA; mail Sells **z** 85634; rural
Alchesay Flat; RMC Place; NAVAJO; ***146** I-12; located on Navajo Nation Ind. Res.; mail Whiteriver **z** 85941; rural
Ali Chuk; RMC Place; PIMA; ***147** N-6; elev. 1,732ft./528m.; mail Sells **z** 85634; rural
Ali Chukson (Little Tucson); RMC Place; PIMA; ***147** N-8; located on Papago Ind. Res.; mail Sells **z** 85634; ● 150
Ali Molina; RMC Place; PIMA; ***147** N-8; elev. 2,679ft./817m.; mail Sells **z** 85634; rural
Allentown; RMC Place; APACHE; ***146** E-14; mail Houck **z** 86506; ● 50
Alpine; RMC Place; APACHE; **146** I-14; elev. 8,021ft./2,445m.; [P]; **z** 85920; ● 350
Amado; CDP; SANTA CRUZ; **147** N-10; elev. 3,070ft./936m.; [P]; **z** 85645 & mail Tumacacori **z** 85640; © 275
Amphitheater; RMC Place; PIMA; ★ **TUC**; pop. incl. with Tucson (Inc. Place)
Andersen Springs; RMC Place; MARICOPA; ★ **PHOE**; mail Chandler **z** 85224, **z** 85246; pop. incl. with Chandler (Inc. Place)
Anegam; RMC Place; PIMA; **147** M-8; located on Papago Ind. Res.; mail Sells **z** 85634; ● 100
Antares; RMC Place; MOHAVE; ***146** E-4; mail Kingman **z** 86401; ● 110
Anthem; RMC Place; MARICOPA; [P]; **z** 85086; pop. incl. with Phoenix (Inc. Place)
Apache; RMC Place; COCHISE; ***147** N-14; elev. 4,382ft./1,336m.; mail Rodeo **z** 88056; rural
APACHE; **146** E-13; Ⓟ 61,591; © 69,423; ◆ 67,681
Apache Flats; RMC Place; COCHISE; mail Fort Huachuca **z** 85613; pop. incl. with Sierra Vista (Inc. Place)
Apache Grove; RMC Place; GREENLEE; ***147** K-14; elev. 3,521ft./1,073m.; mail Duncan **z** 85534; ● 30
Apache Ho; RMC Place; PINAL; ***146** J-9; ★ **PHOE**; mail Apache Junction **z** 85220; pop. incl. with Apache Junction (Inc. Place)
Apache Junction; Inc. Place; PINAL, MARICOPA; **146** J-9; elev. 1,719ft./524m.; [P]; ★ **PHOE**; **z** 85117-20, **z** 85178, **z** 85217-20, **z** 85278, **z** 85290; Ⓟ 18,100; © 31,814; ◆ 48,125
Apache Wells; RMC Place; MARICOPA; ***146** J-8; ★ **PHOE**; mail Mesa **z** 85215; pop. incl. with Mesa (Inc. Place)
Araby; RMC Place; YUMA; ***147** L-2; elev. 212ft./65m.; ★ **YUMA**; mail Yuma **z** 85364; pop. incl. with Yuma (Inc. Place)
Arcadia; RMC Place; MARICOPA; ***146** J-8; ★ **PHOE**; mail Phoenix **z** 85018, **z** 85060; pop. incl. with Phoenix (Inc. Place)
Arcosanti; RMC Place; YAVAPAI; ***146** H-7; mail Mayer **z** 86333; ● 200
Aristuc; RMC Place; MARICOPA; ★ **PHOE**; pop. incl. with Phoenix (Inc. Place)
Arivaca; RMC Place; PIMA; **147** O-9; elev. 3,626ft./1,105m.; [P]; **z** 85601; ● 700
Arivaca Junction (Kinsley Ranch); RMC Place; PIMA; ***147** N-10; mail Tumacacori **z** 85640; ● 750
Arizola; RMC Place; PINAL; ***147** K-8; elev. 1,436ft./438m.; mail Casa Grande **z** 85222; ● 700
Arizona City; CDP; PINAL; **147** L-8; elev. 1,510ft./460m.; [P]; **z** 85123, **z** 85223; Ⓟ 1,940; © 4,385
Arizona Shores; RMC Place; LA PAZ; ***146** H-3; mail Parker **z** 85344; ● 60
Arizona Sun Sites (Sunsites); RMC Place; COCHISE; **147** N-12; mail Pearce **z** 85625
Arizona Village; CDP-Census Area Only; MOHAVE; ***146** F-2; © 351
Arlington; RMC Place; MARICOPA; **146** J-6; [P]; **z** 85322; ● 250
Arrowhead; RMC Place; MARICOPA; mail Glendale **z** 85318; pop. incl. with Glendale (Inc. Place)
Artesa; RMC Place; PIMA; ***147** N-8; located on Papago Ind. Res.; mail Sells **z** 85634; rural
Artesia; RMC Place; GRAHAM; ***147** L-13; mail Safford **z** 85546; ● 200
Asher; RMC Place; YUMA; mail Wellton **z** 85356; rural
Ash Fork; CDP; YAVAPAI; **146** E-7; elev. 5,139ft./1,566m.; [P]; **z** 86320; © 457
Ashurst; RMC Place; GRAHAM; mail Eden **z** 85535; rural
Auction; RMC Place; MARICOPA; ★ **PHOE**; pop. incl. with Phoenix (Inc. Place)
Avondale; Inc. Place; MARICOPA; **146** J-7; elev. 969ft./295m.; [P]; ★ **PHOE**; **z** 85323, **z** 85392; Ⓟ 16,169; © 35,883; ◆ 63,757
Avra Valley; CDP-Census Area Only; PIMA; ***147** M-9; ★ **TUC**; mail Marana **z** 85653; Ⓟ 3,403; © 5,038
Aztec; RMC Place; YUMA; ***147** K-5; mail Dateland **z** 85333

B

Baby Rocks; RMC Place; NAVAJO; ***146** A-12; located on Navajo Nation Ind. Res.; elev. 5,220ft./1,591m.; mail Kayenta **z** 86033; rural
Bacavi (Bacobi); RMC Place; NAVAJO; ***146** H-12; mail Hotevilla **z** 86030; ● 135
Bacobi; NAVAJO; see Bacavi (RMC Place)
Bagdad; CDP; YAVAPAI; **146** G-5; elev. 3,409ft./1,039m.; [P]; **z** 86321; Ⓟ 1,858; © 1,578
Bakerville; RMC Place; COCHISE; ***147** O-12; mail Bisbee **z** 85603; pop. incl. with Bisbee (Inc. Place)
Bapchule; RMC Place; PINAL; **147** K-8; elev. 1,200ft./366m.; [P]; **z** 85121, **z** 85221; ● 100
Beardsley; RMC Place; MARICOPA; ***146** I-7; ★ **PHOE**; mail Sun City **z** 85373; ● 60
Beautys Estates; RMC Place; SANTA CRUZ; ***147** O-10; elev. 3,804ft./1,159m.; ★ **NOGLS**; mail Nogales **z** 85621; pop. incl. with Nogales (Inc. Place)
Beaver Dam; RMC Place; MOHAVE; **145** J-3; mail Littlefield **z** 86432; ● 200
Beaver Valley Estates; RMC Place; GILA; ***146** H-9; elev. 4,800ft./1,463m.; mail Payson **z** 85541; ● 200
Bella Vista Estates; RMC Place; COCHISE; mail Sierra Vista **z** 85635; pop. incl. with Sierra Vista (Inc. Place)
Bellemont; RMC Place; COCONINO; **146** E-8; elev. 7,130ft./2,173m.; [P]; **z** 86015; ● 200
Benson; Inc. Place; COCHISE; **147** N-11; elev. 3,581ft./1,091m.; [P] [H]; **z** 85602; Ⓟ 3,824; © 4,711
Beyerville; RMC Place; SANTA CRUZ; ***147** O-10; elev. 3,640ft./1,109m.; mail Nogales **z** 85621; ● 120
Bidahochi (Bitahochee); RMC Place; NAVAJO; ***146** E-12; located on Navajo Nation Ind. Res.; elev. 5,741ft./1,750m.; mail Indian Wells **z** 86031; rural
Big Park; CDP-Census Area Only; YAVAPAI; ***146** G-8; mail Rimrock **z** 86335; Ⓟ 3,024; © 5,245
Bisbee; Inc. Place; ⊡ COCHISE; **147** O-12; elev. 5,400ft./1,646m.; [P] [H]; **z** 85603; Ⓟ 6,288; © 6,090
Bisbee Junction; RMC Place; COCHISE; **147** O-12; mail Bisbee **z** 85603; ● 30
Bitahochee; NAVAJO; see Bidahochi (RMC Place)
Bitter Springs; CDP; COCONINO; **145** K-10; located on Navajo Nation Ind. Res.; elev. 5,076ft./1,547m.; mail Marble Canyon **z** 86036; © 547
Black Canyon City; CDP; YAVAPAI; **146** H-7; [P]; **z** 85324; Ⓟ 1,811; © 2,697
Black Hills; RMC Place; YAVAPAI; mail Clarkdale **z** 86324; pop. incl. with Clarkdale (Inc. Place)
Black Mountain; RMC Place; APACHE; mail Blue Gap **z** 86520; ● 190
Blackwater; CDP; PINAL; ***147** K-8; located on Gila River Ind. Res.; elev. 1,386ft./422m.; mail Coolidge **z** 85228; Ⓟ 400; © 504
Blue; RMC Place; GREENLEE; **146** I-14; [P]; **z** 85922; ● 30
Blue Gap; RMC Place; APACHE; [P]; **z** 86520; ● 150
Bluewater; CDP-Census Area Only; LA PAZ; ***146** H-3; elev. 400ft./122m.; mail Parker **z** 85344; Ⓟ 505; © 730
Bonita; RMC Place; GRAHAM; **147** L-12; mail Willcox **z** 85643
Bouse; CDP; LA PAZ; **146** I-3; elev. 942ft./287m.; [P]; **z** 85325; © 615
Bowie; RMC Place; COCHISE; **147** M-13; elev. 3,762ft./1,147m.; [P]; **z** 85605; ● 550
Boys Ranch; RMC Place; MARICOPA; ***146** J-8; elev. 1,380ft./421m.; ★ **PHOE**; mail Queen Creek **z** 85242; pop. incl. with Queen Creek (Inc. Place)
Braemer; RMC Place; MARICOPA; ★ **PHOE**; mail Peoria **z** 85345; pop. incl. with Peoria (Inc. Place)
Branding Iron; RMC Place; PIMA; ***147** M-10; elev. 2,470ft./753m.; ★ **TUC**; mail Tucson **z** 85701; ● 600
Brenda; RMC Place; LA PAZ; ***146** I-4; elev. 1,353ft./412m.; mail Salome **z** 85348
Bridgeport; RMC Place; YAVAPAI; ***146** G-8; elev. 3,260ft./994m.; mail Cottonwood **z** 86326; ● 300
Briggs Townsite; RMC Place; COCHISE; mail Bisbee **z** 85603; pop. incl. with Bisbee (Inc. Place)
Bryce; RMC Place; GRAHAM; ***147** K-12; elev. 2,831ft./863m.; mail Pima **z** 85543
Buckeye; Inc. Place; MARICOPA; **146** J-6; elev. 870ft./265m.; [P]; ★ **PHOE**; **z** 85326, **z** 85396; Ⓟ 5,038; © 6,537; Ⓡ 8,497; ◆ 11,018
Buckhorn; RMC Place; MARICOPA; ***146** J-8; ★ **PHOE**; mail Mesa **z** 85205; pop. incl. with Mesa (Inc. Place)
Buena Vista; RMC Place; GRAHAM; ***147** K-13; mail Safford **z** 85546; rural
Bullhead City; Inc. Place; MOHAVE; **147** T-8; elev. 540ft./165m.; [P] [H]; **z** 86426-27, **z** 86429-30, **z** 86439, **z** 86442, **z** 86446; Ⓟ 21,951; © 33,769; ◆ 41,823
Bumble Bee; RMC Place; YAVAPAI; ***146** H-7; elev. 2,573ft./784m.; mail Mayer **z** 86333; rural
Burnside; CDP-Census Area Only; APACHE; ***146** D-13; © 632
Burnt Water; RMC Place; APACHE; ***146** E-13; located on Navajo Nation Ind. Res.; elev. 6,456ft./1,968m.; mail Sanders **z** 86512; rural
Bushman Acres; RMC Place; NAVAJO; ***146** F-10; elev. 4,845ft./1,477m.; mail Winslow **z** 86047; pop. incl. with Winslow (Inc. Place)
Bylas; RMC Place; GRAHAM; **147** K-12; located on San Carlos Ind. Res.; elev. 2,620ft./799m.; [P]; **z** 85530; Ⓟ 1,219; ● 600

C

Cababi; PIMA; see Ko Vaya (RMC Place)
Cactus; RMC Place; MARICOPA; ***146** J-8; ★ **PHOE**; mail Phoenix **z** 85032, **z** 85046, **z** 85078; pop. incl. with Phoenix (Inc. Place)
Cactus Flat; RMC Place; GRAHAM; ***147** L-13; mail Safford **z** 85546; rural
Cactus Forest; RMC Place; PINAL; ***147** K-9; mail Florence **z** 85232; ● 450
Calva; RMC Place; GRAHAM; ***147** K-12; elev. 2,579ft./786m.; mail Bylas **z** 85530; rural
Cameron; CDP; COCONINO; **146** D-9; elev. 4,197ft./1,279m.; [P]; **z** 86016, **z** 86020; Ⓟ 493; © 978
Camp Creek; RMC Place; MARICOPA; ***146** I-8; mail Cave Creek **z** 85331; ● 50
Camp McDowell; MARICOPA; see Fort McDowell (RMC Place)
Campo; RMC Place; MARICOPA; ★ **PHOE**; pop. incl. with Phoenix (Inc. Place)
Camp Verde; Inc. Place; YAVAPAI; **146** G-8; elev. 3,147ft./959m.; [P]; **z** 86322; Ⓟ 6,243; © 9,451
Cane Beds; RMC Place; MOHAVE; ***146** A-6; mail Fredonia **z** 86022
Canelo; RMC Place; SANTA CRUZ; ***147** O-11; mail Elgin **z** 85611; rural
Canyon; RMC Place; MARICOPA; ★ **PHOE**; mail Mesa **z** 85201; pop. incl. with Mesa (Inc. Place)
Canyon Day; CDP; GILA; ***146** I-12; mail Whiteriver **z** 85941; Ⓟ 857; © 1,092
Capitol; RMC Place; MARICOPA; ***146** J-7; ★ **PHOE**; mail Phoenix **z** 85005, **z** 85009; pop. incl. with Phoenix (Inc. Place)
Carefree; Inc. Place; MARICOPA; **146** I-8; elev. 2,389ft./728m.; [P]; ★ **PHOE**; **z** 85377; Ⓟ 1,666; © 2,927
Carmen; RMC Place; SANTA CRUZ; **147** O-10; elev. 3,242ft./988m.; mail Tumacacori **z** 85640; ● 400
Carrizo; RMC Place; GILA; **146** I-11; located on Fort Apache Ind. Res.; mail Show Low **z** 85901, Whiteriver **z** 85941; ● 140
Casa Adobes; RMC Place; PIMA; ★ **TUC**; mail Tucson **z** 85737, **z** 85739-40; pop. incl. with Tucson (Inc. Place)
Casa Blanca; RMC Place; PINAL; ***147** K-8; mail Bapchule **z** 85221; ● 600
Casa Grande; Inc. Place; PINAL; **147** K-8; [P] [H]; **z** 85122, **z** 85130, **z** 85193-94, **z** 85222, **z** 85230, **z** 85293-94; Ⓟ 19,082; © 25,224; ◆ 43,290
Casa Grande Farm Labor Camp; PINAL; see Eleven Mile Corner (RMC Place)
Casas Adobes; CDP; PIMA; ***147** M-10; ★ **TUC**; mail Tucson **z** 85704; © 54,011; ◆ 64,500
Cascabel; RMC Place; COCHISE; ***147** M-11; elev. 3,151ft./960m.; mail Benson **z** 85602; ● 30
Cashion; RMC Place; MARICOPA; ***146** J-7; elev. 986ft./301m.; [P]; ★ **PHOE**; **z** 85329; pop. incl. with Avondale (Inc. Place)
Castle Butte; RMC Place; NAVAJO; mail Winslow **z** 86047; rural
Castle Canyon Mesa; RMC Place; YAVAPAI; ***146** G-7; elev. 5,227ft./1,593m.; mail Prescott **z** 86301; ● 500
Castle Hot Springs; MARICOPA; see Morristown (RMC Place)
Castle Hot Springs (Champie); RMC Place; YAVAPAI; **146** I-7; mail Morristown **z** 85342
Castle Rock Shores; RMC Place; LA PAZ; ***146** H-3; mail Parker **z** 85344; ● 200
Catalina; CDP; PIMA; **147** L-10; elev. 3,138ft./956m.; [P]; ★ **TUC**; **z** 85738 & mail Tucson **z** 85739; Ⓟ 4,864; © 7,025
Catalina Foothills; CDP; PIMA; ***147** M-10; ★ **TUC**; mail Tucson **z** 85718; © 53,794; ◆ 64,247
Cave Creek; Inc. Place; MARICOPA; **146** I-8; elev. 2,196ft./669m.; [P]; ★ **PHOE**; **z** 85327, **z** 85331; Ⓟ 2,925; © 3,728
Cazador; RMC Place; COCHISE; mail Douglas **z** 85608; rural
Cedar Creek; RMC Place; GILA; ***146** I-12; located on Fort Apache Ind. Res.; mail Whiteriver **z** 85941
Cedar Ridge; RMC Place; COCONINO; **146** C-9; located on Navajo Nation Ind. Res.; mail Cameron **z** 86020; ● 40
Cedar Springs; RMC Place; NAVAJO; mail Winslow **z** 86047; ● 100
Centerville; RMC Place; YAVAPAI; ***146** G-8; mail Clarkdale **z** 86324; pop. incl. with Clarkdale (Inc. Place)
Central; RMC Place; GRAHAM; ***147** K-12; elev. 2,900ft./884m.; [P]; **z** 85531; ● 575
Central Heights; RMC Place; GILA; **146** J-10; mail Claypool **z** 85532, Globe **z** 85501; ● 2,000
Central Heights-Midland City; CDP-Census Area Only; GILA; ***146** J-10; mail Claypool **z** 85532; Ⓟ 2,969; © 2,694
Chair Crossing (Lees Ferry); RMC Place; COCONINO; ***146** A-9; elev. 3,135ft./956m.; mail Marble Canyon **z** 86036; rural
Chambers; RMC Place; APACHE; **146** E-13; located on Navajo Nation Ind. Res.; elev. 5,754ft./1,754m.; [P]; **z** 86502; ● 250
Champie; YAVAPAI; see Castle Hot Springs (RMC Place)
Chandler; Inc. Place; MARICOPA; **146** J-8; elev. 1,213ft./370m.; [P] [H]; ★ **PHOE**; **z** 85224-26, **z** 85244, **z** 85246, **z** 85248-49, **z** 85286; Ⓟ 90,533; © 176,581; ◆ 250,632
Chandler Heights; RMC Place; MARICOPA; ***147** K-8; elev. 1,420ft./433m.; [P]; ★ **PHOE**; **z** 85127, **z** 85142, **z** 85227, **z** 85242; ● 850
Chaparral; RMC Place; MARICOPA; ★ **PHOE**; mail Chandler **z** 85224; pop. incl. with Chandler (Inc. Place)
Cherry; RMC Place; YAVAPAI; **146** G-8; mail Dewey **z** 86327
Cheto; APACHE; see Sanders (RMC Place)
Chevelon; RMC Place; COCONINO; ***146** G-10; elev. 7,007ft./2,136m.; mail Flagstaff **z** 86001; ● 80
Chiawuli Tak (Fresnal Village); RMC Place; PIMA; ***147** N-8; located on Papago Ind. Res.; mail Sells **z** 85634; ● 100
Chilchinbito; CDP; NAVAJO; **146** B-12; mail Kayenta **z** 86033; © 462
Childs; RMC Place; PIMA; ***147** L-6; mail Ajo **z** 85321; rural
Chinle; CDP; APACHE; **146** C-13; located on Navajo Nation Ind. Res.; elev. 5,506ft./1,678m.; [P] [H]; **z** 86503, **z** 86507, **z** 86538, **z** 86545, **z** 86547, **z** 86556; location of Indian Agency; Ⓟ 5,059; © 5,366
Chino de Manana; RMC Place; YAVAPAI; ***146** G-7; elev. 4,640ft./1,414m.; mail Chino Valley **z** 86323; pop. incl. with Chino Valley (Inc. Place)
Chino Meadows; RMC Place; YAVAPAI; ***146** G-7; elev. 4,639ft./1,414m.; mail Chino Valley **z** 86323; pop. incl. with Chino Valley (Inc. Place)
Chino Valley; Inc. Place; YAVAPAI; **146** G-7; elev. 4,700ft./1,433m.; [P]; **z** 86323; Ⓟ 4,837; © 7,835
Chloride; RMC Place; MOHAVE; **146** E-3; elev. 4,009ft./1,222m.; [P]; **z** 86431; ● 225
Choulic; RMC Place; PIMA; ***147** N-8; mail Sells **z** 85634; rural
Christmas; RMC Place; GILA; mail Winkelman **z** 85292; rural
Christopher Creek; RMC Place; GILA; ***146** H-10; elev. 5,894ft./1,796m.; mail Payson **z** 85541; ● 110
Chuichu (Chui Chuischu); CDP; PINAL; **147** L-8; located on Papago Ind. Res.; elev. 1,457ft./444m.; mail Casa Grande **z** 85222; Ⓟ 330; © 339
Chui Chuischu; PINAL; see Chuichu (CDP)
Cibecue; CDP; NAVAJO; **146** H-11; located on Fort Apache Ind. Res.; elev. 4,940ft./1,506m.; [P]; **z** 85911; Ⓟ 1,254; © 1,331
Cibola; CDP; LA PAZ; ***146** J-2; [P]; **z** 85328; © 172
Cienega Springs; RMC Place; LA PAZ; ***146** H-3; mail Parker **z** 85344; ● 200
Circle City; RMC Place; MARICOPA; ***146** I-6; mail Morristown **z** 85342; ● 530
Citrus Gardens; RMC Place; MARICOPA; ***146** J-7; ★ **PHOE**; mail Mesa **z** 85201; pop. incl. with Mesa (Inc. Place)
Clarkdale; Inc. Place; YAVAPAI; **146** G-8; elev. 3,545ft./1,081m.; [P]; **z** 86324; Ⓟ 2,144; © 3,422
Claypool; CDP; GILA; **146** J-10; elev. 3,334ft./1,016m.; [P] [H]; **z** 85532; Ⓟ 1,942; © 1,794
Clay Springs; RMC Place; NAVAJO; **146** H-11; elev. 6,312ft./1,924m.; [P]; **z** 85923; ● 250
Cleator; RMC Place; YAVAPAI; ***146** H-7; mail Mayer **z** 86333
Clifton; Inc. Place; ⊡ GREENLEE; **147** K-13; elev. 3,468ft./1,057m.; [P]; **z** 85533; Ⓟ 2,840; © 2,596
Cloud Ridge Terrace; RMC Place; PIMA; ★ **TUC**; pop. incl. with Tucson (Inc. Place)
Coal Mine Mesa; RMC Place; COCONINO; ***146** D-10; located on Hopi Ind. Res.; mail Tuba City **z** 86045; rural
Cobblestone Village; RMC Place; MARICOPA; ★ **PHOE**; mail Peoria **z** 85381; pop. incl. with Peoria (Inc. Place)
Cochise; RMC Place; COCHISE; **147** M-12; elev. 4,225ft./1,288m.; [P]; **z** 85606; ● 100
COCHISE; **147** M-13; Ⓟ 97,624; © 117,755; ◆ 127,949
Cocklebur; PINAL; see Vaiva Vo (RMC Place)
COCONINO; **146** C-8; Ⓟ 96,591; © 116,320; ◆ 132,314
Cocopah Reservation; Indian Reservation; YUMA; ★ **YUMA**; mail Somerton **z** 85350; Ⓟ 355; © 1,025
Colcord Mountain Estates; RMC Place; GILA; ***146** H-10; elev. 6,287ft./1,916m.; mail Payson **z** 85541; rural
Colorado City (Short Creek); Inc. Place; MOHAVE; **146** A-6; elev. 5,000ft./1,524m.; [P]; **z** 86021; Ⓟ 2,426; © 3,334
Colorado River Reservation; Indian Reservation; LA PAZ; Reservation extends into CA; mail Parker **z** 85344; also location of Indian Agency; Ⓟ 6,640; © 7,466
Commerce; RMC Place; MARICOPA; ***146** J-8; ★ **PHOE**; mail Phoenix **z** 85030; pop. incl. with Phoenix (Inc. Place)
Comobabi; RMC Place; PIMA; **147** M-8; located on Papago Ind. Res.; mail Sells **z** 85634
Concho; RMC Place; APACHE; **146** G-13; elev. 5,931ft./1,808m.; [P]; **z** 85924; ● 400
Congress; CDP; YAVAPAI; **146** H-6; elev. 3,036ft./925m.; [P]; **z** 85332; © 1,717
Continental; RMC Place; PIMA; **147** N-10; mail Green Valley **z** 85614, Sahuarita **z** 85629
Coolidge; Inc. Place; PINAL; **147** K-9; elev. 1,430ft./436m.; [P]; **z** 85128, **z** 85228; Ⓟ 6,927; © 7,786
Coolidge Dam; RMC Place; GILA; ***147** K-11; elev. 2,708ft./825m.; mail Peridot **z** 85542; ● 30
Co-op Village; RMC Place; MARICOPA; ***146** J-7; located on Gila River Ind. Res.; ★ **PHOE**; mail Laveen **z** 85339; rural
Copper Mine; RMC Place; COCONINO; **145** K-10; located on Navajo Nation Ind. Res.; mail Page **z** 86040; ● 70
Copper Queen; RMC Place; COCHISE; ***147** O-12; mail Bisbee **z** 85603
Cordes; RMC Place; YAVAPAI; ***146** H-7; elev. 3,771ft./1,149m.; mail Mayer **z** 86333; rural
Cordes Junction; RMC Place; YAVAPAI; ***146** H-7; elev. 2,825ft./861m.; mail Mayer **z** 86333; ● 90
Cordes Lakes; CDP; YAVAPAI; ***146** H-7; elev. 3,680ft./1,122m.; [P]; **z** 86333; © 2,058
Cork; RMC Place; GRAHAM; ***147** K-12; mail Fort Thomas **z** 85536; rural
Cornfields; RMC Place; APACHE; **146** D-12; located on Navajo Nation Ind. Res.; mail Ganado **z** 86505
Cornville; CDP; YAVAPAI; **146** G-8; elev. 3,300ft./1,006m.; [P]; **z** 86325; Ⓟ 2,089; © 3,335
Coronada Foothills Estates; RMC Place; PIMA; ***147** M-10; ★ **TUC**; mail Tucson **z** 85718; ● 1,200
Corona de Tucson; CDP; PIMA; ***147** N-10; elev. 3,350ft./1,021m.; [P]; **z** 85641 & mail Tucson **z** 85747; © 813
Coronado; RMC Place; PIMA; ***147** M-10; ★ **TUC**; mail Tucson **z** 85711, **z** 85732; pop. incl. with Tucson (Inc. Place)
Cortaro; RMC Place; PIMA; **147** M-10; elev. 2,156ft./657m.; [P]; ★ **TUC**; **z** 85652; ● 250
Cotpro; RMC Place; MARICOPA; ★ **PHOE**; pop. incl. with Phoenix (Inc. Place)
Cottonwood (Cottonwood Station); RMC Place; APACHE; ***146** C-12; located on Navajo Nation Ind. Res.; mail Chinle **z** 86503
Cottonwood; Inc. Place; YAVAPAI; **146** G-8; elev. 3,314ft./1,010m.; [P] [H]; **z** 86326; Ⓟ 5,918; © 9,179
Cottonwood Station; APACHE; see Cottonwood (RMC Place)
Cottonwood-Verde Village; CDP-Census Area Only; YAVAPAI; ***146** G-8; mail Cottonwood **z** 86326; Ⓟ 7,037; © 10,610
Country Club Estates; RMC Place; COCHISE; ***147** O-11; elev. 4,528ft./1,380m.; mail Sierra Vista **z** 85650; pop. incl. with Sierra Vista (Inc. Place)
Cove; RMC Place; APACHE; ***146** B-13; located on Navajo Nation Ind. Res.; mail Shiprock **z** 87420; ● 50
Covered Wells; PIMA; see Maish Vaya (RMC Place)
Cowlic; RMC Place; PIMA; ***147** N-8; located on Papago Ind. Res.; elev. 2,098ft./639m.; mail Sells **z** 85634
Cow Springs; RMC Place; COCONINO; **146** C-10; located on Hopi Ind. Res.; mail Tonalea **z** 86044; ● 40
Craycroft; RMC Place; PIMA; ★ **TUC**; mail Tucson **z** 85712; pop. incl. with Tucson (Inc. Place)
Crestview; RMC Place; COCHISE; mail Bisbee **z** 85603; pop. incl. with Bisbee (Inc. Place)
Cross Canyon; RMC Place; APACHE; **146** D-13; located on Navajo Nation Ind. Res.; mail Saint Michaels **z** 86511; ● 30
Crown King; RMC Place; YAVAPAI; **146** H-7; elev. 5,800ft./1,768m.; [P]; **z** 86343; ● 100
Currys Corner; RMC Place; MARICOPA; mail Phoenix **z** 85054; pop. incl. with Scottsdale (Inc. Place)
Curtiss; RMC Place; COCHISE; mail Saint David **z** 85630; ● 300
Cutter; RMC Place; GILA; ***146** J-11; mail Globe **z** 85501; rural

D

Dam View; RMC Place; LA PAZ; ***146** H-3; mail Parker **z** 85344; ● 50
Date (Date Creek); RMC Place; YAVAPAI; ***146** H-6; mail Congress **z** 85332; rural
Date Creek; YAVAPAI; see Date (RMC Place)
Dateland; RMC Place; YUMA; **147** L-4; elev. 440ft./134m.; [P]; **z** 85333
Davis Dam; RMC Place; MOHAVE; ***146** E-2; mail Bullhead City **z** 86430; pop. incl. with Bullhead City (Inc. Place)
Del Rio; RMC Place; YAVAPAI; ***146** F-7; elev. 4,420ft./1,347m.; mail Chino Valley **z** 86323; rural

---

Entries in **UPPERCASE** are counties.
Entries in **bold** have populations of 2,500 or more.
Names in parentheses are alternate names.

Inc. Place	Incorporated Place
RMC Place	Rand McNally Designated Place
CDP	Census Designated Place
MCD	Minor Civil Division
⊡	County Seat
▲	Minor Civil Division
elev.	Elevation
[P]	Post Office
[H]	Hospital
[C]	College
■	Principal Business Center
★	Ranally Metro Area (RMA) Abbreviation
z	Zip Code(s)
Ⓟ	Previous Census Population
Ⓡ	Revised Census Population
Ⓐ	Annexation Population
●	Rand McNally Population Estimate
©	Final Census Population
Ⓢ	Special Census Population
◆	Estimated Population

For additional definitions see Glossary, Volume 1, and Introduction, Volume 2.

Dennehotso (Dinnehotso); CDP; APACHE; **146** A-12; located on Navajo Nation Ind. Res.; 🅿; z 86535; Ⓟ 616; Ⓒ 734
Desert; RMC Place; MARICOPA; ***146** J-8; ★ **PHOE**; mail Mesa z 85206, z 85208, z 85216; pop. incl. with Mesa (Inc. Place)
Desert Dells; RMC Place; PIMA; ★ **TUC**; pop. incl. with Tucson (Inc. Place)
Desert Harbor; RMC Place; MARICOPA; ★ **PHOE**; mail Peoria z 85381; pop. incl. with Peoria (Inc. Place)
Desert Hills; CDP-Census Area Only; MOHAVE; **147** S-10; 🅿; z 85086 & mail Lake Havasu City z 86403; Ⓟ 1,700; Ⓒ 2,183
Desert Sage; MARICOPA; see Twin Knolls (RMC Place)
Desert Sands; RMC Place; MARICOPA; ***146** J-8; elev. 1,400ft./427m.; ★ **PHOE**; mail Mesa z 85208; pop. incl. with Mesa (Inc. Place)
Desert Steppes; RMC Place; PIMA; ★ **TUC**; mail Tucson z 85710; pop. incl. with Tucson (Inc. Place)
Desert View; RMC Place; COCONINO; **146** C-8; elev. 7,438ft./2,267m.; mail Grand Canyon z 86023; ● 60
Dewey; RMC Place; YAVAPAI; **146** G-7; elev. 4,556ft./1,389m.; 🅿; z 86327; ● 700
Dewey-Humboldt; Inc. Place; YAVAPAI; ***146** G-7; mail Dewey z 86327, Humboldt z 86329; incorporated December 20, 2004; not reported in 2000 Census
Dewey-Humboldt; CDP-Census Area Only; YAVAPAI; ***146** G-7; mail Dewey z 86327, Humboldt z 86329; Ⓟ 3,640; Ⓒ 6,295
Diamond Point Summer Homes; RMC Place; GILA; ***146** H-9; elev. 5,600ft./1,707m.; mail Payson z 85541; ● 80
Diamond Star; GILA; see Star Valley (Inc. Place)
Diamond Valley; RMC Place; YAVAPAI; ***146** G-7; elev. 5,292ft./1,613m.; mail Prescott z 86301; ● 700
Dilkon; CDP; NAVAJO; **146** E-11; located on Navajo Nation Ind. Res.; elev. 5,885ft./1,794m.; mail Winslow z 86047; Ⓒ 1,265
Dinnehotso; APACHE; see Dennehotso (CDP)
Dinosaur City; COCONINO; see Grand Canyon Caverns (RMC Place)
Discovery at the Orchard; RMC Place; MARICOPA; ★ **PHOE**; mail Peoria z 85381; pop. incl. with Peoria (Inc. Place)
Dobson; RMC Place; MARICOPA; ★ **PHOE**; mail Mesa z 85202, z 85274; pop. incl. with Mesa (Inc. Place)
Dolan Springs; CDP; MOHAVE; **146** D-3; elev. 4,290ft./1,308m.; 🅿; z 86441; Ⓟ 1,090; Ⓒ 1,867
Dome; RMC Place; YUMA; ***147** L-3; elev. 191ft./58m.; mail Yuma z 85365; rural
Don Luis; RMC Place; COCHISE; ***147** O-12; mail Bisbee z 85603; pop. incl. with Bisbee (Inc. Place)
Dos Cabezas; RMC Place; COCHISE; **147** M-13; elev. 5,071ft./1,546m.; mail Willcox z 85643
Double Adobe; RMC Place; COCHISE; ***147** O-13; mail Mc Neal z 85617; ● 200
Douglas; Inc. Place; COCHISE; **147** O-13; elev. 4,004ft./1,220m.; 🅿 🄷 ■; z 85607-08, z 85655; Ⓟ 13,137; Ⓒ 14,312; ◆ 17,057
Downtown; RMC Place; COCONINO; ***146** F-8; mail Flagstaff z 86001; pop. incl. with Flagstaff (Inc. Place)
Downtown; RMC Place; MARICOPA; ***146** J-7; ★ **PHOE**; mail Phoenix z 85001-04, z 85007; pop. incl. with Phoenix (Inc. Place)
Downtown; RMC Place; MARICOPA; ***146** J-8; ★ **PHOE**; mail Tempe z 85281; pop. incl. with Tempe (Inc. Place)
Downtown; RMC Place; MOHAVE; ***146** F-9; mail Kingman z 86402
Downtown; RMC Place; PIMA; ***147** M-10; ★ **TUC**; mail Tucson z 85701-02; pop. incl. with Tucson (Inc. Place)
Downtown; RMC Place; YUMA; ★ **YUMA**; mail Yuma z 85364, z 85366; pop. incl. with Yuma (Inc. Place)
Dragoon; RMC Place; COCHISE; **147** N-12; elev. 4,615ft./1,407m.; 🅿; z 85609; ● 175
Drake; RMC Place; YAVAPAI; ***146** F-7; mail Paulden z 86334; rural
Dreamland Villa; RMC Place; MARICOPA; ***146** J-8; ★ **PHOE**; mail Mesa z 85205; ● 4,800
Drexel-Alvernon; CDP-Census Area Only; PIMA; ***147** M-10; ★ **TUC**; Ⓒ 4,192
Drexel Heights; CDP; PIMA; ***147** M-10; ★ **TUC**; mail Tucson z 85746; Ⓒ 23,849; ◆ 28,488
Dudleyville; CDP; PINAL; **147** K-10; 🅿; z 85192, z 85292; Ⓟ 1,356; Ⓒ 1,323
Dugas; RMC Place; YAVAPAI; ***146** H-8; elev. 3,937ft./1,200m.; mail Mayer z 86333; rural
Duncan; Inc. Place; GREENLEE; **147** L-14; elev. 759ft./231m.; 🅿; z 85534; Ⓟ 662; Ⓒ 812

E

Eagar; Inc. Place; APACHE; **146** H-13; elev. 7,114ft./2,168m.; 🅿; z 85925; Ⓟ 4,025; Ⓒ 4,033
Eagle Creek; RMC Place; GREENLEE; ***146** J-13; elev. 4,879ft./1,487m.; mail Clifton z 85533; rural
East Flagstaff; RMC Place; COCONINO; ***146** E-8; mail Flagstaff z 86001; pop. incl. with Flagstaff (Inc. Place)
East Fork; CDP; NAVAJO; ***146** I-12; located on Fort Apache Ind. Res.; elev. 5,460ft./1,664m.; mail Whiteriver z 85941; Ⓟ 752; Ⓒ 880
East Mesa; RMC Place; MARICOPA; ★ **PHOE**
East Plantsite; RMC Place; GREENLEE; ***147** K-13; mail Morenci z 85540; pop. incl. with Clifton (Inc. Place)
East Sahuarita; CDP-Census Area Only; PIMA; ***147** N-10; Ⓒ 1,419
Eden; RMC Place; GRAHAM; ***147** K-12; elev. 2,752ft./839m.; 🅿; z 85535 & mail Pima z 85543; rural
Egypt; MARICOPA; see Goodyear (Inc. Place)
Ehrenberg; CDP; LA PAZ; **146** I-2; elev. 310ft./94m.; 🅿; z 85334; Ⓟ 1,226; Ⓒ 1,357
Eleven Mile Corner (Casa Grande Farm Labor Camp); RMC Place; PINAL; ***147** K-9; elev. 1,456ft./444m.; 🅿; z 85122, z 85222; ● 200
Elfrida; RMC Place; COCHISE; **147** N-13; elev. 4,139ft./1,262m.; 🅿; z 85610; ● 600
Elgin; CDP; SANTA CRUZ; **147** N-11; elev. 4,719ft./1,438m.; 🅿; z 85611; Ⓒ 309
Ellison Creek Summer Homes; RMC Place; GILA; ***146** H-9; elev. 5,620ft./1,713m.; mail Payson z 85541; rural
El Mirage; RMC Place; MARICOPA; ***146** J-7; 🅿; ★ **PHOE**; z 85335 & mail Mesa z 85201; pop. incl. with El Mirage (Inc. Place)
El Mirage; Inc. Place; MARICOPA; **145** C-3; elev. 1,130ft./344m.; 🅿; ★ **PHOE**; z 85335; Ⓟ 5,001; Ⓒ 7,609; ◆ 11,645
Eloy; Inc. Place; PINAL; **147** L-9; elev. 1,572ft./479m.; 🅿; z 85131, z 85231; Ⓟ 7,211; Ⓒ 10,375
El Pueblecito; RMC Place; YUMA; ***147** L-2; ★ **YUMA**; mail Yuma z 85364; pop. incl. with Yuma (Inc. Place)
El Rio; RMC Place; PIMA; ★ **TUC**; mail Tucson z 85745; pop. incl. with Tucson (Inc. Place)
Emery Park; RMC Place; PIMA; ***147** M-10; ★ **TUC**; mail Tucson z 85706; pop. incl. with Tucson (Inc. Place)
Emmanuel Mission (Immanuel Mission); RMC Place; APACHE; ***146** A-13; located on Navajo Nation Ind. Res.; mail Teec Nos Pos z 86514; ● 30
Empire Landing; RMC Place; LA PAZ; ***146** H-3; elev. 400ft./122m.; mail Parker z 85344; ● 600

F

Falcon Estates; RMC Place; MARICOPA; ***146** J-8; ★ **PHOE**; mail Mesa z 85203; pop. incl. with Mesa (Inc. Place)
Falcon Field; RMC Place; MARICOPA; ★ **PHOE**; mail Mesa z 85205, z 85207, z 85215, z 85277; pop. incl. with Mesa (Inc. Place)
First Mesa; CDP-Census Area Only; NAVAJO; ***146** D-11; mail Polacca z 86042; Ⓒ 1,124
Fishers Landing; RMC Place; YUMA; ***147** K-2; mail Yuma z 85365; ● 100
Flagstaff; Inc. Place; ⊡ COCONINO; **146** F-8; elev. 6,910ft./2,106m.; 🅿 🄷 🄲 20,562 ■; z 86001-04, z 86011, z 86015, z 86017-18, z 86024, z 86038; Ⓟ 45,857; Ⓒ 52,894; ◆ 63,307
Flecha Caida Estates; RMC Place; PIMA; ***147** M-10; ★ **TUC**; mail Tucson z 85718; ● 1,500
Florence; Inc. Place; ⊡ PINAL; **147** K-9; elev. 1,490ft./454m.; 🅿 🄷; z 85132, z 85232; Ⓟ 7,510; Ⓒ 17,054; Ⓡ 14,466; ◆ 26,610
Florence Junction; RMC Place; PINAL; ***146** J-9; elev. 1,884ft./574m.; mail Apache Junction z 85218; rural
Flowing Wells; CDP-Census Area Only; PIMA; ***147** M-10; ★ **TUC**; mail Tucson z 85705; Ⓟ 14,013; Ⓒ 15,050
Floy; RMC Place; APACHE; ***146** H-12; elev. 6,600ft./2,012m.; mail Concho z 85924; rural
Forbing Park; RMC Place; YAVAPAI; ***146** G-7; mail Prescott z 86301
Forest Lakes Estates; RMC Place; COCONINO; **146** H-10; mail Forest Lakes z 85931; ● 220
Fort Apache; RMC Place; NAVAJO; **146** I-12; located on Fort Apache Ind. Res.; elev. 5,200ft./1,585m.; 🅿; z 85926; ● 200
Fort Apache Junction; RMC Place; GILA; ***146** I-12; mail Whiteriver z 85941; ● 150
Fort Apache Reservation; Indian Reservation; NAVAJO, APACHE, GILA; mail Whiteriver z 85941; also location of Indian Agency; Ⓟ 7,774; Ⓒ 12,429
Fort Defiance; CDP; APACHE; **146** D-14; located on Navajo Nation Ind. Res.; elev. 6,836ft./2,084m.; 🅿 🄷; z 86504; location of Ft. Defiance Indian Agency; Ⓟ 4,489; Ⓒ 4,061
Fort Lowell; RMC Place; PIMA; ***147** M-10; ★ **TUC**; mail Tucson z 85712, z 85715, z 85749; pop. incl. with Tucson (Inc. Place)
Fort McDowell (Camp McDowell); RMC Place; MARICOPA; **146** I-8; located on Fort McDowell Ind. Res.; 🅿; z 85264; ● 175
Fort McDowell Reservation; Indian Reservation; MARICOPA; mail Fort Mcdowell z 85264; Ⓟ 349; Ⓒ 824
Fort Mojave Reservation; Indian Reservation; MOJAVE; Reservation extends into CA and NV; mail Fort Mohave z 86426-27; Ⓟ 183; Ⓒ 773
Fort Rock Ranch; RMC Place; YAVAPAI; ***146** F-5; elev. 4,890ft./1,490m.; mail Seligman z 86337; rural
Fort Thomas; RMC Place; GRAHAM; **147** K-12; elev. 2,713ft./827m.; 🅿; z 85536; ● 170
Fortuna Foothills; CDP-Census Area Only; YUMA; ***147** L-2; ★ **YUMA**; mail Wellton z 85356; Ⓟ 7,737; Ⓒ 20,478; ◆ 23,692
Fort Yuma Reservation; Indian Reservation; YUMA; Reservation extends into CA; Ⓒ 36
Fountain East; RMC Place; MARICOPA; ***146** J-8; ★ **PHOE**; mail Mesa z 85201; pop. incl. with Mesa (Inc. Place)
Fountain Hills; Inc. Place; MARICOPA; **146** J-8; 🅿; ★ **PHOE**; z 85268-69; Ⓟ 10,030; Ⓒ 20,235; ◆ 26,892
Fountain of the Sun; RMC Place; MARICOPA; ***146** J-8; ★ **PHOE**; mail Mesa z 85208; pop. incl. with Mesa (Inc. Place)
Fowler; RMC Place; MARICOPA; ***146** J-7; elev. 1,043ft./318m.; ★ **PHOE**; pop. incl. with Phoenix (Inc. Place)
Foxfire; RMC Place; MARICOPA; ★ **PHOE**; mail Peoria z 85381; pop. incl. with Peoria (Inc. Place)
Foxwood; RMC Place; MARICOPA; ★ **PHOE**; mail Peoria z 85381; pop. incl. with Peoria (Inc. Place)
Franklin; RMC Place; GREENLEE; **147** L-14; elev. 3,787ft./1,154m.; mail Duncan z 85534; ● 50
Fredonia; Inc. Place; COCONINO; **146** A-7; elev. 4,671ft./1,424m.; 🅿; z 86022, z 86052; Ⓟ 1,207; Ⓒ 1,036
Fresnal Canyon; RMC Place; PIMA; **147** N-8; mail Sells z 85634; rural
Fresnal Village; PIMA; see Chiawuli Tak (RMC Place)
Friendly Corners; RMC Place; PINAL; **147** L-9; elev. 1,672ft./510m.; mail Eloy z 85231
Fry; RMC Place; COCHISE; ***147** O-11; mail Sierra Vista z 85635; pop. incl. with Sierra Vista (Inc. Place)

G

Gadsden; CDP; YUMA; **147** L-2; elev. 95ft./29m.; 🅿; ★ **YUMA**; z 85336; Ⓒ 953
Galena; RMC Place; COCHISE; ***147** O-12; mail Bisbee z 85603; pop. incl. with Bisbee (Inc. Place)
Ganado; CDP; APACHE; **146** D-13; located on Navajo Nation Ind. Res.; elev. 6,386ft./1,946m.; 🅿 🄷; z 86505, z 86540; Ⓟ 1,257; Ⓒ 1,505
Geronimo; RMC Place; GRAHAM; ***147** K-12; mail Fort Thomas z 85536; rural
Gibson; RMC Place; PIMA; ***147** M-6; mail Ajo z 85321; ● 2,100
Gila; MARICOPA; see Gila Bend (Inc. Place)
GILA; **146** J-11; Ⓟ 40,216; Ⓒ 51,335; ◆ 52,900
Gila Bend (Gila); Inc. Place; MARICOPA; **147** K-6; elev. 736ft./224m.; 🅿; z 85337; Ⓟ 1,747; Ⓒ 1,980
Gila Crossing; RMC Place; MARICOPA; ***146** J-7; located on Gila River Ind. Res.; elev. 1,037ft./316m.; ★ **PHOE**; mail Laveen z 85339; ● 300
Gila River Ranch; MARICOPA; see Theba (RMC Place)
Gila River Reservation; Indian Reservation; PINAL, MARICOPA; mail Sacaton z 85247; also location of Indian Agency; Ⓟ 7,380; Ⓒ 11,257
Gilbert; Inc. Place; MARICOPA; **146** J-8; elev. 1,230ft./375m.; 🅿; ★ **PHOE**; z 85233-34, z 85295-99; Ⓟ 29,122; Ⓒ 109,697; ◆ 192,464
Gisela; CDP; GILA; ***146** H-9; mail Payson z 85541; Ⓒ 532
Gladden; RMC Place; MARICOPA; ***146** I-5; elev. 2,213ft./675m.; mail Aguila z 85320
Gleeson; RMC Place; COCHISE; **147** N-12; mail Elfrida z 85610; ● 50
Glenbar; RMC Place; GRAHAM; mail Pima z 85543; ● 120
Glendale; Inc. Place; MARICOPA; **146** J-7; elev. 1,150ft./351m.; 🅿 🄷 🄲 4,092 ■; ★ **PHOE**; z 85301-12, z 85318; Ⓟ 147,864; Ⓒ 218,812; ◆ 268,629
Glen Ilah; RMC Place; YAVAPAI; ***146** H-6; mail Yarnell z 85362; ● 125
Globe; Inc. Place; ⊡ GILA; **146** J-10; elev. 3,509ft./1,070m.; 🅿; z 85501-02; Ⓟ 6,062; Ⓒ 7,486
Gold Camp; CDP-Census Area Only; PINAL; ***146** J-9; Ⓒ 6,029
Gold Canyon; RMC Place; PINAL; ***146** J-9; 🅿; z 85118, z 85218 & mail Apache Junction z 85219; ● 250
Golden Shores; RMC Place; MOHAVE; ***146** F-2; elev. 624ft./190m.; mail Topock z 86436; ● 300
Golden Valley; CDP-Census Area Only; MOHAVE; ***146** E-3; elev. 2,860ft./872m.; 🅿; z 86413; Ⓟ 2,619; Ⓒ 4,515
Goldfield; PINAL; see Youngberg (RMC Place)
Goodwin; RMC Place; YAVAPAI; mail Prescott z 86303
Goodyear (Egypt); Inc. Place; MARICOPA; **146** J-7; elev. 963ft./294m.; 🅿; ★ **PHOE**; z 85338, z 85395; Ⓟ 6,258; Ⓒ 18,911; ◆ 32,566
Goodyear Farms; RMC Place; MARICOPA; ★ **PHOE**; mail Litchfield Park z 85340; pop. incl. with Litchfield Park (Inc. Place)
Gordon Canyon Ranch; RMC Place; GILA; ***146** H-10; elev. 6,221ft./1,896m.; mail Payson z 85541; rural
Graham; RMC Place; GRAHAM; ***147** K-12; elev. 2,870ft./875m.; mail Thatcher z 85552; rural
GRAHAM; **147** K-13; Ⓟ 26,554; Ⓒ 33,489; ◆ 38,110
Grand Canyon Caverns (Dinosaur City); RMC Place; COCONINO; ***146** E-5; mail Peach Springs z 86434; ● 60
Grand Canyon Lodge; COCONINO; see North Rim (RMC Place)
Grand Canyon Village; CDP-Census Area Only; COCONINO; **146** C-7; elev. 6,860ft./2,091m.; mail Grand Canyon z 86023; Ⓟ 1,499; Ⓒ 1,460
Grand View; RMC Place; YAVAPAI; ***146** G-6; mail Prescott z 86301; rural
Granite Dells; RMC Place; YAVAPAI; ***146** G-7; elev. 5,104ft./1,556m.; mail Prescott z 86301; ● 145
Grasshopper Flats; YAVAPAI; see West Sedona (RMC Place)
Grasshopper Junction; RMC Place; MOHAVE; ***146** E-3; mail Kingman z 86401; rural
Gray Mountain; RMC Place; COCONINO; **146** D-9; located on Navajo Nation Ind. Res.; elev. 5,030ft./1,533m.; 🅿; z 86016
Greasewood; APACHE; see Upper Greasewood Trading Post (RMC Place)
Greasewood; CDP; NAVAJO; **146** E-12; located on Navajo Nation Ind. Res.; mail Ganado z 86505; Ⓟ 196; Ⓒ 581
Greaterville; RMC Place; PIMA; ***147** N-10; elev. 5,200ft./1,585m.; mail Sonoita z 85637; rural
GREENLEE; **146** J-13; Ⓟ 8,008; Ⓒ 8,547; ◆ 8,316
Green Valley; CDP; PIMA; **147** N-10; elev. 3,193ft./973m.; 🅿; z 85614, z 85622; Ⓟ 13,231; Ⓒ 17,283
Greenway; RMC Place; MARICOPA; ***146** I-7; ★ **PHOE**; mail Glendale z 85306, z 85312; pop. incl. with Glendale (Inc. Place)
Greer; RMC Place; APACHE; **146** H-13; elev. 8,380ft./2,554m.; 🅿; z 85927; ● 100
Gripe; RMC Place; GRAHAM; ***147** L-13; elev. 3,024ft./922m.; mail Safford z 85546; rural
Groom Creek; RMC Place; YAVAPAI; ***146** G-7; 🅿; z 86303; ● 400
Growler; RMC Place; YUMA; mail Roll z 85347; rural
Gu Achi; PIMA; see Santa Rosa (CDP)
Guadalupe; Inc. Place; MARICOPA; **145** E-6; elev. 1,250ft./381m.; 🅿; ★ **PHOE**; z 85283; Ⓟ 5,458; Ⓒ 5,228
Gu Komelik; PINAL; see North Komelik (RMC Place)
Gunsight; RMC Place; PIMA; ***147** M-6; mail Sells z 85634; rural
Gu Oidak; RMC Place; PIMA; ***147** N-8; located on Papago Ind. Res.; elev. 2,044ft./623m.; mail Sells z 85634; rural
Guthrie; RMC Place; GREENLEE; ***147** K-14; mail Clifton z 85533
Gu Vo; RMC Place; PIMA; **147** M-6; located on Papago Ind. Res.; mail Sells z 85634; ● 110

H

Hacienda De Valencia; RMC Place; MARICOPA; ***146** J-8; ★ **PHOE**; mail Mesa z 85201; pop. incl. with Mesa (Inc. Place)
Hackberry; RMC Place; MOHAVE; **146** E-4; elev. 3,580ft./1,091m.; 🅿; z 86411
Haivana Nakya (Havana Nakya); RMC Place; PIMA; **147** N-8; located on Papago Ind. Res.; mail Sells z 85634
Hamilton Corner; RMC Place; MARICOPA; ***146** J-8; elev. 1,219ft./372m.; ★ **PHOE**; mail Chandler z 85248; rural
Hannagan Meadow; RMC Place; GREENLEE; **146** I-13; elev. 9,025ft./2,751m.; mail Alpine z 85920, Blue z 85922; ● 30
Hano; RMC Place; NAVAJO; ***146** D-11; located on Hopi Ind. Res.; mail Polacca z 86042; ● 200
Happy Jack; RMC Place; COCONINO; **146** G-9; elev. 7,500ft./2,286m.; 🅿; z 86024
Harcuvar; RMC Place; LA PAZ; ***146** I-4; elev. 1,925ft./587m.; mail Salome z 85348; ● 50
Hard Rocks; RMC Place; NAVAJO; mail Kykotsmovi Village z 86039; rural
Harmony Villa; RMC Place; MARICOPA; ***146** J-8; ★ **PHOE**; mail Mesa z 85201; pop. incl. with Mesa (Inc. Place)
Hassayampa; RMC Place; MARICOPA; ***146** J-6; elev. 849ft./259m.; mail Palo Verde z 85343; rural
Havana Nakya; PIMA; see Haivana Nakya (RMC Place)
Havasupai Reservation; Indian Reservation; COCONINO; mail Supai z 86435; Ⓟ 282; Ⓒ 503
Hawkins; RMC Place; YAVAPAI; ***146** H-6; elev. 3,255ft./992m.; mail Congress z 85332; rural
Hawley Lake; RMC Place; APACHE; **146** I-12; located on Fort Apache Ind. Res.; elev. 8,200ft./2,499m.; mail McNary z 85930; ● 30
Hayden; Inc. Place; GILA, PINAL; **147** K-10; 🅿; z 85135, z 85235; Ⓟ 909; Ⓒ 892
Hayden Junction; RMC Place; PINAL; ***147** K-10; mail Hayden z 85235; rural
Heber; RMC Place; NAVAJO; **146** G-11; elev. 6,435ft./1,961m.; 🅿; z 85928, z 85931; ● 300
Heber-Overgaard; CDP-Census Area Only; NAVAJO; ***146** G-11; mail Heber z 85928, Overgaard z 85933; Ⓟ 1,581; Ⓒ 2,722
Hereford; RMC Place; COCHISE; **147** O-12; elev. 4,200ft./1,280m.; 🅿; z 85615; ● 300
Hickiwan; RMC Place; PIMA; **147** M-7; located on Papago Ind. Res.; elev. 2,194ft./669m.; mail Sells z 85634
Hidden Springs Mission; RMC Place; COCONINO; ***146** C-9; located on Navajo Nation Ind. Res.; mail Cameron z 86020; rural
Highland Park; RMC Place; COCHISE; ***147** O-12; elev. 6,000ft./1,829m.; mail Bisbee z 85603; rural
Highland Park; RMC Place; YAVAPAI; ***146** G-6; elev. 6,400ft./1,951m.; mail Prescott z 86305; ● 300
Higley; RMC Place; MARICOPA; **145** F-8; elev. 1,298ft./396m.; 🅿; ★ **PHOE**; z 85236; ● 1,000
Hillside; RMC Place; YAVAPAI; **146** G-6; elev. 3,853ft./1,174m.; mail Prescott z 86301
Hilltop; RMC Place; COCHISE; ***147** N-14; mail San Simon z 85632; rural
Holbrook; Inc. Place; ⊡ NAVAJO; **146** F-12; elev. 5,083ft./1,549m.; 🅿; z 86025, z 86028-29, z 86031; Ⓟ 4,686; Ⓒ 4,917
Hollywood; RMC Place; GRAHAM; ***147** K-13; mail Safford z 85546; ● 100
Hope; RMC Place; LA PAZ; ***146** I-4; elev. 1,531ft./467m.; mail Salome z 85348
Hopi; RMC Place; MARICOPA; ***146** J-8; ★ **PHOE**; mail Scottsdale z 85258, z 85261; pop. incl. with Scottsdale (Inc. Place)
Hopi Reservation; Indian Reservation; NAVAJO, COCONINO; mail Kykotsmovi Village z 86039; also location of Indian Agency; Ⓟ 6,906; Ⓒ 6,815
Horn; RMC Place; YUMA; ***147** K-4; mail Dateland z 85333; rural
Horse Mesa; RMC Place; MARICOPA; ***146** J-9; mail Apache Junction z 85219; rural
Hotason Vo; RMC Place; PIMA; ***147** M-6; located on Papago Ind. Res.; elev. 2,091ft./637m.; mail Sells z 85634; ● 30
Hotevilla; RMC Place; NAVAJO; **146** D-10; located on Hopi Ind. Res.; elev. 6,360ft./1,939m.; 🅿; z 86030; Ⓟ 869; ● 600
Hotevilla-Bacavi; CDP-Census Area Only; NAVAJO; ***146** D-10; Ⓒ 767
Houck; CDP; APACHE; **146** E-13; located on Navajo Nation Ind. Res.; elev. 5,984ft./1,824m.; 🅿; z 86506, z 86508; Ⓒ 1,087
Huachuca City (Huachuca Vista); Inc. Place; COCHISE; **147** S-13; elev. 4,289ft./1,307m.; 🅿; z 85616; Ⓟ 1,782; Ⓒ 1,751
Huachuca Terrace; RMC Place; COCHISE; ***147** O-12; mail Bisbee z 85603, Chinle z 86503; pop. incl. with Bisbee (Inc. Place)
Huachuca Vista; COCHISE; see Huachuca City (Inc. Place)
Hualapai; MOHAVE; see Walapai (RMC Place)
Hualapai Reservation; Indian Reservation; COCONINO, MOHAVE, YAVAPAI; mail Hualapai z 86412, Peach Springs z 86434; also location of Indian Agency; Ⓟ 949; Ⓒ 1,353
Humboldt; RMC Place; YAVAPAI; **146** G-7; elev. 4,581ft./1,396m.; 🅿; z 86329; ● 1,300
Hunt; RMC Place; APACHE; **146** G-13; elev. 5,433ft./1,656m.; mail Concho z 85924; ● 50
Hunters Point; RMC Place; APACHE; **146** E-14; located on Navajo Nation Ind. Res.; mail Saint Michaels z 86511; rural
Huntington Park; RMC Place; PIMA; ★ **TUC**; pop. incl. with Tucson (Inc. Place)
Hyder; RMC Place; YUMA; ***147** K-5; mail Dateland z 85333

I

Immanuel Mission; APACHE; see Emmanuel Mission (RMC Place)
Indian Gardens; RMC Place; COCONINO; ***146** F-8; mail Sedona z 86336; ● 125
Indian Pine; RMC Place; NAVAJO; **146** H-12; located on Fort Apache Ind. Res.; mail McNary z 85930, Pinetop z 85935; ● 50
Indian Ridge Estates; RMC Place; PIMA; ***147** M-10; ★ **TUC**; mail Tucson z 85715; ● 1,600
Indian School; RMC Place; MARICOPA; ***146** J-7; ★ **PHOE**; mail Phoenix z 85011, z 85014; pop. incl. with Phoenix (Inc. Place)
Indian Wells; RMC Place; NAVAJO; **146** E-12; located on Navajo Nation Ind. Res.; 🅿; z 86031
Inscription House; RMC Place; COCONINO; ***146** B-10; located on Navajo Nation Ind. Res.; elev. 6,717ft./2,047m.; mail Tonalea z 86044; ● 100
Inspiration; RMC Place; GILA; ***146** J-10; elev. 4,054ft./1,236m.; mail Claypool z 85532; rural
Iron Springs; RMC Place; YAVAPAI; **146** G-7; elev. 5,920ft./1,804m.; 🅿; z 86305, z 86330

J

Jackrabbit; PINAL; see Tat Momoli (RMC Place)
Jacob Lake; RMC Place; COCONINO; ***146** B-7; elev. 7,921ft./2,414m.; mail Fredonia z 86022
Jade Park North; RMC Place; MARICOPA; ★ **PHOE**; mail Glendale z 85308; pop. incl. with Phoenix (Inc. Place)
Jadito; NAVAJO; see Jeddito (CDP)
Jakes Corner; RMC Place; GILA; ***146** I-9; mail Payson z 85541
Jeddito (Jadito); CDP; NAVAJO; **146** D-12; located on Hopi Ind. Res.; mail Keams Canyon z 86034; Ⓒ 390
Jerome; Inc. Place; YAVAPAI; **146** G-7; elev. 4,751ft./1,448m.; 🅿; z 86331; Ⓟ 403; Ⓒ 329
Johnson; RMC Place; COCHISE; ***147** M-12; mail Dragoon z 85609; rural
Joseph City; RMC Place; NAVAJO; **146** F-11; elev. 5,023ft./1,531m.; 🅿; z 86032; ● 1,100
Juniper Heights; RMC Place; YAVAPAI; ***146** G-7; elev. 5,810ft./1,771m.; mail Prescott z 86301; ● 100

K

Kachina Village; CDP-Census Area Only; COCONINO; ***146** F-8; elev. 6,700ft./2,042m.; mail Flagstaff z 86001; Ⓟ 1,711; Ⓒ 2,664
Kaibab; CDP; MOHAVE; **146** A-6; located on Kaibab Ind. Res.; mail Fredonia z 86022; Ⓒ 275
Kaibab Reservation; Indian Reservation; MOJAVE, COCONINO; mail Fredonia z 86022; Ⓟ 173; Ⓒ 196
Kaibito (Lower Kaibito); CDP; COCONINO; **146** B-10; located on Navajo Nation Ind. Res.; mail Kaibeto z 86053; Ⓟ 641; Ⓒ 1,607
Kaihon Kug; RMC Place; PIMA; ***147** N-7; located on Papago Ind. Res.; mail Sells z 85634; rural
Kaka; RMC Place; MARICOPA; ***147** L-7; located on Papago Ind. Res.; mail Ajo z 85321; ● 120
Kansas Settlement; RMC Place; COCHISE; ***147** M-12; mail Willcox z 85643; rural
Katherine; RMC Place; MOHAVE; ***146** E-2; mail Bullhead City z 86429; ● 100
Kayenta; CDP; NAVAJO; **146** B-11; located on Navajo Nation Ind. Res.; elev. 5,641ft./1,719m.; 🅿; z 86033; Ⓟ 4,372; Ⓒ 4,922
Keams Canyon; CDP; NAVAJO; **146** D-11; located on Hopi Ind. Res.; elev. 6,195ft./1,888m.; 🅿 🄷; z 86034; location of Indian Agency; Ⓟ 393; Ⓒ 260
Kearny; Inc. Place; PINAL; **147** K-10; elev. 1,832ft./558m.; 🅿; z 85137, z 85237; Ⓟ 2,262; Ⓒ 2,249
Kelvin; RMC Place; PINAL; **147** K-10; mail Kearny z 85237
Kendall; RMC Place; MARICOPA; ★ **PHOE**; pop. incl. with Phoenix (Inc. Place)
Kendall Square; RMC Place; PIMA; ★ **TUC**; pop. incl. with Tucson (Inc. Place)
Kerwo; RMC Place; PIMA; ***147** M-9; located on Papago Ind. Res.; mail Sells z 85634; rural
Kingman; Inc. Place; ⊡ MOHAVE; **146** F-3; elev. 3,341ft./1,018m.; 🅿 🄷; z 86401-02, z 86409, z 86411-13, z 86437, z 86445; Ⓟ 12,722; Ⓒ 20,069; ◆ 26,489
Kings Ranch; RMC Place; PINAL; ***146** J-9; elev. 2,162ft./659m.; mail Apache Junction z 85217; ● 135
Kingston Knolls Terrace; RMC Place; PIMA; ★ **TUC**; pop. incl. with Tucson (Inc. Place)
Kinlichee; RMC Place; APACHE; ***146** D-13; located on Navajo Nation Ind. Res.; mail Ganado z 86505; ● 200
Kino; RMC Place; PIMA; ***147** M-10; ★ **TUC**; mail Tucson z 85703, z 85705; pop. incl. with Tucson (Inc. Place)
Kino Hills; RMC Place; SANTA CRUZ; ***147** O-10; elev. 3,894ft./1,187m.; mail Nogales z 85621; pop. incl. with Nogales (Inc. Place)
Kino Springs; RMC Place; SANTA CRUZ; ***147** O-10; elev. 4,000ft./1,219m.; mail Nogales z 85621; ● 130
Kinsley Ranch; PIMA; see Arivaca Junction (RMC Place)
Kirkland; RMC Place; YAVAPAI; **146** H-6; elev. 3,935ft./1,199m.; 🅿; z 86332
Kirkland Junction; RMC Place; YAVAPAI; **146** H-6; elev. 4,100ft./1,250m.; mail Kirkland z 86332
Klagetoh; RMC Place; APACHE; **146** E-13; elev. 6,423ft./1,958m.; mail Ganado z 86505; ● 400
Klondyke; RMC Place; GRAHAM; **147** L-11; elev. 3,475ft./1,059m.; mail Willcox z 85643-44; rural
Kohatk; RMC Place; PINAL; **147** L-8; located on Papago Ind. Res.; elev. 1,639ft./500m.; mail Sells z 85634; ● 75
Kohls Ranch; RMC Place; GILA; ***146** H-10; elev. 5,400ft./1,646m.; mail Payson z 85541; ● 100
Komatke; RMC Place; MARICOPA; **146** J-7; located on Gila River Ind. Res.; ★ **PHOE**; mail Laveen z 85339; Ⓟ 1,116; ● 1,000
Komelik; PIMA; see South Komelik (RMC Place)
Ko Vaya (Cababi); RMC Place; PIMA; **147** M-8; located on Papago Ind. Res.; mail Sells z 85634; ● 50
Kupk; RMC Place; PIMA; mail Sells z 85634; rural
Kykotsmovi Village (New Oraibi); CDP-Census Area Only; NAVAJO; **146** D-11; elev. 5,675ft./1,730m.; 🅿; z 86039; Ⓟ 773; Ⓒ 776

L

Lake Havasu City; Inc. Place; MOHAVE; **147** T-12; elev. 600ft./183m.; 🅿 🄷; z 86403-06; Ⓟ 24,363; Ⓒ 41,938; ◆ 52,465
Lake Mohave; RMC Place; MOHAVE; ***146** E-2; mail Bullhead City z 86430; ● 100
Lake Montezuma; CDP; YAVAPAI; **146** G-8; elev. 3,600ft./1,097m.; 🅿; z 86342; Ⓟ 1,841; Ⓒ 3,344
Lakeside; RMC Place; LA PAZ; ***146** H-3; located on Colorado River Ind. Res.; elev. 400ft./122m.; mail Parker z 85344; ● 500
Lakeside; RMC Place; NAVAJO; ***146** H-12; elev. 6,718ft./2,048m.; 🅿; z 85929; pop. incl. with Pinetop-Lakeside (Inc. Place)
Lampliter Village; RMC Place; YAVAPAI; mail Clarkdale z 86324; pop. incl. with Clarkdale (Inc. Place)
La Palma; RMC Place; PINAL; **147** K-9; elev. 1,469ft./448m.; mail Casa Grande z 85222; ● 245
LA PAZ; **146** I-4; Ⓟ 13,844; Ⓒ 19,715; ◆ 20,343
Las Ligas; RMC Place; MARICOPA; ***146** J-7; elev. 948ft./289m.; ★ **PHOE**; mail Avondale z 85323; pop. incl. with Avondale (Inc. Place)
Laveen; RMC Place; MARICOPA; **146** J-7; elev. 1,038ft./316m.; 🅿; ★ **PHOE**; z 85339; ● 1,200
Lechee; CDP-Census Area Only; COCONINO; ***146** A-9; Ⓒ 1,606
LeChee Chapter; RMC Place; COCONINO; ***146** A-9; elev. 4,700ft./1,433m.; mail Page z 86040; ● 240
Lees Ferry; COCONINO; see Chair Crossing (RMC Place)
Lehi; RMC Place; MARICOPA; ***146** J-8; ★ **PHOE**; pop. incl. with Mesa (Inc. Place)
Leisure World; RMC Place; MARICOPA; ***146** J-8; ★ **PHOE**; mail Mesa z 85206; ● 2,100
Leupp; CDP; COCONINO; **146** E-10; located on Navajo Nation Ind. Res.; elev. 4,705ft./1,434m.; 🅿; z 86035; includes separate community of Sunrise; Ⓟ 857; Ⓒ 970
Leupp Corner; RMC Place; COCONINO; **146** F-10; located on Navajo Nation Ind. Res.; mail Winslow z 86047; ● 40
Liberty; RMC Place; MARICOPA; **146** J-7; ★ **PHOE**; mail Buckeye z 85326; ● 150
Ligurta; RMC Place; YUMA; ***147** L-3; elev. 234ft./71m.; mail Wellton z 85356
Linden; RMC Place; NAVAJO; mail Show Low z 85901; ● 150
Litchfield Greens; RMC Place; MARICOPA; ***146** J-7; elev. 1,063ft./324m.; ★ **PHOE**; mail Litchfield Park z 85340; pop. incl. with Litchfield Park (Inc. Place)
Litchfield Park; Inc. Place; MARICOPA; **146** J-7; elev. 1,027ft./313m.; 🅿; ★ **PHOE**; z 85340; Ⓟ 3,303; Ⓒ 3,810
Little Acres; RMC Place; GILA; ***146** J-10; elev. 3,412ft./1,040m.; mail Globe z 85501
Littlefield; RMC Place; MOHAVE; **146** A-4; elev. 1,846ft./563m.; 🅿; z 86432; ● 150
Littletown; CDP; PIMA; ***147** M-10; ★ **TUC**; Ⓒ 1,010
Little Tucson; PIMA; see Ali Chukson (RMC Place)
Lizard Acres; RMC Place; MARICOPA; ***146** I-7; ★ **PHOE**; mail Sun City z 85373; ● 3,000
Lochiel; RMC Place; SANTA CRUZ; ***147** O-11; mail Patagonia z 85624; rural
Lone Star; RMC Place; GRAHAM; ***147** L-13; mail Safford z 85546; ● 200
Long Valley; RMC Place; COCONINO; **146** G-9; elev. 6,950ft./2,118m.; mail Flagstaff z 86001; ● 70
Longview Estates; RMC Place; PIMA; ★ **TUC**; pop. incl. with Tucson (Inc. Place)
Lowell; RMC Place; COCHISE; ***147** O-12; mail Bisbee z 85603
Lower Kaibito; COCONINO; see Kaibito (CDP)
Lower Miami; RMC Place; GILA; ***146** J-10; mail Miami z 85539
Low Mountain; RMC Place; NAVAJO; ***146** D-12; mail Chinle z 86503; ● 400
Lukachukai; CDP; APACHE; **146** B-13; located on Navajo Nation Ind. Res.; elev. 6,421ft./1,957m.; 🅿; z 86507; Ⓟ 113; Ⓒ 1,565
Lukeville; RMC Place; PIMA; **147** N-6; elev. 1,410ft./430m.; 🅿; z 85341
Lupton; RMC Place; APACHE; **146** E-14; located on Navajo Nation Ind. Res.; elev. 6,183ft./1,885m.; 🅿; z 86508; ● 80
Lynx Estates; RMC Place; YAVAPAI; ***146** G-7; elev. 5,500ft./1,676m.; mail Prescott z 86301; rural

M

Madera Canyon; RMC Place; SANTA CRUZ; **147** N-10; 🅿; z 85614 & mail Tucson z 85706
Maine; COCONINO; see Parks (CDP)
Maish Vaya (Covered Wells); RMC Place; PIMA; **147** N-8; located on Papago Ind. Res.; mail Sells z 85634
Mammoth; Inc. Place; PINAL; **147** L-11; elev. 2,353ft./717m.; 🅿; z 85618; Ⓟ 1,845; Ⓒ 1,762
Manana Grande; RMC Place; PIMA; ★ **TUC**; pop. incl. with Tucson (Inc. Place)
Many Farms; CDP; APACHE; **146** C-13; located on Navajo Nation Ind. Res.; elev. 5,301ft./1,616m.; 🅿; z 86538; Ⓟ 1,294; Ⓒ 1,548
Marana; Inc. Place; PIMA; **147** L-9; elev. 1,988ft./606m.; 🅿; ★ **TUC**; z 85653, z 85658; Ⓟ 2,187; Ⓒ 13,556; ◆ 19,537
Marble Canyon; RMC Place; COCONINO; **146** A-8; elev. 3,580ft./1,091m.; 🅿; z 86036
Maricopa; Inc. Place; PINAL; **147** K-8; 🅿; z 85239; incorporated October 15, 2003; not reported in 2000 Census; ◆ 53,473
Maricopa; CDP; PINAL; **147** K-8; elev. 1,180ft./360m.; 🅿; z 85138-39, z 85238-39; Ⓒ 1,040
MARICOPA; **146** I-6; Ⓟ 2,122,101; Ⓒ 3,072,149; ◆ 4,101,715
Maricopa (Ak Chin) Reservation; Indian Reservation; PINAL; mail Maricopa z 85239; Ⓟ 397; Ⓒ 742
Maricopa Village; RMC Place; MARICOPA; ***146** J-7; located on Gila River Ind. Res.; ★ **PHOE**; mail Laveen z 85339; ● 400
Mariposa Manor; RMC Place; SANTA CRUZ; ***147** O-10; elev. 3,880ft./1,183m.; ★ **NOGLS**; mail Nogales z 85621; pop. incl. with Nogales (Inc. Place)
Martinez Lake; RMC Place; YUMA; **147** K-2; elev. 218ft./66m.; 🅿; z 85365; ● 100
Maryvale; RMC Place; MARICOPA; ***146** J-7; ★ **PHOE**; mail Phoenix z 85019, z 85063; pop. incl. with Phoenix (Inc. Place)
Mayer; CDP; YAVAPAI; **146** H-7; elev. 4,401ft./1,341m.; 🅿; z 86333; Ⓒ 1,408
McConnico; RMC Place; MOHAVE; mail Kingman z 86401; ● 250
McDowell; RMC Place; MARICOPA; ***146** J-8; ★ **PHOE**; mail Phoenix z 85008, z 85010; pop. incl. with Phoenix (Inc. Place)
McGuireville; RMC Place; YAVAPAI; ***146** G-8; mail Rimrock z 86335; ● 130
McNary; CDP; APACHE, NAVAJO; **146** H-12; located on Fort Apache Ind. Res.; elev. 7,316ft./2,230m.; 🅿; z 85930; Ⓟ 355; Ⓒ 349
McNeal; RMC Place; COCHISE; **147** O-13; elev. 4,169ft./1,271m.; 🅿; z 85617; ● 100
Meadow Brook; RMC Place; YUMA; ***147** L-2; ★ **YUMA**; mail Yuma z 85364; pop. incl. with Yuma (Inc. Place)
Meadview; RMC Place; MOHAVE; **146** C-3; elev. 900ft./274m.; 🅿; z 86444; ● 1,000
Mesa; Inc. Place; MARICOPA; **146** J-8; elev. 244ft./74m.; 🅿 🄷 🄲 6,873 ■; ★ **PHOE**; z 85201-16, z 85274-75, z 85277 & mail Apache Junction z 85220; Ⓟ 288,104; Ⓒ 396,375; ◆ 475,847
Mesa del Caballo; RMC Place; GILA; ***146** H-9; elev. 5,171ft./1,576m.; mail Payson z 85541; ● 585
Mescal; RMC Place; COCHISE; ***147** N-11; mail Benson z 85602; ● 250
Mesquite Creek; CDP-Census Area Only; MOHAVE; ***146** F-2; Ⓒ 205
Mexican Town; RMC Place; PIMA; ***147** M-6; mail Ajo z 85321; ● 130
Mexican Water; RMC Place; APACHE; **146** A-13; located on Navajo Nation Ind. Res.; mail Teec Nos Pos z 86514; ● 30
Miami; Inc. Place; GILA; **146** J-10; elev. 3,411ft./1,040m.; 🅿; z 85539; Ⓟ 2,018; Ⓒ 1,936
Miami Gardens; RMC Place; GILA; ***146** J-10; mail Miami z 85539; pop. incl. with Globe (Inc. Place)
Middle Verde; RMC Place; YAVAPAI; ***146** G-8; elev. 3,168ft./966m.; mail Camp Verde z 86322; pop. incl. with Camp Verde (Inc. Place)
Midland City; RMC Place; GILA; ***146** J-10; mail Globe z 85501, Miami z 85539; ● 150
Miller Valley; RMC Place; YAVAPAI; ***146** G-7; mail Prescott z 86301, z 86305; pop. incl. with Prescott (Inc. Place)
Miracle Valley; RMC Place; COCHISE; ***147** O-12; elev. 4,367ft./1,331m.; mail Hereford z 85615; ● 600
Miramonte Acres; RMC Place; COCHISE; mail Bisbee z 85603; pop. incl. with Bisbee (Inc. Place)
Mishongnovi; RMC Place; NAVAJO; ***146** D-11; mail Second Mesa z 86043; ● 220
Mission; RMC Place; PIMA; ***147** M-10; ★ **TUC**; mail Tucson z 85706, z 85714, z 85734, z 85746; pop. incl. with Tucson (Inc. Place)
Mobile; RMC Place; MARICOPA; **147** K-7; 🅿; z 85139, z 85239
Moccasin; RMC Place; MOHAVE; **146** A-6; located on Kaibab Ind. Res.; mail Fredonia z 86022; ● 250
Moenave; RMC Place; COCONINO; ***146** C-9; located on Navajo Nation Ind. Res.; elev. 4,794ft./1,461m.; mail Tuba City z 86045; ● 90
Moenkopi; CDP; COCONINO; **146** C-9; located on Navajo Nation Ind. Res.; elev. 4,777ft./1,456m.; mail Tuba City z 86045; Ⓟ 924; Ⓒ 901
MOHAVE; **146** F-4; Ⓟ 93,497; Ⓒ 155,032; ◆ 198,612
Mohave Valley; CDP-Census Area Only; MOHAVE; ***146** F-2; elev. 460ft./140m.; 🅿; z 86440, z 86446; Ⓟ 6,962; Ⓒ 13,694
Mojave Ranch Estates; CDP-Census Area Only; MOHAVE; ***146** F-2; Ⓒ 28
Morenci; CDP; GREENLEE; **147** K-13; 🅿; z 85540; Ⓟ 1,799; Ⓒ 1,879
Mormon Lake; RMC Place; COCONINO; **146** F-9; elev. 7,120ft./2,170m.; 🅿; z 86038; ● 100
Morristown (Castle Hot Springs); RMC Place; MARICOPA; **146** I-6; elev. 1,971ft./601m.; 🅿; z 85342; ● 400
Mountainaire; CDP; COCONINO; **146** F-8; mail Flagstaff z 86001; Ⓒ 1,014
Mountain View; RMC Place; COCHISE; mail Bisbee z 85603; pop. incl. with Bisbee (Inc. Place)
Mountain View; RMC Place; MARICOPA; ***146** J-8; ★ **PHOE**; mail Mesa z 85203, z 85213, z 85275; pop. incl. with Mesa (Inc. Place)
Mountain View; RMC Place; PIMA; mail Vail z 85641; ● 250
Mount Elden; RMC Place; COCONINO; mail Flagstaff z 86001; pop. incl. with Flagstaff (Inc. Place)
Mount Lemmon; PIMA; see Summerhaven (RMC Place)
Mumurva; RMC Place; NAVAJO; ***146** D-10; mail Hotevilla z 86030; rural
Munds Park; CDP; COCONINO; ***146** F-8; elev. 6,459ft./1,969m.; 🅿; z 86017; Ⓒ 1,250

N

Na Ah Tee; RMC Place; NAVAJO; ***146** E-12; located on Navajo Nation Ind. Res.; elev. 6,200ft./1,890m.; mail Holbrook z 86025; rural
Naco; CDP; COCHISE; **147** O-12; elev. 4,615ft./1,407m.; 🅿; z 85620; Ⓒ 833
Navajo; RMC Place; APACHE; **146** F-13; elev. 5,661ft./1,725m.; mail Chambers z 86502
NAVAJO; **146** E-11; Ⓟ 77,658; Ⓒ 97,470; ◆ 110,939
Navajo Agency; APACHE; see Window Rock (CDP)
Navajo Boarding School; NAVAJO; see Shonto (CDP)
Navajo Mountain Mission; RMC Place; COCONINO; ***146** A-10; located on Navajo Nation Ind. Res.; elev. 6,400ft./1,951m.; mail Tonalea z 86044; ● 30
Navajo Nation Reservation; Indian Reservation; APACHE, COCONINO, NAVAJO; Reservation extends into NM and UT; mail Window Rock z 86515; also location of Chinle Indian Agency; Ⓟ 76,042; Ⓒ 104,532
Navajo Station; RMC Place; APACHE; ***146** E-12; mail Ganado z 86505; rural
Nazlini; CDP; APACHE; **146** D-13; located on Navajo Nation Ind. Res.; 🅿; z 86540; Ⓒ 397
Nelson; RMC Place; YAVAPAI; ***146** E-5; mail Peach Springs z 86434
New Kingman-Butler; CDP-Census Area Only; MOHAVE; ***146** E-3; elev. 3,375ft./1,029m.; mail Kingman z 86401; Ⓟ 11,627; Ⓒ 14,810
New Oraibi; NAVAJO; see Kykotsmovi Village (CDP-Census Area Only)
New River; CDP; MARICOPA; ***146** I-7; 🅿; z 85027, z 85087; Ⓒ 10,740
New Tucson; RMC Place; PIMA; ★ **TUC**; mail Tucson z 85747
Nicksville; RMC Place; COCHISE; ***147** O-11; mail Hereford z 85615; ● 350
Nogales; Inc. Place; ⊡ SANTA CRUZ; **147** O-10; elev. 3,869ft./1,179m.; 🅿 🄷 ■; ★ **NOGLS**; z 85621, z 85628, z 85648, z 85662; Ⓟ 19,489; Ⓒ 20,878; ◆ 20,723
Nogales West; RMC Place; SANTA CRUZ; ***147** O-8; elev. 4,000ft./1,219m.; mail Nogales z 85621
Nolia; PIMA; see Nolic (RMC Place)
Nolic (Nolia); RMC Place; PIMA; ***147** N-8; located on Papago Ind. Res.; elev. 2,400ft./732m.; mail Sells z 85634; ● 40
Normal Junction; RMC Place; MARICOPA; ***146** J-8; ★ **PHOE**; mail Tempe z 85281; pop. incl. with Tempe (Inc. Place)
Northeast; RMC Place; MARICOPA; ***146** J-8; ★ **PHOE**; mail Phoenix z 85016, z 85064; pop. incl. with Phoenix (Inc. Place)
Northern Hills; RMC Place; PIMA; ***147** M-10; ★ **TUC**; mail Tucson z 85704; ● 800
North Komelik (Gu Komelik); RMC Place; PINAL; ***147** L-8; located on Papago Ind. Res.; elev. 1,606ft./490m.; mail Sells z 85634; ● 100
North Rim (Grand Canyon Lodge); RMC Place; COCONINO; ***146** C-8; elev. 8,340ft./2,542m.; 🅿; z 86052
Northwest; RMC Place; MARICOPA; ***146** J-8; ★ **PHOE**; mail Phoenix z 85015, z 85017, z 85061, z 85079; pop. incl. with Phoenix (Inc. Place)
Nortons Corner; RMC Place; MARICOPA; **145** F-8; elev. 1,247ft./380m.; ★ **PHOE**; mail Chandler z 85225
Nutrioso; RMC Place; APACHE; **146** I-14; elev. 7,697ft./2,346m.; 🅿; z 85932; ● 100

O

Oak Creek; RMC Place; YAVAPAI; ***146** G-8; elev. 4,120ft./1,256m.; mail Sedona z 86341; ● 1,000
Oak Knoll Village; RMC Place; YAVAPAI; ***146** G-7; elev. 5,899ft./1,798m.; mail Prescott z 86301; ● 120
Oak Ridge; APACHE; see Oak Springs (RMC Place)
Oak Springs (Oak Ridge); RMC Place; APACHE; ***146** E-14; mail Houck z 86506, Saint Michaels z 86511; ● 30
Oasis Park; RMC Place; MARICOPA; ★ **PHOE**; mail Mesa z 85208; pop. incl. with Apache Junction (Inc. Place)
Oatman; RMC Place; MOHAVE; **146** F-3; elev. 2,744ft./836m.; 🅿; z 86433
Ocotillo; RMC Place; MARICOPA; **147** K-8; elev. 1,206ft./368m.; ★ **PHOE**; mail Chandler z 85248; pop. incl. with Chandler (Inc. Place)
Olberg; RMC Place; PINAL; **147** K-8; mail Sacaton z 85247; ● 100
Old Columbine; RMC Place; GRAHAM; ***147** L-12; mail Safford z 85546; rural
Oljato-Monument Valley; CDP-Census Area Only; NAVAJO; ***146** A-11; Ⓒ 155
Oracle; CDP; PINAL; **147** L-10; elev. 4,513ft./1,376m.; 🅿; z 85623; Ⓟ 3,043; Ⓒ 3,563
Oracle Foothills Estates; RMC Place; PIMA; ***147** M-10; ★ **TUC**; mail Tucson z 85704; ● 1,000
Oracle Junction; RMC Place; PINAL; ***147** L-10; elev. 3,308ft./1,008m.; mail Tucson z 85737; ● 135
Oraibi; RMC Place; NAVAJO; ***146** D-10; mail Kykotsmovi Village z 86039; ● 120
Orange Grove Estates; RMC Place; PIMA; ***147** M-10; ★ **TUC**; mail Tucson z 85704; ● 500
Oro Valley; Inc. Place; PIMA; **147** M-10; 🅿; ★ **TUC**; z 85704, z 85737, z 85742, z 85755 & mail Tucson z 85739; Ⓟ 6,670; Ⓒ 29,700; ◆ 39,145
Osborn; RMC Place; MARICOPA; ***146** J-7; ★ **PHOE**; mail Phoenix z 85012-13, z 85067; pop. incl. with Phoenix (Inc. Place)
Overgaard; RMC Place; NAVAJO; **146** H-11; elev. 6,600ft./2,012m.; 🅿; z 85933; ● 400

P

Page; Inc. Place; COCONINO; **146** A-9; located on Navajo Nation Ind. Res.; elev. 4,000ft./1,219m.; 🅿 🄷; z 86040 & mail Marble Canyon z 86036; Ⓟ 6,598; Ⓒ 6,809
Page Springs; RMC Place; YAVAPAI; ***146** G-8; mail Cornville z 86325; ● 300
Palm Springs; RMC Place; PINAL; ***146** J-9; ★ **PHOE**; mail Apache Junction z 85219; pop. incl. with Apache Junction (Inc. Place)
Palominas; RMC Place; COCHISE; **147** O-12; 🅿; z 85615
Palo Verde; RMC Place; MARICOPA; **146** J-6; elev. 840ft./256m.; 🅿; ★ **PHOE**; z 85343; ● 155
Palo Verde Stand; RMC Place; PIMA; mail Sells z 85634; ● 45
Pan Tak; RMC Place; PIMA; **147** N-9; located on Papago Ind. Res.; mail Sells z 85634
Pantano; RMC Place; PIMA; mail Benson z 85602; rural
Papago; RMC Place; MARICOPA; ***147** K-5; mail Scottsdale z 85256-57, z 85271
Papago Agency; PIMA; see Sells (CDP)
Paradise; RMC Place; COCHISE; **147** N-14; 🅿; z 85632; ● 60
Paradise Valley; Inc. Place; MARICOPA; **145** C-6; elev. 1,360ft./415m.; 🅿; ★ **PHOE**; z 85253; Ⓟ 11,773; Ⓒ 13,664
Parker; Inc. Place; ⊡ LA PAZ; **146** H-3; located on Colorado River Ind. Res.; elev. 413ft./126m.; 🅿 🄷; z 85344; location of Indian Agency; Ⓟ 2,897; Ⓒ 3,140
Parker Strip; CDP-Census Area Only; LA PAZ; ***146** H-3; elev. 600ft./183m.; mail Parker z 85344; Ⓟ 1,646; Ⓒ 3,302
Parks (Maine); CDP; COCONINO; **146** E-8; elev. 7,077ft./2,157m.; 🅿; z 86018; Ⓒ 1,137
Pascua Yaqui Reservation; Indian Reservation; PIMA; ★ **TUC**; mail Tucson z 85746; Ⓟ 562; Ⓒ 3,315
Pasqua Village; PIMA; see Yaqui (RMC Place)
Patagonia; Inc. Place; SANTA CRUZ; **147** O-10; elev. 4,057ft./1,237m.; 🅿; z 85624; Ⓟ 888; Ⓒ 881
Paulden; CDP; YAVAPAI; **146** F-7; elev. 4,407ft./1,343m.; 🅿; z 86334; Ⓒ 3,420
Paul Spur; RMC Place; COCHISE; ***147** O-13; mail Douglas z 85607
Payson; Inc. Place; GILA; **146** H-9; elev. 4,887ft./1,490m.; 🅿 🄷; z 85541, z 85547; Ⓟ 8,377; Ⓒ 13,620
Peach Springs; CDP; MOHAVE; **146** E-5; located on Hualapai Ind. Res.; elev. 4,800ft./1,463m.; 🅿; z 86434; Ⓟ 787; Ⓒ 600
Pearce; RMC Place; COCHISE; **147** N-12; elev. 4,375ft./1,334m.; 🅿; z 85625
Peeples Valley; CDP; YAVAPAI; **146** H-6; 🅿; z 86332; Ⓒ 374
Peoria; Inc. Place; MARICOPA; **146** J-7; elev. 1,141ft./348m.; 🅿; ★ **PHOE**; z 85345, z 85380-83, z 85385; Ⓟ 50,675; Ⓒ 108,364; ◆ 176,537
Peralta Estates; RMC Place; PINAL; ***146** J-8; mail Apache Junction z 85218; pop. incl. with Mesa (Inc. Place)
Peridot; CDP; GRAHAM, GILA; **146** J-11; located on San Carlos Ind. Res.; elev. 2,600ft./792m.; 🅿; z 85542; Ⓟ 957; Ⓒ 1,266
Perkinsville; RMC Place; YAVAPAI; ***146** F-7; mail Chino Valley z 86323; rural
Perryville; RMC Place; MARICOPA; ***146** J-7; elev. 979ft./298m.; ★ **PHOE**; mail Goodyear z 85338
Petrie; RMC Place; PIMA; ★ **TUC**; pop. incl. with Tucson (Inc. Place)
Phoenix; Inc. Place; **STATE CAPITAL**; ⊡ MARICOPA; **146** J-8; elev. 1,090ft./332m.; 🅿 🄷 🄲 298,077 ■; ★ **PHOE**; z 85001-46, z 85048, z 85050-51, z 85053-55, z 85060-76, z 85078-80, z 85082-83, z 85085-87, z 85097-99; Ⓟ 983,392; Ⓒ 1,321,045; ◆ 1,675,791
Phoenix Pecos; RMC Place; MARICOPA; mail Phoenix z 85048, z 85070; pop. incl. with Phoenix (Inc. Place)
Pia Oik; RMC Place; PIMA; ***147** N-6; located on Papago Ind. Res.; elev. 1,957ft./596m.; mail Sells z 85634; ● 30
Picacho; RMC Place; PINAL; **147** L-9; elev. 1,624ft./495m.; 🅿; z 85141, z 85241; ● 500
Picture Rocks; CDP-Census Area Only; PIMA; ***147** M-9; ★ **TUC**; mail Marana z 85653; Ⓟ 4,026; Ⓒ 8,139
Pima; Inc. Place; GRAHAM; **147** K-12; elev. 2,848ft./868m.; 🅿; z 85543 & mail Eden z 85535; Ⓟ 1,725; Ⓒ 1,989
PIMA; **147** M-8; Ⓟ 666,880; Ⓒ 843,746; ◆ 1,007,758
PINAL; **147** L-9; Ⓟ 116,379; Ⓒ 179,727; ◆ 355,169
Pine; CDP; GILA; **146** H-9; elev. 5,369ft./1,636m.; 🅿; z 85544; Ⓒ 1,931
Pinedale; RMC Place; NAVAJO; **146** H-11; elev. 6,454ft./1,967m.; 🅿; z 85934; ● 200
Pine Springs; RMC Place; APACHE; ***146** E-13; located on Navajo Nation Ind. Res.; mail Houck z 86506; ● 100
Pinetop; RMC Place; NAVAJO; 🅿; z 85935; pop. incl. with Pinetop-Lakeside (Inc. Place)
Pinetop Country Club; RMC Place; NAVAJO; ***146** H-12; elev. 7,299ft./2,225m.; mail Pinetop z 85935; ● 650
Pinetop-Lakeside; Inc. Place; NAVAJO; **146** H-12; elev. 6,959ft./2,121m.; mail Lakeside z 85929, Pinetop z 85935; Ⓟ 2,422; Ⓒ 3,582
Pinnacle Peak Village; RMC Place; MARICOPA; ***146** I-8; elev. 1,930ft./588m.; ★ **PHOE**; mail Scottsdale z 85255; pop. incl. with Scottsdale (Inc. Place)
Pinon; CDP; NAVAJO; **146** C-11; located on Hopi Ind. Res.; elev. 6,340ft./1,932m.; 🅿; z 86510, z 86520; Ⓟ 468; Ⓒ 1,190
Pioneer; RMC Place; MARICOPA; ★ **PHOE**; mail Mesa z 85210; pop. incl. with Mesa (Inc. Place)
Pipeola; RMC Place; MARICOPA; ★ **PHOE**; pop. incl. with Phoenix (Inc. Place)
Pirtleville; CDP; COCHISE; **147** O-13; elev. 3,960ft./1,207m.; 🅿; z 85626; Ⓟ 1,364; Ⓒ 1,550
Pisinemo; CDP; PIMA; **147** N-7; located on Papago Ind. Res.; elev. 1,895ft./578m.; 🅿; z 85634; Ⓟ 341; Ⓒ 237
Plantsite; RMC Place; GREENLEE; **147** K-13; mail Morenci z 85540; ● 600
Polacca; RMC Place; NAVAJO; **146** D-11; located on Hopi Ind. Res.; 🅿; z 86042; Ⓟ 1,108; ● 700
Poland Junction; RMC Place; YAVAPAI; ***146** G-7; elev. 4,897ft./1,493m.; mail Mayer z 86333; ● 50
Pomerene; RMC Place; COCHISE; ***147** N-11; elev. 3,542ft./1,080m.; 🅿; z 85627; ● 450
Ponderosa Park; RMC Place; YAVAPAI; ***146** G-7; elev. 5,680ft./1,731m.; mail Prescott z 86301; ● 280
Portal; RMC Place; COCHISE; **147** N-14; elev. 4,773ft./1,455m.; 🅿; z 85632
Porter Mountain Estates; RMC Place; NAVAJO; ***146** H-12; elev. 7,036ft./2,145m.; mail Lakeside z 85929; ● 180
Poston; CDP; LA PAZ; **146** H-3; located on Colorado River Ind. Res.; 🅿; z 85371; Ⓟ 480; Ⓒ 389
Potato Patch; RMC Place; YAVAPAI; ***146** G-7; elev. 6,849ft./2,088m.; mail Prescott z 86301; ● 80
Prescott; Inc. Place; ⊡ YAVAPAI; **146** G-7; elev. 5,368ft./1,636m.; 🅿 🄷 🄲 4,827 ■; z 86301-05, z 86313, z 86330; Ⓟ 26,592; Ⓒ 33,938; ◆ 40,148
Prescott Country Club; RMC Place; YAVAPAI; ***146** G-7; elev. 4,700ft./1,433m.; mail Prescott z 86301; ● 500
Prescott Valley (Agua Fria); Inc. Place; YAVAPAI; **146** G-7; elev. 4,900ft./1,494m.; 🅿; z 86312, z 86314-15; Ⓟ 8,858; Ⓒ 23,535; ◆ 39,286
Presidential Estates; RMC Place; COCHISE; ***147** N-11; mail Huachuca City z 85616; ● 110
Pueblo del Sol; RMC Place; COCHISE; ***147** O-11; elev. 4,500ft./1,372m.; mail Sierra Vista z 85635; pop. incl. with Sierra Vista (Inc. Place)
Pueblo del Sol Village I; RMC Place; COCHISE; ***147** O-11; elev. 4,746ft./1,447m.; mail Sierra Vista z 85650
Pueblo Gardens; RMC Place; PIMA; ★ **TUC**; pop. incl. with Tucson (Inc. Place)
Pumpkin Center; GILA; see Punkin Center (RMC Place)
Punkin Center (Pumpkin Center); RMC Place; GILA; ***146** I-9; mail Tonto Basin z 85553; ● 100

Q

Quartzsite; Inc. Place; LA PAZ; **146** I-3; elev. 876ft./267m.; 🅿; z 85346, z 85359; Ⓟ 1,876; Ⓒ 3,354
Queen Creek; Inc. Place; MARICOPA; **146** J-8; elev. 1,400ft./427m.; 🅿; ★ **PHOE**; z 85140, z 85142-43, z 85240, z 85242-43 & mail Chandler Heights z 85227; Ⓟ 2,667; Ⓒ 4,316; ◆ 7,695
Queen Valley; CDP; PINAL; ***146** J-9; elev. 2,150ft./655m.; 🅿; z 85118, z 85218; Ⓒ 820
Querino; RMC Place; APACHE; ***146** E-13; located on Navajo Nation Ind. Res.; elev. 6,101ft./1,860m.; mail Houck z 86506; ● 50

R

Rainbow Valley; RMC Place; MARICOPA; ***146** J-7; elev. 940ft./287m.; mail Buckeye z 85326; pop. incl. with Goodyear (Inc. Place)
Ranch del Sol; RMC Place; MARICOPA; ***146** J-8; ★ **PHOE**; mail Gilbert z 85296; ● 400

Entries in **UPPERCASE** are counties.
Entries in **bold** have populations of 2,500 or more.
Names in parentheses are alternate names.

Inc. Place	Incorporated Place
RMC Place	Rand McNally Designated Place
CDP	Census Designated Place
MCD	Minor Civil Division

⊡	County Seat
▲	Minor Civil Division
elev.	Elevation
🅿	Post Office
🄷	Hospital
🄲	College
■	Principal Business Center
★	Ranally Metro Area (RMA) Abbreviation
z	Zip Code(s)
Ⓟ	Previous Census Population
Ⓡ	Revised Census Population
Ⓐ	Annexation Population
●	Rand McNally Population Estimate
Ⓒ	Final Census Population
Ⓢ	Special Census Population
◆	Estimated Population

For additional definitions see Glossary, Volume 1, and Introduction, Volume 2.

Ranchos Carmela; RMC Place; COCHISE; ***147** O-11; elev. 4,437ft./1,352m.; mail Sierra Vista **Z** 85635
Randolph; RMC Place; PINAL; ***147** K-9; elev. 1,440ft./439m.; mail Casa Grande **Z** 85222; ● 400
Reata Pass; RMC Place; MARICOPA; ***146** I-8; elev. 2,569ft./783m.; ★ **PHOE**; mail Scottsdale **Z** 85255; pop. incl. with Scottsdale (Inc. Place)
Redington; RMC Place; PIMA; ***147** M-11; mail Benson **Z** 85602; rural
Red Lake; RMC Place; COCONINO; **146** E-7; mail Tonalea **Z** 86044; ● 100
Red Mesa; CDP; APACHE; **146** A-13; located on Navajo Nation Ind. Res.; mail Teec Nos Pos **Z** 86514; © 237
Red Rock; RMC Place; APACHE; **146** B-13; located on Navajo Nation Ind. Res.; elev. 1,875ft./572m.; mail Red Valley **Z** 86544, Shiprock **Z** 87420; ● 300
Red Rock (Red Valley); RMC Place; PINAL; **147** L-9; [P]; **Z** 85145, **Z** 85245 & mail Red Valley **Z** 86544
Red Valley; PINAL; see Red Rock (RMC Place)
Rillito; RMC Place; PIMA; **147** M-9; elev. 2,056ft./627m.; [P]; ★ **TUC**; **Z** 85654; ● 400
Rimrock; RMC Place; YAVAPAI; **146** G-8; elev. 3,440ft./1,049m.; [P]; **Z** 86335; rural
Rincon; RMC Place; PIMA; ***147** M-8; elev. 2,586ft./788m.; mail Sells **Z** 85634, Tucson **Z** 85710, **Z** 85730, **Z** 85747-48; rural
Rio Rico; RMC Place; SANTA CRUZ; **147** O-10; [P]; **Z** 85648 & mail Nogales **Z** 85621; ● 1,400
Rio Rico Northeast; CDP-Census Area Only; SANTA CRUZ; ***147** O-10; © 3,164
Rio Rico Northwest; CDP-Census Area Only; SANTA CRUZ; ***147** O-10; © 2,882
Rio Rico Southeast; CDP-Census Area Only; SANTA CRUZ; ***147** O-10; © 1,590
Rio Rico Southwest; CDP-Census Area Only; SANTA CRUZ; ***147** O-10; © 2,777
Rio Salado; RMC Place; MARICOPA; ***146** J-7; ★ **PHOE**; mail Phoenix **Z** 85006, **Z** 85034, **Z** 85036, **Z** 85041, **Z** 85074; pop. incl. with Phoenix (Inc. Place)
Rio Verde; CDP; MARICOPA; **146** I-8; elev. 1,680ft./512m.; [P]; **Z** 85263; © 1,419
Riverside; RMC Place; PINAL; ***147** K-10; elev. 1,800ft./549m.; mail Kearny **Z** 85237; rural
Riviera; RMC Place; MOHAVE; ***146** F-2; elev. 510ft./155m.; mail Bullhead City **Z** 86439, **Z** 86442; pop. incl. with Bullhead City (Inc. Place)
Rock Point; CDP; APACHE; **146** B-13; located on Navajo Nation Ind. Res.; [P]; **Z** 86545; © 724
Rock Springs; RMC Place; YAVAPAI; ***146** H-7; elev. 2,021ft./616m.; [P]; **Z** 85324 & mail Phoenix **Z** 85026
Rocky Point Junction; PIMA; see Why (RMC Place)
Roll; RMC Place; YUMA; **147** L-3; elev. 259ft./79m.; [P]; **Z** 85347
Rolling Hills Country Club Estates; RMC Place; PIMA; ★ **TUC**; mail Tucson **Z** 85710; pop. incl. with Tucson (Inc. Place)
Roosevelt; RMC Place; GILA; **146** I-10; elev. 2,215ft./675m.; [P]; **Z** 85545; ● 50
Roosevelt Lake Estates; RMC Place; GILA; ***146** I-10; elev. 2,200ft./671m.; mail Roosevelt **Z** 85545; ● 540
Roosevelt Resort; RMC Place; GILA; ***146** J-10; elev. 2,484ft./757m.; mail Roosevelt **Z** 85545; ● 170
Rough Rock; CDP; APACHE; **146** C-12; located on Navajo Nation Ind. Res.; mail Chinle **Z** 86503; ℗ 523; © 469
Round Rock; CDP; APACHE; **146** B-13; located on Navajo Nation Ind. Res.; elev. 5,350ft./1,631m.; [P]; **Z** 86547; © 601
Royal Estates; RMC Place; SANTA CRUZ; ***147** O-10; elev. 4,000ft./1,219m.; mail Nogales **Z** 85621; pop. incl. with Nogales (Inc. Place)
Rye; RMC Place; GILA; ***146** H-9; mail Payson **Z** 85541; ● 30

S

Sacaton; CDP; PINAL; **147** K-8; located on Gila River Ind. Res.; elev. 1,284ft./391m.; [P] [H]; **Z** 85147, **Z** 85247; location of Pima Indian Agency; ℗ 1,452; © 1,584
Sacaton Flats; RMC Place; PINAL; ***147** K-8; mail Sacaton **Z** 85247; ● 200
Sacred Mountain; RMC Place; COCONINO; ***146** E-9; elev. 6,320ft./1,926m.; mail Flagstaff **Z** 86001; rural
Safford; Inc. Place; ⊡ GRAHAM; **147** K-13; elev. 2,920ft./890m.; [P] [H]; **Z** 85546, **Z** 85548; ℗ 7,359; © 9,232
Saginaw; RMC Place; COCHISE; ***147** O-12; mail Bisbee **Z** 85603; pop. incl. with Bisbee (Inc. Place)
Sahuarita; Inc. Place; PIMA; **147** N-10; elev. 2,702ft./824m.; [P]; **Z** 85614, **Z** 85629; ℗ 1,629; © 3,242; ◆ 19,454
Sahuarita Heights; RMC Place; PIMA; ***147** N-10; elev. 2,750ft./838m.; mail Sahuarita **Z** 85629; ● 280
Saint David; CDP; COCHISE; **147** N-12; elev. 3,595ft./1,096m.; [P]; **Z** 85630; ℗ 1,468; © 1,744
Saint Johns; Inc. Place; ⊡ APACHE; **146** G-13; elev. 5,686ft./1,733m.; [P]; **Z** 85936; ℗ 3,294; © 3,269
Saint Michaels; CDP; APACHE; **146** D-14; located on Navajo Nation Ind. Res.; elev. 6,800ft./2,073m.; [P]; **Z** 86511; ℗ 1,119; © 1,295
Salado; RMC Place; APACHE; ***146** G-13; mail Saint Johns **Z** 85936; rural
Salina (Salina Springs); RMC Place; APACHE; **146** C-12; located on Navajo Nation Ind. Res.; mail Chinle **Z** 86503
Salina Springs; APACHE; see Salina (RMC Place)
Salome; CDP; LA PAZ; **146** I-4; elev. 1,877ft./572m.; [P]; **Z** 85348; © 1,690
Salt River Reservation; Indian Reservation; MARICOPA; mail Scottsdale **Z** 85256; Indian Agency located in Scottsdale, AZ; ℗ 4,089; © 6,405; Ⓢ 5,910
San Carlos (San Carlos Agency); CDP; GILA; **146** J-11; located on San Carlos Ind. Res.; elev. 2,635ft./803m.; [P] [H]; **Z** 85550; location of Indian Agency; ℗ 2,918; © 3,716
San Carlos Agency; GILA; see San Carlos (CDP)
San Carlos Reservation; Indian Reservation; GRAHAM, GILA, PINAL; mail San Carlos **Z** 85550; also location of Indian Agency; ℗ 6,104; © 9,385
Sanchez; RMC Place; GRAHAM; ***147** K-13; elev. 3,200ft./975m.; mail Safford **Z** 85546; rural
Sanders (Cheto); RMC Place; APACHE; **146** E-13; elev. 5,865ft./1,788m.; [P]; **Z** 86512; ● 550
Sand Springs; RMC Place; COCONINO; ***146** D-10; located on Hopi Ind. Res.; mail Kykotsmovi Village **Z** 86039; rural
San Jose; RMC Place; COCHISE; mail Bisbee **Z** 85603; pop. incl. with Bisbee (Inc. Place)
San Jose; RMC Place; GRAHAM; ***147** K-13; mail Safford **Z** 85546; ● 250
San Lucy Village; RMC Place; MARICOPA; ***147** K-6; elev. 702ft./214m.; mail Gila Bend **Z** 85337
San Luis; RMC Place; PIMA; ***147** M-8; located on Papago Ind. Res.; mail Sells **Z** 85634; ● 60
San Luis; Inc. Place; YUMA; **147** L-2; elev. 131ft./40m.; [P]; ★ **YUMA**; **Z** 85349; ℗ 4,212; © 15,322; ◆ 22,126
San Manuel; CDP; PINAL; **147** L-11; elev. 3,400ft./1,036m.; [P]; **Z** 85631; ℗ 4,009; © 4,375
San Miguel; RMC Place; PIMA; **147** O-8; located on Papago Ind. Res.; elev. 2,477ft./755m.; mail Sells **Z** 85634
San Pedro; RMC Place; PIMA; ***147** M-9; elev. 2,685ft./818m.; mail Sells **Z** 85634
San Rafael Terrace; RMC Place; COCHISE; mail Bisbee **Z** 85603; pop. incl. with Bisbee (Inc. Place)
San Serafin; PIMA; see Ak Chin (RMC Place)
San Simon; RMC Place; COCHISE; **147** M-14; elev. 3,612ft./1,101m.; [P]; **Z** 85632; ● 260
Santa Cruz; RMC Place; PINAL; ***146** J-7; mail Bapchule **Z** 85221; rural
SANTA CRUZ; **147** O-10; ℗ 29,676; © 38,381; ◆ 43,726
Santa Maria; RMC Place; MARICOPA; **145** E-4; elev. 1,015ft./309m.; ★ **PHOE**; mail Phoenix **Z** 85009; pop. incl. with Phoenix (Inc. Place)
Santan; CDP; PINAL; ***147** K-8; located on Gila River Ind. Res.; mail Sacaton **Z** 85247; ℗ 330; © 651
Santa Rita; RMC Place; SANTA CRUZ; ***147** N-10; mail Tumacacori **Z** 85640; rural
Santa Rosa (Gu Achi); CDP; PIMA; **147** M-8; located on Papago Ind. Res.; mail Sells **Z** 85634; ℗ 493; © 438
San Xavier; RMC Place; PIMA; **147** N-10; mail Tucson **Z** 85746; ● 70
Sasabe; RMC Place; PIMA; **147** O-9; elev. 3,566ft./1,087m.; [P]; **Z** 85633
Sawmill; CDP; APACHE; **146** D-14; located on Navajo Nation Ind. Res.; elev. 7,636ft./2,327m.; ℗ 507; © 612
Schuchk; RMC Place; PIMA; ***147** M-8; located on Papago Ind. Res.; mail Sells **Z** 85634; rural
Schuchuli (Sialatuk); RMC Place; PIMA; **147** M-6; located on Papago Ind. Res.; elev. 1,972ft./601m.; mail Sells **Z** 85634
Scottsdale; Inc. Place; MARICOPA; **146** J-8; elev. 1,250ft./381m.; [P] [H] [C] 750 ■; ★ **PHOE**; **Z** 85250-64, **Z** 85266-69, **Z** 85271; location of Salt River Indian Agency; ℗ 130,075; © 202,705; ◆ 239,766
Seba Dalkai; RMC Place; NAVAJO; ***146** E-11; elev. 5,600ft./1,707m.; mail Winslow **Z** 86047; ● 100
Second Mesa; CDP; NAVAJO; **146** D-11; located on Hopi Ind. Res.; elev. 5,680ft./1,731m.; [P]; **Z** 86043; ℗ 929; © 814
Sedona; Inc. Place; COCONINO, YAVAPAI; **146** F-8; elev. 4,400ft./1,341m.; [P]; **Z** 86336, **Z** 86339-41, **Z** 86351; ℗ 7,720; © 10,192
Sehili; APACHE; see Tsaile (CDP)
Seligman; CDP; YAVAPAI; **146** E-6; elev. 5,242ft./1,598m.; [P]; **Z** 86337; © 456
Sells (Papago Agency); CDP; PIMA; **147** N-8; located on Papago Ind. Res.; elev. 2,360ft./719m.; [P] [H]; **Z** 85634; location of Indian Agency; ℗ 2,750; © 2,799
Sentinel; RMC Place; MARICOPA; ***147** K-5; mail Dateland **Z** 85333
Shaw Butte; RMC Place; MARICOPA; ***146** J-7; ★ **PHOE**; mail Phoenix **Z** 85029, **Z** 85071; pop. incl. with Phoenix (Inc. Place)
Sheldon; RMC Place; GREENLEE; ***147** K-14; elev. 3,566ft./1,087m.; mail Duncan **Z** 85534; rural
Sherwood; RMC Place; MARICOPA; ***146** J-8; ★ **PHOE**; mail Mesa **Z** 85204, **Z** 85214; pop. incl. with Mesa (Inc. Place)
Sherwood Village; RMC Place; PIMA; ★ **TUC**; pop. incl. with Tucson (Inc. Place)
Shipolovi; NAVAJO; see Sipaulovi (RMC Place)
Shongopovi; CDP-Census Area Only; NAVAJO; ***146** D-11; located on Hopi Ind. Res.; mail Second Mesa **Z** 86043; ℗ 730; © 632
Shonto (Navajo Boarding School); CDP; NAVAJO; **146** B-10; located on Navajo Nation Ind. Res.; elev. 6,240ft./1,902m.; [P]; **Z** 86054; ℗ 710; © 568
Shopishk; RMC Place; PINAL; ***147** L-8; located on Papago Ind. Res.; mail Sells **Z** 85634; rural
Short Creek; MOHAVE; see Colorado City (Inc. Place)
Show Low; Inc. Place; NAVAJO; **146** H-12; elev. 6,347ft./1,935m.; [P] [H]; **Z** 85901-02, **Z** 85911; ℗ 5,020; © 7,695
Shumway; RMC Place; NAVAJO; **146** H-12; mail Show Low **Z** 85901; ● 200
Shungopavi; RMC Place; NAVAJO; ● 570
Sialatuk; PIMA; see Schuchuli (RMC Place)
Sierra Adobe; RMC Place; MARICOPA; ★ **PHOE**; mail Phoenix **Z** 85023-24, **Z** 85027, **Z** 85050, **Z** 85053-54, **Z** 85080; pop. incl. with Phoenix (Inc. Place)
Sierra Bonita Ranch; RMC Place; GRAHAM; ***147** L-12; elev. 4,391ft./1,338m.; mail Willcox **Z** 85643; ● 30
Sierra Vista; Inc. Place; COCHISE; **147** S-13; [P] [H] ■; **Z** 85613, **Z** 85635-36, **Z** 85650, **Z** 85670-71; ℗ 32,983; © 37,775; ◆ 42,469
Sierra Vista Estates; RMC Place; COCHISE; ***147** O-11; elev. 4,706ft./1,434m.; mail Sierra Vista **Z** 85650
Sierra Vista Southeast; CDP-Census Area Only; COCHISE; ***147** O-12; mail Hereford **Z** 85615; ℗ 9,237; © 14,348
Sil Nakaya; PIMA; see Sil Nakya (RMC Place)
Sil Nakya (Sil Nakaya); RMC Place; PIMA; **147** M-8; located on Papago Ind. Res.; mail Sells **Z** 85634
Silverbell; RMC Place; PIMA; ★ **TUC**; mail Tucson **Z** 85745, **Z** 85754
Sipaulovi (Shipolovi); RMC Place; NAVAJO; ***146** D-11; mail Second Mesa **Z** 86043; ● 230
Site Six; RMC Place; MOHAVE; mail Lake Havasu City **Z** 86403; pop. incl. with Lake Havasu City (Inc. Place)
Skull Valley; RMC Place; YAVAPAI; **146** G-6; elev. 4,253ft./1,296m.; [P]; **Z** 86338
Skyline Bel Aire Estates; RMC Place; PIMA; ***147** M-10; elev. 2,800ft./853m.; ★ **TUC**; mail Tucson **Z** 85718; ● 1,500
Skyway Village; RMC Place; MARICOPA; ***146** J-8; ★ **PHOE**; mail Mesa **Z** 85205; pop. incl. with Mesa (Inc. Place)
Smoke Signal; RMC Place; NAVAJO; ***146** C-12; mail Chinle **Z** 86503; rural
Snowflake; Inc. Place; NAVAJO; **146** G-12; elev. 5,600ft./1,707m.; [P]; **Z** 85937, **Z** 85942; ℗ 3,679; © 4,460
Solomon; RMC Place; GRAHAM; **147** L-13; elev. 2,970ft./905m.; [P]; **Z** 85551; ● 530
Somerton; Inc. Place; YUMA; **147** L-2; [P]; ★ **YUMA**; **Z** 85350; ℗ 5,282; © 7,266
Sonoita; CDP; SANTA CRUZ; **147** N-11; elev. 4,880ft./1,487m.; [P]; **Z** 85637; © 826
Sonora Town; RMC Place; MARICOPA; ***146** J-8; ★ **PHOE**; mail Gilbert **Z** 85233
South Bisbee; RMC Place; COCHISE; ***147** O-12; mail Bisbee **Z** 85603; ● 100
South Central; RMC Place; MARICOPA; ***146** J-7; ★ **PHOE**; mail Phoenix **Z** 85040, **Z** 85066; pop. incl. with Phoenix (Inc. Place)
South Komelik (Komelik); RMC Place; PIMA; ***147** N-8; located on Papago Ind. Res.; mail Sells **Z** 85634; ● 90
South Santan; RMC Place; PINAL; ***147** K-8; elev. 1,296ft./395m.; mail Sacaton **Z** 85247; ● 200
South Tucson; Inc. Place; PIMA; **147** M-10; elev. 2,430ft./741m.; ★ **TUC**; mail Tucson **Z** 85713, **Z** 85725; ℗ 5,093; © 5,490
Springerville; Inc. Place; APACHE; **146** H-13; elev. 6,968ft./2,124m.; [P] [H]; **Z** 85938; ℗ 1,802; © 1,972
Spring Valley; CDP; YAVAPAI; ***146** H-7; elev. 3,910ft./1,192m.; [P]; **Z** 86333; © 1,019
Sprucedale; RMC Place; GREENLEE; ***146** I-13; elev. 7,532ft./2,296m.; mail Alpine **Z** 85920, Blue **Z** 85922; ● 40
Stanfield; CDP; PINAL; **147** K-8; elev. 1,300ft./396m.; [P]; **Z** 85172, **Z** 85272; © 651
Stanton; RMC Place; YAVAPAI; ***146** H-6; mail Congress **Z** 85332; rural
Stargo; RMC Place; GREENLEE; ***147** K-13; mail Morenci **Z** 85540; ● 40
Star Valley (Diamond Star); Inc. Place; GILA; ***146** H-9; [P]; **Z** 85541; incorporated November 1, 2005; not reported in 2000 Census; ● 2,500
Steam; RMC Place; YUMA; mail Yuma **Z** 85364; ● 400
Steamboat; CDP-Census Area Only; APACHE; ***146** D-12; © 233
Steamboat Canyon; RMC Place; APACHE; **146** D-12; located on Navajo Nation Ind. Res.; mail Ganado **Z** 86505; ● 350
Stoneman Lake; RMC Place; COCONINO; ***146** G-9; mail Happy Jack **Z** 86024; rural
Strawberry; CDP; GILA; **146** G-9; [P]; **Z** 85544; © 1,028
Summerhaven (Mount Lemmon); RMC Place; PIMA; **147** M-10; elev. 7,600ft./2,316m.; mail Mount Lemmon **Z** 85619; ● 100
Summit; CDP-Census Area Only; PIMA; ***147** M-10; © 3,702
Sun; RMC Place; PIMA; ***147** M-10; ★ **TUC**; mail Tucson **Z** 85716-17, **Z** 85719, **Z** 85733; pop. incl. with Tucson (Inc. Place)
Sun City; CDP; MARICOPA; **146** J-7; elev. 1,135ft./346m.; [P] [H]; ★ **PHOE**; **Z** 85351, **Z** 85372-75, **Z** 85379, **Z** 85387 & mail Sun City West **Z** 85376, Surprise **Z** 85378; ℗ 38,126; © 38,309; ◆ 51,147
Sun City West; CDP; MARICOPA; **146** I-7; [P] [H]; ★ **PHOE**; **Z** 85375-76, **Z** 85387 & mail Surprise **Z** 85374, **Z** 85379; ℗ 15,997; © 26,344; ◆ 35,183
Sunflower; RMC Place; MARICOPA; ***146** I-9; mail Mesa **Z** 85201; rural
Sunizona; RMC Place; COCHISE; ***147** N-13; mail Pearce **Z** 85625; ● 400
Sun Lakes; CDP; MARICOPA; **147** K-8; [P]; ★ **PHOE**; **Z** 85248; ℗ 6,578; © 11,936
Sunnyslope; RMC Place; MARICOPA; ***146** J-8; ★ **PHOE**; mail Phoenix **Z** 85020, **Z** 85022, **Z** 85068; pop. incl. with Phoenix (Inc. Place)
Sunrise; RMC Place; COCONINO; ***146** E-10; elev. 4,702ft./1,433m.; mail Winslow **Z** 86047; ● 200
Sunrise; RMC Place; YAVAPAI; ***146** G-7; elev. 4,600ft./1,402m.; mail Chino Valley **Z** 86323; pop. incl. with Chino Valley (Inc. Place)
Sunrise Springs; RMC Place; APACHE; **146** E-12; located on Navajo Nation Ind. Res.; elev. 6,069ft./1,850m.; mail Ganado **Z** 86505; rural
Sunset; RMC Place; GRAHAM; ***147** L-12; mail Willcox **Z** 85643; rural
Sunset Acres; RMC Place; COCHISE; ***147** O-12; mail Bisbee **Z** 85603; ● 300
Sunsites; COCHISE; see Arizona Sun Sites (RMC Place)
Suntown; RMC Place; MARICOPA; ★ **PHOE**; mail Peoria **Z** 85345; pop. incl. with Peoria (Inc. Place)
Sun Valley; CDP-Census Area Only; GILA; ***146** H-9; former CDP; became part of Star Valley November 1, 2005; © 1,536
Sun Valley; RMC Place; NAVAJO; **146** F-12; elev. 5,300ft./1,615m.; [P]; **Z** 86029; rural
Supai; CDP; COCONINO; **146** C-6; located on Hualapai Ind. Res.; elev. 3,195ft./974m.; [P]; **Z** 86435; ℗ 423; © 0
Superior; Inc. Place; PINAL; **146** J-10; elev. 2,830ft./863m.; [P]; **Z** 85173, **Z** 85273; ℗ 3,468; © 3,254
Superstition Estates; RMC Place; PINAL; ***146** J-9; ★ **PHOE**; mail Apache Junction **Z** 85220; pop. incl. with Apache Junction (Inc. Place)
Surprise; Inc. Place; MARICOPA; **146** I-7; elev. 1,178ft./359m.; [P]; ★ **PHOE**; **Z** 85374, **Z** 85378-79, **Z** 85387-88; ℗ 7,122; © 30,848; ◆ 54,953
Sweetwater; RMC Place; APACHE; ***146** A-13; located on Navajo Nation Ind. Res.; mail Farmington **Z** 87401; ● 30
Sweetwater; RMC Place; PINAL; ***147** K-8; elev. 1,212ft./369m.; mail Bapchule **Z** 85221; ● 120
Swift Trail Junction; CDP; GRAHAM; ***147** L-13; mail Safford **Z** 85546; ℗ 1,203; © 2,195

T

Tacna; CDP; YUMA; **147** L-4; elev. 347ft./106m.; [P]; **Z** 85352; © 555
Tall Pines; RMC Place; NAVAJO; ***146** H-12; elev. 6,560ft./1,999m.; mail Pinetop **Z** 85935; pop. incl. with Show Low (Inc. Place)
Tanque Verde; CDP; PIMA; ***147** M-10; ★ **TUC**; © 16,195
Tapco; RMC Place; YAVAPAI; ***146** G-8; mail Clarkdale **Z** 86324; rural
Tat Momoli (Jackrabbit); RMC Place; PINAL; ***147** L-8; located on Papago Ind. Res.; mail Sells **Z** 85634
Taylor; Inc. Place; NAVAJO; **146** G-12; elev. 5,629ft./1,716m.; [P]; **Z** 85939; ℗ 2,418; © 3,176
Teec Nos Pos (Tes Nos Pes); CDP; APACHE; **146** A-13; located on Navajo Nation Ind. Res.; elev. 5,240ft./1,597m.; [P]; **Z** 86514, **Z** 86535, **Z** 86544; ℗ 317; © 799
Tees To; NAVAJO; see Tees Toh (RMC Place)
Tees Toh (Tees To); RMC Place; NAVAJO; ***146** E-11; located on Navajo Nation Ind. Res.; elev. 5,745ft./1,751m.; mail Winslow **Z** 86047; ● 100
Tempe; Inc. Place; MARICOPA; **146** J-8; elev. 1,160ft./354m.; [P] [H] [C] 55,768 ■; ★ **PHOE**; **Z** 85280-85, **Z** 85287; ℗ 141,865; © 158,625; ◆ 174,157
Temple Bar; MOHAVE; see Temple Bar Marina (RMC Place)
Temple Bar Marina (Temple Bar); RMC Place; MOHAVE; **146** C-3; elev. 1,279ft./390m.; [P]; **Z** 86443; ● 100
Tes Nez Iah; RMC Place; APACHE; ***146** A-12; mail Kayenta **Z** 86033; ● 30
Tes Nos Pes; APACHE; see Teec Nos Pos (CDP)
Thatcher; Inc. Place; GRAHAM; **147** K-12; elev. 2,932ft./894m.; [P]; **Z** 85552; ℗ 3,763; © 4,022
Theba (Gila River Ranch); RMC Place; MARICOPA; **147** K-6; mail Gila Bend **Z** 85337; ● 100
The Gap; RMC Place; COCONINO; **146** C-9; located on Navajo Nation Ind. Res.; mail Cameron **Z** 86020; ● 100
The Summit Estates; RMC Place; COCHISE; ***147** O-11; elev. 4,600ft./1,402m.; mail Sierra Vista **Z** 85635; pop. incl. with Sierra Vista (Inc. Place)
Three Points; CDP; PIMA; ***147** M-9; elev. 2,339ft./713m.; mail Tucson **Z** 85714; ℗ 2,175; © 5,273
Three Way; RMC Place; GREENLEE; ***147** K-14; elev. 3,600ft./1,097m.; mail Duncan **Z** 85534; rural
Tintown; RMC Place; COCHISE; ***147** O-12; mail Bisbee **Z** 85603
Tohono O'odham Reservation; Indian Reservation; PINAL, MARICOPA, PIMA; © 10,483
Tolani; COCONINO; see Tolani Lake (RMC Place)
Tolani Lake (Tolani); RMC Place; COCONINO; ***146** E-10; located on Navajo Nation Ind. Res.; elev. 4,950ft./1,509m.; mail Winslow **Z** 86047; ● 30
Tolleson; Inc. Place; MARICOPA; **145** E-4; [P]; ★ **PHOE**; **Z** 85353; ℗ 4,434; © 4,974
Toltec; RMC Place; PINAL; ***147** L-8; [P]; **Z** 85131, **Z** 85231; pop. incl. with Eloy (Inc. Place)
Tombstone; Inc. Place; COCHISE; **147** N-12; elev. 4,540ft./1,384m.; [P]; **Z** 85638; ℗ 1,220; © 1,504
Tonalea; CDP-Census Area Only; COCONINO; **146** C-10; located on Hopi Ind. Res.; elev. 5,510ft./1,679m.; [P]; **Z** 86044, **Z** 86053-54; © 562
Tonopah; RMC Place; MARICOPA; **146** J-6; elev. 1,119ft./341m.; [P]; **Z** 85354
Tonto Apache Reservation; Indian Reservation; GILA; © 132
Tonto Basin; CDP-Census Area Only; GILA; **146** I-9; elev. 2,750ft./838m.; [P]; **Z** 85553; © 840
Tonto Hills; MARICOPA; see Tonto Hills Subdivision (RMC Place)
Tonto Hills Subdivision (Tonto Hills); RMC Place; MARICOPA; ***146** I-8; elev. 3,400ft./1,036m.; mail Cave Creek **Z** 85331; ● 220
Tonto Village; RMC Place; GILA; ***146** H-9; elev. 5,739ft./1,749m.; mail Payson **Z** 85541; ● 250
Topawa; RMC Place; PIMA; **147** N-8; located on Papago Ind. Res.; elev. 2,473ft./754m.; [P]; **Z** 85639; ● 325
Topock; RMC Place; MOHAVE; **146** G-3; elev. 528ft./161m.; [P]; **Z** 86436
Top-of-the-World; CDP-Census Area Only; PINAL, GILA; ***146** J-10; © 330
Tortilla Flat; RMC Place; MARICOPA; **146** J-9; elev. 1,752ft./534m.; [P]; **Z** 85190, **Z** 85290 & mail Apache Junction **Z** 85219; rural
Tortolita; CDP; PIMA; ***147** M-10; ★ **TUC**; © 3,740
Totopitk; RMC Place; MARICOPA; ***147** L-7; located on Papago Ind. Res.; elev. 2,064ft./629m.; mail Sells **Z** 85634; rural
Tovrea; RMC Place; MARICOPA; ***146** J-8; ★ **PHOE**; mail Phoenix **Z** 85034; pop. incl. with Phoenix (Inc. Place)
Town and Country; RMC Place; COCHISE; ***147** O-11; elev. 4,678ft./1,426m.; mail Sierra Vista **Z** 85635; pop. incl. with Sierra Vista (Inc. Place)
Toyei; RMC Place; APACHE; ***146** D-12; located on Navajo Nation Ind. Res.; mail Ganado **Z** 86505; ● 200
Tremaine (Tremaine Park); RMC Place; MARICOPA; ***146** J-8; ★ **PHOE**; mail Chandler **Z** 85225; pop. incl. with Gilbert (Inc. Place)
Tremaine Park; MARICOPA; see Tremaine (RMC Place)
Truxton; RMC Place; MOHAVE; **146** E-5; mail Peach Springs **Z** 86434; ● 150
Tsaile (Sehili); CDP; APACHE; **146** C-13; located on Navajo Nation Ind. Res.; [P]; **Z** 86556; ℗ 1,043; © 1,078
Tubac; CDP; SANTA CRUZ; **147** O-10; elev. 3,200ft./975m.; [P]; **Z** 85646 & mail Tumacacori **Z** 85640; © 949
Tuba City; CDP; COCONINO; **146** C-9; elev. 4,936ft./1,504m.; [P] [H]; **Z** 86045; ℗ 7,323; © 8,225
Tucson; Inc. Place; ⊡ PIMA; **147** M-10; elev. 2,386ft./727m.; [P] [H] [C] 38,130 ■; ★ **TUC**; **Z** 85701-26, **Z** 85728, **Z** 85730-52, **Z** 85754-57, **Z** 85775; ℗ 405,371; © 486,699; ◆ 543,984
Tucson Country Club Estates; RMC Place; PIMA; ***147** M-10; ★ **TUC**; mail Tucson **Z** 85715; ● 850
Tucson Estates; CDP; PIMA; ***147** M-10; ★ **TUC**; mail Tucson **Z** 85715; ℗ 2,662; © 9,755
Tucson National Estates; RMC Place; PIMA; ***147** M-10; ★ **TUC**; mail Tucson **Z** 85741; ● 300
Tumacacori; RMC Place; SANTA CRUZ; ***147** O-10; elev. 3,257ft./993m.; [P]; **Z** 85640 & mail Amado **Z** 85645, Tubac **Z** 85646; ● 400
Tumacacori-Carmen; CDP-Census Area Only; SANTA CRUZ; ***147** O-10; © 569
Turkey Flat; RMC Place; GRAHAM; ***147** L-12; mail Safford **Z** 85546
Tusayan; CDP; COCONINO; **146** D-7; mail Grand Canyon **Z** 86023; © 562
Twin Arrows; RMC Place; COCONINO; ***146** F-9; elev. 5,880ft./1,792m.; mail Flagstaff **Z** 86001; rural
Twin Buttes; RMC Place; PIMA; ***147** N-10; mail Sahuarita **Z** 85629; rural
Twin Knolls (Desert Sage); RMC Place; MARICOPA; elev. 1,460ft./445m.; ★ **PHOE**; mail Mesa **Z** 85207
Two Story; RMC Place; APACHE; ***146** D-14; elev. 6,858ft./2,090m.; mail Saint Michaels **Z** 86511; ● 100

U

University of Arizona; RMC Place; PIMA; ★ **TUC**; mail Tucson **Z** 85717; pop. incl. with Tucson (Inc. Place)
Upper Greasewood Trading Post (Greasewood); RMC Place; APACHE; **146** C-13; mail Ganado **Z** 86505, Lukachukai **Z** 86507; ● 10
Upper Wheatfields; RMC Place; APACHE; ***146** C-14; located on Navajo Nation Ind. Res.; mail Lukachukai **Z** 86507, Tsaile **Z** 86556; ● 100
Utting; RMC Place; LA PAZ; ***146** I-4; mail Salome **Z** 85348; rural

V

Vail; CDP; PIMA; **147** M-10; elev. 3,225ft./983m.; [P]; **Z** 85641; © 2,484
Vaiva Vo (Cocklebur); RMC Place; PINAL; ***147** L-8; located on Papago Ind. Res.; mail Sells **Z** 85634; ● 140
Valencia; RMC Place; MARICOPA; ***146** J-6; ★ **PHOE**; mail Buckeye **Z** 85326; pop. incl. with Buckeye (Inc. Place)
Valencia West; CDP-Census Area Only; PIMA; ***147** M-10; ★ **TUC**; mail Tucson **Z** 85746; ℗ 3,277; © 2,380
Valentine; RMC Place; MOHAVE; **146** E-4; located on Hualapai Ind. Res.; elev. 3,800ft./1,158m.; [P]; **Z** 86437; location of Truxton Canon Indian Agency; ● 30
Valle; RMC Place; COCONINO; mail Williams **Z** 86046; ● 140
Valley Farms; RMC Place; PINAL; ***147** K-9; elev. 1,494ft./455m.; [P]; **Z** 85191, **Z** 85291; ● 340
Vamori; RMC Place; PIMA; **147** N-8; located on Papago Ind. Res.; mail Sells **Z** 85634
Vaya Chin; RMC Place; PIMA; **147** M-7; located on Papago Ind. Res.; elev. 2,130ft./649m.; mail Sells **Z** 85634
Velda Rose Estates; RMC Place; MARICOPA; ***146** J-8; ★ **PHOE**; mail Mesa **Z** 85205; ● 3,000
Ventana; RMC Place; PIMA; **147** L-7; located on Papago Ind. Res.; mail Sells **Z** 85634
Ventana Lakes; RMC Place; MARICOPA; ★ **PHOE**; mail Peoria **Z** 85382; pop. incl. with Peoria (Inc. Place)
Venture Out; RMC Place; MARICOPA; ★ **PHOE**; mail Mesa **Z** 85201; pop. incl. with Mesa (Inc. Place)
Verde (Verde Village); RMC Place; YAVAPAI; ***146** G-8; elev. 3,482ft./1,061m.; mail Cottonwood **Z** 86326
Verde Village; YAVAPAI; see Verde (RMC Place)
Vernon; RMC Place; APACHE; **146** H-13; elev. 6,913ft./2,107m.; [P]; **Z** 85940; ● 230
Vicksburg; RMC Place; LA PAZ; ***146** I-4; mail Salome **Z** 85348
Vicksburg Junction; RMC Place; LA PAZ; ***146** I-4; elev. 1,250ft./381m.; mail Salome **Z** 85348; rural
Village Meadows; RMC Place; COCHISE; mail Sierra Vista **Z** 85635; pop. incl. with Sierra Vista (Inc. Place)
Vista Del Sahuaro; RMC Place; PIMA; ★ **TUC**; pop. incl. with Tucson (Inc. Place)
Vista Grande; RMC Place; YAVAPAI; ***146** G-7; elev. 4,728ft./1,441m.; mail Chino Valley **Z** 86323

W

Waddell; RMC Place; MARICOPA; ***146** J-7; elev. 1,251ft./381m.; [P]; ★ **PHOE**; **Z** 85355; ● 500
Wagoner; RMC Place; YAVAPAI; ***146** H-7; mail Kirkland **Z** 86332; rural
Wahak Hotrontk; RMC Place; PIMA; ***147** M-7; elev. 1,939ft./591m.; mail Sells **Z** 85634; ● 110
Wahweap; RMC Place; COCONINO; **145** J-10; elev. 3,728ft./1,136m.; mail Page **Z** 86040; ● 200
Wakefield; RMC Place; PIMA; ★ **TUC**; pop. incl. with Tucson (Inc. Place)
Walapai (Hualapai); RMC Place; MOHAVE; ***146** E-4; elev. 3,400ft./1,036m.; mail Hualapai **Z** 86412; ● 500
Walker; RMC Place; YAVAPAI; **146** G-7; mail Prescott **Z** 86301; ● 80
Walnut Grove; RMC Place; YAVAPAI; ***146** H-7; elev. 3,650ft./1,113m.; mail Kirkland **Z** 86332; rural
Walpi; RMC Place; NAVAJO; ***146** D-11; mail Polacca **Z** 86042; ● 85
Warren; RMC Place; COCHISE; ***147** O-12; mail Bisbee **Z** 85603; pop. incl. with Bisbee (Inc. Place)
Warwick Village; RMC Place; PIMA; ★ **TUC**; pop. incl. with Tucson (Inc. Place)
Washington; RMC Place; MARICOPA; ***146** J-7; ★ **PHOE**; mail Phoenix **Z** 85021, **Z** 85051, **Z** 85069; pop. incl. with Phoenix (Inc. Place)
Washington Camp; RMC Place; SANTA CRUZ; ***147** O-10; mail Patagonia **Z** 85624; rural
Washington Park; RMC Place; GILA; ***146** G-9; elev. 6,000ft./1,829m.; mail Payson **Z** 85541; ● 30
Wellton; Inc. Place; YUMA; **147** L-3; elev. 256ft./78m.; [P]; **Z** 85356; ℗ 1,066; © 1,829
Wenden; CDP; LA PAZ; **146** I-4; elev. 1,869ft./570m.; [P]; **Z** 85357; © 556
Westbrook Village; RMC Place; MARICOPA; ★ **PHOE**; mail Peoria **Z** 85382
West Chandler; RMC Place; MARICOPA; ***146** J-8; elev. 1,165ft./355m.; ★ **PHOE**; mail Chandler **Z** 85224; pop. incl. with Chandler (Inc. Place)
Westfield; RMC Place; MARICOPA; ★ **PHOE**; mail Peoria **Z** 85345; pop. incl. with Peoria (Inc. Place)
Westgreen Estates; RMC Place; MARICOPA; ★ **PHOE**; mail Peoria **Z** 85345; pop. incl. with Peoria (Inc. Place)
Westridge; RMC Place; MARICOPA; ***146** J-7; ★ **PHOE**; mail Phoenix **Z** 85075; pop. incl. with Phoenix (Inc. Place)
West Sedona (Grasshopper Flats); RMC Place; YAVAPAI; ***146** F-8; elev. 4,400ft./1,341m.; mail Sedona **Z** 86340; pop. incl. with Sedona (Inc. Place)
Wheatfields; RMC Place; APACHE; ***146** C-14; located on Navajo Nation Ind. Res.; mail Window Rock **Z** 86515; rural
Whetstone; CDP; COCHISE; ***147** N-11; mail Fort Huachuca **Z** 85613, Huachuca City **Z** 85616; ℗ 1,289; © 2,354
Whipple; RMC Place; YAVAPAI; ***146** G-7; mail Prescott **Z** 86313; pop. incl. with Prescott (Inc. Place)
Whispering Hills; RMC Place; COCHISE; mail Sierra Vista **Z** 85635; pop. incl. with Sierra Vista (Inc. Place)
Whispering Pines; RMC Place; GILA; ***146** H-9; elev. 5,148ft./1,569m.; mail Payson **Z** 85541; ● 150
White Clay; RMC Place; APACHE; ***146** C-13; mail Fort Defiance **Z** 86504; rural
White Cone; RMC Place; NAVAJO; ***146** D-12; located on Hopi Ind. Res.; elev. 6,094ft./1,857m.; mail Holbrook **Z** 86025; rural
White Hills; RMC Place; MOHAVE; mail Dolan Springs **Z** 86441; rural
White Mountain Lakes Estates; RMC Place; NAVAJO; ***146** H-12; elev. 5,993ft./1,827m.; mail White Mountain Lake **Z** 85912; ● 500
Whiteriver; CDP; NAVAJO; **146** I-12; [P] [H]; **Z** 85941; ℗ 3,775; © 5,220
White Tanks; RMC Place; MARICOPA; ***146** J-7; ★ **PHOE**; mail Buckeye **Z** 85326; pop. incl. with Youngtown (Inc. Place)
Why (Rocky Point Junction); RMC Place; PIMA; **147** M-6; elev. 1,784ft./544m.; [P]; **Z** 85321; ● 100
Wickenburg; Inc. Place; MARICOPA; **146** I-6; elev. 2,060ft./628m.; [P] [H]; **Z** 85358, **Z** 85390; ℗ 4,515; © 5,082
Wide Ruin; APACHE; see Wide Ruins (RMC Place)
Wide Ruins (Wide Ruin); RMC Place; APACHE; **146** E-13; located on Navajo Nation Ind. Res.; elev. 6,263ft./1,909m.; mail Chambers **Z** 86502; ● 100
Wikieup; RMC Place; MOHAVE; **146** G-4; elev. 1,970ft./600m.; [P]; **Z** 85360
Wildwood Estates; RMC Place; YAVAPAI; ***146** G-7; elev. 5,400ft./1,646m.; mail Prescott **Z** 86305; ● 130
Wilhoit; CDP; YAVAPAI; **146** H-6; mail Kirkland **Z** 86332; © 664
Willcox; Inc. Place; COCHISE; **147** M-12; elev. 4,167ft./1,270m.; [P] [H]; **Z** 85643-44; ℗ 3,122; © 3,733
Williams; Inc. Place; COCONINO; **146** E-7; elev. 6,754ft./2,059m.; [P]; **Z** 86046; ℗ 2,532; © 2,842
Williamson; CDP-Census Area Only; YAVAPAI; ***146** G-7; © 3,776
Willow Beach; RMC Place; MOHAVE; **146** D-2; [P]; **Z** 86445
Willow Canyon; RMC Place; PIMA; ***147** M-10; elev. 7,000ft./2,134m.; mail Mount Lemmon **Z** 85619; rural
Willow Valley (Willow Valley Estates); CDP-Census Area Only; MOHAVE; ***146** F-2; mail Mohave Valley **Z** 86440; ℗ 355; © 585
Willow Valley Estates; MOHAVE; see Willow Valley (CDP-Census Area Only)
Window Rock (Navajo Agency); CDP; APACHE; **146** D-14; located on Navajo Nation Ind. Res.; elev. 6,880ft./2,097m.; [P]; **Z** 86515; ℗ 3,306; © 3,059
Winkelman; Inc. Place; GILA; **147** K-10; elev. 1,928ft./588m.; [P]; **Z** 85192, **Z** 85292; ℗ 676; © 443
Winona; RMC Place; COCONINO; ***146** E-9; mail Flagstaff **Z** 86001; rural
Winslow; Inc. Place; NAVAJO; **146** F-10; elev. 4,855ft./1,480m.; [P] [H]; **Z** 86047; ℗ 9,095; © 9,520
Winslow West; CDP-Census Area Only; COCONINO; ***146** F-10; elev. 4,950ft./1,509m.; mail Winslow **Z** 86047; © 131
Winwood; RMC Place; COCHISE; ***147** O-12; mail Bisbee **Z** 85603; ● 50
Wittmann; RMC Place; MARICOPA; **146** I-7; elev. 1,696ft./517m.; [P]; ★ **PHOE**; **Z** 85361; ● 1,050
Woodruff; RMC Place; NAVAJO; **146** G-12; elev. 5,160ft./1,573m.; [P]; **Z** 85942; ● 200
Wood Springs; RMC Place; APACHE; ***146** D-13; elev. 6,800ft./2,073m.; mail Ganado **Z** 86505; rural

Y

Yampai; RMC Place; YAVAPAI; mail Seligman **Z** 86337; rural
Yaqui (Pasqua Village); RMC Place; PIMA; ★ **TUC**; mail Tucson **Z** 85746; pop. incl. with Tucson (Inc. Place)
Yarnell; CDP; YAVAPAI; **146** H-6; elev. 4,780ft./1,457m.; [P]; **Z** 85362; © 645
Yava; RMC Place; YAVAPAI; ***146** G-6; mail Prescott **Z** 86301; rural
YAVAPAI; **146** F-6; ℗ 107,714; © 167,517; ◆ 221,745
Yavapai-Apache Nation Reservation; Indian Reservation; YAVAPAI; © 743
Yavapai-Prescott Reservation; Indian Reservation; YAVAPAI; mail Prescott **Z** 86301; ℗ 76; © 182
Yeso; RMC Place; MARICOPA; ★ **PHOE**; pop. incl. with Tempe (Inc. Place)
York; RMC Place; GREENLEE; ***147** K-14; mail Duncan **Z** 85534; ● 30
Young; CDP; GILA; **146** H-10; elev. 5,179ft./1,579m.; [P]; **Z** 85554; © 561
Youngberg (Goldfield); RMC Place; PINAL; ***146** J-9; elev. 2,029ft./618m.; ★ **PHOE**; mail Apache Junction **Z** 85219; rural
Youngtown; Inc. Place; MARICOPA; **145** C-3; elev. 1,135ft./346m.; [P]; ★ **PHOE**; **Z** 85363; ℗ 2,542; © 3,010
Yucca; RMC Place; MOHAVE; **146** F-3; elev. 1,817ft./554m.; [P]; **Z** 86438; ● 150
Yuma; Inc. Place; ⊡ YUMA; **147** L-2; elev. 160ft./49m.; [P] [H] ■; ★ **YUMA**; **Z** 85364-67, **Z** 85369; ℗ 56,966; © 77,515; ◆ 93,000
YUMA; **147** K-3; ℗ 106,895; © 160,026; ◆ 196,352

Z

Zuni Reservation; Indian Reservation; APACHE; Reservation extends into NM; © 0

Entries in **UPPERCASE** are counties.
Entries in **bold** have populations of 2,500 or more.
Names in parentheses are alternate names.
Inc. Place — Incorporated Place
RMC Place — Rand McNally Designated Place
CDP — Census Designated Place
MCD — Minor Civil Division

⊡ County Seat
▲ Minor Civil Division
elev. Elevation
[P] Post Office
[H] Hospital
[C] College
■ Principal Business Center
★ Ranally Metro Area (RMA) Abbreviation
Z Zip Code(s)
℗ Previous Census Population
Ⓡ Revised Census Population
Ⓐ Annexation Population
● Rand McNally Population Estimate
© Final Census Population
Ⓢ Special Census Population
◆ Estimated Population

For additional definitions see Glossary, Volume 1, and Introduction, Volume 2.

ARKANSAS

MO
OK
Little Rock
TN
MS
AL
TX
LA

Statistics

Total area (2000) — 53,179 square miles
Land area (2000) — 52,068 square miles
Water area (2000) — 1,111 square miles
Capital — Little Rock
Admitted as state — June, 1836

Maps

State maps can be found on pages 142-254 in Vol. 1

Ranally Metro Areas (RMAs) and Abbreviations

Fayetteville-Springdale, AR — FAY-
Fort Smith, AR-OK — FTSM
Hot Springs, AR — HTSPR
Jonesboro, AR — JONES
Little Rock, AR — L.R.
Memphis, TN-AR-MS — MEM
Pine Bluff, AR — PNBLF
Texarkana-Texarkana, TX-AR — TEXR-

Principal Places

Place Name	Place Type	County	Population
Little Rock	Inc. Place	PULASKI	◆ 199,559
Fort Smith	Inc. Place	SEBASTIAN	◆ 85,398
Fayetteville	Inc. Place	WASHINGTON	◆ 73,955
Jonesboro	Inc. Place	CRAIGHEAD	◆ 68,292
Springdale	Inc. Place	WASHINGTON	◆ 64,838
North Little Rock	Inc. Place	PULASKI	◆ 62,256
Conway	Inc. Place	FAULKNER	◆ 57,601
Rogers	Inc. Place	BENTON	◆ 56,437
Pine Bluff	Inc. Place	JEFFERSON	◆ 49,260
Hot Springs	Inc. Place	GARLAND	◆ 39,083
Jacksonville	Inc. Place	PULASKI	◆ 32,225
Bentonville	Inc. Place	BENTON	◆ 31,357
Benton	Inc. Place	SALINE	◆ 28,383
Texarkana	Inc. Place	MILLER	◆ 28,333
West Memphis	Inc. Place	CRITTENDEN	◆ 28,097
Paragould	Inc. Place	GREENE	◆ 25,259
Russellville	Inc. Place	POPE	◆ 25,093
Sherwood	Inc. Place	PULASKI	◆ 23,772
Cabot	Inc. Place	LONOKE	◆ 23,278
Van Buren	Inc. Place	CRAWFORD	◆ 23,071
Searcy	Inc. Place	WHITE	◆ 21,785
El Dorado	Inc. Place	UNION	◆ 19,711
Bella Vista	CDP-Census Area Only	BENTON	© 16,582
Bella Vista	Inc. Place	BENTON	● 16,000
Blytheville	Inc. Place	MISSISSIPPI	◆ 15,307
Helena-West Helena	Inc. Place	PHILLIPS	Ⓐ 15,012
Forrest City	Inc. Place	ST. FRANCIS	© 14,774
Harrison	Inc. Place	BOONE	◆ 13,624
Mountain Home	Inc. Place	BAXTER	© 11,012
Arkadelphia	Inc. Place	CLARK	© 10,912
Camden	Inc. Place	OUACHITA	◆ 10,912
Siloam Springs	Inc. Place	BENTON	© 10,843
Hope	Inc. Place	HEMPSTEAD	© 10,616
Maumelle	Inc. Place	PULASKI	© 10,557
Magnolia	Inc. Place	COLUMBIA	◆ 10,203
Bryant	Inc. Place	SALINE	© 9,764
Stuttgart	Inc. Place	ARKANSAS	© 9,745
Batesville	Inc. Place	INDEPENDENCE	◆ 9,314
Monticello	Inc. Place	DREW	© 9,146
Malvern	Inc. Place	HOT SPRING	© 9,021
Marion	Inc. Place	CRITTENDEN	© 8,901
Osceola	Inc. Place	MISSISSIPPI	© 8,875
West Helena	RMC Place	PHILLIPS	© 8,689
Wynne	Inc. Place	CROSS	© 8,615
Hot Springs Village	CDP	GARLAND	© 8,397
Newport	Inc. Place	JACKSON	© 7,811
Clarksville	Inc. Place	JOHNSON	© 7,719
Greenwood	Inc. Place	SEBASTIAN	© 7,112
Trumann	Inc. Place	POINSETT	© 6,889
Morrilton	Inc. Place	CONWAY	© 6,550
Pocahontas	Inc. Place	RANDOLPH	© 6,518
Warren	Inc. Place	BRADLEY	© 6,442
Heber Springs	Inc. Place	CLEBURNE	© 6,432
Helena	RMC Place	PHILLIPS	© 6,323
Crossett	Inc. Place	ASHLEY	© 6,097
De Queen	Inc. Place	SEVIER	© 5,765
Mena	Inc. Place	POLK	© 5,637
East End	CDP	SALINE	© 5,623
Dumas	Inc. Place	DESHA	© 5,238
Marianna	Inc. Place	LEE	© 5,181
Lowell	Inc. Place	BENTON	© 5,013

County Business Data

County	FIPS Code	County Seat	Land Area (Sq. Mi.)	Census Population			Wholesale Trade		Manufacturing, 2002			
				4/1/2000	4/1/1990	% Change 1990-2000	Sales, 2002 ($1,000)	% Change 1997-2002	Establish-ments	Total Employees	Value Added ($1,000)	Ranally Mfg. Units
Arkansas	001	Stuttgart, De Witt	988	20,749	21,653	-4.2	198,279	-14.9	29	3,177	223,007	118
Ashley	003	Hamburg	921	24,209	24,319	-0.5	113,300	(d)	27	(d)	(d)	...
Baxter	005	Mountain Home	554	38,386	31,186	23.1	(d)	(d)	53	3,364	295,157	156
Benton	007	Bentonville	846	153,406	97,499	57.3	(d)	(d)	164	11,325	1,467,484	776
Boone	009	Harrison	591	33,948	28,297	20.0	(d)	(d)	62	2,392	177,463	94
Bradley	011	Warren	651	12,600	11,793	6.8	38,712	51.2	8	1,003	42,649	23
Calhoun	013	Hampton	628	5,744	5,826	-1.4	(d)	(d)	...	(d)	(d)	...
Carroll	015	Berryville, Eureka Springs	630	25,357	18,654	35.9	73,288	186.8	32	(d)	(d)	...
Chicot	017	Lake Village	644	14,117	15,713	-10.2	84,781	-3.3	11	686	65,434	35
Clark	019	Arkadelphia	865	23,546	21,437	9.8	(d)	(d)	30	2,362	135,037	71
Clay	021	Piggott, Corning	639	17,609	18,107	-2.8	71,144	-28.0	23	2,024	87,237	46
Cleburne	023	Heber Springs	553	24,046	19,411	23.9	53,935	-15.6	43	1,489	102,545	54
Cleveland	025	Rison	598	8,571	7,781	10.2	(d)	(d)	...	(d)	(d)	...
Columbia	027	Magnolia	766	25,603	25,691	-0.3	(d)	(d)	35	2,998	352,111	186
Conway	029	Morrilton	556	20,336	19,151	6.2	118,045	(d)	27	1,075	152,459	81
Craighead	031	Jonesboro, Lake City	711	82,148	68,956	19.1	439,880	-13.7	123	6,931	638,672	338
Crawford	033	Van Buren	595	53,247	42,493	25.3	(d)	(d)	58	3,325	301,493	160
Crittenden	035	Marion	610	50,866	49,939	1.9	845,135	(d)	50	1,670	149,883	79
Cross	037	Wynne	616	19,526	19,225	1.6	116,141	13.1	17	1,319	84,869	45
Dallas	039	Fordyce	667	9,210	9,614	-4.2	14,548	(d)	14	737	42,148	22
Desha	041	Arkansas City	765	15,341	16,798	-8.7	106,868	(d)	18	1,116	147,675	78
Drew	043	Monticello	828	18,723	17,369	7.8	200,987	156.5	30	1,312	75,342	40
Faulkner	045	Conway	647	86,014	60,006	43.3	209,214	-13.6	92	6,676	743,340	393
Franklin	047	Ozark, Charleston	610	17,771	14,897	19.3	(d)	(d)	21	1,047	68,620	36
Fulton	049	Salem	618	11,642	10,037	16.0	(d)	(d)	...	(d)	(d)	...
Garland	051	Hot Springs	677	88,068	73,397	20.0	499,783	-48.3	124	4,034	302,916	160
Grant	053	Sheridan	632	16,464	13,948	18.0	(d)	(d)	18	(d)	(d)	...
Greene	055	Paragould	578	37,331	31,804	17.4	620,562	437.1	53	4,849	400,837	212
Hempstead	057	Hope	729	23,587	21,621	9.1	34,988	(d)	32	(d)	(d)	...
Hot Spring	059	Malvern	615	30,353	26,115	16.2	(d)	(d)	40	1,370	153,116	81
Howard	061	Nashville	587	14,300	13,569	5.4	27,919	119.5	27	4,421	399,817	212
Independence	063	Batesville	764	34,233	31,192	9.7	(d)	(d)	53	4,751	454,001	240
Izard	065	Melbourne	581	13,249	11,364	16.6	(d)	(d)	...	(d)	(d)	...
Jackson	067	Newport	634	18,418	18,944	-2.8	67,393	(d)	24	874	103,020	55
Jefferson	069	Pine Bluff	885	84,278	85,487	-1.4	269,927	-12.9	75	(d)	(d)	
Johnson	071	Clarksville	662	22,781	18,221	25.0	8,347	(d)	33	3,020	255,007	135
Lafayette	073	Lewisville	526	8,559	9,643	-11.2	(d)	(d)	...	(d)	(d)	...
Lawrence	075	Walnut Ridge	587	17,774	17,457	1.8	66,704	-21.7	25	973	64,224	34
Lee	077	Marianna	602	12,580	13,053	-3.6	34,171	-46.4	...	(d)	(d)	...
Lincoln	079	Star City	561	14,492	13,690	5.9	(d)	(d)	...	(d)	(d)	...
Little River	081	Ashdown	532	13,628	13,966	-2.4	21,280	-5.2	11	(d)	(d)	...
Logan	083	Paris, Booneville	710	22,486	20,557	9.4	51,856	(d)	25	2,124	144,798	77
Lonoke	085	Lonoke	766	52,828	39,268	34.5	98,848	-31.6	41	1,591	159,648	84
Madison	087	Huntsville	837	14,243	11,618	22.6	(d)	(d)	24	1,394	30,504	16
Marion	089	Yellville	598	16,140	12,001	34.5	1,016	(d)	21	1,666	80,590	43
Miller	091	Texarkana	624	40,443	38,467	5.1	(d)	(d)	25	2,638	372,848	197
Mississippi	093	Blytheville, Osceola	898	51,979	57,525	-9.6	266,658	12.1	47	5,047	999,131	529
Monroe	095	Clarendon	607	10,254	11,333	-9.5	39,854	18.6	...	(d)	(d)	...
Montgomery	097	Mount Ida	781	9,245	7,841	17.9	(d)	(d)	...	(d)	(d)	...
Nevada	099	Prescott	620	9,955	10,101	-1.4	25,168	38.4	5	(d)	(d)	...
Newton	101	Jasper	823	8,608	7,666	12.3	(d)	(d)	...	(d)	(d)	...
Ouachita	103	Camden	732	28,790	30,574	-5.8	(d)	(d)	40	(d)	(d)	...
Perry	105	Perryville	551	10,209	7,969	28.1	(d)	(d)	...	(d)	(d)	...
Phillips	107	Helena	693	26,445	28,838	-8.3	(d)	(d)	14	583	81,238	43
Pike	109	Murfreesboro	603	11,303	10,086	12.1	47,682	4.9	...	(d)	(d)	...
Poinsett	111	Harrisburg	758	25,614	24,664	3.9	138,487	-22.6	24	1,683	113,002	60
Polk	113	Mena	859	20,229	17,347	16.6	(d)	(d)	40	1,747	171,997	91
Pope	115	Russellville	812	54,469	45,883	18.7	235,112	21.3	74	4,346	567,991	301
Prairie	117	Des Arc, De Valls Bluff	646	9,539	9,518	0.2	38,429	107.4	...	(d)	(d)	...
Pulaski	119	Little Rock	771	361,474	349,660	3.4	10,230,833	4.8	391	17,207	1,897,490	1,004
Randolph	121	Pocahontas	652	18,195	16,558	9.9	23,009	-19.2	38	1,443	123,921	66
St. Francis	123	Forrest City	634	29,329	28,497	2.9	489,630	61.2	23	(d)	(d)	...
Saline	125	Benton	723	83,529	64,183	30.1	304,804	49.2	73	1,687	200,769	106
Scott	127	Waldron	894	10,996	10,205	7.8	(d)	(d)	16	(d)	(d)	...
Searcy	129	Marshall	667	8,261	7,841	5.4	(d)	(d)	...	(d)	(d)	...
Sebastian	131	Fort Smith, Greenwood	536	115,071	99,590	15.5	1,382,446	95.1	217	22,084	2,588,712	1,370
Sevier	133	De Queen	564	15,757	13,637	15.5	(d)	(d)	14	2,546	116,360	62
Sharp	135	Ash Flat	604	17,119	14,109	21.3	41,693	(d)	...	(d)	(d)	...
Stone	137	Mountain View	607	11,499	9,775	17.6	19,000	(d)	26	515	21,420	11
Union	139	El Dorado	1,039	45,629	46,719	-2.3	(d)	(d)	62	5,633	803,923	425
Van Buren	141	Clinton	712	16,192	14,008	15.6	(d)	(d)	11	540	29,670	16
Washington	143	Fayetteville	950	157,715	113,409	39.1	(d)	(d)	214	15,427	1,608,089	851
White	145	Searcy	1,034	67,165	54,676	22.8	242,906	-0.1	80	4,466	386,652	205
Woodruff	147	Augusta	587	8,741	9,520	-8.2	68,250	-39.0	...	(d)	(d)	...
Yell	149	Dardanelle, Danville	928	21,139	17,759	19.0	19,018	12.1	24	3,671	235,027	124
The State			**52,068**	**2,673,400**	**2,350,725**	**13.7**	**34,470,795**	**25.3**	**3,185**	**210,394**	**21,965,415**	**11,621**

(d) Data not available. Corresponding percentages or Ranally Manufacturing Units are estimates.
... Represents 0 or amount too minimal to be reported.

Index of Places and Counties

Entries in **UPPERCASE** are counties.
Entries in **bold** have populations of 2,500 or more.
Names in parentheses are alternate names.

Inc. Place	Incorporated Place
RMC Place	Rand McNally Designated Place
CDP	Census Designated Place
MCD	Minor Civil Division
⊡	County Seat
▲	Minor Civil Division
elev.	Elevation
🅿	Post Office
🅷	Hospital
🅲	College
■	Principal Business Center
★	Ranally Metro Area (RMA) Abbreviation
z	Zip Code(s)
Ⓟ	Previous Census Population
Ⓡ	Revised Census Population
Ⓐ	Annexation Population
●	Rand McNally Population Estimate
©	Final Census Population
Ⓢ	Special Census Population
◆	Estimated Population

For additional definitions see Glossary, Volume 1, and Introduction, Volume 2.

Barney; RMC Place; FAULKNER; *148 D-5; mail Enola z 72047
Barton; RMC Place; PHILLIPS; 148 F-8; 🅿; z 72312; ● 200
Bashe; RMC Place; SEBASTIAN; *148 D-1; ★ FTSM; mail Fort Smith z 72901; pop. incl. with Fort Smith (Inc. Place)
Bass; RMC Place; NEWTON; *148 C-4; 🅿; z 72655; rural
Bassett; Inc. Place; MISSISSIPPI; *148 D-9; 🅿; z 72313; Ⓟ 199; Ⓒ 168
Batavia; RMC Place; BOONE; *148 B-3; mail Harrison z 72601; ● 155
Batchelor; RMC Place; PHILLIPS; *148 F-8; elev. 183ft./56m.; mail Marvell z 72366; ● 40
Bates; RMC Place; SCOTT; 148 E-1; elev. 614ft./187m.; 🅿; z 72958; ● 125
Batesville; Inc. Place; ⊡ INDEPENDENCE; 148 C-6; 🅿 🅷 🅲 489 ■; z 72501, z 72503; Ⓟ 9,187; Ⓒ 9,445; ◆ 9,314
Battlefield; RMC Place; HEMPSTEAD; *148 H-2; elev. 324ft./99m.; mail Hope z 71801; ● 30
Baucum; RMC Place; PULASKI; *148 F-5; elev. 252ft./77m.; ★ L.R.; mail North Little Rock z 72117; pop. incl. with North Little Rock (Inc. Place)
Bauxite; Inc. Place; SALINE; 148 F-5; 🅿; ★ L.R.; z 72011; Ⓟ 412; Ⓒ 432
Baxter; RMC Place; DREW; *148 I-7; mail Dermott z 71638; ● 30
BAXTER; 148 B-5; Ⓟ 31,186; Ⓒ 38,386; ◆ 43,025
Bay; Inc. Place; CRAIGHEAD; 148 C-9; 🅿; z 72411; Ⓟ 1,660; Ⓒ 1,800
Bayou Meto; RMC Place; ARKANSAS; *148 G-7; elev. 189ft./58m.; mail Stuttgart z 72160
Bayou Meto; RMC Place; LONOKE; *148 F-6; elev. 225ft./69m.; mail Lonoke z 72086; rural
Bay Village; RMC Place; CROSS, POINSETT; *148 D-8; mail Cherry Valley z 72324; ● 80
Bear; RMC Place; GARLAND; elev. 620ft./189m.; mail Royal z 71968; rural
Bear Creek Springs; RMC Place; BOONE; 148 B-3; mail Harrison z 72601; ● 25
Bearden; Inc. Place; OUACHITA; 148 H-5; elev. 240ft./73m.; 🅿; z 71720; Ⓟ 1,021; Ⓒ 1,125
Beaver; Inc. Place; CARROLL; 148 B-2; 🅿; z 72613; Ⓟ 57; Ⓒ 95
Beaver Shores; RMC Place; BENTON; *148 B-2; mail Rogers z 72756; ● 330
Beck; RMC Place; CRITTENDEN; *148 E-9; mail Hughes z 72348
Becton; RMC Place; WOODRUFF; *148 E-7; elev. 200ft./61m.; mail Cotton Plant z 72036; rural
Beebe; Inc. Place; WHITE; 148 E-6; elev. 246ft./75m.; 🅿; z 72012; Ⓟ 4,455; Ⓒ 4,930
Bee Branch; RMC Place; VAN BUREN; 148 D-5; 🅿; z 72013; ● 130
Beech Grove; RMC Place; DALLAS; *148 H-5; elev. 299ft./91m.; mail Fordyce z 71742; ● 30
Beech Grove; RMC Place; GREENE; 148 B-8; 🅿; z 72412
Beedeville; Inc. Place; JACKSON; 148 D-7; elev. 221ft./67m.; 🅿; z 72014; Ⓟ 141; Ⓒ 105
Beirne; RMC Place; CLARK; 148 H-3; elev. 239ft./73m.; 🅿; z 71721; ● 50
Belfast; RMC Place; GRANT; *148 F-5; ● 50
Bellaire; RMC Place; CHICOT; *148 I-7; elev. 138ft./42m.; mail Dermott z 71638; rural
Bella Vista; Inc. Place; BENTON; 148 B-1; incorporated December 7, 2006; not reported in 2000 Census; ● 16,000
Bella Vista; CDP-Census Area Only; BENTON; 148 B-1; 🅿; z 72714-15; Ⓟ 9,083; Ⓒ 16,582
Bellefonte; Inc. Place; BOONE; 148 B-4; mail Harrison z 72601; Ⓟ 361; Ⓒ 400
Belle Meade; RMC Place; ST. FRANCIS; *148 E-9; elev. 200ft./61m.; mail Hughes z 72348; rural
Belleville; Inc. Place; YELL; 148 E-3; 🅿; z 72824; Ⓟ 390; Ⓒ 371
Bells Chapel; RMC Place; POPE; *148 E-4; elev. 385ft./117m.; mail Atkins z 72823; rural
Bellview; RMC Place; PULASKI; ★ L.R.; pop. incl. with Little Rock (Inc. Place)
Bellville; RMC Place; SEVIER; *148 H-1; elev. 397ft./121m.; mail Lockesburg z 71846
Ben; RMC Place; STONE; *148 C-6; elev. 1,237ft./377m.; mail Drasco z 72530; rural
Ben Gay; RMC Place; SHARP; *148 C-7; mail Smithville z 72466; rural
Ben Hur; RMC Place; NEWTON; *148 C-4; elev. 1,730ft./527m.; mail Pelsor z 72856; rural
Ben Lomond; Inc. Place; SEVIER; 148 H-2; 🅿; z 71823; Ⓟ 157; Ⓒ 126
Benton; Inc. Place; ⊡ SALINE; 148 F-5; elev. 416ft./127m.; 🅿 🅷 ■; ★ L.R.; z 72015, z 72018-19, z 72022, z 72158; Ⓟ 18,177; Ⓒ 21,906; ◆ 28,383
BENTON; 148 B-1; Ⓟ 97,499; Ⓒ 153,406; ◆ 215,170
Bentonville; Inc. Place; ⊡ BENTON; 148 B-1; 🅿 🅷; z 72712, z 72716; Ⓟ 11,257; Ⓒ 19,730; ◆ 31,357
Bentonville Branch Junction; RMC Place; BENTON; mail Rogers z 72756; pop. incl. with Rogers (Inc. Place)
Bergman; Inc. Place; BOONE; 148 B-4; 🅿; z 72615; Ⓟ 324; Ⓒ 407
Berlin; RMC Place; ASHLEY; 148 J-6; elev. 127ft./39m.; mail Hamburg z 71646; rural
Berryville; Inc. Place; ⊡ CARROLL; 148 B-3; elev. 1,205ft./367m.; 🅿 🅷; z 72616; Ⓟ 3,212; Ⓒ 4,433
Beryl; RMC Place; FAULKNER; *148 E-5; elev. 345ft./105m.; mail Conway z 72032; ● 50
Best; RMC Place; BENTON; *148 B-2; elev. 1,194ft./364m.; mail Rogers z 72756; rural
Bestwater; BENTON; see Brightwater (RMC Place)
Bethany; RMC Place; HOWARD; *148 G-2; elev. 466ft./142m.; mail Dierks z 71833; rural
Bethel; RMC Place; GREENE; *148 C-9; mail Paragould z 72450; rural
Bethel Heights; Inc. Place; BENTON; *148 B-2; 🅿; ★ FAY-; z 72764; Ⓟ 281; Ⓒ 714
Bethesda; RMC Place; INDEPENDENCE; *148 C-6; mail Batesville z 72501; ● 55
Beulah; RMC Place; PRAIRIE; *148 E-7; mail Biscoe z 72017
Beverage Town; VAN BUREN; see Gravel Hill (RMC Place)
Bevis Corner; RMC Place; LONOKE; *148 F-6; elev. 241ft./73m.; mail Scott z 72142; rural
Bexar; RMC Place; FULTON; 148 B-6; 🅿; z 72515; ● 10
Bidville; RMC Place; CRAWFORD; *148 C-2; mail Winslow z 72959; rural
Bigelow; Inc. Place; PERRY; 148 E-4; elev. 297ft./91m.; 🅿; z 72016; Ⓟ 340; Ⓒ 329
Big Flat; Inc. Place; BAXTER, SEARCY; 148 C-5; 🅿; z 72617; Ⓟ 93; Ⓒ 104
Big Fork; RMC Place; POLK; *148 F-2; elev. 1,018ft./310m.; mail Mena z 71953
Biggers; Inc. Place; RANDOLPH; 148 B-8; elev. 286ft./87m.; 🅿; z 72413; Ⓟ 337; Ⓒ 355
Big Lake; RMC Place; MISSISSIPPI; *148 C-9; mail Manila z 72442; rural
Big Springs; RMC Place; STONE; *148 C-5; elev. 600ft./183m.; mail Timbo z 72657; rural
Billingsleys Corner; RMC Place; LITTLE RIVER; *148 H-1; elev. 313ft./95m.; mail Winthrop z 71866; rural
Billstown; RMC Place; PIKE; *148 G-3; mail Murfreesboro z 71958
Bingen; RMC Place; HEMPSTEAD; *148 G-2; mail Nashville z 71852; ● 50
Birchwood; RMC Place; PULASKI; ★ L.R.; pop. incl. with Little Rock (Inc. Place)
Birdell; RMC Place; RANDOLPH; *148 B-8; elev. 321ft./98m.; mail Pocahontas z 72455; rural
Birdeye; RMC Place; CROSS; *148 D-8; 🅿; z 72324
Birdsong; Inc. Place; MISSISSIPPI; 148 D-9; mail Tyronza z 72386; Ⓟ 104; Ⓒ 40
Birdtown; RMC Place; CONWAY; *148 D-5; mail Springfield z 72157; ● 30
Birta; RMC Place; YELL; 148 E-4; mail Ola z 72853
Biscoe (Fredonia); Inc. Place; PRAIRIE; 148 E-7; elev. 188ft./57m.; 🅿; z 72017; Ⓟ 484; Ⓒ 476
Bismarck; RMC Place; HOT SPRING; 148 G-3; 🅿; z 71929; ● 410
Blackburn; RMC Place; WASHINGTON; *148 C-1; mail Winslow z 72959; rural
Blackfish; RMC Place; ST. FRANCIS; *148 E-9; mail Heth z 72346; rural
Black Fork; RMC Place; SCOTT; *148 F-1; elev. 810ft./247m.; mail Mena z 71953; rural
Black Oak; Inc. Place; CRAIGHEAD; 148 C-9; elev. 233ft./71m.; 🅿; z 72414; Ⓟ 277; Ⓒ 286
Black Oak; RMC Place; POINSETT; *148 D-9; elev. 221ft./67m.; mail Tyronza z 72386; ● 50
Black Rock; Inc. Place; LAWRENCE; 148 B-7; 🅿; z 72415; Ⓟ 736; Ⓒ 717
Black Springs; Inc. Place; MONTGOMERY; 148 F-2; mail Norman z 71960; Ⓟ 97; Ⓒ 114
Blackton; RMC Place; MONROE; 148 F-7; mail Holly Grove z 72069; ● 30
Blackville; CONWAY; see Blackwell (RMC Place)
Blackville; RMC Place; JACKSON; *148 D-7; mail Newport z 72112; rural
Blackwell (Blackville); RMC Place; CONWAY; 148 E-4; 🅿; z 72823; ● 200
Blakely; RMC Place; GARLAND; *148 F-4; mail Jessieville z 71949; ● 120
Blakemore; RMC Place; LONOKE; 148 F-6; mail England z 72046; rural
Blevins; Inc. Place; HEMPSTEAD; 148 H-3; elev. 424ft./129m.; 🅿; z 71825; Ⓟ 253; Ⓒ 365
Bloomer; RMC Place; SEBASTIAN; *148 D-2; mail Charleston z 72933; ● 240
Bloomfield; RMC Place; BENTON; *148 B-1; elev. 1,187ft./362m.; mail Gentry z 72734
Blossom; RMC Place; ST. FRANCIS; *148 E-8; elev. 207ft./63m.; mail Wheatley z 72392; rural
Blue Ball; RMC Place; SCOTT; *148 E-2; mail Danville z 72833
Blue Eye; Inc. Place; CARROLL; 148 A-3; elev. 1,295ft./395m.; 🅿; z 65611; Ⓟ 38; Ⓒ 36
Blue Hill; RMC Place; PULASKI; *148 E-5; ★ L.R.; mail North Little Rock z 72118; rural
Blue Mountain; Inc. Place; LOGAN; 148 E-2; elev. 506ft./154m.; 🅿; z 72826; Ⓟ 146; Ⓒ 132
Blue Springs; RMC Place; GARLAND; *148 F-4; elev. 774ft./236m.; mail Hot Springs National Park z 71901
Blue Springs Village; RMC Place; WASHINGTON; *148 B-2; elev. 1,200ft./366m.; ★ FAY-; mail Springdale z 72764; ● 50
Bluff City; Inc. Place; NEVADA; 148 H-3; elev. 364ft./111m.; 🅿; z 71722; Ⓟ 227; Ⓒ 158
Bluffton; RMC Place; YELL; 148 E-3; 🅿; z 72827; ● 60
Blytheville; Inc. Place; ⊡ MISSISSIPPI; 148 C-10; 🅿 🅷 ■; z 72315-16, z 72319; Ⓟ 22,906; Ⓒ 18,272; ◆ 15,307
Board Camp; RMC Place; POLK; 148 F-2; elev. 963ft./294m.; 🅿; z 71932; ● 90
Bodcaw; Inc. Place; NEVADA; 148 H-3; elev. 346ft./105m.; mail Rosston z 71858; Ⓟ 161; Ⓒ 154
Bogg Springs; POLK; see Bog Springs (RMC Place)
Bog Springs (Bogg Springs); RMC Place; POLK; *148 G-1; elev. 1,400ft./427m.; mail Grannis z 71944; ● 30
Bolding; RMC Place; UNION; *148 J-5; mail Huttig z 71747; rural
Boles; RMC Place; SCOTT; 148 F-2; elev. 665ft./203m.; 🅿; z 72926; ● 120
Bonanza; Inc. Place; SEBASTIAN; 148 D-1; 🅿; ★ FTSM; z 72916; Ⓟ 520; Ⓒ 514
Bondsville; RMC Place; MISSISSIPPI; *148 C-9; mail Lepanto z 72354
Bonnerdale; RMC Place; HOT SPRING; 148 F-3; elev. 654ft./199m.; 🅿; z 71933; ● 70
Bono; Inc. Place; CRAIGHEAD; 148 C-8; 🅿; z 72416; Ⓟ 1,220; Ⓒ 1,512
Bono; RMC Place; FAULKNER; *148 D-5; mail Greenbrier z 72058
Booker; RMC Place; PULASKI; *148 F-5; ★ L.R.; mail North Little Rock z 72117
BOONE; 148 B-4; Ⓟ 28,297; Ⓒ 33,948; ◆ 37,741
Booneville; Inc. Place; ⊡ LOGAN; 148 E-2; elev. 511ft./156m.; 🅿 🅷; z 72927; Ⓟ 3,804; Ⓒ 4,117
Booster; RMC Place; SEARCY; *148 C-4; mail Leslie z 72645; rural
Boothe (North Boothe); RMC Place; SCOTT; *148 E-2; mail Booneville z 72927; rural
Boston; RMC Place; MADISON; *148 C-3; elev. 2,341ft./714m.; mail Pettigrew z 72752; rural
Boswell; RMC Place; IZARD; 148 C-6; elev. 475ft./145m.; 🅿; z 72556
Botkinburg; RMC Place; VAN BUREN; *148 C-5; mail Clinton z 72031; rural
Boughton; RMC Place; NEVADA; *148 H-3; elev. 236ft./72m.; mail Prescott z 71857
Bowen; RMC Place; PIKE; *148 G-3; elev. 331ft./101m.; mail Delight z 71940; rural
Bowman; RMC Place; CRAIGHEAD; 148 C-9; mail Lake City z 72437
Boxley; RMC Place; NEWTON; *148 C-3; mail Huntsville z 72740
Boyd; RMC Place; MILLER; *148 I-2; mail Fouke z 71837; rural
Boydell; RMC Place; ASHLEY; 148 I-7; mail Montrose z 71658; ● 85
Boyd Hill; RMC Place; LAFAYETTE; *148 I-2; mail Lewisville z 71845; rural
Boydsville; RMC Place; CLAY; 148 B-9; mail Rector z 72461; ● 30
Boynton; RMC Place; MISSISSIPPI; *148 C-9; mail Leachville z 72438; rural
Bradford; Inc. Place; WHITE; 148 D-7; elev. 242ft./74m.; 🅿; z 72020; Ⓟ 874; Ⓒ 800
Bradley; Inc. Place; LAFAYETTE; 148 J-2; elev. 259ft./79m.; 🅿; z 71826; Ⓟ 585; Ⓒ 563
BRADLEY; 148 I-5; Ⓟ 11,793; Ⓒ 12,600; ◆ 11,892
Brady; RMC Place; PULASKI; *148 F-5; ★ L.R.; mail Little Rock z 72205, z 72215; pop. incl. with Little Rock (Inc. Place)
Bragg City; RMC Place; OUACHITA; *148 H-4; mail Chidester z 71726; ● 60
Brakebill; RMC Place; RANDOLPH; *148 B-8; elev. 480ft./146m.; mail Warm Springs z 72478; rural
Branch; Inc. Place; FRANKLIN; *148 D-2; 🅿; z 72928; Ⓟ 299; Ⓒ 357
Brasfield; RMC Place; PRAIRIE; *148 E-7; mail Biscoe z 72017; ● 70
Brashears; RMC Place; MADISON; 148 C-2; elev. 1,470ft./448m.; mail Combs z 72721, Saint Paul z 72760
Breckenridge; RMC Place; PULASKI; ★ L.R.; pop. incl. with Little Rock (Inc. Place)
Bredlow Corner; RMC Place; PULASKI; *148 F-6; elev. 232ft./71m.; mail England z 72046; rural
Brentwood; RMC Place; WASHINGTON; 148 C-2; mail Winslow z 72959
Brewer; RMC Place; CLEBURNE; *148 C-5; mail Edgemont z 72044; rural
Briarcliff; Inc. Place; BAXTER; *148 B-5; mail Mountain Home z 72653; Ⓒ 240
Brickeys; RMC Place; LEE; 148 E-8; 🅿; z 72320; ● 60
Briggsville; RMC Place; YELL; 148 E-3; 🅿; z 72828; ● 100
Brighton; RMC Place; GREENE; *148 B-9; mail Paragould z 72450
Brightstar; RMC Place; MILLER; 148 J-2; elev. 359ft./109m.; mail Doddridge z 71834; ● 30
Brightwater (Bestwater); RMC Place; BENTON; *148 B-2; mail Rogers z 72756; rural
Brinkley; Inc. Place; MONROE; 148 E-7; 🅿; z 72021; Ⓟ 4,234; Ⓒ 3,940
Brister; RMC Place; COLUMBIA; *148 I-3; elev. 274ft./84m.; mail Emerson z 71740; ● 50
Brockett; RMC Place; RANDOLPH; *148 B-8; mail Pocahontas z 72455; rural
Brockwell; RMC Place; IZARD; 148 B-6; 🅿; z 72517
Brookings; RMC Place; CLAY; mail Peach Orchard z 72453
Brookland; Inc. Place; CRAIGHEAD; 148 C-8; 🅿; z 72417; Ⓟ 919; Ⓒ 1,332
Brown Crossing; RMC Place; CHICOT; *148 J-7; elev. 125ft./38m.; mail Eudora z 71640; rural
Brown Springs; RMC Place; HOT SPRING; *148 G-4; mail Malvern z 72104; rural
Brownstown; RMC Place; SEVIER; *148 H-2; mail Lockesburg z 71846
Brownsville; RMC Place; CLEBURNE; *148 D-6; elev. 876ft./267m.; mail Higden z 72067; ● 60
Bruins; RMC Place; CRITTENDEN; *148 E-9; mail Hughes z 72348
Brumley; RMC Place; FAULKNER; *148 E-5; mail Conway z 72032; pop. incl. with Conway (Inc. Place)
Brummitt; RMC Place; LONOKE; *148 F-6; elev. 201ft./61m.; mail Stuttgart z 72160; rural
Bruno; RMC Place; MARION; 148 B-4; 🅿; z 72682
Brush Creek; RMC Place; GRANT; *148 G-4; elev. 272ft./83m.; mail Leola z 72084
Bryant; Inc. Place; SALINE; 148 F-5; 🅿; ★ L.R.; z 72015, z 72019, z 72022, z 72089; Ⓟ 5,269; Ⓒ 9,764
Bryant Addition; RMC Place; YELL; *148 E-3; elev. 391ft./119m.; mail Plainview z 72857; ● 30
Buckeye; RMC Place; MISSISSIPPI; *148 C-9; elev. 239ft./73m.; mail Leachville z 72438; rural
Buckner; Inc. Place; LAFAYETTE; 148 I-3; elev. 260ft./79m.; 🅿; z 71827; Ⓟ 325; Ⓒ 396
Buck Range; RMC Place; HOWARD; *148 H-2; elev. 402ft./123m.; mail Mineral Springs z 71851; rural
Buckville; GARLAND; see Avant (RMC Place)
Buena Vista; RMC Place; OUACHITA; 148 I-4; elev. 283ft./86m.; mail Stephens z 71764; ● 50
Buffalo City; RMC Place; BAXTER; 148 B-5; mail Mountain Home z 72653; ● 40
Buford; RMC Place; BAXTER; *148 B-5; ● 110
Buie; RMC Place; GRANT; *148 G-5; mail Prattsville z 72129; ● 50
Bullfrog Valley; RMC Place; POPE; *148 D-3; mail Dover z 72837; rural
Bull Shoals; Inc. Place; MARION; 148 B-5; 🅿; z 72619; Ⓟ 1,534; Ⓒ 2,000
Bunn; RMC Place; DALLAS; elev. 245ft./75m.; mail Fordyce z 71742; rural
Bunney; RMC Place; CRAIGHEAD; *148 C-9; mail Black Oak z 72414; rural
Burdette; Inc. Place; MISSISSIPPI; 148 C-10; 🅿; z 72321; Ⓟ 148; Ⓒ 129
Burg; RMC Place; HOWARD; *148 G-2; elev. 759ft./231m.; mail Dierks z 71833
Burlington; RMC Place; BOONE; 148 B-3; elev. 1,497ft./456m.; mail Omaha z 72662; ● 70
Burnville; RMC Place; SEBASTIAN; *148 E-1; ★ FTSM; mail Greenwood z 72936
Buroak; RMC Place; SEARCY; *148 C-4; elev. 980ft./299m.; mail Marshall z 72650; rural
Burtsell; RMC Place; CLARK; *148 H-3; elev. 263ft./80m.; mail Okolona z 71962
Busch; RMC Place; CARROLL; *148 B-2; 🅿; z 72631; rural
Bussey; RMC Place; COLUMBIA; *148 I-3; mail Stamps z 71860
Butlerville; RMC Place; LONOKE; 148 E-6; mail Ward z 72176; ● 180
Butterfield; RMC Place; HOT SPRING; *148 F-4; elev. 392ft./119m.; mail Malvern z 72104; ● 170
Byron; RMC Place; FULTON; 148 B-6; elev. 897ft./273m.; mail Salem z 72576

C

Cabanal (Cabanol); RMC Place; CARROLL; *148 B-3; elev. 1,297ft./395m.; mail Berryville z 72616; rural
Cabanol; CARROLL; see Cabanal (RMC Place)
Cabot; Inc. Place; LONOKE; 148 E-6; 🅿; ★ L.R.; z 72023; Ⓟ 8,319; Ⓒ 15,261; ◆ 23,278
Caddo Gap; RMC Place; MONTGOMERY; 148 F-3; elev. 616ft./188m.; 🅿; z 71935; ● 70
Caddo Valley; Inc. Place; CLARK; 148 G-4; elev. 214ft./65m.; 🅿; z 71923; Ⓟ 389; Ⓒ 563
Cades; RMC Place; LINCOLN; elev. 175ft./53m.
Cain; RMC Place; CRAWFORD; *148 D-1; ★ FTSM; mail Mountainburg z 72946; ● 125
Calamine; RMC Place; SHARP; *148 C-7; elev. 315ft./96m.; 🅿; z 72469 & mail Smithville z 72466
Caldwell; Inc. Place; ST. FRANCIS; 148 E-8; elev. 234ft./71m.; 🅿; z 72322; Ⓟ 334; Ⓒ 465
Cale; Inc. Place; NEVADA; 148 H-3; 🅿; z 71828; Ⓟ 70; Ⓒ 75
Caledonia; RMC Place; UNION; *148 J-4; mail Junction City z 71749; rural
Calhoun; RMC Place; COLUMBIA; 148 I-3; mail Magnolia z 71753; ● 30
CALHOUN; 148 I-4; Ⓟ 5,826; Ⓒ 5,744; ◆ 5,413
Calico Rock; Inc. Place; IZARD; 148 B-5; 🅿 🅷; z 72519; Ⓟ 938; Ⓒ 991
Calion; Inc. Place; UNION; 148 I-5; 🅿; z 71724; Ⓟ 558; Ⓒ 516
Calmer; RMC Place; CLEVELAND; *148 H-6; elev. 252ft./77m.; mail Rison z 71665
Calumet; RMC Place; MISSISSIPPI; *148 C-10; elev. 244ft./74m.; mail Blytheville z 72315
Camark; RMC Place; OUACHITA; *148 H-4; mail Camden z 71701; ● 300
Camden; Inc. Place; ⊡ OUACHITA; 148 H-4; elev. 198ft./60m.; 🅿 🅷 ■; z 71701, z 71711; Ⓟ 14,380; Ⓒ 13,154; ◆ 10,912
Cammack; PULASKI; see Cammack Village (Inc. Place)
Cammack Village (Cammack); Inc. Place; PULASKI; 148 L-4; 🅿; ★ L.R.; z 72207; Ⓟ 828; Ⓒ 831
Camp; RMC Place; FULTON; 148 B-6; elev. 623ft./190m.; 🅿; z 72520; ● 200
Campbell Station; Inc. Place; JACKSON; 148 C-7; mail Tuckerman z 72473; Ⓟ 247; Ⓒ 228
Canaan; RMC Place; SEARCY; *148 C-4; mail Marshall z 72650
Canal Gardens; RMC Place; CRITTENDEN; *148 E-9; elev. 200ft./61m.; mail Hughes z 72348; ● 70
Cane Creek; RMC Place; GRANT; *148 F-5; mail Sheridan z 72150; rural
Canehill; RMC Place; WASHINGTON; *148 C-1; 🅿; z 72717; ● 170
Caney; RMC Place; FAULKNER; *148 E-5; elev. 285ft./87m.; mail Conway z 72032; ● 100
Caney; RMC Place; HOT SPRING; *148 G-4; elev. 332ft./101m.; mail Bismarck z 71929
Caney Valley; RMC Place; PIKE; *148 G-3; mail Amity z 71921; rural
Canfield; RMC Place; LAFAYETTE; 148 I-2; elev. 259ft./79m.; mail Lewisville z 71845; ● 40
Cantwell; RMC Place; CLAY; *148 B-9; elev. 290ft./88m.; mail Corning z 72422; rural
Capps; RMC Place; BOONE; *148 B-3; mail Harrison z 72601; ● 95
Capps City (Cappstown); RMC Place; MILLER; *148 J-2; mail Rodessa z 71069; rural
Cappstown; MILLER; see Capps City (RMC Place)
Caraway; Inc. Place; CRAIGHEAD; 148 C-9; 🅿; z 72419; Ⓟ 1,178; Ⓒ 1,349
Carbon City; RMC Place; LOGAN; *148 D-2; mail Paris z 72855; ● 100
Carden Bottoms; RMC Place; YELL; *148 E-4; mail Dardanelle z 72834; rural
Careyville Landing; RMC Place; UNION; *148 I-5; elev. 85ft./26m.; mail Strong z 71765; rural
Carlisle; Inc. Place; LONOKE; 148 F-6; 🅿; z 72024; Ⓟ 2,253; Ⓒ 2,304
Carmel; RMC Place; BRADLEY; *148 I-6; elev. 245ft./75m.; mail Warren z 71671; rural
Carmi; RMC Place; MISSISSIPPI; *148 C-9; mail Leachville z 72438
Carolan; RMC Place; LOGAN; *148 E-2; elev. 525ft./160m.; mail Booneville z 72927; rural
Carpenter; RMC Place; DREW; *148 I-6; elev. 187ft./57m.; mail Fountain Hill z 71642; rural
Carpenter Addition; RMC Place; DREW; *148 H-6; elev. 276ft./84m.; mail Monticello z 71655; pop. incl. with Monticello (Inc. Place)
Carrol Corner (Carroll's Corner); RMC Place; MISSISSIPPI; *148 C-9; mail Manila z 72442; pop. incl. with Etowah (Inc. Place)
Carroll; HOT SPRING; see Midway (Inc. Place)
CARROLL; 148 B-3; Ⓟ 18,654; Ⓒ 25,357; ◆ 27,473
Carroll's Corner; MISSISSIPPI; see Carrol Corner (RMC Place)
Carrollton; RMC Place; CARROLL; 148 B-3; mail Alpena z 72611; ● 75
Carryville; RMC Place; CLAY; *148 B-9; mail Piggott z 72454
Carson; MISSISSIPPI; see Carson Lake (RMC Place)
Carson Lake (Carson); RMC Place; MISSISSIPPI; *148 D-10; mail Osceola z 72370; rural
Carter Cove Public Use Area (Carter Cove Use Area); RMC Place; YELL; *148 E-3; mail Plainview z 72857; ● 250
Carter Cove Use Area; YELL; see Carter Cove Public Use Area (RMC Place)
Carthage; Inc. Place; DALLAS; 148 G-5; 🅿; z 71725; Ⓟ 452; Ⓒ 442
Casa; Inc. Place; PERRY; 148 E-4; 🅿; z 72025; Ⓟ 200; Ⓒ 209
Cash; Inc. Place; CRAIGHEAD; 148 C-8; 🅿; z 72421; Ⓟ 214; Ⓒ 294
Cass; RMC Place; FRANKLIN; 148 C-2; mail Ozark z 72949; ● 140
Casscoe; RMC Place; ARKANSAS; 148 F-7; elev. 204ft./62m.; 🅿; z 72026; ● 134
Catalpa; RMC Place; JOHNSON; *148 C-3; mail Ozone z 72854; ● 25
Catcher; RMC Place; CRAWFORD; *148 D-1; ★ FTSM; mail Van Buren z 72956; rural
Catholic Point; RMC Place; CONWAY; *148 D-5; mail Center Ridge z 72027; ● 50
Cathy Lake; RMC Place; CROSS; *148 E-8; elev. 300ft./91m.; mail Wynne z 72396; rural
Cato; RMC Place; FAULKNER; *148 E-5; elev. 325ft./99m.; mail North Little Rock z 72114, z 72116; ● 200
Catron; RMC Place; PHILLIPS; *148 G-8; elev. 164ft./50m.; mail Mellwood z 72367
Caulksville; Inc. Place; LOGAN; 148 D-2; elev. 390ft./119m.; mail Ratcliff z 72951; Ⓟ 224; Ⓒ 233
Cauthron; RMC Place; LOGAN; *148 E-2; elev. 560ft./171m.; mail Booneville z 72927; ● 30
Cauthron; RMC Place; SCOTT; 148 E-1; elev. 605ft./184m.; mail Waldron z 72958; ● 50
Cavanaugh; RMC Place; SEBASTIAN; *148 D-1; ★ FTSM; mail Fort Smith z 72901; pop. incl. with Fort Smith (Inc. Place)
Cave City; Inc. Place; SHARP, INDEPENDENCE; 148 C-7; 🅿; z 72521; Ⓟ 1,503; Ⓒ 1,946
Cave Creek; RMC Place; INDEPENDENCE; *148 C-6; elev. 600ft./183m.; mail Batesville z 72501; rural
Cave Springs; Inc. Place; BENTON; 148 B-1; 🅿; ★ FAY-; z 72718; Ⓟ 465; Ⓒ 1,103
Cecil; RMC Place; FRANKLIN; 148 D-2; elev. 863ft./263m.; 🅿; z 72930; ● 300
Cedar Creek; RMC Place; SCOTT; 148 F-2; mail Parks z 72950; ● 30
Cedar Grove (Alonzo); RMC Place; INDEPENDENCE; *148 D-6; mail Floral z 72534; ● 30
Cedarville; Inc. Place; CRAWFORD; 148 D-1; elev. 779ft./237m.; 🅿; z 72932; Ⓒ 1,133
Center; RMC Place; SHARP; 148 B-7; mail Hardy z 72542; ● 100
Center Hill; RMC Place; GREENE; *148 C-9; mail Paragould z 72450; pop. incl. with Paragould (Inc. Place)
Center Hill; RMC Place; WHITE; *148 D-6; mail Searcy z 72143; ● 145
Center Point; RMC Place; CLARK; *148 G-3; elev. 231ft./70m.; mail Gurdon z 71743; rural
Center Point; RMC Place; HEMPSTEAD; *148 I-2; elev. 349ft./106m.; mail Hope z 71801; rural
Center Point; RMC Place; HOWARD; 148 G-2; mail Nashville z 71852; ● 120
Center Point; RMC Place; PRAIRIE; *148 E-7; elev. 228ft./69m.; mail Hazen z 72064; rural
Center Ridge; RMC Place; CLARK; *148 G-3; elev. 435ft./133m.; mail Amity z 71921; rural
Center Ridge; RMC Place; CLEBURNE; *148 D-6; elev. 359ft./109m.; mail Heber Springs z 72543; rural
Center Ridge; RMC Place; CONWAY; 148 D-5; 🅿; z 72027; ● 150
Centerton; Inc. Place; BENTON; *148 B-1; 🅿; z 72719; Ⓟ 491; Ⓒ 2,146
Center Valley; RMC Place; POPE; *148 D-4; elev. 445ft./136m.; mail Russellville z 72802; ● 50
Centerville; RMC Place; FAULKNER; *148 D-5; elev. 477ft./145m.; mail Greenbrier z 72058; rural
Centerville; RMC Place; HEMPSTEAD; *148 H-3; elev. 335ft./102m.; mail Emmet z 71835; rural
Centerville; RMC Place; YELL; 148 E-3; 🅿; z 72829; ● 200
Central; RMC Place; CLARK; *148 G-4; elev. 326ft./99m.; mail Arkadelphia z 71923; ● 100
Central; RMC Place; CROSS; *148 D-8; elev. 222ft./68m.; mail Wynne z 72396; ● 50
Central; RMC Place; HOT SPRING; 148 G-4; mail Malvern z 72104; ● 90
Central; RMC Place; SEVIER; *148 H-1; elev. 386ft./118m.; mail Horatio z 71842; ● 85
Central Baptist College; RMC Place; FAULKNER; mail Conway z 72032; pop. incl. with Conway (Inc. Place)
Central City; Inc. Place; SEBASTIAN; *148 D-1; 🅿; ★ FTSM; z 72941 & mail Hot Springs National Park z 71901; Ⓟ 419; Ⓒ 531
Cerrogordo; RMC Place; LITTLE RIVER; *148 H-1; mail Winthrop z 71866; ● 30
Chambersville; RMC Place; CALHOUN; *148 H-5; elev. 314ft./96m.; mail Thornton z 71766; rural
Chanticleer; RMC Place; CHICOT; elev. 125ft./38m.; mail Lake Village z 71653; pop. incl. with Lake Village (Inc. Place)
Chapel Hill; RMC Place; SEVIER; *148 G-1; mail De Queen z 71832; ● 120
Charleston; Inc. Place; ⊡ FRANKLIN; 148 D-2; 🅿; z 72933; Ⓟ 2,128; Ⓒ 2,965
Charlotte; RMC Place; INDEPENDENCE; 148 C-7; elev. 342ft./104m.; 🅿; z 72522; ● 100
Chasewood Landing; RMC Place; MONTGOMERY; *148 F-2; elev. 660ft./201m.; mail Sims z 71969; rural
Chatfield; RMC Place; CRITTENDEN; 148 E-9; mail Hughes z 72348; ● 40
Chelford; RMC Place; MISSISSIPPI; *148 D-9; mail Tyronza z 72386
Cherokee City; RMC Place; BENTON; *148 B-1; elev. 1,161ft./354m.; mail Gentry z 72734
Cherokee Village; Inc. Place; SHARP, FULTON; 148 B-7; 🅿 🅷; z 72525, z 72529; Ⓒ 4,648
Cherry Hill; RMC Place; PERRY; *148 E-4; elev. 355ft./108m.; mail Perryville z 72126; rural
Cherry Hill; RMC Place; POLK; *148 F-2; mail Mena z 71953
Cherry Valley; Inc. Place; CROSS; 148 D-8; 🅿; z 72324; Ⓟ 659; Ⓒ 704
Chester; Inc. Place; CRAWFORD; 148 C-1; 🅿; z 72934; Ⓟ 125; Ⓒ 99
Chickalah; RMC Place; YELL; *148 E-3; mail Dardanelle z 72834
Chicot; RMC Place; CHICOT; 148 I-7; mail Eudora z 71640; rural
CHICOT; 148 I-7; Ⓟ 15,713; Ⓒ 14,117; ◆ 11,925
Chicot Junction; RMC Place; CHICOT; 148 I-7; elev. 126ft./38m.; mail Eudora z 71640; ● 40
Chidester; Inc. Place; OUACHITA; 148 H-4; 🅿; z 71726; Ⓟ 489; Ⓒ 335; Ⓡ 360
Childress; RMC Place; CRAIGHEAD; *148 C-9; mail Des Arc z 72040, Monette z 72447; ● 15
Chimes; RMC Place; VAN BUREN; *148 C-4; mail Leslie z 72645; rural
Chismville; RMC Place; LOGAN; 148 D-2; elev. 606ft./185m.; mail Magazine z 72943; ● 50
Choctaw; RMC Place; VAN BUREN; 148 D-5; 🅿; z 72028; ● 230
Choctaw Acres; RMC Place; VAN BUREN; *148 D-5; elev. 600ft./183m.; mail Clinton z 72031; pop. incl. with Clinton (Inc. Place)
Christy Acres; RMC Place; SALINE; *148 F-5; elev. 322ft./98m.; ★ L.R.; mail Benton z 72015; ● 70
Chula; RMC Place; YELL; *148 F-3; elev. 921ft./281m.; mail Plainview z 72857; rural
Cincinnati; RMC Place; WASHINGTON; 148 B-1; elev. 1,068ft./326m.; mail Summers z 72769; ● 250
Clarendon; Inc. Place; ⊡ MONROE; 148 F-7; elev. 182ft./55m.; 🅿; z 72029; Ⓟ 2,072; Ⓒ 1,960
CLARK; 148 G-3; Ⓟ 21,437; Ⓒ 23,546; ◆ 24,482
Clarkdale; CRITTENDEN; see Clarkedale (Inc. Place)
Clarkedale (Clarkdale); Inc. Place; CRITTENDEN; *148 D-9; elev. 230ft./70m.; 🅿; z 72325; incorporated November 15, 2000; not reported in 2000 Census; ● 200
Clarkridge; RMC Place; BAXTER; 148 B-5; elev. 871ft./265m.; 🅿; z 72623; ● 50
Clarks Corner; RMC Place; ST. FRANCIS; *148 E-8; mail Widener z 72394; rural
Clarksville; Inc. Place; ⊡ JOHNSON; 148 D-3; elev. 379ft./116m.; 🅿 🅷 🅲 622; z 72830; Ⓟ 5,833; Ⓒ 7,719
Clay; RMC Place; WHITE; *148 D-6; elev. 261ft./80m.; mail Searcy z 72143
CLAY; 148 B-9; Ⓟ 18,107; Ⓒ 17,609; ◆ 15,497
Clear Lake; RMC Place; GRANT; *148 G-5; mail Sheridan z 72150; rural
Clear Lake; RMC Place; MISSISSIPPI; *148 C-10; elev. 254ft./77m.; mail Blytheville z 72315; rural
Clear Point; RMC Place; BENTON; *148 B-2; elev. 1,331ft./406m.; mail Rogers z 72756; ● 100
Clear Spring; RMC Place; CLARK; *148 G-3; elev. 395ft./120m.; mail Okolona z 71962; rural
CLEBURNE; 148 D-6; Ⓟ 19,411; Ⓒ 24,046; ◆ 25,473
Cleveland; RMC Place; CONWAY; 148 D-4; elev. 722ft./220m.; 🅿; z 72030; ● 150
CLEVELAND; 148 H-5; Ⓟ 7,781; Ⓒ 8,571; ◆ 8,817
Clifty; RMC Place; MADISON; 148 B-2; mail Rogers z 72756; ● 60
Clinton; Inc. Place; ⊡ VAN BUREN; 148 D-5; 🅿 🅷; z 72027, z 72031; Ⓟ 2,213; Ⓒ 2,283
Clover Bend; RMC Place; LAWRENCE; *148 C-7; mail Hoxie z 72433; ● 60
Cloverdale; RMC Place; PULASKI; *148 F-5; ★ L.R.; mail Little Rock z 72209; pop. incl. with Little Rock (Inc. Place)
Clow; RMC Place; HEMPSTEAD; 148 H-2; mail Ozan z 71855; ● 30
Clyde; RMC Place; WASHINGTON; *148 C-1; mail Canehill z 72717
Coaldale; RMC Place; SCOTT; *148 E-1; mail Heavener z 74937
Coal Hill; Inc. Place; JOHNSON; 148 D-2; elev. 471ft./144m.; 🅿; z 72832; Ⓟ 912; Ⓒ 1,001
Coffeeville; RMC Place; JACKSON; *148 D-7; mail Bradford z 72020; rural
Coffman; RMC Place; GREENE; *148 C-9; elev. 247ft./75m.; mail Paragould z 72450; rural
Coffman; RMC Place; LAWRENCE; *148 C-8; elev. 264ft./80m.; mail Hoxie z 72433; rural
Coldwater; RMC Place; CROSS; *148 D-8; elev. 214ft./65m.; mail Parkin z 72373
Coleman; RMC Place; DREW; *148 H-6; elev. 301ft./92m.; mail Monticello z 71655; rural
Colfax; RMC Place; BAXTER; *148 B-5; elev. 823ft./251m.; mail Mountain Home z 72653; ● 110
College City; Inc. Place; LAWRENCE; *148 B-8; elev. 274ft./84m.; mail Walnut Ridge z 72476; Ⓟ 339; Ⓒ 269
Collegehill; COLUMBIA; see College Hilll (RMC Place)
College Hilll (Collegehill); RMC Place; COLUMBIA; *148 I-3; mail Mc Neil z 71752; rural
College Station (Genevia); CDP; PULASKI; 148 M-6; 🅿; ★ L.R.; z 72053; Ⓒ 766
Collegeville; RMC Place; SALINE; *148 F-5; elev. 423ft./129m.; ★ L.R.; mail Alexander z 72002; ● 190
Collins; RMC Place; DREW; 148 I-7; elev. 170ft./52m.; 🅿; z 71638; ● 60
Colt; Inc. Place; ST. FRANCIS; 148 E-8; 🅿; z 72326; Ⓟ 334; Ⓒ 368
COLUMBIA; 148 J-3; Ⓟ 25,691; Ⓒ 25,603; ◆ 23,746
Columbus; RMC Place; HEMPSTEAD; 148 H-2; 🅿; z 71831; ● 60
Combs; RMC Place; MADISON; *148 C-2; elev. 1,407ft./429m.; 🅿; z 72721; ● 90
Cominto; RMC Place; DREW; 148 I-6; elev. 187ft./57m.; mail Monticello z 71655; ● 30
Compton; RMC Place; NEWTON; 148 B-3; 🅿; z 72624; ● 30
Concord; Inc. Place; CLEBURNE; 148 C-6; elev. 1,004ft./306m.; 🅿; z 72523; Ⓟ 262; Ⓒ 255
Congo; RMC Place; SALINE; 148 F-5; ★ L.R.; mail Benton z 72015; ● 60
Connells Point; RMC Place; PHILLIPS; *148 F-8; elev. 165ft./50m.; mail Marvell z 72366; rural
Conway; Inc. Place; ⊡ FAULKNER; 148 E-5; elev. 316ft./96m.; 🅿 🅷 🅲 13,921 ■; z 72032-35; Ⓟ 26,481; Ⓒ 43,167; ◆ 57,601
CONWAY; 148 D-4; Ⓟ 19,151; Ⓒ 20,336; ◆ 20,970
Copper Mine; RMC Place; BENTON; *148 B-2; mail Rogers z 72756; ● 200
Cord; RMC Place; INDEPENDENCE; 148 C-7; elev. 334ft./102m.; 🅿; z 72524; ● 200
Corinth; Inc. Place; YELL; *148 E-3; mail Belleville z 72824; Ⓟ 63; Ⓒ 65
Corley; RMC Place; LOGAN; *148 E-3; elev. 1,446ft./441m.; mail Paris z 72855; rural
Cornerstone; RMC Place; JEFFERSON; 148 G-6; elev. 194ft./59m.; mail Altheimer z 72004
Cornerville; RMC Place; LINCOLN; 148 H-6; elev. 247ft./75m.; mail Star City z 71667; ● 50
Corning; Inc. Place; ⊡ CLAY; 148 B-8; elev. 292ft./89m.; 🅿; z 72422; Ⓟ 3,323; Ⓒ 3,679
Cotter; Inc. Place; BAXTER; 148 B-5; elev. 615ft./187m.; 🅿; z 72626; Ⓟ 867; Ⓒ 921
Cotterneck; RMC Place; DALLAS; *148 H-5; elev. 211ft./64m.; mail Fordyce z 71742; ● 30
Cottonbelt; RMC Place; OUACHITA; *148 H-5; elev. 251ft./77m.; mail Bearden z 71720; ● 150
Cotton Plant; Inc. Place; WOODRUFF; 148 E-7; elev. 191ft./58m.; 🅿; z 72036; Ⓟ 1,150; Ⓒ 960
Cottonshed Landing; RMC Place; HOWARD; *148 H-2; elev. 284ft./87m.; mail Mineral Springs z 71851; ● 30
Cottonwood Corner; RMC Place; CRAIGHEAD; *148 C-9; elev. 232ft./71m.; mail Monette z 72447; rural
Cottonwood Corner; RMC Place; MISSISSIPPI; *148 C-10; mail Osceola z 72370; pop. incl. with Osceola (Inc. Place)
Council; RMC Place; LEE; *148 E-9; mail Brickeys z 72320; rural
Cove; Inc. Place; POLK; 148 F-1; 🅿; z 71937; Ⓟ 346; Ⓒ 383
Cowell; RMC Place; NEWTON; *148 C-3; mail Pelsor z 72856
Cowlingsville; RMC Place; SEVIER; *148 H-2; elev. 374ft./114m.; mail Lockesburg z 71846
Coy; Inc. Place; LONOKE; 148 F-6; 🅿; z 72037; Ⓟ 142; Ⓒ 116
Cozahome; RMC Place; SEARCY; 148 C-5; 🅿; z 72639; ● 40
Crabapple Point; RMC Place; UNION; *148 I-5; elev. 95ft./29m.; mail Calion z 71724; ● 40
Crabtree; RMC Place; VAN BUREN; 148 D-5; elev. 1,288ft./393m.; mail Clinton z 72031
CRAIGHEAD; 148 C-8; Ⓟ 68,956; Ⓒ 82,148; ◆ 97,411
Cravens; RMC Place; FRANKLIN; *148 D-2; elev. 554ft./169m.; mail Ozark z 72949; rural
CRAWFORD; 148 D-1; Ⓟ 42,493; Ⓒ 53,247; ◆ 60,163
Crawfordsville; Inc. Place; CRITTENDEN; 148 D-9; 🅿; z 72327; Ⓟ 617; Ⓒ 514
Creigh; RMC Place; MONROE, PHILLIPS; *148 F-8; mail Marvell z 72366; rural
Crigler; RMC Place; LINCOLN; *148 H-6; elev. 183ft./56m.; mail Star City z 71667; rural
CRITTENDEN; 148 E-9; Ⓟ 49,939; Ⓒ 50,866; ◆ 52,273
Crockett; RMC Place; CLAY; *148 B-9; mail Piggott z 72454
Crocketts Bluff; RMC Place; ARKANSAS; 148 F-7; 🅿; z 72038; ● 50
Crosby (Armstrong Springs); RMC Place; WHITE; *148 D-6; elev. 264ft./80m.; mail Searcy z 72143
CROSS; 148 D-8; Ⓟ 19,225; Ⓒ 19,526; ◆ 17,950
Crosses; RMC Place; MADISON; *148 C-2; mail Fayetteville z 72701
Crossett; Inc. Place; ASHLEY; 148 J-6; 🅿 🅷; z 71635; Ⓟ 6,282; Ⓒ 6,097
Crossroad; RMC Place; PRAIRIE; *148 E-6; elev. 224ft./68m.; mail Des Arc z 72040; rural
Crossroads; RMC Place; CLEBURNE; *148 D-5; mail Quitman z 72131; rural
Cross Roads; RMC Place; GRANT; 148 G-5; elev. 265ft./81m.; mail Sheridan z 72150
Crossroads; RMC Place; HEMPSTEAD; rural
Cross Roads; RMC Place; HOT SPRING; *148 G-3; elev. 610ft./186m.; mail Bonnerdale z 71933; rural
Crossroads; RMC Place; IZARD; *148 B-6; mail Pineville z 72566; rural
Crossroads; RMC Place; JACKSON; mail Newport z 72112; pop. incl. with Newport (Inc. Place)
Cross Roads; RMC Place; LITTLE RIVER; *148 H-1; elev. 373ft./114m.; mail Winthrop z 71866; ● 50
Cross Roads; LOGAN; see Wilkins (RMC Place)
Cross Roads; RMC Place; MADISON; *148 B-2; elev. 1,601ft./488m.; mail Hindsville z 72738; rural
Cross Roads; RMC Place; MONROE; elev. 162ft./49m.; rural
Crows; RMC Place; SALINE; *148 F-4; elev. 408ft./124m.; mail Benton z 72015, Lonsdale z 72087, Paron z 72122
Crumpler; BOONE; see Crumpler Subdivision (RMC Place)
Crumpler Subdivision (Crumpler); RMC Place; BOONE; *148 B-4; elev. 800ft./244m.; mail Lead Hill z 72644; ● 50
Crumrod; RMC Place; PHILLIPS; 148 G-8; 🅿; z 72328; ● 30
Crystal Hill; RMC Place; PULASKI; *148 E-5; ★ L.R.; mail North Little Rock z 72118; ● 510
Crystal Springs; RMC Place; GARLAND; 148 F-3; mail Royal z 71968
Crystal Springs Landing; RMC Place; GARLAND; *148 F-3; mail Royal z 71968; summer pop. 500
Cullendale; RMC Place; OUACHITA; *148 I-4; mail Camden z 71701; pop. incl. with Camden (Inc. Place)
Culpeper; VAN BUREN; see Culpepper (RMC Place)
Culpepper (Culpeper); RMC Place; VAN BUREN; *148 D-5; elev. 1,035ft./315m.; mail Clinton z 72031; rural
Cumi; RMC Place; BAXTER; *148 B-5; mail Henderson z 72544; rural
Curtis; RMC Place; CLARK; 148 G-4; 🅿; z 71728; ● 300
Cushman; Inc. Place; INDEPENDENCE; 148 C-6; elev. 718ft./219m.; 🅿; z 72526; Ⓟ 428; Ⓒ 461
Cypert; RMC Place; PHILLIPS; *148 F-8; mail Marvell z 72366
Cypress Valley; RMC Place; CONWAY; *148 D-4; elev. 409ft./125m.; mail Solgohachia z 72156; rural

D

Dabney; RMC Place; VAN BUREN; *148 D-4; mail Morrilton z 72110; rural
Daisy; Inc. Place; PIKE; 148 G-2; elev. 628ft./191m.; mail Kirby z 71950; Ⓟ 122; Ⓒ 118
Dalark; RMC Place; DALLAS; 148 G-4; elev. 288ft./88m.; mail Arkadelphia z 71923; ● 70
Dallas; RMC Place; POLK; *148 F-1; elev. 1,101ft./336m.; mail Mena z 71953
DALLAS; 148 H-4; Ⓟ 9,614; Ⓒ 9,210; ◆ 7,936
Dalton; RMC Place; RANDOLPH; 148 B-7; mail Pocahontas z 72455
Damascus; Inc. Place; VAN BUREN, FAULKNER; 148 D-5; 🅿; z 72039; Ⓟ 246; Ⓒ 306
Dansby; RMC Place; LEE; elev. 198ft./60m.
Danville; Inc. Place; ⊡ YELL; 148 E-3; elev. 352ft./107m.; 🅿 🅷; z 72833; Ⓟ 1,585; Ⓒ 2,392
Dardanelle; Inc. Place; ⊡ YELL; 148 E-3; elev. 334ft./102m.; 🅿 🅷; z 72834; Ⓟ 3,722; Ⓒ 4,228
Datto; Inc. Place; CLAY; 148 B-8; 🅿; z 72424; Ⓟ 120; Ⓒ 97
Davis Creek; RMC Place; GRANT; *148 G-5; elev. 261ft./80m.; mail Prattsville z 72129; ● 180
Dawn Hill; RMC Place; BENTON; *148 B-1; elev. 1,096ft./334m.; mail Siloam Springs z 72761; ● 80
Dayton; RMC Place; SEBASTIAN; *148 E-1; mail Huntington z 72940
Dean (Omega); RMC Place; CARROLL; *148 B-3; elev. 1,638ft./499m.; mail Berryville z 72616; rural
De Ann; RMC Place; HEMPSTEAD; *148 H-3; mail Hope z 71801; ● 30
Deans Market; RMC Place; CRAWFORD; *148 D-1; ★ FTSM; mail Alma z 72921; ● 170
Dean Springs; RMC Place; CRAWFORD; *148 D-1; ★ FTSM; mail Alma z 72921; ● 95
Decatur; Inc. Place; BENTON; 148 B-1; elev. 1,230ft./375m.; 🅿; z 72722; Ⓟ 918; Ⓒ 1,314
Deckerville; RMC Place; POINSETT; *148 D-9; elev. 223ft./68m.; mail Tyronza z 72386; rural
Deep Elm; RMC Place; CHICOT; *148 I-7; mail Lake Village z 71653; rural
Deep Elm; RMC Place; MONROE; elev. 168ft./51m.; rural
Deer; RMC Place; NEWTON; 148 C-3; elev. 235ft./72m.; 🅿; z 72628; ● 120
Deerfield; RMC Place; DESHA; *148 G-8; mail Crumrod z 72328; ● 20
Delaney; RMC Place; MADISON; 148 C-2; mail Elkins z 72727
Delaplaine; Inc. Place; GREENE; 148 B-8; 🅿; z 72425; Ⓟ 146; Ⓒ 127
Delaware; RMC Place; LOGAN; 148 D-3; elev. 370ft./113m.; 🅿; z 72835; ● 100
Delfore; RMC Place; CRAIGHEAD; *148 C-9; mail Leachville z 72438; rural
Delight; Inc. Place; PIKE; 148 G-3; 🅿; z 71940; Ⓟ 311; Ⓒ 311
Dell; Inc. Place; MISSISSIPPI; 148 C-10; 🅿; z 72426; Ⓟ 258; Ⓒ 251
Deluce; RMC Place; ARKANSAS; *148 G-7; elev. 179ft./55m.; mail De Witt z 72042; rural
Denmark; RMC Place; JACKSON, WHITE; *148 D-7; mail Bradford z 72020
Dennard; RMC Place; VAN BUREN; 148 C-5; elev. 1,513ft./461m.; 🅿; z 72629; ● 120
Denning; Inc. Place; FRANKLIN; *148 D-2; elev. 449ft./137m.; mail Altus z 72821; Ⓟ 206; Ⓒ 270
Denton; RMC Place; LAWRENCE; *148 B-7; elev. 350ft./107m.; mail Powhatan z 72458; rural
Denver; RMC Place; CARROLL; *148 B-3; elev. 1,025ft./312m.; mail Green Forest z 72638
Denwood; RMC Place; MISSISSIPPI; *148 D-9; mail Tyronza z 72386; ● 40
De Queen; Inc. Place; ⊡ SEVIER; 148 G-1; elev. 432ft./132m.; 🅿 🅷; z 71832; Ⓟ 4,633; Ⓒ 5,765
Dermott; Inc. Place; CHICOT; 148 I-7; 🅿; z 71638; Ⓟ 4,715; Ⓒ 3,292; Ⓡ 3,733
De Roche; RMC Place; HOT SPRING; *148 G-4; elev. 552ft./168m.; mail Bismarck z 71929; rural
Des Arc; Inc. Place; ⊡ PRAIRIE; 148 E-7; 🅿; z 72040; Ⓟ 2,001; Ⓒ 1,933
Desha; RMC Place; INDEPENDENCE; 148 C-6; elev. 325ft./99m.; 🅿; z 72527; ● 750
DESHA; 148 H-7; Ⓟ 16,798; Ⓒ 15,341; ◆ 13,156
Detonti; RMC Place; SALINE; *148 F-5; elev. 351ft./107m.; mail Bauxite z 72011; rural
De Valls Bluff; Inc. Place; ⊡ PRAIRIE; 148 F-7; 🅿; z 72041; Ⓟ 702; Ⓒ 783
Dewey; RMC Place; CHICOT; *148 I-7; elev. 135ft./41m.; mail Dermott z 71638; rural
Dewey; RMC Place; WHITE; *148 D-6; mail Pangburn z 72121
De Witt; Inc. Place; ⊡ ARKANSAS; 148 G-7; elev. 189ft./58m.; 🅿 🅷; z 72042; Ⓟ 3,553; Ⓒ 3,552
Dialion; CLEVELAND; see Mount Zion (RMC Place)
Diamond Bay; RMC Place; BAXTER; *148 B-5; mail Elizabeth z 72531; ● 60
Diamond City (Sugar Loaf); Inc. Place; BOONE; 148 B-4; 🅿; z 72630, z 72644; Ⓟ 601; Ⓒ 730
Diamondhead; RMC Place; HOT SPRING, GARLAND; *148 F-4; ★ HTSPR; mail Hot Springs National Park z 71913; ● 600
Dian; RMC Place; NEVADA; mail Prescott z 71857; pop. incl. with Prescott (Inc. Place)
Diaz; Inc. Place; JACKSON; 148 D-7; 🅿; z 72043; Ⓟ 1,363; Ⓒ 1,284
Dickey Heights; RMC Place; BENTON; *148 A-1; elev. 982ft./299m.; mail Sulphur Springs z 72768; ● 30
Dicus; RMC Place; LAWRENCE; *148 B-8; elev. 269ft./82m.; mail Walnut Ridge z 72476; pop. incl. with Walnut Ridge (Inc. Place)
Dierks; Inc. Place; HOWARD; 148 G-2; elev. 431ft./131m.; 🅿; z 71833; Ⓟ 1,263; Ⓒ 1,230
Dillen; RMC Place; JOHNSON; *148 C-3; mail Ozone z 72854; rural
Dixie; RMC Place; CRAIGHEAD; *148 C-9; elev. 236ft./72m.; mail Lake City z 72437; ● 100
Dixie; RMC Place; PULASKI; *148 F-5; ★ L.R.; mail North Little Rock z 72114; pop. incl. with North Little Rock (Inc. Place)
Dixie; RMC Place; WOODRUFF; 148 E-7; mail Augusta z 72006; ● 30
Doddridge; RMC Place; MILLER; 148 J-2; 🅿; z 71834; ● 40
Dogpatch (Marble Falls); RMC Place; NEWTON; *148 B-4; elev. 997ft./304m.; mail Marble Falls z 72648; ● 30
Dogtown; RMC Place; SEVIER; *148 G-1; elev. 330ft./101m.; mail De Queen z 71832; rural
Dogwood; RMC Place; MISSISSIPPI; *148 C-10; mail Blytheville z 72315; pop. incl. with Blytheville (Inc. Place)
Dogwood Acres; RMC Place; MONTGOMERY; *148 F-3; elev. 600ft./183m.; mail Mount Ida z 71957; rural
Dollarway; RMC Place; JEFFERSON; *148 G-6; ★ PNBLF; mail White Hall z 71602; pop. incl. with Pine Bluff (Inc. Place)
Dolph; RMC Place; IZARD; *148 B-6; 🅿; z 72528; ● 350
Donaldson; Inc. Place; HOT SPRING; 148 G-4; 🅿; z 71941; Ⓟ 225; Ⓒ 326
Dongola; RMC Place; SEARCY; *148 C-4; elev. 934ft./285m.; mail Marshall z 72650; rural
Doniphan; RMC Place; WHITE; *148 D-6; mail Searcy z 72143; ● 30
Dora; RMC Place; CRAWFORD; 148 K-1; ★ FTSM; mail Van Buren z 72956; ● 150
Double Bridges; RMC Place; MISSISSIPPI; mail Luxora z 72358
Douglas; RMC Place; LINCOLN; *148 G-7; elev. 171ft./52m.; mail Gould z 71643; rural
Dover; Inc. Place; POPE; 148 D-4; 🅿; z 72837; Ⓟ 1,055; Ⓒ 1,329
Dowdy; RMC Place; INDEPENDENCE; *148 C-7; mail Cord z 72524; rural
Downtown; RMC Place; PULASKI; mail Little Rock z 72201; pop. incl. with Little Rock (Inc. Place)
Drakes Creek; RMC Place; MADISON; *148 C-2; mail Huntsville z 72740; rural
Drasco; RMC Place; CLEBURNE; 148 D-6; elev. 1,018ft./310m.; 🅿; z 72530; ● 125
DREW; 148 I-6; Ⓟ 17,369; Ⓒ 18,723; ◆ 18,326
Driggs; RMC Place; LOGAN; *148 D-2; mail Magazine z 72943
Dripping Springs; RMC Place; CRAWFORD; *148 D-1; elev. 898ft./274m.; mail Uniontown z 72955
Driver; RMC Place; MISSISSIPPI; 148 D-10; 🅿; z 72329; ● 50
Dryden; RMC Place; CRAIGHEAD; *148 C-8; mail Jonesboro z 72404; rural
Dryfork; RMC Place; CARROLL; *148 B-3; elev. 1,410ft./430m.; mail Huntsville z 72740; rural
Dublin; RMC Place; LOGAN; *148 D-3; elev. 455ft./139m.; mail Scranton z 72863; rural
Duff; RMC Place; SEARCY; *148 C-4; mail Saint Joe z 72675; rural
Dumas; Inc. Place; DESHA; 148 H-7; elev. 163ft./50m.; 🅿 🅷; z 71639; Ⓟ 5,520; Ⓒ 5,238
Durham; RMC Place; WASHINGTON; 148 C-2; mail Elkins z 72727, Fayetteville z 72701
Dutch Mills; RMC Place; WASHINGTON; 148 C-1; mail Lincoln z 72744
Dutton; RMC Place; MADISON; *148 C-2; elev. 1,686ft./514m.; mail Saint Paul z 72760
Dyer; Inc. Place; CRAWFORD; 148 D-2; elev. 424ft./129m.; 🅿; ★ FTSM; z 72935; Ⓟ 502; Ⓒ 585
Dyess; Inc. Place; MISSISSIPPI; 148 D-9; 🅿; z 72330; Ⓟ 466; Ⓒ 515

E

Eagle Mills; RMC Place; OUACHITA; 148 H-4; mail Bearden z 71720; ● 50
Eagle Point; RMC Place; FULTON; *148 B-5; elev. 633ft./193m.; mail Elizabeth z 72531; rural
Eagleton; RMC Place; POLK; *148 F-1; elev. 1,471ft./448m.; mail Mena z 71953
Earle; Inc. Place; CRITTENDEN; 148 D-9; elev. 217ft./66m.; 🅿; z 72331; Ⓟ 3,393; Ⓒ 3,036
East Black Oak; RMC Place; CRITTENDEN; *148 D-9; elev. 218ft./66m.; mail Tyronza z 72386; rural
East Camden; Inc. Place; OUACHITA; 148 H-4; 🅿; z 71701; Ⓟ 783; Ⓒ 902
East End; CDP; SALINE; *148 F-5; elev. 353ft./108m.; ★ L.R.; mail Hensley z 72065; Ⓒ 5,623
Eastview; RMC Place; MISSISSIPPI; *148 C-9; elev. 229ft./70m.; mail Keiser z 72351; ● 50
East Webb Store; CLAY; see Holly Island Community (RMC Place)
Eaton; RMC Place; LAWRENCE; *148 C-7; elev. 300ft./91m.; mail Powhatan z 72458; ● 50
Ebenezer; RMC Place; COLUMBIA; *148 I-4; elev. 342ft./104m.; mail Stephens z 71764; rural
Ebony; RMC Place; CRITTENDEN; *148 E-9; mail Marion z 72364; ● 30
Echo; RMC Place; LOGAN; *148 E-2; mail Booneville z 72927; rural
Economy; RMC Place; POPE; *148 D-4; mail Atkins z 72823
Eden Isle; RMC Place; CLEBURNE; *148 D-6; elev. 500ft./152m.; mail Heber Springs z 72543; ● 320
Edgemont; RMC Place; CLEBURNE; 148 D-5; 🅿; z 72044; ● 140
Edmondson; Inc. Place; CRITTENDEN; 148 E-9; 🅿; z 72332; Ⓟ 372; Ⓒ 513
Eglantine; RMC Place; VAN BUREN; *148 D-5; elev. 869ft./265m.; mail Shirley z 72153; rural
Egypt; Inc. Place; CRAIGHEAD; 148 C-8; 🅿; z 72427; Ⓟ 123; Ⓒ 101
Elaine; Inc. Place; PHILLIPS; 148 G-8; 🅿; z 72333; Ⓟ 846; Ⓒ 865
El Dorado; Inc. Place; ⊡ UNION; 148 I-4; 🅿 🅷 ■; z 71730-31, z 71768; Ⓟ 23,146; Ⓒ 21,530; ◆ 19,711
Elevenpoint; RMC Place; RANDOLPH; *148 B-7; elev. 350ft./107m.; mail Pocahontas z 72455; rural
Elgin; RMC Place; JACKSON; *148 C-7; elev. 234ft./71m.; mail Newport z 72112; rural
Elizabeth; RMC Place; FULTON; *148 B-6; 🅿; z 72531; ● 95
Elkins; Inc. Place; WASHINGTON; 148 C-2; elev. 1,218ft./371m.; 🅿; ★ FAY-; z 72727; Ⓟ 692; Ⓒ 1,251
Elk Ranch; RMC Place; CARROLL; *148 B-2; elev. 954ft./291m.; mail Eureka Springs z 72631-32
Elliott; RMC Place; OUACHITA; *148 I-4; mail Camden z 71701; ● 155
Ellis; BAXTER; see Salesville (Inc. Place)
Ellison; RMC Place; JEFFERSON; *148 G-6; elev. 209ft./64m.; mail Sherrill z 72152; rural
Elm Springs; Inc. Place; WASHINGTON, BENTON; 148 B-1; 🅿; ★ FAY-; z 72728; Ⓟ 893; Ⓒ 1,044
Elm Store; RMC Place; RANDOLPH; *148 B-7; mail Myrtle z 65778; rural
Elmwood; RMC Place; BOONE; *148 B-4; elev. 1,200ft./366m.; mail Harrison z 72601; rural
Elnora; RMC Place; RANDOLPH; *148 B-8; elev. 260ft./79m.; mail Pocahontas z 72455; rural
El Paso; RMC Place; WHITE; 148 E-6; 🅿; z 72045; ● 300
Emanuel; ARKANSAS; see Immanuel (RMC Place)
Emerson; Inc. Place; COLUMBIA; 148 J-3; elev. 310ft./94m.; 🅿; z 71740; Ⓟ 317; Ⓒ 359
Emmet; Inc. Place; NEVADA, HEMPSTEAD; 148 H-3; elev. 332ft./101m.; 🅿; z 71835; Ⓟ 446; Ⓒ 506
Empire; RMC Place; CHICOT; *148 J-7; mail Parkdale z 71661; rural
Enders; RMC Place; FAULKNER; *148 D-5; elev. 579ft./176m.; mail Quitman z 72131; ● 30
Engelberg; RMC Place; RANDOLPH; *148 B-8; mail Pocahontas z 72455
England; Inc. Place; LONOKE; 148 F-6; 🅿; z 72046; Ⓟ 3,351; Ⓒ 2,972; Ⓡ 3,016
English; RMC Place; JEFFERSON; *148 G-6; mail Altheimer z 72004; rural
Enola; Inc. Place; FAULKNER; 148 E-5; 🅿; z 72047; Ⓟ 179; Ⓒ 188
Enterprise; RMC Place; SEBASTIAN; *148 D-1; ★ FTSM; mail Fort Smith z 72901
Eros; RMC Place; MARION; *148 B-4; elev. 1,018ft./310m.; mail Everton z 72633
Erwin; RMC Place; JACKSON; *148 D-7; mail Newport z 72112; ● 160
Ethel; RMC Place; ARKANSAS; 148 G-7; elev. 178ft./54m.; 🅿; z 72048; ● 40
Etna; RMC Place; FRANKLIN; *148 D-2; mail Ozark z 72949; rural
Etowah; Inc. Place; MISSISSIPPI; *148 C-9; 🅿; z 72428; Ⓟ 352; Ⓒ 366
Euclid Heights; RMC Place; GARLAND; *148 F-4; elev. 508ft./155m.; ★ HTSPR; mail Hot Springs National Park z 71901; pop. incl. with Hot Springs (Inc. Place)
Eudora; Inc. Place; CHICOT; 148 J-7; 🅿; z 71640; Ⓟ 3,155; Ⓒ 2,819
Eula; RMC Place; SEARCY; *148 C-4; elev. 768ft./234m.; mail Saint Joe z 72675; rural
Eureka Springs; Inc. Place; ⊡ CARROLL; 148 B-2; elev. 1,329ft./405m.; 🅿 🅷; z 72631-32; Ⓟ 1,900; Ⓒ 2,278
Evansville; RMC Place; WASHINGTON; 148 C-1; elev. 1,150ft./351m.; 🅿; z 72729; ● 100
Evening Shade; RMC Place; HEMPSTEAD; *148 H-3; elev. 398ft./121m.; mail Hope z 71801; rural
Evening Shade; RMC Place; SCOTT; *148 E-2; elev. 700ft./213m.; mail Waldron z 72958; rural
Evening Shade; Inc. Place; SHARP; 148 B-6; 🅿; z 72532; Ⓟ 328; Ⓒ 465
Evening Star; RMC Place; GREENE; *148 B-8; elev. 270ft./82m.; mail Corning z 72422
Everton; Inc. Place; BOONE; *148 B-4; elev. 856ft./261m.; 🅿; z 72633; Ⓟ 150; Ⓒ 170
Excelsior; RMC Place; SEBASTIAN; *148 E-1; ★ FTSM; mail Greenwood z 72936

F

Fairbanks; RMC Place; VAN BUREN; *148 D-5; elev. 872ft./266m.; mail Quitman z 72131; rural
Fairfield; RMC Place; PULASKI; ★ L.R.; mail Little Rock z 72209; pop. incl. with Little Rock (Inc. Place)
Fairfield Bay; Inc. Place; VAN BUREN, CLEBURNE; 148 D-5; 🅿; z 72088; Ⓟ 1,958; Ⓒ 2,460
Fairmont; PRAIRIE; see Fairmount (RMC Place)
Fairmount (Fairmont); RMC Place; PRAIRIE; *148 F-7; elev. 223ft./68m.; mail Stuttgart z 72160
Fair Oaks; RMC Place; CROSS; 148 D-8; elev. 217ft./66m.; 🅿; z 72101; ● 100
Fairview; RMC Place; CHICOT; 148 I-7; mail Lake Village z 71653; ● 40
Fairview; RMC Place; LONOKE; *148 E-6; elev. 249ft./76m.; mail Lonoke z 72086; rural
Fairview; RMC Place; MARION; 148 B-5; elev. 800ft./244m.; mail Marshall z 72650; ● 142
Fairview; RMC Place; OUACHITA; *148 I-4; elev. 177ft./54m.; mail Camden z 71701; pop. incl. with Camden (Inc. Place)
Fairview; RMC Place; SEVIER; *148 G-1; elev. 501ft./153m.; mail Gillham z 71841; rural
Fairwood; RMC Place; GARLAND; *148 F-4; elev. 462ft./141m.; ★ HTSPR; mail Hot Springs National Park z 71913
Falcon; RMC Place; NEVADA; 148 I-3; mail Buckner z 71827; ● 40
Falls Chapel; RMC Place; SEVIER; *148 H-1; mail Lockesburg z 71846
Fallsville; RMC Place; NEWTON; 148 C-3; elev. 2,271ft./692m.; mail Ozone z 72854
Fancy Hill; RMC Place; MONTGOMERY; *148 G-2; elev. 815ft./248m.; mail Caddo Gap z 71935; rural
Fannie; RMC Place; MONTGOMERY; 148 F-3; elev. 690ft./210m.; mail Story z 71970; ● 30
Farelly Lake; RMC Place; JEFFERSON; *148 G-7; elev. 181ft./55m.; mail Stuttgart z 72160; rural
Fargo; Inc. Place; MONROE; 148 E-7; mail Brinkley z 72021; Ⓟ 140; Ⓒ 118
Farmington; Inc. Place; WASHINGTON; 148 C-1; 🅿; ★ FAY-; z 72730; Ⓟ 1,322; Ⓒ 3,605
Farmville; RMC Place; BRADLEY; *148 I-5; elev. 226ft./69m.; mail Warren z 71671; rural
Farrville (Farville); RMC Place; CRAIGHEAD; *148 C-8; elev. 261ft./80m.; ★ JONES; mail Brookland z 72417, Jonesboro z 72401; ● 55
Farville; CRAIGHEAD; see Farrville (RMC Place)
FAULKNER; 148 E-5; Ⓟ 60,006; Ⓒ 86,014; ◆ 112,543
Fayetteville; Inc. Place; ⊡ WASHINGTON; 148 B-2; 🅿 🅷 🅲 17,926 ■; ★ FAY-; z 72701-04, z 72730, z 72764; Ⓟ 42,099; Ⓒ 58,047; ◆ 73,955
Felsenthal; Inc. Place; UNION; 148 J-5; elev. 87ft./27m.; mail Huttig z 71747; Ⓟ 95; Ⓒ 152
Felton; RMC Place; LEE; *148 F-8; mail Marianna z 72360; rural
Fender; RMC Place; RANDOLPH; *148 B-8; mail Walnut Ridge z 72476
Fendley; RMC Place; CLARK; *148 G-3; elev. 548ft./167m.; mail Amity z 71921; rural
Fenter; RMC Place; GRANT; *148 G-4; mail Traskwood z 72167; ● 30
Ferda; RMC Place; JEFFERSON; elev. 226ft./69m.; mail England z 72046; rural
Ferguson; RMC Place; PHILLIPS; *148 G-8; mail Crumrod z 72328
Ferguson Crossroads; RMC Place; MILLER; 148 I-2; ★ TEXR-; mail Fouke z 71837; ● 100
Fern; RMC Place; FRANKLIN; *148 C-2; elev. 1,517ft./462m.; mail Mountainburg z 72946
Ferndale; RMC Place; PULASKI; 148 F-5; mail Paron z 72122
Fianna; RMC Place; SEBASTIAN; ★ FTSM; pop. incl. with Fort Smith (Inc. Place)
Fiftysix; Inc. Place; STONE; 148 C-5; 🅿; z 72533; Ⓟ 156; Ⓒ 163
Figure Five; RMC Place; CRAWFORD; *148 D-1; elev. 920ft./280m.; mail Van Buren z 72956; ● 150
Finch; RMC Place; GREENE; *148 C-8; elev. 491ft./150m.; mail Paragould z 72450; rural

Entries in **UPPERCASE** are counties.
Entries in **bold** have populations of 2,500 or more.
Names in parentheses are alternate names.
Inc. Place — Incorporated Place
RMC Place — Rand McNally Designated Place
CDP — Census Designated Place
MCD — Minor Civil Division

⊡ County Seat
▲ Minor Civil Division
elev. Elevation
🅿 Post Office
🅷 Hospital
🅲 College
■ Principal Business Center
★ Ranally Metro Area (RMA) Abbreviation
z Zip Code(s)
Ⓟ Previous Census Population
Ⓡ Revised Census Population
Ⓐ Annexation Population
● Rand McNally Population Estimate
Ⓒ Final Census Population
Ⓢ Special Census Population
◆ Estimated Population

For additional definitions see Glossary, Volume 1, and Introduction, Volume 2.

Fisher; RMC Place; CRAIGHEAD; *148 C-8; mail Cash z 72421; rural
Fisher; Inc. Place; POINSETT; 148 D-8; 🅿; z 72429; Ⓟ 245; Ⓒ 265
Fitzgerald; RMC Place; JACKSON; *148 C-7; mail Newport z 72112; pop. incl. with Diaz (Inc. Place)
Fitzgerald Crossing; RMC Place; CROSS; *148 E-8; elev. 251ft./77m.; mail Wynne z 72396; rural
Fitzhugh; RMC Place; WOODRUFF; *148 D-7; elev. 221ft./67m.; mail Augusta z 72006
Fivemile; RMC Place; CLEBURNE; *148 C-6; mail Drasco z 72530; rural
Flag; RMC Place; STONE; *148 C-5; elev. 1,150ft./351m.; mail Leslie z 72645; rural
Flat Rock; RMC Place; JOHNSON; *148 D-3; mail London z 72847; rural
Flint Springs; RMC Place; FULTON; *148 B-6; mail Viola z 72583; rural
Flippen; MARION; see Flippin (Inc. Place)
Flippin (Flippen); Inc. Place; MARION; 148 B-5; elev. 650ft./198m.; 🅿; z 72634; Ⓟ 1,006; Ⓒ 1,357
Floodway; RMC Place; MISSISSIPPI; *148 C-9; elev. 246ft./75m.; mail Manila z 72442; rural
Floral; RMC Place; INDEPENDENCE; 148 D-6; 🅿; z 72534; ● 160
Florence; RMC Place; DREW; 148 H-6; elev. 183ft./56m.; mail Monticello z 71655; ● 30
Floyd; RMC Place; WHITE; 148 E-6; elev. 357ft./109m.; mail Searcy z 72143; ● 130
Fomby; RMC Place; LITTLE RIVER; *148 H-2; mail Ashdown z 71822; rural
Fontaine; RMC Place; GREENE; *148 C-8; mail Bono z 72416; rural
Fordyce; Inc. Place; ⊡ DALLAS; 148 H-5; elev. 272ft./83m.; 🅿 🅷; z 71742; Ⓟ 4,729; Ⓒ 4,799
Foreman; Inc. Place; LITTLE RIVER; 148 H-1; elev. 405ft./123m.; 🅿; z 71836; Ⓟ 1,267; Ⓒ 1,125
Forest Grove; RMC Place; COLUMBIA; *148 J-3; mail Emerson z 71740; rural
Forest Grove; RMC Place; LAFAYETTE; *148 I-3; elev. 249ft./76m.; mail Taylor z 71861; rural
Forest Park; RMC Place; PULASKI; *148 F-5; ★ **L.R.**; mail Little Rock z 72207, z 72217; pop. incl. with Little Rock (Inc. Place)
Formosa; RMC Place; VAN BUREN; 148 D-5; elev. 807ft./246m.; mail Clinton z 72031; ● 90
Forrest City; Inc. Place; ⊡ ST. FRANCIS; 148 E-8; elev. 276ft./84m.; 🅿 🅷; z 72335-36; Ⓟ 13,364; Ⓒ 14,774
Fort Douglas; RMC Place; JOHNSON; *148 C-3; mail Ozone z 72854; rural
Fort Lynn; RMC Place; MILLER; *148 I-2; elev. 245ft./75m.; mail Fouke z 71837; rural
Fort Smith; Inc. Place; ⊡ SEBASTIAN; 148 D-1; 🅿 🅷 🅲 6,775 ■; ★ **FTSM**; z 72901-06, z 72908, z 72913-14, z 72916-19; Ⓟ 72,798; Ⓒ 80,268; ◆ 85,398
Fortune; RMC Place; CROSS; *148 D-9; elev. 214ft./65m.; mail Parkin z 72373; rural
Forty Four; RMC Place; IZARD; *148 B-6; elev. 618ft./188m.; mail Wideman z 72585; rural
Forum; RMC Place; MADISON; 148 B-2; mail Huntsville z 72740; ● 40
Fouke; Inc. Place; MILLER; 148 I-2; 🅿; z 71837; Ⓟ 634; Ⓒ 814
Fountain Hill; Inc. Place; ASHLEY; 148 I-6; elev. 196ft./60m.; 🅿; z 71642; Ⓟ 195; Ⓒ 159
Fountain Lake; Inc. Place; GARLAND; 148 F-4; 🅿; z 71901; Ⓒ 409
Fourche; Inc. Place; PERRY; *148 E-5; elev. 289ft./88m.; mail Bigelow z 72016; Ⓟ 55; Ⓒ 59
Fourche Junction; RMC Place; PERRY; 148 E-3; elev. 429ft./131m.; mail Plainview z 72857; rural
Fourche Valley; RMC Place; YELL; *148 E-3; elev. 400ft./122m.; mail Bluffton z 72827
Fourmile Hill; RMC Place; WHITE; *148 D-6; elev. 435ft./133m.; mail Searcy z 72143; ● 40
Fox; RMC Place; STONE; 148 C-5; elev. 1,412ft./430m.; 🅿; z 72051; ● 100
Francis; RMC Place; BOONE; *148 B-3; elev. 1,160ft./354m.; mail Harrison z 72601; rural
Franklin; Inc. Place; IZARD; 148 B-6; 🅿; z 72512, z 72536; Ⓟ 205; Ⓒ 184
FRANKLIN; 148 D-2; Ⓟ 14,897; Ⓒ 17,771; ◆ 18,221
Fredonia; PRAIRIE; see Biscoe (Inc. Place)
Free Hope; RMC Place; COLUMBIA; *148 I-3; elev. 351ft./107m.; mail Magnolia z 71753
Frenchmans Bayou; RMC Place; MISSISSIPPI; 148 D-9; 🅿; z 72338; ● 100
Frenchport; RMC Place; OUACHITA; *148 I-4; mail Camden z 71701; ● 90
Fresno; RMC Place; LINCOLN; *148 H-6; elev. 178ft./54m.; mail Gould z 71643; rural
Friendship; RMC Place; CLEVELAND; *148 G-6; elev. 280ft./85m.; mail Rison z 71665; rural
Friendship; RMC Place; COLUMBIA; *148 I-3; elev. 266ft./81m.; mail Stamps z 71860; rural
Friendship; Inc. Place; HOT SPRING; *148 G-4; 🅿; z 71942; Ⓟ 160; Ⓒ 206
Friley; RMC Place; JOHNSON; *148 C-3; elev. 1,051ft./320m.; mail Pettigrew z 72752; rural
Fritz; RMC Place; GREENE; *148 B-9; elev. 255ft./78m.; mail Rector z 72461; rural
Fryatt; RMC Place; FULTON; *148 B-6; elev. 672ft./205m.; mail Mammoth Spring z 72554; rural
Frys Mill; RMC Place; POINSETT; *148 D-9; mail Tyronza z 72386; rural
Fulton; Inc. Place; HEMPSTEAD; 148 H-2; elev. 269ft./82m.; 🅿; z 71838; Ⓟ 269; Ⓒ 245
FULTON; 148 B-6; Ⓟ 10,037; Ⓒ 11,642; ◆ 11,856
Furlow; RMC Place; LONOKE; 148 E-6; mail Lonoke z 72086; ● 80

G

Gaines Landing; RMC Place; CHICOT; *148 I-7; mail Lake Village z 71653; rural
Gainesville; RMC Place; GREENE; *148 B-9; mail Paragould z 72450; ● 90
Gainsboro; RMC Place; INDEPENDENCE; *148 C-7; elev. 422ft./129m.; mail Batesville z 72501; rural
Gaither; RMC Place; BOONE; *148 B-3; mail Harrison z 72601
Galla Rock; RMC Place; POPE; *148 E-4; mail Atkins z 72823
Gallatin (Gallitin); RMC Place; BENTON; *148 B-1; mail Siloam Springs z 72761; rural
Gallitin; BENTON; see Gallatin (RMC Place)
Galloway; RMC Place; PULASKI; *148 F-5; elev. 252ft./77m.; ★ **L.R.**; mail North Little Rock z 72117; pop. incl. with North Little Rock (Inc. Place)
Gamaliel; RMC Place; BAXTER; 148 B-5; 🅿; z 72537; summer pop. 500; ● 200
Gammon; RMC Place; CRITTENDEN; *148 D-9; elev. 220ft./67m.; mail Marion z 72364; rural
Gardner; RMC Place; UNION; 148 J-5; mail Strong z 71765; ● 200
Garfield; Inc. Place; BENTON; 148 B-2; elev. 1,496ft./456m.; 🅿; z 72732; Ⓟ 308; Ⓒ 490
Garland (Garland City); Inc. Place; MILLER; 148 I-2; mail Garland City z 71839; Ⓟ 415; Ⓒ 352
GARLAND; 148 F-3; Ⓟ 73,397; Ⓒ 88,068; ◆ 97,798
Garland City; MILLER; see Garland (Inc. Place)
Garland Springs; RMC Place; FAULKNER; *148 E-5; mail Mount Vernon z 72111; rural
Garner; Inc. Place; WHITE; 148 E-6; elev. 223ft./68m.; 🅿; z 72052; Ⓟ 191; Ⓒ 284
Garner's Farm; RMC Place; DALLAS; *148 H-5; elev. 250ft./76m.; mail Fordyce z 71742; pop. incl. with Fordyce (Inc. Place)
Garnett; RMC Place; LINCOLN; *148 H-6; elev. 264ft./80m.; mail Star City z 71667; rural
Garret Grove; LEE; see Garrett Grove (RMC Place)
Garrett; RMC Place; JOHNSON; *148 D-3; mail Lamar z 72846; rural
Garrett Bridge; RMC Place; LINCOLN; *148 H-6; mail Dumas z 71639; ● 30
Garrett Grove (Garret Grove); RMC Place; LEE; *148 F-8; elev. 187ft./57m.; mail Moro z 72368; rural
Gassville; Inc. Place; BAXTER; 148 B-5; 🅿; z 72635; Ⓟ 1,167; Ⓒ 1,706
Gateway; Inc. Place; BENTON; 148 A-2; 🅿; z 72733; Ⓟ 65; Ⓒ 116
Gayler (Gaylor); RMC Place; STONE; *148 C-5; mail Timbo z 72657; rural
Gaylor; STONE; see Gayler (RMC Place)
Geneva; RMC Place; SEVIER; *148 G-1; mail De Queen z 71832; rural
Genevia; PULASKI; see College Station (CDP)
Genoa; RMC Place; MILLER; 148 I-2; elev. 367ft./112m.; 🅿; z 71840; ● 250
Gentry; Inc. Place; BENTON; 148 B-1; 🅿; z 72734; Ⓟ 1,726; Ⓒ 2,165
George Creek; MARION; see Georges Creek (RMC Place)
Georges Creek (George Creek); RMC Place; MARION; *148 B-4; elev. 655ft./200m.; mail Yellville z 72687; rural
Georgetown; RMC Place; MADISON; *148 C-2; mail Wesley z 72773
Georgetown; RMC Place; POPE; *148 D-3; mail London z 72847; rural
Georgetown; Inc. Place; WHITE; 148 E-7; 🅿; z 72143; Ⓟ 126; Ⓒ 126
Gepp; RMC Place; FULTON; *148 B-6; 🅿; z 72538; ● 30
Geridge; RMC Place; LONOKE; *148 F-6; mail England z 72046; ● 30
Gertrude (Greenwich Village); RMC Place; MILLER; *148 I-2; elev. 374ft./114m.; ★ **TEXR-**; mail Texarkana z 71854; pop. incl. with Texarkana (Inc. Place)
Gethsemane; RMC Place; JEFFERSON; *148 F-6; elev. 210ft./64m.; mail Altheimer z 72004; rural
Geyer Springs; RMC Place; PULASKI; *148 F-5; ★ **L.R.**; mail Little Rock z 72206; pop. incl. with Little Rock (Inc. Place)
Gibbs; RMC Place; MONTGOMERY; *148 F-3; elev. 750ft./229m.; mail Sims z 71969; rural
Gibson; RMC Place; CRAIGHEAD; *148 C-8; ★ **JONES**; mail Jonesboro z 72404; rural
Gibson; CDP; PULASKI; *148 E-5; elev. 264ft./80m.; ★ **L.R.**; mail North Little Rock z 72116, Sherwood z 72120; Ⓟ 4,288; Ⓒ 4,678
Gieseck; RMC Place; CROSS; *148 E-9; mail Parkin z 72373
Gifford; RMC Place; HOT SPRING; *148 G-4; elev. 320ft./98m.; mail Malvern z 72104; ● 130
Gilbert; Inc. Place; SEARCY; 148 C-4; elev. 595ft./181m.; 🅿; z 72636; Ⓟ 43; Ⓒ 33
Gilchrist (Hillcrest); RMC Place; MISSISSIPPI; *148 C-10; elev. 248ft./76m.; mail Luxora z 72358; rural
Giles Spur; RMC Place; LAWRENCE; *148 B-8; mail Walnut Ridge z 72476; rural
Gill; RMC Place; LEE; mail Marianna z 72360; rural
Gillam Park; RMC Place; PULASKI; *148 F-5; ★ **L.R.**; mail Little Rock z 72206; pop. incl. with Little Rock (Inc. Place)
Gillett; Inc. Place; ARKANSAS; 148 G-7; 🅿; z 72055; Ⓟ 883; Ⓒ 819
Gillham; Inc. Place; SEVIER; 148 G-1; elev. 751ft./229m.; 🅿; z 71841; Ⓟ 210; Ⓒ 188
Gilmore; Inc. Place; CRITTENDEN; 148 D-9; 🅿; z 72339; Ⓟ 331; Ⓒ 292
Gin City; RMC Place; LAFAYETTE; 148 J-2; mail Bradley z 71826; ● 30
Gladden; RMC Place; CROSS; *148 E-9; elev. 208ft./63m.; mail Earle z 72331; rural
Gleason; RMC Place; FAULKNER; *148 E-5; mail Conway z 72032; pop. incl. with Conway (Inc. Place)
Glencoe; RMC Place; FULTON; 148 B-6; elev. 793ft./242m.; 🅿; z 72539; ● 200
Glendale; RMC Place; LINCOLN; 148 H-6; elev. 263ft./80m.; mail Star City z 71667; ● 60
Glen Rose; RMC Place; HOT SPRING; *148 F-4; elev. 329ft./100m.; mail Malvern z 72104; ● 140
Glenview; RMC Place; PULASKI; ★ **L.R.**; mail North Little Rock z 72117; pop. incl. with North Little Rock (Inc. Place)
Glenwood; Inc. Place; PIKE; 148 G-3; elev. 550ft./168m.; 🅿; z 71943; Ⓟ 1,354; Ⓒ 1,751
Gobblers Point; RMC Place; CONWAY; *148 D-4; elev. 658ft./201m.; mail Jerusalem z 72080; rural
Gobell; RMC Place; PHILLIPS; *148 F-8; elev. 175ft./53m.; mail Marvell z 72366; rural
Gold Creek; RMC Place; FAULKNER; *148 E-5; mail Conway z 72032; ● 300
Golden City; RMC Place; LOGAN; *148 E-2; mail Booneville z 72927; rural
Golden Lake; RMC Place; MISSISSIPPI; *148 D-10; mail Wilson z 72395; rural
Gold Lake Estates; RMC Place; FAULKNER; *148 E-5; mail Conway z 72032; ● 30
Goobertown; RMC Place; CRAIGHEAD; *148 C-8; mail Brookland z 72417; rural
Good Hope; RMC Place; OUACHITA; *148 H-4; mail Chidester z 71726; rural
Goodwin; RMC Place; ST. FRANCIS; 148 E-8; elev. 207ft./63m.; 🅿; z 72340; ● 80
Goose Camp; RMC Place; JOHNSON; *148 D-3; mail Hartman z 72840; rural
Goshen; Inc. Place; WASHINGTON; *148 B-2; 🅿; z 72735; Ⓟ 589; Ⓒ 752
Gosnell; Inc. Place; MISSISSIPPI; 148 C-10; 🅿; z 72315, z 72319; Ⓟ 4,255; Ⓒ 3,968
Gould; Inc. Place; LINCOLN; 148 G-7; elev. 167ft./51m.; 🅿; z 71643; Ⓟ 1,470; Ⓒ 1,305
Gourd; RMC Place; LINCOLN; *148 H-7; elev. 176ft./54m.; mail Dumas z 71639, Pickens z 71662; rural
Gourd Neck; RMC Place; JACKSON; *148 D-7; elev. 218ft./66m.; mail Mc Crory z 72101; rural
Grady; Inc. Place; LINCOLN; 148 G-6; 🅿; z 71644; Ⓟ 586; Ⓒ 523
Grand Glaise; RMC Place; JACKSON; *148 D-7; mail Bradford z 72020
Grand Lake; RMC Place; CHICOT; mail Eudora z 71640; rural
Grandview; RMC Place; CARROLL; *148 B-3; elev. 1,147ft./350m.; mail Berryville z 72616, Harrison z 72601; ● 65
Grange; RMC Place; SHARP; *148 C-7; mail Cave City z 72521
Granite Mountain; RMC Place; PULASKI; ★ **L.R.**; pop. incl. with Little Rock (Inc. Place)
Grannis; Inc. Place; POLK; 148 G-1; elev. 927ft./283m.; 🅿; z 71944 & mail Wickes z 71973; Ⓟ 507; Ⓒ 575
GRANT; 148 F-5; Ⓟ 13,948; Ⓒ 16,464; ◆ 17,351
Grapevine; RMC Place; GRANT; 148 G-5; elev. 255ft./78m.; 🅿; z 72057; ● 90
Graphic; RMC Place; CRAWFORD; *148 D-2; mail Alma z 72921
Grassy Lake; CRITTENDEN; see Grassy Lake Bottom (RMC Place)
Grassy Lake Bottom (Grassy Lake); RMC Place; CRITTENDEN; *148 D-9; elev. 211ft./64m.; mail Earle z 72331; rural
Gravel Hill (Beverage Town); RMC Place; VAN BUREN; *148 D-4; elev. 754ft./230m.; mail Cleveland z 72030; rural
Gravel Hill; RMC Place; WHITE; *148 D-6; mail Romance z 72136; rural
Gravelly; RMC Place; YELL; 148 E-2; elev. 464ft./141m.; 🅿; z 72838; ● 210
Gravelridge; RMC Place; BRADLEY; *148 I-5; mail Banks z 71631; rural
Gravel Ridge; CDP; PULASKI; *148 E-5; 🅿; ★ **L.R.**; z 72076 & mail Jacksonville z 72078; Ⓟ 3,846; Ⓒ 3,232
Graves Chapel; RMC Place; SEVIER; *148 H-2; elev. 345ft./105m.; mail Lockesburg z 71846; rural
Gravesville; RMC Place; VAN BUREN; *148 D-5; elev. 776ft./237m.; mail Damascus z 72039
Gravette; Inc. Place; BENTON; 148 B-1; 🅿 🅷; z 72736; Ⓟ 1,412; Ⓒ 1,810
Gray Rock; RMC Place; LOGAN; *148 D-2; elev. 385ft./117m.; mail Paris z 72855; ● 100
Grays; RMC Place; WOODRUFF; 148 E-7; elev. 198ft./60m.; mail Mc Crory z 72101; ● 30
Grayson (Joyland Park); RMC Place; LOGAN; *148 E-2; elev. 496ft./151m.; mail Booneville z 72927; rural
Greasy Corner; RMC Place; ST. FRANCIS; *148 E-9; mail Heth z 72346
Green Acres; RMC Place; BENTON; *148 B-2; elev. 1,340ft./408m.; mail Rogers z 72758; ● 50
Greenbrier; Inc. Place; FAULKNER; 148 E-5; 🅿; z 72058; Ⓟ 2,130; Ⓒ 3,042
GREENE; 148 B-8; Ⓟ 31,804; Ⓒ 37,331; ◆ 40,892
Greenfield; RMC Place; POINSETT; 148 D-8; mail Harrisburg z 72432; ● 60
Green Forest; Inc. Place; CARROLL; 148 B-3; elev. 1,340ft./408m.; 🅿; z 72638; Ⓟ 2,050; Ⓒ 2,717
Green High; RMC Place; GREENE; 148 C-9; mail Paragould z 72450; pop. incl. with Paragould (Inc. Place)
Green Hill; RMC Place; DREW; *148 H-6; mail Wilmar z 71675; ● 30
Greenland; Inc. Place; WASHINGTON; 148 C-2; 🅿; ★ **FAY-**; z 72737; Ⓟ 757; Ⓒ 907
Green Tree; RMC Place; VAN BUREN; *148 D-5; elev. 600ft./183m.; mail Clinton z 72031; rural
Greenway; Inc. Place; CLAY; 148 B-9; 🅿; z 72430; Ⓟ 212; Ⓒ 244
Greenwich Village; MILLER; see Gertrude (RMC Place)
Greenwood; RMC Place; FRANKLIN; *148 D-2; elev. 409ft./125m.; mail Ozark z 72949
Greenwood; Inc. Place; ⊡ SEBASTIAN; 148 E-1; 🅿; ★ **FTSM**; z 72936; Ⓟ 3,984; Ⓒ 7,112
Greers Ferry; Inc. Place; CLEBURNE; 148 D-5; 🅿; z 72067; Ⓟ 724; Ⓒ 930
Gregory; RMC Place; WOODRUFF; 148 E-7; 🅿; z 72059; ● 50
Grider; RMC Place; MISSISSIPPI; *148 C-10; mail Osceola z 72370; rural
Griffith Spring; LINCOLN; see Griffith Springs (RMC Place)
Griffith Springs (Griffith Spring); RMC Place; LINCOLN; *148 G-6; elev. 245ft./75m.; mail Star City z 71667; ● 30
Griffithtown; RMC Place; CLARK; *148 G-4; elev. 192ft./59m.; mail Arkadelphia z 71923; ● 120
Griffithville; Inc. Place; WHITE; 148 E-6; 🅿; z 72060; Ⓟ 237; Ⓒ 262
Grubbs; Inc. Place; JACKSON; 148 C-8; elev. 231ft./70m.; 🅿; z 72431; Ⓟ 528; Ⓒ 438
Guernsey; RMC Place; HEMPSTEAD; *148 H-2; mail Hope z 71801; ● 40
Guion; Inc. Place; IZARD; 148 C-6; 🅿; z 72540; Ⓟ 93; Ⓒ 90
Gum Corner; RMC Place; CHICOT; *148 I-7; elev. 120ft./37m.; mail Eudora z 71640; rural
Gum Log; RMC Place; POPE; *148 D-4; elev. 450ft./137m.; mail Russellville z 72802; rural
Gum Springs; Inc. Place; CLARK; 148 G-4; mail Arkadelphia z 71923; Ⓟ 157; Ⓒ 194
Gum Springs; RMC Place; NEWTON; *148 C-3; elev. 2,097ft./639m.; mail Jasper z 72641; rural
Gurdon; Inc. Place; CLARK; 148 H-3; elev. 210ft./64m.; 🅿; z 71743; Ⓟ 2,199; Ⓒ 2,276
Guy; Inc. Place; FAULKNER; 148 D-5; elev. 685ft./209m.; 🅿; z 72061; Ⓟ 241; Ⓒ 202

H

Hackett; Inc. Place; SEBASTIAN; 148 E-1; elev. 536ft./163m.; 🅿; ★ **FTSM**; z 72937; Ⓟ 490; Ⓒ 694
Hagarville; RMC Place; JOHNSON; 148 D-3; elev. 513ft./156m.; 🅿; z 72839; ● 80
Half Moon; RMC Place; MISSISSIPPI; *148 C-10; mail Blytheville z 72315; rural
Halley; RMC Place; DESHA; 148 I-7; mail Dermott z 71638
Halley Junction; RMC Place; CHICOT; *148 I-7; mail Dermott z 71638
Halliday; RMC Place; GREENE; 148 B-9; mail Marmaduke z 72443; ● 100
Hamburg; Inc. Place; ⊡ ASHLEY; 148 I-6; elev. 174ft./53m.; 🅿; z 71646; Ⓟ 3,098; Ⓒ 3,039
Hamil; RMC Place; RANDOLPH; *148 B-8; elev. 426ft./130m.; mail Ravenden Springs z 72460; rural
Hamilton; RMC Place; LONOKE; *148 F-6; elev. 207ft./63m.; mail Carlisle z 72024; rural
Hamlet; RMC Place; FAULKNER; *148 E-5; ● 160
Hampton; Inc. Place; ⊡ CALHOUN; 148 I-5; elev. 202ft./62m.; 🅿; z 71744; Ⓟ 1,562; Ⓒ 1,579
Hancock; RMC Place; CRAIGHEAD; *148 C-9; elev. 228ft./69m.; mail Caraway z 72419; rural
Hanna; RMC Place; CHICOT; *148 J-7; elev. 135ft./41m.; mail Eudora z 71640; ● 30
Hannaberry; RMC Place; JEFFERSON; *148 G-7; elev. 180ft./55m.; mail Stuttgart z 72160; rural
Hanover; RMC Place; STONE; *148 C-5; 🅿; z 72560; rural
Happy; RMC Place; WHITE; *148 E-6; elev. 215ft./66m.; mail Searcy z 72143; rural
Happy Bend; RMC Place; POPE; *148 D-4; mail Atkins z 72823; rural
Happy Corners; RMC Place; MISSISSIPPI; *148 C-9; elev. 238ft./73m.; mail Leachville z 72438; rural
Hardin; RMC Place; JEFFERSON; *148 G-5; ★ **PNBLF**; mail Pine Bluff z 71601, White Hall z 71602; ● 125
Hardy; Inc. Place; SHARP, FULTON; 148 B-7; elev. 358ft./109m.; 🅿; z 72529, z 72542 & mail Cherokee Village z 72525; Ⓟ 538; Ⓒ 578; Ⓡ 754
Hargrave Corner; RMC Place; CLAY; *148 B-9; mail Rector z 72461; ● 30
Harlow; RMC Place; CALHOUN; *148 H-5; elev. 280ft./85m.; mail Thornton z 71766; rural
Harmon (Harmony); RMC Place; BOONE; *148 B-4; elev. 1,100ft./335m.; mail Harrison z 72601; rural
Harmon; RMC Place; WASHINGTON; *148 B-1; ★ **FAY-**; mail Fayetteville z 72701, z 72704
Harmontown; RMC Place; INDEPENDENCE; *148 C-6; mail Batesville z 72501; ● 30
Harmony; BOONE; see Harmon (RMC Place)
Harmony; RMC Place; COLUMBIA; *148 I-3; elev. 289ft./88m.; mail Magnolia z 71753; rural
Harmony; RMC Place; JOHNSON; *148 D-3; mail Clarksville z 72830
Harmony; RMC Place; MADISON; *148 B-2; mail Huntsville z 72740; rural
Harmony; RMC Place; WHITE; *148 D-6; mail Searcy z 72143; rural
Harmony Grove; RMC Place; OUACHITA; *148 H-4; elev. 116ft./35m.; mail Camden z 71701; ● 65
Harness; RMC Place; STONE; *148 C-5; elev. 1,058ft./322m.; mail Leslie z 72645; rural
Harp; RMC Place; HOT SPRING; *148 G-4; elev. 350ft./107m.; mail Malvern z 72104; ● 150
Harrell; Inc. Place; CALHOUN; 148 I-5; elev. 204ft./62m.; 🅿; z 71745; Ⓟ 258; Ⓒ 293
Harriet; RMC Place; SEARCY; 148 C-5; 🅿; z 72617, z 72639; ● 50
Harrisburg; Inc. Place; ⊡ POINSETT; 148 D-8; 🅿; z 72432; Ⓟ 1,943; Ⓒ 2,192
Harrison; Inc. Place; ⊡ BOONE; 148 B-4; elev. 1,182ft./360m.; 🅿 🅷 ■; z 72601-02; Ⓟ 9,922; Ⓒ 12,152; ◆ 13,624
Hartford; Inc. Place; SEBASTIAN; 148 E-1; 🅿; z 72938; Ⓟ 721; Ⓒ 772
Hartman; Inc. Place; JOHNSON; 148 D-3; elev. 366ft./112m.; 🅿; z 72840; Ⓟ 498; Ⓒ 596
Hartwell; RMC Place; MADISON; *148 B-2; mail Huntsville z 72740
Harvey; RMC Place; SCOTT; 148 E-2; 🅿; z 72841; ● 30
Haskell; Inc. Place; SALINE; 148 F-4; 🅿; z 72015; Ⓟ 1,453; Ⓒ 2,645
Hasty; RMC Place; NEWTON; 148 C-4; 🅿; z 72640; ● 50
Hatchie Coon; RMC Place; POINSETT; *148 D-9; elev. 215ft./66m.; mail Trumann z 72472; ● 50
Hatfield; Inc. Place; POLK; 148 F-1; 🅿; z 71945; Ⓟ 414; Ⓒ 402
Hattieville; RMC Place; CONWAY; 148 D-4; 🅿; z 72063; ● 150
Hatton; RMC Place; POLK; 148 G-1; 🅿; z 71937; ● 100
Havana; Inc. Place; YELL; 148 E-3; elev. 377ft./115m.; 🅿; z 72842; Ⓟ 358; Ⓒ 392
Hayley; RMC Place; PRAIRIE; *148 E-6; elev. 204ft./62m.; mail Des Arc z 72040; rural
Haynes; Inc. Place; LEE; 148 E-8; elev. 222ft./68m.; 🅿; z 72341; Ⓟ 268; Ⓒ 214
Hazen; Inc. Place; PRAIRIE; 148 F-7; elev. 232ft./71m.; 🅿; z 72064; Ⓟ 1,668; Ⓒ 1,637
Heafer; RMC Place; CRITTENDEN; *148 D-9; elev. 217ft./66m.; mail Earle z 72331; ● 50
Healing Springs; RMC Place; BENTON; *148 B-1; elev. 1,124ft./343m.; mail Bentonville z 72712
Heart; RMC Place; FULTON; *148 B-6; elev. 585ft./178m.; mail Glencoe z 72539
Heber Springs; Inc. Place; ⊡ CLEBURNE; 148 D-6; elev. 354ft./108m.; 🅿 🅷; z 72543, z 72545; Ⓟ 5,628; Ⓒ 6,432
Hebron; RMC Place; CLEVELAND; *148 H-5; mail New Edinburg z 71660; rural
Hector; Inc. Place; POPE; 148 D-4; elev. 722ft./220m.; 🅿; z 72843; Ⓟ 478; Ⓒ 506
Helena; RMC Place; ⊡ PHILLIPS; 148 F-8; 🅿 🅷; z 72342; former incorporated place; became part of Helena-West Helena March 11, 2005; Ⓟ 7,491; Ⓒ 6,323
Helena Crossing; RMC Place; PHILLIPS; *148 F-8; mail Helena z 72342; pop. incl. with Helena (RMC Place)
Helena Junction; RMC Place; PHILLIPS; *148 F-8; elev. 213ft./65m.; mail Helena z 72342; rural
Helena-West Helena; Inc. Place; PHILLIPS; *148 F-8; incorporated March 11, 2005; not reported in 2000 Census; includes Helena and West Helena; Ⓐ 15,012
HEMPSTEAD; 148 H-2; Ⓟ 21,621; Ⓒ 23,587; ◆ 23,086
Hempwallace; RMC Place; GARLAND; *148 F-3; ★ **HTSPR**; mail Pearcy z 71964
Henderson; RMC Place; BAXTER; 148 B-5; elev. 673ft./205m.; 🅿; z 72544; summer pop. 600; ● 130
Hendrix College; RMC Place; FAULKNER; *148 E-5; mail Conway z 72032; pop. incl. with Conway (Inc. Place)
Hensley; CDP; PULASKI; *148 F-5; elev. 256ft./78m.; 🅿; z 72065; Ⓒ 150
Herbine; RMC Place; CLEVELAND; *148 H-6; mail Rison z 71665; rural
Hergett; RMC Place; CRAIGHEAD; *148 C-8; mail Jonesboro z 72404; rural
Heritage Estates; RMC Place; BAXTER; *148 B-5; mail Mountain Home z 72653; ● 90
Herman; RMC Place; CRAIGHEAD; *148 C-8; ★ **JONES**; mail Jonesboro z 72404; rural
Hermitage; Inc. Place; BRADLEY; 148 I-5; 🅿; z 71647; Ⓟ 639; Ⓒ 769
Hermitage; RMC Place; PULASKI; ★ **L.R.**; mail Little Rock z 72206; pop. incl. with Little Rock (Inc. Place)
Herndon; RMC Place; CRAIGHEAD; *148 C-8; mail Jonesboro z 72404; rural
Hervey; RMC Place; MILLER; *148 I-2; elev. 249ft./76m.; mail Texarkana z 71854; rural
Heth; RMC Place; ST. FRANCIS; *148 E-9; 🅿; z 72346; ● 20
Hickeytown; RMC Place; JOHNSON; *148 D-3; mail London z 72847; rural
Hickman; RMC Place; MISSISSIPPI; *148 C-10; elev. 256ft./78m.; mail Blytheville z 72315
Hickoria; RMC Place; CLAY; *148 B-9; mail Corning z 72422
Hickory Creek; RMC Place; BENTON; *148 B-2; elev. 1,122ft./342m.; ★ **FAY-**; mail Lowell z 72745; ● 200
Hickory Flat; RMC Place; WHITE; *148 D-6; elev. 625ft./191m.; mail Pangburn z 72121; rural
Hickory Hill; RMC Place; CONWAY; *148 D-4; mail Morrilton z 72110; rural
Hickory Plains; RMC Place; PRAIRIE; 148 E-6; 🅿; z 72066; ● 90
Hickory Ridge (Holly Ridge); RMC Place; CHICOT; *148 I-7; elev. 131ft./40m.; mail Eudora z 71640; ● 30
Hickory Ridge; Inc. Place; CROSS; 148 D-8; 🅿; z 72347; Ⓟ 436; Ⓒ 384
Hickory Valley; RMC Place; INDEPENDENCE; *148 C-7; elev. 601ft./183m.; mail Cave City z 72521; rural
Hicks; RMC Place; PHILLIPS; *148 F-8; mail Fayetteville z 72701, Marvell z 72366; rural
Hicks Station; RMC Place; ST. FRANCIS; *148 E-8; mail Widener z 72394; rural
Hicksville; RMC Place; PHILLIPS; *148 F-8; elev. 186ft./57m.; mail Marvell z 72366; ● 30
Hidden Valley; RMC Place; SHARP; *148 B-7; mail Hardy z 72542; pop. incl. with Highland (Inc. Place)
Higden; Inc. Place; CLEBURNE; 148 D-5; elev. 555ft./169m.; 🅿; z 72067; Ⓟ 92; Ⓒ 101
Higgins; RMC Place; PULASKI; *148 F-5; ★ **L.R.**; mail Little Rock z 72206
Higginson; Inc. Place; WHITE; *148 E-6; elev. 221ft./67m.; 🅿; z 72068; Ⓟ 255; Ⓒ 378
Highfill; Inc. Place; BENTON; 148 B-1; mail Gentry z 72734; Ⓟ 84; Ⓒ 379
Highland; RMC Place; PIKE; *148 G-2; ● 50
Highland; Inc. Place; SHARP; 148 B-7; 🅿; z 72542; Ⓒ 986
Highland Estates; RMC Place; BENTON; *148 B-2; elev. 1,300ft./396m.; ★ **FAY-**; mail Lowell z 72745; ● 100
Hill Creek; RMC Place; CONWAY; *148 E-5; elev. 323ft./98m.; mail Plumerville z 72127; rural
Hillcrest; RMC Place; JOHNSON; *148 D-3; elev. 760ft./232m.; mail Clarksville z 72830; rural
Hillcrest; MISSISSIPPI; see Gilchrist (RMC Place)
Hillcrest; RMC Place; PULASKI; *148 F-5; ★ **L.R.**; mail Little Rock z 72205; pop. incl. with Little Rock (Inc. Place)
Hilleman; WOODRUFF; see Hillemann (RMC Place)
Hillemann (Hilleman); RMC Place; WOODRUFF; 148 E-7; elev. 212ft./65m.; mail Mc Crory z 72101; ● 30
Hillsboro; RMC Place; UNION; *148 I-5; ● 35
Hilltop; RMC Place; SHARP; *148 B-7; elev. 500ft./152m.; mail Williford z 72482; rural
Hilo; RMC Place; BRADLEY; *148 I-5; elev. 136ft./41m.; mail Hermitage z 71647; rural
Hindsville; Inc. Place; MADISON; 148 B-2; elev. 1,365ft./416m.; 🅿; z 72738; Ⓟ 69; Ⓒ 75
Hiram; RMC Place; CLEBURNE; *148 D-6; elev. 417ft./127m.; mail Wilburn z 72179; rural
Hiwasse; RMC Place; BENTON; 148 B-1; 🅿; z 72739; ● 125
Hobbs Spur; CRAWFORD; see Hobbtown (RMC Place)
Hobbtown (Hobbs Spur); RMC Place; CRAWFORD; *148 D-1; elev. 800ft./244m.; mail Rudy z 72952; rural
Hogeye; RMC Place; WASHINGTON; elev. 1,230ft./375m.; mail West Fork z 72774; rural
Holiday Hills; RMC Place; BAXTER; *148 B-5; elev. 875ft./267m.; mail Elizabeth z 72531; ● 30
Holiday Island; RMC Place; CARROLL; *148 A-2; 🅿; z 72631; ● 200
Holland; Inc. Place; FAULKNER; 148 E-5; elev. 365ft./111m.; 🅿; z 72173; Ⓒ 577
Hollis; RMC Place; PERRY; 148 E-4; mail Plainview z 72857; rural
Holly Grove; Inc. Place; MONROE; 148 F-7; elev. 181ft./55m.; 🅿; z 72069; Ⓟ 675; Ⓒ 722
Holly Hills; RMC Place; INDEPENDENCE; *148 C-7; elev. 451ft./137m.; mail Batesville z 72501; ● 80
Holly Island; CLAY; see Holly Island Community (RMC Place)
Holly Island Community (East Webb Store, Holly Island); RMC Place; CLAY; *148 B-9; mail Rector z 72461; rural
Holly Ridge; CHICOT; see Hickory Ridge (RMC Place)
Holly Springs; RMC Place; DALLAS; 148 H-4; mail Sparkman z 71763; ● 30
Holly Springs; RMC Place; WHITE; *148 D-6; elev. 278ft./85m.; mail Searcy z 72143; rural
Hollywood; RMC Place; CLARK; 148 G-3; elev. 254ft./77m.; mail Arkadelphia z 71923; ● 75
Holman; RMC Place; JOHNSON; *148 D-3; mail Lamar z 72846; rural
Holub; LEE; see Holub Crossing (RMC Place)
Holub Crossing (Holub); RMC Place; LEE; *148 E-8; mail Marianna z 72360
Homan; RMC Place; MILLER; *148 H-2; elev. 269ft./82m.; mail Texarkana z 71854; rural
Homewood; RMC Place; PERRY; *148 E-4; mail Casa z 72025; rural
Hon; RMC Place; SCOTT; 148 E-1; elev. 633ft./193m.; mail Waldron z 72958; ● 70
Hooker; RMC Place; GREENE; *148 B-9; mail Paragould z 72450
Hooker; RMC Place; JEFFERSON; *148 G-6; ● 100
Hope; Inc. Place; ⊡ HEMPSTEAD; 148 H-3; 🅿 🅷; z 71801-02; Ⓟ 9,643; Ⓒ 10,616
Hopeville; RMC Place; CALHOUN; *148 H-5; elev. 297ft./91m.; mail Thornton z 71766; rural
Hopewell; RMC Place; CLEBURNE; *148 D-6; elev. 870ft./265m.; mail Rose Bud z 72137
Hopewell; RMC Place; GREENE; *148 B-9; elev. 292ft./89m.; mail Marmaduke z 72443; rural
Hopewell; RMC Place; LAWRENCE; *148 C-7; elev. 249ft./76m.; mail Hoxie z 72433; rural
Hopper; RMC Place; MONTGOMERY; *148 G-2; mail Caddo Gap z 71935
Horatio; Inc. Place; SEVIER; 148 H-1; elev. 348ft./106m.; 🅿; z 71842; Ⓟ 793; Ⓒ 997
Horseshoe; RMC Place; JACKSON; *148 D-7; mail Newport z 72112; rural
Horseshoe Bend; Inc. Place; IZARD, FULTON, SHARP; 148 B-6; 🅿; z 72512; Ⓟ 2,239; Ⓒ 2,278
Horseshoe Lake; Inc. Place; CRITTENDEN; *148 E-9; 🅿; z 72348; Ⓟ 298; Ⓒ 321
Horseshoe Lake; RMC Place; WOODRUFF; *148 D-7; elev. 200ft./61m.; mail Augusta z 72006; ● 50
Horton; RMC Place; ST. FRANCIS; *148 E-8; elev. 218ft./66m.; mail Colt z 72326; rural
HOT SPRING; 148 G-4; Ⓟ 26,115; Ⓒ 30,353; ◆ 32,101
Hot Springs (Hot Springs National Park); Inc. Place; ⊡ GARLAND; 148 F-4; 🅿 🅷 ■; ★ **HTSPR**; z 71901-03, z 71909-10, z 71913-14, z 71951; Ⓟ 32,462; Ⓒ 35,750; ◆ 39,083
Hot Springs Junction; RMC Place; PULASKI; *148 F-5; ★ **L.R.**; pop. incl. with Little Rock (Inc. Place)
Hot Springs National Park; GARLAND; see Hot Springs (Inc. Place)
Hot Springs Village; CDP; GARLAND, SALINE; 148 F-4; 🅿; z 71909-10 & mail Hot Springs National Park z 71901; Ⓟ 6,361; Ⓒ 8,397
Hough (Hugh); RMC Place; CARROLL; *148 B-3; ● 150
Houston; Inc. Place; PERRY; 148 E-4; elev. 299ft./91m.; 🅿; z 72070; Ⓟ 149; Ⓒ 159
HOWARD; 148 G-2; Ⓟ 13,569; Ⓒ 14,300; ◆ 13,591
Howell; RMC Place; WOODRUFF; 148 E-7; 🅿; z 72101; ● 30
Hoxie; Inc. Place; LAWRENCE; 148 C-8; 🅿; z 72433; Ⓟ 2,681; Ⓒ 2,817
Hudspeth; RMC Place; CHICOT; *148 I-7; elev. 135ft./41m.; mail Dermott z 71638; rural
Huff; RMC Place; INDEPENDENCE; *148 D-6; mail Batesville z 72501; rural
Huffman; RMC Place; MISSISSIPPI; *148 C-10; elev. 260ft./79m.; mail Blytheville z 72315
Hugh; CARROLL; see Hough (RMC Place)
Hughes; Inc. Place; ST. FRANCIS; 148 E-9; 🅿; z 72348; Ⓟ 1,810; Ⓒ 1,867
Hulbert; RMC Place; CRITTENDEN; *148 E-9; ★ **MEM**; mail West Memphis z 72301; pop. incl. with West Memphis (Inc. Place)
Humnoke; Inc. Place; LONOKE; 148 F-6; elev. 199ft./61m.; 🅿; z 72072; Ⓟ 311; Ⓒ 280
Humphrey; Inc. Place; ARKANSAS, JEFFERSON; 148 F-6; 🅿; z 72073; Ⓟ 743; Ⓒ 806
Hunt; RMC Place; JOHNSON; 148 D-2; elev. 622ft./190m.; 🅿; z 72840; ● 80
Hunter; Inc. Place; WOODRUFF; 148 E-7; 🅿; z 72074; Ⓟ 137; Ⓒ 152
Huntington; Inc. Place; SEBASTIAN; 148 E-1; elev. 658ft./201m.; 🅿; z 72940; Ⓟ 715; Ⓒ 688
Huntsville; Inc. Place; ⊡ MADISON; 148 B-2; 🅿; z 72740; Ⓟ 1,605; Ⓒ 1,931
Hurricane Grove; RMC Place; MONTGOMERY; 148 F-3; mail Mount Ida z 71957
Hutchinson; RMC Place; INDEPENDENCE; *148 D-6; elev. 836ft./255m.; mail Floral z 72534; rural
Hutson; INDEPENDENCE; see Maple Springs (RMC Place)
Huttig; Inc. Place; UNION; 148 J-5; elev. 108ft./33m.; 🅿; z 71747; Ⓟ 831; Ⓒ 731
Hydrick; RMC Place; POINSETT; *148 D-8; elev. 269ft./82m.; mail Cherry Valley z 72324

I

Ida; RMC Place; CLEBURNE; 148 D-6; elev. 987ft./301m.; 🅿; z 72546; ● 60
Imboden; Inc. Place; LAWRENCE; 148 B-7; 🅿; z 72434; Ⓟ 616; Ⓒ 684
Immanuel (Emanuel); RMC Place; ARKANSAS; *148 F-7; mail Almyra z 72003
INDEPENDENCE; 148 C-6; Ⓟ 31,192; Ⓒ 34,233; ◆ 34,567
Index; RMC Place; MILLER; *148 H-2; elev. 284ft./87m.; mail Texarkana z 71854; rural
Indian; RMC Place; CHICOT; 148 J-7; mail Eudora z 71640; rural
Indian Bay; RMC Place; MONROE; 148 F-8; elev. 160ft./49m.; mail Holly Grove z 72069; ● 40
Indiandale; RMC Place; GARLAND; *148 F-3; ★ **HTSPR**; mail Hot Springs National Park z 71901
Indianhead Lake Estates; RMC Place; PULASKI; ★ **L.R.**; mail North Little Rock z 72116; pop. incl. with North Little Rock (Inc. Place)
Indian Meadows; RMC Place; MARION; *148 B-4; elev. 749ft./228m.; mail Protem z 65733; ● 40
Indian Springs; RMC Place; SALINE; *148 F-5; ★ **L.R.**; mail Bryant z 72022; pop. incl. with Bryant (Inc. Place)
Ingalls; RMC Place; BRADLEY; 148 I-5; mail Hermitage z 71647; ● 40
Ingleside; RMC Place; JACKSON; *148 D-7; mail Newport z 72112; rural
Ingram; RMC Place; RANDOLPH; *148 B-8; mail Warm Springs z 72478; rural
Ink; RMC Place; POLK; *148 F-2; mail Mena z 71953
Ione; RMC Place; LOGAN; *148 E-2; mail Booneville z 72927
Iron Springs; RMC Place; PULASKI; *148 F-5; ★ **L.R.**; mail Little Rock z 72206; ● 500
Island Town; RMC Place; JACKSON; *148 D-7; mail Newport z 72112; ● 70
Iuka; RMC Place; IZARD; *148 B-5; elev. 860ft./262m.; mail Calico Rock z 72519; rural
Ivan; RMC Place; DALLAS; 148 H-5; 🅿; z 71748; ● 50
Ivesville; RMC Place; PULASKI; *148 F-5; ★ **L.R.**; mail Little Rock z 72212; pop. incl. with Little Rock (Inc. Place)
Ivy; RMC Place; DALLAS; *148 G-5; elev. 260ft./79m.; mail Carthage z 71725; rural
IZARD; 148 B-6; Ⓟ 11,364; Ⓒ 13,249; ◆ 12,571

J

Jabb; RMC Place; LONOKE; *148 F-6; elev. 221ft./67m.; mail England z 72046; rural
JACKSON; 148 D-7; Ⓟ 18,944; Ⓒ 18,418; ◆ 16,917
Jackson Heights; RMC Place; PULASKI; ★ **L.R.**; mail Jacksonville z 72076; pop. incl. with Jacksonville (Inc. Place)
Jacksonport; Inc. Place; JACKSON; *148 D-7; 🅿; z 72075; Ⓟ 264; Ⓒ 235
Jacksonville; Inc. Place; PULASKI; 148 E-6; 🅿 🅷 ■; ★ **L.R.**; z 72076, z 72078, z 72099; Ⓟ 29,101; Ⓒ 29,916; ◆ 32,225
James Mill; RMC Place; CRITTENDEN; elev. 220ft./67m.; ★ **MEM**; mail Crawfordsville z 72327, Marion z 72364
Jamestown; RMC Place; INDEPENDENCE; *148 C-6; mail Batesville z 72501; ● 80
Jamestown; RMC Place; JOHNSON; *148 D-3; elev. 401ft./122m.; mail Clarksville z 72830; pop. incl. with Clarksville (Inc. Place)
Japton; RMC Place; MADISON; *148 C-2; mail Huntsville z 72740
Jarrett; RANDOLPH; see Jerrett (RMC Place)
Jasmine; RMC Place; PRAIRIE, WHITE; *148 E-7; elev. 203ft./62m.; mail Griffithville z 72060; rural
Jasper; Inc. Place; ⊡ NEWTON; 148 C-3; elev. 834ft./254m.; 🅿; z 72641; Ⓟ 332; Ⓒ 498
Jefferson; RMC Place; JEFFERSON; *148 G-5; elev. 341ft./104m.; 🅿; z 72079; ● 150
JEFFERSON; 148 G-6; Ⓟ 85,487; Ⓒ 84,278; ◆ 75,192
Jeffersonville; RMC Place; LEE; *148 F-8; elev. 216ft./66m.; mail Marianna z 72360; rural
Jeffrey; RMC Place; PULASKI; *148 E-5; elev. 305ft./93m.; ★ **L.R.**; mail North Little Rock z 72118; rural
Jennette; Inc. Place; CRITTENDEN; *148 E-9; mail Crawfordsville z 72327; Ⓟ 184; Ⓒ 124
Jennie; RMC Place; CHICOT; 148 I-7; 🅿; z 71653; ● 120
Jenny Lind; RMC Place; SEBASTIAN; *148 D-1; ★ **FTSM**; mail Fort Smith z 72916; ● 350
Jenson; RMC Place; SEBASTIAN; *148 E-1; ★ **FTSM**; mail Hackett z 72937; pop. incl. with Rock Island (Inc. Place)
Jericho; Inc. Place; CRITTENDEN; 148 D-9; mail Crawfordsville z 72327; Ⓟ 210; Ⓒ 184
Jerome; Inc. Place; DREW; 148 I-7; mail Dermott z 71638; Ⓟ 47; Ⓒ 46
Jerrett (Jarrett); RMC Place; RANDOLPH; *148 B-8; elev. 307ft./94m.; mail Maynard z 72444; rural
Jersey; RMC Place; BRADLEY; 148 I-5; 🅿; z 71651; ● 30
Jerusalem; RMC Place; CONWAY; 148 D-4; elev. 756ft./230m.; 🅿; z 72080; ● 200
Jessieville; RMC Place; GARLAND; 148 F-4; 🅿; z 71949; ● 100
Jesup; RMC Place; LAWRENCE; *148 C-7; mail Smithville z 72466; ● 40
Jimmerson; RMC Place; PULASKI; ★ **L.R.**; pop. incl. with Little Rock (Inc. Place)
Joan; RMC Place; CLARK; *148 G-4; elev. 281ft./86m.; mail Arkadelphia z 71923
Johnson; Inc. Place; WASHINGTON; *148 B-2; 🅿; ★ **FAY-**; z 72741; Ⓟ 599; Ⓒ 2,319
JOHNSON; 148 D-3; Ⓟ 18,221; Ⓒ 22,781; ◆ 25,323
Johnson Addition; RMC Place; CRAIGHEAD; *148 C-8; elev. 224ft./68m.; mail Bay z 72411; ● 30
Johnstown; RMC Place; JACKSON; *148 D-7; elev. 224ft./68m.; mail Newport z 72112; rural
Johnsville; RMC Place; BRADLEY; 148 I-6; elev. 205ft./62m.; mail Hermitage z 71647; ● 50
Joiner; Inc. Place; MISSISSIPPI; 148 D-9; 🅿; z 72350; Ⓟ 645; Ⓒ 540
Jolliff Store; RMC Place; MISSISSIPPI; *148 C-9; mail Manila z 72442; rural
Jonesboro; Inc. Place; ⊡ CRAIGHEAD; 148 C-8; 🅿 🅷 🅲 10,727 ■; ★ **JONES**; z 72401-04; Ⓟ 46,535; Ⓒ 55,515; ◆ 68,292
Jones Mill; HOT SPRING; see Jones Mills (RMC Place)
Jones Mills (Jones Mill); RMC Place; HOT SPRING; *148 F-4; mail Jones Mill z 72105; ● 450
Jonesville; RMC Place; MILLER; *148 I-2; elev. 226ft./69m.; mail Fouke z 71837; rural
Jonquil; RMC Place; ST. FRANCIS; *148 E-9; elev. 206ft./63m.; mail Heth z 72346; rural
Joplin; RMC Place; MONTGOMERY; 148 F-3; elev. 665ft./203m.; mail Mount Ida z 71957
Jordan; RMC Place; BAXTER; 148 B-5; elev. 848ft./258m.; 🅿; z 72519; ● 50
Joy; RMC Place; WHITE; 148 D-6; elev. 754ft./230m.; mail Searcy z 72143
Joyce City; RMC Place; OUACHITA; *148 I-4; elev. 104ft./32m.; mail Smackover z 71762; ● 50
Joyland Park; LOGAN; see Grayson (RMC Place)
Judd Hill; RMC Place; POINSETT; *148 D-9; mail Trumann z 72472; rural
Judsonia; Inc. Place; WHITE; 148 D-6; 🅿; z 72081; Ⓟ 1,915; Ⓒ 1,982
Julius; RMC Place; CRITTENDEN; *148 E-9; mail Crawfordsville z 72327; ● 60
Jumbo; RMC Place; IZARD; *148 C-6; elev. 513ft./156m.; mail Melbourne z 72556; ● 30
Junction City; Inc. Place; UNION; 148 J-4; see also Junction City, LA; elev. 177ft./54m.; 🅿; z 71749; Ⓟ 674; Ⓒ 721

K

Kansas; RMC Place; CLARK; *148 H-4; elev. 150ft./46m.; mail Whelen Springs z 71772; rural
Kearney; RMC Place; JEFFERSON; *148 F-5; mail Redfield z 72132; rural
Kedron; RMC Place; CLEVELAND; *148 G-5; elev. 205ft./62m.; mail Rison z 71665; rural
Keiser; Inc. Place; MISSISSIPPI; 148 C-9; 🅿; z 72351; Ⓟ 805; Ⓒ 808
Kellum; RMC Place; SEVIER; *148 G-1; elev. 502ft./153m.; mail De Queen z 71832; rural
Kelso; RMC Place; DESHA; 148 H-7; elev. 145ft./44m.; mail Watson z 71674; ● 30
Kenova; RMC Place; UNION; *148 I-4; mail Smackover z 71762; ● 50
Kensett; Inc. Place; WHITE; 148 D-6; elev. 229ft./70m.; 🅿; z 72082; Ⓟ 1,741; Ⓒ 1,791
Kent; RMC Place; OUACHITA; *148 H-4; mail Camden z 71701; rural
Kentucky; RMC Place; SALINE; *148 F-4; ★ **L.R.**; mail Benton z 72015; rural
Kenwood; RMC Place; CONWAY; *148 E-4; mail Atkins z 72823; ● 30
Keo; Inc. Place; LONOKE; 148 F-6; elev. 234ft./71m.; 🅿; z 72083; Ⓟ 154; Ⓒ 235
Kerlin; RMC Place; COLUMBIA; *148 I-3; elev. 310ft./94m.; mail Magnolia z 71753; rural
Kerr; RMC Place; LONOKE; *148 F-6; mail Scott z 72142; rural
Kibler; Inc. Place; CRAWFORD; 148 D-1; ★ **FTSM**; mail Van Buren z 72956; Ⓟ 931; Ⓒ 969
Kimberley; RMC Place; PIKE; *148 G-2; mail Murfreesboro z 71958; rural
Kindall; RMC Place; PHILLIPS; *148 F-8; elev. 196ft./60m.; mail Poplar Grove z 72374
King; RMC Place; SEVIER; 148 G-1; mail Gillham z 71841; ● 90
Kingsland; Inc. Place; CLEVELAND; 148 H-5; elev. 214ft./65m.; 🅿; z 71652; Ⓟ 395; Ⓒ 449
Kingston; RMC Place; MADISON; 148 C-3; elev. 1,351ft./412m.; 🅿; z 72742; ● 60
Kingston; RMC Place; YELL; *148 E-3; mail Ola z 72853; rural
Kingswood Estates; RMC Place; BAXTER; *148 B-5; mail Mountain Home z 72653; ● 110
Kingtown; RMC Place; PHILLIPS; *148 F-8; mail Marvell z 72366; rural
Kingwood; RMC Place; PULASKI; *148 F-5; ★ **L.R.**; mail Little Rock z 72207; pop. incl. with Little Rock (Inc. Place)
Kirby; RMC Place; PIKE; 148 G-2; elev. 671ft./205m.; 🅿; z 71950; ● 125
Kirkland; RMC Place; OUACHITA; *148 I-4; elev. 163ft./50m.; mail Louann z 71751; ● 50
Knob; RMC Place; CLAY; *148 B-9; elev. 347ft./106m.; mail Lafe z 72436; rural
Knobel; Inc. Place; CLAY; 148 B-8; 🅿; z 72435; Ⓟ 317; Ⓒ 358
Knoxville; Inc. Place; JOHNSON; 148 D-3; 🅿; z 72845; Ⓟ 239; Ⓒ 511
Koch Ridge; RMC Place; VAN BUREN; *148 D-5; elev. 1,158ft./353m.; mail Clinton z 72031; rural

L

Lacey; RMC Place; DREW; 148 I-6; elev. 201ft./61m.; mail Monticello z 71655; ● 110
Laconia; RMC Place; DESHA; *148 G-8; mail Snow Lake z 72379; rural
LaCrosse; RMC Place; IZARD; *148 B-6; elev. 766ft./233m.; mail Violet Hill z 72584
Ladd; RMC Place; JEFFERSON; *148 G-6; mail Pine Bluff z 71601
Ladelle; RMC Place; DREW; 148 I-6; mail Monticello z 71655; ● 75
LAFAYETTE; 148 I-2; Ⓟ 9,643; Ⓒ 8,559; ◆ 7,636
Lafe; Inc. Place; GREENE; 148 B-9; 🅿; z 72436; Ⓟ 315; Ⓒ 385
Lafferty; RMC Place; IZARD; *148 C-6; elev. 391ft./119m.; mail Mount Pleasant z 72561; rural
La Grange; Inc. Place; LEE; 148 F-8; 🅿; z 72352; Ⓟ 108; Ⓒ 122
Lake Bull Shoales Estates; RMC Place; MARION; *148 B-4; elev. 800ft./244m.; mail Yellville z 72687; ● 60
Lake Catherine; RMC Place; GARLAND; 148 M-10; ★ **HTSPR**; mail Hot Springs National Park z 71901; ● 870
Lake City; Inc. Place; ⊡ CRAIGHEAD; 148 C-9; 🅿; z 72437; Ⓟ 1,833; Ⓒ 1,956
Lake Dick; RMC Place; JEFFERSON; *148 G-6; mail Altheimer z 72004; ● 50
Lake Elmdale; RMC Place; WASHINGTON; *148 B-1; ★ **FAY-**; mail Springdale z 72764; pop. incl. with Springdale (Inc. Place)
Lake Frances (Lake Francis); RMC Place; BENTON; *148 B-1; elev. 1,170ft./357m.; mail Siloam Springs z 72761; rural
Lake Francis; BENTON; see Lake Frances (RMC Place)
Lakehall; RMC Place; CHICOT; mail Lake Village z 71653; rural
Lake Hamilton; CDP; GARLAND; 148 F-4; 🅿; ★ **HTSPR**; z 71913; Ⓟ 1,331; Ⓒ 1,609
Lake Poinsett; RMC Place; POINSETT; *148 D-8; elev. 350ft./107m.; mail Harrisburg z 72432; ● 200
Lakeport; RMC Place; CHICOT; *148 I-7; mail Lake Village z 71653; rural
Lakeside; RMC Place; GARLAND; ★ **HTSPR**; mail Hot Springs National Park z 71901; pop. incl. with Hot Springs (Inc. Place)
Lakeside; RMC Place; OUACHITA; *148 H-4; elev. 122ft./37m.; mail Camden z 71701; rural
Lakeside; RMC Place; SALINE; *148 F-5; elev. 250ft./76m.; mail Hensley z 72065; summer pop. 100; ● 15
Lakeside Terrace; RMC Place; BAXTER; *148 B-5; mail Mountain Home z 72653; ● 170
Lakeview; Inc. Place; BAXTER; 148 B-5; elev. 789ft./240m.; 🅿; z 72642; Ⓟ 485; Ⓒ 763
Lakeview; RMC Place; CONWAY; *148 E-4; elev. 350ft./107m.; mail Morrilton z 72110; ● 50
Lake View; RMC Place; CRAIGHEAD; *148 C-9; elev. 234ft./71m.; mail Lake City z 72437; rural
Lakeview; Inc. Place; PHILLIPS; 148 F-8; mail Helena z 72342; Ⓟ 526; Ⓒ 531
Lakeview Estates; RMC Place; MONTGOMERY; *148 F-3; elev. 645ft./197m.; mail Story z 71970; ● 30
Lake Village; Inc. Place; ⊡ CHICOT; 148 I-7; 🅿 🅷; z 71653; Ⓟ 2,791; Ⓒ 2,823
Lakeway; RMC Place; MARION; *148 B-4; elev. 1,211ft./369m.; mail Yellville z 72687; rural
Lakewood; RMC Place; JEFFERSON; *148 G-6; elev. 186ft./57m.; mail Altheimer z 72004; rural
Lakewood; RMC Place; PULASKI; *148 F-5; ★ **L.R.**; mail North Little Rock z 72116; pop. incl. with North Little Rock (Inc. Place)
Lakewood Estates; RMC Place; MILLER; *148 I-2; ★ **TEXR-**; mail Texarkana z 75501; pop. incl. with Texarkana (Inc. Place)
Lamar; Inc. Place; JOHNSON; 148 D-3; elev. 407ft./124m.; 🅿; z 72846; Ⓟ 768; Ⓒ 1,415
Lamartine; RMC Place; COLUMBIA; 148 I-3; mail Waldo z 71770; ● 30
Lambert (Marcus); RMC Place; HOT SPRING; *148 G-3; mail Bismarck z 71929
Lambrook; RMC Place; PHILLIPS; 148 G-8; 🅿; z 72353; ● 50
Landers; RMC Place; POINSETT; *148 D-8; mail Trumann z 72472; rural
Landis; RMC Place; SEARCY; *148 C-5; mail Marshall z 72650; rural
Laneburg; RMC Place; NEVADA; 148 H-3; 🅿; z 71857; ● 80
Langford; RMC Place; JEFFERSON; *148 G-7; elev. 182ft./55m.; mail Altheimer z 72004; rural
Langley; RMC Place; PIKE; 148 G-2; elev. 801ft./244m.; 🅿; z 71952; ● 30
Lanieve; CRAIGHEAD; see Pauls Switch (RMC Place)
Lansing; RMC Place; CRITTENDEN; *148 D-9; mail Crawfordsville z 72327; ● 60
Lanty; RMC Place; CONWAY; *148 D-4; elev. 456ft./139m.; mail Hattieville z 72063, Morrilton z 72110; rural
Lapile; RMC Place; UNION; *148 J-5; mail Strong z 71765; ● 40
La Plaza Acres; RMC Place; WHITE; *148 D-6; elev. 319ft./97m.; mail Searcy z 72143; ● 100
Larkin; RMC Place; IZARD; *148 B-6; mail Violet Hill z 72584; rural
Larue; RMC Place; BENTON; *148 B-2; mail Rogers z 72756; ● 30
Latour; RMC Place; PHILLIPS; *148 F-8; mail Lexa z 72355; rural
Lauratown; RMC Place; LAWRENCE; *148 C-7; elev. 260ft./79m.; mail Hoxie z 72433; rural
Lavaca; Inc. Place; SEBASTIAN; 148 D-1; 🅿; ★ **FTSM**; z 72941; Ⓟ 1,253; Ⓒ 1,825
LAWRENCE; 148 C-7; Ⓟ 17,457; Ⓒ 17,774; ◆ 16,754
Lawrenceville; RMC Place; MONROE; mail Holly Grove z 72069; rural
Lawson; RMC Place; UNION; 148 I-5; 🅿; z 71750; ● 100
Lazy Acres; RMC Place; MARION; *148 B-4; elev. 761ft./232m.; mail Protem z 65733; ● 90
Leachville; Inc. Place; MISSISSIPPI; 148 C-9; 🅿; z 72438; Ⓟ 1,743; Ⓒ 1,981
Lead Hill; Inc. Place; BOONE; 148 B-4; 🅿; z 72644 & mail Diamond City z 72630; Ⓟ 283; Ⓒ 287
Lebanon; RMC Place; SEVIER; *148 G-2; mail Lockesburg z 71846; rural
LEE; 148 F-8; Ⓟ 13,053; Ⓒ 12,580; ◆ 10,428
Lehi; RMC Place; CRITTENDEN; *148 E-9; ★ **MEM**; mail Marion z 72364; rural
Leitner; RMC Place; JEFFERSON; *148 G-6; ★ **PNBLF**; mail Pine Bluff z 71601; pop. incl. with Pine Bluff (Inc. Place)
Lemsford (Sandy Ridge); RMC Place; MISSISSIPPI; *148 C-10; elev. 249ft./76m.; mail Blytheville z 72315; rural
Lennie; RMC Place; MISSISSIPPI; elev. 233ft./71m.; mail Manila z 72442
Leola; Inc. Place; GRANT; 148 G-5; 🅿; z 72084; Ⓟ 476; Ⓒ 515
Leonard; RMC Place; CLAY; *148 B-9; mail Rector z 72461
Lepanto (Lepanto Station); Inc. Place; POINSETT; 148 D-9; 🅿; z 72354; Ⓟ 2,033; Ⓒ 2,133
Lepanto Station; POINSETT; see Lepanto (Inc. Place)
Leslie; Inc. Place; SEARCY; 148 C-5; 🅿; z 72645; Ⓟ 446; Ⓒ 482
Lester; RMC Place; CRAIGHEAD; *148 C-9; mail Lake City z 72437; ● 75
Lesterville; RMC Place; RANDOLPH; *148 B-8; ● 40
Letona; Inc. Place; WHITE; 148 D-6; 🅿; z 72085; Ⓟ 218; Ⓒ 201
Levesque; RMC Place; CROSS; *148 D-8; ● 60
Levy; RMC Place; PULASKI; *148 F-5; ★ **L.R.**; mail North Little Rock z 72118; pop. incl. with North Little Rock (Inc. Place)
Lewisville; Inc. Place; ⊡ LAFAYETTE; 148 I-3; elev. 268ft./82m.; 🅿; z 71845; Ⓟ 1,424; Ⓒ 1,285
Lexa; Inc. Place; PHILLIPS; 148 F-8; 🅿; z 72355; Ⓟ 295; Ⓒ 331
Lexington; STONE; see Old Lexington (RMC Place)
Liberty; RMC Place; LOGAN; *148 D-3; elev. 462ft./141m.; mail Delaware z 72835; rural
Liberty Hall; RMC Place; YELL; *148 E-4; mail Dardanelle z 72834; rural
Liberty Valley; RMC Place; WHITE; *148 D-7; elev. 204ft./62m.; mail Bald Knob z 72010; rural
Lick Mountain; RMC Place; CONWAY; *148 D-4; elev. 705ft./215m.; mail Center Ridge z 72027; rural
Light; RMC Place; GREENE; 148 C-8; 🅿; z 72439 & mail Walnut Ridge z 72476; ● 80
Limedale; RMC Place; INDEPENDENCE; *148 C-6; mail Batesville z 72501; rural
Limestone; RMC Place; NEWTON; 148 C-3; elev. 910ft./277m.; mail Deer z 72628
Lincoln; Inc. Place; WASHINGTON; 148 C-1; elev. 1,502ft./458m.; 🅿; z 72744; Ⓟ 1,460; Ⓒ 1,752
LINCOLN; 148 G-6; Ⓟ 13,690; Ⓒ 14,492; ◆ 13,597
Linder; RMC Place; FAULKNER; *148 E-5; mail Greenbrier z 72058; rural
Lisbon; RMC Place; UNION; *148 I-4; elev. 214ft./65m.; mail El Dorado z 71730
Little Bay; RMC Place; CALHOUN; *148 H-5; elev. 320ft./98m.; mail Thornton z 71766; rural
Little Flock; Inc. Place; BENTON; 148 B-2; mail Rogers z 72756; Ⓟ 944; Ⓒ 2,585
Little Garnett; RMC Place; LINCOLN; *148 H-6; elev. 387ft./118m.; mail Star City z 71667; rural
Little Italy; RMC Place; PERRY, PULASKI; *148 E-5; elev. 689ft./210m.; mail Bigelow z 72016
Little Red; RMC Place; WHITE; *148 D-6; elev. 266ft./81m.; mail Pangburn z 72121; rural
Little River; RMC Place; MISSISSIPPI; *148 C-9; mail Manila z 72442; rural
LITTLE RIVER; 148 H-1; Ⓟ 13,966; Ⓒ 13,628; ◆ 12,538
Little River Country Club; RMC Place; LITTLE RIVER; *148 H-1; mail Winthrop z 71866; summer pop. 500; ● 60
Little Rock; Inc. Place; **STATE CAPITAL**; ⊡ PULASKI; 148 F-5; 🅿 🅷 🅲 15,590 ■; ★ **L.R.**; z 72201-07, z 72209-12, z 72214-17, z 72219, z 72221-23, z 72225, z 72227, z 72231, z 72260, z 72295; Ⓟ 175,795; Ⓒ 183,133; ◆ 199,559
Locke; RMC Place; CRAWFORD; 148 C-2; elev. 1,595ft./486m.; mail Mountainburg z 72946; ● 30
Lockesburg; Inc. Place; SEVIER; 148 G-1; elev. 436ft./133m.; 🅿; z 71846; Ⓟ 608; Ⓒ 711
Locust Bayou; RMC Place; CALHOUN; 148 I-4; mail Camden z 71701; ● 140
Locust Grove; RMC Place; INDEPENDENCE; 148 C-6; elev. 318ft./97m.; 🅿; z 72550; ● 85
Lodge Corner; RMC Place; ARKANSAS; *148 G-7; elev. 191ft./58m.; mail Stuttgart z 72160
Lodi; RMC Place; PIKE; *148 G-2; elev. 770ft./235m.; mail Glenwood z 71943
Logan; RMC Place; BENTON; *148 B-1; elev. 1,063ft./324m.; mail Siloam Springs z 72761; rural
LOGAN; 148 E-2; Ⓟ 20,557; Ⓒ 22,486; ◆ 22,506
Lollie; RMC Place; FAULKNER; *148 E-5; mail Mayflower z 72106; rural
London; Inc. Place; POPE; 148 D-3; 🅿; z 72847; Ⓟ 825; Ⓒ 925
Lone Elm (Lonelm); RMC Place; FRANKLIN; *148 D-2; elev. 515ft./157m.; mail Mulberry z 72947; rural
Lonelm; FRANKLIN; see Lone Elm (RMC Place)
Lone Pine; RMC Place; SEARCY; *148 C-5; elev. 1,200ft./366m.; mail Marshall z 72650
Lono; RMC Place; HOT SPRING; *148 G-4; elev. 503ft./153m.; mail Leola z 72084
Lonoke; Inc. Place; ⊡ LONOKE; 148 F-6; elev. 239ft./73m.; 🅿; z 72086; Ⓟ 4,022; Ⓒ 4,287
LONOKE; 148 F-6; Ⓟ 39,268; Ⓒ 52,828; ◆ 66,068
Lonsdale; Inc. Place; GARLAND; *148 F-4; elev. 424ft./129m.; 🅿; z 72087; Ⓟ 127; Ⓒ 118
Lookout; RMC Place; BENTON; *148 B-2; elev. 1,435ft./437m.; mail Rogers z 72756; ● 40
Lookout; RMC Place; MONROE; *148 F-7; elev. 196ft./60m.; mail Roe z 72134; rural
Lorado; RMC Place; GREENE; 148 C-8; mail Jonesboro z 72401; ● 120
Lorine; RMC Place; RANDOLPH; *148 B-8; elev. 477ft./145m.; mail Pocahontas z 72455; rural
Lost Bridge Village; RMC Place; BENTON; *148 B-2; mail Garfield z 72732; ● 270
Lost Cane; RMC Place; MISSISSIPPI; *148 C-9; elev. 236ft./72m.; mail Manila z 72442; rural
Lost Corner; RMC Place; POPE; *148 D-4; elev. 1,677ft./511m.; mail Jerusalem z 72080; rural
Louann; Inc. Place; OUACHITA; 148 I-4; 🅿; z 71751; Ⓟ 158; Ⓒ 195
Louise; RMC Place; CRITTENDEN; *148 E-9; elev. 210ft./64m.; mail Proctor z 72376; rural
Lowell; Inc. Place; BENTON; 148 B-2; elev. 1,343ft./409m.; 🅿; ★ **FAY-**; z 72745; Ⓟ 1,224; Ⓒ 5,013
Lower Boydsville; RMC Place; CLAY; *148 B-9; elev. 302ft./92m.; mail Rector z 72461; rural
Lower Poplar Ridge; CRAIGHEAD; see Poplar Ridge (RMC Place)
Lower White Oak Lake; RMC Place; OUACHITA; *148 H-4; elev. 250ft./76m.; mail Chidester z 71726; ● 150
Low Gap; RMC Place; NEWTON; *148 C-3; elev. 1,755ft./535m.; mail Jasper z 72641; rural
Luber; RMC Place; STONE; *148 C-6; mail Mountain View z 72560; rural
Lucas; RMC Place; LOGAN; *148 E-2; mail Booneville z 72927; rural
Ludwig; RMC Place; JOHNSON; *148 D-3; mail Clarksville z 72830
Lumber; RMC Place; COLUMBIA; *148 I-3; mail Waldo z 71770; ● 30
Luna; RMC Place; CHICOT; *148 I-7; mail Lake Village z 71653; rural
Lundell; RMC Place; PHILLIPS; *148 G-8; mail Mellwood z 72367
Lunenburg; RMC Place; IZARD; *148 C-6; elev. 453ft./138m.; mail Melbourne z 72556
Lunsford; RMC Place; CRAIGHEAD; *148 C-9; mail Lake City z 72437; ● 75
Lurton; RMC Place; NEWTON; 148 C-4; elev. 2,007ft./612m.; mail Pelsor z 72856
Lutherville; RMC Place; JOHNSON; *148 D-3; elev. 895ft./273m.; mail Lamar z 72846
Luxora; Inc. Place; MISSISSIPPI; 148 C-10; 🅿; z 72358; Ⓟ 1,338; Ⓒ 1,317
Lynch; RMC Place; PULASKI; ★ **L.R.**; mail North Little Rock z 72117; pop. incl. with North Little Rock (Inc. Place)
Lynn; Inc. Place; LAWRENCE; 148 C-7; elev. 354ft./108m.; 🅿; z 72440; Ⓟ 299; Ⓒ 315

M

Mabelvale; RMC Place; PULASKI; *148 F-5; elev. 312ft./95m.; 🅿; ★ **L.R.**; z 72103; pop. incl. with Little Rock (Inc. Place)
Macedonia; RMC Place; COLUMBIA; *148 I-3; mail Magnolia z 71753
Macedonia; RMC Place; CONWAY; *148 D-4; mail Hattieville z 72063; rural
Macey; RMC Place; CRAIGHEAD; *148 C-9; mail Monette z 72447; rural
Macks; RMC Place; JACKSON; *148 D-7; mail Newport z 72112; rural

Entries in **UPPERCASE** are counties.
Entries in **bold** have populations of 2,500 or more.
Names in parentheses are alternate names.
Inc. Place — Incorporated Place
RMC Place — Rand McNally Designated Place
CDP — Census Designated Place
MCD — Minor Civil Division

⊡ County Seat
▲ Minor Civil Division
elev. Elevation
🅿 Post Office

🅷 Hospital
🅲 College
■ Principal Business Center
★ Rand McNally Metro Area (RMA) Abbreviation
z Zip Code(s)

Ⓟ Previous Census Population
Ⓡ Revised Census Population
Ⓐ Annexation Population
● Rand McNally Population Estimate
Ⓒ Final Census Population
Ⓢ Special Census Population
◆ Estimated Population

For additional definitions see Glossary, Volume 1, and Introduction, Volume 2.

Macon; RMC Place; PULASKI; 148 E-5; elev. 320ft./98m.; ★ **L.R.**; mail Jacksonville z 72076; ● 960
Macon Lake; RMC Place; CHICOT; *148 I-7; mail Lake Village z 71653; rural
Madding; RMC Place; JEFFERSON; *148 G-6; elev. 200ft./61m.; mail Altheimer z 72004; rural
Madison; Inc. Place; ST. FRANCIS; 148 E-8; elev. 209ft./64m.; 🅿; z 72359; Ⓟ 1,263; Ⓒ 987
MADISON; 148 C-3; Ⓟ 11,618; Ⓒ 14,243; ◆ 15,671
Magazine; Inc. Place; LOGAN; 148 E-2; 🅿; z 72943; Ⓟ 799; Ⓒ 915
Magic Springs; RMC Place; SEARCY; *148 C-4; elev. 1,917ft./584m.; mail Marshall z 72650; rural
Magness; Inc. Place; INDEPENDENCE; 148 C-7; elev. 267ft./81m.; 🅿; z 72553; Ⓟ 158; Ⓒ 191
Magnet; HOT SPRING; see Magnet Cove (Inc. Place)
Magnet Cove (Magnet); Inc. Place; HOT SPRING; 148 F-4; mail Malvern z 72104; incorporated April 27, 2000; not reported in 2000 Census; ● 500
Magnolia; Inc. Place; ⊡ COLUMBIA; 148 I-3; 🅿 🅷 🅲 3,113 ■; z 71753-54; Ⓟ 11,151; Ⓒ 10,858; ◆ 10,203
Main Street; RMC Place; PULASKI; *148 F-5; ★ **L.R.**; mail North Little Rock z 72119; pop. incl. with North Little Rock (Inc. Place)
Mallet Town; RMC Place; CONWAY; *148 D-5; mail Springfield z 72157; rural
Mallory Spur; RMC Place; CRITTENDEN; *148 E-9; elev. 200ft./61m.; mail Hughes z 72348; ● 30
Malvern; Inc. Place; ⊡ HOT SPRING; 148 G-4; 🅿 🅷; z 72104-05; Ⓟ 9,256; Ⓒ 9,021
Mammoth Spring; Inc. Place; FULTON; 148 A-7; 🅿; z 72554; Ⓟ 1,097; Ⓒ 1,147
Mandalay; RMC Place; MISSISSIPPI; *148 C-9; mail Manila z 72442; rural
Mandeville; RMC Place; MILLER; 148 I-2; elev. 318ft./97m.; ★ **TEXR-**; mail Texarkana z 75501; ● 520
Manfred; RMC Place; MONTGOMERY; *148 F-2; mail Caddo Gap z 71935; rural
Mangrum; RMC Place; CRAIGHEAD; *148 C-9; elev. 227ft./69m.; mail Black Oak z 72414; rural
Manila; Inc. Place; MISSISSIPPI; 148 C-9; 🅿; z 72442; Ⓟ 2,635; Ⓒ 3,055
Manning; RMC Place; DALLAS; 148 G-4; elev. 222ft./68m.; 🅿; z 71763; ● 70
Mansfield; Inc. Place; SEBASTIAN, SCOTT; 148 E-1; 🅿; z 72944; Ⓟ 1,018; Ⓒ 1,097
Manson; RMC Place; RANDOLPH; 148 B-7; elev. 267ft./81m.; mail Pocahontas z 72455
Many Island; FULTON; see Many Islands (RMC Place)
Many Islands (Many Island); RMC Place; FULTON; *148 B-7; elev. 422ft./129m.; mail Mammoth Spring z 72554; rural
Maple; RMC Place; CARROLL; *148 B-3; elev. 1,194ft./364m.; mail Berryville z 72616; rural
Maple Corner; RMC Place; PHILLIPS; mail Poplar Grove z 72374
Maple Grove; RMC Place; POINSETT; *148 D-9; mail Trumann z 72472; rural
Maple Springs (Hutson); RMC Place; INDEPENDENCE; *148 D-7; elev. 332ft./101m.; mail Rosie z 72571; rural
Marble; RMC Place; MADISON; 148 B-3; mail Huntsville z 72740; ● 60
Marble Falls; NEWTON; see Dogpatch (RMC Place)
Marcella; RMC Place; STONE; 148 C-6; 🅿; z 72555; ● 80
Marche; RMC Place; PULASKI; *148 E-5; elev. 267ft./81m.; ★ **L.R.**; mail North Little Rock z 72117-18; rural
Marc Lyn Estates; RMC Place; MARION; *148 B-4; elev. 890ft./271m.; mail Yellville z 72687; ● 30
Marcus; HOT SPRING; see Lambert (RMC Place)
Marianna; Inc. Place; ⊡ LEE; 148 F-8; 🅿; z 72360; Ⓟ 5,910; Ⓒ 5,181
Marie; Inc. Place; MISSISSIPPI; 148 D-9; mail Wilson z 72395; Ⓟ 129; Ⓒ 108
Marion; Inc. Place; ⊡ CRITTENDEN; 148 D-9; elev. 225ft./69m.; 🅿; ★ **MEM**; z 72364; Ⓟ 4,391; Ⓒ 8,901
MARION; 148 B-4; Ⓟ 12,001; Ⓒ 16,140; ◆ 16,516
Marked Tree; Inc. Place; POINSETT; 148 D-9; 🅿; z 72365; Ⓟ 3,100; Ⓒ 2,800
Marmaduke; Inc. Place; GREENE; 148 B-9; 🅿; z 72436, z 72443; Ⓟ 1,164; Ⓒ 1,158
Marsden; RMC Place; BRADLEY; *148 I-5; elev. 125ft./38m.; mail Hermitage z 71647; rural
Marsena; RMC Place; SEARCY; *148 C-4; elev. 946ft./288m.; mail Marshall z 72650; rural
Marshall; Inc. Place; ⊡ SEARCY; 148 C-4; 🅿; z 72650; Ⓟ 1,318; Ⓒ 1,313
Mars Hill; RMC Place; LAFAYETTE; *148 I-3; elev. 302ft./92m.; mail Stamps z 71860; rural
Martindale; RMC Place; PULASKI; *148 F-5; ★ **L.R.**; mail Little Rock z 72210; rural
Martinville; RMC Place; FAULKNER, CONWAY; *148 D-5; mail Damascus z 72039, Little Rock z 72204; rural
Marvell; Inc. Place; PHILLIPS; 148 F-8; elev. 210ft./64m.; 🅿; z 72366; Ⓟ 1,545; Ⓒ 1,395
Marvinville; RMC Place; YELL; *148 E-3; elev. 381ft./116m.; mail Havana z 72842; rural
Marysville; RMC Place; UNION; *148 I-4; elev. 284ft./87m.; mail Magnolia z 71753; rural
Mason Valley; RMC Place; BENTON; *148 B-1; mail Bentonville z 72712; rural
Masonville; RMC Place; DESHA; 148 H-7; mail Mc Gehee z 71654; ● 60
Massard; RMC Place; SEBASTIAN; *148 D-1; ★ **FTSM**; mail Fort Smith z 72901; pop. incl. with Fort Smith (Inc. Place)
Maumee; RMC Place; SEARCY; *148 C-4; elev. 900ft./274m.; mail Saint Joe z 72675; rural
Maumelle (Maumelle New Town); Inc. Place; PULASKI; 148 E-5; 🅿 🅷; ★ **L.R.**; z 72113 & mail North Little Rock z 72118; Ⓟ 6,714; Ⓒ 10,557
Maumelle New Town; PULASKI; see Maumelle (Inc. Place)
Maxville; RMC Place; SHARP; *148 C-7; mail Cave City z 72521; rural
Mayfield; RMC Place; WASHINGTON; *148 B-2; elev. 1,200ft./366m.; mail Fayetteville z 72701, z 72703; rural
Mayflower; Inc. Place; FAULKNER; 148 E-5; elev. 288ft./88m.; 🅿; ★ **L.R.**; z 72106; Ⓟ 1,415; Ⓒ 1,631
Maynard; Inc. Place; RANDOLPH; 148 B-8; elev. 381ft./116m.; 🅿; z 72444; Ⓟ 354; Ⓒ 381
Maysville; RMC Place; BENTON; 148 B-1; elev. 1,029ft./314m.; 🅿; z 72747; ● 200
Mazarn; RMC Place; MONTGOMERY; *148 F-3; elev. 596ft./182m.; mail Bonnerdale z 71933; rural
McAlmont; CDP; PULASKI; 148 K-7; ★ **L.R.**; mail North Little Rock z 72117; Ⓒ 1,922
McArthur; RMC Place; DESHA; *148 H-7; mail Mc Gehee z 71654
McBrides; RMC Place; MARION; *148 B-4; elev. 700ft./213m.; mail Protem z 65733; ● 20
McCaskill; Inc. Place; HEMPSTEAD; 148 H-2; elev. 448ft./137m.; 🅿; z 71847; Ⓟ 75; Ⓒ 84
McClelland; RMC Place; WOODRUFF; *148 E-7; elev. 186ft./57m.; mail Augusta z 72006
McCormick; RMC Place; POINSETT; *148 D-8; mail Trumann z 72472; ● 50
McCreanor; RMC Place; LONOKE; *148 F-6; elev. 216ft./66m.; mail Carlisle z 72024; ● 50
McCrory; Inc. Place; WOODRUFF; 148 D-7; 🅿; z 72101; Ⓟ 1,971; Ⓒ 1,850
McDonald; RMC Place; CROSS; *148 D-8; mail Parkin z 72373; rural
McDougal; Inc. Place; CLAY; 148 B-9; 🅿; z 72441; Ⓟ 208; Ⓒ 195
McElroy; RMC Place; CROSS; *148 E-8; elev. 227ft./69m.; mail Wynne z 72396; ● 50
McEntre; RMC Place; LAWRENCE; *148 B-8; elev. 270ft./82m.; mail Walnut Ridge z 72476; pop. incl. with Walnut Ridge (Inc. Place)
McFadden; RMC Place; JACKSON; *148 D-7; elev. 221ft./67m.; mail Hickory Ridge z 72347; rural
McGehee; Inc. Place; DESHA; 148 H-7; 🅿 🅷; z 71654, z 71666; Ⓟ 4,997; Ⓒ 4,570
McGintytown; RMC Place; FAULKNER; *148 D-5; mail Greenbrier z 72058; ● 50
McGregor; RMC Place; WOODRUFF; *148 E-7; elev. 190ft./58m.; mail Cotton Plant z 72036; ● 30
McHue; RMC Place; INDEPENDENCE; *148 C-6; mail Batesville z 72501; ● 50
McJester; RMC Place; CLEBURNE; *148 D-6; mail Pangburn z 72121; rural
McKamie; RMC Place; LAFAYETTE; *148 I-3; mail Stamps z 71860
McMilan Corner; CHICOT; see McMillan Corner (RMC Place)
McMillan Corner (McMilan Corner); RMC Place; CHICOT; 148 I-7; mail Lake Village z 71653; ● 40
McNab; Inc. Place; HEMPSTEAD; 148 H-2; elev. 313ft./95m.; mail Fulton z 71838; Ⓟ 95; Ⓒ 37; Ⓡ 75
McNeil; Inc. Place; COLUMBIA; 148 I-3; 🅿; z 71752; Ⓟ 686; Ⓒ 662
McNutt; RMC Place; LAWRENCE; *148 B-8; elev. 205ft./62m.; mail Walnut Ridge z 72476; pop. incl. with Walnut Ridge (Inc. Place)
McRae; Inc. Place; WHITE; 148 E-6; elev. 233ft./71m.; 🅿; z 72102; Ⓟ 669; Ⓒ 661
Meadowcliff; RMC Place; PULASKI; *148 F-5; ★ **L.R.**; mail Little Rock z 72209; pop. incl. with Little Rock (Inc. Place)
Meadow Cliff; RMC Place; ST. FRANCIS; *148 E-8; mail Forrest City z 72335; ● 165
Meeks Settlement; RMC Place; CLARK; *148 G-3; elev. 323ft./98m.; mail Okolona z 71962; ● 100
Melbourne; Inc. Place; ⊡ IZARD; 148 C-6; elev. 604ft./184m.; 🅿; z 72556; Ⓟ 1,562; Ⓒ 1,673
Mellwood; RMC Place; PHILLIPS; 148 G-8; 🅿; z 72367; ● 100
Melrose; RMC Place; STONE; *148 C-6; mail Locust Grove z 72550; rural
Mena; Inc. Place; ⊡ POLK; 148 F-1; 🅿 🅷; z 71953; Ⓟ 5,475; Ⓒ 5,637
Menifee; Inc. Place; CONWAY; *148 E-5; 🅿; z 72107; Ⓟ 355; Ⓒ 311
Meridian; RMC Place; ASHLEY; *148 J-6; elev. 98ft./30m.; mail Crossett z 71635; ● 30
Meroney; RMC Place; LINCOLN; *148 H-6; elev. 181ft./55m.; mail Gould z 71643; rural
Merrivale; RMC Place; PULASKI; *148 F-5; ★ **L.R.**; mail Little Rock z 72209; pop. incl. with Little Rock (Inc. Place)
Mesa; RMC Place; PRAIRIE; *148 F-7; mail De Valls Bluff z 72041; rural
Metalton; RMC Place; CARROLL; *148 B-3; elev. 1,355ft./413m.; mail Berryville z 72616, Harrison z 72601
Middlebrook; RMC Place; RANDOLPH; 148 B-8; elev. 429ft./131m.; mail Maynard z 72444
Middleton; RMC Place; CONWAY; *148 D-4; mail Center Ridge z 72027; ● 50
Midland; Inc. Place; SEBASTIAN; 148 E-1; 🅿; z 72945; Ⓟ 220; Ⓒ 253
Midway; RMC Place; BAXTER; *148 B-5; 🅿; z 72651; ● 330
Midway (Carroll); Inc. Place; HOT SPRING; 148 G-4; mail Donaldson z 71941; incorporated May 5, 2000; not reported in 2000 Census; ● 300
Midway; RMC Place; HOWARD; *148 H-2; elev. 349ft./106m.; mail Nashville z 71852
Midway; RMC Place; JACKSON; *148 D-8; mail Weiner z 72479; ● 90
Midway; RMC Place; LAFAYETTE; *148 I-2; mail Lewisville z 71845; rural
Midway; RMC Place; LOGAN; 148 D-3; mail Subiaco z 72865
Midway; RMC Place; NEVADA; *148 H-3; elev. 386ft./118m.; mail Prescott z 71857; rural
Midway; RMC Place; WHITE; *148 D-7; elev. 588ft./179m.; mail Pleasant Plains z 72568; ● 50
Midway Corner; RMC Place; CRITTENDEN; *148 E-9; mail Proctor z 72376; ● 50
Milford; RMC Place; SEVIER; *148 H-2; elev. 355ft./108m.; mail Lockesburg z 71846; rural
Mill Creek; RMC Place; POPE; *148 D-3; elev. 400ft./122m.; mail Russellville z 72802; pop. incl. with London (Inc. Place)
Mill Creek; RMC Place; SEBASTIAN; *148 D-1; ★ **FTSM**; mail Fort Smith z 72901; pop. incl. with Fort Smith (Inc. Place)
Mill Creek Estates; RMC Place; MARION; *148 B-4; elev. 700ft./213m.; mail Yellville z 72687; ● 40
MILLER; 148 I-2; Ⓟ 38,467; Ⓒ 40,443; ◆ 42,569
Milligan Ridge; RMC Place; MISSISSIPPI; *148 C-9; mail Manila z 72442; rural
Milltown; RMC Place; SEBASTIAN; *148 E-2; mail Greenwood z 72936
Milo; RMC Place; ASHLEY; *148 I-6; elev. 113ft./34m.; mail Hamburg z 71646; rural
Mimosa Circle; RMC Place; FULTON; *148 B-6; elev. 804ft./245m.; mail Ash Flat z 72513; ● 40
Mineral; RMC Place; SEVIER; *148 G-1; elev. 813ft./248m.; mail Gillham z 71841; rural
Mineral Springs; Inc. Place; HOWARD; 148 H-2; elev. 325ft./99m.; 🅿; z 71851; Ⓟ 1,004; Ⓒ 1,264
Minorca; RMC Place; RANDOLPH; *148 A-8; elev. 350ft./107m.; mail Maynard z 72444; rural
Minturn; Inc. Place; LAWRENCE; 148 C-8; 🅿; z 72445; Ⓟ 124; Ⓒ 114
MISSISSIPPI; 148 C-9; Ⓟ 57,525; Ⓒ 51,979; ◆ 45,992
Mist; RMC Place; ASHLEY; *148 I-6; mail Hamburg z 71646
Mitchell; RMC Place; FULTON; *148 B-6; mail Viola z 72583
Mitchellville; Inc. Place; DESHA; 148 H-7; mail Dumas z 71639; Ⓟ 513; Ⓒ 497
Mixon; RMC Place; LOGAN; *148 E-2; mail Booneville z 72927; rural
Moark; RMC Place; CLAY; *148 B-9; elev. 299ft./91m.; mail Corning z 72422; ● 20
Mohawk; RMC Place; COLUMBIA; *148 J-3; elev. 300ft./91m.; mail Emerson z 71740; rural
Moko; RMC Place; FULTON; 148 B-6; elev. 762ft./232m.; 🅿; z 72576; ● 30
Monarch; RMC Place; MARION; *148 B-4; mail Yellville z 72687; rural
Monette; Inc. Place; CRAIGHEAD; 148 C-9; 🅿; z 72447; Ⓟ 1,115; Ⓒ 1,179
Monkey Run; RMC Place; BAXTER; *148 B-5; mail Gassville z 72635
Monnie Springs; RMC Place; PULASKI; *148 E-5; mail Roland z 72135; ● 50
Monroe; RMC Place; MONROE; 148 F-7; 🅿; z 72108; ● 110
MONROE; 148 F-7; Ⓟ 11,333; Ⓒ 10,254; ◆ 8,218
Montana; RMC Place; JOHNSON; *148 D-3; elev. 400ft./122m.; mail Hartman z 72840; rural
Monte Ne Shores; RMC Place; BENTON; *148 B-2; ★ **FAY-**; mail Rogers z 72758; ● 150
Monterey; RMC Place; CROSS; *148 D-8; mail Parkin z 72373; rural
MONTGOMERY; 148 F-2; Ⓟ 7,841; Ⓒ 9,245; ◆ 8,893
Monticello; Inc. Place; ⊡ DREW; 148 H-6; elev. 298ft./91m.; 🅿 🅷 🅲 3,179; z 71655-57; Ⓟ 8,116; Ⓒ 9,146
Montongo; RMC Place; DREW; *148 H-6; elev. 383ft./117m.; mail Monticello z 71655
Montreal; RMC Place; SEBASTIAN; *148 E-1; mail Huntington z 72940; rural
Montrose; Inc. Place; ASHLEY; 148 I-7; 🅿; z 71658; Ⓟ 528; Ⓒ 526
Moore; RMC Place; NEWTON; *148 C-4; mail Pelsor z 72856; rural
Moore Camp; RMC Place; LITTLE RIVER; *148 H-2; mail Ashdown z 71822; ● 70
Moorefield; Inc. Place; INDEPENDENCE; 148 C-7; elev. 308ft./94m.; mail Batesville z 72501; Ⓟ 160; Ⓒ 160
Moreland; RMC Place; POPE; 148 D-4; elev. 747ft./228m.; mail Russellville z 72802; ● 210
Morgan; RMC Place; PULASKI; *148 E-5; ★ **L.R.**; mail North Little Rock z 72118; rural
Morganton; RMC Place; VAN BUREN; 148 D-5; mail Bee Branch z 72013
Morning Star; RMC Place; GARLAND; *148 F-4; ★ **HTSPR**; mail Hot Springs National Park z 71901
Morning Star; RMC Place; SEARCY; *148 C-5; elev. 1,181ft./360m.; mail Marshall z 72650; ● 30
Morning Sun; RMC Place; WHITE; *148 E-6; mail Searcy z 72143; ● 90
Moro; Inc. Place; LEE; 148 F-8; 🅿; z 72368; Ⓟ 287; Ⓒ 241
Moro Bay; RMC Place; BRADLEY; *148 I-5; mail Jersey z 71651; rural
Morrilton; Inc. Place; ⊡ CONWAY; 148 E-4; elev. 389ft./119m.; 🅿 🅷; z 72110; Ⓟ 6,551; Ⓒ 6,550
Morris; RMC Place; NEVADA; *148 H-3; elev. 254ft./77m.; mail Cale z 71828; rural
Morrison Bluff; Inc. Place; LOGAN; *148 D-3; mail Scranton z 72863; Ⓟ 84; Ⓒ 74
Morriston; RMC Place; FULTON; *148 B-6; mail Salem z 72576
Morrow; RMC Place; WASHINGTON; 148 C-1; 🅿; z 72749; ● 150
Morton; RMC Place; WOODRUFF; 148 D-7; mail Mc Crory z 72101; ● 140
Mosby; PHILLIPS; see Mosby Spur (RMC Place)
Mosby Spur (Mosby); RMC Place; PHILLIPS; *148 G-8; mail Crumrod z 72328
Moscow; RMC Place; JEFFERSON; 148 G-6; elev. 192ft./59m.; 🅿; z 71659; ● 200
Mosley; RMC Place; YELL; *148 E-3; mail Dardanelle z 72834
Mossville; RMC Place; NEWTON; *148 C-3; mail Jasper z 72641; rural
Mounds; RMC Place; CRITTENDEN; *148 E-9; elev. 210ft./64m.; mail Proctor z 72376; rural
Mounds; RMC Place; GREENE; *148 B-9; elev. 254ft./77m.; mail Rector z 72461
Mountainburg; Inc. Place; CRAWFORD; 148 D-2; elev. 737ft./225m.; 🅿; z 72946; Ⓟ 488; Ⓒ 682
Mountain Crest; RMC Place; FRANKLIN; *148 C-2; mail Elkins z 72727; rural
Mountain Fork; RMC Place; POLK; *148 F-1; elev. 1,041ft./317m.; mail Mena z 71953; rural
Mountain Harbor; RMC Place; MONTGOMERY; *148 F-3; elev. 600ft./183m.; mail Mount Ida z 71957; summer pop. 100; ● 30
Mountain Home; Inc. Place; ⊡ BAXTER; 148 B-5; 🅿 🅷; z 72653-54; Ⓟ 9,027; Ⓒ 11,012
Mountain Pine; Inc. Place; GARLAND; 148 F-3; 🅿; z 71956; Ⓟ 866; Ⓒ 772
Mountain Springs; RMC Place; LONOKE; *148 E-6; elev. 400ft./122m.; ★ **L.R.**; mail Cabot z 72023; ● 160
Mountain Top; RMC Place; FRANKLIN; *148 D-2; mail Ozark z 72949; rural
Mountain Valley; RMC Place; GARLAND; *148 F-4; elev. 681ft./208m.; mail Hot Springs National Park z 71901; ● 110
Mountain View; Inc. Place; ⊡ STONE; 148 C-6; elev. 768ft./234m.; 🅿 🅷; z 72533, z 72560; Ⓟ 2,439; Ⓒ 2,876
Mount Elba; RMC Place; CLEVELAND; *148 H-5; mail New Edinburg z 71660; ● 30
Mount Gayler; CRAWFORD; see Mount Gaylor (RMC Place)
Mount Gaylor (Mount Gayler); RMC Place; CRAWFORD; *148 C-2; mail Winslow z 72959; ● 50
Mount George; RMC Place; YELL; 148 E-3; mail Danville z 72833
Mount Hersey; RMC Place; NEWTON; *148 C-4; mail Western Grove z 72685; rural
Mount Holly; RMC Place; UNION; 148 I-4; 🅿; z 71758; ● 150
Mount Ida; Inc. Place; ⊡ MONTGOMERY; 148 F-2; elev. 663ft./202m.; 🅿; z 71957; Ⓟ 775; Ⓒ 981
Mount Judea; RMC Place; NEWTON; 148 C-4; elev. 925ft./282m.; 🅿; z 72655; ● 530
Mount Moriah; RMC Place; PIKE; *148 G-2; mail Murfreesboro z 71958
Mount Olive; RMC Place; BRADLEY; *148 I-6; elev. 198ft./60m.; mail Hermitage z 71647; rural
Mount Olive; RMC Place; CONWAY; *148 E-5; elev. 382ft./116m.; mail Plumerville z 72127; ● 40
Mount Olive; RMC Place; IZARD; *148 C-6; elev. 349ft./106m.; mail Melbourne z 72556; rural
Mount Olive; RMC Place; WASHINGTON; *148 C-2; elev. 1,600ft./488m.; mail Elkins z 72727; rural
Mount Pisgah; RMC Place; WHITE; *148 D-6; elev. 280ft./85m.; mail Searcy z 72143; rural
Mount Pleasant; Inc. Place; IZARD; 148 C-6; 🅿; z 72561; Ⓟ 422; Ⓒ 401
Mount Pleasant; RMC Place; MILLER; *148 I-2; elev. 350ft./107m.; ★ **TEXR-**; mail Texarkana z 71854
Mount Sherman; RMC Place; NEWTON; *148 C-3; elev. 2,111ft./643m.; mail Jasper z 72641; rural
Mount Tabor; RMC Place; GARLAND; *148 F-3; elev. 635ft./194m.; mail Monticello z 71655, Mountain Pine z 71956; rural
Mount Vernon; Inc. Place; FAULKNER; 148 E-5; elev. 434ft./132m.; 🅿; z 72111; Ⓟ 192; Ⓒ 144
Mount Vernon; RMC Place; JOHNSON; *148 D-3; elev. 795ft./242m.; mail Hartman z 72840; rural
Mount Zion (Dialion); RMC Place; CLEVELAND; *148 G-6; mail Rison z 71665; ● 30
Mozart; RMC Place; STONE; *148 C-5; mail Fox z 72051; rural
Muddy Fork; RMC Place; HOWARD; *148 G-2; mail Nashville z 71852; ● 50
Mulberry; Inc. Place; CRAWFORD; 148 D-2; 🅿; z 72947; Ⓟ 1,448; Ⓒ 1,627
Mull; RMC Place; MARION; *148 B-5; elev. 900ft./274m.; mail Yellville z 72687; rural
Murfreesboro; Inc. Place; ⊡ PIKE; 148 G-2; elev. 367ft./112m.; 🅿 🅷; z 71958; Ⓟ 1,542; Ⓒ 1,764
Murphys Corner; RMC Place; JACKSON; *148 D-7; mail Newport z 72112; rural
Mustin Lake; RMC Place; OUACHITA; *148 H-4; elev. 103ft./31m.; mail Camden z 71701; summer pop. 150; ● 80
Myron; RMC Place; IZARD; *148 B-6; mail Ash Flat z 72513; ● 35

N

Nady; RMC Place; ARKANSAS; *148 G-7; mail Tichnor z 72166; rural
Nail; RMC Place; NEWTON; 148 C-3; mail Deer z 72628
Nance; RMC Place; SALINE; *148 F-4; elev. 431ft./131m.; mail Lonsdale z 72087; rural
Nashville; Inc. Place; ⊡ HOWARD; 148 H-2; elev. 383ft./117m.; 🅿 🅷; z 71852; Ⓟ 4,639; Ⓒ 4,878
Nathan; RMC Place; PIKE; *148 G-2; mail Nashville z 71852; ● 50
Natural Dam; RMC Place; CRAWFORD; 148 C-1; 🅿; z 72948; ● 75
Natural Steps; RMC Place; PULASKI; *148 E-5; elev. 278ft./85m.; mail Roland z 72135
Naylor; RMC Place; FAULKNER; 148 E-5; mail Vilonia z 72173; ● 110
Neal Springs; RMC Place; SEVIER; *148 H-1; mail Horatio z 71842; rural
Nebo; RMC Place; LINCOLN; 148 G-6; mail Star City z 71667
Needham; RMC Place; CRAIGHEAD; *148 C-9; ★ **JONES**; mail Lake City z 72437; ● 75
Needmore; RMC Place; SCOTT; 148 E-2; elev. 702ft./214m.; mail Waldron z 72958; ● 40
Nella; RMC Place; SCOTT; *148 F-1; elev. 838ft./255m.; mail Mena z 71953; rural
Nelsonville; RMC Place; SHARP; *148 C-7; elev. 502ft./153m.; mail Smithville z 72466
Nettleton; RMC Place; CRAIGHEAD; *148 C-8; ★ **JONES**; mail Jonesboro z 72402; pop. incl. with Jonesboro (Inc. Place)
Neuhardt; RMC Place; CRITTENDEN; *148 E-9; elev. 206ft./63m.; mail Proctor z 72376
NEVADA; 148 H-3; Ⓟ 10,101; Ⓒ 9,955; ◆ 9,077
Newark; Inc. Place; INDEPENDENCE; 148 C-7; elev. 239ft./73m.; 🅿; z 72562; Ⓟ 1,159; Ⓒ 1,219
New Augusta; RMC Place; WOODRUFF; *148 D-7; mail Augusta z 72006; pop. incl. with Augusta (Inc. Place)
New Blaine; RMC Place; LOGAN; 148 D-3; elev. 349ft./106m.; 🅿; z 72851; ● 150
Newburg; RMC Place; IZARD; *148 B-6; mail Melbourne z 72556; ● 50
New Caledonia; RMC Place; UNION; elev. 180ft./55m.; rural
Newcastle; RMC Place; ST. FRANCIS; mail Colt z 72326; rural
New Dixie; RMC Place; PERRY; *148 E-5; mail Bigelow z 72016; rural
New Edinburg; RMC Place; CLEVELAND; 148 H-5; 🅿; z 71660
Newell; RMC Place; UNION; 148 I-4; mail El Dorado z 71730; ● 50
New Gascony; RMC Place; JEFFERSON; *148 G-6; mail Altheimer z 72004; rural
New Hope; RMC Place; DALLAS; *148 H-4; elev. 269ft./82m.; mail Sparkman z 71763; rural
New Hope; RMC Place; DREW; *148 I-6; mail Monticello z 71655; rural
New Hope; RMC Place; HEMPSTEAD; *148 I-3; elev. 385ft./117m.; mail Hope z 71801; rural
New Hope; RMC Place; INDEPENDENCE; *148 C-6; elev. 425ft./130m.; mail Batesville z 72501; rural
Newhope; RMC Place; PIKE; 148 G-2; elev. 749ft./228m.; 🅿; z 71959; ● 80
New Hope; RMC Place; POPE; *148 E-4; mail Russellville z 72802; rural
New London; RMC Place; UNION; *148 I-5; mail Strong z 71765; ● 40
Newnata; RMC Place; STONE; *148 C-5; mail Timbo z 72680
Newport; Inc. Place; ⊡ JACKSON; 148 D-7; elev. 224ft./68m.; 🅿 🅷; z 72112; Ⓟ 7,459; Ⓒ 7,811
New Salem (Salem); RMC Place; LEE; *148 E-8; elev. 204ft./62m.; mail Moro z 72368, Palestine z 72372; ● 30
New Spadra; RMC Place; JOHNSON; *148 D-3; mail Clarksville z 72830
New Summit; RMC Place; SALINE; ★ **L.R.**; mail Bauxite z 72011; pop. incl. with Benton (Inc. Place)
NEWTON; 148 C-3; Ⓟ 7,666; Ⓒ 8,608; ◆ 8,195
New Town; RMC Place; CRAWFORD; *148 D-1; ★ **FTSM**; mail Alma z 72921; rural
Newtown; RMC Place; JEFFERSON; *148 G-6; mail Altheimer z 72004; pop. incl. with Altheimer (Inc. Place)
Nimmo; RMC Place; WHITE; *148 E-7; mail Searcy z 72143; ● 100
Nimmons; Inc. Place; CLAY; 148 B-9; mail Rector z 72461; Ⓟ 96; Ⓒ 100
Nimrod; RMC Place; PERRY; 148 E-4; elev. 466ft./142m.; mail Perryville z 72126; ● 50
Nine Elms; RMC Place; BENTON; *148 B-1; elev. 1,131ft./345m.; mail Siloam Springs z 72761; ● 100
Noble Lake; RMC Place; JEFFERSON; *148 G-6; mail Pine Bluff z 71601; ● 50
Nodena; RMC Place; MISSISSIPPI; *148 D-10; mail Wilson z 72395; rural
Nola; RMC Place; SCOTT; elev. 511ft./156m.; rural
Noland; RMC Place; RANDOLPH; *148 B-8; mail Pocahontas z 72455; rural
Norfork; Inc. Place; BAXTER; 148 B-5; 🅿; z 72658-59; Ⓟ 394; Ⓒ 484
Norfork Lake Estates; RMC Place; BAXTER; *148 B-5; elev. 781ft./238m.; mail Henderson z 72544; ● 100
Norfork Village; RMC Place; BAXTER; *148 B-5; elev. 500ft./152m.; mail Norfork z 72658; rural
Norman; Inc. Place; MONTGOMERY; 148 F-2; 🅿; z 71960 & mail Caddo Gap z 71935, Mount Ida z 71957; Ⓟ 382; Ⓒ 423
Norphlet; Inc. Place; UNION; 148 I-4; 🅿; z 71759; Ⓟ 706; Ⓒ 822
Norristown; RMC Place; POPE; mail Russellville z 72802; pop. incl. with Russellville (Inc. Place)
North Bingen; RMC Place; HEMPSTEAD; *148 G-2; elev. 440ft./134m.; mail Nashville z 71852; ● 30
North Boothe; SCOTT; see Boothe (RMC Place)
North Cedar; RMC Place; JEFFERSON; *148 G-6; ★ **PNBLF**; mail Pine Bluff z 71601; pop. incl. with Pine Bluff (Inc. Place)
North Crossett; CDP; ASHLEY; 148 I-6; mail Crossett z 71635; Ⓟ 3,358; Ⓒ 3,581
North Dardanelle; RMC Place; POPE; *148 D-4; mail Russellville z 72802; pop. incl. with Russellville (Inc. Place)
Northern Ohio; RMC Place; POINSETT; *148 D-9; mail Marked Tree z 72365; rural
North Heights; RMC Place; MILLER; ★ **TEXR-**; mail Texarkana z 71854; pop. incl. with Texarkana (Inc. Place)
North Hughes; RMC Place; ST. FRANCIS; *148 E-9; elev. 199ft./61m.; mail Hughes z 72348; rural
North Little Rock; Inc. Place; PULASKI; 148 F-5; 🅿 🅷 ■; ★ **L.R.**; z 72113-20, z 72124, z 72190, z 72198-99 & mail Little Rock z 72231; Ⓟ 61,741; Ⓒ 60,433; ◆ 62,256
Northpoint; RMC Place; PULASKI; *148 E-5; mail Roland z 72135; rural
Norvell; RMC Place; CRITTENDEN; *148 D-9; elev. 216ft./66m.; mail Earle z 72331; pop. incl. with Earle (Inc. Place)
Nuckles; RMC Place; JACKSON; *148 D-7; elev. 220ft./67m.; mail Bradford z 72020; rural
Number Nine; RMC Place; MISSISSIPPI; 148 C-10; mail Blytheville z 72315; ● 30
Nunley; RMC Place; POLK; *148 F-1; mail Mena z 71953; rural

O

Oak Bower; RMC Place; HOT SPRING; *148 G-3; elev. 500ft./152m.; mail Bismarck z 71929; rural
Oak Forest; RMC Place; LEE; *148 F-8; mail Marianna z 72360
Oak Forest; RMC Place; PULASKI; *148 F-5; ★ **L.R.**; mail Little Rock z 72204; pop. incl. with Little Rock (Inc. Place)
Oakgrove; Inc. Place; CARROLL; 148 B-3; 🅿; z 72660 & mail Houston z 72070; Ⓟ 231; Ⓒ 376
Oak Grove; RMC Place; CLARK; *148 G-4; mail Curtis z 71728; ● 200
Oak Grove; RMC Place; HOT SPRING; *148 G-4; mail Malvern z 72104; ● 85
Oak Grove; RMC Place; LITTLE RIVER; *148 H-1; elev. 326ft./99m.; mail Ashdown z 71822; ● 30
Oak Grove; RMC Place; LONOKE; *148 E-6; mail Austin z 72007; ● 50
Oak Grove; RMC Place; NEVADA; *148 H-3; mail Rosston z 71858; ● 140
Oak Grove; RMC Place; PERRY; *148 E-4; elev. 310ft./94m.; mail Houston z 72070; rural
Oak Grove; RMC Place; POPE; *148 D-4; mail Russellville z 72802; ● 60
Oak Grove; RMC Place; PULASKI; 148 K-5; elev. 354ft./108m.; ★ **L.R.**; mail North Little Rock z 72118; ● 660
Oak Grove; RMC Place; SEVIER; *148 H-1; elev. 554ft./169m.; mail Lockesburg z 71846; rural
Oak Grove; RMC Place; WASHINGTON; *148 B-2; elev. 1,300ft./396m.; ★ **FAY-**; mail Springdale z 72764; pop. incl. with Springdale (Inc. Place)
Oak Grove Heights; Inc. Place; GREENE; *148 B-9; mail Paragould z 72450; Ⓟ 513; Ⓒ 727
Oakhaven; Inc. Place; HEMPSTEAD; 148 H-2; mail Hope z 71801; Ⓟ 35; Ⓒ 54
Oak Hill; RMC Place; LITTLE RIVER; *148 H-1; elev. 348ft./106m.; mail Ashdown z 71822; rural
Oakland; RMC Place; MARION; 148 B-5; elev. 1,047ft./319m.; 🅿; z 72661; ● 60
Oaklawn; RMC Place; GARLAND; *148 F-4; ★ **HTSPR**; mail Hot Springs National Park z 71901; pop. incl. with Hot Springs (Inc. Place)
Oak Park; RMC Place; JEFFERSON; *148 G-6; ★ **PNBLF**; mail Pine Bluff z 71603; pop. incl. with Pine Bluff (Inc. Place)
Oark; RMC Place; JOHNSON; 148 C-3; elev. 1,028ft./313m.; 🅿; z 72852; ● 50
Oden; Inc. Place; MONTGOMERY; 148 F-2; elev. 761ft./232m.; 🅿; z 71961, z 71966; Ⓟ 126; Ⓒ 220
O'Donnell Bend; RMC Place; MISSISSIPPI; *148 C-10; elev. 253ft./77m.; mail Luxora z 72358; rural
Ogden; Inc. Place; LITTLE RIVER; 148 H-2; 🅿; z 71853; Ⓟ 264; Ⓒ 214
Ogemaw; RMC Place; OUACHITA; 148 I-4; mail Stephens z 71764; ● 50
Oil Trough; Inc. Place; INDEPENDENCE; 148 D-7; elev. 237ft./72m.; 🅿; z 72564; Ⓟ 208; Ⓒ 218
O'Kean; Inc. Place; RANDOLPH; 148 B-8; elev. 271ft./83m.; 🅿; z 72449; Ⓟ 250; Ⓒ 201
Okolona; Inc. Place; CLARK; 148 G-3; elev. 371ft./113m.; 🅿; z 71962; Ⓟ 113; Ⓒ 160
Ola; Inc. Place; YELL; 148 E-3; 🅿; z 72853; Ⓟ 1,090; Ⓒ 1,204
Old Alabam; RMC Place; MADISON; *148 B-2; elev. 1,377ft./420m.; mail Huntsville z 72740; rural
Old Austin; RMC Place; LONOKE; *148 E-6; elev. 321ft./98m.; mail Austin z 72007; pop. incl. with Ward (Inc. Place)
Old Grand Glaise; RMC Place; JACKSON; *148 D-7; mail Bradford z 72020; ● 30
Old Hickory; RMC Place; CONWAY; *148 D-4; mail Hattieville z 72063; rural
Old Jenny Lind; RMC Place; SEBASTIAN; 148 D-1; ★ **FTSM**; mail Fort Smith z 72901; ● 240
Old Joe; RMC Place; BAXTER; *148 B-5; elev. 703ft./214m.; 🅿; z 72658; ● 30
Old Lexington (Lexington); RMC Place; STONE; *148 C-5; elev. 353ft./108m.; mail Clinton z 72031, Shirley z 72153; rural
Old Milo; RMC Place; ASHLEY; 148 I-6; elev. 176ft./54m.; mail Hamburg z 71646
Old Town; RMC Place; PHILLIPS; *148 G-8; elev. 175ft./53m.; mail Wabash z 72389; rural
Old Union; RMC Place; UNION; *148 I-5; elev. 200ft./61m.; mail El Dorado z 71730; ● 200
Old Weona; RMC Place; POINSETT; *148 D-9; mail Trumann z 72472; rural
Olio; RMC Place; SCOTT; *148 E-2; elev. 705ft./215m.; mail Waldron z 72958; ● 30
Oliver; RMC Place; SCOTT; *148 E-1; elev. 665ft./203m.; mail Waldron z 72958; rural
Olmstead; RMC Place; PULASKI; *148 E-5; mail Jacksonville z 72076; ● 30
Olvey; RMC Place; BOONE; *148 B-4; mail Harrison z 72601; ● 70
Olyphant; RMC Place; JACKSON; *148 D-7; elev. 231ft./70m.; mail Bradford z 72020; ● 30
Oma; RMC Place; GARLAND, HOT SPRING; *148 F-3; elev. 600ft./183m.; mail Pearcy z 71964; ● 30
Omaha; Inc. Place; BOONE; 148 B-3; 🅿; z 72662; Ⓟ 207; Ⓒ 165
Omega; CARROLL; see Dean (RMC Place)
Omega; YELL; see Pisgah (RMC Place)
Onda; RMC Place; WASHINGTON; *148 C-1; mail West Fork z 72774; rural
One Horse Store; RMC Place; ARKANSAS; *148 G-7; mail Stuttgart z 72160; rural
Oneida; RMC Place; PHILLIPS; *148 F-8; 🅿; z 72369; ● 80
Onia; RMC Place; STONE; 148 C-5; 🅿; z 72663
Onyx; RMC Place; YELL; *148 E-3; elev. 732ft./223m.; mail Plainview z 72857; rural
Opal; RMC Place; POLK; *148 F-2; elev. 897ft./273m.; mail Board Camp z 71932, Mena z 71953; rural
Opal; RMC Place; WHITE; *148 E-6; elev. 257ft./78m.; mail Beebe z 72012; rural
Oppelo; Inc. Place; CONWAY; 148 E-4; elev. 339ft./103m.; 🅿; z 72110; Ⓟ 643; Ⓒ 725
Optimus; RMC Place; STONE; *148 C-5; elev. 677ft./206m.; mail Calico Rock z 72519; rural
Orion; RMC Place; GRANT; *148 F-5; mail Redfield z 72132; ● 30
Orlando; RMC Place; CLEVELAND; *148 H-5; elev. 196ft./60m.; mail New Edinburg z 71660; rural
Osage; RMC Place; CARROLL; 148 B-3; elev. 1,332ft./406m.; mail Green Forest z 72638; ● 20
Osage Mills; RMC Place; BENTON; *148 B-1; elev. 1,180ft./360m.; mail Bentonville z 72712; rural
Osage Village; RMC Place; FULTON; *148 B-5; elev. 600ft./183m.; mail Elizabeth z 72531; summer pop. 100; ● 20
Osceola; Inc. Place; ⊡ MISSISSIPPI; 148 C-10; 🅿 🅷; z 72370; Ⓟ 8,930; Ⓒ 8,875
Ott; RMC Place; FULTON; *148 A-6; elev. 820ft./250m.; mail Caulfield z 65626; rural
Otter Creek; RMC Place; PULASKI; *148 F-5; ★ **L.R.**; mail Little Rock z 72210; pop. incl. with Little Rock (Inc. Place)
Otto; RMC Place; FAULKNER; *148 E-5; elev. 414ft./126m.; mail Vilonia z 72173
Otwell; RMC Place; CRAIGHEAD; 148 C-8; mail Jonesboro z 72404; ● 140
Ouachita; RMC Place; DALLAS; 148 H-4; mail Sparkman z 71763; ● 30
OUACHITA; 148 H-4; Ⓟ 30,574; Ⓒ 28,790; ◆ 25,266
Overcup; RMC Place; CONWAY; 148 D-4; mail Morrilton z 72110; ● 50
Overcup; RMC Place; WOODRUFF; *148 D-7; mail Mc Crory z 72101; rural
Owensville; RMC Place; SALINE; 148 F-4; elev. 538ft./164m.; mail Lonsdale z 72087; ● 100
Oxford; Inc. Place; IZARD; 148 B-6; elev. 811ft./247m.; 🅿; z 72565; Ⓟ 562; Ⓒ 642
Oxley; RMC Place; SEARCY; *148 C-5; mail Leslie z 72645
Ozan; Inc. Place; HEMPSTEAD; 148 H-2; elev. 382ft./116m.; 🅿; z 71855; Ⓟ 69; Ⓒ 81
Ozark; Inc. Place; ⊡ FRANKLIN; 148 D-2; elev. 397ft./121m.; 🅿 🅷; z 72949; Ⓟ 3,330; Ⓒ 3,525
Ozark Acres; RMC Place; SHARP; *148 B-7; mail Williford z 72482; ● 760
Ozark Lithia; RMC Place; GARLAND; *148 F-4; elev. 635ft./194m.; mail Hot Springs National Park z 71901; rural
Ozone; RMC Place; JOHNSON; 148 D-3; elev. 1,954ft./596m.; 🅿; z 72854; ● 120

P

Pace City; RMC Place; OUACHITA; *148 I-4; mail Louann z 71751; rural
Palatka; RMC Place; CLAY; 148 A-8; elev. 296ft./90m.; mail Corning z 72422
Palestine; Inc. Place; ST. FRANCIS; 148 E-8; 🅿; z 72372; Ⓟ 711; Ⓒ 741
Palmyra; RMC Place; LINCOLN; *148 H-6; elev. 269ft./82m.; mail Star City z 71667; rural
Pangburn; Inc. Place; WHITE; 148 D-6; elev. 335ft./102m.; 🅿; z 72121; Ⓟ 630; Ⓒ 654
Pankey; RMC Place; PULASKI; *148 F-5; ★ **L.R.**; mail Little Rock z 72212; pop. incl. with Little Rock (Inc. Place)
Pansy; RMC Place; CLEVELAND; 148 H-6; elev. 244ft./74m.; mail Rison z 71665
Panther Forest; RMC Place; CHICOT; *148 I-7; elev. 132ft./40m.; mail Lake Village z 71653; rural
Paradise Landing; RMC Place; FAULKNER; *148 E-5; elev. 274ft./84m.; ★ **L.R.**; mail Mayflower z 72106; ● 200
Paragould; Inc. Place; ⊡ GREENE; 148 B-9; 🅿 🅷 ■; z 72450-51; Ⓟ 18,540; Ⓒ 22,017; ◆ 25,259
Paraloma; RMC Place; SEVIER; *148 H-2; mail Lockesburg z 71846
Paris; Inc. Place; ⊡ LOGAN; 148 D-2; elev. 432ft./132m.; 🅿 🅷; z 72855; Ⓟ 3,674; Ⓒ 3,707
Parkdale; Inc. Place; ASHLEY; 148 J-7; 🅿; z 71661; Ⓟ 393; Ⓒ 377
Parkers; RMC Place; PULASKI; *148 F-5; ★ **L.R.**; mail Little Rock z 72206; ● 310
Parkers Chapel; RMC Place; UNION; 148 I-4; mail El Dorado z 71730; ● 500
Parkers-Iron Springs; CDP-Census Area Only; PULASKI; *148 F-5; ★ **L.R.**; mail Little Rock z 72206; Ⓟ 3,611; Ⓒ 3,499
Park Grove; RMC Place; MONROE; *148 F-7; elev. 182ft./55m.; mail Clarendon z 72029; ● 30
Park Hill; RMC Place; PULASKI; *148 F-5; ★ **L.R.**; mail North Little Rock z 72116, z 72190; pop. incl. with North Little Rock (Inc. Place)
Parkin; Inc. Place; CROSS; 148 D-9; 🅿; z 72373; Ⓟ 1,847; Ⓒ 1,602
Park Place; RMC Place; LEE; *148 E-8; mail Brickeys z 72320; rural
Parks; RMC Place; SCOTT; 148 E-2; 🅿; z 72950; ● 90
Parma; RMC Place; STONE; *148 C-5; elev. 1,219ft./372m.; mail Edgemont z 72044; rural
Parmenter Addition; RMC Place; MISSISSIPPI; *148 C-10; elev. 253ft./77m.; mail Blytheville z 72315; pop. incl. with Blytheville (Inc. Place)
Parnell; RMC Place; LONOKE; *148 E-6; elev. 296ft./90m.; ★ **L.R.**; mail Cabot z 72023
Paron; RMC Place; SALINE; 148 F-4; elev. 492ft./150m.; 🅿; z 72122; ● 80
Parthenon; RMC Place; NEWTON; 148 C-3; elev. 925ft./282m.; 🅿; z 72666; ● 300
Pastoria; RMC Place; JEFFERSON; *148 G-6; elev. 219ft./67m.; mail Sherrill z 72152; ● 30
Patmos; Inc. Place; HEMPSTEAD; 148 I-3; elev. 319ft./97m.; mail Hope z 71801; Ⓟ 32; Ⓒ 61
Patrick; RMC Place; MADISON; *148 C-2; mail Elkins z 72727
Patterson; Inc. Place; WOODRUFF; 148 D-7; 🅿; z 72123; Ⓟ 445; Ⓒ 467
Pattsville; RMC Place; BRADLEY; *148 I-6; elev. 186ft./57m.; mail Hermitage z 71647; rural
Pauls Switch (Lanieve); RMC Place; CRAIGHEAD; *148 C-8; mail Bono z 72416; rural
Pawheen; RMC Place; MISSISSIPPI; *148 C-9; elev. 240ft./73m.; mail Leachville z 72438; rural
Payneway; RMC Place; POINSETT; 148 D-9; mail Trumann z 72472
Peach Orchard; Inc. Place; CLAY; 148 B-8; 🅿; z 72435, z 72453; Ⓟ 197; Ⓒ 195
Pearcy; RMC Place; GARLAND; 148 F-3; elev. 618ft./188m.; 🅿; z 71964; ● 175
Pea Ridge; Inc. Place; BENTON; 148 B-2; 🅿; z 72751; Ⓟ 1,620; Ⓒ 2,346
Pea Ridge; RMC Place; DESHA; 148 H-7; elev. 158ft./48m.; mail Watson z 71674; ● 30
Pearson; RMC Place; CLEBURNE; 148 D-5; mail Quitman z 72131
Pecan Point; RMC Place; MISSISSIPPI; *148 D-10; mail Joiner z 72350; rural
Peel; RMC Place; MARION; 148 B-4; elev. 935ft./285m.; 🅿; z 72668; ● 85
Pelsor; POPE; see Sand Gap (RMC Place)
Pencil Bluff; RMC Place; MONTGOMERY; 148 F-2; 🅿; z 71965; ● 150
Pendleton; RMC Place; DESHA; *148 G-7; mail Dumas z 71639; rural
Penjur; RMC Place; ST. FRANCIS; *148 E-9; mail Hughes z 72348
Pennington; RMC Place; JACKSON; *148 D-8; mail Amagon z 72005; rural
Pennys; RMC Place; SEVIER; 148 H-1; mail Lockesburg z 71846; ● 110
Penrose; RMC Place; WOODRUFF; *148 E-8; mail Mc Crory z 72101; rural
Peppers Landing; RMC Place; PRAIRIE; *148 F-7; elev. 213ft./65m.; mail De Valls Bluff z 72041; ● 30
Perla; Inc. Place; HOT SPRING; *148 G-4; elev. 335ft./102m.; mail Malvern z 72104; Ⓟ 145; Ⓒ 115
Perry; Inc. Place; PERRY; 148 E-4; elev. 295ft./90m.; 🅿; z 72125; Ⓟ 228; Ⓒ 314
PERRY; 148 E-4; Ⓟ 7,969; Ⓒ 10,209; ◆ 10,590
Perrytown; Inc. Place; HEMPSTEAD; 148 H-3; mail Hope z 71801; Ⓟ 248; Ⓒ 255
Perryville; Inc. Place; ⊡ PERRY; 148 E-4; 🅿; z 72126; Ⓟ 1,141; Ⓒ 1,458
Peter Pender; RMC Place; FRANKLIN; *148 D-2; mail Charleston z 72933; rural
Peter Rock Acres; RMC Place; VAN BUREN; *148 D-5; elev. 649ft./198m.; mail Clinton z 72031; ● 40
Pettigrew; RMC Place; MADISON; 148 C-3; 🅿; z 72752
Pettus; RMC Place; LONOKE; *148 F-6; elev. 231ft./70m.; mail Lonoke z 72086
Pettyview; RMC Place; GARLAND; ★ **HTSPR**; mail Hot Springs National Park z 71913; rural
Pettyville; RMC Place; MISSISSIPPI; *148 C-9; mail Manila z 72442; rural
Pfeiffer; RMC Place; INDEPENDENCE; *148 C-7; mail Batesville z 72501; ● 130
Philadelphia; RMC Place; CRAIGHEAD; *148 C-8; ★ **JONES**; mail Jonesboro z 72401; pop. incl. with Jonesboro (Inc. Place)
Philander Smith College; RMC Place; PULASKI; *148 F-5; ★ **L.R.**; mail Little Rock z 72202; pop. incl. with Little Rock (Inc. Place)
PHILLIPS; 148 F-8; Ⓟ 28,838; Ⓒ 26,445; ◆ 20,749
Phillips Bayou; RMC Place; LEE; *148 F-8; mail Marianna z 72360; rural
Pickens; RMC Place; DESHA; 148 H-7; 🅿; z 71662; ● 55
Pickens; RMC Place; WHITE; *148 D-6; mail Searcy z 72143
Pickering; RMC Place; UNION; *148 I-4; elev. 235ft./72m.; mail El Dorado z 71730; rural
Piercetown; RMC Place; NEWTON; *148 C-4; elev. 118ft./36m.; mail Jasper z 72641; rural
Piggott; Inc. Place; ⊡ CLAY; 148 B-9; 🅿 🅷; z 72454; Ⓟ 3,777; Ⓒ 3,894
Pike; PIKE; see Pike City (RMC Place)
PIKE; 148 G-3; Ⓟ 10,086; Ⓒ 11,303; ◆ 10,656
Pike City (Pike); RMC Place; PIKE; 148 G-3; mail Delight z 71940, Murfreesboro z 71958; ● 250
Pilgrims Rest; RMC Place; WASHINGTON; *148 B-2; mail Springdale z 72764; rural
Pindall; Inc. Place; SEARCY; 148 C-4; 🅿; z 72669; Ⓟ 135; Ⓒ 95
Pinebergen; RMC Place; JEFFERSON; *148 G-6; ● 60
Pine Bluff; Inc. Place; ⊡ JEFFERSON; 148 G-6; 🅿 🅷 🅲 3,231 ■; ★ **PNBLF**; z 71601-03, z 71611-13; Ⓟ 57,140; Ⓒ 55,085; Ⓡ 55,135; ◆ 49,260
Pine Bluff Southeast; RMC Place; JEFFERSON; ★ **PNBLF**; mail Pine Bluff z 71601; pop. incl. with Pine Bluff (Inc. Place)
Pine City; RMC Place; MONROE; *148 F-7; mail Holly Grove z 72069; ● 110
Pine Grove; RMC Place; DALLAS; *148 H-4; mail Sparkman z 71763; rural
Pine Grove Valley; RMC Place; SCOTT; *148 E-1; mail Mansfield z 72944; rural
Pine Ridge; RMC Place; MONTGOMERY; 148 F-2; 🅿; z 71961, z 71966; ● 50
Pinetree; RMC Place; ST. FRANCIS; *148 E-8; elev. 213ft./65m.; mail Colt z 72326
Pineville; Inc. Place; IZARD; 148 B-6; elev. 697ft./212m.; 🅿; z 72566; Ⓟ 220; Ⓒ 246
Piney; CDP; GARLAND; *148 F-4; ★ **HTSPR**; mail Hot Springs National Park z 71901, z 71913; Ⓟ 2,500; Ⓒ 3,988
Piney; RMC Place; JOHNSON; *148 D-3; mail London z 72847
Piney Grove; RMC Place; LAFAYETTE; *148 I-3; mail Delight z 71940, Lewisville z 71845; rural
Pinnacle; RMC Place; PULASKI; *148 E-5; ★ **L.R.**; mail Roland z 72135; ● 230
Pisgah; RMC Place; PIKE; *148 G-3; elev. 318ft./97m.; mail Delight z 71940; ● 25
Pisgah (Omega); RMC Place; YELL; *148 E-3; elev. 401ft./122m.; mail Dardanelle z 72834; rural
Pitman; RMC Place; RANDOLPH; *148 B-8; mail Maynard z 72444; rural
Pitts; RMC Place; POINSETT; *148 C-8; mail Cash z 72421
Plainfield; RMC Place; COLUMBIA; *148 J-3; elev. 274ft./84m.; mail Emerson z 71740; rural
Plainview; RMC Place; WHITE; *148 D-6; mail Judsonia z 72081; ● 80
Plainview; Inc. Place; YELL; 148 E-3; 🅿; z 72857; Ⓟ 685; Ⓒ 755
Plant; RMC Place; VAN BUREN; *148 C-5; elev. 1,288ft./393m.; mail Clinton z 72031; rural
Pleasant Grove; RMC Place; CRAIGHEAD; *148 C-8; elev. 300ft./91m.; ★ **JONES**; mail Jonesboro z 72401; pop. incl. with Jonesboro (Inc. Place)
Pleasant Grove; RMC Place; STONE; 148 C-6; elev. 474ft./144m.; 🅿; z 72567; ● 220
Pleasant Grove; RMC Place; VAN BUREN; *148 D-5; mail Cleveland z 72030, Scotland z 72141; rural
Pleasant Hill; RMC Place; CRAWFORD; *148 D-2; elev. 460ft./140m.; mail Mulberry z 72947; pop. incl. with Mulberry (Inc. Place)
Pleasant Hill; RMC Place; CROSS; *148 D-8; elev. 314ft./96m.; mail Wynne z 72396; rural
Pleasant Hill; RMC Place; GARLAND; *148 F-3; elev. 531ft./162m.; ★ **HTSPR**; mail Hot Springs National Park z 71901; rural
Pleasant Hill; RMC Place; NEVADA; *148 H-3; mail Prescott z 71857
Pleasant Plains; Inc. Place; INDEPENDENCE; 148 D-6; 🅿; z 72568; Ⓟ 256; Ⓒ 267
Pleasant Ridge; RMC Place; CARROLL; *148 B-3; elev. 1,192ft./363m.; mail Eureka Springs z 72632; rural
Pleasant Ridge; RMC Place; PULASKI; *148 F-5; ★ **L.R.**; mail Little Rock z 72212, z 72222; pop. incl. with Little Rock (Inc. Place)
Pleasant Valley; RMC Place; CARROLL; *148 B-3; elev. 1,200ft./366m.; mail Berryville z 72616; rural
Pleasant Valley; RMC Place; FAULKNER; *148 E-5; mail Greenbrier z 72058; rural
Pleasant Valley; RMC Place; IZARD; *148 B-5; elev. 660ft./201m.; mail Calico Rock z 72519; rural
Pleasant Valley; RMC Place; LAFAYETTE; *148 J-2; elev. 211ft./64m.; mail Bradley z 71826; rural
Pleasant Valley; RMC Place; PERRY; *148 E-4; elev. 298ft./91m.; mail Bigelow z 72016; ● 110
Pleasant Valley; RMC Place; POPE; *148 D-4; elev. 534ft./163m.; mail Dover z 72837; ● 40
Pleasant Valley; RMC Place; PULASKI; ★ **L.R.**; pop. incl. with Little Rock (Inc. Place)
Pleasant View; RMC Place; CONWAY; *148 E-4; elev. 350ft./107m.; mail Morrilton z 72110; ● 70
Pleasant View; RMC Place; FRANKLIN; *148 D-2; mail Ozark z 72949; ● 30
Pleasure Heights; RMC Place; BENTON; *148 B-2; ★ **FAY-**; mail Lowell z 72745; ● 190
Plumerville; Inc. Place; CONWAY; 148 E-4; 🅿; z 72127; Ⓟ 832; Ⓒ 854
Plunketts; RMC Place; PRAIRIE; *148 E-7; elev. 189ft./58m.; mail Biscoe z 72017; rural
Pocahontas; Inc. Place; ⊡ RANDOLPH; 148 B-8; 🅿 🅷; z 72455; Ⓟ 6,151; Ⓒ 6,518
POINSETT; 148 D-8; Ⓟ 24,664; Ⓒ 25,614; ◆ 24,464
Point Cedar; RMC Place; HOT SPRING; 148 G-3; elev. 519ft./158m.; mail Amity z 71921
POLK; 148 F-1; Ⓟ 17,347; Ⓒ 20,229; ◆ 19,916
Pollard; Inc. Place; CLAY; 148 B-9; 🅿; z 72456; Ⓟ 229; Ⓒ 240
Ponca; RMC Place; NEWTON; 148 C-3; elev. 1,068ft./326m.; 🅿; z 72670; ● 30
Ponders; RMC Place; LAWRENCE; *148 C-8; elev. 260ft./79m.; mail Walnut Ridge z 72476; rural
Pontoon; RMC Place; CONWAY; *148 E-4; elev. 325ft./99m.; mail Casa z 72025; ● 30
POPE; 148 D-4; Ⓟ 45,883; Ⓒ 54,469; ◆ 60,450
Poplar Grove; RMC Place; PHILLIPS; 148 F-8; elev. 192ft./59m.; 🅿; z 72374; ● 200
Poplar Ridge (Lower Poplar Ridge); RMC Place; CRAIGHEAD; *148 C-9; elev. 230ft./70m.; mail Black Oak z 72414; rural
Portia; Inc. Place; LAWRENCE; *148 B-8; elev. 264ft./80m.; 🅿; z 72457; Ⓟ 521; Ⓒ 483
Portland; Inc. Place; ASHLEY; 148 I-7; 🅿; z 71663; Ⓟ 560; Ⓒ 552
Posey; RMC Place; ST. FRANCIS; *148 E-7; elev. 210ft./64m.; mail Wheatley z 72392; rural
Possum Grape; RMC Place; JACKSON; 148 D-7; mail Bradford z 72020; ● 130
Possum Trot; CONWAY; see Wesley Chapel (RMC Place)
Possum Trot; OUACHITA, NEVADA; see Reader (RMC Place)
Postelle; RMC Place; PHILLIPS; 148 F-8; mail Marvell z 72366; ● 30
Post Oak; RMC Place; ASHLEY; *148 I-7; elev. 176ft./54m.; mail Montrose z 71658; rural
Potter; RMC Place; POLK; *148 F-1; mail Mena z 71953
Potter Junction; RMC Place; POLK; *148 F-1; mail Mena z 71953
Pottsville; Inc. Place; POPE; *148 D-4; 🅿; z 72858; Ⓟ 984; Ⓒ 1,271
Poughkeepsie; RMC Place; SHARP; 148 B-7; 🅿; z 72569; ● 200
Powhatan; Inc. Place; LAWRENCE; 148 B-7; 🅿; z 72458; Ⓟ 51; Ⓒ 50
Poyen; Inc. Place; GRANT; 148 G-4; 🅿; z 72128; Ⓟ 303; Ⓒ 272
PRAIRIE; 148 E-6; Ⓟ 9,518; Ⓒ 9,539; ◆ 8,419
Prairie Creek; CDP; BENTON; *148 B-2; mail Rogers z 72756; Ⓟ 1,268; Ⓒ 1,849
Prairie Grove; Inc. Place; WASHINGTON; 148 C-1; elev. 1,165ft./355m.; 🅿; z 72753; Ⓟ 1,761; Ⓒ 2,540
Prairie View; RMC Place; LOGAN; *148 D-3; elev. 423ft./129m.; mail Scranton z 72863; ● 100
Prattsville; Inc. Place; GRANT; 148 G-5; elev. 301ft./92m.; 🅿; z 72129; Ⓟ 251; Ⓒ 282
Prescott; Inc. Place; ⊡ NEVADA; 148 H-3; elev. 320ft./98m.; 🅿 🅷; z 71857; Ⓟ 3,673; Ⓒ 3,686
Preston; RMC Place; FAULKNER; *148 E-5; mail Conway z 72032; ● 200
Preston Ferry; RMC Place; ARKANSAS; *148 F-7; mail Roe z 72134
Price Place; RMC Place; MARION; *148 A-5; mail Pontiac z 65729; rural
Prim; RMC Place; CLEBURNE; 148 C-5; elev. 1,220ft./372m.; 🅿; z 72130
Princedale; RMC Place; CROSS; *148 D-8; elev. 208ft./63m.; mail Parkin z 72373; rural
Princeton; RMC Place; DALLAS; 148 G-4; mail Carthage z 71725; ● 50
Process City; RMC Place; SEVIER; *148 G-1; mail De Queen z 71832; ● 50
Proctor; RMC Place; CRITTENDEN; *148 E-9; 🅿; z 72376; ● 60
Promised Land; RMC Place; MISSISSIPPI; *148 C-10; elev. 254ft./77m.; mail Blytheville z 72315; ● 50
Promised Land; RMC Place; POINSETT; *148 D-8; elev. 220ft./67m.; mail Trumann z 72472; rural
Providence; RMC Place; WHITE; 148 D-6; mail Judsonia z 72081; ● 100
Provo; RMC Place; SEVIER; 148 G-2; mail Lockesburg z 71846; ● 90
Pruitt; RMC Place; NEWTON; 148 C-4; elev. 820ft./250m.; mail Marble Falls z 72648; ● 30
Pulaski; RMC Place; PULASKI; *148 F-5; ★ **L.R.**; mail Little Rock z 72207; pop. incl. with Little Rock (Inc. Place)
PULASKI; 148 F-5; Ⓟ 349,660; Ⓒ 361,474; ◆ 383,705
Pulaski Heights; RMC Place; PULASKI; *148 F-5; ★ **L.R.**; mail Little Rock z 72205; pop. incl. with Little Rock (Inc. Place)
Pumpkin Bend; RMC Place; WOODRUFF; *148 D-7; elev. 214ft./65m.; mail Mc Crory z 72101; ● 50
Pyatt; Inc. Place; MARION; *148 B-4; 🅿; z 72672; Ⓟ 185; Ⓒ 253

Q

Quarry Heights; RMC Place; YELL; *148 E-2; elev. 500ft./152m.; mail Blue Mountain z 72826; rural
Quinn; RMC Place; UNION; *148 I-4; mail El Dorado z 71730; ● 50
Quitman; Inc. Place; CLEBURNE, FAULKNER; 148 D-5; elev. 582ft./177m.; 🅿; z 72131; Ⓟ 632; Ⓒ 714

R

Raggio; RMC Place; LEE; *148 E-8; elev. 198ft./60m.; mail Brickeys z 72320; rural
Ragtown; RMC Place; MONROE; *148 F-7; elev. 176ft./54m.; mail Holly Grove z 72069; ● 30
Rainbow Island; RMC Place; CLEBURNE; *148 D-6; mail Pangburn z 72121; ● 200
Ralph; RMC Place; MARION; 148 B-4; elev. 886ft./270m.; mail Yellville z 72687
Rambo Riviera; RMC Place; BENTON; *148 B-2; mail Rogers z 72756; ● 100
Ramsey; RMC Place; DALLAS; *148 H-5; mail Fordyce z 71742; rural
Ramsey Hill; RMC Place; INDEPENDENCE; *148 C-6; mail Batesville z 72501; ● 500
Randall; RMC Place; CLEVELAND; mail Rison z 71665; rural
RANDOLPH; 148 B-7; Ⓟ 16,558; Ⓒ 18,195; ◆ 17,691
Ranger; RMC Place; YELL; *148 E-3; mail Belleville z 72824
Ratcliff; Inc. Place; LOGAN; 148 D-2; 🅿; z 72951; Ⓟ 180; Ⓒ 191
Ratio; RMC Place; PHILLIPS; 148 G-8; mail Elaine z 72333; ● 30
Ravanna; RMC Place; MILLER; 148 J-2; elev. 250ft./76m.; mail Bloomburg z 75556; ● 35
Ravenden; Inc. Place; LAWRENCE; 148 B-7; 🅿; z 72459; Ⓟ 330; Ⓒ 511
Ravenden Springs; Inc. Place; RANDOLPH; 148 B-7; 🅿; z 72460; Ⓟ 131; Ⓒ 137
Rawlinson (Rawlison); RMC Place; ST. FRANCIS; *148 E-8; elev. 200ft./61m.; mail Hughes z 72348; rural
Rawlison; ST. FRANCIS; see Rawlinson (RMC Place)
Ray Lee Addition; RMC Place; POPE; *148 D-4; elev. 400ft./122m.; mail Russellville z 72802; pop. incl. with Russellville (Inc. Place)
Reader (Possum Trot); RMC Place; OUACHITA, NEVADA; 148 H-4; mail Chidester z 71726; disincorporated October 11, 2002; Ⓟ 56; Ⓒ 82
Readland; RMC Place; CHICOT; 148 J-7; elev. 112ft./34m.; mail Eudora z 71640; ● 25
Rea Valley; RMC Place; MARION; *148 B-5; elev. 612ft./187m.; mail Flippin z 72634; rural
Rector; Inc. Place; CLAY; 148 B-9; 🅿; z 72461; Ⓟ 2,268; Ⓒ 2,017
Redfield; Inc. Place; JEFFERSON; 148 F-5; 🅿; z 72132; Ⓟ 1,082; Ⓒ 1,157
Redland; RMC Place; NEVADA; *148 H-3; mail Prescott z 71857; rural
Red Leaf; RMC Place; CHICOT; *148 I-7; elev. 122ft./37m.; mail Lake Village z 71653; rural
Red Onion; RMC Place; CRAIGHEAD; *148 C-9; elev. 243ft./74m.; mail Monette z 72447; rural
Red Springs; RMC Place; CLARK; *148 H-4; elev. 217ft./66m.; mail Gurdon z 71743; rural
Red Star; RMC Place; MADISON; *148 C-3; elev. 2,118ft./646m.; mail Pettigrew z 72752; rural
Red Wing; RMC Place; SEVIER; *148 G-1; mail De Queen z 71832
Reed; Inc. Place; DESHA; 148 H-7; mail Tillar z 71670; Ⓟ 355; Ⓒ 275
Reedville; RMC Place; DESHA; *148 H-7; elev. 163ft./50m.; mail Dumas z 71639; rural
Relfs Bluff; RMC Place; LINCOLN; *148 H-6; mail Star City z 71667; rural
Remmel; RMC Place; JACKSON; *148 D-7; mail Newport z 72112; rural
Rena; RMC Place; CRAWFORD; 148 D-1; ★ **FTSM**; mail Van Buren z 72956
Republican; RMC Place; FAULKNER; *148 D-5; mail Greenbrier z 72058
Revel; RMC Place; WOODRUFF; *148 E-7; mail Augusta z 72006; rural
Rex; RMC Place; VAN BUREN; *148 D-4; elev. 1,645ft./501m.; mail Clinton z 72031; rural
Reydell; RMC Place; JEFFERSON; 148 G-7; elev. 182ft./55m.; 🅿; z 72133; ● 50
Reyno; Inc. Place; RANDOLPH; 148 B-8; 🅿; z 72462; Ⓟ 467; Ⓒ 484
Rhea; RMC Place; WASHINGTON; rural
Rich; RMC Place; MONROE; *148 F-7; elev. 194ft./59m.; mail Brinkley z 72021
Richardson; RMC Place; JEFFERSON; *148 G-6; elev. 193ft./59m.; mail Altheimer z 72004; rural
Richland View; RMC Place; WASHINGTON; *148 B-2; elev. 1,279ft./390m.; mail Elkins z 72727; rural
Richmond; LAWRENCE; see Richwoods (RMC Place)
Richmond; RMC Place; LITTLE RIVER; *148 H-1; mail Ashdown z 71822; ● 60
Rich Mountain; RMC Place; POLK; *148 F-1; ● 60
Richwoods; RMC Place; CLARK; *148 G-4; elev. 215ft./66m.; mail Arkadelphia z 71923; ● 80
Richwoods (Richmond); RMC Place; LAWRENCE; *148 B-8; elev. 265ft./81m.; mail Walnut Ridge z 72476; rural
Ridgeway; RMC Place; BOONE; *148 B-3; elev. 1,387ft./423m.; mail Harrison z 72601
Rio Vista; RMC Place; WHITE; *148 D-7; mail Bald Knob z 72010; rural
Risher; RMC Place; CRAIGHEAD; *148 C-8; mail Cash z 72421; rural
Rison; Inc. Place; ⊡ CLEVELAND; 148 H-5; 🅿; z 71665; Ⓟ 1,258; Ⓒ 1,271
Rivercliff Estates; RMC Place; BENTON; *148 B-2; mail Rogers z 72756; ● 260
Riverdale; RMC Place; SEBASTIAN; *148 D-2; ★ **FTSM**; mail Lavaca z 72941; rural
River Mountain; RMC Place; LOGAN; *148 D-3; elev. 850ft./259m.; mail Delaware z 72835; rural
Riverside; RMC Place; WOODRUFF; *148 D-7; mail Mc Crory z 72101; rural
Rivervale; RMC Place; POINSETT; *148 C-9; 🅿; z 72377; ● 100
Riverview; RMC Place; CONWAY; *148 E-4; elev. 321ft./98m.; mail Morrilton z 72110; ● 50
Riverview; RMC Place; INDEPENDENCE; *148 C-6; elev. 496ft./151m.; mail Batesville z 72501; ● 600
Rixey; RMC Place; PULASKI; *148 E-5; ★ **L.R.**; mail North Little Rock z 72117
Robertsville; RMC Place; CONWAY; *148 D-4; mail Hattieville z 72063; rural
Robinson; RMC Place; BENTON; *148 B-1; mail Siloam Springs z 72761; rural
Robinwood; RMC Place; PULASKI; ★ **L.R.**; pop. incl. with Little Rock (Inc. Place)
Rob Roy; RMC Place; JEFFERSON; *148 G-6; mail Altheimer z 72004; rural
Rock Hill; RMC Place; SEVIER; *148 G-1; mail Lockesburg z 71846; rural
Rockhouse; RMC Place; MADISON; elev. 1,153ft./351m.; mail Eureka Springs z 72632; rural
Rockport; Inc. Place; HOT SPRING; *148 G-4; 🅿; z 72104; Ⓟ 388; Ⓒ 792
Rock Springs; RMC Place; DREW; *148 H-6; elev. 213ft./65m.; mail Wilmar z 71675; rural

Entries in **UPPERCASE** are counties.
Entries in **bold** have populations of 2,500 or more.
Names in parentheses are alternate names.
Inc. Place — Incorporated Place
RMC Place — Rand McNally Designated Place
CDP — Census Designated Place
MCD — Minor Civil Division

⊡ County Seat
▲ Minor Civil Division
elev. Elevation
🅿 Post Office
🅷 Hospital
🅲 College
■ Principal Business Center
★ Ranally Metro Area (RMA) Abbreviation
z Zip Code(s)
Ⓟ Previous Census Population
Ⓡ Revised Census Population
Ⓐ Annexation Population
● Rand McNally Population Estimate
Ⓒ Final Census Population
Ⓢ Special Census Population
◆ Estimated Population

For additional definitions see Glossary, Volume 1, and Introduction, Volume 2.

Rockwell; CDP-Census Area Only; GARLAND; *148 F-3; ★ HTSPR; mail Hot Springs National Park z 71901, z 71913; Ⓟ 2,514; © 3,024
Rocky; RMC Place; POLK; *148 F-1; mail Mena z 71953; rural
Rocky Hill; RMC Place; VAN BUREN; *148 C-5; elev. 1,450ft./442m.; mail Dennard z 72629; rural
Rocky Mound; RMC Place; COLUMBIA; elev. 294ft./90m.; mail Taylor z 71861; rural
Rocky Mound; RMC Place; HEMPSTEAD; *148 H-3; mail Hope z 71801
Rocky Mound; RMC Place; MILLER; *148 I-2; mail Fouke z 71837; rural
Rodney; RMC Place; BAXTER; *148 B-5; mail Calico Rock z 72519; rural
Roe; Inc. Place; MONROE; 148 F-7; 🄿; z 72134; Ⓟ 135; © 124
Rogers; Inc. Place; BENTON; 148 B-2; elev. 1,371ft./418m.; 🄿 🄷 ■; z 72756-58; Ⓟ 24,692; © 38,829; ◆ 56,437
Rogers Avenue; RMC Place; SEBASTIAN; *148 D-1; ★ FTSM; mail Fort Smith z 72903; pop. incl. with Fort Smith (Inc. Place)
Rohwer; RMC Place; DESHA; 148 H-7; 🄿; z 71666; ● 75
Roland; RMC Place; PULASKI; 148 E-5; elev. 284ft./87m.; 🄿; z 72135; ● 200
Rolla; RMC Place; HOT SPRING; *148 G-4; elev. 475ft./145m.; mail Malvern z 72104; ● 30
Romance; RMC Place; WHITE; 148 D-6; elev. 570ft./174m.; 🄿; z 72136; ● 60
Rondo; Inc. Place; LEE; 148 F-8; elev. 214ft./65m.; mail Lexa z 72355; Ⓟ 283; © 237
Rondo; RMC Place; MILLER; *148 I-2; ★ TEXR-; mail Texarkana z 71854; pop. incl. with Texarkana (Inc. Place)
Rosa; RMC Place; MISSISSIPPI; *148 C-10; elev. 252ft./77m.; mail Luxora z 72358
Rosboro; RMC Place; PIKE; *148 G-3; elev. 585ft./178m.; mail Amity z 71921; rural
Rose Bud; Inc. Place; WHITE; 148 D-6; elev. 632ft./193m.; 🄿; z 72137; Ⓟ 156; © 429
Rose City; RMC Place; PULASKI; *148 F-5; ★ L.R.; mail North Little Rock z 72117; pop. incl. with North Little Rock (Inc. Place)
Rose Hill; RMC Place; DREW; *148 H-6; elev. 300ft./91m.; mail Monticello z 71655; rural
Roseland; RMC Place; MISSISSIPPI; *148 C-9; elev. 239ft./73m.; mail Manila z 72442; ● 50
Rose Meadow; RMC Place; PULASKI; ★ L.R.; mail Little Rock z 72206; pop. incl. with Little Rock (Inc. Place)
Roseville; RMC Place; LOGAN; *148 D-2; elev. 384ft./117m.; mail Ozark z 72949; ● 80
Rosie; RMC Place; INDEPENDENCE; 148 C-7; elev. 266ft./81m.; 🄿; z 72571; ● 300
Ross; RMC Place; POPE; *148 D-3; elev. 788ft./240m.; mail Lamar z 72846; rural
Rosston; Inc. Place; NEVADA; 148 H-3; elev. 389ft./119m.; 🄿; z 71858; Ⓟ 262; © 265
Ross Van Ness; RMC Place; CHICOT; *148 J-7; elev. 118ft./36m.; mail Eudora z 71640; rural
Rotan; RMC Place; MISSISSIPPI; *148 D-10; mail Osceola z 72370; ● 50
Round Pond; RMC Place; ST. FRANCIS; *148 E-8; 🄿; z 72394; ● 250
Rover; RMC Place; YELL; 148 E-3; elev. 395ft./120m.; 🄿; z 72860 & mail Briggsville z 72828; ● 260
Rowell; RMC Place; CLEVELAND; *148 H-6; mail Rison z 71665
Roy; RMC Place; PIKE; *148 G-2; mail Nashville z 71852; rural
Royal; RMC Place; GARLAND; 148 F-3; 🄿; ★ HTSPR; z 71968
Royal Oak; RMC Place; SALINE; *148 F-5; ★ L.R.; mail Mabelvale z 72103; ● 200
Rubicon; RMC Place; SALINE; *148 F-4; elev. 400ft./122m.; mail Benton z 72015; rural
Rudd; RMC Place; CARROLL; elev. 1,449ft./442m.; mail Berryville z 72616
Ruddell Hill; RMC Place; INDEPENDENCE; *148 C-6; elev. 400ft./122m.; mail Batesville z 72501; ● 140
Rudy; Inc. Place; CRAWFORD; 148 D-1; elev. 495ft./151m.; 🄿; ★ FTSM; z 72952; Ⓟ 45; © 72
Rule; RMC Place; CARROLL; *148 B-3; mail Green Forest z 72638; rural
Rumley; RMC Place; SEARCY; *148 C-5; elev. 1,000ft./305m.; mail Leslie z 72645; rural
Rupert; RMC Place; VAN BUREN; *148 D-4; mail Clinton z 72031
Rushing; RMC Place; STONE; *148 C-5; mail Fox z 72051, Shirley z 72153
Russell; Inc. Place; WHITE; 148 D-7; elev. 234ft./71m.; 🄿; z 72139; Ⓟ 180; © 228
Russellville; Inc. Place; ⊡ POPE; 148 D-3; elev. 354ft./108m.; 🄿 🄷 🄲 7,038 ■; z 72801-02, z 72811-12; Ⓟ 21,260; © 23,682; ◆ 25,093
Rutherford; RMC Place; INDEPENDENCE; *148 C-7; elev. 276ft./84m.; mail Batesville z 72501; rural
Rye; RMC Place; CLEVELAND; *148 H-6; elev. 184ft./56m.; mail Rison z 71665; rural

S

Sacred Heart; RMC Place; JOHNSON; *148 D-3; elev. 473ft./144m.; mail Hartman z 72840; rural
Saddle; RMC Place; FULTON; 148 B-6; mail Mammoth Spring z 72554
Saffell; RMC Place; LAWRENCE; 148 C-7; 🄿; z 72572; ● 150
Sage; RMC Place; IZARD; 148 C-6; 🄿; z 72573; ● 80
Saginaw; RMC Place; HOT SPRING; *148 G-4; elev. 321ft./98m.; mail Donaldson z 71941; rural
Saint Charles; Inc. Place; ARKANSAS; 148 G-7; 🄿; z 72140; Ⓟ 169; © 261
Saint Francis; Inc. Place; CLAY; 148 B-9; 🄿; z 72464; Ⓟ 201; © 250
ST. FRANCIS; 148 E-8; Ⓟ 28,497; © 29,329; ◆ 26,293
Saint James; RMC Place; STONE; 148 C-6; mail Mountain View z 72560
Saint Joe; Inc. Place; SEARCY; 148 C-4; 🄿; z 72675; © 85
Saint Matthews; RMC Place; COLUMBIA; *148 I-3; elev. 285ft./87m.; mail Mc Neil z 71752; rural
Saint Paul; Inc. Place; MADISON; 148 C-2; 🄿; z 72760; Ⓟ 88; © 163
Saint Vincent; RMC Place; CONWAY; 148 D-4; elev. 606ft./185m.; mail Hattieville z 72063; ● 60
Salado; RMC Place; INDEPENDENCE; 148 C-6; elev. 433ft./132m.; 🄿; z 72575; ● 370
Salem; Inc. Place; ⊡ FULTON; 148 B-6; elev. 668ft./204m.; 🄿 🄷; z 72576; Ⓟ 1,474; © 1,591
Salem; LEE; see New Salem (RMC Place)
Salem; RMC Place; PIKE; 148 G-3; mail Glenwood z 71943; ● 40
Salem; CDP; SALINE; *148 F-5; elev. 474ft./144m.; ★ L.R.; mail Benton z 72015; Ⓟ 2,950; © 2,789
Salesville (Ellis); Inc. Place; BAXTER; 148 B-5; 🄿; z 72653; Ⓟ 374; © 437
SALINE; 148 F-4; Ⓟ 64,183; © 83,529; ◆ 99,743
Saltillo; RMC Place; FAULKNER; *148 E-5; elev. 363ft./111m.; mail Conway z 72032; ● 110
Salus; RMC Place; JOHNSON; 148 C-3; mail Ozone z 72854; ● 20
Sand Gap (Pelsor); RMC Place; POPE; 148 C-4; mail Pelsor z 72856; ● 30
Sand Hill; RMC Place; PRAIRIE; *148 E-7; elev. 186ft./57m.; mail Des Arc z 72040; rural
Sandtown; RMC Place; INDEPENDENCE; *148 C-6; elev. 403ft./123m.; mail Batesville z 72501, Morrilton z 72110
Sandy Bend; RMC Place; UNION; *148 J-5; mail Strong z 71765; rural
Sandy Land; RMC Place; UNION; *148 I-4; mail Smackover z 71762; rural
Sandy Ridge; MISSISSIPPI; see Lemsford (RMC Place)
Sans Souci; RMC Place; MISSISSIPPI; *148 C-10; elev. 243ft./74m.; mail Osceola z 72370; rural
Sarassa; RMC Place; LINCOLN; *148 G-6; elev. 183ft./56m.; mail Grady z 71644; rural
Saratoga; RMC Place; HOWARD, HEMPSTEAD; 148 H-2; 🄿; z 71859; ● 200
Sardis; RMC Place; SALINE; *148 F-5; elev. 370ft./113m.; ★ L.R.; mail Bauxite z 72011
Savoy; RMC Place; WASHINGTON; 148 B-1; elev. 1,038ft./316m.; mail Fayetteville z 72704
Schaal; RMC Place; HOWARD; *148 H-2; elev. 308ft./94m.; mail Mineral Springs z 71851; rural
Schaberg; RMC Place; CRAWFORD; *148 C-2; elev. 1,087ft./331m.; mail Mountainburg z 72946; rural
Schooley; RMC Place; HOWARD; *148 H-2; elev. 345ft./105m.; mail Mineral Springs z 71851; rural
Schug; RMC Place; CRAIGHEAD; *148 C-9; mail Paragould z 72450
Scotland; RMC Place; VAN BUREN; 148 D-5; 🄿; z 72141; ● 130
Scott; CDP; PULASKI, LONOKE; 148 F-6; 🄿; ★ L.R.; z 72142; © 94
SCOTT; 148 E-2; Ⓟ 10,205; © 10,996; ◆ 11,327
Scottsville; RMC Place; POPE; 148 D-4; elev. 496ft./151m.; mail Dover z 72837, Hector z 72843; ● 60
Scott Valley; RMC Place; LEE; *148 F-8; elev. 235ft./72m.; mail Marianna z 72360
Scranton; Inc. Place; LOGAN; 148 D-3; 🄿; z 72863; Ⓟ 218; © 222
Screeton; RMC Place; PRAIRIE; *148 F-6; elev. 236ft./72m.; mail Hazen z 72064; rural
Searcy; Inc. Place; ⊡ WHITE; 148 D-6; 🄿 🄷 🄲 6,108 ■; z 72143, z 72145, z 72149; Ⓟ 15,180; © 18,928; ◆ 21,785
SEARCY; 148 C-4; Ⓟ 7,841; © 8,261; ◆ 8,047
Seaton; RMC Place; LONOKE; *148 F-6; mail England z 72046; ● 30
Seaton Dump; RMC Place; LONOKE; *148 F-6; elev. 206ft./63m.; mail England z 72046
SEBASTIAN; 148 E-1; Ⓟ 99,590; © 115,071; ◆ 123,445
Sedgwick; Inc. Place; LAWRENCE; 148 C-8; 🄿; z 72465; Ⓟ 86; © 112
Sellers Store; RMC Place; SHARP; *148 B-7; elev. 772ft./235m.; mail Hardy z 72542
Selma; RMC Place; DREW; 148 H-7; elev. 186ft./57m.; mail Tillar z 71670; ● 50
SEVIER; 148 H-1; Ⓟ 13,637; © 15,757; ◆ 16,298
Seyppel; RMC Place; CRITTENDEN; *148 E-9; elev. 228ft./69m.; mail Hughes z 72348
Shady; RMC Place; POLK; *148 F-2; elev. 1,100ft./335m.; mail Mena z 71953; rural
Shady Grove; RMC Place; FAULKNER; *148 E-5; elev. 364ft./111m.; mail Greenbrier z 72058
Shady Grove; RMC Place; FULTON; *148 B-6; mail Viola z 72583; rural
Shady Grove; RMC Place; JOHNSON; *148 D-3; elev. 396ft./121m.; mail Clarksville z 72830; pop. incl. with Clarksville (Inc. Place)
Shady Grove; RMC Place; MISSISSIPPI; *148 C-9; elev. 236ft./72m.; mail Manila z 72442; rural
Shady Grove; RMC Place; NEVADA; *148 H-3; elev. 318ft./97m.; mail Prescott z 71857; rural
Shady Grove; RMC Place; POINSETT; *148 C-8; mail Trumann z 72472; rural
Shady Grove; RMC Place; PULASKI; *148 F-5; ★ L.R.; mail Little Rock z 72209; rural
Shakertown; RMC Place; CLARK; *148 H-4; elev. 223ft./68m.; mail Arkadelphia z 71923; rural
Shannon; RMC Place; RANDOLPH; *148 B-8; mail Grady z 71644, Pocahontas z 72455
Shannondale; RMC Place; ST. FRANCIS; *148 E-9; mail Hughes z 72348; rural
Shannon Hills; Inc. Place; SALINE; 148 F-5; 🄿; ★ L.R.; z 72103; Ⓟ 1,755; © 2,005
Shannonville; RMC Place; CRITTENDEN; *148 D-9; elev. 215ft./66m.; mail Earle z 72331; rural
Sharman; RMC Place; COLUMBIA; *148 I-3; mail Stamps z 71860; rural
SHARP; 148 C-7; Ⓟ 14,109; © 17,119; ◆ 17,561
Sharum; RMC Place; RANDOLPH; *148 B-8; mail Pocahontas z 72455; rural
Shaw; RMC Place; SALINE; *148 F-5; elev. 364ft./111m.; mail Benton z 72015; ● 80
Shearerville; RMC Place; CRITTENDEN, ST. FRANCIS; *148 E-9; elev. 205ft./62m.; mail Heth z 72346; rural
Shelbyville; RMC Place; SHARP; *148 C-7; elev. 369ft./112m.; mail Cave City z 72521; rural
Shell Lake; RMC Place; ST. FRANCIS; 148 E-9; mail Heth z 72346; ● 50
Sheppard; RMC Place; HEMPSTEAD; *148 H-2; mail Fulton z 71838; ● 30
Sheridan; Inc. Place; ⊡ GRANT; 148 G-5; elev. 279ft./85m.; 🄿; z 72150; Ⓟ 3,098; © 3,872
Sherrill; Inc. Place; JEFFERSON; 148 G-6; elev. 222ft./68m.; 🄿; z 72152; Ⓟ 55; © 126
Sherwood; Inc. Place; PULASKI; 148 K-6; 🄿 🄷; ★ L.R.; z 72116-17, z 72120, z 72124; Ⓟ 18,893; © 21,511; ◆ 23,772
Sherwood Hills; RMC Place; HOT SPRING; mail Jones Mill z 72105
Shiloh; RMC Place; HOWARD; *148 H-2; mail Mineral Springs z 71851
Shiloh; RMC Place; POPE; *148 D-4; mail Russellville z 72802; pop. incl. with Russellville (Inc. Place)
Shippen; RMC Place; MISSISSIPPI; *148 C-9; elev. 230ft./70m.; mail Keiser z 72351; rural
Shirley; Inc. Place; VAN BUREN; 148 C-5; elev. 542ft./165m.; 🄿; z 72088, z 72153; Ⓟ 363; © 337
Shives; RMC Place; CHICOT; mail Lake Village z 71653; rural
Shoffner; RMC Place; JACKSON; *148 D-7; mail Newport z 72112
Shover Springs; RMC Place; HEMPSTEAD; 148 H-3; elev. 362ft./110m.; mail Hope z 71801; ● 30
Shuler; RMC Place; UNION; 148 I-4; elev. 254ft./77m.; mail El Dorado z 71730; rural
Sidney; Inc. Place; SHARP; 148 C-6; elev. 610ft./186m.; 🄿; z 72577; Ⓟ 271; © 275
Sidon; RMC Place; WHITE; *148 D-6; elev. 715ft./218m.; mail Rose Bud z 72137
Signal Hill; RMC Place; STONE; *148 C-6; mail Mountain View z 72560; rural
Siloam Springs; Inc. Place; BENTON; 148 B-1; 🄿 🄷 🄲 2,010; z 72761; Ⓟ 8,151; © 10,843
Silver; RMC Place; MONTGOMERY; *148 F-3; elev. 606ft./185m.; mail Mount Ida z 71957; rural
Silver Hill; RMC Place; SEARCY; 148 C-4; elev. 937ft./286m.; mail Marshall z 72650, Saint Joe z 72675; ● 30
Silver Ridge; RMC Place; CLEBURNE; *148 D-6; elev. 609ft./186m.; mail Drasco z 72530; ● 80
Silver Ridge; RMC Place; SEVIER; *148 G-2; mail Lockesburg z 71846; rural
Sims; RMC Place; MONTGOMERY; 148 F-2; 🄿; z 71969; ● 250
Simsboro; RMC Place; CRITTENDEN; *148 E-9; elev. 200ft./61m.; mail Hughes z 72348
Sitka; RMC Place; SHARP; *148 B-7; mail Williford z 72482
Skunkhollow; RMC Place; FAULKNER; *148 E-5; elev. 300ft./91m.; mail Conway z 72032; ● 150
Slabtown; RMC Place; GRANT; *148 G-5; mail Sheridan z 72150; ● 430
Slaytonville; RMC Place; SEBASTIAN; *148 E-1; mail Hackett z 72937; rural
Slonikers Mill; RMC Place; ST. FRANCIS; *148 E-8; mail Palestine z 72372; rural
Slovak; RMC Place; PRAIRIE; 148 F-7; mail Stuttgart z 72160; ● 50
Smackover; Inc. Place; UNION; 148 I-4; 🄿; z 71762; Ⓟ 2,232; © 2,005
Smale; RMC Place; MONROE; *148 F-7; mail Brinkley z 72021; ● 30
Smearny (Smyrna); RMC Place; BRADLEY; *148 I-6; elev. 185ft./56m.; mail Hermitage z 71647; rural
Smith Corner (Smiths Corner); RMC Place; LEE; *148 F-8; elev. 205ft./62m.; mail Moro z 72368; rural
Smithdale; RMC Place; CROSS; *148 D-9; elev. 219ft./67m.; mail Parkin z 72373; ● 30
Smiths Corner; LEE; see Smith Corner (RMC Place)
Smithville; Inc. Place; LAWRENCE; 148 B-7; 🄿; z 72466; Ⓟ 86; © 73
Smithville; RMC Place; MILLER; *148 J-2; elev. 250ft./76m.; mail Doddridge z 71834
Smyrna; BRADLEY; see Smearny (RMC Place)
Snow; RMC Place; MARION; *148 B-4; mail Yellville z 72687; rural
Snowball; RMC Place; SEARCY; 148 C-4; elev. 768ft./234m.; mail Marshall z 72650; ● 60
Snow Hill; RMC Place; OUACHITA; 148 I-4; mail Louann z 71751; ● 50
Snow Lake; RMC Place; DESHA; 148 G-8; 🄿; z 72379
Snyder; RMC Place; ASHLEY; 148 I-6; elev. 176ft./54m.; mail Montrose z 71658; ● 170
Social Hill; RMC Place; HOT SPRING; *148 G-4; mail Malvern z 72104
Solgohachia; RMC Place; CONWAY; *148 D-4; elev. 427ft./130m.; 🄿; z 72156; ● 100
Sonora; RMC Place; WASHINGTON; *148 B-2; elev. 1,309ft./399m.; ★ FAY-; mail Springdale z 72764
Soudan; RMC Place; LEE; 148 F-8; mail Marianna z 72360
South Bend; RMC Place; LONOKE; *148 E-6; elev. 250ft./76m.; mail Jacksonville z 72076; ● 950
South Crossett; RMC Place; ASHLEY; *148 J-6; mail Crossett z 71635; pop. incl. with Crossett (Inc. Place)
Southern Hills; RMC Place; BOONE; *148 B-4; mail Harrison z 72601; ● 265
South Fort Smith; RMC Place; SEBASTIAN; *148 D-1; ★ FTSM; mail Fort Smith z 72906; pop. incl. with Fort Smith (Inc. Place)
South Jacksonville; RMC Place; PULASKI; ★ L.R.; mail Jacksonville z 72076; pop. incl. with Jacksonville (Inc. Place)
Southland; RMC Place; CRAIGHEAD; *148 C-9; elev. 230ft./70m.; mail Lake City z 72437; pop. incl. with Lake City (Inc. Place)
Southland; RMC Place; PHILLIPS; *148 F-8; mail Lexa z 72355; rural
South Lead Hill; Inc. Place; BOONE; 148 B-4; elev. 832ft./254m.; mail Lead Hill z 72644; Ⓟ 96; © 88
South Lewisville; RMC Place; LAFAYETTE; *148 I-3; elev. 266ft./81m.; mail Lewisville z 71845; ● 60
South Ozark; RMC Place; FRANKLIN; *148 D-2; mail Ozark z 72949; ● 60
South Shore Park; RMC Place; CLEBURNE; *148 D-6; mail Heber Springs z 72543; ● 100
Southside; RMC Place; INDEPENDENCE; *148 C-6; mail Batesville z 72501; ● 565
South Side; RMC Place; PULASKI; *148 F-5; ★ L.R.; mail Little Rock z 72206; pop. incl. with Little Rock (Inc. Place)
Southside; RMC Place; VAN BUREN; *148 D-5; mail Bee Branch z 72013, Damascus z 72039
Southwick; RMC Place; PULASKI; ★ L.R.; pop. incl. with Little Rock (Inc. Place)
Spadra; RMC Place; JOHNSON; *148 D-3; mail Clarksville z 72830
Sparkman; Inc. Place; DALLAS; 148 H-4; 🄿; z 71763; Ⓟ 553; © 586
Spence Junction; RMC Place; NEWTON; *148 C-4; elev. 2,104ft./641m.; mail Pelsor z 72856; rural
Spirit Lake; RMC Place; LAFAYETTE; *148 I-2; elev. 229ft./70m.; mail Lewisville z 71845; rural
Springdale; Inc. Place; WASHINGTON, BENTON; 148 B-2; elev. 1,329ft./405m.; 🄿 🄷 ■; ★ FAY-; z 72762, z 72764-66; Ⓟ 29,941; © 45,798; ◆ 64,838
Springfield; RMC Place; CONWAY; 148 D-5; elev. 401ft./122m.; 🄿; z 72157; ● 185
Springhill; RMC Place; FAULKNER; *148 E-5; mail Greenbrier z 72058; ● 145
Spring Hill; RMC Place; HEMPSTEAD; 148 H-2; mail Hope z 71801; ● 90
Spring Lake Estates; RMC Place; BAXTER; *148 B-5; mail Mountain Home z 72653; ● 90
Springtown; Inc. Place; BENTON; *148 B-1; 🄿; z 72734; © 114
Spring Valley; RMC Place; INDEPENDENCE; *148 C-7; elev. 400ft./122m.; mail Batesville z 72501; ● 500
Spring Valley; RMC Place; PULASKI; *148 F-5; elev. 449ft./137m.; ★ L.R.; mail Little Rock z 72210; pop. incl. with Little Rock (Inc. Place)
Spring Valley; RMC Place; WASHINGTON; 148 B-2; elev. 1,301ft./397m.; mail Springdale z 72764
Sprudel; RMC Place; HEMPSTEAD; *148 H-2; elev. 250ft./76m.; mail Fulton z 71838; rural
Stacy; RMC Place; CRITTENDEN; *148 D-9; mail Turrell z 72384; ● 50
Stacy; RMC Place; POINSETT; 148 C-8; mail Trumann z 72472; ● 30
Stamps; Inc. Place; LAFAYETTE; 148 I-3; 🄿; z 71860; Ⓟ 2,478; © 2,131
Standard Umpstead (Standard-Umsted); RMC Place; OUACHITA; *148 I-4; mail Smackover z 71762; ● 110
Standard-Umsted; OUACHITA; see Standard Umpstead (RMC Place)
Stanford; RMC Place; GREENE; *148 B-8; mail Paragould z 72450; ● 250
Star City; Inc. Place; ⊡ LINCOLN; 148 H-6; elev. 274ft./84m.; 🄿; z 71667; Ⓟ 2,138; © 2,471
Starks; RMC Place; WASHINGTON; elev. 1,251ft./381m.; ★ FAY-; rural
State Capitol; RMC Place; PULASKI; *148 F-5; ★ L.R.; mail Little Rock z 72201; pop. incl. with Little Rock (Inc. Place)
State Line; RMC Place; COLUMBIA; *148 J-3; elev. 301ft./92m.; mail Emerson z 71740; rural
State Line; RMC Place; LAFAYETTE; *148 J-3; elev. 231ft./70m.; mail Taylor z 71861; rural
Staves; RMC Place; CLEVELAND; 148 G-5; mail Rison z 71665; ● 135
Stelltown; RMC Place; PIKE; *148 G-3; elev. 500ft./152m.; mail Delight z 71940; rural
Stephens; Inc. Place; OUACHITA; 148 I-4; elev. 235ft./72m.; 🄿; z 71764; Ⓟ 1,137; © 1,152
Steprock; RMC Place; WHITE; *148 D-6; elev. 343ft./105m.; 🄿; z 72081; ● 30
Stevens Creek; RMC Place; WHITE; *148 D-6; mail Bald Knob z 72010; rural
Stevens Landing; RMC Place; POINSETT; *148 C-9; elev. 223ft./68m.; mail Trumann z 72472; rural
Stewart (Tully); RMC Place; POINSETT; *148 D-8; elev. 212ft./65m.; mail Trumann z 72472; ● 30
Stokes; RMC Place; RANDOLPH; *148 B-8; elev. 330ft./101m.; mail Pocahontas z 72455
STONE; 148 C-5; Ⓟ 9,775; © 11,499; ◆ 11,835
Stonewall; RMC Place; GREENE; *148 B-9; mail Paragould z 72450
Stony Point; RMC Place; PERRY; *148 E-5; mail Houston z 72070; rural
Story; RMC Place; MONTGOMERY; 148 F-3; 🄿; z 71970; ● 100
Strangers Home; RMC Place; LAWRENCE; *148 C-7; elev. 259ft./79m.; mail Alicia z 72410; rural
Strawberry; RMC Place; JOHNSON; *148 D-3; elev. 613ft./187m.; mail Lamar z 72846; rural
Strawberry; Inc. Place; LAWRENCE; 148 C-7; elev. 327ft./100m.; 🄿; z 72469; Ⓟ 273; © 283
Strickler; RMC Place; WASHINGTON; 148 C-1; elev. 1,514ft./461m.; mail West Fork z 72774; rural
Stringtown; RMC Place; SEVIER; *148 H-1; mail Horatio z 71842; rural
Strong; Inc. Place; UNION; 148 J-5; 🄿; z 71765; Ⓟ 624; © 651
Stump City; RMC Place; ST. FRANCIS; *148 E-9; elev. 205ft./62m.; mail Heth z 72346; rural
Sturkie; RMC Place; FULTON; 148 B-6; 🄿; z 72578; ● 35
Stuttgart; Inc. Place; ⊡ ARKANSAS; 148 F-7; 🄿 🄷; z 72160; Ⓟ 10,420; © 9,745
Subiaco; Inc. Place; LOGAN; 148 D-3; elev. 468ft./143m.; 🄿; z 72865; Ⓟ 538; © 439
Success; Inc. Place; CLAY; 148 B-8; 🄿; z 72470; Ⓟ 170; © 180
Sugar Grove; RMC Place; LOGAN; *148 E-2; elev. 443ft./135m.; mail Booneville z 72927
Sugar Loaf; BOONE; see Diamond City (Inc. Place)
Sugar Loaf Lake; RMC Place; SEBASTIAN; *148 E-1; mail Hackett z 72937; ● 200
Sulphur City; RMC Place; WASHINGTON; *148 C-2; mail Fayetteville z 72701
Sulphur Rock; Inc. Place; INDEPENDENCE; *148 C-7; 🄿; z 72579; Ⓟ 356; © 421
Sulphur Springs; Inc. Place; BENTON; 148 A-1; 🄿; z 72768; Ⓟ 523; © 671
Sulphur Springs; RMC Place; JEFFERSON; 148 G-5; mail Pine Bluff z 71603; ● 100
Sulphur Springs; RMC Place; JOHNSON; *148 D-3; elev. 485ft./148m.; mail Clarksville z 72830; rural
Sulphur Springs; RMC Place; YELL; *148 E-3; mail Dardanelle z 72834; ● 30
Summers; RMC Place; WASHINGTON; 148 C-1; elev. 1,180ft./360m.; 🄿; z 72769; ● 250
Summerville; RMC Place; CALHOUN; *148 I-5; elev. 220ft./67m.; mail Hampton z 71744; rural
Summit; Inc. Place; MARION; 148 B-4; 🄿; z 72677; Ⓟ 480; © 586
Sumpter; RMC Place; BRADLEY; *148 I-6; elev. 246ft./75m.; mail Hermitage z 71647
Sunnydale; RMC Place; WHITE; *148 D-6; mail Judsonia z 72081
Sunny Hill; RMC Place; WHITE; mail Searcy z 72143; pop. incl. with Searcy (Inc. Place)
Sunset; Inc. Place; CRITTENDEN; 148 D-9; elev. 224ft./68m.; ★ MEM; mail Marion z 72364; Ⓟ 571; © 348
Sunset; RMC Place; WASHINGTON; *148 C-2; elev. 2,274ft./693m.; mail Winslow z 72959; rural
Sunshine; RMC Place; ASHLEY; *148 I-7; elev. 119ft./36m.; mail Parkdale z 71661; rural
Sunshine; RMC Place; GARLAND; *148 F-3; elev. 470ft./143m.; ★ HTSPR; mail Royal z 71968; rural
Supply; RMC Place; RANDOLPH; *148 B-8; mail Maynard z 72444
Sutton; RMC Place; NEVADA; *148 H-3; mail Emmet z 71835; ● 40
Swain; RMC Place; NEWTON; 148 C-3; elev. 2,067ft./630m.; mail Deer z 72628
Swan Lake; RMC Place; JEFFERSON; *148 G-6; mail Altheimer z 72004; ● 40
Sweden; RMC Place; JEFFERSON; *148 G-6; elev. 193ft./59m.; mail Altheimer z 72004; rural
Sweethome; RMC Place; MONTGOMERY; *148 F-3; elev. 661ft./201m.; mail Mount Ida z 71957; rural
Sweet Home; CDP; PULASKI; 148 M-6; 🄿; ★ L.R.; z 72164; © 1,070
Swifton; Inc. Place; JACKSON; 148 C-7; 🄿; z 72471; Ⓟ 830; © 871
Sycamore Bend; ST. FRANCIS; see Sycamore Bend Farm (RMC Place)
Sycamore Bend Farm (Sycamore Bend); RMC Place; ST. FRANCIS; *148 E-9; elev. 206ft./63m.; mail Hughes z 72348; rural
Sylamore; RMC Place; IZARD; *148 C-6; elev. 334ft./102m.; mail Melbourne z 72556
Sylvan Hills; RMC Place; PULASKI; *148 E-5; ★ L.R.; mail North Little Rock z 72116; pop. incl. with Sherwood (Inc. Place)
Sylvania; RMC Place; LONOKE; *148 E-6; elev. 287ft./87m.; mail Ward z 72176; ● 90
Sylverino; RMC Place; MILLER; *148 I-2; elev. 300ft./91m.; ★ TEXR-; mail Texarkana z 71854; rural

T

Tafton; RMC Place; PULASKI; *148 F-5; ★ L.R.; mail Wrightsville z 72183; pop. incl. with Wrightsville (Inc. Place)
Talley; RMC Place; COLUMBIA; *148 I-4; elev. 269ft./82m.; mail Emerson z 71740; rural
Tamo; RMC Place; JEFFERSON; *148 G-6; elev. 190ft./58m.; mail Grady z 71644; ● 30
Tanglewood; RMC Place; BENTON; *148 B-2; elev. 1,300ft./396m.; mail Rogers z 72756; ● 50
Tannenbaum; RMC Place; CLEBURNE; *148 D-6; elev. 600ft./183m.; mail Drasco z 72530; rural
Tarry; RMC Place; LINCOLN; 148 G-6; elev. 207ft./63m.; mail Star City z 71667
Tate; RMC Place; LOGAN; *148 E-2; mail Booneville z 72927; rural
Tates Bluff; RMC Place; OUACHITA; *148 H-4; elev. 199ft./61m.; mail Chidester z 71726; ● 30
Taylor; Inc. Place; COLUMBIA; 148 J-3; elev. 243ft./74m.; 🄿; z 71861; Ⓟ 621; © 566
Tennessee; RMC Place; DREW; *148 H-6; elev. 252ft./77m.; mail Monticello z 71655; rural
Terrytown; RMC Place; PULASKI; *148 F-5; ★ L.R.; mail Alexander z 72002; pop. incl. with Little Rock (Inc. Place)
Texarkana; Inc. Place; ⊡ MILLER; 148 I-2; see also Texarkana, TX; elev. 336ft./102m.; 🄿 ■; ★ TEXR-; z 71854; Ⓟ 22,631; © 26,448; ◆ 28,333
Thebes; RMC Place; ASHLEY; *148 I-7; mail Montrose z 71658; rural
Thida; RMC Place; INDEPENDENCE; 148 D-7; 🄿; z 72165; ● 110
Thompson Grove; RMC Place; CRITTENDEN; *148 E-9; mail Hughes z 72348
Thornburg; RMC Place; PERRY; 148 E-4; elev. 740ft./226m.; mail Perryville z 72126; ● 120
Thorney; RMC Place; MADISON; *148 C-2; mail Elkins z 72727; rural
Thornton; Inc. Place; CALHOUN; 148 H-5; elev. 318ft./97m.; 🄿; z 71766; Ⓟ 502; © 517
Three Brothers; RMC Place; BAXTER; *148 B-5; elev. 1,005ft./306m.; mail Mountain Home z 72653
Three Creeks; RMC Place; UNION; 148 J-4; mail Junction City z 71749; ● 50
Three Forks; RMC Place; CRITTENDEN; mail Earle z 72331
Three Way; RMC Place; MISSISSIPPI; *148 C-9; elev. 230ft./70m.; mail Osceola z 72370; pop. incl. with Etowah (Inc. Place)
Tichnor; RMC Place; ARKANSAS; 148 G-7; 🄿; z 72166; ● 85
Tie Plant Spur; RMC Place; PULASKI; ★ L.R.; mail North Little Rock z 72117; pop. incl. with North Little Rock (Inc. Place)
Tillar; Inc. Place; DREW, DESHA; 148 H-7; 🄿; z 71670; Ⓟ 221; © 240
Tilly; RMC Place; POPE; 148 C-4; 🄿; z 72679; ● 50
Tilton; RMC Place; CROSS; 148 D-8; mail Hickory Ridge z 72347; ● 70
Timber Lake Manor; RMC Place; BAXTER; *148 B-5; mail Elizabeth z 72531; ● 30
Timber Lane; RMC Place; HOWARD; *148 G-2; elev. 439ft./134m.; mail Dierks z 71833; pop. incl. with Dierks (Inc. Place)
Timbo; RMC Place; STONE; 148 C-5; 🄿; z 72657, z 72680; ● 240
Tinsman; Inc. Place; CALHOUN; 148 H-5; elev. 173ft./53m.; mail Hampton z 71744; Ⓟ 69; © 75
Tip; RMC Place; WOODRUFF; elev. 200ft./61m.; rural
Toad Suck; RMC Place; PERRY; *148 E-5; elev. 288ft./88m.; mail Bigelow z 72016; ● 90
Togo; RMC Place; CROSS; *148 D-9; mail Parkin z 72373; rural
Tokio; RMC Place; HEMPSTEAD; 148 G-2; mail Nashville z 71852; ● 50
Toledo; RMC Place; CLEVELAND; *148 H-5; elev. 275ft./84m.; mail Rison z 71665; rural
Tollette; Inc. Place; HOWARD; 148 H-2; mail Mineral Springs z 71851; Ⓟ 316; © 324
Tollville; RMC Place; PRAIRIE; *148 F-7; elev. 222ft./68m.; mail De Valls Bluff z 72041; rural
Toltec; RMC Place; LONOKE; *148 F-6; elev. 237ft./72m.; mail Scott z 72142; rural
Tomahawk; RMC Place; SEARCY; *148 C-4; elev. 989ft./301m.; mail Saint Joe z 72675; rural
Tomato; RMC Place; MISSISSIPPI; 148 C-10; mail Luxora z 72358; ● 30
Tomberlin; RMC Place; LONOKE; *148 F-6; mail England z 72046; ● 40
Toneyville; RMC Place; PULASKI; *148 E-6; elev. 285ft./87m.; ★ L.R.; mail Jacksonville z 72076; pop. incl. with Jacksonville (Inc. Place)
Tongin; RMC Place; LEE; *148 E-8; mail Brickeys z 72320; rural
Tontitown; Inc. Place; WASHINGTON; 148 B-1; 🄿; ★ FAY-; z 72770; Ⓟ 460; © 942
Trammellville; RMC Place; CLAY; *148 B-9; mail Rector z 72461; rural
Traskwood; Inc. Place; SALINE; 148 F-4; 🄿; z 72167; Ⓟ 488; © 548
Treasure Hills; RMC Place; FAULKNER; *148 E-5; mail Conway z 72032; ● 250
Treasure Hills; RMC Place; PULASKI; *148 F-5; ★ L.R.; mail Little Rock z 72207, z 72227; pop. incl. with Little Rock (Inc. Place)
Treat; RMC Place; POPE; *148 D-3; mail Ozone z 72854; rural
Trenton; RMC Place; PHILLIPS; *148 F-8; mail Poplar Grove z 72374; ● 50
Troy; RMC Place; OUACHITA; *148 I-4; mail Stephens z 71764; rural
Trumann; Inc. Place; POINSETT; 148 C-9; 🄿; z 72472; Ⓟ 6,304; © 6,889
Tucker; RMC Place; JEFFERSON; 148 F-6; elev. 225ft./69m.; 🄿; z 72168; ● 285
Tuckerman; Inc. Place; JACKSON; 148 C-7; elev. 248ft./76m.; 🄿; z 72473; Ⓟ 2,020; © 1,757
Tuckertown; RMC Place; MISSISSIPPI; *148 C-10; mail Burdette z 72321; pop. incl. with Burdette (Inc. Place)
Tulip; RMC Place; DALLAS; *148 G-4; elev. 481ft./147m.; mail Carthage z 71725
Tull; Inc. Place; GRANT; 148 F-5; elev. 354ft./108m.; 🄿; z 72015; Ⓟ 313; © 358
Tully; POINSETT; see Stewart (RMC Place)
Tulot; RMC Place; POINSETT; *148 D-9; mail Trumann z 72472
Tumbling Shoals; RMC Place; CLEBURNE; 148 D-6; elev. 732ft./223m.; 🄿; z 72581; ● 280
Tupelo; Inc. Place; JACKSON; 148 D-7; 🄿; z 72169; Ⓟ 208; © 177
Turkey Scratch; RMC Place; LEE; *148 F-8; elev. 186ft./57m.; mail Marvell z 72366; rural
Turner; RMC Place; PHILLIPS; 148 F-8; 🄿; z 72383; ● 50
Turrell; Inc. Place; CRITTENDEN; 148 D-9; elev. 220ft./67m.; 🄿; z 72384; Ⓟ 988; © 957
Tuttle; RMC Place; WASHINGTON; *148 C-2; elev. 1,258ft./383m.; ★ FAY-; mail Elkins z 72727
Twentythree; RMC Place; WHITE; *148 D-7; elev. 592ft./180m.; mail Bald Knob z 72010; rural
Twin Groves; Inc. Place; FAULKNER; *148 D-5; 🄿; z 72039; Ⓟ 299; © 276
Twin Lakes; RMC Place; PULASKI; *148 F-5; ★ L.R.; mail Little Rock z 72205; pop. incl. with Little Rock (Inc. Place)
Twin Springs; RMC Place; PULASKI; *148 F-5; ★ L.R.; mail Little Rock z 72211; rural
Twist; RMC Place; CROSS; 148 D-9; 🄿; z 72331; ● 50
Tyro; RMC Place; LINCOLN; 148 H-6; mail Dumas z 71639, Pickens z 71662; ● 30
Tyronza; Inc. Place; POINSETT; 148 D-9; elev. 224ft./68m.; 🄿; z 72386; Ⓟ 858; © 918

U

Ulm; Inc. Place; PRAIRIE; 148 F-7; 🄿; z 72170; Ⓟ 193; © 205
Umpire; RMC Place; HOWARD; 148 G-2; 🄿; z 71971; ● 210
Union; RMC Place; FULTON; *148 B-6; mail Salem z 72576; rural
Union; RMC Place; SEVIER; *148 G-1; mail De Queen z 71832; rural
UNION; 148 J-5; Ⓟ 46,719; © 45,629; ◆ 42,135
Union Hill; RMC Place; INDEPENDENCE; *148 D-7; mail Bradford z 72020; rural
Union Hill; RMC Place; SCOTT; elev. 600ft./183m.; rural
Uniontown; RMC Place; CRAWFORD; 148 D-1; 🄿; z 72955; ● 250
Unity; RMC Place; HOWARD; *148 H-2; elev. 379ft./116m.; mail Nashville z 71852; rural
Uno; RMC Place; POINSETT; *148 D-8; mail Cash z 72421; rural
Upper White Oak Lake; RMC Place; OUACHITA; *148 H-4; elev. 250ft./76m.; mail Chidester z 71726; ● 150
Urbana; RMC Place; UNION; 148 I-5; elev. 148ft./45m.; 🄿; z 71768; ● 300
Urbanette; RMC Place; CARROLL; *148 B-3; elev. 1,282ft./391m.; mail Berryville z 72616, Harrison z 72601; ● 50
Ursula; RMC Place; SEBASTIAN; *148 D-2; mail Charleston z 72933; rural

V

Vaden; RMC Place; CLARK; *148 H-4; elev. 210ft./64m.; mail Arkadelphia z 71923; rural
Vail; RMC Place; MISSISSIPPI, CRAIGHEAD; *148 C-9; elev. 321ft./98m.; mail Leachville z 72438; rural
Valley Gin; RMC Place; MILLER; *148 I-2; elev. 217ft./66m.; mail Fouke z 71837
Valley Springs; Inc. Place; BOONE; 148 B-4; 🄿; z 72682; Ⓟ 200; © 167
Valley View; RMC Place; CRAIGHEAD; *148 C-8; ★ JONES; mail Jonesboro z 72404; pop. incl. with Jonesboro (Inc. Place)
Van; RMC Place; ARKANSAS; *148 G-7; elev. 181ft./55m.; mail De Witt z 72042; rural
Van Buren; Inc. Place; ⊡ CRAWFORD; 148 D-1; elev. 443ft./135m.; 🄿 🄷; ★ FTSM; z 72956-57; Ⓟ 14,979; © 18,986; ◆ 23,071
VAN BUREN; 148 D-5; Ⓟ 14,008; © 16,192; ◆ 16,490
Vandervoort; Inc. Place; POLK; 148 F-1; elev. 1,074ft./327m.; 🄿; z 71972; Ⓟ 111; © 120
Vanndale; RMC Place; CROSS; 148 D-8; 🄿; z 72387; ● 225
Varner; RMC Place; LINCOLN; *148 G-6; ● 45
Vaughn; RMC Place; BENTON; *148 B-1; mail Bentonville z 72712; pop. incl. with Bentonville (Inc. Place)
Velvet Ridge; RMC Place; WHITE; *148 D-7; elev. 639ft./195m.; mail Bald Knob z 72010; ● 120
Vendor; RMC Place; NEWTON; 148 C-4; 🄿; z 72683; ● 30
Verona; RMC Place; MARION; *148 B-4; mail Valley Springs z 72682; rural
Vesta; RMC Place; FRANKLIN; *148 D-2; elev. 436ft./133m.; mail Charleston z 72933
Vick; RMC Place; BRADLEY; 148 I-6; elev. 144ft./44m.; mail Hermitage z 71647; ● 30
Victoria; Inc. Place; MISSISSIPPI; 148 C-9; mail Osceola z 72370; Ⓟ 110; © 59
Village; RMC Place; COLUMBIA; *148 I-4; 🄿; z 71753; ● 100
Vilonia; Inc. Place; FAULKNER; 148 E-5; 🄿; z 72173; Ⓟ 1,133; © 2,106
Vimy Ridge; RMC Place; SALINE; *148 F-5; ★ L.R.; mail Alexander z 72002; ● 165
Vincent; RMC Place; CRITTENDEN; *148 E-9; mail Crawfordsville z 72327; ● 80
Vine Prairie; RMC Place; CRAWFORD; *148 D-2; mail Mulberry z 72947; pop. incl. with Mulberry (Inc. Place)
Vineyard; RMC Place; LEE; *148 F-8; elev. 1,194ft./364m.; mail Lexa z 72355, Marianna z 72360; rural
Viney Grove; RMC Place; WASHINGTON; *148 C-1; elev. 1,167ft./356m.; mail Prairie Grove z 72753
Vinity Corner; RMC Place; WHITE; *148 E-6; elev. 203ft./62m.; mail Searcy z 72143; rural
Viola; Inc. Place; FULTON; 148 B-6; 🄿; z 72583; Ⓟ 320; © 381
Violet Hill; RMC Place; IZARD; *148 B-6; elev. 747ft./228m.; 🄿; z 72584; ● 130
Vista Shores; RMC Place; BENTON; *148 B-2; mail Garfield z 72732; ● 50

W

Wabash; RMC Place; PHILLIPS; 148 F-8; 🄿; z 72389; ● 60
Wabbaseka; Inc. Place; JEFFERSON; 148 G-6; 🄿; z 72175; Ⓟ 332; © 323
Wakefield Village; RMC Place; PULASKI; *148 F-5; ★ L.R.; mail Little Rock z 72209; pop. incl. with Little Rock (Inc. Place)
Walcott; RMC Place; GREENE; *148 C-8; 🄿; z 72474; ● 170
Waldenburg; Inc. Place; POINSETT; 148 D-8; 🄿; z 72475; Ⓟ 103; © 80
Waldo; Inc. Place; COLUMBIA; 148 I-3; 🄿; z 71770; Ⓟ 1,495; © 1,594
Waldron; Inc. Place; ⊡ SCOTT; 148 E-2; elev. 671ft./205m.; 🄿 🄷; z 72958; Ⓟ 3,024; © 3,508
Walker; RMC Place; COLUMBIA; *148 I-3; mail Magnolia z 71753; ● 70
Walker; RMC Place; WHITE; *148 E-6; elev. 209ft./64m.; mail Searcy z 72143
Walker Creek; RMC Place; LAFAYETTE; *148 J-3; elev. 246ft./75m.; mail Taylor z 71861
Walkers Corner; RMC Place; LONOKE, PULASKI; *148 F-6; elev. 246ft./75m.; mail Scott z 72142; rural
Walkerville; RMC Place; COLUMBIA; *148 J-3; elev. 294ft./90m.; mail Emerson z 71740; ● 30
Wallace; RMC Place; LITTLE RIVER; *148 H-1; elev. 416ft./127m.; mail Foreman z 71836; ● 370
Walnut; RMC Place; NEWTON; *148 C-3; mail Ozone z 72854; rural
Walnut Corner; RMC Place; GREENE; *148 C-8; elev. 263ft./80m.; mail Bono z 72416; ● 30
Walnut Corner; RMC Place; PHILLIPS; *148 F-8; elev. 210ft./64m.; mail Barton z 72312
Walnut Grove; RMC Place; CLAY; *148 B-9; elev. 290ft./88m.; mail Knobel z 72435; rural
Walnut Grove; RMC Place; INDEPENDENCE; *148 C-7; elev. 365ft./111m.; mail Cord z 72524; rural
Walnut Grove; RMC Place; VAN BUREN; *148 D-5; mail Clinton z 72031; rural
Walnut Grove; RMC Place; WASHINGTON; *148 C-1; ★ FAY-; mail Farmington z 72730
Walnut Grove; RMC Place; YELL; *148 E-3; mail Havana z 72842; rural
Walnut Hill; RMC Place; LAFAYETTE; *148 J-2; elev. 248ft./76m.; mail Bradley z 71826
Walnut Ridge; Inc. Place; ⊡ LAWRENCE; 148 B-8; 🄿 🄷 🄲 525; z 72476 & mail Light z 72439; Ⓟ 4,388; © 4,925
Walnut Springs; RMC Place; SEVIER; *148 H-1; mail Horatio z 71842
Waltreak; RMC Place; YELL; *148 E-3; elev. 398ft./121m.; mail Danville z 72833
Ward; Inc. Place; LONOKE; 148 E-6; elev. 233ft./71m.; 🄿; z 72176; Ⓟ 1,269; © 2,580
Wardell; RMC Place; MISSISSIPPI; *148 D-9; mail Joiner z 72350; rural
War Eagle; RMC Place; BENTON; *148 B-2; elev. 1,156ft./352m.; mail Rogers z 72756; ● 40
Warm Springs; RMC Place; RANDOLPH; 148 A-8; 🄿; z 72478; ● 30
Warner; RMC Place; OUACHITA; *148 H-4; elev. 114ft./35m.; mail Camden z 71701; rural
Warren; Inc. Place; ⊡ BRADLEY; 148 H-6; elev. 213ft./65m.; 🄿 🄷; z 71671; Ⓟ 6,455; © 6,442
Washburn; RMC Place; SEBASTIAN; *148 E-2; mail Greenwood z 72936
Washington; Inc. Place; HEMPSTEAD; 148 H-2; elev. 445ft./136m.; 🄿; z 71862; Ⓟ 148; © 148
WASHINGTON; 148 C-1; Ⓟ 113,409; © 157,715; ◆ 208,239
Washita; RMC Place; MONTGOMERY; 148 F-3; elev. 602ft./183m.; mail Mount Ida z 71957; ● 90
Watalula; RMC Place; FRANKLIN; *148 D-2; mail Ozark z 72949; rural
Waterloo; RMC Place; NEVADA; 148 I-3; elev. 338ft./103m.; mail Rosston z 71858; ● 50
Watkins Corner; RMC Place; PHILLIPS; *148 F-8; mail Marvell z 72366; ● 30
Watson; Inc. Place; DESHA; 148 H-7; elev. 153ft./47m.; 🄿; z 71674; Ⓟ 282; © 288
Watson Chapel; RMC Place; JEFFERSON; *148 G-6; ★ PNBLF; mail Pine Bluff z 71601; pop. incl. with Pine Bluff (Inc. Place)
Wattensaw; RMC Place; LONOKE; *148 E-6; mail Lonoke z 72086; ● 50
Waveland; RMC Place; YELL; 148 E-3; 🄿; z 72842
Waverly; RMC Place; CRITTENDEN; *148 E-9; elev. 210ft./64m.; mail Proctor z 72376; rural
Wayton; RMC Place; NEWTON; *148 C-3; mail Deer z 72628; rural
Webb City; RMC Place; FRANKLIN; *148 D-2; mail Ozark z 72949; ● 145
Weber; RMC Place; ARKANSAS; 148 G-7; mail Tichnor z 72166; ● 30
Weddington (Wedington); RMC Place; WASHINGTON; *148 B-1; elev. 1,186ft./361m.; mail Fayetteville z 72704
Wedington; WASHINGTON; see Weddington (RMC Place)
Wedington Woods; RMC Place; WASHINGTON; *148 B-1; mail Fayetteville z 72704
Weiner; Inc. Place; POINSETT; 148 D-8; 🄿; z 72479; Ⓟ 655; © 760
Welcome; RMC Place; COLUMBIA; 148 J-3; mail Taylor z 71861; ● 50
Welcome Home; RMC Place; SEARCY; *148 C-4; elev. 1,880ft./573m.; mail Marshall z 72650; rural
Weldon; Inc. Place; JACKSON; 148 D-7; mail Newport z 72112; Ⓟ 106; © 100
Wellford; RMC Place; CHICOT; *148 J-7; elev. 125ft./38m.; mail Eudora z 71640; rural
Welsh; RMC Place; MONTGOMERY; *148 G-3; ● 175
Weona; RMC Place; POINSETT; *148 D-8; mail Trumann z 72472; ● 30
Wesley; RMC Place; MADISON; 148 C-2; elev. 1,262ft./385m.; 🄿; z 72773; ● 50
Wesley Chapel (Possum Trot); RMC Place; CONWAY; *148 D-4; elev. 373ft./114m.; mail Morrilton z 72110; rural
Wesson; RMC Place; UNION; 148 J-4; mail Junction City z 71749; ● 125
West; RMC Place; WASHINGTON; mail Springdale z 72762, z 72766; pop. incl. with Springdale (Inc. Place)
West Camden Heights; RMC Place; OUACHITA; mail Camden z 71701; pop. incl. with Camden (Inc. Place)
West Crossett; CDP; ASHLEY; 148 J-6; mail Crossett z 71635; Ⓟ 2,019; © 1,664
West End; RMC Place; JEFFERSON; *148 G-6; ★ PNBLF; mail Pine Bluff z 71601; pop. incl. with Pine Bluff (Inc. Place)
Western Grove; Inc. Place; NEWTON; 148 B-4; elev. 1,078ft./329m.; 🄿; z 72685; Ⓟ 415; © 407
West Fork; Inc. Place; WASHINGTON; 148 C-1; elev. 1,339ft./408m.; 🄿; z 72774; Ⓟ 1,607; © 2,042
West Gum Springs; RMC Place; CLARK; *148 G-4; mail Arkadelphia z 71923
West Hartford; RMC Place; SEBASTIAN; *148 E-1; mail Hartford z 72938; rural
West Helena; RMC Place; PHILLIPS; 148 F-8; 🄿; z 72390; former incorporated place; became part of Helena-West Helena March 11, 2005; Ⓟ 9,695; © 8,689
West Line; RMC Place; SEVIER; *148 G-1; mail Eagletown z 74734; rural
West Marche; RMC Place; PULASKI; *148 E-5; ★ L.R.; mail North Little Rock z 72118; pop. incl. with Maumelle (Inc. Place)
West Memphis; Inc. Place; CRITTENDEN; 148 E-9; 🄿 🄷 ■; ★ MEM; z 72301, z 72303; Ⓟ 28,259; © 27,666; ◆ 28,097
West Pangburn; RMC Place; CLEBURNE; *148 D-6; elev. 549ft./167m.; mail Pangburn z 72121; rural
West Point; RMC Place; BENTON; *148 B-1; elev. 1,120ft./341m.; mail Gentry z 72734; rural
West Point; Inc. Place; WHITE; 148 E-6; 🄿; z 72178; Ⓟ 146; © 164; Ⓡ 208
West Ridge; RMC Place; MISSISSIPPI; *148 C-9; 🄿; z 72391; ● 250
Westside; RMC Place; PULASKI; mail Little Rock z 72211; pop. incl. with Little Rock (Inc. Place)
Westville; RMC Place; CRAWFORD; *148 D-1; elev. 450ft./137m.; ★ FTSM; mail Van Buren z 72956; rural
Westwood; RMC Place; PULASKI; *148 F-5; elev. 340ft./104m.; ★ L.R.; mail Little Rock z 72204; pop. incl. with Little Rock (Inc. Place)
Wharton; RMC Place; MADISON; *148 C-3; mail Huntsville z 72740; rural
Wheatley; Inc. Place; ST. FRANCIS; 148 E-7; elev. 210ft./64m.; 🄿; z 72392; Ⓟ 413; © 372
Wheeler; RMC Place; WASHINGTON; *148 B-1; elev. 1,119ft./341m.; 🄿; z 72704 & mail Fayetteville z 72703; ● 70
Wheeling; RMC Place; FULTON; *148 B-6; mail Salem z 72576; rural
Whelen Springs; Inc. Place; CLARK; 148 H-3; 🄿; z 71772; Ⓟ 116; © 84
Whisp; RMC Place; MISSISSIPPI; *148 C-9; mail Leachville z 72438; rural
Whispering Springs; RMC Place; CLEBURNE; *148 D-5; elev. 600ft./183m.; mail Higden z 72067; rural
Whistleville; RMC Place; MISSISSIPPI; *148 C-9; mail Manila z 72442; rural
Whitaker; RMC Place; POINSETT; *148 D-8; elev. 223ft./68m.; mail Harrisburg z 72432
White; RMC Place; ASHLEY; 148 J-6; elev. 103ft./31m.; mail Crossett z 71635; ● 30
WHITE; 148 D-6; Ⓟ 54,676; © 67,165; ◆ 74,776
White Cliffs; RMC Place; SEVIER; *148 H-2; elev. 369ft./112m.; mail Lockesburg z 71846; ● 30
White Hall; RMC Place; DREW; *148 H-6; elev. 278ft./85m.; mail Monticello z 71655; rural
White Hall; Inc. Place; JEFFERSON; 148 G-6; 🄿; ★ PNBLF; z 71602, z 71612; Ⓟ 3,849; © 4,732
Whitehall; RMC Place; LEE; *148 F-9; mail Brickeys z 72320; rural
Whitehall; RMC Place; POINSETT; 148 D-8; mail Harrisburg z 72432; ● 50
White Oak; RMC Place; FRANKLIN; *148 D-2; mail Ozark z 72949; rural
White Oak Bluff; RMC Place; CLEVELAND; *148 G-5; elev. 200ft./61m.; mail Rison z 71665; rural
White Rock; RMC Place; WASHINGTON; *148 B-1; elev. 1,253ft./382m.; ★ FAY-; mail Fayetteville z 72701; pop. incl. with Fayetteville (Inc. Place)
Whitetown; RMC Place; MONTGOMERY; *148 F-2; mail Oden z 71961; rural
Whiteville; RMC Place; BAXTER; *148 B-5; mail Gassville z 72635; rural
Whitmore; RMC Place; ST. FRANCIS; *148 E-9; mail Widener z 72394; rural
Whitton; RMC Place; MISSISSIPPI; *148 D-9; mail Tyronza z 72386; ● 50
Wickes; Inc. Place; POLK; 148 G-1; 🄿; z 71973; Ⓟ 570; © 675
Wideman; RMC Place; IZARD; *148 B-6; 🄿; z 72585
Widener; Inc. Place; ST. FRANCIS; 148 E-8; elev. 205ft./62m.; 🄿; z 72394; Ⓟ 381; © 335
Wiederkehr Village; Inc. Place; FRANKLIN; *148 D-2; 🄿; z 72821; Ⓟ 42; © 46
Wilburn; RMC Place; CLEBURNE; 148 D-6; elev. 436ft./133m.; 🄿; z 72179; ● 75
Wild Cherry; RMC Place; FULTON; *148 B-6; mail Salem z 72576; rural
Wildwood; RMC Place; ST. FRANCIS; *148 E-9; elev. 200ft./61m.; mail Heth z 72346; rural
Wilkins (Cross Roads); RMC Place; LOGAN; *148 D-3; elev. 420ft./128m.; mail Scranton z 72863; rural
Williams Junction; RMC Place; PERRY; elev. 441ft./134m.; mail Perryville z 72126; rural
Williamson; RMC Place; SEVIER; *148 H-1; elev. 407ft./124m.; mail Horatio z 71842; rural
Williford; Inc. Place; SHARP; 148 B-7; elev. 322ft./98m.; 🄿; z 72482; Ⓟ 69; © 63
Willisville; Inc. Place; NEVADA; 148 I-3; elev. 350ft./107m.; 🄿; z 71864; Ⓟ 196; © 188
Willow; RMC Place; DALLAS; 148 G-4; mail Leola z 72084; ● 50
Wilmar; Inc. Place; DREW; 148 H-6; elev. 149ft./45m.; 🄿; z 71675; Ⓟ 637; © 571
Wilmot; Inc. Place; ASHLEY; 148 J-7; elev. 115ft./35m.; 🄿; z 71676; Ⓟ 1,047; © 786
Wilson; Inc. Place; MISSISSIPPI; 148 D-10; 🄿; z 72395; Ⓟ 1,068; © 939
Wilson; RMC Place; POPE; *148 E-4; mail Atkins z 72823; rural
Wilton; Inc. Place; LITTLE RIVER; 148 H-1; 🄿; z 71865; Ⓟ 449; © 439
Winchester; Inc. Place; DREW; 148 H-7; elev. 160ft./49m.; 🄿; z 71677; Ⓟ 239; © 191
Windamere; RMC Place; PULASKI; ★ L.R.; mail Little Rock z 72201; pop. incl. with Little Rock (Inc. Place)
Winesburg; RMC Place; CRAIGHEAD; *148 C-8; mail Jonesboro z 72404; rural
Winfield; RMC Place; SCOTT; 148 E-1; elev. 659ft./201m.; mail Waldron z 72958; ● 30
Winfrey; RMC Place; CRAWFORD; *148 C-2; elev. 1,005ft./306m.; mail Winslow z 72959; rural
Wing; RMC Place; YELL; 148 E-3; elev. 477ft./145m.; mail Rover z 72860
Winslow; Inc. Place; WASHINGTON; 148 C-2; elev. 1,731ft./528m.; 🄿; z 72959; Ⓟ 342; © 399
Winston Terrace; RMC Place; PULASKI; ★ L.R.; mail Little Rock z 72201; pop. incl. with Little Rock (Inc. Place)
Winthrop; Inc. Place; LITTLE RIVER; 148 H-1; elev. 323ft./98m.; 🄿; z 71866; Ⓟ 227; © 186
Wirth; RMC Place; SHARP; 148 B-7; elev. 816ft./249m.; mail Mammoth Spring z 72554
Wiseman; RMC Place; IZARD; 148 B-6; 🄿; z 72587; ● 50
Witcherville; RMC Place; SEBASTIAN; 148 E-1; mail Huntington z 72940; ● 200
Witherspoon; RMC Place; CLARK, HOT SPRING; *148 G-4; elev. 196ft./60m.; mail Arkadelphia z 71923; rural
Witter; RMC Place; MADISON; 148 C-2; elev. 1,445ft./440m.; 🄿; z 72776; ● 30
Wittsburg; RMC Place; CROSS; *148 E-8; mail Wynne z 72396; rural
Witts Springs; RMC Place; SEARCY; 148 C-4; elev. 873ft./266m.; 🄿; z 72686; ● 60
Wiville; RMC Place; WOODRUFF; *148 E-7; elev. 221ft./67m.; mail Mc Crory z 72101
Wolf Bayou; RMC Place; CLEBURNE; *148 C-6; mail Drasco z 72530; ● 70
Wonderview; RMC Place; CONWAY; *148 D-4; elev. 700ft./213m.; mail Hattieville z 72063
Woodberry; RMC Place; CALHOUN; 148 H-5; mail Hampton z 71744; ● 40
Woodland; RMC Place; JOHNSON; *148 D-3; mail Clarksville z 72830; rural
Woodland Corner; RMC Place; MISSISSIPPI; *148 C-10; mail Blytheville z 72315; rural
Woodland Heights; RMC Place; PULASKI; *148 F-5; ★ L.R.; mail Little Rock z 72212; pop. incl. with Little Rock (Inc. Place)
Woodland Hills; RMC Place; FULTON; *148 B-7; elev. 567ft./173m.; mail Hardy z 72542; ● 100
Woodland Hills; RMC Place; SALINE; *148 F-5; ★ L.R.; mail Alexander z 72002; ● 900
Woodlawn; RMC Place; CLEVELAND; *148 H-6; elev. 250ft./76m.; mail Rison z 71665; ● 100
Woodlawn; RMC Place; LONOKE; *148 E-6; elev. 263ft./80m.; mail Austin z 72007; ● 30
Woodrow; RMC Place; CLEBURNE; *148 C-6; mail Prim z 72130
WOODRUFF; 148 E-7; Ⓟ 9,520; © 8,741; ◆ 7,173
Woodson; CDP; PULASKI; 148 F-5; elev. 250ft./76m.; 🄿; z 72180; © 445
Wooster; Inc. Place; FAULKNER; 148 E-5; elev. 314ft./96m.; 🄿; z 72181; Ⓟ 414; © 516
Worden; RMC Place; WHITE; 148 D-7; mail Bald Knob z 72010; ● 100
Wright; RMC Place; JEFFERSON; 148 F-6; elev. 220ft./67m.; 🄿; z 72182; ● 350
Wrights Corner; RMC Place; WHITE; *148 D-6; elev. 330ft./101m.; mail Bald Knob z 72010; rural
Wrightsville; Inc. Place; PULASKI; 148 F-5; elev. 257ft./78m.; 🄿; ★ L.R.; z 72183; Ⓟ 1,062; © 1,368
Wycamp; RMC Place; PHILLIPS; *148 F-8; mail West Helena z 72390; rural
Wye; RMC Place; PERRY; *148 E-4; elev. 730ft./223m.; mail Bigelow z 72016; rural
Wyman; RMC Place; WASHINGTON; *148 B-2; elev. 208ft./63m.; ★ FAY-; mail Fayetteville z 72701; rural
Wynne; Inc. Place; ⊡ CROSS; 148 E-8; 🄿 🄷; z 72396; Ⓟ 8,187; © 8,615
Wyola; RMC Place; WASHINGTON; *148 C-2; elev. 1,486ft./453m.; mail Winslow z 72959; rural

Y

Yale; RMC Place; JOHNSON; *148 C-3; elev. 910ft./277m.; mail Pettigrew z 72752; rural
Yancopin; RMC Place; DESHA; *148 H-7; elev. 166ft./51m.; mail Watson z 71674; rural
Yancy; RMC Place; HEMPSTEAD; *148 H-2; elev. 435ft./133m.; mail Ozan z 71855
Yarbro; RMC Place; MISSISSIPPI; 148 C-10; mail Blytheville z 72315; ● 200
Yardelle; RMC Place; NEWTON; *148 C-4; elev. 929ft./283m.; mail Western Grove z 72685; rural
Y City; RMC Place; SCOTT; 148 F-2; mail Boles z 72926, Pencil Bluff z 71965; ● 60
YELL; 148 E-3; Ⓟ 17,759; © 21,139; ◆ 21,736
Yellow Bayou; RMC Place; CHICOT; *148 I-7; elev. 125ft./38m.; mail Lake Village z 71653; rural
Yellville; Inc. Place; ⊡ MARION; 148 B-4; 🄿; z 72687; Ⓟ 1,181; © 1,312
Yocana; RMC Place; POLK; *148 F-2; elev. 928ft./283m.; mail Mena z 71953; rural
Yoestown; RMC Place; CRAWFORD; *148 D-1; ★ FTSM; mail Alma z 72921; rural
Yorktown; RMC Place; LINCOLN; 148 G-6; elev. 190ft./58m.; 🄿; z 71678; ● 30

Z

Zent; RMC Place; MONROE; *148 E-7; elev. 198ft./60m.; mail Brinkley z 72021
Zinc; Inc. Place; BOONE; *148 B-4; mail Harrison z 72601; Ⓟ 91; © 76
Zion; RMC Place; IZARD; 148 B-6; elev. 685ft./209m.; 🄿; z 72556; ● 135
Zion Hill; RMC Place; VAN BUREN; *148 C-4; elev. 1,820ft./555m.; mail Morrilton z 72110; rural

CALIFORNIA

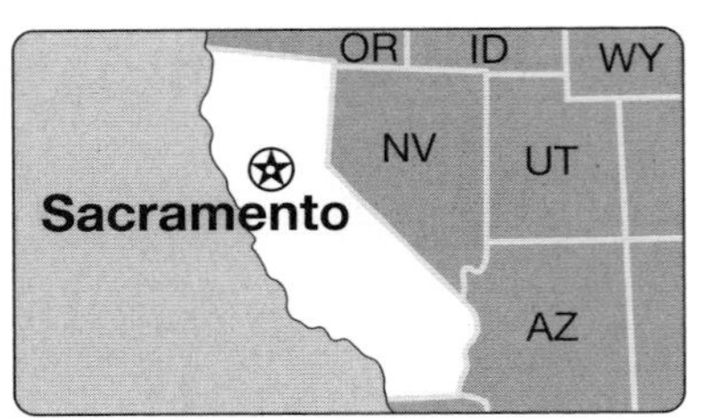

Statistics

Total area (2000) — 163,696 square miles
Land area (2000) — 155,959 square miles
Water area (2000) — 7,737 square miles
Capital — Sacramento
Admitted as state — September, 1850

Maps

State maps can be found on pages 142-254 in Vol. 1

Ranally Metro Areas (RMAs) and Abbreviations

Bakersfield, CA — BAK
Calexico, CA-MEX. — CLEX
Chico, CA — CHICO
Davis, CA — DAV
Eureka-Arcata, CA — EUR-
Fairfield-Vacaville, CA — FRFL-
Fresno, CA — FRES
Hemet, CA — HEM
Hesperia-Apple Valley-Victorville, CA — HESP-
Indio-Coachella, CA — IND-
Lompoc, CA — LOMP
Los Angeles, CA — L.A.
Merced, CA — MRCD
Modesto, CA — MOD
Monterey-Seaside-Marina, CA — MTRY-
Napa, CA — NAPA
Oxnard-Thousand Oaks-Ventura, CA — OXN-
Palm Springs-Cathedral City-Palm Desert, CA — PSPR-
Porterville, CA — PORT
Redding, CA — REDD
Riverside-San Bernadino, CA — RIV-
Sacramento, CA — SAC
Salinas, CA — SLNS
San Diego, CA-MEX. — SDGO
San Francisco-Oakland-San Jose, CA — SF-O-
San Luis Obispo, CA — S.LUIS
Santa Barbara, CA — S.BAR
Santa Cruz, CA — S.CRZ
Santa Maria, CA — S.MAR
Santa Rosa, CA — S.ROS
Stockton, CA — STOC
Visalia, CA — VISL
Watsonville, CA — WATS
Yuba City, CA — YUCY
Yuma, AZ-CA — YUMA

Principal Places

Place Name	Place Type	County	Population
Los Angeles	Inc. Place	LOS ANGELES	◆ 3,812,019
San Diego	Inc. Place	SAN DIEGO	◆ 1,343,698
San Jose	Inc. Place	SANTA CLARA	◆ 993,375
San Francisco	Inc. Place	SAN FRANCISCO	◆ 806,455
Fresno	Inc. Place	FRESNO	◆ 491,328
Long Beach	Inc. Place	LOS ANGELES	◆ 486,798
Sacramento	Inc. Place	SACRAMENTO	◆ 440,443
Oakland	Inc. Place	ALAMEDA	◆ 403,494
Santa Ana	Inc. Place	ORANGE	◆ 350,216
Anaheim	Inc. Place	ORANGE	◆ 345,381
Bakersfield	Inc. Place	KERN	◆ 343,635
Riverside	Inc. Place	RIVERSIDE	◆ 286,237
Stockton	Inc. Place	SAN JOAQUIN	◆ 267,858
Chula Vista	Inc. Place	SAN DIEGO	◆ 212,443
Fremont	Inc. Place	ALAMEDA	◆ 212,286
Glendale	Inc. Place	LOS ANGELES	◆ 203,344
Modesto	Inc. Place	STANISLAUS	◆ 196,523
Huntington Beach	Inc. Place	ORANGE	◆ 194,891
Oxnard	Inc. Place	VENTURA	◆ 194,698
San Bernardino	Inc. Place	SAN BERNARDINO	◆ 184,595
Oceanside	Inc. Place	SAN DIEGO	◆ 183,501
Moreno Valley	Inc. Place	RIVERSIDE	◆ 182,281
Fontana	Inc. Place	SAN BERNARDINO	◆ 179,590
Ontario	Inc. Place	SAN BERNARDINO	◆ 176,410
Garden Grove	Inc. Place	ORANGE	◆ 171,303
Santa Clarita	Inc. Place	LOS ANGELES	◆ 167,484
Corona	Inc. Place	RIVERSIDE	◆ 164,987
Irvine	Inc. Place	ORANGE	◆ 164,490
Pomona	Inc. Place	LOS ANGELES	◆ 161,427
Rancho Cucamonga	Inc. Place	SAN BERNARDINO	◆ 158,857
Salinas	Inc. Place	MONTEREY	◆ 157,293
Santa Rosa	Inc. Place	SONOMA	◆ 155,700
Escondido	Inc. Place	SAN DIEGO	◆ 152,682
Hayward	Inc. Place	ALAMEDA	◆ 146,495
Sunnyvale	Inc. Place	SANTA CLARA	◆ 141,522
Torrance	Inc. Place	LOS ANGELES	◆ 137,713
Orange	Inc. Place	ORANGE	◆ 136,738
Pasadena	Inc. Place	LOS ANGELES	◆ 135,447
Palmdale	Inc. Place	LOS ANGELES	◆ 131,633
Elk Grove	Inc. Place	SACRAMENTO	◆ 129,419
Fullerton	Inc. Place	ORANGE	◆ 128,894
East Los Angeles	CDP	LOS ANGELES	◆ 127,117
Lancaster	Inc. Place	LOS ANGELES	◆ 125,902
Concord	Inc. Place	CONTRA COSTA	◆ 124,976
El Monte	Inc. Place	LOS ANGELES	◆ 121,561
Thousand Oaks	Inc. Place	VENTURA	◆ 121,216
Simi Valley	Inc. Place	VENTURA	◆ 118,052
Vallejo	Inc. Place	SOLANO	◆ 115,723
Visalia	Inc. Place	TULARE	◆ 114,390
Downey	Inc. Place	LOS ANGELES	◆ 113,948
Costa Mesa	Inc. Place	ORANGE	◆ 113,415
Santa Clara	Inc. Place	SANTA CLARA	◆ 111,849
Roseville	Inc. Place	PLACER	◆ 111,787
Inglewood	Inc. Place	LOS ANGELES	◆ 111,222
West Covina	Inc. Place	LOS ANGELES	◆ 110,576
Daly City	Inc. Place	SAN MATEO	◆ 109,232
Norwalk	Inc. Place	LOS ANGELES	◆ 107,495
Richmond	Inc. Place	CONTRA COSTA	◆ 105,858
Antioch	Inc. Place	CONTRA COSTA	◆ 104,674
Arden-Arcade	CDP-Census Area Only	SACRAMENTO	◆ 104,121
Temecula	Inc. Place	RIVERSIDE	◆ 103,609
Ventura	Inc. Place	VENTURA	◆ 103,260
Berkeley	Inc. Place	ALAMEDA	◆ 102,515
South Gate	Inc. Place	LOS ANGELES	◆ 102,487
Burbank	Inc. Place	LOS ANGELES	◆ 102,272
Vista	Inc. Place	SAN DIEGO	◆ 102,167
Fairfield	Inc. Place	SOLANO	◆ 102,124
Rialto	Inc. Place	SAN BERNARDINO	◆ 101,597
El Cajon	Inc. Place	SAN DIEGO	◆ 100,397
Santa Barbara	Inc. Place	SANTA BARBARA	◆ 99,790
Murrieta	Inc. Place	RIVERSIDE	◆ 99,197
San Mateo	Inc. Place	SAN MATEO	◆ 95,258
Mission Viejo	Inc. Place	ORANGE	◆ 94,574
Compton	Inc. Place	LOS ANGELES	◆ 93,714
Carlsbad	Inc. Place	SAN DIEGO	◆ 93,508
Vacaville	Inc. Place	SOLANO	◆ 92,900
Carson	Inc. Place	LOS ANGELES	◆ 91,202
Westminster	Inc. Place	ORANGE	◆ 91,031
Citrus Heights	Inc. Place	SACRAMENTO	◆ 90,552
Hawthorne	Inc. Place	LOS ANGELES	◆ 89,423
Santa Maria	Inc. Place	SANTA BARBARA	◆ 87,664
Redding	Inc. Place	SHASTA	◆ 87,182
Alhambra	Inc. Place	LOS ANGELES	◆ 86,392
Santa Monica	Inc. Place	LOS ANGELES	◆ 86,310
Whittier	Inc. Place	LOS ANGELES	◆ 86,204
Clovis	Inc. Place	FRESNO	◆ 85,777
Buena Park	Inc. Place	ORANGE	◆ 82,403
Chino Hills	Inc. Place	SAN BERNARDINO	◆ 82,235
Indio	Inc. Place	RIVERSIDE	◆ 81,896
San Leandro	Inc. Place	ALAMEDA	◆ 81,527
Lakewood	Inc. Place	LOS ANGELES	◆ 81,226
Victorville	Inc. Place	SAN BERNARDINO	◆ 79,466
Baldwin Park	Inc. Place	LOS ANGELES	◆ 79,456
Livermore	Inc. Place	ALAMEDA	◆ 79,433
Newport Beach	Inc. Place	ORANGE	◆ 79,215
Redwood City	Inc. Place	SAN MATEO	◆ 78,657
Hesperia	Inc. Place	SAN BERNARDINO	◆ 77,980
Bellflower	Inc. Place	LOS ANGELES	◆ 77,255
Napa	Inc. Place	NAPA	◆ 77,077
Chino	Inc. Place	SAN BERNARDINO	◆ 76,688
Tracy	Inc. Place	SAN JOAQUIN	◆ 76,409
Lake Forest	Inc. Place	ORANGE	◆ 74,838
Merced	Inc. Place	MERCED	◆ 74,425
Lynwood	Inc. Place	LOS ANGELES	◆ 74,253
Tustin	Inc. Place	ORANGE	◆ 73,497
Mountain View	Inc. Place	SANTA CLARA	◆ 73,380
Hemet	Inc. Place	RIVERSIDE	◆ 72,588
Alameda	Inc. Place	ALAMEDA	◆ 72,246
Union City	Inc. Place	ALAMEDA	◆ 71,992
Davis	Inc. Place	YOLO	◆ 70,885
Chico	Inc. Place	BUTTE	◆ 70,322
Milpitas	Inc. Place	SANTA CLARA	◆ 69,977
Upland	Inc. Place	SAN BERNARDINO	◆ 69,608
Pleasanton	Inc. Place	ALAMEDA	◆ 68,125
Turlock	Inc. Place	STANISLAUS	◆ 67,203
San Marcos	Inc. Place	SAN DIEGO	◆ 67,161
Folsom	Inc. Place	SACRAMENTO	◆ 67,018
Pico Rivera	Inc. Place	LOS ANGELES	◆ 66,018
Pittsburg	Inc. Place	CONTRA COSTA	◆ 65,625
Laguna Niguel	Inc. Place	ORANGE	◆ 65,623
South San Francisco	Inc. Place	SAN MATEO	◆ 64,713
Redondo Beach	Inc. Place	LOS ANGELES	◆ 64,689
Yorba Linda	Inc. Place	ORANGE	◆ 63,989
Huntington Park	Inc. Place	LOS ANGELES	◆ 63,506
Walnut Creek	Inc. Place	CONTRA COSTA	◆ 63,290
Apple Valley	Inc. Place	SAN BERNARDINO	◆ 63,249
Redlands	Inc. Place	SAN BERNARDINO	◆ 63,214
Montebello	Inc. Place	LOS ANGELES	◆ 63,032
Encinitas	Inc. Place	SAN DIEGO	◆ 62,314

Place Name	Place Type	County	Population
Florence-Graham	CDP-Census Area Only	LOS ANGELES	◆ 61,567
Palo Alto	Inc. Place	SANTA CLARA	◆ 61,398
Yuba City	Inc. Place	SUTTER	◆ 61,050
La Habra	Inc. Place	ORANGE	◆ 60,738
Monterey Park	Inc. Place	LOS ANGELES	◆ 60,285
Gardena	Inc. Place	LOS ANGELES	◆ 60,254
Woodland	Inc. Place	YOLO	◆ 60,231
Rancho Cordova	Inc. Place	SACRAMENTO	◆ 60,167
Elk Grove	CDP-Census Area Only	SACRAMENTO	Ⓒ 59,984
Cupertino	Inc. Place	SANTA CLARA	◆ 59,105
Lodi	Inc. Place	SAN JOAQUIN	◆ 58,755
Castro Valley	CDP	ALAMEDA	◆ 58,615
Paramount	Inc. Place	LOS ANGELES	◆ 58,542
Diamond Bar	Inc. Place	LOS ANGELES	◆ 58,421
Camarillo	Inc. Place	VENTURA	◆ 58,379
Carmichael	CDP	SACRAMENTO	◆ 57,318
Arcadia	Inc. Place	LOS ANGELES	◆ 57,309
Madera	Inc. Place	MADERA	◆ 57,149
Cathedral City	Inc. Place	RIVERSIDE	◆ 57,140
Manteca	Inc. Place	SAN JOAQUIN	◆ 56,954
La Mesa	Inc. Place	SAN DIEGO	◆ 56,940
South Whittier	CDP	LOS ANGELES	◆ 56,448
Tulare	Inc. Place	TULARE	◆ 55,979
Santee	Inc. Place	SAN DIEGO	◆ 55,974
Perris	Inc. Place	RIVERSIDE	◆ 55,963
San Rafael	Inc. Place	MARIN	◆ 55,943
Fountain Valley	Inc. Place	ORANGE	◆ 55,840
Santa Cruz	Inc. Place	SANTA CRUZ	◆ 55,610
Petaluma	Inc. Place	SONOMA	◆ 55,466
National City	Inc. Place	SAN DIEGO	◆ 55,402
Goleta	CDP-Census Area Only	SANTA BARBARA	Ⓒ 55,204
Rancho Cordova	CDP-Census Area Only	SACRAMENTO	Ⓒ 55,060
Arden Town	RMC Place	SACRAMENTO	● 55,000
San Clemente	Inc. Place	ORANGE	◆ 54,663
Palm Desert	Inc. Place	RIVERSIDE	◆ 54,440
Delano	Inc. Place	KERN	◆ 54,361
Hacienda Heights	CDP	LOS ANGELES	◆ 54,331
Rosemead	Inc. Place	LOS ANGELES	◆ 53,682
Rocklin	Inc. Place	PLACER	◆ 52,746
Colton	Inc. Place	SAN BERNARDINO	◆ 52,529
Highland	Inc. Place	SAN BERNARDINO	◆ 51,913
Yucaipa	Inc. Place	SAN BERNARDINO	◆ 51,601
North Highlands	CDP	SACRAMENTO	◆ 50,910
Cerritos	Inc. Place	LOS ANGELES	◆ 50,792
Poway	Inc. Place	SAN DIEGO	◆ 50,657
La Mirada	Inc. Place	LOS ANGELES	◆ 50,174
Gilroy	Inc. Place	SANTA CLARA	◆ 50,103
Watsonville	Inc. Place	SANTA CRUZ	◆ 49,838
Rancho Santa Margarita	Inc. Place	ORANGE	◆ 49,753
Hanford	Inc. Place	KINGS	◆ 49,678
Rowland Heights	CDP	LOS ANGELES	◆ 49,659
Placentia	Inc. Place	ORANGE	◆ 49,655
Glendora	Inc. Place	LOS ANGELES	◆ 48,810
Covina	Inc. Place	LOS ANGELES	◆ 48,554
Novato	Inc. Place	MARIN	◆ 48,370
Azusa	Inc. Place	LOS ANGELES	◆ 47,970
Palm Springs	Inc. Place	RIVERSIDE	◆ 47,490
San Luis Obispo	Inc. Place	SAN LUIS OBISPO	◆ 47,283
Cypress	Inc. Place	ORANGE	◆ 47,005
Porterville	Inc. Place	TULARE	◆ 46,928
Lake Elsinore	Inc. Place	RIVERSIDE	◆ 46,081
San Ramon	Inc. Place	CONTRA COSTA	◆ 45,128
Bell Gardens	Inc. Place	LOS ANGELES	◆ 43,909
Altadena	CDP	LOS ANGELES	◆ 43,576
Newark	Inc. Place	ALAMEDA	◆ 43,471
Lompoc	Inc. Place	SANTA BARBARA	◆ 43,251
La Quinta	Inc. Place	RIVERSIDE	◆ 43,151
Danville	Inc. Place	CONTRA COSTA	◆ 42,925
La Puente	Inc. Place	LOS ANGELES	◆ 42,854
San Gabriel	Inc. Place	LOS ANGELES	◆ 42,174
Parkway-South Sacramento	CDP-Census Area Only	SACRAMENTO	◆ 42,022
Arcade	RMC Place	SACRAMENTO	● 42,000
Rohnert Park	Inc. Place	SONOMA	◆ 41,618
Aliso Viejo	Inc. Place	ORANGE	◆ 41,582
West Sacramento	Inc. Place	YOLO	◆ 41,537
El Centro	Inc. Place	IMPERIAL	◆ 41,289
Rancho Palos Verdes	Inc. Place	LOS ANGELES	◆ 40,946
Rubidoux	CDP	RIVERSIDE	◆ 40,902
San Bruno	Inc. Place	SAN MATEO	◆ 40,310
Aliso Viejo	CDP-Census Area Only	ORANGE	Ⓡ 40,118
Ceres	Inc. Place	STANISLAUS	◆ 39,865
Morgan Hill	Inc. Place	SANTA CLARA	◆ 39,438
Campbell	Inc. Place	SANTA CLARA	◆ 38,989
Stanton	Inc. Place	ORANGE	◆ 38,727
Culver City	Inc. Place	LOS ANGELES	◆ 38,247
Bell	Inc. Place	LOS ANGELES	◆ 37,736
Los Banos	Inc. Place	MERCED	◆ 37,221
Monrovia	Inc. Place	LOS ANGELES	◆ 37,053
Montclair	Inc. Place	SAN BERNARDINO	◆ 37,047
Hollister	Inc. Place	SAN BENITO	◆ 36,994
Coachella	Inc. Place	RIVERSIDE	◆ 36,928
Brea	Inc. Place	ORANGE	◆ 36,903
Pacifica	Inc. Place	SAN MATEO	◆ 36,775
San Juan Capistrano	Inc. Place	ORANGE	◆ 36,359
Temple City	Inc. Place	LOS ANGELES	◆ 36,214
Dana Point	Inc. Place	ORANGE	◆ 35,828
La Presa	CDP	SAN DIEGO	◆ 35,357
Manhattan Beach	Inc. Place	LOS ANGELES	◆ 35,315
Martinez	Inc. Place	CONTRA COSTA	◆ 34,960
Beverly Hills	Inc. Place	LOS ANGELES	◆ 34,924
Willowbrook	CDP-Census Area Only	LOS ANGELES	◆ 34,913
West Hollywood	Inc. Place	LOS ANGELES	◆ 34,718
San Dimas	Inc. Place	LOS ANGELES	◆ 34,691
Claremont	Inc. Place	LOS ANGELES	◆ 34,587
Calexico	Inc. Place	IMPERIAL	◆ 34,390
San Pablo	Inc. Place	CONTRA COSTA	◆ 34,296
Oildale	CDP	KERN	◆ 34,210
Moorpark	Inc. Place	VENTURA	◆ 33,970
Lawndale	Inc. Place	LOS ANGELES	◆ 33,780
San Jacinto	Inc. Place	RIVERSIDE	◆ 33,665
Dublin	Inc. Place	ALAMEDA	◆ 33,518
East Palo Alto	Inc. Place	SAN MATEO	◆ 32,999
La Verne	Inc. Place	LOS ANGELES	◆ 32,688
Seaside	Inc. Place	MONTEREY	◆ 32,594
Westmont	CDP-Census Area Only	LOS ANGELES	◆ 32,342
Fair Oaks	CDP	SACRAMENTO	◆ 32,280
Pleasant Hill	Inc. Place	CONTRA COSTA	◆ 31,933
Florin	CDP	SACRAMENTO	◆ 31,862
Menlo Park	Inc. Place	SAN MATEO	◆ 31,616
Laguna Hills	Inc. Place	ORANGE	◆ 31,484
Fallbrook	CDP	SAN DIEGO	◆ 31,435
Atascadero	Inc. Place	SAN LUIS OBISPO	◆ 30,866
Saratoga	Inc. Place	SANTA CLARA	◆ 30,857
Orangevale	CDP	SACRAMENTO	◆ 30,777
Goleta	Inc. Place	SANTA BARBARA	◆ 30,669
Santa Paula	Inc. Place	VENTURA	◆ 30,358
Brentwood	Inc. Place	CONTRA COSTA	◆ 30,055

Place Name	Place Type	County	Population
Walnut	Inc. Place	LOS ANGELES	◆ 30,053
Orcutt	CDP	SANTA BARBARA	◆ 29,726
Los Gatos	Inc. Place	SANTA CLARA	◆ 29,628
Paso Robles	Inc. Place	SAN LUIS OBISPO	◆ 29,568
Oakley	Inc. Place	CONTRA COSTA	◆ 29,342
Spring Valley	CDP	SAN DIEGO	◆ 28,810
Los Altos	Inc. Place	SANTA CLARA	◆ 28,674
Burlingame	Inc. Place	SAN MATEO	◆ 28,550
Foster City	Inc. Place	SAN MATEO	◆ 27,974
San Carlos	Inc. Place	SAN MATEO	◆ 27,867
Maywood	Inc. Place	LOS ANGELES	◆ 27,718
Soledad	Inc. Place	MONTEREY	◆ 27,661
Imperial Beach	Inc. Place	SAN DIEGO	◆ 27,632
Twentynine Palms	Inc. Place	SAN BERNARDINO	◆ 27,418
Monterey	Inc. Place	MONTEREY	◆ 27,236
Paradise	Inc. Place	BUTTE	◆ 27,141
Desert Hot Springs	Inc. Place	RIVERSIDE	◆ 26,498
Adelanto	Inc. Place	SAN BERNARDINO	◆ 26,419
Rosemont	CDP	SACRAMENTO	◆ 26,391
Benicia	Inc. Place	SOLANO	◆ 26,378
Coronado	Inc. Place	SAN DIEGO	◆ 26,048
West Whittier-Los Nietos	CDP-Census Area Only	LOS ANGELES	◆ 25,704
Eureka	Inc. Place	HUMBOLDT	◆ 25,573
Galt	Inc. Place	SACRAMENTO	◆ 25,405
Lemon Grove	Inc. Place	SAN DIEGO	◆ 25,397
Suisun City	Inc. Place	SOLANO	◆ 25,372
Ridgecrest	Inc. Place	KERN	◆ 25,284
Wasco	Inc. Place	KERN	◆ 25,236
North Tustin	CDP	ORANGE	◆ 25,213
Florence	RMC Place	LOS ANGELES	● 25,000
Reedley	Inc. Place	FRESNO	◆ 24,942
Belmont	Inc. Place	SAN MATEO	◆ 24,728
Norco	Inc. Place	RIVERSIDE	◆ 24,667
Cudahy	Inc. Place	LOS ANGELES	◆ 24,604
South Lake Tahoe	Inc. Place	EL DORADO	◆ 24,412
Banning	Inc. Place	RIVERSIDE	◆ 24,390
Windsor	Inc. Place	SONOMA	◆ 24,278
Seal Beach	Inc. Place	ORANGE	◆ 24,273
South Pasadena	Inc. Place	LOS ANGELES	◆ 24,224
Laguna Beach	Inc. Place	ORANGE	◆ 24,176
San Fernando	Inc. Place	LOS ANGELES	◆ 24,095
Lafayette	Inc. Place	CONTRA COSTA	◆ 23,832
Brawley	Inc. Place	IMPERIAL	◆ 23,622
Selma	Inc. Place	FRESNO	◆ 23,574
Lennox	CDP	LOS ANGELES	◆ 23,480
Lemoore	Inc. Place	KINGS	◆ 23,312
Corcoran	Inc. Place	KINGS	◆ 23,200
West Puente Valley	CDP-Census Area Only	LOS ANGELES	◆ 23,098
Sanger	Inc. Place	FRESNO	◆ 22,924
Bay Point	CDP-Census Area Only	CONTRA COSTA	◆ 22,919
Atwater	Inc. Place	MERCED	◆ 22,660
Port Hueneme	Inc. Place	VENTURA	◆ 22,532
San Lorenzo	CDP	ALAMEDA	◆ 22,404
Valinda	CDP	LOS ANGELES	◆ 22,272
Calabasas	Inc. Place	LOS ANGELES	◆ 22,139
Blythe	Inc. Place	RIVERSIDE	◆ 22,005
El Cerrito	Inc. Place	CONTRA COSTA	◆ 21,780
Rancho San Diego	CDP-Census Area Only	SAN DIEGO	◆ 21,778
West Carson	CDP-Census Area Only	LOS ANGELES	◆ 21,622
Duarte	Inc. Place	LOS ANGELES	◆ 21,590
Ashland	CDP	ALAMEDA	◆ 21,275
South El Monte	Inc. Place	LOS ANGELES	◆ 21,267
La Cañada Flintridge	Inc. Place	LOS ANGELES	◆ 20,849
Barstow	Inc. Place	SAN BERNARDINO	◆ 20,837
South San Jose Hills	CDP-Census Area Only	LOS ANGELES	◆ 20,678
Lincoln	Inc. Place	PLACER	◆ 20,577
Agoura Hills	Inc. Place	LOS ANGELES	◆ 20,499
Millbrae	Inc. Place	SAN MATEO	◆ 20,459
Dinuba	Inc. Place	TULARE	◆ 20,348
Lomita	Inc. Place	LOS ANGELES	Ⓒ 19,975
Hercules	Inc. Place	CONTRA COSTA	◆ 19,830
Winter Gardens	CDP	SAN DIEGO	Ⓒ 19,771
Lakeside	CDP	SAN DIEGO	Ⓒ 19,560
Granite Bay	CDP-Census Area Only	PLACER	Ⓒ 19,388
Bloomington	CDP	SAN BERNARDINO	Ⓒ 19,318
Santa Fe Springs	Inc. Place	LOS ANGELES	◆ 19,185
Riverbank	Inc. Place	STANISLAUS	◆ 19,168
Loma Linda	Inc. Place	SAN BERNARDINO	◆ 19,049
Pinole	Inc. Place	CONTRA COSTA	Ⓒ 19,039
Isla Vista	CDP	SANTA BARBARA	◆ 18,915
Casa de Oro-Mount Helix	CDP-Census Area Only	SAN DIEGO	Ⓒ 18,874
Beaumont	Inc. Place	RIVERSIDE	◆ 18,842
Hermosa Beach	Inc. Place	LOS ANGELES	Ⓒ 18,566
La Crescenta-Montrose	CDP-Census Area Only	LOS ANGELES	Ⓒ 18,532
Yucca Valley	Inc. Place	SAN BERNARDINO	◆ 18,440
El Dorado Hills	CDP-Census Area Only	EL DORADO	Ⓒ 18,016
Marina	Inc. Place	MONTEREY	◆ 17,998
Laguna Woods	Inc. Place	ORANGE	Ⓡ 17,794
Oakdale	Inc. Place	STANISLAUS	O 17,792
Sun City	CDP	RIVERSIDE	Ⓒ 17,773
Mira Loma	CDP	RIVERSIDE	Ⓒ 17,617
Orinda	Inc. Place	CONTRA COSTA	Ⓒ 17,599
Susanville	Inc. Place	LASSEN	Ⓡ 17,428
Foothill Farms	CDP	SACRAMENTO	Ⓒ 17,426
Live Oak	CDP-Census Area Only	SANTA CRUZ	Ⓒ 16,628
Prunedale	CDP	MONTEREY	Ⓡ 16,514
Albany	Inc. Place	ALAMEDA	Ⓒ 16,444
Artesia	Inc. Place	LOS ANGELES	Ⓒ 16,380
Moraga	Inc. Place	CONTRA COSTA	Ⓒ 16,290
Coalinga	Inc. Place	FRESNO	Ⓡ 16,213
Walnut Park	CDP	LOS ANGELES	Ⓒ 16,180
Dixon	Inc. Place	SOLANO	Ⓒ 16,103
Arcata	Inc. Place	HUMBOLDT	◆ 16,053
El Segundo	Inc. Place	LOS ANGELES	◆ 15,914
Arroyo Grande	Inc. Place	SAN LUIS OBISPO	Ⓒ 15,851
Ramona	CDP	SAN DIEGO	Ⓒ 15,691
Alamo	CDP	CONTRA COSTA	Ⓒ 15,626
Pacific Grove	Inc. Place	MONTEREY	Ⓒ 15,522
North Fair Oaks	CDP	SAN MATEO	Ⓒ 15,440
La Palma	Inc. Place	ORANGE	Ⓒ 15,408
Bostonia	CDP	SAN DIEGO	Ⓒ 15,169
Avocado Heights	CDP	LOS ANGELES	Ⓒ 15,148
Vincent	CDP	LOS ANGELES	Ⓒ 15,097
City Terrace	RMC Place	LOS ANGELES	● 15,000
Glen Avon	CDP	RIVERSIDE	Ⓒ 14,853
East Hemet	CDP-Census Area Only	RIVERSIDE	Ⓒ 14,823
Hawaiian Gardens	Inc. Place	LOS ANGELES	Ⓒ 14,779
Avenal	Inc. Place	KINGS	Ⓒ 14,674
Cameron Park	CDP	EL DORADO	Ⓒ 14,549
East San Gabriel	CDP	LOS ANGELES	Ⓒ 14,512
Chowchilla	Inc. Place	MADERA	Ⓡ 14,416
Baywood-Los Osos	CDP-Census Area Only	SAN LUIS OBISPO	Ⓒ 14,351
Rosamond	CDP	KERN	Ⓒ 14,349
Parkway	RMC Place	SACRAMENTO	● 14,280
Carpinteria	Inc. Place	SANTA BARBARA	Ⓒ 14,194
Oroville	Inc. Place	BUTTE	◆ 14,145
Wildomar	CDP	RIVERSIDE	Ⓒ 14,064
Town and Country Village	RMC Place	SACRAMENTO	● 14,000
Ukiah	Inc. Place	MENDOCINO	◆ 13,923

Entries in **UPPERCASE** are counties.
Entries in **bold** have populations of 2,500 or more.
Names in parentheses are alternate names.
Inc. Place — Incorporated Place
RMC Place — Rand McNally Designated Place
CDP — Census Designated Place
MCD — Minor Civil Division

⊡ County Seat
▲ Minor Civil Division
elev. Elevation
Post Office

Hospital
College
■ Principal Business Center
★ Ranally Metro Area (RMA) Abbreviation
z Zip Code(s)

Ⓟ Previous Census Population
Ⓡ Revised Census Population
Ⓐ Annexation Population
● Rand McNally Population Estimate
Ⓒ Final Census Population
Ⓢ Special Census Population
◆ Estimated Population

For additional definitions see Glossary, Volume 1, and Introduction, Volume 2.

Place Name	Place Type	County	Population
Truckee	Inc. Place	NEVADA	© 13,864
Cherryland	CDP-Census Area Only	ALAMEDA	© 13,837
Fillmore	Inc. Place	VENTURA	© 13,643
Mill Valley	Inc. Place	MARIN	© 13,600
McKinleyville	CDP	HUMBOLDT	© 13,599
Alum Rock	CDP	SANTA CLARA	© 13,479
Linda	CDP	YUBA	© 13,474
Palos Verdes Estates	Inc. Place	LOS ANGELES	© 13,340
Stanford	CDP-Census Area Only	SANTA CLARA	© 13,315
Lamont	CDP	KERN	© 13,296
Rancho Mirage	Inc. Place	RIVERSIDE	© 13,249
Red Bluff	Inc. Place	TEHAMA	© 13,147
Alpine	CDP	SAN DIEGO	© 13,143
Clearlake	Inc. Place	LAKE	© 13,142
Marysville	Inc. Place	YUBA	◆ 13,102
Grover Beach	Inc. Place	SAN LUIS OBISPO	© 13,067
Coto de Caza	CDP-Census Area Only	ORANGE	© 13,057
Commerce	Inc. Place	LOS ANGELES	◆ 13,035
La Crescenta	RMC Place	LOS ANGELES	● 13,000
Solana Beach	Inc. Place	SAN DIEGO	© 12,979
Arvin	Inc. Place	KERN	© 12,956
San Marino	Inc. Place	LOS ANGELES	© 12,945
Shafter	Inc. Place	KERN	© 12,736
South Yuba City	CDP-Census Area Only	SUTTER	© 12,651
Greenfield	Inc. Place	MONTEREY	Ⓡ 12,648
Nipomo	CDP	SAN LUIS OBISPO	© 12,626
Malibu	Inc. Place	LOS ANGELES	© 12,575
Salida	CDP	STANISLAUS	© 12,560
Auburn	Inc. Place	PLACER	◆ 12,485
Bonita	CDP	SAN DIEGO	© 12,401
San Anselmo	Inc. Place	MARIN	© 12,378
El Sobrante	CDP	CONTRA COSTA	© 12,260
Larkspur	Inc. Place	MARIN	© 12,014
Casa de Oro	RMC Place	SAN DIEGO	● 12,000
Otterbein	RMC Place	LOS ANGELES	● 12,000
Seguro	RMC Place	KERN	● 12,000
North Auburn	CDP-Census Area Only	PLACER	© 11,847
Half Moon Bay	Inc. Place	SAN MATEO	© 11,842
Grand Terrace	Inc. Place	SAN BERNARDINO	© 11,626
Patterson	Inc. Place	STANISLAUS	© 11,606
Los Alamitos	Inc. Place	ORANGE	© 11,536
Lake Los Angeles	CDP	LOS ANGELES	© 11,523
Scotts Valley	Inc. Place	SANTA CRUZ	© 11,385
Pedley	CDP	RIVERSIDE	© 11,207
King City	Inc. Place	MONTEREY	Ⓡ 11,204
Parlier	Inc. Place	FRESNO	© 11,145
Tehachapi	Inc. Place	KERN	Ⓡ 11,125
Olivehurst	CDP	YUBA	© 11,061
East Tustin	RMC Place	ORANGE	● 11,000
View Park-Windsor Hills	CDP-Census Area Only	LOS ANGELES	© 10,958
Piedmont	Inc. Place	ALAMEDA	© 10,952
Grass Valley	Inc. Place	NEVADA	© 10,922
Foothill Ranch	CDP-Census Area Only	ORANGE	© 10,899
Hillsborough	Inc. Place	SAN MATEO	© 10,825
Clayton	Inc. Place	CONTRA COSTA	© 10,762
Healdsburg	Inc. Place	SONOMA	© 10,722
Tamalpais-Homestead Valley	CDP-Census Area Only	MARIN	© 10,691
Citrus	CDP-Census Area Only	LOS ANGELES	© 10,581
Sierra Madre	Inc. Place	LOS ANGELES	© 10,578
Magalia	CDP	BUTTE	© 10,569
Fortuna	Inc. Place	HUMBOLDT	© 10,497
Valle Vista	CDP	RIVERSIDE	© 10,488
Livingston	Inc. Place	MERCED	© 10,473
Rio Linda	CDP	SACRAMENTO	© 10,466
Lathrop	Inc. Place	SAN JOAQUIN	© 10,445
Morro Bay	Inc. Place	SAN LUIS OBISPO	© 10,350
Rossmoor	CDP	ORANGE	© 10,298
Lindsay	Inc. Place	TULARE	© 10,297
La Riviera	CDP-Census Area Only	SACRAMENTO	© 10,273
Crestline	CDP	SAN BERNARDINO	© 10,218
Ripon	Inc. Place	SAN JOAQUIN	© 10,146
Vineyard	CDP-Census Area Only	SACRAMENTO	© 10,109
Blackhawk-Camino Tassajara	CDP-Census Area Only	CONTRA COSTA	© 10,048
Capitola	Inc. Place	SANTA CRUZ	© 10,033
Montecito	CDP	SANTA BARBARA	© 10,000
Canyon Lake	Inc. Place	RIVERSIDE	© 9,952
Quartz Hill	CDP	LOS ANGELES	© 9,890
McFarland	Inc. Place	KERN	Ⓡ 9,837
American Canyon	Inc. Place	NAPA	© 9,774
Garden Acres	CDP-Census Area Only	SAN JOAQUIN	© 9,747
Placerville	Inc. Place	EL DORADO	© 9,610
East La Mirada	CDP-Census Area Only	LOS ANGELES	© 9,538
Belvedere Gardens	RMC Place	LOS ANGELES	● 9,500
Fairview	CDP-Census Area Only	ALAMEDA	© 9,470
Country Club	CDP-Census Area Only	SAN JOAQUIN	© 9,462
Home Gardens	CDP	RIVERSIDE	© 9,461
Aptos	CDP	SANTA CRUZ	© 9,396
Signal Hill	Inc. Place	LOS ANGELES	© 9,333
East Compton	CDP-Census Area Only	LOS ANGELES	© 9,286
San Diego Country Estates	CDP-Census Area Only	SAN DIEGO	© 9,262
Kingsburg	Inc. Place	FRESNO	© 9,199
Rio del Mar	CDP	SANTA CRUZ	© 9,198
Exeter	Inc. Place	TULARE	© 9,168
Sonoma	Inc. Place	SONOMA	© 9,128
West Athens	CDP-Census Area Only	LOS ANGELES	© 9,101
Corte Madera	Inc. Place	MARIN	© 9,100
Charter Oak	CDP	LOS ANGELES	© 9,027
Anderson	Inc. Place	SHASTA	© 9,022
Del Aire	CDP-Census Area Only	LOS ANGELES	© 9,012
Shasta Lake	Inc. Place	SHASTA	© 9,008
Discovery Bay	CDP	CONTRA COSTA	© 8,981
Lake Arrowhead	CDP	SAN BERNARDINO	© 8,934
Muscoy	CDP	SAN BERNARDINO	© 8,919
Camp Pendleton South	CDP-Census Area Only	SAN DIEGO	© 8,854
Winton	CDP	MERCED	© 8,832
Taft	Inc. Place	KERN	Ⓡ 8,811
Farmersville	Inc. Place	TULARE	© 8,737
Rodeo	CDP	CONTRA COSTA	© 8,717
Oroville East	CDP-Census Area Only	BUTTE	© 8,680
Tiburon	Inc. Place	MARIN	© 8,666
Alondra Park	CDP-Census Area Only	LOS ANGELES	© 8,622
Kerman	Inc. Place	FRESNO	© 8,551
Pismo Beach	Inc. Place	SAN LUIS OBISPO	© 8,551
Rosedale	CDP	KERN	© 8,445
Laguna West-Lakeside	CDP-Census Area Only	SACRAMENTO	© 8,414
Twentynine Palms Base	CDP-Census Area Only	SAN BERNARDINO	© 8,413
California City	Inc. Place	KERN	© 8,385
Westlake Village	Inc. Place	LOS ANGELES	© 8,368
Woodcrest	CDP	RIVERSIDE	© 8,342
Los Nietos	RMC Place	LOS ANGELES	● 8,200
Camp Pendleton North	CDP-Census Area Only	SAN DIEGO	© 8,197
Marina del Rey	CDP-Census Area Only	LOS ANGELES	© 8,176
East Foothills	CDP-Census Area Only	SANTA CLARA	© 8,133
Gold River	CDP-Census Area Only	SACRAMENTO	© 8,023
Delhi	CDP	MERCED	© 8,022
Los Altos Hills	Inc. Place	SANTA CLARA	© 7,902
Mendota	Inc. Place	FRESNO	© 7,890
Ojai	Inc. Place	VENTURA	© 7,862
August	CDP-Census Area Only	SAN JOAQUIN	© 7,808
Mentone	CDP	SAN BERNARDINO	© 7,803
Ellwood	RMC Place	SANTA BARBARA	● 7,800
Sebastopol	Inc. Place	SONOMA	© 7,774
Madera Acres	CDP-Census Area Only	MADERA	© 7,741
Orange Cove	Inc. Place	FRESNO	© 7,722
South Oroville	CDP	BUTTE	© 7,695
Rolling Hills Estates	Inc. Place	LOS ANGELES	© 7,676
South San Gabriel	CDP	LOS ANGELES	© 7,595
Gonzales	Inc. Place	MONTEREY	Ⓡ 7,564
Imperial	Inc. Place	IMPERIAL	© 7,560
Larkfield-Wikiup	CDP-Census Area Only	SONOMA	© 7,479
Golden Hills	CDP-Census Area Only	KERN	© 7,434
Greenacres	RMC Place	KERN	Ⓟ 7,379
Crescent City	Inc. Place	DEL NORTE	Ⓡ 7,347
Sausalito	Inc. Place	MARIN	© 7,330
Interlaken	CDP-Census Area Only	SANTA CRUZ	© 7,328
Valley Center	CDP	SAN DIEGO	© 7,323
Fairfax	Inc. Place	MARIN	© 7,319
Orosi	CDP	TULARE	© 7,318
Bonadelle Ranchos-Madera Ranchos	CDP-Census Area Only	MADERA	© 7,300
Yreka	Inc. Place	SISKIYOU	© 7,290
Calipatria	Inc. Place	IMPERIAL	© 7,289
Oceano	CDP	SAN LUIS OBISPO	© 7,260
Atherton	Inc. Place	SAN MATEO	© 7,194
Mira Monte	CDP	VENTURA	© 7,177
Calimesa	Inc. Place	RIVERSIDE	© 7,139
Ione	Inc. Place	AMADOR	© 7,129
Los Serranos	RMC Place	SAN BERNARDINO	Ⓟ 7,099
Mammoth Lakes	Inc. Place	MONO	© 7,093
Newman	Inc. Place	STANISLAUS	© 7,093
Nadeau	RMC Place	LOS ANGELES	● 7,000
Tamalpais Valley	RMC Place	MARIN	● 7,000
Waterford	Inc. Place	STANISLAUS	© 6,924
Emeryville	Inc. Place	ALAMEDA	© 6,882
Cloverdale	Inc. Place	SONOMA	© 6,831
Fort Bragg	Inc. Place	MENDOCINO	Ⓡ 6,814
Corning	Inc. Place	TEHAMA	© 6,741
East Porterville	CDP-Census Area Only	TULARE	© 6,730
Castroville	CDP	MONTEREY	© 6,724
Boyes Hot Springs	CDP	SONOMA	© 6,665
Woodlake	Inc. Place	TULARE	© 6,651
Earlimart	CDP	TULARE	© 6,583
Ladera Heights	CDP-Census Area Only	LOS ANGELES	© 6,568
Alta Sierra	CDP	NEVADA	© 6,522
Cotati	Inc. Place	SONOMA	© 6,471
Opal Cliffs	CDP	SANTA CRUZ	© 6,458
Mount Helix	RMC Place	SAN DIEGO	● 6,400
Portola Hills	CDP	ORANGE	© 6,391
Roseland	CDP	SONOMA	© 6,369
Lucas Valley-Marinwood	CDP-Census Area Only	MARIN	© 6,357
Kentfield	CDP	MARIN	© 6,351
Huron	Inc. Place	FRESNO	© 6,306
Orland	Inc. Place	GLENN	© 6,281
Loomis	Inc. Place	PLACER	© 6,260
Cambria	CDP	SAN LUIS OBISPO	© 6,232
Bermuda Dunes	CDP-Census Area Only	RIVERSIDE	© 6,229
Live Oak	Inc. Place	SUTTER	© 6,229
Willows	Inc. Place	GLENN	© 6,220
El Rio	CDP	VENTURA	© 6,193
Vandenberg AFB	CDP-Census Area Only	SANTA BARBARA	© 6,151
Winters	Inc. Place	YOLO	© 6,125
West Modesto	CDP-Census Area Only	STANISLAUS	© 6,096
East Pasadena	CDP	LOS ANGELES	© 6,045
Thermalito	CDP	BUTTE	© 6,045
Baywood Park	RMC Place	SAN LUIS OBISPO	● 6,000
Freedom	CDP	SANTA CRUZ	© 6,000
Liberty Acres	RMC Place	LOS ANGELES	● 6,000
Escalon	Inc. Place	SAN JOAQUIN	© 5,963
Villa Park	Inc. Place	ORANGE	Ⓡ 5,952
Saint Helena	Inc. Place	NAPA	© 5,950
Jamul	CDP	SAN DIEGO	© 5,920
Edwards AFB	CDP-Census Area Only	KERN	© 5,909
Cherry Valley	CDP	RIVERSIDE	© 5,891
Vandenberg Village	CDP-Census Area Only	SANTA BARBARA	© 5,802
Big Bear City	CDP	SAN BERNARDINO	© 5,779
Lemoore Station	CDP-Census Area Only	KINGS	© 5,749
Firebaugh	Inc. Place	FRESNO	© 5,743
El Granada	CDP	SAN MATEO	© 5,724
Palermo	CDP	BUTTE	© 5,720
La Habra Heights	Inc. Place	LOS ANGELES	© 5,712
Guadalupe	Inc. Place	SANTA BARBARA	© 5,659
Lakeland Village	CDP	RIVERSIDE	© 5,626
Las Flores	CDP-Census Area Only	ORANGE	© 5,625
Holtville	Inc. Place	IMPERIAL	© 5,612
El Encanto Heights	RMC Place	SANTA BARBARA	● 5,600
Twin Lakes	CDP	SANTA CRUZ	© 5,533
Belvedere	RMC Place	LOS ANGELES	● 5,500
Burkett Gardens	RMC Place	SAN JOAQUIN	● 5,500
View Park	RMC Place	LOS ANGELES	● 5,500
Big Bear Lake	Inc. Place	SAN BERNARDINO	© 5,438
West Compton	CDP-Census Area Only	LOS ANGELES	© 5,435
Colusa	Inc. Place	COLUSA	© 5,402
Mecca	CDP	RIVERSIDE	© 5,402
Gridley	Inc. Place	BUTTE	© 5,382
Woodside	Inc. Place	SAN MATEO	© 5,352
Solvang	Inc. Place	SANTA BARBARA	© 5,332
Tara Hills	CDP	CONTRA COSTA	© 5,332
Strawberry	CDP-Census Area Only	MARIN	© 5,302
Burbank	CDP	SANTA CLARA	© 5,239
Durham	CDP	BUTTE	© 5,220
Calistoga	Inc. Place	NAPA	© 5,190
Shackelford	CDP-Census Area Only	STANISLAUS	© 5,170
Bret Harte	CDP-Census Area Only	STANISLAUS	© 5,161
Waldon	CDP-Census Area Only	CONTRA COSTA	© 5,133
Running Springs	CDP	SAN BERNARDINO	© 5,125
Phoenix Lake-Cedar Ridge	CDP-Census Area Only	TUOLUMNE	© 5,123
Thousand Palms	CDP	RIVERSIDE	© 5,120
Beale AFB	CDP-Census Area Only	YUBA	© 5,115
Mayflower Village	CDP-Census Area Only	LOS ANGELES	© 5,081
Soquel	CDP	SANTA CRUZ	© 5,081
Willits	Inc. Place	MENDOCINO	© 5,073
Bayview-Montalvin	CDP-Census Area Only	CONTRA COSTA	© 5,004
Crafton	RMC Place	SAN BERNARDINO	● 5,000
Los Osos	RMC Place	SAN LUIS OBISPO	● 5,000
Madera Highlands	RMC Place	MADERA	● 5,000
Windsor Hills	RMC Place	LOS ANGELES	● 5,000

County Business Data

County	FIPS Code	County Seat	Land Area (Sq. Mi.)	Census Population			Wholesale Trade		Manufacturing, 2002			
				4/1/2000	4/1/1990	% Change 1990-2000	Sales, 2002 ($1,000)	% Change 1997-2002	Establish-ments	Total Employees	Value Added ($1,000)	Ranally Mfg. Units
Alameda	001	Oakland	738	1,443,741	1,279,182	12.9	41,553,292	-13.1	2,355	94,682	14,628,752	7,740
Alpine	003	Markleeville	739	1,208	1,113	8.5	(d)	(d)	...	(d)	(d)	...
Amador	005	Jackson	593	35,100	30,039	16.8	(d)	(d)	52	557	47,394	25
Butte	007	Oroville	1,639	203,171	182,120	11.6	632,831	-0.8	235	4,427	425,336	225
Calaveras	009	San Andreas	1,020	40,554	31,998	26.7	17,347	(d)	...	(d)	(d)	...
Colusa	011	Colusa	1,151	18,804	16,275	15.5	158,035	3.8	28	828	87,646	46
Contra Costa	013	Martinez	720	948,816	803,732	18.1	18,132,332	21.1	677	20,685	3,971,347	2,101
Del Norte	015	Crescent City	1,008	27,507	23,460	17.3	(d)	(d)	...	(d)	(d)	...
El Dorado	017	Placerville	1,711	156,299	125,995	24.1	(d)	(d)	181	4,224	627,790	332
Fresno	019	Fresno	5,963	799,407	667,490	19.8	(d)	(d)	701	26,639	2,530,737	1,339
Glenn	021	Willows	1,315	26,453	24,798	6.7	213,445	69.6	30	847	114,752	61
Humboldt	023	Eureka	3,572	126,518	119,118	6.2	359,405	-27.2	166	3,636	266,054	141
Imperial	025	El Centro	4,175	142,361	109,303	30.2	945,725	40.4	60	1,811	219,088	116
Inyo	027	Independence	10,203	17,945	18,281	-1.8	(d)	(d)	...	(d)	(d)	...
Kern	029	Bakersfield	8,141	661,645	543,477	21.7	5,872,704	36.1	398	10,968	1,656,177	876
Kings	031	Hanford	1,391	129,461	101,469	27.6	458,982	11.5	79	3,857	689,495	365
Lake	033	Lakeport	1,258	58,309	50,631	15.2	(d)	(d)	...	(d)	(d)	...
Lassen	035	Susanville	4,557	33,828	27,598	22.6	(d)	(d)	...	(d)	(d)	...
Los Angeles	037	Los Angeles	4,061	9,519,338	8,863,164	7.4	198,703,926	12.1	17,205	530,939	55,525,812	29,377
Madera	039	Madera	2,136	123,109	88,090	39.8	(d)	(d)	103	4,414	589,761	312
Marin	041	San Rafael	520	247,289	230,096	7.5	2,960,895	22.6	290	3,428	328,477	174
Mariposa	043	Mariposa	1,451	17,130	14,302	19.8	(d)	(d)	...	(d)	(d)	...
Mendocino	045	Ukiah	3,509	86,265	80,345	7.4	397,135	28.6	152	3,314	311,764	165
Merced	047	Merced	1,929	210,554	178,403	18.0	(d)	(d)	127	8,856	941,111	498
Modoc	049	Alturas	3,944	9,449	9,678	-2.4	(d)	(d)	...	(d)	(d)	...
Mono	051	Bridgeport	3,044	12,853	9,956	29.1	(d)	(d)	...	(d)	(d)	...
Monterey	053	Salinas	3,322	401,762	355,660	13.0	6,571,703	38.4	307	8,431	1,037,074	549
Napa	055	Napa	754	124,279	110,765	12.2	1,208,037	126.6	381	10,910	1,994,584	1,055
Nevada	057	Nevada City	958	92,033	78,510	17.2	(d)	(d)	168	1,901	255,772	135
Orange	059	Santa Ana	789	2,846,289	2,410,556	18.1	109,881,218	16.4	5,621	198,169	21,686,041	11,473
Placer	061	Auburn	1,404	248,399	172,796	43.8	2,683,421	49.7	299	11,316	1,497,416	792
Plumas	063	Quincy	2,554	20,824	19,739	5.5	(d)	(d)	31	529	40,194	21
Riverside	065	Riverside	7,207	1,545,387	1,170,413	32.0	14,081,468	109.7	1,627	54,425	5,989,543	3,169
Sacramento	067	Sacramento	966	1,223,499	1,041,219	17.5	12,852,250	50.2	975	28,979	3,443,846	1,822
San Benito	069	Hollister	1,389	53,234	36,697	45.1	(d)	(d)	77	2,607	248,787	132
San Bernardino	071	San Bernardino	20,052	1,709,434	1,418,380	20.5	21,191,081	48.7	2,177	65,565	7,234,767	3,828
San Diego	073	San Diego	4,200	2,813,833	2,498,016	12.6	31,314,549	18.0	3,473	117,125	14,187,111	7,506
San Francisco	075	San Francisco	47	776,733	723,959	7.3	8,896,586	-27.2	932	15,566	1,818,070	962
San Joaquin	077	Stockton	1,399	563,598	480,628	17.3	8,772,773	14.7	609	23,274	3,515,538	1,860
San Luis Obispo	079	San Luis Obispo	3,304	246,681	217,162	13.6	769,246	37.0	383	6,867	614,992	325
San Mateo	081	Redwood City	449	707,161	649,623	8.9	16,797,756	14.6	858	29,309	5,814,332	3,076
Santa Barbara	083	Santa Barbara	2,737	399,347	369,608	8.0	2,421,920	48.0	532	15,275	1,773,463	938
Santa Clara	085	San Jose	1,291	1,682,585	1,497,577	12.4	(d)	(d)	2,981	170,990	26,640,059	14,094
Santa Cruz	087	Santa Cruz	445	255,602	229,734	11.3	2,293,668	48.8	377	6,694	617,269	327
Shasta	089	Redding	3,785	163,256	147,036	11.0	562,514	-0.7	178	3,342	262,551	139
Sierra	091	Downieville	953	3,555	3,318	7.1	(d)	(d)	...	(d)	(d)	...
Siskiyou	093	Yreka	6,287	44,301	43,531	1.8	(d)	(d)	40	760	80,566	43
Solano	095	Fairfield	829	394,542	340,421	15.9	2,588,902	19.3	303	10,169	1,779,527	941
Sonoma	097	Santa Rosa	1,576	458,614	388,222	18.1	3,474,829	13.2	874	26,678	3,437,229	1,819
Stanislaus	099	Modesto	1,494	446,997	370,522	20.6	2,871,200	26.8	488	24,469	3,284,159	1,738
Sutter	101	Yuba City	603	78,930	64,415	22.5	709,250	(d)	76	1,815	394,495	209
Tehama	103	Red Bluff	2,951	56,039	49,625	12.9	(d)	(d)	56	2,462	180,467	95
Trinity	105	Weaverville	3,179	13,022	13,063	-0.3	(d)	(d)	...	(d)	(d)	...
Tulare	107	Visalia	4,824	368,021	311,921	18.0	2,522,648	-0.2	293	11,340	1,262,113	668
Tuolumne	109	Sonora	2,235	54,501	48,456	12.5	(d)	(d)	81	1,161	105,025	56
Ventura	111	Ventura	1,845	753,197	669,016	12.6	56,451,957	442.7	1,051	33,124	4,525,268	2,394
Yolo	113	Woodland	1,013	168,660	141,092	19.5	6,356,977	27.1	176	6,005	627,400	332
Yuba	115	Marysville	631	60,219	58,228	3.4	120,455	(d)	46	1,332	126,753	67
The State			**155,959**	**33,871,648**	**29,760,021**	**13.8**	**655,954,708**	**19.5**	**48,478**	**1,616,504**	**197,574,490**	**104,530**

(d) Data not available. Corresponding percentages or Ranally Manufacturing Units are estimates. ... Represents 0 or amount too minimal to be reported.

Entries in **UPPERCASE** are counties.
Entries in **bold** have populations of 2,500 or more.
Names in parentheses are alternate names.
Inc. Place — Incorporated Place
RMC Place — Rand McNally Designated Place
CDP — Census Designated Place
MCD — Minor Civil Division

⊡ County Seat
▲ Minor Civil Division
elev. Elevation
P Post Office

H Hospital
C College
■ Principal Business Center
★ Ranally Metro Area (RMA) Abbreviation
z Zip Code(s)

Ⓟ Previous Census Population
Ⓡ Revised Census Population
Ⓐ Annexation Population
● Rand McNally Population Estimate
© Final Census Population
Ⓢ Special Census Population
◆ Estimated Population

For additional definitions see Glossary, Volume 1, and Introduction, Volume 2.

Index of Places and Counties

A

Aberdeen; RMC Place; INYO; *153 SB-11; elev. 3,837ft./1,170m.; mail Independence Z 93526; ● 100
Academy; RMC Place; FRESNO; *152 SB-8; mail Clovis Z 93611
Acampo; RMC Place; SAN JOAQUIN; 150 NL-7; elev. 52ft./16m.; 🅿; ★ STOC; Z 95220; ● 700
Actis; RMC Place; KERN; *153 SG-11; elev. 2,560ft./780m.; mail Mojave Z 93501; ● 200
Acton; CDP; LOS ANGELES; 153 SI-11; 🅿; Z 93510; Ⓟ 1,471; Ⓒ 2,390
Adams; RMC Place; LAKE; *150 NJ-4; mail Cobb Z 95426; rural
Adelaida; RMC Place; SAN LUIS OBISPO; *152 SF-5; mail Paso Robles Z 93446; rural
Adelanto; Inc. Place; SAN BERNARDINO; 153 SH-13; elev. 75ft./23m.; 🅿; ★ HESP-; Z 92301; Ⓟ 6,791; Ⓒ 18,130; ◆ 26,419
Adin; RMC Place; MODOC; 150 NC-8; elev. 4,205ft./1,282m.; 🅿; Z 96006; ● 250
Adobe Corners; RMC Place; SAN BERNARDINO; *153 SI-13; mail Victorville Z 92392; pop. incl. with Victorville (Inc. Place)
Aerial Acres; RMC Place; KERN; *153 SG-12; 🅿; Z 93523; pop. incl. with California City (Inc. Place)
Aetna Springs; RMC Place; NAPA; 150 NJ-5; mail Pope Valley Z 94567; ● 5
Afton; RMC Place; GLENN; *150 NH-6; mail Butte City Z 95920; ● 30
Ager; RMC Place; SISKIYOU; *150 NA-5; elev. 2,376ft./724m.; mail Montague Z 96064; rural
Agnew; RMC Place; SANTA CLARA; *150 NN-6; elev. 22ft./7m.; ★ SF-O-; mail Santa Clara Z 95054, Z 95056; pop. incl. with Santa Clara (Inc. Place)
Agoura; RMC Place; LOS ANGELES; *152 SJ-10; 🅿; ★ L.A.; Z 91301, Z 91376; pop. incl. with Agoura Hills (Inc. Place)
Agoura Hills; Inc. Place; LOS ANGELES; 152 SJ-10; 🅿; ★ OXN-; Z 91301, Z 91376-77; Ⓟ 20,390; Ⓒ 20,537; ◆ 20,499
Agua Caliente; RMC Place; SONOMA; *150 NK-5; elev. 155ft./47m.; mail Sonoma Z 95476; ● 1,200
Agua Caliente Reservation; Indian Reservation; RIVERSIDE; ★ PSPR-; mail Palm Springs Z 92262; Ⓟ 13,743; Ⓒ 21,358
Agua Dulce; RMC Place; LOS ANGELES; 154 N-5; 🅿; Z 91350, Z 91390; ● 1,050
Aguanga; RMC Place; RIVERSIDE; 153 SL-14; elev. 1,940ft./591m.; 🅿; Z 92536; ● 200
Ahwahnee; RMC Place; MADERA; 151 NN-11; elev. 2,321ft./707m.; 🅿; Z 93601; ● 650
Ainsworth Corner; RMC Place; SISKIYOU; mail Tulelake Z 96134; ● 100
Alabama Hills; RMC Place; INYO; *153 SC-11; elev. 4,620ft./1,408m.; mail Lone Pine Z 93545; ● 300
Alameda; Inc. Place; ALAMEDA; 150 NM-5; elev. 30ft./9m.; 🅿 🅷 ■; ★ SF-O-; Z 94501-02; Ⓟ 76,459; Ⓒ 72,259; ◆ 72,246
Alameda; RMC Place; LOS ANGELES; ★ L.A.; mail Los Angeles Z 90012-13; pop. incl. with Los Angeles (Inc. Place)
ALAMEDA; 150 NM-7; Ⓟ 1,279,182; Ⓒ 1,443,741; ◆ 1,477,082
Alamo; CDP; CONTRA COSTA; 151 NE-18; 🅿; ★ SF-O-; Z 94507; Ⓟ 12,277; Ⓒ 15,626
Alamo Oaks; RMC Place; CONTRA COSTA; 151 NE-18; ★ SF-O-; mail Danville Z 94526
Alamorio; RMC Place; IMPERIAL; *153 SM-17; mail Brawley Z 92227; ● 100
Albany; Inc. Place; ALAMEDA; 151 NE-15; 🅿; ★ SF-O-; Z 94706-07, Z 94710; Ⓟ 16,327; Ⓒ 16,444
Alberhill; RMC Place; RIVERSIDE; 155 J-17; mail Lake Elsinore Z 92530; ● 200
Albion; RMC Place; MENDOCINO; 150 NI-2; 🅿; Z 95410; ● 300
Albrae; RMC Place; ALAMEDA; *150 NN-6; elev. 7ft./2m.; ★ SF-O-; mail Fremont Z 94538; pop. incl. with Fremont (Inc. Place)
Alcatraz; RMC Place; SAN FRANCISCO; ★ SF-O-; mail San Francisco Z 94123; pop. incl. with San Francisco (Inc. Place)
Alderbrook Tract; RMC Place; SANTA CLARA; ★ SF-O-; mail Cupertino Z 95014; pop. incl. with Cupertino (Inc. Place)
Aldercroft Heights; RMC Place; SANTA CLARA; *152 SA-2; ★ SF-O-; mail Los Gatos Z 95033; ● 370
Alderpoint; RMC Place; HUMBOLDT; 150 NF-3; 🅿; Z 95511; ● 200
Alder Springs; RMC Place; FRESNO; *152 SB-8; mail Auberry Z 93602; ● 140
Alessandro; RMC Place; RIVERSIDE; *153 SJ-13; ★ RIV-; mail Riverside Z 92508
Alexander Valley; RMC Place; SONOMA; *150 NJ-4; elev. 183ft./56m.; ★ S.ROS; mail Geyserville Z 95441, Healdsburg Z 95448; rural
Alhambra; Inc. Place; LOS ANGELES; 153 SJ-11; elev. 483ft./147m.; 🅿 🅷 🅲 632 ■; ★ L.A.; Z 91801-04, Z 91896, Z 91899; Ⓟ 82,106; Ⓒ 85,804; ◆ 86,392
Alhambra Valley; RMC Place; CONTRA COSTA; *150 NL-6; elev. 300ft./91m.; ★ SF-O-; mail Martinez Z 94553; ● 400
Alisal; RMC Place; MONTEREY; ★ SLNS; mail Salinas Z 93905, Z 93915; pop. incl. with Salinas (Inc. Place)
Aliso Viejo; Inc. Place; ORANGE; 155 L-13; 🅿 🅲 400; ★ L.A.; Z 92653, Z 92656, Z 92698; incorporated July 1, 2001; not reported in 2000 Census; ● 40,300; ◆ 41,582
Aliso Viejo; CDP-Census Area Only; ORANGE; 155 L-13; elev. 300ft./91m.; 🅿; ★ L.A.; Z 92653, Z 92656, Z 92698; Ⓟ 7,612; Ⓒ 40,166; Ⓡ 40,118
Alleghany; RMC Place; SIERRA; 150 NH-8; elev. 4,419ft./1,347m.; 🅿; Z 95910; ● 150
Allendale; RMC Place; SOLANO; 150 NK-6; elev. 118ft./36m.; ★ FRFL-; mail Vacaville Z 95688; ● 1,000
Allensworth; RMC Place; TULARE; 152 SE-8; mail Earlimart Z 93219; ● 200
Alliance; RMC Place; HUMBOLDT; *150 ND-2; ★ EUR-; mail Arcata Z 95521; pop. incl. with Arcata (Inc. Place)
Allied Gardens; RMC Place; SAN DIEGO; *153 SM-14; ★ SDGO; mail San Diego Z 92120; pop. incl. with San Diego (Inc. Place)
Almaden; SANTA CLARA; see New Almaden (RMC Place)
Almaden Valley; RMC Place; SANTA CLARA; ★ SF-O-; mail San Jose Z 95120, Z 95160; pop. incl. with San Jose (Inc. Place)
Almanor; CDP; PLUMAS; 150 NF-8; elev. 4,519ft./1,377m.; mail Chester Z 96020, Greenville Z 95947, Westwood Z 96137; Ⓒ 0
Almonte; RMC Place; MARIN; 151 NE-12; ★ SF-O-; mail Mill Valley Z 94941; pop. incl. with Mill Valley (Inc. Place)
Alondra Park; CDP-Census Area Only; LOS ANGELES; *153 SJ-11; ★ L.A.; mail Gardena Z 90249; Ⓟ 12,215; Ⓒ 8,622
Alpaugh; CDP; TULARE; 152 SE-8; 🅿; Z 93201; Ⓒ 761
Alpine; CDP; SAN DIEGO; 153 SM-14; 🅿; ★ SDGO; Z 91901, Z 91903; Ⓟ 9,695; Ⓒ 13,143
ALPINE; 151 NJ-11; Ⓟ 1,113; Ⓒ 1,208; ◆ 1,100
Alpine Forest; RMC Place; KERN; *152 SG-10; elev. 5,000ft./1,524m.; mail Tehachapi Z 93561; ● 300
Alpine Heights; RMC Place; SAN DIEGO; *153 SM-14; elev. 1,873ft./571m.; ★ SDGO; mail Alpine Z 91901; ● 1,300
Alpine Meadows; RMC Place; PLACER; *150 NI-10; elev. 6,600ft./2,012m.; 🅿; Z 96145-46; ● 500
Alpine Village; CDP-Census Area Only; ALPINE; *151 NJ-11; Ⓒ 136
Alpine Village; RMC Place; RIVERSIDE; *153 SK-15; elev. 4,000ft./1,219m.; mail Palm Springs Z 92262; ● 150
Alpine Village; RMC Place; TULARE; *152 SD-10; elev. 6,000ft./1,829m.; mail Springville Z 93265; ● 30
Alta; RMC Place; PLACER; *150 NI-8; elev. 3,590ft./1,094m.; 🅿; Z 95701, Z 95715; ● 650
Altadena; CDP; LOS ANGELES; 153 SJ-11; elev. 1,342ft./409m.; 🅿; ★ L.A.; Z 91001, Z 91003; Ⓟ 42,658; Ⓒ 42,610; ◆ 43,576
Alta Heights; RMC Place; NAPA; ★ NAPA; mail Napa Z 94559; pop. incl. with Napa (Inc. Place)
Alta Hill; RMC Place; NEVADA; 150 NI-8; mail Grass Valley Z 95945; ● 850
Al Tahoe; RMC Place; EL DORADO; *150 NJ-10; mail South Lake Tahoe Z 96151; pop. incl. with South Lake Tahoe (Inc. Place)
Alta Loma; RMC Place; SAN BERNARDINO; *153 SJ-12; elev. 1,400ft./427m.; 🅿; ★ L.A.; Z 91701, Z 91737; pop. incl. with Rancho Cucamonga (Inc. Place)
Alta Sierra; RMC Place; KERN; 152 SE-10; elev. 5,678ft./1,731m.; mail Wofford Heights Z 93285; ● 70
Alta Sierra; CDP; NEVADA; *150 NI-8; ★ SAC; mail Grass Valley Z 95945, Z 95949; Ⓟ 5,709; Ⓒ 6,522
Altaville; RMC Place; CALAVERAS; *150 NL-9; 🅿; Z 95221; pop. incl. with Angels Camp (Inc. Place)
Alta Vista; RMC Place; INYO; *151 NN-13; elev. 4,540ft./1,384m.; mail Bishop Z 93514; ● 150
Alto; RMC Place; MARIN; *150 NL-5; elev. 27ft./8m.; ★ SF-O-; mail Mill Valley Z 94941; pop. incl. with Mill Valley (Inc. Place)
Alton; RMC Place; HUMBOLDT; *150 NE-1; ★ EUR-; mail Fortuna Z 95540; ● 400
Alturas; Inc. Place; ⊡ MODOC; 150 NC-9; elev. 4,366ft./1,331m.; 🅿 🅷; Z 96101; Ⓟ 3,231; Ⓒ 2,892
Alturas Rancheria; Indian Reservation; MODOC; mail Alturas Z 96101; Ⓒ 2
Alum Rock; CDP; SANTA CLARA; *150 NN-6; ★ SF-O-; Ⓒ 13,479
Alvarado; RMC Place; ALAMEDA; ★ SF-O-; mail Union City Z 94587; pop. incl. with Union City (Inc. Place)
Alviso; RMC Place; SANTA CLARA; *150 NN-6; elev. 4ft./1m.; 🅿; ★ SF-O-; Z 95002; pop. incl. with San Jose (Inc. Place)
AMADOR; 150 NK-10; Ⓟ 30,039; Ⓒ 35,100; ◆ 39,489
Amador City; Inc. Place; AMADOR; 150 NK-8; 🅿; Z 95601; Ⓟ 196; Ⓒ 196
Amarillo Beach; RMC Place; LOS ANGELES; *152 SJ-10; elev. 100ft./30m.; ★ L.A.; mail Malibu Z 90265; pop. incl. with Malibu (Inc. Place)
Ambassador; RMC Place; LOS ANGELES; ★ L.A.; mail Los Angeles Z 90005; pop. incl. with Los Angeles (Inc. Place)
Ambler Park; RMC Place; MONTEREY; *152 SC-3; ★ SLNS; mail Salinas Z 93901; ● 600
Amboy; RMC Place; SAN BERNARDINO; 153 SH-17; elev. 639ft./195m.; 🅿; Z 92304
American Canyon; Inc. Place; NAPA; *150 NL-5; 🅿; ★ SF-O-; Z 94503, Z 94589; Ⓟ 7,734; Ⓒ 9,774
American House; RMC Place; PLUMAS; *150 NH-8; mail Strawberry Valley Z 95981; rural
Amesti; CDP-Census Area Only; SANTA CRUZ; *152 SB-3; ★ WATS; Ⓒ 2,436
Anaheim; Inc. Place; ORANGE; 153 SK-12; elev. 160ft./49m.; 🅿 🅷 🅲 1,841 ■; ★ L.A.; Z 92801-09, Z 92812, Z 92814-17, Z 92825, Z 92850, Z 92899 & mail Atwood Z 92811, Brea Z 92821-23; Ⓟ 266,406; Ⓒ 328,014; ◆ 345,381
Anaheim Hills; RMC Place; ORANGE; ★ L.A.; mail Anaheim Z 92807-09, Z 92817; pop. incl. with Anaheim (Inc. Place)
Ana Verde; RMC Place; LOS ANGELES; *153 SI-11; elev. 3,000ft./914m.; ★ L.A.; mail Palmdale Z 93551
Anchor Bay (Anchor Bay Settlement); RMC Place; MENDOCINO; 150 NJ-2; mail Gualala Z 95445; ● 1,000
Anchor Bay Settlement; MENDOCINO; see Anchor Bay (RMC Place)
Anderson; Inc. Place; SHASTA; 150 NE-5; elev. 430ft./131m.; 🅿; ★ REDD; Z 96007; Ⓟ 8,299; Ⓒ 9,022
Anderson Springs; RMC Place; LAKE; *150 NJ-4; elev. 1,400ft./427m.; mail Middletown Z 95461; ● 200
Andrew Jackson; RMC Place; SAN DIEGO; ★ SDGO; mail San Diego Z 92115, Z 92175, Z 92195; pop. incl. with San Diego (Inc. Place)
Angels; CALAVERAS; see Angels Camp (Inc. Place)
Angels Camp (Angels, Angels City); Inc. Place; CALAVERAS; 150 NL-9; 🅿; Z 95221-22; Ⓟ 2,409; Ⓒ 3,004
Angels City; CALAVERAS; see Angels Camp (Inc. Place)
Angelus Oaks (Camp Angelus); RMC Place; SAN BERNARDINO; *153 SJ-14; 🅿; Z 92305; ● 200
Angiola; RMC Place; TULARE; *152 SE-8; mail Corcoran Z 93212; rural
Angwin (Pacific Union College); CDP; NAPA; 150 NK-5; 🅿 🅲 1,416; Z 94508, Z 94576; Ⓟ 3,503; Ⓒ 3,148
Annapolis; RMC Place; SONOMA; 150 NJ-3; 🅿; Z 95412
Annex Three; RMC Place; LOS ANGELES; ★ L.A.; mail Van Nuys Z 91405-06; pop. incl. with Los Angeles (Inc. Place)
Antelope; RMC Place; SACRAMENTO; 149 B-7; 🅿; ★ SAC; Z 95843; ● 680
Antelope Acres; RMC Place; LOS ANGELES; *153 SH-11; elev. 2,424ft./739m.; ★ L.A.; mail Lancaster Z 93536; ● 1,400
Antioch; Inc. Place; CONTRA COSTA; 150 NL-6; elev. 25ft./8m.; 🅿 🅷 ■; ★ SF-O-; Z 94509, Z 94531; Ⓟ 62,195; Ⓒ 90,532; ◆ 104,674
Antonio; RMC Place; SANTA BARBARA; mail Lompoc Z 93437
Anza; RMC Place; RIVERSIDE; 153 SK-14; elev. 3,918ft./1,194m.; 🅿; Z 92539; ● 700
Applegate; RMC Place; PLACER; 150 NI-8; 🅿; ★ SAC; Z 95703; ● 970
Apple Valley; Inc. Place; SAN BERNARDINO; 153 SI-13; elev. 3,000ft./914m.; 🅿 🅷; ★ HESP-; Z 92307-08; Ⓟ 46,079; Ⓒ 54,239; ◆ 63,249
Aptos; CDP; SANTA CRUZ; 152 SB-3; elev. 100ft./30m.; 🅿; ★ S.CRZ; Z 95001, Z 95003; Ⓟ 9,061; Ⓒ 9,396
Aptos Hills-Larkin Valley; CDP-Census Area Only; SANTA CRUZ; *152 SB-3; elev. 400ft./122m.; ★ WATS; mail Aptos Z 95003; Ⓟ 2,205; Ⓒ 2,361
Arastraville; RMC Place; TUOLUMNE; mail Tuolumne Z 95379; ● 450
Arbolada; RMC Place; VENTURA; *152 SI-9; ★ OXN-; mail Ojai Z 93023
Arbuckle; CDP; COLUSA; 150 NI-6; 🅿; Z 95912; Ⓟ 1,912; Ⓒ 2,332
Arbuckle Tract; SAN LUIS OBISPO; see San Simeon Acres (RMC Place)
Arcade; RMC Place; LOS ANGELES; ★ L.A.; mail Los Angeles Z 90052; pop. incl. with Los Angeles (Inc. Place)
Arcade; RMC Place; SACRAMENTO; 149 C-7; elev. 65ft./20m.; ★ SAC; mail Sacramento Z 95821; ● 42,000
Arcadia; Inc. Place; LOS ANGELES; 154 D-9; elev. 485ft./148m.; 🅿 🅷 ■; ★ L.A.; Z 91006-07, Z 91066, Z 91077; Ⓟ 48,290; Ⓒ 53,054; ◆ 57,309
Arcata; Inc. Place; HUMBOLDT; 150 ND-2; elev. 33ft./10m.; 🅿 🅷 🅲 7,435; ★ EUR-; Z 95518, Z 95521 & mail McKinleyville Z 95519; Ⓟ 15,197; Ⓒ 16,651; ◆ 16,053
Arch Beach Heights; RMC Place; ORANGE; ★ L.A.; mail Laguna Beach Z 92651; pop. incl. with Laguna Beach (Inc. Place)
Arden; SACRAMENTO; see Arden Town (RMC Place)
Arden-Arcade; CDP-Census Area Only; SACRAMENTO; *150 NK-7; ★ SAC; mail Sacramento Z 95821; Ⓟ 92,040; Ⓒ 96,025; ◆ 104,121
Arden Town (Arden); RMC Place; SACRAMENTO; 149 D-7; elev. 60ft./18m.; ★ SAC; mail Sacramento Z 95825, Z 95865-66; ● 55,000
Ardmore; RMC Place; LOS ANGELES; ★ L.A.; mail South Gate Z 90280; pop. incl. with South Gate (Inc. Place)
Arena; RMC Place; MERCED; *150 NN-9; elev. 141ft./43m.; ★ MRCD; mail Atwater Z 95301, Livingston Z 95334; rural
Argus; RMC Place; SAN BERNARDINO; 153 SE-13; elev. 1,648ft./502m.; 🅿; Z 93562; ● 300
Arlanza Village; RMC Place; RIVERSIDE; ★ RIV-; mail Riverside Z 92505; pop. incl. with Riverside (Inc. Place)
Arleta; RMC Place; LOS ANGELES; 🅿; ★ L.A.; Z 91331, Z 91334; pop. incl. with Los Angeles (Inc. Place)
Arlington; RMC Place; RIVERSIDE; *153 SJ-13; elev. 788ft./240m.; ★ RIV-; mail Riverside Z 92503, Z 92513; pop. incl. with Riverside (Inc. Place)
Arlynda Corners; RMC Place; HUMBOLDT; *150 NE-1; elev. 20ft./6m.; mail Ferndale Z 95536; rural
Armistead; RMC Place; KERN; *153 SF-11; elev. 3,063ft./934m.; mail Inyokern Z 93527; rural
Armona; CDP; KINGS; 152 SD-7; elev. 236ft./72m.; 🅿; Z 93202; Ⓟ 3,122; Ⓒ 3,239
Arnold; CDP; CALAVERAS; 150 NL-9; 🅿; Z 95223; Ⓟ 3,788; Ⓒ 4,218
Arnold Heights; RMC Place; RIVERSIDE; ★ RIV-; mail March Air Reserve Base Z 92518, Riverside Z 92508
Aromas; CDP; MONTEREY, SAN BENITO; *152 SB-3; 🅿; ★ WATS; Z 95004; Ⓟ 2,275; Ⓒ 2,797
Arrowbear Lake; RMC Place; SAN BERNARDINO; 155 C-20; elev. 6,087ft./1,855m.; 🅿; ★ RIV-; Z 92382; ● 1,000
Arrowhead Highlands; RMC Place; SAN BERNARDINO; *153 SI-13; ★ RIV-; mail Crestline Z 92325; ● 1,900
Arroyo Grande; Inc. Place; SAN LUIS OBISPO; 152 SG-5; elev. 120ft./37m.; 🅿 🅷; Z 93420-21; Ⓟ 14,378; Ⓒ 15,851
Arroyo Vista; RMC Place; ALAMEDA; ★ SF-O-; mail Pleasanton Z 94566; pop. incl. with Dublin (Inc. Place)
Artesia; Inc. Place; LOS ANGELES; 154 H-9; elev. 50ft./15m.; 🅿 🅷; ★ L.A.; Z 90701-03; Ⓟ 15,464; Ⓒ 16,380
Artois; RMC Place; GLENN; 150 NH-6; 🅿; Z 95913; ● 220
Arvin; Inc. Place; KERN; 152 SG-9; elev. 445ft./136m.; 🅿; Z 93203; Ⓟ 9,286; Ⓒ 12,956
Ashland; CDP; ALAMEDA; 151 NG-17; ★ SF-O-; mail Hayward Z 94541, San Leandro Z 94577; Ⓟ 16,590; Ⓒ 20,793; ◆ 21,275
Asian Village; RMC Place; ORANGE; ★ L.A.; mail Westminster Z 92683; pop. incl. with Westminster (Inc. Place)
Asilomar; RMC Place; MONTEREY; ★ MTRY-; mail Pacific Grove Z 93950; pop. incl. with Pacific Grove (Inc. Place)
Aspendell; RMC Place; INYO; *152 SA-10; elev. 8,400ft./2,560m.; mail Bishop Z 93514; ● 100
Asti; RMC Place; SONOMA; *150 NJ-4; mail Cloverdale Z 95425; rural
Atascadero; Inc. Place; SAN LUIS OBISPO; 152 SF-5; elev. 855ft./261m.; 🅿 🅷; Z 93422-23; Ⓟ 23,138; Ⓒ 26,411; ◆ 30,866
Athens; RMC Place; LOS ANGELES; *153 SJ-11; ★ L.A.; mail Los Angeles Z 90047; ● 600
Atherton; Inc. Place; SAN MATEO; 151 NK-16; elev. 50ft./15m.; 🅿 🅲 778; ★ SF-O-; Z 94027; Ⓟ 7,163; Ⓒ 7,194
Athlone; RMC Place; MERCED; *152 SA-6; mail Le Grand Z 95333; rural
Atlanta; RMC Place; SAN JOAQUIN; *150 NM-8; mail Ripon Z 95366; rural
Atwater; Inc. Place; MERCED; 150 NN-9; elev. 150ft./46m.; 🅿 🅷; ★ MRCD; Z 95301; Ⓟ 22,282; Ⓒ 23,113; ◆ 22,660
Atwood; RMC Place; ORANGE; *153 SK-12; elev. 249ft./76m.; 🅿; ★ L.A.; Z 92811; pop. incl. with Placentia (Inc. Place)
Auberry; CDP; FRESNO; 152 SB-8; 🅿; Z 93602; Ⓟ 1,866; Ⓒ 2,053
Auburn; Inc. Place; ⊡ PLACER; 150 NJ-8; elev. 1,297ft./395m.; 🅿 🅷 ■; ★ SAC; Z 95602-04; Ⓟ 10,592; Ⓒ 12,462; ◆ 12,485
August; CDP-Census Area Only; SAN JOAQUIN; *150 NL-7; ★ STOC; mail Stockton Z 95201; Ⓟ 6,376; Ⓒ 7,808
Augustine Reservation; Indian Reservation; RIVERSIDE; Ⓒ 0
Aukum (Mount Aukum); RMC Place; EL DORADO; *150 NK-9; mail Mount Aukum Z 95656, River Pines Z 95675
Aurora; RMC Place; STANISLAUS; *150 NM-8; elev. 85ft./26m.; ★ MOD; pop. incl. with Modesto (Inc. Place)
Avalon; Inc. Place; LOS ANGELES; 153 SL-11; 🅿 🅷; Z 90704; Ⓟ 2,918; Ⓒ 3,127
Avalon Village; RMC Place; LOS ANGELES; *153 SK-11; elev. 36ft./11m.; ★ L.A.; mail Carson Z 90745; pop. incl. with Carson (Inc. Place)
Avenal; Inc. Place; KINGS; 152 SE-6; 🅿; Z 93204; Ⓟ 9,770; Ⓒ 14,674
Avery; CDP; CALAVERAS; 150 NL-9; elev. 3,387ft./1,032m.; 🅿; Z 95224; Ⓒ 672
Avila Beach; RMC Place; SAN LUIS OBISPO; 152 SG-5; elev. 20ft./6m.; 🅿; Z 93424; ● 300
Avocado Heights; CDP; LOS ANGELES; *153 SJ-11; ★ L.A.; mail La Puente Z 91746; Ⓟ 14,232; Ⓒ 15,148
Azusa; Inc. Place; LOS ANGELES; 155 D-11; elev. 612ft./187m.; 🅿 🅲 8,128; ★ L.A.; Z 91702; Ⓟ 41,333; Ⓒ 44,712; ◆ 47,970

B

Baden; RMC Place; SAN MATEO; ★ SF-O-; mail South San Francisco Z 94080; pop. incl. with South San Francisco (Inc. Place)
Badger; RMC Place; TULARE; 152 SC-9; elev. 3,030ft./924m.; 🅿; Z 93603
Bailey; RMC Place; LOS ANGELES; ★ L.A.; mail Whittier Z 90601, Z 90608; pop. incl. with Whittier (Inc. Place)
Baker; RMC Place; SAN BERNARDINO; 153 SF-16; elev. 923ft./281m.; 🅿; Z 92309, Z 92364; ● 860
Baker Ranch; RMC Place; PLACER; *150 NI-9; elev. 3,693ft./1,126m.; mail Foresthill Z 95631; ● 180
Bakersfield; Inc. Place; ⊡ KERN; 152 SF-9; elev. 408ft./124m.; 🅿 🅷 🅲 7,726 ■; ★ BAK; Z 93301-09, Z 93311-14, Z 93380, Z 93383-90 & mail Shafter Z 93263; Ⓟ 174,978; Ⓒ 247,057; Ⓡ 246,889; ◆ 343,635
Bakersfield East; RMC Place; KERN; *152 SF-9; elev. 500ft./152m.; ★ BAK; mail Bakersfield Z 93305
Bakersfield South; RMC Place; KERN; *152 SF-9; elev. 380ft./116m.; ★ BAK; mail Bakersfield Z 93304; pop. incl. with Bakersfield (Inc. Place)
Balance Rock; RMC Place; TULARE; *152 SE-10; mail Posey Z 93260; rural
Balboa; RMC Place; LOS ANGELES; ★ L.A.; mail Encino Z 91316, Z 91426; pop. incl. with Los Angeles (Inc. Place)
Balboa; RMC Place; ORANGE; *153 SK-12; elev. 5ft./2m.; 🅿; ★ L.A.; Z 92662 & mail Newport Beach Z 92661
Balboa Bay Shores; RMC Place; ORANGE; ★ L.A.; mail Newport Beach Z 92663; pop. incl. with Newport Beach (Inc. Place)
Balboa Island; RMC Place; ORANGE; *153 SK-12; elev. 6ft./2m.; 🅿; ★ L.A.; Z 92662
Balch Camp; RMC Place; FRESNO; *152 SB-9; elev. 1,267ft./386m.; mail Auberry Z 93602
Balderson Station; RMC Place; EL DORADO; *150 NJ-9; elev. 3,288ft./1,002m.; mail Georgetown Z 95634; rural
Baldwin Lake; RMC Place; SAN BERNARDINO; mail Big Bear City Z 92314; ● 300
Baldwin Park; Inc. Place; LOS ANGELES; 154 D-10; elev. 374ft./114m.; 🅿; ★ L.A.; Z 91706; Ⓟ 69,330; Ⓒ 75,837; ◆ 79,456
Baldy Mesa; RMC Place; SAN BERNARDINO; *153 SI-13; elev. 3,406ft./1,038m.; mail Phelan Z 92371, Victorville Z 92392; ● 800
Ballarat; RMC Place; INYO; *153 SD-13; elev. 1,061ft./323m.; mail Trona Z 93562; rural
Ballard; RMC Place; SANTA BARBARA; *152 SH-6; 🅿; Z 93463; ● 500
Ballico; RMC Place; MERCED; 150 NN-9; 🅿; Z 95303; ● 430
Ballou; RMC Place; SAN BERNARDINO; *153 SJ-12; ★ L.A.; mail Ontario Z 91761; pop. incl. with Ontario (Inc. Place)
Balls Ferry; RMC Place; SHASTA; *150 NE-6; mail Anderson Z 96007
Baltimore Park; RMC Place; MARIN; *150 NL-5; ★ SF-O-; mail Larkspur Z 94939; pop. incl. with Larkspur (Inc. Place)
Bandini; RMC Place; LOS ANGELES; *153 SJ-11; elev. 168ft./51m.; ★ L.A.; mail Los Angeles Z 90040; pop. incl. with Commerce (Inc. Place)
Bangor; RMC Place; BUTTE; 150 NH-7; elev. 755ft./230m.; 🅿; Z 95914
Bankhead Springs; RMC Place; SAN DIEGO; *153 SN-16; elev. 3,300ft./1,006m.; mail Jacumba Z 91934; rural
Banner; RMC Place; SAN DIEGO; *153 SM-15; elev. 2,755ft./840m.; mail Julian Z 92036; rural
Banning; Inc. Place; RIVERSIDE; 153 SJ-14; elev. 2,349ft./716m.; 🅿 🅷; Z 92220; Ⓟ 20,570; Ⓒ 23,562; ◆ 24,390
Banta; RMC Place; SAN JOAQUIN; 150 NM-7; elev. 21ft./6m.; 🅿; Z 95304; ● 550
Barber City; RMC Place; ORANGE; *153 SK-11; elev. 28ft./9m.; ★ L.A.; mail Westminster Z 92683; pop. incl. with Westminster (Inc. Place)
Bard; RMC Place; IMPERIAL; 153 SM-19; 🅿; ★ YUMA; Z 92222; ● 230
Bardsdale; RMC Place; VENTURA; *152 SI-9; elev. 426ft./130m.; mail Fillmore Z 93015
Barona; RMC Place; SAN DIEGO; *153 SM-14; elev. 1,360ft./415m.; ★ SDGO; mail Lakeside Z 92040; ● 500
Barona Reservation; Indian Reservation; SAN DIEGO; ★ SDGO; mail Lakeside Z 92040; Ⓟ 300; Ⓒ 536
Barrett; RMC Place; SAN DIEGO; *153 SN-15; mail Dulzura Z 91917; rural
Barrett Junction; RMC Place; SAN DIEGO; mail Dulzura Z 91917; ● 180
Barrington; RMC Place; LOS ANGELES; ★ L.A.; mail Los Angeles Z 90049, Z 90077; pop. incl. with Los Angeles (Inc. Place)
Barron Park; RMC Place; SANTA CLARA; ★ SF-O-; mail Palo Alto Z 94306; pop. incl. with Palo Alto (Inc. Place)
Barstow; RMC Place; FRESNO; *152 SB-7; elev. 271ft./83m.; ★ FRES; mail Fresno Z 93705; rural
Barstow; Inc. Place; SAN BERNARDINO; 153 SH-14; elev. 2,106ft./642m.; 🅿 🅷 ■; Z 92310-12; Ⓟ 21,472; Ⓒ 21,119; ◆ 20,837
Barton; RMC Place; AMADOR; *150 NK-9; mail Pioneer Z 95666; ● 1,600
Barton; RMC Place; FRESNO; ★ FRES; mail Fresno Z 93702; pop. incl. with Fresno (Inc. Place)
Bartonette; RMC Place; FRESNO; ★ FRES; pop. incl. with Fresno (Inc. Place)
Base Line; RMC Place; SAN BERNARDINO; ★ RIV-; mail San Bernardino Z 92410; pop. incl. with San Bernardino (Inc. Place)
Bassett; RMC Place; LOS ANGELES; *153 SJ-11; 🅿; ★ L.A.; Z 91746; ● 2,000
Bassetts; RMC Place; SIERRA; *150 NH-9; mail Sierra City Z 96125; rural
Bass Lake; RMC Place; MADERA; 151 NN-11; elev. 3,425ft./1,044m.; 🅿; Z 93604, Z 93669; ● 260
Batavia; RMC Place; SOLANO; *150 NK-6; ★ FRFL-; mail Dixon Z 95620; rural
Baumberg; RMC Place; ALAMEDA; *150 NM-6; ★ SF-O-; mail Hayward Z 94545; pop. incl. with Hayward (Inc. Place)
Baxter; RMC Place; PLACER; 150 NI-9; mail Alta Z 95701; ● 100
Bay; RMC Place; ORANGE; ★ L.A.; mail Newport Beach Z 92659, Z 92663; pop. incl. with Newport Beach (Inc. Place)
Bay; RMC Place; SAN BERNARDINO; mail Big Bear Lake Z 92315; pop. incl. with Big Bear Lake (Inc. Place)
Bay Cities Annex; RMC Place; LOS ANGELES; ★ L.A.; mail El Segundo Z 90245; pop. incl. with El Segundo (Inc. Place)
Bay Farm Island; RMC Place; ALAMEDA; ★ SF-O-; pop. incl. with Alameda (Inc. Place)
Bayliss; RMC Place; GLENN; *150 NH-6; elev. 109ft./33m.; mail Glenn Z 95943
Bayo Vista; RMC Place; CONTRA COSTA; *150 NL-5; ★ SF-O-; mail Rodeo Z 94572; ● 1,200
Bay Park; RMC Place; SAN DIEGO; *153 SN-13; ★ SDGO; mail San Diego Z 92110; pop. incl. with San Diego (Inc. Place)
Bay Point (West Pittsburg); CDP-Census Area Only; CONTRA COSTA; 151 NC-19; elev. 50ft./15m.; 🅿; ★ SF-O-; Z 94565; Ⓒ 21,534; ◆ 22,919
Bayshore; RMC Place; SAN MATEO; *150 NM-5; ★ SF-O-; pop. incl. with Daly City (Inc. Place)
Bayside; RMC Place; HUMBOLDT; 150 ND-2; 🅿; ★ EUR-; Z 95524; ● 600
Bayside; RMC Place; SANTA CLARA; ★ SF-O-; mail San Jose Z 95131, Z 95134, Z 95164; pop. incl. with San Jose (Inc. Place)
Bayview; CDP; HUMBOLDT; 150 ND-2; ★ EUR-; mail Eureka Z 95503; Ⓟ 1,318; Ⓒ 2,359
Bayview; RMC Place; SAN FRANCISCO; *150 NM-5; ★ SF-O-; mail San Francisco Z 94124; pop. incl. with San Francisco (Inc. Place)
Bayview-Montalvin; CDP-Census Area Only; CONTRA COSTA; *150 NL-5; elev. 38ft./12m.; ★ SF-O-; mail San Pablo Z 94806; Ⓟ 3,988; Ⓒ 5,004
Baywood; RMC Place; SAN MATEO; ★ SF-O-; pop. incl. with San Mateo (Inc. Place)
Baywood-Los Osos; CDP-Census Area Only; SAN LUIS OBISPO; *152 SF-5; mail Los Osos Z 93402; Ⓟ 14,377; Ⓒ 14,351
Baywood Park; RMC Place; SAN LUIS OBISPO; 152 SF-5; elev. 152ft./46m.; mail Los Osos Z 93402; ● 6,000
Beach Center; RMC Place; ORANGE; ★ L.A.; mail Huntington Beach Z 92648; pop. incl. with Huntington Beach (Inc. Place)
Beale AFB; CDP-Census Area Only; YUBA; *150 NI-7; 🅿; Z 95903; Ⓟ 6,912; Ⓒ 5,115
Bear Creek Estates; RMC Place; SANTA CRUZ; *152 SA-2; elev. 581ft./177m.; ★ S.CRZ; mail Boulder Creek Z 95006; ● 200
Bear River Pines; RMC Place; NEVADA; *150 NI-8; mail Grass Valley Z 95945; ● 185
Bear Valley; CDP; ALPINE; 150 NK-10; 🅿; Z 95223; Ⓒ 133
Bear Valley; RMC Place; MARIPOSA; *150 NM-10; mail Mariposa Z 95338
Bear Valley Springs; CDP-Census Area Only; KERN; *152 SG-10; elev. 4,100ft./1,250m.; 🅿; Z 93561; Ⓟ 1,593; Ⓒ 4,232
Beaumont; Inc. Place; RIVERSIDE; 153 SJ-14; elev. 2,573ft./784m.; 🅿; Z 92223; Ⓟ 9,685; Ⓒ 11,384; ◆ 18,842
Beckwourth; CDP; PLUMAS; 150 NG-9; 🅿; Z 96129; Ⓒ 342
Bee Rock; RMC Place; SAN LUIS OBISPO; *152 SE-5; elev. 931ft./284m.; mail Bradley Z 93426; rural
Bel Air; RMC Place; LOS ANGELES; *152 SJ-10; ★ L.A.; mail Los Angeles Z 90024; pop. incl. with Los Angeles (Inc. Place)
Bel Aire Estates; RMC Place; MARIN; ★ SF-O-; mail Belvedere Tiburon Z 94920; pop. incl. with Tiburon (Inc. Place)
Belden; CDP; PLUMAS; 150 NG-8; 🅿; Z 95915; Ⓒ 26
Bell; Inc. Place; LOS ANGELES; 154 F-8; elev. 145ft./44m.; 🅿; ★ L.A.; Z 90201-02, Z 90270; Ⓟ 34,365; Ⓒ 36,664; ◆ 37,736
Bell; RMC Place; MERCED; ★ MRCD; mail Merced Z 95341; pop. incl. with Merced (Inc. Place)
Bella Vista; RMC Place; KERN; *153 SF-11; elev. 2,631ft./802m.; mail Weldon Z 93283; ● 700
Bella Vista; RMC Place; LOS ANGELES; ★ L.A.; mail Los Angeles Z 90022; pop. incl. with Los Angeles (Inc. Place)
Bella Vista; RMC Place; SHASTA; 150 NE-6; elev. 550ft./168m.; 🅿; ★ REDD; Z 96008; ● 400
Belle Haven; RMC Place; SAN MATEO; ★ SF-O-; mail Menlo Park Z 94025; pop. incl. with Menlo Park (Inc. Place)
Belleview; RMC Place; TUOLUMNE; *150 NL-10; mail Sonora Z 95370; ● 250
Bellflower; Inc. Place; LOS ANGELES; 154 G-8; elev. 71ft./22m.; 🅿 🅷 ■; ★ L.A.; Z 90706-07; Ⓟ 61,815; Ⓒ 72,878; ◆ 77,255
Bell Gardens; Inc. Place; LOS ANGELES; 154 F-8; elev. 125ft./38m.; 🅿; ★ L.A.; Z 90201-02; Ⓟ 42,355; Ⓒ 44,054; ◆ 43,909
Bell Mountain; RMC Place; SAN BERNARDINO; *153 SH-13; elev. 3,082ft./939m.; ★ HESP-; mail Victorville Z 92392; pop. incl. with Apple Valley (Inc. Place)
Bellota; RMC Place; SAN JOAQUIN; mail Linden Z 95236; rural
Belltown; RMC Place; RIVERSIDE; 155 E-17; ★ RIV-; mail Riverside Z 92509; ● 1,750
Bel Marin Keys; RMC Place; MARIN; *150 NL-5; ★ SF-O-; mail Novato Z 94947; ● 1,650
Belmont; Inc. Place; SAN MATEO; 151 NJ-15; elev. 35ft./11m.; 🅿 🅷 🅲 1,583; ★ SF-O-; Z 94002; Ⓟ 24,127; Ⓒ 25,123; ◆ 24,728
Belmont Shore; RMC Place; LOS ANGELES; *153 SK-11; ★ L.A.; mail Long Beach Z 90803, Z 90853; pop. incl. with Long Beach (Inc. Place)
Belvedere; RMC Place; LOS ANGELES; *153 SJ-11; elev. 313ft./95m.; ★ L.A.; mail Los Angeles Z 90022; ● 5,500
Belvedere; Inc. Place; MARIN; 151 NE-13; 🅿; ★ SF-O-; Z 94920; Ⓟ 2,147; Ⓒ 2,125
Belvedere Gardens; RMC Place; LOS ANGELES; *152 SJ-11; ★ L.A.; mail Los Angeles Z 90022; ● 9,500
Belvernon Gardens; RMC Place; MARIN; ★ SF-O-; mail Belvedere Tiburon Z 94920; pop. incl. with Tiburon (Inc. Place)
Benali; RMC Place; SACRAMENTO; *150 NJ-7; ★ SAC; pop. incl. with Sacramento (Inc. Place)
Benbow; RMC Place; HUMBOLDT; 150 NF-2; mail Garberville Z 95542; ● 200
Bend; RMC Place; TEHAMA; 150 NF-6; mail Red Bluff Z 96080; ● 565
Ben Hur; RMC Place; MARIPOSA; *150 NN-10; elev. 1,750ft./533m.; mail Raymond Z 93653; rural
Benicia; Inc. Place; SOLANO; 150 NL-5; elev. 33ft./10m.; 🅿; ★ SF-O-; Z 94510; Ⓟ 24,437; Ⓒ 26,865; ◆ 26,378
Ben Lomond; CDP; SANTA CRUZ; 152 SA-2; 🅿; ★ S.CRZ; Z 95005; Ⓟ 7,884; Ⓒ 2,364
Benton (Benton Station); RMC Place; MONO; 151 NM-14; elev. 5,377ft./1,639m.; 🅿; Z 93512; ● 150
Benton Paiute Reservation; Indian Reservation; MONO; Ⓒ 50
Benton Station; MONO; see Benton (RMC Place)
Berenda; RMC Place; MADERA; 152 SB-6; elev. 253ft./77m.; 🅿; Z 93637; rural
Berkeley; Inc. Place; ALAMEDA; 150 NM-5; elev. 152ft./46m.; 🅿 🅷 🅲 33,933 ■; ★ SF-O-; Z 94701-10, Z 94712, Z 94720; Ⓟ 102,724; Ⓒ 102,743; ◆ 102,515
Bermuda Dunes; CDP-Census Area Only; RIVERSIDE; *153 SK-15; elev. 82ft./25m.; 🅿; ★ PSPR-; Z 92203 & mail Indio Z 92201; Ⓟ 4,571; Ⓒ 6,229
Bernal; RMC Place; SAN FRANCISCO; ★ SF-O-; mail San Francisco Z 94110; pop. incl. with San Francisco (Inc. Place)
Berros; SAN LUIS OBISPO; see Los Berros (RMC Place)
Berry Creek; RMC Place; BUTTE; 150 NH-7; 🅿; Z 95916; ● 200
Berry Creek Rancheria; Indian Reservation; BUTTE; Ⓒ 0
Berryessa; RMC Place; SANTA CLARA; *150 NN-6; elev. 144ft./44m.; ★ SF-O-; mail San Jose Z 95132, Z 95152; pop. incl. with San Jose (Inc. Place)
Berryessa Highlands; RMC Place; NAPA; *150 NK-5; elev. 800ft./244m.; mail Napa Z 94558
Berryessa Park; RMC Place; NAPA; *150 NK-5; mail Napa Z 94558; ● 150
Bertsch-Oceanview; CDP-Census Area Only; DEL NORTE; *150 NB-2; Ⓒ 2,238
Bertsch Terrace; RMC Place; DEL NORTE; 150 NB-2; mail Crescent City Z 95531; ● 975
Bethany Park; RMC Place; SANTA CRUZ; *152 SB-2; ★ S.CRZ; mail Scotts Valley Z 95066; pop. incl. with Scotts Valley (Inc. Place)
Bethel Island; CDP; CONTRA COSTA; 150 NL-7; 🅿; ★ SF-O-; Z 94511; Ⓟ 2,115; Ⓒ 2,312
Betteravia; RMC Place; SANTA BARBARA; *152 SH-6; mail Santa Maria Z 93455; rural
Beverly; RMC Place; LOS ANGELES; ★ L.A.; mail Beverly Hills Z 90212; pop. incl. with Beverly Hills (Inc. Place)
Beverly Glen; RMC Place; LOS ANGELES; *152 SJ-10; ★ L.A.; pop. incl. with Los Angeles (Inc. Place)
Beverly Hills; Inc. Place; LOS ANGELES; 152 SJ-10; elev. 225ft./69m.; 🅿 ■; ★ L.A.; Z 90209-13; Ⓟ 31,971; Ⓒ 33,784; ◆ 34,924
Bicentennial; RMC Place; LOS ANGELES; ★ L.A.; mail Los Angeles Z 90048; pop. incl. with Los Angeles (Inc. Place)
Bieber; RMC Place; LASSEN; 150 ND-8; 🅿; Z 96009; ● 215
Big Bar; RMC Place; TRINITY; 150 ND-3; 🅿; Z 96010
Big Bear City; CDP; SAN BERNARDINO; 153 SI-14; elev. 6,750ft./2,057m.; 🅿; Z 92314, Z 92386; Ⓟ 4,920; Ⓒ 5,779
Big Bear Lake; Inc. Place; SAN BERNARDINO; 153 SI-14; elev. 6,754ft./2,059m.; 🅿 🅷; Z 92315; Ⓟ 5,351; Ⓒ 5,438
Big Bend; CDP; SHASTA; 150 ND-6; 🅿; Z 96011; Ⓒ 149
Big Bend Rancheria; Indian Reservation; SHASTA; Ⓒ 0
Big Chief; RMC Place; PLACER; *150 NI-10; elev. 5,991ft./1,826m.; mail Truckee Z 96161; rural
Big Creek; RMC Place; FRESNO; 152 SA-8; 🅿; Z 93605; ● 260
Biggs; Inc. Place; BUTTE; 150 NH-7; elev. 94ft./29m.; 🅿; Z 95917; Ⓟ 1,581; Ⓒ 1,793
Big Lagoon (Big Lagoon Park); RMC Place; HUMBOLDT; *150 NC-2; elev. 80ft./24m.; mail Trinidad Z 95570; ● 100
Big Lagoon Park; HUMBOLDT; see Big Lagoon (RMC Place)
Big Lagoon Rancheria; Indian Reservation; HUMBOLDT; Ⓒ 24
Big Meadow; RMC Place; CALAVERAS; *150 NK-10; mail Arnold Z 95223; rural
Big Oak Flat; RMC Place; TUOLUMNE; 150 NM-10; 🅿; Z 95305; ● 300
Big Pine; CDP; INYO; 153 SA-11; elev. 3,985ft./1,215m.; 🅿; Z 93513; Ⓟ 1,158; Ⓒ 1,350
Big Pine Reservation; Indian Reservation; INYO; mail Big Pine Z 93513; Ⓟ 396; Ⓒ 462
Big Pines; RMC Place; LOS ANGELES; mail Rancho Cucamonga Z 91701; ● 185
Big River; CDP-Census Area Only; SAN BERNARDINO; 153 SI-20; elev. 400ft./122m.; 🅿; Z 92242; Ⓟ 705; Ⓒ 1,266
Big Sandy Rancheria; Indian Reservation; FRESNO; Ⓒ 98
Big Springs (Mayten); RMC Place; SISKIYOU; *150 NB-5; elev. 2,613ft./796m.; mail Montague Z 96064; rural
Big Sur; RMC Place; MONTEREY; 152 SD-3; elev. 155ft./47m.; 🅿; Z 93920; ● 275
Big Valley Rancheria; Indian Reservation; LAKE; Ⓒ 225
Bijou; RMC Place; EL DORADO; *150 NJ-10; mail South Lake Tahoe Z 96156; pop. incl. with South Lake Tahoe (Inc. Place)
Bijou Park; RMC Place; EL DORADO; *150 NJ-10; mail South Lake Tahoe Z 96156; pop. incl. with South Lake Tahoe (Inc. Place)
Binghamton; RMC Place; SOLANO; *150 NK-6; elev. 35ft./11m.; mail Dixon Z 95620; rural
Biola; CDP; FRESNO; 152 SB-7; 🅿; ★ FRES; Z 93606; Ⓒ 1,037
Biola Junction; RMC Place; FRESNO; *152 SB-7; elev. 297ft./91m.; ★ FRES; pop. incl. with Fresno (Inc. Place)
Birch Hill; RMC Place; SAN DIEGO; *153 SL-14; elev. 5,645ft./1,721m.; mail Palomar Mountain Z 92060; ● 20
Birch Meadow Acres; RMC Place; NEVADA; *150 NI-8; elev. 2,200ft./671m.; ★ SAC; mail Grass Valley Z 95945; ● 400
Bird Rock; RMC Place; SAN DIEGO; *153 SM-13; ★ SDGO; mail La Jolla Z 92037; pop. incl. with San Diego (Inc. Place)
Birds Landing; RMC Place; SOLANO; 150 NL-6; elev. 58ft./18m.; 🅿; Z 94512 & mail Suisun City Z 94585
Bishop; Inc. Place; INYO; 151 NN-14; elev. 4,147ft./1,264m.; 🅿 🅷; Z 93512, Z 93514-15; Ⓟ 3,475; Ⓒ 3,575
Bishop Reservation; Indian Reservation; INYO; mail Bishop Z 93514; Ⓟ 1,125; Ⓒ 1,441
Bitterwater; RMC Place; SAN BENITO; 152 SC-4; mail King City Z 93930; rural
Bixby; RMC Place; LOS ANGELES; *153 SK-11; ★ L.A.; mail Long Beach Z 90807; pop. incl. with Long Beach (Inc. Place)
Bixby Knolls; RMC Place; LOS ANGELES; *153 SK-11; elev. 82ft./25m.; ★ L.A.; mail Long Beach Z 90807; pop. incl. with Long Beach (Inc. Place)
Black Bear; RMC Place; SISKIYOU; *150 NC-4; elev. 2,800ft./853m.; mail Forks of Salmon Z 96031; rural
Blackhawk-Camino Tassajara; CDP-Census Area Only; CONTRA COSTA; *150 NM-6; ★ SF-O-; Ⓒ 10,048
Black Meadow Landing; RMC Place; SAN BERNARDINO; *153 SI-20; mail Parker Dam Z 92267; rural
Black Point; RMC Place; MARIN; 151 NA-12; ★ SF-O-; mail Novato Z 94945, Z 94947; ● 470
Black Point-Green Point; CDP-Census Area Only; MARIN; *150 NL-5; ★ SF-O-; Ⓒ 1,143
Blackrock; RMC Place; INYO; *153 SB-11; elev. 3,845ft./1,172m.; mail Independence Z 93526; rural
Blackstone; RMC Place; FRESNO; ★ FRES; mail Fresno Z 93710; pop. incl. with Fresno (Inc. Place)
Blackwells Corner; RMC Place; KERN; *152 SF-7; elev. 644ft./196m.; mail Lost Hills Z 93249; ● 110
Blairsden; CDP; PLUMAS; 150 NG-9; 🅿; Z 96103; Ⓒ 50
Blanco; RMC Place; MONTEREY; *152 SC-3; elev. 32ft./10m.; ★ SLNS; mail Salinas Z 93901; rural
Blocksburg; RMC Place; HUMBOLDT; 150 NF-2; elev. 1,596ft./486m.; 🅿; Z 95514; ● 50
Bloomfield; RMC Place; SONOMA; 150 NK-4; ★ S.ROS; mail Petaluma Z 94952; ● 350
Bloomfield Acres; RMC Place; HUMBOLDT; ★ EUR-; mail Arcata Z 95521; pop. incl. with Arcata (Inc. Place)
Bloomington; CDP; SAN BERNARDINO; 155 E-17; elev. 1,090ft./332m.; 🅿; ★ RIV-; Z 92316; Ⓟ 15,116; Ⓒ 19,318
Blossom Hill; RMC Place; SANTA CLARA; ★ SF-O-; mail San Jose Z 95123, Z 95153; pop. incl. with San Jose (Inc. Place)
Blossom Valley; RMC Place; SANTA CLARA; ★ SF-O-; mail Mountain View Z 94040; pop. incl. with Mountain View (Inc. Place)
Blue Canon; PLACER; see Blue Canyon (RMC Place)
Blue Canyon (Blue Canon); RMC Place; PLACER; 150 NI-9; mail Emigrant Gap Z 95715; ● 75
Blue Hills; RMC Place; SANTA CLARA; *150 NN-6; elev. 318ft./97m.; ★ SF-O-; mail Saratoga Z 95070; pop. incl. with Saratoga (Inc. Place)
Blue Jay; RMC Place; SAN BERNARDINO; 155 B-19; 🅿; ★ RIV-; Z 92317; ● 700
Blue Lake; Inc. Place; HUMBOLDT; 150 ND-2; 🅿; ★ EUR-; Z 95525; Ⓟ 1,235; Ⓒ 1,135
Blue Lake Rancheria; Indian Reservation; HUMBOLDT; Ⓒ 78
Blue Lakes; RMC Place; LAKE; elev. 1,361ft./415m.; mail Witter Springs Z 95493; ● 200
Bluewater; CDP-Census Area Only; SAN BERNARDINO; *153 SI-20; elev. 417ft./127m.; mail Earp Z 92242; Ⓟ 261; Ⓒ 265
Bluff Creek; RMC Place; HUMBOLDT; *150 NC-3; elev. 400ft./122m.; mail Hoopa Z 95546; ● 10
Blythe; Inc. Place; RIVERSIDE; 153 SK-19; elev. 270ft./82m.; 🅿 🅷; Z 92225-26, Z 92280; Ⓟ 8,448; Ⓒ 12,155; Ⓡ 20,463; ◆ 22,005
Bodega; RMC Place; SONOMA; 150 NK-4; elev. 106ft./32m.; 🅿; Z 94922; ● 300
Bodega Bay; CDP; SONOMA; 150 NK-4; elev. 676ft./206m.; 🅿; Z 94923; Ⓟ 1,127; Ⓒ 1,423
Bodfish; CDP; KERN; 152 SF-10; 🅿; Z 93205; Ⓟ 1,283; Ⓒ 1,823
Bolinas; CDP; MARIN; 150 NL-4; elev. 9ft./3m.; 🅿; ★ SF-O-; Z 94924; Ⓟ 1,098; Ⓒ 1,246
Bolsa; RMC Place; ORANGE; ★ L.A.; mail Westminster Z 92683; pop. incl. with Westminster (Inc. Place)
Bolsa Knolls; RMC Place; MONTEREY; 152 SB-3; ★ SLNS; mail Salinas Z 93906; ● 1,950
Bombay Beach; CDP; IMPERIAL; 153 SL-17; mail Niland Z 92257; Ⓒ 366
Bonadelle Ranchos; RMC Place; MADERA; *152 SB-7; elev. 323ft./98m.; mail Madera Z 93637; ● 4,500
Bonadelle Ranchos-Madera Ranchos; CDP-Census Area Only; MADERA; *152 SB-7; mail Madera Z 93637; Ⓟ 5,705; Ⓒ 7,300
Bonds Corner; RMC Place; IMPERIAL; *153 SN-18; elev. 30ft./9m.; mail Holtville Z 92250
Bonita; RMC Place; MADERA; *152 SB-6; elev. 205ft./62m.; mail Madera Z 93637
Bonita; CDP; SAN DIEGO; 156 L-8; 🅿; ★ SDGO; Z 91902, Z 91908; Ⓟ 12,542; Ⓒ 12,401
Bonnefoy; RMC Place; AMADOR; *150 NK-9; mail Jackson Z 95642; rural
Bonny Doon; RMC Place; SANTA CRUZ; *152 SB-2; elev. 1,259ft./384m.; 🅿; ★ S.CRZ; Z 95060; ● 1,100
Bonnyview; RMC Place; SHASTA; ★ REDD; mail Redding Z 96001; pop. incl. with Redding (Inc. Place)
Bonsall; CDP; SAN DIEGO; 153 SL-13; 🅿; ★ SDGO; Z 92003; Ⓟ 1,881; Ⓒ 3,401
Boonville; RMC Place; MENDOCINO; 150 NI-3; 🅿; Z 95415; ● 1,200
Bootjack; CDP; MARIPOSA; *150 NN-10; elev. 2,242ft./683m.; mail Mariposa Z 95338; Ⓟ 1,295; Ⓒ 1,588
Boron; CDP; KERN; 153 SG-12; elev. 2,460ft./750m.; 🅿; Z 93516, Z 93596; Ⓟ 2,101; Ⓒ 2,025
Boronda; CDP-Census Area Only; MONTEREY; *152 SC-3; ★ SLNS; Ⓒ 1,325
Borosolvay; RMC Place; SAN BERNARDINO; *153 SE-13; mail Trona Z 93562; rural
Borrego Springs; CDP; SAN DIEGO; 153 SL-15; elev. 590ft./180m.; 🅿; Z 92004; Ⓟ 2,244; Ⓒ 2,535
Borrego Wells; RMC Place; SAN DIEGO; *153 SM-16; elev. 67ft./20m.; mail Borrego Springs Z 92004; ● 55
Bostonia; CDP; SAN DIEGO; 156 H-10; ★ SDGO; mail El Cajon Z 92021; Ⓟ 13,670; Ⓒ 15,169
Boulder Creek; CDP; SANTA CRUZ; 152 SA-2; elev. 493ft./150m.; 🅿; ★ S.CRZ; Z 95006; Ⓟ 6,725; Ⓒ 4,081
Boulder Oaks; RMC Place; SAN DIEGO; *153 SM-14; elev. 1,474ft./449m.; ★ SDGO; mail Pine Valley Z 91962; ● 40
Boulder Park; RMC Place; IMPERIAL; *153 SN-16; elev. 2,837ft./865m.; mail Jacumba Z 91934; rural
Boulevard; RMC Place; SAN DIEGO; 153 SN-16; 🅿; Z 91905; ● 230
Boulevard Gardens; RMC Place; ORANGE; ★ L.A.; pop. incl. with Huntington Beach (Inc. Place)
Bowles; CDP; FRESNO; *152 SC-7; ★ FRES; Ⓒ 182
Bowman; RMC Place; PLACER; 150 NJ-8; 🅿; ★ SAC; Z 95604; ● 1,100
Box Springs; RMC Place; RIVERSIDE; *153 SJ-13; ★ RIV-; mail Riverside Z 92507; pop. incl. with Moreno Valley (Inc. Place)
Boyes Hot Springs; CDP; SONOMA; 150 NK-5; 🅿; Z 95416; Ⓟ 5,973; Ⓒ 6,665
Boyle; RMC Place; LOS ANGELES; *153 SJ-11; ★ L.A.; mail Los Angeles Z 90033; pop. incl. with Los Angeles (Inc. Place)
Boyle Heights; RMC Place; LOS ANGELES; *153 SJ-11; ★ L.A.; mail Los Angeles Z 90033; pop. incl. with Los Angeles (Inc. Place)
Boys Republic; RMC Place; SAN BERNARDINO; *153 SJ-12; ★ L.A.; mail Chino Z 91710; pop. incl. with Chino Hills (Inc. Place)
Brackney; RMC Place; SANTA CRUZ; *152 SA-2; ★ S.CRZ; mail Ben Lomond Z 95005; ● 400
Bradbury; Inc. Place; LOS ANGELES; 154 D-10; 🅿; ★ L.A.; Z 91008, Z 91010; Ⓟ 829; Ⓒ 855
Bradford; RMC Place; ALAMEDA; ★ SF-O-; mail Hayward Z 94541, Z 94543; pop. incl. with Hayward (Inc. Place)
Bradley; CDP; MONTEREY; 152 SE-5; 🅿; Z 93426; Ⓒ 120
Bradley International; RMC Place; LOS ANGELES; ★ L.A.; mail Los Angeles Z 90045; pop. incl. with Los Angeles (Inc. Place)
Brannan Street Station; RMC Place; SAN FRANCISCO; ★ SF-O-; mail San Francisco Z 94107; pop. incl. with San Francisco (Inc. Place)
Branscomb; RMC Place; MENDOCINO; 150 NG-2; 🅿; Z 95417; ● 100
Brawley; Inc. Place; IMPERIAL; 153 SM-17; elev.-113ft./-34m.; 🅿 🅷; Z 92227; Ⓟ 18,923; Ⓒ 22,052; ◆ 23,622
Bray; RMC Place; SISKIYOU; *150 NB-6; mail Macdoel Z 96058
Brea; Inc. Place; ORANGE; 153 SJ-12; elev. 349ft./106m.; 🅿 🅷 ■; ★ L.A.; Z 92821-23; Ⓟ 32,873; Ⓒ 35,410; ◆ 36,903
Brentwood; Inc. Place; CONTRA COSTA; 150 NL-6; elev. 79ft./24m.; 🅿; ★ SF-O-; Z 94513 & mail Los Angeles Z 90049; Ⓟ 7,563; Ⓒ 23,302; ◆ 30,055
Brentwood; RMC Place; LOS ANGELES; pop. incl. with Los Angeles (Inc. Place)
Brentwood Heights; RMC Place; LOS ANGELES; *152 SJ-10; ★ L.A.; pop. incl. with Los Angeles (Inc. Place)
Brentwood Park; RMC Place; LOS ANGELES; ★ L.A.; pop. incl. with Los Angeles (Inc. Place)
Bret Harte; CDP-Census Area Only; STANISLAUS; *150 NM-8; ★ MOD; Ⓒ 5,161
Briceburg; RMC Place; MARIPOSA; *150 NM-10; mail Midpines Z 95345; rural
Briceland; RMC Place; HUMBOLDT; 150 NF-2; mail Garberville Z 95542; ● 90
Bridgehead; RMC Place; CONTRA COSTA; *150 NL-6; ★ SF-O-; mail Antioch Z 94509, Oakley Z 94561; pop. incl. with Antioch (Inc. Place)
Bridgeport; RMC Place; MARIPOSA; *150 NN-10; mail Mariposa Z 95338; rural
Bridgeport; RMC Place; ⊡ MONO; 151 NL-12; elev. 6,473ft./1,973m.; 🅿; Z 93517; ● 600
Bridgeport; RMC Place; NEVADA; *150 NI-8; elev. 567ft./173m.; mail Smartsville Z 95977; rural
Bridgeport Reservation; Indian Reservation; MONO; Ⓒ 43
Bridgeville; RMC Place; HUMBOLDT; 150 NE-2; elev. 646ft./197m.; 🅿; Z 95526
Brighton; RMC Place; SACRAMENTO; *150 NK-7; ★ SAC; pop. incl. with Sacramento (Inc. Place)
Briones; RMC Place; CONTRA COSTA; ● 100
Brisbane; Inc. Place; SAN MATEO; 151 NH-13; 🅿; ★ SF-O-; Z 94005; Ⓟ 2,952; Ⓒ 3,597
Bristol; RMC Place; ORANGE; ★ L.A.; mail Santa Ana Z 92703; pop. incl. with Santa Ana (Inc. Place)
Broadmoor; CDP; SAN MATEO; 151 NG-12; ★ SF-O-; mail Daly City Z 94015; Ⓟ 3,739; Ⓒ 4,026
Broadway; RMC Place; SACRAMENTO; ★ SAC; mail Sacramento Z 95818; pop. incl. with Sacramento (Inc. Place)
Broadway; RMC Place; SAN MATEO; ★ SF-O-; mail Burlingame Z 94010; pop. incl. with Burlingame (Inc. Place)
Broadway Manchester; RMC Place; LOS ANGELES; ★ L.A.; mail Los Angeles Z 90003; pop. incl. with Los Angeles (Inc. Place)
Brockway; RMC Place; PLACER; 149 B-2; mail Kings Beach Z 96143; ● 370
Broderick; RMC Place; YOLO; 149 D-5; 🅿; ★ SAC; Z 95605; pop. incl. with West Sacramento (Inc. Place)
Brookdale; RMC Place; SANTA CRUZ; *152 SA-2; 🅿; ★ S.CRZ; Z 95007; ● 950
Brookhurst Center; RMC Place; ORANGE; ★ L.A.; mail Anaheim Z 92804, Z 92814; pop. incl. with Anaheim (Inc. Place)
Brooks; RMC Place; YOLO; 150 NJ-6; 🅿; Z 95606; ● 100
Brookside Park; RMC Place; SAN MATEO; ★ SF-O-; mail Portola Valley Z 94028; pop. incl. with Portola Valley (Inc. Place)
Browns Corner; RMC Place; YOLO; *150 NJ-6; elev. 30ft./9m.; mail Woodland Z 95695; pop. incl. with Woodland (Inc. Place)
Browns Flat (Brow's Flat); RMC Place; TUOLUMNE; mail Sonora Z 95370; ● 110
Browns Valley; RMC Place; YUBA; 150 NI-7; 🅿; Z 95918; ● 150
Brownsville; RMC Place; YUBA; 150 NH-7; elev. 2,235ft./681m.; 🅿; Z 95919; ● 700
Brow's Flat; TUOLUMNE; see Browns Flat (RMC Place)
Bruceville; RMC Place; SACRAMENTO; *150 NK-7; elev. 21ft./6m.; mail Elk Grove Z 95758; rural
Brundage; RMC Place; KERN; ★ BAK; mail Bakersfield Z 93307, Z 93387; pop. incl. with Bakersfield (Inc. Place)
Brush Creek; RMC Place; BUTTE; *150 NH-7; elev. 3,540ft./1,079m.; mail Berry Creek Z 95916; ● 80
Bryant; RMC Place; LOS ANGELES; *153 SK-11; ★ L.A.; mail Long Beach Z 90815; pop. incl. with Long Beach (Inc. Place)
Bryant Street Annex; RMC Place; SAN FRANCISCO; ★ SF-O-; mail San Francisco Z 94103, Z 94141; pop. incl. with San Francisco (Inc. Place)
Bryn Mawr; RMC Place; SAN BERNARDINO; *153 SJ-13; elev. 1,202ft./366m.; 🅿; ★ RIV-; Z 92318
Bryson; RMC Place; MONTEREY; 152 SE-4; elev. 978ft./298m.; mail Bradley Z 93426; ● 30
Bryte; RMC Place; YOLO; 149 D-5; 🅿; ★ SAC; Z 95605; pop. incl. with West Sacramento (Inc. Place)
Buckeye; RMC Place; EL DORADO; *150 NJ-8; elev. 2,918ft./889m.; mail Georgetown Z 95634; ● 100
Buckeye; RMC Place; SHASTA; *150 NE-5; ★ REDD; mail Redding Z 96003, Shasta Lake Z 96019
Buckhorn Lodge; RMC Place; AMADOR; *150 NK-9; elev. 3,421ft./1,043m.; mail Pioneer Z 95666; ● 300
Buckingham Park; RMC Place; LAKE; *150 NI-4; mail Kelseyville Z 95451; ● 600
Buck Meadows; RMC Place; MARIPOSA; 150 NM-10; elev. 3,006ft./916m.; mail Groveland Z 95321
Bucks Bar; RMC Place; EL DORADO; *150 NJ-9; mail Placerville Z 95667; ● 100
Bucks Lake; CDP-Census Area Only; PLUMAS; *150 NG-8; mail Quincy Z 95971; Ⓒ 17
Bucks Lodge; RMC Place; PLUMAS; mail Quincy Z 95971; rural
Bucktail; RMC Place; TRINITY; *150 NE-4; elev. 1,804ft./550m.; mail Lewiston Z 96052; ● 30
Buellton; Inc. Place; SANTA BARBARA; 152 SH-6; elev. 361ft./110m.; 🅿; Z 93427; Ⓟ 3,383; Ⓒ 3,828
Buena; RMC Place; SAN DIEGO; 156 I-3; ★ SDGO; mail Vista Z 92083
Buena Park; Inc. Place; ORANGE; 154 H-10; elev. 74ft./23m.; 🅿 🅷 ■; ★ L.A.; Z 90620-24; Ⓟ 68,784; Ⓒ 78,282; ◆ 82,403
Buena Vista; RMC Place; AMADOR; 150 NK-8; elev. 295ft./90m.; mail Ione Z 95640; ● 275
Buena Vista; CDP-Census Area Only; SANTA CLARA; *150 NN-6; ★ SF-O-; Ⓒ 1,704
Buena Vista; RMC Place; SONOMA; *150 NK-5; mail Sonoma Z 95476; ● 600
Buffalo Hill; RMC Place; EL DORADO; *150 NJ-8; elev. 2,488ft./758m.; mail Georgetown Z 95634; ● 330
Buhach; RMC Place; MERCED; *150 NN-9; ★ MRCD; mail Merced Z 95340; ● 900
Bummerville; RMC Place; CALAVERAS; *150 NK-9; elev. 2,949ft./899m.; mail West Point Z 95255; ● 130
Bunker Hill; RMC Place; LOS ANGELES; ★ L.A.; mail Los Angeles Z 90071; pop. incl. with Los Angeles (Inc. Place)
Buntingville; RMC Place; LASSEN; mail Janesville Z 96114; ● 240
Burbank; Inc. Place; LOS ANGELES; 153 SJ-11; elev. 598ft./182m.; 🅿 🅷 🅲 1,481 ■; ★ L.A.; Z 91501-08, Z 91510, Z 91521-23, Z 91526; Ⓟ 93,643; Ⓒ 100,316; ◆ 102,272
Burbank; CDP; SANTA CLARA; *150 NN-6; elev. 122ft./37m.; ★ SF-O-; mail San Jose Z 95128; Ⓟ 4,902; Ⓒ 5,239
Burbank Junction; RMC Place; LOS ANGELES; *153 SJ-11; ★ L.A.; pop. incl. with Burbank (Inc. Place)
Burkett Acres; RMC Place; SAN JOAQUIN; ★ STOC; mail Stockton Z 95215; pop. incl. with Stockton (Inc. Place)
Burkett Gardens; RMC Place; SAN JOAQUIN; 149 H-10; ★ STOC; mail Stockton Z 95205; ● 5,500
Burlingame; Inc. Place; SAN MATEO; 151 NI-14; elev. 34ft./10m.; 🅿 🅷 ■; ★ SF-O-; Z 94010-11; Ⓟ 26,801; Ⓒ 28,158; ◆ 28,550
Burlingame Annex; RMC Place; SAN MATEO; ★ SF-O-; mail Burlingame Z 94011; pop. incl. with Burlingame (Inc. Place)
Burlingame Hills; RMC Place; SAN MATEO; ★ SF-O-; mail Burlingame Z 94010; pop. incl. with Burlingame (Inc. Place)
Burney; CDP; SHASTA; 150 ND-7; elev. 3,173ft./967m.; 🅿; Z 96013; Ⓟ 3,423; Ⓒ 3,217
Burnt Ranch; RMC Place; TRINITY; 150 ND-3; elev. 1,473ft./449m.; 🅿; Z 95527; ● 165
Burrel (Burrell); RMC Place; FRESNO; 152 SC-7; 🅿; Z 93607
Burrell; FRESNO; see Burrel (RMC Place)
Burson (Helisma); RMC Place; CALAVERAS; 150 NL-8; 🅿; Z 95225
Burton; TULARE; see Porterville West (RMC Place)
Butano Park; RMC Place; SAN MATEO; *152 SA-2; elev. 180ft./55m.; mail Pescadero Z 94060; ● 300
BUTTE; 150 NH-6; Ⓟ 182,120; Ⓒ 203,171; ◆ 224,465
Butte City; RMC Place; GLENN; 150 NH-6; 🅿; Z 95920; ● 250
Butte Creek; RMC Place; BUTTE; *150 NF-7; elev. 4,600ft./1,402m.; mail Chico Z 95928; ● 70
Butte Meadows; RMC Place; BUTTE; 150 NF-7; elev. 4,351ft./1,326m.; 🅿; Z 95942; ● 100
Buttonwillow; CDP; KERN; 152 SF-8; elev. 269ft./82m.; 🅿; Z 93206; Ⓟ 1,301; Ⓒ 1,266
Byron; CDP; CONTRA COSTA; 150 NM-7; elev. 26ft./8m.; 🅿; Z 94505, Z 94514; Ⓒ 916
Byron Rumford; RMC Place; ALAMEDA; ★ SF-O-; mail Oakland Z 94612; pop. incl. with Oakland (Inc. Place)
Bystrom; CDP-Census Area Only; STANISLAUS; *150 NM-8; ★ MOD; Ⓒ 4,518

C

Cabazon; CDP; RIVERSIDE; 153 SJ-14; elev. 1,792ft./546m.; 🅿; Z 92230, Z 92282; Ⓟ 1,588; Ⓒ 2,229
Cabazon Reservation; Indian Reservation; RIVERSIDE; mail Indio Z 92201; Ⓟ 815; Ⓒ 806
Cabin Cove; RMC Place; TULARE; *152 SC-10; mail Three Rivers Z 93271; rural
Cabrillo; RMC Place; LOS ANGELES; *153 SK-11; ★ L.A.; mail Long Beach Z 90810; pop. incl. with Long Beach (Inc. Place)
Cache Creek; RMC Place; KERN; *153 SG-11; mail Mojave Z 93501; ● 100
Cachuma Village; RMC Place; SANTA BARBARA; *152 SI-7; mail Santa Barbara Z 93101; ● 100

Entries in **UPPERCASE** are counties.
Entries in **bold** have populations of 2,500 or more.
Names in parentheses are alternate names.
Inc. Place — Incorporated Place
RMC Place — Rand McNally Designated Place
CDP — Census Designated Place
MCD — Minor Civil Division

⊡ County Seat
▲ Minor Civil Division
elev. Elevation
🅿 Post Office
🅷 Hospital
🅲 College
■ Principal Business Center
★ Ranally Metro Area (RMA) Abbreviation
Z Zip Code(s)

Ⓟ Previous Census Population
Ⓡ Revised Census Population
Ⓐ Annexation Population
● Rand McNally Population Estimate
Ⓒ Final Census Population
Ⓢ Special Census Population
◆ Estimated Population

For additional definitions see Glossary, Volume 1, and Introduction, Volume 2.

Cadenassa; YOLO; see Cadenasso (RMC Place)

Cadenasso (Cadenassa); RMC Place; YOLO; mail Capay z 95607; rural

Cadiz; RMC Place; SAN BERNARDINO; **153** SH-17; elev. 791ft./241m.; 🅿; z 92304; rural

Cahuilla; RMC Place; RIVERSIDE; ***153** SK-14; elev. 3,629ft./1,106m.; mail Anza z 92539; rural

Cahuilla Estates; RMC Place; RIVERSIDE; ***153** SK-14; elev. 3,815ft./1,163m.; mail Anza z 92539; ● 150

Cahuilla Hills; RMC Place; RIVERSIDE; ***153** SK-15; ★ **PSPR-**; mail Palm Desert z 92260; ● 140

Cahuilla Reservation; Indian Reservation; RIVERSIDE; mail Hemet z 92543; Ⓟ 56; © 154

Cairns Corner; RMC Place; TULARE; ***152** SD-9; mail Lindsay z 93247; rural

Cajon Junction; RMC Place; SAN BERNARDINO; ***153** SI-13; ★ **RIV-**; mail San Bernardino z 92403, z 92407; rural

Calabasas; Inc. Place; LOS ANGELES; **154** D-2; elev. 928ft./283m.; 🅿; ★ **L.A.**; z 91301-02, z 91372; Ⓟ 16,577; © 20,033; Ⓡ 21,356; ◆ 22,139

Calabasas Highlands; RMC Place; LOS ANGELES; ***152** SJ-10; ★ **L.A.**; mail Calabasas z 91302; pop. incl. with Calabasas (Inc. Place)

Calabasas Hills; RMC Place; LOS ANGELES; ***152** SJ-10; 🅿; ★ **L.A.**; z 91301; pop. incl. with Calabasas (Inc. Place)

Calabasas Park; RMC Place; LOS ANGELES; ***152** SJ-10; elev. 1,439ft./439m.; ★ **L.A.**; mail Calabasas z 91302; pop. incl. with Calabasas (Inc. Place)

Calaveras; RMC Place; SAN JOAQUIN; ★ **STOC**; mail Stockton z 95207, z 95267; pop. incl. with Stockton (Inc. Place)

CALAVERAS; **150** NL-9; Ⓟ 31,998; © 40,554; ◆ 47,171

Calaveras Yacht and Country Club Estates; RMC Place; SAN JOAQUIN; ***150** NL-7; ★ **STOC**; mail Stockton z 95204; ● 1,800

Calaveritas; RMC Place; CALAVERAS; ***150** NL-9; mail San Andreas z 95249; rural

Calavo Gardens; RMC Place; SAN DIEGO; ***153** SN-14; ★ **SDGO**; mail La Mesa z 91941; ● 1,200

Calexico; Inc. Place; IMPERIAL; **153** SN-17; elev. 2ft./1m.; 🅿 🅷 ■; ★ **CLEX**; z 92231-32; Ⓟ 18,633; © 27,109; ◆ 34,390

Calexico Lodge; RMC Place; SAN DIEGO; ***153** SN-15; mail Boulevard z 91905; rural

Cal-Ida; RMC Place; SIERRA; ***150** NH-8; elev. 3,513ft./1,071m.; mail Camptonville z 95922; rural

Caliente; RMC Place; KERN; **152** SG-10; 🅿; z 93518

California City; Inc. Place; KERN; **153** SG-11; 🅿; z 93504-05; Ⓟ 5,955; © 8,385

California Hot Springs; RMC Place; TULARE; **152** SE-10; 🅿; z 93207; ● 100

California Pines; RMC Place; MODOC; mail Alturas z 96101; ● 130

California Rehabilitation Center; RMC Place; RIVERSIDE; ★ **RIV-**; mail Norco z 92860; pop. incl. with Norco (Inc. Place)

California Valley; RMC Place; SAN LUIS OBISPO; ***152** SF-7; mail Santa Margarita z 93453; rural

Calimesa; Inc. Place; RIVERSIDE; **153** SJ-14; 🅿; ★ **RIV-**; z 92320; Ⓟ 6,654; © 7,139

Calipatria; Inc. Place; IMPERIAL; **153** SL-17; elev. 184ft./56m.; 🅿; z 92233; Ⓟ 2,690; © 7,289

Calistoga; Inc. Place; NAPA; **150** NK-5; elev. 362ft./110m.; 🅿; z 94515; Ⓟ 4,468; © 5,190

Calla; RMC Place; SAN JOAQUIN; ***150** NM-8; mail Manteca z 95336; rural

Callahan; RMC Place; SISKIYOU; **150** NC-4; elev. 3,123ft./952m.; 🅿; z 96014; ● 150

Calpella; RMC Place; MENDOCINO; **150** NI-3; 🅿; z 95418; ● 1,000

Calpine (Sierra Valley Lodge); RMC Place; SIERRA; **150** NH-9; elev. 4,958ft./1,511m.; 🅿; z 96124; ● 270

Calville; RMC Place; HUMBOLDT; ***150** ND-2; elev. 15ft./5m.; ★ **EUR-**; mail McKinleyville z 95519; ● 4,000

Calwa; CDP; FRESNO; ***152** SC-7; ★ **FRES**; mail Fresno z 93725, z 93745; © 762

Camarillo; Inc. Place; VENTURA; **152** SJ-9; elev. 160ft./49m.; 🅿 🅷 🅲 2,575 ■; ★ **OXN-**; z 93010-12; Ⓟ 52,303; © 57,077; ◆ 58,379

Camarillo Heights; RMC Place; VENTURA; ***152** SI-9; ★ **OXN-**; mail Camarillo z 93010; pop. incl. with Camarillo (Inc. Place)

Cambria; CDP; SAN LUIS OBISPO; **152** SF-4; elev. 65ft./20m.; 🅿; z 93428; Ⓟ 5,328; © 6,232

Cambrian Park; CDP; SANTA CLARA; **151** NN-19; ★ **SF-O-**; mail San Jose z 95124, z 95154; Ⓟ 2,998; © 3,258

Cambridge; RMC Place; SANTA CLARA; ★ **SF-O-**; mail Palo Alto z 94306; pop. incl. with Palo Alto (Inc. Place)

Camden; RMC Place; FRESNO; ***152** SC-7; elev. 234ft./71m.; mail Laton z 93242, Riverdale z 93656; ● 400

Camellia; RMC Place; SACRAMENTO; ★ **SAC**; mail Sacramento z 95819; pop. incl. with Sacramento (Inc. Place)

Cameo; RMC Place; FRESNO; ***152** SB-7; ★ **FRES**; pop. incl. with Fresno (Inc. Place)

Cameo Acres; RMC Place; CONTRA COSTA; ***150** NM-6; ★ **SF-O-**; mail Danville z 94526; pop. incl. with Danville (Inc. Place)

Cameron Corners; RMC Place; SAN DIEGO; ***153** SN-15; elev. 2,620ft./799m.; mail Campo z 91906; ● 200

Cameron Creek Colony; RMC Place; TULARE; ***152** SD-9; ★ **VISL**; mail Farmersville z 93223; ● 460

Cameron Park; CDP; EL DORADO; **150** NJ-8; 🅿; ★ **SAC**; z 95682; Ⓟ 11,897; © 14,549

Camino; RMC Place; EL DORADO; **150** NJ-9; 🅿; z 95709; ● 1,200

Camino Heights; RMC Place; EL DORADO; ***150** NJ-9; elev. 2,800ft./853m.; mail Camino z 95709; ● 150

Camino Media; RMC Place; KERN; mail Bakersfield z 93390; pop. incl. with Bakersfield (Inc. Place)

Camp Angelus; SAN BERNARDINO; see Angelus Oaks (RMC Place)

Campbell; Inc. Place; SANTA CLARA; **150** NN-6; elev. 195ft./59m.; 🅿 🅷 ■; ★ **SF-O-**; z 95008-09, z 95011; Ⓟ 36,048; © 38,138; ◆ 38,989

Campbell Hot Springs; RMC Place; SIERRA; ***150** NH-9; elev. 5,000ft./1,524m.; mail Sierraville z 96126; ● 30

Camp Connell; RMC Place; CALAVERAS; **150** NK-10; 🅿; z 95223; ● 180

Camp Evers; RMC Place; SANTA CRUZ; ***152** SB-2; elev. 527ft./161m.; ★ **S.CRZ**; mail Scotts Valley z 95066; pop. incl. with Scotts Valley (Inc. Place)

Camp Meeker; RMC Place; SONOMA; ***150** NK-4; 🅿; ★ **S.ROS**; z 95419; ● 750

Camp Nelson; RMC Place; TULARE; **152** SD-10; 🅿; z 93208; ● 200

Campo; RMC Place; SAN DIEGO; **153** SN-15; 🅿; z 91906 & mail Tecate z 91987; ● 350

Campo Reservation; Indian Reservation; SAN DIEGO; mail Campo z 91906; Ⓟ 100; © 351

Campo Seco; RMC Place; CALAVERAS; **150** NL-8; 🅿; z 95226

Camp Pendleton North; CDP-Census Area Only; SAN DIEGO; ***153** SL-13; mail Camp Pendleton z 92055; Ⓟ 10,373; © 8,197

Camp Pendleton South; CDP-Census Area Only; SAN DIEGO; ***153** SL-13; ★ **SDGO**; mail Camp Pendleton z 92055; Ⓟ 11,299; © 8,854

Camp Richardson; RMC Place; EL DORADO; ***150** NJ-10; mail South Lake Tahoe z 96150, z 96156

Camp Saint Michael; RMC Place; MENDOCINO; mail Leggett z 95585; rural

Camp Sierra; RMC Place; FRESNO; ***152** SA-8; mail Shaver Lake z 93664; ● 200

Camptonville; RMC Place; YUBA; **150** NH-8; 🅿; z 95922; ● 250

Camp Wishon; RMC Place; TULARE; ***152** SD-10; mail Springville z 93265; ● 75

Camulos; RMC Place; VENTURA; ***152** SI-10; elev. 740ft./226m.; mail Piru z 93040; rural

Canby; RMC Place; MODOC; **150** NC-8; elev. 4,312ft./1,314m.; 🅿; z 96015; ● 350

Canebrake; RMC Place; KERN; ***153** SE-11; elev. 2,977ft./907m.; mail Onyx z 93255; ● 85

Cannery Row; RMC Place; MONTEREY; ★ **MTRY-**; mail Monterey z 93942; pop. incl. with Monterey (Inc. Place)

Canoga Annex; RMC Place; LOS ANGELES; ★ **L.A.**; mail Canoga Park z 91304; pop. incl. with Los Angeles (Inc. Place)

Canoga Park; RMC Place; LOS ANGELES; ***152** SJ-10; elev. 795ft./242m.; 🅿; ★ **L.A.**; z 91303-09, z 91396; pop. incl. with Los Angeles (Inc. Place)

Cantil; RMC Place; KERN; **153** SF-11; elev. 2,025ft./617m.; 🅿; z 93519

Cantua Creek; CDP; FRESNO; **152** SC-6; elev. 295ft./90m.; 🅿; z 93608; © 655

Canyon; RMC Place; CONTRA COSTA; **151** NE-16; 🅿; ★ **SF-O-**; z 94516; rural

Canyon Acres; RMC Place; ORANGE; ***153** SK-12; ★ **L.A.**; mail Laguna Beach z 92651; pop. incl. with Laguna Beach (Inc. Place)

Canyon Country; RMC Place; LOS ANGELES; ***152** SI-10; 🅿; ★ **L.A.**; z 91351, z 91386-87, z 91390; pop. incl. with Santa Clarita (Inc. Place)

Canyon Crest; RMC Place; RIVERSIDE; ***153** SJ-13; ★ **RIV-**; mail Riverside z 92507, z 92517; pop. incl. with Riverside (Inc. Place)

Canyon Crest Heights; RMC Place; RIVERSIDE; ***153** SJ-13; ★ **RIV-**; mail Riverside z 92507; pop. incl. with Riverside (Inc. Place)

Canyondam; CDP; PLUMAS; **150** NF-8; 🅿; z 95923; © 37

Canyon Lake; Inc. Place; RIVERSIDE; **153** SK-13; 🅿; z 92587; Ⓟ 7,938; © 9,952

Capay; RMC Place; GLENN; ***150** NG-6; elev. 190ft./58m.; mail Orland z 95963; ● 50

Capay; RMC Place; YOLO; **150** NJ-6; elev. 204ft./62m.; 🅿; z 95607; ● 200

Capetown; RMC Place; HUMBOLDT; ***150** NE-1; mail Ferndale z 95536; rural

Capistrano Beach; RMC Place; ORANGE; ***153** SL-12; 🅿; ★ **L.A.**; z 92624; pop. incl. with Dana Point (Inc. Place)

Capistrano Highlands; RMC Place; ORANGE; ***153** SK-12; elev. 400ft./122m.; ★ **L.A.**; mail Laguna Hills z 92653; pop. incl. with Laguna Hills (Inc. Place)

Capital Hill; RMC Place; SAN LUIS OBISPO; ***152** SF-5; mail Paso Robles z 93446; pop. incl. with Paso Robles (Inc. Place)

Capitan Grande Reservation; Indian Reservation; SAN DIEGO; © 0

Capitola; Inc. Place; SANTA CRUZ; **152** SB-2; 🅿; ★ **S.CRZ**; z 95010; Ⓟ 10,171; © 10,033

Capuchino; RMC Place; SAN MATEO; ★ **SF-O-**; mail Burlingame z 94010-11; pop. incl. with Burlingame (Inc. Place)

Carbona; RMC Place; SAN JOAQUIN; ***150** NM-7; mail Tracy z 95376; ● 180

Carbon Beach; RMC Place; LOS ANGELES; ***152** SJ-10; elev. 100ft./30m.; ★ **L.A.**; mail Malibu z 90265; pop. incl. with Malibu (Inc. Place)

Carbon Canyon; RMC Place; SAN BERNARDINO; ★ **L.A.**; mail Chino z 91710; pop. incl. with Chino Hills (Inc. Place)

Cardiff; SAN DIEGO; see Cardiff-by-the-Sea (RMC Place)

Cardiff-by-the-Sea (Cardiff); RMC Place; SAN DIEGO; ***153** SM-13; 🅿; ★ **SDGO**; z 92007; pop. incl. with Encinitas (Inc. Place)

Cardwell; RMC Place; FRESNO; ★ **FRES**; mail Fresno z 93704, z 93755; pop. incl. with Fresno (Inc. Place)

Caribou; CDP; PLUMAS; ***150** NF-8; mail Belden z 95915; © 0

Carlotta; RMC Place; HUMBOLDT; **150** NE-2; elev. 124ft./38m.; 🅿; z 95528; ● 375

Carlsbad; Inc. Place; SAN DIEGO; **153** SL-13; elev. 39ft./12m.; 🅿 ■; ★ **SDGO**; z 92008-11, z 92013, z 92018; Ⓟ 63,126; © 78,247; ◆ 93,508

Carlton; RMC Place; ORANGE; ***153** SJ-12; ★ **L.A.**; pop. incl. with Yorba Linda (Inc. Place)

Carlton Hills; RMC Place; SAN DIEGO; ***153** SM-14; ★ **SDGO**; mail Santee z 92071; pop. incl. with Santee (Inc. Place)

Carmel; MONTEREY; see Carmel-by-the-Sea (Inc. Place)

Carmel-by-the-Sea (Carmel); Inc. Place; MONTEREY; **152** SC-2; 🅿; ★ **MTRY-**; z 93921 & mail Carmel z 93922-23; Ⓟ 4,239; © 4,081

Carmel Highlands; RMC Place; MONTEREY; **152** SC-2; ★ **MTRY-**; mail Carmel z 93923; ● 940

Carmel Hills; RMC Place; MONTEREY; ***152** SC-2; elev. 297ft./91m.; ★ **MTRY-**; mail Carmel z 93923; ● 1,500

Carmel Point; RMC Place; MONTEREY; **149** J-1; elev. 31ft./9m.; ★ **MTRY-**; mail Carmel z 93923; ● 500

Carmel Valley Village; CDP-Census Area Only; MONTEREY; **152** SC-3; ★ **MTRY-**; mail Carmel Valley z 93924; Ⓟ 4,407; © 4,700

Carmel Woods; RMC Place; MONTEREY; **149** I-1; ★ **MTRY-**; mail Carmel z 93923; ● 1,200

Carmenita; RMC Place; LOS ANGELES; ***153** SJ-11; ★ **L.A.**; mail Santa Fe Springs z 90670; pop. incl. with Santa Fe Springs (Inc. Place)

Carmet; RMC Place; SONOMA; ***150** NK-3; mail Bodega Bay z 94923; ● 160

Carmichael; CDP; SACRAMENTO; **150** NJ-7; elev. 123ft./37m.; 🅿 🅷; ★ **SAC**; z 95608-09; Ⓟ 48,702; © 49,742; ◆ 57,318

Carnelian Bay; RMC Place; PLACER; **150** NI-10; elev. 6,238ft./1,901m.; 🅿; z 96140; ● 650

Carpenter; RMC Place; ALAMEDA; ***150** NM-6; ★ **SF-O-**; pop. incl. with Hayward (Inc. Place)

Carpinteria; Inc. Place; SANTA BARBARA; **152** SI-8; elev. 14ft./4m.; 🅿 🅲 651; ★ **S.BAR**; z 93013-14; Ⓟ 13,747; © 14,194

Carquinez Heights; RMC Place; SOLANO; ***150** NL-5; ★ **SF-O-**; mail Vallejo z 94590; pop. incl. with Vallejo (Inc. Place)

Carrick; CDP-Census Area Only; SISKIYOU; ***150** NC-5; © 156

Carrick Addition; RMC Place; SISKIYOU; ***150** NC-5; elev. 3,490ft./1,064m.; mail Weed z 96094; ● 150

Carson; Inc. Place; LOS ANGELES; **154** H-7; elev. 40ft./12m.; 🅿 🅲 12,068 ■; ★ **L.A.**; z 90745-47, z 90749, z 90810, z 90895; Ⓟ 83,995; © 89,730; ◆ 91,202

Carson Hill; RMC Place; CALAVERAS; ***150** NL-9; elev. 1,441ft./439m.; mail Angels Camp z 95222; rural

Cartago; CDP; INYO; **153** SD-11; 🅿; z 93549; © 109

Caruthers; CDP; FRESNO; **152** SC-7; elev. 244ft./74m.; 🅿; ★ **FRES**; z 93609; Ⓟ 1,603; © 2,103

Carvin Creek Homesites; RMC Place; SIERRA; ***150** NH-9; elev. 5,600ft./1,707m.; mail Sierraville z 96126; ● 20

Casa Blanca; RMC Place; RIVERSIDE; ***153** SJ-13; ★ **RIV-**; mail Riverside z 92504; pop. incl. with Riverside (Inc. Place)

Casa Conejo; CDP-Census Area Only; VENTURA; **152** SJ-9; elev. 680ft./207m.; ★ **OXN-**; mail Westlake Village z 91359; Ⓟ 3,286; © 3,180

Casa Correo; RMC Place; CONTRA COSTA; ★ **SF-O-**; mail Concord z 94521; pop. incl. with Concord (Inc. Place)

Casa de Oro; RMC Place; SAN DIEGO; **156** J-9; ★ **SDGO**; mail Spring Valley z 91976-77; ● 12,000

Casa de Oro-Mount Helix; CDP-Census Area Only; SAN DIEGO; ***153** SN-14; ★ **SDGO**; mail Spring Valley z 91977; Ⓟ 30,727; © 18,874

Casa Grande; RMC Place; SONOMA; ★ **SF-O-**; mail Petaluma z 94952, z 94954-55; pop. incl. with Petaluma (Inc. Place)

Cascadel Woods; RMC Place; MADERA; ***152** SA-8; elev. 3,600ft./1,097m.; mail North Fork z 93643; rural

Casino; RMC Place; SANTA CRUZ; ★ **S.CRZ**; pop. incl. with Santa Cruz (Inc. Place)

Casitas Springs; RMC Place; VENTURA; **152** SI-8; elev. 285ft./87m.; ★ **OXN-**; mail Ventura z 93001; ● 800

Casmalia; RMC Place; SANTA BARBARA; ***152** SH-5; elev. 294ft./90m.; 🅿; z 93429; ● 200

Caspar; RMC Place; MENDOCINO; **150** NH-2; 🅿; z 95420; ● 550

Cassel; RMC Place; SHASTA; **150** ND-7; elev. 3,199ft./975m.; 🅿; z 96016; ● 220

Castaic; RMC Place; LOS ANGELES; **152** SI-10; elev. 1,232ft./376m.; 🅿; ★ **L.A.**; z 91310, z 91384; ● 1,200

Castella; RMC Place; SHASTA; **150** NC-5; elev. 1,950ft./594m.; 🅿; z 96017

Castellammare; RMC Place; LOS ANGELES; ★ **L.A.**; mail Pacific Palisades z 90272; pop. incl. with Los Angeles (Inc. Place)

Castle Park; RMC Place; SAN DIEGO; ***153** SN-14; ★ **SDGO**; mail Chula Vista z 91911; pop. incl. with Chula Vista (Inc. Place)

Castle Rock Springs; RMC Place; LAKE; ***150** NJ-4; elev. 2,400ft./732m.; mail Middletown z 95461; rural

Castlewood; RMC Place; ALAMEDA; ***150** NM-6; elev. 600ft./183m.; ★ **SF-O-**; mail Pleasanton z 94588; ● 600

Castro; RMC Place; SANTA CLARA; ***150** NN-6; ★ **SF-O-**; mail Mountain View z 94042; pop. incl. with Mountain View (Inc. Place)

Castro Valley; CDP; ALAMEDA; **150** NM-6; elev. 300ft./91m.; 🅿 🅷; ★ **SF-O-**; z 94546, z 94552; Ⓟ 48,619; © 57,292; ◆ 58,615

Castroville; CDP; MONTEREY; **152** SB-3; elev. 23ft./7m.; 🅿; ★ **SLNS**; z 95012; Ⓟ 5,272; © 6,724

Catalina; RMC Place; LOS ANGELES; ***153** SJ-11; ★ **L.A.**; mail Avalon z 90704, Pasadena z 91116; pop. incl. with Pasadena (Inc. Place)

Cathay; MARIPOSA; see Catheys Valley (RMC Place)

Cathedral City; Inc. Place; RIVERSIDE; **153** SK-15; 🅿 🅷; ★ **PSPR-**; z 92234-35; Ⓟ 30,085; © 42,647; ◆ 57,140

Catheys Valley (Cathay); RMC Place; MARIPOSA; **150** NN-10; elev. 1,321ft./403m.; 🅿; z 95306; ● 350

Cawelo; RMC Place; KERN; ***152** SF-9; mail Bakersfield z 93308; rural

Cayucos; CDP; SAN LUIS OBISPO; **152** SF-5; 🅿; z 93430; Ⓟ 2,960; © 2,943

Cazadero; RMC Place; SONOMA; **150** NK-3; elev. 117ft./36m.; 🅿; z 95421; ● 400

Cecilville; RMC Place; SISKIYOU; ***150** NC-4; mail Forks of Salmon z 96031

Cedar; RMC Place; LOS ANGELES; ★ **L.A.**; mail Lancaster z 93534, z 93584; pop. incl. with Lancaster (Inc. Place)

Cedarbrook; RMC Place; FRESNO; ***152** SC-9; mail Miramonte z 93641; rural

Cedar Crest; RMC Place; FRESNO; ***152** SA-9; mail Big Creek z 93605; rural

Cedar Flat; RMC Place; PLACER; ***150** NI-10; mail Carnelian Bay z 96140; ● 550

Cedar Glen; RMC Place; SAN BERNARDINO; **155** B-20; 🅿; ★ **RIV-**; z 92321; ● 2,100

Cedar Grove; RMC Place; EL DORADO; ***150** NJ-9; mail Camino z 95709; ● 1,200

Cedar Grove; RMC Place; FRESNO; ***152** SB-10; mail Kings Canyon National Pk z 93633

Cedarpines Park; RMC Place; SAN BERNARDINO; **155** B-18; 🅿; ★ **RIV-**; z 92322; ● 850

Cedar Ridge; RMC Place; NEVADA; **150** NI-8; 🅿; z 95924; ● 600

Cedar Ridge; RMC Place; TUOLUMNE; ***150** NL-10; mail Sonora z 95370; ● 750

Cedar Slope; RMC Place; TULARE; ***152** SD-10; mail Springville z 93265; ● 50

Cedar Stock; RMC Place; TRINITY; ***150** ND-4; elev. 2,460ft./750m.; mail Lewiston z 96052; rural

Cedar Valley; RMC Place; MADERA; ***151** NN-11; elev. 3,600ft./1,097m.; mail Oakhurst z 93644; ● 350

Cedarville; RMC Place; MODOC; **150** NB-10; elev. 4,630ft./1,411m.; 🅿 🅷; z 96104; ● 700

Cedarville Rancheria; Indian Reservation; MODOC; © 26

Center Avenue; RMC Place; ORANGE; ★ **L.A.**; mail Huntington Beach z 92605; pop. incl. with Huntington Beach (Inc. Place)

Centerville; RMC Place; ALAMEDA; ★ **SF-O-**; mail Fremont z 94536; pop. incl. with Fremont (Inc. Place)

Centerville; RMC Place; FRESNO; **152** SC-8; ★ **FRES**; mail Sanger z 93657; ● 250

Century City; RMC Place; LOS ANGELES; ***152** SJ-10; 🅿; ★ **L.A.**; z 90067; pop. incl. with Los Angeles (Inc. Place)

Ceres; Inc. Place; STANISLAUS; **150** NM-8; elev. 90ft./27m.; 🅿 🅷; ★ **MOD**; z 95307; Ⓟ 26,314; © 34,609; ◆ 39,865

Cernon; RMC Place; SOLANO; ★ **FRFL-**; mail Vacaville z 95688; pop. incl. with Vacaville (Inc. Place)

Cerritos; Inc. Place; LOS ANGELES; **154** H-9; elev. 45ft./14m.; 🅿 🅷 ■; ★ **L.A.**; z 90701, z 90703; Ⓟ 53,240; © 51,488; ◆ 50,792

Cerro Villa Heights; RMC Place; ORANGE; ***153** SK-12; ★ **L.A.**; mail Villa Park z 92861; pop. incl. with Villa Park (Inc. Place)

Chalfant Valley; RMC Place; MONO; **151** NN-14; 🅿; z 93514; ● 350

Challenge; RMC Place; YUBA; **150** NH-8; 🅿; z 95925; ● 250

Challenge-Brownsville; CDP-Census Area Only; YUBA; ***150** NH-7; elev. 2,500ft./762m.; mail Brownsville z 95919, Challenge z 95925; Ⓟ 1,096; © 1,069

Challenger; RMC Place; LOS ANGELES; ***152** SJ-10; ★ **L.A.**; mail Canoga Park z 91303, z 91305; pop. incl. with Los Angeles (Inc. Place)

Chambless; RMC Place; SAN BERNARDINO; ***153** SH-17; elev. 717ft./219m.; mail Amboy z 92304; rural

Champagne; RMC Place; SAN BERNARDINO; ***153** SJ-12; ★ **L.A.**; pop. incl. with Ontario (Inc. Place)

Champagne Fountain; RMC Place; SANTA CLARA; ***150** NN-6; ★ **SF-O-**; mail Saratoga z 95070; pop. incl. with Saratoga (Inc. Place)

Chandler; RMC Place; LOS ANGELES; ***152** SJ-10; ★ **L.A.**; mail North Hollywood z 91603; pop. incl. with Los Angeles (Inc. Place)

Channel Islands Beach; CDP-Census Area Only; VENTURA; **156** C-2; elev. 10ft./3m.; ★ **OXN-**; mail Oxnard z 93030; Ⓟ 3,317; © 3,142

Chapmantown; RMC Place; BUTTE; ***150** NG-6; ★ **CHICO**; mail Chico z 95928

Chapman Woods; RMC Place; LOS ANGELES; ***153** SJ-11; ★ **L.A.**; mail Pasadena z 91107; ● 1,900

Chappo; RMC Place; SAN DIEGO; elev. 57ft./17m.; mail Camp Pendleton z 92055

Charter Oak; CDP; LOS ANGELES; **155** D-12; elev. 740ft./226m.; ★ **L.A.**; mail Covina z 91724; Ⓟ 8,858; © 9,027

Chatsworth; RMC Place; LOS ANGELES; ***152** SI-10; 🅿; ★ **L.A.**; z 91311, z 91313; pop. incl. with Los Angeles (Inc. Place)

Chatsworth Lake Manor; RMC Place; VENTURA, LOS ANGELES; ***152** SI-10; ★ **L.A.**; mail Chatsworth z 91311; ● 1,100

Cheeseville; RMC Place; SISKIYOU; ***150** NB-4; elev. 2,805ft./855m.; mail Greenview z 96037; ● 30

Chemehuevi Reservation; Indian Reservation; SAN BERNARDINO; mail Needles z 92363; Ⓟ 265; © 345

Chemeketa Park; RMC Place; SANTA CLARA; ***152** SA-2; ★ **SF-O-**; mail Los Gatos z 95033; ● 750

Cherokee; RMC Place; BUTTE; **150** NH-7; mail Nevada City z 95959, Oroville z 95965; ● 80

Cherokee; RMC Place; NEVADA; ***150** NH-8; mail Nevada City z 95959, Oroville z 95965; ● 200

Cherokee Strip; RMC Place; KERN; ***152** SF-8; mail Shafter z 93263; ● 200

Cherry Creek Acres; RMC Place; NEVADA; ***150** NI-8; ★ **SAC**; mail Grass Valley z 95949; ● 130

Cherryland; CDP-Census Area Only; ALAMEDA; ***150** NM-6; ★ **SF-O-**; mail Hayward z 94541; Ⓟ 11,088; © 13,837

Cherry Valley; CDP; RIVERSIDE; **153** SJ-14; 🅿; ★ **RIV-**; z 92223; Ⓟ 5,945; © 5,891

Chester; CDP; PLUMAS; **150** NF-8; elev. 4,528ft./1,380m.; 🅿 🅷; z 96020; Ⓟ 2,082; © 2,316

Chestnut; RMC Place; SAN MATEO; ★ **SF-O-**; mail South San Francisco z 94080; pop. incl. with South San Francisco (Inc. Place)

Chicago Park; RMC Place; NEVADA; ***150** NI-8; elev. 2,313ft./705m.; 🅿; ★ **SAC**; z 95712; ● 750

Chicken Ranch Rancheria; Indian Reservation; TUOLUMNE; © 11

Chico; Inc. Place; BUTTE; **150** NG-6; elev. 200ft./61m.; 🅿 🅷 🅲 16,250 ■; ★ **CHICO**; z 95926-29, z 95973, z 95976; Ⓟ 40,079; © 59,954; Ⓡ 60,516; ◆ 70,322

Chilcoot; RMC Place; PLUMAS; **150** NG-10; 🅿; z 96105; ● 230

Chilcoot-Vinton; CDP-Census Area Only; PLUMAS; ***150** NG-10; © 387

Childs Meadows; RMC Place; TEHAMA; ***150** NF-7; elev. 4,940ft./1,506m.; mail Mill Creek z 96061; rural

Chili Bar; RMC Place; EL DORADO; ***150** NJ-8; elev. 966ft./294m.; mail Placerville z 95667; rural

China; RMC Place; SAN FRANCISCO; ★ **SF-O-**; mail San Francisco z 94108; pop. incl. with San Francisco (Inc. Place)

China Camp; RMC Place; MARIN; ***150** NL-5; elev. 10ft./3m.; ★ **SF-O-**; mail San Rafael z 94901; rural

China Lake; RMC Place; KERN; ***153** SE-12; mail Ridgecrest z 93555; pop. incl. with Ridgecrest (Inc. Place)

China Lake Acres; CDP-Census Area Only; KERN; ***153** SF-12; © 1,761

Chinatown; RMC Place; SAN FRANCISCO; ***150** NM-5; ★ **SF-O-**; mail San Francisco z 94108; pop. incl. with San Francisco (Inc. Place)

Chinese Camp; CDP; TUOLUMNE; **150** NM-9; elev. 1,261ft./384m.; 🅿; z 95309; © 146

Chino; Inc. Place; SAN BERNARDINO; **155** F-14; elev. 720ft./219m.; 🅿 🅷 ■; ★ **L.A.**; z 91708, z 91710 & mail Ontario z 91762; Ⓟ 59,682; © 67,168; ◆ 76,688

Chino Hills; Inc. Place; SAN BERNARDINO; **155** G-13; elev. 734ft./224m.; 🅿; ★ **L.A.**; z 91709; Ⓟ 37,868; © 66,787; ◆ 82,235

Chinowths Corner; RMC Place; TULARE; ***152** SD-8; elev. 313ft./95m.; ★ **VISL**; mail Visalia z 93277; pop. incl. with Visalia (Inc. Place)

Chinquapin; RMC Place; MARIPOSA; ***151** NM-11; elev. 6,040ft./1,841m.; mail Yosemite National Park z 95389; rural

Chiriaco Summit; RMC Place; RIVERSIDE; **153** SK-17; elev. 1,710ft./521m.; 🅿; z 92201

Cholame; RMC Place; SAN LUIS OBISPO; **152** SE-6; elev. 1,157ft./353m.; mail Shandon z 93461; rural

Chowchilla; Inc. Place; MADERA; **152** SA-6; elev. 240ft./73m.; 🅿 🅷; z 93610; Ⓟ 5,930; © 11,127; Ⓡ 14,416

Chrisman; RMC Place; VENTURA; ***152** SI-8; ★ **OXN-**; pop. incl. with Ventura (Inc. Place)

Chrome; RMC Place; GLENN; ***150** NG-5; mail Orland z 95963; rural

Chualar; CDP; MONTEREY; **152** SC-3; 🅿; z 93925; © 1,444

Chula Vista; Inc. Place; SAN DIEGO; **153** SN-14; elev. 75ft./23m.; 🅿 🅷 ■; ★ **SDGO**; z 91909-15, z 91921; Ⓟ 135,163; © 173,556; ◆ 212,443

Cima; RMC Place; SAN BERNARDINO; **153** SF-17; 🅿; z 92323; rural

Cimarron; RMC Place; LOS ANGELES; ★ **L.A.**; mail Los Angeles z 90018; pop. incl. with Los Angeles (Inc. Place)

Cincotta; RMC Place; FRESNO; ***152** SB-7; ★ **FRES**; pop. incl. with Fresno (Inc. Place)

Circle Oaks; RMC Place; NAPA; ***150** NK-5; elev. 1,300ft./396m.; mail Napa z 94558; ● 300

Cisco (Heaton Station); RMC Place; PLACER; **150** NI-9; elev. 5,923ft./1,805m.; mail Soda Springs z 95728

Citrus; CDP-Census Area Only; LOS ANGELES; ***153** SJ-12; ★ **L.A.**; mail Azusa z 91702, North Myrtle Beach z 29582; Ⓟ 9,481; © 10,581

Citrus Heights; Inc. Place; SACRAMENTO; **150** NJ-7; elev. 160ft./49m.; 🅿; ★ **SAC**; z 95610-11, z 95621 & mail Orangevale z 95662; Ⓟ 82,045; © 85,071; ◆ 90,552

City Hall; RMC Place; SAN FRANCISCO; ★ **SF-O-**; mail San Francisco z 94102; pop. incl. with San Francisco (Inc. Place)

City Heights; RMC Place; SAN DIEGO; ***153** SN-14; ★ **SDGO**; mail San Diego z 92105, z 92165; pop. incl. with San Diego (Inc. Place)

City of Industry; LOS ANGELES; see Industry (Inc. Place)

City Terrace; RMC Place; LOS ANGELES; ***153** SJ-11; ★ **L.A.**; mail Los Angeles z 90063; ● 15,000

Civic Center; RMC Place; ALAMEDA; ★ **SF-O-**; mail Oakland z 94604, z 94612; pop. incl. with Oakland (Inc. Place)

Civic Center; RMC Place; FRESNO; ★ **FRES**; mail Fresno z 93707-09, z 93712, z 93714-18, z 93721; pop. incl. with Fresno (Inc. Place)

Civic Center; RMC Place; LOS ANGELES; ***152** SJ-10; ★ **L.A.**; mail Van Nuys z 91401, z 91404, z 91408, z 91411; pop. incl. with Los Angeles (Inc. Place)

Civic Center; RMC Place; ORANGE; ★ **L.A.**; mail La Habra z 90633; pop. incl. with La Habra (Inc. Place)

Civic Center; RMC Place; ORANGE; ★ **L.A.**; mail Santa Ana z 92701, z 92712; pop. incl. with Santa Ana (Inc. Place)

Clairemont; RMC Place; SAN DIEGO; **156** H-5; ★ **SDGO**; mail San Diego z 92117; pop. incl. with San Diego (Inc. Place)

Clam Beach; RMC Place; HUMBOLDT; ***150** ND-2; elev. 19ft./6m.; ★ **EUR-**; mail McKinleyville z 95519; ● 300

Claremont; Inc. Place; LOS ANGELES; **155** D-13; elev. 1,169ft./356m.; 🅿 🅲 7,507; ★ **L.A.**; z 91711; Ⓟ 32,503; © 33,998; ◆ 34,587

Clarksburg; RMC Place; YOLO; **150** NK-7; elev. 14ft./4m.; 🅿; ★ **SAC**; z 95612; ● 525

Clarksville; RMC Place; EL DORADO; ***150** NJ-8; elev. 673ft./205m.; ★ **SAC**; mail Shingle Springs z 95682; rural

Clay; RMC Place; SACRAMENTO; ***150** NK-8; elev. 102ft./31m.; mail Herald z 95638; ● 400

Clayton; Inc. Place; CONTRA COSTA; **150** NL-6; elev. 394ft./120m.; 🅿; ★ **SF-O-**; z 94517; Ⓟ 7,317; © 10,762

Clayton Street Station; RMC Place; SAN FRANCISCO; ★ **SF-O-**; mail San Francisco z 94117; pop. incl. with San Francisco (Inc. Place)

Clear Creek; RMC Place; LASSEN; **150** NF-8; mail Westwood z 96137; ● 200

Clear Creek; RMC Place; SISKIYOU; **150** NB-3; elev. 970ft./296m.; mail Happy Camp z 96039; ● 30

Clearlake; Inc. Place; LAKE; **150** NI-4; 🅿 🅷; z 95422; Ⓟ 11,804; © 13,142

Clearlake Oaks; CDP; LAKE; **150** NI-4; 🅿; z 95423; Ⓟ 2,419; © 2,402

Clearlake Park; RMC Place; LAKE; ***150** NI-4; 🅿; z 95424; pop. incl. with Clearlake (Inc. Place)

Clear Lake Riviera; RMC Place; LAKE; ***150** NI-4; elev. 1,800ft./549m.; mail Kelseyville z 95451; ● 1,100

Clements; RMC Place; SAN JOAQUIN; **150** NL-8; elev. 131ft./40m.; 🅿; z 95227; ● 200

Cleone; RMC Place; MENDOCINO; **150** NH-2; mail Fort Bragg z 95437; ● 100

Cliff Haven; RMC Place; ORANGE; ★ **L.A.**; mail Newport Beach z 92663; pop. incl. with Newport Beach (Inc. Place)

Clifton; RMC Place; LOS ANGELES; ***152** SK-10; elev. 163ft./50m.; ★ **L.A.**; mail Redondo Beach z 90277; pop. incl. with Redondo Beach (Inc. Place)

Clingans Junction; RMC Place; FRESNO; ***152** SB-9; elev. 1,855ft./565m.; mail Squaw Valley z 93675; ● 200

Clinter; RMC Place; FRESNO; ★ **FRES**; mail Fresno z 93703; pop. incl. with Fresno (Inc. Place)

Clinton; RMC Place; AMADOR; ***150** NK-9; mail Jackson z 95642; ● 150

Clio; CDP; PLUMAS; **150** NG-9; 🅿; z 96106; © 90

Clipper Gap; RMC Place; PLACER; **150** NI-8; ★ **SAC**; mail Auburn z 95603; ● 330

Clipper Mills; RMC Place; BUTTE; **150** NH-8; 🅿; z 95930; ● 150

Cloverdale; RMC Place; SHASTA; ***150** NE-5; elev. 892ft./272m.; ★ **REDD**; mail Anderson z 96007

Cloverdale; Inc. Place; SONOMA; **150** NJ-4; elev. 316ft./96m.; 🅿; z 95425; Ⓟ 4,924; © 6,831

Clovis; Inc. Place; FRESNO; **152** SB-7; elev. 361ft./110m.; 🅿 🅷 ■; ★ **FRES**; z 93611-13, z 93619; Ⓟ 50,323; © 68,468; ◆ 85,777

Clyde; CDP; CONTRA COSTA; **151** NC-18; ★ **SF-O-**; mail Concord z 94520; © 694

Coachella; Inc. Place; RIVERSIDE; **153** SK-16; elev. 71ft./22m.; 🅿; ★ **IND-**; z 92236; Ⓟ 16,896; © 22,724; ◆ 36,928

Coalinga; Inc. Place; FRESNO; **152** SD-6; elev. 667ft./203m.; 🅿 🅷; z 93210; Ⓟ 8,212; © 11,668; Ⓡ 16,213

Coarsegold; RMC Place; MADERA; **152** SA-7; elev. 2,206ft./672m.; 🅿; z 93614; ● 2,000

Coarsegold Creek Ranch; RMC Place; MADERA; ***152** SA-7; elev. 2,000ft./610m.; mail Coarsegold z 93614; rural

Coast Guard Island; RMC Place; ALAMEDA; ***150** NM-5; ★ **SF-O-**; mail Alameda z 94501; pop. incl. with Alameda (Inc. Place)

Cobb; CDP; LAKE; **150** NJ-4; 🅿; z 95426; Ⓟ 1,477; © 1,638

Cockatoo Grove; RMC Place; SAN DIEGO; ***153** SN-14; ★ **SDGO**; mail Chula Vista z 91910; pop. incl. with Chula Vista (Inc. Place)

Coddingtown; RMC Place; SONOMA; ★ **S.ROS**; mail Santa Rosa z 95401, z 95406; pop. incl. with Santa Rosa (Inc. Place)

Codora; RMC Place; GLENN; **150** NH-6; mail Princeton z 95970; ● 30

Coffee Creek; RMC Place; TRINITY; ***150** ND-5; elev. 3,200ft./975m.; mail Trinity Center z 96091; ● 100

Cohasset; RMC Place; BUTTE; **150** NG-7; 🅿; z 95973; ● 280

Coit Ranch; RMC Place; FRESNO; ***152** SC-6; elev. 265ft./81m.; mail Mendota z 93640; rural

Cold Fork; RMC Place; TEHAMA; ***150** NF-5; mail Red Bluff z 96080; rural

Cold Springs; RMC Place; TUOLUMNE; 🅿; z 95335; ● 280

Cold Springs Rancheria; Indian Reservation; FRESNO; © 193

Cole; RMC Place; LOS ANGELES; ***153** SJ-11; ★ **L.A.**; mail Los Angeles z 90025, z 90046; pop. incl. with West Hollywood (Inc. Place)

Coleville; RMC Place; MONO; **151** NK-11; 🅿; z 96107

Colfax; Inc. Place; PLACER; **150** NI-8; 🅿; ★ **SAC**; z 95713; Ⓟ 1,306; © 1,496

College City; RMC Place; COLUSA; **150** NI-6; 🅿; z 95912; ● 200

College Heights; RMC Place; KERN; ★ **BAK**; mail Bakersfield z 93305; pop. incl. with Bakersfield (Inc. Place)

College Heights; RMC Place; SAN BERNARDINO; ***153** SJ-12; elev. 1,305ft./398m.; ★ **L.A.**; mail Upland z 91786; pop. incl. with Upland (Inc. Place)

College Heights; RMC Place; SAN DIEGO; ***153** SN-14; ★ **SDGO**; mail San Diego z 92115; pop. incl. with San Diego (Inc. Place)

College Park; RMC Place; SANTA CLARA; ***150** NN-6; ★ **SF-O-**; pop. incl. with San Jose (Inc. Place)

College Park; RMC Place; VENTURA; ★ **OXN-**; mail Thousand Oaks z 91360; pop. incl. with Thousand Oaks (Inc. Place)

Collegeville; RMC Place; SAN JOAQUIN; ***150** NM-8; elev. 59ft./18m.; mail Stockton z 95206; rural

Collier; RMC Place; LOS ANGELES; ★ **L.A.**; mail West Hills z 91307; pop. incl. with Los Angeles (Inc. Place)

Collierville; RMC Place; SAN JOAQUIN; ***150** NL-7; ★ **STOC**; mail Acampo z 95220; ● 1,500

Collinsville; RMC Place; SOLANO; **150** NL-6; elev. 3ft./1m.; mail Suisun City z 94585; ● 90

Colma; Inc. Place; SAN MATEO; **151** NH-13; 🅿; ★ **SF-O-**; z 94014; Ⓟ 1,103; © 1,191; Ⓡ 1,187

Coloma; RMC Place; EL DORADO; **150** NJ-8; 🅿; z 95613; ● 200

Colonial; RMC Place; SACRAMENTO; ★ **SAC**; mail Sacramento z 95820, z 95824; pop. incl. with Sacramento (Inc. Place)

Colonial Acres; RMC Place; SACRAMENTO; ★ **SAC**; pop. incl. with Sacramento (Inc. Place)

Colonial Heights; RMC Place; SACRAMENTO; ★ **SAC**; pop. incl. with Sacramento (Inc. Place)

Colonial Juarez; RMC Place; ORANGE; ★ **L.A.**; mail Fountain Valley z 92708; pop. incl. with Fountain Valley (Inc. Place)

Colonnade; RMC Place; SANTA CLARA; ★ **SF-O-**; mail San Jose z 95172; pop. incl. with San Jose (Inc. Place)

Colony; RMC Place; SAN BERNARDINO; ***153** SH-20; elev. 554ft./169m.; mail Needles z 92363; ● 100

Colorado; RMC Place; LOS ANGELES; ★ **L.A.**; mail Santa Monica z 90404-05, z 90411; pop. incl. with Santa Monica (Inc. Place)

Colorado River Reservation; Indian Reservation; SAN BERNARDINO, RIVERSIDE; Reservation extends into AZ; mail Parker z 85344; Indian Agency located at Parker, AZ; Ⓟ 1,233; © 1,735

Colton; Inc. Place; SAN BERNARDINO; **153** SJ-13; elev. 1,000ft./305m.; 🅿; ★ **RIV-**; z 92324 & mail Grand Terrace z 92313; Ⓟ 40,213; © 47,662; ◆ 52,529

Columbia; CDP; TUOLUMNE; **150** NL-9; elev. 2,143ft./653m.; 🅿; z 95310; Ⓟ 1,799; © 2,405

Columbus; RMC Place; KERN; ★ **BAK**; mail Bakersfield z 93306; pop. incl. with Bakersfield (Inc. Place)

Colusa; Inc. Place; ⊡ COLUSA; **150** NI-6; elev. 61ft./19m.; 🅿 🅷; z 95932; Ⓟ 4,934; © 5,402

COLUSA; **150** NI-6; Ⓟ 16,275; © 18,804; ◆ 21,480

Colusa Junction; RMC Place; SUTTER; ★ **YUCY**; ● 350

Colusa Rancheria; Indian Reservation; COLUSA; © 77

Commerce; Inc. Place; LOS ANGELES; **154** F-8; elev. 140ft./43m.; 🅿 ■; ★ **L.A.**; z 90022-23, z 90040, z 90091; Ⓟ 12,135; © 12,568; ◆ 13,035

Commonwealth; RMC Place; ORANGE; ***153** SK-12; ★ **L.A.**; mail Fullerton z 92832, z 92836; pop. incl. with Fullerton (Inc. Place)

Community Center; RMC Place; VENTURA; ***152** SI-10; ★ **L.A.**; mail Simi Valley z 93065; pop. incl. with Simi Valley (Inc. Place)

Comptche; RMC Place; MENDOCINO; **150** NI-3; 🅿; z 95427; ● 200

Compton; Inc. Place; LOS ANGELES; **154** H-7; elev. 66ft./20m.; 🅿 ■; ★ **L.A.**; z 90220-24; Ⓟ 90,454; © 93,493; ◆ 93,714

Concepcion; RMC Place; SANTA BARBARA; ***152** SI-6; elev. 115ft./35m.; mail Lompoc z 93436; rural

Concord; Inc. Place; CONTRA COSTA; **150** NL-6; elev. 70ft./21m.; 🅿 🅷 ■; ★ **SF-O-**; z 94518-24, z 94527, z 94529; Ⓟ 111,348; © 121,780; ◆ 124,976

Concow; CDP-Census Area Only; BUTTE; ***150** NG-7; elev. 2,600ft./792m.; mail Paradise z 95969; © 1,095

Conejo; RMC Place; FRESNO; **152** SC-7; elev. 263ft./80m.; ★ **FRES**; mail Selma z 93662; ● 300

Conejo Valley; RMC Place; VENTURA; ★ **OXN-**; mail Thousand Oaks z 91358, z 91360; pop. incl. with Thousand Oaks (Inc. Place)

Confidence; RMC Place; TUOLUMNE; ***150** NL-10; mail Twain Harte z 95383; ● 360

CONTRA COSTA; **150** NM-7; Ⓟ 803,732; © 948,816; ◆ 1,009,806

Cool; RMC Place; EL DORADO; **150** NJ-8; elev. 1,525ft./465m.; 🅿; z 95614; ● 1,200

Copco; RMC Place; SISKIYOU; **150** NA-5; mail Montague z 96064; ● 80

Copper Cove Village; RMC Place; CALAVERAS; ***150** NL-9; elev. 751ft./229m.; mail Copperopolis z 95228; ● 350

Copperopolis; CDP; CALAVERAS; **150** NL-9; 🅿; z 95228; © 2,363

Copperwood; RMC Place; SAN DIEGO; ★ **SDGO**; mail Oceanside z 92054; pop. incl. with Oceanside (Inc. Place)

Copsey Creek; RMC Place; LAKE; elev. 1,380ft./421m.; mail Lower Lake z 95457; ● 200

Corcoran; Inc. Place; KINGS; **152** SD-8; elev. 207ft./63m.; 🅿 🅷; z 93212, z 93282; Ⓟ 13,364; © 14,458; Ⓡ 20,835; ◆ 23,200

Cordelia; RMC Place; SOLANO; **150** NL-6; ★ **FRFL-**; mail Suisun City z 94585; ● 170

Cordova; RMC Place; SACRAMENTO; ***150** NK-7; ★ **SAC**; pop. incl. with Sacramento (Inc. Place)

Cornell; RMC Place; LOS ANGELES; ***152** SJ-10; 🅿; ★ **OXN-**; z 91301

Corning; Inc. Place; TEHAMA; **150** NG-6; elev. 272ft./83m.; 🅿; z 96021, z 96029; Ⓟ 5,870; © 6,741

Corona; Inc. Place; RIVERSIDE; **153** SK-12; elev. 678ft./207m.; 🅿 🅷 ■; ★ **RIV-**; z 92877-83; Ⓟ 76,095; © 124,966; ◆ 164,987

Corona Del Mar; RMC Place; ORANGE; ***153** SK-12; 🅿; ★ **L.A.**; z 92625; pop. incl. with Newport Beach (Inc. Place)

Coronado; Inc. Place; SAN DIEGO; **153** SN-13; elev. 25ft./8m.; 🅿 🅷; ★ **SDGO**; z 92118, z 92178; Ⓟ 26,540; © 24,100; ◆ 26,048

Coronet; RMC Place; LOS ANGELES; ★ **L.A.**; pop. incl. with Pasadena (Inc. Place)

Coronita; RMC Place; RIVERSIDE; **155** H-15; ★ **RIV-**; mail Corona z 92880; ● 2,400

Corral Beach; RMC Place; LOS ANGELES; ***152** SJ-10; elev. 100ft./30m.; ★ **L.A.**; mail Malibu z 90265; pop. incl. with Malibu (Inc. Place)

Corralitos; CDP; SANTA CRUZ; ***152** SB-3; 🅿; ★ **WATS**; z 95076; Ⓟ 2,513; © 2,431

Corte Madera; Inc. Place; MARIN; **151** ND-12; elev. 27ft./8m.; 🅿; ★ **SF-O-**; z 94925, z 94976; Ⓟ 8,272; © 9,100

Cortina Rancheria; Indian Reservation; COLUSA; © 19

Coso Junction; RMC Place; INYO; **153** SD-11; elev. 3,368ft./1,027m.; mail Olancha z 93549; ● 20

Costa Mesa; Inc. Place; ORANGE; **155** K-11; elev. 101ft./31m.; 🅿 🅷 🅲 2,156 ■; ★ **L.A.**; z 92626-28; Ⓟ 96,357; © 108,724; ◆ 113,415

Cosumne; RMC Place; SACRAMENTO; ***150** NK-8; elev. 104ft./32m.; ★ **SAC**; mail Sloughhouse z 95683; ● 110

Cotati; Inc. Place; SONOMA; **150** NK-4; 🅿; ★ **S.ROS**; z 94926-28, z 94931; Ⓟ 5,714; © 6,471

Coto de Caza; CDP-Census Area Only; ORANGE; **155** K-15; elev. 1,000ft./305m.; 🅿; ★ **L.A.**; z 92679; Ⓟ 2,853; © 13,057

Cottage Springs; RMC Place; CALAVERAS; ***150** NK-10; elev. 5,800ft./1,768m.; mail Arnold z 95223; rural

Cotton Center; RMC Place; TULARE; ***152** SD-9; ★ **PORT**; mail Porterville z 93257; rural

Cottonwood; CDP; SHASTA; **150** NF-5; elev. 420ft./128m.; 🅿; ★ **REDD**; z 96022; Ⓟ 1,747; © 2,960

Coulterville; RMC Place; MARIPOSA; **150** NM-10; elev. 1,683ft./513m.; 🅿; z 95311; ● 200

Country Club; RMC Place; CONTRA COSTA; ★ **SF-O-**; mail Moraga z 94556; pop. incl. with Moraga (Inc. Place)

Country Club; CDP-Census Area Only; SAN JOAQUIN; ***150** NL-7; ★ **STOC**; mail Stockton z 95204; Ⓟ 9,325; © 9,462

Country Club Acres; RMC Place; MADERA; ***151** NN-11; elev. 3,200ft./975m.; mail Oakhurst z 93644; ● 200

Country Club Estates; RMC Place; SAN LUIS OBISPO; ***152** SG-5; elev. 267ft./81m.; ★ **S.LUIS**; mail San Luis Obispo z 93401; ● 650

Court; RMC Place; CONTRA COSTA; ★ **SF-O-**; mail Martinez z 94553; pop. incl. with Martinez (Inc. Place)

Courtland; RMC Place; SACRAMENTO; **150** NK-7; 🅿; z 95615; ● 300

Covelo; CDP; MENDOCINO; **150** NG-3; elev. 1,398ft./426m.; 🅿; z 95428; Ⓟ 1,057; © 1,175

Covina; Inc. Place; LOS ANGELES; **155** E-11; elev. 546ft./166m.; 🅿 🅷 🅲 900 ■; ★ **L.A.**; z 91722-24; Ⓟ 43,207; © 46,837; ◆ 48,554

Covington Mill; RMC Place; TRINITY; **150** ND-4; mail Lewiston z 96052; ● 30

Cowan Heights; RMC Place; ORANGE; **155** I-12; elev. 113ft./34m.; 🅿; ★ **L.A.**; z 92705; ● 4,000

Cowell; RMC Place; CONTRA COSTA; ***150** NL-6; ★ **SF-O-**; mail Concord z 94518; pop. incl. with Concord (Inc. Place)

Coy Flat; RMC Place; TULARE; mail Camp Nelson z 93208; rural

Coyote; RMC Place; SANTA CLARA; ***152** SA-3; elev. 255ft./78m.; 🅿; ★ **SF-O-**; z 95013; pop. incl. with San Jose (Inc. Place)

Coyote Valley Reservation; Indian Reservation; MENDOCINO; © 104

Cozzens Corner; RMC Place; SONOMA; mail Geyserville z 95441, Healdsburg z 95448; rural

Crafton; RMC Place; SAN BERNARDINO; ***153** SJ-13; elev. 1,752ft./534m.; ★ **RIV-**; mail Mentone z 92359; ● 5,000

Crayold; RMC Place; FRESNO; ★ **FRES**; pop. incl. with Fresno (Inc. Place)

Crenshaw-Imperial; RMC Place; LOS ANGELES; ★ **L.A.**; mail Inglewood z 90303, z 90310; pop. incl. with Inglewood (Inc. Place)

Crescent; RMC Place; LOS ANGELES; ★ **L.A.**; mail Beverly Hills z 90213; pop. incl. with Beverly Hills (Inc. Place)

Crescent City; Inc. Place; ⊡ DEL NORTE; **150** NA-1; elev. 44ft./13m.; 🅿 🅷; z 95531-32, z 95538; Ⓟ 4,380; © 4,006; Ⓡ 7,347

Crescent City North; CDP-Census Area Only; DEL NORTE; ***150** NA-1; mail Crescent City z 95531; Ⓟ 3,853; © 4,028

Crescent Mills; CDP; PLUMAS; **150** NF-8; 🅿; z 95934; © 258

Cressey; RMC Place; MERCED; **150** NN-9; elev. 165ft./50m.; 🅿; ★ **MRCD**; z 95312; ● 370

Crest (Sun Crest); CDP-Census Area Only; SAN DIEGO; **153** SM-14; ★ **SDGO**; mail El Cajon z 92021; © 2,716

Crestline; CDP; SAN BERNARDINO; **155** B-18; elev. 5,000ft./1,524m.; 🅿; ★ **RIV-**; z 92325; Ⓟ 8,594; © 10,218

Crestmore; RMC Place; SAN BERNARDINO; ***153** SJ-13; ★ **RIV-**; mail Bloomington z 92316; ● 4,500

Crestmore Heights; RMC Place; RIVERSIDE; ***153** SJ-13; ★ **RIV-**; mail Riverside z 92509; ● 370

Creston; RMC Place; SAN LUIS OBISPO; **152** SF-6; 🅿; z 93432

Crest Park; RMC Place; SAN BERNARDINO; **155** B-20; 🅿; ★ **RIV-**; z 92326; ● 600

Crestview; RMC Place; MONO; **153** NM-12

C-Road; CDP-Census Area Only; PLUMAS; ***150** NG-9; © 152

Crockett; CDP; CONTRA COSTA; **151** NB-15; elev. 118ft./36m.; 🅿; ★ **SF-O-**; z 94525; Ⓟ 3,228; © 3,194

Cromberg; CDP; PLUMAS; **150** NG-9; 🅿; z 96103; © 290

Crossroads; RMC Place; SONOMA; ★ **S.ROS**; mail Santa Rosa z 95401; pop. incl. with Santa Rosa (Inc. Place)

Crowley Lake; RMC Place; MONO; 🅿; z 93546; pop. incl. with Mammoth Lakes (Inc. Place)

Crown Point; RMC Place; SAN DIEGO; ★ **SDGO**; mail San Diego z 92109; pop. incl. with San Diego (Inc. Place)

Crows Landing; RMC Place; STANISLAUS; **150** NN-8; elev. 111ft./34m.; 🅿; z 95313; ● 300

Crutcher; RMC Place; LOS ANGELES; ★ **L.A.**; mail Paramount z 90723; pop. incl. with Paramount (Inc. Place)

Crystal Cove; RMC Place; ORANGE; **155** L-12; ★ **L.A.**; mail Laguna Beach z 92651; ● 320

Cucamonga; SAN BERNARDINO; see Rancho Cucamonga (Inc. Place)

Cudahy; Inc. Place; LOS ANGELES; **154** G-8; elev. 121ft./37m.; 🅿; ★ **L.A.**; z 90201; Ⓟ 22,817; © 24,208; ◆ 24,604

Cudahy; RMC Place; SAN DIEGO; ★ **SDGO**; pop. incl. with San Diego (Inc. Place)

Cuesta-by-the-Sea; RMC Place; SAN LUIS OBISPO; ***152** SF-5; mail Los Osos z 93402; ● 2,500

Culver City; Inc. Place; LOS ANGELES; **154** F-5; elev. 94ft./29m.; 🅿 🅷 🅲 970 ■; ★ **L.A.**; z 90230-33; Ⓟ 38,793; © 38,816; ◆ 38,247

Cummings; RMC Place; MENDOCINO; ***150** NG-2; mail Laytonville z 95454; rural

Cunningham; RMC Place; SONOMA; ***150** NK-4; ★ **S.ROS**; mail Sebastopol z 95472; ● 480

Cupertino; Inc. Place; SANTA CLARA; **151** NM-17; elev. 236ft./72m.; 🅿 ■; ★ **SF-O-**; z 95014-15; Ⓟ 40,263; © 50,546; ◆ 59,105

Curry Village; RMC Place; MARIPOSA; ***151** NM-11; mail Yosemite National Park z 95389; ● 100

Curtiss Heights; RMC Place; HUMBOLDT; ★ **EUR-**; mail Arcata z 95521; pop. incl. with Arcata (Inc. Place)

Curtner; RMC Place; ALAMEDA; ***150** NN-6; ★ **SF-O-**; mail Fremont z 94539; pop. incl. with Fremont (Inc. Place)

Cutler; CDP; TULARE; **152** SC-8; 🅿; z 93615; Ⓟ 4,450; © 4,491

Cutten; CDP; HUMBOLDT; ***150** ND-1; 🅿; ★ **EUR-**; z 95534 & mail Eureka z 95501; Ⓟ 1,516; © 2,933

Cuyama; RMC Place; SANTA BARBARA; **152** SH-8; elev. 2,261ft./689m.; 🅿; z 93254

Cuyapaipe Reservation; Indian Reservation; SAN DIEGO; © 0

Cypress; Inc. Place; ORANGE; **154** H-9; elev. 36ft./11m.; 🅿 🅲 8,700; ★ **L.A.**; z 90630, z 90720; Ⓟ 42,655; © 46,229; ◆ 47,005

Cypress South; RMC Place; ORANGE; ★ **L.A.**; mail Cypress z 90630; pop. incl. with Cypress (Inc. Place)

D

Daggett; RMC Place; SAN BERNARDINO; **153** SH-14; elev. 2,003ft./611m.; 🅿; z 92327; ● 450

Dairyland; RMC Place; MADERA; ***152** SB-6; elev. 181ft./55m.; mail Chowchilla z 93610; ● 150

Dairyville (Los Robles); RMC Place; TEHAMA; **150** NF-6; mail Red Bluff z 96080; ● 1,000

Dales; RMC Place; TEHAMA; **150** NF-6; elev. 604ft./184m.; mail Red Bluff z 96080

Daly City; Inc. Place; SAN MATEO; **151** NG-13; elev. 400ft./122m.; 🅿 🅷 ■; ★ **SF-O-**; z 94013-17; Ⓟ 92,311; © 103,621; Ⓡ 103,625; ◆ 109,232

Dana; RMC Place; SHASTA; **150** ND-7; elev. 3,336ft./1,017m.; mail Fall River Mills z 96028; ● 100

Dana Point; Inc. Place; ORANGE; **155** N-14; 🅿 🅷; ★ **L.A.**; z 92624, z 92629; Ⓟ 31,896; © 35,110; ◆ 35,828

Danby; RMC Place; SAN BERNARDINO; ***153** SH-17; elev. 1,352ft./412m.; mail Essex z 92332; rural

Danville; Inc. Place; CONTRA COSTA; **150** NM-6; elev. 368ft./112m.; 🅿; ★ **SF-O-**; z 94506, z 94526; Ⓟ 31,306; © 41,715; ◆ 42,925

Danville Square; RMC Place; CONTRA COSTA; ★ **SF-O-**; mail Danville z 94506, z 94526; pop. incl. with Danville (Inc. Place)

Daphnedale Park; RMC Place; MODOC; ***150** NB-9; mail Alturas z 96101; ● 50

Dardanelle; RMC Place; TUOLUMNE; **151** NK-11; 🅿; z 95314; ● 2

Darrah; RMC Place; MARIPOSA; ***151** NN-11; mail Mariposa z 95338; ● 500

Darwin; CDP; INYO; **153** SD-12; elev. 4,746ft./1,447m.; 🅿; z 93522; © 54

Daulton; RMC Place; MADERA; ***152** SA-7; elev. 400ft./122m.; mail Madera z 93637; rural

Davenport; RMC Place; SANTA CRUZ; **152** SB-2; 🅿; ★ **S.CRZ**; z 95017; ● 300

Davis; Inc. Place; YOLO; **150** NK-6; elev. 50ft./15m.; 🅿 🅷 🅲 30,475; ★ **DAV**; z 95616-18; Ⓟ 46,209; © 60,308; ◆ 70,885

Davis Creek; RMC Place; MODOC; **150** NB-10; 🅿; z 96108; ● 110

Day; RMC Place; MODOC; **150** NC-7; elev. 3,655ft./1,114m.; mail McArthur z 96056; ● 50

Dayton; RMC Place; BUTTE; **150** NH-6; ★ **CHICO**; mail Chico z 95928; ● 250

Day Valley; CDP-Census Area Only; SANTA CRUZ; ***152** SB-3; elev. 400ft./122m.; ★ **S.CRZ**; mail Watsonville z 95076; Ⓟ 2,842; © 3,587

Dearborn Park; RMC Place; SAN MATEO; ***150** NN-5; mail Pescadero z 94060; ● 130

Death Valley Junction; RMC Place; INYO; **153** SD-15; mail Death Valley z 92328; ● 20

Decoto; RMC Place; ALAMEDA; ★ **SF-O-**; mail Union City z 94587; pop. incl. with Union City (Inc. Place)

Deep Springs; RMC Place; INYO; ***151** NN-15; mail Dyer z 89010

Deer Creek; RMC Place; TEHAMA; ***150** NF-7; mail Mill Creek z 96061; rural

Deer Lick Springs; RMC Place; TRINITY; mail Platina z 96076; ● 80

Deer Park; CDP-Census Area Only; NAPA; ***150** NK-5; 🅿 🅷; z 94576; Ⓟ 1,825; © 1,433

Del Aire; CDP-Census Area Only; LOS ANGELES; ***153** SJ-11; ★ **L.A.**; mail Hawthorne z 90250; Ⓟ 8,040; © 9,012

Del Amo; RMC Place; LOS ANGELES; ★ **L.A.**; mail Torrance z 90503; pop. incl. with Torrance (Inc. Place)

Delano; Inc. Place; KERN; **152** SE-8; elev. 316ft./96m.; 🅿 🅷; z 93215-16; Ⓟ 22,762; © 38,824; Ⓡ 39,489; ◆ 54,361

Delavan; COLUSA; see Delevan (RMC Place)

Del Cerro; RMC Place; SAN DIEGO; ***153** SM-14; ★ **SDGO**; mail San Diego z 92119; pop. incl. with San Diego (Inc. Place)

Del Dios; RMC Place; SAN DIEGO; ***153** SM-13; ★ **SDGO**; mail Escondido z 92029; ● 355

Delevan (Delavan); RMC Place; COLUSA; **150** NH-6; mail Willows z 95988

Delft Colony; RMC Place; TULARE; ***152** SC-8; mail Dinuba z 93618; ● 750

Delhi; CDP; MERCED; **150** NN-8; 🅿; z 95315; Ⓟ 3,280; © 8,022

Dell; RMC Place; SANTA CLARA; ★ **SF-O-**; mail Los Gatos z 95032; pop. incl. with Campbell (Inc. Place)

Delleker; CDP; PLUMAS; ***150** NG-9; elev. 4,920ft./1,500m.; mail Portola z 96122; © 674

Del Loma; RMC Place; TRINITY; ***150** ND-3; mail Big Bar z 96010; ● 40

Del Mar; Inc. Place; SAN DIEGO; **153** SM-13; 🅿; ★ **SDGO**; z 92014; Ⓟ 4,860; © 4,389

Del Monte; RMC Place; MONTEREY; ★ **MTRY-**; pop. incl. with Monterey (Inc. Place)

Del Monte Forest; CDP-Census Area Only; MONTEREY; ***152** SC-2; elev. 300ft./91m.; ★ **MTRY-**; mail Pebble Beach z 93953; Ⓟ 5,069; © 4,531; Ⓡ 4,536

Del Monte Heights; RMC Place; MONTEREY; ***152** SC-3; ★ **MTRY-**; mail Seaside z 93955; pop. incl. with Seaside (Inc. Place)

Del Monte Park; RMC Place; MONTEREY; ***152** SC-2; ★ **MTRY-**; mail Pacific Grove z 93950; pop. incl. with Pacific Grove (Inc. Place)

DEL NORTE; **150** NB-2; Ⓟ 23,460; © 27,507; ◆ 29,646

Del Paso; RMC Place; SACRAMENTO; ***150** NJ-7; ★ **SAC**; pop. incl. with Sacramento (Inc. Place)

Del Paso Heights; RMC Place; SACRAMENTO; ***150** NJ-7; ★ **SAC**; mail Sacramento z 95838; pop. incl. with Sacramento (Inc. Place)

Del Rey; CDP; FRESNO; **152** SC-8; 🅿; ★ **FRES**; z 93616; Ⓟ 1,150; © 950

Del Rey Oaks; Inc. Place; MONTEREY; **152** SC-3; 🅿; ★ **MTRY-**; z 93940; Ⓟ 1,661; © 1,650

Del Rio; RMC Place; SACRAMENTO; ★ **SAC**; pop. incl. with Sacramento (Inc. Place)

Del Rio; CDP-Census Area Only; STANISLAUS; ***150** NM-8; ★ **MOD**; © 1,168

Del Rio Woods; RMC Place; SONOMA; ***150** NJ-4; ★ **S.ROS**; mail Healdsburg z 95448; rural

Del Rosa; RMC Place; SAN BERNARDINO; ***153** SJ-13; ★ **RIV-**; mail San Bernardino z 92404, z 92413; pop. incl. with San Bernardino (Inc. Place)

Del Sur; RMC Place; LOS ANGELES; ***153** SH-11; elev. 2,422ft./738m.; 🅿; ★ **L.A.**; z 93536 & mail Lancaster z 93534

Delta; RMC Place; SAN JOAQUIN; ★ **STOC**; mail Stockton z 95201-02; pop. incl. with Stockton (Inc. Place)

De Luz; RMC Place; SAN DIEGO; ***153** SL-13; mail Fallbrook z 92028

Del Valle; RMC Place; LOS ANGELES; ***153** SJ-11; ★ **L.A.**; mail Los Angeles z 90015

Denair; CDP; STANISLAUS; **150** NN-8; 🅿; z 95316; Ⓟ 3,693; © 3,446

Denny; RMC Place; TRINITY; **150** ND-3; mail Burnt Ranch z 95527; ● 30

Denverton; RMC Place; SOLANO; ***150** NL-6; elev. 7ft./2m.; mail Suisun City z 94585; rural

Derby Acres; CDP; KERN; **152** SG-8; elev. 1,366ft./416m.; mail Fellows z 93224; © 376

De Sabla; RMC Place; BUTTE; mail Magalia z 95954; ● 500

Descanso; RMC Place; SAN DIEGO; **153** SM-15; elev. 3,396ft./1,035m.; 🅿; z 91916; ● 850

Desert; RMC Place; SAN BERNARDINO; ***153** SF-17; elev. 2,804ft./855m.; mail Nipton z 92364; rural

Desert Beach (North Shore); RMC Place; RIVERSIDE; ***153** SK-16; mail Mecca z 92254; ● 500

Desert Center; RMC Place; RIVERSIDE; **153** SK-17; elev. 906ft./276m.; 🅿; z 92239

Desert Hot Springs; Inc. Place; RIVERSIDE; **153** SJ-15; 🅿; ★ **PSPR-**; z 92240-41; Ⓟ 11,668; © 16,582; ◆ 26,498

Desert Lake; RMC Place; KERN; ***153** SG-12; mail Boron z 93516; ● 630

Desert Shores; CDP; IMPERIAL; **153** SL-16; elev. 200ft./61m.; mail Thermal z 92274; © 792

Desert View Highlands; CDP; LOS ANGELES; **153** SI-11; ★ **L.A.**; mail Palmdale z 93550; Ⓟ 2,154; © 2,337

Des Moines; RMC Place; ORANGE; ***153** SJ-11; ★ **L.A.**; mail La Habra z 90631; pop. incl. with La Habra (Inc. Place)

Devils Den; RMC Place; KERN; ***152** SE-7; elev. 502ft./153m.; mail Avenal z 93204; rural

Devore; RMC Place; SAN BERNARDINO; **153** SJ-13; elev. 2,022ft./616m.; ★ **RIV-**; mail San Bernardino z 92407

Devore Heights; RMC Place; SAN BERNARDINO; ***153** SI-13; elev. 2,492ft./760m.; 🅿; ★ **RIV-**; z 92407; ● 900

Diablo; CDP; CONTRA COSTA; **151** NE-19; 🅿; ★ **SF-O-**; z 94528; © 988

Diamond; RMC Place; ORANGE; ★ **L.A.**; mail Santa Ana z 92704; pop. incl. with Santa Ana (Inc. Place)

Diamond Bar; Inc. Place; LOS ANGELES; **155** F-12; elev. 720ft./219m.; 🅿; ★ **L.A.**; z 91765; Ⓟ 53,672; © 56,287; ◆ 58,421

Diamond Heights; RMC Place; SAN FRANCISCO; ★ **SF-O-**; mail San Francisco z 94131; pop. incl. with San Francisco (Inc. Place)

Diamond Springs; CDP; EL DORADO; **150** NJ-8; elev. 1,778ft./542m.; 🅿; ★ **SAC**; z 95619; Ⓟ 2,872; © 4,888

Di Giorgio; RMC Place; KERN; **152** SG-9; 🅿; z 93203; ● 450

Dillon Beach; CDP; MARIN; **150** NK-4; 🅿; z 94929; © 319

Dimond; RMC Place; ALAMEDA; ★ **SF-O-**; mail Oakland z 94602; pop. incl. with Oakland (Inc. Place)

Dinsmore; RMC Place; HUMBOLDT; **150** NE-3; elev. 2,401ft./732m.; mail Bridgeville z 95526; ● 50

Dinuba; Inc. Place; TULARE; **152** SC-8; elev. 328ft./100m.; 🅿 🅷; z 93618; Ⓟ 12,743; © 16,844; ◆ 20,348

Discovery Bay; CDP; CONTRA COSTA; ***150** NL-7; 🅿; ★ **SF-O-**; z 94505, z 94514 & mail Brentwood z 94513; Ⓟ 5,351; © 8,981

Dixieland; RMC Place; IMPERIAL; ***153** SM-17; elev. 40ft./12m.; mail Imperial z 92251, Seeley z 92273; rural

Dixon; Inc. Place; SOLANO; **150** NK-6; 🅿; ★ **FRFL-**; z 95620; Ⓟ 10,401; © 16,103

Dixon Lane-Meadow Creek; CDP-Census Area Only; INYO; ***151** NN-14; elev. 4,141ft./1,262m.; mail Bishop z 93514; Ⓟ 2,561; © 2,702

Dobbins; RMC Place; YUBA; **150** NH-8; elev. 720ft./219m.; 🅿; z 95935; ● 700

Dockweiler; RMC Place; LOS ANGELES; 🅿; ★ **L.A.**; z 90007 & mail Los Angeles z 90018; pop. incl. with Los Angeles (Inc. Place)

Dogtown; RMC Place; CALAVERAS; ***150** NL-9; elev. 1,237ft./377m.; mail San Andreas z 95249; rural

Entries in **UPPERCASE** are counties.
Entries in **bold** have populations of 2,500 or more.
Names in parentheses are alternate names.

Inc. Place	Incorporated Place
RMC Place	Rand McNally Designated Place
CDP	Census Designated Place
MCD	Minor Civil Division
⊡	County Seat
▲	Minor Civil Division
elev.	Elevation
🅿	Post Office
🅷	Hospital
🅲	College
■	Principal Business Center
★	Ranally Metro Area (RMA) Abbreviation
z	Zip Code(s)
Ⓟ	Previous Census Population
Ⓡ	Revised Census Population
Ⓐ	Annexation Population
●	Rand McNally Population Estimate
©	Final Census Population
Ⓢ	Special Census Population
◆	Estimated Population

For additional definitions see Glossary, Volume 1, and Introduction, Volume 2.

Dollar Point; CDP; PLACER; ***150** NI-10; elev. 6,400ft./1,951m.; mail Tahoe City **z** 96145; Ⓟ 1,449; © 1,539
Dollar Ranch; RMC Place; CONTRA COSTA; ★ **SF-O-**; mail Walnut Creek **z** 94595; pop. incl. with Walnut Creek (Inc. Place)
Dolomite; RMC Place; INYO; ***153** SC-11; elev. 3,673ft./1,120m.; mail Lone Pine **z** 93545; rural
Dominguez; RMC Place; LOS ANGELES; ***153** SK-11; ★ **L.A.**; mail Long Beach **z** 90810; pop. incl. with Carson (Inc. Place)
Dominguez Hills; RMC Place; LOS ANGELES; ***153** SK-11; ★ **L.A.**; pop. incl. with Carson (Inc. Place)
Donlon; RMC Place; VENTURA; ★ **OXN-**; mail Oxnard **z** 93033; pop. incl. with Oxnard (Inc. Place)
Donner; RMC Place; NEVADA; mail Truckee **z** 96162; pop. incl. with Truckee (Inc. Place)
Donner Lake Village; RMC Place; NEVADA; ***150** NI-10; mail Truckee **z** 96161; pop. incl. with Truckee (Inc. Place)
Don Pedro Camp; RMC Place; TUOLUMNE; ***150** NM-9; mail La Grange **z** 95329; ● 40
Dorrington; CDP; CALAVERAS; ***150** NK-10; mail Arnold **z** 95223; © 727
Dorris; Inc. Place; SISKIYOU; **150** NA-6; elev. 4,240ft./1,292m.; 🄿; **z** 96023; Ⓟ 892; © 886
Dos Palos; Inc. Place; MERCED; **152** SB-5; 🄿 🄷; **z** 93620; Ⓟ 4,196; © 4,581
Dos Palos Y; RMC Place; MERCED; ***152** SB-5; mail Santa Rita Park **z** 93661; ● 350
Dos Pueblos; SANTA BARBARA; see Naples (RMC Place)
Dos Rios; RMC Place; MENDOCINO; **150** NG-3; elev. 926ft./282m.; 🄿; **z** 95429; ● 100
Douglas City; RMC Place; TRINITY; **150** NE-4; elev. 1,651ft./503m.; 🄿; **z** 96024; ● 300
Douglas Flat; RMC Place; CALAVERAS; **150** NL-9; elev. 1,965ft./599m.; 🄿; **z** 95229; ● 200
Douglas Park; RMC Place; DEL NORTE; ***150** NA-2; mail Crescent City **z** 95531; ● 150
Downey; Inc. Place; LOS ANGELES; **153** SJ-11; elev. 119ft./36m.; 🄿 🄷 ■; ★ **L.A.**; **z** 90239-42; Ⓟ 91,444; © 107,323; ◆ 113,948
Downieville; RMC Place; ⊡ SIERRA; **150** NH-8; elev. 2,899ft./884m.; 🄿; **z** 95936; ● 200
Downtown; RMC Place; HUMBOLDT; ★ **EUR-**; mail Eureka **z** 95501; pop. incl. with Eureka (Inc. Place)
Downtown; RMC Place; KERN; ★ **BAK**; mail Bakersfield **z** 93302-03; pop. incl. with Bakersfield (Inc. Place)
Downtown; RMC Place; LOS ANGELES; ***152** SJ-10; ★ **L.A.**; mail Manhattan Beach **z** 90266; pop. incl. with Manhattan Beach (Inc. Place)
Downtown; RMC Place; LOS ANGELES; ★ **L.A.**; mail Long Beach **z** 90801-02; pop. incl. with Long Beach (Inc. Place)
Downtown; RMC Place; LOS ANGELES; ★ **L.A.**; mail Burbank **z** 91502-03; pop. incl. with Burbank (Inc. Place)
Downtown; RMC Place; PLACER; ★ **SAC**; mail Auburn **z** 95603; pop. incl. with Auburn (Inc. Place)
Downtown; RMC Place; RIVERSIDE; ★ **RIV-**; mail Riverside **z** 92501-02; pop. incl. with Riverside (Inc. Place)
Downtown; RMC Place; SAN BERNARDINO; ★ **L.A.**; mail Ontario **z** 91761; pop. incl. with Ontario (Inc. Place)
Downtown; RMC Place; SAN BERNARDINO; ★ **RIV-**; mail San Bernardino **z** 92401-02; pop. incl. with San Bernardino (Inc. Place)
Downtown; RMC Place; SAN DIEGO; ***153** SN-13; ★ **SDGO**; mail San Diego **z** 92101, **z** 92112; pop. incl. with San Diego (Inc. Place)
Downtown; RMC Place; SAN MATEO; ***150** NN-5; ★ **SF-O-**; mail Redwood City **z** 94064; pop. incl. with Redwood City (Inc. Place)
Downtown; RMC Place; SHASTA; ★ **REDD**; mail Redding **z** 96001; pop. incl. with Redding (Inc. Place)
Downtown; RMC Place; TUOLUMNE; mail Sonora **z** 95370; pop. incl. with Sonora (Inc. Place)
Doyle; RMC Place; LASSEN; **150** NG-10; elev. 4,267ft./1,301m.; 🄿; **z** 96109; ● 800
Doyle; RMC Place; TULARE; ★ **PORT**; mail Porterville **z** 93258; pop. incl. with Porterville (Inc. Place)
Doyle Colony; TULARE; see East Porterville (CDP-Census Area Only)
Doyles Corner; RMC Place; SHASTA; mail Cassel **z** 96016; rural
Drakesbad; RMC Place; PLUMAS; ***150** NE-7; mail Chester **z** 96020
Drawbridge; RMC Place; ALAMEDA; ***150** NN-6; ★ **SF-O-**; pop. incl. with Fremont (Inc. Place)
Dresser; RMC Place; ALAMEDA; ***150** NM-6; ★ **SF-O-**; pop. incl. with Fremont (Inc. Place)
Dry Creek Rancheria; Indian Reservation; SONOMA; © 53
Drytown; RMC Place; AMADOR; **150** NK-8; 🄿; **z** 95699; ● 140
Duarte; Inc. Place; LOS ANGELES; **154** D-10; elev. 510ft./155m.; 🄿 🄷; ★ **L.A.**; **z** 91008-10; Ⓟ 20,688; © 21,486; ◆ 21,590
Dublin; Inc. Place; ALAMEDA; **150** NM-6; elev. 360ft./110m.; 🄿; ★ **SF-O-**; **z** 94568; Ⓟ 23,229; © 29,973; ◆ 33,518
Ducor; CDP; TULARE; **152** SE-9; elev. 545ft./166m.; 🄿; **z** 93218; © 504
Dulah (Solimar Beach); RMC Place; VENTURA; mail Ventura **z** 93001; ● 320
Dulzura; RMC Place; SAN DIEGO; **153** SN-14; elev. 1,045ft./319m.; 🄿; **z** 91917; ● 220
Dumbarton; RMC Place; ALAMEDA; ★ **SF-O-**; pop. incl. with Fremont (Inc. Place)
Duncans Mills; RMC Place; SONOMA; ***150** NK-4; elev. 29ft./9m.; 🄿; **z** 95430; ● 185
Dunlap; RMC Place; FRESNO; **152** SC-9; elev. 1,914ft./583m.; 🄿; **z** 93621; ● 300
Dunlap Acres; RMC Place; SAN BERNARDINO; ***153** SJ-13; elev. 2,119ft./646m.; ★ **RIV-**; mail Yucaipa **z** 92399; pop. incl. with Yucaipa (Inc. Place)
Dunmovin; RMC Place; INYO; ***153** SD-11; elev. 3,502ft./1,067m.; mail Olancha **z** 93549
Dunneville (Dunneville Corners); RMC Place; SAN BENITO; ***152** SB-4; elev. 187ft./57m.; mail Hollister **z** 95023; rural
Dunneville Corners; SAN BENITO; see Dunneville (RMC Place)
Dunnigan; RMC Place; YOLO; **150** NJ-6; elev. 68ft./21m.; 🄿; **z** 95937; ● 600
Dunsmuir; Inc. Place; SISKIYOU; **150** NC-5; elev. 2,289ft./698m.; 🄿; **z** 96025; Ⓟ 2,129; © 1,923
Durham; CDP; BUTTE; **150** NH-6; elev. 140ft./43m.; 🄿; ★ **CHICO**; **z** 95938, **z** 95958; Ⓟ 4,784; © 5,220
Dustin Acres; CDP; KERN; ***152** SG-8; mail Taft **z** 93268; © 585
Dutch Flat; RMC Place; PLACER; **150** NI-8; elev. 3,144ft./958m.; 🄿; **z** 95714; ● 350

E

Eagle Lake Resort; RMC Place; LASSEN; ***150** NE-8; mail Susanville **z** 96130; rural
Eagle Mountain; RMC Place; RIVERSIDE; **153** SJ-17; 🄿; **z** 92239; ● 580
Eagle Rock; RMC Place; LOS ANGELES; ***153** SJ-11; elev. 566ft./173m.; 🄿; ★ **L.A.**; **z** 90041; pop. incl. with Los Angeles (Inc. Place)
Eagle Station; RMC Place; LASSEN; mail Susanville **z** 96127; pop. incl. with Susanville (Inc. Place)
Eagle Tree; RMC Place; SAN JOAQUIN; ***150** NL-7; mail Walnut Grove **z** 95690; rural
Eagleville; RMC Place; MODOC; **150** NC-10; 🄿; **z** 96110
Earlimart; CDP; TULARE; **152** SE-8; elev. 283ft./86m.; 🄿; **z** 93219; Ⓟ 5,881; © 6,583
Earp; RMC Place; SAN BERNARDINO; **153** SI-20; elev. 388ft./118m.; 🄿; **z** 92242; ● 70
East; RMC Place; LOS ANGELES; ***153** SJ-11; ★ **L.A.**; mail Downey **z** 90239; pop. incl. with Downey (Inc. Place)
East Acres; MADERA; see Eastside Acres (RMC Place)
East Bakersfield; RMC Place; KERN; ★ **BAK**; mail Bakersfield **z** 93305, **z** 93385
East Biggs (Rio Bonito); RMC Place; BUTTE; ***150** NH-7; mail Biggs **z** 95917; rural
East Bluff; RMC Place; ORANGE; ★ **L.A.**; mail Newport Beach **z** 92660; pop. incl. with Newport Beach (Inc. Place)
East Blythe; CDP; RIVERSIDE; **153** SK-19; mail Blythe **z** 92225; Ⓟ 1,511; © 3
East Compton; CDP-Census Area Only; LOS ANGELES; ***153** SJ-11; ★ **L.A.**; mail Compton **z** 90221; Ⓟ 7,967; © 9,286
East Downey; RMC Place; LOS ANGELES; ★ **L.A.**; mail Downey **z** 90239; pop. incl. with Downey (Inc. Place)
East Firebaugh; MADERA; see Eastside Acres (RMC Place)
East Foothills; CDP-Census Area Only; SANTA CLARA; **151** NL-20; elev. 149ft./45m.; ★ **SF-O-**; mail San Jose **z** 95127; Ⓟ 14,898; © 8,133
East Fresno; RMC Place; FRESNO; ***152** SC-7; ★ **FRES**; mail Fresno **z** 93727, **z** 93747
Eastgate; RMC Place; LOS ANGELES; ★ **L.A.**; mail Beverly Hills **z** 90211; pop. incl. with Beverly Hills (Inc. Place)
East Gridley; RMC Place; BUTTE; ***150** NH-7; elev. 95ft./29m.; mail Gridley **z** 95948; rural
East Hemet (Hemet East); CDP-Census Area Only; RIVERSIDE; ***153** SK-14; ★ **HEM**; mail Hemet **z** 92544; Ⓟ 17,611; © 14,823
East Highland; SAN BERNARDINO; see East Highlands (RMC Place)
East Highlands (East Highland); RMC Place; SAN BERNARDINO; **155** D-20; ★ **RIV-**; mail Highland **z** 92346; pop. incl. with Highland (Inc. Place)
East Irvine (Valencia); RMC Place; ORANGE; ***153** SK-12; elev. 195ft./59m.; 🄿; ★ **L.A.**; **z** 92650; pop. incl. with Irvine (Inc. Place)
Eastlake; RMC Place; SAN DIEGO; ★ **SDGO**; mail Chula Vista **z** 91914; pop. incl. with Chula Vista (Inc. Place)
East La Mirada; CDP-Census Area Only; LOS ANGELES; ***153** SJ-11; ★ **L.A.**; mail La Mirada **z** 90638, Whittier **z** 90604; Ⓟ 9,367; © 9,538
East Linda; RMC Place; YUBA; ***150** NI-7; elev. 80ft./24m.; mail Marysville **z** 95901; ● 630
East Long Beach; RMC Place; LOS ANGELES; ***153** SK-11; ★ **L.A.**; mail Long Beach **z** 90804; pop. incl. with Long Beach (Inc. Place)
East Los Angeles; CDP; LOS ANGELES; **154** F-8; elev. 280ft./85m.; 🄿; ★ **L.A.**; **z** 90022; Ⓟ 126,379; © 124,283; ◆ 127,117
East Lynwood; RMC Place; LOS ANGELES; ★ **L.A.**; mail Lynwood **z** 90262; pop. incl. with Lynwood (Inc. Place)
Eastmont; RMC Place; ALAMEDA; ★ **SF-O-**; mail Oakland **z** 94605; pop. incl. with Oakland (Inc. Place)
East Nicolaus; RMC Place; SUTTER; **150** NJ-7; 🄿; **z** 95659; ● 200
East Oakdale; CDP-Census Area Only; STANISLAUS; ***150** NM-8; © 2,742
East Oakland; RMC Place; ALAMEDA; ★ **SF-O-**; pop. incl. with Oakland (Inc. Place)
Easton; CDP; FRESNO; **152** SC-7; elev. 273ft./83m.; ★ **FRES**; mail Fresno **z** 93706; Ⓟ 1,877; © 1,966
East Orosi; CDP; TULARE; ***152** SC-8; elev. 373ft./114m.; mail Orosi **z** 93647; © 426
East Palo Alto; Inc. Place; SAN MATEO; **151** NK-17; elev. 21ft./6m.; 🄿; ★ **SF-O-**; **z** 94303; Ⓟ 23,451; © 29,506; ◆ 32,999
East Pasadena; CDP; LOS ANGELES; **154** D-9; ★ **L.A.**; mail Pasadena **z** 91107, **z** 91117; Ⓟ 5,910; © 6,045
East Porterville (Doyle Colony); CDP-Census Area Only; TULARE; ***152** SD-9; ★ **PORT**; mail Porterville **z** 93257; Ⓟ 5,790; © 6,730
East Quincy; CDP; PLUMAS; **150** NG-8; mail Quincy **z** 95971; © 2,398
East Richmond Heights; CDP-Census Area Only; CONTRA COSTA; **151** ND-14; elev. 404ft./123m.; ★ **SF-O-**; mail Richmond **z** 94805; Ⓟ 3,266; © 3,357
East San Bruno; RMC Place; SAN MATEO; ★ **SF-O-**; pop. incl. with South San Francisco (Inc. Place)
East San Diego; RMC Place; SAN DIEGO; ***153** SN-14; ★ **SDGO**; mail San Diego **z** 92105; pop. incl. with San Diego (Inc. Place)
East San Gabriel; CDP; LOS ANGELES; ***153** SJ-11; elev. 514ft./157m.; ★ **L.A.**; mail San Gabriel **z** 91775; Ⓟ 12,736; © 14,512
East San Luis Obispo; RMC Place; SAN LUIS OBISPO; ★ **S.LUIS**; pop. incl. with San Luis Obispo (Inc. Place)
East San Pedro; RMC Place; LOS ANGELES; ★ **L.A.**; mail San Pedro **z** 90731; pop. incl. with Los Angeles (Inc. Place)
East Santa Barbara; RMC Place; SANTA BARBARA; ★ **S.MAR**; pop. incl. with Santa Barbara (Inc. Place)
East Santa Clara; RMC Place; SANTA CLARA; pop. incl. with Santa Clara (Inc. Place)
East Santa Cruz; RMC Place; SANTA CRUZ; ★ **S.CRZ**; mail Santa Cruz **z** 95060, **z** 95063; pop. incl. with Santa Cruz (Inc. Place)
East Shore; CDP-Census Area Only; PLUMAS; ***150** NF-8; © 177
Eastside Acres (East Acres, East Firebaugh); RMC Place; MADERA; ***152** SB-6; mail Firebaugh **z** 93622; ● 200
Eastside Ranch; RMC Place; MADERA; ***152** SB-6; mail Firebaugh **z** 93622; ● 150
East Sonora; CDP; TUOLUMNE; ***150** NL-9; elev. 1,983ft./604m.; mail Sonora **z** 95370; Ⓟ 1,675; © 2,078
East Stockton; RMC Place; SAN JOAQUIN; ★ **STOC**; mail Stockton **z** 95205, **z** 95215; pop. incl. with Stockton (Inc. Place)
East Tustin; RMC Place; ORANGE; **155** I-12; ★ **L.A.**; mail Santa Ana **z** 92705; ● 11,000
East Vallejo; RMC Place; SOLANO; ★ **SF-O-**; mail Vallejo **z** 94590; pop. incl. with Vallejo (Inc. Place)
East Ventura; RMC Place; VENTURA; ★ **OXN-**; mail Ventura **z** 93003, **z** 93006; pop. incl. with Ventura (Inc. Place)
Eastview; RMC Place; LOS ANGELES; ***153** SK-11; ★ **L.A.**; mail San Pedro **z** 90734; pop. incl. with Rancho Palos Verdes (Inc. Place)
East Watson; RMC Place; LOS ANGELES; ★ **L.A.**; pop. incl. with Carson (Inc. Place)
Eberly; RMC Place; ALAMEDA; ***150** NM-6; ★ **SF-O-**; pop. incl. with Fremont (Inc. Place)
Eblis; RMC Place; SANTA CRUZ; ★ **S.CRZ**; pop. incl. with Santa Cruz (Inc. Place)
Echo Lake; RMC Place; EL DORADO; ***150** NJ-10; 🄿; **z** 95721; ● 100
Echo Park; RMC Place; LOS ANGELES; ★ **L.A.**; mail Los Angeles **z** 90026; pop. incl. with Los Angeles (Inc. Place)
Edendale; RMC Place; LOS ANGELES; ★ **L.A.**; mail Los Angeles **z** 90026; pop. incl. with Los Angeles (Inc. Place)
Edenvale; RMC Place; SANTA CLARA; ***150** NN-6; elev. 182ft./55m.; ★ **SF-O-**; pop. incl. with San Jose (Inc. Place)
Edgemar; RMC Place; SAN MATEO; ***150** NM-5; ★ **SF-O-**; mail Pacifica **z** 94044; pop. incl. with Pacifica (Inc. Place)
Edgemont; RMC Place; RIVERSIDE; ***153** SJ-13; elev. 1,537ft./468m.; ★ **RIV-**; mail Riverside **z** 92508; pop. incl. with Moreno Valley (Inc. Place)
Edgemont Acres; KERN; see North Edwards (CDP)
Edgewood; CDP; SISKIYOU; **150** NC-5; 🄿; **z** 96094; © 67
Edison; RMC Place; KERN; **152** SF-9; elev. 564ft./172m.; 🄿; ★ **BAK**; **z** 93220; ● 400
Edmundson Acres; RMC Place; KERN; ***152** SG-9; mail Arvin **z** 93203; ● 330
Edwards AFB; CDP-Census Area Only; KERN; ***153** SH-11; 🄿; **z** 93524 & mail Edwards **z** 93523; Ⓟ 7,423; © 5,909
Eel Rock; RMC Place; HUMBOLDT; ***150** NF-2; mail Myers Flat **z** 95554
Eighteenth Street Station; RMC Place; SAN FRANCISCO; ★ **SF-O-**; mail San Francisco **z** 94114; pop. incl. with San Francisco (Inc. Place)
Eight Mile House; RMC Place; EL DORADO; mail Camino **z** 95709; ● 280
El Bonita; RMC Place; SONOMA; ***150** NK-4; ★ **S.ROS**; mail Guerneville **z** 95446; ● 200
El Cajon; Inc. Place; SAN DIEGO; **153** SN-14; elev. 435ft./133m.; 🄿 🄷 🄲 905 ■; ★ **SDGO**; **z** 92019-22, **z** 92090; Ⓟ 88,693; © 94,869; ◆ 100,397
El Camino; RMC Place; TEHAMA; ***150** NF-6; mail Gerber **z** 96035; rural
El Casco; RMC Place; RIVERSIDE; **155** F-20; mail Redlands **z** 92373
El Centro; Inc. Place; ⊡ IMPERIAL; **153** SM-17; elev.-40ft./-12m.; 🄿 🄷 ■; **z** 92243-44; Ⓟ 31,384; © 37,835; ◆ 41,289
El Cerrito; Inc. Place; CONTRA COSTA; **150** NL-5; elev. 66ft./20m.; 🄿; ★ **SF-O-**; **z** 94530; Ⓟ 22,869; © 23,171; ◆ 21,780
El Cerrito; CDP; RIVERSIDE; **155** H-16; ★ **RIV-**; mail Corona **z** 92880; Ⓟ 4,490; © 4,590
Elders Corner; RMC Place; PLACER; ***150** NJ-8; elev. 1,354ft./413m.; ★ **SAC**; mail Auburn **z** 95603; ● 450
Elderwood; RMC Place; TULARE; ***152** SC-9; elev. 490ft./149m.; ★ **VISL**; mail Woodlake **z** 93286
El Dorado; RMC Place; EL DORADO; **150** NJ-8; elev. 1,602ft./488m.; 🄿; ★ **SAC**; **z** 95623; ● 1,300
EL DORADO; **150** NJ-10; Ⓟ 125,995; © 156,299; ◆ 170,935
El Dorado Hills; CDP-Census Area Only; EL DORADO; **150** NJ-8; 🄿; ★ **SAC**; **z** 95762; Ⓟ 6,395; © 18,016
Eldridge; CDP; SONOMA; ***150** NK-5; 🄿 🄷; **z** 95431; Ⓟ 1,144; © 1,534
El Encanto Heights; RMC Place; SANTA BARBARA; ***152** SI-7; ★ **S.BAR**; mail Goleta **z** 93117-18; ● 5,600
El Granada; CDP; SAN MATEO; **151** NJ-13; 🄿; ★ **SF-O-**; **z** 94018; Ⓟ 4,426; © 5,724
Elizabeth Lake; RMC Place; LOS ANGELES; ***152** SH-10; elev. 3,331ft./1,015m.; 🄿; **z** 93532; ● 1,000
Elk (Greenwood); RMC Place; MENDOCINO; **150** NI-2; 🄿; **z** 95432
Elk Creek; RMC Place; GLENN; **150** NH-5; 🄿; **z** 95939; ● 200
Elk Grove; Inc. Place; SACRAMENTO; **150** NK-7; elev. 51ft./16m.; 🄿; ★ **SAC**; **z** 95624, **z** 95757-59; incorporated July 1, 2000; not reported in 2000 Census; includes Laguna CDP; ● 81,700; ◆ 129,419
Elk Grove; CDP-Census Area Only; SACRAMENTO; **150** NK-7; elev. 51ft./16m.; 🄿; ★ **SAC**; **z** 95624, **z** 95757-59; former CDP; became part of Elk Grove July 1, 2000; Ⓟ 17,483; © 59,984
Elkhorn; CDP; MONTEREY; ***152** SB-3; ★ **SLNS**; mail Castroville **z** 95012; Ⓟ 1,458; © 1,591; Ⓡ 1,597
Elk River; RMC Place; HUMBOLDT; ***150** ND-1; elev. 55ft./17m.; ★ **EUR-**; mail Eureka **z** 95503; ● 800
Elk River Corners; RMC Place; HUMBOLDT; ***150** ND-1; elev. 108ft./33m.; ★ **EUR-**; mail Eureka **z** 95503; ● 400
Elk Valley Rancheria; Indian Reservation; DEL NORTE; © 77
Ellwood; RMC Place; SANTA BARBARA; **156** B-5; ★ **S.BAR**; mail Goleta **z** 93118; ● 7,800
El Macero; RMC Place; YOLO; ***150** NK-7; 🄿; ★ **DAV**; **z** 95618; ● 650
Elmhurst; RMC Place; ALAMEDA; ★ **SF-O-**; mail Oakland **z** 94603; pop. incl. with Oakland (Inc. Place)
Elmira; CDP; SOLANO; **150** NK-6; 🄿; ★ **FRFL-**; **z** 95625; © 205
El Mirador; RMC Place; TULARE; ***152** SD-9; elev. 480ft./146m.; ★ **PORT**; mail Lindsay **z** 93247; ● 200
El Mirage; RMC Place; SAN BERNARDINO; ***153** SH-12; elev. 2,913ft./888m.; 🄿; **z** 92301
El Modena; RMC Place; ORANGE; ***153** SK-12; elev. 276ft./84m.; ★ **L.A.**; mail Orange **z** 92859, **z** 92862, **z** 92869; pop. incl. with Orange (Inc. Place)
El Monte; RMC Place; CONTRA COSTA; ★ **SF-O-**; mail Concord **z** 94521; pop. incl. with Concord (Inc. Place)
El Monte; Inc. Place; LOS ANGELES; **154** E-10; elev. 283ft./86m.; 🄿 ■; ★ **L.A.**; **z** 91731-35; Ⓟ 106,209; © 115,965; ◆ 121,561
El Monte Park; RMC Place; SAN DIEGO; ***153** SM-14; elev. 520ft./158m.; ★ **SDGO**; mail Lakeside **z** 92040; ● 300
Elm View (Wino's Corner); RMC Place; FRESNO; ***152** SC-7; elev. 255ft./78m.; ★ **FRES**; mail Caruthers **z** 93609
Elmwood; RMC Place; ALAMEDA; ★ **SF-O-**; mail Berkeley **z** 94705; pop. incl. with Berkeley (Inc. Place)
El Nido; RMC Place; LOS ANGELES; ***153** SK-11; elev. 96ft./29m.; ★ **L.A.**
El Nido; RMC Place; MERCED; **152** SA-6; elev. 139ft./42m.; 🄿; **z** 95317; ● 360
El Paso de Robles; SAN LUIS OBISPO; see Paso Robles (Inc. Place)
El Portal; RMC Place; MARIPOSA; **151** NM-11; elev. 1,919ft./585m.; 🄿; **z** 95318; ● 520
El Porto Beach; RMC Place; LOS ANGELES; ★ **L.A.**; mail Manhattan Beach **z** 90266; pop. incl. with Manhattan Beach (Inc. Place)
El Pueblo; RMC Place; CONTRA COSTA; ***150** NL-6; elev. 50ft./15m.; ★ **SF-O-**; mail Pittsburg **z** 94565; pop. incl. with Pittsburg (Inc. Place)
El Rio; CDP; VENTURA; **152** SI-9; elev. 79ft./24m.; ★ **OXN-**; mail Oxnard **z** 93036; Ⓟ 6,419; © 6,193
El Rio Villa; RMC Place; YOLO; ***150** NK-6; mail Winters **z** 95694; ● 400
El Segundo; Inc. Place; LOS ANGELES; **154** G-5; elev. 90ft./27m.; 🄿 ■; ★ **L.A.**; **z** 90245; Ⓟ 15,223; © 16,033; ◆ 15,914
El Sereno; LOS ANGELES; see El Sereno Car (RMC Place)
El Sereno Car (El Sereno); RMC Place; LOS ANGELES; ***153** SJ-11; 🄿; ★ **L.A.**; **z** 90032; pop. incl. with Los Angeles (Inc. Place)
El Sobrante; CDP; CONTRA COSTA; **151** NC-15; elev. 200ft./61m.; 🄿; ★ **SF-O-**; **z** 94803, **z** 94820; Ⓟ 9,852; © 12,260
El Sueno; RMC Place; SANTA BARBARA; **156** B-7; elev. 210ft./64m.; ★ **S.BAR**; mail Santa Barbara **z** 93110; ● 2,000
El Toro; ORANGE; see Lake Forest (Inc. Place)
Elvas; RMC Place; SACRAMENTO; ***150** NK-7; ★ **SAC**; pop. incl. with Sacramento (Inc. Place)
El Verano; CDP; SONOMA; ***150** NK-5; elev. 107ft./33m.; 🄿; **z** 95433; Ⓟ 3,498; © 3,954
Elverta; RMC Place; SACRAMENTO; **150** NJ-7; 🄿; ★ **SAC**; **z** 95626; ● 1,130
El Viejo; RMC Place; STANISLAUS; ★ **MOD**; mail Modesto **z** 95353-54; pop. incl. with Modesto (Inc. Place)
Emandal Resort; RMC Place; MENDOCINO; ***150** NH-3; elev. 1,368ft./417m.; mail Willits **z** 95490; ● 10
Emerald Bay; RMC Place; ORANGE; **155** L-12; ★ **L.A.**; mail Laguna Beach **z** 92651; ● 1,100
Emerald Lake Hills; CDP-Census Area Only; SAN MATEO; ***150** NN-5; ★ **SF-O-**; mail Redwood City **z** 94062; Ⓟ 3,328; © 3,899
Emeryville; Inc. Place; ALAMEDA; **151** NE-15; 🄿 🄲 950; ★ **SF-O-**; **z** 94608, **z** 94662; Ⓟ 5,740; © 6,882
Emigrant Gap; RMC Place; PLACER; **150** NI-9; 🄿; **z** 95715
Empire (Modesto Empire Junction); CDP; STANISLAUS; **150** NM-8; 🄿; ★ **MOD**; **z** 95319; © 3,903
Encanto; RMC Place; SAN DIEGO; ***153** SN-14; ★ **SDGO**; mail San Diego **z** 92114, **z** 92174; pop. incl. with San Diego (Inc. Place)
Encinal; RMC Place; SANTA CLARA; ★ **SF-O-**; mail Sunnyvale **z** 94087; pop. incl. with Sunnyvale (Inc. Place)
Encinitas; Inc. Place; SAN DIEGO; **153** SM-13; elev. 91ft./28m.; 🄿 🄷; ★ **SDGO**; **z** 92023-24; Ⓟ 55,386; © 58,014; ◆ 62,314
Encino; RMC Place; LOS ANGELES; ***152** SJ-10; 🄿; ★ **L.A.**; **z** 91316, **z** 91416, **z** 91426, **z** 91436 & mail Reseda **z** 91335; pop. incl. with Los Angeles (Inc. Place)
Engineer Springs; RMC Place; SAN DIEGO; mail Jamul **z** 91935; ● 370
Enterprise; RMC Place; AMADOR; mail Plymouth **z** 95669; rural
Enterprise; RMC Place; SHASTA; ***150** NE-5; elev. 530ft./162m.; ★ **REDD**; mail Redding **z** 96001; pop. incl. with Redding (Inc. Place)
Enterprise Rancheria; Indian Reservation; BUTTE; © 1
Erwin Lake; SAN BERNARDINO; see Woodlands (RMC Place)
Escalle; RMC Place; MARIN; ★ **SF-O-**; mail Larkspur **z** 94939; pop. incl. with Larkspur (Inc. Place)
Escalon; Inc. Place; SAN JOAQUIN; **150** NM-8; 🄿; ★ **MOD**; **z** 95320; Ⓟ 4,437; © 5,963
Escondido; Inc. Place; SAN DIEGO; **153** SM-14; elev. 684ft./208m.; 🄿 🄷 ■; ★ **SDGO**; **z** 92025-27, **z** 92029-30, **z** 92033, **z** 92046; Ⓟ 108,635; © 133,559; ◆ 152,682
Escondido Junction; RMC Place; SAN DIEGO; ***153** SL-13; ★ **SDGO**; pop. incl. with Oceanside (Inc. Place)
Esparto; CDP; YOLO; **150** NJ-6; elev. 191ft./58m.; 🄿; **z** 95607, **z** 95627; Ⓟ 1,487; © 1,858
Essex; RMC Place; SAN BERNARDINO; **153** SH-18; 🄿; **z** 92332
Estrella; RMC Place; SAN LUIS OBISPO; ***152** SE-5; mail San Miguel **z** 93451
Estudillo; RMC Place; ALAMEDA; ★ **SF-O-**; mail San Leandro **z** 94577; pop. incl. with San Leandro (Inc. Place)
Ethanac; RIVERSIDE; see Romoland (CDP)
Etiwanda; RMC Place; SAN BERNARDINO; ***153** SJ-12; 🄿; ★ **L.A.**; **z** 91739; pop. incl. with Rancho Cucamonga (Inc. Place)
Etna; Inc. Place; SISKIYOU; **150** NB-4; elev. 2,929ft./893m.; 🄿; **z** 96027; Ⓟ 835; © 781
Ettersburg; RMC Place; HUMBOLDT; ***150** NF-2; elev. 679ft./207m.; mail Garberville **z** 95542; rural
Eucalyptus Hills; RMC Place; SAN DIEGO; ***153** SM-14; ★ **SDGO**; mail Lakeside **z** 92040; ● 1,200
Eugene; RMC Place; STANISLAUS; **150** NM-8; elev. 177ft./54m.; mail Farmington **z** 95230; rural
Eureka; Inc. Place; ⊡ HUMBOLDT; **150** ND-1; elev. 44ft./13m.; 🄿 🄷 ■; ★ **EUR-**; **z** 95501-03, **z** 95534; Ⓟ 27,025; © 26,128; ◆ 25,573
Evergreen; RMC Place; SANTA CLARA; ***150** NN-6; ★ **SF-O-**; pop. incl. with San Jose (Inc. Place)
Excelsior Station; RMC Place; SAN FRANCISCO; ★ **SF-O-**; mail San Francisco **z** 94112; pop. incl. with San Francisco (Inc. Place)
Exeter; Inc. Place; TULARE; **152** SD-9; elev. 386ft./118m.; 🄿 🄷; ★ **VISL**; **z** 93221; Ⓟ 7,276; © 9,168

F

Fairbanks Ranch; CDP-Census Area Only; SAN DIEGO; ***153** SM-13; ★ **SDGO**; © 2,244
Fairfax; RMC Place; KERN; ★ **BAK**; mail Bakersfield **z** 93307; ● 900
Fairfax; Inc. Place; MARIN; **150** NL-5; elev. 120ft./37m.; 🄿; ★ **SF-O-**; **z** 94930, **z** 94978; Ⓟ 6,931; © 7,319
Fairfield; Inc. Place; ⊡ SOLANO; **150** NL-6; elev. 15ft./5m.; 🄿 🄷 ■; ★ **FRFL-**; **z** 94533-35 & mail Napa **z** 94558, Suisun City **z** 94585; Ⓟ 77,211; © 96,178; ◆ 102,124
Fairhaven; RMC Place; HUMBOLDT; ***150** ND-1; ★ **EUR-**; mail Samoa **z** 95564; ● 160
Fairmead; RMC Place; MADERA; **152** SB-6; elev. 252ft./77m.; mail Chowchilla **z** 93610; ● 700
Fairmont; RMC Place; LOS ANGELES; ***152** SH-10; elev. 2,784ft./849m.; mail Lancaster **z** 93534, **z** 93536; rural
Fairmont Terrace; RMC Place; ALAMEDA; **151** NG-17; ★ **SF-O-**; mail San Leandro **z** 94577; ● 4,000
Fairmount (Fairmount Avenue); RMC Place; CONTRA COSTA; ★ **SF-O-**; mail El Cerrito **z** 94530; pop. incl. with El Cerrito (Inc. Place)
Fairmount Avenue; CONTRA COSTA; see Fairmount (RMC Place)
Fair Oaks; CDP; SACRAMENTO; **150** NJ-7; elev. 172ft./52m.; 🄿; ★ **SAC**; **z** 95628; Ⓟ 26,867; © 28,008; ◆ 32,280
Fair Oaks; RMC Place; SAN JOAQUIN; ***150** NL-7; ★ **STOC**; mail Stockton **z** 95205; pop. incl. with Stockton (Inc. Place)
Fair Play; RMC Place; EL DORADO; 🄿; **z** 95684; ● 500
Fairview; CDP-Census Area Only; ALAMEDA; ***150** NM-6; elev. 300ft./91m.; ★ **SF-O-**; mail Hayward **z** 94542; Ⓟ 9,045; © 9,470
Fairview; RMC Place; TRINITY; ***150** ND-4; elev. 2,394ft./730m.; mail Lewiston **z** 96052; rural
Fairview; RMC Place; TULARE; **152** SE-10; elev. 3,519ft./1,073m.; mail Kernville **z** 93238; ● 6
Fairway Park; RMC Place; ALAMEDA; ★ **SF-O-**; mail Hayward **z** 94544; pop. incl. with Hayward (Inc. Place)
Falk; RMC Place; HUMBOLDT; ***150** NE-2; ★ **EUR-**; mail Eureka **z** 95503; rural
Fallbrook; CDP; SAN DIEGO; **153** SL-13; elev. 685ft./209m.; 🄿 🄷; ★ **SDGO**; **z** 92028, **z** 92088; Ⓟ 22,095; © 29,100; ◆ 31,435
Fallen Leaf; RMC Place; EL DORADO; ***150** NJ-10; 🄿; **z** 96151; rural
Falling Springs; RMC Place; LOS ANGELES; ***153** SI-12; ★ **L.A.**; mail Azusa **z** 91702; ● 5
Fallon; RMC Place; MARIN; ***150** NK-4; mail Petaluma **z** 94952, Tomales **z** 94971; rural
Fall River Mills; CDP; SHASTA; **150** ND-7; elev. 3,291ft./1,003m.; 🄿 🄷; **z** 96028; © 648
Fallsvale; SAN BERNARDINO; see Forest Falls (RMC Place)
Famoso; RMC Place; KERN; ***152** SF-9; elev. 422ft./129m.; mail Mc Farland **z** 93250
Fancher Ranch; RMC Place; FRESNO; ★ **FRES**; mail Fresno **z** 93727; ● 150
Farmers Market; RMC Place; LOS ANGELES; ★ **L.A.**; mail Los Angeles **z** 90036; pop. incl. with Los Angeles (Inc. Place)
Farmersville; Inc. Place; TULARE; **152** SD-9; elev. 360ft./110m.; 🄿; ★ **VISL**; **z** 93223; Ⓟ 6,235; © 8,737
Farmington; CDP; SAN JOAQUIN; **150** NL-8; 🄿; **z** 95230; © 262
Fawnskin; RMC Place; SAN BERNARDINO; **153** SI-14; elev. 5,756ft./1,754m.; 🄿; **z** 92333; ● 500
Feather Falls; RMC Place; BUTTE; **150** NH-8; 🄿; **z** 95940
Feather River Inn; RMC Place; PLUMAS; ***150** NG-9; elev. 4,401ft./1,341m.; mail Blairsden-Graeagle **z** 96103; ● 30
Feather River Park; RMC Place; PLUMAS; ***150** NG-9; mail Blairsden-Graeagle **z** 96103; ● 150
Federal; RMC Place; LOS ANGELES; ***153** SJ-12; ★ **L.A.**; mail Covina **z** 91723; pop. incl. with Covina (Inc. Place)
Federal; RMC Place; LOS ANGELES; ★ **L.A.**; mail Anaheim **z** 92805, Los Angeles **z** 90012-13; pop. incl. with Los Angeles (Inc. Place)
Federal; RMC Place; ORANGE; ★ **L.A.**; mail Anaheim **z** 92805, **z** 92815, Los Angeles **z** 90012-13; pop. incl. with Anaheim (Inc. Place)
Federal Building; RMC Place; LOS ANGELES; ★ **L.A.**; mail Lawndale **z** 90261; pop. incl. with Lawndale (Inc. Place)
Federal Building; RMC Place; SAN FRANCISCO; ★ **SF-O-**; mail San Francisco **z** 94102; pop. incl. with San Francisco (Inc. Place)
Federal Building; RMC Place; VENTURA; ★ **OXN-**; mail Oxnard **z** 93030; pop. incl. with Oxnard (Inc. Place)
Federal Terrace; RMC Place; SOLANO; ★ **SF-O-**; mail Vallejo **z** 94590; pop. incl. with Vallejo (Inc. Place)
Felicity; RMC Place; IMPERIAL; 🄿; **z** 92283; rural
Fellows; CDP; KERN; **152** SG-8; 🄿; **z** 93224; © 153
Felterwood; RMC Place; DEL NORTE; ***150** NA-2; elev. 40ft./12m.; mail Crescent City **z** 95531; ● 200
Felton; CDP; SANTA CRUZ; **152** SB-2; 🄿; ★ **S.CRZ**; **z** 95018 & mail Mount Hermon **z** 95041; Ⓟ 5,350; © 1,051
Fern; RMC Place; SHASTA; mail Whitmore **z** 96096; ● 200
Fernbridge; RMC Place; HUMBOLDT; ***150** NE-1; ★ **EUR-**; mail Fortuna **z** 95540; ● 200
Fernbrook; RMC Place; SAN DIEGO; **156** E-10; elev. 1,218ft./371m.; ★ **SDGO**; mail Ramona **z** 92065
Ferndale; Inc. Place; HUMBOLDT; **150** NE-1; elev. 50ft./15m.; 🄿; **z** 95536; Ⓟ 1,331; © 1,382
Fern Valley; RMC Place; RIVERSIDE; ***153** SK-14; mail Idyllwild **z** 92549; ● 600
Fernwood; RMC Place; LOS ANGELES; ***152** SJ-10; ★ **L.A.**; mail Topanga **z** 90290; ● 500
Fetters Hot Springs; RMC Place; SONOMA; ***150** NK-5; elev. 137ft./42m.; mail Boyes Hot Springs **z** 95416, Sonoma **z** 95476; ● 600
Fetters Hot Springs-Agua Caliente; CDP-Census Area Only; SONOMA; ***150** NK-5; mail Sonoma **z** 95476; Ⓟ 2,024; © 2,505
Fickle Hill; RMC Place; HUMBOLDT; ***150** ND-2; elev. 1,118ft./341m.; ★ **EUR-**; mail Arcata **z** 95521; ● 250
Fiddletown; RMC Place; AMADOR; **150** NK-9; elev. 1,687ft./514m.; 🄿; **z** 95629
Fieldbrook; RMC Place; HUMBOLDT; **150** ND-2; elev. 186ft./57m.; ★ **EUR-**; mail McKinleyville **z** 95519; ● 1,000
Fields Landing (South Bay); RMC Place; HUMBOLDT; **150** ND-1; 🄿; ★ **EUR-**; **z** 95537; ● 600
Fig Garden; RMC Place; FRESNO; ***152** SB-7; ★ **FRES**; mail Fresno **z** 93704; pop. incl. with Fresno (Inc. Place)
Figueroa; RMC Place; LOS ANGELES; ★ **L.A.**; mail Altadena **z** 91001; pop. incl. with Los Angeles (Inc. Place)
Fillmore; Inc. Place; VENTURA; **152** SI-9; elev. 469ft./143m.; 🄿; **z** 93015-16; Ⓟ 11,992; © 13,643
Fine Gold; RMC Place; MADERA; ***152** SA-8; elev. 1,302ft./397m.; mail North Fork **z** 93643; rural
Finley; RMC Place; LAKE; ***150** NI-4; 🄿; **z** 95435
Firebaugh; Inc. Place; FRESNO; **152** SB-6; elev. 151ft./46m.; 🄿; **z** 93622; Ⓟ 4,429; © 5,743
Fire Mountain; RMC Place; TEHAMA; ***150** NF-7; mail Mill Creek **z** 96061; rural
Firestone; RMC Place; LOS ANGELES; ★ **L.A.**; mail South Gate **z** 90280; pop. incl. with South Gate (Inc. Place)
Firestone Park; RMC Place; LOS ANGELES; ***153** SJ-11; 🄿; ★ **L.A.**; **z** 90001; ● 1,000
First Street; RMC Place; SAN DIEGO; ★ **SDGO**; mail Oceanside **z** 92049, **z** 92054; pop. incl. with Oceanside (Inc. Place)
Fish Camp; RMC Place; MARIPOSA; **151** NN-11; 🄿; **z** 93623; ● 85
Fish Springs; RMC Place; INYO; ***153** SB-11; elev. 3,960ft./1,207m.; mail Big Pine **z** 93513; rural
Fisk; RMC Place; SAN FRANCISCO; ★ **SF-O-**; mail San Francisco **z** 94122; pop. incl. with San Francisco (Inc. Place)
Fitchburg; RMC Place; ALAMEDA; ★ **SF-O-**; mail Oakland **z** 94621; pop. incl. with Oakland (Inc. Place)
Five Brooks; RMC Place; MARIN; ***150** NL-4; mail Olema **z** 94950; rural
Five Corners; RMC Place; SAN JOAQUIN; mail Manteca **z** 95336, Ripon **z** 95366; rural
Five Mile Terrace; RMC Place; EL DORADO; ***150** NJ-9; mail Placerville **z** 95667; ● 300
Five Points; RMC Place; FRESNO; **152** SC-7; 🄿; **z** 93624; ● 110
Five Points; RMC Place; SAN DIEGO; ***153** SN-13; ★ **SDGO**; mail San Diego **z** 92110; pop. incl. with San Diego (Inc. Place)
Flamingo Heights; RMC Place; SAN BERNARDINO; ***153** SI-15; elev. 3,476ft./1,059m.; mail Yucca Valley **z** 92284; ● 950
Fletcher Hills; RMC Place; SAN DIEGO; ***153** SM-14; ★ **SDGO**; mail El Cajon **z** 92020; pop. incl. with El Cajon (Inc. Place)
Flinn Springs; RMC Place; SAN DIEGO; ***153** SM-14; elev. 894ft./272m.; ★ **SDGO**; mail El Cajon **z** 92021; ● 600
Flint; RMC Place; LOS ANGELES; ★ **L.A.**; mail Los Angeles **z** 90057; pop. incl. with Los Angeles (Inc. Place)
Flintridge; RMC Place; LOS ANGELES; ***153** SJ-11; 🄿; ★ **L.A.**; **z** 91011; pop. incl. with La Cañada Flintridge (Inc. Place)
Florence; RMC Place; LOS ANGELES; **154** F-7; elev. 149ft./45m.; ★ **L.A.**; mail Los Angeles **z** 90001; ● 25,000
Florence-Graham; CDP-Census Area Only; LOS ANGELES; ***153** SJ-11; ★ **L.A.**; mail Los Angeles **z** 90001; Ⓟ 57,147; © 60,197; ◆ 61,567
Florin; CDP; SACRAMENTO; **149** E-7; elev. 34ft./10m.; ★ **SAC**; mail Sacramento **z** 95828-29; Ⓟ 24,330; © 27,653; ◆ 31,862
Floriston; RMC Place; NEVADA; ***150** NH-10; 🄿; **z** 96111; ● 110
Flosden Acres; RMC Place; SOLANO; ***150** NL-5; ★ **SF-O-**; mail Vallejo **z** 94590; pop. incl. with Vallejo (Inc. Place)
Flournoy; RMC Place; TEHAMA; **150** NG-5; 🄿; **z** 96029
Fly in Acres; RMC Place; CALAVERAS; ***150** NL-9; mail Arnold **z** 95223; ● 200
Folsom; Inc. Place; SACRAMENTO; **150** NJ-8; elev. 218ft./66m.; 🄿 🄷; ★ **SAC**; **z** 95630, **z** 95762-63 & mail Represa **z** 95671; Ⓟ 29,802; © 51,884; ◆ 67,018
Folsom Junction; RMC Place; SACRAMENTO; ***150** NJ-8; ★ **SAC**; mail Folsom **z** 95630; pop. incl. with Folsom (Inc. Place)
Fontana; Inc. Place; SAN BERNARDINO; **155** D-16; elev. 1,232ft./376m.; 🄿 🄷 ■; ★ **RIV-**; **z** 92331, **z** 92334-37; Ⓟ 87,535; © 128,929; ◆ 179,590
Foothill Farms; CDP; SACRAMENTO; **149** B-8; elev. 131ft./40m.; ★ **SAC**; mail Sacramento **z** 95841; Ⓟ 17,135; © 17,426
Foothill Ranch; CDP-Census Area Only; ORANGE; ***153** SK-12; 🄿; ★ **L.A.**; **z** 92610; © 10,899
Forbestown; RMC Place; BUTTE, YUBA; **150** NH-7; 🄿; **z** 95941 & mail Foothill Ranch **z** 92610; ● 250
Ford City; CDP; KERN; **152** SG-8; mail Taft **z** 93268; Ⓟ 3,781; © 3,512
Forest; RMC Place; SIERRA; **150** NH-8; mail Alleghany **z** 95910; ● 50
Foresta; RMC Place; MARIPOSA; ***151** NM-11; mail Yosemite National Park **z** 95389; ● 100
Forest Falls (Fallsvale, Forest Home); RMC Place; SAN BERNARDINO; **153** SJ-14; 🄿; **z** 92339; ● 550
Forest Glen; RMC Place; TRINITY; **150** NE-3; mail Hayfork **z** 96041; ● 5
Foresthill; CDP; PLACER; **150** NI-8; elev. 3,225ft./983m.; 🄿; ★ **SAC**; **z** 95631; Ⓟ 1,409; © 1,791
Forest Home; SAN BERNARDINO; see Forest Falls (RMC Place)
Forest Knolls; RMC Place; MARIN; ***150** NL-4; elev. 256ft./78m.; 🄿; ★ **SF-O-**; **z** 94933; ● 1,400
Forest Lake; RMC Place; LAKE; ***150** NJ-4; elev. 2,600ft./792m.; mail Cobb **z** 95426; ● 150
Forest Meadows; CDP; CALAVERAS; ***150** NL-9; © 1,197
Forest Park; RMC Place; LOS ANGELES; ***152** SI-10; ★ **L.A.**; mail Santa Clarita **z** 91350; ● 1,450
Forest Park; RMC Place; SANTA CRUZ; ★ **S.CRZ**; mail Boulder Creek **z** 95006; ● 220
Forest Ranch; RMC Place; BUTTE; **150** NG-7; elev. 2,357ft./718m.; 🄿; **z** 95942; ● 365
Forest Springs; RMC Place; SANTA CRUZ; ***152** SA-2; ★ **S.CRZ**; mail Boulder Creek **z** 95006; ● 160
Forestville; CDP; SONOMA; **150** NK-4; 🄿; ★ **S.ROS**; **z** 95436; Ⓟ 2,443; © 2,370
Forks of Salmon; RMC Place; SISKIYOU; **150** NC-3; elev. 1,242ft./379m.; 🄿; **z** 96031; ● 70
Fort Bidwell; RMC Place; MODOC; **150** NB-10; 🄿; **z** 96112; ● 200
Fort Bidwell Reservation; Indian Reservation; MODOC; mail Fort Bidwell **z** 96112; Ⓟ 98; © 108
Fort Bragg; Inc. Place; MENDOCINO; **150** NH-2; 🄿 🄷; **z** 95437 & mail Westport **z** 95488; Ⓟ 6,078; © 7,026; Ⓡ 6,814
Fort Dick; RMC Place; DEL NORTE; **150** NA-2; elev. 47ft./14m.; 🄿; **z** 95538; ● 200
Fort Goff; RMC Place; SISKIYOU; ***150** NA-3; elev. 1,320ft./402m.; mail Seiad Valley **z** 96086; rural
Fort Independence Reservation; Indian Reservation; INYO; mail Independence **z** 93526; Ⓟ 61; © 86
Fort Jones; Inc. Place; SISKIYOU; **150** NB-4; elev. 2,747ft./837m.; 🄿; **z** 96032; Ⓟ 639; © 660
Fort MacArthur; RMC Place; LOS ANGELES; ★ **L.A.**; mail San Pedro **z** 90731; pop. incl. with Los Angeles (Inc. Place)
Fort Mason (Mason); RMC Place; SAN FRANCISCO; ★ **SF-O-**; mail San Francisco **z** 94123; pop. incl. with San Francisco (Inc. Place)
Fort Mojave Reservation; Indian Reservation; SAN BERNARDINO; Reservation extends into AZ and NV; mail Needles **z** 92363; Ⓟ 36; © 21
Fort Ord Village; RMC Place; MONTEREY; ★ **MTRY-**; mail Marina **z** 93933, Seaside **z** 93955; pop. incl. with Seaside (Inc. Place)
Fort Romie; RMC Place; MONTEREY; mail Soledad **z** 93960; ● 300
Fort Seward; RMC Place; HUMBOLDT; **150** NF-2; elev. 322ft./98m.; mail Alderpoint **z** 95511; ● 160
Fort Sutter; RMC Place; SACRAMENTO; ★ **SAC**; mail Sacramento **z** 95816; pop. incl. with Sacramento (Inc. Place)
Fortuna; Inc. Place; HUMBOLDT; **150** NE-1; elev. 61ft./19m.; 🄿 🄷; ★ **EUR-**; **z** 95540; Ⓟ 8,788; © 10,497
Fort Yuma Reservation; Indian Reservation; IMPERIAL; Reservation extends into AZ; mail Winterhaven **z** 92283; Ⓟ 2,346; © 2,340
Foster City; Inc. Place; SAN MATEO; **151** NI-15; 🄿; ★ **SF-O-**; **z** 94404; Ⓟ 28,176; © 28,803; ◆ 27,974
Fountain Springs; RMC Place; TULARE; ***152** SE-9; elev. 790ft./241m.; mail Porterville **z** 93257; rural
Fountain Valley; Inc. Place; ORANGE; **154** J-10; elev. 28ft./9m.; 🄿 🄷 ■; ★ **L.A.**; **z** 92708, **z** 92728; Ⓟ 53,691; © 54,978; ◆ 55,840
Four Corners; RMC Place; MADERA; ***152** SB-7; elev. 457ft./139m.; mail Madera **z** 93637; rural
Four Corners; RMC Place; SAN BERNARDINO; ***153** SJ-16; mail Twentynine Palms **z** 92277; pop. incl. with Twentynine Palms (Inc. Place)
Four Corners; SAN BERNARDINO; see Kramer Junction (RMC Place)
Fouts Springs; RMC Place; COLUSA; **150** NH-4; mail Stonyford **z** 95979
Fowler; Inc. Place; FRESNO; **152** SC-7; 🄿; ★ **FRES**; **z** 93625; Ⓟ 3,208; © 3,979
Fox Hills; RMC Place; LOS ANGELES; ***152** SJ-10; ★ **L.A.**; mail Culver City **z** 90233; pop. incl. with Culver City (Inc. Place)
Foy; RMC Place; LOS ANGELES; ***153** SJ-11; ★ **L.A.**; mail Los Angeles **z** 90017, **z** 90057; pop. incl. with Los Angeles (Inc. Place)
Franciscan Park; RMC Place; SAN MATEO; ★ **SF-O-**; mail Daly City **z** 94014; pop. incl. with Daly City (Inc. Place)
Franklin; RMC Place; NAPA; ★ **NAPA**; mail Napa **z** 94559; pop. incl. with Napa (Inc. Place)
Franklin; RMC Place; SACRAMENTO; ***150** NK-7; elev. 18ft./5m.; ★ **SAC**; mail Elk Grove **z** 95758; ● 250
Frazier Park; CDP; KERN; **152** SH-9; 🄿; **z** 93222, **z** 93225; Ⓟ 2,201; © 2,348
Fredericksburg; RMC Place; ALPINE; ***151** NJ-11; mail Markleeville **z** 96120; rural
Freedom; CDP; SANTA CRUZ; **152** SB-3; 🄿; ★ **WATS**; **z** 95019; Ⓟ 8,361; © 6,000
Freeman (Freeman Junction); RMC Place; KERN; ***153** SF-12; elev. 3,186ft./971m.; mail Inyokern **z** 93527; rural
Freeman Junction; KERN; see Freeman (RMC Place)
Freeport; RMC Place; SACRAMENTO; ***150** NK-7; ★ **SAC**; pop. incl. with Sacramento (Inc. Place)
Freestone; RMC Place; SONOMA; ***150** NK-4; 🄿; ★ **S.ROS**; **z** 95472; ● 170
Freeway Park; RMC Place; ORANGE; ★ **L.A.**; pop. incl. with Anaheim (Inc. Place)
Fremont; Inc. Place; ALAMEDA; **150** NM-6; elev. 53ft./16m.; 🄿 🄷 🄲 4,366 ■; ★ **SF-O-**; **z** 94536-39, **z** 94555; Ⓟ 173,339; © 203,413; ◆ 212,286
French Camp; CDP; SAN JOAQUIN; **150** NM-7; 🄿 🄷; ★ **STOC**; **z** 95231; Ⓟ 3,018; © 4,109
French Corral; RMC Place; NEVADA; ***150** NI-8; elev. 522ft./159m.; mail North San Juan **z** 95960, Smartsville **z** 95977; rural
French Gulch; CDP; SHASTA; **150** NE-5; elev. 1,355ft./413m.; 🄿; **z** 96033; © 254
Fresh Pond; RMC Place; EL DORADO; ***150** NJ-9; mail Pollock Pines **z** 95726; rural
Freshwater; RMC Place; HUMBOLDT; **150** ND-2; ★ **EUR-**; mail Eureka **z** 95503; ● 300
Freshwater Corners; RMC Place; HUMBOLDT; ***150** ND-2; elev. 9ft./3m.; ★ **EUR-**; mail Eureka **z** 95503; ● 350
Fresno; Inc. Place; ⊡ FRESNO; **152** SB-7; elev. 296ft./90m.; 🄿 🄷 🄲 24,625 ■; ★ **FRES**; **z** 93650, **z** 93701-12, **z** 93714-18, **z** 93720-30, **z** 93740-41, **z** 93744-45, **z** 93747, **z** 93750, **z** 93755, **z** 93760-61, **z** 93764-65, **z** 93771-80, **z** 93784, **z** 93786, **z** 93790-94, **z** 93844, **z** 93888; Ⓟ 354,202; © 427,652; ◆ 491,328
FRESNO; **152** SD-6; Ⓟ 667,490; © 799,407; ◆ 914,078
Fresno Flats; MADERA; see Oakhurst (CDP)
Friant; CDP; FRESNO; **152** SB-7; elev. 340ft./104m.; 🄿; ★ **FRES**; **z** 93626; © 519
Friendly Hills; RMC Place; LOS ANGELES; ***153** SJ-11; elev. 318ft./97m.; ★ **L.A.**; pop. incl. with Whittier (Inc. Place)
Fruitdale; CDP-Census Area Only; SANTA CLARA; ***150** NN-6; ★ **SF-O-**; © 895
Fruitland; RMC Place; HUMBOLDT; ***150** NF-2; mail Myers Flat **z** 95554; rural
Fruitridge Manor; RMC Place; SACRAMENTO; **149** E-6; elev. 30ft./9m.; ★ **SAC**; mail Sacramento **z** 95820; pop. incl. with Sacramento (Inc. Place)
Fruit Ridge Manor; RMC Place; SACRAMENTO; ***150** NK-7; ★ **SAC**; pop. incl. with Sacramento (Inc. Place)
Fruitvale; RMC Place; ALAMEDA; ★ **SF-O-**; mail Oakland **z** 94601; pop. incl. with Oakland (Inc. Place)
Fruitvale; RMC Place; KERN; ***152** SF-9; elev. 393ft./120m.; ★ **BAK**; mail Bakersfield **z** 93308; ● 250
Fruto; RMC Place; GLENN; ***150** NH-5; mail Willows **z** 95988; rural
Fuller Acres (Hilltop); RMC Place; KERN; ***152** SG-9; elev. 415ft./126m.; ★ **BAK**; mail Bakersfield **z** 93307; ● 850
Fullerton; Inc. Place; ORANGE; **153** SJ-12; elev. 155ft./47m.; 🄿 🄷 🄲 37,006 ■; ★ **L.A.**; **z** 92831-38; Ⓟ 114,144; © 126,003; ◆ 128,894
Fulton; RMC Place; SONOMA; **150** NK-4; 🄿; ★ **S.ROS**; **z** 95439; ● 1,300
Furnace Creek; CDP-Census Area Only; INYO; **153** SC-14; mail Death Valley **z** 92328; © 31

G

Gabilan; RMC Place; MONTEREY; ★ **SLNS**; mail Salinas **z** 93906; pop. incl. with Salinas (Inc. Place)
Gabilan Acres; RMC Place; MONTEREY; ***152** SB-3; ★ **SLNS**; mail Salinas **z** 93906; ● 1,400
Gallinas; RMC Place; MARIN; ***150** NL-5; ★ **SF-O-**; mail San Rafael **z** 94903; pop. incl. with San Rafael (Inc. Place)
Galt; Inc. Place; SACRAMENTO; **150** NL-7; elev. 47ft./14m.; 🄿; **z** 95632; Ⓟ 8,889; © 19,472; ◆ 25,405
Ganesha; RMC Place; LOS ANGELES; ★ **L.A.**; pop. incl. with Pomona (Inc. Place)
Garberville; RMC Place; HUMBOLDT; **150** NF-2; elev. 533ft./162m.; 🄿 🄷; **z** 95542; ● 800
Garden; RMC Place; SANTA CLARA; ★ **SF-O-**; mail San Jose **z** 95155; pop. incl. with San Jose (Inc. Place)
Gardena; Inc. Place; LOS ANGELES; **154** H-6; elev. 40ft./12m.; 🄿 🄷 ■; ★ **L.A.**; **z** 90247-49; Ⓟ 49,841; © 57,746; ◆ 60,254
Garden Acres; CDP-Census Area Only; SAN JOAQUIN; **149** H-10; ★ **STOC**; mail Stockton **z** 95205; Ⓟ 8,547; © 9,747
Garden Farms; RMC Place; SAN LUIS OBISPO; ***152** SF-5; elev. 952ft./290m.; mail Atascadero **z** 93422; ● 320
Garden Gate Village; RMC Place; SANTA CLARA; ★ **SF-O-**; mail Cupertino **z** 95014; pop. incl. with Cupertino (Inc. Place)
Garden Grove; Inc. Place; ORANGE; **153** SK-12; elev. 90ft./27m.; 🄿 🄷 ■; ★ **L.A.**; **z** 92840-46; Ⓟ 143,050; © 165,196; ◆ 171,303
Gardenland; RMC Place; SACRAMENTO; ***150** NK-7; ★ **SAC**; pop. incl. with Sacramento (Inc. Place)
Garden Valley; RMC Place; EL DORADO; **150** NJ-8; 🄿; **z** 95633; ● 700
Garden Village; RMC Place; SAN MATEO; ★ **SF-O-**; mail Daly City **z** 94015; pop. incl. with Daly City (Inc. Place)
Garey; RMC Place; SANTA BARBARA; **152** SH-6; elev. 379ft./116m.; mail Santa Maria **z** 93454; ● 100
Garfield; RMC Place; KERN; mail Bodfish **z** 93205; ● 700
Garlock; RMC Place; KERN; ***153** SF-12; mail Randsburg **z** 93554; rural
Gasoline Alley; RMC Place; PLACER; ***150** NJ-8; ★ **SAC**; mail Auburn **z** 95603; ● 1,200
Gas Point; RMC Place; SHASTA; **150** NE-5; elev. 607ft./185m.; mail Cottonwood **z** 96022; ● 30
Gasquet; RMC Place; DEL NORTE; **150** NA-2; 🄿; **z** 95543; ● 220
Gateley; RMC Place; CONTRA COSTA; ***150** NL-5; ★ **SF-O-**; pop. incl. with Pinole (Inc. Place)
Gateway; RMC Place; LOS ANGELES; ★ **L.A.**; mail Culver City **z** 90232; pop. incl. with Culver City (Inc. Place)
Gateway (Gateway Park); RMC Place; NEVADA; ***150** NI-10; mail Truckee **z** 96161; pop. incl. with Truckee (Inc. Place)
Gateway Park; NEVADA; see Gateway (RMC Place)
Gateway Station; RMC Place; SAN FRANCISCO; ★ **SF-O-**; mail San Francisco **z** 94126; pop. incl. with San Francisco (Inc. Place)
Gaviota; RMC Place; SANTA BARBARA; **152** SI-6; elev. 98ft./30m.; 🄿; **z** 93117; ● 70
Gazelle; CDP; SISKIYOU; **150** NB-5; 🄿; **z** 96034; © 136
Geary; RMC Place; SAN FRANCISCO; ★ **SF-O-**; mail San Francisco **z** 94121; pop. incl. with San Francisco (Inc. Place)
Gemco; RMC Place; LOS ANGELES; ★ **L.A.**; pop. incl. with Los Angeles (Inc. Place)
Genesee; RMC Place; PLUMAS; **150** NG-9; mail Taylorsville **z** 95983; ● 150
Georgetown; CDP; EL DORADO; **150** NJ-8; 🄿; **z** 95634; © 962
George Washington; RMC Place; SAN DIEGO; ★ **SDGO**; mail San Diego **z** 92103, **z** 92162; pop. incl. with San Diego (Inc. Place)
Gerber; RMC Place; TEHAMA; **150** NF-6; elev. 241ft./73m.; 🄿; **z** 96035; ● 1,100
Gerber-Las Flores; CDP-Census Area Only; TEHAMA; ***150** NF-6; elev. 238ft./73m.; mail Gerber **z** 96035; Ⓟ 1,143; © 1,389
Geyserville; RMC Place; SONOMA; **150** NJ-4; 🄿; **z** 95441; ● 1,000
Giant; RMC Place; CONTRA COSTA; ***150** NL-5; ★ **SF-O-**; pop. incl. with Richmond (Inc. Place)
Gilman Hot Springs; RMC Place; RIVERSIDE; ***153** SK-14; 🄿; ★ **HEM**; **z** 92583; ● 600
Gilroy; Inc. Place; SANTA CLARA; **152** SB-3; elev. 200ft./61m.; 🄿 🄷; ★ **SF-O-**; **z** 95020-21; Ⓟ 31,487; © 41,464; ◆ 50,103
Glamis; RMC Place; IMPERIAL; ***153** SM-18; elev. 335ft./102m.; mail Brawley **z** 92227; rural
Glassell; RMC Place; LOS ANGELES; ***153** SJ-11; 🄿; ★ **L.A.**; **z** 90065; pop. incl. with Los Angeles (Inc. Place)
Glen Arbor; RMC Place; SANTA CRUZ; ***152** SA-2; ★ **S.CRZ**; mail Ben Lomond **z** 95005; ● 350
Glen Avon (Glen Avon Heights); CDP; RIVERSIDE; **155** F-16; ★ **RIV-**; mail Riverside **z** 92509; Ⓟ 12,663; © 14,853
Glen Avon Heights; RIVERSIDE; see Glen Avon (CDP)
Glenbrook; RMC Place; LAKE; ***150** NJ-4; elev. 2,307ft./703m.; mail Middletown **z** 95461; rural
Glenbrook; RMC Place; NEVADA; ***150** NI-8; elev. 2,800ft./853m.; mail Grass Valley **z** 95945; ● 620
Glenburn; RMC Place; SHASTA; **150** ND-7; elev. 3,314ft./1,010m.; mail Fall River Mills **z** 96028; rural
Glencoe; RMC Place; CALAVERAS; **150** NK-9; elev. 2,721ft./829m.; 🄿; **z** 95232; ● 300
Glencove; RMC Place; SOLANO; ***150** NL-5; elev. 10ft./3m.; ★ **SF-O-**; mail Vallejo **z** 94590; pop. incl. with Vallejo (Inc. Place)
Glendale; RMC Place; HUMBOLDT; ***150** ND-2; ★ **EUR-**; mail McKinleyville **z** 95519; ● 500
Glendale; Inc. Place; LOS ANGELES; **153** SJ-11; elev. 571ft./174m.; 🄿 🄷 ■; ★ **L.A.**; **z** 91201-10, **z** 91214, **z** 91221-22, **z** 91224-26; Ⓟ 180,038; © 194,973; ◆ 203,344
Glendora; Inc. Place; LOS ANGELES; **155** D-12; elev. 776ft./237m.; 🄿 🄷 ■; ★ **L.A.**; **z** 91740-41; Ⓟ 47,828; © 49,415; ◆ 48,810
Glen Ellen; CDP; SONOMA; **150** NK-5; elev. 230ft./70m.; 🄿; **z** 95442; Ⓟ 1,191; © 992
Glenhaven; RMC Place; LAKE; **150** NI-4; 🄿; **z** 95443; ● 360
Glen Martin; RMC Place; SAN BERNARDINO; mail Angelus Oaks **z** 92305; ● 120
Glenn; RMC Place; GLENN; **150** NH-6; 🄿; **z** 95943; ● 110
GLENN; **150** NH-5; Ⓟ 24,798; © 26,453; ◆ 28,337
Glennville; RMC Place; KERN; **152** SE-10; elev. 3,188ft./972m.; 🄿; **z** 93226; ● 210
Glenoaks; RMC Place; LOS ANGELES; ★ **L.A.**; mail Burbank **z** 91504, **z** 91508; pop. incl. with Burbank (Inc. Place)
Glenshire-Devonshire; RMC Place; NEVADA; ***150** NI-10; elev. 7,439ft./2,267m.; mail Truckee **z** 96161; Ⓟ 2,133
Glenview; RMC Place; LOS ANGELES; **154** D-3; ★ **L.A.**; mail Topanga **z** 90290; ● 160
Glenview; RMC Place; SAN DIEGO; ***153** SM-14; elev. 597ft./182m.; ★ **SDGO**; mail El Cajon **z** 92021; ● 1,300
Glenwood; RMC Place; SANTA CRUZ; ***152** SA-2; elev. 1,000ft./305m.; mail Scotts Valley **z** 95066; ● 100
Globe; RMC Place; SACRAMENTO; ★ **SAC**; pop. incl. with Sacramento (Inc. Place)
Glorietta; RMC Place; CONTRA COSTA; ***150** NM-5; ★ **SF-O-**; mail Orinda **z** 94563; pop. incl. with Orinda (Inc. Place)
Glorietta; RMC Place; FRESNO; ***152** SB-7; elev. 362ft./110m.; ★ **FRES**; pop. incl. with Clovis (Inc. Place)
Goffs; RMC Place; SAN BERNARDINO; **153** SG-18; elev. 2,587ft./789m.; mail Essex **z** 92332
Golden Gate; RMC Place; SAN FRANCISCO; ★ **SF-O-**; mail San Francisco **z** 94159; pop. incl. with San Francisco (Inc. Place)
Golden Hill; RMC Place; SAN DIEGO; ***153** SN-13; ★ **SDGO**; mail San Diego **z** 92102; pop. incl. with San Diego (Inc. Place)
Golden Hills; RMC Place; CALAVERAS; ***150** NL-9; elev. 1,000ft./305m.; mail San Andreas **z** 95249; rural
Golden Hills; CDP-Census Area Only; KERN; ***152** SG-10; elev. 4,000ft./1,219m.; 🄿; **z** 93561; Ⓟ 5,423; © 7,434
Golden Valley; RMC Place; LOS ANGELES; ★ **L.A.**; mail Santa Clarita **z** 91350; pop. incl. with Santa Clarita (Inc. Place)
Gold Flat; RMC Place; NEVADA; ***150** NI-8; mail Nevada City **z** 95959; rural
Gold Hill; RMC Place; EL DORADO; ***150** NJ-8; elev. 1,605ft./489m.; mail Placerville **z** 95667; ● 460
Goldleaf; RMC Place; FRESNO; ***152** SC-7; elev. 306ft./93m.; ★ **FRES**; pop. incl. with Fresno (Inc. Place)
Gold River; CDP-Census Area Only; SACRAMENTO; ***150** NJ-7; 🄿; ★ **SAC**; **z** 95670; © 8,023
Gold Run; RMC Place; PLACER; **150** NI-8; elev. 3,222ft./982m.; 🄿; **z** 95717; ● 200
Goleta; Inc. Place; SANTA BARBARA; **152** SI-7; 🄿; ★ **S.BAR**; **z** 93110-11, **z** 93116-18, **z** 93199 & mail Santa Barbara **z** 93160; incorporated October 22, 2001; not reported in 2000 Census; ● 28,500; ◆ 30,669
Goleta; CDP-Census Area Only; SANTA BARBARA; **152** SI-7; elev. 40ft./12m.; 🄿; ★ **S.BAR**; **z** 93110-11, **z** 93116-18, **z** 93199 & mail Santa Barbara **z** 93160; © 55,204
Gonzales; Inc. Place; MONTEREY; **152** SC-3; 🄿; **z** 93926; Ⓟ 4,660; © 7,525; Ⓡ 7,564
Goodyears Bar; RMC Place; SIERRA; **150** NH-8; 🄿; **z** 95944; ● 100
Gorda; RMC Place; MONTEREY; ***152** SE-3; elev. 340ft./104m.; mail Big Sur **z** 93920; rural
Gorman; RMC Place; LOS ANGELES; **152** SH-9; elev. 3,811ft./1,162m.; 🄿; **z** 93243; ● 50
Gosford; RMC Place; KERN; ***152** SF-9; elev. 361ft./110m.; ★ **BAK**; pop. incl. with Bakersfield (Inc. Place)
Goshen (Goshen Junction); CDP; TULARE; **152** SD-8; 🄿; ★ **VISL**; **z** 93227; © 2,394
Goshen Junction; TULARE; see Goshen (CDP)
Graeagle; CDP; PLUMAS; **150** NG-9; 🄿; **z** 96103; © 831
Granada Hills; RMC Place; LOS ANGELES; ***152** SI-10; elev. 1,032ft./315m.; 🄿; ★ **L.A.**; **z** 91344, **z** 91394; pop. incl. with Los Angeles (Inc. Place)
Grand Avenue; RMC Place; ORANGE; ★ **L.A.**; mail Santa Ana **z** 92705; pop. incl. with Santa Ana (Inc. Place)
Grand Central; RMC Place; LOS ANGELES; ★ **L.A.**; mail Glendale **z** 91201, **z** 91221; pop. incl. with Glendale (Inc. Place)
Grand Lake; RMC Place; ALAMEDA; ★ **SF-O-**; mail Oakland **z** 94610; pop. incl. with Oakland (Inc. Place)
Grand Terrace; Inc. Place; SAN BERNARDINO; **155** E-18; 🄿; ★ **RIV-**; **z** 92313, **z** 92324; Ⓟ 10,946; © 11,626
Grandview; RMC Place; SAN BERNARDINO; ***153** SH-13; elev. 2,234ft./681m.; mail Barstow **z** 92311; ● 1,400
Grangeville; RMC Place; KINGS; **152** SD-7; mail Hanford **z** 93230; ● 300
Granite Bay; CDP-Census Area Only; PLACER; ***150** NJ-8; 🄿; ★ **SAC**; **z** 95746; © 19,388
Granite Hill; RMC Place; NEVADA; mail Grass Valley **z** 95945; pop. incl. with Grass Valley (Inc. Place)
Granite Hills; CDP-Census Area Only; SAN DIEGO; ***153** SM-14; elev. 600ft./183m.; ★ **SDGO**; mail El Cajon **z** 92019; Ⓟ 3,157; © 3,246
Graniteville; RMC Place; NEVADA; **150** NH-9; mail Nevada City **z** 95959
Grantville; RMC Place; SAN DIEGO; ***153** SM-14; ★ **SDGO**; mail San Diego **z** 92120, **z** 92160, **z** 92190; pop. incl. with San Diego (Inc. Place)
Grapevine; RMC Place; KERN; ***152** SH-9; elev. 1,499ft./457m.; mail Lebec **z** 93243; rural
Grass Valley; Inc. Place; NEVADA; **150** NI-8; elev. 2,411ft./735m.; 🄿 🄷; **z** 95945, **z** 95949; Ⓟ 9,048; © 10,922
Graton; CDP; SONOMA; **150** NK-4; 🄿; ★ **S.ROS**; **z** 95444; Ⓟ 1,409; © 1,815
Gravesboro; RMC Place; FRESNO; ***152** SB-8; elev. 480ft./146m.; mail Sanger **z** 93657; ● 150
Grayson; CDP; STANISLAUS; **150** NM-8; mail Patterson **z** 95363; © 1,077
Greeley Hill; RMC Place; MARIPOSA; **150** NM-10; mail Coulterville **z** 95311; ● 250
Green; RMC Place; LOS ANGELES; ★ **L.A.**; mail Los Angeles **z** 90037; pop. incl. with Los Angeles (Inc. Place)
Greenacres; RMC Place; KERN; **152** SF-9; 🄿; ★ **BAK**; **z** 93312 & mail Bakersfield **z** 93308; pop. incl. with Bakersfield (Inc. Place); Ⓟ 7,379
Green Brae; RMC Place; MARIN; **151** ND-12; elev. 28ft./9m.; 🄿 🄷; ★ **SF-O-**; **z** 94904 & mail Kentfield **z** 94914; ● 3,400
Greenbrook; RMC Place; CONTRA COSTA; ***150** NM-6; ★ **SF-O-**; mail Danville **z** 94526; pop. incl. with Danville (Inc. Place)

Entries in **UPPERCASE** are counties.
Entries in **bold** have populations of 2,500 or more.
Names in parentheses are alternate names.

Inc. Place	Incorporated Place
RMC Place	Rand McNally Designated Place
CDP	Census Designated Place
MCD	Minor Civil Division

⊡ County Seat
▲ Minor Civil Division
elev. Elevation
🄿 Post Office
🄷 Hospital
🄲 College
■ Principal Business Center
★ Ranally Metro Area (RMA) Abbreviation
z Zip Code(s)
Ⓟ Previous Census Population
Ⓡ Revised Census Population
Ⓐ Annexation Population
● Rand McNally Population Estimate
© Final Census Population
Ⓢ Special Census Population
◆ Estimated Population

For additional definitions see Glossary, Volume 1, and Introduction, Volume 2.

Greenfield; RMC Place; KERN; **152** SN-6; ★ **BAK**; mail Bakersfield **z** 93307; ● 1,400
Greenfield; Inc. Place; MONTEREY; **152** SD-4; 🅿; **z** 93927; Ⓟ 7,464; © 12,583; Ⓡ 12,648
Greenhaven Seventy; RMC Place; SACRAMENTO; ★ **SAC**; pop. incl. with Sacramento (Inc. Place)
Greenhorn; CDP-Census Area Only; PLUMAS; ***150** NG-9; © 146
Greenmead; RMC Place; LOS ANGELES; ***153** SJ-11; ★ **L.A.**; mail Los Angeles **z** 90059, **z** 90061
Green Meadows; RMC Place; YOLO; ★ **DAV**; mail Davis **z** 95616; pop. incl. with Davis (Inc. Place)
Greensport; RMC Place; SAN BERNARDINO; ***153** SJ-14; ★ **RIV-**; mail Mentone **z** 92359; ● 1,000
Green Valley (La Joya); RMC Place; LOS ANGELES; ***152** SH-10; elev. 2,928ft./892m.; 🅿; ★ **L.A.**; **z** 91390 & mail Santa Clarita **z** 91350; ● 800
Green Valley; CDP-Census Area Only; SOLANO; ***150** NK-5; ★ **FRFL-**; © 1,859
Green Valley Estates; RMC Place; SOLANO; ***150** NK-5; elev. 120ft./37m.; ★ **FRFL-**; mail Suisun City **z** 94585; ● 1,300
Green Valley Lake; RMC Place; SAN BERNARDINO; **155** B-20; 🅿; **z** 92341; ● 425
Greenview; CDP; SISKIYOU; **150** NB-4; elev. 2,812ft./857m.; 🅿; **z** 96037; © 200
Greenview Acres; RMC Place; HUMBOLDT; ★ **EUR-**; mail Arcata **z** 95521; pop. incl. with Arcata (Inc. Place)
Greenville; CDP; PLUMAS; **150** NF-8; elev. 3,580ft./1,091m.; 🅿 🅷; **z** 95947; Ⓟ 1,396; © 1,160
Greenville Rancheria; Indian Reservation; PLUMAS; © 22
Greenwich Village; RMC Place; VENTURA; ***152** SJ-9; ★ **OXN-**; mail Thousand Oaks **z** 91360; pop. incl. with Thousand Oaks (Inc. Place)
Greenwood; RMC Place; EL DORADO; **150** NJ-8; elev. 1,615ft./492m.; 🅿; **z** 95635; ● 600
Greenwood; MENDOCINO; see Elk (RMC Place)
Grenada; CDP; SISKIYOU; **150** NB-5; 🅿; **z** 96038; © 351
Gridley; Inc. Place; BUTTE; **150** NH-7; elev. 91ft./28m.; 🅿 🅷; **z** 95948; Ⓟ 4,631; © 5,382
Grimes; RMC Place; COLUSA; **150** NI-6; elev. 47ft./14m.; 🅿; **z** 95950; ● 370
Grindstone Rancheria; Indian Reservation; GLENN; © 162
Grizzly Flat (Grizzly Flats); RMC Place; EL DORADO; **150** NK-9; mail Grizzly Flats **z** 95636; ● 400
Grizzly Flats; EL DORADO; see Grizzly Flat (RMC Place)
Grossmont; RMC Place; SAN DIEGO; ***153** SN-14; ★ **SDGO**; mail La Mesa **z** 91942; pop. incl. with La Mesa (Inc. Place)
Groveland; RMC Place; TUOLUMNE; **150** NM-10; elev. 2,846ft./867m.; 🅿; **z** 95321; ● 1,500
Groveland-Big Oak Flat; CDP-Census Area Only; TUOLUMNE; ***150** NM-10; elev. 3,000ft./914m.; mail Big Oak Flat **z** 95305, Groveland **z** 95321; Ⓟ 2,753; © 3,388
Grover Beach (Grover City); Inc. Place; SAN LUIS OBISPO; **152** SG-5; elev. 50ft./15m.; 🅿; **z** 93433, **z** 93483; Ⓟ 11,656; © 13,067
Grover City; SAN LUIS OBISPO; see Grover Beach (Inc. Place)
Guadalupe; Inc. Place; SANTA BARBARA; **152** SG-5; elev. 85ft./26m.; 🅿; **z** 93434; Ⓟ 5,479; © 5,659
Gualala; RMC Place; MENDOCINO; **150** NJ-3; elev. 67ft./20m.; 🅿; **z** 95445; ● 1,500
Guasti; RMC Place; SAN BERNARDINO; ***153** SJ-12; 🅿; ★ **L.A.**; **z** 91743; pop. incl. with Ontario (Inc. Place)
Guatay; RMC Place; SAN DIEGO; ***153** SM-15; 🅿; **z** 91931; ● 300
Guerneville; CDP; SONOMA; **150** NK-4; elev. 56ft./17m.; 🅿; ★ **S.ROS**; **z** 95446 & mail Rio Nido **z** 95471; Ⓟ 1,966; © 2,441
Guernewood Park; RMC Place; SONOMA; ***150** NK-4; ★ **S.ROS**; mail Guerneville **z** 95446; ● 200
Guernsey; RMC Place; KINGS; **152** SD-8; elev. 218ft./66m.; mail Hanford **z** 93230
Guidiville Rancheria; Indian Reservation; MENDOCINO; © 0
Guinda; RMC Place; YOLO; **150** NJ-5; elev. 355ft./108m.; 🅿; **z** 95637; ● 275
Gustine; Inc. Place; MERCED; **152** SA-5; 🅿; **z** 95322; Ⓟ 3,931; © 4,698

H

Hacienda; RMC Place; ALAMEDA; ★ **SF-O-**; mail Pleasanton **z** 94588; pop. incl. with Pleasanton (Inc. Place)
Hacienda; RMC Place; SONOMA; ***150** NK-4; ★ **S.ROS**; mail Forestville **z** 95436; ● 210
Hacienda Heights; CDP; LOS ANGELES; **154** F-10; elev. 400ft./122m.; 🅿; ★ **L.A.**; **z** 91745; Ⓟ 52,354; © 53,122; ◆ 54,331
Hagginwood; RMC Place; SACRAMENTO; ***150** NJ-7; ★ **SAC**; pop. incl. with Sacramento (Inc. Place)
Halcyon; RMC Place; SAN LUIS OBISPO; ***152** SG-5; mail Arroyo Grande **z** 93420-21; ● 250
Hales Grove; RMC Place; MENDOCINO; ***150** NG-2; elev. 1,200ft./366m.; mail Leggett **z** 95585; ● 50
Half Moon Bay; Inc. Place; SAN MATEO; **150** NN-5; elev. 69ft./21m.; 🅿; ★ **SF-O-**; **z** 94019; Ⓟ 8,886; © 11,842
Hall; RMC Place; ALAMEDA; ★ **SF-O-**; mail Union City **z** 94587; pop. incl. with Union City (Inc. Place)
Halloran Springs; RMC Place; SAN BERNARDINO; ***153** SF-16; elev. 907ft./276m.; mail Baker **z** 92309, Nipton **z** 92364; rural
Halls Corner; RMC Place; KINGS; ***152** SD-7; mail Lemoore **z** 93245
Hallwood; RMC Place; YUBA; ***150** NI-7; elev. 91ft./28m.; mail Marysville **z** 95901; ● 50
Hamburg; RMC Place; SISKIYOU; **150** NB-4; elev. 1,592ft./485m.; mail Klamath River **z** 96050; ● 140
Hamilton; GLENN; see Hamilton City (CDP)
Hamilton; RMC Place; SANTA CLARA; ★ **SF-O-**; mail Palo Alto **z** 94301-02; pop. incl. with Palo Alto (Inc. Place)
Hamilton Bay; GLENN; see Hamilton City (CDP)
Hamilton Branch; CDP; PLUMAS; ***150** NF-8; © 587
Hamilton City (Hamilton, Hamilton Bay); CDP; GLENN; **150** NG-6; 🅿; **z** 95951; Ⓟ 1,811; © 1,903
Hammer Ranch; RMC Place; SAN JOAQUIN; ***150** NL-7; ★ **STOC**; mail Stockton **z** 95209, **z** 95219, **z** 95269; pop. incl. with Stockton (Inc. Place)
Hammil; RMC Place; MONO; ***151** NM-14; elev. 4,586ft./1,398m.; mail Bishop **z** 93514; rural
Hammond; RMC Place; FRESNO; ***152** SB-7; ★ **FRES**; pop. incl. with Fresno (Inc. Place)
Hammond; RMC Place; TULARE; mail Three Rivers **z** 93271; ● 500
Hammonton; RMC Place; YUBA; ***150** NI-7; elev. 130ft./40m.; mail Marysville **z** 95901; ● 80
Hancock; RMC Place; LOS ANGELES; ★ **L.A.**; mail Los Angeles **z** 90044; pop. incl. with Los Angeles (Inc. Place)
Hanford; Inc. Place; ⊡ KINGS; **152** SD-8; elev. 246ft./75m.; 🅿 🅷 ■; **z** 93230, **z** 93232; Ⓟ 30,897; © 41,686; ◆ 49,678
Hanford South; KINGS; see Home Garden (CDP-Census Area Only)
Happy Camp; RMC Place; SISKIYOU; **150** NB-3; elev. 1,087ft./331m.; 🅿; **z** 96039; ● 1,200
Harbin Springs; RMC Place; LAKE; ***150** NJ-4; elev. 1,600ft./488m.; mail Middletown **z** 95461; rural
Harbison Canyon; CDP; SAN DIEGO; ***153** SM-14; ★ **SDGO**; mail El Cajon **z** 92020; Ⓟ 2,122; © 3,645
Harbor City; RMC Place; LOS ANGELES; ***153** SK-11; elev. 48ft./15m.; 🅿; ★ **L.A.**; **z** 90710; pop. incl. with Los Angeles (Inc. Place)
Harbor Island; RMC Place; ORANGE; ★ **L.A.**; mail Newport Beach **z** 92660; pop. incl. with Newport Beach (Inc. Place)
Harbor Side; RMC Place; SAN DIEGO; ***153** SN-14; ★ **SDGO**; mail Chula Vista **z** 91911; pop. incl. with Chula Vista (Inc. Place)
Hardman Center; RMC Place; RIVERSIDE; ★ **RIV-**; mail Riverside **z** 92504, **z** 92514; pop. incl. with Riverside (Inc. Place)
Hardwick; RMC Place; KINGS; **152** SC-7; mail Hanford **z** 93230; ● 140
Harlem Springs; RMC Place; SAN BERNARDINO; ***153** SJ-13; elev. 1,411ft./430m.; ★ **RIV-**; mail Highland **z** 92346; pop. incl. with Highland (Inc. Place)
Harmony; RMC Place; SAN LUIS OBISPO; **152** SF-4; elev. 175ft./53m.; 🅿; **z** 93435; rural
Harmony Grove; RMC Place; SAN DIEGO; mail Escondido **z** 92029; ● 640
Harris; RMC Place; HUMBOLDT; ***150** NF-2; mail Garberville **z** 95542; rural
Harrison Park; RMC Place; SAN DIEGO; ***153** SM-15; elev. 4,400ft./1,341m.; mail Julian **z** 92036; ● 300
Hartland; RMC Place; TULARE; ***152** SC-9; mail Badger **z** 93603; rural
Harvard; RMC Place; SAN BERNARDINO; ***153** SG-14; mail Yermo **z** 92398; rural
Harvest; RMC Place; ORANGE; ★ **L.A.**; mail Irvine **z** 92612; pop. incl. with Irvine (Inc. Place)
Harvey; RMC Place; ALAMEDA; ★ **SF-O-**; pop. incl. with Oakland (Inc. Place)
Haskell Creek Homesites; RMC Place; SIERRA; ***150** NH-9; mail Calpine **z** 96124; ● 30
Hat Creek; RMC Place; SHASTA; **150** ND-7; 🅿; **z** 96040; ● 250
Hathaway Pines; RMC Place; CALAVERAS; **150** NL-9; 🅿; **z** 95233; ● 350
Hatton Fields; RMC Place; MONTEREY; ***152** SC-2; elev. 127ft./39m.; ★ **MTRY-**; mail Carmel **z** 93923; ● 650
Havasu Lake (Havasu Landing); RMC Place; SAN BERNARDINO; **147** T-10; mail Needles **z** 92363; ● 410
Havasu Landing; SAN BERNARDINO; see Havasu Lake (RMC Place)
Havilah; RMC Place; KERN; **152** SF-10; 🅿; **z** 93518
Hawaiian Gardens; Inc. Place; LOS ANGELES; **154** H-9; elev. 29ft./9m.; 🅿; ★ **L.A.**; **z** 90716; Ⓟ 13,639; © 14,779
Hawkins Bar; RMC Place; TRINITY; ***150** ND-3; elev. 1,260ft./384m.; mail Burnt Ranch **z** 95527, Salyer **z** 95563; ● 200
Hawkinsville; RMC Place; SISKIYOU; **150** NB-5; mail Yreka **z** 96097; ● 20
Hawthorne; Inc. Place; LOS ANGELES; **154** G-6; elev. 69ft./21m.; 🅿 🅷 ■; ★ **L.A.**; **z** 90250-51; Ⓟ 71,349; © 84,112; ◆ 89,423
Hayfork; CDP; TRINITY; **150** NE-4; elev. 2,327ft./709m.; 🅿; **z** 96041; Ⓟ 2,605; © 2,315
Hayward; Inc. Place; ALAMEDA; **150** NM-6; elev. 111ft./34m.; 🅿 🅷 🅲 13,132 ■; ★ **SF-O-**; **z** 94540-46, **z** 94552, **z** 94557; Ⓟ 111,343; © 140,030; ◆ 146,495
Hayward Highlands; RMC Place; ALAMEDA; ★ **SF-O-**; mail Hayward **z** 94542; pop. incl. with Hayward (Inc. Place)
Hayward Park; RMC Place; SAN MATEO; ***150** NM-5; ★ **SF-O-**; pop. incl. with San Mateo (Inc. Place)
Healdsburg; Inc. Place; SONOMA; **150** NJ-4; elev. 106ft./32m.; 🅿 🅷; ★ **S.ROS**; **z** 95448; Ⓟ 9,469; © 10,722
Heather Glen; RMC Place; PLACER; ***150** NI-8; elev. 2,000ft./610m.; ★ **SAC**; mail Applegate **z** 95703; ● 300
Heaton Station; PLACER; see Cisco (RMC Place)
Heber; CDP; IMPERIAL; **153** SN-17; 🅿; **z** 92249; Ⓟ 2,566; © 2,988
Helena; RMC Place; TRINITY; ***150** ND-4; elev. 1,404ft./428m.; 🅿; **z** 96048; rural
Helendale; RMC Place; SAN BERNARDINO; **153** SH-13; elev. 2,430ft./741m.; 🅿; **z** 92342; ● 700
Helisma; CALAVERAS; see Burson (RMC Place)
Helm; RMC Place; FRESNO; **152** SC-7; elev. 185ft./56m.; 🅿; **z** 93627
Hemet; Inc. Place; RIVERSIDE; **153** SK-14; elev. 1,596ft./486m.; 🅿 🅷 ■; ★ **HEM**; **z** 92543-46; Ⓟ 36,094; © 58,812; ◆ 72,588
Hemet East; RIVERSIDE; see East Hemet (CDP-Census Area Only)
Henderson; RMC Place; SAN MATEO; ***150** NN-5; ★ **SF-O-**; pop. incl. with Menlo Park (Inc. Place)
Henderson; RMC Place; TULARE; ★ **PORT**; mail Porterville **z** 93258; pop. incl. with Porterville (Inc. Place)
Henderson Village; RMC Place; SAN JOAQUIN; **150** NL-7; elev. 29ft./9m.; ★ **STOC**; mail Lodi **z** 95240; ● 200
Henley; RMC Place; SISKIYOU; ***150** NA-5; mail Hornbrook **z** 96044; ● 60
Henleyville; RMC Place; TEHAMA; ***150** NG-5; elev. 435ft./133m.; mail Corning **z** 96021; rural
Herald; RMC Place; SACRAMENTO; **150** NK-7; 🅿; **z** 95638; ● 500
Hercules; Inc. Place; CONTRA COSTA; **151** NC-15; 🅿; ★ **SF-O-**; **z** 94547; Ⓟ 16,829; © 19,488; ◆ 19,830
Heritage Ranch; RMC Place; SAN LUIS OBISPO; ***152** SE-5; elev. 900ft./274m.; 🅿; **z** 93446; ● 900
Heritage Village; RMC Place; SANTA CLARA; ★ **SF-O-**; mail Campbell **z** 95009; pop. incl. with Campbell (Inc. Place)
Herlong; RMC Place; LASSEN; **150** NF-10; 🅿; **z** 96113; ● 1,000
Hermosa Beach; Inc. Place; LOS ANGELES; **154** H-5; elev. 15ft./5m.; 🅿; ★ **L.A.**; **z** 90254; Ⓟ 18,219; © 18,566
Hernandez; RMC Place; SAN BENITO; ***152** SD-5; elev. 2,458ft./749m.; mail Hollister **z** 95023; rural
Herndon; RMC Place; FRESNO; ***152** SB-7; ★ **FRES**; mail Fresno **z** 93711; pop. incl. with Fresno (Inc. Place)
Hesperia; Inc. Place; SAN BERNARDINO; **153** SI-13; elev. 3,191ft./973m.; 🅿; ★ **HESP-**; **z** 92340, **z** 92344-45; Ⓟ 50,418; © 62,582; ◆ 77,980
Hessel; RMC Place; SONOMA; mail Sebastopol **z** 95472; rural
Hewitt; RMC Place; LOS ANGELES; ***152** SJ-10; ★ **L.A.**; pop. incl. with Los Angeles (Inc. Place)
Hickman; CDP; STANISLAUS; **150** NM-9; 🅿; **z** 95323; © 457
Hidden Hills; Inc. Place; LOS ANGELES; **154** D-2; 🅿; ★ **L.A.**; **z** 91302; Ⓟ 1,729; © 1,875
Hidden Meadows; CDP-Census Area Only; SAN DIEGO; ***153** SL-13; ★ **SDGO**; mail Escondido **z** 92025; Ⓟ 2,371; © 3,463
Hidden Valley; RMC Place; PLACER; **150** NJ-8; 🅿; ★ **SAC**; **z** 91361 & mail Loomis **z** 95650; ● 1,400
Hidden Valley Lake; CDP; LAKE; ***150** NJ-5; elev. 1,200ft./366m.; 🅿; **z** 95467 & mail Lower Lake **z** 95457; Ⓟ 1,961; © 3,777
Higgins Corner; RMC Place; NEVADA; mail Auburn **z** 95602, Grass Valley **z** 95949; rural
Highgrove; CDP; RIVERSIDE; **155** F-18; elev. 949ft./289m.; ★ **RIV-**; mail Riverside **z** 92507; Ⓟ 3,175; © 3,445
Highland; Inc. Place; SAN BERNARDINO; **153** SJ-13; elev. 1,315ft./401m.; 🅿; ★ **RIV-**; **z** 92346; Ⓟ 34,439; © 44,605; ◆ 51,913
Highland Park; RMC Place; LOS ANGELES; ***153** SJ-11; 🅿; ★ **L.A.**; **z** 90042; pop. incl. with Los Angeles (Inc. Place)
Highlands; RMC Place; SAN MATEO; ***150** NM-5; mail San Mateo **z** 94402; ● 1,750
Highlands-Baywood Park; CDP-Census Area Only; SAN MATEO; ***150** NM-5; ★ **SF-O-**; © 4,210
Highway City; RMC Place; FRESNO; ***152** SB-7; ★ **FRES**; mail Fresno **z** 93706; pop. incl. with Fresno (Inc. Place)
Highway Highlands; RMC Place; LOS ANGELES; ★ **L.A.**; mail La Crescenta **z** 91214; pop. incl. with Glendale (Inc. Place)
Hilarita; RMC Place; MARIN; ***150** NL-5; elev. 16ft./5m.; ★ **SF-O-**; mail Belvedere Tiburon **z** 94920; pop. incl. with Tiburon (Inc. Place)
Hildreth; RMC Place; MADERA; ***152** SA-8; elev. 1,300ft./396m.; mail O Neals **z** 93645; rural
Hillcrest; RMC Place; LOS ANGELES; ★ **L.A.**; mail Inglewood **z** 90301, **z** 90306-08; pop. incl. with Los Angeles (Inc. Place)
Hillcrest; RMC Place; SAN DIEGO; ***153** SN-13; ★ **SDGO**; mail San Diego **z** 92103, **z** 92163; pop. incl. with San Diego (Inc. Place)
Hillcrest Center; RMC Place; KERN; ***152** SF-9; ★ **BAK**; mail Bakersfield **z** 93306, **z** 93386
Hillsborough; Inc. Place; SAN MATEO; **151** NI-14; elev. 32ft./10m.; 🅿; ★ **SF-O-**; **z** 94010; Ⓟ 10,667; © 10,825
Hillsdale; RMC Place; SAN MATEO; ***150** NM-5; ★ **SF-O-**; mail San Mateo **z** 94403; pop. incl. with San Mateo (Inc. Place)
Hills Flat; RMC Place; NEVADA; ***150** NI-8; mail Grass Valley **z** 95945; pop. incl. with Grass Valley (Inc. Place)
Hilltop; KERN; see Fuller Acres (RMC Place)
Hillview; RMC Place; SANTA CLARA; ★ **SF-O-**; mail San Jose **z** 95121, **z** 95151; pop. incl. with San Jose (Inc. Place)
Hilmar; MERCED; see Hilmar-Irwin (CDP-Census Area Only)
Hilmar-Irwin (Hilmar); CDP-Census Area Only; MERCED; **150** NN-8; mail Hilmar **z** 95324; Ⓟ 3,392; © 4,807
Hilt; RMC Place; SISKIYOU; **150** NA-5; elev. 2,901ft./884m.; mail Hornbrook **z** 96044; ● 30
Hilton; RMC Place; SONOMA; ***150** NK-4; elev. 70ft./21m.; ★ **S.ROS**; mail Forestville **z** 95436; rural
Hinkley; RMC Place; SAN BERNARDINO; **153** SG-13; elev. 2,162ft./659m.; 🅿; **z** 92347; ● 1,000
Hiouchi (Hiouchi Valley); RMC Place; DEL NORTE; ***150** NA-2; mail Crescent City **z** 95531; ● 100
Hiouchi Valley; DEL NORTE; see Hiouchi (RMC Place)
Hirschdale; RMC Place; NEVADA; ***150** NH-10; elev. 5,484ft./1,672m.; mail Truckee **z** 96161; ● 60
Hi Vista; RMC Place; LOS ANGELES; **153** SH-12; 🅿; **z** 93535 & mail Lancaster **z** 93534
Hoaglin; RMC Place; TRINITY; ***150** NE-3; elev. 3,400ft./1,036m.; mail Zenia **z** 95595; rural
Hobart; RMC Place; LOS ANGELES; ***153** SJ-11; ★ **L.A.**; mail Los Angeles **z** 90058; pop. incl. with Vernon (Inc. Place)
Hobart Mills; RMC Place; NEVADA; ***150** NH-10; mail Truckee **z** 96161
Hobergs; RMC Place; LAKE; ***150** NJ-4; elev. 3,026ft./922m.; mail Cobb **z** 95426; ● 100
Hobo Hot Springs; KERN; see Miracle Hot Springs (RMC Place)
Hodge; RMC Place; SAN BERNARDINO; **153** SH-13; elev. 2,273ft./693m.; mail Barstow **z** 92311
Holcomb Village (Sunshine Summit); RMC Place; SAN DIEGO; ***153** SL-14; elev. 3,272ft./997m.; mail Aguanga **z** 92536; ● 180
Holiday; RMC Place; ORANGE; ★ **L.A.**; mail Anaheim **z** 92802, **z** 92812; pop. incl. with Anaheim (Inc. Place)
Holiday Lake; RMC Place; SANTA CLARA; ★ **SF-O-**; mail Morgan Hill **z** 95037; pop. incl. with Morgan Hill (Inc. Place)
Hollister; Inc. Place; ⊡ SAN BENITO; **152** SB-4; elev. 291ft./89m.; 🅿 🅷; **z** 95023-24; Ⓟ 19,212; © 34,413; ◆ 36,994
Hollydale; RMC Place; LOS ANGELES; ***153** SJ-11; ★ **L.A.**; mail South Gate **z** 90280; pop. incl. with South Gate (Inc. Place)
Hollydale; RMC Place; SONOMA; ***150** NK-4; ★ **S.ROS**; mail Forestville **z** 95436; ● 350
Hollywood; RMC Place; LOS ANGELES; ***153** SJ-11; 🅿; ★ **L.A.**; **z** 90028, **z** 90068, **z** 90078 & mail Los Angeles **z** 90027, **z** 90038; pop. incl. with Los Angeles (Inc. Place)
Hollywood Beach; RMC Place; VENTURA; ***152** SJ-8; ★ **OXN-**; mail Oxnard **z** 93035
Hollywood by the Sea; RMC Place; VENTURA; ***152** SJ-9; ★ **OXN-**; mail Oxnard **z** 93035
Hollywood Riviera; RMC Place; LOS ANGELES; ***152** SK-10; ★ **L.A.**; mail Redondo Beach **z** 90277; pop. incl. with Torrance (Inc. Place)
Holmes; RMC Place; HUMBOLDT; ***150** NE-2; mail Redcrest **z** 95569; ● 30
Holt; RMC Place; SAN JOAQUIN; **150** NL-7; elev. 8ft./2m.; 🅿; **z** 95234; rural
Holtville; Inc. Place; IMPERIAL; **153** SM-18; elev.-10ft./-3m.; 🅿; **z** 92250; Ⓟ 4,820; © 5,612
Holy City; RMC Place; SANTA CLARA; ***152** SA-2; 🅿; ★ **SF-O-**; **z** 95026 & mail Redwood Estates **z** 95044; ● 140
Home Garden (Hanford South); CDP-Census Area Only; KINGS; ***152** SD-8; mail Kettleman City **z** 93239; Ⓟ 1,549; © 1,702
Home Gardens; CDP; RIVERSIDE; **155** H-16; ★ **RIV-**; mail Corona **z** 92880; Ⓟ 7,780; © 9,461
Homeland; CDP; RIVERSIDE; **155** I-20; elev. 1,608ft./490m.; 🅿; **z** 92548; Ⓟ 3,312; © 3,710
Homestead; KERN; see Indian Wells (RMC Place)
Homestead; RMC Place; RIVERSIDE; ***153** SK-14; elev. 4,000ft./1,219m.; mail Anza **z** 92539; ● 260
Homestead; RMC Place; SAN JOAQUIN; ★ **STOC**; mail Stockton **z** 95206; pop. incl. with Stockton (Inc. Place)
Homestead Valley; RMC Place; MARIN; **151** NE-12; ★ **SF-O-**; mail Mill Valley **z** 94941; ● 3,500
Homewood; RMC Place; PLACER; **150** NI-10; elev. 6,238ft./1,901m.; 🅿; **z** 96141; ● 350
Homewood Canyon-Valley Wells; CDP-Census Area Only; INYO; ***153** SE-13; © 75
Honby; RMC Place; LOS ANGELES; ★ **L.A.**; mail Santa Clarita **z** 91350; pop. incl. with Santa Clarita (Inc. Place)
Honcut; RMC Place; BUTTE; **150** NI-7; elev. 106ft./32m.; mail Oroville **z** 95965; ● 150
Honda; RMC Place; SANTA BARBARA
Honeydew; RMC Place; HUMBOLDT; **150** NF-1; 🅿; **z** 95545; ● 80
Hood; RMC Place; SACRAMENTO; ***150** NK-7; elev. 7ft./2m.; 🅿; **z** 95639; ● 250
Hooker; RMC Place; TEHAMA; ***150** NF-5; elev. 527ft./161m.; mail Cottonwood **z** 96022
Hookston; RMC Place; CONTRA COSTA; ***150** NL-6; ★ **SF-O-**; mail Pleasant Hill **z** 94523; pop. incl. with Pleasant Hill (Inc. Place)
Hoopa; RMC Place; HUMBOLDT; **150** ND-2; located on Hoopa Valley Ind. Res.; 🅿; **z** 95546; ● 1,200
Hoopa Valley Reservation; Indian Reservation; HUMBOLDT; mail Hoopa **z** 95546; Ⓟ 2,041; © 2,633
Hope Ranch; RMC Place; SANTA BARBARA; **156** B-7; ★ **S.BAR**; mail Santa Barbara **z** 93105; ● 1,600
Hopeton; RMC Place; MERCED; ***150** NN-9; mail Snelling **z** 95369; rural
Hope Valley; RMC Place; ALPINE; ***150** NJ-10; 🅿; **z** 96120; rural
Hopfen; RMC Place; SACRAMENTO; ★ **SAC**; pop. incl. with Sacramento (Inc. Place)
Hopland; RMC Place; MENDOCINO; **150** NI-3; 🅿; **z** 95449; ● 630
Hopland Rancheria; Indian Reservation; MENDOCINO; © 14
Hornbrook; CDP; SISKIYOU; **150** NA-5; elev. 2,154ft./657m.; 🅿; **z** 96044; © 286
Hornitos; RMC Place; MARIPOSA; **150** NN-10; 🅿; **z** 95325
Horse Creek; RMC Place; SISKIYOU; **150** NA-4; 🅿; **z** 96050
Howard Landing; RMC Place; SACRAMENTO; ***150** NL-7; elev. 5ft./2m.; mail Walnut Grove **z** 95690; rural
Howest; RMC Place; SAN MATEO; ★ **SF-O-**; mail Burlingame **z** 94010; pop. incl. with Burlingame (Inc. Place)
Huasna; RMC Place; SAN LUIS OBISPO; mail Arroyo Grande **z** 93420; ● 140
Hub City; RMC Place; LOS ANGELES; ***153** SJ-11; ★ **L.A.**; mail Compton **z** 90220, **z** 90223; pop. incl. with Compton (Inc. Place)
Hudson; RMC Place; ALAMEDA; ★ **SF-O-**; pop. incl. with San Leandro (Inc. Place)
Hudson; RMC Place; STANISLAUS; ★ **MOD**; mail Modesto **z** 95355-57; pop. incl. with Modesto (Inc. Place)
Hughes; RMC Place; FRESNO; ★ **FRES**; mail Fresno **z** 93705, **z** 93790-94; pop. incl. with Fresno (Inc. Place)
Hughson; Inc. Place; STANISLAUS; **150** NM-8; 🅿; ★ **MOD**; **z** 95326; Ⓟ 3,259; © 3,980
HUMBOLDT; **150** NE-2; Ⓟ 119,118; © 126,518; ◆ 129,881
Humboldt Hill; CDP-Census Area Only; HUMBOLDT; ***150** ND-1; ★ **EUR-**; mail Fields Landing **z** 95537; Ⓟ 2,865; © 3,246
Hume; RMC Place; FRESNO; ***152** SB-9; 🅿; **z** 93628
Humphreys Station; RMC Place; FRESNO; ***152** SB-8; elev. 1,028ft./313m.; mail Clovis **z** 93611; rural
Hunters Valley; RMC Place; MARIPOSA; ***150** NM-10; elev. 1,774ft./541m.; mail Hornitos **z** 95325; rural
Huntington; RMC Place; ORANGE; ★ **L.A.**; mail Huntington Beach **z** 92646; pop. incl. with Huntington Beach (Inc. Place)
Huntington Beach; Inc. Place; ORANGE; **153** SK-11; elev. 28ft./9m.; 🅿 🅷 ■; ★ **L.A.**; **z** 92605, **z** 92615, **z** 92646-49; Ⓟ 181,519; © 189,594; ◆ 194,891
Huntington Harbor; RMC Place; ORANGE; ★ **L.A.**; mail Huntington Beach **z** 92649; pop. incl. with Huntington Beach (Inc. Place)
Huntington Park; Inc. Place; LOS ANGELES; **154** F-7; elev. 160ft./49m.; 🅿 🅷 ■; ★ **L.A.**; **z** 90255; Ⓟ 56,065; © 61,348; ◆ 63,506
Huron; Inc. Place; FRESNO; **152** SD-7; elev. 368ft./112m.; 🅿; **z** 93234; Ⓟ 4,766; © 6,306
Hyampom; RMC Place; TRINITY; **150** NE-3; elev. 1,285ft./392m.; 🅿; **z** 96046; ● 150
Hyde Park; RMC Place; LOS ANGELES; ***153** SJ-11; ★ **L.A.**; mail Los Angeles **z** 90043; pop. incl. with Los Angeles (Inc. Place)
Hydesville; CDP; HUMBOLDT; **150** NE-2; 🅿; ★ **EUR-**; **z** 95547; Ⓟ 1,131; © 1,209

I

Ida Jean Haxton; RMC Place; ORANGE; ★ **L.A.**; mail Huntington Beach **z** 92615, **z** 92647; pop. incl. with Huntington Beach (Inc. Place)
Idlewild; RMC Place; TULARE; ***152** SE-10; mail Posey **z** 93260; ● 60
Idria; RMC Place; SAN BENITO; ***152** SC-5; mail Hollister **z** 95023
Idyllwild; RMC Place; RIVERSIDE; **153** SK-14; elev. 5,500ft./1,676m.; 🅿; **z** 92549; ● 2,200
Idyllwild-Pine Cove; CDP-Census Area Only; RIVERSIDE; ***153** SK-14; mail Idyllwild **z** 92549; Ⓟ 2,853; © 3,504
Ignacio; RMC Place; MARIN; **151** NB-12; elev. 24ft./7m.; ★ **SF-O-**; mail Novato **z** 94949; pop. incl. with Novato (Inc. Place)
Igo; RMC Place; SHASTA; **150** NE-5; elev. 1,095ft./334m.; 🅿; **z** 96047
Imperial; Inc. Place; IMPERIAL; **153** SM-17; elev. 60ft./18m.; 🅿; **z** 92251; Ⓟ 4,113; © 7,560
IMPERIAL; **153** SM-19; Ⓟ 109,303; © 142,361; ◆ 164,956
Imperial Beach; Inc. Place; SAN DIEGO; **153** SN-14; elev. 25ft./8m.; 🅿; ★ **SDGO**; **z** 91932-33; Ⓟ 26,512; © 26,992; ◆ 27,632
Imperial Crest; RMC Place; LOS ANGELES; ★ **L.A.**; mail Norwalk **z** 90650; pop. incl. with Norwalk (Inc. Place)
Inaja and Cosmit Reservation; Indian Reservation; SAN DIEGO; © 0
Incline; RMC Place; MARIPOSA; **150** NM-1; mail El Portal **z** 95318; ● 60
Independence; CDP; ⊡ INYO; **153** SB-11; elev. 3,923ft./1,196m.; 🅿; **z** 93526; © 574
Indian Falls; CDP; PLUMAS; ***150** NF-8; mail Crescent Mills **z** 95934; © 37
Indian Lakes Estates; RMC Place; MADERA; ***152** SA-7; elev. 2,300ft./701m.; mail Coarsegold **z** 93614; ● 800
Indian Mission; RMC Place; FRESNO; ***152** SB-8; elev. 2,469ft./753m.; mail Auberry **z** 93602; ● 200
Indianola; RMC Place; HUMBOLDT; ***150** ND-1; ★ **EUR-**; mail Eureka **z** 95503; rural
Indian Springs; RMC Place; MADERA; ***152** SB-7; elev. 3,055ft./931m.; mail Oakhurst **z** 93644; rural
Indian Wells (Homestead); RMC Place; KERN; ***153** SE-12; elev. 2,755ft./840m.; mail Inyokern **z** 93527; rural
Indian Wells; Inc. Place; RIVERSIDE; **153** SK-15; 🅿; ★ **PSPR-**; **z** 92210; Ⓟ 2,647; © 3,816
Indio; Inc. Place; RIVERSIDE; **153** SK-16; elev. 14ft./4m.; 🅿 🅷 ■; ★ **IND-**; **z** 92201-03; Ⓟ 36,793; © 49,116; ◆ 81,896
Industrial; RMC Place; LOS ANGELES; ★ **L.A.**; pop. incl. with Los Angeles (Inc. Place)
Industry (City of Industry); Inc. Place; LOS ANGELES; **154** F-10; ■; ★ **L.A.**; mail Alhambra **z** 91899, City of Industry **z** 91714-16, El Monte **z** 91732, Hacienda Heights **z** 91745, La Puente **z** 91744, **z** 91746, Rowland Heights **z** 91748, Walnut **z** 91789, Whittier **z** 90601; Ⓟ 631; © 777; ◆ 802
Inglenook; RMC Place; MENDOCINO; **150** NH-2; mail Fort Bragg **z** 95437; ● 50
Ingleside; RMC Place; SAN FRANCISCO; ***150** NM-5; ★ **SF-O-**; mail San Francisco **z** 94112; pop. incl. with San Francisco (Inc. Place)
Inglewood; Inc. Place; LOS ANGELES; **153** SJ-11; elev. 118ft./36m.; 🅿 🅷 🅲 435 ■; ★ **L.A.**; **z** 90301-12; Ⓟ 109,602; © 112,580; ◆ 111,222
Ingot; RMC Place; SHASTA; ***150** NE-6; elev. 1,074ft./327m.; mail Bella Vista **z** 96008; rural
Inskip; RMC Place; BUTTE; ***150** NG-7; elev. 4,816ft./1,468m.; mail Stirling City **z** 95978; rural
Interlaken; CDP-Census Area Only; SANTA CRUZ; ***152** SB-3; ★ **WATS**; mail Watsonville **z** 95076; Ⓟ 6,404; © 7,328
Inverness; CDP; MARIN; **150** NL-4; 🅿; **z** 94937; Ⓟ 1,422; © 1,421
Inverness Park; RMC Place; MARIN; ***150** NL-4; mail Point Reyes Station **z** 94956; ● 470
Inwood; RMC Place; SHASTA; ***150** NE-6; elev. 2,046ft./624m.; mail Shingletown **z** 96088; rural
INYO; **153** SB-12; Ⓟ 18,281; © 17,945; ◆ 17,108
Inyokern; CDP; KERN; **153** SF-12; elev. 2,433ft./742m.; 🅿; **z** 93527; © 984
Ione; Inc. Place; AMADOR; **150** NK-8; 🅿; **z** 95640; Ⓟ 6,516; © 7,129
Iowa Hill; RMC Place; PLACER; **150** NI-8; 🅿; **z** 95713
Irish Beach; RMC Place; MENDOCINO; ***150** NI-2; elev. 2,000ft./610m.; mail Manchester **z** 95459; ● 200
Iron Horse; CDP-Census Area Only; PLUMAS; ***150** NG-9; © 321
Iron Mountain; RMC Place; SAN BERNARDINO; ***153** SJ-18; elev. 286ft./87m.; mail Earp **z** 92242, Kirkwood **z** 95646; rural
Irvine; Inc. Place; ORANGE; **153** SK-12; 🅿 🅷 🅲 27,547 ■; ★ **L.A.**; **z** 92602-04, **z** 92606, **z** 92612, **z** 92614, **z** 92616-20, **z** 92623, **z** 92650, **z** 92697; Ⓟ 110,330; © 143,072; ◆ 164,490
Irvington; RMC Place; ALAMEDA; ★ **SF-O-**; mail Fremont **z** 94538; pop. incl. with Fremont (Inc. Place)
Irwin; RMC Place; MERCED; ***150** NN-8; mail Hilmar **z** 95324; ● 1,050
Irwindale; Inc. Place; LOS ANGELES; **155** D-11; elev. 467ft./142m.; 🅿; ★ **L.A.**; **z** 91010, **z** 91702, **z** 91706; Ⓟ 1,050; © 1,446
Irwin Estates; RMC Place; SAN BERNARDINO; ***153** SH-14; elev. 2,123ft./647m.; mail Barstow **z** 92311; ● 600
Island Mountain; RMC Place; TRINITY; ***150** NF-3; mail Garberville **z** 95542; rural
Isla Vista; CDP; SANTA BARBARA; **152** SI-7; 🅿; ★ **S.BAR**; **z** 93117; Ⓟ 20,395; © 18,344; Ⓡ 21,069; ◆ 18,915
Isleton; Inc. Place; SACRAMENTO; **150** NL-7; elev. 5ft./2m.; 🅿; **z** 95641; Ⓟ 833; © 828
Ivanhoe; CDP; TULARE; **152** SC-9; elev. 362ft./110m.; 🅿; ★ **VISL**; **z** 93235; Ⓟ 3,293; © 4,474
Ivanpah; RMC Place; SAN BERNARDINO; ***153** SF-17; elev. 3,508ft./1,069m.; mail Nipton **z** 92364; rural

J

Jacinto Grange; RMC Place; GLENN; ***150** NH-6; mail Glenn **z** 95943; rural
Jackie Robinson; RMC Place; LOS ANGELES; ★ **L.A.**; mail Pasadena **z** 91103-04; pop. incl. with Pasadena (Inc. Place)
Jackson; Inc. Place; ⊡ AMADOR; **150** NK-9; elev. 1,235ft./376m.; 🅿 🅷; **z** 95642, **z** 95654; Ⓟ 3,545; © 3,989
Jackson Gate; RMC Place; AMADOR; ***150** NK-9; mail Jackson **z** 95642
Jackson Rancheria; Indian Reservation; AMADOR; © 2
Jacumba (Jacumba Hot Springs); RMC Place; SAN DIEGO; **153** SN-16; elev. 2,829ft./862m.; 🅿; **z** 91934; ● 600
Jacumba Hot Springs; SAN DIEGO; see Jacumba (RMC Place)
Jalama; RMC Place; SANTA BARBARA; ***152** SI-6; mail Lompoc **z** 93436; ● 50
Jamesburg; RMC Place; MONTEREY; ***152** SC-3; mail Carmel Valley **z** 93924; rural
Jamestown; CDP; TUOLUMNE; **150** NL-9; 🅿; **z** 95327; Ⓟ 2,178; © 3,017
Jamul; CDP; SAN DIEGO; **153** SN-14; elev. 993ft./303m.; 🅿; ★ **SDGO**; **z** 91935; Ⓟ 2,258; © 5,920
Jamul Indian Village; Indian Reservation; SAN DIEGO; © 1
Janesville; RMC Place; LASSEN; **150** NF-9; 🅿; **z** 96114 & mail Wendel **z** 96136; ● 1,000
Jarbo; RMC Place; BUTTE; ***150** NG-7; mail Oroville **z** 95965; ● 50
Jastro; RMC Place; KERN; ***152** SF-9; ★ **BAK**
Jelly Ranch; RMC Place; TEHAMA; mail Red Bluff **z** 96080; rural
Jenner; RMC Place; SONOMA; **150** NK-3; 🅿; **z** 95450; ● 120
Jenny Lind; RMC Place; CALAVERAS; ***150** NL-8; elev. 243ft./74m.; mail Valley Springs **z** 95252; ● 730
Jesmond Dene; RMC Place; SAN DIEGO; ***153** SL-13; ★ **SDGO**; mail Escondido **z** 92026; ● 225
Jimtown; RMC Place; SONOMA; ***150** NJ-4; elev. 174ft./53m.; mail Healdsburg **z** 95448
Johannesburg; CDP; KERN; **153** SF-12; elev. 3,536ft./1,078m.; 🅿; **z** 93528, **z** 93554, **z** 93558; © 176
John Adams; RMC Place; SAN DIEGO; ★ **SDGO**; mail San Diego **z** 92116, **z** 92176; pop. incl. with San Diego (Inc. Place)
Johnsondale; RMC Place; TULARE; **152** SE-10; elev. 4,720ft./1,439m.; mail Kernville **z** 93238
Johnson Park; RMC Place; SHASTA; ***150** ND-7; mail Burney **z** 96013; ● 500
John Steinbeck; RMC Place; MONTEREY; mail Salinas **z** 93901; pop. incl. with Salinas (Inc. Place)
Johnston; RMC Place; SACRAMENTO; ★ **SAC**; pop. incl. with Sacramento (Inc. Place)
Johnstonville; RMC Place; LASSEN; **150** NF-9; mail Susanville **z** 96130; ● 400
Johnstown; RMC Place; SAN DIEGO; ***153** SM-14; ★ **SDGO**; mail El Cajon **z** 92021; ● 1,200
Johnsville; CDP; PLUMAS; ***150** NG-9; mail Blairsden-Graeagle **z** 96103; © 21
Jolon; RMC Place; MONTEREY; ***152** SE-4; located on Fort Hunter Liggett; 🅿; **z** 93928; rural
Jonesville; RMC Place; BUTTE; ***150** NF-7; mail Forest Ranch **z** 95942
Joshua Hills; RMC Place; LOS ANGELES; ***153** SI-11; elev. 2,796ft./852m.; ★ **L.A.**; mail Palmdale **z** 93550; pop. incl. with Palmdale (Inc. Place)
Joshua Tree; CDP; SAN BERNARDINO; **153** SJ-15; elev. 2,728ft./831m.; 🅿 🅷; **z** 92252; Ⓟ 3,898; © 4,207
Julian; CDP; SAN DIEGO; **153** SM-15; elev. 4,220ft./1,286m.; 🅿; **z** 92036; Ⓟ 1,284; © 1,621
Junction City; RMC Place; TRINITY; **150** ND-4; 🅿; **z** 96048; ● 600
Junction Station; RMC Place; LOS ANGELES; ★ **L.A.**; pop. incl. with Los Angeles (Inc. Place)
June Lake; RMC Place; MONO; **151** NM-12; 🅿; **z** 93529; ● 600
June Lake Junction; RMC Place; MONO; ***151** NM-12; elev. 7,684ft./2,342m.; mail June Lake **z** 93529; rural
Juniper Hills; RMC Place; LOS ANGELES; ***153** SI-11; elev. 4,284ft./1,306m.; 🅿; ★ **L.A.**; **z** 93543 & mail Pearblossom **z** 93553; ● 400
Juniper Springs; RMC Place; RIVERSIDE; ***153** SK-14; mail Homeland **z** 92548

K

Kaiser Center; RMC Place; ALAMEDA; ★ **SF-O-**; mail Oakland **z** 94612; pop. incl. with Oakland (Inc. Place)
Karuk Reservation; Indian Reservation; SISKIYOU, HUMBOLDT; © 57
Kaweah; RMC Place; TULARE; ***152** SC-9; 🅿; **z** 93237; ● 330
Keddie; CDP; PLUMAS; **150** NG-8; mail Quincy **z** 95971; © 96
Keeler; CDP; INYO; **153** SC-12; elev. 3,609ft./1,100m.; 🅿; **z** 93530; © 66
Keene; CDP; KERN; **152** SG-10; 🅿; **z** 93531; © 339
Kellogg; RMC Place; SONOMA; mail Calistoga **z** 94515; rural
Kelsey; RMC Place; EL DORADO; **150** NJ-8; elev. 1,925ft./587m.; 🅿; **z** 95667; ● 250
Kelseyville; CDP; LAKE; **150** NI-4; elev. 1,386ft./422m.; 🅿; **z** 95451; Ⓟ 2,861; © 2,928
Kelso; RMC Place; SAN BERNARDINO; **153** SG-17; elev. 2,125ft./648m.; 🅿; **z** 92309
Kennedy; CDP-Census Area Only; SAN JOAQUIN; ***150** NL-7; ★ **STOC**; © 3,275
Kennedy Meadow; RMC Place; TUOLUMNE; ***151** NK-11; mail Sonora **z** 95370; rural
Kensington; CDP; CONTRA COSTA; **151** ND-15; elev. 600ft./183m.; 🅿; ★ **SF-O-**; **z** 94706-08; Ⓟ 4,974; © 4,936
Kensington; RMC Place; SAN DIEGO; ***153** SN-14; ★ **SDGO**; mail San Diego **z** 92116; pop. incl. with San Diego (Inc. Place)
Kentfield; CDP; MARIN; **151** ND-12; elev. 12ft./4m.; 🅿 🅷; ★ **SF-O-**; **z** 94904, **z** 94914; Ⓟ 6,030; © 6,351
Kentwood-In-The-Pines; RMC Place; SAN DIEGO; ***153** SM-15; elev. 4,359ft./1,329m.; mail Julian **z** 92036; ● 460
Kent Woodlands; RMC Place; MARIN; ***152** NL-4; ★ **SF-O-**; mail Greenbrae **z** 94904; ● 1,100
Kenwood; RMC Place; SONOMA; **150** NK-5; elev. 415ft./126m.; 🅿; ★ **S.ROS**; **z** 95409, **z** 95452; ● 900
Keough Hot Springs; RMC Place; INYO; ***152** SA-10; mail Bishop **z** 93514; ● 30
Kerman; Inc. Place; FRESNO; **152** SC-7; 🅿; ★ **FRES**; **z** 93630; Ⓟ 5,448; © 8,551
KERN; **152** SG-9; Ⓟ 543,477; © 661,645; ◆ 811,614
Kern City; RMC Place; KERN; ***152** SF-9; elev. 384ft./117m.; ★ **BAK**; mail Bakersfield **z** 93309; pop. incl. with Bakersfield (Inc. Place)
Kern Junction; RMC Place; KERN; ★ **BAK**; pop. incl. with Bakersfield (Inc. Place)
Kernvale; RMC Place; KERN; ***152** SF-10; mail Lake Isabella **z** 93240; ● 1,600
Kernville; CDP; KERN; **152** SE-10; 🅿; **z** 93238; Ⓟ 1,656; © 1,736
Keswick; RMC Place; SHASTA; ***150** NE-5; ★ **REDD**; mail Redding **z** 96001; ● 370
Kettleman City; CDP; KINGS; **152** SE-7; elev. 234ft./71m.; 🅿; **z** 93239; Ⓟ 1,411; © 1,499
Kevet; RMC Place; VENTURA; ***152** SI-9; ★ **OXN-**; mail Santa Paula **z** 93060
Keyes; CDP; STANISLAUS; **150** NN-8; 🅿; ★ **MOD**; **z** 95328; Ⓟ 2,878; © 4,575
Kilkare Woods; RMC Place; ALAMEDA; ***150** NM-6; ★ **SF-O-**; mail Sunol **z** 94586; ● 350
Kimball; RMC Place; VENTURA; ***152** SI-9; ★ **OXN-**; pop. incl. with Ventura (Inc. Place)
King; RMC Place; ORANGE; ★ **L.A.**; mail Santa Ana **z** 92706; pop. incl. with Santa Ana (Inc. Place)
King City; Inc. Place; MONTEREY; **152** SD-4; elev. 330ft./101m.; 🅿 🅷; **z** 93930; Ⓟ 7,634; © 11,094; Ⓡ 11,204
KINGS; **152** SE-7; Ⓟ 101,469; © 129,461; ◆ 154,323
King Salmon; RMC Place; HUMBOLDT; ***150** ND-1; elev. 13ft./4m.; ★ **EUR-**; mail Eureka **z** 95503; ● 420
Kings Beach; CDP; PLACER; **150** NI-10; elev. 6,247ft./1,904m.; 🅿; **z** 96143; Ⓟ 2,796; © 4,037
Kingsburg; Inc. Place; FRESNO; **152** SC-8; elev. 297ft./91m.; 🅿 🅷; **z** 93631; Ⓟ 7,205; © 9,199
Kingsville; RMC Place; EL DORADO; mail El Dorado **z** 95623, Placerville **z** 95667; ● 600
Kingvale; RMC Place; NEVADA; ***150** NI-9; elev. 6,118ft./1,865m.; mail Soda Springs **z** 95728; ● 100
Kirkville; RMC Place; SUTTER; ***150** NJ-6; elev. 35ft./11m.; mail Knights Landing **z** 95645; rural
Kirkwood (Kirkwood Meadows); CDP; ALPINE; ***150** NJ-10; elev. 7,682ft./2,341m.; 🅿; **z** 95646; © 96
Kirkwood; RMC Place; TEHAMA; **150** NG-6; mail Corning **z** 96021; ● 100
Kirkwood Meadows; ALPINE; see Kirkwood (CDP)
Kit Carson; RMC Place; AMADOR; **150** NJ-10; 🅿; **z** 95644
Klamath; CDP; DEL NORTE; **150** NB-2; elev. 28ft./9m.; 🅿; **z** 95548; Ⓟ 827; © 651
Klamath Glen; RMC Place; DEL NORTE; ***150** NB-2; mail Klamath **z** 95548; ● 290
Klamath River; RMC Place; SISKIYOU; **150** NA-4; 🅿; **z** 96050
Klinefelter; RMC Place; SAN BERNARDINO; ***153** SG-19; elev. 1,233ft./376m.; mail Needles **z** 92363; rural
Kneeland; RMC Place; HUMBOLDT; **150** ND-2; 🅿; **z** 95549; ● 30
Knightsen; CDP; CONTRA COSTA; **150** NL-7; 🅿; ★ **SF-O-**; **z** 94548; © 861
Knights Ferry; RMC Place; STANISLAUS; **150** NM-9; 🅿; **z** 95361; ● 700
Knights Landing; RMC Place; YOLO; **150** NJ-6; elev. 33ft./10m.; 🅿; **z** 95645; ● 1,250
Knob; RMC Place; SHASTA; ***150** NE-4; mail Platina **z** 96076; rural
Knowles; RMC Place; MADERA; ***152** SA-7; mail Raymond **z** 93653
Knowles Corner; RMC Place; SONOMA; mail Sebastopol **z** 95472; ● 800
Kohler; RMC Place; ALAMEDA; ★ **SF-O-**; pop. incl. with Oakland (Inc. Place)
Konocti; RMC Place; LAKE; elev. 1,400ft./427m.; mail Kelseyville **z** 95451; ● 330
Kono Tayee; RMC Place; LAKE; elev. 1,394ft./425m.; mail Glenhaven **z** 95443; ● 110
Korbel; RMC Place; HUMBOLDT; ***150** ND-2; 🅿; **z** 95550; ● 80
Korblex; RMC Place; HUMBOLDT; ***150** ND-2; ★ **EUR-**; pop. incl. with Arcata (Inc. Place)
Kramer Junction (Four Corners); RMC Place; SAN BERNARDINO; **153** SG-12; mail Boron **z** 93516; ● 200
Krug; RMC Place; NAPA; ***150** NK-5; mail Saint Helena **z** 94574; pop. incl. with Saint Helena (Inc. Place)
Kyburz; RMC Place; EL DORADO; **150** NJ-10; elev. 4,047ft./1,234m.; 🅿; **z** 95720; ● 150

L

La Barr Meadows; RMC Place; NEVADA; **150** NI-8; mail Grass Valley **z** 95945, **z** 95949; ● 500
La Canada; RMC Place; LOS ANGELES; ***153** SJ-11; elev. 1,400ft./427m.; 🅿; ★ **L.A.**; **z** 91011-12; pop. incl. with La Cañada Flintridge (Inc. Place)
La Cañada Flintridge; Inc. Place; LOS ANGELES; **154** C-7; 🅿; ★ **L.A.**; **z** 91011-12; Ⓟ 19,378; © 20,318; ◆ 20,849
La Conchita; VENTURA; see Punta (RMC Place)
La Costa; RMC Place; LOS ANGELES; ★ **L.A.**; mail Malibu **z** 90265; pop. incl. with Malibu (Inc. Place)
La Costa; RMC Place; SAN DIEGO; elev. 100ft./30m.; ★ **SDGO**; mail Carlsbad **z** 92008; pop. incl. with Carlsbad (Inc. Place)
La Costa Beach; RMC Place; LOS ANGELES; ***152** SJ-10; elev. 100ft./30m.; ★ **L.A.**; mail Malibu **z** 90265
La Crescenta; RMC Place; LOS ANGELES; **154** C-7; elev. 1,600ft./488m.; 🅿; ★ **L.A.**; **z** 91214, **z** 91224; ● 13,000
La Crescenta-Montrose; CDP-Census Area Only; LOS ANGELES; ***153** SI-11; ★ **L.A.**; mail La Crescenta **z** 91214, Montrose **z** 91020; Ⓟ 16,968; © 18,532
La Cresta; RMC Place; SAN DIEGO; ***153** SM-14; ★ **SDGO**; mail El Cajon **z** 92020; ● 450
Ladera; LOS ANGELES; see Ladera Heights (CDP-Census Area Only)
Ladera; RMC Place; SAN MATEO; **151** NL-16; ★ **SF-O-**; mail Portola Valley **z** 94028; ● 1,540
Ladera Heights (Ladera); CDP-Census Area Only; LOS ANGELES; **154** F-5; ★ **L.A.**; mail Los Angeles **z** 90045; Ⓟ 6,316; © 6,568
Ladera Ranch; RMC Place; ORANGE; ***153** SK-12; 🅿; ★ **L.A.**; **z** 92694; ● 350
Lafayette; Inc. Place; CONTRA COSTA; **151** ND-16; elev. 302ft./92m.; 🅿; ★ **SF-O-**; **z** 94549 & mail Walnut Creek **z** 94596; Ⓟ 23,501; © 23,908; ◆ 23,832
La Grange; RMC Place; STANISLAUS; **150** NM-9; elev. 258ft./79m.; 🅿; **z** 95329
Laguna; CDP-Census Area Only; SACRAMENTO; ***150** NK-7; ★ **SAC**; mail Elk Grove **z** 95758; former CDP; became part of Elk Grove July 1, 2000; Ⓟ 9,828; © 34,309; ◆ 0
Laguna Beach; Inc. Place; ORANGE; **153** SK-12; elev. 40ft./12m.; 🅿 🅲 350; ★ **L.A.**; **z** 92607, **z** 92651-54, **z** 92656, **z** 92677 & mail Aliso Viejo **z** 92698, Laguna Woods **z** 92637; Ⓟ 23,170; © 23,727; ◆ 24,176
Laguna Hills; Inc. Place; ORANGE; **155** L-14; elev. 360ft./110m.; 🅿 🅷; ★ **L.A.**; **z** 92637, **z** 92653-54, **z** 92656; Ⓟ 22,719; © 31,178; Ⓡ 29,939; ◆ 31,484
Laguna Lake; RMC Place; SAN LUIS OBISPO; ★ **S.LUIS**; mail San Luis Obispo **z** 93405; pop. incl. with San Luis Obispo (Inc. Place)
Laguna Niguel; Inc. Place; ORANGE; **155** M-14; 🅿; ★ **L.A.**; **z** 92607, **z** 92677; Ⓟ 44,400; © 61,891; ◆ 65,623
Laguna West; RMC Place; SACRAMENTO; ***150** NK-7; ★ **SAC**; mail Sacramento **z** 95832; ● 2,700
Laguna West-Lakeside; CDP-Census Area Only; SACRAMENTO; ***150** NK-7; ★ **SAC**; © 8,414
Laguna Woods; Inc. Place; ORANGE; **155** L-13; 🅿; ★ **L.A.**; **z** 92637, **z** 92653-54; © 16,507; Ⓡ 17,794
Lagunitas; RMC Place; MARIN; ***150** NL-4; 🅿; ★ **SF-O-**; **z** 94938; ● 435
Lagunitas-Forest Knolls; CDP-Census Area Only; MARIN; ***150** NL-4; ★ **SF-O-**; mail Forest Knolls **z** 94933, Lagunitas **z** 94938; Ⓟ 1,821; © 1,835
La Habra; Inc. Place; ORANGE; **153** SJ-12; elev. 298ft./91m.; 🅿 🅷 ■; ★ **L.A.**; **z** 90631-33; Ⓟ 51,266; © 58,974; ◆ 60,738
La Habra Heights; Inc. Place; LOS ANGELES; **154** F-10; 🅿; ★ **L.A.**; **z** 90631; Ⓟ 6,226; © 5,712
La Honda; RMC Place; SAN MATEO; **150** NN-5; 🅿; **z** 94020; ● 900
Lairport; RMC Place; LOS ANGELES; ***152** SJ-10; ★ **L.A.**; mail El Segundo **z** 90245; pop. incl. with El Segundo (Inc. Place)
La Jolla; RMC Place; ORANGE; **156** H-4; ★ **L.A.**; mail Placentia **z** 92870; pop. incl. with Placentia (Inc. Place)
La Jolla; RMC Place; SAN DIEGO; ***153** SM-13; 🅿 🅷; ★ **SDGO**; **z** 92037-39, **z** 92092-93; pop. incl. with San Diego (Inc. Place)
La Jolla Reservation; Indian Reservation; SAN DIEGO; mail Escondido **z** 92025; also location of Indian Agency; Ⓟ 151; © 390
La Joya; LOS ANGELES; see Green Valley (RMC Place)
LAKE; **150** NI-4; Ⓟ 50,631; © 58,309; ◆ 62,167
Lake Almanor Country Club; CDP-Census Area Only; PLUMAS; ***150** NF-8; © 847
Lake Almanor Peninsula; CDP-Census Area Only; PLUMAS; ***150** NF-8; © 336
Lake Almanor West; CDP-Census Area Only; PLUMAS; ***150** NF-8; © 329
Lake Alpine; RMC Place; ALPINE; ***150** NK-10; mail Arnold **z** 95223
Lake Arrowhead; CDP; SAN BERNARDINO; **155** B-20; 🅿 🅷; ★ **RIV-**; **z** 92352 & mail Blue Jay **z** 92317; Ⓟ 6,539; © 8,934
Lake Christopher; RMC Place; EL DORADO; mail South Lake Tahoe **z** 96150; pop. incl. with South Lake Tahoe (Inc. Place)
Lake City; RMC Place; MODOC; **150** NB-10; elev. 4,559ft./1,390m.; 🅿; **z** 96115; ● 160
Lake Davis; CDP-Census Area Only; PLUMAS; ***150** NG-9; © 23
Lake Earl; RMC Place; DEL NORTE; ***150** NA-2; elev. 40ft./12m.; mail Crescent City **z** 95531; ● 200
Lake Elsinore; Inc. Place; RIVERSIDE; **153** SK-13; 🅿; **z** 92530-32; Ⓟ 18,316; © 28,928; ◆ 46,081
Lake Forest (El Toro); Inc. Place; ORANGE; **153** SK-12; 🅿; ★ **L.A.**; **z** 92609, **z** 92630 & mail Foothill Ranch **z** 92610; Ⓟ 56,065; © 58,707; ◆ 74,838
Lake Forest; RMC Place; PLACER; **149** B-2; elev. 6,264ft./1,909m.; mail Tahoe City **z** 96145; ● 500
Lakehead; RMC Place; SHASTA; **150** ND-5; 🅿; **z** 96051, **z** 96070; ● 545
Lakehead-Lakeshore; CDP-Census Area Only; SHASTA; ***150** ND-5; © 549
Lake Henshaw; RMC Place; SAN DIEGO; ***153** SL-14; elev. 2,840ft./866m.; mail Santa Ysabel **z** 92070; ● 150
Lake Hills Estates; RMC Place; EL DORADO; ***150** NJ-8; ★ **SAC**; mail El Dorado Hills **z** 95762; ● 950
Lake Hughes; RMC Place; LOS ANGELES; **152** SH-10; 🅿; **z** 93532; ● 300
Lake Isabella; CDP; KERN; **152** SF-10; elev. 2,460ft./750m.; 🅿 🅷; **z** 93240; Ⓟ 3,323; © 3,315
Lake Kirkwood; RMC Place; EL DORADO; ***150** NJ-10; elev. 7,682ft./2,341m.; mail Kirkwood **z** 95646; rural
Lakeland Village; CDP; RIVERSIDE; **155** K-18; mail Lake Elsinore **z** 92530; Ⓟ 5,159; © 5,626
Lake Los Angeles; CDP; LOS ANGELES; ***153** SH-12; elev. 2,650ft./808m.; 🅿; **z** 93535, **z** 93550, **z** 93591; Ⓟ 7,977; © 11,523
Lake Madera Country Estates; RMC Place; MADERA; ***152** SB-7; elev. 350ft./107m.; mail Madera **z** 93637; ● 550
Lake Marie Estates; RMC Place; SANTA BARBARA; ***152** SH-6; ★ **S.MAR**; mail Santa Maria **z** 93455; ● 550
Lake Mary; RMC Place; MONO; ***151** NM-12; mail Mammoth Lakes **z** 93546; pop. incl. with Mammoth Lakes (Inc. Place)
Lake Nacimiento; CDP-Census Area Only; SAN LUIS OBISPO; ***152** SE-5; mail Bradley **z** 93426, Paso Robles **z** 93446; Ⓟ 1,556; © 2,176
Lake of the Pines; CDP; NEVADA; ***150** NI-8; ★ **SAC**; mail Auburn **z** 95603; Ⓟ 3,890; © 3,956
Lake of the Woods (West of Frazier Park); CDP; KERN; ***152** SH-9; mail Frazier Park **z** 93225; © 833
Lake Park; RMC Place; SAN DIEGO; ***153** SM-14; ★ **SDGO**; mail San Diego **z** 92119; pop. incl. with San Diego (Inc. Place)
Lakeport; Inc. Place; ⊡ LAKE; **150** NI-4; elev. 1,343ft./409m.; 🅿 🅷; **z** 95453; Ⓟ 4,390; © 4,820
Lake San Marcos; CDP; SAN DIEGO; ***153** SM-13; ★ **SDGO**; mail San Marcos **z** 92069; Ⓟ 3,802; © 4,138
Lakeshore; RMC Place; FRESNO; **152** SA-8; 🅿; **z** 93634 & mail Mono Hot Springs **z** 93642
Lakeside; CDP; SAN DIEGO; **153** SM-14; elev. 406ft./124m.; 🅿; ★ **SDGO**; **z** 92040; Ⓟ 39,412; © 19,560
Lakeside Farms; RMC Place; SAN DIEGO; ***153** SM-14; ★ **SDGO**; mail Lakeside **z** 92040; ● 900
Lake Tamarisk; RMC Place; RIVERSIDE; ***153** SK-17; elev. 746ft./227m.; mail Desert Center **z** 92239; ● 250
Lakeview; RMC Place; KERN; ***152** SG-9; elev. 374ft./114m.; mail Bakersfield **z** 93307; rural
Lakeview; CDP; RIVERSIDE; **153** SK-13; elev. 1,450ft./442m.; 🅿; **z** 92567; Ⓟ 1,448; © 1,619
Lakeview; RMC Place; SAN DIEGO; ***153** SM-14; ★ **SDGO**; mail Lakeside **z** 92040; ● 900
Lake View Terrace; RMC Place; LOS ANGELES; 🅿; ★ **L.A.**; **z** 91342; pop. incl. with Los Angeles (Inc. Place)
Lakeville; RMC Place; SONOMA; ***150** NL-5; mail Petaluma **z** 94952, **z** 94954
Lake Wildwood; CDP; NEVADA; ***150** NI-8; mail Penn Valley **z** 95946; © 4,868
Lake Williams Estates; RMC Place; SAN BERNARDINO; ***153** SI-14; elev. 7,280ft./2,219m.; mail Sugarloaf **z** 92386; ● 250
Lakewood; Inc. Place; LOS ANGELES; **154** H-8; elev. 50ft./15m.; 🅿 🅷 ■; ★ **L.A.**; **z** 90711-16, **z** 90805; Ⓟ 73,557; © 79,345; ◆ 81,226
Lakewood Park; RMC Place; LOS ANGELES; ★ **L.A.**; pop. incl. with Long Beach (Inc. Place)
La Loma; RMC Place; STANISLAUS; ★ **MOD**; mail Modesto **z** 95354; pop. incl. with Modesto (Inc. Place)
Lamanda Park; RMC Place; LOS ANGELES; ***153** SJ-11; ★ **L.A.**; mail Pasadena **z** 91107; pop. incl. with Pasadena (Inc. Place)
La Mesa; Inc. Place; SAN DIEGO; **156** I-8; elev. 540ft./165m.; 🅿 🅷 🅲 514 ■; ★ **SDGO**; **z** 91941-44; Ⓟ 52,931; © 54,749; ◆ 56,940
La Metro; RMC Place; LOS ANGELES; ★ **L.A.**; pop. incl. with Los Angeles (Inc. Place)
La Mirada (Mirada); Inc. Place; LOS ANGELES; **153** SJ-11; elev. 181ft./55m.; 🅿 🅲 5,752 ■; ★ **L.A.**; **z** 90637-39; Ⓟ 40,452; © 46,783; ◆ 50,174
Lamont; CDP; KERN; **152** SG-9; elev. 400ft./122m.; 🅿; ★ **BAK**; **z** 93241; Ⓟ 11,517; © 13,296
Lanare; CDP; FRESNO; **152** SC-7; mail Riverdale **z** 93656; © 540
Lancaster; Inc. Place; LOS ANGELES; **153** SH-11; elev. 2,355ft./718m.; 🅿 🅷 ■; ★ **L.A.**; **z** 93534-36, **z** 93539, **z** 93584, **z** 93586 & mail Palmdale **z** 93551; Ⓟ 97,291; © 118,718; ◆ 125,902
Landers; RMC Place; SAN BERNARDINO; **153** SI-15; elev. 3,083ft./940m.; 🅿; **z** 92285; ● 2,300
Land Park; RMC Place; SACRAMENTO; ★ **SAC**; mail Sacramento **z** 95822; pop. incl. with Sacramento (Inc. Place)
Landscape; RMC Place; ALAMEDA; ★ **SF-O-**; mail Berkeley **z** 94707; pop. incl. with Berkeley (Inc. Place)
Lansdale; RMC Place; MARIN; ★ **SF-O-**; mail San Anselmo **z** 94960; pop. incl. with San Anselmo (Inc. Place)
La Palma; Inc. Place; ORANGE; **154** H-10; elev. 44ft./13m.; 🅿 🅷; ★ **L.A.**; **z** 90623; Ⓟ 15,392; © 15,408
La Panza; RMC Place; SAN LUIS OBISPO; ***152** SF-6; mail Creston **z** 93432; rural
La Patera; RMC Place; SANTA BARBARA; ***152** SI-7; elev. 34ft./10m.; ★ **S.BAR**; mail Goleta **z** 93117; pop. incl. with Goleta (CDP-Census Area Only)
La Playa; RMC Place; SAN DIEGO; ***153** SN-13; ★ **SDGO**; mail San Diego **z** 92106; pop. incl. with San Diego (Inc. Place)
La Porte; CDP; PLUMAS; **150** NH-8; elev. 4,959ft./1,512m.; 🅿; **z** 95981; © 43
La Posta Reservation; Indian Reservation; SAN DIEGO; © 18
La Presa; CDP; SAN DIEGO; ***153** SN-14; elev. 351ft./107m.; ★ **SDGO**; mail Spring Valley **z** 91977; © 32,721; ◆ 35,357
La Puente; Inc. Place; LOS ANGELES; **154** E-10; elev. 330ft./101m.; 🅿; ★ **L.A.**; **z** 91744-49; Ⓟ 36,955; © 41,063; ◆ 42,854
La Quinta; Inc. Place; RIVERSIDE; **153** SK-15; 🅿; ★ **PSPR-**; **z** 92247-48, **z** 92253; Ⓟ 11,215; © 23,694; ◆ 43,151
Larabee; RMC Place; HUMBOLDT; ***150** NE-2; mail Redcrest **z** 95569; ● 30
Larchmont Riviera; SACRAMENTO; see La Riviera (CDP-Census Area Only)
La Riviera (Larchmont Riviera); CDP-Census Area Only; SACRAMENTO; ***150** NK-7; ★ **SAC**; mail Sacramento **z** 95826; Ⓟ 10,986; © 10,273
Larkfield; RMC Place; SONOMA; ***150** NK-4; elev. 160ft./49m.; 🅿; ★ **S.ROS**; **z** 95403; ● 4,300
Larkfield-Wikiup; CDP-Census Area Only; SONOMA; ***150** NK-4; ★ **S.ROS**; mail Santa Rosa **z** 95403; Ⓟ 6,779; © 7,479
Larkspur; Inc. Place; MARIN; **150** NL-5; elev. 43ft./13m.; 🅿; ★ **SF-O-**; **z** 94939, **z** 94977; Ⓟ 11,070; © 12,014
Las Cruces; RMC Place; SANTA BARBARA; **152** SI-6; mail Goleta **z** 93117; ● 70
La Selva Beach; RMC Place; SANTA CRUZ; ***152** SB-3; elev. 76ft./23m.; 🅿; ★ **S.CRZ**; **z** 95076; ● 1,350
Las Flores; RMC Place; LOS ANGELES; ***152** SJ-10; ★ **L.A.**; mail Malibu **z** 90265
Las Flores; CDP-Census Area Only; ORANGE; ***153** SK-12; ★ **L.A.**; © 5,625
Las Flores; RMC Place; TEHAMA; ***150** NF-6; mail Gerber **z** 96035; ● 260
La Sierra; RMC Place; RIVERSIDE; ***153** SJ-13; ★ **RIV-**; mail Riverside **z** 92505, **z** 92515; pop. incl. with Riverside (Inc. Place)
La Sierra Heights; RMC Place; RIVERSIDE; ***153** SJ-13; elev. 800ft./244m.; ★ **RIV-**; mail Riverside **z** 92505; pop. incl. with Riverside (Inc. Place)
Las Lomas; CDP; MONTEREY; ***152** SB-3; ★ **SLNS**; mail Watsonville **z** 95076; Ⓟ 2,127; © 3,078
Las Palmas; RMC Place; FRESNO; ***152** SB-7; elev. 331ft./101m.; ★ **FRES**; pop. incl. with Fresno (Inc. Place)
Las Posas Estates; RMC Place; VENTURA; ***152** SI-9; ★ **OXN-**; mail Camarillo **z** 93010; ● 2,500
LASSEN; **150** NE-9; Ⓟ 27,598; © 33,828; ◆ 36,801
Lathrop; Inc. Place; SAN JOAQUIN; **150** NM-7; 🅿; **z** 95330; Ⓟ 6,841; © 10,445
La Tijera; RMC Place; LOS ANGELES; ★ **L.A.**; mail Los Angeles **z** 90043; pop. incl. with Los Angeles (Inc. Place)
Latin; RMC Place; LOS ANGELES; ★ **L.A.**; pop. incl. with Los Angeles (Inc. Place)
Laton; CDP; FRESNO; ***152** SC-7; 🅿; **z** 93242; Ⓟ 1,415; © 1,236
Latrobe; RMC Place; EL DORADO; ***150** NK-8; 🅿; **z** 95682
Laughlin; RMC Place; MENDOCINO; mail Redwood Valley **z** 95470; ● 340
Laurel; RMC Place; ALAMEDA; ★ **SF-O-**; mail Oakland **z** 94619; pop. incl. with Oakland (Inc. Place)
Laurel Canyon; RMC Place; LOS ANGELES; ★ **L.A.**; mail North Hollywood **z** 91605-06, **z** 91615; pop. incl. with Los Angeles (Inc. Place)
Laurelwood; RMC Place; LOS ANGELES; ★ **L.A.**; mail Studio City **z** 91604; pop. incl. with Los Angeles (Inc. Place)
La Verne; Inc. Place; LOS ANGELES; **153** SJ-12; elev. 1,050ft./320m.; 🅿 🅲 8,328; ★ **L.A.**; **z** 91750; Ⓟ 30,897; © 31,638; ◆ 32,688
La Vina; RMC Place; MADERA; ***152** SB-7; elev. 231ft./70m.; ★ **FRES**; mail Madera **z** 93637; ● 800
Lawndale; Inc. Place; LOS ANGELES; **154** H-5; elev. 55ft./17m.; 🅿; ★ **L.A.**; **z** 90260-61; Ⓟ 27,331; © 31,711; ◆ 33,780

Entries in **UPPERCASE** are counties.
Entries in **bold** have populations of 2,500 or more.
Names in parentheses are alternate names.

Inc. Place	Incorporated Place
RMC Place	Rand McNally Designated Place
CDP	Census Designated Place
MCD	Minor Civil Division

⊡ County Seat
▲ Minor Civil Division
elev. Elevation
🅿 Post Office
🅷 Hospital
🅲 College
■ Principal Business Center
★ Ranally Metro Area (RMA) Abbreviation
z Zip Code(s)
Ⓟ Previous Census Population
Ⓡ Revised Census Population
Ⓐ Annexation Population
● Rand McNally Population Estimate
© Final Census Population
Ⓢ Special Census Population
◆ Estimated Population

For additional definitions see Glossary, Volume 1, and Introduction, Volume 2.

Lawrence; RMC Place; CONTRA COSTA; ★ **SF-O-**; mail Danville **z** 94506; pop. incl. with Danville (Inc. Place)
Laws; RMC Place; INYO; ***151** NN-14; mail Bishop **z** 93514
Laytonville; CDP; MENDOCINO; **150** NG-3; 🅿; **z** 95417, **z** 95454; Ⓟ 1,133; © 1,301
Laytonville Rancheria; Indian Reservation; MENDOCINO; mail Laytonville **z** 95454; © 188
Lebec; CDP; KERN; **152** SH-9; elev. 3,570ft./1,088m.; 🅿; **z** 93243; © 1,285
Lee Vining; RMC Place; MONO; **151** NL-12; elev. 6,781ft./2,067m.; 🅿; **z** 93541; ● 300
Leffingwell; RMC Place; LOS ANGELES; ★ **L.A.**; pop. incl. with Whittier (Inc. Place)
Leggett; RMC Place; MENDOCINO; **150** NG-2; elev. 952ft./290m.; 🅿; **z** 95585; ● 100
Le Grand; CDP; MERCED; **152** SA-6; elev. 253ft./77m.; 🅿; **z** 95333; Ⓟ 1,205; © 1,760
Leisure Town; RMC Place; SOLANO; ★ **FRFL-**; mail Vacaville **z** 95687; pop. incl. with Vacaville (Inc. Place)
Leisure World; RMC Place; CONTRA COSTA; ★ **SF-O-**; pop. incl. with Walnut Creek (Inc. Place)
Leisure World (Rossmore Leisure World); RMC Place; ORANGE; ★ **L.A.**; mail Seal Beach **z** 90740; pop. incl. with Seal Beach (Inc. Place)
Lemon Cove; CDP; TULARE; ***152** SD-9; 🅿; **z** 93244; © 298
Lemon Grove; Inc. Place; SAN DIEGO; **153** SN-14; elev. 450ft./137m.; 🅿; ★ **SDGO**; **z** 91945-46; Ⓟ 23,984; © 24,918; ◆ 25,397
Lemon Heights; RMC Place; ORANGE; **155** I-13; ★ **L.A.**; mail Santa Ana **z** 92705; ● 2,800
Lemoore; Inc. Place; KINGS; **152** SD-7; 🅿 🅷; **z** 93245-46; Ⓟ 13,622; © 19,712; ◆ 23,312
Lemoore Station; CDP-Census Area Only; KINGS; ***152** SD-7; © 5,749
Lennox; CDP; LOS ANGELES; **154** G-6; elev. 71ft./22m.; 🅿; ★ **L.A.**; **z** 90304; Ⓟ 22,757; © 22,950; ◆ 23,480
Lenwood; CDP; SAN BERNARDINO; **153** SH-13; mail Barstow **z** 92311; Ⓟ 3,190; © 3,222
Leona Valley; RMC Place; LOS ANGELES; **154** M-6; elev. 3,133ft./955m.; 🅿; ★ **L.A.**; **z** 93551 & mail Lake Hughes **z** 93532; ● 1,000
Letterman; RMC Place; SAN FRANCISCO; ★ **SF-O-**; mail San Francisco **z** 94129; pop. incl. with San Francisco (Inc. Place)
Leucadia; RMC Place; SAN DIEGO; ***153** SM-13; elev. 54ft./16m.; ★ **SDGO**; mail Encinitas **z** 92024; pop. incl. with Encinitas (Inc. Place)
Lewiston; CDP; TRINITY; **150** NE-4; elev. 1,826ft./557m.; 🅿; **z** 96052; Ⓟ 1,187; © 1,305
Lexington Hills; CDP-Census Area Only; SANTA CLARA; ***152** SA-2; ★ **SF-O-**; mail Holy City **z** 95026, Los Gatos **z** 95030, Redwood Estates **z** 95044; Ⓟ 2,064; © 2,454
Liberty Acres; RMC Place; LOS ANGELES; ***153** SJ-11; elev. 85ft./26m.; ★ **L.A.**; mail Hawthorne **z** 90250; ● 6,000
Liberty Farms; RMC Place; SOLANO; **150** NK-6; 🅿; **z** 95620; rural
Liberty Park; RMC Place; ORANGE; ★ **L.A.**; pop. incl. with Huntington Beach (Inc. Place)
Libfarm; RMC Place; SOLANO; ***150** NK-6; mail Dixon **z** 95620; rural
Lick Observatory; SANTA CLARA; see Mount Hamilton (RMC Place)
Lido Isle; RMC Place; ORANGE; ***153** SK-12; ★ **L.A.**; mail Newport Beach **z** 92663; pop. incl. with Newport Beach (Inc. Place)
Likely; RMC Place; MODOC; **150** NC-9; 🅿; **z** 96116
Likely Rancheria; Indian Reservation; MODOC; © 0
Limco; VENTURA; see Limon (RMC Place)
Limon (Limco); RMC Place; VENTURA; **156** A-3; elev. 300ft./91m.; ★ **OXN-**; mail Santa Paula **z** 93060; ● 500
Lincoln; Inc. Place; PLACER; **150** NJ-7; elev. 164ft./50m.; 🅿; ★ **SAC**; **z** 95648; Ⓟ 7,248; © 11,205; ◆ 20,577
Lincoln Acres; RMC Place; SAN DIEGO; **156** K-8; 🅿; ★ **SDGO**; **z** 91947; ● 1,650
Lincoln Heights; RMC Place; LOS ANGELES; ***153** SJ-11; 🅿; ★ **L.A.**; **z** 90031; pop. incl. with Los Angeles (Inc. Place)
Lincoln Park (Valley Junction); RMC Place; LOS ANGELES; ★ **L.A.**; pop. incl. with Los Angeles (Inc. Place)
Lincoln Village; RMC Place; LOS ANGELES; ***153** SK-11; ★ **L.A.**; mail Long Beach **z** 90810; pop. incl. with Carson (Inc. Place)
Lincoln Village; CDP; SAN JOAQUIN; ***150** NL-7; ★ **STOC**; mail Stockton **z** 95207; Ⓟ 4,236; © 4,216
Linda; CDP; YUBA; **150** NI-7; elev. 70ft./21m.; 🅿; ★ **YUCY**; **z** 95901; Ⓟ 13,033; © 13,474
Linda Mar; RMC Place; SAN MATEO; ★ **SF-O-**; mail Pacifica **z** 94044; pop. incl. with Pacifica (Inc. Place)
Linda Vista; RMC Place; LOS ANGELES; ***153** SJ-11; ★ **L.A.**; mail Pasadena **z** 91103; pop. incl. with Pasadena (Inc. Place)
Linda Vista; RMC Place; SAN DIEGO; ***153** SN-13; ★ **SDGO**; mail San Diego **z** 92111, **z** 92171; pop. incl. with San Diego (Inc. Place)
Lindcove; RMC Place; TULARE; ***152** SD-9; elev. 460ft./140m.; mail Exeter **z** 93221; ● 450
Linden; CDP; SAN JOAQUIN; **150** NL-8; elev. 87ft./27m.; 🅿; ★ **STOC**; **z** 95236; Ⓟ 1,339; © 1,103
Linden; RMC Place; SAN MATEO; ★ **SF-O-**; mail South San Francisco **z** 94080; pop. incl. with South San Francisco (Inc. Place)
Lindenwood; RMC Place; SAN MATEO; ★ **SF-O-**; mail Atherton **z** 94027; pop. incl. with Menlo Park (Inc. Place)
Lindsay; Inc. Place; TULARE; **152** SD-9; elev. 383ft./117m.; 🅿 🅷; **z** 93247; Ⓟ 8,338; © 10,297
Lingard; RMC Place; MERCED; ***152** SA-6; mail Le Grand **z** 95333; rural
Linnell; RMC Place; TULARE; ***152** SD-9; elev. 352ft./107m.; ★ **VISL**; mail Visalia **z** 93292; ● 350
Linns Valley; RMC Place; KERN; ***152** SE-10; elev. 3,000ft./914m.; mail Glennville **z** 93226
Litchfield; RMC Place; LASSEN; **150** NF-9; elev. 4,068ft./1,240m.; 🅿; **z** 96117
Little Grass Valley; CDP-Census Area Only; PLUMAS; ***150** NG-8; © 0
Little Lake; RMC Place; INYO; **153** SE-11; elev. 3,140ft./957m.; 🅿; **z** 93542; ● 50
Little Morongo Heights; RMC Place; SAN BERNARDINO; ***153** SJ-15; ● 200
Little Norway (Phillips); RMC Place; EL DORADO; ***150** NJ-10; mail Echo Lake **z** 95721; ● 120
Little Reed Heights; RMC Place; MARIN; ★ **SF-O-**; mail Belvedere Tiburon **z** 94920; pop. incl. with Tiburon (Inc. Place)
Little River; RMC Place; MENDOCINO; **150** NI-2; 🅿; **z** 95456; ● 400
Littlerock; CDP; LOS ANGELES; **153** SI-11; elev. 2,900ft./884m.; 🅿; ★ **L.A.**; **z** 93543; Ⓟ 1,320; © 1,402
Little Saigon; RMC Place; ORANGE; ★ **L.A.**; mail Westminster **z** 92683; pop. incl. with Westminster (Inc. Place)
Little Shasta; RMC Place; SISKIYOU; ***150** NB-5; elev. 2,705ft./824m.; mail Montague **z** 96064
Little Valley; RMC Place; LASSEN; **150** ND-8; elev. 4,183ft./1,275m.; 🅿; **z** 96056
Live Oak; CDP-Census Area Only; SANTA CRUZ; ***152** SB-2; elev. 97ft./30m.; ★ **S.CRZ**; mail Santa Cruz **z** 95062; Ⓟ 15,212; © 16,628
Live Oak; Inc. Place; SUTTER; **150** NI-7; elev. 75ft./23m.; 🅿; ★ **YUCY**; **z** 95953; Ⓟ 4,320; © 6,229
Live Oak Acres; RMC Place; TEHAMA; ***150** NF-5; elev. 350ft./107m.; mail Red Bluff **z** 96080
Live Oak Acres; RMC Place; VENTURA; ***152** SI-8; ★ **OXN-**; mail Oak View **z** 93022; ● 500
Live Oak Canyon; RMC Place; LOS ANGELES; ***153** SJ-12; elev. 1,400ft./427m.; ★ **L.A.**; mail La Verne **z** 91750; ● 350
Live Oak Springs; RMC Place; SAN DIEGO; **153** SN-15; mail Boulevard **z** 91905; ● 240
Livermore; Inc. Place; ALAMEDA; **150** NM-6; elev. 486ft./148m.; 🅿 🅷 ■; ★ **SF-O-**; **z** 94550-51; Ⓟ 56,741; © 73,345; ◆ 79,433
Livingston; Inc. Place; MERCED; **150** NN-9; 🅿; **z** 95334; Ⓟ 7,317; © 10,473
Llano; RMC Place; LOS ANGELES; ***153** SI-12; 🅿; **z** 93544; rural
Lobitos (Tunitas); RMC Place; SAN MATEO; ***150** NN-5; ★ **SF-O-**; mail Half Moon Bay **z** 94019; ● 100
Lobo; RMC Place; ORANGE; ★ **L.A.**; mail Stanton **z** 90680; pop. incl. with Stanton (Inc. Place)
Loch Lomond; RMC Place; LAKE; **150** NJ-4; 🅿; **z** 95461; ● 300
Locke; RMC Place; SACRAMENTO; ***150** NL-7; mail Walnut Grove **z** 95690; ● 200
Lockeford; CDP; SAN JOAQUIN; **150** NL-8; elev. 104ft./32m.; 🅿; **z** 95237; Ⓟ 2,722; © 3,179
Lockhart; RMC Place; SAN BERNARDINO; ***153** SG-13; mail Hinkley **z** 92347; rural
Lockwood; RMC Place; MONTEREY; **152** SE-4; 🅿; **z** 93932; ● 360
Lodgepole; RMC Place; TULARE; **152** SL-2; elev. 6,720ft./2,048m.; mail Sequoia National Park **z** 93262; rural
Lodi; Inc. Place; SAN JOAQUIN; **150** NL-7; elev. 51ft./16m.; 🅿 🅷 ■; ★ **STOC**; **z** 95240-42; Ⓟ 51,874; © 56,999; ◆ 58,755
Lodoga; RMC Place; COLUSA; **150** NI-5; mail Stonyford **z** 95979
Logan Heights; RMC Place; SAN DIEGO; **156** J-7; ★ **SDGO**; mail San Diego **z** 92113; pop. incl. with San Diego (Inc. Place)
Loleta; RMC Place; HUMBOLDT; **150** NE-1; 🅿; ★ **EUR-**; **z** 95551; ● 600
Loma; RMC Place; LOS ANGELES; ***153** SK-11; ★ **L.A.**; mail Long Beach **z** 90814; pop. incl. with Long Beach (Inc. Place)
Loma Linda; Inc. Place; SAN BERNARDINO; **153** SJ-13; elev. 1,081ft./329m.; 🅿 🅷 🅲 4,029; ★ **RIV-**; **z** 92350, **z** 92354, **z** 92357; Ⓟ 17,400; © 18,681; ◆ 19,049
Loma Mar; RMC Place; SAN MATEO; ***150** NN-5; 🅿; **z** 94021; ● 200
Loma Portal; RMC Place; SAN DIEGO; ***153** SN-13; ★ **SDGO**; mail San Diego **z** 92110; pop. incl. with San Diego (Inc. Place)
Loma Rica; CDP; YUBA; **150** NI-7; 🅿; **z** 95901; Ⓟ 1,852; © 2,075
Lomas Santa Fe; RMC Place; SAN DIEGO; ★ **SDGO**; mail Solana Beach **z** 92075; pop. incl. with Solana Beach (Inc. Place)
Loma Verda; RMC Place; MARIN; ★ **SF-O-**; mail Novato **z** 94949; pop. incl. with Novato (Inc. Place)
Lomita; Inc. Place; LOS ANGELES; **154** I-6; elev. 100ft./30m.; 🅿; ★ **L.A.**; **z** 90717; Ⓟ 19,382; © 20,046; ◆ 19,975
Lomita Park; RMC Place; SAN MATEO; ***150** NM-5; ★ **SF-O-**; mail San Bruno **z** 94066; pop. incl. with San Bruno (Inc. Place)
Lompico; RMC Place; SANTA CRUZ; ***152** SA-2; ★ **S.CRZ**; mail Felton **z** 95018; ● 1,100
Lompoc; Inc. Place; SANTA BARBARA; **152** SH-6; elev. 104ft./32m.; 🅿 🅷 ■; ★ **LOMP**; **z** 93436-38; Ⓟ 37,649; © 41,103; ◆ 43,251
London (New London); CDP; TULARE; **152** SC-8; elev. 295ft./90m.; mail Dinuba **z** 93618; Ⓟ 1,638; © 1,848
Lone Pine; CDP; INYO; **153** SC-11; elev. 3,733ft./1,138m.; 🅿 🅷; **z** 93545; Ⓟ 1,818; © 1,655
Lone Pine Reservation; Indian Reservation; INYO; mail Lone Pine **z** 93545; Ⓟ 248; © 212
Long Barn; RMC Place; TUOLUMNE; **150** NL-10; elev. 4,963ft./1,513m.; 🅿; **z** 95335; ● 250
Long Beach; Inc. Place; LOS ANGELES; **153** SK-11; elev. 29ft./9m.; 🅿 🅷 🅲 30,226 ■; ★ **L.A.**; **z** 90745-47, **z** 90749, **z** 90755, **z** 90801-10, **z** 90813-15, **z** 90822, **z** 90831-35, **z** 90840, **z** 90842, **z** 90844, **z** 90846-48, **z** 90853, **z** 90895, **z** 90899; Ⓟ 429,433; © 461,522; ◆ 486,798
Longvale; RMC Place; MENDOCINO; **150** NH-3; mail Willits **z** 95490; ● 50
Longview; RMC Place; LOS ANGELES; mail Pearblossom **z** 93553; ● 335
Lonoak; RMC Place; MONTEREY; ***152** SD-5; elev. 880ft./268m.; mail King City **z** 93930; rural
Lonoke; RMC Place; SANTA CLARA; ***152** SB-3; ★ **SF-O-**; mail Gilroy **z** 95020; pop. incl. with Gilroy (Inc. Place)
Lookout; RMC Place; MODOC; **150** NC-8; 🅿; **z** 96054; ● 150
Lookout Rancheria; Indian Reservation; MODOC; © 7
Lookout Ranchettes; RMC Place; MODOC; ***150** NC-8; elev. 4,228ft./1,289m.; mail Lookout **z** 96054; ● 100
Loomis; Inc. Place; PLACER; **150** NJ-8; elev. 399ft./122m.; 🅿; ★ **SAC**; **z** 95650; Ⓟ 5,705; © 6,260
Loomis Corners; RMC Place; SHASTA; ***150** NE-5; elev. 550ft./168m.; ★ **REDD**; mail Redding **z** 96003; ● 320
Loraine; RMC Place; KERN; ***152** SG-10; elev. 2,665ft./812m.; mail Caliente **z** 93518
Los Alamitos; Inc. Place; ORANGE; **154** I-9; elev. 22ft./7m.; 🅿 🅷; ★ **L.A.**; **z** 90720-21; Ⓟ 11,676; © 11,536
Los Alamos; CDP; SANTA BARBARA; **152** SH-6; elev. 575ft./175m.; 🅿; **z** 93440; © 1,372
Los Altos; Inc. Place; SANTA CLARA; **150** NN-5; elev. 170ft./52m.; 🅿; ★ **SF-O-**; **z** 94022-24; Ⓟ 26,303; © 27,693; ◆ 28,674
Los Altos Hills; Inc. Place; SANTA CLARA; **151** NL-17; elev. 215ft./66m.; 🅿; ★ **SF-O-**; **z** 94022, **z** 94024; Ⓟ 7,514; © 7,902
Los Altos Terrace; RMC Place; LOS ANGELES; ★ **L.A.**; pop. incl. with Long Beach (Inc. Place)
Los Amigos (Ranchos Los Amigos Hospital); RMC Place; LOS ANGELES; ***153** SJ-11; ★ **L.A.**; mail Downey **z** 90240; pop. incl. with Downey (Inc. Place)
Los Angeles; Inc. Place; ⊡ LOS ANGELES; **153** SJ-11; elev. 330ft./101m.; 🅿 🅷 🅲 154,704 ■; ★ **L.A.**; **z** 90001-84, **z** 90086-91, **z** 90093-96, **z** 90099, **z** 90101, **z** 90103, **z** 90189, **z** 90230 & mail Pacoima **z** 91331, Reseda **z** 91335; Ⓟ 3,485,398; © 3,694,820; Ⓡ 3,694,742; ◆ 3,812,019
LOS ANGELES; **152** SH-10; Ⓟ 8,863,164; © 9,519,338; ◆ 9,736,157
Los Angeles Harbor; RMC Place; LOS ANGELES; ★ **L.A.**; pop. incl. with Los Angeles (Inc. Place)
Los Angeles Junction; RMC Place; LOS ANGELES; ★ **L.A.**; pop. incl. with Los Angeles (Inc. Place)
Los Banos; Inc. Place; MERCED; **152** SB-5; elev. 120ft./37m.; 🅿 🅷; **z** 93635; Ⓟ 14,519; © 25,869; ◆ 37,221
Los Berros (Berros); RMC Place; SAN LUIS OBISPO; ***152** SG-5; mail Arroyo Grande **z** 93420; ● 300
Los Cerritos; RMC Place; LOS ANGELES; ★ **L.A.**; pop. incl. with Long Beach (Inc. Place)
Los Coyotes Reservation; Indian Reservation; SAN DIEGO; mail Warner Springs **z** 92086; also location of Indian Agency; Ⓟ 51; © 70
Los Deltos; RMC Place; FRESNO; ***152** SB-6; elev. 177ft./54m.; mail Firebaugh **z** 93622; rural
Los Feliz; RMC Place; LOS ANGELES; ★ **L.A.**; mail Los Angeles **z** 90027, **z** 90029; pop. incl. with Los Angeles (Inc. Place)
Los Gatos; Inc. Place; SANTA CLARA; **152** SA-2; elev. 385ft./117m.; 🅿 🅷 ■; ★ **SF-O-**; **z** 95030-33; Ⓟ 27,357; © 28,592; ◆ 29,628
Los Molinos; CDP; TEHAMA; **150** NG-6; elev. 220ft./67m.; 🅿; **z** 96055; Ⓟ 1,709; © 1,952
Los Nietos; RMC Place; LOS ANGELES; **154** F-9; elev. 154ft./47m.; 🅿; ★ **L.A.**; **z** 90606, **z** 90610; ● 8,200
Los Olivos; RMC Place; SANTA BARBARA; **152** SH-6; elev. 825ft./251m.; 🅿; **z** 93441; ● 850
Los Osos; RMC Place; SAN LUIS OBISPO; **152** SF-5; elev. 126ft./38m.; 🅿; **z** 93402, **z** 93412; ● 5,000
Los Ranchitos; RMC Place; MARIN; **151** NC-12; ★ **SF-O-**; mail San Rafael **z** 94903; ● 425
Los Robles; TEHAMA; see Dairyville (RMC Place)
Los Serranos; RMC Place; SAN BERNARDINO; **153** SJ-12; ★ **L.A.**; mail Chino Hills **z** 91709; pop. incl. with Chino (Inc. Place); Ⓟ 7,099
Lost Hills; CDP; KERN; **152** SF-7; 🅿; **z** 93249; Ⓟ 1,212; © 1,938
Lost Lake; RMC Place; RIVERSIDE; ***153** SJ-20; mail Blythe **z** 92225; ● 110
Los Trancos Woods; RMC Place; SAN MATEO; ***150** NN-5; ★ **SF-O-**; mail Portola Valley **z** 94028; ● 500
Los Tules; RMC Place; SAN DIEGO; ***153** SL-15; elev. 3,400ft./1,036m.; mail Warner Springs **z** 92086; rural
Lotus; RMC Place; EL DORADO; **150** NJ-8; 🅿; ★ **SAC**; **z** 95651; ● 700
Lovelock; RMC Place; BUTTE; ***150** NG-7; mail Magalia **z** 95954; ● 30
Lower Lake; CDP; LAKE; **150** NJ-5; elev. 1,372ft./418m.; 🅿; **z** 95457; Ⓟ 1,217; © 1,755
Lowrey; RMC Place; TEHAMA; ***150** NG-5; elev. 825ft./251m.; mail Red Bluff **z** 96080; rural
Loyalton; Inc. Place; SIERRA; **150** NH-10; elev. 4,936ft./1,504m.; 🅿 🅷; **z** 96118; Ⓟ 931; © 862
Loyola; CDP-Census Area Only; SANTA CLARA; ***150** NN-6; ★ **SF-O-**; mail Los Altos **z** 94024; Ⓟ 3,076; © 3,478
Lucas Valley; RMC Place; MARIN; ***150** NL-5; ★ **SF-O-**; mail San Rafael **z** 94903; ● 4,000
Lucas Valley-Marinwood; CDP-Census Area Only; MARIN; ***150** NL-5; ★ **SF-O-**; mail San Rafael **z** 94903; Ⓟ 5,982; © 6,357
Lucerne; CDP; LAKE; **150** NI-4; elev. 1,332ft./406m.; 🅿; **z** 95458; Ⓟ 2,011; © 2,870
Lucerne Valley; RMC Place; SAN BERNARDINO; **153** SI-14; elev. 2,946ft./898m.; 🅿; **z** 92356; ● 2,100
Lucia; RMC Place; MONTEREY; ***152** SD-3; elev. 200ft./61m.; mail Big Sur **z** 93920; rural
Ludlow; RMC Place; SAN BERNARDINO; **153** SH-16; elev. 1,775ft./541m.; 🅿; **z** 92338
Lugo; RMC Place; LOS ANGELES; ***153** SJ-11; ★ **L.A.**; mail Los Angeles **z** 90023; pop. incl. with Los Angeles (Inc. Place)
Lugonia; RMC Place; SAN BERNARDINO; ★ **RIV-**; mail Redlands **z** 92375; pop. incl. with Redlands (Inc. Place)
Lunada Bay; RMC Place; LOS ANGELES; ★ **L.A.**; mail Palos Verdes Peninsula **z** 90274; pop. incl. with Palos Verdes Estates (Inc. Place)
Lundy; RMC Place; MONO; ***151** NL-12; mail Lee Vining **z** 93541; rural
Lushmeadows Mountain Estates; RMC Place; MARIPOSA; ***151** NN-11; elev. 3,250ft./991m.; mail Mariposa **z** 95338; ● 460
Luther; RMC Place; SANTA CLARA; ★ **SF-O-**; pop. incl. with San Jose (Inc. Place)
Luther Burbank; RMC Place; SONOMA; ★ **S.ROS**; mail Santa Rosa **z** 95402; pop. incl. with Santa Rosa (Inc. Place)
Lyman Springs; RMC Place; TEHAMA; ***150** NF-6; elev. 3,400ft./1,036m.; mail Paynes Creek **z** 96075; rural
Lynwood; Inc. Place; LOS ANGELES; **154** G-7; elev. 85ft./26m.; 🅿 🅷 ■; ★ **L.A.**; **z** 90262; Ⓟ 61,945; © 69,845; ◆ 74,253
Lynwood Gardens; RMC Place; LOS ANGELES; ***153** SJ-11; elev. 76ft./23m.; ★ **L.A.**; mail Lynwood **z** 90262; pop. incl. with Lynwood (Inc. Place)
Lyons; RMC Place; LOS ANGELES; ★ **L.A.**; mail Newhall **z** 91321-22; pop. incl. with Santa Clarita (Inc. Place)
Lytle Creek; RMC Place; SAN BERNARDINO; **155** B-16; 🅿; **z** 92358; ● 530
Lytton; RMC Place; SONOMA; ***150** NJ-4; elev. 185ft./56m.; mail Healdsburg **z** 95448; ● 275

M

Macdoel; CDP; SISKIYOU; **150** NB-6; 🅿; **z** 96058; © 140
Maclay; RMC Place; LOS ANGELES; ★ **L.A.**; mail San Fernando **z** 91340; pop. incl. with San Fernando (Inc. Place)
Madeline; RMC Place; LASSEN; **150** ND-9; elev. 5,314ft./1,620m.; 🅿; **z** 96119
Madera; Inc. Place; ⊡ MADERA; **152** SB-7; elev. 270ft./82m.; 🅿 🅷; ★ **FRES**; **z** 93636-39; Ⓟ 29,281; © 43,207; ◆ 57,149
MADERA; **152** SB-6; Ⓟ 88,090; © 123,109; ◆ 146,806
Madera Acres; CDP-Census Area Only; MADERA; ***152** SB-7; mail Madera **z** 93637; Ⓟ 5,245; © 7,741
Madera Country Club Estates; RMC Place; MADERA; ***152** SB-7; mail Madera **z** 93637; ● 1,200
Madera Highlands; RMC Place; MADERA; ***152** SB-7; elev. 260ft./79m.; mail Madera **z** 93637; ● 5,000
Madera Ranchos; RMC Place; MADERA; ***152** SB-7; mail Madera **z** 93637; ● 2,600
Madison; RMC Place; YOLO; **150** NJ-6; elev. 151ft./46m.; 🅿; **z** 95653; ● 800
Mad River; RMC Place; TRINITY; **150** NE-3; 🅿; **z** 95526, **z** 95552; ● 200
Madrone; RMC Place; SANTA CLARA; ***152** SA-3; ★ **SF-O-**; mail Morgan Hill **z** 95037; pop. incl. with Morgan Hill (Inc. Place)
Magalia; CDP; BUTTE; **150** NG-7; 🅿; **z** 95954; Ⓟ 8,987; © 10,569
Magnolia; RMC Place; IMPERIAL; ***153** SM-17; elev. 112ft./34m.; mail Brawley **z** 92227; rural
Magnolia; RMC Place; SANTA BARBARA; ★ **S.BAR**; mail Santa Barbara **z** 93111, **z** 93160; pop. incl. with Santa Barbara (Inc. Place)
Magnolia Avenue; RMC Place; RIVERSIDE; ***153** SJ-13; ★ **RIV-**; mail Riverside **z** 92506; pop. incl. with Riverside (Inc. Place)
Magnolia Center; RMC Place; RIVERSIDE; ★ **RIV-**; mail Riverside **z** 92506, **z** 92516; pop. incl. with Riverside (Inc. Place)
Magnolia Park; RMC Place; LOS ANGELES; ***153** SJ-11; ★ **L.A.**; mail Burbank **z** 91505, **z** 91507; pop. incl. with Burbank (Inc. Place)
Magra; RMC Place; PLACER; mail Colfax **z** 95713; ● 340
Malaga; RMC Place; FRESNO; ***152** SC-7; ★ **FRES**; mail Fresno **z** 93725; ● 760
Malibu; Inc. Place; LOS ANGELES; **152** SJ-10; 🅿 🅲 7,593; ★ **L.A.**; **z** 90263-65; © 12,575
Malibu Beach; RMC Place; LOS ANGELES; ★ **L.A.**; mail Malibu **z** 90265; pop. incl. with Malibu (Inc. Place)
Malibu Bowl; RMC Place; LOS ANGELES; ***152** SJ-10; elev. 456ft./139m.; ★ **L.A.**; mail Malibu **z** 90265
Malibu Canyon Homes; RMC Place; LOS ANGELES; ***152** SJ-10; elev. 900ft./274m.; ★ **L.A.**; mail Calabasas **z** 91302; pop. incl. with Calabasas (Inc. Place)
Malibu Junction; RMC Place; LOS ANGELES; ***152** SJ-10; ★ **OXN-**; mail Agoura Hills **z** 91301; pop. incl. with Agoura Hills (Inc. Place)
Mammoth Lakes; Inc. Place; MONO; **151** NM-13; 🅿 🅷; **z** 93546; Ⓟ 4,785; © 7,093
Manchester; RMC Place; MENDOCINO; **150** NI-2; 🅿; **z** 95459; ● 400
Manchester-Point Arena Rancheria; Indian Reservation; MENDOCINO; © 197
Manhattan Beach; Inc. Place; LOS ANGELES; **152** SJ-10; elev. 120ft./37m.; 🅿 ■; ★ **L.A.**; **z** 90266-67; Ⓟ 32,063; © 33,852; ◆ 35,315
Manila (North Samoa); RMC Place; HUMBOLDT; ***150** ND-1; elev. 12ft./4m.; ★ **EUR-**; mail Arcata **z** 95521; ● 770
Mankas Corners; RMC Place; SOLANO; ***150** NK-6; elev. 120ft./37m.; ★ **FRFL-**; mail Suisun City **z** 94585; ● 230
Manlove; RMC Place; SACRAMENTO; ***150** NK-7; ★ **SAC**; mail Sacramento **z** 95826; ● 1,700
Manor; RMC Place; MARIN; ***150** NL-4; ★ **SF-O-**; mail Fairfax **z** 94930; pop. incl. with Fairfax (Inc. Place)
Manteca; Inc. Place; SAN JOAQUIN; **150** NM-8; elev. 35ft./11m.; 🅿 🅷; **z** 95336-37; Ⓟ 40,773; © 49,258; ◆ 56,954
Manton; CDP; TEHAMA; **150** NE-6; 🅿; **z** 96059; © 372
Manuel; RMC Place; LOS ANGELES; ★ **L.A.**; pop. incl. with Long Beach (Inc. Place)
Manzana; RMC Place; SONOMA; ***150** NK-4; ★ **S.ROS**; mail Graton **z** 95444; ● 500
Manzanita; RMC Place; BUTTE; ***150** NH-7; elev. 88ft./27m.; mail Gridley **z** 95948; rural
Manzanita Reservation; Indian Reservation; SAN DIEGO; mail Boulevard **z** 91905; Ⓟ 14; © 69
Maple Creek; RMC Place; HUMBOLDT; ***150** ND-2; elev. 412ft./126m.; mail Korbel **z** 95550; ● 30
Maravilla; RMC Place; LOS ANGELES; ***152** SJ-11; ★ **L.A.**; mail Los Angeles **z** 90022; ● 1,770
Marcelina; RMC Place; LOS ANGELES; ★ **L.A.**; mail Torrance **z** 90501, **z** 90507-08; pop. incl. with Torrance (Inc. Place)
March AFB; CDP-Census Area Only; RIVERSIDE; ***153** SJ-13; ★ **RIV-**; mail Riverside **z** 92508; Ⓟ 5,523; © 370
Marcus Foster; RMC Place; ALAMEDA; ★ **SF-O-**; mail Oakland **z** 94624; pop. incl. with Oakland (Inc. Place)
Maricopa; Inc. Place; KERN; **152** SG-8; elev. 854ft./260m.; 🅿; **z** 93252; Ⓟ 1,193; © 1,111
MARIN; **150** NL-5; Ⓟ 230,096; © 247,289; ◆ 246,713
Marina; Inc. Place; MONTEREY; **152** SC-3; elev. 40ft./12m.; 🅿; ★ **MTRY-**; **z** 93933; Ⓟ 26,436; © 25,101; Ⓡ 18,925; ◆ 17,998
Marina; RMC Place; SAN FRANCISCO; ★ **SF-O-**; mail San Francisco **z** 94123, **z** 94147; pop. incl. with San Francisco (Inc. Place)
Marina del Rey; CDP-Census Area Only; LOS ANGELES; **154** G-4; 🅿 🅷; ★ **L.A.**; **z** 90292, **z** 90295 & mail Venice **z** 90291; Ⓟ 7,431; © 8,176
Marin City; RMC Place; MARIN; **151** NE-12; ★ **SF-O-**; mail Sausalito **z** 94965; ● 2,500
Marin Country Club Estates; RMC Place; MARIN; ★ **SF-O-**; mail Novato **z** 94949; pop. incl. with Novato (Inc. Place)
Mariner; RMC Place; ORANGE; ***153** SK-12; ★ **L.A.**; mail Seal Beach **z** 90740; pop. incl. with Seal Beach (Inc. Place)
Marinwood; RMC Place; MARIN; **151** NB-12; ★ **SF-O-**; mail San Rafael **z** 94903; ● 2,300
Mariposa; CDP; ⊡ MARIPOSA; **150** NN-10; elev. 2,000ft./610m.; 🅿 🅷; **z** 95338; Ⓟ 1,152; © 1,373
MARIPOSA; **150** NN-10; Ⓟ 14,302; © 17,130; ◆ 18,128
Market; RMC Place; LOS ANGELES; ***153** SJ-11; ★ **L.A.**; mail Los Angeles **z** 90021; pop. incl. with Los Angeles (Inc. Place)
Markleeville; CDP; ⊡ ALPINE; **151** NJ-11; elev. 5,501ft./1,677m.; 🅿; **z** 96120; © 197
Mark West Springs; RMC Place; SONOMA; mail Santa Rosa **z** 95404; rural
Marloma; RMC Place; LOS ANGELES; ★ **L.A.**; mail Palos Verdes Peninsula **z** 90274; pop. incl. with Rolling Hills Estates (Inc. Place)
Marne; RMC Place; LOS ANGELES; ***153** SJ-12; elev. 404ft./123m.; ★ **L.A.**; mail Guasti **z** 91743; pop. incl. with Industry (Inc. Place)
Marshall; RMC Place; MARIN; **150** NL-4; elev. 10ft./3m.; 🅿; **z** 94940
Marshall Junction (Marshall Station); RMC Place; FRESNO; ***152** SB-8; elev. 1,225ft./373m.; mail Clovis **z** 93611; rural
Marshall Station; FRESNO; see Marshall Junction (RMC Place)
Martell; RMC Place; AMADOR; **150** NK-8; elev. 1,490ft./454m.; 🅿; **z** 95654
Martinez; Inc. Place; ⊡ CONTRA COSTA; **150** NL-6; elev. 23ft./7m.; 🅿 🅷; ★ **SF-O-**; **z** 94553; Ⓟ 31,808; © 35,866; ◆ 34,960
Martins Beach; RMC Place; SAN MATEO; ***150** NN-5; ★ **SF-O-**; mail Half Moon Bay **z** 94019; ● 130
Mar Vista; RMC Place; LOS ANGELES; ***152** SJ-10; elev. 69ft./21m.; ★ **L.A.**; mail Los Angeles **z** 90066; pop. incl. with Los Angeles (Inc. Place)
Marysville; Inc. Place; ⊡ YUBA; **150** NI-7; elev. 63ft./19m.; 🅿 🅷 ■; ★ **YUCY**; **z** 95901, **z** 95903; Ⓟ 12,324; © 12,268; ◆ 13,102
Mason; SAN FRANCISCO; see Fort Mason (RMC Place)
Massack; RMC Place; PLUMAS; ***150** NG-8; mail Quincy **z** 95971
Maxwell; RMC Place; COLUSA; **150** NI-5; elev. 91ft./28m.; 🅿; **z** 95955; ● 850
Maybury; RMC Place; SANTA CLARA; ★ **SF-O-**; pop. incl. with San Jose (Inc. Place)
Mayfair; RMC Place; LOS ANGELES; ★ **L.A.**; pop. incl. with Lakewood (Inc. Place)
Mayflower Village; CDP-Census Area Only; LOS ANGELES; ***153** SJ-11; ★ **L.A.**; mail Monrovia **z** 91016; Ⓟ 4,978; © 5,081
Mayten; SISKIYOU; see Big Springs (RMC Place)
Maywood; Inc. Place; LOS ANGELES; **154** F-7; elev. 150ft./46m.; 🅿; ★ **L.A.**; **z** 90270; Ⓟ 27,850; © 28,083; ◆ 27,718
McArthur; CDP; SHASTA; **150** ND-7; elev. 3,311ft./1,009m.; 🅿; **z** 96056; © 365
Mcbride; RMC Place; SONOMA; ★ **S.ROS**; mail Santa Rosa **z** 95403; pop. incl. with Santa Rosa (Inc. Place)
McCann; RMC Place; HUMBOLDT; ***150** NF-2; mail Redcrest **z** 95569; rural
McCloud; CDP; SISKIYOU; **150** NC-6; elev. 3,254ft./992m.; 🅿; **z** 96057; Ⓟ 1,555; © 1,343
McFarland; Inc. Place; KERN; **152** SE-8; elev. 350ft./107m.; 🅿; **z** 93250; Ⓟ 7,005; © 9,618; Ⓡ 9,837
McHie; RMC Place; TEHAMA; ***150** NF-6; elev. 272ft./83m.; mail Red Bluff **z** 96080; ● 250
McKeon; RMC Place; PLACER; ***150** NI-8; ★ **SAC**; mail Foresthill **z** 95631; rural
McKinleyville; CDP; HUMBOLDT; **150** ND-2; elev. 140ft./43m.; 🅿; ★ **EUR-**; **z** 95519, **z** 95521; Ⓟ 10,749; © 13,599
McKittrick; CDP; KERN; **152** SG-8; elev. 1,051ft./320m.; 🅿; **z** 93251; © 160
McKnight Acres; RMC Place; NAPA; ***150** NL-5; ★ **SF-O-**; mail Vallejo **z** 94590; pop. incl. with American Canyon (Inc. Place)
Mc Laren; RMC Place; SAN FRANCISCO; ★ **SF-O-**; mail San Francisco **z** 94134; pop. incl. with San Francisco (Inc. Place)
McMillan Manor; RMC Place; VENTURA; ★ **OXN-**; mail Oxnard **z** 93030; pop. incl. with Oxnard (Inc. Place)
McVittie Annex; RMC Place; CONTRA COSTA; ★ **SF-O-**; mail Richmond **z** 94804; pop. incl. with Richmond (Inc. Place)
Meadowbrook; RMC Place; RIVERSIDE; ***153** SK-13; elev. 1,643ft./501m.; mail Perris **z** 92570; ● 100
Meadowbrook Woods; RMC Place; SAN BERNARDINO; ***153** SI-13; ★ **RIV-**; mail Crest Park **z** 92326; ● 700
Meadow Lake Park; RMC Place; NEVADA; mail Truckee **z** 96161; pop. incl. with Truckee (Inc. Place)
Meadow Lakes; RMC Place; FRESNO; ***152** SB-8; mail Auberry **z** 93602; ● 570
Meadowsweet; RMC Place; MARIN; ***150** NL-5; ★ **SF-O-**; mail Corte Madera **z** 94925; pop. incl. with Corte Madera (Inc. Place)
Meadow Valley; CDP; PLUMAS; **150** NG-8; 🅿; **z** 95956; © 575
Meadow Vista; CDP; PLACER; **150** NI-8; 🅿; ★ **SAC**; **z** 95722; Ⓟ 3,067; © 3,096
Mead Valley; RMC Place; RIVERSIDE; ***153** SK-13; elev. 1,653ft./504m.; ★ **RIV-**; mail Perris **z** 92570; ● 4,000
Mecca; CDP; RIVERSIDE; **153** SK-16; elev. 189ft./58m.; 🅿; **z** 92254; Ⓟ 1,966; © 5,402
Meeks Bay; RMC Place; EL DORADO; **150** NI-10; mail Tahoma **z** 96142
Meiners Oaks; CDP; VENTURA; **152** SI-8; ★ **OXN-**; mail Ojai **z** 93023; Ⓟ 3,329; © 3,750
Meloland; RMC Place; IMPERIAL; ***153** SM-17; mail El Centro **z** 92243; rural
Melrose; RMC Place; ALAMEDA; ★ **SF-O-**; pop. incl. with Oakland (Inc. Place)
Melvin; RMC Place; FRESNO; ***152** SB-7; elev. 358ft./109m.; ★ **FRES**; mail Clovis **z** 93611; pop. incl. with Clovis (Inc. Place)
Mendocino; CDP; MENDOCINO; **150** NH-2; 🅿; **z** 95460; © 824
MENDOCINO; **150** NH-3; Ⓟ 80,345; © 86,265; ◆ 82,674
Mendota; Inc. Place; FRESNO; **152** SB-6; 🅿; **z** 93640; Ⓟ 6,821; © 7,890
Menifee (Menifee Valley); RMC Place; RIVERSIDE; **155** J-20; elev. 1,479ft./451m.; 🅿; **z** 92584; ● 130
Menifee Valley; RIVERSIDE; see Menifee (RMC Place)
Menlo Park; Inc. Place; SAN MATEO; **150** NN-5; elev. 70ft./21m.; 🅿 🅷 ■; ★ **SF-O-**; **z** 94025-28; Ⓟ 28,040; © 30,785; ◆ 31,616
Mentone; CDP; SAN BERNARDINO; **155** E-20; 🅿; ★ **RIV-**; **z** 92359; Ⓟ 5,675; © 7,803
Merced; Inc. Place; ⊡ MERCED; **150** NN-9; elev. 172ft./52m.; 🅿 🅷 ■; ★ **MRCD**; **z** 95340-41, **z** 95343-44, **z** 95348; Ⓟ 56,216; © 63,893; ◆ 74,425
MERCED; **152** SB-4; Ⓟ 178,403; © 210,554; ◆ 245,093
Merced Falls; RMC Place; MERCED; **150** NN-9; mail Snelling **z** 95369; rural
Meridian; RMC Place; SUTTER; **150** NI-6; 🅿; **z** 95957; ● 300
Mesa; CDP-Census Area Only; INYO; ***151** NN-13; © 214
Mesa Center; RMC Place; ORANGE; ★ **L.A.**; mail Costa Mesa **z** 92627; pop. incl. with Costa Mesa (Inc. Place)
Mesa Grande; RMC Place; SAN DIEGO; ***153** SL-14; mail Santa Ysabel **z** 92070; rural
Mesa Grande; SONOMA; see Villa Grande (RMC Place)
Mesa Grande Reservation; Indian Reservation; SAN DIEGO; © 75
Mesa Verde (Nicholls Warm Springs); RMC Place; RIVERSIDE; ***153** SK-19; elev. 390ft./119m.; mail Blythe **z** 92225; ● 1,100
Mesa Vista; CDP-Census Area Only; ALPINE; ***151** NJ-11; mail Markleeville **z** 96120; © 182
Metro; RMC Place; SACRAMENTO; ★ **SAC**; mail Sacramento **z** 95812, **z** 95814; pop. incl. with Sacramento (Inc. Place)
Metropolitan; RMC Place; HUMBOLDT; ***150** NE-1; elev. 79ft./24m.; mail Fortuna **z** 95540; rural
Metropolitan; RMC Place; LOS ANGELES; ★ **L.A.**; mail Los Angeles **z** 90014; pop. incl. with Los Angeles (Inc. Place)
Mettler; CDP; KERN; **152** SG-9; elev. 539ft./164m.; mail Bakersfield **z** 93301; © 157
Mexican Colony; RMC Place; KERN; ***152** SF-8; mail Shafter **z** 93263; ● 365
Meyers; RMC Place; EL DORADO; mail South Lake Tahoe **z** 96155; pop. incl. with South Lake Tahoe (Inc. Place)
Michigan Bluff; RMC Place; PLACER; ***150** NI-9; mail Foresthill **z** 95631; ● 60
Mid City; RMC Place; SAN JOAQUIN; ★ **STOC**; mail Stockton **z** 95202; pop. incl. with Stockton (Inc. Place)
Midco; RMC Place; SANTA BARBARA; ***152** SH-6; ★ **S.MAR**; mail Santa Maria **z** 93458
Middle River; RMC Place; SAN JOAQUIN; **150** NL-7; mail Holt **z** 95234; rural
Middletown; CDP; LAKE; **150** NJ-5; elev. 1,105ft./337m.; 🅿; **z** 95461, **z** 95467; © 1,020
Middletown Rancheria; Indian Reservation; LAKE; © 73
Midpines; RMC Place; MARIPOSA; **150** NN-10; 🅿; **z** 95345; ● 200
Midtown; RMC Place; BUTTE; ★ **CHICO**; mail Chico **z** 95928; pop. incl. with Chico (Inc. Place)
Midtown; RMC Place; YOLO; mail Woodland **z** 95695; pop. incl. with Woodland (Inc. Place)
Midway; RMC Place; SHASTA; ***150** NE-6; elev. 2,171ft./662m.; mail Shingletown **z** 96088; ● 100
Midway City; RMC Place; ORANGE; **154** J-10; elev. 40ft./12m.; 🅿; ★ **L.A.**; **z** 92655; pop. incl. with Westminster (Inc. Place)
Mikon; RMC Place; YOLO; ***150** NK-7; ★ **SAC**; mail West Sacramento **z** 95605; pop. incl. with West Sacramento (Inc. Place)
Milford; RMC Place; LASSEN; **150** NF-9; 🅿; **z** 96121; ● 250
Millbrae; Inc. Place; SAN MATEO; **151** NI-13; elev. 25ft./8m.; 🅿; ★ **SF-O-**; **z** 94030; Ⓟ 20,412; © 20,718; ◆ 20,459
Millbrae Meadows; RMC Place; SAN MATEO; ***150** NM-5; ★ **SF-O-**; mail Millbrae **z** 94030; pop. incl. with Millbrae (Inc. Place)
Mill City; RMC Place; MONO; ***151** NM-12; mail Mammoth Lakes **z** 93546; pop. incl. with Mammoth Lakes (Inc. Place)
Mill Creek; RMC Place; TEHAMA; **150** NF-7; 🅿; **z** 96061; ● 17
Millers Corners; RMC Place; MADERA; ***152** SB-7; mail Madera **z** 93637; rural
Mills; SACRAMENTO; see Rancho Cordova (Inc. Place)
Mills College; RMC Place; ALAMEDA; ★ **SF-O-**; mail Oakland **z** 94613; pop. incl. with Oakland (Inc. Place)
Mill Valley; Inc. Place; MARIN; **150** NL-5; elev. 80ft./24m.; 🅿 🅲 1,090; ★ **SF-O-**; **z** 94941-42; Ⓟ 13,038; © 13,600
Millville; CDP; SHASTA; **150** NE-6; elev. 511ft./156m.; 🅿; **z** 96062; © 610
Milo; RMC Place; TULARE; ***152** SD-9; mail Springville **z** 93265
Milpas; RMC Place; SANTA BARBARA; ★ **S.BAR**; mail Santa Barbara **z** 93103, **z** 93140; pop. incl. with Santa Barbara (Inc. Place)
Milpitas; Inc. Place; SANTA CLARA; **150** NN-6; elev. 15ft./5m.; 🅿; ★ **SF-O-**; **z** 95035-36; Ⓟ 50,686; © 62,698; ◆ 69,977
Milton; RMC Place; CALAVERAS; **150** NL-8; mail Farmington **z** 95230
Mineral; CDP; TEHAMA; **150** NF-7; 🅿; **z** 96061, **z** 96063; © 143
Mineral King; RMC Place; TULARE; ***152** SC-10; elev. 7,830ft./2,387m.; mail Three Rivers **z** 93271
Minkler; RMC Place; FRESNO; ***152** SC-8; elev. 395ft./120m.; mail Sanger **z** 93657; ● 400
Mint Canyon; RMC Place; LOS ANGELES; ***152** SI-10; ★ **L.A.**; mail Santa Clarita **z** 91350; pop. incl. with Santa Clarita (Inc. Place)
Minter Village; RMC Place; KERN; ***152** SF-9; elev. 418ft./127m.; mail Bakersfield **z** 93308; pop. incl. with Shafter (Inc. Place)
Mirabel Heights; RMC Place; SONOMA; ***150** NK-4; ★ **S.ROS**; mail Forestville **z** 95436; ● 300
Mirabel Park; RMC Place; SONOMA; ***150** NK-4; ★ **S.ROS**; mail Forestville **z** 95436; ● 200
Miracle Hot Springs (Hobo Hot Springs); RMC Place; KERN; **152** SF-10; elev. 2,396ft./730m.; mail Bakersfield **z** 93301; rural
Miracle Mile; RMC Place; LOS ANGELES; ★ **L.A.**; mail Los Angeles **z** 90036; pop. incl. with Los Angeles (Inc. Place)
Mirada; LOS ANGELES; see La Mirada (Inc. Place)
Miraleste; RMC Place; LOS ANGELES; ***153** SK-11; elev. 770ft./235m.; ★ **L.A.**; mail Palos Verdes Peninsula **z** 90274; pop. incl. with Rancho Palos Verdes (Inc. Place)
Mira Loma; CDP; RIVERSIDE; **153** SJ-12; 🅿; ★ **RIV-**; **z** 91752; Ⓟ 15,786; © 17,617
Miramar; RMC Place; SAN MATEO; ***150** NN-5; ★ **SF-O-**; mail El Granada **z** 94018; pop. incl. with Half Moon Bay (Inc. Place)
Mira Mesa; RMC Place; SAN DIEGO; **156** F-6; ★ **SDGO**; mail San Diego **z** 92126, **z** 92131, **z** 92196; pop. incl. with San Diego (Inc. Place)
Miramonte; RMC Place; FRESNO; ***152** SC-9; elev. 3,095ft./943m.; 🅿; **z** 93603, **z** 93628, **z** 93633, **z** 93641; ● 300
Mira Monte; CDP; VENTURA; **152** SI-8; ★ **OXN-**; mail Ojai **z** 93023; Ⓟ 7,744; © 7,177
Miranda; RMC Place; HUMBOLDT; **150** NF-2; elev. 331ft./101m.; 🅿; **z** 95553; ● 250
Mira Vista; RMC Place; CONTRA COSTA; ★ **SF-O-**; mail Richmond **z** 94805; pop. incl. with Richmond (Inc. Place)
Mission; RMC Place; SAN LUIS OBISPO; ★ **S.LUIS**; mail San Luis Obispo **z** 93406; pop. incl. with San Luis Obispo (Inc. Place)
Mission; RMC Place; SANTA CLARA; ★ **SF-O-**; mail Santa Clara **z** 95051, **z** 95055; pop. incl. with Santa Clara (Inc. Place)
Mission Beach; RMC Place; SAN DIEGO; **156** I-5; ★ **SDGO**; mail San Diego **z** 92109; pop. incl. with San Diego (Inc. Place)
Mission Canyon; CDP-Census Area Only; SANTA BARBARA; ***152** SI-7; ★ **S.BAR**; © 2,610
Mission City Annex; RMC Place; LOS ANGELES; ★ **L.A.**; mail Mission Hills **z** 91346; pop. incl. with Los Angeles (Inc. Place)
Mission Highlands; RMC Place; SONOMA; ***150** NK-5; mail Sonoma **z** 95476; ● 150
Mission Hills; RMC Place; LOS ANGELES; ***152** SI-10; elev. 910ft./277m.; 🅿; ★ **L.A.**; **z** 91345-46, **z** 91395; pop. incl. with Los Angeles (Inc. Place)
Mission Hills; RMC Place; SAN DIEGO; ***153** SN-13; ★ **SDGO**; mail San Diego **z** 92103; pop. incl. with San Diego (Inc. Place)
Mission Hills; CDP-Census Area Only; SANTA BARBARA; **152** SH-6; ★ **LOMP**; mail Lompoc **z** 93436; Ⓟ 3,112; © 3,142
Mission Rafael; RMC Place; MARIN; ★ **SF-O-**; mail San Rafael **z** 94901, **z** 94915; pop. incl. with San Rafael (Inc. Place)
Mission San Jose; RMC Place; ALAMEDA; ★ **SF-O-**; mail Fremont **z** 94539; pop. incl. with Fremont (Inc. Place)
Mission Station; RMC Place; SAN FRANCISCO; ★ **SF-O-**; mail San Francisco **z** 94110, **z** 94140; pop. incl. with San Francisco (Inc. Place)
Mission Viejo; Inc. Place; ORANGE; **153** SK-12; 🅿 🅷; ★ **L.A.**; **z** 92675, **z** 92690-92, **z** 92694; Ⓟ 72,820; © 93,102; ◆ 94,574
Missouri Triangle; RMC Place; KERN; mail Mc Kittrick **z** 93251; rural
Mitchell Mill; RMC Place; CALAVERAS; ***150** NK-9; elev. 3,000ft./914m.; mail Wilseyville **z** 95257; rural
Mitchells Corner; RMC Place; KERN; ***152** SG-9; elev. 461ft./141m.; mail Arvin **z** 93203; rural
Mi-Wuk Village; CDP; TUOLUMNE; **150** NL-10; elev. 4,687ft./1,429m.; 🅿; **z** 95346; Ⓟ 1,175; © 1,485
Moccasin; RMC Place; TUOLUMNE; **150** NM-10; 🅿; **z** 95347
Mococo; RMC Place; CONTRA COSTA; ***150** NL-6; ★ **SF-O-**; mail Martinez **z** 94553; pop. incl. with Martinez (Inc. Place)
Modesto; Inc. Place; ⊡ STANISLAUS; **150** NM-8; elev. 87ft./27m.; 🅿 🅷 ■; ★ **MOD**; **z** 95350-58, **z** 95397; Ⓟ 164,730; © 188,856; ◆ 196,523
Modesto Empire Junction; STANISLAUS; see Empire (CDP)
Modjeska; RMC Place; ORANGE; **155** J-14; ★ **L.A.**; mail Orange **z** 92867, Silverado **z** 92676; ● 500
MODOC; **150** NB-8; Ⓟ 9,678; © 9,449; ◆ 8,887
Mohawk Vista; CDP-Census Area Only; PLUMAS; ***150** NG-9; © 121
Mojave; CDP; KERN; **153** SG-11; elev. 2,757ft./840m.; 🅿; **z** 93501-02, **z** 93519; Ⓟ 3,763; © 3,836
Mojave Heights; RMC Place; SAN BERNARDINO; ***153** SI-13; ★ **HESP-**; mail Victorville **z** 92392; pop. incl. with Victorville (Inc. Place)
Mokelumne Hill; CDP; CALAVERAS; **150** NK-9; elev. 1,474ft./449m.; 🅿; **z** 95245; © 774
Monarch Bay; RMC Place; ORANGE; 🅿; ★ **L.A.**; **z** 92629 & mail Laguna Niguel **z** 92677; pop. incl. with Laguna Niguel (Inc. Place)
Moneta; RMC Place; LOS ANGELES; ★ **L.A.**; pop. incl. with Gardena (Inc. Place)
Monmouth; RMC Place; FRESNO; ***152** SC-7; ★ **FRES**; mail Fresno **z** 93725; rural
MONO; **151** NL-12; Ⓟ 9,956; © 12,853; ◆ 12,331
Mono City; RMC Place; MONO; mail Lee Vining **z** 93541; ● 175
Mono Hot Springs; RMC Place; FRESNO; ***151** NN-12; 🅿; **z** 93642
Mono Lake; RMC Place; MONO; ***151** NL-12; mail Lee Vining **z** 93541; rural
Mono Vista (Tambs Station); CDP; TUOLUMNE; ***150** NL-10; mail Soulsbyville **z** 95372; Ⓟ 2,599; © 3,072
Monrovia; Inc. Place; LOS ANGELES; **154** D-10; elev. 560ft./171m.; 🅿 🅷 🅲 811 ■; ★ **L.A.**; **z** 91016-17; Ⓟ 35,761; © 36,929; ◆ 37,053
Monson; RMC Place; TULARE; ***152** SC-8; mail Dinuba **z** 93618; ● 300
Montague; Inc. Place; SISKIYOU; **150** NB-5; elev. 2,538ft./774m.; 🅿; **z** 96064; Ⓟ 1,415; © 1,456
Montair; RMC Place; CONTRA COSTA; ★ **SF-O-**; mail Danville **z** 94526; pop. incl. with Danville (Inc. Place)
Montalvin Manor; RMC Place; CONTRA COSTA; **151** NC-14; ★ **SF-O-**; mail San Pablo **z** 94806; ● 2,000
Montalvo; RMC Place; VENTURA; ***152** SI-9; elev. 109ft./33m.; ★ **OXN-**; mail Ventura **z** 93003, **z** 93005; pop. incl. with Ventura (Inc. Place)
Montara; CDP; SAN MATEO; **151** NJ-12; elev. 113ft./34m.; 🅿; ★ **SF-O-**; **z** 94037; Ⓟ 2,552; © 2,950
Monta Vista; SANTA CLARA; see Monte Vista (RMC Place)
Montclair; Inc. Place; SAN BERNARDINO; **155** E-13; elev. 977ft./298m.; 🅿 🅷 ■; ★ **L.A.**; **z** 91710, **z** 91762-63; Ⓟ 28,434; © 33,049; ◆ 37,047
Montebello; Inc. Place; LOS ANGELES; **154** F-8; elev. 260ft./79m.; 🅿 🅷 ■; ★ **L.A.**; **z** 90640; Ⓟ 59,564; © 62,150; ◆ 63,032
Montebello Gardens; RMC Place; LOS ANGELES; ★ **L.A.**; mail Pico Rivera **z** 90660; pop. incl. with Pico Rivera (Inc. Place)
Montebello Hills; RMC Place; LOS ANGELES; ★ **L.A.**; mail Montebello **z** 90640; pop. incl. with Montebello (Inc. Place)
Montecito; CDP; SANTA BARBARA; **152** SI-8; elev. 100ft./30m.; 🅿; ★ **S.BAR**; **z** 93108, **z** 93150; © 10,000
Monte Nido; RMC Place; LOS ANGELES; ***152** SJ-10; elev. 590ft./180m.; 🅿; ★ **L.A.**; **z** 91302; ● 850
Monterey; Inc. Place; MONTEREY; **152** SC-2; elev. 40ft./12m.; 🅿 🅷 🅲 2,601 ■; ★ **MTRY-**; **z** 93940, **z** 93942-44; Ⓟ 31,954; © 29,674; Ⓡ 29,696; ◆ 27,236
MONTEREY; **152** SD-5; Ⓟ 355,660; © 401,762; ◆ 402,398
Monterey Acres; RMC Place; LOS ANGELES; ★ **L.A.**; pop. incl. with Lakewood (Inc. Place)
Monterey Park; Inc. Place; LOS ANGELES; **154** E-8; elev. 381ft./116m.; 🅿 🅷 ■; ★ **L.A.**; **z** 91754-56; Ⓟ 60,738; © 60,051; ◆ 60,285
Monte Rio; CDP; SONOMA; **150** NK-4; 🅿; ★ **S.ROS**; **z** 95462; Ⓟ 1,058; © 1,104
Monte Rosa; RMC Place; SONOMA; ★ **S.ROS**; mail Guerneville **z** 95446; rural
Montesano; RMC Place; SONOMA; ***150** NK-4; ★ **S.ROS**; mail Guerneville **z** 95446; rural
Monte Sereno; Inc. Place; SANTA CLARA; **151** NN-18; elev. 503ft./153m.; 🅿; ★ **SF-O-**; **z** 95030; Ⓟ 3,287; © 3,483
Monte Toyon; RMC Place; SANTA CRUZ; ***152** SB-3; elev. 260ft./79m.; ★ **S.CRZ**; mail Aptos **z** 95003; ● 950
Monte Vista (Monta Vista); RMC Place; SANTA CLARA; **151** NM-17; 🅿; ★ **SF-O-**; **z** 95014; pop. incl. with Cupertino (Inc. Place)
Montgomery Creek; CDP; SHASTA; **150** ND-6; elev. 2,140ft./652m.; 🅿; **z** 96065; © 96
Montgomery Creek Rancheria; Indian Reservation; SHASTA; © 5
Montgomery Village; RMC Place; SONOMA; ***150** NK-4; ★ **S.ROS**; mail Santa Rosa **z** 95405; pop. incl. with Santa Rosa (Inc. Place)
Montrose; RMC Place; LOS ANGELES; **154** C-7; elev. 1,350ft./411m.; 🅿; ★ **L.A.**; **z** 91020-21; ● 4,100
Moody; RMC Place; ORANGE; ★ **L.A.**; mail Cypress **z** 90630; pop. incl. with Cypress (Inc. Place)
Moonridge; RMC Place; SAN BERNARDINO; ***153** SI-14; mail Big Bear Lake **z** 92315; pop. incl. with Big Bear Lake (Inc. Place)
Moonstone; RMC Place; HUMBOLDT; ***150** ND-2; ★ **EUR-**; mail Trinidad **z** 95570; ● 150
Mooretown Rancheria; Indian Reservation; BUTTE; © 166
Moorpark; Inc. Place; VENTURA; **152** SI-9; elev. 513ft./156m.; 🅿; ★ **L.A.**; **z** 93020-21; Ⓟ 25,494; © 31,415; ◆ 33,970
Moorpark Home Acres; RMC Place; VENTURA; ***152** SI-9; ★ **L.A.**; mail Moorpark **z** 93021; ● 700
Morada; CDP-Census Area Only; SAN JOAQUIN; **149** G-10; 🅿; ★ **STOC**; **z** 95212; Ⓟ 3,570; © 3,726
Moraga (Moraga Town); Inc. Place; CONTRA COSTA; **151** NE-17; 🅿 🅲 4,172; ★ **SF-O-**; **z** 94556, **z** 94570, **z** 94575; Ⓟ 15,852; © 16,290
Moraga Town; CONTRA COSTA; see Moraga (Inc. Place)
Morena Village; RMC Place; SAN DIEGO; ***153** SN-15; elev. 3,200ft./975m.; mail Campo **z** 91906; ● 700
Moreno; RMC Place; RIVERSIDE; ★ **RIV-**; mail Moreno Valley **z** 92554-55; pop. incl. with Moreno Valley (Inc. Place)
Moreno; RMC Place; SAN DIEGO; ***153** SN-13; ★ **SDGO**; mail Lakeside **z** 92040
Moreno Valley; Inc. Place; RIVERSIDE; **153** SJ-13; elev. 1,597ft./487m.; 🅿 🅷; ★ **RIV-**; **z** 92551-57; Ⓟ 118,779; © 142,381; ◆ 182,281
Morgan Hill; Inc. Place; SANTA CLARA; **152** SA-3; elev. 345ft./105m.; 🅿 🅷; ★ **SF-O-**; **z** 95037-38; Ⓟ 23,928; © 33,556; ◆ 39,438
Mormon Bar; RMC Place; MARIPOSA; **150** NN-10; mail Mariposa **z** 95338; ● 130
Morningside Park; RMC Place; LOS ANGELES; ***153** SJ-11; elev. 215ft./66m.; ★ **L.A.**; mail Inglewood **z** 90305; pop. incl. with Inglewood (Inc. Place)
Morongo Reservation; Indian Reservation; RIVERSIDE; mail Banning **z** 92220; Ⓟ 414; © 954
Morongo Valley; CDP; SAN BERNARDINO; **153** SJ-15; elev. 2,538ft./774m.; 🅿; **z** 92256; Ⓟ 1,544; © 1,929
Morro Bay; Inc. Place; SAN LUIS OBISPO; **152** SF-5; elev. 200ft./61m.; 🅿; **z** 93442-43; Ⓟ 9,664; © 10,350
Moss Beach; CDP; SAN MATEO; **151** NJ-12; 🅿 🅷; ★ **SF-O-**; **z** 94038; Ⓟ 3,002; © 1,953
Mossdale; RMC Place; SAN JOAQUIN; ***150** NM-7; ★ **STOC**; mail Lathrop **z** 95330; pop. incl. with Lathrop (Inc. Place)
Moss Landing; CDP; MONTEREY; ***152** SB-3; 🅿; ★ **SLNS**; **z** 95039; © 300
Mountain Center; RMC Place; RIVERSIDE; **153** SK-14; 🅿; **z** 92561; ● 100
Mountain Gate; RMC Place; SHASTA; **150** NE-5; elev. 886ft./270m.; ★ **REDD**; mail Redding **z** 96003
Mountain Home Village; RMC Place; SAN BERNARDINO; ***153** SJ-14; ★ **RIV-**; mail Mentone **z** 92359; ● 200
Mountain House; RMC Place; ALAMEDA; ***150** NM-7; ★ **SF-O-**; mail Tracy **z** 95376; rural
Mountain House; RMC Place; BUTTE; ***150** NG-7; elev. 3,600ft./1,097m.; mail Berry Creek **z** 95916
Mountain Mesa; CDP; KERN; ***152** SF-10; 🅿; **z** 93240; Ⓟ 1,153; © 716
Mountain Pass; RMC Place; SAN BERNARDINO; **153** SF-17; elev. 4,730ft./1,442m.; 🅿; **z** 92366
Mountain Ranch; CDP; CALAVERAS; ***150** NL-9; elev. 2,117ft./645m.; 🅿; **z** 95246; © 1,557
Mountain Ranch; RMC Place; MADERA; ***152** SA-7; elev. 843ft./257m.; mail Madera **z** 93638; rural
Mountain Rest Station; RMC Place; FRESNO; ***152** SB-8; elev. 4,000ft./1,219m.; mail Shaver Lake **z** 93664; rural
Mountain View; CDP-Census Area Only; CONTRA COSTA; ***150** NL-6; ★ **SF-O-**; © 2,468
Mountain View; Inc. Place; SANTA CLARA; **151** NL-17; elev. 97ft./30m.; 🅿 🅷 ■; ★ **SF-O-**; **z** 94035, **z** 94039-43; Ⓟ 67,460; © 70,708; ◆ 73,380
Mountain View Acres; CDP-Census Area Only; SAN BERNARDINO; ***153** SI-13; ★ **HESP-**; mail Victorville **z** 92392; Ⓟ 2,469; © 2,521
Mount Aukum; EL DORADO; see Aukum (RMC Place)
Mount Baldy; RMC Place; SAN BERNARDINO, LOS ANGELES; **155** B-14; mail Mt Baldy **z** 91759; ● 200
Mount Bullion; RMC Place; MARIPOSA; **150** NN-10; mail Mariposa **z** 95338
Mount Eden; RMC Place; ALAMEDA; ***150** NM-6; 🅿; ★ **SF-O-**; **z** 94557; pop. incl. with Hayward (Inc. Place)
Mount Hamilton (Lick Observatory); RMC Place; SANTA CLARA; ***150** NN-7; elev. 4,213ft./1,284m.; 🅿; **z** 95140; rural
Mount Hannah Lodge; RMC Place; LAKE; ***150** NJ-4; elev. 2,600ft./792m.; mail Kelseyville **z** 95451; ● 100
Mount Hebron; CDP; SISKIYOU; **150** NB-6; elev. 4,256ft./1,297m.; mail Macdoel **z** 96058; © 92
Mount Helix; RMC Place; SAN DIEGO; ***153** SN-14; elev. 1,000ft./305m.; ★ **SDGO**; mail La Mesa **z** 91941; ● 6,400
Mount Hermon; RMC Place; SANTA CRUZ; ***152** SB-2; 🅿; ★ **S.CRZ**; **z** 95041; ● 970
Mount Laguna; RMC Place; SAN DIEGO; ***153** SM-15; 🅿; **z** 91948; rural
Mount Shasta; Inc. Place; SISKIYOU; **150** NC-5; elev. 3,554ft./1,083m.; 🅿 🅷; **z** 96067; Ⓟ 3,460; © 3,621
Mount Signal; RMC Place; IMPERIAL; ***153** SN-17; mail Calexico **z** 92231; rural
Mount View; RMC Place; CONTRA COSTA; **151** NC-17; elev. 36ft./11m.; ★ **SF-O-**; mail Martinez **z** 94553; ● 1,500
Mugginsville; RMC Place; SISKIYOU; **150** NB-4; elev. 2,934ft./894m.; mail Fort Jones **z** 96032; ● 50
Muir; RMC Place; MENDOCINO; ***150** NH-3; mail Willits **z** 95490; pop. incl. with Willits (Inc. Place)
Muir Beach; CDP-Census Area Only; MARIN; **151** NE-11; 🅿; ★ **SF-O-**; **z** 94965; © 295
Mulford; RMC Place; ALAMEDA; ★ **SF-O-**; pop. incl. with San Leandro (Inc. Place)
Mulford Gardens; RMC Place; ALAMEDA; ***150** NM-5; ★ **SF-O-**; pop. incl. with San Leandro (Inc. Place)
Murietta Farm; RMC Place; FRESNO; ***152** SC-6; elev. 255ft./78m.; mail Mendota **z** 93640; rural
Murphys; CDP; CALAVERAS; **150** NL-9; elev. 2,171ft./662m.; 🅿; **z** 95247 & mail Douglas Flat **z** 95229; Ⓟ 1,517; © 2,061
Murray Park; RMC Place; MARIN; ***150** NL-5; elev. 73ft./22m.; ★ **SF-O-**; mail Larkspur **z** 94939
Murrieta; Inc. Place; RIVERSIDE; **153** SK-13; elev. 1,093ft./333m.; 🅿 🅷; **z** 92562-64; Ⓟ 18,557; © 44,282; ◆ 99,197
Murrieta Hot Springs; CDP; RIVERSIDE; ***153** SK-13; mail Murrieta **z** 92562-64; Ⓟ 1,938; © 2,948
Muscatel; RMC Place; FRESNO; ***152** SB-7; ★ **FRES**; pop. incl. with Fresno (Inc. Place)
Muscoy; CDP; SAN BERNARDINO; **155** D-18; elev. 1,385ft./422m.; 🅿; ★ **RIV-**; **z** 92407 & mail San Bernardino **z** 92405; Ⓟ 7,541; © 8,919
Myers Flat; RMC Place; HUMBOLDT; **150** NF-2; elev. 204ft./62m.; 🅿; **z** 95554; ● 120
Myrtletown (Ryans Slough); CDP-Census Area Only; HUMBOLDT; ***150** ND-2; ★ **EUR-**; mail Eureka **z** 95501; Ⓟ 4,413; © 4,459

N

Nacomis Indian Rancheria; RMC Place; MENDOCINO; ***150** NI-4; elev. 739ft./225m.; mail Hopland **z** 95449; ● 100
Nadeau; RMC Place; LOS ANGELES; ***153** SJ-11; ★ **L.A.**; mail Los Angeles **z** 90001; ● 7,000
Nanceville; RMC Place; TULARE; mail Porterville **z** 93257; ● 600
Napa; Inc. Place; ⊡ NAPA; **150** NK-5; elev. 17ft./5m.; 🅿 🅷 ■; ★ **NAPA**; **z** 94558-59, **z** 94581 & mail Suisun City **z** 94585; Ⓟ 61,842; © 72,585; ◆ 77,077
NAPA; **150** NK-5; Ⓟ 110,765; © 124,279; ◆ 130,626
Napa Junction; RMC Place; NAPA; **150** NL-5; elev. 74ft./23m.; ★ **SF-O-**; mail Vallejo **z** 94590; rural
Naples; RMC Place; LOS ANGELES; ***153** SK-11; ★ **L.A.**; mail Long Beach **z** 90803; pop. incl. with Long Beach (Inc. Place)
Naples (Dos Pueblos); RMC Place; SANTA BARBARA; mail Goleta **z** 93117; ● 200
Napoleon Street; RMC Place; SAN FRANCISCO; ★ **SF-O-**; mail San Francisco **z** 94124; pop. incl. with San Francisco (Inc. Place)
Narlon; RMC Place; SANTA BARBARA; elev. 141ft./43m.
Nashville; RMC Place; EL DORADO; ***150** NK-8; ★ **SAC**; mail El Dorado **z** 95623
National City; Inc. Place; SAN DIEGO; **153** SN-14; elev. 25ft./8m.; 🅿 🅷 ■; ★ **SDGO**; **z** 91950-51; Ⓟ 54,249; © 54,260; ◆ 55,402
Navajo; RMC Place; SAN DIEGO; ★ **SDGO**; mail San Diego **z** 92119, **z** 92159; pop. incl. with San Diego (Inc. Place)
Navarro; RMC Place; MENDOCINO; **150** NI-3; elev. 272ft./83m.; 🅿; **z** 95463; ● 250
Navelencia; RMC Place; FRESNO; ***152** SC-8; elev. 419ft./128m.; mail Reedley **z** 93654; ● 300
Nebo; RMC Place; SAN BERNARDINO; mail Barstow **z** 92311
Nebo Center; CDP-Census Area Only; SAN BERNARDINO; ***153** SH-14; mail Barstow **z** 92311; Ⓟ 1,459; © 1,174
Needles; Inc. Place; SAN BERNARDINO; **153** SH-19; elev. 488ft./149m.; 🅿 🅷; **z** 92363; Ⓟ 5,191; © 4,830
Nelson; RMC Place; BUTTE; **150** NH-6; 🅿; **z** 95958; ● 150
Nestor; RMC Place; SAN DIEGO; ***153** SN-14; 🅿; ★ **SDGO**; **z** 92153; pop. incl. with San Diego (Inc. Place)
NEVADA; **150** NH-9; Ⓟ 78,510; © 92,033; ◆ 93,594
Nevada City; Inc. Place; ⊡ NEVADA; **150** NI-8; elev. 2,525ft./770m.; 🅿; **z** 95959; Ⓟ 2,855; © 3,001
New Almaden (Almaden); RMC Place; SANTA CLARA; ***152** SA-3; 🅿; ★ **SF-O-**; **z** 95042; ● 250
Newark; Inc. Place; ALAMEDA; **150** NM-6; elev. 16ft./5m.; 🅿; ★ **SF-O-**; **z** 94560; Ⓟ 37,861; © 42,471; ◆ 43,471
New Auberry; RMC Place; FRESNO; ***152** SB-8; mail Auberry **z** 93602; ● 600
Newberry; SAN BERNARDINO; see Newberry Springs (RMC Place)
Newberry Springs (Newberry); RMC Place; SAN BERNARDINO; **153** SH-14; 🅿; **z** 92338, **z** 92365; ● 1,500
Newburg; RMC Place; HUMBOLDT; ***150** NE-1; elev. 158ft./48m.; ★ **EUR-**; mail Fortuna **z** 95540; rural
Newbury Park; RMC Place; VENTURA; ***152** SJ-9; elev. 700ft./213m.; 🅿; ★ **OXN-**; **z** 91319-20; pop. incl. with Thousand Oaks (Inc. Place)
Newcastle; RMC Place; PLACER; **150** NJ-8; 🅿; ★ **SAC**; **z** 95658; ● 2,200
New Cuyama; RMC Place; SANTA BARBARA; **152** SH-8; 🅿; **z** 93254; ● 360
Newell; RMC Place; MODOC; **150** NA-7; 🅿; **z** 96134; ● 480
New England Mills; PLACER; see Weimar (RMC Place)
Newhall (Santa Clarita); RMC Place; LOS ANGELES; ***152** SI-10; elev. 1,272ft./388m.; 🅿 🅷; ★ **L.A.**; **z** 91321-22, **z** 91381 & mail Santa Clarita **z** 91382; pop. incl. with Santa Clarita (Inc. Place)
Newhall Ranch; RMC Place; LOS ANGELES; ***152** SI-10; ★ **L.A.**; mail Santa Clarita **z** 91350
New Helvetia; RMC Place; SACRAMENTO; ★ **SAC**; mail Sacramento **z** 95815; pop. incl. with Sacramento (Inc. Place)
New London; TULARE; see London (CDP)
Newman; Inc. Place; STANISLAUS; **150** NN-8; elev. 91ft./28m.; 🅿; **z** 95360; Ⓟ 4,151; © 7,093
New Monterey; RMC Place; MONTEREY; ***152** SC-2; ★ **MTRY-**; mail Monterey **z** 93940; pop. incl. with Monterey (Inc. Place)
New Pine Creek; RMC Place; MODOC; ***150** NA-10; 🅿; **z** 97635; ● 210
Newport Beach; Inc. Place; ORANGE; **153** SK-12; 🅿 🅷 🅲 550 ■; ★ **L.A.**; **z** 92657-63; Ⓟ 66,643; © 70,032; ◆ 79,215
Newport Coast; CDP-Census Area Only; ORANGE; ***153** SK-12; 🅿; ★ **L.A.**; **z** 92657; © 2,671

Entries in **UPPERCASE** are counties.
Entries in **bold** have populations of 2,500 or more.
Names in parentheses are alternate names.

Inc. Place	Incorporated Place
RMC Place	Rand McNally Designated Place
CDP	Census Designated Place
MCD	Minor Civil Division
⊡	County Seat
▲	Minor Civil Division
elev.	Elevation
🅿	Post Office
🅷	Hospital
🅲	College
■	Principal Business Center
★	Ranally Metro Area (RMA) Abbreviation
z	Zip Code(s)
Ⓟ	Previous Census Population
Ⓡ	Revised Census Population
Ⓐ	Annexation Population
●	Rand McNally Population Estimate
©	Final Census Population
Ⓢ	Special Census Population
◆	Estimated Population

For additional definitions see Glossary, Volume 1, and Introduction, Volume 2.

Newport Heights; RMC Place; ORANGE; *153 SK-12; ★ L.A.; mail Newport Beach z 92663; pop. incl. with Newport Beach (Inc. Place)

Newport Island; RMC Place; ORANGE; ★ L.A.; mail Newport Beach z 92663; pop. incl. with Newport Beach (Inc. Place)

Newtown; RMC Place; EL DORADO; *150 NJ-9; mail Placerville z 95667; ● 100

Newtown; RMC Place; NEVADA; *150 NI-8; mail Nevada City z 95959; rural

Newville; RMC Place; GLENN; *150 NG-5; mail Orland z 95963; rural

Nicasio; RMC Place; MARIN; 150 NL-4; [P]; z 94946

Nice; CDP; LAKE; 150 NI-4; [P]; z 95464; Ⓟ 2,126; © 2,509

Nicholls Warm Springs; RIVERSIDE; see Mesa Verde (RMC Place)

Nichols; RMC Place; CONTRA COSTA; *150 NL-6; ★ SF-O-; mail Pittsburg z 94565; rural

Nicolaus; RMC Place; SUTTER; 150 NJ-7; elev. 34ft./10m.; [P]; z 95659; ● 150

Nightingale; RIVERSIDE; see Pinyon Pines (RMC Place)

Niguel Terrace; RMC Place; ORANGE; ★ L.A.; mail Laguna Niguel z 92677; pop. incl. with Laguna Niguel (Inc. Place)

Niland; CDP; IMPERIAL; 153 SL-17; elev. 141ft./43m.; [P]; z 92257; Ⓟ 1,183; © 1,143

Niles; RMC Place; ALAMEDA; ★ SF-O-; mail Fremont z 94536; pop. incl. with Fremont (Inc. Place)

Niles Junction; RMC Place; ALAMEDA; *150 NM-6; ★ SF-O-; mail Fremont z 94536; pop. incl. with Fremont (Inc. Place)

Nimshew; RMC Place; BUTTE; *150 NG-7; mail Magalia z 95954; ● 30

Nipinnawasee; RMC Place; MADERA; *151 NN-11; elev. 2,800ft./853m.; mail Ahwahnee z 93601; ● 300

Nipomo; CDP; SAN LUIS OBISPO; 152 SG-6; elev. 330ft./101m.; [P]; ★ S.MAR; z 93444; Ⓟ 7,109; © 12,626

Nipton; RMC Place; SAN BERNARDINO; 153 SF-18; elev. 3,042ft./927m.; [P]; z 92364; ● 25

Nitro; RMC Place; CONTRA COSTA; *150 NL-5; ★ SF-O-; pop. incl. with Richmond (Inc. Place)

Nob Hill; RMC Place; SAN FRANCISCO; ★ SF-O-; mail San Francisco z 94108; pop. incl. with San Francisco (Inc. Place)

Noe Valley; RMC Place; SAN FRANCISCO; ★ SF-O-; mail San Francisco z 94114; pop. incl. with San Francisco (Inc. Place)

No Mirage; RMC Place; IMPERIAL; *153 SN-16; elev. 300ft./91m.; mail Ocotillo z 92259; ● 100

Norco; Inc. Place; RIVERSIDE; 153 SJ-12; elev. 680ft./207m.; [P]; ★ RIV-; z 92860; Ⓟ 23,302; © 24,157; ◆ 24,667

Nord; RMC Place; BUTTE; 150 NG-6; mail Chico z 95973; ● 80

Norden; RMC Place; NEVADA; 150 NI-10; [P]; z 95724

Normal Heights; RMC Place; SAN DIEGO; *153 SN-13; ★ SDGO; mail San Diego z 92116; pop. incl. with San Diego (Inc. Place)

North Auburn; CDP-Census Area Only; PLACER; *150 NJ-8; ★ SAC; mail Auburn z 95603; Ⓟ 10,301; © 11,847

North Beach; RMC Place; SAN FRANCISCO; *150 NM-5; ★ SF-O-; mail San Francisco z 94133; pop. incl. with San Francisco (Inc. Place)

North Belridge; RMC Place; KERN; *152 SF-7; elev. 650ft./198m.; mail Casmalia z 93429; rural

North Berkeley; RMC Place; ALAMEDA; ★ SF-O-; mail Berkeley z 94709; pop. incl. with Berkeley (Inc. Place)

North Bloomfield; RMC Place; NEVADA; 150 NH-8; mail Nevada City z 95959

North Clairemont; RMC Place; SAN DIEGO; *153 SM-13; ★ SDGO; mail San Diego z 92117; pop. incl. with San Diego (Inc. Place)

North Columbia; RMC Place; NEVADA; *150 NH-8; elev. 3,018ft./920m.; mail Nevada City z 95959; rural

Northcrest; RMC Place; DEL NORTE; mail Crescent City z 95531; pop. incl. with Crescent City (Inc. Place)

North Downey; RMC Place; LOS ANGELES; *153 SJ-11; ★ L.A.; mail Downey z 90240; pop. incl. with Downey (Inc. Place)

Northeast Modesto; RMC Place; STANISLAUS; ★ MOD; mail Modesto z 95355; pop. incl. with Modesto (Inc. Place)

North Edwards (Edgemont Acres); CDP; KERN; 153 SG-12; [P]; z 93523; Ⓟ 1,259; © 1,227

North El Monte; CDP-Census Area Only; LOS ANGELES; *153 SJ-11; ★ L.A.; mail Arcadia z 91006; Ⓟ 3,384; © 3,703

North Elsinore; RMC Place; RIVERSIDE; *153 SK-13; elev. 1,275ft./389m.; mail Lake Elsinore z 92530; pop. incl. with Lake Elsinore (Inc. Place)

North Fair Oaks; CDP; SAN MATEO; 151 NK-16; elev. 20ft./6m.; ★ SF-O-; mail Menlo Park z 94025; Ⓟ 13,912; © 15,440

North Fork; RMC Place; MADERA; 152 SA-8; [P]; z 93643; ● 500

North Fork Rancheria; Indian Reservation; MADERA; © 9

Northgate; RMC Place; SACRAMENTO; ★ SAC; pop. incl. with Sacramento (Inc. Place)

North Glendale; RMC Place; LOS ANGELES; *153 SJ-11; elev. 525ft./160m.; ★ L.A.; mail Glendale z 91202, San Diego z 92122; pop. incl. with Glendale (Inc. Place)

North Highlands; CDP; SACRAMENTO; 150 NJ-7; elev. 100ft./30m.; [P]; ★ SAC; z 95660 & mail Mcclellan z 95652, Sacramento z 95821; Ⓟ 42,105; © 44,187; ◆ 50,910

North Hills; RMC Place; LOS ANGELES; *152 SJ-10; [P]; ★ L.A.; z 91343, z 91393; pop. incl. with Los Angeles (Inc. Place)

North Hollywood; RMC Place; LOS ANGELES; *152 SJ-10; [P]; ★ L.A.; z 91601-12, z 91614-18; pop. incl. with Los Angeles (Inc. Place)

North Inglewood; RMC Place; LOS ANGELES; ★ L.A.; mail Inglewood z 90302, z 90309; pop. incl. with Inglewood (Inc. Place)

North Lakeport; CDP-Census Area Only; LAKE; *150 NI-4; elev. 1,339ft./408m.; mail Lakeport z 95453; © 2,879

North Loma Linda; RMC Place; SAN BERNARDINO; ★ RIV-; mail Loma Linda z 92354; pop. incl. with Loma Linda (Inc. Place)

North Long Beach; RMC Place; LOS ANGELES; *153 SK-11; ★ L.A.; mail Long Beach z 90805; pop. incl. with Long Beach (Inc. Place)

North Modesto; RMC Place; STANISLAUS; ★ MOD; mail Modesto z 95356; pop. incl. with Modesto (Inc. Place)

North Oakland; RMC Place; ALAMEDA; ★ SF-O-; mail Oakland z 94609; pop. incl. with Oakland (Inc. Place)

North Palm Springs; RMC Place; RIVERSIDE; *153 SJ-15; [P]; ★ PSPR-; z 92258; ● 550

Northpark; RMC Place; SAN BERNARDINO; ★ RIV-; mail San Bernardino z 92427; pop. incl. with San Bernardino (Inc. Place)

North Park; RMC Place; SAN DIEGO; *153 SN-13; ★ SDGO; mail San Diego z 92104, z 92164; pop. incl. with San Diego (Inc. Place)

North Pomona; RMC Place; LOS ANGELES; *153 SJ-12; ★ L.A.; pop. incl. with Pomona (Inc. Place)

North Redondo Beach; RMC Place; LOS ANGELES; ★ L.A.; mail Redondo Beach z 90278; pop. incl. with Redondo Beach (Inc. Place)

North Richmond; RMC Place; CONTRA COSTA; 151 ND-14; [P]; ★ SF-O-; z 94801 & mail Richmond z 94804; ● 2,200

Northridge; RMC Place; LOS ANGELES; *152 SJ-10; elev. 812ft./247m.; [P]; ★ L.A.; z 91324-30, z 91343; pop. incl. with Los Angeles (Inc. Place)

North Sacramento; RMC Place; SACRAMENTO; *150 NK-7; ★ SAC; mail Sacramento z 95815; pop. incl. with Sacramento (Inc. Place)

North Samoa; HUMBOLDT; see Manila (RMC Place)

North San Jose; RMC Place; SANTA CLARA; ★ SF-O-; pop. incl. with San Jose (Inc. Place)

North San Juan; RMC Place; NEVADA; 150 NH-8; [P]; z 95960; ● 200

North Santa Ana; RMC Place; ORANGE; ★ L.A.; pop. incl. with Santa Ana (Inc. Place)

North Santa Maria; RMC Place; SANTA BARBARA; *152 SG-6; elev. 208ft./63m.; ★ S.MAR; pop. incl. with Santa Maria (Inc. Place)

North Shore; RMC Place; RIVERSIDE; 153 SK-16; mail Mecca z 92254; ● 500

North Shore; RIVERSIDE; see Desert Beach (RMC Place)

Northside; RMC Place; RIVERSIDE; ★ PSPR-; mail Palm Desert z 92260; pop. incl. with Palm Desert (Inc. Place)

North Stanton; RMC Place; ORANGE; ★ L.A.; pop. incl. with Stanton (Inc. Place)

North Torrance; RMC Place; LOS ANGELES; ★ L.A.; mail Torrance z 90504; pop. incl. with Torrance (Inc. Place)

North Tustin (Tustin Foothills); CDP; ORANGE; *153 SK-12; ★ L.A.; mail Tustin z 92782; Ⓟ 24,358; © 24,044; ◆ 25,213

North Woodbridge; CDP-Census Area Only; SAN JOAQUIN; *150 NL-7; ★ STOC; © 1,320

Norwalk; Inc. Place; LOS ANGELES; 153 SJ-11; elev. 93ft./28m.; [P] [H] ■; ★ L.A.; z 90650-52; Ⓟ 94,279; © 103,298; Ⓡ 104,323; ◆ 107,495

Norwalk Manor; RMC Place; LOS ANGELES; *153 SJ-11; ★ L.A.; mail Norwalk z 90650; pop. incl. with Norwalk (Inc. Place)

Novato; Inc. Place; MARIN; 150 NL-5; elev. 18ft./5m.; [P] [H]; ★ SF-O-; z 94945, z 94947-49, z 94998; Ⓟ 47,585; © 47,630; ◆ 48,370

Noyo; RMC Place; MENDOCINO; 150 NH-2; mail Fort Bragg z 95437; pop. incl. with Fort Bragg (Inc. Place)

Nubieber; RMC Place; LASSEN; 150 ND-8; [P]; z 96068

Nuevo; CDP; RIVERSIDE; 155 I-20; [P]; z 92567; Ⓟ 3,010; © 4,135

Number Twenty Three; RMC Place; SAN FRANCISCO; ★ SF-O-; mail San Francisco z 94123; pop. incl. with San Francisco (Inc. Place)

Nut Tree; RMC Place; SOLANO; [P]; ★ FRFL-; z 95696; pop. incl. with Vacaville (Inc. Place)

Nyeland Acres; VENTURA; see Nyland (RMC Place)

Nyland (Nyeland Acres); RMC Place; VENTURA; 156 B-3; ★ OXN-; mail Oxnard z 93036; ● 2,200

O

Oakdale; Inc. Place; STANISLAUS; 150 NM-8; elev. 155ft./47m.; [P] [H]; ★ MOD; z 95361; Ⓟ 11,961; © 15,503; ◆ 17,792

Oak Glen; RMC Place; SAN BERNARDINO; *153 SJ-14; [P]; ★ RIV-; z 92399; ● 300

Oak Grove; RMC Place; BUTTE; *150 NH-7; mail Oroville z 95965-66

Oak Grove; RMC Place; SAN DIEGO; 153 SL-14; elev. 2,787ft./849m.; mail Aguanga z 92536; ● 100

Oak Grove; RMC Place; SAN MATEO; ★ SF-O-; mail Menlo Park z 94025; pop. incl. with Menlo Park (Inc. Place)

Oak Grove; RMC Place; SANTA CLARA; ★ SF-O-; pop. incl. with San Jose (Inc. Place)

Oak Hills; RMC Place; MONTEREY; *152 SB-3; elev. 100ft./30m.; ★ SLNS; mail Salinas z 93907; ● 750

Oakhurst (Fresno Flats); CDP; MADERA; 151 NN-11; elev. 2,289ft./698m.; [P]; z 93644; Ⓟ 2,602; © 2,868

Oak Knoll; RMC Place; NAPA; mail Napa z 94558; ● 400

Oak Knoll Hills; RMC Place; SANTA CLARA; ★ SF-O-; mail Cupertino z 95014; pop. incl. with Cupertino (Inc. Place)

Oak Knolls; RMC Place; SANTA BARBARA; *152 SH-6; ★ S.MAR; mail Santa Maria z 93455; ● 1,600

Oakland; Inc. Place; ⊡ ALAMEDA; 150 NM-5; elev. 42ft./13m.; [P] [H] [C] 4,307 ■; ★ SF-O-; z 94601-15, z 94617-24, z 94649, z 94659-62, z 94666; Ⓟ 372,242; © 399,484; ◆ 403,494

Oakley; Inc. Place; CONTRA COSTA; 150 NL-6; elev. 18ft./5m.; [P]; ★ SF-O-; z 94561 & mail Brentwood z 94513; Ⓟ 18,374; © 25,619; ◆ 29,342

Oakmont; RMC Place; SONOMA; *150 NK-5; ★ S.ROS; mail Santa Rosa z 95409; pop. incl. with Santa Rosa (Inc. Place)

Oak Mountain; SONOMA; see Preston (RMC Place)

Oak Park; RMC Place; SACRAMENTO; *150 NK-7; ★ SAC; mail Sacramento z 95817; pop. incl. with Sacramento (Inc. Place)

Oak Park; RMC Place; SAN LUIS OBISPO; *152 SF-5; mail Paso Robles z 93446; pop. incl. with Paso Robles (Inc. Place)

Oak Park (Oak Valley); CDP; VENTURA; 154 C-1; [P]; ★ OXN-; z 91301, z 91377; Ⓟ 2,412; © 2,320

Oak Park Estates; RMC Place; CALAVERAS; mail San Andreas z 95249; ● 450

Oakridge; RMC Place; SAN JOAQUIN; ★ STOC; mail Stockton z 95207; pop. incl. with Stockton (Inc. Place)

Oak Run; RMC Place; SHASTA; 150 NE-6; [P]; z 96069; ● 250

Oaks; RMC Place; SAN LUIS OBISPO; *152 SG-5; mail Arroyo Grande z 93420; pop. incl. with Arroyo Grande (Inc. Place)

Oak Shores; RMC Place; SAN LUIS OBISPO; *152 SE-4; elev. 1,093ft./333m.; mail Bradley z 93426; ● 235

Oak Valley; VENTURA; see Oak Park (CDP)

Oak View; CDP; VENTURA; 152 SI-8; elev. 520ft./158m.; [P]; ★ OXN-; z 93022; Ⓟ 3,606; © 4,199

Oakville; RMC Place; NAPA; 150 NK-5; elev. 155ft./47m.; [P]; z 94562; ● 220

Oakwood; RMC Place; LOS ANGELES; [P]; ★ L.A.; z 90004; pop. incl. with Los Angeles (Inc. Place)

Oasis; RMC Place; MONO; *151 NN-15; elev. 5,030ft./1,533m.; mail Dyer z 89010; rural

O'Brien; RMC Place; SHASTA; 150 ND-5; [P]; z 96070; ● 30

Occidental; CDP; SONOMA; 150 NK-4; [P]; ★ S.ROS; z 95465 & mail Camp Meeker z 95419; Ⓟ 1,300; © 1,272

Ocean Beach; RMC Place; SAN DIEGO; 156 J-5; ★ SDGO; mail San Diego z 92107, z 92167

Ocean Cove; SONOMA; see Walsh Landing (RMC Place)

Oceano; CDP; SAN LUIS OBISPO; 152 SG-5; elev. 25ft./8m.; [P]; z 93445, z 93475; Ⓟ 6,169; © 7,260

Ocean Park; RMC Place; LOS ANGELES; *152 SJ-10; elev. 23ft./7m.; ★ L.A.; mail Santa Monica z 90405, z 90409; pop. incl. with Santa Monica (Inc. Place)

Oceanside; Inc. Place; SAN DIEGO; 153 SL-13; elev. 47ft./14m.; [P] [H] ■; ★ SDGO; z 92049, z 92051-52, z 92054-58 & mail San Luis Rey z 92068; Ⓟ 128,398; © 161,029; ◆ 183,501

Ocean View; RMC Place; ORANGE; *153 SK-11; elev. 26ft./8m.; ★ L.A.; mail Huntington Beach z 92647; pop. incl. with Huntington Beach (Inc. Place)

Ocean View; RMC Place; SAN FRANCISCO; ★ SF-O-; mail San Francisco z 94112; pop. incl. with San Francisco (Inc. Place)

Ocean View (Wrights Beach); RMC Place; SONOMA; 150 NK-3; mail Bodega Bay z 94923; ● 100

Ockenden; RMC Place; FRESNO; *152 SB-8; elev. 5,600ft./1,707m.; mail Shaver Lake z 93664; ● 100

Ocotillo; CDP; IMPERIAL; 153 SN-16; [P]; z 92259; © 296

Ocotillo Wells; RMC Place; SAN DIEGO; 153 SL-16; elev. 163ft./50m.; mail Borrego Springs z 92004; ● 200

Odd Fellows Park; RMC Place; SONOMA; *150 NK-4; ★ S.ROS; mail Guerneville z 95446; ● 100

Oildale; CDP; KERN; 152 SF-9; elev. 455ft./139m.; ★ BAK; mail Bakersfield z 93308, z 93388; Ⓟ 26,553; © 27,885; ◆ 34,210

Ojai; Inc. Place; VENTURA; 152 SI-8; elev. 746ft./227m.; [P] [H]; ★ OXN-; z 93023-24; Ⓟ 7,613; © 7,862

Olancha; CDP; INYO; 153 SD-11; elev. 3,648ft./1,112m.; [P]; z 93549; © 134

Old Fort Jim; RMC Place; EL DORADO; *150 NJ-9; mail Placerville z 95667; ● 450

Old Gilroy; RMC Place; SANTA CLARA; *152 SB-3; elev. 175ft./53m.; ★ SF-O-; mail Gilroy z 95020; rural

Old Hopland; RMC Place; MENDOCINO; *150 NI-3; mail Hopland z 95449; ● 300

Old Mammoth; RMC Place; MONO; *151 NN-13; mail Mammoth Lakes z 93546; pop. incl. with Mammoth Lakes (Inc. Place)

Old River; RMC Place; KERN; 152 SG-9; ★ BAK; mail Bakersfield z 93309; ● 200

Old Station; RMC Place; SHASTA; 150 NE-7; [P]; z 96071

Old Town; RMC Place; RIVERSIDE; mail Temecula z 92593; pop. incl. with Temecula (Inc. Place)

Old Town; RMC Place; SAN DIEGO; *153 SN-13; ★ SDGO; mail San Diego z 92110; pop. incl. with San Diego (Inc. Place)

Old Towne; RMC Place; KERN; ★ BAK; pop. incl. with Tehachapi (Inc. Place)

Oleander; RMC Place; FRESNO; *152 SC-7; elev. 283ft./86m.; ★ FRES; mail Fresno z 93725; rural

Olema; RMC Place; MARIN; *150 NL-4; [P]; z 94950; ● 100

Olinda; RMC Place; ORANGE; ★ L.A.; mail Brea z 92821; pop. incl. with Brea (Inc. Place)

Olinda; RMC Place; SHASTA; 150 NE-5; elev. 762ft./232m.; ★ REDD; mail Anderson z 96007

Olive; RMC Place; ORANGE; *153 SK-12; elev. 226ft./69m.; ★ L.A.; mail Orange z 92857, z 92865; pop. incl. with Orange (Inc. Place)

Olivehurst; CDP; YUBA; 150 NI-7; elev. 60ft./18m.; [P]; ★ YUCY; z 95961; Ⓟ 9,738; © 11,061

Olivenhain; RMC Place; SAN DIEGO; *153 SM-13; elev. 127ft./39m.; ★ SDGO; mail Encinitas z 92024; pop. incl. with Encinitas (Inc. Place)

Olympia; RMC Place; SANTA CRUZ; *152 SA-2; ★ S.CRZ; mail Felton z 95018; ● 150

Olympic; RMC Place; LOS ANGELES; *152 SJ-10; ★ L.A.; mail Beverly Hills z 90212; pop. incl. with Beverly Hills (Inc. Place)

Olympic Valley (Squaw Valley); RMC Place; PLACER; 149 B-1; elev. 6,240ft./1,902m.; [P]; z 96146; rural

Omo Ranch; RMC Place; EL DORADO; 150 NK-9; mail Somerset z 95684

O'Neals; RMC Place; MADERA; 152 SA-7; elev. 1,313ft./400m.; [P]; z 93645

One Hundred Palms; RMC Place; RIVERSIDE; *153 SK-16; mail Thermal z 92274; ● 600

Ono; RMC Place; SHASTA; 150 NE-5; elev. 981ft./299m.; mail Igo z 96047; ● 60

Ontario; Inc. Place; SAN BERNARDINO; 153 SJ-12; elev. 988ft./301m.; [P] [H] [C] 422 ■; ★ L.A.; z 91710, z 91758, z 91761-62, z 91764; Ⓟ 133,179; © 158,007; ◆ 176,410

Onyx; CDP; KERN; 153 SE-11; [P]; z 93255; © 476

Opal Cliffs; CDP; SANTA CRUZ; *152 SB-2; ★ S.CRZ; mail Santa Cruz z 95062; Ⓟ 5,940; © 6,458

Ophir; RMC Place; PLACER; *150 NJ-8; ★ SAC; mail Auburn z 95603-04, Newcastle z 95658; ● 900

Orange; Inc. Place; ORANGE; 153 SK-12; elev. 187ft./57m.; [P] [H] [C] 5,732 ■; ★ L.A.; z 92856-57, z 92859, z 92861-69 & mail Norco z 92860; Ⓟ 110,658; © 128,821; Ⓡ 128,868; ◆ 136,738

ORANGE; 153 SK-12; Ⓟ 2,410,556; © 2,846,289; ◆ 2,985,498

Orange Center; RMC Place; RIVERSIDE; ★ RIV-; mail Riverside z 92501; pop. incl. with Riverside (Inc. Place)

Orange Cove; Inc. Place; FRESNO; 152 SC-8; elev. 425ft./130m.; [P]; z 93646, z 93675; Ⓟ 5,604; © 7,722

Orange Glen; RMC Place; SAN DIEGO; ★ SDGO; mail Escondido z 92027, z 92030; pop. incl. with Escondido (Inc. Place)

Orange Heights; RMC Place; SAN BERNARDINO; ★ L.A.; mail Upland z 91786; pop. incl. with Upland (Inc. Place)

Orangehurst; RMC Place; ORANGE; ★ L.A.; mail Fullerton z 92833, z 92837; pop. incl. with Fullerton (Inc. Place)

Orange Park Acres; RMC Place; ORANGE; 155 I-13; ★ L.A.; mail Orange z 92869

Orangevale; CDP; SACRAMENTO; 150 NJ-8; elev. 237ft./72m.; [P]; ★ SAC; z 95662; Ⓟ 26,266; © 26,705; ◆ 30,777

Orangewood; RMC Place; LOS ANGELES; ★ L.A.; mail Pasadena z 91115; pop. incl. with Pasadena (Inc. Place)

Orchard Farms; RMC Place; SANTA CLARA; ★ SF-O-; mail San Jose z 95170; pop. incl. with San Jose (Inc. Place)

Orcutt; CDP; SANTA BARBARA; 152 SH-6; [P]; ★ S.MAR; z 93455, z 93457; © 28,830; ◆ 29,726

Ordbend; RMC Place; GLENN; 150 NH-6; mail Glenn z 95943; ● 80

Oregon City; RMC Place; BUTTE; *150 NH-7; mail Oroville z 95965; ● 50

Oregon House; RMC Place; YUBA; 150 NH-7; elev. 1,530ft./466m.; [P]; z 95962; ● 300

Orick; RMC Place; HUMBOLDT; 150 NC-2; elev. 34ft./10m.; [P]; z 95555; ● 400

Orinda; Inc. Place; CONTRA COSTA; 150 NM-5; elev. 485ft./148m.; [P]; ★ SF-O-; z 94563; Ⓟ 16,642; © 17,599

Orinda Village; RMC Place; CONTRA COSTA; *150 NL-5; ★ SF-O-; mail Orinda z 94563; pop. incl. with Orinda (Inc. Place)

Orland; Inc. Place; GLENN; 150 NG-6; elev. 260ft./79m.; [P]; z 95963; Ⓟ 5,052; © 6,281

Orleans; RMC Place; HUMBOLDT; 150 NC-3; elev. 400ft./122m.; [P]; z 95556; ● 375

Ormand; RMC Place; RIVERSIDE; *153 SJ-13; ★ RIV-; mail Riverside z 92509; rural

Oro Fino; RMC Place; SISKIYOU; 150 NB-4; elev. 2,841ft./866m.; mail Fort Jones z 96032; ● 30

Oro Grande; RMC Place; SAN BERNARDINO; 153 SH-13; elev. 2,631ft./802m.; [P]; ★ HESP-; z 92368; ● 310

Oro Loma; RMC Place; FRESNO; *152 SB-5; elev. 171ft./52m.; mail Firebaugh z 93622; rural

Orosi; CDP; TULARE; 152 SC-8; [P]; z 93647; Ⓟ 5,486; © 7,318

Oroville; Inc. Place; ⊡ BUTTE; 150 NH-7; elev. 174ft./53m.; [P] [H] ■; z 95915, z 95940, z 95965-66, z 95980; Ⓟ 11,960; © 13,004; ◆ 14,145

Oroville East; CDP-Census Area Only; BUTTE; *150 NH-7; mail Oroville z 95965; Ⓟ 8,462; © 8,680

Ortonville; RMC Place; VENTURA; mail Ventura z 93001; ● 720

Osbourne; RMC Place; LOS ANGELES; ★ L.A.; mail Los Angeles z 90028; pop. incl. with Los Angeles (Inc. Place)

Otay; RMC Place; SAN DIEGO; 156 M-8; elev. 66ft./20m.; ★ SDGO; mail Chula Vista z 91911; pop. incl. with Chula Vista (Inc. Place)

Otay Mesa; RMC Place; SAN DIEGO; ★ SDGO; mail San Diego z 92153-54; pop. incl. with Chula Vista (Inc. Place)

Otterbein; RMC Place; LOS ANGELES; *153 SJ-12; elev. 508ft./155m.; ★ L.A.; mail Rowland Heights z 91748; ● 12,000

Outingdale; RMC Place; EL DORADO; 150 NK-9; mail Somerset z 95684; ● 400

Oval; RMC Place; TULARE; ★ VISL; mail Visalia z 93291; pop. incl. with Visalia (Inc. Place)

Oxnard; Inc. Place; VENTURA; 152 SJ-9; elev. 52ft./16m.; [P] [H] ■; ★ OXN-; z 93030-36; Ⓟ 142,216; © 170,358; ◆ 194,698

Oxnard Beach; RMC Place; VENTURA; *152 SJ-9; ★ OXN-; mail Oxnard z 93035

P

Pabco; RMC Place; ALAMEDA; ★ SF-O-; pop. incl. with Oakland (Inc. Place)

Pabrico; RMC Place; ALAMEDA; *150 NM-6; ★ SF-O-; mail Union City z 94587; pop. incl. with Union City (Inc. Place)

Pachappa; RMC Place; RIVERSIDE; *153 SJ-13; elev. 900ft./274m.; ★ RIV-; mail Riverside z 92506; pop. incl. with Riverside (Inc. Place)

Pacheco; CDP; CONTRA COSTA; 151 NC-17; [P]; ★ SF-O-; z 94553; Ⓟ 3,325; © 3,562

Pacific (Pacific House); RMC Place; EL DORADO; 150 NJ-9; mail Pollock Pines z 95726

Pacific; RMC Place; LOS ANGELES; *153 SK-11; ★ L.A.; mail Long Beach z 90806; pop. incl. with Long Beach (Inc. Place)

Pacifica; Inc. Place; SAN MATEO; 150 NM-5; elev. 60ft./18m.; [P]; ★ SF-O-; z 94044; Ⓟ 37,670; © 38,390; ◆ 36,775

Pacific Beach; RMC Place; SAN DIEGO; 156 H-5; ★ SDGO; mail San Diego z 92109, z 92169; pop. incl. with San Diego (Inc. Place)

Pacific Gardens; RMC Place; SAN JOAQUIN; *150 NL-7; ★ STOC; mail Stockton z 95204; ● 3,600

Pacific Grove; Inc. Place; MONTEREY; 152 SC-2; elev. 120ft./37m.; [P]; ★ MTRY-; z 93950; Ⓟ 16,117; © 15,522

Pacific Grove Acres; RMC Place; MONTEREY; *152 SC-2; elev. 120ft./37m.; ★ MTRY-; mail Pacific Grove z 93950; pop. incl. with Pacific Grove (Inc. Place)

Pacific House; EL DORADO; see Pacific (RMC Place)

Pacific Manor; RMC Place; HUMBOLDT; ★ EUR-; mail Arcata z 95521; pop. incl. with Arcata (Inc. Place)

Pacific Manor; RMC Place; SAN MATEO; *150 NM-5; ★ SF-O-; mail Pacifica z 94044; pop. incl. with Pacifica (Inc. Place)

Pacific Palisades; RMC Place; LOS ANGELES; *152 SJ-10; [P]; ★ L.A.; z 90272; pop. incl. with Los Angeles (Inc. Place)

Pacific Shores; RMC Place; DEL NORTE; *150 NA-2; elev. 20ft./6m.; mail Crescent City z 95531; rural

Pacific Union College; NAPA; see Angwin (CDP)

Pacific Valley; MONTEREY; see Plaskett (RMC Place)

Pacoima; RMC Place; LOS ANGELES; *152 SI-10; [P]; ★ L.A.; z 91331, z 91333-34; pop. incl. with Los Angeles (Inc. Place)

Paicines; RMC Place; SAN BENITO; 152 SB-4; [P]; z 95043; rural

Paintersville; RMC Place; SACRAMENTO; *150 NK-7; elev. 10ft./3m.; mail Courtland z 95615; ● 200

Pajaro; CDP; MONTEREY; 152 SB-3; [P]; ★ WATS; z 95076; Ⓟ 3,332; © 3,384; Ⓡ 3,420

Pala; RMC Place; SAN DIEGO; 153 SL-14; [P]; z 92059, z 92061; ● 1,050

Pala Mesa; RMC Place; SAN DIEGO; *153 SL-13; elev. 300ft./91m.; ★ SDGO; mail Fallbrook z 92028; ● 300

Pala Reservation; Indian Reservation; SAN DIEGO; mail Pala z 92059; Ⓟ 648; © 1,573

Palermo; CDP; BUTTE; 150 NH-7; elev. 190ft./58m.; [P]; z 95968; Ⓟ 5,260; © 5,720

Palm City; RMC Place; RIVERSIDE; ★ PSPR-; mail Palm Desert z 92211; pop. incl. with Palm Desert (Inc. Place)

Palm City; RMC Place; SAN DIEGO; *153 SN-14; elev. 44ft./13m.; ★ SDGO; mail San Diego z 92154; pop. incl. with San Diego (Inc. Place)

Palmdale; Inc. Place; LOS ANGELES; 153 SI-11; elev. 2,659ft./810m.; [P]; ★ L.A.; z 93550-52, z 93590-91, z 93599; Ⓟ 68,946; © 116,670; ◆ 131,633

Palm Desert; Inc. Place; RIVERSIDE; 153 SK-15; elev. 243ft./74m.; [P]; ★ PSPR-; z 92210-11, z 92255, z 92260-61; Ⓟ 23,252; © 41,155; ◆ 54,440

Palmer Creek; RMC Place; HUMBOLDT; *150 NE-1; elev. 200ft./61m.; ★ EUR-; mail Fortuna z 95540; ● 100

Palms; RMC Place; LOS ANGELES; *152 SJ-10; ★ L.A.; mail Los Angeles z 90034; pop. incl. with Los Angeles (Inc. Place)

Palm Springs; Inc. Place; RIVERSIDE; 153 SK-15; elev. 466ft./142m.; [P] [H] ■; ★ PSPR-; z 92262-64, z 92292; Ⓟ 40,181; © 42,807; ◆ 47,490

Palm Wells; RMC Place; SAN BERNARDINO; ● 600

Palo Alto; Inc. Place; SANTA CLARA; 150 NN-5; elev. 23ft./7m.; [P] [H] [C] 870 ■; ★ SF-O-; z 94301-06, z 94309; Ⓟ 55,900; © 58,598; ◆ 61,398

Palo Cedro; CDP; SHASTA; 150 NE-6; elev. 462ft./141m.; [P]; ★ REDD; z 96073; © 1,247

Paloma; RMC Place; CALAVERAS; 150 NL-9; mail Valley Springs z 95252; ● 300

Palomar Mountain; RMC Place; SAN DIEGO; *153 SL-14; [P]; z 92060; ● 150

Palomar Park; RMC Place; SAN MATEO; 151 NK-15; [P]; ★ SF-O-; z 94062; ● 530

Palos Verdes Estates; Inc. Place; LOS ANGELES; 152 SK-10; elev. 217ft./66m.; [P]; ★ L.A.; z 90274-75; Ⓟ 13,512; © 13,340

Palos Verdes Peninsula; RMC Place; LOS ANGELES; *153 SK-11; [P]; ★ L.A.; z 90274-75; pop. incl. with Rolling Hills Estates (Inc. Place)

Palo Verde; CDP; IMPERIAL; 153 SK-19; elev. 233ft./71m.; [P]; z 92266; © 236

Palo Vista; RMC Place; SAN DIEGO; ★ SDGO; mail Vista z 92083; pop. incl. with Vista (Inc. Place)

Panoche; RMC Place; SAN BENITO; *152 SC-5; elev. 1,220ft./372m.; mail Paicines z 95043; rural

Panorama City; RMC Place; LOS ANGELES; *152 SJ-10; [P]; ★ L.A.; z 91402, z 91412; pop. incl. with Los Angeles (Inc. Place)

Panorama Heights; RMC Place; ORANGE; *153 SK-12; ★ L.A.; mail Santa Ana z 92705; ● 2,500

Panorama Heights; RMC Place; TULARE; *152 SE-10; mail Posey z 93260; ● 60

Paradise; Inc. Place; BUTTE; 150 NG-7; elev. 1,708ft./521m.; [P] [H]; z 95967, z 95969; Ⓟ 25,408; © 26,408; ◆ 27,141

Paradise; RMC Place; STANISLAUS; ★ MOD; mail Modesto z 95351, z 95358; pop. incl. with Modesto (Inc. Place)

Paradise Camp; RMC Place; MONO; *151 NN-13; mail Bishop z 93514; ● 125

Paradise Cay; RMC Place; MARIN; ★ SF-O-; mail Belvedere Tiburon z 94920

Paradise Hills; RMC Place; SAN DIEGO; *153 SN-14; ★ SDGO; mail San Diego z 92139, z 92149; pop. incl. with San Diego (Inc. Place)

Paradise Park; RMC Place; SANTA CRUZ; *152 SB-2; ★ S.CRZ; mail Santa Cruz z 95060; ● 400

Paramount; Inc. Place; LOS ANGELES; 154 H-8; elev. 67ft./20m.; [P] [H]; ★ L.A.; z 90723; Ⓟ 47,669; © 55,266; ◆ 58,542

Parchers Camp; RMC Place; INYO; *152 SA-10; mail Bishop z 93514; ● 30

Parchester Village; RMC Place; CONTRA COSTA; ★ SF-O-; pop. incl. with Richmond (Inc. Place)

Park; RMC Place; ALAMEDA; ★ SF-O-; mail Berkeley z 94702; pop. incl. with Berkeley (Inc. Place)

Park Central; RMC Place; ALAMEDA; ★ SF-O-; mail Alameda z 94501; pop. incl. with Alameda (Inc. Place)

Parker Dam; RMC Place; SAN BERNARDINO; *153 SI-20; [P]; z 92267; ● 100

Parkfield; RMC Place; MONTEREY; *152 SE-6; [P]; z 93451

Parkmoor; RMC Place; SANTA CLARA; ★ SF-O-; mail San Jose z 95128, z 95159

Parksdale; CDP-Census Area Only; MADERA; *152 SB-7; ★ FRES; mail Madera z 93637; Ⓟ 1,911; © 2,688

Parkside; RMC Place; SAN FRANCISCO; ★ SF-O-; mail San Francisco z 94116; pop. incl. with San Francisco (Inc. Place)

Park Siding; RMC Place; SONOMA; ★ SF-O-; mail Petaluma z 94952; pop. incl. with Petaluma (Inc. Place)

Park Village; RMC Place; INYO; *153 SC-14; elev. 200ft./61m.; mail Death Valley z 92328; ● 100

Parkway; RMC Place; SACRAMENTO; 149 E-6; elev. 18ft./5m.; ★ SAC; mail Sacramento z 95823; ● 14,280

Parkway-South Sacramento; CDP-Census Area Only; SACRAMENTO; *150 NK-7; ★ SAC; mail Sacramento z 95823; Ⓟ 31,903; © 36,468; ◆ 42,022

Parkwood; CDP-Census Area Only; MADERA; *152 SB-7; ★ FRES; mail Madera z 93637; Ⓟ 1,659; © 2,119

Parlier; Inc. Place; FRESNO; 152 SC-8; [P]; z 93648; Ⓟ 7,938; © 11,145

Pasadena; Inc. Place; LOS ANGELES; 153 SJ-11; elev. 865ft./264m.; [P] [H] [C] 7,692 ■; ★ L.A.; z 91101-10, z 91114-18, z 91121, z 91123-26, z 91129, z 91182, z 91184-85, z 91188-89, z 91199; Ⓟ 131,591; © 133,936; ◆ 135,447

Pasatiempo; RMC Place; SANTA CRUZ; *152 SB-2; ★ S.CRZ; mail Santa Cruz z 95060; ● 900

Paskenta; RMC Place; TEHAMA; 150 NG-5; elev. 743ft./226m.; [P]; z 96074; ● 100

Paso Robles (El Paso de Robles); Inc. Place; SAN LUIS OBISPO; 152 SF-5; elev. 721ft./220m.; [P]; z 93446-47; Ⓟ 18,583; © 24,297; ◆ 29,568

Patata; RMC Place; LOS ANGELES; ★ L.A.; mail South Gate z 90280; pop. incl. with South Gate (Inc. Place)

Patrick Creek; RMC Place; DEL NORTE; 150 NA-2; mail Gasquet z 95543; rural

Patricks Point; RMC Place; HUMBOLDT; *150 NC-2; elev. 253ft./77m.; mail Trinidad z 95570; ● 160

Patterson; Inc. Place; STANISLAUS; 150 NN-8; elev. 97ft./30m.; [P] [H]; z 95363; Ⓟ 8,626; © 11,606

Patton (Patton State Hospital); RMC Place; SAN BERNARDINO; *153 SJ-13; [P] [H]; ★ RIV-; z 92369; pop. incl. with Highland (Inc. Place)

Patton State Hospital; SAN BERNARDINO; see Patton (RMC Place)

Patton Village (West Patton Village); RMC Place; LASSEN; *150 NF-10; mail Herlong z 96113; ● 750

Pauma and Yuima Reservation; Indian Reservation; SAN DIEGO; mail Pauma Valley z 92061; © 186

Pauma Valley; RMC Place; SAN DIEGO; 153 SL-14; [P]; ★ SDGO; z 92061 & mail Pala z 92059; ● 800

Paxton; CDP; PLUMAS; *150 NG-8; mail Quincy z 95971; © 21

Paynes Creek; RMC Place; TEHAMA; 150 NF-6; elev. 1,850ft./564m.; [P]; z 96075; ● 100

Paynesville; RMC Place; ALPINE; *151 NJ-11; mail Markleeville z 96120

Peanut; RMC Place; TRINITY; *150 NE-4; elev. 2,499ft./762m.; mail Hayfork z 96041; rural

Pearblossom; RMC Place; LOS ANGELES; 153 SI-12; [P]; z 93553, z 93563; ● 700

Peardale; RMC Place; NEVADA; *150 NI-8; elev. 2,716ft./828m.; mail Grass Valley z 95945; ● 450

Pearland; RMC Place; LOS ANGELES; 154 M-8; ★ L.A.; mail Palmdale z 93550; pop. incl. with Palmdale (Inc. Place)

Pearsonville; CDP; INYO; 153 SE-12; [P]; z 93527; © 27

Pebble Beach; RMC Place; MONTEREY; 152 SC-2; [P]; ★ MTRY-; z 93953; ● 2,200

Pechanga Reservation; Indian Reservation; RIVERSIDE; mail Temecula z 92590; Ⓟ 141; © 467

Pecwan; RMC Place; HUMBOLDT; *150 NC-2; elev. 113ft./34m.; mail Hoopa z 95546; ● 50

Pedley; CDP; RIVERSIDE; 155 F-16; ★ RIV-; mail Riverside z 92509; Ⓟ 8,869; © 11,207

Pedro Valley; RMC Place; SAN MATEO; *150 NM-5; ★ SF-O-; mail Pacifica z 94044; pop. incl. with Pacifica (Inc. Place)

Peninsula Village; RMC Place; PLUMAS; *150 NF-8; mail Westwood z 96137; ● 270

Penngrove; RMC Place; SONOMA; 150 NK-4; [P]; ★ SF-O-; z 94951; ● 1,300

Pennington; RMC Place; SUTTER; *150 NI-6; elev. 84ft./26m.; mail Live Oak z 95953

Penn Valley; CDP-Census Area Only; NEVADA; 150 NI-8; [P]; z 95946; Ⓟ 1,242; © 1,387

Penryn; RMC Place; PLACER; 150 NJ-8; elev. 619ft./189m.; [P]; ★ SAC; z 95663; ● 1,200

Pentz; RMC Place; BUTTE; *150 NH-7; mail Oroville z 95965; rural

Pepperwood; RMC Place; HUMBOLDT; 150 NE-2; mail Scotia z 95565; ● 60

Peralta Hills; RMC Place; ORANGE; *153 SK-12; ★ L.A.; mail Orange z 92867; pop. incl. with Anaheim (Inc. Place)

Perkins; RMC Place; SACRAMENTO; *150 NK-7; ★ SAC; mail Sacramento z 95826-27; pop. incl. with Sacramento (Inc. Place)

Perris; Inc. Place; RIVERSIDE; 153 SK-13; elev. 1,457ft./444m.; [P]; ★ RIV-; z 92570-72, z 92599; Ⓟ 21,460; © 36,189; ◆ 55,963

Perry; RMC Place; LOS ANGELES; *153 SJ-11; elev. 73ft./22m.; ★ L.A.; mail Whittier z 90603; pop. incl. with Whittier (Inc. Place)

Pescadero; RMC Place; SAN MATEO; 152 SA-1; [P]; z 94060; ● 1,000

Petaluma; Inc. Place; SONOMA; 150 NK-4; elev. 12ft./4m.; [P] [H] ■; ★ SF-O-; z 94952-55, z 94975, z 94999; Ⓟ 43,184; © 54,548; ◆ 55,466

Peters; RMC Place; SAN JOAQUIN; 150 NL-8; elev. 97ft./30m.; mail Linden z 95236; ● 200

Petrolia; RMC Place; HUMBOLDT; 150 NF-1; [P]; z 95558

Phelan; RMC Place; SAN BERNARDINO; 153 SI-12; elev. 4,112ft./1,253m.; [P]; z 92329, z 92371; ● 2,500

Phillips; EL DORADO; see Little Norway (RMC Place)

Phillipsville; RMC Place; HUMBOLDT; 150 NF-2; elev. 278ft./85m.; [P]; z 95559; ● 170

Philo; RMC Place; MENDOCINO; 150 NI-3; [P]; z 95463, z 95466; ● 250

Phoenix Lake-Cedar Ridge; CDP-Census Area Only; TUOLUMNE; *150 NL-10; mail Sonora z 95370; Ⓟ 3,569; © 5,123

Phoenix Lake County Club Estates; RMC Place; TUOLUMNE; *150 NL-10; elev. 2,702ft./824m.; mail Sonora z 95370; ● 800

Picayune Rancheria; Indian Reservation; MADERA; © 20

Pico; RMC Place; LOS ANGELES; *153 SJ-11; ★ L.A.; mail Pico Rivera z 90660

Pico Heights; RMC Place; LOS ANGELES; ★ L.A.; mail Los Angeles z 90006; pop. incl. with Los Angeles (Inc. Place)

Pico Rivera; Inc. Place; LOS ANGELES; 154 F-9; elev. 161ft./49m.; [P] ■; ★ L.A.; z 90601, z 90660-62; Ⓟ 59,177; © 63,428; ◆ 66,018

Piedmont; Inc. Place; ALAMEDA; 151 NF-15; elev. 300ft./91m.; [P]; ★ SF-O-; z 94602, z 94610-11, z 94618, z 94620; Ⓟ 10,602; © 10,952

Piedra; RMC Place; FRESNO; *152 SB-8; [P]; z 93649; ● 270

Piercy; RMC Place; MENDOCINO; 150 NG-2; [P]; z 95587

Pierpoint Springs; RMC Place; TULARE; *152 SD-10; elev. 5,200ft./1,585m.; mail Camp Nelson z 93208; ● 60

Pike; RMC Place; SIERRA; *150 NH-8; mail North San Juan z 95960; rural

Pilot Hill; RMC Place; EL DORADO; 150 NJ-8; elev. 1,185ft./361m.; [P]; z 95664; ● 800

Pine Cove; RMC Place; RIVERSIDE; *153 SK-14; elev. 6,165ft./1,879m.; mail Idyllwild z 92549; ● 600

Pine Cove; RMC Place; TRINITY; *150 ND-4; elev. 1,935ft./590m.; mail Lewiston z 96052; rural

Pinecrest; RMC Place; TUOLUMNE; 150 NL-10; [P]; z 95314, z 95364, z 95375

Pinedale; RMC Place; FRESNO; *152 SB-7; [P]; ★ FRES; z 93650; pop. incl. with Fresno (Inc. Place)

Pine Flat; RMC Place; TULARE; *152 SE-10; mail California Hot Springs z 93207

Pine Grove; RMC Place; AMADOR; 150 NK-9; [P]; z 95665; ● 1,000

Pine Grove; RMC Place; LAKE; *150 NJ-4; mail Cobb z 95426; ● 160

Pine Grove; RMC Place; MENDOCINO; *150 NH-2; elev. 182ft./55m.; mail Fort Bragg z 95437; rural

Pine Grove; RMC Place; SHASTA; *150 NE-5; ★ REDD; mail Redding z 96003, Shasta Lake z 96079; pop. incl. with Shasta Lake (Inc. Place)

Pine Hills; CDP-Census Area Only; HUMBOLDT; *150 ND-1; ★ EUR-; mail Eureka z 95503; Ⓟ 2,947; © 3,108

Pine Hills; RMC Place; SAN DIEGO; *153 SM-15; mail Julian z 92036; ● 330

Pinehurst; RMC Place; FRESNO; 152 SC-9; mail Miramonte z 93641; ● 150

Pine Mountain Club; CDP; KERN; *152 SH-9; elev. 5,600ft./1,707m.; [P]; z 93222; © 1,600

Pine Mountain Lake; RMC Place; TUOLUMNE; *150 NM-10; mail Groveland z 95321; ● 950

Pineridge; RMC Place; FRESNO; 152 SB-8; mail Auberry z 93602; ● 200

Pine Street; RMC Place; SAN FRANCISCO; ★ SF-O-; mail San Francisco z 94109; pop. incl. with San Francisco (Inc. Place)

Pine Town; RMC Place; LASSEN; mail Westwood z 96137; ● 220

Pine Valley; CDP; SAN DIEGO; 153 SM-15; elev. 3,736ft./1,139m.; [P]; z 91962; Ⓟ 1,297; © 1,501

Pinole; Inc. Place; CONTRA COSTA; 151 NC-14; elev. 21ft./6m.; [P] [H]; ★ SF-O-; z 94564; Ⓟ 17,460; © 19,039

Pinoleville Rancheria; Indian Reservation; MENDOCINO; © 136

Piñon Hills; RMC Place; SAN BERNARDINO; 153 SI-12; [P]; z 92372; ● 1,500

Pinon Pines Estates; RMC Place; KERN; *152 SH-9; elev. 5,400ft./1,646m.; mail Frazier Park z 93225; ● 750

Pinyon Crest; RMC Place; RIVERSIDE; *153 SK-15; elev. 4,200ft./1,280m.; mail Palm Springs z 92262; rural

Pinyon Pines (Nightingale); RMC Place; RIVERSIDE; *153 SK-15; elev. 4,000ft./1,219m.; mail Mountain Center z 92561; ● 240

Pioneer; RMC Place; AMADOR; 150 NK-9; elev. 2,970ft./905m.; [P]; z 95644, z 95646, z 95666; ● 700

Pioneer Point; RMC Place; SAN BERNARDINO; 153 SE-13; elev. 1,658ft./505m.; mail Trona z 93562; ● 1,000

Pioneertown; RMC Place; SAN BERNARDINO; *153 SJ-15; elev. 4,033ft./1,229m.; [P]; z 92268; ● 200

Piru; CDP; VENTURA; 152 SI-9; elev. 692ft./211m.; [P]; z 93040; Ⓟ 1,157; © 1,196

Pismo; SAN LUIS OBISPO; see Pismo Beach (Inc. Place)

Pismo Beach (Pismo); Inc. Place; SAN LUIS OBISPO; 152 SG-5; elev. 33ft./10m.; [P]; z 93448-49 & mail Arroyo Grande z 93420, Grover Beach z 93433; Ⓟ 7,669; © 8,551

Pittsburg; Inc. Place; CONTRA COSTA; 150 NL-6; elev. 28ft./9m.; [P] ■; ★ SF-O-; z 94565; Ⓟ 47,564; © 56,769; ◆ 65,625

Pittville; RMC Place; SHASTA, LASSEN; *150 ND-7; mail McArthur z 96056

Pixley; CDP; TULARE; 152 SE-8; elev. 271ft./83m.; [P]; z 93256; Ⓟ 2,457; © 2,586

Placentia; Inc. Place; ORANGE; 155 H-12; elev. 250ft./76m.; [P] [H]; ★ L.A.; z 92870-71; Ⓟ 41,259; © 46,488; ◆ 49,655

PLACER; 150 NI-9; Ⓟ 172,796; © 248,399; ◆ 346,100

Placerville; Inc. Place; ⊡ EL DORADO; 150 NJ-8; elev. 1,866ft./569m.; [P] [H]; z 95667; Ⓟ 8,355; © 9,610

Plainsburg; RMC Place; MERCED; *152 SA-6; mail Le Grand z 95333, Merced z 95340; ● 130

Plainview; RMC Place; TULARE; 152 SD-9; ★ PORT; mail Strathmore z 93267; ● 1,000

Planada; CDP; MERCED; 150 NN-9; [P]; z 95365; Ⓟ 3,531; © 4,369

Plantation; RMC Place; SONOMA; *150 NJ-3; elev. 742ft./226m.; mail Cazadero z 95421; ● 65

Plaskett (Pacific Valley); RMC Place; MONTEREY; *152 SE-3; elev. 196ft./60m.; mail Big Sur z 93920; rural

Plasse; RMC Place; AMADOR; *150 NJ-10; mail Kirkwood z 95646, Los Angeles z 90026, Pioneer z 95666; rural

Plaster City; RMC Place; IMPERIAL; 153 SM-16; mail El Centro z 92243; ● 60

Platina; RMC Place; SHASTA; 150 NF-4; [P]; z 96076; ● 100

Playa; RMC Place; ORANGE; ★ L.A.; mail Laguna Beach z 92652; pop. incl. with Laguna Beach (Inc. Place)

Playa Del Rey; RMC Place; LOS ANGELES; *152 SJ-10; elev. 47ft./14m.; [P]; ★ L.A.; z 90291, z 90293, z 90296; pop. incl. with Los Angeles (Inc. Place)

Playa Vista; RMC Place; LOS ANGELES; [P]; ★ L.A.; z 90094 & mail Los Angeles z 90045, z 90066; pop. incl. with Los Angeles (Inc. Place)

Pleasant Grove; RMC Place; SUTTER; 150 NJ-7; elev. 48ft./15m.; [P]; z 95668; ● 250

Pleasant Hill; Inc. Place; CONTRA COSTA; 150 NL-6; elev. 50ft./15m.; [P] [C] 1,778 ■; ★ SF-O-; z 94523; Ⓟ 31,585; © 32,837; ◆ 31,933

Pleasanton; Inc. Place; ALAMEDA; 150 NM-6; elev. 352ft./107m.; [P] [H] ■; ★ SF-O-; z 94566, z 94568, z 94588; Ⓟ 50,553; © 63,654; ◆ 68,125

Pleasant Valley; RMC Place; EL DORADO; *150 NJ-9; mail Placerville z 95667; ● 1,100

Pleasant View; RMC Place; TULARE; *152 SE-10; mail Posey z 93260; rural

PLUMAS; 150 NG-10; Ⓟ 19,739; © 20,824; ◆ 20,257

Plumas Eureka; CDP-Census Area Only; PLUMAS; *150 NG-9; © 320

Plymouth; Inc. Place; AMADOR; 150 NK-8; elev. 1,086ft./331m.; [P]; z 95669; Ⓟ 811; © 980

Point Arena; Inc. Place; MENDOCINO; 150 NJ-2; [P]; z 95468; Ⓟ 407; © 474

Point Dume; RMC Place; LOS ANGELES; *152 SJ-9; ★ L.A.; mail Malibu z 90264-65; pop. incl. with Malibu (Inc. Place)

Point Loma; RMC Place; SAN DIEGO; *153 SN-13; ★ SDGO; mail San Diego z 92106, z 92166; pop. incl. with San Diego (Inc. Place)

Point Pleasant; RMC Place; SACRAMENTO; *150 NK-7; mail Elk Grove z 95758; ● 220

Point Reyes Station; CDP; MARIN; 150 NL-4; [P]; z 94956; © 818

Point Richmond; RMC Place; CONTRA COSTA; *150 NL-5; [P]; ★ SF-O-; z 94801 & mail Richmond z 94807; pop. incl. with Richmond (Inc. Place)

Polk; RMC Place; SACRAMENTO; *150 NK-7; elev. 38ft./12m.; ★ SAC; pop. incl. with Sacramento (Inc. Place)

Pollock Pines; CDP; EL DORADO; 150 NJ-9; elev. 3,940ft./1,201m.; [P]; z 95726; Ⓟ 4,291; © 4,728

Pomo; RMC Place; MENDOCINO; mail Potter Valley z 95469; ● 300

Pomona; Inc. Place; LOS ANGELES; 153 SJ-12; elev. 850ft./259m.; [P] [H] [C] 42,955 ■; ★ L.A.; z 91765-69, z 91797; Ⓟ 131,723; © 149,473; ◆ 161,427

Pond; RMC Place; KERN; 152 SE-8; elev. 283ft./86m.; [P]; z 93280; ● 200

Ponderosa Sky Ranch; RMC Place; TEHAMA; *150 NF-6; elev. 3,200ft./975m.; mail Paynes Creek z 96075; ● 120

Pondosa; RMC Place; SISKIYOU; *150 NC-7; mail McCloud z 96057

Pope Valley; RMC Place; NAPA; 150 NJ-5; elev. 706ft./215m.; [P]; z 94567; ● 250

Poplar-Cotton Center; CDP-Census Area Only; TULARE; 152 SD-9; ★ PORT; mail Porterville z 93257-58; Ⓟ 1,901; © 1,496

Port Costa; CDP; CONTRA COSTA; 151 NB-16; elev. 17ft./5m.; [P]; ★ SF-O-; z 94569; © 232

Porter Ranch; RMC Place; LOS ANGELES; [P]; ★ L.A.; z 91326-27; pop. incl. with Los Angeles (Inc. Place)

Porterville; Inc. Place; TULARE; 152 SD-9; elev. 459ft./140m.; [P] [H] ■; ★ PORT; z 93257-58; Ⓟ 29,563; © 39,615; ◆ 46,928

Porterville West (Burton); RMC Place; TULARE; ★ PORT; mail Porterville z 93257; pop. incl. with Porterville (Inc. Place)

Port Hueneme; Inc. Place; VENTURA; 152 SJ-9; elev. 12ft./4m.; [P] [H]; ★ OXN-; z 93041-44; Ⓟ 20,319; © 21,845; ◆ 22,532

Port Kenyon; RMC Place; HUMBOLDT; *150 NE-1; elev. 12ft./4m.; mail Ferndale z 95536; ● 100

Port of Redwood City; SAN MATEO; see Redwood Harbor (RMC Place)

Portola; Inc. Place; PLUMAS; 150 NG-9; elev. 4,834ft./1,473m.; [P] [H]; z 96122, z 96129; Ⓟ 2,193; © 2,227

Portola Hills; CDP; ORANGE; *153 SK-12; elev. 1,300ft./396m.; [P]; ★ L.A.; z 92679; Ⓟ 2,677; © 6,391

Portola Valley; Inc. Place; SAN MATEO; 151 NL-16; [P]; ★ SF-O-; z 94028; Ⓟ 4,194; © 4,462

Port San Luis; RMC Place; SAN LUIS OBISPO; *152 SG-5; mail Avila Beach z 93424; rural

Portuguese Bend; RMC Place; LOS ANGELES; *153 SK-11; ★ L.A.; mail Palos Verdes Peninsula z 90274; pop. incl. with Rancho Palos Verdes (Inc. Place)

Port Watsonvile; RMC Place; SANTA CRUZ; *152 SB-3; elev. 100ft./30m.; ★ WATS; mail Watsonville z 95076; ● 210

Posey; RMC Place; TULARE; *152 SE-10; [P]; z 93260; ● 50

Poso Park; RMC Place; TULARE; *152 SE-10; mail Posey z 93260; ● 5

Potrero; RMC Place; SAN DIEGO; 153 SN-15; elev. 2,323ft./708m.; [P]; z 91963; ● 560

Potrero; RMC Place; SAN FRANCISCO; ★ SF-O-; mail San Francisco z 94110; pop. incl. with San Francisco (Inc. Place)

Potter Valley; RMC Place; MENDOCINO; 150 NH-4; elev. 945ft./288m.; [P]; z 95469; ● 1,025

Poway; Inc. Place; SAN DIEGO; 153 SM-14; elev. 508ft./155m.; [P] [H]; ★ SDGO; z 92064, z 92074; Ⓟ 43,516; © 48,044; ◆ 50,657

Pozo; RMC Place; SAN LUIS OBISPO; 152 SF-6; elev. 145ft./44m.; mail Santa Margarita z 93453

Prather; RMC Place; FRESNO; 152 SB-8; elev. 1,642ft./500m.; [P]; z 93651

Prattville; CDP; PLUMAS; *150 NF-8; elev. 4,535ft./1,382m.; mail Canyon Dam z 95923; © 28

Prenda; RMC Place; RIVERSIDE; *153 SJ-13; ★ RIV-; pop. incl. with Riverside (Inc. Place)

Presidential Heights; RMC Place; ORANGE; ★ L.A.; mail San Clemente z 92672; pop. incl. with San Clemente (Inc. Place)

Presidio; RMC Place; SAN FRANCISCO; ★ SF-O-; mail San Francisco z 94129; pop. incl. with San Francisco (Inc. Place)

Preston (Oak Mountain); RMC Place; SONOMA; mail Cloverdale z 95425; ● 600

Preston Heights; RMC Place; HUMBOLDT; ★ EUR-; mail Arcata z 95521; pop. incl. with Arcata (Inc. Place)

Preuss; RMC Place; LOS ANGELES; ★ L.A.; mail Los Angeles z 90035; pop. incl. with Los Angeles (Inc. Place)

Priest Valley; RMC Place; MONTEREY; *152 SD-5; elev. 2,256ft./688m.; mail Coalinga z 93210; rural

Princeton; RMC Place; COLUSA; 150 NH-6; [P]; z 95970; ● 300

Princeton (Princeton-by-the-Sea); RMC Place; SAN MATEO; *150 NN-5; elev. 13ft./4m.; ★ SF-O-; mail Half Moon Bay z 94019; ● 660

Princeton-by-the-Sea; SAN MATEO; see Princeton (RMC Place)

Proberta; RMC Place; TEHAMA; 150 NF-6; elev. 254ft./77m.; [P]; z 96078; ● 350

Project City; RMC Place; SHASTA; *150 NE-5; [P]; ★ REDD; z 96079; pop. incl. with Shasta Lake (Inc. Place)

Prosser Lakeview Estates; RMC Place; NEVADA; *150 NH-10; elev. 6,000ft./1,829m.; mail Truckee z 96161; pop. incl. with Truckee (Inc. Place)

Prunedale; CDP; MONTEREY; 152 SB-3; elev. 90ft./27m.; [P]; ★ SLNS; z 93907; Ⓟ 7,393; © 16,432; Ⓡ 16,514

Pudding Creek; RMC Place; MENDOCINO; *150 NH-2; elev. 123ft./37m.; mail Fort Bragg z 95437; ● 500

Puente Junction; RMC Place; LOS ANGELES; *153 SJ-11; ★ L.A.; mail La Puente z 91744; pop. incl. with Industry (Inc. Place)

Puerco Beach; RMC Place; LOS ANGELES; *152 SJ-10; elev. 100ft./30m.; ★ L.A.; mail Malibu z 90265

Pulga; RMC Place; BUTTE; 150 NG-7; [P]; z 95965 & mail Port Hueneme z 93044; ● 30

Pumpkin Center; RMC Place; KERN; 152 SG-9; [P]; ★ BAK; z 93313, z 93383 & mail Bakersfield z 93309; ● 520

Punta (La Conchita); RMC Place; VENTURA; mail Ventura z 93001; ● 350

Q

Quail Valley; CDP; RIVERSIDE; 155 J-19; [P]; z 92587; Ⓟ 1,937; © 1,639

Quaking Aspen; RMC Place; TULARE; *152 SD-10; elev. 6,800ft./2,073m.; mail Springville z 93265; rural

Quartz Hill; CDP; LOS ANGELES; 153 SH-11; [P]; ★ L.A.; z 93536, z 93551, z 93586; Ⓟ 9,626; © 9,890

Quartz Valley Reservation; Indian Reservation; SISKIYOU; © 126

Quincy; CDP; ⊡ PLUMAS; 150 NG-8; elev. 3,432ft./1,046m.; [P] [H]; z 95971; © 1,879

Quintette; RMC Place; EL DORADO; *150 NJ-9; elev. 4,050ft./1,234m.; mail Georgetown z 95634; rural

Quito; RMC Place; SANTA CLARA; ★ SF-O-; mail Saratoga z 95070; pop. incl. with Saratoga (Inc. Place)

R

Rackerby; RMC Place; YUBA; 150 NH-7; [P]; z 95972; ● 350

Radec; RMC Place; RIVERSIDE; *153 SL-14; elev. 1,695ft./517m.; mail Hemet z 92543

Rafael Village; RMC Place; MARIN; *150 NL-5; ★ SF-O-; mail Novato z 94949; pop. incl. with Novato (Inc. Place)

Rail Road Flat; CDP; CALAVERAS; 150 NK-9; [P]; z 95248; © 549

Rainbow (Rainbow Valley); CDP; SAN DIEGO; 153 SL-13; elev. 1,050ft./320m.; mail Fallbrook z 92028; Ⓟ 2,006; © 2,026

Rainbow Valley; SAN DIEGO; see Rainbow (CDP)

Raisin City; CDP; FRESNO; 152 SC-7; [P]; ★ FRES; z 93652; © 165

Ralph; RMC Place; TUOLUMNE; *150 NL-10; mail Sonora z 95370; ● 280

Ramirez; RMC Place; LOS ANGELES; ★ L.A.; mail Los Angeles z 90037, z 90082; pop. incl. with Los Angeles (Inc. Place)

Ramona; RMC Place; SACRAMENTO; *150 NK-7; ★ SAC; pop. incl. with Sacramento (Inc. Place)

Ramona; CDP; SAN DIEGO; 153 SM-14; elev. 1,442ft./440m.; [P]; ★ SDGO; z 92065; Ⓟ 13,040; © 15,691

Ramona Acres; RMC Place; SAN LUIS OBISPO; *152 SF-6; elev. 1,200ft./366m.; mail Creston z 93432; rural

Ramona Village; Indian Reservation; RIVERSIDE; © 0

Ranchita; RMC Place; SAN DIEGO; 153 SL-15; elev. 4,065ft./1,239m.; [P]; z 92066; ● 300

Rancho Bernardo; RMC Place; SAN DIEGO; *153 SM-14; ★ SDGO; mail San Diego z 92127-28, z 92198; pop. incl. with San Diego (Inc. Place)

Rancho Buena Ventura; RMC Place; SHASTA; *150 NE-6; ★ REDD; mail Cottonwood z 96022; rural

Rancho Calaveras; CDP-Census Area Only; CALAVERAS; *150 NL-8; © 4,182

Rancho California; RMC Place; RIVERSIDE; *153 SK-13; mail Temecula z 92589-93; pop. incl. with Temecula (Inc. Place)

Rancho Cordova (Mills); Inc. Place; SACRAMENTO; 150 NJ-7; elev. 89ft./27m.; [P]; ★ SAC; z 95670, z 95741-42; incorporated July 1, 2003; not reported in 2000 Census; ◆ 60,167

Rancho Cordova; CDP-Census Area Only; SACRAMENTO; 150 NJ-7; elev. 77ft./23m.; [P]; ★ SAC; z 95670, z 95741-42; Ⓟ 48,731; © 55,060

Rancho Cucamonga (Cucamonga); Inc. Place; SAN BERNARDINO; 155 D-15; elev. 1,110ft./338m.; [P]; ★ L.A.; z 91701, z 91729-30, z 91737, z 91739; Ⓟ 101,409; © 127,743; ◆ 158,857

Rancho Del Mar; RMC Place; NAPA; *150 NL-5; ★ SF-O-; mail Vallejo z 94590; pop. incl. with American Canyon (Inc. Place)

Rancho Del Rey; RMC Place; SAN DIEGO; *153 SN-14; ★ SDGO; mail Chula Vista z 91909, z 91911; pop. incl. with Chula Vista (Inc. Place)

Rancho Dominguez; RMC Place; LOS ANGELES; [P]; ★ L.A.; z 90220, z 90224 & mail Compton z 90221; pop. incl. with Compton (Inc. Place)

Rancho Los Amigos; RMC Place; LOS ANGELES; ★ L.A.; mail Downey z 90242; pop. incl. with Downey (Inc. Place)

Rancho Mirage; Inc. Place; RIVERSIDE; 153 SK-15; [P] [H]; ★ PSPR-; z 92270; Ⓟ 9,778; © 13,249

Rancho Murieta; CDP; SACRAMENTO; 150 NK-8; [P]; z 95683; Ⓟ 2,336; © 4,193

Rancho Palos Verdes; Inc. Place; LOS ANGELES; 154 J-5; [P]; ★ L.A.; z 90275; Ⓟ 41,659; © 41,145; ◆ 40,946

Rancho Park; RMC Place; LOS ANGELES; [P]; ★ L.A.; z 90064; pop. incl. with Los Angeles (Inc. Place)

Rancho Penasquitos; RMC Place; SAN DIEGO; ★ SDGO; mail San Diego z 92129, z 92172; pop. incl. with San Diego (Inc. Place)

Rancho Rinconada; RMC Place; SANTA CLARA; 151 NM-18; ★ SF-O-; mail Cupertino z 95014; pop. incl. with Cupertino (Inc. Place); Ⓟ 4,206

Rancho San Diego; CDP-Census Area Only; SAN DIEGO; *153 SN-14; ★ SDGO; mail La Mesa z 91941, Spring Valley z 91978; Ⓟ 6,977; © 20,155; ◆ 21,778

Rancho Santa Fe; CDP; SAN DIEGO; 153 SM-13; elev. 245ft./75m.; [P]; ★ SDGO; z 92067, z 92091; © 3,252

Rancho Santa Margarita; Inc. Place; ORANGE; 155 K-15; elev. 1,000ft./305m.; [P]; ★ L.A.; z 92688; Ⓟ 11,390; © 47,214; ◆ 49,753

Ranchos Los Amigos Hospital; LOS ANGELES; see Los Amigos (RMC Place)

Rancho Tehama Reserve; CDP-Census Area Only; TEHAMA; *150 NG-5; © 1,406

Randall; RMC Place; SACRAMENTO; *150 NK-7; elev. 10ft./3m.; mail Courtland z 95615; rural

Randolph; RMC Place; SIERRA; *150 NH-9; mail Sierraville z 96126; rural

Randsburg; CDP; KERN; 153 SF-12; [P]; z 93554; © 77

Ravendale; RMC Place; LASSEN; 150 ND-9; elev. 5,299ft./1,615m.; [P]; z 96123

Ravenswood; RMC Place; SAN MATEO; *150 NN-5; ★ SF-O-; mail Palo Alto z 94303; pop. incl. with East Palo Alto (Inc. Place)

Rawhide; RMC Place; TUOLUMNE; *150 NL-9; elev. 1,629ft./497m.; mail Sonora z 95370; ● 100

Rawson; RMC Place; TEHAMA; *150 NF-6; mail Red Bluff z 96080

Raymer; RMC Place; LOS ANGELES; *152 SJ-10; ★ L.A.; pop. incl. with Los Angeles (Inc. Place)

Raymond; RMC Place; MADERA; 152 SA-7; [P]; z 93653; ● 200

Raymus Village Park; RMC Place; SAN JOAQUIN; *150 NM-8; elev. 35ft./11m.; ★ STOC; mail Manteca z 95336; ● 650

Raynor Park; RMC Place; SANTA CLARA; ★ SF-O-; mail Sunnyvale z 94087; pop. incl. with Sunnyvale (Inc. Place)

Red Bank; RMC Place; TEHAMA; *150 NF-5; mail Red Bluff z 96080; rural

Red Bluff; Inc. Place; ⊡ TEHAMA; 150 NF-5; elev. 309ft./94m.; [P] [H]; z 96080; Ⓟ 12,363; © 13,147

Redcrest; RMC Place; HUMBOLDT; 150 NE-2; [P]; z 95569; ● 180

Redding; Inc. Place; ⊡ SHASTA; 150 NE-5; elev. 557ft./170m.; [P] [H] [C] 860 ■; ★ REDD; z 96001-03, z 96049, z 96099; location of Northern California Indian Agency; Ⓟ 66,462; © 80,865; ◆ 87,182

Redding Rancheria; Indian Reservation; SHASTA; © 45

Red Hill; RMC Place; ORANGE; 155 J-12; ★ L.A.; mail Santa Ana z 92705; ● 2,800

Redlands; Inc. Place; SAN BERNARDINO; 153 SJ-13; elev. 1,302ft./397m.; [P] [H] [C] 4,080 ■; ★ RIV-; z 92373-75; Ⓟ 60,394; © 63,591; ◆ 63,214

Red Mountain; RMC Place; SAN BERNARDINO; 153 SF-12; [P]; z 93558; ● 100

Redondo Beach; Inc. Place; LOS ANGELES; 152 SK-10; elev. 59ft./18m.; [P] [H] ■; ★ L.A.; z 90277-78; Ⓟ 60,167; © 63,261; ◆ 64,689

Entries in **UPPERCASE** are counties.
Entries in **bold** have populations of 2,500 or more.
Names in parentheses are alternate names.

Inc. Place	Incorporated Place
RMC Place	Rand McNally Designated Place
CDP	Census Designated Place
MCD	Minor Civil Division
⊡	County Seat
▲	Minor Civil Division
elev.	Elevation
[P]	Post Office
[H]	Hospital
[C]	College
■	Principal Business Center
★	Ranally Metro Area (RMA) Abbreviation
z	Zip Code(s)
Ⓟ	Previous Census Population
Ⓡ	Revised Census Population
Ⓐ	Annexation Population
●	Rand McNally Population Estimate
©	Final Census Population
Ⓢ	Special Census Population
◆	Estimated Population

For additional definitions see Glossary, Volume 1, and Introduction, Volume 2.

Red Top; RMC Place; MADERA; *152 SB-6; elev. 135ft./41m.; mail Merced z 95340; rural
Redway; CDP; HUMBOLDT; 150 NF-2; elev. 538ft./164m.; 🅿; z 95560; ℗ 1,212; © 1,188
Redwood City; Inc. Place; ⊡ SAN MATEO; 150 NN-5; elev. 15ft./5m.; 🅿 🅷 ■; ★ SF-O-; z 94061-65; ℗ 66,072; © 75,402; ◆ 78,657
Redwood Estates; RMC Place; SANTA CLARA; *152 SA-2; 🅿; ★ SF-O-; z 95044; ● 1,300
Redwood Grove; RMC Place; SANTA CRUZ; *152 SA-2; ★ S.CRZ; mail Boulder Creek z 95006; ● 450
Redwood Harbor (Port of Redwood City); RMC Place; SAN MATEO; ★ SF-O-; pop. incl. with Redwood City (Inc. Place)
Redwood Junction; RMC Place; SAN MATEO; *150 NN-5; elev. 22ft./7m.; ★ SF-O-; pop. incl. with Redwood City (Inc. Place)
Redwood Lodge; RMC Place; MENDOCINO; *150 NH-2; mail Fort Bragg z 95437; rural
Redwood Retreat; RMC Place; SANTA CLARA; *152 SB-3; elev. 600ft./183m.; mail Gilroy z 95020; rural
Redwood Shores; RMC Place; SAN MATEO; *150 NM-5; ★ SF-O-; mail Redwood City z 94065; pop. incl. with Redwood City (Inc. Place)
Redwood Terrace; RMC Place; SAN MATEO; *150 NN-5; mail La Honda z 94020; ● 50
Redwood Valley; RMC Place; MENDOCINO; 150 NI-3; elev. 708ft./216m.; 🅿; z 95470; ● 1,900
Redwood Valley Rancheria Reservation; Indian Reservation; MENDOCINO; © 263
Reedley; Inc. Place; FRESNO; 152 SC-8; elev. 348ft./106m.; 🅿 🅷; z 93654; ℗ 15,791; © 20,756; ◆ 24,942
Regina Heights; RMC Place; MENDOCINO; *150 NI-3; elev. 800ft./244m.; mail Ukiah z 95482; ● 800
Relief; RMC Place; NEVADA; *150 NH-8; elev. 4,000ft./1,219m.; mail Nevada City z 95959; rural
Requa; RMC Place; DEL NORTE; *150 NB-2; mail Klamath z 95548; ● 180
Rescue; RMC Place; EL DORADO; 150 NJ-8; elev. 1,208ft./368m.; 🅿; ★ SAC; z 95672; ● 1,200
Reseda; RMC Place; LOS ANGELES; *152 SJ-10; 🅿; ★ L.A.; z 91335, z 91337; pop. incl. with Los Angeles (Inc. Place)
Resighini Rancheria; Indian Reservation; DEL NORTE; mail Hoopa z 95546; © 36
Retreat; RMC Place; MONTEREY; *152 SC-3; ★ MTRY-; pop. incl. with Monterey (Inc. Place)
Rheem; RMC Place; CONTRA COSTA; *150 NL-5; ★ SF-O-; mail Richmond z 94801; pop. incl. with San Pablo (Inc. Place)
Rheem Valley; RMC Place; CONTRA COSTA; *150 NM-6; elev. 602ft./183m.; ★ SF-O-; mail Moraga z 94570; pop. incl. with Moraga (Inc. Place)
Rialto; Inc. Place; SAN BERNARDINO; 153 SJ-13; elev. 1,205ft./367m.; 🅿; ★ RIV-; z 92376-77; ℗ 72,388; © 91,873; ◆ 101,597
Rice; RMC Place; SAN BERNARDINO; *153 SJ-19; elev. 935ft./285m.; mail Vidal z 92280; rural
Richardson Springs; RMC Place; BUTTE; 150 NG-6; mail Chico z 95973; ● 100
Richfield; RMC Place; TEHAMA; 150 NG-6; mail Corning z 96021; ● 450
Richgrove; CDP; TULARE; 152 SE-9; 🅿; z 93261; ℗ 1,899; © 2,723
Richmond; Inc. Place; CONTRA COSTA; 151 ND-14; elev. 55ft./17m.; 🅿 🅷 🅲 642 ■; ★ SF-O-; z 94801-08, z 94820, z 94850 & mail El Cerrito z 94530; ℗ 87,425; © 99,216; ◆ 105,858
Richmond; RMC Place; SAN FRANCISCO; ★ SF-O-; mail San Francisco z 94118, z 94121; pop. incl. with San Francisco (Inc. Place)
Richvale; RMC Place; BUTTE; 150 NH-6; elev. 106ft./32m.; 🅿; z 95974; ● 300
Ridgecrest; Inc. Place; KERN; 153 SF-12; elev. 2,289ft./698m.; 🅿 🅷; z 93555-56; ℗ 27,725; © 24,927; ◆ 25,284
Ridgemark; CDP-Census Area Only; SAN BENITO; *152 SB-4; © 2,741
Rimcrest; RMC Place; RIVERSIDE; ★ PSPR-; mail Palm Springs z 92264; pop. incl. with Palm Springs (Inc. Place)
Rimforest; RMC Place; SAN BERNARDINO; 155 B-19; elev. 5,955ft./1,815m.; 🅿; ★ RIV-; z 92378; ● 700
Rimpau; RMC Place; LOS ANGELES; ★ L.A.; mail Los Angeles z 90019; pop. incl. with Los Angeles (Inc. Place)
Rimrock; RMC Place; SAN BERNARDINO; *153 SJ-15; mail Pioneertown z 92268; rural
Rincon; RMC Place; SAN DIEGO; *153 SL-14; elev. 1,018ft./310m.; ★ SDGO; mail Pauma Valley z 92061; ● 570
Rincon Center; RMC Place; SAN FRANCISCO; ★ SF-O-; mail San Francisco z 94119; pop. incl. with San Francisco (Inc. Place)
Rincon Reservation; Indian Reservation; SAN DIEGO; mail Escondido z 92025; ℗ 490; © 1,495
Rincon Valley; RMC Place; SONOMA; ★ S.ROS; mail Santa Rosa z 95409; pop. incl. with Santa Rosa (Inc. Place)
Rio Bonito; BUTTE; see East Biggs (RMC Place)
Rio Bravo; RMC Place; KERN; *152 SF-8; elev. 312ft./95m.; mail Bakersfield z 93306; rural
Rioco; RMC Place; LOS ANGELES; ★ L.A.; pop. incl. with Long Beach (Inc. Place)
Rio Dell; Inc. Place; HUMBOLDT; 150 NE-1; elev. 126ft./38m.; 🅿; z 95562; ℗ 3,012; © 3,174
Rio Dell; RMC Place; SONOMA; *150 NK-4; ★ S.ROS; mail Forestville z 95436; ● 960
Rio del Mar; CDP; SANTA CRUZ; 152 SB-3; ★ S.CRZ; mail Aptos z 95003; ℗ 8,919; © 9,198
Rio Linda; CDP; SACRAMENTO; 150 NJ-7; elev. 63ft./19m.; 🅿; ★ SAC; z 95673; ℗ 9,481; © 10,466
Rio Nido; RMC Place; SONOMA; *150 NK-4; 🅿; ★ S.ROS; z 95471; ● 320
Rio Oso; RMC Place; SUTTER; 150 NJ-7; elev. 43ft./13m.; 🅿; z 95674; ● 260
Rio Vista; Inc. Place; SOLANO; 150 NL-6; elev. 22ft./7m.; 🅿; z 94571; ℗ 3,316; © 4,571
Ripley; RMC Place; RIVERSIDE; 153 SK-19; elev. 248ft./76m.; 🅿; z 92225; ● 760
Ripon; Inc. Place; SAN JOAQUIN; 150 NM-8; elev. 62ft./19m.; 🅿; z 95366; ℗ 7,455; © 10,146
Ripperdan; RMC Place; MADERA; 152 SB-7; elev. 244ft./74m.; ★ FRES; mail Madera z 93637; ● 350
Ritter Ranch; RMC Place; LOS ANGELES; *153 SH-11; ★ L.A.; mail Palmdale z 93551; pop. incl. with Palmdale (Inc. Place)
Rivera; RMC Place; LOS ANGELES; ★ L.A.; mail Pico Rivera z 90660; pop. incl. with Pico Rivera (Inc. Place)
Riverbank; Inc. Place; STANISLAUS; 150 NM-8; 🅿; ★ MOD; z 95367; ℗ 8,547; © 15,826; ◆ 19,168
Riverdale; CDP; FRESNO; 152 SC-7; 🅿; z 93607, z 93656; ℗ 1,980; © 2,416
Riverdale Park; CDP-Census Area Only; STANISLAUS; *150 NM-8; ★ MOD; © 1,094
Riverkern; RMC Place; KERN; *152 SE-10; elev. 2,800ft./853m.; mail Kernville z 93238; ● 240
River Oaks; RMC Place; SAN BENITO; *152 SB-3; mail San Juan Bautista z 95045; ● 150
River Pines; RMC Place; AMADOR; 150 NK-9; 🅿; z 95675; ● 360
River Road; RMC Place; STANISLAUS; ★ MOD; mail Modesto z 95351; pop. incl. with Modesto (Inc. Place)
River Road Estates; RMC Place; MADERA; *152 SB-7; elev. 335ft./102m.; mail Madera z 93637; ● 350
Riverside; Inc. Place; ⊡ RIVERSIDE; 153 SJ-13; elev. 858ft./262m.; 🅿 🅷 🅲 22,131 ■; ★ RIV-; z 92501-09, z 92513-19, z 92521-22; location of Southern California Indian Agency; ℗ 226,505; © 255,166; ◆ 286,237
RIVERSIDE; 153 SK-19; ℗ 1,170,413; © 1,545,387; ◆ 2,165,994
Riverside Grove; RMC Place; SANTA CRUZ; *152 SA-2; ★ S.CRZ; mail Boulder Creek z 95006; ● 1,300
Riverside Park; RMC Place; HUMBOLDT; *150 NE-2; elev. 256ft./78m.; mail Carlotta z 95528; rural
Rivertown; RMC Place; CONTRA COSTA; ★ SF-O-; mail Antioch z 94509; pop. incl. with Antioch (Inc. Place)
Riverview; RMC Place; SAN DIEGO; *153 SM-14; ★ SDGO; mail Lakeside z 92040; ● 2,000
Riverview Farms; RMC Place; SAN DIEGO; *153 SM-14; ★ SDGO; mail Lakeside z 92040; ● 1,500
Riviera Cliff; RMC Place; SAN JOAQUIN; *150 NL-7; ★ STOC; mail Stockton z 95204; ● 235
Roads End; RMC Place; TULARE; *152 SE-10; mail Kernville z 93238; ● 50
Roaring Creek Rancheria; Indian Reservation; SHASTA; © 9
Robbins; RMC Place; SUTTER; 150 NJ-7; elev. 18ft./5m.; 🅿; z 95676; ● 500
Robert; RMC Place; ALAMEDA; ★ SF-O-; pop. incl. with San Leandro (Inc. Place)
Robertsville; RMC Place; SANTA CLARA; *150 NN-6; elev. 173ft./53m.; ★ SF-O-; mail San Jose z 95118, z 95158; pop. incl. with San Jose (Inc. Place)
Robinson Rancheria; Indian Reservation; LAKE; © 138
Robinsons Corner; RMC Place; BUTTE; *150 NH-7; elev. 101ft./31m.; mail Oroville z 95965; rural
Robla; RMC Place; SACRAMENTO; *150 NJ-7; ★ SAC; pop. incl. with Sacramento (Inc. Place)
Robles Del Rio; RMC Place; MONTEREY; *152 SC-3; ★ MTRY-; mail Carmel Valley z 93924; ● 500
Rob Roy Junction; RMC Place; SANTA CRUZ; *152 SB-3; elev. 150ft./46m.; ★ S.CRZ; mail Aptos z 95003; ● 1,000
Rockaway Beach; RMC Place; SAN MATEO; *150 NM-5; elev. 68ft./21m.; ★ SF-O-; mail Pacifica z 94044; pop. incl. with Pacifica (Inc. Place)
Rock Creek; RMC Place; PLUMAS; *150 NG-7; mail Oroville z 95965, Storrie z 95980; rural
Rock Crest; RMC Place; PLUMAS; *150 NG-7; mail Storrie z 95980; rural
Rock Haven; RMC Place; FRESNO; *152 SA-8; mail Shaver Lake z 93664; rural
Rocking Horse Ranchos; RMC Place; LOS ANGELES; *153 SK-11; elev. 600ft./183m.; ★ L.A.; mail San Pedro z 90731; pop. incl. with Rancho Palos Verdes (Inc. Place)
Rocklin; Inc. Place; PLACER; 150 NJ-8; elev. 248ft./76m.; 🅿 🅲 592; ★ SAC; z 95677, z 95765; ℗ 19,033; © 36,330; ◆ 52,746
Rockport; RMC Place; MENDOCINO; *150 NG-2; mail Westport z 95488
Rockridge; RMC Place; ALAMEDA; ★ SF-O-; mail Oakland z 94618; pop. incl. with Oakland (Inc. Place)
Rockville; RMC Place; SOLANO; *150 NK-6; elev. 60ft./18m.; ★ FRFL-; mail Suisun City z 94585; ● 280
Rodeo; CDP; CONTRA COSTA; 151 NB-15; elev. 15ft./5m.; 🅿; ★ SF-O-; z 94547, z 94572; ℗ 7,589; © 8,717
Rodgers Flat; RMC Place; PLUMAS; *150 NG-8; mail Storrie z 95980; rural
Rohnert Park; Inc. Place; SONOMA; 150 NK-4; elev. 100ft./30m.; 🅿 🅲 8,274; ★ S.ROS; z 94926-28 & mail Cotati z 94931; ℗ 36,326; © 42,236; ◆ 41,618
Rohnerville; RMC Place; HUMBOLDT; 150 NE-2; ★ EUR-; mail Fortuna z 95540; pop. incl. with Fortuna (Inc. Place)
Rohnerville Rancheria; Indian Reservation; HUMBOLDT; © 98
Rolinda; RMC Place; FRESNO; 152 SC-7; ★ FRES; mail Fresno z 93706; ● 200
Rolling Hills; Inc. Place; LOS ANGELES; 154 I-6; 🅿; ★ L.A.; z 90274; ℗ 1,871; © 1,871
Rolling Hills; RMC Place; MADERA; *152 SB-7; elev. 379ft./116m.; ★ FRES; mail Madera z 93637; ● 650
Rolling Hills; RMC Place; RIVERSIDE; *153 SK-15; mail Anza z 92539; ● 200
Rolling Hills Estates; Inc. Place; LOS ANGELES; 154 I-6; elev. 400ft./122m.; 🅿; ★ L.A.; z 90274-75; ℗ 7,789; © 7,676
Rolling Hills Estates; RMC Place; SAN LUIS OBISPO; *152 SG-5; elev. 220ft./67m.; ★ S.LUIS; mail San Luis Obispo z 93401; ● 400
Rolling Hills Riviera; RMC Place; LOS ANGELES; *153 SK-11; ★ L.A.; mail San Pedro z 90731; pop. incl. with Rancho Palos Verdes (Inc. Place)
Rollingwood; CDP-Census Area Only; CONTRA COSTA; 151 NC-14; ★ SF-O-; mail San Pablo z 94806; © 2,900
Romac; RMC Place; SAN MATEO; ★ SF-O-; pop. incl. with San Mateo (Inc. Place)
Romie Lane; RMC Place; MONTEREY; ★ SLNS; mail Salinas z 93901; pop. incl. with Salinas (Inc. Place)
Romoland (Ethanac); CDP; RIVERSIDE; 155 I-20; 🅿; z 92585; ℗ 2,319; © 2,764
Roosevelt; RMC Place; LOS ANGELES; *153 SK-11; ★ L.A.; mail Lancaster z 93534-35
Roosevelt Terrace; RMC Place; SOLANO; 151 NA-15; ★ SF-O-; mail Vallejo z 94590; pop. incl. with Vallejo (Inc. Place)
Rosamond; CDP; KERN; 153 SH-11; 🅿; z 93560; ℗ 7,430; © 14,349
Rose Bowl; RMC Place; LOS ANGELES; ★ L.A.; mail Pasadena z 91103; pop. incl. with Pasadena (Inc. Place)
Rosedale; CDP; KERN; *152 SF-9; ★ BAK; mail Bakersfield z 93308; ℗ 4,673; © 8,445
Roseland; CDP; SONOMA; 149 H-7; ★ S.ROS; mail Santa Rosa z 95407; ℗ 8,779; © 6,369
Rosemead; Inc. Place; LOS ANGELES; 154 E-9; elev. 322ft./98m.; 🅿 🅷 ■; ★ L.A.; z 91770-72; ℗ 51,638; © 53,505; ◆ 53,682
Rosemont; CDP; SACRAMENTO; 149 D-8; ★ SAC; mail Sacramento z 95826; ℗ 22,851; © 22,904; ◆ 26,391
Rosemont; RMC Place; SAN DIEGO; 156 E-10; elev. 1,450ft./442m.; ★ SDGO; mail Ramona z 92065; ● 800
Roseville; Inc. Place; PLACER; 150 NJ-7; elev. 160ft./49m.; 🅿 🅷 ■; ★ SAC; z 95661, z 95678, z 95746-47; ℗ 44,685; © 79,921; ◆ 111,787
Rosewood; RMC Place; HUMBOLDT; *150 ND-1; 🅿; ★ EUR-; z 90222 & mail Eureka z 95503; ● 970
Ross; Inc. Place; MARIN; 151 ND-12; elev. 23ft./7m.; 🅿; ★ SF-O-; z 94957; ℗ 2,123; © 2,329
Ross Corner; RMC Place; IMPERIAL; *153 SM-19; ★ YUMA; mail Bard z 92222; ● 250
Rossmoor; CDP; ORANGE; 154 I-9; 🅿; ★ L.A.; z 90720; ℗ 9,893; © 10,298
Rossmoor Highlands; RMC Place; ORANGE; ★ L.A.; mail Los Alamitos z 90720; pop. incl. with Los Alamitos (Inc. Place)
Rossmore Leisure World; ORANGE; see Leisure World (RMC Place)
Rough And Ready; RMC Place; NEVADA; 150 NI-8; 🅿; z 95975; ● 230
Round Hill Country Club; RMC Place; CONTRA COSTA; *150 NM-6; ★ SF-O-; mail Alamo z 94507; ● 2,600
Round Mountain; CDP; SHASTA; 150 ND-6; 🅿; z 96084; © 122
Round Valley; CDP-Census Area Only; INYO; *151 NN-13; elev. 4,600ft./1,402m.; mail Bishop z 93514; © 278
Round Valley Reservation; Indian Reservation; MENDOCINO, TRINITY; mail Covelo z 95428; also location of Indian Agency; ℗ 1,268; © 82
Rovana; RMC Place; INYO; 151 NN-13; mail Bishop z 93514; ● 450
Rowland; RMC Place; LOS ANGELES; *153 SJ-12; ★ L.A.; mail Guasti z 91743; pop. incl. with Industry (Inc. Place)
Rowland Heights; CDP; LOS ANGELES; 155 F-11; elev. 540ft./165m.; 🅿; ★ L.A.; z 91748; ℗ 42,647; © 48,553; ◆ 49,659
Rubidoux; CDP; RIVERSIDE; 155 F-17; 🅿; ★ RIV-; z 92509 & mail Riverside z 92519; ℗ 24,367; © 29,180; ◆ 40,902
Rucker; RMC Place; SANTA CLARA; *152 SB-3; ★ SF-O-; mail Gilroy z 95020; rural
Rumsey; RMC Place; YOLO; 150 NJ-5; elev. 419ft./128m.; 🅿; z 95679; ● 200
Rumsey Rancheria; Indian Reservation; YOLO; © 36
Running Springs; CDP; SAN BERNARDINO; 153 SJ-13; elev. 6,030ft./1,838m.; 🅿; ★ RIV-; z 92382; ℗ 4,195; © 5,125
Rupert; RMC Place; YUBA; ★ YUCY; mail Marysville z 95901; ● 200
Russell; RMC Place; ALAMEDA; ★ SF-O-; mail Hayward z 94541; pop. incl. with Hayward (Inc. Place)
Russian River Terrace; RMC Place; SONOMA; *150 NK-4; ★ S.ROS; mail Forestville z 95436; ● 300
Ruth; RMC Place; TRINITY; *150 NF-3; 🅿; z 95526; ● 50
Rutherford; RMC Place; NAPA; 150 NK-5; 🅿; z 94573; ● 500
Ryans Slough; HUMBOLDT; see Myrtletown (CDP-Census Area Only)
Ryde; RMC Place; SACRAMENTO; 150 NL-7; elev. 11ft./3m.; 🅿; z 95680; ● 200

S

Sabre City; RMC Place; SACRAMENTO; *150 NJ-7; elev. 130ft./40m.; ★ SAC; mail Roseville z 95678; ● 300
Sacramento; Inc. Place; STATE CAPITAL; ⊡ SACRAMENTO; 150 NK-7; elev. 25ft./8m.; 🅿 🅷 🅲 28,529 ■; ★ SAC; z 94203-09, z 94211, z 94229-30, z 94232, z 94234-37, z 94239-40, z 94244-50, z 94252, z 94254, z 94256-59, z 94261-63, z 94267-69, z 94271, z 94273-74, z 94277-80, z 94282-91, z 94293-99, z 95811-38, z 95840-43, z 95851-53, z 95860, z 95864-67, z 95887, z 95894, z 95899; location of Central California Indian Agency; ℗ 369,365; © 407,018; ◆ 440,443
SACRAMENTO; 150 NK-8; ℗ 1,041,219; © 1,223,499; ◆ 1,409,875
Sage; RMC Place; RIVERSIDE; *153 SK-14; mail Hemet z 92544
Sage Valley; RMC Place; LASSEN; *150 NF-10; elev. 4,050ft./1,234m.; mail Herlong z 96113; ● 350
Saint Bernard; RMC Place; TEHAMA; mail Mill Creek z 96061; rural
Saint Francis Heights; RMC Place; SAN MATEO; ★ SF-O-; mail Daly City z 94015; pop. incl. with Daly City (Inc. Place)
Saint Helena; Inc. Place; NAPA; 150 NK-5; elev. 257ft./78m.; 🅿; z 94574; ℗ 4,990; © 5,950
Saint James Park; RMC Place; SANTA CLARA; ★ SF-O-; mail San Jose z 95103, z 95106, z 95108-09, z 95113, z 95115; pop. incl. with San Jose (Inc. Place)
Saint Johns; RMC Place; TULARE; *152 SD-9; elev. 425ft./130m.; ★ VISL; mail Woodlake z 93286; ● 350
Saint Matthew; RMC Place; SAN MATEO; ★ SF-O-; mail San Mateo z 94401; pop. incl. with San Mateo (Inc. Place)
Salida; CDP; STANISLAUS; 150 NM-8; 🅿; ★ MOD; z 95368; ℗ 4,499; © 12,560
Salinas; Inc. Place; ⊡ MONTEREY; 152 SC-3; elev. 53ft./16m.; 🅿 🅷 ■; ★ SLNS; z 93901-02, z 93905-08, z 93912, z 93915, z 93962; ℗ 108,777; © 151,060; ® 142,685; ◆ 157,293
Salminas Resort; RMC Place; LAKE; *150 NJ-4; elev. 2,600ft./792m.; mail Kelseyville z 95451; ● 140
Salmon Creek; RMC Place; SONOMA; 150 NK-4; mail Bodega Bay z 94923
Salton City; CDP-Census Area Only; IMPERIAL; 153 SL-16; 🅿; z 92275; © 978
Salton Sea Beach; CDP; IMPERIAL; 153 SL-16; mail Thermal z 92274; © 392
Saltus; RMC Place; SAN BERNARDINO; *153 SH-17; mail Amboy z 92304; rural
Salt Works; RMC Place; SAN DIEGO; ★ SDGO; pop. incl. with San Diego (Inc. Place)
Salvador; RMC Place; NAPA; *150 NK-5; ★ NAPA; mail Napa z 94558; pop. incl. with Napa (Inc. Place)
Salyer; RMC Place; TRINITY; 150 ND-3; elev. 600ft./183m.; 🅿; z 95563; ● 500
Samoa; RMC Place; HUMBOLDT; 150 ND-1; 🅿; ★ EUR-; z 95564; ● 270
San Andreas; CDP; ⊡ CALAVERAS; 150 NL-9; elev. 1,008ft./307m.; 🅿 🅷; z 95249 & mail Sheep Ranch z 95250; ℗ 2,115; © 2,615
San Anselmo; Inc. Place; MARIN; 150 NL-5; elev. 45ft./14m.; 🅿 🅲 459; ★ SF-O-; z 94960, z 94979; ℗ 11,743; © 12,378
San Antonio Heights; CDP; SAN BERNARDINO; 155 D-14; ★ L.A.; mail Upland z 91784; ℗ 2,935; © 3,122
San Ardo; CDP; MONTEREY; 152 SD-5; elev. 459ft./140m.; 🅿; z 93450; © 501
San Benito; RMC Place; SAN BENITO; *152 SC-4; elev. 1,400ft./427m.; mail Paicines z 95043; rural
SAN BENITO; 152 SC-5; ℗ 36,697; © 53,234; ◆ 54,266
San Bernardino; Inc. Place; ⊡ SAN BERNARDINO; 153 SJ-13; elev. 1,049ft./320m.; 🅿 🅷 🅲 16,479 ■; ★ RIV-; z 92401-08, z 92410-15, z 92418, z 92423-24, z 92427; ℗ 164,676; © 185,401; ◆ 184,595
SAN BERNARDINO; 153 SH-18; ℗ 1,418,380; © 1,709,434; ◆ 2,023,779
San Bruno; Inc. Place; SAN MATEO; 150 NM-5; elev. 16ft./5m.; 🅿 ■; ★ SF-O-; z 94066; ℗ 38,961; © 40,165; ◆ 40,310
San Buenaventura; VENTURA; see Ventura (Inc. Place)
San Carlos; RMC Place; SAN DIEGO; *153 SM-14; ★ SDGO; mail San Diego z 92119; pop. incl. with San Diego (Inc. Place)
San Carlos; Inc. Place; SAN MATEO; 150 NM-5; elev. 40ft./12m.; 🅿; ★ SF-O-; z 94070; ℗ 26,167; © 27,718; ◆ 27,867
San Clemente; Inc. Place; ORANGE; 153 SL-12; elev. 200ft./61m.; 🅿 🅷; ★ L.A.; z 92672-74; ℗ 41,100; © 49,936; ◆ 54,663
Sand City; Inc. Place; MONTEREY; 149 I-2; 🅿; ★ MTRY-; z 93955; ℗ 192; © 261
Sanderson; RMC Place; RIVERSIDE; ★ HEM; mail Hemet z 92545; pop. incl. with Hemet (Inc. Place)
Sand Hill; RMC Place; CONTRA COSTA; *150 NL-6; elev. 43ft./13m.; ★ SF-O-; mail Oakley z 94561; pop. incl. with Oakley (Inc. Place)
San Diego; Inc. Place; ⊡ SAN DIEGO; 153 SN-13; elev. 42ft./13m.; 🅿 🅷 🅲 106,680 ■; ★ SDGO; z 92101-24, z 92126-32, z 92134-40, z 92142-43, z 92145, z 92147, z 92149-50, z 92152-55, z 92158-79, z 92182, z 92184, z 92186-87, z 92190-99; ℗ 1,110,549; © 1,223,400; ◆ 1,343,698
SAN DIEGO; 153 SL-15; ℗ 2,498,016; © 2,813,833; ◆ 3,040,407
San Diego Country Estates; CDP-Census Area Only; SAN DIEGO; *153 SM-14; ★ SDGO; mail Ramona z 92065; ℗ 6,874; © 9,262
San Dimas; Inc. Place; LOS ANGELES; 155 D-12; elev. 952ft./290m.; 🅿 🅷 🅲 425; ★ L.A.; z 91773; ℗ 32,397; © 34,980; ◆ 34,691
Sandy Korner; RMC Place; RIVERSIDE; *153 SK-16; elev. 96ft./29m.; mail Thermal z 92274; rural
San Felipe; RMC Place; SANTA CLARA; *152 SB-4; elev. 182ft./55m.; mail Hollister z 95023
San Fernando; Inc. Place; LOS ANGELES; 152 SI-10; elev. 1,061ft./323m.; 🅿 🅷; ★ L.A.; z 91340-41, z 91344-46; ℗ 22,580; © 23,564; ◆ 24,095
Sanford; RMC Place; LOS ANGELES; *153 SJ-11; 🅿; ★ L.A.; z 90005 & mail Los Angeles z 90010, z 90020, z 90075-76; pop. incl. with Los Angeles (Inc. Place)
San Francisco; Inc. Place; ⊡ SAN FRANCISCO; 150 NM-5; elev. 63ft./19m.; 🅿 🅷 🅲 63,462 ■; ★ SF-O-; z 94101-05, z 94107-12, z 94114-34, z 94137, z 94139-47, z 94151, z 94153-54, z 94156, z 94158-64, z 94171-72, z 94177, z 94188, z 94199; ℗ 723,959; © 776,733; ◆ 806,455
SAN FRANCISCO; 151 NF-13; ℗ 723,959; © 776,733; ◆ 806,455
San Gabriel; Inc. Place; LOS ANGELES; 154 E-9; elev. 430ft./131m.; 🅿 🅷 ■; ★ L.A.; z 91775-76, z 91778; ℗ 37,120; © 39,804; ◆ 42,174
Sanger; Inc. Place; FRESNO; 152 SC-8; elev. 363ft./111m.; 🅿 🅷; ★ FRES; z 93657; ℗ 16,839; © 18,931; ◆ 22,924
San Geronimo; CDP; MARIN; *150 NL-4; elev. 299ft./91m.; 🅿; ★ SF-O-; z 94963; © 436
San Gregorio; RMC Place; SAN MATEO; 150 NN-5; 🅿; z 94074; ● 200
San Jacinto; Inc. Place; RIVERSIDE; 153 SK-14; elev. 1,567ft./478m.; 🅿; ★ HEM; z 92581-83; ℗ 16,210; © 23,779; ◆ 33,665
San Joaquin; Inc. Place; FRESNO; 152 SC-6; elev. 170ft./52m.; 🅿; z 93660; ℗ 2,311; © 3,270
SAN JOAQUIN; 150 NL-7; ℗ 480,628; © 563,598; ◆ 666,369
San Joaquin Hills; CDP-Census Area Only; ORANGE; *153 SK-12; ★ L.A.; © 2,959
San Joaquin River Club; RMC Place; SAN JOAQUIN; *150 NM-7; mail Vernalis z 95385; ● 980
San Jose; Inc. Place; ⊡ SANTA CLARA; 150 NN-6; elev. 87ft./27m.; 🅿 🅷 🅲 31,318 ■; ★ SF-O-; z 95101, z 95103, z 95106, z 95108-13, z 95115-36, z 95138-41, z 95148, z 95150-61, z 95164, z 95170, z 95172-73, z 95190-94, z 95196; ℗ 782,248; © 894,943; ◆ 993,375
San Jose Recreation Camp; RMC Place; TUOLUMNE; *150 NM-10; elev. 3,000ft./914m.; mail Groveland z 95321; ● 10
San Juan Bautista; Inc. Place; SAN BENITO; 152 SB-3; 🅿; z 95045; ℗ 1,570; © 1,549
San Juan Capistrano; Inc. Place; ORANGE; 153 SL-12; 🅿; ★ L.A.; z 92675, z 92690-93 & mail Ladera Ranch z 92694; ℗ 26,183; © 33,826; ◆ 36,359
San Lawrence Terrace; RMC Place; SAN LUIS OBISPO; *152 SE-5; mail San Miguel z 93451; ● 150
San Leandro; Inc. Place; ALAMEDA; 150 NM-5; elev. 45ft./14m.; 🅿 🅷 ■; ★ SF-O-; z 94577-79; ℗ 68,223; © 79,452; ◆ 81,527
San Lorenzo; CDP; ALAMEDA; 150 NM-5; elev. 35ft./11m.; 🅿; ★ SF-O-; z 94580; ℗ 19,987; © 21,898; ◆ 22,404
San Lorenzo Park; RMC Place; SANTA CRUZ; *152 SA-2; elev. 703ft./214m.; ★ S.CRZ; mail Boulder Creek z 95006; ● 400
San Lucas; CDP; MONTEREY; 152 SD-4; elev. 406ft./124m.; 🅿; z 93954; © 419
San Luis Obispo; Inc. Place; ⊡ SAN LUIS OBISPO; 152 SG-5; elev. 234ft./71m.; 🅿 🅷 🅲 18,722 ■; ★ S.LUIS; z 93401-03, z 93405-10, z 93412; ℗ 41,958; © 44,174; ◆ 47,283
SAN LUIS OBISPO; 152 SF-6; ℗ 217,162; © 246,681; ◆ 273,227
San Luis Rey; RMC Place; SAN DIEGO; 156 I-2; 🅿; ★ SDGO; z 92068; pop. incl. with Oceanside (Inc. Place)
San Luis Rey Heights; RMC Place; SAN DIEGO; *153 SL-13; elev. 300ft./91m.; ★ SDGO; mail Fallbrook z 92028; ● 1,100
San Manuel Reservation; Indian Reservation; SAN BERNARDINO; © 74
San Marcos; Inc. Place; SAN DIEGO; 153 SL-13; 🅿 🅲 8,734; ★ SDGO; z 92069, z 92078-79, z 92096; ℗ 38,974; © 54,977; ◆ 67,161
San Marin; RMC Place; MARIN; ★ SF-O-; mail Novato z 94945; pop. incl. with Novato (Inc. Place)
San Marino; Inc. Place; LOS ANGELES; 154 D-9; elev. 566ft./173m.; 🅿; ★ L.A.; z 91108, z 91118; ℗ 12,959; © 12,945
San Martin; CDP; SANTA CLARA; 152 SA-3; elev. 282ft./86m.; 🅿; ★ SF-O-; z 95046; ℗ 1,713; © 4,230
San Mateo; Inc. Place; SAN MATEO; 151 NI-14; elev. 28ft./9m.; 🅿 🅷 ■; ★ SF-O-; z 94401-04, z 94497; ℗ 85,486; © 92,482; ◆ 95,258
SAN MATEO; 152 SA-2; ℗ 649,623; © 707,161; ® 707,163; ◆ 709,588
San Miguel; CDP; SAN LUIS OBISPO; 152 SE-5; 🅿; z 93451; ℗ 1,123; © 1,427
San Onofre; RMC Place; SAN DIEGO; mail San Clemente z 92672
San Pablo; Inc. Place; CONTRA COSTA; 150 NL-5; elev. 45ft./14m.; 🅿 🅷 ■; ★ SF-O-; z 94803, z 94806; ℗ 25,158; © 30,215; ◆ 34,296
San Pasqual Reservation; Indian Reservation; SAN DIEGO; ★ SDGO; mail Valley Center z 92082; ℗ 209; © 752
San Pedro; RMC Place; LOS ANGELES; *153 SK-11; 🅿; ★ L.A.; z 90731-34; pop. incl. with Los Angeles (Inc. Place)
San Quentin; RMC Place; MARIN; 151 ND-12; elev. 32ft./10m.; 🅿; ★ SF-O-; z 94964, z 94974; ● 100
San Rafael; Inc. Place; ⊡ MARIN; 150 NL-5; elev. 34ft./10m.; 🅿 🅷 🅲 2,045 ■; ★ SF-O-; z 94901, z 94903, z 94912-13, z 94915 & mail Greenbrae z 94904, Kentfield z 94914; ℗ 48,404; © 56,063; ◆ 55,943
San Ramon; Inc. Place; CONTRA COSTA; 150 NM-6; 🅿 🅷; ★ SF-O-; z 94582-83; ℗ 35,303; © 44,722; ◆ 45,128
San Ramon Village; RMC Place; ALAMEDA; ★ SF-O-; mail Dublin z 94568; pop. incl. with Dublin (Inc. Place)
San Roque; RMC Place; SANTA BARBARA; ★ S.BAR; mail Santa Barbara z 93105, z 93130; pop. incl. with Santa Barbara (Inc. Place)
San Simeon; RMC Place; SAN LUIS OBISPO; 152 SF-4; 🅿; z 93452
San Simeon Acres (Arbuckle Tract); RMC Place; SAN LUIS OBISPO; *152 SF-4; elev. 82ft./25m.; mail San Simeon z 93452; ● 400
Santa Ana; Inc. Place; ⊡ ORANGE; 153 SK-12; elev. 110ft./34m.; 🅿 🅷 🅲 6,851 ■; ★ L.A.; z 92701-08, z 92711-12, z 92725, z 92728, z 92735, z 92799; ℗ 293,742; © 337,977; ◆ 350,216
Santa Ana Heights; RMC Place; ORANGE; *153 SK-12; ★ L.A.; mail Santa Ana z 92707; pop. incl. with Costa Mesa (Inc. Place)
Santa Barbara; Inc. Place; ⊡ SANTA BARBARA; 152 SI-7; elev. 42ft./13m.; 🅿 🅷 🅲 26,202 ■; ★ S.BAR; z 93101-03, z 93105-11, z 93116-18, z 93120-21, z 93130, z 93140, z 93150, z 93160, z 93190, z 93199; ℗ 85,571; © 92,325; ® 89,600; ◆ 99,790
SANTA BARBARA; 152 SH-7; ℗ 369,608; © 399,347; ◆ 411,771
Santa Clara; Inc. Place; SANTA CLARA; 151 NL-18; elev. 88ft./27m.; 🅿 🅷 🅲 8,377 ■; ★ SF-O-; z 95050-56; ℗ 93,613; © 102,361; ◆ 111,849
SANTA CLARA; 150 NN-7; ℗ 1,497,577; © 1,682,585; ◆ 1,783,508
Santa Clarita; LOS ANGELES; see Newhall (RMC Place)
Santa Clarita; Inc. Place; LOS ANGELES; 152 SI-10; 🅿 🅲 2,462; ★ L.A.; z 91310, z 91321-22, z 91350-51, z 91354-55, z 91380-87, z 91390; ℗ 110,690; © 151,088; ◆ 167,484
Santa Cruz; Inc. Place; ⊡ SANTA CRUZ; 152 SB-2; elev. 20ft./6m.; 🅿 🅷 🅲 15,360 ■; ★ S.CRZ; z 95060-67; ℗ 49,040; © 54,593; ◆ 55,610
SANTA CRUZ; 152 SA-2; ℗ 229,734; © 255,602; ◆ 255,722
Santa Cruz Gardens; RMC Place; SANTA CRUZ; *152 SB-2; elev. 200ft./61m.; ★ S.CRZ; mail Santa Cruz z 95062; ● 1,850
Santa Fe Springs; Inc. Place; LOS ANGELES; 154 G-9; elev. 130ft./40m.; 🅿 ■; ★ L.A.; z 90670-71 & mail Whittier z 90605; ℗ 15,520; © 17,438; ® 16,413; ◆ 19,185
Santa Margarita; RMC Place; SAN LUIS OBISPO; 152 SF-5; elev. 1,000ft./305m.; 🅿; z 93453; ● 1,200
Santa Maria; Inc. Place; SANTA BARBARA; 152 SG-6; elev. 216ft./66m.; 🅿 🅷 ■; ★ S.MAR; z 93454-58; ℗ 61,284; © 77,423; ◆ 87,664
Santa Monica; Inc. Place; LOS ANGELES; 152 SJ-10; elev. 101ft./31m.; 🅿 🅷 🅲 2,025 ■; ★ L.A.; z 90401-11; ℗ 86,905; © 84,084; ◆ 86,310
Santa Monica Canyon; RMC Place; LOS ANGELES; ★ L.A.; mail Santa Monica z 90402; pop. incl. with Los Angeles (Inc. Place)
Santa Nella; MERCED; see Santa Nella Village (RMC Place)
Santa Nella Village (Santa Nella); RMC Place; MERCED; 152 SA-4; mail Gustine z 95322; ● 1,050
Santa Paula; Inc. Place; VENTURA; 152 SI-9; elev. 274ft./84m.; 🅿 🅷 🅲 361; ★ OXN-; z 93060-61; ℗ 25,062; © 28,598; ◆ 30,358
Santa Rita; RMC Place; MONTEREY; *152 SB-3; ★ SLNS; mail Salinas z 93906; pop. incl. with Salinas (Inc. Place)
Santa Rita; RMC Place; SANTA BARBARA; *152 SH-6; mail Lompoc z 93436; rural
Santa Rita Park; RMC Place; MERCED; 152 SB-5; 🅿; z 93661; ● 170
Santa Rosa; Inc. Place; ⊡ SONOMA; 150 NK-4; elev. 167ft./51m.; 🅿 🅷 ■; ★ S.ROS; z 95401-07, z 95409; ℗ 113,261; © 147,595; ◆ 155,700
Santa Rosa Rancheria; Indian Reservation; KINGS; © 517
Santa Rosa Reservation; Indian Reservation; RIVERSIDE; mail Hemet z 92543; ℗ 12; © 65
Santa Susana; RMC Place; VENTURA; *152 SI-10; elev. 961ft./293m.; 🅿; ★ L.A.; z 93063; pop. incl. with Simi Valley (Inc. Place)
Santa Venetia; CDP; MARIN; 150 NL-5; ★ SF-O-; mail San Rafael z 94901, z 94903; ℗ 3,362; © 4,298
Santa Western; RMC Place; LOS ANGELES; ★ L.A.; mail Los Angeles z 90072; pop. incl. with Los Angeles (Inc. Place)
Santa Ynez; CDP; SANTA BARBARA; 152 SH-7; 🅿; z 93460; ℗ 4,200; © 4,584
Santa Ynez Reservation; Indian Reservation; SANTA BARBARA; © 122
Santa Ysabel; RMC Place; SAN DIEGO; 153 SM-15; elev. 2,984ft./910m.; 🅿; z 92070; ● 100
Santa Ysabel Reservation; Indian Reservation; SAN DIEGO; mail Santa Ysabel z 92070; ℗ 196; © 250
Santee; Inc. Place; SAN DIEGO; 153 SM-14; elev. 369ft./112m.; 🅿; ★ SDGO; z 92071-72; ℗ 52,902; © 52,975; ◆ 55,974
San Ysidro; RMC Place; SAN DIEGO; 156 N-8; 🅿; ★ SDGO; z 92143, z 92173
Saranap; RMC Place; CONTRA COSTA; *150 NM-6; ★ SF-O-; mail Walnut Creek z 94595; ● 1,300
Saratoga; Inc. Place; SANTA CLARA; 152 SA-2; elev. 455ft./139m.; 🅿; ★ SF-O-; z 95070-71; ℗ 28,061; © 29,843; ◆ 30,857
Saratoga Springs; RMC Place; LAKE; *150 NI-4; elev. 1,348ft./411m.; mail Witter Springs z 95493; ● 200
Sather Gate; RMC Place; ALAMEDA; ★ SF-O-; mail Berkeley z 94704; pop. incl. with Berkeley (Inc. Place)
Saticoy; RMC Place; VENTURA; *152 SI-9; elev. 151ft./46m.; ★ OXN-; mail Ventura z 93004, z 93007
Sattley; RMC Place; SIERRA; 150 NH-9; elev. 4,944ft./1,507m.; 🅿; z 96124; ● 100
Saugus; RMC Place; LOS ANGELES; *152 SI-10; 🅿; ★ L.A.; z 91350 & mail Santa Clarita z 91390; pop. incl. with Santa Clarita (Inc. Place)
Sausalito; Inc. Place; MARIN; 151 NE-12; elev. 14ft./4m.; 🅿; ★ SF-O-; z 94965-66; ℗ 7,152; © 7,330
Saviers; RMC Place; VENTURA; ★ OXN-; mail Oxnard z 93033; pop. incl. with Oxnard (Inc. Place)
Sawyers Bar; RMC Place; SISKIYOU; 150 NC-4; 🅿; z 96027; ● 100
Scenic Brook Estates; RMC Place; TUOLUMNE; *150 NL-9; elev. 2,146ft./654m.; mail Sonora z 95370; ● 550
Scenic Center; RMC Place; STANISLAUS; ★ MOD; mail Modesto z 95355; pop. incl. with Modesto (Inc. Place)
Scheideck; RMC Place; VENTURA; *152 SH-8; elev. 3,800ft./1,158m.; mail Maricopa z 93252; ● 20
Schellville; RMC Place; SONOMA; *150 NK-5; mail Sonoma z 95476; ● 200
Scotia; RMC Place; HUMBOLDT; 150 NE-2; elev. 164ft./50m.; 🅿; z 95565; ● 850
Scotland; RMC Place; SAN BERNARDINO; 155 B-16; mail Lytle Creek z 92358; ● 285
Scott Bar; RMC Place; SISKIYOU; 150 NB-4; 🅿; z 96085; ● 150
Scotts Valley; Inc. Place; SANTA CRUZ; 152 SB-2; elev. 570ft./174m.; 🅿 🅲 542; ★ S.CRZ; z 95060, z 95066-67; ℗ 8,615; © 11,385
Scripps Ranch; RMC Place; SAN DIEGO; *153 SM-14; ★ SDGO; mail San Diego z 92128; pop. incl. with San Diego (Inc. Place)
Seabright; RMC Place; SANTA CRUZ; ★ S.CRZ; pop. incl. with Santa Cruz (Inc. Place)
Seacliff; RMC Place; SANTA CRUZ; ★ S.CRZ; mail Aptos z 95003; ● 800
Seahaven; RMC Place; MARIN; *150 NL-4; mail Inverness z 94937; ● 900
Seal Beach; Inc. Place; ORANGE; 154 J-9; elev. 10ft./3m.; 🅿; ★ L.A.; z 90740; ℗ 25,098; © 24,157; ◆ 24,273
Seal Cove; RMC Place; SAN MATEO; *150 NM-5; elev. 50ft./15m.; ★ SF-O-; mail Moss Beach z 94038; ● 300
Sea Ranch; RMC Place; SONOMA; 150 NJ-3; mail Gualala z 95445, The Sea Ranch z 95497; ● 250
Searles Valley; CDP-Census Area Only; SAN BERNARDINO; *153 SE-13; mail Trona z 93562; ℗ 2,740; © 1,885
Seaside; Inc. Place; MONTEREY; 152 SC-3; elev. 20ft./6m.; 🅿 🅲 3,820; ★ MTRY-; z 93955; ℗ 38,901; © 31,696; ® 33,097; ◆ 32,594
Sebastiani; RMC Place; SONOMA; mail Sonoma z 95476; pop. incl. with Sonoma (Inc. Place)
Sebastopol; RMC Place; NEVADA; *150 NH-8; elev. 2,000ft./610m.; mail North San Juan z 95960; rural
Sebastopol; Inc. Place; SONOMA; 150 NK-4; elev. 78ft./24m.; 🅿 🅷; ★ S.ROS; z 95472-73; ℗ 7,004; © 7,774
Sedco Hills; CDP; RIVERSIDE; 155 K-19; elev. 1,275ft./389m.; mail Lake Elsinore z 92530; ℗ 3,008; © 3,078
Seeley; CDP; IMPERIAL; 153 SM-17; elev.-42ft./-13m.; 🅿; z 92273; ℗ 1,228; © 1,624
Seguro; RMC Place; KERN; *152 SF-9; ★ BAK; ● 12,000
Seiad Valley; RMC Place; SISKIYOU; 150 NA-4; elev. 1,371ft./418m.; 🅿; z 96086; ● 270
Selma; Inc. Place; FRESNO; 152 SC-8; elev. 308ft./94m.; 🅿 🅷; ★ FRES; z 93662; ℗ 14,757; © 19,444; ◆ 23,574
Seneca; RMC Place; PLUMAS; *150 NF-8; mail Canyon Dam z 95923
Sentous; RMC Place; LOS ANGELES; *152 SJ-10; elev. 103ft./31m.; ★ L.A.; pop. incl. with Los Angeles (Inc. Place)
Sepulveda; RMC Place; LOS ANGELES; *152 SJ-10; 🅿; ★ L.A.; z 91343, z 91393; pop. incl. with Los Angeles (Inc. Place)
Sequoia Crest; RMC Place; TULARE; *152 SD-10; elev. 6,000ft./1,829m.; mail Springville z 93265; ● 10
Serena Park; RMC Place; SANTA BARBARA; *152 SI-8; ★ S.BAR; mail Carpinteria z 93013; ● 700
Serene Lakes; RMC Place; PLACER; *150 NI-9; elev. 6,997ft./2,133m.; mail Soda Springs z 95728; ● 100
Serra; RMC Place; ORANGE; ★ L.A.; mail Capistrano Beach z 92624; pop. incl. with Dana Point (Inc. Place)
Serra Mesa; RMC Place; SAN DIEGO; *153 SM-13; ★ SDGO; mail San Diego z 92123, z 92193-94; pop. incl. with San Diego (Inc. Place)
Serramonte; RMC Place; SAN MATEO; ★ SF-O-; mail Daly City z 94015; pop. incl. with Daly City (Inc. Place)
Sespe; RMC Place; VENTURA; *152 SI-9; mail Fillmore z 93015; ● 350
Seven Oaks; RMC Place; SAN BERNARDINO; *153 SJ-14; mail Angelus Oaks z 92305; rural
Seven Pines; RMC Place; INYO; *153 SB-11; elev. 1,880ft./573m.; mail Independence z 93526; ● 30
Seven Trees; CDP-Census Area Only; SANTA CLARA; *150 NN-6; ★ SF-O-; © 1,666
Seville; RMC Place; TULARE; *152 SC-9; elev. 353ft./108m.; ★ VISL; mail Visalia z 93291; ● 450
Shackelford; CDP-Census Area Only; STANISLAUS; *150 NM-8; ★ MOD; © 5,170
Shadow Hills; RMC Place; LAKE; *150 NJ-4; elev. 1,400ft./427m.; 🅿; z 91040 & mail Middletown z 95461, Sun Valley z 91352; rural
Shady Glen; RMC Place; PLACER; *150 NI-8; elev. 2,445ft./745m.; ★ SAC; mail Colfax z 95713; ● 450
Shafter; Inc. Place; KERN; 152 SF-8; elev. 345ft./105m.; 🅿; z 93263 & mail Bakersfield z 93314; ℗ 8,409; © 12,736
Shandon; CDP; SAN LUIS OBISPO; 152 SF-6; elev. 1,038ft./316m.; 🅿; z 93461; © 986
Sharon Heights; RMC Place; SAN MATEO; ★ SF-O-; mail Menlo Park z 94025; pop. incl. with Menlo Park (Inc. Place)
Sharp Park; RMC Place; SAN MATEO; *150 NM-5; ★ SF-O-; mail Pacifica z 94044; pop. incl. with Pacifica (Inc. Place)
Shasta; RMC Place; SHASTA; 150 NE-5; elev. 1,026ft./313m.; 🅿; z 96087; ● 950
SHASTA; 150 NE-7; ℗ 147,036; © 163,256; ◆ 178,290
Shasta Lake; Inc. Place; SHASTA; 150 NE-5; 🅿; ★ REDD; z 96019, z 96079, z 96089; ℗ 8,821; © 9,008
Shaver Lake; CDP; FRESNO; *152 SA-8; 🅿; z 93634, z 93642, z 93664; © 705
Shaver Lake Heights; RMC Place; FRESNO; *152 SA-8; mail Shaver Lake z 93664; ● 120
Shaws Flat; RMC Place; TUOLUMNE; mail Sonora z 95370; ● 160
Sheep Ranch; RMC Place; CALAVERAS; 150 NL-9; elev. 2,371ft./723m.; 🅿; z 95246, z 95250; ● 110
Sheldon; RMC Place; SACRAMENTO; *150 NK-7; elev. 74ft./23m.; ★ SAC; mail Elk Grove z 95624; ● 300
Shell Beach; RMC Place; SAN LUIS OBISPO; *152 SG-5; 🅿; z 93448-49; pop. incl. with Pismo Beach (Inc. Place)
Shelter Cove; RMC Place; HUMBOLDT; 150 NF-2; mail Whitethorn z 95589; ● 150
Shelter Cove; RMC Place; SAN MATEO; *150 NM-5; ★ SF-O-; mail Pacifica z 94044
Sheridan; RMC Place; PLACER; 150 NI-7; elev. 115ft./35m.; 🅿; z 95681 & mail Villa Grande z 95486; ● 1,100
Sherman Oaks; RMC Place; LOS ANGELES; *152 SJ-10; elev. 657ft./200m.; 🅿; ★ L.A.; z 91401, z 91403, z 91411, z 91413, z 91423, z 91495; pop. incl. with Los Angeles (Inc. Place)
Sherwood; RMC Place; MONTEREY; ★ SLNS; mail Salinas z 93906; pop. incl. with Salinas (Inc. Place)
Sherwood Forest; RMC Place; CONTRA COSTA; 151 ND-15; ★ SF-O-; mail El Sobrante z 94803; ● 2,600
Sherwood Valley Rancheria; Indian Reservation; MENDOCINO; mail Fort Bragg z 95437; © 179
Shingle Springs; CDP; EL DORADO; 150 NJ-8; 🅿; ★ SAC; z 95682; ℗ 2,049; © 2,643
Shingle Springs Rancheria; Indian Reservation; EL DORADO; © 57
Shingletown; CDP; SHASTA; 150 NE-6; 🅿; z 96088; © 2,222
Shinn; RMC Place; ALAMEDA; *150 NM-6; ★ SF-O-; mail Fremont z 94536; pop. incl. with Fremont (Inc. Place)
Shively; RMC Place; HUMBOLDT; 150 NE-2; mail Scotia z 95565; ● 110
Shore Acres; RMC Place; CONTRA COSTA; 151 NB-18; ★ SF-O-; mail Pittsburg z 94565; ● 4,000
Short Acres; RMC Place; KINGS; *152 SD-8; mail Hanford z 93230; pop. incl. with Hanford (Inc. Place)
Shoshone; CDP; INYO; 153 SE-15; elev. 1,569ft./478m.; 🅿; z 92384; © 52
Sierra; RMC Place; FRESNO; ★ FRES; mail Fresno z 93703; pop. incl. with Fresno (Inc. Place)
SIERRA; 150 NH-9; ℗ 3,318; © 3,555; ◆ 3,176
Sierra Brooks; RMC Place; SIERRA; *150 NH-10; elev. 5,200ft./1,585m.; mail Loyalton z 96118; ● 390
Sierra Cedars; RMC Place; FRESNO; *152 SB-8; elev. 5,800ft./1,768m.; mail Shaver Lake z 93664; ● 200
Sierra City; RMC Place; SIERRA; 150 NH-9; 🅿; z 96125; ● 250
Sierra Heights; RMC Place; TULARE; *152 SD-9; elev. 406ft./124m.; mail Lindsay z 93247; rural
Sierra Madre; Inc. Place; LOS ANGELES; 154 D-9; elev. 840ft./256m.; 🅿; ★ L.A.; z 91024-25; ℗ 10,762; © 10,578
Sierra Sky Park; RMC Place; FRESNO; *152 SB-7; elev. 320ft./98m.; ★ FRES; mail Fresno z 93722; pop. incl. with Fresno (Inc. Place)
Sierra Valley Lodge; SIERRA; see Calpine (RMC Place)
Sierra Village; RMC Place; TUOLUMNE; *150 NL-10; mail Mi Wuk Village z 95346; ● 200
Sierraville; RMC Place; SIERRA; 150 NH-9; elev. 4,952ft./1,509m.; 🅿; z 96126; ● 150
Signal Hill; Inc. Place; LOS ANGELES; 154 I-8; elev. 100ft./30m.; 🅿; ★ L.A.; z 90755, z 90804, z 90807 & mail Long Beach z 90806; ℗ 8,371; © 9,333
Silverado; RMC Place; ORANGE; 155 J-14; 🅿; ★ L.A.; z 92676; ● 800
Silver City; RMC Place; TULARE; 152 SM-2; elev. 6,935ft./2,114m.; mail Three Rivers z 93271; rural
Silver Strand; RMC Place; VENTURA; *152 SJ-9; ★ OXN-; mail Oxnard z 93035; ● 1,200
Simi; VENTURA; see Simi Valley (Inc. Place)
Simi Valley (Simi); Inc. Place; VENTURA; 152 SI-9; elev. 820ft./250m.; 🅿 🅷 ■; ★ L.A.; z 93062-65, z 93094, z 93099; ℗ 100,217; © 111,351; ◆ 118,052
Simmler; RMC Place; SAN LUIS OBISPO; *152 SF-7; elev. 2,049ft./625m.; mail Santa Margarita z 93453; rural
Simms; RMC Place; MARIN; ★ SF-O-; mail San Rafael z 94901; pop. incl. with San Rafael (Inc. Place)
Simms; RMC Place; SAN JOAQUIN; *150 NM-8; mail Ripon z 95366
SISKIYOU; 150 NB-6; ℗ 43,531; © 44,301; ◆ 44,071
Sisquoc; RMC Place; SANTA BARBARA; 152 SH-6; elev. 440ft./134m.; mail Santa Maria z 93454; ● 250
Sites; RMC Place; COLUSA; 150 NI-5; mail Stonyford z 95979
Skyforest; RMC Place; SAN BERNARDINO; 155 B-20; 🅿; ★ RIV-; z 92385; ● 750
Skyhigh; RMC Place; CALAVERAS; *150 NK-10; elev. 7,000ft./2,134m.; mail Arnold z 95223; rural
Skyline East; RMC Place; SAN BERNARDINO; *153 SH-14; mail Barstow z 92311; ● 400
Skyline North; RMC Place; SAN BERNARDINO; *153 SH-14; elev. 2,204ft./672m.; mail Barstow z 92311; ● 650
Sky Londa; RMC Place; SAN MATEO; *150 NN-5; ★ SF-O-; mail Redwood City z 94062; pop. incl. with Woodside (Inc. Place)
Sky Valley; RMC Place; RIVERSIDE; *153 SJ-15; elev. 1,360ft./415m.; ★ PSPR-; mail Desert Hot Springs z 92241; ● 1,000
Slawson; RMC Place; LOS ANGELES; ★ L.A.; mail Pico Rivera z 90662; pop. incl. with Pico Rivera (Inc. Place)
Sleepy Hollow; RMC Place; MARIN; 151 NC-11; ★ SF-O-; mail San Anselmo z 94960; ● 2,400
Sleepy Hollow; RMC Place; SAN BERNARDINO; *153 SJ-12; ★ L.A.; mail Chino z 91710; pop. incl. with Chino Hills (Inc. Place)
Sleepy Valley; RMC Place; LOS ANGELES; mail Santa Clarita z 91350; ● 200
Sloat; RMC Place; PLUMAS; 150 NG-9; mail Blairsden-Graeagle z 96103; ● 100
Sloughhouse; RMC Place; SACRAMENTO; 150 NK-8; 🅿; ★ SAC; z 95683; ● 350
Smartsville (Smartville); RMC Place; YUBA; 150 NI-7; 🅿; z 95977; ● 200
Smartville; YUBA; see Smartsville (RMC Place)
Smeltzer; RMC Place; ORANGE; *153 SK-11; elev. 22ft./7m.; ★ L.A.; pop. incl. with Huntington Beach (Inc. Place)
Smiley Heights; RMC Place; SAN BERNARDINO; ★ RIV-; mail Redlands z 92373; pop. incl. with Redlands (Inc. Place)
Smiley Park; RMC Place; SAN BERNARDINO; *153 SJ-13; ★ RIV-; mail Running Springs z 92382; ● 120
Smith Corner; RMC Place; KERN; *152 SF-8; elev. 328ft./100m.; mail Shafter z 93263; ● 760
Smithflat; RMC Place; EL DORADO; 150 NJ-9; mail Placerville z 95667; ● 250
Smith River; RMC Place; DEL NORTE; 150 NA-2; 🅿; z 95567; ● 950
Smith River Rancheria; Indian Reservation; DEL NORTE; © 62
Smoke Tree; RMC Place; RIVERSIDE; ★ PSPR-; mail Palm Springs z 92262; pop. incl. with Palm Springs (Inc. Place)
Snelling; RMC Place; MERCED; 150 NN-9; elev. 259ft./79m.; 🅿; z 95369; ● 300
Snoboy; RMC Place; ALAMEDA; *150 NN-6; ★ SF-O-; pop. incl. with Fremont (Inc. Place)
Snow Creek; RMC Place; RIVERSIDE; *153 SJ-14; elev. 1,252ft./382m.; mail Whitewater z 92282; ● 60
Snowline Camp; RMC Place; EL DORADO; *150 NJ-9; mail Camino z 95709; rural
Soboba Hot Springs; RMC Place; RIVERSIDE; *153 SK-14; ★ HEM; mail San Jacinto z 92583; ● 200
Soboba Reservation; Indian Reservation; RIVERSIDE; ★ HEM; mail San Jacinto z 92583; ℗ 258; © 522
Soda Bay; RMC Place; LAKE; *150 NI-4; mail Kelseyville z 95451; ● 700
Soda Springs; RMC Place; NEVADA; 150 NI-9; elev. 6,768ft./2,063m.; 🅿; z 95724, z 95728; ● 200
Solana Beach; Inc. Place; SAN DIEGO; 153 SM-13; 🅿; ★ SDGO; z 92075; ℗ 12,962; © 12,979
SOLANO; 150 NK-6; ℗ 340,421; © 394,542; ◆ 402,332
Soledad; Inc. Place; MONTEREY; 152 SC-4; 🅿; z 93960; ℗ 7,161; © 11,263; ® 23,015; ◆ 27,661
Solemint; RMC Place; LOS ANGELES; *152 SI-10; elev. 1,442ft./440m.; ★ L.A.; mail Santa Clarita z 91350; pop. incl. with Santa Clarita (Inc. Place)
Solimar Beach; VENTURA; see Dulah (RMC Place)
Solvang; Inc. Place; SANTA BARBARA; 152 SH-6; 🅿 🅷; z 93463-64; ℗ 4,741; © 5,332
Somerset; RMC Place; EL DORADO; 150 NJ-9; elev. 2,089ft./637m.; 🅿; z 95684; ● 160
Somes Bar; RMC Place; SISKIYOU; 150 NC-3; 🅿; z 95568; ● 150
Somis; RMC Place; VENTURA; 152 SI-9; 🅿; ★ OXN-; z 93066; ● 1,000
Sonoma; Inc. Place; SONOMA; 150 NK-5; elev. 84ft./26m.; 🅿 🅷; z 95476; ℗ 8,121; © 9,128
SONOMA; 150 NJ-4; ℗ 388,222; © 458,614; ◆ 459,348
Sonoma Vista; RMC Place; SONOMA; mail Sonoma z 95476; ● 350
Sonora; Inc. Place; ⊡ TUOLUMNE; 150 NL-9; 🅿 🅷; z 95370, z 95373; ℗ 4,153; © 4,423
Sonora Junction; RMC Place; MONO; *151 NK-11; elev. 6,886ft./2,099m.; mail Bridgeport z 93517; rural
Soquel; CDP; SANTA CRUZ; 152 SB-2; 🅿; ★ S.CRZ; z 95073; ℗ 9,188; © 5,081
Sorensen; RMC Place; ALAMEDA; ★ SF-O-; mail Hayward z 94544; pop. incl. with Hayward (Inc. Place)
Sorensens; RMC Place; ALPINE; 150 NJ-10; mail Markleeville z 96120; ● 50
Sorrento; SAN DIEGO; see Sorrento Valley (RMC Place)
Sorrento Valley (Sorrento); RMC Place; SAN DIEGO; *153 SM-13; ★ SDGO; mail San Diego z 92121, z 92131, z 92191; pop. incl. with San Diego (Inc. Place)
Soto; RMC Place; LOS ANGELES; ★ L.A.; mail Huntington Park z 90255; pop. incl. with Huntington Park (Inc. Place)
Soulsbyville; CDP; TUOLUMNE; 150 NL-10; 🅿; z 95372; ℗ 1,732; © 1,729
South; RMC Place; LOS ANGELES; ★ L.A.; mail Los Angeles z 90061; pop. incl. with Los Angeles (Inc. Place)
South Alhambra; RMC Place; LOS ANGELES; *153 SJ-11; ★ L.A.; mail Alhambra z 91803; pop. incl. with Alhambra (Inc. Place)
South Anaheim; RMC Place; ORANGE; *153 SK-12; ★ L.A.; pop. incl. with Anaheim (Inc. Place)
South Bakersfield; RMC Place; KERN; ★ BAK; mail Bakersfield z 93384; pop. incl. with Bakersfield (Inc. Place)
South Bay; HUMBOLDT; see Fields Landing (RMC Place)
Southbay Pavilion; RMC Place; LOS ANGELES; ★ L.A.; mail Carson z 90745-46; pop. incl. with Carson (Inc. Place)
South Belridge; RMC Place; KERN; *152 SF-7; elev. 825ft./251m.; mail Mc Kittrick z 93251; ● 120
South Berkeley; RMC Place; ALAMEDA; ★ SF-O-; mail Berkeley z 94703; pop. incl. with Berkeley (Inc. Place)
South Brighton; RMC Place; SACRAMENTO; ★ SAC; pop. incl. with Sacramento (Inc. Place)
South Corona; RMC Place; RIVERSIDE; ★ RIV-; mail Corona z 92880; pop. incl. with Corona (Inc. Place)
South Dos Palos; CDP; MERCED; 152 SB-5; elev. 115ft./35m.; 🅿; z 93665; ℗ 1,214; © 1,385
South Downey; RMC Place; LOS ANGELES; ★ L.A.; mail Downey z 90242; pop. incl. with Downey (Inc. Place)
Southeastern; RMC Place; SAN DIEGO; ★ SDGO; mail San Diego z 92113, z 92170; pop. incl. with San Diego (Inc. Place)
South El Monte; Inc. Place; LOS ANGELES; 154 E-9; elev. 244ft./74m.; 🅿 🅷; ★ L.A.; z 91733; ℗ 20,850; © 21,144; ◆ 21,267
South Fontana; RMC Place; SAN BERNARDINO; *153 SJ-13; elev. 1,004ft./306m.; ★ RIV-; mail Fontana z 92337; pop. incl. with Fontana (Inc. Place)
South Fork; RMC Place; HUMBOLDT; *150 NE-2; mail Redcrest z 95569; rural
South Fork; RMC Place; MADERA; *152 SA-8; mail North Fork z 93643; rural
South Fork; RMC Place; MARIPOSA; *150 NM-10; elev. 1,410ft./430m.; mail El Portal z 95318; rural
South Gardena; RMC Place; LOS ANGELES; *153 SJ-11; ★ L.A.; mail Gardena z 90248; pop. incl. with Gardena (Inc. Place)
South Gate; Inc. Place; LOS ANGELES; 154 G-7; elev. 111ft./34m.; 🅿 ■; ★ L.A.; z 90280; ℗ 86,284; © 96,375; ◆ 102,487
South Hills; RMC Place; LOS ANGELES; ★ L.A.; mail West Covina z 91791; pop. incl. with West Covina (Inc. Place)
South Irvine; RMC Place; ORANGE; ★ L.A.; pop. incl. with Irvine (Inc. Place)
South Laguna; RMC Place; ORANGE; *153 SL-12; 🅷; ★ L.A.; mail Laguna Beach z 92651, Laguna Niguel z 92677; pop. incl. with Laguna Beach (Inc. Place)
South Lake; RMC Place; KERN; *152 SF-10; mail Lake Isabella z 93240; ℗ 1,059
South Lake Tahoe; Inc. Place; EL DORADO; 150 NJ-10; elev. 6,260ft./1,908m.; 🅿 🅷 ■; z 96150-52, z 96154-58; ℗ 21,586; © 23,609; ◆ 24,412
South Leggett; RMC Place; MENDOCINO; *150 NG-2; elev. 1,150ft./351m.; mail Leggett z 95585; ● 120
South Los Angeles; RMC Place; LOS ANGELES; *153 SJ-11; ★ L.A.; mail Los Angeles z 90061; pop. incl. with Los Angeles (Inc. Place)
South Main; RMC Place; ORANGE; ★ L.A.; mail Santa Ana z 92707; pop. incl. with Santa Ana (Inc. Place)
South Modesto; RMC Place; STANISLAUS; *150 NM-8; ★ MOD; mail Modesto z 95350
South Oroville; CDP; BUTTE; *150 NH-7; mail Oroville z 95965; ℗ 7,463; © 7,695
South Oxnard; RMC Place; VENTURA; ★ OXN-; pop. incl. with Oxnard (Inc. Place)
South Park; RMC Place; SAN DIEGO; *153 SN-13; ★ SDGO; mail San Diego z 92102; pop. incl. with San Diego (Inc. Place)
South Pasadena; Inc. Place; LOS ANGELES; 154 D-8; elev. 660ft./201m.; 🅿; ★ L.A.; z 91030-31; ℗ 23,936; © 24,292; ◆ 24,224
Southport; RMC Place; YOLO; ★ SAC; mail West Sacramento z 95691; pop. incl. with West Sacramento (Inc. Place)
South Sacramento; RMC Place; SACRAMENTO; ★ SAC; pop. incl. with Sacramento (Inc. Place)
South San Bernardino; RMC Place; SAN BERNARDINO; ★ RIV-; pop. incl. with San Bernardino (Inc. Place)
South San Francisco; Inc. Place; SAN MATEO; 150 NM-5; elev. 19ft./6m.; 🅿 🅷 ■; ★ SF-O-; z 94080, z 94083; ℗ 54,312; © 60,552; ◆ 64,713
South San Gabriel; CDP; LOS ANGELES; 154 E-9; elev. 272ft./83m.; ★ L.A.; mail Rosemead z 91770; ℗ 7,700; © 7,595
South San Jose Hills; CDP-Census Area Only; LOS ANGELES; 155 F-11; ★ L.A.; mail La Puente z 91744; ℗ 17,814; © 20,218; ◆ 20,678
South San Leandro; RMC Place; ALAMEDA; ★ SF-O-; mail San Leandro z 94578; pop. incl. with San Leandro (Inc. Place)
South Santa Ana; RMC Place; ORANGE; *153 SK-12; ★ L.A.; pop. incl. with Santa Ana (Inc. Place)
South Taft; CDP; KERN; 152 SG-8; mail Taft z 93268; ℗ 2,170; © 1,898
South Whittier (Whittier South); CDP; LOS ANGELES; *153 SJ-11; elev. 160ft./49m.; ★ L.A.; mail Whittier z 90605; ℗ 49,524; © 55,193; ◆ 56,448
South Whittier Heights; RMC Place; LOS ANGELES; *153 SJ-11; ★ L.A.; mail Whittier z 90605; ● 1,500
Southwood; RMC Place; SAN MATEO; ★ SF-O-; pop. incl. with South San Francisco (Inc. Place)
South Woodbridge; CDP-Census Area Only; SAN JOAQUIN; *150 NL-7; ★ STOC; © 2,825
South Yuba City; CDP-Census Area Only; SUTTER; *150 NI-7; ★ YUCY; mail Yuba City z 95991; ℗ 8,816; © 12,651
Spadra; RMC Place; LOS ANGELES; *153 SJ-12; ★ L.A.; pop. incl. with Pomona (Inc. Place)
Spalding Tract (Spaulding); RMC Place; LASSEN; 150 NE-9; elev. 5,148ft./1,569m.; mail Susanville z 96130; ● 200
Spanish Flat; RMC Place; EL DORADO; *150 NJ-8; elev. 2,332ft./711m.; mail Garden Valley z 95633; rural
Spanish Flat; RMC Place; NAPA; *150 NK-5; 🅿; z 94558
Spanish Ranch; RMC Place; PLUMAS; 150 NG-8; mail Meadow Valley z 95956, Quincy z 95971; ● 170
Spaulding; LASSEN; see Spalding Tract (RMC Place)
Spicer City; RMC Place; KERN; *152 SF-8; mail Buttonwillow z 93206; rural
Spreckels; CDP; MONTEREY; *152 SC-3; 🅿; ★ SLNS; z 93962; © 485
Spring Creek; RMC Place; EL DORADO; *150 NJ-10; mail South Lake Tahoe z 96158; rural
Springdale; RMC Place; LOS ANGELES; ★ L.A.; pop. incl. with Los Angeles (Inc. Place)
Springfield; RMC Place; TUOLUMNE; *150 NL-9; elev. 2,056ft./627m.; mail Sonora z 95370; ● 900
Spring Garden; CDP; PLUMAS; 150 NG-9; 🅿; z 95971; © 55
Spring Hill; RMC Place; NEVADA; *150 NI-8; mail Grass Valley z 95945; pop. incl. with Grass Valley (Inc. Place)
Springstowne; RMC Place; SOLANO; ★ SF-O-; mail Vallejo z 94591; pop. incl. with Vallejo (Inc. Place)
Spring Valley; CDP; SAN DIEGO; 153 SN-14; elev. 500ft./152m.; 🅿; ★ SDGO; z 91976-79; ℗ 55,331; © 26,663; ◆ 28,810
Spring Valley Lake; RMC Place; SAN BERNARDINO; 🅿; ★ HESP-; z 92392, z 92395; pop. incl. with Apple Valley (Inc. Place)
Springville; CDP; TULARE; 152 SD-9; elev. 1,033ft./315m.; 🅿; z 93208, z 93265; © 1,109
Spruce Point; RMC Place; HUMBOLDT; *150 ND-1; ★ EUR-; mail Eureka z 95503; ● 550
Spurgeon; RMC Place; ORANGE; ★ L.A.; mail Santa Ana z 92701-02; pop. incl. with Santa Ana (Inc. Place)
Squaw Valley; CDP; FRESNO; 152 SB-8; 🅿; z 93646, z 93675; ℗ 2,161; © 2,691
Squaw Valley; PLACER; see Olympic Valley (RMC Place)
Squirrel Mountain Valley; CDP; KERN; *152 SF-10; elev. 2,948ft./899m.; mail Lake Isabella z 93240; © 498
Stadium; RMC Place; ORANGE; ★ L.A.; mail Anaheim z 92825; pop. incl. with Anaheim (Inc. Place)
Stafford; RMC Place; HUMBOLDT; *150 NE-2; elev. 139ft./42m.; mail Scotia z 95565; ● 110

Entries in **UPPERCASE** are counties.
Entries in **bold** have populations of 2,500 or more.
Names in parentheses are alternate names.

Inc. Place	Incorporated Place
RMC Place	Rand McNally Designated Place
CDP	Census Designated Place
MCD	Minor Civil Division
⊡	County Seat
▲	Minor Civil Division
elev.	Elevation
🅿	Post Office
🅷	Hospital
🅲	College
■	Principal Business Center
★	Ranally Metro Area (RMA) Abbreviation
z	Zip Code(s)
℗	Previous Census Population
®	Revised Census Population
Ⓐ	Annexation Population
●	Rand McNally Population Estimate
©	Final Census Population
Ⓢ	Special Census Population
◆	Estimated Population

For additional definitions see Glossary, Volume 1, and Introduction, Volume 2.

Stallion Springs; CDP-Census Area Only; KERN; ***152** SG-10; elev. 3,760ft./1,146m.; [P]; z 93561; Ⓒ 1,522
Standard; RMC Place; TUOLUMNE; ***150** NL-10; [P]; z 95373; ● 200
Standish; RMC Place; LASSEN; **150** NF-9; [P]; z 96128; ● 180
Stanford (Stanford University); CDP-Census Area Only; SANTA CLARA; **151** NK-16; [P] [H] [C] 14,890; ★ **SF-O-**; z 94305, z 94309; Ⓟ 18,097; Ⓒ 13,315
Stanford University; SANTA CLARA; see Stanford (CDP-Census Area Only)
STANISLAUS; **152** SA-4; Ⓟ 370,522; Ⓒ 446,997; ◆ 509,266
Stanton; Inc. Place; ORANGE; **154** I-10; elev. 60ft./18m.; [P]; ★ **L.A.**; z 90680; Ⓟ 30,491; Ⓒ 37,403; ◆ 38,727
Starlight Estates; RMC Place; INYO; ***151** NN-13; elev. 590ft./180m.; mail Bishop z 93514; ● 180
State Capitol; RMC Place; SACRAMENTO; ★ **SAC**; mail Sacramento z 95814; pop. incl. with Sacramento (Inc. Place)
Stateline; RMC Place; EL DORADO; ***150** NJ-10; mail South Lake Tahoe z 96157; pop. incl. with South Lake Tahoe (Inc. Place)
State Street; RMC Place; LOS ANGELES; ★ **L.A.**; mail Huntington Park z 90255; pop. incl. with Huntington Park (Inc. Place)
Stauffer; RMC Place; SAN MATEO; ★ **SF-O-**; pop. incl. with Redwood City (Inc. Place)
Stauffer; RMC Place; VENTURA; mail Frazier Park z 93225; ● 130
Steele Park; RMC Place; NAPA; ***150** NK-5; elev. 600ft./183m.; mail Napa z 94558; ● 150
Stege; RMC Place; CONTRA COSTA; ***150** NL-5; ★ **SF-O-**; pop. incl. with Richmond (Inc. Place)
Steinbeck; RMC Place; MONTEREY; ★ **SLNS**; mail Salinas z 93901; pop. incl. with Salinas (Inc. Place)
Steiner Street Station; RMC Place; SAN FRANCISCO; ★ **SF-O-**; mail San Francisco z 94115; pop. incl. with San Francisco (Inc. Place)
Stent; RMC Place; TUOLUMNE; ***150** NL-9; mail Sonora z 95370; ● 300
Stephens; RMC Place; LOS ANGELES; ★ **L.A.**; mail Santa Fe Springs z 90670; pop. incl. with Santa Fe Springs (Inc. Place)
Sterling Park; RMC Place; SAN MATEO; **151** NG-13; ★ **SF-O-**; mail Daly City z 94017
Stevenson Ranch; RMC Place; LOS ANGELES; ***152** SI-10; [P]; ★ **L.A.**; z 91381
Stevinson; RMC Place; MERCED; **150** NN-8; [P]; z 95374; ● 765
Stewarts Point; RMC Place; SONOMA; **150** NJ-3; elev. 109ft./33m.; [P]; z 95480; ● 100
Stewarts Point Rancheria; Indian Reservation; SONOMA; mail Stewarts Point z 95480; Ⓒ 57
Stewart Springs; RMC Place; SISKIYOU; ***150** NC-5; elev. 4,000ft./1,219m.; mail Weed z 96094; ● 25
Stine Station; RMC Place; KERN; ★ **BAK**; mail Bakersfield z 93309; pop. incl. with Bakersfield (Inc. Place)
Stinson Beach; CDP; MARIN; **150** NL-4; elev. 18ft./5m.; [P]; ★ **SF-O-**; z 94970; Ⓒ 751
Stirling City; RMC Place; BUTTE; **150** NG-7; elev. 3,532ft./1,077m.; [P]; z 95978; ● 300
Stockdale; RMC Place; KERN; ★ **BAK**; mail Bakersfield z 93309, z 93389; pop. incl. with Bakersfield (Inc. Place)
Stockton; Inc. Place; ⊡ SAN JOAQUIN; **150** NL-7; elev. 13ft./4m.; [P] [H] [C] 6,926 ■; ★ **STOC**; z 95201-13, z 95215, z 95219, z 95267, z 95269, z 95296-97; Ⓟ 210,943; Ⓒ 243,771; ◆ 267,858
Stock Yards; RMC Place; ALAMEDA; ★ **SF-O-**; pop. incl. with Oakland (Inc. Place)
Stonegate; RMC Place; SAN MATEO; ★ **SF-O-**; mail Portola Valley z 94028; pop. incl. with Portola Valley (Inc. Place)
Stonehurst; RMC Place; ALAMEDA; ***150** NM-5; ★ **SF-O-**; mail Oakland z 94603; pop. incl. with Oakland (Inc. Place)
Stone Lagoon; RMC Place; HUMBOLDT; ***150** NC-2; elev. 20ft./6m.; mail Trinidad z 95570; rural
Stoneman; RMC Place; LOS ANGELES; ***153** SJ-11; elev. 456ft./139m.; ★ **L.A.**; mail Alhambra z 91801; pop. incl. with Alhambra (Inc. Place)
Stonyford; RMC Place; COLUSA; **150** NH-5; [P]; z 95979; ● 350
Storrie; CDP; PLUMAS; **150** NG-7; [P]; z 95980; Ⓒ 5
Stovepipe Wells; RMC Place; INYO; **153** SC-13; mail Death Valley z 92328; ● 30
Stratford; CDP; KINGS; **152** SD-7; [P]; z 93266; Ⓒ 1,264
Strathmore; CDP; TULARE; **152** SD-9; elev. 402ft./123m.; [P]; ★ **PORT**; z 93267; Ⓟ 2,353; Ⓒ 2,584
Strawberry; RMC Place; EL DORADO; ***150** NJ-10; mail Kyburz z 95720
Strawberry (Strawberry Point); CDP-Census Area Only; MARIN; **151** ND-12; ★ **SF-O-**; mail Mill Valley z 94941; Ⓟ 4,377; Ⓒ 5,302
Strawberry; RMC Place; TUOLUMNE; **150** NL-10; [P]; z 95375; ● 150
Strawberry Point; MARIN; see Strawberry (CDP-Census Area Only)
Strawberry Valley; RMC Place; YUBA; **150** NH-8; [P]; z 95981; ● 100
Stuart; RMC Place; SAN DIEGO; mail Oceanside z 92054
Studebaker; RMC Place; LOS ANGELES; ***153** SJ-11; ★ **L.A.**; mail Norwalk z 90650; pop. incl. with Norwalk (Inc. Place)
Studio City; RMC Place; LOS ANGELES; ***152** SJ-10; [P]; ★ **L.A.**; z 91602, z 91604, z 91607, z 91614; pop. incl. with Los Angeles (Inc. Place)
Sugarloaf; RMC Place; SAN BERNARDINO; ***153** SI-14; elev. 7,024ft./2,141m.; [P]; z 92386; ● 1,700
Sugarloaf Mountain Park; RMC Place; TULARE; ***152** SE-10; mail Posey z 93260; ● 30
Sugar Pine; RMC Place; MADERA; ***151** NN-11; mail Oakhurst z 93644; rural
Sugarpine; RMC Place; TUOLUMNE; ***150** NL-10; mail Twain Harte z 95383; ● 600
Suisun City (Suisun Fairfield); Inc. Place; SOLANO; **150** NL-6; [P]; ★ **FRFL-**; z 94534, z 94585; Ⓟ 22,686; Ⓒ 26,118; ◆ 25,372
Suisun Fairfield; SOLANO; see Suisun City (Inc. Place)
Sulphur Bank Rancheria; Indian Reservation; LAKE; mail Clearlake Oaks z 95423; Ⓒ 69
Sulphur Springs; RMC Place; VENTURA; ***152** SI-9; mail Santa Paula z 93060; ● 100
Sultana; RMC Place; TULARE; **152** SC-8; [P]; z 93666; ● 750
Summer Home; RMC Place; SAN JOAQUIN; ***150** NM-8; elev. 41ft./12m.; ★ **STOC**; mail Manteca z 95336; rural
Summerhome Park; RMC Place; SONOMA; ***150** NK-4; ★ **S.ROS**; mail Forestville z 95436; ● 650
Summerland; CDP; SANTA BARBARA; **152** SI-8; [P]; ★ **S.BAR**; z 93067; Ⓒ 1,545
Summit; RMC Place; SAN BERNARDINO; ***153** SI-13; ★ **RIV-**; mail Hesperia z 92345; rural
Summit City; RMC Place; SHASTA; **150** NE-5; [P]; ★ **REDD**; z 96089; pop. incl. with Shasta Lake (Inc. Place)
Sumner Hill; RMC Place; MADERA; ***152** SB-7; elev. 424ft./129m.; mail Madera z 93637; rural
Sun City; CDP; RIVERSIDE; **153** SK-13; [P] [H]; z 92584-87; Ⓟ 14,930; Ⓒ 17,773
Sun Crest; SAN DIEGO; see Crest (CDP-Census Area Only)
Sunfair; RMC Place; SAN BERNARDINO; ***153** SJ-15; elev. 2,412ft./735m.; mail Joshua Tree z 92252; ● 300
Sunkist; RMC Place; ORANGE; ★ **L.A.**; mail Anaheim z 92806, z 92816; pop. incl. with Anaheim (Inc. Place)
Sunland; RMC Place; LOS ANGELES; ***153** SI-11; elev. 1,503ft./458m.; [P]; ★ **L.A.**; z 91040-41; pop. incl. with Los Angeles (Inc. Place)
Sunny Brae; RMC Place; HUMBOLDT; ***150** ND-2; ★ **EUR-**; mail Arcata z 95521; pop. incl. with Arcata (Inc. Place)
Sunnybrook; RMC Place; AMADOR; ***150** NK-8; mail Ione z 95640
Sunny Hills; RMC Place; ORANGE; ***153** SJ-12; ★ **L.A.**; mail Fullerton z 92835, z 92838; pop. incl. with Fullerton (Inc. Place)
Sunnymead; RMC Place; RIVERSIDE; ***153** SJ-13; ★ **RIV-**; mail Moreno Valley z 92551, z 92553; pop. incl. with Moreno Valley (Inc. Place)
Sunnyside; RMC Place; FRESNO; ***152** SB-7; ★ **FRES**; mail Fresno z 93727; pop. incl. with Fresno (Inc. Place)
Sunnyside; RMC Place; PLACER; ***150** NI-10; elev. 6,256ft./1,907m.; mail Tahoe City z 96145; ● 500
Sunnyside; RMC Place; SAN DIEGO; **156** K-8; ★ **SDGO**; mail Bonita z 91902; ● 1,000
Sunnyside-Tahoe City; CDP-Census Area Only; PLACER; ***150** NI-10; mail Tahoe City z 96145; Ⓟ 1,643; Ⓒ 1,761
Sunnyslope; RMC Place; BUTTE; ***150** NH-7; elev. 500ft./152m.; mail Bangor z 95914; rural
Sunnyslope; CDP; RIVERSIDE; **155** F-17; ★ **RIV-**; mail Riverside z 92509; Ⓟ 3,766; Ⓒ 4,437
Sunnyvale; Inc. Place; SANTA CLARA; **151** NL-18; elev. 130ft./40m.; [P] [C] 341 ■; ★ **SF-O-**; z 94085-89; Ⓟ 117,229; Ⓒ 131,760; ◆ 141,522
Sunny Vista; RMC Place; SAN DIEGO; ***153** SN-14; ★ **SDGO**; mail Chula Vista z 91910; pop. incl. with Chula Vista (Inc. Place)
Sunol; CDP; ALAMEDA; **151** NI-19; [P]; ★ **SF-O-**; z 94586; Ⓒ 1,332
Sunol-Midtown; CDP-Census Area Only; SANTA CLARA; ***150** NN-6; ★ **SF-O-**; Ⓒ 748
Sunrise Vista; RMC Place; LAKE; ***150** NJ-4; elev. 2,600ft./792m.; mail Kelseyville z 95451; ● 80
Sunset; RMC Place; HUMBOLDT; ***150** ND-2; ★ **EUR-**; mail Arcata z 95521; pop. incl. with Arcata (Inc. Place)
Sunset; RMC Place; LOS ANGELES; ★ **L.A.**; mail Los Angeles z 90046, z 90093; pop. incl. with Los Angeles (Inc. Place)
Sunset; RMC Place; SAN FRANCISCO; ★ **SF-O-**; mail San Francisco z 94122, z 94172; pop. incl. with San Francisco (Inc. Place)
Sunset Beach; RMC Place; ORANGE; **154** J-9; [P]; ★ **L.A.**; z 90742; ● 1,000
Sunset Cliffs; RMC Place; SAN DIEGO; ***153** SN-13; ★ **SDGO**; mail San Diego z 92107; pop. incl. with San Diego (Inc. Place)
Sunset View; RMC Place; NEVADA; ***150** NI-8; mail Grass Valley z 95945; ● 600
Sunset Whitney Ranch; RMC Place; PLACER; ***150** NJ-7; ★ **SAC**; mail Rocklin z 95677; pop. incl. with Rocklin (Inc. Place)
Sunshine Summit; SAN DIEGO; see Holcomb Village (RMC Place)
Sun Valley; RMC Place; LOS ANGELES; ***152** SJ-10; [P]; ★ **L.A.**; z 91352-53; pop. incl. with Los Angeles (Inc. Place)
Sun Village; RMC Place; LOS ANGELES; [P]; ★ **L.A.**; z 93543 & mail Palmdale z 93550; pop. incl. with Palmdale (Inc. Place)
Surf; RMC Place; SANTA BARBARA; **152** SH-5; elev. 42ft./13m.; mail Lompoc z 93436
Surfside; RMC Place; ORANGE; ***153** SK-11; [P]; ★ **L.A.**; z 90743; pop. incl. with Seal Beach (Inc. Place)
Susana Knolls; RMC Place; VENTURA; ★ **L.A.**; mail Simi Valley z 93063; pop. incl. with Simi Valley (Inc. Place)
Susanville; Inc. Place; ⊡ LASSEN; **150** NF-9; elev. 4,258ft./1,298m.; [P] [H]; z 96127, z 96130; Ⓟ 7,279; Ⓒ 13,541; Ⓡ 17,428
Susanville Rancheria; Indian Reservation; LASSEN; Ⓒ 298
Sutter; CDP; SUTTER; **150** NI-6; [P]; z 95982; Ⓟ 2,606; Ⓒ 2,885
SUTTER; **150** NI-7; Ⓟ 64,415; Ⓒ 78,930; ◆ 93,248
Sutter Creek; Inc. Place; AMADOR; **150** NK-8; elev. 1,198ft./365m.; [P]; z 95685, z 95699; Ⓟ 1,835; Ⓒ 2,303
Sutter Hill; RMC Place; AMADOR; ***150** NK-8; elev. 1,556ft./474m.; mail Sutter Creek z 95685; ● 100
Sutter Island; RMC Place; SACRAMENTO; ***150** NK-7; mail Courtland z 95615; ● 135
Sutter Street; RMC Place; SAN FRANCISCO; ★ **SF-O-**; mail San Francisco z 94104; pop. incl. with San Francisco (Inc. Place)
Swall Meadows; RMC Place; MONO; ***151** NN-13; elev. 2,012ft./613m.; [P]; z 93514; ● 200
Swanston; RMC Place; SACRAMENTO; ***150** NK-7; ★ **SAC**; pop. incl. with Sacramento (Inc. Place)
Swanton; RMC Place; SANTA CRUZ; ***152** SA-2; mail Davenport z 95017
Sweetbriar (Sweet Brier); RMC Place; SHASTA; mail Castella z 96017; rural
Sweet Brier; SHASTA; see Sweetbriar (RMC Place)
Sweetland; RMC Place; NEVADA; mail Nevada City z 95959; ● 230
Sweetwater Ranch; RMC Place; LAKE; ***150** NJ-4; elev. 1,600ft./488m.; mail Kelseyville z 95451; rural
Sycamore; RMC Place; COLUSA; ***150** NI-6; mail Meridian z 95957
Sycamore; RMC Place; CONTRA COSTA; ★ **SF-O-**; mail Danville z 94526; pop. incl. with Danville (Inc. Place)
Sycuan Reservation; Indian Reservation; SAN DIEGO; Ⓒ 33
Sylmar; RMC Place; LOS ANGELES; ***152** SI-10; [P]; ★ **L.A.**; z 91342, z 91392; pop. incl. with Los Angeles (Inc. Place)
Sylvia Park; RMC Place; LOS ANGELES; **154** D-3; ★ **L.A.**; mail Topanga z 90290; ● 600

T

Table Bluff; RMC Place; HUMBOLDT; ***150** NE-1; elev. 312ft./95m.; ★ **EUR-**; mail Loleta z 95551; rural
Table Bluff Reservation; Indian Reservation; HUMBOLDT; Ⓒ 81
Table Mountain Rancheria; Indian Reservation; FRESNO; Ⓒ 11
Taft; Inc. Place; KERN; **152** SG-8; elev. 984ft./300m.; [P] [H]; z 93268; Ⓟ 5,902; Ⓒ 6,400; Ⓡ 8,811
Taft Heights; CDP; KERN; **152** SG-8; mail Taft z 93268; Ⓟ 2,050; Ⓒ 1,865
Taft Mosswood; CDP-Census Area Only; SAN JOAQUIN; ***150** NL-7; ★ **STOC**; Ⓒ 1,388
Tagus; RMC Place; TULARE; mail Livermore z 94550; rural
Tahoe City; RMC Place; PLACER; **150** NI-10; elev. 6,240ft./1,902m.; [P]; z 96145-46; ● 700
Tahoe Keys; RMC Place; EL DORADO; mail South Lake Tahoe z 96154; pop. incl. with South Lake Tahoe (Inc. Place)
Tahoe Paradise; RMC Place; EL DORADO; elev. 6,340ft./1,932m.; mail South Lake Tahoe z 96155; pop. incl. with South Lake Tahoe (Inc. Place)
Tahoe Pines; RMC Place; PLACER; **150** NI-10; mail Homewood z 96141; ● 110
Tahoe Valley; RMC Place; EL DORADO; ***150** NJ-10; elev. 6,270ft./1,911m.; mail South Lake Tahoe z 96158; pop. incl. with South Lake Tahoe (Inc. Place)
Tahoe Vista; CDP; PLACER; **150** NI-10; elev. 6,232ft./1,900m.; [P]; z 96148; Ⓟ 1,144; Ⓒ 1,668
Tahoma; RMC Place; PLACER, EL DORADO; **150** NI-10; [P]; z 96142; ● 600
Talica; RMC Place; SAN DIEGO; mail Oceanside z 92054; pop. incl. with Oceanside (Inc. Place)
Talmadge Park; RMC Place; SAN DIEGO; ***153** SN-14; ★ **SDGO**; mail San Diego z 92115; pop. incl. with San Diego (Inc. Place)
Talmage; CDP; MENDOCINO; **150** NI-3; [P]; z 95481; Ⓒ 1,141
Tamalpais-Homestead Valley; CDP-Census Area Only; MARIN; ***150** NL-5; ★ **SF-O-**; mail Mill Valley z 94941; Ⓟ 9,601; Ⓒ 10,691
Tamalpais Valley; RMC Place; MARIN; **151** NE-12; elev. 36ft./11m.; ★ **SF-O-**; mail Mill Valley z 94941; ● 7,000
Tamarack; RMC Place; CALAVERAS; ***150** NK-10; mail Arnold z 95223
Tambs Station; TUOLUMNE; see Mono Vista (CDP)
Tanforan; RMC Place; SAN MATEO; ★ **SF-O-**; mail South San Francisco z 94080; pop. incl. with South San Francisco (Inc. Place)
Tangair; RMC Place; SANTA BARBARA; elev. 211ft./64m.; mail Lompoc z 93437
Tara Hills; CDP; CONTRA COSTA; **151** NC-14; ★ **SF-O-**; mail Pinole z 94564, San Pablo z 94806; Ⓟ 4,998; Ⓒ 5,332
Tarpey; RMC Place; FRESNO; ***152** SB-7; ★ **FRES**; mail Fresno z 93727
Tarzana; RMC Place; LOS ANGELES; ***152** SJ-10; [P]; ★ **L.A.**; z 91335, z 91356-57; pop. incl. with Los Angeles (Inc. Place)
Tassajara; RMC Place; CONTRA COSTA; mail Livermore z 94550; rural
Tassajara Hot Springs; RMC Place; MONTEREY; **152** SD-3; mail Carmel Valley z 93924
Taurusa; RMC Place; TULARE; ***152** SC-8; elev. 343ft./105m.; ★ **VISL**; mail Visalia z 93291; rural
Taylorsville; CDP; PLUMAS; **150** NF-8; [P]; z 95983; Ⓒ 154
Tecate; RMC Place; SAN DIEGO; ***153** SN-15; [P]; z 91980, z 91987; ● 200
Tecnor; RMC Place; SISKIYOU; ***150** NB-7; mail Macdoel z 96058; rural
Tecopa; CDP; INYO; **153** SE-15; elev. 1,329ft./405m.; [P]; z 92389; Ⓒ 99
Tecopa Hot Springs; RMC Place; INYO; **153** SE-15; mail Tecopa z 92389; ● 50
Tehachapi; Inc. Place; KERN; **152** SG-10; elev. 3,973ft./1,211m.; [P] [H]; z 93561, z 93581; Ⓟ 5,791; Ⓒ 10,957; Ⓡ 11,125
Tehama; Inc. Place; TEHAMA; **150** NG-6; [P]; z 96090; Ⓟ 401; Ⓒ 432
TEHAMA; **150** NF-5; Ⓟ 49,625; Ⓒ 56,039; ◆ 62,021
Temecula; Inc. Place; RIVERSIDE; **153** SL-13; elev. 1,006ft./307m.; [P]; z 92589-93; Ⓟ 27,099; Ⓒ 57,716; ◆ 103,609
Temelec; CDP; SONOMA; ***150** NK-5; elev. 100ft./30m.; mail Sonoma z 95476; Ⓟ 1,594; Ⓒ 1,556
Temple City; Inc. Place; LOS ANGELES; **154** E-9; elev. 400ft./122m.; [P]; ★ **L.A.**; z 91780; Ⓟ 31,100; Ⓒ 33,377; ◆ 36,214
Templeton; CDP; SAN LUIS OBISPO; **152** SF-5; [P] [H]; z 93465; Ⓟ 2,887; Ⓒ 4,687
Tennant; CDP; SISKIYOU; **150** NB-6; mail Macdoel z 96058; Ⓒ 63
Tent City; RMC Place; SAN DIEGO; ★ **SDGO**; mail Coronado z 92118; pop. incl. with Coronado (Inc. Place)
Terminal Annex; RMC Place; LOS ANGELES; ***153** SJ-11; ★ **L.A.**; mail Los Angeles z 90054, z 90086; pop. incl. with Los Angeles (Inc. Place)
Terminous; RMC Place; SAN JOAQUIN; **150** NL-7; mail Lodi z 95240; ● 600
Termo; RMC Place; LASSEN; **150** ND-9; [P]; z 96132; rural
Terra Bella; CDP; TULARE; **152** SE-9; elev. 487ft./148m.; [P]; ★ **PORT**; z 93270; Ⓟ 2,740; Ⓒ 3,466
Terra Linda; RMC Place; MARIN; ***150** NL-5; elev. 20ft./6m.; ★ **SF-O-**; mail San Rafael z 94903; pop. incl. with San Rafael (Inc. Place)
Textile; RMC Place; LOS ANGELES; ***153** SJ-11; ★ **L.A.**; mail Los Angeles z 90015, z 90055, z 90079; pop. incl. with Los Angeles (Inc. Place)
The Forks; RMC Place; MADERA; mail Bass Lake z 93604; rural
The Forks; RMC Place; MENDOCINO; ***150** NI-3; mail Ukiah z 95482; ● 150
The Geysers; RMC Place; SONOMA; ***150** NJ-4; elev. 1,600ft./488m.; mail Cloverdale z 95425; rural
The Hermitage; RMC Place; MENDOCINO; ***150** NG-2; elev. 1,200ft./366m.; mail Leggett z 95585; rural
The Muirlands; RMC Place; SAN DIEGO; ***153** SM-13; ★ **SDGO**; mail La Jolla z 92037; pop. incl. with San Diego (Inc. Place)
Thenard; RMC Place; LOS ANGELES; ***153** SK-11; ★ **L.A.**; pop. incl. with Los Angeles (Inc. Place)
The Oaks; RMC Place; NEVADA; ***150** NI-8; mail Grass Valley z 95945; ● 450
The Pines; RMC Place; MADERA; mail Bass Lake z 93604; ● 60
Thermal; RMC Place; RIVERSIDE; **153** SK-16; elev. 120ft./37m.; [P]; z 92274-75; ● 1,400
Thermalito; CDP; BUTTE; **150** NH-7; mail Oroville z 95965; Ⓟ 5,646; Ⓒ 6,045
The Shore of Poker Flat; RMC Place; CALAVERAS; ***150** NL-9; mail Copperopolis z 95228; ● 400
Thomas Mountain; RMC Place; RIVERSIDE; ***153** SK-15; mail Mountain Center z 92561; ● 200
Thorn; HUMBOLDT; see Whitethorn (RMC Place)
Thornton; RMC Place; SAN JOAQUIN; **150** NL-7; elev. 11ft./3m.; [P]; z 95686; ● 1,100
Thousand Oaks; Inc. Place; VENTURA; **152** SJ-9; elev. 800ft./244m.; [P] [H] [C] 2,124 ■; ★ **OXN-**; z 91319-20, z 91358-62; Ⓟ 104,352; Ⓒ 117,005; ◆ 121,216
Thousand Palms; CDP; RIVERSIDE; **153** SK-15; [P]; ★ **PSPR-**; z 92276; Ⓟ 4,122; Ⓒ 5,120
Three Arch Bay; RMC Place; ORANGE; ***153** SL-12; ★ **L.A.**; mail Laguna Niguel z 92677; pop. incl. with Dana Point (Inc. Place)
Three Points; RMC Place; LOS ANGELES; ***152** SH-10; elev. 3,424ft./1,044m.; mail Lake Hughes z 93532; ● 120
Three Rivers; CDP; TULARE; **152** SC-9; [P]; z 93271; Ⓒ 2,248
Three Rocks; RMC Place; FRESNO; ***152** SC-6; elev. 417ft./127m.; mail Cantua Creek z 93608; ● 365
Tiburon; Inc. Place; MARIN; **150** NL-5; elev. 90ft./27m.; [P]; ★ **SF-O-**; z 94920; Ⓟ 7,532; Ⓒ 8,666
Tierra Buena; CDP; SUTTER; ***150** NI-7; ★ **YUCY**; mail Yuba City z 95991; Ⓟ 2,878; Ⓒ 4,587
Tierra del Sol; RMC Place; SAN DIEGO; ***153** SN-15; elev. 3,648ft./1,112m.; mail Boulevard z 91905; rural
Tionesta; RMC Place; MODOC; **150** NB-8; [P]; z 96134; ● 30
Tipton; CDP; TULARE; **152** SD-8; elev. 272ft./83m.; [P]; z 93272; Ⓟ 1,383; Ⓒ 1,790
Tobin; CDP; PLUMAS; ***150** NG-7; mail Oroville z 95965, Storrie z 95980; Ⓒ 11
Tocaloma; RMC Place; MARIN; ***150** NL-4; elev. 74ft./23m.; mail Olema z 94950; rural
Todd Valley; RMC Place; PLACER; ***150** NI-8; ★ **SAC**; mail Foresthill z 95631; ● 820
Todos Santos; RMC Place; CONTRA COSTA; ★ **SF-O-**; mail Concord z 94522; pop. incl. with Concord (Inc. Place)
Tollhouse; RMC Place; FRESNO; **152** SB-8; [P]; z 93667; ● 400
Toluca Lake; RMC Place; LOS ANGELES; [P]; ★ **L.A.**; z 91602, z 91610; pop. incl. with Los Angeles (Inc. Place)
Tomales; CDP; MARIN; **150** NK-4; elev. 79ft./24m.; [P]; z 94971; Ⓒ 210
Toms Place; RMC Place; MONO; **151** NM-13; [P]; z 93546 & mail Bishop z 93514; ● 170
Tonyville; RMC Place; TULARE; ***152** SD-9; mail Lindsay z 93247; ● 300
Toolville; RMC Place; TULARE; ***152** SD-9; ★ **VISL**; mail Exeter z 93221; ● 300
Topanga; RMC Place; LOS ANGELES; **152** SJ-10; [P]; ★ **L.A.**; z 90290; ● 700
Topanga Beach; RMC Place; LOS ANGELES; ***154** E-3; mail Malibu z 90265; ● 1,060
Topanga Oaks; RMC Place; LOS ANGELES; ★ **L.A.**; mail Topanga z 90290; ● 500
Topanga Park; RMC Place; LOS ANGELES; **154** D-2; elev. 1,021ft./311m.; ★ **L.A.**; mail Topanga z 90290; ● 600
Topaz (Topaz Post Office); RMC Place; MONO; **151** NK-11; [P]; z 96133; ● 120
Topaz Post Office; MONO; see Topaz (RMC Place)
Top of the World; RMC Place; ORANGE; ***153** SK-12; ★ **L.A.**; mail Laguna Beach z 92651; pop. incl. with Laguna Beach (Inc. Place)
Toro Canyon; CDP-Census Area Only; SANTA BARBARA; ***152** SI-8; ★ **S.BAR**; Ⓒ 1,697
Torrance; Inc. Place; LOS ANGELES; **154** H-5; elev. 84ft./26m.; [P] [H] ■; ★ **L.A.**; z 90501-10; Ⓟ 133,107; Ⓒ 137,946; ◆ 137,713
Torres-Martinez Reservation; Indian Reservation; RIVERSIDE, IMPERIAL; mail Thermal z 92274; Ⓟ 278; Ⓒ 4,146
Tower; RMC Place; FRESNO; ★ **FRES**; mail Fresno z 93728, z 93744; pop. incl. with Fresno (Inc. Place)
Town and Country; RMC Place; RIVERSIDE; ★ **RIV-**; mail Moreno Valley z 92551; pop. incl. with Moreno Valley (Inc. Place)
Town and Country Village; RMC Place; SACRAMENTO; ***150** NK-7; ★ **SAC**; mail Sacramento z 95821; ● 14,000
Town Center; RMC Place; LOS ANGELES; ★ **L.A.**; mail Palmdale z 93550; pop. incl. with Palmdale (Inc. Place)
Town Center; RMC Place; TULARE; ★ **VISL**; mail Visalia z 93279, z 93291; pop. incl. with Visalia (Inc. Place)
Town Square; RMC Place; LOS ANGELES; ★ **L.A.**; mail Palmdale z 93550; pop. incl. with Palmdale (Inc. Place)
Trabuco Canyon; RMC Place; ORANGE; **155** K-15; [P]; ★ **L.A.**; z 92678-79 & mail Rancho Santa Margarita z 92688; ● 800
Trabuco Highlands; RMC Place; ORANGE; ***153** SK-12; elev. 1,200ft./366m.; ★ **L.A.**; mail Mission Viejo z 92691; pop. incl. with Rancho Santa Margarita (Inc. Place); Ⓟ 3,191
Tracy; Inc. Place; SAN JOAQUIN; **150** NM-7; elev. 48ft./15m.; [P] [H]; z 95304, z 95376-78, z 95385, z 95391; Ⓟ 33,558; Ⓒ 56,929; ◆ 76,409
Trade Center; RMC Place; LOS ANGELES; ***153** SK-11; ★ **L.A.**; mail Long Beach z 90831-32; pop. incl. with Long Beach (Inc. Place)
Tranquility; FRESNO; see Tranquillity (CDP)
Tranquillity (Tranquility); CDP; FRESNO; **152** SC-6; [P]; z 93668; Ⓒ 813
Traver; CDP; TULARE; **152** SC-8; elev. 285ft./87m.; [P]; z 93673; Ⓒ 732
Treasure Island; RMC Place; SAN FRANCISCO; ★ **SF-O-**; mail San Francisco z 94130; pop. incl. with San Francisco (Inc. Place)
Tres Pinos; RMC Place; SAN BENITO; **152** SB-4; [P]; z 95075; ● 400
Trevarno; RMC Place; ALAMEDA; ***150** NM-6; elev. 534ft./163m.; ★ **SF-O-**; mail Livermore z 94550; pop. incl. with Livermore (Inc. Place)
Trigo; RMC Place; MADERA; ***152** SB-7; ★ **FRES**; mail Madera z 93637; ● 150
Trimmer; RMC Place; FRESNO; ***152** SB-8; mail Sanger z 93657
Trinidad; Inc. Place; HUMBOLDT; **150** NC-2; [P]; ★ **EUR-**; z 95570; Ⓟ 362; Ⓒ 311
Trinidad Rancheria; Indian Reservation; HUMBOLDT; Ⓒ 52
TRINITY; **150** NF-3; Ⓟ 13,063; Ⓒ 13,022; ◆ 14,562
Trinity Alps; RMC Place; TRINITY; ***150** ND-4; mail Lewiston z 96052; rural
Trinity Center; RMC Place; TRINITY; **150** ND-5; [P]; z 96091; ● 320
Trinity Village; RMC Place; TRINITY; ***150** ND-3; elev. 800ft./244m.; mail Burnt Ranch z 95527, Salyer z 95563; ● 160
Triple R Estates; RMC Place; TULARE; ***152** SD-9; elev. 432ft./132m.; ★ **PORT**; mail Porterville z 93257; ● 600
Trona; RMC Place; SAN BERNARDINO; **153** SE-13; elev. 1,659ft./506m.; [P]; z 93562, z 93592; ● 500
Tropico; RMC Place; KERN; ***153** SH-11; elev. 2,402ft./732m.; mail Rosamond z 93560; ● 250
Tropico; RMC Place; LOS ANGELES; ★ **L.A.**; mail Glendale z 91204-05, z 91208; pop. incl. with Glendale (Inc. Place)
Trowbridge; RMC Place; SUTTER; **150** NJ-7; elev. 48ft./15m.; [P]; z 95659; ● 140
Truckee; Inc. Place; NEVADA; **150** NI-10; elev. 5,820ft./1,774m.; [P] [H]; z 96160-62; Ⓟ 8,848; Ⓒ 13,864
Tudor; RMC Place; SUTTER; mail Yuba City z 95991; ● 200
Tujunga; RMC Place; LOS ANGELES; ***153** SI-11; elev. 1,765ft./538m.; [P]; ★ **L.A.**; z 91042-43; pop. incl. with Los Angeles (Inc. Place)
Tulare; Inc. Place; TULARE; **152** SD-8; elev. 288ft./88m.; [P] [H]; ★ **VISL**; z 93274-75; Ⓟ 33,249; Ⓒ 43,994; ◆ 55,979
TULARE; **152** SC-9; Ⓟ 311,921; Ⓒ 368,021; ◆ 424,628
Tulelake; Inc. Place; SISKIYOU; **150** NA-7; [P]; z 96134; Ⓟ 1,010; Ⓒ 1,020
Tule River Reservation; Indian Reservation; TULARE; mail Porterville z 93257; Ⓟ 453; Ⓒ 566
Tunitas; SAN MATEO; see Lobitos (RMC Place)
Tunnel Inn (Wonderland); RMC Place; SHASTA; ★ **REDD**; mail Redding z 96003; rural
Tuolumne; CDP; TUOLUMNE; **150** NL-10; elev. 2,577ft./785m.; [P]; z 95379; Ⓟ 1,686; Ⓒ 1,865
TUOLUMNE; **151** NL-11; Ⓟ 48,456; Ⓒ 54,501; Ⓡ 54,504; ◆ 54,971
Tuolumne Meadows; RMC Place; TUOLUMNE; ***151** NM-12; [P]; z 95389
Tuolumne Rancheria; Indian Reservation; TUOLUMNE; Ⓒ 165
Tupman; CDP; KERN; ***152** SG-8; [P]; z 93276; Ⓒ 227
Turlock; Inc. Place; STANISLAUS; **150** NN-8; elev. 101ft./31m.; [P] [H] [C] 8,374 ■; ★ **MOD**; z 95380-82; Ⓟ 42,198; Ⓒ 55,810; ◆ 67,203
Turner; RMC Place; SAN JOAQUIN; ***150** NM-8; elev. 30ft./9m.; ★ **STOC**; mail Manteca z 95336; rural
Tustin; Inc. Place; ORANGE; **155** J-12; elev. 130ft./40m.; [P] [H] ■; ★ **L.A.**; z 92780-82; Ⓟ 50,689; Ⓒ 67,504; ◆ 73,497
Tustin Foothills; ORANGE; see North Tustin (CDP)
Tuttle; RMC Place; MERCED; **152** SA-6; ★ **MRCD**; mail Merced z 95340; ● 170
Tuttletown; RMC Place; TUOLUMNE; ***150** NL-9; mail Sonora z 95370
Tuxedo Country Club Estates; RMC Place; SAN JOAQUIN; ***150** NL-7; ★ **STOC**; mail Stockton z 95204; ● 2,100
Tuxedo Park; RMC Place; SAN JOAQUIN; ★ **STOC**; mail Stockton z 95204; pop. incl. with Stockton (Inc. Place)
Twain; CDP; PLUMAS; **150** NG-8; [P]; z 95984; Ⓒ 87
Twain Harte; CDP; TUOLUMNE; **150** NL-10; [P]; z 95383; Ⓟ 2,170; Ⓒ 2,586
Twain Harte Valley; RMC Place; TUOLUMNE; mail Twain Harte z 95383; ● 250
Twenty-Fifth Avenue Station; RMC Place; SAN MATEO; ★ **SF-O-**; mail San Mateo z 94403; pop. incl. with San Mateo (Inc. Place)
Twentynine Palms; Inc. Place; SAN BERNARDINO; **153** SJ-16; elev. 2,001ft./610m.; [P] [H]; z 92277-78; Ⓟ 11,821; Ⓒ 14,764; ◆ 27,418
Twentynine Palms Base; CDP-Census Area Only; SAN BERNARDINO; ***153** SI-16; mail Twentynine Palms z 92278; Ⓟ 10,606; Ⓒ 8,413
Twenty-Nine Palms Reservation; Indian Reservation; RIVERSIDE, SAN BERNARDINO; Ⓒ 0
Twentytwo Mile House; RMC Place; MADERA; ***152** SB-7; elev. 546ft./166m.; mail Madera z 93637; rural
Twin Bridges; RMC Place; EL DORADO; **150** NJ-10; [P]; z 95721, z 95735
Twin Creeks; RMC Place; SANTA CLARA; ***152** SA-3; elev. 624ft./190m.; ★ **SF-O-**; mail San Jose z 95120; ● 110
Twin Lakes; RMC Place; LAKE; ***150** NJ-5; elev. 1,446ft./441m.; mail Lower Lake z 95457; ● 280
Twin Lakes; CDP; SANTA CRUZ; ***152** SB-2; ★ **S.CRZ**; mail Santa Cruz z 95060; Ⓟ 5,379; Ⓒ 5,533
Twin Oaks; RMC Place; SAN DIEGO; ★ **SDGO**; mail San Marcos z 92069; pop. incl. with San Marcos (Inc. Place)
Twin Peaks; RMC Place; SAN BERNARDINO; **155** B-19; [P]; ★ **RIV-**; z 92391; ● 2,100
Two Rivers; RMC Place; PLUMAS; ***150** NG-9; mail Blairsden-Graeagle z 96103; rural
Two Rock (Two Rocks); RMC Place; SONOMA; ***150** NK-4; mail Petaluma z 94952; ● 1,000
Two Rocks; SONOMA; see Two Rock (RMC Place)

U

Ukiah; Inc. Place; ⊡ MENDOCINO; **150** NI-3; elev. 639ft./195m.; [P] [H] ■; z 95418, z 95482; Ⓟ 14,599; Ⓒ 15,497; ◆ 13,923
Ulmar; RMC Place; ALAMEDA; ***150** NM-6; ★ **SF-O-**; mail Livermore z 94550; pop. incl. with Livermore (Inc. Place)
Ultra; RMC Place; TULARE; mail Terra Bella z 93270; ● 300
Union; RMC Place; NAPA; ***150** NK-5; ★ **NAPA**; mail Napa z 94558; pop. incl. with Napa (Inc. Place)
Union City; Inc. Place; ALAMEDA; **151** NI-18; elev. 10ft./3m.; [P]; ★ **SF-O-**; z 94587; Ⓟ 53,762; Ⓒ 66,869; ◆ 71,992
Union Hill; RMC Place; NEVADA; ***150** NI-8; mail Grass Valley z 95945; ● 760
University City; RMC Place; SAN DIEGO; **156** G-5; ★ **SDGO**; mail San Diego z 92122, z 92192; pop. incl. with San Diego (Inc. Place)
University Heights; RMC Place; SAN DIEGO; ***153** SN-13; ★ **SDGO**; mail San Diego z 92104, z 92116; pop. incl. with San Diego (Inc. Place)
University Park; RMC Place; ORANGE; ★ **L.A.**
Upland; Inc. Place; SAN BERNARDINO; **153** SJ-12; elev. 1,245ft./379m.; [P] [H] [C] 1,074 ■; ★ **L.A.**; z 91784-86; Ⓟ 63,374; Ⓒ 68,393; ◆ 69,608
Upper Lake; CDP; LAKE; **150** NI-4; elev. 1,343ft./409m.; [P]; z 95485, z 95493; Ⓒ 989
Upper Lake Rancheria; Indian Reservation; LAKE; Ⓒ 82
Uptown; RMC Place; SAN BERNARDINO; ★ **RIV-**; mail San Bernardino z 92405-06; pop. incl. with San Bernardino (Inc. Place)

V

Vaca; RMC Place; SOLANO; ★ **FRFL-**; mail Vacaville z 95687; pop. incl. with Vacaville (Inc. Place)
Vacation Beach; RMC Place; SONOMA; ★ **S.ROS**; mail Guerneville z 95446; ● 200
Vacaville; Inc. Place; SOLANO; **150** NK-6; elev. 179ft./55m.; [P] [H]; ★ **FRFL-**; z 95687-88, z 95696; Ⓟ 71,479; Ⓒ 88,625; ◆ 92,900
Valencia; RMC Place; LOS ANGELES; ***152** SI-10; [P] [H]; ★ **L.A.**; z 91354-55, z 91380-81, z 91385
Valencia; ORANGE; see East Irvine (RMC Place)
Valerie; RMC Place; RIVERSIDE; mail Thermal z 92274; ● 400
Valinda; CDP; LOS ANGELES; **154** E-10; ★ **L.A.**; mail La Puente z 91744; Ⓟ 18,735; Ⓒ 21,776; ◆ 22,272
Valla; RMC Place; LOS ANGELES; ★ **L.A.**; mail Santa Fe Springs z 90670; pop. incl. with Santa Fe Springs (Inc. Place)
Vallecito; CDP; CALAVERAS; **150** NL-9; elev. 1,745ft./532m.; [P]; z 95229, z 95251; Ⓒ 427
Vallejo; Inc. Place; SOLANO; **150** NL-5; elev. 50ft./15m.; [P] [H] [C] 1,423 ■; ★ **SF-O-**; z 94503, z 94589-92; Ⓟ 109,199; Ⓒ 116,760; ◆ 115,723
Vallemar; RMC Place; SAN MATEO; ***150** NM-5; ★ **SF-O-**; mail Pacifica z 94044; pop. incl. with Pacifica (Inc. Place)
Valle Vista; RMC Place; ALAMEDA; ★ **SF-O-**; mail Hayward z 94541; pop. incl. with Hayward (Inc. Place)
Valle Vista; CDP; RIVERSIDE; **153** SK-14; elev. 1,767ft./539m.; ★ **HEM**; mail Hemet z 92544; Ⓟ 8,751; Ⓒ 10,488
Valley Acres; CDP; KERN; **152** SG-8; mail Taft z 93268; Ⓒ 512
Valley Center; CDP; SAN DIEGO; **153** SL-14; [P]; ★ **SDGO**; z 92082; Ⓟ 1,711; Ⓒ 7,323
Valley Ford; RMC Place; SONOMA; **150** NK-4; elev. 42ft./13m.; [P]; ★ **S.ROS**; z 94972
Valley Home; RMC Place; STANISLAUS; **150** NM-8; [P]; z 95361; ● 450
Valley Junction; LOS ANGELES; see Lincoln Park (RMC Place)
Valley Lake Ranchos; RMC Place; MADERA; ***152** SB-7; mail Madera z 93637; ● 200
Valley of Enchantment; RMC Place; SAN BERNARDINO; ***153** SI-13; ★ **RIV-**; mail Crestline z 92325; ● 1,750
Valley of the Moon; RMC Place; SAN BERNARDINO; ***153** SI-13; ★ **RIV-**; mail Crestline z 92325; ● 300
Valley Ranch; CDP-Census Area Only; PLUMAS; ***150** NG-9; Ⓒ 92
Valley Springs; CDP; CALAVERAS; **150** NL-8; [P]; z 95226, z 95252; Ⓒ 2,560
Valley View Park; RMC Place; SAN BERNARDINO; ***153** SI-13; ★ **RIV-**; mail Crestline z 92325; ● 450
Valley Village; RMC Place; LOS ANGELES; ***152** SJ-10; [P]; ★ **L.A.**; z 91601, z 91607, z 91617; pop. incl. with Los Angeles (Inc. Place)
Valona; RMC Place; CONTRA COSTA; ***150** NL-5; elev. 62ft./19m.; ★ **SF-O-**; mail Crockett z 94525; ● 720
Val Verde (Val Verde Park); CDP; LOS ANGELES; ***152** SI-10; [P]; z 91384; Ⓟ 1,689; Ⓒ 1,472
Val Verde Park; LOS ANGELES; see Val Verde (CDP)
Valyermo; RMC Place; LOS ANGELES; **153** SI-12; [P]; z 93563; ● 100
Vandenberg AFB; CDP-Census Area Only; SANTA BARBARA; ***152** SH-6; [P]; ★ **LOMP**; z 93437; Ⓟ 9,846; Ⓒ 6,151
Vandenberg Village; CDP-Census Area Only; SANTA BARBARA; ***152** SH-6; ★ **LOMP**; mail Lompoc z 93436; Ⓟ 5,971; Ⓒ 5,802
Van Ness; RMC Place; LOS ANGELES; ★ **L.A.**; pop. incl. with Los Angeles (Inc. Place)
Van Nuys; RMC Place; LOS ANGELES; ***152** SJ-10; elev. 708ft./216m.; [P]; ★ **L.A.**; z 91316, z 91401-13, z 91416, z 91423, z 91426, z 91436, z 91470, z 91482, z 91495-96, z 91499; pop. incl. with Los Angeles (Inc. Place)
Vanowen; RMC Place; LOS ANGELES; ★ **L.A.**; mail Van Nuys z 91405, z 91407; pop. incl. with Los Angeles (Inc. Place)
Vasona; RMC Place; SANTA CLARA; ★ **SF-O-**; mail Los Gatos z 95032; pop. incl. with Los Gatos (Inc. Place)
Vega; RMC Place; LOS ANGELES; ***153** SJ-11; ★ **L.A.**; pop. incl. with Burbank (Inc. Place)
Venice; RMC Place; LOS ANGELES; **154** F-4; [P]; ★ **L.A.**; z 90291-96; pop. incl. with Los Angeles (Inc. Place)
Venola; RMC Place; KERN; ***152** SF-9; elev. 370ft./113m.; ★ **BAK**; pop. incl. with Bakersfield (Inc. Place)
Ventucopa; RMC Place; SANTA BARBARA; **152** SH-8; elev. 2,896ft./883m.; mail Maricopa z 93252; ● 50
Ven Tu Park; RMC Place; VENTURA; ★ **OXN-**; mail Newbury Park z 91320; pop. incl. with Thousand Oaks (Inc. Place)
Ventura (San Buenaventura); Inc. Place; ⊡ VENTURA; **152** SI-8; elev. 50ft./15m.; [P] [H] ■; ★ **OXN-**; z 93001-07, z 93009; Ⓟ 92,575; Ⓒ 100,916; ◆ 103,260
VENTURA; **152** SH-9; Ⓟ 669,016; Ⓒ 753,197; ◆ 795,243
Ventura Junction; RMC Place; VENTURA; ★ **OXN-**; pop. incl. with Ventura (Inc. Place)
Verdemont; RMC Place; SAN BERNARDINO; ***153** SJ-13; [P]; ★ **RIV-**; z 92407 & mail San Bernardino z 92402
Verdi Sierra Pines; RMC Place; SIERRA; ***150** NH-10; elev. 5,000ft./1,524m.; mail Verdi z 89439; ● 100
Verdugo City; RMC Place; LOS ANGELES; ***153** SJ-11; [P]; ★ **L.A.**; z 91046; pop. incl. with Glendale (Inc. Place)
Verdugo Viejo; RMC Place; LOS ANGELES; ★ **L.A.**; mail Glendale z 91206-08, z 91226; pop. incl. with Glendale (Inc. Place)
Verdugo Woodlands; RMC Place; LOS ANGELES; ★ **L.A.**; pop. incl. with Glendale (Inc. Place)
Vermont; RMC Place; LOS ANGELES; ***153** SJ-11; ★ **L.A.**; mail Los Angeles z 90029; pop. incl. with Los Angeles (Inc. Place)
Vernalis; RMC Place; SAN JOAQUIN; **150** NM-7; elev. 104ft./32m.; [P]; z 95385; rural
Vernon; Inc. Place; LOS ANGELES; **154** F-7; [P]; ★ **L.A.**; z 90058; Ⓟ 152; Ⓒ 91
Vernon Landing; RMC Place; SUTTER; ***150** NJ-7; elev. 25ft./8m.; mail Nicolaus z 95659; rural
Verona; RMC Place; SUTTER; ***150** NJ-7; mail Nicolaus z 95659
Veteran Heights; RMC Place; NAPA; ***150** NJ-5; mail Angwin z 94508; ● 1,200
Veterans Administration; RMC Place; LOS ANGELES; [P]; ★ **L.A.**; z 90073; pop. incl. with Los Angeles (Inc. Place)
Victor; RMC Place; SAN JOAQUIN; **150** NL-8; [P]; ★ **STOC**; z 95253; ● 300
Victoria Park; RMC Place; LOS ANGELES; ★ **L.A.**; mail Carson z 90746; pop. incl. with Carson (Inc. Place)
Victorville; Inc. Place; SAN BERNARDINO; **153** SI-13; elev. 2,715ft./828m.; [P] [H] ■; ★ **HESP-**; z 92392-95; Ⓟ 40,674; Ⓒ 64,029; ◆ 79,466
Victory Center; RMC Place; LOS ANGELES; ★ **L.A.**; mail North Hollywood z 91609; pop. incl. with Los Angeles (Inc. Place)
Vidal; RMC Place; SAN BERNARDINO; ***153** SJ-19; [P]; z 92280
Vidal Junction; RMC Place; SAN BERNARDINO; ***153** SI-19; mail Vidal z 92280
Viejas Reservation; Indian Reservation; SAN DIEGO; mail Alpine z 91901; Ⓟ 209; Ⓒ 394
View Park; RMC Place; LOS ANGELES; **154** F-6; [P]; ★ **L.A.**; z 90043; ● 5,500
View Park-Windsor Hills; CDP-Census Area Only; LOS ANGELES; ***153** SJ-11; ★ **L.A.**; mail Los Angeles z 90043; Ⓟ 11,769; Ⓒ 10,958
Viking; RMC Place; LOS ANGELES; ***153** SK-11; ★ **L.A.**; mail Long Beach z 90808; pop. incl. with Long Beach (Inc. Place)
Village; RMC Place; SANTA CLARA; ★ **SF-O-**; mail Saratoga z 95071; pop. incl. with Saratoga (Inc. Place)
Village Station; RMC Place; LOS ANGELES; ★ **L.A.**; mail Los Angeles z 90024, z 90067; pop. incl. with Los Angeles (Inc. Place)
Villa Grande (Mesa Grande); RMC Place; SONOMA; ***150** NK-4; [P]; ★ **S.ROS**; z 95486; ● 300
Villa Park; Inc. Place; ORANGE; **155** I-12; [P]; ★ **L.A.**; z 92861, z 92867 & mail Newport Beach z 92661; Ⓟ 6,299; Ⓒ 5,999; Ⓡ 5,952
Villa Verona; RMC Place; BUTTE; ***150** NH-7; mail Oroville z 95965; ● 1,000
Vina; RMC Place; TEHAMA; **150** NG-6; [P]; z 96092; ● 320
Vincent; CDP; LOS ANGELES; ***153** SJ-12; elev. 449ft./137m.; ★ **L.A.**; mail Covina z 91722; Ⓟ 13,713; Ⓒ 15,097
Vineburg; RMC Place; SONOMA; ***150** NK-5; elev. 51ft./16m.; [P]; z 95487; ● 250
Vine Hill; CDP; CONTRA COSTA; **150** NL-6; elev. 23ft./7m.; ★ **SF-O-**; mail Martinez z 94553; Ⓟ 3,214; Ⓒ 3,260
Vineyard; CDP-Census Area Only; SACRAMENTO; ***150** NK-7; ★ **SAC**; Ⓒ 10,109
Vinton; RMC Place; PLUMAS; **150** NG-10; [P]; z 96135; ● 155
Vinvale; RMC Place; LOS ANGELES; ***153** SJ-11; elev. 109ft./33m.; ★ **L.A.**; mail South Gate z 90280; pop. incl. with South Gate (Inc. Place)
Viola; RMC Place; SHASTA; **150** NE-7; mail Shingletown z 96088; ● 30
Virginia Colony; RMC Place; VENTURA; ***152** SI-9; ★ **L.A.**; mail Moorpark z 93021; pop. incl. with Moorpark (Inc. Place)
Visalia; Inc. Place; ⊡ TULARE; **152** SD-8; elev. 331ft./101m.; [P] [H] ■; ★ **VISL**; z 93277-79, z 93290-92; Ⓟ 75,636; Ⓒ 91,565; Ⓡ 91,877; ◆ 114,390
Visitacion; RMC Place; SAN FRANCISCO; ★ **SF-O-**; mail San Francisco z 94134; pop. incl. with San Francisco (Inc. Place)
Vista; Inc. Place; SAN DIEGO; **153** SL-13; elev. 331ft./101m.; [P]; ★ **SDGO**; z 92081, z 92083-85; Ⓟ 71,872; Ⓒ 89,857; ◆ 102,167
Vista del Mar; RMC Place; LOS ANGELES; ***153** SK-11; ★ **L.A.**; pop. incl. with Long Beach (Inc. Place)
Vista Del Mar; RMC Place; ORANGE; ★ **L.A.**; mail San Clemente z 92672; pop. incl. with San Clemente (Inc. Place)
Vista Grande; RMC Place; MADERA; ***152** SB-7; mail Madera z 93637; ● 500
Vista Grande; RMC Place; SAN MATEO; ***150** NM-5; ★ **SF-O-**; mail Daly City z 94014, z 94016
Vista Park; RMC Place; KERN; ***152** SF-9; ★ **BAK**; mail Bakersfield z 93307; ● 950
Volcano; RMC Place; AMADOR; **150** NK-9; elev. 2,053ft./626m.; [P]; z 95689; ● 400
Volcanoville; RMC Place; EL DORADO; ***150** NJ-9; elev. 3,036ft./925m.; mail Georgetown z 95634; rural
Volta; RMC Place; MERCED; **152** SA-5; mail Los Banos z 93635; ● 275
Vorden; RMC Place; SACRAMENTO; ***150** NK-7; mail Walnut Grove z 95690

W

Waddington; RMC Place; HUMBOLDT; ***150** NE-1; elev. 37ft./11m.; ★ **EUR-**; mail Ferndale z 95536
Wagner Branch; RMC Place; LOS ANGELES; ★ **L.A.**; mail Los Angeles z 90047; pop. incl. with Los Angeles (Inc. Place)
Wagy Flats; RMC Place; KERN; ***152** SE-10; elev. 4,473ft./1,363m.; mail Lake Isabella z 93240; rural
Waldon; CDP-Census Area Only; CONTRA COSTA; ***150** NL-6; ★ **SF-O-**; Ⓒ 5,133
Walerga; RMC Place; SACRAMENTO; ***150** NJ-7; ★ **SAC**; mail North Highlands z 95660; ● 3,000
Walker; RMC Place; LOS ANGELES; ★ **L.A.**; mail Bell z 90201; pop. incl. with Bell (Inc. Place)
Walker; RMC Place; MONO; **151** NK-11; mail Coleville z 96107; ● 530
Walker Landing; RMC Place; SACRAMENTO; ***150** NL-7; mail Walnut Grove z 95690; rural
Wallace; CDP; CALAVERAS; **150** NL-8; [P]; z 95254; Ⓒ 220
Walnut; Inc. Place; LOS ANGELES; **155** E-11; elev. 569ft./173m.; [P]; ★ **L.A.**; z 91788-89, z 91795; Ⓟ 29,105; Ⓒ 30,004; ◆ 30,053
Walnut Creek; Inc. Place; CONTRA COSTA; **150** NL-6; elev. 135ft./41m.; [P] [H] ■; ★ **SF-O-**; z 94595-98; Ⓟ 60,569; Ⓒ 64,296; ◆ 63,290
Walnut Creek West; RMC Place; CONTRA COSTA; ***150** NL-6; ★ **SF-O-**; mail Walnut Creek z 94596; pop. incl. with Lafayette (Inc. Place)
Walnut Grove; CDP; SACRAMENTO; **150** NL-7; [P]; z 95690; Ⓒ 669
Walnut Heights; RMC Place; CONTRA COSTA; ***150** NM-6; ★ **SF-O-**; mail Walnut Creek z 94596; ● 1,800
Walnut Park; CDP; LOS ANGELES; **154** F-7; elev. 145ft./44m.; [P]; ★ **L.A.**; z 90255; Ⓟ 14,722; Ⓒ 16,180
Walsh Landing (Ocean Cove); RMC Place; SONOMA; mail Jenner z 95450; ● 200
Walteria; RMC Place; LOS ANGELES; ***153** SK-11; elev. 95ft./29m.; ★ **L.A.**; mail Torrance z 90505; pop. incl. with Torrance (Inc. Place)
Warm Springs; RMC Place; ALAMEDA; ★ **SF-O-**; mail Fremont z 94539; pop. incl. with Fremont (Inc. Place)
Warner Ranch; RMC Place; RIVERSIDE; ★ **RIV-**; mail Moreno Valley z 92551; pop. incl. with Moreno Valley (Inc. Place)
Warner Springs; RMC Place; SAN DIEGO; **153** SL-15; elev. 3,132ft./955m.; [P]; z 92066, z 92086
Wasco; Inc. Place; KERN; **152** SF-8; elev. 333ft./101m.; [P]; z 93280; Ⓟ 12,412; Ⓒ 21,263; ◆ 25,236
Washington; RMC Place; LOS ANGELES; ★ **L.A.**; mail Pasadena z 91114; pop. incl. with Pasadena (Inc. Place)
Washington; RMC Place; LOS ANGELES; ★ **L.A.**; mail Los Angeles z 90011; pop. incl. with Los Angeles (Inc. Place)
Washington; RMC Place; NEVADA; **150** NH-9; [P]; z 95986; ● 200
Washington Manor; RMC Place; ALAMEDA; ★ **SF-O-**; mail San Leandro z 94579; pop. incl. with San Leandro (Inc. Place)
Waterford; Inc. Place; STANISLAUS; **150** NM-9; [P]; ★ **MOD**; z 95386; Ⓟ 4,771; Ⓒ 6,924
Waterloo; RMC Place; SAN JOAQUIN; **150** NL-8; ★ **STOC**; mail Stockton z 95215
Waterman Gardens; RMC Place; SAN BERNARDINO; ★ **RIV-**; mail San Bernardino z 92410; pop. incl. with San Bernardino (Inc. Place)
Watson; RMC Place; LOS ANGELES; ***153** SK-11; elev. 19ft./6m.; ★ **L.A.**; mail Carson z 90745; pop. incl. with Carson (Inc. Place)
Watsonville; Inc. Place; SANTA CRUZ; **152** SB-3; elev. 29ft./9m.; [P] [H] ■; ★ **WATS**; z 95076-77; Ⓟ 31,099; Ⓒ 44,265; ◆ 49,838
Watsonville Junction; RMC Place; MONTEREY; ***152** SB-3; elev. 25ft./8m.; ★ **WATS**; mail Watsonville z 95076; ● 430
Watts; RMC Place; LOS ANGELES; ***153** SJ-11; [P]; ★ **L.A.**; z 90002 & mail Los Angeles z 90044, z 90051, z 90059, z 90061; pop. incl. with Los Angeles (Inc. Place)
Watts Valley; RMC Place; FRESNO; ***152** SB-8; elev. 1,390ft./424m.; mail Tollhouse z 93667; rural
Waukena; RMC Place; TULARE; ***152** SD-8; elev. 192ft./59m.; [P]; z 93282; ● 450
Waverly Heights (Waverly Park); RMC Place; VENTURA; ***152** SJ-9; ★ **OXN-**; mail Thousand Oaks z 91360; pop. incl. with Thousand Oaks (Inc. Place)
Waverly Park; VENTURA; see Waverly Heights (RMC Place)
Wawona; RMC Place; MARIPOSA; **151** NN-11; elev. 4,012ft./1,223m.; [P]; z 95389; ● 200
Weaverville; CDP; ⊡ TRINITY; **150** NE-4; elev. 2,011ft./613m.; [P] [H]; z 96093; Ⓟ 3,370; Ⓒ 3,554
Webster Street; RMC Place; ALAMEDA; ★ **SF-O-**; mail Alameda z 94501; pop. incl. with Alameda (Inc. Place)
Weed; Inc. Place; SISKIYOU; **150** NC-5; elev. 3,466ft./1,056m.; [P]; z 96094; Ⓟ 3,062; Ⓒ 2,978
Weedpatch; CDP-Census Area Only; KERN; **152** SG-9; ★ **BAK**; mail Lamont z 93241; Ⓟ 1,892; Ⓒ 2,726
Weimar (New England Mills); RMC Place; PLACER; **150** NI-8; elev. 2,280ft./695m.; [P]; ★ **SAC**; z 95736; ● 850
Weitchpec; RMC Place; HUMBOLDT; **150** NC-2; mail Hoopa z 95546; ● 30
Weldon; CDP; KERN; **153** SE-11; [P]; z 93283; Ⓒ 2,387
Wendel; RMC Place; LASSEN; **150** NF-10; [P]; z 96136
Weott; RMC Place; HUMBOLDT; **150** NF-2; elev. 338ft./103m.; [P]; z 95571; ● 300
West Adams; RMC Place; LOS ANGELES; ★ **L.A.**; mail Los Angeles z 90016; pop. incl. with Los Angeles (Inc. Place)
West Anaheim; RMC Place; ORANGE; ***153** SK-11; ★ **L.A.**; pop. incl. with Anaheim (Inc. Place)
West Arcadia; RMC Place; LOS ANGELES; ***153** SJ-11; ★ **L.A.**; mail Arcadia z 91006; pop. incl. with Arcadia (Inc. Place)
West Athens; CDP-Census Area Only; LOS ANGELES; ***153** SJ-11; ★ **L.A.**; mail Gardena z 90247, Los Angeles z 90044, z 90047; Ⓟ 8,859; Ⓒ 9,101
West Bishop; CDP-Census Area Only; INYO; ***151** NN-14; elev. 1,325ft./404m.; mail Bishop z 93514; Ⓟ 2,908; Ⓒ 2,807
West Branch; RMC Place; LOS ANGELES; ★ **L.A.**; mail West Hollywood z 90069; pop. incl. with Los Angeles (Inc. Place)
West Butte; RMC Place; SUTTER; ***150** NI-6; mail Live Oak z 95953; rural
West Carson; CDP-Census Area Only; LOS ANGELES; ***153** SK-11; ★ **L.A.**; mail Torrance z 90502; Ⓟ 20,143; Ⓒ 21,138; ◆ 21,622
Westchester; RMC Place; LOS ANGELES; ***152** SJ-10; elev. 120ft./37m.; [P]; ★ **L.A.**; z 90045 & mail Los Angeles z 90083; pop. incl. with Los Angeles (Inc. Place)
West Compton; CDP-Census Area Only; LOS ANGELES; ***153** SJ-11; ★ **L.A.**; mail Compton z 90220; Ⓟ 5,451; Ⓒ 5,435
West Covina; Inc. Place; LOS ANGELES; **155** E-11; elev. 381ft./116m.; [P] [H] ■; ★ **L.A.**; z 91790-93; Ⓟ 96,086; Ⓒ 105,080; ◆ 110,576
Westend; RMC Place; SAN BERNARDINO; **153** SE-13; mail Trona z 93562; rural
Western Pacific Mole; RMC Place; ALAMEDA; ★ **SF-O-**; mail Oakland z 94607; pop. incl. with Oakland (Inc. Place)
West Escondido; RMC Place; SAN DIEGO; ★ **SDGO**; mail Escondido z 92029; pop. incl. with Escondido (Inc. Place)
West Garden Grove; RMC Place; ORANGE; ★ **L.A.**; mail Garden Grove z 92845-46; pop. incl. with Garden Grove (Inc. Place)
Westgate; RMC Place; SANTA CLARA; ★ **SF-O-**; mail San Jose z 95117, z 95170; pop. incl. with San Jose (Inc. Place)
West Glendale; RMC Place; LOS ANGELES; ***153** SJ-11; elev. 461ft./141m.; ★ **L.A.**; pop. incl. with Los Angeles (Inc. Place)
Westhaven; RMC Place; FRESNO; ***152** SD-7; elev. 277ft./84m.; mail Lemoore z 93245; rural
Westhaven; RMC Place; HUMBOLDT; **150** ND-2; elev. 295ft./90m.; [P]; ★ **EUR-**; z 95570; ● 370
Westhaven-Moonstone; CDP-Census Area Only; HUMBOLDT; ***150** NC-2; ★ **EUR-**; mail Trinidad z 95570; Ⓟ 1,109; Ⓒ 1,044
West Hills; RMC Place; LOS ANGELES; ***152** SJ-10; [P]; ★ **L.A.**; z 91304, z 91307-08; pop. incl. with Los Angeles (Inc. Place)
West Hollywood; Inc. Place; LOS ANGELES; **154** E-5; elev. 287ft./87m.; [P]; ★ **L.A.**; z 90038, z 90046, z 90048, z 90069; Ⓟ 36,118; Ⓒ 35,716; Ⓡ 35,794; ◆ 34,718
Westlake; RMC Place; SAN MATEO; ***150** NM-5; ★ **SF-O-**; mail Daly City z 94014-15; pop. incl. with Daly City (Inc. Place)
Westlake Village; Inc. Place; LOS ANGELES; **154** D-1; elev. 900ft./274m.; [P] [H]; ★ **OXN-**; z 91359, z 91361-62; Ⓟ 7,455; Ⓒ 8,368
Westlake Village; RMC Place; VENTURA; [P]; ★ **OXN-**; z 91359, z 91361-62; pop. incl. with Thousand Oaks (Inc. Place)
West Lane; RMC Place; SAN JOAQUIN; ★ **STOC**; mail Stockton z 95208; pop. incl. with Stockton (Inc. Place)
Westley; CDP; STANISLAUS; **150** NM-8; elev. 85ft./26m.; [P]; z 95387; Ⓒ 747
West Los Angeles; RMC Place; LOS ANGELES; ***152** SJ-10; elev. 241ft./73m.; [P]; ★ **L.A.**; z 90025; pop. incl. with Los Angeles (Inc. Place)
West Menlo Park; CDP-Census Area Only; SAN MATEO; ***150** NN-5; [P]; ★ **SF-O-**; z 94025; Ⓟ 3,959; Ⓒ 3,629
Westminster; Inc. Place; ORANGE; **154** J-10; elev. 30ft./9m.; [P] ■; ★ **L.A.**; z 92683-85 & mail Midway City z 92655; Ⓟ 78,118; Ⓒ 88,207; ◆ 91,031
West Modesto; RMC Place; STANISLAUS; ***150** NM-8; ★ **MOD**; mail Modesto z 95351; pop. incl. with Modesto (Inc. Place)
West Modesto; CDP-Census Area Only; STANISLAUS; ***150** NM-8; ★ **MOD**; mail Modesto z 95351; Ⓒ 6,096
Westmont; CDP-Census Area Only; LOS ANGELES; **154** G-6; ★ **L.A.**; mail Los Angeles z 90044; Ⓟ 31,044; Ⓒ 31,623; ◆ 32,342
Westmorland; Inc. Place; IMPERIAL; **153** SM-17; elev. 159ft./48m.; [P]; z 92281; Ⓟ 1,380; Ⓒ 2,131
West of Frazier Park; KERN; see Lake of the Woods (CDP)
West Palm Springs; RMC Place; RIVERSIDE; ***153** SJ-15; elev. 1,131ft./345m.; mail Whitewater z 92282; pop. incl. with Palm Springs (Inc. Place)
West Parlier; RMC Place; FRESNO; ***152** SC-8; mail Parlier z 93648; pop. incl. with Parlier (Inc. Place)
West Patton Village; LASSEN; see Patton Village (RMC Place)
West Pittsburg; CONTRA COSTA; see Bay Point (CDP-Census Area Only)
West Point; CDP; CALAVERAS; **150** NK-9; elev. 2,790ft./850m.; [P]; z 95255; Ⓒ 746
Westport; RMC Place; MENDOCINO; **150** NG-2; [P]; z 95488; ● 160
West Portal; RMC Place; SAN FRANCISCO; ★ **SF-O-**; mail San Francisco z 94127; pop. incl. with San Francisco (Inc. Place)
West Puente Valley; CDP-Census Area Only; LOS ANGELES; ***153** SJ-11; ★ **L.A.**; mail La Puente z 91744; Ⓟ 20,254; Ⓒ 22,589; ◆ 23,098
West Sacramento; Inc. Place; YOLO; **150** NK-7; [P]; ★ **SAC**; z 95605, z 95691, z 95798-99; Ⓟ 28,898; Ⓒ 31,615; ◆ 41,537
West Saticoy; RMC Place; VENTURA; ***152** SI-9; ★ **OXN-**; mail Ventura z 93004; pop. incl. with Ventura (Inc. Place)
Westside; RMC Place; SAN BERNARDINO; ★ **RIV-**; mail San Bernardino z 92411; pop. incl. with San Bernardino (Inc. Place)
Westvern; RMC Place; LOS ANGELES; ***153** SJ-11; ★ **L.A.**; mail Los Angeles z 90062; pop. incl. with Los Angeles (Inc. Place)
West Whittier; RMC Place; LOS ANGELES; ***153** SJ-11; ★ **L.A.**; mail Whittier z 90606; pop. incl. with Whittier (Inc. Place)
West Whittier-Los Nietos; CDP-Census Area Only; LOS ANGELES; ***153** SJ-11; ★ **L.A.**; mail Whittier z 90606; Ⓟ 24,164; Ⓒ 25,129; ◆ 25,704
Westwood; CDP; LASSEN; **150** NF-8; [P]; z 96137; Ⓟ 2,017; Ⓒ 1,998
Westwood; RMC Place; LOS ANGELES; ***152** SJ-10; elev. 300ft./91m.; ★ **L.A.**; mail Los Angeles z 90024; pop. incl. with Los Angeles (Inc. Place)
Westwood Manor; RMC Place; SHASTA; ***150** NE-5; elev. 472ft./144m.; ★ **REDD**; mail Redding z 96001; pop. incl. with Redding (Inc. Place)
Westwood Siding; LOS ANGELES; see Westwood Village (RMC Place)
Westwood Village; RMC Place; HUMBOLDT; ★ **EUR-**; mail Arcata z 95521; pop. incl. with Arcata (Inc. Place)
Westwood Village (Westwood Siding); RMC Place; LOS ANGELES; ***152** SJ-10; ★ **L.A.**; mail Los Angeles z 90024; pop. incl. with Los Angeles (Inc. Place)
Wheatland; Inc. Place; YUBA; **150** NI-7; elev. 87ft./27m.; [P]; z 95692; Ⓟ 1,631; Ⓒ 2,275
Wheeler Ridge; RMC Place; KERN; ***152** SG-9; elev. 964ft./294m.; mail Bakersfield z 93301; rural
Wheeler Springs; RMC Place; VENTURA; rural
Whiskeytown; RMC Place; SHASTA; **150** NE-5; [P]; z 96095; ● 100
Whispering Pines; RMC Place; LAKE; **150** NJ-4; mail Middletown z 95461; ● 100
Whispering Pines; RMC Place; SAN DIEGO; ***153** SM-15; elev. 4,111ft./1,253m.; mail Julian z 92036; ● 350
White Hall; RMC Place; EL DORADO; ***150** NJ-9; mail Pollock Pines z 95726; rural
Whitehawk; CDP-Census Area Only; PLUMAS; ***150** NG-9; Ⓒ 96
White Hills Junction; RMC Place; SANTA BARBARA; ★ **LOMP**; pop. incl. with Lompoc (Inc. Place)
White Oak; RMC Place; LOS ANGELES; ★ **L.A.**; mail Encino z 91416; pop. incl. with Los Angeles (Inc. Place)
White Pines; RMC Place; CALAVERAS; ***150** NL-9; mail Arnold z 95223; ● 170
White River; RMC Place; TULARE; ***152** SE-9; mail Porterville z 93257; rural
White Rock; RMC Place; SACRAMENTO; ***150** NJ-8; elev. 491ft./150m.; ★ **SAC**; mail Folsom z 95630; rural
Whitethorn (Thorn); RMC Place; HUMBOLDT; **150** NF-2; [P]; z 95589; ● 300
White Water; RMC Place; RIVERSIDE; **153** SJ-15; [P]; z 92282
Whitewood; RMC Place; LOS ANGELES; ★ **L.A.**; mail Whittier z 90603; pop. incl. with Whittier (Inc. Place)
Whitley Gardens; RMC Place; SAN LUIS OBISPO; **152** SE-6; mail Paso Robles z 93446; ● 300
Whitlow; RMC Place; HUMBOLDT; ***150** NF-2; mail Myers Flat z 95554; rural
Whitmore; RMC Place; SHASTA; **150** NE-6; elev. 2,233ft./681m.; [P]; z 96096; ● 100
Whitmore Hot Springs; RMC Place; MONO; ***151** NM-13; mail Mammoth Lakes z 93546; rural
Whitner Heights; RMC Place; FRESNO; ***152** SC-8; elev. 331ft./101m.; mail Parlier z 93648; pop. incl. with Parlier (Inc. Place)
Whittier; Inc. Place; LOS ANGELES; **153** SJ-11; elev. 365ft./111m.; [P] [H] [C] 1,945 ■; ★ **L.A.**; z 90601-10; Ⓟ 77,671; Ⓒ 83,680; ◆ 86,204
Whittier South; LOS ANGELES; see South Whittier (CDP)
Wible Orchard; RMC Place; KERN; ***152** SF-9; ★ **BAK**; pop. incl. with Bakersfield (Inc. Place)
Wiest; RMC Place; IMPERIAL; ***153** SM-17; elev. 138ft./42m.; mail Brawley z 92227; rural
Wilbur Springs; RMC Place; COLUSA; **150** NI-5; mail Williams z 95987; rural
Wilcox; RMC Place; LOS ANGELES; ★ **L.A.**; mail Los Angeles z 90038; pop. incl. with Los Angeles (Inc. Place)

Entries in **UPPERCASE** are counties.
Entries in **bold** have populations of 2,500 or more.
Names in parentheses are alternate names.

Inc. Place	Incorporated Place
RMC Place	Rand McNally Designated Place
CDP	Census Designated Place
MCD	Minor Civil Division
⊡	County Seat
▲	Minor Civil Division
elev.	Elevation
[P]	Post Office
[H]	Hospital
[C]	College
■	Principal Business Center
★	Ranally Metro Area (RMA) Abbreviation
z	Zip Code(s)
Ⓟ	Previous Census Population
Ⓡ	Revised Census Population
Ⓐ	Annexation Population
●	Rand McNally Population Estimate
Ⓒ	Final Census Population
Ⓢ	Special Census Population
◆	Estimated Population

For additional definitions see Glossary, Volume 1, and Introduction, Volume 2.

Wildasin; RMC Place; LOS ANGELES; ***153** SJ-11; elev. 137ft./42m.; ★ **L.A.**; pop. incl. with Los Angeles (Inc. Place)
Wildcat Canyon; RMC Place; CONTRA COSTA; ★ **SF-O-**; pop. incl. with Richmond (Inc. Place)
Wildflower; RMC Place; FRESNO; ***152** SC-7; elev. 267ft./81m.; ★ **FRES**; mail Selma **z** 93662; rural
Wildomar; CDP; RIVERSIDE; **155** L-19; 🅿 🅷; **z** 92595; Ⓟ 10,411; © 14,064
Wildwood; RMC Place; SANTA CRUZ; ***152** SA-2; ★ **S.CRZ**; mail Boulder Creek **z** 95006; ● 560
Wildwood; RMC Place; TRINITY; **150** NE-4; elev. 3,504ft./1,068m.; 🅿; **z** 96076; ● 50
Wilfred; RMC Place; SONOMA; ***150** NK-4; elev. 94ft./29m.; ★ **S.ROS**; mail Santa Rosa **z** 95401; pop. incl. with Rohnert Park (Inc. Place)
Wilkerson; CDP-Census Area Only; INYO; ***152** SA-10; elev. 1,350ft./411m.; mail Bishop **z** 93514; © 562
Willaura Estates; RMC Place; NEVADA; ***150** NI-8; elev. 1,700ft./518m.; ★ **SAC**; mail Grass Valley **z** 95945, **z** 95949; ● 200
Williams; Inc. Place; COLUSA; **150** NI-6; elev. 801ft./244m.; 🅿; **z** 95987; Ⓟ 2,297; © 3,670
William Taft; RMC Place; SAN DIEGO; ★ **SDGO**; mail San Diego **z** 92117, **z** 92177, **z** 92197; pop. incl. with San Diego (Inc. Place)
Willits; Inc. Place; MENDOCINO; **150** NH-3; elev. 1,364ft./416m.; 🅿 🅷; **z** 95429, **z** 95490; Ⓟ 5,027; © 5,073
Willowbrook; CDP-Census Area Only; LOS ANGELES; **154** G-7; elev. 80ft./24m.; ★ **L.A.**; mail Compton **z** 90222-23; Ⓟ 32,772; © 34,138; ◆ 34,913
Willow Creek; CDP; HUMBOLDT; **150** ND-3; 🅿; **z** 95573; Ⓟ 1,576; © 1,743
Willow Glen; RMC Place; SANTA CLARA; ***150** NN-6; ★ **SF-O-**; mail San Jose **z** 95125, **z** 95150; pop. incl. with San Jose (Inc. Place)
Willow Ranch; RMC Place; MODOC; ***150** NA-10; elev. 4,738ft./1,444m.; mail Davis Creek **z** 96108; rural
Willows; Inc. Place; ⊡ GLENN; **150** NH-6; elev. 135ft./41m.; 🅿 🅷; **z** 95988; Ⓟ 5,988; © 6,220
Willow Springs; RMC Place; KERN; ***153** SH-11; 🅿; **z** 93560
Willow Springs; RMC Place; MONO; ***151** NL-12; elev. 6,744ft./2,056m.; mail Bridgeport **z** 93517; rural
Willow Springs; RMC Place; TUOLUMNE; ***150** NL-10; mail Soulsbyville **z** 95372; ● 1,100
Will Rogers; RMC Place; LOS ANGELES; ★ **L.A.**; mail Santa Monica **z** 90402, **z** 90408; pop. incl. with Santa Monica (Inc. Place)
Wilmar; RMC Place; LOS ANGELES; ★ **L.A.**; mail Rosemead **z** 91770; pop. incl. with Rosemead (Inc. Place)
Wilmington; RMC Place; LOS ANGELES; ***153** SK-11; 🅿; ★ **L.A.**; **z** 90744, **z** 90748; pop. incl. with Los Angeles (Inc. Place)
Wilmington Park; RMC Place; LOS ANGELES; ★ **L.A.**; mail Wilmington **z** 90744; pop. incl. with Los Angeles (Inc. Place)
Wilseyville; RMC Place; CALAVERAS; **150** NK-9; 🅿; **z** 95257; ● 350
Wilsona Gardens; RMC Place; LOS ANGELES; ***153** SH-12; elev. 2,562ft./781m.; mail Lancaster **z** 93534-35
Wilsonia; RMC Place; TULARE; **152** SK-1; mail Kings Canyon National Pk **z** 93633
Wilton; CDP; SACRAMENTO; **150** NK-7; 🅿; **z** 95693; Ⓟ 3,858; © 4,551
Winchester; CDP; RIVERSIDE; **153** SK-14; elev. 1,474ft./449m.; 🅿; **z** 92596; Ⓟ 1,689; © 2,155
Windsor; Inc. Place; SONOMA; **150** NK-4; elev. 118ft./36m.; 🅿; ★ **S.ROS**; **z** 95492; Ⓟ 12,002; © 22,744; ◆ 24,278
Windsor Hills; RMC Place; LOS ANGELES; **154** F-5; 🅿; ★ **L.A.**; **z** 90043, **z** 90056 & mail Los Angeles **z** 90052; ● 5,000
Wingfoot; RMC Place; LOS ANGELES; ***153** SJ-11; ★ **L.A.**
Winnetka; RMC Place; LOS ANGELES; ***152** SJ-10; 🅿; ★ **L.A.**; **z** 91306, **z** 91396; pop. incl. with Los Angeles (Inc. Place)
Wino's Corner; FRESNO; see Elm View (RMC Place)
Winter Gardens; CDP; SAN DIEGO; ***153** SM-14; ★ **SDGO**; mail Lakeside **z** 92040; © 19,771
Winterhaven; CDP; IMPERIAL; **153** SM-19; 🅿 🅷; ★ **YUMA**; **z** 92283; © 529
Winters; Inc. Place; YOLO; **150** NK-6; elev. 135ft./41m.; 🅿; **z** 95694; Ⓟ 4,639; © 6,125
Wintersburg; RMC Place; ORANGE; ***153** SK-11; ★ **L.A.**; mail Huntington Beach **z** 92647; pop. incl. with Huntington Beach (Inc. Place)
Winterwarm; RMC Place; SAN DIEGO; ***153** SL-13; ★ **SDGO**; mail Fallbrook **z** 92028; ● 1,035
Winton; CDP; MERCED; **150** NN-9; 🅿; ★ **MRCD**; **z** 95388; Ⓟ 7,559; © 8,832
Wise; RMC Place; LOS ANGELES; ★ **L.A.**; mail El Segundo **z** 90245; pop. incl. with El Segundo (Inc. Place)
Wiseburn; RMC Place; LOS ANGELES; ★ **L.A.**; mail Hawthorne **z** 90250; pop. incl. with Hawthorne (Inc. Place)
Wishon; RMC Place; MADERA; **152** SA-8; 🅿; **z** 93669; ● 300
Witch Creek; RMC Place; SAN DIEGO; ***153** SM-14; elev. 2,765ft./843m.; ★ **SDGO**; mail Ramona **z** 92065; rural
Wofford Heights; CDP; KERN; **152** SE-10; 🅿; **z** 93285; Ⓟ 2,270; © 2,276
Wolf; RMC Place; NEVADA; ***150** NI-8; elev. 1,572ft./479m.; ★ **SAC**; mail Auburn **z** 95603; rural
Wonderland; SHASTA; see Tunnel Inn (RMC Place)
Wonder Valley; RMC Place; FRESNO; ***152** SB-8; elev. 662ft./202m.; mail Piedra **z** 93649; ● 140
Woodacre; CDP; MARIN; **150** NL-4; elev. 351ft./107m.; 🅿; ★ **SF-O-**; **z** 94973; Ⓟ 1,478; © 1,393
Woodbridge; RMC Place; SAN JOAQUIN; ***150** NL-7; elev. 46ft./14m.; 🅿; ★ **STOC**; **z** 95258; Ⓟ 3,456; ● 900
Woodcrest; CDP; RIVERSIDE; **155** H-18; elev. 1,529ft./466m.; ★ **RIV-**; mail Riverside **z** 92504; Ⓟ 7,796; © 8,342
Woodfords; RMC Place; ALPINE; **151** NJ-11; mail Markleeville **z** 96120; ● 100
Woodfords Community; Indian Reservation; ALPINE; © 219
Woodlake; Inc. Place; TULARE; **152** SC-9; 🅿; ★ **VISL**; **z** 93286; Ⓟ 5,678; © 6,651
Woodland; Inc. Place; ⊡ YOLO; **150** NJ-6; elev. 65ft./20m.; 🅿 🅷 ■; **z** 95695, **z** 95776; Ⓟ 39,802; © 49,151; ◆ 60,231
Woodland Hills; RMC Place; LOS ANGELES; ***152** SJ-10; 🅿; ★ **L.A.**; **z** 91302-03, **z** 91364-65, **z** 91367, **z** 91371-72; pop. incl. with Los Angeles (Inc. Place)
Woodland Park; RMC Place; LOS ANGELES; ★ **L.A.**; pop. incl. with Lakewood (Inc. Place)
Woodlands (Erwin Lake); RMC Place; SAN BERNARDINO; ***153** SI-14; elev. 6,835ft./2,083m.; mail Sugarloaf **z** 92386; ● 1,400
Woodleaf; RMC Place; YUBA; ***150** NH-8; elev. 3,130ft./954m.; mail Challenge **z** 95925; ● 20
Woodruff Avenue; RMC Place; LOS ANGELES; ★ **L.A.**; mail Bellflower **z** 90706; pop. incl. with Bellflower (Inc. Place)
Woodside; Inc. Place; SAN MATEO; **151** NK-15; elev. 382ft./116m.; 🅿; ★ **SF-O-**; **z** 94061-62; Ⓟ 5,035; © 5,352
Woodside Glens; RMC Place; SAN MATEO; ★ **SF-O-**; mail Redwood City **z** 94062; pop. incl. with Woodside (Inc. Place)
Woodville; RMC Place; MARIN; ***150** NL-4; elev. 180ft./55m.; ★ **SF-O-**; mail Bolinas **z** 94924; rural
Woodville; CDP; TULARE; **152** SD-9; 🅿; **z** 93257 & mail Porterville **z** 93258; Ⓟ 1,557; © 1,678
Woodward Park; RMC Place; FRESNO; ***152** SB-7; ★ **FRES**; mail Fresno **z** 93710, **z** 93720, **z** 93729; pop. incl. with Fresno (Inc. Place)
Woody; RMC Place; KERN; **152** SE-9; elev. 1,647ft./502m.; 🅿; **z** 93287
Woolsey; RMC Place; SONOMA; mail Windsor **z** 95492; ● 200
Workman; RMC Place; LOS ANGELES; ***153** SJ-11; elev. 94ft./29m.; ★ **L.A.**; mail South Gate **z** 90280; pop. incl. with South Gate (Inc. Place)
Wrights Beach; SONOMA; see Ocean View (RMC Place)
Wrightwood; CDP; SAN BERNARDINO; **153** SI-12; elev. 5,931ft./1,808m.; 🅿; **z** 92397; Ⓟ 3,308; © 3,837
Wyandotte; RMC Place; BUTTE; **150** NH-7; elev. 677ft./206m.; mail Oroville **z** 95965; ● 110
Wynola; RMC Place; SAN DIEGO; ***153** SM-15; elev. 3,655ft./1,114m.; mail Santa Ysabel **z** 92070; ● 300
Wyntoon; RMC Place; TRINITY; ***150** ND-5; elev. 2,440ft./744m.; mail Trinity Center **z** 96091; ● 70

X

XL Ranch; Indian Reservation; MODOC; © 14

Y

Yale; RMC Place; RIVERSIDE; ★ **PSPR-**; mail Hemet **z** 92544; pop. incl. with Hemet (Inc. Place)
Yankee Hill; RMC Place; BUTTE; ***150** NG-7; 🅿; **z** 95965; rural
Yankee Jims; RMC Place; PLACER; ***150** NI-8; elev. 2,575ft./785m.; ★ **SAC**; mail Colfax **z** 95713, Foresthill **z** 95631; rural
Yerba Buena Island; RMC Place; SAN FRANCISCO; ★ **SF-O-**; mail San Francisco **z** 94130; pop. incl. with San Francisco (Inc. Place)
Yermo; RMC Place; SAN BERNARDINO; **153** SH-14; elev. 1,926ft./587m.; 🅿; **z** 92398; ● 1,000
Yettem; RMC Place; TULARE; **152** SC-8; 🅿; ★ **VISL**; **z** 93670; ● 500
Ygnacio Valley; RMC Place; CONTRA COSTA; ★ **SF-O-**; mail Walnut Creek **z** 94598; pop. incl. with Walnut Creek (Inc. Place)
Yolanda; RMC Place; MARIN; ★ **SF-O-**; mail San Anselmo **z** 94960; pop. incl. with San Anselmo (Inc. Place)
Yolo; RMC Place; YOLO; **150** NJ-6; 🅿; **z** 95697; ● 450
YOLO; **150** NJ-6; Ⓟ 141,092; © 168,660; ◆ 211,268
Yorba; RMC Place; LOS ANGELES; ★ **L.A.**; mail Pomona **z** 91767; pop. incl. with Pomona (Inc. Place)
Yorba Linda; Inc. Place; ORANGE; **155** G-13; elev. 397ft./121m.; 🅿; ★ **L.A.**; **z** 92885-87; Ⓟ 52,422; © 58,918; ◆ 63,989
York; RMC Place; LOS ANGELES; ***153** SJ-11; ★ **L.A.**; mail Los Angeles **z** 90050; pop. incl. with Los Angeles (Inc. Place)
Yorkville; RMC Place; MENDOCINO; **150** NJ-3; 🅿; **z** 95494; ● 130
Yosemite Forks; RMC Place; MADERA; **151** NN-11; elev. 3,000ft./914m.; mail Oakhurst **z** 93644; ● 210
Yosemite Junction; RMC Place; TUOLUMNE; mail Jamestown **z** 95327; rural
Yosemite Lakes; CDP-Census Area Only; MADERA; ***152** SA-7; elev. 1,500ft./457m.; mail Coarsegold **z** 93614; Ⓟ 2,367; © 4,160
Yosemite Lodge; RMC Place; MARIPOSA; mail Yosemite National Park **z** 95389; pop. incl. with Yosemite Village (RMC Place)
Yosemite Valley; MARIPOSA; see Yosemite Village (RMC Place)
Yosemite Village (Yosemite Valley); RMC Place; MARIPOSA; ***151** NM-11; mail Yosemite National Park **z** 95389; disincorporated since 2000 Census; © 265
Yosemite West; RMC Place; MARIPOSA; ***151** NM-11; elev. 5,600ft./1,707m.; mail Yosemite National Park **z** 95389; ● 100
Yountville; Inc. Place; NAPA; **150** NK-5; elev. 97ft./30m.; 🅿 🅷; ★ **NAPA**; **z** 94599; Ⓟ 3,259; © 2,916; Ⓡ 3,297
Yreka; Inc. Place; ⊡ SISKIYOU; **150** NB-5; elev. 2,625ft./800m.; 🅿 🅷; **z** 96097; Ⓟ 6,948; © 7,290
YUBA; **150** NI-7; Ⓟ 58,228; © 60,219; ◆ 75,463
Yuba City; Inc. Place; ⊡ SUTTER; **150** NI-7; elev. 70ft./21m.; 🅿 🅷 ■; ★ **YUCY**; **z** 95991-93; Ⓟ 27,437; © 36,758; ◆ 61,050
Yucaipa; Inc. Place; SAN BERNARDINO; **153** SJ-14; 🅿; ★ **RIV-**; **z** 92399; Ⓟ 32,824; © 41,207; ◆ 51,601
Yucca Valley; Inc. Place; SAN BERNARDINO; **153** SJ-15; elev. 3,279ft./999m.; 🅿; **z** 92284-86; Ⓟ 16,539; © 16,865; ◆ 18,440
Yurok Reservation; Indian Reservation; HUMBOLDT, DEL NORTE; mail Hoopa **z** 95546; Ⓟ 1,082; © 1,103

Z

Zamora; RMC Place; YOLO; **150** NJ-6; 🅿; **z** 95698; ● 100
Zayante; RMC Place; SANTA CRUZ; ***152** SA-2; ★ **S.CRZ**; mail Felton **z** 95018; ● 660
Zenia; RMC Place; TRINITY; **150** NF-3; elev. 2,969ft./905m.; 🅿; **z** 95595; ● 39

Entries in **UPPERCASE** are counties.
Entries in **bold** have populations of 2,500 or more.
Names in parentheses are alternate names.
Inc. Place — Incorporated Place
RMC Place — Rand McNally Designated Place
CDP — Census Designated Place
MCD — Minor Civil Division

⊡ County Seat
▲ Minor Civil Division
elev. Elevation
🅿 Post Office

🅷 Hospital
🅲 College
■ Principal Business Center
★ Ranally Metro Area (RMA) Abbreviation
z Zip Code(s)

Ⓟ Previous Census Population
Ⓡ Revised Census Population
Ⓐ Annexation Population
● Rand McNally Population Estimate
© Final Census Population
Ⓢ Special Census Population
◆ Estimated Population

For additional definitions see Glossary, Volume 1, and Introduction, Volume 2.

COLORADO

Statistics

Total area (2000) — 104,094 square miles
Land area (2000) — 103,718 square miles
Water area (2000) — 376 square miles
Capital — Denver
Admitted as state — August, 1876

Maps

State maps can be found on pages 142-254 in Vol. 1

Ranally Metro Areas (RMAs) and Abbreviations

Boulder-Longmont, CO — BOUL-
Colorado Springs, CO — CSPG
Denver, CO — DEN
Fort Collins-Loveland, CO — FTCL-
Grand Junction, CO — GDJC
Greeley, CO — GRLY
Pueblo, CO — PUEB

Principal Places

Place Name	Place Type	County	Population
Denver	Inc. Place	DENVER	◆ 632,429
Colorado Springs	Inc. Place	EL PASO	◆ 397,600
Aurora	Inc. Place	ARAPAHOE	◆ 344,560
Lakewood	Inc. Place	JEFFERSON	◆ 148,679
Fort Collins	Inc. Place	LARIMER	◆ 148,391
Westminster	Inc. Place	ADAMS	◆ 118,309
Highlands Ranch	CDP-Census Area Only	DOUGLAS	◆ 116,743
Thornton	Inc. Place	ADAMS	◆ 114,175
Arvada	Inc. Place	JEFFERSON	◆ 106,098
Boulder	Inc. Place	BOULDER	◆ 103,478
Pueblo	Inc. Place	PUEBLO	◆ 101,461
Centennial	Inc. Place	ARAPAHOE	◆ 101,391
Longmont	Inc. Place	BOULDER	◆ 92,479
Greeley	Inc. Place	WELD	◆ 90,235
Loveland	Inc. Place	LARIMER	◆ 65,626
Broomfield	Inc. Place	BROOMFIELD	◆ 57,987
Parker	Inc. Place	DOUGLAS	◆ 51,039
Southglenn	CDP-Census Area Only	ARAPAHOE	◆ 50,107
Grand Junction	Inc. Place	MESA	◆ 49,012
Castle Rock	Inc. Place	DOUGLAS	◆ 42,208
Littleton	Inc. Place	ARAPAHOE	◆ 42,101
Northglenn	Inc. Place	ADAMS	◆ 38,433
Security-Widefield	CDP-Census Area Only	EL PASO	◆ 35,207
Wheat Ridge	Inc. Place	JEFFERSON	◆ 34,269
Englewood	Inc. Place	ARAPAHOE	◆ 32,812
Ken Caryl	CDP-Census Area Only	JEFFERSON	◆ 31,998
Brighton	Inc. Place	ADAMS	◆ 30,994
Lafayette	Inc. Place	BOULDER	◆ 29,841
Castlewood	CDP-Census Area Only	ARAPAHOE	◆ 29,444
Commerce City	Inc. Place	ADAMS	◆ 29,200
Columbine	CDP-Census Area Only	JEFFERSON	◆ 24,968
Louisville	Inc. Place	BOULDER	© 18,937
Sherrelwood	CDP-Census Area Only	ADAMS	© 17,657
Clifton	CDP	MESA	© 17,345
Golden	Inc. Place	JEFFERSON	© 17,159
Pueblo West	CDP-Census Area Only	PUEBLO	© 16,899
Durango	Inc. Place	LA PLATA	◆ 16,388
Cañon City	Inc. Place	FREMONT	© 15,431
Fountain	Inc. Place	EL PASO	© 15,197
Cimarron Hills	CDP-Census Area Only	EL PASO	© 15,194
Black Forest	CDP	EL PASO	© 13,247
Welby	CDP	ADAMS	© 12,973
Sterling	Inc. Place	LOGAN	◆ 12,801
Montrose	Inc. Place	MONTROSE	© 12,344
Federal Heights	Inc. Place	ADAMS	© 12,065
Greenwood Village	Inc. Place	ARAPAHOE	© 11,035
Fort Morgan	Inc. Place	MORGAN	© 11,034
Berkley	CDP-Census Area Only	ADAMS	© 10,743
Fort Carson	CDP	EL PASO	© 10,566
Windsor	Inc. Place	WELD	© 9,896
Steamboat Springs	Inc. Place	ROUTT	© 9,815
Evans	Inc. Place	WELD	© 9,514
Gunbarrel	CDP	BOULDER	© 9,435
Evergreen	CDP	JEFFERSON	© 9,216
Craig	Inc. Place	MOFFAT	© 9,189
Trinidad	Inc. Place	LAS ANIMAS	© 9,078
Superior	Inc. Place	BOULDER	© 9,011
Lamar	Inc. Place	PROWERS	© 8,869
Edwards	CDP	EAGLE	® 8,266
Redlands	CDP	MESA	© 8,043
Cortez	Inc. Place	MONTEZUMA	© 7,977
Alamosa	Inc. Place	ALAMOSA	© 7,960
Glenwood Springs	Inc. Place	GARFIELD	© 7,736
La Junta	Inc. Place	OTERO	© 7,568
United States Air Force Academy	CDP-Census Area Only	EL PASO	© 7,526
The Pinery	CDP-Census Area Only	DOUGLAS	© 7,253
Woodmoor	CDP-Census Area Only	EL PASO	© 7,177
Applewood	CDP-Census Area Only	JEFFERSON	© 7,123
Fruitvale	CDP	MESA	© 6,936
Fort Lupton	Inc. Place	WELD	© 6,787
Rifle	Inc. Place	GARFIELD	© 6,784
Stratmoor	CDP-Census Area Only	EL PASO	© 6,650
Woodland Park	Inc. Place	TELLER	© 6,515
Fruita	Inc. Place	MESA	© 6,478
Orchard Mesa	CDP	MESA	© 6,456
Derby	CDP-Census Area Only	ADAMS	© 6,423
Delta	Inc. Place	DELTA	© 6,400
Twin Lakes	CDP-Census Area Only	ADAMS	© 6,301
Erie	Inc. Place	WELD	© 6,291
Stonegate	CDP-Census Area Only	DOUGLAS	© 6,284
Castle Pines	CDP-Census Area Only	DOUGLAS	© 5,958
Cherry Hills Village	Inc. Place	ARAPAHOE	© 5,958
Aspen	Inc. Place	PITKIN	© 5,914
Avon	Inc. Place	EAGLE	® 5,605
Sheridan	Inc. Place	ARAPAHOE	© 5,600
Salida	Inc. Place	CHAFFEE	© 5,504
Edgewater	Inc. Place	JEFFERSON	© 5,445
Estes Park	Inc. Place	LARIMER	© 5,413
Gunnison	Inc. Place	GUNNISON	© 5,409
Carbondale	Inc. Place	GARFIELD	© 5,196
Brush	Inc. Place	MORGAN	© 5,117

County Business Data

County	FIPS Code	County Seat	Land Area (Sq. Mi.)	Census Population 4/1/2000	Census Population 4/1/1990	Census Population % Change 1990-2000	Wholesale Trade Sales, 2002 ($1,000)	Wholesale Trade % Change 1997-2002	Manufacturing, 2002 Establish-ments	Manufacturing, 2002 Total Employees	Manufacturing, 2002 Value Added ($1,000)	Manufacturing, 2002 Ranally Mfg. Units
Adams[1]	001	Brighton	1,192	363,857	265,038	37.3	10,363,417	47.1	442	12,823	1,144,260	605
Alamosa	003	Alamosa	723	14,966	13,617	9.9	64,393	-6.4	...	(d)	(d)	...
Arapahoe	005	Littleton	803	487,967	391,511	24.6	28,512,637	27.3	511	10,125	1,019,898	540
Archuleta	007	Pagosa Springs	1,350	9,898	5,345	85.2	(d)	(d)	...	(d)	(d)	...
Baca	009	Springfield	2,556	4,517	4,556	-0.9	(d)	(d)	...	(d)	(d)	...
Bent	011	Las Animas	1,514	5,998	5,048	18.8	(d)	(d)	...	(d)	(d)	...
Boulder[1]	013	Boulder	742	291,288	225,339	29.3	4,434,114	13.5	581	16,770	2,191,400	1,159
Broomfield[2]	014	Broomfield	(d)	(d)	(d)	(d)	(d)	(d)	77	5,682	1,079,909	571
Chaffee	015	Salida	1,013	16,242	12,684	28.1	35,672	-4.7	...	(d)	(d)	...
Cheyenne	017	Cheyenne Wells	1,781	2,231	2,397	-6.9	(d)	(d)	...	(d)	(d)	...
Clear Creek	019	Georgetown	395	9,322	7,619	22.4	(d)	(d)	...	(d)	(d)	...
Conejos	021	Conejos	1,287	8,400	7,453	12.7	(d)	(d)	...	(d)	(d)	...
Costilla	023	San Luis	1,227	3,663	3,190	14.8	(d)	(d)	...	(d)	(d)	...
Crowley	025	Ordway	789	5,518	3,946	39.8	(d)	(d)	...	(d)	(d)	...
Custer	027	Westcliffe	739	3,503	1,926	81.9	(d)	(d)	...	(d)	(d)	...
Delta	029	Delta	1,142	27,834	20,980	32.7	60,855	49.3	...	(d)	(d)	...
Denver	031	Denver	153	554,636	467,610	18.6	20,041,482	23.9	895	22,116	2,304,647	1,219
Dolores	033	Dove Creek	1,067	1,844	1,504	22.6	11,269	-52.4	...	(d)	(d)	...
Douglas	035	Castle Rock	840	175,766	60,391	191.0	(d)	(d)	102	1,381	149,623	79
Eagle	037	Eagle	1,688	41,659	21,928	90.0	(d)	(d)	...	(d)	(d)	...
Elbert	039	Kiowa	1,851	19,872	9,646	106.0	32,963	-16.2	...	(d)	(d)	...
El Paso	041	Colorado Springs	2,126	516,929	397,014	30.2	3,525,755	148.7	507	19,254	2,606,368	1,379
Fremont	043	Cañon City	1,533	46,145	32,273	43.0	38,297	-10.5	48	627	67,345	36
Garfield	045	Glenwood Springs	2,947	43,791	29,974	46.1	174,595	54.7	...	(d)	(d)	...
Gilpin	047	Central City	150	4,757	3,070	55.0	(d)	(d)	...	(d)	(d)	...
Grand	049	Hot Sulphur Springs	1,847	12,442	7,966	56.2	13,276	3.1	...	(d)	(d)	...
Gunnison	051	Gunnison	3,239	13,956	10,273	35.9	(d)	(d)	...	(d)	(d)	...
Hinsdale	053	Lake City	1,118	790	467	69.2	(d)	(d)	...	(d)	(d)	...
Huerfano	055	Walsenburg	1,591	7,862	6,009	30.8	(d)	(d)	...	(d)	(d)	...
Jackson	057	Walden	1,613	1,577	1,605	-1.7	(d)	(d)	...	(d)	(d)	...
Jefferson[1]	059	Golden	772	527,056	438,430	20.2	5,238,878	86.7	504	21,241	2,876,528	1,522
Kiowa	061	Eads	1,771	1,622	1,688	-3.9	5,742	-28.0	...	(d)	(d)	...
Kit Carson	063	Burlington	2,161	8,011	7,140	12.2	105,724	-13.7	...	(d)	(d)	...
Lake	065	Leadville	377	7,812	6,007	30.0	(d)	(d)	...	(d)	(d)	...
La Plata	067	Durango	1,692	43,941	32,284	36.1	(d)	(d)	73	654	49,001	26
Larimer	069	Fort Collins	2,601	251,494	186,136	35.1	9,869,002	(d)	390	12,362	1,559,876	825
Las Animas	071	Trinidad	4,773	15,207	13,765	10.5	54,638	61.5	...	(d)	(d)	...
Lincoln	073	Hugo	2,586	6,087	4,529	34.4	13,547	-34.4	...	(d)	(d)	...
Logan	075	Sterling	1,839	20,504	17,567	16.7	102,305	5.1	...	(d)	(d)	...
Mesa	077	Grand Junction	3,328	116,255	93,145	24.8	686,250	29.2	161	2,922	225,575	119
Mineral	079	Creede	876	831	558	48.9	(d)	(d)	...	(d)	(d)	...
Moffat	081	Craig	4,742	13,184	11,357	16.1	43,878	23.4	...	(d)	(d)	...
Montezuma	083	Cortez	2,037	23,830	18,672	27.6	30,886	67.9	...	(d)	(d)	...
Montrose	085	Montrose	2,241	33,432	24,423	36.9	(d)	(d)	64	1,388	100,927	53
Morgan	087	Fort Morgan	1,285	27,171	21,939	23.8	(d)	(d)	27	(d)	(d)	...
Otero	089	La Junta	1,263	20,311	20,185	0.6	284,201	139.1	...	(d)	(d)	...
Ouray	091	Ouray	540	3,742	2,295	63.1	2,279	(d)	...	(d)	(d)	...
Park	093	Fairplay	2,201	14,523	7,174	102.4	(d)	(d)	...	(d)	(d)	...
Phillips	095	Holyoke	688	4,480	4,189	6.9	82,098	-42.3	...	(d)	(d)	...
Pitkin	097	Aspen	970	14,872	12,661	17.5	98,405	24.5	...	(d)	(d)	...
Prowers	099	Lamar	1,640	14,483	13,347	8.5	(d)	(d)	17	768	37,051	20
Pueblo	101	Pueblo	2,389	141,472	123,051	15.0	298,415	-23.5	122	4,088	540,720	286
Rio Blanco	103	Meeker	3,221	5,986	5,972	0.2	(d)	(d)	...	(d)	(d)	...
Rio Grande	105	Del Norte	912	12,413	10,770	15.3	201,165	105.1	...	(d)	(d)	...
Routt	107	Steamboat Springs	2,362	19,690	14,088	39.8	96,446	87.6	...	(d)	(d)	...
Saguache	109	Saguache	3,168	5,917	4,619	28.1	57,845	561.2	...	(d)	(d)	...
San Juan	111	Silverton	387	558	745	-25.1	(d)	(d)	...	(d)	(d)	...
San Miguel	113	Telluride	1,287	6,594	3,653	80.5	(d)	(d)	...	(d)	(d)	...
Sedgwick	115	Julesburg	548	2,747	2,690	2.1	19,534	-47.1	...	(d)	(d)	...
Summit	117	Breckenridge	608	23,548	12,881	82.8	43,671	-25.4	...	(d)	(d)	...
Teller	119	Cripple Creek	557	20,555	12,468	64.9	12,837	-34.1	...	(d)	(d)	...
Washington	121	Akron	2,521	4,926	4,812	2.4	30,153	-43.2	...	(d)	(d)	...
Weld[1]	123	Greeley	3,992	180,936	131,821	37.3	1,276,004	-4.4	231	9,540	1,289,514	682
Yuma	125	Wray	2,366	9,841	8,954	9.9	122,947	9.4	...	(d)	(d)	...
The State			**103,718**	**4,301,261**	**3,294,394**	**30.6**	**92,092,155**	**52.7**	**5,349**	**148,824**	**17,798,062**	**9,416**

(d) Data not available. Corresponding percentages or Ranally Manufacturing Units are estimates.
... Represents 0 or amount too minimal to be reported.

1 Land area and census population include a portion of Broomfield county.
2 Created on November 15, 2001 from parts of Adams, Boulder, Jefferson, and Weld counties.

Index of Places and Counties

A

Abarr; RMC Place; YUMA; mail Yuma **z** 80759; rural
Academy; RMC Place; EL PASO; ***159** H-14; elev. 6,584ft./2,007m.; ★ **CSPG**
Acequia; RMC Place; DOUGLAS; ***159** F-13; mail Littleton **z** 80126; ● 950
Acres Green; CDP-Census Area Only; DOUGLAS; ***159** F-14; ★ **DEN**; mail Lone Tree **z** 80124; © 3,205
ADAMS; **159** E-15; part of Adams county was annexed by Broomfield county on November 15, 2001; Ⓟ 265,038; © 363,857; adjusted 2000 Census population is 348,618; ◆ 439,176
Agate; RMC Place; ELBERT; **159** F-16; elev. 5,458ft./1,664m.; 🅿; **z** 80101; ● 80
Aguilar; Inc. Place; LAS ANIMAS; **159** M-14; elev. 6,400ft./1,951m.; 🅿; **z** 81020; Ⓟ 520; © 593
Air Force Academy; EL PASO; see United States Air Force Academy (CDP-Census Area Only)
Akron; Inc. Place; ⊡ WASHINGTON; **159** D-18; elev. 4,661ft./1,421m.; 🅿; **z** 80720; Ⓟ 1,599; © 1,711
Alameda; RMC Place; JEFFERSON; ★ **DEN**; mail Denver **z** 80215; pop. incl. with Lakewood (Inc. Place)
Alamosa; Inc. Place; ⊡ ALAMOSA; **159** L-11; elev. 7,544ft./2,299m.; 🅿 🄷 🄲 2,813; **z** 81101-02; Ⓟ 7,579; © 7,960
ALAMOSA; **159** L-12; Ⓟ 13,617; © 14,966; ◆ 15,358
Alamosa East (East Alamosa); CDP-Census Area Only; ALAMOSA; **159** L-11; mail Alamosa **z** 81101; Ⓟ 1,389; © 1,528
Alcott; RMC Place; DENVER; ***159** E-13; ★ **DEN**; mail Denver **z** 80212; pop. incl. with Denver (Inc. Place)
Allenspark; CDP; BOULDER; **159** D-12; elev. 8,520ft./2,597m.; 🅿; **z** 80510; © 496
Allison; RMC Place; LA PLATA; **158** N-7; elev. 6,218ft./1,895m.; mail Ignacio **z** 81137; ● 110
Alma; Inc. Place; PARK; **159** G-11; elev. 10,353ft./3,156m.; 🅿; **z** 80420; Ⓟ 148; © 179
Almont; RMC Place; GUNNISON; **158** I-9; elev. 8,018ft./2,444m.; 🅿; **z** 81210; ● 70
Alpine; RMC Place; RIO GRANDE; ***158** L-10; mail South Fork **z** 81154; ● 160
Alta Vista; RMC Place; EL PASO; ***159** H-16; mail Calhan **z** 80808; rural
Altona; RMC Place; BOULDER; ***159** D-13; mail Boulder **z** 80302; ● 400
Altura; RMC Place; ADAMS; ★ **DEN**; mail Aurora **z** 80011; pop. incl. with Aurora (Inc. Place)
Altura Annex; RMC Place; ADAMS; ★ **DEN**; mail Aurora **z** 80011; pop. incl. with Aurora (Inc. Place)
Ames; RMC Place; SAN MIGUEL; ***158** K-6; mail Ophir **z** 81426; rural
Amherst; RMC Place; PHILLIPS; **159** B-20; elev. 3,688ft./1,124m.; 🅿; **z** 80721; ● 80
Andersonville; RMC Place; LARIMER; ★ **FTCL-**; mail Fort Collins **z** 80521; pop. incl. with Fort Collins (Inc. Place)
Angel Acres; RMC Place; JEFFERSON; ***159** F-13; ★ **DEN**; mail Conifer **z** 80433; ● 330
Antares; RMC Place; EL PASO; ★ **CSPG**; mail Colorado Springs **z** 80909, **z** 80932; pop. incl. with Colorado Springs (Inc. Place)
Antelope Hills; RMC Place; GUNNISON; ***158** I-9; mail Gunnison **z** 81230; ● 110
Antlers; RMC Place; GARFIELD; ***158** F-7; elev. 5,387ft./1,642m.; mail Rifle **z** 81650; rural
Anton; RMC Place; WASHINGTON; **159** E-18; elev. 4,870ft./1,484m.; 🅿; **z** 80801; ● 40
Antonito; Inc. Place; CONEJOS; **159** M-11; elev. 7,890ft./2,405m.; 🅿; **z** 81120; Ⓟ 875; © 873
Apache City; RMC Place; HUERFANO; ***159** K-14; mail Walsenburg **z** 81089; rural
Appleton; RMC Place; MESA; ***158** G-5; elev. 4,592ft./1,400m.; ★ **GDJC**; mail Grand Junction **z** 81505; ● 220
Applewood; CDP-Census Area Only; JEFFERSON; ***159** E-13; ★ **DEN**; mail Golden **z** 80401; Ⓟ 11,069; © 7,123
Arabian Acres; RMC Place; TELLER; ***159** H-13; mail Florissant **z** 80816; ● 200
Arapahoe; RMC Place; CHEYENNE; **159** H-20; elev. 4,050ft./1,234m.; 🅿; **z** 80802; ● 100
ARAPAHOE; **159** F-14; Ⓟ 391,511; © 487,967; ® 488,896; ◆ 561,890
Arapahoe East; RMC Place; ARAPAHOE; ***159** F-14; ★ **DEN**; mail Englewood **z** 80112
Arboles; CDP; ARCHULETA; **158** N-7; elev. 6,300ft./1,920m.; 🅿; **z** 81121; © 232
ARCHULETA; **159** M-18; Ⓟ 5,345; © 9,898; ◆ 13,420
Arickaree; RMC Place; WASHINGTON; ***159** E-18; mail Anton **z** 80801, Cope **z** 80812; rural
Aristocrat Ranchettes; CDP-Census Area Only; WELD; ***159** D-14; ★ **DEN**; mail Fort Lupton **z** 80621; © 1,254
Arlington; RMC Place; KIOWA; **159** J-17; elev. 4,240ft./1,292m.; 🅿; **z** 81021; ● 40
Aroya; RMC Place; CHEYENNE; ***159** H-18; mail Wild Horse **z** 80862; rural
Arriba; Inc. Place; LINCOLN; **159** G-18; elev. 5,228ft./1,593m.; 🅿; **z** 80804; Ⓟ 220; © 244
Arriola; RMC Place; MONTEZUMA; **158** L-4; mail Cortez **z** 81321, Dolores **z** 81323; ● 240
Arvada; Inc. Place; JEFFERSON, ADAMS; **159** E-13; elev. 5,340ft./1,628m.; 🅿 ■; ★ **DEN**; **z** 80001-07, **z** 80403 & mail Broomfield **z** 80021; Ⓟ 89,218; © 102,153; ◆ 106,098
Aspen; RMC Place; LARIMER; ★ **FTCL-**; mail Fort Collins **z** 80527; pop. incl. with Fort Collins (Inc. Place)
Aspen; Inc. Place; ⊡ PITKIN; **158** G-9; elev. 7,907ft./2,410m.; 🅿 🄷; **z** 81611-12; Ⓟ 5,049; © 5,914
Aspen-Gerbaz (Gerbaz Dale); RMC Place; PITKIN; ***158** G-9; mail Aspen **z** 81611; ● 490
Aspen Park; CDP; JEFFERSON; ***159** F-13; ★ **DEN**; mail Conifer **z** 80433; © 874
Atwood; CDP; LOGAN; **159** C-17; elev. 3,991ft./1,216m.; 🅿; **z** 80722; © 195

Entries in **UPPERCASE** are counties.
Entries in **bold** have populations of 2,500 or more.
Names in parentheses are alternate names.

Inc. Place	Incorporated Place
RMC Place	Rand McNally Designated Place
CDP	Census Designated Place
MCD	Minor Civil Division
⊡	County Seat
▲	Minor Civil Division
elev.	Elevation
🅿	Post Office
🄷	Hospital
🄲	College
■	Principal Business Center
★	Ranally Metro Area (RMA) Abbreviation
z	Zip Code(s)
Ⓟ	Previous Census Population
®	Revised Census Population
Ⓐ	Annexation Population
●	Rand McNally Population Estimate
©	Final Census Population
Ⓢ	Special Census Population
◆	Estimated Population

For additional definitions see Glossary, Volume 1, and Introduction, Volume 2.

Ault; Inc. Place; WELD; **159** C-14; elev. 4,939ft./1,505m.; 🅿; z 80610; Ⓟ 1,107; © 1,432
Aurora; Inc. Place; ARAPAHOE, ADAMS; **159** E-14; elev. 5,430ft./1,655m.; 🅿 🅷 ■; ★ **DEN**; z 80010-19, z 80040-42, z 80044-47, z 80247 & mail Arvada z 80002, Denver z 80220, z 80230-31; Ⓟ 222,103; © 276,393; ® 275,921; ◆ 344,560
Austin; RMC Place; DELTA; ***158** H-6; elev. 5,040ft./1,536m.; 🅿; z 81410; pop. incl. with Orchard City (Inc. Place)
Avon; Inc. Place; EAGLE; **158** F-10; elev. 7,440ft./2,268m.; 🅿; z 81620; Ⓟ 1,798; © 5,561; ® 5,605
Avondale; CDP; PUEBLO; **159** J-15; elev. 4,556ft./1,389m.; 🅿; z 81022; © 754

B

BACA; **159** M-19; Ⓟ 4,556; © 4,517; ◆ 3,782
Bailey; RMC Place; PARK; **159** F-12; elev. 7,750ft./2,362m.; 🅿; z 80421; ● 150
Bakersville; CLEAR CREEK; see Bakerville (RMC Place)
Bakerville (Bakersville); RMC Place; CLEAR CREEK; ***159** F-11; elev. 9,780ft./2,981m.; mail Silver Plume z 80476; rural
Baldwin; RMC Place; GUNNISON; ***158** H-8; mail Gunnison z 81230; rural
Balltown; RMC Place; LAKE; ***158** G-10; mail Granite z 81228; ● 50
Barnesville; RMC Place; WELD; ***159** C-15; mail Gill z 80624
Barr Lake; RMC Place; ADAMS; **157** F-9; ★ **DEN**; mail Brighton z 80601; ● 100
Bartlett; RMC Place; BACA; ***159** L-20; elev. 3,780ft./1,152m.; mail Walsh z 81090; rural
Barton; RMC Place; PROWERS; ***159** K-20; mail Granada z 81041; rural
Basalt; Inc. Place; EAGLE, PITKIN; **158** F-9; elev. 6,620ft./2,018m.; 🅿; z 81621; Ⓟ 1,128; © 2,681
Basin; RMC Place; SAN MIGUEL; ***158** J-5; mail Redvale z 81431; rural
Battlement Mesa; CDP-Census Area Only; GARFIELD; ***158** F-6; elev. 5,474ft./1,668m.; 🅿; z 81635-36; Ⓟ 1,477; © 3,497
Baxter; RMC Place; PUEBLO; ***159** J-15; ● 840
Baxterville; RMC Place; RIO GRANDE; ***158** L-9; mail Del Norte z 81132; pop. incl. with South Fork (Inc. Place)
Bayfield; Inc. Place; LA PLATA; **158** M-7; elev. 6,892ft./2,101m.; 🅿; z 81122; Ⓟ 1,090; © 1,549; ® 1,551
Beacon Hill; RMC Place; TELLER; ***159** I-13; mail Victor z 80860; rural
Bear Valley; RMC Place; DENVER; ***159** F-13; ★ **DEN**; mail Denver z 80227, z 80232, z 80235-36; pop. incl. with Denver (Inc. Place)
Beaver Point; RMC Place; LARIMER; ***159** C-12; mail Estes Park z 80517
Beaver Ridge; RMC Place; PARK; ***159** G-11; mail Fairplay z 80440; rural
Bedrock; RMC Place; MONTROSE; **158** J-4; elev. 4,980ft./1,518m.; 🅿; z 81411
Beecher Island; RMC Place; YUMA; ***159** E-20; elev. 3,537ft./1,078m.; mail Wray z 80758; rural
Belle Plain; RMC Place; PUEBLO; ★ **PUEB**; mail Pueblo z 81001; pop. incl. with Pueblo (Inc. Place)
Bellvue; RMC Place; LARIMER; **159** C-13; elev. 5,124ft./1,562m.; 🅿; ★ **FTCL-**; z 80512; ● 400
Belmar; RMC Place; JEFFERSON; ***159** F-13; elev. 5,550ft./1,692m.; ★ **DEN**; mail Denver z 80226; pop. incl. with Lakewood (Inc. Place)
Belmont; RMC Place; PUEBLO; ***159** J-14; ★ **PUEB**; mail Pueblo z 81001; pop. incl. with Pueblo (Inc. Place)
Belt Junction; RMC Place; DENVER; ★ **DEN**; pop. incl. with Denver (Inc. Place)
Bendemeer Valley; RMC Place; CLEAR CREEK; ***159** F-12; mail Evergreen z 80439; ● 255
Bennett; Inc. Place; ADAMS, ARAPAHOE; **159** E-15; elev. 5,483ft./1,671m.; 🅿; z 80102; Ⓟ 1,757; © 2,021
BENT; **159** K-18; Ⓟ 5,048; © 5,998; ◆ 5,536
Bergen Park; RMC Place; JEFFERSON; ***159** F-13; elev. 7,791ft./2,375m.; ★ **DEN**; mail Evergreen z 80439; ● 210
Berkley; CDP-Census Area Only; ADAMS; ***159** E-13; ★ **DEN**; © 10,743
Berthoud; Inc. Place; LARIMER, WELD; **159** D-13; elev. 5,030ft./1,533m.; 🅿; ★ **FTCL-**; z 80513 & mail Johnstown z 80534; Ⓟ 2,990; © 4,839
Berthoud Falls; RMC Place; CLEAR CREEK; ***159** E-11; mail Empire z 80438; ● 35
Berthoud Pass; RMC Place; CLEAR CREEK, GRAND; ***159** E-12; mail Idaho Springs z 80452; ● 90
Bethune; Inc. Place; KIT CARSON; **159** G-20; elev. 4,255ft./1,297m.; 🅿; z 80805; Ⓟ 173; © 225
Beulah; RMC Place; PUEBLO; **159** J-13; elev. 6,400ft./1,951m.; 🅿; z 81023; ● 280
Beulah Valley; CDP-Census Area Only; PUEBLO; ***159** K-13; © 1,164
Beverly Heights; RMC Place; JEFFERSON; ***159** E-13; mail Golden z 80401; pop. incl. with Golden (Inc. Place)
Beverly Hills; RMC Place; DOUGLAS; ***159** F-14; ★ **DEN**; mail Castle Rock z 80108; ● 225
Big Bend; RMC Place; BENT; ***159** J-19; mail Wiley z 81092; rural
Big Elk Meadows; RMC Place; LARIMER; ***159** D-12; mail Lyons z 80540; ● 100
Black Forest; CDP; EL PASO; **159** H-14; elev. 7,379ft./2,249m.; ★ **CSPG**; mail Colorado Springs z 80908, Elbert z 80106; Ⓟ 8,143; © 13,247
Black Hawk; Inc. Place; GILPIN; **159** E-12; elev. 8,056ft./2,455m.; 🅿; z 80403, z 80422; Ⓟ 227; © 118
Blakeland; RMC Place; DOUGLAS; ***159** F-13; mail Littleton z 80126; ● 700
Blanca; Inc. Place; COSTILLA; **159** L-12; elev. 7,750ft./2,362m.; 🅿; z 81123; Ⓟ 272; © 391
Blende; RMC Place; PUEBLO; **159** J-14; ★ **PUEB**; mail Pueblo z 81006; ● 1,500
Blue Mountain; RMC Place; MOFFAT; **158** D-4; mail Dinosaur z 81610; ● 15
Blue Mountain Estates; RMC Place; JEFFERSON; ***159** E-13; mail Golden z 80403; ● 160
Blue Ridge; RMC Place; SUMMIT; ***159** F-11; elev. 9,732ft./2,966m.; mail Breckenridge z 80424; ● 180
Blue River; Inc. Place; SUMMIT; **159** F-11; elev. 10,040ft./3,060m.; mail Breckenridge z 80424; Ⓟ 440; © 685
Blue Valley; RMC Place; CLEAR CREEK; ***159** F-12; mail Idaho Springs z 80452; ● 160
Bonanza (Bonanza City); Inc. Place; SAGUACHE; **159** J-11; elev. 9,465ft./2,885m.; mail Villa Grove z 81155; Ⓟ 16; © 14
Bonanza City; SAGUACHE; see Bonanza (Inc. Place)
Boncarbo; RMC Place; LAS ANIMAS; **159** M-14; elev. 6,880ft./2,097m.; 🅿; z 81024; ● 70
Bond; RMC Place; EAGLE; **158** E-9; 🅿; z 80423
Bondad; RMC Place; LA PLATA; **158** M-6; mail Durango z 81301; rural
Boone; Inc. Place; PUEBLO; **159** J-15; elev. 4,476ft./1,364m.; 🅿; z 81025; Ⓟ 341; © 323
Boulder; Inc. Place; ⊡ BOULDER, WELD; **159** D-13; elev. 5,344ft./1,629m.; 🅿 🅷 🅲 30,027 ■; ★ **BOUL-**; z 80301-10, z 80314, z 80321-23, z 80328-29; Ⓟ 83,295; © 94,673; ◆ 103,478
BOULDER; **159** D-13; part of Boulder county was annexed by Broomfield county on November 15, 2001; Ⓟ 225,339; © 291,288; ® 291,290; adjusted 2000 Census population is 269,814; ◆ 307,101
Boulder Heights; RMC Place; BOULDER; ***159** D-13; mail Boulder z 80302; ● 340
Boulder Junction; RMC Place; BOULDER; ***159** E-13; mail Boulder z 80303; pop. incl. with Boulder (Inc. Place)
Bountiful; RMC Place; CONEJOS; ***159** M-11; mail La Jara z 81140; ● 90
Bovina; RMC Place; LINCOLN; ***159** G-17; mail Genoa z 80818; rural
Bowie; RMC Place; DELTA; **158** H-7; mail Paonia z 81428; ● 40
Bow Mar; Inc. Place; ARAPAHOE, JEFFERSON; **157** K-6; elev. 5,515ft./1,681m.; 🅿; ★ **DEN**; z 80123; Ⓟ 854; © 847
Boxelder Estates; RMC Place; LARIMER; ***159** C-13; ★ **FTCL-**; mail Fort Collins z 80521; pop. incl. with Fort Collins (Inc. Place)
Boyero; RMC Place; LINCOLN; **159** H-18; elev. 4,730ft./1,442m.; 🅿; z 80821
Bracewell; RMC Place; WELD; ***159** C-14; elev. 4,730ft./1,442m.; ★ **GRLY**; mail Greeley z 80631; ● 100
Brandon; RMC Place; KIOWA; **159** I-20; elev. 3,925ft./1,196m.; 🅿; z 81071 & mail Eads z 81036; ● 60
Branson; Inc. Place; LAS ANIMAS; **159** N-16; elev. 6,299ft./1,920m.; 🅿; z 81027; Ⓟ 58; © 77
Breckenridge; Inc. Place; ⊡ SUMMIT; **159** F-11; elev. 9,602ft./2,927m.; 🅿; z 80424; Ⓟ 1,285; © 2,408; ® 2,366
Breen; RMC Place; LA PLATA; ***158** M-6; mail Hesperus z 81326
Brewster; RMC Place; FREMONT; ***159** J-13; mail Florence z 81226; rural
Briargate; RMC Place; EL PASO; ★ **CSPG**; mail Colorado Springs z 80920; pop. incl. with Colorado Springs (Inc. Place)
Brigadoon Glen; RMC Place; BOULDER; ***159** D-13; mail Longmont z 80503; ● 300
Briggsdale; RMC Place; WELD; **159** C-15; elev. 4,840ft./1,475m.; 🅿; z 80611; ● 110
Brighton; Inc. Place; ⊡ ADAMS, WELD; **159** E-14; elev. 4,983ft./1,519m.; 🅿 🅷; ★ **DEN**; z 80601-03 & mail Commerce City z 80022; Ⓟ 14,203; © 20,905; ◆ 30,994
Bristol; RMC Place; PROWERS; **159** J-20; elev. 3,567ft./1,087m.; 🅿; z 81047; ● 130
Broadmoor; RMC Place; EL PASO; ***159** H-14; elev. 6,200ft./1,890m.; ★ **CSPG**; mail Colorado Springs z 80906; pop. incl. with Colorado Springs (Inc. Place)
Broadway Estates; RMC Place; ARAPAHOE; ***159** F-13; ★ **DEN**; mail Littleton z 80120; ● 2,400
Broken Arrow Acres; RMC Place; JEFFERSON; ***159** F-13; mail Conifer z 80433; ● 140
Bronquist; RMC Place; PUEBLO; ***159** J-14; mail Pueblo z 81005; rural
Brook Forest; RMC Place; JEFFERSON; ***159** F-12; ★ **DEN**; mail Evergreen z 80439; ● 200
Brook Forest Estates; RMC Place; CLEAR CREEK; ***159** F-12; mail Evergreen z 80439; ● 300
Brookridge; RMC Place; ARAPAHOE; ***159** F-13; ★ **DEN**; mail Littleton z 80120; ● 800
Brookside; Inc. Place; FREMONT; **159** I-13; elev. 5,360ft./1,634m.; mail Canon City z 81212; Ⓟ 183; © 219
Brookvale; RMC Place; CLEAR CREEK; **159** F-12; mail Evergreen z 80439; ● 280
Broomfield; Inc. Place; ⊡ BROOMFIELD; **159** E-13; elev. 5,400ft./1,646m.; 🅿; ★ **DEN**; z 80020-21, z 80023, z 80038 & mail Arvada z 80005, Denver z 80234, Louisville z 80027; became part of Broomfield county in 2001; formerly part of Adams, Boulder, Jefferson, and Weld counties; Ⓟ 24,638; © 38,272; ◆ 57,987
BROOMFIELD; **157** F-6; created November 15, 2001 from parts of Adams, Boulder, Jefferson, and Weld counties; population not reported in 2000 census; ◆ 57,987
Brownlee; RMC Place; JACKSON; ***158** B-10; mail Walden z 80480; rural
Brownsville; RMC Place; BOULDER; ***159** D-13; ★ **BOUL-**; mail Lafayette z 80026; ● 585
Brush; Inc. Place; MORGAN; **159** D-17; elev. 4,231ft./1,290m.; 🅿 🅷; z 80723; Ⓟ 4,165; © 5,117
Buckeye; RMC Place; LARIMER; ***159** B-13; mail Wellington z 80549; rural
Buckingham; RMC Place; LARIMER; ***159** C-13; ★ **FTCL-**; mail Fort Collins z 80521; pop. incl. with Fort Collins (Inc. Place)
Buda; RMC Place; WELD; ***159** D-13; mail Berthoud z 80513; rural
Buena Vista; Inc. Place; CHAFFEE; **159** H-11; elev. 7,955ft./2,425m.; 🅿; z 81211 & mail Granite z 81228, Twin Lakes z 81251; Ⓟ 1,752; © 2,195
Buffalo Creek; RMC Place; JEFFERSON; **159** F-13; elev. 6,680ft./2,036m.; 🅿; z 80425
Buffalo Park Estates; RMC Place; JEFFERSON; ***159** F-13; ★ **DEN**; mail Evergreen z 80439; ● 330
Buford; RMC Place; RIO BLANCO; ***158** E-7; mail Meeker z 81641
Burdett; RMC Place; WASHINGTON; ***159** C-18; mail Akron z 80720; rural
Burland Ranchettes; RMC Place; PARK; ***159** F-12; mail Pine z 80470; ● 550
Burlington; Inc. Place; ⊡ KIT CARSON; **159** G-20; elev. 4,160ft./1,268m.; 🅿 🅷; z 80807; Ⓟ 2,941; © 3,678
Burnham; RMC Place; DENVER; ★ **DEN**; pop. incl. with Denver (Inc. Place)
Burns; RMC Place; EAGLE; **158** E-9; elev. 6,600ft./2,012m.; 🅿; z 80426
Burnt Mill; RMC Place; PUEBLO; ***159** K-14; mail Pueblo z 81005; rural
Buttes; RMC Place; EL PASO; ***159** I-14; mail Fountain z 80817; rural
Byers; CDP; ARAPAHOE; **159** E-15; elev. 5,201ft./1,585m.; 🅿; z 80103; Ⓟ 1,065; © 1,233

C

Caddoa; RMC Place; BENT; **159** J-18; 🅿; z 81044
Cadet; RMC Place; EL PASO; ***159** H-14; ★ **CSPG**; mail USAF Academy z 80841
Cahone; RMC Place; DOLORES; **158** L-4; elev. 6,660ft./2,030m.; 🅿; z 81320; ● 50
Calhan; Inc. Place; EL PASO; **159** H-15; elev. 6,558ft./1,999m.; 🅿; z 80808; Ⓟ 562; © 896
Camp Bird; RMC Place; OURAY; **158** K-7; mail Ouray z 81427
Campion; CDP; LARIMER; **159** D-13; ★ **FTCL-**; mail Loveland z 80537; Ⓟ 1,692; © 1,832
Campo; Inc. Place; BACA; **159** M-19; elev. 4,339ft./1,323m.; 🅿; z 81029; Ⓟ 121; © 150
Canfield; RMC Place; BOULDER; ***159** D-13; ★ **BOUL-**; mail Lafayette z 80026; pop. incl. with Erie (Inc. Place)
Cañon; RMC Place; CONEJOS; ***159** N-11; elev. 8,184ft./2,494m.; mail Antonito z 81120; rural
Cañon City; Inc. Place; ⊡ FREMONT; **159** I-13; elev. 5,332ft./1,625m.; 🅿 🅷; z 81212, z 81215; Ⓟ 12,687; © 15,431
Capitol Hill; RMC Place; DENVER; ★ **DEN**; mail Denver z 80205; pop. incl. with Denver (Inc. Place)
Capitol Hill Annex; RMC Place; DENVER; ***159** E-13; ★ **DEN**; mail Denver z 80203, z 80218; pop. incl. with Denver (Inc. Place)
Capulin; RMC Place; CONEJOS; **159** M-11; 🅿; z 81124; ● 275
Carbondale; Inc. Place; GARFIELD; **158** F-8; elev. 6,170ft./1,881m.; 🅿; z 81623; Ⓟ 3,004; © 5,196
Cardiff; RMC Place; GARFIELD; **158** F-8; mail Glenwood Springs z 81601; pop. incl. with Glenwood Springs (Inc. Place)
Carr; RMC Place; WELD; **159** B-14; elev. 5,706ft./1,739m.; 🅿; z 80612; ● 60
Carriage Club; CDP-Census Area Only; DOUGLAS; ***159** F-14; ★ **DEN**; © 1,002
Cascade; RMC Place; EL PASO; **159** H-13; elev. 7,375ft./2,248m.; 🅿; ★ **CSPG**; z 80809; ● 500
Cascade-Chipita Park; CDP-Census Area Only; EL PASO; ***159** H-13; ★ **CSPG**; mail Cascade z 80809; Ⓟ 1,479; © 1,709
Castle Pines; CDP-Census Area Only; DOUGLAS; ***159** F-14; ★ **DEN**; © 5,958
Castle Rock; Inc. Place; ⊡ DOUGLAS; **159** G-14; elev. 6,200ft./1,890m.; 🅿; ★ **DEN**; z 80104, z 80108-09; Ⓟ 8,710; © 20,224; ◆ 42,208
Castlewood; CDP-Census Area Only; ARAPAHOE; ***159** F-14; ★ **DEN**; mail Littleton z 80120; © 25,567; ◆ 29,444
Cattle Creek; RMC Place; GARFIELD; ***158** F-8; mail Carbondale z 81623; ● 230
Cedar Cove; RMC Place; LARIMER; ***159** C-13; mail Loveland z 80537; ● 85
Cedaredge; Inc. Place; DELTA; **158** H-6; elev. 6,264ft./1,909m.; 🅿; z 81413; Ⓟ 1,380; © 1,854
Centennial; Inc. Place; ARAPAHOE; **159** F-14; 🅿; ★ **DEN**; z 80015-16, z 80111-12, z 80121-22, z 80161; incorporated February 7, 2001; not reported in 2000 Census; ● 101,300; ◆ 101,391
Center; Inc. Place; SAGUACHE, RIO GRANDE; **159** L-11; elev. 7,645ft./2,330m.; 🅿; z 81125; Ⓟ 1,963; © 2,392
Centerville; RMC Place; CHAFFEE; ***159** I-11; mail Nathrop z 81236; rural
Central City; Inc. Place; ⊡ GILPIN, CLEAR CREEK; **159** E-12; elev. 8,496ft./2,590m.; 🅿; z 80427; Ⓟ 335; © 515
Chaddsford; RMC Place; ARAPAHOE; ★ **DEN**; mail Aurora z 80014; pop. incl. with Aurora (Inc. Place)
CHAFFEE; **159** H-11; Ⓟ 12,684; © 16,242; ◆ 17,074
Chama; RMC Place; COSTILLA; **159** M-13; elev. 8,166ft./2,489m.; 🅿; z 81126; ● 245
Chambers Square; RMC Place; ADAMS; ★ **DEN**; mail Aurora z 80011; pop. incl. with Aurora (Inc. Place)
Chapel Hills; RMC Place; EL PASO; ***159** H-14; mail Colorado Springs z 80907; pop. incl. with Colorado Springs (Inc. Place)
Chatfield Estates; RMC Place; JEFFERSON; ***159** F-13; ★ **DEN**; mail Littleton z 80128; ● 730
Chautauqua; RMC Place; BOULDER; ★ **BOUL-**; mail Boulder z 80302; pop. incl. with Boulder (Inc. Place)
Cheney Center; RMC Place; PROWERS; mail Holly z 81047; rural
Cheraw; Inc. Place; OTERO; **159** J-17; elev. 4,130ft./1,259m.; 🅿; z 81030; Ⓟ 265; © 211
Cherry Creek; RMC Place; DENVER; ***159** E-14; ★ **DEN**; mail Denver z 80206; pop. incl. with Denver (Inc. Place)
Cherry Hills Crest; RMC Place; ARAPAHOE; ***159** F-14; ★ **DEN**; mail Littleton z 80120; pop. incl. with Greenwood Village (Inc. Place)
Cherry Hills Manor; RMC Place; ARAPAHOE; ***159** F-14; ★ **DEN**; mail Littleton z 80120; ● 1,100
Cherry Hills Village; Inc. Place; ARAPAHOE; **157** J-7; elev. 5,400ft./1,646m.; 🅿; ★ **DEN**; z 80110-11, z 80113, z 80121; Ⓟ 5,245; © 5,958
Cherry Knolls; RMC Place; ARAPAHOE; **157** K-7; ★ **DEN**; mail Littleton z 80120; ● 1,400
Cherry Park; RMC Place; ARAPAHOE; ***159** F-14; ★ **DEN**; mail Englewood z 80110; ● 770
Cherry Valley; RMC Place; DOUGLAS; ***159** G-14; mail Franktown z 80116; rural
Cherrywood Village; RMC Place; ARAPAHOE; ***159** F-13; ★ **DEN**; mail Littleton z 80120; ● 1,800
CHEYENNE; **159** H-19; Ⓟ 2,397; © 2,231; ◆ 1,614
Cheyenne Canon; RMC Place; EL PASO; ★ **CSPG**; mail Colorado Springs z 80906; pop. incl. with Colorado Springs (Inc. Place)
Cheyenne Wells; Inc. Place; ⊡ CHEYENNE; **159** H-20; elev. 4,296ft./1,309m.; 🅿 🅷; z 80810; Ⓟ 1,128; © 1,010
Chimney Rock; RMC Place; ARCHULETA; **158** M-8; elev. 6,600ft./2,012m.; 🅿; z 81122, z 81127; rural
Chipita Park; RMC Place; EL PASO; **159** H-13; ★ **CSPG**; mail Cascade z 80809; ● 465
Chivington; RMC Place; KIOWA; **159** I-19; elev. 3,889ft./1,185m.; 🅿; z 81036; ● 40
Chromo; RMC Place; ARCHULETA; **158** N-9; elev. 7,286ft./2,221m.; 🅿; z 81128; rural
Churches; JEFFERSON; see Mandalay Gardens (RMC Place)
Cimarron; RMC Place; MONTROSE; **158** I-7; elev. 6,906ft./2,105m.; 🅿; z 81220
Cimarron Hills; CDP-Census Area Only; EL PASO; ***159** H-14; elev. 6,400ft./1,951m.; ★ **CSPG**; mail Colorado Springs z 80906, z 80915-16, z 80922, z 80928-30; Ⓟ 11,160; © 15,194
Clark; RMC Place; ROUTT; **158** B-9; elev. 7,270ft./2,216m.; 🅿; z 80428; summer pop. 1,000
Clark Farms; RMC Place; DOUGLAS; ***159** F-14; ★ **DEN**; mail Parker z 80134; pop. incl. with Parker (Inc. Place)
Clarkville; RMC Place; YUMA; ***159** C-19; mail Yuma z 80759; rural
CLEAR CREEK; **159** F-12; Ⓟ 7,619; © 9,322; ◆ 9,016
Cliff; BOULDER, GILPIN; see Pinecliffe (RMC Place)
Clifton; CDP; MESA; **158** G-5; elev. 4,710ft./1,436m.; 🅿; ★ **GDJC**; z 81520; Ⓟ 12,671; © 17,345
Coal Creek; Inc. Place; FREMONT; **159** J-13; elev. 5,400ft./1,646m.; 🅿; z 81221; Ⓟ 157; © 303
Coal Creek; CDP; JEFFERSON, BOULDER, GILPIN; ***159** E-13; mail Golden z 80403; © 2,323
Coaldale; RMC Place; FREMONT; **159** J-12; elev. 6,500ft./1,981m.; 🅿; z 81222; ● 120
Coalmont; RMC Place; JACKSON; **158** C-10; elev. 8,209ft./2,502m.; 🅿; z 80430; ● 50
Cody Park; RMC Place; JEFFERSON; ***159** E-13; mail Golden z 80401; ● 210
Cokedale; Inc. Place; LAS ANIMAS; **159** M-14; elev. 6,200ft./1,890m.; 🅿; z 81082; Ⓟ 116; © 139
Collbran; Inc. Place; MESA; **158** G-6; elev. 5,987ft./1,825m.; 🅿; z 81624; Ⓟ 228; © 388
College Heights; RMC Place; LA PLATA; ***158** M-6; mail Durango z 81301; pop. incl. with Durango (Inc. Place)
Colona; RMC Place; OURAY; **158** J-7; elev. 6,385ft./1,946m.; mail Montrose z 81401; ● 70
Colorado City; RMC Place; EL PASO; ***159** H-14; ★ **CSPG**; mail Colorado Springs z 80904; pop. incl. with Colorado Springs (Inc. Place)
Colorado City; CDP; PUEBLO; **159** K-14; elev. 5,800ft./1,768m.; 🅿; z 81019; Ⓟ 1,149; © 2,018
Colorado Mountain Estates; RMC Place; TELLER; ***159** H-13; mail Florissant z 80816; ● 80
Colorado Sierra; RMC Place; JEFFERSON; mail Golden z 80403; ● 200
Colorado Springs; Inc. Place; ⊡ EL PASO; **159** H-14; elev. 6,008ft./1,831m.; 🅿 🅷 🅲 12,720 ■; ★ **CSPG**; z 80901-47, z 80949-51, z 80960, z 80962, z 80970, z 80977, z 80995, z 80997; Ⓟ 281,140; © 360,890; ◆ 397,600
Colorado State Veterans Center; RIO GRANDE; see Homelake (RMC Place)
Columbine; CDP-Census Area Only; JEFFERSON, ARAPAHOE; ***159** F-13; ★ **DEN**; mail Littleton z 80128; Ⓟ 23,969; © 24,095; ◆ 24,968
Columbine; RMC Place; ROUTT; ***158** B-9; elev. 8,697ft./2,651m.; mail Clark z 80428
Columbine Hills; RMC Place; JEFFERSON; ***159** F-13; ★ **DEN**; mail Littleton z 80128
Columbine Knolls South; RMC Place; JEFFERSON; ***159** F-13; ★ **DEN**; mail Littleton z 80128
Columbine Manor; RMC Place; ARAPAHOE; ★ **DEN**; mail Littleton z 80128
Columbine Valley; Inc. Place; ARAPAHOE; **157** K-6; elev. 5,350ft./1,631m.; 🅿; ★ **DEN**; z 80123; Ⓟ 1,071; © 1,132
Commerce City; Inc. Place; ADAMS; **157** H-8; elev. 5,170ft./1,576m.; 🅿; ★ **DEN**; z 80022, z 80037 & mail Denver z 80266; Ⓟ 16,466; © 20,991; ◆ 29,200
Como; RMC Place; PARK; **159** G-11; elev. 9,802ft./2,988m.; 🅿; z 80432
Concrete; RMC Place; FREMONT; ***159** J-13; mail Penrose z 81240; ● 150
Conejos; RMC Place; ⊡ CONEJOS; **159** N-11; elev. 7,901ft./2,408m.; 🅿; z 81129; ● 90
CONEJOS; **158** M-10; Ⓟ 7,453; © 8,400; ◆ 7,933
Conifer; RMC Place; JEFFERSON; **159** F-13; elev. 8,240ft./2,512m.; 🅿; ★ **DEN**; z 80433; ● 200
Conifer Mountain; RMC Place; JEFFERSON; ***159** F-13; mail Conifer z 80433; ● 180
Connors; RMC Place; DENVER; ★ **DEN**; pop. incl. with Denver (Inc. Place)
Cope; RMC Place; WASHINGTON; **159** F-19; elev. 4,425ft./1,349m.; 🅿; z 80812; ● 100
Copperdale; RMC Place; BOULDER; ***159** E-13; mail Golden z 80403; ● 200
Copper Mountain (Wheeler); RMC Place; SUMMIT; ***159** F-11; mail Frisco z 80443; winter pop. 1,000; ● 140
Copper Spur; RMC Place; EAGLE; ***158** E-9; elev. 7,000ft./2,134m.; mail Bond z 80423; rural
Cornelia; RMC Place; BENT; ***159** J-18; mail Las Animas z 81054; rural
Cornish; RMC Place; WELD; ***159** C-15; mail Briggsdale z 80611; rural
Coronado; RMC Place; ADAMS; ***159** E-13; ★ **DEN**; mail Denver z 80229; ● 2,250
Cortez; Inc. Place; ⊡ MONTEZUMA; **158** M-5; elev. 6,201ft./1,890m.; 🅿 🅷; z 81321; Ⓟ 7,284; © 7,977
Cory; RMC Place; DELTA; ***158** H-6; elev. 5,180ft./1,579m.; 🅿; z 81414; pop. incl. with Orchard City (Inc. Place)
COSTILLA; **159** M-13; Ⓟ 3,190; © 3,663; ◆ 3,197
Cotopaxi; RMC Place; FREMONT; **159** J-12; elev. 6,400ft./1,951m.; 🅿; z 81223
Cottonwood; CDP-Census Area Only; DOUGLAS; ***159** F-14; ★ **DEN**; © 931
Country Acres; RMC Place; WELD; ***159** D-14; mail Johnstown z 80534; pop. incl. with Johnstown (Inc. Place)
Country Club Estates; RMC Place; LARIMER; ***159** C-13; ★ **FTCL-**; mail Fort Collins z 80521; pop. incl. with Fort Collins (Inc. Place)
Cowdrey; RMC Place; JACKSON; **158** B-10; elev. 7,910ft./2,411m.; 🅿; z 80434; ● 100
Cozy Corner; RMC Place; ADAMS; ***159** E-13; ★ **DEN**; mail Denver z 80234; pop. incl. with Westminster (Inc. Place)
Cragmor; RMC Place; EL PASO; ★ **CSPG**; mail Colorado Springs z 80907; pop. incl. with Colorado Springs (Inc. Place)
Craig; Inc. Place; ⊡ MOFFAT; **158** C-7; elev. 6,186ft./1,885m.; 🅿 🅷; z 81625-26; Ⓟ 8,091; © 9,189
Cranor Acres; RMC Place; GUNNISON; ***158** I-9; mail Gunnison z 81230
Crawford; Inc. Place; DELTA; **158** I-7; elev. 6,520ft./1,987m.; 🅿; z 81415; Ⓟ 221; © 366
Creede; Inc. Place; ⊡ MINERAL; **158** K-9; elev. 8,838ft./2,694m.; 🅿; z 81130; Ⓟ 362; © 377
Crescent (Crescent Village); RMC Place; BOULDER; ***159** E-13; elev. 7,451ft./2,271m.; mail Golden z 80403; ● 330
Crescent Village; RMC Place; BOULDER; ***159** E-13; mail Golden z 80403; ● 250
Crescent Village; BOULDER; see Crescent (RMC Place)
Crested Butte; Inc. Place; GUNNISON; **158** H-9; elev. 8,908ft./2,715m.; 🅿; z 81224-25; Ⓟ 878; © 1,529
Crested Butte South; RMC Place; GUNNISON; ***158** H-9; mail Crested Butte z 81224; ● 100
Crestmoor; RMC Place; ARAPAHOE; ★ **DEN**; mail Denver z 80222; pop. incl. with Glendale (Inc. Place)
Crestone; Inc. Place; SAGUACHE; **159** K-12; elev. 7,920ft./2,414m.; 🅿; z 81131; Ⓟ 39; © 73
Crestview Village; RMC Place; JEFFERSON; ***159** E-13; ★ **DEN**; mail Golden z 80403; ● 670
Crestwoods; RMC Place; SUMMIT; ***159** F-11; elev. 9,800ft./2,987m.; mail Breckenridge z 80424; ● 540
Crews; RMC Place; EL PASO; ***159** I-14; ★ **CSPG**; mail Colorado Springs z 80911
Cripple Creek; Inc. Place; ⊡ TELLER; **159** H-13; elev. 9,508ft./2,898m.; 🅿; z 80813; Ⓟ 584; © 1,115
Crisman; RMC Place; BOULDER; ***159** D-13; ★ **BOUL-**; mail Boulder z 80302; ● 200
Critchell; RMC Place; JEFFERSON; ***159** F-13; mail Conifer z 80433; ● 130
Crook; Inc. Place; LOGAN; **159** B-19; elev. 3,711ft./1,131m.; 🅿; z 80726; Ⓟ 148; © 128
Crowley; Inc. Place; CROWLEY; **159** J-16; elev. 4,347ft./1,325m.; 🅿; z 81033-34; Ⓟ 225; © 187
CROWLEY; **159** J-16; Ⓟ 3,946; © 5,518; ◆ 7,758
Crystola; RMC Place; TELLER; **159** H-13; ★ **CSPG**; mail Woodland Park z 80863; ● 160
Cuchara; RMC Place; HUERFANO; **159** M-13; mail La Veta z 81055
Cuerna Verde; PUEBLO; see Cuerna Verde Park (RMC Place)
Cuerna Verde Park (Cuerna Verde); RMC Place; PUEBLO; ***159** K-13; elev. 7,574ft./2,309m.; mail Rye z 81069; rural
CUSTER; **159** K-13; Ⓟ 1,926; © 3,503; ◆ 4,248

D

Dacono; Inc. Place; WELD; **159** D-14; elev. 5,020ft./1,530m.; 🅿; z 80514; Ⓟ 2,228; © 3,015
Dailey; RMC Place; LOGAN; ***159** B-19; mail Fleming z 80728, Haxtun z 80731
De Beque; Inc. Place; MESA; **158** F-6; elev. 4,954ft./1,510m.; 🅿; z 81630; Ⓟ 257; © 451
Deckers; RMC Place; DOUGLAS; **159** G-13; elev. 5,399ft./1,646m.; 🅿; z 80135
Deer Creek Valley Ranchos; RMC Place; PARK; mail Pine z 80470; rural
Deermont; RMC Place; JEFFERSON; ***159** F-13; mail Littleton z 80127; ● 150
Deer Park; ROUTT; see Haybro (RMC Place)
Deer Trail; Inc. Place; ARAPAHOE; **159** F-16; elev. 5,183ft./1,580m.; 🅿; z 80105; Ⓟ 476; © 598
Delhi; RMC Place; LAS ANIMAS; ***159** L-16; 🅿; z 81059; rural
Del Norte; Inc. Place; ⊡ RIO GRANDE; **158** L-10; elev. 7,880ft./2,402m.; 🅿; z 81132; Ⓟ 1,674; © 1,705
Delta; Inc. Place; ⊡ DELTA; **158** H-6; elev. 4,953ft./1,510m.; 🅿 🅷; z 81416; Ⓟ 3,789; © 6,400
DELTA; **158** H-7; Ⓟ 20,980; © 27,834; ◆ 31,145
Denver; Inc. Place; **STATE CAPITAL**; ⊡ DENVER; **159** E-13; elev. 5,280ft./1,609m.; 🅿 🅷 🅲 67,738 ■; ★ **DEN**; z 80012, z 80014, z 80022, z 80033, z 80123, z 80127, z 80201-12, z 80214-39, z 80241, z 80243-44, z 80246-52, z 80256-57, z 80259-66, z 80271, z 80273-74, z 80279-81, z 80290-91, z 80293-95, z 80299 & mail Arvada z 80002, Aurora z 80010, Westminster z 80030-31; Ⓟ 467,610; © 554,636; ® 553,693; ◆ 632,429
DENVER; **157** I-7; Ⓟ 467,610; © 554,636; ® 553,693; ◆ 632,429
Deora; RMC Place; BACA; ***159** L-18; 🅿; z 81054; rural
Derby; CDP-Census Area Only; ADAMS; ***159** E-14; ★ **DEN**; mail Commerce City z 80022, Henderson z 80640; Ⓟ 6,043; © 6,423
Devine; RMC Place; PUEBLO; ***159** J-15; elev. 4,578ft./1,395m.; ★ **PUEB**; mail Pueblo z 81001
Dillon; Inc. Place; SUMMIT; **159** F-11; elev. 8,858ft./2,700m.; 🅿; z 80435; Ⓟ 553; © 802
Dinosaur; Inc. Place; MOFFAT; **158** D-4; elev. 5,858ft./1,786m.; 🅿; z 81610, z 81633; Ⓟ 324; © 319
Divide; RMC Place; TELLER; **159** H-13; elev. 9,165ft./2,793m.; 🅿; z 80814; ● 50
Dixon; RMC Place; LARIMER; ***159** B-13; mail Wellington z 80549; rural
Dolores; Inc. Place; MONTEZUMA; **158** L-5; elev. 6,936ft./2,114m.; 🅿; z 81323; Ⓟ 866; © 857
DOLORES; **158** K-5; Ⓟ 1,504; © 1,844; ◆ 1,945
Dome Rock; RMC Place; JEFFERSON; ***159** F-13; mail Conifer z 80433; rural
Dominion; RMC Place; BOULDER; ***159** D-13; mail Longmont z 80501; pop. incl. with Longmont (Inc. Place)
Dorey Lakes; RMC Place; GILPIN; ***159** E-12; mail Golden z 80403; ● 230
Dotsero; RMC Place; EAGLE; ***158** F-8; mail Gypsum z 81637; rural
DOUGLAS; **159** G-13; Ⓟ 60,391; © 175,766; ◆ 289,295
Dove Creek; Inc. Place; ⊡ DOLORES; **158** K-4; elev. 6,843ft./2,086m.; 🅿; z 81324; Ⓟ 643; © 698
Downieville; RMC Place; CLEAR CREEK; ***159** E-12; mail Dumont z 80436; ● 120
Downieville-Lawson-Dumont; CDP-Census Area Only; CLEAR CREEK; ***159** E-12; © 364
Downtown; RMC Place; ARAPAHOE; ***159** F-13; ★ **DEN**; mail Englewood z 80110; pop. incl. with Englewood (Inc. Place)
Downtown; RMC Place; DENVER; ★ **DEN**; mail Denver z 80201-02; pop. incl. with Denver (Inc. Place)
Downtown; RMC Place; EL PASO; mail Colorado Springs z 80903; pop. incl. with Colorado Springs (Inc. Place)
Downtown; RMC Place; LARIMER; mail Loveland z 80537; pop. incl. with Loveland (Inc. Place)
Doyleville; RMC Place; GUNNISON; ***158** I-10; mail Gunnison z 81230, Parlin z 81239
Drake; RMC Place; EL PASO; pop. incl. with Colorado Springs (Inc. Place)
Drake; RMC Place; LARIMER; **159** C-13; elev. 6,160ft./1,878m.; 🅿; z 80515; summer pop. 500
Drakes; RMC Place; LARIMER; ***159** C-13; ★ **FTCL-**; mail Fort Collins z 80521; pop. incl. with Fort Collins (Inc. Place)
Dream House Acres; RMC Place; ARAPAHOE; ***159** F-14; ★ **DEN**; mail Littleton z 80120; ● 1,150
Dumont; RMC Place; CLEAR CREEK; ***159** E-12; elev. 7,950ft./2,423m.; 🅿; z 80436; ● 140
Dupont; RMC Place; ADAMS; **157** G-8; elev. 5,150ft./1,570m.; 🅿; ★ **DEN**; z 80024; ● 3,650
Durango; Inc. Place; ⊡ LA PLATA; **158** M-6; elev. 6,523ft./1,988m.; 🅿 🅷 🅲 3,907 ■; z 81301-03; Ⓟ 12,430; © 13,922; ◆ 16,388
Durango West; RMC Place; LA PLATA; **158** M-6; mail Durango z 81303; ● 1,050
Dyke; RMC Place; ARCHULETA; ***158** M-8; mail Pagosa Springs z 81147; ● 215

E

Eads; Inc. Place; ⊡ KIOWA; **159** I-19; elev. 4,213ft./1,284m.; 🅿 🅷; z 81036; Ⓟ 780; © 747
Eagle; Inc. Place; ⊡ EAGLE; **158** F-9; elev. 6,600ft./2,012m.; 🅿; z 81631; Ⓟ 1,580; © 3,032
EAGLE; **158** E-9; Ⓟ 21,928; © 41,659; ® 41,675; ◆ 53,924
Eagle-Vail; CDP-Census Area Only; EAGLE; ***158** F-10; elev. 7,495ft./2,284m.; mail Avon z 81620; Ⓟ 1,922; © 2,887
East Alamosa; ALAMOSA; see Alamosa East (CDP-Census Area Only)
East Canon; RMC Place; FREMONT; ***159** I-13; pop. incl. with Cañon City (Inc. Place)
Eastlake; RMC Place; ADAMS; ***159** E-14; elev. 5,270ft./1,606m.; 🅿; ★ **DEN**; z 80614 & mail Denver z 80241; pop. incl. with Thornton (Inc. Place)
Eastlake; RMC Place; PUEBLO; **157** F-7; ★ **PUEB**; mail Pueblo z 81004; pop. incl. with Pueblo (Inc. Place)
Eastonville; RMC Place; EL PASO; ***159** G-14; mail Peyton z 80831; rural
East Pleasant View; CDP-Census Area Only; JEFFERSON; ***159** E-13; ★ **DEN**; mail Golden z 80401; © 369
East Portal; RMC Place; GILPIN; **159** E-12; mail Rollinsville z 80474
Eastridge; RMC Place; ARAPAHOE; ***159** F-14; ★ **DEN**; mail Aurora z 80014; pop. incl. with Aurora (Inc. Place)
Eastwood; RMC Place; PUEBLO; ★ **PUEB**; mail Pueblo z 81001; pop. incl. with Pueblo (Inc. Place)
Eaton; Inc. Place; WELD; **159** C-14; elev. 4,839ft./1,475m.; 🅿; z 80615; Ⓟ 1,959; © 2,690
Echo Lake; RMC Place; CLEAR CREEK; ***159** F-12; mail Idaho Springs z 80452; rural
Eckert; RMC Place; DELTA; ***158** H-6; elev. 5,560ft./1,695m.; 🅿; z 81418; pop. incl. with Orchard City (Inc. Place)
Eckley; Inc. Place; YUMA; **159** D-19; elev. 3,894ft./1,187m.; 🅿; z 80727; Ⓟ 211; © 278
Eden; RMC Place; PUEBLO; ***159** J-14; ★ **PUEB**; mail Pueblo z 81003; pop. incl. with Pueblo (Inc. Place)
Edgemont; RMC Place; JEFFERSON; ***159** E-13; elev. 5,640ft./1,719m.; ★ **DEN**; mail Golden z 80401; pop. incl. with Lakewood (Inc. Place)
Edgewater; Inc. Place; JEFFERSON; **157** I-6; elev. 5,350ft./1,631m.; 🅿; ★ **DEN**; z 80214; Ⓟ 4,613; © 5,445
Edison; RMC Place; EL PASO; ***159** I-15; mail Yoder z 80864; rural
Edith; RMC Place; ARCHULETA; ***158** N-9; elev. 7,080ft./2,158m.; mail Chromo z 81128; rural
Edler; RMC Place; BACA; ***159** M-19; mail Springfield z 81073; ● 25
Edwards; CDP; EAGLE; **158** F-10; elev. 7,226ft./2,202m.; 🅿; z 81632; © 8,257; ® 8,266
Egnar; RMC Place; SAN MIGUEL; **158** K-4; elev. 7,324ft./2,232m.; 🅿; z 81325
Elba; RMC Place; WASHINGTON; ***159** E-18; mail Akron z 80720; rural
Elbert; RMC Place; ELBERT; **159** G-15; elev. 6,720ft./2,048m.; 🅿; z 80106; ● 120
ELBERT; **159** F-15; Ⓟ 9,646; © 19,872; ◆ 22,684
Eldora; CDP; BOULDER; **159** E-12; elev. 8,641ft./2,634m.; mail Nederland z 80466; © 170
Eldorado Springs; CDP; BOULDER; **159** E-13; elev. 5,760ft./1,756m.; 🅿; ★ **BOUL-**; z 80025; © 557
Elephant Park; RMC Place; JEFFERSON; ***159** F-13; ★ **DEN**; mail Evergreen z 80439; ● 150
Elizabeth; Inc. Place; ELBERT; **159** G-14; elev. 6,448ft./1,965m.; 🅿; z 80107; Ⓟ 818; © 1,434
El Jebel; CDP; EAGLE; **158** F-8; 🅿; z 81623; Ⓟ 2,605; © 4,488
Elk Creek Acres; RMC Place; JEFFERSON; ***159** F-13; mail Pine z 80470; rural
Elk Creek Highlands; RMC Place; PARK; mail Bailey z 80421; rural
Elkdale; RMC Place; GRAND; ***159** D-11; mail Tabernash z 80478; ● 130
Elkhorn Acres; RMC Place; PARK; mail Pine z 80470; ● 100
Elk Springs; RMC Place; MOFFAT; **158** C-5; elev. 6,371ft./1,942m.; 🅿; z 81633; ● 25
Elkton; RMC Place; TELLER; ***159** I-13; mail Victor z 80860; rural
Ellicott; RMC Place; EL PASO; **159** H-15; elev. 6,016ft./1,834m.; mail Calhan z 80808; ● 300
El Moro; RMC Place; LAS ANIMAS; ***159** M-15; elev. 5,930ft./1,807m.; mail Trinidad z 81082
EL PASO; **159** I-15; Ⓟ 397,014; © 516,929; ◆ 609,729
El Rancho; RMC Place; JEFFERSON; ***159** F-13; elev. 7,680ft./2,341m.; ★ **DEN**; mail Golden z 80401; ● 170
El Vado; RMC Place; BOULDER; ***159** E-13; ★ **BOUL-**; mail Boulder z 80302; ● 245
Elwell; RMC Place; WELD; ***159** D-14; elev. 4,939ft./1,505m.; mail Johnstown z 80534; ● 160
Emma; RMC Place; PITKIN; ***158** F-8; mail Basalt z 81621; ● 75
Empire; Inc. Place; CLEAR CREEK; **159** E-12; elev. 8,614ft./2,626m.; 🅿; z 80438; Ⓟ 401; © 355
Englewood; Inc. Place; ARAPAHOE; **159** F-13; elev. 5,369ft./1,636m.; 🅿 🅷 ■; ★ **DEN**; z 80110-13, z 80150-51, z 80155 & mail Denver z 80236; Ⓟ 29,387; © 31,727; ◆ 32,812
Erie; Inc. Place; WELD, BOULDER; **159** D-13; elev. 5,020ft./1,530m.; 🅿; ★ **BOUL-**; z 80514, z 80516; Ⓟ 1,258; © 6,291
Erie Air Park; RMC Place; BOULDER; ★ **BOUL-**; mail Erie z 80516; pop. incl. with Erie (Inc. Place)
Escalante Forks; RMC Place; MESA; ***158** I-5; mail Delta z 81416; rural
Espinosa; RMC Place; CONEJOS; ***159** M-11; mail Manassa z 81141; rural
Estes Park; Inc. Place; LARIMER; **159** C-12; elev. 7,522ft./2,293m.; 🅿 🅷; z 80511, z 80517; Ⓟ 3,184; © 5,413
Estrella; RMC Place; ALAMOSA; ***159** M-11; elev. 7,568ft./2,307m.; mail Alamosa z 81101
Evans; Inc. Place; WELD; **159** C-14; elev. 4,651ft./1,418m.; 🅿; ★ **GRLY**; z 80620, z 80634, z 80645; Ⓟ 5,877; © 9,514
Evanston; RMC Place; WELD; ***159** D-14; mail Frederick z 80530; ● 500
Evergreen; CDP; JEFFERSON; **159** F-13; elev. 7,040ft./2,146m.; 🅿; ★ **DEN**; z 80401, z 80437, z 80439; Ⓟ 7,582; © 9,216
Evergreen Highlands; RMC Place; JEFFERSON; ***159** F-13; ★ **DEN**; mail Evergreen z 80439; ● 900
Ever Green Hills; RMC Place; JEFFERSON; ★ **DEN**; mail Evergreen z 80439
Evergreen Meadows; RMC Place; JEFFERSON; ***159** F-13; ★ **DEN**; mail Evergreen z 80439; ● 430
Evergreen Meadows West; RMC Place; JEFFERSON; ***159** F-13; ★ **DEN**; mail Evergreen z 80439; ● 200
Evergreen Park Estates; RMC Place; JEFFERSON; ***159** F-13; ★ **DEN**; mail Evergreen z 80439; ● 330
Evergreen West; RMC Place; CLEAR CREEK; ***159** F-12; mail Evergreen z 80439; ● 110

F

Fairplay; Inc. Place; ⊡ PARK; **159** G-11; elev. 9,920ft./3,024m.; 🅿; z 80432, z 80440, z 80456; Ⓟ 387; © 610
Fairview; RMC Place; CUSTER; ***159** K-13; mail Rye z 81069; rural
Fairview Estates; RMC Place; JEFFERSON; ***159** F-13; ★ **DEN**; mail Littleton z 80128; ● 960
Fairway Estates; RMC Place; LARIMER; ***159** C-13; ★ **FTCL-**; mail Fort Collins z 80521; ● 370
Falcon; RMC Place; EL PASO; **159** H-14; 🅿; ★ **CSPG**; z 80831 & mail Colorado Springs z 80908; ● 255
Falcon Estates (Falcon Ranch Estates); RMC Place; EL PASO; ***159** H-14; ★ **CSPG**; mail Colorado Springs z 80920; pop. incl. with Colorado Springs (Inc. Place)
Falcon Ranch Estates; EL PASO; see Falcon Estates (RMC Place)
Falfa; RMC Place; LA PLATA; **158** M-7; mail Durango z 81303; ● 100
Fall Creek; RMC Place; SAN MIGUEL; ***158** K-6; mail Placerville z 81430; ● 75
Farisita (Farista); RMC Place; HUERFANO; ***159** L-13; elev. 6,640ft./2,024m.; mail Gardner z 81040, Walsenburg z 81089; rural
Farista; HUERFANO; see Farisita (RMC Place)
Farmers; RMC Place; WELD; ***159** C-14; ★ **GRLY**; mail Greeley z 80631; ● 140
Fearnowville; RMC Place; PUEBLO; ***159** J-14; ★ **PUEB**; pop. incl. with Pueblo (Inc. Place)
Federal Heights; Inc. Place; ADAMS; **157** G-6; elev. 5,520ft./1,682m.; 🅿; ★ **DEN**; z 80221, z 80260 & mail Denver z 80234; Ⓟ 9,342; © 12,065
Fenders; RMC Place; JEFFERSON; ***159** F-13; elev. 7,040ft./2,146m.; ★ **DEN**; mail Morrison z 80465; rural
Ferncliff; RMC Place; BOULDER; **159** D-12; mail Allenspark z 80510; ● 70
Firestone; Inc. Place; WELD; **159** D-14; elev. 4,965ft./1,513m.; 🅿; z 80504, z 80520; Ⓟ 1,358; © 1,908
Firstview; RMC Place; CHEYENNE; ***159** H-19; mail Cheyenne Wells z 80810; rural
Flagler; Inc. Place; KIT CARSON; **159** G-18; elev. 4,931ft./1,503m.; 🅿; z 80815; Ⓟ 564; © 612
Fleming; Inc. Place; LOGAN; **159** B-18; elev. 4,240ft./1,292m.; 🅿; z 80728; Ⓟ 344; © 426
Fletcher; RMC Place; ARAPAHOE; mail Aurora z 80010, z 80040; pop. incl. with Aurora (Inc. Place)
Flintwood Hills; RMC Place; DOUGLAS; ***159** F-14; mail Franktown z 80116; ● 280
Floral; RMC Place; DENVER; ★ **DEN**; pop. incl. with Denver (Inc. Place)
Florence; Inc. Place; FREMONT; **159** J-13; elev. 5,191ft./1,582m.; 🅿; z 81226, z 81290; Ⓟ 2,990; © 3,653
Florissant; RMC Place; TELLER; **159** H-13; elev. 8,160ft./2,487m.; 🅿; z 80816; ● 110
Florissant Heights; RMC Place; TELLER; ***159** H-13; mail Florissant z 80816; ● 90
Fondis; RMC Place; ELBERT; ***159** G-15; elev. 6,177ft./1,883m.; mail Elbert z 80106; rural
Forest Hills; RMC Place; GILPIN; ***159** E-12; mail Golden z 80403; ● 160
Fort Carson; CDP; EL PASO; ***159** H-14; 🅿; ★ **CSPG**; z 80902, z 80913; Ⓟ 11,309; © 10,566
Fort Collins; Inc. Place; ⊡ LARIMER; **159** C-13; elev. 5,003ft./1,525m.; 🅿 🅷 🅲 24,670 ■; ★ **FTCL-**; z 80521-28, z 80553; Ⓟ 87,758; © 118,652; ◆ 148,391
Fort Collins West; LARIMER; see Mountain View (RMC Place)
Fort Garland; CDP; COSTILLA; **159** M-12; elev. 7,932ft./2,418m.; 🅿; z 81133; © 432
Fort Logan; RMC Place; ARAPAHOE; ***159** F-13; elev. 5,420ft./1,652m.; ★ **DEN**; mail Denver z 80236; pop. incl. with Sheridan (Inc. Place)
Fort Lupton (Lupton); Inc. Place; WELD; **159** D-14; elev. 4,906ft./1,495m.; 🅿; ★ **DEN**; z 80621; Ⓟ 5,159; © 6,787
Fort Lyon; RMC Place; BENT; **159** J-18; mail Las Animas z 81054; rural
Fort Morgan; Inc. Place; ⊡ MORGAN; **159** D-16; elev. 4,330ft./1,320m.; 🅿 🅷; z 80701, z 80705 & mail New Raymer z 80742; Ⓟ 9,068; © 11,034
Fort Reynolds; RMC Place; PUEBLO; ***159** J-15; mail Boone z 81025; ● 200
Fountain; Inc. Place; EL PASO; **159** I-14; elev. 5,546ft./1,690m.; 🅿; ★ **CSPG**; z 80817; Ⓟ 10,175; © 15,197
Fountain Valley School; RMC Place; EL PASO; ***159** H-14; elev. 5,780ft./1,762m.; ★ **CSPG**; mail Colorado Springs z 80911; ● 140
Fowler; Inc. Place; OTERO; **159** J-16; elev. 4,341ft./1,323m.; 🅿; z 81039; Ⓟ 1,154; © 1,206
Fox Creek; RMC Place; CONEJOS; ***158** N-10; elev. 8,350ft./2,545m.; mail Antonito z 81120; ● 80
Foxfield; Inc. Place; ARAPAHOE; **159** F-14; 🅿; ★ **DEN**; z 80016; © 746
Foxton; RMC Place; JEFFERSON; **159** F-13; elev. 6,455ft./1,967m.; 🅿; z 80433
Franktown; CDP; DOUGLAS; **159** F-14; elev. 6,153ft./1,875m.; 🅿; z 80116; © 99
Fraser; Inc. Place; GRAND; **159** E-11; elev. 8,574ft./2,613m.; 🅿; z 80442; Ⓟ 575; © 910
Frederick; Inc. Place; WELD; **159** D-14; elev. 4,980ft./1,518m.; 🅿; z 80504, z 80516, z 80530; Ⓟ 988; © 2,467
Freeland; RMC Place; CLEAR CREEK; ***159** E-12; mail Idaho Springs z 80452; rural
FREMONT; **159** I-12; Ⓟ 32,273; © 46,145; ◆ 48,597
Friendship Ranch; RMC Place; PARK; ***159** F-12; mail Pine z 80470; ● 115
Frisco; Inc. Place; SUMMIT; **159** F-11; elev. 9,050ft./2,758m.; 🅿; z 80443; Ⓟ 1,601; © 2,443; ® 2,467
Fruita; Inc. Place; MESA; **158** G-4; elev. 4,500ft./1,372m.; 🅿 🅷; ★ **GDJC**; z 81521; Ⓟ 4,045; © 6,478
Fruitvale; CDP; MESA; **158** G-5; 🅿; ★ **GDJC**; z 81504; Ⓟ 5,222; © 6,936
Fulton Heights; RMC Place; PUEBLO; ★ **PUEB**; mail Pueblo z 81003; pop. incl. with Pueblo (Inc. Place)

G

Galeton; RMC Place; WELD; **159** C-14; elev. 4,770ft./1,454m.; 🅿; z 80622; ● 225
Garcia; RMC Place; COSTILLA; **159** N-12; elev. 7,720ft./2,353m.; 🅿; z 81152; ● 110
Garden City; Inc. Place; WELD; **158** G-2; elev. 4,700ft./1,433m.; 🅿; ★ **GRLY**; z 80631; Ⓟ 199; © 357
Gardner; RMC Place; HUERFANO; **159** K-13; elev. 6,966ft./2,123m.; 🅿; z 81040; ● 100
Garfield (Junction City, Monarch); RMC Place; CHAFFEE; ***158** I-10; elev. 9,600ft./2,926m.; mail Monarch z 81227; rural
GARFIELD; **158** F-6; Ⓟ 29,974; © 43,791; ◆ 57,512
Garo; RMC Place; PARK; ***159** G-11; mail Fairplay z 80440; rural
Gates; RMC Place; WELD; ***159** C-14; mail Eaton z 80615; ● 175
Gateway; RMC Place; ARAPAHOE; ***159** F-14; ★ **DEN**; mail Aurora z 80014, z 80044; pop. incl. with Aurora (Inc. Place)
Gateway; RMC Place; MESA; **158** H-4; elev. 4,595ft./1,401m.; 🅿; z 81522
Gato; ARCHULETA; see Pagosa Junction (RMC Place)
Gaynor Lakes; RMC Place; BOULDER; ***159** D-13; ★ **BOUL-**; mail Longmont z 80501; ● 330
Gem Village; RMC Place; LA PLATA; **158** M-7; mail Bayfield z 81122
Genesee; CDP-Census Area Only; JEFFERSON; ***159** F-13; elev. 7,800ft./2,377m.; ★ **DEN**; mail Golden z 80401; Ⓟ 2,737; © 3,699
Genoa; Inc. Place; LINCOLN; **159** G-17; elev. 5,594ft./1,705m.; 🅿; z 80818; Ⓟ 167; © 211
Georgetown; Inc. Place; ⊡ CLEAR CREEK; **159** E-12; elev. 8,512ft./2,594m.; 🅿; z 80444; Ⓟ 891; © 1,088
Gerbaz Dale; PITKIN; see Aspen-Gerbaz (RMC Place)
Gilcrest; Inc. Place; WELD; **159** D-14; elev. 4,751ft./1,448m.; 🅿; z 80623; Ⓟ 1,084; © 1,162
Gill; RMC Place; WELD; ***159** C-14; elev. 4,680ft./1,426m.; 🅿; z 80624; ● 320
Gilman; RMC Place; EAGLE; ***158** F-10; elev. 8,960ft./2,731m.; 🅿; z 81645
GILPIN; **159** E-12; Ⓟ 3,070; © 4,757; ◆ 5,165
Glade Park; RMC Place; MESA; **158** H-4; elev. 6,901ft./2,103m.; 🅿; z 81523; ● 40
Glen Comfort (Pine Knott); RMC Place; LARIMER; ***159** C-12; mail Drake z 80515; rural
Glendale; Inc. Place; ARAPAHOE; **157** I-7; elev. 5,350ft./1,631m.; 🅿; ★ **DEN**; z 80246 & mail Denver z 80206, z 80222; Ⓟ 2,453; © 4,547
Glendevey; RMC Place; LARIMER; **159** B-11; elev. 8,292ft./2,527m.; mail Jelm z 82063
Gleneagle; CDP-Census Area Only; EL PASO; ***159** H-14; elev. 6,900ft./2,103m.; ★ **CSPG**; mail Monument z 80132; Ⓟ 1,661; © 4,246
Glen Eden; RMC Place; ROUTT; ***158** B-9; mail Clark z 80428; ● 30
Glenelk; RMC Place; JEFFERSON; ***159** F-13; mail Pine z 80470; ● 210
Glen Haven; RMC Place; LARIMER; **159** C-12; elev. 7,240ft./2,207m.; 🅿; z 80532; summer pop. 1,200; ● 130
Glenisle; RMC Place; PARK; ***159** F-12; mail Bailey z 80421; rural
Glen Park; RMC Place; EL PASO; ***159** G-14; ★ **CSPG**; mail Palmer Lake z 80133; pop. incl. with Palmer Lake (Inc. Place)
Glenwood Springs; Inc. Place; ⊡ GARFIELD; **158** F-8; elev. 5,763ft./1,757m.; 🅿 🅷; z 81601-02; Ⓟ 6,561; © 7,736
Goat Hill; RMC Place; PUEBLO; ***159** J-14; ★ **PUEB**; mail Pueblo z 81006; pop. incl. with Pueblo (Inc. Place)
Golden; Inc. Place; ⊡ JEFFERSON; **159** E-13; elev. 5,674ft./1,729m.; 🅿 🅲 4,056; ★ **DEN**; z 80401-03, z 80419, z 80439; Ⓟ 13,116; © 17,159
Goldfield; RMC Place; TELLER; **159** I-13; mail Victor z 80860; ● 55
Gold Hill; CDP; BOULDER; ***159** D-12; elev. 8,296ft./2,529m.; mail Boulder z 80302; © 210
Gooding; RMC Place; BOULDER; ***159** D-13; mail Longmont z 80504; ● 230
Goodnight (Goodnight Place); RMC Place; PUEBLO; ***159** J-14; ★ **PUEB**; mail Pueblo z 81005; ● 1,400
Goodnight Place; PUEBLO; see Goodnight (RMC Place)
Goodrich; RMC Place; MORGAN; **159** C-16; elev. 4,380ft./1,335m.; mail Weldona z 80653; ● 35
Gould; RMC Place; JACKSON; **159** C-11; elev. 8,913ft./2,717m.; mail Walden z 80480; ● 50
Granada; Inc. Place; PROWERS; **159** J-20; elev. 3,484ft./1,062m.; 🅿; z 81041; Ⓟ 513; © 640
Granby; Inc. Place; GRAND; **159** D-11; elev. 7,939ft./2,420m.; 🅿; z 80446; Ⓟ 966; © 1,525
GRAND; **158** D-10; Ⓟ 7,966; © 12,442; ◆ 13,996
Grand Junction; Inc. Place; ⊡ MESA; **158** G-5; elev. 4,597ft./1,401m.; 🅿 🅷 🅲 5,990 ■; ★ **GDJC**; z 81501-07; Ⓟ 29,255; © 41,986; ® 42,666; ◆ 49,012
Grand Lake; Inc. Place; GRAND; **159** D-11; elev. 8,380ft./2,554m.; 🅿; z 80447 & mail Granby z 80446; Ⓟ 259; © 447
Grand Mesa; RMC Place; DELTA; ***158** G-6; elev. 10,125ft./3,086m.; mail Cedaredge z 81413; ● 30
Grand Valley; GARFIELD; see Parachute (Inc. Place)
Grandview; RMC Place; LA PLATA; ***158** M-6; mail Durango z 81303; ● 100
Grand View Estates; CDP; DOUGLAS; ***159** F-14; ★ **DEN**; mail Parker z 80134; © 691
Granite (Yale); RMC Place; CHAFFEE; **158** H-10; elev. 8,928ft./2,721m.; 🅿; z 81228
Grant; RMC Place; PARK; **159** F-12; elev. 8,584ft./2,616m.; 🅿; z 80448
Gray's Mary Greenwood; RMC Place; PUEBLO; ***159** K-14; elev. 7,143ft./2,177m.; mail Rye z 81069; ● 100
Great Divide; RMC Place; MOFFAT; ***158** B-7; mail Craig z 81625; rural
Greeley; Inc. Place; ⊡ WELD; **159** C-14; elev. 4,664ft./1,422m.; 🅿 🅷 🅲 13,031 ■; ★ **GRLY**; z 80631-34, z 80638-39; Ⓟ 60,536; © 76,930; ◆ 90,235
Green Gables; RMC Place; JEFFERSON; ★ **DEN**; mail Denver z 80232; pop. incl. with Lakewood (Inc. Place)
Greenhorn; RMC Place; PUEBLO; ***159** K-14; mail Colorado City z 81019; rural
Greenland; RMC Place; DOUGLAS; ***159** G-14; elev. 6,908ft./2,106m.; mail Larkspur z 80118; rural
Green Mountain; RMC Place; JEFFERSON; ***159** E-13; elev. 5,800ft./1,768m.; ★ **DEN**; mail Denver z 80228
Green Mountain Camp; RMC Place; SUMMIT; **158** E-10; mail Silverthorne z 80498
Green Mountain Estates; RMC Place; JEFFERSON; ***159** F-13; ★ **DEN**; mail Denver z 80228; pop. incl. with Lakewood (Inc. Place)
Green Mountain Falls; Inc. Place; EL PASO, TELLER; **159** H-13; elev. 7,720ft./2,353m.; 🅿; ★ **CSPG**; z 80819; Ⓟ 663; © 773
Green Mountain Village; RMC Place; JEFFERSON; ***159** F-13; ★ **DEN**; mail Denver z 80228; pop. incl. with Lakewood (Inc. Place)
Green Towers; RMC Place; PUEBLO; ***159** K-14; mail Rye z 81069; ● 200
Green Valley Acres; RMC Place; JEFFERSON; ***159** F-13; elev. 8,350ft./2,545m.; mail Conifer z 80433; ● 120
Greenway Park; RMC Place; JEFFERSON; ***159** E-13; mail Broomfield z 80020; pop. incl. with Broomfield (Inc. Place)
Greenwood; RMC Place; CUSTER; **159** J-13; mail Rye z 81069, Wetmore z 81253; ● 140
Greenwood Village; Inc. Place; ARAPAHOE; **157** K-7; elev. 5,450ft./1,661m.; 🅿 🅲 12,591; ★ **DEN**; z 80110-12, z 80121, z 80155 & mail Englewood z 80150; Ⓟ 7,589; © 11,035
Greystone; RMC Place; MOFFAT; ***158** C-5; elev. 6,673ft./2,034m.; mail Maybell z 81640; rural
Greystone Lodge; RMC Place; JEFFERSON; ***159** F-12; ★ **DEN**; mail Evergreen z 80439; ● 150
Grover; Inc. Place; WELD; **159** B-15; elev. 5,071ft./1,546m.; 🅿; z 80729; Ⓟ 135; © 153
Guadalupe; RMC Place; CONEJOS; ***159** N-11; mail Conejos z 81129; ● 100
Guffey; RMC Place; PARK; **159** H-12; elev. 8,680ft./2,646m.; 🅿; z 80820
Gulnare; RMC Place; LAS ANIMAS; **159** M-14; elev. 6,800ft./2,073m.; ● 100
Gunbarrel; CDP; BOULDER; ***159** D-13; ★ **BOUL-**; mail Longmont z 80501; Ⓟ 9,388; © 9,435
Gunbarrel Estates; RMC Place; BOULDER; ***159** D-13; ★ **BOUL-**; mail Longmont z 80503; ● 1,320
Gunbarrel Greens; RMC Place; BOULDER; ***159** D-13; ★ **BOUL-**; mail Boulder z 80301; ● 760
Gunnison; Inc. Place; ⊡ GUNNISON; **158** I-9; elev. 7,703ft./2,348m.; 🅿 🅷 🅲 2,198; z 81230-31, z 81247; Ⓟ 4,636; © 5,409
GUNNISON; **158** H-9; Ⓟ 10,273; © 13,956; ◆ 15,558
Gypsum; Inc. Place; EAGLE; **158** F-9; elev. 6,320ft./1,926m.; 🅿; z 81637; Ⓟ 1,750; © 3,654; ® 3,768

H

Hahns Peak; RMC Place; ROUTT; **158** B-9; elev. 8,128ft./2,477m.; mail Clark z 80428; summer pop. 200; ● 40
Hale; RMC Place; YUMA; ***159** F-20; elev. 3,599ft./1,097m.; 🅿; z 80735; rural
Hamilton; RMC Place; MOFFAT; **158** C-7; elev. 6,239ft./1,902m.; 🅿; z 81638; ● 30
Hanover; RMC Place; EL PASO; ***159** I-15; mail Colorado Springs z 80909; rural
Happy Canyon; RMC Place; DOUGLAS; ***159** F-14; ★ **DEN**; mail Castle Rock z 80108; ● 330
Hardin; RMC Place; WELD; ***159** C-15; elev. 4,527ft./1,380m.; mail Kersey z 80644
Harmony; RMC Place; LARIMER; ***159** C-13; elev. 4,967ft./1,514m.; ★ **FTCL-**; mail Fort Collins z 80521; pop. incl. with Fort Collins (Inc. Place)
Harris Park; RMC Place; ADAMS; ★ **DEN**; mail Westminster z 80036; pop. incl. with Westminster (Inc. Place)
Harris Park; RMC Place; PARK; **159** F-12; mail Pine z 80470; ● 200
Hartman; Inc. Place; PROWERS; **159** J-20; elev. 3,590ft./1,094m.; 🅿; z 81043 & mail Holly z 81047; Ⓟ 108; © 111
Hartsel; RMC Place; PARK; **159** H-11; elev. 8,864ft./2,702m.; 🅿; z 80449; ● 80
Hasty; RMC Place; BENT; **159** J-18; elev. 3,870ft./1,180m.; 🅿; z 81044; ● 200
Haswell; Inc. Place; KIOWA; **159** I-18; elev. 4,538ft./1,383m.; 🅿; z 81045; Ⓟ 62; © 84
Hawley; RMC Place; OTERO; ***159** K-17; mail Rocky Ford z 81067
Haxtun; Inc. Place; PHILLIPS; **159** C-19; elev. 4,039ft./1,231m.; 🅿 🅷; z 80731; Ⓟ 952; © 982
Haybro (Deer Park); RMC Place; ROUTT; ***158** D-9; mail Oak Creek z 80467; rural
Hayden; Inc. Place; ROUTT; **158** C-8; elev. 6,337ft./1,932m.; 🅿; z 81639; Ⓟ 1,444; © 1,634
Hazeltine; RMC Place; ADAMS; ***159** E-14; mail Henderson z 80640; pop. incl. with Commerce City (Inc. Place)
Hazeltine Heights; RMC Place; ADAMS; ***159** E-14; elev. 5,080ft./1,548m.; ★ **DEN**; mail Henderson z 80640; pop. incl. with Commerce City (Inc. Place)
Heartstrong; RMC Place; YUMA; mail Eckley z 80727; rural
Heather Ridge; RMC Place; ARAPAHOE; ***159** F-14; ★ **DEN**; mail Aurora z 80014; pop. incl. with Aurora (Inc. Place)
Heatherwood; RMC Place; BOULDER; ***159** D-13; ★ **BOUL-**; mail Boulder z 80301; ● 1,450
Heeney; RMC Place; SUMMIT; **158** E-10; 🅿; z 80498; summer pop. 300; ● 55
Henderson; RMC Place; ADAMS; **157** F-8; elev. 5,021ft./1,530m.; 🅿; ★ **DEN**; z 80640; ● 600

Entries in **UPPERCASE** are counties.
Entries in **bold** have populations of 2,500 or more.
Names in parentheses are alternate names.

Inc. Place	Incorporated Place
RMC Place	Rand McNally Designated Place
CDP	Census Designated Place
MCD	Minor Civil Division

⊡ County Seat
▲ Minor Civil Division
elev. Elevation
🅿 Post Office
🅷 Hospital
🅲 College
■ Principal Business Center
★ Ranally Metro Area (RMA) Abbreviation
z Zip Code(s)
Ⓟ Previous Census Population
® Revised Census Population
Ⓐ Annexation Population
● Rand McNally Population Estimate
© Final Census Population
Ⓢ Special Census Population
◆ Estimated Population

For additional definitions see Glossary, Volume 1, and Introduction, Volume 2.

Hereford; RMC Place; WELD; **159** B-15; elev. 5,260ft./1,603m.; 🅿; z 80732; ● 60
Heritage Dells; RMC Place; JEFFERSON; ***159** E-13; ★ **DEN**; mail Golden z 80401; pop. incl. with Golden (Inc. Place)
Heritage Hills; CDP-Census Area Only; DOUGLAS; ***159** F-14; ★ **DEN**; Ⓒ 658
Heritage Place; RMC Place; ARAPAHOE; ***159** F-14; ★ **DEN**; mail Englewood z 80110; ● 1,600
Hermosa; RMC Place; LA PLATA; **158** L-6; mail Durango z 81301; ● 260
Herzman Mesa; RMC Place; JEFFERSON; ***159** F-13; ★ **DEN**; mail Evergreen z 80439; ● 350
Hesperus; RMC Place; LA PLATA; **158** M-6; elev. 8,110ft./2,472m.; 🅿; z 81326
Hiawatha; RMC Place; MOFFAT; **158** A-5; mail Rock Springs z 82901; ● 10
Hidden Valley; RMC Place; JEFFERSON; ***159** F-13; ★ **DEN**; mail Evergreen z 80439; ● 190
Hideaway Park; RMC Place; GRAND; ***159** E-12; elev. 8,800ft./2,682m.; mail Winter Park z 80482; pop. incl. with Winter Park (Inc. Place)
High Chateau Ranches; RMC Place; TELLER; ***159** H-13; mail Florissant z 80816; ● 60
Highland; RMC Place; BOULDER; ***159** D-13; mail Longmont z 80504; ● 200
Highland Acres; RMC Place; WELD; mail Greeley z 80631; ● 100
Highland Hills; RMC Place; WELD; ***159** C-14; elev. 4,990ft./1,521m.; ★ **GRLY**; mail Greeley z 80634; pop. incl. with Greeley (Inc. Place)
Highland Lake; RMC Place; WELD; ***159** D-13; elev. 5,067ft./1,544m.; mail Platteville z 80651; ● 120
Highland Lakes; RMC Place; TELLER; ***159** H-13; mail Divide z 80814; ● 200
Highland Park; RMC Place; PARK; **159** F-12; mail Pine z 80470; ● 300
Highland Pines; RMC Place; JEFFERSON; ***159** F-12; mail Pine z 80470; ● 190
Highlands; RMC Place; DENVER; ***159** E-13; ★ **DEN**; mail Denver z 80211, Littleton z 80126, z 80129-30, z 80163, Lone Tree z 80124; pop. incl. with Denver (Inc. Place)
Highlands Ranch; CDP-Census Area Only; DOUGLAS; **157** L-7; elev. 5,900ft./1,798m.; 🅿; ★ **DEN**; z 80124, z 80126, z 80129-30, z 80163; Ⓟ 10,181; Ⓒ 70,931; ◆ 116,743
High-Mar; RMC Place; BOULDER; ***159** E-13; ★ **BOUL-**; mail Boulder z 80303, z 80305, z 80307; pop. incl. with Boulder (Inc. Place)
Hi-Land Acres; RMC Place; ADAMS; ***159** E-14; ★ **DEN**; mail Brighton z 80601; ● 180
Hill and Park; WELD; see Hill N' Park (RMC Place)
Hill N' Park (Hill and Park); RMC Place; WELD; ***159** C-14; ★ **GRLY**; mail Greeley z 80631; ● 1,500
Hillrose; Inc. Place; MORGAN; **159** D-17; elev. 4,165ft./1,269m.; 🅿; z 80733; Ⓟ 169; Ⓒ 254
Hillsboro; RMC Place; WELD; ***159** D-14; mail Milliken z 80543; pop. incl. with Milliken (Inc. Place)
Hillside; RMC Place; FREMONT; **159** J-12; elev. 7,440ft./2,268m.; 🅿; z 81232; rural
Hilltop; RMC Place; DOUGLAS; ***159** F-14; elev. 6,572ft./2,003m.; ★ **DEN**; mail Parker z 80134; ● 300
HINSDALE; **158** K-8; Ⓟ 467; Ⓒ 790; ◆ 874
Hiwan Hills; RMC Place; JEFFERSON; ***159** F-13; ★ **DEN**; mail Evergreen z 80439; ● 1,250
Hoehne (Hoehnes); RMC Place; LAS ANIMAS; **159** M-15; elev. 5,728ft./1,746m.; 🅿; z 81046; ● 85
Hoehnes; LAS ANIMAS; see Hoehne (RMC Place)
Hoffman Heights; RMC Place; ARAPAHOE; ★ **DEN**; mail Aurora z 80012; pop. incl. with Aurora (Inc. Place)
Holiday Acres; RMC Place; ARCHULETA; ***158** M-8; mail Pagosa Springs z 81147; ● 235
Holiday Hills; RMC Place; TELLER; ***159** H-13; mail Woodland Park z 80863; ● 120
Holland Park; RMC Place; EL PASO; ***159** H-14; ★ **CSPG**; mail Colorado Springs z 80907; pop. incl. with Colorado Springs (Inc. Place)
Holly; Inc. Place; PROWERS; **159** J-20; elev. 3,387ft./1,032m.; 🅿; z 81047 & mail Hartman z 81043; Ⓟ 877; Ⓒ 1,048
Holyoke; Inc. Place; ⊡ PHILLIPS; **159** C-20; elev. 3,736ft./1,139m.; 🅿 🅷; z 80734; Ⓟ 1,931; Ⓒ 2,261
Homelake (Colorado State Veterans Center); RMC Place; RIO GRANDE; **159** L-11; elev. 7,630ft./2,326m.; 🅿; z 81135; ● 260
Hooper; Inc. Place; ALAMOSA; **159** L-11; elev. 7,558ft./2,304m.; 🅿; z 81136; Ⓟ 112; Ⓒ 123
Hotchkiss; Inc. Place; DELTA; **158** H-7; elev. 5,351ft./1,631m.; 🅿; z 81419; Ⓟ 744; Ⓒ 968
Hot Sulphur Springs; Inc. Place; ⊡ GRAND; **159** D-11; elev. 7,680ft./2,341m.; 🅿; z 80451; Ⓟ 347; Ⓒ 521
Howard; RMC Place; FREMONT; **159** I-11; elev. 6,720ft./2,048m.; 🅿; z 81233; ● 200
Howells; RMC Place; ARAPAHOE; ***159** F-13; ★ **DEN**; mail Littleton z 80120; pop. incl. with Littleton (Inc. Place)
Hoyt; RMC Place; MORGAN; **159** E-16; elev. 4,764ft./1,452m.; 🅿; z 80654; ● 30
Huajatolla; HUERFANO; see Wahatoya (RMC Place)
Hudson; Inc. Place; WELD; **159** D-14; elev. 5,000ft./1,524m.; 🅿; z 80642; Ⓟ 918; Ⓒ 1,565
HUERFANO; **159** L-13; Ⓟ 6,009; Ⓒ 7,862; ◆ 7,917
Hugo; Inc. Place; ⊡ LINCOLN; **159** G-17; elev. 5,046ft./1,538m.; 🅿 🅷; z 80821; Ⓟ 660; Ⓒ 885
Husted; RMC Place; EL PASO; ★ **CSPG**; mail USAF Academy z 80840
Hyde; RMC Place; WASHINGTON; ***159** D-19; mail Otis z 80743; rural
Hyde Park; RMC Place; PUEBLO; ★ **PUEB**; pop. incl. with Pueblo (Inc. Place)
Hygiene; RMC Place; BOULDER; **159** D-13; elev. 5,097ft./1,554m.; 🅿; z 80533; ● 400
Hyland Hills; RMC Place; CLEAR CREEK; ***159** E-15; mail Evergreen z 80439; ● 100
Hyland Knolls; RMC Place; WELD; ***159** C-14; elev. 4,750ft./1,448m.; ★ **GRLY**; mail Greeley z 80634; pop. incl. with Greeley (Inc. Place)

I

Idaho Springs; Inc. Place; CLEAR CREEK; **159** E-12; elev. 7,524ft./2,293m.; 🅿; z 80452; Ⓟ 1,834; Ⓒ 1,889
Idalia; RMC Place; YUMA; **159** E-20; elev. 3,965ft./1,209m.; 🅿; z 80735; ● 100
Idledale; RMC Place; JEFFERSON; ***159** F-13; elev. 6,466ft./1,971m.; 🅿; ★ **DEN**; z 80453; ● 565
Ignacio; Inc. Place; LA PLATA; **158** M-7; located on Southern Ute Ind. Res.; elev. 6,450ft./1,966m.; 🅿; z 81137; location of Indian Agency; Ⓟ 720; Ⓒ 669
Iliff; Inc. Place; LOGAN; **159** B-18; elev. 3,835ft./1,169m.; 🅿; z 80736; Ⓟ 174; Ⓒ 213
Ilse; RMC Place; FREMONT; ***159** I-13; mail Canon City z 81212; pop. incl. with Cañon City (Inc. Place)
Indian Creek; RMC Place; TELLER; ***159** H-13; mail Florissant z 80816, La Veta z 81055; ● 125
Indian Creek Ranch; RMC Place; DOUGLAS; ***159** F-13; mail Sedalia z 80135; ● 210
Indian Head; RMC Place; GUNNISON; ***158** I-9; mail Parlin z 81239; rural
Indian Hills; CDP; JEFFERSON; **159** F-13; elev. 6,840ft./2,085m.; 🅿; ★ **DEN**; z 80454; Ⓒ 1,197
Indian Springs Village; RMC Place; JEFFERSON; ***159** F-13; elev. 7,200ft./2,195m.; mail Pine z 80470; ● 50
Indian Tree; RMC Place; JEFFERSON; ★ **DEN**; mail Arvada z 80006-07; pop. incl. with Arvada (Inc. Place)
Ione; RMC Place; WELD; ***159** D-14; ★ **DEN**; mail Fort Lupton z 80621
Irondale; RMC Place; ADAMS; **157** G-8; ★ **DEN**; mail Commerce City z 80022, Henderson z 80640; pop. incl. with Commerce City (Inc. Place)
Ivywild; RMC Place; EL PASO; ***159** H-14; ★ **CSPG**; mail Colorado Springs z 80906, z 80926, z 80960; pop. incl. with Colorado Springs (Inc. Place)

J

Jacks Cabin; RMC Place; GUNNISON; ***158** H-9; mail Almont z 81210; rural
JACKSON; **158** C-10; Ⓟ 1,605; Ⓒ 1,577; ◆ 1,336
Jamestown; Inc. Place; BOULDER; **159** D-12; elev. 6,920ft./2,109m.; 🅿; z 80455; Ⓟ 251; Ⓒ 205; Ⓡ 247
Jansen; RMC Place; LAS ANIMAS; **159** M-15; 🅿; z 81082; ● 210
Jaroso; RMC Place; COSTILLA; **159** N-12; elev. 7,575ft./2,309m.; 🅿; z 81138; ● 60
Jefferson; RMC Place; PARK; **159** G-11; elev. 9,499ft./2,895m.; 🅿; z 80456; ● 40
JEFFERSON; **159** F-13; part of Jefferson county was annexed by Broomfield county on November 15, 2001; Ⓟ 438,430; Ⓒ 527,056; adjusted 2000 Census population is 525,507; ◆ 534,949
Jefferson Heights; RMC Place; PARK; ***159** G-11; mail Jefferson z 80456; ● 45
Joes; RMC Place; YUMA; **159** F-19; elev. 4,271ft./1,302m.; 🅿; z 80822; ● 75
Johnson Village; RMC Place; CHAFFEE; **159** H-11; mail Buena Vista z 81211; ● 270
Johnstown; Inc. Place; WELD, LARIMER; **159** D-14; elev. 4,815ft./1,468m.; 🅿; z 80534; Ⓟ 1,579; Ⓒ 3,827
Juanita; RMC Place; ARCHULETA; ***158** N-8; mail Pagosa Springs z 81147; rural
Julesburg; Inc. Place; ⊡ SEDGWICK; **159** A-20; elev. 3,477ft./1,060m.; 🅿 🅷; z 80737; Ⓟ 1,295; Ⓒ 1,467
Junction City; CHAFFEE; see Garfield (RMC Place)

K

Kahler; RMC Place; WELD; ***159** D-13; elev. 5,006ft./1,526m.; mail Berthoud z 80513; rural
Karval; RMC Place; LINCOLN; **159** H-17; elev. 5,070ft./1,545m.; 🅿; z 80823; ● 65
Kassler (Watertown); RMC Place; JEFFERSON; ***159** F-13; mail Littleton z 80125; rural
Keenesburg; Inc. Place; WELD; **159** D-15; elev. 4,958ft./1,511m.; 🅿; z 80643; Ⓟ 570; Ⓒ 855
Kelim; RMC Place; LARIMER; **159** C-14; ★ **FTCL-**; mail Loveland z 80537; ● 90
Kelker; RMC Place; EL PASO; ***159** H-14; elev. 5,854ft./1,784m.; ★ **CSPG**; mail Colorado Springs z 80906; pop. incl. with Colorado Springs (Inc. Place)
Kellytown; RMC Place; DOUGLAS; ***159** F-13; elev. 5,660ft./1,725m.; ★ **DEN**; mail Littleton z 80125; rural
Ken Caryl; CDP-Census Area Only; JEFFERSON; ***159** F-13; ★ **DEN**; mail Littleton z 80123, z 80127; Ⓟ 24,391; Ⓒ 30,887; ◆ 31,998
Keota; RMC Place; WELD; **159** B-16; elev. 4,961ft./1,512m.; mail Grover z 80729
Kersey; Inc. Place; WELD; **159** C-14; elev. 4,617ft./1,407m.; 🅿; z 80644; Ⓟ 980; Ⓒ 1,389
Keystone; CDP; SUMMIT; ***159** F-11; 🅿; z 80435; Ⓒ 825; Ⓡ 819
Kim; Inc. Place; LAS ANIMAS; **159** M-17; elev. 5,690ft./1,734m.; 🅿; z 81049; Ⓟ 76; Ⓒ 65
Kingsborough; RMC Place; ARAPAHOE; ★ **DEN**; mail Aurora z 80017; pop. incl. with Aurora (Inc. Place)
Kingsborough South; RMC Place; ARAPAHOE; ★ **DEN**; mail Aurora z 80012; pop. incl. with Aurora (Inc. Place)
Kings Corner; RMC Place; LARIMER; ***159** C-13; elev. 4,932ft./1,503m.; ★ **FTCL-**; mail Loveland z 80537; pop. incl. with Loveland (Inc. Place)
Kiowa; Inc. Place; ⊡ ELBERT; **159** G-15; elev. 6,360ft./1,939m.; 🅿; z 80117; Ⓟ 275; Ⓒ 581
KIOWA; **159** I-18; Ⓟ 1,688; Ⓒ 1,622; ◆ 1,263
Kipling Hills; RMC Place; JEFFERSON; ★ **DEN**; mail Littleton z 80123
Kipling Villas; RMC Place; JEFFERSON; ***159** F-13; elev. 5,650ft./1,722m.; ★ **DEN**; mail Littleton z 80123; ● 1,200
Kirk; RMC Place; YUMA; **159** F-19; elev. 4,200ft./1,280m.; 🅿; z 80824; ● 80
Kit Carson; Inc. Place; CHEYENNE; **159** H-19; elev. 4,285ft./1,306m.; 🅿; z 80825; Ⓟ 305; Ⓒ 253
KIT CARSON; **159** F-19; Ⓟ 7,140; Ⓒ 8,011; ◆ 7,916
Kittredge; CDP; JEFFERSON; ***159** F-13; elev. 6,840ft./2,085m.; 🅿; ★ **DEN**; z 80457; Ⓒ 954
Kline; RMC Place; LA PLATA; ***158** M-6; mail Hesperus z 81326; ● 130
Knaus; RMC Place; WELD; ***159** C-14; elev. 4,800ft./1,463m.; ★ **GRLY**; mail Greeley z 80634; ● 300
Knob Hill; RMC Place; EL PASO; ***159** H-14; ★ **CSPG**; mail Colorado Springs z 80910; pop. incl. with Colorado Springs (Inc. Place)
Koen; RMC Place; PROWERS; ***159** J-20; elev. 3,511ft./1,070m.; mail Granada z 81041; rural
Kornman; RMC Place; PROWERS; ***159** J-19; elev. 3,685ft./1,123m.; mail Lamar z 81052; rural
Kremmling; Inc. Place; GRAND; **158** D-10; elev. 7,360ft./2,243m.; 🅿 🅷; z 80459; Ⓟ 1,166; Ⓒ 1,578
Kuhlmann Heights; RMC Place; BOULDER, GILPIN; ***159** E-12; mail Golden z 80403; ● 200
Kutch; RMC Place; ELBERT; ***159** H-16; elev. 5,669ft./1,728m.; mail Ramah z 80832; rural

L

Lafayette; Inc. Place; BOULDER; **159** E-13; elev. 5,236ft./1,596m.; 🅿; ★ **BOUL-**; z 80026; Ⓟ 14,548; Ⓒ 23,197; ◆ 29,841
La Foret; RMC Place; EL PASO; ***159** H-14; mail Colorado Springs z 80908; ● 380
La Garita; RMC Place; SAGUACHE; ***158** K-10; mail Del Norte z 81132
Laird; RMC Place; YUMA; **159** D-20; elev. 3,402ft./1,037m.; 🅿; z 80758; ● 70
La Jara; Inc. Place; CONEJOS; **159** M-11; elev. 7,602ft./2,317m.; 🅿 🅷; z 81140; Ⓟ 725; Ⓒ 877
La Junta; Inc. Place; ⊡ OTERO; **159** K-17; elev. 4,066ft./1,239m.; 🅿 🅷; z 81050; Ⓟ 7,637; Ⓒ 7,568
La Junta Gardens; RMC Place; OTERO; ***159** K-17; mail La Junta z 81050
LAKE; **158** G-10; Ⓟ 6,007; Ⓒ 7,812; ◆ 8,267
Lakeborough; RMC Place; JEFFERSON; ***159** F-13; ★ **DEN**; mail Denver z 80235; ● 735
Lake City; Inc. Place; ⊡ HINSDALE; **158** K-8; elev. 8,658ft./2,639m.; 🅿; z 81235; Ⓟ 223; Ⓒ 375
Lake George; RMC Place; PARK; **159** H-13; elev. 7,968ft./2,429m.; 🅿; z 80827; ● 120
Lakeside; Inc. Place; JEFFERSON; ***159** E-13; elev. 5,350ft./1,631m.; ★ **DEN**; mail Denver z 80212; Ⓟ 11; Ⓒ 20
Lake View; RMC Place; GILPIN; ***159** E-12; mail Golden z 80403; ● 300
Lakewood; Inc. Place; JEFFERSON; **157** I-5; elev. 5,450ft./1,661m.; 🅿 🅲 2,357 ■; ★ **DEN**; z 80033, z 80123, z 80214-15, z 80226-28, z 80232, z 80235-36, z 80401 & mail Denver z 80225; Ⓟ 126,481; Ⓒ 144,126; ◆ 148,679
Lamar; Inc. Place; ⊡ PROWERS; **159** J-19; elev. 3,622ft./1,104m.; 🅿 🅷; z 81052; Ⓟ 8,343; Ⓒ 8,869
La Montana Mesa; RMC Place; TELLER; ***159** H-13; mail Florissant z 80816; ● 110
LA PLATA; **158** M-7; Ⓟ 32,284; Ⓒ 43,941; ◆ 51,196
Laporte; CDP; LARIMER; **159** C-13; elev. 5,060ft./1,542m.; 🅿; ★ **FTCL-**; z 80535; Ⓒ 2,691
La Posta; RMC Place; LA PLATA; ***158** M-6; mail Durango z 81301
Lariat; RMC Place; RIO GRANDE; mail Monte Vista z 81144; pop. incl. with Monte Vista (Inc. Place)
LARIMER; **159** C-12; Ⓟ 186,136; Ⓒ 251,494; ◆ 311,227
Larkspur; Inc. Place; DOUGLAS; **159** G-14; elev. 6,720ft./2,048m.; 🅿; z 80118; Ⓟ 232; Ⓒ 234
La Salle; Inc. Place; WELD; **159** D-14; elev. 4,676ft./1,425m.; 🅿; ★ **GRLY**; z 80645; Ⓟ 1,783; Ⓒ 1,849
Las Animas; Inc. Place; ⊡ BENT; **159** K-18; elev. 3,893ft./1,187m.; 🅿; z 81054; Ⓟ 2,481; Ⓒ 2,758
LAS ANIMAS; **159** L-16; Ⓟ 13,765; Ⓒ 15,207; ◆ 16,331
Lasauses (Los Sauces); RMC Place; CONEJOS; ***159** M-12; mail Sanford z 81151
Las Mesitas; RMC Place; CONEJOS; **159** N-11; elev. 8,099ft./2,469m.; mail Antonito z 81120; ● 60
Last Chance; RMC Place; WASHINGTON; **159** E-17; elev. 4,780ft./1,457m.; 🅿; z 80757; ● 25
La Valley (San Francisco); RMC Place; COSTILLA; **159** N-13; mail San Luis z 81152; ● 160
La Veta; Inc. Place; HUERFANO; **159** L-13; elev. 7,013ft./2,138m.; 🅿; z 81055; Ⓟ 726; Ⓒ 924
Lawson; RMC Place; CLEAR CREEK; **159** E-12; elev. 8,089ft./2,466m.; mail Idaho Springs z 80452; ● 320
Lay; RMC Place; MOFFAT; ***158** C-7; elev. 6,171ft./1,881m.; mail Craig z 81625
Lazear; RMC Place; DELTA; **158** H-7; elev. 5,440ft./1,658m.; 🅿; z 81420; ● 140
Leadville; Inc. Place; ⊡ LAKE; **158** G-10; elev. 10,152ft./3,094m.; 🅿 🅷; z 80429, z 80461; Ⓟ 2,629; Ⓒ 2,821
Leadville North; CDP-Census Area Only; LAKE; ***158** G-10; elev. 10,800ft./3,292m.; mail Leadville z 80461; Ⓟ 1,757; Ⓒ 1,942
Leawood; RMC Place; JEFFERSON; ★ **DEN**; mail Littleton z 80128
Lebanon; RMC Place; MONTEZUMA; ***158** L-5; elev. 6,672ft./2,034m.; mail Dolores z 81323; ● 160
Leisure Living; RMC Place; WELD; ***159** E-13; mail Erie z 80516; ● 135
Lewis; RMC Place; MONTEZUMA; **158** L-4; elev. 6,700ft./2,042m.; 🅿; z 81327; ● 160
Leyden; RMC Place; JEFFERSON; ***159** E-13; ★ **DEN**; mail Arvada z 80007; ● 160
Leyner; RMC Place; BOULDER; ***159** D-13; mail Lafayette z 80026; pop. incl. with Erie (Inc. Place)
Liberty Bell (Liberty Bell Village); RMC Place; SAN MIGUEL; ***158** K-7; mail Telluride z 81435
Liberty Bell Village; SAN MIGUEL; see Liberty Bell (RMC Place)
Liggett; RMC Place; BOULDER; ***159** D-13; mail Boulder z 80301; ● 150
Lime; RMC Place; PUEBLO; ***159** J-14; mail Pueblo z 81005; rural
Limon; Inc. Place; LINCOLN; **159** G-17; elev. 5,365ft./1,635m.; 🅿; z 80826, z 80828; Ⓟ 1,831; Ⓒ 2,071
LINCOLN; **159** H-17; Ⓟ 4,529; Ⓒ 6,087; ◆ 5,318
Lincoln Park; CDP; FREMONT; **159** I-13; mail Canon City z 81212; Ⓟ 3,728; Ⓒ 3,904
Lindon; RMC Place; WASHINGTON; **159** E-17; elev. 4,899ft./1,493m.; 🅿; z 80740; ● 120
Littleton; Inc. Place; ⊡ ARAPAHOE, DOUGLAS, JEFFERSON; **159** F-13; elev. 5,389ft./1,643m.; 🅿 🅷 🅲 856 ■; ★ **DEN**; z 80120-30, z 80160-63, z 80165-66; Ⓟ 33,685; Ⓒ 40,340; ◆ 42,101
Livengood Hills; RMC Place; DOUGLAS; ***159** F-14; ★ **DEN**; mail Parker z 80134; ● 210
Livermore; RMC Place; LARIMER; **159** B-13; elev. 5,900ft./1,798m.; 🅿; z 80536; ● 60
Lobatos; RMC Place; CONEJOS; ***159** N-11; elev. 7,786ft./2,373m.; mail Antonito z 81120
Lochbuie; Inc. Place; WELD; **159** E-14; elev. 5,020ft./1,530m.; 🅿; ★ **DEN**; z 80603 & mail Brighton z 80601; Ⓟ 1,168; Ⓒ 2,049
Lochwood; RMC Place; JEFFERSON; ★ **DEN**; mail Denver z 80232; pop. incl. with Lakewood (Inc. Place)
LOGAN; **159** B-17; Ⓟ 17,567; Ⓒ 20,504; Ⓡ 20,574; ◆ 21,366
Loghill Village; CDP-Census Area Only; OURAY; ***158** J-7; Ⓒ 311
Log Lane Village; Inc. Place; MORGAN; **159** D-16; elev. 4,350ft./1,326m.; 🅿; z 80705; Ⓟ 667; Ⓒ 1,006
Loma; RMC Place; MESA; **158** G-4; elev. 4,511ft./1,375m.; 🅿; z 81524; ● 400
Loma Linda; RMC Place; LA PLATA; ***158** M-7; mail Durango z 81303; rural
Lombard Village; RMC Place; PUEBLO; **159** J-15; ★ **PUEB**; mail Pueblo z 81006; ● 600
Lone Pine Estates; RMC Place; JEFFERSON; ***159** F-13; ★ **DEN**; mail Morrison z 80465; ● 300
Lone Star; RMC Place; WASHINGTON; ***159** C-18; mail Otis z 80743; rural
Lonetree; RMC Place; ARCHULETA; ***158** M-8; mail Pagosa Springs z 81147; rural
Lone Tree; Inc. Place; DOUGLAS; ***159** F-14; 🅿; ★ **DEN**; z 80124 & mail Englewood z 80112; Ⓒ 4,873
Longmont; Inc. Place; BOULDER, WELD; **159** D-13; elev. 4,978ft./1,517m.; 🅿 🅷 ■; ★ **BOUL-**; z 80501-04; Ⓟ 51,529; Ⓒ 71,093; ◆ 92,479
Lookout Mountain; RMC Place; JEFFERSON; ***159** E-13; mail Golden z 80401; ● 350
Loretto Heights; RMC Place; DENVER; ***159** F-13; ★ **DEN**; mail Denver z 80236; pop. incl. with Denver (Inc. Place)
Los Fuertes; RMC Place; COSTILLA; ***159** M-12; mail San Luis z 81152; ● 80
Los Sauces; CONEJOS; see Lasauses (RMC Place)
Louisville; Inc. Place; BOULDER; **159** E-13; elev. 5,337ft./1,627m.; 🅿 🅷; ★ **BOUL-**; z 80027-28; Ⓟ 12,363; Ⓒ 18,937
Louviers; CDP; DOUGLAS; **159** F-13; elev. 5,680ft./1,731m.; 🅿; ★ **DEN**; z 80131; Ⓒ 237
Loveland; Inc. Place; LARIMER; **159** C-13; elev. 4,982ft./1,519m.; 🅿 🅷 ■; ★ **FTCL-**; z 80534, z 80537-39; Ⓟ 37,352; Ⓒ 50,608; ◆ 65,626
Loveland Heights; RMC Place; LARIMER; ***159** C-12; mail Drake z 80515; ● 30
Lowe; RMC Place; WELD; ***159** C-14; mail Eaton z 80615; rural
Lubers; RMC Place; BENT; ***159** J-18; elev. 3,875ft./1,181m.; mail Mc Clave z 81057; rural
Lucerne; RMC Place; WELD; **159** C-14; elev. 4,750ft./1,448m.; 🅿; z 80646; ● 160
Ludlow; RMC Place; LAS ANIMAS; ***159** M-14; elev. 6,277ft./1,913m.; mail Trinidad z 81082; rural
Lupton; WELD; see Fort Lupton (Inc. Place)
Lycan; RMC Place; BACA; ***159** L-20; 🅿; z 81084; rural
Lyons; Inc. Place; BOULDER; **159** D-13; elev. 5,360ft./1,634m.; 🅿; z 80540; Ⓟ 1,227; Ⓒ 1,585
Lyons Park Estates; RMC Place; BOULDER; ***159** D-13; mail Lyons z 80540; ● 140

M

Mack; RMC Place; MESA; **158** G-4; elev. 4,520ft./1,378m.; 🅿; z 81525; ● 240
Mad Creek; RMC Place; ROUTT; ***158** C-9; mail Steamboat Springs z 80487; rural
Madison Hill; RMC Place; JEFFERSON; ★ **DEN**; mail Westminster z 80030; pop. incl. with Westminster (Inc. Place)
Madrid; RMC Place; LAS ANIMAS; ***159** M-14; mail Trinidad z 81082; rural
Magnolia; RMC Place; BOULDER; ***159** E-13; ★ **BOUL-**; mail Nederland z 80466; rural
Maher; RMC Place; MONTROSE; **158** I-7; elev. 6,800ft./2,073m.; 🅿; z 81415; ● 100
Manassa; Inc. Place; CONEJOS; **159** M-11; elev. 7,683ft./2,342m.; 🅿; z 81141; Ⓟ 988; Ⓒ 1,042
Mancos; Inc. Place; MONTEZUMA; **158** M-5; elev. 7,030ft./2,143m.; 🅿; z 81328; Ⓟ 842; Ⓒ 1,119
Mandalay Gardens (Churches); RMC Place; JEFFERSON; ***159** E-13; mail Broomfield z 80021; ● 290
Manitou; EL PASO; see Manitou Springs (Inc. Place)
Manitou Springs (Manitou); Inc. Place; EL PASO; **159** H-14; elev. 6,320ft./1,926m.; 🅿; ★ **CSPG**; z 80829; Ⓟ 4,535; Ⓒ 4,980
Manzanola; Inc. Place; OTERO; **159** J-16; elev. 4,252ft./1,296m.; 🅿; z 81058; Ⓟ 437; Ⓒ 525
Marble; Inc. Place; GUNNISON; **158** G-8; elev. 7,960ft./2,426m.; 🅿; z 81623; Ⓟ 64; Ⓒ 105
Marshall; RMC Place; BOULDER; ***159** E-13; elev. 5,509ft./1,679m.; ★ **BOUL-**; mail Boulder z 80302; ● 230
Marshdale (Marshdale Park); RMC Place; JEFFERSON; ***159** F-13; ★ **DEN**; mail Evergreen z 80439; ● 770
Marshdale Park; JEFFERSON; see Marshdale (RMC Place)
Marvel; RMC Place; LA PLATA; **158** M-6; elev. 6,726ft./2,050m.; 🅿; z 81329; ● 65
Mary Jane; RMC Place; GRAND; ***159** E-12; elev. 10,200ft./3,109m.; mail Walden z 80480; pop. incl. with Winter Park (Inc. Place)
Maryvale; RMC Place; GRAND; ***159** E-12; mail Fraser z 80442; pop. incl. with Fraser (Inc. Place)
Mason Corner; RMC Place; WELD; ***159** C-14; elev. 4,730ft./1,442m.; mail Greeley z 80631; rural
Masonic Park; RMC Place; RIO GRANDE; **158** L-9; mail South Fork z 81154; ● 50
Masonville; RMC Place; LARIMER; **159** C-13; elev. 5,380ft./1,640m.; 🅿; z 80541; ● 140
Massadona; RMC Place; MOFFAT; ***158** D-5; mail Dinosaur z 81610; rural
Masters; RMC Place; WELD; ***159** D-15; elev. 4,454ft./1,358m.; mail Orchard z 80649; rural
Matheson; RMC Place; ELBERT; **159** G-16; elev. 5,785ft./1,763m.; 🅿; z 80830
Maxeyville; RMC Place; RIO GRANDE; ***159** L-11; elev. 7,670ft./2,338m.; mail Monte Vista z 81144; rural
Maybell; RMC Place; MOFFAT; **158** C-6; elev. 5,920ft./1,804m.; 🅿; z 81640; ● 100
Mayday; RMC Place; LA PLATA; ***158** M-6; mail Hesperus z 81326
Maysville; RMC Place; CHAFFEE; **159** I-11; elev. 8,225ft./2,507m.; mail Salida z 81201
May Valley; RMC Place; PROWERS; ***159** J-19; mail Lamar z 81052; rural
McClave; RMC Place; BENT; **159** J-19; elev. 3,860ft./1,177m.; 🅿; z 81057; ● 190
McClellands; RMC Place; LARIMER; ★ **FTCL-**; mail Fort Collins z 80521; pop. incl. with Fort Collins (Inc. Place)
McCoy; RMC Place; EAGLE; **158** E-9; elev. 6,690ft./2,039m.; 🅿; z 80463; ● 80
Mead; Inc. Place; WELD; **159** D-13; elev. 5,001ft./1,524m.; 🅿; z 80542; Ⓟ 456; Ⓒ 2,017
Meadow Brook Heights; RMC Place; JEFFERSON; mail Littleton z 80120; ● 400
Meadowood; RMC Place; ARAPAHOE; ★ **DEN**; mail Aurora z 80013; pop. incl. with Aurora (Inc. Place)
Meeker; Inc. Place; ⊡ RIO BLANCO; **158** D-6; elev. 6,239ft./1,902m.; 🅿 🅷; z 81641; Ⓟ 2,098; Ⓒ 2,242
Meeker Park; RMC Place; BOULDER; **159** D-12; elev. 8,489ft./2,587m.; mail Allenspark z 80510; ● 120
Merchant Station; RMC Place; DENVER; ★ **DEN**; mail Denver z 80202; pop. incl. with Denver (Inc. Place)
Meredith; RMC Place; PITKIN; **158** G-9; elev. 7,800ft./2,377m.; 🅿; z 81642
Meridian; CDP-Census Area Only; DOUGLAS; ***159** F-14; ★ **DEN**; Ⓒ 184
Merino; Inc. Place; LOGAN; **159** C-17; elev. 4,035ft./1,230m.; 🅿; z 80741; Ⓟ 238; Ⓒ 246
Mesa; RMC Place; MESA; **158** G-6; elev. 5,639ft./1,719m.; 🅿; z 81643 & mail Pueblo z 81004; ● 240
Mesa; RMC Place; PUEBLO; 🅿; ★ **PUEB**; z 81643 & mail Pueblo z 81004, z 81006; pop. incl. with Pueblo (Inc. Place)
MESA; **158** H-5; Ⓟ 93,145; Ⓒ 116,255; Ⓡ 116,935; ◆ 149,200
Mesa Lakes (Skyway); RMC Place; MESA; **158** G-6; mail Mesa z 81643; ● 30
Mesita; RMC Place; COSTILLA; **159** N-12; elev. 7,668ft./2,337m.; 🅿; z 81152; ● 50
Messex; RMC Place; WASHINGTON; ***159** C-17; mail Merino z 80741
Midland; RMC Place; TELLER; ***159** H-13; mail Divide z 80814; ● 180
Midtown; RMC Place; PUEBLO; mail Pueblo z 81003, z 81008; pop. incl. with Pueblo (Inc. Place)
Midway; RMC Place; LARIMER; ***159** C-13; mail Loveland z 80537; rural
Mile High; RMC Place; DENVER; mail Denver z 80204; pop. incl. with Denver (Inc. Place)
Milliken; Inc. Place; WELD; **159** D-14; elev. 4,750ft./1,448m.; 🅿; z 80543; Ⓟ 1,605; Ⓒ 2,888
Milner; RMC Place; ROUTT; **158** C-9; elev. 6,530ft./1,990m.; mail Steamboat Springs z 80487; ● 200
MINERAL; **158** L-9; Ⓟ 558; Ⓒ 831; ◆ 1,022
Mineral Hot Springs; RMC Place; SAGUACHE; ***159** J-11; mail Moffat z 81143; rural
Minnequa; RMC Place; PUEBLO; ★ **PUEB**; mail Pueblo z 81004; pop. incl. with Pueblo (Inc. Place)
Minnequa Heights; RMC Place; PUEBLO; ★ **PUEB**; mail Pueblo z 81004; pop. incl. with Pueblo (Inc. Place)
Minturn; Inc. Place; EAGLE; **158** F-10; elev. 7,840ft./2,390m.; 🅿; z 81645; Ⓟ 1,066; Ⓒ 1,068
Mission Viejo; RMC Place; ARAPAHOE; ★ **DEN**; mail Aurora z 80013; pop. incl. with Aurora (Inc. Place)
Model; RMC Place; LAS ANIMAS; **159** M-15; elev. 5,610ft./1,710m.; 🅿; z 81059; ● 110
Moffat; Inc. Place; SAGUACHE; **159** K-11; elev. 7,561ft./2,305m.; 🅿; z 81143; Ⓟ 99; Ⓒ 114
MOFFAT; **158** B-7; Ⓟ 11,357; Ⓒ 13,184; ◆ 14,231
Mogote; RMC Place; CONEJOS; **159** N-11; mail Antonito z 81120; ● 85
Molina; RMC Place; MESA; **158** G-6; elev. 5,614ft./1,711m.; 🅿; z 81646; ● 90
Monarch; CHAFFEE; see Garfield (RMC Place)
Montbello; RMC Place; DENVER; ***159** E-14; elev. 5,312ft./1,619m.; 🅿; ★ **DEN**; z 80238 & mail Denver z 80249; pop. incl. with Denver (Inc. Place)
Montclair; RMC Place; DENVER; ***159** E-14; 🅿; ★ **DEN**; z 80230 & mail Denver z 80220; pop. incl. with Denver (Inc. Place)
Monte Vista; Inc. Place; RIO GRANDE; **159** L-11; elev. 7,663ft./2,336m.; 🅿; z 81135, z 81144; Ⓟ 4,324; Ⓒ 4,529
Monte Vista Estates; RMC Place; DOUGLAS; ***159** G-14; ★ **DEN**; mail Castle Rock z 80109; ● 120
Montezuma; Inc. Place; SUMMIT; **159** F-11; elev. 10,300ft./3,139m.; 🅿; z 80435; Ⓟ 60; Ⓒ 42
MONTEZUMA; **158** L-5; Ⓟ 18,672; Ⓒ 23,830; ◆ 25,729
Montrose; Inc. Place; ⊡ MONTROSE; **158** I-7; elev. 5,806ft./1,770m.; 🅿 🅷; z 81401-03; Ⓟ 8,854; Ⓒ 12,344
MONTROSE; **158** J-5; Ⓟ 24,423; Ⓒ 33,432; ◆ 42,303
Monument; Inc. Place; EL PASO; **159** G-14; elev. 6,961ft./2,122m.; 🅿; ★ **CSPG**; z 80132; Ⓟ 1,020; Ⓒ 1,971
Morgan; RMC Place; CONEJOS; ***159** M-11; mail La Jara z 81140; rural
MORGAN; **159** D-16; Ⓟ 21,939; Ⓒ 27,171; ◆ 27,792
Morrison; Inc. Place; JEFFERSON; **159** F-13; elev. 5,800ft./1,768m.; 🅿; ★ **DEN**; z 80465; Ⓟ 465; Ⓒ 430
Mosca; RMC Place; ALAMOSA; **159** L-11; elev. 7,555ft./2,303m.; 🅿; z 81146; ● 130
Mountain View; Inc. Place; JEFFERSON; **157** H-6; elev. 5,379ft./1,640m.; ★ **DEN**; mail Denver z 80212; Ⓟ 550; Ⓒ 569
Mountain View (Fort Collins West); RMC Place; LARIMER; ***159** C-13; ★ **FTCL-**; mail Fort Collins z 80521; ● 1,700
Mountain View Acres; RMC Place; ALAMOSA; mail Alamosa z 81101; rural
Mountain View Lakes; RMC Place; JEFFERSON; ***159** F-12; mail Pine z 80470; ● 220
Mountain Village; Inc. Place; SAN MIGUEL; ***158** K-6; 🅿; z 81435; Ⓒ 978
Mount Crested Butte; Inc. Place; GUNNISON; **158** H-9; elev. 9,280ft./2,829m.; mail Crested Butte z 81225; Ⓟ 264; Ⓒ 707
Mount Massive Lakes; RMC Place; LAKE; ***158** G-10; mail Leadville z 80461; ● 30
Mount Princeton; CHAFFEE; see Mount Princeton Hot Springs (RMC Place)
Mount Princeton Hot Springs (Mount Princeton); RMC Place; CHAFFEE; **159** H-11; mail Nathrop z 81236; summer pop. 130; ● 50
Mount Vernon Club Place; RMC Place; JEFFERSON; ***159** E-13; ★ **DEN**; mail Golden z 80401; ● 465
Mutual; RMC Place; HUERFANO; ***159** L-14; mail Walsenburg z 81089

N

Naturita; Inc. Place; MONTROSE; **158** J-5; elev. 5,431ft./1,655m.; 🅿; z 81422; Ⓟ 434; Ⓒ 635
Nederland; Inc. Place; BOULDER; **159** E-12; elev. 8,233ft./2,509m.; 🅿; z 80466; Ⓟ 1,099; Ⓒ 1,394
Nepesta; RMC Place; PUEBLO; ***159** J-16; mail Boone z 81025; rural
Nevadaville; RMC Place; GILPIN; ***159** E-12; mail Central City z 80427; rural
New Castle; Inc. Place; GARFIELD; **158** F-7; elev. 5,580ft./1,701m.; 🅿; z 81647; Ⓟ 679; Ⓒ 1,984
New Raymer; WELD; see Raymer (Inc. Place)
Nighthawk; RMC Place; DOUGLAS; ***159** G-13; mail Sedalia z 80135; rural
Ninaview; RMC Place; BENT; ***159** L-18; elev. 4,432ft./1,351m.; 🅿; z 81054; rural
Ninemile Corner; RMC Place; BOULDER; ***159** E-13; elev. 5,250ft./1,600m.; ★ **BOUL-**; mail Lafayette z 80026
Niwot; CDP; BOULDER; **159** D-13; elev. 5,095ft./1,553m.; 🅿; ★ **BOUL-**; z 80504, z 80544 & mail Longmont z 80503; Ⓟ 2,666; Ⓒ 4,160
Nob Hill; RMC Place; ARAPAHOE; ***159** F-14; ★ **DEN**; mail Littleton z 80122; ● 1,400
North Avondale; RMC Place; PUEBLO; **159** J-15; elev. 4,516ft./1,376m.; 🅿; z 81022; ● 50
North Cherry Creek Valley; RMC Place; ARAPAHOE; ***159** F-14; ★ **DEN**; mail Denver z 80231; ● 1,550
North Delta; RMC Place; DELTA; ***158** H-6; mail Delta z 81416; pop. incl. with Delta (Inc. Place)
North End; RMC Place; EL PASO; ***159** H-14; ★ **CSPG**; mail Colorado Springs z 80907, z 80933; pop. incl. with Colorado Springs (Inc. Place)
Northglenn; Inc. Place; ADAMS, WELD; **157** F-7; 🅿 ■; ★ **DEN**; z 80233-34, z 80241, z 80260, z 80603 & mail Denver z 80221; Ⓟ 27,195; Ⓒ 31,575; ◆ 38,433
North La Junta; RMC Place; OTERO; ***159** K-17; mail La Junta z 81050
North Pecos; RMC Place; ADAMS; ***159** E-13; elev. 5,250ft./1,600m.; ★ **DEN**; mail Denver z 80221
North Pole; RMC Place; EL PASO; ***159** H-14; elev. 7,600ft./2,316m.; ★ **CSPG**; mail Cascade z 80809; pop. incl. with Colorado Springs (Inc. Place)
North Washington; CDP-Census Area Only; ADAMS; ***159** E-13; ★ **DEN**; Ⓒ 549
North Washington Heights; RMC Place; ADAMS; ***159** E-13; ★ **DEN**; mail Denver z 80229; ● 1,500
North Yard; RMC Place; DENVER; ***159** E-13; ★ **DEN**; pop. incl. with Denver (Inc. Place)
Norwood; Inc. Place; SAN MIGUEL; **158** J-5; elev. 7,006ft./2,135m.; 🅿; z 81423; Ⓟ 429; Ⓒ 438
Nucla; Inc. Place; MONTROSE; **158** J-5; elev. 5,820ft./1,774m.; 🅿; z 81424; Ⓟ 656; Ⓒ 734
Numa; RMC Place; CROWLEY; ***159** J-16; mail Ordway z 81063; rural
Nunn; Inc. Place; WELD; **159** B-14; elev. 5,185ft./1,580m.; 🅿; z 80648; Ⓟ 324; Ⓒ 471
Nutria; RMC Place; ARCHULETA; ***158** M-8; mail Pagosa Springs z 81147; rural

O

Oak Creek; Inc. Place; ROUTT; **158** D-9; elev. 7,414ft./2,260m.; 🅿; z 80467; Ⓟ 673; Ⓒ 849
Oak Grove; RMC Place; MONTROSE; ***158** I-6; mail Montrose z 81401; ● 175
Oehlmann Park; RMC Place; JEFFERSON; ***159** F-13; ★ **DEN**; mail Conifer z 80433; ● 220
Ohio (Ohio City); RMC Place; GUNNISON; ***158** I-10; elev. 8,583ft./2,616m.; mail Ohio City z 81237; ● 40
Ohio City; GUNNISON; see Ohio (RMC Place)
Olathe; Inc. Place; MONTROSE; **158** I-6; elev. 5,356ft./1,633m.; 🅿; z 81425; Ⓟ 1,263; Ⓒ 1,573
Old Town Station; RMC Place; LARIMER; mail Fort Collins z 80522; pop. incl. with Fort Collins (Inc. Place)
Olney Springs; Inc. Place; CROWLEY; **159** J-16; elev. 4,370ft./1,332m.; 🅿; z 81062; Ⓟ 340; Ⓒ 389
Olympus Heights; RMC Place; LARIMER; ***159** C-12; mail Drake z 80515; ● 120
Ophir; Inc. Place; SAN MIGUEL; **158** K-7; elev. 9,680ft./2,950m.; 🅿; z 81426; Ⓟ 69; Ⓒ 113
Orchard; RMC Place; MORGAN; **159** D-15; elev. 4,407ft./1,343m.; 🅿; z 80649; ● 120
Orchard City; Inc. Place; DELTA; **158** H-6; elev. 5,440ft./1,658m.; 🅿; z 81410 & mail Cory z 81414, Eckert z 81418; Ⓟ 2,218; Ⓒ 2,880
Orchard Mesa; CDP; MESA; **158** G-5; ★ **GDJC**; mail Grand Junction z 81501; Ⓟ 5,977; Ⓒ 6,456
Orchard Park; RMC Place; FREMONT; ***159** I-13; mail Canon City z 81212; ● 1,300
Ordway; Inc. Place; ⊡ CROWLEY; **159** J-16; elev. 4,312ft./1,314m.; 🅿; z 81063; Ⓟ 1,025; Ⓒ 1,248
Ormandale; RMC Place; PUEBLO; ★ **PUEB**; mail Pueblo z 81005; ● 160
Orodell; RMC Place; BOULDER; ***159** E-13; mail Boulder z 80302; ● 150
Orsa; RMC Place; DOUGLAS; ***159** F-14; mail Sedalia z 80135; ● 400
Ortiz; RMC Place; CONEJOS; **159** N-11; mail Antonito z 81120; ● 60
OTERO; **159** K-16; Ⓟ 20,185; Ⓒ 20,311; ◆ 18,427
Otis; Inc. Place; WASHINGTON; **159** D-18; elev. 4,335ft./1,321m.; 🅿; z 80743; Ⓟ 451; Ⓒ 534
Ouray; Inc. Place; ⊡ OURAY; **158** K-7; elev. 7,811ft./2,381m.; 🅿; z 81427; Ⓟ 644; Ⓒ 813
OURAY; **158** J-7; Ⓟ 2,295; Ⓒ 3,742; ◆ 4,716
Ovid; Inc. Place; SEDGWICK; **159** B-19; elev. 3,521ft./1,073m.; 🅿; z 80744; Ⓟ 349; Ⓒ 330
Oxford; RMC Place; LA PLATA; ***158** M-7; elev. 6,595ft./2,010m.; mail Ignacio z 81137; ● 90

P

Pactolus; RMC Place; GILPIN; ***159** E-12; mail Golden z 80403; ● 120
Padroni; CDP; LOGAN; **159** B-18; elev. 4,000ft./1,219m.; 🅿; z 80745; Ⓒ 97
Pagosa Junction (Gato); RMC Place; ARCHULETA; **158** N-8; mail Pagosa Springs z 81147; ● 25
Pagosa Springs; Inc. Place; ⊡ ARCHULETA; **158** M-8; elev. 7,105ft./2,166m.; 🅿; z 81147, z 81157; Ⓟ 1,207; Ⓒ 1,591
Paisaje (San Rafael); RMC Place; CONEJOS; ***159** N-11; mail Antonito z 81120; rural
Palisade; Inc. Place; MESA; **158** G-5; elev. 4,720ft./1,439m.; 🅿; ★ **GDJC**; z 81526; Ⓟ 1,871; Ⓒ 2,579
Palmer Lake; Inc. Place; EL PASO; **159** G-14; elev. 7,240ft./2,207m.; 🅿; ★ **CSPG**; z 80133 & mail Larkspur z 80118; Ⓟ 1,480; Ⓒ 2,179
Palos Verdes; RMC Place; ARAPAHOE; ***159** F-14; ★ **DEN**; mail Littleton z 80123; ● 1,850
Palos Verdes East; RMC Place; ARAPAHOE; ***159** F-14; ★ **DEN**; mail Englewood z 80110; ● 860
Pandora; RMC Place; SAN MIGUEL; ***158** K-7; mail Telluride z 81435
Panorama Heights; RMC Place; JEFFERSON; ***159** E-13; ★ **DEN**; mail Golden z 80401; ● 175
Panoview Park; RMC Place; GUNNISON; ***158** I-9; mail Gunnison z 81230
Paoli; Inc. Place; PHILLIPS; **159** C-19; elev. 3,898ft./1,188m.; 🅿; z 80746; Ⓟ 29; Ⓒ 42
Paonia; Inc. Place; DELTA; **158** H-7; elev. 5,645ft./1,721m.; 🅿; z 81428; Ⓟ 1,403; Ⓒ 1,497
Parachute (Grand Valley); Inc. Place; GARFIELD; **158** F-6; elev. 5,090ft./1,551m.; 🅿; z 81635-36; Ⓟ 658; Ⓒ 1,006
Paradise Hills; RMC Place; JEFFERSON; ***159** E-13; mail Golden z 80401; ● 600
Paradox; RMC Place; MONTROSE; **158** I-4; elev. 5,299ft./1,615m.; 🅿; z 81429; ● 70
Paragon Estates; RMC Place; BOULDER; ***159** E-13; elev. 5,450ft./1,661m.; ★ **BOUL-**; mail Boulder z 80303; ● 380
PARK; **159** G-12; Ⓟ 7,174; Ⓒ 14,523; ◆ 17,581
Park Center; RMC Place; FREMONT; ***159** I-13; mail Canon City z 81212; ● 520
Parkdale; RMC Place; FREMONT; ***159** I-13; mail Canon City z 81212; rural
Parker; Inc. Place; DOUGLAS; **159** F-14; elev. 5,865ft./1,788m.; 🅿; ★ **DEN**; z 80134, z 80138; Ⓟ 5,450; Ⓒ 23,558; ◆ 51,039
Park Hill; RMC Place; DENVER; ***159** E-14; ★ **DEN**; mail Denver z 80207; pop. incl. with Denver (Inc. Place)
Park Vista; EL PASO; see Park Vista Estates (RMC Place)
Park Vista Estates (Park Vista); RMC Place; EL PASO; ***159** H-14; ★ **CSPG**; mail Colorado Springs z 80908; ● 620
Parlin; RMC Place; GUNNISON; **158** I-9; elev. 7,939ft./2,420m.; 🅿; z 81239 & mail Ohio City z 81237; ● 50
Parshall; RMC Place; GRAND; **159** D-11; elev. 7,560ft./2,304m.; 🅿; z 80468; ● 130
Peaceful Valley; RMC Place; BOULDER; ***159** D-12; mail Lyons z 80540; ● 35
Peagreen; MONTROSE; see Pea Green Corner (RMC Place)
Pea Green Corner (Peagreen); RMC Place; MONTROSE; ***158** I-6; mail Delta z 81416
Peak Seven West; RMC Place; SUMMIT; ***159** F-11; elev. 9,800ft./2,987m.; mail Breckenridge z 80424; ● 580
Pearl; RMC Place; JACKSON; ***158** B-10; mail Cowdrey z 80434; rural
Peckham; RMC Place; WELD; ***159** D-14; elev. 4,729ft./1,441m.; mail La Salle z 80645; ● 135
Peetz; Inc. Place; LOGAN; **159** B-18; elev. 4,432ft./1,351m.; 🅿; z 80747; Ⓟ 179; Ⓒ 227
Penrose; CDP; FREMONT; **159** I-13; elev. 5,300ft./1,615m.; 🅿; z 81240; Ⓟ 2,235; Ⓒ 4,070
Perry Park; CDP-Census Area Only; DOUGLAS; ***159** G-13; Ⓒ 1,180
Peyton; RMC Place; EL PASO; **159** H-15; elev. 6,780ft./2,067m.; 🅿; z 80831; ● 200
Pheasant Run; RMC Place; ARAPAHOE; ★ **DEN**; mail Aurora z 80015; pop. incl. with Aurora (Inc. Place)
PHILLIPS; **159** C-20; Ⓟ 4,189; Ⓒ 4,480; ◆ 4,419
Phillipsburg; RMC Place; JEFFERSON; ***159** F-13; mail Littleton z 80127; rural
Phippsburg; RMC Place; ROUTT; **158** D-9; elev. 7,424ft./2,263m.; 🅿; z 80469; ● 220
Piedra; RMC Place; ARCHULETA; ***158** M-8; mail Chimney Rock z 81127, Pagosa Springs z 81147; rural
Pierce; Inc. Place; WELD; **159** C-14; elev. 5,039ft./1,536m.; 🅿; z 80650; Ⓟ 823; Ⓒ 884
Pike-San Isabel Village; RMC Place; PARK; ***159** H-12; mail Hartsel z 80449; rural
Pikes Peak Park; RMC Place; EL PASO; ★ **CSPG**; pop. incl. with Colorado Springs (Inc. Place)
Pikeview; RMC Place; EL PASO; ***159** H-14; elev. 6,442ft./1,964m.; ★ **CSPG**; pop. incl. with Colorado Springs (Inc. Place)
Pine; JEFFERSON; see Pine Grove (RMC Place)
Pine Brook Hill (Pinebrook Hills); RMC Place; BOULDER; ***159** D-13; elev. 6,800ft./2,073m.; ★ **BOUL-**; mail Boulder z 80302; ● 400
Pinebrook Hills; BOULDER; see Pine Brook Hill (RMC Place)
Pinecliffe (Cliff); RMC Place; BOULDER, GILPIN; ***159** E-12; elev. 8,000ft./2,438m.; 🅿; z 80471; ● 210
Pine Crest; RMC Place; EL PASO; ***159** G-14; ★ **CSPG**; mail Palmer Lake z 80133; pop. incl. with Palmer Lake (Inc. Place)
Pine Grove (Pine); RMC Place; JEFFERSON; **159** F-13; elev. 6,754ft./2,059m.; mail Pine z 80470; ● 150
Pinehaven; RMC Place; HUERFANO; ***159** M-13; mail La Veta z 81055; rural
Pine Hills; RMC Place; EL PASO; ***159** G-14; elev. 7,020ft./2,140m.; ★ **CSPG**; mail Monument z 80132; ● 265
Pine Junction; RMC Place; JEFFERSON; ***159** F-12; mail Pine z 80470; ● 100
Pine Knott; LARIMER; see Glen Comfort (RMC Place)
Pine Nook; RMC Place; DOUGLAS; ***159** F-13; elev. 7,320ft./2,231m.; mail Sedalia z 80135; rural
Pine Park Estates; RMC Place; JEFFERSON; ***159** F-13; mail Morrison z 80465; ● 220
Pinewood Springs; RMC Place; LARIMER; ***159** D-13; mail Lyons z 80540; ● 230
Pinnacle Park; RMC Place; WELD; ***159** C-14; mail Greeley z 80631; ● 185
Piñon; RMC Place; PUEBLO; ***159** I-14; mail Pueblo z 81008
Piñon Acres; RMC Place; LA PLATA; ***158** M-6; mail Durango z 81301; ● 130
Pinon Canyon; RMC Place; LAS ANIMAS; ***159** M-16; mail Model z 81059, Trinidad z 81082; ● 50
Pinon Hills; RMC Place; CHAFFEE; ***159** I-11; mail Salida z 81201; ● 230
Pitkin; Inc. Place; GUNNISON; **158** I-10; elev. 9,241ft./2,817m.; 🅿; z 81241; Ⓟ 53; Ⓒ 124
PITKIN; **158** G-9; Ⓟ 12,661; Ⓒ 14,872; ◆ 15,388
Placerville; RMC Place; SAN MIGUEL; **158** K-6; elev. 7,300ft./2,225m.; 🅿; z 81430; ● 250
Plateau City; RMC Place; MESA; **158** G-6; elev. 5,960ft./1,817m.; mail Collbran z 81624; pop. incl. with Collbran (Inc. Place)
Platner; RMC Place; WASHINGTON; **159** D-18; elev. 4,432ft./1,351m.; mail Otis z 80743; ● 35
Platoro; RMC Place; CONEJOS; **158** M-10; mail Monte Vista z 81144; ● 100
Platte Springs; RMC Place; PARK; ***159** G-13; mail Lake George z 80827; rural
Platteville; Inc. Place; WELD; **159** D-14; elev. 4,825ft./1,471m.; 🅿; z 80651; Ⓟ 1,515; Ⓒ 2,370
Plaza; RMC Place; RIO GRANDE; mail Del Norte z 81132; rural
Pleasant Valley; RMC Place; EL PASO; ***159** H-14; ★ **CSPG**; mail Colorado Springs z 80904; pop. incl. with Colorado Springs (Inc. Place)
Pleasant View; RMC Place; JEFFERSON; ***159** E-13; elev. 5,768ft./1,758m.; ★ **DEN**; mail Golden z 80401; ● 2,050
Pleasant View; RMC Place; MONTEZUMA; **158** L-4; elev. 6,920ft./2,109m.; 🅿; z 81331; ● 80
Pleasant View Ridge; RMC Place; BOULDER; ***159** D-13; mail Longmont z 80504; rural
Poncha Springs; Inc. Place; CHAFFEE; **159** I-11; elev. 7,465ft./2,275m.; 🅿; z 81242; Ⓟ 244; Ⓒ 466
Ponderosa Hills; RMC Place; DOUGLAS; ***159** F-14; ★ **DEN**; mail Parker z 80134; ● 900
Ponderosa Park; CDP; ELBERT; ***159** F-14; elev. 6,603ft./2,013m.; mail Elizabeth z 80107; Ⓟ 1,640; Ⓒ 3,112
Poudre Park; RMC Place; LARIMER; **159** B-13; elev. 5,676ft./1,730m.; mail Fort Collins z 80521; ● 100
Powars; RMC Place; WELD; ***159** D-14; mail Fort Lupton z 80621; ● 400
Powderhorn; RMC Place; GUNNISON; **158** J-8; elev. 8,080ft./2,463m.; 🅿; z 81243
Powder Wash; RMC Place; MOFFAT; **158** B-6; mail Rock Springs z 82901; ● 55
Pritchett; Inc. Place; BACA; **159** M-19; elev. 4,827ft./1,471m.; 🅿; z 81064; Ⓟ 153; Ⓒ 137
Proctor; RMC Place; LOGAN; ***159** B-18; mail Iliff z 80736
Prospect; WELD; see Prospect Valley (RMC Place)
Prospect Heights; RMC Place; FREMONT; ***159** I-13; elev. 5,440ft./1,658m.; mail Canon City z 81212; ● 260
Prospect Valley (Prospect); RMC Place; WELD; ***159** D-15; mail Keenesburg z 80643; ● 70
Prowers; RMC Place; BENT; ***159** J-19; elev. 3,684ft./1,123m.; mail Lamar z 81052
PROWERS; **159** K-20; Ⓟ 13,347; Ⓒ 14,483; ◆ 12,566
Pryor; RMC Place; HUERFANO; **159** L-14; elev. 6,420ft./1,957m.; mail Walsenburg z 81089; rural
Pueblo; Inc. Place; ⊡ PUEBLO; **159** J-14; elev. 4,662ft./1,421m.; 🅿 🅷 🅲 6,205 ■; ★ **PUEB**; z 81001-12; Ⓟ 98,640; Ⓒ 102,121; ◆ 101,461
PUEBLO; **159** K-15; Ⓟ 123,051; Ⓒ 141,472; ◆ 158,142
Pueblo West; CDP-Census Area Only; PUEBLO; **159** J-14; elev. 5,100ft./1,554m.; 🅿; ★ **PUEB**; z 81007; Ⓟ 4,386; Ⓒ 16,899
Pullman; RMC Place; DENVER; ★ **DEN**; pop. incl. with Denver (Inc. Place)
Pumkin Center; LINCOLN; see Punkin Center (RMC Place)
Punkin Center (Pumkin Center); RMC Place; LINCOLN; ***159** H-17; mail Hugo z 80821, Ordway z 81063; rural
Purcell; RMC Place; WELD; **159** C-14; elev. 5,019ft./1,530m.; mail Pierce z 80650; rural

Q

Quincy; RMC Place; ARAPAHOE; ★ **DEN**; mail Aurora z 80015; pop. incl. with Aurora (Inc. Place)

R

Radium; RMC Place; GRAND; ***158** E-10; mail Bond z 80423
Rainbow Valley; RMC Place; TELLER; ***159** H-13; mail Divide z 80814; ● 120
Ramah; Inc. Place; EL PASO; **159** G-15; elev. 6,120ft./1,865m.; 🅿; z 80832; Ⓟ 94; Ⓒ 117
Rand; RMC Place; JACKSON; **159** C-11; elev. 8,627ft./2,630m.; 🅿; z 80473
Rangely; Inc. Place; RIO BLANCO; **158** D-4; elev. 5,261ft./1,604m.; 🅿 🅷; z 81648; Ⓟ 2,278; Ⓒ 2,096
Rangeview Estates; RMC Place; BOULDER; ***159** D-13; mail Longmont z 80501; ● 420
Range View Estates; RMC Place; WELD; ★ **GRLY**; mail Greeley z 80631; ● 200
Raymer (New Raymer); Inc. Place; WELD; **159** C-16; elev. 4,770ft./1,454m.; mail New Raymer z 80742; Ⓟ 98; Ⓒ 91
Raymond; RMC Place; BOULDER; **159** D-12; mail Lyons z 80540; ● 60
Read; RMC Place; DELTA; ***158** H-6; mail Delta z 81416; rural
Red Cliff; Inc. Place; EAGLE; **158** F-10; elev. 8,800ft./2,682m.; 🅿; z 81649; Ⓟ 297; Ⓒ 289
Red Feather Lakes; CDP; LARIMER; **159** B-12; elev. 8,342ft./2,543m.; 🅿; z 80545 & mail Livermore z 80536; summer pop. 1,000; Ⓒ 525
Redlands; CDP; MESA; ***158** G-5; elev. 4,650ft./1,417m.; ★ **GDJC**; mail Grand Junction z 81503; Ⓟ 9,355; Ⓒ 8,043
Redmesa; RMC Place; LA PLATA; **158** M-6; mail Hesperus z 81326; ● 40
Redmond; RMC Place; LARIMER; ***159** C-13; mail Fort Collins z 80528; ● 370
Red Rock Ranch; RMC Place; EL PASO; ***159** G-14; elev. 7,400ft./2,256m.; ★ **CSPG**; mail Monument z 80132; ● 380
Redstone; RMC Place; PITKIN; **158** G-8; 🅿; z 81623; ● 100
Redvale; RMC Place; MONTROSE; **158** J-5; elev. 6,479ft./1,975m.; 🅿; z 81431; ● 220
Red Wing; RMC Place; HUERFANO; **159** L-13; elev. 7,720ft./2,353m.; ● 40
Rezago; RMC Place; LAS ANIMAS; mail Trinidad z 81082; rural
Richfield; RMC Place; CONEJOS; ***159** M-11; mail La Jara z 81140; rural
Rico; Inc. Place; DOLORES; **158** L-6; elev. 8,827ft./2,690m.; 🅿; z 81332; Ⓟ 92; Ⓒ 205
Ridgeview Hills; RMC Place; ARAPAHOE; ***159** F-14; ★ **DEN**; mail Littleton z 80122; ● 1,650
Ridgway; Inc. Place; OURAY; **158** J-7; elev. 6,985ft./2,129m.; 🅿; z 81432; Ⓟ 423; Ⓒ 713
Rifle; Inc. Place; GARFIELD; **158** F-7; elev. 5,345ft./1,629m.; 🅿 🅷; z 81650; Ⓟ 4,636; Ⓒ 6,784
Rinn; RMC Place; WELD; ***159** D-13; elev. 4,847ft./1,477m.; mail Longmont z 80504; rural
Rio Blanco; RMC Place; RIO BLANCO; ***158** E-6; elev. 7,253ft./2,211m.; mail Rifle z 81650; rural
RIO BLANCO; **158** E-5; Ⓟ 5,972; Ⓒ 5,986; ◆ 6,596
RIO GRANDE; **158** L-10; Ⓟ 10,770; Ⓒ 12,413; ◆ 11,238
Riverside; RMC Place; BOULDER; ***159** D-12; elev. 7,447ft./2,270m.; mail Lyons z 80540; seasonal pop. 200; ● 100
Roberta; RMC Place; OTERO; ***159** K-17; mail La Junta z 81050
Rockrimmon; RMC Place; EL PASO; mail Colorado Springs z 80908, z 80919-21, z 80949, z 80962; pop. incl. with Colorado Springs (Inc. Place)
Rockvale; Inc. Place; FREMONT; **159** J-13; elev. 5,460ft./1,664m.; 🅿; z 81244; Ⓟ 321; Ⓒ 426
Rocky Ford; Inc. Place; OTERO; **159** K-17; elev. 4,178ft./1,273m.; 🅿; z 81067; Ⓟ 4,162; Ⓒ 4,286
Rocky Mountain Station; RMC Place; DENVER; mail Denver z 80249; pop. incl. with Denver (Inc. Place)
Rogers Mesa; RMC Place; DELTA; ***158** H-7; mail Hotchkiss z 81419; ● 120
Roggen; RMC Place; WELD; **159** D-15; elev. 4,707ft./1,435m.; 🅿; z 80652; ● 130
Roland Valley; RMC Place; PARK; ***159** F-12; mail Pine z 80470; ● 200
Rolla; RMC Place; ADAMS; ***159** E-14; mail Henderson z 80640; pop. incl. with Commerce City (Inc. Place)
Rollins; GILPIN; see Rollinsville (RMC Place)
Rollinsville (Rollins); RMC Place; GILPIN; **159** E-12; elev. 8,400ft./2,560m.; 🅿; z 80474 & mail Golden z 80403; ● 150
Romeo; Inc. Place; CONEJOS; **159** M-11; elev. 7,735ft./2,358m.; 🅿; z 81148; Ⓟ 341; Ⓒ 375
Rosedale; RMC Place; JEFFERSON; ***159** F-12; ★ **DEN**; mail Evergreen z 80439; ● 220
Rosedale; RMC Place; WELD; ***159** C-14; elev. 4,700ft./1,433m.; ★ **GRLY**; mail Greeley z 80631; pop. incl. with Garden City (Inc. Place)
Rosita; RMC Place; CUSTER; ***159** J-13; mail Westcliffe z 81252; rural
Roswell; RMC Place; EL PASO; ***159** H-14; ★ **CSPG**; mail Colorado Springs z 80907; pop. incl. with Colorado Springs (Inc. Place)
ROUTT; **158** C-9; Ⓟ 14,088; Ⓒ 19,690; ◆ 23,575
Rowena; RMC Place; BOULDER; ***159** D-12; mail Jamestown z 80455
Roxborough Park; CDP-Census Area Only; DOUGLAS; **157** M-6; elev. 5,550ft./1,692m.; ★ **DEN**; mail Littleton z 80125; Ⓒ 4,446
Royal Gorge; RMC Place; FREMONT; **159** I-13; elev. 6,480ft./1,975m.; rural
Royal Ranch; RMC Place; PARK; mail Bailey z 80421; ● 50
Rulison; RMC Place; GARFIELD; ***158** F-6; elev. 5,186ft./1,581m.; mail Parachute z 81635, Rifle z 81650; rural
Rush; RMC Place; EL PASO; **159** H-16; elev. 6,019ft./1,835m.; 🅿; z 80833; ● 80
Russell Gulch; RMC Place; GILPIN; ***159** E-12; mail Central City z 80427; rural
Russellville (Russelville); RMC Place; DOUGLAS; ***159** G-14; mail Franktown z 80116; ● 240
Russelville; DOUGLAS; see Russellville (RMC Place)
Rustic Hills; RMC Place; EL PASO; ★ **CSPG**; pop. incl. with Colorado Springs (Inc. Place)
Rye; Inc. Place; PUEBLO; **159** K-14; elev. 6,800ft./2,073m.; 🅿; z 81069; Ⓟ 168; Ⓒ 202
Rye Ranchettes; RMC Place; PUEBLO; ***159** K-14; elev. 6,780ft./2,067m.; mail Rye z 81069; ● 100

S

Sable; RMC Place; ADAMS; ***159** E-14; elev. 5,331ft./1,625m.; ★ **DEN**; mail Aurora z 80011; pop. incl. with Aurora (Inc. Place)
Saguache; Inc. Place; ⊡ SAGUACHE; **159** J-11; elev. 7,694ft./2,345m.; 🅿; z 81149; Ⓟ 584; Ⓒ 578
SAGUACHE; **158** J-10; Ⓟ 4,619; Ⓒ 5,917; ◆ 6,910
Saint Charles Mesa; RMC Place; PUEBLO; ***159** J-15; ★ **PUEB**; mail Pueblo z 81006; ● 1,200
Saint Marys; CDP-Census Area Only; CLEAR CREEK; ***159** E-12; Ⓒ 251
Saint Petersburg; RMC Place; LOGAN; ***159** C-19; mail Fleming z 80728; rural
Salida; Inc. Place; ⊡ CHAFFEE; **159** I-11; elev. 7,036ft./2,145m.; 🅿 🅷; z 81201, z 81227, z 81237 & mail Granite z 81228, Twin Lakes z 81251; Ⓟ 4,737; Ⓒ 5,504
Salina; RMC Place; BOULDER; ***159** D-13; elev. 6,581ft./2,006m.; ★ **BOUL-**; mail Boulder z 80302; ● 165
Salt Creek; CDP; PUEBLO; ***159** J-14; ★ **PUEB**; mail Pueblo z 81006; Ⓒ 648
San Acacio; RMC Place; COSTILLA; **159** M-12; elev. 7,731ft./2,356m.; 🅿; z 81151; ● 70
San Antonio; RMC Place; CONEJOS; **159** N-11; elev. 7,938ft./2,420m.; mail Antonito z 81120; ● 190
Sandown; RMC Place; DENVER; ***159** E-14; ★ **DEN**; mail Denver z 80216; pop. incl. with Denver (Inc. Place)
Sanford; Inc. Place; CONEJOS; **159** M-11; elev. 7,600ft./2,316m.; 🅿; z 81151; Ⓟ 750; Ⓒ 817
San Francisco; COSTILLA; see La Valley (RMC Place)
Sangre De Cristo Ranches; RMC Place; COSTILLA; 🅿; z 81133
San Isabel; RMC Place; CUSTER; ***159** K-13; mail Rye z 81069; ● 50
San Juan; RMC Place; LAS ANIMAS; mail Trinidad z 81082; ● 40
SAN JUAN; **158** L-7; Ⓟ 745; Ⓒ 558; ◆ 542
San Luis; Inc. Place; ⊡ COSTILLA; **159** M-12; elev. 7,965ft./2,428m.; 🅿; z 81152; Ⓟ 800; Ⓒ 739
SAN MIGUEL; **158** J-5; Ⓟ 3,653; Ⓒ 6,594; ◆ 8,073
San Pablo; RMC Place; COSTILLA; **159** M-12; elev. 8,090ft./2,466m.; 🅿; z 81152; ● 170
San Rafael; CONEJOS; see Paisaje (RMC Place)
Santa Fe; RMC Place; PUEBLO; ***159** J-14; ★ **PUEB**; mail Pueblo z 81003; pop. incl. with Pueblo (Inc. Place)

Entries in **UPPERCASE** are counties.
Entries in **bold** have populations of 2,500 or more.
Names in parentheses are alternate names.

Inc. Place	Incorporated Place
RMC Place	Rand McNally Designated Place
CDP	Census Designated Place
MCD	Minor Civil Division
⊡	County Seat
▲	Minor Civil Division
elev.	Elevation
🅿	Post Office
🅷	Hospital
🅲	College
■	Principal Business Center
★	Ranally Metro Area (RMA) Abbreviation
z	Zip Code(s)
Ⓟ	Previous Census Population
Ⓡ	Revised Census Population
Ⓐ	Annexation Population
●	Rand McNally Population Estimate
Ⓒ	Final Census Population
Ⓢ	Special Census Population
◆	Estimated Population

For additional definitions see Glossary, Volume 1, and Introduction, Volume 2.

Sapinero; RMC Place; GUNNISON; **158** I-8; elev. 7,620ft./2,323m.; 🅿; z 81247
Sarcillo; RMC Place; LAS ANIMAS; ***159** M-14; mail Weston z 81091; rural
Sarcillo Canon; RMC Place; LAS ANIMAS; ***159** M-14; mail Weston z 81091; rural
Sargents; RMC Place; SAGUACHE; **158** I-10; elev. 8,477ft./2,584m.; 🅿; z 81248
Sargents School; RMC Place; RIO GRANDE; mail Monte Vista z 81144; rural
Satank (Sutank); RMC Place; GARFIELD; ***158** F-8; mail Carbondale z 81623; ● 440
Sawpit; Inc. Place; SAN MIGUEL; **158** K-6; elev. 7,560ft./2,304m.; mail Placerville z 81430, Telluride z 81435; Ⓟ 36; Ⓒ 25
Security; RMC Place; EL PASO; **159** H-14; elev. 5,740ft./1,750m.; ★ **CSPG**; mail Colorado Springs z 80911, z 80925, z 80931; ● 4,400
Security-Widefield; CDP-Census Area Only; EL PASO; ***159** H-14; ★ **CSPG**; mail Colorado Springs z 80911; Ⓟ 23,822; Ⓒ 29,845; ◆ 35,207
Sedalia; CDP; DOUGLAS; **159** F-14; elev. 5,824ft./1,775m.; 🅿; ★ **DEN**; z 80135; Ⓒ 211
Sedgwick; Inc. Place; SEDGWICK; **159** B-19; elev. 3,585ft./1,093m.; 🅿; z 80749; Ⓟ 183; Ⓒ 191
SEDGWICK; **159** B-20; Ⓟ 2,690; Ⓒ 2,747; ◆ 2,168
Segundo; RMC Place; LAS ANIMAS; **159** M-14; elev. 6,580ft./2,006m.; mail Trinidad z 81082; ● 110
Seibert; Inc. Place; KIT CARSON; **159** G-19; elev. 4,710ft./1,436m.; 🅿; z 80834; Ⓟ 181; Ⓒ 180
Severance; Inc. Place; WELD; **159** C-14; elev. 4,886ft./1,489m.; 🅿; z 80546; Ⓟ 106; Ⓒ 597
Shadow Mountain; RMC Place; GRAND; ***159** D-11; mail Grand Lake z 80447; ● 140
Shadow Mountain; RMC Place; JEFFERSON; ***159** F-13; ★ **DEN**; mail Conifer z 80433; ● 310
Shadows North; RMC Place; SUMMIT; ***159** F-11; elev. 9,732ft./2,966m.; mail Breckenridge z 80424; ● 200
Shaffers Crossing; RMC Place; JEFFERSON; ***159** F-13; elev. 7,920ft./2,414m.; mail Conifer z 80433, Rollinsville z 80474; rural
Shamballa Ashrama; DOUGLAS; see Shamballah-Ashrama (RMC Place)
Shamballah-Ashrama (Shamballa Ashrama); RMC Place; DOUGLAS; ***159** G-13; mail Sedalia z 80135; ● 230
Shaw Heights; RMC Place; ADAMS; ***159** E-13; ★ **DEN**; mail Westminster z 80030; ● 1,800
Shaw Heights Mesa; RMC Place; ADAMS; ***159** E-13; ★ **DEN**; mail Westminster z 80030
Shawnee; RMC Place; PARK; **159** F-12; elev. 8,150ft./2,484m.; 🅿; z 80475 & mail Grant z 80448; ● 100
Sheridan; Inc. Place; ARAPAHOE; **157** J-6; elev. 5,320ft./1,622m.; 🅿; ★ **DEN**; z 80110; Ⓟ 4,976; Ⓒ 5,600
Sheridan Lake; Inc. Place; KIOWA; **159** I-20; elev. 4,083ft./1,244m.; 🅿; z 81071; Ⓟ 95; Ⓒ 66
Sherrelwood; CDP-Census Area Only; ADAMS; **157** G-7; ★ **DEN**; mail Denver z 80221; Ⓟ 16,636; Ⓒ 17,657
Silt; Inc. Place; GARFIELD; **158** F-7; elev. 5,440ft./1,658m.; 🅿; z 81652; Ⓟ 1,095; Ⓒ 1,740
Silver Cliff; Inc. Place; CUSTER; **159** J-12; elev. 7,980ft./2,432m.; 🅿; z 81252; Ⓟ 322; Ⓒ 512
Silver Creek; RMC Place; GRAND; ***159** D-11; elev. 8,359ft./2,548m.; mail Granby z 80446; seasonal pop. 2000
Silver Heights; RMC Place; DOUGLAS; ***159** F-14; ★ **DEN**; mail Castle Rock z 80108; ● 300
Silver Plume; Inc. Place; CLEAR CREEK; **159** F-12; elev. 9,120ft./2,780m.; 🅿; z 80476; Ⓟ 134; Ⓒ 203
Silver Shekel; RMC Place; SUMMIT; ***159** F-11; elev. 9,400ft./2,865m.; mail Breckenridge z 80424; pop. incl. with Dillon (Inc. Place) winter pop. 500
Silver Springs; RMC Place; JEFFERSON; ***159** F-12; mail Pine z 80470; rural
Silver Spruce; RMC Place; BOULDER; ***159** E-13; ★ **BOUL-**; mail Boulder z 80301; ● 65
Silverthorne; Inc. Place; SUMMIT; **159** F-11; elev. 8,790ft./2,679m.; 🅿; z 80497-98; Ⓟ 1,768; Ⓒ 3,196
Silverton; Inc. Place; ⊡ SAN JUAN; **158** K-7; elev. 9,305ft./2,836m.; 🅿; z 81433; Ⓟ 716; Ⓒ 531
Simla; Inc. Place; ELBERT; **159** G-16; elev. 6,029ft./1,838m.; 🅿; z 80835; Ⓟ 481; Ⓒ 663
Singleton; RMC Place; PARK; **159** F-12; mail Shawnee z 80475; ● 40
Skyland; RMC Place; GUNNISON; ***158** H-9; mail Crested Butte z 81224-25; ● 110
Skyland Village; RMC Place; ADAMS; ★ **DEN**; mail Westminster z 80030; pop. incl. with Westminster (Inc. Place)
Skyline; RMC Place; ARAPAHOE; ***159** F-14; ★ **DEN**; mail Denver z 80222; ● 2,350
Sky Village; RMC Place; JEFFERSON; ***159** F-13; ★ **DEN**; mail Morrison z 80465; ● 260
Skyway; RMC Place; EL PASO; ***159** H-14; ★ **CSPG**; mail Colorado Springs z 80906; pop. incl. with Colorado Springs (Inc. Place)
Skyway; MESA; see Mesa Lakes (RMC Place)
Skyway Estates; RMC Place; EL PASO; ★ **CSPG**; mail Colorado Springs z 80906; pop. incl. with Colorado Springs (Inc. Place)
Skyway Park; RMC Place; EL PASO; ★ **CSPG**; mail Colorado Springs z 80906; pop. incl. with Colorado Springs (Inc. Place)
Slater; RMC Place; MOFFAT; **158** A-8; elev. 6,540ft./1,993m.; 🅿; z 81653; ● 50
Slick Rock; RMC Place; SAN MIGUEL; **158** J-4; elev. 5,515ft./1,681m.; 🅿; z 81325; rural
Smeltertown; RMC Place; CHAFFEE; ***159** I-11; mail Salida z 81201; ● 210
Smith Hill; RMC Place; GILPIN; ***159** E-12; mail Golden z 80403; rural
Smoky Hill; RMC Place; ARAPAHOE; ★ **DEN**; mail Aurora z 80015, z 80046; pop. incl. with Aurora (Inc. Place)
Snowmass; RMC Place; PITKIN; **158** G-9; elev. 6,880ft./2,097m.; 🅿; z 81654
Snowmass-at-Aspen; PITKIN; see Snowmass Village (Inc. Place)
Snowmass Village (Snowmass-at-Aspen); Inc. Place; PITKIN; **158** G-9; 🅿; z 81615; Ⓟ 1,449; Ⓒ 1,822
Snow Mountain Ranch; RMC Place; GRAND; ***159** E-11; elev. 8,800ft./2,682m.; mail Granby z 80446, Winter Park z 80482; ● 120
Snyder; RMC Place; MORGAN; **159** D-17; elev. 4,190ft./1,277m.; 🅿; z 80750; ● 160
Somerset; RMC Place; GUNNISON; **158** H-7; elev. 6,042ft./1,842m.; 🅿; z 81434
South Canon; RMC Place; FREMONT; mail Canon City z 81212; pop. incl. with Cañon City (Inc. Place)
South Denver; RMC Place; DENVER; ***159** E-13; ★ **DEN**; mail Denver z 80209, z 80223; pop. incl. with Denver (Inc. Place)
Southern Ute Reservation; Indian Reservation; LA PLATA, ARCHULETA, MONTEZUMA; mail Ignacio z 81137; also location of Indian Agency; Ⓟ 5,739; Ⓒ 11,159
South Fork; Inc. Place; RIO GRANDE; **158** L-9; elev. 8,200ft./2,499m.; 🅿; z 81154; Ⓟ 361; Ⓒ 604
Southglenn; CDP-Census Area Only; ARAPAHOE; ***159** F-14; ★ **DEN**; mail Littleton z 80122; Ⓟ 43,087; Ⓒ 43,520; ◆ 50,107
South Golden Road Station; RMC Place; JEFFERSON; mail Golden z 80403; pop. incl. with Golden (Inc. Place)
South Park City; RMC Place; PARK; ***159** G-11; mail Fairplay z 80440; pop. incl. with Fairplay (Inc. Place)
South Platte; RMC Place; JEFFERSON; ***159** F-13; mail Conifer z 80433; rural
South Roggen; RMC Place; WELD; ***159** D-15; mail Roggen z 80652; rural
Southwind; RMC Place; ARAPAHOE; ***159** F-13; ★ **DEN**; mail Littleton z 80120; ● 1,600
Southwood; RMC Place; ARAPAHOE; ***159** F-13; ★ **DEN**; mail Littleton z 80120; ● 1,600
Spanish Peaks; RMC Place; HUERFANO; ***159** M-14; mail La Veta z 81055; rural
Spanish Village; RMC Place; WELD; ***159** C-14; mail Greeley z 80631; ● 300
Sparks; RMC Place; MOFFAT; ***158** B-4; mail Rock Springs z 82901; rural
Sphinx Park; RMC Place; JEFFERSON; ***159** F-13; mail Pine z 80470; ● 70
Springfield; Inc. Place; ⊡ BACA; **159** L-19; elev. 4,365ft./1,330m.; 🅿 🅷; z 81073; Ⓟ 1,475; Ⓒ 1,562
Spring Valley; RMC Place; TELLER; ***159** H-13; mail Divide z 80814; rural
Sprucedale; RMC Place; JEFFERSON; ***159** F-13; ★ **DEN**; mail Evergreen z 80439; ● 410
Stanley Park; RMC Place; JEFFERSON; ***159** F-13; ★ **DEN**; mail Evergreen z 80439; ● 200
Starkville; Inc. Place; LAS ANIMAS; **159** M-15; elev. 6,360ft./1,939m.; 🅿; z 81082; Ⓟ 104; Ⓒ 128
Steamboat Plaza; RMC Place; ROUTT; ***158** C-9; mail Steamboat Springs z 80488; pop. incl. with Steamboat Springs (Inc. Place)
Steamboat Springs; Inc. Place; ⊡ ROUTT; **158** C-9; elev. 6,728ft./2,051m.; 🅿 🅷; z 80477, z 80487-88; Ⓟ 6,695; Ⓒ 9,815
Steamboat Village; RMC Place; ROUTT; ***158** C-9; mail Steamboat Springs z 80477, z 80487-88
Stem Beach; RMC Place; PUEBLO; ***159** J-14; mail Pueblo z 81005; rural
Sterling; Inc. Place; ⊡ LOGAN; **159** C-18; elev. 3,939ft./1,201m.; 🅿 🅷 ■; z 80751; Ⓟ 10,362; Ⓒ 11,360; Ⓡ 12,780; ◆ 12,801
Stockyards; RMC Place; DENVER; ***159** E-13; ★ **DEN**; mail Denver z 80216; pop. incl. with Denver (Inc. Place)
Stonegate; CDP-Census Area Only; DOUGLAS; ***159** F-14; ★ **DEN**; mail Parker z 80134; Ⓒ 6,284
Stoneham; RMC Place; WELD; **159** C-17; elev. 4,573ft./1,394m.; 🅿; z 80754; ● 90
Stoner (Stoner Creek); RMC Place; MONTEZUMA; ***158** L-5; elev. 7,479ft./2,280m.; mail Dolores z 81323
Stoner Creek; MONTEZUMA; see Stoner (RMC Place)
Stonewall; RMC Place; LAS ANIMAS; **159** M-13; mail Weston z 81091; ● 80
Stonington; RMC Place; BACA; **159** M-20; elev. 3,806ft./1,160m.; 🅿; z 81090; ● 30
Strasburg; CDP; ADAMS, ARAPAHOE; **159** E-15; elev. 5,386ft./1,642m.; 🅿; z 80136; Ⓒ 1,402
Stratmoor; CDP-Census Area Only; EL PASO; ***159** H-14; ★ **CSPG**; mail Colorado Springs z 80906; Ⓟ 5,854; Ⓒ 6,650
Stratmoor Hills; RMC Place; EL PASO; **157** I-2; ★ **CSPG**; mail Colorado Springs z 80906; ● 2,350
Stratton; Inc. Place; KIT CARSON; **159** G-19; elev. 4,414ft./1,345m.; 🅿; z 80836; Ⓟ 649; Ⓒ 669
Stratton Meadows; RMC Place; EL PASO; ***159** H-14; ★ **CSPG**; mail Colorado Springs z 80906; pop. incl. with Colorado Springs (Inc. Place)
Stratton Park; RMC Place; EL PASO; ★ **CSPG**; mail Colorado Springs z 80907; pop. incl. with Colorado Springs (Inc. Place)
Stringtown; RMC Place; LAKE; **158** G-10; mail Leadville z 80461; ● 140
Stroh Ranch; RMC Place; DOUGLAS; ***159** F-14; ★ **DEN**; mail Parker z 80134; pop. incl. with Parker (Inc. Place)
Sugar City; Inc. Place; CROWLEY; **159** J-17; elev. 4,300ft./1,311m.; 🅿; z 81076; Ⓟ 252; Ⓒ 279
Sugarloaf; RMC Place; BOULDER; ***159** E-12; elev. 7,842ft./2,390m.; mail Boulder z 80302; ● 150
Sullivan; RMC Place; DENVER; ★ **DEN**; mail Denver z 80231, z 80237; pop. incl. with Denver (Inc. Place)
SUMMIT; **159** F-11; Ⓟ 12,881; Ⓒ 23,548; ◆ 27,540
Summit Cove; RMC Place; SUMMIT; ***159** F-11; mail Dillon z 80435; ● 60
Sunbeam; RMC Place; MOFFAT; ***158** C-6; mail Maybell z 81640
Sunnyside; RMC Place; BOULDER; ***159** E-13; mail Nederland z 80466; rural
Sunnyside; RMC Place; DENVER; ★ **DEN**; mail Denver z 80211; pop. incl. with Denver (Inc. Place)
Sunnyside; RMC Place; LA PLATA; ***158** M-6; mail Durango z 81303; ● 75
Sunset; RMC Place; PUEBLO; ***159** K-15; mail Pueblo z 81004-05
Sunshine; RMC Place; BOULDER; ***159** D-13; ★ **BOUL-**; mail Boulder z 80302; rural
Superior; Inc. Place; BOULDER, JEFFERSON; **159** E-13; elev. 5,490ft./1,673m.; 🅿; ★ **BOUL-**; z 80027; Ⓟ 255; Ⓒ 9,011
Surrey Ridge; RMC Place; DOUGLAS; ***159** F-14; ★ **DEN**; mail Castle Rock z 80108; ● 260
Sutank; GARFIELD; see Satank (RMC Place)
Swallows; RMC Place; PUEBLO; ***159** J-14; mail Pueblo z 81003; rural
Swede Corners; RMC Place; SAGUACHE; ***159** K-11; elev. 7,639ft./2,328m.; mail Saguache z 81149; rural
Sweetwater; RMC Place; EAGLE; ***158** E-8; mail Gypsum z 81637; rural
Swink; Inc. Place; OTERO; **159** K-17; elev. 4,118ft./1,255m.; 🅿; z 81077; Ⓟ 584; Ⓒ 696
Swissvale; RMC Place; FREMONT; ***159** I-11; mail Salida z 81201; ● 50
Switzerland Village; RMC Place; JEFFERSON; ***159** F-13; mail Pine z 80470; rural

T

Tabernash; CDP; GRAND; **159** E-11; elev. 8,326ft./2,538m.; 🅿; z 80478; Ⓒ 165
Tamarron; RMC Place; EL PASO; ***159** H-14; ★ **CSPG**; mail Colorado Springs z 80919; pop. incl. with Colorado Springs (Inc. Place)
Tamarron; RMC Place; LA PLATA; ***158** L-6; mail Durango z 81301; ● 110
Tanglewood Acres; RMC Place; CUSTER; ***159** J-12; mail Westcliffe z 81252; ● 30
Tarryall; RMC Place; PARK; ***159** G-12; mail Lake George z 80827; rural
Taylor Park; RMC Place; GUNNISON; ***158** H-10; mail Almont z 81210, Gunnison z 81230; rural
TELLER; **159** G-13; Ⓟ 12,468; Ⓒ 20,555; ◆ 22,350
Telluride; Inc. Place; ⊡ SAN MIGUEL; **158** K-7; elev. 8,800ft./2,682m.; 🅿; z 81435; Ⓟ 1,309; Ⓒ 2,221
Templeton; RMC Place; EL PASO; ***159** H-14; ★ **CSPG**; mail Colorado Springs z 80917-18; pop. incl. with Colorado Springs (Inc. Place)
Ten Mile Vista; RMC Place; SUMMIT; ***159** F-11; elev. 9,232ft./2,814m.; mail Breckenridge z 80424; winter pop. 400; ● 280
Tennyson Heights; RMC Place; LARIMER; ★ **FTCL-**; mail Fort Collins z 80521; pop. incl. with Fort Collins (Inc. Place)
Texas Creek; RMC Place; FREMONT; ***159** I-12; elev. 6,200ft./1,890m.; mail Cotopaxi z 81223; rural
Thatcher; RMC Place; LAS ANIMAS; ***159** L-16; 🅿; z 81059; rural
The Meadows; RMC Place; JEFFERSON; ***159** F-13; ★ **DEN**; mail Littleton z 80127
The Mesa; RMC Place; EL PASO; ***159** H-14; ★ **CSPG**; mail Colorado Springs z 80904; pop. incl. with Colorado Springs (Inc. Place)
The Pinery; CDP-Census Area Only; DOUGLAS; ***159** F-14; elev. 6,143ft./1,872m.; ★ **DEN**; mail Parker z 80134; Ⓒ 7,253
The Shadows; RMC Place; SUMMIT; ***159** F-11; elev. 9,990ft./3,045m.; mail Breckenridge z 80424; ● 385
The Springs; RMC Place; EL PASO; ***159** H-14; elev. 6,400ft./1,951m.; ★ **CSPG**; mail Colorado Springs z 80906
Thomasville; RMC Place; PITKIN; ***158** G-9; mail Meredith z 81642; rural
Thornton; Inc. Place; ADAMS, WELD; **157** G-7; elev. 5,342ft./1,628m.; 🅿 🅷 ■; ★ **DEN**; z 80023, z 80221, z 80229, z 80233, z 80241, z 80260, z 80602 & mail Brighton z 80601, Broomfield z 80020, Denver z 80234; Ⓟ 55,031; Ⓒ 82,384; ◆ 114,175
Thurman; RMC Place; WASHINGTON; ***159** F-18; mail Anton z 80801, Flagler z 80815; rural
Tiffany; RMC Place; LA PLATA; **158** N-7; mail Ignacio z 81137
Timbers; RMC Place; ARAPAHOE; ★ **DEN**; mail Aurora z 80014; pop. incl. with Aurora (Inc. Place)
Timnath; Inc. Place; LARIMER; **159** C-13; elev. 4,867ft./1,483m.; 🅿; ★ **FTCL-**; z 80547; Ⓟ 190; Ⓒ 223
Timpas; RMC Place; OTERO; ***159** K-16; 🅿; z 81050
Tincup; RMC Place; GUNNISON; ***158** H-10; elev. 10,182ft./3,103m.; mail Almont z 81210
Tiny Town; RMC Place; JEFFERSON; ***159** F-13; elev. 6,840ft./2,085m.; ★ **DEN**; mail Morrison z 80465; ● 90
Todd Creek; CDP-Census Area Only; ADAMS; ***159** E-14; mail Brighton z 80602; Ⓒ 1,299
Toledo Heights; RMC Place; PUEBLO; ★ **PUEB**; pop. incl. with Pueblo (Inc. Place)
Tolland; RMC Place; GILPIN; ***159** E-12; mail Rollinsville z 80474; rural
Tomah; RMC Place; DOUGLAS; ***159** G-14; mail Castle Rock z 80104; rural
Tomichi Heights; RMC Place; GUNNISON; ***158** I-9; mail Gunnison z 81230
Toonerville; RMC Place; BENT; **159** K-18; mail Las Animas z 81054; rural
Toponas; RMC Place; ROUTT; **158** D-9; elev. 8,280ft./2,524m.; 🅿; z 80479
Tordal Estates; RMC Place; SUMMIT; ***159** F-11; elev. 10,800ft./3,292m.; mail Breckenridge z 80424; winter pop. 200; ● 90
Torres; RMC Place; LAS ANIMAS; ***159** N-13; elev. 8,327ft./2,538m.; mail Weston z 81091; rural
Torres; RMC Place; RIO GRANDE; ***158** L-10; elev. 7,703ft./2,348m.; mail Monte Vista z 81144; rural
Towaoc; CDP; MONTEZUMA; **158** M-4; located on Ute Mountain Ind. Res.; elev. 5,880ft./1,792m.; 🅿; z 81334; location of Indian Agency; Ⓟ 700; Ⓒ 1,097
Towner; RMC Place; KIOWA; ***159** I-20; elev. 3,930ft./1,198m.; 🅿; z 81071
Tranquil Acres; RMC Place; TELLER; ***159** H-13; mail Woodland Park z 80863; ● 100
Trimble; RMC Place; LA PLATA; ***158** M-6; mail Durango z 81301; ● 285
Trinchera (Trinchere); RMC Place; LAS ANIMAS; **159** N-16; elev. 5,800ft./1,768m.; 🅿; z 81081; ● 80
Trinchere; LAS ANIMAS; see Trinchera (RMC Place)
Trinidad; Inc. Place; ⊡ LAS ANIMAS; **159** M-15; elev. 6,025ft./1,836m.; 🅿 🅷; z 81082; Ⓟ 8,580; Ⓒ 9,078
Troutdale; RMC Place; JEFFERSON; ***159** F-13; ★ **DEN**; mail Evergreen z 80439
Trout Haven; RMC Place; TELLER; ***159** H-13; mail Divide z 80814; ● 120
Trout Lake; RMC Place; SAN MIGUEL; ***158** K-6; mail Ophir z 81426; rural
Truckton; RMC Place; EL PASO; ***159** H-15; elev. 6,023ft./1,836m.; mail Yoder z 80864; rural
Trujillo; RMC Place; ARCHULETA; ***158** M-8; mail Pagosa Springs z 81147; rural
Trumbull; RMC Place; JEFFERSON; ***159** G-13; mail Sedalia z 80135; rural
Twin Crossing; RMC Place; LA PLATA; ***158** N-6; mail Durango z 81303; rural
Twin Forks; RMC Place; JEFFERSON; ***159** F-13; elev. 6,884ft./2,098m.; ★ **DEN**; mail Indian Hills z 80454; ● 70
Twin Lakes; CDP-Census Area Only; ADAMS; ***159** E-13; ★ **DEN**; Ⓒ 6,301
Twin Lakes; RMC Place; LAKE; **158** G-10; elev. 9,220ft./2,810m.; 🅿; z 81228, z 81251; ● 50
Twin Rock (Twin Rocks); RMC Place; TELLER; ***159** H-13; mail Florissant z 80816; ● 100
Twin Rocks; TELLER; see Twin Rock (RMC Place)
Twin Spruce; RMC Place; JEFFERSON; ***159** E-13; mail Golden z 80403; ● 150
Two Buttes; Inc. Place; BACA; **159** L-20; elev. 4,125ft./1,257m.; 🅿; z 81084; Ⓟ 63; Ⓒ 67
Tyrone; RMC Place; LAS ANIMAS; ***159** L-15; elev. 5,538ft./1,688m.; 🅿; z 81059; rural

U

Unaweep; RMC Place; MESA; ***158** H-5; mail Whitewater z 81527; rural
Uncompahgre; RMC Place; MONTROSE; ***158** I-7; elev. 6,163ft./1,878m.; mail Montrose z 81401; ● 140
Union; RMC Place; MORGAN; ***159** C-17; mail Snyder z 80750; rural
Union Stock Yards; RMC Place; DENVER; ***159** E-13; ★ **DEN**; mail Denver z 80216; pop. incl. with Denver (Inc. Place)
United States Air Force Academy (Air Force Academy); CDP-Census Area Only; EL PASO; ***159** H-14; elev. 7,160ft./2,182m.; 🅷; ★ **CSPG**; mail USAF Academy z 80840-41; Ⓟ 9,062; Ⓒ 7,526
University Park; RMC Place; DENVER; ***159** F-13; ★ **DEN**; mail Denver z 80210, z 80250; pop. incl. with Denver (Inc. Place)
Upper San Juan River; RMC Place; ARCHULETA; ***158** M-8; mail Pagosa Springs z 81147; ● 130
Uravan; RMC Place; MONTROSE; **158** I-4; elev. 4,992ft./1,522m.; mail Naturita z 81422
Ute Heights; RMC Place; CHAFFEE; ***159** I-11; mail Salida z 81201; ● 80
Ute Mountain Reservation; Indian Reservation; MONTEZUMA, LA PLATA; Reservation extends into NM and UT; mail Towaoc z 81334; location of Indian Agency; Ⓟ 1,138; Ⓒ 1,410
Utleyville; RMC Place; BACA; ***159** M-18; 🅿; z 81064; rural

V

Vail; Inc. Place; EAGLE; **158** F-10; elev. 8,160ft./2,487m.; 🅿 🅷; z 81657-58; Ⓟ 3,659; Ⓒ 4,531; Ⓡ 4,585
Valdez; RMC Place; LAS ANIMAS; ***159** M-14; mail Trinidad z 81082; rural
Vallecito; RMC Place; LA PLATA; ***158** M-7; mail Bayfield z 81122; ● 200
Valley of Blue (Valley of the Blue); RMC Place; SUMMIT; ***159** F-11; elev. 10,600ft./3,231m.; mail Breckenridge z 80424; ● 220
Valley of the Blue; SUMMIT; see Valley of Blue (RMC Place)
Valmont; RMC Place; BOULDER; ***159** D-13; mail Boulder z 80301; ● 500
Vancorum; RMC Place; MONTROSE; **158** J-5; mail Naturita z 81422
Velasquez Plaza; RMC Place; LAS ANIMAS; ***159** M-14; elev. 6,680ft./2,036m.; mail Weston z 81091; ● 25
Venetian Village; RMC Place; EL PASO; ★ **CSPG**; mail Colorado Springs z 80907; pop. incl. with Colorado Springs (Inc. Place)
Vernon; RMC Place; YUMA; **159** E-20; elev. 3,937ft./1,200m.; 🅿; z 80755; ● 80
Victor; Inc. Place; TELLER; **159** I-13; elev. 9,695ft./2,955m.; 🅿; z 80860; Ⓟ 258; Ⓒ 445
Viejo San Acacio; RMC Place; COSTILLA; ***159** M-12; elev. 7,791ft./2,375m.; mail Sanford z 81151
Vigil; RMC Place; LAS ANIMAS; **159** M-14; mail Weston z 81091; ● 40
Vilas; Inc. Place; BACA; **159** M-20; elev. 4,158ft./1,267m.; 🅿; z 81087; Ⓟ 105; Ⓒ 110
Village East; RMC Place; ARAPAHOE; ★ **DEN**; mail Aurora z 80012; pop. incl. with Aurora (Inc. Place)
Village Seven; RMC Place; EL PASO; ***159** H-14; ★ **CSPG**; mail Colorado Springs z 80917; pop. incl. with Colorado Springs (Inc. Place)
Villa Grove; RMC Place; SAGUACHE; **159** J-11; elev. 7,980ft./2,432m.; 🅿; z 81155; ● 40
Villegreen; RMC Place; LAS ANIMAS; **159** M-17; elev. 5,640ft./1,719m.; 🅿; z 81049; ● 30
Vineland; RMC Place; PUEBLO; ***159** J-15; ★ **PUEB**; mail Pueblo z 81001, z 81006; ● 140
Virginia Dale; RMC Place; LARIMER; **159** B-13; elev. 7,037ft./2,145m.; 🅿; z 80536; rural
Vista Grande; RMC Place; EL PASO; ★ **CSPG**; mail Colorado Springs z 80918; pop. incl. with Colorado Springs (Inc. Place)
Vista Verde; RMC Place; ARAPAHOE; ***159** F-13; ★ **DEN**; mail Littleton z 80120; ● 1,650
Vollmar; RMC Place; WELD; ***159** D-14; ★ **DEN**; mail Fort Lupton z 80621; ● 100
Vona; Inc. Place; KIT CARSON; **159** G-19; elev. 4,504ft./1,373m.; 🅿; z 80861; Ⓟ 104; Ⓒ 95
Vroman; RMC Place; OTERO; ***159** J-16; mail Rocky Ford z 81067

W

Waconda Hills; RMC Place; EL PASO; ***159** G-14; elev. 7,436ft./2,266m.; ★ **CSPG**; mail Monument z 80132; ● 280
Wagner Manor; RMC Place; BOULDER; mail Boulder z 80302; ● 100
Wagon Wheel Gap; RMC Place; MINERAL; ***158** K-9; mail South Fork z 81154
Wahatoya (Huajatolla); RMC Place; HUERFANO; ***159** M-13; mail La Veta z 81055; rural
Wah Keeney Park; RMC Place; JEFFERSON; ***159** F-13; ★ **DEN**; mail Evergreen z 80439; ● 1,030
Wahketa Village; RMC Place; MORGAN; mail Fort Morgan z 80701; ● 60
Walden; Inc. Place; ⊡ JACKSON; **158** B-10; elev. 8,099ft./2,469m.; 🅿; z 80430, z 80480; Ⓟ 890; Ⓒ 734
Wallstreet; RMC Place; BOULDER; ***159** D-12; mail Boulder z 80302; ● 120
Walnut Hills; RMC Place; ARAPAHOE; ***159** F-14; ★ **DEN**; mail Englewood z 80112; ● 2,100
Walsenburg; Inc. Place; ⊡ HUERFANO; **159** L-14; elev. 6,182ft./1,884m.; 🅿 🅷; z 81089; Ⓟ 3,300; Ⓒ 4,182
Walsh; Inc. Place; BACA; **159** M-20; elev. 3,956ft./1,206m.; 🅿; z 81090; Ⓟ 692; Ⓒ 723
Waltonia; RMC Place; LARIMER; ***159** C-13; mail Drake z 80515; rural
Walts Corner; RMC Place; LAS ANIMAS; ***159** M-16; mail Branson z 81027; rural
Wamblee Park; RMC Place; JEFFERSON; mail Conifer z 80433; rural
Wamblee Valley; RMC Place; JEFFERSON; ***159** F-13; mail Conifer z 80433; rural
Wandcrest Park; RMC Place; JEFFERSON; ***159** F-12; mail Pine z 80470; ● 125
Ward; Inc. Place; BOULDER; **159** D-12; elev. 9,200ft./2,804m.; 🅿; z 80481; Ⓟ 159; Ⓒ 169
WASHINGTON; **159** D-18; Ⓟ 4,812; Ⓒ 4,926; ◆ 4,477
Watertown; JEFFERSON; see Kassler (RMC Place)
Watkins; RMC Place; ADAMS, ARAPAHOE; **159** E-14; elev. 5,520ft./1,682m.; 🅿; ★ **DEN**; z 80137; incorporated June 8, 2004; disincorporated November 30, 2006; ● 1,930
Wattenberg (Wattenburg); RMC Place; WELD; **159** E-14; ★ **DEN**; mail Fort Lupton z 80621; ● 330
Wattenburg; WELD; see Wattenberg (RMC Place)
Waverly; RMC Place; ALAMOSA; ***159** M-11; mail Alamosa z 81101; rural
Waverly; RMC Place; LARIMER; ***159** B-13; mail Fort Collins z 80524, Wellington z 80549; ● 300
Welby; CDP; ADAMS; ***159** E-14; ★ **DEN**; mail Denver z 80229; Ⓟ 10,218; Ⓒ 12,973
WELD; **159** B-15; part of Weld county was annexed by Broomfield county on November 15, 2001; Ⓟ 131,821; Ⓒ 180,936; adjusted 2000 Census population is 180,926; ◆ 258,141
Weldona; RMC Place; MORGAN; **159** D-16; elev. 4,348ft./1,325m.; 🅿; z 80653; ● 170
Wellington; Inc. Place; LARIMER; **159** B-13; elev. 5,200ft./1,585m.; 🅿; ★ **FTCL-**; z 80549; Ⓟ 1,340; Ⓒ 2,672
Wellshire; RMC Place; DENVER; ***159** F-14; ★ **DEN**; mail Denver z 80222, z 80224; pop. incl. with Denver (Inc. Place)
Wellsville; RMC Place; FREMONT; ***159** I-11; mail Salida z 81201; rural
West; RMC Place; WELD; ***159** C-14; ★ **GRLY**; mail Greeley z 80634; pop. incl. with Greeley (Inc. Place)
Westcliffe; Inc. Place; ⊡ CUSTER; **159** J-12; elev. 7,888ft./2,404m.; 🅿; z 81252; Ⓟ 312; Ⓒ 417
Westcreek; CDP; DOUGLAS; ***159** G-13; Ⓒ 105
West End; RMC Place; EL PASO; ***159** H-14; ★ **CSPG**; mail Colorado Springs z 80904, z 80934; pop. incl. with Colorado Springs (Inc. Place)
Western Hills; RMC Place; ADAMS; **157** G-6; ★ **DEN**; mail Denver z 80221; ● 2,600
West Farm; RMC Place; PROWERS; ***159** J-19; elev. 3,588ft./1,094m.; mail Lamar z 81052; rural
Westminster; Inc. Place; ADAMS, JEFFERSON; **159** E-13; elev. 5,300ft./1,615m.; 🅿 🅷 🅲 710 ■; ★ **DEN**; z 80003, z 80005, z 80020-21, z 80023, z 80030-31, z 80035-36, z 80221, z 80234, z 80241, z 80260; Ⓟ 74,625; Ⓒ 100,940; ◆ 118,309
Westminster East; RMC Place; ADAMS; ***159** E-13; ★ **DEN**; mail Denver z 80221; Ⓟ 5,197; ● 3,700
Weston; RMC Place; LAS ANIMAS; **159** M-14; elev. 7,000ft./2,134m.; 🅿; z 81091; ● 85
West Pleasant View; CDP-Census Area Only; JEFFERSON; ***159** E-13; ★ **DEN**; mail Golden z 80401; Ⓒ 3,932
Westridge; RMC Place; WELD; ***159** C-14; elev. 4,950ft./1,509m.; ★ **GRLY**; mail Greeley z 80634; pop. incl. with Greeley (Inc. Place)
West Vail; RMC Place; EAGLE; mail Vail z 81657; pop. incl. with Vail (Inc. Place)
Westwood; RMC Place; DENVER; ***159** F-13; ★ **DEN**; mail Denver z 80219; pop. incl. with Denver (Inc. Place)
Westwood Lake; RMC Place; TELLER; ***159** H-13; mail Woodland Park z 80863; ● 200
Wetmore; RMC Place; CUSTER; **159** J-13; elev. 6,081ft./1,853m.; 🅿; z 81253; ● 60
Wheat Ridge; Inc. Place; JEFFERSON; **157** H-5; elev. 5,410ft./1,649m.; 🅿 🅷 ■; ★ **DEN**; z 80033-34, z 80212, z 80214-15 & mail Arvada z 80002, Golden z 80403; Ⓟ 29,419; Ⓒ 32,913; ◆ 34,269
Wheeler; RMC Place; GILPIN; mail Golden z 80403; rural
Wheeler; SUMMIT; see Copper Mountain (RMC Place)
Wheelman; RMC Place; BOULDER; ***159** E-13; mail Boulder z 80302; rural
Whitepine; RMC Place; GUNNISON; ***158** I-10; elev. 9,791ft./2,984m.; mail Sargents z 81248
Whitewater; RMC Place; MESA; **158** H-5; elev. 4,640ft./1,414m.; 🅿; ★ **GDJC**; z 81527; ● 200
Widefield; RMC Place; EL PASO; **159** H-14; ★ **CSPG**; mail Colorado Springs z 80911; ● 4,200
Wiggins; Inc. Place; MORGAN; **159** D-16; elev. 4,550ft./1,387m.; 🅿; z 80654; Ⓟ 499; Ⓒ 838
Wigwam; RMC Place; EL PASO; ***159** I-14; mail Fountain z 80817; rural
Wild Horse; RMC Place; CHEYENNE; **159** H-18; elev. 4,462ft./1,360m.; 🅿; z 80862; ● 25
Wild Horse; RMC Place; PUEBLO; ***159** J-14; elev. 4,844ft./1,476m.; ★ **PUEB**; mail Pueblo z 81001; ● 100
Wiley; Inc. Place; PROWERS; **159** J-19; elev. 3,735ft./1,138m.; 🅿; z 81092; Ⓟ 406; Ⓒ 483
Willard; RMC Place; LOGAN; **159** C-17; elev. 4,345ft./1,324m.; 🅿; z 80741; ● 40
Williamsburg; Inc. Place; FREMONT; **159** J-13; mail Florence z 81226; Ⓟ 253; Ⓒ 714
Williamsburg; RMC Place; JEFFERSON; ***159** F-13; ★ **DEN**; mail Littleton z 80127
Willis Heights; RMC Place; BOULDER; ***159** D-13; mail Longmont z 80501; ● 480
Willowbrook; RMC Place; JEFFERSON; ***159** F-13; elev. 6,125ft./1,867m.; ★ **DEN**; mail Morrison z 80465; ● 630
Willow Creek; RMC Place; ARAPAHOE; ***159** F-14; ★ **DEN**; mail Englewood z 80110; ● 2,500
Wilmot; RMC Place; JEFFERSON; ***159** F-13; ★ **DEN**; mail Evergreen z 80439
Wilson Lake Estates; RMC Place; TELLER; ***159** H-13; mail Florissant z 80816; ● 215
Windsor; Inc. Place; WELD, LARIMER; **159** C-14; elev. 4,795ft./1,462m.; 🅿; z 80528, z 80550-51; Ⓟ 5,062; Ⓒ 9,896
Windsor Gardens; RMC Place; DENVER; ***159** E-14; ★ **DEN**; mail Denver z 80247; pop. incl. with Denver (Inc. Place)
Winter Park; Inc. Place; GRAND; **159** E-12; elev. 9,040ft./2,755m.; 🅿; z 80482; Ⓟ 528; Ⓒ 662; Ⓡ 658
Wolcott; RMC Place; EAGLE; **158** E-9; elev. 6,984ft./2,129m.; 🅿; z 81655
Wondervu; RMC Place; BOULDER; ***159** E-12; mail Golden z 80403; ● 180
Woodcroft; RMC Place; PUEBLO; ★ **PUEB**; pop. incl. with Pueblo (Inc. Place)
Woodglen; RMC Place; ADAMS; ★ **DEN**; mail Denver z 80233; pop. incl. with Thornton (Inc. Place)
Woodland Acres; RMC Place; PUEBLO; ***159** K-14; mail Rye z 81069; ● 400
Woodland Park; Inc. Place; TELLER; **159** H-13; elev. 8,437ft./2,572m.; 🅿; ★ **CSPG**; z 80863, z 80866; Ⓟ 4,610; Ⓒ 6,515
Woodmar Village; RMC Place; JEFFERSON; ***159** F-13; ★ **DEN**; mail Littleton z 80123; ● 2,250
Woodmoor; CDP-Census Area Only; EL PASO; ***159** G-14; elev. 7,300ft./2,225m.; ★ **CSPG**; mail Colorado Springs z 80908, Monument z 80132; Ⓟ 3,858; Ⓒ 7,177
Woodrow; RMC Place; WASHINGTON; **159** E-17; elev. 4,488ft./1,368m.; 🅿; z 80757; ● 20
Woody Creek; RMC Place; PITKIN; **158** G-9; elev. 7,320ft./2,231m.; 🅿; z 81656; ● 260
Wray; Inc. Place; ⊡ YUMA; **159** D-20; elev. 3,522ft./1,074m.; 🅿 🅷; z 80758; Ⓟ 1,998; Ⓒ 2,187

Y

Yale; CHAFFEE; see Granite (RMC Place)
Yampa; Inc. Place; ROUTT; **158** D-9; elev. 7,892ft./2,405m.; 🅿; z 80483; Ⓟ 317; Ⓒ 443
Yellow Jacket; RMC Place; MONTEZUMA; **158** L-4; elev. 6,900ft./2,103m.; 🅿; z 81335; ● 60
Yoder; RMC Place; EL PASO; **159** H-15; elev. 6,145ft./1,873m.; 🅿; z 80864
Yorkborough; RMC Place; ADAMS; ★ **DEN**; mail Denver z 80229; pop. incl. with Thornton (Inc. Place)
Yuma; Inc. Place; YUMA; **159** D-19; elev. 4,132ft./1,259m.; 🅿 🅷; z 80759; Ⓟ 2,719; Ⓒ 3,285
YUMA; **159** E-20; Ⓟ 8,954; Ⓒ 9,841; ◆ 9,636

CONNECTICUT

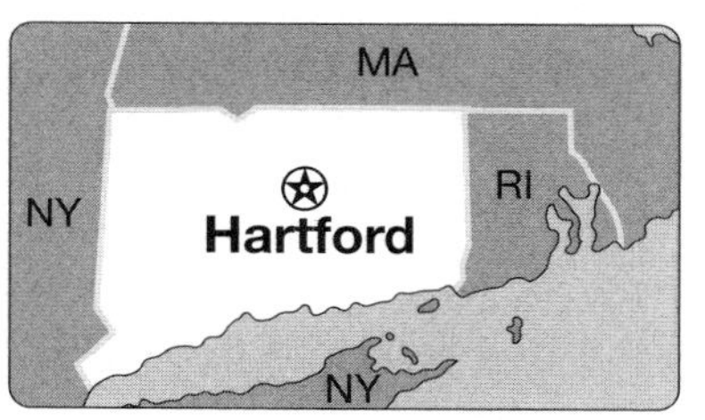

Statistics

Total area (2000) — 5,543 square miles
Land area (2000) — 4,845 square miles
Water area (2000) — 698 square miles
Capital — Hartford
One of Thirteen Original States

Maps

State maps can be found on pages 142-254 in Vol. 1
County Subdivision maps can be found on pages 255-271 in Vol. 1

Ranally Metro Areas (RMAs) and Abbreviations

Hartford-New Britain, CT — H-NB
New Haven, CT — N.HAV
New London-Norwich, CT-RI — N.LON-
New York, NY-NJ-CT — N.Y.
Torrington, CT — TORR
Waterbury, CT — WATB
Worcester, MA-CT — WORC

Principal Places

Place Name	Place Type	County	Population
Bridgeport	Inc. Place	FAIRFIELD	◆ 136,479
Bridgeport	MCD-Town	FAIRFIELD	◆ 136,479
New Haven	Inc. Place	NEW HAVEN	◆ 121,836
New Haven	MCD-Town	NEW HAVEN	◆ 121,836
Hartford	Inc. Place	HARTFORD	◆ 121,044
Hartford	MCD-Town	HARTFORD	◆ 121,044
Stamford	Inc. Place	FAIRFIELD	◆ 119,453
Stamford	MCD-Town	FAIRFIELD	◆ 119,453
Waterbury	Inc. Place	NEW HAVEN	◆ 106,626
Waterbury	MCD-Town	NEW HAVEN	◆ 106,626
Norwalk	Inc. Place	FAIRFIELD	◆ 83,718
Norwalk	MCD-Town	FAIRFIELD	◆ 83,718
Danbury	Inc. Place	FAIRFIELD	◆ 79,021
Danbury	MCD-Town	FAIRFIELD	◆ 79,021
New Britain	Inc. Place	HARTFORD	◆ 70,979
New Britain	MCD-Town	HARTFORD	◆ 70,979
West Hartford	CDP	HARTFORD	◆ 65,937
West Hartford	MCD-Town	HARTFORD	◆ 65,937
Greenwich	MCD-Town	FAIRFIELD	◆ 62,208
Greenwich	RMC Place	FAIRFIELD	● 61,100
Bristol	Inc. Place	HARTFORD	◆ 60,008
Bristol	MCD-Town	HARTFORD	◆ 60,008
Hamden	MCD-Town	NEW HAVEN	◆ 59,271
Fairfield	MCD-Town	FAIRFIELD	◆ 58,399
Meriden	Inc. Place	NEW HAVEN	◆ 58,399
Meriden	MCD-Town	NEW HAVEN	◆ 58,399
Fairfield	RMC Place	FAIRFIELD	● 57,300
Manchester	MCD-Town	HARTFORD	◆ 57,257
Hamden	RMC Place	NEW HAVEN	● 56,900
Milford	MCD-Town	NEW HAVEN	◆ 55,593
Manchester	RMC Place	HARTFORD	● 54,700
Milford	Inc. Place	NEW HAVEN	◆ 53,962
West Haven	Inc. Place	NEW HAVEN	◆ 51,594
West Haven	MCD-Town	NEW HAVEN	◆ 51,594
East Hartford	CDP	HARTFORD	◆ 50,637
East Hartford	MCD-Town	HARTFORD	◆ 50,637
Stratford	CDP	FAIRFIELD	◆ 48,960
Stratford	MCD-Town	FAIRFIELD	◆ 48,960
Enfield	MCD-Town	HARTFORD	◆ 46,267
Wallingford	MCD-Town	NEW HAVEN	◆ 45,115
Middletown	Inc. Place	MIDDLESEX	◆ 44,142
Middletown	MCD-Town	MIDDLESEX	◆ 44,142
Groton	MCD-Town	NEW LONDON	◆ 41,510
Southington	MCD-Town	HARTFORD	◆ 40,901
Shelton	Inc. Place	FAIRFIELD	◆ 38,826
Shelton	MCD-Town	FAIRFIELD	◆ 38,826
Norwich	Inc. Place	NEW LONDON	◆ 37,515
Norwich	MCD-Town	NEW LONDON	◆ 37,515
Torrington	Inc. Place	LITCHFIELD	◆ 35,212
Torrington	MCD-Town	LITCHFIELD	◆ 35,212
Trumbull	CDP	FAIRFIELD	◆ 34,424
Trumbull	MCD-Town	FAIRFIELD	◆ 34,424
Glastonbury	MCD-Town	HARTFORD	◆ 34,082
Naugatuck	Inc. Place	NEW HAVEN	◆ 31,405
Naugatuck	MCD-Town	NEW HAVEN	◆ 31,405
Central Manchester	CDP-Census Area Only	HARTFORD	◆ 31,282
Cheshire	MCD-Town	NEW HAVEN	◆ 30,347
Newington	CDP	HARTFORD	◆ 29,947
Newington	MCD-Town	HARTFORD	◆ 29,947
Branford	MCD-Town	NEW HAVEN	◆ 29,674
East Haven	CDP	NEW HAVEN	◆ 29,206
East Haven	MCD-Town	NEW HAVEN	◆ 29,206
New Milford	MCD-Town	LITCHFIELD	◆ 29,054
Windsor	MCD-Town	HARTFORD	◆ 28,989
Vernon	RMC Place	TOLLAND	● 28,100
Vernon	MCD-Town	TOLLAND	◆ 27,251
Wethersfield	CDP	HARTFORD	◆ 26,656
Wethersfield	MCD-Town	HARTFORD	◆ 26,656
Westport	CDP	FAIRFIELD	◆ 26,571
Westport	MCD-Town	FAIRFIELD	◆ 26,571
New London	Inc. Place	NEW LONDON	◆ 26,178
New London	MCD-Town	NEW LONDON	◆ 26,178

Place Name	Place Type	County	Population
South Windsor	MCD-Town	HARTFORD	◆ 26,132
Newtown	MCD-Town	FAIRFIELD	◆ 25,601
Farmington	MCD-Town	HARTFORD	◆ 25,433
Ridgefield	MCD-Town	FAIRFIELD	◆ 24,719
Simsbury	MCD-Town	HARTFORD	◆ 24,443
Windham	MCD-Town	WINDHAM	◆ 24,357
North Haven	CDP	NEW HAVEN	◆ 23,611
North Haven	MCD-Town	NEW HAVEN	◆ 23,611
Guilford	MCD-Town	NEW HAVEN	◆ 22,553
Mansfield	MCD-Town	TOLLAND	◆ 22,178
Watertown	MCD-Town	LITCHFIELD	◆ 21,507
Bloomfield	MCD-Town	HARTFORD	◆ 20,421
Waterford	MCD-Town	NEW LONDON	◆ 20,387
New Canaan	MCD-Town	FAIRFIELD	◆ 20,035
Darien	MCD-Town	FAIRFIELD	◆ 20,033
Southbury	MCD-Town	NEW HAVEN	◆ 19,908
Montville	MCD-Town	NEW LONDON	◆ 19,792
East Lyme	MCD-Town	NEW LONDON	◆ 19,675
Darien	CDP	FAIRFIELD	© 19,607
Berlin	MCD-Town	HARTFORD	◆ 19,499
Monroe	MCD-Town	FAIRFIELD	◆ 19,444
Stonington	MCD-Town	NEW LONDON	◆ 19,277
Rocky Hill	MCD-Town	HARTFORD	◆ 19,200
Madison	MCD-Town	NEW HAVEN	◆ 18,943
Ansonia	Inc. Place	NEW HAVEN	◆ 18,808
Windsor	RMC Place	HARTFORD	● 18,800
Ansonia	MCD-Town	NEW HAVEN	© 18,554
Bethel	MCD-Town	FAIRFIELD	◆ 18,036
Wilton	MCD-Town	FAIRFIELD	◆ 17,981
New Canaan	RMC Place	FAIRFIELD	● 17,864
Plainville	MCD-Town	HARTFORD	◆ 17,531
Wallingford Center	CDP	NEW HAVEN	© 17,509
Plainville	RMC Place	HARTFORD	● 17,392
Avon	MCD-Town	HARTFORD	◆ 17,058
Brookfield	MCD-Town	FAIRFIELD	◆ 16,629
Rocky Hill	RMC Place	HARTFORD	● 16,554
Killingly	MCD-Town	WINDHAM	© 16,472
Seymour	MCD-Town	NEW HAVEN	◆ 16,348
Colchester	MCD-Town	NEW LONDON	◆ 15,884
Willimantic	CDP	WINDHAM	© 15,823
Wolcott	MCD-Town	NEW HAVEN	◆ 15,706
Ledyard	MCD-Town	NEW LONDON	◆ 15,505
Plainfield	MCD-Town	WINDHAM	◆ 15,209
Ellington	MCD-Town	TOLLAND	◆ 14,788
Suffield	MCD-Town	HARTFORD	◆ 14,637
Tolland	MCD-Town	TOLLAND	◆ 14,385
Seymour	RMC Place	NEW HAVEN	● 14,288
North Branford	MCD-Town	NEW HAVEN	◆ 14,134
South Windsor	RMC Place	HARTFORD	● 14,000
New Fairfield	MCD-Town	FAIRFIELD	◆ 13,846
Cromwell	MCD-Town	MIDDLESEX	◆ 13,657
Orange	MCD-Town	NEW HAVEN	◆ 13,650
Clinton	MCD-Town	MIDDLESEX	◆ 13,349
Orange	CDP	NEW HAVEN	© 13,233
East Hampton	MCD-Town	MIDDLESEX	◆ 13,028
Derby	Inc. Place	NEW HAVEN	◆ 12,499
Derby	MCD-Town	NEW HAVEN	© 12,391
Windsor Locks	MCD-Town	HARTFORD	◆ 12,230
Coventry	MCD-Town	TOLLAND	◆ 12,075
Windsor Locks	CDP	HARTFORD	© 12,043
Somers	MCD-Town	TOLLAND	◆ 11,507
Griswold	MCD-Town	NEW LONDON	◆ 11,496
Plymouth	MCD-Town	LITCHFIELD	◆ 11,206
Granby	MCD-Town	HARTFORD	◆ 11,172
Old Saybrook	MCD-Town	MIDDLESEX	◆ 11,160
Storrs	CDP	TOLLAND	® 11,106
Conning Towers-Nautilus Park	CDP-Census Area Only	NEW LONDON	® 10,981
Stafford	MCD-Town	TOLLAND	◆ 10,923
Oxford	MCD-Town	NEW HAVEN	◆ 10,751
Weston	MCD-Town	FAIRFIELD	◆ 10,218
Winchester	MCD-Town	LITCHFIELD	◆ 10,169

Place Name	Place Type	County	Population
East Windsor	MCD-Town	HARTFORD	◆ 10,141
Woodbury	MCD-Town	LITCHFIELD	◆ 9,845
East Haddam	MCD-Town	MIDDLESEX	◆ 9,713
Canton	MCD-Town	HARTFORD	◆ 9,530
Hebron	MCD-Town	TOLLAND	◆ 9,385
Thompson	MCD-Town	WINDHAM	◆ 9,338
Groton	Inc. Place	NEW LONDON	® 9,288
Portland	MCD-Town	MIDDLESEX	◆ 9,176
Woodbridge	MCD-Town	NEW HAVEN	◆ 9,163
Bethel	CDP	FAIRFIELD	© 9,137
Prospect	MCD-Town	NEW HAVEN	◆ 9,064
Putnam	MCD-Town	WINDHAM	© 9,002
Oakville	CDP	LITCHFIELD	© 8,618
Burlington	MCD-Town	HARTFORD	◆ 8,572
Kensington	CDP	HARTFORD	© 8,541
Monroe	RMC Place	FAIRFIELD	● 8,500
Wallingford	RMC Place	NEW HAVEN	● 8,500
Litchfield	MCD-Town	LITCHFIELD	© 8,316
Redding	MCD-Town	FAIRFIELD	◆ 8,303
Thompsonville	CDP	HARTFORD	© 8,125
Southwood Acres	CDP-Census Area Only	HARTFORD	© 8,067
Glastonbury	RMC Place	HARTFORD	● 8,000
Woodbridge	RMC Place	NEW HAVEN	● 7,860
Old Lyme	MCD-Town	NEW LONDON	◆ 7,851
Prospect	RMC Place	NEW HAVEN	● 7,775
Rockville	CDP	TOLLAND	© 7,708
Thomaston	MCD-Town	LITCHFIELD	◆ 7,659
Haddam	MCD-Town	MIDDLESEX	◆ 7,611
Lebanon	MCD-Town	NEW LONDON	◆ 7,560
Bloomfield	RMC Place	HARTFORD	● 7,500
Wilton	RMC Place	FAIRFIELD	● 7,500
Easton	MCD-Town	FAIRFIELD	◆ 7,493
North Branford	RMC Place	NEW HAVEN	● 7,400
Winsted	CDP	LITCHFIELD	© 7,321
Woodstock	MCD-Town	WINDHAM	© 7,221
Durham	MCD-Town	MIDDLESEX	◆ 7,215
Ridgefield	CDP	FAIRFIELD	© 7,212
Brooklyn	MCD-Town	WINDHAM	© 7,173
Glastonbury Center	CDP-Census Area Only	HARTFORD	© 7,157
Killingworth	MCD-Town	MIDDLESEX	◆ 7,021
Middlebury	MCD-Town	NEW HAVEN	◆ 6,990
Putnam District	CDP-Census Area Only	WINDHAM	© 6,746
New Milford	CDP	LITCHFIELD	© 6,633
Essex	MCD-Town	MIDDLESEX	© 6,505
Wolcott	RMC Place	NEW HAVEN	● 6,400
Watertown	RMC Place	LITCHFIELD	● 6,300
Westbrook	MCD-Town	MIDDLESEX	© 6,292
New Hartford	MCD-Town	LITCHFIELD	◆ 6,072
Plantsville	RMC Place	HARTFORD	● 6,000
Marlborough	MCD-Town	HARTFORD	◆ 5,893
Willington	MCD-Town	TOLLAND	◆ 5,858
Cheshire	RMC Place	NEW HAVEN	● 5,800
Cheshire Village	CDP-Census Area Only	NEW HAVEN	© 5,789
Branford Center	CDP-Census Area Only	NEW HAVEN	© 5,735
Branford	RMC Place	NEW HAVEN	● 5,700
Sherwood Manor	CDP-Census Area Only	HARTFORD	© 5,689
Simsbury Center	CDP-Census Area Only	HARTFORD	© 5,603
Portland	CDP	MIDDLESEX	© 5,534
Pawcatuck	CDP	NEW LONDON	© 5,474
Beacon Falls	MCD-Town	NEW HAVEN	◆ 5,438
Bethany	MCD-Town	NEW HAVEN	◆ 5,430
Terryville	CDP	LITCHFIELD	© 5,360
Simsbury	RMC Place	HARTFORD	● 5,300
Bolton	MCD-Town	TOLLAND	◆ 5,297
North Stonington	MCD-Town	NEW LONDON	◆ 5,288
Harwinton	MCD-Town	LITCHFIELD	◆ 5,214
New Fairfield	RMC Place	FAIRFIELD	● 5,200
Columbia	MCD-Town	TOLLAND	◆ 5,185
East Granby	MCD-Town	HARTFORD	◆ 5,159
Canterbury	MCD-Town	WINDHAM	◆ 5,030
Putnam	RMC Place	WINDHAM	● 5,000

County Business Data

County	FIPS Code	County Seat †	Land Area (Sq. Mi.)	Census Population			Wholesale Trade		Manufacturing, 2002			
				4/1/2000	4/1/1990	% Change 1990-2000	Sales, 2002 ($1,000)	% Change 1997-2002	Establish-ments	Total Employees	Value Added ($1,000)	Ranally Mfg. Units
Fairfield	001		626	882,567	827,645	6.6	51,777,236	7.1	1,164	54,168	9,458,645	5,004
Hartford	003		735	857,183	851,783	0.6	17,040,451	1.2	1,485	61,223	6,460,588	3,418
Litchfield	005		920	182,193	174,092	4.7	(d)	(d)	422	14,173	1,567,864	830
Middlesex	007		369	155,071	143,196	8.3	(d)	(d)	297	11,794	1,313,457	695
New Haven	009		606	824,008	804,219	2.5	9,695,054	20.8	1,455	48,872	5,367,899	2,840
New London	011		666	259,088	254,957	1.6	(d)	(d)	209	13,308	2,226,256	1,178
Tolland	013		410	136,364	128,699	6.0	(d)	(d)	155	4,122	409,318	217
Windham	015		513	109,091	102,525	6.4	466,946	40.2	197	7,250	869,439	460
The State			**4,845**	**3,405,565**	**3,287,116**	**3.6**	**86,932,049**	**14.1**	**5,384**	**214,910**	**27,673,466**	**14,641**

(d) Data not available. Corresponding percentages or Ranally Manufacturing Units are estimates.
... Represents 0 or amount too minimal to be reported.
† Not applicable

Administrative Divisions

Counties: Connecticut's county government was abolished effective October 1, 1960, but the boundaries are retained for certain judicial and elective purposes.

Towns: All of Connecticut's counties are divided into towns. Although legally incorporated, towns are not treated as incorporated places by the U.S. Census because the population often is scattered among several localities and rural areas rather than being concentrated in a single place. Only towns with an active government recognized by the U.S. Census of Governments are printed in this index.

Index of Places and Counties

A

B

Entries in **UPPERCASE** are counties.
Entries in **bold** have populations of 2,500 or more.
Names in parentheses are alternate names.

Inc. Place	Incorporated Place
RMC Place	Rand McNally Designated Place
CDP	Census Designated Place
MCD	Minor Civil Division
⊡	County Seat
▲	Minor Civil Division
elev.	Elevation
🅿	Post Office
🅷	Hospital
🅲	College
■	Principal Business Center
★	Ranally Metro Area (RMA) Abbreviation
Z	Zip Code(s)
Ⓟ	Previous Census Population
®	Revised Census Population
Ⓐ	Annexation Population
●	Rand McNally Population Estimate
©	Final Census Population
Ⓢ	Special Census Population
◆	Estimated Population

For additional definitions see Glossary, Volume 1, and Introduction, Volume 2.

Bethany (Bethany Center); RMC Place; NEW HAVEN; ▲ Bethany; 160 H-7; 🅿; ★ N.HAV; z 06524; ● 1,280

Bethany; MCD-Town; NEW HAVEN; *160 H-7; 🅿; ★ N.HAV; z 06524; ℗ 4,608; © 5,040; ◆ 5,430

Bethany Center; NEW HAVEN; see Bethany (RMC Place)

Bethel; CDP; FAIRFIELD; ▲ Bethel; 160 I-4; 🅿; ★ N.Y.; z 06801; ℗ 8,835; © 9,137

Bethel; MCD-Town; FAIRFIELD; *160 I-4; elev. 384ft./117m.; 🅿; ★ N.Y.; z 06801; ℗ 17,541; © 18,067; ◆ 18,036

Bethlehem; RMC Place; LITCHFIELD; ▲ Bethlehem; ★ WATB; ● 120

Bethlehem; MCD-Town; LITCHFIELD; *160 F-6; 🅿; ★ WATB; z 06751; ℗ 3,071; © 3,422; ◆ 3,558

Bethlehem Village; CDP-Census Area Only; LITCHFIELD; ▲ Bethlehem; 160 F-6; elev. 861ft./262m.; 🅷; ★ WATB; mail Bethlehem z 06751; ℗ 1,976; © 2,022

Birch Groves; RMC Place; LITCHFIELD; ▲ New Milford; *160 G-4; ★ N.Y.; mail New Milford z 06776; ● 180

Birch Hill; RMC Place; LITCHFIELD; ▲ Kent; 160 E-3; mail Kent z 06757; ● 230

Birch Meadow; RMC Place; HARTFORD; ▲ Southington; ★ H-NB; mail Plantsville z 06479

Birchwood; RMC Place; HARTFORD; ▲ Windsor; 160 C-10; ★ H-NB; mail Windsor z 06095; ● 380

Birdland; RMC Place; HARTFORD; ▲ Enfield; ★ H-NB; mail Enfield z 06082

Bishop; RMC Place; WINDHAM; ▲ Plainfield; *161 F-16; elev. 150ft./46m.; ★ N.LON-; mail Plainfield z 06374; rural

Bishops Corner; RMC Place; HARTFORD; ▲ West Hartford; *160 F-8; elev. 189ft./58m.; 🅿; ★ H-NB; z 06137 & mail West Hartford z 06117

Bissell; RMC Place; HARTFORD; ▲ South Windsor; *160 D-10; ★ H-NB; mail South Windsor z 06074

Black Point; RMC Place; NEW LONDON; ▲ East Lyme; 161 J-14; ★ N.LON-; mail Niantic z 06357; ● 17

Black Point Beach Club; RMC Place; NEW LONDON; ▲ East Lyme; 161 J-14; ★ N.LON-; mail Niantic z 06357; ● 1,330

Black Rock; RMC Place; FAIRFIELD; ▲ Bridgeport; *160 K-5; ★ N.Y.; pop. incl. with Bridgeport (Inc. Place)

Bloomfield; RMC Place; HARTFORD; ▲ Bloomfield; 160 D-9; 🅿; ★ H-NB; z 06002; ● 7,500

Bloomfield; MCD-Town; HARTFORD; *160 D-9; 🅿; ★ H-NB; z 06002; ℗ 19,483; © 19,587; ◆ 20,421

Blue Hills; CDP-Census Area Only; HARTFORD; ▲ Bloomfield; 160 D-10; ★ H-NB; mail Hartford z 06112, z 06132; ℗ 3,206; © 3,020

Boardman Bridge (Boardmans Bridge); RMC Place; LITCHFIELD; ▲ New Milford; 160 F-4; ★ N.Y.; mail New Milford z 06776; ● 100

Boardman Manor; RMC Place; LITCHFIELD; ▲ New Milford; ★ N.Y.; mail New Milford z 06776

Boardmans Bridge; LITCHFIELD; see Boardman Bridge (RMC Place)

Bolton (Bolton Notch); RMC Place; TOLLAND; ▲ Bolton; 161 D-12; elev. 583ft./178m.; 🅿; ★ H-NB; z 06043; ● 230

Bolton; MCD-Town; TOLLAND; *161 D-12; elev. 583ft./178m.; 🅿; ★ H-NB; z 06043; ℗ 4,575; © 5,017; ◆ 5,297

Bolton Center; RMC Place; TOLLAND; ▲ Bolton; *161 D-12; elev. 583ft./178m.; ★ H-NB; mail Manchester z 06040; ● 230

Bolton Notch; TOLLAND; see Bolton (RMC Place)

Borough; RMC Place; NEW LONDON; ▲ Groton; *161 I-15; ★ N.LON-; mail Groton z 06340; pop. incl. with Groton (Inc. Place)

Boston (Little Boston); RMC Place; FAIRFIELD; ▲ Redding; *160 J-4; ★ N.Y.; mail Redding Center z 06875; ● 200

Botsford; RMC Place; FAIRFIELD; ▲ Newtown; 160 I-5; 🅿; ★ N.Y.; z 06404; ● 490

Boulder Lake; RMC Place; MIDDLESEX; ▲ Clinton; elev. 25ft./8m.; ★ N.HAV; mail Clinton z 06413

Bozrah; NEW LONDON; see Gilman (RMC Place)

Bozrah; MCD-Town; NEW LONDON; *161 G-14; 🅿; ★ N.LON-; z 06334; ℗ 2,297; © 2,357; ◆ 2,469

Branchville; RMC Place; FAIRFIELD; ▲ Ridgefield; 160 J-4; ★ N.Y.; mail Georgetown z 06829; ● 350

Branford; RMC Place; NEW HAVEN; ▲ Branford; 160 J-9; ★ N.HAV; ● 5,700

Branford; MCD-Town; NEW HAVEN; *160 J-9; 🅿; ★ N.HAV; z 06405; ℗ 27,603; © 28,683; ◆ 29,674

Branford Center; CDP-Census Area Only; NEW HAVEN; ▲ Branford; 161 M-17; 🅷; ★ N.HAV; mail Branford z 06405; ℗ 5,688; © 5,735

Branford Hills; RMC Place; NEW HAVEN; ▲ Branford; *160 J-9; ★ N.HAV; mail Branford z 06405; ● 2,600

Brendan Heights; RMC Place; TOLLAND; ▲ Stafford; ★ H-NB; mail Stafford Springs z 06076

Bretton Heights; RMC Place; MIDDLESEX; ▲ Middletown; *160 G-10; ★ H-NB; mail Middletown z 06457; pop. incl. with Middletown (Inc. Place)

Bridgeport; Inc. Place; FAIRFIELD; ▲ Bridgeport; 161 M-11; 🅿 🅷 🅲 4,018 ■; ★ N.Y.; z 06601-02, z 06604-08, z 06610-12, z 06614-15, z 06650, z 06673, z 06699; ℗ 141,686; © 139,529; ◆ 136,479

Bridgeport; MCD-Town; FAIRFIELD; *160 K-6; 🅿 🅷 🅲 4,018; ★ N.Y.; z 06601-02, z 06604-08, z 06610-12, z 06614-15, z 06650, z 06673, z 06699; coextensive with the City of Bridgeport; ℗ 141,686; © 139,529; ◆ 136,479

Bridgewater; RMC Place; LITCHFIELD; ▲ Bridgewater; 160 G-4; 🅿; ★ N.Y.; z 06752; ● 500

Bridgewater; MCD-Town; LITCHFIELD; *160 G-4; 🅿; ★ N.Y.; z 06752; ℗ 1,654; © 1,824; ◆ 1,886

Brighton Beach; RMC Place; NEW LONDON; ▲ Old Lyme; *161 J-13; elev. 10ft./3m.; ★ N.LON-; mail Old Lyme z 06371; ● 50

Brightview; RMC Place; NEW HAVEN; ▲ New Haven; *160 J-8; ★ N.HAV; pop. incl. with New Haven (Inc. Place)

Bristol; Inc. Place; HARTFORD; ▲ Bristol; 160 E-8; 🅿 🅷 ■; ★ H-NB; z 06010-11; ℗ 60,640; © 60,062; ◆ 60,008

Bristol; MCD-Town; HARTFORD; *160 E-8; 🅿 🅷; ★ H-NB; z 06010-11; coextensive with the City of Bristol; ℗ 60,640; © 60,062; ◆ 60,008

Bristol Terrace; RMC Place; NEW HAVEN; ▲ Naugatuck; ★ WATB; mail Naugatuck z 06770; pop. incl. with Naugatuck (Inc. Place)

Broad Brook; CDP; HARTFORD; ▲ East Windsor; 161 C-11; 🅿; ★ H-NB; z 06016 & mail East Windsor z 06088; ℗ 3,585; © 3,469

Bromica; RMC Place; LITCHFIELD; ▲ Kent; mail Kent z 06757; summer pop. 1,000

Brookfield; RMC Place; FAIRFIELD; ▲ Brookfield; 160 G-4; 🅿; ★ N.Y.; z 06804; ● 1,650

Brookfield; MCD-Town; FAIRFIELD; *160 H-4; 🅿; ★ N.Y.; z 06804; ℗ 14,113; © 15,664; ◆ 16,629

Brookfield Center; RMC Place; FAIRFIELD; ▲ Brookfield; 160 H-4; ★ N.Y.; mail Brookfield z 06804; ● 1,550

Brooklyn; RMC Place; WINDHAM; ▲ Brooklyn; 161 D-16; elev. 280ft./85m.; 🅿; z 06234; ● 1,650

Brooklyn; MCD-Town; WINDHAM; *161 D-16; 🅿; z 06234; ℗ 6,681; © 7,173

Brook Valley; RMC Place; NEW HAVEN; ▲ Naugatuck; ★ WATB; mail Naugatuck z 06770; pop. incl. with Naugatuck (Inc. Place)

Browns Corner; RMC Place; LITCHFIELD; ▲ New Hartford; *160 D-8; elev. 539ft./164m.; ★ H-NB; mail New Hartford z 06057; rural

Bruce Park; RMC Place; FAIRFIELD; ▲ Greenwich; ★ N.Y.; mail Greenwich z 06830

Brush Island; RMC Place; FAIRFIELD; ▲ Darien; elev. 60ft./18m.; ★ N.Y.; mail Darien z 06820

Buckingham; RMC Place; HARTFORD; ▲ Glastonbury; 161 E-11; elev. 420ft./128m.; ★ H-NB; mail Glastonbury z 06033; ● 200

Buckland; RMC Place; HARTFORD; ▲ Manchester; *161 D-11; ★ H-NB; mail Manchester z 06040

Bucks Corners; RMC Place; HARTFORD; ▲ Glastonbury; ★ H-NB; mail South Glastonbury z 06073

Bulls Bridge; RMC Place; LITCHFIELD; ▲ Kent; 160 E-3; mail South Kent z 06785; ● 100

Bunker Hill; RMC Place; NEW HAVEN; ▲ Waterbury; *160 G-7; ★ WATB; mail Waterbury z 06708; pop. incl. with Waterbury (Inc. Place)

Burlington (Burlington Center); RMC Place; HARTFORD; ▲ Burlington; 160 D-8; 🅿; ★ H-NB; z 06013 & mail Unionville z 06085; ● 500

Burlington; MCD-Town; HARTFORD; *160 E-8; 🅿; ★ H-NB; z 06013 & mail Unionville z 06085; ℗ 7,026; © 8,190; ◆ 8,572

Burlington Center; HARTFORD; see Burlington (RMC Place)

Burnside; RMC Place; HARTFORD; ▲ East Hartford; *161 D-11; ★ H-NB; mail East Hartford z 06108

Burrville; RMC Place; LITCHFIELD; ▲ Torrington; *160 C-7; elev. 724ft./221m.; ★ TORR; mail Torrington z 06790; pop. incl. with Torrington (Inc. Place)

Burwells Beach; RMC Place; NEW HAVEN; ▲ Milford; ★ N.Y.; mail Milford z 06460; pop. incl. with Milford (Inc. Place)

Byram; RMC Place; FAIRFIELD; ▲ Greenwich; *160 M-2; ★ N.Y.; mail Greenwich z 06830

Byram Shore; RMC Place; FAIRFIELD; ▲ Greenwich; *160 M-2; elev. 50ft./15m.; ★ N.Y.; mail Greenwich z 06830

C

Camp Bethel; RMC Place; MIDDLESEX; ▲ Haddam; *161 H-12; ★ H-NB; mail Haddam z 06438; summer pop. 60

Camptown; RMC Place; NEW HAVEN; ▲ Derby; ★ N.Y.; mail Derby z 06418; pop. incl. with Derby (Inc. Place)

Canaan; CDP; LITCHFIELD; ▲ North Canaan; 160 B-5; 🅿; z 06018 & mail Falls Village z 06031; ℗ 1,194; © 1,288

Canaan; MCD-Town; LITCHFIELD; *160 B-5; 🅿; z 06018 & mail Falls Village z 06031; ℗ 1,057; © 1,081

Candlewood Echoes; RMC Place; FAIRFIELD; ▲ Sherman; *160 G-3; elev. 552ft./168m.; ★ N.Y.; mail Sherman z 06784

Candlewood Hill; RMC Place; MIDDLESEX; ▲ Haddam; ★ H-NB; mail Higganum z 06441

Candlewood Hills; RMC Place; FAIRFIELD; ▲ New Fairfield; *160 G-3; elev. 700ft./213m.; ★ N.Y.; mail New Fairfield z 06812; summer pop. 1,000; ● 570

Candlewood Isle; RMC Place; FAIRFIELD; ▲ New Fairfield; 160 G-4; ★ N.Y.; mail New Fairfield z 06812; ● 1,260

Candlewood Knolls; RMC Place; FAIRFIELD; ▲ New Fairfield; 160 G-4; ★ N.Y.; mail Danbury z 06810; summer pop. 900; ● 560

Candlewood Lake Club; RMC Place; FAIRFIELD, LITCHFIELD; ▲ New Milford, Brookfield; *160 G-4; elev. 550ft./168m.; ★ N.Y.; mail Brookfield z 06804; ● 1,050

Candlewood Orchards; RMC Place; FAIRFIELD; ▲ Brookfield; *160 H-4; ★ N.Y.; mail Brookfield z 06804; ● 170

Candlewood Point; RMC Place; LITCHFIELD; ▲ New Milford; *160 G-4; ★ N.Y.; mail New Milford z 06776; ● 300

Candlewood Shores; RMC Place; FAIRFIELD; ▲ Brookfield; 160 H-4; ★ N.Y.; mail Brookfield z 06804; ● 1,800

Candlewood Springs; RMC Place; LITCHFIELD; ▲ New Milford; *160 G-4; ★ N.Y.; mail New Milford z 06776; ● 200

Candlewood Trails; RMC Place; LITCHFIELD; ▲ New Milford; *160 G-4; ★ N.Y.; mail New Milford z 06776; ● 100

Cannondale; RMC Place; FAIRFIELD; ▲ Wilton; 160 J-4; ★ N.Y.; mail Wilton z 06897; ● 1,500

Canterbury; RMC Place; WINDHAM; ▲ Canterbury; 161 E-16; 🅿; ★ N.LON-; z 06331 & mail Jewett City z 06351; ● 200

Canterbury; MCD-Town; WINDHAM; *161 E-15; 🅿; ★ N.LON-; z 06331 & mail Jewett City z 06351; ℗ 4,467; © 4,692; ◆ 5,030

Canton; RMC Place; HARTFORD; ▲ Canton; ★ H-NB; ● 480

Canton; HARTFORD; see Canton Valley (CDP-Census Area Only)

Canton; MCD-Town; HARTFORD; *160 C-8; 🅿; ★ H-NB; z 06019; ℗ 8,268; © 8,840; ◆ 9,530

Canton Center; RMC Place; HARTFORD; ▲ Canton; 160 D-8; 🅿; ★ H-NB; z 06020; ● 380

Canton Valley (Canton); CDP-Census Area Only; HARTFORD; ▲ Canton; 160 D-8; elev. 347ft./106m.; ★ H-NB; mail Canton z 06019; ℗ 1,563; © 1,565

Carmel Hill; RMC Place; LITCHFIELD; ▲ Bethlehem; *160 F-5; elev. 1,072ft./327m.; ★ WATB; mail Bethlehem z 06751; rural

Castle Hill; RMC Place; NEW LONDON; ▲ Stonington; *161 I-17; elev. 150ft./46m.; ★ N.LON-; mail Westerly z 02891

Cedar Beach; RMC Place; NEW HAVEN; ▲ Milford; 161 N-13; ★ N.Y.; mail Milford z 06460

Cedar Heights; RMC Place; FAIRFIELD; ▲ Danbury; *160 H-4; ★ N.Y.; mail Danbury z 06810; pop. incl. with Danbury (Inc. Place)

Cedarhurst; RMC Place; FAIRFIELD; ▲ Newtown; *160 H-6; ★ N.Y.; mail Sandy Hook z 06482; summer pop. 300; ● 220

Cedar Knolls; RMC Place; LITCHFIELD; ▲ New Milford; *160 G-4; elev. 246ft./75m.; ★ N.Y.; mail New Milford z 06776; ● 160

Cedar Lake; RMC Place; HARTFORD; ▲ Bristol; ★ H-NB; mail Bristol z 06010; pop. incl. with Bristol (Inc. Place)

Cedar Land; RMC Place; NEW HAVEN; ▲ Southbury; *160 H-5; ★ WATB; mail Southbury z 06488

Center; RMC Place; FAIRFIELD; ▲ Trumbull; *160 J-6; ★ N.Y.; mail Trumbull z 06611

Centerbrook; RMC Place; MIDDLESEX; ▲ Essex; 161 I-12; 🅿; z 06409; ● 1,000

Center Groton; RMC Place; NEW LONDON; ▲ Groton; *161 I-15; ★ N.LON-; mail Groton z 06340

Centerville; RMC Place; NEW HAVEN; ▲ Hamden; 161 K-17; ★ N.HAV; mail Hamden z 06518

Central; RMC Place; HARTFORD; ▲ Hartford; *160 D-10; ★ H-NB; mail Hartford z 06103; pop. incl. with Hartford (Inc. Place)

Central Manchester; CDP-Census Area Only; HARTFORD; ▲ Manchester; *161 D-11; ★ H-NB; mail Manchester z 06040; ℗ 30,934; © 30,595; ◆ 31,282

Central Somers; CDP-Census Area Only; TOLLAND; ▲ Somers; 161 B-12; elev. 272ft./83m.; 🅷; ★ H-NB; mail Somers z 06071; ℗ 1,644; © 1,626

Central Village; RMC Place; WINDHAM; ▲ Plainfield; 161 E-16; 🅿; ★ N.LON-; z 06332; ● 1,800

Central Waterford (Waterford); CDP-Census Area Only; NEW LONDON; ▲ Waterford; 161 M-18; ★ N.LON-; mail Waterford z 06385; ℗ 2,939; © 2,935

Chaffeeville; RMC Place; TOLLAND; ▲ Mansfield; *161 D-14; ★ H-NB; mail Storrs Mansfield z 06268

Chalkers Beach; RMC Place; MIDDLESEX; ▲ Old Saybrook; mail Old Saybrook z 06475

Chaplin; RMC Place; WINDHAM; ▲ Chaplin; 161 D-14; elev. 417ft./127m.; 🅿; ★ H-NB; z 06235; ● 230

Chaplin; MCD-Town; WINDHAM; *161 D-14; 🅿; ★ H-NB; z 06235; ℗ 2,048; © 2,250; ◆ 2,489

Chapman Beach; RMC Place; MIDDLESEX; ▲ Westbrook; mail Westbrook z 06498

Charcoal Ridge; RMC Place; FAIRFIELD; ▲ New Fairfield; *160 H-3; ★ N.Y.; mail New Fairfield z 06812; ● 2,600

Cherry Brook; RMC Place; HARTFORD; ▲ Canton; *160 D-8; ★ H-NB; mail Canton Center z 06020

Cherry Hill; RMC Place; LITCHFIELD; ▲ Cornwall; *160 C-5; elev. 987ft./301m.; mail West Cornwall z 06796; rural

Cherrywood; RMC Place; HARTFORD; ▲ Southington; ★ H-NB; mail Plantsville z 06479

Cheshire; RMC Place; NEW HAVEN; 160 G-8; ★ N.HAV; ● 5,800

Cheshire; MCD-Town; NEW HAVEN; *160 G-8; elev. 262ft./80m.; 🅿; ★ N.HAV; z 06408, z 06410-11; ℗ 25,684; © 28,543; ◆ 30,347

Cheshire Village; CDP-Census Area Only; NEW HAVEN; ▲ Cheshire; 160 G-8; elev. 262ft./80m.; ★ N.HAV; mail Cheshire z 06408, z 06410-11; ℗ 5,759; © 5,789

Chester; RMC Place; MIDDLESEX; ▲ Chester; ● 700

Chester; MCD-Town; MIDDLESEX; *161 H-12; 🅿; z 06412; ℗ 3,417; © 3,743

Chester Center; CDP-Census Area Only; MIDDLESEX; ▲ Chester; 161 H-12; mail Chester z 06412; ℗ 1,563; © 1,546

Chesterfield; RMC Place; NEW LONDON; 161 F-11; elev. 160ft./49m.; ★ N.LON-; mail Oakdale z 06370

Chestnut Hill; NEW LONDON; see Liberty Hill (RMC Place)

Chestnut Hill; RMC Place; TOLLAND; ▲ Columbia; *161 E-13; elev. 389ft./119m.; ★ H-NB; mail Columbia z 06237, Willimantic z 06226

Chickahominy; RMC Place; FAIRFIELD; ▲ Greenwich; ★ N.Y.; mail Greenwich z 06830

Chippens Hill; RMC Place; HARTFORD; ▲ Bristol; ★ H-NB; mail Bristol z 06010; pop. incl. with Bristol (Inc. Place)

Christy Hill Estates; RMC Place; NEW LONDON; ▲ Ledyard; ★ N.LON-; mail Gales Ferry z 06335

Churchwood; RMC Place; NEW LONDON; ▲ East Lyme; ★ N.LON-; mail Niantic z 06357; ● 100

City Point; RMC Place; NEW HAVEN; ▲ New Haven; *160 J-8; ★ N.HAV; pop. incl. with New Haven (Inc. Place)

Clarks Corner; RMC Place; WINDHAM; ▲ Hampton; *161 D-15; mail North Windham z 06256

Clarks Falls; RMC Place; NEW LONDON; ▲ North Stonington; 161 H-17; ★ N.LON-; mail North Stonington z 06359; ● 170

Clarks Village; RMC Place; NEW LONDON; ▲ Stonington; *161 I-17; ★ N.LON-; mail Westerly z 02891

Clearview Heights; RMC Place; TOLLAND; ▲ Stafford; ★ H-NB; mail Stafford Springs z 06076

Clinton; CDP; MIDDLESEX; ▲ Clinton; 161 J-11; elev. 25ft./8m.; 🅿; ★ N.HAV; z 06413; ℗ 3,439; © 3,516

Clinton; MCD-Town; MIDDLESEX; *161 J-11; elev. 25ft./8m.; 🅿; ★ N.HAV; z 06413; ℗ 12,767; © 13,094; ◆ 13,349

Clinton Beach; RMC Place; MIDDLESEX; ▲ Clinton; *161 J-11; elev. 25ft./8m.; ★ N.HAV; mail Clinton z 06413

Clintonville; RMC Place; NEW HAVEN; ▲ North Haven; *160 H-9; ★ N.HAV; mail North Haven z 06473

Cobalt; RMC Place; MIDDLESEX; ▲ East Hampton; 161 G-11; 🅿; ★ H-NB; z 06414; ● 500

Codfish Hill; RMC Place; FAIRFIELD; ▲ Bethel; *160 I-4; elev. 659ft./201m.; ★ N.Y.; mail Bethel z 06801; ● 330

Colburn Hill; RMC Place; TOLLAND; ▲ Stafford; ★ H-NB; mail Stafford Springs z 06076

Colchester; RMC Place; NEW LONDON; ▲ Colchester; 161 F-13; 🅿; ★ H-NB; z 06415, z 06420; ● 4,500

Colchester; MCD-Town; NEW LONDON; *161 G-13; 🅿; ★ H-NB; z 06415, z 06420; ℗ 10,980; © 14,551; ◆ 15,884

Colebrook; RMC Place; LITCHFIELD; ▲ Colebrook; 160 B-7; 🅿; z 06021; ● 400

Colebrook; MCD-Town; LITCHFIELD; *160 B-7; 🅿; z 06021; ℗ 1,365; © 1,471

Collinsville; CDP; HARTFORD; ▲ Canton; 160 D-8; 🅿; ★ H-NB; z 06019, z 06022; ℗ 2,591; © 2,686

Columbia (Columbia Center); RMC Place; TOLLAND; ▲ Columbia; 161 E-13; 🅿; ★ H-NB; z 06237; ● 800

Columbia; MCD-Town; TOLLAND; *161 E-13; 🅿; ★ H-NB; z 06237; ℗ 4,510; © 4,971; ◆ 5,185

Columbia Center; TOLLAND; see Columbia (RMC Place)

Compo Beach; RMC Place; FAIRFIELD; ▲ Westport; elev. 78ft./24m.; ★ N.Y.; mail Westport z 06880

Compo Hill; RMC Place; FAIRFIELD; ▲ Westport; elev. 78ft./24m.; ★ N.Y.; mail Westport z 06880

Conantville; RMC Place; TOLLAND; ▲ Mansfield; *161 E-14; ★ H-NB; mail Willimantic z 06226

Congamond Lakes; RMC Place; HARTFORD; ▲ Suffield; *160 B-9; elev. 75ft./23m.; ★ H-NB; mail West Suffield z 06093; ● 500

Conning Towers-Nautilus Park; CDP-Census Area Only; NEW LONDON; ▲ Groton; *161 I-15; ★ N.LON-; mail Groton z 06340; ℗ 10,013; © 10,241; ® 10,981

Cornwall; RMC Place; LITCHFIELD; ▲ Cornwall; 160 D-5; elev. 718ft./219m.; 🅿; z 06753 & mail West Cornwall z 06796; ● 330

Cornwall; MCD-Town; LITCHFIELD; *160 D-5; 🅿; z 06753 & mail West Cornwall z 06796; ℗ 1,414; © 1,434

Cornwall Bridge; RMC Place; LITCHFIELD; ▲ Cornwall; 160 D-4; elev. 445ft./136m.; 🅿; z 06754; ● 500

Cornwall Center; RMC Place; LITCHFIELD; ▲ Cornwall; *160 C-5; elev. 1,122ft./342m.; mail West Cornwall z 06796

Cornwall Hollow; RMC Place; LITCHFIELD; ▲ Cornwall; *160 C-5; elev. 925ft./282m.; mail Falls Village z 06031; rural

Cos Cob; RMC Place; FAIRFIELD; ▲ Greenwich; 160 M-8; 🅿; ★ N.Y.; z 06807

Cottage Grove; RMC Place; HARTFORD; ▲ Bloomfield; *160 D-10; ★ H-NB; mail Bloomfield z 06002

Coventry; RMC Place; TOLLAND; ▲ Coventry; ★ H-NB; ● 600

Coventry; MCD-Town; TOLLAND; *161 D-13; 🅿; ★ H-NB; z 06238; ℗ 10,063; © 11,504; ® 11,468; ◆ 12,075

Coventry Lake; CDP-Census Area Only; TOLLAND; ▲ Coventry; 161 D-13; ★ H-NB; mail Coventry z 06238; ℗ 2,895; © 2,914

Cranbury; RMC Place; FAIRFIELD; ▲ Norwalk; *160 K-4; ★ N.Y.; mail Norwalk z 06851; pop. incl. with Norwalk (Inc. Place)

Cranska Village; RMC Place; WINDHAM; ▲ Plainfield; ★ N.LON-; mail Moosup z 06354

Crescent Beach; RMC Place; NEW LONDON; ▲ East Lyme; *161 I-14; ★ N.LON-; mail Niantic z 06357

Cromwell; RMC Place; MIDDLESEX; ▲ Cromwell; 160 F-10; 🅿; ★ H-NB; z 06416; ● 2,500

Cromwell; MCD-Town; MIDDLESEX; *160 F-10; 🅿; ★ H-NB; z 06416; ℗ 12,286; © 12,871; ◆ 13,657

Cromwell Hills; RMC Place; MIDDLESEX; ▲ Cromwell; *160 F-10; ★ H-NB; mail Cromwell z 06416; ● 360

Crystal Lake; CDP; TOLLAND; ▲ Ellington; 161 C-12; ★ H-NB; mail Ellington z 06029; ℗ 1,175; © 1,459

D

Damascus; RMC Place; NEW HAVEN; ▲ Branford; *160 J-9; ★ N.HAV; mail Branford z 06405; ● 1,000

Danbury; Inc. Place; FAIRFIELD; ▲ Danbury; 160 H-4; elev. 378ft./115m.; 🅿 🅷 🅲 5,907 ■; ★ N.Y.; z 06810-14, z 06816-17; ℗ 65,585; © 74,848; ◆ 79,021

Danbury; MCD-Town; FAIRFIELD; *160 H-3; 🅿 🅷 🅲 5,907; ★ N.Y.; z 06810-14, z 06816-17; coextensive with the City of Danbury; ℗ 65,585; © 74,848; ◆ 79,021

Danbury West; RMC Place; FAIRFIELD; ▲ Danbury; ★ N.Y.; pop. incl. with Danbury (Inc. Place)

Danielson; Inc. Place; WINDHAM; ▲ Killingly; 161 D-16; elev. 236ft./72m.; 🅿; z 06239; ℗ 4,441; © 4,265

Darien; CDP; FAIRFIELD; ▲ Darien; 160 L-3; elev. 60ft./18m.; 🅿; ★ N.Y.; z 06820; ℗ 18,130; © 19,607

Darien; MCD-Town; FAIRFIELD; *160 L-3; elev. 60ft./18m.; 🅿; ★ N.Y.; z 06820; ℗ 18,196; © 19,607; ◆ 20,033

Dayville; RMC Place; WINDHAM; ▲ Killingly; 161 D-16; elev. 245ft./75m.; 🅿; z 06241; ● 1,650

Dean Corners; RMC Place; LITCHFIELD; ▲ Cornwall; *160 D-5; elev. 700ft./213m.; mail Cornwall z 06753; rural

Deep River; RMC Place; MIDDLESEX; ▲ Deep River; 161 I-12; ● 1,700

Deep River; MCD-Town; MIDDLESEX; *161 I-12; 🅿; z 06417, z 06419; ℗ 4,332; © 4,610

Deep River Center; CDP-Census Area Only; MIDDLESEX; ▲ Deep River; 161 H-12; mail Deep River z 06417, Killingworth z 06419; ℗ 2,520; © 2,470

Deer Island; RMC Place; LITCHFIELD; ▲ Morris; *160 E-5; ★ TORR; mail Lakeside z 06758; ● 100

Deer Run Shores; RMC Place; FAIRFIELD; ▲ Sherman; ★ N.Y.; mail Sherman z 06784; ● 150

Derby (Derby Shelton); Inc. Place; NEW HAVEN; ▲ Derby; 161 K-14; 🅿 🅷 ■; ★ N.Y.; z 06418; ℗ 12,199; © 12,391; ◆ 12,499

Derby; MCD-Town; NEW HAVEN; *160 I-7; 🅿 🅷; ★ N.Y.; z 06418; coextensive with the City of Derby; ℗ 12,199; © 12,391

Derby Junction; RMC Place; NEW HAVEN; ▲ Derby; ★ N.Y.; mail Derby z 06418; pop. incl. with Derby (Inc. Place)

Derby Neck; RMC Place; NEW HAVEN; ▲ Derby; ★ N.Y.; mail Derby z 06418; pop. incl. with Derby (Inc. Place)

Derby Shelton; NEW HAVEN; see Derby (Inc. Place)

Devon; RMC Place; NEW HAVEN; ▲ Milford; 161 M-13; ★ N.Y.; mail Milford z 06460; pop. incl. with Milford (Inc. Place)

Diamond Lake; RMC Place; HARTFORD; ▲ Glastonbury; 161 E-11; ★ H-NB; mail Glastonbury z 06033; ● 400

Dickerman's Corner; RMC Place; HARTFORD; ▲ Southington; ★ H-NB; mail Plantsville z 06479

Doaneville (Doanville); RMC Place; NEW LONDON; ▲ Griswold; *161 F-16; elev. 200ft./61m.; ★ N.LON-; mail Preston z 06365; rural

Doanville; NEW LONDON; see Doaneville (RMC Place)

Dodgingtown; RMC Place; FAIRFIELD; ▲ Newtown; 160 I-5; ★ N.Y.; mail Newtown z 06470; ● 300

Dorlons Point; RMC Place; FAIRFIELD; ▲ Norwalk; ★ N.Y.; pop. incl. with Norwalk (Inc. Place)

Double Beach; RMC Place; NEW HAVEN; ▲ Branford; 161 N-17; ★ N.HAV; mail Branford z 06405; ● 1,100

Dowd's Corner; RMC Place; HARTFORD; ▲ Canton; ★ H-NB; mail Canton z 06019

Downersville; RMC Place; NEW LONDON; ▲ Stonington; ★ N.LON-; mail Westerly z 02891

Drakeville; RMC Place; LITCHFIELD; ▲ Torrington; *160 C-6; ★ TORR; mail Torrington z 06790; pop. incl. with Torrington (Inc. Place)

Durham; CDP; MIDDLESEX; ▲ Durham; 160 H-10; elev. 239ft./73m.; 🅿; ★ H-NB; z 06422; ℗ 2,650; © 2,773

Durham; MCD-Town; MIDDLESEX; *160 H-10; 🅿; ★ H-NB; z 06422; ℗ 5,732; © 6,627; ◆ 7,215

Durham Center; RMC Place; MIDDLESEX; ▲ Durham; *160 H-10; ★ H-NB; mail Durham z 06422

E

Eagleville; RMC Place; TOLLAND; ▲ Mansfield; 161 D-13; ★ H-NB; mail Storrs Mansfield z 06268; ● 460

East Berlin; RMC Place; HARTFORD; ▲ Berlin; 160 F-10; 🅿; ★ H-NB; z 06023; ● 1,100

East Bridgeport; RMC Place; FAIRFIELD; ▲ Bridgeport; 161 M-12; ★ N.Y.; pop. incl. with Bridgeport (Inc. Place)

East Bristol; RMC Place; HARTFORD; ▲ Bristol; *160 F-8; elev. 270ft./82m.; ★ H-NB; mail Bristol z 06010; pop. incl. with Bristol (Inc. Place)

East Brooklyn; CDP; WINDHAM; ▲ Brooklyn; 161 D-16; mail Danielson z 06239; ℗ 1,481; © 1,473

East Canaan; RMC Place; LITCHFIELD; ▲ North Canaan; 160 B-5; elev. 809ft./247m.; 🅿; z 06024; ● 1,000

East Cornwall; RMC Place; LITCHFIELD; ▲ Cornwall; *160 D-5; elev. 1,277ft./389m.; mail Litchfield z 06759; ● 30

East Derby; RMC Place; NEW HAVEN; ▲ Derby; *160 I-7; ★ N.Y.; mail Derby z 06418; pop. incl. with Derby (Inc. Place)

East End; RMC Place; NEW HAVEN; ▲ Waterbury; *160 G-7; ★ WATB; mail Waterbury z 06705; pop. incl. with Waterbury (Inc. Place)

Eastern Point; RMC Place; NEW LONDON; ▲ Groton; ★ N.LON-; mail Groton z 06340; pop. incl. with Groton (Inc. Place)

East Farmington Heights; RMC Place; HARTFORD; ▲ Farmington; 160 E-9; ★ H-NB; mail Farmington z 06032; ● 450

East Farms; RMC Place; NEW HAVEN; ▲ Waterbury; *160 G-7; ★ WATB; mail Waterbury z 06705; pop. incl. with Waterbury (Inc. Place)

Eastford; RMC Place; WINDHAM; ▲ Eastford; 161 C-15; 🅿; z 06242; ● 1,020

Eastford; MCD-Town; WINDHAM; *161 C-15; 🅿; z 06242; ℗ 1,314; © 1,618

East Glastonbury; RMC Place; HARTFORD; ▲ Glastonbury; 161 E-11; elev. 362ft./110m.; 🅿; ★ H-NB; z 06025; ● 300

East Granby; RMC Place; HARTFORD; ▲ East Granby; 160 C-10; elev. 193ft./59m.; 🅿; ★ H-NB; z 06026; ● 1,300

East Granby; MCD-Town; HARTFORD; *160 B-9; 🅿; ★ H-NB; z 06026; ℗ 4,302; © 4,745; ◆ 5,159

East Great Plain; RMC Place; NEW LONDON; ▲ Norwich; ★ N.LON-; mail Norwich z 06360; pop. incl. with Norwich (Inc. Place)

East Haddam; RMC Place; MIDDLESEX; ▲ East Haddam; 161 H-12; elev. 35ft./11m.; 🅿; ★ H-NB; z 06423; ● 800

East Haddam; MCD-Town; MIDDLESEX; *161 H-12; 🅿; ★ H-NB; z 06423; ℗ 6,676; © 8,333; ◆ 9,713

East Haddam Landing; RMC Place; MIDDLESEX; ▲ East Haddam; ★ H-NB; mail East Haddam z 06423

East Hampton; CDP; MIDDLESEX; ▲ East Hampton; 161 F-11; elev. 412ft./126m.; 🅿; ★ H-NB; z 06424, z 06447; ℗ 2,167; © 2,254

East Hampton; MCD-Town; MIDDLESEX; *161 G-11; 🅿; ★ H-NB; z 06424, z 06447; ℗ 10,428; © 13,352; ® 10,956; ◆ 13,028

East Hampton Center; RMC Place; MIDDLESEX; ▲ East Hampton; ★ H-NB; mail East Hampton z 06424

East Hartford; CDP; HARTFORD; ▲ East Hartford; 160 D-10; 🅿; ★ H-NB; z 06108, z 06118, z 06128, z 06138; ℗ 50,452; © 49,575; ◆ 50,637

East Hartford; MCD-Town; HARTFORD; *160 D-10; 🅿 ■; ★ H-NB; z 06108, z 06118, z 06128, z 06138; ℗ 50,452; © 49,575; ◆ 50,637

East Hartland; RMC Place; HARTFORD; ▲ Hartland; 160 B-8; elev. 1,202ft./366m.; 🅿; z 06027; ● 1,200

East Haven; CDP; NEW HAVEN; ▲ East Haven; 161 M-16; elev. 25ft./8m.; 🅿; ★ N.HAV; z 06512-13; ℗ 26,144; © 28,189; ◆ 29,206

East Haven; MCD-Town; NEW HAVEN; *160 J-8; elev. 25ft./8m.; 🅿; ★ N.HAV; z 06512-13; ℗ 26,144; © 28,189; ◆ 29,206

East Hill; RMC Place; HARTFORD; ▲ Canton; ★ H-NB; mail Canton z 06019

East Killingly; RMC Place; WINDHAM; ▲ Killingly; 161 D-17; 🅿; z 06243; ● 770

East Litchfield; RMC Place; LITCHFIELD; ▲ Litchfield; 160 D-6; ★ TORR; mail Litchfield z 06759; ● 180

East Lyme; NEW LONDON; see Flanders (RMC Place)

East Lyme; MCD-Town; NEW LONDON; *161 I-14; 🅿; ★ N.LON-; z 06333; ℗ 15,340; © 18,118; ◆ 19,675

East Meriden; RMC Place; NEW HAVEN; ▲ Meriden; *160 G-9; elev. 350ft./107m.; ★ N.HAV; mail Meriden z 06450; pop. incl. with Meriden (Inc. Place)

East Morris; RMC Place; LITCHFIELD; ▲ Morris; *160 E-6; ★ TORR; mail Morris z 06763

East Mountain; RMC Place; NEW HAVEN; ▲ Waterbury; *160 G-7; ★ WATB; mail Waterbury z 06706; pop. incl. with Waterbury (Inc. Place)

East New London; RMC Place; NEW LONDON; ▲ New London; *161 I-15; ★ N.LON-; mail New London z 06320; pop. incl. with New London (Inc. Place)

East Norwalk; RMC Place; FAIRFIELD; ▲ Norwalk; *160 L-4; ★ N.Y.; mail Bridgeport z 06601, Norwalk z 06855; pop. incl. with Norwalk (Inc. Place)

Easton (Easton Center); RMC Place; FAIRFIELD; ▲ Easton; 161 L-11; 🅿; ★ N.Y.; z 06612; ● 480

Easton; MCD-Town; FAIRFIELD; *160 J-5; 🅿; ★ N.Y.; z 06612; ℗ 6,303; © 7,272; ◆ 7,493

Easton Center; FAIRFIELD; see Easton (RMC Place)

East Plymouth; RMC Place; LITCHFIELD; ▲ Plymouth; ★ H-NB; mail Terryville z 06786

East Port Chester; RMC Place; FAIRFIELD; ▲ Greenwich; ★ N.Y.; mail Greenwich z 06830

East Putnam; RMC Place; WINDHAM; ▲ Putnam; *161 C-17; mail Putnam z 06260

East River; RMC Place; NEW HAVEN; ▲ Madison; 160 J-10; ★ N.HAV; mail Madison z 06443; ● 3,800

East Street; RMC Place; LITCHFIELD; ▲ Cornwall; *160 D-5; elev. 899ft./274m.; mail West Cornwall z 06796; rural

East Thompson; RMC Place; WINDHAM; ▲ Thompson; 161 B-17; elev. 483ft./147m.; ★ WORC; mail Thompson z 06277; ● 640

East Village; RMC Place; FAIRFIELD; ▲ Monroe; 160 I-6; elev. 425ft./130m.; ★ N.Y.; mail Monroe z 06468; ● 100

East Wallingford; RMC Place; NEW HAVEN; ▲ Wallingford; *160 H-9; ★ N.HAV; mail Wallingford z 06492

East Willington; RMC Place; TOLLAND; ▲ Willington; *161 C-13; ★ H-NB; mail Willington z 06279

East Windsor; HARTFORD; see Warehouse Point (RMC Place)

East Windsor; MCD-Town; HARTFORD; *161 C-11; 🅿; ★ H-NB; z 06088 & mail Broad Brook z 06016; ℗ 10,081; © 9,818; ◆ 10,141

East Windsor Hill; RMC Place; HARTFORD; ▲ South Windsor; 161 C-11; 🅿; ★ H-NB; z 06028; ● 450

East Woodstock; RMC Place; WINDHAM; ▲ Woodstock; 161 B-16; 🅿; z 06244; ● 470

Ebbs Corner; RMC Place; HARTFORD; ▲ Suffield; 160 B-9; ★ H-NB; mail West Suffield z 06093; ● 620

Edgewood; RMC Place; FAIRFIELD; ▲ Greenwich; *160 L-2; elev. 150ft./46m.; ★ N.Y.; mail Greenwich z 06830

Edgewood; RMC Place; HARTFORD; ▲ Bristol; *160 E-8; elev. 260ft./79m.; ★ H-NB; mail Bristol z 06010; pop. incl. with Bristol (Inc. Place)

Edgewood; RMC Place; TOLLAND; ▲ Stafford; ★ H-NB; mail Stafford Springs z 06076

Ekonk; RMC Place; WINDHAM; ▲ Sterling; *161 F-17; elev. 638ft./194m.; mail Moosup z 06354

Ellington; RMC Place; TOLLAND; ▲ Ellington; 161 C-12; 🅿; ★ H-NB; z 06029; ● 1,700

Ellington; MCD-Town; TOLLAND; *161 C-12; 🅿; ★ H-NB; z 06029; ℗ 11,197; © 12,921; ◆ 14,788

Elliot; WINDHAM; see Elliotts (RMC Place)

Elliotts (Elliot); RMC Place; WINDHAM; ▲ Pomfret; *161 D-15; mail Pomfret Center z 06259; ● 50

Ellsworth; RMC Place; LITCHFIELD; ▲ Sharon; *160 D-4; mail Sharon z 06069

Elm Hill; RMC Place; HARTFORD; ▲ Newington; ★ H-NB; mail Newington z 06111

Elmville; RMC Place; WINDHAM; ▲ Killingly; 161 D-16; mail Dayville z 06241; ● 330

Elmwood; RMC Place; HARTFORD; ▲ West Hartford; *160 E-10; ★ H-NB; mail West Hartford z 06110, z 06133

Elys Ferry; RMC Place; NEW LONDON; ▲ Lyme; *161 I-13; elev. 48ft./15m.; mail Old Lyme z 06371; rural

Emmons Corners; RMC Place; LITCHFIELD; ▲ Cornwall; *160 C-5; elev. 1,000ft./305m.; mail West Cornwall z 06796; rural

Enders Island; RMC Place; NEW LONDON; ▲ Stonington; *161 I-16; ★ N.LON-; mail Mystic z 06355; ● 50

Enfield; RMC Place; HARTFORD; ▲ Enfield; 161 B-11; 🅿; ★ H-NB; z 06082-83

Enfield; MCD-Town; HARTFORD; *161 B-11; 🅿 ■; ★ H-NB; z 06082-83; ℗ 45,532; © 45,212; ◆ 46,267

Enfield Street; RMC Place; HARTFORD; ▲ Enfield; *161 B-11; ★ H-NB; mail Enfield z 06082

Essex; RMC Place; MIDDLESEX; ▲ Essex; 161 I-12; ● 1,270

Essex; MCD-Town; MIDDLESEX; *161 I-12; 🅿; z 06426; ℗ 5,904; © 6,505

Essex Village; CDP-Census Area Only; MIDDLESEX; ▲ Essex; 161 I-12; mail Essex z 06426; ℗ 2,500; © 2,573

Ethel Acres; RMC Place; NEW LONDON; ▲ Lisbon; *161 F-15; elev. 150ft./46m.; ★ N.LON-; mail Jewett City z 06351; ● 50

Ettadore Park; RMC Place; NEW HAVEN; ▲ Milford; ★ N.Y.; mail Milford z 06460; pop. incl. with Milford (Inc. Place)

F

Fabyan; RMC Place; WINDHAM; ▲ Thompson; 161 B-16; 🅿; ★ WORC; z 06245 & mail North Grosvenordale z 06255; ● 530

Fairfield; RMC Place; FAIRFIELD; ▲ Fairfield; 161 N-11; elev. 15ft./5m.; 🅿 🅲 10,867; ★ N.Y.; z 06824-25, z 06828; ℗ 53,418; ● 57,300

Fairfield; MCD-Town; FAIRFIELD; *160 K-5; 🅿 🅲 10,867 ■; ★ N.Y.; z 06824-25, z 06828; ℗ 53,418; © 57,340; ◆ 58,399

FAIRFIELD; 160 I-4; ℗ 827,645; © 882,567; ◆ 883,681

Fairground; RMC Place; NEW LONDON; ▲ Norwich; ★ N.LON-; mail Norwich z 06360; pop. incl. with Norwich (Inc. Place)

Fair Haven; RMC Place; NEW HAVEN; ▲ New Haven; 161 M-16; ★ N.HAV; mail New Haven z 06513; pop. incl. with New Haven (Inc. Place)

Fair Haven East; RMC Place; NEW HAVEN; ▲ New Haven; 161 M-16; ★ N.HAV; pop. incl. with New Haven (Inc. Place)

Fair Lawn; RMC Place; NEW HAVEN; ▲ Waterbury; 160 C-2; ★ WATB; mail Waterbury z 06705; pop. incl. with Waterbury (Inc. Place)

Fairmount; RMC Place; NEW HAVEN; ▲ Waterbury; *160 F-7; ★ WATB; mail Waterbury z 06706; pop. incl. with Waterbury (Inc. Place)

Fairy Lake; RMC Place; NEW LONDON; ▲ Salem; *161 H-13; elev. 450ft./137m.; ★ N.LON-; mail Oakdale z 06370; ● 300

Fall Mountain; RMC Place; HARTFORD; ▲ Bristol; ★ H-NB; mail Bristol z 06010; pop. incl. with Bristol (Inc. Place)

Fall Mountain Lake; LITCHFIELD; see Allentown (RMC Place)

Falls Switch; RMC Place; NEW LONDON; ▲ Norwich; ★ N.LON-; mail Norwich z 06360; pop. incl. with Norwich (Inc. Place)

Falls Village; RMC Place; LITCHFIELD; ▲ Canaan; 160 B-4; 🅿; z 06031; ● 630

Farmington; RMC Place; HARTFORD; ▲ Farmington; 160 E-9; 🅿 🅷 🅲 325; ★ H-NB; z 06030, z 06032, z 06034 & mail Unionville z 06085; ● 3,100

Farmington; MCD-Town; HARTFORD; *160 E-9; 🅿 🅲 325; ★ H-NB; z 06030, z 06032, z 06034 & mail Unionville z 06085; ℗ 20,608; © 23,641; ◆ 25,433

Farview Beach; RMC Place; NEW HAVEN; ▲ Milford; ★ N.Y.; mail Milford z 06460; pop. incl. with Milford (Inc. Place)

Federal; RMC Place; NEW HAVEN; ▲ New Haven; *160 I-8; ★ N.HAV; mail New Haven z 06510; pop. incl. with New Haven (Inc. Place)

Fenwick; Inc. Place; MIDDLESEX; ▲ Old Saybrook; 161 J-13; mail Old Saybrook z 06475; ℗ 89; © 52

Fenwood; MIDDLESEX; see Fernwood (RMC Place)

Fernwood (Fenwood); RMC Place; MIDDLESEX; ▲ Old Saybrook; *161 J-12; mail Old Saybrook z 06475; ● 300

Ferris Estates; RMC Place; LITCHFIELD; ▲ New Milford; *160 G-4; elev. 450ft./137m.; ★ N.Y.; mail New Milford z 06776; ● 100

Ferry Point; RMC Place; MIDDLESEX; ▲ Old Saybrook; *161 I-13; mail Old Saybrook z 06475; ● 150

Ferry View Heights; RMC Place; NEW LONDON; ▲ Ledyard; *161 H-15; ★ N.LON-; mail Gales Ferry z 06335; ● 1,200

Field Crest Estates; RMC Place; NEW LONDON; ▲ Groton; *161 I-15; ★ N.LON-; mail Mystic z 06355

Firetown; RMC Place; HARTFORD; ▲ Simsbury; *160 C-9; ★ H-NB; mail Simsbury z 06070; ● 160

Fitchville; RMC Place; NEW LONDON; ▲ Bozrah; 161 G-14; ★ N.LON-; mail Bozrah z 06334; ● 300

Five Points; RMC Place; FAIRFIELD; ▲ Redding; *160 I-4; elev. 600ft./183m.; ★ N.Y.; mail Redding Ridge z 06876; ● 50

Five Points; RMC Place; HARTFORD; ▲ Granby; *160 B-9; elev. 258ft./79m.; ★ H-NB; mail Granby z 06035; rural

Flanders; RMC Place; LITCHFIELD; ▲ Kent; 160 E-4; mail Kent z 06757; ● 170

Flanders (East Lyme); RMC Place; NEW LONDON; ▲ East Lyme; 161 I-14; ★ N.LON-; mail East Lyme z 06333; ● 1,330

Flax Hill; RMC Place; FAIRFIELD; ▲ Norwalk; ★ N.Y.; mail Norwalk z 06850; pop. incl. with Norwalk (Inc. Place)

Floral Park; RMC Place; MIDDLESEX; ▲ Old Saybrook; *161 I-13; elev. 20ft./6m.; mail Old Saybrook z 06475; ● 100

Floydville; RMC Place; HARTFORD; ▲ East Granby; *160 C-9; ★ H-NB; mail East Granby z 06026, Granby z 06035; rural

Forbes Village; RMC Place; HARTFORD; ▲ East Hartford; *161 E-11; ★ H-NB; mail East Hartford z 06108

Forest Glen; RMC Place; MIDDLESEX; ▲ Old Saybrook; mail Old Saybrook z 06475

Forest Heights; RMC Place; NEW HAVEN; ▲ Milford; 161 M-14; ★ N.Y.; mail Milford z 06460; pop. incl. with Milford (Inc. Place)

Forest Hills; RMC Place; HARTFORD; ▲ Southington; *160 F-8; elev. 200ft./61m.; ★ H-NB; mail Southington z 06489; ● 470

Forest Park; RMC Place; TOLLAND; ▲ Hebron; *161 E-12; elev. 550ft./168m.; ★ H-NB; mail Hebron z 06248; ● 450

Forestville; RMC Place; HARTFORD; ▲ Bristol; ★ H-NB; mail Bristol z 06010; pop. incl. with Bristol (Inc. Place)

Fort Hill; RMC Place; LITCHFIELD; ▲ New Milford; 160 G-4; ★ N.Y.; mail New Milford z 06776; ● 100

Fort Trumbull Beach; RMC Place; NEW HAVEN; ▲ Milford; ★ N.Y.; mail Milford z 06460; pop. incl. with Milford (Inc. Place)

Fox Den; RMC Place; HARTFORD; ▲ Avon; *160 E-8; elev. 300ft./91m.; ★ H-NB; mail Avon z 06001; ● 300

Foxon; RMC Place; NEW HAVEN; ▲ East Haven; 161 M-17; elev. 25ft./8m.; ★ N.HAV; mail East Haven z 06512

Franklin; RMC Place; NEW LONDON; ▲ Franklin; 161 F-14; ★ N.LON-; mail North Franklin z 06254; ● 140

Franklin; MCD-Town; NEW LONDON; *161 F-14; ★ N.LON-; mail North Franklin z 06254; ℗ 1,810; © 1,835; ◆ 1,915

Franklin Square; RMC Place; NEW LONDON; ▲ Norwich; ★ N.LON-; mail Norwich z 06360; pop. incl. with Norwich (Inc. Place)

Furnace Hollow; RMC Place; TOLLAND; ▲ Stafford; ★ H-NB; mail Stafford Springs z 06076

G

Gales Ferry; RMC Place; NEW LONDON; ▲ Ledyard; 161 H-15; 🅿; ★ N.LON-; z 06335, z 06339; ● 1,200

Gaylordsville; RMC Place; LITCHFIELD; ▲ New Milford; 160 F-3; 🅿; ★ N.Y.; z 06755; ● 730

Georgetown; CDP; FAIRFIELD; ▲ Wilton, Redding, Weston; 160 J-4; 🅿; ★ N.Y.; z 06829; ℗ 1,694; © 1,650

Georgetown; RMC Place; HARTFORD; ▲ Southington; ★ H-NB; mail Plantsville z 06479

Germantown; RMC Place; FAIRFIELD; ▲ Danbury; *160 H-4; ★ N.Y.; mail Danbury z 06810; pop. incl. with Danbury (Inc. Place)

Giants Neck; RMC Place; NEW LONDON; ▲ East Lyme; 161 I-14; ★ N.LON-; mail Niantic z 06357; summer pop. 1,500; ● 1,330

Giants Neck Heights; RMC Place; NEW LONDON; ▲ East Lyme; ★ N.LON-; mail Niantic z 06357

Gildersleeve; RMC Place; MIDDLESEX; ▲ Portland; *160 F-10; ★ H-NB; mail Portland z 06480

Gilead; RMC Place; TOLLAND; ▲ Hebron; 161 E-12; elev. 595ft./181m.; ★ H-NB; mail Hebron z 06248; ● 130

Gilman (Bozrah); RMC Place; NEW LONDON; ▲ Bozrah; 161 F-14; 🅿; ★ N.LON-; z 06336; ● 40

Glasgo; RMC Place; NEW LONDON; ▲ Griswold; 161 G-16; 🅿; ★ N.LON-; z 06384; ● 520

Glastonbury; RMC Place; HARTFORD, HARTFORD; ▲ Glastonbury; 160 E-10; ★ H-NB; ● 8,000

Glastonbury; MCD-Town; HARTFORD; *161 E-11; 🅿; ★ H-NB; z 06033; ℗ 27,901; © 31,876; ◆ 34,082

Glastonbury Center; CDP-Census Area Only; HARTFORD; ▲ Glastonbury; 160 E-10; ★ H-NB; mail Glastonbury z 06033; ℗ 7,082; © 7,157

Glenbrook; RMC Place; FAIRFIELD; ▲ Stamford; 160 L-10; ★ N.Y.; mail Stamford z 06906; pop. incl. with Stamford (Inc. Place)

Glenville; RMC Place; FAIRFIELD; ▲ Greenwich; *160 L-2; ★ N.Y.; mail Greenwich z 06830-31

Golden Hill Reservation; Indian Reservation; NEW LONDON, FAIRFIELD; State Reservation; © 0

Golden Spur; RMC Place; NEW LONDON; ▲ East Lyme; 161 I-14; ★ N.LON-; mail Waterford z 06385; ● 130

Good Hill; RMC Place; LITCHFIELD; ▲ Kent; *160 E-4; elev. 554ft./169m.; mail Kent z 06757; rural

Good Hill; RMC Place; LITCHFIELD; ▲ Roxbury; ★ WATB; mail Roxbury z 06783

Good Hill; RMC Place; NEW HAVEN; ▲ Oxford; 160 H-6; ★ N.Y.; mail Oxford z 06478; ● 330

Goodrich Heights; RMC Place; MIDDLESEX; ▲ Cromwell; *160 F-10; elev. 150ft./46m.; ★ H-NB; mail Cromwell z 06416; ● 50

Goodsell Point; RMC Place; NEW HAVEN; ▲ Branford; ★ N.HAV; mail Branford z 06405

Goshen; RMC Place; LITCHFIELD; ▲ Goshen; 160 D-5; elev. 1,333ft./406m.; 🅿; z 06756; ● 890

Goshen; MCD-Town; LITCHFIELD; *160 D-5; 🅿; z 06756; ℗ 2,329; © 2,697

Goshen; RMC Place; NEW LONDON; ▲ Waterford; *161 I-14; elev. 20ft./6m.; ★ N.LON-; mail Waterford z 06385; ● 600

Goshen Hill; RMC Place; NEW LONDON; ▲ Lebanon; *161 F-13; ★ H-NB; mail Lebanon z 06249; rural

Governor's Hill; RMC Place; NEW HAVEN; ▲ Oxford; ★ N.Y.; mail Oxford z 06478

Granby; RMC Place; HARTFORD; ▲ Granby; ★ H-NB; ● 700

Granby; MCD-Town; HARTFORD; *160 B-9; 🅿; ★ H-NB; z 06035 & mail West Granby z 06090; ℗ 9,369; © 10,347; ◆ 11,172

Granite Bay; RMC Place; NEW HAVEN; ▲ Branford; *160 J-9; elev. 40ft./12m.; ★ N.HAV; mail Branford z 06405; ● 500

Grant Hill; RMC Place; HARTFORD; ▲ Bloomfield; *160 D-9; elev. 250ft./76m.; ★ H-NB; mail Bloomfield z 06002; ● 100

Grappaville; RMC Place; LITCHFIELD; ▲ Litchfield; *160 E-5; ★ TORR; mail Bantam z 06750; rural

Grassy Hill; RMC Place; LITCHFIELD; ▲ Woodbury; *160 G-5; elev. 819ft./250m.; ★ WATB; mail Woodbury z 06798; rural

Grassy Plain; RMC Place; FAIRFIELD; ▲ Bethel; elev. 384ft./117m.; ★ N.Y.; mail Bethel z 06801

Great Hammock Beach; RMC Place; MIDDLESEX; ▲ Old Saybrook; *161 J-12; elev. 8ft./2m.; mail Old Saybrook z 06475; ● 100

Great Harbor; RMC Place; NEW HAVEN; ▲ Guilford; *160 J-10; elev. 50ft./15m.; ★ N.HAV; mail Guilford z 06437; ● 100

Great Meadows; RMC Place; FAIRFIELD; ▲ New Fairfield; ★ N.Y.; mail Danbury z 06810

Greenfield Hill; RMC Place; FAIRFIELD; ▲ Fairfield; *160 K-5; ★ N.Y.

Greenhaven Shores; RMC Place; NEW LONDON; ▲ Stonington; ★ N.LON-; mail Westerly z 02891

Green Manorville; RMC Place; HARTFORD; ▲ Enfield; *161 B-11; ★ H-NB; mail Enfield z 06082

Greens Farms; RMC Place; FAIRFIELD; ▲ Westport; *160 K-5; elev. 78ft./24m.; 🅿; ★ N.Y.; z 06838

Greenville; RMC Place; NEW LONDON; ▲ Norwich; *161 G-15; ★ N.LON-; mail Norwich z 06360; pop. incl. with Norwich (Inc. Place)

Greenwich; RMC Place; FAIRFIELD; ▲ Greenwich; 160 M-8; 🅿 🅷; ★ N.Y.; z 06830-31, z 06836; ℗ 58,441; ● 61,100

Greenwich; MCD-Town; FAIRFIELD; *160 L-2; 🅿 ■; ★ N.Y.; z 06830-31, z 06836, z 98662; ℗ 58,441; © 61,101; ◆ 62,208

Greystone; RMC Place; LITCHFIELD; ▲ Plymouth; 160 F-7; ★ H-NB; mail Terryville z 06786; ● 160

Griswold; MCD-Town; NEW LONDON; *161 F-16; 🅿; ★ N.LON-; z 06351; ℗ 10,384; © 10,807; ◆ 11,496

Griswoldville; RMC Place; HARTFORD; ▲ Wethersfield; ★ H-NB; mail Wethersfield z 06109

Grosvenor Dale; RMC Place; WINDHAM; ▲ Thompson; 161 B-16; 🅿; ★ WORC; z 06246; ● 850

Groton; Inc. Place; NEW LONDON; ▲ Groton; 161 L-20; 🅿 🅷; ★ N.LON-; z 06340, z 06349; ℗ 9,837; © 10,010; ® 9,288

Groton; MCD-Town; NEW LONDON; *161 I-15; 🅿; ★ N.LON-; z 06340, z 06349; ℗ 45,144; © 39,907; ® 39,925; ◆ 41,510

Groton Heights; RMC Place; NEW LONDON; ▲ Groton; ★ N.LON-; mail Groton z 06340; pop. incl. with Groton (Inc. Place)

Groton Lake Shores; RMC Place; NEW LONDON; ▲ East Lyme; ★ N.LON-; mail Niantic z 06357

Groton Long Point; Inc. Place; NEW LONDON; ▲ Groton; 161 I-15; ★ N.LON-; mail Groton z 06340; ℗ 628; summer pop. 4,800; © 667

Grove Beach; RMC Place; MIDDLESEX; ▲ Westbrook, Clinton; *161 J-12; ★ N.HAV; mail Clinton z 06413

Grover Hill; RMC Place; FAIRFIELD; ▲ Bridgeport; *160 K-5; ★ N.Y.; pop. incl. with Bridgeport (Inc. Place)

Gugliotti; RMC Place; HARTFORD; ▲ Southington; ★ H-NB; mail Plantsville z 06479

Guilford; RMC Place; NEW HAVEN, NEW HAVEN; ▲ Guilford; 160 E-10; ★ N.HAV; ● 1,800

Guilford; MCD-Town; NEW HAVEN; *160 I-10; 🅿; ★ N.HAV; z 06437; ℗ 19,848; © 21,398; ◆ 22,553

Guilford Center; CDP-Census Area Only; NEW HAVEN; ▲ Guilford; 160 J-10; ★ N.HAV; mail Guilford z 06437; ℗ 2,588; © 2,603

Guilford Lake; RMC Place; NEW HAVEN; ▲ Guilford; *160 I-10; elev. 100ft./30m.; ★ N.HAV; mail Guilford z 06437; ● 850

Gurleyville; RMC Place; TOLLAND; ▲ Mansfield; 161 D-14; ★ H-NB; mail Storrs Mansfield z 06268; ● 150

H

Haddam; RMC Place; MIDDLESEX; ▲ Haddam; 161 G-11; elev. 89ft./27m.; 🅿; ★ H-NB; z 06438; ● 1,300

Haddam; MCD-Town; MIDDLESEX; *161 H-11; 🅿; ★ H-NB; z 06438; ℗ 6,769; © 7,157; ◆ 7,611

Haddam Neck; RMC Place; MIDDLESEX; ▲ Haddam; 161 G-11; 🅿; ★ H-NB; z 06424; ● 270

Hadlyme; RMC Place; NEW LONDON; ▲ Lyme; 161 H-12; 🅿; z 06439; ● 640

Hale Court; RMC Place; FAIRFIELD; ▲ Westport; *160 K-4; elev. 78ft./24m.; ★ N.Y.; mail Westport z 06880

Halls Hill; RMC Place; NEW LONDON; ▲ Colchester; *161 G-13; elev. 500ft./152m.; ★ H-NB; mail Colchester z 06415

Hallville; RMC Place; NEW LONDON; ▲ Preston; 161 G-15; ★ N.LON-; mail Preston z 06365; ● 160

Hamburg; RMC Place; NEW LONDON; ▲ Lyme; 161 I-13; mail Old Lyme z 06371; ● 110

Hamden; RMC Place; NEW HAVEN; ▲ Hamden; 161 K-17; 🅿 🅲 7,371; ★ N.HAV; z 06511, z 06514, z 06517-18; ℗ 52,434; ● 56,900

Hamden; MCD-Town; NEW HAVEN; *160 H-8; 🅿 🅲 7,371 ■; ★ N.HAV; z 06511, z 06514, z 06517-18; ℗ 52,434; © 56,913; ® 56,763; ◆ 59,271

Hammertown; RMC Place; LITCHFIELD; ▲ Salisbury; *160 A-4; elev. 700ft./213m.; mail Taconic z 06079; rural

Hampton; RMC Place; WINDHAM; ▲ Hampton; 161 D-15; 🅿; z 06247; ● 600

Hampton; MCD-Town; WINDHAM; *161 D-15; 🅿; z 06247; ℗ 1,578; © 1,758

Hanks Hill; RMC Place; TOLLAND; ▲ Mansfield; *161 D-14; elev. 469ft./143m.; ★ H-NB; mail Storrs Mansfield z 06268; rural

Hanover; RMC Place; NEW LONDON; ▲ Sprague; 161 F-15; 🅿; ★ N.LON-; z 06350; ● 500

Happyland; RMC Place; NEW LONDON; ▲ Preston; 161 H-15; ★ N.LON-; mail Preston z 06365; ● 320

Harborview; RMC Place; FAIRFIELD; ▲ Norwalk; *160 L-4; ★ N.Y.; mail Norwalk z 06853; pop. incl. with Norwalk (Inc. Place)

Harbor View; RMC Place; MIDDLESEX; ▲ Clinton; *161 J-11; elev. 25ft./8m.; ★ N.HAV; mail Clinton z 06413

Harrisons; RMC Place; NEW LONDON; ▲ Waterford; *161 I-15; elev. 20ft./6m.; ★ N.LON-; mail Quaker Hill z 06375; rural

Harrisville; RMC Place; WINDHAM; ▲ Woodstock; 161 C-16; mail Woodstock z 06281; ● 90

Hartford; Inc. Place; **STATE CAPITAL**; HARTFORD; ▲ Hartford; 160 D-10; 🅿 🅷 🅲 3,013 ■; ★ H-NB; z 06101-12, z 06114-15, z 06117-20, z 06123, z 06126-29, z 06131-34, z 06137-38, z 06140-47, z 06150-56, z 06160-61, z 06167, z 06176, z 06180, z 06183, z 06199; ℗ 139,739; © 121,578; ® 124,121; ◆ 121,044

Hartford; MCD-Town; HARTFORD; *160 D-10; 🅿 🅷 🅲 3,013; ★ H-NB; z 06101-12, z 06114-15, z 06117-20, z 06123, z 06126-29, z 06131-34, z 06137-38, z 06140-47, z 06150-56, z 06160-61, z 06167, z 06176, z 06180, z 06183, z 06199; coextensive with the City of Hartford; ℗ 139,739; © 121,578; ® 124,121; ◆ 121,044

HARTFORD; 160 C-9; ℗ 851,783; © 857,183; ◆ 876,371

Hartland; MCD-Town; HARTFORD; *160 B-8; mail East Hartland z 06027; ℗ 1,866; © 2,012

Harwinton; RMC Place; LITCHFIELD; ▲ Harwinton; ★ H-NB; ● 400

Harwinton; MCD-Town; LITCHFIELD; *160 E-7; 🅿; ★ H-NB; z 06791-92 & mail Torrington z 06790; ℗ 5,228; © 5,283; ◆ 5,214

Hawks Nest Beach; RMC Place; NEW LONDON; ▲ Old Lyme; *161 J-13; ★ N.LON-; mail Old Lyme z 06371; ● 110

Hawleyville; RMC Place; FAIRFIELD; ▲ Newtown; 160 H-4; 🅿; ★ N.Y.; z 06440; ● 100

Hawthorne Terrace; RMC Place; FAIRFIELD; ▲ Danbury; *160 H-4; ★ N.Y.; mail Danbury z 06810; pop. incl. with Danbury (Inc. Place)

Hayden; RMC Place; HARTFORD; ▲ Windsor; 160 C-10; ★ H-NB; mail Windsor z 06095; ● 110

Hayestown; RMC Place; FAIRFIELD; ▲ Danbury; *160 H-4; ★ N.Y.; mail Danbury z 06810; pop. incl. with Danbury (Inc. Place)

Hazardville; CDP; HARTFORD; ▲ Enfield; 161 B-11; elev. 80ft./24m.; ★ H-NB; mail Enfield z 06082; ℗ 5,179; © 4,900

Headquarters; RMC Place; LITCHFIELD; ▲ Litchfield; *160 E-5; elev. 1,000ft./305m.; ★ TORR; mail Litchfield z 06759; rural

Hebron; RMC Place; TOLLAND; ▲ Hebron; 161 F-12; elev. 542ft./165m.; 🅿; ★ H-NB; z 06248; ● 800

Hebron; MCD-Town; TOLLAND; *161 F-12; 🅿; ★ H-NB; z 06248; ℗ 7,079; © 8,610; ◆ 9,385

Heritage Village; CDP-Census Area Only; NEW HAVEN; ▲ Southbury; *160 G-5; ★ WATB; mail Southbury z 06488; ℗ 3,623; © 3,435

Entries in **UPPERCASE** are counties.
Entries in **bold** have populations of 2,500 or more.
Names in parentheses are alternate names.

Inc. Place	Incorporated Place
RMC Place	Rand McNally Designated Place
CDP	Census Designated Place
MCD	Minor Civil Division

⊡	County Seat
▲	Minor Civil Division
elev.	Elevation
🅿	Post Office
🅷	Hospital
🅲	College
■	Principal Business Center
★	Ranally Metro Area (RMA) Abbreviation
z	Zip Code(s)
℗	Previous Census Population
®	Revised Census Population
Ⓐ	Annexation Population
●	Rand McNally Population Estimate
©	Final Census Population
Ⓢ	Special Census Population
◆	Estimated Population

For additional definitions see Glossary, Volume 1, and Introduction, Volume 2.

Hidden Lake; RMC Place; MIDDLESEX; ▲ Haddam; ***161** H-11; ★ **H-NB**; mail Higganum **z** 06441; ● 370
Higganum; CDP; MIDDLESEX; ▲ Haddam; **161** G-11; 🄿; ★ **H-NB**; **z** 06441; Ⓟ 1,692; © 1,671
Highland Park; RMC Place; HARTFORD; ▲ Manchester; ***161** D-11; ★ **H-NB**; mail Manchester **z** 06040
High Ridge; RMC Place; FAIRFIELD; ▲ Stamford; ***160** K-3; elev. 457ft./139m.; ★ **N.Y.**; pop. incl. with Stamford (Inc. Place)
Hitchcock Lake; RMC Place; NEW HAVEN; ▲ Wolcott; ***160** G-8; ★ **WATB**; mail Wolcott **z** 06716; ● 1,730
Holiday Homes; RMC Place; NEW LONDON; ▲ Colchester; ★ **H-NB**; mail Colchester **z** 06415
Hollywyle Park; RMC Place; FAIRFIELD; ▲ New Fairfield; ***160** H-4; ★ **N.Y.**; mail Danbury **z** 06810; ● 130
Honeypot Glen; RMC Place; NEW HAVEN; ▲ Cheshire; **160** G-8; elev. 262ft./80m.; ★ **N.HAV**; mail Cheshire **z** 06410; ● 1,200
Hopeville; RMC Place; NEW HAVEN; ▲ Waterbury; ***160** G-7; ★ **WATB**; mail Waterbury **z** 06706; pop. incl. with Waterbury (Inc. Place)
Hopeville; RMC Place; NEW LONDON; ▲ Griswold; ***161** F-16; ★ **N.LON-**; mail Jewett City **z** 06351
Horton Hill; RMC Place; NEW HAVEN; ▲ Naugatuck; ★ **WATB**; mail Naugatuck **z** 06770; pop. incl. with Naugatuck (Inc. Place)
Hotchkissville; RMC Place; LITCHFIELD; ▲ Woodbury; **160** G-6; elev. 279ft./85m.; ★ **WATB**; mail Woodbury **z** 06798; ● 350
Huckleberry Hill; RMC Place; HARTFORD; ▲ Avon; ***160** D-8; ★ **H-NB**; mail Avon **z** 06001; ● 700
Hungary Hill; RMC Place; WINDHAM; ▲ Sterling; ***161** E-17; elev. 450ft./137m.; mail Sterling **z** 06377; rural
Huntington; RMC Place; FAIRFIELD; ▲ Shelton; **161** L-13; 🄿; ★ **N.Y.**; **z** 06484; pop. incl. with Shelton (Inc. Place)
Huntsville; RMC Place; LITCHFIELD; ▲ Canaan; ***160** B-5; elev. 746ft./227m.; mail Falls Village **z** 06031; ● 30
Hydeville; RMC Place; TOLLAND; ▲ Stafford; **161** B-13; elev. 639ft./195m.; ★ **H-NB**; mail Stafford **z** 06075; ● 250

I

Indian Cove; RMC Place; NEW HAVEN; ▲ Guilford; ***160** J-10; ★ **N.HAV**; mail Guilford **z** 06437; ● 300
Indian Neck; RMC Place; NEW HAVEN; ▲ Branford; **161** N-17; ★ **N.HAV**; mail Branford **z** 06405; ● 2,500
Ivoryton; RMC Place; MIDDLESEX; ▲ Essex; **161** I-12; 🄿; **z** 06442; ● 2,600

J

Jericho (Jericho Hill); RMC Place; NEW LONDON; ▲ Old Lyme; ***161** I-13; elev. 50ft./15m.; ★ **N.LON-**; mail Old Lyme **z** 06371; ● 200
Jericho Hill; NEW LONDON; see Jericho (RMC Place)
Jewett City; Inc. Place; NEW LONDON; ▲ Griswold; **161** F-16; 🄿; ★ **N.LON-**; **z** 06351; Ⓟ 3,349; © 3,053
Jordan (Jordan Village, Waterford); RMC Place; NEW LONDON; ▲ Waterford; **161** M-18; ★ **N.LON-**; mail Waterford **z** 06385; ● 400
Jordan Village; NEW LONDON; see Jordan (RMC Place)
Joyceville; RMC Place; LITCHFIELD; ▲ Salisbury; ***160** A-4; elev. 784ft./239m.; mail Taconic **z** 06079; rural

K

Kellogg Corners; RMC Place; LITCHFIELD; ▲ Cornwall; ***160** D-5; elev. 1,016ft./310m.; mail West Cornwall **z** 06796; rural
Kelly Corner; RMC Place; LITCHFIELD; ***160** C-6; elev. 1,491ft./454m.; mail Goshen **z** 06756; rural
Kelseytown; RMC Place; MIDDLESEX; ▲ Clinton; ***161** I-11; elev. 42ft./13m.; ★ **N.HAV**; mail Clinton **z** 06413
Kensington; CDP; HARTFORD; ▲ Berlin; **160** F-9; elev. 84ft./26m.; 🄿; ★ **H-NB**; **z** 06037; Ⓟ 8,306; © 8,541
Kent; RMC Place; LITCHFIELD; ▲ Kent; **160** E-3; 🄿; **z** 06757; ● 1,050
Kent; MCD-Town; LITCHFIELD; ***160** E-4; 🄿; **z** 06757; Ⓟ 2,918; © 2,858
Kent Furnace; RMC Place; LITCHFIELD; ▲ Kent; ***160** E-4; mail Kent **z** 06757
Kenyonville; RMC Place; WINDHAM; ▲ Woodstock; ***161** C-15; elev. 615ft./187m.; mail Woodstock Valley **z** 06282
Kilby; RMC Place; NEW HAVEN; ▲ New Haven; ***160** I-8; ★ **N.HAV**; mail New Haven **z** 06519; pop. incl. with New Haven (Inc. Place)
Killingly; MCD-Town; WINDHAM; ***161** D-17; mail Ballouville **z** 06233, Danielson **z** 06239, Dayville **z** 06241, East Killingly **z** 06243, Rogers **z** 06263; Ⓟ 15,889; © 16,472
Killingly Center; RMC Place; WINDHAM; ▲ Killingly; **161** D-16; mail Dayville **z** 06241; ● 110
Killingworth; RMC Place; MIDDLESEX; ▲ Killingworth; **161** I-11; 🄿; ★ **N.HAV**; **z** 06419; ● 300
Killingworth; MCD-Town; MIDDLESEX; ***161** I-11; 🄿; ★ **N.HAV**; **z** 06419; Ⓟ 4,814; © 6,018; ◆ 7,021
Kings Corner; RMC Place; HARTFORD; ▲ Enfield; **161** C-11; ★ **H-NB**; mail East Windsor **z** 06088; ● 270
Knollcrest; RMC Place; FAIRFIELD; ▲ New Fairfield; **160** G-4; ★ **N.Y.**; mail Danbury **z** 06810; ● 400
Knollwood; RMC Place; MIDDLESEX; ▲ Old Saybrook; **161** J-12; mail Old Saybrook **z** 06475; ● 500

L

Lake Bashan; RMC Place; MIDDLESEX; ▲ East Haddam; ★ **H-NB**; mail East Haddam **z** 06423
Lake Beseck; MIDDLESEX; see Beseck Lake (RMC Place)
Lake Bungee; RMC Place; WINDHAM; ▲ Woodstock; ***161** B-15; elev. 771ft./235m.; mail Woodstock Valley **z** 06282; ● 250
Lake Garda; RMC Place; HARTFORD; ▲ Farmington, Burlington; ***160** E-8; ★ **H-NB**; mail Burlington **z** 06013, Unionville **z** 06085; ● 1,200
Lake Hayward; RMC Place; MIDDLESEX; ▲ East Haddam; ***161** G-13; ★ **H-NB**; mail Colchester **z** 06415; ● 360
Lake Plymouth; RMC Place; LITCHFIELD; ▲ Plymouth; ***160** F-7; ★ **H-NB**; mail Plymouth **z** 06782; ● 600
Lake Pocotopaug; CDP; MIDDLESEX; ▲ East Hampton; ***161** F-11; ★ **H-NB**; mail East Hampton **z** 06424; Ⓟ 3,029; © 3,169
Lakeside; RMC Place; LITCHFIELD; ▲ Morris; **160** E-5; 🄿; ★ **TORR**; **z** 06758; ● 550
Lakeside; RMC Place; NEW HAVEN; ▲ Southbury; **160** H-5; ★ **WATB**; mail Southbury **z** 06488; ● 1,340
Lake View Terrace; RMC Place; TOLLAND; ▲ Stafford; **161** B-12; ★ **H-NB**; mail Stafford Springs **z** 06076; ● 100
Lakeville; RMC Place; LITCHFIELD; ▲ Salisbury; **160** B-4; 🄿; **z** 06039; ● 1,900
Lakewood; RMC Place; NEW HAVEN; ▲ Waterbury; ***160** F-7; elev. 484ft./148m.; ★ **WATB**; mail Waterbury **z** 06704; pop. incl. with Waterbury (Inc. Place)
Lanesville; RMC Place; LITCHFIELD; ▲ New Milford; ***160** G-4; elev. 250ft./76m.; ★ **N.Y.**; mail New Milford **z** 06776; ● 30
Lattins Landing; RMC Place; FAIRFIELD; ▲ Danbury; ***160** H-4; ★ **N.Y.**; mail Danbury **z** 06810; pop. incl. with Danbury (Inc. Place)
Laurel; RMC Place; MIDDLESEX; ▲ Middletown; ***161** G-11; ★ **H-NB**; mail Middletown **z** 06457; pop. incl. with Middletown (Inc. Place)
Laurel Beach; RMC Place; NEW HAVEN; ▲ Milford; **161** N-13; ★ **N.Y.**; mail Milford **z** 06460; pop. incl. with Milford (Inc. Place)
Laurel Glen; RMC Place; NEW LONDON; ▲ North Stonington; ***161** H-17; elev. 150ft./46m.; ★ **N.LON-**; mail North Stonington **z** 06359; rural
Laurel Hill; RMC Place; NEW LONDON; ▲ Norwich; ★ **N.LON-**; mail Norwich **z** 06360, Putnam **z** 06260; pop. incl. with Norwich (Inc. Place)
Laysville; RMC Place; NEW LONDON; ▲ Old Lyme; **161** I-13; ★ **N.LON-**; mail Old Lyme **z** 06371; ● 320
Lebanon; RMC Place; NEW LONDON; ▲ Lebanon; **161** F-14; 🄿; ★ **H-NB**; **z** 06249; ● 440
Lebanon; MCD-Town; NEW LONDON; ***161** F-13; 🄿; ★ **H-NB**; **z** 06249; Ⓟ 6,041; © 6,907; ◆ 7,560
Ledyard; NEW LONDON; see Ledyard Center (RMC Place)
Ledyard; MCD-Town; NEW LONDON; ***161** H-15; 🄿; ★ **N.LON-**; **z** 06338-39; Ⓟ 14,913; © 14,687; ◆ 15,505
Ledyard Center (Ledyard); RMC Place; NEW LONDON; ▲ Ledyard; **161** H-15; ★ **N.LON-**; mail Ledyard **z** 06339, Mashantucket **z** 06338; ● 110
Leesville; RMC Place; MIDDLESEX; ▲ East Haddam; **161** G-12; ★ **H-NB**; mail Moodus **z** 06469; ● 160
Leetes Island; RMC Place; NEW HAVEN; ▲ Guilford; **160** J-10; ★ **N.HAV**; mail Guilford **z** 06437; ● 260
Liberty Hill (Chestnut Hill); RMC Place; NEW LONDON; ▲ Lebanon; **161** F-13; elev. 461ft./141m.; ★ **H-NB**; mail Lebanon **z** 06249; ● 250
Lime Rock; RMC Place; LITCHFIELD; ▲ Salisbury; **160** C-4; mail Lakeville **z** 06039; ● 160
Lisbon; MCD-Town; NEW LONDON; ***161** F-15; 🄿; ★ **N.LON-**; **z** 06351; Ⓟ 3,790; © 4,069; ◆ 4,390
Litchfield; Inc. Place; LITCHFIELD; ▲ Litchfield; **160** E-6; elev. 1,086ft./331m.; 🄿; ★ **TORR**; **z** 06759 & mail Bantam **z** 06750; Ⓟ 1,378; © 1,328
Litchfield; MCD-Town; LITCHFIELD; ***160** D-6; 🄿; ★ **TORR**; **z** 06759 & mail Bantam **z** 06750; Ⓟ 8,365; © 8,316
LITCHFIELD; **160** C-5; Ⓟ 174,092; © 182,193; Ⓡ 182,212; ◆ 184,387
Little Boston; FAIRFIELD; see Boston (RMC Place)
Little City; RMC Place; MIDDLESEX; ▲ Haddam; ***161** H-11; elev. 582ft./177m.; ★ **H-NB**; mail Higganum **z** 06441; rural
Long Hill; RMC Place; FAIRFIELD; ▲ Trumbull; **161** L-12; ★ **N.Y.**; mail Trumbull **z** 06611
Long Hill; RMC Place; MIDDLESEX; ▲ Middletown; ★ **H-NB**; mail Middletown **z** 06457; pop. incl. with Middletown (Inc. Place)
Long Hill; RMC Place; NEW HAVEN; ▲ Waterbury; ***160** G-7; ★ **WATB**; mail Waterbury **z** 06704; pop. incl. with Waterbury (Inc. Place)
Long Hill; CDP-Census Area Only; NEW LONDON; ▲ Groton; ***161** I-15; ★ **N.LON-**; mail Groton **z** 06340; © 3,534
Long Ridge; RMC Place; FAIRFIELD; ▲ Stamford; ***160** I-4; ★ **N.Y.**; mail Stamford **z** 06901; pop. incl. with Stamford (Inc. Place)
Lordship; RMC Place; FAIRFIELD; ▲ Stratford; **161** N-12; ★ **N.Y.**; mail Stratford **z** 06615
Lords Point; RMC Place; NEW LONDON; ▲ Stonington; **161** I-16; ★ **N.LON-**; mail Stonington **z** 06378; ● 350
Lower Merryall; RMC Place; LITCHFIELD; ▲ New Milford; ***160** F-4; elev. 462ft./141m.; ★ **N.Y.**; mail New Milford **z** 06776; rural
Lydallville; RMC Place; HARTFORD; ▲ Manchester; ***161** D-11; elev. 350ft./107m.; ★ **H-NB**; mail Manchester **z** 06040
Lyme; NEW LONDON; see Lyme Station (RMC Place)
Lyme; MCD-Town; NEW LONDON; ***161** H-13; 🄿; **z** 06371; Ⓟ 1,949; © 2,016
Lyme Black Hall; NEW LONDON; see Lyme Station (RMC Place)
Lyme Station (Lyme, Lyme Black Hall); RMC Place; NEW LONDON; ▲ Old Lyme; **161** J-13; ★ **N.LON-**; mail Old Lyme **z** 06371; ● 530
Lyons Plain (Lyons Plains); RMC Place; FAIRFIELD; ▲ Weston; **160** J-4; ★ **N.Y.**; mail Westport **z** 06880; ● 350
Lyons Plains; FAIRFIELD; see Lyons Plain (RMC Place)

M

Macedonia; RMC Place; LITCHFIELD; ▲ Kent; **160** E-3; mail Kent **z** 06757; ● 290
Madison; RMC Place; NEW HAVEN; ▲ Madison; ★ **N.HAV**;{; ● 850
Madison; MCD-Town; NEW HAVEN; ***160** I-10; 🄿; ★ **N.HAV**; **z** 06443; Ⓟ 15,485; © 17,858; ◆ 18,943
Madison Center; CDP-Census Area Only; NEW HAVEN; ▲ Madison; **161** J-11; elev. 22ft./7m.; ★ **N.HAV**; mail Madison **z** 06443; Ⓟ 2,139; © 2,222
Main Street; RMC Place; FAIRFIELD; ▲ Danbury; ★ **N.Y.**; mail Danbury **z** 06813; pop. incl. with Danbury (Inc. Place)
Manchester; RMC Place; HARTFORD; ▲ Manchester; **161** D-11; 🄿 🄷; ★ **H-NB**; **z** 06040-43, **z** 06045; Ⓟ 51,618; ● 54,700
Manchester; MCD-Town; HARTFORD; ***161** D-11; 🄿 ■; ★ **H-NB**; **z** 06040-43, **z** 06045; Ⓟ 51,618; © 54,740; ◆ 57,257
Manchester Green; RMC Place; HARTFORD; ▲ Manchester; ***161** D-11; elev. 350ft./107m.; ★ **H-NB**; mail Manchester **z** 06040
Mansfield; TOLLAND; see Mansfield Depot (RMC Place)
Mansfield; TOLLAND; see Mansfield Center (CDP)
Mansfield; MCD-Town; TOLLAND; ***161** D-14; 🄲 28,481; ★ **H-NB**; mail Mansfield Center **z** 06250, Storrs Mansfield **z** 06268; Ⓟ 21,103; © 20,720; Ⓡ 20,816; ◆ 22,178
Mansfield Center (Mansfield); CDP; TOLLAND; ▲ Mansfield; **161** D-14; 🄿 🄷; ★ **H-NB**; **z** 06235, **z** 06250 & mail Storrs Mansfield **z** 06268; © 973
Mansfield City; RMC Place; TOLLAND; ▲ Mansfield; ***161** D-14; ★ **H-NB**; mail Storrs Mansfield **z** 06268
Mansfield Depot (Mansfield); RMC Place; TOLLAND; ▲ Mansfield; **161** D-13; 🄿; ★ **H-NB**; **z** 06251 & mail Mansfield Center **z** 06250, Storrs Mansfield **z** 06268; ● 300
Mansfield Four Corners; RMC Place; TOLLAND; ▲ Mansfield; **161** D-13; ★ **H-NB**; mail Storrs Mansfield **z** 06268; ● 200
Mansfield Hollow; RMC Place; TOLLAND; ▲ Mansfield; ***161** E-14; ★ **H-NB**; mail Mansfield Center **z** 06250
Maple Hill; RMC Place; HARTFORD; ▲ Newington; ***160** E-9; ★ **H-NB**; mail Newington **z** 06111
Maple Hollow; RMC Place; LITCHFIELD; ▲ New Hartford; ***160** D-7; elev. 589ft./180m.; ★ **H-NB**; mail New Hartford **z** 06057; ● 30
Maplewood; RMC Place; NEW HAVEN; ▲ Derby; ***160** I-7; ★ **N.Y.**; mail Derby **z** 06418; pop. incl. with Derby (Inc. Place)
Marble Dale; RMC Place; LITCHFIELD; ▲ Washington; **160** F-4; elev. 515ft./157m.; mail New Preston Marble Dale **z** 06777; ● 220
Margerie Manor; RMC Place; FAIRFIELD; ▲ Danbury; ***160** H-4; ★ **N.Y.**; mail Danbury **z** 06810; pop. incl. with Danbury (Inc. Place)
Marion; RMC Place; HARTFORD; ▲ Southington; **160** G-8; 🄿; ★ **H-NB**; **z** 06444; ● 850
Marlborough; RMC Place; HARTFORD; ▲ Marlborough; ★ **H-NB**; ● 200
Marlborough; MCD-Town; HARTFORD; ***161** F-11; 🄿; ★ **H-NB**; **z** 06447; Ⓟ 5,535; © 5,709; ◆ 5,893
Maromas; RMC Place; MIDDLESEX; ▲ Middletown; ***161** G-11; ★ **H-NB**; mail Middletown **z** 06457; pop. incl. with Middletown (Inc. Place)
Mashantucket Pequot Reservation; Indian Reservation; NEW LONDON; ▲ Ledyard; ★ **N.LON-**; mail Ledyard **z** 06339, Mashantucket **z** 06338; Ⓟ 29; © 315
Mashapaug; RMC Place; TOLLAND; ▲ Union; ***161** B-14; ★ **H-NB**; mail Stafford Springs **z** 06076; rural
Mason Island; RMC Place; NEW LONDON; ▲ Stonington; ***161** I-16; ★ **N.LON-**; mail Mystic **z** 06355; ● 330
Massapeag; RMC Place; NEW LONDON; ▲ Montville; ***161** H-15; ★ **N.LON-**; mail Uncasville **z** 06382; rural
Mayberry Village; RMC Place; HARTFORD; ▲ East Hartford; ***161** D-11; ★ **H-NB**; mail East Hartford **z** 06108
Meads Point; RMC Place; FAIRFIELD; ▲ Greenwich; ***160** M-2; elev. 40ft./12m.; ★ **N.Y.**; mail Greenwich **z** 06830
Mechanicsville; RMC Place; WINDHAM; ▲ Thompson; **161** C-16; ★ **WORC**; mail Thompson **z** 06277; ● 160
Melrose; RMC Place; HARTFORD; ▲ East Windsor; **161** C-11; 🄿; ★ **H-NB**; **z** 06016; ● 300
Melville Village; RMC Place; FAIRFIELD; ▲ Fairfield; ***160** K-5; ★ **N.Y.**
Meriden; Inc. Place; NEW HAVEN; ▲ Meriden; **160** G-9; 🄿 🄷 ■; ★ **N.HAV**; **z** 06450-51; Ⓟ 59,479; © 58,244; ◆ 58,399
Meriden; MCD-Town; NEW HAVEN; ***160** G-9; 🄿 🄷; ★ **N.HAV**; **z** 06450-51, **z** 98662; coextensive with the City of Meriden; Ⓟ 59,479; © 58,244; ◆ 58,399
Merrow; RMC Place; TOLLAND; ▲ Mansfield; **161** D-13; ★ **H-NB**; mail Mansfield Depot **z** 06251; ● 250
Mianus; RMC Place; FAIRFIELD; ▲ Greenwich; **160** L-8; ★ **N.Y.**; mail Cos Cob **z** 06807
Middle Beach; RMC Place; NEW HAVEN; ▲ Madison; ***161** J-11; ★ **N.HAV**; mail Madison **z** 06443
Middlebury; RMC Place; NEW HAVEN; ▲ Middlebury; **160** G-6; 🄿; ★ **WATB**; **z** 06762 & mail Waterbury **z** 06749; ● 4,200
Middlebury; MCD-Town; NEW HAVEN; ***160** G-6; 🄿; ★ **WATB**; **z** 06762 & mail Waterbury **z** 06749; Ⓟ 6,145; © 6,451; ◆ 6,990
Middlefield (Middlefield Center); RMC Place; MIDDLESEX; ▲ Middlefield; **160** G-10; 🄿; ★ **H-NB**; **z** 06455; ● 1,250
Middlefield; MCD-Town; MIDDLESEX; ***160** G-10; 🄿; ★ **H-NB**; **z** 06455; Ⓟ 3,925; © 4,203; ◆ 4,377
Middlefield Center; MIDDLESEX; see Middlefield (RMC Place)
Middle Haddam; RMC Place; MIDDLESEX; ▲ East Hampton; **161** G-11; 🄿; ★ **H-NB**; **z** 06456; ● 450
MIDDLESEX; **161** F-11; Ⓟ 143,196; © 155,071; ◆ 164,905
Middletown; Inc. Place; MIDDLESEX; ▲ Middletown; **160** G-10; 🄿 🄷 🄲 3,433 ■; ★ **H-NB**; **z** 06457, **z** 06459; Ⓟ 42,762; © 43,167; Ⓡ 45,563; ◆ 44,142
Middletown; MCD-Town; MIDDLESEX; ***160** G-10; 🄿 🄷 🄲 3,433; ★ **H-NB**; **z** 06457, **z** 06459; coextensive with the City of Middletown; Ⓟ 42,762; © 43,167; Ⓡ 45,563; ◆ 44,142
Midway; RMC Place; NEW LONDON; ▲ Groton; ***161** I-15; elev. 16ft./5m.; ★ **N.LON-**; mail Groton **z** 06340
Milbrook; RMC Place; FAIRFIELD; ▲ Greenwich; ★ **N.Y.**; mail Greenwich **z** 06830
Milford; Inc. Place; NEW HAVEN; ▲ Milford; **161** M-14; 🄿 🄷 ■; ★ **N.Y.**; **z** 06460-61; Ⓟ 48,168; © 50,594; ◆ 53,962
Milford; MCD-Town; NEW HAVEN; ***160** J-7; 🄿 🄷; ★ **N.Y.**; **z** 06460-61; coextensive with the City of Milford and the Borough of Woodmont; Ⓟ 49,938; © 52,305; ◆ 55,593
Milford Lawns; RMC Place; NEW HAVEN; ▲ Milford; ***160** J-7; ★ **N.Y.**; mail Milford **z** 06460; pop. incl. with Milford (Inc. Place)
Mill Brook; RMC Place; LITCHFIELD; ▲ Colebrook; ***160** B-6; elev. 1,138ft./347m.; mail Winsted **z** 06098; rural
Millbrook; RMC Place; NEW HAVEN; ▲ North Haven; **161** K-17; ★ **N.HAV**; mail Hamden **z** 06518
Milldale; RMC Place; HARTFORD; ▲ Southington; **160** G-8; 🄿; ★ **H-NB**; **z** 06467; ● 900
Mill Hill; RMC Place; FAIRFIELD; ▲ Bridgeport; ***160** K-6; ★ **N.Y.**; pop. incl. with Bridgeport (Inc. Place)
Millington; RMC Place; MIDDLESEX; ▲ East Haddam; **161** G-13; ★ **H-NB**; mail East Haddam **z** 06423; ● 50
Mill Plain; RMC Place; FAIRFIELD; ▲ Danbury; ***160** K-5; ★ **N.Y.**; mail Danbury **z** 06810
Mill Plain; RMC Place; NEW HAVEN; ▲ Waterbury; ***160** G-7; elev. 450ft./137m.; ★ **WATB**; mail Waterbury **z** 06705; pop. incl. with Waterbury (Inc. Place)
Millville; RMC Place; NEW HAVEN; ▲ Naugatuck; ***160** G-7; ★ **WATB**; mail Naugatuck **z** 06770; pop. incl. with Naugatuck (Inc. Place)
Milton; RMC Place; LITCHFIELD; ▲ Litchfield; **160** D-5; ★ **TORR**; mail Litchfield **z** 06759; ● 120
Minortown; RMC Place; LITCHFIELD; **160** D-6; ★ **WATB**; mail Woodbury **z** 06798
Mitcheltown; RMC Place; LITCHFIELD; ▲ Sharon; ***160** C-4; elev. 799ft./244m.; mail Sharon **z** 06069; rural
Mixville; RMC Place; NEW HAVEN; ▲ Cheshire; **160** G-8; elev. 262ft./80m.; ★ **N.HAV**; mail Cheshire **z** 06410; ● 1,400
Mohegan; RMC Place; NEW LONDON; ▲ Montville; **161** H-15; ★ **N.LON-**; mail Uncasville **z** 06382; ● 460
Mohegan Reservation; NEW LONDON; Indian Reservation; © 2
Momauguin; RMC Place; NEW HAVEN; ▲ East Haven; **161** N-16; elev. 25ft./8m.; ★ **N.HAV**; mail East Haven **z** 06512
Monroe; RMC Place; FAIRFIELD; ▲ Monroe; **160** I-6; 🄿; ★ **N.Y.**; **z** 06468; ● 8,500
Monroe; MCD-Town; FAIRFIELD; ***160** I-5; 🄿; ★ **N.Y.**; **z** 06468; Ⓟ 16,896; © 19,247; ◆ 19,444
Monroe Center; RMC Place; FAIRFIELD; ▲ Monroe; ***160** I-6; ★ **N.Y.**; mail Monroe **z** 06468
Montowese; RMC Place; NEW HAVEN; ▲ North Haven; **161** L-17; ★ **N.HAV**; mail North Haven **z** 06473
Montville; NEW LONDON; see Uncasville (RMC Place)
Montville; NEW LONDON; see Palmertown (RMC Place)
Montville; MCD-Town; NEW LONDON; ***161** H-14; 🄿; ★ **N.LON-**; **z** 06353; Ⓟ 16,673; © 18,546; ◆ 19,792
Montville Manor; RMC Place; NEW LONDON; ▲ Montville; ***161** H-14; elev. 560ft./171m.; ★ **N.LON-**; mail Oakdale **z** 06370; ● 950
Moodus; CDP; MIDDLESEX; ▲ East Haddam; **161** G-12; 🄿; ★ **H-NB**; **z** 06469; Ⓟ 1,170; © 1,263
Moosup; CDP; WINDHAM; ▲ Plainfield; **161** E-16; 🄿; ★ **N.LON-**; **z** 06354; Ⓟ 3,289; © 3,237
Morningside; RMC Place; NEW HAVEN; ▲ Milford; ***160** J-7; ★ **N.Y.**; mail Milford **z** 06460; pop. incl. with Milford (Inc. Place)
Morris; RMC Place; LITCHFIELD; ▲ Morris; **160** E-6; elev. 1,099ft./335m.; 🄿; ★ **TORR**; **z** 06763 & mail Lakeside **z** 06758; ● 300
Morris; MCD-Town; LITCHFIELD; ***160** E-6; 🄿; ★ **TORR**; **z** 06763 & mail Lakeside **z** 06758; Ⓟ 2,039; © 2,301
Morris Cove; RMC Place; NEW HAVEN; ▲ East Haven; **161** M-16; elev. 25ft./8m.; ★ **N.HAV**; mail East Haven **z** 06512; pop. incl. with New Haven (Inc. Place)
Mount Carmel; RMC Place; NEW HAVEN; ▲ Hamden; ***160** H-8; ★ **N.HAV**; mail Hamden **z** 06518
Mount Hope; RMC Place; TOLLAND; ▲ Mansfield; **161** D-14; ★ **H-NB**; mail Mansfield Center **z** 06250; ● 200
Murphy Road Carrier Annex; RMC Place; HARTFORD; ▲ Hartford; ***160** E-10; ★ **H-NB**; mail Hartford **z** 06114; pop. incl. with Hartford (Inc. Place)
Murray; RMC Place; FAIRFIELD; ▲ Fairfield; ***160** K-5; elev. 360ft./110m.; ★ **N.Y.**
Myrtle Beach; RMC Place; NEW HAVEN; ▲ Milford; ***160** K-7; ★ **N.Y.**; mail Milford **z** 06460; pop. incl. with Milford (Inc. Place)
Mystic; CDP; NEW LONDON; ▲ Groton, Stonington; **161** I-16; 🄿; ★ **N.LON-**; **z** 06355, **z** 06388; Ⓟ 2,618; © 4,001

N

Naugatuck; Inc. Place; NEW HAVEN; ▲ Naugatuck; **160** G-7; 🄿; ★ **WATB**; **z** 06770; Ⓟ 30,625; © 30,989; ◆ 31,405
Naugatuck; MCD-Town; NEW HAVEN; ***160** G-7; 🄿; ★ **WATB**; **z** 06770; coextensive with the Borough of Naugatuck; Ⓟ 30,625; © 30,989; ◆ 31,405
Naugatuck Gardens; RMC Place; NEW HAVEN; ▲ Naugatuck; ***160** J-7; ★ **WATB**; mail Milford **z** 06460; pop. incl. with Milford (Inc. Place)
Nepaug; RMC Place; LITCHFIELD; ▲ New Hartford; **160** D-7; ★ **H-NB**; mail New Hartford **z** 06057; ● 300
Newberry Corner; RMC Place; LITCHFIELD; ▲ Torrington; ***160** D-6; ★ **TORR**; mail Torrington **z** 06790; pop. incl. with Torrington (Inc. Place)
New Britain; Inc. Place; HARTFORD; ▲ New Britain; **160** F-9; 🄿 🄷 🄲 13,855 ■; ★ **H-NB**; **z** 06050-53; Ⓟ 75,491; © 71,538; ◆ 70,979
New Britain; MCD-Town; HARTFORD; ***160** E-9; 🄿 🄷 🄲 13,855; ★ **H-NB**; **z** 06050-53; coextensive with the City of New Britian; Ⓟ 75,491; © 71,538; ◆ 70,979
New Canaan; RMC Place; FAIRFIELD; ▲ New Canaan; **160** K-3; elev. 300ft./91m.; 🄿 🄷; ★ **N.Y.**; **z** 06840; ● 17,864
New Canaan; MCD-Town; FAIRFIELD; ***160** K-3; elev. 300ft./91m.; 🄿; ★ **N.Y.**; **z** 06840, **z** 98662; Ⓟ 17,864; © 19,395; ◆ 20,035
Newent; RMC Place; NEW LONDON; ▲ Lisbon; ***161** F-15; ★ **N.LON-**; mail Jewett City **z** 06351; ● 390
New Fairfield; RMC Place; FAIRFIELD; ▲ New Fairfield; **160** H-3; 🄿; ★ **N.Y.**; **z** 06812; ● 5,200
New Fairfield; MCD-Town; FAIRFIELD; ***160** G-3; 🄿; ★ **N.Y.**; **z** 06812 & mail Danbury **z** 06810; Ⓟ 12,911; © 13,953; ◆ 13,846
Newfield; RMC Place; FAIRFIELD; ▲ Stamford; ***160** L-3; ★ **N.Y.**; mail Bridgeport **z** 06607; pop. incl. with Stamford (Inc. Place)
Newfield Heights; RMC Place; MIDDLESEX; ▲ Middletown; ***160** G-10; ★ **H-NB**; mail Middletown **z** 06457; pop. incl. with Middletown (Inc. Place)
Newhallville; RMC Place; NEW HAVEN; ▲ New Haven; ★ **N.HAV**; mail New Haven **z** 06511; pop. incl. with New Haven (Inc. Place)
New Hartford; RMC Place; LITCHFIELD; ▲ New Hartford; ★ **H-NB**; ● 620
New Hartford; MCD-Town; LITCHFIELD; ***160** D-7; 🄿; ★ **H-NB**; **z** 06057; Ⓟ 5,769; © 6,088; ◆ 6,072
New Hartford Center; CDP-Census Area Only; LITCHFIELD; ▲ New Hartford; **160** C-7; ★ **H-NB**; mail New Hartford **z** 06057; Ⓟ 1,269; © 1,049
New Haven; Inc. Place; NEW HAVEN; ▲ New Haven; **161** M-16; 🄿 🄷 🄲 25,928 ■; ★ **N.HAV**; **z** 06501-15, **z** 06517-21, **z** 06524-25, **z** 06530-38, **z** 06540 & mail West Haven **z** 06516; Ⓟ 130,474; © 123,626; Ⓡ 123,776; ◆ 121,836
New Haven; MCD-Town; NEW HAVEN; ***160** I-8; 🄿 🄷 🄲 25,928; ★ **N.HAV**; **z** 06501-15, **z** 06517-21, **z** 06524-25, **z** 06530-38, **z** 06540 & mail West Haven **z** 06516; coextensive with the City of New Haven; Ⓟ 130,474; © 123,626; Ⓡ 123,776; ◆ 121,836
NEW HAVEN; **160** H-7; Ⓟ 804,219; © 824,008; ◆ 846,073
Newington; CDP; HARTFORD; ▲ Newington; **160** E-10; 🄿 🄷; ★ **H-NB**; **z** 06111, **z** 06131; Ⓟ 29,208; © 29,306; ◆ 29,947
Newington; MCD-Town; HARTFORD; ***160** E-10; 🄿; ★ **H-NB**; **z** 06111, **z** 06131; Ⓟ 29,208; © 29,306; ◆ 29,947
Newington Junction; RMC Place; HARTFORD; ▲ Newington; ***160** E-9; elev. 60ft./18m.; ★ **H-NB**; mail Newington **z** 06111
New London; Inc. Place; NEW LONDON; ▲ New London; **161** L-19; 🄿 🄷 🄲 3,531 ■; ★ **N.LON-**; **z** 06320; Ⓟ 28,540; © 25,671; Ⓡ 26,185; ◆ 26,178
New London; MCD-Town; NEW LONDON; ***161** I-15; 🄿 🄷 🄲 3,531; ★ **N.LON-**; **z** 06320; coextensive with the City of New London; Ⓟ 28,540; © 25,671; Ⓡ 26,185; ◆ 26,178
NEW LONDON; **161** G-16; Ⓟ 254,957; © 259,088; Ⓡ 259,106; ◆ 275,860
New Milford; CDP; LITCHFIELD; ▲ New Milford; **160** F-4; 🄿; ★ **N.Y.**; **z** 06776; Ⓟ 5,775; © 6,633
New Milford; MCD-Town; LITCHFIELD; ***160** E-3; 🄿 🄷; ★ **N.Y.**; **z** 06776; Ⓟ 23,629; © 27,121; Ⓡ 27,098; ◆ 29,054
New Preston; CDP; LITCHFIELD; ▲ Washington; **160** E-4; 🄿; **z** 06777; Ⓟ 1,217; © 1,110; Ⓡ 1,120
Newtown; Inc. Place; FAIRFIELD; ▲ Newtown; **160** H-5; 🄿; ★ **N.Y.**; **z** 06470; Ⓟ 1,800; © 1,843
Newtown; MCD-Town; FAIRFIELD; ***160** H-5; 🄿; ★ **N.Y.**; **z** 06470; Ⓟ 20,779; © 25,031; ◆ 25,601
New Village; RMC Place; WINDHAM; ▲ Plainfield; ★ **N.LON-**; mail Plainfield **z** 06374
Niantic; CDP; NEW LONDON; ▲ East Lyme; **161** I-14; 🄿; ★ **N.LON-**; **z** 06357 & mail East Lyme **z** 06333; Ⓟ 3,048; © 3,085
Nichols; RMC Place; FAIRFIELD; ▲ Trumbull; **161** L-13; elev. 257ft./78m.; ★ **N.Y.**; mail Trumbull **z** 06611
Noank; CDP; NEW LONDON; ▲ Groton; **161** I-16; ★ **N.LON-**; mail Groton **z** 06340; © 1,830
Noble; RMC Place; FAIRFIELD; ▲ Bridgeport; ***160** K-6; ★ **N.Y.**; mail Bridgeport **z** 06608; pop. incl. with Bridgeport (Inc. Place)
Norfolk; RMC Place; LITCHFIELD; ▲ Norfolk; **160** B-6; 🄿; **z** 06058; ● 1,430
Norfolk; MCD-Town; LITCHFIELD; ***160** B-6; 🄿; **z** 06058; Ⓟ 2,060; © 1,660
Noroton; RMC Place; FAIRFIELD; ▲ Darien; ***160** L-3; elev. 60ft./18m.; ★ **N.Y.**; mail Darien **z** 06820
Noroton Heights; RMC Place; FAIRFIELD; ▲ Darien; ***160** L-3; elev. 60ft./18m.; ★ **N.Y.**; mail Darien **z** 06820
North Ashford; RMC Place; WINDHAM; ▲ Eastford; ***161** B-15; mail Woodstock Valley **z** 06282
North Bloomfield; RMC Place; HARTFORD; ▲ Bloomfield; ***160** C-9; ★ **H-NB**; mail Bloomfield **z** 06002
North Branford; RMC Place; NEW HAVEN; ▲ North Branford; **160** I-9; 🄿; ★ **N.HAV**; **z** 06471 & mail Hamden **z** 06517; ● 7,400
North Branford; MCD-Town; NEW HAVEN; ***160** I-9; 🄿; ★ **N.HAV**; **z** 06471 & mail Hamden **z** 06517; Ⓟ 12,996; © 13,906; ◆ 14,134
North Bridgeport; RMC Place; FAIRFIELD; ▲ Bridgeport; ★ **N.Y.**; mail Bridgeport **z** 06601; pop. incl. with Bridgeport (Inc. Place)
North Canaan; MCD-Town; LITCHFIELD; ***160** B-5; mail Canaan **z** 06018; Ⓟ 3,284; © 3,350
North Canton; RMC Place; HARTFORD; ▲ Canton; **160** C-8; 🄿; ★ **H-NB**; **z** 06059; ● 270
North Colebrook; RMC Place; LITCHFIELD; ▲ Colebrook; ***160** B-6; elev. 1,183ft./361m.; mail Colebrook **z** 06021; rural
North Corners; RMC Place; LITCHFIELD; ▲ Cornwall; ***160** D-5; elev. 1,016ft./310m.; mail West Cornwall **z** 06796; rural
North Cornwall; RMC Place; LITCHFIELD; ▲ Cornwall; ***160** C-5; elev. 1,185ft./361m.; mail West Cornwall **z** 06796; rural
North End; RMC Place; NEW HAVEN; ▲ Waterbury; ★ **WATB**; mail Waterbury **z** 06704; pop. incl. with Waterbury (Inc. Place)
North Farms; RMC Place; NEW HAVEN; ▲ North Branford; ***160** I-8; ★ **N.HAV**; mail North Branford **z** 06471; pop. incl. with New Haven (Inc. Place)
Northfield; RMC Place; LITCHFIELD; ▲ Litchfield; **160** E-6; 🄿; ★ **TORR**; **z** 06778 & mail Thomaston **z** 06787; ● 710
Northford; RMC Place; NEW HAVEN; ▲ North Branford; **160** H-9; 🄿; ★ **N.HAV**; **z** 06472; ● 3,600
North Glenwood; RMC Place; NEW LONDON; ▲ Ledyard; ***161** H-15; elev. 150ft./46m.; ★ **N.LON-**; mail Gales Ferry **z** 06335; ● 300
North Goshen; RMC Place; LITCHFIELD; ▲ Goshen; ***160** C-6; elev. 1,433ft./437m.; mail Goshen **z** 06756; rural
North Granby; CDP; HARTFORD; ▲ Granby; **160** B-9; 🄿; ★ **H-NB**; **z** 06060; Ⓟ 1,455; © 1,720
North Grosvenor Dale; CDP; WINDHAM; ▲ Thompson; **161** B-16; 🄿; ★ **WORC**; **z** 06255; Ⓟ 1,705; © 1,424
North Guilford; RMC Place; NEW HAVEN; ▲ Guilford; ***160** I-10; ★ **N.HAV**; mail Guilford **z** 06437
North Haven; CDP; NEW HAVEN; ▲ North Haven; **161** K-17; elev. 41ft./12m.; 🄿; ★ **N.HAV**; **z** 06473; Ⓟ 22,247; © 23,035; ◆ 23,611
North Haven; MCD-Town; NEW HAVEN; ***160** I-8; 🄿; ★ **N.HAV**; **z** 06473; Ⓟ 22,247; © 23,035; ◆ 23,611
North Kent; RMC Place; LITCHFIELD; ▲ Kent; **160** D-4; mail Kent **z** 06757; ● 170
North Madison; RMC Place; NEW HAVEN; ▲ Madison; ***160** I-10; ★ **N.HAV**; mail Madison **z** 06443
North Mianus; RMC Place; FAIRFIELD; ▲ Greenwich; ***160** L-3; ★ **N.Y.**; mail Cos Cob **z** 06807, Riverside **z** 06878
North Middletown; RMC Place; MIDDLESEX; ▲ Middletown; ★ **H-NB**; pop. incl. with Middletown (Inc. Place)
North Norfolk; RMC Place; LITCHFIELD; ▲ Norfolk; ***160** A-6; elev. 1,150ft./351m.; mail Norfolk **z** 06058; rural
North Plain; RMC Place; MIDDLESEX; ▲ East Haddam; ***161** H-13; elev. 100ft./30m.; ★ **H-NB**; mail East Haddam **z** 06423; rural
North Stamford; RMC Place; FAIRFIELD; ▲ Stamford; ***160** K-3; ★ **N.Y.**; pop. incl. with Stamford (Inc. Place)
North Sterling; RMC Place; WINDHAM; ▲ Sterling; ***161** D-17; elev. 500ft./152m.; mail Sterling **z** 06377; rural
North Stonington; RMC Place; NEW LONDON; ▲ North Stonington; **161** H-16; 🄿; ★ **N.LON-**; **z** 06359; ● 350
North Stonington; MCD-Town; NEW LONDON; ***161** H-16; 🄿; ★ **N.LON-**; **z** 06359; Ⓟ 4,884; © 4,991; ◆ 5,288
North Thompsonville; RMC Place; HARTFORD; ▲ Enfield; ***161** B-11; ★ **H-NB**; mail Enfield **z** 06082; ● 1,500
Northville; RMC Place; LITCHFIELD; ▲ New Milford; **160** F-4; elev. 358ft./109m.; ★ **N.Y.**; mail New Milford **z** 06776; ● 400
North Westchester; RMC Place; NEW LONDON; ▲ Colchester; **161** F-12; 🄿; ★ **H-NB**; **z** 06474; ● 300
Northwest Harwinton; CDP-Census Area Only; LITCHFIELD; ▲ Harwinton; **160** D-7; ★ **H-NB**; mail Harwinton **z** 06791, Torrington **z** 06792; Ⓟ 3,299; © 3,242
North Willimantic; RMC Place; WINDHAM; ▲ Windham; ★ **H-NB**
North Wilton; RMC Place; FAIRFIELD; ▲ Wilton; **160** J-4; ★ **N.Y.**; mail Wilton **z** 06897; ● 100
North Windham; RMC Place; WINDHAM; ▲ Windham; **161** E-14; 🄿; ★ **H-NB**; **z** 06235, **z** 06256 & mail Hampton **z** 06247; ● 1,000
North Woodstock; RMC Place; WINDHAM; **161** B-15; mail Woodstock **z** 06281
Norwalk; Inc. Place; FAIRFIELD; ▲ Norwalk; **160** K-4; 🄿 🄷 ■; ★ **N.Y.**; **z** 06850-60; Ⓟ 78,331; © 82,951; ◆ 83,718
Norwalk; MCD-Town; FAIRFIELD; ***160** L-4; 🄿 🄷; ★ **N.Y.**; **z** 06850-60; coextensive with the City of Norwalk; © 82,951; ◆ 83,718
Norwich; Inc. Place; NEW LONDON; ▲ Norwich; **161** G-15; 🄿 🄷 ■; ★ **N.LON-**; **z** 06360, **z** 06365 & mail Jewett City **z** 06351; Ⓟ 37,391; © 36,117; ◆ 37,515
Norwich; MCD-Town; NEW LONDON; ***161** G-15; 🄿 🄷; ★ **N.LON-**; **z** 06360, **z** 06365 & mail Jewett City **z** 06351; coextensive with the City of Norwich; Ⓟ 37,391; © 36,117; ◆ 37,515
Norwichtown; RMC Place; NEW LONDON; ▲ Norwich; ***161** G-15; ★ **N.LON-**; mail Norwich **z** 06360; pop. incl. with Norwich (Inc. Place)
Nut Plains; RMC Place; NEW HAVEN; ▲ Guilford; ***160** I-10; ★ **N.HAV**; mail Guilford **z** 06437; ● 100

O

Oakdale; RMC Place; NEW LONDON; ▲ Montville; **161** H-14; 🄿; ★ **N.LON-**; **z** 06370; ● 910
Oakdale Heights; RMC Place; NEW LONDON; ▲ Montville; ***161** H-14; ★ **N.LON-**; mail Oakdale **z** 06370; ● 510
Oakdale Manor; RMC Place; NEW HAVEN; ▲ Southbury; **160** H-5; ★ **WATB**; mail Southbury **z** 06488; ● 400
Oakland Gardens; RMC Place; HARTFORD; ▲ Farmington; **161** I-18; ★ **H-NB**; mail Farmington **z** 06032; ● 300
Oakville; CDP; LITCHFIELD; ▲ Watertown; **160** F-7; 🄿; ★ **WATB**; **z** 06779 & mail Watertown **z** 06795; Ⓟ 8,741; © 8,618
Occum; RMC Place; NEW LONDON; ▲ Norwich; ***161** F-15; ★ **N.LON-**; mail Norwich **z** 06360; pop. incl. with Norwich (Inc. Place)
Old Greenwich; RMC Place; FAIRFIELD; ▲ Greenwich; **160** M-9; 🄿; ★ **N.Y.**; **z** 06870
Old Lyme; RMC Place; NEW LONDON; ▲ Old Lyme; **161** I-13; 🄿; ★ **N.LON-**; **z** 06371; ● 480
Old Lyme; MCD-Town; NEW LONDON; ***161** I-13; 🄿; ★ **N.LON-**; **z** 06371; Ⓟ 6,535; © 7,406; ◆ 7,851
Old Lyme Shores; RMC Place; NEW LONDON; ▲ Old Lyme; **161** J-13; ★ **N.LON-**; mail Old Lyme **z** 06371; ● 300
Old Mystic; CDP; NEW LONDON; ▲ Stonington, Groton; **161** H-16; 🄿; ★ **N.LON-**; **z** 06372; © 3,205
Old Saybrook; RMC Place; MIDDLESEX; ▲ Old Saybrook; ● 680
Old Saybrook; MCD-Town; MIDDLESEX; ***161** J-12; 🄿; **z** 06475; Ⓟ 9,552; © 10,367; ◆ 11,160
Old Saybrook Center; CDP-Census Area Only; MIDDLESEX; ▲ Old Saybrook; **161** J-12; mail Old Saybrook **z** 06475; Ⓟ 1,820; © 1,962
Old State House; RMC Place; HARTFORD; ▲ Hartford; ★ **H-NB**; mail Hartford **z** 06123; pop. incl. with Hartford (Inc. Place)
Oneco; RMC Place; WINDHAM; ▲ Sterling; **161** E-17; 🄿; **z** 06373; ● 750
Orange; CDP; NEW HAVEN; ▲ Orange; **161** L-14; 🄿; ★ **N.HAV**; **z** 06477; Ⓟ 12,830; © 13,233
Orange; MCD-Town; NEW HAVEN; ***160** J-7; 🄿 ■; ★ **N.HAV**; **z** 06477; Ⓟ 12,830; © 13,233; ◆ 13,650
Orcutts; RMC Place; TOLLAND; ▲ Stafford; **161** B-13; elev. 545ft./166m.; ★ **H-NB**; mail Stafford Springs **z** 06076; ● 240
Ore Hill; RMC Place; LITCHFIELD; ▲ Salisbury; ***160** B-4; elev. 850ft./259m.; mail Lakeville **z** 06039; ● 30
Oronoke; RMC Place; NEW HAVEN; ▲ Waterbury; ***160** G-7; ★ **WATB**; mail Waterbury **z** 06708
Oronoque; RMC Place; FAIRFIELD; ▲ Stratford; **161** M-13; ★ **N.Y.**; mail Stratford **z** 06614
Oswegatchie; RMC Place; NEW LONDON; ▲ Waterford; **161** I-14; ★ **N.LON-**; mail Waterford **z** 06385; ● 150
Overlook; RMC Place; NEW HAVEN; ▲ Waterbury; ***160** G-7; ★ **WATB**; mail Waterbury **z** 06710; pop. incl. with Waterbury (Inc. Place)
Owenoke; RMC Place; FAIRFIELD; ▲ Westport; ***160** L-4; elev. 78ft./24m.; ★ **N.Y.**; mail Westport **z** 06880
Oxford (Oxford Center); RMC Place; NEW HAVEN; ▲ Oxford; **160** H-6; elev. 351ft./107m.; 🄿; ★ **N.Y.**; **z** 06478; ● 2,100
Oxford; MCD-Town; NEW HAVEN; ***160** H-6; 🄿; ★ **N.Y.**; **z** 06478; Ⓟ 8,685; © 9,821; ◆ 10,751
Oxford Center; NEW HAVEN; see Oxford (RMC Place)
Ox Hill; RMC Place; NEW LONDON; ▲ Norwich; ★ **N.LON-**; mail Norwich **z** 06360; pop. incl. with Norwich (Inc. Place)
Oxoboxo Lake; RMC Place; NEW LONDON; ▲ Montville; ***161** G-14; ★ **N.LON-**; mail Oakdale **z** 06370; ● 180
Oxoboxo River; CDP-Census Area Only; NEW LONDON; ***161** H-14; ★ **N.LON-**; © 2,938

P

Pachaug; RMC Place; NEW LONDON; ▲ Griswold; ***161** F-16; ★ **N.LON-**; mail Jewett City **z** 06351
Palestine; RMC Place; FAIRFIELD; ▲ Newtown; ***160** I-5; ★ **N.Y.**; mail Newtown **z** 06470; ● 200
Palmertown (Montville); RMC Place; NEW LONDON; ▲ Montville; ***161** H-14; ★ **N.LON-**; mail Montville **z** 06353; ● 510
Paradise Green; RMC Place; FAIRFIELD; ▲ Stratford; ★ **N.Y.**; mail Stratford **z** 06614
Parcel Post; RMC Place; NEW HAVEN; ▲ Milford; ***160** I-8; ★ **N.HAV**; mail Milford **z** 06460; pop. incl. with Milford (Inc. Place)
Park Lane; RMC Place; LITCHFIELD; ▲ New Milford; ***160** F-4; elev. 389ft./119m.; ★ **N.Y.**; mail New Milford **z** 06776
Parkville; RMC Place; HARTFORD; ▲ Hartford; ★ **H-NB**; mail Hartford **z** 06106; pop. incl. with Hartford (Inc. Place)
Paucatuck Eastern Pequot Reservation; NEW LONDON; Indian Reservation; State Reservation; © 26
Pawcatuck; CDP; NEW LONDON; ▲ Stonington; **161** I-17; 🄿; ★ **N.LON-**; **z** 06379; Ⓟ 5,289; © 5,474
Pemberwick; RMC Place; FAIRFIELD; ▲ Greenwich; ***160** L-2; ★ **N.Y.**; mail Greenwich **z** 06830
Pequabuck; RMC Place; LITCHFIELD; ▲ Plymouth; ***160** E-7; 🄿; ★ **H-NB**; **z** 06781
Perkins Corner; RMC Place; TOLLAND; ▲ Mansfield; ***161** E-13; elev. 276ft./84m.; ★ **H-NB**; mail Willimantic **z** 06226
Phoenixville; RMC Place; WINDHAM; ▲ Eastford; ***161** C-15; mail Chaplin **z** 06235
Pine Bridge; RMC Place; NEW HAVEN; ▲ Beacon Falls; **160** H-7; ★ **N.Y.**; mail Beacon Falls **z** 06403; ● 1,000
Pine Grove; RMC Place; LITCHFIELD; ▲ Canaan; ***160** B-4; mail Falls Village **z** 06031; ● 60
Pine Grove; RMC Place; NEW LONDON; ▲ East Lyme; ***161** I-14; ★ **N.LON-**; mail Niantic **z** 06357
Pine Meadow; RMC Place; LITCHFIELD; ▲ New Hartford; **160** C-8; 🄿; ★ **H-NB**; **z** 06061; ● 530
Pine Orchard; RMC Place; NEW HAVEN; ▲ Branford; **160** J-9; ★ **N.HAV**; mail Branford **z** 06405; ● 950
Pine Rock Park; RMC Place; FAIRFIELD; ▲ Shelton; **161** L-14; ★ **N.Y.**; mail Shelton **z** 06484; pop. incl. with Shelton (Inc. Place)
Plainfield; RMC Place; WINDHAM; **161** E-16; ★ **N.LON-**; ● 2,600
Plainfield; MCD-Town; WINDHAM; ***161** E-16; 🄿; ★ **N.LON-**; **z** 06374; Ⓟ 14,363; © 14,619; ◆ 15,209
Plainfield Village; CDP-Census Area Only; WINDHAM; ▲ Plainfield; **161** E-16; elev. 203ft./62m.; ★ **N.LON-**; mail Plainfield **z** 06374; Ⓟ 2,856; © 2,638
Plainville; RMC Place; HARTFORD; ▲ Plainville; **160** E-9; elev. 191ft./58m.; 🄿; ★ **H-NB**; **z** 06062; ● 17,392
Plainville; MCD-Town; HARTFORD; ***160** E-8; 🄿; ★ **H-NB**; **z** 06062; Ⓟ 17,392; © 17,328; ◆ 17,531
Plantsville; RMC Place; HARTFORD; ▲ Southington; **160** F-8; 🄿; ★ **H-NB**; **z** 06479; ● 6,000
Platts Mills; RMC Place; NEW HAVEN; ▲ Waterbury; ***160** G-7; ★ **WATB**; mail Waterbury **z** 06706; pop. incl. with Waterbury (Inc. Place)
Pleasant Acres; RMC Place; FAIRFIELD; ▲ Danbury; ***160** H-4; ★ **N.Y.**; mail Danbury **z** 06810; pop. incl. with Danbury (Inc. Place)
Pleasant Valley; RMC Place; LITCHFIELD; ▲ Barkhamsted; **160** C-7; elev. 428ft./130m.; 🄿; ★ **H-NB**; **z** 06063; ● 460
Pleasure Beach; RMC Place; NEW LONDON; ▲ Waterford; **161** N-18; ★ **N.LON-**; mail Waterford **z** 06385; ● 1,450
Plymouth; RMC Place; LITCHFIELD; ▲ Plymouth; **160** E-7; 🄿; ★ **H-NB**; **z** 06782; ● 1,200
Plymouth; MCD-Town; LITCHFIELD; ***160** F-7; 🄿; ★ **H-NB**; **z** 06782; Ⓟ 11,822; © 11,634; ◆ 11,206
Point Beach; RMC Place; NEW HAVEN; ▲ Milford; ★ **N.Y.**; mail Milford **z** 06460; pop. incl. with Milford (Inc. Place)
Point O'Woods; RMC Place; NEW LONDON; ▲ Old Lyme; **161** J-13; ★ **N.LON-**; mail South Lyme **z** 06376; ● 740
Pomfret; RMC Place; WINDHAM; ▲ Pomfret; **161** C-16; elev. 588ft./179m.; 🄿; **z** 06258; ● 670
Pomfret; MCD-Town; WINDHAM; ***161** C-16; 🄿; **z** 06258; Ⓟ 3,102; © 3,798
Pomfret Center; RMC Place; WINDHAM; ▲ Pomfret; **161** C-16; 🄿; **z** 06259; ● 390
Pomfret Landing; RMC Place; WINDHAM; ▲ Pomfret; **161** D-16; mail Pomfret Center **z** 06259; ● 110
Pond Point; RMC Place; NEW HAVEN; ▲ Milford; ★ **N.Y.**; mail Milford **z** 06460; pop. incl. with Milford (Inc. Place)
Ponset; RMC Place; MIDDLESEX; ▲ Haddam; **161** H-11; ★ **H-NB**; mail Higganum **z** 06441; ● 160
Pootatuck Park; RMC Place; FAIRFIELD; ▲ Newtown; ***160** H-5; ★ **N.Y.**; mail Sandy Hook **z** 06482; ● 820
Poquetanuck; RMC Place; NEW LONDON; ▲ Preston; **161** G-15; ★ **N.LON-**; mail Norwich **z** 06360, Preston **z** 06365; ● 220
Poquonock; RMC Place; HARTFORD; ▲ Windsor; **160** C-10; 🄿; ★ **H-NB**; **z** 06064; ● 1,100
Poquonock Bridge; CDP; NEW LONDON; ▲ Groton; **161** I-15; ★ **N.LON-**; mail Groton **z** 06340; Ⓟ 2,770; © 1,592
Portland; CDP; MIDDLESEX; ▲ Portland; **160** G-10; 🄿 🄷; ★ **H-NB**; **z** 06480; Ⓟ 5,645; © 5,534
Portland; MCD-Town; MIDDLESEX; ***161** F-11; 🄿; ★ **H-NB**; **z** 06480; Ⓟ 8,418; © 8,732; ◆ 9,176
Presidential; RMC Place; HARTFORD; ▲ Enfield; ★ **H-NB**; mail Enfield **z** 06082
Preston; NEW LONDON; see Preston City (RMC Place)
Preston; MCD-Town; NEW LONDON; ***161** G-15; 🄿; ★ **N.LON-**; **z** 06365 & mail Jewett City **z** 06351; Ⓟ 5,006; © 4,688; ◆ 4,991
Preston City (Preston); RMC Place; NEW LONDON; ▲ Preston; **161** G-16; ★ **N.LON-**; mail Jewett City **z** 06351, Preston **z** 06365; ● 220
Prospect; RMC Place; NEW HAVEN; ▲ Prospect; **160** G-7; elev. 852ft./260m.; 🄿; ★ **WATB**; **z** 06712; ● 7,775
Prospect; MCD-Town; NEW HAVEN; ***160** G-8; 🄿; ★ **WATB**; **z** 06712; Ⓟ 7,775; © 8,707; ◆ 9,064
Prospect Beach; RMC Place; NEW HAVEN; ▲ West Haven; ★ **N.HAV**; mail West Haven **z** 06516; pop. incl. with West Haven (Inc. Place)
Puddle Town; RMC Place; LITCHFIELD; ▲ New Hartford; ***160** C-8; ★ **H-NB**; mail Collinsville **z** 06022; rural
Putnam; RMC Place; WINDHAM; **161** C-16; ● 5,000
Putnam; MCD-Town; WINDHAM; ***161** C-16; 🄿; **z** 06260; Ⓟ 9,031; © 9,002
Putnam District; CDP-Census Area Only; WINDHAM; ▲ Putnam; **161** C-16; 🄷; mail Putnam **z** 06260; Ⓟ 6,835; © 6,746
Putnam Heights; RMC Place; WINDHAM; ▲ Putnam; **161** C-16; mail Putnam **z** 06260; ● 210
Putney; RMC Place; FAIRFIELD; ▲ Stratford; ***160** J-6; ★ **N.Y.**; mail Stratford **z** 06614

Q

Quaddick; RMC Place; WINDHAM; ▲ Thompson; **161** C-17; elev. 436ft./133m.; ★ **WORC**; mail Thompson **z** 06277; ● 540
Quaker Farms; RMC Place; NEW HAVEN; ▲ Oxford; ***160** H-6; elev. 377ft./115m.; ★ **N.Y.**; mail Oxford **z** 06478
Quaker Hill; RMC Place; NEW LONDON; ▲ Waterford; **161** H-15; 🄿; ★ **N.LON-**; **z** 06375
Quarryville; RMC Place; TOLLAND; ▲ Bolton; **161** D-12; elev. 583ft./178m.; ★ **H-NB**; mail Manchester **z** 06040; ● 410
Quebec; RMC Place; WINDHAM; ▲ Brooklyn; ***161** D-16; mail Danielson **z** 06239
Quinebaug; CDP; WINDHAM; ▲ Thompson; **161** B-16; 🄿; ★ **WORC**; **z** 06262; Ⓟ 1,031; © 1,122
Quinnipiac; RMC Place; NEW HAVEN; ▲ Wallingford; ***160** H-9; elev. 80ft./24m.; ★ **N.HAV**; mail Wallingford **z** 06492

R

Rawson; RMC Place; WINDHAM; ▲ Hampton; ***161** D-15; elev. 650ft./198m.; mail Hampton **z** 06247; rural
Redding (Redding Center); RMC Place; FAIRFIELD; ▲ Redding; ***160** I-4; 🄿; ★ **N.Y.**; **z** 06896 & mail Redding Center **z** 06875; ● 900
Redding; MCD-Town; FAIRFIELD; ***160** I-4; 🄿; ★ **N.Y.**; **z** 06896 & mail Redding Center **z** 06875; Ⓟ 7,927; © 8,270; ◆ 8,303
Redding Center; FAIRFIELD; see Redding (RMC Place)
Redding Ridge; RMC Place; FAIRFIELD; ▲ Redding; **160** I-4; 🄿; ★ **N.Y.**; **z** 06876; ● 550
Reeds Gap; RMC Place; NEW HAVEN; ▲ Wallingford; ***160** H-9; ★ **N.HAV**
Ridgebury; RMC Place; FAIRFIELD; ▲ Ridgefield; **160** I-3; ★ **N.Y.**; mail Ridgefield **z** 06877; ● 220
Ridgefield; CDP; FAIRFIELD; ▲ Ridgefield; **160** J-3; 🄿; ★ **N.Y.**; **z** 06877, **z** 06879; Ⓟ 6,363; © 7,212
Ridgefield; MCD-Town; FAIRFIELD; ***160** I-3; 🄿; ★ **N.Y.**; **z** 06877, **z** 06879; Ⓟ 20,919; © 23,643; ◆ 24,719
Ridgewood; RMC Place; MIDDLESEX; ▲ Clinton; ***161** J-11; elev. 25ft./8m.; ★ **N.HAV**; mail Clinton **z** 06413
Ridgewood (Ridgewood Park); RMC Place; NEW LONDON; ▲ Waterford; ***161** I-15; ★ **N.LON-**; mail Waterford **z** 06385; ● 500
Ridgewood Park; NEW LONDON; see Ridgewood (RMC Place)
Rising Corner; RMC Place; HARTFORD; ▲ Suffield; ***160** B-10; elev. 226ft./69m.; ★ **H-NB**; mail West Suffield **z** 06093; ● 30
Rivercliff; RMC Place; NEW HAVEN; ▲ Milford; **161** M-13; ★ **N.Y.**; mail Milford **z** 06460; pop. incl. with Milford (Inc. Place)
River Glen; RMC Place; HARTFORD; ▲ Farmington; ***160** E-8; ★ **H-NB**; mail Farmington **z** 06032; ● 30
Riverside; RMC Place; FAIRFIELD; ▲ Greenwich; ***160** L-3; 🄿; ★ **N.Y.**; **z** 06878
Riverside; RMC Place; FAIRFIELD; ▲ Newtown; **160** M-8; 🄿; ★ **N.Y.**; **z** 06878 & mail Sandy Hook **z** 06482; ● 270
Riverside; RMC Place; NEW HAVEN; ▲ Oxford; ***160** I-6; ★ **N.Y.**; mail Oxford **z** 06478
Riversville; RMC Place; FAIRFIELD; ▲ Greenwich; ***160** L-2; ★ **N.Y.**; mail Greenwich **z** 06830
Riverton; RMC Place; LITCHFIELD; ▲ Barkhamsted; **160** B-7; 🄿; ★ **H-NB**; **z** 06065; ● 580
Robertsville; RMC Place; LITCHFIELD; ▲ Colebrook; **160** B-7; mail Riverton **z** 06065; ● 280
Rockfall; RMC Place; MIDDLESEX; ▲ Middlefield; **160** G-10; 🄿; ★ **H-NB**; **z** 06481; ● 980
Rock Ridge; RMC Place; FAIRFIELD; ▲ Greenwich; ***160** L-2; ★ **N.Y.**; mail Greenwich **z** 06830
Rockville; CDP; TOLLAND; ***161** C-12; 🄷; ★ **H-NB**; mail Vernon Rockville **z** 06066; © 7,708
Rocky Hill; RMC Place; HARTFORD; ▲ Rocky Hill; **160** F-10; 🄿 🄷; ★ **H-NB**; **z** 06067; ● 16,554
Rocky Hill; MCD-Town; HARTFORD; ***160** F-10; 🄿; ★ **H-NB**; **z** 06067; Ⓟ 16,554; © 17,966; ◆ 19,200
Rogers; RMC Place; WINDHAM; ▲ Killingly; **161** D-16; 🄿; **z** 06263; ● 660
Round Hill; RMC Place; FAIRFIELD; ▲ Greenwich; ***160** L-2; ★ **N.Y.**; mail Greenwich **z** 06830
Rowayton; RMC Place; FAIRFIELD; ▲ Norwalk; ***160** L-4; elev. 36ft./11m.; ★ **N.Y.**; mail Norwalk **z** 06853; pop. incl. with Norwalk (Inc. Place)
Roxbury; RMC Place; FAIRFIELD; ▲ Stamford; ★ **N.Y.**; pop. incl. with Stamford (Inc. Place)
Roxbury; RMC Place; LITCHFIELD; ▲ Roxbury; **160** G-5; elev. 557ft./170m.; 🄿; **z** 06783; ● 500
Roxbury; MCD-Town; LITCHFIELD; ***160** G-5; 🄿; **z** 06783; Ⓟ 1,825; © 2,136; Ⓡ 2,137; ◆ 2,312
Roxbury Falls; RMC Place; LITCHFIELD; ▲ Roxbury; **160** G-5; elev. 303ft./92m.; mail Roxbury **z** 06783; ● 130

S

Sachem Head; RMC Place; NEW HAVEN; ▲ Guilford; **160** J-10; ★ **N.HAV**; mail Guilford **z** 06437; ● 500
Sadds Mill; RMC Place; TOLLAND; ▲ Ellington; ***161** C-11; elev. 187ft./57m.; ★ **H-NB**; mail Ellington **z** 06029; rural
Salem; RMC Place; NEW LONDON; ▲ Salem; **161** G-13; 🄿; ★ **N.LON-**; **z** 06420; ● 40
Salem; MCD-Town; NEW LONDON; ***161** G-13; 🄿; ★ **N.LON-**; **z** 06420; Ⓟ 3,310; © 3,858; ◆ 4,211
Salisbury; RMC Place; LITCHFIELD; ▲ Salisbury; **160** B-4; 🄿; **z** 06068 & mail Taconic **z** 06079; ● 1,700
Salisbury; MCD-Town; LITCHFIELD; ***160** B-4; 🄿; **z** 06068 & mail Taconic **z** 06079; Ⓟ 4,090; © 3,977
Salmon Brook; CDP-Census Area Only; HARTFORD; ▲ Granby; **160** B-9; elev. 215ft./66m.; ★ **H-NB**; mail Granby **z** 06035, West Granby **z** 06090; Ⓟ 2,185; © 2,453
Samp Mortar; RMC Place; FAIRFIELD; ▲ Fairfield; ***160** K-5; ★ **N.Y.**
Sandy Beach; RMC Place; LITCHFIELD; ▲ Morris; ***160** D-5; ★ **TORR**; mail Lakeside **z** 06758; ● 160
Sandy Hook; RMC Place; FAIRFIELD; ▲ Newtown; **160** H-5; 🄿; ★ **N.Y.**; **z** 06482; ● 1,200
Sanfordtown; RMC Place; FAIRFIELD; ▲ Redding; ***160** J-4; elev. 450ft./137m.; ★ **N.Y.**; mail Redding **z** 06896; ● 50
Saugatuck; RMC Place; FAIRFIELD; ▲ Westport; ***160** K-4; elev. 78ft./24m.; ★ **N.Y.**; mail Westport **z** 06880
Saugatuck Shores; RMC Place; FAIRFIELD; ▲ Westport; ***160** L-4; elev. 78ft./24m.; ★ **N.Y.**; mail Westport **z** 06880
Saunders Point; RMC Place; NEW LONDON; ▲ East Lyme; ***161** I-14; ★ **N.LON-**; mail Niantic **z** 06357
Savin Rock; RMC Place; NEW HAVEN; ▲ West Haven; ★ **N.HAV**; mail West Haven **z** 06516; pop. incl. with West Haven (Inc. Place)
Saybrook Manor; CDP; MIDDLESEX; ▲ Old Saybrook; **161** J-12; mail Old Saybrook **z** 06475; Ⓟ 1,073; © 1,133
Saybrook Point; RMC Place; MIDDLESEX; ▲ Old Saybrook; **161** J-13; mail Old Saybrook **z** 06475; ● 300
Scantic; RMC Place; HARTFORD; ▲ East Windsor; **161** C-11; ★ **H-NB**; mail East Windsor **z** 06088; ● 400
Schaghticoke Reservation; Indian Reservation; LITCHFIELD; State Reservation; © 9
Scitico; RMC Place; HARTFORD; ▲ Enfield; ***161** B-11; ★ **H-NB**; mail Enfield **z** 06082
Scotland; RMC Place; WINDHAM; ▲ Scotland; **161** E-15; 🄿; **z** 06264; ● 900
Scotland; MCD-Town; WINDHAM; ***161** E-15; 🄿; **z** 06264; Ⓟ 1,215; © 1,556
Seaview Beach; RMC Place; NEW HAVEN; ▲ Madison; ***161** J-11; ★ **N.HAV**; mail Madison **z** 06443
Secret Lake; RMC Place; HARTFORD; ▲ Avon; ***160** D-8; elev. 650ft./198m.; ★ **H-NB**; mail Avon **z** 06001; ● 400
Seymour; RMC Place; NEW HAVEN; ▲ Seymour; **160** H-7; elev. 100ft./30m.; 🄿; ★ **N.Y.**; **z** 06478, **z** 06483; ● 14,288
Seymour; MCD-Town; NEW HAVEN; ***160** I-7; elev. 100ft./30m.; 🄿; ★ **N.Y.**; **z** 06478, **z** 06483; Ⓟ 14,288; © 15,454; ◆ 16,348

Entries in **UPPERCASE** are counties.
Entries in **bold** have populations of 2,500 or more.
Names in parentheses are alternate names.

Inc. Place	Incorporated Place
RMC Place	Rand McNally Designated Place
CDP	Census Designated Place
MCD	Minor Civil Division
⊡	County Seat
▲	Minor Civil Division
elev.	Elevation
🄿	Post Office
🄷	Hospital
🄲	College
■	Principal Business Center
★	Ranally Metro Area (RMA) Abbreviation
z	Zip Code(s)
Ⓟ	Previous Census Population
Ⓡ	Revised Census Population
Ⓐ	Annexation Population
●	Rand McNally Population Estimate
©	Final Census Population
Ⓢ	Special Census Population
◆	Estimated Population

For additional definitions see Glossary, Volume 1, and Introduction, Volume 2.

Shady Rest; RMC Place; FAIRFIELD; ▲ Newtown; 160 H-5; ★ N.Y.; mail Sandy Hook z 06482; ● 270
Shailerville; RMC Place; MIDDLESEX; ▲ Haddam; *161 H-11; ★ H-NB; mail Haddam z 06438
Sharon; RMC Place; LITCHFIELD; ▲ Sharon; 160 C-4; elev. 714ft./218m.; [P] [H]; z 06069; ● 1,200
Sharon; MCD-Town; LITCHFIELD; *160 C-4; [P]; z 06069; Ⓟ 2,928; Ⓒ 2,968
Sharon Valley; RMC Place; LITCHFIELD; ▲ Sharon; 160 C-3; mail Sharon z 06069; ● 300
Shelton; Inc. Place; FAIRFIELD; ▲ Shelton; 161 L-14; [P]; ★ N.Y.; z 06484; Ⓟ 35,418; Ⓒ 38,101; ◆ 38,826
Shelton; MCD-Town; FAIRFIELD; *160 I-6; [P]; ★ N.Y.; z 06484; coextensive with the City of Shelton; Ⓟ 35,418; Ⓒ 38,101; ◆ 38,826
Sherman; RMC Place; FAIRFIELD; ▲ Sherman; 160 F-3; [P]; ★ N.Y.; z 06784; ● 150
Sherman; MCD-Town; FAIRFIELD; *160 F-3; [P]; ★ N.Y.; z 06784; Ⓟ 2,809; Ⓒ 3,827; ◆ 4,008
Sherman Corner; RMC Place; WINDHAM; ▲ Chaplin; *161 D-14; ★ H-NB; mail North Windham z 06256
Sherwood Manor; CDP-Census Area Only; HARTFORD; ▲ Enfield; *161 B-11; ★ H-NB; mail Enfield z 06082; Ⓟ 6,357; Ⓒ 5,689
Shippan Point; RMC Place; FAIRFIELD; ▲ Stamford; *160 L-3; ★ N.Y.; mail Stamford z 06902; pop. incl. with Stamford (Inc. Place)
Shorehaven; RMC Place; FAIRFIELD; ▲ Norwalk; *160 L-4; ★ N.Y.; pop. incl. with Norwalk (Inc. Place)
Short Beach; RMC Place; NEW HAVEN; ▲ Branford; 161 N-17; ★ N.HAV; mail Branford z 06405; ● 200
Silver Beach; RMC Place; NEW HAVEN; ▲ Milford; *160 K-7; ★ N.Y.; mail Milford z 06460
Silver Lane; RMC Place; HARTFORD; ▲ East Hartford; *161 D-11; [P]; ★ H-NB; z 06138
Silvermine; RMC Place; FAIRFIELD; ▲ Norwalk; *160 K-4; ★ N.Y.; pop. incl. with Norwalk (Inc. Place)
Simsbury; RMC Place; HARTFORD; ▲ Simsbury; 160 C-9; ★ H-NB; ● 5,300
Simsbury; MCD-Town; HARTFORD; *160 C-9; [P]; ★ H-NB; z 06070 & mail Tariffville z 06081, Weatogue z 06089, West Simsbury z 06092; Ⓟ 22,023; Ⓒ 23,234; ◆ 24,443
Simsbury Center; CDP-Census Area Only; HARTFORD; ▲ Simsbury; 160 C-9; elev. 181ft./55m.; ★ H-NB; mail Simsbury z 06070, Tariffville z 06081, Weatogue z 06089, West Simsbury z 06092; Ⓟ 5,577; Ⓒ 5,603
Skiff Mountain; RMC Place; LITCHFIELD; ▲ Kent; *160 D-4; mail Kent z 06757; rural
Somers; RMC Place; TOLLAND; ▲ Somers; 161 B-12; ● 1,000
Somers; MCD-Town; TOLLAND; *161 B-12; [P]; ★ H-NB; z 06071; Ⓟ 9,108; Ⓒ 10,417; ◆ 11,507
Somersville; RMC Place; TOLLAND; ▲ Somers; 161 B-11; [P]; ★ H-NB; z 06072; ● 1,300
Sound View; RMC Place; NEW LONDON; ▲ Old Lyme; 161 J-13; ★ N.LON-; mail Old Lyme z 06371; ● 230
South Britain; RMC Place; NEW HAVEN; ▲ Southbury; 160 H-5; elev. 161ft./49m.; [P]; ★ WATB; z 06487; ● 1,060
Southbury; RMC Place; NEW HAVEN; ▲ Southbury; 160 H-6; [P]; ★ WATB; z 06488; ● 3,400
Southbury; MCD-Town; NEW HAVEN; *160 H-5; [P]; ★ WATB; z 06488; Ⓟ 15,818; Ⓒ 18,567; ◆ 19,908
South Canaan; RMC Place; LITCHFIELD; ▲ Canaan; *160 B-5; mail Falls Village z 06031
South Chaplin; RMC Place; WINDHAM; 161 D-14; ★ H-NB; mail North Windham z 06256
South Coventry; CDP-Census Area Only; TOLLAND; *161 D-13; ★ H-NB; mail Coventry z 06238; Ⓟ 1,257; Ⓒ 1,381
South Ellsworth; RMC Place; LITCHFIELD; ▲ Sharon; *160 D-4; mail Sharon z 06069; rural
South End; RMC Place; FAIRFIELD; ▲ Stamford; *160 L-3; ★ N.Y.; mail Stamford z 06902; pop. incl. with Stamford (Inc. Place)
South End; RMC Place; NEW HAVEN; ▲ East Haven; 161 N-16; elev. 25ft./8m.; ★ N.HAV; mail East Haven z 06512
South Farms; RMC Place; MIDDLESEX; ▲ Middletown; *160 G-10; ★ H-NB; mail Middletown z 06457; pop. incl. with Middletown (Inc. Place)
Southford; RMC Place; NEW HAVEN; ▲ Southbury; *160 H-6; elev. 504ft./154m.; ★ WATB; mail Southbury z 06488; ● 50
South Glastonbury; RMC Place; HARTFORD; ▲ Glastonbury; 161 E-11; [P]; ★ H-NB; z 06073; ● 2,000
South Glenwoods; RMC Place; NEW LONDON; ▲ Ledyard; *161 H-15; elev. 100ft./30m.; ★ N.LON-; mail Gales Ferry z 06335; ● 200
Southington; RMC Place; HARTFORD; ▲ Southington; 160 F-8; [P] [H]; ★ H-NB; z 06489
Southington; MCD-Town; HARTFORD; *160 F-8; [P] ■; ★ H-NB; z 06489; Ⓟ 38,518; Ⓒ 39,728; ◆ 40,901
South Kent; RMC Place; LITCHFIELD; ▲ Kent; 160 E-4; [P]; z 06785; ● 300
South Killingly; RMC Place; WINDHAM; ▲ Killingly; 161 D-17; mail Danielson z 06239; ● 220
South Lyme; RMC Place; NEW LONDON; ▲ Old Lyme; 161 I-13; [P]; ★ N.LON-; z 06376; ● 320
South Manchester; RMC Place; HARTFORD; ▲ Manchester; ★ H-NB; mail Manchester z 06040
South Meriden; RMC Place; NEW HAVEN; ▲ Meriden; *160 G-9; ★ N.HAV; mail Meriden z 06451; pop. incl. with Meriden (Inc. Place)
South Norfolk; RMC Place; LITCHFIELD; ▲ Norfolk; *160 C-6; mail Norfolk z 06058
South Norwalk; RMC Place; FAIRFIELD; ▲ Norwalk; *160 L-4; ★ N.Y.; mail Norwalk z 06854; pop. incl. with Norwalk (Inc. Place)
Southport; RMC Place; FAIRFIELD; ▲ Fairfield; *160 K-5; [P]; ★ N.Y.; z 06890
South Wethersfield; RMC Place; HARTFORD; ▲ Wethersfield; ★ H-NB; mail Wethersfield z 06109
South Willington; RMC Place; TOLLAND; ▲ Willington; 161 C-13; [P]; ★ H-NB; z 06265; ● 320
South Windham; CDP; WINDHAM; ▲ Windham; 161 E-14; [P]; ★ H-NB; z 06266; Ⓟ 1,644; Ⓒ 1,278
South Windsor; RMC Place; HARTFORD; ▲ South Windsor; 161 D-11; elev. 40ft./12m.; [P]; ★ H-NB; z 06074; ● 14,000
South Windsor; MCD-Town; HARTFORD; *161 D-11; [P]; ★ H-NB; z 06074; Ⓟ 22,090; Ⓒ 24,412; ◆ 26,132
Southwood Acres; CDP-Census Area Only; HARTFORD; ▲ Enfield; *161 B-11; ★ H-NB; mail Enfield z 06082; Ⓟ 8,963; Ⓒ 8,067
South Woodstock; CDP; WINDHAM; ▲ Woodstock; 161 C-16; [P]; z 06267; Ⓟ 1,112; Ⓒ 1,211
Sport Hill; RMC Place; FAIRFIELD; ▲ Easton; *160 J-5; ★ N.Y.; mail Easton z 06612; ● 1,800
Sprague; MCD-Town; NEW LONDON; *161 F-15; ★ N.LON-; mail Baltic z 06330; Ⓟ 3,008; Ⓒ 2,971; ◆ 3,051
Springdale; RMC Place; FAIRFIELD; ▲ Stamford; 160 K-10; ★ N.Y.; mail Stamford z 06907; pop. incl. with Stamford (Inc. Place)
Spring Hill; RMC Place; TOLLAND; ▲ Mansfield; 161 D-14; ★ H-NB; mail Storrs Mansfield z 06268; ● 200
Spring Lake Village; RMC Place; HARTFORD; ▲ Southington; ★ H-NB; mail Southington z 06489
Stafford (Stafford Hollow); RMC Place; TOLLAND; ▲ Stafford; 161 B-13; elev. 591ft./180m.; [P]; ★ H-NB; z 06075 & mail Stafford Springs z 06076; ● 720
Stafford; MCD-Town; TOLLAND; *161 B-13; [P]; ★ H-NB; z 06075 & mail Stafford Springs z 06076; Ⓟ 11,091; Ⓒ 11,307; ◆ 10,923
Stafford Hollow; TOLLAND; see Stafford (RMC Place)
Stafford Springs; RMC Place; TOLLAND; ▲ Stafford; 161 B-13; elev. 479ft./146m.; [P] [H]; ★ H-NB; z 06076 & mail Stafford z 06075; ● 4,900
Staffordville; RMC Place; TOLLAND; ▲ Stafford; 161 B-13; [P]; ★ H-NB; z 06077; ● 720
Stamford; Inc. Place; FAIRFIELD; ▲ Stamford; 160 M-9; [P] [H] ■; ★ N.Y.; z 06901-07, z 06910-14, z 06920-22, z 06925-28; Ⓟ 108,056; Ⓒ 117,083; ◆ 119,453
Stamford; MCD-Town; FAIRFIELD; *160 L-3; [P] [H]; ★ N.Y.; z 06901-07, z 06910-14, z 06920-22, z 06925-28; coextensive with the City of Stamford; Ⓟ 108,056; Ⓒ 117,083; ◆ 119,453
Stanwich; RMC Place; FAIRFIELD; ▲ Greenwich; *160 K-2; ★ N.Y.; mail Greenwich z 06830
State Line; RMC Place; LITCHFIELD; ▲ Salisbury; *160 B-3; elev. 748ft./228m.; mail Lakeville z 06039; rural
State Line; RMC Place; TOLLAND; ▲ Stafford; *161 B-13; ★ H-NB; mail Stafford Springs z 06076; ● 100
Stepney; RMC Place; FAIRFIELD; ▲ Monroe; *160 I-5; ★ N.Y.; mail Monroe z 06468; ● 750
Sterling; RMC Place; WINDHAM; ▲ Sterling; 161 E-17; [P]; z 06377; ● 660
Sterling; MCD-Town; WINDHAM; *161 E-17; [P]; z 06377; Ⓟ 2,357; Ⓒ 3,099
Sterling Hill; RMC Place; WINDHAM; ▲ Sterling; *161 E-17; elev. 600ft./183m.; mail Sterling z 06377
Stetson Corner; RMC Place; WINDHAM; ▲ Brooklyn; *161 D-15; elev. 450ft./137m.; mail Brooklyn z 06234; rural
Stevenson; RMC Place; FAIRFIELD; ▲ Monroe; 160 I-6; [P]; ★ N.Y.; z 06491; ● 1,150
Still River; RMC Place; LITCHFIELD; ▲ New Milford; *160 G-4; elev. 400ft./122m.; ★ N.Y.; mail New Milford z 06776; ● 70
Stonington; Inc. Place; NEW LONDON; ▲ Stonington; 161 I-16; [P]; ★ N.LON-; z 06378; Ⓟ 1,100; Ⓒ 1,032
Stonington; MCD-Town; NEW LONDON; *161 I-16; [P]; ★ N.LON-; z 06378; Ⓟ 16,919; Ⓒ 17,906; ◆ 19,277
Stony Corners; RMC Place; HARTFORD; ▲ Avon; *160 D-9; ★ H-NB; mail Avon z 06001; ● 300
Stony Creek; RMC Place; NEW HAVEN; ▲ Branford; 160 J-9; ★ N.HAV; mail Branford z 06405; ● 830
Storrs; CDP; TOLLAND; ▲ Mansfield; 161 D-13; [C] 28,481; ★ H-NB; mail Storrs Mansfield z 06268-69; Ⓟ 12,198; Ⓒ 10,996; Ⓡ 11,106
Straitsville; RMC Place; NEW HAVEN; ▲ Naugatuck; *160 H-7; ★ WATB; mail Naugatuck z 06770; pop. incl. with Naugatuck (Inc. Place)
Stratfield; RMC Place; FAIRFIELD; ▲ Fairfield; 161 M-11; ★ N.Y.
Stratford; CDP; FAIRFIELD; ▲ Stratford; 161 M-13; [P]; ★ N.Y.; z 06614-15; Ⓟ 49,389; Ⓒ 49,976; ◆ 48,960
Stratford; MCD-Town; FAIRFIELD; *160 J-6; [P] ■; ★ N.Y.; z 06614-15, z 98662; Ⓟ 49,389; Ⓒ 49,976; ◆ 48,960
Suffield; RMC Place; HARTFORD; ▲ Suffield; ★ H-NB; ● 600
Suffield; HARTFORD; see Suffield Depot (CDP-Census Area Only)
Suffield; MCD-Town; HARTFORD; *160 B-10; [P]; ★ H-NB; z 06078, z 06080 & mail West Suffield z 06093; Ⓟ 11,427; Ⓒ 13,552; ◆ 14,637
Suffield Depot (Suffield); CDP-Census Area Only; HARTFORD; ▲ Suffield; 160 B-10; ★ H-NB; mail Suffield z 06078, z 06080, West Suffield z 06093; Ⓟ 1,353; Ⓒ 1,244
Summer Hill; RMC Place; NEW HAVEN; ▲ Wallingford; *160 J-9; ★ N.HAV; mail Wallingford z 06492
Sunrise Hill; RMC Place; NEW HAVEN; ▲ Bethany; *160 H-7; elev. 504ft./154m.; ★ N.HAV; mail Woodbridge z 06525; ● 110

T

Taconic; RMC Place; LITCHFIELD; ▲ Salisbury; 160 B-4; [P]; z 06079; ● 350
Taft Station; RMC Place; NEW LONDON; ▲ Norwich; *161 G-15; elev. 10ft./3m.; ★ N.LON-; mail Norwich z 06360; pop. incl. with Norwich (Inc. Place)
Taftville; RMC Place; NEW LONDON; ▲ Norwich; *161 G-15; [P]; ★ N.LON-; z 06380; pop. incl. with Norwich (Inc. Place)
Talcott Village; RMC Place; HARTFORD; ▲ Farmington; *160 E-9; elev. 400ft./122m.; ★ H-NB; mail Farmington z 06032; ● 380
Talcottville; RMC Place; TOLLAND; ▲ Vernon; *161 D-11; ★ H-NB; mail Vernon Rockville z 06066
Talmadge Hill; RMC Place; FAIRFIELD; ▲ New Canaan; *160 K-3; elev. 300ft./91m.; ★ N.Y.; mail New Canaan z 06840
Tariffville; CDP; HARTFORD; ▲ Simsbury; 160 C-9; [P]; ★ H-NB; z 06081; Ⓟ 1,477; Ⓒ 1,371
Terminal; RMC Place; NEW HAVEN; ▲ New Haven; *160 I-8; ★ N.HAV; mail New Haven z 06511; pop. incl. with New Haven (Inc. Place)
Terramuggus; CDP-Census Area Only; HARTFORD; ▲ Marlborough; 161 F-12; ★ H-NB; mail Marlborough z 06447; Ⓟ 1,044; Ⓒ 1,048
Terryville; CDP; LITCHFIELD; ▲ Plymouth; 160 E-7; elev. 609ft./186m.; [P]; ★ H-NB; z 06786; Ⓟ 5,426; Ⓒ 5,360
Thamesville; RMC Place; NEW LONDON; ▲ Norwich; *161 G-15; ★ N.LON-; mail Norwich z 06360; pop. incl. with Norwich (Inc. Place)
The Cedars; RMC Place; LITCHFIELD; ▲ Salisbury; *160 C-4; elev. 712ft./217m.; mail Lakeville z 06039; ● 100
Thomaston; RMC Place; LITCHFIELD; ▲ Thomaston; 160 E-7; elev. 393ft./120m.; [P]; ★ WATB; z 06778, z 06787; ● 4,000
Thomaston; MCD-Town; LITCHFIELD; *160 E-7; [P]; ★ WATB; z 06778, z 06787; Ⓟ 6,947; Ⓒ 7,503; ◆ 7,659
Thompson; RMC Place; WINDHAM; ▲ Thompson; 161 B-17; elev. 584ft./178m.; [P]; ★ WORC; z 06277; ● 960
Thompson; MCD-Town; WINDHAM; *161 B-16; [P]; ★ WORC; z 06277; Ⓟ 8,668; Ⓒ 8,878; ◆ 9,338
Thompsonville; CDP; HARTFORD; ▲ Enfield; 161 B-11; ★ H-NB; mail Enfield z 06082; Ⓟ 8,454; Ⓒ 8,125
Timber Trails; RMC Place; FAIRFIELD; ▲ Sherman; *160 G-3; elev. 950ft./290m.; ★ N.Y.; mail Sherman z 06784; rural
Titicus; RMC Place; FAIRFIELD; ▲ Ridgefield; *160 J-3; ★ N.Y.; mail Ridgefield z 06877
Tokeneke; RMC Place; FAIRFIELD; ▲ Darien; *160 L-4; elev. 60ft./18m.; ★ N.Y.; mail Darien z 06820
Tolland; RMC Place; TOLLAND; ▲ Tolland; 161 C-12; [P]; ★ H-NB; z 06084; ● 1,350
Tolland; MCD-Town; TOLLAND; *161 C-13; [P]; ★ H-NB; z 06084; Ⓟ 11,001; Ⓒ 13,146; Ⓡ 13,086; ◆ 14,385
TOLLAND; 161 D-12; Ⓟ 128,699; Ⓒ 136,364; ◆ 148,733
Torringford; RMC Place; LITCHFIELD; ▲ Torrington; *160 D-7; ★ TORR; mail Torrington z 06790; pop. incl. with Torrington (Inc. Place)
Torrington; Inc. Place; LITCHFIELD; ▲ Torrington; 160 D-6; [P] [H] ■; ★ TORR; z 06790-92; Ⓟ 33,687; Ⓒ 35,202; ◆ 35,212
Torrington; MCD-Town; LITCHFIELD; *160 D-7; [P] [H]; ★ TORR; z 06790-92; coextensive with the City of Torrington; Ⓟ 33,687; Ⓒ 35,202; ◆ 35,212
Town Hill; RMC Place; LITCHFIELD; ▲ New Hartford; *160 C-7; elev. 992ft./302m.; ★ H-NB; mail New Hartford z 06057; ● 240
Town Plot Hill; RMC Place; NEW HAVEN; ▲ Waterbury; *160 G-7; ★ WATB; mail Waterbury z 06708; pop. incl. with Waterbury (Inc. Place)
Trails Corner; RMC Place; NEW LONDON; ▲ Groton; *161 I-15; ★ N.LON-; mail Groton z 06340; rural
Trumbull; CDP; FAIRFIELD; ▲ Trumbull; 161 L-12; [P]; ★ N.Y.; z 06611; Ⓟ 32,016; Ⓒ 34,243; ◆ 34,424
Trumbull; MCD-Town; FAIRFIELD; *160 J-6; [P] ■; ★ N.Y.; z 06611 & mail Easton z 06612; Ⓟ 32,016; Ⓒ 34,243; ◆ 34,424
Turn of the River; RMC Place; FAIRFIELD; ▲ Stamford; *160 L-3; ★ N.Y.; mail Stamford z 06901; pop. incl. with Stamford (Inc. Place)
Turnpike; RMC Place; TOLLAND; ▲ Vernon; *161 D-12; ★ H-NB; mail Vernon Rockville z 06066
Twin Lakes; RMC Place; LITCHFIELD; ▲ Salisbury; 160 B-4; mail Taconic z 06079; ● 380
Tyler Lake Heights; RMC Place; LITCHFIELD; ▲ Goshen; *160 D-5; mail Goshen z 06756

U

Uncasville (Montville); RMC Place; NEW LONDON; ▲ Montville; 161 H-15; [P]; ★ N.LON-; z 06353, z 06382; ● 1,420
Union; RMC Place; TOLLAND; ▲ Union; 161 B-14; [P]; z 06076; ● 60
Union; MCD-Town; TOLLAND; *161 B-14; [P]; z 06076; Ⓟ 612; Ⓒ 693
Union City; RMC Place; NEW HAVEN; ▲ Naugatuck; *160 G-7; ★ WATB; mail Naugatuck z 06770; pop. incl. with Naugatuck (Inc. Place)
Unionville; RMC Place; HARTFORD; ▲ Farmington; 160 E-8; [P]; ★ H-NB; z 06013, z 06085, z 06087; ● 4,400
Upper Merryall; RMC Place; LITCHFIELD; ▲ New Milford; *160 F-4; elev. 644ft./196m.; ★ N.Y.; mail New Milford z 06776; rural
Upper Stepney; RMC Place; FAIRFIELD; ▲ Monroe; 160 I-5; ★ N.Y.; mail Monroe z 06468; ● 1,000

V

Vernon (Vernon-Rockville, Vernon Rockville); RMC Place; TOLLAND; ▲ Vernon; 161 D-11; elev. 350ft./107m.; [P]; ★ H-NB; z 06066; Ⓟ 29,841; ● 28,100
Vernon; MCD-Town; TOLLAND; *161 D-12; [P] ■; ★ H-NB; z 06066; Ⓟ 29,841; Ⓒ 28,063; ◆ 27,251
Vernon Center; RMC Place; TOLLAND; ▲ Vernon; *161 D-12; elev. 300ft./91m.; ★ H-NB; mail Vernon Rockville z 06066
Vernon Rockville; TOLLAND; see Vernon (RMC Place)
Vernon-Rockville; TOLLAND; see Vernon (RMC Place)
Versailles; RMC Place; NEW LONDON; ▲ Sprague, Lisbon; 161 F-15; [P]; ★ N.LON-; z 06383; ● 580
Village Hill; RMC Place; NEW LONDON; ▲ Lebanon; *161 E-13; elev. 615ft./187m.; ★ H-NB; mail Lebanon z 06249; rural
Voluntown; RMC Place; NEW LONDON; ▲ Voluntown; 161 F-17; elev. 271ft./83m.; [P]; z 06384; ● 520
Voluntown; MCD-Town; NEW LONDON; *161 F-17; [P]; z 06384; Ⓟ 2,113; Ⓒ 2,528

W

Wailacks Point; RMC Place; FAIRFIELD; ▲ Stamford; ★ N.Y.; mail Stamford z 06902; pop. incl. with Stamford (Inc. Place)
Wallingford; RMC Place; NEW HAVEN; 160 H-9; [H]; ★ N.HAV; Ⓟ 40,822; ● 8,500
Wallingford; MCD-Town; NEW HAVEN; *160 H-9; [P] ■; ★ N.HAV; z 06492-95; Ⓟ 40,822; Ⓒ 43,026; ◆ 45,115
Wallingford Center; CDP; NEW HAVEN; ▲ Wallingford; 160 H-9; [H]; ★ N.HAV; mail Wallingford z 06492-95; Ⓟ 17,827; Ⓒ 17,509
Walnut Beach; RMC Place; NEW HAVEN; ▲ Milford; *160 K-7; ★ N.Y.; mail Milford z 06460; pop. incl. with Milford (Inc. Place)
Walnut Hill; RMC Place; NEW LONDON; ▲ East Lyme; *161 H-14; elev. 250ft./76m.; ★ N.LON-; mail East Lyme z 06333; ● 150
Wamphassuc Point; RMC Place; NEW LONDON; ▲ Stonington; *161 I-16; ★ N.LON-; mail Stonington z 06378; ● 30
Wapping; RMC Place; HARTFORD; ▲ South Windsor; *161 D-11; elev. 110ft./34m.; ★ H-NB; mail South Windsor z 06074
Warehouse Point (East Windsor); RMC Place; HARTFORD; ▲ East Windsor; 160 C-10; ★ H-NB; mail Broad Brook z 06016, East Windsor z 06088; ● 2,100
Warren; RMC Place; LITCHFIELD; ▲ Warren; 160 E-5; [P]; z 06754, z 06777; ● 240
Warren; MCD-Town; LITCHFIELD; *160 E-5; [P]; z 06754, z 06777 & mail Cornwall z 06753; Ⓟ 1,226; Ⓒ 1,254
Warrenville; RMC Place; WINDHAM; ▲ Ashford; 161 C-14; [P]; ★ H-NB; z 06278; ● 180
Washington (Washington Green); RMC Place; LITCHFIELD; ▲ Washington; 160 F-5; [P]; z 06793 & mail New Preston Marble Dale z 06777, Washington Depot z 06794; ● 700
Washington; MCD-Town; LITCHFIELD; *160 F-5; [P]; z 06793 & mail New Preston Marble Dale z 06777, Washington Depot z 06794; Ⓟ 3,905; Ⓒ 3,596; Ⓡ 3,639; ◆ 3,397
Washington Depot; RMC Place; LITCHFIELD; ▲ Washington; 160 F-5; [P]; z 06777, z 06793-94; ● 700
Washington Green; LITCHFIELD; see Washington (RMC Place)
Washington Hill; RMC Place; LITCHFIELD; ▲ Barkhamsted; *160 C-8; elev. 1,008ft./307m.; ★ H-NB; mail Barkhamsted z 06063, North Canton z 06059; rural
Washington Square; RMC Place; NEW LONDON; ▲ Norwich; ★ N.LON-; mail Norwich z 06360; pop. incl. with Norwich (Inc. Place)
Waterbury; Inc. Place; NEW HAVEN; ▲ Waterbury; 160 G-7; [P] [H] [C] 1,596 ■; ★ WATB; z 06701-06, z 06708, z 06710, z 06712, z 06716, z 06720-26, z 06749; Ⓟ 108,961; Ⓒ 107,271; ◆ 106,626
Waterbury; MCD-Town; NEW HAVEN; *160 G-7; [P] [H] [C] 1,596; ★ WATB; z 06701-06, z 06708, z 06710, z 06712, z 06716, z 06720-26, z 06749; coextensive with the City of Waterbury; Ⓟ 108,961; Ⓒ 107,271; ◆ 106,626
Waterford; NEW LONDON; see Jordan (RMC Place)
Waterford; NEW LONDON; see Central Waterford (CDP-Census Area Only)
Waterford; MCD-Town; NEW LONDON; *161 I-14; [P]; ★ N.LON-; z 06385, z 98662; Ⓟ 17,930; Ⓒ 19,152; Ⓡ 18,638; ◆ 20,387
Waterside; RMC Place; FAIRFIELD; ▲ Stamford; ★ N.Y.; mail Stamford z 06901; pop. incl. with Stamford (Inc. Place)
Watertown; RMC Place; LITCHFIELD; ▲ Watertown; 160 F-6; [P]; ★ WATB; z 06779, z 06795; ● 6,300
Watertown; MCD-Town; LITCHFIELD; *160 F-6; [P]; ★ WATB; z 06779, z 06795; Ⓟ 20,456; Ⓒ 21,661; ◆ 21,507
Waterville; RMC Place; NEW HAVEN; ▲ Waterbury; *160 F-7; elev. 295ft./90m.; ★ WATB; mail Waterbury z 06704; pop. incl. with Waterbury (Inc. Place)
Wauregan; CDP; WINDHAM; ▲ Plainfield; 161 E-16; [P]; ★ N.LON-; z 06387; Ⓟ 1,079; Ⓒ 1,085
Wauwecus Hill; RMC Place; NEW LONDON; ▲ Norwich; ★ N.LON-; mail Norwich z 06360; pop. incl. with Norwich (Inc. Place)
Weatogue; CDP-Census Area Only; HARTFORD; ▲ Simsbury; 160 D-9; [P]; ★ H-NB; z 06089; Ⓟ 2,521; Ⓒ 2,805
Welles Village; RMC Place; HARTFORD; ▲ Glastonbury; *161 E-11; ★ H-NB; mail Glastonbury z 06033
Wells Quarter Village; RMC Place; HARTFORD; ▲ Wethersfield; ★ H-NB; mail Wethersfield z 06109
Wellsville; RMC Place; LITCHFIELD; ▲ New Milford; *160 F-4; elev. 400ft./122m.; ★ N.Y.; mail New Milford z 06776
Wequetequock; RMC Place; NEW LONDON; ▲ Stonington; 161 I-16; ★ N.LON-; mail Westerly z 02891; ● 850
Wesleyan; RMC Place; MIDDLESEX; ▲ Middletown; *160 G-10; ★ H-NB; mail Middletown z 06457, z 06459; pop. incl. with Middletown (Inc. Place)
West Ashford; RMC Place; WINDHAM; ▲ Ashford; *161 C-14; ★ H-NB; mail Mansfield Center z 06250
West Avon; RMC Place; HARTFORD; ▲ Avon; 160 D-8; elev. 293ft./89m.; ★ H-NB; mail Avon z 06001; ● 100
Westbrook; RMC Place; MIDDLESEX; ▲ Westbrook; 161 J-12; ● 1,800
Westbrook; MCD-Town; MIDDLESEX; *161 J-12; [P]; z 06498; Ⓟ 5,414; Ⓒ 6,292
Westbrook Center; CDP-Census Area Only; MIDDLESEX; ▲ Westbrook; 161 J-12; mail Westbrook z 06498; Ⓟ 2,060; Ⓒ 2,238
Westchester (Westchester Corner); RMC Place; NEW LONDON; ▲ Colchester; 161 G-12; ★ H-NB; mail Colchester z 06415; ● 200
Westchester Corner; NEW LONDON; see Westchester (RMC Place)
West Cornwall; RMC Place; LITCHFIELD; ▲ Cornwall; 160 C-4; elev. 531ft./162m.; [P]; z 06796; ● 330
West End; RMC Place; HARTFORD; ▲ Bristol; ★ H-NB; mail Bristol z 06010; pop. incl. with Bristol (Inc. Place)
West Farms Village; RMC Place; HARTFORD; ▲ New Britain; ★ H-NB; mail New Britain z 06050; pop. incl. with New Britain (Inc. Place)
Westfield; RMC Place; MIDDLESEX; ▲ Middletown; *160 F-10; ★ H-NB; mail Middletown z 06457; pop. incl. with Middletown (Inc. Place)
Westford; RMC Place; WINDHAM; ▲ Ashford; 161 C-14; ★ H-NB; mail Ashford z 06278, Stafford Springs z 06076; ● 100
West Goshen; RMC Place; LITCHFIELD; ▲ Goshen; 160 D-5; elev. 1,298ft./396m.; mail Goshen z 06756; ● 700
West Granby; RMC Place; HARTFORD; ▲ Granby; 160 B-9; [P]; ★ H-NB; z 06090; ● 700
West Hartford; CDP; HARTFORD; ▲ West Hartford; 160 E-9; [P] [H] [C] 9,111; ★ H-NB; z 06107, z 06110, z 06117, z 06119, z 06127, z 06133, z 06137 & mail Hartford z 06105-06; Ⓟ 60,110; Ⓒ 63,589; Ⓡ 61,046; ◆ 65,937
West Hartford; MCD-Town; HARTFORD; *160 D-9; [P] [C] 9,111 ■; ★ H-NB; z 06107, z 06110, z 06117, z 06119, z 06127, z 06133, z 06137 & mail Hartford z 06105-06; Ⓟ 60,110; Ⓒ 63,589; Ⓡ 61,046; ◆ 65,937
West Hartland; RMC Place; HARTFORD; ▲ Hartland; 160 B-8; elev. 1,158ft./353m.; [P]; z 06091; ● 400
West Haven; Inc. Place; NEW HAVEN; ▲ West Haven; 161 M-15; [P] [H] [C] 4,649 ■; ★ N.HAV; z 06516; Ⓟ 54,021; Ⓒ 52,360; ◆ 51,594
West Haven; MCD-Town; NEW HAVEN; *160 J-8; [P] [H] [C] 4,649; ★ N.HAV; z 06516; coextensive with the City of West Haven; Ⓟ 54,021; Ⓒ 52,360; ◆ 51,594
West Lakes; RMC Place; NEW HAVEN; ▲ Guilford; *160 I-10; ★ N.HAV; mail Guilford z 06437; ● 1,140
Westminster; RMC Place; WINDHAM; 161 C-13; ★ N.LON-
West Mystic; RMC Place; NEW LONDON; ▲ Groton; 161 I-16; [P]; ★ N.LON-; z 06388; Ⓟ 3,595
West Norfolk; RMC Place; LITCHFIELD; ▲ Norfolk; *160 B-6; mail Norfolk z 06058
West Norwalk; RMC Place; FAIRFIELD; ▲ Norwalk; *160 L-4; ★ N.Y.; mail Norwalk z 06851; pop. incl. with Norwalk (Inc. Place)
Weston; RMC Place; FAIRFIELD; ▲ Weston; 160 J-4; [P]; ★ N.Y.; z 06883; ● 1,460
Weston; MCD-Town; FAIRFIELD; *160 J-4; [P]; ★ N.Y.; z 06883 & mail Westport z 06880; Ⓟ 8,648; Ⓒ 10,037; ◆ 10,218
Westport (Westport Saugatuck); CDP; FAIRFIELD; ▲ Westport; 160 K-4; elev. 78ft./24m.; [P] [H]; ★ N.Y.; z 06880-81, z 06888-89; Ⓟ 24,410; Ⓒ 25,749; ◆ 26,571
Westport; MCD-Town; FAIRFIELD; *160 K-4; elev. 78ft./24m.; [P] ■; ★ N.Y.; z 06880-81, z 06888-89; Ⓟ 24,410; Ⓒ 25,749; ◆ 26,571
Westport Saugatuck; FAIRFIELD; see Westport (CDP)
West Redding; RMC Place; FAIRFIELD; ▲ Redding; 160 I-4; [P]; ★ N.Y.; z 06896; ● 200
West Shore; RMC Place; NEW HAVEN; ▲ West Haven; 161 M-15; ★ N.HAV; mail West Haven z 06516
West Side; RMC Place; NEW LONDON; ▲ Norwich; ★ N.LON-; mail Norwich z 06360; pop. incl. with Norwich (Inc. Place)
West Side Hill; RMC Place; NEW HAVEN; ▲ Waterbury; *160 G-7; ★ WATB; mail Waterbury z 06708; pop. incl. with Waterbury (Inc. Place)
West Simsbury; CDP; HARTFORD; ▲ Simsbury; 160 C-8; elev. 323ft./98m.; [P]; ★ H-NB; z 06092; Ⓟ 2,149; Ⓒ 2,395
West Stafford; RMC Place; TOLLAND; ▲ Stafford; 161 B-12; ★ H-NB; mail Stafford Springs z 06076; ● 600
West Suffield; RMC Place; HARTFORD; ▲ Suffield; 160 B-10; [P]; ★ H-NB; z 06093; ● 860
West Thompson; RMC Place; WINDHAM; ▲ Thompson; 161 B-16; ★ WORC; mail Thompson z 06277; ● 210
West Torrington; RMC Place; LITCHFIELD; ▲ Torrington; *160 D-6; elev. 637ft./194m.; ★ TORR; mail Torrington z 06790; pop. incl. with Torrington (Inc. Place)
Westville; RMC Place; NEW HAVEN; ▲ New Haven; 161 L-16; ★ N.HAV; mail New Haven z 06515; pop. incl. with New Haven (Inc. Place)
West Wauregan; RMC Place; WINDHAM; ▲ Brooklyn; *161 E-16; mail Wauregan z 06387; ● 350
West Willington (Willington); RMC Place; TOLLAND; ▲ Willington; 161 C-13; ★ H-NB; mail Willington z 06279; ● 40
Westwood Park; RMC Place; NEW LONDON; ▲ Norwich; ★ N.LON-; mail Norwich z 06360; pop. incl. with Norwich (Inc. Place)
West Woods; RMC Place; LITCHFIELD; ▲ Sharon; *160 D-4; elev. 1,080ft./329m.; mail Sharon z 06069; rural
West Woodstock; RMC Place; WINDHAM; ▲ Woodstock; *161 B-15; mail Woodstock Valley z 06282
Wethersfield; CDP; HARTFORD; ▲ Wethersfield; 160 E-10; [P]; ★ H-NB; z 06109, z 06129, z 06161; Ⓟ 25,651; Ⓒ 26,271; ◆ 26,656
Wethersfield; MCD-Town; HARTFORD; *160 E-10; [P] ■; ★ H-NB; z 06109, z 06129, z 06161; Ⓟ 25,651; Ⓒ 26,271; ◆ 26,656
Wheeler Farms; RMC Place; NEW HAVEN; ▲ Milford; ★ N.Y.; mail Milford z 06460; pop. incl. with Milford (Inc. Place)
Whigville; RMC Place; HARTFORD; ▲ Burlington; 160 E-8; ★ H-NB; mail Burlington z 06013; ● 450
Whipstick; RMC Place; FAIRFIELD; ▲ Ridgefield; ★ N.Y.; mail Ridgefield z 06877
White Oaks; RMC Place; NEW HAVEN; ▲ Southbury; *160 G-6; elev. 300ft./91m.; ★ WATB; mail Southbury z 06488; ● 50
White Sands Beach; RMC Place; NEW LONDON; ▲ Old Lyme; *161 J-13; ★ N.LON-; mail Old Lyme z 06371; ● 300
Whitneyville; RMC Place; NEW HAVEN; ▲ Hamden; 161 L-16; [P]; ★ N.HAV; z 06517
Wildermere Beach; RMC Place; NEW HAVEN; ▲ Milford; 161 N-13; ★ N.Y.; mail Milford z 06460; pop. incl. with Milford (Inc. Place)
Williams Crossing; RMC Place; NEW LONDON; ▲ Lebanon; *161 F-14; elev. 240ft./73m.; ★ H-NB; mail Lebanon z 06249; rural
Willimantic; CDP; WINDHAM; ▲ Windham; 161 E-14; [P] [H] [C] 5,239; ★ H-NB; z 06226; Ⓟ 14,746; Ⓒ 15,823
Willington; TOLLAND; see West Willington (RMC Place)
Willington; MCD-Town; TOLLAND; *161 C-13; [P]; ★ H-NB; z 06279; Ⓟ 5,979; Ⓒ 5,959; ◆ 5,858
Willington Hill; RMC Place; TOLLAND; ▲ Willington; *161 C-13; elev. 790ft./241m.; ★ H-NB; mail Willington z 06279
Willow Point; RMC Place; NEW LONDON; ▲ Groton; ★ N.LON-; mail West Mystic z 06388
Wilsonville; RMC Place; WINDHAM; ▲ Thompson; 161 B-16; ★ WORC; mail North Grosvenordale z 06255; ● 640
Wilton; RMC Place; FAIRFIELD; ▲ Wilton; 160 K-4; [P]; ★ N.Y.; z 06897; ● 7,500
Wilton; MCD-Town; FAIRFIELD; *160 K-4; [P]; ★ N.Y.; z 06897; Ⓟ 15,989; Ⓒ 17,633; ◆ 17,981
Winchester; LITCHFIELD; see Winchester Center (RMC Place)
Winchester; MCD-Town; LITCHFIELD; *160 C-7; ★ H-NB; mail Winchester Center z 06094, Winsted z 06098; Ⓟ 11,524; Ⓒ 10,664; ◆ 10,169
Winchester Center (Winchester); RMC Place; LITCHFIELD; ▲ Winchester; 160 C-6; [P]; ★ H-NB; z 06094, z 06098; ● 200
Windermere; RMC Place; TOLLAND; ▲ Ellington; *161 C-11; elev. 225ft./69m.; ★ H-NB; mail Ellington z 06029; rural
Windham; RMC Place; WINDHAM; ▲ Windham; 161 E-14; elev. 279ft./85m.; [P]; ★ H-NB; z 06280 & mail North Windham z 06256; ● 1,150
Windham; MCD-Town; WINDHAM; *161 E-14; [P] [C] 5,239; ★ H-NB; z 06280 & mail North Windham z 06256; Ⓟ 22,039; Ⓒ 22,857; ◆ 24,357
WINDHAM; 161 D-15; Ⓟ 102,525; Ⓒ 109,091; ◆ 117,334
Winding Lanes; RMC Place; HARTFORD; ▲ Avon; ★ H-NB; mail Avon z 06001
Windsor; RMC Place; HARTFORD; ▲ Windsor; 160 D-10; elev. 57ft./17m.; [P]; ★ H-NB; z 06006, z 06095; ● 18,800
Windsor; MCD-Town; HARTFORD; *160 C-10; [P]; ★ H-NB; z 06006, z 06095; Ⓟ 27,817; Ⓒ 28,237; ◆ 28,989
Windsor Locks; CDP; HARTFORD; ▲ Windsor Locks; 160 C-10; [P]; ★ H-NB; z 06096; Ⓟ 12,358; Ⓒ 12,043
Windsor Locks; MCD-Town; HARTFORD; *160 C-10; [P]; ★ H-NB; z 06096; Ⓟ 12,358; Ⓒ 12,043; ◆ 12,230
Windsorville; RMC Place; HARTFORD; ▲ East Windsor; 161 C-11; [P]; ★ H-NB; z 06016; ● 350
Winnipauk; RMC Place; FAIRFIELD; ▲ Norwalk; *160 K-4; ★ N.Y.; mail Norwalk z 06851; pop. incl. with Norwalk (Inc. Place)
Winsted; CDP; LITCHFIELD; ▲ Winchester; 160 C-7; elev. 713ft./217m.; [P]; ★ H-NB; z 06063, z 06098 & mail Winchester Center z 06094; Ⓟ 8,254; Ⓒ 7,321
Winthrop; RMC Place; MIDDLESEX; ▲ Deep River; 161 I-11; mail Deep River z 06417; ● 490
Wolcott; RMC Place; NEW HAVEN; ▲ Wolcott; 160 F-8; [P]; ★ WATB; z 06705, z 06716; ● 6,400
Wolcott; MCD-Town; NEW HAVEN; *160 F-8; [P]; ★ WATB; z 06705, z 06716; Ⓟ 13,700; Ⓒ 15,215; ◆ 15,706
Woodbridge; RMC Place; NEW HAVEN; ▲ Woodbridge; 161 K-15; [P]; ★ N.HAV; z 06525; ● 7,860
Woodbridge; MCD-Town; NEW HAVEN; *160 I-7; [P]; ★ N.HAV; z 06525; Ⓟ 7,924; Ⓒ 8,983; ◆ 9,163
Woodbury; RMC Place; LITCHFIELD; ▲ Woodbury; ★ WATB; ● 150
Woodbury; MCD-Town; LITCHFIELD; *160 G-6; [P]; ★ WATB; z 06798; Ⓟ 8,131; Ⓒ 9,198; Ⓡ 9,196; ◆ 9,845
Woodbury Center; CDP-Census Area Only; LITCHFIELD; ▲ Woodbury; 160 G-6; ★ WATB; mail Woodbury z 06798; Ⓟ 1,212; Ⓒ 1,298
Woodmont; Inc. Place; NEW HAVEN; ▲ Milford; 161 M-15; elev. 42ft./13m.; ★ N.Y.; mail Milford z 06460; Ⓟ 1,770; Ⓒ 1,711
Woodstock; RMC Place; WINDHAM; ▲ Woodstock; 161 B-16; elev. 592ft./180m.; [P]; z 06281; ● 410
Woodstock; MCD-Town; WINDHAM; *161 B-15; [P]; z 06281; Ⓟ 6,008; Ⓒ 7,221
Woodstock Valley; RMC Place; WINDHAM; ▲ Woodstock; 161 C-15; [P]; z 06282; ● 350
Woodtick; RMC Place; NEW HAVEN; ▲ Wolcott; 160 F-7; ★ WATB; mail Wolcott z 06716; ● 740
Woodville; RMC Place; LITCHFIELD; ▲ Washington; *160 E-5; mail New Preston Marble Dale z 06777
Wormwood Hill; RMC Place; TOLLAND; ▲ Mansfield; *161 D-14; elev. 600ft./183m.; ★ H-NB; mail Mansfield Center z 06250, Storrs Mansfield z 06268; ● 50

Y

Yale; RMC Place; NEW HAVEN; ▲ New Haven; *160 I-8; ★ N.HAV; mail New Haven z 06520; pop. incl. with New Haven (Inc. Place)
Yalesville; RMC Place; NEW HAVEN; ▲ Wallingford; *160 G-9; [P]; ★ N.HAV; z 06492
Yantic (Yantic-Fitchville); RMC Place; NEW LONDON; ▲ Norwich; *161 G-14; elev. 116ft./35m.; [P]; ★ N.LON-; z 06389; pop. incl. with Norwich (Inc. Place)
Yantic-Fitchville; NEW LONDON; see Yantic (RMC Place)
Yelping Hill; RMC Place; LITCHFIELD; ▲ Cornwall; *160 C-5; elev. 1,350ft./411m.; mail West Cornwall z 06796; rural

Z

Zoar; RMC Place; FAIRFIELD; ▲ Newtown; *160 H-5; elev. 438ft./134m.; ★ N.Y.; mail Sandy Hook z 06482; rural

DELAWARE

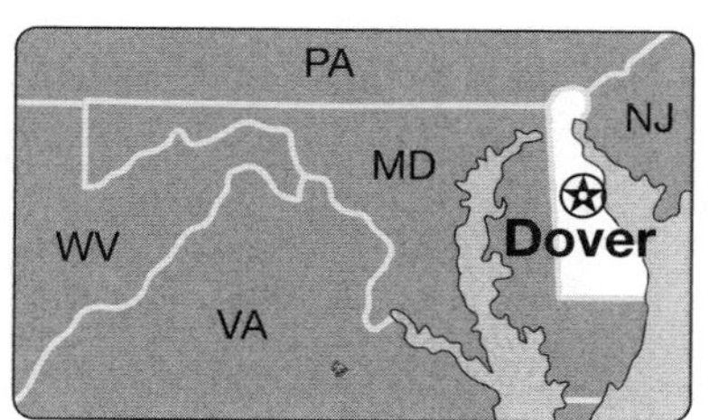

Statistics

Total area (2000) — 2,489 square miles
Land area (2000) — 1,954 square miles
Water area (2000) — 535 square miles
Capital — Dover
One of Thirteen Original States

Maps

State maps can be found on pages 142-254 in Vol. 1

Ranally Metro Areas (RMAs) and Abbreviations

Dover, DE — DOVR
Philadelphia-Trenton-Wilmington, PA-NJ-DE-MD — PHIL-
Salisbury, MD-DE — SLSB

Principal Places

Place Name	Place Type	County	Population
Wilmington	Inc. Place	NEW CASTLE	◆ 73,345
Dover	Inc. Place	KENT	◆ 38,113
Newark	Inc. Place	NEW CASTLE	◆ 29,149
Pike Creek	CDP-Census Area Only	NEW CASTLE	Ⓒ 19,751
Bear	CDP	NEW CASTLE	Ⓒ 17,593
Brookside	CDP	NEW CASTLE	Ⓒ 14,806
Hockessin	CDP	NEW CASTLE	Ⓒ 12,902
Glasgow	CDP	NEW CASTLE	Ⓒ 12,840
Claymont	CDP	NEW CASTLE	Ⓒ 9,220
North Star	CDP	NEW CASTLE	Ⓒ 8,277
Wilmington Manor	CDP	NEW CASTLE	Ⓒ 8,262
Milford	Inc. Place	SUSSEX	Ⓒ 6,732
Seaford	Inc. Place	SUSSEX	Ⓒ 6,699
Middletown	Inc. Place	NEW CASTLE	Ⓒ 6,161
Edgemoor	CDP	NEW CASTLE	Ⓒ 5,992
Elsmere	Inc. Place	NEW CASTLE	Ⓒ 5,800
Smyrna	Inc. Place	KENT	Ⓒ 5,679

County Business Data

County	FIPS Code	County Seat	Land Area (Sq. Mi.)	Census Population			Wholesale Trade		Manufacturing, 2002			
				4/1/2000	4/1/1990	% Change 1990-2000	Sales, 2002 ($1,000)	% Change 1997-2002	Establish-ments	Total Employees	Value Added ($1,000)	Ranally Mfg. Units
Kent	001	Dover	590	126,697	110,993	14.1	(d)	(d)	76	5,789	1,262,907	668
New Castle	003	Wilmington	426	500,265	441,946	13.2	16,360,164	(d)	462	22,384	2,851,516	1,509
Sussex	005	Georgetown	938	156,638	113,229	38.3	(d)	(d)	167	9,114	949,476	502
The State			**1,954**	**783,600**	**666,168**	**17.6**	**17,292,794**	**37.4**	**705**	**37,287**	**5,063,899**	**2,679**

(d) Data not available. Corresponding percentages or Ranally Manufacturing Units are estimates.
... Represents 0 or amount too minimal to be reported.

Index of Places and Counties

A

Adams Crossroads; RMC Place; SUSSEX; ***162** J-2; elev. 38ft./12m.; mail Greenwood **Z** 19950
Adamsville; RMC Place; KENT; ***162** J-2; mail Greenwood **Z** 19950
Afton; RMC Place; NEW CASTLE; ***162** B-3; ★ **PHIL-**; mail Wilmington **Z** 19810; ● 1,200
Alapocas; RMC Place; NEW CASTLE; ***162** C-2; ★ **PHIL-**; mail Wilmington **Z** 19803; ● 350
Albertson Park; RMC Place; NEW CASTLE; ***162** C-2; ★ **PHIL-**; mail Wilmington **Z** 19808; ● 550
Analine Village; NEW CASTLE; see Aniline Village (RMC Place)
Andrewsville (Andrewville); RMC Place; KENT; ***162** J-2; elev. 55ft./17m.; mail Greenwood **Z** 19950
Andrewville; KENT; see Andrewsville (RMC Place)
Anglesey; RMC Place; NEW CASTLE; **162** C-8; ★ **PHIL-**; mail Wilmington **Z** 19807; ● 125
Angola; RMC Place; SUSSEX; ***162** K-5; mail Rehoboth Beach **Z** 19971; rural
Angola by the Bay; RMC Place; SUSSEX; ***162** K-5; mail Rehoboth Beach **Z** 19971; ● 1,200
Aniline Village (Analine Village); RMC Place; NEW CASTLE; ***162** B-3; ★ **PHIL-**; mail Claymont **Z** 19703
Anne Acres; RMC Place; SUSSEX; ***162** K-5; mail Rehoboth Beach **Z** 19971; ● 100
Arden; Inc. Place; NEW CASTLE; **162** B-9; elev. 260ft./79m.; ★ **PHIL-**; mail Wilmington **Z** 19810; Ⓟ 477; Ⓒ 474
Ardencroft; Inc. Place; NEW CASTLE; **162** B-9; ★ **PHIL-**; mail Wilmington **Z** 19810; Ⓟ 282; Ⓒ 267
Ardentown; Inc. Place; NEW CASTLE; **162** B-9; ★ **PHIL-**; mail Wilmington **Z** 19810; Ⓟ 325; Ⓒ 300
Argo Corner; SUSSEX; see Argo Corners (RMC Place)
Argo Corners (Argo Corner, Argos Corner); RMC Place; SUSSEX; **162** I-4; mail Milford **Z** 19963; ● 50
Argos Corner; SUSSEX; see Argo Corners (RMC Place)
Arundel; RMC Place; NEW CASTLE; ***162** C-2; ★ **PHIL-**; mail Wilmington **Z** 19808; ● 1,800
Ashbourne Hills; RMC Place; NEW CASTLE; ***162** B-3; ★ **PHIL-**; mail Claymont **Z** 19703
Ashland; RMC Place; NEW CASTLE; ***162** C-2; ★ **PHIL-**; mail Wilmington **Z** 19807; rural
Ashley; RMC Place; NEW CASTLE; ***162** C-2; ★ **PHIL-**; mail Wilmington **Z** 19804; ● 200
Atlanta; RMC Place; SUSSEX; **162** K-2; mail Bridgeville **Z** 19933; ● 65
Atlanta Estates; RMC Place; SUSSEX; ***162** K-2; mail Seaford **Z** 19973; ● 200
Augustine Beach; RMC Place; NEW CASTLE; ***162** E-2; ★ **PHIL-**; mail Port Penn **Z** 19731; ● 75

B

Bacon; SUSSEX; see Bacons (RMC Place)
Bacons (Bacon); RMC Place; SUSSEX; ***162** L-2; ★ **SLSB**; mail Delmar **Z** 19940; rural
Bakers Choice; RMC Place; KENT; ***162** H-3; ★ **DOVR**; mail Frederica **Z** 19946; ● 150
Bayard; RMC Place; SUSSEX; ***162** L-5; mail Frankford **Z** 19945
Bayberry Dunes; RMC Place; SUSSEX; ***162** L-5; mail Bethany Beach **Z** 19930; ● 10
Bay View Beach; RMC Place; NEW CASTLE; **162** E-2; elev. 5ft./2m.; ★ **PHIL-**; mail Middletown **Z** 19709; summer pop. 300; ● 50
Bay View Park; RMC Place; SUSSEX; ***162** L-5; mail Bethany Beach **Z** 19930; summer pop. 125; ● 40
Bayville; RMC Place; SUSSEX; **162** M-5; mail Selbyville **Z** 19975; ● 100
Bay Vista; RMC Place; SUSSEX; ***162** K-5; mail Rehoboth Beach **Z** 19971; ● 120
Bear; CDP; NEW CASTLE; **162** D-2; elev. 71ft./22m.; 🅿; ★ **PHIL-**; **Z** 19701; Ⓒ 17,593
Beaver Brook Apartments; RMC Place; NEW CASTLE; ***162** D-2; ★ **PHIL-**; mail New Castle **Z** 19720; ● 1,800
Beaver Dam Heights; RMC Place; SUSSEX; ***162** K-2; mail Seaford **Z** 19973; ● 250
Bellefonte; Inc. Place; NEW CASTLE; **162** C-9; elev. 150ft./46m.; ★ **PHIL-**; mail Wilmington **Z** 19809; Ⓟ 1,243; Ⓒ 1,249
Bellemoor; NEW CASTLE; see Belmoor (RMC Place)
Bellevue Manor; RMC Place; NEW CASTLE; **162** C-9; ★ **PHIL-**; mail Wilmington **Z** 19809; ● 200
Belltown; RMC Place; SUSSEX; **162** J-5; mail Lewes **Z** 19958; ● 250
Belmoor (Bellemoor); RMC Place; NEW CASTLE; ***162** C-2; ★ **PHIL-**; mail Wilmington **Z** 19804; ● 900
Belvedere; NEW CASTLE; see Belvidere (RMC Place)
Belvidere (Belvedere); RMC Place; NEW CASTLE; **162** D-8; ★ **PHIL-**; mail Wilmington **Z** 19804; ● 800
Bestfield; RMC Place; NEW CASTLE; ***162** C-2; ★ **PHIL-**; mail Wilmington **Z** 19804; ● 650
Bethany Beach; Inc. Place; SUSSEX; **162** L-5; elev. 8ft./2m.; 🅿; **Z** 19930; Ⓟ 326; Ⓒ 903
Bethany Dunes; RMC Place; SUSSEX; ***162** L-5; mail Bethany Beach **Z** 19930; ● 10
Bethany Village; RMC Place; SUSSEX; ***162** L-5; mail Bethany Beach **Z** 19930; ● 60
Bethel; Inc. Place; SUSSEX; **162** L-2; elev. 20ft./6m.; 🅿; **Z** 19931; Ⓟ 178; Ⓒ 184
Big Mills Bridge; RMC Place; SUSSEX; ***162** L-2; elev. 27ft./8m.; mail Laurel **Z** 19956; pop. incl. with Laurel (Inc. Place)
Big Oak Corners; RMC Place; KENT; ***162** G-2; elev. 45ft./14m.; ★ **DOVR**; mail Smyrna **Z** 19977; ● 60
Big Pine; RMC Place; KENT; ***162** J-2; elev. 50ft./15m.; mail Greenwood **Z** 19950; rural
Big Stone Beach; RMC Place; KENT; **162** I-4; mail Milford **Z** 19963; ● 15
Binns Village; RMC Place; NEW CASTLE; ***162** D-1; ★ **PHIL-**; mail Newark **Z** 19711; pop. incl. with Newark (Inc. Place)
Birchwood Park; RMC Place; NEW CASTLE; **162** D-7; ★ **PHIL-**; mail Newark **Z** 19713; ● 400
Blackbird; RMC Place; NEW CASTLE; ***162** F-2; mail Smyrna **Z** 19977, Townsend **Z** 19734
Blackiston; RMC Place; KENT; ***162** G-2; ★ **DOVR**; mail Clayton **Z** 19938
Blackwater Village; RMC Place; SUSSEX; ***162** L-5; mail Dagsboro **Z** 19939; ● 100
Blades; Inc. Place; SUSSEX; **162** K-2; elev. 20ft./6m.; 🅿; **Z** 19973; Ⓟ 834; Ⓒ 956
Bowers; KENT; see Bowers Beach (Inc. Place)
Bowers Beach (Bowers); Inc. Place; KENT; ***162** H-3; elev. 6ft./2m.; mail Frederica **Z** 19946; Ⓟ 179; summer pop. 400; Ⓒ 305
Boxwood; RMC Place; NEW CASTLE; ***162** C-2; ★ **PHIL-**; mail Wilmington **Z** 19804; ● 500
Brackenville; RMC Place; NEW CASTLE; ***162** C-2; ★ **PHIL-**; mail Hockessin **Z** 19707; ● 1,200
Brack-Ex; RMC Place; NEW CASTLE; ***162** C-2; ★ **PHIL-**; mail Wilmington **Z** 19805; ● 300
Brandywine; RMC Place; NEW CASTLE; **162** B-9; ★ **PHIL-**; mail Wilmington **Z** 19810; ● 1,400
Brandywine Estates; RMC Place; NEW CASTLE; ***162** C-3; ★ **PHIL-**; mail Claymont **Z** 19703
Brandywine Hills; RMC Place; NEW CASTLE; ***162** C-3; ★ **PHIL-**; mail Wilmington **Z** 19802; pop. incl. with Wilmington (Inc. Place)
Brandywine Springs; RMC Place; NEW CASTLE; ***162** C-2; ★ **PHIL-**; mail Wilmington **Z** 19808; ● 700
Brandywood; RMC Place; NEW CASTLE; **162** B-9; ★ **PHIL-**; mail Wilmington **Z** 19810; ● 800
Breezewood; RMC Place; KENT; ***162** H-2; ★ **DOVR**; mail Felton **Z** 19943; ● 50
Breezewood; RMC Place; SUSSEX; ***162** K-5; mail Rehoboth Beach **Z** 19971; ● 250
Breezewood II; RMC Place; NEW CASTLE; ***162** D-2; ★ **PHIL-**; mail Newark **Z** 19713; ● 600
Brenford; RMC Place; KENT; ***162** G-2; ★ **DOVR**; mail Smyrna **Z** 19977
Briar Park; RMC Place; KENT; ***162** H-3; ★ **DOVR**; mail Dover **Z** 19904; ● 250
Bridgeville; Inc. Place; SUSSEX; **162** J-2; elev. 47ft./14m.; 🅿; **Z** 19933; Ⓟ 1,210; Ⓒ 1,436
Broad Acres; RMC Place; SUSSEX; ***162** K-2; mail Seaford **Z** 19973; ● 40
Broad Creek; RMC Place; SUSSEX; ***162** L-2; elev. 42ft./13m.; mail Laurel **Z** 19956
Broadkill Beach; RMC Place; SUSSEX; **162** J-4; mail Milton **Z** 19968; summer pop. 1,100; ● 100
Brookbend; RMC Place; NEW CASTLE; ***162** C-2; ★ **PHIL-**; mail Newark **Z** 19713; ● 450
Brookdale Heights; RMC Place; KENT; ***162** H-3; ★ **DOVR**; mail Camden Wyoming **Z** 19934; ● 250
Brookhaven; RMC Place; NEW CASTLE; ***162** C-2; ★ **PHIL-**; mail Newark **Z** 19711; ● 350
Brookland Terrace; RMC Place; NEW CASTLE; ***162** C-2; ★ **PHIL-**; mail Wilmington **Z** 19805; ● 800
Brookside; CDP; NEW CASTLE; **162** E-6; ★ **PHIL-**; mail Newark **Z** 19713; Ⓟ 15,307; Ⓒ 14,806
Brownsville; RMC Place; KENT; ***162** I-2; mail Harrington **Z** 19952
Bryans Store; RMC Place; SUSSEX; **162** L-3; rural
Bull Pine Corners; RMC Place; SUSSEX; ***162** K-3; elev. 48ft./15m.; mail Georgetown **Z** 19947; rural
Bunting; RMC Place; SUSSEX; ***162** M-5; mail Selbyville **Z** 19975; ● 40

C

Cabbage Corner; RMC Place; SUSSEX; ***162** K-4; mail Georgetown **Z** 19947; ● 125
Camden; Inc. Place; KENT; **162** H-2; elev. 40ft./12m.; 🅿; ★ **DOVR**; **Z** 19934; Ⓟ 1,899; Ⓒ 2,100
Camden Wyoming; RMC Place; KENT; 🅿; ★ **DOVR**; **Z** 19934; pop. incl. with Wyoming (Inc. Place)
Cannon; RMC Place; SUSSEX; **162** K-2; mail Bridgeville **Z** 19933; ● 100
Canterbury; RMC Place; KENT; **162** H-2; ★ **DOVR**; mail Felton **Z** 19943; ● 150
Capitol Green; RMC Place; KENT; ***162** G-3; ★ **DOVR**; mail Dover **Z** 19901; pop. incl. with Dover (Inc. Place)
Capitol Park; RMC Place; KENT; **162** G-9; ★ **DOVR**; mail Dover **Z** 19901; ● 600
Cardiff; RMC Place; NEW CASTLE; ***162** B-3; ★ **PHIL-**; mail Wilmington **Z** 19810; ● 400
Carlisle Village; RMC Place; KENT; **162** F-7; ★ **DOVR**; mail Dover **Z** 19904; ● 200
Carrcroft; RMC Place; NEW CASTLE; **162** C-9; ★ **PHIL-**; mail Wilmington **Z** 19803; ● 500
Carrcroft Crest (Green Acres); RMC Place; NEW CASTLE; **162** B-9; ★ **PHIL-**; mail Wilmington **Z** 19803; ● 900
Carter; RMC Place; KENT; ***162** H-2; ★ **DOVR**; mail Dover **Z** 19901; ● 250
Castle Hills; RMC Place; NEW CASTLE; **162** D-8; ★ **PHIL-**; mail New Castle **Z** 19720; ● 2,000
Catalina Gardens; RMC Place; NEW CASTLE; ***162** D-1; ★ **PHIL-**; mail Newark **Z** 19713; pop. incl. with Newark (Inc. Place)
Cave Colony; RMC Place; SUSSEX; ***162** J-4; mail Milton **Z** 19968; ● 200
Cedar Beach; RMC Place; SUSSEX; ***162** I-4; elev. 7ft./2m.; mail Milford **Z** 19963; pop. incl. with Slaughter Beach (Inc. Place)
Cedarbrook Acres; RMC Place; KENT; ***162** F-2; ★ **DOVR**; mail Smyrna **Z** 19977; ● 75
Cedar Heights; RMC Place; NEW CASTLE; ***162** C-2; ★ **PHIL-**; mail Wilmington **Z** 19804; ● 200
Centerville; RMC Place; NEW CASTLE; **162** B-2; ★ **PHIL-**; mail Wilmington **Z** 19807; ● 500
Chalfonte; RMC Place; NEW CASTLE; **162** B-9; ★ **PHIL-**; mail Wilmington **Z** 19810; ● 1,400
Chalfonte; NEW CASTLE; see Devonshire (RMC Place)
Channin; RMC Place; NEW CASTLE; ***162** B-3; ★ **PHIL-**; mail Wilmington **Z** 19803; ● 250
Chapel Hill; RMC Place; NEW CASTLE; ***162** C-1; ★ **PHIL-**; mail Newark **Z** 19711; ● 750
Chatham; RMC Place; NEW CASTLE; ***162** C-3; ★ **PHIL-**; mail Wilmington **Z** 19810; ● 350
Chelsea Estates; RMC Place; NEW CASTLE; ***162** C-2; ★ **PHIL-**; mail New Castle **Z** 19720; ● 1,500
Chestnut Grove; RMC Place; KENT; ***162** G-2; ★ **DOVR**; mail Dover **Z** 19904; pop. incl. with Dover (Inc. Place)
Chestnut Hill Estates (Christiana); RMC Place; NEW CASTLE; ***162** C-2; ★ **PHIL-**; mail Newark **Z** 19713; ● 1,800
Cheswold; Inc. Place; KENT; **162** G-2; elev. 44ft./13m.; 🅿; ★ **DOVR**; **Z** 19936; Ⓟ 321; Ⓒ 313
Christiana; RMC Place; NEW CASTLE; **162** D-2; 🅿; ★ **PHIL-**; **Z** 19702; ● 500
Christiana; NEW CASTLE; see Chestnut Hill Estates (RMC Place)
Christiana Acres; RMC Place; NEW CASTLE; ***162** C-2; ★ **PHIL-**; mail New Castle **Z** 19720
Christine Manor; NEW CASTLE; see Cristine Manor (RMC Place)
Clarksville; RMC Place; SUSSEX; **162** L-5; elev. 20ft./6m.; 🅿; **Z** 19970; ● 200
Claymont; CDP; NEW CASTLE; **162** C-3; elev. 100ft./30m.; 🅿; ★ **PHIL-**; **Z** 19703; Ⓟ 9,800; Ⓒ 9,220
Clayton; Inc. Place; KENT; **162** F-2; elev. 43ft./13m.; 🅿; ★ **DOVR**; **Z** 19938; Ⓟ 1,163; Ⓒ 1,273
Clearfield; RMC Place; NEW CASTLE; ***162** C-3; ★ **PHIL-**; mail Claymont **Z** 19703
Cleland Heights; RMC Place; NEW CASTLE; **162** D-8; ★ **PHIL-**; mail Wilmington **Z** 19805; ● 900
Cocked Hat; RMC Place; SUSSEX; ***162** J-2; mail Bridgeville **Z** 19933; rural
College Park; RMC Place; NEW CASTLE; ***162** C-1; ★ **PHIL-**; mail Newark **Z** 19711; pop. incl. with Newark (Inc. Place)
Collins Park; RMC Place; NEW CASTLE; **162** D-8; ★ **PHIL-**; mail New Castle **Z** 19720; ● 1,500
Colmar Manor; RMC Place; KENT; ***162** F-2; ★ **DOVR**; mail Smyrna **Z** 19977; ● 70
Colonial Heights; RMC Place; NEW CASTLE; ***162** C-2; ★ **PHIL-**; mail Wilmington **Z** 19805
Columbia; RMC Place; SUSSEX; ***162** L-2; elev. 45ft./14m.; ★ **SLSB**; mail Delmar **Z** 19940; rural
Concord; RMC Place; SUSSEX; **162** K-2; elev. 26ft./8m.; mail Seaford **Z** 19973; ● 250
Cool Spring; RMC Place; SUSSEX; **162** K-4; mail Milton **Z** 19968; ● 50
Cooper Farm; RMC Place; NEW CASTLE; ***162** C-2; ★ **PHIL-**; mail Wilmington **Z** 19808; ● 450
Cottonpatch Hill; SUSSEX; see Cotton Patch Hills (RMC Place)
Cotton Patch Hills (Cottonpatch Hill); RMC Place; SUSSEX; ***162** L-5; mail Bethany Beach **Z** 19930; summer pop. 75; ● 10
Country Club Estates; RMC Place; SUSSEX; ***162** I-3; mail Milford **Z** 19963; ● 500
Country Living; SUSSEX; see Country Living Mobile Home Park (RMC Place)
Country Living Mobile Home Park (Country Living); RMC Place; SUSSEX; ***162** L-4; mail Millsboro **Z** 19966; ● 175
Coventry; RMC Place; NEW CASTLE; **162** E-7; ★ **PHIL-**; mail New Castle **Z** 19720; ● 1,500
Coverdale Crossroads (Coverdales Crossroads); RMC Place; SUSSEX; ***162** K-3; mail Bridgeville **Z** 19933
Coverdales Crossroads; SUSSEX; see Coverdale Crossroads (RMC Place)
Covered Bridge Farms; RMC Place; NEW CASTLE; ***162** C-1; ★ **PHIL-**; mail Newark **Z** 19711; ● 600
Covey Creek; RMC Place; SUSSEX; ***162** J-5; mail Lewes **Z** 19958; ● 250
Cowgills Corner; RMC Place; KENT; ***162** G-3; ★ **DOVR**; mail Dover **Z** 19901; ● 40
Craigs Mill; RMC Place; SUSSEX; ***162** K-2; mail Seaford **Z** 19973; rural
Cranston Heights; RMC Place; NEW CASTLE; ***162** C-2; ★ **PHIL-**; mail Wilmington **Z** 19808; ● 500
Cristine Manor (Christine Manor); RMC Place; NEW CASTLE; ***162** C-1; ★ **PHIL-**; mail Newark **Z** 19711; ● 200
Crossgates; RMC Place; KENT; ***162** G-3; ★ **DOVR**; mail Dover **Z** 19904; pop. incl. with Dover (Inc. Place)
Cross Keys; RMC Place; SUSSEX; ***162** L-4; mail Millsboro **Z** 19966; rural

D

Dagsboro; Inc. Place; SUSSEX; **162** L-4; elev. 25ft./8m.; 🅿; **Z** 19939; Ⓟ 398; Ⓒ 519
Darley Woods; RMC Place; NEW CASTLE; **162** B-9; ★ **PHIL-**; mail Wilmington **Z** 19810; ● 1,300
Dartmouth Woods; RMC Place; NEW CASTLE; ***162** B-3; ★ **PHIL-**; mail Wilmington **Z** 19810; ● 1,100
Deerhurst; RMC Place; NEW CASTLE; ***162** C-3; ★ **PHIL-**; mail Wilmington **Z** 19803; ● 600
Delaney Corner (Delaneys Corner); RMC Place; NEW CASTLE; ***162** F-1; mail Clayton **Z** 19938; rural
Delaneys Corner; NEW CASTLE; see Delaney Corner (RMC Place)
Delaplane Manor; RMC Place; NEW CASTLE; ***162** C-2; ★ **PHIL-**; mail Newark **Z** 19711; ● 225
Delaware City; Inc. Place; NEW CASTLE; **162** D-2; elev. 9ft./3m.; 🅿; ★ **PHIL-**; **Z** 19706; Ⓟ 1,682; Ⓒ 1,453
Delaware Heights; RMC Place; NEW CASTLE; **162** B-8; ★ **PHIL-**; mail Wilmington **Z** 19807; ● 40
Del Haven Estates; RMC Place; KENT; ***162** H-3; ★ **DOVR**; mail Magnolia **Z** 19962; ● 60
Delmar; Inc. Place; SUSSEX; **162** M-2; elev. 55ft./17m.; 🅿; ★ **SLSB**; **Z** 19940; Ⓟ 962; Ⓒ 1,407
Delpark Manor; RMC Place; NEW CASTLE; **162** D-7; ★ **PHIL-**; mail Wilmington **Z** 19808; ● 1,100
Devon; RMC Place; NEW CASTLE; ***162** B-3; ★ **PHIL-**; mail Wilmington **Z** 19810; pop. incl. with Newark (Inc. Place)
Devonshire (Chalfonte); RMC Place; NEW CASTLE; **162** B-9; ★ **PHIL-**; mail Wilmington **Z** 19810; ● 2,200
Devonshire Woods; RMC Place; SUSSEX; ***162** K-2; mail Seaford **Z** 19973; ● 75
Dewey Beach; Inc. Place; SUSSEX; **162** K-5; elev. 10ft./3m.; 🅿; **Z** 19971; Ⓟ 204; Ⓒ 301
Diamond Acres; RMC Place; SUSSEX; ***162** L-4; mail Dagsboro **Z** 19939; ● 150
Dobbinsville; RMC Place; NEW CASTLE; ***162** D-2; ★ **PHIL-**; mail New Castle **Z** 19720; pop. incl. with New Castle (Inc. Place)
Dover; Inc. Place; **STATE CAPITAL**; ⊡ KENT; **162** G-3; elev. 36ft./11m.; 🅿 🄷 🄲 6,181 ■; ★ **DOVR**; **Z** 19901-06; Ⓟ 27,630; Ⓒ 32,135; Ⓡ 32,043; ◆ 38,113
Dover Base Housing; CDP-Census Area Only; KENT; ***162** H-3; ★ **DOVR**; mail Dover AFB **Z** 19902; Ⓟ 4,376; Ⓒ 3,394
Downs Chapel; RMC Place; KENT; **162** G-2; ★ **DOVR**; mail Clayton **Z** 19938; ● 25
Drummond North; RMC Place; NEW CASTLE; ***162** C-2; ★ **PHIL-**; mail Newark **Z** 19711
Dublin Hill; RMC Place; SUSSEX; **162** J-2; elev. 60ft./18m.; mail Bridgeville **Z** 19933; ● 40
Dunleith; RMC Place; NEW CASTLE; **162** D-8; ★ **PHIL-**; mail Wilmington **Z** 19801; ● 2,400
Dunlinden Acres; RMC Place; NEW CASTLE; ***162** C-2; ★ **PHIL-**; mail Wilmington **Z** 19808; ● 1,200
Dupont Manor; RMC Place; KENT; **162** G-3; elev. 43ft./13m.; ★ **DOVR**; mail Dover **Z** 19901; ● 300
Du Ross Heights; RMC Place; NEW CASTLE; **162** D-8; ★ **PHIL-**; mail New Castle **Z** 19720; ● 900
Dutch Acres; RMC Place; SUSSEX; ***162** J-5; mail Lewes **Z** 19958; ● 75

E

Eastman Heights; RMC Place; SUSSEX; ***162** I-3; mail Milford **Z** 19963; ● 400
Eberton; RMC Place; KENT; ***162** G-2; ★ **DOVR**; mail Dover **Z** 19901; ● 150
Eden Park; NEW CASTLE; see Eden Park Gardens (RMC Place)
Eden Park Gardens (Eden Park); RMC Place; NEW CASTLE; ***162** C-3; ★ **PHIL-**; mail New Castle **Z** 19720; ● 600
Edge Hill; RMC Place; KENT; ***162** G-3; ★ **DOVR**; mail Dover **Z** 19901; pop. incl. with Dover (Inc. Place)
Edgehill Acres; RMC Place; KENT; ***162** G-3; ★ **DOVR**; mail Dover **Z** 19901; pop. incl. with Dover (Inc. Place)
Edgemoor; CDP; NEW CASTLE; **162** C-9; elev. 50ft./15m.; 🅿; ★ **PHIL-**; **Z** 19809-10 & mail Wilmington **Z** 19802; Ⓟ 5,853; Ⓒ 5,992
Edgemoor Gardens; RMC Place; NEW CASTLE; ***162** C-3; ★ **PHIL-**; mail Wilmington **Z** 19802
Edgemoor Terrace; RMC Place; NEW CASTLE; ***162** C-3; ★ **PHIL-**; mail Wilmington **Z** 19802
Edgewater; RMC Place; SUSSEX; ***162** J-5; mail Lewes **Z** 19958; ● 200
Edgewater Acres; RMC Place; SUSSEX; ***162** M-5; mail Selbyville **Z** 19975; ● 125
Edgewood Hills; RMC Place; NEW CASTLE; ***162** C-3; ★ **PHIL-**; mail Wilmington **Z** 19802
Edwardsville; RMC Place; KENT; ***162** I-2; ★ **DOVR**; mail Felton **Z** 19943; rural
Ellendale; Inc. Place; SUSSEX; **162** J-3; elev. 52ft./16m.; 🅿; **Z** 19941; Ⓟ 313; Ⓒ 327
Elmhurst; RMC Place; NEW CASTLE; ***162** C-2; ★ **PHIL-**; mail Wilmington **Z** 19804; ● 1,000
Elsmere; Inc. Place; NEW CASTLE; **162** C-2; elev. 80ft./24m.; 🅿; ★ **PHIL-**; **Z** 19805; Ⓟ 5,935; Ⓒ 5,800
Elsmere Junction; RMC Place; NEW CASTLE; ★ **PHIL-**; pop. incl. with Elsmere (Inc. Place)
English Village; RMC Place; NEW CASTLE; ***162** C-2; ★ **PHIL-**; mail Newark **Z** 19711

F

Fairfax; RMC Place; NEW CASTLE; **162** C-9; ★ **PHIL-**; mail Wilmington **Z** 19803; ● 1,600
Fairfield Crest; RMC Place; NEW CASTLE; ***162** C-1; ★ **PHIL-**; pop. incl. with Newark (Inc. Place)
Fairfield Farms; RMC Place; KENT; **162** H-8; ★ **DOVR**; mail Dover **Z** 19901; ● 700
Fairmount; RMC Place; SUSSEX; ***162** K-4; mail Millsboro **Z** 19966; rural
Fairwinds; RMC Place; NEW CASTLE; ***162** D-2; ★ **PHIL-**; mail Bear **Z** 19701; ● 200
Farmington; Inc. Place; KENT; **162** I-2; elev. 63ft./19m.; 🅿; ★ **DOVR**; **Z** 19950; Ⓟ 122; Ⓒ 75
Faulkland (Faulkland Heights); RMC Place; NEW CASTLE; **162** C-7; ★ **PHIL-**; mail Wilmington **Z** 19808; ● 1,300
Faulkland Heights; NEW CASTLE; see Faulkland (RMC Place)
Faulkwoods; NEW CASTLE; see Foulk Woods (RMC Place)
Federal; RMC Place; NEW CASTLE; ***162** C-1; ★ **PHIL-**; mail Newark **Z** 19711, **Z** 19715; pop. incl. with Newark (Inc. Place)
Felton; Inc. Place; KENT; **162** H-2; elev. 67ft./20m.; 🅿; ★ **DOVR**; **Z** 19943; Ⓟ 683; Ⓒ 784
Felton Heights; RMC Place; KENT; ***162** H-2; ★ **DOVR**; mail Felton **Z** 19943; ● 125
Fenwick Island; Inc. Place; SUSSEX; **162** M-5; elev. 4ft./1m.; 🅿; **Z** 19944 & mail Selbyville **Z** 19975; Ⓟ 186; Ⓒ 342
Fieldsboro; RMC Place; NEW CASTLE; ***162** E-2; mail Townsend **Z** 19734
Fleming Corners (Flemings Corners); RMC Place; KENT; ***162** I-2; ★ **DOVR**; mail Harrington **Z** 19952; rural
Flemings Corners; KENT; see Fleming Corners (RMC Place)
Flemings Landing; RMC Place; NEW CASTLE; ***162** F-3; mail Townsend **Z** 19734; rural
Forest Brook Glen; RMC Place; NEW CASTLE; **162** D-8; ★ **PHIL-**; mail Wilmington **Z** 19804; ● 400
Forest Hills Park; RMC Place; NEW CASTLE; **162** C-9; ★ **PHIL-**; mail Wilmington **Z** 19803; ● 650
Foulk Woods (Faulkwoods); RMC Place; NEW CASTLE; ***162** B-3; ★ **PHIL-**; mail Wilmington **Z** 19808; ● 200
Four Seasons; RMC Place; NEW CASTLE; ***162** D-1; ★ **PHIL-**; mail Newark **Z** 19702; ● 1,500
Fox Hall; RMC Place; KENT; **162** F-7; ★ **DOVR**; mail Dover **Z** 19904; pop. incl. with Dover (Inc. Place)
Foxhall Courtside; RMC Place; KENT; ***162** G-2; ★ **DOVR**; mail Dover **Z** 19904; ● 120
Fox Hollow; RMC Place; SUSSEX; ***162** K-5; mail Lewes **Z** 19958; ● 85
Frankford; Inc. Place; SUSSEX; **162** L-4; elev. 30ft./9m.; 🅿; **Z** 19945; Ⓟ 591; Ⓒ 714
Frederica; Inc. Place; KENT; **162** H-3; elev. 20ft./6m.; 🅿; ★ **DOVR**; **Z** 19946; Ⓟ 761; Ⓒ 648

G

Garfield Park; RMC Place; NEW CASTLE; **162** D-8; ★ **PHIL-**; mail New Castle **Z** 19720; ● 400
George Read Village; RMC Place; NEW CASTLE; ***162** C-1; ★ **PHIL-**; pop. incl. with Newark (Inc. Place)
Georgetown; Inc. Place; ⊡ SUSSEX; **162** K-3; elev. 52ft./16m.; 🅿; **Z** 19947; Ⓟ 3,732; Ⓒ 4,643
Ginns Corner; RMC Place; NEW CASTLE; **162** F-2; mail Townsend **Z** 19734; pop. incl. with Townsend (Inc. Place)
Glasgow; CDP; NEW CASTLE; **162** D-1; ★ **PHIL-**; mail Newark **Z** 19702; Ⓒ 12,840
Glasgow Court; RMC Place; NEW CASTLE; ***162** D-2; ★ **PHIL-**; mail Newark **Z** 19702; ● 600
Glasgow Pines; RMC Place; NEW CASTLE; ***162** D-2; ★ **PHIL-**; mail Newark **Z** 19702; ● 900
Glen Berne Estates; RMC Place; NEW CASTLE; ***162** C-2; ★ **PHIL-**; mail Wilmington **Z** 19804; ● 900
Glendale; RMC Place; NEW CASTLE; ***162** D-2; ★ **PHIL-**; mail Newark **Z** 19702; ● 450
Glenville; RMC Place; NEW CASTLE; ***162** C-2; ★ **PHIL-**; mail Wilmington **Z** 19804; ● 650
Gordon Heights; RMC Place; NEW CASTLE; ***162** C-3; ★ **PHIL-**; mail Wilmington **Z** 19802
Gordy Estates; RMC Place; NEW CASTLE; ***162** C-2; ★ **PHIL-**; mail Wilmington **Z** 19804; ● 450
Granogue; RMC Place; NEW CASTLE; ***162** B-2; ★ **PHIL-**; mail Wilmington **Z** 19807
Gravel Hill; RMC Place; SUSSEX; **162** K-4; mail Georgetown **Z** 19947; ● 75
Graylyn Crest; RMC Place; NEW CASTLE; **162** B-9; ★ **PHIL-**; mail Wilmington **Z** 19803; ● 450
Green Acres; RMC Place; NEW CASTLE; **162** B-9; ★ **PHIL-**; mail Wilmington **Z** 19803; ● 1,100
Green Acres; NEW CASTLE; see Carrcroft Crest (RMC Place)
Greenbrier; RMC Place; NEW CASTLE; ***162** D-2; ★ **PHIL-**; mail New Castle **Z** 19720
Greentree; RMC Place; NEW CASTLE; ★ **PHIL-**; mail Claymont **Z** 19703
Greenview; RMC Place; KENT; ***162** H-3; ★ **DOVR**; mail Dover **Z** 19901; ● 300
Greenville; RMC Place; KENT; ***162** I-2; mail Harrington **Z** 19952; rural
Greenville; CDP; NEW CASTLE; **162** C-2; elev. 263ft./80m.; 🅿; ★ **PHIL-**; **Z** 19807, **Z** 19884; Ⓒ 2,332
Greenville Place; RMC Place; NEW CASTLE; **162** C-8; ★ **PHIL-**; mail Wilmington **Z** 19807; ● 1,000
Greenwood; Inc. Place; SUSSEX; **162** J-2; elev. 50ft./15m.; 🅿; **Z** 19950; Ⓟ 578; Ⓒ 837
Gulls Nest; RMC Place; SUSSEX; ***162** L-5; mail Bethany Beach **Z** 19930; summer pop. 80; ● 10
Gumboro; RMC Place; SUSSEX; **162** L-4; mail Frankford **Z** 19945; ● 100
Guyencourt; RMC Place; NEW CASTLE; **162** B-8; ★ **PHIL-**; mail Wilmington **Z** 19807; ● 100
Gwinhurst; RMC Place; NEW CASTLE; **162** B-10; ★ **PHIL-**; mail Wilmington **Z** 19809; ● 400

H

Hall Estates; RMC Place; KENT; ***162** I-3; ★ **DOVR**; mail Milford **Z** 19963; ● 120
Hambys Corner; NEW CASTLE; see Hanbys Corner (RMC Place)
Hamilton Park; RMC Place; NEW CASTLE; **162** D-9; elev. 20ft./6m.; ★ **PHIL-**; mail New Castle **Z** 19720; ● 200
Hanby Corners; NEW CASTLE; see Hanbys Corner (RMC Place)
Hanbys Corner (Hambys Corner, Hanby Corners); RMC Place; NEW CASTLE; ***162** B-3; ★ **PHIL-**; mail Wilmington **Z** 19810
Harbeson; RMC Place; SUSSEX; **162** K-4; elev. 30ft./9m.; 🅿; **Z** 19951; ● 400
Hardscrabble; RMC Place; SUSSEX; ***162** K-3; mail Seaford **Z** 19973; rural
Harmony Hills; RMC Place; NEW CASTLE; **162** D-7; ★ **PHIL-**; mail Newark **Z** 19711; ● 800
Harrington; Inc. Place; KENT; **162** I-2; elev. 63ft./19m.; 🅿; ★ **DOVR**; **Z** 19952; Ⓟ 2,311; Ⓒ 3,174
Hartly; Inc. Place; KENT; **162** G-2; elev. 71ft./22m.; 🅿; ★ **DOVR**; **Z** 19953; Ⓟ 107; Ⓒ 78
Haven Lake Acres; RMC Place; KENT; ***162** I-3; ★ **DOVR**; mail Milford **Z** 19963; ● 40
Hayden Park; RMC Place; NEW CASTLE; ***162** C-2; ★ **PHIL-**; mail Wilmington **Z** 19804
Hazlettville; RMC Place; KENT; ***162** H-2; elev. 65ft./20m.; ★ **DOVR**; mail Hartly **Z** 19953
Hearns Crossroads; RMC Place; SUSSEX; ***162** L-2; elev. 35ft./11m.; mail Laurel **Z** 19956
Hearns Mill; RMC Place; SUSSEX; ***162** K-2; mail Seaford **Z** 19973; ● 130
Heather Woods; RMC Place; NEW CASTLE; ***162** D-2; ★ **PHIL-**; mail Newark **Z** 19702; ● 150
Henlopen Acres; Inc. Place; SUSSEX; **162** K-5; elev. 10ft./3m.; mail Rehoboth Beach **Z** 19971; Ⓟ 107; Ⓒ 139
Henry Clay; RMC Place; NEW CASTLE; ★ **PHIL-**
Heritage Village; RMC Place; SUSSEX; ***162** K-2; mail Seaford **Z** 19973; ● 150
Hickman; RMC Place; KENT; **162** J-1; mail Greenwood **Z** 19950; ● 100
Hickory Hill; RMC Place; SUSSEX; ***162** L-4; mail Millsboro **Z** 19966; rural
Hickory Ridge; RMC Place; KENT; ***162** G-2; ★ **DOVR**; mail Smyrna **Z** 19977; ● 75
Highland Acres; CDP; KENT; ***162** H-3; ★ **DOVR**; mail Dover **Z** 19901; Ⓟ 3,151; Ⓒ 3,379; Ⓡ 3,388
Highland Acres; RMC Place; SUSSEX; ***162** J-5; mail Lewes **Z** 19958; pop. incl. with Lewes (Inc. Place)
Highland West; RMC Place; NEW CASTLE; ***162** C-2; ★ **PHIL-**; mail Wilmington **Z** 19808; ● 600
High Point Park; RMC Place; KENT; ***162** H-3; ★ **DOVR**; mail Frederica **Z** 19946; ● 800
Hillcrest; RMC Place; NEW CASTLE; **162** C-9; ★ **PHIL-**; mail Wilmington **Z** 19809; ● 1,500
Hill N Dale; RMC Place; SUSSEX; ***162** K-2; mail Seaford **Z** 19973; ● 80
Hillside Acres; RMC Place; KENT; ***162** H-3; ★ **DOVR**; mail Felton **Z** 19943; ● 150
Hillside Heights; RMC Place; NEW CASTLE; ***162** C-2; ★ **PHIL-**; mail Newark **Z** 19713; ● 550
Hilltop Manor; RMC Place; NEW CASTLE; ***162** C-3; ★ **PHIL-**; mail Wilmington **Z** 19809; ● 800
Hitchens Crossroads; RMC Place; SUSSEX; ***162** L-3; elev. 47ft./14m.; mail Laurel **Z** 19956
Hockessin; CDP; NEW CASTLE; **162** C-2; elev. 254ft./77m.; 🅿; ★ **PHIL-**; **Z** 19707; Ⓒ 12,902
Holiday Acres; RMC Place; SUSSEX; ***162** L-4; mail Dagsboro **Z** 19939; ● 110
Hollandsville; RMC Place; KENT; ***162** I-2; ★ **DOVR**; mail Felton **Z** 19943; rural
Holletts Corners; RMC Place; KENT; ***162** F-1; ★ **DOVR**; mail Clayton **Z** 19938
Holloway Terrace; RMC Place; NEW CASTLE; **162** D-9; ★ **PHIL-**; mail New Castle **Z** 19720; ● 1,200
Holly Oak; RMC Place; NEW CASTLE; ***162** C-3; ★ **PHIL-**; mail Wilmington **Z** 19809; ● 400
Holly Oak; RMC Place; SUSSEX; ***162** C-3; ★ **SLSB**; mail Seaford **Z** 19973; ● 50
Holly Oak Terrace; RMC Place; NEW CASTLE; ***162** C-3; ★ **PHIL-**; mail Wilmington **Z** 19809; ● 250
Hollyville; RMC Place; SUSSEX; ***162** K-4; mail Harbeson **Z** 19951
Houston; Inc. Place; KENT; **162** I-3; elev. 53ft./16m.; 🅿; ★ **DOVR**; **Z** 19954; Ⓟ 487; Ⓒ 430
Huntley; RMC Place; KENT; **162** H-8; ★ **DOVR**; mail Dover **Z** 19901; ● 100
Hyde Park; RMC Place; NEW CASTLE; ***162** C-2; ★ **PHIL-**; mail Wilmington **Z** 19808; ● 350

I

Indian Beach; RMC Place; SUSSEX; **162** K-5; mail Rehoboth Beach **Z** 19971; summer pop. 200; ● 10
Indian River Acres; RMC Place; SUSSEX; ***162** L-5; mail Dagsboro **Z** 19939; ● 120
Iron Hill; RMC Place; NEW CASTLE; ***162** D-1; ★ **PHIL-**; mail Newark **Z** 19702; ● 500
Ivy Ridge; RMC Place; NEW CASTLE; **162** E-7; ★ **PHIL-**; mail New Castle **Z** 19720; ● 1,800

J

Jefferson Farms; RMC Place; NEW CASTLE; **162** D-8; ★ **PHIL-**; mail New Castle **Z** 19720; ● 2,000
Jimtown; RMC Place; SUSSEX; **162** J-5; mail Lewes **Z** 19958; ● 45
Johnson; RMC Place; SUSSEX; **162** L-5; mail Selbyville **Z** 19975; ● 35
Johnstown; RMC Place; SUSSEX; ***162** J-2; elev. 53ft./16m.; mail Greenwood **Z** 19950; rural
Jones Crossroads; RMC Place; SUSSEX; ***162** K-3; elev. 51ft./16m.; mail Laurel **Z** 19956; rural

K

Keen-Wik; RMC Place; SUSSEX; ***162** M-5; mail Selbyville **Z** 19975; ● 400
Keenwik Sound; RMC Place; SUSSEX; ***162** L-5; mail Selbyville **Z** 19975; ● 250
Keenwik West; RMC Place; SUSSEX; ***162** L-5; mail Selbyville **Z** 19975; ● 250
Kenmore Park; RMC Place; SUSSEX; ***162** K-2; mail Seaford **Z** 19973; ● 50
KENT; **162** H-3; Ⓟ 110,993; Ⓒ 126,697; ◆ 161,564
Kent Acres; CDP; KENT; **162** H-8; ★ **DOVR**; mail Dover **Z** 19901; Ⓟ 1,807; Ⓒ 1,637
Kenton; Inc. Place; KENT; **162** G-2; elev. 68ft./21m.; 🅿; ★ **DOVR**; **Z** 19955; Ⓟ 232; Ⓒ 237
Kiamensi; RMC Place; NEW CASTLE; ★ **PHIL-**
Kirkwood; RMC Place; NEW CASTLE; **162** D-2; elev. 68ft./21m.; 🅿; ★ **PHIL-**; **Z** 19708; ● 150
Kitts Hummock; RMC Place; KENT; **162** H-3; mail Dover **Z** 19901; ● 300

L

Lake Pines; RMC Place; SUSSEX; ***162** L-3; mail Laurel **Z** 19956; ● 125
Lamatan I; RMC Place; NEW CASTLE; ***162** C-1; ★ **PHIL-**; mail Newark **Z** 19711; ● 150
Lancashire; RMC Place; NEW CASTLE; ***162** B-3; ★ **PHIL-**; mail Wilmington **Z** 19810; ● 1,200
Lancaster Avenue Station; RMC Place; NEW CASTLE; ★ **PHIL-**; mail Wilmington **Z** 19805; pop. incl. with Wilmington (Inc. Place)
Lancaster Village; RMC Place; NEW CASTLE; **162** C-8; ★ **PHIL-**; mail Wilmington **Z** 19805; pop. incl. with Elsmere (Inc. Place)
Laurel; Inc. Place; SUSSEX; **162** L-2; elev. 30ft./9m.; 🅿; **Z** 19956; Ⓟ 3,226; Ⓒ 3,668
Lebanon; RMC Place; KENT; **162** H-3; ★ **DOVR**; mail Dover **Z** 19901; ● 120
Leedom Estates; NEW CASTLE; see Leedon Estates (RMC Place)
Leedon Estates (Leedom Estates); RMC Place; NEW CASTLE; ***162** C-2; ★ **PHIL-**; mail New Castle **Z** 19720; ● 800
Leipsic; Inc. Place; KENT; **162** G-3; elev. 10ft./3m.; 🅿; ★ **DOVR**; **Z** 19901; Ⓟ 236; Ⓒ 203
Lewes; Inc. Place; SUSSEX; **162** J-5; elev. 10ft./3m.; 🅿 🄷; **Z** 19958; Ⓟ 2,295; Ⓒ 2,932
Lewes Beach; RMC Place; SUSSEX; ***162** J-5; mail Lewes **Z** 19958; pop. incl. with Lewes (Inc. Place)
Liftwood; RMC Place; NEW CASTLE; ***162** C-3; ★ **PHIL-**; mail Wilmington **Z** 19803; ● 300
Limestone Acres; RMC Place; NEW CASTLE; ***162** C-2; ★ **PHIL-**; mail Wilmington **Z** 19808; ● 800
Limestone Gardene; NEW CASTLE; see Limestone Gardens (RMC Place)

Entries in **UPPERCASE** are counties.
Entries in **bold** have populations of 2,500 or more.
Names in parentheses are alternate names.

Inc. Place	Incorporated Place
RMC Place	Rand McNally Designated Place
CDP	Census Designated Place
MCD	Minor Civil Division
⊡	County Seat
▲	Minor Civil Division
elev.	Elevation
🅿	Post Office
🄷	Hospital
🄲	College
■	Principal Business Center
★	Ranally Metro Area (RMA) Abbreviation
Z	Zip Code(s)
Ⓟ	Previous Census Population
Ⓡ	Revised Census Population
Ⓐ	Annexation Population
●	Rand McNally Population Estimate
Ⓒ	Final Census Population
Ⓢ	Special Census Population
◆	Estimated Population

For additional definitions see Glossary, Volume 1, and Introduction, Volume 2.

Limestone Gardens (Limestone Gardene); RMC Place; NEW CASTLE; ***162** C-2; ★ **PHIL-**; mail Wilmington **z** 19808; ● 1,000
Lincoln; RMC Place; SUSSEX; **162** I-3; elev. 44ft./13m.; 🅿; **z** 19960; ● 500
Lindamere; RMC Place; NEW CASTLE; ***162** C-3; ★ **PHIL-**; mail Wilmington **z** 19809; ● 250
Little Creek; Inc. Place; KENT; **162** G-3; elev. 10ft./3m.; 🅿; ★ **DOVR**; **z** 19961; Ⓟ 167; Ⓒ 195
Little Heaven; RMC Place; KENT; **162** H-3; elev. 29ft./9m.; ★ **DOVR**; mail Frederica **z** 19946; ● 250
Llangollen Estates; RMC Place; NEW CASTLE; **162** E-8; ★ **PHIL-**; mail New Castle **z** 19720; ● 1,400
London Village; RMC Place; KENT; ***162** H-3; ★ **DOVR**; mail Magnolia **z** 19962; ● 350
Long Neck; CDP-Census Area Only; SUSSEX; ***162** K-5; elev. 5ft./2m.; 🅿; **z** 19966; Ⓟ 886; Ⓒ 1,629
Longview Farms; RMC Place; NEW CASTLE; ***162** B-3; ★ **PHIL-**; mail Wilmington **z** 19810
Loveville; RMC Place; NEW CASTLE; ***162** C-2; ★ **PHIL-**; mail Wilmington **z** 19808; ● 500
Lowe; RMC Place; SUSSEX; ***162** L-3; elev. 37ft./11m.; mail Laurel **z** 19956; rural
Lowes Crossroads; RMC Place; SUSSEX; ***162** L-3; elev. 50ft./15m.; mail Millsboro **z** 19966; rural
Lumbrook; RMC Place; NEW CASTLE; ***162** C-1; ★ **PHIL-**; mail Newark **z** 19711; pop. incl. with Newark (Inc. Place)
Lynch Heights; RMC Place; KENT; **162** I-3; ★ **DOVR**; mail Milford **z** 19963; ● 125
Lyndalia; RMC Place; NEW CASTLE; ***162** C-2; ★ **PHIL-**; mail Wilmington **z** 19804; ● 300
Lynnfield; RMC Place; NEW CASTLE; ***162** C-3; ★ **PHIL-**; mail Wilmington **z** 19803; ● 350

M

Magnolia; Inc. Place; KENT; **162** H-3; elev. 30ft./9m.; 🅿; ★ **DOVR**; **z** 19962; Ⓟ 211; Ⓒ 226
Manor; RMC Place; NEW CASTLE; ***162** C-2; elev. 50ft./15m.; 🅿; ★ **PHIL-**; **z** 19720
Manor Park; RMC Place; NEW CASTLE; ***162** C-2; ★ **PHIL-**; mail New Castle **z** 19720; ● 900
Maplecrest; RMC Place; NEW CASTLE; ***162** C-2; ★ **PHIL-**; mail Wilmington **z** 19808; ● 750
Marabou Meadows; RMC Place; NEW CASTLE; ***162** D-1; ★ **PHIL-**; mail Newark **z** 19702; ● 250
Marshallton; RMC Place; NEW CASTLE; **162** D-7; elev. 60ft./18m.; 🅿; ★ **PHIL-**; **z** 19808; ● 1,800
Marvels Crossroads; RMC Place; KENT; ***162** I-3; ★ **DOVR**; mail Harrington **z** 19952
Marydel; RMC Place; KENT; **162** H-1; elev. 59ft./18m.; 🅿; ★ **DOVR**; **z** 19964; ● 100
Massey Landing (Masseys Landing); RMC Place; SUSSEX; ***162** K-5; mail Millsboro **z** 19966; ● 80
Masseys Landing; SUSSEX; see Massey Landing (RMC Place)
Mastens Corner; RMC Place; KENT; **162** I-2; ★ **DOVR**; mail Felton **z** 19943; ● 60
Mayfair; RMC Place; KENT; ***162** H-3; ★ **DOVR**; mail Dover **z** 19904; pop. incl. with Dover (Inc. Place)
Mayfield; RMC Place; NEW CASTLE; ***162** C-3; ★ **PHIL-**; mail Wilmington **z** 19803
McClellandville; RMC Place; NEW CASTLE; **162** C-1; ★ **PHIL-**; mail Newark **z** 19711; ● 120
McDaniel Heights; RMC Place; NEW CASTLE; ***162** C-3; ★ **PHIL-**; mail Wilmington **z** 19803; ● 1,800
Meadowbrook; RMC Place; NEW CASTLE; ***162** C-2; ★ **PHIL-**; mail Wilmington **z** 19804
Meadowbrook Acres; RMC Place; KENT; ***162** H-3; ★ **DOVR**; mail Magnolia **z** 19962; ● 600
Meadowood; RMC Place; NEW CASTLE; **162** D-7; elev. 100ft./30m.; ★ **PHIL-**; mail Newark **z** 19711; ● 600
Mechanicsville; RMC Place; NEW CASTLE; ***162** C-1; ★ **PHIL-**; mail Newark **z** 19711
Meeting House Hill; RMC Place; NEW CASTLE; ***162** C-2; ★ **PHIL-**; mail Newark **z** 19711
Melody Meadows; RMC Place; NEW CASTLE; ***162** D-1; ★ **PHIL-**; mail Newark **z** 19702; ● 500
Mendenhall Village; RMC Place; NEW CASTLE; ***162** C-2; ★ **PHIL-**; mail Newark **z** 19711; ● 1,500
Middleford; RMC Place; SUSSEX; **162** K-2; mail Seaford **z** 19973; ● 150
Middlesex Beach; RMC Place; SUSSEX; **162** L-5; mail Bethany Beach **z** 19930; summer pop. 200; ● 25
Middletown; Inc. Place; NEW CASTLE; **162** E-2; elev. 66ft./20m.; 🅿; ★ **PHIL-**; **z** 19709; Ⓟ 3,834; Ⓒ 6,161
Midvale; RMC Place; NEW CASTLE; ***162** D-2; ★ **PHIL-**; mail New Castle **z** 19720; ● 150
Midway; RMC Place; SUSSEX; **162** K-5; elev. 29ft./9m.; mail Rehoboth Beach **z** 19971; ● 600
Milford; Inc. Place; SUSSEX, KENT; **162** I-3; elev. 21ft./6m.; 🅿 🅷; ★ **SLSB**; **z** 19963; Ⓟ 6,040; Ⓒ 6,732
Milford Crossroads; RMC Place; NEW CASTLE; **162** C-1; ★ **PHIL-**; mail Newark **z** 19711; ● 100
Millpond Acres; RMC Place; SUSSEX; ***162** J-5; mail Lewes **z** 19958; ● 200
Millsboro; Inc. Place; SUSSEX; **162** L-4; elev. 26ft./8m.; 🅿; **z** 19966; Ⓟ 1,643; Ⓒ 2,360
Milltown; RMC Place; NEW CASTLE; ***162** C-2; ★ **PHIL-**; mail Wilmington **z** 19808; ● 800
Millville; Inc. Place; SUSSEX; **162** L-5; elev. 12ft./4m.; 🅿; **z** 19967, **z** 19970; Ⓟ 206; Ⓒ 259
Milton; Inc. Place; SUSSEX; **162** J-4; elev. 30ft./9m.; 🅿; **z** 19968; Ⓟ 1,417; Ⓒ 1,657
Minquadale; RMC Place; NEW CASTLE; **162** D-8; ★ **PHIL-**; mail New Castle **z** 19720; ● 650
Mispillion Light; RMC Place; SUSSEX; ***162** I-4; mail Milford **z** 19963
Mission; RMC Place; SUSSEX; ***162** L-4; elev. 45ft./14m.; mail Millsboro **z** 19966; rural
Montchanin; RMC Place; NEW CASTLE; **162** C-8; elev. 300ft./91m.; 🅿; ★ **PHIL-**; **z** 19710; ● 300
Morris Estates; RMC Place; KENT; ***162** G-3; ★ **DOVR**; mail Dover **z** 19901; pop. incl. with Dover (Inc. Place)
Mount Cuba; RMC Place; NEW CASTLE; ***162** C-2; ★ **PHIL-**; mail Wilmington **z** 19807; rural
Mount Pleasant; RMC Place; NEW CASTLE; **162** E-2; ★ **PHIL-**; mail Middletown **z** 19709; ● 100

N

Naaman (Naamans Corner); RMC Place; NEW CASTLE; ***162** B-3; ★ **PHIL-**; mail Claymont **z** 19703
Naamans Corner; NEW CASTLE; see Naaman (RMC Place)
Naamans Gardens; RMC Place; NEW CASTLE; **162** B-10; ★ **PHIL-**; mail Wilmington **z** 19810; ● 600
Naamans Manor; RMC Place; NEW CASTLE; ***162** B-3; ★ **PHIL-**; mail Wilmington **z** 19810
Nanticoke Acres; RMC Place; SUSSEX; ***162** K-2; mail Seaford **z** 19973; ● 300
Nassau; RMC Place; SUSSEX; **162** J-5; elev. 25ft./8m.; 🅿; **z** 19969; ● 125
Newark; Inc. Place; NEW CASTLE; **162** C-1; elev. 124ft./38m.; 🅿 🅷 🅲 20,380 ■; ★ **PHIL-**; **z** 19702, **z** 19711-18, **z** 19725-26; Ⓟ 25,098; Ⓒ 28,547; ◆ 29,149
New Castle; Inc. Place; NEW CASTLE; **162** D-2; elev. 19ft./6m.; 🅿 🅷 🅲 8,237; ★ **PHIL-**; **z** 19720-21; Ⓟ 4,837; Ⓒ 4,862
NEW CASTLE; **162** F-2; Ⓟ 441,946; Ⓒ 500,265; ◆ 533,474
New Castle Manor; RMC Place; NEW CASTLE; ***162** C-2; ★ **PHIL-**; mail New Castle **z** 19720; pop. incl. with New Castle (Inc. Place)
Newport; Inc. Place; NEW CASTLE; **162** C-2; elev. 50ft./15m.; 🅿; ★ **PHIL-**; **z** 19804; Ⓟ 1,240; Ⓒ 1,122
Newport Heights; RMC Place; NEW CASTLE; ***162** C-2; ★ **PHIL-**; mail Wilmington **z** 19804; pop. incl. with Newport (Inc. Place)
Northcrest; RMC Place; NEW CASTLE; ***162** B-3; ★ **PHIL-**; mail Wilmington **z** 19810; ● 800
North Hills; RMC Place; NEW CASTLE; ***162** C-3; ★ **PHIL-**; mail Wilmington **z** 19809; ● 300
Northridge; RMC Place; KENT; ***162** G-2; ★ **DOVR**; mail Smyrna **z** 19977; ● 200
North Seaford Heights; RMC Place; SUSSEX; ***162** K-2; mail Seaford **z** 19973; pop. incl. with Seaford (Inc. Place)
Northshire; RMC Place; NEW CASTLE; ***162** B-3; ★ **PHIL-**; mail Wilmington **z** 19810; ● 500
North Shore; KENT; see North Shores (RMC Place)
North Shores (North Shore); RMC Place; KENT; ***162** I-3; ★ **DOVR**; mail Milford **z** 19963; ● 180
North Shores; RMC Place; SUSSEX; **162** J-5; mail Rehoboth Beach **z** 19971; ● 100
North Shores; RMC Place; SUSSEX; ***162** K-2; mail Seaford **z** 19973; ● 175
North Star; CDP; NEW CASTLE; **162** C-1; ★ **PHIL-**; mail Newark **z** 19711; Ⓒ 8,277
Northwest Dover Heights; RMC Place; KENT; ***162** G-3; ★ **DOVR**; mail Dover **z** 19904; pop. incl. with Dover (Inc. Place)
Northwood; RMC Place; NEW CASTLE; ***162** C-3; ★ **PHIL-**; mail Wilmington **z** 19803; ● 400
Nottingham Green; RMC Place; NEW CASTLE; ***162** C-1; ★ **PHIL-**; mail Newark **z** 19711; pop. incl. with Newark (Inc. Place)

O

Oak Forest Estates; RMC Place; KENT; ***162** G-2; ★ **DOVR**; mail Hartly **z** 19953; rural
Oak Grove; RMC Place; KENT; ***162** G-3; ★ **DOVR**; mail Dover **z** 19901
Oak Grove; RMC Place; SUSSEX; ***162** K-2; mail Seaford **z** 19973
Oak Hill; RMC Place; NEW CASTLE; ***162** C-2; ★ **PHIL-**; mail Wilmington **z** 19805; ● 600
Oak Lane Manor; RMC Place; NEW CASTLE; **162** B-9; ★ **PHIL-**; mail Wilmington **z** 19803; ● 950
Oakley; RMC Place; SUSSEX; ***162** J-3; elev. 49ft./15m.; mail Ellendale **z** 19941
Oakmont; RMC Place; NEW CASTLE; ***162** C-3; ★ **PHIL-**; mail Wilmington **z** 19801
Oak Orchard; RMC Place; SUSSEX; **162** L-5; mail Millsboro **z** 19966; summer pop. 750; ● 500
Ocean View; Inc. Place; SUSSEX; **162** L-5; elev. 10ft./3m.; 🅿; **z** 19967, **z** 19970; Ⓟ 606; Ⓒ 1,006
Ocean Village; RMC Place; SUSSEX; ***162** L-5; mail Bethany Beach **z** 19930; summer pop. 120; ● 30
Odessa; Inc. Place; NEW CASTLE; **162** E-2; elev. 50ft./15m.; 🅿; ★ **PHIL-**; **z** 19730; Ⓟ 303; Ⓒ 286
Ogletown; RMC Place; NEW CASTLE; **162** C-2; ★ **PHIL-**; mail Newark **z** 19711; ● 175
Old Furnace; RMC Place; SUSSEX; ***162** K-3; elev. 30ft./9m.; mail Georgetown **z** 19947; ● 30
Omar; RMC Place; SUSSEX; ***162** L-5; mail Frankford **z** 19945
Orchard Acres; RMC Place; KENT; ***162** H-3; ★ **DOVR**; mail Felton **z** 19943; ● 100
Overbrook Shores; RMC Place; SUSSEX; ***162** J-4; mail Lewes **z** 19958; ● 175
Overview Gardens; RMC Place; NEW CASTLE; ***162** C-2; ★ **PHIL-**; mail New Castle **z** 19720; ● 900
Owens; RMC Place; SUSSEX; ***162** J-3; elev. 55ft./17m.; mail Greenwood **z** 19950; rural
Owls Nest (Owls Nest Estates); RMC Place; NEW CASTLE; ***162** B-2; ★ **PHIL-**; mail Wilmington **z** 19807; ● 60
Owls Nest Estates; NEW CASTLE; see Owls Nest (RMC Place)

P

Paris Villa; RMC Place; KENT; ***162** H-3; ★ **DOVR**; mail Magnolia **z** 19962; ● 350
Pearsons Corner; RMC Place; KENT; ***162** G-2; ★ **DOVR**; mail Dover **z** 19904
Pembrey; RMC Place; NEW CASTLE; ***162** B-3; ★ **PHIL-**; mail Wilmington **z** 19803; ● 125
Penarth; RMC Place; NEW CASTLE; ***162** B-3; ★ **PHIL-**; mail Wilmington **z** 19803; ● 125
Penn Acres; RMC Place; NEW CASTLE; **162** D-8; ★ **PHIL-**; mail New Castle **z** 19720; ● 2,000
Pennrock; NEW CASTLE; see Penrock (RMC Place)
Pennyhill; RMC Place; NEW CASTLE; **162** C-9; ★ **PHIL-**; mail Wilmington **z** 19809; ● 600
Penrock (Pennrock); RMC Place; NEW CASTLE; ***162** C-3; ★ **PHIL-**; mail Wilmington **z** 19809; ● 200
Pepper; RMC Place; SUSSEX; ***162** L-3; elev. 38ft./12m.; mail Laurel **z** 19956
Pepperbox; RMC Place; SUSSEX; ***162** L-3; elev. 55ft./17m.; mail Laurel **z** 19956; rural
Perth; RMC Place; NEW CASTLE; ***162** C-3; ★ **PHIL-**; mail Wilmington **z** 19803; ● 120
Petersburg; RMC Place; KENT; ***162** H-2; elev. 57ft./17m.; ★ **DOVR**; mail Felton **z** 19943
Phillips Hill; RMC Place; SUSSEX; ***162** L-4; mail Millsboro **z** 19966; rural
Pickering Beach; RMC Place; KENT; ***162** G-3; mail Dover **z** 19901; summer pop. 100
Pike Creek; CDP-Census Area Only; NEW CASTLE; ***162** C-2; elev. 200ft./61m.; ★ **PHIL-**; mail Newark **z** 19711, Wilmington **z** 19808; Ⓟ 10,163; Ⓒ 19,751
Pinetown; RMC Place; SUSSEX; ***162** J-4; mail Lewes **z** 19958; ● 90
Pine Tree Corners; RMC Place; NEW CASTLE; ***162** E-2; mail Townsend **z** 19734
Piney Grove; RMC Place; SUSSEX; ***162** K-3; mail Georgetown **z** 19947; rural
Pleasant Hill; RMC Place; NEW CASTLE; ***162** C-1; ★ **PHIL-**; mail Newark **z** 19711
Pleasanton Acres; RMC Place; KENT; **162** E-9; ★ **DOVR**; mail Dover **z** 19901; ● 50
Pleasantville; RMC Place; NEW CASTLE; ***162** D-2; ★ **PHIL-**; mail New Castle **z** 19720; ● 700
Plymouth; RMC Place; KENT; ***162** H-2; ★ **DOVR**; mail Felton **z** 19943; ● 250
Porter; RMC Place; NEW CASTLE; ***162** D-2; ★ **PHIL-**; mail Bear **z** 19701
Port Mahon; RMC Place; KENT; ***162** G-3; mail Dover **z** 19901; rural
Port Penn; RMC Place; NEW CASTLE; **162** E-2; elev. 11ft./3m.; 🅿; ★ **PHIL-**; **z** 19731; ● 250
Portsville; RMC Place; SUSSEX; ***162** L-2; mail Laurel **z** 19956
Primehook Beach (Shorts Beach); RMC Place; SUSSEX; **162** J-4; mail Milford **z** 19963; summer pop. 150; ● 50

Q

Quaker Heights; SUSSEX; see Quakers Heights (RMC Place)
Quakers Heights (Quaker Heights); RMC Place; SUSSEX; ***162** J-5; mail Lewes **z** 19958; ● 90

R

Radnor Green; RMC Place; NEW CASTLE; ***162** B-3; ★ **PHIL-**; mail Claymont **z** 19703
Rambleton Acres; RMC Place; NEW CASTLE; **162** E-8; ★ **PHIL-**; mail New Castle **z** 19720; ● 1,500
Ramblewood; RMC Place; NEW CASTLE; ***162** B-3; ★ **PHIL-**; mail Wilmington **z** 19810; ● 700
Redden; RMC Place; SUSSEX; ***162** J-3; mail Georgetown **z** 19947; rural
Redden Crossroads; RMC Place; SUSSEX; ***162** J-3; elev. 47ft./14m.; mail Georgetown **z** 19947; rural
Red Lion; RMC Place; NEW CASTLE; ***162** D-2; ★ **PHIL-**; mail Bear **z** 19701
Reeves Crossing; RMC Place; KENT; ***162** I-2; ★ **DOVR**; mail Felton **z** 19943
Rehoboth Beach; Inc. Place; SUSSEX; **162** K-5; elev. 16ft./5m.; 🅿; **z** 19971; Ⓟ 1,234; Ⓒ 1,495
Reliance; RMC Place; SUSSEX; **162** K-2; mail Seaford **z** 19973; total pop., including Reliance, MD: 60; ● 30
Richardson Park; RMC Place; NEW CASTLE; **162** D-8; ★ **PHIL-**; mail Wilmington **z** 19805; ● 500
Rising Sun; RMC Place; KENT; **162** H-3; ★ **DOVR**; mail Camden Wyoming **z** 19934; ● 250
Rising Sun-Lebanon; CDP-Census Area Only; KENT; ***162** H-3; ★ **DOVR**; mail Dover **z** 19901; Ⓟ 2,177; Ⓒ 2,458; Ⓡ 2,459
Riverdale; RMC Place; SUSSEX; **162** L-5; mail Millsboro **z** 19966; summer pop. 750; ● 500
Riverview; CDP; KENT; ***162** H-3; elev. 40ft./12m.; ★ **DOVR**; mail Frederica **z** 19946; Ⓟ 1,138; Ⓒ 1,583
Riverview; RMC Place; SUSSEX; ***162** L-4; mail Millsboro **z** 19966; ● 75
Riverview Gardens; RMC Place; NEW CASTLE; ***162** B-3; ★ **PHIL-**; mail Claymont **z** 19703; ● 300
River Village; SUSSEX; see River Village Mobile Home Park (RMC Place)
River Village Mobile Home Park (River Village); RMC Place; SUSSEX; ***162** K-5; mail Millsboro **z** 19966; ● 250
Robscott Manor; RMC Place; NEW CASTLE; ***162** D-1; ★ **PHIL-**; mail Newark **z** 19713; pop. incl. with Newark (Inc. Place)
Rockland; RMC Place; NEW CASTLE; **162** B-8; elev. 150ft./46m.; 🅿; ★ **PHIL-**; **z** 19732; ● 200
Rodney Square; RMC Place; NEW CASTLE; ★ **PHIL-**; mail Wilmington **z** 19801, **z** 19899; pop. incl. with Wilmington (Inc. Place)
Rodney Village; CDP; KENT; **162** H-3; ★ **DOVR**; mail Dover **z** 19904; Ⓟ 1,745; Ⓒ 1,602; Ⓡ 1,606
Rodric Village; RMC Place; KENT; **162** H-8; ★ **DOVR**; mail Dover **z** 19901; ● 100
Rogers Haven; RMC Place; SUSSEX; ***162** L-5; mail Ocean View **z** 19970; ● 100
Rogers Manor; RMC Place; NEW CASTLE; ***162** C-2; ★ **PHIL-**; mail New Castle **z** 19720; pop. incl. with New Castle (Inc. Place)
Rolling Hills; RMC Place; NEW CASTLE; ***162** C-2; ★ **PHIL-**; mail Wilmington **z** 19804
Rolling Park; RMC Place; NEW CASTLE; ***162** C-3; ★ **PHIL-**; mail Claymont **z** 19703
Rosegate; RMC Place; NEW CASTLE; ***162** C-3; ★ **PHIL-**; mail New Castle **z** 19720; ● 400
Roselle; RMC Place; NEW CASTLE; ***162** C-2; ★ **PHIL-**; mail Wilmington **z** 19805; ● 400
Roseville Park; RMC Place; NEW CASTLE; ***162** C-2; ★ **PHIL-**; mail Newark **z** 19711; ● 300
Roxana; RMC Place; SUSSEX; **162** L-5; mail Frankford **z** 19945; ● 150
Rutherford; RMC Place; NEW CASTLE; ***162** C-2; ★ **PHIL-**; mail Newark **z** 19713; ● 800

S

Saint Georges; RMC Place; NEW CASTLE; **162** D-2; elev. 20ft./6m.; 🅿; ★ **PHIL-**; **z** 19733; ● 350
Sand Dunes Village; RMC Place; SUSSEX; ***162** J-5; mail Lewes **z** 19958; ● 90
Sandtown; RMC Place; KENT; ***162** H-2; elev. 62ft./19m.; ★ **DOVR**; mail Felton **z** 19943
Sandy Brae; RMC Place; SUSSEX; ***162** J-5; mail Lewes **z** 19958; ● 450
Scottfield; RMC Place; NEW CASTLE; ***162** D-1; ★ **PHIL-**; mail Newark **z** 19713; ● 800
Scotts Corner; RMC Place; SUSSEX; ***162** J-2; elev. 47ft./14m.; mail Bridgeville **z** 19933
Sea Air; RMC Place; SUSSEX; ***162** K-5; mail Rehoboth Beach **z** 19971; ● 200
Seabreeze; RMC Place; SUSSEX; ***162** K-5; mail Rehoboth Beach **z** 19971; summer pop. 300; ● 100
Sea Del Estates; RMC Place; SUSSEX; ***162** L-5; mail Bethany Beach **z** 19930; ● 10
Seaford; Inc. Place; SUSSEX; **162** K-2; elev. 29ft./9m.; 🅿 🅷; **z** 19973; Ⓟ 5,689; Ⓒ 6,699
Seaford Heights; RMC Place; SUSSEX; ***162** K-2; mail Seaford **z** 19973; pop. incl. with Seaford (Inc. Place)
Sedgley Farms; RMC Place; NEW CASTLE; **162** C-8; ★ **PHIL-**; mail Wilmington **z** 19807; ● 250
Seeneytown; RMC Place; KENT; ***162** G-2; ★ **DOVR**; mail Clayton **z** 19938; rural
Selbyville; Inc. Place; SUSSEX; **162** M-4; elev. 32ft./10m.; 🅿; **z** 19944, **z** 19975; Ⓟ 1,335; Ⓒ 1,645
Shady Lane; RMC Place; KENT; ***162** H-3; ★ **DOVR**; mail Dover **z** 19901; ● 250
Shaft Ox Corner; RMC Place; SUSSEX; ***162** L-4; elev. 44ft./13m.; mail Millsboro **z** 19966; rural
Sharpley; RMC Place; NEW CASTLE; **162** B-8; ★ **PHIL-**; mail Wilmington **z** 19803; ● 1,400
Shawnee Acres; RMC Place; SUSSEX; ***162** I-3; mail Milford **z** 19963; ● 450
Shell Bridge; RMC Place; SUSSEX; ***162** L-2; elev. 10ft./3m.; ★ **SLSB**; mail Laurel **z** 19956; rural
Shellburne; RMC Place; NEW CASTLE; ***162** C-3; ★ **PHIL-**; mail Wilmington **z** 19803; ● 100
Sherwood; RMC Place; KENT; ***162** G-3; ★ **DOVR**; mail Dover **z** 19904; pop. incl. with Dover (Inc. Place)
Sherwood Acres; RMC Place; SUSSEX; ***162** L-5; mail Frankford **z** 19945; ● 150
Sherwood Forest; RMC Place; NEW CASTLE; ***162** D-2; ★ **PHIL-**; mail Newark **z** 19713; ● 200
Sherwood Park; RMC Place; NEW CASTLE; **162** C-7; ★ **PHIL-**; mail Wilmington **z** 19808; ● 2,000
Shipley Heights; RMC Place; NEW CASTLE; ***162** C-3; ★ **PHIL-**; mail Wilmington **z** 19803; ● 250
Shortly; RMC Place; SUSSEX; ***162** K-3; mail Georgetown **z** 19947
Shorts Beach; SUSSEX; see Primehook Beach (RMC Place)
Silverbrook; RMC Place; NEW CASTLE; **162** C-8; ★ **PHIL-**; mail Wilmington **z** 19805; ● 700
Silverside Heights; RMC Place; NEW CASTLE; **162** B-9; ★ **PHIL-**; mail Wilmington **z** 19809; ● 375
Silview; RMC Place; NEW CASTLE; **162** D-8; ★ **PHIL-**; mail Wilmington **z** 19804; ● 1,500
Simonds Gardens; RMC Place; NEW CASTLE; ***162** C-3; ★ **PHIL-**; mail New Castle **z** 19720; ● 175
Slaughter Beach; Inc. Place; SUSSEX; **162** I-4; elev. 10ft./3m.; mail Milford **z** 19963; Ⓟ 114; summer pop. 600; Ⓒ 198
Smyrna; Inc. Place; KENT, NEW CASTLE; **162** F-2; elev. 36ft./11m.; 🅿; ★ **DOVR**; **z** 19977; Ⓟ 5,231; Ⓒ 5,679
Smyrna Landing; RMC Place; KENT; ***162** F-2; ★ **DOVR**; mail Smyrna **z** 19977
Snug Harbor; RMC Place; SUSSEX; ***162** K-2; mail Seaford **z** 19973; ● 50
South Bethany; Inc. Place; SUSSEX; **162** L-5; elev. 10ft./3m.; mail Bethany Beach **z** 19930; Ⓟ 148; Ⓒ 492
South Bowers; RMC Place; KENT; **162** H-3; mail Frederica **z** 19946; ● 50
Southwood; RMC Place; NEW CASTLE; ***162** C-2; ★ **PHIL-**; mail Hockessin **z** 19707; ● 300
Springfield Crossroads; RMC Place; SUSSEX; ***162** K-4; mail Georgetown **z** 19947; rural
Spruance City; RMC Place; KENT; ***162** F-2; ★ **DOVR**; mail Smyrna **z** 19977; ● 180
Stanton; RMC Place; NEW CASTLE; **162** D-7; 🅿; ★ **PHIL-**; **z** 19804; ● 2,000
Star Hill; RMC Place; KENT; ***162** H-3; elev. 40ft./12m.; ★ **DOVR**; mail Dover **z** 19901; ● 300
Staytonville; RMC Place; SUSSEX; **162** J-3; mail Harrington **z** 19952; ● 40
Stockdale; RMC Place; NEW CASTLE; ***162** C-3; ★ **PHIL-**; mail Claymont **z** 19703
Stockley; RMC Place; SUSSEX; ***162** K-4; mail Georgetown **z** 19947; rural
Stoneybrook Apartments; RMC Place; NEW CASTLE; ***162** B-3; ★ **PHIL-**; mail Claymont **z** 19703
Stratford; RMC Place; NEW CASTLE; **162** E-7; ★ **PHIL-**; mail New Castle **z** 19720; ● 1,100
Summit Bridge; RMC Place; NEW CASTLE; **162** E-1; ★ **PHIL-**; mail Middletown **z** 19709; ● 60
Surrey Park; RMC Place; NEW CASTLE; ***162** C-3; ★ **PHIL-**; mail Wilmington **z** 19803; ● 350
SUSSEX; **162** K-3; Ⓟ 113,229; Ⓒ 156,638; ◆ 192,302
Sussex Shores; RMC Place; SUSSEX; **162** L-5; mail Bethany Beach **z** 19930; summer pop. 75; ● 10
Swain Acres; RMC Place; SUSSEX; ***162** K-3; mail Georgetown **z** 19947; pop. incl. with Georgetown (Inc. Place)
Swann Keys; RMC Place; SUSSEX; ***162** L-5; mail Selbyville **z** 19975; ● 300
Swanwyck; RMC Place; NEW CASTLE; ***162** C-2; ★ **PHIL-**; mail New Castle **z** 19720; ● 1,200
Swanwyck Estates; RMC Place; NEW CASTLE; **162** D-8; ★ **PHIL-**; mail New Castle **z** 19720; ● 800
Swanwyck Gardens; RMC Place; NEW CASTLE; ***162** C-2; ★ **PHIL-**; mail New Castle **z** 19720
Sycamore; RMC Place; SUSSEX; **162** L-3; mail Laurel **z** 19956; ● 20
Sycamore Gardens; RMC Place; NEW CASTLE; ***162** C-2; ★ **PHIL-**; mail Newark **z** 19711; ● 350

T

Talleyville; RMC Place; NEW CASTLE; **162** B-3; 🅿; ★ **PHIL-**; **z** 19803; ● 800
Tarleton; RMC Place; NEW CASTLE; ***162** B-2; ★ **PHIL-**; mail Wilmington **z** 19810; ● 400
Tavistock; RMC Place; NEW CASTLE; ***162** B-2; ★ **PHIL-**; mail Wilmington **z** 19803; ● 900
Taylor Estates; RMC Place; KENT; **162** H-8; ★ **DOVR**; mail Dover **z** 19901; ● 300
Taylors Bridge; RMC Place; NEW CASTLE; ***162** E-2; mail Townsend **z** 19734; rural
The Cedars; RMC Place; NEW CASTLE; **162** C-7; ★ **PHIL-**; mail Wilmington **z** 19808; ● 350
The Island; RMC Place; SUSSEX; ***162** K-2; mail Seaford **z** 19973; ● 90
The Timbers; RMC Place; NEW CASTLE; ***162** B-3; ★ **PHIL-**; mail Wilmington **z** 19803
The Village of Drummond Hill; NEW CASTLE; see Village of Drummond Hill (RMC Place)
Thomas Landing; RMC Place; NEW CASTLE; ***162** E-2; elev. 20ft./6m.; ★ **PHIL-**; mail Townsend **z** 19734; rural
Thompsonville; RMC Place; KENT; ***162** I-3; elev. 10ft./3m.; mail Milford **z** 19963
Tidbury Manor; RMC Place; KENT; ***162** H-3; ★ **DOVR**; mail Dover **z** 19901; ● 125
Todd Estates; RMC Place; NEW CASTLE; ***162** D-2; ★ **PHIL-**; mail Newark **z** 19713; ● 900
Towne Point; RMC Place; KENT; ***162** G-3; ★ **DOVR**; mail Dover **z** 19901; pop. incl. with Dover (Inc. Place)
Townsend; Inc. Place; NEW CASTLE; **162** F-2; elev. 64ft./20m.; 🅿; **z** 19734; Ⓟ 322; Ⓒ 346
Tuxedo Park; RMC Place; NEW CASTLE; **162** D-7; ★ **PHIL-**; mail Wilmington **z** 19804; ● 1,300
Twin Eagle Farms; RMC Place; KENT; ***162** F-2; ★ **DOVR**; mail Clayton **z** 19938; ● 100
Tybrook; RMC Place; NEW CASTLE; ***162** C-2; ★ **PHIL-**; mail Wilmington **z** 19808; ● 650

V

Van Dyke Village; RMC Place; NEW CASTLE; ***162** D-2; ★ **PHIL-**; mail New Castle **z** 19720; pop. incl. with New Castle (Inc. Place)
Varlano; RMC Place; NEW CASTLE; ***162** D-2; ★ **PHIL-**; mail Newark **z** 19702; ● 750
Vernon; RMC Place; KENT; ***162** I-2; ★ **DOVR**; mail Harrington **z** 19952
Village of Drummond Hill (The Village of Drummond Hill); RMC Place; NEW CASTLE; ***162** C-2; ★ **PHIL-**; mail Newark **z** 19711
Village of Westover; RMC Place; KENT; pop. incl. with Dover (Inc. Place)
Villa Monterey; RMC Place; NEW CASTLE; ***162** C-3; ★ **PHIL-**; mail Wilmington **z** 19809; ● 200
Viola; Inc. Place; KENT; **162** H-2; elev. 60ft./18m.; 🅿; ★ **DOVR**; **z** 19979; Ⓟ 153; Ⓒ 156
Voshell Cove; RMC Place; KENT; ***162** G-2; ★ **DOVR**; mail Dover **z** 19901; ● 300

W

Ward; RMC Place; SUSSEX; ***162** L-3; elev. 55ft./17m.; mail Delmar **z** 19940
Warwick; RMC Place; SUSSEX; **162** K-4; mail Millsboro **z** 19966; ● 100
Warwick Park; RMC Place; SUSSEX; ***162** L-4; mail Millsboro **z** 19966; ● 160
Washington Heights; RMC Place; SUSSEX; ***162** K-5; mail Rehoboth Beach **z** 19971; ● 150
Webster Farm; NEW CASTLE; see Webster Farms (RMC Place)
Webster Farms (Webster Farm); RMC Place; NEW CASTLE; ***162** C-3; ★ **PHIL-**; mail Wilmington **z** 19803; ● 600
Wedgewood; RMC Place; NEW CASTLE; ***162** D-2; ★ **PHIL-**; mail New Castle **z** 19720; ● 1,500
Wellington Woods; RMC Place; NEW CASTLE; ***162** D-2; ★ **PHIL-**; mail Newark **z** 19702; ● 150
Welshire; RMC Place; NEW CASTLE; ***162** C-3; ★ **PHIL-**; mail Wilmington **z** 19803; ● 100
West Beach; RMC Place; SUSSEX; ***162** L-5; mail Dagsboro **z** 19939; ● 60
Westfield; RMC Place; NEW CASTLE; ***162** C-2; ★ **PHIL-**; mail Wilmington **z** 19804
West Haven; RMC Place; NEW CASTLE; ***162** C-2; ★ **PHIL-**; mail Wilmington **z** 19807
West Meadow; RMC Place; NEW CASTLE; ***162** C-1; ★ **PHIL-**; mail Newark **z** 19711; ● 100
Westover Hills; RMC Place; NEW CASTLE; **162** C-8; ★ **PHIL-**; mail Wilmington **z** 19807; ● 1,200
West Park; RMC Place; NEW CASTLE; ***162** C-2; ★ **PHIL-**; mail Wilmington **z** 19807
Westview; RMC Place; NEW CASTLE; ***162** C-2; ★ **PHIL-**; mail Wilmington **z** 19804
Westwood Manor; RMC Place; NEW CASTLE; ***162** C-3; ★ **PHIL-**; mail Wilmington **z** 19810; ● 450
Whaleys Corners; RMC Place; SUSSEX; ***162** K-3; elev. 50ft./15m.; mail Laurel **z** 19956; rural
Whaleys Crossroads; RMC Place; SUSSEX; ***162** L-3; elev. 46ft./14m.; mail Laurel **z** 19956
Whiteleysburg; RMC Place; KENT; ***162** I-1; ★ **DOVR**; mail Felton **z** 19943
White Oak Farms; RMC Place; KENT; ***162** G-3; ★ **DOVR**; mail Dover **z** 19901; pop. incl. with Dover (Inc. Place)
Whitesville; RMC Place; SUSSEX; **162** M-3; mail Delmar **z** 19940; ● 50
Williamsville; RMC Place; KENT; ***162** I-3; elev. 52ft./16m.; ★ **DOVR**; mail Houston **z** 19954
Williamsville; RMC Place; SUSSEX; **162** M-5; mail Selbyville **z** 19975; ● 75
Willow Grove; RMC Place; KENT; **162** H-2; ★ **DOVR**; mail Camden Wyoming **z** 19934; ● 75
Willow Run (Wilmington); RMC Place; NEW CASTLE; **162** C-8; ★ **PHIL-**; mail Wilmington **z** 19805; ● 500
Wilmington; NEW CASTLE; see Willow Run (RMC Place)
Wilmington; Inc. Place; ⊡ NEW CASTLE; **162** C-3; elev. 120ft./37m.; 🅿 🅷 🅲 2,415 ■; ★ **PHIL-**; **z** 19801-10, **z** 19850, **z** 19880, **z** 19884-86, **z** 19890-99; Ⓟ 71,529; Ⓒ 72,664; ◆ 73,345
Wilmington Manor; CDP; NEW CASTLE; **162** D-8; ★ **PHIL-**; mail New Castle **z** 19720; Ⓟ 8,568; Ⓒ 8,262
Wilmington Manor Gardens; RMC Place; NEW CASTLE; **162** E-8; ★ **PHIL-**; mail New Castle **z** 19720; ● 1,800
Wilmont; RMC Place; NEW CASTLE; ***162** B-3; ★ **PHIL-**; mail Wilmington **z** 19803
Windermer; RMC Place; NEW CASTLE; ***162** C-2; ★ **PHIL-**; mail Wilmington **z** 19804
Windsor Hills; RMC Place; NEW CASTLE; ***162** C-3; ★ **PHIL-**; mail Wilmington **z** 19803; ● 350
Windy Bush; RMC Place; NEW CASTLE; ***162** C-3; ★ **PHIL-**; mail Wilmington **z** 19810; ● 500
Windy Hills; RMC Place; NEW CASTLE; ***162** C-2; ★ **PHIL-**; mail Newark **z** 19711; ● 1,200
Winterthur; RMC Place; NEW CASTLE; **162** B-8; elev. 300ft./91m.; 🅿; ★ **PHIL-**; **z** 19735; ● 100
Woodbine; RMC Place; NEW CASTLE; ***162** B-3; ★ **PHIL-**; mail Wilmington **z** 19810; ● 250
Woodbrook; RMC Place; KENT; ***162** G-2; ★ **DOVR**; mail Dover **z** 19901
Woodbrook; RMC Place; NEW CASTLE; ***162** C-2; ★ **PHIL-**; mail Wilmington **z** 19803; ● 300
Woodbury; RMC Place; KENT; ***162** H-2; ★ **DOVR**; mail Felton **z** 19943; ● 200
Woodcrest; RMC Place; KENT; ***162** G-3; ★ **DOVR**; mail Dover **z** 19904; pop. incl. with Dover (Inc. Place)
Woodcrest; RMC Place; NEW CASTLE; ***162** C-2; ★ **PHIL-**; mail Wilmington **z** 19804; ● 1,300
Wooddale (Wooddale Quarry); RMC Place; NEW CASTLE; ***162** C-2; ★ **PHIL-**; mail Wilmington **z** 19807; rural
Wooddale Quarry; NEW CASTLE; see Wooddale (RMC Place)
Woodenhawk; RMC Place; SUSSEX; ***162** J-2; mail Greenwood **z** 19950
Woodland; RMC Place; NEW CASTLE; ***162** C-2; ★ **PHIL-**; mail Wilmington **z** 19805; ● 1,000
Woodland; RMC Place; SUSSEX; ***162** L-2; mail Seaford **z** 19973
Woodland Beach; RMC Place; KENT; **162** F-3; mail Smyrna **z** 19977; ● 150
Woodshade; RMC Place; NEW CASTLE; ***162** D-2; ★ **PHIL-**; mail Newark **z** 19702; ● 750
Woods Haven; RMC Place; KENT; ***162** I-3; ★ **DOVR**; mail Milford **z** 19963; ● 400
Woodside; Inc. Place; KENT; **162** H-2; elev. 61ft./19m.; 🅿; ★ **DOVR**; **z** 19980; Ⓟ 140; Ⓒ 184
Woodside East; CDP-Census Area Only; KENT; ***162** H-3; ★ **DOVR**; mail Woodside **z** 19980; Ⓟ 1,655; Ⓒ 2,174
Woods Manor; RMC Place; KENT; ***162** H-3; ★ **DOVR**; mail Dover **z** 19901; ● 400
Workmans Corners; RMC Place; SUSSEX; ***162** L-3; elev. 48ft./15m.; mail Georgetown **z** 19947; rural
Wyoming; Inc. Place; KENT; **162** H-2; elev. 42ft./13m.; 🅿; ★ **DOVR**; **z** 19934; Ⓟ 977; Ⓒ 1,141

Y

York Beach; RMC Place; SUSSEX; ***162** L-5; mail Bethany Beach **z** 19930; pop. incl. with South Bethany (Inc. Place)
Yorklyn; RMC Place; NEW CASTLE; **162** C-2; elev. 177ft./54m.; 🅿; ★ **PHIL-**; **z** 19736; ● 300

Entries in **UPPERCASE** are counties.
Entries in **bold** have populations of 2,500 or more.
Names in parentheses are alternate names.
Inc. Place — Incorporated Place
RMC Place — Rand McNally Designated Place
CDP — Census Designated Place
MCD — Minor Civil Division

⊡ County Seat
▲ Minor Civil Division
elev. Elevation
🅿 Post Office

🅷 Hospital
🅲 College
■ Principal Business Center
★ Ranally Metro Area (RMA) Abbreviation
z Zip Code(s)

Ⓟ Previous Census Population
Ⓡ Revised Census Population
Ⓐ Annexation Population
● Rand McNally Population Estimate
Ⓒ Final Census Population
Ⓢ Special Census Population
◆ Estimated Population

For additional definitions see Glossary, Volume 1, and Introduction, Volume 2.

DISTRICT OF COLUMBIA

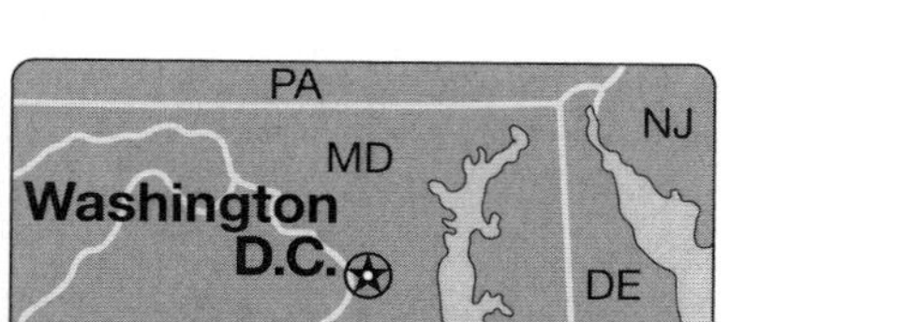

Statistics

Total area (2000) — 68 square miles
Land area (2000) — 61 square miles
Water area (2000) — 7 square miles
Established — March, 1791

Maps

State maps can be found on pages 142-254 in Vol. 1

Ranally Metro Areas (RMAs) and Abbreviations

Washington, DC-MD-VA — WASH

District Business Data

District	FIPS Code	District Seat	Land Area (Sq. Mi.)	Census Population			Wholesale Trade		Manufacturing, 1997			
				4/1/2000	4/1/1990	% Change 1990-2000	Sales, 1997 ($1,000)	% Change 1992-97	Establish-ments	Total Employees	Value Added ($1,000)	Ranally Mfg. Units
District of Columbia	001	Washington	61	572,059	606,900	-5.7	2,971,507	-24.2	146	2,021	163,118	86

(d) Data not available. Corresponding percentages or Ranally Manufacturing Units are estimates.
... Represents 0 or amount too minimal to be reported.

Administrative Divisions

The District of Columbia is treated as a separate entity in tabulations of county of state population. It is considered a municipal government in census statistics on government. The District of Columbia and the city of Washington have been considered co-extensive since 1897.

Index of Places

A

Anacostia; RMC Place; DISTRICT OF COLUMBIA; ***249** G-7; [P]; ★ **WASH**; z 20373 & mail Washington z 20019-20
Anacostia Junction; RMC Place; DISTRICT OF COLUMBIA; ★ **WASH**; pop. incl. with Washington (Inc. Place)

B

Barnaby Terrace; RMC Place; DISTRICT OF COLUMBIA; ***249** H-7; ★ **WASH**; mail Washington z 20032
Barnaby Woods; RMC Place; DISTRICT OF COLUMBIA; ***249** E-6; ★ **WASH**; mail Washington z 20015
Bellevue; RMC Place; DISTRICT OF COLUMBIA; ***249** H-6; ★ **WASH**; mail Washington z 20032
Benjamin Franklin; RMC Place; DISTRICT OF COLUMBIA; ***249** G-6; ★ **WASH**; mail Washington z 20004, z 20044
Benning; RMC Place; DISTRICT OF COLUMBIA; ***249** G-8; ★ **WASH**; mail Washington z 20019, z 20029
Benning Heights; RMC Place; DISTRICT OF COLUMBIA; ***249** G-8; ★ **WASH**; mail Washington z 20019
Blue Plains; RMC Place; DISTRICT OF COLUMBIA; ***249** H-6; ★ **WASH**; mail Washington z 20032
Brightwood; RMC Place; DISTRICT OF COLUMBIA; ***249** E-6; elev. 292ft./89m.; ★ **WASH**; mail Washington z 20011, z 20040
Brightwood Park; RMC Place; DISTRICT OF COLUMBIA; ***249** E-6; ★ **WASH**; mail Washington z 20011
Brookland; RMC Place; DISTRICT OF COLUMBIA; ***249** F-7; ★ **WASH**; mail Washington z 20017
Burleith; RMC Place; DISTRICT OF COLUMBIA; ***249** F-6; ★ **WASH**; mail Washington z 20007

C

Calvert; RMC Place; DISTRICT OF COLUMBIA; ***249** F-6; ★ **WASH**; mail Washington z 20007
Capitol View; RMC Place; DISTRICT OF COLUMBIA; ***249** G-8; ★ **WASH**
Chillum; RMC Place; DISTRICT OF COLUMBIA; ★ **WASH**; pop. incl. with Washington (Inc. Place)
Cleveland Park; RMC Place; DISTRICT OF COLUMBIA; ***249** F-6; ★ **WASH**; mail Washington z 20008
Colonial Village; RMC Place; DISTRICT OF COLUMBIA; ***249** D-6; ★ **WASH**; mail Washington z 20012
Columbia Heights; RMC Place; DISTRICT OF COLUMBIA; ***249** F-6; ★ **WASH**; mail Washington z 20009-10
Congress Heights; RMC Place; DISTRICT OF COLUMBIA; ***249** H-7; ★ **WASH**; mail Washington z 20032, z 20036
Congress Park; RMC Place; DISTRICT OF COLUMBIA; ***249** H-7; ★ **WASH**; mail Washington z 20032
Customs House; RMC Place; DISTRICT OF COLUMBIA; ***249** F-7; ★ **WASH**; mail Washington z 20018

D

Deanewood; RMC Place; DISTRICT OF COLUMBIA; ***249** F-8; ★ **WASH**; mail Washington z 20019
DISTRICT OF COLUMBIA; **249** F-6; Ⓟ 606,900; © 572,059; ◆ 601,816
Douglas Dwellings; RMC Place; DISTRICT OF COLUMBIA; ***249** H-7; ★ **WASH**; mail Washington z 20020

E

Eckington; RMC Place; DISTRICT OF COLUMBIA; ***249** F-7; ★ **WASH**; mail Washington z 20002

F

Fairfax Village; RMC Place; DISTRICT OF COLUMBIA; ***249** G-8; elev. 216ft./66m.; ★ **WASH**; mail Washington z 20020
Farragut; RMC Place; DISTRICT OF COLUMBIA; ***249** F-6; ★ **WASH**; mail Washington z 20033
Fort Davis; RMC Place; DISTRICT OF COLUMBIA; ***249** G-8; ★ **WASH**; mail Washington z 20020
Fort Lincoln New Town; RMC Place; DISTRICT OF COLUMBIA; ★ **WASH**; mail Washington z 20018
Foxhall Village; RMC Place; DISTRICT OF COLUMBIA; ***249** F-5; ★ **WASH**; mail Washington z 20007
Fredrick Douglas; RMC Place; DISTRICT OF COLUMBIA; ★ **WASH**; mail Washington z 20030; pop. incl. with Washington (Inc. Place)
Friendship; RMC Place; DISTRICT OF COLUMBIA; ***249** F-5; ★ **WASH**; mail Washington z 20007-08, z 20016, z 20088

G

Garfield Heights; RMC Place; DISTRICT OF COLUMBIA; ***249** G-7; ★ **WASH**; mail Washington z 20020
Georgetown; RMC Place; DISTRICT OF COLUMBIA; ***249** F-6; ★ **WASH**; mail Washington z 20007
Glover Park; RMC Place; DISTRICT OF COLUMBIA; ***249** F-5; ★ **WASH**; mail Washington z 20007
Good Hope; RMC Place; DISTRICT OF COLUMBIA; ***249** G-7; ★ **WASH**; mail Washington z 20020
Greenway; RMC Place; DISTRICT OF COLUMBIA; ***249** G-8; ★ **WASH**; mail Washington z 20019

H

Hawthorne; RMC Place; DISTRICT OF COLUMBIA; ***249** E-6; ★ **WASH**; mail Washington z 20015
Hillcrest; RMC Place; DISTRICT OF COLUMBIA; ***249** G-7; ★ **WASH**; mail Washington z 20020

I

Ivy City; RMC Place; DISTRICT OF COLUMBIA; ***249** F-7; ★ **WASH**; mail Washington z 20002

K

Kalorama; RMC Place; DISTRICT OF COLUMBIA; ***249** F-6; ★ **WASH**; mail Washington z 20009
Kendall Green; RMC Place; DISTRICT OF COLUMBIA; ***249** F-7; ★ **WASH**; mail Washington z 20002
Kenilworth; RMC Place; DISTRICT OF COLUMBIA; ***249** F-8; ★ **WASH**; mail Washington z 20019
Kent; RMC Place; DISTRICT OF COLUMBIA; ***249** F-5; ★ **WASH**; mail Washington z 20016
Knox Hill Dwellings; RMC Place; DISTRICT OF COLUMBIA; ***249** G-7; ★ **WASH**; mail Washington z 20020

L

Lamond; RMC Place; DISTRICT OF COLUMBIA; ***249** E-7; ★ **WASH**; mail Washington z 20011
Langdon; RMC Place; DISTRICT OF COLUMBIA; ***249** F-7; ★ **WASH**; mail Washington z 20018
Le Droit Park; RMC Place; DISTRICT OF COLUMBIA; ***249** F-6; ★ **WASH**; mail Washington z 20001

M

Manor Park; RMC Place; DISTRICT OF COLUMBIA; ***249** E-6; ★ **WASH**; mail Washington z 20011
Marshall Heights; RMC Place; DISTRICT OF COLUMBIA; ***249** G-8; ★ **WASH**; mail Washington z 20019
McLean Gardens; RMC Place; DISTRICT OF COLUMBIA; ***249** F-5; ★ **WASH**; mail Washington z 20016
McPherson; RMC Place; DISTRICT OF COLUMBIA; ★ **WASH**; mail Washington z 20038; pop. incl. with Washington (Inc. Place)
Mid City; RMC Place; DISTRICT OF COLUMBIA; ***249** F-6; ★ **WASH**; mail Washington z 20005
Mount Pleasant; RMC Place; DISTRICT OF COLUMBIA; ***249** F-6; ★ **WASH**; mail Washington z 20010

N

National Capitol; RMC Place; DISTRICT OF COLUMBIA; ★ **WASH**; mail Washington z 20013; pop. incl. with Washington (Inc. Place)
Naylor Gardens; RMC Place; DISTRICT OF COLUMBIA; ***249** G-7; ★ **WASH**; mail Washington z 20020
Northeast; RMC Place; DISTRICT OF COLUMBIA; ***249** F-7; ★ **WASH**; mail Washington z 20002
North Gate; RMC Place; DISTRICT OF COLUMBIA; ***249** E-6; ★ **WASH**; mail Washington z 20012
Northwest; RMC Place; DISTRICT OF COLUMBIA; ★ **WASH**; mail Washington z 20015; pop. incl. with Washington (Inc. Place)

P

Palisades; RMC Place; DISTRICT OF COLUMBIA; ★ **WASH**; mail Washington z 20016; pop. incl. with Washington (Inc. Place)
Park View; RMC Place; DISTRICT OF COLUMBIA; ***249** F-6; elev. 200ft./61m.; ★ **WASH**; mail Washington z 20010
Petworth; RMC Place; DISTRICT OF COLUMBIA; ***249** E-6; ★ **WASH**; mail Washington z 20011
Potomac Heights; RMC Place; DISTRICT OF COLUMBIA; ***249** F-5; ★ **WASH**; mail Washington z 20016

R

Randall; RMC Place; DISTRICT OF COLUMBIA; ***249** G-7; ★ **WASH**; mail Washington z 20020
River Terrace; RMC Place; DISTRICT OF COLUMBIA; ***249** G-7; ★ **WASH**; mail Washington z 20019

S

Shepherd; RMC Place; DISTRICT OF COLUMBIA; ★ **WASH**; pop. incl. with Washington (Inc. Place)
Southeast; RMC Place; DISTRICT OF COLUMBIA; ***249** G-7; ★ **WASH**; mail Washington z 20003
Southwest; RMC Place; DISTRICT OF COLUMBIA; ***249** G-7; ★ **WASH**; mail Washington z 20024
Spring Valley; RMC Place; DISTRICT OF COLUMBIA; ***249** F-5; ★ **WASH**; mail Washington z 20016

T

Temple Heights; RMC Place; DISTRICT OF COLUMBIA; ***249** F-6; ★ **WASH**; mail Washington z 20009
Tenleytown; RMC Place; DISTRICT OF COLUMBIA; ***249** E-5; ★ **WASH**; mail Washington z 20016
Terra Cotta; RMC Place; DISTRICT OF COLUMBIA; ***249** E-7; elev. 116ft./35m.; ★ **WASH**; mail Washington z 20011
The Palisades; RMC Place; DISTRICT OF COLUMBIA; ***249** F-5; elev. 153ft./47m.; ★ **WASH**; mail Washington z 20016
Trinidad; RMC Place; DISTRICT OF COLUMBIA; ***249** F-7; ★ **WASH**; mail Washington z 20002
T Street; RMC Place; DISTRICT OF COLUMBIA; ***249** F-6; ★ **WASH**; mail Washington z 20009, z 20056
Twentieth Street; RMC Place; DISTRICT OF COLUMBIA; ***249** F-6; ★ **WASH**; mail Washington z 20036-37
Twining; RMC Place; DISTRICT OF COLUMBIA; ***249** G-7; ★ **WASH**; mail Washington z 20020

U

Union Market Yard; RMC Place; DISTRICT OF COLUMBIA; ★ **WASH**; pop. incl. with Washington (Inc. Place)
Union Station; RMC Place; DISTRICT OF COLUMBIA; ★ **WASH**; mail Washington z 20002; pop. incl. with Washington (Inc. Place)

W

Washington; Inc. Place; **NATIONAL CAPITAL**; DISTRICT OF COLUMBIA; **249** E-6; elev. 50ft./15m.; [P] [H] [C] 112,101 ■; ★ **WASH**; z 20001-13, z 20015-20, z 20022-24, z 20026-27, z 20029-30, z 20032-33, z 20035-47, z 20049-53, z 20055-71, z 20073-78, z 20080-82, z 20088, z 20090-91, z 20097-98, z 20201-04, z 20206-08, z 20210-24, z 20226-30, z 20232-33, z 20235, z 20237-42, z 20244-45, z 20250-51, z 20254, z 20260-62, z 20265-66, z 20268, z 20270, z 20277, z 20289, z 20299, z 20301, z 20303, z 20306-07, z 20310, z 20314, z 20317-19, z 20330, z 20340, z 20350, z 20355, z 20370, z 20372-76, z 20380, z 20388-95, z 20398, z 20401-16, z 20418-29, z 20431, z 20433-37, z 20439-42, z 20444, z 20447, z 20451, z 20453, z 20456, z 20460, z 20463, z 20468-70, z 20472, z 20500-11, z 20515, z 20520-44, z 20546-49, z 20551-55, z 20557-60, z 20565-66, z 20570-73, z 20575-81, z 20585-86, z 20590-91, z 20593-94, z 20597, z 20599, z 56901, z 56915, z 56920, z 56933, z 56944, z 56972 & mail Dulles z 20101-04; Ⓟ 606,900; © 572,059; ◆ 601,816
Washington Highlands; RMC Place; DISTRICT OF COLUMBIA; ***249** H-7; ★ **WASH**; mail Washington z 20032
Washington Square; RMC Place; DISTRICT OF COLUMBIA; ***249** F-6; ★ **WASH**; mail Washington z 20035
Watergate; RMC Place; DISTRICT OF COLUMBIA; ***249** G-6; ★ **WASH**; mail Washington z 20037
Wesley Heights; RMC Place; DISTRICT OF COLUMBIA; ***249** F-5; ★ **WASH**; mail Washington z 20016
Woodley Park; RMC Place; DISTRICT OF COLUMBIA; ***249** F-6; ★ **WASH**; mail Washington z 20008
Woodridge; RMC Place; DISTRICT OF COLUMBIA; ***249** F-7; elev. 151ft./46m.; ★ **WASH**; mail Washington z 20018

Entries in **bold** have populations of 2,500 or more.
Names in parentheses are alternate names.
Inc. Place — Incorporated Place
RMC Place — Rand McNally Designated Place
CDP — Census Designated Place
MCD — Minor Civil Division

⊡ District Seat
▲ Minor Civil Division
elev. Elevation
[P] Post Office
[H] Hospital
[C] College
■ Principal Business Center
★ Ranally Metro Area (RMA) Abbreviation
z Zip Code(s)

Ⓟ Previous Census Population
Ⓡ Revised Census Population
Ⓐ Annexation Population
● Rand McNally Population Estimate
© Final Census Population
Ⓢ Special Census Population
◆ Estimated Population

For additional definitions see Glossary, Volume 1, and Introduction, Volume 2.

FLORIDA

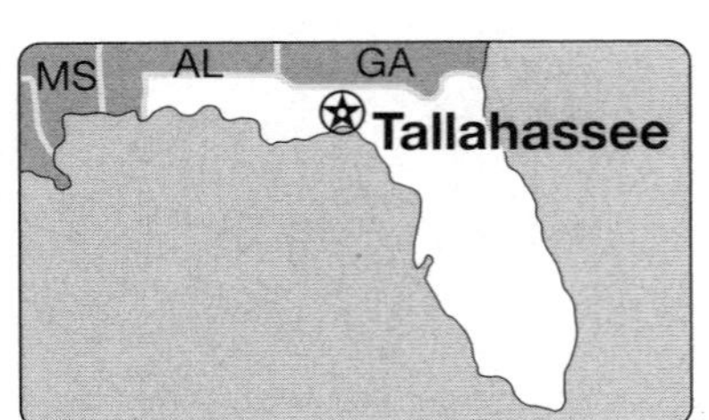

Statistics

Total area (2000) — 65,755 square miles
Land area (2000) — 53,927 square miles
Water area (2000) — 11,828 square miles
Capital — Tallahassee
Admitted as state — March, 1845

Maps

State maps can be found on pages 142-254 in Vol. 1

Ranally Metro Areas (RMAs) and Abbreviations

Daytona Beach, FL — D.BCH
DeLand, FL — DL
Fort Myers-Cape Coral, FL — FTMY-
Fort Pierce, FL — FTPI
Fort Walton Beach, FL — FTWL
Gainesville, FL — GAIN
Jacksonville, FL — JAX
Kissimmee, FL — KISS
Lakeland, FL — LKLD
Melbourne-Palm Bay, FL — MELB-
Miami-Fort Lauderdale, FL — MIA-
Naples, FL — NAP
Ocala, FL — OCA
Orlando, FL — ORL
Panama City, FL — PNCY
Pensacola, FL — PENS
Punta Gorda-Port Charlotte, FL — PUN-
St. Petersburg, FL — ST.PET
Sarasota-Bradenton, FL — SAR-B
Spring Hill, FL — SPR.H
Stuart, FL — STU
Tallahassee, FL — TALL
Tampa, FL — TAM
Titusville, FL — TITUS
Venice, FL — VEN
Vero Beach, FL — VERO
Winter Haven, FL — WNHV

Principal Places

Place Name	Place Type	County	Population
Jacksonville	Inc. Place	DUVAL	◆ 835,957
Miami	Inc. Place	MIAMI-DADE	◆ 377,241
Tampa	Inc. Place	HILLSBOROUGH	◆ 336,461
Saint Petersburg	Inc. Place	PINELLAS	◆ 242,845
Hialeah	Inc. Place	MIAMI-DADE	◆ 227,756
Orlando	Inc. Place	ORANGE	◆ 218,293
Tallahassee	Inc. Place	LEON	◆ 193,699
Pembroke Pines	Inc. Place	BROWARD	◆ 156,975
Cape Coral	Inc. Place	LEE	◆ 153,269
Port Saint Lucie	Inc. Place	ST. LUCIE	◆ 152,918
Fort Lauderdale	Inc. Place	BROWARD	◆ 150,181
Hollywood	Inc. Place	BROWARD	◆ 139,707
Gainesville	Inc. Place	ALACHUA	◆ 129,375
Coral Springs	Inc. Place	BROWARD	◆ 119,952
Clearwater	Inc. Place	PINELLAS	◆ 106,870
Pompano Beach	Inc. Place	BROWARD	◆ 97,647
Palm Bay	Inc. Place	BREVARD	◆ 97,481
Miami Gardens	Inc. Place	MIAMI-DADE	◆ 95,236
Brandon	CDP	HILLSBOROUGH	◆ 94,108
Spring Hill	CDP	HERNANDO	◆ 92,993
West Palm Beach	Inc. Place	PALM BEACH	◆ 90,487
Deltona	Inc. Place	VOLUSIA	◆ 89,926
Miramar	Inc. Place	BROWARD	◆ 89,134
Lakeland	Inc. Place	POLK	◆ 87,947
Town 'n' Country	CDP-Census Area Only	HILLSBOROUGH	◆ 87,619
Davie	Inc. Place	BROWARD	◆ 87,209
Miami Beach	Inc. Place	MIAMI-DADE	◆ 86,595
Sunrise	Inc. Place	BROWARD	◆ 85,663
Boca Raton	Inc. Place	PALM BEACH	◆ 81,528
Plantation	Inc. Place	BROWARD	◆ 79,826
Kendall	CDP	MIAMI-DADE	◆ 78,590
Melbourne	Inc. Place	BREVARD	◆ 75,051
Deerfield Beach	Inc. Place	BROWARD	◆ 71,580
Boynton Beach	Inc. Place	PALM BEACH	◆ 70,438
Palm Coast	Inc. Place	FLAGLER	◆ 67,535
Largo	Inc. Place	PINELLAS	◆ 66,522
Kissimmee	Inc. Place	OSCEOLA	◆ 65,983
Delray Beach	Inc. Place	PALM BEACH	◆ 65,577
Fountainbleau	CDP-Census Area Only	MIAMI-DADE	◆ 62,210
Carol City	CDP	MIAMI-DADE	◆ 62,100
Fort Myers	Inc. Place	LEE	◆ 61,001
Daytona Beach	Inc. Place	VOLUSIA	◆ 60,444
North Miami	Inc. Place	MIAMI-DADE	◆ 60,259
Kendale Lakes	CDP-Census Area Only	MIAMI-DADE	◆ 59,438
Lauderhill	Inc. Place	BROWARD	◆ 59,367
Palm Harbor	CDP	PINELLAS	◆ 58,013
Tamarac	Inc. Place	BROWARD	◆ 57,297
North Fort Myers	CDP	LEE	◆ 57,277
Tamiami	CDP-Census Area Only	MIAMI-DADE	◆ 57,234
Pensacola	Inc. Place	ESCAMBIA	◆ 56,523
Weston	Inc. Place	BROWARD	◆ 55,527
Ocala	Inc. Place	MARION	◆ 53,362
Margate	Inc. Place	BROWARD	◆ 52,773
Pine Hills	CDP	ORANGE	◆ 51,697
Sarasota	Inc. Place	SARASOTA	◆ 51,676
Port Orange	Inc. Place	VOLUSIA	◆ 50,611
Coconut Creek	Inc. Place	BROWARD	◆ 50,569
Bradenton	Inc. Place	MANATEE	◆ 49,688
The Hammocks	CDP-Census Area Only	MIAMI-DADE	◆ 49,490
Port Charlotte	CDP	CHARLOTTE	◆ 48,993
Jupiter	Inc. Place	PALM BEACH	◆ 48,794
Wellington	Inc. Place	PALM BEACH	◆ 48,586
Lehigh Acres	CDP	LEE	◆ 47,615
Sanford	Inc. Place	SEMINOLE	◆ 45,832
Pinellas Park	Inc. Place	PINELLAS	◆ 43,531
Altamonte Springs	Inc. Place	SEMINOLE	◆ 43,490
Bonita Springs	Inc. Place	LEE	◆ 42,912
Titusville	Inc. Place	BREVARD	◆ 41,604
Coral Gables	Inc. Place	MIAMI-DADE	◆ 41,317
Lakeside	CDP-Census Area Only	CLAY	◆ 41,277
North Lauderdale	Inc. Place	BROWARD	◆ 40,932
Merritt Island	CDP	BREVARD	◆ 40,838
North Miami Beach	Inc. Place	MIAMI-DADE	◆ 40,670
Greater Carrollwood	CDP-Census Area Only	HILLSBOROUGH	◆ 40,490
Fort Pierce	Inc. Place	ST. LUCIE	◆ 40,421
Kendall West	CDP-Census Area Only	MIAMI-DADE	◆ 39,739
Egypt Lake-Leto	CDP-Census Area Only	HILLSBOROUGH	◆ 39,606
Palm Beach Gardens	Inc. Place	PALM BEACH	◆ 39,571
Apopka	Inc. Place	ORANGE	◆ 39,041
Country Club	CDP-Census Area Only	MIAMI-DADE	◆ 37,928
Ormond Beach	Inc. Place	VOLUSIA	◆ 37,654
Lake Worth	Inc. Place	PALM BEACH	◆ 37,367
Winter Springs	Inc. Place	SEMINOLE	◆ 37,228
University	CDP-Census Area Only	HILLSBOROUGH	◆ 37,128
Panama City	Inc. Place	BAY	◆ 36,977
Hallandale Beach	Inc. Place	BROWARD	◆ 36,380
Yeehaw Junction	CDP	OSCEOLA	◆ 35,210
South Miami Heights	CDP	MIAMI-DADE	◆ 35,014
Oviedo	Inc. Place	SEMINOLE	◆ 34,817
Lake Magdalene	CDP-Census Area Only	HILLSBOROUGH	◆ 34,742
Plant City	Inc. Place	HILLSBOROUGH	◆ 34,118
Golden Glades	CDP-Census Area Only	MIAMI-DADE	◆ 34,081
North Port	Inc. Place	SARASOTA	◆ 34,048
Homestead	Inc. Place	MIAMI-DADE	◆ 33,961
West Little River	CDP-Census Area Only	MIAMI-DADE	◆ 33,942
Dunedin	Inc. Place	PINELLAS	◆ 33,884
Riviera Beach	Inc. Place	PALM BEACH	◆ 33,086
Ocoee	Inc. Place	ORANGE	◆ 33,061
Winter Haven	Inc. Place	POLK	◆ 32,890
Oakland Park	Inc. Place	BROWARD	◆ 32,154
Lauderdale Lakes	Inc. Place	BROWARD	◆ 32,129
Westchester	CDP	MIAMI-DADE	◆ 31,625
Saint Cloud	Inc. Place	OSCEOLA	◆ 31,424
Greenacres City	Inc. Place	PALM BEACH	◆ 31,336
Holiday	CDP	PASCO	◆ 30,934
Ferry Pass	CDP	ESCAMBIA	◆ 30,283
Bayonet Point	CDP-Census Area Only	PASCO	◆ 30,211
Land O' Lakes	CDP	PASCO	◆ 29,621
Richmond West	CDP-Census Area Only	MIAMI-DADE	◆ 29,337
East Lake	CDP-Census Area Only	PINELLAS	◆ 28,773
Aventura	Inc. Place	MIAMI-DADE	◆ 28,557
Cooper City	Inc. Place	BROWARD	◆ 27,851
University Park	CDP-Census Area Only	MIAMI-DADE	◆ 27,725
Oak Ridge	CDP-Census Area Only	ORANGE	◆ 27,671
Winter Park	Inc. Place	ORANGE	◆ 27,494
Dania Beach	Inc. Place	BROWARD	◆ 27,048
De Land	Inc. Place	VOLUSIA	◆ 27,038
Wekiva Springs	CDP-Census Area Only	SEMINOLE	◆ 26,270
South Bradenton	CDP-Census Area Only	MANATEE	◆ 26,023
Cutler Bay	Inc. Place	MIAMI-DADE	◆ 25,889
Cutler Ridge	CDP	MIAMI-DADE	◆ 25,889
Coral Terrace	CDP-Census Area Only	MIAMI-DADE	◆ 25,473
Royal Palm Beach	Inc. Place	PALM BEACH	◆ 25,108
Brent	CDP	ESCAMBIA	◆ 24,797
Greater Northdale	CDP-Census Area Only	HILLSBOROUGH	◆ 24,721
The Crossings	CDP-Census Area Only	MIAMI-DADE	◆ 24,615
West Pensacola	CDP	ESCAMBIA	◆ 24,449
Citrus Park	CDP	HILLSBOROUGH	◆ 24,444
Vero Beach South	CDP-Census Area Only	INDIAN RIVER	◆ 24,346
Boca Del Mar	CDP-Census Area Only	PALM BEACH	◆ 24,108
Rockledge	Inc. Place	BREVARD	◆ 24,061
Norland	CDP	MIAMI-DADE	◆ 24,024
Bellview	CDP	ESCAMBIA	◆ 23,778
Wright	CDP	OKALOOSA	◆ 23,366
Golden Gate	CDP	COLLIER	◆ 23,338
Temple Terrace	Inc. Place	HILLSBOROUGH	◆ 23,263
Leisure City	CDP	MIAMI-DADE	◆ 23,138
Casselberry	Inc. Place	SEMINOLE	◆ 23,099
New Smyrna Beach	Inc. Place	VOLUSIA	◆ 22,792
Miami Lakes	CDP-Census Area Only	MIAMI-DADE	© 22,676
Jacksonville Beach	Inc. Place	DUVAL	◆ 22,536
Doral	Inc. Place	MIAMI-DADE	◆ 22,461
Palmetto Bay	Inc. Place	MIAMI-DADE	◆ 22,440
Palm City	CDP	MARTIN	◆ 21,972
Key West	Inc. Place	MONROE	◆ 21,921
Miami Lakes	Inc. Place	MIAMI-DADE	◆ 21,327
West and East Lealman	CDP-Census Area Only	PINELLAS	◆ 21,301
Winter Garden	Inc. Place	ORANGE	◆ 21,248
Tarpon Springs	Inc. Place	PINELLAS	◆ 21,101
Sebastian	Inc. Place	INDIAN RIVER	◆ 20,600
Doral	CDP-Census Area Only	MIAMI-DADE	© 20,438
Edgewater	Inc. Place	VOLUSIA	◆ 20,363
Palm Valley	CDP	ST. JOHNS	© 19,860
Bloomingdale	CDP	HILLSBOROUGH	© 19,839
Immokalee	CDP	COLLIER	© 19,763
Fort Walton Beach	Inc. Place	OKALOOSA	◆ 19,429
Hialeah Gardens	Inc. Place	MIAMI-DADE	© 19,297
Pinecrest	Inc. Place	MIAMI-DADE	© 19,055
Leesburg	Inc. Place	LAKE	◆ 18,993
Naples	Inc. Place	COLLIER	◆ 18,960
Ensley	CDP	ESCAMBIA	© 18,752
New Port Richey	Inc. Place	PASCO	◆ 18,696
Lake Worth Corridor	CDP-Census Area Only	PALM BEACH	© 18,663
Venice	Inc. Place	SARASOTA	◆ 18,321
Jasmine Estates	CDP-Census Area Only	PASCO	© 18,213
Palm River-Clair Mel	CDP-Census Area Only	HILLSBOROUGH	© 17,589
Ives Estates	CDP	MIAMI-DADE	© 17,586
Cutler	CDP	MIAMI-DADE	© 17,390
Bayshore Gardens	CDP	MANATEE	© 17,350
Myrtle Grove	CDP	ESCAMBIA	© 17,211
Safety Harbor	Inc. Place	PINELLAS	© 17,203
Sunset	CDP-Census Area Only	MIAMI-DADE	© 17,150
Lutz	CDP	HILLSBOROUGH	© 17,081
Vero Beach	Inc. Place	INDIAN RIVER	◆ 16,750
Ojus	CDP	MIAMI-DADE	© 16,642
Sandalfoot Cove	CDP-Census Area Only	PALM BEACH	© 16,582
Bellair-Meadowbrook Terrace	CDP-Census Area Only	CLAY	© 16,539
Pinewood	CDP-Census Area Only	MIAMI-DADE	© 16,523
Greater Sun Center	CDP-Census Area Only	HILLSBOROUGH	© 16,321
Parkland	Inc. Place	BROWARD	◆ 16,320
San Carlos Park	CDP	LEE	© 16,317
Glenvar Heights	CDP	MIAMI-DADE	© 16,243
Englewood	CDP	SARASOTA	© 16,196
Stuart	Inc. Place	MARTIN	◆ 16,089
Fruit Cove	CDP	ST. JOHNS	© 16,077
Sarasota Springs	CDP-Census Area Only	SARASOTA	© 15,875
Punta Gorda	Inc. Place	CHARLOTTE	◆ 15,798
DeBary	Inc. Place	VOLUSIA	© 15,559
Bartow	Inc. Place	POLK	© 15,340
Sunny Isles Beach	Inc. Place	MIAMI-DADE	© 15,315
Florida Ridge	CDP-Census Area Only	INDIAN RIVER	© 15,217
Warrington	CDP	ESCAMBIA	© 15,207
Eustis	Inc. Place	LAKE	© 15,106
Cocoa	Inc. Place	BREVARD	◆ 14,988
Opa-locka	Inc. Place	MIAMI-DADE	© 14,951
Belle Glade	Inc. Place	PALM BEACH	© 14,906
Marco	Inc. Place	COLLIER	© 14,879
Crestview	Inc. Place	OKALOOSA	© 14,766
Keystone	CDP	HILLSBOROUGH	© 14,627
Gladeview	CDP-Census Area Only	MIAMI-DADE	© 14,468
Scott Lake	CDP-Census Area Only	MIAMI-DADE	© 14,401
Conway	CDP	ORANGE	© 14,394
Brownsville	CDP-Census Area Only	MIAMI-DADE	© 14,393
Callaway	Inc. Place	BAY	© 14,233
Sweetwater	Inc. Place	MIAMI-DADE	© 14,226
Buenaventura Lakes	RMC Place	OSCEOLA	● 14,000
Fairview Shores	CDP	ORANGE	© 13,898
Longwood	Inc. Place	SEMINOLE	© 13,745
Miami Springs	Inc. Place	MIAMI-DADE	© 13,712
West Park	Inc. Place	BROWARD	● 13,700
Palmetto Estates	CDP-Census Area Only	MIAMI-DADE	© 13,675
Poinciana	CDP-Census Area Only	OSCEOLA	© 13,647
South Venice	CDP	SARASOTA	© 13,539
Olympia Heights	CDP	MIAMI-DADE	© 13,452
North Naples	RMC Place	COLLIER	© 13,422
Atlantic Beach	Inc. Place	DUVAL	© 13,368
South Daytona	Inc. Place	VOLUSIA	© 13,177
Haines City	Inc. Place	POLK	© 13,174
Elfers	CDP	PASCO	© 13,161
Lockhart	CDP	ORANGE	© 12,944
Goldenrod	CDP	ORANGE	© 12,871
Hudson	CDP	PASCO	© 12,765
Fruitville	CDP	SARASOTA	© 12,741
Wilton Manors	Inc. Place	BROWARD	© 12,697
Forest City	CDP	SEMINOLE	© 12,612
Palmetto	Inc. Place	MANATEE	© 12,571
Lakeland Highlands	CDP-Census Area Only	POLK	© 12,557
Gulfport	Inc. Place	PINELLAS	© 12,527
Lake City	Inc. Place	COLUMBIA	◆ 12,490
Cocoa Beach	Inc. Place	BREVARD	© 12,482
Homosassa Springs	CDP	CITRUS	© 12,458
Lynn Haven	Inc. Place	BAY	© 12,451
Kings Point	CDP-Census Area Only	PALM BEACH	© 12,207
Holly Hill	Inc. Place	VOLUSIA	© 12,119
Port Saint John	CDP-Census Area Only	BREVARD	© 12,112
Cypress Lake	CDP-Census Area Only	LEE	© 12,072
North Palm Beach	Inc. Place	PALM BEACH	© 12,064
Riverview	CDP	HILLSBOROUGH	® 12,040
Maitland	Inc. Place	ORANGE	© 12,019
Citrus Ridge	CDP	LAKE	© 12,015
Westwood Lakes	CDP	MIAMI-DADE	© 12,005
Oldsmar	Inc. Place	PINELLAS	© 11,910
Key Largo	CDP	MONROE	© 11,886
Lady Lake	Inc. Place	LAKE	© 11,828
Iona	CDP	LEE	© 11,756
Palm Springs	Inc. Place	PALM BEACH	© 11,699
Niceville	Inc. Place	OKALOOSA	© 11,684
Gulf Gate Estates	CDP-Census Area Only	SARASOTA	© 11,647
Lake Mary	Inc. Place	SEMINOLE	© 11,458
Hobe Sound	CDP	MARTIN	© 11,376
Gonzalez	CDP	ESCAMBIA	© 11,365
Villas	CDP-Census Area Only	LEE	© 11,346
Hamptons at Boca Raton	CDP-Census Area Only	PALM BEACH	© 11,306
Meadow Woods	CDP-Census Area Only	ORANGE	© 11,286
Saint Augustine	Inc. Place	ST. JOHNS	◆ 11,131
Destin	Inc. Place	OKALOOSA	© 11,119
Westchase	CDP	HILLSBOROUGH	© 11,116
Jensen Beach	CDP	MARTIN	© 11,100
Azalea Park	CDP	ORANGE	© 11,073
Auburndale	Inc. Place	POLK	© 11,032
Seminole	Inc. Place	PINELLAS	© 10,890
Upper Grand Lagoon	CDP-Census Area Only	BAY	© 10,889
Zephyrhills	Inc. Place	PASCO	© 10,833
Lighthouse Point	Inc. Place	BROWARD	© 10,767
South Miami	Inc. Place	MIAMI-DADE	© 10,741
Country Walk	CDP-Census Area Only	MIAMI-DADE	© 10,653
Hammocks	RMC Place	MIAMI-DADE	● 10,650
Fernandina Beach	Inc. Place	NASSAU	© 10,549
Key Biscayne	Inc. Place	MIAMI-DADE	© 10,507
Lakewood Park	CDP	ST. LUCIE	© 10,458
Miami Shores	Inc. Place	MIAMI-DADE	© 10,380
Middleburg	CDP	CLAY	© 10,338
Palm Beach	Inc. Place	PALM BEACH	◆ 10,336
Marathon	Inc. Place	MONROE	© 10,255
Lake Wales	Inc. Place	POLK	© 10,194
Union Park	CDP	ORANGE	© 10,191
Palatka	Inc. Place	PUTNAM	◆ 10,170
Port Salerno	CDP	MARTIN	© 10,141
Princeton	CDP	MIAMI-DADE	© 10,090
Saint Pete Beach	Inc. Place	PINELLAS	© 9,929
New Port Richey East	CDP-Census Area Only	PASCO	© 9,916
West Melbourne	Inc. Place	BREVARD	© 9,824
Tavares	Inc. Place	LAKE	© 9,700
Westview	CDP-Census Area Only	MIAMI-DADE	© 9,692
Sebring	Inc. Place	HIGHLANDS	© 9,667
North Andrews Gardens	CDP-Census Area Only	BROWARD	© 9,656
Satellite Beach	Inc. Place	BREVARD	© 9,577
Doctor Phillips	CDP-Census Area Only	ORANGE	© 9,548
Estero	CDP	LEE	© 9,503
Micco	CDP	BREVARD	© 9,498
Mount Dora	Inc. Place	LAKE	© 9,418
Lantana	Inc. Place	PALM BEACH	® 9,404
Hunters Creek	CDP-Census Area Only	ORANGE	© 9,369
Clermont	Inc. Place	LAKE	® 9,338
Mims	CDP	BREVARD	© 9,147
Lake Lucerne	CDP	MIAMI-DADE	© 9,132
Orange Park	Inc. Place	CLAY	© 9,081
Lake Park	Inc. Place	PALM BEACH	◆ 9,059
Lakes by the Bay	CDP-Census Area Only	MIAMI-DADE	© 9,055
Winston	CDP	POLK	© 9,024
Sun City Center	RMC Place	HILLSBOROUGH	● 9,000
South Patrick Shores	CDP-Census Area Only	BREVARD	© 8,913
Cypress Gardens	CDP	POLK	© 8,844
Mango	CDP	HILLSBOROUGH	© 8,842
South Highpoint	CDP-Census Area Only	PINELLAS	© 8,839
Cape Canaveral	Inc. Place	BREVARD	© 8,829
Springfield	Inc. Place	BAY	© 8,810
Pine Castle	CDP	ORANGE	© 8,803
Gibsonton	CDP	HILLSBOROUGH	© 8,752
Bee Ridge	CDP	SARASOTA	© 8,744
West Perrine	CDP-Census Area Only	MIAMI-DADE	© 8,600
Avon Park	Inc. Place	HIGHLANDS	© 8,542
Del Rio	RMC Place	HILLSBOROUGH	● 8,500
Andover	CDP-Census Area Only	MIAMI-DADE	© 8,489
Richmond Heights	CDP	MIAMI-DADE	© 8,479
Ormond-By-The-Sea	CDP	VOLUSIA	© 8,430
Laurel	CDP	SARASOTA	© 8,393
Yulee	CDP	NASSAU	© 8,392
The Villages	CDP	SUMTER	© 8,333
Ruskin	CDP	HILLSBOROUGH	© 8,321
Fern Park	CDP	SEMINOLE	© 8,318
Beverly Hills	CDP	CITRUS	© 8,317
Hernando	CDP	CITRUS	© 8,253
Seminole Park	RMC Place	PINELLAS	● 8,200
Tropical Gulf Acres	RMC Place	CHARLOTTE	● 8,200
Indian Harbour Beach	Inc. Place	BREVARD	© 8,152
Westgate-Belvedere Homes	CDP-Census Area Only	PALM BEACH	© 8,134
Eglin AFB	CDP-Census Area Only	OKALOOSA	© 8,082
Florida City	Inc. Place	MIAMI-DADE	© 7,843
Shady Hills	CDP-Census Area Only	PASCO	© 7,798
Collier Manor-Cresthaven	CDP-Census Area Only	BROWARD	© 7,741
West Vero Corridor	CDP-Census Area Only	INDIAN RIVER	© 7,695
Panama City Beach	Inc. Place	BAY	© 7,671
Century Village	CDP-Census Area Only	PALM BEACH	© 7,616
Longboat Key	Inc. Place	MANATEE	© 7,603
Cheval	CDP-Census Area Only	HILLSBOROUGH	© 7,602
Gifford	CDP	INDIAN RIVER	© 7,599
Clair-Mel City	RMC Place	HILLSBOROUGH	● 7,500
Venice Gardens	CDP	SARASOTA	© 7,466
Southgate	CDP-Census Area Only	SARASOTA	© 7,455
Goulds	CDP	MIAMI-DADE	© 7,453
Treasure Island	Inc. Place	PINELLAS	© 7,450
Apollo Beach	CDP-Census Area Only	HILLSBOROUGH	© 7,444
Pace	CDP	SANTA ROSA	© 7,393
Fort Pierce North	CDP-Census Area Only	ST. LUCIE	© 7,386
Neptune Beach	Inc. Place	DUVAL	© 7,270
Brooksville	Inc. Place	HERNANDO	© 7,264
Memphis	CDP	MANATEE	© 7,264
Beacon Square	CDP	PASCO	© 7,263
Siesta Key	CDP	SARASOTA	© 7,150
McGregor	CDP-Census Area Only	LEE	© 7,136
Melrose Park	CDP	BROWARD	© 7,114
Lake Lorraine	CDP-Census Area Only	OKALOOSA	© 7,106
Southwest Ranches	Inc. Place	BROWARD	● 7,100
East Perrine	CDP-Census Area Only	MIAMI-DADE	© 7,079
Lake Butter	CDP-Census Area Only	ORANGE	© 7,062
Milton	Inc. Place	SANTA ROSA	© 7,045
Quincy	Inc. Place	GADSDEN	© 6,982
Three Lakes	CDP-Census Area Only	MIAMI-DADE	© 6,955
Inwood	CDP	POLK	© 6,925
Perry	Inc. Place	TAYLOR	© 6,847
Islamorada	Inc. Place	MONROE	© 6,846
Broadview Park	CDP	BROWARD	© 6,798
Inverness	Inc. Place	CITRUS	© 6,789
Naples Park	CDP	COLLIER	© 6,741
North Sarasota	CDP-Census Area Only	SARASOTA	© 6,738
Williamsburg	CDP-Census Area Only	ORANGE	© 6,736
North Bay Village	Inc. Place	MIAMI-DADE	© 6,733
Golden Lakes	CDP-Census Area Only	PALM BEACH	© 6,694
Silver Springs Shores	CDP	MARION	© 6,690
Medulla	CDP	POLK	© 6,637
Arcadia	Inc. Place	DESOTO	© 6,604
Orange City	Inc. Place	VOLUSIA	© 6,604
Sweetwater Creek	RMC Place	HILLSBOROUGH	● 6,600
Rotonda	CDP	CHARLOTTE	© 6,574
Fort Myers Beach	Inc. Place	LEE	© 6,561
Valrico	CDP	HILLSBOROUGH	® 6,556
Pompano Beach Highlands	CDP	BROWARD	© 6,505
Bellair	RMC Place	CLAY	● 6,500
Live Oak	Inc. Place	SUWANNEE	© 6,480
Clewiston	Inc. Place	HENDRY	© 6,460
Sugarmill Woods	CDP-Census Area Only	CITRUS	© 6,409

Entries in **UPPERCASE** are counties.
Entries in **bold** have populations of 2,500 or more.
Names in parentheses are alternate names.
Inc. Place — Incorporated Place
RMC Place — Rand McNally Designated Place
CDP — Census Designated Place
MCD — Minor Civil Division

⊡ County Seat
▲ Minor Civil Division
elev. Elevation
▣ Post Office
Hospital
College
■ Principal Business Center
★ Ranally Metro Area (RMA) Abbreviation
z Zip Code(s)
Ⓟ Previous Census Population
® Revised Census Population
Ⓐ Annexation Population
● Rand McNally Population Estimate
© Final Census Population
Ⓢ Special Census Population
◆ Estimated Population

For additional definitions see Glossary, Volume 1, and Introduction, Volume 2.

Place Name	Place Type	County	Population
Valparaiso	Inc. Place	OKALOOSA	© 6,408
Marianna	Inc. Place	JACKSON	© 6,230
Opa-Locka North	CDP-Census Area Only	MIAMI-DADE	© 6,224
Dade City	Inc. Place	PASCO	© 6,188
Alachua	Inc. Place	ALACHUA	© 6,098
Thonotosassa	CDP	HILLSBOROUGH	© 6,091
Sanibel	Inc. Place	LEE	© 6,064
Southeast Arcadia	CDP-Census Area Only	DESOTO	© 6,064
Orlovista	CDP	ORANGE	© 6,047
Pahokee	Inc. Place	PALM BEACH	© 5,985
Cocoa West	CDP-Census Area Only	BREVARD	© 5,921
Boyette	CDP	HILLSBOROUGH	Ⓡ 5,890
West Miami	Inc. Place	MIAMI-DADE	© 5,863
Timber Pines	CDP-Census Area Only	HERNANDO	© 5,840
South Apopka	CDP	ORANGE	© 5,800
Fort Myers Shores	CDP	LEE	© 5,793
Indian River Estates	CDP-Census Area Only	ST. LUCIE	© 5,793
Inverness Highlands South	CDP-Census Area Only	CITRUS	© 5,781
South Pasadena	Inc. Place	PINELLAS	© 5,778
East Lake-Orient Park	CDP-Census Area Only	HILLSBOROUGH	© 5,703
Fort Meade	Inc. Place	POLK	© 5,691
Wesley Chapel	CDP	PASCO	© 5,691
Pelican Bay	CDP-Census Area Only	COLLIER	© 5,686
Fort Pierce South	CDP-Census Area Only	ST. LUCIE	© 5,672
Gulf Breeze	Inc. Place	SANTA ROSA	© 5,665
South Gate Ridge	CDP-Census Area Only	SARASOTA	© 5,655
Sky Lake	CDP	ORANGE	© 5,651
Jan Phyl Village	CDP	POLK	© 5,633
Fort Myers Villas	RMC Place	LEE	● 5,600
Ocean City	CDP	OKALOOSA	© 5,594
Starke	Inc. Place	BRADFORD	© 5,593
Indiantown	CDP	MARTIN	© 5,588
Belle Isle	Inc. Place	ORANGE	© 5,531
West Samoset	CDP-Census Area Only	MANATEE	© 5,507
Pine Ridge	CDP-Census Area Only	CITRUS	© 5,490
Seffner	CDP	HILLSBOROUGH	© 5,467
Palm Springs North	CDP	MIAMI-DADE	© 5,460
Combee Settlement	CDP-Census Area Only	POLK	© 5,436
Minneola	Inc. Place	LAKE	© 5,435
Pembroke Park	Inc. Place	BROWARD	Ⓡ 5,384
Green Cove Springs	Inc. Place	CLAY	© 5,378
Okeechobee	Inc. Place	OKEECHOBEE	© 5,376
Cedar Grove	Inc. Place	BAY	© 5,367
Crystal Lake	CDP-Census Area Only	POLK	© 5,341
Broadview-Pompano Park	CDP-Census Area Only	BROWARD	© 5,314
South Sarasota	CDP-Census Area Only	SARASOTA	© 5,314
Fussels Corner	CDP-Census Area Only	POLK	© 5,313
Vamo	CDP	SARASOTA	© 5,285
Tequesta	Inc. Place	PALM BEACH	© 5,273
Zephyrhills West	CDP-Census Area Only	PASCO	© 5,242
Pine Island Ridge	CDP-Census Area Only	BROWARD	© 5,199
Naples Manor	CDP	COLLIER	© 5,186
Bay Hill	CDP-Census Area Only	ORANGE	© 5,177
Port Saint Lucie-River Park	CDP-Census Area Only	ST. LUCIE	© 5,175
Lecanto	CDP	CITRUS	© 5,161
Bay Harbor Islands	Inc. Place	MIAMI-DADE	© 5,146
Whisper Walk	CDP-Census Area Only	PALM BEACH	© 5,135
Indian Rocks Beach	Inc. Place	PINELLAS	Ⓡ 5,127
De Funiak Springs	Inc. Place	WALTON	© 5,089
Saint Augustine South	CDP-Census Area Only	ST. JOHNS	© 5,035
Big Pine Key	CDP	MONROE	© 5,032
Ridge Wood Heights	CDP-Census Area Only	SARASOTA	© 5,028
Meadowbrook Terrace	RMC Place	CLAY	● 5,000
Palm River	RMC Place	HILLSBOROUGH	● 5,000

County Business Data

County	FIPS Code	County Seat	Land Area (Sq. Mi.)	Census Population			Wholesale Trade		Manufacturing, 2002			
				4/1/2000	4/1/1990	% Change 1990-2000	Sales, 2002 ($1,000)	% Change 1997-2002	Establish-ments	Total Employees	Value Added ($1,000)	Ranally Mfg. Units
Alachua	001	Gainesville	874	217,955	181,596	20.0	(d)	(d)	154	3,873	393,735	208
Baker	003	Macclenny	585	22,259	18,486	20.4	(d)	(d)	...	(d)	(d)	...
Bay	005	Panama City	764	148,217	126,994	16.7	478,815	13.4	133	3,671	404,555	214
Bradford	007	Starke	293	26,088	22,515	15.9	29,818	-4.1	...	(d)	(d)	...
Brevard	009	Titusville	1,018	476,230	398,978	19.4	2,412,569	77.1	459	18,347	2,580,956	1,366
Broward	011	Fort Lauderdale	1,205	1,623,018	1,255,488	29.3	35,028,568	34.1	1,836	32,179	3,751,169	1,985
Calhoun	013	Blountstown	567	13,017	11,011	18.2	(d)	(d)	...	(d)	(d)	...
Charlotte	015	Punta Gorda	694	141,627	110,975	27.6	(d)	(d)	86	638	64,113	34
Citrus	017	Inverness	584	118,085	93,515	26.3	138,239	52.9	62	546	26,709	14
Clay	019	Green Cove Springs	601	140,814	105,986	32.9	237,703	7.8	71	(d)	(d)	...
Collier	021	Naples	2,025	251,377	152,099	65.3	1,040,455	27.9	252	2,733	235,764	125
Columbia	023	Lake City	797	56,513	42,613	32.6	(d)	(d)	39	836	60,758	32
DeSoto	027	Arcadia	637	32,209	23,865	35.0	(d)	(d)	...	(d)	(d)	...
Dixie	029	Cross City	704	13,827	10,585	30.6	(d)	(d)	...	(d)	(d)	...
Duval	031	Jacksonville	774	778,879	672,971	15.7	18,867,449	13.7	690	27,340	3,975,300	2,103
Escambia	033	Pensacola	662	294,410	262,798	12.0	2,013,186	24.6	223	5,927	812,864	430
Flagler	035	Bunnell	485	49,832	28,701	73.6	63,288	-33.1	50	1,628	165,543	88
Franklin	037	Apalachicola	544	11,057	8,967	23.3	(d)	(d)	...	(d)	(d)	...
Gadsden	039	Quincy	516	45,087	41,105	9.7	244,379	(d)	33	1,352	77,692	41
Gilchrist	041	Trenton	349	14,437	9,667	49.3	(d)	(d)	...	(d)	(d)	...
Glades	043	Moore Haven	774	10,576	7,591	39.3	(d)	(d)	...	(d)	(d)	...
Gulf	045	Port Saint Joe	555	13,332	11,504	15.9	(d)	(d)	...	(d)	(d)	...
Hamilton	047	Jasper	515	13,327	10,930	21.9	(d)	(d)	3	(d)	(d)	...
Hardee	049	Wauchula	637	26,938	19,499	38.2	158,529	71.5	...	(d)	(d)	...
Hendry	051	La Belle	1,153	36,210	25,773	40.5	(d)	(d)	15	(d)	(d)	...
Hernando	053	Brooksville	478	130,802	101,115	29.4	(d)	(d)	75	885	118,485	63
Highlands	055	Sebring	1,028	87,366	68,432	27.7	(d)	(d)	49	996	96,027	51
Hillsborough	057	Tampa	1,051	998,948	834,054	19.8	24,551,768	3.7	930	29,054	3,157,296	1,670
Holmes	059	Bonifay	482	18,564	15,778	17.7	(d)	(d)	...	(d)	(d)	...
Indian River	061	Vero Beach	503	112,947	90,208	25.2	(d)	(d)	100	2,408	184,361	98
Jackson	063	Marianna	916	46,755	41,375	13.0	(d)	(d)	18	620	70,419	37
Jefferson	065	Monticello	598	12,902	11,296	14.2	(d)	(d)	...	(d)	(d)	...
Lafayette	067	Mayo	543	7,022	5,578	25.9	(d)	(d)	...	(d)	(d)	...
Lake	069	Tavares	953	210,528	152,104	38.4	(d)	(d)	165	3,847	333,511	176
Lee	071	Fort Myers	804	440,888	335,113	31.6	2,009,534	38.6	403	6,726	582,985	308
Leon	073	Tallahassee	667	239,452	192,493	24.4	893,786	(d)	103	1,833	149,246	79
Levy	075	Bronson	1,118	34,450	25,923	32.9	43,257	14.7	...	(d)	(d)	...
Liberty	077	Bristol	836	7,021	5,569	26.1	(d)	(d)	...	(d)	(d)	...
Madison	079	Madison	692	18,733	16,569	13.1	23,425	-61.5	10	(d)	(d)	...
Manatee	081	Bradenton	741	264,002	211,707	24.7	1,290,926	18.7	268	9,640	1,009,947	534
Marion	083	Ocala	1,579	258,916	194,833	32.9	1,392,032	39.3	245	9,065	724,731	383
Martin	085	Stuart	556	126,731	100,900	25.6	584,752	38.0	152	2,586	214,640	114
Miami-Dade	086	Miami	1,946	2,253,362	1,937,094	16.3	39,021,392	(d)	2,608	50,316	5,021,323	2,657
Monroe	087	Key West	997	79,589	78,024	2.0	185,125	-14.9	...	(d)	(d)	...
Nassau	089	Fernandina Beach	652	57,663	43,941	31.2	(d)	(d)	36	1,314	300,417	159
Okaloosa	091	Crestview	936	170,498	143,776	18.6	397,090	59.9	125	2,338	203,117	107
Okeechobee	093	Okeechobee	774	35,910	29,627	21.2	111,989	(d)	...	(d)	(d)	...
Orange	095	Orlando	907	896,344	677,491	32.3	29,640,652	23.0	827	29,196	4,072,426	2,155
Osceola	097	Kissimmee	1,322	172,493	107,728	60.1	(d)	(d)	83	1,565	124,227	66
Palm Beach	099	West Palm Beach	1,974	1,131,184	863,518	31.0	14,804,170	28.2	1,078	18,234	1,718,538	909
Pasco	101	Dade City	745	344,765	281,131	22.6	(d)	(d)	208	3,047	229,564	121
Pinellas	103	Clearwater	280	921,482	851,659	8.2	17,745,138	53.5	1,240	39,396	3,923,790	2,076
Polk	105	Bartow	1,874	483,924	405,382	19.4	6,542,016	56.7	452	16,088	2,229,138	1,179
Putnam	107	Palatka	722	70,423	65,070	8.2	69,106	(d)	38	2,309	363,832	192
St. Johns	109	Saint Augustine	609	123,135	83,829	46.9	893,844	108.9	92	1,841	172,392	91
St. Lucie	111	Fort Pierce	572	192,695	150,171	28.3	747,068	28.5	146	2,384	322,990	171
Santa Rosa	113	Milton	1,017	117,743	81,608	44.3	171,246	66.2	62	987	108,545	57
Sarasota	115	Sarasota	572	325,957	277,776	17.3	1,432,109	38.3	386	7,803	631,906	334
Seminole	117	Sanford	308	365,196	287,529	27.0	4,761,803	29.8	431	11,768	1,316,175	696
Sumter	119	Bushnell	546	53,345	31,577	68.9	(d)	(d)	25	821	62,949	33
Suwannee	121	Live Oak	688	34,844	26,780	30.1	121,621	(d)	21	1,616	32,970	17
Taylor	123	Perry	1,042	19,256	17,111	12.5	(d)	(d)	24	1,604	227,781	121
Union	125	Lake Butler	240	13,442	10,252	31.1	(d)	(d)	...	(d)	(d)	...
Volusia	127	De Land	1,103	443,343	370,712	19.6	2,036,909	25.0	383	8,609	687,362	364
Wakulla	129	Crawfordville	607	22,863	14,202	61.0	(d)	(d)	...	(d)	(d)	...
Walton	131	De Funiak Springs	1,058	40,601	27,760	46.3	139,978	42.5	31	700	71,348	38
Washington	133	Chipley	580	20,973	16,919	24.0	(d)	(d)	9	(d)	(d)	...
The State			**53,927**	**15,982,378**	**12,937,926**	**23.5**	**219,490,896**	**17.3**	**15,202**	**377,137**	**41,912,600**	**22,175**

(d) Data not available. Corresponding percentages or Ranally Manufacturing Units are estimates.
... Represents 0 or amount too minimal to be reported.

Index of Places and Counties

Entries in **UPPERCASE** are counties.
Entries in **bold** have populations of 2,500 or more.
Names in parentheses are alternate names.

Inc. Place	Incorporated Place
RMC Place	Rand McNally Designated Place
CDP	Census Designated Place
MCD	Minor Civil Division
⊡	County Seat
▲	Minor Civil Division
elev.	Elevation
[P]	Post Office
[H]	Hospital
[C]	College
■	Principal Business Center
★	Ranally Metro Area (RMA) Abbreviation
z	Zip Code(s)
Ⓟ	Previous Census Population
Ⓡ	Revised Census Population
Ⓐ	Annexation Population
●	Rand McNally Population Estimate
©	Final Census Population
Ⓢ	Special Census Population
◆	Estimated Population

For additional definitions see Glossary, Volume 1, and Introduction, Volume 2.

Beachwood; RMC Place; DUVAL; ***164** C-10; ★ **JAX**; mail Jacksonville z 32246; pop. incl. with Jacksonville (Inc. Place)
Beacon Beach; RMC Place; BAY; ***165** S-6; ★ **PNCY**; mail Panama City z 32403; ● 350
Beacon Groves; RMC Place; PINELLAS; ***164** J-6; elev. 15ft./5m.; ★ **ST.PET**; mail Palm Harbor z 34683
Beacon Hill; RMC Place; GULF; **165** T-7; mail Port Saint Joe z 32456; ● 230
Beacon Hills; RMC Place; DUVAL; ***164** C-9; elev. 30ft./9m.; ★ **JAX**; mail Jacksonville z 32225; pop. incl. with Jacksonville (Inc. Place)
Beacon Lakes; RMC Place; PASCO; ***164** I-6; ★ **ST.PET**; mail Holiday z 34691; ● 2,400
Beacon Square; CDP; PASCO; ***164** I-6; ★ **ST.PET**; mail Holiday z 34691; Ⓟ 6,265; Ⓒ 7,263
Bealsville; RMC Place; HILLSBOROUGH; ***164** J-8; ★ **TAM**; mail Plant City z 33567; ● 490
Bean City; RMC Place; PALM BEACH; ***165** N-12; elev. 22ft./7m.; mail Clewiston z 33440; ● 185
Bear Creek; RMC Place; BAY; ***165** S-6; ★ **PNCY**; mail Panama City z 32401, Youngstown z 32466; ● 400
Bear Lake; RMC Place; SEMINOLE; ***164** H-10; ★ **ORL**; mail Apopka z 32703; ● 1,700
Beauclere Gardens; RMC Place; DUVAL; ***164** C-9; ★ **JAX**; mail Jacksonville z 32257; pop. incl. with Jacksonville (Inc. Place)
Beaver Creek; RMC Place; OKALOOSA; ***165** Q-3; mail Baker z 32531; rural
Becker; RMC Place; NASSAU; ***164** B-9; mail Yulee z 32097
Beckhamtown; RMC Place; ALACHUA; ***164** E-8; elev. 145ft./44m.; mail Hawthorne z 32640; rural
Beeghly Heights; RMC Place; DUVAL; ***164** B-9; ★ **JAX**; mail Jacksonville z 32218; pop. incl. with Jacksonville (Inc. Place)
Bee Ridge; CDP; SARASOTA; **165** L-7; ★ **SAR-B**; mail Sarasota z 34233; Ⓟ 6,406; Ⓒ 8,744
Belair; RMC Place; LEON; ***164** C-2; mail Tallahassee z 32310-11; ● 400
Bel-Air; RMC Place; SEMINOLE; ***164** G-10; ★ **ORL**; mail Sanford z 32771; pop. incl. with Sanford (Inc. Place)
Bell; Inc. Place; GILCHRIST; **164** E-6; elev. 70ft./21m.; 🅿; z 32619; Ⓟ 267; Ⓒ 349
Bellair; RMC Place; CLAY; ***164** C-9; elev. 65ft./20m.; ★ **JAX**; mail Orange Park z 32073; ● 6,500
Bellair-Meadowbrook Terrace; CDP-Census Area Only; CLAY; ***164** C-9; ★ **JAX**; mail Orange Park z 32073; Ⓟ 15,606; Ⓒ 16,539
Belleair; Inc. Place; PINELLAS; **163** C-1; 🅿; ★ **ST.PET**; z 33756; Ⓟ 3,968; Ⓒ 4,067
Belleair Beach; Inc. Place; PINELLAS; **163** C-1; elev. 6ft./2m.; 🅿; ★ **ST.PET**; z 33785-86; Ⓟ 2,070; Ⓒ 1,751; Ⓡ 1,632
Belleair Bluffs; Inc. Place; PINELLAS; **163** C-1; elev. 65ft./20m.; 🅿; ★ **ST.PET**; z 33770; Ⓟ 2,128; Ⓒ 2,243
Belleair Shore; PINELLAS; see Belleair Shores (Inc. Place)
Belleair Shores (Belleair Shore); Inc. Place; PINELLAS; **163** C-1; elev. 20ft./6m.; 🅿; ★ **ST.PET**; z 33786; Ⓟ 60; Ⓒ 0; Ⓡ 75
Belle Glade (Belleglade-Chosen); Inc. Place; PALM BEACH; **165** N-12; elev. 20ft./6m.; 🅿 🅷; z 33430; Ⓟ 16,177; Ⓒ 14,906
Belle Glade Camp; CDP-Census Area Only; PALM BEACH; ***165** N-12; mail Belle Glade z 33430; Ⓟ 1,616; Ⓒ 1,141
Belleglade-Chosen; PALM BEACH; see Belle Glade (Inc. Place)
Belle Isle; Inc. Place; ORANGE; **165** O-4; elev. 97ft./30m.; 🅿; ★ **ORL**; z 32809, z 32812; Ⓟ 5,272; Ⓒ 5,531
Belle Meade; RMC Place; COLLIER; ***165** P-9; elev. 4ft./1m.; mail Naples z 34113-14; ● 260
Belleview; Inc. Place; MARION; **164** G-8; elev. 82ft./25m.; 🅿; ★ **OCA**; z 34420-21; Ⓟ 2,666; Ⓒ 3,478
Belleview Heights; RMC Place; MARION; ***164** G-8; elev. 69ft./21m.; ★ **OCA**; mail Belleview z 34420; ● 300
Bellview; CDP; ESCAMBIA; **162** L-8; 🅿; ★ **PENS**; z 32526 & mail Pensacola z 32506; Ⓟ 19,386; Ⓒ 21,201; ◆ 23,778
Bellville; RMC Place; HAMILTON; ***164** B-5; mail Pinetta z 32350; ● 100
Bellwood; RMC Place; BREVARD; ***164** H-12; ★ **TITUS**; mail Titusville z 32780; ● 500
Belmore; RMC Place; CLAY; ***164** D-9; mail Keystone Heights z 32656; rural
Belvedere Homes; RMC Place; PALM BEACH; **163** B-10; ★ **MIA-**; mail West Palm Beach z 33409; ● 4,000
Benbow; RMC Place; GLADES; ***165** M-11; mail Clewiston z 33440; ● 75
Bennett; RMC Place; BAY; ***165** S-6; mail Youngstown z 32466
Benson Junction; RMC Place; VOLUSIA; pop. incl. with DeBary (Inc. Place)
Ben White Raceway; RMC Place; ORANGE; ★ **ORL**; mail Orlando z 32810; pop. incl. with Orlando (Inc. Place)
Beresford; RMC Place; VOLUSIA; ***164** G-10; ★ **DL**; mail DeLand z 32720; ◐ 260
Berkeley; RMC Place; HERNANDO; ***164** H-7; mail Spring Hill z 34606-07; ◐ 100
Berry; RMC Place; POLK; ***164** I-9; elev. 118ft./36m.; mail Polk City z 33868; rural
Berrydale; RMC Place; SANTA ROSA; **165** Q-3; elev. 241ft./73m.; mail Jay z 32565; ● 200
Bertha; RMC Place; SEMINOLE; ***164** H-10; elev. 70ft./21m.; ★ **ORL**; mail Winter Park z 32792; ● 370
Bethany; RMC Place; MANATEE; ***165** K-8; mail Myakka City z 34251; rural
Bethel; RMC Place; WAKULLA; ***164** C-2; mail Crawfordville z 32327; ● 130
Bethlehem; RMC Place; HOLMES; ***165** Q-6; elev. 148ft./45m.; mail Bonifay z 32425; rural
Bethune Beach; RMC Place; VOLUSIA; ***164** G-11; ★ **D.BCH**; mail New Smyrna Beach z 32169; ● 500
Betton Hills; RMC Place; LEON; ***164** B-2; ★ **TALL**; mail Tallahassee z 32308, z 32312; pop. incl. with Tallahassee (Inc. Place)
Beulah; RMC Place; ESCAMBIA; ***165** R-2; ★ **PENS**; mail Pensacola z 32526; ● 400
Beulah; RMC Place; ORANGE; **165** N-2; ★ **ORL**; mail Winter Garden z 34787; ● 200
Beverley Terrace; RMC Place; SARASOTA; ***165** L-7; ★ **SAR-B**; mail Sarasota z 34234; ● 1,400
Beverly Beach; Inc. Place; FLAGLER; **164** E-11; elev. 5ft./2m.; mail Flagler Beach z 32136; Ⓟ 312; Ⓒ 547
Beverly Hills; CDP; CITRUS; **164** G-7; 🅿; z 34464-65; Ⓟ 6,163; Ⓒ 8,317
Beverly Hills; RMC Place; DUVAL; ***164** B-9; ★ **JAX**; mail Jacksonville z 32208; pop. incl. with Jacksonville (Inc. Place)
Bevilles Corner; RMC Place; SUMTER; ***164** H-8; elev. 89ft./27m.; mail Bushnell z 33513; rural
Bib Town; RMC Place; POLK; ★ **LKLD**; pop. incl. with Lakeland (Inc. Place)
Big Bayou; RMC Place; PINELLAS; ***165** K-7; ★ **ST.PET**; mail Saint Petersburg z 33705; pop. incl. with Saint Petersburg (Inc. Place)
Big Coppitt Key; CDP-Census Area Only; MONROE; **165** T-9; mail Key West z 33040; Ⓟ 2,388; Ⓒ 2,595
Big Cypress Reservation; Indian Reservation; HENDRY, BROWARD; mail Clewiston z 33440; Ⓟ 387; Ⓒ 142
Big Pine Key; CDP; MONROE; **165** T-10; 🅿; z 33043; Ⓟ 4,206; Ⓒ 5,032
Big Scrub; RMC Place; MARION; ***164** G-9; mail Ocklawaha z 32179; ● 300
Biltmore; RMC Place; DUVAL; ***164** C-9; ★ **JAX**; mail Jacksonville z 32254; pop. incl. with Jacksonville (Inc. Place)
Biltmore Beach; RMC Place; BAY; ***165** S-6; ★ **PNCY**; mail Panama City z 32408; ● 600
Bimini; RMC Place; FLAGLER; ***164** E-10; rural
Bird Key; RMC Place; SARASOTA; ***165** L-7; ★ **SAR-B**; mail Sarasota z 34236; pop. incl. with Sarasota (Inc. Place)
Biscayne Gardens; RMC Place; MIAMI-DADE; **163** K-8; ★ **MIA-**; mail Miami z 33168-69; ● 1,150
Biscayne One; RMC Place; MIAMI-DADE; ***165** Q-13; ★ **MIA-**; mail Miami z 33111, z 33131; pop. incl. with Miami (Inc. Place)
Biscayne Park; Inc. Place; MIAMI-DADE; **163** K-9; elev. 10ft./3m.; 🅿; ★ **MIA-**; z 33161 & mail Miami z 33181, z 33261; Ⓟ 3,068; Ⓒ 3,269
Bithlo; CDP; ORANGE; **164** H-11; elev. 68ft./21m.; ★ **ORL**; mail Orlando z 32807; Ⓟ 4,834; Ⓒ 4,626
Black Diamond; CDP-Census Area Only; CITRUS; ***164** G-7; Ⓒ 694
Blackman (Elm Mission); RMC Place; OKALOOSA; ***165** Q-4; mail Baker z 32531
Black Point; RMC Place; FLAGLER; ***164** E-10; rural
Bland; RMC Place; ALACHUA; ***164** D-7; mail Alachua z 32615; ● 250
Blanton; RMC Place; PASCO; ***164** I-8; elev. 97ft./30m.; mail Dade City z 33523; ● 640
Blitchton; RMC Place; MARION; ***164** F-7; mail Ocala z 34482; rural
Blitchville; RMC Place; GILCHRIST; ***164** E-6; mail Trenton z 32693; ● 160
Blocker; RMC Place; LEON; ***164** B-2; mail Tallahassee z 32312; ● 300
Bloomingdale; CDP; HILLSBOROUGH; **163** C-5; ★ **TAM**; mail Brandon z 33511, Valrico z 33594; Ⓟ 13,912; Ⓒ 19,839
Blountstown; Inc. Place; ⊡ CALHOUN; **165** S-7; elev. 69ft./21m.; 🅿 🅷; z 32424; Ⓟ 2,404; Ⓒ 2,444
Bloxham; RMC Place; LEON; ***164** C-1; mail Tallahassee z 32310; ● 200
Blue Gulf Beach; RMC Place; WALTON; ***165** S-5; mail Santa Rosa Beach z 32459; ● 120
Blue Lake; RMC Place; VOLUSIA; ***164** G-10; ★ **DL**; mail DeLand z 32720; ● 350
Blue Lakes Ridge; RMC Place; LAKE; ***164** G-10; mail Paisley z 32767; ● 200
Blue Mountain Beach; RMC Place; WALTON; ***165** S-5; mail Santa Rosa Beach z 32459; ● 80
Blue Springs; RMC Place; LAKE; mail Yalaha z 34797
Bluff Springs; RMC Place; ESCAMBIA; **165** Q-2; mail Century z 32535; ● 220
Boardman; RMC Place; MARION; ***164** E-8; ★ **OCA**; mail Evinston z 32633, Mc Intosh z 32664, Micanopy z 32667; ● 255
Boca Del Mar; CDP-Census Area Only; PALM BEACH; ***165** O-13; ★ **MIA-**; mail Boca Raton z 33433; Ⓟ 17,754; Ⓒ 21,832; ◆ 24,108
Boca Grande; RMC Place; LEE; **165** N-8; elev. 7ft./2m.; 🅿; z 33921; ● 700
Boca Pointe; CDP-Census Area Only; PALM BEACH; **163** F-9; ★ **MIA-**; mail Boca Raton z 33433; Ⓟ 2,174; Ⓒ 3,302
Boca Raton; Inc. Place; PALM BEACH; **165** O-14; elev. 16ft./5m.; 🅿 🅷 🅲 29,420 ■; ★ **MIA-**; z 33427-29, z 33431-34, z 33464, z 33481, z 33486-88, z 33496-99; Ⓟ 61,492; Ⓒ 74,764; ◆ 81,528
Boca West; RMC Place; PALM BEACH; **163** F-9; ★ **MIA-**; mail Boca Raton z 33434; Ⓟ 2,847; ● 2,100
Bogia; RMC Place; ESCAMBIA; ***165** Q-2; mail Mc David z 32568; rural
Bohemia; RMC Place; ESCAMBIA; ***165** R-3; mail Pensacola z 32504; pop. incl. with Pensacola (Inc. Place)
Bokeelia; CDP; LEE; **165** N-8; elev. 3ft./1m.; 🅿; z 33922; Ⓒ 1,997
Bonaventure; RMC Place; BREVARD; ***164** I-12; mail Rockledge z 32955; ● 380
Bonaventure; RMC Place; BROWARD; ***165** P-13; ★ **MIA-**; mail Fort Lauderdale z 33326; pop. incl. with Weston (Inc. Place)
Bonifay; Inc. Place; ⊡ HOLMES; **165** R-6; elev. 160ft./49m.; 🅿 🅷; z 32425; Ⓟ 2,612; Ⓒ 4,078; Ⓡ 2,665
Bonita Beach; RMC Place; LEE; **165** O-9; ★ **NAP**; mail Bonita Springs z 34134; pop. incl. with Bonita Springs (Inc. Place)
Bonita Shores; RMC Place; LEE, COLLIER; **165** O-9; mail Bonita Springs z 34134; pop. incl. with Bonita Springs (Inc. Place)
Bonita Springs; Inc. Place; LEE; **165** O-9; elev. 10ft./3m.; 🅿; ★ **NAP**; z 34133-36; Ⓒ 32,797; ◆ 42,912
Bonnie Lock; RMC Place; BROWARD; ***165** O-14; ★ **MIA-**; mail Pompano Beach z 33064; ● 2,000
Bonnie Lock-Woodsetter North; CDP-Census Area Only; BROWARD; ***165** O-14; ★ **MIA-**; Ⓒ 4,275
Bon Terra; RMC Place; FLAGLER; ***164** E-10; rural
Bookertown; RMC Place; SEMINOLE; ***164** G-10; ★ **ORL**; mail Sanford z 32771; ● 235
Bostwick; RMC Place; PUTNAM; **164** D-9; elev. 36ft./11m.; 🅿; z 32007; ● 300
Boulevard; RMC Place; HILLSBOROUGH; ★ **TAM**; pop. incl. with Tampa (Inc. Place)
Boulevard Gardens; CDP-Census Area Only; BROWARD; ***165** O-13; ★ **MIA-**; Ⓒ 1,415
Boulogne; RMC Place; NASSAU; **164** A-8; mail Hilliard z 32046; ● 260
Bowden; RMC Place; DUVAL; ***164** C-9; ★ **JAX**; mail Jacksonville z 32216; pop. incl. with Jacksonville (Inc. Place)
Bowling Green; Inc. Place; HARDEE; **165** K-9; elev. 95ft./29m.; 🅿; z 33834; Ⓟ 1,836; Ⓒ 2,892
Boyd; RMC Place; TAYLOR; ***164** C-4; mail Perry z 32347; ● 50
Boyette; CDP; HILLSBOROUGH; ***164** J-8; ★ **TAM**; mail Lithia z 33547; Ⓒ 5,895; Ⓡ 5,890
Boynton Beach; Inc. Place; PALM BEACH; **165** N-14; elev. 16ft./5m.; 🅿 🅷; ★ **MIA-**; z 33424-26, z 33435-37, z 33472-74; Ⓟ 46,194; Ⓒ 60,389; ◆ 70,438
Boys Ranch; RMC Place; SUWANNEE; ***164** B-6; 🅿; z 32064 & mail Live Oak z 32060; ● 100
Braden Castle; RMC Place; MANATEE; ***165** K-7; ★ **SAR-B**; mail Bradenton z 34208; pop. incl. with Bradenton (Inc. Place)
Bradenton; Inc. Place; ⊡ MANATEE; **165** K-7; elev. 23ft./7m.; 🅿 🅷 ■; ★ **SAR-B**; z 34201-12, z 34280-82; Ⓟ 43,779; Ⓒ 49,504; ◆ 49,688
Bradenton Beach; Inc. Place; MANATEE; **165** L-6; elev. 5ft./2m.; 🅿; ★ **SAR-B**; z 34217-18; Ⓟ 1,657; Ⓒ 1,482
BRADFORD; **164** D-8; Ⓟ 22,515; Ⓒ 26,088; ◆ 29,622
Bradfordville; RMC Place; LEON; **164** B-2; elev. 237ft./72m.; mail Tallahassee z 32309; ● 470
Bradley; POLK; see Bradley Junction (RMC Place)
Bradley Junction (Bradley); RMC Place; POLK; **164** J-8; elev. 136ft./41m.; mail Bradley z 33835; ● 600
Branchborough; RMC Place; POLK; ***164** I-8; rural
Branchton; RMC Place; HILLSBOROUGH; ***164** I-8; mail Thonotosassa z 33592; ● 250
Brandon; CDP; HILLSBOROUGH; **164** J-8; elev. 48ft./15m.; 🅿 🅷; ★ **TAM**; z 33508-11; Ⓟ 57,985; Ⓒ 77,895; Ⓡ 77,871; ◆ 94,108
Branford; Inc. Place; SUWANNEE; **164** D-6; elev. 41ft./12m.; 🅿; z 32008; Ⓟ 670; Ⓒ 695
Brannonville; RMC Place; BAY; ***165** S-6; ★ **PNCY**; mail Panama City z 32401; pop. incl. with Cedar Grove (Inc. Place)
Bratt; RMC Place; ESCAMBIA; **165** Q-2; mail Century z 32535; ● 200
Brent; CDP; ESCAMBIA; **162** L-9; ★ **PENS**; mail Pensacola z 32503, z 32505; Ⓟ 21,624; Ⓒ 22,257; ◆ 24,797
Brentwood; RMC Place; DUVAL; ***164** C-9; ★ **JAX**; mail Jacksonville z 32206; pop. incl. with Jacksonville (Inc. Place)
Brentwood; RMC Place; SARASOTA; ***165** L-7; ★ **SAR-B**; mail Sarasota z 34232
BREVARD; **164** J-12; Ⓟ 398,978; Ⓒ 476,230; ◆ 538,865
Brewster; RMC Place; POLK; ***165** K-8; mail Mulberry z 33860; rural
Bridgeport; RMC Place; PINELLAS; ***164** J-6; mail Safety Harbor z 34695; pop. incl. with Safety Harbor (Inc. Place)
Bridgeport; RMC Place; PUTNAM; ***164** D-9; mail Palatka z 32177; ● 370
Bright; RMC Place; MIAMI-DADE; ***165** P-13; ★ **MIA-**; mail Hialeah z 33013; pop. incl. with Hialeah (Inc. Place)
Brighton; RMC Place; HIGHLANDS; ***165** L-11; elev. 33ft./10m.; mail Okeechobee z 34972; rural
Brighton Reservation; Indian Reservation; GLADES; mail Moore Haven z 33471; Ⓟ 338; Ⓒ 566
Briny Breezes; Inc. Place; PALM BEACH; **163** D-10; elev. 3ft./1m.; 🅿; ★ **MIA-**; z 33435; Ⓟ 400; Ⓒ 411
Bristol; Inc. Place; ⊡ LIBERTY; **165** S-8; elev. 168ft./51m.; 🅿; z 32321; Ⓟ 937; Ⓒ 845
Broadview Park; CDP; BROWARD; ***165** P-13; ★ **MIA-**; mail Fort Lauderdale z 33317; Ⓟ 6,109; Ⓒ 6,798
Broadview-Pompano Park; CDP-Census Area Only; BROWARD; ***165** O-13; ★ **MIA-**; mail Fort Lauderdale z 33319, z 33359, Pompano Beach z 33068; Ⓟ 5,230; Ⓒ 5,314
Broadwater; RMC Place; PINELLAS; ***165** K-6; ★ **ST.PET**; mail Saint Petersburg z 33711; pop. incl. with Saint Petersburg (Inc. Place)
Brock Crossroad; RMC Place; WASHINGTON; ***165** R-6; elev. 48ft./15m.; mail Wausau z 32463; rural
Bronson; Inc. Place; ⊡ LEVY; **164** E-7; elev. 61ft./19m.; 🅿; z 32621; Ⓟ 875; Ⓒ 964
Brooker; Inc. Place; BRADFORD; **164** D-7; 🅿; z 32622; Ⓟ 312; Ⓒ 352
Brooklyn; RMC Place; DUVAL; ***164** C-9; ★ **JAX**; mail Jacksonville z 32204; pop. incl. with Jacksonville (Inc. Place)
Brookridge; CDP-Census Area Only; HERNANDO; ***164** H-7; ★ **SPR.H**; mail Brooksville z 34613; Ⓟ 2,805; Ⓒ 3,279
Brooksville; Inc. Place; ⊡ HERNANDO; **164** H-7; elev. 209ft./64m.; 🅿 🅷; ★ **SPR.H**; z 34601-11, z 34613-14; Ⓟ 7,440; Ⓒ 7,264
BROWARD; **165** O-12; Ⓟ 1,255,488; Ⓒ 1,623,018; ◆ 1,701,866
Browardale; RMC Place; BROWARD; ***165** O-13; ★ **MIA-**; mail Fort Lauderdale z 33311; Ⓟ 6,257; ● 1,100
Broward Estates; CDP-Census Area Only; BROWARD; ***165** O-13; ★ **MIA-**; Ⓒ 3,416
Brownsdale; RMC Place; SANTA ROSA; ***165** Q-2; mail Jay z 32565; ● 185
Browns Farm; RMC Place; PALM BEACH; ***165** N-12; elev. 15ft./5m.; mail Belle Glade z 33430; rural
Brownsville; RMC Place; ESCAMBIA; ***165** R-2; ★ **PENS**; mail Pensacola z 32505
Brownsville; CDP-Census Area Only; MIAMI-DADE; **163** L-8; ★ **MIA-**; mail Miami z 33142; Ⓟ 15,607; Ⓒ 14,393
Browntown; RMC Place; JACKSON; ***165** Q-7; mail Graceville z 32440; rural
Brownville; RMC Place; DESOTO; **165** L-9; mail Arcadia z 34266; ● 80
Bruce; RMC Place; WALTON; **165** R-5; elev. 45ft./14m.; 🅿; z 32455; ● 200
Bruceville; RMC Place; MARION; ***164** F-8; mail Silver Springs z 34488; rural
Bryant; RMC Place; PALM BEACH; **165** M-12; 🅿; z 33438-39; ● 180
Bryceville; RMC Place; NASSAU; **164** C-8; elev. 69ft./21m.; 🅿; z 32009; ● 180
Brynwood; RMC Place; LEE; ***165** N-9; ★ **FTMY-**; mail Fort Myers z 33912; ● 400
Buccaneer Estates; RMC Place; MIAMI-DADE; **163** J-8; ★ **MIA-**; mail Opa Locka z 33054; ● 1,000
Bucell Junction; RMC Place; TAYLOR; ***164** D-4; mail Perry z 32347; ● 150
Buchanan; RMC Place; HARDEE; ***165** L-9; elev. 76ft./23m.; mail Zolfo Springs z 33890
Buckhead Ridge; CDP; GLADES; **165** L-11; mail Okeechobee z 34974; Ⓟ 1,275; Ⓒ 1,390
Buckhorn; RMC Place; WAKULLA; ***164** D-2; mail Sopchoppy z 32358; rural
Buckingham; CDP; LEE; ***165** N-9; elev. 12ft./4m.; ★ **FTMY-**; mail Fort Myers z 33905; Ⓒ 3,742
Buckingham West; RMC Place; ALACHUA; ***164** E-7; elev. 150ft./46m.; ★ **GAIN**; mail Gainesville z 32601; ● 640
Buckville; RMC Place; LAFAYETTE; ***164** C-5; mail Mayo z 32066; rural
Buenaventura Lakes; RMC Place; OSCEOLA; **165** P-4; 🅿; ★ **KISS**; z 34743; Ⓟ 14,148; ● 14,000
Buena Vista; RMC Place; JACKSON; ***165** Q-7; elev. 106ft./32m.; mail Sneads z 32460; rural
Buena Vista; RMC Place; MIAMI-DADE; ***165** P-13; ★ **MIA-**; mail Miami z 33137; pop. incl. with Miami (Inc. Place)
Buena Vista; RMC Place; PASCO; ***164** I-6; ★ **ST.PET**; mail Holiday z 34691
Buffalo Bluff; RMC Place; PUTNAM; ***164** E-9; elev. 10ft./3m.; mail Satsuma z 32189; ● 320
Bunche Park; CDP; MIAMI-DADE; **163** K-8; ★ **MIA-**; mail Opa Locka z 33054; Ⓟ 4,388; Ⓒ 3,972
Bunnell; Inc. Place; ⊡ FLAGLER; **164** E-10; elev. 20ft./6m.; 🅿 🅷; z 32110; Ⓟ 1,873; Ⓒ 2,122
Burbank; RMC Place; MARION; ***164** F-8; mail Fort Mc Coy z 32134; rural
Burnetts Lake; RMC Place; ALACHUA; ***164** D-7; elev. 74ft./23m.; ★ **GAIN**; mail Alachua z 32615; pop. incl. with Alachua (Inc. Place)
Burnt Store Marina; CDP-Census Area Only; LEE; ***165** N-8; Ⓒ 1,271
Bushnell; Inc. Place; ⊡ SUMTER; **164** H-8; elev. 79ft./24m.; 🅿; z 33513; Ⓟ 1,998; Ⓒ 2,050
Butler Beach; CDP-Census Area Only; ST. JOHNS; ***164** D-10; mail Saint Augustine z 32080; Ⓟ 3,377; Ⓒ 4,436
Byrd; RMC Place; ST. JOHNS; ***164** E-10; rural
Byrneville (Byrnville); RMC Place; ESCAMBIA; ***165** Q-2; mail Century z 32535; ● 300
Byrnville; ESCAMBIA; see Byrneville (RMC Place)

C

Cadillac; RMC Place; ALACHUA; ***164** E-7; mail Alachua z 32615; ● 200
Cairo; RMC Place; BAY; ***165** S-6; mail Panama City z 32404; ● 340
CALHOUN; **165** S-7; Ⓟ 11,011; Ⓒ 13,017; ◆ 13,920
Callahan; Inc. Place; NASSAU; **164** B-9; elev. 19ft./6m.; 🅿; ★ **JAX**; z 32011; Ⓟ 946; Ⓒ 962
Callaway; Inc. Place; BAY; **165** S-6; 🅿; ★ **PNCY**; z 32404; Ⓟ 12,253; Ⓒ 14,233
Calphos; RMC Place; CITRUS; ***164** G-7; mail Hernando z 34442; ● 500
Camellia Gardens; RMC Place; ORANGE; ***164** H-10; ★ **ORL**; mail Orlando z 32809; ● 1,500
Camelot Park; RMC Place; LEON; ***164** B-2; ★ **TALL**; mail Tallahassee z 32301; pop. incl. with Tallahassee (Inc. Place)
Cameron City; RMC Place; SEMINOLE; **165** L-5; ★ **ORL**; mail Sanford z 32771; ● 180
Campbell (Campbell City); CDP; OSCEOLA; **164** I-10; elev. 73ft./22m.; ★ **KISS**; mail Kissimmee z 34746; Ⓟ 3,884; Ⓒ 2,677
Campbell City; OSCEOLA; see Campbell (CDP)
Campbellton; Inc. Place; JACKSON; **165** Q-7; elev. 157ft./48m.; 🅿; z 32426; Ⓟ 202; Ⓒ 212
Camps; RMC Place; HERNANDO; ***164** H-7; mail Brooksville z 34601; rural
Campton; RMC Place; OKALOOSA; **165** Q-4; mail Laurel Hill z 32567; ● 125
Campville; RMC Place; ALACHUA; **164** E-8; mail Hawthorne z 32640; ● 200
Canaan; RMC Place; SEMINOLE; ***164** G-10; ★ **ORL**; mail Sanford z 32771
Canal Point; CDP; PALM BEACH; **165** M-12; elev. 26ft./8m.; 🅿; z 33438-39; Ⓒ 525
Candler; RMC Place; MARION; **164** G-8; 🅿; ★ **OCA**; z 32111; ● 370
Cannon Town; RMC Place; OKALOOSA; ***165** Q-4; elev. 235ft./72m.; mail Baker z 32531; ● 50
Canova Beach; RMC Place; BREVARD; **164** I-12; elev. 10ft./3m.; pop. incl. with Indian Harbour Beach (Inc. Place)
Cantonment; RMC Place; ESCAMBIA; **165** R-2; elev. 150ft./46m.; 🅿; ★ **PENS**; z 32533; ● 2,800
Cape Canaveral; Inc. Place; BREVARD; **164** I-12; elev. 9ft./3m.; 🅿; ★ **MELB-**; z 32920; Ⓟ 8,014; Ⓒ 8,829
Cape Coral; Inc. Place; LEE; **165** N-8; 🅿 🅷; ★ **FTMY-**; z 33904, z 33909-10, z 33914-15, z 33990-91, z 33993; Ⓟ 74,991; Ⓒ 102,286; ◆ 153,269
Cape Coral Central; RMC Place; LEE; ***165** N-8; ★ **FTMY-**; mail Cape Coral z 33904, z 33914-15, z 33990-91, z 33993; pop. incl. with Cape Coral (Inc. Place)
Cape Haze; RMC Place; CHARLOTTE; **165** M-8; elev. 7ft./2m.; 🅿; ★ **VEN**; z 33946-47; ● 400
Capital Hills; RMC Place; LEON; ***164** B-2; ★ **TALL**; mail Tallahassee z 32308; pop. incl. with Tallahassee (Inc. Place)
Capitola; RMC Place; LEON; **164** B-3; mail Tallahassee z 32311; ● 165
Capps; RMC Place; JEFFERSON; **164** C-3; mail Lamont z 32336; ● 20
Capri Isle; RMC Place; PINELLAS; ***165** K-6; ★ **ST.PET**; mail Saint Petersburg z 33706; pop. incl. with Treasure Island (Inc. Place)
Captiva (Captiva Island); CDP; LEE; **165** N-8; elev. 7ft./2m.; 🅿; z 33924; Ⓒ 379
Captiva Island; LEE; see Captiva (CDP)
Cara; RMC Place; MARION; ***164** F-8; mail Reddick z 32686; ● 160
Carleton; RMC Place; PUTNAM; mail Hawthorne z 32640; rural
Carl Fisher; RMC Place; MIAMI-DADE; ***165** Q-14; 🅿; ★ **MIA-**; z 33139, z 33239; pop. incl. with Miami Beach (Inc. Place)
Carlson; RMC Place; SUMTER; ***164** G-8; mail Lake Panasoffkee z 33538; ● 150
Carlton Village; RMC Place; LAKE; ***164** G-9; mail Lady Lake z 32159; ● 630
Carol City; CDP; MIAMI-DADE; ***165** P-13; 🅿; ★ **MIA-**; z 33055-56; Ⓟ 53,331; Ⓒ 59,443; ◆ 62,100
Carr; RMC Place; CALHOUN; ***165** S-7; mail Altha z 32421, Clarksville z 32430; rural
Carrabelle; Inc. Place; FRANKLIN; **164** D-1; elev. 12ft./4m.; 🅿; z 32322; Ⓟ 1,200; Ⓒ 1,303
Carrabelle Beach; RMC Place; FRANKLIN; ***165** T-8; mail Carrabelle z 32322; ● 150
Carraway; RMC Place; PUTNAM; ***164** E-9; mail Palatka z 32177; rural
Carrollwood; RMC Place; HILLSBOROUGH; **163** B-3; 🅿; ★ **TAM**; z 33618, z 33625, z 33688 & mail Tampa z 33624; Ⓟ 7,195; ● 3,100
Carters Corner; RMC Place; POLK; **163** J-3; ★ **LKLD**; mail Auburndale z 33823; ● 250
Carver; RMC Place; DUVAL; ***164** C-9; ★ **JAX**; mail Jacksonville z 32209; pop. incl. with Jacksonville (Inc. Place)
Carver Manor; RMC Place; DUVAL; ***164** C-9; ★ **JAX**; mail Jacksonville z 32209; pop. incl. with Jacksonville (Inc. Place)
Carver Ranches; CDP; BROWARD; ***165** P-13; ★ **MIA-**; mail Hollywood z 33023; Ⓒ 4,299
Caryville; Inc. Place; WASHINGTON; **165** R-6; elev. 58ft./18m.; 🅿; z 32425, z 32427; Ⓟ 631; Ⓒ 218
Casa Blanco; RMC Place; JEFFERSON; ***164** B-3; mail Monticello z 32344; rural
Casa Cola; RMC Place; ST. JOHNS; ***164** D-10; mail Saint Augustine z 32095; ● 500
Casey Key; RMC Place; SARASOTA; ***165** L-7; ★ **VEN**; mail Nokomis z 34275; ● 150
Cason Inglis Acres; RMC Place; LEVY; ***164** G-6; mail Inglis z 34449; ● 200
Cassadaga; RMC Place; VOLUSIA; ***164** G-10; elev. 43ft./13m.; 🅿; ★ **ORL**; z 32706
Casselberry; Inc. Place; SEMINOLE; **164** H-10; elev. 85ft./26m.; 🅿; ★ **ORL**; z 32707-08, z 32718-19, z 32730; Ⓟ 18,849; Ⓒ 22,629; Ⓡ 23,438; ◆ 23,099
Cassia; RMC Place; LAKE; **164** G-10; mail Eustis z 32726; ● 90
Catawba; RMC Place; CITRUS; ***164** H-7; mail Floral City z 34436; ● 180
Causeway; RMC Place; BROWARD; ★ **MIA-**; mail Fort Lauderdale z 33316, z 33346; pop. incl. with Fort Lauderdale (Inc. Place)
Causeway Isles; RMC Place; PINELLAS; ***165** K-6; ★ **ST.PET**; mail Saint Petersburg z 33707; pop. incl. with Saint Petersburg (Inc. Place)
Cedar Creek; RMC Place; MARION; ***164** F-9; mail Silver Springs z 34488; ● 230
Cedar Grove; Inc. Place; BAY; **165** S-6; ★ **PNCY**; mail Panama City z 32401, z 32405; Ⓟ 1,479; Ⓒ 5,367
Cedar Hammock; RMC Place; MANATEE; ***165** L-7; ★ **SAR-B**; mail Bradenton z 34205, z 34207
Cedar Hills Estates; RMC Place; DUVAL; ***164** C-9; elev. 25ft./8m.; ★ **JAX**; mail Jacksonville z 32210; pop. incl. with Jacksonville (Inc. Place)
Cedar Key; Inc. Place; LEVY; **164** F-5; elev. 5ft./2m.; 🅿; z 32625; Ⓟ 668; Ⓒ 790
Cedar Point; RMC Place; DUVAL; ***164** B-10; ★ **JAX**; mail Jacksonville z 32226; pop. incl. with Jacksonville (Inc. Place)
Cedar Shores; RMC Place; MARION; ***164** F-8; ★ **OCA**; mail Ocala z 34471; pop. incl. with Ocala (Inc. Place)
Celebration; CDP; OSCEOLA; ***164** I-10; 🅿; ★ **KISS**; z 34747; Ⓒ 2,736
Center Hill; Inc. Place; SUMTER; **164** H-8; elev. 102ft./31m.; 🅿; z 33514; Ⓟ 735; Ⓒ 910
Center Ridge; RMC Place; WALTON; ***165** R-5; mail Defuniak Springs z 32433; ● 135
Centerville Station; RMC Place; LEON; ***164** B-2; ★ **TALL**; mail Tallahassee z 32308, z 32312, z 32317; pop. incl. with Tallahassee (Inc. Place)
Central; RMC Place; PINELLAS; ★ **ST.PET**; mail Saint Petersburg z 33713-14, z 33784; pop. incl. with Saint Petersburg (Inc. Place)
Century; Inc. Place; ESCAMBIA; **165** Q-2; 🅿; z 32535; Ⓟ 1,989; Ⓒ 1,714
Century Village; CDP-Census Area Only; PALM BEACH; **163** B-9; ★ **MIA-**; mail Boca Raton z 33434, West Palm Beach z 33417; Ⓟ 8,363; Ⓒ 7,616
Cerrogordo; RMC Place; HOLMES; ***165** R-6; elev. 83ft./25m.; mail Westville z 32464; ● 50
Chain O'Lakes; RMC Place; LAKE; ***164** G-10; mail Paisley z 32767; ● 180
Chaires; RMC Place; LEON; **164** B-3; elev. 58ft./18m.; ★ **TALL**; mail Tallahassee z 32311; ● 100
Chambers Estates; CDP-Census Area Only; BROWARD; ***165** P-13; ★ **MIA-**; Ⓒ 3,556
Chancey; RMC Place; LAFAYETTE; ***164** C-5; mail Mayo z 32066; ● 120
Chapman; RMC Place; HILLSBOROUGH; ***164** J-7; mail Lutz z 33549; ● 500
Charleston Park; CDP-Census Area Only; LEE; ***165** N-10; Ⓒ 411
CHARLOTTE; **165** M-9; Ⓟ 110,975; Ⓒ 141,627; ◆ 149,378
Charlotte Beach; RMC Place; CHARLOTTE; ***165** M-8; ★ **VEN**; mail El Jobean z 33927; ● 600
Charlotte Harbor; CDP; CHARLOTTE; **165** M-8; ★ **PUN-**; mail Punta Gorda z 33980; Ⓟ 3,327; Ⓒ 3,647
Charlotte Park; CDP; CHARLOTTE; ***165** M-8; ★ **PUN-**; mail Punta Gorda z 33950; Ⓟ 2,225; Ⓒ 2,182
Chaseville; RMC Place; DUVAL; ***164** C-9; ★ **JAX**; pop. incl. with Jacksonville (Inc. Place)
Chason; RMC Place; CALHOUN; ***165** R-7; elev. 128ft./39m.; mail Altha z 32421
Chassahowitzka; RMC Place; CITRUS; **164** H-7; mail Homosassa Springs z 34447; ● 850
Chatmar; MARION; see Chatmire (RMC Place)
Chatmire (Chatmar); RMC Place; MARION; ***164** G-7; elev. 55ft./17m.; mail Dunnellon z 34432; ● 400
Chattahoochee; Inc. Place; GADSDEN; **165** R-8; elev. 200ft./61m.; 🅿 🅷; z 32324; Ⓟ 4,382; Ⓒ 3,287
Cherry Lake; RMC Place; MADISON; **164** B-4; elev. 117ft./36m.; mail Madison z 32340, Pinetta z 32350
Chester; RMC Place; NASSAU; **164** B-9; mail Yulee z 32097; ● 370
Cheval; CDP-Census Area Only; HILLSBOROUGH; ***164** I-7; ★ **TAM**; Ⓒ 7,602
Chiefland; Inc. Place; LEVY; **164** E-6; elev. 31ft./9m.; 🅿; z 32626, z 32644; Ⓟ 1,917; Ⓒ 1,993
Chipley; Inc. Place; ⊡ WASHINGTON; **165** R-6; elev. 119ft./36m.; 🅿 🅷; z 32428; Ⓟ 3,866; Ⓒ 3,592
Chipola; RMC Place; CALHOUN; ***165** R-7; mail Altha z 32421
Chipola Park; RMC Place; CALHOUN; **165** S-7; mail Wewahitchka z 32449; ● 20
Chipola Terrace; RMC Place; JACKSON; ***165** R-7; elev. 115ft./35m.; mail Marianna z 32448; ● 75
Choctaw; RMC Place; WALTON; ***165** S-5; mail Santa Rosa Beach z 32459; ● 100
Choctaw Bay Estates; RMC Place; WALTON; ***165** S-5; mail Santa Rosa Beach z 32459; ● 260
Choctaw Beach; RMC Place; WALTON; ***165** R-4; 🅿; z 32578 & mail Freeport z 32439; ● 1,050
Chokoloskee; CDP; COLLIER; **165** Q-10; elev. 10ft./3m.; 🅿; z 34138; summer pop. 1,800; Ⓒ 404
Christina; RMC Place; POLK; ***164** J-8; ★ **LKLD**; mail Lakeland z 33813; ● 2,100
Christmas; CDP; ORANGE; **164** H-11; elev. 44ft./13m.; 🅿; z 32709; Ⓒ 1,162
Chula Vista; CDP-Census Area Only; BROWARD; ***165** P-13; ★ **MIA-**; Ⓒ 573
Chuluota; CDP; SEMINOLE; **164** H-11; elev. 58ft./18m.; 🅿; ★ **ORL**; z 32766; Ⓟ 1,441; Ⓒ 1,921
Chumuckla; RMC Place; SANTA ROSA; ***165** R-2; elev. 204ft./62m.; mail Jay z 32565, Milton z 32571; rural
Cinco Bayou; Inc. Place; OKALOOSA; ***165** S-4; elev. 23ft./7m.; ★ **FTWL**; mail Fort Walton Beach z 32548; Ⓟ 322; Ⓒ 377
Cisky Park; RMC Place; LAKE; ***164** G-9; elev. 75ft./23m.; mail Leesburg z 34748; ● 360
Citra; RMC Place; MARION; **164** F-8; 🅿; ★ **OCA**; z 32113; ● 950
Citronelle; RMC Place; CITRUS; ***164** G-7; elev. 28ft./9m.; mail Dunnellon z 34433; ● 430
Citrus; RMC Place; CITRUS; ***164** G-7; mail Inverness z 34450; pop. incl. with Inverness (Inc. Place)
CITRUS; **164** G-7; Ⓟ 93,515; Ⓒ 118,085; ◆ 143,977
Citrus Center; RMC Place; GLADES; ***165** M-10; mail Moore Haven z 33471; rural
Citrus Hills; CDP-Census Area Only; CITRUS; ***164** G-7; 🅿; z 34442; Ⓒ 4,029
Citrus Park; CDP; HILLSBOROUGH; **163** A-3; ★ **TAM**; mail Tampa z 33624; Ⓒ 20,226; ◆ 24,444
Citrus Ridge; CDP; LAKE, ORANGE, OSCEOLA, POLK; ***164** I-9; 🅿; ★ **KISS**; z 32966, z 32968-69; Ⓒ 12,015
Citrus Springs; CDP; CITRUS; **164** G-7; 🅿; z 34433-34; Ⓟ 2,213; Ⓒ 4,157
City of Sunrise; BROWARD; see Sunrise (Inc. Place)
City Point; RMC Place; BREVARD; ***164** I-12; rural
Clair Mel; HILLSBOROUGH; see Clair-Mel City (RMC Place)
Clair-Mel City (Clair Mel); RMC Place; HILLSBOROUGH; **163** C-4; 🅿; ★ **TAM**; z 33619; ● 7,500
Clarcona; RMC Place; ORANGE; **165** M-2; elev. 100ft./30m.; 🅿; ★ **ORL**; z 32710; ● 800
Clark; RMC Place; ALACHUA; ***164** D-7; mail High Springs z 32643; pop. incl. with High Springs (Inc. Place)
Clarksville; RMC Place; CALHOUN; **165** S-7; 🅿; z 32430; ● 150
Clarkwild; RMC Place; HILLSBOROUGH; ***164** J-7; mail Thonotosassa z 33592; ● 470
CLAY; **164** D-9; Ⓟ 105,986; Ⓒ 140,814; ◆ 187,954
Clay Landing; RMC Place; PUTNAM; ***164** D-9; mail Palatka z 32177; ● 180
Clear Springs; RMC Place; OKALOOSA; ***165** Q-4; mail Laurel Hill z 32567; rural
Clear Springs; RMC Place; WALTON; ***165** Q-5; mail Laurel Hill z 32567; ● 200
Clearwater; Inc. Place; ⊡ PINELLAS; **164** J-6; elev. 24ft./7m.; 🅿 🅷 🅲 1,393 ■; ★ **ST.PET**; z 33755-67, z 33769; Ⓟ 98,784; Ⓒ 108,787; Ⓡ 108,789; ◆ 106,870
Clearwater Beach; RMC Place; PINELLAS; ***164** J-6; 🅿; ★ **ST.PET**; z 33767; pop. incl. with Clearwater (Inc. Place)
Clermont; Inc. Place; LAKE; **164** H-9; elev. 112ft./34m.; 🅿 🅷; z 34711-15; Ⓟ 6,910; Ⓒ 9,333; Ⓡ 9,338
Cleveland; CDP; CHARLOTTE; **165** M-8; ★ **PUN-**; mail Punta Gorda z 33982; Ⓟ 2,896; Ⓒ 3,268
Cleveland Street; RMC Place; PINELLAS; ***164** J-6; ★ **ST.PET**; mail Clearwater z 33755, z 33757; pop. incl. with Clearwater (Inc. Place)
Clewiston; Inc. Place; HENDRY; **165** N-11; elev. 18ft./5m.; 🅿 🅷; z 33440; Ⓟ 6,085; Ⓒ 6,460
Clifton; RMC Place; DUVAL; ***164** C-9; ★ **JAX**; mail Jacksonville z 32211; pop. incl. with Jacksonville (Inc. Place)
Clifton; RMC Place; SEMINOLE; ***164** H-10; mail Winter Springs z 32708; pop. incl. with Winter Springs (Inc. Place)
Clinton Heights; RMC Place; PASCO; ***164** I-8; mail Dade City z 33525; ● 870
Cloud Lake; Inc. Place; PALM BEACH; **163** B-10; 🅿; ★ **MIA-**; z 33406; Ⓟ 121; Ⓒ 167
Cluster Springs; RMC Place; WALTON; ***165** Q-5; elev. 219ft./67m.; mail Defuniak Springs z 32433; rural
Cobbtown; RMC Place; SANTA ROSA; ***165** Q-3; elev. 181ft./55m.; mail Jay z 32565; rural
Cocoa (Cocoa Rockledge); Inc. Place; BREVARD; **164** I-12; elev. 25ft./8m.; 🅿 ■; ★ **MELB-**; z 32922-24, z 32926-27; Ⓟ 17,722; Ⓒ 16,412; ◆ 14,988
Cocoa Beach; Inc. Place; BREVARD; **164** I-12; elev. 12ft./4m.; 🅿 🅷; ★ **MELB-**; z 32931-32; Ⓟ 12,123; Ⓒ 12,482
Cocoa Rockledge; BREVARD; see Cocoa (Inc. Place)
Cocoa West; CDP-Census Area Only; BREVARD; ***164** I-12; ★ **MELB-**; mail Cocoa z 32922; Ⓟ 6,160; Ⓒ 5,921
Coconut Creek; Inc. Place; BROWARD; **163** G-9; elev. 10ft./3m.; 🅿; ★ **MIA-**; z 33063, z 33066, z 33073, z 33093, z 33097; Ⓟ 27,485; Ⓒ 43,566; ◆ 50,569
Coconut Creek Reservation; Indian Reservation; BROWARD; Ⓒ 0
Coconut Grove; RMC Place; MIAMI-DADE; ***165** Q-13; 🅿; ★ **MIA-**; z 33133, z 33146 & mail Miami z 33134, z 33233; pop. incl. with Miami (Inc. Place)
Cody; RMC Place; JEFFERSON; ***164** C-3; elev. 40ft./12m.; mail Monticello z 32344; rural
Codys Corner; RMC Place; FLAGLER; ***164** F-10; mail Bunnell z 32110; ● 110
Coker; RMC Place; HARDEE; ***165** K-9; mail Wauchula z 33873; ● 200
Colee; RMC Place; BROWARD; ***165** P-14; ★ **MIA-**; mail Fort Lauderdale z 33301, z 33303; pop. incl. with Fort Lauderdale (Inc. Place)
Coleman; Inc. Place; SUMTER; **164** G-8; elev. 60ft./18m.; 🅿; z 33521; Ⓟ 857; Ⓒ 647
College Park; RMC Place; DUVAL; ***164** C-9; ★ **JAX**; mail Jacksonville z 32209; pop. incl. with Jacksonville (Inc. Place)
College Park; RMC Place; MARION; ***164** F-8; ★ **OCA**; mail Ocala z 34474; pop. incl. with Ocala (Inc. Place)
College Park; RMC Place; ORANGE; ***164** H-10; ★ **ORL**; mail Orlando z 32804, z 32854; pop. incl. with Orlando (Inc. Place)
College Point; RMC Place; BAY; ***165** S-6; ★ **PNCY**; mail Lynn Haven z 32444; ● 800
COLLIER; **165** O-10; Ⓟ 152,099; Ⓒ 251,377; ◆ 317,662
Collier City; RMC Place; BROWARD; ***165** O-13; ★ **MIA-**; mail Pompano Beach z 33069; pop. incl. with Pompano Beach (Inc. Place)
Collier Manor-Cresthaven; CDP-Census Area Only; BROWARD; ***165** O-14; ★ **MIA-**; mail Pompano Beach z 33064; Ⓟ 7,322; Ⓒ 7,741
Collins Park Estates; RMC Place; ST. LUCIE; ***165** L-13; ● 450
Colonial Gables; RMC Place; SARASOTA; ***165** L-7; ★ **SAR-B**; mail Sarasota z 34232
Colonial Manor; RMC Place; DUVAL; ***164** C-9; ★ **JAX**; mail Jacksonville z 32207; pop. incl. with Jacksonville (Inc. Place)
Colonialtown; RMC Place; ORANGE; ***164** H-10; ★ **ORL**; mail Orlando z 32803, z 32853; pop. incl. with Orlando (Inc. Place)
Columbia; RMC Place; COLUMBIA; ***164** D-6; mail Lake City z 32055; ● 300
COLUMBIA; **164** C-7; Ⓟ 42,613; Ⓒ 56,513; ◆ 77,233
Combee Settlement; CDP-Census Area Only; POLK; ***164** J-9; ★ **LKLD**; mail Lakeland z 33801; Ⓟ 5,463; Ⓒ 5,436
Commerce; RMC Place; HILLSBOROUGH; ★ **TAM**; mail Tampa z 33602, z 33672; pop. incl. with Tampa (Inc. Place)
Compass Lake; RMC Place; JACKSON; **165** R-7; elev. 208ft./63m.; mail Alford z 32420; ● 200
Conant; RMC Place; LAKE; ***164** G-8; elev. 95ft./29m.; mail Lady Lake z 32159; pop. incl. with Lady Lake (Inc. Place)
Conch Key; RMC Place; MONROE; ***165** T-12; elev. 7ft./2m.; 🅿; z 33050 & mail Long Key z 33001; ● 140
Concord; RMC Place; GADSDEN; **164** B-2; elev. 232ft./71m.; mail Havana z 32333; ● 125
Conner; RMC Place; MARION; ***164** F-8; mail Silver Springs z 34488; rural
Connersville; RMC Place; POLK; ***164** J-9; elev. 122ft./37m.; mail Bartow z 33830-31; ● 220
Conway; CDP; ORANGE; **164** H-10; ★ **ORL**; mail Orlando z 32806, z 32812; Ⓟ 13,159; Ⓒ 14,394
Cooks Hammock; RMC Place; LAFAYETTE; ***164** D-5; mail Mayo z 32066; rural
Cooper City; Inc. Place; BROWARD; **163** I-8; elev. 9ft./3m.; 🅿; ★ **MIA-**; z 33328-30 & mail Fort Lauderdale z 33326, Hollywood z 33024, z 33026; Ⓟ 21,335; Ⓒ 27,939; Ⓡ 27,914; ◆ 27,851
Copeland; RMC Place; COLLIER; **165** P-10; 🅿; z 34137; ● 30
Copeland Settlement; RMC Place; ALACHUA; ***164** E-8; ★ **GAIN**; mail Gainesville z 32609; ● 350
Coquina Key; RMC Place; PINELLAS; ***165** K-7; ★ **ST.PET**; mail Saint Petersburg z 33705; pop. incl. with Saint Petersburg (Inc. Place)
Cora; RMC Place; SANTA ROSA; mail Jay z 32565; rural
Coral Cove; RMC Place; SARASOTA; **165** L-7; ★ **SAR-B**; mail Sarasota z 34231; ● 1,160
Coral Gables; Inc. Place; MIAMI-DADE; **165** Q-13; 🅿 🅷 🅲 15,351 ■; ★ **MIA-**; z 33114, z 33124, z 33133-34, z 33143, z 33145-46, z 33156, z 33158, z 33234 & mail Miami z 33144; Ⓟ 40,091; Ⓒ 42,249; ◆ 41,317
Coral Gardens; RMC Place; MARTIN; ***165** L-13; ★ **STU**; mail Stuart z 34997; ● 1,300
Coral Springs; Inc. Place; BROWARD; **165** O-13; 🅿 🅷; ★ **MIA-**; z 33065, z 33067, z 33071, z 33073, z 33075-77; Ⓟ 79,443; Ⓒ 117,549; ◆ 119,952
Coral Terrace; CDP-Census Area Only; MIAMI-DADE; ***165** Q-13; ★ **MIA-**; mail Miami z 33144, z 33156; Ⓟ 23,255; Ⓒ 24,380; ◆ 25,473
Coral Way Village; RMC Place; MIAMI-DADE; **163** M-7; ★ **MIA-**; mail Miami z 33155; ● 3,200
Cordova; RMC Place; ESCAMBIA; mail Pensacola z 32503; pop. incl. with Pensacola (Inc. Place)
Cordova Lakes; RMC Place; MANATEE; ***165** K-7; ★ **SAR-B**; mail Bradenton z 34209; pop. incl. with Bradenton (Inc. Place)
Corkscrew; RMC Place; COLLIER; **165** O-10; mail Immokalee z 34142
Cornwell; RMC Place; HIGHLANDS; ***165** L-11; elev. 41ft./12m.; mail Lorida z 33857; rural
Coronet; RMC Place; HILLSBOROUGH; ***164** J-8; elev. 134ft./41m.; ★ **TAM**; mail Plant City z 33566; ● 670
Cortez; CDP; MANATEE; **163** G-2; 🅿; ★ **SAR-B**; z 34215; Ⓟ 4,509; Ⓒ 4,491
Cortez Road; RMC Place; MANATEE; ***165** L-7; ★ **SAR-B**; mail Bradenton z 34210
Cottage Hill; RMC Place; ESCAMBIA; **165** R-2; elev. 124ft./38m.; ★ **PENS**; mail Cantonment z 32533; ● 1,050
Cottondale; Inc. Place; JACKSON; **165** R-7; elev. 135ft./41m.; 🅿; z 32431; Ⓟ 900; Ⓒ 869
Cotton Plant; RMC Place; MARION; ***164** F-7; ★ **OCA**; mail Ocala z 34474; rural
Country Club; CDP-Census Area Only; MIAMI-DADE; ***165** P-13; ★ **MIA-**; mail Hialeah z 33015; Ⓒ 36,310; ◆ 37,928
Country Club Acres; RMC Place; PALM BEACH; ***165** N-14; ★ **MIA-**; mail Delray Beach z 33484; ● 1,230
Country Club Estates; RMC Place; COLUMBIA; ***164** C-7; mail Lake City z 32055; pop. incl. with Lake City (Inc. Place)
Country Club Estates; RMC Place; POLK; ***164** J-9; ★ **LKLD**; mail Lakeland z 33801; ● 1,550
Country Club Manor; RMC Place; SEMINOLE; ***164** G-10; elev. 35ft./11m.; ★ **ORL**; mail Sanford z 32771; pop. incl. with Sanford (Inc. Place)
Country Estates; CDP-Census Area Only; BROWARD; ***165** P-13; ★ **MIA-**; Ⓒ 1,910
Countryside; RMC Place; MARION; ★ **OCA**; mail Ocala z 34481
Countryside; RMC Place; PINELLAS; ***164** J-6; ★ **ST.PET**; mail Clearwater z 33761; pop. incl. with Clearwater (Inc. Place)
Country Walk; CDP-Census Area Only; MIAMI-DADE; ***165** Q-13; ★ **MIA-**; Ⓒ 10,653
Courtenay; RMC Place; BREVARD; ***164** H-12; ★ **MELB-**; mail Merritt Island z 32952; ● 470
Cove; RMC Place; BAY; ***165** S-6; ★ **PNCY**; mail Panama City z 32401; pop. incl. with Panama City (Inc. Place)
Cox; RMC Place; CALHOUN; ***165** R-7; elev. 202ft./62m.; mail Blountstown z 32424; rural
Coytown; ORANGE; see Crown Point (RMC Place)
Crackertown; RMC Place; LEVY; ***164** G-6; elev. 12ft./4m.; mail Inglis z 34449; pop. incl. with Inglis (Inc. Place)
Crandall; RMC Place; NASSAU; ***164** B-9; mail Yulee z 32097; ● 100
Crawford; RMC Place; NASSAU; ***164** B-9; elev. 87ft./27m.; mail Bryceville z 32009, Jacksonville z 32208
Crawfordville; RMC Place; ⊡ WAKULLA; **164** C-2; elev. 30ft./9m.; 🅿; z 32326-27; ● 1,400
Crescent Beach; RMC Place; SARASOTA; ***165** L-7; ★ **SAR-B**; mail Sarasota z 34242; pop. incl. with Sarasota (Inc. Place)
Crescent Beach; CDP; ST. JOHNS; **164** D-10; mail Saint Augustine z 32080; Ⓟ 1,081; Ⓒ 985
Crescent City; Inc. Place; PUTNAM; **164** E-10; elev. 53ft./16m.; 🅿; z 32112; Ⓟ 1,859; Ⓒ 1,776
Crescent City Station; RMC Place; PUTNAM; ***164** F-10; rural
Crestview; Inc. Place; ⊡ OKALOOSA; **165** R-4; elev. 236ft./72m.; 🅿 🅷; z 32531, z 32536, z 32539; Ⓟ 9,886; Ⓒ 14,766
Crewsville; RMC Place; HARDEE; ***165** L-9; elev. 98ft./30m.; mail Zolfo Springs z 33890; rural
Crooked Lake Park; CDP; POLK; ***164** J-9; mail Lake Wales z 33859; Ⓟ 1,575; Ⓒ 1,682
Croom; RMC Place; HERNANDO; ***164** H-8; mail Brooksville z 34602, Nobleton z 34661; rural
Cross City; Inc. Place; ⊡ DIXIE; **164** E-5; elev. 42ft./13m.; 🅿; z 32628; Ⓟ 2,041; Ⓒ 1,775
Cross Creek; RMC Place; ALACHUA; **164** E-8; elev. 69ft./21m.; 🅿; z 32640; ● 270
Crossroads; RMC Place; PINELLAS; ***164** J-7; ★ **ST.PET**; mail Saint Petersburg z 33709-10, z 33743; pop. incl. with Saint Petersburg (Inc. Place)
Crown Point (Coytown); RMC Place; ORANGE; ***164** H-9; ★ **ORL**; mail Orlando z 32803
Crows Bluff; RMC Place; LAKE; **164** G-10; elev. 12ft./4m.; mail DeLand z 32720; rural
Crystal Beach; RMC Place; PINELLAS; **163** A-1; elev. 8ft./2m.; 🅿; ★ **ST.PET**; z 34681; ● 1,350
Crystal Lake; CDP-Census Area Only; BROWARD; ***165** O-14; ★ **MIA-**; Ⓒ 0
Crystal Lake; CDP-Census Area Only; POLK; ***164** J-9; ★ **LKLD**; mail Lakeland z 33801, z 33803; Ⓟ 5,300; Ⓒ 5,341
Crystal Lake; RMC Place; WASHINGTON; **165** S-6; mail Panama City z 32409; ● 135
Crystal River; Inc. Place; CITRUS; **164** G-7; elev. 4ft./1m.; 🅿 🅷; z 34423, z 34428-29; Ⓟ 4,044; Ⓒ 3,485
Crystal Springs; CDP; PASCO; **164** I-8; elev. 73ft./22m.; 🅿; z 33524; Ⓒ 1,175
Cubitis; RMC Place; DESOTO; ***165** L-9; mail Arcadia z 34266; ● 60
Cudjoe Key; CDP-Census Area Only; MONROE; ***165** T-10; 🅿; z 33042; Ⓟ 1,714; Ⓒ 1,695
Cunningham Estates; RMC Place; PASCO; ***164** I-8; mail Zephyrhills z 33541; ● 260
Curlew; RMC Place; PINELLAS; **163** B-2; ★ **ST.PET**; mail Palm Harbor z 34683; ● 780
Curtis; RMC Place; GILCHRIST; ***164** E-6; mail Bell z 32619; ● 100
Curtis Mill; RMC Place; WAKULLA; ***164** D-2; mail Sopchoppy z 32358; rural
Cutler; CDP; MIAMI-DADE; ***165** Q-13; ★ **MIA-**; mail Miami z 33157-58; former CDP; became part of Palmetto Bay September 11, 2002; Ⓟ 16,201; Ⓒ 17,390
Cutler Bay; Inc. Place; MIAMI-DADE; ***165** Q-13; incorporated November 9, 2005; not reported in 2000 Census; includes Cutler Ridge CDP and Lakes by the Bay CDP; ● 40,000; ◆ 25,889
Cutler Ridge; CDP; MIAMI-DADE; **165** Q-13; 🅿; ★ **MIA-**; z 33157 & mail Miami z 33170, z 33189-90; former CDP; became part of Cutler Bay November 9, 2005; Ⓟ 21,268; Ⓒ 24,781; ◆ 25,889
Cutlers; RMC Place; CITRUS; ***164** G-7; mail Crystal River z 34429, Homosassa z 34448; ● 700
Cypress; RMC Place; BROWARD; ***165** O-14; ★ **MIA-**; mail Pompano Beach z 33060; pop. incl. with Pompano Beach (Inc. Place)
Cypress; RMC Place; JACKSON; **165** R-7; elev. 135ft./41m.; 🅿; z 32432; ● 250
Cypress Gardens; CDP; POLK; **163** K-5; 🅿; ★ **WNHV**; z 33884; Ⓟ 9,188; Ⓒ 8,844
Cypress Lake; CDP-Census Area Only; LEE; ***165** N-9; ★ **FTMY-**; mail Fort Myers z 33919; Ⓟ 10,491; Ⓒ 12,072
Cypress Lake Estates; RMC Place; VOLUSIA; ***164** G-10; ● 65
Cypress Lakes; CDP-Census Area Only; PALM BEACH; ***165** N-14; ★ **MIA-**; mail West Palm Beach z 33417; Ⓟ 1,260; Ⓒ 1,468
Cypress Point; RMC Place; PUTNAM; ***164** E-9; mail East Palatka z 32131; ● 100
Cypress Quarters; CDP; OKEECHOBEE; **165** L-12; mail Okeechobee z 34972; Ⓟ 1,343; Ⓒ 1,150
Cyprus Village; RMC Place; MIAMI-DADE; ★ **MIA-**; mail Hialeah z 33014; pop. incl. with Miami Lakes (CDP-Census Area Only)

D

Dade City; Inc. Place; ⊡ PASCO; **164** I-8; elev. 78ft./24m.; 🅿 🅷; z 33523, z 33525-26; Ⓟ 5,633; Ⓒ 6,188
Dade City North; CDP-Census Area Only; PASCO; ***164** I-8; mail Dade City z 33523; Ⓟ 3,058; Ⓒ 3,319
Dahoma; RMC Place; NASSAU; ***164** B-8; mail Bryceville z 32009, Callahan z 32011; ● 170
Daisy Lake; RMC Place; VOLUSIA; ***164** G-10; ● 100
Dalhousie Acres; RMC Place; LAKE; ***164** G-9; rural
Dalkeith; RMC Place; GULF; ***165** T-7; mail Wewahitchka z 32465
Dallas; RMC Place; MARION; ***164** G-8; ★ **OCA**; mail Summerfield z 34491; ● 75
Dames Point; RMC Place; DUVAL; ***164** C-9; ★ **JAX**; mail Jacksonville z 32226; pop. incl. with Jacksonville (Inc. Place)
Dames Point Junction; RMC Place; DUVAL; ★ **JAX**; pop. incl. with Jacksonville (Inc. Place)
Dana; RMC Place; UNION; ***164** D-7; mail Lake Butler z 32054; ● 140
Dania; BROWARD; see Dania Beach (Inc. Place)
Dania Beach (Dania); Inc. Place; BROWARD; **165** P-14; elev. 11ft./3m.; 🅿; ★ **MIA-**; z 33004 & mail Fort Lauderdale z 33312, z 33314; Ⓟ 13,024; Ⓒ 20,061; ◆ 27,048
Danks Corner; RMC Place; MARION; ***164** G-8; elev. 71ft./22m.; ★ **OCA**; mail Summerfield z 34491; rural
Darby; RMC Place; PASCO; **164** I-7; elev. 114ft./35m.; mail Dade City z 33525; ● 375
Darlington; RMC Place; WALTON; ***165** Q-5; mail Westville z 32464; ● 170
Darsey; RMC Place; GADSDEN; ***164** B-2; mail Havana z 32333; ● 300
Davenport; Inc. Place; POLK; **164** I-9; elev. 136ft./41m.; 🅿; z 33836-37, z 33896-97; Ⓟ 1,529; Ⓒ 1,924
Davie; Inc. Place; BROWARD; **165** P-13; elev. 5ft./2m.; 🅿; ★ **MIA-**; z 33312, z 33314, z 33317, z 33324-26, z 33328-32, z 33355 & mail Hollywood z 33024; Ⓟ 47,217; Ⓒ 75,720; ◆ 87,209
Davis Islands; RMC Place; HILLSBOROUGH; ***164** J-7; ★ **TAM**; mail Tampa z 33606; pop. incl. with Tampa (Inc. Place)
Davis Shores; RMC Place; ST. JOHNS; ***164** D-10; mail Saint Augustine z 32084; pop. incl. with Saint Augustine (Inc. Place)
Day; RMC Place; LAFAYETTE; **164** C-5; elev. 84ft./26m.; 🅿; z 32013; ● 130
Daytona Beach; Inc. Place; VOLUSIA; **164** F-11; elev. 10ft./3m.; 🅿 🅷 🅲 24,800 ■; ★ **D.BCH**; z 32114-26, z 32198 & mail Port Orange z 32127-29; Ⓟ 61,921; Ⓒ 64,112; ◆ 60,444
Daytona Beach Shores; Inc. Place; VOLUSIA; **164** F-11; 🅿; ★ **D.BCH**; z 32116, z 32118; Ⓟ 2,335; Ⓒ 4,299
Daytona Highridge Estates; RMC Place; VOLUSIA; ***164** F-11; mail Daytona Beach z 32114; ● 460
Daytona Park Estates; RMC Place; VOLUSIA; ***164** G-10; ★ **DL**; mail DeLand z 32720; ● 1,200
DeBary; Inc. Place; VOLUSIA; **164** G-10; elev. 76ft./23m.; 🅿; ★ **ORL**; z 32713, z 32753; Ⓟ 7,176; Ⓒ 15,559
Deep Creek; RMC Place; COLUMBIA; ***164** C-7; mail Lake City z 32055; ● 90
Deerfield Beach; Inc. Place; BROWARD; **165** O-14; elev. 12ft./4m.; 🅿; ★ **MIA-**; z 33441-43 & mail Pompano Beach z 33064, z 33069, z 33073; Ⓟ 46,325; Ⓒ 64,583; Ⓡ 64,585; ◆ 71,580
Deering Bay; RMC Place; MIAMI-DADE; ***165** Q-13; ★ **MIA-**; mail Miami z 33158; pop. incl. with Coral Gables (Inc. Place)
Deerland; RMC Place; OKALOOSA; ***165** R-4; mail Crestview z 32536; ● 30
Deer Park; RMC Place; OSCEOLA; ***164** J-11; elev. 43ft./13m.; mail Melbourne z 32901
Deerwood; RMC Place; DUVAL; ***164** C-9; ★ **JAX**; mail Jacksonville z 32256; pop. incl. with Jacksonville (Inc. Place)
De Funiak Springs; Inc. Place; ⊡ WALTON; **165** R-5; elev. 260ft./79m.; 🅿 🅷; z 32433, z 32435; Ⓟ 5,120; Ⓒ 5,089
Dekle Beach; RMC Place; TAYLOR; **164** D-4; mail Perry z 32347; ● 50
De Land; Inc. Place; ⊡ VOLUSIA; **164** G-10; elev. 77ft./23m.; 🅿 🅷 🅲 3,762 ■; ★ **DL**; z 32720-24; Ⓟ 16,491; Ⓒ 20,904; ◆ 27,038
De Land Highlands; RMC Place; VOLUSIA; ***164** G-10; ★ **DL**; mail DeLand z 32720; ● 900
De Land Southwest; CDP-Census Area Only; VOLUSIA; ***164** G-10; ★ **DL**; mail DeLand z 32720; Ⓟ 1,249; Ⓒ 1,169
De Leon Springs; CDP; VOLUSIA; **164** F-10; elev. 43ft./13m.; 🅿; ★ **DL**; z 32130; Ⓟ 1,481; Ⓒ 2,358
Delespine; RMC Place; BREVARD; ***164** H-12; ★ **MELB-**; mail Cocoa z 32927; ● 1,400
Dellwood; RMC Place; JACKSON; **165** R-7; elev. 117ft./36m.; mail Grand Ridge z 32442; ● 75
Dellwood; RMC Place; LEON; ***164** B-2; ★ **TALL**; mail Tallahassee z 32303; pop. incl. with Tallahassee (Inc. Place)
Delray Beach; Inc. Place; PALM BEACH; **165** N-14; elev. 20ft./6m.; 🅿 🅷 ■; ★ **MIA-**; z 33444-46, z 33448, z 33482-84; Ⓟ 47,181; Ⓒ 60,020; ◆ 65,577
Delray Gardens; RMC Place; PALM BEACH; **163** D-9; ★ **MIA-**; mail Delray Beach z 33484; ● 460
Del Rio; RMC Place; HILLSBOROUGH; ***164** J-7; ★ **TAM**; mail Tampa z 33617; Ⓟ 8,248; ● 8,500
Deltona; Inc. Place; VOLUSIA; **164** G-10; 🅿; ★ **ORL**; z 32725, z 32728, z 32738-39; Ⓟ 50,828; Ⓒ 69,543; ◆ 89,926
Deltona Pines; RMC Place; VOLUSIA; ★ **ORL**; mail Deltona z 32738; pop. incl. with Deltona (Inc. Place)
Denaud (Fort Denaud); RMC Place; HENDRY; ***165** N-10; mail Labelle z 33935; rural
Denham; RMC Place; PASCO; ***164** I-7; mail Land O Lakes z 34639; ● 200
Denver; RMC Place; PUTNAM; ***164** F-10; elev. 70ft./21m.; mail Crescent City z 32112; rural
DESOTO; **165** L-9; Ⓟ 23,865; Ⓒ 32,209; ◆ 34,352
De Soto City; RMC Place; HIGHLANDS; **165** K-10; mail Sebring z 33870; ● 600
Desoto Lakes; CDP-Census Area Only; SARASOTA; **163** G-4; ★ **SAR-B**; mail Sarasota z 34235; Ⓟ 2,807; Ⓒ 3,198
Destin; Inc. Place; OKALOOSA; **165** S-4; elev. 33ft./10m.; 🅿; ★ **FTWL**; z 32540-41, z 32550; Ⓟ 8,080; Ⓒ 11,119
Devils Garden; RMC Place; HENDRY; ***165** N-11; elev. 29ft./9m.; mail Clewiston z 33440; rural
Dickerson City; RMC Place; SANTA ROSA; ***165** R-3; mail Milton z 32583; rural
Dickert; RMC Place; SUWANNEE; ***164** C-5; mail Live Oak z 32060; ● 200
Dills (Sheffield); RMC Place; JEFFERSON; ***164** B-4; elev. 124ft./38m.; mail Monticello z 32344; rural
Dinsmore; RMC Place; DUVAL; ***164** C-9; 🅿; ★ **JAX**; z 32219; pop. incl. with Jacksonville (Inc. Place)
Dirego Park; RMC Place; BAY; ***165** S-6; ★ **PNCY**; mail Panama City z 32405; pop. incl. with Cedar Grove (Inc. Place)
Dixie; RMC Place; HERNANDO, PASCO; ***164** I-7; mail Brooksville z 34602; ● 260
DIXIE; **164** E-5; Ⓟ 10,585; Ⓒ 13,827; ◆ 15,025
Dixieland; RMC Place; POLK; ***164** J-8; ★ **LKLD**; mail Lakeland z 33803, z 33806; pop. incl. with Lakeland (Inc. Place)
Dixie Ranch Acres; RMC Place; OKEECHOBEE; **165** L-11; mail Okeechobee z 34972; ● 335
Dixietown; RMC Place; DIXIE; ***164** E-6; mail Old Town z 32680; ● 225
Dixie Village; RMC Place; ORANGE; ***164** H-10; ★ **ORL**; mail Orlando z 32806, z 32856
Dixon; RMC Place; WALTON; ***165** R-5; mail Defuniak Springs z 32433; pop. incl. with De Funiak Springs (Inc. Place)
Doctor Phillips; CDP-Census Area Only; ORANGE; **165** O-2; elev. 105ft./32m.; ★ **ORL**; mail Orlando z 32819; Ⓟ 7,963; Ⓒ 9,548
Doctors Inlet; RMC Place; CLAY; **164** C-9; elev. 9ft./3m.; 🅿; ★ **JAX**; z 32030; ● 1,800
Dogtown; RMC Place; GADSDEN; ***164** B-2; mail Quincy z 32352; rural
Dogwood Lakes Estates; RMC Place; HOLMES; ***165** Q-6; mail Bonifay z 32425; ● 200
Dona Vista; RMC Place; LAKE; ***164** G-9; elev. 82ft./25m.; 🅿; z 32784; ● 640
Doral; Inc. Place; MIAMI-DADE; ***165** P-13; elev. 3ft./1m.; 🅿; ★ **MIA-**; z 33122, z 33126, z 33166, z 33172, z 33178, z 33182; incorporated June 23, 2003; not reported in 2000 Census; ◆ 22,461
Doral; CDP-Census Area Only; MIAMI-DADE; ***165** P-13; 🅿; ★ **MIA-**; z 33122, z 33126, z 33166, z 33172, z 33178, z 33182; Ⓟ 3,126; Ⓒ 20,438
Dorcas; RMC Place; OKALOOSA; ***165** R-4; mail Crestview z 32539
Douglas City; RMC Place; GADSDEN; ***164** B-1; mail Quincy z 32351; rural
Douglas Crossroads; WALTON; see Douglass Crossroads (RMC Place)
Douglass Crossroads (Douglas Crossroads); RMC Place; WALTON; ***165** R-5; mail Ponce de Leon z 32455; rural
Dover; CDP; HILLSBOROUGH; **164** J-8; elev. 102ft./31m.; 🅿; ★ **TAM**; z 33527; Ⓟ 2,606; Ⓒ 2,798
Dover Shores; RMC Place; ORANGE; ***164** H-10; ★ **ORL**; mail Orlando z 32806; pop. incl. with Orlando (Inc. Place)
Dowling Park; RMC Place; SUWANNEE; **164** C-5; 🅿; z 32060, z 32064; ● 500
Drayton Island; RMC Place; PUTNAM; mail Georgetown z 32139; rural
Dreamworld; RMC Place; SEMINOLE; ***164** G-10; elev. 45ft./14m.; ★ **ORL**; mail Sanford z 32771; pop. incl. with Sanford (Inc. Place)
Drew Park; RMC Place; HILLSBOROUGH; ***164** J-7; ★ **TAM**; mail Tampa z 33614; pop. incl. with Tampa (Inc. Place)
Drexel; RMC Place; PASCO; ***164** I-7; mail Land O Lakes z 34639; ● 540
Drifton; RMC Place; JEFFERSON; **164** B-3; mail Monticello z 32344; ● 25

Entries in **UPPERCASE** are counties.
Entries in **bold** have populations of 2,500 or more.
Names in parentheses are alternate names.
Inc. Place — Incorporated Place
RMC Place — Rand McNally Designated Place
CDP — Census Designated Place
MCD — Minor Civil Division

⊡ County Seat
▲ Minor Civil Division
elev. Elevation
🅿 Post Office

🅷 Hospital
🅲 College
■ Principal Business Center
★ Ranally Metro Area (RMA) Abbreviation
z Zip Code(s)

Ⓟ Previous Census Population
Ⓡ Revised Census Population
Ⓐ Annexation Population
● Rand McNally Population Estimate
Ⓒ Final Census Population
Ⓢ Special Census Population
◆ Estimated Population

For additional definitions see Glossary, Volume 1, and Introduction, Volume 2.

Druid Hills; RMC Place; SEMINOLE; *164 H-10; ★ ORL; mail Maitland z 32751; ● 880
Dublin; RMC Place; LAKE; *164 G-9; mail Mount Dora z 32757; pop. incl. with Mount Dora (Inc. Place)
Duck Key; CDP-Census Area Only; MONROE; 165 T-11; 🅿; z 33050; © 443
Duette; RMC Place; MANATEE; *165 K-8; 🅿; z 33834, z 34219; rural
Dukes; RMC Place; UNION; *164 D-7; mail Lake Butler z 32054, Worthington Springs z 32697; ● 200
Dundee; Inc. Place; POLK; 164 J-9; elev. 128ft./39m.; 🅿; ★ WNHV; z 33838; Ⓟ 2,335; © 2,912
Dune Allen Beach; RMC Place; WALTON; *165 S-5; mail Santa Rosa Beach z 32459; ● 70
Dunedin; Inc. Place; PINELLAS; 164 J-6; 🅿 🅷 🅲 862; ★ ST.PET; z 34697-98; Ⓟ 34,012; © 35,691; ◆ 33,884
Dunedin Isles; RMC Place; PINELLAS; *164 J-6; ★ ST.PET; mail Dunedin z 34698; pop. incl. with Dunedin (Inc. Place)
Dunes Road; CDP-Census Area Only; PALM BEACH; *165 N-14; ★ MIA-; © 391
Dunnellon; Inc. Place; MARION; 164 G-7; elev. 55ft./17m.; 🅿; z 34430-34; Ⓟ 1,624; © 1,898
Dupont; RMC Place; FLAGLER; *164 E-10; mail Bunnell z 32110; rural
Dupont Center; RMC Place; ST. JOHNS; *164 D-10; elev. 30ft./9m.; mail Saint Augustine z 32086; ● 150
Dupree Gardens; RMC Place; PASCO; *164 I-7; mail Land O Lakes z 34639; ● 420
Durant; RMC Place; HILLSBOROUGH; 164 J-8; elev. 47ft./14m.; 🅿; ★ TAM; z 33530; ● 225
Durbin; RMC Place; ST. JOHNS; *164 C-10; mail Ponte Vedra Beach z 32082, Saint Augustine z 32095; ● 170
Duval; RMC Place; DUVAL; *164 B-9; ★ JAX; mail Jacksonville z 32218; pop. incl. with Jacksonville (Inc. Place)
DUVAL; 164 C-9; Ⓟ 672,971; © 778,879; ◆ 870,146
Dyal; RMC Place; NASSAU; *164 B-9; elev. 48ft./15m.; mail Callahan z 32011; ● 120

E

Eagle Lake; Inc. Place; POLK; 163 K-4; elev. 172ft./52m.; 🅿; ★ WNHV; z 33839; Ⓟ 1,758; © 2,496
Earleton; RMC Place; ALACHUA; 164 E-8; 🅿; z 32631; ● 320
Early Bird; RMC Place; MARION; *164 F-7; mail Dunnellon z 34432, Ocala z 34482; ● 45
East Avenue; RMC Place; SARASOTA; *165 L-7; ★ SAR-B; mail Sarasota z 34237; pop. incl. with Sarasota (Inc. Place)
East Bronson; CDP-Census Area Only; LEVY; *164 E-7; © 1,075
Eastbrook; RMC Place; SEMINOLE; *164 H-10; ★ ORL; mail Winter Park z 32792; ● 3,200
East Dunbar; CDP-Census Area Only; LEE; *165 N-9; ★ FTMY-; © 1,935
Eastern Shores; RMC Place; MIAMI-DADE; *165 P-14; ★ MIA-; mail North Miami Beach z 33160; pop. incl. with North Miami Beach (Inc. Place)
Eastgate; RMC Place; LEON; *164 B-2; ★ TALL; mail Tallahassee z 32308; pop. incl. with Tallahassee (Inc. Place)
Eastgate; RMC Place; ORANGE; *164 H-10; ★ ORL; mail Winter Park z 32792; pop. incl. with Winter Park (Inc. Place)
Eastgate; RMC Place; SARASOTA; *165 M-7; mail Venice z 34292; pop. incl. with Venice (Inc. Place)
East Hill; RMC Place; ESCAMBIA; *165 R-2; ★ PENS; mail Pensacola z 32503; pop. incl. with Pensacola (Inc. Place)
East Lake (East Lake Park); RMC Place; HILLSBOROUGH; *164 J-7; ★ TAM; mail Tampa z 33610; ● 3,300
East Lake; CDP-Census Area Only; PINELLAS; *164 J-6; ★ ST.PET; © 29,394; ◆ 28,773
East Lake-Orient Park; CDP-Census Area Only; HILLSBOROUGH; *164 J-7; ★ TAM; mail Tampa z 33610, z 33619; Ⓟ 6,171; © 5,703
East Lake Park; HILLSBOROUGH; see East Lake (RMC Place)
East Lake Weir; RMC Place; MARION; 164 G-9; 🅿; ★ OCA; z 32133; ● 140
East Milton; RMC Place; SANTA ROSA; *165 R-3; ★ PENS; mail Milton z 32583; ● 1,100
East Mims; RMC Place; BREVARD; *164 H-11; ● 175
East Naples; RMC Place; COLLIER; 165 P-9; ★ NAP; mail Naples z 34112; Ⓟ 22,951; ● 2,050
East Palatka; CDP; PUTNAM; 164 E-9; elev. 16ft./5m.; 🅿; z 32131; Ⓟ 1,989; © 1,707
East Perrine; CDP-Census Area Only; MIAMI-DADE; *165 Q-13; ★ MIA-; © 7,079
Eastpoint; CDP; FRANKLIN; 165 T-8; elev. 10ft./3m.; 🅿; z 32328; Ⓟ 1,577; © 2,158
East Rockland Key; RMC Place; MONROE; *165 T-9; 🅿; z 33040; ● 100
East Side; RMC Place; SEMINOLE; *164 H-10; ★ ORL; mail Altamonte Springs z 32715; pop. incl. with Altamonte Springs (Inc. Place)
East Silver Springs Shore; RMC Place; MARION; *164 G-9; ★ OCA; mail Ocklawaha z 32179; ● 70
East Tampa; RMC Place; HILLSBOROUGH; 163 C-4; elev. 11ft./3m.; ★ TAM; mail Tampa z 33619; ● 750
East Tampa Junction; RMC Place; HILLSBOROUGH; ★ TAM
East Williston; CDP-Census Area Only; LEVY; 164 F-7; mail Williston z 32696; © 966
Eastwood; RMC Place; POLK; *164 J-9; mail Winter Haven z 33884; ● 150
Eaton Park; RMC Place; POLK; 163 K-2; 🅿; ★ LKLD; z 33840; ● 900
Eatonville; Inc. Place; ORANGE; 165 M-3; elev. 101ft./31m.; 🅿; ★ ORL; z 32751; Ⓟ 2,170; © 2,432
Eau Gallie; RMC Place; BREVARD; *164 I-12; 🅿; ★ MELB-; z 32934, z 32936 & mail Melbourne z 32935, z 32940; pop. incl. with Melbourne (Inc. Place)
Ebb; RMC Place; MADISON; *164 C-4; mail Greenville z 32331; rural
Ebro; Inc. Place; WASHINGTON; 165 S-6; elev. 68ft./21m.; 🅿; z 32437; Ⓟ 255; © 250
Eden; RMC Place; ST. LUCIE; *165 L-13; mail Jensen Beach z 34957; ● 300
Edgar; RMC Place; PUTNAM; 164 E-8; elev. 100ft./30m.; 🅿; z 32149; ● 50
Edgewater; CDP-Census Area Only; BROWARD; *165 P-13; ★ MIA-; © 803
Edgewater; RMC Place; MIAMI-DADE; *165 P-13; ★ MIA-; mail Miami z 33137; pop. incl. with Miami (Inc. Place)
Edgewater; Inc. Place; VOLUSIA; 164 G-11; elev. 6ft./2m.; 🅿; ★ D.BCH; z 32132, z 32141; Ⓟ 15,337; © 18,668; ◆ 20,363
Edgewater Gulf Beach; RMC Place; BAY; *165 S-6; ★ PNCY; mail Panama City Beach z 32407; pop. incl. with Panama City Beach (Inc. Place)
Edgewater Junction; RMC Place; VOLUSIA; *164 G-11; rural
Edgewood; RMC Place; DUVAL; ★ JAX; pop. incl. with Jacksonville (Inc. Place)
Edgewood; Inc. Place; ORANGE; 165 N-4; 🅿; ★ ORL; z 32809, z 32839; Ⓟ 1,062; © 1,901
Edgewood Manor; RMC Place; DUVAL; *164 C-9; ★ JAX; mail Jacksonville z 32209; pop. incl. with Jacksonville (Inc. Place)
Edison; RMC Place; HILLSBOROUGH; *164 J-8; mail Lithia z 33547; ● 600
Edison Center; RMC Place; MIAMI-DADE; *165 P-13; ★ MIA-; mail Miami z 33151; pop. incl. with Miami (Inc. Place)
Eglin AFB; CDP-Census Area Only; OKALOOSA; *165 R-4; 🅿; ★ FTWL; z 32542; Ⓟ 8,347; © 8,082
Eglin Village; RMC Place; OKALOOSA; ★ FTWL; mail Hurlburt Field z 32544
Egypt Lake; RMC Place; HILLSBOROUGH; 163 B-3; ★ TAM; mail Tampa z 33614; Ⓟ 14,580; ● 3,500
Egypt Lake-Leto; CDP-Census Area Only; HILLSBOROUGH; *164 J-7; ★ TAM; © 32,782; ◆ 39,606
Ehren; RMC Place; PASCO; *164 I-7; mail Land O Lakes z 34639; ● 155
El Chico; RMC Place; MONROE; *165 T-9; mail Key West z 33040
Elder Springs; RMC Place; SEMINOLE; *164 H-10; ★ ORL; mail Sanford z 32773; ● 150
El Destinado; RMC Place; LEON; *164 B-2; mail Tallahassee z 32312; ● 550
Eldorado; RMC Place; LAKE; *164 G-9; ● 85
Eldridge; RMC Place; VOLUSIA; *164 F-10; mail Pierson z 32180; ● 140
Electra; RMC Place; MARION; *164 F-9; mail Ocklawaha z 32179; ● 170
Elfers; CDP; PASCO; 164 I-6; 🅿; ★ ST.PET; z 34680 & mail New Port Richey z 34652; Ⓟ 12,356; © 13,161
El Jobean; RMC Place; CHARLOTTE; 165 M-8; elev. 6ft./2m.; 🅿; ★ PUN-; z 33927; ● 600
Elkton; RMC Place; ST. JOHNS; 164 D-10; elev. 36ft./11m.; 🅿; z 32033
Ellaville; RMC Place; JACKSON; *165 Q-7; elev. 140ft./43m.; mail Campbellton z 32426; rural
Ellaville; RMC Place; SUWANNEE; *164 C-5; mail Live Oak z 32060; rural
Ellenton; CDP; MANATEE; 165 K-7; elev. 9ft./3m.; 🅿; ★ SAR-B; z 34222; Ⓟ 2,573; © 3,142
Ellerslie; RMC Place; PASCO; *164 I-8; elev. 130ft./40m.; mail Dade City z 33525; ● 200
Ellinor Village; RMC Place; VOLUSIA; *164 F-11; ★ D.BCH; mail Ormond Beach z 32175; pop. incl. with Ormond Beach (Inc. Place)
Ellison Acres; RMC Place; VOLUSIA; mail New Smyrna Beach z 32168; ● 120
Ellisville; RMC Place; COLUMBIA; *164 D-7; mail Lake City z 32055; ● 150
Ellsworth Junction; RMC Place; LAKE; *164 H-9; mail Astatula z 34705; ● 270
Ellzey; RMC Place; LEVY; *164 F-6; mail Otter Creek z 32683; rural
Elm Mission; OKALOOSA; see Blackman (RMC Place)
Eloise; RMC Place; POLK; 163 K-4; elev. 160ft./49m.; 🅿; ★ WNHV; z 33880; ● 250
Eloise Woods; RMC Place; POLK; *164 J-9; ★ WNHV; mail Winter Haven z 33884; ● 1,900
El Portal; Inc. Place; MIAMI-DADE; 163 L-9; elev. 10ft./3m.; 🅿; ★ MIA-; z 33138, z 33150; Ⓟ 2,457; © 2,505
Elsi De Monde Heights; RMC Place; JACKSON; mail Marianna z 32448; ● 25
Elwood Park; RMC Place; MANATEE; *165 K-7; ★ SAR-B; mail Bradenton z 34208; ● 1,200
Emathla; RMC Place; MARION; *164 F-7; mail Ocala z 34482; ● 130
Empire Point; RMC Place; DUVAL; *164 C-9; ★ JAX; mail Jacksonville z 32207; pop. incl. with Jacksonville (Inc. Place)
Emporia; RMC Place; VOLUSIA; 164 F-10; mail Pierson z 32180; ● 300
Englewood; RMC Place; DUVAL; *164 C-9; ★ JAX; mail Jacksonville z 32207; pop. incl. with Jacksonville (Inc. Place)
Englewood; CDP; SARASOTA, CHARLOTTE; 165 M-7; elev. 13ft./4m.; 🅿 🅷; ★ VEN; z 34223-24, z 34295; Ⓟ 15,025; © 16,196
Englewood Beach; CHARLOTTE; see Punta Gorda Beach (RMC Place)
English Estates; RMC Place; SEMINOLE; *164 H-10; ★ ORL; mail Casselberry z 32730, Maitland z 32751
Enon; RMC Place; ESCAMBIA; *165 Q-2; mail Mc David z 32568
Ensley; CDP; ESCAMBIA; 165 R-2; elev. 133ft./41m.; ★ PENS; mail Pensacola z 32514, z 32534; Ⓟ 16,362; © 18,752
Enterprise; RMC Place; VOLUSIA; 164 G-10; 🅿; ★ ORL; z 32725; ● 2,000
Eppes Heights; RMC Place; LEON; *164 B-2; ★ TALL; mail Tallahassee z 32304; pop. incl. with Tallahassee (Inc. Place)
Eridu; RMC Place; TAYLOR; 164 C-4; mail Greenville z 32331; ● 60
Erie; RMC Place; MANATEE; *165 K-7; mail Parrish z 34219; rural
Errol Estates; RMC Place; ORANGE; *164 H-10; ★ ORL; mail Apopka z 32712; pop. incl. with Apopka (Inc. Place)
ESCAMBIA; 165 Q-2; Ⓟ 262,798; © 294,410; ◆ 328,051
Escambia Farms; RMC Place; OKALOOSA; *165 Q-4; elev. 216ft./66m.; mail Baker z 32531; rural
Espanola; RMC Place; FLAGLER; 164 E-10; mail Bunnell z 32110; ● 100
Esperenza; RMC Place; PUTNAM; *164 E-9; mail East Palatka z 32131; ● 50
Estates of Fort Lauderdale; CDP-Census Area Only; BROWARD; *165 P-13; ★ MIA-; © 1,791
Estero; CDP; LEE; 165 O-9; elev. 16ft./5m.; 🅿; ★ FTMY-; z 33928-29 & mail Melbourne z 32912; © 9,503
Estiffanulga; RMC Place; LIBERTY; 165 S-7; mail Bristol z 32321; ● 120
Esto; Inc. Place; HOLMES; 165 Q-6; elev. 237ft./72m.; 🅿; z 32425; Ⓟ 253; © 356
Eucheeanna; RMC Place; WALTON; *165 R-5; mail Defuniak Springs z 32433; rural
Euclid; RMC Place; PINELLAS; *164 J-7; ★ ST.PET; mail Saint Petersburg z 33704, z 33734; pop. incl. with Saint Petersburg (Inc. Place)
Eugene; RMC Place; DIXIE; *164 E-5; mail Cross City z 32628; ● 220
Eureka; RMC Place; MARION; *164 F-9; mail Fort Mc Coy z 32134; ● 130
Eustis; Inc. Place; LAKE; 164 G-9; elev. 67ft./20m.; 🅿 🅷; z 32726-27, z 32736; Ⓟ 12,967; © 15,106
Eva; RMC Place; POLK; *164 I-9; mail Lakeland z 33809
Everglades; COLLIER; see Everglades City (Inc. Place)
Everglades City (Everglades); Inc. Place; COLLIER; 165 P-10; elev. 3ft./1m.; 🅿; z 34139; Ⓟ 321; © 479
Evergreen; RMC Place; NASSAU; *164 B-9; mail Yulee z 32097; ● 130
Evinston; RMC Place; ALACHUA; 164 E-8; elev. 102ft./31m.; 🅿; z 32633; ● 240
Ewing; RMC Place; HILLSBOROUGH; ★ TAM; pop. incl. with Tampa (Inc. Place)

F

Facil; RMC Place; HAMILTON; *164 C-6; mail White Springs z 32096; rural
Fairbanks; RMC Place; ALACHUA; 164 E-8; elev. 166ft./51m.; mail Gainesville z 32601; ● 500
Fairfield; RMC Place; MARION; 164 F-8; elev. 114ft./35m.; 🅿; ★ OCA; z 32634; ● 45
Fairlane Estates; RMC Place; SEMINOLE; *164 H-10; mail Ochlocknee z 31773; pop. incl. with Sanford (Inc. Place)
Fair Meadows; RMC Place; LEON; *164 B-2; ★ TALL; mail Tallahassee z 32304; pop. incl. with Tallahassee (Inc. Place)
Fairmont; RMC Place; PINELLAS; *165 K-6; ★ ST.PET; mail Saint Petersburg z 33711; pop. incl. with Saint Petersburg (Inc. Place)
Fairview Shores; CDP; ORANGE; 165 M-3; ★ ORL; mail Orlando z 32804; Ⓟ 13,192; © 13,898
Fairvilla; RMC Place; ORANGE; *164 H-10; ★ ORL; mail Orlando z 32804
Fairyland; RMC Place; BREVARD; ★ MELB-; mail Merritt Island z 32952
Falmouth; RMC Place; SUWANNEE; *164 C-5; mail Live Oak z 32060
Fanlew; RMC Place; JEFFERSON; *164 C-3; elev. 35ft./11m.; mail Monticello z 32344; rural
Fanning Springs; Inc. Place; LEVY, GILCHRIST; 164 E-6; elev. 32ft./10m.; 🅿; z 32693 & mail Old Town z 32680; Ⓟ 493; © 737
Farm Hill; RMC Place; ESCAMBIA; *165 R-2; mail Cantonment z 32533; ● 550
Favoretta (Favorita); RMC Place; FLAGLER; *164 F-10; elev. 25ft./8m.; mail Bunnell z 32110
Favorita; FLAGLER; see Favoretta (RMC Place)
Feather Sound; CDP-Census Area Only; PINELLAS; *164 J-7; ★ ST.PET; mail Clearwater z 33762; Ⓟ 2,690; © 3,597
Federal Point; RMC Place; PUTNAM; 164 D-9; mail East Palatka z 32131; ● 260
Fedhaven; RMC Place; POLK; 164 J-10; elev. 65ft./20m.; 🅿; z 33854; ● 250
Felda; RMC Place; HENDRY; 165 N-10; 🅿; z 33930; ● 200
Felicia; RMC Place; CITRUS; *164 G-7; mail Hernando z 34442; ● 80
Fellowship; RMC Place; MARION; *164 F-7; elev. 178ft./54m.; mail Ocala z 34482
Fellowship Park; RMC Place; CLAY; *164 D-9; mail Green Cove Springs z 32043; ● 300
Fellsmere; Inc. Place; INDIAN RIVER; 164 J-12; elev. 25ft./8m.; 🅿; z 32948; Ⓟ 2,179; © 3,813
Fenholloway; RMC Place; TAYLOR; *164 D-4; elev. 56ft./17m.; mail Perry z 32347
Fernandina Beach; Inc. Place; ⊡ NASSAU; 164 B-10; elev. 19ft./6m.; 🅿 🅷; z 32034-35; Ⓟ 8,765; © 10,549
Ferndale; CDP; LAKE; 164 H-9; elev. 103ft./31m.; 🅿; z 34729; © 233; Ⓡ 232
Fern Park; CDP; SEMINOLE; 165 M-4; elev. 99ft./30m.; 🅿; ★ ORL; z 32730; Ⓟ 8,294; © 8,318
Ferry Pass; CDP; ESCAMBIA; 162 L-9; ★ PENS; mail Pensacola z 32504, z 32514; Ⓟ 26,301; © 27,176; ◆ 30,283
Festus; RMC Place; JEFFERSON; *164 B-3; elev. 99ft./30m.; mail Monticello z 32344; rural
Fiddlesticks; RMC Place; LEE; *165 N-9; ★ FTMY-; mail Fort Myers z 33912; ● 400
Fidelis; RMC Place; SANTA ROSA; *165 Q-3; mail Jay z 32565; rural
Fisher Island; CDP-Census Area Only; MIAMI-DADE; *165 Q-14; ★ MIA-; mail Miami Beach z 33109, z 33139; © 467
Fish Hawk; CDP-Census Area Only; HILLSBOROUGH; *164 J-8; ★ TAM; © 1,991
Fish Lake; RMC Place; OSCEOLA; *164 I-10; ★ KISS; mail Kissimmee z 34744; ● 570
Fivay Junction; RMC Place; PASCO; *164 I-7; mail Land O Lakes z 34639; ● 35
Five Points; RMC Place; BREVARD; *164 I-12; ★ MELB-; mail Cocoa z 32924
Five Points; CDP; COLUMBIA; *164 C-7; elev. 169ft./52m.; mail Lake City z 32055; Ⓟ 1,136; © 1,362
Five Points; RMC Place; WASHINGTON; *165 R-6; elev. 70ft./21m.; mail Caryville z 32427; rural
Flagami; RMC Place; MIAMI-DADE; *165 R-13; mail Miami z 33126
Flagler; RMC Place; MIAMI-DADE; *165 Q-13; ★ MIA-; mail Miami z 33101, z 33128-32, z 33136; pop. incl. with Miami (Inc. Place)
Flagler; RMC Place; MONROE; *165 T-9; mail Key West z 33040, z 33045; pop. incl. with Key West (Inc. Place)
FLAGLER; 164 E-10; Ⓟ 28,701; © 49,832; ◆ 98,847
Flagler Beach; Inc. Place; FLAGLER; 164 E-11; elev. 18ft./5m.; 🅿; ★ D.BCH; z 32136; Ⓟ 3,820; © 4,954
Flagler-Tamiami; RMC Place; MIAMI-DADE; *165 Q-13; ★ MIA-; mail Miami z 33126, z 33144; pop. incl. with Miami (Inc. Place)
Flamingo; RMC Place; MONROE; 165 R-11; mail Homestead z 33030, z 33034
Flamingo Bay; RMC Place; LEE; 165 N-8; ★ FTMY-; mail Saint James City z 33956; ● 880
Flemington; RMC Place; MARION; *164 F-7; elev. 94ft./29m.; mail Reddick z 32686; rural
Fletcher; RMC Place; DIXIE; *164 E-6; mail Old Town z 32680; ● 170
Florahome; RMC Place; PUTNAM; 164 E-9; elev. 125ft./38m.; 🅿; z 32140; ● 430
Floral Bluff; RMC Place; DUVAL; *164 C-9; ★ JAX; mail Jacksonville z 32211; pop. incl. with Jacksonville (Inc. Place)
Floral City; CDP; CITRUS; 164 H-7; elev. 68ft./21m.; 🅿; z 34436; Ⓟ 2,609; © 4,989
Floral Park; RMC Place; PALM BEACH; *165 N-14; ★ MIA-; mail Lake Worth z 33462; ● 700
Florence Villa; RMC Place; POLK; *164 J-9; 🅿; ★ WNHV; z 33885 & mail Winter Haven z 33880-81; pop. incl. with Winter Haven (Inc. Place)
Florida A and M University; RMC Place; LEON; *164 B-2; 🅿; ★ TALL; z 32307; pop. incl. with Tallahassee (Inc. Place)
Florida City; Inc. Place; MIAMI-DADE; 165 R-13; elev. 6ft./2m.; 🅿; ★ MIA-; z 33034 & mail Homestead z 33035; Ⓟ 5,806; © 7,843
Florida Gardens; RMC Place; PALM BEACH; *165 N-13; ★ MIA-; mail Lake Worth z 33460; ● 1,100
Florida Hills; RMC Place; LAKE; *164 G-10; ● 100
Floridana Beach (Floridiana); RMC Place; BREVARD; 164 J-12; ★ MELB-; mail Melbourne Beach z 32951; ● 500
Florida Ridge; CDP-Census Area Only; INDIAN RIVER; *165 K-13; ★ VERO; mail Vero Beach z 32962; Ⓟ 12,218; © 15,217
Florida State University; RMC Place; LEON; *164 B-2; 🅿; ★ TALL; z 32313; pop. incl. with Tallahassee (Inc. Place)
Floridiana; BREVARD; see Floridana Beach (RMC Place)
Floritan; RMC Place; POLK; *164 J-9; mail Lake Wales z 33853; ● 230
Florosa; RMC Place; OKALOOSA; 165 S-4; ★ FTWL; mail Mary Esther z 32569; ● 1,000
Flowersville; RMC Place; WALTON; *165 Q-5; elev. 287ft./87m.; mail Laurel Hill z 32567; ● 210
Fluffy Landing; RMC Place; WALTON; *165 S-5; mail Freeport z 32439; ● 160
Foley; RMC Place; TAYLOR; *164 D-4; mail Perry z 32347; ● 220
Footman; RMC Place; BREVARD; *164 I-12; ★ MELB-; mail Merritt Island z 32952
Forest City; CDP; SEMINOLE; 165 M-3; 🅿; ★ ORL; z 32714; Ⓟ 10,638; © 12,612
Forest Heights; RMC Place; LEON; *164 B-2; ★ TALL; mail Tallahassee z 32303; pop. incl. with Tallahassee (Inc. Place)
Forest Hills; RMC Place; HILLSBOROUGH; *164 J-7; ★ TAM; mail Tampa z 33612, z 33682; pop. incl. with Tampa (Inc. Place)
Forest Hills; RMC Place; LAKE; *164 G-10; elev. 75ft./23m.; mail DeLand z 32720; ● 550
Forest Hills; RMC Place; PASCO; *164 I-6; ★ ST.PET; mail Holiday z 34690
Forest Hills; RMC Place; VOLUSIA; ★ D.BCH; mail Ormond Beach z 32174; ● 400
Forest Lakes; RMC Place; SARASOTA; *165 L-7; ★ SAR-B; mail Sarasota z 34232
Forest Lakes Park; RMC Place; MARION; *164 G-9; mail Ocklawaha z 32179; ● 200
Forest Ridge Village; RMC Place; NASSAU; mail Fernandina Beach z 32034; pop. incl. with Fernandina Beach (Inc. Place)
Formosa; RMC Place; ORANGE; ★ ORL; mail Orlando z 32804; pop. incl. with Orlando (Inc. Place)
Fort Basinger; RMC Place; HIGHLANDS; *165 L-11; mail Okeechobee z 34972; rural
Fort Braden; RMC Place; LEON; *164 B-2; mail Tallahassee z 32310; ● 220
Fort Caroline Club Estates; RMC Place; DUVAL; *164 C-9; ★ JAX; mail Jacksonville z 32277; pop. incl. with Jacksonville (Inc. Place)
Fort Denaud; HENDRY; see Denaud (RMC Place)
Fort Drum; RMC Place; OKEECHOBEE; 165 K-12; mail Okeechobee z 34972; ● 140
Fort George Island; RMC Place; DUVAL; *164 C-10; ★ JAX; mail Jacksonville z 32226; pop. incl. with Jacksonville (Inc. Place)
Fort Green; RMC Place; HARDEE; 165 K-8; elev. 116ft./35m.; mail Bowling Green z 33834
Fort Green Springs; RMC Place; HARDEE; 165 K-8; mail Bowling Green z 33834; ● 100
Fort Hamer; RMC Place; MANATEE; *165 K-7; mail Parrish z 34219; ● 120
Fort King Acres; RMC Place; PASCO; *164 I-8; mail Zephyrhills z 33541; ● 480
Fort Lauderdale; Inc. Place; ⊡ BROWARD; 165 O-14; elev. 10ft./3m.; 🅿 🅷 🅲 40,068 ■; ★ MIA-; z 33301-32, z 33334-40, z 33345-46, z 33348-49, z 33351, z 33355, z 33359, z 33388, z 33394; Ⓟ 149,377; © 152,397; ◆ 150,181
Fort Lonesome; RMC Place; HILLSBOROUGH; *165 K-8; elev. 122ft./37m.; mail Lithia z 33547; rural
Fort Mason; RMC Place; LAKE; *164 G-9; mail Eustis z 32726; pop. incl. with Eustis (Inc. Place)
Fort McCoy; RMC Place; MARION; 164 F-8; elev. 74ft./23m.; 🅿; z 32134; ● 300
Fort Meade; Inc. Place; POLK; 165 K-9; elev. 131ft./40m.; 🅿; z 33841; Ⓟ 4,993; © 5,691
Fort Myers; Inc. Place; ⊡ LEE; 165 N-9; elev. 10ft./3m.; 🅿 🅷 🅲 8,316 ■; ★ FTMY-; z 33900-03, z 33905-08, z 33911-13, z 33916-19, z 33965-67, z 33993-94; Ⓟ 45,206; © 48,208; ◆ 61,001
Fort Myers Beach; Inc. Place; LEE; 165 O-8; elev. 5ft./2m.; 🅿; ★ FTMY-; z 33931-32; Ⓟ 9,284; © 6,561
Fort Myers Shores; CDP; LEE; *165 N-9; ★ FTMY-; mail Fort Myers z 33905; Ⓟ 5,460; © 5,793
Fort Myers Villas; RMC Place; LEE; 165 N-9; ★ FTMY-; mail Fort Myers z 33912; ● 5,600
Fort Ogden; RMC Place; DESOTO; 165 M-8; elev. 40ft./12m.; 🅿; z 34267; ● 300
Fort Pierce; Inc. Place; ⊡ ST. LUCIE; 165 K-13; elev. 24ft./7m.; 🅿 🅷 ■; ★ FTPI; z 34945-54, z 34979, z 34981-88; Ⓟ 36,830; © 37,516; ◆ 40,421
Fort Pierce Beach; RMC Place; ST. LUCIE; *165 K-13; ★ FTPI; mail Fort Pierce z 34949
Fort Pierce North; CDP-Census Area Only; ST. LUCIE; *165 K-13; ★ FTPI; mail Fort Pierce z 34946-47; Ⓟ 5,833; © 7,386
Fort Pierce Reservation; Indian Reservation; ST. LUCIE; © 2
Fort Pierce Shores; RMC Place; ST. LUCIE; *165 K-13; ★ FTPI; mail Fort Pierce z 34949; ● 800
Fort Pierce South; CDP-Census Area Only; ST. LUCIE; *165 L-13; ★ FTPI; mail Fort Pierce z 34981-82; Ⓟ 5,320; © 5,672
Fort Taylor; RMC Place; MONROE; *165 T-9; mail Key West z 33040; historic fort located on U.S. Naval Reservation, Key West; pop. incl. with Key West (Inc. Place)
Fort Union; RMC Place; SUWANNEE; *164 C-5; mail Live Oak z 32060; rural
Fort Walton Beach; Inc. Place; OKALOOSA; 165 S-4; elev. 23ft./7m.; 🅿 🅷 ■; ★ FTWL; z 32547-49; Ⓟ 21,471; © 19,973; ◆ 19,429
Fort White; Inc. Place; COLUMBIA; 164 D-6; elev. 72ft./22m.; 🅿; z 32038; Ⓟ 268; © 409
Fountain; RMC Place; BAY; 165 R-7; elev. 184ft./56m.; 🅿; z 32438; ● 450
Fountainbleau; CDP-Census Area Only; MIAMI-DADE; *165 Q-13; ★ MIA-; © 59,549; ◆ 62,210
Fountain Heights; RMC Place; POLK; *164 J-8; pop. incl. with Lakeland (Inc. Place)
Fowler Bluff; LEVY; see Fowlers Bluff (RMC Place)
Fowlers Bluff (Fowler Bluff); RMC Place; LEVY; 164 F-6; mail Chiefland z 32626; ● 90
Foxcroft; RMC Place; LEON; *164 B-2; elev. 100ft./30m.; ★ TALL; mail Tallahassee z 32308; pop. incl. with Tallahassee (Inc. Place)
Fox Town; RMC Place; POLK; 163 I-2; ★ LKLD; mail Lakeland z 33809; ● 300
Francis; RMC Place; PUTNAM; *164 E-9; mail Palatka z 32177; ● 1,000
FRANKLIN; 164 D-1; Ⓟ 8,967; © 11,057; Ⓡ 9,829; ◆ 11,572
Franklin Park; CDP-Census Area Only; BROWARD; *165 O-13; ★ MIA-; © 943
Franklin Park; RMC Place; LEE; 163 M-2; ★ FTMY-; mail Fort Myers z 33916; ● 2,400
Franklintown; RMC Place; NASSAU; *164 B-10; mail Fernandina Beach z 32034; ● 500
Freeport; Inc. Place; WALTON; 165 R-5; elev. 32ft./10m.; 🅿; z 32439; Ⓟ 843; © 1,190
Fremd Village-Padgett Island; CDP-Census Area Only; PALM BEACH; *165 M-12; © 2,264
Frink; RMC Place; CALHOUN; *165 S-7; mail Clarksville z 32430; rural
Frontenac; RMC Place; BREVARD; 164 H-12; elev. 18ft./5m.; ★ MELB-; mail Cocoa z 32927; ● 680
Frostproof; Inc. Place; POLK; 165 K-10; elev. 102ft./31m.; 🅿; z 33843; Ⓟ 2,808; © 2,975
Fruit Cove; CDP; ST. JOHNS; 164 C-9; 🅿; ★ JAX; z 32259; Ⓟ 5,904; © 16,077
Fruitland; RMC Place; PUTNAM; *164 F-9; elev. 26ft./8m.; mail Crescent City z 32112; ● 500
Fruitland Park; Inc. Place; LAKE; 164 G-9; elev. 113ft./34m.; 🅿; z 34731; Ⓟ 2,754; © 3,186
Fruitville; CDP; SARASOTA; 165 L-7; 🅿; ★ SAR-B; z 34232; Ⓟ 9,808; © 12,741
Fuller Heights; RMC Place; POLK; *164 J-8; elev. 115ft./35m.; ★ LKLD; mail Mulberry z 33860; ● 700
Fullers; RMC Place; ORANGE; *164 H-9; mail Ocoee z 34761, Winter Garden z 34787; ● 200
Fussels Corner; CDP-Census Area Only; POLK; 163 J-3; ★ LKLD; mail Auburndale z 33823; Ⓟ 3,840; © 5,313

G

Gaberonne; RMC Place; ESCAMBIA; *165 R-3; mail Pensacola z 32504; pop. incl. with Pensacola (Inc. Place)
Gabriella; RMC Place; SEMINOLE; *164 H-10; mail Oviedo z 32765; ● 500
GADSDEN; 164 B-1; Ⓟ 41,105; © 45,087; ◆ 48,039
Gainesville; Inc. Place; ⊡ ALACHUA; 164 E-7; elev. 185ft./56m.; 🅿 🅷 🅲 51,239 ■; ★ GAIN; z 32601-14, z 32627, z 32635, z 32641, z 32653; Ⓟ 84,770; © 95,447; ◆ 129,375
Galliver; RMC Place; OKALOOSA; *165 R-4; mail Holt z 32564; ● 50
Galloway; RMC Place; POLK; 163 J-1; ★ LKLD; mail Lakeland z 33810; ● 150
Galt City; RMC Place; SANTA ROSA; *165 R-3; ★ PENS; mail Milton z 32583
Galt Ocean Mile; RMC Place; BROWARD; *165 O-14; ★ MIA-; mail Fort Lauderdale z 33308; pop. incl. with Fort Lauderdale (Inc. Place)
Gandy; CDP-Census Area Only; PINELLAS; *164 J-7; ★ ST.PET; mail Saint Petersburg z 33702; Ⓟ 3,164; © 2,031
Garden City; RMC Place; DUVAL; *164 B-9; ★ JAX; mail Jacksonville z 32218; pop. incl. with Jacksonville (Inc. Place)
Garden City; RMC Place; OKALOOSA; 165 Q-4; mail Crestview z 32536, z 32539; ● 150
Garden Grove (Garden Grove Estates); RMC Place; HERNANDO; 164 H-7; mail Brooksville z 34604; ● 480
Garden Grove Estates; HERNANDO; see Garden Grove (RMC Place)
Gardenville; RMC Place; HILLSBOROUGH; *164 J-7; elev. 9ft./3m.; ★ TAM; mail Gibsonton z 33534
Gardner; RMC Place; HARDEE; 165 L-9; mail Zolfo Springs z 33890; ● 130
Garnier; RMC Place; OKALOOSA; *165 R-4; mail Fort Walton Beach z 32547; ● 260
Gary; RMC Place; HILLSBOROUGH; *164 J-7; ★ TAM; pop. incl. with Tampa (Inc. Place)
Gaskin; RMC Place; WALTON; 165 Q-5; elev. 217ft./66m.; mail Defuniak Springs z 32433; ● 150
Gateway; RMC Place; BROWARD; *165 O-14; ★ MIA-; mail Fort Lauderdale z 33338; pop. incl. with Fort Lauderdale (Inc. Place)
Gateway; CDP-Census Area Only; LEE; *165 N-9; © 2,943
Geneva; CDP; SEMINOLE; 164 H-11; elev. 79ft./24m.; 🅿; z 32732; © 2,601
Georgetown; RMC Place; PUTNAM; 164 F-9; elev. 24ft./7m.; 🅿; z 32139; ● 450
Georgiana; RMC Place; BREVARD; *164 I-12; elev. 13ft./4m.; ★ MELB-; mail Merritt Island z 32952; ● 280
Gibson; RMC Place; GADSDEN; *164 B-2; elev. 134ft./41m.; mail Havana z 32333; ● 80
Gibsonia; CDP; POLK; 163 I-1; ★ LKLD; mail Lakeland z 33805, z 33809-10; Ⓟ 5,168; © 4,507
Gibsonton; CDP; HILLSBOROUGH; 164 J-7; 🅿; ★ TAM; z 33534; Ⓟ 7,706; © 8,752
Gifford; CDP; INDIAN RIVER; 165 K-13; ★ VERO; mail Vero Beach z 32960-61, z 32967; Ⓟ 6,278; © 7,599
Gilberts Mill; RMC Place; WASHINGTON; *165 R-6; mail Chipley z 32428; rural
GILCHRIST; 164 D-6; Ⓟ 9,667; © 14,437; ◆ 17,783
Gillett; MANATEE; see Gillette (RMC Place)
Gillette (Gillett); RMC Place; MANATEE; *165 K-7; ★ SAR-B; mail Palmetto z 34221; rural
Gilmore; RMC Place; DUVAL; *164 C-9; ★ JAX; pop. incl. with Jacksonville (Inc. Place)
GLADES; 165 M-10; Ⓟ 7,591; © 10,576; ◆ 10,796
Gladeview; CDP-Census Area Only; MIAMI-DADE; *165 P-13; ★ MIA-; mail Miami z 33147, z 33150; Ⓟ 15,637; © 14,468
Glencoe; CDP; VOLUSIA; *164 G-11; ★ D.BCH; mail New Smyrna Beach z 32168; Ⓟ 2,282; © 2,485
Glendale; RMC Place; LEON; *164 B-2; ★ TALL; mail Tallahassee z 32303; pop. incl. with Tallahassee (Inc. Place)
Glendale; RMC Place; WALTON; 165 Q-5; elev. 289ft./88m.; mail Defuniak Springs z 32433; ● 110
Glen Oaks; RMC Place; SARASOTA; *165 L-7; ★ SAR-B; mail Sarasota z 34232; pop. incl. with Sarasota (Inc. Place)
Glen Ridge; Inc. Place; PALM BEACH; 163 B-10; elev. 15ft./5m.; 🅿; ★ MIA-; z 33406; Ⓟ 207; © 276
Glen Saint Mary; Inc. Place; BAKER; 164 C-8; elev. 134ft./41m.; 🅿; z 32040; Ⓟ 480; © 473
Glenvar Heights; CDP; MIAMI-DADE; 163 M-7; ★ MIA-; mail Miami z 33143, z 33155; Ⓟ 14,823; © 16,243
Glenwood; RMC Place; NASSAU; *164 B-9; mail Yulee z 32097; ● 340
Glenwood; RMC Place; VOLUSIA; 164 G-10; elev. 83ft./25m.; 🅿; ★ DL; z 32722 & mail DeLand z 32720; ● 600
Glory; RMC Place; GADSDEN; mail Quincy z 32352; rural
Glynlea Park; RMC Place; DUVAL; *164 C-9; ★ JAX; mail Jacksonville z 32216; pop. incl. with Jacksonville (Inc. Place)
Godfrey Road; CDP-Census Area Only; BROWARD; *165 O-13; ★ MIA-; © 172
Golden Beach; Inc. Place; MIAMI-DADE; 163 J-9; 🅿; ★ MIA-; z 33160; Ⓟ 774; © 919
Golden Gate; CDP; COLLIER; 165 O-9; ★ NAP; mail Naples z 34116, z 34119; Ⓟ 14,148; © 20,951; ◆ 23,338
Golden Gate; RMC Place; MARTIN; *165 L-13; ★ STU; mail Stuart z 34997; ● 2,650
Golden Gates Estates; RMC Place; COLLIER; *165 O-9; ★ NAP; mail Naples z 34117, z 34119-20; rural
Golden Glades; CDP-Census Area Only; MIAMI-DADE; *165 P-13; ★ MIA-; mail Miami z 33161-62, z 33167-69; Ⓟ 25,474; © 32,623; ◆ 34,081
Golden Heights; CDP-Census Area Only; BROWARD; *165 O-13; ★ MIA-; © 501
Golden Hills; RMC Place; MARION; *164 F-8; ★ OCA; mail Ocala z 34482; ● 420
Golden Isles; RMC Place; BROWARD; *165 P-14; ★ MIA-; mail Hallandale z 33008-09; pop. incl. with Hallandale Beach (Inc. Place)
Golden Lakes; CDP-Census Area Only; PALM BEACH; 163 B-9; ★ MIA-; mail West Palm Beach z 33411; Ⓟ 3,867; © 6,694
Goldenrod; CDP; ORANGE, SEMINOLE; 165 M-4; 🅿; ★ ORL; z 32733; Ⓟ 12,362; © 12,871
Golden Shores; RMC Place; MIAMI-DADE; *165 P-14; ★ MIA-; mail North Miami Beach z 33160; pop. incl. with Aventura (Inc. Place)
Golf (Village of Golf); Inc. Place; PALM BEACH; *165 N-14; ★ MIA-; mail Boynton Beach z 33436; Ⓟ 234; © 230
Golfview; RMC Place; PALM BEACH; 163 B-9; elev. 18ft./5m.; ★ MIA-; mail West Palm Beach z 33406; Ⓟ 153; ● 600
Gomez; RMC Place; MARTIN; *165 M-13; ★ STU; mail Hobe Sound z 33455; ● 600
Gonzalez (Roberts); CDP; ESCAMBIA; 165 R-2; elev. 155ft./47m.; 🅿; ★ PENS; z 32560; Ⓟ 7,669; © 11,365
Goodbys; RMC Place; DUVAL; *164 C-9; ★ JAX; mail Jacksonville z 32257; pop. incl. with Jacksonville (Inc. Place)
Good Hope; RMC Place; OKALOOSA; *165 Q-4; mail Baker z 32531; rural
Goodland; CDP; COLLIER; 165 P-9; 🅿; z 34140; © 320
Gopher Ridge; RMC Place; ST. JOHNS; *164 E-10; elev. 35ft./11m.; mail Hastings z 32145; rural
Gordon; RMC Place; WALTON; *165 Q-5; elev. 283ft./86m.; mail Defuniak Springs z 32433; rural
Gordon Chapel; RMC Place; PUTNAM; mail Hawthorne z 32640; rural
Gordonville; RMC Place; POLK; *164 J-9; elev. 118ft./36m.; ★ WNHV; mail Bartow z 33830-31; ● 1,500
Gotha; CDP; ORANGE; 165 N-2; elev. 138ft./42m.; 🅿; ★ ORL; z 34734; © 731
Goulding; CDP; ESCAMBIA; 162 M-9; ★ PENS; mail Pensacola z 32501; Ⓟ 4,159; © 4,484
Goulds; CDP; MIAMI-DADE; 165 Q-13; elev. 11ft./3m.; 🅿; ★ MIA-; z 33170; Ⓟ 7,284; © 7,453
Graceville; Inc. Place; JACKSON; 165 Q-6; elev. 161ft./49m.; 🅿 🅷 🅲 598; z 32440; Ⓟ 2,675; © 2,402
Graham; RMC Place; BRADFORD; 164 D-8; 🅿; z 32042; ● 200
Grahamsville; RMC Place; MARION; *164 F-8; mail Silver Springs z 34488; rural
Grand Crossing; RMC Place; DUVAL; *164 C-9; ★ JAX; mail Jacksonville z 32209; pop. incl. with Jacksonville (Inc. Place)
Grandin; RMC Place; PUTNAM; 164 E-8; 🅿; z 32138
Grand Island; RMC Place; LAKE; 164 G-9; elev. 125ft./38m.; 🅿; z 32735; ● 1,200
Grand Park; RMC Place; DUVAL; *164 C-9; ★ JAX; mail Jacksonville z 32209; pop. incl. with Jacksonville (Inc. Place)
Grand Ridge; Inc. Place; JACKSON; 165 R-8; elev. 32ft./10m.; 🅿; z 32442; Ⓟ 536; © 792
Grandview; RMC Place; PUTNAM; *164 E-9; mail East Palatka z 32131; ● 150
Grangers Mill; RMC Place; COLUMBIA; mail Lake City z 32055; ● 400
Grant; BREVARD; see Grant-Valkaria (Inc. Place)
Grant-Valkaria (Grant, Valkaria); Inc. Place; BREVARD; 164 J-12; elev. 8ft./2m.; 🅿; ★ MELB-; z 32949; incorporated July 26, 2006; not reported in 2000 Census; ● 2,900
Grassy Key; RMC Place; MONROE; *165 T-11; 🅿; z 33050; pop. incl. with Marathon (Inc. Place)
Gratigny; RMC Place; MIAMI-DADE; *165 P-13; ★ MIA-; mail Miami z 33168; pop. incl. with North Miami (Inc. Place)
Grayton Beach; RMC Place; WALTON; 165 S-5; mail Santa Rosa Beach z 32459; ● 150
Grayvic; MONROE; see Grayvik (RMC Place)
Grayvik (Grayvic); RMC Place; MONROE; *165 R-13; elev. 3ft./1m.; mail Key Largo z 33037; ● 125
Greater Carrollwood; CDP-Census Area Only; HILLSBOROUGH; *164 J-7; ★ TAM; © 33,519; ◆ 40,490
Greater Northdale; CDP-Census Area Only; HILLSBOROUGH; *164 J-7; ★ TAM; mail Tampa z 33624; Ⓟ 16,318; © 20,461; ◆ 24,721
Greater Sun Center; CDP-Census Area Only; HILLSBOROUGH; *165 K-7; © 16,321
Greenacres; PALM BEACH; see Greenacres City (Inc. Place)
Greenacres City (Greenacres); Inc. Place; PALM BEACH; 165 N-14; elev. 19ft./6m.; ★ MIA-; mail Lake Worth z 33454, z 33463, z 33467, West Palm Beach z 33413, z 33415; Ⓟ 18,683; © 27,569; ◆ 31,336
Greenbriar; RMC Place; SEMINOLE; *164 G-10; ★ ORL; mail Sanford z 32771; ● 680
Green Cove Springs; Inc. Place; ⊡ CLAY; 164 D-9; elev. 17ft./5m.; 🅿 🅷; ★ JAX; z 32043; Ⓟ 4,497; © 5,378
Greenfield; RMC Place; PASCO; *164 I-7; mail Spring Hill z 34610; ● 130
Greenhead; RMC Place; WASHINGTON; *165 R-6; mail Chipley z 32428
Green Hills; RMC Place; BAY; *165 S-7; mail Fountain z 32438
Greenland; RMC Place; DUVAL; *164 C-9; ★ JAX; mail Jacksonville z 32256, z 32258; pop. incl. with Jacksonville (Inc. Place)
Green Meadow; CDP-Census Area Only; BROWARD; *165 P-13; ★ MIA-; © 1,874
Green Point; RMC Place; FRANKLIN; *165 T-8; mail Eastpoint z 32328; ● 200
Greensboro; Inc. Place; GADSDEN; 164 B-1; elev. 263ft./80m.; 🅿; z 32330; Ⓟ 586; © 619
Greenville; Inc. Place; MADISON; 164 B-4; elev. 98ft./30m.; 🅿; z 32331; Ⓟ 950; © 837
Greenwood; Inc. Place; JACKSON; 165 Q-7; elev. 115ft./35m.; 🅿; z 32443; Ⓟ 474; © 735
Greenwood; RMC Place; SANTA ROSA; *165 Q-3; mail Jay z 32565; rural
Grenelefe; RMC Place; POLK; *164 J-10; mail Haines City z 33844-45; ● 700
Gretna; Inc. Place; GADSDEN; 164 B-1; elev. 284ft./87m.; 🅿; z 32332; Ⓟ 1,981; © 1,709
Griffin; RMC Place; POLK; 163 J-1; ★ LKLD; mail Lakeland z 33810; pop. incl. with Lakeland (Inc. Place)
Griffins Corner; RMC Place; HARDEE; *165 K-9; ● 200
Gritney; RMC Place; HOLMES; *165 R-6; mail Caryville z 32427; ● 200
Grosh; RMC Place; WALTON; *165 S-5; mail Santa Rosa Beach z 32459; ● 400
Gross; RMC Place; NASSAU; *164 B-9; elev. 24ft./7m.; mail Yulee z 32097; rural
Grove City; CDP; CHARLOTTE; 165 M-7; elev. 12ft./4m.; 🅿; ★ VEN; z 34224; Ⓟ 2,374; © 2,092
Groveland; Inc. Place; LAKE; 164 H-9; elev. 105ft./32m.; 🅿; z 34736-37; Ⓟ 2,300; © 2,360; Ⓡ 2,394
Grove Park; RMC Place; ALACHUA; *164 E-8; mail Hawthorne z 32640; ● 140
Grove Park; RMC Place; DUVAL; *164 C-9; ★ JAX; mail Jacksonville z 32216; pop. incl. with Jacksonville (Inc. Place)
GULF; 165 T-7; Ⓟ 11,504; © 13,332; Ⓡ 14,560; ◆ 15,838
Gulf Beach; ESCAMBIA; see Perdido Key (RMC Place)
Gulf Beach Heights; RMC Place; ESCAMBIA; *165 S-2; ★ PENS; mail Pensacola z 32507; ● 1,600
Gulf Breeze; Inc. Place; SANTA ROSA; 165 S-3; 🅿 🅷; ★ PENS; z 32561-63, z 32566; Ⓟ 5,530; © 5,665
Gulf City; RMC Place; HILLSBOROUGH; 163 E-4; mail Ruskin z 33570; ● 550
Gulf Gate Estates; CDP-Census Area Only; SARASOTA; 163 H-3; ★ SAR-B; mail Sarasota z 34231; Ⓟ 11,622; © 11,647
Gulf Hammock; RMC Place; LEVY; 164 F-6; elev. 12ft./4m.; 🅿; z 32639; ● 250
Gulf Harbors; RMC Place; PASCO; 164 I-6; ★ ST.PET; mail New Port Richey z 34652; ● 3,300
Gulf Lagoon Beach; RMC Place; BAY; *165 S-6; mail Panama City z 32408; ● 450
Gulf Pine; RMC Place; PASCO; *164 I-7; mail Odessa z 33556; ● 110
Gulf Pines; RMC Place; WALTON; *165 S-4; mail Santa Rosa Beach z 32459; ● 60
Gulfport; Inc. Place; PINELLAS; 165 K-6; elev. 11ft./3m.; 🅿; ★ ST.PET; z 33707, z 33711, z 33737; Ⓟ 11,727; © 12,527
Gulf Resort Beach; RMC Place; BAY; *165 S-5; ★ PNCY; mail Panama City Beach z 32407; pop. incl. with Panama City Beach (Inc. Place)
Gulf Stream; Inc. Place; PALM BEACH; 165 N-14; elev. 7ft./2m.; 🅿; ★ MIA-; z 33483; Ⓟ 690; © 716
Gulfwinds; RMC Place; PINELLAS; *165 K-6; ★ ST.PET; mail Saint Petersburg z 33711, z 33747; pop. incl. with Saint Petersburg (Inc. Place)
Gun Club Estates; CDP-Census Area Only; PALM BEACH; *165 N-14; ★ MIA-; © 711

H

Hague; RMC Place; ALACHUA; 164 D-7; ★ GAIN; mail Alachua z 32615, Gainesville z 32601; ● 400
Haines City; Inc. Place; POLK; 164 I-9; elev. 161ft./49m.; 🅿 🅷; z 33844-45; Ⓟ 11,683; © 13,174
Hainesworth; RMC Place; ALACHUA; *164 D-7; elev. 175ft./53m.; mail Alachua z 32615; rural
Halifax Estates; RMC Place; VOLUSIA; *164 F-11; pop. incl. with Daytona Beach Shores (Inc. Place)
Hallandale; BROWARD; see Hallandale Beach (Inc. Place)
Hallandale Beach (Hallandale); Inc. Place; BROWARD; 165 P-14; elev. 11ft./3m.; 🅿 ■; ★ MIA-; z 33009 & mail Hallandale z 33008; Ⓟ 30,996; © 34,282; ◆ 36,380
Hall City; RMC Place; GLADES; *165 M-10; elev. 34ft./10m.; mail Moore Haven z 33471; ● 145
Hamilton; RMC Place; BROWARD; *165 O-14; ★ MIA-; mail Pompano Beach z 33072; pop. incl. with Pompano Beach (Inc. Place)
HAMILTON; 164 B-6; Ⓟ 10,930; © 13,327; ◆ 14,504
Hammock; RMC Place; FLAGLER; mail Palm Coast z 32137; pop. incl. with Palm Coast (Inc. Place)
Hammocks; RMC Place; MIAMI-DADE; *165 Q-13; ★ MIA-; mail Miami z 33196; Ⓟ 10,897; ● 10,650
Hammond; RMC Place; PUTNAM; *164 F-10; mail Crescent City z 32112; ● 140
Hampton; Inc. Place; BRADFORD; 164 D-8; elev. 146ft./45m.; 🅿; z 32044; Ⓟ 296; © 431
Hampton Beach; RMC Place; BRADFORD; *164 D-8; mail Hampton z 32044; ● 300
Hamptons at Boca Raton; CDP-Census Area Only; PALM BEACH; *165 O-13; ★ MIA-; mail Boca Raton z 33434; Ⓟ 11,686; © 11,306
Hampton Springs; RMC Place; TAYLOR; 164 D-4; elev. 27ft./8m.; mail Perry z 32348
Hanson; RMC Place; MADISON; *164 B-5; mail Madison z 32340
Harbinwood Estates; RMC Place; LEON; *164 B-2; ★ TALL; mail Tallahassee z 32303; ● 1,900
Harbor Bluffs; CDP-Census Area Only; PINELLAS; *164 J-6; ★ ST.PET; mail Largo z 33770; Ⓟ 2,659; © 2,807
Harbor Oaks; RMC Place; VOLUSIA; *164 F-11; ★ D.BCH; mail Port Orange z 32127; pop. incl. with Port Orange (Inc. Place)
Harbor Shores; RMC Place; LAKE; *164 G-9; elev. 65ft./20m.; mail Leesburg z 34748; ● 380
Harbor View; RMC Place; CHARLOTTE; *165 M-8; ★ PUN-; mail Punta Gorda z 33980; ● 600
Harbor View; RMC Place; DUVAL; *164 C-9; ★ JAX; mail Jacksonville z 32209; pop. incl. with Jacksonville (Inc. Place)
Harbour Heights; CDP; CHARLOTTE; *165 M-8; elev. 15ft./5m.; ★ PUN-; mail Punta Gorda z 33983; Ⓟ 2,569; © 2,873
Hardaway; RMC Place; GADSDEN; *165 R-8; mail Chattahoochee z 32324; rural
HARDEE; 165 L-8; Ⓟ 19,499; © 26,938; ◆ 29,665
Hardeetown; RMC Place; LEVY; *164 E-6; mail Chiefland z 32626; pop. incl. with Chiefland (Inc. Place)
Hardin Heights; RMC Place; GADSDEN; *165 R-8; mail Chattahoochee z 32324; ● 75
Harlem; CDP; HENDRY; 165 N-11; mail Clewiston z 33440; Ⓟ 2,826; © 2,730
Harlem Heights; CDP-Census Area Only; LEE; *165 N-9; ★ ORL; © 1,065
Harlem Heights; RMC Place; ORANGE; *164 H-9; ● 200
Harmony Heights; RMC Place; ST. LUCIE; *165 K-13; ★ FTPI; mail Fort Pierce z 34946; ● 885
Harold; RMC Place; SANTA ROSA; 165 R-3; elev. 149ft./45m.; mail Gulf Breeze z 32563; ● 200
Harris; RMC Place; OKALOOSA; *165 S-4; mail Mary Esther z 32569; ● 700
Harshaw; RMC Place; PINELLAS; *165 K-6; ★ ST.PET; mail Saint Petersburg z 33713; pop. incl. with Saint Petersburg (Inc. Place)
Hastings; Inc. Place; ST. JOHNS; 164 E-10; elev. 10ft./3m.; 🅿; z 32145; Ⓟ 595; © 521
Hatchbend; RMC Place; LAFAYETTE; *164 D-6; mail Branford z 32008; rural
Hathaway Mill; RMC Place; HOLMES; *165 R-6; mail Caryville z 32427; ● 120
Havana; Inc. Place; GADSDEN; 164 B-2; elev. 245ft./75m.; 🅿; z 32333; Ⓟ 1,654; © 1,713
Haverhill; Inc. Place; PALM BEACH; 165 N-14; elev. 17ft./5m.; 🅿; ★ MIA-; z 33409, z 33415, z 33417, z 33422; Ⓟ 1,058; © 1,454
Hawthorne; Inc. Place; ALACHUA; 164 E-8; elev. 153ft./47m.; 🅿; z 32640; Ⓟ 1,305; © 1,415
Haynes; RMC Place; JACKSON; *165 Q-8; mail Sneads z 32460; ● 100
Heathrow; CDP; SEMINOLE; 164 G-10; 🅿; ★ ORL; z 32746; © 4,068
Hedges; RMC Place; NASSAU; 164 B-9; ★ JAX; mail Yulee z 32097; ● 800
Heilbronn (Hillburn); RMC Place; BRADFORD; *164 D-8; mail Starke z 32091; rural
Henderson Creek; RMC Place; COLLIER; *165 P-9; ★ NAP; mail Naples z 34114; ● 800
Henderson Mill; RMC Place; CALHOUN; *165 R-7; mail Altha z 32421; ● 145
HENDRY; 165 N-10; Ⓟ 25,773; © 36,210; ◆ 39,741
Hernando; CDP; CITRUS; 164 G-7; elev. 48ft./15m.; 🅿; z 34442; Ⓟ 2,103; © 8,253
HERNANDO; 164 H-7; Ⓟ 101,115; © 130,802; ◆ 176,093
Hernando Beach; CDP-Census Area Only; HERNANDO; *164 H-7; 🅿; ★ SPR.H; z 34607; Ⓟ 1,767; © 2,185
Herndon; RMC Place; ORANGE; *164 H-10; ★ ORL; mail Orlando z 32803, z 32814; pop. incl. with Orlando (Inc. Place)
Hero; RMC Place; NASSAU; *164 B-9; ★ JAX; mail Yulee z 32097; ● 170
Hesperides; RMC Place; POLK; *164 J-10; mail Lake Wales z 33853
Hialeah; Inc. Place; MIAMI-DADE; 165 P-13; 🅿 🅷 ■; ★ MIA-; z 33002, z 33010-18 & mail Opa Locka z 33054; Ⓟ 188,004; © 226,419; ◆ 227,756
Hialeah Gardens; Inc. Place; MIAMI-DADE; 163 K-7; elev. 5ft./2m.; 🅿; ★ MIA-; z 33016, z 33018 & mail Hialeah z 33010; Ⓟ 7,713; © 19,297
Hialeah Lakes; RMC Place; MIAMI-DADE; *165 P-13; ★ MIA-; mail Hialeah z 33014-15, z 33018; pop. incl. with Hialeah (Inc. Place)
Hibernia; RMC Place; CLAY; *164 D-9; ★ JAX; mail Green Cove Springs z 32043; ● 1,400
Hibiscus; RMC Place; LAKE; *164 G-9; mail Miami z 33124, z 33146, Mount Dora z 32757
Hickory Hill; RMC Place; HOLMES; *165 R-5; elev. 128ft./39m.; mail Westville z 32464; rural
Hidden Lake Villas; RMC Place; SEMINOLE; *164 G-11; mail Sanford z 32773
Hidden River; RMC Place; SARASOTA; *165 L-8; mail Sarasota z 34240; ● 90
Highland; RMC Place; CLAY; *164 C-8; elev. 198ft./60m.; ★ JAX; mail Lawtey z 32058
Highland Beach; Inc. Place; PALM BEACH; 165 O-14; elev. 6ft./2m.; 🅿; ★ MIA-; z 33487; Ⓟ 3,209; © 3,775
Highland City; CDP; POLK; 164 J-9; elev. 158ft./48m.; 🅿; ★ LKLD; z 33846; Ⓟ 1,919; © 2,051
Highland Lakes; RMC Place; HIGHLANDS; *165 K-10; mail Avon Park z 33825; ● 850
Highland Lakes; RMC Place; PINELLAS; *164 I-6; ★ ST.PET; ● 3,700
Highland Park; RMC Place; FRANKLIN; 164 J-9; mail Apalachicola z 32320; ● 100
Highland Park; Inc. Place; POLK; *164 J-9; elev. 150ft./46m.; mail Lake Wales z 33853, z 33898; Ⓟ 155; © 244
Highland Park; RMC Place; SEMINOLE; *164 G-10; ★ ORL; mail Sanford z 32771; pop. incl. with Sanford (Inc. Place)
Highlands; RMC Place; DUVAL; *164 B-9; ★ JAX; mail Jacksonville z 32218; pop. incl. with Jacksonville (Inc. Place)
HIGHLANDS; 165 K-10; Ⓟ 68,432; © 87,366; ◆ 101,903
Highlands Park Estates; RMC Place; HIGHLANDS; *165 L-10; mail Lake Placid z 33852; ● 1,100
Highland View; RMC Place; GULF; 165 T-7; mail Port Saint Joe z 32456; ● 450
High Point; CDP-Census Area Only; HERNANDO; *164 H-7; ★ SPR.H; mail Brooksville z 34613; Ⓟ 2,814; © 2,973
High Point; CDP-Census Area Only; PALM BEACH; *165 N-14; ★ MIA-; mail Delray Beach z 33484; Ⓟ 2,288; © 2,191
Highpoint; RMC Place; PINELLAS; 163 C-2; ★ ST.PET; mail Clearwater z 33759-60; ● 2,300
High Springs; Inc. Place; ALACHUA; 164 D-7; elev. 71ft./22m.; 🅿; z 32643, z 32655; Ⓟ 3,144; © 3,863
Hiland Park; CDP; BAY; 165 S-6; ★ PNCY; mail Panama City z 32405; Ⓟ 3,865; © 999
Hildreth; RMC Place; SUWANNEE; *164 D-6; mail Branford z 32008
Hill and Dale; HERNANDO; see Hill 'n Dale (CDP)
Hillburn; BRADFORD; see Heilbronn (RMC Place)
Hillcoat; RMC Place; HAMILTON; *164 B-6; mail Jasper z 32052; ● 140
Hillcrest Heights; Inc. Place; POLK; 164 J-10; elev. 241ft./73m.; mail Babson Park z 33827; Ⓟ 221; © 266
Hilldale; RMC Place; HILLSBOROUGH; *164 J-7; ★ TAM; mail Tampa z 33614, z 33634, z 33684; pop. incl. with Tampa (Inc. Place)
Hilliard; Inc. Place; NASSAU; 164 B-8; elev. 70ft./21m.; 🅿; z 32046; Ⓟ 1,751; © 2,702
Hilliardville; RMC Place; WAKULLA; *164 C-2; mail Crawfordville z 32327; ● 255
Hill 'n Dale (Hill and Dale); CDP; HERNANDO; *164 H-7; mail Brooksville z 34602; © 1,436
Hillsboro; RMC Place; HILLSBOROUGH; ★ TAM
Hillsboro Beach; Inc. Place; BROWARD; 163 G-10; elev. 16ft./5m.; 🅿; ★ MIA-; z 33062 & mail Pompano Beach z 33072; Ⓟ 1,748; © 2,163
Hillsboro Pines; CDP-Census Area Only; BROWARD; *165 O-13; ★ MIA-; © 406
Hillsboro Ranches; CDP-Census Area Only; BROWARD; *165 O-13; ★ MIA-; © 47
HILLSBOROUGH; 164 J-8; Ⓟ 834,054; © 998,948; ◆ 1,206,830
Hinson; RMC Place; GADSDEN; 164 B-2; mail Havana z 32333; ● 150
Hinsons Crossroads; RMC Place; WASHINGTON; *165 R-6; mail Caryville z 32427; rural
Hobe Sound; CDP; MARTIN; 165 M-13; 🅿; ★ STU; z 33455, z 33475; Ⓟ 11,507; © 11,376
Hodgson; RMC Place; LEVY; *164 F-7; mail Williston z 32696; ● 160
Hog Valley; RMC Place; MARION; *164 E-9; mail Fort Mc Coy z 32134; ● 250
Holden Heights; CDP-Census Area Only; ORANGE; *164 H-10; ★ ORL; mail Orlando z 32805, z 32839; Ⓟ 4,387; © 3,856
Holder; RMC Place; CITRUS; 164 G-7; elev. 58ft./18m.; 🅿; z 34445; ● 200
Holiday; CDP; PASCO; 164 I-6; 🅿; ★ ST.PET; z 34690-92; Ⓟ 19,360; © 21,904; ◆ 30,934
Holiday Harbor; RMC Place; DUVAL; *164 C-10; ★ JAX; mail Jacksonville z 32224; pop. incl. with Jacksonville (Inc. Place)
Holiday Heights; RMC Place; MONROE; mail Key Largo z 33037
Holiday Manor; RMC Place; POLK; 163 I-5; ★ WNHV; mail Haines City z 33844; ● 100
Holland Crossroads; RMC Place; HOLMES; *165 Q-6; mail Bonifay z 32425; pop. incl. with Esto (Inc. Place)
Holley; RMC Place; SANTA ROSA; 165 R-3; elev. 14ft./4m.; mail Gulf Breeze z 32561; ● 400
Holliday Hills; RMC Place; DUVAL; *164 C-9; ★ JAX; mail Jacksonville z 32216; pop. incl. with Jacksonville (Inc. Place)
Hollister; RMC Place; PUTNAM; 164 E-9; elev. 80ft./24m.; 🅿; z 32147; ● 400
Holly Ford; RMC Place; DUVAL; *164 B-9; ★ JAX; mail Jacksonville z 32218; pop. incl. with Jacksonville (Inc. Place)
Holly Hill; Inc. Place; VOLUSIA; 164 F-11; elev. 6ft./2m.; 🅿; ★ D.BCH; z 32117, z 32125; Ⓟ 11,141; © 12,119
Holly Hills; RMC Place; LEON; *164 B-2; ★ TALL; mail Tallahassee z 32303; pop. incl. with Tallahassee (Inc. Place)
Holly Point; RMC Place; CLAY; *164 C-9; ★ JAX; mail Orange Park z 32073; pop. incl. with Orange Park (Inc. Place)
Hollywood; Inc. Place; BROWARD; 165 P-14; elev. 11ft./3m.; 🅿 🅷 ■; ★ MIA-; z 33019-29, z 33081, z 33083-84 & mail Fort Lauderdale z 33312, z 33314, z 33316, z 33332, Pembroke Pines z 33082; location of Seminole Indian Agency; Ⓟ 121,697; © 139,357; Ⓡ 139,368; ◆ 139,707
Hollywood Beach; RMC Place; BAY; *165 S-5; ★ PNCY; mail Panama City Beach z 32413; ● 700
Hollywood Beach Gardens; RMC Place; BROWARD; *165 P-13; ★ MIA-; mail Hollywood z 33021; pop. incl. with Hollywood (Inc. Place)
Hollywood Hills; RMC Place; BROWARD; *165 P-11; mail Hollywood z 33021, z 33081
Hollywood Reservation; Indian Reservation; BROWARD; ★ MIA-; mail Hollywood z 33024; Ⓟ 2,592; © 2,051
HOLMES; 165 Q-6; Ⓟ 15,778; © 18,564; ◆ 19,357
Holmes Beach; Inc. Place; MANATEE; 165 K-6; elev. 5ft./2m.; 🅿; ★ SAR-B; z 34217-18; Ⓟ 4,810; © 4,966
Holopaw; RMC Place; OSCEOLA; 164 I-11; mail Melbourne z 32901; ● 240
Holt; RMC Place; OKALOOSA; 165 R-4; elev. 200ft./61m.; 🅿; z 32564 & mail Gulf Breeze z 32563; ● 300
Homeland; RMC Place; POLK; 164 J-9; elev. 143ft./44m.; 🅿; z 33847; ● 200
Homestead; Inc. Place; MIAMI-DADE; 165 Q-13; 🅿 🅷 ■; ★ MIA-; z 33030-35, z 33039, z 33090, z 33092; Ⓟ 26,866; © 31,909; ◆ 33,961
Homestead Base; CDP-Census Area Only; MIAMI-DADE; *165 Q-13; ★ MIA-; mail Homestead z 33039; © 446
Homestead Ridge; RMC Place; LEON; *164 B-3; elev. 150ft./46m.; mail Tallahassee z 32308; ● 280
Homosassa; CDP; CITRUS; 164 G-7; elev. 4ft./1m.; 🅿; z 34446, z 34448, z 34487; Ⓟ 2,113; © 2,294
Homosassa Springs; CDP; CITRUS; 164 G-7; 🅿; z 34447; Ⓟ 6,271; © 12,458
Honeyville; RMC Place; GULF; 165 T-7; mail Wewahitchka z 32465; ● 240
Hooker Point; RMC Place; HENDRY; *165 N-11; mail Clewiston z 33440; ● 1,000
Hooker Point; RMC Place; HILLSBOROUGH; *164 J-7; ★ TAM; mail Tampa z 33605; pop. incl. with Tampa (Inc. Place)
Hopewell; RMC Place; HILLSBOROUGH; *164 J-8; elev. 101ft./31m.; ★ TAM; mail Plant City z 33566; rural
Hopewell; RMC Place; MADISON; *164 C-4; mail Madison z 32340; rural
Hornsville; RMC Place; JACKSON; *165 Q-8; mail Bascom z 32423; ● 100
Horseshoe Beach; Inc. Place; DIXIE; 164 E-5; elev. 6ft./2m.; 🅿; z 32648; Ⓟ 252; © 206
Hosford; RMC Place; LIBERTY; 165 S-8; elev. 95ft./29m.; 🅿; z 32334; ● 450
Houston; RMC Place; SUWANNEE; *164 C-6; mail Live Oak z 32060; ● 200
Howard; RMC Place; MIAMI-DADE; 163 N-7; ★ MIA-; mail Miami z 33176; ● 780
Howey Height; RMC Place; LAKE; *164 H-9; mail Clermont z 34711; ● 80
Howey In The Hills; Inc. Place; LAKE; 164 H-9; elev. 82ft./25m.; 🅿; z 34737, z 34797; Ⓟ 724; © 956
Hoyt; RMC Place; MARION; *164 F-7; mail Dunnellon z 34432, Ocala z 34481; ● 300
Hudson; CDP; PASCO; 164 I-6; elev. 11ft./3m.; 🅿 🅷; ★ ST.PET; z 34667, z 34669, z 34674; Ⓟ 7,344; © 12,765
Hull; RMC Place; DESOTO; *165 M-8; mail Arcadia z 34269
Hunt Club; RMC Place; SEMINOLE; *164 H-10; ★ ORL; mail Apopka z 32703; ● 950
Hunters Creek; CDP-Census Area Only; ORANGE; *164 I-10; ★ ORL; © 9,369
Huntington; RMC Place; MARION; *164 F-8; mail Ocala z 34471; ● 500
Huntington; RMC Place; PUTNAM; *164 E-9; elev. 60ft./18m.; mail Crescent City z 32112; rural
Huntington Woods; RMC Place; LEON; *164 B-2; ★ TALL; mail Tallahassee z 32303; pop. incl. with Tallahassee (Inc. Place)
Hutchinson Island South; CDP-Census Area Only; ST. LUCIE; *165 L-13; ★ STU; mail Fort Pierce z 34949; Ⓟ 3,893; © 4,846

Entries in **UPPERCASE** are counties.
Entries in **bold** have populations of 2,500 or more.
Names in parentheses are alternate names.
Inc. Place — Incorporated Place
RMC Place — Rand McNally Designated Place
CDP — Census Designated Place
MCD — Minor Civil Division

⊡ County Seat
▲ Minor Civil Division
elev. Elevation
🅿 Post Office
🅷 Hospital
🅲 College
■ Principal Business Center
★ Ranally Metro Area (RMA) Abbreviation
z Zip Code(s)

Ⓟ Previous Census Population
Ⓡ Revised Census Population
Ⓐ Annexation Population
● Rand McNally Population Estimate
© Final Census Population
Ⓢ Special Census Population
◆ Estimated Population

For additional definitions see Glossary, Volume 1, and Introduction, Volume 2.

Hyde Grove; RMC Place; DUVAL; *164 C-9; ★ JAX; mail Jacksonville z 32210; pop. incl. with Jacksonville (Inc. Place)
Hyde Park; RMC Place; DUVAL; *164 C-9; ★ JAX; mail Jacksonville z 32210; pop. incl. with Jacksonville (Inc. Place)
Hyde Park; RMC Place; HILLSBOROUGH; *164 J-7; ★ TAM; mail Tampa z 33606, z 33609; pop. incl. with Tampa (Inc. Place)
Hyde Park; RMC Place; WAKULLA; *164 C-2; mail Crawfordville z 32327; ● 200
Hypoluxo; Inc. Place; PALM BEACH; 165 N-14; elev. 9ft./3m.; [P]; ★ MIA-; z 33462; Ⓟ 830; Ⓒ 2,015

I

Iddo; RMC Place; TAYLOR; *164 C-4; elev. 53ft./16m.; mail Greenville z 32331
Immokalee; CDP; COLLIER; 165 O-10; [P]; z 34142-43; Ⓟ 14,120; Ⓒ 19,763
Immokalee Reservation; Indian Reservation; COLLIER; Ⓒ 175
Indialantic; Inc. Place; BREVARD; 164 I-12; elev. 18ft./5m.; [P]; ★ MELB-; z 32903; Ⓟ 2,844; Ⓒ 2,944
Indian Bluff Island; RMC Place; PINELLAS; *164 J-6; ★ ST.PET; mail Palm Harbor z 34683; ● 390
Indian Creek; MIAMI-DADE; see Indian Creek Village (Inc. Place)
Indian Creek Village (Indian Creek); Inc. Place; MIAMI-DADE; 163 K-9; elev. 7ft./2m.; [P]; ★ MIA-; z 33154; Ⓟ 44; Ⓒ 33
Indian Harbour Beach; Inc. Place; BREVARD; 164 I-12; elev. 15ft./5m.; [P]; ★ MELB-; z 32937; Ⓟ 6,933; Ⓒ 8,152
Indian Head Acres; RMC Place; LEON; *164 B-2; ★ TALL; mail Tallahassee z 32301; pop. incl. with Tallahassee (Inc. Place)
Indian Hills; RMC Place; BREVARD; *164 I-12; ★ MELB-; mail Cocoa z 32922; pop. incl. with Cocoa (Inc. Place)
Indian Lake Estates; RMC Place; POLK; 164 J-10; elev. 64ft./20m.; [P]; z 33855; ● 200
Indian Mound Village; RMC Place; SEMINOLE; *164 G-10; elev. 10ft./3m.; ★ ORL; mail Sanford z 32771; ● 70
Indianola; RMC Place; BREVARD; *164 I-12; ★ MELB-; mail Merritt Island z 32952
Indian Pass (McNeil); RMC Place; GULF; *165 T-7; mail Port Saint Joe z 32456; rural
INDIAN RIVER; 165 K-12; Ⓟ 90,208; Ⓒ 112,947; ◆ 135,083
Indian River City; RMC Place; BREVARD; *164 H-12; ★ TITUS; mail Titusville z 32780; pop. incl. with Titusville (Inc. Place)
Indian River Estates; CDP-Census Area Only; ST. LUCIE; *165 L-13; ★ FTPI; mail Fort Pierce z 34982; Ⓟ 4,858; Ⓒ 5,793
Indian River Shores; Inc. Place; INDIAN RIVER; 165 K-13; [P]; ★ VERO; z 32963; Ⓟ 2,278; Ⓒ 3,448
Indian Rocks Beach; Inc. Place; PINELLAS; 164 J-6; elev. 22ft./7m.; [P]; ★ ST.PET; z 33785-86; Ⓟ 3,963; Ⓒ 5,072; Ⓡ 5,127
Indian Shores; Inc. Place; PINELLAS; 163 C-1; [P]; ★ ST.PET; z 33785; Ⓟ 1,405; Ⓒ 1,705
Indiantown; CDP; MARTIN; 165 M-13; elev. 37ft./11m.; [P]; z 34956; Ⓟ 4,794; Ⓒ 5,588
Indrio; RMC Place; ST. LUCIE; 165 K-13; ★ FTPI; mail Fort Pierce z 34946; ● 330
Inglis; Inc. Place; LEVY; 164 G-6; elev. 15ft./5m.; [P]; z 34449; Ⓟ 1,241; Ⓒ 1,491
Inlet Beach; RMC Place; WALTON, BAY; 165 S-5; [P]; ★ PNCY; z 32413 & mail Rosemary Beach z 32461; ● 400
Innisbrook; RMC Place; PINELLAS; *164 J-6; ★ ST.PET; mail Palm Harbor z 34684; ● 2,150
Interbay; RMC Place; HILLSBOROUGH; *164 J-7; ★ TAM; mail Tampa z 33611, z 33629, z 33681; pop. incl. with Tampa (Inc. Place)
Intercession City; RMC Place; OSCEOLA; 164 I-10; elev. 71ft./22m.; [P]; ★ KISS; z 33848; ● 630
Interlachen; Inc. Place; PUTNAM; 164 E-9; elev. 104ft./32m.; [P]; z 32148-49; Ⓟ 1,160; Ⓒ 1,475
Inverness; Inc. Place; ⊡ CITRUS; 164 G-7; elev. 50ft./15m.; [P] [H]; z 34450-53; Ⓟ 5,797; Ⓒ 6,789
Inverness Highlands North; CDP-Census Area Only; CITRUS; *164 G-7; Ⓒ 1,470
Inverness Highlands South; CDP-Census Area Only; CITRUS; *164 G-7; Ⓒ 5,781
Inwood; RMC Place; JACKSON; *165 R-8; elev. 170ft./52m.; mail Sneads z 32460; rural
Inwood; CDP; POLK; 164 J-4; ★ WNHV; mail Winter Haven z 33881; Ⓟ 6,824; Ⓒ 6,925
Iona; CDP; LEE; *165 N-8; ★ FTMY-; mail Fort Myers z 33908; Ⓟ 9,565; Ⓒ 11,756
Irvine; RMC Place; MARION; *164 F-8; ★ OCA; mail Reddick z 32686; rural
Islamorada (Islamorada, Village of Islands); Inc. Place; MONROE; 165 S-12; [P]; z 33036 & mail Tavernier z 33070; Ⓟ 1,220; Ⓒ 6,846
Islamorada, Village of Islands; MONROE; see Islamorada (Inc. Place)
Island Estates; RMC Place; PINELLAS; *164 J-6; ★ ST.PET; mail Clearwater Beach z 33767; pop. incl. with Clearwater (Inc. Place)
Island Grove; RMC Place; ALACHUA; 164 E-8; elev. 75ft./23m.; [P]; z 32654; ● 100
Islandia; RMC Place; MIAMI-DADE; 165 R-13; mail Miami z 33131; former incorporated place; disincorporated 2002; Ⓟ 13; Ⓒ 6
Isleboro; RMC Place; VOLUSIA; *164 G-11; ★ D.BCH; mail New Smyrna Beach z 32168; pop. incl. with New Smyrna Beach (Inc. Place)
Isle of Palms; RMC Place; DUVAL; *164 C-10; ★ JAX; mail Jacksonville Beach z 32250; pop. incl. with Jacksonville (Inc. Place)
Isle of Palms; RMC Place; PINELLAS; *165 K-6; ★ ST.PET; mail Saint Petersburg z 33706; pop. incl. with Treasure Island (Inc. Place)
Isle of Palms South; RMC Place; DUVAL; *164 C-10; ★ JAX; mail Jacksonville Beach z 32250; pop. incl. with Jacksonville (Inc. Place)
Isles of Capri; RMC Place; COLLIER; *165 P-9; ★ NAP; mail Naples z 34113; ● 850
Isleworth; RMC Place; ORANGE; 165 O-2; ★ ORL; mail Windermere z 34786; ● 700
Istachatta; CDP; HERNANDO; 164 H-8; elev. 56ft./17m.; [P]; z 34636; Ⓒ 65
Istokpoga; RMC Place; HIGHLANDS; *165 L-10; mail Sebring z 33870; ● 170
Istokpoga Shores; RMC Place; HIGHLANDS; *165 L-10; mail Lorida z 33857; ● 340
Italia; RMC Place; NASSAU; *164 B-9; mail Callahan z 32011; ● 150
Ivan; RMC Place; WAKULLA; *164 C-2; mail Crawfordville z 32327; ● 160
Ivanhoe Estates; CDP-Census Area Only; BROWARD; *165 P-13; ★ MIA-; Ⓒ 279
Ives Estates; CDP; MIAMI-DADE; 163 J-9; ★ MIA-; mail Miami z 33162, z 33179; Ⓟ 13,531; Ⓒ 17,586
Izagora; RMC Place; HOLMES; *165 Q-6; elev. 83ft./25m.; mail Caryville z 32427; rural

J

JACKSON; 165 Q-7; Ⓟ 41,375; Ⓒ 46,755; ◆ 49,409
Jacksonville; Inc. Place; ⊡ DUVAL; 164 C-9; [P] [H] [C] 22,592 ■; ★ JAX; z 32099, z 32201-12, z 32214-41, z 32244-47, z 32250, z 32254-60, z 32266, z 32277; Ⓟ 635,230; Ⓒ 735,617; ◆ 835,957
Jacksonville Beach; Inc. Place; DUVAL; 164 C-10; elev. 9ft./3m.; [P] [H]; ★ JAX; z 32240, z 32250 & mail Jacksonville z 32227; Ⓟ 17,839; Ⓒ 20,990; ◆ 22,536
Jacksonville Heights; RMC Place; DUVAL; *164 C-9; ★ JAX; mail Jacksonville z 32210; pop. incl. with Jacksonville (Inc. Place)
Jacksonville Junction; RMC Place; DUVAL; pop. incl. with Jacksonville (Inc. Place)
Jacob City; JACKSON; see Jacobs (Inc. Place)
Jacobs (Jacob City); Inc. Place; JACKSON; 165 Q-7; mail Cottondale z 32431; Ⓟ 261; Ⓒ 281
Jamestown; RMC Place; SEMINOLE; *164 H-10; ● 500
Jan Phyl Village; CDP; POLK; 163 K-4; elev. 154ft./47m.; ★ WNHV; mail Winter Haven z 33880; Ⓟ 5,308; Ⓒ 5,633
Jarrett (Jarrot); RMC Place; JEFFERSON; *164 B-3; mail Monticello z 32344; rural
Jarrot; JEFFERSON; see Jarrett (RMC Place)
Jasmine Estates; CDP-Census Area Only; PASCO; *164 I-6; ★ ST.PET; mail Port Richey z 34668; Ⓟ 17,136; Ⓒ 18,213
Jasper; Inc. Place; ⊡ HAMILTON; 164 B-6; elev. 154ft./47m.; [P] [H]; z 32052; Ⓟ 2,099; Ⓒ 1,780
Jay; Inc. Place; SANTA ROSA; 165 Q-3; elev. 252ft./77m.; [P] [H]; z 32565; Ⓟ 666; Ⓒ 579
Jay Jay; RMC Place; BREVARD; *164 H-11; ● 30
JEFFERSON; 164 C-3; Ⓟ 11,296; Ⓒ 12,902; ◆ 14,228
Jena; RMC Place; DIXIE; 164 E-5; mail Steinhatchee z 32359; ● 200
Jennings; Inc. Place; HAMILTON; 164 B-5; elev. 149ft./45m.; [P]; z 32053; Ⓟ 712; Ⓒ 833
Jensen Beach; CDP; MARTIN; 165 L-13; elev. 50ft./15m.; [P]; ★ STU; z 34957-58; Ⓟ 9,884; Ⓒ 11,100
Jerome; RMC Place; COLLIER; *165 P-10; [P]; z 34141 & mail Copeland z 34137
Jessamine; RMC Place; PASCO; *164 I-8; mail Dade City z 33523; rural
Johnson; RMC Place; PUTNAM; 164 E-8; elev. 104ft./32m.; mail Hawthorne z 32640; ● 300
Johnsons Corner; RMC Place; LAKE; *164 G-9; mail Paisley z 32767; ● 55
Jonathan's Landing; RMC Place; PALM BEACH; *165 M-14; ★ MIA-; mail Jupiter z 33477; ● 800
Jones Corner; RMC Place; POLK; *164 J-9; mail Auburndale z 33823, Winter Haven z 33880; ● 100
Jonesville; RMC Place; ALACHUA; *164 E-7; elev. 96ft./29m.; [P]; z 32669; ● 150
Judson; RMC Place; LEVY; *164 E-6; mail Trenton z 32693; rural
Julington Forest; RMC Place; DUVAL; *164 C-9; ★ JAX; mail Jacksonville z 32258; pop. incl. with Jacksonville (Inc. Place)
Jumeau; RMC Place; CITRUS; *164 H-7; mail Floral City z 34436; ● 550
June Park; CDP; BREVARD; 164 J-12; ★ MELB-; mail Melbourne z 32901; Ⓟ 4,080; Ⓒ 4,367
Jungle; RMC Place; PINELLAS; *165 K-6; ★ ST.PET; mail Saint Petersburg z 33710; pop. incl. with Saint Petersburg (Inc. Place)
Juniper; RMC Place; GADSDEN; *165 R-8; elev. 245ft./75m.; mail Greensboro z 32330; rural
Juno Beach; Inc. Place; PALM BEACH; 165 M-14; elev. 25ft./8m.; [P]; ★ MIA-; z 33408; Ⓟ 2,121; Ⓒ 3,262
Juno Ridge; CDP-Census Area Only; PALM BEACH; *165 M-14; ★ MIA-; Ⓒ 742
Jupiter; Inc. Place; PALM BEACH; 165 M-14; elev. 8ft./2m.; [P] [H]; ★ MIA-; z 33458, z 33468-69, z 33477-78; Ⓟ 24,907; Ⓒ 39,328; ◆ 48,794
Jupiter Inlet Beach Colony (Jupiter Inlet Colony); Inc. Place; PALM BEACH; 165 M-14; elev. 17ft./5m.; ★ MIA-; mail Jupiter z 33469; Ⓟ 405; Ⓒ 368
Jupiter Inlet Colony; PALM BEACH; see Jupiter Inlet Beach Colony (Inc. Place)
Jupiter Island; Inc. Place; MARTIN; 165 M-14; elev. 13ft./4m.; ★ STU; mail Hobe Sound z 33455; Ⓟ 549; Ⓒ 620

K

Kalamazoo; RMC Place; VOLUSIA; *164 G-11; ● 120
Kathleen; CDP; POLK; 164 I-8; elev. 160ft./49m.; [P]; ★ LKLD; z 33849; Ⓟ 2,743; Ⓒ 3,280
Keaton Beach; RMC Place; TAYLOR; 164 D-4; mail Perry z 32347; ● 75
Keela; RMC Place; PALM BEACH; *165 N-11; elev. 13ft./4m.; mail Clewiston z 33440; ● 40
Keene; RMC Place; NASSAU; *164 B-9; mail Callahan z 32011; ● 100
Kenansville; RMC Place; OSCEOLA; 164 J-11; elev. 74ft./23m.; [P]; z 34739; ● 160
Kendale Lakes; CDP-Census Area Only; MIAMI-DADE; *165 Q-13; ★ MIA-; mail Miami z 33175, z 33183; Ⓟ 48,524; Ⓒ 56,901; ◆ 59,438
Kendall; CDP; MIAMI-DADE; 165 Q-13; [P]; ★ MIA-; z 33156, z 33183, z 33256 & mail Miami z 33143, z 33158, z 33173, z 33176, z 33186, z 33193, z 33196, z 33283, z 33296; Ⓟ 87,271; Ⓒ 75,226; ◆ 78,590
Kendall Green; CDP; BROWARD; *165 O-14; ★ MIA-; mail Pompano Beach z 33064; Ⓟ 3,815; Ⓒ 3,084
Kendall West; CDP-Census Area Only; MIAMI-DADE; *165 Q-13; ★ MIA-; Ⓒ 38,034; ◆ 39,739
Kendrick; RMC Place; MARION; 164 F-8; ★ OCA; mail Ocala z 34475
Kennedy Hill; RMC Place; HILLSBOROUGH; *164 J-7; mail Seffner z 33584; ● 970
Kenneth City; Inc. Place; PINELLAS; 163 D-2; elev. 18ft./5m.; [P]; ★ ST.PET; z 33709; Ⓟ 4,462; Ⓒ 4,400
Kenny; RMC Place; BAKER; *164 C-8; mail Glen Saint Mary z 32040; ● 100
Kensington Park; CDP-Census Area Only; SARASOTA; 163 G-3; ★ SAR-B; mail Sarasota z 34235; Ⓒ 3,720
Kerr City; RMC Place; MARION; *164 F-9; mail Fort Mc Coy z 32134; ● 80
Keuka; RMC Place; PUTNAM; *164 E-8; mail Interlachen z 32148; ● 50
Key Biscayne; Inc. Place; MIAMI-DADE; 165 Q-14; [P]; ★ MIA-; z 33149; Ⓟ 8,854; Ⓒ 10,507
Key Colony Beach; Inc. Place; MONROE; 165 T-11; [P]; z 33051; Ⓟ 977; Ⓒ 788
Key Largo; CDP; MONROE; 165 S-13; [P]; z 33037; Ⓟ 11,336; Ⓒ 11,886
Key Largo Park; RMC Place; MONROE; *165 S-13; mail Key Largo z 33037
Key Largo Village; RMC Place; MONROE; mail Key Largo z 33037
Keystone; CDP; HILLSBOROUGH; *164 I-7; ★ TAM; Ⓒ 14,627
Keystone Heights; Inc. Place; CLAY; 164 D-8; elev. 136ft./41m.; [P]; z 32656; Ⓟ 1,315; Ⓒ 1,349; Ⓡ 1,345
Keystone Islands; RMC Place; MIAMI-DADE; *165 P-14; ★ MIA-; mail Miami z 33161, z 33181, z 33261; pop. incl. with North Miami (Inc. Place)
Keysville; RMC Place; HILLSBOROUGH; *164 J-8; elev. 81ft./25m.; ★ TAM; mail Lithia z 33547; ● 300
Key West; Inc. Place; ⊡ MONROE; 165 T-9; elev. 5ft./2m.; [P] [H] ■; z 33040-41, z 33045; Ⓟ 24,832; Ⓒ 25,478; ◆ 21,921
Killarney; RMC Place; ORANGE; 165 N-1; elev. 125ft./38m.; [P]; ★ ORL; z 34740
Killearn Estates; RMC Place; LEON; *164 B-2; ★ TALL; mail Tallahassee z 32308; pop. incl. with Tallahassee (Inc. Place)
Killearn Lakes; RMC Place; LEON; *164 B-2; elev. 200ft./61m.; mail Tallahassee z 32312; ● 1,550
Kinard; RMC Place; CALHOUN; 165 S-7; elev. 66ft./20m.; [P]; z 32449; ● 50
Kincaid Hills; RMC Place; ALACHUA; *164 E-8; elev. 153ft./47m.; ★ GAIN; mail Gainesville z 32601; ● 670
Kings Bay; RMC Place; MIAMI-DADE; *165 Q-13; elev. 14ft./4m.; ★ MIA-; mail Miami z 33158; ● 800
Kings Ferry; RMC Place; NASSAU; *164 A-9; mail Hilliard z 32046
Kingsford; RMC Place; POLK; *164 J-8; mail Mulberry z 33860; ● 35
Kingsley Village; RMC Place; CLAY; *164 D-8; elev. 200ft./61m.; mail Starke z 32091; ● 300
Kings Point; CDP-Census Area Only; PALM BEACH; *165 O-14; ★ MIA-; mail Delray Beach z 33446, z 33484; Ⓟ 12,422; Ⓒ 12,207
Kings Road; RMC Place; DUVAL; *164 C-9; ★ JAX; mail Jacksonville z 32254; pop. incl. with Jacksonville (Inc. Place)
Kingswood Manor; RMC Place; ORANGE; *164 H-10; ★ ORL; mail Orlando z 32804; ● 3,300
Kirkwood; RMC Place; ALACHUA; *164 E-7; mail Gainesville z 32608, Micanopy z 32667; rural
Kissimmee; Inc. Place; ⊡ OSCEOLA; 164 I-10; elev. 65ft./20m.; [P] [H] ■; ★ KISS; z 34741-47, z 34758-59; Ⓟ 30,050; Ⓒ 47,814; ◆ 65,983
Kissimmee Park; RMC Place; OSCEOLA; 164 I-10; elev. 60ft./18m.; ★ KISS; mail Saint Cloud z 34772; ● 160
Knights; RMC Place; HILLSBOROUGH; *164 J-8; ★ TAM; mail Plant City z 33565
Koerber; RMC Place; WALTON; *165 R-5; mail Defuniak Springs z 32433; ● 185
Kolokee; RMC Place; SEMINOLE; *164 H-11; mail Geneva z 32732; ● 100
Korona; RMC Place; FLAGLER; 164 F-10; mail Bunnell z 32110; ● 75
Kossuthville; RMC Place; POLK; 163 J-3; ★ LKLD; mail Auburndale z 33823; ● 400
Kuhlman; RMC Place; HIGHLANDS; *165 L-10; mail Sebring z 33870, z 33872; ● 500
Kynesville; RMC Place; JACKSON; 165 R-7; mail Cottondale z 32431; ● 120

L

La Belle; Inc. Place; ⊡ HENDRY; 165 N-10; elev. 16ft./5m.; [P]; z 33935, z 33975; Ⓟ 2,703; Ⓒ 4,210
Lacoochee; CDP; PASCO; 164 H-8; elev. 74ft./23m.; [P]; z 33537; Ⓟ 2,072; Ⓒ 1,345
La Crosse; Inc. Place; ALACHUA; 164 D-7; elev. 46ft./14m.; [P]; z 32658; Ⓟ 122; Ⓒ 143
Lacy; RMC Place; DUVAL; pop. incl. with Jacksonville (Inc. Place)
Lady Lake; Inc. Place; LAKE; 164 G-8; elev. 72ft./22m.; [P]; z 32158-59, z 32162; Ⓟ 8,071; Ⓒ 11,828
LAFAYETTE; 164 D-5; Ⓟ 5,578; Ⓒ 7,022; ◆ 7,977
La Gorce Island; RMC Place; MIAMI-DADE; *165 P-14; ★ MIA-; mail Miami Beach z 33139, z 33141; pop. incl. with Miami Beach (Inc. Place)
La Grange; RMC Place; BREVARD; 164 C-12; elev. 26ft./8m.; ★ TITUS; mail Titusville z 32796; pop. incl. with Titusville (Inc. Place)
Laguna Beach; CDP; BAY; 165 S-5; elev. 20ft./6m.; ★ PNCY; mail Panama City Beach z 32413; Ⓟ 1,876; Ⓒ 2,909
LAKE; 164 I-9; Ⓟ 152,104; Ⓒ 210,528; Ⓡ 210,527; ◆ 321,758
Lake Alfred; Inc. Place; POLK; 164 J-9; elev. 170ft./52m.; [P]; ★ WNHV; z 33850; Ⓟ 3,622; Ⓒ 3,890
Lake Ashby Shores; RMC Place; VOLUSIA; *164 G-11; mail New Smyrna Beach z 32168; ● 100
Lake Belvedere Estates; CDP-Census Area Only; PALM BEACH; *165 N-13; ★ MIA-; Ⓒ 1,525
Lake Bird; RMC Place; TAYLOR; 164 C-4; mail Perry z 32347; ● 50
Lake Brantley; RMC Place; SEMINOLE; 165 L-3; ★ ORL; mail Longwood z 32750; ● 3,000
Lake Buena Vista; Inc. Place; ORANGE; 164 I-10; [P]; z 32830; Ⓟ 1,776; Ⓒ 16
Lake Butler; Inc. Place; ⊡ UNION; 164 D-7; elev. 136ft./41m.; [P] [H]; z 32054 & mail Lulu z 32061; Ⓟ 2,116; Ⓒ 1,927
Lake Butter; CDP-Census Area Only; ORANGE; *164 H-9; ★ ORL; Ⓒ 7,062
Lake Cain Hills; RMC Place; ORANGE; 165 N-3; elev. 116ft./35m.; ★ ORL; mail Orlando z 32805; ● 1,600
Lake Charm; RMC Place; SEMINOLE; *164 H-10; ★ ORL; mail Oviedo z 32765; pop. incl. with Oviedo (Inc. Place)
Lake City; Inc. Place; ⊡ COLUMBIA; 164 C-7; elev. 196ft./60m.; [P] [H] ■; z 32024-25, z 32055-56; Ⓟ 10,005; Ⓒ 9,980; ◆ 12,490
Lake Clarke Shores; Inc. Place; PALM BEACH; 163 B-10; elev. 16ft./5m.; [P]; ★ MIA-; z 33406; Ⓟ 3,364; Ⓒ 3,451
Lake Como; RMC Place; PUTNAM; 164 E-9; [P]; z 32157; ● 500
Lake Fern; RMC Place; HILLSBOROUGH; *164 I-7; mail Lutz z 33549, Odessa z 33556; ● 150
Lake Forest; CDP; BROWARD; *165 P-13; ★ MIA-; mail Hollywood z 33023; Ⓒ 4,994
Lake Forest; RMC Place; DUVAL; *164 C-9; ★ JAX; mail Jacksonville z 32208; pop. incl. with Jacksonville (Inc. Place)
Lake Forest Hills; RMC Place; DUVAL; *164 C-9; ★ JAX; mail Jacksonville z 32208; pop. incl. with Jacksonville (Inc. Place)
Lake Frances; RMC Place; LAKE; *164 G-9; mail Tavares z 32778; pop. incl. with Tavares (Inc. Place)
Lake Garfield; RMC Place; POLK; *164 J-9; mail Bartow z 33830-31; ● 1,800
Lake Geneva; RMC Place; CLAY; 164 D-8; elev. 137ft./42m.; [P]; z 32160; ● 1,200
Lake Grove; RMC Place; GULF; *165 S-7; mail Wewahitchka z 32465; pop. incl. with Wewahitchka (Inc. Place)
Lake Hamilton; Inc. Place; POLK; 164 J-9; elev. 145ft./44m.; [P]; ★ WNHV; z 33851; Ⓟ 1,128; Ⓒ 1,304
Lake Harbor; CDP; PALM BEACH; 165 N-12; elev. 17ft./5m.; [P]; z 33459; Ⓒ 195
Lake Hart; CDP-Census Area Only; ORANGE; *164 I-10; ★ ORL; Ⓒ 557
Lake Helen; Inc. Place; VOLUSIA; 164 G-10; elev. 81ft./25m.; [P]; ★ ORL; z 32744; Ⓟ 2,344; Ⓒ 2,743
Lake Jem; RMC Place; LAKE; 164 H-9; elev. 88ft./27m.; ● 340
Lake Joanna; RMC Place; LAKE; *164 G-9; mail Eustis z 32726; ● 1,100
Lake Kathryn; CDP-Census Area Only; LAKE; *164 G-10; Ⓒ 845
Lake Kathryn Heights; RMC Place; LAKE; *164 G-10; mail DeLand z 32720; ● 520
Lakeland; Inc. Place; POLK; 164 J-8; elev. 219ft./67m.; [P] [H] [C] 6,075 ■; ★ LKLD; z 33801-07, z 33809-13, z 33815; Ⓟ 70,576; Ⓒ 78,452; ◆ 87,947
Lakeland Highlands; CDP-Census Area Only; POLK; *164 J-8; ★ LKLD; mail Lakeland z 33813; Ⓟ 9,972; Ⓒ 12,557
Lake Lindsey; CDP-Census Area Only; HERNANDO; *164 H-7; mail Brooksville z 34601; Ⓒ 49
Lake Lorraine; CDP-Census Area Only; OKALOOSA; *165 S-4; ★ FTWL; mail Shalimar z 32579; Ⓟ 6,779; Ⓒ 7,106
Lake Lucerne; CDP; MIAMI-DADE; *165 P-13; ★ MIA-; mail Miami z 33169, Opa Locka z 33055-56; Ⓟ 9,478; Ⓒ 9,132
Lake Lucina; RMC Place; DUVAL; *164 C-9; ★ JAX; mail Jacksonville z 32277; pop. incl. with Jacksonville (Inc. Place)
Lake Mack-Forest Hills; CDP-Census Area Only; LAKE; *164 G-10; Ⓒ 989
Lake Mack Park; RMC Place; LAKE; *164 G-10; mail DeLand z 32720; ● 450
Lake Magdalene; CDP-Census Area Only; HILLSBOROUGH; 163 B-4; ★ TAM; mail Tampa z 33612-13; Ⓟ 15,973; Ⓒ 28,755; Ⓡ 28,873; ◆ 34,742
Lake Marian Highlands; RMC Place; OSCEOLA; 164 J-11; mail Kenansville z 34739; ● 370
Lake Mary; Inc. Place; SEMINOLE; 164 G-10; elev. 63ft./19m.; [P]; ★ ORL; z 32746, z 32795; Ⓟ 5,929; Ⓒ 11,458
Lake Mendelin Estates; RMC Place; ORANGE; *164 H-10; ★ ORL; mail Apopka z 32703; ● 700
Lake Monroe; RMC Place; SEMINOLE; 164 G-10; elev. 20ft./6m.; [P]; ★ ORL; z 32747; ● 270
Lakemont; RMC Place; HIGHLANDS; *165 K-10; mail Avon Park z 33825; ● 300
Lake Mystic; RMC Place; LIBERTY; *165 S-8; mail Bristol z 32321; ● 150
Lake of the Hills; RMC Place; POLK; *164 J-9; elev. 165ft./50m.; ★ WNHV; mail Lake Wales z 33853, z 33898; ● 580
Lake Panasoffkee; CDP; SUMTER; 164 H-8; elev. 62ft./19m.; [P]; z 33538; Ⓟ 2,705; winter pop. 5,000; Ⓒ 3,413
Lake Park; Inc. Place; PALM BEACH; 165 M-14; elev. 13ft./4m.; [P] ■; ★ MIA-; z 33403, z 33408, z 33410; Ⓟ 6,704; Ⓒ 8,721; ◆ 9,059
Lake Pasadena Heights; RMC Place; PASCO; *164 I-8; mail Dade City z 33525; ● 550
Lake Placid; Inc. Place; HIGHLANDS; 165 L-10; elev. 136ft./41m.; [P]; z 33852, z 33862; Ⓟ 1,158; Ⓒ 1,668
Lakeport; RMC Place; GLADES; 165 M-11; mail Moore Haven z 33471; ● 300
Lake Sarasota; CDP-Census Area Only; SARASOTA; *165 L-7; ★ SAR-B; mail Sarasota z 34241; Ⓟ 4,117; Ⓒ 4,458
Lakes by the Bay; CDP-Census Area Only; MIAMI-DADE; *165 Q-13; ★ MIA-; mail Miami z 33157, z 33189-90; Ⓟ 5,615; Ⓒ 9,055
Lake Shore; RMC Place; DUVAL; *164 C-9; ★ JAX; mail Jacksonville z 32210, z 32238; pop. incl. with Jacksonville (Inc. Place)
Lakeside; CDP-Census Area Only; CLAY; *164 C-9; ★ JAX; mail Orange Park z 32073; Ⓟ 29,137; Ⓒ 30,927; ◆ 41,277
Lakeside Green; CDP-Census Area Only; PALM BEACH; 163 A-9; ★ MIA-; mail West Palm Beach z 33417; Ⓟ 2,994; Ⓒ 3,311
Lake Suzy; RMC Place; DESOTO; 165 M-8; [P]; z 34266, z 34269; ● 1,040
Lake View Point; RMC Place; GADSDEN; *164 B-1; mail Quincy z 32351; ● 150
Lakeville; RMC Place; LEE; *165 N-9; mail North Fort Myers z 33917; ● 160
Lake Wales; Inc. Place; POLK; 164 J-9; elev. 147ft./45m.; [P] [H] [C] 1,035; z 33853-56, z 33859, z 33867, z 33898; Ⓟ 9,670; Ⓒ 10,194
Lake Weir; RMC Place; MARION; *164 G-8; ★ OCA; mail Ocklawaha z 32179, Summerfield z 34491; ● 3,800
Lakewood; RMC Place; DUVAL; *164 C-9; ★ JAX; mail Jacksonville z 32207; pop. incl. with Jacksonville (Inc. Place)
Lakewood; RMC Place; LEON; *164 B-2; elev. 100ft./30m.; ★ TALL; mail Tallahassee z 32303; ● 1,900
Lakewood; RMC Place; WALTON; *165 Q-5; elev. 345ft./105m.; mail Defuniak Springs z 32433; rural
Lakewood Heights; RMC Place; LEON; *164 C-2; ★ TALL; mail Tallahassee z 32311; pop. incl. with Tallahassee (Inc. Place)
Lakewood Park; CDP; ST. LUCIE; 165 K-13; ★ FTPI; mail Fort Pierce z 34951; Ⓟ 7,211; Ⓒ 10,458
Lake Worth; Inc. Place; PALM BEACH; 165 N-14; elev. 19ft./6m.; [P] ■; ★ MIA-; z 33449, z 33454, z 33460-63, z 33465-67 & mail Boca Raton z 33464; Ⓟ 28,564; Ⓒ 35,133; ◆ 37,367
Lake Worth Corridor; CDP-Census Area Only; PALM BEACH; *165 N-14; ★ MIA-; Ⓒ 18,663
Lamont; RMC Place; JEFFERSON; 164 C-3; [P]; z 32336; ● 150
Lamplighter; RMC Place; ALACHUA; *164 E-8; ★ GAIN; mail Gainesville z 32609; pop. incl. with Gainesville (Inc. Place)
Lanark Village; RMC Place; FRANKLIN; 164 D-1; elev. 30ft./9m.; [P]; z 32323; ● 600
Lancaster; RMC Place; SUWANNEE; *164 C-5; mail Live Oak z 32060; ● 150
Land O' Lakes; CDP; PASCO; 164 I-7; elev. 81ft./25m.; [P]; ★ TAM; z 34637-39; Ⓟ 7,892; Ⓒ 20,971; ◆ 29,621
Lane; RMC Place; DUVAL; mail Jacksonville z 32254; pop. incl. with Jacksonville (Inc. Place)
Lane Park; RMC Place; LAKE; *164 G-9; mail Tavares z 32778; ● 600
Lansing; RMC Place; DESOTO; *165 L-9; elev. 56ft./17m.; mail Arcadia z 34266; ● 100
Lantana; Inc. Place; PALM BEACH; 165 N-14; elev. 10ft./3m.; [P] [H]; ★ MIA-; z 33460, z 33462, z 33465 & mail Boca Raton z 33464; Ⓟ 8,392; Ⓒ 9,437; Ⓡ 9,404
Largo; Inc. Place; PINELLAS; 164 J-6; elev. 57ft./17m.; [P] [H] ■; ★ ST.PET; z 33770-71, z 33773-74, z 33776-79 & mail Seminole z 33772, z 33775; Ⓟ 65,674; Ⓒ 69,371; ◆ 66,522
Larkin Fish Camp; RMC Place; LIBERTY; *165 S-7; mail Bristol z 32321; ● 30
Lauderdale-by-the-Sea; Inc. Place; BROWARD; 163 H-10; elev. 10ft./3m.; [P]; ★ MIA-; z 33308 & mail Pompano Beach z 33062; Ⓟ 2,990; Ⓒ 2,563; Ⓡ 3,221
Lauderdale Lakes; Inc. Place; BROWARD; 163 H-8; elev. 7ft./2m.; [P] ■; ★ MIA-; z 33309, z 33311, z 33313, z 33319 & mail Fort Lauderdale z 33330; Ⓟ 27,341; Ⓒ 31,705; ◆ 32,129
Lauderhill; Inc. Place; BROWARD; 163 H-8; elev. 7ft./2m.; [P] ■; ★ MIA-; z 33311, z 33313, z 33319, z 33351 & mail Fort Lauderdale z 33321; Ⓟ 49,708; Ⓒ 57,585; ◆ 59,367
Laurel; CDP; SARASOTA; 165 L-7; [P]; ★ VEN; z 34272 & mail Nokomis z 34275, Osprey z 34229; Ⓟ 8,245; Ⓒ 8,393
Laurel Grove; RMC Place; CLAY; *164 C-9; ★ JAX; mail Orange Park z 32073; pop. incl. with Orange Park (Inc. Place)
Laurel Hill; Inc. Place; OKALOOSA; 165 Q-4; elev. 289ft./88m.; [P]; z 32567; Ⓟ 543; Ⓒ 549
Laurel Park; RMC Place; ESCAMBIA; ★ PENS; mail Pensacola z 32505
Lawtey; Inc. Place; BRADFORD; 164 D-8; elev. 162ft./49m.; [P]; z 32058; Ⓟ 676; Ⓒ 656
Layton; Inc. Place; MONROE; 165 T-12; mail Long Key z 33001; Ⓟ 183; Ⓒ 186
Lazy Lake; Inc. Place; BROWARD; *165 O-14; elev. 5ft./2m.; [P]; ★ MIA-; z 33305; Ⓟ 33; Ⓒ 38
Lealman (Lellman); RMC Place; PINELLAS; 163 D-2; elev. 49ft./15m.; ★ ST.PET; mail Saint Petersburg z 33714; Ⓟ 21,748; ● 4,200
Lebanon; RMC Place; LEVY; 164 F-7; mail Dunnellon z 34431; ● 30
Lecanto; CDP; CITRUS; 164 G-7; elev. 49ft./15m.; [P] [H]; z 34460-61; Ⓟ 1,243; Ⓒ 5,161
Lee; Inc. Place; MADISON; 164 B-5; elev. 94ft./29m.; [P]; z 32059; Ⓟ 306; Ⓒ 352
LEE; 165 N-9; Ⓟ 335,113; Ⓒ 440,888; ◆ 627,898
Lee Cypress; RMC Place; COLLIER; *165 P-10; mail Copeland z 34137
Leesburg; Inc. Place; LAKE; 164 G-9; elev. 79ft./24m.; [P] [H] ■; z 34748-49, z 34788-89; Ⓟ 14,903; Ⓒ 15,956; ◆ 18,993
Lehigh; RMC Place; LEON; *164 B-2; ★ TALL; mail Tallahassee z 32301; pop. incl. with Tallahassee (Inc. Place)
Lehigh Acres; CDP; LEE; 165 N-9; elev. 26ft./8m.; [P] [H]; ★ FTMY-; z 33936, z 33970-74, z 33976; Ⓟ 13,611; Ⓒ 33,430; ◆ 47,615
Leisure City; CDP; MIAMI-DADE; 165 Q-13; ★ MIA-; mail Homestead z 33030, z 33033; Ⓟ 19,379; Ⓒ 22,152; ◆ 23,138
Leisureville; CDP-Census Area Only; BROWARD; *165 O-14; ★ MIA-; Ⓒ 1,147
Lellman; PINELLAS; see Lealman (RMC Place)
Lely; CDP-Census Area Only; COLLIER; *165 P-9; ★ NAP; mail Naples z 34113; Ⓟ 3,014; Ⓒ 3,857
Lely Resort; CDP-Census Area Only; COLLIER; *165 P-9; ★ NAP; Ⓒ 1,426
Lemon Bluff; RMC Place; VOLUSIA; *164 G-11; elev. 10ft./3m.; mail Osteen z 32764; ● 70
Lemon City; RMC Place; MIAMI-DADE; *165 P-13; ★ MIA-; mail Miami z 33127, z 33137; pop. incl. with Miami (Inc. Place)
Lemon Grove; RMC Place; HARDEE; *165 K-9; elev. 127ft./39m.; mail Wauchula z 33873, Zolfo Springs z 33890; rural
Leno; RMC Place; CLAY; *164 D-9; mail Green Cove Springs z 32043; ● 150
LEON; 164 B-3; Ⓟ 192,493; Ⓒ 239,452; ◆ 291,214
Leonia; RMC Place; HOLMES; 165 Q-5; mail Westville z 32464; ● 150
Leon Station; RMC Place; LEON; *164 B-2; ★ TALL; mail Tallahassee z 32303, z 32315; pop. incl. with Tallahassee (Inc. Place)
Leonton; RMC Place; JEFFERSON; mail Monticello z 32344; rural
Lessie; RMC Place; NASSAU; *164 B-9; elev. 17ft./5m.; mail Hilliard z 32046; rural
LEVY; 164 F-7; Ⓟ 25,923; Ⓒ 34,450; ◆ 40,091
Liberty; RMC Place; WALTON; 165 R-5; mail Defuniak Springs z 32433; ● 100
LIBERTY; 164 C-1; Ⓟ 5,569; Ⓒ 7,021; ◆ 7,929
Liberty City; RMC Place; MIAMI-DADE; *165 P-13; ★ MIA-; mail Miami z 33142; pop. incl. with Miami (Inc. Place)
Liberty Square; RMC Place; MIAMI-DADE; *165 P-13; ★ MIA-; mail Miami z 33147; pop. incl. with Miami (Inc. Place)
Lido Key; RMC Place; SARASOTA; *165 L-7; ★ SAR-B; mail Sarasota z 34239; pop. incl. with Sarasota (Inc. Place)
Lighthouse Point; Inc. Place; BROWARD; 165 O-14; elev. 6ft./2m.; [P]; ★ MIA-; z 33064, z 33074; Ⓟ 10,378; Ⓒ 10,767
Lighthouse Point; RMC Place; MARTIN; *165 L-13; ★ STU; mail Stuart z 34994; ● 800
Lily; RMC Place; HARDEE; *165 L-8; elev. 77ft./23m.; mail Ona z 33865; ● 60
Limestone; RMC Place; HARDEE; 165 L-9; mail Ona z 33865; ● 60
Limestone; RMC Place; JEFFERSON; *164 C-3; elev. 38ft./12m.; mail Monticello z 32344; rural
Limestone Creek; CDP-Census Area Only; PALM BEACH; *165 M-13; ★ MIA-; Ⓒ 569
Limona; RMC Place; HILLSBOROUGH; *164 J-7; ★ TAM; mail Brandon z 33510
Lincoln City; RMC Place; BRADFORD; *164 D-8; mail Starke z 32091
Lincoln Estates; RMC Place; ALACHUA; *164 E-7; ★ GAIN; mail Gainesville z 32601; pop. incl. with Gainesville (Inc. Place)
Lincoln Park; RMC Place; SUMTER; *164 H-8; mail Bushnell z 33513, Webster z 33597
Linden; RMC Place; SUMTER; 164 H-8; mail Webster z 33597; ● 120
Lisbon; CDP; LAKE; 164 G-9; mail Leesburg z 34788; Ⓒ 273
Lithia; RMC Place; HILLSBOROUGH; 164 J-8; elev. 110ft./34m.; [P]; ★ TAM; z 33547; rural
Little Havana; RMC Place; MIAMI-DADE; *165 Q-13; ★ MIA-; mail Miami z 33125; pop. incl. with Miami (Inc. Place)
Little Hollywood; RMC Place; BREVARD; *164 J-13; ★ MELB-; ● 1,200
Little Lake City; RMC Place; GILCHRIST; *164 D-6; mail Bell z 32619; ● 220
Little River; RMC Place; MIAMI-DADE; *165 P-13; ★ MIA-; mail Miami z 33138, z 33238; pop. incl. with Miami (Inc. Place)
Little Torch Key; RMC Place; MONROE; *165 T-10; [P]; z 33042; ● 700
Live Oak; Inc. Place; ⊡ SUWANNEE; 164 C-6; elev. 102ft./31m.; [P] [H]; z 32060, z 32064; Ⓟ 6,332; Ⓒ 6,480
Live Oak; RMC Place; WASHINGTON; *165 R-6; mail Vernon z 32462; rural
Live Oak Island (Live Oak Point); RMC Place; WAKULLA; *164 D-2; mail Crawfordville z 32327; ● 120
Live Oak Point; WAKULLA; see Live Oak Island (RMC Place)
Lloyd; RMC Place; JEFFERSON; 164 B-3; elev. 74ft./23m.; [P]; z 32337; ● 250
Loch Lommond; RMC Place; CLAY; *164 D-8; mail Keystone Heights z 32656; ● 655
Loch Lomond; CDP-Census Area Only; BROWARD; *165 O-14; ★ MIA-; Ⓒ 3,537
Lochloosa; RMC Place; ALACHUA; 164 E-8; elev. 66ft./20m.; [P]; z 32662; ● 260
Lochmoor; RMC Place; LEE; 163 M-1; ★ FTMY-; mail North Fort Myers z 33903; ● 1,200
Lochmoor Waterway Estates; CDP-Census Area Only; LEE; *165 N-9; ★ FTMY-; mail North Fort Myers z 33903; Ⓟ 4,091; Ⓒ 3,858
Lock Arbor; RMC Place; SEMINOLE; *164 G-10; elev. 50ft./15m.; ★ ORL; mail Sanford z 32773
Lockhart; CDP; ORANGE; 165 M-3; elev. 97ft./30m.; [P]; ★ ORL; z 32810 & mail Orlando z 32860; Ⓟ 11,636; Ⓒ 12,944
Lockwood; RMC Place; ORANGE; *164 H-11; mail Orlando z 32828, z 32833; ● 400
Lois; RMC Place; JEFFERSON; *164 B-3; mail Monticello z 32344; ● 270
Londonderry; RMC Place; ORANGE; *164 H-10; ★ ORL; mail Orlando z 32808
Longboat Key; Inc. Place; MANATEE, SARASOTA; 165 L-6; elev. 9ft./3m.; [P]; ★ SAR-B; z 34228; Ⓟ 5,937; Ⓒ 7,603
Long Hammock; RMC Place; SUMTER; *164 G-8; elev. 64ft./20m.; mail Oxford z 34484; ● 120
Long Point; RMC Place; BAY; *165 S-6; mail Panama City z 32404; pop. incl. with Parker (Inc. Place)
Longwood; RMC Place; OKALOOSA; *165 R-4; ★ FTWL; mail Shalimar z 32579; ● 1,100
Longwood; Inc. Place; SEMINOLE; 164 H-10; elev. 75ft./23m.; [P] [H]; ★ ORL; z 32750, z 32752, z 32779, z 32791; Ⓟ 13,316; Ⓒ 13,745
Lorida; RMC Place; HIGHLANDS; 165 L-10; elev. 49ft./15m.; [P]; z 33857; ● 340
Lorraine; RMC Place; MANATEE; *165 L-7; mail Bradenton z 34202; rural
Lotus; RMC Place; BREVARD; *164 I-12; ★ MELB-; mail Merritt Island z 32952
Loughman; CDP; POLK; 164 I-9; elev. 101ft./31m.; [P]; ★ KISS; z 33858; Ⓟ 1,214; Ⓒ 1,385
Lovedale; RMC Place; JACKSON; *165 Q-7; mail Bascom z 32423; rural
Lovett; RMC Place; MADISON; *164 B-4; elev. 126ft./38m.; mail Greenville z 32331; rural
Lovewood; RMC Place; JACKSON; *165 R-7; mail Cottondale z 32431; rural
Lowell; RMC Place; MARION; 164 F-8; elev. 110ft./34m.; [P]; ★ OCA; z 32663; ● 220
Lower Clay Landing; RMC Place; LEVY; *164 E-6; mail Chiefland z 32626; ● 50
Lower Grand Lagoon; CDP-Census Area Only; BAY; *165 S-6; ★ PNCY; mail Panama City z 32401; Ⓟ 3,329; Ⓒ 4,082
Lower Matecumbe Beach; RMC Place; MONROE; *165 S-12; mail Islamorada z 33036
Loxahatchee; PALM BEACH; see Loxahatchee Groves (Inc. Place)
Loxahatchee Groves (Loxahatchee); Inc. Place; PALM BEACH; 165 N-13; elev. 22ft./7m.; [P] [H]; ★ MIA-; z 33470; incorporated November 6, 2006; not reported in 2000 Census; ● 3,000
Loyce; RMC Place; PASCO; *164 I-7; mail Spring Hill z 34610; ● 175
Lucerne Avenue; RMC Place; PALM BEACH; *165 N-14; ★ MIA-; mail Lake Worth z 33460; pop. incl. with Lake Worth (Inc. Place)
Lucerne Park; RMC Place; POLK; *164 J-9; ★ WNHV; mail Winter Haven z 33881; pop. incl. with Winter Haven (Inc. Place)
Ludlam; RMC Place; MIAMI-DADE; *165 T-13; [P]; z 33255 & mail Miami z 33155
Lullwater Beach; RMC Place; BAY; *165 S-5; ★ PNCY; mail Panama City Beach z 32407; pop. incl. with Panama City Beach (Inc. Place)
Lulu; RMC Place; COLUMBIA; 164 C-7; elev. 155ft./47m.; [P]; z 32061 & mail Lake Butler z 32054; ● 100
Lumberton; RMC Place; PASCO; 164 I-8; elev. 83ft./25m.; mail Zephyrhills z 33540; ● 220
Lundy; RMC Place; PUTNAM; *164 E-9; mail Palatka z 32177; ● 150
Luraville; RMC Place; SUWANNEE; *164 C-5; elev. 55ft./17m.; mail Live Oak z 32060
Lutz; CDP; HILLSBOROUGH; 164 I-7; elev. 73ft./22m.; [P] [H]; ★ TAM; z 33548-49, z 33558-59; Ⓟ 10,552; Ⓒ 17,081
Lyle Corner; RMC Place; POLK; *164 J-9; mail Bartow z 33830, Lakeland z 33813
Lynchburg; RMC Place; POLK; *164 J-9; mail Winter Haven z 33881
Lynne; RMC Place; MARION; 164 F-9; mail Silver Springs z 34488; ● 200
Lynn Haven; Inc. Place; BAY; 165 S-6; elev. 14ft./4m.; [P]; ★ PNCY; z 32444; Ⓟ 9,298; Ⓒ 12,451

M

Mabel; RMC Place; SUMTER; *164 H-8; mail Center Hill z 33514; rural
Mabry Manor; RMC Place; LEON; *164 B-2; ★ TALL; mail Tallahassee z 32310; pop. incl. with Tallahassee (Inc. Place)
Macclenny (Maclenny); Inc. Place; ⊡ BAKER; 164 C-8; elev. 135ft./41m.; [P] [H]; z 32063; Ⓟ 3,966; Ⓒ 4,459
Macedonia; RMC Place; CALHOUN; *165 R-7; elev. 113ft./34m.; mail Blountstown z 32424; rural
Maclenny; BAKER; see Macclenny (Inc. Place)
Madeira Beach; Inc. Place; PINELLAS; 164 J-6; elev. 5ft./2m.; [P]; ★ ST.PET; z 33708, z 33738; Ⓟ 4,225; Ⓒ 4,511
Madison; Inc. Place; ⊡ MADISON; 164 B-5; elev. 191ft./58m.; [P] [H]; z 32340-41; Ⓟ 3,345; Ⓒ 3,061
MADISON; 164 C-4; Ⓟ 16,569; Ⓒ 18,733; ◆ 18,904
Magnolia Beach; RMC Place; BAY; *165 S-6; ★ PNCY; mail Panama City z 32408; ● 500
Magnolia Bluffs; RMC Place; FRANKLIN; *165 T-8; mail Eastpoint z 32328; ● 330
Magnolia Gardens; RMC Place; DUVAL; *164 C-9; ★ JAX; mail Jacksonville z 32209; pop. incl. with Jacksonville (Inc. Place)
Magnolia Springs; RMC Place; CLAY; *164 D-9; ★ JAX; mail Green Cove Springs z 32043; ● 1,100
Mainland; RMC Place; VOLUSIA; *164 F-11; ★ D.BCH; mail Ormond Beach z 32174; pop. incl. with Ormond Beach (Inc. Place)
Mainlands Center; RMC Place; PINELLAS; *164 J-6; ★ ST.PET; mail Pinellas Park z 33782; pop. incl. with Pinellas Park (Inc. Place)
Main Street; RMC Place; ALACHUA; ★ GAIN; mail Gainesville z 32601-02, z 32605, z 32611, z 32613, z 32627; pop. incl. with Gainesville (Inc. Place)
Maitland; Inc. Place; ORANGE; 164 H-10; elev. 89ft./27m.; [P]; ★ ORL; z 32751, z 32794 & mail Winter Park z 32789; Ⓟ 9,110; Ⓒ 12,019
Malabar; Inc. Place; BREVARD; 164 J-12; elev. 27ft./8m.; [P]; ★ MELB-; z 32950; Ⓟ 1,977; Ⓒ 2,622
Malone; Inc. Place; JACKSON; 165 Q-7; elev. 138ft./42m.; [P]; z 32445; Ⓟ 765; Ⓒ 2,007
Manalapan; Inc. Place; PALM BEACH; 163 C-10; elev. 20ft./6m.; [P]; ★ MIA-; z 33462; Ⓟ 312; Ⓒ 321
Manasota; RMC Place; SARASOTA; 165 M-7; [P]; ★ VEN; z 34260; ● 540
Manasota Key; CDP-Census Area Only; CHARLOTTE; *165 M-7; ★ VEN; mail Englewood z 34223; Ⓟ 1,395; Ⓒ 1,345
Manatee; RMC Place; MANATEE; *165 K-7; ★ SAR-B; mail Bradenton z 34208; pop. incl. with Bradenton (Inc. Place)
MANATEE; 165 L-8; Ⓟ 211,707; Ⓒ 264,002; ◆ 318,176
Manattee Road; CDP-Census Area Only; LEVY; *164 E-6; Ⓒ 1,937
Mandarin; RMC Place; DUVAL; *164 C-9; ★ JAX; mail Jacksonville z 32223, z 32241; pop. incl. with Jacksonville (Inc. Place)
Mango; CDP; HILLSBOROUGH; 163 B-5; [P]; ★ TAM; z 33550 & mail Seffner z 33584; Ⓟ 8,700; Ⓒ 8,842
Mango Hills; RMC Place; HILLSBOROUGH; *164 J-8; ★ TAM; mail Seffner z 33584; ● 1,300
Mangonia Park; Inc. Place; PALM BEACH; 163 A-10; elev. 18ft./5m.; ★ MIA-; mail West Palm Beach z 33407; Ⓟ 1,453; Ⓒ 1,283
Manhattan; RMC Place; MANATEE; *165 K-7; mail Myakka City z 34251, Parrish z 34219; ● 40
Mannville; RMC Place; PUTNAM; *164 E-9; mail Interlachen z 32148; ● 450
Marathon; Inc. Place; MONROE; 165 T-11; [P] [H]; z 33050-52; Ⓟ 8,857; winter pop. 20,000; Ⓒ 10,255
Marathon Shores; RMC Place; MONROE; *165 T-11; elev. 5ft./2m.; [P]; z 33050, z 33052
Maravilla; RMC Place; ST. LUCIE; *165 L-13; ★ FTPI; mail Fort Pierce z 34982; pop. incl. with Fort Pierce (Inc. Place)
Marco (Marco Island); Inc. Place; COLLIER; 165 P-9; mail Marco Island z 34145-46; Ⓟ 9,493; Ⓒ 14,879
Marco Island; COLLIER; see Marco (Inc. Place)
Margate; Inc. Place; BROWARD; 165 O-13; elev. 13ft./4m.; [P] [H]; ★ MIA-; z 33063, z 33065, z 33068, z 33073, z 33093 & mail Pompano Beach z 33076; Ⓟ 42,985; Ⓒ 53,909; ◆ 52,773
Marianna; Inc. Place; ⊡ JACKSON; 165 R-7; elev. 117ft./36m.; [P] [H] [C] 2,232; z 32446-48; Ⓟ 6,292; Ⓒ 6,230
Maricamp; RMC Place; MARION; *164 F-8; ★ OCA; mail Ocala z 34471-72, z 34480; pop. incl. with Ocala (Inc. Place)
Marietta; RMC Place; DUVAL; *164 C-9; ★ JAX; mail Jacksonville z 32220; pop. incl. with Jacksonville (Inc. Place)
Marineland; Inc. Place; FLAGLER, ST. JOHNS; 164 E-10; elev. 11ft./3m.; mail Saint Augustine z 32086; Ⓟ 21; Ⓒ 6
MARION; 164 F-7; Ⓟ 194,833; Ⓒ 258,916; ◆ 341,671
Marion Oaks; RMC Place; MARION; 164 G-8; elev. 22ft./7m.; ★ OCA; mail Ocala z 34473; ● 4,200
Martel; RMC Place; MARION; 164 F-8; ★ OCA; mail Ocala z 34475; ● 200
Martin; RMC Place; MARION; *164 F-8; ★ OCA; mail Anthony z 32617; ● 70
MARTIN; 165 M-13; Ⓟ 100,900; Ⓒ 126,731; ◆ 138,546
Marvina; RMC Place; HILLSBOROUGH; *164 J-8; mail Valrico z 33594; ● 75
Mary Esther; Inc. Place; OKALOOSA; 165 S-4; [P]; ★ FTWL; z 32569; Ⓟ 4,139; Ⓒ 4,055
Masaryktown; CDP; HERNANDO; 164 H-7; elev. 64ft./20m.; [P]; ★ SPR.H; z 34604; Ⓒ 920
Mascotte; Inc. Place; LAKE; 164 H-9; elev. 128ft./39m.; [P]; z 34753; Ⓟ 1,761; Ⓒ 2,687
Mason; RMC Place; COLUMBIA; *164 D-7; mail Lake City z 32055; ● 200
Matlacha; CDP; LEE; 165 N-8; elev. 4ft./1m.; [P]; ★ FTMY-; z 33993 & mail Cape Coral z 33909; Ⓒ 735
Matlacha Isles-Matlacha Shores; CDP-Census Area Only; LEE; *165 N-8; ★ FTMY-; mail Cape Coral z 33991; Ⓒ 304
Matoaka; RMC Place; MANATEE; *165 L-7; mail Sarasota z 34243; ● 150
Maxcy Quarters; RMC Place; POLK; *165 K-10; mail Frostproof z 33843; ● 560
Maximo Moorings; RMC Place; PINELLAS; *165 K-6; elev. 5ft./2m.; ★ ST.PET; mail Saint Petersburg z 33711; pop. incl. with Saint Petersburg (Inc. Place)
Maxville; RMC Place; DUVAL; *164 C-8; [P]; ★ JAX; z 32234; pop. incl. with Jacksonville (Inc. Place)
Mayo; Inc. Place; ⊡ LAFAYETTE; 164 D-5; elev. 79ft./24m.; [P]; z 32066; Ⓟ 917; Ⓒ 988
Mayo Junction; RMC Place; LAFAYETTE; *164 C-5; elev. 65ft./20m.; mail Mayo z 32066; rural
Mayport; RMC Place; DUVAL; *164 C-10; [P]; ★ JAX; z 32233 & mail Jacksonville z 32227-28; pop. incl. with Jacksonville (Inc. Place)
McAllaster Landing; RMC Place; BAY; *165 S-6; mail Youngstown z 32466; ● 180
McAlpin; RMC Place; SUWANNEE; 164 C-6; elev. 101ft./31m.; [P]; z 32062; ● 165
McColsky; RMC Place; COLUMBIA; *164 C-7; mail Lake City z 32055; ● 110
McDavid; RMC Place; ESCAMBIA; 165 Q-2; [P]; z 32568; ● 100
McGregor; CDP-Census Area Only; LEE; *165 N-9; ★ FTMY-; mail Fort Myers z 33919; Ⓟ 6,504; Ⓒ 7,136
McIntosh; Inc. Place; MARION; 164 E-8; elev. 109ft./33m.; [P]; ★ OCA; z 32664; Ⓟ 411; Ⓒ 453
McKinnon (McKinnonville); RMC Place; ESCAMBIA; *165 Q-2; mail Mc David z 32568
McKinnonville; ESCAMBIA; see McKinnon (RMC Place)
McLellan; RMC Place; SANTA ROSA; *165 Q-3; mail Milton z 32570; rural
McMeekin; RMC Place; PUTNAM; *164 E-8; mail Hawthorne z 32640; ● 400
McNeil; GULF; see Indian Pass (RMC Place)
Meadowbrook; RMC Place; ORANGE; *164 H-10; ★ ORL; mail Orlando z 32808; ● 1,600
Meadowbrook Terrace; RMC Place; CLAY; *164 C-9; ★ JAX; mail Orange Park z 32073; ● 5,000
Meadowlawn; RMC Place; PINELLAS; *164 J-7; ★ ST.PET; mail Saint Petersburg z 33702; pop. incl. with Saint Petersburg (Inc. Place)
Meadow Woods; CDP-Census Area Only; ORANGE; 165 P-3; ★ ORL; mail Orlando z 32824; Ⓟ 4,876; Ⓒ 11,286
Mecca; RMC Place; SEMINOLE; *164 H-10; ★ ORL; mail Sanford z 32771; ● 200
Medart; RMC Place; WAKULLA; 164 C-2; mail Crawfordville z 32327; ● 150
Medley; Inc. Place; MIAMI-DADE; 163 K-7; elev. 5ft./2m.; [P]; ★ MIA-; z 33166, z 33178 & mail Hialeah z 33016; Ⓟ 663; Ⓒ 1,098
Medulla; CDP; POLK; 163 K-4; ★ LKLD; mail Lakeland z 33811; Ⓟ 3,977; Ⓒ 6,637
Melbourne; Inc. Place; BREVARD; 164 J-12; elev. 21ft./6m.; [P] [H] [C] 5,656 ■; ★ MELB-; z 32901-12, z 32919, z 32934-37, z 32940-41, z 32951; Ⓟ 59,646; Ⓒ 71,382; ◆ 75,051
Melbourne Beach; Inc. Place; BREVARD; 164 J-12; elev. 12ft./4m.; [P]; ★ MELB-; z 32951; Ⓟ 3,021; Ⓒ 3,335
Melbourne Shores; RMC Place; BREVARD; 164 J-12; ★ MELB-; mail Melbourne Beach z 32951; ● 600
Melbourne Village; Inc. Place; BREVARD; 164 G-13; elev. 25ft./8m.; [P]; ★ MELB-; z 32904; Ⓟ 591; Ⓒ 706
Melody Hills; RMC Place; LEON; *164 B-2; ★ TALL; mail Tallahassee z 32308; pop. incl. with Tallahassee (Inc. Place)
Melrose; RMC Place; PUTNAM, ALACHUA; 164 E-8; elev. 161ft./49m.; [P]; z 32666; ● 1,100
Melrose Park; CDP; BROWARD; 163 I-8; ★ MIA-; mail Fort Lauderdale z 33312; Ⓟ 6,477; Ⓒ 7,114
Memphis; CDP; MANATEE; 163 F-3; ★ SAR-B; mail Palmetto z 34221; Ⓟ 6,760; Ⓒ 7,264
Memphis Heights; RMC Place; MANATEE; *165 K-7; ★ SAR-B; mail Palmetto z 34221
Mercer; RMC Place; SUWANNEE; *164 C-5; mail Live Oak z 32060; ● 230
Merediths; RMC Place; LEVY; *164 E-7; mail Archer z 32618, Bronson z 32621; ● 200
Merritt Island; CDP; BREVARD; 164 I-12; [P]; ★ MELB-; z 32952-54; Ⓟ 32,886; Ⓒ 36,090; ◆ 40,838
Mexico Beach; Inc. Place; BAY; 165 T-7; elev. 10ft./3m.; [P]; z 32410, z 32456; Ⓟ 992; Ⓒ 1,017
Miami; Inc. Place; ⊡ MIAMI-DADE; 165 Q-13; [P] [H] [C] 96,190 ■; ★ MIA-; z 33101-02, z 33109, z 33111-12, z 33114, z 33116, z 33119, z 33122, z 33124-47, z 33149-70, z 33172-90, z 33193-94, z 33196-97, z 33199, z 33222, z 33231, z 33233-34, z 33238-39, z 33242-43, z 33245, z 33247, z 33255-57, z 33261, z 33265-66, z 33269, z 33280, z 33283, z 33296, z 33299 & mail Hialeah z 33010-18, Opa Locka z 33054-56; Ⓟ 358,548; Ⓒ 362,470; ◆ 377,241
Miami Beach; Inc. Place; MIAMI-DADE; 165 P-14; elev. 6ft./2m.; [P] [H] ■; ★ MIA-; z 33109, z 33119, z 33139-41, z 33154, z 33239; Ⓟ 92,639; Ⓒ 87,933; ◆ 86,595
MIAMI-DADE; 165 Q-12; Ⓟ 1,937,094; Ⓒ 2,253,362; Ⓡ 2,253,779; ◆ 2,353,924
Miami Gardens; CDP; BROWARD; *165 P-13; [P]; ★ MIA-; z 33014-15, z 33017, z 33054-56, z 33169, z 33179 & mail Hollywood z 33023; Ⓒ 2,706
Miami Gardens; Inc. Place; MIAMI-DADE; 165 P-13; [P] [C] 4,386; ★ MIA-; z 33014-15, z 33017, z 33054-56, z 33169, z 33179; incorporated May 13, 2003; not reported in 2000 Census; Ⓡ 100,809; ◆ 95,236
Miami Lakes; Inc. Place; MIAMI-DADE; 163 K-7; [P]; ★ MIA-; z 33014, z 33016, z 33018 & mail Castlewood z 24224; incorporated December 5, 2000; not reported in 2000 Census; ● 22,800; ◆ 21,327
Miami Lakes; CDP-Census Area Only; MIAMI-DADE; 163 K-7; [P]; ★ MIA-; z 33014, z 33016, z 33018 & mail Hialeah z 33015; Ⓟ 12,750; Ⓒ 22,676
Miami Shores; Inc. Place; MIAMI-DADE; 163 K-9; elev. 8ft./2m.; [P] [C] 8,885; ★ MIA-; z 33138, z 33150, z 33153, z 33161, z 33167-68 & mail Miami z 33162; Ⓟ 10,084; Ⓒ 10,380
Miami Springs; Inc. Place; MIAMI-DADE; 165 P-13; elev. 5ft./2m.; [P]; ★ MIA-; z 33166, z 33266; Ⓟ 13,268; Ⓒ 13,712
Micanopy; Inc. Place; ALACHUA; 164 E-8; elev. 125ft./38m.; [P]; z 32667; Ⓟ 612; Ⓒ 653
Micco; CDP; BREVARD; 164 J-12; [P]; ★ MELB-; z 32976 & mail Sebastian z 32958; Ⓟ 8,757; Ⓒ 9,498
Miccosukee; RMC Place; LEON; 164 B-3; elev. 220ft./67m.; [P]; z 32309; ● 285
Miccosukee Hills; RMC Place; LEON; *164 B-2; ★ TALL; mail Tallahassee z 32308; pop. incl. with Tallahassee (Inc. Place)
Miccosukee Reservation; Indian Reservation; BROWARD, MIAMI-DADE; mail Clewiston z 33440; Ⓟ 276; Ⓒ 0
Mickler Landing; RMC Place; ST. JOHNS; *164 C-10; mail Ponte Vedra Beach z 32082; ● 1,100
Middleburg; CDP; CLAY; 164 D-9; [P]; ★ JAX; z 32050, z 32068; Ⓟ 6,233; Ⓒ 10,338
Mid Florida; RMC Place; SEMINOLE; *164 G-10; [P]; ★ ORL; z 32745, z 32799; pop. incl. with Lake Mary (Inc. Place)
Midriver (Mid River Farms); RMC Place; BROWARD; pop. incl. with Fort Lauderdale (Inc. Place)
Mid River Farms; BROWARD; see Midriver (RMC Place)
Midway; Inc. Place; GADSDEN; 164 B-2; elev. 191ft./58m.; [P]; z 32343; Ⓟ 852; Ⓒ 1,446
Midway; RMC Place; HILLSBOROUGH; *164 J-8; ★ TAM; mail Plant City z 33565; rural
Midway; CDP; SEMINOLE; 164 G-10; ★ ORL; mail Sanford z 32771; Ⓒ 1,714
Mikesville; RMC Place; COLUMBIA; *164 D-7; ● 100
Millcreek; RMC Place; ST. JOHNS; mail Saint Augustine z 32092; rural
Miller; RMC Place; UNION; *164 D-7; mail Lake Butler z 32054; ● 110
Miller Crossroads; RMC Place; HOLMES; *165 Q-6; mail Bonifay z 32425; ● 135
Millers Ferry; RMC Place; WASHINGTON; *165 R-6; mail Vernon z 32462; ● 65
Milligan; RMC Place; OKALOOSA; 165 R-4; elev. 100ft./30m.; [P]; z 32537; ● 350
Milltown; RMC Place; GULF; *165 T-7; mail Wewahitchka z 32465; ● 150
Millview; RMC Place; ESCAMBIA; 162 M-7; ★ PENS; mail Pensacola z 32506; ● 1,100
Millville; RMC Place; BAY; *165 S-6; ★ PNCY; mail Panama City z 32401; pop. incl. with Panama City (Inc. Place)
Millwood; RMC Place; MARION; *164 F-8; mail Reddick z 32686; ● 325
Milton; Inc. Place; ⊡ SANTA ROSA; 165 R-3; elev. 17ft./5m.; [P] [H]; ★ PENS; z 32570-72, z 32583; Ⓟ 7,216; Ⓒ 7,045
Mims; CDP; BREVARD; 164 H-11; [P]; ★ TITUS; z 32754 & mail Titusville z 32796; Ⓟ 9,412; Ⓒ 9,147
Mineral Springs; RMC Place; SANTA ROSA; *165 Q-2; mail Jay z 32565; rural
Minneola; Inc. Place; LAKE; 164 H-9; elev. 118ft./36m.; [P]; z 34715, z 34755; Ⓟ 1,515; Ⓒ 5,435
Minorville; RMC Place; ORANGE; *164 H-10; mail Gotha z 34734, Ocoee z 34761; pop. incl. with Ocoee (Inc. Place)
Miracle Mile; RMC Place; LEE; *165 N-9; ★ FTMY-; mail Fort Myers z 33901, z 33911; pop. incl. with Fort Myers (Inc. Place)
Miramar; Inc. Place; BROWARD; 165 P-13; elev. 6ft./2m.; [P] [C] 960; ★ MIA-; z 33023, z 33025, z 33027, z 33029 & mail Hollywood z 33028, z 33083; Ⓟ 40,663; Ⓒ 72,739; ◆ 89,134
Miramar Beach; CDP; WALTON; *165 S-4; [P]; z 32550 & mail Destin z 32541; Ⓟ 1,644; Ⓒ 2,435
Miramar Terrace; RMC Place; DUVAL; *164 C-9; ★ JAX; mail Jacksonville z 32207; pop. incl. with Jacksonville (Inc. Place)
Mission Bay; CDP-Census Area Only; PALM BEACH; *165 O-13; ★ MIA-; mail Boca Raton z 33428; Ⓟ 1,227; Ⓒ 2,926
Mission City; RMC Place; VOLUSIA; 164 G-11; ★ D.BCH; mail New Smyrna Beach z 32168; ● 1,700
Mission Hills; RMC Place; PINELLAS; *164 J-6; ★ ST.PET; mail Clearwater z 33759; pop. incl. with Clearwater (Inc. Place)
Mobile Gardens; RMC Place; CHARLOTTE; *165 M-7; ★ VEN; mail Englewood z 34224
Moffitt; RMC Place; HARDEE; *165 L-9; elev. 70ft./21m.; mail Zolfo Springs z 33890; ● 80
Mohawk; RMC Place; LAKE; *164 H-9; elev. 150ft./46m.; mail Clermont z 34711; pop. incl. with Minneola (Inc. Place)
Molino; CDP; ESCAMBIA; 165 R-2; [P]; z 32577; Ⓟ 1,207; Ⓒ 1,312
Molino Crossroads; RMC Place; ESCAMBIA; *165 R-2; mail Molino z 32577; ● 360
Monarch; RMC Place; SUMTER; *164 G-8; mail Wildwood z 34785; pop. incl. with Wildwood (Inc. Place)
MONROE; 165 R-11; Ⓟ 78,024; Ⓒ 79,589; ◆ 70,157
Monroes Corner; RMC Place; MARION; *164 G-8; ★ OCA; mail Summerfield z 34491; rural
Monroe Station; RMC Place; COLLIER; 165 P-11; rural
Montague; RMC Place; MARION; *164 F-8; mail Ocala z 34471, z 34480; ● 80
Montbrook; RMC Place; LEVY; *164 F-7; mail Williston z 32696
Montclair; RMC Place; LAKE; *164 G-9; mail Leesburg z 34748; pop. incl. with Leesburg (Inc. Place)
Monteocha; RMC Place; ALACHUA; *164 D-7; mail Gainesville z 32609; ● 100
Monterey; RMC Place; DUVAL; *164 C-9; ★ JAX; mail Jacksonville z 32211; pop. incl. with Jacksonville (Inc. Place)
Monticello; Inc. Place; ⊡ JEFFERSON; 164 B-3; elev. 235ft./72m.; [P]; z 32344-45; Ⓟ 2,573; Ⓒ 2,533
Montivilla; RMC Place; JEFFERSON; *164 B-3; mail Monticello z 32344; ● 170
Montverde; Inc. Place; LAKE; 165 M-1; [P]; z 34729, z 34756; Ⓟ 890; Ⓒ 882
Monument Lakes; RMC Place; DUVAL; *164 C-10; ★ JAX; mail Jacksonville z 32225; pop. incl. with Jacksonville (Inc. Place)
Moore Haven; Inc. Place; ⊡ GLADES; 165 M-11; elev. 10ft./3m.; [P]; z 33471; Ⓟ 1,432; Ⓒ 1,635
Moreland Park; RMC Place; SUMTER; *164 G-8; mail Wildwood z 34785; ● 500
Morningside; RMC Place; MIAMI-DADE; *165 P-13; ★ MIA-; mail Miami z 33137; pop. incl. with Miami (Inc. Place)
Morningside Park; RMC Place; ORANGE; 165 O-3; ★ ORL; mail Orlando z 32809; ● 500
Morriston; RMC Place; LEVY; 164 F-7; elev. 63ft./19m.; [P]; z 32668; ● 300
Morse Shores; RMC Place; LEE; *165 N-9; ★ FTMY-; mail Fort Myers z 33905; Ⓟ 3,771; ● 3,300
Mosley Hall; RMC Place; MADISON; *164 C-4; mail Greenville z 32331; rural
Moss Bluff; RMC Place; MARION; 164 G-9; mail Ocklawaha z 32179; ● 120
Moss Town; RMC Place; PASCO; mail Lacoochee z 33537
Mossy Head; RMC Place; WALTON; 165 R-5; elev. 251ft./77m.; [P]; z 32434; ● 250
Moultrie; RMC Place; ST. JOHNS; *164 D-10; mail Saint Augustine z 32086
Moultrie Junction; RMC Place; ST. JOHNS; *164 D-10
Mountain Lake Station; RMC Place; POLK; *164 J-9; mail Lake Wales z 33853; ● 140
Mountain Park; RMC Place; HERNANDO; *164 H-7; ★ SPR.H; mail Brooksville z 34601; ● 240
Mount Carmel; RMC Place; SANTA ROSA; *165 Q-3; mail Jay z 32565
Mount Dora; Inc. Place; LAKE; 164 G-9; elev. 167ft./51m.; [P]; z 32756-57; Ⓟ 7,196; Ⓒ 9,418
Mount Homer; RMC Place; LAKE; *164 G-9; mail Eustis z 32726, Tavares z 32778; pop. incl. with Eustis (Inc. Place)
Mount Pleasant; RMC Place; GADSDEN; 164 B-1; [P]; z 32352; ● 75
Mount Pleasant; RMC Place; WAKULLA; *164 C-2; mail Crawfordville z 32327; ● 300
Mount Plymouth; CDP; LAKE; 164 G-10; [P]; z 32776; Ⓟ 1,752; Ⓒ 2,814
Mount Royal; RMC Place; PUTNAM; *164 E-10; mail Welaka z 32193; rural
Muce; RMC Place; GLADES; *165 M-10; elev. 47ft./14m.; mail Labelle z 33935; ● 160
Mulberry; Inc. Place; POLK; 164 J-8; elev. 112ft./34m.; [P]; ★ LKLD; z 33860; Ⓟ 2,988; Ⓒ 3,230
Mullis City; RMC Place; HILLSBOROUGH; *164 J-7; mail Tampa z 33618, z 33624; ● 530
Munson; RMC Place; SANTA ROSA; *165 Q-3; elev. 210ft./64m.; mail Milton z 32570

Entries in **UPPERCASE** are counties.
Entries in **bold** have populations of 2,500 or more.
Names in parentheses are alternate names.

Inc. Place	Incorporated Place
RMC Place	Rand McNally Designated Place
CDP	Census Designated Place
MCD	Minor Civil Division

⊡ County Seat
▲ Minor Civil Division
elev. Elevation
[P] Post Office
[H] Hospital
[C] College
■ Principal Business Center
★ Ranally Metro Area (RMA) Abbreviation
z Zip Code(s)
Ⓟ Previous Census Population
Ⓡ Revised Census Population
Ⓐ Annexation Population
● Rand McNally Population Estimate
Ⓒ Final Census Population
Ⓢ Special Census Population
◆ Estimated Population

For additional definitions see Glossary, Volume 1, and Introduction, Volume 2.

Murat Hills; LEON; see Norfleet (RMC Place)
Murdock; RMC Place; CHARLOTTE; ***165** M-8; elev. 10ft./3m.; 🅿; ★ **PUN-**; **z** 33938
Murray Hill; RMC Place; DUVAL; ***164** C-9; ★ **JAX**; mail Jacksonville **z** 32205, **z** 32236, **z** 32254; pop. incl. with Jacksonville (Inc. Place)
Muscogee; RMC Place; ESCAMBIA; ***165** R-2; mail Cantonment **z** 32533; ● 300
Myakka; SARASOTA; see Old Myakka (RMC Place)
Myakka City; RMC Place; MANATEE; **165** L-8; elev. 44ft./13m.; 🅿; **z** 34251; ● 170
Myakka Head; RMC Place; MANATEE; ***165** K-8; elev. 91ft./28m.; mail Myakka City **z** 34251; ● 100
Myrtis; RMC Place; COLUMBIA; ***164** D-7; elev. 129ft./39m.; mail Lake City **z** 32055; rural
Myrtle Grove; CDP; ESCAMBIA; **165** R-2; ★ **PENS**; mail Pensacola **z** 32506, **z** 32516; Ⓟ 17,402; Ⓒ 17,211

N

Nalcrest; RMC Place; POLK; **164** J-10; elev. 63ft./19m.; 🅿; **z** 33856; ● 500
Naples; Inc. Place; ⊡ COLLIER; **165** O-9; elev. 9ft./3m.; 🅿 🅷 🅲 2,227 ■; ★ **NAP**; **z** 34101-10, **z** 34112-14, **z** 34116-17, **z** 34119-20; Ⓟ 19,505; Ⓒ 20,976; ◆ 18,960
Naples Manor; CDP; COLLIER; **165** P-9; ★ **NAP**; mail Naples **z** 34113; Ⓟ 4,571; Ⓒ 5,186
Naples Park; CDP; COLLIER; **165** O-9; ★ **NAP**; mail Naples **z** 34108; Ⓟ 8,002; Ⓒ 6,741
Naranja; CDP; MIAMI-DADE; **165** Q-13; 🅿; ★ **MIA-**; **z** 33032, **z** 33092 & mail Homestead **z** 33033; Ⓟ 5,790; Ⓒ 4,034
Narcoossee; RMC Place; OSCEOLA; **164** I-10; elev. 80ft./24m.; ★ **ORL**; mail Saint Cloud **z** 34771; ● 200
Nash; RMC Place; JEFFERSON; ***164** B-3; elev. 216ft./66m.; mail Lamont **z** 32336; rural
Nashua; RMC Place; PUTNAM; ***164** E-9; elev. 90ft./27m.; mail Satsuma **z** 32189; ● 100
NASSAU; **164** B-9; Ⓟ 43,941; Ⓒ 57,663; ◆ 71,828
Nassau Village; RMC Place; NASSAU; 3 mi. SE of Callahan; ★ **JAX**; mail Callahan **z** 32011; ● 2,200
Nassau Village-Ratliff; CDP-Census Area Only; NASSAU; ***164** B-9; ★ **JAX**; mail Callahan **z** 32011; Ⓟ 4,047; Ⓒ 4,667
Nassauville; RMC Place; NASSAU; **164** B-9; mail Fernandina Beach **z** 32034; ● 1,900
National Gardens; RMC Place; VOLUSIA; **164** F-11; ★ **D.BCH**; mail Ormond Beach **z** 32174; ● 400
Navair; RMC Place; COLUMBIA; ***164** C-7; mail Lake City **z** 32055; ● 150
Navarre; RMC Place; SANTA ROSA; **165** S-3; 🅿; ★ **PENS**; **z** 32566; ● 900
Navy Point; RMC Place; ESCAMBIA; ***165** S-2; ★ **PENS**; mail Pensacola **z** 32507
Neals; RMC Place; GILCHRIST; ***164** D-6; mail Trenton **z** 32693; ● 230
Neptune Beach; Inc. Place; DUVAL; **164** C-10; elev. 10ft./3m.; 🅿; ★ **JAX**; **z** 32266; Ⓟ 6,816; Ⓒ 7,270
Neptune Shores; RMC Place; OSCEOLA; mail Kissimmee **z** 34744; ● 90
Nevins; RMC Place; INDIAN RIVER; ***165** K-13; mail Vero Beach **z** 32962; ● 150
New Berlin; RMC Place; DUVAL; ***164** C-9; ★ **JAX**; mail Jacksonville **z** 32226; pop. incl. with Jacksonville (Inc. Place)
Newberry; Inc. Place; ALACHUA; **164** E-7; elev. 77ft./23m.; 🅿; **z** 32669; Ⓟ 1,644; Ⓒ 3,316
Newburn; RMC Place; SUWANNEE; ***164** C-5; mail Live Oak **z** 32060
New Eden; RMC Place; OSCEOLA; ***164** I-11; ★ **ORL**; mail Saint Cloud **z** 34771; ● 450
New Harmony; RMC Place; WALTON; ***165** Q-5; elev. 261ft./80m.; mail Defuniak Springs **z** 32433; rural
New Hope; RMC Place; HOLMES; ***165** Q-6; mail Westville **z** 32464; ● 50
New Hope; RMC Place; WASHINGTON; **165** R-6; mail Vernon **z** 32462; ● 110
Newnans Lake Homesites; RMC Place; ALACHUA; ***164** E-8; ★ **GAIN**; mail Gainesville **z** 32601; ● 430
New Point Comfort; RMC Place; CHARLOTTE; ***165** M-7; mail Englewood **z** 34223-24; ● 400
Newport; RMC Place; MONROE; ***165** S-13; elev. 12ft./4m.; mail Key Largo **z** 33037
Newport; RMC Place; WAKULLA; **164** C-2; mail Crawfordville **z** 32327
New Port Richey; Inc. Place; PASCO; **164** I-6; elev. 11ft./3m.; 🅿 🅷 ■; ★ **ST.PET**; **z** 34652-56; Ⓟ 14,044; Ⓒ 16,117; ◆ 18,696
New Port Richey East; CDP-Census Area Only; PASCO; ***164** I-6; ★ **ST.PET**; mail New Port Richey **z** 34653; Ⓟ 9,683; Ⓒ 9,916
New River; RMC Place; BROWARD; ***165** P-14; ★ **MIA-**; mail Fort Lauderdale **z** 33301-02; pop. incl. with Fort Lauderdale (Inc. Place)
New Smyrna Beach; Inc. Place; VOLUSIA; **164** G-11; elev. 8ft./2m.; 🅿 🅷; ★ **D.BCH**; **z** 32168-70; Ⓟ 16,543; Ⓒ 20,048; ◆ 22,792
Newton; RMC Place; LEVY; ***164** E-6; mail Chiefland **z** 32626; rural
Niceville; Inc. Place; OKALOOSA; **165** R-4; elev. 51ft./16m.; 🅿 🅷 🅲 8,938; ★ **FTWL**; **z** 32578, **z** 32588; Ⓟ 10,507; Ⓒ 11,684
Nichols; RMC Place; POLK; **164** J-8; elev. 116ft./35m.; 🅿; ★ **LKLD**; **z** 33863; ● 130
Nixon; RMC Place; BAY; ***165** S-6; mail Youngstown **z** 32466; ● 270
Nobles; RMC Place; ESCAMBIA; ***165** R-3; ★ **PENS**; mail Pensacola **z** 32504, **z** 32514; pop. incl. with Pensacola (Inc. Place)
Nobleton; CDP; HERNANDO; **164** H-8; elev. 50ft./15m.; 🅿; **z** 34661; Ⓒ 160
Nocatee; RMC Place; DESOTO; **165** L-9; elev. 40ft./12m.; 🅿; **z** 34268 & mail Ponte Vedra **z** 32081; ● 1,600
Nokomis; CDP; SARASOTA; **165** M-7; elev. 11ft./3m.; 🅿; ★ **VEN**; **z** 34274-75; Ⓟ 3,448; Ⓒ 3,334
Noma; Inc. Place; HOLMES; **165** Q-6; elev. 181ft./55m.; 🅿; **z** 32452; Ⓟ 207; Ⓒ 213
Norfleet (Murat Hills); RMC Place; LEON; ***164** B-2; ★ **TALL**; mail Tallahassee **z** 32304
Norland; CDP; MIAMI-DADE; **163** K-8; ★ **MIA-**; mail Miami **z** 33169, **z** 33179; Ⓟ 22,109; Ⓒ 22,995; ◆ 24,024
Norman; RMC Place; HERNANDO; ***164** H-7; mail Brooksville **z** 34613; ● 425
Normandy; RMC Place; DUVAL; ***164** C-9; ★ **JAX**; mail Jacksonville **z** 32205; pop. incl. with Jacksonville (Inc. Place)
Normandy (Normandy Isle); RMC Place; MIAMI-DADE; ***165** P-14; ★ **MIA-**; mail Miami Beach **z** 33141; pop. incl. with Miami Beach (Inc. Place)
Normandy Isle; MIAMI-DADE; see Normandy (RMC Place)
Normandy Manor; RMC Place; DUVAL; ***164** C-9; ★ **JAX**; mail Jacksonville **z** 32221; pop. incl. with Jacksonville (Inc. Place)
Normandy Village; RMC Place; DUVAL; ***164** C-9; ★ **JAX**; mail Jacksonville **z** 32221; pop. incl. with Jacksonville (Inc. Place)
North Andrews Gardens; CDP-Census Area Only; BROWARD; ***165** O-14; ★ **MIA-**; mail Fort Lauderdale **z** 33309, **z** 33334; Ⓟ 9,002; Ⓒ 9,656
North Babcock; RMC Place; BREVARD; ***164** J-12; ★ **MELB-**; mail Melbourne **z** 32901; pop. incl. with Melbourne (Inc. Place)
North Bay Village; Inc. Place; MIAMI-DADE; **163** L-9; elev. 6ft./2m.; 🅿; ★ **MIA-**; **z** 33141; Ⓟ 5,383; Ⓒ 6,733
North Beach; CDP-Census Area Only; INDIAN RIVER; ***164** J-13; Ⓒ 243
North Biscayne; RMC Place; MIAMI-DADE; ***165** P-13; ★ **MIA-**; mail Miami **z** 33161; pop. incl. with North Miami (Inc. Place)
North Brooksville; CDP-Census Area Only; HERNANDO; ***164** H-7; ★ **SPR.H**; mail Brooksville **z** 34601; Ⓟ 1,459; Ⓒ 1,461
Northcrest; RMC Place; ORANGE; ***164** H-10; ★ **ORL**; mail Apopka **z** 32703; ● 100
North De Land; CDP-Census Area Only; VOLUSIA; ***164** G-10; ★ **DL**; mail DeLand **z** 32720; Ⓟ 1,493; Ⓒ 1,327
North Fort Myers; CDP; LEE; **165** N-9; 🅿; ★ **FTMY-**; **z** 33903, **z** 33917-18; Ⓟ 30,027; Ⓒ 40,214; ◆ 57,277
North Jacksonville; RMC Place; DUVAL; ★ **JAX**; mail Jacksonville **z** 32218, **z** 32226; pop. incl. with Jacksonville (Inc. Place)
North Key Largo; CDP-Census Area Only; MONROE; ***165** R-13; mail Key Largo **z** 33037; Ⓟ 1,490; Ⓒ 1,049
North La Belle; RMC Place; HENDRY; ● 1,000
North Lauderdale; Inc. Place; BROWARD; **163** G-8; elev. 10ft./3m.; 🅿; ★ **MIA-**; **z** 33068 & mail Fort Lauderdale **z** 33309, **z** 33319; Ⓟ 26,506; Ⓒ 32,264; ◆ 40,932
North Meadowbrook Terrace; RMC Place; CLAY; ***164** C-9; ★ **JAX**; mail Orange Park **z** 32073; ● 2,100
North Miami; Inc. Place; MIAMI-DADE; **163** K-9; elev. 10ft./3m.; 🅿 🅷 🅲 725 ■; ★ **MIA-**; **z** 33161, **z** 33167-68, **z** 33181, **z** 33261 & mail Miami **z** 33162, **z** 33169, **z** 33179; Ⓟ 49,998; Ⓒ 59,880; ◆ 60,259
North Miami Beach; Inc. Place; MIAMI-DADE; **165** P-13; elev. 10ft./3m.; 🅿 🅷 ■; ★ **MIA-**; **z** 33160, **z** 33162, **z** 33169, **z** 33179, **z** 33181 & mail Miami **z** 33161, **z** 33180, **z** 33261, **z** 33280; Ⓟ 35,359; Ⓒ 40,786; ◆ 40,670
North Naples; RMC Place; COLLIER; **165** O-9; ★ **NAP**; mail Naples **z** 34108, **z** 34110; Ⓟ 13,422
North Oak Hill; RMC Place; DUVAL; ***164** C-9; ★ **JAX**; mail Jacksonville **z** 32210; pop. incl. with Jacksonville (Inc. Place)
North Palm Beach; Inc. Place; PALM BEACH; **165** M-14; elev. 25ft./8m.; 🅿; ★ **MIA-**; **z** 33403, **z** 33408, **z** 33410; Ⓟ 11,284; Ⓒ 12,064
North Port; Inc. Place; SARASOTA; **165** M-8; 🅿; ★ **PUN-**; **z** 34286-91; Ⓟ 11,973; Ⓒ 22,797; ◆ 34,048
North Redington Beach; Inc. Place; PINELLAS; **163** D-1; elev. 5ft./2m.; 🅿; ★ **ST.PET**; **z** 33708; Ⓟ 1,135; Ⓒ 1,474
North River Shores; CDP; MARTIN; **165** L-13; ★ **STU**; mail Stuart **z** 34994; Ⓟ 3,250; Ⓒ 3,101
North Sarasota; CDP-Census Area Only; SARASOTA; ***165** L-7; ★ **SAR-B**; mail Sarasota **z** 34234; Ⓟ 6,702; Ⓒ 6,738
North Shore; RMC Place; DUVAL; ***164** C-9; ★ **JAX**; mail Jacksonville **z** 32208; pop. incl. with Jacksonville (Inc. Place)
North Shore Junction; RMC Place; DUVAL; ★ **JAX**; pop. incl. with Jacksonville (Inc. Place)
North Side; RMC Place; BAY; ***165** S-6; ★ **PNCY**; mail Panama City **z** 32406; pop. incl. with Panama City (Inc. Place)
North Weeki Wachee; CDP-Census Area Only; HERNANDO; ***164** H-7; Ⓒ 4,253
Northwest Saint Johns; RMC Place; ST. JOHNS; ★ **JAX**; mail Jacksonville **z** 32260, Saint Johns **z** 32259
Northwood; RMC Place; PALM BEACH; ***165** N-14; ★ **MIA-**; mail West Palm Beach **z** 33407; pop. incl. with West Palm Beach (Inc. Place)
Northwood Pines; RMC Place; ALACHUA; ***164** E-7; elev. 183ft./56m.; ★ **GAIN**; mail Gainesville **z** 32605; pop. incl. with Gainesville (Inc. Place)
Norwalk; RMC Place; PUTNAM; ***164** E-9; rural
Norwood; RMC Place; DUVAL; ***164** C-9; ★ **JAX**; mail Jacksonville **z** 32208; pop. incl. with Jacksonville (Inc. Place)
Nubbin Ridge; RMC Place; OKALOOSA; ***165** Q-4; mail Baker **z** 32531; rural
Nutall Rise; RMC Place; TAYLOR; ***164** C-3; mail Lamont **z** 32336; ● 50

O

Oak; RMC Place; MARION; ***164** F-8; elev. 75ft./23m.; ★ **OCA**; mail Ocala **z** 34479; ● 1,050
Oakbrook; RMC Place; MARION; ***164** F-8; ★ **OCA**; mail Ocala **z** 34470; pop. incl. with Ocala (Inc. Place)
Oak Crest; RMC Place; ALACHUA; mail Hawthorne **z** 32640; rural
Oakcrest; RMC Place; MARION; ***164** F-8; ★ **OCA**; mail Ocala **z** 34479
Oakdale; RMC Place; JACKSON; **165** R-7; elev. 88ft./27m.; mail Marianna **z** 32448; ● 50
Oak Grove; RMC Place; ESCAMBIA; ***165** Q-2; mail Mc David **z** 32568; rural
Oak Grove; RMC Place; GADSDEN; ***165** R-8; elev. 286ft./87m.; mail Chattahoochee **z** 32324; rural
Oak Grove; RMC Place; GULF; **165** T-7; mail Port Saint Joe **z** 32456; ● 300
Oak Grove; RMC Place; HARDEE; ***165** K-9; elev. 93ft./28m.; mail Wauchula **z** 33873; rural
Oak Grove; RMC Place; OKALOOSA; ***165** Q-4; mail Baker **z** 32531; rural
Oak Grove; RMC Place; SUMTER; ***164** H-8; mail Webster **z** 33597; ● 200
Oak Harbor; RMC Place; DUVAL; ***164** C-10; ★ **JAX**; mail Atlantic Beach **z** 32233; pop. incl. with Jacksonville (Inc. Place)
Oakhaven; RMC Place; DUVAL; ***164** C-9; ★ **JAX**; mail Jacksonville **z** 32211; pop. incl. with Jacksonville (Inc. Place)
Oak Hill; Inc. Place; VOLUSIA; **164** G-11; elev. 14ft./4m.; 🅿; ★ **D.BCH**; **z** 32759; Ⓟ 917; Ⓒ 1,378
Oak Hill Park; RMC Place; DUVAL; ***164** C-9; ★ **JAX**; mail Jacksonville **z** 32244; pop. incl. with Jacksonville (Inc. Place)
Oakland; Inc. Place; ORANGE; **164** H-9; elev. 124ft./38m.; 🅿; ★ **ORL**; **z** 34740, **z** 34760, **z** 34787; Ⓟ 700; Ⓒ 936
Oakland Park; Inc. Place; BROWARD; **165** O-14; elev. 5ft./2m.; 🅿 ■; ★ **MIA-**; **z** 33304-09, **z** 33311, **z** 33334 & mail Fort Lauderdale **z** 33310; Ⓟ 26,326; Ⓒ 30,966; ◆ 32,154
Oakland Park; RMC Place; LAKE; ***164** G-9; mail Mount Dora **z** 32757; Ⓟ 1,743; ● 2,100
Oak Point; CDP-Census Area Only; BROWARD; ***165** P-13; ★ **MIA-**; Ⓒ 145
Oak Ridge; CDP-Census Area Only; ORANGE; ***164** H-10; ★ **ORL**; mail Orlando **z** 32809, **z** 32839; Ⓟ 15,388; Ⓒ 22,349; ◆ 27,671
Oak Run; RMC Place; MARION; ★ **OCA**; ● 250
Oak Street; RMC Place; OSCEOLA; ***164** I-10; ★ **KISS**; mail Kissimmee **z** 34741, **z** 34746-47; pop. incl. with Kissimmee (Inc. Place)
Oak Terrace; RMC Place; POLK; ***164** J-8; ★ **LKLD**; mail Mulberry **z** 33860; ● 50
Oakwood Villa; RMC Place; DUVAL; ***164** C-9; ★ **JAX**; mail Jacksonville **z** 32211; pop. incl. with Jacksonville (Inc. Place)
O'Brien; RMC Place; SUWANNEE; **164** D-6; elev. 54ft./16m.; 🅿; **z** 32071; ● 120
Ocala; Inc. Place; ⊡ MARION; **164** F-8; elev. 47ft./14m.; 🅿 🅷 🅲 410 ■; ★ **OCA**; **z** 34470-83; Ⓟ 42,045; Ⓒ 45,943; ◆ 53,362
Ocala Estates; RMC Place; MARION; ***164** F-7; mail Ocala **z** 34482; ● 1,700
Ocala Highlands; RMC Place; MARION; ***164** F-8; ★ **OCA**; mail Ocala **z** 34471; pop. incl. with Ocala (Inc. Place)
Ocala Highlands Estates; RMC Place; MARION; ***164** F-8; ★ **OCA**; mail Ocala **z** 34482; ● 600
Ocala Park Ranch; RMC Place; MARION; ***164** F-8; ★ **OCA**; mail Ocala **z** 34482; ● 2,100
Ocala Ridge; RMC Place; MARION; ***164** F-8; ★ **OCA**; mail Ocala **z** 34474; ● 1,250
Ocala Waterway; RMC Place; MARION; ***164** G-8; ★ **OCA**; mail Ocala **z** 34474; ● 200
Ocala West; RMC Place; MARION; ★ **OCA**; mail Ocala **z** 34474-75; pop. incl. with Ocala (Inc. Place)
Ocean Breeze Park; Inc. Place; MARTIN; ***165** L-13; elev. 14ft./4m.; ★ **STU**; mail Jensen Beach **z** 34957; Ⓟ 519; Ⓒ 463
Ocean City; CDP; OKALOOSA; ***165** S-4; ★ **FTWL**; mail Fort Walton Beach **z** 32547-48; Ⓟ 5,422; Ⓒ 5,594
Ocean Reef Club (Upper Key Largo); RMC Place; MONROE; ***165** R-13; mail Key Largo **z** 33037; ● 900
Ocean Ridge; Inc. Place; PALM BEACH; **165** N-14; elev. 3ft./1m.; 🅿; ★ **MIA-**; **z** 33435; Ⓟ 1,570; Ⓒ 1,636
Ocean View; RMC Place; MIAMI-DADE; ***165** P-14; ★ **MIA-**; mail Miami Beach **z** 33140; pop. incl. with Miami Beach (Inc. Place)
Oceanway; RMC Place; DUVAL; ***164** B-9; ★ **JAX**; mail Jacksonville **z** 32218; pop. incl. with Jacksonville (Inc. Place)
Ocheesee; RMC Place; CALHOUN; ***165** R-8; elev. 125ft./38m.; mail Grand Ridge **z** 32442; rural
Ocheesee Gardens; RMC Place; JACKSON; ***165** R-8; mail Grand Ridge **z** 32442; ● 160
Ochopee; RMC Place; COLLIER; **165** P-10; 🅿; **z** 34141; rural
Ocklawaha (Oklawaha); RMC Place; MARION; **164** G-8; 🅿; ★ **OCA**; **z** 32179, **z** 32183; ● 860
Ocoee; Inc. Place; ORANGE; **164** H-9; elev. 127ft./39m.; 🅿 🅷; ★ **ORL**; **z** 34761; Ⓟ 12,778; Ⓒ 24,391; ◆ 33,061
Octahatchee; RMC Place; HAMILTON; ***164** B-5; mail Jennings **z** 32053; ● 130
Odessa; CDP; PASCO; **164** I-7; elev. 58ft./18m.; 🅿; ★ **TAM**; **z** 33556; Ⓒ 3,173
Ojus; CDP; MIAMI-DADE; **165** P-14; 🅿; ★ **MIA-**; **z** 33163 & mail Miami **z** 33179-80; Ⓟ 15,519; Ⓒ 16,642
Okahumpka; CDP; LAKE; **164** H-9; elev. 92ft./28m.; 🅿; **z** 34762; Ⓒ 251
OKALOOSA; **165** R-4; Ⓟ 143,776; Ⓒ 170,498; ◆ 183,634
Okaloosa Island; RMC Place; OKALOOSA; ***165** S-4; 🅿; ★ **FTWL**; **z** 32548; ● 1,100
Okeechobee; Inc. Place; ⊡ OKEECHOBEE; **165** L-12; elev. 29ft./9m.; 🅿 🅷; **z** 34972-74; Ⓟ 4,943; Ⓒ 5,376
OKEECHOBEE; **165** K-11; Ⓟ 29,627; Ⓒ 35,910; ◆ 40,550
Okeelanta; RMC Place; PALM BEACH; ***165** N-12; elev. 23ft./7m.; mail Belle Glade **z** 33430, South Bay **z** 33493; rural
Oklawaha; MARION; see Ocklawaha (RMC Place)
Old Bay View; RMC Place; WALTON; ***165** S-5; mail Freeport **z** 32439; ● 350
Old Fernandina; RMC Place; NASSAU; ***164** B-10; mail Fernandina Beach **z** 32034; pop. incl. with Fernandina Beach (Inc. Place)
Old Marco Junction; RMC Place; COLLIER; ***165** P-9; elev. 4ft./1m.; mail Naples **z** 34113-14; ● 400
Old Myakka (Myakka); RMC Place; SARASOTA; ***165** L-8; elev. 52ft./16m.; mail Sarasota **z** 34240; ● 200
Oldsmar; Inc. Place; PINELLAS; **164** J-7; elev. 8ft./2m.; 🅿; ★ **ST.PET**; **z** 34677; Ⓟ 8,361; Ⓒ 11,910
Old Town; RMC Place; DIXIE; **164** E-6; elev. 23ft./7m.; 🅿; **z** 32680; ● 250
Olga; CDP; LEE; ***165** N-9; ★ **FTMY-**; mail Fort Myers **z** 33905; Ⓒ 1,398
Olive; RMC Place; ESCAMBIA; ***165** R-2; ★ **PENS**
Olustee; RMC Place; BAKER; **164** C-7; 🅿; **z** 32072; ● 300
Olympia Heights; CDP; MIAMI-DADE; ***165** Q-13; elev. 10ft./3m.; 🅿; ★ **MIA-**; **z** 33165, **z** 33175, **z** 33185, **z** 33265 & mail Miami **z** 33155, **z** 33174, **z** 33184; Ⓟ 37,792; Ⓒ 13,452
Ona; RMC Place; HARDEE; **165** K-9; elev. 90ft./27m.; 🅿; **z** 33865
Oneco; RMC Place; MANATEE; **165** L-7; elev. 35ft./11m.; 🅿; ★ **SAR-B**; **z** 34264 & mail Bradenton **z** 34203; ● 3,200
O'Neil; RMC Place; NASSAU; **164** B-9; elev. 14ft./4m.; mail Fernandina Beach **z** 32034; ● 455
Opa-locka; Inc. Place; MIAMI-DADE; **165** P-13; elev. 10ft./3m.; 🅿; ★ **MIA-**; **z** 33054-56 & mail Hialeah **z** 33014; Ⓟ 15,283; Ⓒ 14,951
Opa-Locka North; CDP-Census Area Only; MIAMI-DADE; ***165** P-13; ★ **MIA-**; mail Hialeah **z** 33014, Opa Locka **z** 33054; Ⓟ 6,568; Ⓒ 6,224
Open Air; RMC Place; PINELLAS; ***165** K-7; ★ **ST.PET**; mail Saint Petersburg **z** 33701, **z** 33731-32; pop. incl. with Saint Petersburg (Inc. Place)
Orange; RMC Place; LIBERTY; **165** S-7; mail Bristol **z** 32321; ● 60
ORANGE; **164** I-11; Ⓟ 677,491; Ⓒ 896,344; ◆ 1,109,559
Orange Avenue; RMC Place; ST. LUCIE; ★ **FTPI**; mail Fort Pierce **z** 34954; pop. incl. with Fort Pierce (Inc. Place)
Orange Bend; RMC Place; LAKE; ***164** G-9; mail Leesburg **z** 34788; rural
Orange Blossom; RMC Place; ORANGE; ***164** H-10; ★ **ORL**; mail Orlando **z** 32805, **z** 32855; pop. incl. with Orlando (Inc. Place)
Orange Blossom Hills; RMC Place; MARION; ***164** G-8; ★ **OCA**; mail Summerfield **z** 34491
Orange Blossom Hills South; RMC Place; LAKE; ***164** G-8; pop. incl. with Lady Lake (Inc. Place)
Orange City; Inc. Place; VOLUSIA; **164** G-10; elev. 35ft./11m.; 🅿; ★ **ORL**; **z** 32763, **z** 32774; Ⓟ 5,347; Ⓒ 6,604
Orange City Hills; RMC Place; VOLUSIA; ***164** G-10; ★ **ORL**; mail Orange City **z** 32763; ● 1,600
Orangedale; RMC Place; POLK; ***164** I-9; elev. 139ft./42m.; ★ **LKLD**; mail Lakeland **z** 33809
Orangedale; RMC Place; ST. JOHNS; **164** D-9; elev. 20ft./6m.; ★ **JAX**; mail Saint Augustine **z** 32092; ● 400
Orange Grove Villas; RMC Place; PASCO; ***164** I-8; mail Zephyrhills **z** 33541; ● 340
Orange Harbor; RMC Place; LEE; ***165** N-9; ★ **FTMY-**; mail Fort Myers **z** 33905
Orange Heights; RMC Place; ALACHUA; **164** E-8; mail Hawthorne **z** 32640; ● 130
Orange Hill Corners; RMC Place; WASHINGTON; ***165** R-6; mail Chipley **z** 32428; ● 130
Orange Home; RMC Place; SUMTER; ***164** G-8; mail Wildwood **z** 34785; ● 450
Orange Lake; RMC Place; MARION; **164** F-8; elev. 86ft./26m.; 🅿; ★ **OCA**; **z** 32681; ● 700
Orange Mills; RMC Place; PUTNAM; **164** E-9; elev. 12ft./4m.; mail East Palatka **z** 32131; ● 200
Orange Mountain; RMC Place; LAKE; ***164** H-9; elev. 170ft./52m.; mail Clermont **z** 34711; pop. incl. with Clermont (Inc. Place)
Orange Park; Inc. Place; CLAY; **164** C-9; elev. 24ft./7m.; 🅿 🅷; ★ **JAX**; **z** 32003, **z** 32006, **z** 32065, **z** 32067, **z** 32073; Ⓟ 9,488; Ⓒ 9,081
Orange River Hills; RMC Place; LEE; ***165** N-9; ★ **FTMY-**; mail Fort Myers **z** 33905
Orange Springs; RMC Place; MARION; **164** E-8; 🅿; **z** 32182
Orangetree; CDP-Census Area Only; COLLIER; ***165** O-10; Ⓒ 950
Orchid; Inc. Place; INDIAN RIVER; ***164** J-13; 🅿; ★ **VERO**; **z** 32963 & mail Vero Beach **z** 32960; Ⓟ 10; Ⓒ 140
Orienta Gardens; RMC Place; SEMINOLE; ***164** H-10; mail Altamonte Springs **z** 32701; ● 2,300
Orient Park; RMC Place; HILLSBOROUGH; ***164** J-7; ★ **TAM**; mail Tampa **z** 33619; ● 2,300
Oriole Beach; RMC Place; SANTA ROSA; **165** S-3; ★ **PENS**; mail Gulf Breeze **z** 32561; ● 600
Orlando; Inc. Place; ⊡ ORANGE; **164** H-10; elev. 106ft./32m.; 🅿 🅷 🅲 56,010 ■; ★ **ORL**; **z** 32801-12, **z** 32814-22, **z** 32824-37, **z** 32839, **z** 32853-62, **z** 32867-69, **z** 32872, **z** 32877-78, **z** 32885-87, **z** 32891, **z** 32896-97, **z** 32899; Ⓟ 164,693; Ⓒ 185,951; ◆ 218,293
Orlovista; CDP; ORANGE; **164** H-10; 🅿; ★ **ORL**; **z** 32811 & mail Orlando **z** 32835, **z** 32861; Ⓟ 5,990; Ⓒ 6,047
Ormond Beach; Inc. Place; VOLUSIA; **164** F-11; elev. 22ft./7m.; 🅿 🅷; ★ **D.BCH**; **z** 32173-76; Ⓟ 29,721; Ⓒ 36,301; ◆ 37,654
Ormond-By-The-Sea; CDP; VOLUSIA; **164** F-11; ★ **D.BCH**; mail Ormond Beach **z** 32174; Ⓟ 8,157; Ⓒ 8,430
Ortega; RMC Place; DUVAL; ***164** C-9; ★ **JAX**; mail Jacksonville **z** 32210; pop. incl. with Jacksonville (Inc. Place)
Ortega Farms; RMC Place; DUVAL; ***164** C-9; elev. 15ft./5m.; ★ **JAX**; mail Jacksonville **z** 32210; pop. incl. with Jacksonville (Inc. Place)
Ortega Forest; RMC Place; DUVAL; ***164** C-9; ★ **JAX**; mail Jacksonville **z** 32210; pop. incl. with Jacksonville (Inc. Place)
Ortega Hills; RMC Place; DUVAL; ***164** C-9; ★ **JAX**; mail Jacksonville **z** 32244; pop. incl. with Jacksonville (Inc. Place)
Ortega Terrace; RMC Place; DUVAL; ***164** C-9; elev. 10ft./3m.; ★ **JAX**; mail Jacksonville **z** 32210; pop. incl. with Jacksonville (Inc. Place)
Ortona; RMC Place; GLADES; ***165** M-10; elev. 25ft./8m.; mail Moore Haven **z** 33471; rural
Ortona; RMC Place; VOLUSIA; ***164** F-11; pop. incl. with Daytona Beach (Inc. Place)
Osceola; RMC Place; SEMINOLE; ***164** G-11; rural
OSCEOLA; **164** I-11; Ⓟ 107,728; Ⓒ 172,493; ◆ 278,889
Osceola Heights; RMC Place; LEON; ***164** B-2; ★ **TALL**; mail Tallahassee **z** 32301; pop. incl. with Tallahassee (Inc. Place)
Oslo; RMC Place; INDIAN RIVER; ***165** K-13; mail Vero Beach **z** 32962; ● 400
Osowaw Junction; RMC Place; OKEECHOBEE; ***165** K-11; rural
Osprey; CDP; SARASOTA; **165** L-7; elev. 17ft./5m.; 🅿; ★ **SAR-B**; **z** 34229; Ⓟ 2,597; Ⓒ 4,143
Osteen; RMC Place; VOLUSIA; **164** G-11; elev. 50ft./15m.; 🅿; **z** 32764; ● 550
Otis; RMC Place; DUVAL; ***164** C-9; ★ **JAX**; pop. incl. with Jacksonville (Inc. Place)
Otter Creek; Inc. Place; LEVY; **164** F-6; elev. 29ft./9m.; 🅿; **z** 32683; Ⓟ 136; Ⓒ 121
Overstreet; RMC Place; GULF; **165** T-7; 🅿; **z** 32456; ● 70
Oviedo; Inc. Place; SEMINOLE; **164** H-10; elev. 48ft./15m.; 🅿 🅲 605; ★ **ORL**; **z** 32762, **z** 32765-66; Ⓟ 11,114; Ⓒ 26,316; ◆ 34,817
Oxford; RMC Place; SUMTER; **164** G-8; elev. 114ft./35m.; 🅿; **z** 34484; ● 360
Ozello; RMC Place; CITRUS; ***164** G-7; mail Crystal River **z** 34429; ● 300
Ozona; RMC Place; PINELLAS; **164** J-6; elev. 8ft./2m.; 🅿; ★ **ST.PET**; **z** 34660; ● 1,900

P

Pace; CDP; SANTA ROSA; **165** R-3; 🅿; ★ **PENS**; **z** 32571; Ⓟ 6,277; Ⓒ 7,393
Packwood Place; RMC Place; VOLUSIA; ***164** G-11; mail Edgewater **z** 32141, New Smyrna Beach **z** 32169; ● 1,500
Padlock; RMC Place; SUWANNEE; ***164** C-6; mail Live Oak **z** 32060; ● 365
Page Field; RMC Place; LEE; ★ **FTMY-**; mail Fort Myers **z** 33906-07, **z** 33994; pop. incl. with Fort Myers (Inc. Place)
Page Park; CDP; LEE; ***165** N-9; ★ **FTMY-**; mail Fort Myers **z** 33907; Ⓒ 524
Pahokee; Inc. Place; PALM BEACH; **165** M-12; 🅿 🅷; **z** 33476; Ⓟ 6,822; Ⓒ 5,985
Painters Hill; RMC Place; FLAGLER; **164** E-11; elev. 10ft./3m.; mail Flagler Beach **z** 32136; ● 50
Paisley; CDP; LAKE; **164** G-9; 🅿; **z** 32767; Ⓒ 734
Palatka; Inc. Place; ⊡ PUTNAM; **164** E-9; elev. 22ft./7m.; 🅿 🅷 ■; **z** 32177-78; Ⓟ 10,201; Ⓒ 10,033; ◆ 10,170
Palma Ceia; RMC Place; HILLSBOROUGH; ***164** J-7; 🅿; ★ **TAM**; **z** 33629, **z** 33690 & mail Tampa **z** 33609; pop. incl. with Tampa (Inc. Place)
Palm Aire; CDP-Census Area Only; BROWARD; ***165** O-13; ★ **MIA-**; Ⓒ 1,539
Palma Sola; RMC Place; MANATEE; **163** F-2; 🅿; ★ **SAR-B**; **z** 34209, **z** 34280; ● 3,100
Palma Sola Park; RMC Place; MANATEE; ***165** K-7; ★ **SAR-B**; mail Bradenton **z** 34209
Palm Bay; Inc. Place; BREVARD; **164** J-12; elev. 20ft./6m.; 🅿; ★ **MELB-**; **z** 32905-11; Ⓟ 62,632; Ⓒ 79,413; ◆ 97,481
Palm Bay West; RMC Place; BREVARD; ★ **MELB-**; mail Palm Bay **z** 32907-11; pop. incl. with Palm Bay (Inc. Place)
Palm Beach; Inc. Place; PALM BEACH; **165** N-14; elev. 15ft./5m.; 🅿 ■; ★ **MIA-**; **z** 33480; Ⓟ 9,814; Ⓒ 10,468; Ⓡ 9,676; ◆ 10,336
PALM BEACH; **165** N-12; Ⓟ 863,518; Ⓒ 1,131,184; Ⓡ 1,131,191; ◆ 1,249,392
Palm Beach Gardens; Inc. Place; PALM BEACH; **165** M-14; elev. 14ft./4m.; 🅿 🅷; ★ **MIA-**; **z** 33403, **z** 33408, **z** 33410, **z** 33412, **z** 33418, **z** 33420; Ⓟ 22,990; Ⓒ 35,058; ◆ 39,571
Palm Beach Shores; Inc. Place; PALM BEACH; **165** M-14; 🅿; ★ **MIA-**; **z** 33404; Ⓟ 1,040; Ⓒ 1,269
Palm City; CDP; MARTIN; **165** L-13; 🅿; ★ **STU**; **z** 34990-91; Ⓟ 3,925; Ⓒ 20,097; ◆ 21,972
Palm Coast; Inc. Place; FLAGLER; **164** E-10; elev. 20ft./6m.; 🅿; **z** 32135, **z** 32137, **z** 32142-43, **z** 32164; Ⓟ 14,287; Ⓒ 32,732; ◆ 67,535
Palmdale; RMC Place; GLADES; **165** M-10; elev. 42ft./13m.; 🅿; **z** 33944; ● 100
Palmetto; Inc. Place; MANATEE; **165** K-7; 🅿; ★ **SAR-B**; **z** 34220-21; Ⓟ 9,268; Ⓒ 12,571
Palmetto Bay; Inc. Place; MIAMI-DADE; ***165** Q-13; elev. 10ft./3m.; 🅿; ★ **MIA-**; **z** 33157-58, **z** 33176; incorporated September 11, 2002; not reported in 2000 Census; ◆ 22,440
Palmetto Estates; CDP-Census Area Only; MIAMI-DADE; ***165** Q-13; ★ **MIA-**; mail Miami **z** 33157; Ⓟ 12,293; Ⓒ 13,675
Palmetto Lakes; RMC Place; MIAMI-DADE; ★ **MIA-**; mail Hialeah **z** 33014; pop. incl. with Hialeah (Inc. Place)
Palm Grove Colony; RMC Place; HERNANDO; ***164** H-7; ★ **SPR.H**; mail Spring Hill **z** 34607; ● 300
Palm Harbor; CDP; PINELLAS; **164** J-6; 🅿; ★ **ST.PET**; **z** 34682-85; Ⓟ 50,256; Ⓒ 59,248; ◆ 58,013
Palmona Park; CDP; LEE; ***165** N-9; ★ **FTMY-**; Ⓒ 1,353
Palm River; RMC Place; COLLIER; ***165** O-9; ★ **NAP**; mail Naples **z** 34110; Ⓟ 9,960; ● 2,400
Palm River; RMC Place; HILLSBOROUGH; ***164** J-7; ★ **TAM**; mail Tampa **z** 33619; ● 5,000
Palm River-Clair Mel; CDP-Census Area Only; HILLSBOROUGH; ***164** J-7; ★ **TAM**; mail Tampa **z** 33619; Ⓟ 13,691; Ⓒ 17,589
Palm Shadows; RMC Place; SEMINOLE; ***164** G-11; ● 100
Palm Shores; Inc. Place; BREVARD; **164** I-12; 🅿; ★ **MELB-**; **z** 32940 & mail Melbourne **z** 32935; Ⓟ 210; Ⓒ 794
Palm Springs; Inc. Place; PALM BEACH; **163** B-10; elev. 18ft./5m.; 🅿; ★ **MIA-**; **z** 33406, **z** 33461; Ⓟ 9,763; Ⓒ 11,699
Palm Springs Estates; RMC Place; MIAMI-DADE; ***165** P-13; ★ **MIA-**; pop. incl. with Hialeah (Inc. Place)
Palm Springs North; CDP; MIAMI-DADE; **163** K-7; ★ **MIA-**; mail Hialeah **z** 33015; Ⓟ 5,300; Ⓒ 5,460
Palms West; RMC Place; PALM BEACH; ★ **MIA-**; mail West Palm Beach **z** 33421; pop. incl. with Royal Palm Beach (Inc. Place)
Palm Valley; CDP; ST. JOHNS; **164** C-10; ★ **JAX**; mail Ponte Vedra Beach **z** 32082; Ⓟ 9,960; Ⓒ 19,860
Palm View; RMC Place; MANATEE; ***165** K-7; ★ **SAR-B**; mail Palmetto **z** 34221; ● 400
Palm Village; RMC Place; MIAMI-DADE; ***165** P-13; ★ **MIA-**; mail Hialeah **z** 33012; pop. incl. with Hialeah (Inc. Place)
Panacea; RMC Place; WAKULLA; **164** D-2; elev. 2ft./1m.; 🅿; **z** 32346; ● 900
Panacea Park; RMC Place; WAKULLA; ***164** D-2; mail Panacea **z** 32346
Panacoochee Retreats; RMC Place; SUMTER; ***164** G-8; elev. 46ft./14m.; mail Lake Panasoffkee **z** 33538
Panama City; Inc. Place; ⊡ BAY; **165** S-6; 🅿 🅷 ■; ★ **PNCY**; **z** 32401-09, **z** 32411-13, **z** 32417, **z** 32461; Ⓟ 34,378; Ⓒ 36,417; ◆ 36,977
Panama City Beach; Inc. Place; BAY; **165** S-6; 🅿; ★ **PNCY**; **z** 32401, **z** 32407-08, **z** 32413, **z** 32417 & mail Panama City **z** 32411; Ⓟ 4,051; Ⓒ 7,671
Panama Park; RMC Place; DUVAL; ***164** C-9; ★ **JAX**; mail Jacksonville **z** 32208; pop. incl. with Jacksonville (Inc. Place)
Paola; RMC Place; SEMINOLE; ***164** G-10; ★ **ORL**; mail Sanford **z** 32771; ● 300
Paradise Bay; RMC Place; MANATEE; ***165** L-7; ★ **SAR-B**; mail Bradenton **z** 34210; ● 1,000
Paradise Beach; RMC Place; ESCAMBIA; ***165** S-2; ★ **PENS**; mail Pensacola **z** 32506; ● 500
Paradise Heights; CDP-Census Area Only; ORANGE; **165** M-2; ★ **ORL**; mail Apopka **z** 32703; Ⓒ 1,310
Paradise Island; RMC Place; PINELLAS; ***165** K-6; ★ **ST.PET**; mail Saint Petersburg **z** 33706; pop. incl. with Treasure Island (Inc. Place)
Paradise Palms; RMC Place; PALM BEACH; ***165** O-14; elev. 13ft./4m.; ★ **MIA-**; mail Boca Raton **z** 33486; pop. incl. with Boca Raton (Inc. Place)
Paradise Park; RMC Place; ST. LUCIE; ***165** K-13; ★ **FTPI**; mail Fort Pierce **z** 34946; ● 1,200
Paradise Point; RMC Place; CITRUS; ***164** G-7; mail Crystal River **z** 34429; pop. incl. with Crystal River (Inc. Place)
Park Avenue Station; RMC Place; LEON; ***164** B-2; ★ **TALL**; mail Tallahassee **z** 32302; pop. incl. with Tallahassee (Inc. Place)
Parker; Inc. Place; BAY; **165** S-6; elev. 23ft./7m.; ★ **PNCY**; mail Panama City **z** 32404; Ⓟ 4,598; Ⓒ 4,623
Parkland; Inc. Place; BROWARD; **163** F-8; 🅿; ★ **MIA-**; **z** 33067, **z** 33073, **z** 33076; Ⓟ 3,558; Ⓒ 13,835; ◆ 16,320
Parkside; RMC Place; LEON; ***164** B-2; ★ **TALL**; mail Tallahassee **z** 32303; pop. incl. with Tallahassee (Inc. Place)
Parmalee; RMC Place; MANATEE; ***165** L-8; elev. 68ft./21m.; mail Myakka City **z** 34251; rural
Parramore; RMC Place; JACKSON; ***165** Q-8; elev. 94ft./29m.; mail Bascom **z** 32423; rural
Parrish; RMC Place; MANATEE; **165** K-7; elev. 44ft./13m.; 🅿; **z** 34219; ● 460
Pasadena; RMC Place; PINELLAS; ***165** K-6; ★ **ST.PET**; mail Saint Petersburg **z** 33707; pop. incl. with Saint Petersburg (Inc. Place)
Pasadena Shores; RMC Place; PASCO; ***164** I-8; mail Dade City **z** 33525; ● 230
Pasco; RMC Place; PASCO; ***164** I-7; mail Land O Lakes **z** 34639, San Antonio **z** 33576; ● 400
PASCO; **164** I-7; Ⓟ 281,131; Ⓒ 344,765; Ⓡ 344,768; ◆ 487,021
Pass A Grill Beach (Pass-a-Grille, Pass-a-Grille Beach); RMC Place; PINELLAS; ***165** K-6; ★ **ST.PET**; mail Saint Petersburg **z** 33706, **z** 33741; pop. incl. with Saint Pete Beach (Inc. Place)
Pass-a-Grille; PINELLAS; see Pass A Grill Beach (RMC Place)
Pass-a-Grille Beach; PINELLAS; see Pass A Grill Beach (RMC Place)
Patersonville; RMC Place; PUTNAM; ***164** E-9; mail East Palatka **z** 32131; rural
Paxton; Inc. Place; WALTON; **165** Q-5; elev. 327ft./100m.; 🅿; **z** 32538; Ⓟ 600; Ⓒ 656
Peaceful Acres; RMC Place; LEVY; mail Dunnellon **z** 34431; ● 200
Peace River Shores; RMC Place; CHARLOTTE; ***165** M-8; ★ **PUN-**; mail Punta Gorda **z** 33982; ● 770
Peach Orchard; RMC Place; ALACHUA; ***164** E-7; elev. 84ft./26m.; mail Archer **z** 32618; ● 130
Pebble Creek; CDP-Census Area Only; HILLSBOROUGH; ***164** I-7; ★ **TAM**; Ⓒ 4,824
Pecan Park; RMC Place; DUVAL; ***164** B-9; ★ **JAX**; mail Jacksonville **z** 32218; pop. incl. with Jacksonville (Inc. Place)
Pedro; RMC Place; MARION; ***164** G-8; elev. 80ft./24m.; ★ **OCA**; mail Summerfield **z** 34491; ● 360
Pelican Bay; CDP-Census Area Only; COLLIER; ***165** O-9; ★ **NAP**; mail Naples **z** 34108; Ⓒ 5,686
Pelican Lake; RMC Place; PALM BEACH; ***165** M-12; mail Canal Point **z** 33438; ● 100
Pembroke; BROWARD; see Pembroke Park (Inc. Place)
Pembroke; RMC Place; POLK; ***164** J-9; pop. incl. with Fort Meade (Inc. Place)
Pembroke Park (Pembroke); Inc. Place; BROWARD; **163** J-9; elev. 10ft./3m.; 🅿; ★ **MIA-**; **z** 33021, **z** 33023 & mail Hallandale **z** 33009; Ⓟ 4,933; Ⓒ 6,299; Ⓡ 5,384
Pembroke Pines; Inc. Place; BROWARD; **163** J-7; 🅿 🅷; ★ **MIA-**; **z** 33023-29, **z** 33082, **z** 33084 & mail Fort Lauderdale **z** 33330-32, Hollywood **z** 33019-20, **z** 33022, **z** 33081, **z** 33083; Ⓟ 65,452; Ⓒ 137,427; ◆ 156,975
Peniel; RMC Place; PUTNAM; ***164** E-9; mail Palatka **z** 32177; ● 800
Peninsula; RMC Place; HILLSBOROUGH; ***164** J-7; ★ **TAM**; mail Tampa **z** 33609, **z** 33679; pop. incl. with Tampa (Inc. Place)
Peninsula; RMC Place; VOLUSIA; ★ **D.BCH**; mail Daytona Beach **z** 32118; pop. incl. with Daytona Beach (Inc. Place)
Penney Farms; Inc. Place; CLAY; **164** D-9; elev. 100ft./30m.; 🅿; ★ **JAX**; **z** 32079; Ⓟ 609; Ⓒ 580
Pennsuco; RMC Place; MIAMI-DADE; **163** K-6; elev. 8ft./2m.; ★ **MIA-**; mail Hialeah **z** 33010
Pensacola; Inc. Place; ⊡ ESCAMBIA; **165** R-2; elev. 11ft./3m.; 🅿 🅷 🅲 9,819 ■; ★ **PENS**; **z** 32501-09, **z** 32511-14, **z** 32516, **z** 32520-24, **z** 32526, **z** 32534, **z** 32559, **z** 32590-92; Ⓟ 58,165; Ⓒ 56,255; ◆ 56,523
Pensacola Beach; RMC Place; ESCAMBIA; **165** S-3; 🅿; ★ **PENS**; **z** 32561; summer pop. 5,000; ● 1,200
Pensacola Heights; RMC Place; ESCAMBIA; ***165** R-3; ★ **PENS**; mail Pensacola **z** 32503; pop. incl. with Pensacola (Inc. Place)
Perdido Bay; RMC Place; ESCAMBIA; ***165** S-2; ★ **PENS**; mail Pensacola **z** 32507; ● 1,050
Perdido Key (Gulf Beach); RMC Place; ESCAMBIA; **162** N-7; ★ **PENS**; mail Pensacola **z** 32507; ● 450
Perrine; RMC Place; MIAMI-DADE; **165** Q-13; 🅿; ★ **MIA-**; **z** 33157, **z** 33257 & mail Miami **z** 33170, **z** 33177, **z** 33187, **z** 33189-90; Ⓟ 15,576; ● 1,370
Perry; Inc. Place; ⊡ TAYLOR; **164** C-4; elev. 42ft./13m.; 🅿 🅷; **z** 32347-48; Ⓟ 7,151; Ⓒ 6,847
Pickettville; RMC Place; DUVAL; ***164** C-9; ★ **JAX**; mail Jacksonville **z** 32254; pop. incl. with Jacksonville (Inc. Place)
Picnic; RMC Place; HILLSBOROUGH; ***165** K-8; elev. 72ft./22m.; mail Lithia **z** 33547
Picolata; RMC Place; ST. JOHNS; ***164** D-9; mail Saint Augustine **z** 32092; rural
Piedmont; RMC Place; LEON; ***164** B-2; ★ **TALL**; mail Tallahassee **z** 32308, **z** 32312; pop. incl. with Tallahassee (Inc. Place)
Piedmont; RMC Place; ORANGE, SEMINOLE; **165** M-3; elev. 132ft./40m.; ★ **ORL**; mail Apopka **z** 32703; ● 450
Pierce; RMC Place; POLK; **164** J-8; ★ **LKLD**; mail Mulberry **z** 33860; ● 115
Pierson; Inc. Place; VOLUSIA; **164** F-10; elev. 78ft./24m.; 🅿; **z** 32180; Ⓟ 2,988; Ⓒ 2,596
Pine Bluff; RMC Place; ST. JOHNS; ***164** C-9; mail Jacksonville **z** 32258, Saint Johns **z** 32259; ● 1,400
Pine Castle; CDP; ORANGE; **165** O-4; 🅿; ★ **ORL**; **z** 32809, **z** 32839 & mail Orlando **z** 32859; Ⓟ 8,276; Ⓒ 8,803
Pinecraft; RMC Place; SARASOTA; ***165** L-7; 🅿; ★ **SAR-B**; **z** 34239, **z** 34278; ● 1,250
Pinecrest; RMC Place; HILLSBOROUGH; ***164** J-7; ★ **TAM**; mail Lithia **z** 33547; ● 150
Pinecrest; Inc. Place; MIAMI-DADE; ***165** Q-13; 🅿; ★ **MIA-**; **z** 33156, **z** 33256 & mail Miami **z** 33158, **z** 33173, **z** 33176; Ⓒ 19,055
Pineda; RMC Place; BREVARD; ***164** I-12; elev. 32ft./10m.; ★ **MELB-**; mail Melbourne **z** 32935; ● 750
Pine Dale; RMC Place; POLK; ***164** J-8; ★ **LKLD**; mail Mulberry **z** 33860; ● 160
Pine Forest; RMC Place; ESCAMBIA; ***165** R-2; ★ **PENS**; mail Pensacola **z** 32506; ● 2,500
Pine Grove; RMC Place; OSCEOLA; ***164** I-11; ★ **ORL**; mail Saint Cloud **z** 34771; ● 500
Pine Hill Estates; RMC Place; ALACHUA; ***164** E-7; ★ **GAIN**; mail Gainesville **z** 32601; ● 400
Pine Hills; RMC Place; LAKE; ***164** G-10; mail Eustis **z** 32736; rural
Pine Hills; CDP; ORANGE; **164** H-10; 🅿; ★ **ORL**; **z** 32808, **z** 32818; Ⓟ 35,322; Ⓒ 41,764; ◆ 51,697
Pine Island; RMC Place; CALHOUN; ***165** S-7; mail Blountstown **z** 32424; ● 330
Pine Island; CDP; HERNANDO; ***164** H-7; mail Spring Hill **z** 34607; Ⓒ 64
Pine Island Center; CDP; LEE; ***165** N-8; elev. 9ft./3m.; ★ **FTMY-**; mail Pineland **z** 33945; Ⓒ 1,721
Pine Island Ridge; CDP-Census Area Only; BROWARD; **163** I-8; ★ **MIA-**; mail Fort Lauderdale **z** 33324; Ⓟ 5,244; Ⓒ 5,199
Pine Lakes; CDP; LAKE; ***164** G-10; mail Eustis **z** 32736; Ⓒ 755
Pineland; CDP; LEE; **165** N-8; elev. 5ft./2m.; 🅿; **z** 33945; Ⓒ 444
Pineland Gardens; RMC Place; DUVAL; ***164** C-9; ★ **JAX**; mail Jacksonville **z** 32216; pop. incl. with Jacksonville (Inc. Place)
Pine Level; RMC Place; DESOTO; ***165** L-8; mail Arcadia **z** 34266; rural
PINELLAS; **165** K-6; Ⓟ 851,659; Ⓒ 921,482; Ⓡ 921,495; ◆ 902,256
Pinellas Park; Inc. Place; PINELLAS; **164** J-6; elev. 15ft./5m.; 🅿 ■; ★ **ST.PET**; **z** 33780-82; Ⓟ 43,426; Ⓒ 45,658; ◆ 43,531
Pine Log; RMC Place; BAY; ***165** S-5; mail Ebro **z** 32437; rural
Pine Manor; CDP; LEE; ***165** N-9; ★ **FTMY-**; mail Fort Myers **z** 33907; Ⓒ 3,785
Pineola; RMC Place; CITRUS; ***164** H-8; mail Floral City **z** 34436
Pine Ridge; CDP-Census Area Only; CITRUS; ***164** G-7; 🅿; **z** 34465; Ⓒ 5,490
Pine Ridge; CDP-Census Area Only; COLLIER; ***165** O-9; ★ **NAP**; mail Naples **z** 34108; Ⓒ 1,965
Pinesville; RMC Place; ALACHUA; ***164** E-7; elev. 83ft./25m.; mail Archer **z** 32618; rural
Pinetta; RMC Place; MADISON; **164** B-5; elev. 148ft./45m.; 🅿; **z** 32350; ● 300
Pineville; RMC Place; ESCAMBIA; ***165** Q-2; mail Mc David **z** 32568; rural
Pinewood; CDP-Census Area Only; MIAMI-DADE; ***165** P-13; ★ **MIA-**; mail Miami **z** 33147, **z** 33150, **z** 33167-68; Ⓟ 15,518; Ⓒ 16,523
Pinewood Park; RMC Place; MIAMI-DADE; **163** K-8; ★ **MIA-**; mail Miami **z** 33147, **z** 33150; ● 3,400
Pinland; RMC Place; TAYLOR; ***164** D-4; mail Perry **z** 32347; rural
Pirate Harbor; RMC Place; CHARLOTTE; **165** N-8; mail Punta Gorda **z** 33955; ● 260
Pirates Cove; RMC Place; MONROE; ***165** T-10; elev. 4ft./1m.; mail Summerland Key **z** 33042; ● 170
Pittman; RMC Place; HOLMES; ***165** Q-6; elev. 102ft./31m.; mail Caryville **z** 32427
Pittman; CDP; LAKE; ***164** G-9; elev. 75ft./23m.; mail Altoona **z** 32702; Ⓒ 192
Placida; RMC Place; CHARLOTTE; **165** M-8; elev. 5ft./2m.; 🅿; ★ **VEN**; **z** 33946-47; ● 220
Placid Lakes; CDP-Census Area Only; HIGHLANDS; **165** L-10; mail Lake Placid **z** 33852; Ⓟ 2,045; Ⓒ 3,054
Plantation; Inc. Place; BROWARD; **163** I-8; elev. 7ft./2m.; 🅿 🅷 ■; ★ **MIA-**; **z** 33311, **z** 33313, **z** 33317-18, **z** 33322-25, **z** 33388 & mail Fort Lauderdale **z** 33312, **z** 33326-27, **z** 33337; Ⓟ 66,692; Ⓒ 82,934; ◆ 79,826
Plantation; RMC Place; MONROE; **165** S-12; mail Islamorada **z** 33036, Tavernier **z** 33070; pop. incl. with Islamorada (Inc. Place); Ⓟ 4,405
Plantation; CDP-Census Area Only; SARASOTA; ***165** M-7; ★ **VEN**; mail Venice **z** 34293; Ⓟ 1,885; Ⓒ 4,168
Plantation Island; CDP; COLLIER; ***165** P-10; Ⓒ 202
Plantation Mobile Home Park; CDP-Census Area Only; PALM BEACH; ***165** N-13; ★ **MIA-**; Ⓒ 1,218
Plant City; Inc. Place; HILLSBOROUGH; **164** J-8; elev. 130ft./40m.; 🅿 🅷; ★ **TAM**; **z** 33563-67; Ⓟ 22,754; Ⓒ 29,915; Ⓡ 29,760; ◆ 34,118
Playland Estates; RMC Place; BROWARD; ***165** P-13; ★ **MIA-**; mail Hollywood **z** 33021; pop. incl. with Hollywood (Inc. Place)
Playland Isles; RMC Place; BROWARD; **163** I-8; ★ **MIA-**; mail Fort Lauderdale **z** 33312; ● 1,000
Pleasant Grove; RMC Place; ESCAMBIA; **162** N-8; elev. 86ft./26m.; ★ **PENS**; mail Pensacola **z** 32507; ● 1,000
Pleasant Grove; RMC Place; HILLSBOROUGH; ***164** J-8; elev. 64ft./20m.; ★ **TAM**; mail Dover **z** 33527, Durant **z** 33530; ● 260
Pleasant Grove; RMC Place; WALTON; ***165** Q-4; mail Laurel Hill **z** 32567; ● 200
Pleasant Ridge; RMC Place; WALTON; ***165** R-5; mail Defuniak Springs **z** 32433; rural
Plummer; RMC Place; DUVAL; ***164** B-9; elev. 23ft./7m.; ★ **JAX**; mail Jacksonville **z** 32219; pop. incl. with Jacksonville (Inc. Place)
Plymouth; RMC Place; ORANGE; **164** H-9; 🅿; ★ **ORL**; **z** 32768; ● 1,250
Poinciana; CDP-Census Area Only; OSCEOLA; ***164** I-10; 🅿; ★ **KISS**; **z** 34758-59; Ⓟ 3,618; Ⓒ 13,647
Poinciana Park; RMC Place; INDIAN RIVER; ***165** K-13; elev. 24ft./7m.; ★ **VERO**; mail Vero Beach **z** 32962; ● 760
Poinciana Place; PALM BEACH; see Poincianna Place (RMC Place)
Poincianna Place (Poinciana Place); RMC Place; PALM BEACH; **164** I-10; elev. 19ft./6m.; ★ **MIA-**; mail Lake Worth **z** 33467; ● 1,100
Poinsettia Park; RMC Place; POLK; ***164** J-9; mail Winter Haven **z** 33881; ● 220
Point Baker; RMC Place; SANTA ROSA; ***165** R-3; ★ **PENS**; mail Milton **z** 32570; ● 350
Point Brittany; RMC Place; PINELLAS; ***165** K-6; ★ **ST.PET**; mail Saint Petersburg **z** 33715; pop. incl. with Saint Petersburg (Inc. Place)
Point O'Rocks; RMC Place; SARASOTA; ***165** L-7; ★ **SAR-B**; mail Sarasota **z** 34242; ● 400
Point Pleasant; RMC Place; MARION; ***164** F-9; mail Fort Mc Coy **z** 32134; ● 210
Point Washington; RMC Place; WALTON; **165** S-5; elev. 17ft./5m.; 🅿; **z** 32459; ● 220
POLK; **164** I-8; Ⓟ 405,382; Ⓒ 483,924; ◆ 600,097
Polk City; Inc. Place; POLK; **164** I-9; elev. 173ft./53m.; 🅿; **z** 33868; Ⓟ 1,439; Ⓒ 1,516
Polly Town; RMC Place; DUVAL; ***164** B-9; ★ **JAX**; mail Jacksonville **z** 32218; pop. incl. with Jacksonville (Inc. Place)
Pomona Park; Inc. Place; PUTNAM; **164** E-9; elev. 52ft./16m.; 🅿; **z** 32181; Ⓟ 663; Ⓒ 789
Pompano Beach; Inc. Place; BROWARD; **165** O-14; 🅿 🅷 🅲 1,510 ■; ★ **MIA-**; **z** 33060-69, **z** 33071-77, **z** 33093, **z** 33097; Ⓟ 72,411; Ⓒ 78,191; ◆ 97,647
Pompano Beach Highlands; CDP; BROWARD; ***165** O-14; ★ **MIA-**; mail Pompano Beach **z** 33064; Ⓟ 17,915; Ⓒ 6,505
Pompano Estates; CDP-Census Area Only; BROWARD; ***165** O-14; ★ **MIA-**; Ⓒ 3,367
Pompano Park; RMC Place; BROWARD; ***165** O-13; ★ **MIA-**; mail Fort Lauderdale **z** 33319
Ponce de Leon; Inc. Place; HOLMES; **165** R-5; elev. 65ft./20m.; 🅿; **z** 32455; Ⓟ 406; Ⓒ 457
Ponce Inlet; Inc. Place; VOLUSIA; **164** F-11; 🅿; ★ **D.BCH**; **z** 32127; Ⓟ 1,704; Ⓒ 2,513
Ponte Vedra; RMC Place; ST. JOHNS; ***164** C-10; 🅿; ★ **JAX**; **z** 32004, **z** 32081-82
Ponte Vedra Beach; RMC Place; ST. JOHNS; **164** C-10; elev. 16ft./5m.; 🅿; ★ **JAX**; **z** 32004, **z** 32081-82; ● 3,000
Poplar Head; RMC Place; WASHINGTON; ***165** R-6; mail Bonifay **z** 32425; rural
Port Boca Grande; RMC Place; LEE; ***165** N-8; mail Boca Grande **z** 33921; ● 160
Port Charlotte; CDP; CHARLOTTE; **165** M-8; 🅿 🅷; ★ **PUN-**; **z** 33948-49, **z** 33952-54, **z** 33980-81, **z** 33983; Ⓟ 41,535; Ⓒ 46,451; ◆ 48,993
Port Denison; RMC Place; BROWARD; pop. incl. with Fort Lauderdale (Inc. Place)
Port Everglades; RMC Place; BROWARD; ***165** P-14; ★ **MIA-**; mail Fort Lauderdale **z** 33316; pop. incl. with Fort Lauderdale (Inc. Place)
Port Everglades Junction; RMC Place; BROWARD; ***165** P-13; ★ **MIA-**
Port La Belle; CDP-Census Area Only; HENDRY; ***165** N-10; mail Labelle **z** 33935; Ⓟ 1,512; Ⓒ 3,050
Portland; RMC Place; WALTON; **165** R-5; mail Freeport **z** 32439; ● 230
Port Malabar; RMC Place; BREVARD; ***164** J-12; ★ **MELB-**; mail Palm Bay **z** 32905; pop. incl. with Palm Bay (Inc. Place)
Port Mayaca; RMC Place; MARTIN; **165** M-12; mail Canal Point **z** 33438; rural
Port Orange; Inc. Place; VOLUSIA; **164** F-11; elev. 10ft./3m.; 🅿 🅲 632; ★ **D.BCH**; **z** 32123, **z** 32127-29 & mail Daytona Beach **z** 32118-19, **z** 32124; Ⓟ 35,317; Ⓒ 45,823; ◆ 50,611
Port Palm Beach; RMC Place; PALM BEACH; ★ **MIA-**; pop. incl. with Riviera Beach (Inc. Place)
Port Palm Beach Junction; RMC Place; PALM BEACH; ★ **MIA-**; pop. incl. with Riviera Beach (Inc. Place)
Port Richey; Inc. Place; PASCO; **164** I-6; elev. 11ft./3m.; 🅿; ★ **ST.PET**; **z** 34667-69, **z** 34673-74; Ⓟ 2,523; Ⓒ 3,021
Port Saint Joe; Inc. Place; ⊡ GULF; **165** T-7; elev. 7ft./2m.; 🅿 🅷; **z** 32456-57 & mail Mexico Beach **z** 32410; Ⓟ 4,044; Ⓒ 3,644
Port Saint John; CDP-Census Area Only; BREVARD; **164** H-12; 🅿; ★ **MELB-**; **z** 32927; Ⓟ 8,933; Ⓒ 12,112
Port Saint Lucie; Inc. Place; ST. LUCIE; **165** L-13; elev. 10ft./3m.; 🅿 🅷; ★ **FTPI**; **z** 34952-53, **z** 34983-88; Ⓟ 55,866; Ⓒ 88,769; ◆ 152,918
Port Saint Lucie-River Park; CDP-Census Area Only; ST. LUCIE; ***165** L-13; ★ **FTPI**; mail Port Saint Lucie **z** 34983; Ⓟ 4,874; Ⓒ 5,175
Port Salerno (Salerno); CDP; MARTIN; **165** L-13; elev. 15ft./5m.; 🅿; ★ **STU**; **z** 34992; Ⓟ 7,786; Ⓒ 10,141
Port Sewall; RMC Place; MARTIN; **165** L-13; ★ **STU**; mail Stuart **z** 34996; pop. incl. with Sewall's Point (Inc. Place)
Port Sutton; RMC Place; HILLSBOROUGH; ***164** J-7; mail Tampa **z** 33619; ● 45
Port Tampa; RMC Place; HILLSBOROUGH; ***164** J-7; ★ **TAM**; mail Tampa **z** 33616, **z** 33686; pop. incl. with Tampa (Inc. Place)
Pottsburg; RMC Place; DUVAL; ***164** C-9; ★ **JAX**; mail Jacksonville **z** 32216, **z** 32245-46; pop. incl. with Jacksonville (Inc. Place)
Powell; RMC Place; HERNANDO; ***164** H-7; elev. 103ft./31m.; mail Spring Hill **z** 34609; ● 300
Power Park; RMC Place; DUVAL; ***164** B-9; ★ **JAX**; pop. incl. with Jacksonville (Inc. Place)
Pretty Bayou; CDP-Census Area Only; BAY; ***165** S-6; ★ **PNCY**; mail Panama City **z** 32401; Ⓟ 3,839; Ⓒ 3,519
Princeton; CDP; MIAMI-DADE; **165** Q-13; elev. 10ft./3m.; 🅿; ★ **MIA-**; **z** 33032, **z** 33092; Ⓟ 7,073; Ⓒ 10,090
Produce; RMC Place; HILLSBOROUGH; ***164** J-7; ★ **TAM**; mail Tampa **z** 33610, **z** 33680; pop. incl. with Tampa (Inc. Place)
Progress Village; CDP; HILLSBOROUGH; **163** C-4; ★ **TAM**; mail Tampa **z** 33619; Ⓒ 2,482
Prospect; RMC Place; BROWARD; ***165** O-13; ★ **MIA-**; mail Fort Lauderdale **z** 33309; pop. incl. with Oakland Park (Inc. Place)
Prospect Road; RMC Place; BROWARD; ★ **MIA-**; mail Fort Lauderdale **z** 33309; pop. incl. with Oakland Park (Inc. Place)
Prosperity; RMC Place; HOLMES; **165** Q-5; elev. 148ft./45m.; mail Westville **z** 32464; ● 50
Providence; RMC Place; POLK; **164** I-8; ★ **LKLD**; mail Lakeland **z** 33809; ● 100
Providence; RMC Place; UNION; **164** D-7; elev. 153ft./47m.; mail Lake Butler **z** 32054; ● 250
Pumpkin Center; RMC Place; LAKE; ***164** H-9; elev. 88ft./27m.; mail Yalaha **z** 34797; rural
Punta Gorda; Inc. Place; ⊡ CHARLOTTE; **165** M-8; elev. 61ft./19m.; 🅿 🅷; ★ **PUN-**; **z** 33950-51, **z** 33955, **z** 33980, **z** 33982-83 & mail El Jobean **z** 33927; Ⓟ 10,747; Ⓒ 14,344; ◆ 15,798
Punta Gorda Beach (Englewood Beach); RMC Place; CHARLOTTE; **165** M-7; elev. 13ft./4m.; ★ **VEN**; ● 400
Punta Gorda Isles; RMC Place; CHARLOTTE; ***165** M-8; ★ **PUN-**; mail Punta Gorda **z** 33950; pop. incl. with Punta Gorda (Inc. Place)
Punta Rassa; CDP; LEE; **165** N-8; ★ **FTMY-**; mail Fort Myers **z** 33908; Ⓟ 1,493; Ⓒ 1,731
PUTNAM; **164** E-9; Ⓟ 65,070; Ⓒ 70,423; ◆ 73,216
Putnam Hall; RMC Place; PUTNAM; **164** E-8; elev. 97ft./30m.; 🅿; **z** 32185; ● 400

Q

Quail Heights; RMC Place; MIAMI-DADE; ***165** K-13; 🅿; ★ **MIA-**; **z** 33170, **z** 33177, **z** 33187, **z** 33189-90, **z** 33197 & mail Miami **z** 33257; rural
Queens Cove; RMC Place; ST. LUCIE; ***165** K-13; ★ **FTPI**; mail Fort Pierce **z** 34947; ● 500
Queens Park; RMC Place; MARTIN; ***165** L-13; mail Stuart **z** 34997; ● 900
Quinavista; RMC Place; ESCAMBIA; ***165** S-2; mail Pensacola **z** 32507; ● 350
Quincy; Inc. Place; ⊡ GADSDEN; **164** B-1; elev. 187ft./57m.; 🅿 🅷; **z** 32351-53; Ⓟ 7,444; Ⓒ 6,982
Quinlan; RMC Place; DUVAL; ★ **JAX**; pop. incl. with Jacksonville (Inc. Place)

R

Raccoon Key; RMC Place; MONROE; ***165** T-9; mail Key West **z** 33040; ● 850
Raiford; Inc. Place; UNION; **164** D-8; 🅿; **z** 32026, **z** 32083; Ⓟ 198; Ⓒ 187
Rainbow Lakes; MARION; see Rainbow Lakes Estates (RMC Place)
Rainbow Lakes; RMC Place; PALM BEACH; **163** C-9; ★ **MIA-**; mail Boynton Beach **z** 33437; Ⓟ 1,496; ● 1,550
Rainbow Lakes Estates (Rainbow Lakes); RMC Place; MARION; ***164** F-7; mail Dunnellon **z** 34431; ● 1,050
Rainbow Springs; RMC Place; MARION; **164** F-7; ● 2,500
Raleigh; RMC Place; LEVY; **164** E-7; elev. 74ft./23m.; mail Williston **z** 32696; ● 150
Ramblewood; RMC Place; SEMINOLE; ***164** G-10; ★ **ORL**; mail Sanford **z** 32773; pop. incl. with Sanford (Inc. Place)
Ramblewood East; CDP-Census Area Only; BROWARD; ***165** O-13; ★ **MIA-**; Ⓒ 1,395
Ramrod Key; RMC Place; MONROE; **165** T-10; 🅿; **z** 33042; ● 700
Ratliff; RMC Place; NASSAU; ***164** B-9; elev. 18ft./5m.; ★ **JAX**; mail Callahan **z** 32011; ● 2,000
Ravenna Park; RMC Place; SEMINOLE; ***164** G-10; ★ **ORL**; mail Sanford **z** 32771; ● 600
Ravenswood Estates; CDP-Census Area Only; BROWARD; ***165** P-13; ★ **MIA-**; Ⓒ 960
Reavills Corner; RMC Place; LAKE; ***164** H-9; elev. 135ft./41m.; mail Clermont **z** 34711; ● 750
Redbay; RMC Place; WALTON; **165** R-5; 🅿; **z** 32455; ● 150
Reddick; Inc. Place; MARION; **164** F-8; elev. 65ft./20m.; 🅿; ★ **OCA**; **z** 32686; Ⓟ 554; Ⓒ 571
Red Head; RMC Place; WASHINGTON; **165** R-6; mail Ebro **z** 32437; ● 100
Redington Beach; Inc. Place; PINELLAS; **163** D-1; elev. 5ft./2m.; 🅿; ★ **ST.PET**; **z** 33708; Ⓟ 1,626; Ⓒ 1,539
Redington Shores; Inc. Place; PINELLAS; **164** J-6; elev. 5ft./2m.; 🅿; ★ **ST.PET**; **z** 33708; Ⓟ 2,366; Ⓒ 2,338
Redland; RMC Place; MIAMI-DADE; ***165** Q-13; 🅿; ★ **MIA-**; **z** 33031-32; ● 210
Red Level; RMC Place; CITRUS; ***164** G-7; elev. 14ft./4m.; mail Crystal River **z** 34428; rural
Regal Park; RMC Place; MARION; ***164** F-8; ★ **OCA**; mail Ocala **z** 34475; ● 300
Regency; RMC Place; DUVAL; ***164** C-9; ★ **JAX**; mail Jacksonville **z** 32211; pop. incl. with Jacksonville (Inc. Place)
Remlap; RMC Place; HILLSBOROUGH; ***164** J-7; mail Gibsonton **z** 33534; ● 650
Rerdell; RMC Place; HERNANDO; ***164** H-8; elev. 76ft./23m.; mail Webster **z** 33597; ● 40
Resota Beach; RMC Place; BAY; ***165** S-6; ★ **PNCY**; mail Panama City **z** 32409; ● 350
Rex; RMC Place; ALACHUA; ***164** E-8; mail Hawthorne **z** 32640; ● 170
Ribault Manor; RMC Place; DUVAL; ***164** C-9; ★ **JAX**; mail Jacksonville **z** 32208; pop. incl. with Jacksonville (Inc. Place)
Rice Creek; RMC Place; PUTNAM; ***164** E-9; elev. 10ft./3m.; mail Palatka **z** 32177; rural
Rich Bay; RMC Place; GADSDEN; ***164** B-2; mail Havana **z** 32333; ● 50
Richey Lakes; RMC Place; PASCO; ★ **ST.PET**; mail New Port Richey **z** 34653
Richland; RMC Place; PASCO; ***164** I-8; 🅿; **z** 33525 & mail Zephyrhills **z** 33540; ● 430
Richloam; RMC Place; HERNANDO; ***164** H-8; mail Webster **z** 33597; rural
Richmond Heights; CDP; MIAMI-DADE; **165** Q-13; ★ **MIA-**; mail Miami **z** 33156, **z** 33158, **z** 33176; Ⓟ 8,583; Ⓒ 8,479
Richmond West; CDP-Census Area Only; MIAMI-DADE; ***165** Q-13; ★ **MIA-**; Ⓒ 28,082; ◆ 29,337
Richter Crossroads; RMC Place; JACKSON; ***165** R-6; elev. 156ft./48m.; mail Graceville **z** 32440; rural
Ridgecrest; CDP-Census Area Only; PINELLAS; ***164** J-6; ★ **ST.PET**; Ⓒ 2,453
Ridge Harbor; RMC Place; CHARLOTTE; ***165** M-8; ★ **PUN-**; mail Punta Gorda **z** 33982; ● 350
Ridge Manor; CDP; HERNANDO; **164** H-8; elev. 69ft./21m.; 🅿; **z** 33523; Ⓟ 1,947; Ⓒ 4,108
Ridgewood; RMC Place; CLAY; ***164** C-9; ★ **JAX**; mail Orange Park **z** 32065; ● 1,100
Ridgewood Estates; RMC Place; SARASOTA; ***165** L-7; ★ **SAR-B**; mail Sarasota **z** 34232
Ridge Wood Heights; CDP-Census Area Only; SARASOTA; ***165** L-7; ★ **SAR-B**; mail Sarasota **z** 34231; Ⓟ 4,851; Ⓒ 5,028
Rio; CDP; MARTIN; ***165** L-13; ★ **STU**; mail Jensen Beach **z** 34957; Ⓟ 1,054; Ⓒ 1,028
Riomar; RMC Place; INDIAN RIVER; ***165** K-13; elev. 5ft./2m.; ★ **VERO**; mail Vero Beach **z** 32963; pop. incl. with Vero Beach (Inc. Place)
Riverdale; RMC Place; HERNANDO; ***164** H-8; mail Dade City **z** 33523; ● 330
Riverdale; RMC Place; ST. JOHNS; ***164** D-9; mail Saint Augustine **z** 32095; ● 260
River Forest; RMC Place; DUVAL; ***164** C-9; ★ **JAX**; mail Jacksonville **z** 32211; pop. incl. with Jacksonville (Inc. Place)
River Isles; RMC Place; MANATEE; ***165** K-7; ★ **SAR-B**; mail Bradenton **z** 34208; pop. incl. with Bradenton (Inc. Place)
Riverland Village; CDP-Census Area Only; BROWARD; ***165** P-13; ★ **MIA-**; Ⓒ 2,108
River Park; RMC Place; ST. LUCIE; ***165** L-13; elev. 15ft./5m.; ★ **FTPI**; mail Port Saint Lucie **z** 34983; ● 2,200
River Ranch; RMC Place; POLK; ***165** K-11; 🅿; **z** 33867; ● 100
Riverside; RMC Place; DUVAL; ***164** C-9; ★ **JAX**; mail Jacksonville **z** 32204; pop. incl. with Jacksonville (Inc. Place)
Riverside; RMC Place; MIAMI-DADE; ***165** Q-13; ★ **MIA-**; mail Miami **z** 33135; pop. incl. with Miami (Inc. Place)
Riverside; RMC Place; VOLUSIA; ***164** G-10; mail DeLand **z** 32720; ● 650
Riverside Acres; RMC Place; ORANGE; ***164** H-10; ● 500
Riverview; RMC Place; DUVAL; ***164** C-9; ★ **JAX**; mail Jacksonville **z** 32208; pop. incl. with Jacksonville (Inc. Place)
Riverview; RMC Place; ESCAMBIA; ***165** R-3; mail Pensacola **z** 32514; ● 600
Riverview; CDP; HILLSBOROUGH; **164** J-7; 🅿; ★ **TAM**; **z** 33568-69, **z** 33578-79; Ⓟ 6,478; Ⓒ 12,035; Ⓡ 12,040

Entries in **UPPERCASE** are counties.
Entries in **bold** have populations of 2,500 or more.
Names in parentheses are alternate names.

Inc. Place	Incorporated Place
RMC Place	Rand McNally Designated Place
CDP	Census Designated Place
MCD	Minor Civil Division

⊡ County Seat
▲ Minor Civil Division
elev. Elevation
🅿 Post Office
🅷 Hospital
🅲 College
■ Principal Business Center
★ Ranally Metro Area (RMA) Abbreviation
z Zip Code(s)
Ⓟ Previous Census Population
Ⓡ Revised Census Population
Ⓐ Annexation Population
● Rand McNally Population Estimate
Ⓒ Final Census Population
Ⓢ Special Census Population
◆ Estimated Population

For additional definitions see Glossary, Volume 1, and Introduction, Volume 2.

Riviera Beach; Inc. Place; PALM BEACH; 165 M-14; elev. 11ft./3m.; 🅿; ★ MIA-; z 33403-04, z 33407, z 33410, z 33418-19; Ⓟ 27,639; © 29,884; ◆ 33,086
Roan; RMC Place; LAKE; *164 H-9; mail Clermont z 34711, Winter Garden z 34787; ● 500
Roberts; ESCAMBIA; see Gonzalez (CDP)
Robin Hill; RMC Place; SEMINOLE; *164 H-10; ★ ORL; mail Altamonte Springs z 32701; ● 760
Robinson Heights; RMC Place; ALACHUA; *164 E-8; mail Micanopy z 32667; ● 250
Rochelle; RMC Place; ALACHUA; *164 E-8; mail Gainesville z 32601
Rock Bluff; RMC Place; LIBERTY; 165 R-8; elev. 282ft./86m.; mail Bristol z 32321; ● 90
Rockdale; RMC Place; MIAMI-DADE; *165 Q-13; elev. 15ft./5m.; ★ MIA-; mail Miami z 33157
Rock Harbor; RMC Place; MONROE; *165 S-13; mail Key Largo z 33037
Rock Hill; RMC Place; WALTON; *165 R-5; mail Defuniak Springs z 32433; rural
Rock Island; CDP-Census Area Only; BROWARD; *165 O-13; ★ MIA-; © 3,076
Rockledge; Inc. Place; BREVARD; 164 I-12; elev. 40ft./12m.; 🅿 🅷; ★ MELB-; z 32955-56; Ⓟ 16,023; © 20,170; ◆ 24,061
Rock Ridge; RMC Place; POLK; *164 I-8; mail Lakeland z 33809; ● 30
Rocksprings; RMC Place; MARION; *164 F-7; mail Dunnellon z 34431; rural
Rock Springs; RMC Place; ORANGE; *164 H-10; ★ ORL; mail Apopka z 32703; ● 560
Rockwell; RMC Place; BREVARD; *164 I-12; ● 300
Rocky Creek; RMC Place; HILLSBOROUGH; 163 B-3; ★ TAM; mail Tampa z 33615; ● 40
Rocky Point; RMC Place; ALACHUA; *164 E-7; mail Gainesville z 32608; rural
Roeville; RMC Place; SANTA ROSA; *165 R-3; mail Milton z 32583; ● 150
Ro-Len Lake Gardens; RMC Place; BROWARD; *165 P-13; ★ MIA-; mail Hallandale z 33009; pop. incl. with Hallandale Beach (Inc. Place)
Rolling Acres; RMC Place; HERNANDO; *164 H-7; mail Brooksville z 34602; ● 300
Rolling Hills; RMC Place; DUVAL; *164 C-9; ★ JAX; mail Jacksonville z 32221; pop. incl. with Jacksonville (Inc. Place)
Rolling Hills; RMC Place; MARION; *164 F-7; ★ OCA; mail Ocala z 34474; ● 80
Rolling Hills; RMC Place; POLK; *164 J-8; ★ LKLD; mail Mulberry z 33860; ● 90
Rolling Oaks; CDP-Census Area Only; BROWARD; *165 P-13; ★ MIA-; © 1,291
Rolling Ranches; RMC Place; MARION; *164 G-7; ★ OCA; mail Dunnellon z 34431; ● 400
Romeo; RMC Place; MARION; *164 F-7; mail Dunnellon z 34432; rural
Roosevelt Gardens; CDP-Census Area Only; BROWARD; *165 O-13; ★ MIA-; © 1,923
Rosedale; RMC Place; GADSDEN; 165 R-8; mail Chattahoochee z 32324; ● 100
Roseland; CDP; INDIAN RIVER; 164 J-12; elev. 21ft./6m.; 🅿; z 32957; Ⓟ 1,379; © 1,775
Rosemont; RMC Place; ORANGE; *164 H-10; pop. incl. with Orlando (Inc. Place)
Rosewood; RMC Place; LEVY; *164 F-6; mail Cedar Key z 32625; rural
Rotonda; CDP; CHARLOTTE; 165 M-8; elev. 6ft./2m.; ★ VEN; mail Englewood z 34224, Placida z 33946; Ⓟ 3,576; © 6,574
Rotonda West; CHARLOTTE; see Rotunda-West (RMC Place)
Rotunda-West (Rotonda West); RMC Place; CHARLOTTE; *165 M-8; ★ VEN; mail Placida z 33946, Rotonda West z 33947
Round Lake; RMC Place; JACKSON; 165 R-7; elev. 254ft./77m.; mail Alford z 32420; ● 50
Royal; RMC Place; SUMTER; *164 G-8; mail Wildwood z 34785; ● 370
Royal Gardens Estates; RMC Place; MANATEE; *165 L-7; ★ SAR-B; mail Bradenton z 34209; ● 900
Royal Palm Beach; Inc. Place; PALM BEACH; 165 N-13; elev. 20ft./6m.; 🅿; ★ MIA-; z 33411-12, z 33414, z 33421; Ⓟ 14,589; © 21,523; ◆ 25,108
Royal Palm Estates; CDP-Census Area Only; PALM BEACH; *165 N-14; ★ MIA-; © 3,583
Royal Palm Ranches; CDP-Census Area Only; BROWARD; *165 P-13; ★ MIA-; © 294
Royal Pal Village; RMC Place; LEE; *165 N-9; ★ FTMY-; mail Fort Myers z 33908; ● 700
Royal Poinciana Park; RMC Place; INDIAN RIVER; *165 K-13; ● 800
Royals Crossroads; RMC Place; HOLMES; *165 Q-5; elev. 181ft./55m.; mail Westville z 32464; rural
Royal Terrace; RMC Place; DUVAL; *164 C-9; ★ JAX; mail Jacksonville z 32209; pop. incl. with Jacksonville (Inc. Place)
Rubonia; RMC Place; MANATEE; *165 K-7; 🅿; ★ SAR-B; z 34221; ● 500
Runyon; RMC Place; PALM BEACH; *165 N-12; elev. 12ft./4m.; mail Belle Glade z 33430; ● 160
Ruskin; CDP; HILLSBOROUGH; 165 K-7; elev. 11ft./3m.; 🅿; z 33570-73, z 33575; Ⓟ 6,046; © 8,321
Russell; RMC Place; CLAY; 164 D-9; ★ JAX; mail Green Cove Springs z 32043; ● 500
Rutland; RMC Place; SUMTER; *164 G-8; mail Lake Panasoffkee z 33538
Rye; RMC Place; MANATEE; *165 K-7; elev. 25ft./8m.; mail Bradenton z 34202, Parrish z 34219; ● 40

S

Sabal Palm Estates; BROWARD; see Sabal Palms Estates (RMC Place)
Sabal Palms Estates (Sabal Palm Estates); RMC Place; BROWARD; *165 O-13; ★ MIA-; mail Fort Lauderdale z 33319, Pompano Beach z 33068
Safety Harbor; Inc. Place; PINELLAS; 163 B-2; elev. 14ft./4m.; 🅿 🅷; ★ ST.PET; z 34695; Ⓟ 15,124; © 17,203
Saint Andrews; RMC Place; BAY; *165 S-6; ★ PNCY; mail Panama City z 32401; pop. incl. with Panama City (Inc. Place)
Saint Armands; RMC Place; SARASOTA; *165 L-7; ★ SAR-B; mail Sarasota z 34236; pop. incl. with Sarasota (Inc. Place)
Saint Augustine; Inc. Place; ⊡ ST. JOHNS; 164 D-10; elev. 6ft./2m.; 🅿 🅷 🅲 3,292 ■; z 32080, z 32084-86, z 32092, z 32095; Ⓟ 11,692; © 11,592; ◆ 11,131
Saint Augustine Beach; Inc. Place; ST. JOHNS; 164 D-10; mail Saint Augustine z 32080, z 32084; Ⓟ 3,657; © 4,683
Saint Augustine Shores; CDP; ST. JOHNS; 164 D-10; mail Saint Augustine z 32086; Ⓟ 4,411; © 4,922
Saint Augustine South; CDP-Census Area Only; ST. JOHNS; *164 D-10; mail Saint Augustine z 32086; Ⓟ 4,218; © 5,035
Saint Catherine; RMC Place; SUMTER; 164 H-8; elev. 70ft./21m.; mail Bushnell z 33513; ● 225
Saint Cloud; Inc. Place; OSCEOLA; 164 I-10; elev. 63ft./19m.; 🅿 🅷; ★ KISS; z 34769-73; Ⓟ 12,453; © 20,074; ◆ 31,424
Saint George; CDP-Census Area Only; BROWARD; *165 O-13; ★ MIA-; © 2,450
Saint George; RMC Place; PINELLAS; *164 J-6; ★ ST.PET; mail Palm Harbor z 34684; ● 3,700
Saint George Island; RMC Place; FRANKLIN; *165 T-8; 🅿; z 32328; ● 450
Saint James; RMC Place; FRANKLIN; *164 D-1; elev. 10ft./3m.; mail Sopchoppy z 32358; ● 150
Saint James City; CDP; LEE; 165 N-8; elev. 5ft./2m.; 🅿; ★ FTMY-; z 33956; Ⓟ 1,904; © 4,105
Saint Joe Beach; RMC Place; GULF; *165 T-7; elev. 20ft./6m.; mail Port Saint Joe z 32456; ● 850
ST. JOHNS; 164 D-10; Ⓟ 83,829; © 123,135; ◆ 187,577
Saint Johns Park; RMC Place; DUVAL; *164 C-9; ★ JAX; mail Jacksonville z 32210; pop. incl. with Jacksonville (Inc. Place)
Saint Johns Park; RMC Place; FLAGLER; *164 E-10; mail Bunnell z 32110; ● 100
Saint Johns River Estates; RMC Place; SEMINOLE; *164 G-10; elev. 5ft./2m.; ★ ORL; mail Sanford z 32771; ● 150
Saint Joseph; RMC Place; PASCO; *164 I-8; mail Dade City z 33523, z 33525; ● 375
Saint Josephs; RMC Place; SEMINOLE; *164 G-10; elev. 25ft./8m.; ★ ORL; mail Sanford z 32771; ● 200
Saint Leo; Inc. Place; PASCO; 164 I-8; elev. 178ft./54m.; 🅿 🅲 14,179; z 33574; Ⓟ 1,009; © 595; Ⓡ 590
Saint Lucie; Inc. Place; ST. LUCIE; 165 K-13; elev. 2ft./1m.; ★ FTPI; mail Fort Pierce z 34946, Port Saint Lucie z 34953, z 34983, z 34986-88; Ⓟ 584; © 604
ST. LUCIE; 165 L-12; Ⓟ 150,171; © 192,695; ◆ 276,889
Saint Marks; Inc. Place; WAKULLA; 164 C-2; 🅿; z 32355; Ⓟ 307; © 272
Saint Nicholas; RMC Place; DUVAL; *164 C-9; ★ JAX; mail Jacksonville z 32207; pop. incl. with Jacksonville (Inc. Place)
Saint Pete Beach (St. Petersburg Beach); Inc. Place; PINELLAS; 165 K-6; elev. 5ft./2m.; 🅿; ★ ST.PET; z 33706 & mail Saint Petersburg z 33707, z 33736; Ⓟ 9,200; © 9,929
Saint Petersburg; Inc. Place; PINELLAS; 165 K-7; elev. 44ft./13m.; 🅿 🅷 🅲 27,133 ■; ★ ST.PET; z 33701-16, z 33729-34, z 33736-38, z 33740-43, z 33747, z 33784; Ⓟ 238,629; © 248,232; ◆ 242,845
St. Petersburg Beach; PINELLAS; see Saint Pete Beach (Inc. Place)
Saint Teresa; RMC Place; FRANKLIN; 164 D-2; 🅿; z 32358
Salem; RMC Place; TAYLOR; 164 D-4; elev. 41ft./12m.; 🅿; z 32356; ● 100
Salerno; MARTIN; see Port Salerno (CDP)
Salt Springs; RMC Place; MARION; 164 F-9; 🅿; z 32134; ● 600
Salvista; RMC Place; LEE; *165 N-9; ● 800
Samoset; CDP; MANATEE; 165 K-7; ★ SAR-B; mail Bradenton z 34208; Ⓟ 3,119; © 3,440
Sampson (Sampson City); RMC Place; BRADFORD; 164 D-8; mail Starke z 32091; ● 35
Sampson City; BRADFORD; see Sampson (RMC Place)
Samsula; RMC Place; VOLUSIA; 164 G-11; elev. 27ft./8m.; ★ D.BCH; mail New Smyrna Beach z 32168; ● 1,260
Samsula-Spruce Creek; CDP-Census Area Only; VOLUSIA; *164 G-11; ★ D.BCH; mail New Smyrna Beach z 32168; Ⓟ 3,404; © 4,877
San Antonio; Inc. Place; PASCO; 164 I-8; elev. 146ft./45m.; 🅿; z 33576; Ⓟ 776; © 655; Ⓡ 684
San Blas; RMC Place; BAY; *165 T-6; elev. 20ft./6m.; ★ PNCY; mail Port Saint Joe z 32456; ● 200
Sanborn; RMC Place; WAKULLA; rural
San Carlos Park; CDP; LEE; 165 N-9; ★ FTMY-; mail Fort Myers z 33912; Ⓟ 11,785; © 16,317
Sandalfoot Cove; CDP-Census Area Only; PALM BEACH; *165 O-13; ★ MIA-; mail Boca Raton z 33428, z 33433; Ⓟ 14,214; © 16,582
Sandalwood; RMC Place; DUVAL; *164 C-9; ★ JAX; mail Jacksonville z 32246; pop. incl. with Jacksonville (Inc. Place)
Sand Cut; RMC Place; PALM BEACH; *165 M-12; mail Canal Point z 33438; rural
Sanderson; RMC Place; BAKER; 164 C-8; elev. 156ft./48m.; 🅿; z 32087; ● 470
Sandestin; RMC Place; WALTON; *165 S-4; 🅿; z 32550; summer pop. 2,000; ● 300
Sand Lake; RMC Place; ORANGE; *164 H-10; 🅿; ★ ORL; z 32819 & mail Orlando z 32821, z 32836-37, z 32869
Sandy; RMC Place; MANATEE; *165 L-8; elev. 62ft./19m.; mail Myakka City z 34251; rural
Sandy Point; RMC Place; SUWANNEE; *164 D-6; mail Branford z 32008; ● 80
Sanford; Inc. Place; ⊡ SEMINOLE; 164 G-10; elev. 29ft./9m.; 🅿 🅷 ■; ★ ORL; z 32771-73; Ⓟ 32,387; © 38,291; ◆ 45,832
Sanibel; Inc. Place; LEE; 165 O-8; elev. 5ft./2m.; 🅿; z 33957; Ⓟ 5,468; © 6,064
San Jose; RMC Place; DUVAL; *164 C-9; ★ JAX; mail Jacksonville z 32217; pop. incl. with Jacksonville (Inc. Place)
San Marco; RMC Place; DUVAL; *164 C-9; ★ JAX; mail Jacksonville z 32207; pop. incl. with Jacksonville (Inc. Place)
San Mateo; RMC Place; DUVAL; *164 B-9; ★ JAX; mail Jacksonville z 32218; pop. incl. with Jacksonville (Inc. Place)
San Mateo; RMC Place; PUTNAM; 164 E-9; elev. 85ft./26m.; 🅿; z 32187; ● 1,100
San Souci Estates; RMC Place; MIAMI-DADE; *165 P-14; ★ MIA-; mail Miami z 33181; pop. incl. with North Miami (Inc. Place)
San Souci Lakes; RMC Place; LEE; *165 N-9; ★ FTMY-; mail North Fort Myers z 33917; ● 1,500
Sans Souci; RMC Place; CHARLOTTE; *165 M-8; ★ PUN-; mail Punta Gorda z 33982; ● 100
Sans Souci; RMC Place; DUVAL; *164 C-9; ★ JAX; mail Jacksonville z 32216; pop. incl. with Jacksonville (Inc. Place)
Santa Fe; RMC Place; ALACHUA; 164 D-7; elev. 145ft./44m.; 🅿; z 32615; ● 110
Santa Monica; RMC Place; BAY; *165 S-5; ★ PNCY; mail Panama City Beach z 32413; summer pop. 500
Santa Rosa; WALTON; see Santa Rosa Beach (RMC Place)
SANTA ROSA; 165 Q-3; Ⓟ 81,608; © 117,743; ◆ 151,779
Santa Rosa Beach (Santa Rosa); RMC Place; WALTON; 165 S-5; 🅿; z 32459; ● 600
Santos; RMC Place; MARION; *164 F-8; ★ OCA; mail Ocala z 34474; ● 350
Sarabay Acres; RMC Place; SARASOTA; ★ SAR-B; mail Osprey z 34229
Sarasota; Inc. Place; ⊡ SARASOTA; 165 L-7; elev. 27ft./8m.; 🅿 🅷 🅲 3,354 ■; ★ SAR-B; z 34230-43, z 34260, z 34276-78; Ⓟ 50,961; © 52,715; ◆ 51,676
SARASOTA; 165 L-8; Ⓟ 277,776; © 325,957; Ⓡ 325,961; ◆ 376,498
Sarasota Colony; RMC Place; GLADES; *165 M-11; mail Okeechobee z 34974; ● 90
Sarasota Heights; RMC Place; SARASOTA; *165 L-7; ★ SAR-B; mail Sarasota z 34239; pop. incl. with Sarasota (Inc. Place)
Sarasota Springs; CDP-Census Area Only; SARASOTA; 163 H-4; ★ SAR-B; mail Sarasota z 34232; Ⓟ 16,088; © 15,875
Saratoga; RMC Place; PUTNAM; *164 E-9; mail Satsuma z 32189; rural
Satellite Beach; Inc. Place; BREVARD; 164 I-12; elev. 12ft./4m.; 🅿; ★ MELB-; z 32937; Ⓟ 9,889; © 9,577
Satsuma; RMC Place; PUTNAM; 164 E-9; elev. 74ft./23m.; 🅿; z 32189; ● 1,000
Sawdust; RMC Place; GADSDEN; *165 R-8; elev. 247ft./75m.; mail Quincy z 32351; rural
Sawgrass; CDP-Census Area Only; ST. JOHNS; *164 C-10; ★ JAX; mail Ponte Vedra Beach z 32082; Ⓟ 2,999; © 4,942
Saxton; RMC Place; BRADFORD; *164 D-8; mail Lawtey z 32058; ● 180
Scenic Heights; RMC Place; LEON; *164 B-2; ★ TALL; mail Tallahassee z 32303; pop. incl. with Tallahassee (Inc. Place)
Schall Circle; CDP-Census Area Only; PALM BEACH; *165 N-14; ★ MIA-; © 965
Scotland; RMC Place; GADSDEN; *164 B-2; elev. 226ft./69m.; mail Havana z 32333; rural
Scott Lake; CDP-Census Area Only; MIAMI-DADE; *165 P-13; ★ MIA-; mail Miami z 33169, Opa Locka z 33056; Ⓟ 14,588; © 14,401
Scotts Ferry; RMC Place; CALHOUN; *165 S-7; mail Blountstown z 32424
Scottsmoor; RMC Place; BREVARD; 164 G-11; 🅿; ★ TITUS; z 32775; ● 1,340
Seabreeze; RMC Place; VOLUSIA; *164 F-11; mail Daytona Beach z 32118; pop. incl. with Daytona Beach (Inc. Place)
Seaglades; RMC Place; ESCAMBIA; 162 N-7; ★ PENS; mail Pensacola z 32507; ● 900
Seagrove Beach; RMC Place; WALTON; 165 S-5; mail Santa Rosa Beach z 32459; ● 250
Sea Ranch Lakes; Inc. Place; BROWARD; 163 H-10; elev. 6ft./2m.; 🅿; ★ MIA-; z 33308 & mail Pompano Beach z 33062; Ⓟ 619; © 1,392; Ⓡ 734
Seascape; RMC Place; WALTON; *165 S-4; mail Miramar Beach z 32550; summer pop. 1,500; ● 930
Seaside; RMC Place; WALTON; *165 S-5; mail Santa Rosa Beach z 32459
Sebastian; Inc. Place; INDIAN RIVER; 164 J-12; elev. 20ft./6m.; 🅿 🅷; z 32958, z 32976, z 32978; Ⓟ 10,205; © 16,181; ◆ 20,600
Sebastian Highlands; RMC Place; INDIAN RIVER; mail Sebastian z 32958; pop. incl. with Sebastian (Inc. Place)
Sebring; Inc. Place; ⊡ HIGHLANDS; 165 K-10; elev. 131ft./40m.; 🅿 🅷; z 33870-72, z 33875-76; Ⓟ 8,900; © 9,667
Sebring Shores; RMC Place; HIGHLANDS; *165 K-10; mail Sebring z 33870; ● 400
Secotan; RMC Place; TAYLOR; *164 C-4; mail Perry z 32347; ● 175
Seffner; CDP; HILLSBOROUGH; 163 B-5; 🅿; ★ TAM; z 33583-84; Ⓟ 5,371; © 5,467
Selman; RMC Place; CALHOUN; *165 R-7; mail Blountstown z 32424; ● 150
Seminole; RMC Place; OKALOOSA; *165 R-4; ★ FTWL; mail Niceville z 32578; ● 1,200
Seminole; Inc. Place; PINELLAS; 163 C-1; elev. 31ft./9m.; 🅿 🅷; ★ ST.PET; z 33772, z 33775-78 & mail Largo z 33773-74; Ⓟ 9,251; © 10,890
SEMINOLE; 164 H-11; Ⓟ 287,529; © 365,196; Ⓡ 365,199; ◆ 414,064
Seminole Heights; RMC Place; HILLSBOROUGH; *164 J-7; ★ TAM; mail Tampa z 33603, z 33673; pop. incl. with Tampa (Inc. Place)
Seminole Manor; RMC Place; LEON; *164 B-2; ★ TALL; mail Tallahassee z 32310; pop. incl. with Tallahassee (Inc. Place)
Seminole Manor; CDP-Census Area Only; PALM BEACH; 163 C-9; ★ MIA-; mail Lake Worth z 33460; © 2,546
Seminole Park; RMC Place; PINELLAS; *164 J-6; ★ ST.PET; mail Seminole z 33777; ● 8,200
Seminole Shores; RMC Place; MARTIN; *165 L-13; mail Stuart z 34996; ● 800
Seminole Springs; RMC Place; LAKE; *164 G-10; mail Sorrento z 32776; rural
Seven Springs; RMC Place; PASCO; *164 I-7; ★ ST.PET; mail New Port Richey z 34655; ● 2,000
Seville; RMC Place; VOLUSIA; 164 F-10; elev. 55ft./17m.; 🅿; z 32190; ● 530
Sewall's Point; Inc. Place; MARTIN; 165 L-13; elev. 37ft./11m.; 🅿; ★ STU; z 34996; Ⓟ 1,588; © 1,946
Shadeville; RMC Place; WAKULLA; *164 C-2; mail Crawfordville z 32327; ● 200
Shady; RMC Place; MARION; *164 G-8; elev. 102ft./31m.; ★ OCA; mail Ocala z 34474; ● 800
Shady Grove; RMC Place; JACKSON; *165 R-8; mail Grand Ridge z 32442; rural
Shady Grove; RMC Place; TAYLOR; 164 C-4; elev. 86ft./26m.; 🅿; z 32357; ● 100
Shady Hills; CDP-Census Area Only; PASCO; *164 I-7; 🅿; ★ ST.PET; z 34610; © 7,798
Shady Rest; RMC Place; GADSDEN; *164 B-2; mail Havana z 32333; ● 100
Shalimar; Inc. Place; OKALOOSA; 165 S-4; 🅿; ★ FTWL; z 32579; Ⓟ 341; © 718
Shamrock; RMC Place; DIXIE; 164 E-5; mail Cross City z 32628; ● 150
Shannon Forest; RMC Place; LEON; *164 B-2; elev. 150ft./46m.; ★ TALL; mail Tallahassee z 32308; pop. incl. with Tallahassee (Inc. Place)
Shannon Wood; RMC Place; ALACHUA; *164 E-7; elev. 75ft./23m.; ★ GAIN; mail Gainesville z 32607; ● 750
Sharpes; CDP; BREVARD; 164 H-12; 🅿; ★ MELB-; z 32959 & mail Cocoa z 32922; Ⓟ 3,348; © 3,415
Shawnee (Shawnee Farms); RMC Place; GLADES; *165 N-11; mail Clewiston z 33440
Shawnee Farms; GLADES; see Shawnee (RMC Place)
Sheffield; JEFFERSON; see Dills (RMC Place)
Shell Island; RMC Place; WAKULLA; *164 C-2; mail Crawfordville z 32327; pop. incl. with Saint Marks (Inc. Place)
Shell Point; RMC Place; WAKULLA; ● 400
Shenandoah; RMC Place; MIAMI-DADE; *165 Q-13; ★ MIA-; mail Miami z 33245; pop. incl. with Miami (Inc. Place)
Sherman; RMC Place; OKEECHOBEE; *165 L-12; mail Okeechobee z 34974; ● 175
Sherwood Forest; RMC Place; DUVAL; *164 C-9; ★ JAX; mail Jacksonville z 32219; pop. incl. with Jacksonville (Inc. Place)
Sherwood Forest; RMC Place; OSCEOLA; 165 P-2; ★ KISS; ● 700
Sherwood Park; RMC Place; PALM BEACH; *165 O-14; ★ MIA-; mail Delray Beach z 33445; pop. incl. with Delray Beach (Inc. Place)
Shilow; RMC Place; HILLSBOROUGH; *164 J-8; mail Plant City z 33565; pop. incl. with Plant City (Inc. Place)
Shore Acres; RMC Place; PINELLAS; *164 J-7; ★ ST.PET; mail Saint Petersburg z 33705; pop. incl. with Saint Petersburg (Inc. Place)
Siesta Key; CDP; SARASOTA; 163 H-3; 🅿; ★ SAR-B; z 34242; Ⓟ 7,772; © 7,150
Siesta Lago; RMC Place; OSCEOLA; 165 P-3; ★ KISS; ● 1,800
Silver Beach Heights; RMC Place; LAKE; *164 G-9; mail Umatilla z 32784; ● 200
Silver Lake; CDP-Census Area Only; LAKE; *164 G-9; mail Leesburg z 34788; Ⓟ 1,573; © 1,882
Silver Sands; RMC Place; BAY; *165 S-6; ★ PNCY; mail Panama City Beach z 32407
Silver Springs; RMC Place; MARION; 164 F-8; elev. 98ft./30m.; 🅿; ★ OCA; z 34488-89; ● 1,050
Silver Springs; RMC Place; OKALOOSA; *165 R-4; elev. 248ft./76m.; mail Crestview z 32536; rural
Silver Springs Shores; CDP; MARION; 164 F-8; ★ OCA; mail Ocala z 34472; Ⓟ 6,421; © 6,690
Simmons Point; RMC Place; WAKULLA; *164 D-2; elev. 7ft./2m.; mail Panacea z 32346
Singer Island; RMC Place; PALM BEACH; *165 M-14; 🅿; ★ MIA-; z 33404; pop. incl. with Riviera Beach (Inc. Place)
Sink Creek; RMC Place; JACKSON; 165 R-7; mail Marianna z 32448; ● 35
Sirmans; RMC Place; MADISON; *164 C-4; mail Greenville z 32331; rural
Sisco; RMC Place; PUTNAM; *164 E-9; mail Pomona Park z 32181; rural
Sixmile Creek; RMC Place; HILLSBOROUGH; *164 J-7; mail Tampa z 33619; ● 50
Skycrest; RMC Place; PINELLAS; *164 J-6; ★ ST.PET; mail Clearwater z 33755; pop. incl. with Clearwater (Inc. Place)
Sky Lake; CDP; ORANGE; 165 O-3; ★ ORL; mail Orlando z 32809; Ⓟ 6,202; © 5,651
Skyline Hills; RMC Place; LAKE; *164 G-9; mail Lady Lake z 32159; pop. incl. with Lady Lake (Inc. Place)
Slater; RMC Place; LEE; *165 N-9; mail North Fort Myers z 33917; ● 500
Slavia; RMC Place; SEMINOLE; *164 H-10; ★ ORL; mail Oviedo z 32765; ● 1,000
Slones Ridge; RMC Place; LAKE; *164 H-8; mail Groveland z 34736; ● 70
Smith Crossroads; RMC Place; HOLMES; *165 Q-6; mail Bonifay z 32425; rural
Sneads; Inc. Place; JACKSON; 165 R-8; elev. 115ft./35m.; 🅿; z 32460; Ⓟ 1,746; © 1,919
Snell Isle; RMC Place; PINELLAS; *164 J-7; ★ ST.PET; mail Saint Petersburg z 33705; pop. incl. with Saint Petersburg (Inc. Place)
Snow Hill; RMC Place; SEMINOLE; *164 H-11; mail Oviedo z 32765
Snug Harbor; RMC Place; MARTIN; pop. incl. with Stuart (Inc. Place)
Socrum; RMC Place; POLK; *164 I-8; ★ LKLD; mail Lakeland z 33810; rural
Solana; CDP; CHARLOTTE; 165 M-8; ★ PUN-; mail Punta Gorda z 33950; Ⓟ 1,128; © 1,011
Sopchoppy; Inc. Place; WAKULLA; 164 D-2; elev. 28ft./9m.; 🅿; z 32358; Ⓟ 367; © 426
Sorrento; CDP; LAKE; 164 G-9; elev. 68ft./21m.; 🅿; z 32776; © 765
South Apopka; CDP; ORANGE; 165 M-2; ★ ORL; mail Apopka z 32703; Ⓟ 6,360; © 5,800
South Bay; Inc. Place; PALM BEACH; 165 N-12; elev. 21ft./6m.; 🅿; z 33493; Ⓟ 3,558; © 3,859
South Beach; CDP-Census Area Only; INDIAN RIVER; *165 K-13; ★ VERO; mail Vero Beach z 32963; Ⓟ 2,754; © 3,457
South Beach; RMC Place; MIAMI-DADE; *165 Q-12; mail Miami Beach z 33139
Southboro; RMC Place; PALM BEACH; *165 N-14; ★ MIA-; mail West Palm Beach z 33405; pop. incl. with West Palm Beach (Inc. Place)
South Bradenton; CDP-Census Area Only; MANATEE; 163 G-3; ★ SAR-B; mail Bradenton z 34205; Ⓟ 20,398; © 21,587; ◆ 26,023
South Brooksville; CDP-Census Area Only; HERNANDO; *164 H-7; ★ SPR.H; mail Brooksville z 34601; Ⓟ 1,586; © 1,376
Southchase; CDP-Census Area Only; ORANGE; *164 I-10; ★ ORL; © 4,633
South Clermont; RMC Place; LAKE; *164 H-9; mail Clermont z 34711; ● 300
South Clewiston; RMC Place; HENDRY; *165 N-11; elev. 14ft./4m.; mail Clewiston z 33440; rural
South Clinton Heights; RMC Place; PASCO; *164 I-8; mail Dade City z 33525; ● 460
South Cocoa Beach; RMC Place; BREVARD; *164 I-12
South Daytona; Inc. Place; VOLUSIA; 164 F-11; elev. 11ft./3m.; 🅿; ★ D.BCH; z 32119, z 32121; Ⓟ 12,482; © 13,177
Southeast Arcadia; CDP-Census Area Only; DESOTO; *165 L-9; mail Arcadia z 34266; Ⓟ 4,145; © 6,064
Southfort; RMC Place; DESOTO; *165 M-8; mail Arcadia z 34266; ● 250
South Fort Meade; RMC Place; POLK; pop. incl. with Fort Meade (Inc. Place)
Southgate; CDP-Census Area Only; SARASOTA; 163 H-3; ★ SAR-B; mail Sarasota z 34239, z 34277; Ⓟ 7,324; © 7,455
South Gate Ridge; CDP-Census Area Only; SARASOTA; *165 L-7; ★ SAR-B; mail Sarasota z 34231, z 34233; Ⓟ 5,924; © 5,655
South Highpoint; CDP-Census Area Only; PINELLAS; *164 J-6; ★ ST.PET; © 8,839
South Jacksonville; RMC Place; DUVAL; *164 C-9; ★ JAX; mail Jacksonville z 32207, z 32247; pop. incl. with Jacksonville (Inc. Place)
South Masaryktown; RMC Place; PASCO; *164 I-7; mail Spring Hill z 34610; ● 400
South Merritt Estates; RMC Place; BREVARD; ★ MELB-; mail Merritt Island z 32952
South Miami; Inc. Place; MIAMI-DADE; 165 Q-13; elev. 10ft./3m.; 🅿 🅷; ★ MIA-; z 33143, z 33146, z 33243 & mail Miami z 33155-56, z 33173, z 33176, z 33183, z 33256; Ⓟ 10,404; © 10,741
South Miami Heights; CDP; MIAMI-DADE; *165 Q-13; ★ MIA-; mail Miami z 33157, z 33177; Ⓟ 30,030; © 33,522; ◆ 35,014
South Mulberry; RMC Place; POLK; *164 J-8; ★ LKLD; mail Mulberry z 33860; ● 180
South Palm Beach; Inc. Place; PALM BEACH; 163 C-10; elev. 24ft./7m.; 🅿; ★ MIA-; z 33480; Ⓟ 1,480; © 699; Ⓡ 1,531
South Pasadena; Inc. Place; PINELLAS; 163 D-2; 🅿; ★ ST.PET; z 33707; Ⓟ 5,644; © 5,778
South Patrick; RMC Place; BREVARD; *164 I-12; ● 600
South Patrick Shores; CDP-Census Area Only; BREVARD; *164 I-12; ★ MELB-; mail Satellite Beach z 32937; Ⓟ 10,249; © 8,913
South Pine Lakes; RMC Place; LAKE; *164 G-10; mail Eustis z 32736; ● 340
Southpoint; RMC Place; DUVAL; mail Jacksonville z 32256; pop. incl. with Jacksonville (Inc. Place)
South Ponte Vedra Beach; RMC Place; ST. JOHNS; 164 D-10; ★ JAX; mail Ponte Vedra Beach z 32082; ● 200
Southport; RMC Place; BAY; 165 S-6; elev. 16ft./5m.; 🅿; ★ PNCY; z 32409; ● 1,500
South Port; RMC Place; OSCEOLA; *164 I-10; elev. 60ft./18m.; ★ KISS; mail Kissimmee z 34746; rural
South Punta Gorda Heights; RMC Place; CHARLOTTE; 165 M-8; ★ PUN-; mail Punta Gorda z 33955; ● 940
South Sarasota; CDP-Census Area Only; SARASOTA; *165 L-7; ★ SAR-B; mail Sarasota z 34231; Ⓟ 5,298; © 5,314
Southside; RMC Place; BROWARD; *165 P-14; ★ MIA-; mail Fort Lauderdale z 33315-16, z 33335; pop. incl. with Fort Lauderdale (Inc. Place)
Southside; RMC Place; POLK; *164 J-8; ★ LKLD; mail Lakeland z 33807, z 33811, z 33813; pop. incl. with Lakeland (Inc. Place)
Southside Estates; RMC Place; DUVAL; *164 C-9; ★ JAX; mail Jacksonville z 32246; pop. incl. with Jacksonville (Inc. Place)
South Venice; CDP; SARASOTA; 165 M-7; ★ VEN; mail Venice z 34293; Ⓟ 11,951; © 13,539
South Weeki Wachee; RMC Place; HERNANDO; *164 H-7; ★ SPR.H; mail Spring Hill z 34606; ● 1,650
Southwest Ranches; Inc. Place; BROWARD; 163 I-7; elev. 10ft./3m.; 🅿; z 33330-32; incorporated June 6, 2000; not reported in 2000 Census; ● 7,100
Southwood; RMC Place; ORANGE; 165 O-3; elev. 15ft./5m.; ★ ORL; mail Orlando z 32809; ● 1,700
Sparr; RMC Place; MARION; 164 F-8; 🅿; ★ OCA; z 32192; ● 400
Spivey; RMC Place; HILLSBOROUGH; *164 J-7; ● 400
Spring Creek; RMC Place; WAKULLA; 164 C-2; mail Crawfordville z 32327; ● 100
Springfield; Inc. Place; BAY; 165 S-6; elev. 32ft./10m.; ★ PNCY; mail Panama City z 32401; Ⓟ 8,715; © 8,810
Springfield; RMC Place; DUVAL; *164 C-9; ★ JAX; mail Jacksonville z 32206; pop. incl. with Jacksonville (Inc. Place)
Spring Glen; RMC Place; DUVAL; *164 C-9; ★ JAX; mail Jacksonville z 32207; pop. incl. with Jacksonville (Inc. Place)
Springhead; RMC Place; HILLSBOROUGH; *164 J-8; ★ TAM; mail Plant City z 33566; rural
Spring Hill; CDP; HERNANDO; 164 H-7; elev. 209ft./64m.; 🅿 🅷; ★ SPR.H; z 34604, z 34606-11, z 34613; Ⓟ 31,117; © 69,078; ◆ 92,993
Spring Hill; RMC Place; LEON; *164 C-2; mail Tallahassee z 32310; ● 250
Spring Lake; CDP; HERNANDO; 164 H-7; elev. 122ft./37m.; mail Brooksville z 34602; © 327
Spring Lake; RMC Place; HIGHLANDS; 165 L-10; mail Sebring z 33870; ● 1,100
Spring Oaks; RMC Place; SEMINOLE; *164 H-10; ★ ORL; mail Altamonte Springs z 32714; pop. incl. with Altamonte Springs (Inc. Place)
Springside; RMC Place; PUTNAM; *164 E-9; mail Palatka z 32177; rural
Springside Park; RMC Place; PUTNAM; *164 E-9; mail Palatka z 32177; ● 500
Spuds; RMC Place; ST. JOHNS; 164 E-10; mail Elkton z 32033; ● 100
Stacey Street; CDP-Census Area Only; PALM BEACH; *165 N-14; ★ MIA-; © 958
Stanton; RMC Place; MARION; *164 G-8; mail Weirsdale z 32195; ● 220
Starke; Inc. Place; ⊡ BRADFORD; 164 D-8; elev. 160ft./49m.; 🅿 🅷; z 32091; Ⓟ 5,226; © 5,593
Starkes Ferry; RMC Place; MARION; *164 G-9; mail Ocklawaha z 32179; ● 65
Starr; RMC Place; SUWANNEE; *164 C-5; mail Live Oak z 32060; ● 120
State Capitol; RMC Place; LEON; ★ TALL; mail Tallahassee z 32399; pop. incl. with Tallahassee (Inc. Place)
State Line; RMC Place; JACKSON; *165 Q-7; elev. 150ft./46m.; mail Campbellton z 32426; rural
Steele City; RMC Place; JACKSON; *165 R-7; mail Cottondale z 32431; ● 200
Steinhatchee; RMC Place; TAYLOR; 164 E-5; elev. 15ft./5m.; 🅿; z 32359; ● 600
Stetson University; RMC Place; VOLUSIA; *164 G-10; ★ DL; mail DeLand z 32720; pop. incl. with De Land (Inc. Place)
Steward City; RMC Place; DIXIE; *164 E-5; mail Steinhatchee z 32359; ● 110
Stock Island; CDP-Census Area Only; MONROE; 165 T-9; 🅿; z 33040 & mail Key West z 33041; Ⓟ 3,613; © 4,410
Stuart; Inc. Place; ⊡ MARTIN; 165 L-13; elev. 13ft./4m.; 🅿 🅷 ■; ★ STU; z 34994-97; Ⓟ 11,936; © 14,633; ◆ 16,089
Sugarloaf Shores; RMC Place; MONROE; *165 T-10; mail Summerland Key z 33042; ● 700
Sugarmill Woods; CDP-Census Area Only; CITRUS; *164 H-7; mail Homosassa z 34446; Ⓟ 4,073; © 6,409
Sulphur Springs; RMC Place; HILLSBOROUGH; *164 J-7; elev. 27ft./8m.; ★ TAM; mail Tampa z 33604, z 33674; pop. incl. with Tampa (Inc. Place)
Sumatra; RMC Place; LIBERTY; 165 T-8; elev. 28ft./9m.; 🅿; z 32335; ● 130
Summerbrooke; RMC Place; LEON; *164 B-2; ★ TALL; mail Tallahassee z 32312; pop. incl. with Tallahassee (Inc. Place)
Summerfield; RMC Place; MARION; 164 G-8; elev. 90ft./27m.; 🅿; ★ OCA; z 34491-92; ● 320
Summer Haven; RMC Place; ST. JOHNS; 164 E-10; mail Saint Augustine z 32080; ● 200
Summerland Key; RMC Place; MONROE; 165 T-10; 🅿; z 33042-43; ● 950
Summerport Beach; RMC Place; ORANGE; 165 N-2; ★ ORL; mail Windermere z 34786; ● 150
Sumner; RMC Place; LEVY; *164 F-6; mail Cedar Key z 32625
SUMTER; 164 G-8; Ⓟ 31,577; © 53,345; ◆ 79,129
Sumterville; RMC Place; SUMTER; 164 H-8; elev. 76ft./23m.; 🅿; z 33585; ● 260
Sun City; RMC Place; HILLSBOROUGH; 165 K-7; elev. 25ft./8m.; 🅿; z 33586; ● 150
Sun City Center; RMC Place; HILLSBOROUGH; 165 K-7; elev. 50ft./15m.; 🅿 🅷; z 33571, z 33573, z 33575 & mail Ruskin z 33570; Ⓟ 8,326; ● 9,000
Suncoast Estates; CDP-Census Area Only; LEE; *165 N-9; ★ FTMY-; mail North Fort Myers z 33917; Ⓟ 4,483; © 4,867
Sun Haven; RMC Place; SARASOTA; *165 L-7; ★ SAR-B; mail Sarasota z 34231
Suniland; RMC Place; MIAMI-DADE; ★ MIA-; mail Miami z 33156; pop. incl. with Pinecrest (Inc. Place)
Sunland Estates; RMC Place; SEMINOLE; *164 H-10; ★ ORL; mail Sanford z 32771; pop. incl. with Sanford (Inc. Place)
Sunland Gardens; RMC Place; ST. LUCIE; 165 K-13; ★ FTPI; mail Fort Pierce z 34947; ● 1,600
Sunniland; RMC Place; COLLIER; *165 O-10; elev. 20ft./6m.; mail Immokalee z 34142; rural
Sunniland; RMC Place; MIAMI-DADE; ★ MIA-; mail Miami z 33156
Sun 'n' Lakes; RMC Place; HIGHLANDS; *165 K-10; mail Sebring z 33870; ● 1,000
Sunny Hills; RMC Place; WASHINGTON; *165 R-6; 🅿; z 32428; rural
Sunny Isles Beach; Inc. Place; MIAMI-DADE; 163 K-9; 🅿; ★ MIA-; z 33160; Ⓟ 11,772; © 15,315
Sunnyland; RMC Place; SARASOTA; *165 L-7; ★ SAR-B; mail Sarasota z 34233; ● 400
Sunnyside (Sunnyside Beach); RMC Place; BAY; *165 S-5; elev. 20ft./6m.; ★ PNCY; mail Rosemary Beach z 32461; summer pop. 3,000; ● 700
Sunnyside; RMC Place; LAKE; *164 G-9; mail Leesburg z 34748; ● 190
Sunnyside Beach; BAY; see Sunnyside (RMC Place)
Sun Ray Homes; RMC Place; POLK; *165 K-9; mail Frostproof z 33843; ● 100
Sunrise (City of Sunrise); Inc. Place; BROWARD; 163 H-8; elev. 8ft./2m.; 🅿 🅷; ★ MIA-; z 33313, z 33319, z 33322-23, z 33325-26, z 33345, z 33351 & mail Fort Lauderdale z 33304, z 33321, z 33338, z 33355; Ⓟ 64,407; © 85,779; Ⓡ 85,787; ◆ 85,663
Sunrise; RMC Place; SARASOTA; *165 L-7; mail Sarasota z 34241; ● 300
Sunset; CDP-Census Area Only; MIAMI-DADE; *165 Q-13; ★ MIA-; mail Miami z 33173, z 33183, z 33193; Ⓟ 15,810; © 17,150
Sunset Harbor; RMC Place; MARION; *164 G-8; ★ OCA; mail Summerfield z 34491
Sunset Islands; RMC Place; MIAMI-DADE; *165 P-14; ★ MIA-; mail Miami Beach z 33140; pop. incl. with Miami Beach (Inc. Place)
Sunset Point; RMC Place; MONROE; 165 S-13; mail Key Largo z 33037; ● 600
Sunshine Acres; CDP-Census Area Only; BROWARD; *165 P-13; ★ MIA-; © 827
Sunshine Ranches; CDP; BROWARD; *165 P-13; ★ MIA-; © 1,704
Suntree; RMC Place; BREVARD; *164 I-12; ★ MELB-; mail Melbourne z 32934, z 32940-41; ● 700
Sun Valley; RMC Place; PALM BEACH; 163 D-9; ★ MIA-; mail Boynton Beach z 33437; Ⓟ 2,735; ● 1,300
Surf; RMC Place; WAKULLA; *164 D-2; elev. 7ft./2m.; mail Panacea z 32346; ● 140
Surfside; Inc. Place; MIAMI-DADE; 165 P-14; elev. 5ft./2m.; 🅿; ★ MIA-; z 33154; Ⓟ 4,108; © 4,909
Sutherlands Still; RMC Place; PUTNAM; *164 E-9; mail San Mateo z 32187, Satsuma z 32189; ● 1,700
Suwannee; RMC Place; DIXIE; 164 F-5; 🅿; z 32692; ● 450
SUWANNEE; 164 C-5; Ⓟ 26,780; © 34,844; ◆ 40,778
Suwannee Springs; RMC Place; SUWANNEE; *164 C-6; mail Live Oak z 32060
Suwannee Valley; RMC Place; COLUMBIA; *164 C-6; mail Lake City z 32055; ● 200
Svea; RMC Place; OKALOOSA; 165 Q-4; mail Laurel Hill z 32567; ● 75
Sweet Gum Head; RMC Place; HOLMES; *165 Q-5; mail Westville z 32464; rural
Sweetwater; RMC Place; LIBERTY; *165 R-8; mail Bristol z 32321; rural
Sweetwater; Inc. Place; MIAMI-DADE; 165 Q-13; elev. 5ft./2m.; ★ MIA-; mail Miami z 33144, z 33172, z 33174, z 33182, z 33184, z 33194; Ⓟ 13,909; © 14,226
Sweetwater Creek; RMC Place; HILLSBOROUGH; *164 J-7; ★ TAM; mail Tampa z 33615; ● 6,600
Sweetwater Oaks; RMC Place; SEMINOLE; 165 L-3; ★ ORL; mail Longwood z 32750; ● 1,100
Switzerland; RMC Place; ST. JOHNS; 164 C-9; 🅿; ★ JAX; z 32259 & mail Green Cove Springs z 32043; ● 2,900
Sycamore; RMC Place; GADSDEN; *165 R-8; elev. 286ft./87m.; mail Quincy z 32351; rural
Sydney; RMC Place; HILLSBOROUGH; 163 B-6; elev. 90ft./27m.; 🅿; ★ TAM; z 33587; ● 440
Sylvania; RMC Place; WASHINGTON; *165 R-6; mail Vernon z 32462; rural
Sylvan Shores; CDP-Census Area Only; HIGHLANDS; 165 L-10; mail Lake Placid z 33852; Ⓟ 2,155; © 2,424
Sylvan Shores; RMC Place; LAKE; *164 G-12; mail Mount Dora z 32757; ● 40

T

Taft; CDP; ORANGE; 164 I-10; elev. 97ft./30m.; ★ ORL; mail Orlando z 32824; © 1,938
Talisman; RMC Place; HERNANDO; *164 H-8; mail Dade City z 33523; ● 400
Tallahassee; Inc. Place; STATE CAPITAL; ⊡ LEON; 164 B-2; elev. 190ft./58m.; 🅿 🅷 🅲 51,886 ■; ★ TALL; z 32301-18, z 32395, z 32399; Ⓟ 124,773; © 150,624; ◆ 193,699
Tallavast; MANATEE; see Tallevast (RMC Place)
Tallevast (Tallavast); RMC Place; MANATEE; 165 L-7; elev. 30ft./9m.; 🅿; ★ SAR-B; z 34270; ● 200
Talleyrand; RMC Place; DUVAL; *164 C-9; ★ JAX; mail Jacksonville z 32206; pop. incl. with Jacksonville (Inc. Place)
Tamarac; Inc. Place; BROWARD; 165 O-13; elev. 10ft./3m.; 🅿 🅷; ★ MIA-; z 33309, z 33319-21, z 33351, z 33359 & mail Fort Lauderdale z 33323; Ⓟ 44,822; © 55,588; ◆ 57,297
Tamiami; CDP-Census Area Only; MIAMI-DADE; *165 Q-13; ★ MIA-; mail Miami z 33175, z 33182, z 33184; Ⓟ 33,845; © 54,788; ◆ 57,234
Tampa; Inc. Place; ⊡ HILLSBOROUGH; 164 J-7; elev. 57ft./17m.; 🅿 🅷 🅲 54,408 ■; ★ TAM; z 33601-26, z 33629-31, z 33633-35, z 33637, z 33646-47, z 33650, z 33655, z 33660-64, z 33672-75, z 33677, z 33679-82, z 33684-90, z 33694; Ⓟ 280,015; © 303,447; ◆ 336,461
Tampa Reservation; Indian Reservation; HILLSBOROUGH; © 0
Tancrede; RMC Place; POLK; *164 J-8; mail Lakeland z 33811; ● 90
Tangelo Park; CDP; ORANGE; 165 O-3; ★ ORL; mail Orlando z 32819; Ⓟ 2,663; © 2,430
Tangerine; CDP; ORANGE; 164 G-9; elev. 149ft./45m.; 🅿; ★ ORL; z 32777; © 826
Tang-O-Mar Beach; RMC Place; WALTON; *165 S-4; mail Miramar Beach z 32550; ● 125
Tarpon; RMC Place; HILLSBOROUGH; *164 J-7; mail Tampa z 33615, z 33625; ● 180
Tarpon Lake Villages; RMC Place; PINELLAS; *164 I-6; ★ ST.PET; ● 1,200
Tarpon Point; RMC Place; SARASOTA; *165 M-8; mail Venice z 34293; ● 140
Tarpon Springs; Inc. Place; PINELLAS; 164 I-6; elev. 10ft./3m.; 🅿 🅷; ★ ST.PET; z 34688-91; Ⓟ 17,906; © 21,003; ◆ 21,101
Tarrytown; RMC Place; SUMTER; 164 H-8; elev. 88ft./27m.; mail Webster z 33597; ● 200
Tatum Ridge; RMC Place; SARASOTA; *165 L-7; mail Sarasota z 34240; ● 200
Tavares; Inc. Place; ⊡ LAKE; 164 G-9; elev. 77ft./23m.; 🅿; z 32778; Ⓟ 7,383; © 9,700
Tavernier; CDP; MONROE; 165 S-13; elev. 11ft./3m.; 🅿 🅷; z 33070; Ⓟ 2,433; © 2,173
Taylor; RMC Place; BAKER; 164 B-7; mail Sanderson z 32087; ● 200
TAYLOR; 164 D-4; Ⓟ 17,111; © 19,256; ◆ 23,001
Taylor Creek; CDP-Census Area Only; OKEECHOBEE; 165 L-12; mail Okeechobee z 34974; Ⓟ 4,081; © 4,289
Tedder; CDP-Census Area Only; BROWARD; *165 O-14; ★ MIA-; © 2,079
Tee and Green Estates; RMC Place; CHARLOTTE; *165 M-8; ★ PUN-; mail Punta Gorda z 33982; ● 880
Telogia; RMC Place; LIBERTY; 165 S-8; elev. 116ft./35m.; 🅿; z 32360; ● 330
Temple Terrace; Inc. Place; HILLSBOROUGH; 164 J-7; elev. 56ft./17m.; 🅿 🅲 513; ★ TAM; z 33617, z 33637, z 33687; Ⓟ 16,444; © 20,918; ◆ 23,263
Tenille; TAYLOR; see Tennille (RMC Place)
Tennille (Tenille); RMC Place; TAYLOR; *164 D-5; mail Salem z 32356
Tensulate; RMC Place; DUVAL; *164 C-9; ★ JAX; mail Jacksonville z 32209; pop. incl. with Jacksonville (Inc. Place)
Tequesta; Inc. Place; PALM BEACH; 165 M-14; elev. 13ft./4m.; 🅿 🅷; ★ MIA-; z 33469; Ⓟ 4,499; © 5,273
Terra Ceia; RMC Place; MANATEE; 165 K-7; elev. 9ft./3m.; 🅿; ★ SAR-B; z 34250; ● 220
Terra Mar; CDP; BROWARD; *165 O-14; ★ MIA-; © 2,631
Thames; RMC Place; GILCHRIST; *164 E-6; mail Trenton z 32693; ● 180
The Crossings; CDP-Census Area Only; MIAMI-DADE; *165 Q-13; ★ MIA-; © 23,557; ◆ 24,615
The Fountains; RMC Place; PALM BEACH; *165 N-13; elev. 19ft./6m.; ★ MIA-; mail Lake Worth z 33467; ● 1,300
The Hammocks; CDP-Census Area Only; MIAMI-DADE; *165 Q-13; ★ MIA-; © 47,379; ◆ 49,490
The Meadows; CDP-Census Area Only; SARASOTA; 163 G-4; ★ SAR-B; mail Sarasota z 34235; Ⓟ 3,437; © 4,423
Theressa; RMC Place; BRADFORD; 164 D-8; mail Starke z 32091; ● 100
The Villages; CDP; SUMTER; 164 G-8; elev. 75ft./23m.; 🅿; z 32159, z 32162-63 & mail Lady Lake z 32158, Oxford z 34484; © 8,333
Thomas City; RMC Place; JEFFERSON; *164 C-3; elev. 40ft./12m.; mail Monticello z 32344
Thompson; RMC Place; MONROE; *165 S-13; elev. 8ft./2m.; mail Key Largo z 33037; ● 280
Thonotosassa; CDP; HILLSBOROUGH; 164 J-7; elev. 41ft./12m.; 🅿; ★ TAM; z 33592; © 6,091
Three Lakes; CDP-Census Area Only; MIAMI-DADE; *165 Q-13; ★ MIA-; © 6,955
Three Oaks; CDP-Census Area Only; LEE; *165 O-9; ★ FTMY-; © 2,255
Three Rivers; RMC Place; FRANKLIN; *165 T-8; elev. 13ft./4m.; mail Carrabelle z 32322; pop. incl. with Carrabelle (Inc. Place)
Tice; CDP; LEE; 165 N-9; 🅿; ★ FTMY-; z 33905; Ⓟ 3,971; © 4,538
Tierra Verde; CDP; PINELLAS; 163 E-2; 🅿; ★ ST.PET; z 33715; © 3,574
Tiger Point; RMC Place; SANTA ROSA; *165 S-3; ★ PENS; mail Gulf Breeze z 32561, z 32563; ● 1,500
Tildenville; CDP; ORANGE; *164 H-9; ★ ORL; mail Winter Garden z 34787; © 513
Timber Pines; CDP-Census Area Only; HERNANDO; *164 H-7; ★ SPR.H; mail Spring Hill z 34606; Ⓟ 3,182; © 5,840
Tisonia; RMC Place; DUVAL; *164 B-9; ★ JAX; mail Jacksonville z 32218; pop. incl. with Jacksonville (Inc. Place)
Titusville; Inc. Place; ⊡ BREVARD; 164 H-11; elev. 18ft./5m.; 🅿 🅷 ■; ★ TITUS; z 32780-83, z 32796; Ⓟ 39,394; © 40,670; ◆ 41,604
Tocoi; RMC Place; ST. JOHNS; *164 D-9; mail Elkton z 32033; rural
Tolson; RMC Place; POLK; ★ LKLD; pop. incl. with Lakeland (Inc. Place)
Tommytown; RMC Place; PASCO; *164 I-8; mail Dade City z 33523
Tomoka Estates; RMC Place; VOLUSIA; *164 F-11; ★ D.BCH; mail Ormond Beach z 32174; ● 850
Tooke Lake Junction; RMC Place; HERNANDO; *164 H-7; mail Brooksville z 34601; ● 200
Torrey; RMC Place; HARDEE; 165 K-9; mail Bowling Green z 33834; ● 650
Town 'n' Country; CDP-Census Area Only; HILLSBOROUGH; *164 J-7; 🅿; ★ TAM; z 33615 & mail Tampa z 33635; Ⓟ 60,946; © 72,523; ◆ 87,619
Town Park Estates; RMC Place; MIAMI-DADE; *165 Q-13; ★ MIA-; mail Miami z 33165, z 33174; ● 1,860
Trailer Estates; RMC Place; MANATEE; *165 L-7; 🅿; ★ SAR-B; z 34281; ● 1,300
Trailer Haven; RMC Place; BREVARD; *164 J-12; ★ MELB-; mail Melbourne z 32901; pop. incl. with Melbourne (Inc. Place)
Trapnell; RMC Place; HILLSBOROUGH; *164 J-8; elev. 123ft./37m.; ★ TAM; mail Plant City z 33566; ● 600
Treasure Hill Park; RMC Place; ESCAMBIA; *165 S-2; mail Pensacola z 32507; ● 750
Treasure Island; RMC Place; MIAMI-DADE; *165 P-14; ★ MIA-; mail Miami Beach z 33141; pop. incl. with North Bay Village (Inc. Place)
Treasure Island; Inc. Place; PINELLAS; 165 K-6; elev. 5ft./2m.; 🅿; ★ ST.PET; z 33706, z 33740; Ⓟ 7,266; © 7,450
Trenton; Inc. Place; ⊡ GILCHRIST; 164 E-6; elev. 56ft./17m.; 🅿; z 32693; Ⓟ 1,287; © 1,617
Triangle Acres; RMC Place; LAKE; mail Mount Dora z 32757; ● 250
Trilby; RMC Place; PASCO; 164 H-8; elev. 74ft./23m.; 🅿; z 33593; ● 100
Trinity; CDP-Census Area Only; PASCO; *164 I-7; 🅿; ★ ST.PET; z 34655; © 4,279
Tropic; RMC Place; BREVARD; *164 I-12; ★ MELB-; mail Merritt Island z 32952
Tropical Gulf Acres; RMC Place; CHARLOTTE; 165 M-8; ★ PUN-; mail Punta Gorda z 33955; ● 8,200
Tropical Park; RMC Place; MARTIN; *165 L-13; mail Palm City z 34990; ● 875
Tropical Shores Manor; RMC Place; LAKE; mail Tavares z 32778; ● 75
Tropic Palms; RMC Place; PALM BEACH; *165 O-14; ★ MIA-; mail Delray Beach z 33444
Tropic Vista; RMC Place; MARTIN; *165 M-14; ★ MIA-; mail Jupiter z 33469; ● 900
Truckland; RMC Place; LEE; *165 N-8; ★ FTMY-; mail Fort Myers z 33908; ● 500
Tully; RMC Place; WAKULLA; *164 C-2; mail Crawfordville z 32327; ● 500
Turkey Creek; RMC Place; HILLSBOROUGH; *164 J-8; ★ TAM; mail Plant City z 33567; ● 700
Turnbull; RMC Place; BREVARD; *164 H-11; ● 200
Turquoise Beach; RMC Place; WALTON; *165 S-5; mail Santa Rosa Beach z 32459; ● 350
Tuscannoga (Tuscannooga); RMC Place; LAKE; *164 H-8; mail Groveland z 34736; ● 175
Tuscannooga; LAKE; see Tuscannoga (RMC Place)
Tuskawilla; RMC Place; SEMINOLE; *164 H-10; ★ ORL; mail Winter Springs z 32708; pop. incl. with Winter Springs (Inc. Place)
Twin Lakes; CDP; BROWARD; *165 O-13; ★ MIA-; © 1,875
Two Egg; RMC Place; JACKSON; *165 R-7; mail Bascom z 32423
Tyndall AFB; CDP-Census Area Only; BAY; *165 T-6; 🅿; ★ PNCY; z 32403; Ⓟ 4,318; © 2,757

U

Uceta Yard; RMC Place; HILLSBOROUGH; *164 J-7; ★ TAM; pop. incl. with Tampa (Inc. Place)
Uleta; RMC Place; MIAMI-DADE; 163 K-9; elev. 10ft./3m.; 🅿; ★ MIA-; z 33162, z 33164; ● 2,300
Ulmerton; RMC Place; PINELLAS; *164 J-6; mail Largo z 33771, z 33773; ● 1,000
Umatilla; Inc. Place; LAKE; 164 G-9; elev. 98ft./30m.; 🅿; z 32784; Ⓟ 2,350; © 2,214
UNION; 164 D-7; Ⓟ 10,252; © 13,442; ◆ 15,827
Union Park; CDP; ORANGE; 164 H-10; elev. 73ft./22m.; 🅿; ★ ORL; z 32817 & mail Orlando z 32822, z 32867, z 32872; Ⓟ 6,890; © 10,191
University; CDP-Census Area Only; HILLSBOROUGH; *164 J-7; ★ TAM; © 30,736; Ⓡ 30,618; ◆ 37,128
University of Tampa; RMC Place; HILLSBOROUGH; *164 J-7; 🅿; ★ TAM; z 33606; pop. incl. with Tampa (Inc. Place)
University Park; RMC Place; DUVAL; *164 C-9; ★ JAX; mail Jacksonville z 32277; pop. incl. with Jacksonville (Inc. Place)
University Park; CDP-Census Area Only; MIAMI-DADE; *165 Q-13; ★ MIA-; © 26,538; ◆ 27,725
University Park; RMC Place; ORANGE; 165 N-5; ★ ORL; mail Orlando z 32817; ● 600
Upper Grand Lagoon; CDP-Census Area Only; BAY; *165 S-6; ★ PNCY; mail Panama City z 32411, Panama City Beach z 32407; Ⓟ 7,855; © 10,889
Upper Key Largo; MONROE; see Ocean Reef Club (RMC Place)
Usina Beach; RMC Place; ST. JOHNS; *164 D-10; mail Ponte Vedra Beach z 32082, Saint Augustine z 32095; ● 700
Utopia; CDP-Census Area Only; BROWARD; *165 P-13; ★ MIA-; © 714

V

Valdez; RMC Place; VOLUSIA; *164 G-10; elev. 19ft./6m.; ★ ORL; mail Debary z 32713; pop. incl. with DeBary (Inc. Place)
Valkaria; BREVARD; see Grant-Valkaria (Inc. Place)
Valparaiso; Inc. Place; OKALOOSA; 165 R-4; elev. 97ft./30m.; 🅿; ★ FTWL; z 32580; Ⓟ 4,672; © 6,408
Valrico; CDP; HILLSBOROUGH; *164 J-8; 🅿; ★ TAM; z 33594-96; © 6,582; Ⓡ 6,556
Vamo; CDP; SARASOTA; *165 L-7; ★ SAR-B; mail Sarasota z 34231; Ⓟ 3,325; © 5,285
Vanderbilt Beach; RMC Place; COLLIER; *165 O-9; elev. 8ft./2m.; 🅿; ★ NAP; z 34107
Vandolah; RMC Place; HARDEE; *165 K-9; mail Ona z 33865, Wauchula z 33873; rural
Venetia; RMC Place; DUVAL; *164 C-9; elev. 10ft./3m.; ★ JAX; mail Jacksonville z 32210; pop. incl. with Jacksonville (Inc. Place)
Venetian Islands; RMC Place; MIAMI-DADE; *165 Q-14; ★ MIA-; mail Miami Beach z 33139; pop. incl. with Miami Beach (Inc. Place)
Venetian Isles; RMC Place; PINELLAS; *164 J-7; ★ ST.PET; mail Saint Petersburg z 33705; pop. incl. with Saint Petersburg (Inc. Place)
Venetia Terrace; RMC Place; DUVAL; *164 C-9; ★ JAX; mail Jacksonville z 32244; pop. incl. with Jacksonville (Inc. Place)
Venice; Inc. Place; SARASOTA; 165 M-7; elev. 18ft./5m.; 🅿 🅷 ■; ★ VEN; z 34284-87, z 34290-93 & mail North Port z 34288-89; Ⓟ 16,922; © 17,764; Ⓡ 17,864; ◆ 18,321
Venice East; RMC Place; SARASOTA; *165 M-7; ★ VEN; mail Venice z 34293; ● 2,100
Venice Gardens; CDP; SARASOTA; 165 M-7; ★ VEN; mail Venice z 34293; Ⓟ 7,701; © 7,466
Venice Groves; RMC Place; SARASOTA; *165 M-7; mail Venice z 34293; ● 190
Venus; RMC Place; HIGHLANDS; 165 M-10; 🅿; z 33960; ● 50
Verdie; RMC Place; NASSAU; *164 B-8; mail Bryceville z 32009; ● 120
Vermont Heights; RMC Place; ST. JOHNS; 164 D-10; elev. 48ft./15m.; mail Elkton z 32033; ● 200
Verna; RMC Place; MANATEE; *165 L-8; elev. 93ft./28m.; mail Myakka City z 34251
Vernon; Inc. Place; WASHINGTON; 165 R-6; elev. 47ft./14m.; 🅿; z 32462; Ⓟ 778; © 743
Vero Beach; Inc. Place; ⊡ INDIAN RIVER; 165 K-13; elev. 20ft./6m.; 🅿 🅷 ■; ★ VERO; z 32960-69; Ⓟ 17,350; © 17,705; ◆ 16,750
Vero Beach Highlands; RMC Place; INDIAN RIVER; *165 K-13; ★ VERO; mail Vero Beach z 32962; ● 2,100
Vero Beach South; CDP-Census Area Only; INDIAN RIVER; *165 K-13; ★ VERO; mail Vero Beach z 32960, z 32962, z 32966, z 32968; Ⓟ 16,973; © 20,362; ◆ 24,346
Vero Lake Estates; RMC Place; INDIAN RIVER; 165 K-12; mail Vero Beach z 32967; ● 1,600
Vero Shores; RMC Place; INDIAN RIVER; *165 K-13; ★ VERO; mail Vero Beach z 32962; ● 960
Vicksburg; RMC Place; BAY; *165 S-6; mail Panama City z 32401
Viera; RMC Place; BREVARD; 164 I-12; 🅿; ★ MELB-; z 32940, z 32955; ● 200
Viking; RMC Place; ST. LUCIE; *165 K-13; rural
Vilas; RMC Place; LIBERTY; *165 S-8; elev. 82ft./25m.; mail Hosford z 32334; rural
Village; RMC Place; BROWARD; *165 O-14; ★ MIA-; mail Deerfield Beach z 33442; pop. incl. with Deerfield Beach (Inc. Place)
Village Green; RMC Place; BREVARD; *164 I-12; ★ MELB-; mail Rockledge z 32955; pop. incl. with Rockledge (Inc. Place)
Village Green; RMC Place; MANATEE; *165 K-7; ★ SAR-B; mail Bradenton z 34209; pop. incl. with Bradenton (Inc. Place)
Village of Golf; PALM BEACH; see Golf (Inc. Place)
Village Park; CDP-Census Area Only; BROWARD; *165 O-13; ★ MIA-; © 895
Villages of Oriole; CDP-Census Area Only; PALM BEACH; 163 E-9; ★ MIA-; mail Delray Beach z 33446; Ⓟ 5,698; © 4,758
Villano Beach; CDP-Census Area Only; ST. JOHNS; 164 D-10; mail Saint Augustine z 32095; Ⓟ 1,867; © 2,533
Villa Rica; RMC Place; PALM BEACH; ★ MIA-; pop. incl. with Boca Raton (Inc. Place)
Villas; CDP-Census Area Only; LEE; *165 N-9; ★ FTMY-; mail Fort Myers z 33912; Ⓟ 9,898; © 11,346
Villa Sabine; RMC Place; ESCAMBIA; *165 S-3; ★ PENS; mail Gulf Breeze z 32561
Villa Tasso; RMC Place; WALTON; *165 R-4; mail Niceville z 32578; ● 580
Vina del Mar; RMC Place; PINELLAS; *165 K-6; ★ ST.PET; mail Saint Petersburg z 33706; pop. incl. with Saint Pete Beach (Inc. Place)
Vineland; RMC Place; ORANGE; *164 I-10; elev. 115ft./35m.; mail Orlando z 32836; ● 440
Vineyards; CDP-Census Area Only; COLLIER; *165 O-9; ★ NAP; © 2,232
Virginia Gardens; Inc. Place; MIAMI-DADE; 163 L-7; elev. 5ft./2m.; 🅿; ★ MIA-; z 33166; Ⓟ 2,212; © 2,348
Vista; RMC Place; LEVY; *164 F-5; mail Cedar Key z 32625, Chiefland z 32626; ● 40
Volusia; RMC Place; VOLUSIA; *164 F-10; mail Astor z 32102; ● 280
VOLUSIA; 164 G-11; Ⓟ 370,712; © 443,343; ◆ 507,337

W

Wabasso; CDP; INDIAN RIVER; 164 J-13; elev. 14ft./4m.; 🅿; ★ VERO; z 32970; Ⓟ 1,145; © 918
Wabasso Beach; CDP; INDIAN RIVER; *165 K-13; ★ VERO; © 1,075
Wacahoota; RMC Place; ALACHUA; *164 E-7; mail Micanopy z 32667; rural
Wacissa; RMC Place; JEFFERSON; 164 C-3; elev. 41ft./12m.; 🅿; z 32361; ● 350
Wadesboro; RMC Place; LEON; *164 B-3; elev. 116ft./35m.; mail Tallahassee z 32308; ● 175
Wagner; RMC Place; SEMINOLE; *164 H-10; mail Winter Springs z 32708; pop. incl. with Winter Springs (Inc. Place)
Wahneta; CDP; POLK; 163 K-4; 🅿; ★ WNHV; z 33880; Ⓟ 4,024; © 4,731
Wahoo; RMC Place; SUMTER; *164 H-8; mail Bushnell z 33513; rural
Wakulla; RMC Place; WAKULLA; 164 C-2; mail Crawfordville z 32327; ● 135
WAKULLA; 164 C-2; Ⓟ 14,202; © 22,863; ◆ 32,088
Wakulla Gardens; RMC Place; WAKULLA; *164 C-2; mail Crawfordville z 32327; ● 500
Wakulla Springs; RMC Place; WAKULLA; *164 C-2; 🅿; z 32327 & mail Tallahassee z 32305; ● 75
Waldo; Inc. Place; ALACHUA; 164 D-8; elev. 154ft./47m.; 🅿; z 32694; Ⓟ 1,017; © 821
Walkill; RMC Place; CLAY; *164 D-9; mail Green Cove Springs z 32043; ● 130
Wallace; RMC Place; SANTA ROSA; *165 R-3; elev. 179ft./55m.; ★ PENS; mail Milton z 32571
Wall Springs; RMC Place; PINELLAS; *164 J-6; mail Palm Harbor z 34683; ● 825
Walnut Hill; RMC Place; ESCAMBIA; 165 Q-2; 🅿; z 32568; ● 350
Walsingham; RMC Place; PINELLAS; *164 J-6; ★ ST.PET; mail Largo z 33774; ● 1,650
Walton; RMC Place; ST. LUCIE; 165 L-13; ★ STU; mail Jensen Beach z 34957; ● 200
WALTON; 165 R-5; Ⓟ 27,760; © 40,601; ◆ 55,347
Wannee; RMC Place; GILCHRIST; 164 E-6; mail Bell z 32619; ● 130
Ward Ridge; RMC Place; GULF; 165 T-7; mail Port Saint Joe z 32456; pop. incl. with Port Saint Joe (Inc. Place)
Warm Mineral Springs; CDP; SARASOTA; *165 M-8; ★ PUN-; mail North Port z 34287; Ⓟ 4,041; © 4,811
Warrington; CDP; ESCAMBIA; 165 S-2; ★ PENS; mail Pensacola z 32507; Ⓟ 16,040; © 15,207
WASHINGTON; 165 R-6; Ⓟ 16,919; © 20,973; ◆ 23,824
Washington Lake Estates; RMC Place; DUVAL; *164 C-9; ★ JAX; mail Jacksonville z 32218; pop. incl. with Jacksonville (Inc. Place)
Washington Park; CDP-Census Area Only; BROWARD; *165 O-13; ★ MIA-; mail Fort Lauderdale z 33311; Ⓟ 6,930; © 1,257
Washington Shores; RMC Place; ORANGE; ★ ORL; mail Orlando z 32805; pop. incl. with Orlando (Inc. Place)
Waterbury; RMC Place; MANATEE; *165 L-7; mail Bradenton z 34202, Myakka City z 34251; ● 60
Waters Lake; RMC Place; GILCHRIST; *164 E-6; mail Trenton z 32693; ● 100
Watertown; CDP; COLUMBIA; 164 C-7; mail Lake City z 32055; Ⓟ 3,340; © 2,837
Waterway Estates; RMC Place; LEE; *165 N-9; ★ FTMY-; mail North Fort Myers z 33903; ● 2,000
Watson; RMC Place; PALM BEACH; *165 N-12; elev. 13ft./4m.; mail Clewiston z 33440; ● 40
Wauchula; Inc. Place; ⊡ HARDEE; 165 K-9; elev. 109ft./33m.; 🅿; z 33873; Ⓟ 3,253; © 4,368
Wauchula Hills; RMC Place; HARDEE; *165 K-9; mail Wauchula z 33873; ● 950
Waukeenah; RMC Place; JEFFERSON; *164 C-3; elev. 196ft./60m.; mail Monticello z 32344

Entries in **UPPERCASE** are counties.
Entries in **bold** have populations of 2,500 or more.
Names in parentheses are alternate names.
Inc. Place — Incorporated Place
RMC Place — Rand McNally Designated Place
CDP — Census Designated Place
MCD — Minor Civil Division

⊡ County Seat
▲ Minor Civil Division
elev. Elevation
🅿 Post Office
🅷 Hospital
🅲 College
■ Principal Business Center
★ Ranally Metro Area (RMA) Abbreviation
z Zip Code(s)

Ⓟ Previous Census Population
Ⓡ Revised Census Population
Ⓐ Annexation Population
● Rand McNally Population Estimate
© Final Census Population
Ⓢ Special Census Population
◆ Estimated Population

For additional definitions see Glossary, Volume 1, and Introduction, Volume 2.

Wausau; Inc. Place; WASHINGTON; **165** R-6; elev. 103ft./31m.; 🅿; **z** 32463; Ⓟ 313; Ⓒ 398

Waveland; RMC Place; ST. LUCIE; ***165** L-13; mail Jensen Beach **z** 34957; ● 850

Waverly; CDP; POLK; **164** J-9; elev. 129ft./39m.; 🅿; ★ **WNHV**; **z** 33877; Ⓟ 2,071; Ⓒ 1,927

Waverly Hills; RMC Place; LEON; ***164** B-2; ★ **TALL**; mail Tallahassee **z** 32308, **z** 32312; pop. incl. with Tallahassee (Inc. Place)

Weathersfield; RMC Place; SEMINOLE; ***164** H-10; elev. 83ft./25m.; ★ **ORL**; mail Altamonte Springs **z** 32714; pop. incl. with Altamonte Springs (Inc. Place)

Webster; Inc. Place; SUMTER; **164** H-8; elev. 90ft./27m.; 🅿; **z** 33597; Ⓟ 746; Ⓒ 805

Wedgefield; CDP-Census Area Only; ORANGE; ***164** H-11; Ⓒ 2,700

Weeki Wachee (Weeki Wachee Springs); Inc. Place; HERNANDO; **164** H-7; 🅿; ★ **SPR.H**; **z** 34606-07, **z** 34613-14 & mail Spring Hill **z** 34610; Ⓟ 53; Ⓒ 12

Weeki Wachee Acres; RMC Place; HERNANDO; ***164** H-7; ★ **SPR.H**; mail Spring Hill **z** 34606; Ⓟ 1,394; ● 2,100

Weeki Wachee Gardens; CDP-Census Area Only; HERNANDO; ***164** H-7; ★ **SPR.H**; mail Spring Hill **z** 34607; Ⓟ 1,170; Ⓒ 1,140

Weeki Wachee Springs; HERNANDO; see Weeki Wachee (Inc. Place)

Weirsdale; RMC Place; MARION; **164** G-8; elev. 97ft./30m.; 🅿; ★ **OCA**; **z** 32195; ● 840

Wekiva Springs; CDP-Census Area Only; SEMINOLE; **165** L-3; 🅿; ★ **ORL**; **z** 32779, **z** 32791 & mail Longwood **z** 32750; Ⓟ 23,026; Ⓒ 23,169; ◆ 26,270

Wekiwa Manor; RMC Place; ORANGE; ***164** H-10; ★ **ORL**; mail Apopka **z** 32703; ● 750

Welaka; Inc. Place; PUTNAM; **164** E-9; elev. 25ft./8m.; 🅿; **z** 32193; Ⓟ 533; Ⓒ 586

Welcome; RMC Place; HILLSBOROUGH; ***164** J-8; mail Lithia **z** 33547; rural

Wellborn; RMC Place; SUWANNEE; **164** C-6; elev. 190ft./58m.; 🅿; **z** 32094; ● 400

Wellington; Inc. Place; PALM BEACH; **163** B-8; 🅿; ★ **MIA-**; **z** 33411, **z** 33414, **z** 33421, **z** 33449, **z** 33467, **z** 33470; Ⓟ 20,670; Ⓒ 38,216; ◆ 48,586

Wesconnett; RMC Place; DUVAL; ***164** C-9; ★ **JAX**; mail Jacksonville **z** 32244; pop. incl. with Jacksonville (Inc. Place)

Wesley Chapel; CDP; PASCO; **164** I-7; 🅿; ★ **TAM**; **z** 33543-45; Ⓒ 5,691

Wesley Chapel South; CDP-Census Area Only; PASCO; ***164** I-7; Ⓒ 3,245

Wesley Manor; RMC Place; ST. JOHNS; ***164** C-9; ★ **JAX**; mail Jacksonville **z** 32223; ● 440

West and East Lealman; CDP-Census Area Only; PINELLAS; ***164** J-6; ★ **ST.PET**; Ⓒ 21,753; ◆ 21,301

West Atlantic; RMC Place; BROWARD; ***165** O-13; ★ **MIA-**; mail Pompano Beach **z** 33071, **z** 33077; pop. incl. with Coral Springs (Inc. Place)

West Bay; RMC Place; BAY; **165** S-6; elev. 9ft./3m.; ★ **PNCY**; mail Panama City Beach **z** 32413; ● 300

West Bradenton; CDP-Census Area Only; MANATEE; **163** F-2; ★ **SAR-B**; mail Bradenton **z** 34205, **z** 34209; Ⓟ 4,528; Ⓒ 4,444

Westchase; CDP; HILLSBOROUGH; ***164** J-7; 🅿; ★ **TAM**; **z** 33626; Ⓒ 11,116

Westchester; CDP; MIAMI-DADE; **163** M-7; ★ **MIA-**; mail Miami **z** 33144, **z** 33155, **z** 33165, **z** 33174; Ⓟ 29,883; Ⓒ 30,271; ◆ 31,625

West De Land; CDP-Census Area Only; VOLUSIA; ***164** G-10; ★ **DL**; mail DeLand **z** 32720; Ⓟ 3,389; Ⓒ 3,424

West End; RMC Place; JACKSON; ***165** R-7; mail Marianna **z** 32446; pop. incl. with Marianna (Inc. Place)

Western Acres; RMC Place; LEE; ★ **FTMY-**; mail North Fort Myers **z** 33903

West Farm; RMC Place; MADISON; ***164** B-5; mail Madison **z** 32340; rural

West Frostproof; RMC Place; POLK; **165** K-9; mail Frostproof **z** 33843; ● 200

Westgate; RMC Place; MANATEE; ***165** K-7; ★ **SAR-B**; mail Bradenton **z** 34205; pop. incl. with Bradenton (Inc. Place)

Westgate; RMC Place; PALM BEACH; ***165** N-14; elev. 14ft./4m.; ★ **MIA-**; mail West Palm Beach **z** 33409; pop. incl. with West Palm Beach (Inc. Place)

Westgate-Belvedere Homes; CDP-Census Area Only; PALM BEACH; ***165** N-14; ★ **MIA-**; mail West Palm Beach **z** 33409; Ⓟ 6,880; Ⓒ 8,134

West Holly Hill; RMC Place; VOLUSIA; 1 mi. W of Holly Hill; ★ **D.BCH**; mail Daytona Beach **z** 32117; ● 4,500

West Hollywood; RMC Place; BROWARD; ***165** P-13; 🅿; ★ **MIA-**; **z** 33023 & mail Hollywood **z** 33083; pop. incl. with Hollywood (Inc. Place)

West Jacksonville; RMC Place; DUVAL; ***164** C-9; ★ **JAX**; mail Jacksonville **z** 32254; pop. incl. with Jacksonville (Inc. Place)

West Kendall; RMC Place; MIAMI-DADE; ★ **MIA-**; mail Miami **z** 33183, **z** 33296

West Ken-Lark; CDP-Census Area Only; BROWARD; ***165** O-13; ★ **MIA-**; Ⓒ 3,412

Westlake; RMC Place; DUVAL; ★ **JAX**; pop. incl. with Jacksonville (Inc. Place)

West Lake; RMC Place; HAMILTON; ***164** B-5; mail Jennings **z** 32053; ● 150

West Lake Wales; RMC Place; POLK; ***164** J-9; mail Bartow **z** 33830; ● 130

West Lantana; RMC Place; PALM BEACH; ***165** N-14; ★ **MIA-**; mail Lake Worth **z** 33462; pop. incl. with Lantana (Inc. Place)

West Little River; CDP-Census Area Only; MIAMI-DADE; ***165** P-13; ★ **MIA-**; mail Miami **z** 33147, **z** 33150; Ⓟ 33,575; Ⓒ 32,498; ◆ 33,942

West Melbourne; Inc. Place; BREVARD; **164** J-12; elev. 32ft./10m.; 🅿; ★ **MELB-**; **z** 32904, **z** 32912; Ⓟ 8,399; Ⓒ 9,824

West Miami; Inc. Place; MIAMI-DADE; **163** M-7; elev. 10ft./3m.; 🅿; ★ **MIA-**; **z** 33144 & mail Miami **z** 33155, **z** 33172, **z** 33174, **z** 33182, **z** 33194; Ⓟ 5,727; Ⓒ 5,863

Weston; Inc. Place; BROWARD; **165** O-13; 🅿 🅲 1,485; ★ **MIA-**; **z** 33326-27, **z** 33331-32; Ⓒ 49,286; ◆ 55,527

West Palm Beach; Inc. Place; ⊡ PALM BEACH; **165** N-14; elev. 21ft./6m.; 🅿 🅷 🅲 3,949 ■; ★ **MIA-**; **z** 33401-22; Ⓟ 67,643; Ⓒ 82,103; ◆ 90,487

West Palmetto Park; RMC Place; PALM BEACH; ***165** O-14; ★ **MIA-**; mail Boca Raton **z** 33427, **z** 33486; pop. incl. with Boca Raton (Inc. Place)

West Panama City Beach; RMC Place; BAY; ***165** S-6; ★ **PNCY**; mail Panama City Beach **z** 32413; pop. incl. with Panama City Beach (Inc. Place)

West Park; Inc. Place; BROWARD; ***165** P-14; 🅿; **z** 33023; ● 13,700

West Pensacola; CDP; ESCAMBIA; **165** R-2; ★ **PENS**; mail Pensacola **z** 32505; Ⓟ 22,107; Ⓒ 21,939; ◆ 24,449

West Perrine; CDP-Census Area Only; MIAMI-DADE; ***165** Q-13; ★ **MIA-**; Ⓒ 8,600

West Samoset; CDP-Census Area Only; MANATEE; ***165** K-7; ★ **SAR-B**; mail Bradenton **z** 34208; Ⓟ 3,819; Ⓒ 5,507

West Scenic Park; RMC Place; POLK; ***164** J-9; mail Lake Wales **z** 33853; ● 730

West Tampa; RMC Place; HILLSBOROUGH; ***164** J-7; ★ **TAM**; mail Tampa **z** 33607, **z** 33677; pop. incl. with Tampa (Inc. Place)

West Tocoi; RMC Place; CLAY; ***164** D-9; mail Green Cove Springs **z** 32043; rural

West Vero Corridor; CDP-Census Area Only; INDIAN RIVER; ***165** K-12; ★ **VERO**; Ⓒ 7,695

Westview; CDP-Census Area Only; MIAMI-DADE; ***165** P-13; ★ **MIA-**; mail Miami **z** 33167; Ⓟ 9,668; Ⓒ 9,692

Westville; Inc. Place; HOLMES; **165** R-6; elev. 66ft./20m.; 🅿; **z** 32464; Ⓟ 257; Ⓒ 221

Westwood; RMC Place; DUVAL; ***164** C-9; ★ **JAX**; mail Jacksonville **z** 32244; pop. incl. with Jacksonville (Inc. Place)

Westwood; RMC Place; ORANGE; ***164** H-10; ★ **ORL**; mail Orlando **z** 32808; ● 1,000

Westwood Lake; MIAMI-DADE; see Westwood Lakes (CDP)

Westwood Lakes (Westwood Lake); CDP; MIAMI-DADE; **163** M-7; elev. 45ft./14m.; ★ **MIA-**; mail Miami **z** 33165; Ⓟ 11,522; Ⓒ 12,005

Wetumpka; RMC Place; GADSDEN; ***164** B-1; mail Quincy **z** 32351; ● 100

Wewahitchka; Inc. Place; GULF; **165** S-7; 🅿; **z** 32449, **z** 32465; Ⓟ 1,779; Ⓒ 1,722

Whiskey Creek; CDP-Census Area Only; LEE; ***165** N-9; ★ **FTMY-**; mail Fort Myers **z** 33919; Ⓟ 5,061; Ⓒ 4,806

Whispering Hills Golf Estates; RMC Place; BREVARD; pop. incl. with Titusville (Inc. Place)

Whispering Pines; RMC Place; OKEECHOBEE; ***165** L-12; mail Okeechobee **z** 34972; ● 980

Whisper Walk; CDP-Census Area Only; PALM BEACH; ***165** O-13; ★ **MIA-**; mail Boca Raton **z** 33496; Ⓟ 3,037; Ⓒ 5,135

White Beach; RMC Place; SARASOTA; ***165** L-7; mail Sarasota **z** 34242; ● 100

White City; RMC Place; GULF; **165** T-7; mail Wewahitchka **z** 32465; ● 400

White City; CDP; ST. LUCIE; **165** L-13; ★ **FTPI**; mail Fort Pierce **z** 34981; Ⓟ 4,645; Ⓒ 4,221

Whitehouse; RMC Place; DUVAL; ***164** C-9; ★ **JAX**; mail Jacksonville **z** 32220; pop. incl. with Jacksonville (Inc. Place)

Whites Ford; RMC Place; ST. JOHNS; ***164** D-9; mail Saint Augustine **z** 32092; ● 200

Whites Landing; RMC Place; SEMINOLE; ***164** H-10; mail Oviedo **z** 32765; ● 130

White Springs; Inc. Place; HAMILTON; **164** C-6; elev. 138ft./42m.; 🅿; **z** 32096; Ⓟ 704; Ⓒ 819

White Springs; RMC Place; LIBERTY; ***165** S-8; mail Bristol **z** 32321; ● 120

Whiteville; RMC Place; PUTNAM; mail Hawthorne **z** 32640; ● 300

Whitfield; CDP-Census Area Only; MANATEE; ***165** L-7; ★ **SAR-B**; mail Sarasota **z** 34243; Ⓟ 3,152; Ⓒ 2,984

Whitney; RMC Place; LAKE; ***164** G-8; mail Leesburg **z** 34748; ● 200

Whitney Beach; RMC Place; MANATEE; ***165** L-6; ★ **SAR-B**; mail Longboat Key **z** 34228; pop. incl. with Longboat Key (Inc. Place)

Wilbur-By-The-Sea; RMC Place; VOLUSIA; **164** F-11; 🅿; ★ **D.BCH**; **z** 32127; ● 1,300

Wilcox; RMC Place; GILCHRIST; ***164** E-6; mail Trenton **z** 32693; ● 140

Wild Island; RMC Place; HIGHLANDS; ***165** L-11; rural

Wildwood; Inc. Place; SUMTER; **164** G-8; elev. 64ft./20m.; 🅿; **z** 34785; Ⓟ 3,421; Ⓒ 3,924

Wiley; RMC Place; BREVARD; ***164** H-11; ● 50

Williamsburg; CDP-Census Area Only; ORANGE; **165** O-3; ★ **ORL**; mail Orlando **z** 32821; Ⓟ 3,093; Ⓒ 6,736

Williams Point; RMC Place; BREVARD; ***164** H-12; elev. 34ft./10m.; ★ **MELB-**; mail Sharpes **z** 32959; ● 1,000

Willis Landing; RMC Place; GULF; ***165** T-7; mail Wewahitchka **z** 32465; rural

Williston; Inc. Place; LEVY; **164** F-7; elev. 76ft./23m.; 🅿 🅷; **z** 32696; Ⓟ 2,179; Ⓒ 2,297

Williston Highlands; CDP; LEVY; ***164** F-7; mail Williston **z** 32696; Ⓒ 1,386

Willow Oak; CDP; POLK; ***164** J-8; ★ **LKLD**; mail Mulberry **z** 33860; Ⓟ 4,017; Ⓒ 4,917

Wilson Corners; RMC Place; SUMTER; ***164** H-8; mail Webster **z** 33597; rural

Wilton Manors; Inc. Place; BROWARD; **163** H-9; elev. 5ft./2m.; 🅿; ★ **MIA-**; **z** 33305-06, **z** 33311, **z** 33334; Ⓟ 11,804; Ⓒ 12,697

Wimauma; CDP; HILLSBOROUGH; **165** K-8; elev. 102ft./31m.; 🅿; **z** 33598; Ⓟ 2,932; Ⓒ 4,246

Windermere; Inc. Place; ORANGE; **164** H-10; 🅿; ★ **ORL**; **z** 34786; Ⓟ 1,371; Ⓒ 1,897

Windsor; RMC Place; ALACHUA; ***164** E-8; mail Gainesville **z** 32601; ● 100

Winfield; RMC Place; COLUMBIA; ***164** C-6; mail Lake City **z** 32055; ● 155

Winston; CDP; POLK; **163** J-1; ★ **LKLD**; mail Lakeland **z** 33811; Ⓟ 9,118; Ⓒ 9,024

Winter Beach; CDP; INDIAN RIVER; **165** K-13; elev. 13ft./4m.; 🅿; ★ **VERO**; **z** 32971; Ⓒ 965

Winter Garden; Inc. Place; ORANGE; **164** H-9; elev. 126ft./38m.; 🅿 🅷; ★ **ORL**; **z** 34777-78, **z** 34787; Ⓟ 9,745; Ⓒ 14,351; ◆ 21,248

Winter Haven; Inc. Place; POLK; **164** J-9; elev. 170ft./52m.; 🅿 🅷 ■; ★ **WNHV**; **z** 33880-85, **z** 33888; Ⓟ 24,725; Ⓒ 26,487; ◆ 32,890

Winter Park; Inc. Place; ORANGE; **164** H-10; elev. 94ft./29m.; 🅿 🅷 🅲 8,332 ■; ★ **ORL**; **z** 32789-90, **z** 32792-93; Ⓟ 22,623; Ⓒ 24,090; ◆ 27,494

Winter Springs; Inc. Place; SEMINOLE; **165** L-4; elev. 49ft./15m.; 🅿; ★ **ORL**; **z** 32708, **z** 32719; Ⓟ 22,151; Ⓒ 31,666; Ⓡ 30,860; ◆ 37,228

Wiscon; RMC Place; HERNANDO; ***164** H-7; ★ **SPR.H**; mail Spring Hill **z** 34609; ● 320

Woodland; RMC Place; PALM BEACH; ★ **MIA-**; mail Boca Raton **z** 33431, **z** 33481; pop. incl. with Boca Raton (Inc. Place)

Woodland Drives; RMC Place; LEON; ***164** B-2; ★ **TALL**; mail Tallahassee **z** 32301; pop. incl. with Tallahassee (Inc. Place)

Woodlawn; RMC Place; BAY; ***165** S-6; ★ **PNCY**; mail Panama City Beach **z** 32407; ● 1,000

Woodlawn; RMC Place; PINELLAS; ***165** K-7; ★ **ST.PET**; mail Saint Petersburg **z** 33704; pop. incl. with Saint Petersburg (Inc. Place)

Woodlawn; RMC Place; ST. JOHNS; ***164** D-10; mail Saint Augustine **z** 32095; ● 330

Woodlawn Beach; RMC Place; SANTA ROSA; ***165** S-3; elev. 6ft./2m.; ★ **PENS**; mail Gulf Breeze **z** 32561; ● 300

Woodmere; RMC Place; SARASOTA; ***165** M-7; mail Englewood **z** 34223; ● 220

Woodmont; RMC Place; BROWARD; ***165** O-13; ★ **MIA-**; mail Fort Lauderdale **z** 33321; pop. incl. with Tamarac (Inc. Place)

Woods; RMC Place; LIBERTY; **165** S-8; mail Bristol **z** 32321; ● 130

Woods and Lakes; RMC Place; MARION; ***164** F-9; mail Ocklawaha **z** 32179; ● 400

Woodville; CDP; LEON; **164** C-2; elev. 59ft./18m.; 🅿; ★ **TALL**; **z** 32362; Ⓟ 2,760; Ⓒ 3,006

Woodward Avenue; RMC Place; LEON; ***164** B-2; ★ **TALL**; mail Tallahassee **z** 32304, **z** 32316; pop. incl. with Tallahassee (Inc. Place)

Worthington Springs; Inc. Place; UNION; **164** D-7; elev. 84ft./26m.; 🅿; **z** 32697; Ⓟ 178; Ⓒ 193

Wright; CDP; OKALOOSA; ***165** S-4; ★ **FTWL**; mail Fort Walton Beach **z** 32547; Ⓟ 18,945; Ⓒ 21,697; ◆ 23,366

Wulfert; RMC Place; LEE; ***165** O-8; mail Sanibel **z** 33957; pop. incl. with Sanibel (Inc. Place)

Wynnehaven Beach; RMC Place; OKALOOSA; ***165** S-3; ★ **FTWL**; mail Mary Esther **z** 32569; ● 2,300

Wynwood; RMC Place; MIAMI-DADE; ***165** P-13; ★ **MIA-**; mail Miami **z** 33127

Wynwood; RMC Place; SEMINOLE; ***164** G-10; ★ **ORL**; mail Sanford **z** 32771; pop. incl. with Sanford (Inc. Place)

Y

Yalaha; CDP; LAKE; **164** H-9; elev. 82ft./25m.; 🅿; **z** 34797; Ⓟ 1,168; Ⓒ 1,175

Yankeetown; Inc. Place; LEVY; **164** G-6; elev. 5ft./2m.; 🅿; **z** 34498; Ⓟ 635; Ⓒ 629

Ybor City; RMC Place; HILLSBOROUGH; ***164** J-7; 🅿; ★ **TAM**; **z** 33605, **z** 33675; pop. incl. with Tampa (Inc. Place)

Yeehaw; RMC Place; INDIAN RIVER; ***165** K-11; 🅿; **z** 34972; ● 200

Yeehaw Junction; CDP; OSCEOLA; ***164** I-10; 🅿; ★ **KISS**; **z** 34972; Ⓒ 21,778; ◆ 35,210

Yelvington; RMC Place; PUTNAM, ST. JOHNS; ***164** E-10; mail East Palatka **z** 32131; ● 100

Yeoman Yard; RMC Place; HILLSBOROUGH; ★ **TAM**; pop. incl. with Tampa (Inc. Place)

Yniestra; RMC Place; ESCAMBIA; ***165** R-3; mail Pensacola **z** 32504; ● 450

York; RMC Place; MARION; ***164** F-7; ★ **OCA**; mail Ocala **z** 34474; rural

Youmans; RMC Place; HILLSBOROUGH; **163** B-7; elev. 142ft./43m.; ★ **TAM**; mail Plant City **z** 33566; ● 600

Youngstown; RMC Place; BAY; **165** S-7; elev. 88ft./27m.; 🅿; **z** 32466; ● 150

Yukon; RMC Place; DUVAL; ***164** C-9; ★ **JAX**; mail Jacksonville **z** 32244; pop. incl. with Jacksonville (Inc. Place)

Yulee; CDP; NASSAU; **164** B-9; elev. 35ft./11m.; 🅿; ★ **JAX**; **z** 32041, **z** 32097; Ⓟ 6,915; Ⓒ 8,392

Yulee Heights; RMC Place; NASSAU; ***164** B-9; ★ **JAX**; mail Yulee **z** 32097; ● 300

Z

Zana; RMC Place; MARTIN; ***165** L-12; mail Indiantown **z** 34956; ● 220

Zellwood; CDP; ORANGE; **164** H-9; elev. 99ft./30m.; 🅿; ★ **ORL**; **z** 32798; winter pop. 3,000; Ⓒ 2,540

Zephyrhills; Inc. Place; PASCO; **164** I-8; elev. 97ft./30m.; 🅿 🅷; **z** 33539-45; Ⓟ 8,220; Ⓒ 10,833

Zephyrhills North; CDP-Census Area Only; PASCO; ***164** I-8; mail Zephyrhills **z** 33540; Ⓟ 2,320; Ⓒ 2,544

Zephyrhills South; CDP-Census Area Only; PASCO; ***164** I-8; mail Zephyrhills **z** 33540-41; Ⓟ 2,514; Ⓒ 4,435

Zephyrhills West; CDP-Census Area Only; PASCO; ***164** I-8; mail Zephyrhills **z** 33541; Ⓟ 4,249; Ⓒ 5,242

Zolfo Springs; Inc. Place; HARDEE; **165** K-9; elev. 64ft./20m.; 🅿; **z** 33890; Ⓟ 1,219; Ⓒ 1,641

Zuber; RMC Place; MARION; ***164** F-8; ★ **OCA**; mail Ocala **z** 34475; ● 125

GEORGIA

Statistics

Total area (2000) — 59,425 square miles
Land area (2000) — 57,906 square miles
Water area (2000) — 1,519 square miles
Capital — Atlanta
One of Thirteen Original States

Maps

State maps can be found on pages 142-254 in Vol. 1

Ranally Metro Areas (RMAs) and Abbreviations

Albany, GA — ALB
Athens, GA — ATH
Atlanta, GA — ATL
Augusta, GA-SC — AUG
Brunswick, GA — BRUNS
Chattanooga, TN-GA — CHTN
Columbus, GA-AL — COL
Macon, GA — MAC
Rome, GA — ROME
Savannah, GA — SAV
Valdosta, GA — VALD

Principal Places

Place Name	Place Type	County	Population
Atlanta	Inc. Place	FULTON	◆ 514,055
Augusta	Inc. Place	RICHMOND	◆ 208,238
Columbus	Inc. Place	MUSCOGEE	◆ 192,560
Savannah	Inc. Place	CHATHAM	◆ 133,005
Athens	Inc. Place	CLARKE	◆ 117,272
Roswell	Inc. Place	FULTON	◆ 105,134
Sandy Springs	Inc. Place	FULTON	◆ 100,041
Macon	Inc. Place	BIBB	◆ 93,953
Sandy Springs	CDP-Census Area Only	FULTON	© 85,781
Albany	Inc. Place	DOUGHERTY	◆ 78,664
Marietta	Inc. Place	COBB	◆ 72,011
Warner Robins	Inc. Place	HOUSTON	◆ 62,536
Johns Creek	Inc. Place	FULTON	● 61,100
Smyrna	Inc. Place	COBB	◆ 50,446
East Point	Inc. Place	FULTON	◆ 48,765
Valdosta	Inc. Place	LOWNDES	◆ 47,912
Alpharetta	Inc. Place	FULTON	◆ 46,742
North Atlanta	CDP	DEKALB	◆ 44,044
Gainesville	Inc. Place	HALL	◆ 39,950
Redan	CDP	DEKALB	◆ 38,632
Dunwoody	CDP	DEKALB	◆ 37,455
Rome	Inc. Place	FLOYD	◆ 37,370
Martinez	CDP	COLUMBIA	◆ 35,122
Mableton	CDP	COBB	◆ 34,923
Dalton	Inc. Place	WHITFIELD	◆ 34,192
Peachtree City	Inc. Place	FAYETTE	◆ 34,156
Hinesville	Inc. Place	LIBERTY	◆ 33,431
Douglasville	Inc. Place	DOUGLAS	◆ 32,941
Candler-McAfee	CDP-Census Area Only	DEKALB	◆ 32,296
Kennesaw	Inc. Place	COBB	◆ 31,909
Duluth	Inc. Place	GWINNETT	◆ 31,441
Tucker	CDP	DEKALB	◆ 30,296
Newnan	Inc. Place	COWETA	◆ 29,475
La Grange	Inc. Place	TROUP	◆ 28,859
Lawrenceville	Inc. Place	GWINNETT	◆ 28,339
Forest Park	Inc. Place	CLAYTON	◆ 27,418
Carrollton	Inc. Place	CARROLL	◆ 26,501
Statesboro	Inc. Place	BULLOCH	◆ 25,643
Griffin	Inc. Place	SPALDING	◆ 25,506
Woodstock	Inc. Place	CHEROKEE	◆ 22,779
College Park	Inc. Place	FULTON	◆ 21,600
Snellville	Inc. Place	GWINNETT	◆ 20,757
Milledgeville	Inc. Place	BALDWIN	◆ 19,959
Cartersville	Inc. Place	BARTOW	◆ 19,795
Thomasville	Inc. Place	THOMAS	◆ 19,145
Belvedere Park	CDP	DEKALB	© 18,945
North Druid Hills	CDP	DEKALB	© 18,852
Decatur	Inc. Place	DEKALB	◆ 18,251
Canton	Inc. Place	CHEROKEE	◆ 18,195
Evans	CDP	COLUMBIA	© 17,727
Americus	Inc. Place	SUMTER	© 17,013
Brunswick	Inc. Place	GLYNN	◆ 16,980
Dublin	Inc. Place	LAURENS	◆ 16,833
Tifton	Inc. Place	TIFT	◆ 16,776
Milton	Inc. Place	FULTON	● 15,500
North Decatur	CDP	DEKALB	© 15,270
Union City	Inc. Place	FULTON	◆ 15,140
Waycross	Inc. Place	WARE	◆ 15,051
Moultrie	Inc. Place	COLQUITT	◆ 14,643
Wilmington Island	CDP-Census Area Only	CHATHAM	© 14,213
Saint Marys	Inc. Place	CAMDEN	© 13,761
Acworth	Inc. Place	COBB	© 13,422
Saint Simons	CDP	GLYNN	© 13,381
Druid Hills	CDP	DEKALB	© 12,741
Powder Springs	Inc. Place	COBB	© 12,481
Riverdale	Inc. Place	CLAYTON	© 12,478
East Marietta	RMC Place	COBB	● 12,000
Panthersville	CDP	DEKALB	© 11,791
Mountain Park	CDP-Census Area Only	GWINNETT	© 11,753
Fort Benning South	CDP-Census Area Only	CHATTAHOOCHEE	© 11,737
Bainbridge	Inc. Place	DECATUR	© 11,722
Cordele	Inc. Place	CRISP	© 11,608
Covington	Inc. Place	NEWTON	© 11,547
Monroe	Inc. Place	WALTON	© 11,407
Sugar Hill	Inc. Place	GWINNETT	© 11,399
Lilburn	Inc. Place	GWINNETT	© 11,307
Fort Stewart	CDP-Census Area Only	LIBERTY	© 11,205
Doraville	Inc. Place	DEKALB	◆ 11,191
Fayetteville	Inc. Place	FAYETTE	© 11,148
Chamblee	Inc. Place	DEKALB	◆ 11,041
Conyers	Inc. Place	ROCKDALE	© 10,689
Buford	Inc. Place	GWINNETT	© 10,668
Calhoun	Inc. Place	GORDON	© 10,667
Douglas	Inc. Place	COFFEE	© 10,639
Georgetown	CDP	CHATHAM	© 10,599
Kingsland	Inc. Place	CAMDEN	© 10,506
Vidalia	Inc. Place	TOOMBS	© 10,491
Winder	Inc. Place	BARROW	© 10,201
Garden City	Inc. Place	CHATHAM	® 10,160
Stockbridge	Inc. Place	HENRY	© 9,853
Scottdale	CDP	DEKALB	© 9,803
Vinings	CDP	COBB	© 9,677
Perry	Inc. Place	HOUSTON	© 9,602
Cedartown	Inc. Place	POLK	© 9,470
Thomaston	Inc. Place	UPSON	© 9,411
Toccoa	Inc. Place	STEPHENS	© 9,323
Jesup	Inc. Place	WAYNE	© 9,279
Cairo	Inc. Place	GRADY	© 9,239
Gresham Park	CDP-Census Area Only	DEKALB	© 9,215
Fitzgerald	Inc. Place	BEN HILL	© 8,758
Suwanee	Inc. Place	GWINNETT	© 8,725
McDonough	Inc. Place	HENRY	© 8,493
Fair Oaks	CDP	COBB	© 8,443
Norcross	Inc. Place	GWINNETT	© 8,410
Fort Valley	Inc. Place	PEACH	© 8,005
Dunaire	RMC Place	DEKALB	● 8,000
Irondale	CDP-Census Area Only	CLAYTON	© 7,727
Country Club Estates	CDP-Census Area Only	GLYNN	© 7,594
Clarkston	Inc. Place	DEKALB	© 7,231
Stone Mountain	Inc. Place	DEKALB	© 7,145
Brookhaven	RMC Place	DEKALB	● 7,000
Richmond Hill	Inc. Place	BRYAN	© 6,959
Dock Junction	CDP-Census Area Only	GLYNN	© 6,951
Swainsboro	Inc. Place	EMANUEL	© 6,943
Fort Oglethorpe	Inc. Place	CATOOSA	© 6,940
Skidaway Island	CDP-Census Area Only	CHATHAM	© 6,914
Auburn	Inc. Place	BARROW	© 6,904
Thomson	Inc. Place	MCDUFFIE	© 6,828
Eatonton	Inc. Place	PUTNAM	© 6,764
LaFayette	Inc. Place	WALKER	© 6,702
Fairview	CDP	WALKER	© 6,601
Pooler	Inc. Place	CHATHAM	© 6,239
Conley	CDP	CLAYTON	© 6,188
Hapeville	Inc. Place	FULTON	© 6,180
Sandersville	Inc. Place	WASHINGTON	© 6,144
Grovetown	Inc. Place	COLUMBIA	© 6,089
Belvedere	RMC Place	DEKALB	● 6,000
Sylvester	Inc. Place	WORTH	© 5,990
Barnesville	Inc. Place	LAMAR	© 5,972
Whitemarsh Island	CDP-Census Area Only	CHATHAM	© 5,824
Waynesboro	Inc. Place	BURKE	© 5,813
Blakely	Inc. Place	EARLY	© 5,696
Morrow	Inc. Place	CLAYTON	◆ 5,694
Camilla	Inc. Place	MITCHELL	© 5,669
Fairburn	Inc. Place	FULTON	© 5,464
Eastman	Inc. Place	DODGE	© 5,440
Loganville	Inc. Place	WALTON	© 5,435
Austell	Inc. Place	COBB	© 5,359
Adel	Inc. Place	COOK	© 5,307
Commerce	Inc. Place	JACKSON	© 5,292
Glenwood Hills	RMC Place	DEKALB	● 5,200
Midway-Hardwick	CDP-Census Area Only	BALDWIN	© 5,135
Dawson	Inc. Place	TERRELL	© 5,058
Dallas	Inc. Place	PAULDING	© 5,056
Blackwells	RMC Place	COBB	● 5,000
La Vista	RMC Place	DEKALB	● 5,000
Pendley Hills	RMC Place	DEKALB	● 5,000

County Business Data

County	FIPS Code	County Seat	Land Area (Sq. Mi.)	Census Population 4/1/2000	Census Population 4/1/1990	Census Population % Change 1990-2000	Wholesale Trade Sales, 2002 ($1,000)	Wholesale Trade % Change 1997-2002	Manufacturing, 2002 Establish-ments	Manufacturing, 2002 Total Employees	Manufacturing, 2002 Value Added ($1,000)	Manufacturing, 2002 Ranally Mfg. Units
Appling	001	Baxley	509	17,419	15,744	10.6	33,201	-19.0	25	733	104,612	55
Atkinson	003	Pearson	338	7,609	6,213	22.5	(d)	(d)	14	975	73,648	39
Bacon	005	Alma	285	10,103	9,566	5.6	(d)	(d)	12	501	38,312	20
Baker	007	Newton	343	4,074	3,615	12.7	(d)	(d)	...	(d)	(d)	...
Baldwin	009	Milledgeville	258	44,700	39,530	13.1	(d)	(d)	20	(d)	(d)	...
Banks	011	Homer	234	14,422	10,308	39.9	15,288	-65.8	...	(d)	(d)	...
Barrow	013	Winder	162	46,144	29,721	55.3	277,383	275.9	58	2,134	173,816	92
Bartow	015	Cartersville	459	76,019	55,911	36.0	549,048	112.7	119	8,252	1,421,853	752
Ben Hill	017	Fitzgerald	252	17,484	16,245	7.6	39,852	(d)	30	3,254	204,828	108
Berrien	019	Nashville	452	16,235	14,153	14.7	(d)	(d)	19	1,749	79,060	42
Bibb	021	Macon	250	153,887	149,967	2.6	1,517,753	0.4	156	(d)	(d)	...
Bleckley	023	Cochran	217	11,666	10,430	11.9	(d)	(d)	7	(d)	(d)	...
Brantley	025	Nahunta	444	14,629	11,077	32.1	(d)	(d)	...	(d)	(d)	...
Brooks	027	Quitman	494	16,450	15,398	6.8	(d)	(d)	13	(d)	(d)	...
Bryan	029	Pembroke	442	23,417	15,438	51.7	(d)	(d)	...	(d)	(d)	...
Bulloch	031	Statesboro	682	55,983	43,125	29.8	252,939	-24.1	51	2,348	182,838	97
Burke	033	Waynesboro	830	22,243	20,579	8.1	(d)	(d)	15	1,000	80,759	43
Butts	035	Jackson	187	19,522	15,326	27.4	(d)	(d)	15	1,079	160,834	85
Calhoun	037	Morgan	280	6,320	5,013	26.1	23,760	26.3	...	(d)	(d)	...
Camden	039	Woodbine	630	43,664	30,167	44.7	(d)	(d)	18	1,304	192,728	102
Candler	043	Metter	247	9,577	7,744	23.7	(d)	(d)	...	(d)	(d)	...
Carroll	045	Carrollton	499	87,268	71,422	22.2	1,931,571	50.2	123	6,521	738,564	391
Catoosa	047	Ringgold	162	53,282	42,464	25.5	(d)	(d)	53	2,382	203,406	108
Charlton	049	Folkston	781	10,282	8,496	21.0	21,847	-74.3	...	(d)	(d)	...
Chatham	051	Savannah	438	232,048	216,935	7.0	2,789,968	14.1	189	12,187	1,863,091	986
Chattahoochee	053	Cusseta	249	14,882	16,934	-12.1	(d)	(d)	...	(d)	(d)	...
Chattooga	055	Summerville	313	25,470	22,242	14.5	38,568	211.5	22	3,869	320,027	169
Cherokee	057	Canton	424	141,903	90,204	57.3	1,068,083	117.6	167	3,936	267,277	141
Clarke	059	Athens	121	101,489	87,594	15.9	1,311,023	(d)	98	6,966	603,968	320
Clay	061	Fort Gaines	195	3,357	3,364	-0.2	1,337	-64.6	...	(d)	(d)	...
Clayton	063	Jonesboro	143	236,517	182,052	29.9	4,451,421	33.1	148	5,853	876,343	464
Clinch	065	Homerville	809	6,878	6,160	11.7	(d)	(d)	10	771	101,858	54
Cobb	067	Marietta	340	607,751	447,745	35.7	21,812,823	-6.1	597	22,158	3,057,777	1,618
Coffee	069	Douglas	599	37,413	29,592	26.4	(d)	(d)	43	4,683	282,776	150
Colquitt	071	Moultrie	552	42,053	36,645	14.8	212,521	35.9	56	2,051	103,889	55
Columbia	073	Appling	290	89,288	66,031	35.2	3,424,830	(d)	56	4,474	716,558	379
Cook	075	Adel	229	15,771	13,456	17.2	140,803	63.7	30	1,171	71,623	38
Coweta	077	Newnan	443	89,215	53,853	65.7	1,078,796	110.1	84	4,989	530,239	281
Crawford	079	Knoxville	325	12,495	8,991	39.0	(d)	(d)	...	(d)	(d)	...
Crisp	081	Cordele	274	21,996	20,011	9.9	217,952	-18.3	26	2,235	145,019	77
Dade	083	Trenton	174	15,154	13,147	15.3	(d)	(d)	24	894	78,538	42
Dawson	085	Dawsonville	211	15,999	9,429	69.7	(d)	(d)	21	709	55,509	29
Decatur	087	Bainbridge	597	28,240	25,511	10.7	189,587	-44.4	24	2,068	220,956	117
DeKalb	089	Decatur	268	665,865	545,837	22.0	12,918,395	-32.8	588	20,728	4,006,557	2,120
Dodge	091	Eastman	500	19,171	17,607	8.9	12,387	(d)	...	(d)	(d)	...
Dooly	093	Vienna	393	11,525	9,901	16.4	53,716	-5.2	9	(d)	(d)	...
Dougherty	095	Albany	330	96,065	96,311	-0.3	974,203	(d)	80	7,340	2,554,112	1,351
Douglas	097	Douglasville	199	92,174	71,120	29.6	932,046	-15.3	112	4,055	302,349	160
Early	099	Blakely	511	12,354	11,854	4.2	48,603	-63.5	13	1,083	356,744	189
Echols	101	Statenville	404	3,754	2,334	60.8	(d)	(d)	...	(d)	(d)	...
Effingham	103	Springfield	479	37,535	25,687	46.1	(d)	(d)	16	2,022	474,394	251
Elbert	105	Elberton	369	20,511	18,949	8.2	70,111	2.9	119	2,875	274,256	145
Emanuel	107	Swainsboro	686	21,837	20,546	6.3	103,210	-18.3	34	1,977	153,492	81
Evans	109	Claxton	185	10,495	8,724	20.3	7,676	-78.1	14	1,870	172,159	91
Fannin	111	Blue Ridge	386	19,798	15,992	23.8	25,706	22.0	27	732	46,019	24
Fayette	113	Fayetteville	197	91,263	62,415	46.2	535,718	-1.8	104	4,475	476,570	252
Floyd	115	Rome	513	90,565	81,251	11.5	464,928	-11.1	119	7,553	735,657	389
Forsyth	117	Cumming	226	98,407	44,083	123.2	2,547,488	123.3	169	6,712	815,225	431
Franklin	119	Carnesville	263	20,285	16,650	21.8	(d)	(d)	47	2,351	320,078	169
Fulton	121	Atlanta	529	816,006	648,951	25.7	84,705,048	51.5	794	30,562	6,126,659	3,241
Gilmer	123	Ellijay	427	23,456	13,368	75.5	56,231	26.5	31	2,841	129,857	69
Glascock	125	Gibson	144	2,556	2,357	8.4	(d)	(d)	...	(d)	(d)	...
Glynn	127	Brunswick	422	67,568	62,496	8.1	503,865	9.2	68	3,030	412,139	218
Gordon	129	Calhoun	356	44,104	35,072	25.8	277,232	84.1	109	8,346	932,129	493
Grady	131	Cairo	458	23,659	20,279	16.7	128,714	2.8	16	724	68,725	36
Greene	133	Greensboro	388	14,406	11,793	22.2	68,447	-32.9	15	662	81,177	43
Gwinnett	135	Lawrenceville	433	588,448	352,910	66.7	36,028,796	23.7	762	25,437	2,350,716	1,244
Habersham	137	Clarkesville	278	35,902	27,621	30.0	87,907	150.7	67	4,294	270,093	143
Hall	139	Gainesville	394	139,277	95,428	45.9	1,984,915	11.7	240	17,738	1,777,531	940
Hancock	141	Sparta	473	10,076	8,908	13.1	(d)	(d)	...	(d)	(d)	...

Entries in UPPERCASE are counties.
Entries in **bold** have populations of 2,500 or more.
Names in parentheses are alternate names.
Inc. Place — Incorporated Place
RMC Place — Rand McNally Designated Place
CDP — Census Designated Place
MCD — Minor Civil Division

⊡ County Seat
▲ Minor Civil Division
elev. Elevation
🅿 Post Office

🅷 Hospital
🅲 College
■ Principal Business Center
★ Ranally Metro Area (RMA) Abbreviation
z Zip Code(s)

Ⓟ Previous Census Population
® Revised Census Population
Ⓐ Annexation Population
● Rand McNally Population Estimate
© Final Census Population
Ⓢ Special Census Population
◆ Estimated Population

For additional definitions see Glossary, Volume 1, and Introduction, Volume 2.

County	FIPS Code	County Seat	Land Area (Sq. Mi.)	Census Population			Wholesale Trade		Maunfacturing, 2002			
				4/1/2000	4/1/1990	% Change 1990-2000	Sales, 2002 ($1,000)	% Change 1997-2002	Establish-ments	Total Employees	Value Added ($1,000)	Ranally Mfg. Units
Haralson	143	Buchanan	282	25,690	21,966	17.0	70,325	38.5	33	2,123	145,833	77
Harris	145	Hamilton	464	23,695	17,788	33.2	(d)	(d)	21	(d)	(d)	...
Hart	147	Hartwell	232	22,997	19,712	16.7	(d)	(d)	29	2,064	101,444	54
Heard	149	Franklin	296	11,012	8,628	27.6	(d)	(d)	...	(d)	(d)	...
Henry	151	McDonough	323	119,341	58,741	103.2	881,969	133.9	81	3,225	561,182	297
Houston	153	Perry	377	110,765	89,208	24.2	156,736	-33.7	58	2,868	619,016	328
Irwin	155	Ocilla	357	9,931	8,649	14.8	18,615	39.5	...	(d)	(d)	...
Jackson	157	Jefferson	342	41,589	30,005	38.6	533,822	6.3	67	4,319	403,792	214
Jasper	159	Monticello	370	11,426	8,453	35.2	(d)	(d)	25	949	73,703	39
Jeff Davis	161	Hazlehurst	333	12,684	12,032	5.4	(d)	(d)	25	1,632	173,352	92
Jefferson	163	Louisville	528	17,266	17,408	-0.8	60,782	1.7	26	1,559	134,464	71
Jenkins	165	Millen	350	8,575	8,247	4.0	(d)	(d)	8	1,090	53,429	28
Johnson	167	Wrightsville	304	8,560	8,329	2.8	(d)	(d)	...	(d)	(d)	...
Jones	169	Gray	394	23,639	20,739	14.0	21,572	(d)	...	(d)	(d)	...
Lamar	171	Barnesville	185	15,912	13,038	22.0	(d)	(d)	13	509	38,748	21
Lanier	173	Lakeland	187	7,241	5,531	30.9	(d)	(d)	...	(d)	(d)	...
Laurens	175	Dublin	812	44,874	39,988	12.2	203,499	62.4	44	4,107	496,500	263
Lee	177	Leesburg	356	24,757	16,250	52.4	(d)	(d)	...	(d)	(d)	...
Liberty	179	Hinesville	519	61,610	52,745	16.8	(d)	(d)	16	(d)	(d)	...
Lincoln	181	Lincolnton	211	8,348	7,442	12.2	2,406	-41.2	...	(d)	(d)	...
Long	183	Ludowici	401	10,304	6,202	66.1	(d)	(d)	...	(d)	(d)	...
Lowndes	185	Valdosta	504	92,115	75,981	21.2	537,644	18.7	104	4,659	532,212	282
Lumpkin	187	Dahlonega	284	21,016	14,573	44.2	30,693	279.0	16	900	49,712	26
Macon	193	Oglethorpe	403	14,074	13,114	7.3	34,911	-45.1	15	804	134,916	71
Madison	195	Danielsville	284	25,730	21,050	22.2	(d)	(d)	23	531	43,726	23
Marion	197	Buena Vista	367	7,144	5,590	27.8	(d)	(d)	5	(d)	(d)	...
McDuffie	189	Thomson	260	21,231	20,119	5.5	32,152	(d)	30	1,622	93,137	49
McIntosh	191	Darien	433	10,847	8,634	25.6	(d)	(d)	...	(d)	(d)	...
Meriwether	199	Greenville	503	22,534	22,411	0.5	5,149	68.1	16	1,359	161,538	85
Miller	201	Colquitt	283	6,383	6,280	1.6	21,677	(d)	...	(d)	(d)	...
Mitchell	205	Camilla	512	23,932	20,275	18.0	130,294	-12.3	20	2,471	94,751	50
Monroe	207	Forsyth	396	21,757	17,113	27.1	(d)	(d)	...	(d)	(d)	...
Montgomery	209	Mount Vernon	245	8,270	7,163	15.5	(d)	(d)	...	(d)	(d)	...
Morgan	211	Madison	350	15,457	12,883	20.0	69,721	4.6	26	1,581	113,093	60
Murray	213	Chatsworth	344	36,506	26,147	39.6	(d)	(d)	94	5,398	300,660	159
Muscogee	215	Columbus	216	186,291	179,278	3.9	1,059,263	-19.5	141	11,116	1,213,141	642
Newton	217	Covington	276	62,001	41,808	48.3	380,107	(d)	85	5,703	1,363,200	721
Oconee	219	Watkinsville	186	26,225	17,618	48.9	148,527	(d)	31	843	82,678	44
Oglethorpe	221	Lexington	441	12,635	9,763	29.4	(d)	(d)	...	(d)	(d)	...
Paulding	223	Dallas	313	81,678	41,611	96.3	195,511	98.3	48	1,097	93,799	50
Peach	225	Fort Valley	151	23,668	21,189	11.7	112,793	(d)	28	2,745	110,407	58
Pickens	227	Jasper	232	22,983	14,432	59.3	84,944	(d)	35	942	69,577	37
Pierce	229	Blackshear	343	15,636	13,328	17.3	(d)	(d)	...	(d)	(d)	...
Pike	231	Zebulon	218	13,688	10,224	33.9	(d)	(d)	...	(d)	(d)	...
Polk	233	Cedartown	311	38,127	33,815	12.8	(d)	(d)	37	2,662	258,971	137
Pulaski	235	Hawkinsville	247	9,588	8,108	18.3	61,824	-62.0	...	(d)	(d)	...
Putnam	237	Eatonton	345	18,812	14,137	33.1	114,912	80.3	26	1,718	111,455	59
Quitman	239	Georgetown	152	2,598	2,209	17.6	(d)	(d)	...	(d)	(d)	...
Rabun	241	Clayton	371	15,050	11,648	29.2	(d)	(d)	29	1,533	147,702	78
Randolph	243	Cuthbert	429	7,791	8,023	-2.9	23,110	-31.0	...	(d)	(d)	...
Richmond	245	Augusta	324	199,775	189,719	5.3	792,550	4.7	144	10,672	2,106,998	1,115
Rockdale	247	Conyers	131	70,111	54,091	29.6	1,305,402	6.1	97	6,156	740,767	392
Schley	249	Ellaville	168	3,766	3,588	5.0	(d)	(d)	9	601	83,912	44
Screven	251	Sylvania	648	15,374	13,842	11.1	6,152	-37.3	17	1,046	59,825	32
Seminole	253	Donalsonville	238	9,369	9,010	4.0	49,909	-39.9	...	(d)	(d)	...
Spalding	255	Griffin	198	58,417	54,457	7.3	(d)	(d)	64	5,297	653,759	346
Stephens	257	Toccoa	179	25,435	23,257	9.4	52,382	3.0	57	2,944	238,648	126
Stewart	259	Lumpkin	459	5,252	5,654	-7.1	(d)	(d)	...	(d)	(d)	...
Sumter	261	Americus	485	33,200	30,228	9.8	(d)	(d)	34	2,397	311,183	165
Talbot	263	Talbotton	393	6,498	6,524	-0.4	(d)	(d)	...	(d)	(d)	...
Taliaferro	265	Crawfordville	195	2,077	1,915	8.5	(d)	(d)	...	(d)	(d)	...
Tattnall	267	Reidsville	484	22,305	17,722	25.9	74,752	28.1	...	(d)	(d)	...
Taylor	269	Butler	377	8,815	7,642	15.3	(d)	(d)	...	(d)	(d)	...
Telfair	271	McRae	441	11,794	11,000	7.2	47,658	-11.1	11	(d)	(d)	...
Terrell	273	Dawson	335	10,970	10,653	3.0	52,049	-58.6	...	(d)	(d)	...
Thomas	275	Thomasville	548	42,737	38,986	9.6	318,763	8.8	59	3,499	239,922	127
Tift	277	Tifton	265	38,407	34,998	9.7	383,364	-16.6	57	3,461	271,607	144
Toombs	279	Lyons	367	26,067	24,072	8.3	(d)	(d)	34	1,528	74,710	40
Towns	281	Hiawassee	167	9,319	6,754	38.0	3,605	(d)	...	(d)	(d)	...
Treutlen	283	Soperton	201	6,854	5,994	14.3	(d)	(d)	...	(d)	(d)	...
Troup	285	Lagrange	414	58,779	55,536	5.8	(d)	(d)	100	8,724	899,387	476
Turner	287	Ashburn	286	9,504	8,703	9.2	83,551	-59.0	...	(d)	(d)	...
Twiggs	289	Jeffersonville	360	10,590	9,806	8.0	(d)	(d)	...	(d)	(d)	...
Union	291	Blairsville	323	17,289	11,993	44.2	59,260	58.8	...	(d)	(d)	...
Upson	293	Thomaston	325	27,597	26,300	4.9	(d)	(d)	23	2,423	222,421	118
Walker	295	La Fayette	447	61,053	58,340	4.7	(d)	(d)	71	6,313	538,472	285
Walton	297	Monroe	329	60,687	38,586	57.3	258,434	7.7	49	2,095	218,962	116
Ware	299	Waycross	902	35,483	35,471	0.0	(d)	(d)	35	1,541	89,830	48
Warren	301	Warrenton	286	6,336	6,078	4.2	(d)	(d)	5	634	28,237	15
Washington	303	Sandersville	680	21,176	19,112	10.8	34,359	-9.1	...	(d)	(d)	...
Wayne	305	Jesup	645	26,565	22,356	18.8	59,506	17.4	25	1,662	278,291	147
Webster	307	Preston	210	2,390	2,263	5.6	2,037	(d)	...	(d)	(d)	...
Wheeler	309	Alamo	298	6,179	4,903	26.0	3,492	(d)	...	(d)	(d)	...
White	311	Cleveland	242	19,944	13,006	53.3	41,850	77.4	31	598	58,134	31
Whitfield	313	Dalton	290	83,525	72,462	15.3	(d)	(d)	354	22,462	2,563,777	1,356
Wilcox	315	Abbeville	380	8,577	7,008	22.4	5,405	(d)	...	(d)	(d)	...
Wilkes	317	Washington	471	10,687	10,597	0.8	27,678	-55.0	21	846	78,526	42
Wilkinson	319	Irwinton	447	10,220	10,228	-0.1	(d)	(d)	13	1,110	275,823	146
Worth	321	Sylvester	570	21,967	19,745	11.3	86,914	-26.8	...	(d)	(d)	...
The State			**57,906**	**8,186,453**	**6,478,216**	**26.4**	**201,091,040**	**22.8**	**8,805**	**452,625**	**59,651,286**	**31,560**

(d) Data not available. Corresponding percentages or Ranally Manufacturing Units are estimates.
... Represents 0 or amount too minimal to be reported.

Index of Places and Counties

A

Aaron; RMC Place; BULLOCH; ***166** I-11; elev. 264ft./80m.; mail Portal Z 30450; rural
Abba; RMC Place; IRWIN; ***167** L-7; mail Fitzgerald Z 31750; rural
Abbeville; Inc. Place; ⊡ WILCOX; **167** K-7; elev. 259ft./79m.; 🅿; Z 31001; Ⓟ 907; Ⓒ 2,298
Abbottsford; RMC Place; TROUP; ***166** H-2; mail Lagrange Z 30240; rural
Abercorn Heights; RMC Place; CHATHAM; ***167** K-13; ★ **SAV**; pop. incl. with Savannah (Inc. Place)
Aberdeen; RMC Place; FAYETTE; ***166** G-4; elev. 908ft./277m.; ★ **ATL**; mail Peachtree City Z 30269; pop. incl. with Peachtree City (Inc. Place)
Acree; RMC Place; DOUGHERTY; **167** L-5; elev. 232ft./71m.; ★ **ALB**; mail Sylvester Z 31791; ● 130
Acworth; Inc. Place; COBB; **166** E-4; elev. 913ft./278m.; 🅿; ★ **ATL**; Z 30101-02; Ⓟ 4,519; Ⓒ 13,422
Adairsville; Inc. Place; BARTOW; **166** D-3; elev. 714ft./218m.; 🅿; Z 30103; Ⓟ 2,131; Ⓒ 2,542
Adams Park; RMC Place; TWIGGS; ***166** I-7; mail Dry Branch Z 31020; rural
Adamsville; RMC Place; FULTON; ***166** E-4; ★ **ATL**; mail Atlanta Z 30331; pop. incl. with Atlanta (Inc. Place)
Adasburg; RMC Place; WILKES; ***166** F-9; elev. 524ft./160m.; mail Washington Z 30673; rural
Adel; Inc. Place; ⊡ COOK; **167** N-7; elev. 240ft./73m.; 🅿 🅷; Z 31620; Ⓟ 5,093; Ⓒ 5,307
Adgateville; RMC Place; JASPER; **166** G-6; elev. 660ft./201m.; mail Hillsboro Z 31038; ● 25
Adrian; Inc. Place; EMANUEL, JOHNSON; **166** I-9; elev. 286ft./87m.; 🅿; Z 31002; Ⓟ 615; Ⓒ 579
Agnes Scott College; RMC Place; DEKALB; ***166** E-5; ★ **ATL**; mail Decatur Z 30030; pop. incl. with Decatur (Inc. Place)
Agricola; RMC Place; GLASCOCK; ***166** G-9; mail Mitchell Z 30820; rural
Ailey; Inc. Place; MONTGOMERY; **166** J-9; elev. 254ft./77m.; 🅿; Z 30410; Ⓟ 579; Ⓒ 394; Ⓡ 527
Air Line; RMC Place; HART; **166** D-8; mail Bowersville Z 30516; ● 150
Akin; BULLOCH; see Akins (RMC Place)
Akins (Akin); RMC Place; BULLOCH; ***166** J-12; mail Brooklet Z 30415; rural
Alamo; Inc. Place; ⊡ WHEELER; **167** K-9; elev. 235ft./72m.; 🅿; Z 30411; Ⓟ 855; Ⓒ 1,943
Alapaha; Inc. Place; BERRIEN; **167** M-8; elev. 293ft./89m.; 🅿; Z 31622; Ⓟ 812; Ⓒ 682
Albany; Inc. Place; ⊡ DOUGHERTY; **167** L-5; elev. 208ft./63m.; 🅿 🅷 🅲 3,605 ■; ★ **ALB**; Z 31701-08, Z 31721; Ⓟ 78,122; Ⓒ 76,939; ◆ 78,664
Albion Acres; RMC Place; RICHMOND; ***166** F-11; ★ **AUG**; mail Augusta Z 30906; pop. incl. with Augusta (Inc. Place)
Alcovy; RMC Place; NEWTON; ***166** F-6; elev. 715ft./218m.; ★ **ATL**; mail Covington Z 30014; rural
Alcovy Shores; RMC Place; JASPER; ***166** G-6; mail Monticello Z 31064; ● 175
Aldora; Inc. Place; LAMAR; **166** H-5; elev. 870ft./265m.; mail Barnesville Z 30204; Ⓟ 127; Ⓒ 98
Alexander; RMC Place; BURKE; **166** H-11; elev. 289ft./88m.; mail Sardis Z 30456; ● 100
Alfords; RMC Place; WORTH; ***167** M-6; mail Sylvester Z 31791; rural
Aline; RMC Place; CANDLER; **166** J-10; mail Cobbtown Z 30420; ● 50
Allendale; RMC Place; GWINNETT; **167** T-1; ★ **ATL**; mail Lawrenceville Z 30045; ● 500
Allendale; RMC Place; MUSCOGEE; ***166** I-3; ★ **COL**; mail Columbus Z 31909; pop. incl. with Columbus (Inc. Place)
Allenhurst; Inc. Place; LIBERTY; **167** L-12; elev. 60ft./18m.; 🅿; Z 31301; Ⓟ 594; Ⓒ 788
Allentown; Inc. Place; WILKINSON, BLECKLEY, LAURENS, TWIGGS; **166** I-7; elev. 411ft./125m.; 🅿; Z 31003; Ⓟ 273; Ⓒ 287
Allenville; RMC Place; BERRIEN; ***167** N-8; elev. 231ft./70m.; mail Nashville Z 31639; rural
Allenwood; RMC Place; BALDWIN; ***166** H-7; mail Milledgeville Z 31061; pop. incl. with Milledgeville (Inc. Place)
Allie; RMC Place; MERIWETHER; ***166** H-4; mail Greenville Z 30222; rural
Alma; Inc. Place; ⊡ BACON; **167** M-10; elev. 201ft./61m.; 🅿 🅷; Z 31510; Ⓟ 3,663; Ⓒ 3,236
Almon; RMC Place; NEWTON; **166** F-6; elev. 704ft./215m.; ★ **ATL**; mail Covington Z 30014; ● 500
Alpharetta; Inc. Place; FULTON; **166** D-5; elev. 1,137ft./347m.; 🅿 🅲 743; ★ **ATL**; Z 30004-05, Z 30009, Z 30022-23; Ⓟ 13,002; Ⓒ 34,854; ◆ 46,742
Alpine; RMC Place; CHATTOOGA; ***166** C-2; mail Menlo Z 30731; rural
Alps Road; RMC Place; CLARKE; ***166** E-7; ★ **ATH**; mail Athens Z 30604; pop. incl. with Athens (Inc. Place)
Alston; Inc. Place; MONTGOMERY; **167** K-10; elev. 227ft./69m.; 🅿; Z 30412; Ⓟ 160; Ⓒ 159
Altamaha; RMC Place; TATTNALL; ***167** K-10; mail Reidsville Z 30453; rural
Alta Vista; RMC Place; MUSCOGEE; **167** T-2; ★ **COL**; mail Columbus Z 31907; pop. incl. with Columbus (Inc. Place)
Altman; RMC Place; SCREVEN, BANKS; **166** I-12; mail Sylvania Z 30467; ● 70
Alto; Inc. Place; HABERSHAM, BANKS; **166** C-7; elev. 1,394ft./425m.; 🅿; Z 30510; Ⓟ 651; Ⓒ 876
Alto Park; RMC Place; FLOYD; ***166** D-2; ★ **ROME**; mail Rome Z 30165; ● 500
Alvaton; RMC Place; MERIWETHER; **166** G-4; elev. 760ft./232m.; mail Gay Z 30218; ● 100
Amboy; RMC Place; TURNER; ***167** L-6; mail Ashburn Z 31714; rural
Ambrose; Inc. Place; COFFEE; **167** L-8; elev. 306ft./93m.; 🅿; Z 31512; Ⓟ 288; Ⓒ 320
Americus; Inc. Place; ⊡ SUMTER; **167** K-5; elev. 355ft./108m.; 🅿 🅷 🅲 2,457; Z 31709, Z 31719; Ⓟ 16,512; Ⓒ 17,013
Amity; RMC Place; LINCOLN; ***166** F-9; elev. 455ft./139m.; mail Lincolnton Z 30817; rural
Amos Mill; RMC Place; DADE; ***166** B-2; elev. 825ft./251m.; mail Fort Payne Z 35967; rural
Amsterdam; RMC Place; DECATUR; **167** O-4; mail Climax Z 39834; ● 100
Anderson City (Minton); RMC Place; WORTH; **167** M-6; elev. 410ft./125m.; mail Doerun Z 31744; ● 30
Andersonville; Inc. Place; SUMTER; **166** J-5; elev. 390ft./119m.; 🅿; Z 31711; Ⓟ 277; Ⓒ 331
Andrew Wood; RMC Place; MUSCOGEE; ***166** J-3; ★ **COL**; mail Columbus Z 31903; pop. incl. with Columbus (Inc. Place)
Anguilla; RMC Place; GLYNN; ***167** M-12; mail Brunswick Z 31525; rural
Ansley; RMC Place; WARREN; ***166** G-9; mail Warrenton Z 30828; rural
Anthony Terrace; RMC Place; BIBB; ★ **MAC**; mail Macon Z 31206; pop. incl. with Macon (Inc. Place)
Antioch; RMC Place; POLK; ***166** E-2; mail Cedartown Z 30125; rural
Antioch; RMC Place; TROUP; ***166** H-2; elev. 746ft./227m.; mail Lagrange Z 30240; rural
Aonia; RMC Place; WILKES; ***166** F-9; elev. 502ft./153m.; mail Washington Z 30673; rural
Apalachee; MONTGOMERY; see Uvalda (Inc. Place)
Apalachee; RMC Place; MORGAN; **166** F-7; elev. 643ft./196m.; mail Madison Z 30650; ● 160
Apple Valley; RMC Place; JACKSON; ***166** D-7; elev. 820ft./250m.; ★ **ATH**; mail Commerce Z 30529; rural
Appling; RMC Place; ⊡ COLUMBIA; **166** F-10; elev. 263ft./80m.; 🅿; Z 30802; ● 500
APPLING; **167** L-10; Ⓟ 15,744; Ⓒ 17,419; ◆ 18,297
Arabi; Inc. Place; CRISP; **167** L-6; elev. 445ft./136m.; 🅿; Z 31712; Ⓟ 433; Ⓒ 456
Aragon; Inc. Place; POLK; **166** E-3; elev. 748ft./228m.; 🅿; Z 30104; Ⓟ 902; Ⓒ 1,039
Aragon Park; RMC Place; RICHMOND; ***166** G-11; ★ **AUG**; mail Augusta Z 30901; pop. incl. with Augusta (Inc. Place)
Arcade; Inc. Place; JACKSON; **166** E-7; elev. 880ft./268m.; ★ **ATH**; mail Jefferson Z 30549; Ⓟ 697; Ⓒ 1,643
Arch City; RMC Place; GORDON; mail Calhoun Z 30701; ● 400
Arco; RMC Place; GLYNN; **167** S-12; elev. 17ft./5m.; ★ **BRUNS**; mail Brunswick Z 31520
Arcola; RMC Place; BULLOCH; ***166** J-12; elev. 126ft./38m.; mail Brooklet Z 30415
Ardick; RMC Place; MCINTOSH; ***167** M-12; elev. 16ft./5m.; mail Townsend Z 31331; ● 50
Ardmore; RMC Place; EFFINGHAM; ***166** I-12; mail Springfield Z 31329; rural
Ardsley Park; RMC Place; CHATHAM; ★ **SAV**; mail Savannah Z 31405; pop. incl. with Savannah (Inc. Place)
Argyle; Inc. Place; CLINCH; **167** N-9; elev. 162ft./49m.; 🅿; Z 31623; Ⓟ 206; Ⓒ 151
Arkwright (Holton); RMC Place; BIBB; ***166** H-6; ★ **MAC**; mail Macon Z 31204; ● 90
Arlington; RMC Place; BIBB; ★ **MAC**; mail Macon Z 31217; pop. incl. with Macon (Inc. Place)
Arlington; Inc. Place; CALHOUN, EARLY; **167** M-3; elev. 293ft./89m.; 🅿 🅷; Z 39813; Ⓟ 1,513; Ⓒ 1,602
Arlington Park; RMC Place; BIBB; ★ **MAC**; mail Macon Z 31204; pop. incl. with Macon (Inc. Place)
Armuchee; RMC Place; FLOYD; **166** C-2; elev. 643ft./196m.; 🅿; ★ **ROME**; Z 30105; ● 200
Arnco Mills; RMC Place; COWETA; **166** G-3; mail Newnan Z 30263; ● 500
Arnoldsville; Inc. Place; OGLETHORPE; **166** E-8; elev. 778ft./237m.; 🅿; ★ **ATH**; Z 30619; Ⓟ 275; Ⓒ 312
Arp; RMC Place; IRWIN; ***167** L-7; mail Rebecca Z 31783; ● 30
Arrowhead Village; RMC Place; CLAYTON; ***166** F-4; ★ **ATL**; mail Jonesboro Z 30236; ● 1,870
Ascalon; RMC Place; WALKER; ***166** B-2; elev. 1,935ft./590m.; ★ **CHTN**; mail Rising Fawn Z 30738; rural
Ashburn; Inc. Place; ⊡ TURNER; **167** L-6; elev. 450ft./137m.; 🅿; Z 31714; Ⓟ 4,827; Ⓒ 4,419
Ashford Park; RMC Place; DEKALB; ★ **ATL**; mail Atlanta Z 30319
Ashintilly; RMC Place; MCINTOSH; ***167** M-12; mail Townsend Z 31331; ● 100
Ashland; RMC Place; FRANKLIN; ***166** D-7; mail Carnesville Z 30521; rural
Ashley Estates; RMC Place; CLAYTON; ***166** F-4; elev. 933ft./284m.; ★ **ATL**; mail Riverdale Z 30274; ● 300
Athens (Athens-Clarke County); Inc. Place; ⊡ CLARKE; **166** E-7; elev. 775ft./236m.; 🅿 🅷 🅲 33,959 ■; ★ **ATH**; Z 30601-09, Z 30612; Ⓟ 45,734; Ⓒ 100,266; ◆ 117,272
Athens-Clarke County; CLARKE; see Athens (Inc. Place)
Atkinson; RMC Place; BRANTLEY; **167** N-11; mail Hortense Z 31543; ● 135
ATKINSON; **167** M-8; Ⓟ 6,213; Ⓒ 7,609; ◆ 8,387
Atlanta; Inc. Place; **STATE CAPITAL**; ⊡ FULTON, DEKALB; **166** E-4; elev. 1,050ft./320m.; 🅿 🅷 🅲 75,132 ■; ★ **ATL**; Z 30301-22, Z 30324-34, Z 30336-50, Z 30353-64, Z 30366, Z 30368-71, Z 30374-80, Z 30384-85, Z 30388, Z 30390, Z 30392, Z 30394, Z 30396, Z 30398, Z 31106-07, Z 31119, Z 31126, Z 31131, Z 31136, Z 31139, Z 31141, Z 31145-46, Z 31150, Z 31156, Z 31192-93, Z 31195-96, Z 39901; Ⓟ 394,017; Ⓒ 416,474; Ⓡ 416,267; ◆ 514,055
Attapulgus; Inc. Place; DECATUR; **167** O-4; elev. 310ft./94m.; 🅿; Z 39815; Ⓟ 380; Ⓒ 492
Attapulgus Station; RMC Place; DECATUR; ***167** O-4; elev. 180ft./55m.; mail Attapulgus Z 39815; ● 50
Attica; RMC Place; JACKSON; ***166** E-7; elev. 859ft./262m.; ★ **ATH**; mail Athens Z 30607; rural
Auburn; Inc. Place; BARROW, GWINNETT; **166** E-6; elev. 1,035ft./315m.; 🅿; Z 30011; Ⓟ 3,139; Ⓒ 6,904
Audubon; RMC Place; GORDON; ***166** C-3; elev. 691ft./211m.; mail Resaca Z 30735; rural
Augusta (Augusta-Richmond County); Inc. Place; ⊡ RICHMOND; **166** C-13; elev. 414ft./126m.; 🅿 🅷 🅲 9,713 ■; ★ **AUG**; Z 30901, Z 30903-07, Z 30909, Z 30912-14, Z 30916-17, Z 30919, Z 30999; Ⓟ 44,639; Ⓒ 195,182; ◆ 208,238
Augusta-Richmond County; RICHMOND; see Augusta (Inc. Place)
Aumond Heights; RMC Place; RICHMOND; ***166** F-11; elev. 344ft./105m.; ★ **AUG**; mail Augusta Z 30909; pop. incl. with Augusta (Inc. Place)
Auraria; RMC Place; LUMPKIN; **166** C-5; mail Dawsonville Z 30534; ● 50
Austell; Inc. Place; COBB, DOUGLAS; **166** E-4; elev. 918ft./280m.; 🅿 🅷; ★ **ATL**; Z 30106, Z 30168; Ⓟ 4,173; Ⓒ 5,359
Autreyville; RMC Place; COLQUITT; **167** N-6; elev. 249ft./76m.; mail Moultrie Z 31768, Z 31788; ● 75
Autumn Forest; RMC Place; CLAYTON; ***166** F-5; ★ **ATL**; mail Jonesboro Z 30236; ● 470
Avallon; RMC Place; FULTON; ***166** E-4; ★ **ATL**; mail Atlanta Z 30328; ● 160
Avalon; RMC Place; CHATHAM; ★ **SAV**; mail Savannah Z 31419; pop. incl. with Savannah (Inc. Place)
Avalon; Inc. Place; STEPHENS; **166** C-8; elev. 924ft./282m.; mail Martin Z 30557; Ⓟ 159; Ⓒ 278
Avans (Stephensville); RMC Place; DADE; ***166** B-2; ★ **CHTN**; mail Trenton Z 30752; rural
Avants; RMC Place; WHEELER; ***167** K-8; mail Alamo Z 30411; rural
Avera; Inc. Place; JEFFERSON; **166** G-9; 🅿; Z 30803; Ⓟ 215; Ⓒ 217
Avert Acres; RMC Place; DOUGHERTY; ***167** L-5; ★ **ALB**; mail Albany Z 31705; pop. incl. with Albany (Inc. Place)
Avery; RMC Place; CHEROKEE; ***166** D-4; elev. 1,124ft./343m.; ★ **ATL**; mail Canton Z 30115; rural
Avondale; RMC Place; BIBB; ***166** I-6; ★ **MAC**; mail Macon Z 31216; rural
Avondale; DEKALB; see Avondale Estates (Inc. Place)
Avondale; RMC Place; MCDUFFIE; ***166** G-10; mail Harlem Z 30814; rural
Avondale; RMC Place; MUSCOGEE; ***166** J-3; ★ **COL**; mail Columbus Z 31903; pop. incl. with Columbus (Inc. Place)
Avondale Estates (Avondale); Inc. Place; DEKALB; **168** E-5; elev. 1,075ft./328m.; 🅿; ★ **ATL**; Z 30002; Ⓟ 2,209; Ⓒ 2,609
Avondale Heights; RMC Place; MUSCOGEE; ***166** J-3; ★ **COL**; mail Columbus Z 31903; pop. incl. with Columbus (Inc. Place)
Avondale Park; RMC Place; CHATHAM; ***167** K-13; ★ **SAV**; mail Savannah Z 31404; pop. incl. with Savannah (Inc. Place)
Axson; RMC Place; ATKINSON; **167** M-9; elev. 178ft./54m.; 🅿; Z 31624; ● 200
Ayersville; RMC Place; STEPHENS; ***166** C-7; mail Toccoa Z 30577; rural
Azalea Park; RMC Place; BIBB; ★ **MAC**; mail Macon Z 31204; pop. incl. with Macon (Inc. Place)

B

Babcock; RMC Place; MILLER; **167** N-4; mail Colquitt Z 39837; ● 40
Bachlott; RMC Place; BRANTLEY; ***167** N-11; mail Nahunta Z 31553; rural
BACON; **167** L-9; Ⓟ 9,566; Ⓒ 10,103; ◆ 10,806
Baconton; Inc. Place; MITCHELL; **167** M-5; elev. 170ft./52m.; 🅿; Z 31716; Ⓟ 623; Ⓒ 804
Bainbridge; Inc. Place; ⊡ DECATUR; **167** O-4; elev. 135ft./41m.; 🅿 🅷; Z 39817-19; Ⓟ 10,712; Ⓒ 11,722
Bairdstown; RMC Place; OGLETHORPE; **166** F-8; mail Union Point Z 30669; ● 40
BAKER; **167** M-4; Ⓟ 3,615; Ⓒ 4,074; ◆ 3,467
Baker Village; RMC Place; MUSCOGEE; ***166** J-3; ★ **COL**; mail Columbus Z 31903; pop. incl. with Columbus (Inc. Place)
Baldwin; Inc. Place; HABERSHAM, BANKS; **166** C-7; elev. 1,470ft./448m.; 🅿; Z 30511; Ⓟ 1,439; Ⓒ 2,425
BALDWIN; **166** G-7; Ⓟ 39,530; Ⓒ 44,700; ◆ 47,269
Baldwin Park; RMC Place; CHATHAM; ***167** K-13; ★ **SAV**; mail Savannah Z 31401; pop. incl. with Savannah (Inc. Place)
Baldwinville; RMC Place; TALBOT; ***166** I-4; elev. 729ft./222m.; mail Junction City Z 31812; rural
Ball Ground; Inc. Place; CHEROKEE; **166** D-5; elev. 1,098ft./335m.; 🅿; Z 30107; Ⓟ 905; Ⓒ 730
Ball Ground; RMC Place; MURRAY; ***166** C-4; mail Chatsworth Z 30705; rural
Baltimore; RMC Place; WILKES; mail Washington Z 30673; pop. incl. with Washington (Inc. Place)
BANKS; **166** D-7; Ⓟ 10,308; Ⓒ 14,422; ◆ 17,135
Banks Crossing; RMC Place; BANKS; ***166** D-7; mail Commerce Z 30529; ● 200
Banning; RMC Place; CARROLL; **166** F-3; mail Whitesburg Z 30185; ● 150
Bannockburn; RMC Place; BERRIEN; ***167** M-8; elev. 226ft./69m.; mail Nashville Z 31639; rural
Barksdale; RMC Place; WASHINGTON; mail Sandersville Z 31082; rural
Barnesville; Inc. Place; ⊡ LAMAR; **166** H-5; elev. 870ft./265m.; 🅿; Z 30204; Ⓟ 4,747; Ⓒ 5,972
Barnett; RMC Place; WARREN; **166** F-9; mail Norwood Z 30821; ● 45
Barnett Shoals; RMC Place; OCONEE; ***166** E-7; ★ **ATH**; mail Athens Z 30605; rural
Barney; RMC Place; BROOKS; **167** N-7; elev. 239ft./73m.; 🅿; Z 31625; ● 150
Barneyville; RMC Place; COOK; ***167** N-7; mail Sparks Z 31647; rural
Barnhill; RMC Place; TREUTLEN; ***166** J-9; mail Soperton Z 30457; rural
Barnsley; RMC Place; BARTOW; ***166** D-3; mail Kingston Z 30145; rural
Barr; RMC Place; DOUGHERTY; pop. incl. with Albany (Inc. Place)
Barrett Parkway; RMC Place; COBB; ★ **ATL**; mail Kennesaw Z 30144; pop. incl. with Kennesaw (Inc. Place)
Barretts; RMC Place; LOWNDES; ***167** N-8; elev. 249ft./76m.; ★ **VALD**; mail Valdosta Z 31605; ● 100
Barrettsville; RMC Place; DAWSON; ***166** D-5; mail Dawsonville Z 30534; rural
BARROW; **166** E-6; Ⓟ 29,721; Ⓒ 46,144; ◆ 74,360
Barrow Heights; RMC Place; BARROW; ***166** E-6; mail Winder Z 30680; ● 210
Bartletts Ferry; RMC Place; HARRIS; ***166** I-3; mail Fortson Z 31808; ● 100
Barton Village; RMC Place; RICHMOND; ***166** G-11; ★ **AUG**; mail Augusta Z 30906; pop. incl. with Augusta (Inc. Place)
Bartonwoods; RMC Place; DEKALB; ★ **ATL**; mail Atlanta Z 30307; ● 400
Bartow; Inc. Place; JEFFERSON; **166** H-10; elev. 245ft./75m.; 🅿; Z 30413; Ⓟ 292; Ⓒ 223; Ⓡ 304
BARTOW; **166** D-3; Ⓟ 55,911; Ⓒ 76,019; ◆ 95,528
Barwick; Inc. Place; THOMAS, BROOKS; **167** O-6; elev. 250ft./76m.; 🅿; Z 31720; Ⓟ 385; Ⓒ 444
Bascom; RMC Place; SCREVEN; ***166** H-12; elev. 118ft./36m.; mail Sylvania Z 30467; rural
Bass Crossroads (Draneville); RMC Place; TROUP; ***166** G-3; elev. 723ft./220m.; mail Hogansville Z 30230; rural
Batesville; RMC Place; HABERSHAM; ***166** B-7; elev. 1,676ft./511m.; mail Clarkesville Z 30523; rural
Bath; RMC Place; RICHMOND; ***166** G-10; ★ **AUG**; mail Blythe Z 30805; pop. incl. with Augusta (Inc. Place)
Battery Point; RMC Place; CHATHAM; ★ **SAV**; mail Savannah Z 31404
Battle Forest; RMC Place; DEKALB; ***166** F-5; ★ **ATL**; mail Decatur Z 30034; ● 200
Baughs Crossroads; RMC Place; TROUP; ***166** H-3; elev. 727ft./222m.; mail West Point Z 31833; rural
Baxley; Inc. Place; ⊡ APPLING; **167** L-10; elev. 206ft./63m.; 🅿 🅷; Z 31513, Z 31515; Ⓟ 3,841; Ⓒ 4,150
Bay; RMC Place; COLQUITT; ***167** N-6; mail Hartsfield Z 31756, Moultrie Z 31768; ● 100

Entries in **UPPERCASE** are counties.
Entries in **bold** have populations of 2,500 or more.
Names in parentheses are alternate names.

Inc. Place	Incorporated Place
RMC Place	Rand McNally Designated Place
CDP	Census Designated Place
MCD	Minor Civil Division
⊡	County Seat
▲	Minor Civil Division
elev.	Elevation
🅿	Post Office
🅷	Hospital
🅲	College
■	Principal Business Center
★	Ranally Metro Area (RMA) Abbreviation
Z	Zip Code(s)
Ⓟ	Previous Census Population
Ⓡ	Revised Census Population
Ⓐ	Annexation Population
●	Rand McNally Population Estimate
Ⓒ	Final Census Population
Ⓢ	Special Census Population
◆	Estimated Population

For additional definitions see Glossary, Volume 1, and Introduction, Volume 2.

Bay Branch; RMC Place; SCREVEN; *166 I-11; mail Sylvania z 30467; rural
Bayview; RMC Place; LONG; mail Ludowici z 31316; rural
Beach; RMC Place; WARE; *167 M-9; elev. 168ft./51m.; mail Nicholls z 31554; rural
Beachton; RMC Place; GRADY; *167 O-5; elev. 276ft./84m.; mail Thomasville z 31792; rural
Beacon Heights; RMC Place; MORGAN; 166 F-7; mail Madison z 30650; pop. incl. with Madison (Inc. Place)
Beallwood; RMC Place; MUSCOGEE; *166 I-3; ★ COL; mail Columbus z 31904; pop. incl. with Columbus (Inc. Place)
Beaulieu; RMC Place; CHATHAM; *167 K-13; ★ SAV; mail Savannah z 31406; ● 275
Beaumont; CATOOSA; see Beaumount (RMC Place)
Beaumount (Beaumont); RMC Place; CATOOSA; *166 B-2; ★ CHTN; mail Ringgold z 30736; rural
Beaverdale; RMC Place; WHITFIELD; *166 B-3; mail Dalton z 30721; rural
Bedingfield; RMC Place; BIBB; ★ MAC; mail Macon z 31206; pop. incl. with Macon (Inc. Place)
Belair; RMC Place; RICHMOND; *166 G-10; elev. 306ft./93m.; ★ AUG; mail Augusta z 30907; pop. incl. with Augusta (Inc. Place)
Belair Hills Estates; RMC Place; RICHMOND; *166 F-10; ★ AUG; mail Augusta z 30909; pop. incl. with Augusta (Inc. Place)
Belfast; RMC Place; BRYAN; 167 L-13; elev. 15ft./5m.; mail Richmond Hill z 31324; ● 250
Bellemeade; RMC Place; RICHMOND; *166 G-11; ★ AUG; mail Augusta z 30906; pop. incl. with Augusta (Inc. Place)
Bellevue; RMC Place; BIBB; 167 R-5; ★ MAC; pop. incl. with Macon (Inc. Place)
Bellton; RMC Place; HALL, BANKS; mail Lula z 30554; pop. incl. with Lula (Inc. Place)
Bellville; RMC Place; CLAY; 167 L-3; mail Bluffton z 39824; rural
Bellville; Inc. Place; EVANS; 167 K-11; elev. 185ft./56m.; 🅿; z 30414; Ⓟ 192; Ⓒ 130
Bellville Bluff; RMC Place; MCINTOSH; mail Townsend z 31331; ● 200
Belmont; RMC Place; DEKALB; *166 F-5; elev. 958ft./292m.; ★ ATL; mail Stone Mountain z 30086; ● 300
Belmont; RMC Place; HALL; *166 D-6; elev. 1,137ft./347m.; mail Gainesville z 30507; ● 150
Belvedere; RMC Place; DEKALB; 168 E-5; ★ ATL; mail Decatur z 30032; ● 6,000
Belvedere Park; CDP; DEKALB; *166 F-5; elev. 1,000ft./305m.; ★ ATL; mail Decatur z 30032; Ⓟ 18,089; Ⓒ 18,945
Belvins Acres; CATOOSA; see Blevins Acre (RMC Place)
Bemiss; RMC Place; LOWNDES; 167 N-7; elev. 242ft./74m.; ★ VALD; mail Valdosta z 31605; ● 200
Benedict; RMC Place; POLK; *166 E-2; mail Cedartown z 30125; ● 400
Benevolence; RMC Place; RANDOLPH; 167 K-3; elev. 530ft./162m.; mail Cuthbert z 39840; ● 50
Ben Hill; RMC Place; FULTON; *166 F-4; elev. 962ft./293m.; ★ ATL; mail Atlanta z 30331, z 31131; pop. incl. with Atlanta (Inc. Place)
BEN HILL; 167 L-8; Ⓟ 16,245; Ⓒ 17,484; ◆ 17,961
Benning Hills; RMC Place; MUSCOGEE; 167 S-3; ★ COL; mail Columbus z 31903; pop. incl. with Columbus (Inc. Place)
Bentley Place; RMC Place; WALKER; mail Rossville z 30741; ● 300
Benton; RMC Place; FLOYD; *166 D-2; ★ ROME; mail Rome z 30165; ● 600
Bent Tree; RMC Place; PICKENS; *166 C-5; mail Jasper z 30143; ● 200
Berckman Hills; RMC Place; RICHMOND; *166 F-11; elev. 250ft./76m.; ★ AUG; mail Augusta z 30909; pop. incl. with Augusta (Inc. Place)
Berckman Village; RMC Place; RICHMOND; *166 F-11; ★ AUG; mail Augusta z 30909; pop. incl. with Augusta (Inc. Place)
Berkeley Lake; Inc. Place; GWINNETT; *166 E-5; elev. 1,050ft./320m.; 🅿; ★ ATL; z 30092, z 30096; Ⓟ 791; Ⓒ 1,695
Berkshire Woods; RMC Place; CHATHAM; ★ SAV; mail Savannah z 31419; pop. incl. with Savannah (Inc. Place)
Berlin; Inc. Place; COLQUITT; 167 N-6; elev. 266ft./81m.; 🅿; z 31722; Ⓟ 480; Ⓒ 595
Berner; RMC Place; MONROE; *166 G-6; mail Forsyth z 31029; rural
BERRIEN; 167 M-7; Ⓟ 14,153; Ⓒ 16,235; ◆ 16,684
Berryton; RMC Place; CHATTOOGA; 166 C-2; elev. 640ft./195m.; mail Summerville z 30747; ● 100
Berzelia; RMC Place; COLUMBIA; *166 G-10; ★ AUG; mail Harlem z 30814; ● 60
Bethany; RMC Place; BAKER; *167 M-4; elev. 207ft./63m.; mail Leary z 39862; rural
Bethel; RMC Place; JASPER; *166 G-6; elev. 728ft./222m.; mail Monticello z 31064; rural
Bethel; RMC Place; RANDOLPH; mail Cuthbert z 39840; rural
Bethesda; RMC Place; CHATHAM; *167 K-13; ★ SAV; mail Savannah z 31406; rural
Bethesda; RMC Place; GREENE; *166 F-8; mail Union Point z 30669; rural
Bethesda; RMC Place; GWINNETT; *166 E-5; ★ ATL; mail Lawrenceville z 30045; ● 2,400
Bethlehem; Inc. Place; BARROW; 166 E-6; elev. 833ft./254m.; 🅿; z 30620; Ⓟ 348; Ⓒ 716
Between; Inc. Place; WALTON; 166 E-6; ★ ATL; mail Monroe z 30656; Ⓟ 82; Ⓒ 148
Beulah (Sheba); RMC Place; HANCOCK; *166 G-8; elev. 680ft./207m.; mail Sparta z 31087; rural
Beulah; RMC Place; LINCOLN, WILKES; 166 E-9; elev. 467ft./142m.; mail Tignall z 30668; ● 80
Beulah; RMC Place; PAULDING; *166 E-3; mail Rockmart z 30153; rural
Beulah Heights; RMC Place; FULTON; *166 F-5; ★ ATL; mail Atlanta z 30316; pop. incl. with Atlanta (Inc. Place)
Beverly Hills; RMC Place; WALKER; *166 B-2; ★ CHTN; mail Rossville z 30741; ● 1,000
Bexton; RMC Place; COWETA; *166 G-4; mail Moreland z 30259; rural
BIBB; 166 I-6; Ⓟ 149,967; Ⓒ 153,887; ◆ 153,419
Bibb City; RMC Place; MUSCOGEE; 167 R-2; elev. 300ft./91m.; ★ COL; mail Columbus z 31904; former incorporated place; became part of Columbus January 1, 2001; pop. incl. with Columbus (Inc. Place); Ⓟ 597; Ⓒ 510
Bibb Mills (Ensign Mills); RMC Place; MONROE; mail Forsyth z 31029; ● 200
Bickley; RMC Place; WARE; *167 M-9; elev. 163ft./50m.; mail Nicholls z 31554; rural
Big Canoe; RMC Place; PICKENS, DAWSON; *166 C-5; 🅿; z 30143; rural
Big Creek; RMC Place; FORSYTH; *166 D-5; ★ ATL; mail Cumming z 30041; rural
Big Sandy; WILKINSON; see Nicklesville (RMC Place)
Big Spring; TROUP; see Big Springs (RMC Place)
Big Springs (Big Spring); RMC Place; TROUP; *166 H-3; elev. 788ft./240m.; mail Lagrange z 30241; rural
Billarp; RMC Place; DOUGLAS; 166 F-3; elev. 1,104ft./336m.; ★ ATL; mail Winston z 30187; ● 30
Bingville; RMC Place; CHATHAM; *167 K-13; ★ SAV; mail Savannah z 31403, z 31405; pop. incl. with Savannah (Inc. Place)
Birdie; RMC Place; SPALDING; *166 G-5; mail Griffin z 30223; rural
Birmingham; RMC Place; FULTON; 166 D-5; elev. 1,063ft./324m.; ★ ATL; mail Alpharetta z 30004; ● 200
Bishop; Inc. Place; OCONEE; 166 E-7; elev. 782ft./238m.; 🅿; ★ ATH; z 30621; Ⓟ 158; Ⓒ 146
Blackjack; RMC Place; COWETA; *166 G-4; mail Senoia z 30276; rural
Blackshear; Inc. Place; ⊡ PIERCE; 167 M-10; elev. 120ft./37m.; 🅿; z 31516; Ⓟ 3,263; Ⓒ 3,283
Blackshear Place; RMC Place; HALL; 166 D-6; elev. 1,270ft./387m.; mail Gainesville z 30507; ● 500
Blacksville; CDP; HENRY; 166 G-5; ★ ATL; mail McDonough z 30253; Ⓟ 1,112; Ⓒ 4
Blackville; RMC Place; TREUTLEN; *166 J-9; mail Soperton z 30457; rural
Blackwells; RMC Place; COBB; 166 E-4; elev. 1,116ft./340m.; ★ ATL; mail Marietta z 30066; ● 5,000
Blackwood; RMC Place; GORDON; *166 C-3; mail Calhoun z 30701; rural
Blaine; RMC Place; PICKENS; *166 C-4; elev. 1,110ft./338m.; mail Talking Rock z 30175; rural
Blairsville; Inc. Place; ⊡ UNION; 166 B-6; elev. 1,892ft./577m.; 🅿 🅷; z 30512, z 30514; Ⓟ 564; Ⓒ 659
Blair Village; RMC Place; FULTON; *166 F-4; ★ ATL; mail Atlanta z 30354; pop. incl. with Atlanta (Inc. Place)
Blakely; Inc. Place; ⊡ EARLY; 167 M-3; elev. 275ft./84m.; 🅿 🅷; z 39823; Ⓟ 5,595; Ⓒ 5,696
Blalock; RABUN; see Persimmon (RMC Place)
Blandford; RMC Place; EFFINGHAM; *166 J-13; ★ SAV; mail Rincon z 31326
Bland Villa; RMC Place; CRISP; 167 K-6; mail Cordele z 31015; pop. incl. with Cordele (Inc. Place)
Blandy; RMC Place; BALDWIN; *166 H-7; mail Milledgeville z 31061
BLECKLEY; 166 J-7; Ⓟ 10,430; Ⓒ 11,666; ◆ 13,234
Blevins Acre (Belvins Acres); RMC Place; CATOOSA; *166 B-2; ★ CHTN; mail Ringgold z 30736; ● 600
Blitchton; RMC Place; BRYAN; 166 J-12; elev. 76ft./23m.; mail Ellabell z 31308; ● 250
Bloomfield Gardens; RMC Place; BIBB; *166 I-6; ★ MAC; mail Macon z 31216; pop. incl. with Macon (Inc. Place)
Bloomingdale; Inc. Place; CHATHAM; 167 K-13; elev. 22ft./7m.; 🅿; ★ SAV; z 31302; Ⓟ 2,271; Ⓒ 2,665
Blount; RMC Place; MONROE; *166 G-6; mail Forsyth z 31029; rural
Blowing Spring (Blowing Springs); RMC Place; WALKER; *166 B-2; ★ CHTN; mail Flintstone z 30725; ● 75
Blowing Springs; WALKER; see Blowing Spring (RMC Place)
Blue Ridge; Inc. Place; ⊡ FANNIN; 166 B-5; elev. 1,750ft./533m.; 🅿 🅷; z 30513; Ⓟ 1,336; Ⓒ 1,210
Blue Spring; RMC Place; CATOOSA; *166 B-2; ★ CHTN; mail Ringgold z 30736; rural
Blue Springs; RMC Place; DOUGHERTY; *167 M-5; ★ ALB; mail Albany z 31707; ● 500
Blue Springs; RMC Place; SCREVEN; *166 I-12; mail Newington z 30446; rural
Bluffton; Inc. Place; CLAY; 167 M-3; elev. 331ft./101m.; 🅿; z 39824; Ⓟ 138; Ⓒ 118
Blun; RMC Place; EMANUEL; *166 I-10; elev. 301ft./92m.; mail Swainsboro z 30401; rural
Blundale; RMC Place; EMANUEL; *166 I-10; elev. 387ft./118m.; mail Swainsboro z 30401; rural
Blythe; Inc. Place; RICHMOND, BURKE; 166 G-10; 🅿; z 30805; Ⓟ 300; Ⓒ 718
Bogart; Inc. Place; OCONEE, CLARKE; 166 E-7; elev. 820ft./250m.; 🅿; ★ ATH; z 30622; Ⓟ 1,018; Ⓒ 1,049; Ⓡ 1,086
Bold Spring; WALTON; see Bold Springs (RMC Place)
Bold Springs (Bold Spring); RMC Place; WALTON; *166 E-6; mail Monroe z 30656; rural
Bolingbroke; RMC Place; MONROE; 166 H-6; elev. 568ft./173m.; 🅿; z 31004; ● 150
Bolton; RMC Place; FULTON; *166 E-4; ★ ATL; mail Atlanta z 30318; pop. incl. with Atlanta (Inc. Place)
Bona Bella; RMC Place; CHATHAM; *167 K-13; elev. 25ft./8m.; ★ SAV; mail Savannah z 31406; ● 1,100
Bonair; RMC Place; COLUMBIA; *166 F-10; ★ AUG; mail Augusta z 30907
Bonaire; RMC Place; HOUSTON; 166 I-7; elev. 348ft./106m.; 🅿; ★ MAC; z 31005; ● 900
Bonanza; CDP; CLAYTON; *166 F-5; ★ ATL; mail Jonesboro z 30238; Ⓟ 2,010; Ⓒ 2,904
Bond; RMC Place; MADISON; *166 D-8; mail Danielsville z 30633; rural
Boneville; RMC Place; MCDUFFIE; 166 G-10; elev. 462ft./141m.; 🅿; z 30806; ● 230
Bonny Brook Estates; RMC Place; FULTON; *166 F-4; ★ ATL; mail Atlanta z 30311; pop. incl. with Atlanta (Inc. Place)
Booker Washington Heights; RMC Place; MUSCOGEE; ★ COL; mail Columbus z 31909; pop. incl. with Columbus (Inc. Place)
Boozeville; RMC Place; FLOYD; *166 D-2; elev. 690ft./210m.; ★ ROME; mail Lindale z 30147; ● 70
Boston; Inc. Place; THOMAS; 167 O-6; elev. 200ft./61m.; 🅿; z 31626; Ⓟ 1,395; Ⓒ 1,417
Bostwick; Inc. Place; MORGAN; 166 F-7; elev. 755ft./230m.; 🅿; z 30623; Ⓟ 307; Ⓒ 322
Bowden Hills; RMC Place; BIBB; *166 H-7; ★ MAC; mail Macon z 31217
Bowdon; Inc. Place; CARROLL; 166 F-2; elev. 1,096ft./334m.; 🅿 🅷; z 30108; Ⓟ 1,981; Ⓒ 1,959
Bowdon Junction; RMC Place; CARROLL; 166 F-2; elev. 1,244ft./379m.; 🅿; z 30109; ● 400
Bowens Mill; RMC Place; BEN HILL; 167 L-8; mail Fitzgerald z 31750; ● 90
Bowersville; Inc. Place; HART; 166 D-8; elev. 934ft./285m.; 🅿; z 30516; Ⓟ 311; Ⓒ 334
Bowman; Inc. Place; ELBERT; 166 D-8; elev. 783ft./239m.; 🅿; z 30624; Ⓟ 791; Ⓒ 898
Box Springs; RMC Place; TALBOT; 166 I-4; 🅿; z 31801; ● 200
Boyd Highlands; RMC Place; CATOOSA; *166 B-2; elev. 400ft./122m.; ★ CHTN; mail Ringgold z 30736; ● 150
Boydville; RMC Place; STEPHENS; *166 C-7; elev. 836ft./255m.; mail Toccoa z 30577; rural
Boykin; RMC Place; MILLER; 167 N-4; elev. 136ft./41m.; mail Colquitt z 39837; ● 150
Boynton; RMC Place; CATOOSA; *166 B-2; ★ CHTN; mail Ringgold z 30736; ● 300
Boys Estate; RMC Place; GLYNN; *167 M-12; ★ BRUNS; mail Brunswick z 31523; ● 80
Bradley; RMC Place; JONES; 166 H-7; elev. 624ft./190m.; ★ MAC; mail Gray z 31032; ● 90
Branchville; RMC Place; MITCHELL; *167 N-5; mail Camilla z 31730; rural
Brantley; RMC Place; MARION; *166 J-4; mail Buena Vista z 31803; rural
BRANTLEY; 167 M-11; Ⓟ 11,077; Ⓒ 14,629; ◆ 15,377
Braselton; Inc. Place; JACKSON; 166 D-6; 🅿; z 30517; Ⓟ 418; Ⓒ 1,206
Braswell; Inc. Place; POLK, PAULDING; 166 E-3; elev. 1,056ft./322m.; mail Rockmart z 30153; Ⓟ 247; Ⓒ 80
Bremen; Inc. Place; HARALSON, CARROLL; 166 F-2; elev. 1,424ft./434m.; 🅿 🅷; z 30110; Ⓟ 4,356; Ⓒ 4,579
Brent; RMC Place; MONROE; *166 H-5; mail Forsyth z 31029; rural
Brentwood; RMC Place; DOUGHERTY; *167 L-5; ★ ALB; mail Albany z 31721; pop. incl. with Albany (Inc. Place)
Brentwood; RMC Place; FULTON; *166 F-4; ★ ATL; mail Atlanta z 30331; pop. incl. with Atlanta (Inc. Place)
Brentwood; RMC Place; WAYNE; *167 L-11; elev. 167ft./51m.; mail Odum z 31555; rural
Brest; MITCHELL; see Lester (RMC Place)
Brewton; RMC Place; LAURENS; 166 I-9; elev. 240ft./73m.; mail Dublin z 31021; ● 200
Briarcliff; RMC Place; DEKALB; *166 E-5; elev. 997ft./304m.; ★ ATL; mail Atlanta z 30329, z 30345, z 30359
Briarwood; RMC Place; CHATHAM; ★ SAV; mail Savannah z 31408; pop. incl. with Savannah (Inc. Place)
Briarwood; RMC Place; COLUMBIA; *166 F-10; ★ AUG; mail Augusta z 30907
Briarwood; RMC Place; ROCKDALE; *166 F-5; ★ ATL; mail Conyers z 30094; ● 200
Briar Wood Estates; RMC Place; COBB; 168 A-1; ★ ATL; mail Marietta z 30068; ● 750
Brick Store; RMC Place; NEWTON; *166 F-6; elev. 849ft./259m.; mail Social Circle z 30025; rural
Bridgeboro; RMC Place; WORTH; 167 M-5; elev. 410ft./125m.; 🅿; z 31705; ● 100
Bridgeman Heights; RMC Place; BIBB; *166 H-7; ★ MAC; mail Macon z 31217; ● 200
Brighton; RMC Place; TIFT; *167 M-7; mail Tifton z 31794; rural
Brighton Woods; RMC Place; CHATHAM; *167 K-13; ★ SAV; mail Pooler z 31322; pop. incl. with Pooler (Inc. Place)
Brinson; Inc. Place; DECATUR; 167 N-3; elev. 120ft./37m.; 🅿; z 39825; Ⓟ 238; Ⓒ 225
Brisbon; RMC Place; BRYAN; *167 K-13; mail Richmond Hill z 31324; rural
Bristol; RMC Place; PIERCE; 167 M-10; elev. 148ft./45m.; 🅿; z 31518; ● 200
Bristol Forest; RMC Place; BIBB; *166 H-7; ★ MAC; mail Macon z 31217; pop. incl. with Macon (Inc. Place)
Bristol Woods; RMC Place; ROCKDALE; *166 F-5; elev. 790ft./241m.; ★ ATL; mail Conyers z 30094; ● 250
Broad; RMC Place; WILKES; *166 E-9; elev. 529ft./161m.; mail Tignall z 30668; rural
Broadhurst; RMC Place; WAYNE; *167 M-11; mail Jesup z 31545; rural
Broadview; RMC Place; FULTON; *166 E-5; ★ ATL; mail Atlanta z 30324, z 30376; pop. incl. with Atlanta (Inc. Place)
Brockton; RMC Place; JACKSON; *166 D-7; elev. 818ft./249m.; ★ ATH; mail Jefferson z 30549; rural
Bronco; RMC Place; WALKER; *166 C-2; mail La Fayette z 30728; rural
Bronwood; Inc. Place; TERRELL; 167 L-4; elev. 367ft./112m.; 🅿; z 39826; Ⓟ 513; Ⓒ 513
Brookfield; RMC Place; TIFT; 167 M-7; elev. 328ft./100m.; 🅿; z 31727; ● 450
Brookfield West; RMC Place; RICHMOND; *166 F-11; ★ AUG; mail Augusta z 30907; pop. incl. with Augusta (Inc. Place)
Brookhaven; RMC Place; BIBB; *166 H-6; ★ MAC; mail Macon z 31206; ● 130
Brookhaven; RMC Place; DEKALB; 168 C-4; ★ ATL; mail Atlanta z 30319; ● 7,000
Brookhaven; RMC Place; FULTON; ★ ATL; mail Atlanta z 31119; pop. incl. with Atlanta (Inc. Place)
Brookhaven; RMC Place; MUSCOGEE; *166 I-3; ★ COL; mail Columbus z 31906; pop. incl. with Columbus (Inc. Place)
Brooklet; Inc. Place; BULLOCH; 166 J-12; elev. 156ft./48m.; 🅿; z 30415; Ⓟ 1,013; Ⓒ 1,113
Brooklyn; RMC Place; STEWART; 166 J-4; mail Richland z 31825; ● 65
Brooks; Inc. Place; FAYETTE; 166 G-4; elev. 830ft./253m.; 🅿; z 30205; Ⓟ 328; Ⓒ 553
BROOKS; 167 O-7; Ⓟ 15,398; Ⓒ 16,450; ◆ 16,338
Brookstone; RMC Place; COBB; ★ ATL; mail Acworth z 30101; pop. incl. with Acworth (Inc. Place)
Brookstone; RMC Place; MUSCOGEE; *166 I-3; ★ COL; mail Columbus z 31904; pop. incl. with Columbus (Inc. Place)
Brookstore Place; RMC Place; FULTON; ★ ATL; mail Atlanta z 30342; rural
Brooksville; RMC Place; RANDOLPH; *167 K-4; mail Cuthbert z 39840; rural
Brookton; RMC Place; HALL; *166 C-6; mail Gainesville z 30506; ● 70
Brookvale Estates; RMC Place; CATOOSA; *166 B-2; ★ CHTN; mail Ringgold z 30736; ● 960
Brookview; RMC Place; CHATHAM; *167 K-13; ★ SAV; mail Savannah z 31406; pop. incl. with Savannah (Inc. Place)
Brookwood; DEKALB; see Eastwood (RMC Place)
Brookwood; RMC Place; FORSYTH; *166 D-5; ★ ATL; mail Alpharetta z 30005; rural
Brookwood; RMC Place; LAURENS; mail Dublin z 31021; pop. incl. with Dublin (Inc. Place)
Brookwood; RMC Place; RICHMOND; *166 G-11; ★ AUG; mail Augusta z 30909; pop. incl. with Augusta (Inc. Place)
Brookwood Apartments; RMC Place; BIBB; ★ MAC; pop. incl. with Macon (Inc. Place)
Brown Crossing (Browns); RMC Place; BALDWIN; *166 H-7; mail Milledgeville z 31061; rural
Browndale; RMC Place; PULASKI; *166 J-7; mail Hawkinsville z 31036; rural
Browns; BALDWIN; see Brown Crossing (RMC Place)
Browns; RMC Place; DADE; mail Trenton z 30752; rural
Brownsville; RMC Place; PAULDING; *166 E-3; elev. 1,050ft./320m.; ★ ATL; mail Douglasville z 30133; rural
Browntown; RMC Place; BRANTLEY; *167 M-11; mail Hortense z 31543; rural
Brownwood; RMC Place; MORGAN; *166 F-7; elev. 682ft./208m.; mail Madison z 30650; rural
Broxton; Inc. Place; COFFEE; 167 L-8; elev. 265ft./81m.; 🅿; z 31519; Ⓟ 1,211; Ⓒ 1,428
Brunswick; Inc. Place; ⊡ GLYNN; 167 N-12; elev. 10ft./3m.; 🅿 🅷 ■; ★ BRUNS; z 31520-25, z 31527, z 31561; Ⓟ 16,433; Ⓒ 15,600; ◆ 16,980
BRYAN; 167 K-12; Ⓟ 15,438; Ⓒ 23,417; ◆ 32,420
Brynwood; RMC Place; RICHMOND; *166 F-11; ★ AUG; mail Augusta z 30909; pop. incl. with Augusta (Inc. Place)
Buchanan; Inc. Place; ⊡ HARALSON; 166 E-2; elev. 1,258ft./383m.; 🅿; z 30113; Ⓟ 1,009; Ⓒ 941
Buckhead; RMC Place; FULTON; *166 E-5; ★ ATL; mail Atlanta z 30326; pop. incl. with Atlanta (Inc. Place)
Buckhead; Inc. Place; MORGAN; 166 F-7; elev. 626ft./191m.; 🅿; z 30625; Ⓟ 176; Ⓒ 205
Bucktown; RMC Place; CARROLL; *166 F-2; mail Bowdon z 30108; rural
Budapest; RMC Place; HARALSON; *166 F-2; mail Tallapoosa z 30176; rural
Buena Vista; Inc. Place; ⊡ MARION; 166 J-4; elev. 657ft./200m.; 🅿; z 31803; Ⓟ 1,472; Ⓒ 1,664
Buffington; RMC Place; CHEROKEE; *166 D-4; ★ ATL; mail Canton z 30114
Buford; Inc. Place; GWINNETT, HALL; 166 D-5; elev. 1,187ft./362m.; 🅿; ★ ATL; z 30515, z 30518-19; Ⓟ 8,771; Ⓒ 10,668
Bullard; RMC Place; TWIGGS; 166 I-7; elev. 372ft./113m.; mail Dry Branch z 31020; ● 100
BULLOCH; 166 J-11; Ⓟ 43,125; Ⓒ 55,983; ◆ 68,697
Bulloch Crossroads; RMC Place; MERIWETHER; *166 H-4; elev. 883ft./269m.; mail Manchester z 31816; pop. incl. with Manchester (Inc. Place)
Bumphead; RMC Place; SCHLEY; *166 J-5; mail Americus z 31719, Ellaville z 31806; rural
Bunker Hill; RMC Place; UNION; *166 B-5; mail Blairsville z 30512
BURKE; 166 H-11; Ⓟ 20,579; Ⓒ 22,243; ◆ 22,757
Burning Bush; RMC Place; CATOOSA; *166 B-2; ★ CHTN; mail Ringgold z 30736; rural
Burnside; RMC Place; CHATHAM; *167 K-13; elev. 5ft./2m.; ★ SAV; mail Savannah z 31406; ● 175
Burnside Island; RMC Place; CHATHAM; *167 K-13; elev. 17ft./5m.; ★ SAV; mail Savannah z 31406; ● 500
Burroughs; RMC Place; CHATHAM; 167 Q-11; ★ SAV; mail Savannah z 31405; ● 300
Burwell; RMC Place; CARROLL; *166 F-2; mail Carrollton z 30117; rural
Bushnell; RMC Place; COFFEE; *167 L-8; elev. 294ft./90m.; mail Douglas z 31533; rural
Butler; RMC Place; DOUGHERTY; ★ ALB; mail Albany z 31705; ● 50
Butler; Inc. Place; ⊡ TAYLOR; 166 I-5; elev. 628ft./191m.; 🅿; z 31006; Ⓟ 1,673; Ⓒ 1,907
Butler Manor; RMC Place; RICHMOND; *166 G-11; ★ AUG; mail Augusta z 30905; pop. incl. with Augusta (Inc. Place)
Butts; RMC Place; JENKINS; *166 I-11; elev. 238ft./73m.; mail Millen z 30442; rural
BUTTS; 166 G-5; Ⓟ 15,326; Ⓒ 19,522; Ⓡ 19,552; ◆ 24,601
Byers Crossroads; RMC Place; CARROLL; *166 F-3; elev. 870ft./265m.; mail Whitesburg z 30185; rural
Byne Crossroads; RMC Place; LEE; *167 L-5; mail Leesburg z 31763; rural
Byromville; Inc. Place; DOOLY; 166 J-6; elev. 354ft./108m.; 🅿; z 31007; Ⓟ 452; Ⓒ 415
Byron; Inc. Place; PEACH; 166 I-6; elev. 505ft./154m.; 🅿; ★ MAC; z 31008; Ⓟ 2,276; Ⓒ 2,887

C

Cabaniss; RMC Place; MONROE; *166 G-6; elev. 572ft./174m.; mail Forsyth z 31029; rural
Cadley; RMC Place; WARREN; 166 F-9; mail Norwood z 30821; ● 50
Cadwell; Inc. Place; LAURENS; 166 J-8; elev. 345ft./105m.; 🅿; z 31009; Ⓟ 458; Ⓒ 329
Cagle; RMC Place; PICKENS; *166 C-4; mail Jasper z 30143; rural
Cairo; Inc. Place; ⊡ GRADY; 167 O-5; elev. 244ft./74m.; 🅿 🅷; z 39827-28; Ⓟ 9,035; Ⓒ 9,239
Caleb; RMC Place; GWINNETT; *166 E-5; elev. 952ft./290m.; ★ ATL; mail Lithonia z 30058; rural
Calhoun; Inc. Place; ⊡ GORDON; 166 C-3; elev. 715ft./218m.; 🅿 🅷; z 30701, z 30703; Ⓟ 7,135; Ⓒ 10,667
CALHOUN; 167 M-4; Ⓟ 5,013; Ⓒ 6,320; ◆ 5,909
Callaway; RMC Place; WILKES; *166 E-8; mail Rayle z 30660; rural
Calvary; RMC Place; GRADY; 167 O-4; 🅿; z 39829; ● 350
Camak; Inc. Place; WARREN; 166 F-9; elev. 613ft./187m.; 🅿; z 30807; Ⓟ 220; Ⓒ 165
CAMDEN; 167 N-11; Ⓟ 30,167; Ⓒ 43,664; ◆ 50,333
Camellia Terrace; RMC Place; CHATHAM; ★ SAV; mail Savannah z 31404; pop. incl. with Savannah (Inc. Place)
Camelot; RMC Place; CLARKE; *166 E-7; ★ ATH; mail Athens z 30606; pop. incl. with Athens (Inc. Place)
Cameron; RMC Place; SCREVEN; *166 I-12; mail Sylvania z 30467; rural
Camilla; Inc. Place; ⊡ MITCHELL; 167 N-5; elev. 180ft./55m.; 🅿 🅷; z 31730; Ⓟ 5,008; Ⓒ 5,669
Campania; RMC Place; COLUMBIA; 166 G-10; ★ AUG; mail Harlem z 30814; ● 400
Campbellton; RMC Place; FULTON; *166 F-4; ★ ATL; mail Fairburn z 30213; ● 75
Campton; RMC Place; WALTON; 166 E-6; mail Monroe z 30655; ● 100
Canal Lake; RMC Place; UNION; *166 B-6; mail Blairsville z 30512; rural
Candler; RMC Place; HALL; *166 D-6; mail Gainesville z 30507; rural
CANDLER; 166 J-11; Ⓟ 7,744; Ⓒ 9,577; ◆ 10,897
Candler-McAfee; CDP-Census Area Only; DEKALB; *166 F-5; ★ ATL; mail Decatur z 30032; Ⓟ 29,491; Ⓒ 28,294; ◆ 32,296
Cannon Crossing; RMC Place; WALKER; *166 B-2; elev. 869ft./265m.; ★ CHTN; mail Fort Oglethorpe z 30742; ● 400
Cannon Gate; RMC Place; COLUMBIA, RICHMOND; ★ AUG; mail Augusta z 30907
Cannonville; RMC Place; TROUP; 166 H-2; elev. 661ft./201m.; mail Lagrange z 30240; ● 100
Canon; Inc. Place; FRANKLIN, HART; 166 D-8; elev. 925ft./282m.; 🅿; z 30520; Ⓟ 737; Ⓒ 755
Canoochee; RMC Place; EMANUEL; 166 I-10; elev. 366ft./112m.; mail Twin City z 30471; ● 40
Canton; Inc. Place; ⊡ CHEROKEE; 166 D-4; elev. 868ft./265m.; 🅿 🅷; ★ ATL; z 30114-15, z 30169; Ⓟ 4,817; Ⓒ 7,709; ◆ 18,195
Capel; RMC Place; GRADY; *167 N-5; mail Brookfield z 31727; rural
Capitol Hill; RMC Place; FULTON; *166 F-4; ★ ATL; mail Atlanta z 30334; pop. incl. with Atlanta (Inc. Place)
Captola; SCREVEN; see Captolo (RMC Place)
Captolo (Captola); RMC Place; SCREVEN; *166 I-12; elev. 196ft./60m.; mail Sylvania z 30467; rural
Carbondale; RMC Place; WHITFIELD; *166 C-3; mail Dalton z 30721
Carey Park; RMC Place; FULTON; *166 E-4; ★ ATL; mail Atlanta z 30318; pop. incl. with Atlanta (Inc. Place)
Carl; Inc. Place; BARROW; 166 E-6; elev. 1,080ft./329m.; mail Auburn z 30011; Ⓟ 263; Ⓒ 205
Carlton; Inc. Place; MADISON; 166 E-8; elev. 570ft./174m.; 🅿; z 30627; Ⓟ 282; Ⓒ 233
Carmichael Crossroads; RMC Place; CHEROKEE; *166 D-4; elev. 93ft./28m.; ★ ATL; mail Canton z 30115; rural
Carnegie; RMC Place; RANDOLPH; 167 L-3; elev. 397ft./121m.; mail Cuthbert z 39840; ● 35
Carnes Creek; RMC Place; STEPHENS; *166 C-7; mail Toccoa z 30577; pop. incl. with Toccoa (Inc. Place)
Carnesville; Inc. Place; ⊡ FRANKLIN; 166 D-8; elev. 712ft./217m.; 🅿; z 30521; Ⓟ 514; Ⓒ 541
Carnigan; RMC Place; MCINTOSH; 167 M-13; mail Meridian z 31319; ● 100
Carns Mill; RMC Place; PICKENS; *166 C-4; elev. 1,073ft./327m.; mail Talking Rock z 30175; rural
Caroline Park; RMC Place; MUSCOGEE; ★ COL; mail Columbus z 31904; pop. incl. with Columbus (Inc. Place)
CARROLL; 166 F-3; Ⓟ 71,422; Ⓒ 87,268; ◆ 120,599
Carrollton; Inc. Place; ⊡ CARROLL; 166 F-3; elev. 1,116ft./340m.; 🅿 🅷 🅲 10,163 ■; z 30112, z 30116-19; Ⓟ 16,029; Ⓒ 19,843; ◆ 26,501
Carrs; HANCOCK; see Carrs Station (RMC Place)
Carrs Station (Carrs); RMC Place; HANCOCK; *166 G-8; mail Sparta z 31087; rural
Carsonville; RMC Place; TAYLOR; *166 I-5; mail Butler z 31006; rural
Cartecay; RMC Place; GILMER; *166 C-5; mail Ellijay z 30540
Carter Acres; RMC Place; MUSCOGEE; *166 I-3; ★ COL; mail Columbus z 31903; pop. incl. with Columbus (Inc. Place)
Carters; RMC Place; MURRAY; 166 C-4; elev. 694ft./212m.; mail Chatsworth z 30705; ● 30
Carters Grove; RMC Place; TALIAFERRO; *166 F-8; mail Rayle z 30660; rural
Cartersville; Inc. Place; ⊡ BARTOW; 166 D-3; elev. 787ft./240m.; 🅿 🅷 ■; z 30120-21; Ⓟ 12,035; Ⓒ 15,925; ◆ 19,795
Carver Heights; RMC Place; MUSCOGEE; *166 J-3; ★ COL; mail Columbus z 31906; pop. incl. with Columbus (Inc. Place)
Carver Village; RMC Place; CHATHAM; *167 K-13; ★ SAV; mail Savannah z 31415; pop. incl. with Savannah (Inc. Place)
Cary; RMC Place; BLECKLEY; 166 I-7; elev. 426ft./130m.; mail Cochran z 31014; ● 120
Cascade Heights; RMC Place; FULTON; *166 F-4; ★ ATL; mail Atlanta z 30311; pop. incl. with Atlanta (Inc. Place)
Cascade Hills; RMC Place; MUSCOGEE; ★ COL; mail Columbus z 31904; pop. incl. with Columbus (Inc. Place)
Cash; RMC Place; GORDON; *166 C-3; mail Calhoun z 30701; rural
Cassandra; RMC Place; WALKER; *166 B-2; mail Chickamauga z 30707; rural
Cassville; RMC Place; BARTOW; 166 D-3; elev. 808ft./246m.; 🅿; z 30123; ● 650
Castlewood; RMC Place; MUSCOGEE; *166 I-3; ★ COL; mail Columbus z 31907; pop. incl. with Columbus (Inc. Place)
Cataula; RMC Place; HARRIS; 166 I-3; elev. 690ft./210m.; 🅿; z 31804; ● 550
Catlett; RMC Place; WALKER; *166 B-2; mail La Fayette z 30728; rural
CATOOSA; 166 B-2; Ⓟ 42,464; Ⓒ 53,282; ◆ 64,450
Cave Spring; Inc. Place; FLOYD; 166 D-2; elev. 636ft./194m.; 🅿; z 30124; Ⓟ 950; Ⓒ 975
Cecil; Inc. Place; COOK; 167 N-7; elev. 240ft./73m.; 🅿; z 31627; Ⓟ 376; Ⓒ 265
Cedar Creek; RMC Place; CLAYTON; *166 F-4; ★ ATL; mail Riverdale z 30274; ● 600
Cedar Creek Park; RMC Place; CLARKE; *166 E-7; ★ ATH; mail Athens z 30605; pop. incl. with Athens (Inc. Place)
Cedar Crossing; RMC Place; TOOMBS; 167 K-10; mail Lyons z 30436; ● 50
Cedar Grove; RMC Place; CHATHAM; *167 K-13; ★ SAV; mail Savannah z 31419; pop. incl. with Savannah (Inc. Place)
Cedar Grove; RMC Place; DEKALB; 168 G-5; ★ ATL; mail Conley z 30288, Ellenwood z 30294; ● 2,000
Cedar Grove; RMC Place; FULTON; *166 F-4; elev. 881ft./269m.; ★ ATL; mail Fairburn z 30213; rural
Cedar Grove; RMC Place; LAURENS; *166 J-8; mail Dublin z 31021; rural
Cedar Grove; RMC Place; WALKER; *166 B-2; mail Chickamauga z 30707; rural
Cedar Hammock; RMC Place; CHATHAM; *167 K-13; ★ SAV; mail Savannah z 31406; rural
Cedar Hills; RMC Place; MUSCOGEE; *166 J-3; ★ COL; mail Columbus z 31907; pop. incl. with Columbus (Inc. Place)
Cedar Point; RMC Place; MCINTOSH; *167 M-13; mail Meridian z 31319; ● 65
Cedar Springs; RMC Place; EARLY; 167 N-3; elev. 155ft./47m.; 🅿; z 39832; ● 200
Cedartown; Inc. Place; ⊡ POLK; 166 E-2; elev. 802ft./244m.; 🅿 🅷; z 30125; Ⓟ 7,978; Ⓒ 9,470
Celanese Village; FLOYD; see Riverside (RMC Place)
Celeste; RMC Place; WILKES; *166 E-9; elev. 638ft./194m.; mail Washington z 30673
Cenchat; RMC Place; WALKER; *166 B-2; ★ CHTN; mail Chickamauga z 30707; ● 45
Centennial; RMC Place; MORGAN; *166 F-6; mail Rutledge z 30663; rural
Center; RMC Place; BARTOW; *166 D-4; mail Cartersville z 30121; ● 150
Center; RMC Place; JACKSON; 166 E-7; elev. 807ft./246m.; ★ ATH; mail Athens z 30601; ● 150
Center; RMC Place; TOOMBS; *167 K-10; elev. 248ft./76m.; mail Vidalia z 30474; rural
Center Hill; RMC Place; COLQUITT; *167 N-6; mail Moultrie z 31768; rural
Center Hill; RMC Place; FULTON; *166 E-4; ★ ATL; mail Atlanta z 30318; pop. incl. with Atlanta (Inc. Place)
Center Point; RMC Place; CARROLL; 166 F-3; elev. 1,183ft./361m.; mail Temple z 30179; ● 75
Center Post; RMC Place; WALKER; *166 C-2; mail La Fayette z 30728; rural
Centerville; RMC Place; ELBERT; *166 D-8; mail Elberton z 30635; ● 30
Centerville; RMC Place; GWINNETT; *166 E-5; elev. 926ft./282m.; ★ ATL; mail Lithonia z 30058, Snellville z 30039; ● 600
Centerville; Inc. Place; HOUSTON; 166 I-6; elev. 462ft./141m.; 🅿; ★ MAC; z 31028; Ⓟ 3,251; Ⓒ 4,278
Centerville; RMC Place; TALBOT; *166 I-4; elev. 588ft./179m.; mail Junction City z 31812; rural
Central City; RMC Place; FULTON; *166 F-4; ★ ATL; mail Atlanta z 30302; pop. incl. with Atlanta (Inc. Place)
Central City Retail; RMC Place; FULTON; mail Atlanta z 30302; pop. incl. with Atlanta (Inc. Place)
Centralhatchee; Inc. Place; HEARD; 166 G-3; elev. 849ft./259m.; mail Franklin z 30217; Ⓟ 301; Ⓒ 383
Central Junction; RMC Place; CHATHAM; *167 K-13; ★ SAV; mail Savannah z 31408; pop. incl. with Garden City (Inc. Place)
Century; RMC Place; LEE; *167 L-5; elev. 243ft./74m.; ★ ALB; mail Leesburg z 31763; rural
Chalybeate Springs; RMC Place; MERIWETHER; 166 H-4; elev. 791ft./241m.; mail Manchester z 31816; ● 250
Chamberlain; RMC Place; WALKER; mail La Fayette z 30728; rural
Chamblee; Inc. Place; DEKALB; 166 E-5; elev. 1,000ft./305m.; 🅿 ■; ★ ATL; z 30341, z 30366, z 39901; Ⓟ 7,668; Ⓒ 9,552; ◆ 11,041
Chambliss; RMC Place; SUMTER; mail Americus z 31709; rural
Chapel Hill; RMC Place; DOUGLAS; *166 F-4; elev. 966ft./294m.; ★ ATL; mail Douglasville z 30134; rural
Chappel; RMC Place; LAMAR; *166 G-5; mail Milner z 30257; rural
Charing; RMC Place; TAYLOR; 166 J-4; mail Mauk z 31058; ● 30
Charles; RMC Place; STEWART; 167 K-3; mail Lumpkin z 31815; ● 90
Charles; RMC Place; TOOMBS; *166 J-10; elev. 280ft./85m.; mail Vidalia z 30474; pop. incl. with Vidalia (Inc. Place)
Charlotteville; RMC Place; MONTGOMERY; 167 K-9; mail Uvalda z 30473; ● 35
CHARLTON; 167 O-10; Ⓟ 8,496; Ⓒ 10,282; ◆ 10,209
Charter Oaks; RMC Place; MUSCOGEE; *166 I-3; ★ COL; mail Columbus z 31909; pop. incl. with Columbus (Inc. Place)
Chaserville; RMC Place; COOK; *167 N-7; mail Sparks z 31647; ● 40
Chastain; RMC Place; THOMAS; *167 N-6; mail Coolidge z 31738; rural
CHATHAM; 167 K-13; Ⓟ 216,935; Ⓒ 232,048; Ⓡ 232,347; ◆ 261,223
Chatham City; RMC Place; CHATHAM; *167 K-13; ★ SAV; mail Savannah z 31408; pop. incl. with Garden City (Inc. Place)
Chatham Villa; RMC Place; CHATHAM; ★ SAV; mail Savannah z 31408; pop. incl. with Garden City (Inc. Place)
Chatsworth; Inc. Place; ⊡ MURRAY; 166 B-3; elev. 752ft./229m.; 🅿 🅷; z 30705; Ⓟ 2,865; Ⓒ 3,531
Chattahoochee; RMC Place; FULTON; *166 E-4; ★ ATL; mail Atlanta z 30318; pop. incl. with Atlanta (Inc. Place)
CHATTAHOOCHEE; 166 J-3; Ⓟ 16,934; Ⓒ 14,882; ◆ 14,477
Chattahoochee Hill Country; FULTON; see Chattahoochee Hills (Inc. Place)
Chattahoochee Hills (Chattahoochee Hill Country, Chatt Hills); Inc. Place; FULTON; *166 F-3; incorporated June 19, 2007; not reported in 2000 Census; ● 2,200
Chattahoochee Plantation; RMC Place; COBB; 168 A-3; elev. 1,000ft./305m.; ★ ATL; mail Marietta z 30067; ● 150
Chattanooga Valley; CDP; WALKER; *166 B-2; elev. 206ft./63m.; ★ CHTN; mail Flintstone z 30725; Ⓟ 4,088; Ⓒ 4,065
Chatterton; RMC Place; COFFEE; *167 M-9; elev. 231ft./70m.; mail Nicholls z 31554; rural
Chatt Hills; FULTON; see Chattahoochee Hills (Inc. Place)
CHATTOOGA; 166 C-2; Ⓟ 22,242; Ⓒ 25,470; ◆ 28,022
Chattoogaville; RMC Place; CHATTOOGA; 166 D-2; elev. 625ft./191m.; mail Lyerly z 30730; ● 125
Chauncey; Inc. Place; DODGE; 167 K-8; elev. 300ft./91m.; 🅿; z 31011; Ⓟ 312; Ⓒ 295
Checkero; RMC Place; RABUN; mail Clayton z 30525; rural
Chelsea; RMC Place; CHATTOOGA; *166 C-2; mail Menlo z 30731; rural
Chennault; RMC Place; LINCOLN; *166 E-9; elev. 471ft./144m.; mail Tignall z 30668; rural
Cherokee; RMC Place; BIBB; ★ MAC; mail Macon z 31204
CHEROKEE; 166 D-4; Ⓟ 90,204; Ⓒ 141,903; ◆ 221,484
Cherokee Forest; RMC Place; CHEROKEE; *166 D-4; ★ ATL; mail Woodstock z 30188; ● 950
Cherokee Heights; RMC Place; BIBB; ★ MAC; pop. incl. with Macon (Inc. Place)
Cherry Log; RMC Place; GILMER; 166 B-4; elev. 1,552ft./473m.; 🅿; z 30522; ● 140
Chestatee; RMC Place; FORSYTH; *166 D-5; elev. 1,263ft./385m.; ★ ATL; mail Cumming z 30040; rural
Chester; Inc. Place; DODGE; 166 J-8; elev. 376ft./115m.; 🅿; z 31012; Ⓟ 1,072; Ⓒ 305; Ⓡ 1,310
Chestnut Mountain; RMC Place; HALL; 166 D-6; elev. 1,139ft./347m.; 🅿; ★ ATL; z 30502; ● 250
Chickamauga; Inc. Place; WALKER; 166 B-2; elev. 119ft./36m.; 🅿; ★ CHTN; z 30707; Ⓟ 2,149; Ⓒ 2,245
Chickasawhatchee; RMC Place; TERRELL; *167 L-4; mail Dawson z 39842; rural
Chicopee; RMC Place; HALL; 166 D-6; mail Gainesville z 30507; ● 750
China Hill; RMC Place; TELFAIR; *167 L-8; elev. 221ft./67m.; mail Rhine z 31077; rural
Chipley; HARRIS; see Pine Mountain (Inc. Place)
Chippewa Terrace; RMC Place; CHATHAM; *167 K-13; ★ SAV; mail Savannah z 31406; pop. incl. with Savannah (Inc. Place)
Choestoe; RMC Place; UNION; *166 B-6; mail Blairsville z 30512; rural
Chubbtown; RMC Place; FLOYD; *166 D-2; mail Cave Spring z 30124; rural
Chula; RMC Place; TIFT; 167 M-7; elev. 395ft./120m.; 🅿; z 31733; ● 250
Cinderella Hills; RMC Place; CATOOSA; *166 B-2; ★ CHTN; mail Ringgold z 30736; ● 700
Cisco; RMC Place; MURRAY; 166 B-4; 🅿; z 30708; ● 300
Civic Center; RMC Place; FULTON; *166 E-4; ★ ATL; mail Atlanta z 30308, z 30379; pop. incl. with Atlanta (Inc. Place)
Clarkdale; RMC Place; COBB; 166 E-4; elev. 960ft./293m.; 🅿; ★ ATL; z 30111; ● 500
CLARKE; 166 E-7; Ⓟ 87,594; Ⓒ 101,489; ◆ 115,721
Clarke Dale; RMC Place; CLARKE; *166 E-7; ★ ATH; mail Athens z 30605; pop. incl. with Athens (Inc. Place)
Clarkesville; Inc. Place; ⊡ HABERSHAM; 166 C-7; elev. 1,361ft./415m.; 🅿; z 30523; Ⓟ 1,151; Ⓒ 1,248
Clarksboro; RMC Place; JACKSON; *166 E-7; elev. 855ft./261m.; ★ ATH; mail Athens z 30607; ● 70
Clarkston; Inc. Place; DEKALB; 168 D-6; elev. 1,000ft./305m.; 🅿; ★ ATL; z 30021; Ⓟ 5,385; Ⓒ 7,231
Clarkview; RMC Place; BIBB; *166 H-6; ★ MAC; mail Macon z 31204; pop. incl. with Macon (Inc. Place)
Claxton; Inc. Place; ⊡ EVANS; 167 K-11; elev. 187ft./57m.; 🅿 🅷; z 30417 & mail Bellville z 30414, Manassas z 30438; Ⓟ 2,464; Ⓒ 2,276
CLAY; 167 L-3; Ⓟ 3,364; Ⓒ 3,357; ◆ 3,233
Clayfields; RMC Place; WILKINSON; *166 H-7; mail Mc Intyre z 31054; rural
Clayton; Inc. Place; ⊡ RABUN; 166 B-7; elev. 1,925ft./587m.; 🅿 🅷; z 30525; Ⓟ 1,613; Ⓒ 2,019
CLAYTON; 166 F-4; Ⓟ 182,052; Ⓒ 236,517; ◆ 272,689
Clearview; RMC Place; CHATHAM; *167 K-13; ★ SAV; mail Savannah z 31415; pop. incl. with Savannah (Inc. Place)
Clem; RMC Place; CARROLL; 166 F-3; mail Carrollton z 30116; ● 150
Cleola; HARRIS; see Oak Mountain (RMC Place)
Clermont; Inc. Place; HALL; 166 C-6; elev. 1,400ft./427m.; 🅿; z 30527; Ⓟ 402; Ⓒ 419; Ⓡ 429
Cleveland; Inc. Place; ⊡ WHITE; 166 C-6; elev. 1,570ft./479m.; 🅿 🅲 409; z 30528; Ⓟ 1,653; Ⓒ 1,907
Cliftondale (Tell); RMC Place; FULTON; *166 F-4; ★ ATL; mail Atlanta z 30337; ● 50
Climax; Inc. Place; DECATUR; 167 O-4; elev. 280ft./85m.; 🅿; z 39834; Ⓟ 226; Ⓒ 297
CLINCH; 167 N-9; Ⓟ 6,160; Ⓒ 6,878; ◆ 7,059
Clinchfield; RMC Place; HOUSTON; 166 J-6; elev. 268ft./82m.; 🅿; z 31013; ● 125
Clinton; RMC Place; JONES; 166 H-7; elev. 559ft./170m.; ★ MAC; mail Gray z 31032; ● 80
Cloudland; RMC Place; CHATTOOGA; 166 C-2; elev. 1,578ft./481m.; 🅿; z 30731; ● 300
Cloverdale; RMC Place; DADE; *166 B-2; mail Rising Fawn z 30738; rural
Clubview Heights; RMC Place; MUSCOGEE; ★ COL; mail Columbus z 31906; pop. incl. with Columbus (Inc. Place)
Clyatteville; LOWNDES; see Clyattville (RMC Place)
Clyattville (Clyatteville); RMC Place; LOWNDES; 167 O-7; elev. 202ft./62m.; 🅿; ★ VALD; z 31601; ● 300
Clyo; RMC Place; EFFINGHAM; 166 I-13; elev. 72ft./22m.; 🅿; z 31303; ● 370
CNN Center; RMC Place; FULTON; ★ ATL; mail Atlanta z 30303; pop. incl. with Atlanta (Inc. Place)
Coal Mountain; RMC Place; FORSYTH; 166 D-5; ★ ATL; mail Cumming z 30040; ● 100
Cobb; RMC Place; SUMTER; 167 K-5; elev. 297ft./91m.; 🅿; z 31735; ● 150
COBB; 166 E-4; Ⓟ 447,745; Ⓒ 607,751; ◆ 713,777
Cobbtown; Inc. Place; TATTNALL; 166 J-10; elev. 245ft./75m.; 🅿; z 30420; Ⓟ 338; Ⓒ 311
Cochran; Inc. Place; ⊡ BLECKLEY; 166 J-7; elev. 342ft./104m.; 🅿 🅷; z 31014; Ⓟ 4,390; Ⓒ 4,455
Coffee; RMC Place; BACON; *167 M-10; elev. 179ft./55m.; mail Mershon z 31551; rural
COFFEE; 167 L-9; Ⓟ 29,592; Ⓒ 37,413; ◆ 40,668
Coffee Bluff Plantation; RMC Place; CHATHAM; *167 K-13; ★ SAV; mail Savannah z 31419; pop. incl. with Savannah (Inc. Place)
Cogdell; RMC Place; CLINCH; 167 N-9; elev. 185ft./56m.; 🅿; z 31634; ● 50
Cohutta; Inc. Place; WHITFIELD; 166 B-3; elev. 866ft./264m.; 🅿; z 30710; Ⓟ 529; Ⓒ 582
Cohutta Springs; RMC Place; MURRAY; *166 B-4; mail Crandall z 30711; ● 30
Colbert; Inc. Place; MADISON; 166 E-8; elev. 745ft./227m.; 🅿; z 30628; Ⓟ 443; Ⓒ 488
Cole City; RMC Place; DADE; *166 B-1; ★ CHTN; mail Trenton z 30752; rural
Coleman; RMC Place; RANDOLPH; 167 L-3; elev. 385ft./117m.; 🅿; z 39836; disincorporated January 1, 2007; Ⓟ 137; Ⓒ 149
Colemans Lake; RMC Place; EMANUEL; 166 H-10; elev. 200ft./61m.; mail Midville z 30441; ● 45
Colesburg; RMC Place; CAMDEN; *167 N-12; elev. 20ft./6m.; mail Woodbine z 31569
College Heights; RMC Place; DOUGHERTY; ★ ALB; mail Albany z 31705; ● 100
College Heights; RMC Place; MUSCOGEE; ★ COL; mail Columbus z 31906; pop. incl. with Columbus (Inc. Place)
College Park; Inc. Place; FULTON, CLAYTON; 166 F-4; elev. 1,057ft./322m.; 🅿; ★ ATL; z 30337, z 30349; Ⓟ 20,457; Ⓒ 20,382; ◆ 21,600
Collins; Inc. Place; TATTNALL; 166 J-11; elev. 235ft./72m.; 🅿; z 30421; Ⓟ 528; Ⓒ 528
Collinsville; RMC Place; DEKALB; *166 F-5; elev. 900ft./274m.; ★ ATL; mail Lithonia z 30058; rural
Colomokee; RMC Place; EARLY; *167 M-3; mail Blakely z 39823; rural
Colonial Oaks; RMC Place; CHATHAM; ★ SAV; mail Savannah z 31419; pop. incl. with Savannah (Inc. Place)
Colonial Place; RMC Place; DOUGHERTY; *167 M-5; ★ ALB; mail Albany z 31705; pop. incl. with Albany (Inc. Place)
Colonial Village; RMC Place; CHATHAM; ★ SAV; mail Savannah z 31406; pop. incl. with Savannah (Inc. Place)
Colony Park; RMC Place; RICHMOND; *166 F-11; elev. 350ft./107m.; ★ AUG; mail Augusta z 30909; pop. incl. with Augusta (Inc. Place)
Colquitt; Inc. Place; ⊡ MILLER; 167 N-3; elev. 175ft./53m.; 🅿 🅷; z 39837; Ⓟ 1,991; Ⓒ 1,939
COLQUITT; 167 N-6; Ⓟ 36,645; Ⓒ 42,053; ◆ 45,559
COLUMBIA; 166 F-10; Ⓟ 66,031; Ⓒ 89,288; ◆ 113,011
Columbia Heights; RMC Place; COLUMBIA; *166 F-10; ★ AUG; mail Augusta z 30907; ● 2,500
Columbus; Inc. Place; ⊡ MUSCOGEE; 167 T-2; elev. 249ft./76m.; 🅿 🅷 🅲 7,597 ■; ★ COL; z 31829, z 31901-09, z 31914, z 31917, z 31993, z 31995, z 31997-99; Ⓟ 178,681; Ⓒ 185,781; Ⓐ 186,291; ◆ 192,560
Columbus Heights; RMC Place; BIBB; *166 H-6; ★ MAC; mail Macon z 31204; pop. incl. with Macon (Inc. Place)
Colwell; RMC Place; FANNIN; *166 B-4; mail Epworth z 30541; rural
Comer; Inc. Place; MADISON; 166 E-8; elev. 17ft./5m.; 🅿; z 30629; Ⓟ 939; Ⓒ 1,052
Commerce; Inc. Place; JACKSON; 166 D-7; elev. 931ft./284m.; 🅿 🅷; z 30529-30, z 30599; Ⓟ 4,108; Ⓒ 5,292
Concord; RMC Place; JASPER; *166 G-6; mail Monticello z 31064; rural
Concord; Inc. Place; PIKE; 166 H-4; elev. 816ft./249m.; 🅿; z 30206; Ⓟ 211; Ⓒ 336
Concord; RMC Place; SCHLEY; *166 J-5; elev. 533ft./162m.; mail Ellaville z 31806; rural
Concord; RMC Place; SUMTER; *167 K-4; mail Americus z 31719; rural
Coney; RMC Place; CRISP; *167 K-6; mail Cordele z 31015; ● 45
Conley; CDP; CLAYTON; 168 G-4; elev. 850ft./259m.; 🅿; ★ ATL; z 30288; Ⓟ 5,528; Ⓒ 6,188
Constitution; RMC Place; DEKALB; 168 F-4; ★ ATL; mail Atlanta z 30316; ● 600
Conyers; Inc. Place; ⊡ ROCKDALE; 166 F-5; elev. 904ft./276m.; 🅿 🅷; ★ ATL; z 30012-13, z 30094; Ⓟ 7,380; Ⓒ 10,689
COOK; 167 N-7; Ⓟ 13,456; Ⓒ 15,771; ◆ 16,705
Cooksville; RMC Place; HEARD; *166 G-3; mail Hogansville z 30230; rural
Cooktown; RMC Place; MILLER; *167 N-4; mail Colquitt z 39837; rural
Coolidge; Inc. Place; THOMAS; 167 N-6; elev. 717ft./219m.; 🅿; z 31738; Ⓟ 610; Ⓒ 552
Cool Spring; COLQUITT; see Cool Springs (RMC Place)
Cool Springs (Cool Spring); RMC Place; COLQUITT; *167 N-6; mail Norman Park z 31771; rural
Cooper Creek Park; RMC Place; MUSCOGEE; ★ COL; mail Columbus z 31907; pop. incl. with Columbus (Inc. Place)
Cooper Heights; RMC Place; WALKER; *166 B-2; ★ CHTN; mail Chickamauga z 30707
Coopers; RMC Place; BALDWIN; 166 H-7; elev. 389ft./119m.; mail Gordon z 31031; ● 300
Coosa; RMC Place; FLOYD; 166 D-2; elev. 603ft./184m.; 🅿; ★ ROME; z 30129 & mail Rome z 30165; ● 350
Copeland; RMC Place; DODGE; *167 K-7; elev. 182ft./55m.; mail Rhine z 31077; ● 50
Cora; NEWTON; see Kings (RMC Place)
Cordele; Inc. Place; ⊡ CRISP; 167 K-6; elev. 319ft./97m.; 🅿 🅷; z 31010, z 31015; Ⓟ 10,321; Ⓒ 11,608
Corinth; RMC Place; HEARD, COWETA; 166 G-3; elev. 759ft./231m.; mail Hogansville z 30230; disincorporated May 1, 2000; Ⓟ 136; Ⓒ 213
Cornelia; Inc. Place; HABERSHAM; 166 C-7; elev. 1,500ft./457m.; 🅿; z 30531; Ⓟ 3,219; Ⓒ 3,674
Cotton; RMC Place; MITCHELL; 167 N-5; elev. 250ft./76m.; 🅿; z 31739; ● 100
Cotton Hill; RMC Place; CLAY; *167 L-3; mail Morris z 39867; rural
Council; RMC Place; CLINCH; 167 O-10; mail Fargo z 31631; ● 80
Country Club Estates; CDP-Census Area Only; GLYNN; *167 N-12; elev. 4ft./1m.; ★ BRUNS; mail Brunswick z 31520; Ⓟ 7,500; Ⓒ 7,594
Country Club Hills; RMC Place; RICHMOND; *166 F-11; ★ AUG; mail Augusta z 30904; pop. incl. with Augusta (Inc. Place)
Country Park; RMC Place; RICHMOND; *166 G-11; ★ AUG; mail Augusta z 30906; pop. incl. with Augusta (Inc. Place)
Country Place; RMC Place; COLUMBIA; *166 F-10; ★ AUG; mail Evans z 30809; ● 115
Country Side; RMC Place; CHATHAM; ★ SAV; mail Savannah z 31406; pop. incl. with Savannah (Inc. Place)
County Line; RMC Place; BARROW; *166 E-6; mail Winder z 30680; rural
County Line; RMC Place; DEKALB; *166 F-5; elev. 916ft./279m.; ★ ATL; mail Decatur z 30032; ● 600
Court Square; RMC Place; LAURENS; *166 I-8; mail Dublin z 31021; pop. incl. with Dublin (Inc. Place)
Covena; RMC Place; EMANUEL; 166 J-10; elev. 203ft./62m.; 🅿; z 30401; ● 50
Coverdale; RMC Place; TURNER; 167 L-6; mail Ashburn z 31714; ● 30
Covington; Inc. Place; ⊡ NEWTON; 166 F-6; elev. 747ft./228m.; 🅿 🅷; ★ ATL; z 30014-16; Ⓟ 10,026; Ⓒ 11,547
Covington Mills; RMC Place; NEWTON; *166 F-6; ★ ATL; mail Covington z 30014; pop. incl. with Covington (Inc. Place)
COWETA; 166 G-3; Ⓟ 53,853; Ⓒ 89,215; ◆ 125,684
Cox; RMC Place; MCINTOSH; 167 M-12; elev. 17ft./5m.; mail Townsend z 31331; ● 75
Coxs Crossing; RMC Place; CLAYTON; *166 F-4; ★ ATL; mail Atlanta z 30321
Crabapple; RMC Place; FULTON; 166 D-5; ★ ATL; mail Alpharetta z 30004; ● 300
Crandall; RMC Place; MURRAY; 166 B-4; elev. 894ft./272m.; 🅿; z 30711; ● 250
Crane Eater; RMC Place; GORDON; *166 C-3; elev. 667ft./203m.; mail Calhoun z 30701; rural
Cravey; RMC Place; TELFAIR; mail Milan z 31060; rural
Crawford; Inc. Place; OGLETHORPE; 166 E-8; elev. 770ft./235m.; 🅿; z 30630; Ⓟ 694; Ⓒ 807
CRAWFORD; 166 I-5; Ⓟ 8,991; Ⓒ 12,495; ◆ 12,307
Crawfordville; Inc. Place; ⊡ TALIAFERRO; 166 F-8; elev. 600ft./183m.; 🅿; z 30631; Ⓟ 577; Ⓒ 572
Crescent; RMC Place; MCINTOSH; 167 M-13; elev. 30ft./9m.; 🅿; z 31304; ● 500
Crest; RMC Place; UPSON; *166 H-4; mail Thomaston z 30286
Cresthill; RMC Place; CHATHAM; *167 K-13; elev. 15ft./5m.; ★ SAV; mail Savannah z 31406; ● 150
Crest Hill Gardens; RMC Place; CHATHAM; ★ SAV; mail Savannah z 31406; pop. incl. with Savannah (Inc. Place)
Crestview; RMC Place; BAKER; *167 M-4; elev. 244ft./74m.; mail Arlington z 39813; rural
Crestwell Heights; RMC Place; BIBB; *166 H-6; ★ MAC; mail Macon z 31204; ● 120
CRISP; 167 K-6; Ⓟ 20,011; Ⓒ 21,996; ◆ 22,504
Crosland; RMC Place; COLQUITT; 167 M-6; elev. 271ft./83m.; mail Norman Park z 31771; ● 150
Cross Keys; RMC Place; BIBB; 167 R-7; ★ MAC; mail Macon z 31217; pop. incl. with Macon (Inc. Place)
Cross Roads; RMC Place; HART; *166 D-8; elev. 923ft./281m.; mail Bowersville z 30516; rural
Crossroads; RMC Place; LIBERTY; 167 L-12; mail Riceboro z 31323; pop. incl. with Riceboro (Inc. Place)
Cruse; RMC Place; GWINNETT; ★ ATL; mail Lawrenceville z 30045; rural
Crystal Springs; RMC Place; BIBB; *166 H-7; ★ MAC; mail Macon z 31217; ● 1,300
Crystal Springs; RMC Place; FLOYD; *166 C-2; ★ ROME; mail Armuchee z 30105
Crystal Valley; RMC Place; MUSCOGEE; 167 T-1; ★ COL; mail Columbus z 31907; pop. incl. with Columbus (Inc. Place)
Culloden; Inc. Place; MONROE; 166 H-5; elev. 711ft./217m.; 🅿; z 31016; Ⓟ 242; Ⓒ 223
Culverton; RMC Place; HANCOCK; 166 G-8; mail Sparta z 31087; ● 45
Cumming; Inc. Place; ⊡ FORSYTH; 166 D-5; elev. 1,315ft./401m.; 🅿 🅷; ★ ATL; z 30028, z 30040-41; Ⓟ 2,828; Ⓒ 4,220
Curryville; RMC Place; GORDON; *166 C-3; mail Calhoun z 30701; rural
Curtis; RMC Place; FANNIN; *166 B-5; mail Blue Ridge z 30513; rural
Cusseta (Cusseta-Chattahoochee County); Inc. Place; ⊡ CHATTAHOOCHEE; 166 J-3; elev. 480ft./146m.; 🅿; ★ COL; z 31805; the governments of the city of Cusseta and the county of Chattahoochee merged on November 5, 2003; Ⓟ 1,107; Ⓒ 1,196
Cusseta-Chattahoochee County; CHATTAHOOCHEE; see Cusseta (Inc. Place)
Cuthbert; Inc. Place; ⊡ RANDOLPH; 167 L-3; elev. 473ft./144m.; 🅿 🅷; z 39840; Ⓟ 3,730; Ⓒ 3,731
Cypress Mills; RMC Place; GLYNN; 167 S-13; ★ BRUNS; mail Brunswick z 31520; pop. incl. with Brunswick (Inc. Place)

D

Dacula; Inc. Place; GWINNETT; 166 E-6; elev. 1,052ft./321m.; 🅿; ★ ATL; z 30019; Ⓟ 2,217; Ⓒ 3,848
DADE; 166 B-2; Ⓟ 13,147; Ⓒ 15,154; ◆ 16,266
Daffin Heights; RMC Place; CHATHAM; *167 K-13; ★ SAV; mail Savannah z 31404; pop. incl. with Savannah (Inc. Place)
Dahlonega; Inc. Place; ⊡ LUMPKIN; 166 C-6; elev. 1,454ft./443m.; 🅿 🅷 🅲 4,922; z 30533, z 30597; Ⓟ 3,086; Ⓒ 3,638
Daisy; Inc. Place; EVANS; 167 K-11; elev. 177ft./54m.; 🅿; z 30423; Ⓟ 138; Ⓒ 126
Dakota; RMC Place; TURNER; 167 L-6; elev. 397ft./121m.; mail Ashburn z 31714; ● 100
Dallas; Inc. Place; ⊡ PAULDING; 166 E-3; elev. 1,050ft./320m.; 🅿 🅷; ★ ATL; z 30132, z 30157; Ⓟ 2,810; Ⓒ 5,056
Dallas Heights; RMC Place; RICHMOND; *166 G-11; ★ AUG; mail Augusta z 30906; pop. incl. with Augusta (Inc. Place)
Dallondale; RMC Place; CATOOSA; *166 B-2; ★ CHTN; mail Rossville z 30741; ● 300
Dalton; Inc. Place; ⊡ WHITFIELD; 166 B-3; elev. 759ft./231m.; 🅿 🅷 🅲 4,267 ■; z 30719-22; Ⓟ 21,761; Ⓒ 27,912; ◆ 34,192
Damascus; Inc. Place; EARLY; 167 M-3; elev. 226ft./69m.; 🅿; z 39841; Ⓟ 290; Ⓒ 277
Damascus; RMC Place; GORDON; *166 C-3; mail Calhoun z 30701; ● 120
Dames Ferry; RMC Place; MONROE; *166 H-6; mail Juliette z 31046; rural
Dan; RMC Place; RICHMOND; ★ AUG; pop. incl. with Augusta (Inc. Place)
Danburg; RMC Place; WILKES; 166 E-9; elev. 564ft./172m.; 🅿; z 30668; ● 130
Daniel; RMC Place; BRYAN; *167 K-13; mail Richmond Hill z 31324; rural
Daniel Springs; RMC Place; GREENE; *166 F-8; elev. 482ft./147m.; mail Union Point z 30669; rural
Danielsville; Inc. Place; ⊡ MADISON; 166 D-8; elev. 735ft./224m.; 🅿; z 30633; Ⓟ 318; Ⓒ 457
Danville; Inc. Place; TWIGGS, WILKINSON; 166 I-7; elev. 451ft./137m.; 🅿; z 31017; Ⓟ 480; Ⓒ 373
Darien; Inc. Place; ⊡ MCINTOSH; 167 M-12; 🅿; z 31305; Ⓟ 1,783; Ⓒ 1,719
Dasher; Inc. Place; LOWNDES; 167 O-8; elev. 177ft./54m.; ★ VALD; mail Valdosta z 31601; Ⓟ 688; Ⓒ 834
Davisboro; Inc. Place; WASHINGTON; 166 H-9; elev. 302ft./92m.; 🅿; z 31018; Ⓟ 407; Ⓒ 1,544
Davis Crossroads; RMC Place; WALKER; *166 B-2; mail Chickamauga z 30707; rural
Dawesville; RMC Place; THOMAS; *167 N-5; mail Thomasville z 31792; rural
Dawnville; RMC Place; WHITFIELD; *166 B-3; mail Dalton z 30721; ● 150
Dawson; Inc. Place; ⊡ TERRELL; 167 L-4; elev. 355ft./108m.; 🅿; z 39842; Ⓟ 5,295; Ⓒ 5,058
DAWSON; 166 D-5; Ⓟ 9,429; Ⓒ 15,999; ◆ 23,238
Dawsonville; Inc. Place; ⊡ DAWSON; 166 C-5; elev. 1,375ft./419m.; 🅿; z 30534; Ⓟ 467; Ⓒ 619
Days Crossroads; RMC Place; CLAY; *167 L-3; elev. 273ft./83m.; mail Fort Gaines z 39851; rural
Dearing; Inc. Place; MCDUFFIE; 166 G-10; elev. 470ft./143m.; 🅿; z 30808; Ⓟ 547; Ⓒ 441
De Bruce; RMC Place; RICHMOND; *166 G-11; ★ AUG; pop. incl. with Augusta (Inc. Place)
Decatur; Inc. Place; ⊡ DEKALB; 166 E-5; elev. 1,048ft./319m.; 🅿 🅷 🅲 3,645 ■; ★ ATL; z 30030-37; Ⓟ 17,336; Ⓒ 18,147; ◆ 18,251
DECATUR; 167 O-4; Ⓟ 25,511; Ⓒ 28,240; ◆ 28,755
Deenwood; CDP; WARE; 167 N-10; mail Waycross z 31503; Ⓟ 2,055; Ⓒ 1,836
Deepstep; Inc. Place; WASHINGTON; 166 H-8; elev. 300ft./91m.; 🅿; z 31082; Ⓟ 111; Ⓒ 132
Deer Run; RMC Place; ROCKDALE; *166 F-5; elev. 700ft./213m.; ★ ATL; mail Conyers z 30094; ● 470
Deerwood Forest; RMC Place; RICHMOND; *166 G-11; ★ AUG; mail Augusta z 30906; pop. incl. with Augusta (Inc. Place)
Deerwood Park; RMC Place; DEKALB; 168 E-5; ★ ATL; mail Decatur z 30032; ● 3,000
DEKALB; 166 F-5; Ⓟ 545,837; Ⓒ 665,865; Ⓡ 666,072; ◆ 760,154
Delhi; RMC Place; WILKES; *166 E-9; elev. 519ft./158m.; mail Tignall z 30668; rural
Dellwood; RMC Place; EMANUEL; *166 I-10; mail Swainsboro z 30401; ● 200
Demorest; Inc. Place; HABERSHAM; 166 C-7; elev. 1,400ft./427m.; 🅿 🅷 🅲 2,118; z 30535, z 30544; Ⓟ 1,088; Ⓒ 1,465
Denmark; RMC Place; BULLOCH; 166 J-12; elev. 181ft./55m.; mail Brooklet z 30415; ● 50
Dennis; RMC Place; PUTNAM; *166 G-7; mail Eatonton z 31024; rural
Denton; Inc. Place; JEFF DAVIS; 167 L-9; elev. 259ft./79m.; 🅿; z 31532; Ⓟ 335; Ⓒ 269
Denver; RMC Place; HEARD; *166 G-2; elev. 834ft./254m.; mail Franklin z 30217; rural
Deptford; RMC Place; CHATHAM; ★ SAV; mail Savannah z 31404; pop. incl. with Savannah (Inc. Place)

Entries in **UPPERCASE** are counties.
Entries in **bold** have populations of 2,500 or more.
Names in parentheses are alternate names.

Inc. Place	Incorporated Place
RMC Place	Rand McNally Designated Place
CDP	Census Designated Place
MCD	Minor Civil Division
⊡	County Seat
▲	Minor Civil Division
elev.	Elevation
🅿	Post Office
🅷	Hospital
🅲	College
■	Principal Business Center
★	Ranally Metro Area (RMA) Abbreviation
z	Zip Code(s)
Ⓟ	Previous Census Population
Ⓡ	Revised Census Population
Ⓐ	Annexation Population
●	Rand McNally Population Estimate
Ⓒ	Final Census Population
Ⓢ	Special Census Population
◆	Estimated Population

For additional definitions see Glossary, Volume 1, and Introduction, Volume 2.

DeSoto; Inc. Place; SUMTER; 167 K-5; elev. 305ft./93m.; 🅿; z 31743; Ⓟ 258; Ⓒ 214
De Soto Park; RMC Place; FLOYD; *166 D-2; ★ **ROME**; mail Rome z 30161; ● 1,200
Desser; RMC Place; SEMINOLE; *167 O-3; mail Donalsonville z 39845; ● 50
Devereux; RMC Place; HANCOCK; 166 G-8; elev. 577ft./176m.; mail Sparta z 31087; ● 70
Dewberry; RMC Place; WALKER; *166 B-2; ★ **CHTN**; mail Rossville z 30741; pop. incl. with Fort Oglethorpe (Inc. Place)
Dewey Rose; ELBERT; see Dewy Rose (RMC Place)
Dewy Rose (Dewey Rose); RMC Place; ELBERT; 166 D-8; elev. 727ft./222m.; 🅿; z 30634; ● 220
Dexter; Inc. Place; LAURENS; 166 J-8; elev. 273ft./83m.; 🅿; z 31019; Ⓟ 475; Ⓒ 509
Dial; RMC Place; FANNIN; *166 B-5; mail Blue Ridge z 30513; ● 100
Dialtown; RMC Place; NEWTON; *166 F-6; ★ **ATL**; mail Oxford z 30054; ● 150
Diamond Hill; RMC Place; MADISON; 166 E-7; mail Colbert z 30628; ● 75
Dickey; RMC Place; CALHOUN; *167 L-4; elev. 285ft./87m.; mail Edison z 39846
Digbey; RMC Place; SPALDING; *166 G-4; mail Brooks z 30205; rural
Dillard; Inc. Place; RABUN; 166 B-7; elev. 2,144ft./653m.; 🅿; z 30537; Ⓟ 199; Ⓒ 198
Dillon; RMC Place; THOMAS; *167 O-6; mail Thomasville z 31757; rural
Dinglewood; RMC Place; MUSCOGEE; ★ **COL**; mail Columbus z 31906; pop. incl. with Columbus (Inc. Place)
Dixie; RMC Place; BROOKS; 167 O-6; elev. 160ft./49m.; 🅿; z 31629; ● 200
Dixie; RMC Place; NEWTON; *166 F-6; ★ **ATL**; mail Covington z 30014; rural
Dixie Heights; RMC Place; DOUGHERTY; ★ **ALB**; mail Albany z 31705; pop. incl. with Albany (Inc. Place)
Dixie Union; RMC Place; WARE; 167 M-10; elev. 158ft./48m.; mail Waycross z 31503; ● 250
Dock Junction; CDP-Census Area Only; GLYNN; 167 S-12; ★ **BRUNS**; mail Brunswick z 31520; Ⓟ 7,094; Ⓒ 6,951
Doctortown; RMC Place; WAYNE; *167 L-11; mail Jesup z 31545; rural
DODGE; 166 J-7; Ⓟ 17,607; Ⓒ 19,171; ◆ 20,180
Doerun; Inc. Place; COLQUITT; 167 M-6; elev. 399ft./122m.; 🅿; z 31744; Ⓟ 899; Ⓒ 828
Doles; RMC Place; WORTH; 167 L-6; elev. 276ft./84m.; mail Sylvester z 31791; ● 100
Donald; RMC Place; LONG; 167 L-11; elev. 83ft./25m.; mail Ludowici z 31316; ● 75
Donalsonville; Inc. Place; ⊡ SEMINOLE; 167 N-3; elev. 150ft./46m.; 🅿 🅷; z 39845; Ⓟ 2,761; Ⓒ 2,796
Donegal; RMC Place; BULLOCH; *166 I-12; mail Statesboro z 30461; rural
Donovan; RMC Place; JOHNSON; *166 I-9; mail Wrightsville z 31096; rural
Doogan; RMC Place; MURRAY; *166 B-4; mail Cisco z 30708; rural
Dooling; Inc. Place; DOOLY; 166 J-6; mail Montezuma z 31063; Ⓟ 28; Ⓒ 163
DOOLY; 167 K-6; Ⓟ 9,901; Ⓒ 11,525; ◆ 11,174
Doraville; Inc. Place; DEKALB; 166 E-5; elev. 1,069ft./326m.; 🅿 ■; ★ **ATL**; z 30340, z 30360, z 30362; Ⓟ 7,626; Ⓒ 9,862; ◆ 11,191
Dorchester; RMC Place; LIBERTY; *167 L-12; elev. 18ft./5m.; mail Midway z 31320; pop. incl. with Midway (Inc. Place)
Dorchester; RMC Place; RICHMOND; *166 F-11; elev. 250ft./76m.; ★ **AUG**; mail Augusta z 30909; pop. incl. with Augusta (Inc. Place)
Dot; RMC Place; CARROLL; *166 F-2; mail Bowdon z 30108; rural
Double Branches; RMC Place; LINCOLN; *166 F-10; mail Lincolnton z 30817; ● 200
Doublegate; RMC Place; DOUGHERTY; *167 L-5; ★ **ALB**; mail Albany z 31721; pop. incl. with Albany (Inc. Place)
Double Run; RMC Place; WILCOX; *167 L-7; elev. 349ft./106m.; mail Pitts z 31072; rural
Dougherty; RMC Place; DAWSON; *166 D-5; mail Dawsonville z 30534; rural
DOUGHERTY; 167 L-4; Ⓟ 96,311; Ⓒ 96,065; ◆ 96,929
Douglas; Inc. Place; ⊡ COFFEE; 167 M-9; elev. 259ft./79m.; 🅿 🅷; z 31533-35; Ⓟ 10,464; Ⓒ 10,639
DOUGLAS; 166 F-3; Ⓟ 71,120; Ⓒ 92,174; ◆ 133,774
Douglasville; Inc. Place; ⊡ DOUGLAS; 166 F-3; elev. 1,209ft./369m.; 🅿 🅷; ★ **ATL**; z 30133-35, z 30154; Ⓟ 11,635; Ⓒ 20,065; ◆ 32,941
Dove Creek; RMC Place; ELBERT; *166 E-8; mail Elberton z 30635; rural
Dover; RMC Place; SCREVEN; 166 I-12; elev. 102ft./31m.; 🅿; z 30424; ● 85
Doverel; RMC Place; TERRELL; *167 L-4; elev. 336ft./102m.; mail Dawson z 39842; rural
Downs; RMC Place; WASHINGTON; *166 H-9; mail Davisboro z 31018; rural
Downtown; RMC Place; MUSCOGEE; *166 J-3; ★ **COL**; mail Columbus z 31901; pop. incl. with Columbus (Inc. Place)
Doyle; RMC Place; MARION; *166 J-4; mail Buena Vista z 31803; rural
Drakes Still; RMC Place; SEMINOLE; *167 O-3; mail Donalsonville z 39845; ● 55
Draketown; RMC Place; HARALSON; 166 E-3; mail Temple z 30179; ● 180
Dranesville; MARION; see Draneville (RMC Place)
Draneville (Dranesville); RMC Place; MARION; *166 J-4; mail Buena Vista z 31803; rural
Draneville; TROUP; see Bass Crossroads (RMC Place)
Drayton; RMC Place; DOOLY; *167 K-6; mail Vienna z 31092; rural
Dresden; RMC Place; COWETA; *166 G-3; mail Newnan z 30263; rural
Drew; RMC Place; FORSYTH; *166 D-5; elev. 1,147ft./350m.; ★ **ATL**; mail Cumming z 30040; rural
Druid Hills; CDP; DEKALB; 168 E-4; ★ **ATL**; mail Atlanta z 30322, z 30333; Ⓟ 12,174; Ⓒ 12,741
Dry Branch (Youley); RMC Place; JENKINS; mail Perkins z 30822; rural
Dry Branch; RMC Place; TWIGGS, BIBB; 166 I-7; elev. 361ft./110m.; 🅿; ★ **MAC**; z 31020; ● 400
Dry Pond; RMC Place; JACKSON; *166 D-7; elev. 916ft./279m.; mail Commerce z 30529; rural
Dublin; Inc. Place; ⊡ LAURENS; 166 I-8; elev. 228ft./69m.; 🅿 🅷 ■; z 31021, z 31027, z 31040; Ⓟ 16,312; Ⓒ 15,857; ◆ 16,833
Dubois; RMC Place; DODGE; *166 J-7; mail Cochran z 31014; rural
Ducktown; RMC Place; FORSYTH; *166 D-5; elev. 1,252ft./382m.; ★ **ATL**; mail Cumming z 30040
Dudley; Inc. Place; LAURENS; 166 I-8; 🅿; z 31022; Ⓟ 430; Ⓒ 447
Due West; RMC Place; COBB; *166 E-4; elev. 1,093ft./333m.; ★ **ATL**; mail Marietta z 30064; rural
Duffee; RMC Place; MITCHELL; *167 M-5; mail Camilla z 31730; rural
Dugdown; RMC Place; HARALSON; *166 E-2; mail Buchanan z 30113; rural
Duluth; Inc. Place; GWINNETT; 166 E-5; elev. 1,100ft./335m.; 🅿 🅷 🅲 437; ★ **ATL**; z 30026, z 30029, z 30095-99; Ⓟ 9,029; Ⓒ 22,122; ◆ 31,441
Dumas; RMC Place; WEBSTER; *167 K-4; mail Preston z 31824; rural
Dunaire; RMC Place; DEKALB; 168 D-6; elev. 900ft./274m.; ★ **ATL**; mail Decatur z 30032; ● 8,000
Duncan Park; RMC Place; CATOOSA; *166 B-2; ★ **CHTN**; mail Chattanooga z 37412; ● 850
Dunwoody; CDP; DEKALB; 168 A-4; 🅿; ★ **ATL**; z 30338, z 30346, z 30356, z 30360; Ⓟ 26,302; Ⓒ 32,808; ◆ 37,455
Du Pont; Inc. Place; CLINCH; 167 N-8; elev. 182ft./55m.; 🅿; z 31630; Ⓟ 177; Ⓒ 139
Durand; RMC Place; MERIWETHER; 166 H-3; elev. 841ft./256m.; mail Warm Springs z 31830; ● 200
Dutch Island; RMC Place; CHATHAM; *167 K-13; ★ **SAV**; mail Savannah z 31406; ● 200

E

Eagle Cliff; RMC Place; WALKER; *166 B-2; ★ **CHTN**; mail Flintstone z 30725; ● 120
Eagle Grove; RMC Place; HART; *166 D-8; elev. 827ft./252m.; mail Canon z 30520; rural
EARLY; 167 M-3; Ⓟ 11,854; Ⓒ 12,354; ◆ 11,519
Eason; RMC Place; THOMAS; *167 O-6; mail Thomasville z 31757; rural
East Albany; RMC Place; DOUGHERTY; *167 L-5; ★ **ALB**; mail Albany z 31701; pop. incl. with Albany (Inc. Place)
Eastanollee; RMC Place; STEPHENS; 166 C-7; elev. 962ft./293m.; 🅿; z 30538; ● 450
East Armuchee; RMC Place; WALKER; *166 C-3; mail La Fayette z 30728; rural
East Athens; RMC Place; CLARKE; ★ **ATH**; mail Winterville z 30683; pop. incl. with Athens (Inc. Place)
East Atlanta; RMC Place; DEKALB; *166 F-5; ★ **ATL**; mail Atlanta z 30316; pop. incl. with Atlanta (Inc. Place)
East Boynton; RMC Place; CATOOSA; *166 B-2; ★ **CHTN**; mail Ringgold z 30736
East Cobb; RMC Place; COBB; ★ **ATL**; mail Marietta z 30007; pop. incl. with Marietta (Inc. Place)
East Columbus; RMC Place; MUSCOGEE; ★ **COL**; mail Columbus z 31907; rural
East Dublin; Inc. Place; LAURENS; 166 I-9; elev. 260ft./79m.; 🅿; z 31027 & mail Dublin z 31021; Ⓟ 2,524; Ⓒ 2,484
East Edgewood; RMC Place; MUSCOGEE; ★ **COL**; mail Columbus z 31907; pop. incl. with Columbus (Inc. Place)
East Ellijay; Inc. Place; GILMER; 166 C-4; elev. 1,320ft./402m.; 🅿; z 30539-40; Ⓟ 303; Ⓒ 707
East Griffin; CDP; SPALDING; *166 G-5; mail Griffin z 30223; Ⓟ 1,746; Ⓒ 1,635
East Highlands; RMC Place; MUSCOGEE; ★ **COL**; mail Columbus z 31901; pop. incl. with Columbus (Inc. Place)
East Juliette; RMC Place; JONES; 166 H-6; elev. 376ft./115m.; mail Juliette z 31046; ● 170
East Lake; RMC Place; DEKALB; *166 F-5; ★ **ATL**; mail Atlanta z 30317; pop. incl. with Atlanta (Inc. Place)
Eastman; Inc. Place; ⊡ DODGE; 166 J-8; elev. 362ft./110m.; 🅿 🅷; z 31023; Ⓟ 5,153; Ⓒ 5,440
East Marietta; RMC Place; COBB; 168 A-2; ★ **ATL**; mail Marietta z 30062; ● 12,000
East Meadow; RMC Place; CLARKE; *166 E-7; ★ **ATH**; mail Athens z 30605; pop. incl. with Athens (Inc. Place)
East Newnan; CDP; COWETA; 166 G-3; mail Newnan z 30263; Ⓟ 1,173; Ⓒ 1,305
East Point; Inc. Place; FULTON; 166 F-4; elev. 1,055ft./322m.; 🅿 🅷 🅲 452 ■; ★ **ATL**; z 30344, z 30364; Ⓟ 34,402; Ⓒ 39,595; ◆ 48,765
East Savannah; RMC Place; CHATHAM; ★ **SAV**; mail Savannah z 31404; pop. incl. with Savannah (Inc. Place)
East Side; RMC Place; WHITFIELD; *166 B-3; mail Dalton z 30719; pop. incl. with Dalton (Inc. Place)
East Thomasville; RMC Place; THOMAS; mail Thomasville z 31757; pop. incl. with Thomasville (Inc. Place)
East Town; RMC Place; DOUGHERTY; ★ **ALB**; mail Albany z 31705; pop. incl. with Albany (Inc. Place)
East Trion; RMC Place; CHATTOOGA; *166 C-2; mail Trion z 30753
Eastview; RMC Place; RICHMOND; *166 F-11; ★ **AUG**; mail Augusta z 30901; pop. incl. with Augusta (Inc. Place)
Eastville; RMC Place; OCONEE; 166 E-7; elev. 822ft./251m.; mail Bishop z 30621, Bogart z 30622, Watkinsville z 30677; ● 170
Eastwood (Brookwood); RMC Place; DEKALB; *166 F-5; ★ **ATL**; mail Atlanta z 30317; pop. incl. with Atlanta (Inc. Place)
Eastwood; RMC Place; DEKALB; ★ **ATL**; mail Atlanta z 30317; pop. incl. with Atlanta (Inc. Place)
Eatonton; Inc. Place; ⊡ PUTNAM; 166 G-7; elev. 575ft./175m.; 🅿 🅷; z 31024, z 31026; Ⓟ 4,737; Ⓒ 6,764
Ebenezer; RMC Place; WALTON; *166 F-6; mail Social Circle z 30025; rural
Echeconnee; RMC Place; PEACH; *166 I-6; ★ **MAC**; mail Byron z 31008; rural
ECHOLS; 167 O-8; Ⓟ 2,334; Ⓒ 3,754; ◆ 4,114
Echota; RMC Place; GORDON; 166 C-3; mail Calhoun z 30701; pop. incl. with Calhoun (Inc. Place)
Eden; RMC Place; EFFINGHAM; 166 J-12; elev. 36ft./11m.; 🅿; ★ **SAV**; z 31307; ● 750
Edgehill; Inc. Place; GLASCOCK; 166 G-9; elev. 450ft./137m.; 🅿; z 30810; Ⓟ 22; Ⓒ 30
Edgemoor East; RMC Place; CLAYTON; *166 F-4; ★ **ATL**; mail Jonesboro z 30236; ● 350
Edgemoor West; RMC Place; CLAYTON; *166 F-4; ★ **ATL**; mail Jonesboro z 30236; ● 300
Edgewater; RMC Place; CHATHAM; ★ **SAV**; mail Savannah z 31406; pop. incl. with Savannah (Inc. Place)
Edgewater Park; RMC Place; CHATHAM; ★ **SAV**; mail Savannah z 31406; pop. incl. with Savannah (Inc. Place)
Edgewood; RMC Place; COLUMBIA; 167 S-2; ★ **AUG**; mail Augusta z 30907; ● 4,000
Edgewood; RMC Place; DEKALB; *166 E-5; ★ **ATL**; mail Atlanta z 30307; pop. incl. with Atlanta (Inc. Place)
Edgewood; RMC Place; MUSCOGEE; *166 I-3; ★ **COL**; mail Columbus z 31907; pop. incl. with Columbus (Inc. Place)
Edison; Inc. Place; CALHOUN; 167 L-3; elev. 289ft./88m.; 🅿; z 39846; Ⓟ 1,182; Ⓒ 1,340
Edith; RMC Place; CLINCH; 167 O-9; mail Fargo z 31631; ● 50
Ednaville; RMC Place; JACKSON; *166 D-6; mail Braselton z 30517; ● 130
EFFINGHAM; 166 J-12; Ⓟ 25,687; Ⓒ 37,535; ◆ 54,836
Egypt; RMC Place; EFFINGHAM; 166 J-12; elev. 134ft./41m.; mail Springfield z 31329; ● 75
ELBERT; 166 E-8; Ⓟ 18,949; Ⓒ 20,511; ◆ 20,270
Elberta; RMC Place; HOUSTON; 166 I-6; ★ **MAC**; mail Warner Robins z 31093; ● 950
Elberton; Inc. Place; ⊡ ELBERT; 166 D-8; elev. 701ft./214m.; 🅿 🅷; z 30635; Ⓟ 5,682; Ⓒ 4,743
Elder; RMC Place; OCONEE; *166 F-7; mail Watkinsville z 30677; rural
Eldora; RMC Place; BRYAN; *166 J-12; mail Ellabell z 31308; ● 100
Eldorado; RMC Place; TIFT; 167 M-7; elev. 331ft./101m.; mail Tifton z 31794; ● 100
Eldorendo; RMC Place; DECATUR; 167 N-4; elev. 131ft./40m.; mail Colquitt z 39837; ● 100
Eleanor Village; RMC Place; DOUGHERTY; *167 L-5; ★ **ALB**; mail Albany z 31705; ● 200
Elim; RMC Place; LONG; *167 L-12; elev. 92ft./28m.; mail Ludowici z 31316; rural
Elizabeth; RMC Place; COBB; *166 E-4; elev. 1,187ft./362m.; ★ **ATL**; mail Marietta z 30060; pop. incl. with Marietta (Inc. Place)
Elko; RMC Place; HOUSTON; 166 J-6; elev. 416ft./127m.; 🅿; z 31025; ● 160
Ellabell; RMC Place; BRYAN; 167 K-12; elev. 82ft./25m.; 🅿; z 31308; ● 500
Ella Gap; RMC Place; GILMER; *166 C-4; mail Ellijay z 30540; rural
Ellaville; Inc. Place; ⊡ SCHLEY; 166 J-5; elev. 565ft./172m.; 🅿; z 31806; Ⓟ 1,724; Ⓒ 1,609
Ellenton; Inc. Place; COLQUITT; 167 N-7; elev. 267ft./81m.; 🅿; z 31747; Ⓟ 227; Ⓒ 336
Ellenwood; RMC Place; CLAYTON; 168 H-5; elev. 850ft./259m.; 🅿; ★ **ATL**; z 30294; ● 400
Ellerslie; RMC Place; HARRIS; 166 I-3; elev. 730ft./223m.; 🅿; z 31807; ● 200
Ellijay; Inc. Place; ⊡ GILMER; 166 C-4; elev. 1,312ft./400m.; 🅿 🅷; z 30536, z 30540; Ⓟ 1,178; Ⓒ 1,584
Elliotts Bluff; RMC Place; CAMDEN; *167 O-12; mail Saint Marys z 31558; rural
Ellwood; RMC Place; RICHMOND; *166 G-10; ★ **AUG**; mail Blythe z 30805; pop. incl. with Augusta (Inc. Place)
Elmodel; RMC Place; BAKER; 167 M-4; mail Newton z 39870; ● 75
Elza; RMC Place; TATTNALL; *167 K-10; mail Reidsville z 30453; rural
EMANUEL; 166 I-10; Ⓟ 20,546; Ⓒ 21,837; ◆ 22,356
Embry Hills; RMC Place; DEKALB; 168 C-6; elev. 950ft./290m.; ★ **ATL**; mail Atlanta z 31141; ● 1,600
Emerson; Inc. Place; BARTOW; 166 D-3; 🅿; ★ **ATL**; z 30137; Ⓟ 1,201; Ⓒ 1,092
Emerson Park; RMC Place; WARE; *167 N-10; mail Waycross z 31503; ● 750
Emit; RMC Place; BULLOCH; *166 J-11; mail Statesboro z 30458; rural
Emma; RMC Place; DAWSON; *166 C-5; mail Dawsonville z 30534; rural
Emmalane; RMC Place; JENKINS; 166 I-11; elev. 207ft./63m.; mail Millen z 30442; ● 30
Empire; RMC Place; DODGE; 166 J-7; elev. 386ft./118m.; 🅿; z 31014; ● 200
Englewood; RMC Place; MUSCOGEE; *166 J-3; ★ **COL**; mail Columbus z 31907; pop. incl. with Columbus (Inc. Place)
Enigma; Inc. Place; BERRIEN; 167 M-7; elev. 314ft./96m.; 🅿; z 31749; Ⓟ 611; Ⓒ 869
Enon Grove; RMC Place; HEARD; 166 G-3; elev. 839ft./256m.; mail Franklin z 30217; ● 60
Ensign Mills; MONROE; see Bibb Mills (RMC Place)
Enterprise; RMC Place; OGLETHORPE; 166 E-8; mail Carlton z 30627; ● 50
Ephesus (Loftin); Inc. Place; HEARD; 166 G-2; elev. 1,200ft./366m.; mail Franklin z 30217, Roopville z 30170; Ⓟ 324; Ⓒ 388
Epworth; RMC Place; FANNIN; 166 B-4; elev. 1,800ft./549m.; 🅿; z 30541; ● 650
Epworth Acres; RMC Place; GLYNN; *167 N-12; ★ **BRUNS**; mail Saint Simons Island z 31522; ● 100
Eric; WHEELER; see Erick (RMC Place)
Erick (Eric); RMC Place; WHEELER; *167 K-9; mail Alamo z 30411; rural
Esom Hill; RMC Place; POLK; 166 E-2; elev. 908ft./277m.; 🅿; z 30138; ● 250
Etna; RMC Place; POLK; 166 E-2; mail Cedartown z 30125; ● 60
Eton; Inc. Place; MURRAY; 166 B-4; elev. 725ft./221m.; 🅿; z 30724; Ⓟ 315; Ⓒ 319
Eudora; JASPER; see Prospect (RMC Place)
Euharlee; Inc. Place; BARTOW; 166 D-3; elev. 680ft./207m.; 🅿; z 30120, z 30145; Ⓟ 850; Ⓒ 3,208
Eulonia; RMC Place; MCINTOSH; 167 M-12; elev. 10ft./3m.; mail Townsend z 31331; ● 100
Evans; CDP; COLUMBIA; 166 F-10; elev. 426ft./130m.; 🅿; ★ **AUG**; z 30809; Ⓟ 13,713; Ⓒ 17,727
EVANS; 166 J-11; Ⓟ 8,724; Ⓒ 10,495; ◆ 11,591
Evansville; RMC Place; TROUP; *166 H-2; mail Lagrange z 30240; rural
Everett; RMC Place; GLYNN; 167 M-12; elev. 16ft./5m.; mail Brunswick z 31523, z 31525; ● 350
Everett Springs; RMC Place; FLOYD; *166 C-3; mail Armuchee z 30105
Evergreen; RMC Place; DOUGHERTY; *167 L-5; ★ **ALB**; mail Albany z 31721; pop. incl. with Albany (Inc. Place)
Excelsior; RMC Place; CANDLER; *166 J-11; elev. 168ft./51m.; mail Metter z 30439; ● 30
Executive Park; RMC Place; DEKALB; *166 E-5; ★ **ATL**; mail Atlanta z 30347
Experiment; CDP; SPALDING; 166 G-5; 🅿; z 30212 & mail Griffin z 30223; Ⓟ 3,762; Ⓒ 3,233

F

Faceville; RMC Place; DECATUR; 167 O-4; elev. 302ft./92m.; ● 200
Fairburn; Inc. Place; FULTON; 166 F-4; elev. 1,016ft./310m.; 🅿; ★ **ATL**; z 30213; Ⓟ 4,013; Ⓒ 5,464
Fairchild; RMC Place; SEMINOLE; *167 O-3; elev. 130ft./40m.; mail Donalsonville z 39845; ● 30
Fairfax; RMC Place; WARE; *167 M-9; elev. 163ft./50m.; mail Millwood z 31552; rural
Fairfield; RMC Place; CHATHAM; *167 K-13; ★ **SAV**; mail Savannah z 31404; pop. incl. with Savannah (Inc. Place)
Fairlawn Acres; RMC Place; CATOOSA; *166 B-2; ★ **CHTN**; mail Rossville z 30741; pop. incl. with Fort Oglethorpe (Inc. Place)
Fairmount; Inc. Place; GORDON; 166 C-4; elev. 758ft./231m.; 🅿; z 30139; Ⓟ 657; Ⓒ 745
Fair Oaks; CDP; COBB; 168 B-1; elev. 1,100ft./335m.; ★ **ATL**; mail Marietta z 30060; Ⓟ 6,996; Ⓒ 8,443
Fairplay; RMC Place; DOUGLAS; 166 F-3; elev. 1,170ft./357m.; ★ **ATL**; mail Winston z 30187; ● 200
Fairplay; RMC Place; MORGAN; 166 F-7; elev. 781ft./238m.; mail Rutledge z 30663; ● 75
Fairview; RMC Place; FRANKLIN; *166 C-8; mail Lavonia z 30553; rural
Fairview; RMC Place; HABERSHAM; *166 C-7; mail Demorest z 30535; rural
Fairview; RMC Place; JACKSON; *166 D-6; mail Pendergrass z 30567; rural
Fairview; CDP; WALKER; *166 B-2; ★ **CHTN**; mail Rossville z 30741; Ⓟ 6,444; Ⓒ 6,601
Fairway Oaks; RMC Place; CHATHAM; *167 K-13; ★ **SAV**; mail Savannah z 31406; pop. incl. with Savannah (Inc. Place)
Fairway Village; RMC Place; RICHMOND; *166 G-11; ★ **AUG**; mail Augusta z 30906; pop. incl. with Augusta (Inc. Place)
Fairyland; WALKER; see Lookout Mountain (Inc. Place)
Fancy Hall; RMC Place; BRYAN; *167 L-13; mail Richmond Hill z 31324; rural
FANNIN; 166 B-4; Ⓟ 15,992; Ⓒ 19,798; ◆ 23,049
Fantasy Hills; RMC Place; WALKER; *166 B-2; ★ **CHTN**; mail Flintstone z 30725; ● 350
Fargo; Inc. Place; CLINCH; 167 O-9; elev. 118ft./36m.; 🅿; z 31631; Ⓟ 414; Ⓒ 380
Farmdale; RMC Place; SCREVEN; *166 I-12; mail Sylvania z 30467; rural
Farmers High; RMC Place; CARROLL; *166 F-2; elev. 1,123ft./342m.; mail Carrollton z 30117; rural
Farmington; RMC Place; OCONEE; 166 E-7; elev. 740ft./226m.; 🅿; z 30638; ● 200
Farmville; RMC Place; GORDON; *166 C-3; mail Calhoun z 30701; rural
Farrar; RMC Place; JASPER; *166 F-6; mail Shady Dale z 31085; rural
Fashion; RMC Place; MURRAY; *166 B-3; elev. 763ft./233m.; mail Chatsworth z 30705; rural
Faulkner; RMC Place; PICKENS; mail Ball Ground z 30107; rural
FAYETTE; 166 G-4; Ⓟ 62,415; Ⓒ 91,263; ◆ 104,625
Fayetteville; Inc. Place; ⊡ FAYETTE; 166 F-4; elev. 937ft./286m.; 🅿; ★ **ATL**; z 30214-15, z 30270; Ⓟ 5,827; Ⓒ 11,148
Federal Center; RMC Place; FULTON; ★ **ATL**; mail Atlanta z 30301; pop. incl. with Atlanta (Inc. Place)
Federal Station; RMC Place; DOUGHERTY; *167 L-5; ★ **ALB**; mail Albany z 31702; pop. incl. with Albany (Inc. Place)
Fellwood Homes; RMC Place; CHATHAM; *167 K-13; ★ **SAV**; mail Savannah z 31415; pop. incl. with Savannah (Inc. Place)
Felton; RMC Place; HARALSON; 166 E-2; elev. 1,184ft./361m.; 🅿; z 30140; ● 200
Fernwood; RMC Place; CHATHAM; *167 K-13; ★ **SAV**; mail Savannah z 31404; pop. incl. with Savannah (Inc. Place)
Ficklin; RMC Place; WILKES; *166 F-9; mail Washington z 30673; rural
Fickling Mill (Ficklings Mill); RMC Place; TAYLOR; *166 I-5; mail Butler z 31006; rural
Ficklings Mill; TAYLOR; see Fickling Mill (RMC Place)
Fidele; GORDON; see Fidelle (RMC Place)
Fidelle (Fidele); RMC Place; GORDON; *166 C-3; mail Resaca z 30735; rural
Fife; RMC Place; FULTON; *166 F-4; ★ **ATL**; mail Fairburn z 30213; ● 100
Fincherville; RMC Place; BUTTS; *166 G-6; elev. 712ft./217m.; mail Jackson z 30233; rural
Findlay; RMC Place; DOOLY; 167 K-6; elev. 372ft./113m.; mail Pinehurst z 31070; ● 70
Finleyson; RMC Place; PULASKI; 167 K-7; elev. 225ft./69m.; mail Pineview z 31071; ● 100
Fish; POLK; see Fish Creek (RMC Place)
Fish Creek (Fish); RMC Place; POLK; *166 E-3; elev. 334ft./102m.; mail Cedartown z 30125; ● 200
Fitzgerald; Inc. Place; ⊡ BEN HILL, IRWIN; 167 L-7; elev. 338ft./103m.; 🅿 🅷; z 31750; Ⓟ 8,612; Ⓒ 8,758
Fitzgerald Cotton Mill; RMC Place; BEN HILL; mail Fitzgerald z 31750; ● 250
Fitzpatrick; RMC Place; TWIGGS; *166 I-7; mail Jeffersonville z 31044; rural
Five Forks; RMC Place; GWINNETT; 166 E-5; ★ **ATL**; mail Lawrenceville z 30045; ● 3,200
Five Forks (Five Points); RMC Place; THOMAS; *167 O-6; mail Boston z 31626; rural
Fivemile Still; RMC Place; CLINCH; *167 N-9; mail Homerville z 31634
Five Points; RMC Place; DOUGHERTY; *167 L-5; ★ **ALB**; pop. incl. with Albany (Inc. Place)
Five Points; RMC Place; FULTON; *166 F-4; ★ **ATL**; mail Atlanta z 30303; pop. incl. with Atlanta (Inc. Place)
Five Points; RMC Place; LOWNDES; *167 O-7; ★ **VALD**; mail Valdosta z 31602; pop. incl. with Valdosta (Inc. Place)
Five Points; RMC Place; MACON; *166 J-6; mail Montezuma z 31063; rural
Five Points; RMC Place; MARION; *166 J-4; mail Buena Vista z 31803; rural
Five Points; RMC Place; RANDOLPH; *167 L-4; elev. 326ft./99m.; mail Shellman z 39886; rural
Five Points; RMC Place; TAYLOR; *166 I-5; mail Butler z 31006; rural
Five Points; THOMAS; see Five Forks (RMC Place)
Five Points; RMC Place; TREUTLEN; *166 J-10; elev. 301ft./92m.; mail Soperton z 30457; rural
Five Springs; RMC Place; WHITFIELD; *166 B-3; mail Dalton z 30721; rural
Flat Rock; RMC Place; MUSCOGEE; ★ **COL**; mail Columbus z 31907; pop. incl. with Columbus (Inc. Place)
Flat Rock; RMC Place; PUTNAM; *166 G-7; mail Eatonton z 31024; rural
Flat Shoals; RMC Place; HART; *166 D-8; elev. 825ft./251m.; mail Bowersville z 30516; ● 150
Fleetwood; RMC Place; CHATHAM; *167 K-13; ★ **SAV**; mail Savannah z 31404; pop. incl. with Savannah (Inc. Place)
Fleming; RMC Place; LIBERTY; *167 K-12; elev. 21ft./6m.; 🅿; z 31309; ● 200
Fleming Heights; RMC Place; RICHMOND; *166 G-11; ★ **AUG**; mail Augusta z 30906; pop. incl. with Augusta (Inc. Place)
Flemington; Inc. Place; LIBERTY; 167 K-12; elev. 24ft./7m.; mail Hinesville z 31313; Ⓟ 279; Ⓒ 369
Flint; RMC Place; MITCHELL; *167 M-5; elev. 181ft./55m.; mail Baconton z 31716; rural
Flint Hill; RMC Place; TALBOT; *166 H-4; mail Shiloh z 31826; rural
Flint River; RMC Place; SUMTER; mail Andersonville z 31711; rural
Flint River Estates; RMC Place; CLAYTON; *166 F-4; ★ **ATL**; mail Jonesboro z 30238; ● 2,000
Flintside; RMC Place; SUMTER; 167 K-6; mail Cobb z 31735; ● 50
Flintstone; RMC Place; WALKER; *166 B-2; elev. 679ft./207m.; 🅿; ★ **CHTN**; z 30725; ● 350
Flintwoods; RMC Place; CLAYTON; *166 F-4; elev. 880ft./268m.; ★ **ATL**; mail Riverdale z 30274; ● 1,500
Flippen; RMC Place; HENRY; 166 F-5; elev. 855ft./261m.; ★ **ATL**; mail McDonough z 30253; ● 250
Floral Hill; RMC Place; WILKES; *166 E-9; mail Tignall z 30668; rural
Florence; RMC Place; STEWART; *167 K-3; mail Omaha z 31821
Florida Rock; MUSCOGEE; see Fortson (RMC Place)
Flovilla; Inc. Place; BUTTS; 166 G-6; elev. 586ft./179m.; 🅿; z 30216; Ⓟ 602; Ⓒ 652
Flowery Branch; Inc. Place; HALL; 166 D-6; 🅿; ★ **ATL**; z 30542; Ⓟ 1,251; Ⓒ 1,806
Floyd; RMC Place; COBB; *166 E-4; ★ **ATL**; mail Mableton z 30126
FLOYD; 166 D-2; Ⓟ 81,251; Ⓒ 90,565; ◆ 95,532
Floyd Springs; RMC Place; FLOYD; *166 C-2; mail Armuchee z 30105; rural
Folkston; Inc. Place; ⊡ CHARLTON; 167 O-11; elev. 81ft./25m.; 🅿 🅷; z 31537; Ⓟ 2,285; Ⓒ 2,178; Ⓡ 3,230
Folsom; RMC Place; BARTOW; 166 D-3; mail Adairsville z 30103; ● 200
Forest Estates; RMC Place; RICHMOND; *166 F-11; elev. 300ft./91m.; ★ **AUG**; mail Augusta z 30909; pop. incl. with Augusta (Inc. Place)
Forest Hills; RMC Place; MUSCOGEE; *166 I-3; ★ **COL**; mail Columbus z 31907; pop. incl. with Columbus (Inc. Place)
Forest Hills; RMC Place; RICHMOND; *166 F-11; ★ **AUG**; mail Augusta z 30909, z 30919; pop. incl. with Augusta (Inc. Place)
Forest Lake; RMC Place; BIBB; *166 H-6; ★ **MAC**; mail Macon z 31210; pop. incl. with Macon (Inc. Place)
Forest Park; Inc. Place; CLAYTON; 166 F-4; elev. 999ft./304m.; 🅿; ★ **ATL**; z 30297-98; Ⓟ 16,925; Ⓒ 21,447; ◆ 27,418
Forest Park; RMC Place; DOUGHERTY; *167 M-5; ★ **ALB**; mail Albany z 31701; pop. incl. with Albany (Inc. Place)
Forest Park; RMC Place; RICHMOND; *166 F-11; ★ **AUG**; mail Augusta z 30904; pop. incl. with Augusta (Inc. Place)
Forest River Farms; RMC Place; CHATHAM; ★ **SAV**; mail Savannah z 31406; pop. incl. with Savannah (Inc. Place)
Forrest Hills; RMC Place; CHATHAM; *167 K-13; ★ **SAV**; mail Savannah z 31404; pop. incl. with Savannah (Inc. Place)
Forsyth; Inc. Place; ⊡ MONROE; 166 H-6; elev. 705ft./215m.; 🅿 🅷; z 31029; Ⓟ 4,268; Ⓒ 3,776; Ⓡ 4,094
FORSYTH; 166 D-5; Ⓟ 44,083; Ⓒ 98,407; ◆ 174,061
Fort Benning Junction; RMC Place; MUSCOGEE; *166 J-3; ★ **COL**; pop. incl. with Columbus (Inc. Place)
Fort Benning South; CDP-Census Area Only; CHATTAHOOCHEE; *166 J-3; ★ **COL**; mail Fort Benning z 31905; Ⓟ 14,617; Ⓒ 11,737
Fort Gaines; Inc. Place; ⊡ CLAY; 167 L-3; elev. 245ft./75m.; 🅿; z 39851; Ⓟ 1,248; Ⓒ 1,110
Fort Lamar; RMC Place; MADISON; 166 D-7; elev. 668ft./204m.; mail Danielsville z 30633; ● 85
Fort McAllister; RMC Place; BRYAN; 167 K-13; mail Richmond Hill z 31324; ● 300
Fort Oglethorpe; Inc. Place; CATOOSA, WALKER; 166 B-2; elev. 700ft./213m.; 🅿 🅷; ★ **CHTN**; z 30742; Ⓟ 5,880; Ⓒ 6,940
Fort Screven; RMC Place; CHATHAM; *167 K-14; ★ **SAV**; mail Tybee Island z 31328; pop. incl. with Tybee Island (Inc. Place)
Fortson (Florida Rock); RMC Place; MUSCOGEE; *166 I-3; elev. 516ft./157m.; 🅿; ★ **COL**; z 31808; pop. incl. with Columbus (Inc. Place)
Fortsonia; RMC Place; ELBERT; 166 E-9; mail Elberton z 30635; ● 90
Fort Stewart; CDP-Census Area Only; LIBERTY; *167 K-12; 🅿; z 31313-15; Ⓟ 13,774; Ⓒ 11,205
Fort Valley; Inc. Place; ⊡ PEACH; 166 I-6; elev. 525ft./160m.; 🅿 🅷 🅲 2,204; z 31030; Ⓟ 8,198; Ⓒ 8,005
Foster Hills; RMC Place; CATOOSA; *166 B-2; ★ **CHTN**; mail Ringgold z 30736; ● 150
Foster Mills (Fosters Mills); RMC Place; FLOYD; *166 D-2; mail Rome z 30161; rural
Fosters Mills; FLOYD; see Foster Mills (RMC Place)
Four Points; RMC Place; DOUGHERTY; *167 L-5; ★ **ALB**; mail Albany z 31705; pop. incl. with Albany (Inc. Place)
Four Seasons; RMC Place; ROCKDALE; *166 F-5; elev. 857ft./261m.; ★ **ATL**; mail Conyers z 30094; ● 300
Fowlstown; RMC Place; DECATUR; 167 O-4; elev. 290ft./88m.; 🅿; z 39852; ● 140
Fox; RMC Place; FLOYD; ★ **ROME**; mail Rome z 30161; pop. incl. with Rome (Inc. Place)
Foxboro; RMC Place; LOWNDES; *167 O-7; elev. 150ft./46m.; ★ **VALD**; mail Valdosta z 31602; ● 100
Frances Hollow; RMC Place; ROCKDALE; *166 F-5; elev. 899ft./274m.; ★ **ATL**; mail Conyers z 30094; ● 200
Franklin; Inc. Place; ⊡ HEARD; 166 G-3; elev. 696ft./212m.; 🅿; z 30217 & mail Glenn z 30219; Ⓟ 876; Ⓒ 902
FRANKLIN; 166 C-7; Ⓟ 16,650; Ⓒ 20,285; ◆ 22,005
Franklin Springs; Inc. Place; FRANKLIN; 166 D-8; elev. 755ft./230m.; 🅿 🅲 676; z 30639; Ⓟ 475; Ⓒ 762
Franklinton; RMC Place; BIBB; *166 I-7; ★ **MAC**; mail Dry Branch z 31020; ● 75
Frazier; RMC Place; BLECKLEY; *166 J-7; mail Cochran z 31014; ● 90
Free Home; RMC Place; CHEROKEE; *166 D-5; elev. 1,253ft./382m.; ★ **ATL**; mail Canton z 30115; rural
Friendship; RMC Place; POLK; *166 E-2; mail Cedartown z 30125; rural
Friendship; RMC Place; SUMTER; *167 K-4; elev. 548ft./167m.; mail Americus z 31719
Frolona; RMC Place; HEARD; *166 G-2; mail Franklin z 30217; rural
Fruitland; RMC Place; ECHOLS; 167 O-9; elev. 160ft./49m.; mail Du Pont z 31630; ● 35
Fry; RMC Place; FANNIN; *166 B-5; elev. 1,600ft./488m.; mail Mc Caysville z 30555; ● 60
Fullwood Springs; RMC Place; POLK; *166 E-2; mail Cedartown z 30125; rural
FULTON; 166 F-4; Ⓟ 648,951; Ⓒ 816,006; Ⓡ 815,806; ◆ 1,050,801
Funston; Inc. Place; COLQUITT; 167 N-6; elev. 346ft./105m.; 🅿; z 31753; Ⓟ 248; Ⓒ 426
Furniture City; RMC Place; COBB; ★ **ATL**; mail Mableton z 30126

G

Gabbettville; RMC Place; TROUP; 166 H-2; mail Lagrange z 30240; ● 75
Gaddistown; RMC Place; UNION; *166 C-5; mail Suches z 30572; rural
Gaillard; RMC Place; CRAWFORD; 166 I-5; elev. 406ft./124m.; mail Roberta z 31078; ● 30
Gaines School; RMC Place; CLARKE; *166 E-7; ★ **ATH**; mail Athens z 30605; pop. incl. with Athens (Inc. Place)
Gainesville; Inc. Place; ⊡ HALL; 166 D-6; elev. 1,249ft./381m.; 🅿 🅷 🅲 2,407 ■; z 30501, z 30503-04, z 30506-07; Ⓟ 17,885; Ⓒ 25,578; ◆ 39,950
Gainesville Cotton Mills; HALL; see Gainesville Mills (RMC Place)
Gainesville Mills (Gainesville Cotton Mills); RMC Place; HALL; *166 D-6; mail Gainesville z 30501; Ⓟ 1,329
Galloway; RMC Place; FANNIN; *166 B-5; mail Blue Ridge z 30513; rural
Garden Acres Estates; RMC Place; CHATHAM; ★ **SAV**; mail Pooler z 31322; pop. incl. with Pooler (Inc. Place)
Garden City; Inc. Place; CHATHAM; 167 S-9; elev. 19ft./6m.; 🅿; ★ **SAV**; z 31405, z 31408, z 31415, z 31418 & mail Savannah z 31407; Ⓟ 7,410; Ⓒ 11,289; Ⓡ 10,160
Garden Lakes; RMC Place; FLOYD; 166 D-2; ★ **ROME**; mail Rome z 30165; ● 4,000
Garden Valley; RMC Place; MACON; *166 J-5; mail Ideal z 31041; rural
Gardi; RMC Place; WAYNE; 167 M-11; elev. 64ft./20m.; mail Jesup z 31545; ● 100
Gardner; RMC Place; WASHINGTON; *166 H-8; mail Oconee z 31067; pop. incl. with Oconee (Inc. Place)
Garfield; Inc. Place; EMANUEL; 166 I-11; elev. 225ft./69m.; 🅿; z 30425; Ⓟ 255; Ⓒ 152
Garland; RMC Place; LUMPKIN; *166 C-6; mail Dahlonega z 30533; rural
Garnersville; RMC Place; CLAY; *167 L-3; mail Morris z 39867; rural
Garretta; RMC Place; LAURENS; *166 J-8; mail Dublin z 31021; rural
Gasco; RMC Place; FULTON; ★ **ATL**; pop. incl. with Atlanta (Inc. Place)
Gate City; RMC Place; FULTON; *166 F-4; ★ **ATL**; mail Atlanta z 30312; pop. incl. with Atlanta (Inc. Place)
Gay; Inc. Place; MERIWETHER; 166 H-4; elev. 200ft./61m.; 🅿; z 30218; Ⓟ 133; Ⓒ 149
Geneva; Inc. Place; TALBOT; 166 I-4; elev. 580ft./177m.; 🅿; z 31810; Ⓟ 182; Ⓒ 114
Gentian; RMC Place; MUSCOGEE; 167 T-1; ★ **COL**; mail Columbus z 31907; pop. incl. with Columbus (Inc. Place)
Georgetown; CDP; CHATHAM; *167 K-13; ★ **SAV**; mail Savannah z 31405; Ⓟ 5,554; Ⓒ 10,599
Georgetown (Georgetown-Quitman County); Inc. Place; ⊡ QUITMAN; 167 K-2; elev. 297ft./91m.; 🅿; z 39854; Ⓟ 913; Ⓒ 973
Georgetown Estates; RMC Place; RICHMOND; *166 G-11; ★ **AUG**; mail Augusta z 30906; pop. incl. with Augusta (Inc. Place)
Georgetown-Quitman County; QUITMAN; see Georgetown (Inc. Place)
Georgia Industrial Institute; HABERSHAM; see Raoul (CDP)
Georgia Southern; RMC Place; BULLOCH; *166 J-11; mail Statesboro z 30460; pop. incl. with Statesboro (Inc. Place)
Germany; RMC Place; RABUN; *166 B-7; mail Clayton z 30525; rural
Gibson; Inc. Place; ⊡ GLASCOCK; 166 G-9; elev. 540ft./165m.; 🅿; z 30810; Ⓟ 679; Ⓒ 694
Gill; RMC Place; LINCOLN; *166 E-9; mail Tignall z 30668; rural
Gillis Springs; RMC Place; TREUTLEN; *166 J-9; elev. 297ft./91m.; mail Soperton z 30457; rural
Gillsville; Inc. Place; BANKS, HALL; 166 D-6; elev. 940ft./287m.; 🅿; z 30543; Ⓟ 113; Ⓒ 195
GILMER; 166 B-4; Ⓟ 13,368; Ⓒ 23,456; ◆ 28,886
Girard; Inc. Place; BURKE; 166 H-12; elev. 241ft./73m.; 🅿; z 30426; Ⓟ 195; Ⓒ 227
Gladesville; RMC Place; JASPER; *166 G-6; elev. 504ft./154m.; mail Monticello z 31064; rural
Gladys; RMC Place; BERRIEN; *167 M-7; mail Alapaha z 31622; rural
GLASCOCK; 166 G-9; Ⓟ 2,357; Ⓒ 2,556; ◆ 2,854
Glasgow; RMC Place; THOMAS; *167 O-6; mail Boston z 31626; rural
Gleason Heights; RMC Place; CHATHAM; *167 K-13; ★ **SAV**; mail Pooler z 31322; pop. incl. with Pooler (Inc. Place)
Glencliff; RMC Place; UPSON; *166 H-4; mail Thomaston z 30286; ● 120
Glen Cove; RMC Place; BIBB; ★ **MAC**; pop. incl. with Macon (Inc. Place)
Glenhaven; RMC Place; BIBB; ★ **MAC**; pop. incl. with Macon (Inc. Place)
Glen Haven; RMC Place; DEKALB; *166 F-5; ★ **ATL**; mail Decatur z 30032; ● 3,000
Glenloch; RMC Place; HEARD; *166 G-3; elev. 1,043ft./318m.; mail Franklin z 30217
Glenloch Village; RMC Place; FAYETTE; mail Peachtree City z 30269; pop. incl. with Peachtree City (Inc. Place)
Glenmore; RMC Place; WARE; *167 N-9; mail Waycross z 31503; rural
Glenn; RMC Place; HEARD; 166 G-2; elev. 819ft./250m.; 🅿; z 30219; ● 90
Glenn Hills; RMC Place; RICHMOND; *166 G-11; ★ **AUG**; mail Augusta z 30906; pop. incl. with Augusta (Inc. Place)
Glennville; Inc. Place; TATTNALL; 167 K-11; elev. 175ft./53m.; 🅿; z 30427; Ⓟ 3,676; Ⓒ 3,641; Ⓡ 4,829
Glenridge; RMC Place; FULTON; mail Atlanta z 30342; pop. incl. with Atlanta (Inc. Place)
Glenwood; RMC Place; FLOYD; *166 D-2; ★ **ROME**; mail Rome z 30165; ● 1,500
Glenwood; Inc. Place; WHEELER; 167 K-9; elev. 191ft./58m.; 🅿 🅷; z 30428; Ⓟ 881; Ⓒ 884
Glenwood Hills; RMC Place; DEKALB; *166 F-5; elev. 1,019ft./311m.; ★ **ATL**; mail Decatur z 30032; ● 5,200
Glory; RMC Place; BERRIEN; *167 M-8; mail Alapaha z 31622; rural
Gloster; RMC Place; GWINNETT; *166 E-5; ★ **ATL**; mail Lawrenceville z 30045
GLYNN; 167 M-12; Ⓟ 62,496; Ⓒ 67,568; ◆ 77,175
Glynn Haven; RMC Place; GLYNN; 167 S-14; elev. 15ft./5m.; ★ **BRUNS**; mail Saint Simons Island z 31522; ● 450
Goat Town; RMC Place; WASHINGTON; *166 H-8; mail Sandersville z 31082; rural
Gobblers Hill; RMC Place; CHATTAHOOCHEE; *166 J-3; mail Cusseta z 31805; rural
Gober; RMC Place; CHEROKEE; *166 D-4; mail Ball Ground z 30107; rural
Godfrey; RMC Place; MORGAN; 166 F-7; elev. 550ft./168m.; mail Madison z 30650; ● 130
Godwinsville; RMC Place; DODGE; *167 K-8; elev. 310ft./94m.; mail Eastman z 31023; rural
Goggins; RMC Place; LAMAR; *166 H-5; mail Barnesville z 30204; rural
Golden Isle; RMC Place; CHATHAM; ★ **SAV**; mail Savannah z 31410
Goldmine; RMC Place; HART; *166 D-8; mail Canon z 30520
Goldsboro; RMC Place; BLECKLEY; *166 J-7; elev. 398ft./121m.; mail Cochran z 31014; rural
Goldson; RMC Place; TAYLOR; *166 I-5; mail Butler z 31006; rural
Goodes; RMC Place; FULTON; *166 F-4; elev. 926ft./282m.; mail Palmetto z 30268; rural
Good Hope; Inc. Place; WALTON; 166 E-7; elev. 794ft./242m.; 🅿; z 30641; Ⓟ 181; Ⓒ 210
Goolsby; RMC Place; JASPER; *166 G-6; mail Monticello z 31064; rural
Gordon; Inc. Place; WILKINSON; 166 H-7; elev. 346ft./105m.; 🅿; z 31031; Ⓟ 2,468; Ⓒ 2,152
GORDON; 166 C-3; Ⓟ 35,072; Ⓒ 44,104; ◆ 53,727
Gordonston; RMC Place; CHATHAM; *167 K-13; ★ **SAV**; mail Savannah z 31404; pop. incl. with Savannah (Inc. Place)
Gordy; RMC Place; WORTH; 167 M-6; mail Sylvester z 31791; ● 50
Gore; RMC Place; CHATTOOGA; *166 C-2; mail Summerville z 30747; rural
Goss; RMC Place; ELBERT; *166 D-8; elev. 715ft./218m.; mail Elberton z 30635; ● 150
Gough; RMC Place; BURKE; 166 H-10; elev. 400ft./122m.; 🅿; z 30811; ● 300
Graball; RMC Place; LINCOLN; *166 E-9; mail Tignall z 30668; rural
Gracewood; RMC Place; RICHMOND; *166 G-11; elev. 305ft./93m.; 🅿 🅷; ★ **AUG**; z 30812; pop. incl. with Augusta (Inc. Place)
GRADY; 167 N-5; Ⓟ 20,279; Ⓒ 23,659; ◆ 25,376
Graham; Inc. Place; APPLING; 167 L-9; elev. 244ft./74m.; mail Baxley z 31513; Ⓟ 293; Ⓒ 312
Grandview; RMC Place; PICKENS; *166 C-4; mail Jasper z 30143; ● 100
Grange; RMC Place; JEFFERSON; 166 H-9; mail Louisville z 30434; ● 30
Granite Hill; RMC Place; HANCOCK; *166 G-8; mail Sparta z 31087; rural
Grantville; Inc. Place; COWETA; 166 G-3; elev. 872ft./266m.; 🅿; z 30220; Ⓟ 1,180; Ⓒ 1,309
Gratis; RMC Place; WALTON; 166 E-6; elev. 821ft./250m.; mail Monroe z 30655; ● 80
Graves; RMC Place; TERRELL; 167 L-4; elev. 350ft./107m.; mail Dawson z 39842; ● 60
Gray; Inc. Place; ⊡ JONES; 166 H-7; elev. 603ft./184m.; 🅿; ★ **MAC**; z 31032; Ⓟ 2,189; Ⓒ 1,811; Ⓡ 1,931
Gray Hill; RMC Place; TROUP; *166 H-3; mail West Point z 31833; rural
Graymont; RMC Place; EMANUEL; mail Twin City z 30471; pop. incl. with Twin City (Inc. Place)
Grays; CHATHAM; see Riverside (RMC Place)
Grayson; Inc. Place; GWINNETT; 166 E-6; elev. 1,088ft./332m.; 🅿; ★ **ATL**; z 30017; Ⓟ 529; Ⓒ 765
Graysville; RMC Place; CATOOSA; 166 B-3; elev. 697ft./212m.; 🅿; ★ **CHTN**; z 30726; ● 500
Green Acres; RMC Place; CATOOSA; *166 B-2; ★ **CHTN**; mail Rossville z 30741; pop. incl. with Fort Oglethorpe (Inc. Place)
Green Acres; RMC Place; CHATHAM; *167 K-13; ★ **SAV**; mail Savannah z 31404; pop. incl. with Savannah (Inc. Place)
Green Acres; RMC Place; CLARKE; *166 E-7; ★ **ATH**; mail Athens z 30605; pop. incl. with Athens (Inc. Place)
Green Acres Estate; RMC Place; LAURENS; mail Dublin z 31021; pop. incl. with Dublin (Inc. Place)
GREENE; 166 F-8; Ⓟ 11,793; Ⓒ 14,406; ◆ 16,030
Green Island Hills; RMC Place; MUSCOGEE; *166 I-3; ★ **COL**; mail Columbus z 31904; pop. incl. with Columbus (Inc. Place)
Greenough; RMC Place; MITCHELL; *167 M-5; elev. 292ft./89m.; mail Baconton z 31716; rural
Greensboro; Inc. Place; ⊡ GREENE; 166 F-8; elev. 598ft./182m.; 🅿 🅷; z 30642; Ⓟ 2,860; Ⓒ 3,238
Greens Cut; RMC Place; BURKE; *166 G-11; mail Augusta z 30906
Greenville; Inc. Place; ⊡ MERIWETHER; 166 H-4; elev. 870ft./265m.; 🅿; z 30222; Ⓟ 1,167; Ⓒ 946
Greenville Street; RMC Place; COWETA; mail Newnan z 30264; pop. incl. with Newnan (Inc. Place)
Greenway; RMC Place; EMANUEL; mail Midville z 30441; rural
Greenway; RMC Place; FULTON; *166 E-4; elev. 1,156ft./352m.; ★ **ATL**; mail Roswell z 30075; pop. incl. with Roswell (Inc. Place)
Greenwood; RMC Place; HENRY; *166 G-5; elev. 857ft./261m.; ★ **ATL**; mail McDonough z 30253; rural
Greenwood; RMC Place; LANIER; *167 N-8; mail Stockton z 31649; rural
Greenwood; RMC Place; MITCHELL; *167 N-4; elev. 151ft./46m.; mail Camilla z 31730; rural
Greenwood Forest; RMC Place; CLINCH; mail Stockton z 31649; rural
Gregory (Gregorys Mill); RMC Place; MURRAY; *166 B-3; mail Crandall z 30711; rural
Gregorys Mill; MURRAY; see Gregory (RMC Place)
Gresham Park; CDP-Census Area Only; DEKALB; 168 F-4; ★ **ATL**; mail Atlanta z 30316; Ⓟ 9,000; Ⓒ 9,215
Gresham Road; RMC Place; COBB; *166 E-4; ★ **ATL**; mail Marietta z 30067; pop. incl. with Marietta (Inc. Place)
Greshamville; RMC Place; GREENE; *166 F-7; elev. 632ft./193m.; mail Madison z 30650; ● 80
Gresston; RMC Place; DODGE; 166 J-7; mail Eastman z 31023; ● 115
Griffin; Inc. Place; ⊡ SPALDING; 166 G-5; elev. 977ft./298m.; 🅿 🅷 ■; z 30223-24; Ⓟ 21,347; Ⓒ 23,451; ◆ 25,506
Grimball Park; RMC Place; CHATHAM; ★ **SAV**; mail Savannah z 31406
Griswold; JONES; see Griswoldville (RMC Place)
Griswoldville (Griswold); RMC Place; JONES; *166 H-7; ★ **MAC**; mail Macon z 31217; rural
Grizzletown; RMC Place; BARTOW; mail Acworth z 30101; ● 180
Grooverville; RMC Place; BROOKS; *167 O-6; mail Boston z 31626; rural
Grovania; RMC Place; HOUSTON; 166 J-6; mail Hawkinsville z 31036; ● 125
Groveland; RMC Place; BRYAN; 167 K-12; mail Pembroke z 31321; ● 50
Groveland; RMC Place; CHATHAM; *167 K-13; ★ **SAV**; mail Savannah z 31405; pop. incl. with Savannah (Inc. Place)
Groveland Park; RMC Place; BIBB; ★ **MAC**; pop. incl. with Macon (Inc. Place)
Grove Park; RMC Place; CHATHAM; *167 K-13; ★ **SAV**; mail Savannah z 31406; pop. incl. with Savannah (Inc. Place)
Grove Park; RMC Place; FULTON; *166 E-4; ★ **ATL**; mail Atlanta z 30318; pop. incl. with Atlanta (Inc. Place)
Grove Point; RMC Place; CHATHAM; *167 K-13; ★ **SAV**; mail Savannah z 31405; ● 60
Grovetown; Inc. Place; COLUMBIA; 166 F-10; 🅿; ★ **AUG**; z 30813; Ⓟ 3,596; Ⓒ 6,089
Gum Branch; Inc. Place; LIBERTY; 167 L-12; mail Hinesville z 31313; Ⓟ 291; Ⓒ 273
Gumlog (Gumlong); CDP; FRANKLIN; *166 C-8; elev. 700ft./213m.; mail Lavonia z 30553; Ⓟ 1,470; Ⓒ 2,025
Gum Log; RMC Place; UNION; *166 B-6; mail Blairsville z 30512; ● 100
Gumlong; FRANKLIN; see Gumlog (CDP)
Guysie; RMC Place; BACON; *167 M-9; mail Alma z 31510; rural
Guyton; Inc. Place; EFFINGHAM; 166 J-12; elev. 80ft./24m.; 🅿; z 31312; Ⓟ 740; Ⓒ 917
GWINNETT; 166 E-6; Ⓟ 352,910; Ⓒ 588,448; ◆ 811,358

H

Habersham; RMC Place; HABERSHAM; 166 C-7; 🅿; z 30544; ● 75
HABERSHAM; 166 C-7; Ⓟ 27,621; Ⓒ 35,902; ◆ 44,494
Haddock; RMC Place; JONES; 166 H-7; elev. 500ft./152m.; 🅿; z 31033; ● 750
Hagan; Inc. Place; EVANS; 167 K-11; 🅿; z 30429; Ⓟ 787; Ⓒ 898
Haggards Crossroads; RMC Place; MADISON; *166 D-7; mail Danielsville z 30633; rural
Hahira; Inc. Place; LOWNDES; 167 N-7; elev. 225ft./69m.; 🅿 🅷; z 31632; Ⓟ 1,353; Ⓒ 1,626
Halcyon Bluff (Halycon Bluff); RMC Place; CHATHAM; *167 K-13; ★ **SAV**; mail Savannah z 31401; ● 500
Halcyondale; RMC Place; SCREVEN; *166 I-12; elev. 113ft./34m.; mail Sylvania z 30467; rural
Hale Gap; RMC Place; DADE; *166 B-2; ★ **CHTN**; mail Trenton z 30752; rural
Halfmoon Landing; RMC Place; LIBERTY; 167 L-13; mail Midway z 31320; ● 150
HALL; 166 D-6; Ⓟ 95,428; Ⓒ 139,277; Ⓡ 139,281; ◆ 192,923
Halls (Linwood); RMC Place; BARTOW; 166 D-3; mail Kingston z 30145; ● 50
Halls Crossing; RMC Place; WASHINGTON; *166 H-9; mail Davisboro z 31018; rural
Hallwood; RMC Place; PUTNAM; *166 G-7; mail Eatonton z 31024; rural
Halycon Bluff; CHATHAM; see Halcyon Bluff (RMC Place)
Hamilton; Inc. Place; ⊡ HARRIS; 166 I-3; elev. 762ft./232m.; 🅿; z 31811; Ⓟ 454; Ⓒ 307; Ⓡ 446
Hammett; RMC Place; CRAWFORD; *166 I-5; elev. 388ft./118m.; mail Roberta z 31078; rural
Hampton; Inc. Place; HENRY; 166 G-5; elev. 890ft./271m.; 🅿; ★ **ATL**; z 30228; Ⓟ 2,694; Ⓒ 3,857
HANCOCK; 166 G-8; Ⓟ 8,908; Ⓒ 10,076; ◆ 9,711
Handy; RMC Place; COWETA; *166 G-3; mail Newnan z 30263; rural
Hanes Manor; RMC Place; FULTON; *166 E-4; ★ **ATL**; mail Atlanta z 30305; pop. incl. with Atlanta (Inc. Place)
Haney; RMC Place; FLOYD; *166 D-2; mail Cave Spring z 30124; rural
Hannah; RMC Place; DOUGLAS; *166 F-3; mail Winston z 30187; rural
Hannahs Mill; CDP; UPSON; *166 H-5; mail Thomaston z 30286; Ⓒ 3,267
Hannatown; RMC Place; DECATUR; *167 O-4; elev. 291ft./89m.; rural
Hansell; RMC Place; THOMAS; *167 N-5; mail Meigs z 31765; rural
Hapeville; Inc. Place; FULTON; 168 G-3; elev. 1,001ft./305m.; 🅿; ★ **ATL**; z 30354; Ⓟ 5,483; Ⓒ 6,180
Haralson; Inc. Place; COWETA, MERIWETHER; 166 G-4; elev. 810ft./247m.; 🅿; z 30229; Ⓟ 139; Ⓒ 144
HARALSON; 166 E-2; Ⓟ 21,966; Ⓒ 25,690; ◆ 29,545
Harbin (Harbins); RMC Place; GWINNETT; *166 E-6; ★ **ATL**; mail Bethlehem z 30620; rural
Harbins; GWINNETT; see Harbin (RMC Place)
Harbor Creek; RMC Place; CHATHAM; *167 K-14; ★ **SAV**; mail Savannah z 31410
Hard Cash; RMC Place; ELBERT; *166 D-8; elev. 714ft./218m.; mail Dewy Rose z 30634; rural
Hardwick (Midway); RMC Place; BALDWIN; 166 H-7; elev. 450ft./137m.; 🅿; z 31034; pop. incl. with Milledgeville (Inc. Place)
Hardwicke; RMC Place; BRYAN; *167 K-13; mail Richmond Hill z 31324; ● 120
Harlem; Inc. Place; COLUMBIA; 166 G-10; elev. 520ft./158m.; 🅿; ★ **AUG**; z 30814 & mail Appling z 30802; Ⓟ 2,199; Ⓒ 1,814
Harmony; RMC Place; PUTNAM; *166 F-7; mail Eatonton z 31024; rural
Harp; RMC Place; FAYETTE; *166 G-4; elev. 745ft./227m.; ★ **ATL**; mail Fayetteville z 30215; rural
Harrietts Bluff; RMC Place; CAMDEN; 167 O-12; mail Woodbine z 31569; ● 100
Harrington; RMC Place; GLYNN; 167 R-14; ★ **BRUNS**; mail Saint Simons Island z 31522; ● 125
HARRIS; 166 I-3; Ⓟ 17,788; Ⓒ 23,695; ◆ 30,351
Harrisburg; RMC Place; WALKER; *166 C-2; mail Summerville z 30747; rural
Harris City; RMC Place; MERIWETHER; 166 H-4; mail Greenville z 30222; ● 85
Harrison; Inc. Place; WASHINGTON; 166 H-9; elev. 400ft./122m.; 🅿; z 31035; Ⓟ 414; Ⓒ 509
Harrisonville; RMC Place; TROUP; 166 G-3; mail Hogansville z 30230; ● 120
Harrock Hall; RMC Place; CHATHAM; *167 K-13; ★ **SAV**; mail Savannah z 31406; ● 350
HART; 166 D-8; Ⓟ 19,712; Ⓒ 22,997; Ⓡ 23,000; ◆ 24,109
Hartford; RMC Place; PULASKI; 166 J-7; elev. 233ft./71m.; mail Hawkinsville z 31036; ● 250
Harts; RMC Place; GLASCOCK; *166 G-9; mail Gibson z 30810; rural
Hartsfield; RMC Place; COLQUITT; 167 N-5; 🅿; z 31756; ● 150
Hartwell; Inc. Place; ⊡ HART; 166 D-8; elev. 818ft./249m.; 🅿 🅷; z 30643; Ⓟ 4,555; Ⓒ 4,188; Ⓡ 4,191
Harvest; RMC Place; HABERSHAM; *166 C-7; elev. 1,476ft./450m.; mail Clarkesville z 30523; rural
Haskins; LAURENS; see Haskins Crossing (RMC Place)
Haskins Crossing (Haskins); RMC Place; LAURENS; *166 I-8; mail Dudley z 31022; rural
Hassier Mill; RMC Place; WHITFIELD; mail Rocky Face z 30740
Hatcher; RMC Place; QUITMAN; *167 L-3; mail Georgetown z 39854; rural
Hatchers Store; RMC Place; BURKE; *166 H-11; mail Waynesboro z 30830; ● 20
Hatley; RMC Place; CRISP; 167 K-6; mail Cordele z 31015; ● 60
Hawkinsville; Inc. Place; ⊡ PULASKI; 166 J-7; elev. 245ft./75m.; 🅿 🅷; z 31036; Ⓟ 3,527; Ⓒ 3,280; Ⓡ 4,255
Haylow; RMC Place; ECHOLS; 167 O-8; elev. 167ft./51m.; mail Du Pont z 31630; ● 25
Hayneville; RMC Place; HOUSTON; 166 J-6; elev. 436ft./133m.; mail Hawkinsville z 31036; ● 200
Hayston; RMC Place; NEWTON; *166 F-6; mail Mansfield z 30055; rural
Hazlehurst; Inc. Place; ⊡ JEFF DAVIS; 167 K-9; elev. 253ft./77m.; 🅿 🅷; z 31539; Ⓟ 4,202; Ⓒ 3,787
Head River; RMC Place; DADE; *166 C-2; mail Menlo z 30731; rural
HEARD; 166 G-2; Ⓟ 8,628; Ⓒ 11,012; ◆ 11,379
Heardsville; FORSYTH; see Heardville (RMC Place)
Heardville (Heardsville); RMC Place; FORSYTH; *166 D-5; ★ **ATL**; mail Cumming z 30040; rural
Hebardville; RMC Place; WARE; *167 M-10; elev. 135ft./41m.; mail Waycross z 31503; ● 300
Helen; Inc. Place; WHITE; 166 C-6; elev. 1,446ft./441m.; 🅿; z 30545; Ⓟ 300; Ⓒ 430
Helena; Inc. Place; TELFAIR, WHEELER; 167 K-8; elev. 248ft./76m.; 🅿; z 31037; Ⓟ 1,256; Ⓒ 2,307
Hemp; RMC Place; FANNIN; *166 B-5; mail Morganton z 30560
Henderson; RMC Place; HOUSTON; 166 J-6; mail Elko z 31025; ● 220
HENRY; 166 F-5; Ⓟ 58,741; Ⓒ 119,341; ◆ 201,169
Hentown; RMC Place; EARLY; *167 M-3; elev. 192ft./59m.; mail Blakely z 39823; rural
Hephzibah; Inc. Place; RICHMOND; 166 G-11; elev. 435ft./133m.; 🅿; ★ **AUG**; z 30815; Ⓟ 2,466; Ⓒ 3,880
Herndon; RMC Place; JENKINS; 166 H-10; elev. 178ft./54m.; mail Midville z 30441, Millen z 30442; ● 75
Herod; RMC Place; TERRELL; 167 L-4; elev. 303ft./92m.; mail Dawson z 39842; ● 30
Hiawassee; Inc. Place; ⊡ TOWNS; 166 B-6; elev. 1,980ft./604m.; 🅿 🅷; z 30546; Ⓟ 547; Ⓒ 808
Hickory Bluff; RMC Place; CAMDEN; *167 N-12; mail Waverly z 31565; ● 60
Hickory Flat; RMC Place; BANKS; *166 D-7; mail Lula z 30554; rural
Hickory Flat; RMC Place; CHEROKEE; *166 D-4; elev. 1,039ft./317m.; ★ **ATL**; mail Canton z 30115; rural
Hickory Level; RMC Place; CARROLL; *166 F-3; elev. 1,080ft./329m.; mail Carrollton z 30116; rural
Hickory Ridge; RMC Place; BIBB; ★ **MAC**; mail Macon z 31204; pop. incl. with Macon (Inc. Place)
Hickox; RMC Place; BRANTLEY; 167 N-11; elev. 60ft./18m.; mail Nahunta z 31553; ● 100
Hicks Circle; RMC Place; ROCKDALE; *166 F-5; elev. 543ft./166m.; ★ **ATL**; mail Conyers z 30012; pop. incl. with Conyers (Inc. Place)
Hidden Acres; RMC Place; ROCKDALE; *166 F-5; elev. 860ft./262m.; ★ **ATL**; mail Conyers z 30094; ● 700
Hidden Lake; RMC Place; CHATHAM; *167 K-13; ★ **SAV**; mail Savannah z 31419; pop. incl. with Savannah (Inc. Place)
Higdon; RMC Place; FANNIN; *166 B-4; mail Epworth z 30541; rural
Higgston; Inc. Place; MONTGOMERY; 166 J-10; elev. 293ft./89m.; mail Ailey z 30410; Ⓟ 274; Ⓒ 316
High Falls; RMC Place; MONROE; 166 G-5; elev. 660ft./201m.; mail Jackson z 30233; ● 300
Highgate; RMC Place; RICHMOND; *166 F-11; elev. 205ft./62m.; ★ **AUG**; mail Augusta z 30909; pop. incl. with Augusta (Inc. Place)
Highland Circle; RMC Place; BIBB; ★ **MAC**; mail Macon z 31211; pop. incl. with Macon (Inc. Place)
Highland Heights; RMC Place; LOWNDES; *167 O-7; elev. 636ft./194m.; ★ **VALD**; mail Americus z 31709; ● 200
Highland Mills; RMC Place; SPALDING; 166 G-5; mail Griffin z 30223; ● 700
Highland Park; RMC Place; CHATHAM; *167 K-13; ★ **SAV**; mail Savannah z 31406; pop. incl. with Savannah (Inc. Place)
Highland Pines; RMC Place; MUSCOGEE; *166 I-4; mail Columbus z 31909; pop. incl. with Columbus (Inc. Place)
High Point; RMC Place; NEWTON; *166 F-6; elev. 793ft./242m.; ★ **ATL**; mail Covington z 30016; ● 300
High Point; RMC Place; WALKER; *166 B-2; ★ **CHTN**; mail Chickamauga z 30707; rural
High Shoals; RMC Place; MORGAN, OCONEE, WALTON; 166 E-7; 🅿; z 30645; pop. incl. with North High Shoals (Inc. Place)
Hightower; RMC Place; FORSYTH; *166 D-5; mail Cumming z 30040; rural
Hill City; RMC Place; GORDON; *166 C-3; mail Resaca z 30735; ● 135
Hillcrest; RMC Place; TROUP; *166 G-3; elev. 742ft./226m.; mail Lagrange z 30240; rural
Hillcrest Heights; RMC Place; BIBB; *166 H-6; ★ **MAC**; mail Macon z 31204; pop. incl. with Macon (Inc. Place)
Hillman; RMC Place; TALIAFERRO; *166 F-9; mail Crawfordville z 30631; rural
Hillsboro; RMC Place; JASPER; 166 G-6; elev. 633ft./193m.; 🅿; z 31038; ● 200
Hillsdale; RMC Place; TIFT; *167 M-6; mail Tifton z 31794; rural
Hilltonia; SCREVEN; see Hiltonia (Inc. Place)

Entries in **UPPERCASE** are counties.
Entries in **bold** have populations of 2,500 or more.
Names in parentheses are alternate names.

Inc. Place	Incorporated Place
RMC Place	Rand McNally Designated Place
CDP	Census Designated Place
MCD	Minor Civil Division

⊡ County Seat
▲ Minor Civil Division
elev. Elevation
🅿 Post Office
🅷 Hospital
🅲 College
■ Principal Business Center
★ Ranally Metro Area (RMA) Abbreviation
z Zip Code(s)
Ⓟ Previous Census Population
Ⓡ Revised Census Population
Ⓐ Annexation Population
● Rand McNally Population Estimate
Ⓒ Final Census Population
Ⓢ Special Census Population
◆ Estimated Population

For additional definitions see Glossary, Volume 1, and Introduction, Volume 2.

Hilltop; CDP-Census Area Only; PIKE; *166 H-4; © 401
Hilton; RMC Place; EARLY; 167 M-3; elev. 218ft./66m.; mail Blakely Z 39823; ● 100
Hilton Heights; RMC Place; MUSCOGEE; ★ COL; mail Columbus Z 31906; pop. incl. with Columbus (Inc. Place)
Hiltonia (Hilltonia); Inc. Place; SCREVEN; 166 H-12; elev. 182ft./55m.; 🅿; Z 30467; Ⓟ 402; © 421
Hinesville; Inc. Place; ⊡ LIBERTY; 167 K-12; elev. 70ft./21m.; 🅿 🅷; Z 31310, Z 31313, Z 31315 & mail Fort Stewart Z 31314; Ⓟ 21,603; © 30,392; ◆ 33,431
Hinkles; RMC Place; WALKER; *166 B-2; ★ CHTN; mail Rising Fawn Z 30738; rural
Hinsonton; RMC Place; MITCHELL; 167 N-5; mail Meigs Z 31765; ● 100
Hinton; RMC Place; PICKENS; *166 C-4; mail Jasper Z 30143; rural
Hiram; Inc. Place; PAULDING; 166 E-3; elev. 1,005ft./306m.; 🅿; ★ ATL; Z 30141; Ⓟ 1,389; © 1,361
Hi-Roc Lake; ROCKDALE; see Hi Roc Shores (RMC Place)
Hi Roc Shores (Hi-Roc Lake); RMC Place; ROCKDALE; *166 F-6; ★ ATL; mail Conyers Z 30012; ● 600
Hobby; RMC Place; TURNER; *167 L-6; mail Ashburn Z 31714; rural
Hoboken; Inc. Place; BRANTLEY; 167 N-10; elev. 131ft./40m.; 🅿; Z 31542; Ⓟ 440; © 463
Hogansville; Inc. Place; TROUP; 166 G-3; elev. 716ft./218m.; 🅿; Z 30230; Ⓟ 2,976; © 2,774
Hoggard Mill; RMC Place; BAKER; *167 N-4; mail Newton Z 39870; rural
Hog Hammock; RMC Place; MCINTOSH; *167 M-13; mail Sapelo Island Z 31327; rural
Holbrook; RMC Place; CHEROKEE; *166 D-5; ★ ATL; mail Cumming Z 30040; rural
Holcomb Bridge; RMC Place; FULTON; *166 E-5; ★ ATL; mail Roswell Z 30076; pop. incl. with Roswell (Inc. Place)
Holland; RMC Place; CHATTOOGA; 166 D-2; elev. 698ft./213m.; mail Lyerly Z 30730; ● 150
Hollingsworth; RMC Place; BANKS; *166 C-7; mail Alto Z 30510
Hollis; RMC Place; THOMAS; *167 N-6; mail Pavo Z 31778; rural
Hollonville; RMC Place; PIKE; 166 G-4; elev. 823ft./251m.; mail Williamson Z 30292; ● 75
Holly Hills; RMC Place; MUSCOGEE; ★ COL; mail Columbus Z 31906; pop. incl. with Columbus (Inc. Place)
Holly Springs; Inc. Place; CHEROKEE; 166 D-4; elev. 1,100ft./335m.; 🅿; ★ ATL; Z 30114-15, Z 30142, Z 30188; Ⓟ 2,406; © 3,195
Holly Springs; RMC Place; JACKSON; *166 D-6; mail Maysville Z 30558, Pendergrass Z 30567; rural
Hollywood; RMC Place; HABERSHAM; *166 C-7; elev. 1,523ft./464m.; mail Clarkesville Z 30523; ● 300
Holt; RMC Place; IRWIN; 167 L-8; mail Wray Z 31798; ● 50
Holton; BIBB; see Arkwright (RMC Place)
Homeland; Inc. Place; CHARLTON; 167 O-11; elev. 97ft./30m.; 🅿; Z 31537; Ⓟ 981; © 765
Homer; Inc. Place; ⊡ BANKS; 166 D-7; 🅿; Z 30547; Ⓟ 742; © 950
Homerville; Inc. Place; ⊡ CLINCH; 167 N-9; elev. 178ft./54m.; 🅿 🅷; Z 31634; Ⓟ 2,560; © 2,803
Hooker; RMC Place; DADE; *166 B-2; ★ CHTN; mail Trenton Z 30752; rural
Hopeful; RMC Place; MITCHELL; *167 N-4; mail Camilla Z 31730
Hopeulikit; RMC Place; BULLOCH; *166 I-11; mail Statesboro Z 30458
Hopewell; RMC Place; CHEROKEE; mail Canton Z 30115; rural
Hopewell; RMC Place; HARRIS; *166 H-3; elev. 838ft./255m.; mail Pine Mountain Z 31822; rural
Horns; RMC Place; CRAWFORD; 166 I-5; mail Roberta Z 31078; ● 75
Hornsby; RMC Place; RICHMOND; *166 F-11; ★ AUG; mail Augusta Z 30901; pop. incl. with Augusta (Inc. Place)
Horseleg; FLOYD; see Horseleg Estates (RMC Place)
Horseleg Estates (Horseleg); RMC Place; FLOYD; *166 D-2; ★ ROME; mail Rome Z 30165; pop. incl. with Rome (Inc. Place)
Hortense; RMC Place; BRANTLEY; 167 M-11; elev. 56ft./17m.; 🅿; Z 31543; ● 400
Hoschton; Inc. Place; JACKSON; 166 D-6; elev. 918ft./280m.; 🅿; Z 30548; Ⓟ 642; © 1,070
HOUSTON; 166 J-6; Ⓟ 89,208; © 110,765; ◆ 137,278
Houston Heights; RMC Place; BIBB; ★ MAC; pop. incl. with Macon (Inc. Place)
Houston Lake; RMC Place; HOUSTON; 166 I-6; ★ MAC; mail Kathleen Z 31047; ● 100
Howard; RMC Place; TAYLOR; 166 I-4; elev. 634ft./193m.; 🅿; Z 31039; ● 80
Howell; RMC Place; ECHOLS; 167 O-8; elev. 170ft./52m.; mail Lake Park Z 31636; ● 75
Howell Mill; RMC Place; FULTON; *166 E-4; ★ ATL; mail Atlanta Z 30325; pop. incl. with Atlanta (Inc. Place)
Howells Transfer; RMC Place; FULTON; ★ ATL; pop. incl. with Atlanta (Inc. Place)
Howell Tower; RMC Place; FULTON; ★ ATL; pop. incl. with Atlanta (Inc. Place)
Huber; RMC Place; TWIGGS; *166 I-7; elev. 260ft./79m.; 🅿; Z 31201 & mail Macon Z 31217; ● 35
Hubert; RMC Place; BULLOCH; *166 J-12; mail Brooklet Z 30415; rural
Huffer; RMC Place; COFFEE; *167 L-9; mail Douglas Z 31533; rural
Hughland; RMC Place; TATTNALL; *167 K-11; mail Manassas Z 30438; rural
Hulett; RMC Place; CARROLL; *166 F-3; mail Carrollton Z 30116; rural
Hull; Inc. Place; MADISON; 166 E-7; elev. 811ft./247m.; 🅿; ★ ATH; Z 30646; Ⓟ 156; © 160
Hunter; SCREVEN; see Hunters (RMC Place)
Hunters (Hunter); RMC Place; SCREVEN; 166 I-12; mail Sylvania Z 30467; ● 40
Hunters Point; RMC Place; MUSCOGEE; *166 F-3; mail Columbus Z 31909
Huntington; RMC Place; SUMTER; *167 K-5; mail Americus Z 31709; rural
Hunts Corner; RMC Place; GORDON; *166 C-3; mail Calhoun Z 30701; rural
Hurst; RMC Place; FANNIN; *166 B-5; mail Morganton Z 30560; rural
Hutchings; OGLETHORPE; see Hutchins (RMC Place)
Hutchins (Hutchings); RMC Place; OGLETHORPE; 166 E-8; mail Crawford Z 30630; ● 50

I

Ideal; Inc. Place; MACON; 166 J-5; elev. 400ft./122m.; 🅿; Z 31041; Ⓟ 554; © 518
Ila; Inc. Place; MADISON; 166 D-7; elev. 815ft./248m.; 🅿; Z 30647; Ⓟ 297; © 328
Imlac; RMC Place; MERIWETHER; *166 H-4; mail Woodbury Z 30293; rural
Imperial (Imperial Mills); RMC Place; PUTNAM; 166 G-7; mail Eatonton Z 31024; pop. incl. with Eatonton (Inc. Place)
Imperial Mills; PUTNAM; see Imperial (RMC Place)
Inaha; RMC Place; TURNER; *167 L-6; elev. 403ft./123m.; mail Sycamore Z 31790; rural
Indian Hills Estates; RMC Place; CLAYTON; *166 F-5; ★ ATL; mail Jonesboro Z 30236
Indianola; RMC Place; LOWNDES; *167 O-8; mail Valdosta Z 31602; rural
Indian Springs; RMC Place; BUTTS; 166 G-6; elev. 635ft./194m.; mail Flovilla Z 30216; ● 200
Indian Springs; CDP; CATOOSA; *166 B-3; ★ CHTN; mail Ringgold Z 30736; Ⓟ 1,273; © 1,982
Industrial City (Industrial City of Gordon, Murray and Whitfield Counties, Tri-Counties Industrial City); RMC Place; GORDON, MURRAY, WHITFIELD; 166 C-3; elev. 700ft./213m.; mail Chatsworth Z 30705; ● 800
Industrial City of Gordon, Murray and Whitfield Counties; GORDON, MURRAY, WHITFIELD; see Industrial City (RMC Place)
Ingleside; RMC Place; BIBB; 167 R-5; ★ MAC; mail Macon Z 31204; pop. incl. with Macon (Inc. Place)
Inman; RMC Place; FAYETTE; *166 G-4; elev. 875ft./267m.; ★ ATL; ● 300
Inman Park; RMC Place; FULTON; *166 F-5; ★ ATL; mail Atlanta Z 30306; pop. incl. with Atlanta (Inc. Place)
Iron City; Inc. Place; SEMINOLE; 167 N-3; elev. 145ft./44m.; 🅿; Z 39859; Ⓟ 503; © 321
Irondale; CDP-Census Area Only; CLAYTON; *166 F-5; elev. 924ft./282m.; ★ ATL; mail Jonesboro Z 30238; Ⓟ 3,352; © 7,727
IRWIN; 167 L-7; Ⓟ 8,649; © 9,931; ◆ 9,253
Irwins Crossroads; RMC Place; WASHINGTON; *166 H-9; mail Tennille Z 31089; rural
Irwinton; Inc. Place; ⊡ WILKINSON; 166 I-8; elev. 450ft./137m.; 🅿; Z 31042; Ⓟ 641; © 587
Irwinville; RMC Place; IRWIN; 167 L-7; elev. 334ft./102m.; 🅿; Z 31760; ● 200
Isabella; RMC Place; WORTH; 167 L-6; elev. 447ft./136m.; mail Sylvester Z 31791; ● 225
Islandwood; RMC Place; CHATHAM; *167 K-14; ★ SAV; mail Savannah Z 31410
Isle of Hope; CDP; CHATHAM; 167 T-11; ★ SAV; mail Savannah Z 31406; © 2,605
Ivey; Inc. Place; WILKINSON; 166 H-7; elev. 316ft./96m.; 🅿; Z 31031; Ⓟ 1,053; © 1,100
Ivylog; RMC Place; UNION; *166 B-5; mail Blairsville Z 30512

J

Jackson; Inc. Place; ⊡ BUTTS; 166 G-6; elev. 700ft./213m.; 🅿 🅷; Z 30233; Ⓟ 4,076; © 3,934; ® 3,964
JACKSON; 166 D-7; Ⓟ 30,005; © 41,589; ◆ 66,106
Jacksons Crossroads; RMC Place; WILKES; *166 E-9; elev. 607ft./185m.; mail Tignall Z 30668; rural
Jacksons Store; RMC Place; WILKES; *166 E-8; elev. 596ft./182m.; mail Tignall Z 30668; rural
Jacksonville; Inc. Place; TELFAIR; 167 L-8; elev. 206ft./63m.; 🅿; Z 31544; Ⓟ 128; © 118
Jacksonville; RMC Place; TOWNS; 166 B-6; mail Young Harris Z 30582; ● 60
Jake; RMC Place; CARROLL; 166 F-2; mail Waco Z 30182; ● 120
Jakin; Inc. Place; EARLY; 167 N-3; elev. 148ft./45m.; 🅿; Z 39861; Ⓟ 137; © 157
Jamaica Estates; RMC Place; COLUMBIA; *166 F-10; ★ AUG; mail Augusta Z 30907; ● 100
James; RMC Place; JONES; 166 H-7; elev. 490ft./149m.; mail Gray Z 31032; ● 100
Jamestown; RMC Place; WARE; *167 M-10; mail Waycross Z 31503; ● 750
Jarrell; RMC Place; TAYLOR; *166 I-5; elev. 637ft./194m.; mail Butler Z 31006; rural
Jasper; Inc. Place; ⊡ PICKENS; 166 C-4; elev. 1,480ft./451m.; 🅿; Z 30143; Ⓟ 1,772; © 2,167
JASPER; 166 G-6; Ⓟ 8,453; © 11,426; ◆ 14,046
Jay Bird Springs; RMC Place; DODGE; *167 K-8; elev. 202ft./62m.; mail Chauncey Z 31011; rural
JEFF DAVIS; 167 L-9; Ⓟ 12,032; © 12,684; ◆ 13,357
Jefferson; Inc. Place; ⊡ JACKSON; 166 D-7; elev. 802ft./244m.; 🅿; ★ ATH; Z 30549; Ⓟ 2,763; © 3,825
JEFFERSON; 166 H-9; Ⓟ 17,408; © 17,266; ® 17,263; ◆ 16,107
Jefferson Hills; RMC Place; BIBB; ★ MAC; pop. incl. with Macon (Inc. Place)
Jeffersonville; Inc. Place; ⊡ TWIGGS; 166 I-7; elev. 524ft./160m.; 🅿; Z 31044; Ⓟ 1,545; © 1,209
JENKINS; 166 H-11; Ⓟ 8,247; © 8,575; ◆ 8,469
Jenkinsburg; Inc. Place; BUTTS; 166 G-5; elev. 770ft./235m.; 🅿; Z 30234; Ⓟ 213; © 203
Jersey; Inc. Place; WALTON; 166 F-6; elev. 820ft./250m.; 🅿; ★ ATL; Z 30018; Ⓟ 149; © 163
Jerusalem; RMC Place; CAMDEN; 167 N-11; mail White Oak Z 31568; ● 150
Jerusalem; RMC Place; PICKENS; *166 C-4; elev. 215ft./66m.; mail Jasper Z 30143; rural
Jesup; Inc. Place; ⊡ WAYNE; 167 L-11; elev. 102ft./31m.; 🅿 🅷; Z 31545-46, Z 31598-99; Ⓟ 8,958; © 9,279
Jewell (Jewell's Mills); RMC Place; WARREN; 166 G-9; elev. 450ft./137m.; 🅿; Z 31045; ● 100
Jewell's Mills; WARREN; see Jewell (RMC Place)
Jewelville (Nails Creek); RMC Place; BANKS; *166 D-7; mail Carnesville Z 30521; rural
Jewtown; RMC Place; GLYNN; *167 N-12; ★ BRUNS; mail Saint Simons Island Z 31522
Jinks; RMC Place; DECATUR; *167 O-3; elev. 90ft./27m.; rural
Johns Creek; Inc. Place; FULTON; *166 E-5; incorporated December 1,2006; not reported in 2000 Census; ● 61,100
JOHNSON; 166 I-9; Ⓟ 8,329; © 8,560; ◆ 10,400
Johnson Corner; RMC Place; TOOMBS; 167 K-10; mail Lyons Z 30436; ● 50
Johnson Crossroads; RMC Place; MERIWETHER; *166 H-4; elev. 883ft./269m.; mail Pine Mountain Z 31822; rural
Johnstonville; RMC Place; LAMAR; *166 H-5; mail Barnesville Z 30204; rural
Jolly; RMC Place; PIKE; *166 H-4; elev. 874ft./266m.; mail Williamson Z 30292; rural
Jones; RMC Place; MCINTOSH; 167 L-12; elev. 15ft./5m.; mail Riceboro Z 31323; ● 75
JONES; 166 H-7; Ⓟ 20,739; © 23,639; ◆ 27,521
Jones Acres; RMC Place; JONES; *166 H-7; ★ MAC; mail Macon Z 31217; ● 300
Jonesboro; Inc. Place; ⊡ CLAYTON; 166 F-5; elev. 921ft./281m.; 🅿; ★ ATL; Z 30236-38; Ⓟ 3,635; © 3,829
Jones Creek; RMC Place; UNION; *166 B-5; mail Blairsville Z 30512; rural
Jones Crossroads; RMC Place; HARRIS, TROUP; *166 H-3; mail Pine Mountain Z 31822; rural
Jonesville; RMC Place; CARROLL; 166 F-2; mail Bowdon Z 30108; ● 150
Jordan; RMC Place; WHEELER; *167 K-9; mail Alamo Z 30411; rural
Jordan City; RMC Place; MUSCOGEE; ★ COL; mail Columbus Z 31904; pop. incl. with Columbus (Inc. Place)
Jot Em Down Store; RMC Place; PIERCE; *167 M-10; elev. 124ft./38m.; mail Blackshear Z 31516; rural
Joy Lake; RMC Place; CLAYTON; *166 F-5; ★ ATL; mail Morrow Z 30260; ● 250
Julia; STEWART; see Union (RMC Place)
Juliette; RMC Place; MONROE; 166 H-6; elev. 385ft./117m.; 🅿; Z 31046; ● 300
Junction City; Inc. Place; TALBOT; 166 I-4; elev. 678ft./207m.; 🅿; Z 31812; Ⓟ 182; © 179
Juniper; RMC Place; MARION, TALBOT; *166 I-4; elev. 398ft./121m.; 🅿; Z 31801
Juno; RMC Place; DAWSON; 166 C-5; mail Dawsonville Z 30534; ● 100
Junta; RMC Place; BARTOW; pop. incl. with Cartersville (Inc. Place)

K

Kansas; RMC Place; CARROLL; 166 F-2; mail Waco Z 30182; ● 150
Kathleen; RMC Place; HOUSTON; 166 J-7; elev. 320ft./98m.; 🅿; ★ MAC; Z 31047; ● 400
Keith; RMC Place; CATOOSA; *166 B-3; mail Tunnel Hill Z 30755; ● 250
Keithsburg; RMC Place; CHEROKEE; *166 D-4; elev. 1,013ft./309m.; ★ ATL; mail Canton Z 30114; rural
Keller; RMC Place; BRYAN; 167 L-13; mail Richmond Hill Z 31324; ● 200
Kelleytown; RMC Place; HENRY; *166 F-5; ★ ATL; mail McDonough Z 30252; ● 100
Kelly; RMC Place; JASPER; *166 G-6; elev. 687ft./209m.; mail Shady Dale Z 31085; rural
Kemp; RMC Place; EMANUEL; mail Swainsboro Z 30401; rural
Kennesaw; Inc. Place; COBB; 166 E-4; elev. 1,092ft./333m.; 🅿 🅷 🅲 19,854; ★ ATL; Z 30144, Z 30152, Z 30156, Z 30160; Ⓟ 8,936; © 21,675; ◆ 31,909
Kensington; RMC Place; WALKER; *166 B-2; mail Chickamauga Z 30707; ● 100
Kensington Park; RMC Place; CHATHAM; *167 K-13; ★ SAV; mail Savannah Z 31405; pop. incl. with Savannah (Inc. Place)
Kenwood; RMC Place; FAYETTE; 166 F-4; ★ ATL; mail Fayetteville Z 30214; ● 170
Kenwood; RMC Place; MUSCOGEE; ★ COL; mail Columbus Z 31909; pop. incl. with Columbus (Inc. Place)
Keysville; Inc. Place; BURKE, JEFFERSON; 166 G-10; elev. 265ft./81m.; 🅿; Z 30816 & mail Gough Z 30811; Ⓟ 284; © 180
Kibbee; RMC Place; MONTGOMERY; *166 J-9; mail Vidalia Z 30474
Kiker; RMC Place; GILMER; 166 C-4; elev. 1,255ft./383m.; mail Ellijay Z 30540; ● 60
Kildare; RMC Place; EFFINGHAM; 166 I-12; mail Newington Z 30446; ● 30
Killarney; RMC Place; EARLY; *167 N-3; mail Jakin Z 39861; rural
Kimbrough; RMC Place; WEBSTER; *167 K-4; elev. 560ft./171m.; mail Richland Z 31825; rural
Kinderlou; RMC Place; LOWNDES; *167 O-7; ★ VALD; mail Valdosta Z 31601; rural
Kings (Cora); RMC Place; NEWTON; *166 F-5; ★ ATL; mail Covington Z 30016; rural
Kings Bay; CAMDEN; see Kings Bay Base (CDP-Census Area Only)
Kings Bay Base (Kings Bay); CDP-Census Area Only; CAMDEN; *167 O-12; elev. 8ft./2m.; mail Kings Bay Z 31547; Ⓟ 3,463; © 2,599
Kingsboro; RMC Place; HARRIS; *166 I-3; mail Hamilton Z 31811; rural
Kingsland; Inc. Place; CAMDEN; 167 O-12; elev. 35ft./11m.; 🅿; Z 31548; Ⓟ 5,474; © 10,506
Kingsridge; RMC Place; CHEROKEE; *166 D-4; ★ ATL; mail Woodstock Z 30188; ● 1,000
Kingston; Inc. Place; BARTOW; 166 D-3; elev. 699ft./213m.; 🅿; Z 30145; Ⓟ 616; © 659
Kingston; RMC Place; MUSCOGEE; *166 I-3; ★ COL; mail Columbus Z 31904; pop. incl. with Columbus (Inc. Place)
Kingston; RMC Place; RICHMOND; *166 F-11; elev. 356ft./109m.; ★ AUG; mail Augusta Z 30909; pop. incl. with Augusta (Inc. Place)
Kings Wood; RMC Place; CHATHAM; *167 K-13; ★ SAV; mail Savannah Z 31401; ● 250
Kingswood; RMC Place; CLARKE; *166 E-7; ★ ATH; mail Athens Z 30606; pop. incl. with Athens (Inc. Place)
Kings Wood; RMC Place; RICHMOND; ★ AUG; mail Augusta Z 30904; pop. incl. with Augusta (Inc. Place)
Kirkland; RMC Place; ATKINSON; 167 M-8; elev. 225ft./69m.; mail Pearson Z 31642; ● 60
Kirkland; RMC Place; JEFF DAVIS; *167 L-9; elev. 290ft./88m.; mail Hazlehurst Z 31539; rural
Kirkwood; RMC Place; COLQUITT; mail Moultrie Z 31768; pop. incl. with Moultrie (Inc. Place)
Kirkwood; RMC Place; DEKALB; *166 F-5; ★ ATL; mail Atlanta Z 30317; pop. incl. with Atlanta (Inc. Place)
Kirkwood; RMC Place; MUSCOGEE; *166 I-3; ★ COL; mail Columbus Z 31904; pop. incl. with Columbus (Inc. Place)
Kite; Inc. Place; JOHNSON; 166 I-9; elev. 250ft./76m.; 🅿; Z 31049; Ⓟ 297; © 241
Klondike; RMC Place; DEKALB; *166 F-5; elev. 774ft./236m.; ★ ATL; mail Lithonia Z 30058
Klondike; RMC Place; HOUSTON; *166 J-7; mail Hawkinsville Z 31036; rural
Knott; RMC Place; TROUP; *166 H-3; mail Lagrange Z 30241; rural
Knoxville; RMC Place; ⊡ CRAWFORD; 166 I-5; elev. 500ft./152m.; 🅿; Z 31050; ● 100
Kramer; RMC Place; WILCOX; *167 K-7; mail Abbeville Z 31001; rural

L

La Crosse; RMC Place; SCHLEY; *166 J-5; elev. 525ft./160m.; mail Ellaville Z 31806; rural
LaFayette; Inc. Place; ⊡ WALKER; 166 B-2; elev. 823ft./251m.; 🅿; Z 30728; Ⓟ 6,313; © 6,702
La Grange; Inc. Place; ⊡ TROUP; 166 H-3; elev. 772ft./235m.; 🅿 🅷 🅲 1,137 ■; Z 30240-41, Z 30261; Ⓟ 25,597; © 25,998; ◆ 28,859
Lake; RMC Place; POLK; mail Cedartown Z 30125; rural
Lake Arrowhead; RMC Place; CHEROKEE; *166 D-4; mail Waleska Z 30183; ● 225
Lake Capri (Lake Capri Estates); RMC Place; ROCKDALE; *166 F-5; ★ ATL; mail Lithonia Z 30058; ● 630
Lake Capri Estates; ROCKDALE; see Lake Capri (RMC Place)
Lake Cindy; RMC Place; HENRY; *166 G-5; ★ ATL; mail Hampton Z 30228; ● 750
Lake City; Inc. Place; CLAYTON; 168 H-4; elev. 950ft./290m.; 🅿; ★ ATL; Z 30260; Ⓟ 2,733; © 2,886
Lake Creek; RMC Place; POLK; *166 D-2; mail Cedartown Z 30125; rural
Lakehills; RMC Place; COWETA; *166 G-3; mail Newnan Z 30263; ● 300
Lake Howard; RMC Place; WALKER; mail La Fayette Z 30728; rural
Lake Jodeco; RMC Place; CLAYTON; *166 F-5; ★ ATL; mail Jonesboro Z 30236; ● 600
Lakeland; Inc. Place; ⊡ LANIER; 167 N-8; elev. 199ft./61m.; 🅿 🅷; Z 31635; Ⓟ 2,467; © 2,730
Lake Lanier Islands; RMC Place; HALL; ★ ATL; mail Buford Z 30518; summer pop. 1,000; ● 50
Lake Lucerne; RMC Place; GWINNETT; *166 E-5; ★ ATL; mail Lilburn Z 30047; ● 900
Lakemont; RMC Place; RABUN; 166 B-7; elev. 1,630ft./497m.; 🅿; Z 30552; ● 500
Lakemont; RMC Place; RICHMOND; *166 F-11; ★ AUG; mail Augusta Z 30901; pop. incl. with Augusta (Inc. Place)
Lake Park; Inc. Place; LOWNDES; 167 O-8; elev. 160ft./49m.; 🅿; ★ VALD; Z 31636; Ⓟ 500; © 549
Lakeshore Estates; RMC Place; HALL; *166 D-6; mail Gainesville Z 30501; pop. incl. with Gainesville (Inc. Place)
Lakeside Hills; RMC Place; BIBB; 167 S-7; ★ MAC; mail Macon Z 31217; pop. incl. with Macon (Inc. Place)
Lakeside Park; RMC Place; CHATHAM; *167 K-13; ★ SAV; mail Savannah Z 31406; ● 500
Lake Talmadge; RMC Place; HENRY; *166 G-5; ★ ATL; mail Hampton Z 30228; ● 240
Lake Tara; RMC Place; CLAYTON; *166 F-5; ★ ATL; mail Jonesboro Z 30236; pop. incl. with Jonesboro (Inc. Place)
Lakeview; RMC Place; BLECKLEY; *166 J-7; mail Cochran Z 31014; ● 250
Lakeview; CDP; CATOOSA, WALKER; *166 B-2; ★ CHTN; mail Rossville Z 30741; Ⓟ 5,237; © 4,820
Lakeview; RMC Place; PEACH; *166 I-6; elev. 465ft./142m.; ★ MAC; mail Fort Valley Z 31030; ● 150
Lakeview Estates; CDP; ROCKDALE; *166 F-5; ★ ATL; mail Conyers Z 30012; Ⓟ 1,477; © 2,637
Lakewood; RMC Place; CLARKE; *166 E-7; ★ ATH; mail Athens Z 30605; pop. incl. with Athens (Inc. Place)
Lakewood; RMC Place; FULTON; *166 F-4; ★ ATL; mail Atlanta Z 30315; pop. incl. with Atlanta (Inc. Place)
Lakewood Heights; RMC Place; FULTON; *166 F-4; ★ ATL; mail Atlanta Z 30315; pop. incl. with Atlanta (Inc. Place)
Lamar; RMC Place; SUMTER; *167 K-5; mail Americus Z 31709; rural
LAMAR; 166 H-5; Ⓟ 13,038; © 15,912; ◆ 17,428
Lamara Heights; RMC Place; CHATHAM; *167 K-13; ★ SAV; mail Savannah Z 31405; pop. incl. with Savannah (Inc. Place)
Lamarville; RMC Place; CHATHAM; *167 K-13; ★ SAV; mail Savannah Z 31405
Landrum; RMC Place; DAWSON; *166 C-5; mail Dawsonville Z 30534; rural
Lanier; RMC Place; BRYAN; 167 K-12; elev. 70ft./21m.; mail Pembroke Z 31321; ● 300
LANIER; 167 N-8; Ⓟ 5,531; © 7,241; ◆ 8,481
Laroche Park; RMC Place; CHATHAM; ★ SAV; mail Savannah Z 31404; pop. incl. with Savannah (Inc. Place)
Lashley; RMC Place; HOUSTON; *166 I-6; ★ MAC; mail Bonaire Z 31005; ● 400
Lathemtown; RMC Place; CHEROKEE; 166 D-5; ★ ATL; mail Canton Z 30115; ● 200
Laurel Hills; RMC Place; MUSCOGEE; ★ COL; mail Columbus Z 31904; pop. incl. with Columbus (Inc. Place)
LAURENS; 166 J-8; Ⓟ 39,988; © 44,874; ◆ 47,738
Lavender; RMC Place; FLOYD; *166 D-2; elev. 659ft./201m.; ★ ROME; mail Rome Z 30165; rural
La Vista; RMC Place; DEKALB; *166 E-5; ★ ATL; mail Atlanta Z 30329; ● 5,000
Lavonia; Inc. Place; FRANKLIN; 166 C-8; elev. 853ft./260m.; 🅿; Z 30553; Ⓟ 1,840; © 1,827
Lawrenceville; Inc. Place; ⊡ GWINNETT; 166 E-6; elev. 1,080ft./329m.; 🅿 🅷 ■; ★ ATL; Z 30042-46, Z 30049; Ⓟ 16,848; © 22,397; ◆ 28,339
Lax; RMC Place; COFFEE, IRWIN; 167 M-8; mail Ocilla Z 31774; ● 120
Leaf; RMC Place; WHITE; *166 C-6; elev. 1,404ft./428m.; mail Cleveland Z 30528
Leafmore; RMC Place; DEKALB; *166 E-5; ★ ATL; mail Decatur Z 30033; ● 300
Leah; RMC Place; COLUMBIA; 166 F-10; elev. 343ft./105m.; mail Appling Z 30802; ● 110
Leary; Inc. Place; CALHOUN; 167 M-4; elev. 210ft./64m.; 🅿; Z 39862; Ⓟ 701; © 666
Leathersville (Woodlawn); RMC Place; LINCOLN; *166 F-10; elev. 398ft./121m.; mail Lincolnton Z 30817; rural
Lebanon (Toonigh); RMC Place; CHEROKEE; 166 D-4; elev. 996ft./304m.; 🅿; ★ ATL; Z 30146; ● 650
Lee; RMC Place; CLAYTON; *166 F-5; ★ ATL; pop. incl. with Lake City (Inc. Place)
LEE; 167 L-5; Ⓟ 16,250; © 24,757; ◆ 34,508
Leefield; RMC Place; BULLOCH; *166 J-12; mail Brooklet Z 30415
Lee Pope; RMC Place; CRAWFORD; *166 I-6; mail Fort Valley Z 31030; rural
Leesburg; Inc. Place; ⊡ LEE; 167 L-5; elev. 255ft./78m.; 🅿; Z 31763; Ⓟ 1,452; © 2,633; ® 2,296
Lees Crossing; RMC Place; TROUP; *166 H-3; mail Lagrange Z 30240; pop. incl. with La Grange (Inc. Place)
Lees Mill; RMC Place; FAYETTE; *166 F-4; ★ ATL; mail Fayetteville Z 30214; ● 90
Leland; RMC Place; COBB; *166 E-4; ★ ATL; mail Mableton Z 30126
Leliaton; RMC Place; ATKINSON; *167 M-8; elev. 224ft./68m.; mail Willacoochee Z 31650; ● 45
Lena; RMC Place; COBB; ★ ATL; mail Acworth Z 30101; rural
Lenox; Inc. Place; COOK; 167 M-7; elev. 284ft./87m.; 🅿; Z 31637; Ⓟ 783; © 889
Lenox Square; RMC Place; FULTON; *166 E-5; elev. 100ft./30m.; ★ ATL; mail Atlanta Z 30326; pop. incl. with Atlanta (Inc. Place)
LePageville; RMC Place; CHATHAM; *167 K-13; ★ SAV
Leslie (Leslie Desoto); Inc. Place; SUMTER; 167 K-5; elev. 344ft./105m.; 🅿; Z 31764; Ⓟ 445; © 455
Leslie Desoto; SUMTER; see Leslie (Inc. Place)
Lester (Brest); RMC Place; MITCHELL; *167 M-5; mail Baconton Z 31716; rural
Lewis; RMC Place; SCREVEN; *166 I-12; elev. 152ft./46m.; mail Sylvania Z 30467; rural
Lewis Corner; RMC Place; GORDON; *166 C-3; mail Calhoun Z 30701; rural
Lewiston; RMC Place; COLUMBIA; *166 F-10; ★ AUG; mail Evans Z 30809; ● 80
Lexington; Inc. Place; ⊡ OGLETHORPE; 166 E-8; elev. 684ft./208m.; 🅿; Z 30648; Ⓟ 230; © 239
Lexsy; RMC Place; EMANUEL; 166 J-10; elev. 208ft./63m.; mail Swainsboro Z 30401; ● 50
Liberty; RMC Place; GREENE; *166 G-8; elev. 562ft./171m.; mail White Plains Z 30678; rural
LIBERTY; 167 K-11; Ⓟ 52,745; © 61,610; ◆ 60,210
Liberty City; RMC Place; CHATHAM; *167 K-13; ★ SAV; mail Savannah Z 31405; pop. incl. with Savannah (Inc. Place)
Liberty Hill; RMC Place; LAMAR; *166 G-5; elev. 754ft./230m.; mail Milner Z 30257; ● 75
Lifsey; RMC Place; PIKE; *166 H-4; mail Zebulon Z 30295; rural
Lilburn; Inc. Place; GWINNETT; 166 E-5; elev. 940ft./287m.; 🅿; ★ ATL; Z 30047-48; Ⓟ 9,301; © 11,307
Lilly; Inc. Place; DOOLY; 167 K-6; 🅿; Z 31051; Ⓟ 138; © 221
Lillypond; GORDON; see Lily Pond (RMC Place)
Lily Pond (Lillypond); RMC Place; GORDON; *166 C-3; mail Calhoun Z 30701; rural
Limestone; RMC Place; BLECKLEY; mail Cochran Z 31014; rural
Limestone; RMC Place; HALL; mail Gainesville Z 30501; pop. incl. with Gainesville (Inc. Place)
LINCOLN; 166 E-9; Ⓟ 7,442; © 8,348; ◆ 7,957
Lincoln Hills; RMC Place; MUSCOGEE; *166 I-3; ★ COL; mail Columbus Z 31909; pop. incl. with Columbus (Inc. Place)
Lincoln Park; CDP; UPSON; 166 H-5; mail Thomaston Z 30286; © 1,122
Lincolnton; Inc. Place; ⊡ LINCOLN; 166 E-10; elev. 400ft./122m.; 🅿; Z 30817 & mail Thomson Z 30824; Ⓟ 1,476; © 1,595
Lindale; CDP; FLOYD; 166 D-2; 🅿; ★ ROME; Z 30147; Ⓟ 4,187; © 4,088
Lindsey Creek; RMC Place; MUSCOGEE; *166 I-3; ★ COL; mail Columbus Z 31907, Z 31917; pop. incl. with Columbus (Inc. Place)
Lindsley Park; RMC Place; BIBB; *166 I-6; ★ MAC; mail Macon Z 31216; pop. incl. with Macon (Inc. Place)
Linesville; RMC Place; WILKES; *166 E-8; elev. 602ft./183m.; mail Crawfordville Z 30631; rural
Linton; RMC Place; HANCOCK; 166 H-8; mail Sparta Z 31087; ● 40
Linwood; BARTOW; see Halls (RMC Place)
Linwood; RMC Place; WALKER; *166 B-2; elev. 840ft./256m.; mail La Fayette Z 30728; pop. incl. with LaFayette (Inc. Place)
Lions Gate; RMC Place; FULTON; ★ ATL; mail Atlanta Z 30327; ● 50
Listonia; RMC Place; CRISP; *167 K-6; mail Cordele Z 31015; rural
Lithia Springs; RMC Place; DOUGLAS; 166 E-4; elev. 1,043ft./318m.; 🅿 🅷; ★ ATL; Z 30122; disincorporated June 21, 2001; Ⓟ 2,437; © 2,072
Lithonia; Inc. Place; DEKALB; 166 F-5; elev. 939ft./286m.; 🅿 🅲 1,000; ★ ATL; Z 30038, Z 30058 & mail Snellville Z 30039; Ⓟ 2,448; © 2,187
Little Five Points; RMC Place; DEKALB; *166 E-5; elev. 1,023ft./312m.; ★ ATL; mail Atlanta Z 30307, Z 31107; pop. incl. with Atlanta (Inc. Place)
Little Hope; RMC Place; SEMINOLE; *167 N-3; mail Donalsonville Z 39845; ● 45
Little Miami; RMC Place; LOWNDES; 167 O-7; ★ VALD; mail Valdosta Z 31601; ● 200
Livingston; RMC Place; FLOYD; *166 D-2; ★ ROME; mail Rome Z 30161; ● 50
Lizella; RMC Place; BIBB; 166 I-6; elev. 561ft./171m.; 🅿; ★ MAC; Z 31052; ● 600
Loco; RMC Place; LINCOLN; *166 F-9; mail Lincolnton Z 30817; rural
Locust Grove; Inc. Place; HENRY; 166 G-5; elev. 847ft./258m.; 🅿; Z 30248; Ⓟ 1,681; © 2,322
Loftin; HEARD; see Ephesus (Inc. Place)
Loftin; RMC Place; MERIWETHER; *166 H-4; mail Manchester Z 31816; rural
Loganville; Inc. Place; WALTON, GWINNETT; 166 E-6; elev. 1,003ft./306m.; 🅿; ★ ATL; Z 30052; Ⓟ 3,180; © 5,435
Lone Oak; Inc. Place; MERIWETHER; 166 G-3; elev. 855ft./261m.; mail Hogansville Z 30230; Ⓟ 161; © 104
LONG; 167 L-12; Ⓟ 6,202; © 10,304; ◆ 11,488
Long Cane; RMC Place; TROUP; *166 H-2; elev. 702ft./214m.; mail Lagrange Z 30240; rural
Lookout Mountain (Fairyland); Inc. Place; WALKER; 166 B-2; elev. 1,800ft./549m.; 🅿 🅲 1,282; ★ CHTN; Z 30750; Ⓟ 1,636; © 1,617
Lorane; RMC Place; BIBB; *166 H-6; elev. 548ft./167m.; ★ MAC; mail Macon Z 31210; rural
Lorenzo; RMC Place; EFFINGHAM; *166 J-12; mail Springfield Z 31329; rural
Lorwood; RMC Place; CHATHAM; ★ SAV; mail Savannah Z 31406; pop. incl. with Savannah (Inc. Place)
Lost Mountain; RMC Place; COBB; *166 E-4; elev. 1,218ft./371m.; ★ ATL; mail Powder Springs Z 30127; rural
Lothair; RMC Place; TREUTLEN; *166 J-9; mail Soperton Z 30457
Lotts; RMC Place; COFFEE; *167 L-8; mail Broxton Z 31519; rural
Louise; RMC Place; TROUP; 166 H-3; mail Hogansville Z 30230; ● 150
Louisville; Inc. Place; ⊡ JEFFERSON; 166 H-10; elev. 320ft./98m.; 🅿 🅷; Z 30434; Ⓟ 2,429; © 2,712
Louvale; RMC Place; STEWART; 166 J-3; elev. 383ft./117m.; 🅿; Z 31814; ● 300
Lovejoy; Inc. Place; CLAYTON; 166 G-5; elev. 953ft./290m.; 🅿; ★ ATL; Z 30250; Ⓟ 754; © 2,495
Lovett; RMC Place; LAURENS; 166 I-9; elev. 333ft./101m.; mail Dublin Z 31021; ● 100
Loving; RMC Place; FANNIN; *166 B-5; mail Morganton Z 30560; rural
Lowell; RMC Place; CARROLL; *166 F-3; elev. 1,061ft./323m.; mail Carrollton Z 30116
LOWNDES; 167 N-7; Ⓟ 75,981; © 92,115; ® 92,121; ◆ 109,030
Lowry; RMC Place; FAYETTE; *166 G-4; mail Fayetteville Z 30215; ● 200
Lucile; RMC Place; EARLY, MILLER; *167 M-3; elev. 218ft./66m.; mail Blakely Z 39823
Lucius; RMC Place; GILMER; *166 B-5; mail Cherry Log Z 30522; rural
Ludowici; Inc. Place; ⊡ LONG; 167 L-12; elev. 70ft./21m.; 🅿; Z 31316; Ⓟ 1,291; © 1,440
Ludville; RMC Place; PICKENS; 166 C-4; mail Talking Rock Z 30175; ● 150
Luella; RMC Place; HENRY; *166 G-5; elev. 860ft./262m.; ★ ATL; mail Locust Grove Z 30248; rural
Lula; Inc. Place; HALL, BANKS; 166 D-6; elev. 1,304ft./397m.; 🅿; Z 30554; Ⓟ 1,018; © 1,438
Lulaton; RMC Place; BRANTLEY; *167 N-11; mail Nahunta Z 31553; rural
Lumber City; Inc. Place; TELFAIR; 167 K-9; elev. 147ft./45m.; 🅿; Z 31549; Ⓟ 1,429; © 1,247
Lumpkin; Inc. Place; ⊡ STEWART; 167 K-3; elev. 593ft./181m.; 🅿; Z 31815; Ⓟ 1,250; © 1,369
LUMPKIN; 166 C-5; Ⓟ 14,573; © 21,016; ◆ 27,625
Lundberg; RMC Place; WILKES; *166 F-9; mail Washington Z 30673; rural
Luthersville (Lutherville); Inc. Place; MERIWETHER; 166 G-3; elev. 931ft./284m.; 🅿; Z 30251; Ⓟ 741; © 783
Lutherville; MERIWETHER; see Luthersville (Inc. Place)
Luvdale; RMC Place; DOUGHERTY; ★ ALB; mail Albany Z 31701; rural
Luxomni; RMC Place; GWINNETT; *166 E-5; elev. 880ft./268m.; ★ ATL; mail Lilburn Z 30047; ● 100
Lyerly; Inc. Place; CHATTOOGA; 166 C-2; elev. 614ft./187m.; 🅿; Z 30730; Ⓟ 493; © 488
Lyn Hills; RMC Place; MUSCOGEE; ★ COL; mail Columbus Z 31909; pop. incl. with Columbus (Inc. Place)
Lynhurst; RMC Place; CHATHAM; *167 K-13; elev. 16ft./5m.; ★ SAV; mail Savannah Z 31406; pop. incl. with Savannah (Inc. Place)
Lynmore Estates; RMC Place; BIBB; *166 I-6; ★ MAC; mail Macon Z 31216; pop. incl. with Macon (Inc. Place)
Lynn; RMC Place; DECATUR; *167 N-4; rural
Lynnwood; RMC Place; CATOOSA; ★ CHTN; mail Rossville Z 30741
Lyons; Inc. Place; ⊡ TOOMBS; 166 J-10; elev. 224ft./68m.; 🅿; Z 30436; Ⓟ 4,502; © 4,169
Lytle; RMC Place; WALKER; *166 B-2; ★ CHTN; mail Chickamauga Z 30707; rural

M

Mableton; CDP; COBB; 166 E-4; 🅿; ★ ATL; Z 30126; Ⓟ 25,725; © 29,733; ◆ 34,923
Macedonia; RMC Place; CHEROKEE; *166 D-5; ★ ATL; mail Canton Z 30115; ● 150
Macedonia; RMC Place; TOWNS; *166 B-6; mail Hiawassee Z 30546; rural
Machen; RMC Place; JASPER; 166 G-7; elev. 623ft./190m.; mail Monticello Z 31064; ● 50
Macland; RMC Place; COBB; *166 E-4; elev. 1,019ft./311m.; ★ ATL; mail Powder Springs Z 30127; ● 600
Macon; Inc. Place; ⊡ BIBB, JONES; 167 S-6; elev. 325ft./99m.; 🅿 🅷 🅲 13,889 ■; ★ MAC; Z 31201-13, Z 31216-17, Z 31220-21, Z 31294-97; Ⓟ 106,612; © 97,255; ◆ 93,953
MACON; 166 J-5; Ⓟ 13,114; © 14,074; ◆ 13,275
Macon Yard; RMC Place; BIBB; ★ MAC; pop. incl. with Macon (Inc. Place)
Madison; Inc. Place; ⊡ MORGAN; 166 F-7; elev. 667ft./203m.; 🅿 🅷; Z 30650; Ⓟ 3,483; © 3,636
MADISON; 166 D-7; Ⓟ 21,050; © 25,730; ◆ 28,632
Madola; RMC Place; FANNIN; *166 B-4; mail Epworth Z 30541; rural
Madras; RMC Place; COWETA; 166 F-4; elev. 992ft./302m.; mail Newnan Z 30263; ● 50
Madray Springs; RMC Place; WAYNE; 167 L-11; elev. 160ft./49m.; mail Jesup Z 31545; ● 75
Magby Gap; RMC Place; DADE; *166 B-2; ★ CHTN; mail Trenton Z 30752; rural
Magnet; RMC Place; ROCKDALE; 166 F-5; ★ ATL; mail Conyers Z 30013, Z 30094; ● 300
Magnolia; RMC Place; CHATHAM; *167 K-13; ★ SAV; mail Savannah Z 31406; pop. incl. with Savannah (Inc. Place)
Magnolia; RMC Place; FULTON; pop. incl. with Atlanta (Inc. Place)
Magruder; RMC Place; BURKE; 166 H-10; mail Midville Z 30441; ● 15
Mallorysville; RMC Place; WILKES; *166 E-9; elev. 597ft./182m.; mail Tignall Z 30668; rural
Manassas; Inc. Place; TATTNALL; 167 K-11; elev. 210ft./64m.; 🅿; Z 30438; Ⓟ 123; © 100
Manchester; Inc. Place; MERIWETHER, TALBOT; 166 H-4; elev. 883ft./269m.; 🅿; Z 31816; Ⓟ 4,104; © 3,988
Manningtown; RMC Place; WAYNE; 167 M-11; mail Jesup Z 31545; ● 75
Manor; RMC Place; WARE; 167 N-9; elev. 156ft./48m.; 🅿; Z 31550; ● 400
Mansfield; Inc. Place; NEWTON; 166 F-6; elev. 772ft./235m.; 🅿; Z 30055; Ⓟ 341; © 392
Manta; RMC Place; CHATTAHOOCHEE; *166 J-4; mail Cusseta Z 31805; rural
Marblehill; RMC Place; PICKENS; 166 C-5; elev. 1,048ft./319m.; 🅿; Z 30148; ● 350
Maretts; RMC Place; HART; *166 C-8; mail Lavonia Z 30553; rural
Margret; RMC Place; FANNIN; *166 B-5; mail Suches Z 30572; rural
Maridale Estates; RMC Place; MUSCOGEE; *166 I-3; ★ COL; mail Columbus Z 31904; pop. incl. with Columbus (Inc. Place)
Marietta; Inc. Place; ⊡ COBB; 166 E-4; elev. 1,128ft./344m.; 🅿 🅷 🅲 5,869 ■; ★ ATL; Z 30006-08, Z 30060-69, Z 30090; Ⓟ 44,129; © 58,748; ◆ 72,011
Marietta Campground; RMC Place; COBB; *166 E-4; ★ ATL; mail Marietta Z 30062; ● 3,000
Marion; RMC Place; TWIGGS; *166 I-7; elev. 383ft./117m.; mail Dry Branch Z 31020; rural
MARION; 166 J-4; Ⓟ 5,590; © 7,144; ◆ 6,881
Marlborough; RMC Place; CLAYTON; *166 F-4; ★ ATL; mail Jonesboro Z 30238; ● 1,600
Marlow; RMC Place; EFFINGHAM; 166 J-12; elev. 71ft./22m.; mail Guyton Z 31312; ● 350
Marshallville; Inc. Place; MACON; 166 J-6; elev. 500ft./152m.; 🅿; Z 31030, Z 31057; Ⓟ 1,457; © 1,335
Mars Hill; RMC Place; COBB; *166 E-4; ★ ATL; mail Acworth Z 30101; ● 300
Martech; RMC Place; FULTON; *166 E-4; ★ ATL; mail Atlanta Z 30318, Z 30377; pop. incl. with Atlanta (Inc. Place)
Martin; Inc. Place; STEPHENS, FRANKLIN; 166 C-8; elev. 90ft./27m.; 🅿; Z 30557; Ⓟ 243; © 311
Martinez; CDP; COLUMBIA, RICHMOND; 166 A-11; elev. 347ft./106m.; 🅿; ★ AUG; Z 30907; Ⓟ 24,738; © 27,749; ◆ 35,122
Massee; RMC Place; COOK; *167 N-7; elev. 236ft./72m.; mail Adel Z 31620; rural
Matt; RMC Place; FORSYTH; 166 D-5; mail Cumming Z 30040; ● 90
Matthews; RMC Place; JEFFERSON; 166 G-10; elev. 395ft./120m.; 🅿; Z 30818; ● 150
Mattox; RMC Place; CHARLTON; *167 N-11; mail Folkston Z 31537; rural
Mauk; RMC Place; TAYLOR; 166 I-4; elev. 780ft./238m.; 🅿; Z 31058; ● 60
Maura Estates; RMC Place; RICHMOND; *166 G-11; ★ AUG; mail Augusta Z 30906; pop. incl. with Augusta (Inc. Place)
Maxeys; Inc. Place; OGLETHORPE; 166 F-8; elev. 753ft./230m.; 🅿; Z 30671; Ⓟ 180; © 210
Maxim; RMC Place; LINCOLN; *166 E-10; mail Lincolnton Z 30817; rural
Maxwell; RMC Place; JASPER; *166 G-6; mail Shady Dale Z 31085; rural
Mayday; RMC Place; ECHOLS; *167 O-8; mail Lake Park Z 31636
Mayfair; RMC Place; CHATHAM; ★ SAV; mail Savannah Z 31406; pop. incl. with Savannah (Inc. Place)
Mayfield; RMC Place; HANCOCK; 166 G-9; elev. 418ft./127m.; 🅿; Z 31087; ● 150
Mayhaw; RMC Place; MILLER; *167 N-3; elev. 191ft./58m.; mail Blakely Z 39823; rural
Maysville; Inc. Place; BANKS, JACKSON; 166 D-7; elev. 907ft./276m.; 🅿; Z 30558; Ⓟ 728; © 1,247
McAfee; RMC Place; DEKALB; ★ ATL; mail Decatur Z 30032
McBean; RMC Place; RICHMOND; *166 G-11; elev. 140ft./43m.; mail Augusta Z 30906; pop. incl. with Augusta (Inc. Place)
McBride; RMC Place; COWETA; *166 G-3; pop. incl. with Newnan (Inc. Place)
McCaysville; Inc. Place; FANNIN; 166 B-5; elev. 1,487ft./453m.; 🅿; Z 30555; Ⓟ 1,065; © 1,071
McCollum; RMC Place; COWETA; *166 F-4; elev. 981ft./299m.; mail Newnan Z 30263; rural
McDaniels (McHenry); RMC Place; GORDON; *166 C-3; mail Calhoun Z 30701; rural
McDonald; CATOOSA; see McDonald Acres (RMC Place)
McDonald Acres (McDonald); RMC Place; CATOOSA; *166 B-2; ★ CHTN; mail Rossville Z 30741; ● 300
McDonough; Inc. Place; ⊡ HENRY; 166 F-5; elev. 803ft./245m.; 🅿; ★ ATL; Z 30252-53; Ⓟ 2,929; © 8,493
MCDUFFIE; 166 G-9; Ⓟ 20,119; © 21,231; ◆ 21,337
McElroys Mill; RMC Place; ROCKDALE; *166 E-6; ★ ATL; mail Loganville Z 30052; rural
McGregor; RMC Place; MONTGOMERY; *166 J-9; mail Ailey Z 30410, Brooklet Z 30415; ● 50
McHenry; GORDON; see McDaniels (RMC Place)
McIntosh; RMC Place; LIBERTY; 167 L-12; mail Midway Z 31320; ● 250
MCINTOSH; 167 M-12; Ⓟ 8,634; © 10,847; ◆ 11,943
McIntosh Mill Village; RMC Place; COWETA; mail Newnan Z 30263; ● 150
McIntyre; Inc. Place; WILKINSON; 166 H-8; elev. 256ft./78m.; 🅿; Z 31054; Ⓟ 552; © 718
McKinnon; RMC Place; WAYNE; 167 M-11; mail Jesup Z 31545; ● 75
McPherson; RMC Place; PAULDING; *166 E-3; elev. 1,015ft./309m.; ★ ATL; mail Dallas Z 30132; rural
McRae; Inc. Place; ⊡ TELFAIR; 167 K-8; elev. 258ft./79m.; 🅿 🅷; Z 31055; Ⓟ 3,007; © 2,682
McWhorter; RMC Place; DOUGLAS; *166 F-3; mail Douglasville Z 30134; rural
Mead; RMC Place; BIBB; ★ MAC; pop. incl. with Macon (Inc. Place)
Meadowbrook; RMC Place; BIBB; ★ MAC; mail Macon Z 31204; pop. incl. with Macon (Inc. Place)
Meadow Grove; RMC Place; RICHMOND; *166 G-11; ★ AUG; mail Augusta Z 30906; pop. incl. with Augusta (Inc. Place)
Meansville; Inc. Place; PIKE; 166 H-5; elev. 800ft./244m.; 🅿; Z 30256; Ⓟ 250; © 192
Mechanicsville; RMC Place; GWINNETT; *166 E-5; ★ ATL; mail Atlanta Z 30340; ● 1,600
Meeks; RMC Place; JOHNSON; 166 I-9; mail Kite Z 31049; ● 90
Meigs; Inc. Place; THOMAS, MITCHELL; 167 N-5; elev. 347ft./106m.; 🅿; Z 31765; Ⓟ 1,120; © 1,090
Meinhard; RMC Place; CHATHAM; *166 J-13; elev. 17ft./5m.; ★ SAV; mail Savannah Z 31407; pop. incl. with Port Wentworth (Inc. Place)
Meldrim; RMC Place; EFFINGHAM; 167 K-12; elev. 32ft./10m.; 🅿; ★ SAV; Z 31318; ● 450
Melrose; RMC Place; LOWNDES; *167 O-8; mail Lake Park Z 31636; rural
Memorial; RMC Place; DEKALB; ★ ATL; mail Stone Mountain Z 30083; pop. incl. with Stone Mountain (Inc. Place)
Mendes; RMC Place; TATTNALL; 167 K-11; mail Glennville Z 30427; ● 130
Menlo; Inc. Place; CHATTOOGA; 166 C-2; elev. 793ft./242m.; 🅿; Z 30731; Ⓟ 538; © 485
Mercer University; RMC Place; BIBB; *166 H-6; 🅿; ★ MAC; Z 31207 & mail Macon Z 31204; pop. incl. with Macon (Inc. Place)
Meridian; RMC Place; MCINTOSH; 167 M-13; elev. 19ft./6m.; 🅿; Z 31319; ● 250
MERIWETHER; 166 H-3; Ⓟ 22,411; © 22,534; ◆ 22,189
Merrillville; RMC Place; THOMAS; 167 N-6; mail Coolidge Z 31738; ● 120
Mershon; RMC Place; PIERCE; 167 M-10; elev. 162ft./49m.; 🅿; Z 31551; ● 200
Mesena; RMC Place; WARREN; 166 F-9; 🅿; Z 30819; ● 250
Metasville; RMC Place; WILKES; 166 E-9; elev. 561ft./171m.; mail Washington Z 30673; ● 80
Metcalf; RMC Place; THOMAS; 167 O-5; elev. 175ft./53m.; 🅿; Z 31792; ● 130
Metter; Inc. Place; ⊡ CANDLER; 166 J-11; elev. 200ft./61m.; 🅿 🅷; Z 30439; Ⓟ 3,707; © 3,879
Meyer; RMC Place; MUSCOGEE; ★ COL; pop. incl. with Columbus (Inc. Place)
Mica; RMC Place; CHEROKEE; *166 D-5; mail Ball Ground Z 30107; rural
Middleton; RMC Place; ELBERT; *166 D-9; elev. 524ft./160m.; mail Elberton Z 30635; ● 60
Midland; RMC Place; MUSCOGEE; *166 I-3; elev. 546ft./166m.; 🅿; ★ COL; Z 31820; pop. incl. with Columbus (Inc. Place)
Midtown; RMC Place; FULTON; *166 E-4; ★ ATL; mail Atlanta Z 30309, Z 30357; pop. incl. with Atlanta (Inc. Place)
Midville; Inc. Place; BURKE; 166 H-10; elev. 189ft./58m.; 🅿; Z 30441; Ⓟ 620; © 457
Midway; BALDWIN; see Hardwick (RMC Place)
Midway; RMC Place; CATOOSA; *166 B-2; ★ CHTN; mail Rossville Z 30741; pop. incl. with Fort Oglethorpe (Inc. Place)
Midway; RMC Place; CLINCH; *167 N-9; mail Homerville Z 31634; rural
Midway; Inc. Place; LIBERTY; 167 L-12; elev. 20ft./6m.; 🅿; Z 31320; Ⓟ 863; © 1,100
Midway; RMC Place; TATTNALL; *167 K-11; mail Glennville Z 30427
Midway-Hardwick; CDP-Census Area Only; BALDWIN; *166 H-7; mail Milledgeville Z 31061; Ⓟ 4,910; © 5,135
Milan; Inc. Place; TELFAIR, DODGE; 167 K-8; elev. 282ft./86m.; 🅿; Z 31060; Ⓟ 1,056; © 1,012
Miles Park; RMC Place; RICHMOND; ★ AUG; mail Augusta Z 30906; pop. incl. with Augusta (Inc. Place)
Milford; RMC Place; BAKER; 167 M-4; elev. 180ft./55m.; mail Leary Z 39862; ● 60
Mill Creek; RMC Place; WHITFIELD; *166 B-3; mail Rocky Face Z 30740; rural
Mill Creek Estates; RMC Place; HALL; mail Gainesville Z 30506; ● 150
Milledgeville; Inc. Place; ⊡ BALDWIN; 166 H-8; elev. 335ft./102m.; 🅿 🅷 🅲 6,040 ■; Z 31059, Z 31061-62; Ⓟ 17,727; © 18,757; ◆ 19,959
Millen; Inc. Place; ⊡ JENKINS; 166 I-11; elev. 160ft./49m.; 🅿 🅷; Z 30442; Ⓟ 3,808; © 3,492
MILLER; 167 N-4; Ⓟ 6,280; © 6,383; ◆ 6,196
Millers Mill; RMC Place; HENRY; *166 F-5; elev. 700ft./213m.; ★ ATL; mail Stockbridge Z 30281; rural
Millhaven; RMC Place; SCREVEN; *166 H-12; elev. 119ft./36m.; mail Sylvania Z 30467; rural
Millwood; RMC Place; WARE; 167 M-9; elev. 160ft./49m.; 🅿; Z 31552; ● 180
Milner; Inc. Place; LAMAR; 166 H-5; elev. 835ft./255m.; 🅿; Z 30257; Ⓟ 321; © 522
Milstead; RMC Place; ROCKDALE; 166 F-5; ★ ATL; mail Conyers Z 30012; ● 1,500
Milton; Inc. Place; FULTON; *166 D-4; incorporated December 1, 2006; not reported in 2000 Census; ● 15,500
Mina; RMC Place; FULTON; ★ ATL; pop. incl. with Atlanta (Inc. Place)
Mineola; RMC Place; LOWNDES; 167 N-7; mail Valdosta Z 31602; ● 150
Mineral Bluff; RMC Place; FANNIN; 166 B-5; elev. 1,600ft./488m.; 🅿; Z 30559; Ⓟ 153
Minish; RMC Place; MADISON; *166 D-7; mail Hull Z 30646; rural
Minnesota; RMC Place; COLQUITT; *167 M-6; mail Doerun Z 31744; ● 30
Minton; WORTH; see Anderson City (RMC Place)
Mission Ridge; RMC Place; WALKER; ★ CHTN; mail Rossville Z 30741; pop. incl. with Rossville (Inc. Place)
Mitchell; RMC Place; DODGE; *167 K-7; mail Eastman Z 31023; rural
Mitchell; Inc. Place; GLASCOCK; 166 G-9; elev. 539ft./164m.; 🅿; Z 30820; Ⓟ 181; © 173
MITCHELL; 167 M-5; Ⓟ 20,275; © 23,932; ◆ 24,726
Mize; RMC Place; STEPHENS; *166 C-7; mail Toccoa Z 30577; rural
Mizell; RMC Place; TAYLOR; *166 I-5; elev. 633ft./193m.; mail Butler Z 31006; rural
Mock Road; RMC Place; DOUGHERTY; mail Albany Z 31705; pop. incl. with Albany (Inc. Place)
Modoc; RMC Place; EMANUEL; 166 I-10; elev. 271ft./83m.; mail Swainsboro Z 30401; ● 40
Molena; Inc. Place; PIKE; 166 H-4; elev. 772ft./235m.; 🅿; Z 30258; Ⓟ 439; © 475
Moncrief; RMC Place; GRADY; *167 O-5; mail Tallahassee Z 32301
Moniac; RMC Place; CHARLTON; *167 P-10; mail Saint George Z 31562; rural
Monroe; Inc. Place; ⊡ WALTON; 166 E-6; elev. 900ft./274m.; 🅿 🅷; Z 30655-56; Ⓟ 9,759; © 11,407
MONROE; 166 H-5; Ⓟ 17,113; © 21,757; ® 21,774; ◆ 26,538
Montclair; RMC Place; RICHMOND; *166 F-11; ★ AUG; mail Augusta Z 30907; pop. incl. with Augusta (Inc. Place)
Monteith; RMC Place; CHATHAM; *166 J-13; elev. 17ft./5m.; ★ SAV; mail Savannah Z 31407; pop. incl. with Port Wentworth (Inc. Place)
Montevideo (Montivedio); RMC Place; ELBERT, HART; *166 D-9; mail Elberton Z 30635; rural
Montezuma; Inc. Place; MACON; 166 J-5; elev. 184ft./56m.; 🅿 🅷; Z 31063; Ⓟ 4,506; © 3,999
Montgomery; CDP; CHATHAM; *167 K-13; elev. 4ft./1m.; ★ SAV; mail Savannah Z 31406; Ⓟ 4,327; © 4,134
MONTGOMERY; 167 K-9; Ⓟ 7,163; © 8,270; ◆ 8,894
Monticello; Inc. Place; ⊡ JASPER; 166 G-6; elev. 683ft./208m.; 🅿 🅷; Z 31064; Ⓟ 2,289; © 2,428
Monticello; RMC Place; RICHMOND; *166 G-11; ★ AUG; mail Augusta Z 30906; pop. incl. with Augusta (Inc. Place)
Montivedio; ELBERT, HART; see Montevideo (RMC Place)
Montreal; RMC Place; DEKALB; ★ ATL; mail Decatur Z 30033
Montrose; Inc. Place; LAURENS; 166 I-8; elev. 388ft./118m.; 🅿; Z 31065; Ⓟ 117; © 154
Moody AFB; CDP-Census Area Only; LOWNDES; *167 N-8; 🅿; ★ VALD; Z 31699; Ⓟ 1,288; © 993
Moons; RMC Place; WALKER; *166 B-2; ★ CHTN; mail Flintstone Z 30725; ● 200
Moores; RMC Place; LAURENS; *166 I-8; elev. 254ft./77m.; mail Dublin Z 31021; rural
Mora; RMC Place; ATKINSON, COFFEE; 167 M-8; mail Willacoochee Z 31650; ● 75
Moreland; Inc. Place; COWETA; 166 G-3; elev. 940ft./287m.; 🅿; Z 30259; Ⓟ 366; © 393
Morgan; Inc. Place; ⊡ CALHOUN; 167 M-4; elev. 247ft./75m.; 🅿; Z 39866; Ⓟ 252; © 1,464
Morgan; RMC Place; HARALSON; *166 F-3; mail Bremen Z 30110; rural
MORGAN; 166 F-7; Ⓟ 12,883; © 15,457; ◆ 18,776
Morganton; Inc. Place; FANNIN; 166 B-5; elev. 1,807ft./551m.; 🅿; Z 30560; Ⓟ 295; © 299
Morganville; RMC Place; DADE; *166 B-2; ★ CHTN; mail Wildwood Z 30757; ● 100
Morningside; RMC Place; FULTON; *166 E-5; ★ ATL; mail Atlanta Z 30324; pop. incl. with Atlanta (Inc. Place)
Morningside; RMC Place; MUSCOGEE; ★ COL; mail Columbus Z 31909; pop. incl. with Columbus (Inc. Place)
Morning Side Hills; RMC Place; HALL; *166 D-6; mail Gainesville Z 30501; ● 300
Morris; RMC Place; QUITMAN; 167 L-3; elev. 242ft./74m.; 🅿; Z 39867; ● 75
Morris Brown; RMC Place; FULTON; *166 F-4; ★ ATL; mail Atlanta Z 30314; pop. incl. with Atlanta (Inc. Place)
Morris Estates; RMC Place; CATOOSA; *166 B-2; ★ CHTN; mail Ringgold Z 30736; ● 1,000
Morris Siding; RMC Place; FULTON; ★ ATL; pop. incl. with Atlanta (Inc. Place)
Morrow; Inc. Place; CLAYTON; 166 F-5; elev. 929ft./283m.; 🅿 🅲 6,081 ■; ★ ATL; Z 30260, Z 30287; Ⓟ 5,168; © 4,882; ◆ 5,694
Mortons; RMC Place; CHATHAM; *167 K-13; ★ SAV; mail Savannah Z 31405; ● 80
Morven; Inc. Place; BROOKS; 167 N-7; elev. 222ft./68m.; 🅿; Z 31638; Ⓟ 536; © 634
Mossy Creek; RMC Place; WHITE; *166 C-6; mail Cleveland Z 30528; rural
Moultrie; Inc. Place; ⊡ COLQUITT; 167 N-6; elev. 340ft./104m.; 🅿 🅷 ■; Z 31768, Z 31776, Z 31788; Ⓟ 14,865; © 14,387; ◆ 14,643
Mountainbrook; RMC Place; HARRIS; *166 H-3; elev. 926ft./282m.; mail Pine Mountain Z 31822; pop. incl. with Pine Mountain (Inc. Place)
Mountain City; Inc. Place; RABUN; 166 B-7; elev. 2,168ft./661m.; 🅿; Z 30562; Ⓟ 784; © 829
Mountain Hill; RMC Place; HARRIS; *166 I-3; elev. 716ft./218m.; mail Hamilton Z 31811; rural
Mountain Park; Inc. Place; FULTON, CHEROKEE; 166 E-5; elev. 917ft./280m.; ★ ATL; mail Roswell Z 30075; Ⓟ 554; © 506; ® 541
Mountain Park; CDP-Census Area Only; GWINNETT; *166 E-5; ★ ATL; mail Stone Mountain Z 30087; Ⓟ 11,025; © 11,753
Mountaintown; RMC Place; GILMER; *166 B-4; mail Ellijay Z 30540; rural
Mountain View; RMC Place; CLAYTON; 168 G-3; elev. 995ft./303m.; ★ ATL; mail Atlanta Z 30321; ● 1,100
Mountain View; RMC Place; WALKER; *166 B-2; ★ CHTN; mail Rossville Z 30741; ● 1,550
Mount Airy; Inc. Place; HABERSHAM; 166 C-7; elev. 1,560ft./475m.; 🅿; Z 30563; Ⓟ 543; © 604
Mount Berry; RMC Place; FLOYD; 166 D-2; elev. 500ft./152m.; 🅿 🅲 1,842; ★ ROME; Z 30149; pop. incl. with Rome (Inc. Place)
Mount Bethel; RMC Place; COBB; *166 E-4; ★ ATL; mail Marietta Z 30067-68; ● 200
Mount Carmel; RMC Place; WALKER; 166 C-2; mail La Fayette Z 30728; ● 30
Mount Olivet; RMC Place; HART; *166 D-8; mail Hartwell Z 30643; rural
Mount Pleasant; RMC Place; BANKS; *166 D-7; mail Homer Z 30547; rural
Mount Pleasant; RMC Place; WAYNE; 167 M-12; mail Hortense Z 31543; ● 60
Mount Vernon; Inc. Place; ⊡ MONTGOMERY; 166 J-9; elev. 229ft./70m.; 🅿 🅲 1,119; Z 30445; Ⓟ 1,914; © 2,082; ® 1,949
Mount Vernon; RMC Place; WALTON; *166 E-6; mail Monroe Z 30655; rural
Mount Vernon; RMC Place; WHITFIELD; 166 B-3; mail Rocky Face Z 30740; ● 400
Mountville; RMC Place; TROUP; 166 H-3; elev. 918ft./280m.; 🅿; Z 30261; ● 200
Mount Zion; Inc. Place; CARROLL; 166 F-2; elev. 1,100ft./335m.; 🅿; Z 30150; Ⓟ 511; © 1,275
Moxley; RMC Place; JEFFERSON; *166 H-10; elev. 323ft./98m.; mail Wadley Z 30477; ● 100
Mulberry; RMC Place; BARROW; *166 E-6; mail Winder Z 30680; rural
Mulberry Grove; RMC Place; HARRIS; 166 I-3; mail Cataula Z 31804; ● 100
Mulberry Heights; RMC Place; DOUGHERTY; ★ ALB; mail Albany Z 31705; pop. incl. with Albany (Inc. Place)
Mulberry Street; RMC Place; BIBB; *166 H-6; ★ MAC; mail Macon Z 31201; pop. incl. with Macon (Inc. Place)
Munnerlyn; RMC Place; BURKE; 166 H-11; elev. 266ft./81m.; mail Waynesboro Z 30830; ● 50
Murphy; RMC Place; COLQUITT; 167 N-6; mail Coolidge Z 31738; ● 100
MURRAY; 166 B-4; Ⓟ 26,147; © 36,506; ◆ 40,242
Murray Hills; RMC Place; RICHMOND; *166 F-11; elev. 350ft./107m.; ★ AUG; mail Augusta Z 30909; pop. incl. with Augusta (Inc. Place)
Murrays Crossroads; RMC Place; SCHLEY; *166 J-5; elev. 437ft./133m.; mail Ellaville Z 31806; rural
Murrayville; RMC Place; HALL; 166 C-6; elev. 1,295ft./395m.; 🅿; Z 30564; ● 800
MUSCOGEE; 166 J-3; Ⓟ 179,278; © 186,291; ◆ 182,591
Muscogee Junction; RMC Place; MUSCOGEE; ★ COL; pop. incl. with Columbus (Inc. Place)
Musella; RMC Place; CRAWFORD; 166 I-5; elev. 592ft./180m.; 🅿; Z 31066; ● 40
Myrtle Grove; RMC Place; BRYAN; *167 K-13; mail Richmond Hill Z 31324; rural
Mystic; RMC Place; IRWIN; 167 L-7; elev. 368ft./112m.; 🅿; Z 31769; ● 300

N

Nahunta; Inc. Place; ⊡ BRANTLEY; 167 N-11; elev. 65ft./20m.; 🅿; Z 31553; Ⓟ 1,049; © 930
Nails Creek; BANKS; see Jewelville (RMC Place)
Nance Springs; RMC Place; WHITFIELD; *166 C-3; mail Dalton Z 30721; rural
Nankipooh; RMC Place; MUSCOGEE; ★ COL; mail Columbus Z 31909; pop. incl. with Columbus (Inc. Place)
Naomi; RMC Place; WALKER; 166 B-2; mail La Fayette Z 30728; ● 60
Nashville; Inc. Place; ⊡ BERRIEN; 167 N-7; elev. 240ft./73m.; 🅿 🅷; Z 31639; Ⓟ 4,782; © 4,697
National Hills; RMC Place; RICHMOND; *166 F-11; ★ AUG; mail Augusta Z 30904; pop. incl. with Augusta (Inc. Place)
Naylor; RMC Place; LOWNDES; 167 O-8; elev. 192ft./59m.; 🅿; Z 31641; Ⓟ 111
Neal; RMC Place; PIKE; *166 H-4; elev. 816ft./249m.; mail Concord Z 30206; rural
Nebo; RMC Place; PAULDING; *166 E-3; ★ ATL; mail Dallas Z 30132; rural
Neco; RICHMOND; see Sherwood (RMC Place)
Needmore; RMC Place; ECHOLS; *167 O-9; elev. 135ft./41m.; mail Fargo Z 31631
Neese; RMC Place; MADISON; *166 E-7; ★ ATH; mail Hull Z 30646; ● 130
Nelson; Inc. Place; PICKENS, CHEROKEE; 166 D-5; elev. 1,245ft./379m.; 🅿; Z 30151; Ⓟ 486; © 626
Nevils; RMC Place; BULLOCH; 166 J-11; 🅿; Z 31321; ● 185

Entries in **UPPERCASE** are counties.
Entries in **bold** have populations of 2,500 or more.
Names in parentheses are alternate names.

Inc. Place	Incorporated Place
RMC Place	Rand McNally Designated Place
CDP	Census Designated Place
MCD	Minor Civil Division

⊡	County Seat
▲	Minor Civil Division
elev.	Elevation
🅿	Post Office
🅷	Hospital
🅲	College
■	Principal Business Center
★	Ranally Metro Area (RMA) Abbreviation
Z	Zip Code(s)
Ⓟ	Previous Census Population
®	Revised Census Population
Ⓐ	Annexation Population
●	Rand McNally Population Estimate
©	Final Census Population
Ⓢ	Special Census Population
◆	Estimated Population

For additional definitions see Glossary, Volume 1, and Introduction, Volume 2.

Newark; RMC Place; THOMAS; *__167__ O-6; mail Thomasville z 31757; rural
Newborn; Inc. Place; NEWTON, JACKSON; **166** F-6; elev. 740ft./226m.; 🅿; z 30056; Ⓟ 404; © 520
New Branch; RMC Place; TOOMBS; **167** K-10; mail Lyons z 30436; ● 60
New Elm; RMC Place; COLQUITT; *__167__ M-6; mail Moultrie z 31768
New England; RMC Place; DADE; **166** B-2; ★ **CHTN**; mail Trenton z 30752; ● 175
New Era; RMC Place; SUMTER; *__167__ K-5; mail Americus z 31709
New Georgia; RMC Place; PAULDING; *__166__ E-3; ★ **ATL**; mail Dallas z 30157
New Holland; RMC Place; HALL; **166** D-6; mail Gainesville z 30501; ● 1,200
New Home; RMC Place; DADE; *__166__ B-2; ★ **CHTN**; mail Trenton z 30752; rural
New Hope; RMC Place; GILMER; *__166__ B-4; mail Ellijay z 30540; rural
New Hope; RMC Place; GWINNETT; *__166__ E-6; elev. 961ft./293m.; ★ **ATL**; mail Lawrenceville z 30045; rural
New Hope; RMC Place; LINCOLN; *__166__ F-10; mail Lincolnton z 30817
New Hope; RMC Place; PAULDING; **166** E-3; ★ **ATL**; mail Dallas z 30132; ● 150
Newington; Inc. Place; SCREVEN; **166** I-12; elev. 140ft./43m.; 🅿; z 30446; Ⓟ 319; © 322
Newnan; Inc. Place; ⊡ COWETA; **166** G-3; elev. 1,001ft./305m.; 🅿 🅷; z 30263-65, z 30271; Ⓟ 12,497; © 16,242; ◆ 29,475
New Point; RMC Place; SUMTER; *__167__ K-5; mail Plains z 31780; rural
New Salem; RMC Place; BANKS; *__166__ D-7; mail Homer z 30547; rural
Newton; Inc. Place; ⊡ BAKER; **167** M-4; elev. 145ft./44m.; 🅿; z 39870; Ⓟ 703; © 851
NEWTON; **166** F-6; Ⓟ 41,808; © 62,001; ◆ 104,660
Newtown; RMC Place; FULTON; *__166__ E-5; elev. 1,130ft./344m.; ★ **ATL**; mail Alpharetta z 30023; rural
New Town; RMC Place; GORDON; *__166__ C-3; mail Calhoun z 30701; ● 600
New Town; RMC Place; WILKES; *__166__ E-9; mail Washington z 30673; rural
New York; RMC Place; POLK; mail Rockmart z 30153; pop. incl. with Aragon (Inc. Place)
Neyami; RMC Place; LEE; *__167__ L-5; elev. 300ft./91m.; mail Leesburg z 31763; rural
Nicholasville; RMC Place; EARLY; *__167__ M-4; elev. 254ft./77m.; mail Arlington z 39813; rural
Nicholls; Inc. Place; COFFEE; **167** M-9; elev. 186ft./57m.; 🅿; z 31554; Ⓟ 1,003; © 1,008; Ⓡ 2,024
Nicholson; Inc. Place; JACKSON; **166** D-7; elev. 840ft./256m.; 🅿; ★ **ATH**; z 30565; Ⓟ 535; © 1,247
Nickelsville; RMC Place; GORDON; *__166__ C-3; elev. 698ft./213m.; mail Calhoun z 30701; ● 80
Nicklesville (Big Sandy); RMC Place; WILKINSON; *__166__ I-8; mail Irwinton z 31042; rural
Nickleville; RMC Place; GRADY; *__167__ O-4; elev. 279ft./85m.; mail Whigham z 39897; rural
Nickville; RMC Place; ELBERT; *__166__ D-8; mail Dewy Rose z 30634; rural
Nixon; RMC Place; RICHMOND; *__166__ G-11; ★ **AUG**; pop. incl. with Augusta (Inc. Place)
Noah (Noah's Station); RMC Place; JEFFERSON; *__166__ G-10; mail Matthews z 30818; rural
Noah's Station; JEFFERSON; see Noah (RMC Place)
Noble; RMC Place; WALKER; *__166__ B-2; elev. 891ft./272m.; ★ **CHTN**; mail La Fayette z 30728; ● 150
Noonday; RMC Place; COBB; *__166__ E-4; ★ **ATL**; mail Marietta z 30066; ● 1,000
Norcross; Inc. Place; GWINNETT; **166** E-5; elev. 1,057ft./322m.; 🅿; ★ **ATL**; z 30003, z 30010, z 30071, z 30091-93; Ⓟ 5,947; © 8,410
Norman; RMC Place; WILKES; *__166__ E-9; elev. 495ft./151m.; mail Tignall z 30668; rural
Norman Park; Inc. Place; COLQUITT; **167** M-6; elev. 325ft./99m.; 🅿; z 31771; Ⓟ 711; © 849
Normantown; RMC Place; TOOMBS; **166** J-10; elev. 216ft./66m.; mail Vidalia z 30474; ● 45
Norris; RMC Place; WARREN; *__166__ G-9; mail Warrenton z 30828
Norristown; RMC Place; EMANUEL; **166** I-9; elev. 245ft./75m.; 🅿; z 30447; ● 150
North Albany; RMC Place; DOUGHERTY; ★ **ALB**; pop. incl. with Albany (Inc. Place)
North Atlanta; CDP; DEKALB; *__166__ E-5; ★ **ATL**; mail Atlanta z 30319; Ⓟ 27,812; © 38,579; ◆ 44,044
North Canton; RMC Place; CHEROKEE; **166** D-4; ★ **ATL**; mail Canton z 30114; pop. incl. with Canton (Inc. Place)
North Columbus; RMC Place; MUSCOGEE; ★ **COL**; pop. incl. with Columbus (Inc. Place)
North Decatur; CDP; DEKALB; **168** D-5; elev. 950ft./290m.; ★ **ATL**; mail Decatur z 30033; Ⓟ 13,936; © 15,270
North Druid Hills; CDP; DEKALB; **168** D-5; ★ **ATL**; mail Decatur z 30033; Ⓟ 14,170; © 18,852
North Dublin; RMC Place; LAURENS; mail Dublin z 31021; pop. incl. with Dublin (Inc. Place)
North Elberton; RMC Place; ELBERT; **166** D-8; mail Elberton z 30635; ● 150
Northgate; RMC Place; MUSCOGEE; ★ **COL**; mail Columbus z 31907; pop. incl. with Columbus (Inc. Place)
North Highland; RMC Place; FULTON; *__166__ E-5; ★ **ATL**; mail Atlanta z 30306, z 31106; pop. incl. with Atlanta (Inc. Place)
North Highlands; RMC Place; MUSCOGEE; ★ **COL**; mail Columbus z 31904; pop. incl. with Columbus (Inc. Place)
North High Shoals; Inc. Place; OCONEE; **166** E-7; elev. 700ft./213m.; mail High Shoals z 30645; Ⓟ 268; © 439
North Kirkwood; RMC Place; DEKALB; *__166__ E-5; ★ **ATL**; mail Atlanta z 30307; pop. incl. with Atlanta (Inc. Place)
Northlake; RMC Place; DEKALB; *__166__ E-5; ★ **ATL**; mail Atlanta z 30345, z 31145
Northridge; RMC Place; ROCKDALE; ★ **ATL**; mail Conyers z 30012; pop. incl. with Conyers (Inc. Place)
North Savannah; RMC Place; CHATHAM; ★ **SAV**; pop. incl. with Savannah (Inc. Place)
Northside; RMC Place; HOUSTON; mail Warner Robins z 31093; pop. incl. with Warner Robins (Inc. Place)
North West Point; RMC Place; TROUP; **166** H-2; mail West Point z 31833; ● 700
Norton Acres; RMC Place; RICHMOND; *__166__ G-11; ★ **AUG**; mail Augusta z 30906; pop. incl. with Augusta (Inc. Place)
Norwood; Inc. Place; WARREN; **166** F-9; elev. 609ft./186m.; 🅿; z 30821; Ⓟ 238; © 299
Note; RMC Place; PUTNAM; *__166__ G-7; mail Eatonton z 31024; rural
Nuberg; RMC Place; HART; **166** D-8; elev. 720ft./219m.; mail Dewy Rose z 30634; ● 130
Nunez; Inc. Place; EMANUEL; **166** J-10; elev. 251ft./77m.; 🅿; z 30448; Ⓟ 135; © 131
Nyson; FAYETTE; see Starrs Mill (RMC Place)

O

Oakdale; RMC Place; CHATHAM; ★ **SAV**; mail Savannah z 31405; pop. incl. with Savannah (Inc. Place)
Oakdale; RMC Place; COBB; **168** C-2; elev. 850ft./259m.; ★ **ATL**; mail Smyrna z 30080
Oakfield; RMC Place; WORTH; **167** L-5; elev. 267ft./81m.; 🅿; z 31772; ● 200
Oak Forest; RMC Place; CHATHAM; *__167__ K-13; ★ **SAV**; mail Savannah z 31404; ● 150
Oak Forest; RMC Place; CLAYTON; *__166__ F-5; ★ **ATL**; mail Jonesboro z 30236; ● 800
Oak Grove; RMC Place; CARROLL; *__166__ F-3; elev. 1,172ft./357m.; mail Carrollton z 30117; rural
Oak Grove; RMC Place; CHEROKEE; *__166__ D-4; ★ **ATL**; mail Acworth z 30102; ● 600
Oak Grove; RMC Place; DEKALB; **168** D-5; ★ **ATL**; mail Decatur z 30033; ● 2,850
Oak Grove; RMC Place; TROUP; *__166__ H-3; elev. 839ft./256m.; mail Pine Mountain z 31822; rural
Oakhaven; RMC Place; DOUGHERTY; ★ **ALB**; mail Albany z 31701, z 31721; ● 350
Oak Hill; RMC Place; GILMER; *__166__ C-4; mail Ellijay z 30540; rural
Oak Hill; RMC Place; NEWTON; *__166__ F-5; ★ **ATL**; mail Covington z 30016; rural
Oakhurst; RMC Place; CHATHAM; *__167__ K-13; ★ **SAV**; mail Savannah z 31406; pop. incl. with Savannah (Inc. Place)
Oakhurst Siding; RMC Place; DEKALB; *__166__ E-5; ★ **ATL**; pop. incl. with Decatur (Inc. Place)
Oakland; RMC Place; MERIWETHER; *__166__ H-4; mail Gay z 30218
Oakland City; RMC Place; FULTON; ★ **ATL**; pop. incl. with Atlanta (Inc. Place)
Oakland Heights; RMC Place; BARTOW; **166** D-3; mail Cartersville z 30121
Oakland Park; RMC Place; CHATHAM; ★ **SAV**; mail Savannah z 31404; pop. incl. with Savannah (Inc. Place)
Oakland Park; RMC Place; MUSCOGEE; *__166__ J-3; ★ **COL**; mail Columbus z 31903; pop. incl. with Columbus (Inc. Place)
Oaklawn; RMC Place; COWETA; *__166__ G-3; mail Newnan z 30263; rural
Oakleaf Plantation; RMC Place; COBB; ★ **ATL**; mail Marietta z 30067; ● 150
Oakman; RMC Place; GORDON; **166** C-4; elev. 745ft./227m.; 🅿; z 30732; ● 150
Oak Mountain (Cleola); RMC Place; HARRIS; *__166__ I-4; elev. 676ft./206m.; mail Shiloh z 31826; rural
Oak Park; Inc. Place; EMANUEL; **166** J-10; elev. 250ft./76m.; 🅿; z 30401 & mail Ailey z 30410; Ⓟ 269; © 366
Oakwood; Inc. Place; HALL; **166** D-6; elev. 1,149ft./350m.; 🅿; z 30502, z 30566; Ⓟ 1,464; © 2,689
Oasis; RMC Place; FANNIN; *__166__ B-4; mail Blue Ridge z 30513; rural
Oatland Island; RMC Place; CHATHAM; *__167__ K-13; ★ **SAV**; mail Savannah z 31410; ● 150
Ocee; RMC Place; FULTON; *__166__ E-5; ★ **ATL**; mail Alpharetta z 30023; ● 50
Ochillee; RMC Place; CHATTAHOOCHEE; ★ **COL**; mail Fort Benning z 31905
Ochlocknee; Inc. Place; THOMAS; **167** N-5; elev. 270ft./82m.; 🅿; z 31773; Ⓟ 588; © 605
Ochwalkee; RMC Place; WHEELER; *__166__ J-9; elev. 50ft./15m.; mail Glenwood z 30428; rural
Ocilla; Inc. Place; ⊡ IRWIN; **167** L-7; elev. 327ft./100m.; 🅿 🅷; z 31774; Ⓟ 3,182; © 3,270
Oconee; Inc. Place; WASHINGTON; **166** H-8; elev. 218ft./66m.; 🅿; z 31067; Ⓟ 234; © 280
OCONEE; **166** E-7; Ⓟ 17,618; © 26,225; ◆ 32,993
Oconee Heights; RMC Place; CLARKE; *__166__ E-7; ★ **ATH**; mail Athens z 30607; pop. incl. with Athens (Inc. Place)
Odessadale; RMC Place; MERIWETHER; *__166__ H-3; elev. 900ft./274m.; mail Greenville z 30222; ● 150
Odum; Inc. Place; WAYNE; **167** L-11; elev. 156ft./48m.; 🅿; z 31555; Ⓟ 388; © 414
Offerman; Inc. Place; PIERCE; **167** M-11; elev. 106ft./32m.; 🅿; z 31556; © 403
Ogeechee; RMC Place; SCREVEN; *__166__ I-11; elev. 112ft./34m.; mail Sylvania z 30467; rural
Ogeechee Farms; RMC Place; CHATHAM; *__167__ K-13; elev. 15ft./5m.; ★ **SAV**; mail Savannah z 31405; ● 300
Ogeechee Road; RMC Place; CHATHAM; *__167__ K-13; elev. 10ft./3m.; ★ **SAV**; mail Savannah z 31405; pop. incl. with Savannah (Inc. Place)
Ogeecheeton; RMC Place; CHATHAM; *__167__ K-13; ★ **SAV**; mail Savannah z 31415; pop. incl. with Savannah (Inc. Place)
Oglethorpe; RMC Place; CHATHAM; *__167__ K-13; elev. 20ft./6m.; ★ **SAV**; mail Savannah z 31406, z 31411, z 31416; pop. incl. with Savannah (Inc. Place)
Oglethorpe; Inc. Place; ⊡ MACON; **166** J-5; elev. 299ft./91m.; 🅿; z 31068; Ⓟ 1,302; © 1,200
OGLETHORPE; **166** E-8; Ⓟ 9,763; © 12,635; ◆ 14,338
Oglethorpe Park; RMC Place; CHATHAM; ★ **SAV**; mail Savannah z 31406; pop. incl. with Savannah (Inc. Place)
Ogletree Woods; RMC Place; MUSCOGEE; *__166__ I-3; ★ **COL**; mail Columbus z 31909; pop. incl. with Columbus (Inc. Place)
Ohoopee; RMC Place; TOOMBS; **166** J-10; elev. 189ft./58m.; mail Lyons z 30436; ● 70
Okefenokee; RMC Place; WARE; *__167__ N-10; elev. 125ft./38m.; mail Waycross z 31501, z 31503; rural
Ola; RMC Place; HENRY; *__166__ G-5; elev. 805ft./245m.; mail McDonough z 30252; ● 200
Old Damascus; RMC Place; EARLY; *__167__ M-3; elev. 186ft./57m.; mail Damascus z 39841
Old National; RMC Place; FULTON; *__166__ F-4; ★ **ATL**; mail Atlanta z 30349
Old South; RMC Place; CLAYTON; *__166__ F-5; ★ **ATL**; mail Jonesboro z 30236; ● 750
Olive Branch; RMC Place; TALBOT; *__166__ I-4; mail Talbotton z 31827; rural
Oliver; Inc. Place; SCREVEN; **166** I-12; elev. 120ft./37m.; 🅿; z 30449; Ⓟ 242; © 253
Olney; RMC Place; BULLOCH; *__166__ J-12; elev. 72ft./22m.; mail Ellabell z 31308; rural
Omaha; RMC Place; STEWART; **167** K-3; elev. 240ft./73m.; 🅿; z 31821; ● 115
Omega; Inc. Place; TIFT, COLQUITT; **167** M-7; elev. 325ft./99m.; 🅿; z 31775; Ⓟ 912; © 1,340
Oostanaula; RMC Place; GORDON; *__166__ C-3; mail Calhoun z 30701; rural
Ophir; RMC Place; CHEROKEE; *__166__ D-5; ★ **ATL**; mail Ball Ground z 30107; rural
Orange; RMC Place; CHEROKEE; *__166__ D-5; ★ **ATL**; mail Canton z 30115; rural
Orchard Hill; Inc. Place; SPALDING; **166** G-5; elev. 871ft./265m.; 🅿; z 30266; Ⓟ 239; © 230
Orchard Hills; RMC Place; WALKER; *__166__ B-2; ★ **CHTN**; mail Rossville z 30741; ● 900
Orianna; RMC Place; LAURENS; *__166__ J-9; mail Adrian z 31002; rural
Orland; RMC Place; TREUTLEN; *__166__ J-9; mail Soperton z 30457; rural
Ormewood; RMC Place; FULTON; *__166__ F-5; ★ **ATL**; mail Atlanta z 30316; pop. incl. with Atlanta (Inc. Place)
Oscarville; RMC Place; FORSYTH; *__166__ D-6; elev. 1,188ft./362m.; ★ **ATL**; mail Gainesville z 30506; ● 100
Osierfield; RMC Place; IRWIN; **167** L-8; elev. 339ft./103m.; mail Fitzgerald z 31750; ● 100
Other; RMC Place; PAULDING; *__166__ E-3; elev. 1,080ft./329m.; ★ **ATL**; mail Dallas z 30157; rural
Ottawa Estates; RMC Place; CHATHAM; ★ **SAV**; mail Bloomingdale z 31302; pop. incl. with Bloomingdale (Inc. Place)
Ottley; RMC Place; FULTON; ★ **ATL**; pop. incl. with Atlanta (Inc. Place)
Owen; RMC Place; PIERCE; *__167__ M-10; mail Blackshear z 31516; rural
Owensboro; RMC Place; WILCOX; *__167__ K-7; elev. 403ft./123m.; mail Rochelle z 31079; rural
Owltown; RMC Place; UNION; *__166__ B-6; mail Blairsville z 30512; rural
Oxford; Inc. Place; NEWTON; **166** F-6; elev. 740ft./226m.; 🅿; ★ **ATL**; z 30054; Ⓟ 1,945; © 1,892

P

Pace; RMC Place; NEWTON; *__166__ F-6; elev. 846ft./258m.; ★ **ATL**; mail Covington z 30014
Pachitla (Pachitta); RMC Place; RANDOLPH; *__167__ L-4; mail Cuthbert z 39840; rural
Pachitta; RANDOLPH; see Pachitla (RMC Place)
Padena; RMC Place; FANNIN; *__166__ B-5; mail Morganton z 30560; rural
Paintertown; FANNIN; see Pantertown (RMC Place)
Palato; RMC Place; JASPER; *__166__ G-6; mail Monticello z 31064; rural
Palmetto; Inc. Place; FULTON, COWETA; **166** F-4; elev. 1,027ft./313m.; 🅿; z 30268; Ⓟ 2,612; © 3,400
Palmetto; RMC Place; OGLETHORPE; *__166__ E-8; mail Carlton z 30627; rural
Palmyra; RMC Place; LEE; **167** L-5; ★ **ALB**; mail Leesburg z 31763; ● 60
Pancras; RMC Place; BALDWIN; *__166__ H-7; mail Milledgeville z 31061; rural
Panhandle; RMC Place; TAYLOR; *__166__ I-5; elev. 597ft./182m.; mail Reynolds z 31076; rural
Pannell; RMC Place; WALTON; *__166__ E-6; mail Monroe z 30655; rural
Panola; RMC Place; DEKALB; *__166__ F-5; ★ **ATL**; mail Lithonia z 30058; ● 200
Pantertown (Paintertown); RMC Place; FANNIN; **166** B-5; mail Mineral Bluff z 30559; ● 150
Panthersville (South De Kalb); CDP; DEKALB; **166** F-5; ★ **ATL**; mail Decatur z 30034; Ⓟ 9,874; © 11,791
Paoli; RMC Place; MADISON; *__166__ D-8; mail Comer z 30629; rural
Paradise Park; RMC Place; CHATHAM; ★ **SAV**; mail Savannah z 31406; pop. incl. with Savannah (Inc. Place)
Paradise Park; RMC Place; WAYNE; *__167__ L-12; mail Jesup z 31545; ● 60
Paradise Valley; RMC Place; CLARKE; *__166__ E-7; ★ **ATH**; mail Athens z 30607; pop. incl. with Athens (Inc. Place)
Parhams; RMC Place; FRANKLIN; *__166__ C-7; mail Carnesville z 30521; rural
Parkchester; RMC Place; MUSCOGEE; ★ **COL**; mail Columbus z 31906; pop. incl. with Columbus (Inc. Place)
Park City; RMC Place; WALKER; *__166__ B-2; ★ **CHTN**; mail Rossville z 30741; pop. incl. with Fort Oglethorpe (Inc. Place)
Parkers; RMC Place; SCREVEN; *__166__ I-11; mail Sylvania z 30467; rural
Parkersburg; RMC Place; CHATHAM; **167** T-11; ★ **SAV**; mail Savannah z 31406; ● 1,000
Parkerville; RMC Place; WORTH; *__167__ M-6; elev. 445ft./136m.; mail Doerun z 31744
Park Hill; RMC Place; HALL; mail Gainesville z 30501; pop. incl. with Gainesville (Inc. Place)
Parkwood; RMC Place; CHATHAM; *__167__ K-13; ★ **SAV**; mail Savannah z 31404; pop. incl. with Savannah (Inc. Place)
Parrott; Inc. Place; TERRELL; **167** K-4; elev. 469ft./143m.; 🅿; z 39877; Ⓟ 140; © 156
Pateville; RMC Place; CRISP; *__167__ L-6; mail Cordele z 31015; rural
Patillo; RMC Place; LAMAR; *__166__ G-5; elev. 723ft./220m.; mail Jackson z 30233; rural
Patten; RMC Place; THOMAS; *__167__ N-6; mail Boston z 31626; rural
Patterson; Inc. Place; PIERCE; **167** M-10; elev. 104ft./32m.; 🅿; z 31557; Ⓟ 626; © 627
PAULDING; **166** E-3; Ⓟ 41,611; © 81,678; ◆ 140,019
Pavo; Inc. Place; THOMAS, BROOKS; **167** N-6; elev. 252ft./77m.; 🅿; z 31778; Ⓟ 774; © 711
Payne; Inc. Place; BIBB; **167** R-5; elev. 507ft./155m.; ★ **MAC**; mail Macon z 31201; Ⓟ 192; © 178
Payne; RMC Place; CHEROKEE; *__166__ D-4; elev. 985ft./300m.; ★ **ATL**; mail Acworth z 30102; rural
PEACH; **166** I-6; Ⓟ 21,189; © 23,668; ◆ 28,155
Peach Orchard; RMC Place; RICHMOND; *__166__ F-11; elev. 150ft./46m.; ★ **AUG**; mail Augusta z 30906; pop. incl. with Augusta (Inc. Place)
Peachtree Center; RMC Place; FULTON; *__166__ E-4; ★ **ATL**; mail Atlanta z 30343; pop. incl. with Atlanta (Inc. Place)
Peachtree City; Inc. Place; FAYETTE; **166** G-4; elev. 920ft./280m.; 🅿; ★ **ATL**; z 30269-70; Ⓟ 19,027; © 31,580; ◆ 34,156
Peachtree Hills; RMC Place; FULTON; *__166__ E-4; ★ **ATL**; mail Atlanta z 30305; pop. incl. with Atlanta (Inc. Place)
Pearly; RMC Place; LAURENS; mail Dublin z 31021; rural
Pearson; Inc. Place; ⊡ ATKINSON; **167** M-9; elev. 205ft./62m.; 🅿; z 31642; Ⓟ 1,714; © 1,805
Pebble City; RMC Place; MITCHELL; *__167__ M-5; mail Sale City z 31784; rural
Pedenville; RMC Place; PIKE; *__166__ H-4; elev. 764ft./233m.; mail Concord z 30206; rural
Pelham; Inc. Place; MITCHELL; **167** N-5; elev. 365ft./111m.; 🅿; z 31779; Ⓟ 3,869; © 4,126
Pembroke; Inc. Place; ⊡ BRYAN; **167** K-12; elev. 95ft./29m.; 🅿; z 31321; Ⓟ 1,503; © 2,379
Pendergrass; Inc. Place; JACKSON; **166** D-6; elev. 866ft./264m.; 🅿; z 30567; Ⓟ 298; © 431
Pendley Hills; RMC Place; DEKALB; **168** E-6; ★ **ATL**; mail Decatur z 30032; ● 5,000
Penfield; RMC Place; GREENE; **166** F-8; elev. 653ft./199m.; mail Union Point z 30669; ● 150
Penia; RMC Place; CRISP; *__167__ K-6; mail Cordele z 31015; rural
Pennick; RMC Place; GLYNN; *__167__ M-12; ★ **BRUNS**; mail Brunswick z 31525; rural
Pennington; RMC Place; MORGAN; *__166__ F-7; mail Madison z 30650; rural
Pennville; RMC Place; CHATTOOGA; **166** C-2; mail Summerville z 30747; ● 250
Peoples Still; RMC Place; GRADY; *__167__ N-5; mail Whigham z 39897; rural
Pepperton; RMC Place; BUTTS; *__166__ G-6; elev. 721ft./220m.; mail Jackson z 30233
Perkins; RMC Place; JENKINS; **166** H-11; elev. 327ft./100m.; 🅿; z 30822; ● 200
Perry; Inc. Place; ⊡ HOUSTON, PEACH; **166** J-6; elev. 337ft./103m.; 🅿 🅷; z 31069; Ⓟ 9,452; © 9,602
Persimmon (Blalock); RMC Place; RABUN; *__166__ B-7; mail Clayton z 30525; rural
Petross; RMC Place; MONTGOMERY; *__167__ K-10; mail Vidalia z 30474
Pharr Road; RMC Place; FULTON; *__166__ E-4; elev. 900ft./274m.; ★ **ATL**; mail Atlanta z 30305, z 30355; pop. incl. with Atlanta (Inc. Place)
Phelps; RMC Place; WHITFIELD; *__166__ C-3; mail Dalton z 30720; rural
Phillipsburg; CDP; TIFT; **167** M-7; mail Tifton z 31794; Ⓟ 1,044; © 887
Philomath; RMC Place; OGLETHORPE; **166** F-8; elev. 632ft./193m.; 🅿; z 30660; ● 150
Phinizy; RMC Place; COLUMBIA; **166** F-10; elev. 447ft./136m.; mail Appling z 30802; ● 50
Phoenix; RMC Place; FULTON; *__166__ F-4; ★ **ATL**; mail Atlanta z 30301, z 30370; pop. incl. with Atlanta (Inc. Place)
Phoenix; RMC Place; PUTNAM; *__166__ G-7; elev. 392ft./119m.; mail Eatonton z 31024; rural
Pickard; RMC Place; UPSON; *__166__ H-4; mail Thomaston z 30286; rural
PICKENS; **166** C-4; Ⓟ 14,432; © 22,983; ◆ 32,777
Piedmont; RMC Place; LAMAR; *__166__ H-5; mail Barnesville z 30204, The Rock z 30285; rural
PIERCE; **167** M-10; Ⓟ 13,328; © 15,636; ◆ 18,622
Pierceville; RMC Place; FANNIN; *__166__ B-4; mail Copperhill z 37317; rural
PIKE; **166** H-4; Ⓟ 10,224; © 13,688; ◆ 18,285
Pineboro; RMC Place; COLQUITT; *__167__ N-6; mail Moultrie z 31768; rural
Pine Chapel; RMC Place; GORDON; mail Calhoun z 30701; rural
Pine Gardens; RMC Place; CHATHAM; *__167__ K-13; ★ **SAV**; mail Savannah z 31404; pop. incl. with Savannah (Inc. Place)
Pine Grove; RMC Place; APPLING; **167** L-10; elev. 228ft./69m.; mail Baxley z 31513; ● 50
Pine Harbor; RMC Place; MCINTOSH; **167** L-13; mail Townsend z 31331; ● 125
Pine Hill; RMC Place; MUSCOGEE; ★ **COL**; mail Columbus z 31903; pop. incl. with Columbus (Inc. Place)
Pinehurst; Inc. Place; DOOLY; **166** J-6; elev. 378ft./115m.; 🅿; z 31070; Ⓟ 388; © 307
Pinehurst; RMC Place; HENRY; *__166__ F-5; ★ **ATL**; mail Stockbridge z 30281; ● 120
Pine Lake; Inc. Place; DEKALB; *__166__ E-5; elev. 1,009ft./308m.; 🅿; ★ **ATL**; z 30072; Ⓟ 810; © 621
Pineland; RMC Place; ECHOLS; *__167__ O-9; elev. 143ft./44m.; mail Fargo z 31631; rural
Pine Log; RMC Place; BARTOW; **166** D-4; elev. 870ft./265m.; mail Rydal z 30171; ● 150
Pine Mountain; RMC Place; DEKALB; *__166__ F-5; ★ **ATL**; mail Lithonia z 30058; ● 100
Pine Mountain (Chipley); Inc. Place; HARRIS; **166** H-3; elev. 935ft./285m.; 🅿; z 31822; Ⓟ 875; © 1,141
Pine Mountain; RMC Place; RABUN; *__166__ B-8; elev. 1,661ft./506m.; mail Mountain Rest z 29664; rural
Pine Mountain Valley; RMC Place; HARRIS; **166** H-3; elev. 860ft./262m.; 🅿; z 31823; ● 950
Pineora; RMC Place; EFFINGHAM; **166** J-12; elev. 74ft./23m.; mail Guyton z 31312; ● 300
Pine Park; RMC Place; GRADY; **167** O-5; elev. 232ft./71m.; ● 200
Pine Valley; RMC Place; COOK; *__167__ N-7; mail Adel z 31620; ● 25
Pine Valley; RMC Place; RICHMOND; *__166__ G-11; ★ **AUG**; mail Augusta z 30904; pop. incl. with Augusta (Inc. Place)
Pineview; Inc. Place; WILCOX; **167** K-7; elev. 280ft./85m.; 🅿; z 31071; Ⓟ 594; © 532
Pinewood Shores; RMC Place; ROCKDALE; *__166__ F-5; elev. 735ft./224m.; ★ **ATL**; mail Conyers z 30094; ● 500
Piney Bluff; RMC Place; CAMDEN; *__167__ N-12; mail Waverly z 31565; rural
Piney Grove; RMC Place; HARRIS; *__166__ I-3; mail Fortson z 31808; rural
Pin Point; RMC Place; CHATHAM; *__167__ K-13; ★ **SAV**; mail Savannah z 31406; ● 500
Pinson; RMC Place; FLOYD; *__166__ D-3; ★ **ROME**; mail Rome z 30161; rural
Pio Nono; RMC Place; BIBB; *__166__ H-6; ★ **MAC**; mail Macon z 31203; pop. incl. with Macon (Inc. Place)
Pirkle Woods; RMC Place; FORSYTH; *__166__ D-5; ★ **ATL**; mail Cumming z 30040; pop. incl. with Cumming (Inc. Place)
Pitts; Inc. Place; WILCOX; **167** K-7; elev. 384ft./117m.; 🅿; z 31072; Ⓟ 214; © 308
Pittsburg; RMC Place; DEKALB; *__166__ E-5; ★ **ATL**; mail Tucker z 30084
Plainfield; RMC Place; DODGE; **166** J-8; elev. 355ft./108m.; 🅿; z 31023; ● 140
Plains; Inc. Place; SUMTER; **167** K-4; elev. 499ft./152m.; 🅿; z 31780; Ⓟ 716; © 637
Plainview; RMC Place; FRANKLIN; *__166__ D-7; mail Carnesville z 30521; rural
Plainview; RMC Place; WHITFIELD; *__166__ B-3; elev. 751ft./229m.; mail Dalton z 30720; ● 125
Plainville; Inc. Place; GORDON; **166** C-3; elev. 680ft./207m.; 🅿; z 30733; Ⓟ 231; © 257
Planter; RMC Place; MADISON; *__166__ D-7; mail Hull z 30646; rural
Pleasant Hill; RMC Place; FULTON; *__166__ F-4; ★ **ATL**; mail Atlanta z 30337; rural
Pleasant Hill; RMC Place; GWINNETT; *__166__ E-5; elev. 944ft./288m.; ★ **ATL**; mail Duluth z 30096; ● 800
Pleasant Hill; RMC Place; TALBOT; **166** I-4; mail Woodland z 31836; ● 50
Pleasant Hill; RMC Place; TERRELL; *__167__ K-4; mail Dawson z 39842; rural
Pleasant Valley; RMC Place; BARTOW; *__166__ D-3; mail Adairsville z 30103; rural
Pleasant Valley; RMC Place; DOOLY; mail Vienna z 31092; rural
Pocatalago; MADISON; see Pocataligo (RMC Place)
Pocataligo (Pocatalago); RMC Place; MADISON; **166** D-7; elev. 881ft./269m.; mail Danielsville z 30633; ● 100
Pointe South; RMC Place; CLAYTON; *__166__ F-4; ★ **ATL**; mail Jonesboro z 30238; ● 400
Point Peter; RMC Place; OGLETHORPE; **166** E-8; mail Carlton z 30627; ● 50
POLK; **166** E-2; Ⓟ 33,815; © 38,127; ◆ 42,263
Pollards Corner; RMC Place; COLUMBIA; *__166__ F-10; mail Appling z 30802; rural
Pomona; RMC Place; SPALDING; *__166__ G-5; mail Griffin z 30223; ● 150
Pond Spring; RMC Place; WALKER; *__166__ B-2; ★ **CHTN**; mail Chickamauga z 30707; rural
Pooler; Inc. Place; CHATHAM; **167** Q-9; elev. 22ft./7m.; 🅿; ★ **SAV**; z 31322; Ⓟ 4,453; © 6,239
Pope City; RMC Place; WILCOX; *__167__ K-7; mail Rochelle z 31079; rural
Popes Ferry; RMC Place; MONROE; **166** H-6; mail Juliette z 31046; ● 30
Poplar Springs; RMC Place; HARALSON; *__166__ E-2; mail Buchanan z 30113; rural
Poplar Springs; RMC Place; OCONEE; *__166__ E-7; mail Watkinsville z 30677; rural
Portal; Inc. Place; BULLOCH; **166** I-11; elev. 295ft./90m.; 🅿; z 30450; Ⓟ 522; © 597
Porter; RMC Place; BLECKLEY; *__166__ J-7; mail Cochran z 31014; ● 80
Porterdale; Inc. Place; NEWTON; **166** F-6; elev. 700ft./213m.; 🅿; ★ **ATL**; z 30014, z 30016, z 30070; Ⓟ 1,278; © 1,281
Porter Springs; RMC Place; LUMPKIN; *__166__ C-6; mail Dahlonega z 30533; rural
Portland; RMC Place; POLK; *__166__ E-3; mail Aragon z 30104; rural
Port Royal; RMC Place; BRYAN; *__167__ K-13; elev. 182ft./55m.; mail Richmond Hill z 31324; rural
Port Wentworth; Inc. Place; CHATHAM; **167** S-8; elev. 20ft./6m.; 🅿; ★ **SAV**; z 31407; Ⓟ 4,012; © 3,276
Port Wentworth Junction; RMC Place; CHATHAM; *__167__ K-13; ★ **SAV**; mail Savannah z 31407; pop. incl. with Port Wentworth (Inc. Place)
Postell; RMC Place; JONES; *__166__ H-7; elev. 536ft./163m.; ★ **MAC**; mail Macon z 31217; rural
Potterville; RMC Place; TAYLOR; **166** I-5; mail Reynolds z 31076; ● 170
Poulan; Inc. Place; WORTH; **167** M-6; elev. 361ft./110m.; 🅿; z 31781; Ⓟ 962; © 946
Powder Springs; Inc. Place; COBB; **166** E-4; elev. 979ft./298m.; 🅿; ★ **ATL**; z 30127; Ⓟ 6,893; © 12,481
Powell Place; RMC Place; DOUGHERTY; *__167__ L-5; ★ **ALB**; mail Albany z 31701; pop. incl. with Albany (Inc. Place)
Powelton; RMC Place; HANCOCK; **166** G-8; elev. 597ft./182m.; mail Sparta z 31087; ● 40
Powers Lake; RMC Place; FULTON; *__166__ E-4; ★ **ATL**; mail Atlanta z 30327; ● 300
Powersville; RMC Place; PEACH; **166** I-6; elev. 416ft./127m.; 🅿; ★ **MAC**; z 31008; ● 110
Prather; RMC Place; WILKES; *__166__ E-9; mail Washington z 30673; rural
Prattsburg; RMC Place; TALBOT; *__166__ I-4; elev. 530ft./162m.; mail Talbotton z 31827; rural
Presley; RMC Place; TOWNS; *__166__ B-6; mail Hiawassee z 30546; rural
Preston; Inc. Place; ⊡ WEBSTER; **167** K-4; elev. 450ft./137m.; 🅿; z 31824; Ⓟ 388; © 453
Pretoria; RMC Place; DOUGHERTY; *__167__ M-5; elev. 189ft./58m.; ★ **ALB**; mail Albany z 31701
Price; RMC Place; HALL; *__166__ D-6; mail Gainesville z 30506; rural
Pridgen; RMC Place; COFFEE; **167** L-8; mail Broxton z 31519; ● 50
Primrose; RMC Place; MERIWETHER; **166** G-3; elev. 886ft./270m.; mail Greenville z 30222; ● 100
Princeton; RMC Place; CLARKE; *__166__ E-7; ★ **ATH**; mail Athens z 30601; pop. incl. with Athens (Inc. Place)
Pringle; RMC Place; WASHINGTON; *__166__ I-9; elev. 372ft./113m.; mail Wrightsville z 31096; rural
Prior; RMC Place; POLK; *__166__ E-2; mail Cedartown z 30125; rural
Pritchetts; RMC Place; WORTH; *__167__ M-6; mail Doerun z 31744; rural
Privette Heights; RMC Place; COBB; **168** B-1; ★ **ATL**; mail Marietta z 30008; ● 420
Prospect (Eudora); RMC Place; JASPER; *__166__ G-6; mail Monticello z 31064
Pulaski; Inc. Place; CANDLER; **166** J-11; elev. 211ft./64m.; 🅿; z 30451; Ⓟ 264; © 261
PULASKI; **166** J-7; Ⓟ 8,108; © 9,588; ◆ 9,825
Pumpkin Center; RMC Place; COLUMBIA; *__166__ F-10; ★ **AUG**; mail Harlem z 30814; ● 50
Putnam; RMC Place; MARION; *__166__ J-4; mail Buena Vista z 31803; rural
PUTNAM; **166** G-7; Ⓟ 14,137; © 18,812; ◆ 20,714
Putney; CDP; DOUGHERTY; **167** M-5; elev. 189ft./58m.; 🅿; ★ **ALB**; z 31782; Ⓟ 3,108; © 2,998
Pyles Marsh; RMC Place; GLYNN; *__167__ M-12; ★ **BRUNS**; mail Brunswick z 31525; rural
Pyne; RMC Place; TROUP; *__166__ H-2; mail Lagrange z 30240; rural

Q

Queensland; RMC Place; BEN HILL; **167** L-7; mail Fitzgerald z 31750; ● 140
Quitman; Inc. Place; ⊡ BROOKS; **167** O-7; elev. 192ft./59m.; 🅿 🅷; z 31643; Ⓟ 5,292; © 4,638
QUITMAN; **167** K-3; Ⓟ 2,209; © 2,598; ◆ 2,670

R

Rabbit Hill; RMC Place; BRYAN; *__167__ K-13; mail Richmond Hill z 31324; rural
RABUN; **166** B-7; Ⓟ 11,648; © 15,050; ◆ 16,731
Rabun Gap; RMC Place; RABUN; *__166__ B-7; elev. 2,140ft./652m.; 🅿; z 30568; ● 200
Racepond; RMC Place; CHARLTON; **167** N-11; mail Folkston z 31537; ● 130
Radium Springs; RMC Place; DOUGHERTY; **167** M-5; ★ **ALB**; mail Albany z 31702, z 31705; ● 1,400
Ragsdale; RMC Place; DOUGHERTY; ★ **ALB**; pop. incl. with Albany (Inc. Place)
Raines; RMC Place; CRISP; *__167__ K-6; mail Cordele z 31015; rural
Raleigh; RMC Place; MERIWETHER; **166** H-4; elev. 800ft./244m.; mail Woodbury z 30293; ● 75
Ramhurst; RMC Place; MURRAY; *__166__ C-4; mail Chatsworth z 30705
Randall; RMC Place; STEWART; *__167__ K-3; mail Lumpkin z 31815; pop. incl. with Richland (Inc. Place)
RANDOLPH; **167** L-3; Ⓟ 8,023; © 7,791; ◆ 7,124
Ranger; Inc. Place; GORDON; **166** C-4; elev. 760ft./232m.; 🅿; z 30734; Ⓟ 153; © 85
Raoul (Georgia Industrial Institute); CDP; HABERSHAM; *__166__ C-7; mail Alto z 30510; Ⓟ 1,666; © 1,816
Raulerson; RMC Place; BRANTLEY; mail Patterson z 31557; rural
Raulerson; RMC Place; PIERCE; *__167__ M-11; mail Patterson z 31557; ● 60
Ravenwood; RMC Place; RICHMOND; *__166__ F-11; ★ **AUG**; mail Augusta z 30907; pop. incl. with Augusta (Inc. Place)
Raybon; RMC Place; BRANTLEY; **167** M-11; elev. 58ft./18m.; mail Nahunta z 31553; ● 200
Ray City; Inc. Place; BERRIEN; **167** N-8; elev. 189ft./58m.; 🅿; z 31645; Ⓟ 603; © 746
Rayle; Inc. Place; WILKES; **166** E-8; 🅿; z 30660; Ⓟ 107; © 139
Raymond; RMC Place; COWETA; **166** G-4; elev. 804ft./245m.; 🅿; z 30263 & mail Newnan z 30265; ● 300
Raytown; RMC Place; TALIAFERRO; *__166__ F-9; elev. 570ft./174m.; mail Crawfordville z 30631; rural
Rebecca; Inc. Place; TURNER; **167** L-7; elev. 352ft./107m.; 🅿; z 31783; Ⓟ 148; © 246
Rebie; RMC Place; BLECKLEY; *__166__ J-8; elev. 330ft./101m.; mail Chester z 31012; rural
Recovery; RMC Place; DECATUR; *__167__ O-3; elev. 220ft./67m.; mail Chattahoochee z 32324; ● 30
Redan; CDP; DEKALB; *__166__ F-5; elev. 977ft./298m.; 🅿; ★ **ATL**; z 30074; Ⓟ 24,376; © 33,841; ◆ 38,632
Redbud; RMC Place; GORDON; *__166__ C-3; elev. 666ft./203m.; mail Calhoun z 30701; ● 100
Red Clay; RMC Place; WHITFIELD; *__166__ B-3; mail Cohutta z 30710; ● 85
Red Hill; RMC Place; FRANKLIN; *__166__ C-7; mail Carnesville z 30521; rural
Red Hill; RMC Place; STEWART; *__167__ K-4; mail Richland z 31825; rural
Red Lane; RMC Place; HALL; mail Gainesville z 30501; rural
Red Oak; RMC Place; FULTON; **168** H-2; elev. 1,027ft./313m.; 🅿; ★ **ATL**; z 30272; ● 2,800
Red Rock (Terry); RMC Place; PAULDING; mail Acworth z 30101; rural
Red Rock; RMC Place; WORTH; **167** L-6; elev. 335ft./102m.; mail Sylvester z 31791; ● 85
Red Stone; RMC Place; JACKSON; *__166__ E-7; ★ **ATH**; mail Jefferson z 30549; rural
Red Store Crossroads; RMC Place; BAKER; *__167__ M-5; mail Newton z 39870; rural
Reed Creek; CDP; HART; **166** C-8; mail Hartwell z 30643; Ⓟ 1,854; © 2,148
Reese; RMC Place; WARREN; *__166__ G-9; mail Warrenton z 30828; rural
Reeves; RMC Place; GORDON; *__166__ C-3; mail Calhoun z 30701; rural
Register; Inc. Place; BULLOCH; **166** J-11; elev. 171ft./52m.; 🅿; z 30452; Ⓟ 195; © 164
Rehoboth; RMC Place; DEKALB; **168** D-6; ★ **ATL**; mail Decatur z 30033; ● 1,300
Reidsboro; RMC Place; PIKE; *__166__ G-4; mail Williamson z 30292; rural
Reidsville; Inc. Place; ⊡ TATTNALL; **167** K-10; elev. 207ft./63m.; 🅿 🅷; z 30453, z 30499; Ⓟ 2,469; © 2,235
Reka; RMC Place; BRYAN; *__167__ K-12; mail Pembroke z 31321; rural
Relay; RMC Place; FLOYD; *__166__ D-2; elev. 912ft./278m.; ★ **ROME**; mail Cedartown z 30125; rural
Remerton; Inc. Place; LOWNDES; **167** O-7; elev. 200ft./61m.; ★ **VALD**; mail Valdosta z 31601; Ⓟ 463; © 847
Renfroe; RMC Place; CHATTAHOOCHEE; *__166__ J-4; mail Cusseta z 31805
Reno; RMC Place; GRADY; **167** O-5; elev. 268ft./82m.; ● 100
Rentz; Inc. Place; LAURENS; **166** J-8; elev. 310ft./94m.; 🅿; z 31075; Ⓟ 364; © 304
Reo; RMC Place; WALKER; *__166__ B-3; mail Rocky Face z 30740
Resaca; Inc. Place; GORDON; **166** C-3; elev. 644ft./196m.; 🅿; z 30735; Ⓟ 410; © 815
Resseaus Crossroads; RMC Place; PUTNAM; *__166__ G-7; elev. 468ft./143m.; mail Eatonton z 31024; rural
Rest Haven; Inc. Place; GWINNETT, HALL; *__166__ D-6; elev. 1,100ft./335m.; ★ **ATL**; mail Buford z 30518; Ⓟ 176; © 151
Retreat; RMC Place; LIBERTY; **167** L-12; mail Riceboro z 31323; pop. incl. with Riceboro (Inc. Place)
Rex; RMC Place; CLAYTON; *__166__ F-5; elev. 780ft./238m.; 🅿; ★ **ATL**; z 30273; ● 950
Reynolds; Inc. Place; TAYLOR; **166** I-5; elev. 429ft./131m.; 🅿; z 31076; Ⓟ 1,166; © 1,036
Reynoldsville; RMC Place; SEMINOLE; **167** O-3; elev. 107ft./33m.; mail Donalsonville z 39845; ● 50
Rhine; Inc. Place; DODGE; **167** K-8; elev. 225ft./69m.; 🅿; z 31077; Ⓟ 466; © 422
Riceboro; Inc. Place; LIBERTY; **167** L-12; elev. 20ft./6m.; 🅿; z 31323; Ⓟ 745; © 736
Richfield; RMC Place; CHATHAM; *__167__ K-13; ★ **SAV**; mail Savannah z 31405; pop. incl. with Savannah (Inc. Place)
Richland; Inc. Place; STEWART; **167** K-4; elev. 598ft./182m.; 🅿 🅷; z 31825; Ⓟ 1,668; © 1,794
RICHMOND; **166** G-10; Ⓟ 189,719; © 199,775; ◆ 201,693
Richmond Hill; Inc. Place; BRYAN; **167** K-13; elev. 17ft./5m.; 🅿; z 31324; Ⓟ 2,934; © 6,959
Richwood; RMC Place; DOOLY; *__167__ K-6; mail Vienna z 31092; rural
Rico; RMC Place; FULTON; **166** F-3; elev. 835ft./255m.; mail Palmetto z 30268; ● 70
Riddleville; Inc. Place; WASHINGTON; **166** H-9; elev. 450ft./137m.; mail Davisboro z 31018, Harrison z 31035; Ⓟ 79; © 124
Ridgefield Heights; RMC Place; MUSCOGEE; ★ **COL**; mail Columbus z 31907; pop. incl. with Columbus (Inc. Place)
Ridgeville; RMC Place; MCINTOSH; **167** M-12; elev. 24ft./7m.; mail Townsend z 31331; ● 300
Ridgewood; RMC Place; CHATHAM; *__167__ K-13; ★ **SAV**; pop. incl. with Savannah (Inc. Place)
Ridgewood; RMC Place; RICHMOND; *__166__ F-11; elev. 375ft./114m.; ★ **AUG**; mail Augusta z 30909; pop. incl. with Augusta (Inc. Place)
Rincon; Inc. Place; EFFINGHAM; **166** J-13; elev. 73ft./22m.; 🅿; ★ **SAV**; z 31326; Ⓟ 2,697; © 4,376
Ringgold; Inc. Place; ⊡ CATOOSA; **166** B-3; elev. 781ft./238m.; 🅿; ★ **CHTN**; z 30736; Ⓟ 1,675; © 2,422
Rio; RMC Place; SPALDING; *__166__ G-4; mail Griffin z 30223; rural
Rio Vista; RMC Place; CHATHAM; *__167__ K-13; ★ **SAV**; mail Savannah z 31406
Rio Vista; RMC Place; DOUGHERTY; ★ **ALB**; mail Albany z 31705; pop. incl. with Albany (Inc. Place)
Rising Fawn; RMC Place; DADE; **166** B-2; elev. 100ft./30m.; 🅿; z 30738; ● 110
Riverdale; Inc. Place; CLAYTON; **166** F-4; elev. 924ft./282m.; 🅿 🅷; ★ **ATL**; z 30274, z 30296; Ⓟ 9,359; © 12,478
Riverland Terrace; RMC Place; MUSCOGEE; **167** S-3; ★ **COL**; mail Columbus z 31903; pop. incl. with Columbus (Inc. Place)
River Oaks; RMC Place; CHATHAM; *__167__ K-14; ★ **SAV**; mail Savannah z 31410
River Road; RMC Place; DOUGHERTY; *__167__ M-5; ★ **ALB**; mail Albany z 31707; pop. incl. with Albany (Inc. Place)
Rivers End; RMC Place; CHATHAM; *__167__ K-13; ★ **SAV**; mail Savannah z 31406; pop. incl. with Savannah (Inc. Place)
Riverside (Grays); RMC Place; CHATHAM; *__167__ K-13; ★ **SAV**; mail Savannah z 31404; ● 600
Riverside; Inc. Place; COLQUITT; **167** N-6; elev. 300ft./91m.; mail Moultrie z 31768; Ⓟ 74; © 57
Riverside (Celanese Village); RMC Place; FLOYD; *__166__ D-2; ★ **ROME**; mail Rome z 30161; ● 950
Riverside; RMC Place; FULTON; *__166__ E-4; ★ **ATL**; mail Atlanta z 30318; pop. incl. with Atlanta (Inc. Place)
Rivertown; RMC Place; FULTON; *__166__ F-4; elev. 830ft./253m.; ★ **ATL**; mail Fairburn z 30213; ● 150
Riverturn; RMC Place; SEMINOLE; *__167__ N-3; elev. 167ft./51m.; mail Donalsonville z 39845; rural
Riverview; RMC Place; BIBB; ★ **MAC**; mail Macon z 31204; pop. incl. with Macon (Inc. Place)
Rivoli Park; RMC Place; BIBB; *__166__ H-6; ★ **MAC**; mail Macon z 31210; pop. incl. with Macon (Inc. Place)
Roanoke Acres; RMC Place; BEN HILL; *__167__ L-7; mail Fitzgerald z 31750; ● 250
Roberta; Inc. Place; CRAWFORD; **166** I-5; elev. 500ft./152m.; 🅿; z 31078; Ⓟ 939; © 808
Robertstown; RMC Place; WHITE; **166** B-6; mail Helen z 30545; ● 250
Robertsville; RMC Place; WALKER; *__166__ B-2; ★ **CHTN**; mail Chickamauga z 30707; rural
Robins AFB; CDP-Census Area Only; HOUSTON; *__166__ I-7; 🅿; ★ **MAC**; z 31098; Ⓟ 3,092; © 3,949
Robinson; RMC Place; TALIAFERRO; *__166__ F-8; elev. 625ft./191m.; mail Union Point z 30669; rural
Rochelle; Inc. Place; WILCOX; **167** K-7; elev. 371ft./113m.; 🅿; z 31079; Ⓟ 1,510; © 1,415
Rock Branch; RMC Place; ELBERT; *__166__ D-9; mail Elberton z 30635; rural
Rock Chapel; RMC Place; DEKALB; *__166__ F-5; ★ **ATL**; mail Lithonia z 30058; ● 150
Rockdale; RMC Place; FULTON; *__166__ E-4; ★ **ATL**; mail Atlanta z 30318; pop. incl. with Atlanta (Inc. Place)
ROCKDALE; **166** F-5; Ⓟ 54,091; © 70,111; ◆ 85,106
Rock Hill; RMC Place; EARLY; *__167__ M-3; mail Blakely z 39823; rural
Rockingham; RMC Place; BACON; **167** M-10; mail Alma z 31510; ● 30
Rockledge; RMC Place; LAURENS; **166** J-9; elev. 214ft./65m.; 🅿; z 30454; ● 250
Rockmart; Inc. Place; POLK; **166** E-3; elev. 750ft./229m.; 🅿; z 30153; Ⓟ 3,356; © 3,870
Rock Spring (Rock Springs); RMC Place; WALKER; **166** B-2; elev. 850ft./259m.; 🅿; ★ **CHTN**; z 30739; ● 300
Rock Springs; WALKER; see Rock Spring (RMC Place)
Rockville; RMC Place; PUTNAM; *__166__ G-8; mail Eatonton z 31024; ● 60
Rocky Face; RMC Place; WHITFIELD; **166** B-3; elev. 770ft./235m.; 🅿; z 30740; ● 1,000
Rocky Ford; Inc. Place; SCREVEN; **166** I-11; elev. 132ft./40m.; 🅿; z 30455; Ⓟ 197; © 186
Rocky Mount; RMC Place; MERIWETHER; **166** G-4; elev. 900ft./274m.; mail Luthersville z 30251; ● 55
Rocky Plains; RMC Place; NEWTON; *__166__ F-6; mail Covington z 30016; rural
Roddy; RMC Place; DODGE; *__166__ J-7; mail Cochran z 31014; ● 100
Rogers; RMC Place; MADISON; *__166__ D-7; elev. 824ft./251m.; mail Commerce z 30529; rural
Rolling Green; RMC Place; ROCKDALE; *__166__ F-5; ★ **ATL**; mail Conyers z 30094; ● 300
Rolling Meadows; RMC Place; RICHMOND; *__166__ G-11; ★ **AUG**; mail Augusta z 30905; pop. incl. with Augusta (Inc. Place)
Rome; Inc. Place; ⊡ FLOYD; **166** D-2; elev. 605ft./184m.; 🅿 🅷 🅲 2,604 ■; ★ **ROME**; z 30149, z 30161-65; Ⓟ 30,326; © 34,980; ◆ 37,370
Roopville; Inc. Place; CARROLL; **166** F-2; elev. 1,253ft./382m.; 🅿; z 30170; Ⓟ 248; © 177
Roosterville; RMC Place; HEARD; *__166__ G-2; elev. 1,026ft./313m.; mail Roopville z 30170; rural
Roper; RMC Place; JEFF DAVIS; *__167__ L-9; elev. 251ft./77m.; mail Hazlehurst z 31539; rural
Ropers Crossroads; RMC Place; COLUMBIA; *__166__ F-10; ★ **AUG**; mail Evans z 30809; ● 1,500
Roscoe; RMC Place; COWETA; **166** F-3; elev. 857ft./261m.; mail Newnan z 30263; ● 200
Rosebud; RMC Place; GWINNETT; *__166__ E-6; ★ **ATL**; mail Loganville z 30052; rural
Rosedale; RMC Place; FLOYD; *__166__ C-3; mail Calhoun z 30701; rural
Rose Dhu; RMC Place; CHATHAM; ★ **SAV**; mail Savannah z 31406; rural
Rose Hill; RMC Place; CHATHAM; *__167__ K-13; ★ **SAV**; mail Savannah z 31406; pop. incl. with Savannah (Inc. Place)
Rose Hill; RMC Place; PIKE; *__166__ H-5; mail Meansville z 30256; rural
Rose Hill Heights; RMC Place; MUSCOGEE; ★ **COL**; mail Columbus z 31904; pop. incl. with Columbus (Inc. Place)
Rosemont; RMC Place; COLUMBIA; *__166__ F-10; mail Appling z 30802; rural
Rosemont Park; RMC Place; FLOYD; *__166__ D-2; ★ **ROME**; mail Rome z 30161; ● 2,000
Rosier; RMC Place; BURKE; *__166__ H-10; elev. 345ft./105m.; mail Louisville z 30434; rural
Rossignol Hill; RMC Place; CHATHAM; *__167__ K-13; ★ **SAV**; mail Savannah z 31408; pop. incl. with Garden City (Inc. Place)
Rossville; Inc. Place; WALKER; **166** B-2; elev. 696ft./212m.; 🅿; ★ **CHTN**; z 30741-42; Ⓟ 3,601; © 3,511
Roswell; Inc. Place; FULTON; **166** E-5; elev. 1,059ft./323m.; 🅿 🅷 ■; ★ **ATL**; z 30075-77; Ⓟ 47,923; © 79,334; Ⓡ 79,309; ◆ 105,134
Round Oak; RMC Place; JONES; **166** H-6; elev. 629ft./192m.; 🅿; z 31038; ● 200
Roundtop; RMC Place; GILMER; *__166__ C-4; mail Ellijay z 30540; rural
Rover; RMC Place; SPALDING; *__166__ G-5; elev. 974ft./297m.; mail Williamson z 30292; rural
Rowena; RMC Place; EARLY; *__167__ M-3; mail Arlington z 39813; rural
Roxana (Roxanna); RMC Place; PAULDING; *__166__ E-3; mail Dallas z 30132; rural
Roxanna; PAULDING; see Roxana (RMC Place)
Roy; RMC Place; BIBB; ★ **MAC**; pop. incl. with Macon (Inc. Place)
Royston; Inc. Place; FRANKLIN, HART, MADISON; **166** D-8; elev. 905ft./276m.; 🅿 🅷; z 30662; Ⓟ 2,758; © 2,493
Ruckersville; RMC Place; ELBERT; **166** D-9; mail Elberton z 30635; ● 75
Rudden; RMC Place; PUTNAM; *__166__ G-7; mail Eatonton z 31024; rural
Rupert; RMC Place; TAYLOR; **166** J-5; elev. 437ft./133m.; 🅿; z 31081; ● 100
Russell; RMC Place; BARROW; **166** E-6; elev. 980ft./299m.; mail Winder z 30680; ● 850
Russellville; RMC Place; MONROE; *__166__ H-5; mail Culloden z 31016; rural
Rutledge; Inc. Place; MORGAN; **166** F-7; elev. 718ft./219m.; 🅿; z 30663; Ⓟ 659; © 707
Rydal; RMC Place; BARTOW; **166** D-4; 🅿; z 30171; ● 200
Ryo; RMC Place; GORDON; *__166__ C-4; mail Fairmount z 30139, Ranger z 30734; ● 30

S

Saginaw; RMC Place; COFFEE; *__167__ M-9; mail Nicholls z 31554; rural
Saint Charles; RMC Place; COWETA; *__166__ G-3; mail Moreland z 30259; rural
Saint Clair; RMC Place; BURKE; **166** G-10; mail Keysville z 30816; ● 150
Saint George; RMC Place; CHARLTON; **167** P-11; elev. 77ft./23m.; 🅿; z 31562; ● 350
Saint Marks; RMC Place; MERIWETHER; **166** G-3; elev. 876ft./267m.; mail Hogansville z 30230; ● 45
Saint Marys; Inc. Place; CAMDEN; **167** O-12; elev. 10ft./3m.; 🅿 🅷; z 31558; Ⓟ 8,187; © 13,761
Saint Marys Hills; RMC Place; MUSCOGEE; ★ **COL**; mail Columbus z 31906; pop. incl. with Columbus (Inc. Place)
Saint Simons; CDP; GLYNN; **167** S-14; elev. 11ft./3m.; 🅷; ★ **BRUNS**; mail Saint Simons Island z 31522; Ⓟ 12,026; © 13,381
Saint Simons Island; RMC Place; GLYNN; ★ **BRUNS**; ● 570
Sale City; Inc. Place; MITCHELL; **167** M-5; elev. 377ft./115m.; 🅿; z 31784; Ⓟ 324; © 319
Salem; CDP-Census Area Only; UPSON; *__166__ I-5; © 339
Salem Arms; RMC Place; RICHMOND; *__166__ G-11; ★ **AUG**; mail Augusta z 30906; pop. incl. with Augusta (Inc. Place)
Sanborn; RMC Place; DOUGHERTY; ★ **ALB**; mail Albany z 31705; ● 100
Sandalwood; RMC Place; DOUGHERTY; *__167__ L-5; ★ **ALB**; mail Albany z 31701; pop. incl. with Albany (Inc. Place)
Sand Bed; RMC Place; HOUSTON; *__166__ J-6; mail Kathleen z 31047; rural
Sandersville; Inc. Place; ⊡ WASHINGTON, MERIWETHER; **166** H-9; elev. 446ft./136m.; 🅿 🅷; z 31082; Ⓟ 6,290; © 6,144
Sandfly; RMC Place; CHATHAM; **167** T-11; ★ **SAV**; mail Savannah z 31406; ● 1,200
Sand Hill; RMC Place; BROOKS; *__167__ N-6; mail Pavo z 31778; rural
Sand Hill; RMC Place; CARROLL; **166** F-3; mail Villa Rica z 30180; ● 200
Sand Hills; RMC Place; RICHMOND; *__166__ G-11; ★ **AUG**; mail Augusta z 30904; pop. incl. with Augusta (Inc. Place)
Sandtown; RMC Place; WILKES; *__166__ E-9; elev. 575ft./175m.; mail Washington z 30673; rural
Sandy Cross; RMC Place; FRANKLIN; **166** D-8; elev. 848ft./258m.; mail Royston z 30662; ● 260
Sandy Cross; RMC Place; OGLETHORPE; *__166__ E-8; mail Carlton z 30627; rural
Sandy Plains; RMC Place; COBB; *__166__ E-4; elev. 1,090ft./332m.; ★ **ATL**; mail Roswell z 30075; ● 2,950
Sandy Springs; Inc. Place; FULTON; **166** E-4; ★ **ATL**; incorporated December 1, 2005; not reported in 2000 Census; ● 85,800; ◆ 100,041
Sandy Springs; CDP-Census Area Only; FULTON; **166** E-4; 🅿; ★ **ATL**; z 30328, z 30342, z 30350, z 30358; former CDP; incorporated December 1, 2005; Ⓟ 67,842; © 85,781
Sanford; RMC Place; MADISON; *__166__ E-7; ★ **ATH**; mail Hull z 30646; rural
Sanford; RMC Place; STEWART; *__167__ K-3; mail Lumpkin z 31815; rural
Sangrena Woods; RMC Place; CHATHAM; *__167__ K-13; ★ **SAV**; mail Pooler z 31322; pop. incl. with Pooler (Inc. Place)
Santa Claus; Inc. Place; TOOMBS; **167** K-10; elev. 235ft./72m.; mail Lyons z 30436; Ⓟ 154; © 237
Sapelo Island; RMC Place; MCINTOSH; **167** M-13; elev. 10ft./3m.; 🅿; z 31327; ● 150
Sapp; RMC Place; BLECKLEY; mail Cochran z 31014; rural
Sardis; Inc. Place; BURKE; **166** H-11; elev. 234ft./71m.; 🅿; z 30456; Ⓟ 1,116; © 1,171
Sargent; RMC Place; COWETA; **166** F-3; elev. 760ft./232m.; 🅿; z 30275; ● 900
Sasser; Inc. Place; TERRELL; **167** L-4; elev. 310ft./94m.; 🅿; z 39885; Ⓟ 335; © 393
Satolah; RMC Place; RABUN; **166** B-8; mail Clayton z 30525; ● 30
Sautee (Sautee-Nacoochee, Sautee Nacoochee); RMC Place; WHITE; *__166__ C-6; elev. 1,385ft./422m.; mail Sautee Nacoochee z 30571; ● 500
Sautee Nacoochee; WHITE; see Sautee (RMC Place)
Sautee-Nacoochee; WHITE; see Sautee (RMC Place)
Savannah; Inc. Place; ⊡ CHATHAM; **167** R-10; elev. 42ft./13m.; 🅿 🅷 🅲 22,205 ■; ★ **SAV**; z 31401-12, z 31414-16, z 31418-21 & mail Pooler z 31322; Ⓟ 137,560; © 131,510; Ⓡ 132,985; ◆ 133,005
Savannah Beach; CHATHAM; see Tybee Island (Inc. Place)
Savannah Gardens; RMC Place; CHATHAM; ★ **SAV**; mail Savannah z 31404; pop. incl. with Savannah (Inc. Place)
Sawdust; RMC Place; COLUMBIA; *__166__ G-10; ★ **AUG**; mail Harlem z 30814; pop. incl. with Harlem (Inc. Place)
Sawhatchee; RMC Place; EARLY; *__167__ M-3; elev. 202ft./62m.; mail Blakely z 39823; rural
Scarboro; RMC Place; JENKINS; **166** I-11; elev. 152ft./46m.; mail Millen z 30442; ● 40
Scarbrough Cross Roads; RMC Place; HENRY; *__166__ F-5; elev. 899ft./274m.; ★ **ATL**; mail Ellenwood z 30294
Scarlet; RMC Place; CAMDEN; *__167__ N-11; mail Woodbine z 31569; rural
Schatulga; RMC Place; MUSCOGEE; *__166__ I-3; ★ **COL**; mail Midland z 31820; pop. incl. with Columbus (Inc. Place)
Schlatterville; RMC Place; BRANTLEY; *__167__ N-10; mail Waycross z 31501; rural
Schley; RMC Place; COLQUITT; *__167__ M-6; elev. 304ft./93m.; mail Moultrie z 31768
SCHLEY; **166** J-4; Ⓟ 3,588; © 3,766; ◆ 4,339
Scotland; Inc. Place; TELFAIR, WHEELER; **167** K-9; elev. 143ft./44m.; 🅿; z 31083; Ⓟ 244; © 300
Scott; RMC Place; JOHNSON, LAURENS; **166** I-9; elev. 359ft./109m.; mail Adrian z 31002; ● 140
Scottdale; CDP; DEKALB; **168** D-6; elev. 1,035ft./315m.; 🅿; ★ **ATL**; z 30079; Ⓟ 8,636; © 9,803
Scottsboro; RMC Place; BALDWIN; **166** H-8; mail Milledgeville z 31061; ● 100
Screven; Inc. Place; WAYNE; **167** M-11; elev. 124ft./38m.; 🅿; z 31560; Ⓟ 819; © 702
SCREVEN; **166** H-11; Ⓟ 13,842; © 15,374; ◆ 14,990
Screven Fork; RMC Place; LIBERTY; *__167__ L-12; mail Midway z 31320; rural
Screvens Point; RMC Place; CHATHAM; *__167__ K-14; ★ **SAV**; mail Savannah z 31410; ● 100
Seabrook; RMC Place; LIBERTY; *__167__ L-13; mail Midway z 31320; rural
Seagraves; RMC Place; MADISON; *__166__ D-7; mail Hull z 30646; rural
Sea Island; RMC Place; GLYNN; **167** S-14; elev. 11ft./3m.; 🅿; ★ **BRUNS**; z 31561; ● 700
Sea Palms; RMC Place; GLYNN; *__167__ N-13; ★ **BRUNS**; mail Saint Simons Island z 31522
Sells; RMC Place; JACKSON; *__166__ E-6; mail Hoschton z 30548; rural
SEMINOLE; **167** N-3; Ⓟ 9,010; © 9,369; ◆ 8,973
Seney; RMC Place; POLK; *__166__ D-3; mail Aragon z 30104
Senoia; Inc. Place; COWETA; **166** G-4; elev. 863ft./263m.; 🅿; z 30276; Ⓟ 956; © 1,738
Sessoms; RMC Place; BACON; *__167__ M-9; mail Nicholls z 31554; rural
Seville; RMC Place; WILCOX; **167** K-6; elev. 374ft./114m.; 🅿; z 31084; ● 200
Shady Dale; Inc. Place; JASPER; **166** G-7; elev. 620ft./189m.; 🅿; z 31085; Ⓟ 180; © 242
Shake Rag; RMC Place; FULTON; *__166__ E-5; ★ **ATL**; mail Suwanee z 30024; ● 100
Shannon; CDP; FLOYD; **166** D-3; elev. 696ft./212m.; 🅿; ★ **ROME**; z 30172; Ⓟ 1,703; © 1,682
Sharon; Inc. Place; TALIAFERRO; **166** F-9; elev. 608ft./185m.; 🅿; z 30664; Ⓟ 94; © 105
Sharon Park; RMC Place; CHATHAM; *__167__ K-13; ★ **SAV**; mail Savannah z 31408; pop. incl. with Garden City (Inc. Place)
Sharpe; RMC Place; WALKER; *__166__ C-2; mail La Fayette z 30728; rural
Sharphagen; RMC Place; SEMINOLE; *__167__ N-3; mail Donalsonville z 39845; ● 40
Sharpsboro; COWETA; see Sharpsburg (Inc. Place)
Sharpsburg (Sharpsboro); Inc. Place; COWETA; **166** G-4; elev. 900ft./274m.; 🅿; z 30277; Ⓟ 224; © 316
Sharps Spur; RMC Place; MONTGOMERY; *__167__ K-10; mail Ailey z 30410; rural
Sharp Top; RMC Place; CHEROKEE; *__166__ D-4; mail Canton z 30114; rural
Shawnee; RMC Place; EFFINGHAM; **166** J-12; elev. 123ft./37m.; mail Springfield z 31329; ● 70
Sheba; HANCOCK; see Beulah (RMC Place)
Shell Bluff; RMC Place; BURKE; *__166__ G-11; elev. 922ft./281m.; mail Waynesboro z 30830; rural
Shellman; Inc. Place; RANDOLPH; **167** L-4; elev. 395ft./120m.; 🅿; z 39886; Ⓟ 1,162; © 1,166
Shellman Bluff; RMC Place; MCINTOSH; **167** L-13; 🅿; z 31331; ● 450
Shelly; RMC Place; THOMAS; *__167__ N-6; mail Pavo z 31778; rural
Shenandoah; RMC Place; COWETA; *__166__ G-3; mail Newnan z 30265; ● 45
Sheppards; RMC Place; SCREVEN; *__166__ I-12; mail Sylvania z 30467; rural
Sherwood (Neco); RMC Place; RICHMOND; *__166__ G-11; ★ **AUG**; mail Augusta z 30904; pop. incl. with Augusta (Inc. Place)
Sherwood Forest; RMC Place; BIBB; *__166__ I-6; ★ **MAC**; mail Macon z 31216; pop. incl. with Macon (Inc. Place)
Sherwood Forest; RMC Place; CLAYTON; *__166__ F-5; ★ **ATL**; mail Jonesboro z 30236; ● 1,000
Sherwood Forest; RMC Place; COWETA; *__166__ G-3; mail Newnan z 30263; ● 250
Sherwood Forest; RMC Place; DEKALB; *__166__ F-5; ★ **ATL**; mail Decatur z 30032; ● 400
Sherwood Forest; RMC Place; FLOYD; *__166__ D-3; ★ **ROME**; mail Rome z 30161; ● 2,000
Shields Crossroads; RMC Place; WALKER; *__166__ B-2; ★ **CHTN**; mail Chickamauga z 30707; ● 400
Shiloh; Inc. Place; HARRIS; **166** I-4; elev. 900ft./274m.; 🅿; z 31826; Ⓟ 329; © 423
Shiloh; RMC Place; LOWNDES; *__167__ N-7; mail Homerville z 31634; ● 50
Shiloh; RMC Place; MADISON; *__166__ D-8; mail Danielsville z 30633; rural
Shiloh; RMC Place; SUMTER; *__167__ K-5; mail Americus z 31719; rural
Shingler; RMC Place; WORTH; **167** L-6; mail Poulan z 31781; ● 60
Shirley Hills; RMC Place; BIBB; ★ **MAC**; mail Macon z 31211; pop. incl. with Macon (Inc. Place)
Shirley Park; RMC Place; CHATHAM; *__167__ K-13; ★ **SAV**; mail Savannah z 31404; pop. incl. with Savannah (Inc. Place)
Shoal Creek; RMC Place; HART; *__166__ C-8; mail Lavonia z 30553; rural
Shurlington; RMC Place; BIBB; *__166__ H-7; ★ **MAC**; mail Macon z 31211; pop. incl. with Macon (Inc. Place)
Sigsbee; RMC Place; COLQUITT; **167** M-6; mail Doerun z 31744; ● 30
Silco; RMC Place; DOUGHERTY; mail Folkston z 31537; rural
Silica Hills; RMC Place; DOUGHERTY; ★ **ALB**; mail Albany z 31705; ● 30
Silk Hope; RMC Place; CHATHAM; *__167__ K-13; ★ **SAV**; mail Savannah z 31401; pop. incl. with Garden City (Inc. Place)
Silk Mills; RMC Place; ELBERT; *__166__ D-9; mail Elberton z 30635; ● 200
Siloam; Inc. Place; GREENE; **166** F-8; elev. 720ft./219m.; 🅿; z 30665; Ⓟ 329; © 331
Silver City; RMC Place; FORSYTH; *__166__ D-5; mail Gainesville z 30506; rural
Silver Creek; RMC Place; FLOYD; **166** D-2; elev. 681ft./208m.; 🅿; ★ **ROME**; z 30173; ● 500
Silver Crest; RMC Place; RICHMOND; *__166__ G-11; ★ **AUG**; mail Augusta z 30906; pop. incl. with Augusta (Inc. Place)
Silver Pines; RMC Place; BIBB; *__166__ I-6; ★ **MAC**; mail Macon z 31216; ● 250
Simpson; RMC Place; HEARD; *__166__ G-2; mail Franklin z 30217; rural
Six Mile; RMC Place; FLOYD; *__166__ D-2; ★ **ROME**; mail Rome z 30165

Entries in **UPPERCASE** are counties.
Entries in **bold** have populations of 2,500 or more.
Names in parentheses are alternate names.

Inc. Place	Incorporated Place
RMC Place	Rand McNally Designated Place
CDP	Census Designated Place
MCD	Minor Civil Division
⊡	County Seat
▲	Minor Civil Division
elev.	Elevation
🅿	Post Office
🅷	Hospital
🅲	College
■	Principal Business Center
★	Ranally Metro Area (RMA) Abbreviation
z	Zip Code(s)
Ⓟ	Previous Census Population
Ⓡ	Revised Census Population
Ⓐ	Annexation Population
●	Rand McNally Population Estimate
©	Final Census Population
Ⓢ	Special Census Population
◆	Estimated Population

For additional definitions see Glossary, Volume 1, and Introduction, Volume 2.

Skidaway; RMC Place; CHATHAM; ***167** K-13; ★ **SAV**; mail Savannah **z** 31404, **z** 31414; pop. incl. with Savannah (Inc. Place)
Skidaway Island; CDP-Census Area Only; CHATHAM; ***167** K-13; ★ **SAV**; mail Savannah **z** 31411; Ⓟ 4,495; Ⓒ 6,914
Skipperton; RMC Place; BIBB; ***166** I-6; elev. 454ft./138m.; ★ **MAC**; mail Macon **z** 31216; rural
Skyland; RMC Place; DEKALB; **168** C-5; ★ **ATL**; mail Atlanta **z** 30319; ● 2,500
Skyland Terrace; RMC Place; CHATHAM; ★ **SAV**; mail Savannah **z** 31401; pop. incl. with Savannah (Inc. Place)
Sky Valley; Inc. Place; RABUN; ***166** B-7; 🅿; **z** 30537 & mail Clayton **z** 30525; Ⓟ 187; Ⓒ 221
Smarr; RMC Place; MONROE; **166** H-6; elev. 620ft./189m.; 🅿; **z** 31086; ● 350
Smithonia (Smithsonia); RMC Place; OGLETHORPE; ***166** E-8; elev. 710ft./216m.; mail Colbert **z** 30628; ● 25
Smiths Crossroad (Smiths Crossroads); RMC Place; TROUP; ***166** H-3; mail Lagrange **z** 30240; rural
Smiths Crossroads; RMC Place; HARRIS; ***166** H-3; elev. 838ft./255m.; mail Pine Mountain Valley **z** 31823; rural
Smiths Crossroads; TROUP; see Smiths Crossroad (RMC Place)
Smithsonia; OGLETHORPE; see Smithonia (RMC Place)
Smithville; Inc. Place; LEE, SUMTER; **167** K-5; elev. 327ft./100m.; 🅿; **z** 31787; Ⓟ 804; Ⓒ 774
Smyrna; Inc. Place; COBB; **166** E-4; elev. 1,063ft./324m.; 🅿 🅷 ■; ★ **ATL**; **z** 30080-82 & mail Atlanta **z** 30339; Ⓟ 30,981; Ⓒ 40,999; ◆ 50,446
Snake Nation; RMC Place; FANNIN; ***166** B-5; mail Blue Ridge **z** 30513; rural
Snapfinger; RMC Place; DEKALB; ***166** F-5; ★ **ATL**; mail Decatur **z** 30035, Lithonia **z** 30058; ● 300
Snapping Shoals; RMC Place; NEWTON; ***166** F-6; ★ **ATL**; mail Covington **z** 30016; rural
Snead; RMC Place; COLUMBIA; ***166** F-10; ★ **AUG**; mail Evans **z** 30809; rural
Snellville; Inc. Place; GWINNETT; **166** E-5; elev. 1,062ft./324m.; 🅿 🅷; ★ **ATL**; **z** 30039, **z** 30078; Ⓟ 12,084; Ⓒ 15,351; ◆ 20,757
Snipesville; RMC Place; JEFF DAVIS; **167** L-9; elev. 280ft./85m.; mail Denton **z** 31532; ● 50
Snow Spring; RMC Place; DOOLY; ***166** J-6; mail Unadilla **z** 31091; rural
Snug Harbor Estates; RMC Place; HALL; mail Gainesville **z** 30504; ● 200
Soapstick; RMC Place; GORDON; ***166** C-3; elev. 679ft./207m.; mail Calhoun **z** 30701; ● 90
Social Circle; Inc. Place; WALTON, NEWTON; **166** F-6; elev. 861ft./262m.; 🅿; **z** 30025; Ⓟ 2,755; Ⓒ 3,379
Sofkee; RMC Place; BIBB; ***166** I-6; ★ **MAC**; mail Macon **z** 31216; rural
Somerset Park; RMC Place; CHATHAM; ★ **SAV**; mail Savannah **z** 31419; pop. incl. with Savannah (Inc. Place)
Sonoraville; RMC Place; GORDON; ***166** C-3; elev. 73ft./22m.; mail Calhoun **z** 30701
Soperton; Inc. Place; ⊡ TREUTLEN; **166** J-9; elev. 294ft./90m.; 🅿; **z** 30457; Ⓟ 2,797; Ⓒ 2,824
South Augusta; RMC Place; RICHMOND; ***166** G-11; ★ **AUG**; pop. incl. with Augusta (Inc. Place)
South Canton; RMC Place; CHEROKEE; ***166** D-4; ★ **ATL**; pop. incl. with Canton (Inc. Place)
South Cobb; RMC Place; COBB; ***166** E-4; ★ **ATL**; mail Austell **z** 30106; ● 4,400
South Columbus; RMC Place; MUSCOGEE; ★ **COL**; pop. incl. with Columbus (Inc. Place)
Southdale; RMC Place; RICHMOND; ***166** G-11; ★ **AUG**; mail Augusta **z** 30906; pop. incl. with Augusta (Inc. Place)
South De Kalb; DEKALB; see Panthersville (CDP)
South Glen; RMC Place; CLAYTON; ***166** F-5; ★ **ATL**; mail Jonesboro **z** 30236; ● 400
South Kirkwood; RMC Place; DEKALB; ***166** F-5; ★ **ATL**; mail Atlanta **z** 30317; pop. incl. with Atlanta (Inc. Place)
South Macon; RMC Place; BIBB; **167** S-6; ★ **MAC**; mail Macon **z** 31205-06, **z** 31216; pop. incl. with Macon (Inc. Place)
South Moultrie; RMC Place; COLQUITT; ***167** N-6; mail Moultrie **z** 31768
South Nellieville; RMC Place; RICHMOND; ***166** G-11; ★ **AUG**; mail Augusta **z** 30901; pop. incl. with Augusta (Inc. Place)
South Newport; RMC Place; MCINTOSH; ***167** L-12; elev. 21ft./6m.; mail Riceboro **z** 31323
Southover; RMC Place; CHATHAM; ***167** K-13; ★ **SAV**; mail Savannah **z** 31405; pop. incl. with Savannah (Inc. Place)
South Pooler; RMC Place; CHATHAM; ★ **SAV**; mail Pooler **z** 31322; ● 530
Southside; RMC Place; CHATHAM; ***167** K-13; ★ **SAV**; mail Savannah **z** 31419-20; pop. incl. with Savannah (Inc. Place)
Spalding; RMC Place; MACON; ***166** J-5; mail Montezuma **z** 31063; ● 60
SPALDING; **166** G-5; Ⓟ 54,457; Ⓒ 58,417; ◆ 64,328
Spanish Trace; RMC Place; RICHMOND; ***166** G-11; ★ **AUG**; mail Augusta **z** 30906; pop. incl. with Augusta (Inc. Place)
Spann; RMC Place; JOHNSON; ***166** I-9; mail Wrightsville **z** 31096; rural
Sparks; Inc. Place; COOK; **167** N-7; elev. 230ft./70m.; 🅿; **z** 31647; Ⓟ 1,205; Ⓒ 1,755
Sparta; Inc. Place; ⊡ HANCOCK; **166** G-8; elev. 660ft./201m.; 🅿 🅷; **z** 31087; Ⓟ 1,710; Ⓒ 1,522
Spence; RMC Place; GRADY; ***167** N-5; elev. 322ft./98m.; mail Pelham **z** 31779; rural
Spencer Hills; RMC Place; WALKER; ***166** B-2; ★ **CHTN**; mail Rossville **z** 30741; ● 1,000
Split Silk; RMC Place; WALTON; ***166** E-6; ★ **ATL**; mail Loganville **z** 30052; rural
Spout Spring Crossroads; RMC Place; HALL; ***166** D-6; elev. 1,187ft./362m.; ★ **ATL**; mail Flowery Branch **z** 30542; rural
Spring Bluff; RMC Place; CAMDEN; ***167** N-12; elev. 20ft./6m.; mail Waverly **z** 31565
Springfield; Inc. Place; ⊡ EFFINGHAM; **166** J-13; elev. 75ft./23m.; 🅿 🅷; **z** 31329; Ⓟ 1,415; Ⓒ 1,821
Spring Hill; RMC Place; CHATHAM; ★ **SAV**; mail Savannah **z** 31404; pop. incl. with Savannah (Inc. Place)
Spring Hill; RMC Place; WHEELER; ***167** K-9; mail Alamo **z** 30411; rural
Spring Lake; RMC Place; MUSCOGEE; ***166** I-3; ★ **COL**; mail Columbus **z** 31909; pop. incl. with Columbus (Inc. Place)
Spring Place; RMC Place; MURRAY; **166** B-3; elev. 730ft./223m.; mail Chatsworth **z** 30705; ● 270
Springvale; RMC Place; RANDOLPH; **167** L-3; elev. 387ft./118m.; mail Morris **z** 39867; ● 60
Springvale Station; RMC Place; RANDOLPH; ***167** L-3; mail Morris **z** 39867; rural
Spring Valley; RMC Place; MUSCOGEE; ***166** I-3; ★ **COL**; mail Columbus **z** 31909; pop. incl. with Columbus (Inc. Place)
Springview Acres; RMC Place; HALL; mail Gainesville **z** 30501; pop. incl. with Gainesville (Inc. Place)
Staley Heights; RMC Place; CHATHAM; ***167** K-13; ★ **SAV**; mail Savannah **z** 31405; pop. incl. with Savannah (Inc. Place)
Stanleys Store; RMC Place; TOOMBS; ***167** K-10; mail Lyons **z** 30436; rural
Stapleton; Inc. Place; JEFFERSON; **166** G-10; elev. 440ft./134m.; 🅿; **z** 30823; Ⓟ 330; Ⓒ 318
Stark; RMC Place; BUTTS; **166** G-6; mail Jackson **z** 30233; ● 100
Starr; RMC Place; ROCKDALE; ***166** F-5; elev. 899ft./274m.; ★ **ATL**; mail Conyers **z** 30094; ● 150
Starrs Mill (Nyson); RMC Place; FAYETTE; ***166** G-4; mail Fayetteville **z** 30215
Starrsville; RMC Place; NEWTON; ***166** F-6; elev. 694ft./212m.; mail Covington **z** 30014
Statenville (Statesville); RMC Place; ⊡ ECHOLS; **167** O-8; elev. 138ft./42m.; 🅿; **z** 31648; ● 650
Statesboro; Inc. Place; ⊡ BULLOCH; **166** J-11; elev. 258ft./79m.; 🅿 🅷 🅲 16,425 ■; **z** 30458-61; Ⓟ 15,854; Ⓒ 22,698; ◆ 25,643
Statesville; ECHOLS; see Statenville (RMC Place)
Statham; Inc. Place; BARROW; **166** E-7; elev. 884ft./269m.; 🅿; ★ **ATH**; **z** 30666; Ⓟ 1,360; Ⓒ 2,040
Staunton; RMC Place; COOK; ***167** M-7; mail Lenox **z** 31637; rural
Steadham Store; RMC Place; DECATUR; rural
Steadman; RMC Place; HARALSON; ***166** E-2; mail Tallapoosa **z** 30176; rural
Steam Mill; RMC Place; SEMINOLE; ***167** N-3; elev. 147ft./45m.; mail Donalsonville **z** 39845; ● 25
Steffen Wood Estates; RMC Place; CHATHAM; ***167** K-13; ★ **SAV**; mail Pooler **z** 31322; pop. incl. with Pooler (Inc. Place)
Stellaville; RMC Place; JEFFERSON; **166** G-10; mail Wrens **z** 30833; ● 50
Stephens; RMC Place; OGLETHORPE; **166** E-8; elev. 772ft./235m.; 🅿; **z** 30667 & mail Maxeys **z** 30671; ● 110
STEPHENS; **166** C-7; Ⓟ 23,257; Ⓒ 25,435; ◆ 25,180
Stephensville; DADE; see Avans (RMC Place)
Sterling; RMC Place; GLYNN; **167** M-12; elev. 12ft./4m.; ★ **BRUNS**; mail Brunswick **z** 31523, **z** 31525; ● 130
Stevens Pottery; RMC Place; BALDWIN; **166** H-7; elev. 500ft./152m.; mail Gordon **z** 31031; ● 100
Stewart; RMC Place; NEWTON; ***166** G-6; elev. 678ft./207m.; mail Covington **z** 30016
STEWART; **167** K-3; Ⓟ 5,654; Ⓒ 5,252; ◆ 4,505
Stewart Town; RMC Place; DADE; ***166** B-1; mail Trenton **z** 30752; rural
Stilesboro; RMC Place; BARTOW; **166** D-3; elev. 754ft./230m.; mail Cartersville **z** 30120, Taylorsville **z** 30178; ● 150
Stillmore; Inc. Place; EMANUEL; **166** J-10; elev. 271ft./83m.; 🅿; **z** 30464; Ⓟ 615; Ⓒ 730
Stillwell; RMC Place; EFFINGHAM; **166** J-13; elev. 69ft./21m.; 🅿; **z** 31329; ● 30
Stilson; RMC Place; BULLOCH; **166** J-12; elev. 102ft./31m.; mail Brooklet **z** 30415; ● 150
Stockbridge; Inc. Place; HENRY; **166** F-5; elev. 799ft./244m.; 🅿 🅷; ★ **ATL**; **z** 30281; Ⓟ 3,359; Ⓒ 9,853
Stockton; RMC Place; LANIER; **167** N-8; elev. 183ft./56m.; 🅿; **z** 31649; ● 200
Stockwood; RMC Place; CHEROKEE; ★ **ATL**; mail Woodstock **z** 30188; ● 400
Stone Mountain; Inc. Place; DEKALB; **166** E-5; elev. 1,043ft./318m.; 🅿; ★ **ATL**; **z** 30083, **z** 30086-88; Ⓟ 6,494; Ⓒ 7,145
Stonewall; RMC Place; FULTON; ***166** F-4; elev. 1,043ft./318m.; ★ **ATL**; mail Atlanta **z** 30349
Stoney Point; RMC Place; CARROLL; ***166** F-2; mail Roopville **z** 30170; rural
Stovall; RMC Place; HABERSHAM; mail Cornelia **z** 30531; pop. incl. with Cornelia (Inc. Place)
Stovall; RMC Place; MERIWETHER; **166** H-3; elev. 820ft./250m.; 🅿; **z** 30222; ● 130
Stratford; RMC Place; FULTON; ***166** F-4; ★ **ATL**; mail Atlanta **z** 30311; pop. incl. with Atlanta (Inc. Place)
Strouds; RMC Place; MONROE; ***166** H-5; mail Culloden **z** 31016; ● 45
Stuckey; RMC Place; WHEELER; ***167** K-9; mail Glenwood **z** 30428; rural
Subligna; RMC Place; CHATTOOGA; **166** C-2; elev. 778ft./237m.; mail Summerville **z** 30747; ● 60
Suches; RMC Place; UNION; **166** C-5; elev. 2,797ft./853m.; 🅿; **z** 30572; ● 160
Sudie; RMC Place; PAULDING; ***166** E-3; ★ **ATL**; mail Dallas **z** 30157; rural
Sugar Hill; Inc. Place; GWINNETT; **166** D-5; 🅿; ★ **ATL**; **z** 30518; Ⓟ 4,557; Ⓒ 11,399
Sugar Hill; RMC Place; HALL; ***166** D-6; mail Gainesville **z** 30507; rural
Sugartown; RMC Place; CATOOSA; ***166** B-3; mail Tunnel Hill **z** 30755; ● 200
Sugar Valley; RMC Place; GORDON; **166** C-3; elev. 630ft./192m.; 🅿; **z** 30746; ● 300
Sulphur Springs; RMC Place; DADE; ***166** B-2; mail Rising Fawn **z** 30738; rural
Sulphur Springs Station; RMC Place; DADE; ***166** C-2; elev. 838ft./255m.; mail Trenton **z** 30752; rural
Sumac (Sumach); RMC Place; MURRAY; ***166** B-3; mail Chatsworth **z** 30705; ● 100
Sumach; MURRAY; see Sumac (RMC Place)
Summertown; Inc. Place; EMANUEL; **166** I-10; elev. 251ft./77m.; 🅿; **z** 30401; Ⓟ 153; Ⓒ 140
Summerville; Inc. Place; ⊡ CHATTOOGA; **166** C-2; elev. 648ft./198m.; 🅿 🅷; **z** 30747; Ⓟ 5,025; Ⓒ 4,556
Summit; RMC Place; EMANUEL; mail Twin City **z** 30471; pop. incl. with Twin City (Inc. Place)
Sumner; Inc. Place; WORTH; **167** M-6; elev. 384ft./117m.; 🅿; **z** 31789; Ⓟ 209; Ⓒ 309
Sumter; RMC Place; SUMTER; **167** K-5; mail Americus **z** 31709; ● 35
SUMTER; **167** K-5; Ⓟ 30,228; Ⓒ 33,200; ◆ 32,565
Sunbury; RMC Place; LIBERTY; **167** L-13; mail Midway **z** 31320; ● 150
Sunny Acres; RMC Place; DOUGHERTY; ***167** M-5; ★ **ALB**; mail Albany **z** 31701; pop. incl. with Albany (Inc. Place)
Sunnydale Acres; RMC Place; BIBB; ***166** H-7; ★ **MAC**; mail Macon **z** 31217; pop. incl. with Macon (Inc. Place)
Sunny Side; Inc. Place; SPALDING; **166** G-5; elev. 929ft./283m.; 🅿; **z** 30284; Ⓟ 215; Ⓒ 142
Sunnyside; CDP-Census Area Only; WARE; ***167** M-10; mail Waycross **z** 31501; Ⓟ 1,506; Ⓒ 1,385
Sunset; RMC Place; COLQUITT; ***167** N-6; mail Moultrie **z** 31768; pop. incl. with Moultrie (Inc. Place)
Sunset Heights; RMC Place; HALL; ***166** D-6; mail Gainesville **z** 30501; pop. incl. with Gainesville (Inc. Place)
Sunset Park; RMC Place; CHATHAM; ***167** K-13; ★ **SAV**; mail Savannah **z** 31404; pop. incl. with Savannah (Inc. Place)
Sunset Village; CDP; UPSON; **166** H-4; elev. 752ft./229m.; mail Thomaston **z** 30286; Ⓒ 871
Sunshine Acres; RMC Place; MUSCOGEE; ***166** I-3; ★ **COL**; mail Columbus **z** 31909; pop. incl. with Columbus (Inc. Place)
Sunsweet; RMC Place; TIFT; ***167** L-7; mail Tifton **z** 31794; rural
Surrency; Inc. Place; APPLING; **167** L-10; elev. 187ft./57m.; 🅿; **z** 31563; Ⓟ 253; Ⓒ 237
Sutalee; CHEROKEE; see Sutallee (RMC Place)
Sutallee (Sutalee); RMC Place; CHEROKEE; ***166** D-4; mail White **z** 30184; rural
Suttles Mill; RMC Place; WALKER; ***166** C-2; mail La Fayette **z** 30728; rural
Suttons Corner; RMC Place; CLAY; ***167** L-3; elev. 394ft./120m.; mail Bluffton **z** 39824; rural
Suwanee; Inc. Place; GWINNETT; **166** E-5; elev. 1,013ft./309m.; 🅿; ★ **ATL**; **z** 30024; Ⓟ 2,412; Ⓒ 8,725
Swainsboro; Inc. Place; ⊡ EMANUEL; **166** I-10; elev. 332ft./101m.; 🅿 🅷; **z** 30401; Ⓟ 7,361; Ⓒ 6,943
Swan Lake; RMC Place; HENRY; ***166** F-5; ★ **ATL**; mail Stockbridge **z** 30281; ● 200
Swords; RMC Place; MORGAN; **166** F-7; mail Buckhead **z** 30625; ● 90
Sybert; RMC Place; LINCOLN; ***166** E-9; elev. 589ft./180m.; mail Lincolnton **z** 30817; rural
Sycamore; Inc. Place; TURNER; **167** L-6; elev. 415ft./126m.; 🅿; **z** 31790; Ⓟ 417; Ⓒ 496
Sylvan Hills; RMC Place; FULTON; ***166** F-4; ★ **ATL**; mail Atlanta **z** 30310; pop. incl. with Atlanta (Inc. Place)
Sylvania; Inc. Place; ⊡ SCREVEN; **166** I-12; elev. 236ft./72m.; 🅿 🅷; **z** 30467; Ⓟ 2,871; Ⓒ 2,675
Sylvester; Inc. Place; ⊡ WORTH; **167** M-6; elev. 426ft./130m.; 🅿 🅷; **z** 31791; Ⓟ 5,702; Ⓒ 5,990

T

Tails Creek; RMC Place; GILMER; ***166** C-4; mail Ellijay **z** 30540; rural
Talahi Island; RMC Place; CHATHAM; ***167** K-14; mail Savannah **z** 31410; ● 500
TALBOT; **166** I-4; Ⓟ 6,524; Ⓒ 6,498; ◆ 6,640
Talbotton; Inc. Place; ⊡ TALBOT; **166** I-4; elev. 700ft./213m.; 🅿; **z** 31827; Ⓟ 1,046; Ⓒ 1,019
TALIAFERRO; **166** F-8; Ⓟ 1,915; Ⓒ 2,077; ◆ 1,873
Talking Rock; Inc. Place; PICKENS; **166** C-4; elev. 1,100ft./335m.; 🅿; **z** 30175; Ⓟ 62; Ⓒ 49
Tallapoosa; Inc. Place; HARALSON; **166** F-2; elev. 1,134ft./346m.; 🅿; **z** 30176; Ⓟ 2,805; Ⓒ 2,789
Tallulah Falls; Inc. Place; HABERSHAM, RABUN; **166** B-7; elev. 1,570ft./479m.; 🅿; **z** 30573; Ⓟ 147; Ⓒ 164
Tallulah Lodge; RMC Place; HABERSHAM; ***166** B-7; mail Tallulah Falls **z** 30573; pop. incl. with Tallulah Falls (Inc. Place)
Talmo; Inc. Place; JACKSON; **166** D-6; elev. 921ft./281m.; 🅿; **z** 30575; Ⓟ 189; Ⓒ 477
Talmo; RMC Place; WARE; **167** M-9; rural
Talona; RMC Place; GILMER; ***166** C-4; mail Talking Rock **z** 30175; rural
Tama Reservation; Indian Reservation; State Reservation; GRADY; Ⓒ 57
Tanglewood; RMC Place; CLARKE; ***166** E-7; ★ **ATH**; mail Athens **z** 30606; pop. incl. with Athens (Inc. Place)
Tanglewood; RMC Place; RICHMOND; ***166** F-11; ★ **AUG**; mail Augusta **z** 30909; pop. incl. with Augusta (Inc. Place)
Tarboro; RMC Place; CAMDEN; **167** N-11; mail White Oak **z** 31568; ● 150
Tarrytown; Inc. Place; MONTGOMERY; **166** J-9; elev. 310ft./94m.; 🅿; **z** 30470; Ⓟ 130; Ⓒ 100
Tarver; RMC Place; ECHOLS; ***167** O-8; mail Fargo **z** 31631; rural
Tarversville; RMC Place; TWIGGS; ***166** I-7; mail Dry Branch **z** 31020; rural
Tate; RMC Place; PICKENS; **166** C-4; elev. 1,276ft./389m.; 🅿; **z** 30177; ● 1,000
Tate City; RMC Place; TOWNS; ***166** B-7; mail Clayton **z** 30525; rural
TATTNALL; **167** K-10; Ⓟ 17,722; Ⓒ 22,305; ◆ 22,995
Tatumsville; RMC Place; CHATHAM; ***167** K-13; ★ **SAV**; mail Savannah **z** 31405; pop. incl. with Savannah (Inc. Place)
Tax; TALBOT; see Tax Crossroads (RMC Place)
Tax Crossroads (Tax); RMC Place; TALBOT; ***166** H-4; mail Shiloh **z** 31826; rural
TAYLOR; **166** I-4; Ⓟ 7,642; Ⓒ 8,815; ◆ 8,816
Taylorsville; Inc. Place; BARTOW, POLK; **166** D-3; elev. 729ft./222m.; 🅿; **z** 30178; Ⓟ 269; Ⓒ 229
Tazewell; RMC Place; MARION; **166** J-4; elev. 487ft./148m.; 🅿; **z** 31803; ● 130
TELFAIR; **167** K-8; Ⓟ 11,000; Ⓒ 11,794; ◆ 13,432
Tell; FULTON; see Cliftondale (RMC Place)
Teloga; RMC Place; CHATTOOGA; ***166** C-2; mail Summerville **z** 30747; rural
Temperance; RMC Place; TELFAIR; ***167** K-8; mail Rhine **z** 31077; rural
Temple; Inc. Place; CARROLL; **166** F-3; elev. 1,169ft./356m.; 🅿; **z** 30179; Ⓟ 1,870; Ⓒ 2,383
Temple Grove; RMC Place; MURRAY; ***166** B-4; mail Crandall **z** 30711; rural
Tennga; RMC Place; MURRAY; **166** B-4; elev. 852ft./260m.; 🅿; **z** 30751; ● 400
Tennille; Inc. Place; WASHINGTON; **166** H-9; elev. 466ft./142m.; 🅿; **z** 31089; Ⓟ 1,552; Ⓒ 1,505
Terrace Manor; RMC Place; RICHMOND; ***166** G-11; ★ **AUG**; mail Augusta **z** 30906; pop. incl. with Augusta (Inc. Place)
Terrell; RMC Place; WORTH; ***167** L-6; elev. 414ft./126m.; mail Ashburn **z** 31714, Sumner **z** 31789; rural
TERRELL; **167** L-4; Ⓟ 10,653; Ⓒ 10,970; ◆ 9,899
Terry; PAULDING; see Red Rock (RMC Place)
Texas; RMC Place; HEARD; ***166** G-2; elev. 940ft./287m.; mail Franklin **z** 30217
Thalmann; RMC Place; GLYNN; **167** M-12; mail Brunswick **z** 31523; ● 50
The Hill; RMC Place; RICHMOND; ***167** K-13; ★ **SAV**; mail Augusta **z** 30904; pop. incl. with Augusta (Inc. Place)
The Landings; RMC Place; CHATHAM; ***167** K-13; elev. 15ft./5m.; ★ **SAV**; mail Savannah **z** 31411; ● 950
The Rock; RMC Place; UPSON; **166** H-5; elev. 810ft./247m.; 🅿; **z** 30285; Ⓟ 88
THOMAS; **167** N-6; Ⓟ 38,986; Ⓒ 42,737; ◆ 45,967
Thomasboro; RMC Place; SCREVEN; ***166** I-11; elev. 235ft./72m.; mail Rocky Ford **z** 30455; rural
Thomaston; Inc. Place; ⊡ UPSON; **166** H-5; elev. 76ft./23m.; 🅿 🅷; **z** 30286; Ⓟ 9,127; Ⓒ 9,411
Thomasville; RMC Place; FULTON; ***166** F-5; elev. 916ft./279m.; ★ **ATL**; mail Atlanta **z** 30315; pop. incl. with Atlanta (Inc. Place)
Thomasville; Inc. Place; ⊡ THOMAS; **167** O-5; elev. 285ft./87m.; 🅿 🅷 🅲 691 ■; **z** 31757-58, **z** 31792, **z** 31799; Ⓟ 17,457; Ⓒ 18,162; ◆ 19,145
Thomas Woods; RMC Place; RICHMOND; ***166** G-11; ★ **AUG**; mail Augusta **z** 30906; pop. incl. with Augusta (Inc. Place)
Thompson; RMC Place; LOWNDES; ***167** O-7; elev. 236ft./72m.; ★ **VALD**; mail Valdosta **z** 31601; ● 500
Thompsonville; RMC Place; WALKER; ***166** B-2; elev. 1,935ft./590m.; ★ **CHTN**; mail Rising Fawn **z** 30738; rural
Thomson; Inc. Place; ⊡ MCDUFFIE; **166** F-9; elev. 532ft./162m.; 🅿 🅷; **z** 30824 & mail Appling **z** 30802; Ⓟ 6,862; Ⓒ 6,828
Thornhedge; RMC Place; CLAYTON; ***166** F-4; elev. 900ft./274m.; ★ **ATL**; mail Riverdale **z** 30296; ● 400
Thornton Estates; RMC Place; CLAYTON; ***166** F-5; ★ **ATL**; mail Jonesboro **z** 30236; ● 200
Thrift; RMC Place; JENKINS; ***166** I-11; elev. 269ft./82m.; mail Millen **z** 30442
Thunderbolt; Inc. Place; CHATHAM; **167** T-10; elev. 21ft./6m.; 🅿; ★ **SAV**; **z** 31404, **z** 31410; Ⓟ 2,786; Ⓒ 2,340
Thurmack (Thurmock); RMC Place; JACKSON; ***166** D-6; mail Pendergrass **z** 30567; rural
Thurmock; JACKSON; see Thurmack (RMC Place)
Thurston; RMC Place; GREENE; ***166** F-8; mail Greensboro **z** 30642; pop. incl. with Greensboro (Inc. Place)
Thyatira; RMC Place; JACKSON; **166** D-7; ★ **ATH**; mail Jefferson **z** 30549; ● 150
Ticknor; RMC Place; COLQUITT; ***167** M-6; mail Doerun **z** 31744; rural
TIFT; **167** M-7; Ⓟ 34,998; Ⓒ 38,407; ◆ 42,998
Tifton; Inc. Place; ⊡ TIFT; **167** M-7; elev. 357ft./109m.; 🅿 🅷 ■; **z** 31793-94; Ⓟ 14,215; Ⓒ 15,060; ◆ 16,776
Tiger; Inc. Place; RABUN; **166** B-7; elev. 1,963ft./598m.; 🅿; **z** 30576; Ⓟ 301; Ⓒ 316
Tignall; Inc. Place; WILKES; **166** E-9; elev. 641ft./195m.; 🅿; **z** 30668; Ⓟ 711; Ⓒ 653
Tilford; RMC Place; FULTON; ★ **ATL**; pop. incl. with Atlanta (Inc. Place)
Tilton; RMC Place; WHITFIELD; ***166** C-3; mail Dalton **z** 30720
Timothy Estates; RMC Place; CLARKE; ★ **ATH**; mail Athens **z** 30606; pop. incl. with Athens (Inc. Place)
Tippettville; RMC Place; DOOLY; ***167** K-6; elev. 351ft./107m.; mail Vienna **z** 31092; rural
Tison; RMC Place; TATTNALL; ***167** K-11; mail Glennville **z** 30427; rural
Titus; RMC Place; TOWNS; ***166** B-6; mail Hiawassee **z** 30546; rural
Toccoa; Inc. Place; ⊡ STEPHENS; **166** C-7; elev. 1,017ft./310m.; 🅿 🅷; **z** 30577 & mail Toccoa Falls **z** 30598; Ⓟ 8,266; Ⓒ 9,323
Toccoa Falls; RMC Place; STEPHENS; **166** C-7; elev. 900ft./274m.; 🅿 🅲 943; **z** 30598; ● 900
Toco Hills; RMC Place; DEKALB; **168** D-5; ★ **ATL**; mail Atlanta **z** 30329; ● 3,200
Toledo; RMC Place; CHARLTON; ***167** O-11; elev. 58ft./18m.; mail Saint George **z** 31562; rural
Tom; RMC Place; JOHNSON; ***166** I-9; mail Kite **z** 31049; rural
Toms Creek; RMC Place; STEPHENS; ***166** C-7; mail Martin **z** 30557; rural
Toney Valley; RMC Place; DEKALB; ***166** F-5; ★ **ATL**; mail Decatur **z** 30032; ● 600
TOOMBS; **167** K-10; Ⓟ 24,072; Ⓒ 26,067; ◆ 28,667
Toomsboro; Inc. Place; WILKINSON; **166** H-8; elev. 236ft./72m.; 🅿; **z** 31090; Ⓟ 617; Ⓒ 622
Toonigh; CHEROKEE; see Lebanon (RMC Place)
Topeka Junction; RMC Place; UPSON; ***166** H-5; elev. 816ft./249m.; mail The Rock **z** 30285; rural
Town and Country; RMC Place; RICHMOND; ***166** G-10; ★ **AUG**; mail Hephzibah **z** 30815; pop. incl. with Augusta (Inc. Place)
Town and Country Acres; RMC Place; DOUGHERTY; ***167** L-5; ★ **ALB**; mail Albany **z** 31721; pop. incl. with Albany (Inc. Place)
Towns; RMC Place; TELFAIR; **167** K-9; mail Mc Rae **z** 31055; ● 90
TOWNS; **166** B-6; Ⓟ 6,754; Ⓒ 9,319; ◆ 11,338
Townsend; RMC Place; MCINTOSH; **167** L-12; elev. 21ft./6m.; 🅿; **z** 31331; ● 200
Traders Hill; RMC Place; CHARLTON; **167** O-11; elev. 76ft./23m.; mail Folkston **z** 31537; ● 150
Tranquilla Woods; RMC Place; CHATHAM; ***167** K-13; ★ **SAV**; mail Savannah **z** 31419; pop. incl. with Savannah (Inc. Place)
Trans; RMC Place; WALKER; mail La Fayette **z** 30728; rural
Travisville; RMC Place; CLINCH; ***167** N-9; mail Homerville **z** 31634; ● 100
Tremont; RMC Place; CRISP; ***167** K-6; mail Cordele **z** 31015; rural
Tremont; RMC Place; RICHMOND; ★ **AUG**; mail Augusta **z** 30907; pop. incl. with Augusta (Inc. Place)
Tremont Park; RMC Place; CHATHAM; ***167** K-13; ★ **SAV**; mail Savannah **z** 31405; pop. incl. with Savannah (Inc. Place)
Trenton; Inc. Place; ⊡ DADE; **166** B-2; elev. 730ft./223m.; 🅿; ★ **CHTN**; **z** 30752; Ⓟ 1,994; Ⓒ 1,942
TREUTLEN; **166** J-9; Ⓟ 5,994; Ⓒ 6,854; ◆ 7,088
Trice; RMC Place; UPSON; mail Thomaston **z** 30286; rural
Trickum; RMC Place; GWINNETT; ★ **ATL**
Trickum; RMC Place; WHITFIELD; ***166** B-3; mail Tunnel Hill **z** 30755; rural
Tri-Counties Industrial City; GORDON, MURRAY, WHITFIELD; see Industrial City (RMC Place)
Trimble; RMC Place; TROUP; **166** G-3; mail Hogansville **z** 30230; ● 60
Trion; Inc. Place; CHATTOOGA; **166** C-2; elev. 664ft./202m.; 🅿; **z** 30753; Ⓟ 1,661; Ⓒ 1,993
TROUP; **166** G-3; Ⓟ 55,536; Ⓒ 58,779; ◆ 64,477
Troutman; RMC Place; STEWART; **167** K-4; elev. 515ft./157m.; mail Cuthbert **z** 39840; ● 50
Trudie; RMC Place; BRANTLEY; ***167** M-11; mail Patterson **z** 31557; rural
Tucker; CDP; DEKALB; **166** E-5; 🅿; ★ **ATL**; **z** 30084-85; Ⓟ 25,781; Ⓒ 26,532; ◆ 30,296
Tugaloo; RMC Place; HABERSHAM; ***166** C-7; mail Tallulah Falls **z** 30573; pop. incl. with Tallulah Falls (Inc. Place)
Tulakes; RMC Place; MUSCOGEE; ***166** I-3; ★ **COL**; mail Columbus **z** 31904; pop. incl. with Columbus (Inc. Place)
Tunnel Hill; Inc. Place; WHITFIELD; **166** B-3; elev. 840ft./256m.; 🅿; **z** 30755; Ⓟ 970; Ⓒ 1,209
Turin; Inc. Place; COWETA; **166** G-4; elev. 903ft./275m.; 🅿; **z** 30289; Ⓟ 189; Ⓒ 165
TURNER; **167** L-7; Ⓟ 8,703; Ⓒ 9,504; ◆ 9,160
Turner City; RMC Place; DOUGHERTY; ***167** L-5; ★ **ALB**; mail Albany **z** 31705; pop. incl. with Albany (Inc. Place)
Turners Corner; RMC Place; LUMPKIN; ***166** C-6; mail Cleveland **z** 30528; rural
Turners Rock; RMC Place; CHATHAM; ***167** K-13; ★ **SAV**; mail Savannah **z** 31406
Turnerville; RMC Place; HABERSHAM; **166** C-7; 🅿; **z** 30580; ● 300
Tusculum; RMC Place; EFFINGHAM; ***166** J-12; elev. 122ft./37m.; mail Guyton **z** 31312, Springfield **z** 31329
TWIGGS; **166** I-7; Ⓟ 9,806; Ⓒ 10,590; ◆ 10,091
Twin City; Inc. Place; EMANUEL; **166** I-10; elev. 309ft./94m.; 🅿; **z** 30471; Ⓟ 1,466; Ⓒ 1,752
Twin Lakes; RMC Place; LOWNDES; **167** O-8; elev. 180ft./55m.; ★ **VALD**; mail Lake Park **z** 31636; ● 950
Tybee Island (Savannah Beach); Inc. Place; CHATHAM; **167** K-14; elev. 17ft./5m.; 🅿; ★ **SAV**; **z** 31328; Ⓟ 2,842; Ⓒ 3,392
Tyler; RMC Place; JASPER; ***166** G-6; mail Monticello **z** 31064; rural
Tyrone; Inc. Place; FAYETTE; **166** F-4; elev. 993ft./303m.; 🅿; ★ **ATL**; **z** 30290; Ⓟ 2,724; Ⓒ 3,916
Tyrone; RMC Place; WILKES; ***166** F-8; elev. 980ft./299m.; mail Washington **z** 30673
Ty Ty; Inc. Place; TIFT; **167** M-6; elev. 330ft./101m.; 🅿; **z** 31795; Ⓟ 579; Ⓒ 716
Tyus; RMC Place; CARROLL; **166** F-2; mail Bowdon **z** 30108; ● 100

U

Unadilla; Inc. Place; DOOLY; **166** J-6; elev. 395ft./120m.; 🅿; **z** 31091; Ⓟ 1,620; Ⓒ 2,772
Union; RMC Place; MARION; ***166** J-4; mail Buena Vista **z** 31803; rural
Union; RMC Place; PAULDING; ***166** E-3; mail Temple **z** 30179
Union; RMC Place; QUITMAN; ***167** K-3; mail Morris **z** 39867; rural
Union (Julia); RMC Place; STEWART; ***167** K-3; elev. 254ft./77m.; mail Omaha **z** 31821; rural
UNION; **166** B-5; Ⓟ 11,993; Ⓒ 17,289; ◆ 22,165
Unionburg; RMC Place; TIFT; mail Tifton **z** 31794
Union City; Inc. Place; FULTON; **166** F-4; elev. 1,024ft./312m.; 🅿 ■; ★ **ATL**; **z** 30291; Ⓟ 8,887; Ⓒ 11,621; ◆ 15,140
Union Hill; RMC Place; CHEROKEE; ***166** D-4; elev. 1,073ft./327m.; ★ **ATL**; mail Alpharetta **z** 30004; rural
Union Point; Inc. Place; GREENE; **166** F-8; elev. 685ft./209m.; 🅿; **z** 30669; Ⓟ 1,753; Ⓒ 1,669
Unionville; RMC Place; BIBB; ★ **MAC**; mail Macon **z** 31204; pop. incl. with Macon (Inc. Place)
Unionville; CDP; TIFT; **167** M-7; mail Tifton **z** 31794; Ⓟ 2,710; Ⓒ 2,074
Unity; RMC Place; FRANKLIN; ***166** D-7; mail Carnesville **z** 30521; rural
University Heights; RMC Place; CLARKE; ***166** E-7; ★ **ATH**; mail Athens **z** 30605; pop. incl. with Athens (Inc. Place)
Upatoi; RMC Place; MUSCOGEE; ***166** I-3; 🅿; ★ **COL**; **z** 31829; pop. incl. with Columbus (Inc. Place)
UPSON; **166** H-5; Ⓟ 26,300; Ⓒ 27,597; ◆ 27,645
Upton; RMC Place; COFFEE; ***167** M-8; mail Douglas **z** 31533; rural
Uptonville; RMC Place; CHARLTON; ***167** O-11; mail Folkston **z** 31537; rural
Uvalda (Apalachee); Inc. Place; MONTGOMERY; **167** K-9; elev. 185ft./56m.; 🅿; **z** 30473; Ⓟ 561; Ⓒ 530

V

Vada; RMC Place; DECATUR, MITCHELL; **167** N-4; elev. 148ft./45m.; mail Climax **z** 39834; ● 80
Valdosta; Inc. Place; ⊡ LOWNDES; **167** O-7; elev. 229ft./70m.; 🅿 🅷 🅲 10,888 ■; ★ **VALD**; **z** 31601-06, **z** 31698 & mail Moody AFB **z** 31699; Ⓟ 39,806; Ⓒ 43,724; Ⓡ 44,268; ◆ 47,912
Valley Forge; RMC Place; RICHMOND; ***166** G-11; ★ **AUG**; mail Augusta **z** 30906; pop. incl. with Augusta (Inc. Place)
Valley View; RMC Place; WALKER; ***166** B-2; ★ **CHTN**; mail Flintstone **z** 30725; ● 200
Valona; RMC Place; MCINTOSH; **167** M-13; elev. 10ft./3m.; 🅿; **z** 31319; ● 75
Vanceville; RMC Place; TIFT; ***167** M-7; mail Tifton **z** 31794; ● 150
Vandiver Heights; RMC Place; COBB; ***166** E-4; ★ **ATL**; mail Marietta **z** 30066; ● 650
Vanna; RMC Place; HART; **166** D-8; elev. 835ft./255m.; mail Royston **z** 30662; ● 150
Vans Valley; RMC Place; FLOYD; ***166** D-2; elev. 631ft./192m.; mail Rome **z** 30161; rural
Van Wert; RMC Place; POLK; **166** E-3; mail Rockmart **z** 30153; ● 275
Varnell; Inc. Place; WHITFIELD; **166** B-3; elev. 809ft./247m.; 🅿; **z** 30756; Ⓟ 358; Ⓒ 1,491; Ⓡ 1,531
Vaughn; RMC Place; SPALDING; ***166** G-4; elev. 790ft./241m.; mail Griffin **z** 30223; ● 150
Veal; RMC Place; CARROLL; **166** F-2; elev. 1,187ft./362m.; mail Bowdon **z** 30108; ● 90
Veazey; RMC Place; GREENE; **166** F-8; mail Greensboro **z** 30642; ● 50
Vega; RMC Place; PIKE; ***166** H-5; mail Meansville **z** 30256; rural
Veribest; RMC Place; OGLETHORPE; ***166** E-8; elev. 660ft./201m.; mail Carlton **z** 30627; rural
Vernonburg; Inc. Place; CHATHAM; **167** S-11; elev. 10ft./3m.; ★ **SAV**; mail Savannah **z** 31406; Ⓟ 74; Ⓒ 138
Vernon View; RMC Place; CHATHAM; ***167** K-13; ★ **SAV**; mail Savannah **z** 31406
Vesta; RMC Place; OGLETHORPE; **166** E-8; elev. 635ft./194m.; mail Carlton **z** 30627; ● 60
Victoria; RMC Place; CHEROKEE; ***166** D-4; ★ **ATL**; mail Woodstock **z** 30189; ● 300
Victory; RMC Place; CARROLL; **166** F-2; mail Bowdon **z** 30108; ● 40
Victory Heights; RMC Place; CHATHAM; ***167** K-13; ★ **SAV**; mail Savannah **z** 31404; pop. incl. with Savannah (Inc. Place)
Vidalia; Inc. Place; TOOMBS, MONTGOMERY; **166** J-10; elev. 298ft./91m.; 🅿 🅷; **z** 30474-75; Ⓟ 11,078; Ⓒ 10,491
Vidette; Inc. Place; BURKE; **166** H-10; elev. 353ft./108m.; mail Louisville **z** 30434; Ⓟ 98; Ⓒ 112
Vienna; Inc. Place; ⊡ DOOLY; **167** K-6; elev. 338ft./103m.; 🅿 🅷; **z** 31092; Ⓟ 2,708; Ⓒ 2,973
View; RMC Place; HABERSHAM; ***166** C-7; elev. 1,434ft./437m.; mail Cornelia **z** 30531; rural
Villanow; RMC Place; WALKER; ***166** C-3; mail La Fayette **z** 30728
Villa Rica; Inc. Place; CARROLL, DOUGLAS; **166** F-3; elev. 1,100ft./335m.; 🅿 🅷; ★ **ATL**; **z** 30180; Ⓟ 6,542; Ⓒ 4,134
Vineland; RMC Place; RICHMOND; ***166** F-11; elev. 250ft./76m.; ★ **AUG**; mail Augusta **z** 30909; pop. incl. with Augusta (Inc. Place)
Vineville; RMC Place; BIBB; ★ **MAC**; mail Macon **z** 31204; pop. incl. with Macon (Inc. Place)
Vinings; CDP; COBB; **168** C-2; ★ **ATL**; mail Atlanta **z** 30339; Ⓟ 7,417; Ⓒ 9,677
Vinson Village; RMC Place; BIBB; ***166** I-6; ★ **MAC**; mail Macon **z** 31216; pop. incl. with Macon (Inc. Place)
Vista Grove; RMC Place; DEKALB; **168** D-5; elev. 1,000ft./305m.; ★ **ATL**; mail Decatur **z** 30033; ● 3,000
Vulcan; RMC Place; WALKER; mail Rising Fawn **z** 30738; rural

W

Waco; Inc. Place; HARALSON; **166** F-2; 🅿; **z** 30182; Ⓟ 461; Ⓒ 469
Wadley; Inc. Place; JEFFERSON; **166** H-10; elev. 234ft./71m.; 🅿; **z** 30477; Ⓟ 2,473; Ⓒ 2,088; Ⓡ 2,085
Wagon Wheel; RMC Place; COOK; ***167** M-7; mail Sparks **z** 31647; rural
Wahoo; RMC Place; LUMPKIN; ***166** C-6; mail Dahlonega **z** 30533; rural
Walden; RMC Place; BIBB; ***166** I-6; elev. 371ft./113m.; ★ **MAC**; mail Macon **z** 31216
Waleska; Inc. Place; CHEROKEE; **166** D-4; elev. 1,151ft./351m.; 🅿 🅲 1,060; **z** 30183; Ⓟ 700; Ⓒ 616
WALKER; **166** C-2; Ⓟ 58,340; Ⓒ 61,053; ◆ 65,357
Walker Park; RMC Place; WALTON; ***166** E-6; mail Monroe **z** 30655; ● 65
Walkersville; RMC Place; PIERCE; ***167** M-10; mail Blackshear **z** 31516; rural
Wallace; RMC Place; PULASKI; ***166** J-7; elev. 311ft./95m.; mail Hawkinsville **z** 31036; rural
Wallaceville; RMC Place; WALKER; ***166** B-2; ★ **CHTN**; mail Chickamauga **z** 30707, Rossville **z** 30741; ● 500
Walls Crossing; RMC Place; SCHLEY; ***166** J-4; mail Ellaville **z** 31806; rural
Walnut Grove; RMC Place; WALKER; ***166** C-2; mail La Fayette **z** 30728; rural
Walnut Grove; Inc. Place; WALTON; **166** F-6; elev. 928ft./283m.; ★ **ATL**; mail Covington **z** 30014; Ⓟ 458; Ⓒ 1,241
Walthourville; Inc. Place; LIBERTY; **167** L-12; elev. 91ft./28m.; 🅿; **z** 31333; Ⓟ 2,024; Ⓒ 4,030
WALTON; **166** E-6; Ⓟ 38,586; Ⓒ 60,687; ◆ 90,243
Wanona Park; WARE; see Winona Park (RMC Place)
WARE; **167** N-9; Ⓟ 35,471; Ⓒ 35,483; ◆ 36,254
Waresboro; RMC Place; WARE; **167** M-10; elev. 144ft./44m.; 🅿; **z** 31564; ● 400
Wares Crossroads; RMC Place; TROUP; **166** H-3; elev. 752ft./229m.; mail Lagrange **z** 30240; ● 50
Waresville; RMC Place; HEARD; ***166** G-2; elev. 928ft./283m.; mail Franklin **z** 30217
Waring; RMC Place; WHITFIELD; ***166** B-3; mail Dalton **z** 30720; ● 150
Warm Springs; Inc. Place; MERIWETHER; **166** H-4; elev. 930ft./283m.; 🅿 🅷; **z** 31830; Ⓟ 407; Ⓒ 485
Warner Robins; Inc. Place; HOUSTON, PEACH; **166** I-7; elev. 360ft./110m.; 🅿 🅷 ■; ★ **MAC**; **z** 31088, **z** 31093, **z** 31095, **z** 31098-99; Ⓟ 43,726; Ⓒ 48,804; ◆ 62,536
WARREN; **166** G-9; Ⓟ 6,078; Ⓒ 6,336; ◆ 5,768
Warren Terrace; RMC Place; WALKER; ***166** B-2; ★ **CHTN**; mail Rossville **z** 30741; ● 650
Warrenton; Inc. Place; ⊡ WARREN; **166** G-9; elev. 500ft./152m.; 🅿; **z** 30828; Ⓟ 2,056; Ⓒ 2,013; Ⓡ 2,118
Warsaw; RMC Place; FULTON; ***166** E-5; ★ **ATL**; mail Alpharetta **z** 30005; rural
Warthen; RMC Place; WASHINGTON; **166** H-9; 🅿; **z** 31094; ● 250
Warwick; Inc. Place; WORTH; **167** L-6; elev. 275ft./84m.; 🅿; **z** 31796; Ⓟ 501; Ⓒ 430
Washington; Inc. Place; ⊡ WILKES; **166** F-9; elev. 618ft./188m.; 🅿 🅷; **z** 30673; Ⓟ 4,279; Ⓒ 4,295
WASHINGTON; **166** H-9; Ⓟ 19,112; Ⓒ 21,176; ◆ 21,590
Waterloo; RMC Place; IRWIN; ***167** L-7; elev. 369ft./112m.; mail Chula **z** 31733; rural
Waterport; RMC Place; WALTON; mail Loganville **z** 30052; rural
Waters; RMC Place; SCREVEN; ***166** I-12; mail Sylvania **z** 30467; rural
Watkinsville; Inc. Place; ⊡ OCONEE; **166** E-7; elev. 750ft./229m.; 🅿; ★ **ATH**; **z** 30677; Ⓟ 1,600; Ⓒ 2,097
Waverly; RMC Place; CAMDEN; **167** N-12; elev. 20ft./6m.; 🅿; **z** 31565; ● 400
Waverly; RMC Place; RICHMOND; ***166** F-11; ★ **AUG**; mail Augusta **z** 30909; pop. incl. with Augusta (Inc. Place)
Waverly Hall; Inc. Place; HARRIS; **166** I-3; elev. 750ft./229m.; 🅿; **z** 31831; Ⓟ 769; Ⓒ 709
Waverly Heights; RMC Place; BIBB; ***166** I-6; ★ **MAC**; mail Macon **z** 31216; pop. incl. with Macon (Inc. Place)
Waverly Park; RMC Place; CATOOSA; ***166** B-2; ★ **CHTN**; mail Rossville **z** 30741
Wax; RMC Place; FLOYD; **166** D-3; elev. 738ft./225m.; ★ **ROME**; mail Aragon **z** 30104; ● 100
Wayback; RMC Place; CALHOUN; mail Edison **z** 39846; rural
Waycross; Inc. Place; ⊡ WARE, PIERCE; **167** N-10; elev. 135ft./41m.; 🅿 🅷 ■; **z** 31501-03; Ⓟ 16,410; Ⓒ 15,333; ◆ 15,051
WAYNE; **167** L-11; Ⓟ 22,356; Ⓒ 26,565; ◆ 29,664
Waynesboro; Inc. Place; ⊡ BURKE; **166** H-11; elev. 295ft./90m.; 🅿 🅷; **z** 30830; Ⓟ 5,701; Ⓒ 5,813
Waynesville; RMC Place; BRANTLEY; **167** M-11; elev. 57ft./17m.; 🅿; **z** 31566; ● 450
Wayside; RMC Place; JONES; **166** H-7; elev. 641ft./195m.; mail Gray **z** 31032; ● 130
Webb; RMC Place; FULTON; ***166** D-5; ★ **ATL**; mail Alpharetta **z** 30004; rural
Webb Bridge; RMC Place; FULTON; ★ **ATL**; mail Alpharetta **z** 30023; pop. incl. with Alpharetta (Inc. Place)
Weber; RMC Place; BERRIEN; ***167** M-8; mail Nashville **z** 31639
WEBSTER; **167** K-4; Ⓟ 2,263; Ⓒ 2,390; ◆ 2,271
Welcome; RMC Place; COWETA; **166** G-3; mail Newnan **z** 30263; ● 200
Welcome Hill; RMC Place; CHATTOOGA; ***166** C-2; elev. 816ft./249m.; mail Trion **z** 30753; ● 100
Wenona; RMC Place; CRISP; **167** K-6; mail Cordele **z** 31015; ● 200
Weracoba Heights; RMC Place; MUSCOGEE; ★ **COL**; mail Columbus **z** 31906; pop. incl. with Columbus (Inc. Place)
Wesley; RMC Place; EMANUEL; **166** J-10; elev. 243ft./74m.; mail Swainsboro **z** 30401; ● 50
Wesley; RMC Place; TAYLOR; ***166** I-5; elev. 697ft./212m.; mail Butler **z** 31006, Junction City **z** 31812; rural
Wesleyan Estates; RMC Place; BIBB; ***166** H-6; ★ **MAC**; mail Macon **z** 31204; ● 290
Wesleyan Woods; RMC Place; BIBB; ***166** H-6; ★ **MAC**; mail Macon **z** 31210; pop. incl. with Macon (Inc. Place)
West Albany; RMC Place; DOUGHERTY; pop. incl. with Albany (Inc. Place)
West Bainbridge; RMC Place; DECATUR; ***167** N-4; mail Bainbridge **z** 39817; pop. incl. with Bainbridge (Inc. Place)
West Brow; RMC Place; DADE; ***166** B-2; ★ **CHTN**; mail Lookout Mountain **z** 30750, Rising Fawn **z** 30738; rural
West Crossing; RMC Place; HARALSON; ***166** F-2; mail Tallapoosa **z** 30176; rural
West Dublin; RMC Place; LAURENS; mail Dublin **z** 31021; pop. incl. with Dublin (Inc. Place)
West End; RMC Place; FLOYD; ***166** D-2; ★ **ROME**; mail Rome **z** 30165; pop. incl. with Rome (Inc. Place)
West End; RMC Place; FULTON; ***166** F-4; ★ **ATL**; mail Atlanta **z** 30310; pop. incl. with Atlanta (Inc. Place)
Westfield; RMC Place; BIBB; ★ **MAC**; pop. incl. with Macon (Inc. Place)
Westgate; RMC Place; COBB; ★ **ATL**; mail Marietta **z** 30060; pop. incl. with Marietta (Inc. Place)
Westgate; RMC Place; DOUGHERTY; ★ **ALB**; mail Albany **z** 31707, **z** 31721; pop. incl. with Albany (Inc. Place)
Westgate Park; RMC Place; CLARKE; ★ **ATH**; mail Athens **z** 30607; pop. incl. with Athens (Inc. Place)
West Green; RMC Place; COFFEE; **167** L-9; elev. 254ft./77m.; 🅿; **z** 31567; ● 300
Westhampton; RMC Place; COLUMBIA; ***166** F-11; ★ **AUG**; mail Augusta **z** 30907; ● 1,800
West Hills; RMC Place; RICHMOND; ***166** F-11; ★ **AUG**; mail Augusta **z** 30907; pop. incl. with Augusta (Inc. Place)
Westmont; RMC Place; COLUMBIA; ***166** F-10; ★ **AUG**; mail Augusta **z** 30907; ● 1,700
Westoak; RMC Place; COBB; ***166** E-4; elev. 1,139ft./347m.; ★ **ATL**; mail Marietta **z** 30062; ● 900
Weston; Inc. Place; WEBSTER; **167** K-4; elev. 528ft./161m.; 🅿; **z** 31832; Ⓟ 42; Ⓒ 75
Westover; RMC Place; RICHMOND; ***166** G-11; ★ **AUG**; pop. incl. with Augusta (Inc. Place)
West Point; Inc. Place; TROUP, HARRIS; **166** H-2; elev. 578ft./176m.; 🅿; **z** 31833; Ⓟ 3,571; Ⓒ 3,382
West Rome; RMC Place; FLOYD; ★ **ROME**; mail Rome **z** 30164; pop. incl. with Rome (Inc. Place)
West Savannah; RMC Place; CHATHAM; ★ **SAV**; mail Savannah **z** 31415; pop. incl. with Savannah (Inc. Place)
Westside; RMC Place; CATOOSA; ***166** B-2; ★ **CHTN**; mail Rossville **z** 30741; pop. incl. with Fort Oglethorpe (Inc. Place)
Westside; RMC Place; HALL; ***166** D-6; elev. 1,200ft./366m.; mail Gainesville **z** 30501; Ⓟ 2,180
West Valdosta; RMC Place; LOWNDES; ***167** O-7; elev. 210ft./64m.; ★ **VALD**; mail Valdosta **z** 31601; ● 60
West Vidalia; RMC Place; TOOMBS; mail Vidalia **z** 30474; pop. incl. with Vidalia (Inc. Place)
Westwood; RMC Place; BEN HILL; ***167** L-7; mail Fitzgerald **z** 31750; ● 100
Wexwood; RMC Place; CLAYTON; ***166** F-4; elev. 910ft./277m.; ★ **ATL**; mail Riverdale **z** 30296; ● 800
Wheat Hill; RMC Place; CHATHAM; ***167** K-13; ★ **SAV**; mail Savannah **z** 31408; pop. incl. with Garden City (Inc. Place)
WHEELER; **167** K-9; Ⓟ 4,903; Ⓒ 6,179; ◆ 6,626
Wheeler Heights; RMC Place; BIBB; **167** S-7; ★ **MAC**; mail Macon **z** 31217; ● 275
Wheless; RMC Place; RICHMOND; ***166** F-11; ★ **AUG**; pop. incl. with Augusta (Inc. Place)
Whigham; Inc. Place; GRADY; **167** O-5; elev. 270ft./82m.; 🅿; **z** 39897; Ⓟ 605; Ⓒ 631
Whistleville; RMC Place; BARROW; ***166** E-6; mail Winder **z** 30680; rural
Whitaker; RMC Place; BRANTLEY; ***167** M-12; mail Hortense **z** 31543; rural
White; Inc. Place; BARTOW; **166** D-4; elev. 840ft./256m.; 🅿; **z** 30184; Ⓟ 542; Ⓒ 693
WHITE; **166** C-6; Ⓟ 13,006; Ⓒ 19,944; ◆ 25,752
White Bluff; RMC Place; CHATHAM; ***167** K-13; ★ **SAV**; mail Savannah **z** 31406; pop. incl. with Savannah (Inc. Place)
White City; RMC Place; DOUGLAS; ***166** F-3; elev. 1,177ft./359m.; ★ **ATL**; mail Winston **z** 30187; ● 100
White Hall; RMC Place; CLARKE; ***166** E-7; elev. 686ft./209m.; ★ **ATH**; mail Athens **z** 30605; pop. incl. with Athens (Inc. Place)
Whitehouse; RMC Place; HENRY; ***166** F-5; ★ **ATL**; mail McDonough **z** 30252
Whitemarsh Island; CDP-Census Area Only; CHATHAM; ***167** K-13; elev. 5ft./2m.; ★ **SAV**; mail Savannah **z** 31404; Ⓟ 2,824; Ⓒ 5,824
White Oak; RMC Place; CAMDEN; **167** N-12; elev. 14ft./4m.; 🅿; **z** 31568; ● 250
White Plains; Inc. Place; GREENE; **166** F-8; elev. 664ft./202m.; 🅿; **z** 30678; Ⓟ 286; Ⓒ 283
Whitesburg; Inc. Place; CARROLL; **166** F-3; elev. 852ft./260m.; 🅿; **z** 30185; Ⓟ 643; Ⓒ 596
Whitestone; RMC Place; GILMER, PICKENS; **166** C-4; elev. 1,118ft./341m.; mail Talking Rock **z** 30175; ● 150
White Sulphur Springs; RMC Place; MERIWETHER; ***166** H-3; elev. 800ft./244m.; mail Pine Mountain **z** 31822; ● 100
Whitesville; RMC Place; HARRIS; **166** H-3; elev. 735ft./224m.; mail West Point **z** 31833; ● 100
WHITFIELD; **166** B-3; Ⓟ 72,462; Ⓒ 83,525; ◆ 93,649
Whitworth; RMC Place; FRANKLIN; ***166** C-8; elev. 833ft./254m.; mail Lavonia **z** 30553; ● 600
Wilbanks Store; RMC Place; MURRAY; mail Crandall **z** 30711; ● 200
WILCOX; **167** K-7; Ⓟ 7,008; Ⓒ 8,577; ◆ 8,456
Wildwood; RMC Place; DADE; **166** B-2; elev. 714ft./218m.; 🅿 🅷; ★ **CHTN**; **z** 30757; ● 200
Wiley; RMC Place; RABUN; **166** B-7; 🅿; **z** 30581; ● 200
WILKES; **166** E-9; Ⓟ 10,597; Ⓒ 10,687; ◆ 10,115
WILKINSON; **166** I-8; Ⓟ 10,228; Ⓒ 10,220; ◆ 10,073
Willacoochee; Inc. Place; ATKINSON; **167** M-8; elev. 247ft./75m.; 🅿; **z** 31650; Ⓟ 1,205; Ⓒ 1,434
Willard; RMC Place; PUTNAM; ***166** G-7; mail Eatonton **z** 31024; rural
Williamsburg Manor; RMC Place; CHATHAM; ***167** K-13; ★ **SAV**; mail Savannah **z** 31419; pop. incl. with Savannah (Inc. Place)
Williamson; Inc. Place; PIKE; **166** G-5; elev. 921ft./281m.; 🅿; **z** 30292; Ⓟ 295; Ⓒ 297
Wilmington; CHATHAM; see Wilmington Island (CDP-Census Area Only)
Wilmington Island (Wilmington); CDP-Census Area Only; CHATHAM; ***167** K-14; elev. 14ft./4m.; ★ **SAV**; mail Savannah **z** 31410; Ⓟ 11,230; Ⓒ 14,213
Wilmington Park; RMC Place; CHATHAM; ★ **SAV**; mail Savannah **z** 31410
Wilshire; RMC Place; CHATHAM; ★ **SAV**; mail Savannah **z** 31419; pop. incl. with Savannah (Inc. Place)
Wilshire Estates; RMC Place; CHATHAM; ★ **SAV**; mail Savannah **z** 31419; pop. incl. with Savannah (Inc. Place)
Wilsons Church; RMC Place; JACKSON; ***166** D-7; mail Maysville **z** 30558; rural
Wilsonville; RMC Place; COFFEE; ***167** M-9; mail Nicholls **z** 31554; rural
Wimberly on the Marsh; RMC Place; CHATHAM; ★ **SAV**; mail Savannah **z** 31406
Wimbish Woods; RMC Place; BIBB; ***166** H-6; ★ **MAC**; mail Macon **z** 31210; pop. incl. with Macon (Inc. Place)
Winchester; RMC Place; MACON; ***166** J-6; elev. 456ft./139m.; mail Marshallville **z** 31057; rural
Winchester Hills; RMC Place; ROCKDALE; ***166** F-5; elev. 800ft./244m.; ★ **ATL**; mail Conyers **z** 30012; ● 335
Winder; Inc. Place; ⊡ BARROW; **166** E-6; elev. 984ft./300m.; 🅿 🅷; **z** 30680; Ⓟ 7,373; Ⓒ 10,201
Windermere; RMC Place; RICHMOND; ***166** G-10; ★ **AUG**; mail Augusta **z** 30904; pop. incl. with Augusta (Inc. Place)
Windsor; RMC Place; WALTON; ***166** E-6; elev. 889ft./271m.; ★ **ATL**; mail Loganville **z** 30052; rural
Windsor Estates; RMC Place; COWETA; ***166** G-3; mail Newnan **z** 30263; ● 300
Windsor Forest; RMC Place; CHATHAM; ***167** K-13; elev. 15ft./5m.; ★ **SAV**; mail Savannah **z** 31419; pop. incl. with Savannah (Inc. Place)
Windsor Forest; RMC Place; RICHMOND; ***166** F-11; elev. 200ft./61m.; ★ **AUG**; mail Augusta **z** 30904; pop. incl. with Augusta (Inc. Place)
Windsor Park; RMC Place; LOWNDES; ***167** O-7; ★ **VALD**; mail Valdosta **z** 31601; pop. incl. with Valdosta (Inc. Place)
Windsor Park; RMC Place; MUSCOGEE; ***166** I-3; ★ **COL**; mail Columbus **z** 31909; pop. incl. with Columbus (Inc. Place)
Windward; RMC Place; CHATHAM; ***167** K-13; ★ **SAV**; mail Savannah **z** 31419; pop. incl. with Savannah (Inc. Place)
Windy Ridge; RMC Place; FANNIN; ***166** B-5; mail Mineral Bluff **z** 30559; rural
Winfield; RMC Place; COLUMBIA; ***166** F-10; elev. 497ft./151m.; mail Appling **z** 30802, Thomson **z** 30824; rural
Winokur; RMC Place; CHARLTON; **167** N-11; elev. 71ft./22m.; mail Folkston **z** 31537; ● 100
Winona Park (Wanona Park); RMC Place; WARE; ***167** N-10; mail Waycross **z** 31503; ● 700
Winship Gardens; RMC Place; BIBB; ***166** H-6; ★ **MAC**; mail Macon **z** 31204; pop. incl. with Macon (Inc. Place)
Winston; RMC Place; DOUGLAS; **166** F-3; elev. 1,200ft./366m.; 🅿; ★ **ATL**; **z** 30187; ● 350
Winterville; Inc. Place; CLARKE; **166** E-7; elev. 804ft./245m.; 🅿; ★ **ATH**; **z** 30683; Ⓟ 876; Ⓒ 1,068
Withers; RMC Place; CLINCH; ***167** O-8; elev. 166ft./51m.; mail Du Pont **z** 31630; rural
Woodbine; Inc. Place; ⊡ CAMDEN; **167** N-12; elev. 16ft./5m.; 🅿; **z** 31569; Ⓟ 1,212; Ⓒ 1,218
Woodbury; Inc. Place; MERIWETHER; **166** H-4; elev. 779ft./237m.; 🅿; **z** 30293; Ⓟ 1,429; Ⓒ 1,184
Woodcliff; RMC Place; SCREVEN; **166** I-11; mail Sylvania **z** 30467; ● 100
Woodlake; RMC Place; RICHMOND; ***166** G-11; ★ **AUG**; mail Augusta **z** 30906; pop. incl. with Augusta (Inc. Place)
Woodland; Inc. Place; TALBOT; **166** I-4; elev. 760ft./232m.; 🅿; **z** 31836; Ⓟ 552; Ⓒ 432
Woodland Hills; RMC Place; LAURENS; mail Dublin **z** 31021; ● 30
Woodland Hills; RMC Place; WALKER; ***166** B-2; ★ **CHTN**; mail Rossville **z** 30741; ● 200
Woodlawn; RMC Place; CHATHAM; ★ **SAV**; mail Savannah **z** 31406; pop. incl. with Savannah (Inc. Place)
Woodlawn; LINCOLN; see Leathersville (RMC Place)
Woodlawn Estates; RMC Place; MUSCOGEE; **167** T-2; ★ **COL**; mail Columbus **z** 31907; pop. incl. with Columbus (Inc. Place)
Woodlawn Terrace; RMC Place; CHATHAM; ***167** K-13; ★ **SAV**; mail Savannah **z** 31406; pop. incl. with Garden City (Inc. Place)
Woodridge Estates; RMC Place; CHATHAM; ***167** K-14; ★ **SAV**; mail Savannah **z** 31410
Woods Grove; RMC Place; TOWNS; ***166** B-6; mail Young Harris **z** 30582; rural
Wood Station; RMC Place; CATOOSA; ***166** B-3; ★ **CHTN**; mail Ringgold **z** 30736; rural
Woodstock; Inc. Place; CHEROKEE; **166** D-4; elev. 968ft./295m.; 🅿; ★ **ATL**; **z** 30188-89; Ⓟ 4,361; Ⓒ 10,050; ◆ 22,779
Woodville; RMC Place; CHATHAM; ***167** K-13; ★ **SAV**; mail Savannah **z** 31415; pop. incl. with Savannah (Inc. Place)
Woodville; Inc. Place; GREENE; **166** F-8; elev. 693ft./211m.; 🅿; **z** 30669; Ⓟ 415; Ⓒ 400
Woolsey; Inc. Place; FAYETTE; **166** G-4; 🅿; **z** 30214 & mail Fayetteville **z** 30215; Ⓟ 120; Ⓒ 175
Wooster; RMC Place; MERIWETHER; ***166** G-4; mail Gay **z** 30218; rural
Wormsloe; RMC Place; CHATHAM; ***167** K-13; ★ **SAV**; mail Savannah **z** 31406
Worth; RMC Place; TURNER; ***167** L-6; mail Ashburn **z** 31714; rural
WORTH; **167** M-6; Ⓟ 19,745; Ⓒ 21,967; ◆ 20,786
Worthville; RMC Place; BUTTS; **166** G-6; elev. 659ft./201m.; mail Jackson **z** 30233; ● 100
Wray; RMC Place; IRWIN; **167** L-8; elev. 309ft./94m.; 🅿; **z** 31798; ● 100
Wrayswood; RMC Place; GREENE; ***166** F-7; mail Watkinsville **z** 30677; rural
Wrens; Inc. Place; JEFFERSON; **166** G-10; elev. 425ft./130m.; 🅿; **z** 30818, **z** 30833; Ⓟ 2,414; Ⓒ 2,314
Wright Landing; RMC Place; CLAYTON; ***166** F-5; ★ **ATL**; mail Jonesboro **z** 30236; ● 150
Wright Square; RMC Place; CHATHAM; ***167** K-13; ★ **SAV**; mail Savannah **z** 31401; pop. incl. with Savannah (Inc. Place)
Wrightsville; Inc. Place; ⊡ JOHNSON; **166** I-9; elev. 322ft./98m.; 🅿; **z** 31096; Ⓟ 2,331; Ⓒ 2,223
Wymberly; RMC Place; CHATHAM; ★ **SAV**; mail Savannah **z** 31406
Wynngate; RMC Place; COLUMBIA; ***166** F-11; ★ **AUG**; mail Augusta **z** 30907; ● 1,200
Wynnton; RMC Place; MUSCOGEE; **167** S-2; ★ **COL**; mail Columbus **z** 31906; pop. incl. with Columbus (Inc. Place)

Y

Yahoola; RMC Place; LUMPKIN; ***166** C-3; mail Dahlonega **z** 30533; rural
Yates; RMC Place; COWETA; **166** F-3; mail Newnan **z** 30263; ● 30
Yatesville; Inc. Place; UPSON; **166** H-5; elev. 771ft./235m.; 🅿; **z** 31097; Ⓟ 409; Ⓒ 408
Yellow Bluff Fishing Village; RMC Place; LIBERTY; ***167** L-13; mail Midway **z** 31320; ● 75
Yeomans; RMC Place; TERRELL; ***167** L-4; mail Dawson **z** 39842; rural
Yonah; RMC Place; HALL; mail Alto **z** 30510; rural
Yonkers; RMC Place; DODGE; ***166** J-8; mail Cochran **z** 31014; ● 40
Yorktown; RMC Place; MUSCOGEE; ***166** J-3; ★ **COL**; mail Columbus **z** 31907; pop. incl. with Columbus (Inc. Place)
Yorkville; RMC Place; PAULDING; **166** E-3; mail Dallas **z** 30157; ● 200
Youley; JENKINS; see Dry Branch (RMC Place)
Young Harris; Inc. Place; TOWNS; **166** B-6; elev. 1,908ft./582m.; 🅿; **z** 30582; Ⓟ 604; Ⓒ 604
Youngs; RMC Place; POLK; ***166** E-2; mail Cedartown **z** 30125; rural
Youngstown; RMC Place; UNION; ***166** B-6; mail Blairsville **z** 30512; rural
Youth; RMC Place; WALTON; **166** E-6; ★ **ATL**; mail Loganville **z** 30052; ● 75

Z

Zaidee; RMC Place; TREUTLEN; ***166** J-9; mail Soperton **z** 30457; rural
Zebina; RMC Place; JEFFERSON; ***166** G-10; mail Wrens **z** 30833
Zebulon; Inc. Place; ⊡ PIKE; **166** H-5; elev. 860ft./262m.; 🅿; **z** 30295; Ⓟ 1,035; Ⓒ 1,181
Zeigler; RMC Place; SCREVEN; ***166** I-11; mail Sylvania **z** 30467; rural
Zenith; RMC Place; CRAWFORD; **166** I-6; elev. 575ft./175m.; mail Roberta **z** 31078; ● 50
Zetella; RMC Place; SPALDING; ***166** G-4; elev. 849ft./259m.; mail Griffin **z** 30223-24; rural
Zetto; RMC Place; CLAY; ***167** L-3; elev. 389ft./119m.; mail Fort Gaines **z** 39851; rural
Zingara; RMC Place; ROCKDALE; ***166** F-6; ★ **ATL**; mail Conyers **z** 30012; rural

---

Entries in **UPPERCASE** are counties.
Entries in **bold** have populations of 2,500 or more.
Names in parentheses are alternate names.
Inc. Place — Incorporated Place
RMC Place — Rand McNally Designated Place
CDP — Census Designated Place
MCD — Minor Civil Division

⊡ County Seat
▲ Minor Civil Division
elev. Elevation
🅿 Post Office

🅷 Hospital
🅲 College
■ Principal Business Center
★ Ranally Metro Area (RMA) Abbreviation
z Zip Code(s)

Ⓟ Previous Census Population
Ⓡ Revised Census Population
Ⓐ Annexation Population
● Rand McNally Population Estimate

Ⓒ Final Census Population
Ⓢ Special Census Population
◆ Estimated Population

For additional definitions see Glossary, Volume 1, and Introduction, Volume 2.

HAWAII

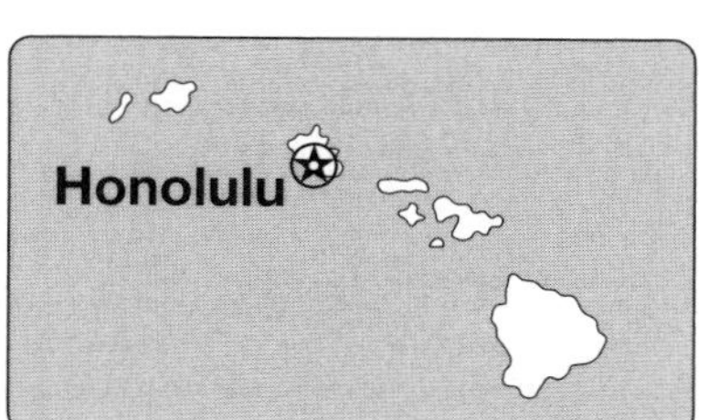

Statistics

Total area (2000) — 10,931 square miles
Land area (2000) — 6,423 square miles
Water area (2000) — 4,508 square miles
Capital — Honolulu
Admitted as state — August, 1959

Maps

State maps can be found on pages 142-254 in Vol. 1

Ranally Metro Areas (RMAs) and Abbreviations

Hilo, HI — HILO
Honolulu, HI — HON

Principal Places

Place Name	Place Type	County	Population
Honolulu	CDP	HONOLULU	◆ 383,787
Hilo	CDP	HAWAII	◆ 48,393
Kailua	CDP	HONOLULU	◆ 37,321
Kāne'ohe	CDP	HONOLULU	◆ 35,745
Waipahu	CDP	HONOLULU	◆ 33,830
Pearl City	CDP	HONOLULU	◆ 31,658
Waimalu	CDP-Census Area Only	HONOLULU	◆ 30,016
Mililani Town	CDP	HONOLULU	◆ 29,241
Kahului	CDP	MAUI	◆ 22,484
K›hei	CDP	MAUI	© 16,749
Wahiawā	CDP	HONOLULU	© 16,151
'Ewa Beach	CDP	HONOLULU	© 14,650
Schofield Barracks	CDP-Census Area Only	HONOLULU	© 14,428
Hālawa	CDP	HONOLULU	© 13,891
Wailuku	CDP	MAUI	◆ 13,715
Makakilo City	CDP	HONOLULU	© 13,156
Kaneohe Station	CDP-Census Area Only	HONOLULU	© 11,827
Waipi'o	CDP	HONOLULU	© 11,672
Nānākuli	CDP	HONOLULU	© 10,814
Wai¤anae	CDP	HONOLULU	© 10,506
Lahaina	CDP	MAUI	◆ 10,177
Kailua	CDP	HAWAII	© 9,870
Village Park	CDP-Census Area Only	HONOLULU	© 9,625
Kapa'a	CDP	KAUAI	© 9,472
¤Aiea	CDP	HONOLULU	◆ 9,210
'Āhuimanu	CDP	HONOLULU	© 8,506
Mākaha	CDP	HONOLULU	© 7,753
Pukalani	CDP	MAUI	© 7,380
Waihee-Waiehu	CDP-Census Area Only	MAUI	© 7,310
Hawaiian Paradise Park	CDP-Census Area Only	HAWAII	© 7,051
Waimea	CDP	HAWAII	© 7,028
Kaimuki	RMC Place	HONOLULU	● 6,800
Kalaoa	CDP	HAWAII	© 6,794
Napili-Honokowai	CDP-Census Area Only	MAUI	© 6,788
Haiku-Pauwela	CDP-Census Area Only	MAUI	© 6,578
Makawao	CDP	MAUI	© 6,327
Lihue	CDP	KAUAI	◆ 6,246
Hōlualoa	CDP	HAWAII	© 6,107
Mā'ili	CDP	HONOLULU	© 5,943
Wailea-Makena	CDP-Census Area Only	MAUI	© 5,671
Pacific Palisades	RMC Place	HONOLULU	● 5,600
Hickam Housing	CDP-Census Area Only	HONOLULU	© 5,471
Waipi'o Acres	CDP	HONOLULU	© 5,298

County Business Data

County	FIPS Code	County Seat	Land Area (Sq. Mi.)	Census Population 4/1/2000	Census Population 4/1/1990	Census Population % Change 1990-2000	Wholesale Trade Sales, 2002 ($1,000)	Wholesale Trade % Change 1997-2002	Manufacturing, 2002 Establish-ments	Manufacturing, 2002 Total Employees	Manufacturing, 2002 Value Added ($1,000)	Manufacturing, 2002 Ranally Mfg. Units
Hawaii	001	Hilo	4,028	148,677	120,317	23.6	605,605	32.4	114	1,246	97,719	52
Honolulu	003	Honolulu	600	876,156	836,231	4.8	8,579,151	41.1	683	10,253	948,546	502
Kalawao	005		13	147	130	13.1	(d)	(d)	...	(d)	(d)	...
Kauai	007	Lihue	622	58,463	51,177	14.2	238,711	35.1	...	(d)	(d)	...
Maui	009	Wailuku	1,159	128,094	100,374	27.6	562,888	29.8	93	1,491	157,060	83
The State			**6,423**	**1,211,537**	**1,108,229**	**9.3**	**9,986,355**	**39.7**	**929**	**13,200**	**1,217,728**	**644**

(d) Data not available. Corresponding percentages or Ranally Manufacturing Units are estimates.
... Represents 0 or amount too minimal to be reported.

Administrative Divisions

Hawaii's local administrative divisions differ considerably from those found in most of the other states. The number of administrative units is quite small, and the state government conducts some functions that elsewhere would be handled by city or minor civil division governments.

Counties: Three of Hawaii's counties, Hawaii, Kauai, and Maui, have county governments similar to those in other states. Honolulu County, however, is legally known as the City and County of Honolulu and, in effect, has one municipal government exercising jurisdiction over the entire island of Oahu. The small outlying islands northwest of Kauai are part of the City and County of Honolulu. Kalawao county, on the island of Molokai, has no county government and is often shown as a district of Maui county for statistical purposes. Kalawao county is not shown on the maps in this atlas.

Cities: The only incorporated city in Hawaii is Honolulu, which is officially known as the City and County of Honolulu. The Honolulu District is sometimes regarded as the "city" for statistical purposes, although it has no municipal or other government separate from that of the City and County as a whole. The U.S. Bureau of the Census recognizes a Honolulu "census designated place" with boundaries nearly identical to those of the Honolulu District. All data for Honolulu (city) in this atlas refer only to the area of the Honolulu census designated place.

In cooperation with the State Department of Planning and Economic Development, the U.S. Census has defined boundaries for the most important population concentrations, treating them as census designated places. Statistical and other information is usually based upon these boundaries.

Index of Places and Counties

A

'Āhuimanu; CDP; HONOLULU; ***168** L-5; ★ **HON**; mail Kaneohe **z** 96744; Ⓟ 8,387; © 8,506
'Aiea; CDP; HONOLULU; **168** M-4; 🄿 ■; ★ **HON**; **z** 96701; Ⓟ 8,906; © 9,019; ◆ 9,210
'Aiea Heights; RMC Place; HONOLULU; ***168** M-4; ★ **HON**; mail Aiea **z** 96701; ● 1,300
'Āina Haina; RMC Place; HONOLULU; ***168** N-5; ★ **HON**; mail Honolulu **z** 96821, **z** 96824; ● 500
Ainaloa; CDP-Census Area Only; HAWAII; ***168** M-10; © 1,910
Akasaki Camp; RMC Place; HAWAII; ***168** L-9; elev. 600ft./183m.; mail Ookala **z** 96774; rural
'Ālewa Heights; RMC Place; HONOLULU; ***168** M-4; ★ **HON**; mail Honolulu **z** 96819; ● 1,300
'Amauulu Camp; RMC Place; HAWAII; ***168** M-10; ★ **HILO**; mail Hilo **z** 96720; rural
Anahola; CDP; KAUAI; **168** I-2; elev. 20ft./6m.; 🄿; **z** 96703; Ⓟ 1,181; © 1,932
Andrade Camp; RMC Place; HAWAII; ***168** M-10; elev. 600ft./183m.; ★ **HILO**; mail Pepeekeo **z** 96783; ● 340

B

Barbers Point; HONOLULU; see Barbers Point Housing (CDP-Census Area Only)
Barbers Point Housing (Barbers Point); CDP-Census Area Only; HONOLULU; ***168** N-2; ★ **HON**; Ⓟ 2,218; © 67
Black Sand Beach; HAWAII; see Kaimu (RMC Place)

C

Camp One Hundred Six; RMC Place; HAWAII; ***168** L-9; mail Honokaa **z** 96727; ● 120
Captain Cook; CDP; HAWAII; **168** M-8; elev. 1,320ft./402m.; 🄿; **z** 96704 & mail Ocean View **z** 96737; Ⓟ 2,595; © 3,206
Chinatown; RMC Place; HONOLULU; ***168** N-4; ★ **HON**; mail Honolulu **z** 96817, **z** 96827; ● 3,500
Chin Chuck (Chin Chuck Camps); RMC Place; HAWAII; ***168** L-10; ★ **HILO**; mail Hakalau **z** 96710; rural
Chin Chuck Camps; HAWAII; see Chin Chuck (RMC Place)
Crestview; RMC Place; HONOLULU; ***168** M-3; elev. 229ft./70m.; ★ **HON**; mail Waipahu **z** 96797; ● 2,300

E

Eden Roc; CDP-Census Area Only; HAWAII; ***168** M-10; © 451
Eight and One-half Mile Camp; RMC Place; HAWAII; ***168** M-10; mail Keaau **z** 96749; ● 80
Eleele; CDP; KAUAI; ***168** I-2; elev. 40ft./12m.; 🄿; **z** 96705; Ⓟ 1,489; © 2,040
Elevenmile Homestead; RMC Place; HAWAII; ***168** M-10; elev. 771ft./235m.; mail Kurtistown **z** 96760; ● 80
'Ewa; HONOLULU; see 'Ewa Villages (CDP)
'Ewa Beach; CDP; HONOLULU; **168** N-3; elev. 5ft./2m.; 🄿 🄷; ★ **HON**; **z** 96706; Ⓟ 14,315; © 14,650
'Ewa Gentry; CDP; HONOLULU; ***168** M-3; elev. 44ft./13m.; ★ **HON**; mail Ewa Beach **z** 96706; Ⓟ 1,992; © 4,939
'Ewa Villages ('Ewa); CDP; HONOLULU; **168** M-3; elev. 49ft./15m.; ★ **HON**; mail Ewa Beach **z** 96706; Ⓟ 3,780; © 4,741

F

Fern Acres; CDP-Census Area Only; HAWAII; ***168** M-10; © 756
Fernandez Village; RMC Place; HONOLULU; ***168** M-3; ★ **HON**; mail Ewa Beach **z** 96706; ● 1,800
Fern Forest; CDP-Census Area Only; HAWAII; ***168** M-10; © 480
Ford Island; RMC Place; HONOLULU; ***168** M-4; ★ **HON**; mail Honolulu **z** 96818; ● 370
Foster Village; RMC Place; HONOLULU; ***168** M-4; ★ **HON**; mail Honolulu **z** 96818; ● 4,800

G

Glenwood; RMC Place; HAWAII; ***168** M-10; elev. 2,302ft./702m.; mail Mountain View **z** 96771; rural

H

Haaheo; RMC Place; HAWAII; ***168** M-10; ★ **HILO**; mail Hilo **z** 96720; ● 35
Hā'ena; RMC Place; KAUAI; ***168** I-2; mail Hanalei **z** 96714; rural
Haiku; RMC Place; MAUI; **168** I-9; elev. 512ft./156m.; 🄿; **z** 96708; ● 1,150
Haiku-Pauwela; CDP-Census Area Only; MAUI; ***168** I-9; elev. 534ft./163m.; mail Haiku **z** 96708; Ⓟ 4,509; © 6,578
Haina; RMC Place; HAWAII; ***168** L-9; elev. 520ft./158m.; mail Honokaa **z** 96727; ● 190
Hakalau; RMC Place; HAWAII; **168** L-10; 🄿; ★ **HILO**; **z** 96710; ● 100
Halaula (Kohala Mills); CDP; HAWAII; **168** L-9; mail Kapaau **z** 96755; Ⓟ 496; © 495
Halawa; RMC Place; HAWAII; ***168** L-9; mail Kapaau **z** 96755; ● 460
Hālawa; CDP; HONOLULU; ***168** M-4; ★ **HON**; mail Aiea **z** 96701; Ⓟ 13,408; © 13,891
Hālawa; RMC Place; MAUI; ***168** J-7; elev. 26ft./8m.; mail Kaunakakai **z** 96748; rural
Hālawa Heights; RMC Place; HONOLULU; **168** M-4; ★ **HON**; mail Aiea **z** 96701; ● 4,000
Hālawa Hills; RMC Place; HONOLULU; ***168** M-4; ★ **HON**; mail Aiea **z** 96701; ● 180
Hale'iwa; CDP; HONOLULU; **168** I-4; elev. 20ft./6m.; 🄿; ★ **HON**; **z** 96712; Ⓟ 2,442; © 2,225
Haliimaile; CDP; MAUI; **168** I-9; elev. 1,073ft./327m.; mail Makawao **z** 96768; Ⓟ 841; © 895
Hāmoa; RMC Place; MAUI; ***168** J-10; mail Hana **z** 96713; ● 60
Hāna; CDP; MAUI; **168** K-8; elev. 98ft./30m.; 🄿; **z** 96713; Ⓟ 683; © 709
Hanalei; CDP; KAUAI; **168** I-2; elev. 13ft./4m.; 🄿; **z** 96714; Ⓟ 461; © 478
Hanamaulu; CDP; KAUAI; **168** I-2; elev. 188ft./57m.; 🄿; **z** 96715; Ⓟ 3,611; © 3,272
Hanapēpē; CDP; KAUAI; **168** I-2; elev. 40ft./12m.; 🄿; **z** 96716; Ⓟ 1,395; © 2,153
Hanapepe Heights; RMC Place; KAUAI; ***168** I-2; elev. 142ft./43m.; mail Hanapepe **z** 96716; ● 750
Hā'ō'ū; RMC Place; MAUI; ***168** J-10; mail Hana **z** 96713; rural
Happy Valley; RMC Place; MAUI; ***168** I-8; mail Wailuku **z** 96793; ● 630
Hau'ula; CDP; HONOLULU; **168** K-4; elev. 20ft./6m.; 🄿; ★ **HON**; **z** 96717; Ⓟ 3,479; © 3,651
HAWAII; **168** L-10; Ⓟ 120,317; © 148,677; ◆ 176,513
Hawaiian Acres; CDP-Census Area Only; HAWAII; ***168** M-10; © 1,776
Hawaiian Beaches; CDP-Census Area Only; HAWAII; ***168** M-10; elev. 290ft./88m.; mail Pahoa **z** 96778; Ⓟ 2,846; © 3,709
Hawaiian Ocean View; CDP-Census Area Only; HAWAII; ***168** N-9; elev. 3,400ft./1,036m.; mail Captain Cook **z** 96704, Ocean View **z** 96737; Ⓟ 969; © 2,178
Hawaiian Paradise Park; CDP-Census Area Only; HAWAII; ***168** M-10; elev. 160ft./49m.; mail Pahoa **z** 96778; Ⓟ 3,389; © 7,051
Hawaiian Village; RMC Place; MAUI; ***168** I-9; mail Honolulu **z** 96813; rural
Hawai'i Kai; RMC Place; HONOLULU; ***168** N-6; ★ **HON**; mail Honolulu **z** 96825; ● 1,150
Hawi; CDP; HAWAII; **168** L-8; elev. 600ft./183m.; 🄿; **z** 96719; Ⓟ 924; © 938
He'eia; CDP; HONOLULU; ***168** M-5; ★ **HON**; mail Kaneohe **z** 96744; Ⓟ 5,010; © 4,944
Hickam Housing; CDP-Census Area Only; HONOLULU; ***168** M-4; ★ **HON**; mail Honolulu **z** 96818; Ⓟ 6,553; © 5,471
Hilo; CDP; ⊡ HAWAII; **168** M-10; elev. 38ft./12m.; 🄿 🄷 🄲 3,517 ■; ★ **HILO**; **z** 96720-21; Ⓟ 37,808; © 40,759; ◆ 48,393
Hōlualoa; CDP; HAWAII; **168** M-8; elev. 1,372ft./418m.; 🄿; **z** 96725; Ⓟ 3,834; © 6,107
Homestead; KAUAI; see Kalaheo (CDP)
Honalo; CDP; HAWAII; ***168** M-8; mail Kealakekua **z** 96750; Ⓟ 1,926; © 1,987
Hōnaunau; RMC Place; HAWAII; **168** M-8; elev. 1,080ft./329m.; 🄿; **z** 96726; rural
Honaunau-Napoopoo; CDP-Census Area Only; HAWAII; ***168** M-8; elev. 80ft./24m.; mail Honaunau **z** 96726; Ⓟ 2,373; © 2,414
Honohina; RMC Place; HAWAII; ***168** L-10; mail Hakalau **z** 96710; rural
Honoka'a; CDP; HAWAII; **168** L-9; elev. 1,114ft./340m.; 🄿 🄷; **z** 96727; Ⓟ 2,186; © 2,233
Honokahua; RMC Place; MAUI; **168** I-8; mail Lahaina **z** 96761; ● 400
Honokai Hale; RMC Place; HONOLULU; ***168** M-2; ★ **HON**; mail Kapolei **z** 96707; ● 1,670
Honokohau; RMC Place; HAWAII; ***168** M-8; mail Holualoa **z** 96725, Kailua Kona **z** 96740; rural
Honokowai; RMC Place; MAUI; **168** K-7; mail Lahaina **z** 96761; ● 2,200
Honolulu; CDP; **STATE CAPITAL**; ⊡ HONOLULU; **168** J-5; elev. 18ft./5m.; 🄿 🄷 🄲 32,275 ■; ★ **HON**; **z** 96801-28, **z** 96830, **z** 96836-41, **z** 96843-44, **z** 96846-50 & mail Pearl Harbor **z** 96860; Ⓟ 365,272; © 371,657; ◆ 383,787
HONOLULU; **168** I-5; Ⓟ 836,231; © 876,156; ◆ 895,466
Honomakau; RMC Place; HAWAII; ***168** L-8; mail Kapaau **z** 96755; ● 50
Honomu; CDP; HAWAII; **168** L-10; elev. 300ft./91m.; 🄿; ★ **HILO**; **z** 96728; Ⓟ 532; © 541
Honouliuli; RMC Place; HONOLULU; **168** M-3; ★ **HON**; mail Ewa Beach **z** 96706; ● 520
Honu'apo; RMC Place; HAWAII; ***168** N-9; elev. 22ft./7m.; mail Naalehu **z** 96772
Hookena; RMC Place; HAWAII; ***168** M-8; mail Captain Cook **z** 96704; rural
Ho'olehua; RMC Place; MAUI; **168** J-6; elev. 640ft./195m.; 🄿; **z** 96729; ● 270
Hoopuloa; RMC Place; HAWAII; ***168** N-8; elev. 20ft./6m.; mail Honaunau **z** 96726; rural
Huehue (Huehue Ranch); RMC Place; HAWAII; ***168** M-8; mail Holualoa **z** 96725, Kailua Kona **z** 96740; ● 55
Huehue Ranch; HAWAII; see Huehue (RMC Place)
Huelo; RMC Place; MAUI; ***168** I-9; mail Haiku **z** 96708; ● 170

I

Iroquois Point; CDP-Census Area Only; HONOLULU; ***168** N-3; ★ **HON**; mail Ewa Beach **z** 96706; Ⓟ 4,188; © 2,462
Iwasaki Camp; RMC Place; HAWAII; ***168** M-10; elev. 643ft./196m.; mail Kurtistown **z** 96760; ● 300
Iwilei; RMC Place; HONOLULU; ***168** N-4; ★ **HON**; mail Honolulu **z** 96817; ● 50

K

Ka'a'awa; CDP; HONOLULU; **168** K-4; 🄿; ★ **HON**; **z** 96730; Ⓟ 1,138; © 1,324
Kaalawai; RMC Place; HONOLULU; ***168** N-5; ★ **HON**; mail Honolulu **z** 96821; ● 1,000
Kā'anapali; CDP; MAUI; ***168** I-8; mail Lahaina **z** 96761; Ⓟ 579; © 1,375
Kaawanui Village; RMC Place; KAUAI; ***168** I-2; mail Makaweli **z** 96769; ● 150
Ka'elekū; RMC Place; MAUI; ***168** I-10; rural
Kahakuloa; RMC Place; MAUI; ***168** I-8; mail Wailuku **z** 96793; rural
Kahala; RMC Place; HONOLULU; ***168** N-5; ★ **HON**; ● 800
Kahaluu; RMC Place; HAWAII; ***168** M-8; mail Holualoa **z** 96725; ● 550
Kahalu'u (Libbyville); CDP; HONOLULU; **168** L-5; ★ **HON**; mail Kaneohe **z** 96744; Ⓟ 3,068; © 2,935
Kahaluu-Keauhou; CDP-Census Area Only; HAWAII; ***168** M-8; elev. 200ft./61m.; mail Holualoa **z** 96725; Ⓟ 1,990; © 2,414
Kahana; RMC Place; HONOLULU; **168** I-5; ★ **HON**; mail Hauula **z** 96717; ● 50
Kahana; RMC Place; MAUI; ***168** I-8; mail Lahaina **z** 96761; ● 670
Kahua; RMC Place; HAWAII; ***168** L-9; mail Kamuela **z** 96743, Kapaau **z** 96755; rural
Kahuku (Kahuku Ranch); RMC Place; HAWAII; ***168** N-9; mail Naalehu **z** 96772; ● 10
Kahuku; CDP; HONOLULU; **168** I-5; elev. 20ft./6m.; 🄿 🄷; ★ **HON**; **z** 96731; Ⓟ 2,063; © 2,097
Kahuku Ranch; HAWAII; see Kahuku (RMC Place)
Kahului; CDP; MAUI; **168** K-7; elev. 7ft./2m.; 🄿 ■; **z** 96732-33; Ⓟ 16,889; © 20,146; ◆ 22,484
Kailua (Kailua Kona); CDP; HAWAII; **168** M-8; elev. 40ft./12m.; mail Kailua Kona **z** 96740, **z** 96745, Keauhou **z** 96739; Ⓟ 9,126; © 9,870
Kailua; CDP; HONOLULU; **168** J-5; elev. 10ft./3m.; 🄿 🄷 ■; ★ **HON**; **z** 96734; Ⓟ 36,818; © 36,513; ◆ 37,321
Kailua; RMC Place; MAUI; ***168** I-9; mail Haiku **z** 96708; ● 160
Kailua Kona; HAWAII; see Kailua (CDP)
Kai Malino; HAWAII; see Kealia (RMC Place)
Kaimu (Black Sand Beach); RMC Place; HAWAII; ***168** M-10; mail Pahoa **z** 96778; ● 50
Kaimuki; RMC Place; HONOLULU; ***168** N-5; ★ **HON**; mail Honolulu **z** 96816; ● 6,800
Kainaliu; RMC Place; HAWAII; ***168** M-8; mail Kealakekua **z** 96750; ● 290
Kainalu; RMC Place; MAUI; ***168** J-7; mail Kaunakakai **z** 96748; rural
Kala'e; RMC Place; MAUI; ***168** J-6; mail Kualapuu **z** 96757; rural
Kalaheo (Homestead); CDP; KAUAI; **168** I-2; elev. 700ft./213m.; 🄿; **z** 96741; Ⓟ 3,592; © 3,913
Kalaoa; CDP; HAWAII; ***168** M-8; elev. 1,600ft./488m.; mail Kailua Kona **z** 96740; Ⓟ 4,490; © 6,794
Kalapana; RMC Place; HAWAII; ***168** M-10; elev. 11ft./3m.; mail Pahoa **z** 96778; community destroyed by lava from Kilauea Volcano, 1990; rural
Kalauao; RMC Place; HONOLULU; ***168** M-4; ★ **HON**; mail Aiea **z** 96701; ● 1,200
Kalaupapa; RMC Place; KALAWAO; **168** J-6; elev. 10ft./3m.; 🄿; **z** 96742; ● 120
KALAWAO; ***168** J-6; Ⓟ 130; © 147; ◆ 116
Kalihi; RMC Place; HONOLULU; ***168** M-4; ★ **HON**; mail Honolulu **z** 96819; ● 1,900
Kalihi Kai; RMC Place; HONOLULU; ***168** N-4; ★ **HON**; mail Honolulu **z** 96818; ● 780
Kalihiwai; CDP; KAUAI; ***168** I-2; mail Kilauea **z** 96754; Ⓟ 435; © 717
Kalua'aha; RMC Place; MAUI; ***168** J-7; mail Kaunakakai **z** 96748; rural
Kamalō; RMC Place; MAUI; ***168** J-7; elev. 5ft./2m.; mail Kaunakakai **z** 96748; ● 60
Kamehameha Heights; RMC Place; HONOLULU; ***168** M-4; ★ **HON**; mail Honolulu **z** 96819; ● 1,100
Kamiloloa; RMC Place; MAUI; ***168** J-6; mail Kaunakakai **z** 96748; ● 590
Kamo'oloa; RMC Place; HONOLULU; ***168** K-2; ★ **HON**; mail Waialua **z** 96791; ● 1,200
Kamuela; HAWAII; see Waimea (CDP)
Kāne'ohe; CDP; HONOLULU; **168** J-5; elev. 40ft./12m.; 🄿 🄷 ■; ★ **HON**; **z** 96744; Ⓟ 35,448; © 34,970; ◆ 35,745
Kaneohe Station; CDP-Census Area Only; HONOLULU; ***168** L-5; ★ **HON**; mail MCBHKaneohe Bay **z** 96863; Ⓟ 11,662; © 11,827
Kaniahiku Village; RMC Place; HAWAII; ***168** M-10; elev. 660ft./201m.; mail Pahoa **z** 96778; rural
Kapa'a; CDP; KAUAI; **168** I-2; elev. 20ft./6m.; 🄿 🄷; **z** 96746; Ⓟ 8,149; © 9,472
Kapaau (Kohala); CDP; HAWAII; ***168** L-8; elev. 481ft./147m.; 🄿 🄷; **z** 96755; Ⓟ 1,083; © 1,159
Kapaia; RMC Place; KAUAI; ***168** I-2; mail Lihue **z** 96766; ● 60
Kapaka; RMC Place; KAUAI; ***168** I-2; mail Kaumakani **z** 96747; ● 75
Kapālama; RMC Place; HONOLULU; ***168** M-4; ★ **HON**; mail Honolulu **z** 96817; ● 1,650
Kapalua; CDP-Census Area Only; MAUI; ***168** I-8; elev. 80ft./24m.; mail Lahaina **z** 96761; Ⓟ 408; © 467
Kapoho; RMC Place; HAWAII; ***168** M-10; elev. 166ft./51m.; mail Pahoa **z** 96778; rural
Kapolei; RMC Place; HONOLULU; ***168** M-3; 🄿; ★ **HON**; **z** 96707, **z** 96709; ● 60
Kapulena; RMC Place; HAWAII; ***168** L-9; mail Honokaa **z** 96727; ● 110
KAUAI; **168** I-2; Ⓟ 51,177; © 58,463; ◆ 64,367
Kaumakani; CDP; KAUAI; ***168** I-2; elev. 196ft./60m.; 🄿; **z** 96747; Ⓟ 803; © 607
Kaumalapau; RMC Place; MAUI; ***168** K-6; mail Lanai City **z** 96763
Kaumana; RMC Place; HAWAII; ***168** M-10; elev. 1,123ft./342m.; ★ **HILO**; mail Hilo **z** 96720; ● 280
Kaunakakai; CDP; MAUI; **168** J-6; elev. 5ft./2m.; 🄿 🄷; **z** 96748; Ⓟ 2,658; © 2,726
Kaupakulua; RMC Place; MAUI; ***168** I-9; mail Haiku **z** 96708; ● 350
Kaupō; RMC Place; MAUI; **168** J-10; elev. 281ft./86m.; mail Hana **z** 96713; rural
Kawaihae; RMC Place; HAWAII; ***168** L-8; mail Kamuela **z** 96743; rural
Kawaihau; RMC Place; KAUAI; ***168** I-2; mail Kapaa **z** 96746; ● 330
Kawailoa Beach; RMC Place; HONOLULU; **168** K-2; ★ **HON**; mail Haleiwa **z** 96712; ● 300
Kawainui; RMC Place; HAWAII; ***168** M-10; elev. 315ft./96m.; ★ **HILO**; mail Pepeekeo **z** 96783; ● 70
Kawela; RMC Place; MAUI; ***168** J-6; mail Kaunakakai **z** 96748; ● 100
Kawela Bay; CDP-Census Area Only; HONOLULU; **168** J-3; ★ **HON**; mail Kahuku **z** 96731; Ⓟ 366; © 410
Kea'au; CDP; HAWAII; **168** M-10; elev. 359ft./109m.; 🄿; ★ **HILO**; **z** 96749; Ⓟ 1,584; © 2,010
Kea'au Camp; RMC Place; HAWAII; ***168** M-10; mail Keaau **z** 96749; ● 100
Kea'au Ranch; RMC Place; HAWAII; ***168** M-10; mail Keaau **z** 96749; ● 30
Kealakekua; CDP; HAWAII; **168** M-8; elev. 1,571ft./479m.; 🄿 🄷; **z** 96750; Ⓟ 1,453; © 1,645
Kealia (Kai Malino); RMC Place; HAWAII; ***168** M-8; mail Captain Cook **z** 96704; ● 120
Kealia; RMC Place; KAUAI; ***168** I-2; elev. 11ft./3m.; 🄿; **z** 96751; ● 400
Ke'anae; RMC Place; MAUI; **168** K-8; mail Haiku **z** 96708; ● 50
Keauhou; RMC Place; HAWAII; ***168** M-8; 🄿; **z** 96739; ● 200
Keaukaha; RMC Place; HAWAII; ***168** M-10; ★ **HILO**; mail Hilo **z** 96720; ● 450
Keawakapu; RMC Place; MAUI; ***168** J-9; elev. 29ft./9m.; mail Kihei **z** 96753; ● 120
Keei; RMC Place; HAWAII; ***168** M-8; mail Honaunau **z** 96726; ● 70
Kehena; RMC Place; HAWAII; ***168** M-10; mail Pahoa **z** 96778; ● 85
Kekaha; CDP; KAUAI; **168** I-2; 🄿; **z** 96752; Ⓟ 3,506; © 3,175
Kelawea; RMC Place; MAUI; ***168** I-8; mail Lahaina **z** 96761; ● 1,650
Keokea; RMC Place; HAWAII; ***168** M-8; mail Captain Cook **z** 96704; ● 90
Keokea; RMC Place; MAUI; **168** K-8; mail Kula **z** 96790; rural
Keolu Hills; RMC Place; HONOLULU; ***168** M-6; ★ **HON**; mail Kailua **z** 96734; ● 1,850
Kīhei; CDP; MAUI; **168** K-7; 🄿; **z** 96753; Ⓟ 11,107; © 16,749
Kilauea; CDP; KAUAI; **168** I-2; 🄿; **z** 96754 & mail Princeville **z** 96722; Ⓟ 1,685; © 2,092
Kīpahulu; RMC Place; MAUI; **168** J-10; mail Hana **z** 96713; rural
Kipu; RMC Place; KAUAI; ***168** I-2; mail Lihue **z** 96766; rural
Kīpū; RMC Place; MAUI; ***168** J-6; mail Kualapuu **z** 96757; ● 230
Koali; RMC Place; MAUI; ***168** J-10; mail Hana **z** 96713; rural
Koele; RMC Place; MAUI; ***168** K-7; mail Lanai City **z** 96763; ● 110
Kohala; HAWAII; see Kapaau (CDP)
Kohala Mills; HAWAII; see Halaula (CDP)
Kokohahi; RMC Place; HONOLULU; ***168** M-5; ★ **HON**; mail Kaneohe **z** 96744; ● 560
Kokomo; RMC Place; MAUI; **168** I-9; mail Haiku **z** 96708; ● 320
Koloa; CDP; KAUAI; **168** I-2; elev. 200ft./61m.; 🄿; **z** 96756; Ⓟ 1,791; © 1,942
Kualapu'u; CDP; MAUI; **168** J-6; elev. 878ft./268m.; 🄿; **z** 96757; Ⓟ 1,661; © 1,936
Kualoa; RMC Place; HONOLULU; ***168** L-5; elev. 10ft./3m.; ★ **HON**; mail Kaaawa **z** 96730; ● 60
Kuhio Village; RMC Place; HAWAII; ***168** L-9; mail Kamuela **z** 96743; ● 330
Kuiaha; MAUI; see Pauwela (RMC Place)
Kūka'iau; RMC Place; HAWAII; ***168** L-9; mail Paauilo **z** 96776; rural
Kukaiau Ranch; HAWAII; see 'Umikoa (RMC Place)
Kukui; RMC Place; HAWAII; ***168** M-10; mail Mountain View **z** 96771; ● 120
Kukuihaele; CDP; HAWAII; **168** L-9; elev. 30ft./9m.; mail Honokaa **z** 96727; Ⓟ 316; © 317
Kukuiula; RMC Place; KAUAI; ***168** I-2; elev. 11ft./3m.; mail Koloa **z** 96756; ● 120
Kukui Village; RMC Place; HAWAII; ***168** L-9; mail Ookala **z** 96774; ● 80
Kula; MAUI; see Waiakoa (RMC Place)
Kuli'ou'ou; RMC Place; HONOLULU; ***168** N-6; ★ **HON**; ● 375
Kumukumu; RMC Place; KAUAI; ***168** I-2; mail Anahola **z** 96703; rural
Kunia; HONOLULU; see Kunia Camp (RMC Place)
Kunia Camp (Kunia); RMC Place; HONOLULU; **168** L-3; ★ **HON**; mail Kunia **z** 96759; ● 580
Kupolo; RMC Place; KAUAI; ***168** I-2; mail Lihue **z** 96766; ● 1,100
Kurtistown; CDP; HAWAII; **168** M-10; elev. 651ft./198m.; 🄿; **z** 96760; Ⓟ 910; © 1,157

L

Lahaina; CDP; MAUI; **168** K-7; elev. 9ft./3m.; 🄿 ■; **z** 96761, **z** 96767; Ⓟ 9,073; © 9,118; ◆ 10,177
Lā'ie; CDP; HONOLULU; **168** J-4; elev. 20ft./6m.; 🄿 🄲 2,471; ★ **HON**; **z** 96762; Ⓟ 5,577; © 4,585
Lalakoa; RMC Place; MAUI; ***168** K-7; elev. 1,640ft./500m.; mail Lanai City **z** 96763; ● 200
Lalamilo; HAWAII; see Puako (CDP)
Lanai City; CDP; MAUI; **168** K-7; elev. 1,624ft./495m.; 🄿 🄷; **z** 96763; Ⓟ 2,400; © 3,164
Lanikai; RMC Place; HONOLULU; ***168** M-6; ★ **HON**; mail Kailua **z** 96734; ● 1,150
Laupāhoehoe; CDP; HAWAII; **168** L-9; elev. 380ft./116m.; 🄿; **z** 96764; Ⓟ 508; © 473
Lawai; CDP; KAUAI; ***168** I-2; 🄿; **z** 96765; Ⓟ 1,787; © 1,984
Leilani Estates; CDP-Census Area Only; HAWAII; ***168** M-10; © 1,046
Libbyville; HONOLULU; see Kahalu'u (CDP)
Lihue; CDP; ⊡ KAUAI; **168** I-2; elev. 206ft./63m.; 🄿 🄷 ■; **z** 96766; Ⓟ 5,536; © 5,674; ◆ 6,246
Lower Paia; RMC Place; MAUI; **168** I-9; elev. 17ft./5m.; mail Paia **z** 96779; ● 220
Lower Village; RMC Place; HONOLULU; ***168** M-3; ★ **HON**; mail Ewa Beach **z** 96706; ● 3,300

M

Maalaea; CDP; MAUI; **168** I-8; mail Wailuku **z** 96793; Ⓟ 443; © 454
Mā'ili; CDP; HONOLULU; **168** M-2; ★ **HON**; mail Waianae **z** 96792; Ⓟ 6,059; © 5,943
Mākaha; CDP; HONOLULU; **168** L-1; ★ **HON**; mail Waianae **z** 96792; Ⓟ 7,990; © 7,753
Mākaha Valley; CDP; HONOLULU; ***168** L-1; elev. 600ft./183m.; ★ **HON**; mail Waianae **z** 96792; Ⓟ 1,012; © 1,289
Makakilo City; CDP; HONOLULU; **168** M-2; ★ **HON**; mail Ewa Beach **z** 96706; Ⓟ 9,828; © 13,156
Makapala; RMC Place; HAWAII; ***168** L-9; mail Kapaau **z** 96755; ● 230
Makawao; CDP; MAUI; **168** I-9; 🄿; **z** 96768; Ⓟ 5,405; © 6,327
Makaweli; KAUAI; see Pakala Village (CDP)
Makena; RMC Place; MAUI; ***168** J-9; elev. 11ft./3m.; mail Kihei **z** 96753; rural
Makiki Heights; RMC Place; HONOLULU; ***168** N-5; ★ **HON**; mail Honolulu **z** 96822; ● 790
Mānā; RMC Place; KAUAI; **168** I-2; mail Kekaha **z** 96752
MAUI; **168** J-7; Ⓟ 100,374; © 128,094; ◆ 142,937
Maunalani Heights; RMC Place; HONOLULU; ***168** N-5; ★ **HON**; mail Honolulu **z** 96816; ● 700
Maunaloa; CDP; MAUI; **168** J-6; elev. 1,050ft./320m.; 🄿; **z** 96770; Ⓟ 405; © 230
Maunawili; CDP; HONOLULU; **168** M-5; ★ **HON**; mail Kailua **z** 96734; Ⓟ 4,847; © 4,869
Mililani; HONOLULU; see Mililani Town (CDP)
Mililani Town (Mililani); CDP; HONOLULU; **168** L-3; ★ **HON**; mail Mililani **z** 96789; Ⓟ 29,359; © 28,608; ◆ 29,241
Miloli'i; RMC Place; HAWAII; **168** N-8; mail Honaunau **z** 96726; rural
Milo Village; RMC Place; HAWAII; ***168** L-9; mail Ookala **z** 96774; ● 140
Moanalua; RMC Place; HONOLULU; ***168** M-4; ★ **HON**; mail Honolulu **z** 96819; ● 300
Mō'ili'ili; RMC Place; HONOLULU; ***168** N-5; ★ **HON**; mail Honolulu **z** 96814, **z** 96828; ● 2,600
Mokuleia; CDP; HONOLULU; ***168** K-2; ★ **HON**; mail Waialua **z** 96791; Ⓟ 1,776; © 1,839
Mountain View; CDP; HAWAII; **168** M-10; elev. 1,398ft./426m.; 🄿; **z** 96771; Ⓟ 3,075; © 2,799
Mū'olea; RMC Place; MAUI; ***168** J-10; elev. 335ft./102m.; mail Hana **z** 96713; ● 40

N

Nā'ālehu; CDP; HAWAII; **168** N-9; elev. 674ft./205m.; 🄿; **z** 96772; Ⓟ 1,027; © 919
Nānākuli; CDP; HONOLULU; **168** J-4; elev. 20ft./6m.; ★ **HON**; mail Waianae **z** 96792; Ⓟ 9,575; © 10,814
Nanawale Estates; CDP-Census Area Only; HAWAII; ***168** M-10; © 1,073
Napili; RMC Place; MAUI; ***168** I-9; mail Lahaina **z** 96761; ● 2,400
Napili-Honokowai; CDP-Census Area Only; MAUI; ***168** I-8; mail Lahaina **z** 96761; Ⓟ 4,332; © 6,788
Napoopoo (Napupu); RMC Place; HAWAII; ***168** M-8; mail Captain Cook **z** 96704; ● 230
Napupu; HAWAII; see Napoopoo (RMC Place)
Nawiliwili; RMC Place; KAUAI; ***168** I-2; elev. 10ft./3m.; mail Lihue **z** 96766; ● 75
Ninemile Camp (Nine Miles); RMC Place; HAWAII; ***168** M-10; mail Keaau **z** 96749; ● 200
Nine Miles; HAWAII; see Ninemile Camp (RMC Place)
Nīnole; RMC Place; HAWAII; ***168** L-10; elev. 240ft./73m.; 🄿; **z** 96773; ● 70
Niu; RMC Place; HONOLULU; ***168** N-5; ★ **HON**; mail Honolulu **z** 96821; ● 570
Niuli'i; RMC Place; HAWAII; ***168** L-9; mail Kapaau **z** 96755; ● 150
Niumalu; RMC Place; KAUAI; ***168** I-2; mail Lihue **z** 96766; ● 100
Niu Village; RMC Place; HAWAII; ***168** L-9; mail Ookala **z** 96774; ● 60
Numila; RMC Place; KAUAI; ***168** I-2; mail Eleele **z** 96705; ● 70

Entries in **UPPERCASE** are counties.
Entries in **bold** have populations of 2,500 or more.
Names in parentheses are alternate names.

Inc. Place	Incorporated Place
RMC Place	Rand McNally Designated Place
CDP	Census Designated Place
MCD	Minor Civil Division
⊡	County Seat
▲	Minor Civil Division
elev.	Elevation
🄿	Post Office
🄷	Hospital
🄲	College
■	Principal Business Center
★	Ranally Metro Area (RMA) Abbreviation
z	Zip Code(s)
Ⓟ	Previous Census Population
Ⓡ	Revised Census Population
Ⓐ	Annexation Population
●	Rand McNally Population Estimate
©	Final Census Population
Ⓢ	Special Census Population
◆	Estimated Population

For additional definitions see Glossary, Volume 1, and Introduction, Volume 2.

O

Olinda; RMC Place; MAUI; ***168** I-9; mail Makawao **z** 96768; rural
Olomana; RMC Place; HONOLULU; ***168** M-5; ★ **HON**; mail Kailua **z** 96734; ● 450
Olowalu; RMC Place; MAUI; **168** I-8; mail Lahaina **z** 96761; ● 50
Omao; CDP; KAUAI; ***168** I-2; elev. 514ft./157m.; mail Koloa **z** 96756; Ⓟ 1,142; Ⓒ 1,221
Omapio; RMC Place; MAUI; ***168** I-9; elev. 1,900ft./579m.; mail Kula **z** 96790; ● 100
Onomea; RMC Place; HAWAII; ***168** M-10; ★ **HILO**; mail Papaikou **z** 96781; ● 40
ʻŌʻōkala; RMC Place; HAWAII; **168** L-9; 🅿; **z** 96774; ● 150
Opihikao; RMC Place; HAWAII; ***168** M-10; elev. 46ft./14m.; mail Pahoa **z** 96778
Orchidlands Estates; CDP-Census Area Only; HAWAII; ***168** M-10; Ⓒ 1,731
Orpheum Village; RMC Place; MAUI; ***168** I-9; mail Paia **z** 96779; rural

P

Paauhau; RMC Place; HAWAII; **168** L-9; elev. 20ft./6m.; 🅿; **z** 96727; ● 270
Paauhau Mauka; RMC Place; HAWAII; ***168** L-9; mail Honokaa **z** 96727; ● 30
Paʻauilo; CDP; HAWAII; **168** L-9; elev. 766ft./233m.; 🅿; **z** 96776; Ⓟ 620; Ⓒ 571
Pacific Heights; RMC Place; HONOLULU; ***168** N-5; ★ **HON**; mail Honolulu **z** 96817; ● 650
Pacific Palisades; RMC Place; HONOLULU; **168** M-3; ★ **HON**; mail Pearl City **z** 96782; ● 5,600
Pāhala; CDP; HAWAII; **168** N-9; elev. 900ft./274m.; 🅿 🅷; **z** 96777; Ⓟ 1,520; Ⓒ 1,378
Pāhoa; CDP; HAWAII; **168** M-10; elev. 655ft./200m.; 🅿; **z** 96778; Ⓟ 1,027; Ⓒ 962
Pahoehoe; RMC Place; HAWAII; ***168** M-8; mail Captain Cook **z** 96704; rural
Paia; CDP; MAUI; **168** I-9; elev. 295ft./90m.; 🅿; **z** 96779; Ⓟ 2,091; Ⓒ 2,499
Pakala Village (Makaweli); CDP; KAUAI; ***168** I-2; elev. 20ft./6m.; mail Makaweli **z** 96769; Ⓟ 565; Ⓒ 478
Palama; RMC Place; HONOLULU; ***168** N-4; ★ **HON**; mail Honolulu **z** 96817; ● 1,200
Palani Junction; RMC Place; HAWAII; ***168** M-8; mail Holualoa **z** 96725; ● 350
Pāpā; RMC Place; HAWAII; ***168** N-8; mail Captain Cook **z** 96704
Pāpaʻaloa; RMC Place; HAWAII; **168** L-10; elev. 240ft./73m.; 🅿; **z** 96780; ● 320
Pāpaʻikou; CDP; HAWAII; **168** M-10; elev. 200ft./61m.; 🅿; ★ **HILO**; **z** 96781; Ⓟ 1,634; Ⓒ 1,414
Paukaa; CDP; HAWAII; ***168** M-10; elev. 155ft./47m.; ★ **HILO**; mail Hilo **z** 96720; Ⓟ 495; Ⓒ 495
Paukukalo; RMC Place; MAUI; ***168** I-8; mail Wailuku **z** 96793; ● 900
Pauwela (Kuiaha); RMC Place; MAUI; **168** K-8; mail Haiku **z** 96708; ● 500
Pearl City; CDP; HONOLULU; **168** J-5; 🅿 🅲 866; ★ **HON**; **z** 96782; Ⓟ 30,993; Ⓒ 30,976; ◆ 31,658
Pepeekeo; CDP; HAWAII; **168** M-10; elev. 487ft./148m.; 🅿; ★ **HILO**; **z** 96783; Ⓟ 1,813; Ⓒ 1,697
Pepeekeo Mill; RMC Place; HAWAII; ***168** M-10; elev. 100ft./30m.; ★ **HILO**; mail Pepeekeo **z** 96783; rural
Piʻihonua; RMC Place; HAWAII; ***168** M-10; elev. 877ft./267m.; ★ **HILO**; mail Hilo **z** 96720; ● 60
Pōhākupu; RMC Place; HONOLULU; ***168** M-5; ★ **HON**; mail Kailua **z** 96734; ● 2,100
Pohoiki; RMC Place; HAWAII; ***168** M-10; elev. 10ft./3m.; mail Pahoa **z** 96778
Poipu; CDP; KAUAI; ***168** I-2; mail Koloa **z** 96756; Ⓟ 975; Ⓒ 1,075
Pomoho (Pomoho Camp); RMC Place; HONOLULU; **168** L-3; ★ **HON**; mail Wahiawa **z** 96786; ● 480
Pomoho Camp; HONOLULU; see Pomoho (RMC Place)
Port Allen; RMC Place; KAUAI; ***168** I-2; mail Eleele **z** 96705; ● 100
Portlock; RMC Place; HONOLULU; ***168** N-6; ★ **HON**; mail Honolulu **z** 96825; ● 270
Princeville; CDP-Census Area Only; KAUAI; ***168** I-2; 🅿; **z** 96722 & mail Hanalei **z** 96714; Ⓟ 1,244; Ⓒ 1,698
Puako (Lalamilo); CDP; HAWAII; ***168** L-8; mail Kamuela **z** 96743; Ⓟ 397; Ⓒ 429
Pua Loke; RMC Place; KAUAI; ***168** I-2; mail Lihue **z** 96766; ● 430
Puhi; CDP; KAUAI; ***168** I-2; elev. 340ft./104m.; mail Lihue **z** 96766; Ⓟ 1,210; Ⓒ 1,186
Pukalani; CDP; MAUI; **168** K-8; elev. 1,622ft./494m.; 🅿; **z** 96788; Ⓟ 5,879; Ⓒ 7,380
Pūkoʻo; RMC Place; MAUI; ***168** J-7; mail Kaunakakai **z** 96748; rural
Pūlehu; RMC Place; MAUI; ***168** I-9; mail Kula **z** 96790; ● 570
Punaluʻu; RMC Place; HAWAII; **168** K-4; mail Pahala **z** 96777
Punaluʻu; CDP; HONOLULU; ***168** K-4; ★ **HON**; mail Hauula **z** 96717; Ⓟ 672; Ⓒ 881
Pūʻōhala Village; RMC Place; HONOLULU; ***168** M-5; ★ **HON**; mail Kaneohe **z** 96744; ● 900
Pūpūkea; CDP; HONOLULU; ***168** J-3; elev. 600ft./183m.; ★ **HON**; mail Haleiwa **z** 96712; Ⓟ 4,111; Ⓒ 4,250
Puʻuanahulu (Puu Anahulu Homesteads); RMC Place; HAWAII; **168** M-8; mail Holualoa **z** 96725, Kailua Kona **z** 96740; rural
Puu Anahulu Homesteads; HAWAII; see Puʻuanahulu (RMC Place)
Puʻuʻeo; RMC Place; HAWAII; ***168** M-10; elev. 1,445ft./440m.; mail Hilo **z** 96720; ● 220
Puu Hue (Puuhue Ranch); RMC Place; HAWAII; ***168** L-8; mail Hawi **z** 96719; rural
Puuhue Ranch; HAWAII; see Puu Hue (RMC Place)
Puʻuiki; RMC Place; MAUI; **168** J-10; elev. 152ft./46m.; mail Hana **z** 96713; rural
Puukolii; RMC Place; MAUI; ***168** I-8; ● 200
Puunene; RMC Place; MAUI; ***168** I-9; elev. 76ft./23m.; 🅿; **z** 96784; rural
Puunoa; RMC Place; MAUI; ***168** I-8; mail Lahaina **z** 96761; ● 550
Puʻunui; RMC Place; HONOLULU; ***168** M-5; ★ **HON**; mail Honolulu **z** 96819; ● 1,300
Puuohala Village; RMC Place; MAUI; ***168** I-9; mail Wailuku **z** 96793; ● 170
Puu Waawaa Ranch; RMC Place; HAWAII; ***168** M-8; mail Kailua Kona **z** 96740; ● 50
Puʻuwai; RMC Place; KAUAI; ***168** I-1; mail Makaweli **z** 96769; rural

R

Renton Village; RMC Place; HONOLULU; ***168** N-5; ★ **HON**; mail Ewa Beach **z** 96706; ● 235
Royal Hawaiian; RMC Place; HONOLULU; ***168** N-5; ★ **HON**; mail Honolulu **z** 96815; ● 50

S

Saint Louis Heights; RMC Place; HONOLULU; ***168** N-5; ★ **HON**; mail Honolulu **z** 96816; ● 1,000
Schofield Barracks; CDP-Census Area Only; HONOLULU; ***168** L-3; 🅿; ★ **HON**; **z** 96857; Ⓟ 19,597; Ⓒ 14,428
Spanish B Village; RMC Place; MAUI; ***168** I-9; mail Puunene **z** 96784; ● 300
Spreckelsville; RMC Place; MAUI; **168** I-9; elev. 88ft./27m.; mail Paia **z** 96779; rural
Sunset Beach; RMC Place; HONOLULU; **168** J-3; ★ **HON**; mail Haleiwa **z** 96712; ● 660

T

Tantalus; RMC Place; HONOLULU; ***168** M-5; ★ **HON**; mail Honolulu **z** 96822; ● 140
Tenney Village; RMC Place; HONOLULU; ***168** M-3; ★ **HON**; mail Ewa Beach **z** 96706; ● 360
Timber Town; RMC Place; HONOLULU; ***168** N-5; ★ **HON**; mail Honolulu **z** 96826; ● 870

U

ʻUalapuʻe; RMC Place; MAUI; ***168** J-7; mail Kaunakakai **z** 96748; ● 80
Ulumalu; RMC Place; MAUI; ***168** I-9; elev. 820ft./250m.; mail Haiku **z** 96708; rural
Ulupalakua; RMC Place; MAUI; **168** K-7; mail Kula **z** 96790; ● 75
ʻUmikoa (Kukaiau Ranch); RMC Place; HAWAII; ***168** L-9; elev. 3,513ft./1,071m.; mail Paauilo **z** 96776; rural
Union Mill; RMC Place; HAWAII; ***168** L-8; mail Hawi **z** 96719, Kapaau **z** 96755; ● 285

V

Varona Village; RMC Place; HONOLULU; ***168** M-3; ★ **HON**; mail Ewa Beach **z** 96706; ● 180
Village Park; CDP-Census Area Only; HONOLULU; ***168** M-3; elev. 320ft./98m.; ★ **HON**; mail Waipahu **z** 96797; Ⓟ 7,407; Ⓒ 9,625
Volcano; CDP; HAWAII; **168** M-9; elev. 3,723ft./1,135m.; 🅿; **z** 96785; Ⓟ 1,516; Ⓒ 2,231

W

Wahiawā (Wahiawa City); CDP; HONOLULU; **168** J-5; elev. 900ft./274m.; 🅿 🅷; ★ **HON**; **z** 96786; Ⓟ 17,386; Ⓒ 16,151
Wahiawa City; HONOLULU; see Wahiawā (CDP)
Waiāhole; RMC Place; HONOLULU; ***168** L-4; ★ **HON**; mail Kaneohe **z** 96744; ● 170
Waiaka; RMC Place; HAWAII; ***168** L-9; elev. 2,400ft./732m.; mail Kamuela **z** 96743; ● 380
Waiākea; RMC Place; HAWAII; ***168** M-10; ★ **HILO**; mail Hilo **z** 96720; ● 560
Waiakea Camps; RMC Place; HAWAII; ***168** M-9; ★ **HILO**; mail Hilo **z** 96720; rural
Waiakoa (Kula); RMC Place; MAUI; **168** J-9; 🅷; mail Kula **z** 96790; ● 900
Waiʻalae; RMC Place; HONOLULU; ***168** N-5; ★ **HON**; mail Honolulu **z** 96816; ● 700
Waialua; CDP; HONOLULU; **168** K-2; elev. 35ft./11m.; 🅿; ★ **HON**; **z** 96791; Ⓟ 3,943; Ⓒ 3,761
Waialua; RMC Place; MAUI; **168** J-7; mail Kaunakakai **z** 96748; rural
Waianae; RMC Place; HONOLULU; ***168** L-2; 🅿; ★ **HON**; **z** 96792; ● 2,400
Waiʻanae; CDP; HONOLULU; **168** J-4; 🅿; ★ **HON**; **z** 96792; Ⓟ 8,758; Ⓒ 10,506
Waiau; RMC Place; HONOLULU; ***168** M-4; ★ **HON**; mail Pearl City **z** 96782; ● 500
Waiehu; RMC Place; MAUI; **168** I-8; mail Wailuku **z** 96793; ● 600
Waiehu Village; RMC Place; MAUI; ***168** I-8; mail Wailuku **z** 96793; ● 90
Waihee; RMC Place; MAUI; ***168** I-8; mail Wailuku **z** 96793; ● 500
Waihee-Waiehu; CDP-Census Area Only; MAUI; ***168** I-8; elev. 200ft./61m.; mail Wailuku **z** 96793; Ⓟ 4,004; Ⓒ 7,310
Waikāne; CDP; HONOLULU; ***168** L-4; ★ **HON**; mail Kaneohe **z** 96744; Ⓟ 717; Ⓒ 726
Waikapu; CDP; MAUI; **168** K-7; mail Wailuku **z** 96793; Ⓟ 729; Ⓒ 1,115
Waikiʻi; RMC Place; HAWAII; ***168** M-9; rural
Waikīkī; RMC Place; HONOLULU; ***168** N-5; ★ **HON**; mail Honolulu **z** 96815, **z** 96830; ● 3,000
Waikoloa; HAWAII; see Waikoloa Village (CDP-Census Area Only)
Waikoloa Village (Waikoloa); CDP-Census Area Only; HAWAII; ***168** L-8; mail Waikoloa **z** 96738; Ⓟ 2,248; Ⓒ 4,806
Wailea; RMC Place; HAWAII; **168** J-9; ★ **HILO**; mail Hakalau **z** 96710; ● 140
Wailea-Makena; CDP-Census Area Only; MAUI; ***168** J-9; mail Kihei **z** 96753; Ⓟ 3,799; Ⓒ 5,671
Wailua; CDP; KAUAI; **168** I-2; mail Kapaa **z** 96746; Ⓟ 2,018; Ⓒ 2,083
Wailua; RMC Place; MAUI; **168** I-10; mail Haiku **z** 96708, Kihei **z** 96753; ● 120
Wailua Homesteads; CDP-Census Area Only; KAUAI; ***168** I-2; elev. 320ft./98m.; mail Kapaa **z** 96746; Ⓟ 3,870; Ⓒ 4,567
Wailuku; CDP; ⊡ MAUI; **168** K-7; elev. 331ft./101m.; 🅿 🅷 ■; **z** 96793; Ⓟ 10,688; Ⓒ 12,296; ◆ 13,715
Wailupe; RMC Place; HONOLULU; ***168** N-5; ★ **HON**; mail Honolulu **z** 96821; ● 790
Waimalu; CDP-Census Area Only; HONOLULU; ***168** M-4; ★ **HON**; mail Aiea **z** 96701; Ⓟ 29,967; Ⓒ 29,371; ◆ 30,016
Waimānalo; CDP; HONOLULU; **168** J-5; elev. 30ft./9m.; 🅿; ★ **HON**; **z** 96795; Ⓟ 3,508; Ⓒ 3,664
Waimānalo Beach; CDP; HONOLULU; **168** M-6; ★ **HON**; mail Waimanalo **z** 96795; Ⓟ 4,185; Ⓒ 4,271
Waimea (Kamuela); CDP; HAWAII; **168** L-9; elev. 2,669ft./814m.; mail Kamuela **z** 96743; Ⓟ 5,972; Ⓒ 7,028
Waimea; RMC Place; HONOLULU; **168** J-3; ★ **HON**; mail Haleiwa **z** 96712; ● 650
Waimea; CDP; KAUAI; **168** I-2; elev. 9ft./3m.; 🅿 🅷; **z** 96796; Ⓟ 1,840; Ⓒ 1,787
Wainaku; CDP; HAWAII; ***168** M-10; ★ **HILO**; mail Hilo **z** 96720; Ⓟ 1,243; Ⓒ 1,227
Wainee; RMC Place; MAUI; ***168** I-8; mail Lahaina **z** 96761; rural
Wainiha; RMC Place; KAUAI; ***168** I-2; mail Hanalei **z** 96714; ● 100
Waiʻōhinu; RMC Place; HAWAII; ***168** N-9; elev. 1,056ft./322m.; mail Naalehu **z** 96772; ● 150
Waipahu; CDP; HONOLULU; **168** M-3; elev. 20ft./6m.; 🅿; ★ **HON**; **z** 96797; Ⓟ 31,435; Ⓒ 33,108; ◆ 33,830
Waipio; RMC Place; HAWAII; ***168** L-9; mail Honokaa **z** 96727; rural
Waipiʻo; CDP; HONOLULU; ***168** M-3; elev. 299ft./91m.; ★ **HON**; mail Waipahu **z** 96797; Ⓟ 11,812; Ⓒ 11,672
Waipiʻo Acres; CDP; HONOLULU; **168** L-3; ★ **HON**; mail Wahiawa **z** 96786; Ⓟ 5,304; Ⓒ 5,298
Waipouli; RMC Place; KAUAI; ***168** I-2; mail Kapaa **z** 96746; ● 265
Welokā; RMC Place; HAWAII; ***168** L-10; mail Papaaloa **z** 96780; rural
Wheeler AFB (Wheeler Army Field); CDP-Census Area Only; HONOLULU; ***168** L-3; ★ **HON**; mail Wheeler Army Airfield **z** 96854; Ⓟ 2,600; Ⓒ 2,829
Wheeler Army Field; HONOLULU; see Wheeler AFB (CDP-Census Area Only)
Whitmore; HONOLULU; see Whitmore Village (CDP)
Whitmore Village (Whitmore); CDP; HONOLULU; **168** L-3; elev. 1,002ft./305m.; ★ **HON**; mail Wahiawa **z** 96786; Ⓟ 3,373; Ⓒ 4,057
Wilhelmina Rise; RMC Place; HONOLULU; ***168** N-5; ★ **HON**; mail Honolulu **z** 96816; ● 620
Woodlawn; RMC Place; HONOLULU; ***168** N-5; ★ **HON**; mail Honolulu **z** 96822; ● 1,200
Wood Valley; RMC Place; HAWAII; ***168** N-9; elev. 2,260ft./689m.; mail Pahala **z** 96777; ● 60

IDAHO

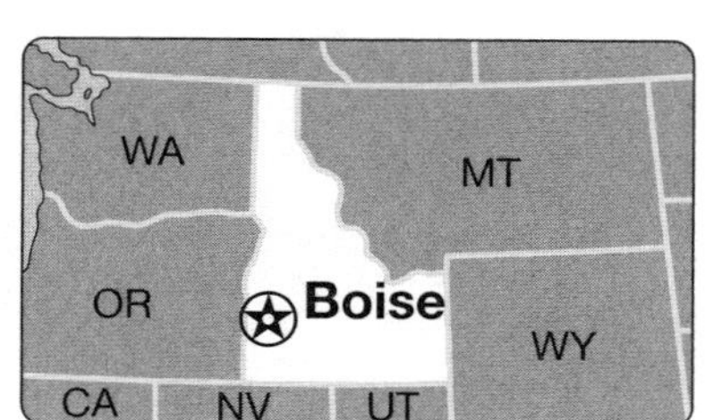

Statistics

Total area (2000) — 83,570 square miles
Land area (2000) — 82,747 square miles
Water area (2000) — 823 square miles
Capital — Boise (Boise City)
Admitted as state — July, 1890

Maps

State maps can be found on pages 142-254 in Vol. 1

Ranally Metro Areas (RMAs) and Abbreviations

Boise, ID — BOIS
Idaho Falls, ID — IDFL
Lewiston, ID-WA — LEW
Pocatello, ID — POC
Spokane, WA-ID — SPOK

Principal Places

Place Name	Place Type	County	Population
Boise	Inc. Place	ADA	◆ 217,984
Nampa	Inc. Place	CANYON	◆ 87,530
Meridian	Inc. Place	ADA	◆ 60,773
Idaho Falls	Inc. Place	BONNEVILLE	◆ 57,826
Pocatello	Inc. Place	BANNOCK	◆ 54,995
Coeur d'Alene	Inc. Place	KOOTENAI	◆ 43,718
Caldwell	Inc. Place	CANYON	◆ 42,961
Twin Falls	Inc. Place	TWIN FALLS	◆ 35,994
Lewiston	Inc. Place	NEZ PERCE	◆ 33,058
Rexburg	Inc. Place	MADISON	◆ 26,021

Place Name	Place Type	County	Population
Post Falls	Inc. Place	KOOTENAI	◆ 25,699
Moscow	Inc. Place	LATAH	◆ 22,340
Mountain Home	Inc. Place	ELMORE	© 11,143
Eagle	Inc. Place	ADA	© 11,085
Garden City	Inc. Place	ADA	© 10,624
Blackfoot	Inc. Place	BINGHAM	© 10,419
Chubbuck	Inc. Place	BANNOCK	© 9,700
Burley	Inc. Place	CASSIA	© 9,316
Hayden	Inc. Place	KOOTENAI	© 9,159
Mountain Home AFB	CDP-Census Area Only	ELMORE	© 8,894

Place Name	Place Type	County	Population
Jerome	Inc. Place	JEROME	© 7,780
Payette	Inc. Place	PAYETTE	© 7,054
Sandpoint	Inc. Place	BONNER	© 6,835
Hailey	Inc. Place	BLAINE	© 6,200
Ammon	Inc. Place	BONNEVILLE	© 6,187
Rupert	Inc. Place	MINIDOKA	© 5,645
Emmett	Inc. Place	GEM	© 5,490
Kuna	Inc. Place	ADA	© 5,382
Weiser	Inc. Place	WASHINGTON	© 5,343

County Business Data

County	FIPS Code	County Seat	Land Area (Sq. Mi.)	Census Population: 4/1/2000	Census Population: 4/1/1990	Census Population: % Change 1990-2000	Wholesale Trade: Sales, 2002 ($1,000)	Wholesale Trade: % Change 1997-2002	Manufacturing, 2002: Establish-ments	Manufacturing, 2002: Total Employees	Manufacturing, 2002: Value Added ($1,000)	Manufacturing, 2002: Ranally Mfg. Units
Ada	001	Boise	1,055	300,904	205,775	46.2	5,349,555	-0.2	405	20,195	3,437,063	1,818
Adams	003	Council	1,365	3,476	3,254	6.8	(d)	(d)	...	(d)	(d)	...
Bannock	005	Pocatello	1,113	75,565	66,026	14.4	283,310	0.3	72	(d)	(d)	...
Bear Lake	007	Paris	971	6,411	6,084	5.4	27,167	34.5	...	(d)	(d)	...
Benewah	009	Saint Maries	776	9,171	7,937	15.5	52,159	196.8	9	528	40,682	22
Bingham	011	Blackfoot	2,095	41,735	37,583	11.0	288,624	52.4	48	2,366	228,967	121
Blaine	013	Hailey	2,645	18,991	13,552	40.1	149,983	-12.9	...	(d)	(d)	...
Boise	015	Idaho City	1,902	6,670	3,509	90.1	(d)	(d)	...	(d)	(d)	...
Bonner	017	Sandpoint	1,738	36,835	26,622	38.4	(d)	(d)	89	1,581	135,838	72
Bonneville	019	Idaho Falls	1,868	82,522	72,207	14.3	(d)	(d)	120	2,160	246,476	130
Boundary	021	Bonners Ferry	1,269	9,871	8,332	18.5	13,341	-20.2	...	(d)	(d)	...
Butte	023	Arco	2,233	2,899	2,918	-0.7	(d)	(d)	...	(d)	(d)	...
Camas	025	Fairfield	1,075	991	727	36.3	(d)	(d)	...	(d)	(d)	...
Canyon	027	Caldwell	590	131,441	90,076	45.9	900,722	62.2	201	9,937	751,995	398
Caribou	029	Soda Springs	1,766	7,304	6,963	4.9	51,032	101.9	10	(d)	(d)	...
Cassia	031	Burley	2,566	21,416	19,532	9.6	148,715	-32.0	30	(d)	(d)	...
Clark	033	Dubois	1,765	1,022	762	34.1	(d)	(d)	...	(d)	(d)	...
Clearwater	035	Orofino	2,461	8,930	8,505	5.0	(d)	(d)	...	(d)	(d)	...
Custer	037	Challis	4,925	4,342	4,133	5.1	(d)	(d)	...	(d)	(d)	...
Elmore	039	Mountain Home	3,078	29,130	21,205	37.4	18,746	-6.8	...	(d)	(d)	...
Franklin	041	Preston	665	11,329	9,232	22.7	58,733	95.1	...	(d)	(d)	...
Fremont	043	Saint Anthony	1,867	11,819	10,937	8.1	68,549	-17.4	...	(d)	(d)	...
Gem	045	Emmett	563	15,181	11,844	28.2	(d)	(d)	...	(d)	(d)	...
Gooding	047	Gooding	731	14,155	11,633	21.7	(d)	(d)	...	(d)	(d)	...
Idaho	049	Grangeville	8,485	15,511	13,783	12.5	22,052	-42.9	31	519	38,992	21
Jefferson	051	Rigby	1,095	19,155	16,543	15.8	(d)	(d)	31	796	52,587	28
Jerome	053	Jerome	600	18,342	15,138	21.2	254,195	0.9	28	670	162,376	86
Kootenai	055	Coeur d'Alene	1,245	108,685	69,795	55.7	567,990	41.0	218	4,050	274,972	145
Latah	057	Moscow	1,077	34,935	30,617	14.1	91,074	-18.4	...	(d)	(d)	...
Lemhi	059	Salmon	4,564	7,806	6,899	13.1	6,947	-12.7	...	(d)	(d)	...
Lewis	061	Nezperce	479	3,747	3,516	6.6	21,781	-19.8	...	(d)	(d)	...
Lincoln	063	Shoshone	1,206	4,044	3,308	22.2	(d)	(d)	...	(d)	(d)	...
Madison	065	Rexburg	472	27,467	23,674	16.0	171,539	81.8	27	1,392	198,219	105
Minidoka	067	Rupert	760	20,174	19,361	4.2	276,067	74.3	26	(d)	(d)	...
Nez Perce	069	Lewiston	849	37,410	33,754	10.8	(d)	(d)	45	(d)	(d)	...
Oneida	071	Malad City	1,200	4,125	3,492	18.1	1,547	(d)	...	(d)	(d)	...
Owyhee	073	Murphy	7,678	10,644	8,392	26.8	(d)	(d)	...	(d)	(d)	...
Payette	075	Payette	408	20,578	16,434	25.2	(d)	(d)	23	(d)	(d)	...
Power	077	American Falls	1,406	7,538	7,086	6.4	63,121	-13.4	7	(d)	(d)	...
Shoshone	079	Wallace	2,634	13,771	13,931	-1.1	9,879	-70.1	...	(d)	(d)	...
Teton	081	Driggs	450	5,999	3,439	74.4	15,128	(d)	...	(d)	(d)	...
Twin Falls	083	Twin Falls	1,925	64,284	53,580	20.0	408,292	-9.4	102	3,132	307,077	162
Valley	085	Cascade	3,678	7,651	6,109	25.2	(d)	(d)	...	(d)	(d)	...
Washington	087	Weiser	1,456	9,977	8,550	16.7	39,664	-15.1	...	(d)	(d)	...
The State			**82,747**	**1,293,953**	**1,006,749**	**28.5**	**11,458,012**	**13.1**	**1,814**	**61,538**	**7,440,111**	**3,936**

(d) Data not available. Corresponding percentages or Ranally Manufacturing Units are estimates.
... Represents 0 or amount too minimal to be reported.

Index of Places and Counties

Entries in **UPPERCASE** are counties.
Entries in **bold** have populations of 2,500 or more.
Names in parentheses are alternate names.

Inc. Place	Incorporated Place
RMC Place	Rand McNally Designated Place
CDP	Census Designated Place
MCD	Minor Civil Division
⊡	County Seat
▲	Minor Civil Division
elev.	Elevation
🅿	Post Office
🄷	Hospital
🄲	College
■	Principal Business Center
★	Ranally Metro Area (RMA) Abbreviation
z	Zip Code(s)
Ⓟ	Previous Census Population
Ⓡ	Revised Census Population
Ⓐ	Annexation Population
●	Rand McNally Population Estimate
©	Final Census Population
Ⓢ	Special Census Population
◆	Estimated Population

For additional definitions see Glossary, Volume 1, and Introduction, Volume 2.

E

Eagle; Inc. Place; ADA; **169** K-2; elev. 2,550ft./777m.; 🅿; ★ **BOIS**; z 83616; Ⓟ 3,327; © 11,085

Eagle; RMC Place; SHOSHONE; ***169** D-3; mail Murray z 83874; rural

Eagle Rock; BONNEVILLE; see Gerrard (RMC Place)

Easley Hot Springs; RMC Place; BLAINE; ***169** K-4; mail Ketchum z 83340; rural

East Hope; Inc. Place; BONNER; **169** C-2; elev. 2,089ft./637m.; mail Hope z 83836; Ⓟ 215; © 200

East Kamiah; RMC Place; IDAHO; ***169** F-2; mail Kamiah z 83536; rural

East Lewiston; RMC Place; NEZ PERCE; ★ **LEW**; mail Lewiston z 83501; pop. incl. with Lewiston (Inc. Place)

Eastport; RMC Place; BOUNDARY; **169** A-2; elev. 2,633ft./803m.; 🅿; z 83826

Eaton; RMC Place; WASHINGTON; ***169** J-1; elev. 2,104ft./641m.; mail Weiser z 83672; rural

Echo Beach; RMC Place; KOOTENAI; ***169** C-1; mail Rathdrum z 83858; rural

Eddyville; RMC Place; KOOTENAI; ***169** D-2; mail Coeur D Alene z 83814; ● 130

Eden; Inc. Place; JEROME; **169** M-5; elev. 3,950ft./1,204m.; 🅿; z 83325; Ⓟ 314; © 411

Edgemere; RMC Place; BONNER; ***169** C-2; mail Priest River z 83856; rural

Edmonds; RMC Place; MADISON; ***169** J-8; elev. 4,858ft./1,481m.; mail Rexburg z 83440

Egin; RMC Place; FREMONT; ***169** J-8; mail Saint Anthony z 83445; ● 50

Elba; RMC Place; CASSIA; **169** M-6; elev. 5,130ft./1,564m.; 🅿; z 83342

Elk City; RMC Place; IDAHO; **169** G-3; elev. 4,000ft./1,219m.; 🅿; z 83525; ● 300

Elk River; Inc. Place; CLEARWATER; **169** E-2; elev. 2,841ft./866m.; 🅿; z 83827; Ⓟ 149; © 156

Ellis; RMC Place; CUSTER; **169** I-5; elev. 4,648ft./1,417m.; 🅿; z 83235; ● 40

Elmira; RMC Place; BONNER; ***169** B-2; elev. 2,149ft./655m.; rural

ELMORE; **169** L-3; Ⓟ 21,205; © 29,130; ◆ 30,141

Emida; RMC Place; BENEWAH; **169** E-2; elev. 2,850ft./869m.; mail Saint Maries z 83861; ● 100

Emmett; Inc. Place; ⊡ GEM; **169** J-2; elev. 2,379ft./725m.; 🅿 🅷; z 83617; Ⓟ 4,601; © 5,490

Enaville; RMC Place; SHOSHONE; ***169** D-2; mail Kingston z 83839; rural

Enrose; RMC Place; CANYON; ***169** K-1; mail Caldwell z 83605; rural

Evergreen; RMC Place; ADAMS; ***169** I-2; mail New Meadows z 83654; rural

Excelsior Beach; RMC Place; KOOTENAI; ***169** C-1; mail Rathdrum z 83858; rural

F

Fairfield; Inc. Place; ⊡ CAMAS; **169** K-4; elev. 5,060ft./1,542m.; 🅿; z 83322, z 83327; Ⓟ 371; © 395

Fairview; RMC Place; FRANKLIN; ***169** N-8; elev. 4,517ft./1,377m.; mail Preston z 83263

Fairview; RMC Place; TWIN FALLS; ***169** M-4; elev. 3,918ft./1,194m.; mail Buhl z 83316

Fall Creek; RMC Place; IDAHO; ***169** G-3; mail Grangeville z 83530; rural

Falls City; RMC Place; JEROME; ***169** M-4; elev. 3,838ft./1,170m.; mail Jerome z 83338; rural

Featherville; RMC Place; ELMORE; **169** K-3; 🅿; z 83647

Felt; RMC Place; TETON; **169** J-9; elev. 6,040ft./1,841m.; 🅿; z 83424

Fenn; RMC Place; IDAHO; **169** G-2; 🅿; z 83531; ● 30

Ferdinand; Inc. Place; IDAHO; **169** F-2; elev. 3,728ft./1,136m.; 🅿; z 83526; Ⓟ 135; © 145

Fernan Lake Village; Inc. Place; KOOTENAI; **169** D-2; elev. 2,160ft./658m.; mail Coeur D Alene z 83814; Ⓟ 170; © 186

Fernwood; RMC Place; BENEWAH; **169** E-2; elev. 2,707ft./825m.; 🅿; z 83830 & mail Clarkia z 83812; ● 425

Filer; Inc. Place; TWIN FALLS; **169** M-4; elev. 3,756ft./1,145m.; 🅿; z 83328; Ⓟ 1,511; © 1,620

Firth; Inc. Place; BINGHAM; **169** K-7; elev. 4,555ft./1,388m.; 🅿; z 83236; Ⓟ 429; © 408

Fish Haven; RMC Place; BEAR LAKE; **169** N-8; elev. 5,951ft./1,814m.; 🅿; z 83287; ● 50

Florence; RMC Place; IDAHO; ***169** H-2; mail Lucile z 83542; rural

Fort Hall; CDP; BANNOCK, BINGHAM; ***169** L-7; elev. 4,448ft./1,356m.; 🅿; z 83203; Ⓟ 2,681; © 3,193

Fort Hall Reservation; Indian Reservation; BINGHAM, BANNOCK, CARIBOU, POWER; mail Fort Hall z 83203; also location of Indian Agency; Ⓟ 4,783; © 5,760

Fort Wilson; RMC Place; PAYETTE; mail Payette z 83661; rural

Fox Creek; RMC Place; TETON; ***169** K-9; mail Victor z 83455

Franklin; RMC Place; ADA; ★ **BOIS**; mail Boise z 83704; pop. incl. with Boise (Inc. Place)

Franklin; Inc. Place; FRANKLIN; **169** N-8; elev. 4,504ft./1,373m.; 🅿; z 83237; Ⓟ 478; © 641

FRANKLIN; **169** M-8; Ⓟ 9,232; © 11,329; ◆ 12,514

Franklin Park; RMC Place; ADA; ★ **BOIS**; mail Boise z 83704; pop. incl. with Boise (Inc. Place)

Fraser; RMC Place; CLEARWATER; ***169** F-2; elev. 3,100ft./945m.; mail Orofino z 83544; rural

Freedom; RMC Place; CARIBOU; ***169** L-9; 🅿; z 83120; total pop., including Freedom, WY, 550; ● 100

FREMONT; **169** J-8; Ⓟ 10,937; © 11,819; ◆ 12,794

Frisco; RMC Place; SHOSHONE; ***169** D-3; mail Wallace z 83873; rural

Fruitland; Inc. Place; PAYETTE; **169** J-1; elev. 3,083ft./940m.; 🅿; z 83619; Ⓟ 2,400; © 3,805

Fruitvale; RMC Place; ADAMS; **169** I-2; elev. 2,226ft./678m.; 🅿; z 83612; ● 100

G

Galena; RMC Place; BLAINE; ***169** J-4; mail Ketchum z 83340

Gannett; RMC Place; BLAINE; ***169** K-5; 🅿; z 83313

Gardena; RMC Place; BOISE; ***169** J-2; elev. 2,670ft./814m.; mail Horseshoe Bend z 83629

Garden City; Inc. Place; ADA; **169** B-5; elev. 2,650ft./808m.; 🅿; ★ **BOIS**; z 83703, z 83714; Ⓟ 6,369; © 10,624

Garden Valley; RMC Place; BOISE; **169** J-2; elev. 3,120ft./951m.; 🅿; z 83622; ● 200

Garfield (Midas); RMC Place; BONNER; ***169** C-2; mail Sandpoint z 83864; ● 170

Garfield; RMC Place; JEFFERSON; ***169** K-8; ★ **IDFL**; mail Rigby z 83442; rural

Garwood; RMC Place; KOOTENAI; ***169** C-2; mail Hayden z 83835; rural

Gem; RMC Place; SHOSHONE; ***169** D-3; mail Wallace z 83873; rural

GEM; **169** J-2; Ⓟ 11,844; © 15,181; ◆ 16,899

Genesee; Inc. Place; LATAH; **169** F-1; elev. 2,675ft./815m.; 🅿; z 83832; Ⓟ 725; © 946

Geneva; RMC Place; BEAR LAKE; **169** M-9; 🅿; z 83238; rural

Georgetown; Inc. Place; BEAR LAKE; **169** M-8; elev. 6,006ft./1,831m.; 🅿; z 83239; Ⓟ 558; © 538

Gerrard (Eagle Rock); RMC Place; BONNEVILLE; ***169** K-7; mail Idaho Falls z 83402

Gibbonsville; RMC Place; LEMHI; **169** G-5; elev. 4,600ft./1,402m.; 🅿; z 83463

Gibson; RMC Place; BINGHAM; ***169** L-7; located on Fort Hall Ind. Res.; mail Blackfoot z 83221, Fort Hall z 83203; rural

Gibson City; RMC Place; SHOSHONE; mail Pinehurst z 83850; pop. incl. with Pinehurst (Inc. Place)

Gifford; RMC Place; NEZ PERCE; ***169** F-2; mail Lenore z 83541

Givens Hot Springs; RMC Place; OWYHEE; **169** K-1; elev. 2,315ft./706m.; mail Melba z 83641; ● 120

Glendale; RMC Place; FRANKLIN; ***169** N-8; mail Preston z 83263; rural

Glengary; RMC Place; BONNER; ***169** C-2; mail Sandpoint z 83864

Glenns Ferry; Inc. Place; ELMORE; **169** L-3; elev. 2,560ft./780m.; 🅿; z 83623 & mail King Hill z 83633; Ⓟ 1,304; © 1,611

Glenwood; RMC Place; CLEARWATER; mail Orofino z 83544; pop. incl. with Orofino (Inc. Place)

Glenwood; RMC Place; IDAHO; ***169** F-3; elev. 3,130ft./954m.; mail Kamiah z 83536; rural

Golden; RMC Place; IDAHO; ***169** G-3; mail Grangeville z 83530

Gooding; Inc. Place; ⊡ GOODING; **169** L-4; elev. 3,573ft./1,089m.; 🅿 🅷; z 83330; Ⓟ 2,820; © 3,384; Ⓡ 3,387

GOODING; **169** L-4; Ⓟ 11,633; © 14,155; Ⓡ 14,158; ◆ 14,357

Goodrich; RMC Place; ADAMS; ***169** I-2; mail Council z 83612

Goshen; RMC Place; BINGHAM; ***169** K-7; mail Shelley z 83274

Grace; Inc. Place; CARIBOU; **169** M-8; elev. 5,533ft./1,686m.; 🅿; z 83241, z 83283; Ⓟ 973; © 990

Grandview; RMC Place; BINGHAM; ***169** L-7; mail Aberdeen z 83210; rural

Grand View; Inc. Place; OWYHEE; **169** L-2; elev. 2,365ft./721m.; 🅿; z 83624; Ⓟ 330; © 470

Grangemont; RMC Place; CLEARWATER; ***169** F-2; elev. 3,235ft./986m.; mail Orofino z 83544; rural

Grangeville; Inc. Place; ⊡ IDAHO; **169** G-2; elev. 3,390ft./1,033m.; 🅿 🅷; z 83530-31; Ⓟ 3,226; © 3,228

Granite; RMC Place; BONNER; ***169** C-2; mail Athol z 83801; rural

Grant; RMC Place; JEFFERSON; ***169** K-8; elev. 4,785ft./1,458m.; mail Rigby z 83442; rural

Grasmere; RMC Place; OWYHEE; ***169** M-2; 🅿; z 83604; rural

Gray; RMC Place; BONNEVILLE; ***169** L-8; mail Soda Springs z 83276, Wayan z 83285; rural

Greencreek; RMC Place; IDAHO; **169** F-2; elev. 3,183ft./970m.; 🅿; z 83533; ● 30

Greenleaf; Inc. Place; CANYON; **169** K-1; elev. 2,421ft./738m.; 🅿; z 83626; Ⓟ 648; © 862

Greenwood; RMC Place; JEROME; ***169** M-5; elev. 4,101ft./1,250m.; mail Hazelton z 83335; rural

Greer; RMC Place; CLEARWATER; **169** F-2; located on Nez Perce Ind. Res.; mail Orofino z 83544

Gross; RMC Place; GEM; ***169** J-2; mail Ola z 83657; rural

Groveland; RMC Place; BINGHAM; ***169** L-7; mail Blackfoot z 83221; ● 350

Gwenford; RMC Place; ONEIDA; ***169** N-7; elev. 4,440ft./1,353m.; mail Malad City z 83252; rural

H

Hagerman; Inc. Place; GOODING; **169** L-4; elev. 2,959ft./902m.; 🅿; z 83332; Ⓟ 600; © 656

Hailey; Inc. Place; ⊡ BLAINE; **169** K-5; elev. 5,330ft./1,625m.; 🅿 🅷; z 83333; Ⓟ 3,687; © 6,200

Hamer; Inc. Place; JEFFERSON; **169** J-7; elev. 4,814ft./1,467m.; 🅿; z 83425; Ⓟ 79; © 12

Hamilton Corner; RMC Place; PAYETTE; mail New Plymouth z 83655; rural

Hammett; RMC Place; ELMORE; **169** L-3; elev. 2,531ft./771m.; 🅿; z 83627; ● 300

Hampton; RMC Place; LATAH; ***169** E-1; mail Princeton z 83857; ● 35

Hansen; Inc. Place; TWIN FALLS; **169** M-5; elev. 4,030ft./1,228m.; 🅿; z 83334; Ⓟ 848; © 970

Harpster; RMC Place; IDAHO; **169** G-2; 🅿; z 83552 & mail Kooskia z 83539; ● 50

Harrison; Inc. Place; KOOTENAI; **169** D-2; elev. 2,135ft./651m.; 🅿; z 83833 & mail Medimont z 83842; Ⓟ 226; © 267

Harvard; RMC Place; LATAH; **169** E-2; elev. 2,600ft./792m.; 🅿; z 83834; ● 55

Hatch; RMC Place; CARIBOU; ***169** L-8; mail Bancroft z 83217; rural

Hatwai; RMC Place; NEZ PERCE; ***169** F-1; elev. 785ft./239m.; ★ **LEW**; mail Lewiston z 83501; rural

Hauser (Hauser Lake); Inc. Place; KOOTENAI; ***169** C-1; elev. 2,200ft./671m.; 🅿; z 83854; Ⓟ 380; © 668

Hauser Lake; KOOTENAI; see Hauser (Inc. Place)

Havens; RMC Place; BINGHAM; ***169** L-7; mail Blackfoot z 83221; rural

Hawkins; RMC Place; BANNOCK; ***169** M-7; mail Arimo z 83214, Downey z 83234; rural

Hayden; Inc. Place; KOOTENAI; **169** C-2; elev. 2,276ft./694m.; 🅿; z 83835; Ⓟ 3,744; © 9,159

Hayden Lake; Inc. Place; KOOTENAI; **169** C-2; elev. 2,280ft./695m.; 🅿; z 83835; Ⓟ 338; © 494

Hazelton; Inc. Place; JEROME; **169** M-5; elev. 4,080ft./1,244m.; 🅿; z 83335; Ⓟ 394; © 687

Headquarters; RMC Place; CLEARWATER; **169** E-3; elev. 3,136ft./956m.; 🅿; z 83546; ● 35

Heglar; RMC Place; CASSIA; ***169** M-6; elev. 4,726ft./1,440m.; mail American Falls z 83211; rural

Heise; RMC Place; JEFFERSON; ***169** K-8; elev. 5,000ft./1,524m.; mail Ririe z 83443

Helmer; RMC Place; LATAH; **169** E-2; mail Deary z 83823

Heman; RMC Place; FREMONT; ***169** J-8; mail Saint Anthony z 83445; rural

Henry; RMC Place; CARIBOU; ***169** L-8; mail Conda z 83230

Heyburn; Inc. Place; MINIDOKA; **169** M-5; elev. 4,150ft./1,265m.; 🅿; z 83336; Ⓟ 2,714; © 2,899

Hibbard; RMC Place; MADISON; ***169** J-8; mail Rexburg z 83440

Highlands; RMC Place; ADA; ***169** K-2; ★ **BOIS**; mail Boise z 83702; pop. incl. with Boise (Inc. Place)

Hill City; RMC Place; CAMAS; **169** K-4; elev. 5,092ft./1,552m.; 🅿; z 83337

Hillview; RMC Place; BONNEVILLE; ***169** K-8; ★ **IDFL**; mail Idaho Falls z 83401

Holbrook; RMC Place; ONEIDA; **169** M-7; elev. 4,779ft./1,457m.; 🅿; z 83243

Hollister; Inc. Place; TWIN FALLS; **169** M-4; elev. 4,520ft./1,378m.; 🅿; z 83301; Ⓟ 144; © 237

Home Acres; RMC Place; ADA; ★ **BOIS**; mail Boise z 83704; pop. incl. with Boise (Inc. Place)

Homedale; Inc. Place; OWYHEE; **169** K-1; elev. 2,230ft./680m.; 🅿; z 83628; Ⓟ 1,963; © 2,528

Honeysuckle Hills; RMC Place; KOOTENAI; ***169** C-2; mail Hayden z 83835; ● 120

Hop; RMC Place; CANYON; mail Greenleaf z 83626; pop. incl. with Greenleaf (Inc. Place)

Hope; Inc. Place; BONNER; **169** C-2; elev. 2,200ft./671m.; 🅿; z 83836; Ⓟ 99; © 79

Horseshoe Bend; Inc. Place; BOISE; **169** J-2; elev. 2,604ft./794m.; 🅿; z 83629; Ⓟ 643; © 770

Hot Springs; RMC Place; OWYHEE; ***169** L-3; mail Bruneau z 83604; rural

Howe; RMC Place; BUTTE; **169** K-6; elev. 4,824ft./1,470m.; 🅿; z 83244; ● 80

Hoyt; RMC Place; SHOSHONE; ***169** D-3; mail Avery z 83802; ● 40

Huetter; Inc. Place; KOOTENAI; ***169** D-1; elev. 2,167ft./661m.; ★ **SPOK**; mail Post Falls z 83854; Ⓟ 82; © 96

Humphrey; RMC Place; CLARK; ***169** I-7; mail Spencer z 83446; rural

Hunt; RMC Place; JEROME; ***169** M-5; mail Eden z 83325, Hazelton z 83335; rural

Huston; RMC Place; CANYON; ***169** K-1; elev. 2,500ft./762m.; 🅿; z 83630; ● 150

I

IDAHO; **169** G-3; Ⓟ 13,783; © 15,511; ◆ 15,545

Idaho City; Inc. Place; ⊡ BOISE; **169** K-3; elev. 3,906ft./1,191m.; 🅿; z 83631 & mail Atlanta z 83601; Ⓟ 322; © 458

Idaho Falls; Inc. Place; ⊡ BONNEVILLE; **169** K-7; elev. 4,710ft./1,436m.; 🅿 🅷 ■; ★ **IDFL**; z 83401-06, z 83415; Ⓟ 43,929; © 50,730; ◆ 57,826

Idahome; RMC Place; CASSIA; ***169** M-6; elev. 4,422ft./1,348m.; mail Declo z 83323; rural

Idmon; RMC Place; CLARK; ***169** J-8; mail Dubois z 83423; rural

Indian Cove; RMC Place; OWYHEE; ***169** L-3; mail Hammett z 83627

Indian Hills; RMC Place; BANNOCK; ★ **POC**; mail Pocatello z 83204; pop. incl. with Pocatello (Inc. Place)

Indian Valley; RMC Place; ADAMS; **169** I-2; elev. 3,002ft./915m.; 🅿; z 83632; ● 75

Inkom; Inc. Place; BANNOCK; **169** L-7; elev. 4,520ft./1,378m.; 🅿; z 83245; Ⓟ 769; © 738

Iona; Inc. Place; BONNEVILLE; **169** K-8; elev. 4,782ft./1,458m.; 🅿; ★ **IDFL**; z 83427; Ⓟ 1,049; © 1,201

Irwin; Inc. Place; BONNEVILLE; **169** K-8; elev. 5,326ft./1,623m.; 🅿; z 83428; Ⓟ 108; © 157

Island Park; Inc. Place; FREMONT; **169** I-8; elev. 6,290ft./1,917m.; 🅿; z 83429, z 83433; Ⓟ 159; © 215

J

Jackson; RMC Place; CASSIA; ***169** M-5; elev. 4,160ft./1,268m.; 🅿; z 83350; rural

Jacques; RMC Place; NEZ PERCE; ***169** F-2; mail Culdesac z 83524; rural

JEFFERSON; **169** J-7; Ⓟ 16,543; © 19,155; ◆ 24,733

Jerome; Inc. Place; ⊡ JEROME; **169** M-4; elev. 3,781ft./1,152m.; 🅿 🅷; z 83338; Ⓟ 6,529; © 7,780

JEROME; **169** L-5; Ⓟ 15,138; © 18,342; ◆ 20,829

Joel; RMC Place; LATAH; **169** E-1; mail Moscow z 83843; ● 100

Johnny Creek; RMC Place; BANNOCK; ★ **POC**; mail Pocatello z 83204; pop. incl. with Pocatello (Inc. Place)

Jonathan; RMC Place; WASHINGTON; ***169** J-1; mail Weiser z 83672; rural

Joseph; RMC Place; IDAHO; ***169** G-2; mail Cottonwood z 83522; rural

Judge Town; RMC Place; CLEARWATER; ***169** F-3; mail Pierce z 83546; ● 35

Juliaetta; Inc. Place; LATAH; **169** F-2; elev. 1,075ft./328m.; 🅿; z 83535; Ⓟ 488; © 609

Juniper; RMC Place; ONEIDA; ***169** N-6; mail Snowville z 84336; rural

K

Kamiah; Inc. Place; LEWIS, IDAHO; **169** F-2; located on Nez Perce Ind. Res.; elev. 1,195ft./364m.; 🅿; z 83536; Ⓟ 1,157; © 1,160

Kellogg (Kellogg Wardner); Inc. Place; SHOSHONE; **169** D-2; elev. 2,308ft./703m.; 🅿 🅷; z 83837; Ⓟ 2,591; © 2,395

Kellogg Wardner; SHOSHONE; see Kellogg (Inc. Place)

Kendrick; Inc. Place; LATAH; **169** E-2; elev. 1,242ft./379m.; 🅿; z 83537; Ⓟ 325; © 369

Ketchum; Inc. Place; BLAINE; **169** K-4; elev. 5,820ft./1,774m.; 🅿; z 83340; Ⓟ 2,523; © 3,003

Keuterville; RMC Place; IDAHO; ***169** G-2; elev. 4,170ft./1,271m.; 🅿; z 83522; ● 30

Kidder; RMC Place; IDAHO; ***169** F-3; elev. 3,298ft./1,005m.; mail Kooskia z 83539; rural

Kilgore; RMC Place; CLARK; ***169** I-8; mail Dubois z 83423

Kimball; RMC Place; BINGHAM; ***169** L-7; mail Firth z 83236

Kimberly; Inc. Place; TWIN FALLS; **169** M-4; elev. 3,920ft./1,195m.; 🅿; z 83341; Ⓟ 2,367; © 2,614

King Hill; RMC Place; ELMORE; **169** L-3; elev. 2,529ft./771m.; 🅿; z 83633; ● 100

Kings Corner; RMC Place; CANYON; ***169** K-2; ★ **BOIS**; mail Nampa z 83686

Kingston; RMC Place; SHOSHONE; **169** D-2; 🅿; z 83839; ● 800

Knowlton Heights; RMC Place; CANYON; ***169** K-1; elev. 2,367ft./721m.; mail Caldwell z 83605; rural

Knull; RMC Place; TWIN FALLS; mail Twin Falls z 83301; ● 200

Kooskia; Inc. Place; IDAHO; **169** F-2; elev. 1,252ft./382m.; 🅿; z 83539; Ⓟ 692; © 675

Kootenai; Inc. Place; BONNER; **169** B-2; elev. 2,112ft./644m.; 🅿; z 83840; Ⓟ 327; © 441

KOOTENAI; **169** C-2; Ⓟ 69,795; © 108,685; ◆ 140,843

Kootenai Reservation; Indian Reservation; BOUNDARY; © 75

Kuna; Inc. Place; ADA; **169** K-2; 🅿; ★ **BOIS**; z 83634; Ⓟ 1,955; © 5,382

L

Labelle; RMC Place; JEFFERSON; ***169** K-8; ★ **IDFL**; mail Rigby z 83442

Laclede; RMC Place; BONNER; **169** C-2; elev. 2,100ft./640m.; 🅿; z 83841; ● 400

Lake Fork; RMC Place; VALLEY; **169** I-2; elev. 4,980ft./1,518m.; 🅿; z 83635; ● 120

Lakeview; RMC Place; BONNER; **169** C-2; mail Bayview z 83803; ● 40

Lamb Creek; RMC Place; BONNER; ***169** B-1; mail Priest River z 83856; ● 120

Lamont; RMC Place; FREMONT; ***169** J-9; mail Ashton z 83420; rural

Lanark; RMC Place; BEAR LAKE; ***169** M-8; elev. 5,953ft./1,814m.; mail Montpelier z 83254; rural

Lancaster Terrace; RMC Place; ADA; ★ **BOIS**; mail Boise z 83702; pop. incl. with Boise (Inc. Place)

Lane; RMC Place; KOOTENAI; ***169** D-2; mail Cataldo z 83810; rural

Lapwai; Inc. Place; NEZ PERCE; **169** F-1; located on Nez Perce Ind. Res.; elev. 964ft./294m.; 🅿; z 83540; location of Northern Idaho Indian Agency; Ⓟ 932; © 1,134

Lardo; RMC Place; VALLEY; mail McCall z 83638; pop. incl. with McCall (Inc. Place)

Last Chance Resort; RMC Place; FREMONT; mail Island Park z 83429; pop. incl. with Island Park (Inc. Place)

LATAH; **169** E-2; Ⓟ 30,617; © 34,935; ◆ 35,307

Lava Hot Springs; Inc. Place; BANNOCK; **169** M-8; 🅿; z 83246; Ⓟ 420; © 521

Leadore; Inc. Place; LEMHI; **169** I-6; elev. 5,989ft./1,825m.; 🅿; z 83464; Ⓟ 74; © 90

Leland; RMC Place; NEZ PERCE; ***169** F-2; mail Kendrick z 83537; ● 25

Lemhi; RMC Place; LEMHI; **169** I-5; elev. 5,200ft./1,585m.; 🅿; z 83465; ● 30

LEMHI; **169** H-5; Ⓟ 6,899; © 7,806; ◆ 7,643

Lenore; RMC Place; NEZ PERCE; **169** F-2; elev. 920ft./280m.; 🅿; z 83541

Leslie; RMC Place; CUSTER; ***169** J-6; elev. 5,700ft./1,737m.; mail Moore z 83255

Letha; RMC Place; GEM; **169** J-1; elev. 2,285ft./696m.; 🅿; z 83636; ● 240

LEWIS; **169** F-2; Ⓟ 3,516; © 3,747; ◆ 3,484

Lewiston; Inc. Place; ⊡ NEZ PERCE; **169** F-1; elev. 739ft./225m.; 🅿 🅷 🅲 3,394 ■; ★ **LEW**; z 83501; Ⓟ 28,082; © 30,904; ◆ 33,058

Lewiston Orchards; RMC Place; NEZ PERCE; ***169** F-1; ★ **LEW**; mail Lewiston z 83501; pop. incl. with Lewiston (Inc. Place)

Lewisville; Inc. Place; JEFFERSON; **169** K-7; elev. 4,795ft./1,462m.; 🅿; z 83431; Ⓟ 471; © 467

Liberty; RMC Place; BEAR LAKE; **169** M-8; elev. 5,980ft./1,823m.; mail Montpelier z 83254

Lidy Hot Springs; RMC Place; CLARK; ***169** J-7; mail Dubois z 83423; rural

Lincoln; RMC Place; BONNEVILLE; **169** K-8; elev. 4,754ft./1,449m.; ★ **IDFL**; mail Idaho Falls z 83401; ● 500

LINCOLN; **169** L-5; Ⓟ 3,308; © 4,044; ◆ 4,685

Lone Pine; RMC Place; CLARK; ***169** J-6; mail Leadore z 83464; rural

Lorenzo; RMC Place; JEFFERSON; **169** K-8; ★ **IDFL**; mail Rigby z 83442; ● 100

Lost River; RMC Place; BUTTE; **169** K-5; elev. 6,160ft./1,878m.; mail Moore z 83255; disincorporated since 2000 Census; Ⓟ 29; © 26

Lost River; RMC Place; BUTTE; ***169** K-6; mail Moore z 83255; rural

Lowell; RMC Place; IDAHO; **169** F-3; mail Kooskia z 83539; ● 25

Lower Stanley; RMC Place; CUSTER; ***169** J-4; mail Stanley z 83278; ● 25

Lowman; RMC Place; BOISE; **169** J-3; elev. 3,850ft./1,173m.; 🅿; z 83637; ● 50

Lucile; RMC Place; IDAHO; **169** G-2; elev. 1,689ft./515m.; 🅿; z 83542; ● 100

Lund; RMC Place; CARIBOU; ***169** M-8; elev. 5,485ft./1,672m.; mail Bancroft z 83217; rural

Lyman; RMC Place; MADISON; ***169** K-8; mail Rexburg z 83440

M

Mace; RMC Place; SHOSHONE; ***169** D-3; mail Wallace z 83873; rural

Mackay; Inc. Place; CUSTER; **169** J-5; elev. 5,900ft./1,798m.; 🅿; z 83251; Ⓟ 574; © 566

Macks Inn; RMC Place; FREMONT; ***169** I-8; 🅿; z 83433

MADISON; **169** K-8; Ⓟ 23,674; © 27,467; ◆ 38,096

Magic City; RMC Place; BLAINE; ***169** K-4; mail Bellevue z 83313, Hailey z 83333

Malad; ONEIDA; see Malad City (Inc. Place)

Malad City (Malad); Inc. Place; ⊡ ONEIDA; **169** M-7; elev. 4,700ft./1,433m.; 🅿 🅷; z 83252; Ⓟ 1,946; © 2,158

Malta; Inc. Place; CASSIA; **169** M-6; 🅿; z 83342; Ⓟ 171; © 177

Mapleton; RMC Place; FRANKLIN; ***169** N-8; elev. 4,691ft./1,430m.; mail Preston z 83263

Marble Creek; RMC Place; SHOSHONE; ***169** D-2; elev. 2,301ft./701m.; mail Calder z 83808; ● 25

Marion; RMC Place; CASSIA; ***169** M-5; elev. 4,477ft./1,365m.; mail Oakley z 83346; rural

Marley; RMC Place; LINCOLN; mail Richfield z 83349; rural

Marsing; Inc. Place; OWYHEE; **169** K-1; elev. 2,249ft./685m.; 🅿; z 83639; Ⓟ 798; © 890

Marysville; RMC Place; FREMONT; **169** J-8; mail Ashton z 83420; ● 180

May; RMC Place; LEMHI; **169** I-5; elev. 5,068ft./1,545m.; 🅿; z 83253; ● 50

McArthur; RMC Place; BOUNDARY; ***169** B-2; mail Naples z 83847; rural

McCall; Inc. Place; VALLEY; **169** I-2; elev. 5,030ft./1,533m.; 🅿 🅷; z 83635, z 83638; Ⓟ 2,005; © 2,084

McCammon; Inc. Place; BANNOCK; **169** M-7; elev. 4,719ft./1,438m.; 🅿; z 83250; Ⓟ 722; © 805

McGuire (McGuires); RMC Place; KOOTENAI; ***169** C-1; ★ **SPOK**; mail Post Falls z 83854

McGuires; KOOTENAI; see McGuire (RMC Place)

Meadow Creek; RMC Place; BOUNDARY; ***169** B-2; mail Bonners Ferry z 83805; rural

Meadows; RMC Place; ADAMS; **169** H-2; elev. 3,981ft./1,213m.; mail New Meadows z 83654; ● 190

Meadowville; RMC Place; CARIBOU; ***169** L-8; mail Soda Springs z 83276; rural

Medimont; RMC Place; KOOTENAI; **169** D-2; elev. 2,140ft./652m.; 🅿; z 83842

Melba; Inc. Place; CANYON; **169** K-2; 🅿; z 83641; Ⓟ 252; © 439

Menan; Inc. Place; JEFFERSON; **169** K-8; elev. 4,795ft./1,462m.; 🅿; z 83434; Ⓟ 601; © 707

Meridian; Inc. Place; ADA; **169** K-2; elev. 2,607ft./795m.; 🅿; ★ **BOIS**; z 83642, z 83646, z 83680; Ⓟ 9,596; © 34,919; ◆ 60,773

Mesa; RMC Place; ADAMS; **169** I-2; elev. 3,243ft./988m.; 🅿; z 83643; ● 65

Mica; RMC Place; KOOTENAI; ***169** D-1; elev. 2,575ft./785m.; mail Coeur D Alene z 83814; rural

Midas; BONNER; see Garfield (RMC Place)

Middleton; Inc. Place; CANYON; **169** K-2; elev. 2,398ft./731m.; 🅿; z 83644; Ⓟ 1,851; © 2,978

Midvale; Inc. Place; WASHINGTON; **169** I-1; elev. 2,552ft./778m.; 🅿; z 83645; Ⓟ 110; © 176

Midway; BINGHAM; see Atomic City (Inc. Place)

Midway; RMC Place; CANYON; ***169** K-2; ★ **BOIS**; mail Nampa z 83651; rural

Miller Creek Settlement; RMC Place; OWYHEE; ***169** N-2; mail Owyhee z 89832; rural

Milltown; RMC Place; BENEWAH; ***169** D-2; mail Saint Maries z 83861; ● 100

Milo; RMC Place; BONNEVILLE; ***169** K-8; ★ **IDFL**; mail Idaho Falls z 83401, Rigby z 83442

Minidoka; Inc. Place; MINIDOKA; **169** L-6; elev. 4,286ft./1,306m.; 🅿; z 83343, z 83350; Ⓟ 67; © 129

MINIDOKA; **169** L-5; Ⓟ 19,361; © 20,174; ◆ 18,615

Mink Creek; RMC Place; FRANKLIN; ***169** M-8; mail Preston z 83263

Mohler; RMC Place; LEWIS; ***169** F-2; located on Nez Perce Ind. Res.; mail Craigmont z 83523; rural

Montana Junction; RMC Place; BANNOCK; ★ **POC**; mail Pocatello z 83201; pop. incl. with Pocatello (Inc. Place)

Monteview; RMC Place; JEFFERSON; **169** J-7; elev. 4,789ft./1,460m.; 🅿; z 83435; rural

Montour; RMC Place; GEM; ***169** J-2; 🅿; z 83617; rural

Montpelier; Inc. Place; BEAR LAKE; **169** M-8; elev. 5,964ft./1,818m.; 🅿 🅷; z 83254 & mail Bern z 83220, Dingle z 83233; Ⓟ 2,656; © 2,785

Moore; Inc. Place; BUTTE; **169** K-6; elev. 5,500ft./1,676m.; 🅿; z 83255; Ⓟ 190; © 196

Mora; RMC Place; ADA; ***169** K-2; mail Kuna z 83634; rural

Moravia; RMC Place; BOUNDARY; ***169** B-2; mail Bonners Ferry z 83805

Moreland; RMC Place; BINGHAM; **169** L-7; elev. 4,460ft./1,359m.; 🅿; z 83256; ● 500

Morgans Alley; RMC Place; NEZ PERCE; ★ **LEW**; mail Lewiston z 83501; pop. incl. with Lewiston (Inc. Place)

Moscow; Inc. Place; ⊡ LATAH; **169** E-1; elev. 2,583ft./787m.; 🅿 🅷 🅲 11,739 ■; z 83843-44; Ⓟ 18,519; © 21,291; ◆ 22,340

Mountain Home; Inc. Place; ⊡ ELMORE; **169** L-3; elev. 3,143ft./958m.; 🅿 🅷; z 83647; Ⓟ 7,913; © 11,143

Mountain Home AFB; CDP-Census Area Only; ELMORE; ***169** L-2; 🅿; z 83648; Ⓟ 5,936; © 8,894

Mountain View; RMC Place; ADA; ***169** K-2; ★ **BOIS**; mail Boise z 83704; pop. incl. with Boise (Inc. Place)

Mount Idaho; RMC Place; IDAHO; ***169** G-2; mail Grangeville z 83530

Moyie Springs; Inc. Place; BOUNDARY; **169** B-2; elev. 2,200ft./671m.; 🅿; z 83845; Ⓟ 415; © 656

Mud Lake; Inc. Place; JEFFERSON; **169** J-7; elev. 4,785ft./1,458m.; mail Terreton z 83450; Ⓟ 179; © 270

Mullan; Inc. Place; SHOSHONE; **169** D-3; elev. 3,277ft./999m.; 🅿; z 83846; Ⓟ 821; © 840

Murphy; RMC Place; ⊡ OWYHEE; **169** L-2; elev. 2,823ft./860m.; 🅿; z 83650; ● 100

Murray; RMC Place; SHOSHONE; **169** D-3; elev. 2,800ft./853m.; 🅿; z 83874; ● 75

Murtaugh; Inc. Place; TWIN FALLS; **169** M-5; elev. 4,082ft./1,244m.; 🅿; z 83344; Ⓟ 134; © 139

Myrtle; RMC Place; NEZ PERCE; ***169** F-2; mail Juliaetta z 83535

N

Naf; RMC Place; CASSIA; ***169** N-6; elev. 5,260ft./1,603m.; mail Malta z 83342; rural

Nampa; Inc. Place; CANYON; **169** K-2; elev. 2,490ft./759m.; 🅿 🅷 🅲 1,755 ■; ★ **BOIS**; z 83651-53, z 83686-87; Ⓟ 28,365; © 51,867; ◆ 87,530

Naples; RMC Place; BOUNDARY; **169** B-2; elev. 2,038ft./621m.; 🅿; z 83847; ● 450

Neeley; RMC Place; POWER; ***169** L-6; elev. 4,317ft./1,316m.; mail American Falls z 83211

New Centerville; RMC Place; BOISE; **169** J-2; elev. 4,122ft./1,256m.; 🅿; z 83631; rural

Newdale; Inc. Place; FREMONT; **169** J-8; elev. 5,068ft./1,545m.; 🅿; z 83436; Ⓟ 377; © 358

New Meadows; Inc. Place; ADAMS; **169** H-2; elev. 3,868ft./1,179m.; 🅿; z 83654; Ⓟ 534; © 533

New Plymouth; Inc. Place; PAYETTE; **169** J-1; elev. 2,255ft./687m.; 🅿; z 83655 & mail Letha z 83636; Ⓟ 1,313; © 1,400

Nezperce; Inc. Place; ⊡ LEWIS; **169** F-2; located on Nez Perce Ind. Res.; elev. 3,150ft./960m.; 🅿; z 83543; Ⓟ 453; © 523

NEZ PERCE; **169** F-1; Ⓟ 33,754; © 37,410; ◆ 39,628

Nez Perce Reservation; Indian Reservation; NEZ PERCE, CLEARWATER, IDAHO, LEWIS; mail Lapwai z 83540; also location of Indian Agency; Ⓟ 17,806; © 17,959

Niter; RMC Place; CARIBOU; ***169** M-8; mail Grace z 83241

Nordman; RMC Place; BONNER; **169** B-1; elev. 2,650ft./808m.; 🅿; z 83848

Norland; RMC Place; MINIDOKA; ***169** L-5; mail Minidoka z 83343; rural

North Avenue; RMC Place; KOOTENAI; mail Coeur D Alene z 83815; pop. incl. with Coeur d'Alene (Inc. Place)

North Fork; RMC Place; LEMHI; **169** H-5; elev. 3,850ft./1,173m.; 🅿; z 83466, z 83469

North Lewiston; RMC Place; NEZ PERCE; ***169** F-1; elev. 735ft./224m.; ★ **LEW**; mail Lewiston z 83501; pop. incl. with Lewiston (Inc. Place)

Northside; RMC Place; ADA; ***169** K-2; ★ **BOIS**; mail Boise z 83702; pop. incl. with Boise (Inc. Place)

Northside; RMC Place; GEM; ***169** J-2; mail Emmett z 83617

Notus; Inc. Place; CANYON; **169** K-1; elev. 2,308ft./703m.; 🅿; z 83656; Ⓟ 380; © 458

Nounan; RMC Place; BEAR LAKE; ***169** M-8; mail Montpelier z 83254

O

Oakley; Inc. Place; CASSIA; **169** M-5; 🅿; z 83346; Ⓟ 635; © 668

Obsidian; RMC Place; CUSTER; ***169** J-4; mail Ketchum z 83340; rural

Ola; RMC Place; GEM; **169** J-2; elev. 3,000ft./914m.; 🅿; z 83657

Oldtown; Inc. Place; BONNER; ***169** C-1; elev. 2,109ft./643m.; 🅿; z 83822; Ⓟ 151; © 190

Onaway; Inc. Place; LATAH; **169** E-1; elev. 2,640ft./805m.; 🅿; z 83855; Ⓟ 203; © 230

ONEIDA; **169** M-6; Ⓟ 3,492; © 4,125; ◆ 4,130

Oreana; RMC Place; OWYHEE; ***169** L-2; elev. 2,828ft./862m.; 🅿; z 83650; rural

Orofino; Inc. Place; ⊡ CLEARWATER; **169** F-2; located on Nez Perce Ind. Res.; elev. 1,027ft./313m.; 🅿 🅷; z 83544; Ⓟ 2,868; © 3,247

Orogrande; RMC Place; IDAHO; ***169** G-3; mail Elk City z 83525

Osburn; Inc. Place; SHOSHONE; **169** D-2; elev. 2,530ft./771m.; 🅿; z 83849; Ⓟ 1,579; © 1,545

Osgood; RMC Place; BONNEVILLE; ***169** K-7; mail Idaho Falls z 83401-02

Outlet Bay; RMC Place; BONNER; ***169** B-1; mail Priest River z 83856

Ovid; RMC Place; BEAR LAKE; **169** M-8; elev. 5,935ft./1,809m.; 🅿; z 83254

OWYHEE; **169** M-2; Ⓟ 8,392; © 10,644; ◆ 10,940

Oxford; Inc. Place; FRANKLIN; **169** M-8; elev. 4,798ft./1,462m.; mail Preston z 83263; Ⓟ 44; © 53

P

Page; RMC Place; SHOSHONE; ***169** D-2; mail Smelterville z 83868; ● 100

Palisades; RMC Place; BONNEVILLE; **169** K-9; 🅿; z 83428; ● 100

Palisades Corner; RMC Place; PAYETTE; mail Fruitland z 83619; rural

Palmetto; RMC Place; ADA; mail Eagle z 83616; pop. incl. with Eagle (Inc. Place)

Paradise Hot Springs; RMC Place; ELMORE; ***169** K-3; 🅿; z 83647; rural

Paris; Inc. Place; ⊡ BEAR LAKE; **169** M-8; elev. 5,968ft./1,819m.; 🅿; z 83261, z 83287; Ⓟ 581; © 576

Park; RMC Place; LATAH; rural

Parker; Inc. Place; FREMONT; **169** J-8; elev. 4,924ft./1,501m.; 🅿; z 83438; Ⓟ 288; © 319

Parkline; RMC Place; BENEWAH; ***169** D-2; mail Saint Maries z 83861; disincorporated September 7, 2001; © 65

Parma; Inc. Place; CANYON; **169** K-1; elev. 2,245ft./684m.; 🅿; z 83660; Ⓟ 1,597; © 1,771

Patterson; RMC Place; LEMHI; **169** I-5; 🅿; z 83253; ● 5

Paul; Inc. Place; MINIDOKA; **169** M-5; elev. 4,150ft./1,265m.; 🅿; z 83347; Ⓟ 901; © 998

Payette; Inc. Place; ⊡ PAYETTE; **169** J-1; elev. 2,150ft./655m.; 🅿; z 83661; Ⓟ 5,592; © 7,054

PAYETTE; **169** J-2; Ⓟ 16,434; © 20,578; ◆ 23,973

Payette Heights; RMC Place; PAYETTE; ***169** J-1; pop. incl. with Payette (Inc. Place)

Peck; Inc. Place; NEZ PERCE; **169** F-2; elev. 1,200ft./366m.; 🅿; z 83545; Ⓟ 160; © 186

Pedee; RMC Place; BENEWAH; ***169** D-2; mail Plummer z 83851

Pegram; RMC Place; BEAR LAKE; ***169** M-9; mail Montpelier z 83254

Pella; RMC Place; CASSIA; ***169** M-5; mail Burley z 83318; rural

Picabo; RMC Place; BLAINE; **169** K-5; elev. 4,875ft./1,486m.; 🅿; z 83348; ● 100

Pierce; Inc. Place; CLEARWATER; **169** F-3; elev. 3,087ft./941m.; 🅿; z 83546; Ⓟ 746; © 617

Pine; RMC Place; ELMORE; **169** K-3; elev. 4,218ft./1,286m.; 🅿; z 83647

Pinehurst; RMC Place; ADAMS; ***169** H-2; mail New Meadows z 83654; ● 50

Pinehurst; Inc. Place; SHOSHONE; **169** D-2; elev. 2,240ft./683m.; 🅿; z 83850; Ⓟ 1,722; © 1,661

Pine Ridge; RMC Place; ADAMS; ***169** I-2; mail Council z 83612

Pingree; RMC Place; BINGHAM; **169** L-7; elev. 4,450ft./1,356m.; 🅿; z 83262; ● 150

Pinto Point; RMC Place; BONNER; mail Coolin z 83821

Pioneerville; RMC Place; BOISE; ***169** J-3; 🅿; z 83631; rural

Placerville; Inc. Place; BOISE; **169** J-2; elev. 4,320ft./1,317m.; 🅿; z 83666; Ⓟ 14; © 60

Plano; RMC Place; MADISON; ***169** J-8; elev. 4,845ft./1,477m.; mail Rexburg z 83440; ● 100

Pleasant Valley; RMC Place; ADA; mail Kuna z 83634; rural

Pleasantview; RMC Place; ONEIDA; **169** M-7; mail Malad City z 83252; ● 220

Plummer; Inc. Place; BENEWAH; **169** D-1; located on Coeur d'Alene Ind. Res.; elev. 2,722ft./830m.; 🅿; z 83851; Ⓟ 804; © 990

Pocatello; Inc. Place; ⊡ BANNOCK, POWER; **169** L-7; elev. 4,464ft./1,361m.; 🅿 🅷 🅲 12,679 ■; ★ **POC**; z 83201-06, z 83209; Ⓟ 46,080; © 51,466; ◆ 54,995

Polaris; RMC Place; SHOSHONE; mail Osburn z 83849; pop. incl. with Osburn (Inc. Place)

Pollock; RMC Place; IDAHO; **169** H-2; elev. 2,352ft./717m.; 🅿; z 83547; ● 140

Ponderay; Inc. Place; BONNER; **169** B-2; 🅿; z 83852; Ⓟ 449; © 638

Ponds Resort; RMC Place; FREMONT; mail Island Park z 83429; pop. incl. with Island Park (Inc. Place)

Porthill; RMC Place; BOUNDARY; **169** A-2; elev. 1,800ft./549m.; 🅿; z 83853

Post Falls; Inc. Place; KOOTENAI; **169** C-1; elev. 2,172ft./662m.; 🅿; ★ **SPOK**; z 83854, z 83877; Ⓟ 7,349; © 17,247; ◆ 25,699

Potlatch; Inc. Place; LATAH; **169** E-1; elev. 2,519ft./768m.; 🅿; z 83855; Ⓟ 790; © 791

Potlatch Junction; RMC Place; LATAH; ***169** E-1; mail Potlatch z 83855; ● 35

POWER; **169** M-7; Ⓟ 7,086; © 7,538; ◆ 7,660

Prairie; RMC Place; ELMORE; ***169** K-3; 🅿; z 83647

Preston; Inc. Place; ⊡ FRANKLIN; **169** N-8; elev. 4,720ft./1,439m.; 🅿 🅷; z 83263; Ⓟ 3,710; © 4,682

Prichard; RMC Place; SHOSHONE; ***169** D-3; elev. 2,405ft./733m.; 🅿; z 83873

Priest River; Inc. Place; BONNER; **169** C-1; elev. 2,080ft./634m.; 🅿; z 83856; Ⓟ 1,560; © 1,754

Princeton; RMC Place; LATAH; **169** E-1; elev. 2,514ft./766m.; 🅿; z 83857; ● 75

R

Raft River; RMC Place; CASSIA; ***169** M-6; mail American Falls z 83211; rural

Ramey; RMC Place; PAYETTE; mail Fruitland z 83619; ● 200

Ramsdell; RMC Place; BENEWAH; ***169** D-2; mail Plummer z 83851

Rathdrum; Inc. Place; KOOTENAI; **169** C-1; elev. 2,196ft./669m.; 🅿; z 83858; Ⓟ 2,000; © 4,816

Raymond; RMC Place; BEAR LAKE; ***169** M-9; 🅿; z 83114 & mail Geneva z 83238

Red River Hot Springs; RMC Place; IDAHO; ***169** G-3; mail Elk City z 83525; rural

Reno; RMC Place; CLARK; ***169** J-7; mail Dubois z 83423; rural

Reubens; Inc. Place; LEWIS; **169** F-2; located on Nez Perce Ind. Res.; elev. 3,520ft./1,073m.; 🅿; z 83548; Ⓟ 46; © 72

Rexburg; Inc. Place; ⊡ MADISON; **169** J-8; elev. 4,865ft./1,483m.; 🅿 🅷 🅲 14,116; z 83440-41, z 83460; Ⓟ 14,302; © 17,257; ◆ 26,021

Reynolds; RMC Place; OWYHEE; ***169** L-1; mail Murphy z 83650; rural

Richfield; Inc. Place; LINCOLN; **169** L-5; elev. 4,325ft./1,318m.; 🅿; z 83349; Ⓟ 383; © 412

Riddle; RMC Place; OWYHEE; **169** M-2; 🅿; z 83604; rural

Rigby; Inc. Place; ⊡ JEFFERSON; **169** K-8; elev. 4,858ft./1,481m.; 🅿; ★ **IDFL**; z 83442; Ⓟ 2,681; © 2,998

Riggins; Inc. Place; IDAHO; **169** H-2; elev. 1,800ft./549m.; 🅿; z 83549; Ⓟ 443; © 410

Ririe; Inc. Place; JEFFERSON, BONNEVILLE; **169** K-8; elev. 4,960ft./1,512m.; 🅿; z 83443; Ⓟ 596; © 545

Riverdale; RMC Place; FRANKLIN; ***169** M-8; mail Preston z 83263; rural

Riverside; RMC Place; BINGHAM; **169** L-7; elev. 4,455ft./1,358m.; mail Blackfoot z 83221; ● 225

Riverside; RMC Place; CANYON; ***169** K-1; mail Caldwell z 83605; rural

Riverside; RMC Place; CLEARWATER; ***169** F-2; elev. 996ft./304m.; mail Orofino z 83544; pop. incl. with Orofino (Inc. Place)

Roberts; Inc. Place; JEFFERSON; **169** K-7; elev. 4,775ft./1,455m.; 🅿; z 83444; Ⓟ 557; © 647

Robin; RMC Place; BANNOCK; ***169** M-7; mail Arimo z 83214; rural

Rock Creek; RMC Place; TWIN FALLS; ***169** M-5; mail Hansen z 83334

Rockford; RMC Place; BINGHAM; ***169** L-7; elev. 4,463ft./1,360m.; mail Blackfoot z 83221; ● 175

Rockford Bay; RMC Place; KOOTENAI; ***169** D-1; mail Coeur D Alene z 83814; ● 100

Rockland; Inc. Place; POWER; **169** M-6; elev. 4,671ft./1,424m.; 🅿; z 83271; Ⓟ 264; © 316

Rocky Bar; RMC Place; ELMORE; ***169** K-3; 🅿; z 83647

Rocky Point; RMC Place; BENEWAH; ***169** D-2; mail Plummer z 83851

Rocky Point; RMC Place; BONNER; mail Coolin z 83821

Rogerson; RMC Place; TWIN FALLS; **169** M-4; elev. 4,897ft./1,493m.; 🅿; z 83302; ● 100

Rose; RMC Place; BINGHAM; ***169** L-7; elev. 4,518ft./1,377m.; mail Blackfoot z 83221; rural

Rose; RMC Place; CARIBOU; mail Soda Springs z 83276; rural

Roseberry; RMC Place; VALLEY; ***169** I-2; mail Donnelly z 83615; rural

Rose Lake; RMC Place; KOOTENAI; **169** D-2; mail Cataldo z 83810

Roseworth; RMC Place; TWIN FALLS; ***169** M-4; mail Castleford z 83321; rural

Roswell; RMC Place; CANYON; ***169** K-1; mail Parma z 83660; ● 200

Roy; RMC Place; POWER; ***169** M-6; elev. 5,104ft./1,556m.; mail Rockland z 83271; rural

Rupert; Inc. Place; ⊡ MINIDOKA; **169** M-5; elev. 4,158ft./1,267m.; 🅿 🅷; z 83343, z 83350; Ⓟ 5,455; © 5,645

S

Sagle; RMC Place; BONNER; ***169** C-2; elev. 2,160ft./658m.; 🅿; z 83860 & mail Careywood z 83809; ● 150

Saint Anthony; Inc. Place; ⊡ FREMONT; **169** J-8; elev. 4,972ft./1,515m.; 🅿; z 83445; Ⓟ 3,010; © 3,342

Saint Charles; Inc. Place; BEAR LAKE; **169** N-8; elev. 5,944ft./1,812m.; 🅿; z 83272; Ⓟ 189; © 156

Saint Joe; RMC Place; BENEWAH; ***169** D-2; mail Saint Maries z 83861

Saint John; ONEIDA; see Saint Johns (RMC Place)

Saint Johns (Saint John); RMC Place; ONEIDA; ***169** M-7; mail Malad City z 83252; ● 180

Saint Leon; RMC Place; BONNEVILLE; ***169** K-8; ★ **IDFL**; mail Idaho Falls z 83401; rural

Saint Maries; Inc. Place; ⊡ BENEWAH; **169** D-2; elev. 2,216ft./675m.; 🅿 🅷; z 83861; Ⓟ 2,442; © 2,652

Salem; RMC Place; MADISON; ***169** J-8; mail Rexburg z 83440; ● 200

Salmon; Inc. Place; ⊡ LEMHI; **169** H-5; elev. 4,004ft./1,220m.; 🅿 🅷; z 83467; Ⓟ 2,941; © 3,122

Samaria; RMC Place; ONEIDA; **169** N-7; mail Malad City z 83252; ● 100

Samuels; RMC Place; BONNER; **169** B-2; ● 150

Sanders; RMC Place; BENEWAH; ***169** E-1; located on Coeur d'Alene Ind. Res.; mail Tensed z 83870

Sandpoint; Inc. Place; ⊡ BONNER; **169** B-2; elev. 2,085ft./636m.; 🅿 🅷; z 83864 & mail Careywood z 83809, Colburn z 83865, Kootenai z 83840; Ⓟ 5,203; © 6,835

Sandy Shores Addition; RMC Place; BONNER; mail Coolin z 83821

Santa; RMC Place; BENEWAH; **169** E-2; elev. 2,681ft./817m.; 🅿; z 83866; ● 100

Selle; RMC Place; BONNER; ***169** B-2; elev. 2,176ft./663m.; mail Sandpoint z 83864; rural

Setters; RMC Place; KOOTENAI; ***169** D-1; mail Worley z 83876; rural

Sharon; RMC Place; BEAR LAKE; ***169** M-8; mail Montpelier z 83254; rural

Shelley; Inc. Place; BINGHAM; **169** K-7; elev. 4,629ft./1,411m.; 🅿; z 83274; Ⓟ 3,536; © 3,813

Sherwood Beach; RMC Place; BONNER; mail Coolin z 83821

Shoshone; Inc. Place; ⊡ LINCOLN; **169** L-4; elev. 3,970ft./1,210m.; 🅿; z 83324, z 83352; Ⓟ 1,249; © 1,398

SHOSHONE; **169** D-3; Ⓟ 13,931; © 13,771; ◆ 12,695

Shoup; RMC Place; LEMHI; **169** H-5; elev. 3,384ft./1,031m.; 🅿; z 83469; ● 60

Silver Beach; RMC Place; KOOTENAI; mail Spirit Lake z 83869; ● 80

Silver City; RMC Place; OWYHEE; ***169** L-1; mail Murphy z 83650

Silver Sands Beach; RMC Place; KOOTENAI; ***169** C-1; mail Rathdrum z 83858; rural

Silverton; RMC Place; SHOSHONE; **169** D-3; elev. 2,720ft./829m.; 🅿; z 83867; ● 300

Skyline; RMC Place; BONNEVILLE; ***169** K-7; ★ **IDFL**; mail Idaho Falls z 83401-02; pop. incl. with Idaho Falls (Inc. Place)

Slate Creek; RMC Place; IDAHO; ***169** G-2; mail White Bird z 83554

Slickpoo; RMC Place; LEWIS; ***169** F-2; mail Culdesac z 83524; rural

Small; RMC Place; CLARK; ***169** J-7; elev. 5,281ft./1,610m.; mail Dubois z 83423; rural

Smelter Heights; RMC Place; SHOSHONE; ***169** D-2; mail Kellogg z 83837

Smelterville; Inc. Place; SHOSHONE; **169** D-2; elev. 2,219ft./676m.; 🅿; z 83868; Ⓟ 464; © 651

Smiths Ferry; RMC Place; VALLEY; **169** J-2; mail Cascade z 83611

Soda Springs; Inc. Place; ⊡ CARIBOU; **169** M-8; elev. 5,773ft./1,760m.; 🅿 🅷; z 83230, z 83276, z 83285; Ⓟ 3,111; © 3,381

Soldier; RMC Place; CAMAS; ***169** K-4; mail Fairfield z 83327

Soldiers Home; RMC Place; ADA; ★ **BOIS**; mail Boise z 83704; pop. incl. with Boise (Inc. Place)

South Boise; RMC Place; ADA; ★ **BOIS**; mail Boise z 83706; pop. incl. with Boise (Inc. Place)

South Park; RMC Place; BANNOCK; ★ **POC**; mail Pocatello z 83204; pop. incl. with Pocatello (Inc. Place)

Southside; RMC Place; ADA; ***169** K-2; ★ **BOIS**; mail Boise z 83706; pop. incl. with Boise (Inc. Place)

Southwick; RMC Place; NEZ PERCE; **169** F-2; mail Kendrick z 83537; ● 40

Spalding; RMC Place; NEZ PERCE; **169** F-1; elev. 800ft./244m.; 🅿; z 83540

Spencer; Inc. Place; CLARK; **169** J-7; elev. 5,883ft./1,793m.; 🅿; z 83446; Ⓟ 11; © 38

Spirit Lake; Inc. Place; KOOTENAI; **169** C-1; elev. 2,567ft./782m.; 🅿; z 83869; Ⓟ 790; © 1,376

Springdale; RMC Place; CASSIA; ***169** M-5; mail Burley z 83318; rural

Springfield; RMC Place; BINGHAM; **169** L-7; elev. 4,425ft./1,349m.; 🅿; z 83277; ● 100

Squirrel; RMC Place; FREMONT; ***169** J-8; elev. 5,580ft./1,701m.; ● 25

Standrod; RMC Place; CASSIA; ***169** N-6; mail Malta z 83342; rural

Stanley; Inc. Place; CUSTER; **169** J-4; elev. 6,260ft./1,908m.; 🅿; z 83278; Ⓟ 71; © 100

Star; Inc. Place; ADA; **169** K-2; elev. 2,470ft./753m.; 🅿; z 83669; Ⓟ 648; © 1,795

Starkey; RMC Place; ADAMS; ***169** I-2; rural

Starrhs Ferry; RMC Place; CASSIA; ***169** M-5; mail Burley z 83318

State Line; KOOTENAI; see State Line Village (Inc. Place)

State Line Village (State Line); Inc. Place; KOOTENAI; ***169** D-1; elev. 2,120ft./646m.; ★ **SPOK**; mail Post Falls z 83854; Ⓟ 26; © 28

Sterling; RMC Place; BINGHAM; ***169** L-7; elev. 4,370ft./1,332m.; 🅿; z 83210

Stites; Inc. Place; IDAHO; **169** F-2; elev. 1,319ft./402m.; 🅿; z 83552; Ⓟ 204; © 226

Stoddard; RMC Place; CANYON; ***169** K-2; mail Melba z 83641, Nampa z 83686; rural

Stone; RMC Place; ONEIDA; **169** N-7; elev. 4,550ft./1,387m.; 🅿; z 83252; rural

Sturgeon; RMC Place; KOOTENAI; mail Rathdrum z 83858; rural

Sublett; RMC Place; CASSIA; mail Malta z 83342; rural

Sugar City; Inc. Place; MADISON; **169** J-8; elev. 4,891ft./1,491m.; 🅿; z 83448; Ⓟ 1,275; © 1,242

Sunbeam; RMC Place; CUSTER; **169** J-4; mail Stanley z 83278; ● 40

Sunnydell; RMC Place; MADISON; ***169** K-8; mail Rexburg z 83440

Sunnyside; RMC Place; BONNER; ***169** B-2; mail Sandpoint z 83864; ● 100

Sunnyslope; RMC Place; CANYON; ***169** K-1; elev. 2,402ft./732m.; mail Caldwell z 83605; rural

Sun Valley; Inc. Place; BLAINE; **169** K-4; elev. 5,920ft./1,804m.; 🅿 🅷; z 83353-54; Ⓟ 938; © 1,427

Swan Falls; RMC Place; ADA; ***169** L-2; mail Kuna z 83634; rural

Swanlake; RMC Place; BANNOCK; **169** M-8; elev. 4,779ft./1,457m.; 🅿; z 83281

Swan Valley; Inc. Place; BONNEVILLE; **169** K-8; elev. 5,277ft./1,608m.; 🅿; z 83449; Ⓟ 141; © 213

Sweet; RMC Place; GEM; **169** J-2; elev. 2,548ft./777m.; 🅿; z 83670; ● 200

Sweetwater; RMC Place; NEZ PERCE; ***169** F-1; mail Lapwai z 83540

Syringa; RMC Place; IDAHO; **169** F-3; mail Kooskia z 83539; ● 30

T

Taber; RMC Place; BINGHAM; ***169** K-7; mail Blackfoot z 83221; rural

Talache; RMC Place; BONNER; ***169** C-2; mail Sagle z 83860

Talmage; RMC Place; CARIBOU; mail Bancroft z 83217; rural

Tamarack; RMC Place; ADAMS; ***169** H-2; elev. 4,104ft./1,251m.; 🅿; z 83615 & mail Council z 83612; rural

Taylorville; RMC Place; BONNEVILLE; mail Idaho Falls z 83401; rural

Teakean; RMC Place; CLEARWATER; ***169** F-2; mail Lenore z 83541; rural

Tendoy; RMC Place; LEMHI; **169** I-5; elev. 4,836ft./1,474m.; 🅿; z 83468; rural

Tenmile; RMC Place; ADA; ***169** K-2; ★ **BOIS**; mail Meridian z 83642

Tensed; Inc. Place; BENEWAH; **169** E-1; located on Coeur d'Alene Ind. Res.; elev. 2,557ft./779m.; 🅿; z 83870; Ⓟ 90; © 126

Terreton; RMC Place; JEFFERSON; **169** J-7; elev. 4,787ft./1,459m.; 🅿; z 83450

Teton; Inc. Place; FREMONT; **169** J-8; elev. 4,949ft./1,508m.; 🅿; z 83451; Ⓟ 570; © 569

TETON; **169** K-8; Ⓟ 3,439; © 5,999; ◆ 9,400

Tetonia; Inc. Place; TETON; **169** J-9; 🅿; z 83424, z 83452; Ⓟ 132; © 247

Thama; RMC Place; BONNER; mail Priest River z 83856; rural

Thatcher; RMC Place; FRANKLIN; **169** M-8; elev. 4,897ft./1,493m.; 🅿; z 83283

The String; RMC Place; TETON; mail Victor z 83455; ● 100

Thomas; RMC Place; BINGHAM; ***169** L-7; elev. 4,446ft./1,355m.; mail Blackfoot z 83221; ● 250

Thornton; RMC Place; MADISON; **169** K-8; mail Rexburg z 83440; ● 100

Three Creek; RMC Place; OWYHEE; ***169** N-3; mail Rogerson z 83302, Twin Falls z 83301; rural

Transfer; RMC Place; NEZ PERCE; ***169** F-1; ★ **LEW**; mail Lewiston z 83501; pop. incl. with Lewiston (Inc. Place)

Travers; RMC Place; MINIDOKA; mail Rupert z 83350; rural

Treasureton; RMC Place; FRANKLIN; ***169** M-8; elev. 5,076ft./1,547m.; mail Preston z 83263; rural

Trestle Creek; RMC Place; BONNER; ***169** B-2; mail Hope z 83836

Triumph; RMC Place; BLAINE; **169** K-5; 🅿; z 83333

Troy; Inc. Place; LATAH; **169** E-2; elev. 2,460ft./750m.; 🅿; z 83871; Ⓟ 699; © 798

Turner; RMC Place; CARIBOU; mail Grace z 83241; rural

Tuttle; RMC Place; GOODING; ***169** L-4; elev. 3,309ft./1,009m.; mail Bliss z 83314, Hagerman z 83332; rural

Twin Falls; Inc. Place; ⊡ TWIN FALLS; **169** M-4; elev. 3,745ft./1,141m.; 🅿 🅷 ■; z 83301-03; Ⓟ 27,591; © 34,469; ◆ 35,994

TWIN FALLS; **169** M-4; Ⓟ 53,580; © 64,284; ◆ 68,704

Twin Groves; RMC Place; FREMONT; ***169** J-8; mail Saint Anthony z 83445; rural

Twin Lakes; RMC Place; KOOTENAI; 🅿; z 83858; rural

Twinlow; RMC Place; KOOTENAI; ***169** C-1; mail Rathdrum z 83858

Tyhee; RMC Place; BANNOCK; ***169** L-7; ★ **POC**; mail Pocatello z 83201; rural

U

Ucon; Inc. Place; BONNEVILLE; **169** K-8; elev. 4,808ft./1,465m.; 🅿; ★ **IDFL**; z 83454; Ⓟ 895; © 943

Unity; RMC Place; CASSIA; ***169** M-5; mail Burley z 83318; rural

Ustick; RMC Place; ADA; **169** B-4; elev. 2,645ft./806m.; ★ **BOIS**; mail Boise z 83704, z 83713; pop. incl. with Boise (Inc. Place)

V

VALLEY; **169** I-3; Ⓟ 6,109; © 7,651; ◆ 9,480

Valley View Heights; RMC Place; NEZ PERCE; ***169** F-1; ★ **LEW**; mail Lewiston z 83501

Victor; Inc. Place; TETON; **169** K-9; elev. 6,207ft./1,892m.; 🅿; z 83455; Ⓟ 292; © 840

View; RMC Place; CASSIA; ***169** M-5; mail Burley z 83318; rural

Viola; RMC Place; LATAH; **169** E-1; elev. 2,640ft./805m.; 🅿; z 83872; ● 150

Virginia; RMC Place; BANNOCK; ***169** M-7; mail Downey z 83234

W

Waha; RMC Place; NEZ PERCE; ***169** F-1; elev. 3,420ft./1,042m.; mail Lewiston z 83501

Wallace; Inc. Place; ⊡ SHOSHONE; **169** D-3; elev. 2,744ft./836m.; 🅿; z 83873-74; Ⓟ 1,010; © 960

Wapello; RMC Place; BINGHAM; ***169** L-7; mail Blackfoot z 83221

Wardboro; RMC Place; BEAR LAKE; ***169** M-9; elev. 5,948ft./1,813m.; mail Montpelier z 83254

Wardner; Inc. Place; SHOSHONE; ***169** D-2; 🅿; z 83837; Ⓟ 246; © 215

Warm Lake; RMC Place; VALLEY; **169** I-3; elev. 5,280ft./1,609m.; mail Cascade z 83611

Warm River; Inc. Place; FREMONT; **169** J-8; mail Ashton z 83420; Ⓟ 9; © 10

Warren; RMC Place; IDAHO; **169** H-3; elev. 5,907ft./1,800m.; 🅿; z 83671; ● 45

Warrens; RMC Place; CANYON; mail Melba z 83641; rural

WASHINGTON; **169** I-1; Ⓟ 8,550; © 9,977; ◆ 10,203

Washoe; RMC Place; PAYETTE; ***169** J-1; mail Payette z 83661

Wayan; RMC Place; CARIBOU; **169** L-8; elev. 6,437ft./1,962m.; 🅿; z 83285; ● 35

Webb; RMC Place; NEZ PERCE; ***169** F-1; mail Lapwai z 83540; rural

Weippe; Inc. Place; CLEARWATER; **169** F-3; elev. 3,020ft./920m.; 🅿; z 83553; Ⓟ 532; © 416

Weiser; Inc. Place; ⊡ WASHINGTON; **169** J-1; elev. 2,117ft./645m.; 🅿 🅷; z 83672; Ⓟ 4,571; © 5,343

Weitz; RMC Place; CANYON; ***169** K-1; mail Caldwell z 83605; rural

Wendell; Inc. Place; GOODING; **169** L-4; elev. 3,467ft./1,057m.; 🅿; z 83355; Ⓟ 1,963; © 2,338

Westgate Acres; RMC Place; ADA; ★ **BOIS**; mail Boise z 83704; pop. incl. with Boise (Inc. Place)

Westlake; RMC Place; IDAHO; ***169** F-2; mail Ferdinand z 83526; rural

---

Entries in **UPPERCASE** are counties.
Entries in **bold** have populations of 2,500 or more.
Names in parentheses are alternate names.

Inc. Place	Incorporated Place
RMC Place	Rand McNally Designated Place
CDP	Census Designated Place
MCD	Minor Civil Division

⊡	County Seat
▲	Minor Civil Division
elev.	Elevation
🅿	Post Office
🅷	Hospital
🅲	College
■	Principal Business Center
★	Ranally Metro Area (RMA) Abbreviation
z	Zip Code(s)
Ⓟ	Previous Census Population
Ⓡ	Revised Census Population
Ⓐ	Annexation Population
●	Rand McNally Population Estimate
©	Final Census Population
Ⓢ	Special Census Population
◆	Estimated Population

For additional definitions see Glossary, Volume 1, and Introduction, Volume 2.

Westland Acres; RMC Place; ADA; ★ **BOIS**; pop. incl. with Boise (Inc. Place)
Westmond; RMC Place; BONNER; ***169** C-2; mail Sagle **z** 83860; ● 150
Westmoreland; RMC Place; ADA; ★ **BOIS**; mail Boise **z** 83704; pop. incl. with Boise (Inc. Place)
West Mountain; RMC Place; VALLEY; ***169** I-2; elev. 4,840ft./1,475m.; mail Cascade **z** 83611; rural
Weston; Inc. Place; FRANKLIN; **169** N-8; elev. 4,743ft./1,446m.; 🅿; **z** 83286; Ⓟ 390; © 425
White Bird; Inc. Place; IDAHO; **169** G-2; elev. 1,560ft./475m.; 🅿; **z** 83554; Ⓟ 108; © 106
Whitney; RMC Place; ADA; ***169** K-2; ★ **BOIS**; mail Boise **z** 83705; pop. incl. with Boise (Inc. Place)
Whitney; RMC Place; FRANKLIN; **169** N-8; mail Preston **z** 83263; ● 200
Wilder; Inc. Place; CANYON; **169** K-1; elev. 2,424ft./739m.; 🅿; **z** 83676; Ⓟ 1,232; © 1,462
Wilford; RMC Place; FREMONT; ***169** J-8; mail Saint Anthony **z** 83445; rural
Winchester; Inc. Place; LEWIS; **169** F-2; elev. 3,968ft./1,209m.; 🅿; **z** 83555; Ⓟ 262; © 308
Winder; RMC Place; FRANKLIN; ***169** M-8; mail Preston **z** 83263; rural
Winona; RMC Place; IDAHO; ***169** F-2; mail Kooskia **z** 83539; rural
Wolf Lodge; RMC Place; KOOTENAI; ***169** D-2; elev. 2,160ft./658m.; mail Coeur D Alene **z** 83814; ● 100
Wolverine; RMC Place; BINGHAM; ***169** K-8; elev. 5,590ft./1,704m.; mail Firth **z** 83236; rural
Wood; RMC Place; PAYETTE; mail Payette **z** 83661; rural
Woodland; RMC Place; IDAHO; ***169** F-2; elev. 3,010ft./917m.; mail Kamiah **z** 83536; rural
Woodland Park; RMC Place; SHOSHONE; ***169** D-3; mail Wallace **z** 83873; ● 230
Woodruff; RMC Place; ONEIDA; ***169** N-7; mail Malad City **z** 83252
Woodville; RMC Place; BINGHAM; ***169** K-7; mail Shelley **z** 83274; ● 300
Worley; Inc. Place; KOOTENAI; **169** D-1; elev. 2,654ft./809m.; 🅿; **z** 83876; Ⓟ 182; © 223
Wrencoe; RMC Place; BONNER; mail Sandpoint **z** 83864; rural

Y

Yellow Pine; RMC Place; VALLEY; **169** H-3; elev. 4,762ft./1,451m.; 🅿; **z** 83677

Entries in **UPPERCASE** are counties.
Entries in **bold** have populations of 2,500 or more.
Names in parentheses are alternate names.
Inc. Place Incorporated Place
RMC Place Rand McNally Designated Place
CDP Census Designated Place
MCD Minor Civil Division

⊡ County Seat
▲ Minor Civil Division
elev. Elevation
🅿 Post Office

⊞ Hospital
⊠ College
■ Principal Business Center
★ Ranally Metro Area (RMA) Abbreviation
z Zip Code(s)

Ⓟ Previous Census Population
Ⓡ Revised Census Population
Ⓐ Annexation Population
● Rand McNally Population Estimate
© Final Census Population
Ⓢ Special Census Population
◆ Estimated Population

For additional definitions see Glossary, Volume 1, and Introduction, Volume 2.

ILLINOIS

Statistics

Total area (2000) — 57,914 square miles
Land area (2000) — 55,584 square miles
Water area (2000) — 2,330 square miles
Capital — Springfield
Admitted as state — December, 1818

Ranally Metro Areas (RMAs) and Abbreviations

Bloomington-Normal, IL — BLOOM-
Carbondale-Marion, IL — CARB-
Champaign-Urbana, IL — CH-U
Chicago, IL-IN-WI — CHI
Clinton, IA-IL — CLNT
Danville, IL — DANV
Davenport-Rock Island-Moline, IA-IL — D-RI-M
Decatur, IL — DEC
De Kalb, IL — DKLB
Dubuque, IA-WI-IL — DUB
Galesburg, IL — GLSB
Kankakee, IL — KANK
Paducah, KY-IL — PAD
Peoria, IL — PEOR
Quincy, IL — QUIN
Rockford, IL-WI — RKFD
St. Louis, MO-IL — ST.L
Springfield, IL — SPRG

Maps

State Maps can be found on pages 142-254 in Vol. 1
County Subdivision maps can be found on pages 255-271 in Vol. 1

Principal Places

Place Name	Place Type	County	Population
Chicago	Inc. Place	COOK	◆ 2,868,472
Aurora	Inc. Place	KANE	◆ 187,118
Thornton	MCD-Township	COOK	© 180,802
Rockford	MCD-Township	WINNEBAGO	© 178,853
Rockford	Inc. Place	WINNEBAGO	◆ 159,746
Wheeling	MCD-Township	COOK	® 155,904
Proviso	MCD-Township	COOK	© 155,831
Worth	MCD-Township	COOK	© 152,239
Downers Grove	MCD-Township	DUPAGE	© 148,110
Joliet	Inc. Place	WILL	◆ 144,888
Naperville	Inc. Place	DUPAGE	◆ 139,514
Maine	MCD-Township	COOK	© 135,623
Schaumburg	MCD-Township	COOK	© 134,114
York	MCD-Township	DUPAGE	© 124,553
Milton	MCD-Township	DUPAGE	© 118,616
Lisle	MCD-Township	DUPAGE	© 117,604
Springfield	Inc. Place	SANGAMON	◆ 117,122
Aurora	MCD-Township	KANE	© 115,553
Elgin	Inc. Place	KANE	◆ 114,976
Peoria	Inc. Place	PEORIA	◆ 114,037
Peoria City	MCD-Township	PEORIA	© 112,936
Palatine	MCD-Township	COOK	© 112,740
Bloomingdale	MCD-Township	DUPAGE	© 111,709
Capital	MCD-Township	SANGAMON	® 111,372
Bremen	MCD-Township	COOK	© 109,575
Lyons	MCD-Township	COOK	© 109,264
Niles	MCD-Township	COOK	© 102,638
Elk Grove	MCD-Township	COOK	© 94,969
Waukegan	Inc. Place	LAKE	◆ 94,749
Leyden	MCD-Township	COOK	© 94,685
Bloom	MCD-Township	COOK	© 93,901
Waukegan	MCD-Township	LAKE	© 92,805
Orland	MCD-Township	COOK	© 91,418
Elgin	MCD-Township	KANE	© 90,384
Addison	MCD-Township	DUPAGE	© 88,900
Cicero	Inc. Place	COOK	◆ 88,292
Joliet	MCD-Township	WILL	© 86,468
Algonquin	MCD-Township	MCHENRY	® 86,217
Naperville	MCD-Township	DUPAGE	© 85,736
Hanover	MCD-Township	COOK	© 83,471
Northfield	MCD-Township	COOK	© 82,880
Decatur	Inc. Place	MACON	◆ 77,914
Bloomington	Inc. Place	MCLEAN	◆ 76,555
Champaign	Inc. Place	CHAMPAIGN	◆ 74,849
Evanston	Inc. Place	COOK	◆ 74,751
Evanston	MCD-Township	COOK	© 74,239
Arlington Heights	Inc. Place	COOK	◆ 72,184
Schaumburg	Inc. Place	COOK	◆ 71,748
Du Page	MCD-Township	WILL	© 71,745
Palatine	Inc. Place	COOK	◆ 70,098
Champaign City	MCD-Township	CHAMPAIGN	® 67,959
Rich	MCD-Township	COOK	© 67,623
Skokie	Inc. Place	COOK	◆ 67,027
Vernon	MCD-Township	LAKE	® 65,362
Bloomington City	MCD-Township	MCLEAN	© 64,808
Wayne	MCD-Township	DUPAGE	© 63,776
Bolingbrook	Inc. Place	WILL	◆ 62,629
Des Plaines	Inc. Place	COOK	◆ 59,481
Warren	MCD-Township	LAKE	© 59,424
Decatur	MCD-Township	MACON	© 58,355
New Trier	MCD-Township	COOK	© 56,716
Mount Prospect	Inc. Place	COOK	◆ 55,799
Avon	MCD-Township	LAKE	© 54,957
Wheaton	Inc. Place	DUPAGE	◆ 54,505
Berwyn	MCD-Township	COOK	© 54,016
Berwyn	Inc. Place	COOK	◆ 53,597
Palos	MCD-Township	COOK	© 53,419
Dundee	MCD-Township	KANE	© 53,207
Oak Park	MCD-Township	COOK	© 52,524
Normal	Inc. Place	MCLEAN	◆ 52,179
Oak Lawn	Inc. Place	COOK	◆ 51,214
Orland Park	Inc. Place	COOK	◆ 50,445
Hoffman Estates	Inc. Place	COOK	◆ 49,606
Libertyville	MCD-Township	LAKE	© 48,904
Tinley Park	Inc. Place	COOK	◆ 48,859
Downers Grove	Inc. Place	DUPAGE	◆ 48,672
Oak Park	Inc. Place	COOK	◆ 48,034
Plainfield	MCD-Township	WILL	© 45,691
Normal	MCD-Township	MCLEAN	© 45,637
DeKalb	Inc. Place	DEKALB	◆ 45,253
Winfield	MCD-Township	DUPAGE	© 45,155
Crystal Lake	Inc. Place	MCHENRY	◆ 44,651
Wheatland	MCD-Township	WILL	© 44,349
Moline	Inc. Place	ROCK ISLAND	◆ 43,993
Elmhurst	Inc. Place	DUPAGE	◆ 43,599
Shields	MCD-Township	LAKE	© 43,382
Belleville	Inc. Place	ST. CLAIR	◆ 42,746
Carpentersville	Inc. Place	KANE	◆ 42,512
Glenview	Inc. Place	COOK	◆ 42,233
DeKalb	MCD-Township	DEKALB	© 42,189
St. Charles	MCD-Township	KANE	© 42,051
Lockport	MCD-Township	WILL	© 42,048
Lombard	Inc. Place	DUPAGE	◆ 41,821
McHenry	MCD-Township	MCHENRY	© 41,740
Belleville	MCD-Township	ST. CLAIR	® 41,570
Frankfort	MCD-Township	WILL	© 41,292
Buffalo Grove	Inc. Place	COOK	◆ 41,267
Carol Stream	Inc. Place	DUPAGE	◆ 41,245
Quincy	MCD-Township	ADAMS	© 40,366
Urbana	MCD-Township	CHAMPAIGN	© 40,257
Rock Island	Inc. Place	ROCK ISLAND	◆ 39,770
Ela	MCD-Township	LAKE	© 39,688
Bartlett	Inc. Place	COOK	◆ 39,619
Calumet City	Inc. Place	COOK	◆ 39,111
Hanover Park	Inc. Place	COOK	◆ 39,041
Quincy	Inc. Place	ADAMS	◆ 38,785
Stickney	MCD-Township	COOK	© 38,673
Oswego	Inc. Place	KENDALL	◆ 38,062
Cunningham	MCD-Township	CHAMPAIGN	® 37,362
Park Ridge	Inc. Place	COOK	◆ 36,800
Addison	Inc. Place	DUPAGE	◆ 36,693
Streamwood	Inc. Place	COOK	◆ 36,598
South Moline	MCD-Township	ROCK ISLAND	© 36,586
Harlem	MCD-Township	WINNEBAGO	© 36,171
Wheeling	Inc. Place	COOK	◆ 35,911
Nunda	MCD-Township	MCHENRY	© 35,104
Moraine	MCD-Township	LAKE	® 34,694
Pekin	Inc. Place	TAZEWELL	◆ 34,519
North Chicago	Inc. Place	LAKE	◆ 34,455
Danville	MCD-Township	VERMILION	© 34,094
Mundelein	Inc. Place	LAKE	◆ 34,078
Edwardsville	MCD-Township	MADISON	© 33,731
Lake Villa	MCD-Township	LAKE	© 33,721
Galesburg City	MCD-Township	KNOX	© 33,706
Gurnee	Inc. Place	LAKE	◆ 33,691
Wood River	MCD-Township	MADISON	© 33,410
Bourbonnais	MCD-Township	KANKAKEE	© 33,061
Collinsville	MCD-Township	MADISON	© 32,954
Saint Charles	Inc. Place	KANE	◆ 32,931
Elk Grove Village	Inc. Place	COOK	◆ 32,890
Northbrook	Inc. Place	COOK	◆ 32,638
Glendale Heights	Inc. Place	DUPAGE	◆ 31,858
West Deerfield	MCD-Township	LAKE	® 31,856
Granite City	Inc. Place	MADISON	◆ 31,854
Woodridge	Inc. Place	DUPAGE	◆ 31,817
St. Clair	MCD-Township	ST. CLAIR	® 31,782
Galesburg	Inc. Place	KNOX	◆ 31,769
Chicago Heights	Inc. Place	COOK	◆ 31,682
East St. Louis	MCD-Township	ST. CLAIR	© 31,542
Granite City	MCD-Township	MADISON	© 31,301
Danville	Inc. Place	VERMILION	◆ 31,043
Highland Park	Inc. Place	LAKE	◆ 31,000
Pekin	MCD-Township	TAZEWELL	© 30,600
Alton	MCD-Township	MADISON	® 30,504
East Saint Louis	Inc. Place	ST. CLAIR	◆ 30,476
Alton	Inc. Place	MADISON	◆ 30,380
Belvidere	Inc. Place	BOONE	◆ 30,287
Lake in the Hills	Inc. Place	MCHENRY	◆ 30,196
Batavia	MCD-Township	KANE	© 30,137
Algonquin	Inc. Place	MCHENRY	◆ 29,862
New Lenox	MCD-Township	WILL	© 29,730
Carbondale	MCD-Township	JACKSON	® 29,416
Niles	Inc. Place	COOK	◆ 29,018
Homer	MCD-Township	WILL	© 28,992
Centreville	MCD-Township	ST. CLAIR	© 28,711
Harvey	Inc. Place	COOK	◆ 28,689
Round Lake Beach	Inc. Place	LAKE	◆ 28,560
Oswego	MCD-Township	KENDALL	© 28,417
Kankakee	Inc. Place	KANKAKEE	◆ 28,347
Kankakee	MCD-Township	KANKAKEE	© 28,029
Troy	MCD-Township	WILL	© 27,970
Wilmette	Inc. Place	COOK	◆ 27,755
Batavia	Inc. Place	KANE	◆ 27,557
Grafton	MCD-Township	MCHENRY	© 27,547
Glen Ellyn	Inc. Place	DUPAGE	◆ 27,546
Romeoville	Inc. Place	WILL	◆ 27,155
Burbank	Inc. Place	COOK	◆ 27,147
Plainfield	Inc. Place	WILL	◆ 27,117
McHenry	Inc. Place	MCHENRY	◆ 27,003
Collinsville	Inc. Place	MADISON	◆ 26,760
Oak Forest	Inc. Place	COOK	◆ 26,682
Freeport	MCD-Township	STEPHENSON	© 26,443
Lansing	Inc. Place	COOK	◆ 26,302
Maywood	Inc. Place	COOK	◆ 26,232
Norwood Park	MCD-Township	COOK	© 26,176
Caseyville	MCD-Township	ST. CLAIR	© 25,987
Elmwood Park	Inc. Place	COOK	◆ 25,638
Dolton	Inc. Place	COOK	◆ 25,621
Carbondale	Inc. Place	JACKSON	◆ 25,605
Belvidere	MCD-Township	BOONE	© 25,212
West Chicago	Inc. Place	DUPAGE	◆ 25,204
Woodstock	Inc. Place	MCHENRY	◆ 25,140
Rolling Meadows	Inc. Place	COOK	◆ 25,118
Westmont	Inc. Place	DUPAGE	◆ 25,067
Freeport	Inc. Place	STEPHENSON	◆ 24,837
New Lenox	Inc. Place	WILL	◆ 24,674
Geneva	Inc. Place	KANE	◆ 24,611
Homer Glen	Inc. Place	WILL	◆ 24,224
O'Fallon	Inc. Place	ST. CLAIR	◆ 24,056
Zion	Inc. Place	LAKE	◆ 23,963
Fremont	MCD-Township	LAKE	© 23,955
Machesney Park	Inc. Place	WINNEBAGO	◆ 23,873
Blue Island	Inc. Place	COOK	◆ 23,689
Moline	MCD-Township	ROCK ISLAND	© 23,594
Crete	MCD-Township	WILL	© 23,589
Vernon Hills	Inc. Place	LAKE	◆ 23,528
Edwardsville	Inc. Place	MADISON	◆ 23,509
Roselle	Inc. Place	DUPAGE	◆ 23,470
Loves Park	Inc. Place	WINNEBAGO	◆ 23,326
Geneva	MCD-Township	KANE	© 23,268
Melrose Park	Inc. Place	COOK	◆ 23,233
Charleston	MCD-Township	COLES	® 23,011
Zion	MCD-Township	LAKE	© 22,866
Darien	Inc. Place	DUPAGE	◆ 22,737
East Peoria	Inc. Place	TAZEWELL	◆ 22,697
Calumet	MCD-Township	COOK	© 22,374
Grayslake	Inc. Place	LAKE	◆ 22,351
Lockport	Inc. Place	WILL	◆ 22,306
Bloomingdale	Inc. Place	DUPAGE	◆ 22,233
Morton Grove	Inc. Place	COOK	◆ 21,986
Antioch	MCD-Township	LAKE	© 21,879
O'Fallon	MCD-Township	ST. CLAIR	© 21,859
Villa Park	Inc. Place	DUPAGE	◆ 21,666
Hampton	MCD-Township	ROCK ISLAND	® 21,638
Lisle	Inc. Place	DUPAGE	◆ 21,603
Park Forest	Inc. Place	COOK	◆ 21,548
South Holland	Inc. Place	COOK	◆ 21,471
South Elgin	Inc. Place	KANE	◆ 21,096
Charleston	Inc. Place	COLES	◆ 21,063
Bensenville	Inc. Place	DUPAGE	◆ 21,027
Lake Forest	Inc. Place	LAKE	◆ 20,973
Libertyville	Inc. Place	LAKE	◆ 20,961
Macomb	Inc. Place	MCDONOUGH	◆ 19,985
Evergreen Park	Inc. Place	COOK	◆ 19,854
East Moline	Inc. Place	ROCK ISLAND	◆ 19,823
Bellwood	Inc. Place	COOK	◆ 19,733
Alsip	Inc. Place	COOK	◆ 19,725
Franklin Park	Inc. Place	COOK	◆ 19,489
Washington	MCD-Township	TAZEWELL	© 19,427
Limestone	MCD-Township	PEORIA	© 19,374
South Rock Island	MCD-Township	ROCK ISLAND	© 19,174
Brookfield	Inc. Place	COOK	© 19,085
Lake Zurich	Inc. Place	LAKE	◆ 18,993
Homewood	Inc. Place	COOK	◆ 18,840
Jacksonville	Inc. Place	MORGAN	◆ 18,691
Sterling	MCD-Township	WHITESIDE	® 18,677
Macomb City	MCD-Township	MCDONOUGH	© 18,558
Deerfield	Inc. Place	LAKE	© 18,420
Groveland	MCD-Township	TAZEWELL	© 18,376
Ottawa	Inc. Place	LA SALLE	◆ 18,309
Hinsdale	Inc. Place	DUPAGE	◆ 18,197
Dorr	MCD-Township	MCHENRY	© 18,157
Lemont	MCD-Township	COOK	© 18,002
Dixon	MCD-Township	LEE	© 17,925
Rock Island	MCD-Township	ROCK ISLAND	© 17,763
Mattoon	Inc. Place	COLES	◆ 17,757
Cherry Valley	MCD-Township	WINNEBAGO	© 17,692
Crest Hill	Inc. Place	WILL	◆ 17,681
Palos Hills	Inc. Place	COOK	© 17,665
Hickory Point	MCD-Township	MACON	© 17,603
Benton	MCD-Township	LAKE	© 17,413
Grant	MCD-Township	LAKE	© 17,397
Goodings Grove	CDP	WILL	© 17,084
Marion	Inc. Place	WILLIAMSON	◆ 17,079
Prospect Heights	Inc. Place	COOK	® 17,061
Westchester	Inc. Place	COOK	© 16,824
Centralia	MCD-Township	MARION	© 16,533
Wauconda	MCD-Township	LAKE	® 16,403
Cahokia	Inc. Place	ST. CLAIR	© 16,391
Morton	MCD-Township	TAZEWELL	© 16,335
Godfrey	Inc. Place	MADISON	© 16,286
Godfrey	MCD-Township	MADISON	© 16,286
Mattoon	MCD-Township	COLES	© 16,184
Country Club Hills	Inc. Place	COOK	© 16,169
Mount Vernon	Inc. Place	JEFFERSON	◆ 16,149
Fairview Heights	Inc. Place	ST. CLAIR	◆ 16,107
Canton	MCD-Township	FULTON	© 16,075
Dixon	Inc. Place	LEE	© 15,941
Cuba	MCD-Township	LAKE	® 15,751
Riverside	MCD-Township	COOK	© 15,704
Forest Park	Inc. Place	COOK	© 15,688
La Grange	Inc. Place	COOK	© 15,608
Cary	Inc. Place	MCHENRY	© 15,531
Lincoln	Inc. Place	LOGAN	© 15,369
Bridgeview	Inc. Place	COOK	© 15,335
Bourbonnais	Inc. Place	KANKAKEE	© 15,256
Morton	Inc. Place	TAZEWELL	© 15,198
Canton	Inc. Place	FULTON	◆ 15,101
Sterling	Inc. Place	WHITESIDE	◆ 15,058
Riverdale	Inc. Place	COOK	© 15,055
Hazel Crest	Inc. Place	COOK	© 14,816
Mokena	Inc. Place	WILL	© 14,583
Mount Vernon	MCD-Township	JEFFERSON	© 14,443
Midlothian	Inc. Place	COOK	© 14,315
Norridge	Inc. Place	COOK	◆ 14,263
Chicago Ridge	Inc. Place	COOK	© 14,127
Campton	MCD-Township	KANE	© 14,072
Barrington	MCD-Township	COOK	® 14,030
Hickory Hills	Inc. Place	COOK	© 13,926
Newell	MCD-Township	VERMILION	© 13,835
LaSalle	MCD-Township	LA SALLE	© 13,744
Roscoe	MCD-Township	WINNEBAGO	© 13,578
Wood Dale	Inc. Place	DUPAGE	© 13,535
Rockton	MCD-Township	WINNEBAGO	© 13,534
Streator	Inc. Place	LA SALLE	◆ 13,513
Bruce	MCD-Township	LA SALLE	© 13,489
Centralia	Inc. Place	MARION	◆ 13,364
Warrenville	Inc. Place	DUPAGE	© 13,363
La Grange Park	Inc. Place	COOK	© 13,295
Monee	MCD-Township	WILL	© 13,294
Flagg	MCD-Township	OGLE	© 13,276
Pontiac	MCD-Township	LIVINGSTON	© 13,148
Fondulac	MCD-Township	TAZEWELL	© 13,138
Lemont	Inc. Place	COOK	© 13,098
Kewanee	Inc. Place	HENRY	© 12,944
Rantoul	Inc. Place	CHAMPAIGN	® 12,918
Woodside	MCD-Township	SANGAMON	® 12,828
Matteson	Inc. Place	COOK	◆ 12,826
Bradley	Inc. Place	KANKAKEE	© 12,784
Douglas	MCD-Township	EFFINGHAM	© 12,698
Taylorville	MCD-Township	CHRISTIAN	© 12,659
Markham	Inc. Place	COOK	© 12,620
Lindenhurst	Inc. Place	LAKE	© 12,539
Richton Park	Inc. Place	COOK	© 12,533
Western Springs	Inc. Place	COOK	© 12,493
Winnetka	Inc. Place	COOK	© 12,419
Lincolnwood	Inc. Place	COOK	© 12,359
Justice	Inc. Place	COOK	© 12,193
Effingham	Inc. Place	EFFINGHAM	◆ 12,188
Ottawa	MCD-Township	LA SALLE	© 12,177
Jarvis	MCD-Township	MADISON	© 12,062
Sycamore	Inc. Place	DEKALB	© 12,020
Canteen	MCD-Township	ST. CLAIR	® 11,929
Morris	Inc. Place	GRUNDY	© 11,928
Northlake	Inc. Place	COOK	© 11,878
Pontiac	Inc. Place	LIVINGSTON	© 11,864
Schiller Park	Inc. Place	COOK	© 11,850
Coloma	MCD-Township	WHITESIDE	© 11,844
Harrisburg	MCD-Township	SALINE	© 11,658
River Forest	Inc. Place	COOK	© 11,635
River Forest	MCD-Township	COOK	© 11,635
Champaign	MCD-Township	CHAMPAIGN	© 11,591
Taylorville	Inc. Place	CHRISTIAN	© 11,427
Herrin	Inc. Place	WILLIAMSON	© 11,298
Wood River	Inc. Place	MADISON	© 11,296
Palos Heights	Inc. Place	COOK	© 11,260
Rantoul	MCD-Township	CHAMPAIGN	® 11,257
Crestwood	Inc. Place	COOK	© 11,251
Nameoki	MCD-Township	MADISON	© 11,186
Worth	Inc. Place	COOK	© 11,047
Campton Hills	Inc. Place	KANE	● 11,000
Washington	Inc. Place	TAZEWELL	© 10,841
Monmouth	MCD-Township	WARREN	® 10,799
Murphysboro	MCD-Township	JACKSON	® 10,778
Paris	MCD-Township	EDGAR	© 10,692
Greenwood	MCD-Township	MCHENRY	© 10,677
River Grove	Inc. Place	COOK	© 10,668
Summit	Inc. Place	COOK	© 10,637
Blackhawk	MCD-Township	ROCK ISLAND	® 10,616
North Aurora	Inc. Place	KANE	© 10,585
Swansea	Inc. Place	ST. CLAIR	® 10,563
Long Creek	MCD-Township	MACON	© 10,547
Glen Carbon	Inc. Place	MADISON	© 10,425
Gages Lake	CDP-Census Area Only	LAKE	© 10,415
Sauk Village	Inc. Place	COOK	© 10,411
Burr Ridge	Inc. Place	DUPAGE	© 10,408
Sycamore	MCD-Township	DEKALB	© 10,401
Frankfort	Inc. Place	WILL	© 10,391
Kewanee	MCD-Township	HENRY	© 10,364
Peru	MCD-Township	LA SALLE	© 10,272
Lyons	Inc. Place	COOK	© 10,255
Stookey	MCD-Town	ST. CLAIR	© 10,185
Barrington	Inc. Place	COOK	© 10,168
Robinson	MCD-Township	CRAWFORD	© 10,138
Mahomet	MCD-Township	CHAMPAIGN	© 10,113
Beach Park	Inc. Place	LAKE	© 10,072
Shiloh Valley	MCD-Township	ST. CLAIR	® 10,048
Olney	MCD-Township	RICHLAND	© 9,883
Harrisburg	Inc. Place	SALINE	© 9,860
Salem	MCD-Township	MARION	© 9,849
Monmouth	Inc. Place	WARREN	© 9,841
Huntley	Inc. Place	MCHENRY	◆ 9,820
Steger	Inc. Place	COOK	® 9,679
Peru	Inc. Place	LA SALLE	◆ 9,602
Sugar Grove	MCD-Township	KANE	© 9,595
La Salle	Inc. Place	LA SALLE	◆ 9,594
Rock Falls	Inc. Place	WHITESIDE	© 9,580
Jersey	MCD-Township	JERSEY	© 9,496
Bethalto	Inc. Place	MADISON	© 9,454
Wauconda	Inc. Place	LAKE	© 9,448
Rochelle	Inc. Place	OGLE	© 9,424
Flossmoor	Inc. Place	COOK	© 9,301
East Lincoln	MCD-Township	LOGAN	© 9,209
Fox Lake	Inc. Place	LAKE	© 9,178

Entries in **UPPERCASE** are counties.
Entries in **bold** have populations of 2,500 or more.
Names in parentheses are alternate names.
Inc. Place — Incorporated Place
RMC Place — Rand McNally Designated Place
CDP — Census Designated Place
MCD — Minor Civil Division

⊡ County Seat
▲ Minor Civil Division
elev. Elevation
Post Office
Hospital
College
■ Principal Business Center
★ Ranally Metro Area (RMA) Abbreviation
z Zip Code(s)

Ⓟ Previous Census Population
® Revised Census Population
Ⓐ Annexation Population
● Rand McNally Population Estimate
© Final Census Population
Ⓢ Special Census Population
◆ Estimated Population

For additional definitions see Glossary, Volume 1, and Introduction, Volume 2.

Place Name	Place Type	County	Population
Princeton	MCD-Township	BUREAU	© 9,164
Paris	Inc. Place	EDGAR	© 9,077
Glenwood	Inc. Place	COOK	© 9,000
Willowbrook	Inc. Place	DUPAGE	© 8,967
Riverside	Inc. Place	COOK	© 8,895
Cincinnati	MCD-Township	TAZEWELL	© 8,862
Antioch	Inc. Place	LAKE	© 8,788
Glencoe	Inc. Place	COOK	© 8,762
Chemung	MCD-Township	MCHENRY	© 8,761
Winfield	Inc. Place	DUPAGE	© 8,718
Murphysboro	Inc. Place	JACKSON	® 8,694
Oak Brook	Inc. Place	DUPAGE	◆ 8,654
Chatham	Inc. Place	SANGAMON	© 8,583
Benton	MCD-Township	FRANKLIN	® 8,570
Troy	Inc. Place	MADISON	© 8,524
Calumet Park	Inc. Place	COOK	© 8,516
Highland	Inc. Place	MADISON	© 8,438
Chester	Inc. Place	RANDOLPH	® 8,378
Channahon	MCD-Township	WILL	© 8,339
Itasca	Inc. Place	DUPAGE	© 8,302
Harwood Heights	Inc. Place	COOK	© 8,297
Broadview	Inc. Place	COOK	© 8,264
Hall	MCD-Township	BUREAU	© 8,245
Chillicothe	MCD-Township	PEORIA	© 8,233
South Ottawa	MCD-Township	LA SALLE	© 8,222
West Frankfort	Inc. Place	FRANKLIN	© 8,196
Boulder Hill	CDP-Census Area Only	KENDALL	© 8,169
Clear Lake	MCD-Township	SANGAMON	© 8,155
Hillside	Inc. Place	COOK	© 8,155
Island Lake	Inc. Place	LAKE	© 8,153
Helvetia	MCD-Township	MADISON	© 8,145
Georgetown	MCD-Township	VERMILION	© 8,083
Urbana	MCD-Township	CHAMPAIGN	® 8,063
West Lincoln	MCD-Township	LOGAN	© 8,042
Chouteau	MCD-Township	MADISON	© 8,010
Harvard	Inc. Place	MCHENRY	© 7,996
Jerseyville	Inc. Place	JERSEY	© 7,984
Mount Carmel	Inc. Place	WABASH	© 7,982
Olney	Inc. Place	RICHLAND	◆ 7,952
Central	MCD-Township	BOND	© 7,941
Clintonia	MCD-Township	DE WITT	© 7,926
Columbia	Inc. Place	MONROE	© 7,922
Salem	Inc. Place	MARION	© 7,909
Manteno	MCD-Township	KANKAKEE	© 7,846
Morris	MCD-Township	GRUNDY	© 7,781
Frankfort Square	CDP-Census Area Only	WILL	© 7,766
Crete	Inc. Place	WILL	® 7,712
Fort Russell	MCD-Township	MADISON	© 7,710
Shorewood	Inc. Place	WILL	© 7,686
Bristol	MCD-Township	KENDALL	© 7,677
Little Rock	MCD-Township	KENDALL	© 7,662
Shiloh	Inc. Place	ST. CLAIR	© 7,643
Waterloo	Inc. Place	MONROE	© 7,614
Clarendon Hills	Inc. Place	DUPAGE	© 7,610
Mendota	MCD-Township	LA SALLE	© 7,539
Hillsboro	MCD-Township	MONTGOMERY	® 7,504
Princeton	Inc. Place	BUREAU	© 7,501
Clinton	Inc. Place	DE WITT	© 7,485
Wonder Lake	CDP-Census Area Only	MCHENRY	© 7,463
Lynwood	Inc. Place	COOK	© 7,377
Channahon	Inc. Place	WILL	© 7,344

Place Name	Place Type	County	Population
Worth	MCD-Township	WOODFORD	© 7,285
Mendota	Inc. Place	LA SALLE	© 7,272
Silvis	Inc. Place	ROCK ISLAND	© 7,269
Geneseo	MCD-Township	HENRY	© 7,255
Marengo	MCD-Township	MCHENRY	© 7,239
Frankfort	MCD-Township	FRANKLIN	® 7,149
Sugar Loaf	MCD-Township	ST. CLAIR	® 7,102
Springfield	MCD-Township	SANGAMON	© 7,046
Carmi	MCD-Township	WHITE	© 6,996
Cortland	MCD-Township	DEKALB	© 6,986
Vandalia	Inc. Place	FAYETTE	© 6,975
Greenville	Inc. Place	BOND	© 6,955
Sandwich	MCD-Township	DEKALB	© 6,920
Carlinville	MCD-Township	MACOUPIN	© 6,910
Benton	Inc. Place	FRANKLIN	® 6,879
Pana	MCD-Township	CHRISTIAN	© 6,860
Lawrence	MCD-Township	LAWRENCE	© 6,831
East Alton	Inc. Place	MADISON	© 6,830
Robinson	Inc. Place	CRAWFORD	© 6,822
Litchfield	Inc. Place	MONTGOMERY	© 6,815
Venice	MCD-Township	MADISON	© 6,783
Orland Hills	Inc. Place	COOK	© 6,779
Inverness	Inc. Place	COOK	© 6,749
Long Grove	Inc. Place	LAKE	© 6,735
North Riverside	Inc. Place	COOK	◆ 6,728
Colona	MCD-Township	HENRY	© 6,699
Grant	MCD-Township	VERMILION	© 6,672
Winthrop Harbor	Inc. Place	LAKE	© 6,670
Vandalia	MCD-Township	FAYETTE	® 6,667
University Park	Inc. Place	WILL	© 6,662
Northville	MCD-Township	LA SALLE	© 6,642
Park City	Inc. Place	LAKE	© 6,637
Peoria Heights	Inc. Place	PEORIA	© 6,635
Robbins	Inc. Place	COOK	© 6,635
Beardstown	MCD-Township	CASS	© 6,611
Richwoods	MCD-Township	PEORIA	© 6,539
Sandwich	Inc. Place	DEKALB	© 6,509
Metropolis	Inc. Place	MASSAC	© 6,482
Harter	MCD-Township	CLAY	© 6,481
Geneseo	Inc. Place	HENRY	© 6,480
Mascoutah	MCD-Township	ST. CLAIR	© 6,474
Du Quoin	Inc. Place	PERRY	© 6,448
Manteno	Inc. Place	KANKAKEE	© 6,414
Medina	MCD-Township	PEORIA	© 6,388
Marengo	Inc. Place	MCHENRY	© 6,355
East Eldorado	MCD-Township	SALINE	© 6,349
Shiloh	MCD-Township	JEFFERSON	© 6,345
Mount Zion	MCD-Township	MACON	© 6,324
Bartonville	Inc. Place	PEORIA	© 6,310
Melrose	MCD-Township	ADAMS	© 6,305
Roscoe	Inc. Place	WINNEBAGO	© 6,244
Yorkville	Inc. Place	KENDALL	© 6,189
Stickney	Inc. Place	COOK	© 6,148
Lincolnshire	Inc. Place	LAKE	© 6,108
Blackberry	MCD-Township	KANE	© 6,071
Lake Bluff	Inc. Place	LAKE	© 6,056
Reed	MCD-Township	WILL	© 6,051
Wilmington	MCD-Township	WILL	© 6,050
Round Lake Park	Inc. Place	LAKE	© 6,038
Auburn	MCD-Township	SANGAMON	© 6,020
Chatham	MCD-Township	SANGAMON	© 6,019

Place Name	Place Type	County	Population
Hawthorn Woods	Inc. Place	LAKE	® 6,015
Chillicothe	Inc. Place	PEORIA	© 5,996
Countryside	Inc. Place	COOK	© 5,991
Hoopeston	Inc. Place	VERMILION	© 5,965
Centreville	Inc. Place	ST. CLAIR	© 5,951
Washington Park	Inc. Place	ST. CLAIR	® 5,942
Sullivan	MCD-Township	MOULTRIE	© 5,874
Lake Villa	Inc. Place	LAKE	© 5,864
Round Lake	Inc. Place	LAKE	© 5,842
Byron	MCD-Township	OGLE	© 5,840
Aroma	MCD-Township	KANKAKEE	© 5,835
Beardstown	Inc. Place	CASS	© 5,766
Staunton	MCD-Township	MACOUPIN	© 5,731
Carlinville	Inc. Place	MACOUPIN	© 5,685
Watseka	Inc. Place	IROQUOIS	© 5,670
Mascoutah	Inc. Place	ST. CLAIR	© 5,659
Manlius	MCD-Township	LA SALLE	© 5,652
Plano	Inc. Place	KENDALL	© 5,633
Pontoon Beach	Inc. Place	MADISON	© 5,620
Manhattan	MCD-Township	WILL	© 5,615
Pana	Inc. Place	CHRISTIAN	© 5,614
Monticello	MCD-Township	PIATT	© 5,604
Brookside	MCD-Township	CLINTON	© 5,576
Looking Glass	MCD-Township	CLINTON	© 5,555
Millstadt	MCD-Township	ST. CLAIR	© 5,493
Montgomery	Inc. Place	KANE	© 5,471
Highwood	Inc. Place	LAKE	® 5,470
Pinckneyville	Inc. Place	PERRY	© 5,464
Creve Coeur	Inc. Place	TAZEWELL	© 5,448
West Dundee	Inc. Place	KANE	© 5,428
Carmi	Inc. Place	WHITE	© 5,422
Fairfield	Inc. Place	WAYNE	© 5,421
Patton	MCD-Township	FORD	© 5,413
Knox	MCD-Township	KNOX	© 5,407
Spring Valley	Inc. Place	BUREAU	© 5,398
South Beloit	Inc. Place	WINNEBAGO	© 5,397
Johnsburg	Inc. Place	MCHENRY	© 5,391
Tuscola	MCD-Township	DOUGLAS	© 5,390
Northfield	Inc. Place	COOK	© 5,389
Milan	Inc. Place	ROCK ISLAND	© 5,348
Genoa	MCD-Township	DEKALB	© 5,342
Oregon-Nashua	MCD-Township	OGLE	© 5,310
Havana	MCD-Township	MASON	© 5,303
Rockton	Inc. Place	WINNEBAGO	© 5,296
Mount Pleasant	MCD-Township	WHITESIDE	© 5,291
Berkeley	Inc. Place	COOK	© 5,245
Braidwood	Inc. Place	WILL	© 5,203
Colona	Inc. Place	HENRY	© 5,173
Winnebago	MCD-Township	WINNEBAGO	© 5,142
Monticello	Inc. Place	PIATT	© 5,138
Anna	Inc. Place	UNION	© 5,136
North Litchfield	MCD-Township	MONTGOMERY	© 5,135
Wilmington	Inc. Place	WILL	© 5,134
Sugar Creek	MCD-Township	CLINTON	© 5,133
Stone Park	Inc. Place	COOK	© 5,127
Freeburg	MCD-Township	ST. CLAIR	© 5,124
Flora	Inc. Place	CLAY	© 5,086
Breese	MCD-Township	CLINTON	© 5,044
Staunton	Inc. Place	MACOUPIN	© 5,030
Willow Springs	Inc. Place	COOK	© 5,027
Tyrone	MCD-Township	FRANKLIN	® 5,008

County Business Data

County	FIPS Code	County Seat	Land Area (Sq. Mi.)	Census Population			Wholesale Trade		Manufacturing, 2002			
				4/1/2000	4/1/1990	% Change 1990-2000	Sales, 2002 ($1,000)	% Change 1997-2002	Establish-ments	Total Employees	Value Added ($1,000)	Ranally Mfg. Units
Adams	001	Quincy	857	68,277	66,090	3.3	(d)	(d)	91	(d)	(d)	...
Alexander	003	Cairo	236	9,590	10,626	-9.7	(d)	(d)	...	(d)	(d)	...
Bond	005	Greenville	380	17,633	14,991	17.6	(d)	(d)	11	736	65,564	35
Boone	007	Belvidere	281	41,786	30,806	35.6	(d)	(d)	65	4,174	631,473	334
Brown	009	Mount Sterling	306	6,950	5,836	19.1	(d)	(d)	...	(d)	(d)	...
Bureau	011	Princeton	869	35,503	35,688	-0.5	1,023,926	(d)	48	2,520	262,369	139
Calhoun	013	Hardin	254	5,084	5,322	-4.5	(d)	(d)	...	(d)	(d)	...
Carroll	015	Mount Carroll	444	16,674	16,805	-0.8	(d)	(d)	27	1,113	144,565	76
Cass	017	Virginia	376	13,695	13,437	1.9	(d)	(d)	11	(d)	(d)	...
Champaign	019	Urbana	997	179,669	173,025	3.8	2,613,361	8.0	151	9,469	1,495,778	791
Christian	021	Taylorville	709	35,372	34,418	2.8	(d)	(d)	24	2,002	192,861	102
Clark	023	Marshall	502	17,008	15,921	6.8	125,021	19.3	20	1,434	155,051	82
Clay	025	Louisville	469	14,560	14,460	0.7	97,233	15.5	20	2,206	182,167	96
Clinton	027	Carlyle	474	35,535	33,944	4.7	(d)	(d)	44	1,141	120,730	64
Coles	029	Charleston	508	53,196	51,644	3.0	(d)	(d)	48	(d)	(d)	...
Cook	031	Chicago	946	5,376,741	5,105,067	5.3	117,324,662	-2.7	6,937	282,373	33,292,244	17,614
Crawford	033	Robinson	444	20,452	19,464	5.1	290,890	17.9	19	2,215	520,591	275
Cumberland	035	Toledo	346	11,253	10,670	5.5	(d)	(d)	...	(d)	(d)	...
DeKalb	037	Sycamore	634	88,969	77,932	14.2	431,831	-50.5	139	5,308	596,251	315
De Witt	039	Clinton	398	16,798	16,516	1.7	113,168	-18.0	12	641	79,009	42
Douglas	041	Tuscola	417	19,922	19,464	2.4	185,524	-8.8	89	2,538	252,208	133
DuPage	043	Wheaton	334	904,161	781,666	15.7	92,529,975	24.5	1,985	67,071	7,707,637	4,078
Edgar	045	Paris	624	19,704	19,595	0.6	145,260	-11.3	27	1,718	137,197	73
Edwards	047	Albion	222	6,971	7,440	-6.3	76,673	-27.5	6	(d)	(d)	...
Effingham	049	Effingham	479	34,264	31,704	8.1	761,452	186.4	68	4,777	564,109	298
Fayette	051	Vandalia	716	21,802	20,893	4.4	193,115	3.7	19	1,008	84,286	45
Ford	053	Paxton	486	14,241	14,275	-0.2	(d)	(d)	20	(d)	(d)	...
Franklin	055	Benton	412	39,018	40,319	-3.2	78,327	7.9	37	1,323	120,579	64
Fulton	057	Lewistown	866	38,250	38,080	0.4	(d)	(d)	...	(d)	(d)	...
Gallatin	059	Shawneetown	324	6,445	6,909	-6.7	28,620	(d)	...	(d)	(d)	...
Greene	061	Carrollton	543	14,761	15,317	-3.6	92,436	31.9	...	(d)	(d)	...
Grundy	063	Morris	420	37,535	32,337	16.1	477,467	23.3	45	1,602	566,152	300
Hamilton	065	McLeansboro	435	8,621	8,499	1.4	(d)	(d)	...	(d)	(d)	...
Hancock	067	Carthage	795	20,121	21,373	-5.9	339,041	60.0	26	1,616	100,266	53
Hardin	069	Elizabethtown	178	4,800	5,189	-7.5	(d)	(d)	...	(d)	(d)	...
Henderson	071	Oquawka	379	8,213	8,096	1.4	32,437	50.3	...	(d)	(d)	...
Henry	073	Cambridge	823	51,020	51,159	-0.3	(d)	(d)	52	4,105	330,740	175
Iroquois	075	Watseka	1,116	31,334	30,787	1.8	263,210	-35.1	28	814	70,369	37
Jackson	077	Murphysboro	588	59,612	61,067	-2.4	(d)	(d)	35	839	75,255	40
Jasper	079	Newton	494	10,117	10,609	-4.6	111,766	-7.0	...	(d)	(d)	...
Jefferson	081	Mount Vernon	571	40,045	37,020	8.2	(d)	(d)	42	(d)	(d)	...
Jersey	083	Jerseyville	369	21,668	20,539	5.5	(d)	(d)	...	(d)	(d)	...
Jo Daviess	085	Galena	601	22,289	21,821	2.1	91,208	-30.0	43	1,504	156,389	83
Johnson	087	Vienna	345	12,878	11,347	13.5	(d)	(d)	...	(d)	(d)	...
Kane	089	Geneva	520	404,119	317,471	27.3	11,434,376	33.6	908	37,647	4,240,714	2,244
Kankakee	091	Kankakee	677	103,833	96,255	7.9	(d)	(d)	116	6,308	967,841	512
Kendall	093	Yorkville	321	54,544	39,413	38.4	(d)	(d)	73	2,405	300,841	159
Knox	095	Galesburg	716	55,836	56,393	-1.0	199,680	-47.7	44	4,150	338,378	179
Lake	097	Waukegan	448	644,356	516,418	24.8	(d)	(d)	928	51,336	8,552,279	4,525
La Salle	099	Ottawa	1,135	111,509	106,913	4.3	1,201,496	-7.0	150	5,955	837,138	443
Lawrence	101	Lawrenceville	372	15,452	15,972	-3.3	(d)	(d)	15	(d)	(d)	...
Lee	103	Dixon	725	36,062	34,392	4.9	(d)	(d)	37	4,056	425,582	225
Livingston	105	Pontiac	1,044	39,678	39,301	1.0	(d)	(d)	55	4,531	613,722	325
Logan	107	Lincoln	618	31,183	30,798	1.3	172,601	-31.6	24	1,427	198,922	105
Macon	115	Decatur	581	114,706	117,206	-2.1	3,308,329	1.8	126	8,826	1,760,168	931
Macoupin	117	Carlinville	864	49,019	47,679	2.8	247,894	3.7	44	833	67,240	36
Madison	119	Edwardsville	725	258,941	249,238	3.9	2,331,913	3.0	212	15,142	2,215,881	1,172
Marion	121	Salem	572	41,691	41,561	0.3	148,648	-10.8	57	3,914	443,355	235
Marshall	123	Lacon	386	13,180	12,846	2.6	(d)	(d)	18	854	106,808	57
Mason	125	Havana	539	16,038	16,269	-1.4	228,610	-25.1	...	(d)	(d)	...
Massac	127	Metropolis	239	15,161	14,752	2.8	(d)	(d)	9	603	104,930	56
McDonough	109	Macomb	589	32,913	35,244	-6.6	(d)	(d)	30	1,510	102,313	54
McHenry	111	Woodstock	604	260,077	183,241	41.9	7,688,122	167.5	592	21,107	2,092,055	1,107
McLean	113	Bloomington	1,184	150,433	129,180	16.5	2,557,582	89.7	113	6,574	1,039,530	550
Menard	129	Petersburg	314	12,486	11,164	11.8	(d)	(d)	...	(d)	(d)	...
Mercer	131	Aledo	561	16,957	17,290	-1.9	(d)	(d)	...	(d)	(d)	...
Monroe	133	Waterloo	388	27,619	22,422	23.2	183,853	(d)	...	(d)	(d)	...
Montgomery	135	Hillsboro	704	30,652	30,728	-0.2	177,695	-17.4	37	1,491	122,283	65
Morgan	137	Jacksonville	569	36,616	36,397	0.6	(d)	(d)	27	(d)	(d)	...
Moultrie	139	Sullivan	336	14,287	13,930	2.6	66,870	-35.2	21	1,896	167,236	88
Ogle	141	Oregon	759	51,032	45,957	11.0	(d)	(d)	71	4,957	399,771	212
Peoria	143	Peoria	620	183,433	182,827	0.3	2,150,765	-63.4	170	11,783	1,549,477	820
Perry	145	Pinckneyville	441	23,094	21,412	7.9	63,353	(d)	27	1,899	132,812	70
Piatt	147	Monticello	440	16,365	15,548	5.3	(d)	(d)	...	(d)	(d)	...
Pike	149	Pittsfield	830	17,384	17,577	-1.1	(d)	(d)	...	(d)	(d)	...
Pope	151	Golconda	371	4,413	4,373	0.9	(d)	(d)	...	(d)	(d)	...
Pulaski	153	Mound City	201	7,348	7,523	-2.3	(d)	(d)	...	(d)	(d)	...
Putnam	155	Hennepin	160	6,086	5,730	6.2	57,345	(d)	...	(d)	(d)	...
Randolph	157	Chester	578	33,893	34,583	-2.0	(d)	(d)	31	2,720	203,894	108
Richland	159	Olney	360	16,149	16,545	-2.4	(d)	(d)	39	611	89,912	48
Rock Island	161	Rock Island	427	149,374	148,723	0.4	3,060,713	49.8	169	8,098	1,325,275	701

Entries in **UPPERCASE** are counties.
Entries in **bold** have populations of 2,500 or more.
Names in parentheses are alternate names.
Inc. Place — Incorporated Place
RMC Place — Rand McNally Designated Place
CDP — Census Designated Place
MCD — Minor Civil Division

⊡ County Seat
▲ Minor Civil Division
elev. Elevation
🅿 Post Office

H Hospital
C College
■ Principal Business Center
★ Ranally Metro Area (RMA) Abbreviation
z Zip Code(s)

Ⓟ Previous Census Population
® Revised Census Population
Ⓐ Annexation Population
● Rand McNally Population Estimate
© Final Census Population
Ⓢ Special Census Population
◆ Estimated Population

For additional definitions see Glossary, Volume 1, and Introduction, Volume 2.

County	FIPS Code	County Seat	Land Area (Sq. Mi.)	Census Population			Wholesale Trade		Manufacturing, 2002			
				4/1/2000	4/1/1990	% Change 1990-2000	Sales, 2002 ($1,000)	% Change 1997-2002	Establish-ments	Total Employees	Value Added ($1,000)	Ranally Mfg. Units
St. Clair	163	Belleville	664	256,082	262,852	-2.6	1,096,769	-32.1	204	7,117	795,578	421
Saline	165	Harrisburg	383	26,733	26,551	0.7	(d)	(d)	...	(d)	(d)	...
Sangamon	167	Springfield	868	188,951	178,386	5.9	(d)	(d)	130	(d)	(d)	...
Schuyler	169	Rushville	437	7,189	7,498	-4.1	(d)	(d)	...	(d)	(d)	...
Scott	171	Winchester	251	5,537	5,644	-1.9	(d)	(d)	...	(d)	(d)	...
Shelby	173	Shelbyville	759	22,893	22,261	2.8	143,466	-6.3	15	1,327	128,565	68
Stark	175	Toulon	288	6,332	6,534	-3.1	(d)	(d)	...	(d)	(d)	...
Stephenson	177	Freeport	564	48,979	48,052	1.9	(d)	(d)	65	4,858	515,051	272
Tazewell	179	Pekin	649	128,485	123,692	3.9	5,816,120	(d)	124	5,964	856,974	453
Union	181	Jonesboro	416	18,293	17,619	3.8	(d)	(d)	...	(d)	(d)	...
Vermilion	183	Danville	899	83,919	88,257	-4.9	(d)	(d)	108	5,899	587,220	311
Wabash	185	Mount Carmel	223	12,937	13,111	-1.3	54,726	4.6	16	1,189	47,393	25
Warren	187	Monmouth	543	18,735	19,181	-2.3	152,738	-7.1	26	1,521	47,303	25
Washington	189	Nashville	563	15,148	14,965	1.2	197,517	53.2	16	1,840	223,633	118
Wayne	191	Fairfield	714	17,151	17,241	-0.5	72,033	-36.4	16	(d)	(d)	...
White	193	Carmi	495	15,371	16,522	-7.0	129,289	23.4	...	(d)	(d)	...
Whiteside	195	Morrison	685	60,653	60,186	0.8	553,438	14.8	100	4,550	415,400	220
Will	197	Joliet	837	502,266	357,313	40.6	6,640,965	68.3	593	25,992	3,774,946	1,997
Williamson	199	Marion	423	61,296	57,733	6.2	219,717	16.1	50	2,713	206,176	109
Winnebago	201	Rockford	514	278,418	252,913	10.1	(d)	(d)	720	31,172	3,864,987	2,045
Woodford	203	Eureka	528	35,469	32,653	8.6	(d)	(d)	47	2,009	386,249	204
The State			**55,584**	**12,419,293**	**11,430,602**	**8.6**	**317,467,059**	**15.0**	**16,860**	**741,908**	**91,825,126**	**48,582**

(d) Data not available. Corresponding percentages or Ranally Manufacturing Units are estimates.
... Represents 0 or amount too minimal to be reported.

Administrative Divisions

Townships: Eighty-six of Illinois' 102 counties are divided into townships. Every place within these counties, except for the city of Chicago, is within some township. Townships may levy taxes, elect certain officials, and perform limited governmental functions. Only townships with an active government recognized by the U.S. Census of Governments are printed in this index.

Precincts: The remaining 16 counties are divided into precincts for convenience in local administration. The precincts do not possess governmental and taxing powers, and they are not listed in this index.

Index of Places and Counties

A

Abingdon; Inc. Place; KNOX; **170** G-6; elev. 753ft./230m.; 🄿; ★ **GLSB**; **z** 61410; Ⓟ 3,597; Ⓒ 3,612
Abington; MCD-Township; MERCER; ***170** F-4; mail Seaton **z** 61476; Ⓟ 468; Ⓒ 453
Absher; WILLIAMSON; see Dykersburg (RMC Place)
Acacia Acres; RMC Place; COOK; ★ **CHI**; mail La Grange **z** 60525
Acme Station; RMC Place; PEORIA; ★ **PEOR**; mail Peoria **z** 61607; pop. incl. with Bartonville (Inc. Place)
Adair; RMC Place; MCDONOUGH; **170** H-5; elev. 650ft./198m.; 🄿; **z** 61411; ● 230
Adams (Newtown); RMC Place; ADAMS; **170** J-3; mail Liberty **z** 62347; ● 50
Adams; MCD-Township; LA SALLE; ***170** D-10; mail Leland **z** 60531; Ⓟ 1,353; Ⓒ 1,589
ADAMS; **170** J-4; Ⓟ 66,090; Ⓒ 68,277; ◆ 66,575
Adams Corner; RMC Place; WABASH; ***171** O-13; mail Allendale **z** 62410; rural
Addieville; Inc. Place; WASHINGTON; **171** P-8; elev. 466ft./142m.; 🄿; **z** 62214; Ⓟ 257; Ⓒ 267
Addison; Inc. Place; DUPAGE; ▲ Addison; **172** H-5; elev. 691ft./211m.; 🄿 🄲 1,440 ■; ★ **CHI**; **z** 60101; Ⓟ 32,058; Ⓒ 35,914; ◆ 36,693
Addison; MCD-Township; DUPAGE; ***170** C-12; 🄿 🄲 1,440; ★ **CHI**; **z** 60101; Ⓟ 82,727; Ⓒ 88,900
Adeline; Inc. Place; OGLE; **170** B-8; elev. 796ft./243m.; mail Leaf River **z** 61047; Ⓟ 141; Ⓒ 139
Aden; RMC Place; HAMILTON; ***171** P-11; mail Wayne City **z** 62895; rural
Adrian; RMC Place; HANCOCK; **170** H-3; elev. 700ft./213m.; 🄿; **z** 62330; ● 60
Aero Estates; RMC Place; DUPAGE; ***170** C-12; ★ **CHI**; mail Naperville **z** 60564; ● 160
Aetna; COLES; see Etna (RMC Place)
Aetna; MCD-Township; LOGAN; ***170** I-9; mail Kenney **z** 61749; Ⓟ 540; Ⓒ 524
Afolkey; RMC Place; STEPHENSON; ***170** A-8; elev. 913ft./278m.; mail Dakota **z** 61018; ● 35
Afton; MCD-Township; DEKALB; ***170** C-10; mail DeKalb **z** 60115; Ⓟ 665; Ⓒ 640
Agnew; RMC Place; WHITESIDE; ***170** C-7; mail Sterling **z** 61081; rural
Airport; CARROLL; see Ayers (RMC Place)
Airport Heights; RMC Place; PEORIA; ★ **PEOR**; mail Peoria **z** 61607; ● 370
Akin; RMC Place; FRANKLIN; **171** Q-10; elev. 473ft./144m.; 🄿; **z** 62805; ● 110
Akron; MCD-Township; PEORIA; ***170** F-7; mail Princeville **z** 61559; Ⓟ 859; Ⓒ 984
Alan Dale (Allendale); RMC Place; MADISON; ***171** N-6; ★ **ST.L**; mail Godfrey **z** 62035; pop. incl. with Godfrey (Inc. Place)
Alba; MCD-Township; HENRY; ***170** D-7; mail Atkinson **z** 61235; Ⓟ 268; Ⓒ 190
Albany; Inc. Place; WHITESIDE; ▲ Albany; **170** C-6; 🄿; ★ **CLNT**; **z** 61230; Ⓟ 835; Ⓒ 895
Albany; MCD-Township; WHITESIDE; ***170** C-6; 🄿; **z** 61230; Ⓟ 994; Ⓒ 1,060
Albany Park; RMC Place; COOK; mail Chicago **z** 60625, **z** 60630; pop. incl. with Chicago (Inc. Place)
Albers; Inc. Place; CLINTON; **171** O-8; elev. 434ft./132m.; 🄿; ★ **ST.L**; **z** 62215; Ⓟ 700; Ⓒ 878
Albion; Inc. Place; ⊡ EDWARDS; **171** P-12; elev. 500ft./152m.; 🄿; **z** 62806; Ⓟ 2,116; Ⓒ 1,933
Albright Acres; RMC Place; JERSEY; ***171** M-6; ★ **ST.L**; mail Cottage Hills **z** 62018; ● 50
Alden; RMC Place; MCHENRY; ▲ Alden; **170** A-11; elev. 962ft./293m.; 🄿; **z** 60001 & mail Harvard **z** 60033; ● 250
Alden; MCD-Township; MCHENRY; ***170** A-11; 🄿; **z** 60001 & mail Harvard **z** 60033; Ⓟ 1,457; Ⓒ 1,534
Alderson; FAYETTE; see Woodyard (RMC Place)
Aldridge; RMC Place; UNION; ***171** S-8; mail Wolf Lake **z** 62998; rural
Aledo; Inc. Place; ⊡ MERCER; **170** E-5; elev. 731ft./223m.; 🄿 🄷; **z** 61231; Ⓟ 3,681; Ⓒ 3,613
Alexander; RMC Place; MORGAN; **171** K-6; elev. 660ft./201m.; 🄿; **z** 62601; ● 300
ALEXANDER; **171** T-8; Ⓟ 10,626; Ⓒ 9,590; ◆ 7,918
Alexis; Inc. Place; WARREN, MERCER; **170** F-5; elev. 700ft./213m.; 🄿; **z** 61412; Ⓟ 908; Ⓒ 863
Algonquin; Inc. Place; MCHENRY, KANE; **170** B-11; elev. 844ft./257m.; 🄿; ★ **CHI**; **z** 60102, **z** 60156; Ⓟ 11,693; Ⓒ 23,276; ◆ 29,862
Algonquin; MCD-Township; MCHENRY; ***170** B-11; 🄿; ★ **CHI**; **z** 60102, **z** 60156; includes part of the village of Algonquin; Ⓟ 57,746; Ⓒ 86,219; Ⓡ 86,217
Algonquin Shores; RMC Place; KANE, MCHENRY; ***170** B-11; ★ **CHI**; mail Algonquin **z** 60102; pop. incl. with Algonquin (Inc. Place)
Algonquin Trails; RMC Place; COOK; ★ **CHI**; mail Mount Prospect **z** 60056; pop. incl. with Mount Prospect (Inc. Place)
Alhambra; Inc. Place; MADISON; ▲ Alhambra; **171** N-7; 🄿; **z** 62001; Ⓟ 709; Ⓒ 630; Ⓡ 638
Alhambra; MCD-Township; MADISON; ***171** N-7; 🄿; **z** 62001; Ⓟ 1,445; Ⓒ 1,475; Ⓡ 1,476
Allen; MCD-Township; LA SALLE; ***170** E-10; mail Ransom **z** 60470; Ⓟ 690; Ⓒ 638
Allen; RMC Place; MASON; ***170** I-8; elev. 533ft./162m.; mail San Jose **z** 62682; rural
Allen; RMC Place; WHITESIDE; ***170** C-7; mail Rock Falls **z** 61071; ● 500
Allendale; MADISON; see Alan Dale (RMC Place)
Allendale; Inc. Place; WABASH; **171** O-13; elev. 480ft./146m.; 🄿; **z** 62410; Ⓟ 476; Ⓒ 528
Allens Corners; RMC Place; KANE; ***170** B-11; ★ **CHI**; mail Hampshire **z** 60140; ● 30
Allens Grove; MCD-Township; MASON; ***170** I-8; mail San Jose **z** 62682; Ⓟ 669; Ⓒ 699
Allentown; RMC Place; TAZEWELL; ***170** H-8; ★ **PEOR**; mail Tremont **z** 61568; ● 60
Allenville; Inc. Place; MOULTRIE; **171** K-11; elev. 650ft./198m.; 🄿; **z** 61951; Ⓟ 166; Ⓒ 154
Allerton; Inc. Place; VERMILION, CHAMPAIGN; **170** J-12; elev. 700ft./213m.; 🄿; **z** 61810; Ⓟ 274; Ⓒ 293
Allin; MCD-Township; MCLEAN; ***170** H-9; mail Stanford **z** 61774; Ⓟ 996; Ⓒ 1,047
Allison; MCD-Township; LAWRENCE; ***171** N-13; mail Lawrenceville **z** 62439; Ⓟ 308; Ⓒ 307
Alma; Inc. Place; MARION; **171** N-10; elev. 625ft./191m.; 🄿; **z** 62807; Ⓟ 388; Ⓒ 386
Alma; MCD-Township; MARION; ***171** N-10; 🄿; **z** 62807; Ⓟ 845; Ⓒ 837
Almora; RMC Place; KANE; ***170** B-11; elev. 860ft./262m.; ★ **CHI**; mail Elgin **z** 60123; rural
Almora Heights; RMC Place; KANE; ***170** B-11; elev. 850ft./259m.; ★ **CHI**; mail Elgin **z** 60123; ● 230
Alorton; Inc. Place; ST. CLAIR; **195** F-8; elev. 420ft./128m.; 🄿; ★ **ST.L**; **z** 62207; Ⓟ 2,960; Ⓒ 2,749
Alpha; Inc. Place; HENRY; **170** E-6; elev. 803ft./245m.; 🄿; **z** 61413; Ⓟ 753; Ⓒ 726
Alsey; Inc. Place; SCOTT; **171** K-5; elev. 627ft./191m.; 🄿; **z** 62610; Ⓟ 253; Ⓒ 246
Alsip; Inc. Place; COOK; **172** K-8; elev. 600ft./183m.; 🄿; ★ **CHI**; **z** 60803; Ⓟ 18,227; Ⓒ 19,725
Alsip Woods; RMC Place; COOK; ★ **CHI**; mail Alsip **z** 60803; pop. incl. with Alsip (Inc. Place)
Alta; RMC Place; PEORIA; **170** G-8; ★ **PEOR**; mail Peoria **z** 61615; ● 400
Altamont; Inc. Place; EFFINGHAM; **171** M-10; elev. 619ft./189m.; 🄿; **z** 62411; Ⓟ 2,296; Ⓒ 2,283
Altamont; RMC Place; MADISON; ***171** N-6; ★ **ST.L**; mail Godfrey **z** 62035; pop. incl. with Godfrey (Inc. Place)
Altgeld Gardens; RMC Place; COOK; ***170** D-13; ★ **CHI**; pop. incl. with Chicago (Inc. Place)
Alto; MCD-Township; LEE; ***170** C-9; mail Steward **z** 60553; Ⓟ 568; Ⓒ 577
Alton; Inc. Place; MADISON; **171** N-6; elev. 500ft./152m.; 🄿 🄷 ■; ★ **ST.L**; **z** 62002; Ⓟ 32,905; Ⓒ 30,496; Ⓡ 30,504; ◆ 30,380
Alton; MCD-Township; MADISON; ***171** N-6; 🄿 🄷; ★ **ST.L**; **z** 62002; coextensive with the City of Alton; Ⓟ 32,905; Ⓒ 30,496; Ⓡ 30,504
Altona; Inc. Place; KNOX; **170** F-6; elev. 750ft./229m.; 🄿; **z** 61414; Ⓟ 559; Ⓒ 570
Alto Pass; Inc. Place; UNION; **171** R-8; elev. 757ft./231m.; 🄿; **z** 62905; Ⓟ 417; Ⓒ 388
Altorf; RMC Place; KANKAKEE; ***170** E-12; ★ **KANK**; mail Bourbonnais **z** 60914; ● 100
Alvan; VERMILION; see Alvin (Inc. Place)
Alvin (Alvan); Inc. Place; VERMILION; **170** I-13; elev. 667ft./203m.; 🄿; **z** 61811; Ⓟ 339; Ⓒ 316
Alworth; RMC Place; WINNEBAGO; ***170** B-9; ★ **RKFD**; mail Winnebago **z** 61088; rural
Amboy; Inc. Place; LEE; ▲ Amboy, Marion; **170** C-8; elev. 743ft./226m.; 🄿; **z** 61310; Ⓟ 2,377; Ⓒ 2,561
Amboy; MCD-Township; LEE; ***170** C-8; 🄿; **z** 61310; Ⓟ 3,047; Ⓒ 3,230
Amenia; RMC Place; PIATT; ***170** J-10; mail Monticello **z** 61856; ● 45
America; RMC Place; PULASKI; ***171** T-9; mail Villa Ridge **z** 62996; ● 30
Americana Village; RMC Place; DUPAGE; ★ **CHI**; mail Glendale Heights **z** 60139; pop. incl. with Glendale Heights (Inc. Place)
Ames; RMC Place; MONROE; ***171** P-6; mail Prairie Du Rocher **z** 62277; ● 50
Amity; MCD-Township; LIVINGSTON; ***170** F-10; mail Cornell **z** 61319; Ⓟ 968; Ⓒ 869
Anchor; Inc. Place; MCLEAN; ▲ Anchor; ***170** H-11; 🄿; **z** 61720; Ⓟ 178; Ⓒ 175
Anchor; MCD-Township; MCLEAN; ***170** H-11; 🄿; **z** 61720; Ⓟ 393; Ⓒ 376
Ancient Tree; RMC Place; COOK; ★ **CHI**; mail Northbrook **z** 60062; pop. incl. with Northbrook (Inc. Place)
Ancona; RMC Place; LIVINGSTON; ***170** F-10; elev. 626ft./191m.; 🄿; **z** 61311; ● 80
Andalusia; Inc. Place; ROCK ISLAND; ▲ Andalusia; **170** D-5; 🄿; ★ **D-RI-M**; **z** 61232; Ⓟ 1,052; Ⓒ 1,050
Andalusia; MCD-Township; ROCK ISLAND; ***170** D-5; 🄿; ★ **D-RI-M**; **z** 61232; Ⓟ 1,899; Ⓒ 2,176
Anderman Acres; RMC Place; WILL; ***170** D-12; ★ **CHI**; mail Plainfield **z** 60544; ● 250
Anderson; MCD-Township; CLARK; ***171** L-13; mail Marshall **z** 62441; Ⓟ 335; Ⓒ 397
Anderson Lake; RMC Place; FULTON; ***170** I-6; elev. 468ft./143m.; mail Astoria **z** 61501; ● 60
Andersonville; RMC Place; COOK; ***170** B-13; ★ **CHI**; mail Chicago **z** 60640; pop. incl. with Chicago (Inc. Place)
Andover; Inc. Place; HENRY; **170** E-6; elev. 776ft./237m.; 🄿; **z** 61233; Ⓟ 579; Ⓒ 594
Andover; MCD-Township; HENRY; ***170** E-6; 🄿; **z** 61233; Ⓟ 1,003; Ⓒ 984
Andres; RMC Place; WILL; ***170** E-12; elev. 725ft./221m.; mail Peotone **z** 60468; ● 50
Andrew; RMC Place; SANGAMON; ***170** J-8; 🄿; ★ **SPRG**; **z** 62707; ● 200
Anna; Inc. Place; UNION; **171** S-9; elev. 631ft./192m.; 🄿 🄷; **z** 62906; Ⓟ 4,805; Ⓒ 5,136
Annapolis; RMC Place; CRAWFORD; **171** M-13; elev. 570ft./174m.; 🄿; **z** 62413; ● 150
Annawan; Inc. Place; HENRY; ▲ Annawan; **170** E-7; elev. 625ft./191m.; 🄿; **z** 61234; Ⓟ 802; Ⓒ 868
Annawan; MCD-Township; HENRY; ***170** E-7; 🄿; **z** 61234; Ⓟ 1,164; Ⓒ 1,146
Antioch; Inc. Place; LAKE; ▲ Antioch, Newport; **170** A-12; 🄿; ★ **CHI**; **z** 60002; Ⓟ 6,105; Ⓒ 8,788
Antioch; MCD-Township; LAKE; ***170** A-12; 🄿; ★ **CHI**; **z** 60002; Ⓟ 18,046; Ⓒ 21,879
Appanoose; MCD-Township; HANCOCK; ***170** G-3; mail Nauvoo **z** 62354; Ⓟ 672; Ⓒ 350
Apple Canyon Lake; RMC Place; JO DAVIESS; ***170** A-6; elev. 860ft./262m.; mail Apple River **z** 61001; ● 380
Applegate; RMC Place; COOK; mail Schaumburg **z** 60193; pop. incl. with Schaumburg (Inc. Place)
Apple River; Inc. Place; JO DAVIESS; ▲ Apple River; **170** A-6; 🄿; **z** 61001; Ⓟ 414; Ⓒ 379
Apple River; MCD-Township; JO DAVIESS; ***170** A-6; 🄿; **z** 61001; Ⓟ 535; Ⓒ 525
Appleton; RMC Place; KNOX; ***170** F-6; elev. 603ft./184m.; mail Dahinda **z** 61428; rural
Appletree; RMC Place; COOK; ★ **CHI**; mail Country Club Hills **z** 60478; pop. incl. with Country Club Hills (Inc. Place)
Appolalooosa West; RMC Place; KANE; ***170** C-11; elev. 850ft./259m.; ★ **CHI**; mail Elburn **z** 60119; ● 60
Arboretum East; RMC Place; DUPAGE; ***170** C-12; ★ **CHI**; mail Glen Ellyn **z** 60137; ● 400
Arboretum Villages; RMC Place; DUPAGE; ★ **CHI**; mail Lisle **z** 60532; pop. incl. with Lisle (Inc. Place)
Arboretum West; RMC Place; DUPAGE; ***170** C-12; ★ **CHI**; mail Glen Ellyn **z** 60137; ● 650
Arbor Trails; RMC Place; WILL; ★ **CHI**; mail Park Forest **z** 60466; pop. incl. with Park Forest (Inc. Place)
Arbury Hills; RMC Place; WILL; **172** M-7; ★ **CHI**; mail Mokena **z** 60448; ● 1,770
Arcadia; RMC Place; MORGAN; ***170** J-6; elev. 608ft./185m.; 🄿; **z** 62650; ● 30
Archer; RMC Place; SANGAMON; ***170** J-7; 🄿; **z** 62707
Archer Heights; RMC Place; COOK; ★ **CHI**; mail Chicago **z** 60632; pop. incl. with Chicago (Inc. Place)
Archie; RMC Place; VERMILION; ***170** J-13; mail Sidell **z** 61876
Arcola; Inc. Place; DOUGLAS; ▲ Arcola; **171** K-11; elev. 678ft./207m.; 🄿; **z** 61910; Ⓟ 2,678; Ⓒ 2,652
Arcola; MCD-Township; DOUGLAS; ***171** K-11; 🄿; **z** 61910; Ⓟ 3,132; Ⓒ 3,301
Arenzville; Inc. Place; CASS; ▲ Arenzville; **170** J-6; 🄿; **z** 62611; Ⓟ 432; Ⓒ 419
Arenzville; MCD-Township; CASS; ***170** J-6; 🄿; **z** 62611; Ⓟ 857; Ⓒ 839
Argenta; Inc. Place; MACON; **170** J-10; elev. 610ft./186m.; 🄿; **z** 62501; Ⓟ 940; Ⓒ 921
Argo; CARROLL; see Argo Fay (RMC Place)
Argo; RMC Place; COOK; ***170** C-13; elev. 603ft./184m.; 🄿; ★ **CHI**; **z** 60501; pop. incl. with Summit (Inc. Place)
Argo Fay (Argo); RMC Place; CARROLL; ***170** B-7; mail Mount Carroll **z** 61053, Thomson **z** 61285; ● 100
Argyle; RMC Place; BOONE, WINNEBAGO; **170** A-10; mail Caledonia **z** 61011; ● 100
Arispie; MCD-Township; BUREAU; ***170** E-8; mail Tiskilwa **z** 61368; Ⓟ 806; Ⓒ 835
Arlingdale; RMC Place; COOK; ★ **CHI**; pop. incl. with Arlington Heights (Inc. Place)
Arlington; Inc. Place; BUREAU; **170** D-9; elev. 750ft./229m.; 🄿; **z** 61312; Ⓟ 200; Ⓒ 211
Arlington Acres; RMC Place; COOK; ★ **CHI**; pop. incl. with Arlington Heights (Inc. Place)
Arlington Countryside; RMC Place; COOK; ★ **CHI**; pop. incl. with Arlington Heights (Inc. Place)
Arlington Farms; RMC Place; COOK; ★ **CHI**; pop. incl. with Arlington Heights (Inc. Place)
Arlington Heights; Inc. Place; COOK, LAKE; **170** B-12; elev. 700ft./213m.; 🄿 🄷 ■; ★ **CHI**; **z** 60004-06; Ⓟ 75,460; Ⓒ 76,031; Ⓡ 76,079; ◆ 72,184
Arlington Ridge; RMC Place; COOK; ★ **CHI**; mail Arlington Heights **z** 60004; pop. incl. with Arlington Heights (Inc. Place)
Armington; Inc. Place; TAZEWELL; **170** H-9; elev. 630ft./192m.; 🄿; **z** 61721; Ⓟ 348; Ⓒ 368
Armour Square; RMC Place; COOK; ★ **CHI**; mail Chicago **z** 60609, **z** 60616; pop. incl. with Chicago (Inc. Place)
Armstrong; RMC Place; VERMILION; **170** I-12; elev. 696ft./212m.; 🄿; **z** 61812; ● 200
Arnold; RMC Place; MORGAN; ***171** K-6; elev. 643ft./196m.; 🄿; **z** 62650; rural
Aroma; MCD-Township; KANKAKEE; ***170** F-13; ★ **KANK**; mail Kankakee **z** 60901; Ⓟ 5,565; Ⓒ 5,835
Aroma Park; Inc. Place; KANKAKEE; **170** F-13; elev. 610ft./186m.; 🄿; ★ **KANK**; **z** 60910; Ⓟ 690; Ⓒ 821
Aroma Park Northwest; RMC Place; KANKAKEE; ***170** F-13; elev. 607ft./185m.; ★ **KANK**; mail Kankakee **z** 60901; ● 1,200
Arrington; MCD-Township; WAYNE; ***171** P-11; mail Sims **z** 62886; Ⓟ 519; Ⓒ 444
Arrowhead; RMC Place; DUPAGE; ***170** C-12; ★ **CHI**; mail Wheaton **z** 60187; ● 1,750
Arrowhead; RMC Place; KANKAKEE; ***170** E-12; elev. 700ft./213m.; ★ **KANK**; mail Bourbonnais **z** 60914; ● 250
Arrowhead Hills; RMC Place; KENDALL; ***170** D-11; elev. 750ft./229m.; ★ **CHI**; mail Oswego **z** 60543; ● 100
Arrowsmith; Inc. Place; MCLEAN; ▲ Arrowsmith; **170** H-10; elev. 881ft./269m.; 🄿; **z** 61722; Ⓟ 313; Ⓒ 298
Arrowsmith; MCD-Township; MCLEAN; ***170** H-10; 🄿; **z** 61722 & mail Shirley **z** 61772; Ⓟ 549; Ⓒ 569
Arrow Wood; RMC Place; MADISON; ***171** N-6; ★ **ST.L**; mail Godfrey **z** 62035; pop. incl. with Godfrey (Inc. Place)
Artesia; MCD-Township; IROQUOIS; ***170** G-12; mail Buckley **z** 60918; Ⓟ 977; Ⓒ 957
Arthur; Inc. Place; DOUGLAS, MOULTRIE; **171** K-11; elev. 662ft./202m.; 🄿; **z** 61911; Ⓟ 2,112; Ⓒ 2,203
Asbury; MCD-Township; GALLATIN; ***171** Q-12; mail Omaha **z** 62871; Ⓟ 158; Ⓒ 146
Ashburn; RMC Place; COOK; ***170** C-13; ★ **CHI**; mail Chicago **z** 60652; pop. incl. with Chicago (Inc. Place)
Ash Grove; MCD-Township; IROQUOIS; ***170** G-13; mail Milford **z** 60953; Ⓟ 793; Ⓒ 766
Ash Grove; MCD-Township; SHELBY; ***171** L-11; mail Windsor **z** 61957; Ⓟ 502; Ⓒ 544
Ashkum; Inc. Place; IROQUOIS; ▲ Ashkum; **170** G-12; 🄿; **z** 60911; Ⓟ 650; Ⓒ 724
Ashkum; MCD-Township; IROQUOIS; ***170** F-12; 🄿; **z** 60911; Ⓟ 1,484; Ⓒ 1,535
Ashland; Inc. Place; CASS; ▲ Ashland; **170** J-7; 🄿; **z** 62612; Ⓟ 1,257; Ⓒ 1,361
Ashland; MCD-Township; CASS; ***170** J-6; 🄿; **z** 62612; Ⓟ 1,356; Ⓒ 1,440
Ashland Avenue; RMC Place; COOK; ***170** C-13; ★ **CHI**; pop. incl. with Chicago (Inc. Place)
Ashley; Inc. Place; WASHINGTON; ▲ Ashley; **171** P-9; 🄿; **z** 62808; Ⓟ 583; Ⓒ 613
Ashley; MCD-Township; WASHINGTON; ***171** P-9; 🄿; **z** 62808; Ⓟ 847; Ⓒ 922
Ashmore; Inc. Place; COLES; ▲ Ashmore; **171** K-12; elev. 696ft./212m.; 🄿; **z** 61912; Ⓟ 800; Ⓒ 809
Ashmore; MCD-Township; COLES; ***171** K-12; 🄿; **z** 61912; Ⓟ 1,467; Ⓒ 1,447
Ashton; Inc. Place; LEE; ▲ Ashton; **170** C-9; 🄿; **z** 61006; Ⓟ 1,042; Ⓒ 1,142
Ashton; MCD-Township; LEE; ***170** C-9; 🄿; **z** 61006; Ⓟ 1,260; Ⓒ 1,317
Assumption; Inc. Place; CHRISTIAN; ▲ Assumption; **171** K-9; elev. 647ft./197m.; 🄿; **z** 62510; Ⓟ 1,244; Ⓒ 1,261
Assumption; MCD-Township; CHRISTIAN; ***171** K-9; 🄿; **z** 62510; Ⓟ 1,595; Ⓒ 1,509
Astoria; Inc. Place; FULTON; ▲ Astoria; **170** I-6; 🄿; **z** 61501; Ⓟ 1,205; Ⓒ 1,193
Astoria; MCD-Township; FULTON; ***170** I-5; 🄿; **z** 61501; Ⓟ 1,608; Ⓒ 1,517
Athens; Inc. Place; MENARD; **170** J-7; elev. 606ft./185m.; 🄿; **z** 62613; Ⓟ 1,404; Ⓒ 1,726
Athensville; RMC Place; GREENE; ▲ Athensville; **171** L-6; mail Roodhouse **z** 62082; ● 50
Athensville; MCD-Township; GREENE; ***171** L-6; mail Roodhouse **z** 62082; Ⓟ 391; Ⓒ 351
Atkinson; Inc. Place; HENRY; ▲ Atkinson; **170** E-7; 🄿; **z** 61235; Ⓟ 950; Ⓒ 1,001
Atkinson; MCD-Township; HENRY; ***170** D-7; 🄿; **z** 61235; includes part of the Town of Atkinson; Ⓟ 1,296; Ⓒ 1,318
Atlanta; Inc. Place; LOGAN; ▲ Atlanta; **170** I-9; 🄿; **z** 61723; Ⓟ 1,616; Ⓒ 1,649
Atlanta; MCD-Township; LOGAN; ***170** I-9; 🄿; **z** 61723; Ⓟ 1,884; Ⓒ 1,888
Atlas; RMC Place; PIKE; ▲ Atlas; **171** K-4; mail Rockport **z** 62370; ● 50
Atlas; MCD-Township; PIKE; ***171** K-4; mail Rockport **z** 62370; Ⓟ 641; Ⓒ 655
Atlee Ogles; ST. CLAIR; see Ogles (RMC Place)
Atterberry (Atterbury); RMC Place; MENARD; **170** I-7; 🄿; **z** 62675; ● 120
Atterbury; MENARD; see Atterberry (RMC Place)
Attila; RMC Place; WILLIAMSON; ***171** R-10; elev. 562ft./171m.; mail Pittsburg **z** 62974; ● 30
Atwater; RMC Place; MACOUPIN; **171** L-7; elev. 635ft./194m.; ● 100
Atwood; Inc. Place; DOUGLAS, PIATT; **170** J-11; elev. 670ft./204m.; 🄿; **z** 61913; Ⓟ 1,253; Ⓒ 1,290
Atwood Heights; RMC Place; COOK; ★ **CHI**; mail Alsip **z** 60803; pop. incl. with Alsip (Inc. Place)
Auburn; MCD-Township; CLARK; ***171** L-13; mail Marshall **z** 62441; Ⓟ 278; Ⓒ 289
Auburn; Inc. Place; SANGAMON; ▲ Auburn; **171** K-7; elev. 626ft./191m.; 🄿; **z** 62615; Ⓟ 3,724; Ⓒ 4,317
Auburn; MCD-Township; SANGAMON; ***171** K-7; 🄿; **z** 62615; Ⓟ 5,208; Ⓒ 6,020
Auburn Gresham; RMC Place; COOK; ★ **CHI**; mail Chicago **z** 60620; pop. incl. with Chicago (Inc. Place)
Auburn Park; RMC Place; COOK; ***170** C-13; ★ **CHI**; mail Chicago **z** 60620; pop. incl. with Chicago (Inc. Place)
Auburn Woods; RMC Place; COOK; ***170** B-12; elev. 750ft./229m.; ★ **CHI**; mail Palatine **z** 60067; pop. incl. with Palatine (Inc. Place)
Audubon; MCD-Township; MONTGOMERY; ***171** L-9; mail Nokomis **z** 62075; Ⓟ 627; Ⓒ 495; Ⓡ 570
Augsburg; RMC Place; FAYETTE; ***171** N-9; elev. 563ft./172m.; mail Shobonier **z** 62885; rural
Augusta; Inc. Place; HANCOCK; ▲ Augusta; **170** I-4; elev. 668ft./204m.; 🄿; **z** 62311; Ⓟ 614; Ⓒ 657
Augusta; MCD-Township; HANCOCK; ***170** I-4; 🄿; **z** 62311; Ⓟ 867; Ⓒ 923
Aurora; Inc. Place; KANE, DUPAGE, KENDALL, WILL; **170** C-11; elev. 676ft./206m.; 🄿 🄷 🄲 3,791 ■; ★ **CHI**; **z** 60502-07, **z** 60568, **z** 60572, **z** 60598 & mail Fox Valley **z** 60599; Ⓟ 99,556; Ⓒ 142,990; ◆ 187,118
Aurora; MCD-Township; KANE; ***170** C-11; 🄿 🄲 3,791; ★ **CHI**; **z** 60502-07, **z** 60568, **z** 60572, **z** 60598 & mail Fox Valley **z** 60599; includes part of the City of Aurora; Ⓟ 101,769; Ⓒ 115,553
Aurora East; RMC Place; KANE; ★ **CHI**; mail Aurora **z** 60598; pop. incl. with Aurora (Inc. Place)
Austin; RMC Place; COOK; ***170** C-13; ★ **CHI**; mail Chicago **z** 60644; pop. incl. with Chicago (Inc. Place)
Austin; MCD-Township; MACON; ***170** J-9; mail Warrensburg **z** 62573; Ⓟ 263; Ⓒ 240
Austin Park; RMC Place; COOK; ★ **CHI**; pop. incl. with Oak Park (Inc. Place)
Austin View; RMC Place; COOK; ***170** D-13; ★ **CHI**; mail Alsip **z** 60803; pop. incl. with Alsip (Inc. Place)
Aux Sable; MCD-Township; GRUNDY; ***170** E-11; ★ **CHI**; mail Minooka **z** 60447; Ⓟ 3,284; Ⓒ 4,525
Ava; Inc. Place; JACKSON; **171** Q-8; elev. 600ft./183m.; 🄿; **z** 62907; Ⓟ 674; Ⓒ 662
Avalon Park; RMC Place; COOK; ★ **CHI**; mail Chicago **z** 60617, **z** 60619; pop. incl. with Chicago (Inc. Place)
Avena; RMC Place; FAYETTE; ***171** M-10; mail Saint Elmo **z** 62458
Avena; MCD-Township; FAYETTE; ***171** M-10; mail Saint Elmo **z** 62458; Ⓟ 2,091; Ⓒ 1,964
Avery Hill; RMC Place; ST. CLAIR; ***171** O-6; ★ **ST.L**; mail Belleville **z** 62223; pop. incl. with Belleville (Inc. Place)
Aviston; Inc. Place; CLINTON; ▲ Breese; **171** O-8; elev. 473ft./144m.; 🄿; ★ **ST.L**; **z** 62216; Ⓟ 924; Ⓒ 1,231
Avoca; MCD-Township; LIVINGSTON; ***170** G-11; mail Fairbury **z** 61739; Ⓟ 406; Ⓒ 386
Avon; Inc. Place; FULTON; **170** G-5; elev. 641ft./195m.; 🄿; **z** 61415; Ⓟ 957; Ⓒ 915
Avon; MCD-Township; LAKE; ***170** A-12; ★ **CHI**; mail Grayslake **z** 60030; Ⓟ 35,989; Ⓒ 54,957
Avondale; RMC Place; COOK; ★ **CHI**; mail Chicago **z** 60618, **z** 60641; pop. incl. with Chicago (Inc. Place)
Ayers (Airport); RMC Place; CARROLL; ***170** B-6; elev. 610ft./186m.; mail Savanna **z** 61074; ● 30
Ayers; MCD-Township; CHAMPAIGN; ***170** J-12; mail Broadlands **z** 61816; Ⓟ 481; Ⓒ 441

B

Babcock (Meersman); RMC Place; ROCK ISLAND; ***170** D-6; ★ **D-RI-M**; mail East Moline **z** 61244; pop. incl. with East Moline (Inc. Place)
Babson; RMC Place; KANE; ★ **CHI**; mail Saint Charles **z** 60175; pop. incl. with Saint Charles (Inc. Place)
Babylon; RMC Place; FULTON; ***170** H-6; elev. 514ft./157m.; mail Ellisville **z** 61431; rural
Baden Baden; BOND; see Pierron (RMC Place)
Bader; RMC Place; SCHUYLER; ***170** I-6; elev. 617ft./188m.; 🄿; **z** 62624; ● 50
Baileyville; RMC Place; OGLE; ***170** B-8; elev. 913ft./278m.; 🄿; **z** 61007; ● 200
Bainbridge; MCD-Township; SCHUYLER; ***170** I-5; mail Frederick **z** 62639; Ⓟ 526; Ⓒ 540
Baker; RMC Place; LA SALLE; ***170** D-10; mail Leland **z** 60531; ● 40
Baker Lake; RMC Place; COOK; ***170** B-12; elev. 854ft./260m.; ★ **CHI**; mail Barrington **z** 60010; ● 330
Bakerville; RMC Place; JEFFERSON; ***171** P-10; mail Mount Vernon **z** 62864; rural
Balcom; RMC Place; UNION; **171** S-9; elev. 496ft./151m.; mail Anna **z** 62906; ● 70
Bald Bluff; MCD-Township; HENDERSON; ***170** F-4; mail Seaton **z** 61476; Ⓟ 317; Ⓒ 283
Bald Hill; MCD-Township; JEFFERSON; ***171** P-9; mail Scheller **z** 62883; Ⓟ 781; Ⓒ 793
Baldwin; Inc. Place; RANDOLPH; **171** P-7; elev. 460ft./140m.; 🄿; **z** 62217; Ⓟ 426; Ⓒ 3,627; Ⓡ 434
Baldwin Beach; RMC Place; MASON; ***170** H-7; mail Havana **z** 62644; ● 45
Baldwin Heights; WASHINGTON; see Suburban Heights (RMC Place)
Bales Lake (Bayles Lake); RMC Place; IROQUOIS; mail Loda **z** 60948; summer pop. 600; ● 200
Ball; MCD-Township; SANGAMON; ***171** K-8; ★ **SPRG**; mail Chatham **z** 62629; Ⓟ 3,475; Ⓒ 4,573
Ballou; RMC Place; WILL; ***170** E-12; elev. 602ft./183m.; mail Wilmington **z** 60481; rural
Banner; MCD-Township; EFFINGHAM; ***171** M-10; mail Shumway **z** 62461; Ⓟ 539; Ⓒ 545
Banner; Inc. Place; FULTON; ▲ Banner; **170** H-7; elev. 475ft./145m.; 🄿; **z** 61520; Ⓟ 160; Ⓒ 149
Banner; MCD-Township; FULTON; ***170** H-7; 🄿; **z** 61520; Ⓟ 424; Ⓒ 370
Bannister; RMC Place; MARION; ***171** O-10; mail Salem **z** 62881; rural
Bannockburn; Inc. Place; LAKE; **172** D-7; elev. 685ft./209m.; 🄿; ★ **CHI**; **z** 60015; Ⓟ 1,388; Ⓒ 1,429
Barclay; RMC Place; SANGAMON; ***170** J-8; 🄿; ★ **SPRG**; **z** 62684; ● 30
Bardolph; Inc. Place; MCDONOUGH; **170** H-5; elev. 660ft./201m.; 🄿; **z** 61416; Ⓟ 301; Ⓒ 253
Bargerville; RMC Place; MASSAC; mail Metropolis **z** 62960; ● 60
Barnett; MCD-Township; DE WITT; ***170** I-9; mail Clinton **z** 61727; Ⓟ 493; Ⓒ 478
Barnett; RMC Place; MONTGOMERY; ***171** L-7; mail Litchfield **z** 62056; ● 40
Barnhill; RMC Place; WAYNE; ▲ Barnhill; **171** P-11; 🄿; **z** 62809 & mail Fairfield **z** 62837; ● 80
Barnhill; MCD-Township; WAYNE; ***171** P-11; 🄿; **z** 62809 & mail Fairfield **z** 62837; Ⓟ 493; Ⓒ 561
Barr; MCD-Township; MACOUPIN; ***171** L-6; 🄿; **z** 62674; Ⓟ 395; Ⓒ 351
Barr; RMC Place; SANGAMON; ***170** J-7; ★ **SPRG**; mail Athens **z** 62613; rural
Barren; MCD-Township; FRANKLIN; ***171** Q-9; mail Benton **z** 62812; Ⓟ 467; Ⓒ 456
Barreville; RMC Place; MCHENRY; ***170** A-11; ★ **CHI**; mail Crystal Lake **z** 60012; pop. incl. with Prairie Grove (Inc. Place)
Barrington; Inc. Place; COOK, LAKE; **170** B-12; elev. 880ft./268m.; 🄿 🄷; ★ **CHI**; **z** 60010-11; Ⓟ 9,504; Ⓒ 10,168
Barrington; MCD-Township; COOK; ***170** B-12; 🄿; ★ **CHI**; **z** 60010-11; includes part of the Village of Barrington; Ⓟ 13,034; Ⓒ 14,026; Ⓡ 14,030
Barrington Center; RMC Place; COOK; ***170** B-12; elev. 859ft./262m.; ★ **CHI**; mail Barrington **z** 60010; pop. incl. with Barrington Hills (Inc. Place)
Barrington Downtown; RMC Place; COOK; ★ **CHI**; mail Barrington **z** 60010-11; pop. incl. with Barrington (Inc. Place)
Barrington Highlands; RMC Place; LAKE; ★ **CHI**; mail Barrington **z** 60010; ● 200
Barrington Hills; Inc. Place; COOK, KANE, LAKE, MCHENRY; **172** E-3; elev. 850ft./259m.; ★ **CHI**; mail Algonquin **z** 60102, Barrington **z** 60010, Dundee **z** 60118, Fox River Grove **z** 60021; Ⓟ 4,202; Ⓒ 3,915; Ⓡ 3,930
Barrington Square; RMC Place; COOK; ★ **CHI**; mail Schaumburg **z** 60195; pop. incl. with Hoffman Estates (Inc. Place)
Barrington Woods; RMC Place; COOK; ***170** B-12; ★ **CHI**; mail Palatine **z** 60074; ● 400
Barrow; RMC Place; GREENE; ***171** K-5; elev. 653ft./199m.; mail Roodhouse **z** 62082; ● 40
Barry; Inc. Place; PIKE; ▲ Barry; **171** K-4; 🄿; **z** 62312; Ⓟ 1,391; Ⓒ 1,368
Barry; MCD-Township; PIKE; ***171** K-4; 🄿; **z** 62312; includes part of the City of Barry; Ⓟ 1,800; Ⓒ 1,751
Barstow; RMC Place; ROCK ISLAND; **171** S-6; elev. 570ft./174m.; 🄿; ★ **D-RI-M**; **z** 61236; ● 140
Bartelso; Inc. Place; CLINTON; **171** O-8; elev. 449ft./137m.; 🄿; **z** 62218; Ⓟ 412; Ⓒ 593
Bartlett; Inc. Place; COOK, DUPAGE, KANE; **172** G-3; elev. 800ft./244m.; 🄿; ★ **CHI**; **z** 60103, **z** 60133 & mail Bloomingdale **z** 60108; Ⓟ 19,373; Ⓒ 36,706; ◆ 39,619
Bartonville; Inc. Place; PEORIA; **170** G-8; elev. 460ft./140m.; 🄿; ★ **PEOR**; **z** 61607; Ⓟ 5,643; Ⓒ 6,310
Basco; Inc. Place; HANCOCK; ***170** H-3; elev. 635ft./194m.; 🄿; **z** 62313; Ⓟ 99; Ⓒ 107
Batavia; Inc. Place; KANE, DUPAGE; **170** C-11; elev. 716ft./218m.; 🄿; ★ **CHI**; **z** 60510, **z** 60539; Ⓟ 17,076; Ⓒ 23,866; ◆ 27,557
Batavia; MCD-Township; KANE; ***170** C-11; 🄿; ★ **CHI**; **z** 60510, **z** 60539; includes part of the City of Batavia; Ⓟ 20,306; Ⓒ 30,137
Batchtown; Inc. Place; CALHOUN; **171** M-5; elev. 593ft./181m.; 🄿; **z** 62006; Ⓟ 225; Ⓒ 218
Bates; RMC Place; SANGAMON; ***171** K-7; elev. 641ft./195m.; 🄿; **z** 62670; ● 30
Batestown; RMC Place; VERMILION; ***170** I-13; elev. 651ft./198m.; ★ **DANV**; mail Danville **z** 61834
Bath; Inc. Place; MASON; ▲ Bath; **170** I-6; elev. 462ft./141m.; 🄿; **z** 62617; Ⓟ 388; Ⓒ 310
Bath; MCD-Township; MASON; ***170** I-6; 🄿; **z** 62617; Ⓟ 864; Ⓒ 860
Bay City; RMC Place; POPE; ***171** T-11; elev. 361ft./110m.; mail Golconda **z** 62938
Bayle; FAYETTE; see Bayle City (RMC Place)
Bayle City (Bayle); RMC Place; FAYETTE; ***171** M-9; mail Ramsey **z** 62080; ● 50
Bayles Lake; IROQUOIS; see Bales Lake (RMC Place)
Baylestown; RMC Place; MACOUPIN; ***171** M-7; mail Gillespie **z** 62033; rural
Baylis; Inc. Place; PIKE; **171** K-4; elev. 841ft./256m.; 🄿; **z** 62314; Ⓟ 257; Ⓒ 265
Baytown; CALHOUN; see Mozier (RMC Place)
Bay View Garden (Bay View Gardens); Inc. Place; WOODFORD; ***170** G-8; elev. 550ft./168m.; ★ **PEOR**; mail East Peoria **z** 61611; Ⓟ 418; Ⓒ 366
Bay View Gardens; WOODFORD; see Bay View Garden (Inc. Place)
Beach Park; Inc. Place; LAKE; ▲ Newport, Warren; **170** A-12; 🄿; ★ **CHI**; **z** 60083, **z** 60087, **z** 60099; Ⓟ 9,492; Ⓒ 10,072
Beacon Hill; RMC Place; COOK; ★ **CHI**; mail Chicago Heights **z** 60411; pop. incl. with Chicago Heights (Inc. Place)
Bear Creek; MCD-Township; CHRISTIAN; ***171** L-8; mail Palmer **z** 62556; Ⓟ 607; Ⓒ 575
Bear Creek; MCD-Township; HANCOCK; ***170** H-3; mail Basco **z** 62313; Ⓟ 399; Ⓒ 379
Beardstown; Inc. Place; CASS; ▲ Beardstown; **170** J-5; 🄿; **z** 62618; Ⓟ 5,270; Ⓒ 5,766
Beardstown; MCD-Township; CASS; ***170** J-5; 🄿; **z** 62618; Ⓟ 6,280; Ⓒ 6,611
Bear Grove; MCD-Township; FAYETTE; ***171** M-9; mail Vandalia **z** 62471; Ⓟ 623; Ⓒ 598
Bearsdale; RMC Place; MACON; ***170** J-9; 🄿; ★ **DEC**; **z** 62526; rural
Beason; RMC Place; LOGAN; **170** I-9; elev. 644ft./196m.; 🄿; **z** 62512; ● 250
Beau Bien; RMC Place; DUPAGE; ***170** C-12; ★ **CHI**; mail Lisle **z** 60532; pop. incl. with Lisle (Inc. Place)
Beaucoup; RMC Place; WASHINGTON; ▲ Beaucoup; **171** P-9; mail Nashville **z** 62263; ● 80
Beaucoup; MCD-Township; WASHINGTON; ***171** P-8; mail Nashville **z** 62263; Ⓟ 493; Ⓒ 596
Beaver; MCD-Township; IROQUOIS; ***170** F-13; mail Donovan **z** 60931; Ⓟ 613; Ⓒ 584
Beaver Creek (Wisetown); RMC Place; BOND; ***171** N-8; mail Greenville **z** 62246; ● 35
Beaver Creek; MCD-Township; HAMILTON; ***171** P-11; mail Springerton **z** 62887; Ⓟ 286; Ⓒ 283
Beaver Valley; RMC Place; BOONE; ***170** A-10; elev. 850ft./259m.; ★ **RKFD**; mail Belvidere **z** 61008; ● 150
Beaver Valley (Skunk Hollow); RMC Place; COOK; ***170** D-12; elev. 713ft./217m.; ★ **CHI**; mail Orland Park **z** 60467; ● 350
Beaverville; Inc. Place; IROQUOIS; ▲ Beaverville; **170** F-13; 🄿; **z** 60912; Ⓟ 278; Ⓒ 391
Beaverville; MCD-Township; IROQUOIS; ***170** F-13; 🄿; **z** 60912; Ⓟ 672; Ⓒ 656
Beckemeyer; Inc. Place; CLINTON; **171** O-8; elev. 454ft./138m.; 🄿; **z** 62219; Ⓟ 1,070; Ⓒ 1,043; Ⓡ 1,072
Bedford; RMC Place; PIKE; ***171** K-5; elev. 428ft./130m.; mail Pearl **z** 62361; rural
Bedford; MCD-Township; WAYNE; ***171** O-11; mail Cisne **z** 62823; Ⓟ 1,063; Ⓒ 1,094
Bedford Park; Inc. Place; COOK; **172** J-7; elev. 615ft./187m.; 🄿; ★ **CHI**; **z** 60455, **z** 60458-59, **z** 60499, **z** 60501, **z** 60629, **z** 60638; Ⓟ 566; Ⓒ 574
Beecher; Inc. Place; WILL; **170** E-13; elev. 736ft./224m.; 🄿; ★ **CHI**; **z** 60401; Ⓟ 2,032; Ⓒ 2,033
Beecher City; Inc. Place; EFFINGHAM; **171** M-10; elev. 610ft./186m.; 🄿; **z** 62414, **z** 62444; Ⓟ 437; Ⓒ 493
Beechville; RMC Place; CALHOUN; ***171** M-5; elev. 546ft./166m.; mail Batchtown **z** 62006; ● 30
Bee Creek; RMC Place; PIKE; ***171** L-5; mail Pearl **z** 62361
Beh Lake Estates; RMC Place; MCHENRY; ***170** B-10; mail Garden Prairie **z** 61038; ● 45
Belgium; Inc. Place; VERMILION; **170** J-13; elev. 652ft./199m.; ★ **DANV**; mail Westville **z** 61883; Ⓟ 511; Ⓒ 466
Belgium Row; RMC Place; VERMILION; ***170** I-13; elev. 644ft./196m.; ★ **DANV**; mail Oakwood **z** 61858; rural
Belknap; Inc. Place; JOHNSON; **171** S-10; elev. 341ft./104m.; 🄿; **z** 62908; Ⓟ 125; Ⓒ 133
Bellair; RMC Place; CRAWFORD; **171** M-12; elev. 549ft./167m.; mail Oblong **z** 62449; ● 25
Belle Prairie; HAMILTON; see Belle Prairie City (Inc. Place)
Belle Prairie; MCD-Township; LIVINGSTON; ***170** G-11; mail Cropsey **z** 61731; Ⓟ 161; Ⓒ 91
Belle Prairie City (Belle Prairie); Inc. Place; HAMILTON; **171** P-11; elev. 447ft./136m.; mail Dahlgren **z** 62828; Ⓟ 64; Ⓒ 60
Belle Rive; Inc. Place; JEFFERSON; **171** P-10; elev. 478ft./146m.; 🄿; **z** 62810; Ⓟ 396; Ⓒ 371
Belleview; RMC Place; CALHOUN; **171** L-4; mail Nebo **z** 62355; ● 25
Belleville; Inc. Place; ⊡ ST. CLAIR; **171** O-7; elev. 529ft./161m.; 🄿 🄷 ■; ★ **ST.L**; **z** 62220-23, **z** 62226, **z** 62269 & mail Scott Air Force Base **z** 62225; Ⓟ 42,785; Ⓒ 41,410; ◆ 42,746
Belleville; MCD-Township; ST. CLAIR; ***171** O-7; elev. 529ft./161m.; 🄿 🄷; ★ **ST.L**; **z** 62220-23, **z** 62226, **z** 62269 & mail Scott Air Force Base **z** 62225; coextensive with the City of Belleville; Ⓟ 42,785; Ⓒ 41,410; Ⓡ 41,570
Bellevue; Inc. Place; PEORIA; **173** C-15; elev. 690ft./210m.; 🄿; ★ **PEOR**; **z** 61604; Ⓟ 1,491; Ⓒ 1,887
Bellevue Park; RMC Place; ST. CLAIR; ★ **ST.L**; pop. incl. with Belleville (Inc. Place)
Bellflower; Inc. Place; MCLEAN; ▲ Bellflower; **170** H-11; 🄿; **z** 61724; Ⓟ 405; Ⓒ 408
Bellflower; MCD-Township; MCLEAN; ***170** H-11; 🄿; **z** 61724; Ⓟ 702; Ⓒ 682
Bellmont; Inc. Place; WABASH; **171** P-12; elev. 430ft./131m.; 🄿; **z** 62811; Ⓟ 271; Ⓒ 297
Bell Plain; MCD-Township; MARSHALL; ***170** F-9; mail La Rose **z** 61541; Ⓟ 459; Ⓒ 436
Bell Ridge; RMC Place; EDGAR; ***171** K-13; elev. 661ft./201m.; mail Paris **z** 61944; rural
Belltown (New Providence); RMC Place; GREENE; **171** L-5; mail White Hall **z** 62092; ● 40
Bellwood; Inc. Place; COOK; **172** H-7; elev. 630ft./192m.; 🄿; ★ **CHI**; **z** 60104; Ⓟ 20,241; Ⓒ 20,535; ◆ 19,733
Bel-Mar Estates; RMC Place; BOONE; ***170** B-10; elev. 780ft./238m.; mail Belvidere **z** 61008; ● 150
Belmont; RMC Place; DUPAGE; ***170** C-12; ★ **CHI**; mail Downers Grove **z** 60515; pop. incl. with Downers Grove (Inc. Place)
Belmont; MCD-Township; IROQUOIS; ***170** G-13; mail Watseka **z** 60970; Ⓟ 2,439; Ⓒ 2,600
Belmont Acres; RMC Place; IROQUOIS; ***170** G-13; elev. 645ft./197m.; mail Watseka **z** 60970; ● 150
Belmont-Cragin; RMC Place; COOK; ★ **CHI**; mail Chicago **z** 60634, **z** 60639, **z** 60641; pop. incl. with Chicago (Inc. Place)
Belmont Road; RMC Place; DUPAGE; ★ **CHI**; mail Downers Grove **z** 60515; pop. incl. with Downers Grove (Inc. Place)
Belmont Village; RMC Place; MADISON; ★ **ST.L**; mail Godfrey **z** 62035; pop. incl. with Godfrey (Inc. Place)
Beltrees; RMC Place; JERSEY; ***171** M-6; ★ **ST.L**; mail Dow **z** 62022; rural
Belvidere; Inc. Place; ⊡ BOONE; ▲ Belvidere, Spring; **170** A-10; 🄿 🄷; ★ **RKFD**; **z** 61008; Ⓟ 15,958; Ⓒ 20,820; ◆ 30,287
Belvidere; MCD-Township; BOONE; ***170** A-10; 🄿; ★ **RKFD**; **z** 61008; includes part of the City of Belvidere; Ⓟ 19,782; Ⓒ 25,212
Bement; Inc. Place; PIATT; ▲ Bement; **170** J-11; 🄿; **z** 61813; Ⓟ 1,668; Ⓒ 1,784
Bement; MCD-Township; PIATT; ***170** J-11; 🄿; **z** 61813; Ⓟ 1,928; Ⓒ 1,979
Benedale Green; RMC Place; DUPAGE; ★ **CHI**; mail Lisle **z** 60532; pop. incl. with Lisle (Inc. Place)
Benevolent Heights; RMC Place; ST. CLAIR; ***171** O-7; ★ **ST.L**; mail Belleville **z** 62220; ● 350
Benjaminville; MCLEAN; see Ben Town (RMC Place)
Benld; Inc. Place; MACOUPIN; **171** M-7; elev. 642ft./196m.; 🄿; **z** 62009; Ⓟ 1,604; Ⓒ 1,541
Bennington (Blood); RMC Place; EDWARDS; ***171** O-12; mail West Salem **z** 62476; ● 30
Bennington; MCD-Township; MARSHALL; ***170** F-9; mail Toluca **z** 61369; Ⓟ 1,633; Ⓒ 1,630
Bensenville; Inc. Place; DUPAGE, COOK; **172** G-6; elev. 675ft./206m.; 🄿; ★ **CHI**; **z** 60105-06, **z** 60399; Ⓟ 17,767; Ⓒ 20,703; ◆ 21,027
Benson; Inc. Place; WOODFORD; **170** G-9; elev. 760ft./232m.; 🄿; **z** 61516; Ⓟ 410; Ⓒ 408
Bentley; Inc. Place; HANCOCK; **170** H-4; elev. 670ft./204m.; mail Carthage **z** 62321; Ⓟ 36; Ⓒ 43
Benton; Inc. Place; ⊡ FRANKLIN; **171** Q-10; elev. 470ft./143m.; 🄿 🄷; **z** 62812; Ⓟ 7,216; Ⓒ 6,880; Ⓡ 6,879
Benton; MCD-Township; FRANKLIN; ***171** Q-10; 🄿; **z** 62812; includes part of the City of Benton; Ⓟ 9,190; Ⓒ 8,561; Ⓡ 8,570
Benton; MCD-Township; LAKE; ***170** A-12; ★ **CHI**; mail Winthrop Harbor **z** 60096; Ⓟ 15,815; Ⓒ 17,413
Benton Park (Lake Benton); RMC Place; FRANKLIN; ***171** Q-10; mail Benton **z** 62812; pop. incl. with Benton (Inc. Place)
Ben Town (Benjaminville); RMC Place; MCLEAN; ***170** H-10; elev. 853ft./260m.; mail Bloomington **z** 61701; rural
Bent Tree Village; RMC Place; COOK; ★ **CHI**; mail Elgin **z** 60120; pop. incl. with Elgin (Inc. Place)
Berdan; RMC Place; GREENE; **171** L-5; mail Carrollton **z** 62016; ● 50
Bergen; RMC Place; BOONE; ***170** A-10; elev. 950ft./290m.; mail Clinton **z** 53525; rural
Berkeley; Inc. Place; COOK; **172** H-6; elev. 675ft./206m.; 🄿; ★ **CHI**; **z** 60163; Ⓟ 5,137; Ⓒ 5,245
Berkland Heights; RMC Place; LA SALLE; ***170** E-10; elev. 641ft./195m.; mail Marseilles **z** 61341; ● 70
Berkley Square; RMC Place; COOK; ★ **CHI**; pop. incl. with Arlington Heights (Inc. Place)
Berlin; Inc. Place; SANGAMON; **171** K-7; elev. 640ft./195m.; 🄿; **z** 62670; Ⓟ 180; Ⓒ 140; Ⓡ 149
Bernadotte; RMC Place; FULTON; ▲ Bernadotte; **170** H-6; mail Ipava **z** 61441; ● 100
Bernadotte; MCD-Township; FULTON; ***170** H-6; mail Ipava **z** 61441; Ⓟ 313; Ⓒ 306
Bernice; RMC Place; COOK; ***170** D-13; ★ **CHI**; mail Lansing **z** 60438; pop. incl. with Lansing (Inc. Place)
Berreman; MCD-Township; JO DAVIESS; ***170** B-7; mail Mount Carroll **z** 61053; Ⓟ 161; Ⓒ 174
Berry; RMC Place; SANGAMON; **171** K-8; 🄿; **z** 62563; ● 70
Berry; MCD-Township; WAYNE; ***171** O-11; mail Johnsonville **z** 62850; Ⓟ 349; Ⓒ 373
Berryville; RMC Place; RICHLAND; **171** O-12; elev. 502ft./153m.; mail Calhoun **z** 62419; ● 30
Berryville; RMC Place; UNION; ***171** S-9; elev. 500ft./152m.; mail Jonesboro **z** 62952; ● 40
Bertinetti Lake; RMC Place; CHRISTIAN; ***171** K-9; elev. 600ft./183m.; mail Taylorville **z** 62568; ● 250
Berwick; RMC Place; WARREN; ▲ Berwick; **170** G-5; elev. 710ft./216m.; 🄿; **z** 61417; ● 160
Berwick; MCD-Township; WARREN; ***170** G-5; 🄿; **z** 61417; Ⓟ 435; Ⓒ 379
Berwyn; Inc. Place; COOK; **172** I-8; elev. 610ft./186m.; 🄿 🄷 ■; ★ **CHI**; **z** 60402; Ⓟ 45,426; Ⓒ 54,016; ◆ 53,597
Berwyn; MCD-Township; COOK; ***170** C-13; 🄿 🄷; ★ **CHI**; **z** 60402; coextensive with the City of Berwyn; Ⓟ 45,426; Ⓒ 54,016
Bethalto; Inc. Place; MADISON; **171** N-6; elev. 520ft./158m.; 🄿; ★ **ST.L**; **z** 62010; Ⓟ 9,507; Ⓒ 9,454
Bethany; Inc. Place; MOULTRIE; **171** K-10; elev. 655ft./200m.; 🄿; **z** 61914; Ⓟ 1,369; Ⓒ 1,287
Bethel; MCD-Township; MCDONOUGH; ***170** H-5; mail Avon **z** 61415; Ⓟ 302; Ⓒ 383
Bethel; RMC Place; MORGAN; ***170** J-5; mail Chapin **z** 62628; rural
Bethel; RMC Place; VERMILION; ***170** J-13; elev. 675ft./206m.; mail Ridge Farm **z** 61870; rural
Bethlehem; RMC Place; EFFINGHAM; mail Altamont **z** 62411; rural
Beulah Heights; RMC Place; SALINE; mail Eldorado **z** 62930; pop. incl. with Eldorado (Inc. Place)
Be-Ver Kreek; RMC Place; BOONE; ***170** A-10; elev. 826ft./252m.; ★ **RKFD**; mail Belvidere **z** 61008; ● 300
Beverly; RMC Place; ADAMS; ▲ Beverly; **170** J-4; elev. 840ft./256m.; mail Barry **z** 62312, Liberty **z** 62347; ● 30

Entries in **UPPERCASE** are counties.
Entries in **bold** have populations of 2,500 or more.
Names in parentheses are alternate names.

Inc. Place	Incorporated Place
RMC Place	Rand McNally Designated Place
CDP	Census Designated Place
MCD	Minor Civil Division

⊡ County Seat
▲ Minor Civil Division
elev. Elevation
🄿 Post Office
🄷 Hospital
🄲 College
■ Principal Business Center
★ Ranally Metro Area (RMA) Abbreviation
z Zip Code(s)
Ⓟ Previous Census Population
Ⓡ Revised Census Population
Ⓐ Annexation Population
● Rand McNally Population Estimate
Ⓒ Final Census Population
Ⓢ Special Census Population
◆ Estimated Population

For additional definitions see Glossary, Volume 1, and Introduction, Volume 2.

Beverly; MCD-Township; ADAMS; *170 J-4; mail Barry z 62312; Ⓟ 363; © 338
Beverly; RMC Place; COOK; ★ CHI; mail Chicago z 60620, z 60643; pop. incl. with Chicago (Inc. Place)
Beverly Manor; RMC Place; TAZEWELL; *170 G-8; ★ PEOR; mail Washington z 61571; pop. incl. with Washington (Inc. Place)
Beyers Lake Addition; RMC Place; SHELBY; *171 L-9; mail Pana z 62557; ● 60
Bible Grove; RMC Place; CLAY; ▲ Bible Grove; 171 N-11; 🅿; z 62858; ● 100
Bible Grove; MCD-Township; CLAY; *171 N-11; 🅿; z 62858; Ⓟ 417; © 384
Biddleborn; RMC Place; WASHINGTON; *171 P-7; mail Marissa z 62257; rural
Big Bay (McNoel); RMC Place; MASSAC; *171 S-10; mail Metropolis z 62960; ● 40
Big Foot; MCHENRY; see Big Foot Prairie (RMC Place)
Big Foot Prairie (Big Foot); RMC Place; MCHENRY; 170 A-10; mail Harvard z 60033; ● 75
Big Grove; MCD-Township; KENDALL; *170 D-11; mail Newark z 60541; Ⓟ 1,430; © 1,526
Biggs; RMC Place; MASON; *170 I-7; 🅿; z 62633; rural
Biggsville; Inc. Place; HENDERSON; ▲ Biggsville; 170 G-4; elev. 650ft./198m.; 🅿; z 61418; Ⓟ 349; © 343
Biggsville; MCD-Township; HENDERSON; *170 G-4; 🅿; z 61418; Ⓟ 627; © 586
Big Hollow; RMC Place; LAKE; ★ CHI; mail Ingleside z 60041; rural
Big Mound; MCD-Township; WAYNE; *171 P-11; mail Fairfield z 62837; Ⓟ 1,825; © 1,792
Bigneck; RMC Place; ADAMS; *170 I-3; mail Loraine z 62349; rural
Big Rock (Village of Big Rock); Inc. Place; KANE; ▲ Big Rock; 170 C-11; 🅿; z 60511; incorporated July 26, 2001; not reported in 2000 Census; ● 700
Big Rock; MCD-Township; KANE; *170 C-11; 🅿; z 60511; Ⓟ 1,948; © 1,938
Big Spring; MCD-Township; SHELBY; *171 L-11; mail Neoga z 62447; Ⓟ 658; © 699
Billet; LAWRENCE; see Billett (RMC Place)
Billett (Billet); RMC Place; LAWRENCE; *171 O-13; mail Lawrenceville z 62439; ● 75
Bingham; Inc. Place; FAYETTE; 171 M-9; elev. 600ft./183m.; 🅿; z 62011; Ⓟ 98; © 117
Binghampton; RMC Place; LEE; *170 C-9; mail Amboy z 61310; ● 100
Binney; RMC Place; MADISON; *171 M-7; mail New Douglas z 62074; rural
Bird; MCD-Township; MACOUPIN; *171 L-7; mail Chesterfield z 62630; Ⓟ 323; © 279
Birds; Inc. Place; LAWRENCE; 171 N-13; elev. 440ft./134m.; 🅿; z 62427; Ⓟ 160; © 51
Birkbeck; RMC Place; DE WITT; *170 I-10; mail Clinton z 61727; rural
Birmingham; RMC Place; SCHUYLER; ▲ Birmingham; *170 I-4; mail Plymouth z 62367; ● 30
Birmingham; MCD-Township; SCHUYLER; *170 I-4; mail Plymouth z 62367; Ⓟ 169; © 150
Bishop; MCD-Township; EFFINGHAM; *171 M-11; mail Dieterich z 62424; Ⓟ 1,200; © 1,407
Bishop; RMC Place; MASON; *170 H-7; mail Forest City z 61532
Bishop Hill; Inc. Place; HENRY; 170 E-6; elev. 780ft./238m.; 🅿; z 61419; Ⓟ 131; © 125
Bishop Quarter Lane; RMC Place; COOK; *170 C-13; elev. 625ft./191m.; ★ CHI; mail Oak Park z 60302; pop. incl. with Oak Park (Inc. Place)
Bismarck; Inc. Place; VERMILION; 170 I-13; elev. 660ft./201m.; 🅿; ★ DANV; z 61814; © 542
Bissell; RMC Place; SANGAMON; *170 J-8; 🅿; ★ SPRG; z 62707
Black; RMC Place; EDWARDS; *171 O-12; elev. 461ft./141m.; mail Albion z 62806; rural
Blackberry; MCD-Township; KANE; *170 C-11; ★ CHI; mail Elburn z 60119; Ⓟ 3,658; © 6,071
Blackberry Heights; RMC Place; KANE; *170 C-11; ★ CHI; mail Montgomery z 60538; ● 500
Blackberry Woods; RMC Place; KANE; *170 C-11; elev. 720ft./219m.; ★ CHI; mail Sugar Grove z 60554; ● 150
Blackhawk; RMC Place; COOK; *170 B-11; ★ CHI; mail Elgin z 60120; pop. incl. with Elgin (Inc. Place)
Blackhawk; MCD-Township; ROCK ISLAND; *170 D-5; ★ D-RI-M; mail Milan z 61264; Ⓟ 10,991; © 10,612; Ⓡ 10,616
Blackhawk Heights; RMC Place; DUPAGE; ★ CHI; mail Clarendon Hills z 60514; pop. incl. with Clarendon Hills (Inc. Place)
Blackhawk Island; RMC Place; WINNEBAGO; *170 B-9; ★ RKFD; mail Rockford z 61102; ● 30
Black Hawk Springs; RMC Place; KENDALL; *170 D-11; elev. 575ft./175m.; ★ CHI; mail Plano z 60545; ● 60
Blackstone; RMC Place; LIVINGSTON; 170 F-10; elev. 730ft./223m.; 🅿; z 61313; ● 100
Blaine; RMC Place; BOONE; *170 A-10; mail Poplar Grove z 61065
Blair; MCD-Township; CLAY; *171 N-11; mail Louisville z 62858; Ⓟ 589; © 619
Blair; RMC Place; LIVINGSTON; *170 F-11; elev. 613ft./187m.; mail Reddick z 60961; rural
Blair; RMC Place; RANDOLPH; *171 Q-7; elev. 498ft./152m.; mail Sparta z 62286; ● 35
Blairsville; RMC Place; HAMILTON; *171 P-11; elev. 385ft./117m.; mail Mc Leansboro z 62859; rural
Blairsville; RMC Place; WILLIAMSON; *171 R-9; elev. 399ft./122m.; ★ CARB-; mail Carterville z 62918; ● 200
Blandinsville; Inc. Place; MCDONOUGH; 170 H-4; elev. 729ft./222m.; 🅿; z 61420, z 61475; Ⓟ 762; © 777
Blandinsville; MCD-Township; MCDONOUGH; *170 G-4; 🅿; z 61420, z 61475; includes part of the Village of Blandinsville; Ⓟ 1,003; © 1,003
Blissville; MCD-Township; JEFFERSON; *171 P-9; mail Waltonville z 62894; Ⓟ 355; © 402
Block; RMC Place; CHAMPAIGN; *170 J-12; elev. 710ft./216m.; mail Sidney z 61877; rural
Blodgett; RMC Place; LAKE; *170 B-13; ★ CHI; mail Highland Park z 60035; pop. incl. with Highland Park (Inc. Place)
Blodgett; RMC Place; WILL; *170 E-12; ★ CHI; mail Elwood z 60421; ● 100
Blood; EDWARDS; see Bennington (RMC Place)
Bloom; MCD-Township; COOK; *170 D-13; ★ CHI; mail Chicago Heights z 60411; Ⓟ 95,029; © 93,901
Bloomfield; RMC Place; EDGAR; *171 K-13; elev. 635ft./194m.; mail Chrisman z 61924
Bloomfield; RMC Place; JOHNSON; *171 S-10; mail Vienna z 62995
Bloomfield; RMC Place; SCOTT; *171 K-5; mail Winchester z 62694; rural
Bloomingdale; Inc. Place; DUPAGE; 170 C-12; elev. 758ft./231m.; 🅿 ■; ★ CHI; z 60108, z 60117; Ⓟ 16,614; © 21,675; ◆ 22,233
Bloomingdale; MCD-Township; DUPAGE; *170 C-12; 🅿; ★ CHI; z 60108, z 60117; Ⓟ 96,050; © 111,709
Bloomington; Inc. Place; ⊡ MCLEAN; 170 H-9; elev. 829ft./253m.; 🅿 🄷 🄲 2,145 ■; ★ BLOOM-; z 61701-02, z 61704-05, z 61709-10, z 61791, z 61799; Ⓟ 51,889; © 64,808; ◆ 76,555
Bloomington; MCD-Township; MCLEAN; *170 H-9; 🅿 🄲 2,145; ★ BLOOM-; z 61701-02, z 61704-05, z 61709-10, z 61791, z 61799; does not include City of Bloomington; Ⓟ 3,835; © 3,176
Bloomington City; MCD-Township; MCLEAN; *170 H-9; 🄷; ★ BLOOM-; mail Bloomington z 61701-02, z 61704, z 61709-10, z 61791, z 61799; coextensive with the City of Bloomington; Ⓟ 51,889; © 64,808
Bloomington Heights; RMC Place; MCLEAN; *170 H-9; ★ BLOOM-; mail Bloomington z 61701, z 61704; ● 50
Blossom Hill; RMC Place; MCHENRY; ★ CHI; mail Cary z 60013; pop. incl. with Cary (Inc. Place)
Blount; MCD-Township; VERMILION; *170 I-13; mail Danville z 61834; Ⓟ 3,122; © 3,325
Blue Fountain; RMC Place; MADISON; *171 N-6; ★ ST.L; mail Godfrey z 62035; pop. incl. with Godfrey (Inc. Place)
Blue Island; Inc. Place; COOK; 172 L-9; elev. 608ft./185m.; 🅿 🄷; ★ CHI; z 60406 & mail Riverdale z 60827; Ⓟ 21,203; © 23,463; ◆ 23,689
Blue Island Junction; RMC Place; COOK; ★ CHI; mail Blue Island z 60406; pop. incl. with Blue Island (Inc. Place)
Blue Island Junction; RMC Place; COOK; ★ CHI; mail Chicago z 60617; pop. incl. with Chicago (Inc. Place)
Blue Mound; Inc. Place; MACON; ▲ Pleasant View; 171 K-9; elev. 620ft./189m.; 🅿; z 62513; Ⓟ 1,161; © 1,129
Blue Mound; MCD-Township; MACON; *171 K-9; 🅿; z 62513 & mail Boody z 62514; does not include Village of Blue Mound; Ⓟ 916; © 917
Blue Mound; MCD-Township; MCLEAN; *170 H-10; mail Cooksville z 61730; Ⓟ 478; © 473
Blue Point; RMC Place; EFFINGHAM; *171 M-10; mail Effingham z 62401; rural
Blue Ridge; RMC Place; PIATT; ▲ Blue Ridge; *170 I-11; elev. 788ft./240m.; mail Mansfield z 61854; rural
Blue Ridge; MCD-Township; PIATT; *170 I-11; mail Mansfield z 61854; Ⓟ 1,407; © 1,414
Bluff City; RMC Place; FAYETTE; 171 M-9; elev. 515ft./157m.; mail Vandalia z 62471; ● 300
Bluff City; RMC Place; SCHUYLER; *170 I-6; elev. 462ft./141m.; 🅿; z 62624; ● 40
Bluffdale; MCD-Township; GREENE; *171 L-5; mail Eldred z 62027; Ⓟ 694; © 580
Bluffdale; RMC Place; HENDERSON; *170 G-4; elev. 567ft./173m.; mail Gladstone z 61437; ● 70
Bluff Hall; RMC Place; ADAMS; *170 J-3; mail Payson z 62360; rural
Bluffs; Inc. Place; SCOTT; 171 K-5; elev. 474ft./144m.; 🅿; z 62621; Ⓟ 774; © 748
Bluffside; RMC Place; ST. CLAIR; *171 O-6; ★ ST.L; mail Columbia z 62236; rural
Bluff Springs; RMC Place; CASS; ▲ Bluff Springs; 170 J-6; 🅿; z 62622; ● 120
Bluff Springs; MCD-Township; CASS; *170 J-6; 🅿; z 62622; Ⓟ 751; © 856
Bluff View Park; RMC Place; ST. CLAIR; ★ ST.L; mail Caseyville z 62232; pop. incl. with Caseyville (Inc. Place)
Bluford; Inc. Place; JEFFERSON; 171 P-10; elev. 519ft./158m.; 🅿; z 62814; Ⓟ 747; © 785
Blyton; RMC Place; FULTON; 170 H-6; elev. 629ft./192m.; mail Smithfield z 61477; ● 25
Boaz; RMC Place; MASSAC; *171 T-10; mail Karnak z 62956
Boden; RMC Place; MERCER; 170 E-5; mail Sherrard z 61281; ● 100
Bogota; RMC Place; JASPER; 171 N-12; mail Newton z 62448; ● 60
Bohleysville; RMC Place; ST. CLAIR; *171 O-6; ★ ST.L; mail Millstadt z 62260; rural
Bois; WASHINGTON; see Du Bois (Inc. Place)
Bois d'Arc; MCD-Township; MONTGOMERY; *171 L-8; mail Farmersville z 62533; Ⓟ 1,047; © 1,050
Boles; JOHNSON; see West Vienna (RMC Place)
Bolingbrook; Inc. Place; WILL, DUPAGE; 170 D-12; elev. 703ft./214m.; 🅿; ★ CHI; z 60440, z 60490 & mail Lemont z 60439; Ⓟ 40,843; © 56,321; ◆ 62,629
Boling Green; RMC Place; WILL; ★ CHI; mail Bolingbrook z 60440; pop. incl. with Bolingbrook (Inc. Place)
Bolivia; RMC Place; CHRISTIAN; *171 K-8; 🅿; z 62545; ● 35
Bolo; MCD-Town; WASHINGTON; *171 P-8; mail Ashley z 62808; Ⓟ 396; © 390
Bolton; RMC Place; STEPHENSON; *170 B-7; mail Freeport z 61032; ● 30
Bond; MCD-Township; LAWRENCE; *171 N-13; mail Lawrenceville z 62439; Ⓟ 844; © 776
BOND; 171 M-8; Ⓟ 14,991; © 17,633; ◆ 18,755
Bondville; Inc. Place; CHAMPAIGN; *170 I-11; elev. 719ft./219m.; 🅿; z 61815; Ⓟ 446; © 455
Bone Gap; Inc. Place; EDWARDS; 171 O-12; elev. 462ft./141m.; 🅿; z 62815; Ⓟ 271; © 272
Bonfield; Inc. Place; KANKAKEE; 170 E-12; elev. 625ft./191m.; 🅿; z 60913; Ⓟ 299; © 364
Bongard; RMC Place; CHAMPAIGN; *170 J-12; elev. 681ft./208m.; mail Philo z 61864; rural
Bonnie; Inc. Place; JEFFERSON; 171 P-10; elev. 430ft./131m.; 🅿; z 62816; Ⓟ 411; © 424
Bonnie Brea; RMC Place; WILL; *170 D-12; ★ CHI; mail Lockport z 60441; pop. incl. with Lockport (Inc. Place)
Bonpas; MCD-Township; RICHLAND; *171 O-12; mail Calhoun z 62419; Ⓟ 404; © 365
Bonus; MCD-Township; BOONE; *170 A-10; mail Garden Prairie z 61038; Ⓟ 1,951; © 2,662
Boody; RMC Place; MACON; 171 K-9; elev. 680ft./207m.; 🅿; z 62514; ● 370
Boone; MCD-Township; BOONE; *170 A-10; mail Capron z 61012; Ⓟ 1,410; © 1,671
BOONE; 170 A-10; Ⓟ 30,806; © 41,786; ◆ 56,557
Boos; RMC Place; JASPER; *171 N-12; mail Newton z 62448; rural
Booster Station; RMC Place; ST. CLAIR; ★ ST.L; mail O Fallon z 62269; rural
Borton; RMC Place; EDGAR; 171 K-12; mail Brocton z 61917; ● 60
Boskydell; RMC Place; JACKSON; 171 R-9; elev. 409ft./125m.; ★ CARB-; mail Carbondale z 62901; ● 30
Boulder; RMC Place; CLINTON; 171 N-9; mail Carlyle z 62231; ● 100
Boulder Hill; CDP-Census Area Only; KENDALL; *170 C-11; elev. 650ft./198m.; ★ CHI; mail Montgomery z 60538; Ⓟ 8,894; © 8,169
Boulevard Manor; RMC Place; COOK; ★ CHI; mail Cicero z 60804; pop. incl. with Cicero (Inc. Place)
Bourbon; RMC Place; DOUGLAS; ▲ Bourbon; 171 K-11; elev. 667ft./203m.; mail Tuscola z 61953; ● 140
Bourbon; MCD-Township; DOUGLAS; *171 K-11; mail Tuscola z 61953; Ⓟ 3,318; © 3,662
Bourbonnais; Inc. Place; KANKAKEE; ▲ Bourbonnais, Manteno; 170 E-12; elev. 663ft./202m.; 🅿 🄲 4,495; ★ KANK; z 60914; Ⓟ 13,929; © 15,256
Bourbonnais; MCD-Township; KANKAKEE; *170 E-13; 🅿 🄲 4,495; ★ KANK; z 60914; Ⓟ 29,129; © 33,061
Bowdre; MCD-Township; DOUGLAS; *171 K-12; mail Arcola z 61910; Ⓟ 811; © 755
Bowen; Inc. Place; HANCOCK; 170 I-4; elev. 680ft./207m.; 🅿; z 62316; Ⓟ 462; © 535
Bowes; RMC Place; KANE; *170 B-11; elev. 858ft./262m.; ★ CHI; mail Elgin z 60123; rural
Bowlesville; MCD-Township; GALLATIN; *171 R-12; mail Shawneetown z 62984; Ⓟ 216; © 190
Bowling; MCD-Township; ROCK ISLAND; *170 E-5; ★ D-RI-M; mail Milan z 61264; Ⓟ 3,135; © 4,150; Ⓡ 3,501
Bowling Green; MCD-Township; FAYETTE; *171 M-10; mail Cowden z 62422; Ⓟ 425; © 433
Boxtown; MONROE; see Kidd (RMC Place)
Boyd; RMC Place; JEFFERSON; *171 O-9; elev. 524ft./160m.; mail Dix z 62830; ● 45
Boyleston; RMC Place; WAYNE; *171 P-11; elev. 435ft./133m.; mail Fairfield z 62837; ● 60
Boynton; MCD-Township; TAZEWELL; *170 H-8; mail Delavan z 61734; Ⓟ 266; © 265
Braceville; Inc. Place; GRUNDY; ▲ Braceville; 170 E-11; 🅿; ★ CHI; z 60407; Ⓟ 587; © 792
Braceville; MCD-Township; GRUNDY; *170 E-11; 🅿; ★ CHI; z 60407; Ⓟ 3,637; © 4,895
Bradbury; RMC Place; CUMBERLAND; *171 L-12; elev. 607ft./185m.; mail Toledo z 62468; rural
Bradford; MCD-Township; LEE; *170 C-9; mail Ashton z 61006; Ⓟ 332; © 362
Bradford; Inc. Place; STARK; 170 E-8; elev. 810ft./247m.; 🅿; z 61421; Ⓟ 678; © 787
Bradfordton; RMC Place; SANGAMON; *170 J-7; elev. 590ft./180m.; 🅿; ★ SPRG; z 62707; rural
Bradley; RMC Place; GRUNDY; *170 E-11; mail Morris z 60450; ● 200
Bradley; MCD-Township; JACKSON; *171 Q-8; mail Ava z 62907; Ⓟ 1,659; © 1,757
Bradley; Inc. Place; KANKAKEE; ▲ Manteno; 170 F-13; elev. 632ft./193m.; 🅿; ★ KANK; z 60915; Ⓟ 10,918; © 12,784
Braeside; RMC Place; LAKE; ★ CHI; mail Highland Park z 60035; pop. incl. with Highland Park (Inc. Place)
Braidwood; Inc. Place; WILL; 170 E-12; elev. 575ft./175m.; 🅿; ★ CHI; z 60408; Ⓟ 3,584; © 5,203
Branding; RMC Place; CALHOUN; *171 M-5; elev. 430ft./131m.; mail Brussels z 62013; summer pop. 100; ● 40
Brandywine; RMC Place; DUPAGE; 172 I-6; ★ CHI; mail Villa Park z 60181; ● 3,100
Branigar Estates; RMC Place; COOK; *170 B-12; ★ CHI; mail Elk Grove Village z 60007; ● 400
Breckenridge; RMC Place; SANGAMON; *171 K-8; 🅿; z 62563; ● 40
Breeds; RMC Place; FULTON; *170 H-7; mail Canton z 61520; ● 50
Breese; Inc. Place; CLINTON; ▲ Breese; 171 O-8; elev. 452ft./138m.; 🅿 🄷; ★ ST.L; z 62230 & mail Aviston z 62216; Ⓟ 3,567; © 4,048
Breese; MCD-Township; CLINTON; *171 O-8; 🅿; ★ ST.L; z 62230 & mail Aviston z 62216; Ⓟ 4,612; © 5,044
Bremen; MCD-Township; COOK; *170 D-13; ★ CHI; mail Harvey z 60426; Ⓟ 107,803; © 109,575
Bremen; RMC Place; RANDOLPH; 171 Q-7; elev. 565ft./172m.; mail Chester z 62233; ● 50
Brenton; MCD-Township; FORD; *170 G-12; mail Piper City z 60959; Ⓟ 994; © 929
Brentwood; RMC Place; COOK; *170 B-12; elev. 760ft./232m.; ★ CHI; mail Palatine z 60074; ● 190
Brereton; RMC Place; FULTON; *170 G-7; mail Canton z 61520; ● 120
Briar Bluff; RMC Place; HENRY; *170 D-6; ★ D-RI-M; mail Coal Valley z 61240; rural
Briarbrook Village; RMC Place; DUPAGE; ★ CHI; mail Wheaton z 60187; pop. incl. with Wheaton (Inc. Place)
Briarcliffe; RMC Place; DUPAGE; ★ CHI; mail Wheaton z 60187; pop. incl. with Wheaton (Inc. Place)
Briarcliffe Knolls; RMC Place; DUPAGE; ★ CHI; mail Wheaton z 60187; pop. incl. with Wheaton (Inc. Place)
Briarcliff Estates; RMC Place; KANKAKEE; *170 E-12; elev. 675ft./206m.; ★ KANK; mail Bourbonnais z 60914; pop. incl. with Bourbonnais (Inc. Place)
Briarwick; RMC Place; COLES; *171 L-11; mail Mattoon z 61938; ● 110
Briarwoods Estates; RMC Place; LAKE; ★ CHI; mail Deerfield z 60015; pop. incl. with Deerfield (Inc. Place)
Briarwood Trace; RMC Place; WILLIAMSON; mail Carbondale z 62901; ● 40
Brickman Manor; RMC Place; COOK; ★ CHI; mail Mount Prospect z 60056; pop. incl. with Mount Prospect (Inc. Place)
Bridge Junction; RMC Place; ST. CLAIR; ★ ST.L; pop. incl. with East Saint Louis (Inc. Place)
Bridgelane; RMC Place; ROCK ISLAND; ★ D-RI-M; mail Moline z 61265; ● 200
Bridgeport; RMC Place; COOK; ★ CHI; mail Chicago z 60608-09, z 60616; pop. incl. with Chicago (Inc. Place)
Bridgeport; Inc. Place; LAWRENCE; 171 N-13; elev. 446ft./136m.; 🅿; z 62417; Ⓟ 2,118; © 2,168
Bridgeport; MCD-Township; LAWRENCE; *171 N-13; 🅿; z 62417; Ⓟ 2,588; © 2,655
Bridgeview; Inc. Place; COOK; 172 J-7; elev. 617ft./188m.; 🅿; ★ CHI; z 60455; Ⓟ 14,402; © 15,335
Bridgeway Addition; RMC Place; ROCK ISLAND; *170 D-5; ★ D-RI-M; mail Moline z 61265; pop. incl. with Moline (Inc. Place)
Bridle Creek Estates; RMC Place; KANE; *170 C-11; elev. 800ft./244m.; ★ CHI; mail Saint Charles z 60175; ● 40
Brierwood; RMC Place; KANE; *170 C-11; elev. 890ft./271m.; ★ CHI; mail Saint Charles z 60175; ● 150
Bright Oaks; RMC Place; MCHENRY; ★ CHI; mail Cary z 60013; pop. incl. with Cary (Inc. Place)
Brighton; Inc. Place; MACOUPIN, JERSEY; 171 M-6; elev. 653ft./199m.; 🅿; ★ ST.L; z 62012; Ⓟ 2,270; © 2,196
Brighton; MCD-Township; MACOUPIN; *171 M-6; 🅿; ★ ST.L; z 62012; includes part of the Village of Brighton; Ⓟ 3,814; © 4,149
Brighton Park; RMC Place; COOK; ★ CHI; mail Chicago z 60632; pop. incl. with Chicago (Inc. Place)
Brimfield; Inc. Place; PEORIA; ▲ Brimfield; 170 G-7; elev. 707ft./215m.; 🅿; z 61517; Ⓟ 797; © 933
Brimfield; MCD-Township; PEORIA; *170 G-7; 🅿; z 61517; includes part of the village of Brimfield; Ⓟ 1,177; © 1,281
Brisbane; RMC Place; WILL; *170 D-12; ★ CHI; mail New Lenox z 60451; rural
Bristol (Bristol Station); RMC Place; KENDALL; ▲ Bristol; 170 D-11; 🅿; ★ CHI; z 60512; ● 500
Bristol; MCD-Township; KENDALL; *170 D-11; 🅿; ★ CHI; z 60512; Ⓟ 5,598; © 7,677
Bristol Lake; RMC Place; KENDALL; *170 D-11; elev. 644ft./196m.; ★ CHI; mail Yorkville z 60560; ● 100
Bristol Ridge; RMC Place; KENDALL; *170 D-11; elev. 649ft./198m.; ★ CHI; mail Yorkville z 60560; ● 160
Bristol Station; KENDALL; see Bristol (RMC Place)
Broadlands; Inc. Place; CHAMPAIGN; 170 J-12; elev. 683ft./208m.; 🅿; z 61816; Ⓟ 340; © 312
Broadmoor; RMC Place; MARSHALL; *170 F-8; mail Bradford z 61421; ● 25
Broadview; Inc. Place; COOK; 172 I-7; elev. 625ft./191m.; 🅿; ★ CHI; z 60153, z 60155; Ⓟ 8,713; © 8,264
Broadwell; Inc. Place; LOGAN; ▲ Broadwell; 170 I-8; 🅿; z 62634; Ⓟ 146; © 169
Broadwell; MCD-Township; LOGAN; *170 I-8; 🅿; z 62634; Ⓟ 2,200; © 2,961
Brocton; Inc. Place; EDGAR; 171 K-12; elev. 660ft./201m.; 🅿; z 61917; Ⓟ 322; © 322
Brooke Estates; RMC Place; LAKE; ★ CHI; mail Highland Park z 60035; pop. incl. with Highland Park (Inc. Place)
Brookeridge; RMC Place; DUPAGE; *170 C-12; ★ CHI; mail Downers Grove z 60515; ● 600
Brookfield; Inc. Place; COOK; 172 I-7; elev. 620ft./189m.; 🅿; ★ CHI; z 60513; Ⓟ 18,876; © 19,085
Brookfield; MCD-Township; LA SALLE; *170 E-10; mail Ransom z 60470; Ⓟ 823; © 936
Brook Forest; RMC Place; DUPAGE; ★ CHI; mail Oak Brook z 60523; pop. incl. with Oak Brook (Inc. Place)
Brookforest North; RMC Place; WILL; *170 D-12; ★ CHI; mail Joliet z 60435; pop. incl. with Shorewood (Inc. Place)
Brookhaven; RMC Place; WHITESIDE; mail Prophetstown z 61277; ● 100
Brookhaven Manor; RMC Place; DUPAGE; ★ CHI; mail Darien z 60561; pop. incl. with Darien (Inc. Place)
Brookhill; RMC Place; LAKE; *170 A-12; ★ CHI; mail Libertyville z 60048; ● 240
Brooklyn; MCD-Township; LEE; *170 D-9; mail Compton z 61318; Ⓟ 886; © 876
Brooklyn; RMC Place; SCHUYLER; ▲ Brooklyn; 170 I-4; elev. 551ft./168m.; mail Plymouth z 62367; ● 100
Brooklyn; MCD-Township; SCHUYLER; *170 I-5; mail Plymouth z 62367; Ⓟ 234; © 213
Brooklyn (Lovejoy); Inc. Place; ST. CLAIR; 195 E-7; elev. 411ft./125m.; 🅿; ★ ST.L; z 62059; Ⓟ 1,144; © 676
Brookport; Inc. Place; MASSAC; 171 T-10; elev. 340ft./104m.; 🅿; ★ PAD; z 62910; Ⓟ 1,070; © 1,054
Brooks; RMC Place; MADISON; *171 N-6; ★ ST.L; mail Granite City z 62040
Brookside; MCD-Township; CLINTON; *171 O-9; mail Centralia z 62801; Ⓟ 5,458; © 5,576
Brookside; RMC Place; KANE; *170 C-11; elev. 900ft./274m.; ★ CHI; mail Saint Charles z 60175; ● 50
Brooks Isle; RMC Place; OGLE; mail Oregon z 61061; ● 50
Brookview; RMC Place; PEORIA; *170 G-8; ★ PEOR; mail Peoria z 61614; ● 400
Brookville; RMC Place; OGLE; ▲ Brookville; 170 B-8; mail Polo z 61064; ● 80
Brookville; MCD-Township; OGLE; *170 B-8; mail Polo z 61064; Ⓟ 286; © 253
Brookville; VERMILION; see Grape Creek (RMC Place)
Brookwood; RMC Place; COOK; ★ CHI; mail Rolling Meadows z 60008; pop. incl. with Rolling Meadows (Inc. Place)
Brookwood; RMC Place; COOK; ★ CHI; mail Prospect Heights z 60070; pop. incl. with Prospect Heights (Inc. Place)
Brookwood; RMC Place; KANE; *170 C-11; elev. 700ft./213m.; ★ CHI; mail Saint Charles z 60174; ● 150
Brookwood Estates; RMC Place; DUPAGE; ★ CHI; mail Wood Dale z 60191; pop. incl. with Wood Dale (Inc. Place)
Brothers (Brothers Station); RMC Place; VERMILION; *170 I-13; elev. 653ft./199m.; ★ DANV; mail Oakwood z 61858; rural
Brothers Station; VERMILION; see Brothers (RMC Place)
Broughton; Inc. Place; HAMILTON; 171 Q-11; elev. 378ft./115m.; 🅿; z 62817; Ⓟ 218; © 193
Broughton; MCD-Township; LIVINGSTON; *170 F-11; mail Emington z 60934; Ⓟ 330; © 290
Brouilletts Creek; MCD-Township; EDGAR; *171 K-13; mail Chrisman z 61924; Ⓟ 253; © 261
Brown; MCD-Township; CHAMPAIGN; *170 H-11; mail Foosland z 61845; Ⓟ 1,488; © 2,966; Ⓡ 1,495
BROWN; 170 J-5; Ⓟ 5,836; © 6,950; ◆ 6,399
Brownfield; RMC Place; POPE; 171 S-11; elev. 338ft./103m.; 🅿; z 62938; ● 75
Browning; MCD-Township; FRANKLIN; *171 Q-9; mail Benton z 62812; Ⓟ 2,318; © 2,420; Ⓡ 2,418
Browning; Inc. Place; SCHUYLER; ▲ Browning; 170 I-6; 🅿; z 62624; Ⓟ 193; © 130
Browning; MCD-Township; SCHUYLER; *170 I-5; 🅿; z 62624; Ⓟ 556; © 456
Browns; Inc. Place; EDWARDS; 171 P-12; elev. 400ft./122m.; 🅿; z 62818; Ⓟ 207; © 175
Brownstown; Inc. Place; FAYETTE; 171 M-10; elev. 586ft./179m.; 🅿; z 62418; Ⓟ 668; © 705
Brownsville; RMC Place; WHITE; 171 Q-12; elev. 416ft./127m.; mail Carmi z 62821; ● 50
Brownwood; RMC Place; TAZEWELL; *170 H-8; mail Hopedale z 61747; rural
Brubaker; RMC Place; MARION; *171 N-10; mail Salem z 62881
Bruce; MCD-Township; LA SALLE; *170 E-10; mail Streator z 61364; Ⓟ 14,070; © 13,489
Bruce; RMC Place; MOULTRIE; 171 K-11; mail Sullivan z 61951; ● 50
Brunning; RMC Place; WILL; *170 D-12; ★ CHI; mail Lockport z 60441; ● 980
Brushy; MCD-Township; SALINE; *171 R-10; mail Galatia z 62935; Ⓟ 795; © 838
Brushy Mound; MCD-Township; MACOUPIN; *171 M-7; mail Gillespie z 62033; Ⓟ 697; © 751
Brussels; Inc. Place; CALHOUN; 171 M-5; elev. 527ft./161m.; 🅿; z 62013; Ⓟ 125; © 141
Bryant; Inc. Place; FULTON; 170 H-6; elev. 619ft./189m.; 🅿; z 61519; Ⓟ 273; © 255
Bryce; RMC Place; IROQUOIS; *170 G-13; mail Milford z 60953
Bryn Mawr; RMC Place; COOK; ★ CHI; mail Chicago z 60649; pop. incl. with Chicago (Inc. Place)
Bryn Mawr; RMC Place; DUPAGE; ★ CHI; pop. incl. with Chicago (Inc. Place)
Buck; MCD-Township; EDGAR; *171 K-13; mail Paris z 61944; Ⓟ 366; © 346
Buckeye; MCD-Township; STEPHENSON; *170 A-8; mail Cedarville z 61013; Ⓟ 1,458; © 1,365
Buckhart; MCD-Township; CHRISTIAN; *171 K-8; mail Edinburg z 62531; Ⓟ 1,730; © 1,868
Buckhart; RMC Place; SANGAMON; *171 K-8; elev. 566ft./173m.; mail Mechanicsburg z 62545, Rochester z 62563; ● 30
Buckheart; MCD-Township; FULTON; *170 H-6; mail Saint David z 61563; Ⓟ 1,577; © 1,515
Buckhorn; RMC Place; BROWN; *170 J-4; mail Mount Sterling z 62353; rural
Buckhorn; MCD-Township; BROWN; *170 J-4; mail Timewell z 62375; Ⓟ 103; © 107
Buckingham; Inc. Place; KANKAKEE; 170 F-12; elev. 654ft./199m.; 🅿; z 60917; Ⓟ 340; © 237
Buckley; Inc. Place; IROQUOIS; 170 H-12; elev. 699ft./213m.; 🅿; z 60918; Ⓟ 557; © 593
Buckner; Inc. Place; FRANKLIN; *171 Q-9; elev. 410ft./125m.; 🅿; z 62819; Ⓟ 478; © 479; Ⓡ 477
Bucks; RMC Place; DE WITT; *170 I-9; mail Wapella z 61777; rural
Buda; Inc. Place; BUREAU; 170 E-8; elev. 752ft./229m.; 🅿; z 61314; Ⓟ 563; © 592
Budd; RMC Place; LIVINGSTON; *170 F-10; elev. 703ft./214m.; mail Blackstone z 61313; rural
Buena Vista; RMC Place; SALINE; *171 R-11; elev. 402ft./123m.; mail Harrisburg z 62946; pop. incl. with Harrisburg (Inc. Place)
Buena Vista; MCD-Township; SCHUYLER; *170 I-5; mail Rushville z 62681; Ⓟ 1,433; © 1,426
Buena Vista; RMC Place; STEPHENSON; *170 A-8; mail Freeport z 61032; ● 35
Buffalo; MCD-Township; OGLE; *170 B-8; mail Polo z 61064; Ⓟ 3,003; © 2,941
Buffalo; Inc. Place; SANGAMON; 170 J-8; elev. 611ft./186m.; 🅿; z 62515; Ⓟ 503; © 491
Buffalo Grove; Inc. Place; COOK, LAKE; 172 D-6; elev. 680ft./207m.; 🅿; ★ CHI; z 60089; Ⓟ 36,427; © 42,909; Ⓡ 42,963; ◆ 41,267
Buffalo Grove; RMC Place; OGLE; *170 B-8; mail Polo z 61064; ● 60
Buffalo Hart; RMC Place; SANGAMON; ▲ Buffalo Hart; 170 J-8; 🅿; z 62515; ● 25
Buffalo Hart; MCD-Township; SANGAMON; *170 J-8; 🅿; z 62515; Ⓟ 226; © 195
Buffalo Prairie; RMC Place; ROCK ISLAND; ▲ Buffalo Prairie; *170 E-4; elev. 755ft./230m.; 🅿; z 61237; ● 60
Buffalo Prairie; MCD-Township; ROCK ISLAND; *170 E-4; 🅿; z 61237; Ⓟ 838; © 936
Bull Creek; RMC Place; LAKE; *170 A-12; ★ CHI; mail Libertyville z 60048; ● 150
Bullock Addition; RMC Place; HENRY; *170 D-6; elev. 600ft./183m.; ★ D-RI-M; mail Colona z 61241; ● 100
Bull Valley; Inc. Place; MCHENRY; 172 B-2; 🅿; ★ CHI; z 60012, z 60050, z 60097-98; © 726
Bulpitt; Inc. Place; CHRISTIAN; *171 K-8; elev. 597ft./182m.; 🅿; z 62517; Ⓟ 206; © 206
Buncombe; Inc. Place; JOHNSON; 171 S-9; elev. 495ft./151m.; 🅿; z 62912; Ⓟ 208; © 186
Bungay; RMC Place; HAMILTON; 171 P-11; mail Springerton z 62887; ● 45
Bunker Hill; Inc. Place; MACOUPIN; ▲ Bunker Hill; 171 M-7; elev. 668ft./204m.; 🅿; z 62014; Ⓟ 1,722; © 1,801
Bunker Hill; MCD-Township; MACOUPIN; *171 M-7; 🅿; z 62014; Ⓟ 3,052; © 3,352
Bunkum; RMC Place; ST. CLAIR; *171 O-6; ★ ST.L; mail Fairview Heights z 62208; pop. incl. with Fairview Heights (Inc. Place)
Bunsenville; RMC Place; VERMILION; *170 J-13; ★ DANV; mail Georgetown z 61846; ● 70
Burbank; Inc. Place; COOK; 172 J-8; elev. 619ft./189m.; 🅿; ★ CHI; z 60459; Ⓟ 27,600; © 27,902; ◆ 27,147
Burches; RMC Place; KANKAKEE; *170 E-13; elev. 675ft./206m.; ★ KANK; mail Bourbonnais z 60914; ● 500
Bureau (Bureau Junction); Inc. Place; BUREAU; ▲ Leepertown; *170 E-8; elev. 485ft./148m.; 🅿; z 61315; Ⓟ 350; © 368
Bureau; MCD-Township; BUREAU; *170 D-8; 🅿; z 61315 & mail Wyanet z 61379; Ⓟ 316; © 282
BUREAU; 170 D-8; Ⓟ 35,688; © 35,503; ◆ 34,824
Bureau Junction; BUREAU; see Bureau (Inc. Place)
Burgess; MCD-Township; BOND; *171 N-8; mail Pocahontas z 62275; Ⓟ 2,163; © 2,391
Burgess; RMC Place; MERCER; 170 F-5; mail Aledo z 61231; ● 50
Burksville; RMC Place; MONROE; 171 P-6; elev. 654ft./199m.; mail Waterloo z 62298; ● 80
Burksville Station; RMC Place; MONROE; *171 P-6; mail Waterloo z 62298; ● 40
Burlington; Inc. Place; KANE; ▲ Burlington; 170 B-11; 🅿; z 60109; Ⓟ 400; © 452
Burlington; MCD-Township; KANE; *170 B-11; 🅿; z 60109; Ⓟ 1,555; © 1,834
Burnham; Inc. Place; COOK; 172 L-10; elev. 585ft./178m.; 🅿; ★ CHI; z 60633; Ⓟ 3,916; © 4,170
Burnham Mill; RMC Place; KANE; ★ CHI; mail Elgin z 60123; pop. incl. with Elgin (Inc. Place)
Burns; MCD-Township; HENRY; *170 E-7; mail Kewanee z 61443; Ⓟ 353; © 307
Burnside; RMC Place; COOK; *170 C-13; ★ CHI; mail Chicago z 60619; pop. incl. with Chicago (Inc. Place)
Burnside; RMC Place; HANCOCK; *170 H-4; elev. 647ft./197m.; 🅿; z 62330; ● 130
Burnside's Lakewood; RMC Place; COOK; ★ CHI; mail Richton Park z 60471; pop. incl. with Richton Park (Inc. Place)
Burnt Prairie (Liberty); Inc. Place; WHITE; ▲ Burnt Prairie; 171 P-11; elev. 450ft./137m.; 🅿; z 62820; Ⓟ 71; © 58
Burnt Prairie; MCD-Township; WHITE; *171 P-12; 🅿; z 62820 & mail Carmi z 62821; Ⓟ 473; © 402
Burritt; MCD-Township; WINNEBAGO; *170 A-9; mail Winnebago z 61088; Ⓟ 932; © 1,026
Burr Oak; RMC Place; COOK; ★ CHI; pop. incl. with Arlington Heights (Inc. Place)
Burr Oak; RMC Place; COOK; ★ CHI; mail Blue Island z 60406; pop. incl. with Blue Island (Inc. Place)
Burr Oaks; RMC Place; WILL; ★ CHI; mail Joliet z 60435; pop. incl. with Joliet (Inc. Place)
Burr Ridge; Inc. Place; DUPAGE, COOK; 172 J-6; elev. 700ft./213m.; 🅿; ★ CHI; z 60527 & mail Hinsdale z 60521, La Grange z 60525; Ⓟ 7,684; © 10,408
Burt; RMC Place; TAZEWELL; *170 H-8; mail Armington z 61721; rural
Burton; RMC Place; ADAMS; ▲ Burton; *170 J-3; mail Quincy z 62301, z 62305; ● 70
Burton; MCD-Township; ADAMS; *170 J-3; mail Quincy z 62301, z 62305; Ⓟ 815; © 843
Burton; MCD-Township; MCHENRY; *170 A-11; ★ CHI; mail Spring Grove z 60081; Ⓟ 2,144; © 3,997
Burtons Bridge; RMC Place; MCHENRY; 172 B-3; ★ CHI; mail McHenry z 60050; ● 700
Burton View; RMC Place; LOGAN; *170 I-8; mail Lincoln z 62656
Bush; RMC Place; JACKSON; *171 R-9; elev. 450ft./137m.; ★ CARB-; mail De Soto z 62924; ● 100
Bush; Inc. Place; WILLIAMSON; *171 R-9; elev. 410ft./125m.; ★ CARB-; mail De Soto z 62924; Ⓟ 351; © 257
Bushnell; Inc. Place; MCDONOUGH; ▲ Bushnell; 170 H-5; elev. 661ft./201m.; 🅿; z 61422; Ⓟ 3,288; © 3,221
Bushnell; MCD-Township; MCDONOUGH; *170 H-5; 🅿; z 61422; Ⓟ 3,511; © 3,444
Bushton; RMC Place; COLES; 171 K-12; mail Charleston z 61920; ● 100
Butler; Inc. Place; MONTGOMERY; 171 M-8; elev. 640ft./195m.; 🅿; z 62015; Ⓟ 156; © 197
Butler; MCD-Township; VERMILION; *170 H-13; mail Rankin z 60960; Ⓟ 1,249; © 1,154
Butler Grove; MCD-Township; MONTGOMERY; *171 M-8; mail Butler z 62015; Ⓟ 723; © 709
Butterfield; RMC Place; DUPAGE; 172 I-5; ★ CHI; mail Lombard z 60148; ● 3,750
Butterfield West; RMC Place; DUPAGE; *170 C-12; ★ CHI; mail Glen Ellyn z 60137; ● 1,400
Button; MCD-Township; FORD; *170 H-12; mail Rankin z 60960; Ⓟ 299; © 290
Buysse Addition; RMC Place; HENRY; *170 D-6; elev. 721ft./220m.; ★ D-RI-M; mail Coal Valley z 61240; ● 100
Buzzville; RMC Place; MASON; *170 H-7; mail Havana z 62644; summer pop. 200; ● 130
Byron; Inc. Place; OGLE; ▲ Byron; 170 B-9; elev. 729ft./222m.; 🅿; ★ RKFD; z 61010; Ⓟ 2,284; © 2,917
Byron; MCD-Township; OGLE; *170 B-9; 🅿; ★ RKFD; z 61010; Ⓟ 4,221; © 5,840
Byron Hills; RMC Place; OGLE; *170 B-9; ★ RKFD; mail Byron z 61010; ● 300
Byron Hills; RMC Place; ROCK ISLAND; *170 E-6; mail Port Byron z 61275; ● 200

C

Cabbage Patch; SANGAMON; see Mildred (RMC Place)
Cabery; Inc. Place; FORD, KANKAKEE; 170 F-12; elev. 698ft./213m.; 🅿; z 60919; Ⓟ 268; © 263
Cable; RMC Place; MERCER; 170 E-5; mail Sherrard z 61281; ● 120
Cache; RMC Place; ALEXANDER; 171 T-9; elev. 326ft./99m.; 🅿; z 62914; ● 50
Cadiz; RMC Place; HARDIN; *171 R-12; elev. 565ft./172m.; mail Elizabethtown z 62931; rural
Cadwell; RMC Place; MOULTRIE; *171 K-11; elev. 674ft./205m.; mail Arthur z 61911; ● 65
Cahokia; MCD-Township; MACOUPIN; *171 M-7; mail Eagarville z 62023; Ⓟ 3,266; © 3,389
Cahokia; Inc. Place; ST. CLAIR; 171 O-6; elev. 411ft./125m.; 🅿; ★ ST.L; z 62206; Ⓟ 17,550; © 16,391
Cairo; Inc. Place; ⊡ ALEXANDER; 171 T-9; elev. 314ft./96m.; 🅿; z 62914; Ⓟ 4,846; © 3,632
Caledonia; Inc. Place; BOONE; ▲ Caledonia; 170 A-10; 🅿; z 61011; © 199
Caledonia; MCD-Township; BOONE; *170 A-10; 🅿; z 61011; Ⓟ 1,491; © 4,416
Calhoun; Inc. Place; RICHLAND; 171 O-12; elev. 530ft./162m.; 🅿; z 62419; Ⓟ 232; © 222
CALHOUN; 171 L-4; Ⓟ 5,322; © 5,084; ◆ 5,151
Calumet; RMC Place; COOK; ★ CHI; mail Hazel Crest z 60429; pop. incl. with East Hazel Crest (Inc. Place)
Calumet; MCD-Township; COOK; *170 D-13; ★ CHI; mail Blue Island z 60406; Ⓟ 21,000; © 22,374
Calumet City (Calumet Park); Inc. Place; COOK; ▲ Thornton; 172 L-10; elev. 589ft./180m.; 🅿 ■; ★ CHI; z 60409 & mail Chicago z 60643, Riverdale z 60827; Ⓟ 37,840; © 39,071; ◆ 39,111
Calumet Harbor; RMC Place; COOK; ★ CHI; mail Chicago z 60633; pop. incl. with Chicago (Inc. Place)
Calumet Heights; RMC Place; COOK; ★ CHI; mail Chicago z 60617; pop. incl. with Chicago (Inc. Place)
Calumet Park; Inc. Place; COOK; 172 L-9; elev. 604ft./184m.; 🅿; ★ CHI; z 60643, z 60827; Ⓟ 8,418; © 8,516
Calumet Park; COOK; see Calumet City (Inc. Place)
Calumet Western Junction; RMC Place; COOK; ★ CHI; pop. incl. with Chicago (Inc. Place)
Calumet Yard; RMC Place; COOK; ★ CHI; mail Chicago z 60617; pop. incl. with Chicago (Inc. Place)
Calvin; RMC Place; WHITE; 171 P-12; mail Crossville z 62827; ● 30
Camargo; Inc. Place; DOUGLAS; ▲ Camargo; 170 J-12; 🅿; z 61919; Ⓟ 372; © 469
Camargo; MCD-Township; DOUGLAS; *170 J-12; 🅿; z 61919; Ⓟ 3,716; © 3,576
Cambria; Inc. Place; WILLIAMSON; 171 R-9; elev. 418ft./127m.; 🅿; ★ CARB-; z 62915; Ⓟ 1,230; © 1,330
Cambridge; Inc. Place; ⊡ HENRY; ▲ Cambridge; 170 E-6; 🅿; z 61238; Ⓟ 2,124; © 2,180
Cambridge; MCD-Township; HENRY; *170 E-6; 🅿; z 61238; Ⓟ 2,601; © 2,618
Cambridge; RMC Place; LAKE; ★ CHI; mail Libertyville z 60048; pop. incl. with Libertyville (Inc. Place)
Camden; Inc. Place; SCHUYLER; ▲ Camden; 170 I-4; 🅿; z 62319; Ⓟ 115; © 97
Camden; MCD-Township; SCHUYLER; *170 I-5; 🅿; z 62319; Ⓟ 317; © 270
Camelot; RMC Place; EFFINGHAM; *171 M-11; mail Effingham z 62401; ● 60
Camelot; RMC Place; WILL; *170 D-12; ★ CHI; mail Joliet z 60431; ● 250
Cameron; RMC Place; WARREN; 170 F-5; elev. 775ft./236m.; 🅿; z 61423; ● 200
Campbell (Farmington); RMC Place; COLES; *171 L-12; mail Lerna z 62440; ● 25
Campbell Hill; Inc. Place; JACKSON; 171 Q-8; elev. 552ft./168m.; 🅿; z 62916; Ⓟ 351; © 333
Campbells Island; RMC Place; ROCK ISLAND; *170 D-5; ★ D-RI-M; mail East Moline z 61244; ● 450
Camp Epworth (Epworth Park); RMC Place; BOONE; *170 B-10; mail Garden Prairie z 61038; ● 50
Camp Ground; RMC Place; JEFFERSON; *171 P-10; mail Mount Vernon z 62864; ● 30
Camp Grove; RMC Place; MARSHALL; 170 F-8; elev. 850ft./259m.; 🅿; z 61424; ● 120
Camp Point; Inc. Place; ADAMS; ▲ Camp Point; 170 I-4; elev. 743ft./226m.; 🅿; z 62320; Ⓟ 1,230; © 1,244
Camp Point; MCD-Township; ADAMS; *170 I-4; 🅿; z 62320; Ⓟ 1,622; © 1,709
Campton; MCD-Township; KANE; *170 C-11; ★ CHI; mail Wasco z 60183; Ⓟ 9,473; © 14,072
Campton Hills; Inc. Place; KANE; ▲ Campton, Elgin, Plato, St. Charles; 172 H-1; 🅿; z 60175; incorporated April 17, 2007; not reported in 2000 Census; ● 11,000
Campus; Inc. Place; LIVINGSTON; 170 F-11; elev. 658ft./201m.; 🅿; z 60920; Ⓟ 137; © 145
Campus Walk; RMC Place; KANE; ★ CHI; mail Elgin z 60120; pop. incl. with Elgin (Inc. Place)
Candlewood Estates; RMC Place; CHAMPAIGN; *170 I-11; elev. 746ft./227m.; mail Mahomet z 61853; ● 1,000
Canoe Creek; MCD-Township; ROCK ISLAND; *170 D-6; mail Hillsdale z 61257; Ⓟ 761; © 864
Canteen; MCD-Township; ST. CLAIR; *171 O-6; ★ ST.L; mail East Saint Louis z 62204; Ⓟ 15,029; © 12,032; Ⓡ 11,929
Cantera Village; RMC Place; DUPAGE; *170 C-12; ★ CHI; mail Warrenville z 60555; pop. incl. with Warrenville (Inc. Place)
Canterbury Lane; RMC Place; COOK; ★ CHI; mail Glenview z 60025; pop. incl. with Glenview (Inc. Place)
Canton; Inc. Place; FULTON; 170 H-7; elev. 655ft./200m.; 🅿 ■; z 61520; Ⓟ 13,922; © 15,288; ◆ 15,101
Canton; MCD-Township; FULTON; *170 H-6; 🅿 🄷; z 61520; includes part of the City of Canton; Ⓟ 14,880; © 16,075
Cantrall; Inc. Place; SANGAMON; 170 J-8; elev. 595ft./181m.; 🅿; ★ SPRG; z 62625; Ⓟ 123; © 139
Capital; MCD-Township; SANGAMON; *170 J-8; ★ SPRG; mail Springfield z 62701-07; Ⓟ 104,126; © 111,471; Ⓡ 111,372
Capitol; RMC Place; SANGAMON; *170 J-8; ★ SPRG; mail Springfield z 62701; pop. incl. with Springfield (Inc. Place)
Capri Village; RMC Place; COOK; *170 B-12; ★ CHI; mail Palatine z 60074; pop. incl. with Palatine (Inc. Place)
Capron; Inc. Place; BOONE; 170 A-10; elev. 903ft./275m.; 🅿; z 61012; Ⓟ 682; © 961
Carbon; RMC Place; ST. CLAIR; *171 O-7; ★ ST.L; mail O Fallon z 62269; pop. incl. with O'Fallon (Inc. Place)
Carbon Cliff; Inc. Place; ROCK ISLAND; 171 T-5; elev. 575ft./175m.; 🅿; ★ D-RI-M; z 61239; Ⓟ 1,492; © 1,689
Carbondale; Inc. Place; JACKSON, WILLIAMSON; ▲ Makanda, Murphysboro; 171 R-9; elev. 415ft./126m.; 🅿 🄷 🄲 21,003 ■; ★ CARB-; z 62901-03; Ⓟ 27,033; © 20,681; Ⓡ 25,597; ◆ 25,605
Carbondale; MCD-Township; JACKSON; *171 R-9; 🅿 🄲 21,003; ★ CARB-; z 62901-03; Ⓟ 31,252; © 24,586; Ⓡ 29,416
Carbon Hill; Inc. Place; GRUNDY; *170 E-11; elev. 570ft./174m.; 🅿; ★ CHI; z 60416; Ⓟ 362; © 392
Cardiff; RMC Place; LIVINGSTON; *170 F-11; elev. 631ft./192m.; mail Dwight z 60420; ● 30
Carle Springs; RMC Place; DE WITT; *170 I-9; mail Wapella z 61777; rural
Carlinville; Inc. Place; ⊡ MACOUPIN; ▲ Carlinville, Brushy Mound; 171 L-7; 🅿 🄷 🄲 605; z 62626; Ⓟ 5,416; © 5,685
Carlinville; MCD-Township; MACOUPIN; *171 L-7; 🅿 🄲 605; z 62626; Ⓟ 6,553; © 6,910
Carlock; Inc. Place; MCLEAN; 170 H-9; elev. 780ft./238m.; 🅿; z 61725; Ⓟ 418; © 456
Carlsburg; RMC Place; MACOUPIN; *171 M-7; elev. 690ft./210m.; mail Mount Olive z 62069; ● 60
Carlyle; Inc. Place; ⊡ CLINTON; ▲ Carlyle; 171 O-8; 🅿; z 62231; Ⓟ 3,474; © 3,406
Carlyle; MCD-Township; CLINTON; *171 O-8; 🅿; z 62231; Ⓟ 3,951; © 3,938
Carlysle; RMC Place; COOK; ★ CHI; mail Schaumburg z 60194; pop. incl. with Schaumburg (Inc. Place)
Carman; RMC Place; HENDERSON; ▲ Carman; 170 G-4; 🅿; z 61425; ● 100
Carman; MCD-Township; HENDERSON; *170 G-4; 🅿; z 61425; Ⓟ 398; © 366
Carmi; Inc. Place; ⊡ WHITE; ▲ Carmi; 171 Q-12; elev. 383ft./117m.; 🅿 🄷; z 62821; Ⓟ 5,626; © 5,422
Carmi; MCD-Township; WHITE; *171 Q-12; 🅿; z 62821; Ⓟ 7,327; © 6,996
Carol Stream; Inc. Place; DUPAGE; 172 H-4; elev. 768ft./234m.; 🅿; ★ CHI; z 60116, z 60122, z 60128, z 60132, z 60188, z 60197, z 60199; Ⓟ 31,759; © 40,438; ◆ 41,245
Carol Stream Main; RMC Place; DUPAGE; ★ CHI; mail Carol Stream z 60197; pop. incl. with Carol Stream (Inc. Place)
Carol Stream Main; RMC Place; DUPAGE; *170 C-12; ★ CHI; mail Carol Stream z 60188, z 60197; pop. incl. with Carol Stream (Inc. Place)
Carpenter; RMC Place; MADISON; 195 A-10; mail Edwardsville z 62025; ● 100
Carpentersville; Inc. Place; KANE; 170 B-11; elev. 866ft./264m.; 🅿; ★ CHI; z 60110; Ⓟ 23,049; © 30,586; Ⓡ 30,579; ◆ 42,512
Carriage Creek; RMC Place; COOK; ★ CHI; mail Richton Park z 60471; pop. incl. with Richton Park (Inc. Place)
Carriage Park; RMC Place; KENDALL; *170 D-11; elev. 655ft./200m.; ★ CHI; mail Oswego z 60543; ● 100
Carriage Way Court; RMC Place; COOK; *170 B-12; ★ CHI; mail Palatine z 60074; pop. incl. with Palatine (Inc. Place)
Carrier Mills; Inc. Place; SALINE; ▲ Carrier Mills; 171 R-10; 🅿; z 62917; Ⓟ 1,991; © 1,886
Carrier Mills; MCD-Township; SALINE; *171 R-10; 🅿; z 62917; Ⓟ 2,732; © 2,573
Carrigan; RMC Place; CLINTON; *171 O-9; elev. 474ft./144m.; mail Carlyle z 62231; ● 45
Carrigan; MCD-Township; MARION; *171 N-9; mail Patoka z 62875; Ⓟ 437; © 434
Carroll; MCD-Township; VERMILION; *170 J-13; mail Ridge Farm z 61870; Ⓟ 715; © 557; Ⓡ 562
CARROLL; 170 B-7; Ⓟ 16,805; © 16,674; ◆ 15,614
Carroll Addition; RMC Place; CHAMPAIGN; *170 I-12; elev. 720ft./219m.; ★ CH-U; mail Urbana z 61802; ● 210
Carroll Addition; RMC Place; FORD; *170 H-11; mail Gibson City z 60936; ● 30
Carrollton; Inc. Place; ⊡ GREENE; ▲ Carrollton; 171 L-5; 🅿 🄷; z 62016; Ⓟ 2,507; © 2,605
Carrollton; MCD-Township; GREENE; *171 L-5; 🅿; z 62016; Ⓟ 3,075; © 3,142
Carson; MCD-Township; FAYETTE; *171 M-9; mail Ramsey z 62080; Ⓟ 170; © 148
Carterville; Inc. Place; WILLIAMSON; 171 R-9; elev. 457ft./139m.; 🅿; ★ CARB-; z 62918; Ⓟ 3,630; © 4,616
Carthage; Inc. Place; ⊡ HANCOCK; ▲ Carthage; 170 H-3; 🅿 🄷; z 62321; Ⓟ 2,657; © 2,725
Carthage; MCD-Township; HANCOCK; *170 H-4; 🅿; z 62321; Ⓟ 3,122; © 3,175
Carthage Lake; RMC Place; HENDERSON; *170 G-4; mail Carman z 61425
Cartter; RMC Place; MARION; *171 O-10; mail Kell z 62853; ● 50
Cartwright; MCD-Township; SANGAMON; *170 J-7; mail Pleasant Plains z 62677; Ⓟ 1,381; © 1,507
Cary; Inc. Place; MCHENRY; 170 B-11; elev. 825ft./251m.; 🅿; ★ CHI; z 60013; Ⓟ 10,043; © 15,531
Casey; Inc. Place; CLARK, CUMBERLAND; 171 L-12; elev. 650ft./198m.; 🅿; z 62420; Ⓟ 2,914; © 2,942
Casey; MCD-Township; CLARK; *171 L-12; 🅿; z 62420; includes part of the City of Casey; Ⓟ 4,021; © 4,176
Caseyville; Inc. Place; ST. CLAIR; 171 O-6; elev. 425ft./130m.; 🅿; ★ ST.L; z 62232; Ⓟ 4,419; © 4,310
Caseyville; MCD-Township; ST. CLAIR; *171 O-7; 🅿; ★ ST.L; z 62232; includes part of the Village of Caseyville; Ⓟ 24,981; © 25,987
Casner; MCD-Township; JEFFERSON; *171 P-9; mail Woodlawn z 62898; Ⓟ 998; © 1,235
Casner; RMC Place; MACON; 170 J-10; ★ DEC; mail Argenta z 62501; ● 50
Cass; MCD-Township; FULTON; *170 H-6; mail Smithfield z 61477; Ⓟ 647; © 642
CASS; 170 J-6; Ⓟ 13,437; © 13,695; ◆ 13,731
Castellean Lower; RMC Place; LEE; *170 C-8; mail Dixon z 61021; ● 130
Castellean Upper; RMC Place; LEE; *170 C-8; mail Dixon z 61021; ● 80
Castleton; RMC Place; STARK; 170 F-7; elev. 787ft./240m.; 🅿; z 61426; ● 130
Catatoga; RMC Place; KANE; *170 B-11; elev. 810ft./247m.; ★ CHI; mail Elgin z 60123; ● 350
Catatoga 2; RMC Place; KANE; *170 B-11; elev. 850ft./259m.; ★ CHI; mail Elgin z 60123; ● 200
Catino; RMC Place; COOK; ★ CHI; pop. incl. with Arlington Heights (Inc. Place)
Catlin; Inc. Place; VERMILION; ▲ Catlin; 170 I-13; elev. 657ft./200m.; 🅿; ★ DANV; z 61817; Ⓟ 2,173; © 2,087
Catlin; MCD-Township; VERMILION; *170 I-13; 🅿; ★ DANV; z 61817; Ⓟ 3,402; © 3,153
Cave; MCD-Township; FRANKLIN; *171 Q-10; mail Thompsonville z 62890; Ⓟ 1,580; © 1,592
Cave-In-Rock; Inc. Place; HARDIN; 171 S-12; elev. 380ft./116m.; 🅿; z 62919; Ⓟ 381; © 346
Cayuga; RMC Place; LIVINGSTON; *170 F-11; mail Pontiac z 61764
Cazenovia; RMC Place; WOODFORD; ▲ Cazenovia; 170 G-8; 🅿; z 61545; ● 100
Cazenovia; MCD-Township; WOODFORD; *170 G-8; 🅿; z 61545; Ⓟ 1,841; © 1,788
Cedar; MCD-Township; KNOX; *170 G-6; ★ GLSB; mail Abingdon z 61410; Ⓟ 3,589; © 3,454
Cedarbrook; RMC Place; COOK; ★ CHI; pop. incl. with Arlington Heights (Inc. Place)
Cedar Glen; RMC Place; COOK; ★ CHI; pop. incl. with Arlington Heights (Inc. Place)
Cedar Glen; RMC Place; KENDALL; ★ CHI; mail Oswego z 60543
Cedar Grove (Dogwalk); RMC Place; WILLIAMSON; *171 R-10; ★ CARB-; mail Marion z 62959; ● 250
Cedar Island; RMC Place; LAKE; *170 A-12; ★ CHI; mail Fox Lake z 60020; ● 30
Cedar Meadows; RMC Place; ST. CLAIR; *171 O-7; elev. 556ft./169m.; ★ ST.L; mail O Fallon z 62269; pop. incl. with O'Fallon (Inc. Place)
Cedar Park; RMC Place; MADISON; *171 N-6; ★ ST.L; mail Granite City z 62040; ● 250
Cedar Point; Inc. Place; LA SALLE; 170 E-9; elev. 660ft./201m.; 🅿; z 61316; Ⓟ 275; © 262
Cedar Run; RMC Place; COOK; ★ CHI; mail Wheeling z 60090; pop. incl. with Wheeling (Inc. Place)
Cedarville; Inc. Place; STEPHENSON; 170 A-8; elev. 850ft./259m.; 🅿; z 61013; Ⓟ 751; © 719
Centaur Estate; RMC Place; BOONE; *170 A-10; elev. 800ft./244m.; ★ RKFD; mail Belvidere z 61008; ● 110
Center Hill; RMC Place; CARROLL; *170 B-7; mail Mount Carroll z 61053; rural
Centerville; RMC Place; CALHOUN; *171 N-5; elev. 536ft./163m.; mail Golden Eagle z 62036; rural
Centerville; RMC Place; PIATT; *170 I-11; mail Mansfield z 61854, White Heath z 61884; rural
Centerville; RMC Place; WHITE; 171 P-12; mail Carmi z 62821; ● 50
Central; MCD-Township; BOND; *171 N-8; mail Greenville z 62246; Ⓟ 6,023; © 7,941
Central City; RMC Place; GRUNDY; *170 E-11; elev. 576ft./176m.; ★ CHI; mail Braceville z 60407; ● 40
Central City; Inc. Place; MARION; 171 O-9; elev. 475ft./145m.; mail Centralia z 62801; Ⓟ 1,390; © 1,371
Centralia; Inc. Place; MARION, CLINTON, JEFFERSON, WASHINGTON; 171 O-9; elev. 499ft./152m.; 🅿 🄷 ■; z 62801; Ⓟ 14,274; © 14,136; ◆ 13,364
Centralia; MCD-Township; MARION; *171 O-9; 🅿; z 62801; includes part of the City of Centralia; Ⓟ 16,834; © 16,533
Central Park; RMC Place; VERMILION; *170 I-13; ★ DANV; mail Danville z 61832; pop. incl. with Tilton (Inc. Place)
Central Street; RMC Place; COOK; *170 B-13; ★ CHI; mail Evanston z 60201; pop. incl. with Evanston (Inc. Place)
Centreville; Inc. Place; ST. CLAIR; ▲ Centreville; 195 F-8; 🅿 🄷; ★ ST.L; z 62203, z 62205, z 62207; Ⓟ 7,489; © 5,951
Centreville; MCD-Township; ST. CLAIR; *171 O-6; 🅿; ★ ST.L; z 62203, z 62205, z 62207; Ⓟ 32,425; © 28,711
Century Oaks; RMC Place; KANE; ★ CHI; mail Elgin z 60123; pop. incl. with Elgin (Inc. Place)
Century Oaks West; RMC Place; KANE; ★ CHI; mail Elgin z 60123; pop. incl. with Elgin (Inc. Place)
Cerro Gordo; Inc. Place; PIATT; ▲ Cerro Gordo; 170 J-10; 🅿; z 61818; Ⓟ 1,436; © 1,436
Cerro Gordo; MCD-Township; PIATT; *170 J-10; 🅿; z 61818; Ⓟ 2,208; © 2,199
Chadwick; Inc. Place; CARROLL; 170 B-7; elev. 791ft./241m.; 🅿; z 61014; Ⓟ 557; © 505
Chalfin Bridge; RMC Place; MONROE; *171 P-6; mail Fults z 62244
Chalmers; MCD-Township; MCDONOUGH; *170 H-5; mail Macomb z 61455; Ⓟ 804; © 740
Chambersburg; RMC Place; PIKE; ▲ Chambersburg; 170 J-5; 🅿; z 62323; ● 100
Chambersburg; MCD-Township; PIKE; *170 J-5; 🅿; z 62323; Ⓟ 203; © 200
Chambord; RMC Place; DUPAGE; ★ CHI; mail Oak Brook z 60523; pop. incl. with Oak Brook (Inc. Place)
Chamnesstown; RMC Place; JACKSON; *171 Q-9; mail Elkville z 62932; ● 25
Champaign; Inc. Place; CHAMPAIGN; 170 I-11; elev. 742ft./226m.; 🅿 🄷 🄲 30,457 ■; ★ CH-U; z 61820-22, z 61824-26; Ⓟ 63,502; © 67,518; Ⓡ 67,959; ◆ 74,849
Champaign; MCD-Township; CHAMPAIGN; *170 I-11; 🅿 🄲 30,457; ★ CH-U; z 61820-22, z 61824-26; does not include City of Champaign; Ⓟ 8,864; © 11,591
CHAMPAIGN; 170 I-11; Ⓟ 173,025; © 179,669; ◆ 199,125
Champaign City; MCD-Township; CHAMPAIGN; *170 I-11; 🄷; ★ CH-U; mail Champaign z 61820-22, z 61824-26; coextensive with the City of Champaign; Ⓟ 63,502; © 67,518; Ⓡ 67,959
Chana; RMC Place; OGLE; 170 C-9; elev. 782ft./238m.; 🅿; z 61015; ● 200
Chandlerville; Inc. Place; CASS; 170 I-6; elev. 464ft./141m.; 🅿; z 62627; Ⓟ 689; © 704
Chandlerville; MCD-Township; CASS; *170 I-6; 🅿; z 62627; includes part of the Village of Chandlerville; Ⓟ 715; © 623
Channahon; Inc. Place; WILL, GRUNDY; ▲ Channahon, Goose Lake, Saratoga; 170 D-12; 🅿; ★ CHI; z 60410; Ⓟ 4,266; © 7,344
Channahon; MCD-Township; WILL; *170 E-12; 🅿; ★ CHI; z 60410; Ⓟ 5,386; © 8,339
Channel Lake; CDP; LAKE; *170 A-12; ★ CHI; mail Antioch z 60002; Ⓟ 1,660; © 1,785
Chantilly; RMC Place; LAKE; ★ CHI; mail Highland Park z 60035; pop. incl. with Highland Park (Inc. Place)
Chapin; Inc. Place; MORGAN; 171 K-5; elev. 628ft./191m.; 🅿; z 62628; Ⓟ 632; © 592
Chapman; RMC Place; MONTGOMERY; *171 M-8; mail Fillmore z 62032
Charleston; Inc. Place; ⊡ COLES; 171 L-12; elev. 686ft./209m.; 🅿 🄲 12,349; z 61920; Ⓟ 20,398; © 21,039; Ⓡ 21,149; ◆ 21,063
Charleston; MCD-Township; COLES; *171 L-12; 🅿 🄲 12,349; z 61920; Ⓟ 22,031; © 22,901; Ⓡ 23,011
Charlotte; RMC Place; LIVINGSTON; ▲ Charlotte; 170 G-11; elev. 663ft./202m.; mail Chatsworth z 60921; ● 25
Charlotte; MCD-Township; LIVINGSTON; *170 G-11; mail Chatsworth z 60921; Ⓟ 168; © 192
Charlotte Hills; RMC Place; PERRY; *171 Q-8; elev. 420ft./128m.; mail Lake Villa z 60046, Pinckneyville z 62274; pop. incl. with Pinckneyville (Inc. Place)
Charter Grove; RMC Place; DEKALB; *170 B-10; ★ DKLB; mail Sycamore z 60178
Chasco (Whitehill); RMC Place; JOHNSON; *171 S-9; mail Cypress z 62923; rural
Chateau Terrace; RMC Place; ST. CLAIR; *171 O-7; ★ ST.L; mail Belleville z 62221; pop. incl. with Fairview Heights (Inc. Place)
Chatelaine South; RMC Place; COOK; ★ CHI; pop. incl. with Arlington Heights (Inc. Place)
Chatham; RMC Place; COOK; ★ CHI; mail Chicago z 60619; pop. incl. with Chicago (Inc. Place)
Chatham; Inc. Place; SANGAMON; 171 K-7; elev. 606ft./185m.; 🅿; ★ SPRG; z 62629; Ⓟ 6,074; © 8,583
Chatham; MCD-Township; SANGAMON; *171 K-7; 🅿; ★ SPRG; z 62629; includes part of the Village of Chatham; Ⓟ 4,961; © 6,019
Chatham Manor; RMC Place; COOK; *170 B-12; ★ CHI; mail Buffalo Grove z 60089; pop. incl. with Buffalo Grove (Inc. Place)
Chatsworth; Inc. Place; LIVINGSTON; ▲ Chatsworth; 170 G-11; elev. 735ft./224m.; 🅿; z 60921; Ⓟ 1,186; © 1,265
Chatsworth; MCD-Township; LIVINGSTON; *170 G-11; 🅿; z 60921; Ⓟ 1,444; © 1,468
Chatton; RMC Place; ADAMS; *170 I-4; elev. 710ft./216m.; mail La Prairie z 62346; rural
Chauncey; RMC Place; LAWRENCE; 171 N-13; elev. 490ft./149m.; mail Sumner z 62466; ● 80
Chautauqua; RMC Place; JERSEY; *171 M-5; ★ ST.L; mail Elsah z 62028; summer pop. 500
Chautauqua Park; RMC Place; MASON; *170 I-6; mail Havana z 62644; ● 150
Chautauqua Park; RMC Place; MENARD; mail Petersburg z 62675; summer pop. 250; ● 150
Chebanse; MCD-Township; IROQUOIS; *170 F-12; 🅿; ★ KANK; z 60922 & mail Clifton z 60927; includes part of the Village of Chebanse; Ⓟ 3,074; © 3,061
Chebanse; Inc. Place; KANKAKEE, IROQUOIS; 170 F-12; elev. 672ft./205m.; 🅿; ★ KANK; z 60922; Ⓟ 1,082; © 1,148
Checkrow; RMC Place; FULTON; *170 H-6; elev. 619ft./189m.; mail Avon z 61415; rural
Chelsea Cove; RMC Place; COOK; ★ CHI; mail Wheeling z 60090; pop. incl. with Wheeling (Inc. Place)
Cheltenham; RMC Place; COOK; ★ CHI; mail Chicago z 60649; pop. incl. with Chicago (Inc. Place)
Chemung; RMC Place; MCHENRY; 170 A-10; mail Harvard z 60033; ● 275
Chemung; MCD-Township; MCHENRY; *170 A-10; mail Harvard z 60033; Ⓟ 6,660; © 8,761
Cheney's Grove; MCD-Township; MCLEAN; *170 H-11; mail Saybrook z 61770; Ⓟ 1,051; © 1,069
Cheneyville; RMC Place; VERMILION; 170 H-13; elev. 725ft./221m.; mail Hoopeston z 60942; ● 80
Chenoa; Inc. Place; MCLEAN; ▲ Chenoa; 170 G-10; 🅿; z 61726; Ⓟ 1,732; © 1,845
Chenoa; MCD-Township; MCLEAN; *170 G-10; 🅿; z 61726; Ⓟ 2,228; © 2,305
Chenot Place; RMC Place; ST. CLAIR; *171 O-7; ★ ST.L; mail Belleville z 62221; ● 1,970
Cherry; Inc. Place; BUREAU; 170 E-9; elev. 682ft./208m.; 🅿; z 61317; Ⓟ 487; © 509
Cherry Grove-Shannon; MCD-Township; CARROLL; *170 B-7; mail Lanark z 61046; Ⓟ 1,535; © 1,556
Cherry Hill; RMC Place; WILL; *170 D-12; elev. 632ft./193m.; ★ CHI; mail Joliet z 60431; pop. incl. with New Lenox (Inc. Place)
Cherry Hills; RMC Place; CHAMPAIGN; *170 I-11; elev. 750ft./229m.; ★ CH-U; mail Champaign z 61822; ● 400
Cherry Hills; RMC Place; KANE; ★ CHI; mail Aurora z 60506; pop. incl. with Aurora (Inc. Place)

Entries in **UPPERCASE** are counties.
Entries in **bold** have populations of 2,500 or more.
Names in parentheses are alternate names.
Inc. Place — Incorporated Place
RMC Place — Rand McNally Designated Place
CDP — Census Designated Place
MCD — Minor Civil Division

⊡ County Seat
▲ Minor Civil Division
elev. Elevation
🅿 Post Office

🄷 Hospital
🄲 College
■ Principal Business Center
★ Ranally Metro Area (RMA) Abbreviation
z Zip Code(s)

Ⓟ Previous Census Population
Ⓡ Revised Census Population
Ⓐ Annexation Population
● Rand McNally Population Estimate
© Final Census Population
Ⓢ Special Census Population
◆ Estimated Population

For additional definitions see Glossary, Volume 1, and Introduction, Volume 2.

Cherry Point; RMC Place; EDGAR; *170 J-13; mail Chrisman z 61924; rural
Cherry Valley; Inc. Place; WINNEBAGO, BOONE; ▲ Belvidere, Flora; 170 B-9; elev. 735ft./224m.; 🅿; ★ RKFD; z 61016; ℗ 1,615; © 2,191
Cherry Valley; MCD-Township; WINNEBAGO; *170 B-9; 🅿; ★ RKFD; z 61016; ℗ 15,828; © 17,692
Cherrywood; RMC Place; CHRISTIAN; *171 K-9; elev. 610ft./186m.; mail Taylorville z 62568; pop. incl. with Taylorville (Inc. Place)
Cherrywood; RMC Place; WILL; *170 D-12; ★ CHI; mail Bolingbrook z 60440; pop. incl. with Bolingbrook (Inc. Place)
Chesney Shores; RMC Place; LAKE; *170 A-12; ★ CHI; mail Lake Villa z 60046
Chester; MCD-Township; LOGAN; *170 I-9; mail Lincoln z 62656; ℗ 680; © 723
Chester; Inc. Place; ⊡ RANDOLPH; 171 Q-7; elev. 646ft./197m.; 🅿 🅷; z 62233; ℗ 8,194; © 5,185; Ⓡ 8,378
Chesterfield; Inc. Place; MACOUPIN; ▲ Chesterfield; 171 L-6; elev. 585ft./178m.; 🅿; z 62630; ℗ 230; © 223
Chesterfield; MCD-Township; MACOUPIN; *171 M-6; 🅿; z 62630; ℗ 951; © 943
Chesterville; RMC Place; DOUGLAS; *171 K-11; elev. 651ft./198m.; mail Arthur z 61911; ● 110
Chestline; RMC Place; ADAMS; *170 J-4; elev. 700ft./213m.; mail Baylis z 62314, Liberty z 62347; rural
Chestnut; MCD-Township; KNOX; *170 G-6; mail London Mills z 61544; ℗ 335; © 250
Chestnut; RMC Place; LOGAN; 170 J-9; elev. 620ft./189m.; 🅿; z 62518; ● 350
Chestnut Street; RMC Place; COOK; mail Chicago z 60610; pop. incl. with Chicago (Inc. Place)
Chicago; Inc. Place; ⊡ COOK, DUPAGE; 170 C-13; elev. 596ft./182m.; 🅿 🅷 🅲 171,164 ■; ★ CHI; z 60290, z 60601-26, z 60628-34, z 60636-47, z 60649, z 60651-57, z 60659-61, z 60664, z 60666, z 60668-70, z 60673-75, z 60677-78, z 60680-82, z 60684-91, z 60693-97, z 60699, z 60701, z 60706-07, z 60803-05, z 60827; ℗ 2,783,726; © 2,896,016; ◆ 2,868,472
Chicago Heights; Inc. Place; COOK; 170 D-13; elev. 689ft./210m.; 🅿 🅷 ■; ★ CHI; z 60411-12; ℗ 33,072; © 32,776; ◆ 31,682
Chicago Lawn; RMC Place; COOK; *170 C-13; ★ CHI; mail Chicago z 60629; pop. incl. with Chicago (Inc. Place)
Chicago Ridge; Inc. Place; COOK; 172 K-8; elev. 600ft./183m.; 🅿; ★ CHI; z 60415; ℗ 13,643; © 14,127
Chicken Bristle; RMC Place; DOUGLAS; *170 J-11; elev. 668ft./204m.; mail Tuscola z 61953; rural
Child City; KANE; see Mooseheart (RMC Place)
Childers Acres; RMC Place; OGLE; *170 C-9; mail Rochelle z 61068; ● 150
Chili; RMC Place; HANCOCK; *170 I-3; elev. 684ft./208m.; mail West Point z 62380; rural
Chili; MCD-Township; HANCOCK; *170 I-4; mail West Point z 62380; ℗ 693; © 718
Chillicothe; Inc. Place; PEORIA; ▲ Chillicothe; 170 F-8; 🅿; ★ PEOR; z 61523; ℗ 5,959; © 5,996
Chillicothe; MCD-Township; PEORIA; *170 F-8; 🅿; ★ PEOR; z 61523; ℗ 8,254; © 8,233
Chilon Chalet; RMC Place; COOK; ★ CHI; mail Chicago Heights z 60411; pop. incl. with Chicago Heights (Inc. Place)
China; LEE; see Franklin Grove (MCD-Township)
Chinatown; RMC Place; COOK; ★ CHI; mail Chicago z 60616; pop. incl. with Chicago (Inc. Place)
Chinatown; RMC Place; MADISON; *171 N-7; ★ ST.L; mail Maryville z 62062; pop. incl. with Maryville (Inc. Place)
Chippendale; RMC Place; LAKE; ★ CHI; mail Barrington z 60010; pop. incl. with Barrington (Inc. Place)
Chippewa; RMC Place; COOK; *170 D-13; ★ CHI; mail Alsip z 60803; pop. incl. with Alsip (Inc. Place)
Chippewa Ridge; RMC Place; COOK; ★ CHI; mail Alsip z 60803; pop. incl. with Alsip (Inc. Place)
Chittenden; RMC Place; LAKE; ★ CHI; mail Gurnee z 60031; pop. incl. with Gurnee (Inc. Place)
Chittyville; RMC Place; WILLIAMSON; *171 R-9; ★ CARB-; mail Herrin z 62948; pop. incl. with Herrin (Inc. Place)
Chouteau; MCD-Township; MADISON; *171 N-6; ★ ST.L; mail Granite City z 62040; ℗ 7,792; © 8,010
Chrisman; Inc. Place; EDGAR; 170 J-13; elev. 645ft./197m.; 🅿; z 61924; ℗ 1,136; © 1,318
CHRISTIAN; 171 L-8; ℗ 34,418; © 35,372; ◆ 34,335
Christopher; Inc. Place; FRANKLIN; 171 Q-9; elev. 443ft./135m.; 🅿; ★ CARB-; z 62822; ℗ 2,774; © 2,836; Ⓡ 2,833
Christy; MCD-Township; LAWRENCE; *171 N-13; mail Sumner z 62466; ℗ 1,679; © 1,579
Churchill; RMC Place; COOK; ★ CHI; mail Schaumburg z 60195; pop. incl. with Hoffman Estates (Inc. Place)
Churchville; RMC Place; DUPAGE; *170 C-12; ★ CHI; mail Elmhurst z 60126
Cicero; Inc. Place; COOK; 170 C-13; elev. 606ft./185m.; 🅿 ■; ★ CHI; z 60804; ℗ 67,436; © 85,616; ◆ 88,292
Cimic; RMC Place; SANGAMON; *171 K-8; 🅿; z 62530
Cincinnati; MCD-Township; PIKE; *171 K-3; mail Hull z 62343; ℗ 73; © 37
Cincinnati; MCD-Township; TAZEWELL; *170 H-8; ★ PEOR; mail Pekin z 61554; ℗ 6,722; © 8,862
Cincinnati Landing; RMC Place; PIKE; *171 K-3; mail New Canton z 62356; rural
Cinnamon Creek; RMC Place; WILL; *170 D-12; ★ CHI; mail Bolingbrook z 60440; pop. incl. with Bolingbrook (Inc. Place)
Circle Drive; RMC Place; LA SALLE; *170 F-10; mail Streator z 61364; ● 200
Circle Park; RMC Place; SHELBY; *171 L-10; elev. 670ft./204m.; mail Shelbyville z 62565; ● 50
Cisco; Inc. Place; PIATT; 170 J-10; elev. 689ft./210m.; 🅿; z 61830; ℗ 282; © 264; Ⓡ 286
Cisne; Inc. Place; WAYNE; 171 O-11; elev. 460ft./140m.; 🅿; z 62823; ℗ 645; © 673
Cissna Park; Inc. Place; IROQUOIS; 170 H-12; elev. 666ft./203m.; 🅿; z 60924; ℗ 805; © 811
Citation Lake Estates; RMC Place; COOK; *170 B-12; ★ CHI; mail Northbrook z 60062; ● 350
Clank; RMC Place; ALEXANDER; *171 T-8; elev. 343ft./105m.; mail Tamms z 62988; rural
Clare; RMC Place; DEKALB; 170 B-10; elev. 870ft./265m.; 🅿; z 60111; ● 75
Claremont; Inc. Place; RICHLAND; ▲ Claremont; 171 N-12; 🅿; z 62421; ℗ 256; © 212
Claremont; MCD-Township; RICHLAND; *171 N-12; 🅿; z 62421; ℗ 914; © 934
Clarence; RMC Place; FORD; 170 H-12; elev. 763ft./233m.; 🅿; z 60960; ● 80
Clarendon Hills; Inc. Place; DUPAGE; 172 I-6; elev. 725ft./221m.; 🅿; ★ CHI; z 60514 & mail Willowbrook z 60527; ℗ 6,994; © 7,610
Clarion; MCD-Township; BUREAU; *170 D-9; mail La Moille z 61330; ℗ 446; © 421
CLARK; 171 L-13; ℗ 15,921; © 17,008; ◆ 16,853
Clark Center; RMC Place; CLARK; *171 L-13; elev. 616ft./188m.; mail Marshall z 62441; ● 50
Clarksburg; RMC Place; SHELBY; ▲ Clarksburg; 171 L-10; 🅿; z 62565; ● 50
Clarksburg; MCD-Township; SHELBY; *171 L-10; 🅿; z 62565; ℗ 371; © 378
Clarksdale; RMC Place; CHRISTIAN; *171 L-8; 🅿; z 62556; ● 50
Clarksville; RMC Place; CLARK; 171 L-13; mail Marshall z 62441; ● 100
Clarksville; RMC Place; MCLEAN; *170 G-10; elev. 756ft./230m.; mail Lexington z 61753; ● 80
Clarmin; RMC Place; WASHINGTON; *171 P-7; mail Marissa z 62257; ● 160
CLAY; 171 N-11; ℗ 14,460; © 14,560; ◆ 13,504
Clay City; Inc. Place; CLAY; ▲ Clay City; 171 N-11; elev. 433ft./132m.; 🅿; z 62824; ℗ 929; © 1,000
Clay City; MCD-Township; CLAY; *171 O-11; 🅿; z 62824; ℗ 1,356; © 1,407
Clays Prairie; RMC Place; EDGAR; *171 K-13; elev. 612ft./187m.; mail Paris z 61944; rural
Clayton; Inc. Place; ADAMS; ▲ Clayton; 170 J-4; elev. 736ft./224m.; 🅿; z 62324; ℗ 726; © 904
Clayton; MCD-Township; ADAMS; *170 I-4; 🅿; z 62324; ℗ 990; © 1,185
Clayton; MCD-Township; WOODFORD; *170 F-9; mail Benson z 61516; ℗ 701; © 698
Claytonville; RMC Place; IROQUOIS; 170 H-13; elev. 662ft./202m.; 🅿; z 60926; ● 130
Clearing; RMC Place; COOK; *170 C-13; ★ CHI; mail Chicago z 60638; pop. incl. with Chicago (Inc. Place)
Clear Lake; RMC Place; CASS; *170 I-6; elev. 435ft./133m.; mail Bluff Springs z 62622
Clear Lake; Inc. Place; SANGAMON; ▲ Clear Lake; 173 F-18; ★ SPRG; mail Springfield z 62707; ℗ 193; © 267
Clear Lake; MCD-Township; SANGAMON; *170 J-8; ★ SPRG; mail Springfield z 62707; ℗ 7,780; © 8,155
Cleburne; RMC Place; FRANKLIN; *171 Q-9; elev. 421ft./128m.; ★ CARB-; mail Mulkeytown z 62865; ● 150
Clement; MCD-Township; CLINTON; *171 O-9; mail Huey z 62252; ℗ 502; © 515
Clements; RMC Place; MORGAN; *171 K-6; 🅿; z 62638; rural
Cleone; RMC Place; CLARK; *171 L-12; mail Martinsville z 62442
Cleveland; Inc. Place; HENRY; *170 D-6; elev. 576ft./176m.; 🅿; ★ D-RI-M; z 61241; ℗ 283; © 253
Clifton; Inc. Place; IROQUOIS; 170 F-12; elev. 661ft./201m.; 🅿 🅷; ★ KANK; z 60927; ℗ 1,347; © 1,317
Clifton Terrace; RMC Place; MADISON; *171 N-6; ★ ST.L; mail Godfrey z 62035; pop. incl. with Godfrey (Inc. Place)
Clifty Heights; RMC Place; WILLIAMSON; *171 R-10; ★ CARB-; mail Marion z 62959; ● 80
Clinch; RMC Place; PERRY; *171 Q-9; mail Du Quoin z 62832; rural
Clinton; Inc. Place; ⊡ DE WITT; 170 I-9; elev. 744ft./227m.; 🅿; z 61727; ℗ 7,437; © 7,485
Clinton; MCD-Township; DEKALB; *170 C-10; 🅷; mail Waterman z 60556; ℗ 1,521; © 1,663
CLINTON; 171 N-8; ℗ 33,944; © 35,535; Ⓡ 35,531; ◆ 36,511
Clintonia; MCD-Township; DE WITT; *170 I-9; mail Clinton z 61727; ℗ 7,860; © 7,926
Clover; MCD-Township; HENRY; *170 E-6; mail Woodhull z 61490; ℗ 1,027; © 975
Cloverdale; RMC Place; DUPAGE; *170 C-12; ★ CHI; mail Bartlett z 60103; pop. incl. with Bloomingdale (Inc. Place)
Cloverdale; RMC Place; TAZEWELL; *170 G-8; ★ PEOR; mail East Peoria z 61611; pop. incl. with East Peoria (Inc. Place)
Cloverleaf; RMC Place; MADISON; 195 E-7; ★ ST.L; mail Madison z 62060; ● 100
Clyde; RMC Place; COOK; ★ CHI; mail Cicero z 60804; pop. incl. with Cicero (Inc. Place)
Clyde; MCD-Township; WHITESIDE; *170 C-7; mail Morrison z 61270; ℗ 454; © 495
Coach Homes of Willow Bend; RMC Place; COOK; ★ CHI; mail Rolling Meadows z 60008; pop. incl. with Rolling Meadows (Inc. Place)
Coach Light Manor; RMC Place; COOK; ★ CHI; mail Mount Prospect z 60056; pop. incl. with Mount Prospect (Inc. Place)
Coal City; Inc. Place; GRUNDY, WILL; 170 E-11; elev. 565ft./172m.; 🅿; ★ CHI; z 60416; ℗ 3,907; © 4,797
Coal Hollow; RMC Place; BUREAU; *170 E-8; mail Princeton z 61356; rural
Coalton; Inc. Place; MONTGOMERY; 171 L-8; elev. 660ft./201m.; mail Nokomis z 62075; ℗ 359; © 307
Coal Valley; Inc. Place; ROCK ISLAND, HENRY; ▲ Coal Valley; 170 D-5; 🅿; ★ D-RI-M; z 61240; ℗ 2,683; © 3,606
Coal Valley; MCD-Township; ROCK ISLAND; *170 D-5; 🅿; ★ D-RI-M; z 61240; ℗ 4,695; © 4,561
Coatsburg; Inc. Place; ADAMS; 170 J-3; elev. 761ft./232m.; 🅿; z 62325; ℗ 201; © 226
Cobblestone; RMC Place; COOK; *170 B-12; elev. 654ft./199m.; ★ CHI; mail Glenview z 60025; ● 250
Cobblewood; RMC Place; COOK; ★ CHI; mail Northbrook z 60062; pop. incl. with Northbrook (Inc. Place)
Cobden; Inc. Place; UNION; 171 S-9; elev. 616ft./188m.; 🅿; z 62920; ℗ 1,090; © 1,116
Coe; MCD-Township; ROCK ISLAND; *170 D-6; mail Port Byron z 61275; ℗ 1,538; © 1,542
Coello (North City); Inc. Place; FRANKLIN; 171 Q-9; elev. 470ft./143m.; 🅿; ★ CARB-; z 62825; ℗ 538; © 630
Coffeen; Inc. Place; MONTGOMERY; 171 M-8; elev. 633ft./193m.; 🅿; z 62017; ℗ 736; © 709; Ⓡ 706
Colby Point; RMC Place; MCHENRY; *170 A-11; ★ CHI; mail McHenry z 60050; ● 60
Colchester; Inc. Place; MCDONOUGH; ▲ Colchester; 170 H-4; elev. 697ft./212m.; 🅿; z 62326; ℗ 1,645; © 1,493
Colchester; MCD-Township; MCDONOUGH; *170 H-4; 🅿; z 62326; ℗ 2,168; © 1,959
Coldbrook; RMC Place; WARREN; *170 F-5; elev. 771ft./235m.; mail Cameron z 61423; rural
Coldbrook; MCD-Township; WARREN; *170 F-5; mail Galesburg z 61401; ℗ 516; © 483
Cold Spring; MCD-Township; SHELBY; *171 L-9; mail Tower Hill z 62571; ℗ 372; © 425
Colehour; RMC Place; COOK; ★ CHI; mail Chicago z 60617; pop. incl. with Chicago (Inc. Place)
Coles; RMC Place; MOULTRIE, COLES; *171 K-11; mail Mattoon z 61938; ● 40
COLES; 171 K-11; ℗ 51,644; © 53,196; ◆ 52,139
Coleta; Inc. Place; WHITESIDE; 170 C-7; elev. 815ft./248m.; 🅿; z 61081; ℗ 154; © 155
Colfax; MCD-Township; CHAMPAIGN; *170 J-11; mail Ivesdale z 61851; ℗ 271; © 250
Colfax; Inc. Place; MCLEAN; 170 H-10; elev. 756ft./230m.; 🅿; z 61728; ℗ 854; © 989
College Avenue; RMC Place; DUPAGE; ★ CHI; pop. incl. with Wheaton (Inc. Place)
College Green; RMC Place; KANE; *170 B-11; ★ CHI; mail Elgin z 60123; pop. incl. with Elgin (Inc. Place)
College Park; RMC Place; KANE; ★ CHI; mail Elgin z 60123; pop. incl. with Elgin (Inc. Place)
College View; RMC Place; WILL; *170 D-12; ★ CHI; mail Lockport z 60441; pop. incl. with Lockport (Inc. Place)
Collins; RMC Place; WILL; ★ CHI; mail Plainfield z 60544; ● 50
Collins; RMC Place; WINNEBAGO; ★ RKFD; mail South Beloit z 61080; ● 50
Collinsville; Inc. Place; MADISON, ST. CLAIR; 171 N-7; elev. 550ft./168m.; 🅿; ★ ST.L; z 62234; ℗ 22,446; © 24,707; ◆ 26,760
Collinsville; MCD-Township; MADISON; *171 N-7; 🅿; ★ ST.L; z 62234; includes part of the City of Collinsville; ℗ 29,842; © 32,954
Collison; RMC Place; VERMILION; 170 I-13; elev. 677ft./206m.; 🅿; z 61831; ● 100
Colmar; RMC Place; MCDONOUGH; 170 H-4; elev. 556ft./169m.; 🅿; z 62367; ● 70
Coloma; MCD-Township; WHITESIDE; *170 C-8; mail Rock Falls z 61071; ℗ 12,083; © 11,844
Colona; Inc. Place; HENRY; ▲ Colona; 171 T-6; 🅿; ★ D-RI-M; z 61241; ℗ 4,852; © 5,173
Colona; MCD-Township; HENRY; *170 D-6; 🅿; ★ D-RI-M; z 61241; ℗ 6,728; © 6,699
Colonial Gardens; RMC Place; WINNEBAGO; ★ RKFD; mail Machesney Park z 61115; pop. incl. with Machesney Park (Inc. Place)
Colonial Manor; RMC Place; COOK; ★ CHI; mail Mount Prospect z 60056; pop. incl. with Mount Prospect (Inc. Place)
Colonial Ridge; RMC Place; COOK; *170 B-12; ★ CHI; mail Des Plaines z 60016; ● 850
Colonial Village; RMC Place; MADISON; *171 N-6; ★ ST.L; mail Godfrey z 62035; pop. incl. with Godfrey (Inc. Place)
Colonial Village; RMC Place; WILL; ★ CHI; mail Bolingbrook z 60440; pop. incl. with Bolingbrook (Inc. Place)
Colony Grove; RMC Place; CHAMPAIGN; *170 I-11; elev. 750ft./229m.; mail Mahomet z 61853; pop. incl. with Mahomet (Inc. Place)
Colony Park; RMC Place; DUPAGE; ★ CHI; mail Carol Stream z 60188; pop. incl. with Carol Stream (Inc. Place)
Colony Point; RMC Place; LAKE; ★ CHI; mail Deerfield z 60015; pop. incl. with Deerfield (Inc. Place)
Colp; Inc. Place; WILLIAMSON; *171 R-9; elev. 400ft./122m.; 🅿; ★ CARB-; z 62921; ℗ 235; © 224
Columbia; Inc. Place; MONROE, ST. CLAIR; 171 O-6; elev. 503ft./153m.; 🅿; ★ ST.L; z 62236; ℗ 5,524; © 7,922
Columbia Heights; RMC Place; KNOX; *170 F-6; ★ GLSB; mail East Galesburg z 61430; pop. incl. with East Galesburg (Inc. Place)
Columbia Village; RMC Place; CHAMPAIGN; *170 I-12; elev. 710ft./216m.; ★ CH-U; mail Urbana z 61802; ● 600
Columbus; Inc. Place; ADAMS; 170 J-3; elev. 725ft./221m.; 🅿; z 62320 & mail Quincy z 62305; ℗ 88; © 112
Columbus; MCD-Township; ADAMS; *170 J-4; 🅿; z 62320 & mail Quincy z 62305; includes part of the Village of Columbus; ℗ 500; © 578
Columbus Manor; RMC Place; COOK; ★ CHI; mail Oak Lawn z 60453; pop. incl. with Oak Lawn (Inc. Place)
Colusa; RMC Place; HANCOCK; *170 H-3; elev. 650ft./198m.; 🅿; z 62329; ● 100
Colvin Park; RMC Place; DEKALB; *170 B-10; mail Kingston z 60145; rural
Como; RMC Place; WHITESIDE; *170 C-7; mail Sterling z 61081; ● 350
Compromise; MCD-Township; CHAMPAIGN; *170 I-12; mail Penfield z 61862; ℗ 1,525; © 1,422
Compton; Inc. Place; LEE; 170 D-9; elev. 970ft./296m.; 🅿; z 61318; ℗ 343; © 347
Compton Pines; RMC Place; KANE; *170 C-11; elev. 841ft./256m.; ★ CHI; mail Saint Charles z 60175; ● 100
Comstock; RMC Place; MADISON; *171 N-6; ★ ST.L; mail Edwardsville z 62025; ● 50
Conant; RMC Place; PERRY; *171 Q-8; mail Pinckneyville z 62274; ● 30
Concord; MCD-Township; ADAMS; *170 J-4; mail Clayton z 62324; ℗ 231; © 293
Concord; MCD-Township; BUREAU; *170 E-8; mail Sheffield z 61361; ℗ 1,722; © 1,724
Concord; MCD-Township; IROQUOIS; *170 G-13; mail Iroquois z 60945; ℗ 524; © 551
Concord; Inc. Place; MORGAN; 170 J-6; elev. 595ft./181m.; 🅿; z 62631; ℗ 172; © 176
Condit; MCD-Township; CHAMPAIGN; *170 I-11; mail Dewey z 61840; ℗ 467; © 511
Cone; RMC Place; ST. CLAIR; ★ ST.L; pop. incl. with East Saint Louis (Inc. Place)
Confidence; RMC Place; FAYETTE; *171 N-10; mail Brownstown z 62418; rural
Congerville; Inc. Place; WOODFORD; 170 G-9; elev. 722ft./220m.; 🅿; z 61729; ℗ 397; © 466
Congress Park; RMC Place; COOK; ★ CHI; mail Brookfield z 60513; pop. incl. with Brookfield (Inc. Place)
Conlogue; RMC Place; EDGAR; *171 K-13; mail Paris z 61944; rural
Conover; RMC Place; KENDALL; *170 D-11; ★ CHI; mail Yorkville z 60560; ● 300
Conrad; RMC Place; CALHOUN; *171 N-5; elev. 622ft./190m.; mail Golden Eagle z 62036; rural
Continental Village; RMC Place; LAKE; ★ CHI; mail Waukegan z 60085; pop. incl. with Waukegan (Inc. Place)
COOK; 170 D-12; ℗ 5,105,067; © 5,376,741; Ⓡ 5,376,815; ◆ 5,266,525
Cooks Mills; RMC Place; COLES; 171 K-11; mail Humboldt z 61931; ● 200
Cooksville; Inc. Place; MCLEAN; 170 H-10; elev. 765ft./233m.; 🅿; z 61730; ℗ 211; © 213
Cooper; MCD-Township; SANGAMON; *171 K-8; mail Rochester z 62563; ℗ 771; © 820
Cooper; RMC Place; TAZEWELL; *170 G-8; ★ PEOR; mail Washington z 61571; rural
Cooperstown; RMC Place; BROWN; ▲ Cooperstown; *170 J-5; mail Mount Sterling z 62353; ● 50
Cooperstown; MCD-Township; BROWN; *170 J-5; mail Mount Sterling z 62353; ℗ 360; © 334
Copley; MCD-Township; KNOX; *170 F-6; mail Victoria z 61485; ℗ 388; © 433
Cora; RMC Place; JACKSON; 171 R-7; mail Rockwood z 62280; ● 25
Coral; RMC Place; MCHENRY; ▲ Coral; *170 B-11; ★ CHI; mail Marengo z 60152; ● 100
Coral; MCD-Township; MCHENRY; *170 B-11; ★ CHI; mail Marengo z 60152, Union z 60180; ℗ 2,549; © 3,020
Coral Gable; RMC Place; ST. CLAIR; *171 O-7; ★ ST.L; mail O Fallon z 62269; pop. incl. with O'Fallon (Inc. Place)
Cordova; Inc. Place; ROCK ISLAND; 170 D-6; elev. 604ft./184m.; 🅿; ★ D-RI-M; z 61242; ℗ 638; © 633; Ⓡ 651
Cordova; MCD-Township; ROCK ISLAND; *170 C-6; 🅿; z 61242; includes part of the Village of Cordova; ℗ 944; © 923
Corinth; RMC Place; WILLIAMSON; 171 R-10; elev. 519ft./158m.; mail Thompsonville z 62890; ● 30
Cornell; Inc. Place; LIVINGSTON; 170 F-10; elev. 638ft./194m.; 🅿; z 61319; ℗ 556; © 511
Cornerville; RMC Place; SALINE; mail Galatia z 62935; rural
Cornland; RMC Place; LOGAN; 170 J-8; elev. 600ft./183m.; 🅿; z 62519; ● 130
Cornwall; MCD-Township; HENRY; *170 E-7; mail Atkinson z 61235; ℗ 323; © 315
Cortese; RMC Place; KANKAKEE; *170 F-12; elev. 623ft./190m.; ★ KANK; mail Kankakee z 60901
Cortland; Inc. Place; DEKALB; ▲ Cortland; 170 C-10; 🅿; ★ DKLB; z 60112; ℗ 963; © 2,066
Cortland; MCD-Township; DEKALB; *170 C-10; 🅿; ★ DKLB; z 60112; ℗ 4,637; © 6,986
Corwin; MCD-Township; LOGAN; *170 I-8; mail Middletown z 62666; ℗ 727; © 723
Corwith; RMC Place; COOK; ★ CHI; pop. incl. with Chicago (Inc. Place)
Cottage; MCD-Township; SALINE; *171 R-11; mail Harrisburg z 62946; ℗ 254; © 356
Cottagegrove; RMC Place; SALINE; *171 R-11; elev. 408ft./124m.; mail Eldorado z 62930; rural
Cottage Hills; RMC Place; MADISON; 195 A-8; elev. 500ft./152m.; 🅿; ★ ST.L; z 62018; ● 980
Cotton Hill; MCD-Township; SANGAMON; *171 K-8; mail Rochester z 62563; ℗ 954; © 1,065
Cottonwood; MCD-Township; CUMBERLAND; *171 L-11; mail Toledo z 62468; ℗ 529; © 508
Cottonwood; RMC Place; GALLATIN; *171 Q-12; mail Omaha z 62871; ● 40
Coulterville; Inc. Place; RANDOLPH; 171 P-8; elev. 541ft./165m.; 🅿; z 62237; ℗ 984; © 1,230
Council Hill; RMC Place; JO DAVIESS; ▲ Council Hill; *170 A-6; elev. 925ft./282m.; mail Scales Mound z 61075
Council Hill; MCD-Township; JO DAVIESS; *170 A-6; mail Scales Mound z 61075; ℗ 181; © 179
Council Hill Station; RMC Place; JO DAVIESS; *170 A-6; elev. 800ft./244m.; mail Scales Mound z 61075; rural
Country Acres; RMC Place; LA SALLE; *170 E-10; elev. 600ft./183m.; mail Seneca z 61360; ● 200
Country Acres; RMC Place; ST. CLAIR; *171 O-7; ★ ST.L; mail Belleville z 62220; pop. incl. with Swansea (Inc. Place)
Country Aire; RMC Place; JEFFERSON; *171 P-10; elev. 550ft./168m.; mail Mount Vernon z 62864; ● 200
Country Aire; RMC Place; KANE; ★ CHI; mail Elgin z 60120; pop. incl. with Elgin (Inc. Place)
Country Club; RMC Place; COLES; *171 L-11; mail Mattoon z 61938; pop. incl. with Mattoon (Inc. Place)
Country Club Acres; RMC Place; MACOUPIN; *171 L-7; elev. 600ft./183m.; mail Carlinville z 62626; ● 30
Country Club Heights; RMC Place; COLES; *171 L-11; mail Mattoon z 61938; pop. incl. with Mattoon (Inc. Place)
Country Club Hills; Inc. Place; COOK; 172 M-8; elev. 675ft./206m.; 🅿; ★ CHI; z 60478 & mail Tinley Park z 60477; ℗ 15,431; © 16,169
Country Club Manor; RMC Place; COOK; ★ CHI; mail Country Club Hills z 60478; pop. incl. with Country Club Hills (Inc. Place)
Country Club Place; RMC Place; ST. CLAIR; *171 O-6; ★ ST.L; mail Belleville z 62223; ● 600
Country Club Terrace; RMC Place; ST. CLAIR; ★ ST.L; mail Belleville z 62220
Country Courts; RMC Place; ROCK ISLAND; ★ D-RI-M; mail Moline z 61265; ● 500
Country Estates; RMC Place; HENRY; *170 D-6; elev. 646ft./197m.; mail Geneseo z 61254; ● 100
Country Gardens; RMC Place; COOK; ★ CHI; mail Prospect Heights z 60070; pop. incl. with Prospect Heights (Inc. Place)
Country Heights; RMC Place; JEFFERSON; *171 P-10; elev. 500ft./152m.; mail Mount Vernon z 62864; pop. incl. with Mount Vernon (Inc. Place)
Country Knolls; RMC Place; KANE; ★ CHI; mail Elgin z 60123; pop. incl. with Elgin (Inc. Place)
Country Knolls; RMC Place; KNOX; *170 G-6; elev. 730ft./223m.; ★ GLSB; mail Abingdon z 61410; ● 50
Country Lake; RMC Place; DUPAGE; *170 C-11; ★ CHI; mail Naperville z 60563; pop. incl. with Naperville (Inc. Place)
Country Lake Estates; RMC Place; MENARD; *170 J-7; elev. 600ft./183m.; mail Athens z 62613; ● 200
Country Manor; RMC Place; COLES; *171 L-11; mail Mattoon z 61938; pop. incl. with Mattoon (Inc. Place)
Country Manor; RMC Place; EFFINGHAM; *171 M-11; mail Effingham z 62401; ● 50
Country Manor; RMC Place; HENRY; *170 D-6; elev. 650ft./198m.; mail Geneseo z 61254; pop. incl. with Geneseo (Inc. Place)
Country Oaks; RMC Place; MCLEAN; *170 H-9; mail Heyworth z 61745; ● 150
Country Orchard; RMC Place; COLES; *171 K-11; mail Mattoon z 61938; ● 250
Countryside; Inc. Place; COOK; 172 J-7; elev. 653ft./199m.; 🅿; ★ CHI; z 60525; ℗ 5,716; © 5,991
Countryside; RMC Place; KANE; *170 C-11; elev. 665ft./203m.; ★ CHI; mail Yorkville z 60560; ● 100
Countryside; RMC Place; KENDALL; *170 D-11; ★ CHI; mail Yorkville z 60560; pop. incl. with Yorkville (Inc. Place)
Countryside Estates; RMC Place; KANKAKEE; *170 F-12; elev. 625ft./191m.; ★ KANK; mail Chebanse z 60922; ● 200
Countryside Lake; RMC Place; LAKE; *170 A-12; ★ CHI; mail Mundelein z 60060; ● 320
Countryside Manor; RMC Place; LAKE; *170 A-12; ★ CHI; mail Libertyville z 60048; ● 700
Country Squire; RMC Place; CHAMPAIGN; *170 I-12; elev. 725ft./221m.; ★ CH-U; mail Urbana z 61801; pop. incl. with Urbana (Inc. Place)
Country Squire Estates; RMC Place; STEPHENSON; *170 A-8; elev. 800ft./244m.; mail Freeport z 61032; ● 100
Countryview Estates; RMC Place; KANE; *170 B-11; elev. 921ft./281m.; ★ CHI; mail Dundee z 60118; ● 40
Country View Estates; RMC Place; WILL; *170 C-12; ★ CHI; mail Naperville z 60564; pop. incl. with Naperville (Inc. Place)
Covel; MCLEAN; see Covell (RMC Place)
Covell (Covel); RMC Place; MCLEAN; *170 H-9; mail Bloomington z 61701, z 61704; ● 120
Coventry; RMC Place; MCHENRY; ★ CHI; mail Crystal Lake z 60014; pop. incl. with Crystal Lake (Inc. Place)
Coventry East; RMC Place; MCHENRY; ★ CHI; mail Crystal Lake z 60014; pop. incl. with Crystal Lake (Inc. Place)
Covington; RMC Place; WASHINGTON; ▲ Covington; *171 O-8; mail Okawville z 62271; ● 30
Covington; MCD-Township; WASHINGTON; *171 O-8; mail Okawville z 62271; ℗ 437; © 412
Covington Manor; RMC Place; COOK; *170 B-12; ★ CHI; mail Arlington Heights z 60004, Buffalo Grove z 60089
Cow Bell Lane; RMC Place; PERRY; *171 Q-8; elev. 420ft./128m.; mail Pinckneyville z 62274; ● 65
Cowden; Inc. Place; SHELBY; 171 L-10; elev. 590ft./180m.; 🅿; z 62422 & mail Lakewood z 62438; ℗ 599; © 612
Cowling; RMC Place; WABASH; 171 P-12; mail Mount Carmel z 62863; ● 120
Coyne Center; CDP; ROCK ISLAND; *170 E-5; ★ D-RI-M; mail Milan z 61264; © 906
Crab Orchard; RMC Place; WILLIAMSON; 171 R-10; mail Marion z 62959; ● 450
Crab Orchard Estates; RMC Place; WILLIAMSON; *171 R-9; ★ CARB-; mail Carbondale z 62901; ● 600
Cragin; RMC Place; COOK; *170 C-13; ★ CHI; mail Chicago z 60639; pop. incl. with Chicago (Inc. Place)
Craig; PERRY; see Winkle (RMC Place)
Craig Manor; RMC Place; COOK; ★ CHI; mail Des Plaines z 60016; pop. incl. with Des Plaines (Inc. Place)
Crainville; Inc. Place; WILLIAMSON; *171 R-9; elev. 473ft./144m.; ★ CARB-; mail Carterville z 62918; ℗ 1,019; © 992
Cramer (Cramers); RMC Place; PEORIA; *170 G-7; mail Elmwood z 61529
Cramers; PEORIA; see Cramer (RMC Place)
Crane Creek; MCD-Township; MASON; *170 I-7; mail Easton z 62633; ℗ 195; © 158
Cravat; RMC Place; JEFFERSON; *171 O-9; mail Centralia z 62801; ● 50
CRAWFORD; 171 M-13; ℗ 19,464; © 20,452; ◆ 19,371
Crawford Countryside; RMC Place; COOK; *170 D-13; ★ CHI; mail Matteson z 60443; pop. incl. with Matteson (Inc. Place)
Creal Springs; Inc. Place; WILLIAMSON; 171 R-10; elev. 500ft./152m.; 🅿; z 62922; ℗ 791; © 702
Creek; MCD-Township; DE WITT; *170 I-10; mail Lane z 61750; ℗ 412; © 402
Creekside; RMC Place; COOK; ★ CHI; mail Matteson z 60443; pop. incl. with Matteson (Inc. Place)
Creekwood; RMC Place; COOK, WILL; *170 D-12; elev. 675ft./206m.; ★ CHI; mail Lemont z 60439; ● 200
Crenshaw; RMC Place; WILLIAMSON; *171 R-9; ★ CARB-; mail Marion z 62959; ● 50
Crescent; MCD-Township; IROQUOIS; *170 G-13; mail Milford z 60953; ℗ 680; © 644
Crescent City; Inc. Place; IROQUOIS; 170 G-13; elev. 636ft./194m.; 🅿; z 60928; ℗ 541; © 631
Cress Creek; RMC Place; DUPAGE; ★ CHI; mail Naperville z 60563; pop. incl. with Naperville (Inc. Place)
Crest Haven; RMC Place; ST. CLAIR; *171 O-7; ★ ST.L; mail Belleville z 62221; pop. incl. with Fairview Heights (Inc. Place)
Crest Hill; Inc. Place; WILL; 172 M-4; elev. 625ft./191m.; 🅿; ★ CHI; z 60403, z 60435; ℗ 10,643; © 13,329; ◆ 17,681
Creston; Inc. Place; OGLE; 170 C-9; elev. 889ft./271m.; 🅿; z 60113; ℗ 535; © 543
Crestview; RMC Place; IROQUOIS; *170 G-13; elev. 657ft./200m.; mail Watseka z 60970; ● 40
Crestview Terrace; RMC Place; WAYNE; mail Fairfield z 62837; pop. incl. with Fairfield (Inc. Place)
Crestwood; Inc. Place; COOK; 172 L-8; elev. 604ft./184m.; 🅿; ★ CHI; z 60445; ℗ 10,823; © 11,251
Crestwood Estates; RMC Place; WILLIAMSON; ★ CARB-; mail Marion z 62959; ● 100
Crete; Inc. Place; WILL; ▲ Crete; 170 D-13; 🅿; ★ CHI; z 60417; ℗ 6,773; © 7,346; Ⓡ 7,712
Crete; MCD-Township; WILL; *170 D-13; 🅿; ★ CHI; z 60417; ℗ 21,512; © 23,589
Creve Coeur; Inc. Place; TAZEWELL; 170 G-8; elev. 690ft./210m.; 🅿; ★ PEOR; z 61610; ℗ 5,938; © 5,448
Cricket Hill; RMC Place; COOK; ★ CHI; mail Matteson z 60443; pop. incl. with Matteson (Inc. Place)
Crisp; RMC Place; WAYNE; *171 O-11; mail Wayne City z 62895
Crittenden; MCD-Township; CHAMPAIGN; *170 J-12; mail Tolono z 61880; ℗ 315; © 345
Crocketts Estates; RMC Place; LAKE; ★ CHI; mail Ingleside z 60041
Crook; MCD-Township; HAMILTON; *171 Q-11; mail Mc Leansboro z 62859; ℗ 366; © 347
Crooked Creek; MCD-Township; CUMBERLAND; *171 M-12; mail Greenup z 62428; ℗ 414; © 427
Crooked Creek; MCD-Township; JASPER; *171 M-12; mail Hidalgo z 62432; ℗ 820; © 735
Crooked Lake; RMC Place; LAKE; *170 A-12; ★ CHI; mail Lake Villa z 60046; ● 250
Cropsey; RMC Place; MCLEAN; ▲ Cropsey; 170 H-11; elev. 798ft./243m.; 🅿; z 61731; ● 120
Cropsey; MCD-Township; MCLEAN; *170 H-11; 🅿; z 61731; ℗ 240; © 256
Crossroads; RMC Place; JOHNSON; *171 S-10; elev. 444ft./135m.; mail Vienna z 62995; rural
Crossroads; RMC Place; ST. CLAIR; *171 O-7; elev. 564ft./172m.; ★ ST.L; mail Caseyville z 62232; pop. incl. with Fairview Heights (Inc. Place)
Crossroad Terrace; RMC Place; ST. CLAIR; ★ ST.L; mail Caseyville z 62232; pop. incl. with Fairview Heights (Inc. Place)
Crossville; Inc. Place; WHITE; 171 P-12; elev. 398ft./121m.; 🅿; z 62827; ℗ 805; © 782
Crotty; LA SALLE, GRUNDY; see Seneca (Inc. Place)
Crouch; MCD-Township; HAMILTON; *171 P-11; mail Wayne City z 62895; ℗ 395; © 408
Cruger; RMC Place; WOODFORD; ▲ Cruger; *170 G-9; ★ PEOR; mail Eureka z 61530
Cruger; MCD-Township; WOODFORD; *170 G-9; ★ PEOR; mail Eureka z 61530; ℗ 1,125; © 1,363
Crystal Gardens; RMC Place; MCHENRY; *170 B-11; ★ CHI; mail Crystal Lake z 60014
Crystal Lake; RMC Place; JERSEY; *171 M-6; mail Brighton z 62012; ● 40
Crystal Lake; RMC Place; MADISON; ★ ST.L; mail Godfrey z 62035; ● 50
Crystal Lake; Inc. Place; MCHENRY; 170 B-11; elev. 934ft./285m.; 🅿 ■; ★ CHI; z 60012, z 60014, z 60039; ℗ 24,512; © 38,000; ◆ 44,651
Crystal Lake Estates; RMC Place; MCHENRY; *170 B-11; ★ CHI; mail Crystal Lake z 60014; ● 720
Crystal Lawns; CDP-Census Area Only; WILL; 172 M-4; ★ CHI; mail Joliet z 60435; ℗ 3,037; © 2,933
Crystal Manor; RMC Place; MCHENRY; *170 B-11; ★ CHI; mail Crystal Lake z 60014
Crystal Vista; RMC Place; MCHENRY; *170 B-11; ★ CHI; mail Crystal Lake z 60014; pop. incl. with Crystal Lake (Inc. Place)
Cuba; Inc. Place; FULTON; 170 H-6; elev. 678ft./207m.; 🅿; z 61427; ℗ 1,440; © 1,418
Cuba; MCD-Township; LAKE; *170 B-12; ★ CHI; mail Barrington z 60010; ℗ 14,118; © 15,749; Ⓡ 15,751
Cullom; Inc. Place; LIVINGSTON; 170 G-11; elev. 689ft./210m.; 🅿; z 60929; ℗ 568; © 563
Cumberland; RMC Place; COOK; ★ CHI; mail Des Plaines z 60016; pop. incl. with Des Plaines (Inc. Place)
CUMBERLAND; 171 L-11; ℗ 10,670; © 11,253; ◆ 10,688
Cumberland Green; RMC Place; KANE; ★ CHI; mail Saint Charles z 60174; pop. incl. with Saint Charles (Inc. Place)
Cumberland Highlands; RMC Place; COOK; ★ CHI; mail Des Plaines z 60016; pop. incl. with Des Plaines (Inc. Place)
Cunningham; MCD-Township; CHAMPAIGN; *170 I-12; 🅷; ★ CH-U; mail Urbana z 61801-03; coextensive with the City of Urbana; ℗ 36,344; © 36,395; Ⓡ 37,362
Cunningham Courts; RMC Place; COOK; ★ CHI; mail Palatine z 60074; pop. incl. with Palatine (Inc. Place)
Curran; Inc. Place; SANGAMON; ▲ Curran; 171 K-7; elev. 626ft./191m.; 🅿; z 62670; incorporated April 5, 2005; not reported in 2000 Census; ● 300
Curran; MCD-Township; SANGAMON; *171 K-7; 🅿; z 62670; ℗ 1,505; © 1,678
Custer; MCD-Township; WILL; *170 E-12; mail Wilmington z 60481; ℗ 1,110; © 1,463
Custer Park; RMC Place; WILL; 170 E-12; elev. 564ft./172m.; 🅿; z 60481; ● 300
Cutler; Inc. Place; PERRY; 171 Q-8; elev. 500ft./152m.; 🅿; z 62238; ℗ 523; © 543
Cypress; Inc. Place; JOHNSON; 171 S-9; elev. 432ft./132m.; 🅿; z 62923; ℗ 275; © 271
Cypress Gardens; RMC Place; WILLIAMSON; *171 R-9; elev. 414ft./126m.; ★ CARB-; mail Carbondale z 62901; ● 50

D

D'Adrian Gardens; RMC Place; MADISON; *171 N-6; ★ ST.L; mail Godfrey z 62035; pop. incl. with Godfrey (Inc. Place)
Daggetts; RMC Place; CARROLL; *170 B-7; mail Mount Carroll z 61053; rural
Dahinda; RMC Place; KNOX; 170 F-6; elev. 596ft./182m.; 🅿; z 61428; ● 150
Dahlgren; Inc. Place; HAMILTON; ▲ Dahlgren; 171 P-10; elev. 500ft./152m.; 🅿; z 62828; ℗ 512; © 514
Dahlgren; MCD-Township; HAMILTON; *171 P-10; elev. 500ft./152m.; 🅿; z 62828; ℗ 1,232; © 1,224
Dailey; RMC Place; CHAMPAIGN; *170 I-12; mail Penfield z 61862; rural
Dakota; Inc. Place; STEPHENSON; ▲ Dakota; 170 A-8; 🅿; z 61018; ℗ 549; © 499
Dakota; MCD-Township; STEPHENSON; *170 A-8; 🅿; z 61018; ℗ 914; © 841
Dale; RMC Place; HAMILTON; 171 Q-11; elev. 400ft./122m.; 🅿; z 62829; ● 150
Dale; MCD-Township; MCLEAN; *170 H-9; mail Shirley z 61772; ℗ 1,192; © 1,276
Dale Valley; RMC Place; CHAMPAIGN; *170 I-11; elev. 775ft./236m.; mail Mahomet z 61853; pop. incl. with Mahomet (Inc. Place)
Dallasania; RMC Place; SALINE; mail Carrier Mills z 62917; rural
Dallas City; Inc. Place; HANCOCK, HENDERSON; 170 G-3; elev. 537ft./164m.; 🅿; z 62330; ℗ 1,037; © 1,055
Dallas City; MCD-Township; HANCOCK; *170 G-3; 🅿; z 62330; includes part of the City of Dallas City; ℗ 1,082; © 1,089
Dalton City; Inc. Place; MOULTRIE; 171 K-10; elev. 690ft./210m.; 🅿; z 61925; ℗ 573; © 581
Dalzell; Inc. Place; BUREAU, LA SALLE; 170 E-9; elev. 650ft./198m.; 🅿; z 61320; ℗ 587; © 717
Damiansville; Inc. Place; CLINTON; *171 O-8; 🅿; ★ ST.L; z 62215; ℗ 379; © 368
Dana; Inc. Place; LA SALLE; 170 F-10; elev. 660ft./201m.; 🅿; z 61321; ℗ 165; © 171
Danada North; RMC Place; DUPAGE; ★ CHI; mail Wheaton z 60187; pop. incl. with Wheaton (Inc. Place)
Danada West; RMC Place; DUPAGE; ★ CHI; mail Wheaton z 60187; pop. incl. with Wheaton (Inc. Place)
Danforth; Inc. Place; IROQUOIS; ▲ Danforth; 170 G-12; 🅿; z 60930; ℗ 457; © 587
Danforth; MCD-Township; IROQUOIS; *170 G-12; 🅿; z 60930; ℗ 972; © 951
Danley; RMC Place; RANDOLPH; *171 Q-6; mail Modoc z 62261; ● 40
Danvers; Inc. Place; MCLEAN; ▲ Danvers; 170 H-9; 🅿; z 61732; ℗ 981; © 1,183
Danvers; MCD-Township; MCLEAN; *170 H-9; 🅿; z 61732; ℗ 1,692; © 1,953
Danville; Inc. Place; ⊡ VERMILION; 170 I-13; elev. 597ft./182m.; 🅿 🅷 ■; ★ DANV; z 61832-34; ℗ 33,828; © 33,904; ◆ 31,043
Danville; MCD-Township; VERMILION; *170 I-13; 🅿; ★ DANV; z 61832-34; includes part of the City of Danville; ℗ 37,025; © 34,094
Danville Junction; RMC Place; VERMILION; ★ DANV; mail Danville z 61832; pop. incl. with Danville (Inc. Place)
Danway; RMC Place; LA SALLE; *170 D-10; mail Marseilles z 61341; rural
Darien; Inc. Place; DUPAGE; 172 J-5; elev. 756ft./230m.; 🅿; ★ CHI; z 60561; ℗ 18,140; © 22,860; ◆ 22,737
Darmstadt; RMC Place; ST. CLAIR; 171 P-7; elev. 424ft./129m.; mail Lenzburg z 62255; ● 130
Darrow; RMC Place; IROQUOIS; *170 G-13; elev. 686ft./209m.; mail Sheldon z 60966; rural
Darwin; RMC Place; CLARK; ▲ Darwin; 171 L-13; elev. 462ft./141m.; mail West Union z 62477; ● 60
Darwin; MCD-Township; CLARK; *171 L-13; mail West Union z 62477; ℗ 372; © 378
David Acres; RMC Place; JERSEY; *171 M-6; ★ ST.L; mail Brighton z 62012; ● 200
Davis; Inc. Place; STEPHENSON; 170 A-8; elev. 900ft./274m.; 🅿; z 61019; ℗ 541; © 662
Davis Junction; Inc. Place; OGLE; 170 B-9; elev. 789ft./240m.; 🅿; z 61020; ℗ 246; © 491
Dawson; MCD-Township; MCLEAN; *170 H-10; mail Ellsworth z 61737; ℗ 649; © 668
Dawson; Inc. Place; SANGAMON; *170 J-8; elev. 599ft./183m.; 🅿; z 62520; ℗ 536; © 466
Dawson Park; RMC Place; IROQUOIS; *170 G-13; elev. 708ft./216m.; mail Milford z 60953; rural
Daysville; RMC Place; OGLE; 170 C-9; mail Oregon z 61061; ● 150
Dayton; RMC Place; HENRY; *170 D-6; ★ D-RI-M; mail Colona z 61241; ● 160
Dayton; RMC Place; LA SALLE; ▲ Dayton; 170 E-10; elev. 542ft./165m.; mail Ottawa z 61350; ● 200
Dayton; MCD-Township; LA SALLE; *170 E-10; mail Ottawa z 61350; ℗ 1,453; © 1,685
Decatur; Inc. Place; ⊡ MACON; 170 J-10; elev. 670ft./204m.; 🅿 🅷 🅲 2,488 ■; ★ DEC; z 62521-26; ℗ 83,885; © 81,860; ◆ 77,914
Decatur; MCD-Township; MACON; *170 J-9; 🅿 🅲 2,488; ★ DEC; z 62521-26; includes part of the City of Decatur; ℗ 61,907; © 58,355
Decker; MCD-Township; RICHLAND; *171 O-12; mail Noble z 62868; ℗ 415; © 395
Decorra; RMC Place; HENDERSON; *170 G-4; mail Stronghurst z 61480
Deep Lake; RMC Place; LAKE; *170 A-12; ★ CHI; mail Lake Villa z 60046; ● 250
Deep Spring Woods; RMC Place; MCHENRY; ★ CHI; mail Wonder Lake z 60097
Deep Woods; RMC Place; LAKE; ★ CHI; mail Mundelein z 60060; pop. incl. with Mundelein (Inc. Place)
Deer Creek; Inc. Place; TAZEWELL, WOODFORD; 170 G-8; elev. 755ft./230m.; 🅿; z 61733; ℗ 630; © 605
Deer Creek; MCD-Township; TAZEWELL; *170 G-8; 🅿; z 61733; includes part of the Village of Deer Creek; ℗ 1,098; © 1,156
Deerfield; MCD-Township; FULTON; *170 H-6; mail Ellisville z 61431; ℗ 343; © 313
Deerfield; Inc. Place; LAKE, COOK; 172 D-7; elev. 675ft./206m.; 🅿 🅲 2,855; ★ CHI; z 60015; ℗ 17,327; © 18,420
Deerfield; LAKE; see Moraine (MCD-Township)
Deer Grove; Inc. Place; WHITESIDE; 170 D-8; elev. 647ft./197m.; 🅿; z 61243; ℗ 44; © 48
Deering; RMC Place; COOK; ★ CHI; mail Chicago z 60610; pop. incl. with Chicago (Inc. Place)
Deering City; RMC Place; FRANKLIN; *171 Q-10; elev. 393ft./120m.; ★ CARB-; mail West Frankfort z 62896; ● 150
Deer Lake; RMC Place; COOK; *170 B-12; elev. 888ft./271m.; ★ CHI; mail Barrington z 60010; ● 200
Deer Park; MCD-Township; LA SALLE; *170 E-9; mail Oglesby z 61348; ℗ 548; © 467
Deer Park; Inc. Place; LAKE, COOK; 172 D-4; elev. 850ft./259m.; 🅿; ★ CHI; z 60010; ℗ 2,887; © 3,102
Deer Plain; RMC Place; CALHOUN; 171 N-5; mail Brussels z 62013; ● 80
Deer Run; RMC Place; KANE; *170 C-11; elev. 830ft./253m.; ★ CHI; mail Saint Charles z 60175; ● 50
Deerwood Estates; RMC Place; FAYETTE; *171 M-9; elev. 550ft./168m.; mail Vandalia z 62471; ● 100
Degognia; MCD-Township; JACKSON; *171 R-8; mail Jacob z 62950; ℗ 174; © 200; Ⓡ 163
DeKalb; Inc. Place; DEKALB; ▲ DeKalb; 170 C-10; 🅿 🅷 🅲 25,313 ■; ★ DKLB; z 60115; ℗ 34,925; © 39,018; ◆ 45,253
DeKalb; MCD-Township; DEKALB; *170 C-10; 🅿 🅲 25,313; ★ DKLB; z 60115; ℗ 38,710; © 42,189
DEKALB; 170 C-10; ℗ 77,932; © 88,969; ◆ 110,727
Delafield; RMC Place; HAMILTON; 171 P-10; mail Mc Leansboro z 62859; ● 40
De Land; Inc. Place; PIATT; 170 I-10; elev. 700ft./213m.; 🅿; z 61839; ℗ 458; © 475
Delavan; Inc. Place; TAZEWELL; ▲ Delavan; 170 H-8; elev. 609ft./186m.; 🅿; z 61734; ℗ 1,642; © 1,825
Delavan; MCD-Township; TAZEWELL; *170 H-8; 🅿; z 61734; ℗ 2,019; © 2,206
Del-Bar; RMC Place; FULTON; *170 H-7; mail Canton z 61520; ● 150
Delhi; RMC Place; JERSEY; *171 M-6; elev. 600ft./183m.; ★ ST.L; mail Jerseyville z 62052; ● 50
Dellwood Highlands; RMC Place; WILL; *170 D-12; ★ CHI; mail Lockport z 60441; ● 680
Del Mar Woods; RMC Place; LAKE; 172 D-7; ★ CHI; mail Deerfield z 60015; ● 120
DeLong; RMC Place; KNOX; *170 G-6; 🅿; z 61436; ● 130
Delrey; RMC Place; IROQUOIS; *170 G-12; mail Thawville z 60968; ● 25
Delwood; RMC Place; POPE; *171 R-11; mail Harrisburg z 62946
Dement; MCD-Township; OGLE; *170 C-9; mail Rochelle z 61068; ℗ 956; © 825
Denison; MCD-Township; LAWRENCE; *171 O-13; mail Saint Francisville z 62460; ℗ 1,806; © 1,714
Denmark; RMC Place; PERRY; *171 Q-8; mail Cutler z 62238; rural
Denning; MCD-Township; FRANKLIN; *171 Q-9; ★ CARB-; mail West Frankfort z 62896; ℗ 5,261; © 4,910; Ⓡ 4,921
Dennison; RMC Place; CLARK; 171 L-13; elev. 580ft./177m.; 🅿; z 62423; ● 100
Denny; RMC Place; PERRY; *171 Q-8; mail Du Quoin z 62832; rural
Denver; RMC Place; HANCOCK; 170 I-4; mail Carthage z 62321; ● 120
Denver; MCD-Township; RICHLAND; *171 N-12; mail Noble z 62868; ℗ 428; © 414
Depue; Inc. Place; BUREAU; 170 E-9; elev. 472ft./144m.; 🅿; z 61322; ℗ 1,729; © 1,842
Derby; RMC Place; FORD; *170 H-11; elev. 761ft./232m.; mail Gibson City z 60936; rural
Derby; RMC Place; SALINE; *171 R-11; elev. 477ft./145m.; mail Herod z 62947; rural
Derinda; MCD-Township; JO DAVIESS; *170 B-6; mail Elizabeth z 61028; ℗ 328; © 318
Derinda Center; RMC Place; JO DAVIESS; *170 A-6; elev. 803ft./245m.; mail Elizabeth z 61028; rural
Derry; MCD-Township; PIKE; *171 K-4; mail Barry z 62312; ℗ 292; © 274
Deselm; RMC Place; KANKAKEE; *170 E-12; elev. 682ft./208m.; mail Manteno z 60950
De Soto; Inc. Place; JACKSON; ▲ De Soto; 171 R-9; 🅿; z 62924; ℗ 1,500; © 1,653
De Soto; MCD-Township; JACKSON; *171 R-9; 🅿; z 62924; ℗ 2,073; © 2,231
Des Plaines; Inc. Place; COOK; 170 B-12; elev. 642ft./196m.; 🅿 🅷 ■; ★ CHI; z 60016-19; ℗ 53,223; © 58,720; Ⓡ 56,945; ◆ 59,481
Des Plaines Manor; RMC Place; COOK; ★ CHI; mail Des Plaines z 60016; pop. incl. with Des Plaines (Inc. Place)
Des Plaines Terrace; RMC Place; COOK; ★ CHI; mail Des Plaines z 60016; pop. incl. with Des Plaines (Inc. Place)
Detroit; Inc. Place; PIKE; 171 K-5; elev. 639ft./195m.; 🅿; z 62363; ℗ 126; © 93
Detroit; MCD-Township; PIKE; *171 K-5; 🅿; z 62363; ℗ 353; © 354
Devereux Heights; RMC Place; SANGAMON; *170 J-8; ★ SPRG; mail Springfield z 62707; pop. incl. with Springfield (Inc. Place)
Devon Avenue; RMC Place; COOK; pop. incl. with Chicago (Inc. Place)
Devonshire; RMC Place; COOK; ★ CHI; mail Des Plaines z 60018; pop. incl. with Des Plaines (Inc. Place)
Dewey; RMC Place; CHAMPAIGN; 170 I-11; elev. 728ft./222m.; 🅿; z 61840; ● 150
De Witt; Inc. Place; DE WITT; ▲ De Witt; 170 I-10; 🅿; z 61735; ℗ 122; © 188
De Witt; MCD-Township; DE WITT; *170 I-10; mail Dewitt z 61735; ℗ 417; © 465
DE WITT; 170 I-9; ℗ 16,516; © 16,798; ◆ 16,165
Dewmaine; RMC Place; WILLIAMSON; *171 R-9; elev. 434ft./132m.; ★ CARB-; mail Carterville z 62918; pop. incl. with Carterville (Inc. Place)
Dexter; RMC Place; EFFINGHAM; *171 M-10; elev. 599ft./183m.; mail Altamont z 62411; ● 35
Diamond; Inc. Place; GRUNDY, WILL; 170 E-11; elev. 563ft./172m.; 🅿; ★ CHI; z 60416; ℗ 1,077; © 1,393
Diamond City; RMC Place; HAMILTON; *171 Q-11; mail Mc Leansboro z 62859; pop. incl. with McLeansboro (Inc. Place)
Diamond Lake; RMC Place; LAKE; 172 C-5; ★ CHI; mail Mundelein z 60060; ● 1,500
Diamond Town; RMC Place; PERRY; *171 Q-8; elev. 450ft./137m.; mail Pinckneyville z 62274; pop. incl. with Pinckneyville (Inc. Place)
Dieterich; Inc. Place; EFFINGHAM; 171 M-11; elev. 591ft./180m.; 🅿; z 62424; ℗ 568; © 591
Dillon; RMC Place; TAZEWELL; ▲ Dillon; 170 H-8; mail Tremont z 61568; ● 60
Dillon; MCD-Township; TAZEWELL; *170 H-8; mail Tremont z 61568; ℗ 916; © 962
Dillsburg; RMC Place; CHAMPAIGN; *170 I-12; mail Rantoul z 61866
Dimmick; MCD-Township; LA SALLE; *170 E-9; mail La Salle z 61301; ℗ 611; © 693
Diona; RMC Place; COLES, CUMBERLAND; *171 L-12; mail Greenup z 62428; rural
Disco; RMC Place; HANCOCK; *170 G-4; mail Dallas City z 62330, La Harpe z 61450; ● 50
Diswood; RMC Place; ALEXANDER; *171 T-8; elev. 360ft./110m.; mail Tamms z 62988; rural
Divernon; Inc. Place; SANGAMON; ▲ Divernon; 171 K-8; elev. 617ft./188m.; 🅿; z 62530; ℗ 1,178; © 1,201
Divernon; MCD-Township; SANGAMON; *171 K-8; 🅿; z 62530; ℗ 1,484; © 1,548
Divide; RMC Place; JEFFERSON; *171 O-10; elev. 541ft./165m.; mail Texico z 62889; rural
Division Street; RMC Place; COOK; *170 C-13; ★ CHI; mail Chicago z 60651; pop. incl. with Chicago (Inc. Place)
Dix; MCD-Township; FORD; *170 H-11; mail Elliott z 60933; ℗ 711; © 686
Dix (Rome); Inc. Place; JEFFERSON; 171 O-10; elev. 580ft./177m.; 🅿; z 62830; ℗ 456; © 494
Dixmoor; Inc. Place; COOK; 172 L-9; elev. 600ft./183m.; 🅿; ★ CHI; z 60426 & mail Blue Island z 60406; ℗ 3,647; © 3,934
Dixon; Inc. Place; ⊡ LEE; 170 C-8; elev. 659ft./201m.; 🅿 🅷; z 61021; ℗ 15,144; © 15,941
Dixon; MCD-Township; LEE; *170 C-8; 🅿; z 61021; includes part of the City of Dixon; ℗ 17,166; © 17,925
Dixon Springs; RMC Place; POPE; 171 S-10; mail Grantsburg z 62943; ● 50
Dobbins Downs; RMC Place; CHAMPAIGN; *170 I-11; ★ CH-U; mail Champaign z 61821; ● 780
Dodds; MCD-Township; JEFFERSON; *171 P-10; mail Mount Vernon z 62864; ℗ 2,666; © 2,720
Doddsville; RMC Place; MCDONOUGH, SCHUYLER; *170 I-5; elev. 682ft./208m.; mail Littleton z 61452
Dogwalk; WILLIAMSON; see Cedar Grove (RMC Place)
Dollville; RMC Place; SHELBY; *171 L-9; 🅿; z 62571
Dolson; MCD-Township; CLARK; *171 L-13; mail Paris z 61944; ℗ 310; © 352
Dolton; Inc. Place; COOK; 172 L-10; elev. 600ft./183m.; 🅿; ★ CHI; z 60419; ℗ 23,930; © 25,614; ◆ 25,621
Dongola; Inc. Place; UNION; 171 S-9; elev. 388ft./118m.; 🅿; z 62926; ℗ 728; © 806
Donnellson; Inc. Place; MONTGOMERY, BOND; 171 M-8; elev. 611ft./186m.; 🅿; z 62019; ℗ 167; © 243
Donovan; Inc. Place; IROQUOIS; 170 F-13; elev. 673ft./205m.; 🅿; z 60931; ℗ 361; © 351
Dora; MCD-Township; MOULTRIE; *171 K-10; mail Dalton City z 61925; ℗ 911; © 845
Dorans; RMC Place; COLES; *171 K-11; mail Mattoon z 61938; ● 30
Dorchester; Inc. Place; MACOUPIN; *171 M-7; elev. 660ft./201m.; 🅿; z 62033; ℗ 145; © 142
Dorchester; MCD-Township; MACOUPIN; *171 M-7; 🅿; z 62033 & mail Benld z 62009; includes part of the Village of Dorchester; ℗ 1,517; © 1,546
Dorr; MCD-Township; MCHENRY; *170 A-11; ★ CHI; mail Woodstock z 60098; ℗ 14,231; © 18,157
Dorris Heights; RMC Place; SALINE; *171 R-11; mail Harrisburg z 62946; pop. incl. with Harrisburg (Inc. Place)
Dorsey (Dorsey's); RMC Place; MADISON; 171 M-7; elev. 550ft./168m.; 🅿; ★ ST.L; z 62021; ● 200
Dorsey's; MADISON; see Dorsey (RMC Place)
Douglas; MCD-Township; CLARK; *171 L-13; mail Marshall z 62441; ℗ 166; © 161
Douglas; RMC Place; COOK; ★ CHI; mail Chicago z 60616; pop. incl. with Chicago (Inc. Place)
Douglas; MCD-Township; EFFINGHAM; *171 M-11; mail Effingham z 62401; ℗ 12,566; © 12,698
Douglas; MCD-Township; IROQUOIS; *170 G-12; mail Gilman z 60938; ℗ 2,112; © 2,098
Douglas; RMC Place; KNOX; *170 G-6; mail Yates City z 61572; ● 80
Douglas; RMC Place; ST. CLAIR; *171 O-7; ★ ST.L; mail Freeburg z 62243; ● 80
DOUGLAS; 171 K-11; ℗ 19,464; © 19,922; ◆ 19,312
Douglas Park; RMC Place; WHITESIDE; *170 C-7; elev. 651ft./198m.; mail Sterling z 61081; ● 200
Dover; Inc. Place; BUREAU; 170 D-8; elev. 740ft./226m.; 🅿; z 61323; ℗ 163; © 172
Dover; MCD-Township; BUREAU; *170 D-8; 🅿; z 61323 & mail Princeton z 61356; includes part of the Village of Dover; ℗ 632; © 585
Dow; RMC Place; JERSEY; *171 M-6; elev. 669ft./204m.; 🅿; z 62022; ● 160
Dowell; Inc. Place; JACKSON; 171 Q-9; elev. 400ft./122m.; 🅿; z 62927; ℗ 465; © 441
Downers Fairview; RMC Place; DUPAGE; ★ CHI; mail Downers Grove z 60515; pop. incl. with Downers Grove (Inc. Place)
Downers Grove; Inc. Place; DUPAGE; 172 I-5; elev. 725ft./221m.; 🅿 🅷 🅲 1,978 ■; ★ CHI; z 60515-17; ℗ 46,858; © 48,724; ◆ 48,672
Downers Grove; MCD-Township; DUPAGE; *170 C-12; 🅿 🅲 1,978; ★ CHI; z 60515-17 & mail Westmont z 60559; includes part of the Village of Downers Grove; ℗ 137,862; © 148,110
Downers Grove Estates; RMC Place; DUPAGE; *170 C-12; ★ CHI; mail Downers Grove z 60515; ● 500
Downey; RMC Place; LAKE; *170 A-12; elev. 700ft./213m.; 🅿; ★ CHI; z 60064; pop. incl. with North Chicago (Inc. Place)
Downs; Inc. Place; MCLEAN; 170 H-10; elev. 795ft./242m.; 🅿; z 61736; ℗ 620; © 776
Downs; MCD-Township; MCLEAN; *170 H-10; 🅿; z 61736; includes part of the Village of Downs; ℗ 992; © 1,079
Downtown; RMC Place; COOK; *170 B-12; ★ CHI; mail Des Plaines z 60016; pop. incl. with Des Plaines (Inc. Place)
Downtown; RMC Place; DUPAGE; ★ CHI; mail Villa Park z 60181; pop. incl. with Villa Park (Inc. Place)
Downtown; RMC Place; DUPAGE; *170 C-12; ★ CHI; mail Glen Ellyn z 60137; pop. incl. with Glen Ellyn (Inc. Place)
Downtown; RMC Place; JACKSON; *171 R-9; ★ CARB-; mail Carbondale z 62901; pop. incl. with Carbondale (Inc. Place)
Downtown; RMC Place; LA SALLE; *170 E-9; mail La Salle z 61301; pop. incl. with La Salle (Inc. Place)
Downtown; RMC Place; MCLEAN; *170 I-9; mail Bloomington z 61701; pop. incl. with Bloomington (Inc. Place)
Downtown; RMC Place; SANGAMON; *170 J-8; ★ SPRG; mail Springfield z 62701, z 62705; pop. incl. with Springfield (Inc. Place)
Dozaville (Pujol); RMC Place; RANDOLPH; *171 Q-7; mail Saint Mary z 63673; ● 20
Drake (Hank's Station); RMC Place; GREENE; *171 L-5; mail White Hall z 62092; ● 25
Dresden Acres; RMC Place; GRUNDY; mail Morris z 60450; ● 300
Drexel; RMC Place; COOK; ★ CHI; mail Cicero z 60804; pop. incl. with Cicero (Inc. Place)
Drivers; RMC Place; JEFFERSON; *171 P-9; mail Woodlawn z 62898; rural
Druce Lake; RMC Place; LAKE; 172 A-5; ★ CHI; mail Lake Villa z 60046; ● 200
Drummer; MCD-Township; FORD; *170 H-11; mail Gibson City z 60936; ℗ 3,897; © 3,898
Drury; MCD-Township; ROCK ISLAND; *170 E-4; mail Muscatine z 52761; ℗ 715; © 806
Dry Grove; MCD-Township; MCLEAN; *170 H-9; mail Danvers z 61732; ℗ 1,494; © 1,649
Dry Point; MCD-Township; SHELBY; *171 L-10; mail Cowden z 62422; ℗ 1,096; © 1,085
Du Bois (Bois); Inc. Place; WASHINGTON; ▲ Du Bois; 171 P-9; 🅿; z 62831; ℗ 216; © 222
Du Bois; MCD-Township; WASHINGTON; *171 P-9; 🅿; z 62831; ℗ 732; © 952
Duck Lake Woods; RMC Place; LAKE; 172 A-4; ★ CHI; mail Ingleside z 60041; ● 400
Dudley; RMC Place; EDGAR; *171 K-13; mail Paris z 61944; ● 90
Dudleyville; RMC Place; BOND; *171 N-8; mail Greenville z 62246; rural
Duncan; MCD-Township; MERCER; *170 E-4; mail Aledo z 61231; ℗ 337; © 299
Duncan; RMC Place; STARK; *170 F-7; mail Princeville z 61559; ● 30
Duncans Mills; RMC Place; FULTON; 170 H-6; mail Lewistown z 61542; ● 60
Duncanville; RMC Place; CRAWFORD; *171 M-13; mail Robinson z 62454; ● 50
Dundas; RMC Place; RICHLAND; 171 N-12; elev. 478ft./146m.; 🅿; z 62425; ● 250
Dundee; RMC Place; KANE; 🅿; ★ CHI; z 60118; pop. incl. with West Dundee (Inc. Place)
Dundee; KANE; see West Dundee (Inc. Place)
Dundee; MCD-Township; KANE; *170 B-11; 🅿; ★ CHI; z 60118; ℗ 39,070; © 53,207
Dunfermline; Inc. Place; FULTON; 170 H-7; elev. 640ft./195m.; 🅿; z 61524; ℗ 259; © 262
Dunham; MCD-Township; MCHENRY; *170 A-10; mail Harvard z 60033; ℗ 2,001; © 2,375
Dunhurst; RMC Place; COOK; ★ CHI; mail Wheeling z 60090; pop. incl. with Wheeling (Inc. Place)
Dunkel; RMC Place; CHRISTIAN; *171 L-9; elev. 660ft./201m.; 🅿; z 62557; rural
Dunlap; Inc. Place; PEORIA; 170 G-8; elev. 720ft./219m.; 🅿; z 61525; ℗ 851; © 926
Dunlap Lake; RMC Place; MADISON; ★ ST.L; mail Edwardsville z 62025; pop. incl. with Edwardsville (Inc. Place)
Dunleith; MCD-Township; JO DAVIESS; *170 A-5; ★ DUB; mail East Dubuque z 61025; ℗ 3,877; © 3,872
Dunn; RMC Place; MOULTRIE; *171 K-10; elev. 656ft./200m.; mail Sullivan z 61951
Dunning; RMC Place; COOK; *170 C-13; elev. 638ft./194m.; ★ CHI; mail Chicago z 60634; pop. incl. with Chicago (Inc. Place)
Du Page; MCD-Township; WILL; *170 D-12; ★ CHI; mail Lockport z 60441; ℗ 55,444; © 71,745
DUPAGE; 170 C-12; ℗ 781,666; © 904,161; ◆ 920,255
Dupo; Inc. Place; ST. CLAIR; 171 O-6; elev. 415ft./126m.; 🅿; ★ ST.L; z 62239; ℗ 3,164; © 3,933; Ⓡ 3,930
Du Quoin; Inc. Place; PERRY; 171 Q-9; elev. 468ft./143m.; 🅿 🅷; z 62832; ℗ 6,697; © 6,448
Durand; Inc. Place; WINNEBAGO; ▲ Durand; 170 A-8; 🅿; z 61024; ℗ 1,100; © 1,081
Durand; MCD-Township; WINNEBAGO; *170 A-8; 🅿; z 61024; ℗ 1,910; © 2,184
Durham; RMC Place; HANCOCK; *170 G-4; elev. 648ft./198m.; mail Dallas City z 62330; rural
Durham; MCD-Township; HANCOCK; *170 G-4; mail Dallas City z 62330; ℗ 333; © 302
Durley Camp; RMC Place; BOND; *171 N-8; elev. 550ft./168m.; mail Greenville z 62246; summer pop. 100; rural
Dutch Creek Woodlands; RMC Place; MCHENRY; ★ CHI; mail McHenry z 60050; rural
Dutch Hollow; RMC Place; ST. CLAIR; *171 O-6; ★ ST.L; mail Belleville z 62221
Duvall; RMC Place; SHELBY; *171 L-10; 🅿; z 62565; rural
Dwight; Inc. Place; LIVINGSTON, GRUNDY; ▲ Dwight; 170 F-11; elev. 640ft./195m.; 🅿; z 60420; ℗ 4,230; © 4,363
Dwight; MCD-Township; LIVINGSTON; *170 F-11; 🅿; z 60420; includes part of the village of Dwight; ℗ 4,511; © 5,625; Ⓡ 4,616
Dykersburg (Absher); RMC Place; WILLIAMSON; *171 R-10; elev. 556ft./169m.; mail Stonefort z 62987; ● 50

Entries in **UPPERCASE** are counties.
Entries in **bold** have populations of 2,500 or more.
Names in parentheses are alternate names.

Inc. Place	Incorporated Place
RMC Place	Rand McNally Designated Place
CDP	Census Designated Place
MCD	Minor Civil Division
⊡	County Seat
▲	Minor Civil Division
elev.	Elevation
🅿	Post Office
🅷	Hospital
🅲	College
■	Principal Business Center
★	Ranally Metro Area (RMA) Abbreviation
z	Zip Code(s)
℗	Previous Census Population
Ⓡ	Revised Census Population
Ⓐ	Annexation Population
●	Rand McNally Population Estimate
©	Final Census Population
Ⓢ	Special Census Population
◆	Estimated Population

For additional definitions see Glossary, Volume 1, and Introduction, Volume 2.

E

Eagarville; MACOUPIN; see Eagerville (Inc. Place)
Eagerville (Eagarville); Inc. Place; MACOUPIN; 171 M-7; mail Eagarville z 62023; Ⓟ 127; Ⓒ 128
Eagle; MCD-Township; LA SALLE; *170 F-10; mail Streator z 61364; Ⓟ 1,854; Ⓒ 1,845
Eagle Creek; MCD-Township; GALLATIN; *171 R-11; mail Equality z 62934; Ⓟ 207; Ⓒ 194
Eagle Heights; RMC Place; KANE; *170 B-11; elev. 881ft./269m.; ★ CHI; mail Elgin z 60123; ● 250
Eagle Lake; RMC Place; WILL; *170 E-13; ★ CHI; mail Beecher z 60401; ● 40
Eagle Park; RMC Place; MADISON; *171 O-6; ★ ST.L; mail Madison z 62060; pop. incl. with Madison (Inc. Place)
Eagle Point; MCD-Township; OGLE; *170 C-8; mail Polo z 61064; Ⓟ 288; Ⓒ 249
Eagle Point Bay; RMC Place; JOHNSON, WILLIAMSON; *171 R-10; mail Goreville z 62939; ● 350
Earl; MCD-Township; LA SALLE; *170 D-10; mail Earlville z 60518; Ⓟ 2,305; Ⓒ 2,653
Earl Estates; RMC Place; KANE; *170 C-11; elev. 730ft./223m.; ★ CHI; mail Sugar Grove z 60554; ● 75
Earlville; Inc. Place; LA SALLE; ▲ Earl; 170 D-10; elev. 705ft./215m.; 🄿; z 60518; Ⓟ 1,435; Ⓒ 1,778
East Alton; Inc. Place; MADISON; 171 N-6; elev. 440ft./134m.; 🄿; ★ ST.L; z 62024; Ⓟ 7,063; Ⓒ 6,830
East Bend; MCD-Township; CHAMPAIGN; *170 H-11; mail Dewey z 61840; Ⓟ 814; Ⓒ 880
East Brooklyn; Inc. Place; GRUNDY; *170 E-11; elev. 582ft./177m.; mail South Wilmington z 60474; Ⓟ 80; Ⓒ 123
East Cape Girardeau; Inc. Place; ALEXANDER; 171 T-8; elev. 349ft./106m.; mail Mc Clure z 62957; Ⓟ 451; Ⓒ 437
East Carondelet; Inc. Place; ST. CLAIR; 195 G-7; elev. 405ft./123m.; 🄿; ★ ST.L; z 62240; Ⓟ 630; Ⓒ 267; Ⓡ 318
East Chicago Heights; COOK; see Ford Heights (Inc. Place)
East Clinton; RMC Place; WHITESIDE; *170 C-6; ★ CLNT; mail Fulton z 61252
East Dubuque; Inc. Place; JO DAVIESS; 170 A-5; elev. 620ft./189m.; 🄿; ★ DUB; z 61025; Ⓟ 1,914; Ⓒ 1,995
East Dundee; Inc. Place; KANE, COOK; 172 E-2; elev. 800ft./244m.; 🄿; ★ CHI; z 60118; Ⓟ 2,721; Ⓒ 2,955
East Eldorado; MCD-Township; SALINE; *171 R-11; mail Eldorado z 62930; Ⓟ 6,526; Ⓒ 6,349
Eastern; MCD-Township; FRANKLIN; *171 Q-10; mail Benton z 62812; Ⓟ 602; Ⓒ 498
East Fork; MCD-Township; CLINTON; *171 N-9; Ⓟ 435; Ⓒ 409
East Fork; MCD-Township; MONTGOMERY; *171 M-8; mail Coffeen z 62017; Ⓟ 2,228; Ⓒ 2,403; Ⓡ 2,328
East Fulton (East Okie); RMC Place; WHITESIDE; ★ CLNT; mail Fulton z 61252; ● 300
East Galena; MCD-Township; JO DAVIESS; *170 A-6; mail Galena z 61036; Ⓟ 1,063; Ⓒ 1,192
East Galesburg; Inc. Place; KNOX; 170 F-6; elev. 700ft./213m.; 🄿; ★ GLSB; z 61430; Ⓟ 813; Ⓒ 839
Eastgate; RMC Place; MARION; *171 O-10; elev. 525ft./160m.; mail Salem z 62881; ● 100
East Gillespie; Inc. Place; MACOUPIN; *171 M-7; elev. 660ft./201m.; mail Gillespie z 62033; Ⓟ 205; Ⓒ 234
East Grove; MCD-Township; LEE; *170 D-8; mail Ohio z 61349; Ⓟ 292; Ⓒ 267
East Hannibal; RMC Place; PIKE; 171 K-3; elev. 463ft./141m.; mail Hull z 62343; ● 35
East Hardin; RMC Place; GREENE; 171 M-5; mail Fieldon z 62031; ● 30
East Hazel Crest; Inc. Place; COOK; 172 M-9; elev. 625ft./191m.; ★ CHI; mail Hazel Crest z 60429; Ⓟ 1,570; Ⓒ 1,607
East Joliet; RMC Place; WILL; *170 D-12; ★ CHI; pop. incl. with Joliet (Inc. Place)
East Keokuk; RMC Place; HANCOCK; mail Hamilton z 62341; pop. incl. with Hamilton (Inc. Place)
East Lincoln; MCD-Township; LOGAN; *170 I-9; mail Lincoln z 62656; Ⓟ 8,887; Ⓒ 9,209
East Loon Lake; RMC Place; LAKE; *170 A-12; ★ CHI; mail Antioch z 60002; ● 450
East Lynn; RMC Place; VERMILION; 170 H-13; elev. 697ft./212m.; 🄿; z 60932; ● 200
East Meadowbrook; RMC Place; MADISON; mail Moro z 62067
East Meadowview; RMC Place; KANKAKEE; ★ KANK; mail Bradley z 60915; pop. incl. with Bradley (Inc. Place)
East Moline; Inc. Place; ROCK ISLAND; 170 D-6; elev. 570ft./174m.; 🄿 🄷; ★ D-RI-M; z 61244; Ⓟ 20,147; Ⓒ 20,333; Ⓡ 21,431; ◆ 19,823
East Nelson; MCD-Township; MOULTRIE; *171 K-11; mail Sullivan z 61951; Ⓟ 997; Ⓒ 1,035
East Newbern; RMC Place; JERSEY; *171 M-6; elev. 638ft./194m.; mail Dow z 62022
East Oakland; MCD-Township; COLES; *171 K-12; mail Oakland z 61943; Ⓟ 1,447; Ⓒ 1,710; Ⓡ 1,600
East Okie; WHITESIDE; see East Fulton (RMC Place)
Easton; Inc. Place; MASON; 170 I-7; elev. 510ft./155m.; 🄿; z 62633; Ⓟ 351; Ⓒ 373
East Peoria; Inc. Place; TAZEWELL; 170 G-8; elev. 450ft./137m.; 🄿; ★ PEOR; z 61611, z 61630, z 61635; Ⓟ 21,378; Ⓒ 22,638; ◆ 22,697
East River; RMC Place; KANKAKEE; *170 F-13; ★ KANK; mail Saint Anne z 60964
East Rockford; RMC Place; WINNEBAGO; *170 A-9; ★ RKFD; mail Rockford z 61110; pop. incl. with Rockford (Inc. Place)
East Saint Louis; Inc. Place; ST. CLAIR; 171 O-6; elev. 410ft./125m.; 🄿 🄷 ■; ★ ST.L; z 62201-08; Ⓟ 40,944; Ⓒ 31,542; ◆ 30,476
East St. Louis; MCD-Township; ST. CLAIR; *171 O-6; 🄿 🄷; ★ ST.L; z 62201-08; coextensive with the City of East St. Louis; Ⓟ 40,944; Ⓒ 31,542
East Side; RMC Place; COOK; *170 C-13; ★ CHI; mail Chicago z 60617; pop. incl. with Chicago (Inc. Place)
East Side; RMC Place; KANKAKEE; *170 E-13; elev. 633ft./193m.; ★ KANK; mail Momence z 60954; ● 300
East Wenona; RMC Place; LA SALLE; *170 F-9; mail Wenona z 61377; ● 40
Eastwood; RMC Place; COOK; ★ CHI; pop. incl. with Arlington Heights (Inc. Place)
Eastwood Manor; RMC Place; MCHENRY; 172 A-3; ★ CHI; mail McHenry z 60050; ● 950
Eaton; RMC Place; CRAWFORD; 171 M-13; mail Robinson z 62454; ● 100
Eberle; RMC Place; EFFINGHAM; *171 N-11; elev. 549ft./167m.; mail Dieterich z 62424
Echo Lake; RMC Place; LAKE; 172 C-4; ★ CHI; mail Lake Zurich z 60047; ● 550
Eckard; RMC Place; MASON; *170 I-7; elev. 475ft./145m.; 🄿; z 62644; rural
Eco Park; RMC Place; DEKALB; *170 C-10; ★ DKLB; mail DeKalb z 60115; pop. incl. with DeKalb (Inc. Place)
Eddyville; Inc. Place; POPE; 171 S-11; elev. 662ft./202m.; 🄿; z 62928; Ⓟ 151; Ⓒ 153
Edelstein; RMC Place; PEORIA; 170 F-8; elev. 800ft./244m.; 🄿; z 61526; ● 160
Eden; MCD-Township; LA SALLE; *170 E-9; mail Tonica z 61370; Ⓟ 1,409; Ⓒ 1,318
Eden; RMC Place; PEORIA; *170 G-7; elev. 739ft./225m.; ★ PEOR; mail Hanna City z 61536; ● 50
Eden; RMC Place; RANDOLPH; 171 Q-7; mail Sparta z 62286; ● 220
Edford; MCD-Township; HENRY; *170 D-6; mail Geneseo z 61254; Ⓟ 664; Ⓒ 670
Edgar; RMC Place; EDGAR; ▲ Edgar; 171 K-13; mail Chrisman z 61924; ● 40
Edgar; MCD-Township; EDGAR; *171 K-13; mail Chrisman z 61924; Ⓟ 547; Ⓒ 508
EDGAR; 171 K-13; Ⓟ 19,595; Ⓒ 19,704; ◆ 18,673
Edgebrook; RMC Place; COOK; *170 B-13; ★ CHI; mail Chicago z 60646; pop. incl. with Chicago (Inc. Place)
Edgebrook; RMC Place; DEKALB; *170 C-10; elev. 850ft./259m.; ★ DKLB; mail Sycamore z 60178; pop. incl. with DeKalb (Inc. Place)
Edgemont; RMC Place; ST. CLAIR; *171 O-6; ★ ST.L; mail East Saint Louis z 62203; pop. incl. with East Saint Louis (Inc. Place)
Edgewater; RMC Place; COOK; ★ CHI; mail Chicago z 60640, z 60660; pop. incl. with Chicago (Inc. Place)
Edgewater Beach; RMC Place; CLINTON; *171 O-8; elev. 462ft./141m.; mail Carlyle z 62231; ● 60
Edgewood; RMC Place; CHAMPAIGN; *170 I-12; ★ CH-U; mail Urbana z 61802; ● 300
Edgewood; Inc. Place; EFFINGHAM; 171 N-10; elev. 564ft./172m.; 🄿; z 62426; Ⓟ 502; Ⓒ 527
Edgewood Heights; RMC Place; BOONE; *170 A-10; elev. 800ft./244m.; ★ RKFD; mail Belvidere z 61008; ● 140
Edgington; RMC Place; ROCK ISLAND; ▲ Edgington; 170 E-5; 🄿; z 61284; ● 450
Edgington; MCD-Township; ROCK ISLAND; *170 E-5; 🄿; z 61284; Ⓟ 1,619; Ⓒ 1,547
Edinburg; Inc. Place; CHRISTIAN; 171 K-8; elev. 590ft./180m.; 🄿; z 62531; Ⓟ 982; Ⓒ 1,135
Edison Park; RMC Place; COOK; ★ CHI; pop. incl. with Chicago (Inc. Place)
Edison Square; RMC Place; LAKE; *170 A-12; ★ CHI; mail Waukegan z 60079, z 60085; pop. incl. with Waukegan (Inc. Place)
Edwards; RMC Place; PEORIA; 170 G-7; elev. 504ft./154m.; 🄿; ★ PEOR; z 61528; ● 350
EDWARDS; 171 O-12; Ⓟ 7,440; Ⓒ 6,971; ◆ 6,579
Edwardsville; Inc. Place; ⊡ MADISON; 171 N-7; elev. 552ft./168m.; 🄿 🄲 13,449; ★ ST.L; z 62025-26; Ⓟ 14,579; Ⓒ 21,491; ◆ 23,509
Edwardsville; MCD-Township; MADISON; *171 N-7; 🄿 🄲 13,449; ★ ST.L; z 62025-26; includes part of the City of Edwardsville; Ⓟ 26,665; Ⓒ 33,731
Effingham; Inc. Place; ⊡ EFFINGHAM; 171 M-11; elev. 592ft./180m.; 🄿 🄷 ■; z 62401; Ⓟ 11,851; Ⓒ 12,384; ◆ 12,188
EFFINGHAM; 171 M-10; Ⓟ 31,704; Ⓒ 34,264; ◆ 33,889
Effner; RMC Place; IROQUOIS; *170 G-13; elev. 680ft./207m.; mail Sheldon z 60966; ● 20
Egan; RMC Place; OGLE; 170 B-8; elev. 826ft./252m.; 🄿; z 61047; ● 50
Egyptian Hills; RMC Place; WILLIAMSON; mail Creal Springs z 62922; ● 400
Egyptian Shores; RMC Place; WILLIAMSON; *171 R-10; mail Creal Springs z 62922; ● 300
Eight Mile Prairie; RMC Place; WILLIAMSON; *171 R-9; elev. 434ft./132m.; ★ CARB-; mail Carterville z 62918; ● 50
Eiker Addition; RMC Place; KNOX; *170 F-6; elev. 744ft./227m.; ★ GLSB; mail Knoxville z 61448; ● 200
Eileen; RMC Place; GRUNDY; *170 E-11; elev. 560ft./171m.; ★ CHI; mail Coal City z 60416; pop. incl. with Coal City (Inc. Place)
Ela; MCD-Township; LAKE; *170 B-12; ★ CHI; mail Lake Zurich z 60047; Ⓟ 32,433; Ⓒ 39,688
Elam Lake; RMC Place; MOULTRIE; *171 K-10; mail Sullivan z 61951; ● 150
Elba; RMC Place; GALLATIN; *171 R-11; mail Omaha z 62871; rural
Elba; MCD-Township; KNOX; *170 G-6; mail Williamsfield z 61489; Ⓟ 281; Ⓒ 278
Elba Center; RMC Place; KNOX; *170 G-7; elev. 706ft./215m.; mail Yates City z 61572; rural
Elbridge; RMC Place; EDGAR; 171 K-13; elev. 685ft./209m.; mail Paris z 61944; ● 80
Elbridge; MCD-Township; EDGAR; *171 K-13; mail Paris z 61944; Ⓟ 672; Ⓒ 798
Elburn; Inc. Place; KANE; 170 C-11; elev. 850ft./259m.; 🄿; ★ CHI; z 60119; Ⓟ 1,275; Ⓒ 2,756
Elco; RMC Place; ALEXANDER; 171 T-9; elev. 420ft./128m.; 🄿; z 62988; ● 150
El Dara; Inc. Place; PIKE; *171 K-4; elev. 741ft./226m.; mail Barry z 62312; Ⓟ 94; Ⓒ 89
Eldena; RMC Place; LEE; *170 C-8; elev. 787ft./240m.; 🄿; z 61324; ● 150
Elderville; RMC Place; HANCOCK; *170 H-3; elev. 673ft./205m.; mail Basco z 62313; rural
Eldorado; MCD-Township; MCDONOUGH; *170 H-5; mail Adair z 61411; Ⓟ 250; Ⓒ 227
Eldorado; Inc. Place; SALINE; 171 R-11; elev. 389ft./119m.; 🄿 🄷; z 62930; Ⓟ 4,536; Ⓒ 4,534
Eldred; Inc. Place; GREENE; 171 L-5; elev. 454ft./138m.; 🄿; z 62027; Ⓟ 254; Ⓒ 211
Eleanor; RMC Place; WARREN; *170 F-5; mail Little York z 61453; rural
Eleroy; RMC Place; STEPHENSON; 170 A-7; elev. 912ft./278m.; 🄿; z 61027; ● 120
Elgin; Inc. Place; KANE, COOK; ▲ Rutland, Campton, Plato; 170 B-11; elev. 752ft./229m.; 🄿 🄷 🄲 1,300 ■; ★ CHI; z 60120-21, z 60123-24 & mail Carol Stream z 60122; Ⓟ 77,010; Ⓒ 94,487; ◆ 114,976
Elgin; MCD-Township; KANE; *170 B-11; 🄿 🄲 1,300; ★ CHI; z 60120-21, z 60123-24; includes part of the City of Elgin; Ⓟ 72,355; Ⓒ 90,384
Elgin Estates; RMC Place; KANE; *170 B-11; elev. 821ft./250m.; ★ CHI; mail Elgin z 60123; ● 260
Eliza; RMC Place; MERCER; ▲ Eliza; *170 E-4; elev. 694ft./212m.; mail New Boston z 61272; ● 30
Eliza; MCD-Township; MERCER; *170 E-4; mail New Boston z 61272; Ⓟ 438; Ⓒ 398
Elizabeth; Inc. Place; JO DAVIESS; ▲ Elizabeth; 170 A-6; 🄿; z 61028; Ⓟ 641; Ⓒ 682
Elizabeth; MCD-Township; JO DAVIESS; *170 A-6; 🄿; z 61028; Ⓟ 1,050; Ⓒ 1,063
Elizabethtown; Inc. Place; ⊡ HARDIN; 171 S-11; elev. 357ft./109m.; 🄿; z 62931; Ⓟ 427; Ⓒ 348
Elk; MCD-Township; JACKSON; *171 Q-9; mail Elkville z 62932; Ⓟ 2,091; Ⓒ 2,001; Ⓡ 1,988
Elk Grove; MCD-Township; COOK; *170 B-12; ★ CHI; mail Elk Grove Village z 60007; Ⓟ 87,857; Ⓒ 94,969
Elk Grove Village; Inc. Place; COOK, DUPAGE; ▲ Elk Grove; 172 F-5; 🄿 🄷 ■; ★ CHI; z 60007, z 60009; Ⓟ 33,429; Ⓒ 34,727; ◆ 32,890
Elkhart; Inc. Place; LOGAN; 170 J-8; elev. 592ft./180m.; 🄿; z 62634; Ⓟ 475; Ⓒ 443
Elkhart; MCD-Township; LOGAN; *170 J-8; 🄿; z 62634; includes part of the village of Elkhart; Ⓟ 656; Ⓒ 582
Elkhorn; MCD-Township; BROWN; *170 J-5; mail Mount Sterling z 62353; Ⓟ 282; Ⓒ 285
Elkhorn Grove; MCD-Township; CARROLL; *170 C-7; mail Milledgeville z 61051; Ⓟ 243; Ⓒ 299
Elk Prairie; MCD-Township; JEFFERSON; *171 P-9; mail Bonnie z 62816; Ⓟ 754; Ⓒ 721
Elk Ridge Villa; RMC Place; COOK; ★ CHI; mail Mount Prospect z 60056; pop. incl. with Mount Prospect (Inc. Place)
Elkton; RMC Place; WASHINGTON; *171 P-8; mail Oakdale z 62268; ● 70
Elkville; Inc. Place; JACKSON; ▲ Elk; 171 Q-9; elev. 401ft./122m.; 🄿; z 62932; Ⓟ 958; Ⓒ 1,001; Ⓡ 988
Ellery; RMC Place; EDWARDS, WAYNE; 171 P-12; elev. 427ft./130m.; 🄿; z 62833; ● 50
Ellington; RMC Place; ADAMS; *170 J-3; elev. 724ft./221m.; ★ QUIN; mail Quincy z 62305; ● 40
Ellington; MCD-Township; ADAMS; *170 J-3; ★ QUIN; mail Quincy z 62305; Ⓟ 2,796; Ⓒ 2,911
Elliott; Inc. Place; FORD; 170 H-11; elev. 781ft./238m.; 🄿; z 60933; Ⓟ 309; Ⓒ 341
Elliottstown; RMC Place; EFFINGHAM; *171 M-11; elev. 568ft./173m.; mail Dieterich z 62424; ● 40
Ellis; RMC Place; VERMILION; *170 H-12; elev. 760ft./232m.; mail Potomac z 61865
Ellis Grove; Inc. Place; RANDOLPH; 171 Q-7; elev. 540ft./165m.; 🄿; z 62241; Ⓟ 353; Ⓒ 381
Ellison; MCD-Township; WARREN; *170 G-5; mail Smithshire z 61478; Ⓟ 360; Ⓒ 339
Ellisville; Inc. Place; FULTON; ▲ Ellisville; 170 G-6; 🄿; z 61431; Ⓟ 116; Ⓒ 87
Ellisville; MCD-Township; FULTON; *170 G-6; 🄿; z 61431; Ⓟ 222; Ⓒ 178
Ellsworth; Inc. Place; MCLEAN; *170 H-10; elev. 874ft./266m.; 🄿; z 61737; Ⓟ 224; Ⓒ 271
Ellwood Greens; RMC Place; DEKALB; *170 B-10; mail Genoa z 60135; ● 100
Elm Grove; MCD-Township; TAZEWELL; *170 H-8; ★ PEOR; mail Pekin z 61554; Ⓟ 2,675; Ⓒ 3,007
Elmhurst; Inc. Place; DUPAGE, COOK; 170 C-12; elev. 680ft./207m.; 🄿 🄷 🄲 3,107 ■; ★ CHI; z 60126; Ⓟ 42,029; Ⓒ 42,762; ◆ 43,599
Elmira; RMC Place; STARK; ▲ Elmira; 170 E-7; elev. 783ft./239m.; mail Toulon z 61483; ● 50
Elmira; MCD-Township; STARK; *170 E-7; mail Toulon z 61483; Ⓟ 412; Ⓒ 391
Elmore; RMC Place; PEORIA; *170 F-7; mail Laura z 61451; ● 100
El Morro; RMC Place; COOK; ★ CHI; mail Oak Forest z 60452; pop. incl. with Oak Forest (Inc. Place)
Elm River; MCD-Township; WAYNE; *171 O-11; mail Geff z 62842; Ⓟ 340; Ⓒ 319
Elmwood; Inc. Place; PEORIA; ▲ Elmwood; 170 G-7; elev. 643ft./196m.; 🄿; z 61529; Ⓟ 1,841; Ⓒ 1,945
Elmwood; MCD-Township; PEORIA; *170 G-7; 🄿; z 61529; Ⓟ 2,284; Ⓒ 2,392
Elmwood Park; Inc. Place; COOK; 172 H-7; elev. 625ft./191m.; 🄿; ★ CHI; z 60707; Ⓟ 23,206; Ⓒ 25,405; ◆ 25,638
El Paso; Inc. Place; WOODFORD; ▲ El Paso; 170 G-9; elev. 752ft./229m.; 🄿; z 61738; Ⓟ 2,499; Ⓒ 2,695
El Paso; MCD-Township; WOODFORD; *170 G-9; 🄿; z 61738; Ⓟ 2,985; Ⓒ 3,402
El-Rancho; RMC Place; KANKAKEE; *170 F-12; elev. 631ft./192m.; ★ KANK; mail Kankakee z 60901; ● 200
Elsah; Inc. Place; JERSEY; ▲ Elsah; 171 M-6; 🄿 🄲 502; ★ ST.L; z 62028; Ⓟ 851; Ⓒ 635
Elsah; MCD-Township; JERSEY; *171 M-6; 🄿 🄲 502; ★ ST.L; z 62028; Ⓟ 2,553; Ⓒ 2,425
Elsdon; RMC Place; COOK; *170 C-13; elev. 602ft./183m.; ★ CHI; mail Chicago z 60632; pop. incl. with Chicago (Inc. Place)
El Sierra; RMC Place; DUPAGE; ★ CHI; mail Downers Grove z 60515; pop. incl. with Downers Grove (Inc. Place)
Elva; RMC Place; DEKALB; *170 C-10; mail DeKalb z 60115; ● 30
Elvaston; Inc. Place; HANCOCK; 170 H-3; elev. 650ft./198m.; 🄿; z 62334; Ⓟ 198; Ⓒ 152
Elvira; RMC Place; JOHNSON; *171 S-9; elev. 450ft./137m.; mail Buncombe z 62912; rural
El Vista; RMC Place; COOK; ★ CHI; mail Oak Forest z 60452; pop. incl. with Oak Forest (Inc. Place)
El Vista; RMC Place; PEORIA; *170 G-8; ★ PEOR; mail Peoria z 61604; pop. incl. with Peoria (Inc. Place)
Elwin; RMC Place; MACON; 171 K-9; elev. 716ft./218m.; 🄿; ★ DEC; z 62532; ● 150
Elwood; MCD-Township; VERMILION; *170 J-13; ★ DANV; mail Ridge Farm z 61870; Ⓟ 1,773; Ⓒ 1,672
Elwood; Inc. Place; WILL; 170 E-12; elev. 650ft./198m.; 🄿; ★ CHI; z 60421; Ⓟ 951; Ⓒ 1,620
Embarrass; MCD-Township; EDGAR; *171 K-12; mail Redmon z 61949; Ⓟ 696; Ⓒ 658
Emden; Inc. Place; LOGAN; 170 I-8; elev. 590ft./180m.; 🄿; z 62635; Ⓟ 459; Ⓒ 515
Emerald Green; RMC Place; DUPAGE; ★ CHI; mail Warrenville z 60555; pop. incl. with Warrenville (Inc. Place)
Emerald Park; RMC Place; MCHENRY; 172 A-3; ★ CHI; mail McHenry z 60050; ● 400
Emerald Terrace; RMC Place; ST. CLAIR; *171 O-7; ★ ST.L; mail Belleville z 62226; pop. incl. with Swansea (Inc. Place)
Emerson; RMC Place; WHITESIDE; *170 C-7; mail Sterling z 61081; ● 100
Emerson City; RMC Place; JEFFERSON; *171 P-9; elev. 470ft./143m.; mail Scheller z 62883; rural
Eminence; MCD-Township; LOGAN; *170 I-8; mail Armington z 61721; Ⓟ 506; Ⓒ 507
Emington; Inc. Place; LIVINGSTON; 170 F-11; elev. 700ft./213m.; 🄿; z 60934; Ⓟ 135; Ⓒ 120
Emma; RMC Place; WHITE; ▲ Emma; 171 Q-12; 🄿; z 62834; ● 90
Emma; MCD-Township; WHITE; *171 Q-12; 🄿; z 62834; Ⓟ 507; Ⓒ 473
Emmet; MCD-Township; MCDONOUGH; *170 H-5; mail Macomb z 61455; Ⓟ 1,497; Ⓒ 1,318
Empire; MCD-Township; MCLEAN; *170 H-10; mail Le Roy z 61752; Ⓟ 3,379; Ⓒ 3,845
Empire Hills; RMC Place; KANE; *170 C-11; elev. 870ft./265m.; ★ CHI; mail Saint Charles z 60175; ● 50
Enchanted Forest; RMC Place; PEORIA; *170 G-8; ★ PEOR; mail Peoria z 61604; ● 1,190
Energy; Inc. Place; WILLIAMSON; 171 R-9; elev. 450ft./137m.; 🄿; ★ CARB-; z 62933; Ⓟ 1,106; Ⓒ 1,175
Enfield; Inc. Place; WHITE; ▲ Enfield; 171 Q-11; 🄿; z 62835; Ⓟ 683; Ⓒ 625
Enfield; MCD-Township; WHITE; *171 Q-11; 🄿; z 62835; Ⓟ 1,145; Ⓒ 1,017
Engelmann; MCD-Township; ST. CLAIR; *171 O-7; mail Mascoutah z 62258; Ⓟ 576; Ⓒ 654
England Heights; RMC Place; JACKSON; *171 R-9; elev. 532ft./162m.; ★ CARB-; mail Carbondale z 62901; ● 50
Englewood; RMC Place; COOK; *170 C-13; elev. 595ft./181m.; ★ CHI; mail Chicago z 60621; pop. incl. with Chicago (Inc. Place)
English; MCD-Township; JERSEY; *171 M-5; mail Jerseyville z 62052; Ⓟ 417; Ⓒ 480
Enion; RMC Place; FULTON; *170 I-6; elev. 461ft./141m.; 🄿; z 62644; rural
Enos; RMC Place; MACOUPIN; *171 L-7; 🄿; z 62626; rural
Enright; RMC Place; MCLEAN; *170 G-9; mail El Paso z 61738; rural
Enterprise; RMC Place; WAYNE; 171 O-11; mail Cisne z 62823; ● 40
Eola; RMC Place; DUPAGE; 172 J-3; elev. 720ft./219m.; 🄿; ★ CHI; z 60519; ● 100
Eppards Point; MCD-Township; LIVINGSTON; *170 G-10; mail Pontiac z 61764; Ⓟ 508; Ⓒ 472
Epworth; RMC Place; WHITE; *171 Q-12; mail Carmi z 62821
Epworth Park; BOONE; see Camp Epworth (RMC Place)
Equality; Inc. Place; GALLATIN; ▲ Equality; 171 R-11; 🄿; z 62934; Ⓟ 748; Ⓒ 721
Equality; MCD-Township; GALLATIN; *171 R-11; 🄿; z 62934; Ⓟ 1,023; Ⓒ 1,047
Erie; Inc. Place; WHITESIDE; ▲ Erie; 170 D-6; 🄿; z 61250; Ⓟ 1,572; Ⓒ 1,589
Erie; MCD-Township; WHITESIDE; *170 D-6; 🄿; z 61250; Ⓟ 2,032; Ⓒ 2,014
Erienna; MCD-Township; GRUNDY; *170 E-11; mail Morris z 60450; Ⓟ 924; Ⓒ 1,420
Erin; MCD-Township; STEPHENSON; *170 A-7; mail Eleroy z 61027; Ⓟ 482; Ⓒ 405
Erontenac; RMC Place; KANE; *170 B-11; elev. 800ft./244m.; ★ CHI; mail Dundee z 60118; ● 60
Esmen; MCD-Township; LIVINGSTON; *170 F-10; mail Odell z 60460; Ⓟ 360; Ⓒ 367
Esmond; RMC Place; DEKALB; *170 B-10; elev. 820ft./250m.; 🄿; z 60129; ● 100
Essex; Inc. Place; KANKAKEE; ▲ Essex; 170 E-12; elev. 590ft./180m.; 🄿; z 60935; Ⓟ 482; Ⓒ 554
Essex; MCD-Township; KANKAKEE; *170 E-12; 🄿; z 60935; Ⓟ 994; Ⓒ 1,294
Essex; MCD-Township; STARK; *170 F-7; mail Wyoming z 61491; Ⓟ 672; Ⓒ 675
Estate Lane; RMC Place; COOK; ★ CHI; mail Glenview z 60025; pop. incl. with Glenview (Inc. Place)
Etherton; RMC Place; JACKSON; *171 R-8; elev. 400ft./122m.; mail Murphysboro z 62966; rural
Etna (Aetna); RMC Place; COLES; 171 L-11; mail Mattoon z 61938; ● 60
Euclid Lake; RMC Place; COOK; ★ CHI; mail Mount Prospect z 60056; pop. incl. with Mount Prospect (Inc. Place)
Eureka; Inc. Place; ⊡ WOODFORD; 170 G-9; elev. 739ft./225m.; 🄿 🄲 575; ★ PEOR; z 61530; Ⓟ 4,435; Ⓒ 4,871
Evans; RMC Place; MARSHALL; *170 F-9; mail Wenona z 61377; rural
Evans; MCD-Township; MARSHALL; *170 F-9; mail Wenona z 61377; Ⓟ 1,219; Ⓒ 1,346
Evanston; Inc. Place; COOK; 170 B-13; elev. 600ft./183m.; 🄿 🄷 🄲 18,804 ■; ★ CHI; z 60201-04, z 60208-09; Ⓟ 73,233; Ⓒ 74,239; ◆ 74,751
Evanston; MCD-Township; COOK; *170 B-13; 🄿 🄷 🄲 18,804; ★ CHI; z 60201-04, z 60208-09; coextensive with the City of Evanston; Ⓟ 73,233; Ⓒ 74,239
Evanston North; RMC Place; COOK; *170 B-13; ★ CHI; mail Evanston z 60201; pop. incl. with Evanston (Inc. Place)
Evanston South; RMC Place; COOK; *170 B-13; ★ CHI; mail Evanston z 60202; pop. incl. with Evanston (Inc. Place)
Evansville; Inc. Place; RANDOLPH; 171 Q-7; elev. 400ft./122m.; 🄿; z 62242; Ⓟ 844; Ⓒ 724
Evarts; RMC Place; STEPHENSON; *170 B-8; mail Ridott z 61067
Evergreen Park; Inc. Place; COOK; 172 K-8; elev. 625ft./191m.; 🄿 🄷 ■; ★ CHI; z 60805; Ⓟ 20,874; Ⓒ 20,821; ◆ 19,854
Ewbanks; RMC Place; ADAMS; *170 J-3; elev. 712ft./217m.; ★ QUIN; mail Quincy z 62305; rural
Ewing; Inc. Place; FRANKLIN; ▲ Ewing; 171 Q-10; elev. 471ft./144m.; 🄿; z 62836; Ⓟ 264; Ⓒ 310
Ewing; MCD-Township; FRANKLIN; *171 Q-10; 🄿; z 62836; Ⓟ 1,263; Ⓒ 1,391
Exeter; Inc. Place; SCOTT; *171 K-5; elev. 520ft./158m.; 🄿; z 62621; Ⓟ 59; Ⓒ 70
Exline; RMC Place; KANKAKEE; *170 E-13; elev. 637ft./194m.; ★ KANK; mail Kankakee z 60901; rural
Expo Park; RMC Place; COOK, KANE; *170 B-12; ★ CHI; mail Hoffman Estates z 60192; pop. incl. with Hoffman Estates (Inc. Place)
Eylar; RMC Place; LIVINGSTON; *170 F-11; mail Saunemin z 61769; rural
Ezra; FRANKLIN; see Pershing (RMC Place)

F

Fairbanks; RMC Place; MOULTRIE; *171 K-11; elev. 679ft./207m.; mail Lovington z 61937; rural
Fairbury; Inc. Place; LIVINGSTON; 170 G-11; elev. 689ft./210m.; 🄿; z 61739; Ⓟ 3,643; Ⓒ 3,968
Fair City; UNION; see Valley Mission (RMC Place)
Fairdale; RMC Place; DEKALB; 170 B-10; elev. 776ft./237m.; mail Kirkland z 60146; ● 200
Fairfield; MCD-Township; BUREAU; *170 D-7; mail Tampico z 61283; Ⓟ 427; Ⓒ 380
Fairfield; RMC Place; LAKE; *170 B-12; elev. 858ft./262m.; ★ CHI; mail Lake Zurich z 60047; pop. incl. with Hawthorn Woods (Inc. Place)
Fairfield; Inc. Place; ⊡ WAYNE; 171 P-11; elev. 441ft./134m.; 🄿 🄷; z 62837; Ⓟ 5,439; Ⓒ 5,421
Fairfield Heights; RMC Place; STEPHENSON; *170 A-8; elev. 834ft./254m.; mail Freeport z 61032; ● 200
Fairgrange; RMC Place; COLES; *171 K-12; mail Charleston z 61920; ● 60
Fair Haven; RMC Place; CARROLL; ▲ Fairhaven; 170 C-7; elev. 795ft./242m.; mail Chadwick z 61014; ● 30
Fairhaven; MCD-Township; CARROLL; *170 B-7; mail Chadwick z 61014; Ⓟ 994; Ⓒ 888
Fairland; RMC Place; DOUGLAS; *170 J-12; mail Villa Grove z 61956; ● 80
Fairman; RMC Place; MARION; *171 N-9; mail Sandoval z 62882; ● 30
Fairmont; CDP; WILL; 172 M-4; ★ CHI; mail Lockport z 60441; Ⓟ 2,894; Ⓒ 2,563
Fairmont City; Inc. Place; ST. CLAIR, MADISON; ▲ Stites; 195 E-8; elev. 420ft./128m.; 🄿; ★ ST.L; z 62201; Ⓟ 2,140; Ⓒ 2,436
Fairmount; RMC Place; MADISON; *171 N-6; ★ ST.L; mail Godfrey z 62035; pop. incl. with Godfrey (Inc. Place)
Fairmount; RMC Place; MASSAC; mail Metropolis z 62960; ● 270
Fairmount; MCD-Township; PIKE; *170 J-4; mail Baylis z 62314; Ⓟ 265; Ⓒ 193
Fairmount; Inc. Place; VERMILION; 170 J-13; elev. 665ft./203m.; 🄿; z 61841; Ⓟ 678; Ⓒ 640
Fair Oaks; RMC Place; COOK; ★ CHI; mail Streamwood z 60107; pop. incl. with Streamwood (Inc. Place)
Fair Oaks; RMC Place; DUPAGE; *170 C-12; ★ CHI; mail West Chicago z 60185; ● 200
Fair Oaks; RMC Place; KANE; *170 C-11; elev. 850ft./259m.; ★ CHI; mail Saint Charles z 60175; ● 30
Fairview; RMC Place; CHRISTIAN; *171 K-9; elev. 611ft./186m.; mail Taylorville z 62568
Fairview; Inc. Place; FULTON; ▲ Fairview; 170 G-6; elev. 745ft./227m.; 🄿; z 61432; Ⓟ 510; Ⓒ 493
Fairview; MCD-Township; FULTON; *170 G-6; 🄿; z 61432; Ⓟ 702; Ⓒ 708
Fairview; RMC Place; ST. CLAIR; *171 O-6; ★ ST.L; mail Caseyville z 62232
Fairview Addition; RMC Place; SALINE; *171 R-11; elev. 408ft./124m.; mail Eldorado z 62930; ● 100
Fairview Gardens; RMC Place; COOK; ★ CHI; mail Mount Prospect z 60056; pop. incl. with Mount Prospect (Inc. Place)
Fairview Heights; Inc. Place; ST. CLAIR; 171 O-7; elev. 595ft./181m.; 🄿 ■; ★ ST.L; z 62208 & mail Caseyville z 62232; Ⓟ 14,351; Ⓒ 15,034; ◆ 16,107
Fairway; RMC Place; KNOX; *170 F-6; elev. 788ft./240m.; ★ GLSB; mail Galesburg z 61401; ● 30
Fairway Estates; RMC Place; COOK; ★ CHI; mail Orland Park z 60462; pop. incl. with Orland Park (Inc. Place)
Fairway Estates; RMC Place; DUPAGE; ★ CHI; mail Wheaton z 60187; pop. incl. with Wheaton (Inc. Place)
Fairweather; ADAMS; see Kingston (RMC Place)
Fall Creek; RMC Place; ADAMS; ▲ Fall Creek; 170 J-3; mail Payson z 62360; ● 40
Fall Creek; MCD-Township; ADAMS; *170 J-3; mail Payson z 62360; Ⓟ 568; Ⓒ 620
Fall River; MCD-Township; LA SALLE; *170 E-10; mail Ottawa z 61350; Ⓟ 885; Ⓒ 850
Falmouth; RMC Place; JASPER; *171 M-12; elev. 544ft./166m.; mail Newton z 62448; ● 30
Fancher; RMC Place; SHELBY; 171 L-10; elev. 616ft./188m.; mail Mode z 62444; ● 75
Fancy Creek; MCD-Township; SANGAMON; *170 J-8; ★ SPRG; mail Sherman z 62684; Ⓟ 3,293; Ⓒ 4,145
Fancy Prairie; RMC Place; MENARD; 170 J-8; elev. 618ft./188m.; 🄿; z 62613; ● 100
Fandon; RMC Place; MCDONOUGH; 170 H-5; mail Colchester z 62326; ● 60
Fargo; RMC Place; BROWN; *170 J-4; mail Timewell z 62375; rural
Farina; Inc. Place; FAYETTE, MARION; 171 N-10; elev. 580ft./177m.; 🄿; z 62838; Ⓟ 575; Ⓒ 558
Farmer City; Inc. Place; DE WITT; 170 I-10; elev. 724ft./221m.; 🄿; z 61842; Ⓟ 2,114; Ⓒ 2,055
Farmers; MCD-Township; FULTON; *170 H-6; mail Table Grove z 61482; Ⓟ 429; Ⓒ 400
Farmersville; Inc. Place; MONTGOMERY; 171 L-8; elev. 643ft./196m.; 🄿; z 62533; Ⓟ 698; Ⓒ 768
Farmingdale; RMC Place; DUPAGE; 172 J-6; ★ CHI; mail Darien z 60561; ● 970
Farmingdale; RMC Place; SANGAMON; *170 J-7; elev. 587ft./179m.; 🄿; ★ SPRG; z 62677; ● 50
Farmingdale South; RMC Place; DUPAGE; ★ CHI; mail Darien z 60561; pop. incl. with Darien (Inc. Place)
Farmingdale Terrace; RMC Place; DUPAGE; ★ CHI; mail Darien z 60561; pop. incl. with Darien (Inc. Place)
Farmingdale Village; RMC Place; DUPAGE; ★ CHI; mail Darien z 60561; pop. incl. with Darien (Inc. Place)
Farmington; COLES; see Campbell (RMC Place)
Farmington; Inc. Place; FULTON, PEORIA; ▲ Farmington, Trivoli; 170 G-7; elev. 752ft./229m.; 🄿; z 61531; Ⓟ 2,535; Ⓒ 2,601
Farmington; MCD-Township; FULTON; *170 G-6; 🄿; z 61531; Ⓟ 3,469; Ⓒ 3,358
Farmington; RMC Place; KANE; *170 C-11; elev. 727ft./222m.; ★ CHI; mail Saint Charles z 60174; ● 180
Farm Ridge; MCD-Township; LA SALLE; *170 E-10; mail Grand Ridge z 61325; Ⓟ 971; Ⓒ 898
Farmsted; RMC Place; DUPAGE; ★ CHI; mail Naperville z 60565; pop. incl. with Naperville (Inc. Place)
Farnsworth; RMC Place; LAKE; ★ CHI; mail Great Lakes z 60088; pop. incl. with Waukegan (Inc. Place)
Farrington; MCD-Township; JEFFERSON; *171 O-10; mail Bluford z 62814; Ⓟ 538; Ⓒ 552
Farrow; RMC Place; PEORIA; *170 G-8; ★ PEOR; mail Peoria z 61605; ● 680
Fayette; RMC Place; GREENE; *171 L-6; elev. 563ft./172m.; mail Greenfield z 62044; ● 40
Fayette; MCD-Township; LIVINGSTON; *170 G-11; mail Strawn z 61775; Ⓟ 322; Ⓒ 264
FAYETTE; 171 M-9; Ⓟ 20,893; Ⓒ 21,802; ◆ 20,720
Fayetteville; Inc. Place; ST. CLAIR; ▲ Fayetteville; 171 P-7; 🄿; z 62258; Ⓟ 371; Ⓒ 384
Fayetteville; MCD-Township; ST. CLAIR; *171 P-7; 🄿; z 62258; Ⓟ 1,599; Ⓒ 1,656
Fayville; RMC Place; ALEXANDER; *171 T-8; mail Thebes z 62990
Feehanville; RMC Place; COOK; ★ CHI; mail Mount Prospect z 60056; pop. incl. with Mount Prospect (Inc. Place)
Felix; MCD-Township; GRUNDY; *170 E-11; ★ CHI; mail Coal City z 60416; Ⓟ 3,869; Ⓒ 4,009
Felker; RMC Place; TAZEWELL; ★ PEOR; mail Washington z 61571; pop. incl. with Washington (Inc. Place)
Fenton; RMC Place; WHITESIDE; ▲ Fenton; 170 C-7; 🄿; z 61251; ● 170
Fenton; MCD-Township; WHITESIDE; *170 C-7; 🄿; z 61251; Ⓟ 557; Ⓒ 547
Fergestown; RMC Place; WILLIAMSON; *171 R-9; elev. 451ft./137m.; ★ CARB-; mail Johnston City z 62951, Marion z 62959; ● 200
Ferrel; RMC Place; EDGAR; *171 K-13; elev. 600ft./183m.; mail Paris z 61944; rural
Ferrin; RMC Place; CLINTON; *171 O-9; mail Carlyle z 62231; ● 60
Ferris; Inc. Place; HANCOCK; 170 H-3; elev. 680ft./207m.; 🄿; z 62336; Ⓟ 177; Ⓒ 168
Fetzer; RMC Place; SANGAMON; ★ SPRG; pop. incl. with Springfield (Inc. Place)
Fiatt; RMC Place; FULTON; 170 H-6; elev. 680ft./207m.; 🄿; z 61433; ● 200
Ficklin; RMC Place; DOUGLAS; *170 J-11; elev. 677ft./206m.; mail Tuscola z 61953; rural
Fiday View; RMC Place; WILL; *170 D-12; ★ CHI; mail Joliet z 60435; pop. incl. with Joliet (Inc. Place)
Fidelity; Inc. Place; JERSEY; ▲ Fidelity; *171 M-6; elev. 630ft./192m.; 🄿; z 62030; Ⓟ 66; Ⓒ 105
Fidelity; MCD-Township; JERSEY; *171 M-6; 🄿; z 62030; Ⓟ 655; Ⓒ 674
Field; MCD-Township; JEFFERSON; *171 O-10; mail Texico z 62889; Ⓟ 1,159; Ⓒ 1,460
Fieldcrest; RMC Place; COOK; ★ CHI; mail Oak Forest z 60452; pop. incl. with Oak Forest (Inc. Place)
Fieldon; Inc. Place; JERSEY; 171 M-5; elev. 700ft./213m.; 🄿; z 62031; Ⓟ 277; Ⓒ 271
Fields West; RMC Place; CHAMPAIGN; *170 I-11; elev. 723ft./220m.; ★ CH-U; mail Champaign z 61822; ● 230
Fillmore; Inc. Place; MONTGOMERY; ▲ Fillmore; 171 M-9; 🄿; z 62032; Ⓟ 326; Ⓒ 362
Fillmore; MCD-Township; MONTGOMERY; *171 M-9; 🄿; z 62032; Ⓟ 739; Ⓒ 660
Filson; RMC Place; DOUGLAS; *171 K-12; elev. 648ft./198m.; mail Arcola z 61910; ● 30
Findlay; Inc. Place; SHELBY; 171 K-10; elev. 673ft./205m.; 🄿; z 62534; Ⓟ 787; Ⓒ 723
Finney Heights; RMC Place; CLINTON; mail Centralia z 62801; ● 250
Fisher; Inc. Place; CHAMPAIGN; 170 I-11; elev. 740ft./226m.; 🄿; z 61843; Ⓟ 1,526; Ⓒ 1,647
Fishhook; RMC Place; PIKE; 170 J-4; elev. 756ft./230m.; mail Baylis z 62314; ● 30
Fithian; Inc. Place; VERMILION; 170 I-12; elev. 659ft./201m.; 🄿; z 61844; Ⓟ 512; Ⓒ 506
Five Islands Park; RMC Place; KANE; 172 G-2; ★ CHI; mail South Elgin z 60177; ● 220
Flag Center; RMC Place; OGLE; 170 C-9; mail Rochelle z 61068; ● 100
Flagg; RMC Place; OGLE; ▲ Flagg; *170 C-9; elev. 783ft./239m.; mail Rochelle z 61068; ● 30
Flagg; MCD-Township; OGLE; *170 C-9; mail Rochelle z 61068; Ⓟ 11,841; Ⓒ 13,276
Flamingo Estates; RMC Place; RANDOLPH; *171 Q-8; elev. 490ft./149m.; mail Sparta z 62286; ● 30
Flanagan; Inc. Place; LIVINGSTON; 170 G-10; elev. 666ft./203m.; 🄿; z 61740; Ⓟ 987; Ⓒ 1,083
Flannigan; MCD-Township; HAMILTON; *171 Q-10; mail Thompsonville z 62890; Ⓟ 258; Ⓒ 301
Flat Branch; MCD-Township; SHELBY; *171 K-9; mail Moweaqua z 62550; Ⓟ 438; Ⓒ 463
Flat Rock; Inc. Place; CRAWFORD; 171 N-13; elev. 493ft./150m.; 🄿; z 62427; Ⓟ 421; Ⓒ 415
Flatville; RMC Place; CHAMPAIGN; 170 I-12; elev. 685ft./209m.; mail Thomasboro z 61878; ● 60
Flat Woods; RMC Place; JOHNSON; *171 S-10; elev. 526ft./160m.; mail Simpson z 62985; rural
Fletcher; RMC Place; MCLEAN; *170 H-10; mail Bloomington z 61701, Cooksville z 61730; rural
Flickerville; RMC Place; KANKAKEE; *170 E-12; ★ KANK; mail Bourbonnais z 60914; rural
Flint; MCD-Township; PIKE; *171 K-5; mail Griggsville z 62340; Ⓟ 118; Ⓒ 108
Flora; MCD-Township; BOONE; *170 B-10; mail Belvidere z 61008; Ⓟ 1,698; Ⓒ 2,175
Flora; Inc. Place; CLAY; 171 O-11; elev. 497ft./151m.; 🄿 🄷; z 62839; Ⓟ 5,054; Ⓒ 5,086
Floraville; RMC Place; ST. CLAIR; 171 P-6; ★ ST.L; mail Waterloo z 62298; ● 100
Florence; Inc. Place; PIKE; 171 K-5; elev. 438ft./134m.; mail Pittsfield z 62363; Ⓟ 45; Ⓒ 71
Florence (Florence Station); RMC Place; STEPHENSON; ▲ Florence; *170 B-8; mail Freeport z 61032; ● 100
Florence; MCD-Township; STEPHENSON; *170 B-8; mail Freeport z 61032; Ⓟ 1,332; Ⓒ 1,305
Florence; MCD-Township; WILL; *170 E-12; mail Wilmington z 60481; Ⓟ 720; Ⓒ 642
Florence Station; STEPHENSON; see Florence (RMC Place)
Florid; RMC Place; PUTNAM; *170 E-9; mail Hennepin z 61327; ● 30
Flossmoor; Inc. Place; COOK; 172 M-9; elev. 674ft./205m.; 🄿; ★ CHI; z 60422; Ⓟ 8,651; Ⓒ 9,301
Flossmoor Highlands; RMC Place; COOK; *170 D-13; ★ CHI; mail Flossmoor z 60422; pop. incl. with Flossmoor (Inc. Place)
Floyd; MCD-Township; WARREN; *170 G-5; mail Cameron z 61423; Ⓟ 535; Ⓒ 514
Fondulac; MCD-Township; TAZEWELL; *170 G-8; ★ PEOR; mail East Peoria z 61611; Ⓟ 12,821; Ⓒ 13,138
Fon-Du-Lac; RMC Place; WILL; ★ CHI; mail Plainfield z 60544; ● 200
Foosland; Inc. Place; CHAMPAIGN; *170 H-11; elev. 740ft./226m.; 🄿; z 61845; Ⓟ 132; Ⓒ 90
FORD; 170 H-11; Ⓟ 14,275; Ⓒ 14,241; ◆ 14,298
Fordham; RMC Place; COOK; ★ CHI; mail Chicago z 60619; pop. incl. with Chicago (Inc. Place)
Ford Heights (East Chicago Heights); Inc. Place; COOK; 172 N-10; elev. 637ft./194m.; 🄿; ★ CHI; z 60411; Ⓟ 4,259; Ⓒ 3,456
Forest City; Inc. Place; MASON; ▲ Forest City; 170 H-7; 🄿; z 61532; Ⓟ 321; Ⓒ 287
Forest City; MCD-Township; MASON; *170 H-7; 🄿; z 61532; Ⓟ 670; Ⓒ 697
Forest Estates; RMC Place; COOK; *170 B-12; ★ CHI; mail Palatine z 60067; ● 550
Forest Gardens; RMC Place; LAKE; *170 A-12; ★ CHI; mail Wauconda z 60084; ● 80
Forest Glen; RMC Place; COOK; ★ CHI; mail Chicago z 60646; pop. incl. with Chicago (Inc. Place)
Foresthaven; RMC Place; LAKE; *170 A-12; ★ CHI; mail Lake Forest z 60045; ● 250
Forest Heights; RMC Place; COOK; ★ CHI; mail Chicago Heights z 60411; pop. incl. with Chicago Heights (Inc. Place)
Forest Hill; RMC Place; COOK; ★ CHI; mail Chicago z 60652; pop. incl. with Chicago (Inc. Place)
Forest Hills Estates; RMC Place; FAYETTE; *171 M-9; elev. 575ft./175m.; mail Vandalia z 62471; ● 120
Forest Homes; RMC Place; MADISON; 195 A-8; ★ ST.L; mail Cottage Hills z 62018; ● 1,700
Forest Lake; CDP; LAKE; 172 C-5; ★ CHI; mail Lake Zurich z 60047; Ⓟ 1,371; Ⓒ 1,530
Forest Manor; RMC Place; WILL; *170 D-12; ★ CHI; mail Lockport z 60441; ● 350
Forest Park; Inc. Place; COOK; 172 I-7; elev. 620ft./189m.; 🄿 🄷; ★ CHI; z 60130; Ⓟ 14,918; Ⓒ 15,688
Forest Park; RMC Place; WILL; *170 D-12; ★ CHI; pop. incl. with Joliet (Inc. Place)
Forest View; Inc. Place; COOK; 172 I-8; elev. 600ft./183m.; 🄿; ★ CHI; z 60402 & mail Chicago z 60638; Ⓟ 743; Ⓒ 778
Forest View Hills; RMC Place; COOK; ★ CHI; mail Oak Forest z 60452; pop. incl. with Oak Forest (Inc. Place)
Forman; RMC Place; JOHNSON; *171 S-10; elev. 352ft./107m.; mail Belknap z 62908; rural
Forrest; Inc. Place; LIVINGSTON; ▲ Forrest; 170 G-11; elev. 688ft./210m.; 🄿; z 61741; Ⓟ 1,124; Ⓒ 1,225
Forrest; MCD-Township; LIVINGSTON; *170 G-11; 🄿; z 61741; Ⓟ 1,521; Ⓒ 1,597
Forrestal Village; RMC Place; LAKE; ★ CHI; mail Great Lakes z 60088; pop. incl. with North Chicago (Inc. Place)
Forreston; Inc. Place; OGLE; ▲ Forreston; 170 B-8; elev. 937ft./286m.; 🄿; z 61030; Ⓟ 1,361; Ⓒ 1,469
Forreston; MCD-Township; OGLE; *170 B-8; 🄿; z 61030; Ⓟ 2,032; Ⓒ 2,122
Forsyth; Inc. Place; MACON; 170 J-10; elev. 678ft./207m.; 🄿; ★ DEC; z 62535; Ⓟ 1,275; Ⓒ 2,434
Fort Dearborn; RMC Place; COOK; *170 C-13; ★ CHI; mail Chicago z 60610-11; pop. incl. with Chicago (Inc. Place)
Fort Gage; RMC Place; RANDOLPH; *171 Q-7; elev. 400ft./122m.; mail Ellis Grove z 62241; ● 30
Fort Russell; MCD-Township; MADISON; *171 N-7; ★ ST.L; mail Bethalto z 62010; Ⓟ 6,534; Ⓒ 7,710
Forty-Seventh Street; RMC Place; COOK; pop. incl. with Chicago (Inc. Place)
Foss Acres; RMC Place; LAKE; ★ CHI; mail Great Lakes z 60088; pop. incl. with Waukegan (Inc. Place)
Foster; MCD-Township; MADISON; *171 M-6; ★ ST.L; mail Alton z 62002; Ⓟ 3,719; Ⓒ 4,172
Foster; MCD-Township; MARION; *171 N-9; mail Alma z 62807; Ⓟ 342; Ⓒ 405
Fosterburg; RMC Place; MADISON; 171 M-6; ★ ST.L; mail Alton z 62002, Bethalto z 62010; ● 250
Foster Pond; RMC Place; MONROE; *171 P-6; mail Waterloo z 62298
Fountain; RMC Place; MONROE; *171 P-6; mail Valmeyer z 62295
Fountain Bluff; MCD-Township; JACKSON; *171 R-8; mail Jacob z 62950; Ⓟ 304; Ⓒ 276
Fountain Creek; RMC Place; IROQUOIS; ▲ Fountain Creek; *170 H-13; elev. 679ft./207m.; mail Hoopeston z 60942; rural
Fountain Creek; MCD-Township; IROQUOIS; *170 H-13; mail Hoopeston z 60942; Ⓟ 414; Ⓒ 440
Fountain Gap; RMC Place; MONROE; *171 P-6; mail Columbia z 62236; rural
Fountain Green; RMC Place; HANCOCK; ▲ Fountain Green; 170 H-4; mail Carthage z 62321, La Harpe z 61450; ● 120
Fountain Green; MCD-Township; HANCOCK; *170 H-4; mail Carthage z 62321; Ⓟ 381; Ⓒ 329
Four Lakes; RMC Place; DUPAGE; *170 C-12; ★ CHI; mail Lisle z 60532; ● 2,000
Four Mile; MCD-Township; WAYNE; *171 P-10; mail Wayne City z 62895; Ⓟ 551; Ⓒ 584
Fowler; RMC Place; ADAMS; 170 J-3; elev. 725ft./221m.; 🄿; z 62338; ● 400
Fox; MCD-Township; JASPER; *171 N-12; mail Newton z 62448; Ⓟ 593; Ⓒ 515
Fox; RMC Place; KENDALL; ▲ Fox; *170 D-11; mail Yorkville z 60560; rural
Fox; MCD-Township; KENDALL; *170 D-11; mail Yorkville z 60560; Ⓟ 1,146; Ⓒ 1,257
Fox Chase; RMC Place; KANE; *170 C-11; elev. 760ft./232m.; ★ CHI; mail Saint Charles z 60174; pop. incl. with Saint Charles (Inc. Place)
Foxfield; RMC Place; KANE; *170 C-11; elev. 900ft./274m.; ★ CHI; mail Saint Charles z 60175; ● 100
Fox Lake; Inc. Place; LAKE, MCHENRY; 170 A-12; elev. 750ft./229m.; 🄿; ★ CHI; z 60020; Ⓟ 7,478; Ⓒ 9,178
Fox Lake Hills; CDP; LAKE; *170 A-12; ★ CHI; mail Lake Villa z 60046; Ⓟ 2,681; Ⓒ 2,561
Fox Lake Vista; RMC Place; LAKE; *170 A-12; ★ CHI; mail Spring Grove z 60081; pop. incl. with Fox Lake (Inc. Place)
Fox Lawn; RMC Place; KENDALL; *170 D-11; elev. 652ft./199m.; ★ CHI; mail Yorkville z 60560; ● 240
Fox Point; RMC Place; COOK, LAKE; *170 B-12; elev. 830ft./253m.; ★ CHI; mail Barrington z 60010; pop. incl. with Barrington (Inc. Place)
Fox River Bluffs 2; RMC Place; KANE; *170 B-11; elev. 850ft./259m.; ★ CHI; mail Dundee z 60118; ● 120
Fox River Estates; RMC Place; KANE; *170 C-11; ★ CHI; mail Saint Charles z 60174; ● 500
Fox River Gardens; RMC Place; KENDALL; *170 D-11; elev. 600ft./183m.; ★ CHI; mail Yorkville z 60560; ● 300
Fox River Grove; Inc. Place; MCHENRY, LAKE; 170 B-11; elev. 750ft./229m.; 🄿; ★ CHI; z 60021; Ⓟ 3,551; Ⓒ 4,862
Fox River Heights; RMC Place; KANE; ★ CHI; mail Saint Charles z 60174
Fox River Valley Gardens; MCHENRY, LAKE; see Port Barrington (Inc. Place)
Fox Valley East; RMC Place; DUPAGE; *170 C-12; ★ CHI; mail Aurora z 60505; pop. incl. with Aurora (Inc. Place)
Fox Valley Villages; RMC Place; DUPAGE; ★ CHI; mail Aurora z 60505; pop. incl. with Aurora (Inc. Place)
Frankfort; MCD-Township; FRANKLIN; *171 Q-10; ★ CARB-; mail West Frankfort z 62896; Ⓟ 7,317; Ⓒ 7,153; Ⓡ 7,149
Frankfort; Inc. Place; WILL; ▲ Frankfort, Green Garden, Monee; 170 D-12; elev. 767ft./234m.; 🄿; ★ CHI; z 60423; Ⓟ 7,180; Ⓒ 10,391
Frankfort; MCD-Township; WILL; *170 D-13; 🄿; ★ CHI; z 60423; Ⓟ 25,755; Ⓒ 41,292
Frankfort Heights; RMC Place; FRANKLIN; *171 Q-10; elev. 400ft./122m.; 🄿; ★ CARB-; z 62840; pop. incl. with West Frankfort (Inc. Place)
Frankfort Square; CDP-Census Area Only; WILL; ▲ Frankfort; *170 D-13; elev. 700ft./213m.; ★ CHI; mail Frankfort z 60423; Ⓟ 6,227; Ⓒ 7,766
Franklin; MCD-Township; DEKALB; *170 B-10; mail Kirkland z 60146; Ⓟ 1,879; Ⓒ 2,026
Franklin; Inc. Place; MORGAN; 171 K-6; elev. 678ft./207m.; 🄿; z 62638; Ⓟ 634; Ⓒ 586
FRANKLIN; 171 Q-10; Ⓟ 40,319; Ⓒ 39,018; Ⓡ 39,029; ◆ 39,296
Franklin Grove; Inc. Place; LEE; 170 C-9; elev. 810ft./247m.; 🄿; z 61031; Ⓟ 968; Ⓒ 1,052
Franklin Grove (China); MCD-Township; LEE; *170 C-9; mail Amboy z 61310; Ⓟ 1,389; Ⓒ 1,472
Franklin Park; Inc. Place; COOK; 172 G-7; elev. 641ft./195m.; 🄿 ■; ★ CHI; z 60131; Ⓟ 18,485; Ⓒ 19,434; ◆ 19,489
Franklin Square; RMC Place; WILL; *170 D-13; ★ CHI; mail Frankfort z 60423; ● 1,200
Franklinville; RMC Place; MCHENRY; *170 A-11; mail Woodstock z 60098
Frederick; RMC Place; SCHUYLER; 170 I-5; elev. 448ft./137m.; 🄿; z 62639; ● 100
Frederick; MCD-Township; SCHUYLER; *170 I-5; 🄿; z 62639; Ⓟ 164; Ⓒ 181
Freeburg; Inc. Place; ST. CLAIR; 171 O-7; elev. 518ft./158m.; 🄿; ★ ST.L; z 62243; Ⓟ 3,115; Ⓒ 3,872
Freeburg; MCD-Township; ST. CLAIR; *171 O-7; 🄿; ★ ST.L; z 62243; Ⓟ 4,710; Ⓒ 5,124
Freedom; MCD-Township; CARROLL; *170 B-7; mail Lanark z 61046; Ⓟ 433; Ⓒ 609
Freedom; MCD-Township; LA SALLE; *170 D-10; mail Ottawa z 61350; Ⓟ 635; Ⓒ 696
Freeman Spur; Inc. Place; WILLIAMSON, FRANKLIN; *171 Q-9; elev. 427ft./130m.; 🄿; ★ CARB-; z 62841; Ⓟ 290; Ⓒ 273
Freeport; Inc. Place; ⊡ STEPHENSON; 170 A-8; elev. 780ft./238m.; 🄿 🄷 ■; z 61032; Ⓟ 25,840; Ⓒ 26,443; ◆ 24,837
Freeport; MCD-Township; STEPHENSON; *170 A-8; 🄿 🄷; z 61032; coextensive with the City of Freeport; Ⓟ 25,840; Ⓒ 26,443
Fremont; MCD-Township; LAKE; *170 A-12; ★ CHI; mail Mundelein z 60060; Ⓟ 14,280; Ⓒ 23,955
Fremont Center; RMC Place; LAKE; *170 A-12; elev. 790ft./241m.; ★ CHI; mail Mundelein z 60060; rural
Fremont Junction; RMC Place; COOK; ★ CHI; mail Hanover Park z 60133; pop. incl. with Hanover Park (Inc. Place)
Frenchman's Cove; RMC Place; COOK; ★ CHI; mail Arlington Heights z 60004; pop. incl. with Arlington Heights (Inc. Place)
French Village; RMC Place; ST. CLAIR; *171 O-6; ★ ST.L; mail Fairview Heights z 62208; pop. incl. with Fairview Heights (Inc. Place)
Frentress Lake; RMC Place; JO DAVIESS; *170 A-5; elev. 617ft./188m.; ★ DUB; mail East Dubuque z 61025; ● 200
Friends Creek; MCD-Township; MACON; *170 J-10; mail Argenta z 62501; Ⓟ 1,429; Ⓒ 1,456
Friendsville; RMC Place; WABASH; *171 O-13; elev. 475ft./145m.; mail Mount Carmel z 62863; ● 80
Frisco; RMC Place; FRANKLIN; *171 Q-10; elev. 464ft./141m.; mail Ewing z 62836; rural
Frog City; RMC Place; ALEXANDER; *171 T-9; elev. 320ft./98m.; mail Cairo z 62914; rural
Frogtown; RMC Place; CLINTON; *171 O-8; elev. 456ft./139m.; mail Carlyle z 62231; rural
Frogtown; RMC Place; WASHINGTON; *171 O-8; mail Okawville z 62271; rural
Frontenac; RMC Place; DUPAGE; *170 C-11; elev. 711ft./217m.; ★ CHI; mail Naperville z 60563; pop. incl. with Aurora (Inc. Place)
Frontenac Place; RMC Place; MADISON; mail Godfrey z 62035; ● 80
Frost; RMC Place; JACKSON; *171 R-9; elev. 450ft./137m.; ★ CARB-; mail Carbondale z 62901
Fruit; RMC Place; MADISON; *171 N-7; mail Edwardsville z 62025
Fruitland; RMC Place; ROCK ISLAND; *170 D-5; elev. 573ft./175m.; ★ D-RI-M; mail Moline z 61265; ● 1,300
Fuller Park; RMC Place; COOK; ★ CHI; mail Chicago z 60609; pop. incl. with Chicago (Inc. Place)
Fulton; Inc. Place; WHITESIDE; ▲ Fulton; 170 C-6; 🄿; ★ CLNT; z 61252; Ⓟ 3,698; Ⓒ 3,881
Fulton; MCD-Township; WHITESIDE; *170 C-6; 🄿; ★ CLNT; z 61252; Ⓟ 4,373; Ⓒ 4,602
FULTON; 170 H-6; Ⓟ 38,080; Ⓒ 38,250; ◆ 36,481
Fults; Inc. Place; MONROE; 171 P-6; elev. 390ft./119m.; 🄿; z 62244; Ⓟ 45; Ⓒ 28
Funkhouser; RMC Place; EFFINGHAM; *171 M-10; elev. 584ft./178m.; mail Effingham z 62401
Funks Grove; RMC Place; MCLEAN; ▲ Funks Grove; *170 H-9; mail Mc Lean z 61754
Funks Grove; MCD-Township; MCLEAN; *170 H-9; mail Mc Lean z 61754; Ⓟ 302; Ⓒ 293
Future City; RMC Place; ALEXANDER; 171 T-9; mail Cairo z 62914; ● 150
Fyre Lake; RMC Place; MERCER; *170 E-5; mail Sherrard z 61281; ● 200

G

Gage Park; RMC Place; COOK; mail Chicago z 60629, z 60632; pop. incl. with Chicago (Inc. Place)
Gages Lake; CDP-Census Area Only; LAKE; 172 A-5; elev. 800ft./244m.; 🄿; ★ CHI; z 60030; Ⓟ 8,349; Ⓒ 10,415
Galatia; Inc. Place; SALINE; ▲ Galatia; 171 R-10; elev. 397ft./121m.; 🄿; z 62935; Ⓟ 983; Ⓒ 1,013
Galatia; MCD-Township; SALINE; *171 R-10; 🄿; z 62935; Ⓟ 1,345; Ⓒ 1,386
Gale; RMC Place; ALEXANDER; *171 T-8; elev. 400ft./122m.; 🄿; z 62990
Galena; Inc. Place; ⊡ JO DAVIESS; 170 A-6; 🄿 🄷; z 61036; Ⓟ 3,647; Ⓒ 3,460
Galena Oaks; RMC Place; JO DAVIESS; *170 A-6; elev. 800ft./244m.; mail Elizabeth z 61028; ● 60
Galesburg; Inc. Place; ⊡ KNOX; 170 F-6; elev. 773ft./236m.; 🄿 🄷 🄲 1,339 ■; ★ GLSB; z 61401-02; Ⓟ 33,530; Ⓒ 33,706; ◆ 31,769
Galesburg; MCD-Township; KNOX; *170 F-6; 🄿 🄲 1,339; ★ GLSB; z 61401-02; Ⓟ 526; Ⓒ 436
Galesburg City; MCD-Township; KNOX; *170 F-6; 🄷; ★ GLSB; mail Galesburg z 61401-02; coextensive with the City of Galesburg; Ⓟ 33,530; Ⓒ 33,706
Galesville; RMC Place; PIATT; *170 I-11; mail Mansfield z 61854; ● 50
Galewood; RMC Place; COOK; ★ CHI; pop. incl. with Chicago (Inc. Place)
Gallagher; RMC Place; RICHLAND; *171 O-12; mail Olney z 62450; rural
GALLATIN; 171 R-12; Ⓟ 6,909; Ⓒ 6,445; ◆ 5,906
Galt; RMC Place; WHITESIDE; 170 C-7; elev. 639ft./195m.; 🄿; z 61037; ● 210
Galton; RMC Place; DOUGLAS; 171 K-11; elev. 651ft./198m.; mail Arcola z 61910; ● 20
Galva; Inc. Place; HENRY; 170 E-7; elev. 850ft./259m.; 🄿; z 61434; Ⓟ 2,742; Ⓒ 2,758
Galva; MCD-Township; HENRY; *170 E-7; 🄿; z 61434; Ⓟ 3,118; Ⓒ 3,076
Ganeer; MCD-Township; KANKAKEE; *170 E-13; ★ KANK; mail Momence z 60954; Ⓟ 3,146; Ⓒ 3,222
Ganntown; RMC Place; JOHNSON; 171 S-10; mail Grantsburg z 62943; ● 35
Garber; RMC Place; FORD; *170 H-11; mail Gibson City z 60936; rural
Gardena; RMC Place; TAZEWELL; *170 G-8; ★ PEOR; mail East Peoria z 61611; pop. incl. with East Peoria (Inc. Place)
Garden Heights; RMC Place; SALINE; *171 R-11; mail Harrisburg z 62946; pop. incl. with Harrisburg (Inc. Place)
Garden Hill; MCD-Township; WAYNE; *171 O-10; mail Xenia z 62899; Ⓟ 138; Ⓒ 144
Garden Hills; RMC Place; CHAMPAIGN; *170 I-11; elev. 752ft./229m.; ★ CH-U; mail Champaign z 61821; pop. incl. with Champaign (Inc. Place)
Garden of Eden; RMC Place; KANKAKEE; *170 E-13; mail Momence z 60954; ● 140
Garden Plain; RMC Place; WHITESIDE; ▲ Garden Plain; 170 C-6; mail Fulton z 61252; ● 80
Garden Plain; MCD-Township; WHITESIDE; *170 C-6; mail Fulton z 61252; Ⓟ 1,048; Ⓒ 1,055
Garden Prairie; RMC Place; BOONE; 170 B-10; elev. 779ft./237m.; 🄿; z 61038; ● 400
Garden Quarter; RMC Place; KANE; ★ CHI; mail Elgin z 60123; pop. incl. with Elgin (Inc. Place)
Gardner; Inc. Place; GRUNDY; 170 E-11; elev. 590ft./180m.; 🄿; z 60424; Ⓟ 1,237; Ⓒ 1,406
Gardner; MCD-Township; SANGAMON; *170 J-7; ★ SPRG; mail Pleasant Plains z 62677; Ⓟ 3,870; Ⓒ 4,250
Gards Point; RMC Place; WABASH; *171 O-12; elev. 428ft./130m.; mail Mount Carmel z 62863; rural
Garfield; MCD-Township; GRUNDY; *170 E-11; mail Gardner z 60424; Ⓟ 1,404; Ⓒ 1,543
Garfield; RMC Place; LA SALLE; *170 F-10; mail Wenona z 61377
Garfield Park; RMC Place; COOK; *170 C-13; ★ CHI; mail Chicago z 60624; pop. incl. with Chicago (Inc. Place)
Garfield Ridge; RMC Place; COOK; ★ CHI; mail Chicago z 60638; pop. incl. with Chicago (Inc. Place)
Garland; RMC Place; EDGAR; *171 K-13; elev. 671ft./205m.; mail Brocton z 61917; rural
Garrett; Inc. Place; DOUGLAS; ▲ Garrett; 170 J-11; mail Atwood z 61913; Ⓟ 169; Ⓒ 198
Garrett; MCD-Township; DOUGLAS; *170 J-11; mail Atwood z 61913; Ⓟ 1,466; Ⓒ 1,478
Gary Gardens; RMC Place; DUPAGE; ★ CHI; mail Carol Stream z 60188; ● 300
Gateway Yard; RMC Place; ST. CLAIR; *171 O-6; ★ ST.L; mail East Saint Louis z 62207; pop. incl. with East Saint Louis (Inc. Place)
Gays; Inc. Place; MOULTRIE; 171 L-11; elev. 755ft./230m.; 🄿; z 61928; Ⓟ 237; Ⓒ 259
Geff (Jeffersonville); Inc. Place; WAYNE; 171 O-11; elev. 457ft./139m.; 🄿; z 62842; Ⓟ 311; Ⓒ 366
Genesee; MCD-Township; WHITESIDE; *170 C-7; mail Morrison z 61270; Ⓟ 856; Ⓒ 806
Geneseo; Inc. Place; HENRY; ▲ Geneseo; 170 D-6; 🄿 🄷; z 61254; Ⓟ 5,990; Ⓒ 6,480
Geneseo; MCD-Township; HENRY; *170 D-6; 🄿; z 61254; Ⓟ 6,804; Ⓒ 7,255
Geneseo Hills; RMC Place; HENRY; *170 D-6; elev. 665ft./203m.; mail Geneseo z 61254; ● 200
Geneva; Inc. Place; ⊡ KANE; ▲ Geneva; 170 C-11; 🄿 🄷; ★ CHI; z 60134; Ⓟ 12,617; Ⓒ 19,515; ◆ 24,611
Geneva; MCD-Township; KANE; *170 C-11; 🄿; ★ CHI; z 60134; Ⓟ 16,025; Ⓒ 23,268
Genoa; Inc. Place; DEKALB; ▲ Genoa; 170 B-10; 🄿; z 60135; Ⓟ 3,083; Ⓒ 4,169
Genoa; MCD-Township; DEKALB; *170 B-10; 🄿; z 60135; Ⓟ 4,210; Ⓒ 5,342
Gent City; RMC Place; WILLIAMSON; ★ CARB-; mail Marion z 62959; ● 80
Gentry Acres; RMC Place; WILLIAMSON; *171 R-9; elev. 450ft./137m.; ★ CARB-; mail Carterville z 62918; pop. incl. with Carterville (Inc. Place)
Georgetown; RMC Place; CARROLL; *170 B-7; mail Lanark z 61046
Georgetown; RMC Place; MCDONOUGH; *170 H-5; mail Macomb z 61455; ● 400
Georgetown; Inc. Place; VERMILION; ▲ Georgetown; 170 J-13; 🄿; ★ DANV; z 61846; Ⓟ 3,678; Ⓒ 3,628
Georgetown; MCD-Township; VERMILION; *170 J-13; 🄿; ★ DANV; z 61846; Ⓟ 8,286; Ⓒ 8,083
Gerald; RMC Place; VERMILION; mail Armstrong z 61812; rural
Gerlaw; RMC Place; WARREN; 170 F-5; elev. 728ft./222m.; 🄿; z 61435; ● 150
German; MCD-Township; RICHLAND; *171 N-12; mail Claremont z 62421; Ⓟ 406; Ⓒ 394
German Corner; RMC Place; HENRY; *170 E-7; mail Cambridge z 61238; rural
Germantown; Inc. Place; CLINTON; ▲ Germantown, Breese; 171 O-8; elev. 432ft./132m.; 🄿; z 62245 & mail Aviston z 62216; Ⓟ 1,167; Ⓒ 1,118
Germantown; MCD-Township; CLINTON; *171 O-8; 🄿; z 62245 & mail Aviston z 62216; Ⓟ 1,931; Ⓒ 1,990
Germantown Hills (Oak Grove Park); Inc. Place; WOODFORD; 170 G-8; elev. 800ft./244m.; 🄿; ★ PEOR; z 61548; Ⓟ 1,195; Ⓒ 2,111
German Valley; Inc. Place; STEPHENSON; 170 B-8; 🄿; z 61039; Ⓟ 480; Ⓒ 481
Germanville; MCD-Township; LIVINGSTON; *170 G-11; mail Chatsworth z 60921; Ⓟ 91; Ⓒ 73
Gibson; FORD; see Gibson City (Inc. Place)
Gibson City (Gibson); Inc. Place; FORD; 170 H-11; elev. 752ft./229m.; 🄿 🄷; z 60936; Ⓟ 3,396; Ⓒ 3,373
Gibsonia; RMC Place; GALLATIN; *171 R-12; elev. 365ft./111m.; mail Junction z 62954; rural
Gifford; Inc. Place; CHAMPAIGN; 170 I-12; elev. 780ft./238m.; 🄿; z 61847; Ⓟ 845; Ⓒ 815; Ⓡ 838
Gila; RMC Place; JASPER; 171 M-11; elev. 578ft./176m.; mail Montrose z 62445; ● 35
Gilberts; Inc. Place; KANE; 172 E-1; elev. 900ft./274m.; 🄿; ★ CHI; z 60136; Ⓟ 987; Ⓒ 1,279
Gilchrist; RMC Place; MERCER; *170 E-5; mail Viola z 61486; ● 50
Gilead; RMC Place; CALHOUN; 171 M-5; elev. 469ft./143m.; mail Batchtown z 62006; ● 30
Gillespie; Inc. Place; MACOUPIN; 171 M-7; elev. 660ft./201m.; 🄿; z 62033; Ⓟ 3,645; Ⓒ 3,412
Gillespie; MCD-Township; MACOUPIN; *171 M-7; 🄿; z 62033; includes part of the City of Gillespie; Ⓟ 4,159; Ⓒ 4,114
Gillespie Lakes; RMC Place; MACOUPIN; *171 M-7; elev. 650ft./198m.; mail Gillespie z 62033; ● 80
Gillum; RMC Place; MCLEAN; *170 H-10; elev. 826ft./252m.; mail Bloomington z 61701, z 61704; ● 40
Gilman; Inc. Place; IROQUOIS; 170 G-12; elev. 646ft./197m.; 🄿; z 60938; Ⓟ 1,816; Ⓒ 1,793
Gilmer; MCD-Township; ADAMS; *170 J-3; Ⓟ 1,107; Ⓒ 1,143
Gilmore; RMC Place; EFFINGHAM; *171 M-10; mail Mason z 62443; rural
Gilmore Lake; RMC Place; MONROE; *171 O-6; mail Columbia z 62236; ● 150
Gilson; RMC Place; KNOX; 170 G-6; elev. 689ft./210m.; 🄿; z 61436; ● 220
Ginger Creek; RMC Place; DUPAGE; ★ CHI; mail Oak Brook z 60523; pop. incl. with Oak Brook (Inc. Place)
Ginger Hill; RMC Place; ROCK ISLAND; *170 D-5; ★ D-RI-M; mail Milan z 61264; pop. incl. with Milan (Inc. Place)
Girard; Inc. Place; MACOUPIN; ▲ Girard; 171 L-7; 🄿; z 62640; Ⓟ 2,164; Ⓒ 2,245
Girard; MCD-Township; MACOUPIN; *171 L-7; 🄿; z 62640; Ⓟ 2,454; Ⓒ 2,582
Givins; RMC Place; COOK; ★ CHI; mail Chicago z 60620; pop. incl. with Chicago (Inc. Place)

Entries in **UPPERCASE** are counties.
Entries in **bold** have populations of 2,500 or more.
Names in parentheses are alternate names.

Inc. Place	Incorporated Place
RMC Place	Rand McNally Designated Place
CDP	Census Designated Place
MCD	Minor Civil Division
⊡	County Seat
▲	Minor Civil Division
elev.	Elevation
🄿	Post Office
🄷	Hospital
🄲	College
■	Principal Business Center
★	Ranally Metro Area (RMA) Abbreviation
z	Zip Code(s)
Ⓟ	Previous Census Population
Ⓒ	Final Census Population
Ⓡ	Revised Census Population
Ⓢ	Special Census Population
Ⓐ	Annexation Population
●	Rand McNally Population Estimate
◆	Estimated Population

For additional definitions see Glossary, Volume 1, and Introduction, Volume 2.

Gladstone; Inc. Place; HENDERSON; ▲ Gladstone; **170** F-4; 🅿; **z** 61437; Ⓟ 270; © 284
Gladstone; MCD-Township; HENDERSON; ***170** G-4; 🅿; **z** 61437; Ⓟ 1,166; © 1,169
Gladstone Park; RMC Place; COOK; ★ **CHI**; mail Chicago **z** 60630; pop. incl. with Chicago (Inc. Place)
Glasford; Inc. Place; PEORIA; **170** H-7; elev. 620ft./189m.; 🅿; **z** 61533; Ⓟ 1,115; © 1,076
Glasgow; Inc. Place; SCOTT; **171** K-5; elev. 587ft./179m.; mail Winchester **z** 62694; Ⓟ 163; © 170
Glass Works; RMC Place; MADISON; ★ **ST.L**; mail Alton **z** 62002; pop. incl. with Alton (Inc. Place)
Glen Acres; RMC Place; COOK; ★ **CHI**; mail Des Plaines **z** 60018; pop. incl. with Rosemont (Inc. Place)
Glenarm; RMC Place; SANGAMON; **171** K-8; elev. 601ft./183m.; 🅿; ★ **SPRG**; **z** 62536; ● 200
Glen Arms; RMC Place; LAKE; ★ **CHI**; mail Ingleside **z** 60041; ● 150
Glenavon; RMC Place; MCLEAN; ***170** H-11; mail Bellflower **z** 61724; rural
Glenayre; RMC Place; COOK; ★ **CHI**; mail Glenview **z** 60025; pop. incl. with Glenview (Inc. Place)
Glenayre Gardens; RMC Place; COOK; ★ **CHI**; mail Glenview **z** 60025; pop. incl. with Glenview (Inc. Place)
Glenbard South; RMC Place; DUPAGE; ***170** C-12; elev. 751ft./229m.; ★ **CHI**; mail Lisle **z** 60532; Ⓟ 3,957
Glenbrook Countryside; RMC Place; COOK; ***170** B-13; ★ **CHI**; mail Northbrook **z** 60062
Glenburn; RMC Place; VERMILION; ***170** I-13; elev. 589ft./180m.; ★ **DANV**; mail Oakwood **z** 61858; ● 30
Glen Carbon; Inc. Place; MADISON; ▲ Pin Oak; **195** C-9; elev. 446ft./136m.; 🅿; ★ **ST.L**; **z** 62034; Ⓟ 7,774; © 10,425
Glencoe; Inc. Place; COOK; **170** B-13; elev. 675ft./206m.; 🅿; ★ **CHI**; **z** 60022 & mail Winnetka **z** 60093; Ⓟ 8,499; © 8,762
Glendale; RMC Place; POPE; **171** S-10; elev. 388ft./118m.; mail Simpson **z** 62985; ● 50
Glendale; RMC Place; ROCK ISLAND; ***170** D-6; ★ **D-RI-M**; mail Silvis **z** 61282; pop. incl. with Silvis (Inc. Place)
Glendale Gardens; RMC Place; MADISON; ★ **ST.L**; mail Wood River **z** 62095; pop. incl. with Wood River (Inc. Place)
Glendale Heights; Inc. Place; DUPAGE; **172** H-4; elev. 762ft./232m.; 🅿 🅷; ★ **CHI**; **z** 60137, **z** 60139; Ⓟ 27,973; © 31,765; ◆ 31,858
Glen Ellyn; Inc. Place; DUPAGE; **172** H-5; elev. 750ft./229m.; 🅿; ★ **CHI**; **z** 60137-38; Ⓟ 24,919; © 26,999; ◆ 27,546
Glen Ellyn Countryside; RMC Place; DUPAGE; **172** H-4; ★ **CHI**; mail Glen Ellyn **z** 60137; ● 2,500
Glen Ellyn Downtown; RMC Place; DUPAGE; ★ **CHI**; mail Glen Ellyn **z** 60138; pop. incl. with Glen Ellyn (Inc. Place)
Glen Ellyn Woods; RMC Place; DUPAGE; ***170** C-12; ★ **CHI**; mail Glen Ellyn **z** 60137; ● 400
Glengarry; RMC Place; KANE; ***170** C-11; elev. 750ft./229m.; ★ **CHI**; mail Geneva **z** 60134; pop. incl. with Geneva (Inc. Place)
Glenn; RMC Place; JACKSON; ***171** R-8; elev. 391ft./119m.; mail Rockwood **z** 62280
Glen Oak; RMC Place; DUPAGE; ***170** C-12; ★ **CHI**; mail Glen Ellyn **z** 60137; ● 200
Glen Park; RMC Place; LA SALLE; ***170** D-10; elev. 625ft./191m.; mail Sheridan **z** 60551; ● 30
Glen Ridge; RMC Place; COOK; ★ **CHI**; mail Matteson **z** 60443, Sandoval **z** 62882; pop. incl. with Matteson (Inc. Place)
Glenridge; MARION; see Junction City (Inc. Place)
Glenshire; RMC Place; COOK; ★ **CHI**; mail Glenview **z** 60025; pop. incl. with Glenview (Inc. Place)
Glenview; Inc. Place; COOK; **172** E-7; elev. 635ft./194m.; 🅿 ■; ★ **CHI**; **z** 60025-26; Ⓟ 37,052; © 41,847; ◆ 42,233
Glen View; RMC Place; ST. CLAIR; ***171** O-7; ★ **ST.L**; mail O Fallon **z** 62269; pop. incl. with O'Fallon (Inc. Place)
Glenview Countryside; RMC Place; COOK; **172** F-7; ★ **CHI**; mail Glenview **z** 60025; ● 1,950
Glenview Estates; RMC Place; COOK; ***170** B-13; ★ **CHI**; mail Glenview **z** 60025; pop. incl. with Glenview (Inc. Place)
Glenview Terrace; RMC Place; COOK; ★ **CHI**; mail Glenview **z** 60025; pop. incl. with Glenview (Inc. Place)
Glenview Woodlands; RMC Place; COOK; ***170** B-13; ★ **CHI**; mail Glenview **z** 60025; pop. incl. with Glenview (Inc. Place)
Glenwood; Inc. Place; COOK; **172** M-10; elev. 624ft./190m.; 🅿; ★ **CHI**; **z** 60425; Ⓟ 9,289; © 9,000
Glenwood Estates; RMC Place; COOK; ★ **CHI**; mail Glenwood **z** 60425; pop. incl. with Glenwood (Inc. Place)
Godfrey; Inc. Place; MADISON; **171** M-6; 🅿; ★ **ST.L**; **z** 62035; Ⓟ 15,671; © 16,286
Godfrey; MCD-Township; MADISON; ***171** M-6; 🅿; ★ **ST.L**; **z** 62035; © 16,286
Godley; Inc. Place; WILL, GRUNDY; ***170** E-11; elev. 585ft./178m.; 🅿; ★ **CHI**; **z** 60407; Ⓟ 322; © 594
Golconda; Inc. Place; ⊡ POPE; **171** S-11; elev. 352ft./107m.; 🅿; **z** 62938; Ⓟ 823; © 726
Gold; MCD-Township; BUREAU; ***170** D-7; mail Mineral **z** 61344; Ⓟ 216; © 199
Golden; Inc. Place; ADAMS; **170** I-4; elev. 781ft./238m.; 🅿; **z** 62339; Ⓟ 565; © 629
Golden Acres; RMC Place; COOK; ***170** B-13; ★ **CHI**; mail Glenview **z** 60025; pop. incl. with Glenview (Inc. Place)
Golden Acres; RMC Place; PEORIA; ***170** G-8; ★ **PEOR**; pop. incl. with Peoria (Inc. Place)
Golden Eagle; RMC Place; CALHOUN; **171** N-5; elev. 670ft./204m.; 🅿; **z** 62036; ● 50
Golden Gardens; RMC Place; ST. CLAIR; ***171** O-6; ★ **ST.L**; mail East Saint Louis **z** 62206; pop. incl. with Centreville (Inc. Place)
Golden Gate; Inc. Place; WAYNE; **171** P-12; elev. 386ft./118m.; 🅿; **z** 62843; Ⓟ 71; © 100
Golden Highridge; RMC Place; COOK; ★ **CHI**; mail Des Plaines **z** 60016; pop. incl. with Des Plaines (Inc. Place)
Golden Manor; RMC Place; COOK; ★ **CHI**; mail Des Plaines **z** 60016; pop. incl. with Des Plaines (Inc. Place)
Gold Hill; MCD-Township; GALLATIN; ***171** R-12; mail Shawneetown **z** 62984; Ⓟ 2,123; © 1,934
Golena Knolls; RMC Place; PEORIA; ★ **PEOR**; mail Chillicothe **z** 61523; ● 70
Golf; Inc. Place; COOK; **172** F-8; elev. 640ft./195m.; 🅿; ★ **CHI**; **z** 60029; Ⓟ 454; © 451
Golfview Hills; RMC Place; DUPAGE; ***170** C-12; ★ **CHI**; mail Hinsdale **z** 60521; ● 800
Goode; MCD-Township; FRANKLIN; ***171** Q-9; mail Sesser **z** 62884; Ⓟ 2,844; © 2,855
Goodenow; RMC Place; WILL; **170** E-13; ★ **CHI**; mail Beecher **z** 60401; ● 140
Goodfarm; MCD-Township; GRUNDY; ***170** F-11; mail Gardner **z** 60424; Ⓟ 324; © 392
Goodfield; Inc. Place; WOODFORD, TAZEWELL; **170** G-9; elev. 748ft./228m.; 🅿; **z** 61742; Ⓟ 454; © 686
Good Hope; Inc. Place; MCDONOUGH; **170** H-5; elev. 715ft./218m.; 🅿; **z** 61438; Ⓟ 416; © 415
Goodings Grove; CDP; WILL; ▲ Lockport; ***170** D-12; elev. 750ft./229m.; ★ **CHI**; mail Lockport **z** 60441; Ⓟ 14,054; © 17,084
Goodrich; RMC Place; KANKAKEE; ***170** F-12; elev. 636ft./194m.; mail Bonfield **z** 60913; rural
Goodwine; RMC Place; IROQUOIS; **170** H-13; elev. 662ft./202m.; 🅿; **z** 60939; ● 80
Goofy Ridge; RMC Place; MASON; ***170** H-7; mail Topeka **z** 61567; summer pop. 400; ● 200
Goose Creek; MCD-Township; PIATT; ***170** I-10; mail De Land **z** 61839; Ⓟ 848; © 852
Goose Lake; MCD-Township; GRUNDY; ***170** E-11; mail Mazon **z** 60444; Ⓟ 1,483; © 1,784
Gordon (Gordons); RMC Place; CRAWFORD; ***171** M-13; mail Robinson **z** 62454; ● 20
Gordons; CRAWFORD; see Gordon (RMC Place)
Goreville; Inc. Place; JOHNSON; **171** S-9; elev. 740ft./226m.; 🅿; **z** 62939; Ⓟ 872; © 938
Gorham; Inc. Place; JACKSON; **171** R-8; elev. 364ft./111m.; 🅿; **z** 62940; Ⓟ 290; © 256
Goshen; MCD-Township; STARK; ***170** F-7; mail Toulon **z** 61483; Ⓟ 760; © 751
Gossett; RMC Place; WHITE; ***171** Q-11; mail Norris City **z** 62869
Graceland; RMC Place; COOK; mail Chicago **z** 60657; pop. incl. with Chicago (Inc. Place)
Grafton; Inc. Place; JERSEY; **171** M-5; elev. 429ft./131m.; 🅿; **z** 62037; Ⓟ 918; © 609
Grafton; MCD-Township; MCHENRY; ***170** B-11; ★ **CHI**; mail Huntley **z** 60142; Ⓟ 9,946; © 27,547
Grand Chain; PULASKI; see New Grand Chain (Inc. Place)
Grand Crossing; RMC Place; COOK; ***170** C-13; ★ **CHI**; mail Chicago **z** 60619; pop. incl. with Chicago (Inc. Place)
Grand Detour; RMC Place; OGLE; ▲ Grand Detour; **170** C-8; mail Dixon **z** 61021; ● 600
Grand Detour; MCD-Township; OGLE; ***170** C-8; mail Dixon **z** 61021; Ⓟ 771; © 742
Grand Prairie; MCD-Township; JEFFERSON; ***171** O-9; mail Woodlawn **z** 62898; Ⓟ 898; © 1,032
Grand Rapids; MCD-Township; LA SALLE; ***170** E-10; mail Grand Ridge **z** 61325; Ⓟ 361; © 315
Grand Ridge; Inc. Place; LA SALLE; **170** E-10; elev. 644ft./196m.; 🅿; **z** 61325; Ⓟ 560; © 546
Grand Tower; Inc. Place; JACKSON; ▲ Grand Tower; **171** R-8; elev. 361ft./110m.; 🅿; **z** 62942; Ⓟ 775; © 624
Grand Tower; MCD-Township; JACKSON; ***171** R-8; 🅿; **z** 62942; Ⓟ 903; © 735
Grandview; RMC Place; CARROLL; ***170** B-6; elev. 620ft./189m.; mail Thomson **z** 61285; ● 60
Grandview; RMC Place; EDGAR; ▲ Grandview; **171** K-13; mail Paris **z** 61944; ● 110
Grandview; MCD-Township; EDGAR; ***171** K-13; mail Paris **z** 61944; Ⓟ 601; © 574
Grandview; Inc. Place; SANGAMON; **173** F-17; elev. 600ft./183m.; 🅿; ★ **SPRG**; **z** 62702; Ⓟ 1,647; © 1,537
Grandview; RMC Place; WOODFORD; ★ **PEOR**; mail East Peoria **z** 61611; ● 200
Grandview Park; RMC Place; COOK; ★ **CHI**; mail Oak Lawn **z** 60453; pop. incl. with Oak Lawn (Inc. Place)
Grandville; MCD-Township; JASPER; ***171** M-12; mail Yale **z** 62481; Ⓟ 410; © 392
Grandwood Park; CDP-Census Area Only; LAKE; **172** A-5; ★ **CHI**; mail Gurnee **z** 60031; Ⓟ 2,470; © 4,521
Grange; RMC Place; CHAMPAIGN; ***170** J-11; mail Sadorus **z** 61872; rural
Granite City; Inc. Place; MADISON; ▲ Chouteau, Granite City, Nameoki, Venice; **171** N-6; elev. 420ft./128m.; 🅿 🅷 ■; ★ **ST.L**; **z** 62040; Ⓟ 32,766; © 31,301; ◆ 31,854
Granite City; MCD-Township; MADISON; ***171** N-6; 🅿 🅷; ★ **ST.L**; **z** 62040; coextensive with the City of Granite City; Ⓟ 32,766; © 31,301
Grant; MCD-Township; LAKE; ***170** A-12; ★ **CHI**; mail Ingleside **z** 60041; Ⓟ 14,423; © 17,397
Grant; MCD-Township; VERMILION; ***170** H-13; mail Hoopeston **z** 60942; Ⓟ 6,673; © 6,672
Grantfork; Inc. Place; MADISON; **171** N-7; elev. 548ft./167m.; mail Highland **z** 62249; Ⓟ 273; © 254
Grant Park; Inc. Place; KANKAKEE; **170** E-13; elev. 700ft./213m.; 🅿; **z** 60940; Ⓟ 1,024; © 1,358
Grantsburg; RMC Place; JOHNSON; **171** S-10; elev. 365ft./111m.; 🅿; **z** 62943; ● 150
Granville; Inc. Place; PUTNAM; ▲ Granville; **170** E-9; 🅿; **z** 61326; Ⓟ 1,407; © 1,414
Granville; MCD-Township; PUTNAM; ***170** E-9; 🅿; **z** 61326; Ⓟ 2,835; © 3,023
Grape Creek (Brookville); RMC Place; VERMILION; ***170** I-13; ★ **DANV**; mail Danville **z** 61834; ● 150
Grass Lake; RMC Place; LAKE; ***170** A-12; elev. 720ft./219m.; ★ **CHI**; mail Antioch **z** 60002; ● 900
Gray; MCD-Township; WHITE; ***171** P-12; mail Grayville **z** 62844; Ⓟ 1,362; © 1,238
Graymont; RMC Place; LIVINGSTON; **170** G-10; elev. 650ft./198m.; 🅿; **z** 61743; ● 130
Graymoor; RMC Place; COOK; ★ **CHI**; mail Olympia Fields **z** 60461; pop. incl. with Olympia Fields (Inc. Place)
Grayslake; Inc. Place; LAKE; **172** B-5; elev. 790ft./241m.; 🅿; ★ **CHI**; **z** 60030; Ⓟ 7,388; © 18,506; ◆ 22,351
Grays Siding; RMC Place; VERMILION; mail Oakwood **z** 61858; ● 60
Grayville; Inc. Place; WHITE, EDWARDS; **171** P-12; elev. 398ft./121m.; 🅿; **z** 62844; Ⓟ 2,043; © 1,725
Green Acres; RMC Place; MCDONOUGH; mail Macomb **z** 61455; ● 100
Green Acres; RMC Place; SANGAMON; ***170** J-7; ★ **SPRG**; mail Springfield **z** 62707; ● 110
Greenbriar; RMC Place; WILL; ★ **CHI**; mail New Lenox **z** 60451; pop. incl. with New Lenox (Inc. Place)
Greenbriar Addition; RMC Place; WILLIAMSON; ***171** R-9; elev. 436ft./133m.; ★ **CARB-**; mail Carterville **z** 62918; pop. incl. with Carterville (Inc. Place)
Greenbrier; RMC Place; COOK; ★ **CHI**; pop. incl. with Arlington Heights (Inc. Place)
Greenbrook Country; RMC Place; COOK; ★ **CHI**; mail Hanover Park **z** 60133; pop. incl. with Hanover Park (Inc. Place)
Greenbush; RMC Place; WARREN; ▲ Greenbush; ***170** G-5; mail Avon **z** 61415; ● 100
Greenbush; MCD-Township; WARREN; ***170** G-5; mail Avon **z** 61415; Ⓟ 610; © 569
Green Creek (Saint Marys); RMC Place; EFFINGHAM; ***171** M-11; mail Effingham **z** 62401; rural
Greene; MCD-Township; MERCER; ***170** E-5; mail Viola **z** 61486; Ⓟ 1,651; © 1,622
Greene; MCD-Township; WOODFORD; ***170** G-9; mail Benson **z** 61516; Ⓟ 390; © 459
GREENE; **171** L-5; Ⓟ 15,317; © 14,761; ◆ 13,391
Greenfield; Inc. Place; GREENE; **171** L-6; elev. 590ft./180m.; 🅿; **z** 62044; Ⓟ 1,162; © 1,179
Greenfield; MCD-Township; GRUNDY; ***170** E-11; mail South Wilmington **z** 60474; Ⓟ 969; © 940
Green Garden; MCD-Township; WILL; ***170** D-13; mail Frankfort **z** 60423; Ⓟ 1,722; © 2,556
Greenleaf Hills; RMC Place; DE WITT; ***170** I-10; elev. 726ft./221m.; mail Farmer City **z** 61842; ● 100
Green Meadows; RMC Place; COOK; ★ **CHI**; pop. incl. with Arlington Heights (Inc. Place)
Green Meadows; RMC Place; COOK; ★ **CHI**; mail Streamwood **z** 60107; pop. incl. with Streamwood (Inc. Place)
Green Oak; RMC Place; BUREAU; ***170** D-8; elev. 700ft./213m.; mail Princeton **z** 61356; rural
Green Oaks; Inc. Place; LAKE; **172** B-6; elev. 700ft./213m.; ★ **CHI**; mail Lake Bluff **z** 60044, Lake Forest **z** 60045, Libertyville **z** 60048; Ⓟ 2,101; © 3,572
Greenpond; RMC Place; PIKE; ***171** K-5; elev. 660ft./201m.; mail Pearl **z** 62361; rural
Green River; RMC Place; HENRY; ***170** D-6; ★ **D-RI-M**; mail Colona **z** 61241; ● 110
Green Rock; RMC Place; HENRY; ***170** D-6; elev. 585ft./178m.; 🅿; ★ **D-RI-M**; **z** 61241; pop. incl. with Colona (Inc. Place)
Green's Switch; RMC Place; MACON; ***170** J-10; ★ **DEC**; pop. incl. with Decatur (Inc. Place)
Greentree; RMC Place; LAKE; ★ **CHI**; mail Libertyville **z** 60048; pop. incl. with Libertyville (Inc. Place)
Greenup; Inc. Place; CUMBERLAND; ▲ Greenup; **171** L-12; elev. 543ft./166m.; 🅿; **z** 62428; Ⓟ 1,616; © 1,532
Greenup; MCD-Township; CUMBERLAND; ***171** L-12; 🅿; **z** 62428; Ⓟ 2,500; © 2,411
Green Valley; RMC Place; DUPAGE; ★ **CHI**; mail Lombard **z** 60148; pop. incl. with Lombard (Inc. Place)
Green Valley; Inc. Place; TAZEWELL; **170** H-8; elev. 540ft./165m.; 🅿; **z** 61534; Ⓟ 745; © 728
Greenview; Inc. Place; MENARD; **170** I-7; elev. 550ft./168m.; 🅿; **z** 62642; Ⓟ 848; © 862
Greenville; Inc. Place; ⊡ BOND; **171** N-8; elev. 619ft./189m.; 🅿 🅷 🅲 1,451; **z** 62246; Ⓟ 4,806; © 6,955
Greenville; MCD-Township; BUREAU; ***170** D-7; mail Walnut **z** 61376; Ⓟ 370; © 397
Greenwich; RMC Place; KANKAKEE; ***170** F-12; elev. 623ft./190m.; ★ **KANK**; mail Kankakee **z** 60901; ● 230
Greenwood; MCD-Township; CHRISTIAN; ***171** L-9; mail Morrisonville **z** 62546; Ⓟ 242; © 232
Greenwood; Inc. Place; MCHENRY; ▲ Greenwood; ***170** A-11; elev. 838ft./255m.; ★ **CHI**; mail Woodstock **z** 60098; © 244
Greenwood; MCD-Township; MCHENRY; ***170** A-11; ★ **CHI**; mail Woodstock **z** 60098; Ⓟ 8,317; © 10,677
Greenwood Acres; RMC Place; CHAMPAIGN; ***170** H-11; mail Dewey **z** 61840; ● 80
Greenwood Meadows; RMC Place; MADISON; ***171** N-6; ★ **ST.L**; mail Godfrey **z** 62035; pop. incl. with Godfrey (Inc. Place)
Greer; RMC Place; IROQUOIS; ***170** H-13; elev. 755ft./230m.; mail Wellington **z** 60973
Gresham; RMC Place; COOK; ★ **CHI**; mail Chicago **z** 60620; pop. incl. with Chicago (Inc. Place)
Gridley; Inc. Place; MCLEAN; ▲ Gridley; **170** G-10; 🅿; **z** 61744; Ⓟ 1,304; © 1,411
Gridley; MCD-Township; MCLEAN; ***170** G-10; 🅿; **z** 61744; Ⓟ 1,813; © 1,914
Grigg; RMC Place; RANDOLPH; ***171** P-7; elev. 421ft./128m.; mail Red Bud **z** 62278; rural
Griggsville; Inc. Place; PIKE; ▲ Griggsville; **171** K-5; 🅿; **z** 62340; Ⓟ 1,218; © 1,258
Griggsville; MCD-Township; PIKE; ***171** K-5; 🅿; **z** 62340; Ⓟ 1,497; © 1,479
Grimes Addition; RMC Place; WHITESIDE; ***170** C-7; mail Sterling **z** 61081; ● 200
Grimsby; RMC Place; JACKSON; ***171** R-8; elev. 361ft./110m.; mail Gorham **z** 62940
Grinnell; RMC Place; MASSAC; ***171** T-10; elev. 366ft./112m.; mail Belknap **z** 62908; rural
Grisham; MCD-Township; MONTGOMERY; ***171** M-8; mail Panama **z** 62077; Ⓟ 648; © 633
Griswold; RMC Place; LIVINGSTON; ***170** F-11; mail Cullom **z** 60929; rural
Gromers Woods; RMC Place; COOK; ***170** B-12; elev. 840ft./256m.; ★ **CHI**; mail Elgin **z** 60120; ● 100
Gross; RMC Place; HARDIN; ***171** S-11; mail Elizabethtown **z** 62931; rural
Grove; MCD-Township; JASPER; ***171** M-11; mail Newton **z** 62448; Ⓟ 608; © 623
Grove City; RMC Place; CHRISTIAN; ***171** K-9; mail Edinburg **z** 62531; ● 25
Groveland; MCD-Township; LA SALLE; ***170** F-9; mail Rutland **z** 61358; Ⓟ 739; © 725
Groveland; RMC Place; TAZEWELL; ▲ Groveland; **170** H-8; elev. 779ft./237m.; 🅿; ★ **PEOR**; **z** 61535; ● 500
Groveland; MCD-Township; TAZEWELL; ***170** G-8; 🅿; ★ **PEOR**; **z** 61535; Ⓟ 19,608; © 18,376
Grover; MCD-Township; WAYNE; ***171** P-11; mail Fairfield **z** 62837; Ⓟ 4,113; © 4,051
GRUNDY; **170** E-10; Ⓟ 32,337; © 37,535; ◆ 49,822
Grupe; RMC Place; EFFINGHAM; ***171** M-11; mail Effingham **z** 62401; ● 100
Guilford; RMC Place; JO DAVIESS; ***170** A-6; mail Galena **z** 61036; rural
Guilford; MCD-Township; JO DAVIESS; ***170** A-6; mail Elizabeth **z** 61028; Ⓟ 411; © 916
Gulfport; Inc. Place; HENDERSON; ***170** G-4; elev. 525ft./160m.; mail Burlington **z** 52601, Carman **z** 61425; Ⓟ 209; © 207
Gurnee; Inc. Place; LAKE; **172** A-6; elev. 700ft./213m.; 🅿; ★ **CHI**; **z** 60031; Ⓟ 13,701; © 28,834; ◆ 33,691
Guthrie; RMC Place; FORD; ***170** H-11; mail Gibson City **z** 60936; ● 40

H

Hadley; RMC Place; PIKE; ▲ Hadley; ***171** K-4; elev. 756ft./230m.; mail Barry **z** 62312; rural
Hadley; MCD-Township; PIKE; ***171** K-4; mail Barry **z** 62312; Ⓟ 242; © 255
Haegers Bend; RMC Place; MCHENRY; ***170** B-11; ★ **CHI**; mail Algonquin **z** 60102; ● 250
Hafer; RMC Place; WILLIAMSON; ***171** R-9; ★ **CARB-**; mail Carterville **z** 62918; pop. incl. with Herrin (Inc. Place)
Hagaman; RMC Place; MACOUPIN; ***171** L-6; 🅿; **z** 62630; ● 25
Hagarstown; RMC Place; FAYETTE; **171** N-9; elev. 529ft./161m.; 🅿; **z** 62247; ● 100
Hagener; MCD-Township; CASS; ***170** J-5; mail Beardstown **z** 62618; Ⓟ 432; © 406
Hahnaman; MCD-Township; WHITESIDE; ***170** D-8; mail Deer Grove **z** 61243, Tampico **z** 61283; Ⓟ 393; © 394
Haines; MCD-Township; MARION; ***171** O-10; mail Kell **z** 62853; Ⓟ 852; © 917
Hainesville; Inc. Place; LAKE; **172** A-5; elev. 800ft./244m.; 🅿; ★ **CHI**; **z** 60030, **z** 60073; Ⓟ 134; © 2,129
Haldane; RMC Place; OGLE; ***170** B-8; elev. 904ft./276m.; mail Forreston **z** 61030; ● 70
Hale; MCD-Township; WARREN; ***170** F-5; mail Monmouth **z** 61462; Ⓟ 381; © 421
Half Day; RMC Place; LAKE; **172** D-6; elev. 654ft./199m.; ★ **CHI**; mail Lincolnshire **z** 60069; pop. incl. with Vernon Hills (Inc. Place)
Hall; MCD-Township; BUREAU; ***170** E-9; mail Spring Valley **z** 61362; Ⓟ 8,094; © 8,245
Hallidayboro; RMC Place; JACKSON; ***171** Q-9; mail Elkville **z** 62932; ● 100
Hallock; RMC Place; IROQUOIS; ***170** H-13; mail Wellington **z** 60973; rural
Hallock; MCD-Township; PEORIA; ***170** F-8; mail Edelstein **z** 61526; Ⓟ 1,485; © 1,532
Hallsville (Hallville); RMC Place; DE WITT; **170** I-9; mail Clinton **z** 61727; ● 80
Hallville; DE WITT; see Hallsville (RMC Place)
Halsey Village; RMC Place; LAKE; ★ **CHI**; mail Great Lakes **z** 60088; pop. incl. with Waukegan (Inc. Place)
Hamburg; RMC Place; BOND; ***171** N-9; elev. 510ft./155m.; mail Smithboro **z** 62284
Hamburg; Inc. Place; CALHOUN; **171** L-5; elev. 445ft./136m.; 🅿; **z** 62045; Ⓟ 150; © 126
Hamel; Inc. Place; MADISON; ▲ Hamel; **171** N-7; 🅿; **z** 62046; Ⓟ 530; © 570
Hamel; MCD-Township; MADISON; ***171** N-7; 🅿; **z** 62046; Ⓟ 1,685; © 2,027
Hamilton; Inc. Place; HANCOCK; **170** H-3; elev. 637ft./194m.; 🅿; **z** 62341; Ⓟ 3,281; © 3,029
Hamilton; MCD-Township; LEE; ***170** D-8; mail Ohio **z** 61349; Ⓟ 224; © 236
HAMILTON; **171** Q-11; Ⓟ 8,499; © 8,621; ◆ 8,061
Hamlet; RMC Place; MERCER; ***170** E-5; elev. 808ft./246m.; mail Aledo **z** 61231; ● 60
Hamletsburg; RMC Place; POPE; ***171** T-11; elev. 394ft./120m.; 🅿; **z** 62910; Ⓟ 85
Hammond; Inc. Place; PIATT; **170** J-10; elev. 678ft./207m.; 🅿; **z** 61929; Ⓟ 527; © 518
Hampshire; Inc. Place; KANE; ▲ Hampshire, Rutland; **170** B-11; 🅿; **z** 60140; Ⓟ 1,843; © 2,900
Hampshire; MCD-Township; KANE; ***170** B-11; 🅿; **z** 60140; Ⓟ 3,398; © 4,793
Hampton; Inc. Place; ROCK ISLAND; ▲ Hampton; **171** S-5; elev. 580ft./177m.; 🅿; ★ **D-RI-M**; **z** 61256; Ⓟ 1,601; © 1,626
Hampton; MCD-Township; ROCK ISLAND; ***170** D-6; 🅿; ★ **D-RI-M**; **z** 61256; Ⓟ 20,498; © 20,540; ® 21,638
Hampton Court; RMC Place; COOK; ★ **CHI**; mail Country Club Hills **z** 60478; pop. incl. with Country Club Hills (Inc. Place)
Hanaford; FRANKLIN; see Logan (Inc. Place)
Hancock; MCD-Township; HANCOCK; ***170** H-4; mail Carthage **z** 62321; Ⓟ 255; © 254
HANCOCK; **170** I-3; Ⓟ 21,373; © 20,121; ® 20,125; ◆ 18,602
Hank's Station; GREENE; see Drake (RMC Place)
Hanna; MCD-Township; HENRY; ***170** D-6; ★ **D-RI-M**; mail Geneseo **z** 61254; Ⓟ 2,134; © 2,427
Hanna; PEORIA; see Hanna City (Inc. Place)
Hanna City (Hanna); Inc. Place; PEORIA; **170** G-7; elev. 724ft./221m.; 🅿; ★ **PEOR**; **z** 61536; Ⓟ 1,205; © 1,013
Hannon; RMC Place; CHRISTIAN; ***171** K-9; elev. 610ft./186m.; mail Taylorville **z** 62568; pop. incl. with Taylorville (Inc. Place)
Hanover; MCD-Township; COOK; ***170** B-12; ★ **CHI**; mail Bartlett **z** 60103; Ⓟ 62,308; © 83,471
Hanover; Inc. Place; JO DAVIESS; ▲ Hanover; **170** A-6; 🅿; **z** 61041; Ⓟ 908; © 836
Hanover; MCD-Township; JO DAVIESS; ***170** B-6; 🅿; **z** 61041; Ⓟ 1,394; © 1,229
Hanover Highlands; RMC Place; COOK; ★ **CHI**; mail Hanover Park **z** 60133; pop. incl. with Hanover Park (Inc. Place)
Hanover Park; Inc. Place; COOK, DUPAGE; **172** G-4; elev. 800ft./244m.; 🅿; ★ **CHI**; **z** 60133 & mail Bartlett **z** 60103, Bloomingdale **z** 60108; Ⓟ 32,918; © 38,278; ◆ 39,041
Hanover Square; RMC Place; COOK; ★ **CHI**; mail Hanover Park **z** 60133; pop. incl. with Hanover Park (Inc. Place)
Hanson; RMC Place; SHELBY; ***171** M-9; mail Ramsey **z** 62080; rural
Happy Hollow Lake; RMC Place; KNOX; ***170** F-6; elev. 600ft./183m.; mail Dahinda **z** 61428; ● 100
Harbor Estates; RMC Place; LAKE; ***170** B-12; ★ **CHI**; mail Barrington **z** 60010; pop. incl. with Lake Barrington (Inc. Place)
Harco; RMC Place; SALINE; **171** R-10; 🅿; **z** 62935; ● 100
Hardin; Inc. Place; ⊡ CALHOUN; **171** M-5; 🅿; **z** 62047; Ⓟ 1,071; © 959
Hardin; MCD-Township; PIKE; ***171** K-4; elev. 436ft./133m.; mail Nebo **z** 62355; Ⓟ 254; © 239
HARDIN; **171** S-11; Ⓟ 5,189; © 4,800; ◆ 4,324
Harding; RMC Place; LA SALLE; **170** D-10; mail Earlville **z** 60518; ● 120
Hardinville; RMC Place; CRAWFORD; ***171** N-13; mail Oblong **z** 62449, Robinson **z** 62454
Harlem; MCD-Township; STEPHENSON; ***170** A-8; mail Freeport **z** 61032; Ⓟ 2,344; © 2,402
Harlem; RMC Place; WINNEBAGO; ▲ Harlem; ***170** A-9; ★ **RKFD**; mail Loves Park **z** 61111; pop. incl. with Loves Park (Inc. Place)
Harlem; MCD-Township; WINNEBAGO; ***170** A-9; ★ **RKFD**; mail Loves Park **z** 61111; Ⓟ 28,453; © 36,171
Harmon; Inc. Place; LEE; ▲ Harmon; **170** C-8; elev. 675ft./206m.; 🅿; **z** 61042; Ⓟ 186; © 149
Harmon; MCD-Township; LEE; ***170** C-8; 🅿; **z** 61042; Ⓟ 510; © 400
Harmony; MCD-Township; HANCOCK; ***170** H-4; mail Carthage **z** 62321; Ⓟ 413; © 421
Harmony; RMC Place; JEFFERSON; ***171** O-10; elev. 540ft./165m.; mail Bluford **z** 62814; rural
Harmony; RMC Place; MCHENRY; ***170** B-11; elev. 924ft./282m.; ★ **CHI**; mail Hampshire **z** 60140; rural
Harmony Village; RMC Place; COOK; ★ **CHI**; mail Wheeling **z** 60090; pop. incl. with Wheeling (Inc. Place)
Harp; MCD-Township; DE WITT; ***170** I-10; mail Clinton **z** 61727; Ⓟ 250; © 335
Harper; RMC Place; OGLE; **170** B-8; elev. 942ft./287m.; mail Forreston **z** 61030; ● 30
Harpster; RMC Place; FORD; ***170** H-11; mail Foosland **z** 61845; rural
Harris; MCD-Township; FULTON; ***170** H-6; mail Marietta **z** 61459; Ⓟ 421; © 410
Harris; RMC Place; PIATT; ***170** I-11; elev. 724ft./221m.; mail Farmer City **z** 61842; rural
Harrisburg; Inc. Place; ⊡ SALINE; ▲ Harrisburg; **171** R-11; elev. 403ft./123m.; 🅿 🅷; **z** 62946; Ⓟ 9,289; © 9,860
Harrisburg; MCD-Township; SALINE; ***171** R-11; 🅿; **z** 62946; Ⓟ 11,375; © 11,658
Harrison; RMC Place; JACKSON; ***171** R-8; elev. 407ft./124m.; ★ **CARB-**; mail Murphysboro **z** 62966; ● 250
Harrison; RMC Place; WINNEBAGO; ▲ Harrison; **170** A-9; mail Rockton **z** 61072; ● 160
Harrison; MCD-Township; WINNEBAGO; ***170** A-9; mail Rockton **z** 61072; Ⓟ 697; © 713
Harrisonville; RMC Place; GRUNDY; ***170** E-11; elev. 563ft./172m.; ★ **CHI**; mail Coal City **z** 60416; ● 50
Harrisonville; RMC Place; MONROE; ***171** P-6; mail Valmeyer **z** 62295
Harristown; Inc. Place; MACON; ▲ Harristown; **170** J-9; 🅿; ★ **DEC**; **z** 62537; Ⓟ 1,319; © 1,338
Harristown; MCD-Township; MACON; ***170** J-9; 🅿; ★ **DEC**; **z** 62537; Ⓟ 1,956; © 1,913
Harter; MCD-Township; CLAY; ***171** O-11; mail Flora **z** 62839; Ⓟ 6,591; © 6,481
Hartford; Inc. Place; MADISON; **195** B-8; elev. 420ft./128m.; 🅿; ★ **ST.L**; **z** 62048; Ⓟ 1,676; © 1,545
Hartland; RMC Place; MCHENRY; ▲ Hartland; ***170** A-11; elev. 919ft./280m.; mail Woodstock **z** 60098; ● 90
Hartland; MCD-Township; MCHENRY; ***170** A-11; mail Woodstock **z** 60098; Ⓟ 1,911; © 2,063
Hartsburg; Inc. Place; LOGAN; **170** I-8; elev. 600ft./183m.; 🅿; **z** 62643; Ⓟ 306; © 358
Harvard; Inc. Place; MCHENRY; **170** A-10; elev. 966ft./294m.; 🅿 🅷; **z** 60033; Ⓟ 5,975; © 7,996
Harvard Hills; RMC Place; TAZEWELL; ***170** G-8; ★ **PEOR**; mail Washington **z** 61571; ● 170
Harvel; Inc. Place; MONTGOMERY, CHRISTIAN; **171** L-8; elev. 640ft./195m.; 🅿; **z** 62538; Ⓟ 213; © 235
Harvel; MCD-Township; MONTGOMERY; ***171** L-8; 🅿; **z** 62538; includes part of the Village of Harvel; Ⓟ 272; © 274
Harvey; Inc. Place; COOK; **170** D-13; elev. 600ft./183m.; 🅿 🅷 ■; ★ **CHI**; **z** 60426, **z** 60428; Ⓟ 29,771; © 30,000; ◆ 28,689
Harwood; MCD-Township; CHAMPAIGN; ***170** H-12; mail Gifford **z** 61847; Ⓟ 589; © 618
Harwood Heights; Inc. Place; COOK; **172** G-7; elev. 650ft./198m.; 🅿; ★ **CHI**; **z** 60656, **z** 60706 & mail Chicago **z** 60630, **z** 60634; Ⓟ 7,680; © 8,297
Hastings; RMC Place; VERMILION; ***170** J-12; mail Sidell **z** 61876; rural
Hatcher Woods; RMC Place; GRUNDY; ***170** E-11; mail Morris **z** 60450; pop. incl. with Morris (Inc. Place)
Hatton; CLARK; see Snyder (RMC Place)
Havana; Inc. Place; ⊡ MASON; ▲ Havana; **170** I-6; 🅿 🅷; **z** 62644; Ⓟ 3,610; © 3,577
Havana; MCD-Township; MASON; ***170** I-7; 🅿; **z** 62644; Ⓟ 5,593; © 5,303
Haw Creek; MCD-Township; KNOX; ***170** G-6; mail Maquon **z** 61458; Ⓟ 561; © 498
Hawthorne; RMC Place; COOK; ***170** C-13; ★ **CHI**; mail Chicago **z** 60623; pop. incl. with Chicago (Inc. Place)
Hawthorne; MCD-Township; WHITE; ***171** Q-12; mail Carmi **z** 62821; Ⓟ 413; © 360
Hawthorn Woods; Inc. Place; LAKE; **172** C-5; elev. 800ft./244m.; 🅿; ★ **CHI**; **z** 60047; Ⓟ 4,423; © 6,002; ® 6,015
Hawthrone Hills; RMC Place; JEFFERSON; ***171** P-10; elev. 550ft./168m.; mail Mount Vernon **z** 62864; ● 50
Hayes; RMC Place; DOUGLAS; ***170** J-11; mail Tuscola **z** 61953; rural
Hayford; RMC Place; COOK; mail Chicago **z** 60652; pop. incl. with Chicago (Inc. Place)
Haymarket; RMC Place; COOK; ***170** C-13; ★ **CHI**; mail Chicago **z** 60606; pop. incl. with Chicago (Inc. Place)
Haypress; RMC Place; GREENE; ***171** L-5; mail Eldred **z** 62027, Hillview **z** 62050; rural
Hazel Crest; Inc. Place; COOK; **172** M-9; elev. 648ft./198m.; 🅿 🅷; ★ **CHI**; **z** 60429; Ⓟ 13,334; © 14,816
Hazelcrest Highlands; RMC Place; COOK; ★ **CHI**; mail Hazel Crest **z** 60429; pop. incl. with Hazel Crest (Inc. Place)
Hazel Dell; RMC Place; CUMBERLAND; **171** M-12; elev. 600ft./183m.; 🅿; **z** 62428; ● 100
Hazelgreen; RMC Place; COOK; ***170** D-13; elev. 608ft./185m.; ★ **CHI**; mail Worth **z** 60482; pop. incl. with Alsip (Inc. Place)
Hazelhurst; RMC Place; OGLE, CARROLL; ***170** C-8; mail Polo **z** 61064; ● 30
Hazelwood; RMC Place; HENRY; ***170** D-6; elev. 694ft./212m.; mail Geneseo **z** 61254; ● 250
Hazelwood Heights; RMC Place; HENRY; ***170** D-6; elev. 685ft./209m.; ★ **D-RI-M**; mail Geneseo **z** 61254; ● 120
Hazelwood West; RMC Place; HENRY; ***170** D-6; elev. 650ft./198m.; ★ **D-RI-M**; mail Geneseo **z** 61254; ● 50
Headyville; RMC Place; EFFINGHAM; mail Dieterich **z** 62424; rural
Heapsville; RMC Place; HENDERSON; ***170** G-4; elev. 520ft./158m.; mail Carman **z** 61425
Heartland Meadows; RMC Place; KANE; ***170** B-11; ★ **CHI**; mail South Elgin **z** 60177
Heartville; RMC Place; EFFINGHAM; ***171** M-11; mail Effingham **z** 62401; ● 150
Heathercrest; RMC Place; COOK; ★ **CHI**; mail Northbrook **z** 60062; pop. incl. with Northbrook (Inc. Place)
Heatherfield; RMC Place; GRUNDY; ***170** E-11; elev. 548ft./167m.; mail Morris **z** 60450; ● 100
Heatherlea; RMC Place; COOK; ***170** B-12; elev. 750ft./229m.; ★ **CHI**; mail Palatine **z** 60067; pop. incl. with Palatine (Inc. Place)
Heathsville; RMC Place; CRAWFORD; ***171** N-13; mail Flat Rock **z** 62427; rural
Hebron; Inc. Place; MCHENRY; ▲ Hebron; **170** A-11; 🅿; **z** 60034; Ⓟ 809; © 1,038
Hebron; MCD-Township; MCHENRY; ***170** A-11; 🅿; **z** 60034; Ⓟ 1,817; © 2,166
Hecker; Inc. Place; MONROE; **171** P-7; elev. 460ft./140m.; 🅿; **z** 62248; Ⓟ 534; © 475
Hegeler; RMC Place; VERMILION; **170** I-13; ★ **DANV**; mail Danville **z** 61832, **z** 61834; ● 1,900
Hegewisch; RMC Place; COOK; ***170** D-13; ★ **CHI**; mail Chicago **z** 60633; pop. incl. with Chicago (Inc. Place)
Helena; RMC Place; LAWRENCE; ***171** O-13; mail Sumner **z** 62466; rural
Helmar; RMC Place; KENDALL; ***170** D-11; elev. 710ft./216m.; ★ **CHI**; mail Newark **z** 60541; ● 50
Helvetia; MCD-Township; MADISON; ***171** N-8; mail Highland **z** 62249; Ⓟ 7,238; © 8,145
Heman; RMC Place; MACON; ***170** J-9; elev. 610ft./186m.; 🅿; **z** 62573; rural
Henderson; Inc. Place; KNOX; ▲ Henderson; **170** F-6; elev. 815ft./248m.; 🅿; ★ **GLSB**; **z** 61439; Ⓟ 290; © 319
Henderson; MCD-Township; KNOX; ***170** F-6; 🅿; **z** 61439; Ⓟ 1,290; © 1,269
Henderson; RMC Place; MACOUPIN; ***171** M-7; elev. 665ft./203m.; mail Gillespie **z** 62033; rural
HENDERSON; **170** G-4; Ⓟ 8,096; © 8,213; ◆ 7,437
Henderson Grove (Soperville); RMC Place; KNOX; ***170** F-6; mail Galesburg **z** 61401; rural
Hendryx Manor; RMC Place; PEORIA; ***170** G-8; ★ **PEOR**; mail Peoria **z** 61614; ● 600
Hennepin; Inc. Place; ⊡ PUTNAM; ▲ Hennepin; **170** E-8; 🅿; **z** 61327; Ⓟ 669; © 707
Hennepin; MCD-Township; PUTNAM; ***170** E-9; 🅿; **z** 61327; Ⓟ 1,111; © 1,212
Henning; Inc. Place; VERMILION; **170** I-13; elev. 685ft./209m.; 🅿; **z** 61848; Ⓟ 273; © 241
Henry; Inc. Place; MARSHALL; ▲ Henry; **170** F-8; 🅿; **z** 61537; Ⓟ 2,591; © 2,540
Henry; MCD-Township; MARSHALL; ***170** F-8; 🅿; **z** 61537; Ⓟ 2,877; © 2,865
HENRY; **170** E-6; Ⓟ 51,159; © 51,020; ◆ 49,604
Hensley; MCD-Township; CHAMPAIGN; ***170** I-11; mail Champaign **z** 61820; Ⓟ 1,073; © 1,111
Henton; RMC Place; SHELBY; ***171** L-10; 🅿; **z** 62565; ● 60
Herald; RMC Place; WHITE; **171** Q-12; elev. 420ft./128m.; 🅿; **z** 62869; ● 80
Heralds Prairie; MCD-Township; WHITE; ***171** Q-12; mail Norris City **z** 62869; Ⓟ 641; © 663
Herbert; RMC Place; BOONE; **170** B-10; mail Kingston **z** 60145; ● 100
Herborn; RMC Place; SHELBY; ***171** L-10; mail Strasburg **z** 62465
Heritage Estates; RMC Place; KANKAKEE; ***170** E-12; elev. 691ft./211m.; ★ **KANK**; mail Bourbonnais **z** 60914; pop. incl. with Bourbonnais (Inc. Place)
Hermon; RMC Place; KNOX; **170** G-6; mail Maquon **z** 61458; ● 50
Hermosa; RMC Place; COOK; ★ **CHI**; mail Chicago **z** 60639; pop. incl. with Chicago (Inc. Place)
Herod; RMC Place; POPE; **171** R-11; elev. 426ft./130m.; 🅿; **z** 62947; ● 70
Herrick; Inc. Place; SHELBY; ▲ Herrick; **171** M-9; 🅿; **z** 62431; Ⓟ 466; © 524
Herrick; MCD-Township; SHELBY; ***171** L-9; 🅿; **z** 62431; Ⓟ 628; © 687
Herrin; Inc. Place; WILLIAMSON; **171** R-9; elev. 420ft./128m.; 🅿 🅷; ★ **CARB-**; **z** 62948; Ⓟ 10,857; © 11,298
Herscher; Inc. Place; KANKAKEE; **170** F-12; elev. 660ft./201m.; 🅿; **z** 60941; Ⓟ 1,278; © 1,523
Hersman; RMC Place; BROWN; **170** J-5; mail Mount Sterling **z** 62353; ● 80
Hervey City; RMC Place; MACON; ***171** K-10; elev. 699ft./213m.; 🅿; ★ **DEC**; **z** 62549; rural
Hettick; Inc. Place; MACOUPIN; **171** L-6; elev. 590ft./180m.; 🅿; **z** 62649; Ⓟ 211; © 182
Hewittsville; CHRISTIAN; see Hewittville (RMC Place)
Hewittville (Hewittsville); RMC Place; CHRISTIAN; **171** K-8; mail Taylorville **z** 62568; ● 450
Heyworth; Inc. Place; MCLEAN; **170** I-9; elev. 749ft./228m.; 🅿; **z** 61745; Ⓟ 1,629; © 2,431
Hickory; MCD-Township; SCHUYLER; ***170** I-6; mail Browning **z** 62624; Ⓟ 210; © 172
Hickory Falls; RMC Place; MCHENRY; ***170** A-11; ★ **CHI**; mail Wonder Lake **z** 60097; ● 700
Hickory Grove; RMC Place; ADAMS; ***170** J-3; ★ **QUIN**; mail Quincy **z** 62305; ● 400
Hickory Hill; MCD-Township; WAYNE; ***171** O-10; mail Wayne City **z** 62895; Ⓟ 417; © 444
Hickory Hills; Inc. Place; COOK; **172** K-7; elev. 675ft./206m.; 🅿; ★ **CHI**; **z** 60457 & mail Justice **z** 60458; Ⓟ 13,021; © 13,926
Hickory Hills; RMC Place; PIATT; ***170** I-11; elev. 697ft./212m.; mail White Heath **z** 61884; ● 100
Hickory Hollow; RMC Place; KANE; ***170** B-11; elev. 850ft./259m.; ★ **CHI**; mail Dundee **z** 60118; ● 100
Hickory Point; MCD-Township; MACON; ***170** J-9; ★ **DEC**; mail Forsyth **z** 62535; Ⓟ 16,556; © 17,603
Hickory Point; RMC Place; SHELBY; ***171** L-10; elev. 672ft./205m.; mail Shelbyville **z** 62565; ● 50
Hickoryville; RMC Place; RANDOLPH; ***171** Q-7; elev. 370ft./113m.; mail Saint Mary **z** 63673; rural
Hicks; RMC Place; HARDIN; ***171** S-11; mail Herod **z** 62947; rural
Hidalgo; Inc. Place; JASPER; **171** M-12; elev. 583ft./178m.; 🅿; **z** 62432; Ⓟ 122; © 123
Hidden Creek; RMC Place; COOK; ***170** B-12; ★ **CHI**; mail Palatine **z** 60074; pop. incl. with Palatine (Inc. Place)
Hidden Hill; RMC Place; KANE; ***170** B-11; ★ **CHI**; mail Elgin **z** 60123; ● 100
Hidden Hills; RMC Place; MCDONOUGH; mail Macomb **z** 61455; ● 150
Higginsville; RMC Place; VERMILION; ***170** I-13; mail Potomac **z** 61865; rural
High Knob; RMC Place; DUPAGE; ***170** C-12; ★ **CHI**; mail Wheaton **z** 60187; pop. incl. with Wheaton (Inc. Place)
High Lake; RMC Place; DUPAGE; ***170** C-12; ★ **CHI**; mail West Chicago **z** 60185; ● 600
Highland; MCD-Township; GRUNDY; ***170** F-11; mail Kinsman **z** 60437; Ⓟ 363; © 314
Highland; Inc. Place; MADISON; **171** N-7; elev. 545ft./166m.; 🅿 🅷; **z** 62249; Ⓟ 7,525; © 8,438
Highlander; RMC Place; JACKSON; ***171** R-9; elev. 532ft./162m.; ★ **CARB-**; mail Carbondale **z** 62901; ● 60
Highland Glen; RMC Place; KANE; ***170** B-11; ★ **CHI**; mail Elgin **z** 60123; pop. incl. with Elgin (Inc. Place)
Highland Haven; RMC Place; KANE; ***170** B-11; elev. 881ft./269m.; ★ **CHI**; mail Elgin **z** 60123; ● 100
Highland Hills; RMC Place; DUPAGE; **172** I-5; ★ **CHI**; mail Lombard **z** 60148; pop. incl. with Lombard (Inc. Place)
Highland Lake; RMC Place; LAKE; **172** A-5; ★ **CHI**; mail Grayslake **z** 60030; pop. incl. with Round Lake Park (Inc. Place)
Highland Park; Inc. Place; LAKE; **170** B-13; elev. 690ft./210m.; 🅿 🅷 ■; ★ **CHI**; **z** 60035, **z** 60037; Ⓟ 30,575; © 31,365; ® 30,262; ◆ 31,000
Highland Park; RMC Place; MARION; ***171** O-10; elev. 574ft./175m.; mail Salem **z** 62881; ● 120
Highlands; RMC Place; COOK; ★ **CHI**; pop. incl. with Arlington Heights (Inc. Place)
Highlands; RMC Place; DUPAGE; ★ **CHI**; mail Hinsdale **z** 60521; pop. incl. with Hinsdale (Inc. Place)
Highlands-Clarks; RMC Place; KENDALL; ***170** D-11; elev. 650ft./198m.; ★ **CHI**; mail Oswego **z** 60543; ● 200
Highland Shores; RMC Place; MCHENRY; ***170** A-11; ★ **CHI**; mail Wonder Lake **z** 60097; ● 950
Highlawn; RMC Place; COOK; ★ **CHI**; mail Riverdale **z** 60827; pop. incl. with Riverdale (Inc. Place)
High Meadows; RMC Place; PEORIA; ★ **PEOR**; mail Peoria **z** 61607; ● 200
High Point; RMC Place; COOK; ★ **CHI**; mail Schaumburg **z** 60195; pop. incl. with Hoffman Estates (Inc. Place)
Highway Village; RMC Place; TAZEWELL; ***170** G-8; ★ **PEOR**; mail East Peoria **z** 61611; pop. incl. with East Peoria (Inc. Place)
Highwood; Inc. Place; LAKE; **170** B-13; elev. 685ft./209m.; 🅿; ★ **CHI**; **z** 60040; Ⓟ 5,331; © 4,143; ® 5,470
Highwood; RMC Place; ST. CLAIR; ★ **ST.L**; mail Belleville **z** 62221; pop. incl. with Belleville (Inc. Place)
Highwood Terrace; RMC Place; ST. CLAIR; ★ **ST.L**; mail Belleville **z** 62221; pop. incl. with Belleville (Inc. Place)
Hilcrest; RMC Place; MONTGOMERY; mail Taylor Springs **z** 62089; ● 300
Hildreth; RMC Place; EDGAR; ***170** J-13; mail Sidell **z** 61876
Hillcrest; RMC Place; CALHOUN; ***171** L-5; mail Nebo **z** 62355; rural
Hillcrest; RMC Place; CHRISTIAN; ***171** K-9; elev. 629ft./192m.; mail Taylorville **z** 62568; pop. incl. with Taylorville (Inc. Place)
Hillcrest; RMC Place; DOUGLAS; ***170** J-11; mail Tuscola **z** 61953; ● 200
Hillcrest; RMC Place; HENRY; ***170** D-6; elev. 650ft./198m.; mail Geneseo **z** 61254; pop. incl. with Geneseo (Inc. Place)
Hillcrest; Inc. Place; OGLE; **170** C-9; mail Rochelle **z** 61068; Ⓟ 828; © 1,158
Hilldale Villages; RMC Place; COOK; ★ **CHI**; mail Schaumburg **z** 60195; pop. incl. with Hoffman Estates (Inc. Place)
Hillerman; RMC Place; MASSAC; **171** T-10; elev. 380ft./116m.; mail Grand Chain **z** 62941; ● 35
Hillery; RMC Place; VERMILION; ***170** I-13; ★ **DANV**; mail Danville **z** 61834; ● 300
Hillsboro; Inc. Place; ⊡ MONTGOMERY; **171** M-8; elev. 630ft./192m.; 🅿 🅷; **z** 62049; Ⓟ 4,400; © 4,359
Hillsboro; MCD-Township; MONTGOMERY; ***171** M-8; 🅿; **z** 62049; includes part of the City of Hillsboro; Ⓟ 6,726; © 5,515; ® 7,504
Hillsdale; Inc. Place; ROCK ISLAND; **170** D-6; elev. 587ft./179m.; 🅿; **z** 61257; Ⓟ 489; © 588
Hillside; Inc. Place; COOK; **172** H-6; elev. 659ft./201m.; 🅿; ★ **CHI**; **z** 60162-63; Ⓟ 7,672; © 8,155
Hillside Manor; RMC Place; KANKAKEE; ***170** F-12; elev. 655ft./200m.; ★ **KANK**; mail Kankakee **z** 60901; ● 330
Hill Top; RMC Place; MCLEAN; ***170** G-10; mail Lexington **z** 61753; pop. incl. with Lexington (Inc. Place)
Hill Top; RMC Place; MENARD; ***170** J-7; mail Petersburg **z** 62675; rural
Hillview; Inc. Place; GREENE; **171** L-5; elev. 439ft./134m.; 🅿; **z** 62050; Ⓟ 271; © 179
Hillyard; MCD-Township; MACOUPIN; ***171** M-7; mail Shipman **z** 62685; Ⓟ 792; © 733
Himrod; RMC Place; VERMILION; ***170** J-13; ★ **DANV**; mail Westville **z** 61883; rural
Hinckley; Inc. Place; DEKALB; **170** C-10; elev. 750ft./229m.; 🅿; **z** 60520; Ⓟ 1,682; © 1,994
Hindsboro; Inc. Place; DOUGLAS; **171** K-12; elev. 649ft./198m.; 🅿; **z** 61930; Ⓟ 346; © 361
Hinsdale; Inc. Place; DUPAGE, COOK; **172** I-6; elev. 725ft./221m.; 🅿 🅷 ■; ★ **CHI**; **z** 60521-23; Ⓟ 16,029; © 17,349; ◆ 18,197
Hinswood; RMC Place; DUPAGE; ★ **CHI**; mail Darien **z** 60561; pop. incl. with Darien (Inc. Place)
Hire; MCD-Township; MCDONOUGH; ***170** H-4; mail Colchester **z** 62326; Ⓟ 269; © 246
Hitt; RMC Place; CARROLL; ***170** B-7; elev. 747ft./228m.; mail Milledgeville **z** 61051; rural
Hittle; MCD-Township; TAZEWELL; ***170** H-8; mail Armington **z** 61721; Ⓟ 650; © 658
Hodgetown; RMC Place; FRANKLIN; ***171** Q-9; elev. 460ft./140m.; ★ **CARB-**; mail Mulkeytown **z** 62865; ● 70
Hodgkins; Inc. Place; COOK; **172** J-7; elev. 600ft./183m.; 🅿; ★ **CHI**; **z** 60525; Ⓟ 1,963; © 2,134
Hoffman; Inc. Place; CLINTON; **171** O-9; elev. 457ft./139m.; 🅿; **z** 62250; Ⓟ 492; © 460
Hoffman Estates; Inc. Place; COOK; **172** F-3; elev. 790ft./241m.; 🅿 🅷; ★ **CHI**; **z** 60010, **z** 60067, **z** 60169, **z** 60173, **z** 60179, **z** 60192, **z** 60194-96 & mail Elgin **z** 60120; Ⓟ 46,561; © 49,495; ® 49,489; ◆ 49,606
Hoffmann Edition; RMC Place; IROQUOIS; ***170** H-12; mail Cissna Park **z** 60924; ● 30
Holbrook; RMC Place; COOK; ***170** D-13; ★ **CHI**; mail Chicago Heights **z** 60411
Holcomb; RMC Place; OGLE; **170** B-9; elev. 841ft./256m.; 🅿; **z** 61043; ● 270
Holcombville Corners; RMC Place; MCHENRY; ***170** A-11; ★ **CHI**; mail Crystal Lake **z** 60012; ● 100
Holden; RMC Place; PERRY; ***171** Q-9; mail Du Quoin **z** 62832; rural
Holder; RMC Place; MCLEAN; **170** H-10; elev. 838ft./255m.; 🅿; **z** 61736; ● 60
Holiday; FAYETTE, SHELBY; see Holliday (RMC Place)
Holiday Hills; Inc. Place; MCHENRY; **172** B-3; elev. 750ft./229m.; 🅿; ★ **CHI**; **z** 60050-51; Ⓟ 807; © 831
Holiday Lake; LA SALLE; see Lake Holiday (RMC Place)
Holiday Shores; RMC Place; MADISON; ***171** N-7; ★ **ST.L**; mail Edwardsville **z** 62025; ● 600
Holland; RMC Place; SHELBY, EFFINGHAM; ***171** M-10; mail Beecher City **z** 62414; ● 30
Holland; MCD-Township; SHELBY; ***171** L-10; mail Beecher City **z** 62414; Ⓟ 408; © 423
Hollandia; RMC Place; ST. CLAIR; ***171** O-7; ★ **ST.L**; mail Belleville **z** 62221; pop. incl. with Fairview Heights (Inc. Place)
Hollenback; RMC Place; GRUNDY; ***170** E-11; elev. 517ft./158m.; mail Morris **z** 60450; ● 300
Hollendale; RMC Place; COOK; ★ **CHI**; mail South Holland **z** 60473; pop. incl. with South Holland (Inc. Place)
Holliday (Holiday); RMC Place; FAYETTE, SHELBY; ***171** M-10; mail Beecher City **z** 62414; ● 30
Hollis; RMC Place; PEORIA; ***170** H-8; mail Peoria **z** 61607; rural
Hollis; MCD-Township; PEORIA; ***170** H-7; mail Peoria **z** 61607; Ⓟ 1,603; © 1,707
Hollowayville; Inc. Place; BUREAU; ***170** E-9; elev. 650ft./198m.; 🅿; **z** 61356; Ⓟ 37; © 90
Hollydale; RMC Place; COOK; ★ **CHI**; mail Homewood **z** 60430; pop. incl. with Homewood (Inc. Place)
Hollywood Heights; RMC Place; ST. CLAIR; **195** E-9; ★ **ST.L**; mail Caseyville **z** 62232; ● 1,060
Holmes Center; RMC Place; PEORIA; mail Chillicothe **z** 61523; ● 100
Homberg; RMC Place; POPE; ***171** S-11; mail Golconda **z** 62938
Home Gardens; RMC Place; VERMILION; ★ **DANV**; mail Danville **z** 61832; pop. incl. with Danville (Inc. Place)
Homer; Inc. Place; CHAMPAIGN; **170** J-12; elev. 673ft./205m.; 🅿; **z** 61849; Ⓟ 1,264; © 1,200
Homer; MCD-Township; WILL; ***170** D-12; ★ **CHI**; mail Lockport **z** 60441; Ⓟ 21,464; © 28,992
Homer Glen; Inc. Place; WILL; ▲ Homer; **172** L-6; 🅿; ★ **CHI**; **z** 60441, **z** 60491; incorporated April 7, 2001; not reported in 2000 Census; ● 22,800; ◆ 24,224
Homerican Villas; RMC Place; COOK; ★ **CHI**; mail Des Plaines **z** 60016; pop. incl. with Des Plaines (Inc. Place)
Homestead; RMC Place; ST. CLAIR; ★ **ST.L**; mail O Fallon **z** 62269; pop. incl. with O'Fallon (Inc. Place)
Hometown; Inc. Place; COOK; **172** K-8; elev. 620ft./189m.; 🅿; ★ **CHI**; **z** 60456; Ⓟ 4,769; © 4,467
Homewood; Inc. Place; COOK; **172** M-9; elev. 650ft./198m.; 🅿 ■; ★ **CHI**; **z** 60422, **z** 60430; Ⓟ 19,278; © 19,543; ◆ 18,840
Homewood; RMC Place; ROCK ISLAND; ★ **D-RI-M**; mail Moline **z** 61265; pop. incl. with Moline (Inc. Place)
Homewood Acres; RMC Place; COOK; ★ **CHI**; mail Homewood **z** 60430; ● 200
Homewood Shores; RMC Place; COOK; ★ **CHI**; mail Homewood **z** 60430; pop. incl. with Homewood (Inc. Place)
Homewood Terrace; RMC Place; COOK; ★ **CHI**; mail Homewood **z** 60430; pop. incl. with Homewood (Inc. Place)
Honegger; RMC Place; LIVINGSTON; mail Forrest **z** 61741; rural
Honey Bend; RMC Place; MONTGOMERY; ***171** L-8; mail Litchfield **z** 62056; ● 50
Honey Creek; MCD-Township; ADAMS; ***170** I-3; mail Coatsburg **z** 62325; Ⓟ 700; © 738
Honey Creek; MCD-Township; CRAWFORD; ***171** N-13; mail Flat Rock **z** 62427; Ⓟ 1,497; © 1,566
Honey Creek; RMC Place; OGLE; ***170** B-9; mail Chana **z** 61015; ● 30
Honey Point; MCD-Township; MACOUPIN; ***171** M-7; mail Litchfield **z** 62056; Ⓟ 290; © 225
Honeytree; RMC Place; WILL; ★ **CHI**; pop. incl. with Romeoville (Inc. Place)
Hononegah Heights; RMC Place; WINNEBAGO; ***170** A-9; ★ **RKFD**; mail Roscoe **z** 61073; ● 100
Hoodville; RMC Place; HAMILTON; ***171** Q-11; elev. 450ft./137m.; mail Mc Leansboro **z** 62859
Hookdale; RMC Place; BOND; ***171** N-8; mail Smithboro **z** 62284; ● 60
Hoopeston; Inc. Place; VERMILION; **170** H-13; elev. 718ft./219m.; 🅿 🅷; **z** 60942; Ⓟ 5,871; © 5,965
Hooppole; Inc. Place; HENRY; **170** D-7; elev. 620ft./189m.; 🅿; **z** 61258; Ⓟ 196; © 162
Hoosier; MCD-Township; CLAY; ***171** N-11; mail Louisville **z** 62858; Ⓟ 409; © 357
Hope; MCD-Township; LA SALLE; ***170** F-9; mail Lostant **z** 61334; Ⓟ 747; © 684
Hope; RMC Place; VERMILION; ***170** I-12; elev. 715ft./218m.; mail Armstrong **z** 61812
Hopedale; Inc. Place; TAZEWELL; ▲ Hopedale; **170** H-8; 🅿 🅷; **z** 61747; Ⓟ 805; © 929
Hopedale; MCD-Township; TAZEWELL; ***170** H-8; 🅿; **z** 61747; Ⓟ 1,679; © 1,921
Hopewell; Inc. Place; MARSHALL; **170** F-8; 🅿; **z** 61565; Ⓟ 343; © 396
Hopewell; MCD-Township; MARSHALL; ***170** F-8; 🅿; **z** 61565 & mail Lacon **z** 61540; Ⓟ 511; © 552
Hop Hollow; RMC Place; MADISON; ***171** N-6; ★ **ST.L**; mail Godfrey **z** 62035; pop. incl. with Godfrey (Inc. Place)
Hopkins; MCD-Township; WHITESIDE; ***170** C-7; mail Sterling **z** 61081; Ⓟ 2,308; © 2,381
Hopkins Park (Pembroke); Inc. Place; KANKAKEE; ▲ Pembroke; **170** F-13; 🅿; **z** 60944 & mail Pembroke Township **z** 60958; Ⓟ 601; © 711
Hopper; RMC Place; HENDERSON; ***170** G-4; elev. 572ft./174m.; mail Stronghurst **z** 61480; rural
Horace; RMC Place; EDGAR; ***171** K-13; elev. 657ft./200m.; mail Chrisman **z** 61924; ● 25
Hord; RMC Place; CLAY; **171** N-11; mail Louisville **z** 62858; ● 175
Hornsby; RMC Place; MACOUPIN; ***171** M-7; mail Litchfield **z** 62056; ● 50
Horseshoe; RMC Place; SALINE; ***171** R-11; elev. 364ft./111m.; mail Equality **z** 62934; rural
Houston; MCD-Township; ADAMS; ***170** I-4; mail Golden **z** 62339; Ⓟ 287; © 250
Houston; RMC Place; RANDOLPH; ***171** P-7; mail Sparta **z** 62286; ● 50
Howardton; RMC Place; JACKSON; ***171** R-8; elev. 359ft./109m.; mail Grand Tower **z** 62942; ● 30
Howe; RMC Place; BUREAU; mail Depue **z** 61322; pop. incl. with Depue (Inc. Place)
Howe Terrace; RMC Place; COOK; ***170** B-12; elev. 867ft./264m.; ★ **CHI**; mail Barrington **z** 60010; ● 280
Hoyleton; Inc. Place; WASHINGTON; ▲ Hoyleton; **171** O-9; 🅿; **z** 62803; Ⓟ 508; © 520
Hoyleton; MCD-Township; WASHINGTON; ***171** O-8; 🅿; **z** 62803; Ⓟ 1,214; © 1,187
Hubbard Woods; RMC Place; COOK; ***170** B-13; ★ **CHI**; mail Winnetka **z** 60093; pop. incl. with Winnetka (Inc. Place)
Hubbard Woods; RMC Place; MARION; ***171** O-9; mail Centralia **z** 62801; ● 60
Hubly; RMC Place; MENARD; ***170** I-8; 🅿; **z** 62642; rural
Hudgens; RMC Place; WILLIAMSON; ***171** R-10; mail Marion **z** 62959; rural
Hudson; Inc. Place; MCLEAN; ▲ Hudson; **170** H-9; elev. 765ft./233m.; 🅿; **z** 61748; Ⓟ 1,006; © 1,510
Hudson; MCD-Township; MCLEAN; ***170** G-9; 🅿; **z** 61748; Ⓟ 1,853; © 2,318
Huegely; RMC Place; WASHINGTON; ***171** O-8; elev. 496ft./151m.; mail Hoyleton **z** 62803; rural
Huey; Inc. Place; CLINTON; **171** O-9; elev. 454ft./138m.; 🅿; **z** 62252; Ⓟ 210; © 196
Hugh's Addition; RMC Place; SANGAMON; mail Sherman **z** 62684; ● 30
Hugo; RMC Place; DOUGLAS; ***171** K-12; mail Tuscola **z** 61953
Hull (Hulls); Inc. Place; PIKE; **171** K-3; elev. 469ft./143m.; 🅿; **z** 62343; Ⓟ 514; © 474
Hulls; PIKE; see Hull (Inc. Place)
Humboldt; Inc. Place; COLES; ▲ Humboldt; **171** K-11; 🅿; **z** 61931; Ⓟ 470; © 481
Humboldt; MCD-Township; COLES; ***171** K-11; 🅿; **z** 61931; Ⓟ 1,346; © 1,341
Humbolt Park; RMC Place; COOK; ★ **CHI**; mail Chicago **z** 60651; pop. incl. with Chicago (Inc. Place)
Hume; Inc. Place; EDGAR; **170** J-13; elev. 651ft./198m.; 🅿; **z** 61932; Ⓟ 406; © 382
Hume; MCD-Township; WHITESIDE; ***170** C-7; mail Rock Falls **z** 61071; Ⓟ 514; © 472
Humm Wye; RMC Place; HARDIN; **171** S-11; elev. 451ft./137m.; mail Golconda **z** 62938; ● 25
Humrick; RMC Place; VERMILION; ***170** J-13; elev. 650ft./198m.; mail Ridge Farm **z** 61870; ● 50
Hunt; JASPER; see Hunt City (RMC Place)
Hunt City (Hunt); RMC Place; JASPER; ▲ Hunt City; **171** M-12; mail Willow Hill **z** 62480; ● 90
Hunt City; MCD-Township; JASPER; ***171** M-12; mail Willow Hill **z** 62480; Ⓟ 444; © 294
Hunter; RMC Place; BOONE; ***170** A-10; mail Caledonia **z** 61011; rural
Hunter; RMC Place; EDGAR; ***171** K-13; elev. 612ft./187m.; mail Paris **z** 61944; rural
Hunter; MCD-Township; EDGAR; ***171** K-13; mail Paris **z** 61944; Ⓟ 269; © 263
Hunter Trail; RMC Place; DUPAGE; ★ **CHI**; mail Oak Brook **z** 60523; pop. incl. with Oak Brook (Inc. Place)
Huntington; RMC Place; DUPAGE; ★ **CHI**; mail Naperville **z** 60540; pop. incl. with Naperville (Inc. Place)
Huntington Commons; RMC Place; COOK; ★ **CHI**; mail Mount Prospect **z** 60056; pop. incl. with Mount Prospect (Inc. Place)
Huntington Park; RMC Place; COOK; ★ **CHI**; mail Elgin **z** 60120; pop. incl. with Elgin (Inc. Place)
Huntinton Park; RMC Place; MADISON; ***171** N-6; ★ **ST.L**; mail Godfrey **z** 62035; pop. incl. with Godfrey (Inc. Place)
Huntley; Inc. Place; MCHENRY, KANE; **170** B-11; elev. 900ft./274m.; 🅿; ★ **CHI**; **z** 60142; Ⓟ 2,453; © 5,730; ◆ 9,820
Huntsville; RMC Place; SCHUYLER; ▲ Huntsville; ***170** I-4; elev. 654ft./199m.; 🅿; **z** 62344; ● 40
Huntsville; MCD-Township; SCHUYLER; ***170** I-4; 🅿; **z** 62344; Ⓟ 189; © 160
Hurlbut; MCD-Township; LOGAN; ***170** J-8; mail Elkhart **z** 62634; Ⓟ 363; © 367
Hurricane; MCD-Township; FAYETTE; ***171** M-9; mail Ramsey **z** 62080; Ⓟ 235; © 247
Hurst; Inc. Place; WILLIAMSON; **171** R-9; elev. 390ft./119m.; 🅿; ★ **CARB-**; **z** 62949; Ⓟ 842; © 805
Hutchins Park; RMC Place; WINNEBAGO; ***170** A-9; ★ **RKFD**; mail Rockford **z** 61103; ● 190
Hutsonville; Inc. Place; CRAWFORD; ▲ Hutsonville; **171** M-13; 🅿; **z** 62433; Ⓟ 622; © 568; ® 631
Hutsonville; MCD-Township; CRAWFORD; ***171** M-13; 🅿; **z** 62433; Ⓟ 1,333; © 1,303
Hutton (Salisbury); RMC Place; COLES; ▲ Hutton; **171** L-12; mail Charleston **z** 61920; ● 50
Hutton; MCD-Township; COLES; ***171** L-12; mail Charleston **z** 61920; Ⓟ 778; © 841
Hyde Park; RMC Place; COOK; ***170** C-13; ★ **CHI**; mail Chicago **z** 60615, **z** 60653; pop. incl. with Chicago (Inc. Place)

I

Idaville Corner; RMC Place; IROQUOIS; ***170** G-12; mail Cissna Park **z** 60924; rural
Ideal; RMC Place; CARROLL; ***170** C-7; elev. 860ft./262m.; mail Thomson **z** 61285; rural
Idlewild; RMC Place; LAKE; ***170** A-12; ★ **CHI**; mail Grayslake **z** 60030
Idlewood; RMC Place; JEFFERSON; ***171** P-10; mail Mount Vernon **z** 62864; rural
Iliana; RMC Place; VERMILION; ***170** I-13; ★ **DANV**; mail State Line **z** 47982; ● 50
Illiana Heights; RMC Place; KANKAKEE; ***170** E-13; mail Momence **z** 60954; ● 300
Illini; MCD-Township; MACON; ***170** J-9; mail Warrensburg **z** 62573; Ⓟ 1,517; © 1,563
Illinois City; RMC Place; ROCK ISLAND; **170** E-4; elev. 768ft./234m.; 🅿; **z** 61259; ● 250
Illinois Veterans Home; RMC Place; ADAMS; ***170** J-3; ★ **QUIN**; mail Quincy **z** 62301; pop. incl. with Quincy (Inc. Place)
Illiopolis; Inc. Place; SANGAMON; ▲ Illiopolis; **170** J-9; elev. 602ft./183m.; 🅿; **z** 62539; Ⓟ 934; © 916
Illiopolis; MCD-Township; SANGAMON; ***170** J-9; 🅿; **z** 62539; Ⓟ 1,366; © 1,302
Imbs; RMC Place; ST. CLAIR; ***171** O-6; ★ **ST.L**; mail East Carondelet **z** 62240; rural
Imperial; RMC Place; LAKE; ★ **CHI**; mail Libertyville **z** 60048; ● 150
Ina; Inc. Place; JEFFERSON; **171** P-10; elev. 433ft./132m.; 🅿; **z** 62846; Ⓟ 489; © 2,455
Inclose; RMC Place; EDGAR; ***171** L-12; mail Kansas **z** 61933; rural
Independence; RMC Place; PIKE; ***171** K-4; mail Pittsfield **z** 62363; rural
Independence; MCD-Township; SALINE; ***171** R-11; mail Harrisburg **z** 62946; Ⓟ 1,100; © 1,221
Indian Creek; Inc. Place; LAKE; **172** C-6; elev. 741ft./226m.; 🅿; ★ **CHI**; **z** 60061; Ⓟ 247; © 194
Indian Creek; MCD-Township; WHITE; ***171** Q-11; mail Norris City **z** 62869; Ⓟ 2,373; © 2,129
Indian Grove; MCD-Township; LIVINGSTON; ***170** G-11; mail Fairbury **z** 61739; Ⓟ 4,139; © 4,315
Indian Head Park; Inc. Place; COOK; **172** J-6; elev. 650ft./198m.; 🅿; ★ **CHI**; **z** 60525; Ⓟ 3,503; © 3,685
Indian Hill; RMC Place; COOK; ***170** D-13; ★ **CHI**; mail Winnetka **z** 60093; pop. incl. with Winnetka (Inc. Place)
Indian Hill; RMC Place; DUPAGE; ★ **CHI**; mail Naperville **z** 60563; pop. incl. with Naperville (Inc. Place)
Indian Hills; RMC Place; COOK; ★ **CHI**; mail Chicago Heights **z** 60411; pop. incl. with Sauk Village (Inc. Place)
Indian Hills; RMC Place; JO DAVIESS; ***170** A-5; elev. 800ft./244m.; ★ **DUB**; mail East Dubuque **z** 61025; ● 130
Indian Hills; LAKE; see Round Lake Heights (Inc. Place)
Indian Oaks; RMC Place; KANKAKEE; **170** E-13; elev. 691ft./211m.; ★ **KANK**; mail Bourbonnais **z** 60914; ● 500
Indian Oaks; RMC Place; WILL; ★ **CHI**; mail Bolingbrook **z** 60440; pop. incl. with Bolingbrook (Inc. Place)
Indianola; Inc. Place; VERMILION; **170** J-13; elev. 674ft./205m.; 🅿; **z** 61850; Ⓟ 336; © 207; ® 224
Indian Point; MCD-Township; KNOX; ***170** G-6; mail Abingdon **z** 61410; Ⓟ 1,781; © 1,682
Indian Point; RMC Place; LAKE; ★ **CHI**; mail Antioch **z** 60002; ● 300
Indian Point; RMC Place; MENARD; ***170** J-7; elev. 581ft./177m.; mail Athens **z** 62613; ● 40
Indian Prairie; MCD-Township; WAYNE; ***171** O-11; mail Cisne **z** 62823; Ⓟ 571; © 573

Entries in **UPPERCASE** are counties.
Entries in **bold** have populations of 2,500 or more.
Names in parentheses are alternate names.

Inc. Place	Incorporated Place
RMC Place	Rand McNally Designated Place
CDP	Census Designated Place
MCD	Minor Civil Division

⊡ County Seat
▲ Minor Civil Division
elev. Elevation
🅿 Post Office

🅷 Hospital
🅲 College
■ Principal Business Center
★ Ranally Metro Area (RMA) Abbreviation
z Zip Code(s)

Ⓟ Previous Census Population
® Revised Census Population
Ⓐ Annexation Population
● Rand McNally Population Estimate
© Final Census Population
Ⓢ Special Census Population
◆ Estimated Population

For additional definitions see Glossary, Volume 1, and Introduction, Volume 2.

Indian Ridge; RMC Place; MCHENRY; 6 mi. NW of McHenry; ★ CHI; mail Wonder Lake Z 60097; ● 1,000
Indian Ridge; RMC Place; PIATT; *170 I-11; elev. 697ft./212m.; mail White Heath Z 61884; ● 50
Indiantown; MCD-Township; BUREAU; *170 E-8; mail Bradford Z 61421; Ⓟ 781; Ⓒ 732
Indian Trail Estates; RMC Place; LAKE; *170 B-12; ★ CHI; mail Deerfield Z 60015; pop. incl. with Lincolnshire (Inc. Place)
Industrial Park; RMC Place; JEFFERSON; *171 P-10; elev. 450ft./137m.; mail Mount Vernon Z 62864; pop. incl. with Mount Vernon (Inc. Place)
Industry; Inc. Place; MCDONOUGH; ▲ Industry; 170 H-5; 🅿; Z 61440; Ⓟ 571; Ⓒ 540
Industry; MCD-Township; MCDONOUGH; *170 H-5; 🅿; Z 61440; Ⓟ 885; Ⓒ 851
Ingalls Park; CDP; WILL; 172 N-5; ★ CHI; mail Joliet Z 60431; Ⓟ 3,173; Ⓒ 3,082
Ingalton; RMC Place; DUPAGE; *170 C-12; ★ CHI; mail West Chicago Z 60185; rural
Ingleside; RMC Place; LAKE; 172 A-4; 🅿; ★ CHI; Z 60041; ● 1,700
Ingleside Shores; RMC Place; LAKE; ★ CHI; mail Ingleside Z 60041
Ingraham; RMC Place; CLAY; 171 N-11; elev. 480ft./146m.; 🅿; Z 62434; ● 150
Ingram Hill; RMC Place; SALINE; mail Harrisburg Z 62946; rural
International Village; RMC Place; COOK; ★ CHI; mail Schaumburg Z 60173; pop. incl. with Schaumburg (Inc. Place)
International Village; RMC Place; WILL; ★ CHI; mail Bolingbrook Z 60440; pop. incl. with Bolingbrook (Inc. Place)
Inverness; Inc. Place; COOK; 172 E-5; elev. 853ft./260m.; 🅿; ★ CHI; Z 60010, Z 60067; Ⓟ 6,516; Ⓒ 6,749
Inverness on the Ponds; RMC Place; COOK; *170 B-12; ★ CHI; mail Palatine Z 60067; pop. incl. with Inverness (Inc. Place)
Iola; Inc. Place; CLAY; 171 N-10; elev. 524ft./160m.; 🅿; Z 62838; Ⓟ 163; Ⓒ 171
Iowa Junction; RMC Place; PEORIA; ★ PEOR; pop. incl. with Peoria (Inc. Place)
Ipava; Inc. Place; FULTON; 170 H-6; elev. 660ft./201m.; 🅿; Z 61441; Ⓟ 483; Ⓒ 506
Irene; RMC Place; BOONE; *170 B-10; mail Cherry Valley Z 61016
Irishtown; MCD-Township; CLINTON; *171 N-8; mail Keyesport Z 62253; Ⓟ 889; Ⓒ 1,078
Irondale; RMC Place; COOK; ★ CHI; mail Chicago Z 60617; pop. incl. with Chicago (Inc. Place)
Iroquois; Inc. Place; IROQUOIS; ▲ Concord; 170 G-13; elev. 660ft./201m.; 🅿; Z 60945; Ⓟ 199; Ⓒ 207
Iroquois; MCD-Township; IROQUOIS; *170 G-13; 🅿; Z 60945 & mail Crescent City Z 60928; Ⓟ 591; Ⓒ 652
IROQUOIS; 170 G-12; Ⓟ 30,787; Ⓒ 31,334; ◆ 30,294
Irving; Inc. Place; MONTGOMERY; ▲ Irving; 171 M-8; 🅿; Z 62051; Ⓟ 516; Ⓒ 2,484; Ⓡ 495
Irving; MCD-Township; MONTGOMERY; *171 M-8; 🅿; Z 62051; Ⓟ 1,074; Ⓒ 2,983; Ⓡ 994
Irving Park; RMC Place; COOK; *170 C-13; ★ CHI; mail Chicago Z 60641; pop. incl. with Chicago (Inc. Place)
Irvington; Inc. Place; WASHINGTON; ▲ Irvington; 171 O-9; elev. 530ft./162m.; 🅿; Z 62848; Ⓟ 827; Ⓒ 736
Irvington; MCD-Township; WASHINGTON; *171 O-9; 🅿; Z 62848; Ⓟ 1,624; Ⓒ 1,496
Irwin; Inc. Place; KANKAKEE; *170 F-12; elev. 662ft./202m.; mail Kankakee Z 60901; Ⓟ 50; Ⓒ 92
Isabel; RMC Place; EDGAR; *171 K-12; mail Oakland Z 61943; ● 50
Isabel; MCD-Township; FULTON; *170 I-6; mail Lewistown Z 61542; Ⓟ 247; Ⓒ 206
Island Grove; RMC Place; JASPER; mail Teutopolis Z 62467; rural
Island Grove; MCD-Township; SANGAMON; *171 K-7; mail Pleasant Plains Z 62677; Ⓟ 494; Ⓒ 532; Ⓡ 535
Island Lake; Inc. Place; LAKE, MCHENRY; 172 B-3; elev. 780ft./238m.; 🅿; ★ CHI; Z 60042; Ⓟ 4,449; Ⓒ 8,153
Israelite Farm; RMC Place; PULASKI; *171 T-9; mail Ullin Z 62992; ● 100
Itasca; Inc. Place; DUPAGE; 172 G-5; elev. 686ft./209m.; 🅿; ★ CHI; Z 60143; Ⓟ 6,947; Ⓒ 8,302
Itasca Ranchettes; RMC Place; DUPAGE; *170 C-12; ★ CHI; mail Itasca Z 60143; ● 650
Iuka; Inc. Place; MARION; ▲ Iuka; 171 O-10; elev. 518ft./158m.; 🅿; Z 62849; Ⓟ 388; Ⓒ 598
Iuka; MCD-Township; MARION; *171 O-10; 🅿; Z 62849; Ⓟ 965; Ⓒ 1,100
Ivanhoe; RMC Place; LAKE; 172 B-5; ★ CHI; mail Mundelein Z 60060; ● 100
Ivanhoe; RMC Place; WILL; ★ CHI; mail Bolingbrook Z 60440; pop. incl. with Bolingbrook (Inc. Place)
Ivanhoe Estates; RMC Place; CHAMPAIGN; *170 I-12; elev. 710ft./216m.; ★ CH-U; mail Urbana Z 61802; ● 700
Ivesdale; Inc. Place; CHAMPAIGN, PIATT; 170 J-11; elev. 694ft./212m.; 🅿; Z 61851; Ⓟ 339; Ⓒ 288
Ivy Glen; RMC Place; KANE; ★ CHI; mail Aurora Z 60506; pop. incl. with Aurora (Inc. Place)
Ivy Heights; RMC Place; MADISON; ★ ST.L; mail East Alton Z 62024
Ivy Hill; RMC Place; COOK; ★ CHI; pop. incl. with Arlington Heights (Inc. Place)

J

Jackson; MCD-Township; EFFINGHAM; *171 M-10; mail Effingham Z 62401; Ⓟ 1,023; Ⓒ 1,178
Jackson; MCD-Township; WILL; *170 D-12; ★ CHI; mail Elwood Z 60421; Ⓟ 2,700; Ⓒ 3,541
JACKSON; 171 Q-8; Ⓟ 61,067; Ⓒ 59,612; Ⓡ 59,627; ◆ 56,637
Jackson Park; RMC Place; COOK; *170 C-13; ★ CHI; mail Chicago Z 60637; pop. incl. with Chicago (Inc. Place)
Jacksonville; Inc. Place; ⊡ MORGAN; 171 K-6; elev. 613ft./187m.; 🅿 🅷 🅲 1,724 ■; Z 62650-51; Ⓟ 19,324; Ⓒ 18,940; Ⓡ 19,939; ◆ 18,691
Jacksonville Junction; RMC Place; MORGAN; pop. incl. with Jacksonville (Inc. Place)
Jacob; RMC Place; JACKSON; *171 R-8; elev. 360ft./110m.; 🅿; Z 62950; ● 50
Jalapa; RMC Place; GREENE; *171 L-6; elev. 495ft./151m.; mail Kane Z 62054; rural
Jamaica; RMC Place; VERMILION; ▲ Jamaica; *170 J-13; elev. 677ft./206m.; mail Fairmount Z 61841; ● 60
Jamaica; MCD-Township; VERMILION; *170 J-13; mail Fairmount Z 61841; Ⓟ 229; Ⓒ 206
Jamesburg; RMC Place; VERMILION; *170 I-13; elev. 682ft./208m.; mail Potomac Z 61865; ● 50
Jamestown; RMC Place; CLINTON; 171 N-8; mail Pocahontas Z 62275; ● 120
Jamestown; RMC Place; PERRY; *171 Q-8; mail Cutler Z 62238; rural
Janesville; RMC Place; CUMBERLAND, COLES; 171 L-11; elev. 695ft./212m.; 🅿; Z 62435; ● 150
Jarvis; MCD-Township; MADISON; *171 N-7; ★ ST.L; mail Troy Z 62294; Ⓟ 9,360; Ⓒ 12,062
Jasper; MCD-Township; WAYNE; *171 O-11; mail Fairfield Z 62837; Ⓟ 1,746; Ⓒ 1,726
JASPER; 171 M-12; Ⓟ 10,609; Ⓒ 10,117; ◆ 9,598
Jefferson; MCD-Township; STEPHENSON; *170 B-7; mail Pearl City Z 61062; Ⓟ 277; Ⓒ 301
JEFFERSON; 171 O-9; Ⓟ 37,020; Ⓒ 40,045; ◆ 39,933
Jefferson Park; RMC Place; COOK; *170 C-13; 🅿; ★ CHI; Z 60630; pop. incl. with Chicago (Inc. Place)
Jeffersonville; WAYNE; see Geff (Inc. Place)
Jeffries; RMC Place; WILLIAMSON; *171 R-9; ★ CARB-; mail Johnston City Z 62951; ● 30
Jeiseyville; CHRISTIAN; see Jeisyville (Inc. Place)
Jeisyville (Jeiseyville); Inc. Place; CHRISTIAN; *171 K-8; elev. 582ft./177m.; mail Taylorville Z 62568; Ⓟ 126; Ⓒ 128
Jenkins; RMC Place; DE WITT; *170 I-9; elev. 735ft./224m.; mail Clinton Z 61727; rural
Jerome; Inc. Place; SANGAMON; 173 G-16; elev. 600ft./183m.; 🅿; ★ SPRG; Z 62704; Ⓟ 1,206; Ⓒ 1,414
Jersey; MCD-Township; JERSEY; *171 M-6; mail Jerseyville Z 62052; Ⓟ 9,022; Ⓒ 9,496
JERSEY; 171 M-5; Ⓟ 20,539; Ⓒ 21,668; ◆ 22,494
Jerseyville; Inc. Place; ⊡ JERSEY; ▲ Jersey; 171 M-6; elev. 663ft./202m.; 🅿 🅷; Z 62052; Ⓟ 7,382; Ⓒ 7,984
Jewett; Inc. Place; CUMBERLAND; 171 M-12; elev. 584ft./178m.; 🅿; Z 62436; Ⓟ 194; Ⓒ 232
JO DAVIESS; 170 A-6; Ⓟ 21,821; Ⓒ 22,289; ◆ 21,867
Johannisburg; RMC Place; WASHINGTON; ▲ Johannisburg; *171 P-8; mail Addieville Z 62214; ● 30
Johannisburg; MCD-Township; WASHINGTON; *171 P-8; mail Addieville Z 62214; Ⓟ 572; Ⓒ 588
Johnsburg; Inc. Place; MCHENRY; 172 A-3; 🅿; ★ CHI; Z 60050-51; Ⓒ 5,391
Johnson; MCD-Township; CHRISTIAN; *171 L-8; mail Taylorville Z 62568; Ⓟ 565; Ⓒ 680
Johnson; MCD-Township; CLARK; *171 M-12; mail Casey Z 62420; Ⓟ 363; Ⓒ 376
JOHNSON; 171 S-10; Ⓟ 11,347; Ⓒ 12,878; ◆ 13,784
Johnsonville; Inc. Place; WAYNE; 171 O-11; elev. 548ft./167m.; 🅿; Z 62850; Ⓟ 68; Ⓒ 69
Johnston City; Inc. Place; WILLIAMSON; 171 R-10; elev. 432ft./132m.; 🅿; ★ CARB-; Z 62951; Ⓟ 3,706; Ⓒ 3,557
Johnstown; RMC Place; CUMBERLAND; *171 L-11; mail Lerna Z 62440; ● 20
Joliet; Inc. Place; ⊡ WILL; 170 D-12; elev. 564ft./172m.; 🅿 🅷 🅲 3,709 ■; ★ CHI; Z 60403-04, Z 60431-36; Ⓟ 76,836; Ⓒ 106,221; ◆ 144,888
Joliet; MCD-Township; WILL; *170 D-12; 🅿 🅲 3,709; ★ CHI; Z 60403-04, Z 60431-36; includes part of the City of Joliet; Ⓟ 84,243; Ⓒ 86,468
Jonathan Creek; MCD-Township; MOULTRIE; *171 K-11; mail Arthur Z 61911; Ⓟ 676; Ⓒ 841
Jones; RMC Place; COLES; *171 L-11; elev. 727ft./222m.; mail Mattoon Z 61938; rural
Jonesboro; Inc. Place; ⊡ UNION; 171 S-9; elev. 568ft./173m.; 🅿; Z 62952; Ⓟ 1,728; Ⓒ 1,853
Jones Ridge; RMC Place; JACKSON; *171 R-8; mail Rockwood Z 62280; ● 30
Jonesville; RMC Place; LA SALLE; *170 E-9; mail Oglesby Z 61348; ● 200
Joppa; Inc. Place; MASSAC; 171 T-10; elev. 350ft./107m.; 🅿; Z 62953; Ⓟ 492; Ⓒ 409
Jordan; MCD-Township; WHITESIDE; *170 C-8; mail Sterling Z 61081; Ⓟ 860; Ⓒ 918
Joshua; MCD-Township; FULTON; *170 H-6; mail Fairview Z 61432; Ⓟ 495; Ⓒ 529
Joslin; RMC Place; ROCK ISLAND; 170 D-6; mail Hillsdale Z 61257; ● 100
Joy; Inc. Place; MERCER; 170 E-4; elev. 688ft./210m.; 🅿; Z 61260; Ⓟ 452; Ⓒ 373
Joywood Farms Estates; RMC Place; JERSEY; *171 M-6; elev. 550ft./168m.; ★ ST.L; mail Elsah Z 62028; ● 200
Jubilee; MCD-Township; PEORIA; *170 G-7; mail Princeville Z 61559; Ⓟ 1,187; Ⓒ 1,423
Junction; Inc. Place; GALLATIN; 171 R-12; elev. 363ft./111m.; 🅿; Z 62954; Ⓟ 201; Ⓒ 139
Junction City (Glenridge); Inc. Place; MARION; *171 O-9; elev. 494ft./151m.; mail Sandoval Z 62882; Ⓟ 539; Ⓒ 559
Justice; Inc. Place; COOK; 172 J-7; elev. 624ft./190m.; 🅿; ★ CHI; Z 60458; Ⓟ 11,137; Ⓒ 12,193

K

Kampsville; Inc. Place; CALHOUN; 171 L-5; elev. 438ft./134m.; 🅿; Z 62053; Ⓟ 399; Ⓒ 302
Kane; Inc. Place; GREENE; ▲ Kane; 171 M-6; 🅿; Z 62054; Ⓟ 456; Ⓒ 459
Kane; MCD-Township; GREENE; *171 M-5; 🅿; Z 62054; Ⓟ 1,044; Ⓒ 1,059
KANE; 170 B-11; Ⓟ 317,471; Ⓒ 404,119; ◆ 514,417
Kaneville; Inc. Place; KANE; ▲ Kaneville; 170 C-11; 🅿; Z 60144; incorporated November 7, 2006; not reported in 2000 Census; ● 600
Kaneville; MCD-Township; KANE; *170 C-11; 🅿; Z 60144; Ⓟ 1,367; Ⓒ 1,292
Kangley; Inc. Place; LA SALLE; 170 F-10; elev. 633ft./193m.; mail Streator Z 61364; Ⓟ 250; Ⓒ 287
Kankakee; Inc. Place; ⊡ KANKAKEE; 170 F-13; elev. 663ft./202m.; 🅿 🅷 ■; ★ KANK; Z 60901; Ⓟ 27,541; Ⓒ 27,491; ◆ 28,347
Kankakee; MCD-Township; KANKAKEE; *170 F-13; 🅿; ★ KANK; Z 60901; includes part of the City of Kankakee; Ⓟ 28,502; Ⓒ 28,029
KANKAKEE; 170 F-13; Ⓟ 96,255; Ⓒ 103,833; ◆ 113,719
Kankakee Valley; RMC Place; KANKAKEE; ★ KANK; mail Saint Anne Z 60964
Kansas; Inc. Place; EDGAR; ▲ Kansas; 171 K-12; 🅿; Z 61933; Ⓟ 887; Ⓒ 842
Kansas; MCD-Township; EDGAR; *171 K-12; 🅿; Z 61933; Ⓟ 1,114; Ⓒ 1,101
Kansas; MCD-Township; WOODFORD; *170 G-9; mail Carlock Z 61725; Ⓟ 319; Ⓒ 346
Kappa; Inc. Place; WOODFORD; 170 G-9; elev. 735ft./224m.; 🅿; Z 61738; Ⓟ 134; Ⓒ 170
Karbers Ridge; RMC Place; HARDIN; 171 R-11; elev. 604ft./184m.; 🅿; Z 62955; ● 45
Karnak; Inc. Place; PULASKI; 171 T-9; elev. 339ft./103m.; 🅿; Z 62956; Ⓟ 581; Ⓒ 619
Kasbeer; RMC Place; BUREAU; 170 D-8; 🅿; Z 61328; ● 85
Kaskaskia; MCD-Township; FAYETTE; *171 N-9; mail Vernon Z 62892; Ⓟ 593; Ⓒ 618
Kaskaskia; Inc. Place; RANDOLPH; 171 Q-7; mail Saint Mary Z 63673; Ⓟ 32; Ⓒ 9
Kaskaskia Heights; RMC Place; RANDOLPH; *171 P-7; elev. 395ft./120m.; mail Baldwin Z 62217; ● 60
Kaskaskia River; RMC Place; CLINTON; *171 O-8; elev. 420ft./128m.; mail Carlyle Z 62231; rural
Kaufman; RMC Place; MADISON; *171 N-7; mail Alhambra Z 62001; rural
Kedron; RMC Place; GALLATIN; *171 R-11; elev. 383ft./117m.; mail Equality Z 62934; rural
Kedzie Grace; RMC Place; COOK; *170 C-13; ★ CHI; mail Chicago Z 60618; pop. incl. with Chicago (Inc. Place)
Keene; MCD-Township; ADAMS; *170 I-3; mail Loraine Z 62349; Ⓟ 634; Ⓒ 652
Keenes; Inc. Place; WAYNE; 171 P-10; elev. 450ft./137m.; 🅿; Z 62851; Ⓟ 62; Ⓒ 99
Keeneyville; RMC Place; DUPAGE; 172 G-4; elev. 773ft./236m.; ★ CHI; mail Roselle Z 60172; ● 300
Keensburg; Inc. Place; WABASH; 171 P-13; elev. 425ft./130m.; 🅿; Z 62852 & mail Mount Carmel Z 62863; Ⓟ 238; Ⓒ 252
Keith; MCD-Township; WAYNE; *171 O-11; mail Rinard Z 62878; Ⓟ 379; Ⓒ 368
Keithsburg; Inc. Place; MERCER; ▲ Keithsburg; 170 F-4; elev. 549ft./167m.; 🅿; Z 61442; Ⓟ 747; Ⓒ 714
Keithsburg; MCD-Township; MERCER; *170 F-4; 🅿; Z 61442; Ⓟ 885; Ⓒ 821
Kell; Inc. Place; MARION; 171 O-10; elev. 615ft./187m.; 🅿; Z 62853; Ⓟ 213; Ⓒ 231
Kellart Lake; RMC Place; IROQUOIS; *170 G-12; mail Cissna Park Z 60924; ● 120
Kellerville; RMC Place; ADAMS; 170 J-4; elev. 734ft./224m.; mail Clayton Z 62324; ● 30
Kelleyville; RMC Place; VERMILION; ★ DANV; mail Westville Z 61883; pop. incl. with Westville (Inc. Place)
Kelly; MCD-Township; WARREN; *170 F-5; mail Alexis Z 61412; Ⓟ 491; Ⓒ 398
Kemp; RMC Place; DOUGLAS; *171 K-12; mail Arcola Z 61910; ● 40
Kemper; RMC Place; JERSEY; 171 L-6; elev. 524ft./160m.; mail Medora Z 62063; ● 70
Kempton; Inc. Place; FORD; 170 F-11; elev. 740ft./226m.; 🅿; Z 60946; Ⓟ 219; Ⓒ 235
Kendall; MCD-Township; KENDALL; *170 D-11; ★ CHI; mail Yorkville Z 60560; Ⓟ 3,417; Ⓒ 4,636
KENDALL; 170 D-11; Ⓟ 39,413; Ⓒ 54,544; ◆ 113,878
Kendall Hills; RMC Place; MADISON; *171 N-6; ★ ST.L; mail East Alton Z 62024; ● 600
Keneddy; RMC Place; WINNEBAGO; ★ RKFD; mail South Beloit Z 61080; ● 100
Kenilwicke; RMC Place; COOK; *170 B-12; ★ CHI; mail Palatine Z 60074; pop. incl. with Palatine (Inc. Place)
Kenilworth; Inc. Place; COOK; 172 E-8; elev. 615ft./187m.; 🅿; ★ CHI; Z 60043; Ⓟ 2,402; Ⓒ 2,494
Kenney; Inc. Place; DE WITT; 170 I-9; elev. 650ft./198m.; 🅿; Z 61749; Ⓟ 390; Ⓒ 374
Ken Rock; RMC Place; WINNEBAGO; *170 B-9; ★ RKFD; mail Rockford Z 61109; pop. incl. with Rockford (Inc. Place)
Kensington; RMC Place; COOK; *170 D-13; ★ CHI; mail Chicago Z 60628; pop. incl. with Chicago (Inc. Place)
Kensington Junction; RMC Place; COOK; ★ CHI; mail Chicago Z 60628; pop. incl. with Chicago (Inc. Place)
Kent; RMC Place; STEPHENSON; ▲ Kent; 170 A-7; 🅿; Z 61044; ● 100
Kent; MCD-Township; STEPHENSON; *170 A-7; 🅿; Z 61044; Ⓟ 763; Ⓒ 701
Kenton; RMC Place; COOK; ★ CHI; mail Chicago Z 60644; pop. incl. with Chicago (Inc. Place)
Kentucky; RMC Place; EDGAR; *171 K-13; elev. 683ft./208m.; mail Paris Z 61944; rural
Kenwood; RMC Place; CHAMPAIGN; *170 I-11; ★ CH-U; mail Champaign Z 61821; pop. incl. with Champaign (Inc. Place)
Kenwood; RMC Place; COOK; ★ CHI; mail Chicago Z 60615; pop. incl. with Chicago (Inc. Place)
Keptown; RMC Place; EFFINGHAM; 171 M-10; elev. 692ft./211m.; mail Altamont Z 62411; ● 45
Kernan; RMC Place; LA SALLE; *170 F-10; elev. 668ft./204m.; mail Streator Z 61364; ● 80
Kerr; MCD-Township; CHAMPAIGN; *170 H-12; mail Gifford Z 61847; Ⓟ 200; Ⓒ 173
Kerton; MCD-Township; FULTON; *170 I-6; mail Havana Z 62644; Ⓟ 123; Ⓒ 144
Kewanee; Inc. Place; HENRY; 170 E-7; elev. 820ft./250m.; 🅿 🅷; Z 61443; Ⓟ 12,969; Ⓒ 12,944
Kewanee; MCD-Township; HENRY; *170 E-7; 🅿; Z 61443; includes part of the City of Kewanee; Ⓟ 10,536; Ⓒ 10,364
Keyesport; Inc. Place; CLINTON, BOND; 171 N-9; elev. 453ft./138m.; 🅿; Z 62253; Ⓟ 440; Ⓒ 481
Keyesport Landing; RMC Place; BOND; *171 N-9; elev. 469ft./143m.; mail Keyesport Z 62253; ● 25
Kickapoo; RMC Place; PEORIA; ▲ Kickapoo; 170 G-7; ★ PEOR; mail Edwards Z 61528; ● 400
Kickapoo; MCD-Township; PEORIA; *170 G-7; ★ PEOR; mail Edwards Z 61528; Ⓟ 3,207; Ⓒ 3,573
Kidd (Boxtown); RMC Place; MONROE; *171 P-6; mail Prairie Du Rocher Z 62277; rural
Kidley; RMC Place; EDGAR; *171 K-13; elev. 613ft./187m.; mail Chrisman Z 61924; rural
Kilbourne; Inc. Place; MASON; ▲ Kilbourne; 170 I-7; 🅿; Z 62655; Ⓟ 350; Ⓒ 375
Kilbourne; MCD-Township; MASON; *170 I-7; 🅿; Z 62655; Ⓟ 633; Ⓒ 588
Kildeer; Inc. Place; LAKE; 172 D-5; elev. 780ft./238m.; 🅿; ★ CHI; Z 60010, Z 60047, Z 60074; Ⓟ 2,257; Ⓒ 3,460
Kimball Farms; RMC Place; KANE; *170 B-11; ★ CHI; mail Carpentersville Z 60110; pop. incl. with Carpentersville (Inc. Place)
Kimberly Heights; RMC Place; COOK; *170 D-13; ★ CHI; mail Oak Forest Z 60452; pop. incl. with Oak Forest (Inc. Place)
Kincaid; Inc. Place; CHRISTIAN; 171 K-8; elev. 601ft./183m.; 🅿; Z 62540; Ⓟ 1,353; Ⓒ 1,441
Kinderhook; Inc. Place; PIKE; ▲ Kinderhook; 171 K-3; elev. 478ft./146m.; 🅿; Z 62345; Ⓟ 257; Ⓒ 249
Kinderhook; MCD-Township; PIKE; *171 K-3; 🅿; Z 62345; Ⓟ 1,071; Ⓒ 937
King; MCD-Township; CHRISTIAN; *171 L-8; mail Morrisonville Z 62546; Ⓟ 271; Ⓒ 264
Kingdom; RMC Place; LEE; *170 C-8; elev. 675ft./206m.; mail Dixon Z 61021; rural
Kingman; RMC Place; SHELBY; *171 L-11; mail Stewardson Z 62463; rural
Kings; RMC Place; OGLE; 170 B-9; elev. 888ft./271m.; 🅿; Z 61068; ● 250
Kings Cove; RMC Place; LAKE; ★ CHI; mail Deerfield Z 60015; pop. incl. with Deerfield (Inc. Place)
Kings Island; RMC Place; LAKE; *170 A-12; ★ CHI; mail Fox Lake Z 60020; pop. incl. with Fox Lake (Inc. Place)
Kings Park; RMC Place; WILL; ★ CHI; mail Bolingbrook Z 60440; pop. incl. with Bolingbrook (Inc. Place)
Kingston (Fairweather); RMC Place; ADAMS; 170 J-4; elev. 815ft./248m.; mail Barry Z 62312, Liberty Z 62347; ● 30
Kingston; Inc. Place; DEKALB; ▲ DeKalb; 170 B-10; elev. 791ft./241m.; 🅿; Z 60145; Ⓟ 562; Ⓒ 980
Kingston; MCD-Township; DEKALB; *170 B-10; 🅿; Z 60145; Ⓟ 1,955; Ⓒ 2,577
Kingston Mines; Inc. Place; PEORIA; 170 H-7; elev. 460ft./140m.; 🅿; Z 61539; Ⓟ 293; Ⓒ 259
Kingswood; RMC Place; KANE; *170 C-11; elev. 900ft./274m.; ★ CHI; mail Saint Charles Z 60175; ● 40
Kinkaid; MCD-Township; JACKSON; *171 R-8; mail Ava Z 62907; Ⓟ 365; Ⓒ 368
Kinmundy; Inc. Place; MARION; ▲ Kinmundy; 171 N-10; elev. 619ft./189m.; 🅿; Z 62854; Ⓟ 879; Ⓒ 892
Kinmundy; MCD-Township; MARION; *171 N-10; 🅿; Z 62854; Ⓟ 1,306; Ⓒ 1,244
Kinsman; Inc. Place; GRUNDY; 170 E-11; elev. 650ft./198m.; 🅿; Z 60437; Ⓟ 112; Ⓒ 109
Kirkland; Inc. Place; DEKALB; 170 B-10; elev. 764ft./233m.; 🅿; Z 60146; Ⓟ 1,011; Ⓒ 1,166
Kirksville; RMC Place; MOULTRIE; 171 K-10; 🅿; Z 61951; ● 50
Kirkwood; Inc. Place; WARREN; 170 F-5; elev. 758ft./231m.; 🅿; Z 61447; Ⓟ 884; Ⓒ 794
Kishwaukee Glen; RMC Place; WINNEBAGO; ★ RKFD; mail Rockford Z 61109; rural
Klein Acres; RMC Place; CHAMPAIGN; *170 I-12; elev. 730ft./223m.; mail Rantoul Z 61866; pop. incl. with Rantoul (Inc. Place)
Klendworth Addition; RMC Place; WHITESIDE; *170 D-6; elev. 590ft./180m.; mail Erie Z 61250; ● 80
Klines Corner; RMC Place; WAYNE; *171 P-11; mail Fairfield Z 62837; rural
Klondike; RMC Place; ALEXANDER; *171 T-9; mail Cairo Z 62914
Klondike; RMC Place; LAKE; *170 A-12; ★ CHI; mail Antioch Z 60002; ● 350
Klondyke; RMC Place; LAWRENCE; mail Sumner Z 62466; rural
Knapp's Noll; RMC Place; WINNEBAGO; *170 A-9; ★ RKFD; mail Rockton Z 61072; ● 180
Knight Prairie; MCD-Township; HAMILTON; *171 Q-10; mail Mc Leansboro Z 62859; Ⓟ 490; Ⓒ 549
Knollcrest; RMC Place; PEORIA; ★ PEOR; pop. incl. with Peoria (Inc. Place)
Knolle Hill; RMC Place; CALHOUN; *171 M-5; elev. 621ft./189m.; mail Golden Eagle Z 62036; rural
Knollwood (Lincoln Trail); RMC Place; CHRISTIAN; *171 K-9; elev. 600ft./183m.; mail Taylorville Z 62568; ● 100
Knollwood; RMC Place; LAKE; 172 B-7; ★ CHI; mail Lake Bluff Z 60044; ● 1,500
Knollwood; RMC Place; SANGAMON; *170 J-8; mail Sherman Z 62684; ● 90
Knottingham; RMC Place; DUPAGE; ★ CHI; mail Downers Grove Z 60515; pop. incl. with Downers Grove (Inc. Place)
Knox; MCD-Township; KNOX; *170 F-6; ★ GLSB; mail Knoxville Z 61448; Ⓟ 5,463; Ⓒ 5,407
KNOX; 170 F-6; Ⓟ 56,393; Ⓒ 55,836; ◆ 51,255
Knoxville; Inc. Place; KNOX; 170 F-6; elev. 755ft./230m.; 🅿; ★ GLSB; Z 61448; Ⓟ 3,243; Ⓒ 3,183
Kortcamp; RMC Place; MONTGOMERY; mail Hillsboro Z 62049; pop. incl. with Schram City (Inc. Place)
Kraft Addition; RMC Place; FRANKLIN; *171 Q-10; elev. 420ft./128m.; mail Benton Z 62812; ● 80
Kriegh Addition; RMC Place; KNOX; *170 F-6; elev. 750ft./229m.; ★ GLSB; mail Knoxville Z 61448; ● 100
Kristal Lake Ranch; RMC Place; STEPHENSON; *170 A-7; elev. 850ft./259m.; mail Freeport Z 61032; ● 40
Kuhn; RMC Place; MADISON; *171 N-7; mail Edwardsville Z 62025; rural
Kumler; RMC Place; MCLEAN; *170 I-11; mail Bellflower Z 61724; rural

L

La Clede; RMC Place; FAYETTE; ▲ La Clede; 171 N-10; 🅿; Z 62426; ● 100
La Clede; MCD-Township; FAYETTE; *171 N-10; mail Edgewood Z 62426; Ⓟ 925; Ⓒ 917
Lacon; Inc. Place; ⊡ MARSHALL; ▲ Lacon; 170 F-8; elev. 495ft./151m.; 🅿; Z 61540; Ⓟ 1,986; Ⓒ 1,979
Lacon; MCD-Township; MARSHALL; *170 F-8; 🅿; Z 61540; Ⓟ 2,442; Ⓒ 2,492
La Crosse; RMC Place; HANCOCK; *170 H-4; elev. 649ft./198m.; mail La Harpe Z 61450; rural
Ladd; Inc. Place; BUREAU; 170 E-9; elev. 651ft./198m.; 🅿; Z 61329; Ⓟ 1,283; Ⓒ 1,313
Laenna; MCD-Township; LOGAN; *170 J-9; mail Mount Pulaski Z 62548; Ⓟ 810; Ⓒ 617
Lafayette; MCD-Township; COLES; *171 L-11; mail Mattoon Z 61938; Ⓟ 3,991; Ⓒ 4,448
Lafayette; MCD-Township; OGLE; *170 C-9; mail Ashton Z 61006; Ⓟ 206; Ⓒ 180
Lafayette; Inc. Place; STARK; 170 F-7; elev. 780ft./238m.; 🅿; Z 61449; Ⓟ 231; Ⓒ 227
La Fontaine; RMC Place; COOK; ★ CHI; mail Glenview Z 60025; pop. incl. with Glenview (Inc. Place)
La Fox; RMC Place; KANE; *170 C-11; elev. 800ft./244m.; 🅿; ★ CHI; Z 60147; ● 250
Lagrange; MCD-Township; BOND; *171 M-8; mail Donnellson Z 62019; Ⓟ 803; Ⓒ 942
La Grange; RMC Place; BROWN; *170 J-5; mail Versailles Z 62378
La Grange; Inc. Place; COOK; 172 I-7; elev. 650ft./198m.; 🅿 🅷; ★ CHI; Z 60525; Ⓟ 15,362; Ⓒ 15,608
La Grange Highlands; RMC Place; COOK; 172 J-6; elev. 683ft./208m.; 🅿; ★ CHI; Z 60525; ● 3,650
La Grange Park; Inc. Place; COOK; 172 I-7; elev. 625ft./191m.; 🅿; ★ CHI; Z 60526; Ⓟ 12,861; Ⓒ 13,295
La Grange Road; RMC Place; COOK; ★ CHI; mail La Grange Z 60525; pop. incl. with La Grange (Inc. Place)
Laguna Woods; RMC Place; COOK; *170 D-13; elev. 700ft./213m.; ★ CHI; mail Orland Park Z 60462; pop. incl. with Orland Park (Inc. Place)
La Harpe; Inc. Place; HANCOCK; ▲ La Harpe; 170 H-4; elev. 697ft./212m.; 🅿; Z 61450; Ⓟ 1,407; Ⓒ 1,385
La Harpe; MCD-Township; HANCOCK; *170 G-4; 🅿; Z 61450; Ⓟ 1,686; Ⓒ 1,653
La Hogue; RMC Place; IROQUOIS; 170 G-12; mail Gilman Z 60938; ● 30
Lake; RMC Place; CLINTON; *171 N-9; elev. 469ft./143m.; ● 90
Lake; MCD-Township; CLINTON; *171 O-8; mail Centralia Z 62801; Ⓟ 943; Ⓒ 958
LAKE; 170 B-12; Ⓟ 516,418; Ⓒ 644,356; Ⓡ 644,599; ◆ 703,084
Lake Barrington; Inc. Place; LAKE; 172 C-4; elev. 760ft./232m.; 🅿; ★ CHI; Z 60010, Z 60084; Ⓟ 3,855; Ⓒ 4,757
Lake Benton; FRANKLIN; see Benton Park (RMC Place)
Lake Bluff; Inc. Place; LAKE; 170 A-13; elev. 671ft./205m.; 🅿; ★ CHI; Z 60044; Ⓟ 5,513; Ⓒ 6,056
Lake Boulevard Addition; RMC Place; VERMILION; *170 I-13; ★ DANV; mail Danville Z 61834; ● 600
Lake Bracken; RMC Place; KNOX; *170 G-6; elev. 750ft./229m.; ★ GLSB; mail Galesburg Z 61401; ● 550
Lake Briarwood; RMC Place; COOK; *170 B-12; elev. 684ft./208m.; ★ CHI; mail Arlington Heights Z 60005; pop. incl. with Arlington Heights (Inc. Place)
Lake Camelot; RMC Place; PEORIA; *170 G-7; ★ PEOR; mail Mapleton Z 61547; ● 200
Lake Carlinville; RMC Place; MACOUPIN; *171 L-7; mail Carlinville Z 62626; ● 75
Lake Catherine; CDP; LAKE; *170 A-12; ★ CHI; mail Antioch Z 60002; Ⓟ 1,515; Ⓒ 1,490
Lake Centralia; RMC Place; MARION; *171 O-9; mail Centralia Z 62801, Rockbridge Z 62081; summer pop. 400; ● 200
Lake Charleston; RMC Place; COLES; *171 L-12; mail Charleston Z 61920; pop. incl. with Charleston (Inc. Place)
Lake Charlotte; RMC Place; KANE; *170 C-11; elev. 800ft./244m.; ★ CHI; mail Saint Charles Z 60174; ● 400
Lake City; RMC Place; MOULTRIE; 171 K-10; elev. 690ft./210m.; mail Lovington Z 61937; ● 110
Lakecrest; RMC Place; MONTGOMERY; mail Hillsboro Z 62049
Lake Crest; RMC Place; WILLIAMSON; *171 R-10; mail Creal Springs Z 62922; ● 40
Lake Estates; RMC Place; WILLIAMSON; *171 R-10; ★ CARB-; mail Marion Z 62959; ● 200
Lake Forest; Inc. Place; LAKE; 170 B-13; elev. 713ft./217m.; 🅿 🅷 🅲 2,210; ★ CHI; Z 60045; Ⓟ 17,836; Ⓒ 20,059; Ⓡ 20,057; ◆ 20,973
Lake Forest Estates; RMC Place; ST. CLAIR; ★ ST.L; mail Belleville Z 62221; pop. incl. with Belleville (Inc. Place)
Lake Fork; RMC Place; LOGAN; ▲ Mount Pulaski; 170 J-8; elev. 600ft./183m.; 🅿; Z 62541; ● 100
Lake Fork; MCD-Township; LOGAN; *170 J-9; 🅿; Z 62541 & mail Mount Pulaski Z 62548; Ⓟ 173; Ⓒ 142
Lake Holiday (Holiday Lake); RMC Place; LA SALLE; *170 D-10; mail Sandwich Z 60548, Somonauk Z 60552; ● 4,900
Lake in the Hills; Inc. Place; MCHENRY; 172 D-2; elev. 850ft./259m.; 🅿; ★ CHI; Z 60102, Z 60156; Ⓟ 5,866; Ⓒ 23,152; ◆ 30,196
Lake in the Woods; RMC Place; DUPAGE; ★ CHI; mail Downers Grove Z 60515; ● 900
Lake Iroquois; RMC Place; IROQUOIS; mail Loda Z 60948; summer pop. 200; ● 150
Lake Ka-ho; Inc. Place; MACOUPIN; *171 M-7; elev. 660ft./201m.; mail Mount Olive Z 62069; incorporated March 24, 2000; not reported in 2000 Census; ● 300
Lake Killarney; RMC Place; MCHENRY; 172 C-3; ★ CHI; mail Cary Z 60013; ● 700
Lake Lancelot; RMC Place; PEORIA; *170 G-7; ★ PEOR; mail Mapleton Z 61547
Lakeland Hills; RMC Place; JACKSON; *171 R-9; elev. 387ft./118m.; ★ CARB-; mail Carbondale Z 62901; ● 70
Lakeland Hills; RMC Place; ST. CLAIR; *171 O-7; ★ ST.L; mail Belleville Z 62221; pop. incl. with Fairview Heights (Inc. Place)
Lakeland Park; RMC Place; MCHENRY; *170 A-11; ★ CHI; mail McHenry Z 60050
Lake Lawrence; RMC Place; LAWRENCE; *171 N-13; elev. 415ft./126m.; mail Lawrenceville Z 62439; summer pop. 200; ● 150
Lake Louise; RMC Place; OGLE; *170 B-9; elev. 688ft./210m.; ★ RKFD; mail Byron Z 61010; ● 60
Lake Lynwood; RMC Place; COOK; ★ CHI; mail Chicago Heights Z 60411; pop. incl. with Lynwood (Inc. Place)
Lake Lynwood; RMC Place; HENRY; *170 E-6; elev. 750ft./229m.; mail Lynn Center Z 61262; ● 75
Lake Mantero; RMC Place; KANKAKEE; *170 E-13; elev. 684ft./208m.; ★ KANK; mail Manteno Z 60950; ● 50
Lake Marie; RMC Place; LAKE; ★ CHI; mail Antioch Z 60002
Lake Marion; RMC Place; KANE; *170 B-11; elev. 850ft./259m.; ★ CHI; mail Carpentersville Z 60110; pop. incl. with Carpentersville (Inc. Place)
Lake Mattoon; RMC Place; SHELBY, CUMBERLAND; *171 L-11; mail Neoga Z 62447; ● 1,000
Lakemoor; Inc. Place; MCHENRY, LAKE; 170 A-12; elev. 750ft./229m.; 🅿; ★ CHI; Z 60050-51; Ⓟ 1,322; Ⓒ 2,788
Lake Oakland; RMC Place; COLES; *171 K-12; mail Oakland Z 61943; ● 150
Lake of the Winds; RMC Place; COOK; ★ CHI; mail Wheeling Z 60090; pop. incl. with Wheeling (Inc. Place)
Lake of the Woods; CDP-Census Area Only; CHAMPAIGN; 170 I-11; elev. 700ft./213m.; mail Champaign Z 61820, Mahomet Z 61853; Ⓟ 2,748; Ⓒ 3,026
Lake of the Woods; RMC Place; PEORIA; *170 G-8; ★ PEOR; mail Dunlap Z 61525; ● 1,100
Lake Pana; RMC Place; CHRISTIAN; *171 L-9; mail Pana Z 62557; summer pop. 150; ● 50
Lake Park; RMC Place; CHAMPAIGN; *170 I-11; elev. 719ft./219m.; ★ CH-U; mail Champaign Z 61822; pop. incl. with Savoy (Inc. Place)
Lake Park Estates; RMC Place; COOK; *170 B-12; ★ CHI; mail Palatine Z 60067; ● 350
Lake Park Forest; RMC Place; COOK; ★ CHI; mail Palatine Z 60067; ● 250
Lake Petersburg; RMC Place; MENARD; *170 J-7; mail Petersburg Z 62675; ● 700
Lake Piasa; RMC Place; JERSEY; *171 M-6; ★ ST.L; mail Brighton Z 62012; ● 200
Lake Sara; RMC Place; EFFINGHAM; *171 M-10; mail Effingham Z 62401; summer pop. 500; ● 300
Lakeshore Acres; RMC Place; CLINTON; *171 O-8; elev. 468ft./143m.; mail Carlyle Z 62231; ● 80
Lakeside Knolls; RMC Place; MONTGOMERY; mail Hillsboro Z 62049; ● 75
Lakeside Villas; RMC Place; COOK; ★ CHI; mail Wheeling Z 60090; pop. incl. with Wheeling (Inc. Place)
Lake Summerset; CDP; STEPHENSON, WINNEBAGO; *170 A-8; elev. 870ft./265m.; mail Davis Z 61019; Ⓟ 1,296; Ⓒ 2,061
Lake Tacoma; RMC Place; WILLIAMSON; *171 R-9; mail Carbondale Z 62901; rural
Lake Tara Estates; RMC Place; KANE; *170 B-11; elev. 850ft./259m.; ★ CHI; mail Dundee Z 60118; ● 80
Lake Thunderbird; RMC Place; PUTNAM; mail Putnam Z 61560; summer pop. 300; ● 150
Laketown; RMC Place; SANGAMON; ★ SPRG; mail Springfield Z 62703; pop. incl. with Springfield (Inc. Place)
Lakeview; RMC Place; COOK; *170 C-13; ★ CHI; mail Chicago Z 60613, Z 60657; pop. incl. with Chicago (Inc. Place)
Lakeview Acres; RMC Place; MADISON; *171 N-7; ★ ST.L; mail Collinsville Z 62234; ● 300
Lakeview Estate; RMC Place; MARION; *171 O-10; elev. 559ft./170m.; mail Salem Z 62881; pop. incl. with Salem (Inc. Place)
Lakeview Estates; RMC Place; JEFFERSON; *171 P-10; elev. 550ft./168m.; mail Mount Vernon Z 62864; ● 45
Lake View Estates (Lakeview Farm Estates); RMC Place; WILLIAMSON; mail Makanda Z 62958; ● 100
Lakeview Farm Estates; WILLIAMSON; see Lake View Estates (RMC Place)
Lake Villa; RMC Place; CLINTON; *171 N-9; ● 60
Lake Villa; Inc. Place; LAKE; ▲ Lake Villa; 170 A-12; 🅿; ★ CHI; Z 60046; Ⓟ 2,857; Ⓒ 5,864
Lake Villa; MCD-Township; LAKE; *170 A-12; 🅿; ★ CHI; Z 60046; Ⓟ 20,764; Ⓒ 33,721
Lake Wildwood; RMC Place; MARSHALL; *170 F-9; mail Magnolia Z 61336, Varna Z 61375; ● 500
Lake Williamson; RMC Place; MACOUPIN; *171 L-7; elev. 640ft./195m.; mail Carlinville Z 62626; ● 150
Lakewood; RMC Place; COOK; ★ CHI; mail Richton Park Z 60471; pop. incl. with Richton Park (Inc. Place)
Lakewood; RMC Place; DUPAGE; *170 C-12; ★ CHI; mail West Chicago Z 60185; ● 250
Lakewood; RMC Place; MADISON; ★ ST.L; mail Glen Carbon Z 62034; pop. incl. with Glen Carbon (Inc. Place)
Lakewood (Village of Lakewood); Inc. Place; MCHENRY; 172 C-1; elev. 894ft./272m.; ★ CHI; mail Crystal Lake Z 60014; Ⓟ 1,609; Ⓒ 2,337
Lakewood; RMC Place; SHELBY; ▲ Lakewood; 171 L-10; 🅿; Z 62438 & mail Crystal Lake Z 60014; ● 100
Lakewood; MCD-Township; SHELBY; *171 L-10; 🅿; Z 62438 & mail Crystal Lake Z 60014; Ⓟ 415; Ⓒ 409
Lakewood Park; RMC Place; WILLIAMSON; *171 R-9; ★ CARB-; mail Carbondale Z 62901; ● 100
Lakewood Shores; CDP; WILL; *170 E-12; mail Wilmington Z 60481; Ⓟ 1,606; Ⓒ 1,487
Lake Zurich; Inc. Place; LAKE; 170 B-12; elev. 860ft./262m.; 🅿; ★ CHI; Z 60047, Z 60049; Ⓟ 14,947; Ⓒ 18,104; Ⓡ 18,093; ◆ 18,993
Lamard; MCD-Township; WAYNE; *171 O-11; mail Geff Z 62842; Ⓟ 1,343; Ⓒ 1,460
Lamb; RMC Place; HARDIN; *171 S-12; mail Cave In Rock Z 62919; ● 25
La Moille; Inc. Place; BUREAU; 170 D-9; elev. 800ft./244m.; 🅿; Z 61330; Ⓟ 654; Ⓒ 773
La Moille; MCD-Township; BUREAU; *170 D-8; 🅿; Z 61330 & mail Ohio Z 61349; includes part of the Village of La Moille; Ⓟ 1,103; Ⓒ 1,156
Lamoine; MCD-Township; MCDONOUGH; *170 H-4; mail Avon Z 61415; Ⓟ 321; Ⓒ 400
Lamotte; MCD-Township; CRAWFORD; *171 M-13; mail Palestine Z 62451; Ⓟ 2,413; Ⓒ 2,093
Lamplighter; RMC Place; MCLEAN; *170 H-10; mail Towanda Z 61776
Lanark; Inc. Place; CARROLL; 170 B-7; elev. 851ft./259m.; 🅿; Z 61046; Ⓟ 1,382; Ⓒ 1,584
Lancaster; MCD-Township; STEPHENSON; *170 A-8; mail Freeport Z 61032; Ⓟ 1,643; Ⓒ 1,612
Lancaster; RMC Place; WABASH; 171 O-13; elev. 490ft./149m.; 🅿; Z 62855; ● 150
Landers; RMC Place; COOK; mail Chicago Z 60652; pop. incl. with Chicago (Inc. Place)
Landes; RMC Place; CRAWFORD; *171 N-13; elev. 461ft./141m.; mail Sumner Z 62466
Lane; RMC Place; DE WITT; 170 I-10; elev. 724ft./221m.; 🅿; Z 61750; ● 130
Lanesville; RMC Place; SANGAMON; ▲ Lanesville; *170 J-8; 🅿; Z 62515; ● 30
Lanesville; MCD-Township; SANGAMON; *170 J-8; 🅿; Z 62515; Ⓟ 225; Ⓒ 199
Langleyville; RMC Place; CHRISTIAN; 171 K-8; elev. 610ft./186m.; 🅿; Z 62568; ● 380
Lansdowne; RMC Place; ST. CLAIR; ★ ST.L; mail East Saint Louis Z 62204; pop. incl. with East Saint Louis (Inc. Place)
Lansing; Inc. Place; COOK; 172 M-10; elev. 630ft./192m.; 🅿; ★ CHI; Z 60438; Ⓟ 28,086; Ⓒ 28,332; ◆ 26,302
Laona; MCD-Township; WINNEBAGO; *170 A-9; mail Durand Z 61024; Ⓟ 912; Ⓒ 1,167
LaPlace; RMC Place; PIATT; 170 J-10; elev. 700ft./213m.; 🅿; Z 61936; ● 400
La Prairie; Inc. Place; ADAMS; *170 I-4; elev. 708ft./216m.; 🅿; Z 62346; Ⓟ 68; Ⓒ 60
La Prairie; MCD-Township; MARSHALL; *170 F-8; mail Chillicothe Z 61523; Ⓟ 381; Ⓒ 388
La Prairie Center; RMC Place; MARSHALL; *170 F-8; mail Sparland Z 61565; rural
Larchland; RMC Place; WARREN; *170 G-5; elev. 734ft./224m.; mail Monmouth Z 61462
Larkdale; RMC Place; LAKE; ★ CHI; mail Wauconda Z 60084; pop. incl. with Wauconda (Inc. Place)
Larkdale; RMC Place; MACON; *170 J-10; ★ DEC; mail Decatur Z 62521; pop. incl. with Decatur (Inc. Place)
Larkinsburg; MCD-Township; CLAY; *171 N-10; mail Edgewood Z 62426; Ⓟ 634; Ⓒ 647
La Rose; Inc. Place; MARSHALL; 170 F-9; elev. 683ft./208m.; 🅿; Z 61541; Ⓟ 130; Ⓒ 159
La Salle; Inc. Place; LA SALLE; ▲ LaSalle; 170 E-9; 🅿 ■; Z 61301; Ⓟ 9,717; Ⓒ 9,796; ◆ 9,594
LaSalle; MCD-Township; LA SALLE; *170 E-9; 🅿; Z 61301; Ⓟ 13,768; Ⓒ 13,744
LA SALLE; 170 E-9; Ⓟ 106,913; Ⓒ 111,509; ◆ 111,486
Latham; Inc. Place; LOGAN; 170 J-9; elev. 610ft./186m.; 🅿; Z 62543; Ⓟ 482; Ⓒ 371
Latona; RMC Place; JASPER; *171 M-11; elev. 555ft./169m.; mail Wheeler Z 62479; ● 30
Laura; RMC Place; PEORIA; 170 F-7; elev. 729ft./222m.; 🅿; Z 61451; ● 150
Lawndale; RMC Place; COOK; mail Chicago Z 60623; pop. incl. with Chicago (Inc. Place)
Lawndale; RMC Place; LOGAN; 170 I-9; elev. 596ft./182m.; 🅿; Z 61751; ● 150
Lawndale; MCD-Township; MCLEAN; *170 G-10; mail Colfax Z 61728; Ⓟ 237; Ⓒ 227
Lawn Ridge; RMC Place; MARSHALL; *170 F-8; mail Edelstein Z 61526; ● 50
Lawrence; MCD-Township; LAWRENCE; *171 N-13; mail Lawrenceville Z 62439; Ⓟ 7,041; Ⓒ 6,831
Lawrence; RMC Place; MCHENRY; *170 A-10; mail Harvard Z 60033; ● 200
LAWRENCE; 171 O-13; Ⓟ 15,972; Ⓒ 15,452; ◆ 17,026
Lawrenceville; Inc. Place; ⊡ LAWRENCE; ▲ Lawrence; 171 N-13; 🅿 🅷; Z 62439; Ⓟ 4,897; Ⓒ 4,745
Leaf River; Inc. Place; OGLE; ▲ Leaf River; 170 B-8; elev. 709ft./216m.; 🅿; Z 61047; Ⓟ 546; Ⓒ 555
Leaf River; MCD-Township; OGLE; *170 B-8; 🅿; Z 61047; Ⓟ 1,282; Ⓒ 1,260
Leaverton Park; RMC Place; CRAWFORD; *171 M-13; elev. 440ft./134m.; mail Palestine Z 62451; rural
Lebanon; Inc. Place; ST. CLAIR; 171 O-7; elev. 515ft./157m.; 🅿 🅲 2,559; ★ ST.L; Z 62254; Ⓟ 3,688; Ⓒ 3,523
Lebanon; MCD-Township; ST. CLAIR; *171 O-7; 🅿 🅲 2,559; ★ ST.L; Z 62254; includes part of the City of Lebanon; Ⓟ 4,381; Ⓒ 4,096
Leclaire; RMC Place; MADISON; *171 N-7; ★ ST.L; mail Edwardsville Z 62025
Ledford; RMC Place; SALINE; *171 R-11; mail Harrisburg Z 62946; ● 220
Lee; MCD-Township; BROWN; *170 J-4; mail Timewell Z 62375; Ⓟ 372; Ⓒ 342
Lee; MCD-Township; FULTON; *170 H-6; mail Prairie City Z 61470; Ⓟ 310; Ⓒ 257
Lee; Inc. Place; LEE, DEKALB; 170 C-10; elev. 940ft./287m.; 🅿; Z 60530; Ⓟ 319; Ⓒ 313
LEE; 170 C-8; Ⓟ 34,392; Ⓒ 36,062; ◆ 35,360
Lee Center; RMC Place; LEE; ▲ Lee Center; 170 C-9; 🅿; Z 61331; ● 250
Lee Center; MCD-Township; LEE; *170 C-9; 🅿; Z 61331; Ⓟ 537; Ⓒ 593
Leech; MCD-Township; WAYNE; *171 P-12; mail Ellery Z 62833; Ⓟ 538; Ⓒ 535
Leeds; RMC Place; LA SALLE; *170 F-9; elev. 679ft./207m.; mail Wenona Z 61377; rural
Leef; MCD-Township; MADISON; *171 N-8; mail Highland Z 62249; Ⓟ 488; Ⓒ 507
Leepertown; MCD-Township; BUREAU; *170 E-8; mail Bureau Z 61315; Ⓟ 398; Ⓒ 408
Leesburg; RMC Place; FULTON; *170 I-6; elev. 647ft./197m.; mail Astoria Z 61501
Leesville; RMC Place; KANKAKEE; 170 F-13; mail Saint Anne Z 60964; ● 100
Lehigh; RMC Place; KANKAKEE; *170 F-12; ★ KANK; mail Kankakee Z 60901; rural
Leisure Lea; RMC Place; KENDALL; *170 D-11; elev. 720ft./219m.; ★ CHI; mail Oswego Z 60543; ● 140
Leisure Village; RMC Place; LAKE; ★ CHI; mail Fox Lake Z 60020; pop. incl. with Fox Lake (Inc. Place)
Leland; Inc. Place; LA SALLE; 170 D-10; elev. 692ft./211m.; 🅿; Z 60531; Ⓟ 862; Ⓒ 970
Leland Grove; Inc. Place; SANGAMON; 173 F-16; elev. 600ft./183m.; 🅿; ★ SPRG; Z 62704; Ⓟ 1,626; Ⓒ 1,592
Leland Lake; RMC Place; MORGAN; *171 K-6; mail Jacksonville Z 62650; ● 100
Lemont; Inc. Place; COOK, DUPAGE, WILL; 172 K-5; elev. 606ft./185m.; 🅿 🅷; ★ CHI; Z 60439 & mail Bolingbrook Z 60440, Z 60490; Ⓟ 7,359; Ⓒ 13,098
Lemont; MCD-Township; COOK; *170 D-12; 🅿; ★ CHI; Z 60439 & mail Bolingbrook Z 60440, Z 60490; includes the Village of Lemont; Ⓟ 11,537; Ⓒ 18,002
Lena; Inc. Place; STEPHENSON; 170 A-7; elev. 950ft./290m.; 🅿; Z 61048; Ⓟ 2,605; Ⓒ 2,887
Lenox; MCD-Township; WARREN; *170 G-5; mail Monmouth Z 61462; Ⓟ 354; Ⓒ 312
Lenzburg; Inc. Place; ST. CLAIR; 171 P-7; elev. 443ft./135m.; 🅿; Z 62255; Ⓟ 510; Ⓒ 577
Lenzburg; MCD-Township; ST. CLAIR; *171 P-7; 🅿; Z 62255 & mail Marissa Z 62257; includes the Village of Lenzburg; Ⓟ 1,053; Ⓒ 1,148
Leonard; RMC Place; IROQUOIS; *170 G-12; mail Gilman Z 60938; rural
Leon Corners; RMC Place; WHITESIDE; *170 D-7; mail Prophetstown Z 61277; rural
Leonore; Inc. Place; LA SALLE; 170 E-9; elev. 682ft./208m.; 🅿; Z 61332; Ⓟ 134; Ⓒ 110
L'Erable; RMC Place; IROQUOIS; *170 F-13; elev. 627ft./191m.; ★ KANK; mail Clifton Z 60927; ● 90
Lerna; Inc. Place; COLES; 171 L-11; elev. 754ft./230m.; 🅿; Z 62440; Ⓟ 301; Ⓒ 322
LeRoy; MCD-Township; BOONE; *170 A-10; mail Capron Z 61012; Ⓟ 519; Ⓒ 542
Le Roy; Inc. Place; MCLEAN; 170 H-10; elev. 796ft./243m.; 🅿; Z 61752; Ⓟ 2,777; Ⓒ 3,332
Levan; MCD-Township; JACKSON; *171 R-8; mail Murphysboro Z 62966; Ⓟ 596; Ⓒ 775
Levee; MCD-Township; PIKE; *171 K-3; mail Hull Z 62343; Ⓟ 175; Ⓒ 61
Leverett; RMC Place; CHAMPAIGN; *170 I-12; elev. 732ft./223m.; mail Champaign Z 61822, Urbana Z 61801; rural
Lewistown; Inc. Place; ⊡ FULTON; ▲ Lewistown; 170 H-6; 🅿; Z 61542; Ⓟ 2,572; Ⓒ 2,522
Lewistown; MCD-Township; FULTON; *170 H-6; 🅿; Z 61542; Ⓟ 3,243; Ⓒ 3,151
Lewood; RMC Place; WILL; *170 D-12; ★ CHI; mail Plainfield Z 60544; ● 300
Lexington; Inc. Place; MCLEAN; ▲ Lexington; 170 G-10; elev. 754ft./230m.; 🅿; Z 61753; Ⓟ 1,809; Ⓒ 1,912
Lexington; MCD-Township; MCLEAN; *170 G-10; 🅿; Z 61753; Ⓟ 2,271; Ⓒ 2,331
Leyden; MCD-Township; COOK; *170 C-12; ★ CHI; mail Franklin Park Z 60131; Ⓟ 89,142; Ⓒ 94,685
Liberty; Inc. Place; ADAMS; ▲ Liberty; 170 J-4; elev. 757ft./231m.; 🅿; Z 62347; Ⓟ 541; Ⓒ 519
Liberty; MCD-Township; ADAMS; *170 J-4; 🅿; Z 62347; Ⓟ 1,156; Ⓒ 1,217
Liberty; MCD-Township; EFFINGHAM; *171 M-10; mail Beecher City Z 62414; Ⓟ 734; Ⓒ 816
Liberty; RMC Place; SALINE; *171 R-11; elev. 435ft./133m.; mail Harrisburg Z 62946; ● 200
Liberty; WHITE; see Burnt Prairie (Inc. Place)
Liberty Acres; RMC Place; LAKE; *170 A-12; ★ CHI; mail Libertyville Z 60048; ● 110
Liberty Hill; RMC Place; CUMBERLAND; *171 M-12; mail Greenup Z 62428; rural
Liberty Lake; RMC Place; LAKE; ★ CHI; mail Libertyville Z 60048; pop. incl. with Libertyville (Inc. Place)
Liberty Park; RMC Place; DUPAGE; *170 C-12; ★ CHI; mail Westmont Z 60559; ● 1,300
Libertyville; Inc. Place; LAKE; ▲ Libertyville; 170 A-12; 🅿 🅷 ■; ★ CHI; Z 60048, Z 60092; Ⓟ 19,174; Ⓒ 20,742; ◆ 20,961
Libertyville; MCD-Township; LAKE; *170 A-12; 🅿; ★ CHI; Z 60048, Z 60092; Ⓟ 42,436; Ⓒ 48,904
Libertyville Estates; LAKE; see North Libertyville Estates (RMC Place)
Lick; RMC Place; SANGAMON; ★ SPRG; mail Chatham Z 62629; rural
Lick Creek; RMC Place; UNION; 171 S-9; mail Buncombe Z 62912; ● 60
Licking; MCD-Township; CRAWFORD; *171 M-13; mail Oblong Z 62449; Ⓟ 324; Ⓒ 384
Lidice; RMC Place; WILL; *170 D-12; ★ CHI; mail Joliet Z 60435; pop. incl. with Crest Hill (Inc. Place)
Lightsville; RMC Place; OGLE; *170 B-8; mail Leaf River Z 61047; ● 50
Lilac Circle Homes; RMC Place; DUPAGE; ★ CHI; mail Lombard Z 60148; pop. incl. with Lombard (Inc. Place)
Lilly; RMC Place; TAZEWELL; *170 H-9; elev. 800ft./244m.; mail Mackinaw Z 61755; ● 60
Lily Cache; RMC Place; WILL; *170 D-12; ★ CHI; mail Plainfield Z 60544
Lily Cache Acres; RMC Place; WILL; *170 D-12; ★ CHI; mail Plainfield Z 60544; ● 300
Lily Lake; Inc. Place; KANE; 170 C-11; elev. 962ft./293m.; ★ CHI; mail Maple Park Z 60151, Saint Charles Z 60175; Ⓒ 825
Lilymoor; RMC Place; MCHENRY; 172 B-3; ★ CHI; mail McHenry Z 60050; ● 450
Lima; Inc. Place; ADAMS; ▲ Lima; 170 I-3; elev. 659ft./201m.; 🅿; Z 62348; Ⓟ 120; Ⓒ 159
Lima; MCD-Township; ADAMS; *170 I-3; 🅿; Z 62348; Ⓟ 569; Ⓒ 588
Limestone; Inc. Place; KANKAKEE; *170 G-7; elev. 460ft./140m.; ★ PEOR; mail Peoria Z 61607; incorporated December 7, 2006; not reported in 2000 Census; ● 1,600
Limestone; MCD-Township; KANKAKEE; *170 F-12; ★ KANK; mail Kankakee Z 60901; Ⓟ 4,358; Ⓒ 4,659
Limestone; MCD-Township; PEORIA; *170 G-7; ★ PEOR; mail Peoria Z 61604; Ⓟ 19,072; Ⓒ 19,374
Lincoln; Inc. Place; ⊡ LOGAN; 170 I-8; elev. 591ft./180m.; 🅿 🅷 🅲 2,146; Z 62656; Ⓟ 15,418; Ⓒ 15,369
Lincoln; MCD-Township; OGLE; *170 B-8; mail Polo Z 61064; Ⓟ 526; Ⓒ 502
Lincoln Addition; RMC Place; MADISON; ★ ST.L; mail Wood River Z 62095; pop. incl. with Wood River (Inc. Place)
Lincoln Estates; RMC Place; WILL; *170 D-13; ★ CHI; mail Frankfort Z 60423; ● 600
Lincoln Gardens; RMC Place; MADISON; ★ ST.L; mail Alton Z 62002; pop. incl. with Alton (Inc. Place)
Lincoln Hills; RMC Place; DUPAGE; *170 C-12; ★ CHI; mail Glen Ellyn Z 60137; ● 300
Lincoln Park; RMC Place; COOK; *170 C-13; ★ CHI; mail Chicago Z 60614, Z 60657; pop. incl. with Chicago (Inc. Place)
Lincolnshire; Inc. Place; LAKE; 172 D-6; elev. 675ft./206m.; 🅿; ★ CHI; Z 60069; Ⓟ 4,931; Ⓒ 6,108
Lincolnshire; RMC Place; WILL; ★ CHI; mail Crete Z 60417; pop. incl. with Crete (Inc. Place)
Lincolnshire Fields; RMC Place; CHAMPAIGN; *170 I-11; elev. 725ft./221m.; ★ CH-U; mail Champaign Z 61822; ● 450
Lincoln Square; RMC Place; COOK; ★ CHI; mail Chicago Z 60625; pop. incl. with Chicago (Inc. Place)
Lincoln Trail; CHRISTIAN; see Knollwood (RMC Place)
Lincolnwood; Inc. Place; COOK; 172 F-8; elev. 600ft./183m.; 🅿; ★ CHI; Z 60645-46, Z 60659, Z 60712; Ⓟ 11,365; Ⓒ 12,359
Lincolnwood Hills; RMC Place; WILL; *170 D-12; ★ CHI; mail New Lenox Z 60451; ● 400
Lindenhurst; Inc. Place; LAKE; 170 A-12; elev. 800ft./244m.; 🅿; ★ CHI; Z 60046; Ⓟ 8,038; Ⓒ 12,539
Lindenhurst Estates; RMC Place; LAKE; ★ CHI; mail Lake Villa Z 60046; pop. incl. with Lindenhurst (Inc. Place)
Lindenwood; RMC Place; OGLE; 170 B-9; elev. 770ft./235m.; 🅿; Z 61049; ● 300
Linder; MCD-Township; GREENE; *171 L-6; mail Carrollton Z 62016; Ⓟ 300; Ⓒ 309
Linn; WABASH; see Orio (RMC Place)
Linn; MCD-Township; WOODFORD; *170 G-9; mail Washburn Z 61570; Ⓟ 375; Ⓒ 307
Linrose Heights; RMC Place; CLINTON; *171 O-8; elev. 468ft./143m.; ★ ST.L; mail Aviston Z 62216; pop. incl. with Aviston (Inc. Place)
Lintner; RMC Place; PIATT; *170 J-10; mail Hammond Z 61929; ● 25
Lioncrest; RMC Place; COOK; ★ CHI; mail Richton Park Z 60471; pop. incl. with Richton Park (Inc. Place)
Lis; RMC Place; JASPER; *171 M-11; elev. 565ft./172m.; mail Newton Z 62448
Lisbon; Inc. Place; KENDALL; 170 D-11; elev. 675ft./206m.; mail Newark Z 60541; Ⓟ 216; Ⓒ 248
Lisbon; MCD-Township; KENDALL; *170 D-11; mail Newark Z 60541; includes part of the Village of Lisbon; Ⓟ 784; Ⓒ 851
Lisbon Center; RMC Place; KENDALL; *170 D-11; elev. 643ft./196m.; mail Newark Z 60541; rural
Lisle; Inc. Place; DUPAGE; 170 C-12; elev. 682ft./208m.; 🅿 🅲 3,924; ★ CHI; Z 60532; Ⓟ 19,512; Ⓒ 21,182; ◆ 21,603
Lisle; MCD-Township; DUPAGE; *170 C-12; 🅿 🅲 3,924; ★ CHI; Z 60532; includes part of the Village of Lisle; Ⓟ 108,452; Ⓒ 117,604
Litchfield; Inc. Place; MONTGOMERY; 171 M-8; elev. 680ft./207m.; 🅿 🅷; Z 62056; Ⓟ 6,883; Ⓒ 6,815
Literberry; RMC Place; MORGAN; 170 J-6; elev. 602ft./183m.; 🅿; Z 62660; ● 100
Little America; RMC Place; FULTON; 170 H-7; mail Lewistown Z 61542; ● 200
Little Indian; RMC Place; CASS; *170 J-6; 🅿; Z 62691; rural
Little Mackinaw; MCD-Township; TAZEWELL; *170 H-8; mail Minier Z 61759; Ⓟ 1,483; Ⓒ 1,590
Little Rock; RMC Place; KENDALL; *170 C-11; ★ CHI; mail Plano Z 60545; ● 60
Little Rock; MCD-Township; KENDALL; *170 D-11; ★ CHI; mail Plano Z 60545; Ⓟ 7,081; Ⓒ 7,662
Little Swan Lake; RMC Place; WARREN; *170 G-5; elev. 684ft./208m.; mail Avon Z 61415; ● 100
Littleton; Inc. Place; SCHUYLER; ▲ Littleton; 170 I-5; 🅿; Z 61452; Ⓟ 181; Ⓒ 197
Littleton; MCD-Township; SCHUYLER; *170 I-5; 🅿; Z 61452; Ⓟ 386; Ⓒ 372
Little York; Inc. Place; WARREN; 170 F-5; elev. 620ft./189m.; 🅿; Z 61453; Ⓟ 349; Ⓒ 269
Lively Grove; RMC Place; WASHINGTON; ▲ Johannisburg, Lively Grove; 171 P-8; mail Oakdale Z 62268; ● 45
Lively Grove; MCD-Township; WASHINGTON; *171 P-8; mail Oakdale Z 62268; Ⓟ 728; Ⓒ 702
Liverpool; Inc. Place; FULTON; ▲ Liverpool; 170 H-7; 🅿; Z 61543; Ⓟ 129; Ⓒ 119
Liverpool; MCD-Township; FULTON; *170 H-7; 🅿; Z 61543; Ⓟ 730; Ⓒ 664
Livingston; RMC Place; CLARK; *171 L-13; mail Marshall Z 62441; ● 90
Livingston; Inc. Place; MADISON; 171 M-7; elev. 600ft./183m.; 🅿; Z 62058; Ⓟ 928; Ⓒ 825
LIVINGSTON; 170 F-10; Ⓟ 39,301; Ⓒ 39,678; ◆ 37,609
Loami; Inc. Place; SANGAMON; ▲ Loami; 171 K-7; 🅿; Z 62661; Ⓟ 802; Ⓒ 804
Loami; MCD-Township; SANGAMON; *171 K-7; 🅿; Z 62661; Ⓟ 1,071; Ⓒ 1,118
Loch Lomond; RMC Place; LAKE; ★ CHI; mail Mundelein Z 60060
Lockhaven; RMC Place; JERSEY; *171 N-6; ★ ST.L; mail Godfrey Z 62035; rural
Lockport; Inc. Place; WILL; ▲ Lockport; 170 D-12; 🅿; ★ CHI; Z 60441, Z 60491 & mail Romeoville Z 60446; Ⓟ 9,401; Ⓒ 15,191; ◆ 22,306
Lockport; MCD-Township; WILL; *170 D-12; 🅿; ★ CHI; Z 60441, Z 60491 & mail Romeoville Z 60446; Ⓟ 32,336; Ⓒ 42,048
Locust; MCD-Township; CHRISTIAN; *171 L-9; mail Owaneco Z 62555; Ⓟ 656; Ⓒ 1,856
Loda; Inc. Place; IROQUOIS; ▲ Loda; 170 H-12; elev. 781ft./238m.; 🅿; Z 60948; Ⓟ 390; Ⓒ 419
Loda; MCD-Township; IROQUOIS; *170 H-12; 🅿; Z 60948; Ⓟ 1,254; Ⓒ 1,392
Lodge; RMC Place; PIATT; 170 I-11; 🅿; Z 61856; ● 100
Logan; RMC Place; EDGAR; *171 K-13; elev. 629ft./192m.; mail Chrisman Z 61924
Logan (Hanaford); Inc. Place; FRANKLIN; 171 Q-10; elev. 479ft./146m.; 🅿; Z 62856; Ⓟ 380; Ⓒ 55; Ⓡ 214
Logan; MCD-Township; PEORIA; *170 G-7; ★ PEOR; mail Hanna City Z 61536; Ⓟ 3,041; Ⓒ 3,091
LOGAN; 170 I-8; Ⓟ 30,798; Ⓒ 31,183; ◆ 29,598
Logan Square; RMC Place; COOK; *170 C-13; ★ CHI; mail Chicago Z 60647; pop. incl. with Chicago (Inc. Place)
Lomax; Inc. Place; HENDERSON; ▲ Lomax; 170 G-4; 🅿; Z 61454; Ⓟ 473; Ⓒ 477
Lomax; MCD-Township; HENDERSON; *170 G-4; 🅿; Z 61454; Ⓟ 989; Ⓒ 936
Lombard; Inc. Place; DUPAGE; 172 H-5; elev. 700ft./213m.; 🅿 🅲 582 ■; ★ CHI; Z 60148; Ⓟ 39,408; Ⓒ 42,322; ◆ 41,821
Lombardville; RMC Place; STARK; *170 E-8; elev. 750ft./229m.; mail Bradford Z 61421; ● 30
London Mills; Inc. Place; FULTON, KNOX; 170 G-6; elev. 533ft./162m.; 🅿; Z 61544; Ⓟ 485; Ⓒ 447
Lone Grove; MCD-Township; FAYETTE; *171 N-10; mail Saint Peter Z 62880; Ⓟ 725; Ⓒ 707
Lone Tree; RMC Place; BUREAU; *170 E-8; elev. 707ft./215m.; mail Tiskilwa Z 61368; rural
Long Branch; MCD-Township; SALINE; *171 Q-11; mail Galatia Z 62935; Ⓟ 265; Ⓒ 189
Long Creek; Inc. Place; MACON; 170 J-10; ★ DEC; mail Decatur Z 62521; Ⓒ 1,364
Long Creek; MCD-Township; MACON; *170 J-10; ★ DEC; mail Decatur Z 62521; Ⓟ 10,628; Ⓒ 10,547
Long Grove; Inc. Place; LAKE; 172 D-5; elev. 725ft./221m.; 🅿; ★ CHI; Z 60047, Z 60049, Z 60060; Ⓟ 4,740; Ⓒ 6,735
Long Lake; CDP; LAKE; 172 A-4; ★ CHI; mail Ingleside Z 60041, Round Lake Z 60073; Ⓟ 2,888; Ⓒ 3,356
Long Meadow; RMC Place; DUPAGE; ★ CHI; mail Downers Grove Z 60515; pop. incl. with Downers Grove (Inc. Place)
Long Point; Inc. Place; LIVINGSTON; ▲ Long Point; 170 F-10; 🅿; Z 61333; Ⓟ 208; Ⓒ 247
Long Point; MCD-Township; LIVINGSTON; *170 F-10; 🅿; Z 61333; Ⓟ 541; Ⓒ 542
Longview; Inc. Place; CHAMPAIGN; 170 J-12; elev. 680ft./207m.; 🅿; Z 61852; Ⓟ 180; Ⓒ 153
Longview Addition; RMC Place; MCLEAN; *170 H-9; mail Heyworth Z 61745; ● 50
Longwood Farms; RMC Place; COOK; ★ CHI; mail Chicago Heights Z 60411; pop. incl. with Chicago Heights (Inc. Place)
Longwood Manor (Scot Plains); RMC Place; DUPAGE; *170 C-12; ★ CHI; mail Naperville Z 60563; ● 1,250
Loogootee; RMC Place; FAYETTE; 171 N-10; elev. 600ft./183m.; 🅿; Z 62838, Z 62857; ● 70
Looking Glass; MCD-Township; CLINTON; *171 O-8; ★ ST.L; mail New Baden Z 62265; Ⓟ 5,096; Ⓒ 5,555
Lookout Point; RMC Place; MCHENRY; *170 A-11; ★ CHI; mail Wonder Lake Z 60097; ● 500
Loon Lake; RMC Place; LAKE; *170 A-12; ★ CHI; mail Antioch Z 60002; ● 400
Loop; RMC Place; COOK; *170 C-13; ★ CHI; mail Chicago Z 60601-05, Z 60690-91; pop. incl. with Chicago (Inc. Place)
Loraine; Inc. Place; ADAMS; 170 I-3; elev. 648ft./198m.; 🅿; Z 62349; Ⓟ 331; Ⓒ 363
Loraine; MCD-Township; HENRY; *170 D-7; mail Prophetstown Z 61277; Ⓟ 364; Ⓒ 315
Loran; RMC Place; STEPHENSON; ▲ Loran; 170 B-7; mail Pearl City Z 61062; ● 40
Loran; MCD-Township; STEPHENSON; *170 B-7; mail Pearl City Z 61062; Ⓟ 1,276; Ⓒ 1,389
Lords' Park Manor; RMC Place; COOK; ★ CHI; mail Elgin Z 60120; pop. incl. with Elgin (Inc. Place)
Lorenzo; RMC Place; WILL; *170 E-12; ★ CHI; mail Wilmington Z 60481; rural
Loretto; RMC Place; LIVINGSTON; *170 F-11; elev. 709ft./216m.; mail Odell Z 60460; rural
Lorraine Park; RMC Place; DUPAGE; ★ CHI; mail Wheaton Z 60187; pop. incl. with Wheaton (Inc. Place)
Lostant; Inc. Place; LA SALLE; 170 F-9; elev. 703ft./214m.; 🅿; Z 61334; Ⓟ 510; Ⓒ 486
Lost Lake; RMC Place; STEPHENSON; *170 A-8; elev. 800ft./244m.; mail Rock City Z 61070; ● 50
Lost Nation; RMC Place; OGLE; *170 C-8; mail Dixon Z 61021; rural
Lotus; RMC Place; CHAMPAIGN; *170 I-11; elev. 743ft./226m.; mail Foosland Z 61845; ● 30
Lotus Woods; RMC Place; LAKE; *170 A-12; ★ CHI; mail Spring Grove Z 60081; ● 750
Lou Del; RMC Place; MONROE; mail Waterloo Z 62298; ● 300
Loudon; MCD-Township; FAYETTE; *171 M-10; mail Beecher City Z 62414; Ⓟ 826; Ⓒ 676
Louisville; Inc. Place; ⊡ CLAY; ▲ Louisville; 171 N-11; 🅿; Z 62858; Ⓟ 1,098; Ⓒ 1,242
Louisville; MCD-Township; CLAY; *171 N-11; 🅿; Z 62858; Ⓟ 1,676; Ⓒ 1,865
Love; MCD-Township; VERMILION; *170 J-13; mail Ridge Farm Z 61870; Ⓟ 321; Ⓒ 223
Lovejoy; MCD-Township; IROQUOIS; *170 H-13; mail Wellington Z 60973; Ⓟ 514; Ⓒ 462
Lovejoy; ST. CLAIR; see Brooklyn (Inc. Place)
Loves Park; Inc. Place; WINNEBAGO; 170 A-9; elev. 740ft./226m.; 🅿; ★ RKFD; Z 61111, Z 61115, Z 61130-32; Ⓟ 15,462; Ⓒ 20,044; ◆ 23,326
Lovington; Inc. Place; MOULTRIE; ▲ Lovington; 171 K-10; elev. 679ft./207m.; 🅿; Z 61937; Ⓟ 1,143; Ⓒ 1,222
Lovington; MCD-Township; MOULTRIE; *171 K-10; 🅿; Z 61937; Ⓟ 1,671; Ⓒ 1,684
Lowder; RMC Place; SANGAMON; 171 K-7; elev. 690ft./210m.; 🅿; Z 62662; ● 100
Lowe; MCD-Township; MOULTRIE; *171 K-11; mail Arthur Z 61911; Ⓟ 1,523; Ⓒ 1,622
Lowell; RMC Place; LA SALLE; 170 E-9; mail Tonica Z 61370; ● 50
Low Point; RMC Place; WOODFORD; 170 G-9; elev. 723ft./220m.; 🅿; Z 61545; ● 200
Loxa; RMC Place; COLES; *171 L-11; elev. 674ft./205m.; mail Mattoon Z 61938; ● 100
Lucas; MCD-Township; EFFINGHAM; *171 M-11; mail Dieterich Z 62424; Ⓟ 439; Ⓒ 480
Ludlow; Inc. Place; CHAMPAIGN; ▲ Ludlow; 170 H-12; 🅿; Z 60949; Ⓟ 323; Ⓒ 324
Ludlow; MCD-Township; CHAMPAIGN; *170 H-12; 🅿; Z 60949; Ⓟ 4,744; Ⓒ 4,766
Lukin; MCD-Township; LAWRENCE; *171 O-13; mail Bridgeport Z 62417; Ⓟ 397; Ⓒ 414

Entries in **UPPERCASE** are counties.
Entries in **bold** have populations of 2,500 or more.
Names in parentheses are alternate names.

Inc. Place	Incorporated Place
RMC Place	Rand McNally Designated Place
CDP	Census Designated Place
MCD	Minor Civil Division

⊡	County Seat
▲	Minor Civil Division
elev.	Elevation
🅿	Post Office
🅷	Hospital
🅲	College
■	Principal Business Center
★	Ranally Metro Area (RMA) Abbreviation
Z	Zip Code(s)
Ⓟ	Previous Census Population
Ⓡ	Revised Census Population
Ⓐ	Annexation Population
●	Rand McNally Population Estimate
Ⓒ	Final Census Population
Ⓢ	Special Census Population
◆	Estimated Population

For additional definitions see Glossary, Volume 1, and Introduction, Volume 2.

Lumaghi Heights; RMC Place; MADISON; *171 N-7; ★ **ST.L**; mail Collinsville z 62234; ● 70
Luther; RMC Place; MASON; *170 I-8; 🅿; z 62664; rural
Lyman; MCD-Township; FORD; *170 G-12; mail Roberts z 60962; Ⓟ 617; © 578
Lynchburg; MCD-Township; MASON; *170 I-6; 🅿; z 62617; Ⓟ 254; © 274
Lyndon; Inc. Place; WHITESIDE; ▲ Lyndon; 170 C-7; 🅿; z 61261; Ⓟ 615; © 566
Lyndon; MCD-Township; WHITESIDE; *170 C-7; 🅿; z 61261; Ⓟ 1,004; © 1,036
Lynn; HENRY; see Lynn Center (RMC Place)
Lynn; MCD-Township; HENRY; *170 E-6; mail Lynn Center z 61262; Ⓟ 789; © 755
Lynn; MCD-Township; KNOX; *170 F-7; mail Altona z 61414; Ⓟ 340; © 316
Lynn Center (Lynn); RMC Place; HENRY; ▲ Lynn; 170 E-6; elev. 756ft./230m.; 🅿; z 61262; ● 150
Lynn Gardens; RMC Place; KANKAKEE; *170 F-12; elev. 625ft./191m.; ★ **KANK**; mail Kankakee z 60901; ● 100
Lynnville; Inc. Place; MORGAN; 171 K-6; elev. 618ft./188m.; 🅿; z 62650; Ⓟ 125; © 137
Lynnville; MCD-Township; OGLE; *170 B-9; mail Lindenwood z 61049; Ⓟ 552; © 614
Lynnwood; RMC Place; KENDALL; *170 D-11; ★ **CHI**; mail Oswego z 60543; ● 400
Lynnwood; RMC Place; LA SALLE; *170 E-9; elev. 600ft./183m.; mail Peru z 61354; ● 60
Lynwood; Inc. Place; COOK; 172 N-10; elev. 633ft./193m.; 🅿; ★ **CHI**; z 60411; Ⓟ 6,535; © 7,377
Lynwood Estates; RMC Place; CARROLL; mail Thomson z 61285; ● 100
Lyons; Inc. Place; COOK; 172 I-7; elev. 625ft./191m.; 🅿; ★ **CHI**; z 60534; Ⓟ 9,828; © 10,255
Lyons; MCD-Township; COOK; *170 C-12; 🅿; ★ **CHI**; z 60534 & mail La Grange z 60525; includes part of the Village of Lyons; Ⓟ 105,004; © 109,264
Lyons; RMC Place; VERMILION; ★ **DANV**; mail Westville z 61883; pop. incl. with Belgium (Inc. Place)

M

Macedonia; Inc. Place; HAMILTON, FRANKLIN; 171 Q-10; elev. 480ft./146m.; 🅿; z 62860; Ⓟ 58; © 51
Machesney Park; Inc. Place; WINNEBAGO; 170 A-9; 🅿; ★ **RKFD**; z 61103, z 61111, z 61115; Ⓟ 19,033; © 20,759; ◆ 23,873
MacIntoch; RMC Place; LA SALLE; *170 F-10; mail Streator z 61364; pop. incl. with Streator (Inc. Place)
Mackinaw; Inc. Place; TAZEWELL; ▲ Mackinaw; 170 H-8; 🅿; z 61755; Ⓟ 1,331; © 1,452
Mackinaw; MCD-Township; TAZEWELL; *170 H-8; 🅿; z 61755; Ⓟ 2,772; © 3,769
Mackler Heights; RMC Place; COOK; ★ **CHI**; mail Chicago Heights z 60411; pop. incl. with Chicago Heights (Inc. Place)
Macomb; Inc. Place; ⊡ MCDONOUGH; 170 H-5; elev. 700ft./213m.; 🅿 🅷 🅲 13,602 ■; z 61455; Ⓟ 19,952; © 18,558; ◆ 19,985
Macomb; MCD-Township; MCDONOUGH; *170 H-5; 🅿 🅲 13,602; z 61455 & mail Good Hope z 61438; does not include the City of Macomb; Ⓟ 729; © 608
Macomb City; MCD-Township; MCDONOUGH; *170 H-5; 🅷; mail Macomb z 61455; coextensive with the City of Macomb; Ⓟ 19,952; © 18,558
Macon; MCD-Township; BUREAU; *170 E-7; mail Buda z 61314; Ⓟ 271; © 252
Macon; Inc. Place; MACON; 171 K-9; elev. 714ft./218m.; 🅿; z 62544; Ⓟ 1,282; © 1,213
MACON; 170 J-9; Ⓟ 117,206; © 114,706; ◆ 107,373
Macoupin; RMC Place; MACOUPIN; *171 M-7; mail Shipman z 62685
MACOUPIN; 171 M-7; Ⓟ 47,679; © 49,019; ◆ 48,119
Madison; Inc. Place; MADISON, ST. CLAIR; 195 D-7; elev. 410ft./125m.; 🅿; ★ **ST.L**; z 62060; Ⓟ 4,629; © 4,545
Madison; MCD-Township; RICHLAND; *171 O-12; mail Olney z 62450; Ⓟ 920; © 910
MADISON; 171 N-7; Ⓟ 249,238; © 258,941; Ⓡ 258,950; ◆ 270,869
Madonnaville; RMC Place; MONROE; *171 P-6; mail Waterloo z 62298; rural
Maeystown; Inc. Place; MONROE; *171 P-6; elev. 500ft./152m.; 🅿; z 62256; Ⓟ 116; © 148
Magnet; RMC Place; COLES; *171 L-11; elev. 750ft./229m.; mail Mattoon z 61938; ● 30
Magnolia; Inc. Place; PUTNAM; ▲ Magnolia; 170 F-9; elev. 673ft./205m.; 🅿; z 61336; Ⓟ 261; © 279
Magnolia; MCD-Township; PUTNAM; *170 F-9; 🅿; z 61336; Ⓟ 1,215; © 1,166
Mahomet; Inc. Place; CHAMPAIGN; ▲ Mahomet; 170 I-11; elev. 714ft./218m.; 🅿; z 61853; Ⓟ 3,103; © 4,877
Mahomet; MCD-Township; CHAMPAIGN; *170 I-11; 🅿; z 61853; Ⓟ 8,440; © 10,113
Maine; MCD-Township; COOK; *170 B-12; ★ **CHI**; mail Des Plaines z 60016; Ⓟ 128,837; © 135,623
Maine; MCD-Township; GRUNDY; *170 E-11; mail Mazon z 60444; Ⓟ 222; © 242
Main Street; RMC Place; COOK; *170 B-13; ★ **CHI**; mail Evanston z 60202; pop. incl. with Evanston (Inc. Place)
Makanda; Inc. Place; JACKSON; ▲ Makanda; 171 R-9; elev. 437ft./133m.; 🅿; ★ **CARB-**; z 62958; Ⓟ 404; © 419
Makanda; MCD-Township; JACKSON; *171 R-9; 🅿; ★ **CARB-**; z 62958; Ⓟ 3,700; © 4,062; Ⓡ 4,059
Malden; Inc. Place; BUREAU; *170 E-8; elev. 704ft./215m.; 🅿; z 61337; Ⓟ 370; © 343
Malibu Village; RMC Place; JACKSON; *171 R-9; elev. 450ft./137m.; ★ **CARB-**; mail Carbondale z 62901; pop. incl. with Carbondale (Inc. Place)
Malone; MCD-Township; TAZEWELL; *170 H-8; mail Green Valley z 61534; Ⓟ 285; © 297
Malta; Inc. Place; DEKALB; ▲ Malta; 170 C-10; 🅿; z 60150; Ⓟ 865; © 969
Malta; MCD-Township; DEKALB; *170 C-10; 🅿; z 60150; Ⓟ 1,335; © 1,402
Malvern; RMC Place; WHITESIDE; *170 C-7; elev. 698ft./213m.; mail Morrison z 61270; ● 50
Manchester; MCD-Township; BOONE; *170 A-10; mail Caledonia z 61011; Ⓟ 939; © 931
Manchester; Inc. Place; SCOTT; 171 K-6; elev. 696ft./212m.; 🅿; z 62663; Ⓟ 347; © 354
Manhattan; Inc. Place; WILL; ▲ Manhattan; 170 E-12; 🅿; ★ **CHI**; z 60442; Ⓟ 2,059; © 3,330
Manhattan; MCD-Township; WILL; *170 D-12; 🅿; ★ **CHI**; z 60442; Ⓟ 3,963; © 5,615
Manito; Inc. Place; MASON; ▲ Manito; 170 H-7; 🅿; z 61546; Ⓟ 1,711; © 1,733
Manito; MCD-Township; MASON; *170 H-7; 🅿; z 61546; Ⓟ 2,593; © 2,522
Manlius; Inc. Place; BUREAU; ▲ Manlius; 170 D-8; 🅿; z 61338; Ⓟ 365; © 355
Manlius; MCD-Township; BUREAU; *170 D-8; 🅿; z 61338; Ⓟ 731; © 692
Manlius; MCD-Township; LA SALLE; *170 E-10; mail Seneca z 61360; Ⓟ 5,267; © 5,652
Mannheim; RMC Place; COOK; ★ **CHI**; mail Franklin Park z 60131; pop. incl. with Franklin Park (Inc. Place)
Mannon; RMC Place; MERCER; *170 E-4; elev. 572ft./174m.; mail New Boston z 61272
Mansfield; Inc. Place; PIATT; 170 I-11; elev. 730ft./223m.; 🅿; z 61854; Ⓟ 929; © 949
Manteno; Inc. Place; KANKAKEE; ▲ Manteno; 170 E-13; 🅿; ★ **KANK**; z 60950; Ⓟ 3,488; © 6,414
Manteno; MCD-Township; KANKAKEE; *170 E-13; 🅿; ★ **KANK**; z 60950; Ⓟ 5,059; © 7,846
Manville; RMC Place; LIVINGSTON; 170 F-10; elev. 612ft./187m.; 🅿; z 61319; ● 50
Maplebrook; RMC Place; DUPAGE; ★ **CHI**; mail Naperville z 60565; pop. incl. with Naperville (Inc. Place)
Maple Grove; RMC Place; EDWARDS; *171 O-12; elev. 447ft./136m.; mail West Salem z 62476; rural
Maple Hill; RMC Place; DUPAGE; *170 C-12; ★ **CHI**; mail Warrenville z 60555; pop. incl. with Warrenville (Inc. Place)
Maple Lane; RMC Place; WHITESIDE; *170 C-7; mail Sterling z 61081; ● 80
Maple Park; Inc. Place; KANE, DEKALB; 170 C-10; elev. 860ft./262m.; 🅿; z 60151; Ⓟ 641; © 765
Maple Point; RMC Place; CUMBERLAND; *171 L-12; mail Greenup z 62428; rural
Maples Mill; RMC Place; FULTON; *170 H-7; mail Canton z 61520, Lewistown z 61542; ● 40
Mapleton; Inc. Place; PEORIA; 170 H-7; elev. 461ft./141m.; 🅿; z 61547; Ⓟ 216; © 227
Maplewood; RMC Place; COOK; ★ **CHI**; mail Chicago z 60647; pop. incl. with Chicago (Inc. Place)
Maplewood; RMC Place; ST. CLAIR; ★ **ST.L**; mail East Saint Louis z 62206; pop. incl. with Cahokia (Inc. Place)
Maplewood Estates; RMC Place; FULTON; *170 H-7; mail Canton z 61520; rural
Maquon; Inc. Place; KNOX; ▲ Maquon; 170 G-6; 🅿; z 61458; Ⓟ 331; © 318
Maquon; MCD-Township; KNOX; *170 G-6; 🅿; z 61458; Ⓟ 647; © 608
Marblehead; RMC Place; ADAMS; 170 J-3; mail Quincy z 62301, z 62305; ● 100
Marcelline; RMC Place; ADAMS; 170 I-3; mail Ursa z 62376; ● 100
Marcoe; RMC Place; JEFFERSON; *171 P-9; mail Mount Vernon z 62864; rural
Mardell Manor; RMC Place; PEORIA; *170 G-8; ★ **PEOR**; mail Peoria z 61607; ● 700
Marengo; Inc. Place; MCHENRY; ▲ Coral, Marengo; 170 B-10; elev. 837ft./255m.; 🅿; z 60152; Ⓟ 4,768; © 6,355
Marengo; MCD-Township; MCHENRY; *170 A-10; 🅿; z 60152; includes part of the City of Marengo; Ⓟ 5,723; © 7,239
Marietta; Inc. Place; FULTON; 170 H-6; elev. 640ft./195m.; 🅿; z 61459; Ⓟ 142; © 150
Marigold; RMC Place; RANDOLPH; *171 Q-6; elev. 564ft./172m.; mail Evansville z 62242; rural
Marina Terrace; RMC Place; KENDALL; *170 C-11; ★ **CHI**; mail Oswego z 60543; ● 280
Marina Village; RMC Place; KENDALL; ★ **CHI**; mail Oswego z 60543; ● 250
Marine; Inc. Place; MADISON; ▲ Marine; 171 N-7; 🅿; z 62061; Ⓟ 972; © 910
Marine; MCD-Township; MADISON; *171 N-7; 🅿; z 62061; Ⓟ 1,852; © 1,922
Marion; MCD-Township; LEE; *170 C-8; mail Amboy z 61310; Ⓟ 301; © 268
Marion; MCD-Township; OGLE; *170 B-9; mail Chana z 61015; Ⓟ 2,740; © 3,671
Marion; Inc. Place; ⊡ WILLIAMSON, JOHNSON; 171 R-10; elev. 448ft./137m.; 🅿 🅷 ■; ★ **CARB-**; z 62959; Ⓟ 14,545; © 16,035; ◆ 17,079
MARION; 171 O-10; Ⓟ 41,561; © 41,691; ◆ 39,192
Marion Circle; RMC Place; KANE; *170 C-11; elev. 730ft./223m.; ★ **CHI**; mail Sugar Grove z 60554; ● 40
Marion Country Club; RMC Place; WILLIAMSON; *171 R-10; elev. 500ft./152m.; mail Marion z 62959; ● 50
Marion Hills; RMC Place; DUPAGE; ★ **CHI**; mail Darien z 60561; pop. incl. with Darien (Inc. Place)
Marissa; Inc. Place; ST. CLAIR; ▲ Marissa; 171 P-7; 🅿; z 62257; Ⓟ 2,375; © 2,141
Marissa; MCD-Township; ST. CLAIR; *171 P-7; 🅿; z 62257; Ⓟ 2,875; © 2,664
Mark; Inc. Place; PUTNAM; *170 E-9; elev. 650ft./198m.; 🅿; z 61340; Ⓟ 391; © 491
Markham; Inc. Place; COOK; 172 L-9; elev. 615ft./187m.; 🅿; ★ **CHI**; z 60426, z 60428; Ⓟ 13,136; © 12,620
Markham; RMC Place; MORGAN; *171 K-6; mail Chapin z 62628; rural
Markham City; RMC Place; JEFFERSON; *171 P-10; mail Bluford z 62814; pop. incl. with Bluford (Inc. Place)
Marley; RMC Place; EDGAR; *171 K-13; elev. 643ft./196m.; mail Paris z 61944; rural
Marley; RMC Place; WILL; 172 M-6; ★ **CHI**; mail Mokena z 60448; ● 100
Marlow; RMC Place; JEFFERSON; *171 P-10; mail Opdyke z 62872; ● 45
Marnico Village; RMC Place; MORGAN; *171 K-6; mail Jacksonville z 62650; ● 80
Maroa; Inc. Place; MACON; ▲ Maroa; 170 J-10; 🅿; z 61756; Ⓟ 1,602; © 1,654
Maroa; MCD-Township; MACON; *170 J-9; 🅿; z 61756; Ⓟ 1,898; © 1,988
Marquette Heights; Inc. Place; TAZEWELL; *170 G-8; elev. 600ft./183m.; 🅿; ★ **PEOR**; z 61554; Ⓟ 3,077; © 2,794
Marrowbone; MCD-Township; MOULTRIE; *171 K-10; mail Bethany z 61914; Ⓟ 1,784; © 1,705
Mars; RMC Place; COOK; ★ **CHI**; mail Chicago z 60639; pop. incl. with Chicago (Inc. Place)
Marseilles; Inc. Place; LA SALLE; 170 E-10; elev. 504ft./154m.; 🅿; z 61341; Ⓟ 4,811; © 4,655
Marshall; Inc. Place; ⊡ CLARK; ▲ Marshall; 171 L-13; elev. 641ft./195m.; 🅿; z 62441; Ⓟ 3,555; © 3,771
Marshall; MCD-Township; CLARK; *171 L-13; 🅿; z 62441; includes part of the City of Marshall; Ⓟ 4,491; © 4,734
MARSHALL; 170 F-8; Ⓟ 12,846; © 13,180; ◆ 12,789
Marston; RMC Place; MERCER; *170 E-4; mail Reynolds z 61279; rural
Martin; MCD-Township; CRAWFORD; *171 N-13; mail Robinson z 62454; Ⓟ 606; © 607
Martin; MCD-Township; MCLEAN; *170 H-10; mail Colfax z 61728; Ⓟ 1,154; © 1,229
Martinsburg; RMC Place; PIKE; ▲ Martinsburg; *171 K-4; mail Pittsfield z 62363; ● 40
Martinsburg; MCD-Township; PIKE; *171 K-4; mail Pittsfield z 62363; Ⓟ 380; © 435
Martinsville; Inc. Place; CLARK; ▲ Martinsville; 171 L-13; 🅿; z 62442; Ⓟ 1,161; © 1,225
Martinsville; MCD-Township; CLARK; *171 L-13; 🅿; z 62442; Ⓟ 1,624; © 1,688
Martinton; Inc. Place; IROQUOIS; ▲ Martinton; 170 F-13; 🅿; z 60951; Ⓟ 299; © 375
Martinton; MCD-Township; IROQUOIS; *170 F-13; 🅿; z 60951; Ⓟ 1,004; © 1,063
Mary Crest; RMC Place; COOK; ★ **CHI**; mail Country Club Hills z 60478; pop. incl. with Country Club Hills (Inc. Place)
Mary Crest; RMC Place; WILL; ★ **CHI**; mail Joliet z 60436; pop. incl. with Joliet (Inc. Place)
Marydale; RMC Place; CLINTON; *171 N-8; elev. 463ft./141m.; mail Carlyle z 62231; rural
Marydale Manor; RMC Place; COOK; ★ **CHI**; mail Dolton z 60419; pop. incl. with Dolton (Inc. Place)
Maryland; RMC Place; OGLE; ▲ Lincoln; *170 B-8; mail Polo z 61064; ● 40
Maryland; MCD-Township; OGLE; *170 B-8; mail Baileyville z 61007; Ⓟ 670; © 610
Mary Meadows; RMC Place; KANE; *170 C-11; elev. 903ft./275m.; ★ **CHI**; mail Saint Charles z 60175; ● 60
Maryville; Inc. Place; MADISON; 195 D-10; elev. 582ft./177m.; 🅿 🅷; ★ **ST.L**; z 62062; Ⓟ 2,576; © 4,651
Mascoutah; Inc. Place; ST. CLAIR; ▲ Mascoutah; 171 O-7; elev. 424ft./129m.; 🅿; ★ **ST.L**; z 62258; Ⓟ 5,511; © 5,659
Mascoutah; MCD-Township; ST. CLAIR; *171 O-7; 🅿; ★ **ST.L**; z 62258, z 98662; Ⓟ 6,340; © 6,474
Mason; Inc. Place; EFFINGHAM; ▲ Mason; 171 N-10; 🅿; z 62443; Ⓟ 387; © 396
Mason; MCD-Township; EFFINGHAM; *171 M-10; 🅿; z 62443; Ⓟ 1,411; © 1,510
MASON; 170 I-7; Ⓟ 16,269; © 16,038; ◆ 14,949
Mason City; Inc. Place; MASON; ▲ Mason City; 170 I-7; 🅿; z 62664; Ⓟ 2,323; © 2,558
Mason City; MCD-Township; MASON; *170 I-8; 🅿; z 62664; Ⓟ 2,729; © 2,832
MASSAC; 171 T-10; Ⓟ 14,752; © 15,161; ◆ 15,026
Massbach; RMC Place; JO DAVIESS; *170 B-6; elev. 945ft./288m.; mail Elizabeth z 61028; ● 25
Massilon; MCD-Township; WAYNE; *171 O-12; mail Scheller z 62883; Ⓟ 195; © 161
Matanzas Beach; RMC Place; MASON; *170 I-6; mail Havana z 62644; summer pop. 500; ● 200
Matherville; Inc. Place; MERCER; 170 E-5; elev. 750ft./229m.; 🅿; z 61263; Ⓟ 708; © 772
Matteson; Inc. Place; COOK, WILL; 172 N-8; elev. 693ft./211m.; 🅿 ■; ★ **CHI**; z 60443; Ⓟ 11,378; © 12,928; ◆ 12,826
Mattoon; Inc. Place; COLES; 171 L-11; elev. 726ft./221m.; 🅿 🅷 ■; z 61938; Ⓟ 18,441; © 18,291; ◆ 17,757
Mattoon; MCD-Township; COLES; *171 L-11; 🅿; z 61938; includes part of the City of Mattoon; Ⓟ 16,560; © 16,184
Maud; RMC Place; WABASH; *171 O-13; elev. 428ft./130m.; mail Mount Carmel z 62863; rural
Maunie; Inc. Place; WHITE; 171 Q-12; elev. 374ft./114m.; 🅿; z 62861; Ⓟ 119; © 177
Maxwell; MCD-Township; SANGAMON; *171 K-7; mail Loami z 62661; Ⓟ 215; © 194
May; MCD-Township; CHRISTIAN; *171 K-9; mail Stonington z 62567; Ⓟ 1,307; © 1,436
May; MCD-Township; LEE; *170 D-8; mail Sublette z 61367; Ⓟ 344; © 395
Mayberry; MCD-Township; HAMILTON; *171 Q-11; mail Broughton z 62817; Ⓟ 548; © 526
Mayfair; RMC Place; COOK; ★ **CHI**; mail Chicago z 60630; pop. incl. with Chicago (Inc. Place)
Mayfair; RMC Place; TAZEWELL; *170 G-8; ★ **PEOR**; mail Morton z 61550; ● 80
Mayfield; MCD-Township; DEKALB; *170 B-10; mail Sycamore z 60178; Ⓟ 741; © 810
Maynard Lake; RMC Place; CHAMPAIGN; *170 I-11; elev. 720ft./219m.; ★ **CH-U**; mail Champaign z 61822; ● 450
Mays; RMC Place; EDGAR; *171 K-13; mail Paris z 61944; rural
Maysville; RMC Place; PIKE; *171 K-4; elev. 714ft./218m.; mail Griggsville z 62340; rural
Maytown; RMC Place; LEE; *170 D-8; mail Amboy z 61310; rural
Mayview; RMC Place; CHAMPAIGN; *170 I-12; ★ **CH-U**; mail Urbana z 61802; ● 50
Maywood; Inc. Place; COOK; 172 H-7; elev. 626ft./191m.; 🅿 🅷; ★ **CHI**; z 60153, z 60155; Ⓟ 27,139; © 26,987; ◆ 26,232
Mazon; Inc. Place; GRUNDY; ▲ Mazon; 170 E-11; elev. 586ft./179m.; 🅿; z 60444; Ⓟ 764; © 904
Mazon; MCD-Township; GRUNDY; *170 E-11; 🅿; z 60444; Ⓟ 1,287; © 1,377
McCall; RMC Place; HANCOCK; *170 H-3; elev. 698ft./213m.; mail Carthage z 62321; rural
McClellan; MCD-Township; JEFFERSON; *171 P-9; mail Waltonville z 62894; Ⓟ 1,183; © 1,239
McClure; Inc. Place; ALEXANDER; 171 S-8; elev. 343ft./105m.; 🅿; z 62957; incorporated November 2, 2004; not reported in 2000 Census; ● 600
McClusky; RMC Place; JERSEY; *171 M-6; elev. 639ft./195m.; mail Jerseyville z 62052; ● 25
McConnell; RMC Place; STEPHENSON; 170 A-7; elev. 777ft./237m.; 🅿; z 61050; ● 250
McCook; Inc. Place; COOK; 172 J-7; elev. 650ft./198m.; 🅿; ★ **CHI**; z 60525; Ⓟ 235; © 254
McCormick; RMC Place; POPE; *171 S-10; elev. 725ft./221m.; mail Stonefort z 62987
McCullom Lake; Inc. Place; MCHENRY; 172 A-2; elev. 763ft./233m.; 🅿; ★ **CHI**; z 60050; Ⓟ 1,033; © 1,038
McCully; RMC Place; LIVINGSTON; *170 F-10; mail Pontiac z 61764; ● 100
MCDONOUGH; 170 H-4; Ⓟ 35,244; © 32,913; ◆ 33,163
McDowell; RMC Place; LIVINGSTON; *170 G-11; elev. 665ft./203m.; mail Pontiac z 61764
McGirr; RMC Place; DEKALB; *170 C-10; mail Waterman z 60556; rural
McHenry; Inc. Place; MCHENRY; ▲ McHenry; 170 A-11; elev. 761ft./232m.; 🅿 🅷; ★ **CHI**; z 60050-51; Ⓟ 16,343; © 21,501; ◆ 27,003
McHenry; MCD-Township; MCHENRY; *170 A-11; 🅿; ★ **CHI**; z 60050-51; Ⓟ 37,034; © 41,740
MCHENRY; 170 A-10; Ⓟ 183,241; © 260,077; Ⓡ 260,075; ◆ 322,331
McHenry Shores; RMC Place; MCHENRY; *170 A-11; elev. 750ft./229m.; ★ **CHI**; mail McHenry z 60050; pop. incl. with McHenry (Inc. Place)
McIntosh; RMC Place; KANE; *170 B-11; elev. 850ft./259m.; ★ **CHI**; mail Elgin z 60123; pop. incl. with Elgin (Inc. Place)
McKee; MCD-Township; ADAMS; *170 J-4; mail Liberty z 62347; Ⓟ 205; © 193
McKeen; RMC Place; CLARK; *171 L-13; elev. 583ft./178m.; mail Marshall z 62441; ● 30
McKendree; MCD-Township; VERMILION; *170 J-13; mail Danville z 61834; Ⓟ 791; © 743
McKinley Park; RMC Place; COOK; ★ **CHI**; mail Chicago z 60608-09; pop. incl. with Chicago (Inc. Place)
McLean; Inc. Place; MCLEAN; 170 I-9; elev. 700ft./213m.; 🅿; z 61754; Ⓟ 797; © 808
MCLEAN; 170 G-10; Ⓟ 129,180; © 150,433; ◆ 169,927
McLeansboro; Inc. Place; ⊡ HAMILTON; ▲ McLeansboro; 171 Q-11; 🅿 🅷; z 62859; Ⓟ 2,677; © 2,945
McLeansboro; MCD-Township; HAMILTON; *171 Q-11; mail Mc Leansboro z 62859; Ⓟ 3,728; © 3,917
McNabb; Inc. Place; PUTNAM; 170 E-9; 🅿; z 61335; Ⓟ 310; © 310
McNoel; MASSAC; see Big Bay (RMC Place)
McQueen; RMC Place; DUPAGE; *170 C-11; ★ **CHI**; mail West Chicago z 60185; ● 150
McVey; RMC Place; MACOUPIN; *171 L-7; 🅿; z 62640; rural
Meacham; MCD-Township; MARION; *171 N-10; mail Kinmundy z 62854; Ⓟ 374; © 374
Meadowbrook; RMC Place; COOK; ★ **CHI**; mail Wheeling z 60090; pop. incl. with Wheeling (Inc. Place)
Meadowbrook; RMC Place; MADISON; 195 A-9; ★ **ST.L**; mail Bethalto z 62010, Eldred z 62027; ● 1,000
Meadowbrook; RMC Place; MCDONOUGH; *170 H-5; mail Macomb z 61455; ● 350
Meadow Heights; RMC Place; ST. CLAIR; ★ **ST.L**; mail Collinsville z 62234; pop. incl. with Collinsville (Inc. Place)
Meadowlake; RMC Place; CHAMPAIGN; *170 I-11; elev. 750ft./229m.; mail Champaign z 61821; ● 120
Meadows; RMC Place; MCLEAN; 170 G-10; mail Chenoa z 61726; ● 300
Meadowview; RMC Place; KANE; *170 C-11; elev. 950ft./290m.; ★ **CHI**; mail Saint Charles z 60175; pop. incl. with Lily Lake (Inc. Place)
Meadowview; RMC Place; KANKAKEE; ★ **KANK**; mail Kankakee z 60901; pop. incl. with Kankakee (Inc. Place)
Mechanicsburg; Inc. Place; SANGAMON; ▲ Mechanicsburg; 170 J-8; 🅿; z 62545; Ⓟ 538; © 456
Mechanicsburg; MCD-Township; SANGAMON; *170 J-8; 🅿; z 62545; Ⓟ 2,261; © 2,116
Medalist Park; RMC Place; COOK; ★ **CHI**; mail Palatine z 60067; pop. incl. with Palatine (Inc. Place)
Media; Inc. Place; HENDERSON; ▲ Media; 170 G-4; 🅿; z 61460; Ⓟ 146; © 130
Media; MCD-Township; HENDERSON; *170 G-4; 🅿; z 61460; Ⓟ 484; © 468
Medina; MCD-Township; PEORIA; *170 G-8; ★ **PEOR**; mail Chillicothe z 61523; Ⓟ 6,124; © 6,388
Medinah; RMC Place; DUPAGE; 172 G-5; elev. 717ft./219m.; 🅿; ★ **CHI**; z 60157; Ⓟ 2,512
Medinah on the Lake; RMC Place; DUPAGE; ★ **CHI**; mail Bloomingdale z 60108; pop. incl. with Bloomingdale (Inc. Place)
Medora; Inc. Place; MACOUPIN; 171 M-6; elev. 600ft./183m.; 🅿; z 62063; Ⓟ 420; © 501
Meeks; RMC Place; VERMILION; *170 J-13; elev. 692ft./211m.; mail Georgetown z 61846; rural
Meersman; ROCK ISLAND; see Babcock (RMC Place)
Meersman; RMC Place; ROCK ISLAND; ★ **D-RI-M**; mail East Moline z 61244
Melrose; MCD-Township; ADAMS; *170 J-3; ★ **QUIN**; mail Quincy z 62305; Ⓟ 6,098; © 6,305
Melrose; RMC Place; CLARK; ▲ Melrose; *171 L-13; mail West Union z 62477
Melrose; MCD-Township; CLARK; *171 M-13; mail West York z 62478; Ⓟ 371; © 395
Melrose Park; Inc. Place; COOK; 172 H-7; elev. 640ft./195m.; 🅿 🅷 ■; ★ **CHI**; z 60160-61, z 60163-65; Ⓟ 20,859; © 23,171; ◆ 23,233
Melville; RMC Place; MADISON; *171 N-6; ★ **ST.L**; mail Godfrey z 62035; pop. incl. with Godfrey (Inc. Place)
Melvin; Inc. Place; FORD; 170 H-11; elev. 800ft./244m.; 🅿; z 60952; Ⓟ 466; © 465
Memorial; RMC Place; MACON; ★ **DEC**; mail Decatur z 62526; pop. incl. with Decatur (Inc. Place)
MENARD; 170 I-7; Ⓟ 11,164; © 12,486; ◆ 12,658
Mendon; Inc. Place; ADAMS; ▲ Mendon; 170 I-3; 🅿; z 62351; Ⓟ 854; © 883
Mendon; MCD-Township; ADAMS; *170 I-3; 🅿; z 62351; Ⓟ 1,475; © 1,553
Mendota; Inc. Place; LA SALLE; 170 D-9; elev. 740ft./226m.; 🅿 🅷; z 61342; Ⓟ 7,018; © 7,272
Mendota; MCD-Township; LA SALLE; *170 D-9; 🅿; z 61342; includes part of the City of Mendota; Ⓟ 7,217; © 7,539
Menominee; Inc. Place; JO DAVIESS; ▲ Menominee; 170 A-5; mail East Dubuque z 61025; Ⓟ 187; © 237
Menominee; MCD-Township; JO DAVIESS; *170 A-5; mail East Dubuque z 61025; Ⓟ 998; © 1,020
Meppen; RMC Place; CALHOUN; 171 M-5; elev. 470ft./143m.; 🅿; z 62013; ● 60
Mercer; MCD-Township; MERCER; *170 E-5; mail Aledo z 61231; Ⓟ 4,227; © 4,172
MERCER; 170 E-5; Ⓟ 17,290; © 16,957; ◆ 16,278
Merchandise Mart; RMC Place; COOK; *170 C-13; ★ **CHI**; mail Chicago z 60654; pop. incl. with Chicago (Inc. Place)
Meredosia; Inc. Place; MORGAN; 170 J-5; elev. 446ft./136m.; 🅿; z 62665; Ⓟ 1,134; © 1,041
Meriden; RMC Place; LA SALLE; ▲ Meriden; 170 D-9; mail Mendota z 61342; ● 50
Meriden; MCD-Township; LA SALLE; *170 D-9; mail Mendota z 61342; Ⓟ 338; © 318
Meridian; MCD-Township; CLINTON; *171 O-9; Ⓟ 684; © 607
Meridian Heights; RMC Place; PULASKI; mail Mounds z 62964; pop. incl. with Mounds (Inc. Place)
Mermet; RMC Place; MASSAC; *171 T-10; mail Belknap z 62908
Merna; RMC Place; MCLEAN; 170 H-10; elev. 809ft./247m.; 🅿; z 61758, z 61761; ● 40
Merriam; RMC Place; WAYNE; *171 P-11; elev. 415ft./126m.; mail Fairfield z 62837; ● 25
Merrimac; RMC Place; MONROE; *171 P-6; mail Valmeyer z 62295; rural
Merrionette Park; Inc. Place; COOK; 172 K-9; elev. 620ft./189m.; 🅿; ★ **CHI**; z 60655, z 60803; Ⓟ 2,065; © 1,999
Merritt; RMC Place; SCOTT; *171 K-5; 🅿; z 62650; ● 50
Merry Oaks; RMC Place; ROCK ISLAND; ★ **D-RI-M**; mail East Moline z 61244; ● 500
Mesa Lake; RMC Place; WABASH; *171 O-13; mail Lancaster z 62855, Mount Carmel z 62863; ● 150
Metamora; Inc. Place; WOODFORD; ▲ Metamora; 170 G-8; elev. 821ft./250m.; 🅿; ★ **PEOR**; z 61548; Ⓟ 2,520; © 2,700
Metamora; MCD-Township; WOODFORD; *170 G-8; 🅿; ★ **PEOR**; z 61548; Ⓟ 3,320; © 3,462
Metcalf; Inc. Place; EDGAR; 170 J-13; elev. 663ft./202m.; 🅿; z 61940; Ⓟ 227; © 213
Metropolis; Inc. Place; ⊡ MASSAC; 171 T-10; elev. 345ft./105m.; 🅿 🅷; ★ **PAD**; z 62960; Ⓟ 6,734; © 6,482
Mettawa; Inc. Place; LAKE; 172 C-6; elev. 675ft./206m.; 🅿; ★ **CHI**; z 60045 & mail Libertyville z 60048; Ⓟ 348; © 367
Meyer; RMC Place; ADAMS; 170 I-2; elev. 486ft./148m.; mail Warsaw z 62379; ● 50
Meyer; RMC Place; KANKAKEE; *170 F-12; elev. 623ft./190m.; ★ **KANK**; mail Kankakee z 60901
Meyerbrook; RMC Place; KENDALL; *170 D-11; elev. 650ft./198m.; ★ **CHI**; mail Plano z 60545; ● 100
Meyers Bay; RMC Place; LAKE; ★ **CHI**; mail Fox Lake z 60020; pop. incl. with Fox Lake (Inc. Place)
Michael; RMC Place; CALHOUN; 171 L-5; 🅿; z 62065; ● 50
Middlebury; RMC Place; COOK, KANE, MCHENRY; *170 B-11; elev. 850ft./259m.; ★ **CHI**; mail Barrington z 60010; pop. incl. with Barrington Hills (Inc. Place)
Middle Creek; RMC Place; HANCOCK; *170 H-4; elev. 613ft./187m.; mail Plymouth z 62367; rural
Middlecreek; RMC Place; KANE; *170 C-11; elev. 790ft./241m.; ★ **CHI**; mail Saint Charles z 60175; ● 350
Middlefork; MCD-Township; VERMILION; *170 I-13; mail Potomac z 61865; Ⓟ 1,543; © 1,404
Middlegrove; RMC Place; FULTON; *170 G-6; elev. 721ft./220m.; 🅿; z 61531; ● 150
Middleport; MCD-Township; IROQUOIS; *170 G-13; mail Watseka z 60970; Ⓟ 4,653; © 4,784
Middlesworth; RMC Place; SHELBY; *171 L-10; elev. 699ft./213m.; 🅿; z 62565; ● 30
Middletown; Inc. Place; LOGAN; 170 I-8; elev. 583ft./178m.; 🅿; z 62666; Ⓟ 436; © 434
Midland City; RMC Place; DE WITT; *170 I-9; mail Clinton z 61727; ● 60
Midland Hills; RMC Place; JACKSON; *171 R-9; elev. 560ft./171m.; ★ **CARB-**; mail Makanda z 62958; rural
Midlothian; Inc. Place; COOK; 172 L-8; elev. 615ft./187m.; 🅿; ★ **CHI**; z 60445; Ⓟ 14,372; © 14,315
Midway; RMC Place; MADISON; *171 N-7; ★ **ST.L**; mail Moro z 62067; ● 150
Midway; RMC Place; MASSAC; 171 T-10; elev. 548ft./167m.; mail Metropolis z 62960; ● 25
Midway; RMC Place; TAZEWELL; 170 H-8; ★ **PEOR**; mail Pekin z 61554; ● 330
Midway; RMC Place; VERMILION; *170 J-13; elev. 675ft./206m.; ★ **DANV**; mail Westville z 61883; ● 100
Midwest; RMC Place; COOK; *170 C-13; ★ **CHI**; mail Chicago z 60612; pop. incl. with Chicago (Inc. Place)
Midwest Club; RMC Place; DUPAGE; ★ **CHI**; mail Oak Brook z 60523; pop. incl. with Oak Brook (Inc. Place)
Milam; MCD-Township; MACON; *171 K-10; mail Macon z 62544; Ⓟ 104; © 95
Milan; MCD-Township; DEKALB; *170 C-10; mail Shabbona z 60550; Ⓟ 373; © 364
Milan; Inc. Place; ROCK ISLAND; 171 T-3; elev. 570ft./174m.; 🅿; ★ **D-RI-M**; z 61264; Ⓟ 5,831; © 5,348
Mildred (Cabbage Patch); RMC Place; SANGAMON; *171 K-8; ★ **SPRG**; mail Springfield z 62707; ● 1,600
Miles Station; RMC Place; MACOUPIN; *171 M-6; ★ **ST.L**; mail Brighton z 62012; rural
Milford; Inc. Place; IROQUOIS; ▲ Milford; 170 G-13; 🅿; z 60953; Ⓟ 1,512; © 1,369
Milford; MCD-Township; IROQUOIS; *170 G-13; 🅿; z 60953; Ⓟ 2,026; © 1,800
Milks Grove; MCD-Township; IROQUOIS; *170 F-12; mail Herscher z 60941; Ⓟ 221; © 177
Millbrook; Inc. Place; KENDALL; *170 D-11; elev. 635ft./194m.; 🅿; z 60536; incorporated November 5, 2002; not reported in 2000 Census; ● 300
Millbrook; MCD-Township; PEORIA; *170 F-7; mail Laura z 61451; Ⓟ 500; © 490
Millburn; RMC Place; LAKE; *170 A-12; ★ **CHI**; mail Wadsworth z 60083; ● 50
Mill Creek; RMC Place; JERSEY; *171 M-6; ★ **ST.L**; mail Dow z 62022; ● 60
Mill Creek; Inc. Place; UNION; 171 S-9; elev. 374ft./114m.; 🅿; z 62961; Ⓟ 87; © 76
Milledgeville; Inc. Place; CARROLL; 170 C-7; elev. 749ft./228m.; 🅿; z 61051; Ⓟ 1,076; © 1,016
Miller; MCD-Township; LA SALLE; *170 E-10; mail Seneca z 61360; Ⓟ 522; © 617
Miller Addition; RMC Place; WHITESIDE; *170 D-6; elev. 585ft./178m.; mail Erie z 61250; ● 75
Miller City; RMC Place; ALEXANDER; *171 T-8; elev. 335ft./102m.; 🅿; z 62962; ● 70
Miller Lake; RMC Place; JEFFERSON; *171 O-10; elev. 541ft./165m.; mail Mount Vernon z 62864; ● 50
Millersburg; RMC Place; MERCER; ▲ Millersburg; 170 E-4; mail Aledo z 61231, Joy z 61260; ● 100
Millersburg; MCD-Township; MERCER; *170 E-4; mail Joy z 61260; Ⓟ 848; © 777
Millersville; RMC Place; CHRISTIAN; 171 L-9; 🅿; z 62557; ● 65
Miller Woods; RMC Place; COOK; *170 D-13; ★ **CHI**; mail Chicago Heights z 60411; pop. incl. with Chicago Heights (Inc. Place)
Millhurst; RMC Place; KENDALL; *170 D-11; mail Plano z 60545; rural
Millington; Inc. Place; KENDALL, LA SALLE; *170 D-10; elev. 560ft./171m.; 🅿; z 60537; Ⓟ 470; © 458
Mills; MCD-Township; BOND; *171 N-8; mail Greenville z 62246; Ⓟ 487; © 554
Mill Shoals; Inc. Place; WHITE, WAYNE; 171 P-11; elev. 380ft./116m.; 🅿; z 62862; Ⓟ 247; © 235
Mill Shoals; MCD-Township; WHITE; *171 P-11; 🅿; z 62862; includes part of the Village of Mill Shoals; Ⓟ 893; © 780
Mill Spring; RMC Place; MADISON; *171 M-6; ★ **ST.L**; mail Godfrey z 62035; pop. incl. with Godfrey (Inc. Place)
Millstadt; Inc. Place; ST. CLAIR; ▲ Millstadt; 171 O-6; 🅿; ★ **ST.L**; z 62260; Ⓟ 2,566; © 2,794
Millstadt; MCD-Township; ST. CLAIR; *171 O-6; 🅿; ★ **ST.L**; z 62260; Ⓟ 4,979; © 5,493
Milmine; RMC Place; PIATT; *170 J-10; elev. 710ft./216m.; 🅿; z 61855; ● 120
Milo; RMC Place; BUREAU; *170 E-8; mail Bradford z 61421; rural
Milo; MCD-Township; BUREAU; *170 E-8; mail Bradford z 61421; Ⓟ 232; © 223
Milton; MCD-Township; DUPAGE; *170 C-12; ★ **CHI**; mail Wheaton z 60187; Ⓟ 108,148; © 118,616
Milton; Inc. Place; PIKE; 171 K-5; elev. 660ft./201m.; 🅿; z 62352; Ⓟ 270; © 274
Mindale; RMC Place; SCHUYLER; *170 I-4; elev. 678ft./207m.; mail Huntsville z 62344; rural
Mineral; Inc. Place; BUREAU; ▲ Mineral; 170 E-7; 🅿; z 61344; Ⓟ 250; © 272
Mineral; MCD-Township; BUREAU; *170 E-7; 🅿; z 61344; Ⓟ 603; © 521
Minier; Inc. Place; TAZEWELL; 170 H-9; elev. 630ft./192m.; 🅿; z 61759; Ⓟ 1,155; © 1,244
Minonk; Inc. Place; WOODFORD; ▲ Minonk; 170 F-9; 🅿; z 61760; Ⓟ 1,982; © 2,168
Minonk; MCD-Township; WOODFORD; *170 F-9; 🅿; z 61760; includes part of the City of Minonk; Ⓟ 2,334; © 2,407
Minooka; Inc. Place; GRUNDY, WILL; 170 D-11; elev. 590ft./180m.; 🅿; ★ **CHI**; z 60447 & mail Channahon z 60410; Ⓟ 2,561; © 3,971
Missal; RMC Place; LIVINGSTON; *170 F-10; mail Streator z 61364; rural
Mission; MCD-Township; LA SALLE; *170 D-10; mail Sheridan z 60551; Ⓟ 3,160; © 4,178
Mission Hills; RMC Place; COOK; *170 B-12; elev. 675ft./206m.; ★ **CHI**; mail Northbrook z 60062; ● 500
Mississippi; MCD-Township; JERSEY; *171 M-6; mail Dow z 62022; Ⓟ 1,758; © 1,992
Missouri; MCD-Township; BROWN; *170 I-5; mail Mount Sterling z 62353; Ⓟ 157; © 162
Mitchell; RMC Place; MADISON; 195 C-8; elev. 426ft./130m.; 🅿; ★ **ST.L**; z 62040; ● 1,300
Mitchellsville; RMC Place; SALINE; 171 R-11; elev. 385ft./117m.; mail Carrier Mills z 62917; ● 100
Mitchie; RMC Place; MONROE; *171 P-6; mail Valmeyer z 62295; rural
Mobet Meadows; RMC Place; ROCK ISLAND; *170 D-6; ★ **D-RI-M**; mail Port Byron z 61275; ● 430
Mobile City; RMC Place; KNOX; *170 F-6; elev. 775ft./236m.; ★ **GLSB**; mail Galesburg z 61401; ● 200
Moccasin; RMC Place; EFFINGHAM; ▲ Moccasin; *171 M-10; elev. 613ft./187m.; mail Altamont z 62411; ● 40
Moccasin; MCD-Township; EFFINGHAM; *171 M-10; mail Altamont z 62411; Ⓟ 454; © 522
Mode; RMC Place; SHELBY; *171 L-10; elev. 620ft./189m.; 🅿; z 62444; ● 100
Modena; RMC Place; STARK; *170 F-7; mail Wyoming z 61491; rural
Modesto; Inc. Place; MACOUPIN; 171 L-7; elev. 685ft./209m.; 🅿; z 62667; Ⓟ 240; © 252
Modoc; RMC Place; RANDOLPH; 171 Q-6; elev. 400ft./122m.; 🅿; z 62261; ● 100
Moecherville; RMC Place; KANE; 172 J-2; ★ **CHI**; mail Aurora z 60505; pop. incl. with Aurora (Inc. Place)
Mokena; Inc. Place; WILL; 172 M-6; elev. 706ft./215m.; 🅿; ★ **CHI**; z 60448 & mail New Lenox z 60451; Ⓟ 6,128; © 14,583
Moline; Inc. Place; ROCK ISLAND; 170 D-5; elev. 580ft./177m.; 🅿 🅷 ■; ★ **D-RI-M**; z 61265-66; Ⓟ 43,202; © 43,768; ◆ 43,993
Moline; MCD-Township; ROCK ISLAND; *170 D-5; 🅿; ★ **D-RI-M**; z 61265-66; includes part of the City of Moline; Ⓟ 23,484; © 23,594
Momence; Inc. Place; KANKAKEE; 170 E-13; elev. 626ft./191m.; 🅿; ★ **KANK**; z 60954; Ⓟ 2,968; © 3,171
Momence; MCD-Township; KANKAKEE; *170 E-13; 🅿; z 60954; includes part of the City of Momence; Ⓟ 3,570; © 3,884
Mona; MCD-Township; FORD; *170 F-12; mail Saint Anne z 60964; Ⓟ 383; © 387
Monee; Inc. Place; WILL; ▲ Monee; 170 E-13; 🅿; ★ **CHI**; z 60449; Ⓟ 1,044; © 2,924
Monee; MCD-Township; WILL; *170 D-13; 🅿; ★ **CHI**; z 60449; Ⓟ 10,765; © 13,294
Money Creek; MCD-Township; MCLEAN; *170 G-10; mail Lexington z 61753; Ⓟ 824; © 1,084
Monica; RMC Place; PEORIA; 170 F-7; mail Princeville z 61559; ● 80
Monmouth; Inc. Place; ⊡ WARREN; ▲ Monmouth; 170 F-5; elev. 770ft./235m.; 🅿 🅷 🅲 1,359; z 61462; Ⓟ 9,489; © 9,841
Monmouth; MCD-Township; WARREN; *170 F-5; 🅿 🅲 1,359; z 61462; Ⓟ 10,546; © 10,799
Monroe; MCD-Township; OGLE; *170 B-9; mail Monroe Center z 61052; Ⓟ 1,378; © 1,570
MONROE; 171 P-6; Ⓟ 22,422; © 27,619; ◆ 33,141
Monroe Center; Inc. Place; OGLE; ▲ Monroe; 170 B-9; 🅿; z 61052; incorporated March 18, 2004; not reported in 2000 Census; ● 500
Monroe City; RMC Place; MONROE; *171 P-6; mail Waterloo z 62298; ● 60
Mont; RMC Place; MADISON; *171 N-7; ★ **ST.L**; mail Glen Carbon z 62034; rural
Montague Forest; RMC Place; KANE; *170 B-11; elev. 890ft./271m.; ★ **CHI**; mail Elgin z 60123; ● 300
Montclare; RMC Place; COOK; ★ **CHI**; mail Chicago z 60634; pop. incl. with Chicago (Inc. Place)
Montebello; MCD-Township; HANCOCK; *170 H-3; mail Hamilton z 62341; Ⓟ 3,929; © 3,632
Monterey; RMC Place; FULTON; *170 H-7; elev. 605ft./184m.; mail Canton z 61520; ● 40
Monterey Village; RMC Place; WILL; ★ **CHI**; mail Park Forest z 60466; pop. incl. with University Park (Inc. Place)
Montezuma; RMC Place; PIKE; *171 K-5; elev. 436ft./133m.; mail Pearl z 62361; rural
Montezuma; MCD-Township; PIKE; *171 K-5; mail Pearl z 62361; Ⓟ 548; © 543
Montgomery; MCD-Township; CRAWFORD; *171 N-13; mail Flat Rock z 62427; Ⓟ 676; © 736
Montgomery; Inc. Place; KANE, KENDALL; 170 C-11; elev. 642ft./196m.; 🅿; ★ **CHI**; z 60538; Ⓟ 4,268; © 5,471
Montgomery; MCD-Township; WOODFORD; *170 G-9; mail Deer Creek z 61733; Ⓟ 1,863; © 2,099
MONTGOMERY; 171 L-8; Ⓟ 30,728; © 30,652; ◆ 29,459
Monticello; Inc. Place; ⊡ PIATT; ▲ Monticello; 170 J-11; elev. 675ft./206m.; 🅿 🅷; z 61856; Ⓟ 4,549; © 5,138
Monticello; MCD-Township; PIATT; *170 J-11; 🅿; z 61856; Ⓟ 5,339; © 5,604
Montmorency; MCD-Township; WHITESIDE; *170 C-8; mail Rock Falls z 61071; Ⓟ 2,451; © 2,538
Montrose; Inc. Place; EFFINGHAM, CUMBERLAND; 171 M-11; elev. 600ft./183m.; 🅿; z 62445; Ⓟ 306; © 257
Moon Lake Village; RMC Place; COOK; mail Schaumburg z 60194; pop. incl. with Hoffman Estates (Inc. Place)
Moonshine; RMC Place; CLARK; *171 M-12; elev. 566ft./173m.; mail Martinsville z 62442; rural
Moores Prairie; MCD-Township; JEFFERSON; *171 P-10; mail Belle Rive z 62810; Ⓟ 371; © 391
Mooseheart (Child City); RMC Place; KANE; 170 C-11; elev. 710ft./216m.; 🅿; ★ **CHI**; z 60539; ● 100
Moraine (Deerfield); MCD-Township; LAKE; *170 B-13; ★ **CHI**; mail Deerfield z 60015, Highland Park z 60035; includes part of the Village of Deerfield; Ⓟ 34,814; © 34,538; Ⓡ 34,694
Moraine Valley Facility; RMC Place; COOK; *170 C-13; ★ **CHI**; mail Bridgeview z 60455; pop. incl. with Bridgeview (Inc. Place)
Morea; RMC Place; CRAWFORD; *171 N-13; elev. 558ft./170m.; mail Palestine z 62451; rural
Morehaven; RMC Place; WINNEBAGO; *170 A-9; ★ **RKFD**; mail Roscoe z 61073; ● 100
Morgan; MCD-Township; COLES; *171 K-12; mail Oakland z 61943; Ⓟ 403; © 367
MORGAN; 170 J-6; Ⓟ 36,397; © 36,616; ◆ 35,156
Morgan Park; RMC Place; COOK; *170 D-13; ★ **CHI**; mail Chicago z 60643; pop. incl. with Chicago (Inc. Place)
Morgan's Gate; RMC Place; COOK; *170 B-12; elev. 819ft./250m.; ★ **CHI**; mail Palatine z 60067; pop. incl. with Palatine (Inc. Place)
Moriah; RMC Place; CLARK; *171 M-12; mail Casey z 62420; rural
Moro; RMC Place; MADISON; ▲ Moro; *171 N-6; 🅿; ★ **ST.L**; z 62067; ● 500
Moro; MCD-Township; MADISON; *171 M-7; 🅿; ★ **ST.L**; z 62067; Ⓟ 2,768; © 3,294
Morris; Inc. Place; ⊡ GRUNDY; 170 E-11; elev. 519ft./158m.; 🅿 🅷; z 60450; Ⓟ 10,270; © 11,928
Morris; MCD-Township; GRUNDY; *170 E-11; 🅿; z 60450; Ⓟ 7,876; © 7,781
Morris Hills; RMC Place; ST. CLAIR; ★ **ST.L**; mail Collinsville z 62234; pop. incl. with Collinsville (Inc. Place)
Morrison; Inc. Place; ⊡ WHITESIDE; 170 C-7; elev. 716ft./218m.; 🅿 🅷; z 61270; Ⓟ 4,363; © 4,447
Morrisonville; Inc. Place; CHRISTIAN; 171 L-8; elev. 625ft./191m.; 🅿; z 62546; Ⓟ 1,113; © 1,068
Morristown; RMC Place; HENRY; *170 E-6; elev. 733ft./223m.; mail Osco z 61274; rural
Morristown; WINNEBAGO; see New Milford (Inc. Place)
Morseville (Plum River); RMC Place; JO DAVIESS; *170 A-7; elev. 866ft./264m.; mail Stockton z 61085
Mortimer; RMC Place; EDGAR; *170 J-13; mail Chrisman z 61924; rural
Morton; Inc. Place; TAZEWELL; ▲ Morton; 170 G-8; 🅿; ★ **PEOR**; z 61550; Ⓟ 13,799; © 15,198
Morton; MCD-Township; TAZEWELL; *170 G-8; 🅿; ★ **PEOR**; z 61550; Ⓟ 14,975; © 16,335
Morton Grove; Inc. Place; COOK; 172 F-8; elev. 625ft./191m.; 🅿 ■; ★ **CHI**; z 60053; Ⓟ 22,408; © 22,451; ◆ 21,986
Morton Park; RMC Place; COOK; ★ **CHI**; mail Cicero z 60804; pop. incl. with Cicero (Inc. Place)
Moser Highlands; RMC Place; DUPAGE; ★ **CHI**; mail Naperville z 60540; pop. incl. with Naperville (Inc. Place)
Moses Lake; RMC Place; FRANKLIN; *171 Q-10; mail Benton z 62812; ● 60
Mosquito; MCD-Township; CHRISTIAN; *171 K-9; mail Mount Auburn z 62547; Ⓟ 420; © 362
Mossville; RMC Place; PEORIA; *170 G-8; elev. 471ft./144m.; 🅿; ★ **PEOR**; z 61552; ● 600
MOULTRIE; 171 K-10; Ⓟ 13,930; © 14,287; ◆ 14,423
Mound; MCD-Township; EFFINGHAM; *171 M-10; mail Altamont z 62411; Ⓟ 3,413; © 3,434
Mound; MCD-Township; MCDONOUGH; *170 H-5; mail Macomb z 61455; Ⓟ 365; © 279
Mound City; Inc. Place; ⊡ PULASKI; 171 T-9; elev. 320ft./98m.; 🅿; z 62963; Ⓟ 765; © 692
Mounds; Inc. Place; PULASKI; 171 T-9; elev. 324ft./99m.; 🅿; z 62964; Ⓟ 1,407; © 1,117
Mound Station; BROWN; see Timewell (Inc. Place)
Mountain; MCD-Township; SALINE; *171 R-11; mail Harrisburg z 62946; Ⓟ 349; © 323
Mountain Glen; RMC Place; UNION; *171 S-9; mail Cobden z 62920; ● 35
Mount Auburn; Inc. Place; CHRISTIAN; ▲ Mount Auburn; 171 K-9; elev. 628ft./191m.; 🅿; z 62547; Ⓟ 544; © 515
Mount Auburn; MCD-Township; CHRISTIAN; *171 K-8; 🅿; z 62547; Ⓟ 1,112; © 1,031
Mount Carbon; RMC Place; JACKSON; *171 R-8; ★ **CARB-**; mail Murphysboro z 62966; ● 200
Mount Carmel; Inc. Place; ⊡ WABASH; 171 O-13; elev. 450ft./137m.; 🅿 🅷; z 62863; Ⓟ 8,287; © 7,982
Mount Carroll; Inc. Place; ⊡ CARROLL; 170 B-7; elev. 798ft./243m.; 🅿; z 61053; Ⓟ 1,726; © 1,832
Mount Carroll; MCD-Township; CARROLL; *170 B-7; 🅿; z 61053; includes part of the City of Mount Carroll; Ⓟ 2,467; © 2,473
Mount Clair; RMC Place; MADISON; *171 M-6; ★ **ST.L**; mail Godfrey z 62035; pop. incl. with Godfrey (Inc. Place)
Mount Clare; Inc. Place; MACOUPIN; *171 M-7; elev. 641ft./195m.; mail Gillespie z 62033; Ⓟ 297; © 433
Mount Erie; Inc. Place; WAYNE; ▲ Mount Erie; 171 O-12; 🅿; z 62446; Ⓟ 137; © 105
Mount Erie; MCD-Township; WAYNE; *171 O-12; 🅿; z 62446; Ⓟ 463; © 407
Mount Greenwood; RMC Place; COOK; *170 D-13; 🅿; ★ **CHI**; z 60655; pop. incl. with Chicago (Inc. Place)
Mount Hope; MCD-Township; MCLEAN; *170 H-9; mail Mc Lean z 61754; Ⓟ 1,130; © 1,172
Mount Joy; RMC Place; LOGAN; *170 I-9; mail Atlanta z 61723; rural
Mount Morris; Inc. Place; OGLE; ▲ Mount Morris; 170 B-8; elev. 916ft./279m.; 🅿; z 61054; Ⓟ 2,919; © 3,013
Mount Morris; MCD-Township; OGLE; *170 B-8; 🅿; z 61054; Ⓟ 4,042; © 4,065
Mount Olive; Inc. Place; MACOUPIN; ▲ Mount Olive; 171 M-7; elev. 684ft./208m.; 🅿; z 62069; Ⓟ 2,126; © 2,150
Mount Olive; MCD-Township; MACOUPIN; *171 M-7; 🅿; z 62069; Ⓟ 3,443; © 3,379
Mount Palatine; RMC Place; PUTNAM; *170 E-9; mail Lostant z 61334; ● 40
Mount Pleasant; RMC Place; UNION; 171 S-9; elev. 494ft./151m.; mail Buncombe z 62912; ● 50
Mount Pleasant; MCD-Township; WHITESIDE; *170 C-7; mail Morrison z 61270; Ⓟ 5,371; © 5,291
Mount Prospect; Inc. Place; COOK; 172 F-6; elev. 675ft./206m.; 🅿 ■; ★ **CHI**; z 60056; Ⓟ 53,170; © 56,265; Ⓡ 56,268; ◆ 55,799
Mount Prospect Gardens; RMC Place; COOK; ★ **CHI**; mail Mount Prospect z 60056; pop. incl. with Mount Prospect (Inc. Place)
Mount Pulaski; Inc. Place; LOGAN; ▲ Mount Pulaski; 170 J-9; 🅿; z 62548; Ⓟ 1,610; © 1,701
Mount Pulaski; MCD-Township; LOGAN; *170 J-9; 🅿; z 62548; Ⓟ 2,256; © 2,242
Mount Sterling; Inc. Place; ⊡ BROWN; ▲ Mount Sterling; 170 J-4; 🅿; z 62353; Ⓟ 1,922; © 2,070
Mount Sterling; MCD-Township; BROWN; *170 J-5; 🅿; z 62353; Ⓟ 3,408; © 4,562
Mount Vernon; Inc. Place; ⊡ JEFFERSON; 171 P-10; elev. 500ft./152m.; 🅿 🅷 ■; z 62864; Ⓟ 16,988; © 16,269; ◆ 16,149
Mount Vernon; MCD-Township; JEFFERSON; *171 P-10; 🅿; z 62864; includes part of the City of Mount Vernon; Ⓟ 15,059; © 14,443
Mount Vernon; RMC Place; JO DAVIESS; *170 A-5; elev. 865ft./264m.; ★ **DUB**; mail East Dubuque z 61025; ● 250
Mount Zion; Inc. Place; MACON; ▲ Mount Zion; 171 K-10; 🅿; ★ **DEC**; z 62549; Ⓟ 4,522; © 4,845
Mount Zion; MCD-Township; MACON; *171 K-10; 🅿; ★ **DEC**; z 62549; Ⓟ 5,922; © 6,324
Moweaqua; Inc. Place; SHELBY, CHRISTIAN; 171 K-9; elev. 620ft./189m.; 🅿; z 62550; Ⓟ 1,785; © 1,923
Moweaqua; MCD-Township; SHELBY; *171 K-10; 🅿; z 62550; includes part of the Village Moweaqua; Ⓟ 2,001; © 2,110
Mozier (Baytown); RMC Place; CALHOUN; 171 L-4; elev. 495ft./151m.; 🅿; z 62070; ● 50
Mozier Landing; RMC Place; CALHOUN; *171 L-5; elev. 459ft./140m.; mail Hamburg z 62045; ● 50
Muddy; Inc. Place; SALINE; 171 R-11; elev. 370ft./113m.; 🅿; z 62965; Ⓟ 87; © 78
Mulberry Grove; Inc. Place; BOND; ▲ Mulberry Grove; 171 N-9; 🅿; z 62262; Ⓟ 660; © 671
Mulberry Grove; MCD-Township; BOND; *171 M-8; 🅿; z 62262; Ⓟ 1,247; © 1,360
Mulkeytown; RMC Place; FRANKLIN; 171 Q-9; elev. 451ft./137m.; 🅿; ★ **CARB-**; z 62865; ● 400
Muncie; Inc. Place; VERMILION; *170 I-13; elev. 659ft./201m.; 🅿; z 61857; Ⓟ 182; © 155
Mundelein; Inc. Place; LAKE; 172 C-5; elev. 750ft./229m.; 🅿; ★ **CHI**; z 60060; Ⓟ 21,215; © 30,935; ◆ 34,078
Mundelein Ridge Estates; RMC Place; LAKE; ★ **CHI**; mail Mundelein z 60060; pop. incl. with Mundelein (Inc. Place)
Munson; MCD-Township; HENRY; *170 E-6; mail Cambridge z 61238; Ⓟ 566; © 488
Munster; RMC Place; LA SALLE; mail Streator z 61364; rural
Murdock; RMC Place; DOUGLAS; ▲ Murdock; *170 J-12; 🅿; z 61941; ● 150
Murdock; MCD-Township; DOUGLAS; *170 J-12; 🅿; z 61941; Ⓟ 374; © 267
Murphy Acres; RMC Place; WILL; ★ **CHI**; mail Joliet z 60435
Murphysboro; Inc. Place; ⊡ JACKSON; 171 R-8; elev. 396ft./121m.; 🅿 🅷; ★ **CARB-**; z 62966; Ⓟ 9,176; © 13,295; Ⓡ 8,694
Murphysboro; MCD-Township; JACKSON; *171 R-8; 🅿; ★ **CARB-**; z 62966; includes part of the City of Murphysboro; Ⓟ 11,316; © 15,540; Ⓡ 10,778
Murrayville; Inc. Place; MORGAN; 171 K-6; elev. 687ft./209m.; 🅿; z 62668; Ⓟ 673; © 644
Myers Lake; RMC Place; CHRISTIAN; *171 K-9; elev. 613ft./187m.; mail Taylorville z 62568; rural
Mylith Park; RMC Place; LAKE; *170 A-12; ★ **CHI**; mail McHenry z 60050; ● 230
Myrtle; RMC Place; OGLE; *170 B-8; elev. 769ft./234m.; mail Leaf River z 61047; rural

N

Na-Au-Say; MCD-Township; KENDALL; *170 D-11; mail Yorkville z 60560; Ⓟ 1,067; © 1,672
Nachusa; RMC Place; LEE; ▲ Nachusa; 170 C-8; 🅿; z 61057; ● 270
Nachusa; MCD-Township; LEE; *170 C-8; 🅿; z 61057; Ⓟ 584; © 497
Nameoki; RMC Place; MADISON; *171 N-6; ★ **ST.L**; mail Granite City z 62040; pop. incl. with Granite City (Inc. Place)
Nameoki; MCD-Township; MADISON; *171 N-6; ★ **ST.L**; mail Granite City z 62040; Ⓟ 12,492; © 11,186
Nantucket Cove; RMC Place; COOK; mail Schaumburg z 60193; pop. incl. with Schaumburg (Inc. Place)
Naperville; Inc. Place; DUPAGE, WILL; 170 C-12; elev. 700ft./213m.; 🅿 🅷 🅲 2,556 ■; ★ **CHI**; z 60540, z 60563-67; Ⓟ 85,351; © 128,358; ◆ 139,514
Naperville; MCD-Township; DUPAGE; *170 C-12; 🅿 🅲 2,556; ★ **CHI**; z 60540, z 60563-67; includes part of the City of Naperville; Ⓟ 49,533; © 85,736
Naplate; Inc. Place; LA SALLE; *170 E-10; elev. 488ft./149m.; mail Ottawa z 61350; Ⓟ 609; © 523
Naples; Inc. Place; SCOTT; 171 K-5; elev. 440ft./134m.; 🅿; z 62665; Ⓟ 130; © 134
Nashville; Inc. Place; ⊡ WASHINGTON; ▲ Nashville; 171 P-8; 🅿 🅷; z 62263; Ⓟ 3,202; © 3,147
Nashville; MCD-Township; WASHINGTON; *171 P-8; 🅿; z 62263; Ⓟ 3,675; © 3,514
Nason; Inc. Place; JEFFERSON; 171 P-9; elev. 420ft./128m.; 🅿; z 62866; Ⓟ 235; © 234
Natalie Estates; RMC Place; COOK; ★ **CHI**; mail Oak Forest z 60452; pop. incl. with Oak Forest (Inc. Place)
National City; RMC Place; ST. CLAIR; 195 E-7; elev. 415ft./126m.; ★ **ST.L**; mail National Stock Yards z 62071; Ⓟ 57
Natrona; RMC Place; MASON; *170 I-8; mail San Jose z 62682; rural
Nauvoo; Inc. Place; HANCOCK; 170 H-3; elev. 659ft./201m.; 🅿; z 62354; Ⓟ 1,108; © 1,063; Ⓡ 1,071
Nauvoo; MCD-Township; HANCOCK; *170 H-3; 🅿; z 62354; includes part of the City of Nauvoo; Ⓟ 1,108; © 1,090; Ⓡ 1,091
Navajo Hills; RMC Place; COOK; ★ **CHI**; mail Palos Heights z 60463; pop. incl. with Palos Heights (Inc. Place)
Neadmore; RMC Place; CLARK; *171 L-13; elev. 593ft./181m.; mail Martinsville z 62442; rural
Near North Side; RMC Place; COOK; ★ **CHI**; mail Chicago z 60610-11; pop. incl. with Chicago (Inc. Place)
Near South Side; RMC Place; COOK; ★ **CHI**; mail Chicago z 60616; pop. incl. with Chicago (Inc. Place)
Nebo; Inc. Place; PIKE; 171 L-4; elev. 483ft./147m.; 🅿; z 62355; Ⓟ 402; © 408
Nebraska; MCD-Township; LIVINGSTON; *170 F-10; mail Flanagan z 61740; Ⓟ 1,424; © 1,494
Neelys (Neelyville); RMC Place; MORGAN; *171 K-5; elev. 566ft./173m.; mail Bluffs z 62621; rural
Neelyville; MORGAN; see Neelys (RMC Place)
Neil Street; RMC Place; CHAMPAIGN; ★ **CH-U**; mail Champaign z 61820, z 61824; pop. incl. with Champaign (Inc. Place)
Nekoma; RMC Place; HENRY; 170 E-6; mail Woodhull z 61490; ● 30
Nelson; Inc. Place; LEE; ▲ Nelson; 170 C-8; 🅿; z 61021; Ⓟ 200; © 163
Nelson; MCD-Township; LEE; *170 C-8; 🅿; z 61021; Ⓟ 881; © 854
Neoga; Inc. Place; CUMBERLAND; 171 L-11; elev. 650ft./198m.; 🅿; z 62447; Ⓟ 1,678; © 1,854
Neoga; MCD-Township; CUMBERLAND; *171 L-11; 🅿; z 62447; Ⓟ 2,952; © 3,291
Neponset; Inc. Place; BUREAU; ▲ Neponset; 170 E-7; 🅿; z 61345; Ⓟ 529; © 519
Neponset; MCD-Township; BUREAU; *170 E-7; 🅿; z 61345; Ⓟ 819; © 785
Nerska; RMC Place; COOK; mail Chicago z 60632; pop. incl. with Chicago (Inc. Place)
Nettle Creek; MCD-Township; GRUNDY; *170 E-11; mail Newark z 60541; Ⓟ 345; © 467
Neunert; RMC Place; JACKSON; 171 R-8; elev. 357ft./109m.; mail Jacob z 62950; ● 25
Nevada; MCD-Township; LIVINGSTON; *170 F-11; mail Odell z 60460; Ⓟ 930; © 212; Ⓡ 1,221
Nevins; RMC Place; EDGAR; *171 K-13; elev. 689ft./210m.; mail Paris z 61944; ● 30
Newark; Inc. Place; KENDALL; 170 D-11; elev. 663ft./202m.; 🅿; z 60541; Ⓟ 840; © 887
New Athens; Inc. Place; ST. CLAIR; ▲ New Athens; 171 P-7; 🅿; ★ **ST.L**; z 62264; Ⓟ 2,010; © 1,981
New Athens; MCD-Township; ST. CLAIR; *171 P-7; 🅿; ★ **ST.L**; z 62264; Ⓟ 2,588; © 2,620
New Baden; Inc. Place; CLINTON, ST. CLAIR; 171 O-7; elev. 462ft./141m.; 🅿; ★ **ST.L**; z 62265; Ⓟ 2,602; © 3,001
New Bedford; Inc. Place; BUREAU; 170 D-7; elev. 645ft./197m.; 🅿; z 61346; Ⓟ 65; © 95
New Berlin; Inc. Place; SANGAMON; ▲ New Berlin; 171 K-7; elev. 654ft./199m.; 🅿; z 62670; Ⓟ 797; © 1,030
New Berlin; MCD-Township; SANGAMON; *171 K-7; 🅿; z 62670; Ⓟ 990; © 1,262
Newbern; RMC Place; JERSEY; 171 M-6; elev. 654ft./199m.; mail Dow z 62022; ● 100
New Blossom Hill; RMC Place; MCHENRY; ★ **CHI**; mail Cary z 60013; pop. incl. with Cary (Inc. Place)
New Boston; Inc. Place; MERCER; ▲ New Boston; 170 E-4; 🅿; z 61272; Ⓟ 620; © 632
New Boston; MCD-Township; MERCER; *170 E-4; 🅿; z 61272; Ⓟ 1,225; © 1,207
Newburg; RMC Place; MACON; *170 J-10; 🅿; z 62501; rural
Newburg; MCD-Township; PIKE; *171 K-5; mail Pittsfield z 62363; Ⓟ 944; © 983; Ⓡ 978
New Burnside; Inc. Place; JOHNSON; 171 R-10; elev. 550ft./168m.; 🅿; z 62967; Ⓟ 259; © 242
Newby; RMC Place; COLES; *171 L-11; elev. 743ft./226m.; mail Mattoon z 61938; rural
New Camp; RMC Place; WILLIAMSON; *171 R-9; ★ **CARB-**; mail Colp z 62921; pop. incl. with Colp (Inc. Place)
New Canton; Inc. Place; PIKE; 171 K-4; elev. 469ft./143m.; 🅿; z 62356; Ⓟ 405; © 417
Newcastle; RMC Place; SALINE; *171 R-10; elev. 424ft./129m.; mail Stonefort z 62987; rural
New Century Town; RMC Place; LAKE; ★ **CHI**; mail Vernon Hills z 60061; pop. incl. with Vernon Hills (Inc. Place)
New City; RMC Place; COOK; ★ **CHI**; mail Chicago z 60609; pop. incl. with Chicago (Inc. Place)
New City; RMC Place; SANGAMON; *171 K-8; elev. 592ft./180m.; 🅿; z 62563
New Columbia; RMC Place; MASSAC; 171 S-10; mail Grantsburg z 62943; ● 150
Newcomb; MCD-Township; CHAMPAIGN; *170 I-11; mail Mahomet z 61853; Ⓟ 921; © 1,004
New Delhi; RMC Place; JERSEY; 171 M-6; mail Jerseyville z 62052; ● 40
New Dennison; RMC Place; WILLIAMSON; *171 R-10; ★ **CARB-**; mail Marion z 62959; ● 100
New Douglas; Inc. Place; MADISON; ▲ New Douglas; 171 M-7; elev. 619ft./189m.; 🅿; z 62074; Ⓟ 387; © 369
New Douglas; MCD-Township; MADISON; *171 M-7; 🅿; z 62074; Ⓟ 644; © 580
Newell; MCD-Township; VERMILION; *170 I-13; ★ **DANV**; mail Danville z 61834; Ⓟ 13,930; © 13,835
New Grand Chain (Grand Chain); Inc. Place; PULASKI; 171 T-9; elev. 404ft./123m.; mail Grand Chain z 62941; Ⓟ 273; © 233
New Hanover; RMC Place; MONROE; 171 P-6; elev. 575ft./175m.; mail Waterloo z 62298; ● 60
New Hartford; RMC Place; PIKE; *171 K-4; mail Pittsfield z 62363; ● 75
New Haven; Inc. Place; GALLATIN; ▲ New Haven; 171 Q-12; 🅿; z 62867; Ⓟ 459; © 477
New Haven; MCD-Township; GALLATIN; *171 Q-12; 🅿; z 62867; Ⓟ 545; © 552
New Hebron; RMC Place; CRAWFORD; 171 M-13; elev. 534ft./163m.; mail Robinson z 62454; ● 50
New Holland; Inc. Place; LOGAN; 170 I-8; elev. 550ft./168m.; 🅿; z 62671; Ⓟ 330; © 318
New Lebanon; RMC Place; DEKALB; *170 B-10; mail Hampshire z 60140; rural
New Lenox; Inc. Place; WILL; 170 D-12; elev. 675ft./206m.; 🅿; ★ **CHI**; z 60451; Ⓟ 9,698; © 17,771; ◆ 24,674
New Lenox; MCD-Township; WILL; *170 D-12; 🅿; ★ **CHI**; z 60451; includes part of the Village of New Lenox; Ⓟ 20,716; © 29,730
New Liberty; RMC Place; POPE; 171 T-11; 🅿; z 62910; ● 70
Newman; Inc. Place; DOUGLAS; ▲ Newman; 170 J-12; elev. 646ft./197m.; 🅿; z 61942; Ⓟ 960; © 956
Newman; MCD-Township; DOUGLAS; *170 J-12; 🅿; z 61942; Ⓟ 1,248; © 1,200
Newmansville; RMC Place; CASS; ▲ Newmansville; *170 J-7; 🅿; z 62612; rural
Newmansville; MCD-Township; CASS; *170 J-7; 🅿; z 62612; Ⓟ 64; © 61
New Memphis; RMC Place; CLINTON; 171 O-7; elev. 420ft./128m.; 🅿; ★ **ST.L**; z 62266; ● 300
New Milford (Morristown, New Millford); Inc. Place; WINNEBAGO; 170 B-9; ★ **RKFD**; mail Rockford z 61109; Ⓟ 463; © 541
New Millford; WINNEBAGO; see New Milford (Inc. Place)
New Minden; Inc. Place; WASHINGTON; 171 O-8; elev. 460ft./140m.; mail Nashville z 62263; Ⓟ 219; © 204
New Palestine; RMC Place; RANDOLPH; *171 Q-7; mail Walsh z 62297; ● 25
New Philadelphia; RMC Place; MCDONOUGH; 170 H-5; mail Marietta z 61459; ● 100
Newport; MCD-Township; LAKE; *170 A-12; ★ **CHI**; mail Wadsworth z 60083; Ⓟ 3,561; © 4,142
Newport; RMC Place; MADISON; *171 N-6; ★ **ST.L**; mail Madison z 62060; pop. incl. with Madison (Inc. Place)
New Providence; GREENE; see Belltown (RMC Place)
New Salem; MCD-Township; MCDONOUGH; *170 H-5; mail Table Grove z 61482; Ⓟ 481; © 412
New Salem; Inc. Place; PIKE; ▲ New Salem; 171 K-4; 🅿; z 62357; Ⓟ 147; © 136
New Salem; MCD-Township; PIKE; *171 K-4; 🅿; z 62357; Ⓟ 651; © 675
Newton; Inc. Place; ⊡ JASPER; 171 M-12; elev. 535ft./163m.; 🅿; z 62448; Ⓟ 3,154; © 3,069

Entries in **UPPERCASE** are counties.
Entries in **bold** have populations of 2,500 or more.
Names in parentheses are alternate names.

Inc. Place	Incorporated Place
RMC Place	Rand McNally Designated Place
CDP	Census Designated Place
MCD	Minor Civil Division

⊡ County Seat
▲ Minor Civil Division
elev. Elevation
🅿 Post Office
🅷 Hospital
🅲 College
■ Principal Business Center
★ Ranally Metro Area (RMA) Abbreviation
z Zip Code(s)
Ⓟ Previous Census Population
Ⓡ Revised Census Population
Ⓐ Annexation Population
● Rand McNally Population Estimate
© Final Census Population
Ⓢ Special Census Population
◆ Estimated Population

For additional definitions see Glossary, Volume 1, and Introduction, Volume 2.

Newton; MCD-Township; WHITESIDE; ***170** C-6; mail Erie **z** 61250; Ⓟ 476; © 420
Newtown; ADAMS; see Adams (RMC Place)
Newtown; MCD-Township; LIVINGSTON; ***170** F-10; mail Ancona **z** 61311; Ⓟ 805; © 723
Newtown; RMC Place; VERMILION; ***170** I-13; elev. 730ft./223m.; mail Oakwood **z** 61858; ● 40
New Trier; MCD-Township; COOK; ***170** B-13; ★ **CHI**; mail Winnetka **z** 60093; Ⓟ 54,705; © 56,716
New Virginia; RMC Place; WILLIAMSON; ***171** R-10; mail Johnston City **z** 62951; ● 60
New Windsor (Windsor); Inc. Place; MERCER; **170** E-5; elev. 790ft./241m.; 🄿; **z** 61465; Ⓟ 774; © 720
Niantic; Inc. Place; MACON; ▲ Niantic; **170** J-9; 🄿; **z** 62551; Ⓟ 647; © 738
Niantic; MCD-Township; MACON; ***170** J-9; 🄿; **z** 62551; Ⓟ 850; © 896
Niles; Inc. Place; COOK; **172** F-7; elev. 650ft./198m.; 🄿 ■; ★ **CHI**; **z** 60714; Ⓟ 28,284; © 30,068; ◆ 29,018
Niles; MCD-Township; COOK; ***170** B-13; 🄿; ★ **CHI**; **z** 60714 & mail Skokie **z** 60076; includes part of the Village of Niles; Ⓟ 96,412; © 102,638
Nilwood; Inc. Place; MACOUPIN; **171** L-7; elev. 660ft./201m.; 🄿; **z** 62672; Ⓟ 238; © 284
Nilwood; MCD-Township; MACOUPIN; ***171** L-7; 🄿; **z** 62672 & mail Girard **z** 62640; includes part of the Town of Nilwood; Ⓟ 633; © 699
Nineteenth Avenue; RMC Place; COOK; ***170** C-12; ★ **CHI**; mail Melrose Park **z** 60160; pop. incl. with Melrose Park (Inc. Place)
Niota; RMC Place; HANCOCK; **170** G-3; elev. 530ft./162m.; 🄿; **z** 62358; ● 300
Nippersink Terrace; RMC Place; LAKE; ***170** A-12; ★ **CHI**; mail Spring Grove **z** 60081; ● 200
Nixon; MCD-Township; DE WITT; ***170** I-10; mail Weldon **z** 61882; Ⓟ 579; © 590
Nixon's Greenwood-Central; RMC Place; COOK; ***170** B-12; ★ **CHI**; mail Glenview **z** 60025; pop. incl. with Glenview (Inc. Place)
Noble; Inc. Place; RICHLAND; ▲ Noble; **171** N-12; elev. 478ft./146m.; 🄿; **z** 62868; Ⓟ 756; © 746
Noble; MCD-Township; RICHLAND; ***171** N-12; 🄿; **z** 62868; Ⓟ 1,582; © 1,509
Nokomis; Inc. Place; MONTGOMERY; ▲ Nokomis; **171** L-9; elev. 670ft./204m.; 🄿; **z** 62075; Ⓟ 2,534; © 2,389
Nokomis; MCD-Township; MONTGOMERY; ***171** L-9; 🄿; **z** 62075; Ⓟ 3,372; © 3,079
Nora; Inc. Place; JO DAVIESS; ▲ Nora; **170** A-7; 🄿; **z** 61059; Ⓟ 162; © 118
Nora; MCD-Township; JO DAVIESS; ***170** A-7; 🄿; **z** 61059; Ⓟ 443; © 404
Nordic Acres; RMC Place; BOONE; ***170** A-10; elev. 792ft./241m.; ★ **RKFD**; mail Belvidere **z** 61008
Nordic Park; RMC Place; DUPAGE; ***170** C-12; ★ **CHI**; mail Itasca **z** 60143; ● 700
Nordic Woods; RMC Place; OGLE; ***170** B-9; mail Byron **z** 61010; ● 250
Normal; Inc. Place; MCLEAN; ▲ Normal; **170** H-9; 🄿 🄷 🄲 20,521 ■; ★ **BLOOM-**; **z** 61761, **z** 61790; Ⓟ 40,023; © 45,386; ◆ 52,179
Normal; MCD-Township; MCLEAN; ***170** H-9; 🄿 🄲 20,521; ★ **BLOOM-**; **z** 61761, **z** 61790; Ⓟ 40,449; © 45,637
Norman; MCD-Township; GRUNDY; ***170** E-11; mail Morris **z** 60450; Ⓟ 213; © 269
Normandale; RMC Place; TAZEWELL; ★ **PEOR**; mail Pekin **z** 61554; ● 450
Normandy; RMC Place; BUREAU; **170** D-8; elev. 658ft./201m.; 🄿; **z** 61376; ● 30
Normandy Heights; RMC Place; JEFFERSON; ***171** P-10; elev. 550ft./168m.; mail Mount Vernon **z** 62864; ● 40
Normandy Hill; RMC Place; COOK; ★ **CHI**; mail Northbrook **z** 60062; pop. incl. with Northbrook (Inc. Place)
Normandy Villa; RMC Place; COOK; ★ **CHI**; mail Chicago Heights **z** 60411; pop. incl. with Chicago Heights (Inc. Place)
Norpaul; RMC Place; COOK; ★ **CHI**; mail Franklin Park **z** 60131; pop. incl. with Franklin Park (Inc. Place)
Norridge; Inc. Place; COOK; **172** G-7; elev. 650ft./198m.; 🄿 ■; ★ **CHI**; **z** 60634, **z** 60656, **z** 60706; Ⓟ 14,459; © 14,582; ◆ 14,263
Norris; Inc. Place; FULTON; **170** G-7; elev. 732ft./223m.; 🄿; **z** 61553; Ⓟ 212; © 194
Norris City; Inc. Place; WHITE; **171** Q-11; elev. 443ft./135m.; 🄿; **z** 62869; Ⓟ 1,341; © 1,057
North Alton; RMC Place; MADISON; ***171** N-6; ★ **ST.L**; mail Alton **z** 62002; pop. incl. with Alton (Inc. Place)
North Arm; RMC Place; EDGAR; ***171** K-13; elev. 695ft./212m.; mail Paris **z** 61944; rural
North Aurora; Inc. Place; KANE; **170** C-11; elev. 689ft./210m.; 🄿; ★ **CHI**; **z** 60542; Ⓟ 5,940; © 10,585
North Barrington; Inc. Place; LAKE; **172** C-4; elev. 780ft./238m.; 🄿; ★ **CHI**; **z** 60010; Ⓟ 1,787; © 2,918
Northbelt Homesites; RMC Place; ST. CLAIR; ★ **ST.L**; mail Belleville **z** 62221; pop. incl. with Belleville (Inc. Place)
Northbrook; Inc. Place; COOK; **172** E-7; elev. 650ft./198m.; 🄿 ■; ★ **CHI**; **z** 60062, **z** 60065; Ⓟ 32,308; © 33,435; ◆ 32,638
Northbrook Downtown; RMC Place; COOK; ★ **CHI**; mail Northbrook **z** 60062, **z** 60065; pop. incl. with Northbrook (Inc. Place)
Northbrook Knolls; RMC Place; COOK; ★ **CHI**; mail Northbrook **z** 60062; pop. incl. with Northbrook (Inc. Place)
Northbrook West; RMC Place; COOK; ***170** B-12; ★ **CHI**; mail Northbrook **z** 60062; ● 750
North Center; RMC Place; COOK; ***170** C-13; ★ **CHI**; mail Chicago **z** 60618; pop. incl. with Chicago (Inc. Place)
North Chicago; Inc. Place; LAKE; **170** A-12; elev. 650ft./198m.; 🄿 🄷 🄲 1,700; ★ **CHI**; **z** 60064, **z** 60086, **z** 60088; Ⓟ 34,978; © 35,918; ◆ 34,455
North Chillicothe; RMC Place; PEORIA; ***170** F-8; ★ **PEOR**; mail Chillicothe **z** 61523; pop. incl. with Chillicothe (Inc. Place)
North City; FRANKLIN; see Coello (Inc. Place)
North Dixon; RMC Place; LEE; mail Dixon **z** 61021; pop. incl. with Dixon (Inc. Place)
North Dupo (Prairie du Pont); RMC Place; ST. CLAIR; ***171** O-6; ★ **ST.L**; mail East Carondelet **z** 62240; ● 1,380
Northeast; MCD-Township; ADAMS; ***170** I-4; mail Golden **z** 62339; Ⓟ 869; © 949
Northern; MCD-Township; FRANKLIN; ***171** Q-10; mail Macedonia **z** 62860; Ⓟ 393; © 458
Northern Heights; RMC Place; OGLE; ***170** B-9; ★ **RKFD**; mail Byron **z** 61010; ● 50
Northern Hills; RMC Place; STEPHENSON; ***170** A-8; elev. 800ft./244m.; mail Freeport **z** 61032; ● 150
Northfield; Inc. Place; COOK; **172** E-8; elev. 625ft./191m.; 🄿; ★ **CHI**; **z** 60093; Ⓟ 4,635; © 5,389
Northfield; MCD-Township; COOK; ***170** B-13; 🄿; ★ **CHI**; **z** 60093 & mail Glenview **z** 60025; includes part of the Village of Northfield; Ⓟ 78,186; © 82,880
Northfield; RMC Place; GRUNDY; ***170** E-11; mail Morris **z** 60450; ● 100
Northfield Woods; RMC Place; COOK; ***170** B-12; ★ **CHI**; mail Glenview **z** 60025; pop. incl. with Glenview (Inc. Place)
North Fork; MCD-Township; GALLATIN; ***171** R-11; mail Ridgway **z** 62979; Ⓟ 592; © 523
Northgate; RMC Place; COOK; ★ **CHI**; pop. incl. with Arlington Heights (Inc. Place)
Northgate; RMC Place; COOK; ★ **CHI**; mail Hanover Park **z** 60133; pop. incl. with Hanover Park (Inc. Place)
North Glen Ellyn; RMC Place; DUPAGE; **172** H-5; ★ **CHI**; mail Glen Ellyn **z** 60137; ● 1,400
North Hampton; RMC Place; PEORIA; ***170** F-8; mail Chillicothe **z** 61523
North Henderson; Inc. Place; MERCER; ▲ North Henderson; **170** F-5; elev. 774ft./236m.; 🄿; **z** 61466; Ⓟ 184; © 187
North Henderson; MCD-Township; MERCER; ***170** F-5; 🄿; **z** 61466; Ⓟ 472; © 444
North Hills; RMC Place; LAKE; ***170** A-12; ★ **CHI**; mail Mundelein **z** 60060; pop. incl. with Mundelein (Inc. Place)
Northlake; Inc. Place; COOK; **172** H-6; elev. 650ft./198m.; 🄿; ★ **CHI**; **z** 60164; Ⓟ 12,505; © 11,878
North Lakewood; RMC Place; MARION; ***171** O-10; elev. 535ft./163m.; mail Salem **z** 62881; pop. incl. with Salem (Inc. Place)
North Libertyville Estates (Libertyville Estates); RMC Place; LAKE; ***170** A-12; ★ **CHI**; mail Libertyville **z** 60048; ● 120
North Litchfield; MCD-Township; MONTGOMERY; ***171** M-8; mail Litchfield **z** 62056; Ⓟ 5,240; © 5,135
Northmore; RMC Place; MADISON; ★ **ST.L**; mail Godfrey **z** 62035; pop. incl. with Godfrey (Inc. Place)
Northmore Heights; RMC Place; EFFINGHAM; mail Effingham **z** 62401; pop. incl. with Effingham (Inc. Place)
North Mounds; RMC Place; PULASKI; ***171** T-9; mail Mounds **z** 62964; ● 300
North Muddy; MCD-Township; JASPER; ***171** M-11; mail Wheeler **z** 62479; Ⓟ 809; © 765
North Okaw; MCD-Township; COLES; ***171** K-11; mail Mattoon **z** 61938; Ⓟ 849; © 918
North Oregon; RMC Place; OGLE; ***170** B-8; mail Oregon **z** 61061; ● 130
North Otter; MCD-Township; MACOUPIN; ***171** L-7; mail Virden **z** 62690; Ⓟ 721; © 840
North Palmyra; MCD-Township; MACOUPIN; ***171** L-7; mail Modesto **z** 62667; Ⓟ 905; © 974
North Park; RMC Place; COOK; ★ **CHI**; mail Chicago **z** 60625, **z** 60659; pop. incl. with Chicago (Inc. Place)
North Park; RMC Place; WINNEBAGO; ***170** A-9; ★ **RKFD**; mail Machesney Park **z** 61115; pop. incl. with Machesney Park (Inc. Place)
North Pekin; Inc. Place; TAZEWELL; ***170** G-8; elev. 470ft./143m.; 🄿; ★ **PEOR**; **z** 61554; Ⓟ 1,556; © 1,574
Northpoint Estates; RMC Place; KANKAKEE; ***170** E-13; elev. 658ft./201m.; ★ **KANK**; mail Bourbonnais **z** 60914
North Prairie Acres; RMC Place; DOUGLAS; ***170** J-11; mail Tuscola **z** 61953; ● 150
North Riverside; Inc. Place; COOK; **172** I-7; elev. 620ft./189m.; 🄿 ■; ★ **CHI**; **z** 60546; Ⓟ 6,005; © 6,688; ◆ 6,728
North Shore; RMC Place; MCHENRY; ***170** B-11; ★ **CHI**; mail Crystal Lake **z** 60014; pop. incl. with Crystal Lake (Inc. Place)
North Shoreland; RMC Place; WILLIAMSON; ***171** R-10; ★ **CARB-**; mail Marion **z** 62959; ● 150
Northtown; RMC Place; COOK; ***170** B-13; ★ **CHI**; mail Chicago **z** 60645, **z** 60659; pop. incl. with Chicago (Inc. Place)
North Utica; LA SALLE; see Utica (Inc. Place)
Northville; MCD-Township; LA SALLE; ***170** D-10; mail Sheridan **z** 60551; Ⓟ 4,393; © 6,642
Northwest Highlands; RMC Place; COOK; ★ **CHI**; pop. incl. with Arlington Heights (Inc. Place)
Northwood; RMC Place; CHAMPAIGN; ***170** I-12; elev. 725ft./221m.; ★ **CH-U**; mail Urbana **z** 61802; ● 250
Northwoods; RMC Place; DEKALB; ***170** B-10; elev. 840ft./256m.; mail Genoa **z** 60135; pop. incl. with Chamblee (Inc. Place)
North Woods; RMC Place; DUPAGE; ***170** C-12; 🄿; ★ **CHI**; **z** 60185; ● 220
Northwoods; RMC Place; ST. CLAIR; ***171** O-7; elev. 556ft./169m.; ★ **ST.L**; mail O Fallon **z** 62269; pop. incl. with O'Fallon (Inc. Place)
Norton; MCD-Township; KANKAKEE; ***170** F-12; mail Buckingham **z** 60917; Ⓟ 1,129; © 1,067
Nortonville; RMC Place; MORGAN; **171** K-6; 🄿; **z** 62668; ● 50
Norway; RMC Place; LA SALLE; **170** D-10; mail Sheridan **z** 60551; ● 300
Norwood; RMC Place; MERCER; ***170** F-5; mail Alexis **z** 61412; rural
Norwood; Inc. Place; PEORIA; ***170** G-7; elev. 650ft./198m.; ★ **PEOR**; mail Peoria **z** 61604; Ⓟ 495; © 473
Norwood Park; RMC Place; COOK; ***170** B-13; ★ **CHI**; mail Chicago **z** 60631; pop. incl. with Chicago (Inc. Place)
Norwood Park; MCD-Township; COOK; ***170** C-13; ★ **CHI**; mail Chicago **z** 60631, **z** 60656; Ⓟ 25,600; © 26,176
Nottingham Park; RMC Place; COOK; ***170** C-13; ★ **CHI**; mail Chicago **z** 60638; pop. incl. with Bridgeview (Inc. Place)
Nottingham Woods; RMC Place; KANE; ***170** C-11; ★ **CHI**; mail Elburn **z** 60119; ● 140
Novak Park; RMC Place; KANE; ***170** C-11; ★ **CHI**; mail Saint Charles **z** 60175; ● 150
Nubbin Ridge; RMC Place; WHITE; mail Enfield **z** 62835; rural
Nunda; MCD-Township; MCHENRY; ***170** A-11; ★ **CHI**; mail Crystal Lake **z** 60012; Ⓟ 24,759; © 35,104
Nutwood; RMC Place; JERSEY; **171** M-5; elev. 451ft./137m.; mail Fieldon **z** 62031; ● 120

O

Oak; RMC Place; POPE; ***171** R-11; elev. 765ft./233m.; mail Herod **z** 62947; rural
Oak Bluff Estates; RMC Place; BOONE; ***170** A-10; elev. 808ft./246m.; mail Garden Prairie **z** 61038; ● 100
Oak Brook; Inc. Place; DUPAGE, COOK; **172** I-6; elev. 660ft./201m.; 🄿 ■; ★ **CHI**; **z** 60521-23 & mail Darien **z** 60561; Ⓟ 9,178; © 8,702; ◆ 8,654
Oakbrook; RMC Place; MACOUPIN; ***171** L-7; elev. 600ft./183m.; mail Carlinville **z** 62626; pop. incl. with Carlinville (Inc. Place)
Oakbrook Terrace; Inc. Place; DUPAGE; **172** I-6; elev. 700ft./213m.; 🄿; ★ **CHI**; **z** 60181; Ⓟ 1,907; © 2,300
Oakdale; RMC Place; COOK; ★ **CHI**; mail Chicago **z** 60619; pop. incl. with Chicago (Inc. Place)
Oakdale; Inc. Place; WASHINGTON; ▲ Oakdale; **171** P-8; 🄿; **z** 62268; Ⓟ 179; © 213
Oakdale; MCD-Township; WASHINGTON; ***171** P-8; 🄿; **z** 62268; Ⓟ 620; © 643
Oakdale Woods; RMC Place; DUPAGE; ★ **CHI**; mail Bensenville **z** 60106; ● 400
Oakford; Inc. Place; MENARD; **170** I-7; elev. 495ft./151m.; 🄿; **z** 62673; Ⓟ 246; © 309
Oak Forest; Inc. Place; COOK; **172** L-8; elev. 660ft./201m.; 🄿 🄷; ★ **CHI**; **z** 60452; Ⓟ 26,202; © 28,051; ◆ 26,682
Oak Glen; RMC Place; COOK; ***170** D-13; ★ **CHI**; pop. incl. with Lansing (Inc. Place)
Oak Grove; RMC Place; MADISON; mail Godfrey **z** 62035; ● 190
Oak Grove (Oak Grove Park); Inc. Place; ROCK ISLAND; **170** E-5; elev. 721ft./220m.; ★ **D-RI-M**; mail Milan **z** 61264; Ⓟ 626; © 1,318; Ⓡ 728
Oak Grove Park; ROCK ISLAND; see Oak Grove (Inc. Place)
Oak Grove Park; WOODFORD; see Germantown Hills (Inc. Place)
Oak Hill; RMC Place; PEORIA; **170** G-7; elev. 590ft./180m.; mail Brimfield **z** 61517; ● 100
Oak Hills; RMC Place; ST. CLAIR; ***171** O-7; ★ **ST.L**; mail Caseyville **z** 62232; ● 1,150
Oak Hills Estates; RMC Place; BOONE; ***170** A-10; elev. 835ft./255m.; ★ **RKFD**; mail Belvidere **z** 61008; ● 150
Oak Knolls; RMC Place; KANE; ***170** B-11; elev. 931ft./284m.; ★ **CHI**; mail Dundee **z** 60118; ● 60
Oakland; Inc. Place; COLES; **171** K-12; elev. 656ft./200m.; 🄿; **z** 61943; Ⓟ 996; © 996
Oakland; RMC Place; COOK; ★ **CHI**; mail Chicago **z** 60653; pop. incl. with Chicago (Inc. Place)
Oakland; MCD-Township; SCHUYLER; ***170** I-5; mail Rushville **z** 62681; Ⓟ 201; © 176
Oak Lawn; Inc. Place; COOK; **170** C-13; elev. 615ft./187m.; 🄿 🄷 ■; ★ **CHI**; **z** 60453-59; Ⓟ 56,182; © 55,245; ◆ 51,214
Oaklawn; RMC Place; VERMILION; ★ **DANV**; mail Danville **z** 61832; pop. incl. with Danville (Inc. Place)
Oakley; RMC Place; MACON; ▲ Oakley; ***170** J-10; 🄿; **z** 62501; ● 160
Oakley; MCD-Township; MACON; ***170** J-10; 🄿; **z** 62501; Ⓟ 1,060; © 1,177
Oak Manor; RMC Place; KENDALL; ***170** D-11; elev. 675ft./206m.; ★ **CHI**; mail Plano **z** 60545; ● 40
Oak Meadows; RMC Place; DUPAGE; ***170** C-12; ★ **CHI**; mail West Chicago **z** 60185; ● 1,400
Oak Park; Inc. Place; COOK; **170** C-13; elev. 620ft./189m.; 🄿 🄷 ■; ★ **CHI**; **z** 60301-04; Ⓟ 53,648; © 52,524; ◆ 48,034
Oak Park; MCD-Township; COOK; ***170** C-13; 🄿 🄷; ★ **CHI**; **z** 60301-04; coextensive with the Village of Oak Park; Ⓟ 53,648; © 52,524
Oak Park South; RMC Place; COOK; ***170** C-13; ★ **CHI**; mail Oak Park **z** 60304; pop. incl. with Oak Park (Inc. Place)
Oak Ridge; RMC Place; WOODFORD; ***170** G-8; ★ **PEOR**; mail Metamora **z** 61548; ● 250
Oak Run; RMC Place; KNOX; **170** F-6; mail Dahinda **z** 61428; ● 200
Oak Spring Woods; RMC Place; LAKE; ***170** A-12; ★ **CHI**; mail Libertyville **z** 60048; ● 770
Oakwood; RMC Place; DUPAGE; ★ **CHI**; mail Westmont **z** 60559; pop. incl. with Westmont (Inc. Place)
Oakwood; RMC Place; HENDERSON; ***170** G-4; elev. 570ft./174m.; mail Gladstone **z** 61437; ● 50
Oakwood; RMC Place; PEORIA; ***170** G-8; ★ **PEOR**; mail Peoria **z** 61605; ● 1,000
Oakwood; Inc. Place; VERMILION; **170** I-13; elev. 645ft./197m.; 🄿; ★ **DANV**; **z** 61858; Ⓟ 1,533; © 1,502
Oakwood; MCD-Township; VERMILION; ***170** I-13; 🄿; **z** 61858; Ⓟ 3,538; © 3,423
Oakwood Acres; RMC Place; HENRY; ***170** D-6; elev. 650ft./198m.; mail Geneseo **z** 61254; pop. incl. with Geneseo (Inc. Place)
Oakwood Hills; Inc. Place; MCHENRY; **172** C-3; elev. 800ft./244m.; 🄿; ★ **CHI**; **z** 60013; Ⓟ 1,498; © 2,194
Oakwood Shores; RMC Place; MCHENRY; ***170** A-11; ★ **CHI**; mail Wonder Lake **z** 60097; ● 250
Obed; RMC Place; SHELBY; ***171** K-10; elev. 703ft./214m.; mail Assumption **z** 62510; rural
Oblong; Inc. Place; CRAWFORD; ▲ Oblong; **171** M-12; elev. 524ft./160m.; 🄿; **z** 62449; Ⓟ 1,616; © 1,580
Oblong; MCD-Township; CRAWFORD; ***171** M-13; 🄿; **z** 62449; Ⓟ 2,977; © 2,918
Oconee; Inc. Place; SHELBY; ▲ Oconee; **171** L-9; 🄿; **z** 62553; Ⓟ 201; © 202
Oconee; MCD-Township; SHELBY; ***171** L-9; 🄿; **z** 62553; Ⓟ 796; © 848
Ocoya; RMC Place; LIVINGSTON; ***170** G-10; elev. 669ft./204m.; mail Pontiac **z** 61764; ● 25
Odell; Inc. Place; LIVINGSTON; ▲ Odell; **170** F-11; 🄿; **z** 60460; Ⓟ 1,030; © 1,014
Odell; MCD-Township; LIVINGSTON; ***170** F-11; 🄿; **z** 60460; Ⓟ 1,234; © 1,208
Odgen; RMC Place; WABASH; ***171** O-13; elev. 489ft./149m.; mail Mount Carmel **z** 62863; rural
Odin; Inc. Place; MARION; ▲ Odin; **171** O-9; 🄿; **z** 62870; Ⓟ 1,150; © 1,122
Odin; MCD-Township; MARION; ***171** O-9; 🄿; **z** 62870; Ⓟ 1,758; © 1,711
O'Fallon; Inc. Place; ST. CLAIR; **171** O-7; elev. 550ft./168m.; 🄿; ★ **ST.L**; **z** 62269; Ⓟ 16,073; © 21,910; ◆ 24,056
O'Fallon; MCD-Township; ST. CLAIR; ***171** O-7; ★ **ST.L**; mail O Fallon **z** 62269; includes part of the City of O'Fallon; Ⓟ 16,660; © 21,859
Ogden; Inc. Place; CHAMPAIGN; ▲ Ogden; **170** I-12; 🄿; **z** 61859; Ⓟ 671; © 743
Ogden; MCD-Township; CHAMPAIGN; ***170** I-12; 🄿; **z** 61859; Ⓟ 1,397; © 1,601
Ogden Park; RMC Place; COOK; ***170** C-13; ★ **CHI**; mail Chicago **z** 60636; pop. incl. with Chicago (Inc. Place)
OGLE; **170** B-9; Ⓟ 45,957; © 51,032; ◆ 55,452
Ogles (Atlee Ogles); RMC Place; ST. CLAIR; ***171** O-6; ★ **ST.L**; mail Belleville **z** 62223; ● 1,350
Oglesby; Inc. Place; LA SALLE; **170** E-9; elev. 636ft./194m.; 🄿; **z** 61348; Ⓟ 3,619; © 3,647
Ohio; Inc. Place; BUREAU; ▲ Ohio; **170** D-8; 🄿; **z** 61349; Ⓟ 426; © 540
Ohio; MCD-Township; BUREAU; ***170** D-8; 🄿; **z** 61349; Ⓟ 897; © 897
Ohio Grove; MCD-Township; MERCER; ***170** F-5; mail Aledo **z** 61231; Ⓟ 337; © 302
Ohlman; Inc. Place; MONTGOMERY; **171** L-9; elev. 720ft./219m.; 🄿; **z** 62076; Ⓟ 82; © 0; Ⓡ 75
Oil Center; RMC Place; MARION; mail Centralia **z** 62801; pop. incl. with Centralia (Inc. Place)
Oilfield; RMC Place; CLARK; ***171** L-12; elev. 665ft./203m.; mail Casey **z** 62420; rural
Okaw; MCD-Township; SHELBY; ***171** L-10; mail Findlay **z** 62534; Ⓟ 914; © 857
Okawville; Inc. Place; WASHINGTON; ▲ Okawville; **171** O-8; 🄿; **z** 62271; Ⓟ 1,274; © 1,355
Okawville; MCD-Township; WASHINGTON; ***171** O-8; 🄿; **z** 62271; Ⓟ 1,831; © 1,909
Oklahoma Addition; RMC Place; CRAWFORD; ***171** M-13; elev. 450ft./137m.; mail Palestine **z** 62451; ● 30
Old Camp; RMC Place; WILLIAMSON; ***171** R-9; ★ **CARB-**; mail Colp **z** 62921; ● 300
Old Du Quoin; RMC Place; PERRY; ***171** Q-9; mail Du Quoin **z** 62832; ● 100
Oldenburg; RMC Place; MADISON; ***171** N-6; ★ **ST.L**; mail East Alton **z** 62024; rural
Olde Salem; RMC Place; COOK; ★ **CHI**; mail Hanover Park **z** 60133; pop. incl. with Hanover Park (Inc. Place)
Old Farm; RMC Place; DUPAGE; ★ **CHI**; mail Naperville **z** 60565; pop. incl. with Naperville (Inc. Place)
Old Gilchrist; RMC Place; MERCER; ***170** E-5; mail Aledo **z** 61231; rural
Old Kane; RMC Place; GREENE; ***171** M-6; elev. 585ft./178m.; mail Kane **z** 62054
Old Marissa; RMC Place; ST. CLAIR; ***171** P-7; mail Marissa **z** 62257; pop. incl. with Marissa (Inc. Place)
Old Mill Creek; Inc. Place; LAKE; ***170** A-12; elev. 709ft./216m.; 🄿; ★ **CHI**; **z** 60002, **z** 60083; Ⓟ 73; © 251
Old Pearl; RMC Place; PIKE; ***171** L-5; mail Pearl **z** 62361; rural
Old Ripley; Inc. Place; BOND; ▲ Old Ripley; **171** N-8; mail Pocahontas **z** 62275, Sorento **z** 62086; Ⓟ 95; © 127
Old Ripley; MCD-Township; BOND; ***171** N-8; mail Pocahontas **z** 62275; Ⓟ 784; © 796
Old Shawneetown; Inc. Place; GALLATIN; **171** R-12; elev. 370ft./113m.; mail Shawneetown **z** 62984; Ⓟ 356; © 278
Old Stonington; RMC Place; CHRISTIAN; ***171** K-9; elev. 611ft./186m.; mail Stonington **z** 62567; rural
Oldtown; MCD-Township; MCLEAN; ***170** H-10; mail Bloomington **z** 61701; Ⓟ 1,738; © 2,692
Oldtown; RMC Place; SALINE; ***171** R-10; elev. 437ft./133m.; mail Stonefort **z** 62987; rural
Olena; RMC Place; HENDERSON; ***170** G-4; mail Stronghurst **z** 61480; rural
Olio; MCD-Township; WOODFORD; ***170** G-9; ★ **PEOR**; mail Eureka **z** 61530; Ⓟ 4,630; © 4,868
Olive; MCD-Township; MADISON; ***171** M-7; mail Livingston **z** 62058; Ⓟ 1,820; © 1,746
Olive Branch; RMC Place; ALEXANDER; **171** T-8; elev. 340ft./104m.; 🄿; **z** 62969; ● 600
Oliver; RMC Place; EDGAR; **171** L-13; mail Marshall **z** 62441; ● 110
Olivet; RMC Place; VERMILION; ***170** J-13; elev. 673ft./205m.; ★ **DANV**; mail Georgetown **z** 61846; ● 360
Olmsted; Inc. Place; PULASKI; **171** T-9; elev. 360ft./110m.; 🄿; **z** 62970; Ⓟ 358; © 299
Olney; Inc. Place; ⊡ RICHLAND; ▲ Olney; **171** N-12; 🄿 🄷 ■; **z** 62450; Ⓟ 8,662; © 8,631; ◆ 7,952
Olney; MCD-Township; RICHLAND; ***171** N-12; 🄿; **z** 62450; Ⓟ 10,170; © 9,883
Olympia Fields; Inc. Place; COOK; **172** N-9; elev. 700ft./213m.; 🄿 🄷; ★ **CHI**; **z** 60461; Ⓟ 4,248; © 4,732
Olympia Gardens; RMC Place; COOK; ***170** D-13; ★ **CHI**; mail Flossmoor **z** 60422; pop. incl. with Flossmoor (Inc. Place)
Olympic Terrace; RMC Place; DUPAGE; ★ **CHI**; mail Naperville **z** 60565; pop. incl. with Naperville (Inc. Place)
Olympic Village; RMC Place; COOK; ★ **CHI**; mail Chicago Heights **z** 60411; pop. incl. with Chicago Heights (Inc. Place)
Omaha; Inc. Place; GALLATIN; ▲ Omaha; **171** Q-11; 🄿; **z** 62871; Ⓟ 273; © 263
Omaha; MCD-Township; GALLATIN; ***171** Q-11; 🄿; **z** 62871; Ⓟ 484; © 473
Omega; RMC Place; MARION; ▲ Omega; **171** N-10; elev. 558ft./170m.; mail Iuka **z** 62849, Kinmundy **z** 62854; ● 50
Omega; MCD-Township; MARION; ***171** N-10; mail Iuka **z** 62849; Ⓟ 472; © 471
Omphghent; MCD-Township; MADISON; ***171** M-7; mail Worden **z** 62097; Ⓟ 1,995; © 2,063
Onarga; Inc. Place; IROQUOIS; ▲ Onarga; **170** G-12; elev. 667ft./203m.; 🄿; **z** 60955; Ⓟ 1,281; © 1,438
Onarga; MCD-Township; IROQUOIS; ***170** G-12; 🄿; **z** 60955; includes only part of the Village of Onarga; Ⓟ 1,678; © 1,844
Oneco; RMC Place; STEPHENSON; ▲ Oneco; **170** A-8; mail Orangeville **z** 61060; ● 50
Oneco; MCD-Township; STEPHENSON; ***170** A-8; mail Orangeville **z** 61060; Ⓟ 1,200; © 1,345
Oneida; Inc. Place; KNOX; **170** F-6; elev. 810ft./247m.; 🄿; **z** 61467; Ⓟ 723; © 752
Ontario; MCD-Township; KNOX; ***170** F-6; mail Oneida **z** 61467; Ⓟ 1,044; © 1,047
Ontario Street; RMC Place; COOK; ***170** C-13; ★ **CHI**; mail Chicago **z** 60611; pop. incl. with Chicago (Inc. Place)
Ontarioville; RMC Place; DUPAGE; **172** G-4; 🄿; ★ **CHI**; **z** 60103 & mail Hanover Park **z** 60133; pop. incl. with Hanover Park (Inc. Place)
Opdyke; RMC Place; JEFFERSON; **171** P-10; elev. 520ft./158m.; 🄿; **z** 62872; ● 300
Opheim; HENRY; see Ophiem (RMC Place)
Ophiem (Opheim); RMC Place; HENRY; **170** E-6; elev. 712ft./217m.; 🄿; **z** 61468; ● 170
Ophir; MCD-Township; LA SALLE; ***170** D-9; mail Mendota **z** 61342; Ⓟ 555; © 529
Oquawka; Inc. Place; ⊡ HENDERSON; ▲ Oquawka; **170** F-4; elev. 562ft./171m.; 🄿; **z** 61469; Ⓟ 1,442; © 1,539
Oquawka; MCD-Township; HENDERSON; ***170** F-4; 🄿; **z** 61469; Ⓟ 2,100; © 2,350
Ora; MCD-Township; JACKSON; ***171** Q-8; mail Oraville **z** 62971; Ⓟ 365; © 427
Oran; MCD-Township; LOGAN; ***170** I-9; mail Beason **z** 62512; Ⓟ 437; © 452
Orange; MCD-Township; CLARK; ***171** L-13; mail Martinsville **z** 62442; Ⓟ 257; © 251
Orange; MCD-Township; KNOX; ***170** G-6; mail Gilson **z** 61436; Ⓟ 650; © 573
Orange Prairie; RMC Place; PEORIA; ***170** G-8; ★ **PEOR**; mail Peoria **z** 61614; pop. incl. with Peoria (Inc. Place)
Orangeville; Inc. Place; STEPHENSON; **170** A-8; elev. 820ft./250m.; 🄿; **z** 61060; Ⓟ 451; © 751
Oraville; RMC Place; JACKSON; ▲ Ora; **171** Q-8; elev. 395ft./120m.; 🄿; **z** 62971; ● 100
Orchard; MCD-Township; WAYNE; ***171** O-10; mail Johnsonville **z** 62850; Ⓟ 555; © 534
Orchard Acres; RMC Place; MCHENRY; ***170** B-11; ★ **CHI**; mail Crystal Lake **z** 60014; ● 150
Orchard Estates; RMC Place; DUPAGE; ***170** C-12; ★ **CHI**; mail Wheaton **z** 60187; ● 250
Orchard Heights; RMC Place; RICHLAND; mail Olney **z** 62450; ● 300
Orchard Mines; RMC Place; PEORIA; ***170** H-8; mail Peoria **z** 61607; rural
Orchard Valley; RMC Place; LAKE; ***170** A-12; ★ **CHI**; mail Gurnee **z** 60031; ● 170
Orchardville; RMC Place; WAYNE; **171** O-10; elev. 506ft./154m.; mail Johnsonville **z** 62850, Xenia **z** 62899; ● 100
Oreana; Inc. Place; MACON; **170** J-10; elev. 688ft./210m.; 🄿; ★ **DEC**; **z** 62554; Ⓟ 847; © 892
Oregon; Inc. Place; ⊡ OGLE; ▲ Oregon-Nashua; **170** B-8; 🄿; **z** 61061; Ⓟ 3,891; © 4,060
Oregon-Nashua; MCD-Township; OGLE; ***170** C-9; mail Oregon **z** 61061; Ⓟ 5,191; © 5,310
Orel; MCD-Township; WAYNE; ***171** P-11; mail Wayne City **z** 62895; Ⓟ 1,523; © 1,467
Orient; Inc. Place; FRANKLIN; **171** Q-9; elev. 450ft./137m.; 🄿; ★ **CARB-**; **z** 62874; Ⓟ 428; © 296
Orio (Linn); RMC Place; WABASH; ***171** O-13; mail Allendale **z** 62410
Orion; MCD-Township; FULTON; ***170** H-7; mail Canton **z** 61520; Ⓟ 1,105; © 1,003
Orion; Inc. Place; HENRY; **170** E-6; elev. 785ft./239m.; 🄿; ★ **D-RI-M**; **z** 61273; Ⓟ 1,821; © 1,713
Orland; MCD-Township; COOK; ***170** D-13; ★ **CHI**; mail Orland Park **z** 60462; Ⓟ 69,542; © 91,418
Orland Hills; Inc. Place; COOK; **172** M-7; elev. 710ft./216m.; 🄿; ★ **CHI**; **z** 60477, **z** 60487; Ⓟ 5,510; © 6,779
Orland Park; Inc. Place; COOK, WILL; **170** D-12; elev. 725ft./221m.; 🄿 ■; ★ **CHI**; **z** 60462, **z** 60467; Ⓟ 35,720; © 51,077; ◆ 50,445
Orleans; RMC Place; MORGAN; ***171** K-6; elev. 659ft./201m.; mail Alexander **z** 62601; rural
Orleans Terrace; RMC Place; DUPAGE; ★ **CHI**; mail Addison **z** 60101; pop. incl. with Addison (Inc. Place)
Orvil; MCD-Township; LOGAN; ***170** I-8; mail Emden **z** 62635; Ⓟ 1,155; © 1,116
Osage; RMC Place; FRANKLIN; ***171** Q-9; ★ **CARB-**; mail Royalton **z** 62983; rural
Osage; MCD-Township; LA SALLE; ***170** F-9; mail Wenona **z** 61377; Ⓟ 328; © 207
Osbernville; RMC Place; CHRISTIAN; ***171** K-9; mail Blue Mound **z** 62513; ● 25
Osborn; RMC Place; ROCK ISLAND; ***170** D-6; mail Hillsdale **z** 61257; ● 140
Osceola; RMC Place; STARK; ▲ Elmira; **170** E-7; elev. 777ft./237m.; mail Bradford **z** 61421, Neponset **z** 61345; ● 50
Osceola; MCD-Township; STARK; ***170** E-7; mail Bradford **z** 61421; Ⓟ 1,084; © 1,038
Osco; RMC Place; HENRY; ▲ Osco; ***170** E-6; 🄿; **z** 61274; ● 130
Osco; MCD-Township; HENRY; ***170** E-6; 🄿; **z** 61274; Ⓟ 538; © 504
Oskaloosa; RMC Place; CLAY; ▲ Oskaloosa; ***171** N-10; mail Xenia **z** 62899
Oskaloosa; MCD-Township; CLAY; ***171** N-10; mail Xenia **z** 62899; Ⓟ 335; © 307
Osman; RMC Place; MCLEAN; ***170** I-11; elev. 748ft./228m.; mail Fisher **z** 61843
Ospur; RMC Place; DE WITT; ***170** I-10; mail Clinton **z** 61727; rural
Ossami Lake; RMC Place; TAZEWELL; ★ **PEOR**; mail Morton **z** 61550; pop. incl. with Morton (Inc. Place)
Oswego; Inc. Place; KENDALL; ▲ Oswego, Bristol; **170** D-11; elev. 646ft./197m.; 🄿; ★ **CHI**; **z** 60543; Ⓟ 3,876; © 13,326; ◆ 38,062
Oswego; MCD-Township; KENDALL; ***170** D-11; 🄿; ★ **CHI**; **z** 60543; Ⓟ 18,078; © 28,417
Otego; MCD-Township; FAYETTE; ***171** M-9; mail Brownstown **z** 62418; Ⓟ 1,347; © 1,438
Ottawa; Inc. Place; ⊡ LA SALLE; **170** E-10; elev. 480ft./146m.; 🄿 🄷 ■; **z** 61350; Ⓟ 17,528; © 18,307; ◆ 18,309
Ottawa; MCD-Township; LA SALLE; ***170** E-10; 🄿; **z** 61350; includes part of the City of Ottawa; Ⓟ 12,271; © 12,177
Otter Creek; MCD-Township; JERSEY; ***171** M-5; mail Jerseyville **z** 62052; Ⓟ 742; © 898
Otter Creek; MCD-Township; LA SALLE; ***170** F-10; mail Streator **z** 61364; Ⓟ 3,003; © 2,819
Otterville; Inc. Place; JERSEY; **171** M-5; elev. 622ft./190m.; 🄿; **z** 62052 & mail Grafton **z** 62037; Ⓟ 115; © 120
Otto; RMC Place; KANKAKEE; ▲ Otto; ***170** F-12; ★ **KANK**; mail Chebanse **z** 60922; ● 50
Otto; MCD-Township; KANKAKEE; ***170** F-12; mail Chebanse **z** 60922; Ⓟ 2,558; © 2,430
Ottville; RMC Place; BUREAU; ***170** E-9; elev. 650ft./198m.; mail Spring Valley **z** 61362; rural
Outter Creek; RMC Place; JERSEY; ***171** M-5; elev. 440ft./134m.; mail Fieldon **z** 62031; ● 40
Owaneco; Inc. Place; CHRISTIAN; **171** L-9; elev. 624ft./190m.; 🄿; **z** 62555; Ⓟ 260; © 256
Owego; MCD-Township; LIVINGSTON; ***170** F-11; mail Pontiac **z** 61764; Ⓟ 302; © 336
Owen; MCD-Township; WINNEBAGO; ***170** A-9; ★ **RKFD**; mail Rockford **z** 61103; Ⓟ 2,995; © 3,306
Oxford; MCD-Township; HENRY; ***170** E-6; mail Alpha **z** 61413; Ⓟ 1,290; © 1,236
Oxville; RMC Place; SCOTT; **171** K-5; mail Bluffs **z** 62621; ● 30
Ozark; RMC Place; JOHNSON; **171** S-10; elev. 696ft./212m.; 🄿; **z** 62972; ● 110

P

Pacesetter Park; RMC Place; COOK; ★ **CHI**; mail South Holland **z** 60473; pop. incl. with South Holland (Inc. Place)
Paderborn; RMC Place; ST. CLAIR; ***171** P-6; ★ **ST.L**; mail Waterloo **z** 62298; ● 30
Padua; RMC Place; MCLEAN; ***170** H-10; elev. 838ft./255m.; mail Ellsworth **z** 61737; rural
Paines Point; OGLE; see Paynes Point (RMC Place)
Painesville; WILLIAMSON; see Paineville (RMC Place)
Paineville (Painesville); RMC Place; WILLIAMSON; ***171** R-9; ★ **CARB-**; mail Herrin **z** 62948; ● 30
Palatine; Inc. Place; COOK; ▲ Palatine; **170** B-12; elev. 741ft./226m.; 🄿; ★ **CHI**; **z** 60038, **z** 60055, **z** 60067, **z** 60074, **z** 60078, **z** 60094-95; Ⓟ 38,894; © 65,479; ◆ 70,098
Palatine; MCD-Township; COOK; ***170** B-12; 🄿; ★ **CHI**; **z** 60038, **z** 60055, **z** 60067, **z** 60074, **z** 60078, **z** 60094-95; Ⓟ 103,273; © 112,740
Palatine Processing & Distribution Center; RMC Place; COOK; ***170** B-12; ★ **CHI**; mail Palatine **z** 60095; pop. incl. with Palatine (Inc. Place)
Palermo; RMC Place; EDGAR; ***170** J-13; elev. 712ft./217m.; mail Sidell **z** 61876; rural
Palestine; Inc. Place; CRAWFORD; **171** M-13; elev. 450ft./137m.; 🄿; **z** 62451; Ⓟ 1,619; © 1,366
Palestine; MCD-Township; WOODFORD; ***170** G-9; mail Secor **z** 61771; Ⓟ 892; © 987
Palmer; Inc. Place; CHRISTIAN; **171** L-8; elev. 621ft./189m.; 🄿; **z** 62556; Ⓟ 275; © 248
Palmyra; RMC Place; LEE; ***170** C-8; elev. 812ft./247m.; mail Dixon **z** 61021; ● 50
Palmyra; MCD-Township; LEE; ***170** C-8; mail Dixon **z** 61021; Ⓟ 2,188; © 2,610
Palmyra; Inc. Place; MACOUPIN; **171** L-7; elev. 678ft./207m.; 🄿; **z** 62674; Ⓟ 722; © 733
Paloma; RMC Place; ADAMS; ***170** J-3; elev. 742ft./226m.; 🄿; **z** 62359; ● 200
Palos; MCD-Township; COOK; ***170** D-13; ★ **CHI**; mail Palos Park **z** 60464; Ⓟ 50,916; © 53,419
Palos Heights; Inc. Place; COOK; **172** L-7; elev. 625ft./191m.; 🄿 🄷 🄲 1,310; ★ **CHI**; **z** 60463; Ⓟ 11,478; © 11,260
Palos Hills; Inc. Place; COOK; **172** K-7; elev. 600ft./183m.; 🄿; ★ **CHI**; **z** 60465; Ⓟ 17,803; © 17,665
Palos Park; Inc. Place; COOK; **172** K-7; elev. 700ft./213m.; 🄿; ★ **CHI**; **z** 60464 & mail Palos Heights **z** 60463; Ⓟ 4,199; © 4,689
Palos Westgate; RMC Place; COOK; ★ **CHI**; mail Palos Heights **z** 60463; pop. incl. with Palos Heights (Inc. Place)
Palsgrove; RMC Place; CARROLL; ***170** B-7; elev. 652ft./199m.; mail Mount Carroll **z** 61053; rural
Pam Anne Estates; RMC Place; COOK; ***170** B-12; ★ **CHI**; mail Glenview **z** 60025; pop. incl. with Glenview (Inc. Place)
Pana; Inc. Place; CHRISTIAN; ▲ Pana; **171** L-9; elev. 700ft./213m.; 🄿 🄷; **z** 62557; Ⓟ 5,796; © 5,614
Pana; MCD-Township; CHRISTIAN; ***171** L-9; 🄿; **z** 62557; Ⓟ 7,081; © 6,860
Panama; Inc. Place; BOND, MONTGOMERY; **171** M-8; elev. 596ft./182m.; 🄿; **z** 62077; Ⓟ 294; © 323
Pankeyville; RMC Place; SALINE; **171** R-11; mail Harrisburg **z** 62946; ● 200
Panola; Inc. Place; WOODFORD; ▲ Panola; **170** G-9; elev. 734ft./224m.; 🄿; **z** 61738; Ⓟ 43; © 33
Panola; MCD-Township; WOODFORD; ***170** G-9; 🄿; **z** 61738; Ⓟ 366; © 359
Panther Creek; MCD-Township; CASS; ***170** J-6; 🄿; **z** 62627; Ⓟ 289; © 365
Papineau; Inc. Place; IROQUOIS; ▲ Papineau; **170** F-13; 🄿; **z** 60956; Ⓟ 142; © 196
Papineau; MCD-Township; IROQUOIS; ***170** F-13; 🄿; **z** 60956; Ⓟ 565; © 647
Paradise; RMC Place; COLES; ▲ Paradise; ***171** L-11; mail Mattoon **z** 61938; ● 130
Paradise; MCD-Township; COLES; ***171** L-11; mail Mattoon **z** 61938; Ⓟ 1,156; © 1,324
Paradise Acres; RMC Place; WILLIAMSON; ***171** R-9; elev. 420ft./128m.; ★ **CARB-**; mail Carterville **z** 62918; pop. incl. with Cambria (Inc. Place)
Paris; Inc. Place; ⊡ EDGAR; ▲ Paris; **171** K-13; elev. 726ft./221m.; 🄿 🄷; **z** 61944; Ⓟ 8,987; © 9,077
Paris; MCD-Township; EDGAR; ***171** K-13; 🄿; **z** 61944; Ⓟ 10,380; © 10,692
Park City; Inc. Place; LAKE; **172** A-7; elev. 700ft./213m.; 🄿; ★ **CHI**; **z** 60085; Ⓟ 4,677; © 6,637
Parker; MCD-Township; CLARK; ***171** L-12; mail Westfield **z** 62474; Ⓟ 218; © 242
Parker; RMC Place; JOHNSON; ***171** R-10; elev. 547ft./167m.; mail Creal Springs **z** 62922; ● 70
Parkersburg; Inc. Place; RICHLAND; **171** O-12; elev. 480ft./146m.; 🄿; **z** 62452; Ⓟ 211; © 234
Parkfield Terrace; RMC Place; ST. CLAIR; ***171** O-6; ★ **ST.L**; mail East Saint Louis **z** 62206; ● 1,100
Park Forest; Inc. Place; COOK, WILL; **170** D-13; elev. 720ft./219m.; 🄿; ★ **CHI**; **z** 60466, **z** 60484; Ⓟ 24,656; © 23,462; ◆ 21,548
Park Forest South; WILL, COOK; see University Park (Inc. Place)
Park Hill Estates; RMC Place; WILL; ★ **CHI**; pop. incl. with Joliet (Inc. Place)
Park Hills; RMC Place; EFFINGHAM; mail Effingham **z** 62401; pop. incl. with Effingham (Inc. Place)
Parkhome; RMC Place; COOK; ★ **CHI**; mail Cicero **z** 60804; pop. incl. with Cicero (Inc. Place)
Parkland; RMC Place; TAZEWELL; ***170** H-7; mail Manito **z** 61546; rural
Park Lane; RMC Place; KANKAKEE; ***170** F-13; ★ **KANK**; mail Saint Anne **z** 60964; ● 140
Park Meadows; RMC Place; COOK; ★ **CHI**; mail Rolling Meadows **z** 60008; pop. incl. with Rolling Meadows (Inc. Place)
Park Ridge; Inc. Place; COOK; **172** F-7; elev. 640ft./195m.; 🄿 🄷 ■; ★ **CHI**; **z** 60068; Ⓟ 36,175; © 37,775; ◆ 36,800
Parkville; RMC Place; CHAMPAIGN; ***170** J-11; mail Sadorus **z** 61872
Parkway; RMC Place; COOK; ★ **CHI**; mail Riverside **z** 60546; pop. incl. with North Riverside (Inc. Place)
Parkwood; RMC Place; KANE; ★ **CHI**; mail Elgin **z** 60120; pop. incl. with Elgin (Inc. Place)
Parkwood Village; RMC Place; COOK; ★ **CHI**; mail Elgin **z** 60120; pop. incl. with Elgin (Inc. Place)
Parnell; RMC Place; DE WITT; ***170** I-10; mail Farmer City **z** 61842; ● 30
Parrish; RMC Place; FRANKLIN; ***171** Q-10; mail Thompsonville **z** 62890; ● 100
Parrish Addition; RMC Place; SALINE; ***171** R-11; elev. 400ft./122m.; mail Eldorado **z** 62930; pop. incl. with Eldorado (Inc. Place)
Partridge; MCD-Township; WOODFORD; ***170** F-8; mail Lowpoint **z** 61545, Metamora **z** 61548; Ⓟ 472; © 511
Partridge Hill; RMC Place; COOK; ★ **CHI**; mail Schaumburg **z** 60194; pop. incl. with Hoffman Estates (Inc. Place)
Passport; RMC Place; RICHLAND; **171** N-12; elev. 467ft./142m.; mail Noble **z** 62868; ● 30
Patoka; Inc. Place; MARION; ▲ Patoka; **171** N-9; elev. 507ft./155m.; 🄿; **z** 62875; Ⓟ 656; © 633
Patoka; MCD-Township; MARION; ***171** N-9; 🄿; **z** 62875; Ⓟ 1,228; © 1,164
Patterson (Wilmington); Inc. Place; GREENE; ▲ Patterson; ***171** L-5; 🄿; **z** 62078; Ⓟ 129; © 120
Patterson; MCD-Township; GREENE; ***171** L-5; 🄿; **z** 62078; Ⓟ 795; © 644
Patterson Heights; RMC Place; MADISON; ★ **ST.L**; mail Godfrey **z** 62035; pop. incl. with Godfrey (Inc. Place)
Patterson Springs; RMC Place; DOUGLAS; ***170** J-12; elev. 655ft./200m.; mail Camargo **z** 61919, Tuscola **z** 61953; ● 50
Patton; MCD-Township; FORD; ***170** H-12; mail Paxton **z** 60957; Ⓟ 5,226; © 5,413
Patton; RMC Place; WABASH; **171** O-13; elev. 413ft./126m.; mail Mount Carmel **z** 62863; ● 90
Pattonsburg; RMC Place; MARSHALL; ***170** F-9; mail Toluca **z** 61369
Paulton; RMC Place; WILLIAMSON; ***171** R-10; elev. 538ft./164m.; mail Marion **z** 62959; ● 150
Pavillion; RMC Place; KENDALL; ***170** D-11; elev. 750ft./229m.; ★ **CHI**; mail Yorkville **z** 60560; ● 150
Pawnee; Inc. Place; SANGAMON; ▲ Pawnee; **171** K-8; 🄿; ★ **SPRG**; **z** 62558; Ⓟ 2,384; © 2,647
Pawnee; MCD-Township; SANGAMON; ***171** K-8; 🄿; ★ **SPRG**; **z** 62558; Ⓟ 2,775; © 2,948
Paw Paw; MCD-Township; DEKALB; ***170** D-10; mail Earlville **z** 60518; Ⓟ 384; © 306
Paw Paw; Inc. Place; LEE; **170** D-9; elev. 940ft./287m.; 🄿; **z** 61353; Ⓟ 791; © 852
Paxton; Inc. Place; ⊡ FORD; **170** H-12; elev. 792ft./241m.; 🄿; **z** 60957; Ⓟ 4,289; © 4,525
Paynes Point (Paines Point); RMC Place; OGLE; ***170** B-9; mail Chana **z** 61015
Payson; Inc. Place; ADAMS; ▲ Payson; **170** J-3; 🄿; **z** 62360; Ⓟ 1,114; © 1,066
Payson; MCD-Township; ADAMS; ***170** J-3; 🄿; **z** 62360; Ⓟ 1,926; © 1,920
Peach Orchard; MCD-Township; FORD; ***170** H-11; mail Melvin **z** 60952; Ⓟ 654; © 614
Pea Ridge; MCD-Township; BROWN; ***170** I-4; mail Timewell **z** 62375; Ⓟ 167; © 188
Pearl; Inc. Place; PIKE; ▲ Pearl; **171** L-5; 🄿; **z** 62361; Ⓟ 177; © 187
Pearl; MCD-Township; PIKE; ***171** L-5; 🄿; **z** 62361; Ⓟ 372; © 313
Pearl City; Inc. Place; STEPHENSON; **170** A-7; elev. 823ft./251m.; 🄿; **z** 61062; Ⓟ 670; © 780
Pecan Grove; RMC Place; JERSEY; ***171** M-5; elev. 423ft./129m.; mail Fieldon **z** 62031; ● 30
Pecatonica; Inc. Place; WINNEBAGO; ▲ Pecatonica; **170** A-8; elev. 759ft./231m.; 🄿; **z** 61063; Ⓟ 1,760; © 1,997
Pecatonica; MCD-Township; WINNEBAGO; ***170** A-8; 🄿; **z** 61063; Ⓟ 2,592; © 2,998
Peerless; RMC Place; WILL; ***170** D-12; ★ **CHI**; mail Plainfield **z** 60544; ● 300
Pekin; Inc. Place; ⊡ TAZEWELL, PEORIA; **170** H-8; elev. 502ft./153m.; 🄿 🄷 ■; ★ **PEOR**; **z** 61554-55, **z** 61558; Ⓟ 32,254; © 33,857; ◆ 34,519
Pekin; MCD-Township; TAZEWELL; ***170** H-8; 🄿; ★ **PEOR**; **z** 61554-55, **z** 61558; includes part of the City of Pekin; Ⓟ 31,135; © 30,600
Pekin Heights; RMC Place; TAZEWELL; ***170** H-8; ★ **PEOR**; mail Pekin **z** 61554; pop. incl. with Pekin (Inc. Place)
Pella; MCD-Township; FORD; ***170** G-12; mail Piper City **z** 60959; Ⓟ 206; © 220
Pembroke; KANKAKEE; see Hopkins Park (Inc. Place)
Pembroke; MCD-Township; KANKAKEE; ***170** F-13; mail Pembroke Township **z** 60958, Saint Anne **z** 60964; Ⓟ 3,320; © 2,784
Pendleton; MCD-Township; JEFFERSON; ***171** P-10; mail Belle Rive **z** 62810; Ⓟ 1,062; © 1,083
Penfield; RMC Place; CHAMPAIGN; **170** I-12; elev. 710ft./216m.; 🄿; **z** 61862; ● 250
Penn; MCD-Township; SHELBY; ***171** K-10; mail Moweaqua **z** 62550; Ⓟ 136; © 118
Penn; MCD-Township; STARK; ***170** F-7; mail Bradford **z** 61421; Ⓟ 402; © 362
Pennsylvania; MCD-Township; MASON; ***170** I-7; mail Mason City **z** 62664; Ⓟ 238; © 200
Penrose; RMC Place; WHITESIDE; ***170** C-8; elev. 717ft./219m.; mail Sterling **z** 61081; ● 25
Peoria; Inc. Place; ⊡ PEORIA; **170** G-8; elev. 510ft./155m.; 🄿 🄷 🄲 6,743 ■; ★ **PEOR**; **z** 61601-07, **z** 61610-16, **z** 61625, **z** 61629-30, **z** 61633-39, **z** 61641, **z** 61643, **z** 61650-56; Ⓟ 113,504; © 112,936; ◆ 114,037
PEORIA; **170** F-7; Ⓟ 182,827; © 183,433; ◆ 183,606
Peoria City; MCD-Township; PEORIA; ***170** G-8; 🄷; ★ **PEOR**; mail Creve Coeur **z** 61610, East Peoria **z** 61611, Peoria **z** 61601-07, **z** 61612-15, **z** 61625, **z** 61629-30, **z** 61633-39, **z** 61641, **z** 61643, **z** 61650-56, Peoria Heights **z** 61616; coextensive with the City of Peoria; Ⓟ 113,504; © 112,936
Peoria Heights; Inc. Place; PEORIA, TAZEWELL, WOODFORD; **170** G-8; elev. 789ft./240m.; 🄿; ★ **PEOR**; **z** 61616 & mail Peoria **z** 61603, **z** 61614; Ⓟ 6,930; © 6,635
Peotone; Inc. Place; WILL; ▲ Peotone; **170** E-13; elev. 702ft./214m.; 🄿; **z** 60468; Ⓟ 2,947; © 3,385
Peotone; MCD-Township; WILL; ***170** E-13; 🄿; **z** 60468; Ⓟ 3,613; © 3,938
Pepper Tree; RMC Place; COOK; ***170** B-12; ★ **CHI**; mail Palatine **z** 60067; pop. incl. with Palatine (Inc. Place)
Pequot; RMC Place; GRUNDY; ★ **CHI**; mail Coal City **z** 60416; pop. incl. with Coal City (Inc. Place)
Percy; Inc. Place; RANDOLPH; **171** Q-8; elev. 490ft./149m.; 🄿; **z** 62272; Ⓟ 925; © 942
Perdueville; RMC Place; FORD; ***170** H-12; elev. 767ft./234m.; mail Paxton **z** 60957; rural
Perks; RMC Place; PULASKI; ***171** S-9; elev. 346ft./105m.; 🄿; **z** 62973; ● 200
Perry; Inc. Place; PIKE; ▲ Perry; **170** J-5; 🄿; **z** 62362; Ⓟ 491; © 437
Perry; MCD-Township; PIKE; ***170** J-5; 🄿; **z** 62362; Ⓟ 703; © 636
PERRY; **171** Q-8; Ⓟ 21,412; © 23,094; ◆ 22,427
Perryton; MCD-Township; MERCER; ***170** E-5; mail Reynolds **z** 61279; Ⓟ 513; © 497
Perryville; RMC Place; WINNEBAGO; ***170** B-9; elev. 764ft./233m.; ★ **RKFD**; mail Cherry Valley **z** 61016; rural
Pershing (Ezra); RMC Place; FRANKLIN; ***171** Q-9; ★ **CARB-**; mail West Frankfort **z** 62896; ● 200
Persifer; MCD-Township; KNOX; ***170** F-6; mail Gilson **z** 61436; Ⓟ 892; © 960
Peru; Inc. Place; LA SALLE; **170** E-9; elev. 500ft./152m.; 🄿 🄷 ■; **z** 61354; Ⓟ 9,302; © 9,835; ◆ 9,602
Peru; MCD-Township; LA SALLE; ***170** E-9; 🄿; **z** 61354; includes part of the City of Peru; Ⓟ 10,326; © 10,272
Pesotum; Inc. Place; CHAMPAIGN; ▲ Pesotum; **170** J-11; 🄿; **z** 61863; Ⓟ 558; © 521
Pesotum; MCD-Township; CHAMPAIGN; ***170** J-11; 🄿; **z** 61863; Ⓟ 931; © 849
Petersburg (Petersbury); Inc. Place; ⊡ MENARD; **170** J-7; elev. 524ft./160m.; 🄿; **z** 62675 & mail Lincolns New Salem **z** 62659; Ⓟ 2,261; © 2,299
Petersburg; RMC Place; ST. CLAIR; ***171** O-7; ★ **ST.L**; mail O Fallon **z** 62269; pop. incl. with O'Fallon (Inc. Place)
Petersbury; MENARD; see Petersburg (Inc. Place)
Peters Creek; RMC Place; HARDIN; ***171** S-12; elev. 453ft./138m.; mail Elizabethtown **z** 62931
Peterson Avenue; RMC Place; COOK; ***170** B-13; ★ **CHI**; mail Chicago **z** 60646; pop. incl. with Chicago (Inc. Place)
Petite Lake; RMC Place; LAKE; ***170** A-12; ★ **CHI**; mail Antioch **z** 60002, Lake Villa **z** 60046; ● 1,200
Petrolia; RMC Place; LAWRENCE; **171** N-13; elev. 449ft./137m.; mail Bridgeport **z** 62417; ● 90
Petty; MCD-Township; LAWRENCE; ***171** N-13; mail Sumner **z** 62466; Ⓟ 827; © 708
Pharoah's Gardens; RMC Place; WILLIAMSON; ★ **CARB-**; mail Elkville **z** 62932; ● 300
Pheasant Creek; RMC Place; COOK; ★ **CHI**; mail Northbrook **z** 60062; pop. incl. with Northbrook (Inc. Place)
Pheasant Hollow; RMC Place; DUPAGE; ***170** C-12; ★ **CHI**; mail Wheaton **z** 60187; ● 200
Pheasant Meadows; RMC Place; WILL; ★ **CHI**; mail Beecher **z** 60401; ● 60
Pheasant Ridge; RMC Place; WILL; ★ **CHI**; mail Mokena **z** 60448; pop. incl. with Mokena (Inc. Place)
Pheasant Ridge; RMC Place; WILL; ***170** D-11; ★ **CHI**; mail Plainfield **z** 60544; ● 80
Phelps; RMC Place; ST. CLAIR; ***171** O-6; ★ **ST.L**; mail East Carondelet **z** 62240; pop. incl. with Dupo (Inc. Place)
Phenix; MCD-Township; HENRY; ***170** D-6; mail Geneseo **z** 61254; Ⓟ 1,502; © 1,710
Philadelphia; RMC Place; CASS; ▲ Philadelphia; **170** J-6; elev. 626ft./191m.; mail Ashland **z** 62612; ● 60
Philadelphia; MCD-Township; CASS; ***170** J-6; mail Ashland **z** 62612; Ⓟ 270; © 235
Phillips; MCD-Township; WHITE; ***171** P-12; mail Crossville **z** 62827; Ⓟ 1,388; © 1,313
Phillipstown; Inc. Place; WHITE; **171** P-12; elev. 487ft./148m.; mail Crossville **z** 62827; Ⓟ 48; © 28
Philo; Inc. Place; CHAMPAIGN; ▲ Philo; **170** J-12; elev. 737ft./225m.; 🄿; **z** 61864; Ⓟ 1,028; © 1,314
Philo; MCD-Township; CHAMPAIGN; ***170** J-12; 🄿; **z** 61864; Ⓟ 1,480; © 1,768
Phinney; RMC Place; CHAMPAIGN; ***170** I-11; ★ **CH-U**; mail Champaign **z** 61821; ● 600
Phoenix; Inc. Place; COOK; **172** L-9; elev. 600ft./183m.; 🄿; ★ **CHI**; **z** 60426; Ⓟ 2,217; © 2,157
Piasa; MCD-Township; JERSEY; ***171** M-6; ★ **ST.L**; mail Brighton **z** 62012; Ⓟ 2,660; © 3,054
Piasa; RMC Place; MACOUPIN; **171** M-6; elev. 593ft./181m.; 🄿; **z** 62079; ● 200
Piasa Hills; RMC Place; MADISON; ***171** M-6; ★ **ST.L**; mail Godfrey **z** 62035; pop. incl. with Godfrey (Inc. Place)
PIATT; **170** I-10; Ⓟ 15,548; © 16,365; Ⓡ 16,369; ◆ 16,340
Picadilly Terrace; RMC Place; DUPAGE; ***170** C-12; ★ **CHI**; mail Clarendon Hills **z** 60514; ● 900
Pickaway; MCD-Township; SHELBY; ***171** K-10; mail Bethany **z** 61914; Ⓟ 203; © 193
Pierce; MCD-Township; DEKALB; ***170** C-10; mail Maple Park **z** 60151; Ⓟ 506; © 473
Pierceburg; RMC Place; CRAWFORD; ***171** N-12; elev. 457ft./139m.; mail Oblong **z** 62449
Pierron (Baden Baden); RMC Place; BOND; ***171** N-8; mail Pocahontas **z** 62275
Pierron; Inc. Place; BOND, MADISON; **171** N-8; 🄿; **z** 62273; Ⓟ 554; © 653
Pierson; RMC Place; PIATT; ***170** J-11; mail Hammond **z** 61929; ● 100
Piety Hill; RMC Place; LA SALLE; ***170** E-9; elev. 600ft./183m.; mail Oglesby **z** 61348; ● 100
Pigeon Grove; MCD-Township; IROQUOIS; ***170** H-12; mail Cissna Park **z** 60924; Ⓟ 1,122; © 1,160
Pike; MCD-Township; LIVINGSTON; ***170** G-10; mail Chenoa **z** 61726; Ⓟ 295; © 303
Pike (Pike Station); RMC Place; PIKE; **171** L-4; elev. 454ft./138m.; mail Rockport **z** 62370; ● 30
PIKE; **171** K-4; Ⓟ 17,577; © 17,384; Ⓡ 17,379; ◆ 16,942
Pike Station; PIKE; see Pike (RMC Place)
Pilot; MCD-Township; KANKAKEE; ***170** F-12; mail Herscher **z** 60941; Ⓟ 1,917; © 2,065
Pilot; MCD-Township; VERMILION; ***170** I-13; mail Collison **z** 61831; Ⓟ 668; © 658
Pilot Grove; MCD-Township; HANCOCK; ***170** H-4; mail Dallas City **z** 62330; Ⓟ 339; © 299
Pilot Knob; MCD-Township; WASHINGTON; ***171** P-8; mail Nashville **z** 62263; Ⓟ 395; © 466
Pilsen; RMC Place; COOK; ***170** C-13; ★ **CHI**; mail Chicago **z** 60608; pop. incl. with Chicago (Inc. Place)
Pinckneyville; Inc. Place; ⊡ PERRY; **171** Q-8; elev. 439ft./134m.; 🄿 🄷; **z** 62274; Ⓟ 3,372; © 5,464
Pine Creek; MCD-Township; OGLE; ***170** C-8; mail Polo **z** 61064; Ⓟ 726; © 719
Pinecrest; RMC Place; WILL; ***170** D-12; ★ **CHI**; mail Joliet **z** 60435; ● 300
Pinegate Manor; RMC Place; COOK; ★ **CHI**; pop. incl. with Arlington Heights (Inc. Place)
Pinehurst Manor; RMC Place; COOK; ***170** B-12; ★ **CHI**; mail Palatine **z** 60074; pop. incl. with Palatine (Inc. Place)
Pine Meadow; RMC Place; WILL; ★ **CHI**; mail Bolingbrook **z** 60440; pop. incl. with Bolingbrook (Inc. Place)
Pine Ridge; RMC Place; HENRY; ***170** D-6; elev. 700ft./213m.; mail Geneseo **z** 61254; ● 40
Pine Rock; MCD-Township; OGLE; ***170** C-9; mail Chana **z** 61015; Ⓟ 883; © 979
Pingree Grove; Inc. Place; KANE; **170** B-11; elev. 912ft./278m.; 🄿; ★ **CHI**; **z** 60140; Ⓟ 138; © 124
Pinkstaff; RMC Place; LAWRENCE; **171** N-13; mail Lawrenceville **z** 62439; ● 150
Pin Oak; MCD-Township; MADISON; ***171** N-7; mail Edwardsville **z** 62025; Ⓟ 2,007; © 2,607
Pioneer Acres; RMC Place; JO DAVIESS; ***170** A-5; elev. 700ft./213m.; ★ **DUB**; mail East Dubuque **z** 61025; ● 300
Pioneer Estates; RMC Place; COOK; ★ **CHI**; pop. incl. with Arlington Heights (Inc. Place)
Pioneer Terrace; RMC Place; DEKALB; ***170** C-10; elev. 900ft./274m.; ★ **DKLB**; mail DeKalb **z** 60115; ● 100
Piopolis; RMC Place; HAMILTON; ***171** P-11; mail Mc Leansboro **z** 62859
Piper City; Inc. Place; FORD; **170** G-12; elev. 668ft./204m.; 🄿; **z** 60959; Ⓟ 760; © 781
Pisgah; RMC Place; MORGAN; ***171** K-6; 🄿; **z** 62650
Pistakee Bay; RMC Place; LAKE, MCHENRY; ***170** A-12; ★ **CHI**; mail McHenry **z** 60050; ● 970
Pistakee Heights; RMC Place; LAKE; ★ **CHI**; mail McHenry **z** 60050; pop. incl. with Fox Lake (Inc. Place)
Pistakee Highlands; CDP; MCHENRY; ***170** A-12; ★ **CHI**; mail McHenry **z** 60050; Ⓟ 3,848; © 3,812
Pistakee Hills; RMC Place; MCHENRY; ***170** A-11; ★ **CHI**; mail McHenry **z** 60050; ● 1,400
Pistaqua Heights; RMC Place; LAKE, MCHENRY; ★ **CHI**; mail McHenry **z** 60050; ● 700
Pitchin; RMC Place; IROQUOIS; ***170** G-13; mail Cissna Park **z** 60924; rural
Pitman; MCD-Township; MONTGOMERY; ***171** L-8; mail Waggoner **z** 62572; Ⓟ 547; © 507
Pittsburg; RMC Place; FAYETTE; ***171** N-9; elev. 529ft./161m.; mail Vandalia **z** 62471
Pittsburg; Inc. Place; WILLIAMSON; **171** R-10; elev. 466ft./142m.; 🄿; ★ **CARB-**; **z** 62974 & mail Vandalia **z** 62471; Ⓟ 602; © 575
Pittsfield; Inc. Place; ⊡ PIKE; ▲ Pittsfield; **171** K-4; 🄿 🄷; **z** 62363; Ⓟ 4,231; © 4,211; Ⓡ 4,614
Pittsfield; MCD-Township; PIKE; ***171** K-4; 🄿; **z** 62363; Ⓟ 4,100; © 4,450
Pittwood; RMC Place; IROQUOIS; ***170** G-13; mail Watseka **z** 60970; ● 100
Pixley; MCD-Township; CLAY; ***171** N-11; mail Noble **z** 62868; Ⓟ 712; © 765
Plainfield; Inc. Place; WILL; ▲ Plainfield; **170** D-12; 🄿; ★ **CHI**; **z** 60544, **z** 60585-86; Ⓟ 4,557; © 13,038; ◆ 27,117
Plainfield; MCD-Township; WILL; ***170** D-12; 🄿; ★ **CHI**; **z** 60544, **z** 60585-86; Ⓟ 15,392; © 45,691
Plainfield Acres; RMC Place; WILL; ***170** D-12; ★ **CHI**; mail Plainfield **z** 60544; pop. incl. with Plainfield (Inc. Place)
Plainview; RMC Place; MACOUPIN; **171** M-7; elev. 617ft./188m.; 🄿; **z** 62685; ● 150
Plainville; Inc. Place; ADAMS; **170** J-3; elev. 693ft./211m.; 🄿; **z** 62365; Ⓟ 261; © 248
Plano; Inc. Place; KENDALL; **170** D-11; elev. 650ft./198m.; 🄿; ★ **CHI**; **z** 60545; Ⓟ 5,104; © 5,633
Plato; MCD-Township; KANE; ***170** B-11; ★ **CHI**; mail Elgin **z** 60123, Hampshire **z** 60140; Ⓟ 3,469; © 4,018
Plato Center; RMC Place; KANE; **172** F-1; elev. 920ft./280m.; 🄿; ★ **CHI**; **z** 60124, **z** 60170; ● 120
Plattville; Inc. Place; KENDALL; **170** D-11; mail Yorkville **z** 60560; incorporated March 21, 2006; not reported in 2000 Census; ● 200
Playfield; RMC Place; COOK; ★ **CHI**; mail Midlothian **z** 60445; pop. incl. with Crestwood (Inc. Place)
Pleasant; MCD-Township; FULTON; ***170** I-6; mail Ipava **z** 61441; Ⓟ 839; © 809
Pleasant Dale; RMC Place; COOK; ***170** C-12; ★ **CHI**; mail La Grange **z** 60525; pop. incl. with Burr Ridge (Inc. Place)
Pleasantdale Estates; RMC Place; DUPAGE; ***170** C-12; ★ **CHI**; mail Lemont **z** 60439; ● 1,000
Pleasant Grove; MCD-Township; COLES; ***171** L-11; mail Lerna **z** 62440; Ⓟ 1,283; © 1,403
Pleasant Grove; RMC Place; JOHNSON; ***171** S-9; mail Buncombe **z** 62912; rural
Pleasant Hill; RMC Place; DUPAGE; ***170** C-12; ★ **CHI**; mail Carol Stream **z** 60188; ● 3,700
Pleasant Hill; RMC Place; JACKSON; ***171** R-9; elev. 450ft./137m.; ★ **CARB-**; mail Carbondale **z** 62901; ● 30
Pleasant Hill; RMC Place; MCLEAN; ***170** G-10; mail Lexington **z** 61753; ● 25
Pleasant Hill; Inc. Place; PIKE; ▲ Pleasant Hill; **171** L-4; 🄿; **z** 62366; Ⓟ 1,030; © 1,047
Pleasant Hill; MCD-Township; PIKE; ***171** L-4; 🄿; **z** 62366; Ⓟ 1,387; © 1,355
Pleasant Hills; RMC Place; COOK; ***170** B-12; ★ **CHI**; mail Roselle **z** 60172; ● 450
Pleasant Mound; RMC Place; BOND; ▲ Pleasant Mound; **171** N-9; mail Smithboro **z** 62284; ● 100
Pleasant Mound; MCD-Township; BOND; ***171** N-8; mail Smithboro **z** 62284; Ⓟ 1,106; © 1,178
Pleasant Plains; Inc. Place; SANGAMON; **170** J-7; elev. 615ft./187m.; 🄿; **z** 62677; Ⓟ 701; © 777
Pleasant Ridge; MCD-Township; LIVINGSTON; ***170** G-11; mail Forrest **z** 61741; Ⓟ 288; © 302
Pleasant Ridge; RMC Place; MADISON; ***171** N-7; ★ **ST.L**; mail Maryville **z** 62062; pop. incl. with Maryville (Inc. Place)
Pleasant Run; RMC Place; COOK; ★ **CHI**; mail Wheeling **z** 60090; pop. incl. with Wheeling (Inc. Place)
Pleasant Vale; MCD-Township; PIKE; ***171** K-4; mail New Canton **z** 62356; Ⓟ 658; © 673
Pleasant Valley; MCD-Township; JO DAVIESS; ***170** B-7; mail Stockton **z** 61085; Ⓟ 291; © 260
Pleasant View; MCD-Township; MACON; ***171** K-9; mail Blue Mound **z** 62513; Ⓟ 1,486; © 1,428
Pleasant View; RMC Place; SCHUYLER; ***170** I-5; 🄿; **z** 62681; ● 80
Plumfield; RMC Place; FRANKLIN; ***171** Q-9; elev. 399ft./122m.; ★ **CARB-**; mail West Frankfort **z** 62896; ● 150
Plum Grove Countryside; RMC Place; COOK; ★ **CHI**; mail Palatine **z** 60067; pop. incl. with Palatine (Inc. Place)
Plum Grove Estates; RMC Place; COOK; ***170** B-12; ★ **CHI**; mail Palatine **z** 60067; ● 990
Plum Grove Hills; RMC Place; COOK; ★ **CHI**; mail Rolling Meadows **z** 60008; pop. incl. with Rolling Meadows (Inc. Place)
Plum Grove Village; RMC Place; COOK; ★ **CHI**; mail Rolling Meadows **z** 60008; pop. incl. with Rolling Meadows (Inc. Place)
Plum Grove Woods; RMC Place; COOK; ★ **CHI**; mail Palatine **z** 60067; ● 200
Plum Hill; RMC Place; WASHINGTON; ▲ Plum Hill; ***171** P-8; mail Addieville **z** 62214; ● 20
Plum Hill; MCD-Township; WASHINGTON; ***171** P-8; mail Addieville **z** 62214; Ⓟ 539; © 541
Plum Hollow; RMC Place; LEE; ***170** C-8; mail Dixon **z** 61021; ● 30
Plum River; JO DAVIESS; see Morseville (RMC Place)
Plymouth; Inc. Place; HANCOCK, MCDONOUGH; **170** I-4; elev. 656ft./200m.; 🄿; **z** 62367; Ⓟ 521; © 562
Plymouth Farms; RMC Place; LAKE; ★ **CHI**; mail Vernon Hills **z** 60061; pop. incl. with Vernon Hills (Inc. Place)
Poag; RMC Place; MADISON; **195** C-9; ★ **ST.L**; mail Edwardsville **z** 62025; ● 60
Pocahontas; Inc. Place; BOND; **171** N-8; elev. 570ft./174m.; 🄿; **z** 62275; Ⓟ 837; © 727
Point Pleasant; MCD-Township; WARREN; ***170** G-5; mail Roseville **z** 61473; Ⓟ 193; © 173
Polk; MCD-Township; MACOUPIN; ***171** M-7; mail Carlinville **z** 62626; Ⓟ 467; © 514
Polo; Inc. Place; OGLE; **170** B-8; elev. 874ft./266m.; 🄿; **z** 61064; Ⓟ 2,514; © 2,477
Pomona; RMC Place; JACKSON; ▲ Pomona; ***171** R-8; 🄿; **z** 62975; ● 80
Pomona; MCD-Township; JACKSON; ***171** R-8; 🄿; **z** 62975; Ⓟ 769; © 843
Pond; RMC Place; JOHNSON; ***171** S-10; elev. 528ft./161m.; mail Vienna **z** 62995; rural

Entries in **UPPERCASE** are counties.
Entries in **bold** have populations of 2,500 or more.
Names in parentheses are alternate names.
Inc. Place — Incorporated Place
RMC Place — Rand McNally Designated Place
CDP — Census Designated Place
MCD — Minor Civil Division

⊡ County Seat
▲ Minor Civil Division
elev. Elevation
🄿 Post Office
🄷 Hospital
🄲 College
■ Principal Business Center
★ Ranally Metro Area (RMA) Abbreviation
z Zip Code(s)
Ⓟ Previous Census Population
Ⓡ Revised Census Population
Ⓐ Annexation Population
● Rand McNally Population Estimate
© Final Census Population
Ⓢ Special Census Population
◆ Estimated Population

For additional definitions see Glossary, Volume 1, and Introduction, Volume 2.

Pontiac; Inc. Place; ⊡ LIVINGSTON; ▲ Pontiac; **170** G-10; elev. 642ft./196m.; 🅿 🅷; **z** 61764; Ⓟ 11,428; Ⓒ 11,864
Pontiac; MCD-Township; LIVINGSTON; ***170** F-10; 🅿; **z** 61764; Ⓟ 12,923; Ⓒ 13,148
Pontiac; RMC Place; ST. CLAIR; ***171** O-7; ★ **ST.L**; mail Caseyville **z** 62232; pop. incl. with Fairview Heights (Inc. Place)
Pontiac Station; RMC Place; ST. CLAIR; ★ **ST.L**; mail Fairview Heights **z** 62208; pop. incl. with Fairview Heights (Inc. Place)
Pontoon Beach; Inc. Place; MADISON; **195** D-8; elev. 415ft./126m.; 🅿; ★ **ST.L**; **z** 62040; Ⓟ 4,013; Ⓒ 5,620
Pontoosuc; Inc. Place; HANCOCK; ▲ Pontoosuc; **170** G-3; 🅿; **z** 62330; Ⓟ 264; Ⓒ 171
Pontoosuc; MCD-Township; HANCOCK; ***170** G-3; 🅿; **z** 62330; Ⓟ 473; Ⓒ 423
Pope; MCD-Township; FAYETTE; ***171** N-9; mail Patoka **z** 62875; Ⓟ 250; Ⓒ 226
POPE; **171** S-11; Ⓟ 4,373; Ⓒ 4,413; ◆ 4,106
Poplar City; RMC Place; MASON; ***170** I-7; 🅿; **z** 62633; rural
Poplar Creek; RMC Place; COOK; ★ **CHI**; pop. incl. with Elgin (Inc. Place)
Poplar Grove; Inc. Place; BOONE; ▲ Poplar Grove, Belvidere; **170** A-10; 🅿; **z** 61065; Ⓟ 743; Ⓒ 1,368
Poplar Grove; MCD-Township; BOONE; ***170** A-10; 🅿; **z** 61065; Ⓟ 1,984; Ⓒ 3,176
Poplar Grove; RMC Place; ROCK ISLAND; ***170** D-5; elev. 564ft./172m.; ★ **D-RI-M**; mail East Moline **z** 61244; pop. incl. with Moline (Inc. Place)
Poplar Ridge; RMC Place; WILL; ★ **CHI**; pop. incl. with Romeoville (Inc. Place)
Portage Park; RMC Place; COOK; ★ **CHI**; mail Chicago **z** 60641; pop. incl. with Chicago (Inc. Place)
Port Barrington (Fox River Valley Gardens); Inc. Place; MCHENRY, LAKE; **172** C-3; elev. 740ft./226m.; 🅿; ★ **CHI**; **z** 60010; Ⓟ 665; Ⓒ 788; Ⓡ 804
Port Byron; Inc. Place; ROCK ISLAND; ▲ Port Byron; **170** D-6; 🅿; ★ **D-RI-M**; **z** 61275; Ⓟ 1,002; Ⓒ 1,535
Port Byron; MCD-Township; ROCK ISLAND; ***170** D-6; 🅿; ★ **D-RI-M**; **z** 61275; includes part of the Village of Port Byron; Ⓟ 1,114; Ⓒ 1,396
Portland (Portland Corners); RMC Place; WHITESIDE; ***170** D-7; mail Prophetstown **z** 61277
Portland; MCD-Township; WHITESIDE; ***170** D-7; mail Prophetstown **z** 61277; Ⓟ 471; Ⓒ 437
Portland Corners; WHITESIDE; see Portland (RMC Place)
Port Ridge; RMC Place; WILL; ★ **CHI**; mail Lockport **z** 60441; pop. incl. with Lockport (Inc. Place)
Posen; Inc. Place; COOK; **172** L-9; elev. 600ft./183m.; 🅿; ★ **CHI**; **z** 60469; Ⓟ 4,226; Ⓒ 4,730
Posen; RMC Place; WASHINGTON; ***171** P-8; mail Nashville **z** 62263
Posey; RMC Place; CLINTON; **171** O-8; elev. 466ft./142m.; mail Carlyle **z** 62231; ● 75
Post Oak; RMC Place; FAYETTE; ***171** M-10; elev. 602ft./183m.; mail Brownstown **z** 62418; rural
Potomac; Inc. Place; VERMILION; **170** I-13; elev. 670ft./204m.; 🅿; **z** 61865; Ⓟ 753; Ⓒ 681
Pottawatawi Highlands; RMC Place; COOK; ***170** D-13; elev. 700ft./213m.; ★ **CHI**; mail Tinley Park **z** 60477; pop. incl. with Tinley Park (Inc. Place)
Pottstown; RMC Place; PEORIA; **173** B-15; ★ **PEOR**; mail Peoria **z** 61614; ● 70
Powder Creek; RMC Place; ST. CLAIR; ★ **ST.L**; mail Belleville **z** 62223
Powder Mill Woods; RMC Place; ST. CLAIR; ★ **ST.L**; mail Belleville **z** 62220
Powellton; RMC Place; HANCOCK; ***170** H-3; elev. 694ft./212m.; mail Niota **z** 62358; rural
Prairie; MCD-Township; CRAWFORD; ***171** M-13; mail Martinsville **z** 62442; Ⓟ 694; Ⓒ 631
Prairie; MCD-Township; EDGAR; ***170** J-13; mail Chrisman **z** 61924; Ⓟ 315; Ⓒ 370
Prairie; MCD-Township; HANCOCK; ***170** H-3; mail Carthage **z** 62321; Ⓟ 449; Ⓒ 385
Prairie; RMC Place; RANDOLPH; ***171** P-7; mail Burnt Prairie **z** 62820, Red Bud **z** 62278; ● 50
Prairie; MCD-Township; SHELBY; ***171** L-10; mail Stewardson **z** 62463; Ⓟ 1,219; Ⓒ 1,267
Prairie Center; RMC Place; LA SALLE; ***170** D-10; mail Ottawa **z** 61350; ● 30
Prairie City; Inc. Place; MCDONOUGH; ▲ Prairie City; **170** G-5; elev. 667ft./203m.; 🅿; **z** 61470; Ⓟ 497; Ⓒ 461
Prairie City; MCD-Township; MCDONOUGH; ***170** G-5; 🅿; **z** 61470; Ⓟ 651; Ⓒ 595
Prairie Creek; MCD-Township; LOGAN; ***170** I-8; mail Emden **z** 62635; Ⓟ 556; Ⓒ 533
Prairie Du Long; MCD-Township; ST. CLAIR; ***171** P-7; mail Freeburg **z** 62243; Ⓟ 1,025; Ⓒ 1,352
Prairie du Pont; ST. CLAIR; see North Dupo (RMC Place)
Prairie du Rocher; Inc. Place; RANDOLPH; **171** Q-6; elev. 396ft./121m.; 🅿; **z** 62261, **z** 62277; Ⓟ 540; Ⓒ 613
Prairie Estates; RMC Place; MENARD; ***170** J-7; elev. 600ft./183m.; mail Petersburg **z** 62675; ● 30
Prairie Green; MCD-Township; IROQUOIS; ***170** H-13; mail Hoopeston **z** 60942; Ⓟ 268; Ⓒ 233
Prairie Grove; Inc. Place; MCHENRY; **172** C-3; elev. 847ft./258m.; ★ **CHI**; mail Crystal Lake **z** 60012, McHenry **z** 60050; Ⓟ 654; Ⓒ 960
Prairie Home; RMC Place; SHELBY; ***171** K-10; elev. 698ft./213m.; mail Moweaqua **z** 62550; rural
Prairieton; MCD-Township; CHRISTIAN; ***171** K-9; mail Moweaqua **z** 62550; Ⓟ 537; Ⓒ 492
Prairietown; RMC Place; MADISON; ***171** M-7; mail Worden **z** 62097; ● 250
Prairie View; RMC Place; LAKE; **172** D-6; elev. 675ft./206m.; 🅿; ★ **CHI**; **z** 60069; pop. incl. with Buffalo Grove (Inc. Place)
Prairieville; RMC Place; LEE; ***170** C-8; elev. 717ft./219m.; mail Dixon **z** 61021; ● 60
Preemption; RMC Place; MERCER; ▲ Preemption; **170** E-5; elev. 806ft./246m.; 🅿; **z** 61276; ● 350
Preemption; MCD-Township; MERCER; ***170** E-5; 🅿; **z** 61276; Ⓟ 1,796; Ⓒ 1,837
Prentice; RMC Place; MORGAN; **170** J-6; 🅿; **z** 62612; ● 30
Presswood Hills; RMC Place; PERRY; ***171** Q-8; elev. 481ft./147m.; mail Pinckneyville **z** 62274; ● 70
Prestbury; RMC Place; KANE; ***170** C-11; elev. 710ft./216m.; ★ **CHI**; mail Aurora **z** 60506; ● 600
Preston; RMC Place; RANDOLPH; ***171** Q-7; mail Evansville **z** 62242; ● 40
Preston; MCD-Township; RICHLAND; ***171** N-12; mail Olney **z** 62450; Ⓟ 1,306; Ⓒ 1,345
Preston Heights; CDP; WILL; **172** N-4; ★ **CHI**; mail Joliet **z** 60431; Ⓟ 2,750; Ⓒ 2,527
Prestwick; RMC Place; WILL; ***170** D-13; ★ **CHI**; mail Frankfort **z** 60423; pop. incl. with Frankfort (Inc. Place)
Prickett; RMC Place; MADISON; ★ **ST.L**; mail Edwardsville **z** 62025; pop. incl. with Edwardsville (Inc. Place)
Princeton; Inc. Place; ⊡ BUREAU; ▲ Princeton; **170** E-8; 🅿 🅷; **z** 61356; Ⓟ 7,197; Ⓒ 7,501
Princeton; MCD-Township; BUREAU; ***170** E-8; 🅿; **z** 61356; includes part of the City of Princeton; Ⓟ 8,966; Ⓒ 9,164
Princeville; Inc. Place; PEORIA; **170** F-7; elev. 740ft./226m.; 🅿; **z** 61559; Ⓟ 1,421; Ⓒ 1,621
Princeville; MCD-Township; PEORIA; ***170** F-7; 🅿; **z** 61559; includes part of the Village of Princeville; Ⓟ 1,564; Ⓒ 1,599
Proctor; RMC Place; FORD; ***170** H-11; elev. 741ft./226m.; mail Gibson City **z** 60936; rural
Prophetstown; Inc. Place; WHITESIDE; ▲ Prophetstown; **170** D-7; elev. 618ft./188m.; 🅿; **z** 61277; Ⓟ 1,749; Ⓒ 2,023
Prophetstown; MCD-Township; WHITESIDE; ***170** D-7; 🅿; **z** 61277; Ⓟ 2,569; Ⓒ 2,642
Prospect; RMC Place; CHAMPAIGN; ***170** I-12; mail Rantoul **z** 61866; rural
Prospect Heights; Inc. Place; COOK; **172** E-6; elev. 668ft./204m.; 🅿; ★ **CHI**; **z** 60070; Ⓟ 15,239; Ⓒ 17,081; Ⓡ 17,061
Prospect Meadows; RMC Place; COOK; ***170** B-12; ★ **CHI**; mail Mount Prospect **z** 60056; pop. incl. with Mount Prospect (Inc. Place)
Prospect Park; RMC Place; COOK; ★ **CHI**; pop. incl. with Arlington Heights (Inc. Place)
Prospect Park; RMC Place; ST. CLAIR; ★ **ST.L**; mail Fairview Heights **z** 62208; pop. incl. with Fairview Heights (Inc. Place)
Providence; RMC Place; BUREAU; ***170** E-8; mail Tiskilwa **z** 61368; rural
Provincetown; RMC Place; COOK; ★ **CHI**; mail Country Club Hills **z** 60478; pop. incl. with Country Club Hills (Inc. Place)
Proviso; MCD-Township; COOK; ***170** C-12; ★ **CHI**; mail Melrose Park **z** 60160; Ⓟ 152,443; Ⓒ 155,831
Pruett; RMC Place; FAYETTE; ***171** M-10; mail Saint Elmo **z** 62458; rural
Pujol; RANDOLPH; see Dozaville (RMC Place)
Pulaski; Inc. Place; PULASKI; **171** T-9; elev. 343ft./105m.; 🅿; **z** 62976; Ⓟ 361; Ⓒ 274
PULASKI; **171** T-9; Ⓟ 7,523; Ⓒ 7,348; ◆ 6,306
Pulleys Mill; RMC Place; WILLIAMSON; **171** R-9; mail Goreville **z** 62939; ● 60
Pullman; RMC Place; COOK; ***170** D-13; elev. 589ft./180m.; ★ **CHI**; mail Chicago **z** 60628; pop. incl. with Chicago (Inc. Place)
Pullman Junction; RMC Place; COOK; ★ **CHI**; mail Chicago **z** 60617; pop. incl. with Chicago (Inc. Place)
Putman; MCD-Township; FULTON; ***170** H-6; mail Cuba **z** 61427; Ⓟ 2,169; Ⓒ 2,198
Putnam; RMC Place; PUTNAM; **170** E-8; elev. 515ft./157m.; 🅿; **z** 61560; ● 200
PUTNAM; **170** E-8; Ⓟ 5,730; Ⓒ 6,086; ◆ 6,168

Q

Quarry; MCD-Township; JERSEY; ***171** M-5; mail Grafton **z** 62037; Ⓟ 1,294; Ⓒ 1,090
Quatoga; RMC Place; MADISON; mail Godfrey **z** 62035; ● 150
Quincy; Inc. Place; ⊡ ADAMS; **170** J-3; elev. 601ft./183m.; 🅿 🅷 🅲 1,250 ■; ★ **QUIN**; **z** 62301, **z** 62305-06; Ⓟ 39,682; Ⓒ 40,366; ◆ 38,785
Quincy; MCD-Township; ADAMS; ***170** J-3; 🅿 🅷 🅲 1,250; ★ **QUIN**; **z** 62301, **z** 62305-06; coextensive with the City of Quincy; Ⓟ 39,682; Ⓒ 40,366
Quiver; MCD-Township; MASON; ***170** H-7; mail Havana **z** 62644; Ⓟ 969; Ⓒ 1,049
Quiver Beach; RMC Place; MASON; ***170** H-6; mail Havana **z** 62644; ● 250

R

Raccoon; MCD-Township; MARION; ***171** O-9; mail Centralia **z** 62801; Ⓟ 1,386; Ⓒ 1,395
Raddle; RMC Place; JACKSON; ***171** R-8; mail Jacob **z** 62950; rural
Radford; RMC Place; CHRISTIAN; ***171** K-9; 🅿; **z** 62550; rural
Radnor; MCD-Township; PEORIA; ***170** G-7; mail Dunlap **z** 61525; Ⓟ 2,044; Ⓒ 2,433
Radom; Inc. Place; WASHINGTON; **171** P-9; elev. 531ft./162m.; 🅿; **z** 62876; Ⓟ 174; Ⓒ 395
Railport; RMC Place; COOK; pop. incl. with Chicago (Inc. Place)
Rainbow Hills; RMC Place; KANE; ***170** C-11; elev. 800ft./244m.; ★ **CHI**; mail Saint Charles **z** 60175; ● 130
Rakers Addition; RMC Place; CLINTON; ***171** O-8; elev. 450ft./137m.; ★ **ST.L**; mail Aviston **z** 62216; pop. incl. with Aviston (Inc. Place)
Raleigh; Inc. Place; SALINE; ▲ Raleigh; **171** R-11; 🅿; **z** 62977; Ⓟ 305; Ⓒ 330
Raleigh; MCD-Township; SALINE; ***171** R-11; 🅿; **z** 62977; Ⓟ 1,150; Ⓒ 1,124
Ramona Place; RMC Place; MADISON; ★ **ST.L**; mail Godfrey **z** 62035; pop. incl. with Godfrey (Inc. Place)
Ramsey; Inc. Place; FAYETTE; ▲ Ramsey; **171** M-9; 🅿; **z** 62080; Ⓟ 963; Ⓒ 1,056
Ramsey; MCD-Township; FAYETTE; ***171** M-9; 🅿; **z** 62080; Ⓟ 1,743; Ⓒ 1,885
Randall Ridge; RMC Place; KANE; ***170** B-11; ★ **CHI**; mail Elgin **z** 60123; pop. incl. with Elgin (Inc. Place)
Randolph; RMC Place; MCLEAN; ▲ Randolph; ***170** H-9; elev. 789ft./240m.; mail Heyworth **z** 61745; rural
Randolph; MCD-Township; MCLEAN; ***170** H-9; mail Heyworth **z** 61745; Ⓟ 2,934; Ⓒ 3,856
RANDOLPH; **171** P-7; Ⓟ 34,583; Ⓒ 33,893; ◆ 32,318
Range; RMC Place; JEFFERSON; mail Mount Vernon **z** 62864; rural
Rankin; Inc. Place; VERMILION; **170** H-12; elev. 710ft./216m.; 🅿; **z** 60960; Ⓟ 619; Ⓒ 617
Ransom; Inc. Place; LA SALLE; **170** E-10; elev. 700ft./213m.; 🅿; **z** 60470; Ⓟ 438; Ⓒ 409
Rantoul; Inc. Place; CHAMPAIGN; **170** I-12; elev. 748ft./228m.; 🅿; **z** 61866; Ⓟ 17,212; Ⓒ 12,857; Ⓡ 12,918
Rantoul; MCD-Township; CHAMPAIGN; ***170** I-12; 🅿; **z** 61866; Ⓟ 15,691; Ⓒ 11,196; Ⓡ 11,257
Rapatee; RMC Place; KNOX; **170** G-6; mail London Mills **z** 61544; ● 80
Rapids City; Inc. Place; ROCK ISLAND; **170** D-6; elev. 593ft./181m.; 🅿; ★ **D-RI-M**; **z** 61278; Ⓟ 932; Ⓒ 953
Rardin; RMC Place; COLES; **171** K-12; elev. 664ft./202m.; mail Charleston **z** 61920; ● 160
Raritan; Inc. Place; HENDERSON; ▲ Raritan; **170** G-4; 🅿; **z** 61471; Ⓟ 146; Ⓒ 140
Raritan; MCD-Township; HENDERSON; ***170** G-4; 🅿; **z** 61471; Ⓟ 345; Ⓒ 322
Rasmussen Addition; RMC Place; FORD; ***170** H-11; mail Gibson City **z** 60936; ● 100
Raven; RMC Place; EDGAR; ***170** J-13; elev. 625ft./191m.; mail Chrisman **z** 61924; rural
Ravenswood; RMC Place; COOK; ***170** C-13; ★ **CHI**; mail Chicago **z** 60625; pop. incl. with Chicago (Inc. Place)
Ravinia; RMC Place; LAKE; ***170** B-13; ★ **CHI**; mail Highland Park **z** 60035; pop. incl. with Highland Park (Inc. Place)
Ravinia Park; RMC Place; LAKE; ★ **CHI**; mail Highland Park **z** 60035; pop. incl. with Highland Park (Inc. Place)
Rawalts; RMC Place; FULTON; ***170** H-7; elev. 627ft./191m.; mail Canton **z** 61520; rural
Rawlins; MCD-Township; JO DAVIESS; ***170** A-5; mail Galena **z** 61036; Ⓟ 344; Ⓒ 360
Ray; RMC Place; SCHUYLER; ***170** I-5; elev. 535ft./163m.; 🅿; **z** 62681; ● 30
Raymond; MCD-Township; CHAMPAIGN; ***170** J-12; mail Longview **z** 61852; Ⓟ 459; Ⓒ 437
Raymond; Inc. Place; MONTGOMERY; ▲ Raymond; **171** L-8; 🅿; **z** 62560; Ⓟ 820; Ⓒ 927
Raymond; MCD-Township; MONTGOMERY; ***171** L-8; 🅿; **z** 62560; Ⓟ 1,179; Ⓒ 1,204
Raynor Park; RMC Place; WILL; ***170** D-12; ★ **CHI**; pop. incl. with Joliet (Inc. Place)
Reader; RMC Place; MACOUPIN; ***171** L-6; elev. 584ft./178m.; mail Chesterfield **z** 62630; rural
Reading; RMC Place; LIVINGSTON; ▲ Reading; ***170** F-10; mail Ancona **z** 61311; ● 30
Reading; MCD-Township; LIVINGSTON; ***170** F-10; mail Ancona **z** 61311; Ⓟ 2,379; Ⓒ 2,247
Rector; MCD-Township; SALINE; ***171** Q-11; mail Eldorado **z** 62930; Ⓟ 76; Ⓒ 81
Red Bud; Inc. Place; RANDOLPH; **171** P-7; elev. 479ft./146m.; 🅿 🅷; **z** 62278; Ⓟ 2,918; Ⓒ 3,422
Reddick; Inc. Place; KANKAKEE, LIVINGSTON; **170** F-11; elev. 610ft./186m.; 🅿; **z** 60961; Ⓟ 208; Ⓒ 219
Redmon; Inc. Place; EDGAR; **171** K-13; elev. 690ft./210m.; 🅿; **z** 61949; Ⓟ 201; Ⓒ 199
Red Oak; RMC Place; STEPHENSON; ***170** A-8; mail Freeport **z** 61032; ● 90
Red Oak Terrace; RMC Place; LAKE; ★ **CHI**; mail Highland Park **z** 60035; pop. incl. with Highland Park (Inc. Place)
Reed; MCD-Township; WILL; ***170** E-12; ★ **CHI**; mail Braidwood **z** 60408; Ⓟ 4,086; Ⓒ 6,051
Reed City; RMC Place; PEORIA; mail Mapleton **z** 61547; rural
Reeds Station; RMC Place; JACKSON; ***171** R-9; elev. 409ft./125m.; mail De Soto **z** 62924; rural
Rees; RMC Place; MORGAN; ***171** K-6; elev. 696ft./212m.; 🅿; **z** 62638; rural
Reevesville; RMC Place; JOHNSON; ***171** S-10; mail Grantsburg **z** 62943; ● 160
Regency Grove; RMC Place; DUPAGE; ***170** C-12; ★ **CHI**; mail Downers Grove **z** 60515; ● 430
Regency Terrace; RMC Place; DUPAGE; ★ **CHI**; mail Bloomingdale **z** 60108; pop. incl. with Bloomingdale (Inc. Place)
Reilly; RMC Place; VERMILION; ***170** H-13; elev. 750ft./229m.; mail Rankin **z** 60960
Reily Lake; RMC Place; RANDOLPH; ***171** Q-7; mail Ellis Grove **z** 62241; rural
Rellswood Hills; RMC Place; BOONE; ***170** A-10; elev. 863ft./263m.; ★ **RKFD**; mail Belvidere **z** 61008; ● 60
Renault; RMC Place; MONROE; **171** P-6; elev. 684ft./208m.; 🅿; **z** 62279; ● 200
Renchville; RMC Place; PEORIA; ★ **PEOR**; mail Chillicothe **z** 61523; ● 150
Rend; FRANKLIN; see Rend City (RMC Place)
Rend City (Rend); RMC Place; FRANKLIN; ***171** Q-9; mail Benton **z** 62812; ● 50
Reno; RMC Place; BOND; ***171** M-8; mail Greenville **z** 62246, Sorento **z** 62086; ● 50
Rentchler; RMC Place; ST. CLAIR; ***171** O-7; ★ **ST.L**; mail Belleville **z** 62221; ● 100
Reseda; RMC Place; COOK; ★ **CHI**; mail Palatine **z** 60067; pop. incl. with Palatine (Inc. Place)
Resthaven; RMC Place; WILL; ***170** E-12; mail Wilmington **z** 60481; ● 350
Reynolds; MCD-Township; LEE; ***170** C-9; mail Ashton **z** 61006; Ⓟ 345; Ⓒ 333
Reynolds; Inc. Place; ROCK ISLAND, MERCER; **170** E-5; elev. 800ft./244m.; 🅿; **z** 61279; Ⓟ 583; Ⓒ 508
Reynoldsburg; RMC Place; JOHNSON; ***171** S-10; mail Ozark **z** 62972; ● 20
Reynoldsville; RMC Place; UNION; ***171** S-8; mail Jonesboro **z** 62952
Rice; MCD-Township; JO DAVIESS; ***170** A-6; mail Galena **z** 61036; Ⓟ 296; Ⓒ 306
Rice; RMC Place; PERRY; **171** P-8; mail Pinckneyville **z** 62274; ● 100
Rice Lake; RMC Place; KNOX; ***170** F-6; elev. 788ft./240m.; ★ **GLSB**; mail Galesburg **z** 61401; ● 50
Rich; MCD-Township; COOK; ***170** D-13; ★ **CHI**; mail Richton Park **z** 60471; Ⓟ 61,458; Ⓒ 67,623
Richards; RMC Place; GRUNDY; ***170** E-11; elev. 525ft./160m.; mail Morris **z** 60450; ● 130
Richards; RMC Place; LA SALLE; ***170** E-10; elev. 639ft./195m.; mail Streator **z** 61364; rural
Richardson; RMC Place; KANE; ***170** C-11; mail Maple Park **z** 60151; rural
Richardson Estates; RMC Place; CHAMPAIGN; ***170** I-12; elev. 725ft./221m.; ★ **CH-U**; mail Urbana **z** 61802; ● 150
Richfield; RMC Place; ADAMS; ▲ Richfield; ***170** J-3; mail Liberty **z** 62347, Plainville **z** 62365; ● 40
Richfield; MCD-Township; ADAMS; ***170** J-4; mail Plainville **z** 62365; Ⓟ 431; Ⓒ 419
Richland; MCD-Township; LA SALLE; ***170** F-9; mail Lostant **z** 61334; Ⓟ 437; Ⓒ 354
Richland; MCD-Township; MARSHALL; ***170** F-8; mail Washburn **z** 61570; Ⓟ 493; Ⓒ 477
Richland; RMC Place; SANGAMON; ***170** J-7; 🅿; **z** 62677; rural
Richland; MCD-Township; SHELBY; ***171** L-10; mail Strasburg **z** 62465; Ⓟ 777; Ⓒ 915
RICHLAND; **171** O-12; Ⓟ 16,545; Ⓒ 16,149; ◆ 15,509
Richland Grove; MCD-Township; MERCER; ***170** E-5; mail Sherrard **z** 61281; Ⓟ 2,192; Ⓒ 2,294
Richmond; Inc. Place; MCHENRY; ▲ Richmond; **170** A-11; 🅿; ★ **CHI**; **z** 60071; Ⓟ 1,016; Ⓒ 1,091
Richmond; MCD-Township; MCHENRY; ***170** A-11; 🅿; ★ **CHI**; **z** 60071; Ⓟ 3,286; Ⓒ 4,934
Richton; COOK; see Richton Park (Inc. Place)
Richton Hills; RMC Place; COOK; ★ **CHI**; mail Richton Park **z** 60471; pop. incl. with Richton Park (Inc. Place)
Richton Park (Richton); Inc. Place; COOK; **170** D-13; elev. 710ft./216m.; 🅿; ★ **CHI**; **z** 60471; Ⓟ 10,523; Ⓒ 12,533
Richview; Inc. Place; WASHINGTON; ▲ Richview; **171** P-9; 🅿; **z** 62877; Ⓟ 307; Ⓒ 308
Richview; MCD-Township; WASHINGTON; ***171** P-9; 🅿; **z** 62877; Ⓟ 428; Ⓒ 407
Richwood; MCD-Township; JERSEY; ***171** M-5; mail Fieldon **z** 62031; Ⓟ 644; Ⓒ 702
Richwoods; RMC Place; CRAWFORD; ***171** M-13; elev. 459ft./140m.; mail Palestine **z** 62451; ● 35
Richwoods; MCD-Township; PEORIA; ***170** G-8; ★ **PEOR**; mail Peoria **z** 61614; Ⓟ 6,890; Ⓒ 6,539
Ricks; MCD-Township; CHRISTIAN; ***171** L-8; mail Morrisonville **z** 62546; Ⓟ 1,348; Ⓒ 1,272
Riddle Hill; RMC Place; SANGAMON; ***170** J-7; 🅿; ★ **SPRG**; **z** 62707; ● 100
Ridge; MCD-Township; SHELBY; ***171** L-10; mail Shelbyville **z** 62565; Ⓟ 512; Ⓒ 454
Ridgecrest; RMC Place; GRUNDY; ***170** E-11; elev. 550ft./168m.; mail Morris **z** 60450; ● 350
Ridge Farm; Inc. Place; VERMILION; **170** J-13; elev. 700ft./213m.; 🅿; ★ **DANV**; **z** 61870; Ⓟ 939; Ⓒ 912
Ridgefield; RMC Place; MCHENRY; **172** B-1; ★ **CHI**; mail Crystal Lake **z** 60012; ● 120
Ridgeland; MCD-Township; IROQUOIS; ***170** G-12; mail Thawville **z** 60968; Ⓟ 374; Ⓒ 403
Ridgemoor; RMC Place; DUPAGE; ★ **CHI**; mail Hinsdale **z** 60521; pop. incl. with Willowbrook (Inc. Place)
Ridge Prairie Heights; RMC Place; ST. CLAIR; ★ **ST.L**; mail O Fallon **z** 62269; pop. incl. with O'Fallon (Inc. Place)
Ridgeville; RMC Place; IROQUOIS; ***170** G-12; mail Onarga **z** 60955
Ridgewood; RMC Place; COOK; ***170** C-12; ★ **CHI**; mail Western Springs **z** 60558; pop. incl. with Western Springs (Inc. Place)
Ridgewood; RMC Place; WILL; ***170** D-12; ★ **CHI**
Ridgewood East; RMC Place; COOK; ***170** D-13; elev. 675ft./206m.; ★ **CHI**; mail Oak Forest **z** 60452; pop. incl. with Oak Forest (Inc. Place)
Ridgewood West; RMC Place; COOK; ***170** D-13; elev. 700ft./213m.; ★ **CHI**; mail Oak Forest **z** 60452; pop. incl. with Oak Forest (Inc. Place)
Ridgway; Inc. Place; GALLATIN; **171** R-12; elev. 380ft./116m.; 🅿; **z** 62979; Ⓟ 1,103; Ⓒ 928
Ridgway; MCD-Township; GALLATIN; ***171** R-12; 🅿; **z** 62979; includes part of the Village of Ridgway; Ⓟ 1,094; Ⓒ 1,033
Ridott; Inc. Place; STEPHENSON; ▲ Ridott; **170** A-8; 🅿; **z** 61067; Ⓟ 156; Ⓒ 159
Ridott; MCD-Township; STEPHENSON; ***170** A-8; 🅿; **z** 61067; Ⓟ 1,656; Ⓒ 1,510
Rieuf's Meadows; RMC Place; LA SALLE; ***170** E-10; elev. 733ft./223m.; mail Marseilles **z** 61341; ● 50
Riffel; RMC Place; CLAY; ***171** N-11; mail Louisville **z** 62858; rural
Riggston; RMC Place; SCOTT; **171** K-5; elev. 600ft./183m.; 🅿; **z** 62694; ● 40
Riley; MCD-Township; MCHENRY; ***170** B-10; mail Garden Prairie **z** 61038; Ⓟ 1,431; Ⓒ 1,811
Riley Center; RMC Place; MCHENRY; mail Marengo **z** 60152; rural
Rinard; RMC Place; WAYNE; **171** O-11; elev. 458ft./140m.; 🅿; **z** 62878; ● 110
Ring Neck; RMC Place; KENDALL; ***170** D-11; elev. 720ft./219m.; ★ **CHI**; mail Oswego **z** 60543; ● 110
Ringwood; Inc. Place; MCHENRY; **170** A-11; elev. 840ft./256m.; 🅿; ★ **CHI**; **z** 60072; Ⓒ 471
Rio; Inc. Place; KNOX; ▲ Rio; **170** F-6; elev. 778ft./237m.; 🅿; **z** 61472; Ⓟ 260; Ⓒ 240
Rio; MCD-Township; KNOX; ***170** F-6; 🅿; **z** 61472; Ⓟ 622; Ⓒ 545
Ripley; Inc. Place; BROWN; ▲ Ripley; **170** J-5; elev. 557ft./170m.; mail Mount Sterling **z** 62353; Ⓟ 103; Ⓒ 103
Ripley; MCD-Township; BROWN; ***170** J-5; mail Mount Sterling **z** 62353; Ⓟ 133; Ⓒ 121
Rising Sun; RMC Place; WHITE; **171** Q-12; mail Carmi **z** 62821; ● 35
Risk; RMC Place; LIVINGSTON
Ritchason Addition; RMC Place; FRANKLIN; ***171** Q-10; elev. 400ft./122m.; ★ **CARB-**; mail West Frankfort **z** 62896; ● 50
Ritchie; RMC Place; WILL; **170** E-12; mail Wilmington **z** 60481; ● 60
Riverair; RMC Place; MADISON; ***171** N-6; ★ **ST.L**; mail Godfrey **z** 62035; pop. incl. with Godfrey (Inc. Place)
Riverdale; Inc. Place; COOK; **172** L-9; elev. 600ft./183m.; 🅿; ★ **CHI**; **z** 60827; Ⓟ 13,671; Ⓒ 15,055
Riverdale; RMC Place; WINNEBAGO; ***170** A-9; elev. 716ft./218m.; ★ **RKFD**; mail Roscoe **z** 61073; ● 250
River Forest; Inc. Place; COOK; **172** H-7; elev. 628ft./191m.; 🅿 🅲 4,366; ★ **CHI**; **z** 60305; Ⓟ 11,669; Ⓒ 11,635
River Forest; MCD-Township; COOK; ***170** C-13; 🅿 🅲 4,366; ★ **CHI**; **z** 60305; coextensive with the Village of River Forest; Ⓟ 11,669; Ⓒ 11,635
River Glen; RMC Place; LAKE; ★ **CHI**; mail Barrington **z** 60010; ● 200
River Grange Lakes; RMC Place; KANE; ***170** C-11; elev. 800ft./244m.; ★ **CHI**; mail Saint Charles **z** 60175; ● 150
River Grove; Inc. Place; COOK; **172** H-7; elev. 629ft./192m.; 🅿; ★ **CHI**; **z** 60171; Ⓟ 9,961; Ⓒ 10,668
River Heights; RMC Place; VERMILION; ★ **DANV**; mail Danville **z** 61832; pop. incl. with Danville (Inc. Place)
River Isle; RMC Place; KANKAKEE; ***170** E-13; elev. 622ft./190m.; ★ **KANK**; mail Momence **z** 60954; ● 90
River Reach; RMC Place; BOONE; ***170** B-10; elev. 782ft./238m.; mail Belvidere **z** 61008; ● 120
River Ridge; RMC Place; KENDALL; ***170** D-11; elev. 647ft./197m.; ★ **CHI**; mail Yorkville **z** 60560; rural
River Road; RMC Place; STEPHENSON; ***170** A-8; mail Ridott **z** 61067; ● 200
Riverside; MCD-Township; ADAMS; ***170** J-3; ★ **QUIN**; mail Quincy **z** 62305; Ⓟ 2,016; Ⓒ 2,397
Riverside; Inc. Place; COOK; **172** I-7; elev. 615ft./187m.; 🅿; ★ **CHI**; **z** 60546; Ⓟ 8,774; Ⓒ 8,895
Riverside; MCD-Township; COOK; ***170** C-13; 🅿; ★ **CHI**; **z** 60546; includes part of the Village of Riverside; Ⓟ 15,240; Ⓒ 15,704
Riverside Island; RMC Place; LAKE; ★ **CHI**; mail Fox Lake **z** 60020; pop. incl. with Fox Lake (Inc. Place)
Riverside Lawns; RMC Place; COOK; ***170** C-13; elev. 600ft./183m.; ★ **CHI**; mail Riverside **z** 60546; pop. incl. with Lyons (Inc. Place)
Riverside Park; RMC Place; MCHENRY; ★ **CHI**; mail McHenry **z** 60050; ● 100
Riverton; Inc. Place; SANGAMON; **170** J-8; elev. 552ft./168m.; 🅿; ★ **SPRG**; **z** 62561; Ⓟ 2,638; Ⓒ 3,048
Riverview; RMC Place; CARROLL; ***170** B-6; mail Thomson **z** 61285; ● 200
Riverview; RMC Place; LEE; ***170** C-8; mail Dixon **z** 61021; ● 80
Riverview; RMC Place; WHITESIDE; mail Rock Falls **z** 61071; ● 100
Riverview Heights; RMC Place; KENDALL; ★ **CHI**; mail Oswego **z** 60543; ● 230
Riverwoods; Inc. Place; LAKE; **172** D-7; elev. 650ft./198m.; 🅿; ★ **CHI**; **z** 60015; Ⓟ 2,868; Ⓒ 3,843
Rivoli; MCD-Township; MERCER; ***170** E-5; mail New Windsor **z** 61465; Ⓟ 1,171; Ⓒ 1,149
Roaches; RMC Place; JEFFERSON; ***171** P-9; mail Woodlawn **z** 62898; rural
Roachtown; RMC Place; ST. CLAIR; ***171** O-6; ★ **ST.L**; mail Millstadt **z** 62260; ● 30
Roanoke; Inc. Place; WOODFORD; ▲ Roanoke; **170** G-9; 🅿; **z** 61561; Ⓟ 1,910; Ⓒ 1,994
Roanoke; MCD-Township; WOODFORD; ***170** G-9; 🅿; **z** 61561; Ⓟ 2,500; Ⓒ 2,576
Robbins; Inc. Place; COOK; **172** L-9; elev. 600ft./183m.; 🅿; ★ **CHI**; **z** 60472; Ⓟ 7,498; Ⓒ 6,635
Robbs; RMC Place; POPE; ***171** S-10; elev. 449ft./137m.; 🅿; **z** 62985; ● 80
Robein; RMC Place; TAZEWELL; ***170** G-8; ★ **PEOR**; mail East Peoria **z** 61611; pop. incl. with East Peoria (Inc. Place)
Roberts; Inc. Place; FORD; **170** G-12; elev. 777ft./237m.; 🅿; **z** 60962; Ⓟ 397; Ⓒ 387
Roberts; MCD-Township; MARSHALL; ***170** F-9; mail Varna **z** 61375; Ⓟ 910; Ⓒ 970
Robin Hill; RMC Place; WILL; ★ **CHI**; mail Joliet **z** 60431; pop. incl. with Joliet (Inc. Place)
Robinson; Inc. Place; ⊡ CRAWFORD; ▲ Robinson; **171** M-13; 🅿 🅷; **z** 62454; Ⓟ 6,740; Ⓒ 6,822
Robinson; MCD-Township; CRAWFORD; ***171** M-13; 🅿; **z** 62454; Ⓟ 8,842; Ⓒ 10,138
Rob Roy Country Club; RMC Place; COOK; ***170** B-12; elev. 651ft./198m.; ★ **CHI**; mail Prospect Heights **z** 60070; pop. incl. with Prospect Heights (Inc. Place)
Roby; RMC Place; CHRISTIAN; **171** K-8; elev. 588ft./179m.; 🅿; **z** 62545; ● 80
Rochelle; Inc. Place; OGLE; **170** C-9; elev. 823ft./251m.; 🅿 🅷; **z** 61068; Ⓟ 8,769; Ⓒ 9,424
Rochester; Inc. Place; SANGAMON; **171** K-8; elev. 577ft./176m.; 🅿; ★ **SPRG**; **z** 62563; Ⓟ 2,676; Ⓒ 2,893
Rochester; MCD-Township; SANGAMON; ***171** K-8; 🅿; ★ **SPRG**; **z** 62563; Ⓟ 4,432; Ⓒ 4,486
Rochester; RMC Place; WABASH; ***171** P-13; elev. 395ft./120m.; mail Mount Carmel **z** 62863
Rock; RMC Place; POPE; ***171** S-10; mail Golconda **z** 62938; rural
Rockbridge; Inc. Place; GREENE; ▲ Rockbridge; **171** L-6; elev. 542ft./165m.; 🅿; **z** 62081; Ⓟ 212; Ⓒ 189
Rockbridge; MCD-Township; GREENE; ***171** L-6; 🅿; **z** 62081; Ⓟ 1,797; Ⓒ 1,775
Rock City; Inc. Place; STEPHENSON; **170** A-8; elev. 900ft./274m.; 🅿; **z** 61070; Ⓟ 286; Ⓒ 313
Rock Creek; MCD-Township; HANCOCK; ***170** H-3; mail Carthage **z** 62321; Ⓟ 431; Ⓒ 383
Rock Creek; RMC Place; HARDIN; ***171** S-12; elev. 562ft./171m.; mail Cave In Rock **z** 62919; rural
Rock Creek-Lima; MCD-Township; CARROLL; ***170** B-7; mail Lanark **z** 61046; Ⓟ 2,016; Ⓒ 2,171
Rockdale; Inc. Place; WILL; **172** N-4; elev. 550ft./168m.; 🅿; ★ **CHI**; **z** 60436; Ⓟ 1,709; Ⓒ 1,888
Rockdale Junction; RMC Place; WILL; ***170** D-12; ★ **CHI**; mail Joliet **z** 60436; pop. incl. with Crest Hill (Inc. Place)
Rock Falls; Inc. Place; WHITESIDE; **170** C-8; elev. 641ft./195m.; 🅿; **z** 61071; Ⓟ 9,654; Ⓒ 9,580
Rockford; Inc. Place; ⊡ WINNEBAGO; ▲ Rockford; **170** A-9; 🅿 🅷 🅲 1,110 ■; ★ **RKFD**; **z** 61101-10, **z** 61112, **z** 61114, **z** 61125-26; Ⓟ 140,003; Ⓒ 150,115; ◆ 159,746
Rockford; MCD-Township; WINNEBAGO; ***170** B-9; 🅿 🅲 1,110; ★ **RKFD**; **z** 61101-10, **z** 61112, **z** 61114, **z** 61125-26; includes part of the City of Rockford; Ⓟ 173,645; Ⓒ 178,853
Rockford Broadway; RMC Place; WINNEBAGO; ***170** B-9; ★ **RKFD**; mail Rockford **z** 61106; pop. incl. with Rockford (Inc. Place)
Rockford Main; RMC Place; WINNEBAGO; ★ **RKFD**; mail Rockford **z** 61125-26; pop. incl. with Rockford (Inc. Place)
Rockgate Estates; RMC Place; MADISON; ***171** N-6; ★ **ST.L**; mail Godfrey **z** 62035; ● 260
Rock Grove; RMC Place; STEPHENSON; ▲ Rock Grove; **170** A-8; elev. 942ft./287m.; mail Rock City **z** 61070; ● 150
Rock Grove; MCD-Township; STEPHENSON; ***170** A-8; mail Rock City **z** 61070; Ⓟ 1,134; Ⓒ 1,402
Rock Island; Inc. Place; ⊡ ROCK ISLAND; **170** D-5; elev. 560ft./171m.; 🅿 🅷 🅲 2,443 ■; ★ **D-RI-M**; **z** 61201, **z** 61204, **z** 61299; Ⓟ 40,552; Ⓒ 39,684; ◆ 39,770
Rock Island; MCD-Township; ROCK ISLAND; ***170** D-5; 🅿 🅲 2,443; ★ **D-RI-M**; **z** 61201, **z** 61204, **z** 61299; includes part of the City of Rock Island; Ⓟ 18,140; Ⓒ 17,763
ROCK ISLAND; **170** E-4; Ⓟ 148,723; Ⓒ 149,374; Ⓡ 149,388; ◆ 146,597
Rock Island Arsenal; CDP-Census Area Only; ROCK ISLAND; ***170** D-5; ★ **D-RI-M**; Ⓒ 145
Rock Island Junction; RMC Place; COOK; ★ **CHI**; pop. incl. with Chicago (Inc. Place)
Rockport; RMC Place; PIKE; **171** K-4; elev. 489ft./149m.; 🅿; **z** 62370; ● 200
Rock River Terrace; RMC Place; OGLE; ***170** B-9; mail Byron **z** 61010; ● 230
Rock Run; MCD-Township; STEPHENSON; ***170** A-8; mail Davis **z** 61019; Ⓟ 1,936; Ⓒ 2,252
Rockton; Inc. Place; WINNEBAGO; ▲ Rockton, Roscoe; **170** A-9; 🅿; ★ **RKFD**; **z** 61072; Ⓟ 2,928; Ⓒ 5,296
Rockton; MCD-Township; WINNEBAGO; ***170** A-9; 🅿; ★ **RKFD**; **z** 61072; Ⓟ 10,470; Ⓒ 13,534
Rockvale; MCD-Township; OGLE; ***170** B-8; mail Oregon **z** 61061; Ⓟ 1,336; Ⓒ 1,748
Rock Vale Heights; RMC Place; OGLE; ***170** B-9; mail Oregon **z** 61061; ● 50
Rockville; MCD-Township; KANKAKEE; ***170** E-12; mail Manteno **z** 60950; Ⓟ 614; Ⓒ 786
Rockwell; RMC Place; LA SALLE; mail La Salle **z** 61301; pop. incl. with La Salle (Inc. Place)
Rockwood; Inc. Place; RANDOLPH; **171** R-7; elev. 380ft./116m.; 🅿; **z** 62280; Ⓟ 45; Ⓒ 41
Rocky Run; MCD-Township; HANCOCK; ***170** I-3; mail Warsaw **z** 62379; Ⓟ 202; Ⓒ 158
Rodden; RMC Place; JO DAVIESS; ***170** A-6; mail Hanover **z** 61041; rural
Rogers; MCD-Township; FORD; ***170** F-12; mail Kempton **z** 60946; Ⓟ 460; Ⓒ 414
Rogers Park; RMC Place; COOK; ***170** B-13; ★ **CHI**; mail Chicago **z** 60626, **z** 60660; pop. incl. with Chicago (Inc. Place)
Rohrer; RMC Place; MORGAN; ***171** K-7; mail Waverly **z** 62692; rural
Rolling Acres; RMC Place; CHAMPAIGN; ***170** H-12; elev. 740ft./226m.; mail Rantoul **z** 61866
Rolling Acres; RMC Place; PEORIA; ***170** G-8; ★ **PEOR**; mail Peoria **z** 61614; pop. incl. with Peoria (Inc. Place)
Rolling Green; RMC Place; COLES; ***171** L-11; mail Mattoon **z** 61938; ● 250
Rolling Hills; RMC Place; CLINTON; ***171** O-7; elev. 495ft./151m.; ★ **ST.L**; mail Trenton **z** 62293; ● 30
Rolling Hills; RMC Place; PIATT; ***170** I-11; elev. 697ft./212m.; mail White Heath **z** 61884; ● 40
Rolling Meadows; Inc. Place; COOK; **172** E-5; elev. 700ft./213m.; 🅿; ★ **CHI**; **z** 60008; Ⓟ 22,591; Ⓒ 24,604; ◆ 25,118
Rollo; RMC Place; DEKALB; ***170** D-10; elev. 753ft./230m.; mail Earlville **z** 60518
Rome; JEFFERSON; see Dix (Inc. Place)
Rome; MCD-Township; JEFFERSON; ***171** O-9; mail Dix **z** 62830; Ⓟ 1,552; Ⓒ 1,831
Rome; CDP; PEORIA; **170** G-8; elev. 465ft./142m.; 🅿; ★ **PEOR**; **z** 61562; Ⓟ 1,902; Ⓒ 1,776
Rome Heights; RMC Place; PEORIA; ★ **PEOR**; mail Chillicothe **z** 61523; ● 150
Romeo; WILL; see Romeoville (Inc. Place)
Romeoville (Romeo); Inc. Place; WILL; **170** D-12; elev. 614ft./187m.; 🅿 🅲 5,290; ★ **CHI**; **z** 60446 & mail Lockport **z** 60441; Ⓟ 14,074; Ⓒ 21,153; ◆ 27,155
Romine; MCD-Township; MARION; ***171** O-10; mail Iuka **z** 62849; Ⓟ 409; Ⓒ 456
Rondout; RMC Place; LAKE; **172** B-7; ★ **CHI**; mail Lake Bluff **z** 60044; pop. incl. with Green Oaks (Inc. Place)
Ron Lee; RMC Place; WILL; ***170** D-12; ★ **CHI**; mail Joliet **z** 60431; ● 150
Roodhouse; Inc. Place; GREENE; ▲ Roodhouse; **171** L-6; 🅿; **z** 62082; Ⓟ 2,139; Ⓒ 2,214
Roodhouse; MCD-Township; GREENE; ***171** K-6; 🅿; **z** 62082; Ⓟ 2,542; Ⓒ 2,634
Rooks Creek; MCD-Township; LIVINGSTON; ***170** F-10; mail Pontiac **z** 61764; Ⓟ 483; Ⓒ 568
Rooney Heights; RMC Place; WILL; ***170** D-12; ★ **CHI**; mail Joliet **z** 60435; pop. incl. with Joliet (Inc. Place)
Roosevelt Road; RMC Place; COOK; mail Chicago **z** 60607; pop. incl. with Chicago (Inc. Place)
Roots; RMC Place; RANDOLPH; ***171** Q-7; mail Modoc **z** 62261; rural
Root Spring; RMC Place; MCHENRY; ***170** B-11; ★ **CHI**; mail Cary **z** 60013; pop. incl. with Fox River Grove (Inc. Place)
Ropers Landing; RMC Place; POPE; ***171** S-11; mail Golconda **z** 62938; rural
Rosamond; RMC Place; CHRISTIAN; ▲ Rosamond; **171** L-9; elev. 714ft./218m.; 🅿; **z** 62083; ● 200
Rosamond; MCD-Township; CHRISTIAN; ***171** L-9; 🅿; **z** 62083; Ⓟ 443; Ⓒ 400
Roscoe; Inc. Place; WINNEBAGO; ▲ Roscoe; **170** A-9; elev. 741ft./226m.; 🅿; ★ **RKFD**; **z** 61073; Ⓟ 2,079; Ⓒ 6,244
Roscoe; MCD-Township; WINNEBAGO; ***170** A-9; 🅿; ★ **RKFD**; **z** 61073; includes part of the City of Roscoe; Ⓟ 9,230; Ⓒ 13,578
Rose; MCD-Township; SHELBY; ***171** L-10; mail Shelbyville **z** 62565; Ⓟ 1,799; Ⓒ 1,789
Rosebud; RMC Place; POPE; ***171** T-11; mail Golconda **z** 62938; rural
Rosecrans; RMC Place; LAKE; ***170** A-12; elev. 720ft./219m.; ★ **CHI**; mail Wadsworth **z** 60083; ● 35
Rosedale; RMC Place; JERSEY; ▲ Rosedale; **171** M-5; elev. 454ft./138m.; mail Fieldon **z** 62031; ● 40
Rosedale; MCD-Township; JERSEY; ***171** M-5; mail Fieldon **z** 62031; Ⓟ 497; Ⓒ 476
Rosefield; MCD-Township; PEORIA; ***170** G-7; mail Elmwood **z** 61529; Ⓟ 1,021; Ⓒ 1,133
Rose Hill; RMC Place; COOK; ★ **CHI**; mail Chicago **z** 60640; pop. incl. with Chicago (Inc. Place)
Rose Hill; RMC Place; DUPAGE; ***170** C-12; ★ **CHI**; mail Downers Grove **z** 60515; ● 150
Rose Hill; Inc. Place; JASPER; **171** M-12; elev. 563ft./172m.; mail Hidalgo **z** 62432; Ⓟ 78; Ⓒ 79
Rose Lake; RMC Place; ST. CLAIR; ***171** O-6; ★ **ST.L**; mail East Saint Louis **z** 62201; pop. incl. with Fairmont City (Inc. Place)
Roseland; RMC Place; COOK; ***170** D-13; ★ **CHI**; mail Chicago **z** 60628; pop. incl. with Chicago (Inc. Place)
Roselle; Inc. Place; DUPAGE, COOK; **170** B-12; elev. 780ft./238m.; 🅿; ★ **CHI**; **z** 60172; Ⓟ 20,819; Ⓒ 23,115; ◆ 23,470
Rosemont; Inc. Place; COOK; **172** G-7; elev. 640ft./195m.; 🅿; ★ **CHI**; **z** 60018-19; Ⓟ 3,995; Ⓒ 4,224
Rosemont; RMC Place; ST. CLAIR; ***171** O-6; ★ **ST.L**; mail East Saint Louis **z** 62204; pop. incl. with Washington Park (Inc. Place)
Roseville; Inc. Place; WARREN; ▲ Roseville; **170** G-5; 🅿; **z** 61473; Ⓟ 1,151; Ⓒ 1,083
Roseville; MCD-Township; WARREN; ***170** G-5; 🅿; **z** 61473; Ⓟ 1,453; Ⓒ 1,341
Rosewood; RMC Place; MADISON; ***171** N-6; ★ **ST.L**; mail East Alton **z** 62024
Rosewood Heights; CDP; MADISON; **195** A-8; ★ **ST.L**; mail East Alton **z** 62024; Ⓟ 4,821; Ⓒ 4,262
Rosiclare; Inc. Place; HARDIN; **171** S-11; elev. 400ft./122m.; 🅿 🅷; **z** 62982; Ⓟ 1,378; Ⓒ 1,213
Roslyn; RMC Place; CUMBERLAND; ***171** L-11; elev. 617ft./188m.; mail Sigel **z** 62462, Toledo **z** 62468; rural
Ross; MCD-Township; EDGAR; ***170** J-13; mail Chrisman **z** 61924; Ⓟ 1,556; Ⓒ 1,563
Ross; MCD-Township; PIKE; ***171** L-4; mail Pleasant Hill **z** 62366; Ⓟ 134; Ⓒ 101
Ross; MCD-Township; VERMILION; ***170** H-13; mail Rossville **z** 60963; Ⓟ 1,601; Ⓒ 1,476
Rossville; Inc. Place; VERMILION; **170** H-13; elev. 706ft./215m.; 🅿; **z** 60963; Ⓟ 1,334; Ⓒ 1,217
Round Barn; RMC Place; CHAMPAIGN; ***170** I-11; ★ **CH-U**; mail Champaign **z** 61821; pop. incl. with Champaign (Inc. Place)
Round Grove; MCD-Township; LIVINGSTON; ***170** F-11; mail Dwight **z** 60420; Ⓟ 445; Ⓒ 411
Round Grove; RMC Place; WHITESIDE; ***170** C-7; mail Morrison **z** 61270; ● 150
Round Knob; RMC Place; MASSAC; **171** T-10; elev. 395ft./120m.; mail Metropolis **z** 62960; ● 50
Round Lake; Inc. Place; LAKE; **172** A-4; elev. 800ft./244m.; 🅿; ★ **CHI**; **z** 60073; Ⓟ 3,550; Ⓒ 5,842
Round Lake Beach; Inc. Place; LAKE; **172** A-4; elev. 780ft./238m.; 🅿; ★ **CHI**; **z** 60073; Ⓟ 16,434; Ⓒ 25,859; ◆ 28,560
Round Lake Heights (Indian Hills); Inc. Place; LAKE; **172** A-4; 🅿; ★ **CHI**; **z** 60073; Ⓟ 1,251; Ⓒ 1,347
Round Lake Park; Inc. Place; LAKE; **172** A-4; elev. 800ft./244m.; 🅿; ★ **CHI**; **z** 60073; Ⓟ 4,045; Ⓒ 6,038
Round Prairie; RMC Place; WAYNE; ***171** O-11; elev. 468ft./143m.; mail Cisne **z** 62823; rural
Rountree; MCD-Township; MONTGOMERY; ***171** L-8; mail Witt **z** 62094; Ⓟ 335; Ⓒ 272
Rowe; RMC Place; LIVINGSTON; ***170** F-10; elev. 641ft./195m.; mail Pontiac **z** 61764; ● 40
Roxana; Inc. Place; MADISON; **171** N-6; elev. 445ft./136m.; 🅿; ★ **ST.L**; **z** 62084; Ⓟ 1,562; Ⓒ 1,547
Roxanne; RMC Place; JACKSON; ***171** R-9; elev. 450ft./137m.; ★ **CARB-**; mail Carbondale **z** 62901; pop. incl. with Carbondale (Inc. Place)
Roxbury; RMC Place; LEE; ***170** D-9; mail Paw Paw **z** 61353; rural
Royal; Inc. Place; CHAMPAIGN; **170** I-12; elev. 680ft./207m.; 🅿; **z** 61871; Ⓟ 217; Ⓒ 279
Royal Lake (Royal Lakes); Inc. Place; MACOUPIN; ***171** M-7; mail Shipman **z** 62685; Ⓟ 272; Ⓒ 190
Royal Lake Resort; RMC Place; BOND; ***171** N-9; mail Mulberry Grove **z** 62262; ● 400
Royal Lake Resort; RMC Place; CLINTON; ***171** O-8; elev. 452ft./138m.; mail Carlyle **z** 62231; ● 100
Royal Lakes; MACOUPIN; see Royal Lake (Inc. Place)
Royal Lakes; RMC Place; MARION; ***171** O-9; elev. 525ft./160m.; mail Odin **z** 62870; ● 100
Royal Oaks; RMC Place; STEPHENSON; ***170** A-8; elev. 840ft./256m.; mail Freeport **z** 61032; ● 100
Royalton; Inc. Place; FRANKLIN; **171** Q-9; elev. 391ft./119m.; 🅿; ★ **CARB-**; **z** 62983; Ⓟ 1,191; Ⓒ 1,130
Rozetta; RMC Place; HENDERSON; ***170** F-4; elev. 707ft./215m.; mail Kirkwood **z** 61447, Oquawka **z** 61469
Rozetta; MCD-Township; HENDERSON; ***170** F-4; mail Kirkwood **z** 61447; Ⓟ 310; Ⓒ 290
Rubicon; MCD-Township; GREENE; ***171** L-6; mail Greenfield **z** 62044; Ⓟ 339; Ⓒ 355
Rudement; RMC Place; SALINE; ***171** R-11; elev. 396ft./121m.; mail Harrisburg **z** 62946
Ruma; Inc. Place; RANDOLPH; **171** P-7; elev. 442ft./135m.; 🅿; **z** 62278; Ⓟ 256; Ⓒ 260
Rural; MCD-Township; ROCK ISLAND; ***170** E-5; mail Coal Valley **z** 61240; Ⓟ 1,207; Ⓒ 1,517; Ⓡ 1,078
Rural; MCD-Township; SHELBY; ***171** L-9; mail Assumption **z** 62510; Ⓟ 354; Ⓒ 327
Rush; MCD-Township; JO DAVIESS; ***170** A-7; mail Stockton **z** 61085; Ⓟ 428; Ⓒ 427
Rushville; Inc. Place; ⊡ SCHUYLER; **170** I-5; elev. 676ft./206m.; 🅿 🅷; **z** 62681; Ⓟ 3,229; Ⓒ 3,212
Rushville; MCD-Township; SCHUYLER; ***170** I-5; 🅿; **z** 62681; includes part of the City of Rushville; Ⓟ 2,776; Ⓒ 2,760
Russell; RMC Place; LAKE; ***170** A-12; elev. 696ft./212m.; 🅿; ★ **CHI**; **z** 60075; ● 130
Russell; MCD-Township; LAWRENCE; ***171** N-13; mail Vincennes **z** 47591; Ⓟ 482; Ⓒ 468
Russellville; Inc. Place; LAWRENCE; ▲ Russell; **171** N-14; elev. 425ft./130m.; mail Vincennes **z** 47591; Ⓟ 133; Ⓒ 119
Rutland; MCD-Township; KANE; ***170** B-11; ★ **CHI**; mail Elgin **z** 60120; Ⓟ 2,549; Ⓒ 3,959
Rutland; Inc. Place; LA SALLE; ▲ Groveland; **170** F-9; elev. 706ft./215m.; 🅿; **z** 61358; Ⓟ 391; Ⓒ 354
Rutland; MCD-Township; LA SALLE; ***170** E-10; 🅿; **z** 61358 & mail Marseilles **z** 61341; Ⓟ 3,292; Ⓒ 3,527
Rutledge; MCD-Township; DE WITT; ***170** I-10; mail Le Roy **z** 61752; Ⓟ 189; Ⓒ 201
Ruyle; MCD-Township; JERSEY; ***171** M-6; mail Medora **z** 62063; Ⓟ 297; Ⓒ 381

S

Sabina; RMC Place; MCLEAN; ***170** H-10; mail Arrowsmith **z** 61722
Sacramento; RMC Place; WHITE; ***171** Q-11; elev. 437ft./133m.; mail Enfield **z** 62835; rural
Sadorus; Inc. Place; CHAMPAIGN; ▲ Sadorus; **170** J-11; elev. 690ft./210m.; 🅿; **z** 61872; Ⓟ 469; Ⓒ 426
Sadorus; MCD-Township; CHAMPAIGN; ***170** J-11; 🅿; **z** 61872; Ⓟ 1,126; Ⓒ 1,039
Sag Bridge; RMC Place; COOK; ***170** D-12; elev. 622ft./190m.; ★ **CHI**; mail Lemont **z** 60439; rural
Saidora; RMC Place; MASON; ***170** I-6; elev. 472ft./144m.; mail Chandlerville **z** 62627
Sailor Springs; Inc. Place; CLAY; **171** N-11; elev. 451ft./137m.; 🅿; **z** 62879; Ⓟ 136; Ⓒ 128
St. Albans; MCD-Township; HANCOCK; ***170** I-3; mail West Point **z** 62380; Ⓟ 503; Ⓒ 414
Saint Anne; Inc. Place; KANKAKEE; ▲ St. Anne; **170** F-13; 🅿; ★ **KANK**; **z** 60964; Ⓟ 1,153; Ⓒ 1,212
St. Anne; MCD-Township; KANKAKEE; ***170** F-13; ★ **KANK**; mail Saint Anne **z** 60964; Ⓟ 2,196; Ⓒ 2,108
Saint Anne Woods; RMC Place; KANKAKEE; ***170** F-13; mail Saint Anne **z** 60964; ● 200
Saint Augustine; Inc. Place; KNOX; **170** G-6; elev. 680ft./207m.; 🅿; **z** 61474; Ⓟ 151; Ⓒ 152
Saint Charles; Inc. Place; KANE, DUPAGE; **170** C-11; elev. 697ft./212m.; 🅿 ■; ★ **CHI**; **z** 60174-75; Ⓟ 22,501; Ⓒ 27,896; ◆ 32,931
St. Charles; MCD-Township; KANE; ***170** C-11; ★ **CHI**; mail Saint Charles **z** 60174; includes part of the City of Saint Charles; Ⓟ 33,112; Ⓒ 42,051
St. Clair; MCD-Township; ST. CLAIR; ***171** O-7; ★ **ST.L**; mail Belleville **z** 62221; Ⓟ 27,024; Ⓒ 31,798; Ⓡ 31,782
ST. CLAIR; **171** O-6; Ⓟ 262,852; Ⓒ 256,082; Ⓡ 256,067; ◆ 261,523
Saint David; Inc. Place; FULTON; **170** H-6; elev. 630ft./192m.; 🅿; **z** 61563; Ⓟ 603; Ⓒ 587
Saint Elmo; Inc. Place; FAYETTE; **171** M-10; elev. 620ft./189m.; 🅿; **z** 62458; Ⓟ 1,473; Ⓒ 1,456
Sainte Marie (Ste. Marie); Inc. Place; JASPER; **171** N-12; 🅿; **z** 62459; Ⓟ 281; Ⓒ 261
St. Francis; MCD-Township; EFFINGHAM; ***171** M-11; mail Teutopolis **z** 62467; Ⓟ 1,263; Ⓒ 1,330
Saint Francisville; Inc. Place; LAWRENCE; **171** O-13; elev. 451ft./137m.; 🅿; **z** 62460; Ⓟ 851; Ⓒ 759
Saint George; RMC Place; KANKAKEE; ***170** E-13; ★ **KANK**; mail Bourbonnais **z** 60914; ● 60
Saint Jacob; Inc. Place; MADISON; ▲ St. Jacob; **171** N-7; elev. 518ft./158m.; 🅿; **z** 62281; Ⓟ 752; Ⓒ 801
St. Jacob; MCD-Township; MADISON; ***171** N-7; mail Saint Jacob **z** 62281; Ⓟ 1,756; Ⓒ 2,102
Saint James; RMC Place; FAYETTE; ***171** M-10; elev. 600ft./183m.; mail Loogootee **z** 62857; ● 50
Saint James Estates; RMC Place; COOK; ★ **CHI**; mail Chicago Heights **z** 60411; pop. incl. with Sauk Village (Inc. Place)
Saint Joe; RMC Place; MONROE; ***171** P-6; mail Waterloo **z** 62298; rural
Saint Johns; Inc. Place; PERRY; **171** Q-9; elev. 462ft./141m.; mail Du Quoin **z** 62832; Ⓟ 262; Ⓒ 218
Saint Joseph; Inc. Place; CHAMPAIGN; ▲ St. Joseph; **170** I-12; 🅿; ★ **CH-U**; **z** 61873; Ⓟ 2,052; Ⓒ 2,912
St. Joseph; MCD-Township; CHAMPAIGN; ***170** I-12; ★ **CH-U**; mail Saint Joseph **z** 61873; Ⓟ 3,694; Ⓒ 4,611
Saint Libory; Inc. Place; ST. CLAIR; **171** P-7; elev. 420ft./128m.; 🅿; **z** 62282; Ⓟ 525; Ⓒ 583
Ste. Marie; JASPER; see Sainte Marie (Inc. Place)
Ste. Marie; MCD-Township; JASPER; ***171** N-12; mail Sainte Marie **z** 62459; Ⓟ 659; Ⓒ 615
Saint Mary; RMC Place; HANCOCK; ▲ St. Mary; ***170** H-4; elev. 575ft./175m.; mail Plymouth **z** 62367; ● 30
St. Mary; MCD-Township; HANCOCK; ***170** H-4; mail Plymouth **z** 62367; Ⓟ 701; Ⓒ 714
Saint Marys; EFFINGHAM; see Green Creek (RMC Place)
Saint Morgan; RMC Place; MADISON; ***171** O-7; elev. 504ft./154m.; mail Trenton **z** 62293; rural
Saint Paul; RMC Place; FAYETTE; ***171** N-10; elev. 569ft./173m.; mail Saint Peter **z** 62880, Shobonier **z** 62885
Saint Peter; Inc. Place; FAYETTE; **171** N-10; elev. 591ft./180m.; 🅿; **z** 62880; Ⓟ 353; Ⓒ 386
Saint Regis; RMC Place; DUPAGE; ★ **CHI**; mail Lombard **z** 60148; pop. incl. with Lombard (Inc. Place)
Saint Rose; RMC Place; CLINTON; ▲ St. Rose; **171** N-8; elev. 504ft./154m.; mail Breese **z** 62230; ● 250
St. Rose; MCD-Township; CLINTON; ***171** N-8; mail Trenton **z** 62293; Ⓟ 1,230; Ⓒ 1,319
Salem; MCD-Township; CARROLL; ***170** B-7; mail Lanark **z** 61046; Ⓟ 396; Ⓒ 387
Salem; MCD-Township; KNOX; ***170** G-7; mail Yates City **z** 61572; Ⓟ 1,129; Ⓒ 992
Salem; Inc. Place; ⊡ MARION; ▲ Salem; **171** O-10; elev. 544ft./166m.; 🅿 🅷; **z** 62881; Ⓟ 7,470; Ⓒ 7,909
Salem; MCD-Township; MARION; ***171** O-9; 🅿; **z** 62881; Ⓟ 9,614; Ⓒ 9,849
Salina; MCD-Township; KANKAKEE; ***170** E-12; mail Bonfield **z** 60913; Ⓟ 1,189; Ⓒ 1,317
Saline; MCD-Township; MADISON; ***171** N-8; mail Highland **z** 62249; Ⓟ 3,421; Ⓒ 4,372
SALINE; **171** Q-11; Ⓟ 26,551; Ⓒ 26,733; ◆ 26,151
Saline Landing; RMC Place; HARDIN; ***171** R-12; elev. 370ft./113m.; mail Cave In Rock **z** 62919; ● 40
Saline Mines; RMC Place; GALLATIN; **171** R-12; mail Shawneetown **z** 62984; ● 25
Salisbury; COLES; see Hutton (RMC Place)
Salisbury; RMC Place; SANGAMON; **170** J-7; 🅿; ★ **SPRG**; **z** 62677; ● 160
Salt Creek; MCD-Township; MASON; ***170** I-7; mail Mason City **z** 62664; Ⓟ 239; Ⓒ 241
Sammons Point; RMC Place; KANKAKEE; incorporated March 21, 2006; disincorporated August 8, 2007; ● 300
Samoth; RMC Place; MASSAC; ***171** S-10; mail Grantsburg **z** 62943; ● 30
Samsville; RMC Place; EDWARDS; ***171** O-12; elev. 476ft./145m.; mail Albion **z** 62806, West Salem **z** 62476
Sand Barrens; RMC Place; LAWRENCE; ***171** O-13; mail Saint Francisville **z** 62460; rural
Sandburg Village; RMC Place; COOK; ★ **CHI**; mail Chicago **z** 60610; pop. incl. with Chicago (Inc. Place)
Sandoval; Inc. Place; MARION; ▲ Sandoval; **171** O-9; 🅿; **z** 62882; Ⓟ 1,535; Ⓒ 1,434
Sandoval; MCD-Township; MARION; ***171** O-9; 🅿; **z** 62882; Ⓟ 2,708; Ⓒ 2,652
Sandpebble Walk; RMC Place; COOK; ★ **CHI**; mail Wheeling **z** 60090; pop. incl. with Wheeling (Inc. Place)
Sand Prairie; MCD-Township; TAZEWELL; ***170** H-8; mail Green Valley **z** 61534; Ⓟ 1,515; Ⓒ 1,477
Sandra Heights; RMC Place; COOK; ★ **CHI**; mail Chicago Heights **z** 60411; pop. incl. with Chicago Heights (Inc. Place)
Sand Ridge; RMC Place; JACKSON; ▲ Sand Ridge; ***171** R-8; elev. 368ft./112m.; mail Gorham **z** 62940; ● 40
Sand Ridge; MCD-Township; JACKSON; ***171** R-8; mail Gorham **z** 62940; Ⓟ 800; Ⓒ 810
Sandusky; RMC Place; ALEXANDER; **171** T-9; mail Tamms **z** 62988; ● 250
Sandwich; Inc. Place; DEKALB, KENDALL; **170** D-10; elev. 670ft./204m.; 🅿 🅷; ★ **CHI**; **z** 60548; Ⓟ 5,567; Ⓒ 6,509
Sandwich; MCD-Township; DEKALB; ***170** D-10; 🅿; ★ **CHI**; **z** 60548; includes part of the City of Sandwich; Ⓟ 5,990; Ⓒ 6,920
Sangamon; RMC Place; MACON; ***170** J-10; ★ **DEC**; mail Decatur **z** 62521; rural
Sangamon; MCD-Township; PIATT; ***170** I-11; mail White Heath **z** 61884; Ⓟ 1,481; Ⓒ 2,041
SANGAMON; **171** K-7; Ⓟ 178,386; Ⓒ 188,951; Ⓡ 188,954; ◆ 194,891
Sangamon Heights; RMC Place; CHAMPAIGN; ***170** I-11; elev. 704ft./215m.; mail Mahomet **z** 61853; pop. incl. with Mahomet (Inc. Place)
Sangamon Valley; MCD-Township; CASS; ***170** J-6; mail Beardstown **z** 62618; Ⓟ 380; Ⓒ 328
San Jose; Inc. Place; MASON, LOGAN; **170** I-8; elev. 573ft./175m.; 🅿; **z** 62682; Ⓟ 519; Ⓒ 696
Sankoty; RMC Place; PEORIA; ***170** G-8; ★ **PEOR**; pop. incl. with Peoria (Inc. Place)
Santa Anna; MCD-Township; DE WITT; ***170** I-10; mail Farmer City **z** 61842; Ⓟ 2,550; Ⓒ 2,487
Santa Fe; MCD-Township; CLINTON; ***171** O-8; mail Bartelso **z** 62218; Ⓟ 1,112; Ⓒ 1,127
Santa Fe Park; RMC Place; COOK; ***170** C-12; elev. 620ft./189m.; ★ **CHI**; mail Hinsdale **z** 60521; ● 120
Saratoga; MCD-Township; GRUNDY; ***170** E-11; mail Morris **z** 60450; Ⓟ 3,181; Ⓒ 4,448
Saratoga; MCD-Township; MARSHALL; ***170** F-8; mail Henry **z** 61537; Ⓟ 353; Ⓒ 320
Saratoga; RMC Place; UNION; **171** S-9; mail Anna **z** 62906; ● 50
Sargent; MCD-Township; DOUGLAS; ***171** K-12; mail Oakland **z** 61943; Ⓟ 343; Ⓒ 293
Sato; RMC Place; JACKSON; ***171** Q-8; elev. 469ft./143m.; mail Ava **z** 62907; ● 40
Sauganash; RMC Place; COOK; ***170** B-13; ★ **CHI**; mail Chicago **z** 60646; pop. incl. with Chicago (Inc. Place)
Sauget; Inc. Place; ST. CLAIR; **195** F-7; elev. 410ft./125m.; 🅿; ★ **ST.L**; **z** 62201, **z** 62206; Ⓟ 197; Ⓒ 249
Sauk Village; Inc. Place; COOK, WILL; **172** N-10; elev. 650ft./198m.; 🅿; ★ **CHI**; **z** 60411; Ⓟ 9,926; Ⓒ 10,411
Saunemin; Inc. Place; LIVINGSTON; ▲ Saunemin; **170** F-11; elev. 690ft./210m.; 🅿; **z** 61769; Ⓟ 399; Ⓒ 456
Saunemin; MCD-Township; LIVINGSTON; ***170** F-11; 🅿; **z** 61769; Ⓟ 683; Ⓒ 690
Savanna; Inc. Place; CARROLL; ▲ Savanna; **170** B-6; elev. 606ft./185m.; 🅿; **z** 61074; Ⓟ 3,819; Ⓒ 3,542
Savanna; MCD-Township; CARROLL; ***170** B-6; 🅿; **z** 61074; Ⓟ 4,483; Ⓒ 4,214
Savoy; Inc. Place; CHAMPAIGN; **170** J-11; elev. 738ft./225m.; 🅿; ★ **CH-U**; **z** 61874; Ⓟ 2,674; Ⓒ 4,476
Sawyerville; Inc. Place; MACOUPIN; ***171** M-7; elev. 629ft./192m.; 🅿; **z** 62085; Ⓟ 312; Ⓒ 295
Say Brook; RMC Place; DUPAGE; ★ **CHI**; mail Naperville **z** 60563; pop. incl. with Naperville (Inc. Place)
Saybrook; Inc. Place; MCLEAN; **170** H-11; elev. 790ft./241m.; 🅿; **z** 61770; Ⓟ 767; Ⓒ 764
Scales Mound; Inc. Place; JO DAVIESS; ▲ Scales Mound; **170** A-6; elev. 950ft./290m.; 🅿; **z** 61075; Ⓟ 388; Ⓒ 401
Scales Mound; MCD-Township; JO DAVIESS; ***170** A-6; 🅿; **z** 61075; Ⓟ 619; Ⓒ 635
Scarboro; RMC Place; LEE; ***170** C-9; mail Steward **z** 60553; ● 50
Scarsdale; RMC Place; COOK; ★ **CHI**; pop. incl. with Arlington Heights (Inc. Place)
Schaeferville (Shaferville); RMC Place; TAZEWELL; ***170** H-8; ★ **PEOR**; mail Pekin **z** 61554; ● 430
Schapville; RMC Place; JO DAVIESS; **170** A-6; mail Elizabeth **z** 61028; ● 50
Schaumburg; Inc. Place; COOK, DUPAGE; **172** F-4; elev. 799ft./244m.; 🅿 🅲 1,852 ■; ★ **CHI**; **z** 60159, **z** 60168-69, **z** 60173, **z** 60179, **z** 60192-96; Ⓟ 68,586; Ⓒ 75,386; ◆ 71,748
Schaumburg; MCD-Township; COOK; ***170** B-12; 🅿 🅲 1,852; ★ **CHI**; **z** 60159, **z** 60168-69, **z** 60173, **z** 60179, **z** 60192-96; includes part of the Village of Schaumburg; Ⓟ 127,625; Ⓒ 134,114
Schaumburg Green; RMC Place; COOK; ★ **CHI**; mail Schaumburg **z** 60194; pop. incl. with Schaumburg (Inc. Place)
Scheller; RMC Place; JEFFERSON; ***171** P-9; elev. 504ft./154m.; 🅿; **z** 62883; ● 200
Schiller Park; Inc. Place; COOK; **172** G-7; elev. 640ft./195m.; 🅿; ★ **CHI**; **z** 60131, **z** 60176; Ⓟ 11,189; Ⓒ 11,850
Schoper; RMC Place; MACOUPIN; ***171** L-7; rural
Schram City; Inc. Place; MONTGOMERY; **171** M-8; elev. 645ft./197m.; mail Hillsboro **z** 62049; Ⓟ 692; Ⓒ 653
Schrodt; WABASH; see Schrodts Station (RMC Place)
Schrodts Station (Schrodt, Sugar Creek); RMC Place; WABASH; ***171** P-13; mail Mount Carmel **z** 62863; rural
Schuline (Schulines); RMC Place; RANDOLPH; ***171** Q-7; mail Sparta **z** 62286; ● 80
Schulines; RANDOLPH; see Schuline (RMC Place)
SCHUYLER; **170** I-4; Ⓟ 7,498; Ⓒ 7,189; ◆ 6,944
Schwer; RMC Place; IROQUOIS; ***170** G-13; elev. 662ft./202m.; mail Milford **z** 60953; rural
Sciota; Inc. Place; MCDONOUGH; ▲ Sciota; **170** H-5; elev. 753ft./230m.; 🅿; **z** 61475; Ⓟ 68; Ⓒ 58
Sciota; MCD-Township; MCDONOUGH; ***170** H-5; 🅿; **z** 61475; Ⓟ 622; Ⓒ 574
Scioto Mills; RMC Place; STEPHENSON; ***170** A-8; elev. 771ft./235m.; 🅿; **z** 61032; ● 100
Scotland; RMC Place; EDGAR; **170** J-13; mail Chrisman **z** 61924; ● 110
Scotland; MCD-Township; MCDONOUGH; ***170** H-5; mail Macomb **z** 61455; Ⓟ 521; Ⓒ 444
Scot Plains; DUPAGE; see Longwood Manor (RMC Place)
Scotsboro; RMC Place; WILLIAMSON; ★ **CARB-**; mail Marion **z** 62959; ● 300
Scott; MCD-Township; CHAMPAIGN; ***170** I-11; mail Seymour **z** 61875; Ⓟ 1,059; Ⓒ 1,157
Scott; MCD-Township; OGLE; ***170** B-9; mail Davis Junction **z** 61020; Ⓟ 1,418; Ⓒ 1,671
SCOTT; **171** K-5; Ⓟ 5,644; Ⓒ 5,537; ◆ 5,134
Scott AFB; CDP-Census Area Only; ST. CLAIR; ***171** O-7; 🅿; ★ **ST.L**; **z** 62225; Ⓟ 7,245; Ⓒ 2,707
Scottsburg; RMC Place; MCDONOUGH; ***170** H-5; mail Bushnell **z** 61422; rural
Scottswood; RMC Place; CHAMPAIGN; ***170** I-12; elev. 725ft./221m.; ★ **CH-U**; mail Urbana **z** 61801; ● 1,650
Scottville; Inc. Place; MACOUPIN; ▲ Scottville; **171** L-6; 🅿; **z** 62683; Ⓟ 165; Ⓒ 140
Scottville; MCD-Township; MACOUPIN; ***171** L-6; 🅿; **z** 62683; Ⓟ 387; Ⓒ 356
Seaton; Inc. Place; MERCER; **170** F-4; elev. 600ft./183m.; 🅿; **z** 61476; Ⓟ 221; Ⓒ 242
Seatonville; Inc. Place; BUREAU; **170** E-9; elev. 600ft./183m.; 🅿; **z** 61359; Ⓟ 259; Ⓒ 303
Seco Park; RMC Place; DEKALB; ***170** C-10; elev. 880ft./268m.; ★ **DKLB**; mail DeKalb **z** 60115; pop. incl. with DeKalb (Inc. Place)
Secor; Inc. Place; WOODFORD; **170** G-9; elev. 730ft./223m.; 🅿; **z** 61771; Ⓟ 389; Ⓒ 379
Seeger; RMC Place; COOK; ★ **CHI**; mail Des Plaines **z** 60016; pop. incl. with Des Plaines (Inc. Place)
Seehorn; RMC Place; PIKE; ***170** J-3; elev. 477ft./145m.; mail Hull **z** 62343; rural
Sefton; RMC Place; FAYETTE; ***171** M-10; mail Brownstown **z** 62418; ● 70
Sefton; MCD-Township; FAYETTE; ***171** M-9; mail Brownstown **z** 62418; Ⓟ 577; Ⓒ 605
Selby; MCD-Township; BUREAU; ***170** E-8; mail Depue **z** 61322; Ⓟ 2,461; Ⓒ 2,489
Selmaville; RMC Place; MARION; ***171** O-9; mail Salem **z** 62881; ● 50
Seminary; MCD-Township; FAYETTE; ***171** N-9; mail Vandalia **z** 62471; Ⓟ 529; Ⓒ 538
Seminary; RMC Place; RICHLAND; ***171** O-12; elev. 437ft./133m.; mail Olney **z** 62450; rural
Senachwine; MCD-Township; PUTNAM; ***170** E-8; mail Putnam **z** 61560; Ⓟ 569; Ⓒ 685
Seneca (Crotty); Inc. Place; LA SALLE, GRUNDY; **170** E-10; elev. 500ft./152m.; 🅿; **z** 61360; Ⓟ 1,878; Ⓒ 2,053
Seneca; MCD-Township; MCHENRY; ***170** A-11; mail Woodstock **z** 60098; Ⓟ 2,229; Ⓒ 2,733
Sepo; RMC Place; FULTON; ***170** H-6; mail Lewistown **z** 61542; rural
Serena; RMC Place; LA SALLE; ▲ Serena; **170** D-10; 🅿; **z** 60549; ● 250
Serena; MCD-Township; LA SALLE; ***170** D-10; 🅿; **z** 60549; Ⓟ 846; Ⓒ 980
Sesser; Inc. Place; FRANKLIN; **171** Q-9; elev. 460ft./140m.; 🅿; **z** 62884; Ⓟ 2,087; Ⓒ 2,128

Entries in **UPPERCASE** are counties.
Entries in **bold** have populations of 2,500 or more.
Names in parentheses are alternate names.

Inc. Place	Incorporated Place
RMC Place	Rand McNally Designated Place
CDP	Census Designated Place
MCD	Minor Civil Division

⊡	County Seat
▲	Minor Civil Division
elev.	Elevation
🅿	Post Office
🅷	Hospital
🅲	College
■	Principal Business Center
★	Ranally Metro Area (RMA) Abbreviation
z	Zip Code(s)
Ⓟ	Previous Census Population
Ⓡ	Revised Census Population
Ⓐ	Annexation Population
●	Rand McNally Population Estimate
Ⓒ	Final Census Population
Ⓢ	Special Census Population
◆	Estimated Population

For additional definitions see Glossary, Volume 1, and Introduction, Volume 2.

Seven Hickory; MCD-Township; COLES; ***171** K-12; mail Charleston **z** 61920; ℗ 333; © 312
Seville; RMC Place; FULTON; ***170** H-6; mail Smithfield **z** 61477; rural
Seward; MCD-Township; KENDALL; ***170** D-11; mail Minooka **z** 60447; ℗ 812; © 846
Seward; RMC Place; WINNEBAGO; ▲ Seward; **170** B-8; 🅿; **z** 61077; ● 300
Seward; MCD-Township; WINNEBAGO; ***170** B-8; 🅿; **z** 61077; ℗ 1,001; © 946
Sexson Corner; RMC Place; SHELBY; ***171** L-11; mail Gays **z** 61928; rural
Seymour; RMC Place; CHAMPAIGN; **170** I-11; elev. 700ft./213m.; 🅿; **z** 61875; ● 450
Shabbona; Inc. Place; DEKALB; ▲ Shabbona; **170** C-10; 🅿; **z** 60550; ℗ 897; © 929
Shabbona; MCD-Township; DEKALB; ***170** C-10; 🅿; **z** 60550; ℗ 1,379; © 1,454
Shabbona Grove; RMC Place; DEKALB; ***170** C-10; mail Earlville **z** 60518
Shadetree; RMC Place; COOK; ★ **CHI**; mail Oak Forest **z** 60452; pop. incl. with Oak Forest (Inc. Place)
Shadow Lawn; RMC Place; KANKAKEE; ***170** E-13; mail Momence **z** 60954; ● 100
Shady Acres; RMC Place; MORGAN; ***170** J-5; elev. 445ft./136m.; mail Meredosia **z** 62665; ● 30
Shady Beach; RMC Place; HENRY; ***170** D-6; elev. 600ft./183m.; mail Geneseo **z** 61254; rural
Shady Grove; RMC Place; MASSAC; ***171** T-11; mail Brookport **z** 62910; rural
Shady Hill; RMC Place; LAKE; ***170** B-12; ★ **CHI**; mail Barrington **z** 60010; ● 300
Shaferville; TAZEWELL; see Schaeferville (RMC Place)
Shafter; RMC Place; FAYETTE; ***171** M-9; elev. 562ft./171m.; mail Vandalia **z** 62471; rural
Shafter; MCD-Township; FAYETTE; ***171** M-9; mail Vandalia **z** 62471; ℗ 416; © 468
Shakerag; RMC Place; WILLIAMSON; ***171** R-10; elev. 422ft./129m.; ★ **CARB-**; mail Johnston City **z** 62951; ● 120
Shale City; RMC Place; MERCER; ***170** E-5; mail Aledo **z** 61231
Shanghai City; RMC Place; WARREN; ***170** F-5; mail Alexis **z** 61412; rural
Shangrila; RMC Place; OGLE; ***170** C-9; mail Rochelle **z** 61068; ● 400
Shannon; Inc. Place; CARROLL; **170** B-7; elev. 907ft./276m.; 🅿; **z** 61078; ℗ 887; © 854
Sharon; MCD-Township; FAYETTE; ***171** M-9; mail Ramsey **z** 62080; ℗ 1,837; © 940; Ⓡ 2,377
Sharp Rock Falls; RMC Place; JACKSON; ***171** Q-8; mail Ava **z** 62907; ● 50
Sharpsburg; RMC Place; CHRISTIAN; ***171** K-8; 🅿; **z** 62568; ● 70
Shattuc; RMC Place; CLINTON; **171** O-9; elev. 475ft./145m.; 🅿; **z** 62231; ● 220
Shaw; RMC Place; LAKE; ★ **CHI**; mail Round Lake **z** 60073
Shawnee; MCD-Township; GALLATIN; ***171** R-12; mail Shawneetown **z** 62984; ℗ 467; © 353
Shawneetown; Inc. Place; ⊡ GALLATIN; **171** R-12; elev. 405ft./123m.; 🅿; **z** 62984; ℗ 1,575; © 1,410
Shaws; RMC Place; LEE; ***170** C-9; mail Amboy **z** 61310; ● 40
Shaws Point; MCD-Township; MACOUPIN; ***171** L-7; ℗ 489; © 490
Sheffield; Inc. Place; BUREAU; **170** E-7; elev. 717ft./219m.; 🅿; **z** 61361; ℗ 951; © 946
Sheffield Park; RMC Place; COOK; ★ **CHI**; mail Schaumburg **z** 60194; pop. incl. with Schaumburg (Inc. Place)
SHELBY; **171** K-10; ℗ 22,261; © 22,893; ◆ 21,359
Shelbyville; Inc. Place; ⊡ SHELBY; **171** L-10; elev. 650ft./198m.; 🅿 🅷; **z** 62565; ℗ 4,943; © 4,971
Shelbyville; MCD-Township; SHELBY; ***171** L-10; 🅿; **z** 62565; includes part of the City of Shelbyville; ℗ 4,797; © 4,944
Sheldon; Inc. Place; IROQUOIS; ▲ Sheldon; **170** G-13; elev. 687ft./209m.; 🅿; **z** 60966; ℗ 1,109; © 1,232
Sheldon; MCD-Township; IROQUOIS; ***170** G-13; 🅿; **z** 60966; ℗ 1,422; © 1,531
Sheldons Grove; RMC Place; SCHUYLER; ***170** I-6; elev. 464ft./141m.; mail Browning **z** 62624
Shepherd; RMC Place; PIKE; ***171** K-3; elev. 462ft./141m.; mail Hull **z** 62343; ● 25
Sherburnville; RMC Place; KANKAKEE; **170** E-13; elev. 675ft./206m.; mail Grant Park **z** 60940; ● 80
Sheridan; Inc. Place; LA SALLE; **170** D-10; elev. 592ft./180m.; 🅿; **z** 60551; ℗ 1,288; © 2,411
Sheridan; MCD-Township; LOGAN; ***170** I-8; mail New Holland **z** 62671; ℗ 593; © 555
Sherman; MCD-Township; MASON; ***170** I-7; mail Easton **z** 62633; ℗ 623; © 615
Sherman; Inc. Place; SANGAMON; **170** J-8; elev. 580ft./177m.; 🅿; ★ **SPRG**; **z** 62684; ℗ 2,080; © 2,871
Sherrard; Inc. Place; MERCER; **170** E-5; elev. 800ft./244m.; 🅿; **z** 61281; ℗ 697; © 694
Sherwood; RMC Place; COOK; ★ **CHI**; pop. incl. with Arlington Heights (Inc. Place)
Sherwood Forest; RMC Place; DUPAGE; ★ **CHI**; mail Wood Dale **z** 60191; pop. incl. with Wood Dale (Inc. Place)
Sherwood Forest; RMC Place; PEORIA; ★ **PEOR**; mail Peoria **z** 61614; pop. incl. with Peoria (Inc. Place)
Sherwood Oaks; RMC Place; COOK; ***170** B-11; elev. 800ft./244m.; ★ **CHI**; mail Elgin **z** 60120; ● 170
Sherwood on the Fox; RMC Place; KANE; ★ **CHI**; mail Carpentersville **z** 60110; pop. incl. with Carpentersville (Inc. Place)
Shields; MCD-Township; LAKE; ***170** A-12; ★ **CHI**; mail Lake Forest **z** 60045; ℗ 43,414; © 43,382
Shiloh; MCD-Township; EDGAR; ***171** K-13; mail Brocton **z** 61917; ℗ 247; © 193
Shiloh; MCD-Township; JEFFERSON; ***171** P-9; mail Mount Vernon **z** 62864; ℗ 6,119; © 6,345
Shiloh; Inc. Place; ST. CLAIR; **195** F-10; elev. 650ft./198m.; 🅿; ★ **ST.L**; **z** 62269 & mail Belleville **z** 62221; ℗ 2,655; © 7,643
Shiloh Hill; RMC Place; RANDOLPH; ***171** Q-8; mail Campbell Hill **z** 62916; ● 40
Shiloh Valley; MCD-Township; ST. CLAIR; ***171** O-7; ★ **ST.L**; mail Belleville **z** 62221; ℗ 10,984; © 10,108; Ⓡ 10,048
Shipman; Inc. Place; MACOUPIN; ▲ Shipman; **171** M-6; 🅿; **z** 62685; ℗ 624; © 655
Shipman; MCD-Township; MACOUPIN; ***171** M-6; 🅿; **z** 62685; ℗ 1,407; © 1,507
Shippingsport; RMC Place; LA SALLE; ***170** E-9; elev. 500ft./152m.; mail Oglesby **z** 61348; rural
Shires of Inverness; RMC Place; COOK; ***170** B-12; ★ **CHI**; mail Palatine **z** 60067; pop. incl. with Inverness (Inc. Place)
Shirland; RMC Place; WINNEBAGO; ▲ Shirland; **170** A-9; 🅿; **z** 61079; ● 200
Shirland; MCD-Township; WINNEBAGO; ***170** A-9; 🅿; **z** 61079; ℗ 1,011; © 1,108
Shirley; RMC Place; MCLEAN; **170** H-9; elev. 760ft./232m.; 🅿; **z** 61772; ● 150
Shoal Creek; MCD-Township; BOND; ***171** M-8; mail Sorento **z** 62086; ℗ 1,803; © 1,896
Shobonier; RMC Place; FAYETTE; **171** N-9; elev. 516ft./157m.; 🅿; **z** 62885; ● 250
Shokokon; RMC Place; HENDERSON; ***170** G-4; mail Carman **z** 61425; rural
Shops; RMC Place; SANGAMON; ★ **SPRG**; pop. incl. with Springfield (Inc. Place)
Shore Acres; RMC Place; WHITESIDE; mail Rock Falls **z** 61071; ● 350
Shore Heights Manor; RMC Place; KENDALL; ***170** D-11; elev. 650ft./198m.; ★ **CHI**; mail Oswego **z** 60543; ● 300
Shore Hills; RMC Place; MCHENRY; ***170** A-11; ★ **CHI**; mail Wonder Lake **z** 60097; ● 300
Shores of Shining Waters; RMC Place; DUPAGE; ★ **CHI**; mail Carol Stream **z** 60188; pop. incl. with Carol Stream (Inc. Place)
Shorewood; RMC Place; KANKAKEE; ***170** F-13; elev. 625ft./191m.; ★ **KANK**; mail Saint Anne **z** 60964; ● 400
Shorewood; Inc. Place; WILL; **170** D-12; elev. 581ft./177m.; 🅿; ★ **CHI**; **z** 60404, **z** 60431, **z** 60435-36; ℗ 6,264; © 7,686
Shull's Urban Estates; RMC Place; CHAMPAIGN; mail Rantoul **z** 61866; pop. incl. with Rantoul (Inc. Place)
Shumway; Inc. Place; EFFINGHAM; **171** M-10; elev. 655ft./200m.; 🅿; **z** 62461; ℗ 243; © 217
Sibley; Inc. Place; FORD; **170** H-11; elev. 813ft./248m.; 🅿; **z** 61773; ℗ 359; © 329
Sicily; RMC Place; CHRISTIAN; ***171** K-8; 🅿; **z** 62558; ● 20
Sidell; Inc. Place; VERMILION; ▲ Sidell; **170** J-13; elev. 685ft./209m.; 🅿; **z** 61876; ℗ 584; © 626
Sidell; MCD-Township; VERMILION; ***170** J-13; 🅿; **z** 61876; ℗ 1,077; © 1,105
Sidney; Inc. Place; CHAMPAIGN; ▲ Sidney; **170** J-12; elev. 672ft./205m.; 🅿; **z** 61877; ℗ 1,027; © 1,062
Sidney; MCD-Township; CHAMPAIGN; ***170** J-12; 🅿; **z** 61877; ℗ 1,521; © 1,609
Sigel; Inc. Place; SHELBY; ▲ Sigel; **171** M-11; 🅿; **z** 62462; ℗ 344; © 386
Sigel; MCD-Township; SHELBY; ***171** L-11; 🅿; **z** 62462; ℗ 738; © 788
Signal Hill; RMC Place; ST. CLAIR; **195** F-8; elev. 592ft./180m.; ★ **ST.L**; mail Belleville **z** 62223; pop. incl. with Belleville (Inc. Place)
Silver Creek; MCD-Township; STEPHENSON; ***170** B-8; mail Freeport **z** 61032; ℗ 1,027; © 739
Silver Lake; RMC Place; MCHENRY; **172** C-3; ★ **CHI**; mail Cary **z** 60013; ● 800
Silver Ridge; RMC Place; OGLE; ***170** B-8; mail Oregon **z** 61061; ● 50
Silvis; Inc. Place; ROCK ISLAND; **171** S-5; elev. 700ft./213m.; 🅿 🅷; ★ **D-RI-M**; **z** 61282; ℗ 6,926; © 7,269
Silvis Heights; RMC Place; ROCK ISLAND; ★ **D-RI-M**; mail Silvis **z** 61282; pop. incl. with Silvis (Inc. Place)
Simpson; Inc. Place; JOHNSON; **171** S-10; elev. 444ft./135m.; 🅿; **z** 62985; ℗ 61; © 54
Simpson; RMC Place; WHITE; mail Crossville **z** 62827; rural
Sims; Inc. Place; WAYNE; **171** P-11; elev. 415ft./126m.; 🅿; **z** 62886; ℗ 338; © 273
Sims Western Acres; RMC Place; SANGAMON; mail Springfield **z** 62707; ● 300
Sinclair; RMC Place; MORGAN; ***170** J-6; 🅿; **z** 62650
Six Mile; MCD-Township; FRANKLIN; ***171** Q-9; ★ **CARB-**; mail Zeigler **z** 62999; ℗ 3,846; © 3,713
Sixty Six Court; RMC Place; COOK; ***170** D-13; elev. 665ft./203m.; ★ **CHI**; mail Oak Forest **z** 60452; ● 40
Skokie; Inc. Place; COOK; **170** B-13; elev. 623ft./190m.; 🅿 🅷 🅲 427 ■; ★ **CHI**; **z** 60076-77; ℗ 59,432; © 63,348; ◆ 67,027
Skunk Hollow; COOK; see Beaver Valley (RMC Place)
Slap Out; RMC Place; MARION; mail Iuka **z** 62849; rural
Sleepy Hollow; Inc. Place; KANE; **172** E-2; elev. 750ft./229m.; 🅿; ★ **CHI**; **z** 60118; ℗ 3,241; © 3,553
Smallwood; MCD-Township; JASPER; ***171** N-12; mail Newton **z** 62448; ℗ 461; © 422
Smithboro; Inc. Place; BOND; ***171** N-8; elev. 560ft./171m.; 🅿; **z** 62284; ℗ 201; © 200
Smithfield; Inc. Place; FULTON; **170** H-6; elev. 650ft./198m.; 🅿; **z** 61477; ℗ 277; © 214
Smithshire; RMC Place; WARREN; **170** G-4; elev. 730ft./223m.; 🅿; **z** 61478; ● 200
Smithton; Inc. Place; ST. CLAIR; ▲ Smithton; **171** O-7; 🅿; ★ **ST.L**; **z** 62285; ℗ 1,587; © 2,248
Smithton; MCD-Township; ST. CLAIR; ***171** O-7; 🅿; ★ **ST.L**; **z** 62285; ℗ 2,883; © 3,392
Smithville; RMC Place; PEORIA; ***170** G-7; elev. 719ft./219m.; ★ **PEOR**; mail Hanna City **z** 61536; ● 100
Snicarte; RMC Place; MASON; ***170** I-6; 🅿; **z** 62617; ● 30
Snyder (Hatton); RMC Place; CLARK; ***171** L-13; elev. 531ft./162m.; mail West Union **z** 62477
Sollitt; RMC Place; KANKAKEE; ***170** E-13; mail Beecher **z** 60401; ● 50
Solon Mills; RMC Place; MCHENRY; ***170** A-11; elev. 780ft./238m.; 🅿; ★ **CHI**; **z** 60071; ● 200
Solvay; RMC Place; COOK; pop. incl. with Chicago (Inc. Place)
Somer; MCD-Township; CHAMPAIGN; ***170** I-12; mail Champaign **z** 61820; ℗ 1,282; © 1,421
Somerset; RMC Place; DUPAGE; ★ **CHI**; mail Hinsdale **z** 60521; pop. incl. with Hinsdale (Inc. Place)
Somerset; MCD-Township; JACKSON; ***171** R-8; ★ **CARB-**; mail Murphysboro **z** 62966; ℗ 4,021; © 4,115; Ⓡ 4,276
Somerset; RMC Place; MCHENRY; ★ **CHI**; mail Crystal Lake **z** 60014; pop. incl. with Crystal Lake (Inc. Place)
Somerset; RMC Place; SALINE; ***171** R-11; mail Harrisburg **z** 62946; rural
Somonauk; Inc. Place; DEKALB, LA SALLE; ▲ Somonauk; **170** D-10; 🅿; ★ **CHI**; **z** 60552; ℗ 1,263; © 1,295
Somonauk; MCD-Township; DEKALB; ***170** D-10; 🅿; ★ **CHI**; **z** 60552; ℗ 1,543; © 1,805
Songer; MCD-Township; CLAY; ***171** N-10; mail Xenia **z** 62899; ℗ 375; © 369
Sonora; MCD-Township; HANCOCK; ***170** H-3; mail Nauvoo **z** 62354; ℗ 537; © 489; Ⓡ 492
Soperville; KNOX; see Henderson Grove (RMC Place)
Sorento; Inc. Place; BOND; **171** M-8; elev. 537ft./164m.; 🅿; **z** 62086; ℗ 596; © 601
South Addison; RMC Place; DUPAGE; ***170** C-12; elev. 704ft./215m.; ★ **CHI**; mail Villa Park **z** 60181; pop. incl. with Villa Park (Inc. Place)
South Barrington; Inc. Place; COOK; **172** E-4; elev. 858ft./262m.; 🅿; ★ **CHI**; **z** 60010; ℗ 2,937; © 3,760
South Beloit; Inc. Place; WINNEBAGO; **170** A-9; elev. 745ft./227m.; 🅿; ★ **RKFD**; **z** 61080; ℗ 4,072; © 5,397
South Chicago; RMC Place; COOK; ***170** C-13; ★ **CHI**; mail Chicago **z** 60617; pop. incl. with Chicago (Inc. Place)
South Chicago Heights; Inc. Place; COOK; **172** N-9; elev. 717ft./219m.; 🅿; ★ **CHI**; **z** 60411 & mail Steger **z** 60475; ℗ 3,597; © 3,970
South Crouch; MCD-Township; HAMILTON; ***171** P-11; mail Mc Leansboro **z** 62859; ℗ 263; © 249
South Danville; RMC Place; VERMILION; ***170** I-13; ★ **DANV**; mail Danville **z** 61832; pop. incl. with Danville (Inc. Place)
South Deering; RMC Place; COOK; ***170** D-13; ★ **CHI**; mail Chicago **z** 60617; pop. incl. with Chicago (Inc. Place)
South Dixon; MCD-Township; LEE; ***170** C-8; mail Dixon **z** 61021; ℗ 820; © 828
South Elgin; Inc. Place; KANE; **172** G-2; elev. 715ft./218m.; 🅿; ★ **CHI**; **z** 60177; ℗ 7,474; © 16,100; ◆ 21,096
Southern Hills; RMC Place; JACKSON; ***171** R-9; ★ **CARB-**; mail Carbondale **z** 62901; pop. incl. with Carbondale (Inc. Place)
Southern View; Inc. Place; SANGAMON; **173** G-16; elev. 610ft./186m.; 🅿; ★ **SPRG**; **z** 62703; ℗ 2,044; © 1,695
South Fillmore; MCD-Township; MONTGOMERY; ***171** M-9; mail Fillmore **z** 62032; ℗ 238; © 246
South Flannigan; MCD-Township; HAMILTON; ***171** Q-10; mail Thompsonville **z** 62890; ℗ 155; © 139
South Fork; MCD-Township; CHRISTIAN; ***171** K-8; mail Kincaid **z** 62540; ℗ 2,629; © 2,696
South Grove; MCD-Township; DEKALB; ***170** B-10; mail Kirkland **z** 60146; ℗ 461; © 535
South Holland; Inc. Place; COOK; **172** M-10; elev. 600ft./183m.; 🅿; ★ **CHI**; **z** 60473; ℗ 22,105; © 22,147; ◆ 21,471
South Homer; MCD-Township; CHAMPAIGN; ***170** J-12; mail Homer **z** 61849; ℗ 1,624; © 1,585
South Hurricane; MCD-Township; FAYETTE; ***171** M-9; mail Bingham **z** 62011; ℗ 330; © 335
South Jacksonville; Inc. Place; MORGAN; **171** K-6; elev. 621ft./189m.; mail Jacksonville **z** 62650; ℗ 3,187; © 3,475
Southlawn; RMC Place; SANGAMON; ***171** K-8; ★ **SPRG**; pop. incl. with Springfield (Inc. Place)
South Litchfield; MCD-Township; MONTGOMERY; ***171** M-8; mail Litchfield **z** 62056; ℗ 3,678; © 3,476
South Lockport; RMC Place; WILL; ***170** D-12; ★ **CHI**; mail Lockport **z** 60441; pop. incl. with Lockport (Inc. Place)
South Macon; MCD-Township; MACON; ***171** K-9; mail Macon **z** 62544; ℗ 1,633; © 1,545
South Moline; MCD-Township; ROCK ISLAND; ***170** D-5; ★ **D-RI-M**; mail East Moline **z** 61244; ℗ 36,781; © 36,586
Southmoor; MADISON; see Southmore (RMC Place)
Southmore (Southmoor); RMC Place; MADISON; ***171** N-6; ★ **ST.L**; mail Godfrey **z** 62035; pop. incl. with Godfrey (Inc. Place)
Southmore Heights; RMC Place; EFFINGHAM; ***171** M-10; mail Altamont **z** 62411; pop. incl. with Altamont (Inc. Place)
South Mounds; RMC Place; PULASKI; mail Mounds **z** 62964; pop. incl. with Mounds (Inc. Place)
South Muddy; MCD-Township; JASPER; ***171** N-11; mail Newton **z** 62448; ℗ 365; © 322
South Ottawa; MCD-Township; LA SALLE; ***170** E-10; mail Ottawa **z** 61350; ℗ 7,684; © 8,222
South Otter; MCD-Township; MACOUPIN; ***171** L-7; mail Palmyra **z** 62674; ℗ 426; © 395
South Palmyra; MCD-Township; MACOUPIN; ***171** L-7; mail Palmyra **z** 62674; ℗ 846; © 819
South Pekin; Inc. Place; TAZEWELL; **170** H-8; elev. 514ft./157m.; 🅿; ★ **PEOR**; **z** 61564; ℗ 1,184; © 1,162
Southport; RMC Place; PEORIA; ***170** G-7; mail Brimfield **z** 61517; rural
South Rock Island; MCD-Township; ROCK ISLAND; ***170** D-5; ★ **D-RI-M**; mail Rock Island **z** 61201; ℗ 19,678; © 19,174
South Rome; RMC Place; PEORIA; ***170** G-8; ★ **PEOR**; mail Chillicothe **z** 61523; ● 350
South Ross; MCD-Township; VERMILION; ***170** I-13; mail Henning **z** 61848; ℗ 1,226; © 1,109
South Roxana; Inc. Place; MADISON; **195** B-8; elev. 440ft./134m.; 🅿; ★ **ST.L**; **z** 62087; ℗ 1,961; © 1,888
South Shore; RMC Place; COOK; ***170** C-13; ★ **CHI**; mail Chicago **z** 60649; pop. incl. with Chicago (Inc. Place)
South Standard; RMC Place; MACOUPIN; ***171** L-7; pop. incl. with Standard City (Inc. Place)
South Streator; RMC Place; LIVINGSTON; **170** F-10; mail Streator **z** 61364; pop. incl. with Streator (Inc. Place)
South Twigg; MCD-Township; HAMILTON; ***171** Q-11; mail Broughton **z** 62817; ℗ 184; © 129
South Waukegan; RMC Place; LAKE; ★ **CHI**; mail North Chicago **z** 60064; pop. incl. with North Chicago (Inc. Place)
Southwest; MCD-Township; CRAWFORD; ***171** N-13; mail Sumner **z** 62466; ℗ 102; © 76
Southwest Station; RMC Place; SANGAMON; ★ **SPRG**; mail Springfield **z** 62704, **z** 62707; pop. incl. with Springfield (Inc. Place)
South Wheatland; MCD-Township; MACON; ***170** J-9; ★ **DEC**; mail Elwin **z** 62532; ℗ 4,340; © 4,185
South Wilmington; Inc. Place; GRUNDY; **170** E-11; elev. 590ft./180m.; 🅿; **z** 60474; ℗ 698; © 621
Space Valley; RMC Place; DUPAGE; ★ **CHI**; mail Hinsdale **z** 60521; ● 100
Spankey; RMC Place; JERSEY; ***171** M-5; elev. 454ft./138m.; mail Fieldon **z** 62031
Sparks Hill; RMC Place; HARDIN; ***171** R-11; mail Elizabethtown **z** 62931; rural
Sparland; Inc. Place; MARSHALL; **170** F-8; elev. 468ft./143m.; 🅿; **z** 61565; ℗ 412; © 504
Sparta; MCD-Township; KNOX; ***170** F-6; mail Wataga **z** 61488; ℗ 1,226; © 1,183
Sparta; Inc. Place; RANDOLPH; **171** Q-7; elev. 541ft./165m.; 🅿 🅷; **z** 62286; ℗ 4,853; © 4,486
Spaulding; RMC Place; COOK; ***170** B-11; ★ **CHI**; mail Elgin **z** 60120; rural
Spaulding; Inc. Place; SANGAMON; ***170** J-8; elev. 578ft./176m.; 🅿; ★ **SPRG**; **z** 62561; ℗ 440; © 559
Speer; RMC Place; STARK; **170** F-8; elev. 746ft./227m.; 🅿; **z** 61479; ● 100
Spencer; RMC Place; WILL; ***170** D-12; ★ **CHI**; mail New Lenox **z** 60451; ● 70
Spencer Heights; RMC Place; PULASKI; ***171** T-9; mail Mounds **z** 62964; ● 100
Spillertown; Inc. Place; WILLIAMSON; ***171** R-10; elev. 483ft./147m.; ★ **CARB-**; mail Marion **z** 62959; ℗ 249; © 220
Spin Lake; RMC Place; MCLEAN; mail Danvers **z** 61732; rural
Sportsman Lake; RMC Place; MARION; mail Salem **z** 62881; rural
Spring; MCD-Township; BOONE; ***170** B-10; mail Belvidere **z** 61008; ℗ 1,032; © 1,001
Spring Arbor Lake; RMC Place; JACKSON; ***171** R-9; elev. 550ft./168m.; ★ **CARB-**; mail Carbondale **z** 62901; ● 85
Spring Bay; Inc. Place; WOODFORD; **170** G-8; elev. 471ft./144m.; 🅿; ★ **PEOR**; **z** 61611; ℗ 439; © 436
Spring Bay; MCD-Township; WOODFORD; ***170** G-8; 🅿; ★ **PEOR**; **z** 61611; ℗ 2,658; © 2,552
Spring Creek; MCD-Township; PIKE; ***171** L-4; mail Nebo **z** 62355; ℗ 716; © 677
Springerton; Inc. Place; WHITE; **171** P-11; elev. 384ft./117m.; 🅿; **z** 62887; ℗ 166; © 134
Springfield; Inc. Place; **STATE CAPITAL**; ⊡ SANGAMON; **170** J-8; elev. 600ft./183m.; 🅿 🅷 🅲 4,761 ■; ★ **SPRG**; **z** 62701-08, **z** 62711-12, **z** 62715-16, **z** 62719, **z** 62721-23, **z** 62726, **z** 62736, **z** 62739, **z** 62746, **z** 62756-57, **z** 62761-67, **z** 62769, **z** 62776-77, **z** 62781, **z** 62786, **z** 62791, **z** 62794, **z** 62796; ℗ 105,417; © 111,454; Ⓡ 111,355; ◆ 117,122
Springfield; MCD-Township; SANGAMON; ***170** J-8; 🅿 🅲 4,761; ★ **SPRG**; **z** 62701-08, **z** 62711-12, **z** 62715-16, **z** 62719, **z** 62721-23, **z** 62726, **z** 62736, **z** 62739, **z** 62746, **z** 62756-57, **z** 62761-67, **z** 62769, **z** 62776-77, **z** 62781, **z** 62786, **z** 62791, **z** 62794, **z** 62796, **z** 98662; includes a small part of the City of Springfield; ℗ 7,857; © 7,046
Spring Garden; RMC Place; JEFFERSON; ▲ Spring Garden; **171** P-10; mail Ina **z** 62846; ● 50
Spring Garden; MCD-Township; JEFFERSON; ***171** P-10; mail Ina **z** 62846; ℗ 1,441; © 3,454
Spring Grove; Inc. Place; MCHENRY; **170** A-11; elev. 793ft./242m.; 🅿; ★ **CHI**; **z** 60081; ℗ 1,066; © 3,880
Spring Grove; MCD-Township; WARREN; ***170** F-5; mail Alexis **z** 61412; ℗ 1,133; © 1,120
Springhaven; RMC Place; MADISON; ***171** M-6; ★ **ST.L**; mail Godfrey **z** 62035; pop. incl. with Godfrey (Inc. Place)
Spring Hill; RMC Place; WHITESIDE; **170** D-7; elev. 637ft./194m.; mail Erie **z** 61250; ● 50
Spring Lake; RMC Place; CHAMPAIGN; ***170** I-11; elev. 700ft./213m.; mail Mahomet **z** 61853; pop. incl. with Mahomet (Inc. Place)
Spring Lake; RMC Place; TAZEWELL; ***170** H-7; mail Manito **z** 61546; ● 80
Spring Lake; MCD-Township; TAZEWELL; ***170** H-7; mail Manito **z** 61546; ℗ 1,745; © 2,011
Spring Point; MCD-Township; CUMBERLAND; ***171** L-11; mail Sigel **z** 62462; ℗ 1,131; © 1,207
Spring Valley; Inc. Place; BUREAU; **170** E-9; elev. 570ft./174m.; 🅿 🅷; **z** 61362; ℗ 5,246; © 5,398
Squaw Grove; MCD-Township; DEKALB; ***170** C-10; mail Hinckley **z** 60520; ℗ 2,387; © 2,712
Squaw Prairie Estate; RMC Place; BOONE; ***170** A-10; elev. 820ft./250m.; ★ **RKFD**; mail Belvidere **z** 61008; ● 60
Stable; RMC Place; WILLIAMSON; ***171** R-9; elev. 450ft./137m.; ★ **CARB-**; mail Carterville **z** 62918; pop. incl. with Carterville (Inc. Place)
Stainfield; RMC Place; KENDALL; ***170** C-11; elev. 675ft./206m.; ★ **CHI**; mail Plano **z** 60545; ● 50
Staley (Staleys); RMC Place; CHAMPAIGN; ***170** I-11; elev. 732ft./223m.; ★ **CH-U**; mail Champaign **z** 61822; rural
Staleys; CHAMPAIGN; see Staley (RMC Place)
Standard; Inc. Place; PUTNAM; ***170** E-9; elev. 650ft./198m.; 🅿; **z** 61363; ℗ 260; © 256
Standard City; Inc. Place; MACOUPIN; **171** L-7; elev. 640ft./195m.; 🅿; **z** 62640; ℗ 128; © 138
Stanford; MCD-Township; CLAY; ***171** O-11; mail Clay City **z** 62824; ℗ 680; © 654
Stanford; Inc. Place; MCLEAN; **170** H-9; elev. 680ft./207m.; 🅿; **z** 61774; ℗ 620; © 670
Stanton; MCD-Township; CHAMPAIGN; ***170** I-12; mail Saint Joseph **z** 61873; ℗ 474; © 474
Stanton Point; RMC Place; LAKE; ★ **CHI**; mail Ingleside **z** 60041
Stark; RMC Place; STARK; ***170** F-7; mail Princeville **z** 61559; ● 80
STARK; **170** F-7; ℗ 6,534; © 6,332; ◆ 6,170
Starks; RMC Place; KANE; ***170** B-11; elev. 916ft./279m.; ★ **CHI**; mail Hampshire **z** 60140; pop. incl. with Pingree Grove (Inc. Place)
Starne (Starnes); RMC Place; SANGAMON; ***170** J-8; ★ **SPRG**; mail Springfield **z** 62702; ● 80
Starnes; SANGAMON; see Starne (RMC Place)
State Line; RMC Place; CLARK; ***171** L-13; elev. 564ft./172m.; mail Dennison **z** 62423; ● 30
State Park Place; RMC Place; MADISON, ST. CLAIR; **195** E-9; ★ **ST.L**; mail Collinsville **z** 62234, East Saint Louis **z** 62201; ● 2,600
State Street; RMC Place; COOK; ★ **CHI**; mail Chicago **z** 60628; pop. incl. with Chicago (Inc. Place)
Staunton; Inc. Place; MACOUPIN; ▲ Staunton; **171** M-7; elev. 622ft./190m.; 🅿 🅷; **z** 62088; ℗ 4,806; © 5,030
Staunton; MCD-Township; MACOUPIN; ***171** M-7; 🅿; **z** 62088; ℗ 5,482; © 5,731
Stavanger; RMC Place; LA SALLE; ***170** E-10; elev. 672ft./205m.; mail Seneca **z** 61360; ● 40
Steel City; RMC Place; FRANKLIN; **171** Q-10; mail Benton **z** 62812; ● 150
Steeleville; Inc. Place; RANDOLPH; **171** Q-7; elev. 410ft./125m.; 🅿; **z** 62288; ℗ 2,059; © 2,077
Steeple Run; RMC Place; DUPAGE; ***170** C-12; ★ **CHI**; mail Naperville **z** 60540; ● 1,150
Steger; Inc. Place; COOK, WILL; **170** D-13; elev. 715ft./218m.; 🅿; ★ **CHI**; **z** 60475; ℗ 8,592; © 9,682; Ⓡ 9,679
Stelle; RMC Place; FORD; **170** F-12; mail Cabery **z** 60919; ● 100
STEPHENSON; **170** A-7; ℗ 48,052; © 48,979; ◆ 45,799
Sterling; Inc. Place; WHITESIDE; **170** C-8; elev. 645ft./197m.; 🅿 🅷 ■; **z** 61081; ℗ 15,132; © 15,451; Ⓡ 15,596; ◆ 15,058
Sterling; MCD-Township; WHITESIDE; ***170** C-8; 🅿; **z** 61081; ℗ 18,329; © 18,679; Ⓡ 18,677
Sterling Place; RMC Place; ST. CLAIR; ***171** O-6; ★ **ST.L**; mail Caseyville **z** 62232; pop. incl. with Caseyville (Inc. Place)
Steuben; MCD-Township; MARSHALL; ***170** F-8; mail Sparland **z** 61565; ℗ 1,190; © 1,328
Stevenson; MCD-Township; MARION; ***171** O-10; mail Salem **z** 62881; ℗ 1,090; © 1,116
Steward; Inc. Place; LEE; **170** C-9; elev. 819ft./250m.; 🅿; **z** 60553; ℗ 282; © 271
Stewardson; Inc. Place; SHELBY; **171** L-10; elev. 640ft./195m.; 🅿; **z** 62463; ℗ 660; © 747
Stickney; Inc. Place; COOK; ▲ Stickney; **172** I-8; elev. 604ft./184m.; 🅿; ★ **CHI**; **z** 60402 & mail Chicago **z** 60638; ℗ 5,678; © 6,148
Stickney; MCD-Township; COOK; ***170** C-13; 🅿; ★ **CHI**; **z** 60402 & mail Chicago **z** 60638; ℗ 37,297; © 38,673
Stillman Valley; Inc. Place; OGLE; **170** B-9; elev. 720ft./219m.; 🅿; **z** 61084; ℗ 848; © 1,048
Stillmeadow; RMC Place; KANE; ***170** C-11; elev. 816ft./249m.; ★ **CHI**; mail Elburn **z** 60119; ● 130
Stillwell; RMC Place; HANCOCK; **170** I-3; mail West Point **z** 62380; ● 80
Stiritz; RMC Place; WILLIAMSON; ***171** R-10; ★ **CARB-**; mail West Frankfort **z** 62896; ● 200
Stites; MCD-Township; ST. CLAIR; ***171** O-6; ★ **ST.L**; mail Lovejoy **z** 62059; ℗ 1,201; © 679
Stockland; RMC Place; IROQUOIS; **170** G-13; elev. 689ft./210m.; 🅿; **z** 60967; ● 150
Stockland; MCD-Township; IROQUOIS; ***170** G-13; 🅿; **z** 60967; ℗ 341; © 343
Stockton; Inc. Place; JO DAVIESS; ▲ Stockton; **170** A-7; 🅿; **z** 61085; ℗ 1,871; © 1,926
Stockton; MCD-Township; JO DAVIESS; ***170** A-7; 🅿; **z** 61085; ℗ 2,485; © 2,555
Stock Yards; RMC Place; COOK; ***170** C-13; ★ **CHI**; mail Chicago **z** 60609; pop. incl. with Chicago (Inc. Place)
Stolletown; RMC Place; CLINTON; ***171** N-8; elev. 464ft./141m.; mail Carlyle **z** 62231
Stone; RMC Place; HARDIN; ***171** S-11; elev. 400ft./122m.; mail Elizabethtown **z** 62931; ● 50
Stone Avenue; RMC Place; COOK; ***170** C-12; ★ **CHI**; pop. incl. with La Grange (Inc. Place)
Stone Church; RMC Place; WASHINGTON; ***171** P-8; elev. 454ft./138m.; mail Addieville **z** 62214; ● 50
Stonefort; Inc. Place; SALINE, WILLIAMSON; **171** R-10; elev. 400ft./122m.; 🅿; **z** 62987; ℗ 311; © 292
Stonefort; MCD-Township; SALINE; ***171** R-10; 🅿; **z** 62987; includes part of the Village of Stonefort; ℗ 346; © 379
Stonehenge; RMC Place; DEKALB; ***170** C-10; elev. 850ft./259m.; ★ **DKLB**; mail Sycamore **z** 60178
Stonelake; RMC Place; MCHENRY; ★ **CHI**; mail Woodstock **z** 60098; pop. incl. with Woodstock (Inc. Place)
Stone Park; Inc. Place; COOK; **172** H-7; elev. 640ft./195m.; 🅿; ★ **CHI**; **z** 60165; ℗ 4,383; © 5,127
Stoneyville; RMC Place; LA SALLE; ***170** E-10; mail Ottawa **z** 61350; ● 30
Stonington; Inc. Place; CHRISTIAN; ▲ Stonington; **171** K-9; 🅿; **z** 62567; ℗ 1,006; © 960
Stonington; MCD-Township; CHRISTIAN; ***171** K-9; 🅿; **z** 62567; ℗ 1,280; © 1,180
Stookey; MCD-Town; ST. CLAIR; ***171** O-6; ★ **ST.L**; mail Belleville **z** 62221; ℗ 10,737; © 10,185
Storeyland; RMC Place; MADISON; ***171** N-6; ★ **ST.L**; mail Godfrey **z** 62035; pop. incl. with Godfrey (Inc. Place)
Storybrook; RMC Place; KENDALL; ***170** D-11; elev. 649ft./198m.; ★ **CHI**; mail Bristol **z** 60512; ● 150
Stoy; Inc. Place; CRAWFORD; **171** M-13; elev. 467ft./142m.; 🅿; **z** 62464; ℗ 135; © 119
Strasburg; Inc. Place; SHELBY; **171** L-10; elev. 642ft./196m.; 🅿; **z** 62465; ℗ 473; © 603
Stratford; RMC Place; OGLE; **170** B-8; mail Polo **z** 61064; ● 50
Stratford Park; RMC Place; CHAMPAIGN; ***170** I-11; elev. 720ft./219m.; ★ **CH-U**; mail Champaign **z** 61821; pop. incl. with Champaign (Inc. Place)
Stratton; MCD-Township; EDGAR; ***171** K-13; mail Paris **z** 61944; ℗ 594; © 531
Stratton; RMC Place; JEFFERSON; ***171** O-10; mail Bluford **z** 62814, Keenes **z** 62851; rural
Strawberry Hill; RMC Place; WHITESIDE; ***170** C-7; mail Morrison **z** 61270; rural
Strawn; Inc. Place; LIVINGSTON; **170** G-11; elev. 767ft./234m.; 🅿; **z** 61775; ℗ 132; © 104
Streamwood; Inc. Place; COOK; **172** F-3; elev. 800ft./244m.; 🅿 🅷; ★ **CHI**; **z** 60107; ℗ 30,987; © 36,407; ◆ 36,598
Streator; Inc. Place; LA SALLE, LIVINGSTON; **170** F-10; elev. 626ft./191m.; 🅿 🅷 ■; **z** 61364; ℗ 14,121; © 14,190; ◆ 13,513
Streator Junction; RMC Place; WOODFORD; ★ **PEOR**; mail Eureka **z** 61530; pop. incl. with Eureka (Inc. Place)
Stringtown; RMC Place; RICHLAND; ***171** N-12; mail Olney **z** 62450, Shobonier **z** 62885; rural
Stronghurst; Inc. Place; HENDERSON; **170** G-4; elev. 672ft./205m.; 🅿; **z** 61480; ℗ 799; © 896
Stronghurst; MCD-Township; HENDERSON; ***170** G-4; 🅿; **z** 61480; includes part of the Village of Stronghurst; ℗ 1,055; © 1,164
Stubblefield; RMC Place; BOND; ***171** N-8; elev. 540ft./165m.; mail Greenville **z** 62246; rural
Sublette; Inc. Place; LEE; ▲ Sublette; **170** D-9; elev. 927ft./283m.; 🅿; **z** 61367; ℗ 394; © 456
Sublette; MCD-Township; LEE; ***170** D-9; 🅿; **z** 61367; ℗ 745; © 807
Suburban Estates; RMC Place; DUPAGE; ***170** C-12; ★ **CHI**; mail Downers Grove **z** 60515; ● 350
Suburban Heights (Baldwin Heights); RMC Place; WASHINGTON; ***171** O-9; mail Centralia **z** 62801; ● 90
Suez; MCD-Township; MERCER; ***170** F-5; mail Alexis **z** 61412; ℗ 730; © 685
Sugar Brook; RMC Place; WILL; ***170** D-12; ★ **CHI**; mail Bolingbrook **z** 60440; pop. incl. with Bolingbrook (Inc. Place)
Sugar Creek; MCD-Township; CLINTON; ***171** O-8; ★ **ST.L**; mail Trenton **z** 62293; ℗ 4,775; © 5,133
Sugar Creek; WABASH; see Schrodts Station (RMC Place)
Sugar Grove; Inc. Place; KANE; ▲ Sugar Grove; **170** C-11; 🅿; ★ **CHI**; **z** 60554; ℗ 2,005; © 3,909
Sugar Grove; MCD-Township; KANE; ***170** C-11; 🅿; ★ **CHI**; **z** 60554; ℗ 5,514; © 9,595
Sugar Grove; RMC Place; MERCER; ***170** E-5; mail Aledo **z** 61231; ● 30
Sugar Island; RMC Place; KANKAKEE; ***170** F-13; elev. 619ft./189m.; ★ **KANK**; mail Chebanse **z** 60922; ● 60
Sugar Loaf (Sugar Loaf Heights); RMC Place; ST. CLAIR; ★ **ST.L**; mail East Carondelet **z** 62240; pop. incl. with Dupo (Inc. Place)
Sugar Loaf; MCD-Township; ST. CLAIR; ***171** O-6; ★ **ST.L**; mail East Carondelet **z** 62240; ℗ 7,073; © 7,098; Ⓡ 7,102
Sugar Loaf Heights; RMC Place; ST. CLAIR; ***171** O-6; elev. 423ft./129m.; ★ **ST.L**; pop. incl. with Dupo (Inc. Place)
Sugar Loaf Heights; ST. CLAIR; see Sugar Loaf (RMC Place)
Sullivan; MCD-Township; LIVINGSTON; ***170** F-11; mail Cullom **z** 60929; ℗ 782; © 738
Sullivan; Inc. Place; ⊡ MOULTRIE; ▲ Sullivan; **171** K-10; 🅿; **z** 61951; ℗ 4,354; © 4,326
Sullivan; MCD-Township; MOULTRIE; ***171** K-10; 🅿; **z** 61951; ℗ 5,690; © 5,874
Sullivant; MCD-Township; FORD; ***170** H-11; mail Sibley **z** 61773; ℗ 608; © 594
Summerdale; RMC Place; COOK; ★ **CHI**; mail Chicago **z** 60640; pop. incl. with Chicago (Inc. Place)
Summerfield; Inc. Place; ST. CLAIR; **171** O-7; elev. 478ft./146m.; 🅿; ★ **ST.L**; **z** 62289; ℗ 509; © 472
Summerhill; RMC Place; COOK; ★ **CHI**; mail Northbrook **z** 60062; pop. incl. with Northbrook (Inc. Place)
Summer Hill; RMC Place; COOK; ★ **CHI**; mail Elgin **z** 60120; pop. incl. with Elgin (Inc. Place)
Summer Hill; RMC Place; PIKE; **171** K-4; elev. 755ft./230m.; 🅿; **z** 62363; ● 100
Summerlakes; RMC Place; DUPAGE; ★ **CHI**; mail Warrenville **z** 60555; pop. incl. with Warrenville (Inc. Place)
Summersville; RMC Place; JEFFERSON; ***171** P-10; mail Mount Vernon **z** 62864; pop. incl. with Mount Vernon (Inc. Place)
Summerville; RMC Place; MACOUPIN; ***171** M-6; mail Medora **z** 62063; ● 50
Summit; Inc. Place; COOK; **172** J-7; elev. 610ft./186m.; 🅿; ★ **CHI**; **z** 60501; ℗ 9,971; © 10,637
Summit; MCD-Township; EFFINGHAM; ***171** M-10; mail Shumway **z** 62461; ℗ 2,665; © 3,431
Summit Argo; RMC Place; COOK; 🅿; ★ **CHI**; **z** 60501; pop. incl. with Summit (Inc. Place)
Summit Heights; RMC Place; MONTGOMERY; mail Taylor Springs **z** 62089
Summum; RMC Place; FULTON; **170** I-6; mail Astoria **z** 61501; ● 150
Sumner; MCD-Township; KANKAKEE; ***170** E-13; mail Grant Park **z** 60940; ℗ 799; © 879
Sumner; Inc. Place; LAWRENCE; **171** N-13; elev. 459ft./140m.; 🅿; **z** 62466; ℗ 1,083; © 1,022
Sumner; MCD-Township; WARREN; ***170** F-5; mail Little York **z** 61453; ℗ 673; © 551
Sumpter; MCD-Township; CUMBERLAND; ***171** L-11; mail Toledo **z** 62468; ℗ 1,872; © 1,967
Sunbeam; RMC Place; MERCER; ***170** F-5; mail Aledo **z** 61231; rural
Sunbury; MCD-Township; LIVINGSTON; ***170** F-10; mail Blackstone **z** 61313; ℗ 258; © 235
Sunfield; RMC Place; PERRY; **171** Q-9; mail Du Quoin **z** 62832; ● 220
Sunny Acres; RMC Place; CHAMPAIGN; ***170** I-11; elev. 725ft./221m.; mail Mahomet **z** 61853; pop. incl. with Mahomet (Inc. Place)
Sunny Acres; RMC Place; KANKAKEE; ***170** E-13; elev. 681ft./208m.; ★ **KANK**; mail Manteno **z** 60950; ● 200
Sunny Crest; RMC Place; COOK; ***170** D-13; elev. 703ft./214m.; ★ **CHI**; mail Homewood **z** 60430; pop. incl. with Flossmoor (Inc. Place)
Sunnydale; RMC Place; LEE; ***170** C-8; mail Dixon **z** 61021; ● 40
Sunny Hill; RMC Place; HENRY; **170** E-6; elev. 732ft./223m.; ★ **D-RI-M**; mail Orion **z** 61273; ● 400
Sunny Hills Estates; RMC Place; DUPAGE; ★ **CHI**; mail Downers Grove **z** 60515; ● 200
Sunnyland; RMC Place; TAZEWELL; ***170** G-8; elev. 680ft./207m.; ★ **PEOR**; mail Washington **z** 61571
Sunny Land; RMC Place; WILL; ★ **CHI**; mail Joliet **z** 60435; pop. incl. with Crest Hill (Inc. Place)
Sunnyside; RMC Place; MCHENRY; ***170** A-11; elev. 800ft./244m.; ★ **CHI**; mail McHenry **z** 60050; pop. incl. with Johnsburg (Inc. Place)
Sunnyside; RMC Place; WILLIAMSON; ***171** R-9; ★ **CARB-**; mail Herrin **z** 62948; pop. incl. with Herrin (Inc. Place)
Sunnyside Acres; RMC Place; CHRISTIAN; ***171** K-8; elev. 582ft./177m.; mail Edinburg **z** 62531; ● 30
Sunrise Ridge; RMC Place; WILL; ★ **CHI**; mail Lockport **z** 60441; pop. incl. with Romeoville (Inc. Place)
Sun River Terrace; Inc. Place; KANKAKEE; **170** F-13; ★ **KANK**; mail Saint Anne **z** 60964; ℗ 532; © 383
Sunset Acres; RMC Place; LAKE; ★ **CHI**; mail Libertyville **z** 60048; ● 90
Sunset Acres; RMC Place; STEPHENSON; ***170** A-8; elev. 800ft./244m.; mail Freeport **z** 61032; ● 160
Sunset Harbor; RMC Place; WILLIAMSON; mail Marion **z** 62959
Sunset Hills; RMC Place; COOK; ***170** B-12; ★ **CHI**; mail Roselle **z** 60172; ● 200
Sunset Lake; RMC Place; MACOUPIN; ***171** L-7; mail Girard **z** 62640; ● 500
Sutter; RMC Place; HANCOCK; ***170** I-3; elev. 656ft./200m.; 🅿; **z** 62373
Sutton; RMC Place; COOK; ***170** B-12; ★ **CHI**; mail Barrington **z** 60010; rural
Sutton Point; RMC Place; COOK; ★ **CHI**; mail Northbrook **z** 60062; pop. incl. with Northbrook (Inc. Place)
Swan; MCD-Township; WARREN; ***170** G-5; mail Roseville **z** 61473; ℗ 324; © 296
Swan Creek; RMC Place; WARREN; **170** G-5; mail Roseville **z** 61473; ● 90
Swansea; Inc. Place; ST. CLAIR; **171** O-7; elev. 550ft./168m.; 🅿; ★ **ST.L**; **z** 62220-21, **z** 62223, **z** 62226; ℗ 8,201; © 10,579; Ⓡ 10,563
Swanwick; RMC Place; PERRY; **171** P-8; elev. 572ft./174m.; 🅿; **z** 62237; ● 100
Swedona; RMC Place; MERCER; ***170** E-5; mail Lynn Center **z** 61262; ● 100
Sweet Water; RMC Place; MENARD; ***170** I-7; elev. 610ft./186m.; 🅿; **z** 62642 & mail Meredosia **z** 62665; ● 100
Swiss Valley; RMC Place; WILL; ★ **CHI**; mail Crete **z** 60417; pop. incl. with Crete (Inc. Place)
Swissville; RMC Place; LEE; mail Dixon **z** 61021; pop. incl. with Dixon (Inc. Place)
Swygert; RMC Place; LIVINGSTON; ***170** F-11; elev. 733ft./223m.; mail Pontiac **z** 61764; ● 25
Sycamore; Inc. Place; ⊡ DEKALB; **170** B-10; elev. 877ft./267m.; 🅿 🅷; ★ **DKLB**; **z** 60178; ℗ 9,708; © 12,020
Sycamore; MCD-Township; DEKALB; ***170** B-10; 🅿; ★ **DKLB**; **z** 60178; includes part of the City of Sycamore; ℗ 8,843; © 10,401
Sylvan Hill; RMC Place; COOK; ***170** D-13; elev. 700ft./213m.; ★ **CHI**; mail Orland Park **z** 60462; ● 200
Sylvan Lake; RMC Place; LAKE; **172** C-5; ★ **CHI**; mail Mundelein **z** 60060; ● 430
Symerton; Inc. Place; WILL; **170** E-12; elev. 635ft./194m.; mail Wilmington **z** 60481; ℗ 110; © 106
Symmes; MCD-Township; EDGAR; ***171** K-13; mail Paris **z** 61944; ℗ 1,136; © 1,077

T

Table Grove; Inc. Place; FULTON; **170** H-5; elev. 734ft./224m.; 🅿; **z** 61482; ℗ 408; © 396
Tabor; RMC Place; DE WITT; ***170** I-9; mail Waynesville **z** 61778; rural
Taggert Woods; RMC Place; MACOUPIN; ***171** L-7; elev. 600ft./183m.; mail Carlinville **z** 62626; ● 200
Talbott; RMC Place; TAZEWELL; ***170** H-7; mail Manito **z** 61546; ● 400
Talkington; MCD-Township; SANGAMON; ***171** K-7; mail Waverly **z** 62692; ℗ 257; © 263
Tallula; Inc. Place; MENARD; **170** J-7; elev. 620ft./189m.; 🅿; **z** 62688; ℗ 598; © 638
Tamalco; RMC Place; BOND; ▲ Tamalco; **171** N-9; elev. 481ft./147m.; mail Keyesport **z** 62253; ● 40
Tamalco; MCD-Township; BOND; ***171** N-8; mail Keyesport **z** 62253; ℗ 575; © 575
Tamarac; RMC Place; COOK; ★ **CHI**; mail Flossmoor **z** 60422; pop. incl. with Flossmoor (Inc. Place)
Tamaroa; Inc. Place; PERRY; **171** P-9; elev. 504ft./154m.; 🅿; **z** 62888; ℗ 780; © 740
Tamms; Inc. Place; ALEXANDER; **171** T-9; elev. 338ft./103m.; 🅿; **z** 62988, **z** 62993; ℗ 748; © 724; Ⓡ 1,192
Tampico; Inc. Place; WHITESIDE; ▲ Tampico; **170** D-7; 🅿; **z** 61283; ℗ 833; © 772
Tampico; MCD-Township; WHITESIDE; ***170** D-7; 🅿; **z** 61283; ℗ 1,253; © 1,151
Tanbark; RMC Place; COOK; ***170** D-13; elev. 700ft./213m.; ★ **CHI**; mail Tinley Park **z** 60477; pop. incl. with Tinley Park (Inc. Place)
Tanglewood; RMC Place; COOK; ★ **CHI**; mail Hanover Park **z** 60133; pop. incl. with Hanover Park (Inc. Place)
Tate; MCD-Township; SALINE; ***171** Q-10; mail Galatia **z** 62935; ℗ 238; © 256
Tatumville; RMC Place; ALEXANDER; ***171** T-9; elev. 340ft./104m.; mail Tamms **z** 62988; rural
Taylor; MCD-Township; OGLE; ***170** C-8; mail Dixon **z** 61021; ℗ 547; © 784
Taylor Ridge; RMC Place; ROCK ISLAND; **170** E-5; elev. 770ft./235m.; 🅿; ★ **D-RI-M**; **z** 61284; ● 200
Taylor Springs; Inc. Place; MONTGOMERY; **171** M-8; elev. 620ft./189m.; 🅿; **z** 62089; ℗ 670; © 583
Taylorville; Inc. Place; ⊡ CHRISTIAN; **171** K-9; elev. 634ft./193m.; 🅿 🅷; **z** 62568; ℗ 11,133; © 11,427
Taylorville; MCD-Township; CHRISTIAN; ***171** K-8; 🅿; **z** 62568; includes part of the City of Taylorville; ℗ 12,595; © 12,659
TAZEWELL; **170** H-8; ℗ 123,692; © 128,485; ◆ 132,058
Techny; RMC Place; COOK; ***170** B-13; elev. 665ft./203m.; 🅿; ★ **CHI**; **z** 60082
Teheran; RMC Place; MASON; ***170** I-7; 🅿; **z** 62664
Temple Hill; RMC Place; POPE; **171** T-10; 🅿; **z** 62938; ● 35
Tenerelli; RMC Place; KANE; ***170** C-11; elev. 704ft./215m.; mail Big Rock **z** 60511; ● 50
Tennessee; Inc. Place; MCDONOUGH; ▲ Tennessee; **170** H-4; 🅿; **z** 62374; ℗ 127; © 144
Tennessee; MCD-Township; MCDONOUGH; ***170** H-4; 🅿; **z** 62374; ℗ 414; © 408
Terra Cotta (Terre Cotta); RMC Place; MCHENRY; ***170** A-11; ★ **CHI**; mail Crystal Lake **z** 60014; ● 150
Terre Cotta; MCHENRY; see Terra Cotta (RMC Place)
Terre Haute; RMC Place; HENDERSON; ▲ Terre Haute; **170** G-4; elev. 714ft./218m.; mail Lomax **z** 61454; ● 150
Terre Haute; MCD-Township; HENDERSON; ***170** G-4; mail Lomax **z** 61454; ℗ 305; © 279
Teutopolis; Inc. Place; EFFINGHAM; **171** M-11; elev. 604ft./184m.; 🅿; **z** 62467; ℗ 1,417; © 1,559
Teutopolis; MCD-Township; EFFINGHAM; ***171** M-11; 🅿; **z** 62467; includes part of the Village of Teutopolis; ℗ 2,332; © 2,515
Texas; MCD-Township; DE WITT; ***170** I-9; mail Clinton **z** 61727; ℗ 1,028; © 1,284
Texas City; RMC Place; SALINE; ***171** Q-11; elev. 367ft./112m.; mail Eldorado **z** 62930
Texico; RMC Place; JEFFERSON; **171** O-10; elev. 510ft./155m.; 🅿; **z** 62889; ● 160
Thackeray; RMC Place; HAMILTON; **171** Q-11; mail Mc Leansboro **z** 62859; ● 50
Thawville; Inc. Place; IROQUOIS; **170** G-12; elev. 690ft./210m.; 🅿; **z** 60968; ℗ 241; © 258
Thayer; Inc. Place; SANGAMON; **171** K-7; elev. 650ft./198m.; 🅿; **z** 62689; ℗ 730; © 750
Thebes; Inc. Place; ALEXANDER; **171** T-8; elev. 413ft./126m.; 🅿; **z** 62990; ℗ 461; © 478
Thebes Junction; RMC Place; ALEXANDER; mail Thebes **z** 62990; pop. incl. with Thebes (Inc. Place)
The Burg; RMC Place; LEE; ***170** C-9; mail Compton **z** 61318; rural
The Clusters; RMC Place; WILL; ★ **CHI**; mail Bolingbrook **z** 60440; pop. incl. with Bolingbrook (Inc. Place)
The Covered Bridges; RMC Place; DUPAGE; ★ **CHI**; mail Carol Stream **z** 60188; pop. incl. with Carol Stream (Inc. Place)
The Fairway of Country Lakes; RMC Place; DUPAGE; ★ **CHI**; mail Naperville **z** 60563; pop. incl. with Naperville (Inc. Place)
The Greens of Woodgate; RMC Place; COOK; ★ **CHI**; mail Matteson **z** 60443; pop. incl. with Matteson (Inc. Place)
The Knolls; RMC Place; KANE; ***170** C-11; elev. 912ft./278m.; ★ **CHI**; mail Saint Charles **z** 60175; ● 30
The Laurels; RMC Place; COOK; ★ **CHI**; mail Justice **z** 60458; pop. incl. with Justice (Inc. Place)
The Ledges; RMC Place; WINNEBAGO; ***170** A-9; elev. 800ft./244m.; ★ **RKFD**; mail Roscoe **z** 61073; ● 800
The Meadows; RMC Place; DUPAGE; ***170** C-12; ★ **CHI**; mail Lisle **z** 60532; ● 2,650
The Old Farm; RMC Place; CHAMPAIGN; ***170** I-11; elev. 725ft./221m.; ★ **CH-U**; mail Champaign **z** 61821; pop. incl. with Champaign (Inc. Place)
Third Lake; Inc. Place; LAKE; **172** A-5; elev. 770ft./235m.; 🅿; ★ **CHI**; **z** 60030 & mail Lake Villa **z** 60046; ℗ 1,248; © 1,355
Thomas; RMC Place; BUREAU; ***170** D-7; elev. 629ft./192m.; mail Tampico **z** 61283
Thomas Addition; RMC Place; LA SALLE; ***170** F-10; mail Streator **z** 61364; ● 250
Thomasboro; Inc. Place; CHAMPAIGN; **170** I-12; elev. 732ft./223m.; 🅿; **z** 61878; ℗ 1,250; © 1,233
Thomas Prairie; WAYNE; see Toms Prairie (RMC Place)
Thomasville; RMC Place; MONTGOMERY; ***171** L-8; mail Farmersville **z** 62533; rural
Thompson; MCD-Township; JO DAVIESS; ***170** A-6; mail Apple River **z** 61001; ℗ 585; © 708
Thompson Addition; RMC Place; HENRY; ***170** D-6; elev. 664ft./202m.; ★ **D-RI-M**; mail Colona **z** 61241; ● 70
Thompsonville; Inc. Place; FRANKLIN; **171** Q-10; elev. 501ft./153m.; 🅿; **z** 62890; ℗ 602; © 571
Thomson; Inc. Place; CARROLL; **170** C-6; elev. 601ft./183m.; 🅿; **z** 61285; ℗ 538; © 559
Thornhill; RMC Place; DUPAGE; ★ **CHI**; mail Wheaton **z** 60187; pop. incl. with Carol Stream (Inc. Place)
Thornton; Inc. Place; COOK; ▲ Thornton; **172** M-10; elev. 603ft./184m.; 🅿; ★ **CHI**; **z** 60476; ℗ 2,778; © 2,582
Thornton; MCD-Township; COOK; ***170** D-13; 🅿; ★ **CHI**; **z** 60476; ℗ 175,896; © 180,802
Thornton Junction; RMC Place; COOK; ***170** D-13; ★ **CHI**; mail South Holland **z** 60473; pop. incl. with South Holland (Inc. Place)
Thornwilde; RMC Place; DUPAGE; ★ **CHI**; mail Warrenville **z** 60555; pop. incl. with Warrenville (Inc. Place)
Thunderbird Lake; RMC Place; JERSEY; ***171** M-6; ★ **ST.L**; mail Brighton **z** 62012; ● 300
Tice; RMC Place; MENARD; ***170** J-7; 🅿; **z** 62675; rural
Ticona; RMC Place; LA SALLE; ***170** E-9; elev. 645ft./197m.; mail Tonica **z** 61370; rural
Tierra Grande; RMC Place; COOK; ★ **CHI**; mail Country Club Hills **z** 60478; pop. incl. with Country Club Hills (Inc. Place)
Tilden; Inc. Place; RANDOLPH; **171** P-7; elev. 522ft./159m.; 🅿; **z** 62292; ℗ 919; © 922
Tilton; Inc. Place; VERMILION; **170** I-13; elev. 648ft./198m.; 🅿; ★ **DANV**; **z** 61833; ℗ 2,729; © 2,976
Timber; MCD-Township; PEORIA; ***170** H-7; mail Glasford **z** 61533; ℗ 2,531; © 2,528
Timberbrook; RMC Place; HENRY; ***170** D-6; elev. 702ft./214m.; mail Geneseo **z** 61254; ● 90
Timbercrest; RMC Place; COOK; ★ **CHI**; mail Schaumburg **z** 60193; pop. incl. with Schaumburg (Inc. Place)
Timber Lake; RMC Place; CARROLL; ***170** B-7; elev. 800ft./244m.; mail Mount Carroll **z** 61053; summer pop. 100; rural
Timber Lake; RMC Place; LAKE; ★ **CHI**; mail Barrington **z** 60010
Timberlake Estate; RMC Place; CHRISTIAN; ***171** K-9; elev. 613ft./187m.; mail Taylorville **z** 62568; ● 80
Timberlake Estates; RMC Place; DUPAGE; ***170** C-12; ★ **CHI**; mail Hinsdale **z** 60521; ● 400
Timberlake Village; RMC Place; COOK; ★ **CHI**; mail Mount Prospect **z** 60056; pop. incl. with Mount Prospect (Inc. Place)
Timberlane; Inc. Place; BOONE; **170** A-10; elev. 850ft./259m.; mail Belvidere **z** 61008; © 234
Timberline; RMC Place; WILL; ***170** D-12; ★ **CHI**; mail Joliet **z** 60435; ● 350
Timber Ridge; RMC Place; DUPAGE; ***170** C-12; ★ **CHI**; mail Winfield **z** 60190; ● 100
Timber Terrace; RMC Place; DEKALB; ***170** C-10; elev. 850ft./259m.; ★ **DKLB**; mail DeKalb **z** 60115; pop. incl. with DeKalb (Inc. Place)
Timber Trails; RMC Place; DUPAGE; ★ **CHI**; mail Hinsdale **z** 60521; pop. incl. with Oak Brook (Inc. Place)
Timberview; RMC Place; CHAMPAIGN; ***170** I-11; elev. 725ft./221m.; mail Mahomet **z** 61853; pop. incl. with Mahomet (Inc. Place)
Timber View; RMC Place; CHAMPAIGN; ***170** I-12; elev. 700ft./213m.; ★ **CH-U**; mail Urbana **z** 61802; ● 30
Time; Inc. Place; PIKE; ***171** K-5; elev. 692ft./211m.; mail Pittsfield **z** 62363; ℗ 36; © 29
Timewell (Mound Station); Inc. Place; BROWN; **170** J-4; elev. 753ft./230m.; 🅿; **z** 62375; ℗ 147; © 127
Timothy; RMC Place; CUMBERLAND; ***171** L-12; mail Greenup **z** 62428; rural
Tinley Park; Inc. Place; COOK, WILL; **170** D-13; elev. 698ft./213m.; 🅿 🅷 🅲 1,261; ★ **CHI**; **z** 60477-78, **z** 60487; ℗ 37,121; © 48,401; ◆ 48,859
Tinley Terrace; RMC Place; COOK; ★ **CHI**; mail Tinley Park **z** 60477; pop. incl. with Tinley Park (Inc. Place)
Tioga; RMC Place; HANCOCK; **170** I-3; mail Mendon **z** 62351; ● 100
Tipton; RMC Place; MONROE; ***171** P-6; mail Waterloo **z** 62298; rural
Tiskilwa; Inc. Place; BUREAU; **170** E-8; elev. 512ft./156m.; 🅿; **z** 61368; ℗ 830; © 787
Todds Mill; RMC Place; PERRY; ***171** P-8; elev. 494ft./151m.; mail Nashville **z** 62263, Pinckneyville **z** 62274; rural
Todds Point; RMC Place; SHELBY; ▲ Todds Point; ***171** K-10; elev. 659ft./201m.; mail Bethany **z** 61914; ● 30
Todds Point; MCD-Township; SHELBY; ***171** K-10; mail Bethany **z** 61914; ℗ 496; © 501
Toledo; Inc. Place; ⊡ CUMBERLAND; **171** L-11; elev. 593ft./181m.; 🅿; **z** 62468; ℗ 1,199; © 1,166
Tolono; Inc. Place; CHAMPAIGN; ▲ Tolono; **170** J-11; 🅿; ★ **CH-U**; **z** 61880; ℗ 2,605; © 2,700
Tolono; MCD-Township; CHAMPAIGN; ***170** J-11; 🅿; ★ **CH-U**; **z** 61880; ℗ 3,574; © 3,757
Toluca; Inc. Place; MARSHALL; **170** F-9; elev. 700ft./213m.; 🅿; **z** 61369; ℗ 1,315; © 1,339
Tomahawk Bluff; RMC Place; LA SALLE; ***170** E-9; elev. 630ft./192m.; mail La Salle **z** 61301; ● 50
Tompkins; MCD-Township; WARREN; ***170** G-5; mail Kirkwood **z** 61447; ℗ 1,177; © 1,040
Toms Prairie (Thomas Prairie); RMC Place; WAYNE; ***171** O-11; elev. 446ft./136m.; mail Fairfield **z** 62837; rural
Tonica; Inc. Place; LA SALLE; **170** E-9; 🅿; **z** 61370; ℗ 715; © 685
Tonti; RMC Place; MARION; ▲ Tonti; ***171** O-9; mail Salem **z** 62881; rural
Tonti; MCD-Township; MARION; ***171** N-9; mail Salem **z** 62881; ℗ 941; © 1,033
Topeka; Inc. Place; MASON; **170** H-7; elev. 480ft./146m.; 🅿; **z** 61567; ℗ 93; © 90
Toronto; RMC Place; SANGAMON; ***171** K-8; 🅿; ★ **SPRG**; **z** 62707; rural
Toulon; Inc. Place; ⊡ STARK; **170** F-7; elev. 720ft./219m.; 🅿; **z** 61483; ℗ 1,328; © 1,400
Toulon; MCD-Township; STARK; ***170** F-7; 🅿; **z** 61483; ℗ 2,464; © 2,446
Tovey; Inc. Place; CHRISTIAN; **171** K-8; elev. 607ft./185m.; 🅿; **z** 62570; ℗ 533; © 516
Towanda; Inc. Place; MCLEAN; ▲ Towanda; **170** H-10; elev. 776ft./237m.; 🅿; **z** 61776; ℗ 856; © 493
Towanda; MCD-Township; MCLEAN; ***170** H-10; 🅿; **z** 61776; ℗ 1,191; © 1,024
Tower Hill; Inc. Place; SHELBY; ▲ Tower Hill; **171** L-9; elev. 658ft./201m.; 🅿; **z** 62571; ℗ 601; © 609
Tower Hill; MCD-Township; SHELBY; ***171** L-9; 🅿; **z** 62571; ℗ 1,133; © 1,150
Tower Lake (Tower Lakes); Inc. Place; LAKE; **172** C-4; elev. 760ft./232m.; ★ **CHI**; mail Barrington **z** 60010; ℗ 1,333; © 1,310
Tower Lakes; LAKE; see Tower Lake (Inc. Place)
Town and Country; RMC Place; JACKSON; ***171** R-9; elev. 450ft./137m.; ★ **CARB-**; mail Carbondale **z** 62901; pop. incl. with Carbondale (Inc. Place)
Towne Oaks; RMC Place; TAZEWELL; ***170** H-8; ★ **PEOR**; mail Groveland **z** 61535; ● 200
Tradewinds; RMC Place; DEKALB; ***170** C-10; elev. 900ft./274m.; ★ **DKLB**; mail DeKalb **z** 60115; ● 100
Trago Lake; RMC Place; CLAY; ***171** N-11; elev. 522ft./159m.; mail Flora **z** 62839; summer pop. 200
Tremont; RMC Place; MADISON; ***171** M-6; ★ **ST.L**; mail Godfrey **z** 62035; pop. incl. with Godfrey (Inc. Place)
Tremont; Inc. Place; TAZEWELL; **170** H-8; elev. 650ft./198m.; 🅿; ★ **PEOR**; **z** 61568; ℗ 2,088; © 2,029
Tremont; MCD-Township; TAZEWELL; ***170** H-8; 🅿; ★ **PEOR**; **z** 61568; includes part of the village of Tremont; ℗ 2,421; © 2,428
Trenton; Inc. Place; CLINTON; **171** O-7; elev. 497ft./151m.; 🅿; ★ **ST.L**; **z** 62293 & mail Aviston **z** 62216, Breese **z** 62230; ℗ 2,481; © 2,610
Trenton Corners; RMC Place; KNOX; ***170** F-6; mail Dahinda **z** 61428; rural
Trilla; RMC Place; COLES, CUMBERLAND; **171** L-11; elev. 650ft./198m.; 🅿; **z** 62469; ● 250
Trimble; RMC Place; CRAWFORD; ***171** M-13; mail Robinson **z** 62454; ● 40
Triple Lance Heights; RMC Place; WILLIAMSON; mail Carbondale **z** 62901; ● 100
Tri-State Village; RMC Place; DUPAGE; **172** J-6; ★ **CHI**; mail Hinsdale **z** 60521; ● 1,200
Triumph; RMC Place; LA SALLE; **170** D-9; elev. 660ft./201m.; 🅿; **z** 61371; ● 150
Triumvera; RMC Place; COOK; ***170** B-12; ★ **CHI**; mail Glenview **z** 60025; ● 350
Trivoli; RMC Place; PEORIA; ▲ Trivoli; **170** G-7; elev. 752ft./229m.; 🅿; **z** 61569; ● 450
Trivoli; MCD-Township; PEORIA; ***170** G-7; 🅿; **z** 61569; ℗ 1,166; © 1,035
Trout Valley; Inc. Place; MCHENRY; ***170** B-11; 🅿; ★ **CHI**; **z** 60013; ℗ 612; © 599
Trowbridge; RMC Place; SHELBY; **171** L-11; mail Neoga **z** 62447; ● 50
Troxel; RMC Place; KANE; ***170** C-10; mail Maple Park **z** 60151; rural
Troy; Inc. Place; MADISON; **171** N-7; elev. 546ft./166m.; 🅿; ★ **ST.L**; **z** 62294; ℗ 6,046; © 8,524
Troy; MCD-Township; WILL; ***170** D-12; ★ **CHI**; mail Joliet **z** 60435; ℗ 21,642; © 27,970
Troy Grove; Inc. Place; LA SALLE; ▲ Troy Grove; **170** D-9; 🅿; **z** 61372; ℗ 259; © 305
Troy Grove; MCD-Township; LA SALLE; ***170** D-9; 🅿; **z** 61372; ℗ 1,316; © 1,269
Tru Lock Acres; RMC Place; MCDONOUGH; mail Macomb **z** 61455; ● 50
Trumbull; RMC Place; WHITE; ***171** Q-12; mail Carmi **z** 62821; rural
Truro; MCD-Township; KNOX; ***170** F-7; mail Williamsfield **z** 61489; ℗ 897; © 903
Tullamore; RMC Place; LAKE; ★ **CHI**; mail Mundelein **z** 60060; pop. incl. with Mundelein (Inc. Place)
Tunbridge; MCD-Township; DE WITT; ***170** I-9; mail Kenney **z** 61749; ℗ 789; © 784
Tunnel Hill; RMC Place; JOHNSON; ***171** S-10; elev. 650ft./198m.; 🅿; **z** 62972; ● 90
Turnberry; RMC Place; MCHENRY; ***170** B-11; ★ **CHI**; mail Crystal Lake **z** 60014; pop. incl. with Lakewood (Inc. Place)
Tuscarora; RMC Place; PEORIA; ***170** G-8; ★ **PEOR**; mail Peoria **z** 61607; ● 90
Tuscola; Inc. Place; ⊡ DOUGLAS; ▲ Tuscola; **170** J-11; 🅿; **z** 61953; ℗ 4,155; © 4,448
Tuscola; MCD-Township; DOUGLAS; ***170** J-11; 🅿; **z** 61953; ℗ 5,056; © 5,390
Twelvemile Corner; RMC Place; LEE; ***170** C-9; elev. 787ft./240m.; mail Compton **z** 61318; rural
Twenty-Second Street; RMC Place; COOK; ***170** C-13; ★ **CHI**; mail Chicago **z** 60616; pop. incl. with Chicago (Inc. Place)
Twigg; MCD-Township; HAMILTON; ***171** Q-11; mail Dale **z** 62829; ℗ 594; © 549
Twilight Terrace; RMC Place; ST. CLAIR; ***171** O-7; ★ **ST.L**; mail Belleville **z** 62221; pop. incl. with Swansea (Inc. Place)
Twin City; RMC Place; CHAMPAIGN; ***170** I-12; ★ **CH-U**; mail Urbana **z** 61801; pop. incl. with Champaign (Inc. Place)
Twin Grove; RMC Place; MCLEAN; ***170** H-9; elev. 816ft./249m.; mail Bloomington **z** 61704; rural
Twin Lakes; RMC Place; MADISON; ***171** N-7; ★ **ST.L**; mail Troy **z** 62294; ● 300
Twin Oaks; RMC Place; WILL; ★ **CHI**; mail Joliet **z** 60431; pop. incl. with Joliet (Inc. Place)
Two Hundred Eleventh Street; RMC Place; COOK; ★ **CHI**; pop. incl. with Olympia Fields (Inc. Place)
Tyrone; MCD-Township; FRANKLIN; ***171** Q-9; ★ **CARB-**; mail Christopher **z** 62822; ℗ 5,238; © 5,011; Ⓡ 5,008

U

Udina; RMC Place; KANE; **172** F-1; elev. 900ft./274m.; ★ **CHI**; mail Elgin **z** 60123; ● 120
Ulah; RMC Place; HENRY; ***170** E-6; mail Cambridge **z** 61238
Ullin; Inc. Place; PULASKI; **171** T-9; elev. 341ft./104m.; 🅿; **z** 62992; ℗ 402; © 779
Union; MCD-Township; CUMBERLAND; ***171** L-12; mail Greenup **z** 62428; ℗ 698; © 758
Union; MCD-Township; EFFINGHAM; ***171** M-11; mail Dieterich **z** 62424; ℗ 534; © 768
Union; MCD-Township; FULTON; ***170** G-6; mail Avon **z** 61415; ℗ 1,205; © 1,132
Union; MCD-Township; LIVINGSTON; ***170** F-11; mail Odell **z** 60460; ℗ 271; © 253
Union; RMC Place; LOGAN; ***170** I-8; mail Emden **z** 62635; ● 30
Union; Inc. Place; MCHENRY; **170** B-11; elev. 842ft./257m.; 🅿; ★ **CHI**; **z** 60180; ℗ 542; © 576
UNION; **171** S-9; ℗ 17,619; © 18,293; ◆ 18,219
Union Center; RMC Place; CUMBERLAND; ***171** L-12; elev. 615ft./187m.; mail Greenup **z** 62428

Entries in **UPPERCASE** are counties.
Entries in **bold** have populations of 2,500 or more.
Names in parentheses are alternate names.

Inc. Place	Incorporated Place
RMC Place	Rand McNally Designated Place
CDP	Census Designated Place
MCD	Minor Civil Division
⊡	County Seat
▲	Minor Civil Division
elev.	Elevation
🅿	Post Office
🅷	Hospital
🅲	College
■	Principal Business Center
★	Ranally Metro Area (RMA) Abbreviation
z	Zip Code(s)
℗	Previous Census Population
Ⓡ	Revised Census Population
Ⓐ	Annexation Population
●	Rand McNally Population Estimate
©	Final Census Population
Ⓢ	Special Census Population
◆	Estimated Population

For additional definitions see Glossary, Volume 1, and Introduction, Volume 2.

Union Grove; RMC Place; WHITESIDE; ▲ Union Grove; *170 C-7; elev. 677ft./206m.; mail Morrison z 61270; ● 50
Union Grove; MCD-Township; WHITESIDE; *170 C-7; mail Morrison z 61270; Ⓟ 1,146; © 1,247
Union Hill; Inc. Place; KANKAKEE; 170 F-12; elev. 619ft./189m.; 🅿; z 60969; Ⓟ 37; © 66
Union Hill; RMC Place; ST. CLAIR; *171 O-7; ★ ST.L; mail Caseyville z 62232; pop. incl. with Fairview Heights (Inc. Place)
Union Stock Yards; RMC Place; COOK; ★ CHI; mail Chicago z 60609; pop. incl. with Chicago (Inc. Place)
Uniontown (Unionville); RMC Place; KNOX; *170 G-6; mail Farmington z 61531; rural
Unionville; KNOX; see Uniontown (RMC Place)
Unionville; RMC Place; MASSAC; 171 T-11; mail Brookport z 62910; ● 70
Unionville; RMC Place; VERMILION; *170 J-13; ★ DANV; mail Westville z 61883
Unionville; RMC Place; WHITESIDE; 170 C-7; mail Morrison z 61270; ● 200
Unity; RMC Place; ALEXANDER; 171 T-9; elev. 337ft./103m.; 🅿; z 62993; ● 200
Unity; MCD-Township; PIATT; *170 J-11; mail Atwood z 61913; Ⓟ 1,605; © 1,560
University Heights; RMC Place; COLES; mail Charleston z 61920; pop. incl. with Charleston (Inc. Place)
University Park (Park Forest South); Inc. Place; WILL, COOK; 170 D-13; elev. 750ft./229m.; 🅿 🅲 5,382; ★ CHI; z 60466, z 60484; Ⓟ 6,204; © 6,662
Upper Alton; RMC Place; MADISON; *171 N-6; ★ ST.L; mail Alton z 62002; pop. incl. with Alton (Inc. Place)
Uptown; RMC Place; COOK; *170 C-13; ★ CHI; mail Chicago z 60640; pop. incl. with Chicago (Inc. Place)
Urbain; RMC Place; FRANKLIN; *171 Q-9; elev. 416ft./127m.; ★ CARB-; mail Mulkeytown z 62865; pop. incl. with Christopher (Inc. Place)
Urban; RMC Place; CHRISTIAN; *171 K-9; elev. 614ft./187m.; mail Taylorville z 62568; pop. incl. with Taylorville (Inc. Place)
Urbana; Inc. Place; ⊡ CHAMPAIGN; 170 I-12; elev. 727ft./222m.; 🅿 🅷 ■; ★ CH-U; z 61801-03; Ⓟ 36,344; © 36,395; Ⓡ 37,362; ◆ 40,257
Urbana; MCD-Township; CHAMPAIGN; *170 I-12; 🅿; ★ CH-U; z 61801-03; does not include City of Urbana; Ⓟ 8,675; © 8,061; Ⓡ 8,063
Urbandale; RMC Place; ALEXANDER; 171 T-9; elev. 311ft./95m.; mail Cairo z 62914; ● 200
Ursa; Inc. Place; ADAMS; ▲ Ursa; 170 I-3; 🅿; z 62376; Ⓟ 506; © 595
Ursa; MCD-Township; ADAMS; *170 I-3; 🅿; z 62376; Ⓟ 1,051; © 1,110
Ustick; MCD-Township; WHITESIDE; *170 C-7; mail Morrison z 61270; Ⓟ 644; © 624
Utica (North Utica); Inc. Place; LA SALLE; ▲ Utica; 170 E-9; 🅿; z 61373; Ⓟ 848; © 977
Utica; MCD-Township; LA SALLE; *170 E-9; 🅿; z 61373; Ⓟ 1,414; © 1,638

V

Vale Vue Acres; RMC Place; MORGAN; *170 J-6; mail Jacksonville z 62650; ● 60
Valier; Inc. Place; FRANKLIN; 171 Q-9; elev. 420ft./128m.; 🅿; ★ CARB-; z 62891; Ⓟ 708; © 662
Valley; MCD-Township; STARK; *170 F-7; mail Wyoming z 61491; Ⓟ 398; © 349
Valley City; Inc. Place; PIKE; 171 K-5; elev. 460ft./140m.; mail Griggsville z 62340; Ⓟ 23; © 14
Valley Creek; RMC Place; KANE; *170 B-11; ★ CHI; mail Elgin z 60123; pop. incl. with Elgin (Inc. Place)
Valley Lo; RMC Place; COOK; ★ CHI; mail Glenview z 60025; pop. incl. with Glenview (Inc. Place)
Valley Mission (Fair City); RMC Place; UNION; *171 S-8; elev. 400ft./122m.; mail Jonesboro z 62952; ● 50
Valley View; RMC Place; DEKALB; *170 B-10; mail Kingston z 60145, Saint Charles z 60174; ● 150
Valley View; RMC Place; DUPAGE; *170 C-12; elev. 755ft./230m.; ★ CHI; mail Glen Ellyn z 60137; ● 2,100
Valley View; RMC Place; KANE; 172 G-2; elev. 700ft./213m.; ★ CHI; mail Kingston z 60145, Saint Charles z 60174; ● 700
Valley View; RMC Place; TAZEWELL; ★ PEOR; mail East Peoria z 61611; pop. incl. with East Peoria (Inc. Place)
Valmeyer; Inc. Place; MONROE; 171 P-6; elev. 401ft./122m.; 🅿; z 62295; Ⓟ 897; © 608
Van Burensburg; RMC Place; MONTGOMERY; 171 M-9; mail Fillmore z 62032; ● 50
Vance; MCD-Township; VERMILION; *170 J-13; mail Fairmount z 61841; Ⓟ 1,088; © 1,027
Vandalia; Inc. Place; ⊡ FAYETTE; ▲ Vandalia; 171 M-9; 🅿 🅷; z 62471; Ⓟ 6,114; © 6,975
Vandalia; MCD-Township; FAYETTE; *171 M-9; 🅿; z 62471; Ⓟ 6,339; © 8,104; Ⓡ 6,667
Van Orin; RMC Place; BUREAU; 170 D-8; elev. 810ft./247m.; 🅿; z 61374; ● 120
Varna; Inc. Place; MARSHALL; 170 F-9; elev. 729ft./222m.; 🅿; z 61375; Ⓟ 405; © 436
Velma; RMC Place; CHRISTIAN; *171 K-9; elev. 626ft./191m.; mail Taylorville z 62568; rural
Venedy; Inc. Place; WASHINGTON; ▲ Venedy; 171 O-8; 🅿; z 62214; Ⓟ 158; © 137
Venedy; MCD-Township; WASHINGTON; *171 O-8; 🅿; z 62214; Ⓟ 434; © 423
Venetian Village; CDP; LAKE; *170 A-12; ★ CHI; mail Lake Villa z 60046; Ⓟ 3,133; © 3,082
Venice; Inc. Place; MADISON; ▲ Venice; 195 E-7; 🅿; ★ ST.L; z 62090; Ⓟ 3,571; © 2,528
Venice; MCD-Township; MADISON; *171 N-6; 🅿; ★ ST.L; z 62090; Ⓟ 8,657; © 6,783
Vera; RMC Place; FAYETTE; 171 M-9; mail Ramsey z 62080; ● 100
Vergennes; Inc. Place; JACKSON; ▲ Vergennes; 171 Q-8; 🅿; z 62994; Ⓟ 314; © 491; Ⓡ 330
Vergennes; MCD-Township; JACKSON; *171 Q-8; 🅿; z 62994; Ⓟ 679; © 886; Ⓡ 725
Vermilion; Inc. Place; EDGAR; 171 K-13; elev. 668ft./204m.; 🅿; z 61955; Ⓟ 283; © 239
VERMILION; 170 H-13; Ⓟ 88,257; © 83,919; Ⓡ 83,924; ◆ 79,539
Vermilion Grove; RMC Place; VERMILION; *170 J-13; elev. 675ft./206m.; ★ DANV; mail Ridge Farm z 61870; ● 150
Vermilion Heights; RMC Place; VERMILION; *170 I-13; elev. 605ft./184m.; ★ DANV; mail Danville z 61834; pop. incl. with Danville (Inc. Place)
Vermilionville; RMC Place; LA SALLE; *170 E-9; elev. 646ft./197m.; mail Tonica z 61370; rural
Vermillion; MCD-Township; LA SALLE; *170 E-9; mail Tonica z 61370; Ⓟ 313; © 325
Vermillion Estates; RMC Place; LIVINGSTON; *170 F-10; mail Pontiac z 61764; pop. incl. with Pontiac (Inc. Place)
Vermont; Inc. Place; FULTON; ▲ Vermont; 170 H-5; elev. 697ft./212m.; 🅿; z 61484; Ⓟ 806; © 792
Vermont; MCD-Township; FULTON; *170 I-6; 🅿; z 61484; Ⓟ 1,112; © 1,035
Vernon; MCD-Township; LAKE; *170 B-12; ★ CHI; mail Lincolnshire z 60069; Ⓟ 51,141; © 65,355; Ⓡ 65,362
Vernon; Inc. Place; MARION; 171 N-9; elev. 515ft./157m.; 🅿; z 62892; Ⓟ 207; © 178
Vernon Hills; Inc. Place; LAKE; 172 C-6; elev. 683ft./208m.; 🅿 ■; ★ CHI; z 60061; Ⓟ 15,319; © 20,120; ◆ 23,528
Verona; Inc. Place; GRUNDY; 170 E-11; elev. 630ft./192m.; 🅿; z 60479; Ⓟ 242; © 257
Versailles; Inc. Place; BROWN; ▲ Versailles; 170 J-5; 🅿; z 62378; Ⓟ 480; © 567
Versailles; MCD-Township; BROWN; *170 J-5; 🅿; z 62378; Ⓟ 854; © 849
Versailles-on-the-Lake; RMC Place; COOK; ★ CHI; mail Schaumburg z 60173; pop. incl. with Schaumburg (Inc. Place)
Vets Row; RMC Place; PEORIA; ★ PEOR; mail Chillicothe z 61523; ● 60
Vevay Park; RMC Place; CUMBERLAND; *171 L-12; elev. 615ft./187m.; mail Casey z 62420; rural
Vicic; RMC Place; TAZEWELL; ★ PEOR; mail East Peoria z 61611; pop. incl. with East Peoria (Inc. Place)
Victor; MCD-Township; DEKALB; *170 D-10; mail Waterman z 60556; Ⓟ 413; © 364
Victoria; Inc. Place; KNOX; 170 F-6; elev. 830ft./253m.; 🅿; z 61485; Ⓟ 299; © 323
Victoria; MCD-Township; KNOX; *170 F-7; 🅿; z 61485; includes part of the Village of Victoria; Ⓟ 376; © 432
Vienna; MCD-Township; GRUNDY; *170 E-11; mail Verona z 60479; Ⓟ 556; © 638
Vienna; Inc. Place; ⊡ JOHNSON; 171 S-10; elev. 404ft./123m.; 🅿; z 62995; Ⓟ 1,446; © 1,234
Village Green; RMC Place; DUPAGE; *170 C-12; ★ CHI; mail Warrenville z 60555; pop. incl. with Warrenville (Inc. Place)
Village of Big Rock; KANE; see Big Rock (Inc. Place)
Village of Lakewood; MCHENRY; see Lakewood (Inc. Place)
Village Square; RMC Place; DUPAGE; *170 C-12; ★ CHI; mail Downers Grove z 60515; pop. incl. with Downers Grove (Inc. Place)
Villa Grove; Inc. Place; DOUGLAS; 170 J-12; elev. 650ft./198m.; 🅿; z 61956; Ⓟ 2,734; © 2,553
Villa Grove Junction; RMC Place; DOUGLAS; mail Villa Grove z 61956; pop. incl. with Villa Grove (Inc. Place)
Villa Hills; RMC Place; ST. CLAIR; 195 G-8; ★ ST.L; mail Belleville z 62223; ● 1,410
Villa Marie; RMC Place; MADISON; ★ ST.L; mail Godfrey z 62035; pop. incl. with Godfrey (Inc. Place)
Villa Park; Inc. Place; DUPAGE; 172 H-5; elev. 700ft./213m.; 🅿 ■; ★ CHI; z 60181; Ⓟ 22,253; © 22,075; ◆ 21,666
Villa Ridge; RMC Place; PULASKI; 171 T-9; elev. 398ft./121m.; 🅿; z 62996; ● 500
Villas Salceda; RMC Place; COOK; ★ CHI; mail Northbrook z 60062; pop. incl. with Northbrook (Inc. Place)
Villa Verde; RMC Place; COOK; ★ CHI; mail Buffalo Grove z 60089; pop. incl. with Buffalo Grove (Inc. Place)
Villa West; RMC Place; COOK; *170 D-13; ★ CHI; mail Palos Park z 60464; pop. incl. with Palos Park (Inc. Place)
Vincennes Trail; RMC Place; KANKAKEE; *170 E-13; elev. 625ft./191m.; ★ KANK; mail Momence z 60954; ● 200
Vinegar Hill; MCD-Township; JO DAVIESS; *170 A-5; mail Galena z 61036; Ⓟ 267; © 250
Viner; RMC Place; ST. CLAIR; ★ ST.L; pop. incl. with East Saint Louis (Inc. Place)
Viola; MCD-Township; LEE; *170 C-9; mail Compton z 61318; Ⓟ 300; © 279
Viola; Inc. Place; MERCER; 170 E-5; elev. 790ft./241m.; 🅿; z 61486; Ⓟ 964; © 956
Virden; Inc. Place; MACOUPIN, SANGAMON; ▲ Virden; 171 K-7; 🅿; z 62690; Ⓟ 3,635; © 3,488
Virden; MCD-Township; MACOUPIN; *171 K-7; 🅿; z 62690; includes part of the City of Virden; Ⓟ 3,944; © 3,689
Virgil; Inc. Place; KANE; ▲ Virgil; 170 C-11; 🅿; z 60151; © 266
Virgil; MCD-Township; KANE; *170 C-11; 🅿; z 60151; Ⓟ 1,903; © 1,947
Virginia; Inc. Place; ⊡ CASS; 170 J-6; elev. 622ft./190m.; 🅿; z 62691; Ⓟ 1,767; © 1,728
Virginia; MCD-Township; CASS; *170 J-6; 🅿; z 62691; includes part of the City of Virginia; Ⓟ 2,043; © 1,931
Volo; Inc. Place; LAKE; 170 A-12; 🅿; ★ CHI; z 60020, z 60030, z 60041, z 60051, z 60073 & mail McHenry z 60050; Ⓟ 193; © 180
Vonachen Knolls; RMC Place; PEORIA; mail Chillicothe z 61523; ● 200
Voorhies; RMC Place; PIATT; *170 J-11; elev. 677ft./206m.; mail Bement z 61813
Vulcan; RMC Place; ST. CLAIR; *171 O-6; ★ ST.L; mail East Carondelet z 62240; pop. incl. with East Carondelet (Inc. Place)

W

Wabash; MCD-Township; CLARK; *171 L-13; mail Marshall z 62441; Ⓟ 1,670; © 2,102
WABASH; 171 O-13; Ⓟ 13,111; © 12,937; ◆ 11,818
Wacker; RMC Place; CARROLL; 170 B-7; mail Mount Carroll z 61053; ● 50
Wacker; RMC Place; KENDALL; *170 D-11; elev. 634ft./193m.; ★ CHI; mail Yorkville z 60560; ● 90
Wacker Drive; RMC Place; COOK; ★ CHI; mail Chicago z 60607; pop. incl. with Chicago (Inc. Place)
Waddams; MCD-Township; STEPHENSON; *170 A-7; mail Mc Connell z 61050; Ⓟ 892; © 872
Waddams Grove; RMC Place; STEPHENSON; 170 A-7; mail Lena z 61048; ● 60
Wade; MCD-Township; CLINTON; *171 O-8; mail Carlyle z 62231; Ⓟ 1,792; © 1,740; Ⓡ 1,736
Wade; MCD-Township; JASPER; *171 M-12; mail Newton z 62448; Ⓟ 4,835; © 4,734
Wadsworth; Inc. Place; LAKE; 170 A-12; elev. 670ft./204m.; 🅿; ★ CHI; z 60083; Ⓟ 1,826; © 3,083
Waggoner; Inc. Place; MONTGOMERY; 171 L-8; elev. 639ft./195m.; 🅿; z 62572; Ⓟ 221; © 245
Wakefield; RMC Place; RICHLAND; 171 N-12; mail Newton z 62448; ● 50
Waldo; MCD-Township; LIVINGSTON; *170 G-10; mail Gridley z 61744; Ⓟ 329; © 259
Walker; MCD-Township; HANCOCK; *170 I-3; mail Basco z 62313; Ⓟ 371; © 315
Walker; RMC Place; MACON; *171 K-9; mail Macon z 62544; rural
Walkerville; RMC Place; GREENE; ▲ Walkerville; *171 L-5; elev. 575ft./175m.; mail Hillview z 62050, White Hall z 62092; ● 30
Walkerville; MCD-Township; GREENE; *171 L-5; mail Hillview z 62050, White Hall z 62092; Ⓟ 244; © 227
Wall; MCD-Township; FORD; *170 H-12; mail Loda z 60948; Ⓟ 220; © 218
Wallace; MCD-Township; LA SALLE; *170 E-10; mail Ottawa z 61350; Ⓟ 489; © 529
Walla Walla; RMC Place; CUMBERLAND; *171 M-12; mail Greenup z 62428; rural
Wallingford; RMC Place; WILL; *170 E-12; mail Manhattan z 60442; rural
Walmar; RMC Place; ST. CLAIR; ★ ST.L; pop. incl. with Belleville (Inc. Place)
Walnut; Inc. Place; BUREAU; ▲ Walnut; 170 D-8; 🅿; z 61376; Ⓟ 1,463; © 1,461
Walnut; MCD-Township; BUREAU; *170 D-8; 🅿; z 61376; Ⓟ 1,894; © 1,821
Walnut Grove; MCD-Township; KNOX; *170 F-6; mail Altona z 61414; Ⓟ 826; © 864
Walnut Grove; RMC Place; MCDONOUGH; ▲ Walnut Grove, Prairie City; 170 G-5; elev. 712ft./217m.; mail Good Hope z 61438, Prairie City z 61470; ● 50
Walnut Grove; MCD-Township; MCDONOUGH; *170 H-5; mail Good Hope z 61438, Prairie City z 61470; Ⓟ 499; © 464
Walnut Hill; Inc. Place; MARION; 171 O-9; elev. 560ft./171m.; 🅿; z 62893; Ⓟ 133; © 109
Walnut Park; RMC Place; CLINTON; *171 O-8; elev. 468ft./143m.; mail Carlyle z 62231; ● 50
Walnut Prairie; RMC Place; CLARK; *171 L-13; mail West Union z 62477
Walpole; RMC Place; HAMILTON; 171 Q-11; elev. 440ft./134m.; mail Broughton z 62817; ● 50
Walsh; RMC Place; RANDOLPH; 171 Q-7; elev. 480ft./146m.; 🅿; z 62297; ● 140
Walshville; Inc. Place; MONTGOMERY; ▲ Walshville; 171 M-8; 🅿; z 62091; Ⓟ 44; © 89
Walshville; MCD-Township; MONTGOMERY; *171 M-8; 🅿; z 62091; Ⓟ 359; © 365
Waltham; RMC Place; LA SALLE; *170 D-9; elev. 693ft./211m.; mail Utica z 61373
Waltham; MCD-Township; LA SALLE; *170 E-9; mail Utica z 61373; Ⓟ 520; © 490
Walton; RMC Place; LEE; *170 C-8; mail Dixon z 61021; ● 40
Waltonville; Inc. Place; JEFFERSON; 171 P-9; elev. 466ft./142m.; 🅿; z 62894; Ⓟ 396; © 422
Wamac; Inc. Place; MARION, CLINTON, WASHINGTON; 171 O-9; elev. 491ft./150m.; mail Centralia z 62801; Ⓟ 1,501; © 1,378
Wanda; RMC Place; MADISON; 195 B-9; ★ ST.L; mail Edwardsville z 62025; ● 80
Wanlock; RMC Place; MERCER; *170 E-5; mail Aledo z 61231; rural
Wapella; Inc. Place; DE WITT; ▲ Wapella; 170 I-9; elev. 748ft./228m.; 🅿; z 61777; Ⓟ 608; © 651
Wapella; MCD-Township; DE WITT; *170 I-9; 🅿; z 61777; Ⓟ 1,031; © 1,004
Wards Grove; MCD-Township; JO DAVIESS; *170 A-7; mail Lena z 61048; Ⓟ 282; © 280
Ware; RMC Place; UNION; 171 S-8; elev. 347ft./106m.; mail Jonesboro z 62952; ● 260
Warner; RMC Place; HENRY; *170 E-6; ★ D-RI-M; mail Orion z 61273; rural
Warren; Inc. Place; JO DAVIESS; ▲ Warren; 170 A-7; elev. 1,012ft./308m.; 🅿; z 61087; Ⓟ 1,550; © 1,496
Warren; MCD-Township; JO DAVIESS; *170 A-7; 🅿; z 61087; Ⓟ 1,760; © 1,675
Warren; MCD-Township; LAKE; *170 A-12; ★ CHI; mail Gurnee z 60031; Ⓟ 34,785; © 59,424
WARREN; 170 G-5; Ⓟ 19,181; © 18,735; ◆ 17,685
Warrenhurst; RMC Place; DUPAGE; *170 C-12; ★ CHI; mail Warrenville z 60555; pop. incl. with Warrenville (Inc. Place)
Warren Park; RMC Place; COOK; ★ CHI; mail Cicero z 60804; pop. incl. with Cicero (Inc. Place)
Warrensburg; Inc. Place; MACON; 170 J-9; elev. 692ft./211m.; 🅿; z 62573; Ⓟ 1,274; © 1,289
Warrenville; Inc. Place; DUPAGE; 172 I-3; elev. 700ft./213m.; 🅿; ★ CHI; z 60555; Ⓟ 11,333; © 13,363
Warrington; RMC Place; EDGAR; *171 K-12; mail Kansas z 61933; rural
Warsaw; Inc. Place; HANCOCK; 170 H-3; elev. 577ft./176m.; 🅿; z 62379; Ⓟ 1,882; © 1,793
Warsaw; MCD-Township; HANCOCK; *170 H-3; 🅿; z 62379; coextensive with the City of Warsaw; Ⓟ 1,882; © 1,793
Wartburg; RMC Place; MONROE; *171 P-6; mail Waterloo z 62298; ● 55
Wartrace; RMC Place; JOHNSON; *171 S-10; elev. 495ft./151m.; mail Grantsburg z 62943; rural
Wasco; RMC Place; KANE; 172 G-1; elev. 820ft./250m.; 🅿; ★ CHI; z 60183; ● 300
Washburn; Inc. Place; WOODFORD, MARSHALL; 170 F-9; elev. 680ft./207m.; 🅿; z 61570; Ⓟ 1,075; © 1,147
Washington; MCD-Township; CARROLL; *170 B-6; mail Savanna z 61074; Ⓟ 445; © 381
Washington; Inc. Place; TAZEWELL; ▲ Washington; 170 G-8; 🅿; ★ PEOR; z 61571; Ⓟ 10,099; © 10,841
Washington; MCD-Township; TAZEWELL; *170 G-8; 🅿; ★ PEOR; z 61571; Ⓟ 18,907; © 19,427
Washington; MCD-Township; WILL; *170 E-13; ★ CHI; mail Beecher z 60401; Ⓟ 3,724; © 3,948
WASHINGTON; 171 P-8; Ⓟ 14,965; © 15,148; ◆ 14,519
Washington Heights; RMC Place; COOK; ★ CHI; mail Chicago z 60620, z 60643; pop. incl. with Chicago (Inc. Place)
Washington Park; RMC Place; COOK; ★ CHI; mail Chicago z 60615, z 60637; pop. incl. with Chicago (Inc. Place)
Washington Park; Inc. Place; ST. CLAIR; 195 E-8; elev. 420ft./128m.; ★ ST.L; mail East Saint Louis z 62204-05; Ⓟ 7,431; © 5,345; Ⓡ 5,942
Wasson; RMC Place; SALINE; 171 R-11; elev. 381ft./116m.; mail Eldorado z 62930, Harrisburg z 62946; ● 200
Wataga; Inc. Place; KNOX; 170 F-6; elev. 820ft./250m.; 🅿; z 61488; Ⓟ 879; © 857
Waterford; RMC Place; DUPAGE; ★ CHI; mail Hinsdale z 60521; pop. incl. with Willowbrook (Inc. Place)
Waterford; MCD-Township; FULTON; *170 H-6; mail Lewistown z 61542; Ⓟ 236; © 188
Waterloo; Inc. Place; ⊡ MONROE; 171 P-6; elev. 717ft./219m.; 🅿; z 62298; Ⓟ 5,072; © 7,614
Waterman; Inc. Place; DEKALB; 170 C-10; elev. 820ft./250m.; 🅿; z 60556; Ⓟ 1,074; © 1,224
Watertown; RMC Place; ROCK ISLAND; ★ D-RI-M; mail East Moline z 61244; pop. incl. with East Moline (Inc. Place)
Watervalley; RMC Place; UNION; *171 S-9; elev. 570ft./174m.; mail Cobden z 62920; rural
Watseka; Inc. Place; ⊡ IROQUOIS; 170 G-13; elev. 637ft./194m.; 🅿 🅷; z 60970; Ⓟ 5,424; © 5,670
Watson; Inc. Place; EFFINGHAM; ▲ Watson; 171 M-11; elev. 561ft./171m.; 🅿; z 62473; Ⓟ 646; © 729
Watson; MCD-Township; EFFINGHAM; *171 M-11; 🅿; z 62473; Ⓟ 2,711; © 3,186
Wauconda; Inc. Place; LAKE; ▲ Wauconda; 170 A-12; 🅿; ★ CHI; z 60084; Ⓟ 6,294; © 9,448
Wauconda; MCD-Township; LAKE; *170 A-12; 🅿; ★ CHI; z 60084; Ⓟ 12,859; © 16,387; Ⓡ 16,403
Waukegan; Inc. Place; ⊡ LAKE; 170 A-12; elev. 644ft./196m.; 🅿 🅷 ■; ★ CHI; z 60079, z 60085, z 60087 & mail North Chicago z 60086; Ⓟ 69,392; © 87,901; ◆ 94,749
Waukegan; MCD-Township; LAKE; *170 A-12; 🅿; ★ CHI; z 60079, z 60085, z 60087; includes part of the City of Waukegan; Ⓟ 78,185; © 92,805
Wauponsee; MCD-Township; GRUNDY; *170 E-11; mail Morris z 60450; Ⓟ 2,400; © 2,491
Waverly; Inc. Place; MORGAN; 171 K-7; elev. 670ft./204m.; 🅿; z 62692; Ⓟ 1,402; © 1,346
Waycinden Park; RMC Place; COOK; *170 B-12; ★ CHI; mail Des Plaines z 60018; pop. incl. with Des Plaines (Inc. Place)
Wayne; MCD-Township; DUPAGE; *170 C-12; 🅿; ★ CHI; z 60184 & mail West Chicago z 60185; includes part of the Village of Wayne; Ⓟ 40,379; © 63,776
Wayne; Inc. Place; KANE, DUPAGE; 172 G-3; elev. 750ft./229m.; 🅿; ★ CHI; z 60184; Ⓟ 1,541; © 2,137
WAYNE; 171 O-11; Ⓟ 17,241; © 17,151; ◆ 16,712
Wayne Center; RMC Place; DUPAGE; *170 C-12; elev. 776ft./237m.; ★ CHI; mail West Chicago z 60185; pop. incl. with Bartlett (Inc. Place)
Wayne City; Inc. Place; WAYNE; 171 P-11; elev. 437ft./133m.; 🅿; z 62895; Ⓟ 1,099; © 1,089
Waynesville; Inc. Place; DE WITT; ▲ Waynesville; 170 I-9; 🅿; z 61778; Ⓟ 440; © 452
Waynesville; MCD-Township; DE WITT; *170 I-9; 🅿; z 61778; Ⓟ 768; © 687
Wayside; RMC Place; UNION; *171 R-9; mail Goreville z 62939, Makanda z 62958; rural
Weathersfield; RMC Place; COOK; ★ CHI; mail Schaumburg z 60194; pop. incl. with Schaumburg (Inc. Place)
Weaver; RMC Place; CLARK; *171 L-13; elev. 545ft./166m.; mail Dennison z 62423; rural
Webber; MCD-Township; JEFFERSON; *171 P-10; mail Bluford z 62814; Ⓟ 2,084; © 2,344
Webster; RMC Place; HANCOCK; *170 H-4; mail Carthage z 62321; ● 50
Webster Park; RMC Place; BUREAU; mail Spring Valley z 61362; pop. incl. with Spring Valley (Inc. Place)
Wedgewood Estates; RMC Place; CLINTON; *171 O-7; elev. 495ft./151m.; ★ ST.L; mail Trenton z 62293; ● 35
Wedron; RMC Place; LA SALLE; 170 D-10; elev. 521ft./159m.; 🅿; z 60557; ● 300
Weedman; RMC Place; MCLEAN; *170 I-10; mail Farmer City z 61842; rural
Wee-Ma-Tuk Hills; RMC Place; FULTON; *170 H-6; mail Canton z 61520, Cuba z 61427; summer pop. 500; ● 200
Weldon; Inc. Place; DE WITT; 170 I-10; elev. 710ft./216m.; 🅿; z 61882; Ⓟ 361; © 440
Welge; RMC Place; RANDOLPH; *171 Q-7; elev. 410ft./125m.; mail Steeleville z 62288; ● 40
Weller; MCD-Township; HENRY; *170 E-6; mail Cambridge z 61238; Ⓟ 492; © 474
Wellington; Inc. Place; IROQUOIS; 170 H-13; elev. 700ft./213m.; 🅿; z 60973; Ⓟ 294; © 264
Wellington Heights; RMC Place; WILL; *170 D-12; ★ CHI; mail Joliet z 60435; ● 250
Wendelin; RMC Place; CLAY; 171 N-11; mail Newton z 62448; ● 60
Wenona; Inc. Place; MARSHALL, LA SALLE; 170 F-9; elev. 699ft./213m.; 🅿; z 61377; Ⓟ 950; © 1,065
Wenonah; Inc. Place; MONTGOMERY; 171 L-9; elev. 670ft./204m.; mail Nokomis z 62075; Ⓟ 40; © 44
Wentworth Avenue; RMC Place; COOK; *170 D-13; ★ CHI; mail Calumet City z 60409; pop. incl. with Calumet City (Inc. Place)
Wesley; RMC Place; TAZEWELL; *170 G-8; ★ PEOR; mail East Peoria z 61611; pop. incl. with Creve Coeur (Inc. Place)
Wesley; MCD-Township; WILL; *170 E-12; mail Wilmington z 60481; Ⓟ 2,540; © 2,568
West; MCD-Township; EFFINGHAM; *171 M-10; mail Saint Elmo z 62458; Ⓟ 420; © 444
West; MCD-Township; MCLEAN; *170 H-10; mail Arrowsmith z 61722; Ⓟ 264; © 278
Westaway; RMC Place; KANE; *170 C-11; elev. 680ft./207m.; ★ CHI; mail Aurora z 60506; ● 600
Westbrook; RMC Place; CHAMPAIGN; *170 I-11; elev. 750ft./229m.; mail Mahomet z 61853; ● 75
Westbrook Estates; RMC Place; ST. CLAIR; ★ ST.L; mail O Fallon z 62269; pop. incl. with O'Fallon (Inc. Place)
West Brooklyn; Inc. Place; LEE; 170 D-9; elev. 950ft./290m.; 🅿; z 61378; Ⓟ 164; © 174
Westbury; RMC Place; WILL; ★ CHI; mail Bolingbrook z 60440; pop. incl. with Bolingbrook (Inc. Place)
Westchester; Inc. Place; COOK; 172 I-6; elev. 625ft./191m.; 🅿; ★ CHI; z 60154; Ⓟ 17,301; © 16,824
West Chicago; Inc. Place; DUPAGE; 172 H-3; elev. 784ft./239m.; 🅿; ★ CHI; z 60185-86; Ⓟ 14,796; © 23,469; ◆ 25,204
West City; Inc. Place; FRANKLIN; 171 Q-10; elev. 450ft./137m.; mail Benton z 62812; Ⓟ 747; © 716
West Clinton Estates; RMC Place; CLINTON; *171 O-7; elev. 450ft./137m.; ★ ST.L; mail New Baden z 62265; ● 200
Westdale Gardens; RMC Place; COOK; *170 C-12; elev. 675ft./206m.; ★ CHI; mail Elmhurst z 60126; ● 350
West Deerfield; MCD-Township; LAKE; *170 B-12; ★ CHI; mail Deerfield z 60015; Ⓟ 29,580; © 31,794; Ⓡ 31,856
West Dundee (Dundee); Inc. Place; KANE; 170 B-11; elev. 750ft./229m.; 🅿; ★ CHI; z 60118; Ⓟ 3,728; © 5,428
West Elsdon; RMC Place; COOK; ★ CHI; mail Chicago z 60629, z 60632; pop. incl. with Chicago (Inc. Place)
West End; RMC Place; SALINE; *171 Q-10; mail Thompsonville z 62890
West Englewood; RMC Place; COOK; ★ CHI; mail Chicago z 60636; pop. incl. with Chicago (Inc. Place)
Western; MCD-Township; HENRY; *170 E-6; ★ D-RI-M; mail Orion z 61273; Ⓟ 3,121; © 2,920
Western Avenue; RMC Place; COOK; pop. incl. with Chicago (Inc. Place)
Western Knolls; RMC Place; SANGAMON; mail Springfield z 62707; ● 150
Western Mound; MCD-Township; MACOUPIN; *171 L-6; mail Chesterfield z 62630; Ⓟ 266; © 302
Western Springs; Inc. Place; COOK; 172 I-6; elev. 673ft./205m.; 🅿; ★ CHI; z 60558; Ⓟ 11,984; © 12,493
Westervelt; RMC Place; SHELBY; 171 L-10; elev. 661ft./201m.; 🅿; z 62565; ● 200
Westfield; MCD-Township; BUREAU; *170 D-9; mail Arlington z 61312; Ⓟ 1,044; © 1,014
Westfield; Inc. Place; CLARK; ▲ Westfield; 171 L-12; 🅿; z 62474; Ⓟ 676; © 678
Westfield; MCD-Township; CLARK; *171 L-12; 🅿; z 62474; Ⓟ 824; © 816
Westfield; RMC Place; WILL; ★ CHI; mail Joliet z 60431; pop. incl. with Joliet (Inc. Place)
West Frankfort; Inc. Place; FRANKLIN; 171 Q-10; elev. 401ft./122m.; 🅿 🅷; ★ CARB-; z 62896; Ⓟ 8,526; © 8,196
West Frankfort Lake; RMC Place; FRANKLIN; mail West Frankfort z 62896; ● 100
West Galena; MCD-Township; JO DAVIESS; *170 A-5; mail Galena z 61036; Ⓟ 3,362; © 3,364
Westgate; RMC Place; WILLIAMSON; ★ CARB-; mail Marion z 62959; ● 100
West Glen; RMC Place; PEORIA; *170 G-8; ★ PEOR; mail Peoria z 61612, z 61614; pop. incl. with Peoria (Inc. Place)
West Glenview; RMC Place; COOK; *170 B-13; ★ CHI; mail Glenview z 60025; ● 1,000
West Hallock; RMC Place; PEORIA; *170 F-8; elev. 755ft./230m.; mail Edelstein z 61526; rural
West Harrisburg; RMC Place; SALINE; pop. incl. with Harrisburg (Inc. Place)
West Hinsdale; RMC Place; DUPAGE; ★ CHI; mail Hinsdale z 60521; pop. incl. with Hinsdale (Inc. Place)
West Jersey; RMC Place; STARK; ▲ West Jersey; 170 F-7; mail Toulon z 61483; ● 50
West Jersey; MCD-Township; STARK; *170 F-7; mail Toulon z 61483; Ⓟ 342; © 320
West Kankakee; RMC Place; KANKAKEE; *170 F-12; ★ KANK; mail Kankakee z 60901; pop. incl. with Kankakee (Inc. Place)
West Lake; RMC Place; CRAWFORD; mail Robinson z 62454; ● 80
Westlake; RMC Place; DUPAGE; ★ CHI; mail Glendale Heights z 60139; pop. incl. with Glendale Heights (Inc. Place)
West Lake Forest; RMC Place; LAKE; *170 B-12; ★ CHI; mail Lake Forest z 60045; pop. incl. with Lake Forest (Inc. Place)
West Lawn; RMC Place; COOK; ★ CHI; mail Chicago z 60629; pop. incl. with Chicago (Inc. Place)
West Liberty; RMC Place; JASPER; 171 N-12; elev. 481ft./147m.; 🅿; z 62475; ● 180
West Lincoln; MCD-Township; LOGAN; *170 I-8; mail Lincoln z 62656; Ⓟ 8,375; © 8,042
West Meadowview; RMC Place; KANKAKEE; ★ KANK; mail Kankakee z 60901; pop. incl. with Kankakee (Inc. Place)
West Miltmore; RMC Place; LAKE; *170 A-12; ★ CHI; mail Lake Villa z 60046; ● 1,800
Westmont; Inc. Place; DUPAGE; 172 J-5; elev. 750ft./229m.; 🅿; ★ CHI; z 60559 & mail Darien z 60561; Ⓟ 21,228; © 24,554; ◆ 25,067
Westmore; RMC Place; DUPAGE; ★ CHI; mail Lombard z 60148; pop. incl. with Lombard (Inc. Place)
Westmoreland; RMC Place; WINNEBAGO; ★ RKFD; mail Rockford z 61102
Weston; RMC Place; MCLEAN; 170 G-10; mail Chenoa z 61726; ● 100
West Peoria; Inc. Place; PEORIA; 173 C-16; 🅿; ★ PEOR; z 61604; Ⓟ 5,309; © 4,762
West Peoria; MCD-Township; PEORIA; *170 G-8; 🅿; ★ PEOR; z 61604; © 4,762
West Point; Inc. Place; HANCOCK; 170 I-3; elev. 670ft./204m.; 🅿; z 62380; Ⓟ 214; © 195
West Point; RMC Place; MORGAN; *171 K-6; mail Jacksonville z 62650; ● 50
West Point; MCD-Township; STEPHENSON; *170 A-7; mail Lena z 61048; Ⓟ 3,156; © 3,375
Westport; RMC Place; KNOX; *170 F-5; elev. 756ft./230m.; ★ GLSB; mail Galesburg z 61401; ● 200
Westport; RMC Place; LAWRENCE; *171 N-13; mail Lawrenceville z 62439; ● 35
West Pullman; RMC Place; COOK; *170 D-13; ★ CHI; mail Chicago z 60628; pop. incl. with Chicago (Inc. Place)
West Ridge; RMC Place; COOK; ★ CHI; mail Chicago z 60659; pop. incl. with Chicago (Inc. Place)
West Ridge; RMC Place; DOUGLAS; *170 J-12; mail Tuscola z 61953; rural
West Salem; Inc. Place; EDWARDS; 171 O-12; elev. 501ft./153m.; 🅿; z 62476; Ⓟ 1,042; © 1,001
West Sandford; RMC Place; EDGAR; *171 K-13; elev. 620ft./189m.; mail Paris z 61944; rural
West Side; RMC Place; COOK; ★ CHI; mail Chicago z 60607-08, z 60612; pop. incl. with Chicago (Inc. Place)
West Town; RMC Place; COOK; mail Chicago z 60622; pop. incl. with Chicago (Inc. Place)
West Union; RMC Place; CLARK; 171 M-13; elev. 480ft./146m.; 🅿; z 62477; ● 440
West Vienna (Boles); RMC Place; JOHNSON; 171 S-9; elev. 375ft./114m.; mail Boles z 62909; ● 90
Westville; Inc. Place; VERMILION; 170 J-13; elev. 671ft./205m.; 🅿; ★ DANV; z 61883; Ⓟ 3,387; © 3,175
West Waukegan; RMC Place; LAKE; pop. incl. with Waukegan (Inc. Place)
Westwood; RMC Place; DUPAGE; ★ CHI; mail Addison z 60101; pop. incl. with Addison (Inc. Place)
West York; RMC Place; CRAWFORD; 171 M-13; elev. 508ft./155m.; 🅿; z 62478; ● 220
Wetaug; RMC Place; PULASKI; 171 S-9; elev. 356ft./109m.; mail Dongola z 62926; ● 50
Wethersfield; MCD-Township; HENRY; *170 E-7; mail Prophetstown z 61277; Ⓟ 3,972; © 3,845
Wetzel; RMC Place; EDGAR; *171 K-13; elev. 650ft./198m.; mail Paris z 61944; rural
Wheatfield; MCD-Township; CLINTON; *171 N-8; mail Carlyle z 62231; Ⓟ 534; © 546
Wheatland; MCD-Township; BUREAU; *170 E-8; mail Tiskilwa z 61368; Ⓟ 155; © 129
Wheatland; MCD-Township; FAYETTE; *171 M-10; mail Brownstown z 62418; Ⓟ 510; © 490
Wheatland; MCD-Township; WILL; *170 D-12; ★ CHI; mail Plainfield z 60544; Ⓟ 10,746; © 44,349
Wheatland View; RMC Place; WILL; *170 C-12; ★ CHI; mail Naperville z 60564; ● 700
Wheaton; Inc. Place; ⊡ DUPAGE; 170 C-12; elev. 753ft./230m.; 🅿 🅷 🅲 2,924; ★ CHI; z 60187, z 60189 & mail Carol Stream z 60188; Ⓟ 51,464; © 55,416; ◆ 54,505
Wheaton Center; RMC Place; DUPAGE; ★ CHI; mail Wheaton z 60187; pop. incl. with Wheaton (Inc. Place)
Wheaton South; RMC Place; DUPAGE; *170 C-12; ★ CHI; mail Wheaton z 60187; pop. incl. with Wheaton (Inc. Place)
Wheeler; Inc. Place; JASPER; 171 M-11; elev. 573ft./175m.; 🅿; z 62479; Ⓟ 161; © 119
Wheeling; Inc. Place; COOK, LAKE; 172 E-6; elev. 650ft./198m.; 🅿; ★ CHI; z 60090 & mail Prospect Heights z 60070; Ⓟ 29,911; © 34,496; Ⓡ 34,488; ◆ 35,911
Wheeling; MCD-Township; COOK; *170 B-12; 🅿; ★ CHI; z 60090 & mail Prospect Heights z 60070; includes part of the Village of Wheeling; Ⓟ 148,641; © 155,834; Ⓡ 155,904
Whiskey Corners; RMC Place; MCHENRY; ★ CHI; mail Richmond z 60071; rural
Whiskey Creek; RMC Place; DUPAGE; *170 C-12; ★ CHI; mail West Chicago z 60185; ● 850
Whispering Hills; RMC Place; MCHENRY; ★ CHI; mail McHenry z 60050
Whispering Oaks; RMC Place; LAKE; ★ CHI; mail Groveland z 61535, Lake Forest z 60045; pop. incl. with Lake Forest (Inc. Place)
Whitaker; RMC Place; KANKAKEE; *170 E-13; mail Grant Park z 60940; ● 40
WHITE; 171 P-11; Ⓟ 16,522; © 15,371; ◆ 14,311
White Ash; Inc. Place; WILLIAMSON; *171 R-10; elev. 439ft./134m.; ★ CARB-; mail Marion z 62959; Ⓟ 249; © 268
White City; Inc. Place; MACOUPIN; 171 M-7; elev. 652ft./199m.; mail Mount Olive z 62069; Ⓟ 229; © 221
White Cliffs; RMC Place; MADISON; ★ ST.L; mail Godfrey z 62035; ● 30
Whitefield; RMC Place; MARSHALL, BUREAU; ▲ Whitefield; mail Henry z 61537; ● 40
Whitefield; MCD-Township; MARSHALL; *170 F-8; mail Henry z 61537; Ⓟ 378; © 376
Whitehall; RMC Place; COOK; ★ CHI; mail Mount Prospect z 60056; pop. incl. with Mount Prospect (Inc. Place)
White Hall; Inc. Place; GREENE; ▲ White Hall; 171 L-5; 🅿; z 62092; Ⓟ 2,814; © 2,629
White Hall; MCD-Township; GREENE; *171 L-5; 🅿; z 62092; Ⓟ 3,296; © 3,036
White Heath; RMC Place; PIATT; 170 I-11; elev. 699ft./213m.; 🅿; z 61884; ● 500
Whitehill; JOHNSON; see Chasco (RMC Place)
White Oak; RMC Place; MASON; *170 I-6; mail Havana z 62644; rural
White Oak; MCD-Township; MCLEAN; *170 H-9; mail Carlock z 61725; Ⓟ 803; © 807
White Oaks; RMC Place; LEE; *170 C-8; mail Dixon z 61021; ● 200
White Oaks Bay; RMC Place; MCHENRY; *170 A-11; ★ CHI; mail Wonder Lake z 60097; ● 500
White Pigeon; RMC Place; WHITESIDE; *170 C-7; mail Morrison z 61270; ● 40
White Pines; RMC Place; DUPAGE; *170 C-12; ★ CHI; mail Bensenville z 60106; pop. incl. with Elmhurst (Inc. Place)
White Post; RMC Place; MACOUPIN; *171 M-7; elev. 650ft./198m.; mail Wilsonville z 62093; pop. incl. with Wilsonville (Inc. Place)
White Rock; RMC Place; LEE; *170 C-8; mail Dixon z 61021; ● 150
White Rock; RMC Place; OGLE; ▲ White Rock; *170 B-9; mail Rochelle z 61068; ● 100
White Rock; MCD-Township; OGLE; *170 B-9; mail Rochelle z 61068; Ⓟ 717; © 709
Whites Addition; RMC Place; ROCK ISLAND; ★ D-RI-M; mail East Moline z 61244; ● 60
WHITESIDE; 170 C-7; Ⓟ 60,186; © 60,653; Ⓡ 60,651; ◆ 58,611
Whitley; MCD-Township; MOULTRIE; *171 L-11; mail Gays z 61928; Ⓟ 678; © 681
Whitmore; MCD-Township; MACON; *170 J-10; ★ DEC; mail Argenta z 62501; Ⓟ 4,741; © 4,474
Whittington; RMC Place; FRANKLIN; 171 Q-10; elev. 445ft./136m.; 🅿; z 62897; ● 200
Wichert; RMC Place; KANKAKEE; *170 F-13; elev. 634ft./193m.; ★ KANK; mail Saint Anne z 60964; ● 120
Wicker Park; RMC Place; COOK; *170 C-13; 🅿; ★ CHI; z 60642 & mail Chicago z 60622; pop. incl. with Chicago (Inc. Place)
Wickmore; RMC Place; MADISON; *171 M-6; ★ ST.L; mail Godfrey z 62035; pop. incl. with Godfrey (Inc. Place)
Wideview; RMC Place; KANE; *170 C-11; elev. 850ft./259m.; ★ CHI; mail Saint Charles z 60175; ● 200
Wieisbrook; RMC Place; WILLIAMSON; *171 R-9; elev. 450ft./137m.; ★ CARB-; mail Carterville z 62918; pop. incl. with Carterville (Inc. Place)
Wilbern; RMC Place; MARSHALL; *170 F-8; mail Washburn z 61570; ● 40
Wilberton; MCD-Township; FAYETTE; *171 N-9; mail Shobonier z 62885; Ⓟ 402; © 465
Wilbur Heights; RMC Place; CHAMPAIGN; *170 I-12; mail Champaign z 61822; ● 300
Wilcox; MCD-Township; HANCOCK; *170 H-3; mail Warsaw z 62379; Ⓟ 263; © 164
Wildrose; RMC Place; KANE; *170 C-11; elev. 750ft./229m.; ★ CHI; mail Saint Charles z 60174; ● 600
Wildwood; RMC Place; KANE; 172 A-5; elev. 699ft./213m.; ★ CHI; mail Aurora z 60506; ● 40
Wildwood; RMC Place; LAKE; *170 A-12; ★ CHI; mail Grayslake z 60030
Wildwood Addition; RMC Place; ROCK ISLAND; ★ D-RI-M; mail Moline z 61265; pop. incl. with Moline (Inc. Place)
Wildwood Valley; RMC Place; KANE; *170 B-11; elev. 930ft./283m.; ★ CHI; mail Elgin z 60123; ● 200
Will; MCD-Township; WILL; *170 E-13; mail Peotone z 60468; Ⓟ 1,323; © 1,568
WILL; 170 D-12; Ⓟ 357,313; © 502,266; ◆ 682,797
Willard; RMC Place; ALEXANDER; *171 T-8; mail Miller City z 62962
Willard; RMC Place; ST. CLAIR; *171 O-7; ★ ST.L; mail O Fallon z 62269; ● 80
Willeys; RMC Place; CHRISTIAN; *171 K-9; elev. 633ft./193m.; 🅿; z 62568; ● 30
Williams; MCD-Township; SANGAMON; *170 J-8; mail Williamsville z 62693; Ⓟ 2,797; © 3,310
Williamsburg; RMC Place; MOULTRIE; *171 K-11; elev. 693ft./211m.; mail Lovington z 61937; rural
Williamsfield; Inc. Place; KNOX; 170 F-7; elev. 711ft./217m.; 🅿; z 61489; Ⓟ 571; © 620
Williamson; Inc. Place; MADISON; *171 M-7; elev. 600ft./183m.; mail Staunton z 62088; Ⓟ 278; © 251
WILLIAMSON; 171 R-10; Ⓟ 57,733; © 61,296; ◆ 65,344
Williams Park; RMC Place; LAKE; *170 A-12; ★ CHI; mail Wauconda z 60084; ● 400
Williams Place; RMC Place; MADISON; ★ ST.L; mail Godfrey z 62035; ● 100
Williamsville; Inc. Place; SANGAMON; 170 J-8; elev. 600ft./183m.; 🅿; z 62693; Ⓟ 1,140; © 1,439
Willisville; Inc. Place; PERRY; 171 Q-8; elev. 500ft./152m.; 🅿; z 62997; Ⓟ 577; © 694
Willow; RMC Place; JO DAVIESS; *170 A-7; mail Stockton z 61085; rural
Willoway; RMC Place; DUPAGE; ★ CHI; mail Naperville z 60540; pop. incl. with Naperville (Inc. Place)
Willoway Manor; RMC Place; DUPAGE; ★ CHI; mail Hinsdale z 60521; pop. incl. with Willowbrook (Inc. Place)
Willow Branch; MCD-Township; PIATT; *170 J-10; mail Cisco z 61830; Ⓟ 732; © 716; Ⓡ 720
Willowbrook; Inc. Place; DUPAGE; 172 J-5; elev. 710ft./216m.; 🅿; ★ CHI; z 60527 & mail Clarendon Hills z 60514, Hinsdale z 60521; Ⓟ 8,598; © 8,967
Willowbrook; RMC Place; KENDALL; *170 C-11; elev. 650ft./198m.; ★ CHI; mail Bristol z 60512; ● 250
Willowbrook; CDP-Census Area Only; WILL; ▲ Crete; *170 D-13; elev. 700ft./213m.; ★ CHI; mail Crete z 60417; Ⓟ 1,808; © 2,130
Willow Brooke; RMC Place; WINNEBAGO; ★ RKFD; mail South Beloit z 61080; ● 40
Willow Creek; MCD-Township; LEE; *170 C-9; mail Lee z 60530; Ⓟ 550; © 700
Willow Estates; RMC Place; DEKALB; *170 B-10; mail Genoa z 60135; ● 90
Willow Estates; RMC Place; IROQUOIS; *170 F-13; elev. 675ft./206m.; mail Beaverville z 60912; ● 100
Willow Hill; Inc. Place; JASPER; ▲ Willow Hill; 171 M-12; elev. 502ft./153m.; 🅿; z 62480; Ⓟ 268; © 250
Willow Hill; MCD-Township; JASPER; *171 M-12; 🅿; z 62480; Ⓟ 605; © 700
Willow Springs; Inc. Place; COOK, DUPAGE; 172 K-7; elev. 618ft./188m.; 🅿; ★ CHI; z 60480; Ⓟ 4,509; © 5,027
Willow Wood; RMC Place; COOK; ★ CHI; mail Palatine z 60074; pop. incl. with Palatine (Inc. Place)
Wilmette; Inc. Place; COOK; 170 B-13; elev. 610ft./186m.; 🅿; ★ CHI; z 60091; Ⓟ 26,690; © 27,651; ◆ 27,755
Wilmington; GREENE; see Patterson (Inc. Place)
Wilmington; Inc. Place; WILL; ▲ Wilmington, Wesley; 170 E-12; 🅿; ★ CHI; z 60481; Ⓟ 4,743; © 5,134
Wilmington; MCD-Township; WILL; *170 E-12; 🅿; ★ CHI; z 60481; includes part of the City of Wilmington; Ⓟ 5,736; © 6,050
Wilshire Bluffs Estate; RMC Place; BOONE; *170 A-10; elev. 799ft./244m.; mail Belvidere z 61008; ● 200
Wilsman; RMC Place; LA SALLE; *170 E-10; elev. 643ft./196m.; mail Streator z 61364; rural
Wilson; MCD-Township; DE WITT; *170 I-10; mail Wapella z 61777; Ⓟ 150; © 155
Wilson Avenue; RMC Place; COOK; *170 C-13; ★ CHI; pop. incl. with Chicago (Inc. Place)
Wilson Heights; RMC Place; MADISON; *171 N-7; ★ ST.L; mail Collinsville z 62234; ● 180
Wilsonville; Inc. Place; MACOUPIN; 171 M-7; 🅿; z 62093; Ⓟ 609; © 604
Wilton; MCD-Township; WILL; *170 E-12; mail Manhattan z 60442; Ⓟ 675; © 819
Wilton Center; RMC Place; WILL; 170 E-12; elev. 665ft./203m.; 🅿; z 60442; ● 100
Winchester; Inc. Place; ⊡ SCOTT; 171 K-5; elev. 546ft./166m.; 🅿; z 62694; Ⓟ 1,769; © 1,650
Winden Oak; RMC Place; KANE; *170 C-11; elev. 803ft./245m.; ★ CHI; mail Elburn z 60119; ● 70
Windham Manor; RMC Place; COOK; ★ CHI; mail Northbrook z 60062; pop. incl. with Northbrook (Inc. Place)
Windings; RMC Place; KANE; *170 C-11; elev. 950ft./290m.; ★ CHI; mail Saint Charles z 60175; ● 250
Windsor; MERCER; see New Windsor (Inc. Place)
Windsor; Inc. Place; SHELBY; ▲ Windsor; 171 L-10; elev. 711ft./217m.; 🅿; z 61957; Ⓟ 1,143; © 1,125
Windsor; MCD-Township; SHELBY; *171 L-10; 🅿; z 61957; Ⓟ 1,498; © 1,519
Windsor Estates West; RMC Place; COOK; ★ CHI; mail Mount Prospect z 60056; pop. incl. with Mount Prospect (Inc. Place)
Windsor Park; RMC Place; CHAMPAIGN; *170 I-11; ★ CH-U; mail Champaign z 61822; ● 580
Windsor Park; RMC Place; COOK; ★ CHI; mail Chicago z 60649; pop. incl. with Chicago (Inc. Place)
Wine Hill; RMC Place; RANDOLPH; *171 Q-7; elev. 593ft./181m.; mail Steeleville z 62288; rural
Winfield; Inc. Place; DUPAGE; 172 H-4; elev. 750ft./229m.; 🅿 🅷; ★ CHI; z 60190; Ⓟ 7,096; © 8,718
Winfield; MCD-Township; DUPAGE; *170 C-12; 🅿; ★ CHI; z 60190 & mail West Chicago z 60185; includes part of the Village of Winfield; Ⓟ 37,969; © 45,155
Wing; RMC Place; LIVINGSTON; *170 G-11; mail Forrest z 61741; ● 50
Winkle (Craig); RMC Place; PERRY; *171 P-8; mail Coulterville z 62237; ● 30
Winnebago; Inc. Place; WINNEBAGO; ▲ Winnebago; 170 A-9; elev. 869ft./265m.; 🅿; ★ RKFD; z 61088; Ⓟ 1,840; © 2,958
Winnebago; MCD-Township; WINNEBAGO; *170 B-9; 🅿; ★ RKFD; z 61088; Ⓟ 3,237; © 5,142
WINNEBAGO; 170 A-9; Ⓟ 252,913; © 278,418; ◆ 304,327
Winneshiek; RMC Place; STEPHENSON; *170 A-8; mail Freeport z 61032; rural
Winnetka; Inc. Place; COOK; 170 B-13; elev. 658ft./201m.; 🅿; ★ CHI; z 60093 & mail Glencoe z 60022; Ⓟ 12,174; © 12,419
Winslow; Inc. Place; STEPHENSON; ▲ Winslow; 170 A-7; 🅿; z 61089; Ⓟ 317; © 345
Winslow; MCD-Township; STEPHENSON; *170 A-7; 🅿; z 61089; Ⓟ 722; © 720
Winston Hills; RMC Place; DUPAGE; ★ CHI; mail Downers Grove z 60515; pop. incl. with Woodridge (Inc. Place)
Winston Park; RMC Place; COOK; ★ CHI; mail Palatine z 60074; pop. incl. with Palatine (Inc. Place)
Winston Park South; RMC Place; COOK; ★ CHI; mail Country Club Hills z 60478; pop. incl. with Country Club Hills (Inc. Place)
Winston Village; RMC Place; WILL; *170 C-12; ★ CHI; mail Bolingbrook z 60440; pop. incl. with Bolingbrook (Inc. Place)
Winston Woods; RMC Place; WILL; *170 C-12; ★ CHI; mail Bolingbrook z 60440; pop. incl. with Bolingbrook (Inc. Place)
Winterrowd; RMC Place; EFFINGHAM; *171 N-11; mail Dieterich z 62424; rural
Winthrop Harbor; Inc. Place; LAKE; 170 A-13; elev. 633ft./193m.; 🅿; ★ CHI; z 60096; Ⓟ 6,240; © 6,670
Wireton; RMC Place; COOK; ★ CHI; mail Blue Island z 60406; pop. incl. with Blue Island (Inc. Place)
Wisetown; BOND; see Beaver Creek (RMC Place)
Witt; Inc. Place; MONTGOMERY; 171 L-8; elev. 666ft./203m.; 🅿; z 62094; Ⓟ 866; © 991
Witt; MCD-Township; MONTGOMERY; *171 M-9; 🅿; z 62094; includes part of the City of Witt; Ⓟ 1,251; © 1,247
Woburn; RMC Place; BOND; *171 M-8; elev. 577ft./176m.; mail Greenville z 62246; ● 25
Wolf Lake; RMC Place; UNION; 171 S-8; elev. 353ft./108m.; 🅿; z 62998; ● 300
Womac; RMC Place; MACOUPIN; *171 L-7; 🅿; z 62626; rural
Wonder Lake; Inc. Place; MCHENRY; 170 A-11; elev. 850ft./259m.; 🅿; ★ CHI; z 60097; Ⓟ 1,024; © 1,345
Wonder Lake; CDP-Census Area Only; MCHENRY; *170 A-11; 🅿; ★ CHI; z 60097; Ⓟ 6,664; © 7,463
Wonder View; RMC Place; MCHENRY; *170 A-11; ★ CHI; mail Wonder Lake z 60097; ● 500
Wonder Woods; RMC Place; MCHENRY; *170 A-11; ★ CHI; mail Wonder Lake z 60097; ● 500
Woodbine; RMC Place; JO DAVIESS; ▲ Woodbine; 170 A-6; mail Stockton z 61085; ● 140
Woodbine; MCD-Township; JO DAVIESS; *170 A-6; mail Stockton z 61085; Ⓟ 661; © 577
Woodborough; RMC Place; COOK; ★ CHI; mail Homewood z 60430; pop. incl. with Homewood (Inc. Place)
Woodbridge; RMC Place; KANE; *170 B-11; ★ CHI; mail Elgin z 60123; pop. incl. with Elgin (Inc. Place)
Woodburn; RMC Place; MACOUPIN; 171 M-7; mail Bunker Hill z 62014; ● 170
Woodbury; RMC Place; CUMBERLAND; ▲ Woodbury; 171 M-11; mail Montrose z 62445; ● 70
Woodbury; MCD-Township; CUMBERLAND; *171 M-11; mail Montrose z 62445; Ⓟ 574; © 684
Wood Dale; Inc. Place; DUPAGE; 172 G-6; elev. 696ft./212m.; 🅿; ★ CHI; z 60191, z 60399; Ⓟ 12,425; © 13,535
Wooddale; RMC Place; PEORIA; ★ PEOR; mail Peoria z 61607; ● 200
Wooded Shores; RMC Place; MCHENRY; *170 A-11; ★ CHI; mail Wonder Lake z 60097; ● 600
Woodford; RMC Place; WOODFORD; *170 G-9; mail Minonk z 61760; rural
WOODFORD; 170 G-9; Ⓟ 32,653; © 35,469; ◆ 39,022
Woodford Heights; RMC Place; WOODFORD; *170 G-8; elev. 814ft./248m.; ★ PEOR; mail Metamora z 61548; ● 100
Woodgate; RMC Place; DEKALB; *170 C-10; elev. 870ft./265m.; ★ DKLB; mail Sycamore z 60178; pop. incl. with Sycamore (Inc. Place)
Woodgate Estate; RMC Place; JERSEY; *171 M-6; ★ ST.L; mail Brighton z 62012; ● 80
Woodhill Estates; RMC Place; BOONE; *170 A-10; elev. 800ft./244m.; mail Garden Prairie z 61038; ● 40
Woodhull; Inc. Place; HENRY; 170 E-6; elev. 819ft./250m.; 🅿; z 61490; Ⓟ 808; © 809
Woodland; MCD-Township; CARROLL; *170 B-7; mail Mount Carroll z 61053; Ⓟ 376; © 430
Woodland; MCD-Township; FULTON; *170 I-6; mail Astoria z 61501; Ⓟ 485; © 423
Woodland; Inc. Place; IROQUOIS; 170 G-13; elev. 640ft./195m.; 🅿; z 60974; Ⓟ 313; © 319
Woodland; RMC Place; KANKAKEE; *170 E-13; elev. 625ft./191m.; mail Momence z 60954; ● 50
Woodland Addition; RMC Place; LA SALLE; *170 E-10; mail Ottawa z 61350; ● 45
Woodland Heights; RMC Place; COOK; ★ CHI; mail Streamwood z 60107; pop. incl. with Streamwood (Inc. Place)
Woodland Hills; RMC Place; KANE; *170 C-11; ★ CHI; mail Batavia z 60510; pop. incl. with Batavia (Inc. Place)
Woodland Lake; RMC Place; VERMILION; *170 I-13; ★ DANV; mail Catlin z 61817; ● 120
Woodland Shores; RMC Place; LEE; *170 C-8; mail Dixon z 61021; ● 100
Woodlawn; RMC Place; COOK; ★ CHI; mail Chicago z 60637; pop. incl. with Chicago (Inc. Place)
Woodlawn; Inc. Place; JEFFERSON; 171 P-9; elev. 494ft./151m.; 🅿; z 62898; Ⓟ 582; © 630
Woodlawn Acres; RMC Place; OGLE; *170 C-9; mail Rochelle z 61068; ● 300
Woodlawn Heights; RMC Place; WHITESIDE; mail Sterling z 61081; ● 350
Woodmere; RMC Place; LAKE; ★ CHI; mail Libertyville z 60048; pop. incl. with Libertyville (Inc. Place)
Woodridge; Inc. Place; DUPAGE, COOK, WILL; 172 J-5; elev. 750ft./229m.; 🅿; ★ CHI; z 60517 & mail Naperville z 60540; Ⓟ 26,359; © 30,934; ◆ 31,817
Wood River; Inc. Place; MADISON; ▲ Wood River; 171 N-6; 🅿 🅷; ★ ST.L; z 62095; Ⓟ 11,490; © 11,296
Wood River; MCD-Township; MADISON; *171 N-6; 🅿; ★ ST.L; z 62095; Ⓟ 35,506; © 33,410
Woods Edge; RMC Place; CHAMPAIGN; *170 I-12; elev. 725ft./221m.; ★ CH-U; mail Urbana z 61802; ● 250
Woodside; MCD-Township; SANGAMON; *171 K-8; ★ SPRG; mail Springfield z 62703; Ⓟ 14,612; © 12,729; Ⓡ 12,828
Woodside Estates; RMC Place; DUPAGE; ★ CHI; mail Oak Brook z 60523; pop. incl. with Oak Brook (Inc. Place)
Woodson; Inc. Place; MORGAN; 171 K-6; elev. 677ft./206m.; 🅿; z 62695; Ⓟ 472; © 559
Woodstock; Inc. Place; ⊡ MCHENRY; 170 A-11; elev. 942ft./287m.; 🅿 🅷; ★ CHI; z 60098; Ⓟ 14,353; © 20,151; ◆ 25,140
Woodstock; MCD-Township; SCHUYLER; *170 I-5; mail Rushville z 62681; Ⓟ 337; © 313
Woodville; MCD-Township; GREENE; *171 M-5; mail Eldred z 62027; Ⓟ 454; © 301
Woodworth; RMC Place; IROQUOIS; 170 G-13; elev. 668ft./204m.; mail Milford z 60953; ● 100
Woody; RMC Place; GREENE; *171 L-5; mail Carrollton z 62016; rural
Woodyard; RMC Place; EDGAR; *170 J-13; elev. 672ft./205m.; mail Chrisman z 61924; rural
Woodyard (Alderson); RMC Place; FAYETTE; mail Shobonier z 62885; rural
Wooster Lake; RMC Place; LAKE; ★ CHI; mail Ingleside z 60041
Woosung; RMC Place; OGLE; ▲ Woosung; 170 C-8; 🅿; z 61091; ● 180
Woosung; MCD-Township; OGLE; *170 C-8; 🅿; z 61091; Ⓟ 345; © 392
Worden; Inc. Place; MADISON; 171 N-7; elev. 570ft./174m.; 🅿; z 62097; Ⓟ 896; © 905
Worth; Inc. Place; COOK; 172 K-8; elev. 600ft./183m.; 🅿; ★ CHI; z 60482; Ⓟ 11,208; © 11,047
Worth; MCD-Township; COOK; *170 D-13; 🅿; ★ CHI; z 60482; includes part of the Village of Worth; Ⓟ 151,144; © 152,239
Worth; MCD-Township; WOODFORD; *170 G-8; ★ PEOR; mail Metamora z 61548; Ⓟ 5,882; © 7,285
Wrights; RMC Place; GREENE; ▲ Wrights; 171 L-6; 🅿; z 62098; ● 100
Wrights; MCD-Township; GREENE; *171 L-6; 🅿; z 62098; Ⓟ 346; © 348
Wrights Corner; RMC Place; FAYETTE; *171 M-10; mail Beecher City z 62414; rural
Wyanet; Inc. Place; BUREAU; ▲ Wyanet; 170 E-8; 🅿; z 61379; Ⓟ 1,017; © 1,028
Wyanet; MCD-Township; BUREAU; *170 E-8; 🅿; z 61379; Ⓟ 1,483; © 1,348
Wynoose; RMC Place; RICHLAND, WAYNE; 171 O-12; elev. 428ft./130m.; mail Noble z 62868; ● 40
Wyoming; MCD-Township; LEE; *170 D-9; mail Paw Paw z 61353; Ⓟ 1,123; © 1,236
Wyoming; Inc. Place; STARK; 170 F-7; elev. 707ft./215m.; 🅿; z 61491; Ⓟ 1,462; © 1,424
Wysox; MCD-Township; CARROLL; *170 C-7; mail Milledgeville z 61051; Ⓟ 1,549; © 1,465
Wythe; MCD-Township; HANCOCK; *170 H-3; mail Warsaw z 62379; Ⓟ 282; © 269

X

Xenia; Inc. Place; CLAY; ▲ Xenia; 171 O-10; 🅿; z 62899; Ⓟ 424; © 407
Xenia; MCD-Township; CLAY; *171 O-10; 🅿; z 62899; Ⓟ 686; © 705

Y

Yale; Inc. Place; JASPER; 171 M-12; elev. 555ft./169m.; 🅿; z 62481; Ⓟ 94; © 97
Yankee Ridge; RMC Place; CHAMPAIGN; *170 I-12; elev. 725ft./221m.; ★ CH-U; mail Urbana z 61802; ● 200
Yantisville; RMC Place; SHELBY; *171 K-10; elev. 709ft./216m.; 🅿; z 62534
Yard Center; RMC Place; COOK; ★ CHI; mail Dolton z 60419; pop. incl. with Dolton (Inc. Place)
Yates; MCD-Township; MCLEAN; *170 G-10; mail Chenoa z 61726; Ⓟ 375; © 340
Yates City; Inc. Place; KNOX; 170 G-7; elev. 673ft./205m.; 🅿; z 61572; Ⓟ 760; © 725
Yatesville; RMC Place; MORGAN; *170 J-6; 🅿; z 62612; rural
Yellowhead; MCD-Township; KANKAKEE; *170 E-13; mail Grant Park z 60940; Ⓟ 2,210; © 2,567
Yeoward Addition (Yeowardville); RMC Place; WHITESIDE; *170 C-8; mail Rock Falls z 61071; ● 650
Yeowardville; WHITESIDE; see Yeoward Addition (RMC Place)
York; MCD-Township; CARROLL; *170 C-7; mail Thomson z 61285; Ⓟ 1,868; © 1,801
York; RMC Place; CLARK; ▲ York; 171 M-13; elev. 448ft./137m.; mail West Union z 62477; ● 100
York; MCD-Township; CLARK; *171 L-13; mail West Union z 62477; Ⓟ 621; © 651
York; MCD-Township; DUPAGE; *170 C-12; ★ CHI; mail Villa Park z 60181; Ⓟ 120,546; © 124,553
York Center; RMC Place; DUPAGE; 172 I-5; ★ CHI; mail Lombard z 60148; Ⓟ 4,818
Yorkfield; RMC Place; DUPAGE; 172 I-6; ★ CHI; mail Elmhurst z 60126; pop. incl. with Elmhurst (Inc. Place)
Yorkshire Woods; RMC Place; DUPAGE; ★ CHI; mail Oak Brook z 60523; pop. incl. with Oak Brook (Inc. Place)
Yorktown; RMC Place; BUREAU; 170 D-7; mail Tampico z 61283; ● 100
Yorktown; MCD-Township; HENRY; *170 D-7; mail Prophetstown z 61277; Ⓟ 506; © 429
Yorkville; Inc. Place; ⊡ KENDALL; 170 D-11; elev. 643ft./196m.; 🅿; ★ CHI; z 60560; Ⓟ 3,925; © 6,189
Young America; MCD-Township; EDGAR; *170 J-13; mail Metcalf z 61940; Ⓟ 849; © 769
Young Hickory; MCD-Township; FULTON; *170 G-6; mail London Mills z 61544; Ⓟ 746; © 719
Youngstown; RMC Place; WARREN; *170 G-5; elev. 758ft./231m.; mail Roseville z 61473; ● 25

Z

Zanesville; MCD-Township; MONTGOMERY; *171 L-8; mail Waggoner z 62572; Ⓟ 445; © 399
Zearing; RMC Place; BUREAU; *170 D-9; mail Malden z 61337; ● 40
Zeigler; Inc. Place; FRANKLIN; 171 Q-9; elev. 410ft./125m.; 🅿; ★ CARB-; z 62999; Ⓟ 1,746; © 1,669
Zenith; RMC Place; WAYNE; *171 O-10; elev. 491ft./150m.; mail Xenia z 62899
Zif; MCD-Township; WAYNE; *171 O-11; mail Clay City z 62824; Ⓟ 120; © 114
Zion; RMC Place; CARROLL; mail Savanna z 61074; rural
Zion; Inc. Place; LAKE; 170 A-13; elev. 634ft./193m.; 🅿 🅷; ★ CHI; z 60099; Ⓟ 19,775; © 22,866; ◆ 23,963
Zion; MCD-Township; LAKE; *170 A-12; 🅿 🅷; ★ CHI; z 60099; coextensive with the City of Zion; Ⓟ 19,775; © 22,866
Zuma; MCD-Township; ROCK ISLAND; *170 D-6; mail Hillsdale z 61257; Ⓟ 686; © 687
Zurich Heights; RMC Place; LAKE; ★ CHI; mail Lake Zurich z 60047; pop. incl. with Lake Zurich (Inc. Place)

Entries in **UPPERCASE** are counties.
Entries in **bold** have populations of 2,500 or more.
Names in parentheses are alternate names.

Inc. Place	Incorporated Place
RMC Place	Rand McNally Designated Place
CDP	Census Designated Place
MCD	Minor Civil Division

⊡ County Seat
▲ Minor Civil Division
elev. Elevation
🅿 Post Office
🅷 Hospital
🅲 College
■ Principal Business Center
★ Ranally Metro Area (RMA) Abbreviation
z Zip Code(s)
Ⓟ Previous Census Population
Ⓡ Revised Census Population
Ⓐ Annexation Population
● Rand McNally Population Estimate
© Final Census Population
Ⓢ Special Census Population
◆ Estimated Population

For additional definitions see Glossary, Volume 1, and Introduction, Volume 2.

INDIANA

IA
MI
OH
IL
Indianapolis
MO
KY
WV

Statistics

Total area (2000) — 36,418 square miles
Land area (2000) — 35,867 square miles
Water area (2000) — 551 square miles
Capital — Indianapolis
Admitted as state — December, 1816

Maps

State maps can be found on pages 142-254 in Vol. 1
County Subdivision maps can be found on pages 255-271 in Vol. 1

Ranally Metro Areas (RMAs) and Abbreviations

Anderson, IN — AND
Bloomington, IN — BLMNG
Chicago, IL-IN-WI — CHI
Cincinnati, OH-KY-IN — CIN
Columbus, IN — COL
Elkhart, IN-MI — ELK
Evansville, IN-KY — EV
Fort Wayne, IN — FTWA
Indianapolis, IN — IND
Kokomo, IN — KOK
Lafayette-West Lafayette, IN — LAF-
Louisville, KY-IN — LOU
Marion, IN — MRN
Michigan City, IN — MICH
Muncie, IN — MUN
Richmond, IN-OH — RICH
South Bend, IN-MI — S.B.
Terre Haute, IN — T.H.

Principal Places

Place Name	Place Type	County	Population
Indianapolis	Inc. Place	MARION	◆811,560
Fort Wayne	Inc. Place	ALLEN	◆213,506
Center	MCD-Township	MARION	©167,055
North	MCD-Township	LAKE	©165,656
Wayne	MCD-Township	MARION	®133,477
Washington	MCD-Township	MARION	©132,927
Calumet	MCD-Township	LAKE	©127,800
Evansville	Inc. Place	VANDERBURGH	◆116,851
Lawrence	MCD-Township	MARION	©111,961
Wayne	MCD-Township	ALLEN	©111,117
South Bend	Inc. Place	ST. JOSEPH	◆108,904
Gary	Inc. Place	LAKE	◆99,455
Portage	MCD-Township	ST. JOSEPH	®96,080
Warren	MCD-Township	MARION	©93,941
Perry	MCD-Township	MARION	©92,838
Fishers	Inc. Place	HAMILTON	◆80,191
Hammond	Inc. Place	LAKE	◆79,917
Bloomington	Inc. Place	MONROE	®78,719
Pike	MCD-Township	MARION	®71,449
Lafayette	Inc. Place	TIPPECANOE	◆71,222
Center	MCD-Township	DELAWARE	©71,120
St. Joseph	MCD-Township	ALLEN	©68,276
Knight	MCD-Township	VANDERBURGH	©67,491
Muncie	Inc. Place	DELAWARE	◆65,581
Carmel	Inc. Place	HAMILTON	◆64,711
Clay	MCD-Township	HAMILTON	©64,709
Penn	MCD-Township	ST. JOSEPH	©64,322
Terre Haute	Inc. Place	VIGO	◆63,268
Anderson	Inc. Place	MADISON	◆60,070
Anderson	MCD-Township	MADISON	©60,026
Jeffersonville	MCD-Township	CLARK	©56,695
Concord	MCD-Township	ELKHART	©55,377
St. John	MCD-Township	LAKE	©53,701
Elkhart	Inc. Place	ELKHART	◆52,406
Harrison	MCD-Township	VIGO	©51,898
Wabash	MCD-Township	TIPPECANOE	®51,275
Fairfield	MCD-Township	TIPPECANOE	©49,970
New Albany	MCD-Township	FLOYD	©48,476
Greenwood	Inc. Place	JOHNSON	◆47,651
Center	MCD-Township	HOWARD	©47,619
Mishawaka	Inc. Place	ST. JOSEPH	◆47,470
Kokomo	Inc. Place	HOWARD	◆44,378
Portage	MCD-Township	PORTER	©43,956
Lawrence	Inc. Place	MARION	◆43,883
Wayne	MCD-Township	WAYNE	©43,742
Columbus	MCD-Township	BARTHOLOMEW	©41,194
Bloomington	MCD-Township	MONROE	©41,032
Columbus	Inc. Place	BARTHOLOMEW	◆40,853
Perry	MCD-Township	MONROE	©40,508
Pleasant	MCD-Township	JOHNSON	©39,901
Noblesville	Inc. Place	HAMILTON	◆39,707
Hobart	MCD-Township	LAKE	©39,636
Ross	MCD-Township	LAKE	©38,685
Center	MCD-Township	PORTER	©38,186
New Albany	Inc. Place	FLOYD	◆38,012
Clay	MCD-Township	ST. JOSEPH	®37,981
Richmond	Inc. Place	WAYNE	◆37,278
Portage	Inc. Place	PORTER	◆36,864
White River	MCD-Township	JOHNSON	©35,539
Noblesville	MCD-Township	HAMILTON	©34,534
Elkhart	MCD-Township	ELKHART	©33,986
Pigeon	MCD-Township	VANDERBURGH	©33,682
Washington	MCD-Township	ALLEN	©33,105
Goshen	Inc. Place	ELKHART	◆32,921
Merrillville	Inc. Place	LAKE	◆32,406
Michigan City	Inc. Place	LAPORTE	◆32,332
Center	MCD-Township	VANDERBURGH	©32,220
West Lafayette	Inc. Place	TIPPECANOE	◆32,219
Franklin	MCD-Township	MARION	©32,080
Adams	MCD-Township	ALLEN	©31,394
East Chicago	Inc. Place	LAKE	◆31,212
Ohio	MCD-Township	WARRICK	©31,002
Jeffersonville	Inc. Place	CLARK	◆30,668
Valparaiso	Inc. Place	PORTER	◆29,776
Michigan	MCD-Township	LAPORTE	©29,326
Aboite	MCD-Township	ALLEN	©28,338
Delaware	MCD-Township	HAMILTON	©28,268
Granger	CDP	ST. JOSEPH	◆28,148
Marion	Inc. Place	GRANT	◆27,849
Franklin	Inc. Place	JOHNSON	◆26,776
Osolo	MCD-Township	ELKHART	©26,369
Washington	MCD-Township	HENDRICKS	©26,319
Center	MCD-Township	LAKE	©26,191
Hobart	Inc. Place	LAKE	◆26,028
Schererville	Inc. Place	LAKE	◆25,690
Wayne	MCD-Township	KOSCIUSKO	©25,262
Center	MCD-Township	GRANT	©24,833
Decatur	MCD-Township	MARION	©24,726
Center	MCD-Township	LAPORTE	©24,405
Henry	MCD-Township	HENRY	©23,859
Union	MCD-Township	MONTGOMERY	©23,837
Perry	MCD-Township	VANDERBURGH	©23,687
Vincennes	MCD-Township	KNOX	©23,372
Highland	Inc. Place	LAKE	◆23,077
Guilford	MCD-Township	HENDRICKS	©22,895
Clarksville	Inc. Place	CLARK	◆22,521
Plainfield	Inc. Place	HENDRICKS	◆22,184
Wea	MCD-Township	TIPPECANOE	©22,102
LaPorte	Inc. Place	LAPORTE	◆21,676
Munster	Inc. Place	LAKE	◆21,582
Huntington	MCD-Township	HUNTINGTON	©21,262
Crown Point	Inc. Place	LAKE	◆21,012
Shawswick	MCD-Township	LAWRENCE	©20,598
Eel	MCD-Township	CASS	©20,115
Center	MCD-Township	HANCOCK	©20,096
Addison	MCD-Township	SHELBY	©19,943
Harris	MCD-Township	ST. JOSEPH	©19,873
Jackson	MCD-Township	JACKSON	©19,578
Shelbyville	Inc. Place	SHELBY	◆19,160
Lincoln	MCD-Township	HENDRICKS	©18,967
Franklin	MCD-Township	JOHNSON	©18,752
Logansport	Inc. Place	CASS	◆18,693
Vincennes	Inc. Place	KNOX	◆18,417
Washington	MCD-Township	HAMILTON	©18,358
Perry	MCD-Township	ALLEN	©18,170
Westchester	MCD-Township	PORTER	©18,133
Seymour	Inc. Place	JACKSON	©18,101
Washington	MCD-Township	MORGAN	©17,978
Center	MCD-Township	CLINTON	©17,505
Huntington	Inc. Place	HUNTINGTON	©17,450
Griffith	Inc. Place	LAKE	©17,334
New Castle	Inc. Place	HENRY	◆17,226
Center	MCD-Township	BOONE	©17,102
Fall Creek	MCD-Township	HAMILTON	©17,079
Madison	MCD-Township	JEFFERSON	©16,770
Frankfort	Inc. Place	CLINTON	©16,662
Noble	MCD-Township	WABASH	©15,580
Connersville	Inc. Place	FAYETTE	©15,411
Crawfordsville	Inc. Place	MONTGOMERY	◆15,356
Washington	MCD-Township	DAVIESS	©15,110
Bainbridge	MCD-Township	DUBOIS	©14,950
Coolspring	MCD-Township	LAPORTE	©14,910
Beech Grove	Inc. Place	MARION	©14,880
Center	MCD-Township	MARSHALL	©14,721
Greenfield	Inc. Place	HANCOCK	©14,600
Brownsburg	Inc. Place	HENDRICKS	©14,520
Honey Creek	MCD-Township	VIGO	©14,280
Centre	MCD-Township	ST. JOSEPH	©14,236
Lebanon	Inc. Place	BOONE	©14,222
Lake Station	Inc. Place	LAKE	©13,948
Eagle	MCD-Township	BOONE	©13,910
Dyer	Inc. Place	LAKE	©13,895
Pipe Creek	MCD-Township	MADISON	©13,762
Westfield	Inc. Place	HAMILTON	◆13,572
Brown	MCD-Township	MORGAN	©13,491
Fall Creek	MCD-Township	MADISON	©13,363
Pleasant	MCD-Township	STEUBEN	©13,312
Bedford	Inc. Place	LAWRENCE	◆13,290
Connersville	MCD-Township	FAYETTE	©13,163
Jasper	Inc. Place	DUBOIS	◆13,057
Peru	Inc. Place	MIAMI	©12,994
Speedway	Inc. Place	MARION	©12,881
Boon	MCD-Township	WARRICK	©12,844
Warsaw	Inc. Place	KOSCIUSKO	◆12,752
Union	MCD-Township	DE KALB	©12,716
Peru	MCD-Township	MIAMI	©12,666
Mount Pleasant	MCD-Township	DELAWARE	©12,591
Greencastle	MCD-Township	PUTNAM	©12,491
New Haven	Inc. Place	ALLEN	©12,406
Richland	MCD-Township	MONROE	©12,349
Washington	MCD-Township	DECATUR	©12,206
Sugar Creek	MCD-Township	HANCOCK	©12,165
Troy	MCD-Township	PERRY	©12,129
Auburn	Inc. Place	DE KALB	©12,074
Madison	Inc. Place	JEFFERSON	◆12,035
Wabash	Inc. Place	WABASH	©11,743
Martinsville	Inc. Place	MORGAN	©11,698
Patoka	MCD-Township	GIBSON	©11,502
Charlestown	MCD-Township	CLARK	©11,457
Van Buren	MCD-Township	MONROE	©11,434
Mill	MCD-Township	GRANT	©11,271
Washington	Inc. Place	DAVIESS	◆11,229
Notre Dame	RMC Place	ST. JOSEPH	●11,000
Cedar Creek	MCD-Township	LAKE	©10,649
Washington	MCD-Township	ADAMS	©10,528
Chesterton	Inc. Place	PORTER	©10,488
Union	MCD-Township	WHITE	©10,436
Lawrenceburg	MCD-Township	DEARBORN	©10,434
Wayne	MCD-Township	NOBLE	©10,365
Harrison	MCD-Township	HARRISON	©10,303
Black	MCD-Township	POSEY	©10,288
Cedar Creek	MCD-Township	ALLEN	©10,288
Greensburg	Inc. Place	DECATUR	©10,260
Monroe	MCD-Township	MADISON	©10,233
Rochester	MCD-Township	FULTON	©9,992
Washington	MCD-Township	WASHINGTON	©9,955
Jackson	MCD-Township	HAMILTON	©9,919
Lost Creek	MCD-Township	VIGO	©9,907
Greencastle	Inc. Place	PUTNAM	©9,880
Plymouth	Inc. Place	MARSHALL	©9,840
Center	MCD-Township	HENDRICKS	©9,744
Elwood	Inc. Place	MADISON	©9,737
Cleveland	MCD-Township	ELKHART	©9,729
Kendallville	Inc. Place	NOBLE	©9,616
Columbia	MCD-Township	WHITLEY	©9,582
Clinton	MCD-Township	VERMILLION	©9,544
Bluffton	Inc. Place	WELLS	©9,536
Taylor	MCD-Township	HOWARD	©9,536
Decatur	Inc. Place	ADAMS	©9,528
Marion	MCD-Township	LAWRENCE	©9,491
Silver Creek	MCD-Township	CLARK	©9,399
Union	MCD-Township	MADISON	©9,287
Cedar Lake	Inc. Place	LAKE	©9,279
Mooresville	Inc. Place	MORGAN	©9,273
Vienna	MCD-Township	SCOTT	©9,160
Otter Creek	MCD-Township	VIGO	©9,059
Turkey Creek	MCD-Township	KOSCIUSKO	©9,032
Keener	MCD-Township	JASPER	©8,826
Zionsville	Inc. Place	BOONE	©8,775
Stockton	MCD-Township	GREENE	©8,722
Hanover	MCD-Township	LAKE	©8,692
Licking	MCD-Township	BLACKFORD	©8,689
Harrison	MCD-Township	WELLS	©8,616
Miller	MCD-Township	DEARBORN	©8,605
Center	MCD-Township	JENNINGS	©8,593
German	MCD-Township	MARSHALL	©8,584
German	MCD-Township	ST. JOSEPH	©8,518
Brazil	MCD-Township	CLAY	®8,504
Harrison	MCD-Township	HOWARD	©8,498
Porter	MCD-Township	PORTER	©8,459
Saint John	Inc. Place	LAKE	©8,382
Cicero	MCD-Township	TIPTON	©8,350
Georgetown	MCD-Township	FLOYD	©8,337
Rushville	MCD-Township	RUSH	©8,264
Brazil	Inc. Place	CLAY	®8,176
Princeton	Inc. Place	GIBSON	©8,175
Union	MCD-Township	PORTER	©8,166
Wayne	MCD-Township	JAY	©8,162
Brown	MCD-Township	HENDRICKS	©8,142
Sugar Creek	MCD-Township	VIGO	©8,121
Franklin	MCD-Township	GRANT	©8,108
Chester	MCD-Township	WABASH	©8,044
Tell City	Inc. Place	PERRY	©7,845
White River	MCD-Township	RANDOLPH	©7,661
Baugo	MCD-Township	ELKHART	©7,646
Lowell	Inc. Place	LAKE	©7,505
Mount Vernon	Inc. Place	POSEY	©7,478
Geneva	MCD-Township	JENNINGS	©7,469
Madison	MCD-Township	MORGAN	©7,391
German	MCD-Township	VANDERBURGH	©7,354
Angola	Inc. Place	STEUBEN	©7,344
Center	MCD-Township	WAYNE	©7,331
Lakes of the Four Seasons	CDP	LAKE	®7,296
Marion	MCD-Township	JASPER	©7,227
Plain	MCD-Township	KOSCIUSKO	®7,192
New Durham	MCD-Civil Township	LAPORTE	®7,190
Patoka	MCD-Township	DUBOIS	©7,178
Hamilton	MCD-Township	DELAWARE	©7,163
Keyser	MCD-Township	DE KALB	©7,090
Hamilton	MCD-Township	SULLIVAN	©7,083
Columbia City	Inc. Place	WHITLEY	©7,077
German	MCD-Township	BARTHOLOMEW	©7,062
Middlebury	MCD-Township	ELKHART	©7,028
Washington	MCD-Township	ELKHART	©7,019
Jennings	MCD-Township	SCOTT	©6,997
Pleasant	MCD-Township	GRANT	©6,941
Hartford City	Inc. Place	BLACKFORD	©6,928
Vernon	MCD-Township	HANCOCK	©6,894
Winfield	MCD-Township	LAKE	©6,878
Allen	MCD-Township	NOBLE	©6,847
Harrison	MCD-Township	FAYETTE	©6,836
Boonville	Inc. Place	WARRICK	©6,834
Liberty	MCD-Township	PORTER	©6,727
Nappanee	Inc. Place	ELKHART	©6,710
Pipe Creek	MCD-Township	MIAMI	©6,677
Buck Creek	MCD-Township	HANCOCK	©6,659
Perry	MCD-Township	NOBLE	©6,600
Jefferson	MCD-Township	ELKHART	©6,545
North Vernon	Inc. Place	JENNINGS	©6,515
Tippecanoe	MCD-Township	KOSCIUSKO	©6,493
Portland	Inc. Place	JAY	©6,437
Warren	MCD-Township	ST. JOSEPH	©6,430
Danville	Inc. Place	HENDRICKS	©6,418
Rochester	Inc. Place	FULTON	©6,414
Washington	MCD-Township	OWEN	©6,399
Lafayette	MCD-Township	FLOYD	©6,378
Greenville	MCD-Township	FLOYD	©6,340
Center	MCD-Township	STARKE	©6,271
Alexandria	Inc. Place	MADISON	©6,260
North Manchester	Inc. Place	WABASH	©6,260
Avon	Inc. Place	HENDRICKS	©6,248
Salem	Inc. Place	WASHINGTON	©6,172
Sellersburg	Inc. Place	CLARK	©6,071
Scottsburg	Inc. Place	SCOTT	©6,040
Batesville	Inc. Place	RIPLEY	©6,033
Rushville	Inc. Place	RUSH	©5,995
Charlestown	Inc. Place	CLARK	©5,993
Gas City	Inc. Place	GRANT	©5,940
Tippecanoe	MCD-Township	TIPPECANOE	®5,937
Paoli	MCD-Township	ORANGE	©5,890
Dunlap	CDP	ELKHART	©5,887
Boone	MCD-Township	PORTER	©5,884
Wabash	MCD-Township	ADAMS	©5,854
Jefferson	MCD-Township	GRANT	©5,850
Union	MCD-Township	ELKHART	©5,827
Garrett	Inc. Place	DE KALB	©5,803
Brookville	MCD-Township	FRANKLIN	©5,800
Linton	Inc. Place	GREENE	©5,774
Monticello	Inc. Place	WHITE	©5,723
Jefferson	MCD-Township	WELLS	©5,676
South Haven	CDP	PORTER	©5,619
Huntingburg	Inc. Place	DUBOIS	©5,598
Bloomfield	MCD-Township	LAGRANGE	©5,512
Cumberland	Inc. Place	MARION	©5,500
Scott	MCD-Township	VANDERBURGH	©5,445
Center	MCD-Township	DEARBORN	©5,431
Lafayette	MCD-Township	MADISON	©5,431
Lancaster	MCD-Township	WELLS	©5,411
Hanover	MCD-Township	JEFFERSON	©5,409
Bright	CDP	DEARBORN	©5,405
Adams	MCD-Township	PARKE	©5,399
Oak Park	CDP	CLARK	©5,379
Perry	MCD-Township	TIPPECANOE	©5,322
Brownstown	MCD-Township	JACKSON	©5,301
Rensselaer	Inc. Place	JASPER	©5,294
Tipton	Inc. Place	TIPTON	©5,251
Jackson	MCD-Township	HARRISON	©5,213
Westville	Inc. Place	LAPORTE	®5,211
Blue River	MCD-Township	JOHNSON	©5,189
Richland	MCD-Township	MADISON	©5,173
Whiting	Inc. Place	LAKE	©5,137
Clinton	Inc. Place	VERMILLION	©5,126
Ohio	MCD-Township	SPENCER	©5,092
Ellettsville	Inc. Place	MONROE	©5,078
Liberty	MCD-Township	HENDRICKS	©5,072
Smith	MCD-Township	WHITLEY	©5,050
Winchester	Inc. Place	RANDOLPH	©5,037
Liberty	MCD-Township	HOWARD	©5,032
Richland	MCD-Township	GREENE	©5,008

County Business Data

County	FIPS Code	County Seat	Land Area (Sq. Mi.)	Census Population			Wholesale Trade		Manufacturing, 2002			
				4/1/2000	4/1/1990	% Change 1990-2000	Sales, 2002 ($1,000)	% Change 1997-2002	Establish-ments	Total Employees	Value Added ($1,000)	Ranally Mfg. Units
Adams	001	Decatur	339	33,625	31,095	8.1	131,252	-13.3	68	5,711	742,573	393
Allen	003	Fort Wayne	657	331,849	300,836	10.3	6,794,125	3.2	551	27,683	5,174,437	2,738
Bartholomew	005	Columbus	407	71,435	63,657	12.2	590,566	-17.3	136	11,502	1,522,537	806
Benton	007	Fowler	406	9,421	9,441	-0.2	72,269	-33.7	16	558	29,213	15
Blackford	009	Hartford City	165	14,048	14,067	-0.1	65,526	215.5	28	1,919	146,170	77
Boone	011	Lebanon	423	46,107	38,147	20.9	437,120	-12.7	85	2,157	197,119	104
Brown	013	Nashville	312	14,957	14,080	6.2	(d)	(d)	...	(d)	(d)	...
Carroll	015	Delphi	372	20,165	18,809	7.2	137,663	-5.6	32	2,136	140,515	74
Cass	017	Logansport	413	40,930	38,413	6.6	238,938	8.6	47	5,750	444,426	235
Clark	019	Jeffersonville	375	96,472	87,777	9.9	835,383	21.7	173	(d)	(d)	...

Entries in **UPPERCASE** are counties.
Entries in **bold** have populations of 2,500 or more.
Names in parentheses are alternate names.
Inc. Place — Incorporated Place
RMC Place — Rand McNally Designated Place
CDP — Census Designated Place
MCD — Minor Civil Division

⊡ County Seat
▲ Minor Civil Division
elev. Elevation
🅿 Post Office

Ⓗ Hospital
Ⓒ College
■ Principal Business Center
★ Ranally Metro Area (RMA) Abbreviation
z Zip Code(s)

Ⓟ Previous Census Population
® Revised Census Population
Ⓐ Annexation Population
● Rand McNally Population Estimate
© Final Census Population
Ⓢ Special Census Population
◆ Estimated Population

For additional definitions see Glossary, Volume 1, and Introduction, Volume 2.

County	FIPS Code	County Seat	Land Area (Sq. Mi.)	Census Population			Wholesale Trade		Manufacturing, 2002			
				4/1/2000	4/1/1990	% Change 1990-2000	Sales, 2002 ($1,000)	% Change 1997-2002	Establish-ments	Total Employees	Value Added ($1,000)	Ranally Mfg. Units
Clay	021	Brazil	358	26,556	24,705	7.5	(d)	(d)	31	1,462	128,523	68
Clinton	023	Frankfort	405	33,866	30,974	9.3	143,071	(d)	50	4,503	1,052,397	557
Crawford	025	English	306	10,743	9,914	8.4	(d)	(d)	...	(d)	(d)	...
Daviess	027	Washington	431	29,820	27,533	8.3	100,879	31.7	58	1,903	142,280	75
Dearborn	029	Lawrenceburg	305	46,109	38,835	18.7	(d)	(d)	40	(d)	(d)	...
Decatur	031	Greensburg	373	24,555	23,645	3.8	(d)	(d)	54	5,796	709,465	375
De Kalb	033	Auburn	363	40,285	35,324	14.0	239,795	-5.8	115	10,767	1,415,209	749
Delaware	035	Muncie	393	118,769	119,659	-0.7	714,773	9.4	162	7,642	777,890	412
Dubois	037	Jasper	430	39,674	36,616	8.4	815,319	4.3	113	11,748	1,084,555	574
Elkhart	039	Goshen	464	182,791	156,198	17.0	2,902,523	29.2	906	58,176	4,607,324	2,438
Fayette	041	Connersville	215	25,588	26,015	-1.6	(d)	(d)	32	3,708	55,957	30
Floyd	043	New Albany	148	70,823	64,404	10.0	986,054	230.9	119	6,451	764,387	404
Fountain	045	Covington	396	17,954	17,808	0.8	68,083	(d)	23	2,065	205,719	109
Franklin	047	Brookville	386	22,151	19,580	13.1	(d)	(d)	19	(d)	(d)	...
Fulton	049	Rochester	369	20,511	18,840	8.9	51,492	-26.5	55	2,592	232,770	123
Gibson	051	Princeton	489	32,500	31,913	1.8	(d)	(d)	45	(d)	(d)	...
Grant	053	Marion	414	73,403	74,169	-1.0	(d)	(d)	79	7,862	736,785	390
Greene	055	Bloomfield	542	33,157	30,410	9.0	126,305	41.7	26	(d)	(d)	...
Hamilton	057	Noblesville	398	182,740	108,936	67.7	3,954,613	-23.5	200	5,911	568,049	301
Hancock	059	Greenfield	306	55,391	45,527	21.7	706,323	173.0	70	3,000	359,070	190
Harrison	061	Corydon	485	34,325	29,890	14.8	(d)	(d)	47	(d)	(d)	...
Hendricks	063	Danville	408	104,093	75,717	37.5	2,968,504	(d)	91	2,377	240,756	127
Henry	065	New Castle	393	48,508	48,139	0.8	187,586	-4.9	45	2,894	323,514	171
Howard	067	Kokomo	293	84,964	80,827	5.1	772,899	(d)	79	(d)	(d)	...
Huntington	069	Huntington	383	38,075	35,427	7.5	388,011	46.4	72	5,763	618,226	327
Jackson	071	Brownstown	509	41,335	37,730	9.6	257,600	25.0	83	6,733	914,914	484
Jasper	073	Rensselaer	560	30,043	24,960	20.4	235,509	-17.0	41	1,344	162,061	86
Jay	075	Portland	384	21,806	21,512	1.4	110,483	-9.9	37	3,047	261,594	138
Jefferson	077	Madison	361	31,705	29,797	6.4	53,169	32.0	54	3,505	344,682	182
Jennings	079	Vernon	377	27,554	23,661	16.5	(d)	(d)	44	2,026	166,445	88
Johnson	081	Franklin	320	115,209	88,109	30.8	1,193,703	80.9	138	6,472	547,476	290
Knox	083	Vincennes	516	39,256	39,884	-1.6	331,526	-11.3	40	1,454	158,514	84
Kosciusko	085	Warsaw	538	74,057	65,294	13.4	393,755	5.8	193	14,723	3,123,359	1,652
LaGrange	087	Lagrange	380	34,909	29,477	18.4	285,486	115.7	111	5,793	529,728	280
Lake	089	Crown Point	497	484,564	475,594	1.9	3,538,212	-8.7	412	27,275	4,524,870	2,394
LaPorte	091	La Porte	598	110,106	107,066	2.8	(d)	(d)	195	9,095	924,395	489
Lawrence	093	Bedford	449	45,922	42,836	7.2	(d)	(d)	68	4,210	435,850	231
Madison	095	Anderson	452	133,358	130,669	2.1	353,715	-17.5	130	8,230	874,696	463
Marion	097	Indianapolis	396	860,454	797,159	7.9	21,180,806	-0.5	1,074	61,143	13,631,065	7,212
Marshall	099	Plymouth	444	45,128	42,182	7.0	297,954	12.2	126	5,745	550,777	291
Martin	101	Shoals	336	10,369	10,369	0.0	(d)	(d)	14	587	71,221	38
Miami	103	Peru	376	36,082	36,897	-2.2	(d)	(d)	57	3,290	276,874	146
Monroe	105	Bloomington	394	120,563	108,978	10.6	651,463	(d)	123	6,789	647,366	343
Montgomery	107	Crawfordsville	505	37,629	34,436	9.3	(d)	(d)	62	5,906	960,177	508
Morgan	109	Martinsville	406	66,689	55,920	19.3	154,558	2.7	73	2,225	265,189	140
Newton	111	Kentland	402	14,566	13,551	7.5	(d)	(d)	26	1,144	83,694	44
Noble	113	Albion	411	46,275	37,877	22.2	134,912	-35.2	145	10,380	935,096	495
Ohio	115	Rising Sun	87	5,623	5,315	5.8	(d)	(d)	...	(d)	(d)	...
Orange	117	Paoli	400	19,306	18,409	4.9	38,596	15.5	27	1,548	103,891	55
Owen	119	Spencer	385	21,786	17,281	26.1	13,705	5.8	29	(d)	(d)	...
Parke	121	Rockville	445	17,241	15,410	11.9	(d)	(d)	18	755	43,815	23
Perry	123	Tell City	381	18,899	19,107	-1.1	44,504	-42.5	28	1,647	182,346	96
Pike	125	Petersburg	336	12,837	12,509	2.6	35,540	-4.2	...	(d)	(d)	...
Porter	127	Valparaiso	418	146,798	128,932	13.9	1,109,723	17.8	152	11,293	1,657,586	877
Posey	129	Mount Vernon	409	27,061	25,968	4.2	(d)	(d)	32	3,287	1,266,749	670
Pulaski	131	Winamac	434	13,755	12,643	8.8	100,470	-39.9	19	1,012	136,942	72
Putnam	133	Greencastle	480	36,019	30,315	18.8	(d)	(d)	28	2,907	237,753	126
Randolph	135	Winchester	453	27,401	27,148	0.9	(d)	(d)	62	3,072	302,701	160
Ripley	137	Versailles	446	26,523	24,616	7.7	(d)	(d)	40	3,447	744,221	394
Rush	139	Rushville	408	18,261	18,129	0.7	106,750	-10.3	31	1,323	176,884	94
St. Joseph	141	South Bend	457	265,559	247,052	7.5	3,659,573	8.0	452	19,242	2,671,007	1,413
Scott	143	Scottsburg	190	22,960	20,991	9.4	(d)	(d)	36	2,441	424,077	224
Shelby	145	Shelbyville	413	43,445	40,307	7.8	206,756	-4.1	93	6,304	654,386	346
Spencer	147	Rockport	399	20,391	19,490	4.6	232,171	6.7	25	1,967	1,017,061	538
Starke	149	Knox	309	23,556	22,747	3.6	37,348	-50.7	21	792	63,876	34
Steuben	151	Angola	309	33,214	27,446	21.0	(d)	(d)	101	5,349	505,865	268
Sullivan	153	Sullivan	447	21,751	18,993	14.5	82,729	-27.2	...	(d)	(d)	...
Switzerland	155	Vevay	221	9,065	7,738	17.1	(d)	(d)	...	(d)	(d)	...
Tippecanoe	157	Lafayette	500	148,955	130,598	14.1	319,610	(d)	127	16,183	1,887,822	999
Tipton	159	Tipton	260	16,577	16,119	2.8	(d)	(d)	22	(d)	(d)	...
Union	161	Liberty	162	7,349	6,976	5.3	(d)	(d)	...	(d)	(d)	...
Vanderburgh	163	Evansville	235	171,922	165,058	4.2	(d)	(d)	275	15,512	1,972,320	1,043
Vermillion	165	Newport	257	16,788	16,773	0.1	(d)	(d)	13	(d)	(d)	...
Vigo	167	Terre Haute	403	105,848	106,107	-0.2	444,872	-34.8	132	7,746	1,424,267	754
Wabash	169	Wabash	413	34,960	35,069	-0.3	(d)	(d)	76	5,239	427,423	226
Warren	171	Williamsport	365	8,419	8,176	3.0	61,404	-17.9	...	(d)	(d)	...
Warrick	173	Boonville	384	52,383	44,920	16.6	(d)	(d)	54	(d)	(d)	...
Washington	175	Salem	514	27,223	23,717	14.8	(d)	(d)	39	(d)	(d)	...
Wayne	177	Richmond	404	71,097	71,951	-1.2	499,716	-60.2	129	7,736	934,318	494
Wells	179	Bluffton	370	27,600	25,948	6.4	(d)	(d)	51	(d)	(d)	...
White	181	Monticello	505	25,267	23,265	8.6	183,656	-6.6	48	2,359	224,680	119
Whitley	183	Columbia City	336	30,707	27,651	11.1	(d)	(d)	74	(d)	(d)	...
The State			**35,867**	**6,080,485**	**5,544,159**	**9.7**	**79,806,006**	**20.3**	**9,223**	**565,559**	**78,023,817**	**41,280**

(d) Data not available. Corresponding percentages or Ranally Manufacturing Units are estimates.
... Represents 0 or amount too minimal to be reported.

Administrative Divisions

Townships: All Indiana counties are divided into townships. Townships may levy taxes, elect certain officials, and carry on limited governmental functions. Only townships with an active government recognized by the U.S. Census of Governments are printed in this index.

Index of Places and Counties

A

Aberdeen; RMC Place; OHIO; **175** O-13; elev. 882ft./269m.; mail Rising Sun **z** 47040; ● 90
Abington; RMC Place; WAYNE; ▲ Abington; **174** J-13; mail Centerville **z** 47330; ● 80
Abington; MCD-Township; WAYNE; ***174** J-13; mail Centerville **z** 47330; Ⓟ 865; Ⓒ 919
Aboite; RMC Place; ALLEN; **174** D-12; ★ **FTWA**; mail Roanoke **z** 46783; ● 50
Aboite; MCD-Township; ALLEN; ***174** D-12; ★ **FTWA**; mail Fort Wayne **z** 46804; Ⓟ 18,490; Ⓒ 28,338
Abydel; RMC Place; ORANGE; **175** P-7; mail Paoli **z** 47454; ● 30
Acme; RMC Place; JACKSON; **175** N-9; mail Seymour **z** 47274; ● 30
Acton; RMC Place; MARION; ***175** K-9; elev. 794ft./242m.; 🅿; ★ **IND**; **z** 46259; pop. incl. with Indianapolis (Inc. Place)
Adams; MCD-Township; ALLEN; ***174** D-13; ★ **FTWA**; mail Fort Wayne **z** 46806, **z** 46816; Ⓟ 31,023; Ⓒ 31,394
Adams; MCD-Township; CARROLL; ***174** F-7; mail Monticello **z** 47960; Ⓟ 461; Ⓒ 464
Adams; MCD-Township; CASS; ***174** E-8; mail Twelve Mile **z** 46988; Ⓟ 873; Ⓒ 1,127
Adams; RMC Place; DECATUR; **175** L-11; elev. 885ft./270m.; mail Greensburg **z** 47240; ● 175
Adams; MCD-Township; DECATUR; ***175** L-11; mail Greensburg **z** 47240, Saint Paul **z** 47272; Ⓟ 1,889; Ⓒ 1,910
Adams; MCD-Township; HAMILTON; ***174** H-9; ★ **IND**; mail Sheridan **z** 46069; Ⓟ 4,504; Ⓒ 4,892
Adams; MCD-Township; MADISON; ***174** I-11; ★ **AND**; mail Markleville **z** 46056; Ⓟ 3,688; Ⓒ 3,780
Adams; RMC Place; MORGAN; ***175** L-8; ★ **IND**; mail Martinsville **z** 46151; ● 150
Adams; MCD-Township; MORGAN; ***175** K-7; mail Martinsville **z** 46151; Ⓟ 972; Ⓒ 1,231
Adams; MCD-Township; PARKE; ***174** J-5; mail Rockville **z** 47872; Ⓟ 4,628; Ⓒ 5,399
Adams; MCD-Township; RIPLEY; ***175** M-13; mail Sunman **z** 47041; Ⓟ 3,553; Ⓒ 4,325
Adams; MCD-Township; WARREN; ***174** G-5; mail Pine Village **z** 47975; Ⓟ 493; Ⓒ 561
ADAMS; **174** F-13; Ⓟ 31,095; Ⓒ 33,625; ◆ 33,642
Adamsboro; RMC Place; CASS; ***174** E-8; mail Logansport **z** 46947
Adams Lake; RMC Place; LAGRANGE; ***174** B-12; mail Wolcottville **z** 46795; summer pop. 1,000; ● 500
Adams Mill; RMC Place; CARROLL; ***174** G-7; mail Cutler **z** 46920; rural
Addison; MCD-Township; SHELBY; ***175** L-10; mail Shelbyville **z** 46176; Ⓟ 17,577; Ⓒ 19,943
Addmore; RMC Place; CLARK; ***175** Q-10; ★ **LOU**; mail Clarksville **z** 47129; pop. incl. with Clarksville (Inc. Place)
Ade; RMC Place; NEWTON; **174** E-4; elev. 662ft./202m.; mail Brook **z** 47922; ● 20
Advance; Inc. Place; BOONE; **174** I-7; elev. 934ft./285m.; 🅿; **z** 46102; Ⓟ 520; Ⓒ 562
Aetna; RMC Place; LAKE; ***174** A-4; ★ **CHI**; mail Gary **z** 46402; pop. incl. with Gary (Inc. Place)
Ainsworth; RMC Place; LAKE; **175** N-14; ★ **CHI**; mail Hobart **z** 46342; pop. incl. with Hobart (Inc. Place)
Akron; Inc. Place; FULTON; **174** D-9; elev. 859ft./262m.; 🅿; **z** 46910; Ⓟ 1,001; Ⓒ 1,076
Alamo; Inc. Place; MONTGOMERY; **174** I-5; elev. 811ft./247m.; 🅿; **z** 47916; Ⓟ 112; Ⓒ 137
Albany; Inc. Place; DELAWARE, RANDOLPH; **174** H-12; elev. 948ft./289m.; 🅿; ★ **MUN**; **z** 47320; Ⓟ 2,357; Ⓒ 2,368
Albion; Inc. Place; ⊡ NOBLE; ▲ Albion; **174** B-11; elev. 963ft./294m.; 🅿; **z** 46701; Ⓟ 1,823; Ⓒ 2,284
Albion; MCD-Township; NOBLE; ***174** B-11; 🅿; **z** 46701; Ⓟ 1,951; Ⓒ 2,382
Aldine; RMC Place; STARKE; ***174** C-7; mail North Judson **z** 46366
Alert; RMC Place; DECATUR; **175** M-10; mail Westport **z** 47283; ● 90
Alexandria; Inc. Place; MADISON; **174** H-11; elev. 866ft./264m.; 🅿; ★ **AND**; **z** 46001; Ⓟ 5,709; Ⓒ 6,260
Alfont; RMC Place; MADISON; ***174** I-10; ★ **IND**; mail Fortville **z** 46040
Alford; RMC Place; PIKE; **175** Q-4; mail Petersburg **z** 47567; ● 90
Alfordsville; Inc. Place; DAVIESS; **175** P-6; elev. 492ft./150m.; mail Loogootee **z** 47553; Ⓟ 74; Ⓒ 112
Algers; PIKE; see Algiers (RMC Place)
Algiers (Algers); RMC Place; PIKE; ***175** Q-5; mail Petersburg **z** 47567; ● 50
Alida; RMC Place; LAPORTE; ***174** B-6; mail Westville **z** 46391; rural
Allen; MCD-Township; MIAMI; ***174** D-9; mail Macy **z** 46951; Ⓟ 697; Ⓒ 746
Allen; MCD-Township; NOBLE; ***174** B-12; mail Avilla **z** 46710, Kendallville **z** 46755; Ⓟ 5,132; Ⓒ 6,847
ALLEN; **174** C-13; Ⓟ 300,836; Ⓒ 331,849; ◆ 351,864
Allendale; RMC Place; VIGO; **175** L-4; ★ **T.H.**; mail Terre Haute **z** 47802; ● 250
Allens Acres; RMC Place; BOONE; ***174** I-8; ★ **IND**; mail Zionsville **z** 46077; ● 60
Allensville; RMC Place; SWITZERLAND; ***175** O-13; elev. 873ft./266m.; mail Bennington **z** 47011; rural
Allisonville; RMC Place; MARION; ***174** J-9; ★ **IND**; mail Indianapolis **z** 46250; pop. incl. with Indianapolis (Inc. Place)
Allman; RMC Place; MORGAN; ***175** K-8; ★ **IND**; mail Mooresville **z** 46158; ● 200
Alpine; RMC Place; FAYETTE; **175** K-12; mail Connersville **z** 47331; ● 40
Alquina; RMC Place; FAYETTE; **175** K-13; mail Connersville **z** 47331; ● 130
Alta; RMC Place; VERMILLION; ***174** J-4; mail Hillsdale **z** 47854
Alto; RMC Place; HOWARD; **174** G-9; elev. 842ft./257m.; ★ **KOK**; mail Kokomo **z** 46902; ● 400
Alton; Inc. Place; CRAWFORD; **175** R-8; elev. 425ft./130m.; 🅿; **z** 47137; Ⓟ 57; Ⓒ 53
Altona; Inc. Place; DE KALB; **174** C-12; elev. 900ft./274m.; mail Garrett **z** 46738; Ⓟ 156; Ⓒ 198
Alvarado; RMC Place; STEUBEN; ***174** A-14; mail Hamilton **z** 46742
Amberley; RMC Place; BARTHOLOMEW; ***175** M-10; ★ **COL**; mail Columbus **z** 47201; ● 125
Amber Valley; RMC Place; VIGO; ★ **T.H.**; mail Terre Haute **z** 47803; ● 50
Ambia; Inc. Place; BENTON; **174** G-4; 🅿; **z** 47917; Ⓟ 249; Ⓒ 197
Amboy; Inc. Place; MIAMI; **174** F-10; elev. 815ft./248m.; 🅿; **z** 46911; Ⓟ 370; Ⓒ 360
Americus; RMC Place; TIPPECANOE; **174** G-6; ★ **LAF-**; mail Lafayette **z** 47905; ● 100
Ames; RMC Place; MONTGOMERY; pop. incl. with Crawfordsville (Inc. Place)
Amity; RMC Place; JOHNSON; **175** L-9; ★ **IND**; mail Franklin **z** 46131; ● 225
Amo; Inc. Place; HENDRICKS; **175** K-7; elev. 822ft./251m.; 🅿; **z** 46103; Ⓟ 380; Ⓒ 414
Anderson; Inc. Place; ⊡ MADISON; **174** I-10; 🅿 🄷 🄲 2,730 ■; ★ **AND**; **z** 46011-18; Ⓟ 59,459; Ⓒ 59,734; ◆ 60,070
Anderson; MCD-Township; MADISON; ***174** I-10; elev. 883ft./269m.; 🅿 🄲 2,730; ★ **AND**; **z** 46011-18; includes part of the City of Anderson; Ⓟ 59,892; Ⓒ 60,026
Anderson; MCD-Township; PERRY; ***175** S-7; mail Tell City **z** 47586; Ⓟ 1,340; Ⓒ 1,536
Anderson; MCD-Township; RUSH; ***175** L-11; mail Milroy **z** 46156; Ⓟ 1,342; Ⓒ 1,363
Anderson; MCD-Township; WARRICK; ***175** S-4; mail Newburgh **z** 47630; Ⓟ 1,056; Ⓒ 1,265
Andersonville; RMC Place; FRANKLIN; **175** L-12; mail Laurel **z** 47024; ● 250
Andrews; Inc. Place; HUNTINGTON; **174** E-11; elev. 737ft./225m.; 🅿; **z** 46702; Ⓟ 1,118; Ⓒ 1,290
Angola; Inc. Place; ⊡ STEUBEN; **174** A-13; elev. 1,055ft./322m.; 🅿 🄷 🄲 1,450; **z** 46703; Ⓟ 5,824; Ⓒ 7,344
Annandale Estates; RMC Place; BROWN; ***175** M-8; mail Nashville **z** 47448; ● 100
Annapolis; RMC Place; PARKE; **174** J-5; mail Bloomingdale **z** 47832; ● 100
Anoka; RMC Place; CASS; **174** F-8; mail Logansport **z** 46947; ● 60
Ansley Acres; RMC Place; ALLEN; ***174** D-12; ★ **FTWA**; mail Fort Wayne **z** 46804; ● 300
Anthony; RMC Place; DELAWARE; **174** H-11; elev. 910ft./277m.; ★ **MUN**; mail Muncie **z** 47303; ● 50
Antioch; RMC Place; CLINTON; **174** H-7; mail Frankfort **z** 46041; ● 150
Antiville; RMC Place; JAY; ***174** G-13; mail Portland **z** 47371; rural
Apache Acres; RMC Place; VIGO; ***175** K-4; ★ **T.H.**; mail Terre Haute **z** 47805; ● 400
Arba; RMC Place; RANDOLPH; **174** I-14; mail Lynn **z** 47355; ● 40
Arcadia; Inc. Place; HAMILTON; **174** H-9; elev. 860ft./262m.; 🅿; ★ **IND**; **z** 46030; Ⓟ 1,468; Ⓒ 1,747
Arcana; RMC Place; GRANT; ***174** G-11; mail Marion **z** 46952; rural
Arcola; RMC Place; ALLEN; **174** D-12; elev. 884ft./269m.; 🅿; **z** 46704; ● 180
Arctic Springs; RMC Place; CLARK; ***175** R-10; ★ **LOU**; mail Jeffersonville **z** 47130; pop. incl. with Jeffersonville (Inc. Place)
Arda; RMC Place; PIKE; ***175** P-4; elev. 520ft./158m.; mail Petersburg **z** 47567; ● 50
Ardmore; RMC Place; ST. JOSEPH; **173** B-18; ★ **S.B.**; mail South Bend **z** 46628; ● 2,200
Argos; Inc. Place; MARSHALL; **174** C-8; elev. 828ft./252m.; 🅿; **z** 46501; Ⓟ 1,642; Ⓒ 1,613
Ari; RMC Place; ALLEN, NOBLE; **174** C-12; ★ **FTWA**; mail Churubusco **z** 46723; ● 30
Arlington; RMC Place; MONROE; ***175** M-7; ★ **BLMNG**; mail Bloomington **z** 47404; ● 100
Arlington; RMC Place; RUSH; **175** K-11; elev. 922ft./281m.; 🅿; **z** 46104; ● 500
Arlington Park; RMC Place; ALLEN; ***174** H-13; ★ **FTWA**; mail Fort Wayne **z** 46835; ● 250
Armiesburg; RMC Place; PARKE; mail Montezuma **z** 47862; rural
Armstrong; RMC Place; VANDERBURGH; ▲ Armstrong; ***175** R-3; elev. 470ft./143m.; mail Evansville **z** 47720
Armstrong; MCD-Township; VANDERBURGH; ***175** R-3; mail Evansville **z** 47720; Ⓟ 1,694; Ⓒ 1,651
Armuth Acres; RMC Place; BARTHOLOMEW; ***175** M-10; mail Columbus **z** 47203; ● 200
Arney; RMC Place; OWEN; ***175** M-6; mail Freedom **z** 47431; rural
Aroma; RMC Place; HAMILTON; ***174** H-10; mail Atlanta **z** 46031; ● 50
Arrowhead Park; RMC Place; KOSCIUSKO; ***174** C-10; mail Warsaw **z** 46580; ● 100
Art; RMC Place; CLAY; ***175** L-5; mail Brazil **z** 47834, Cory **z** 47846
Arthur; RMC Place; PIKE; **175** Q-4; mail Winslow **z** 47598; ● 75
Artic; RMC Place; DE KALB; ***174** B-14; mail Butler **z** 46721; rural
Ashboro; RMC Place; CLAY; ***175** L-5; mail Centerpoint **z** 47840; ● 40
Asherville; RMC Place; CLAY; ***175** L-5; mail Brazil **z** 47834; ● 30
Ash Grove; RMC Place; TIPPECANOE; ***174** F-6; ★ **LAF-**; mail Battle Ground **z** 47920
Ashland; RMC Place; HENRY; **174** J-12; mail New Castle **z** 47362; ● 80
Ashland; MCD-Township; MORGAN; ***175** L-7; mail Martinsville **z** 46151; Ⓟ 1,212; Ⓒ 1,482
Ashley (Ashley Hudson); Inc. Place; STEUBEN, DE KALB; **174** B-13; elev. 1,000ft./305m.; 🅿; **z** 46705; Ⓟ 767; Ⓒ 1,010
Ashley Hudson; STEUBEN, DE KALB; see Ashley (Inc. Place)
Athens; RMC Place; FULTON; **174** D-9; elev. 810ft./247m.; 🅿; **z** 46912; ● 130
Atherton; RMC Place; VIGO; **175** K-4; ★ **T.H.**; mail Rosedale **z** 47874; ● 45
Atkinsonville; RMC Place; OWEN; ***175** L-6; elev. 882ft./269m.; mail Poland **z** 47868; rural
Atlanta; Inc. Place; HAMILTON; **174** H-9; elev. 862ft./263m.; 🅿; ★ **IND**; **z** 46031; Ⓟ 703; Ⓒ 761
Attica; Inc. Place; FOUNTAIN; **174** H-5; elev. 547ft./167m.; 🅿; **z** 47918; Ⓟ 3,457; Ⓒ 3,491
Atwood; RMC Place; KOSCIUSKO; **174** C-9; 🅿; **z** 46502; ● 300
Atwood Lake; RMC Place; LAGRANGE; ***174** B-11; mail Wolcottville **z** 46795; summer pop. 500; ● 100
Aubbeenaubbee; MCD-Township; FULTON; ***174** D-8; mail Rochester **z** 46975; Ⓟ 1,262; Ⓒ 1,501
Auburn; Inc. Place; ⊡ DE KALB; **174** B-13; elev. 870ft./265m.; 🅿 🄷; **z** 46706; Ⓟ 9,379; Ⓒ 12,074
Auburn Junction; RMC Place; DE KALB; ***174** B-13; mail Auburn **z** 46706; pop. incl. with Auburn (Inc. Place)
Augusta; RMC Place; PIKE; ***175** Q-5; mail Winslow **z** 47598; ● 50
Aultshire; RMC Place; DELAWARE; ***174** H-12; ★ **MUN**; mail Muncie **z** 47303; pop. incl. with Muncie (Inc. Place)
Aurora; Inc. Place; DEARBORN; **175** N-13; elev. 501ft./153m.; 🅿; ★ **CIN**; **z** 47001; Ⓟ 3,825; Ⓒ 3,965
Austin; Inc. Place; SCOTT; **175** O-10; elev. 548ft./167m.; 🅿; **z** 47102; Ⓟ 4,310; Ⓒ 4,724
Avalon; RMC Place; ALLEN; ***174** D-12; ★ **FTWA**; mail Fort Wayne **z** 46819; pop. incl. with Fort Wayne (Inc. Place)
Avalon Hills; RMC Place; MARION; ***174** J-9; ★ **IND**; mail Indianapolis **z** 46220; pop. incl. with Indianapolis (Inc. Place)
Avery; RMC Place; CLINTON; ***174** H-8; mail Frankfort **z** 46041
Avilla; Inc. Place; NOBLE; **174** B-12; elev. 972ft./296m.; 🅿; **z** 46710; Ⓟ 1,366; Ⓒ 2,049
Avoca; RMC Place; LAWRENCE; **175** O-7; elev. 554ft./169m.; 🅿; ★ **BLMNG**; **z** 47420; ● 300
Avon; Inc. Place; HENDRICKS; **174** J-8; elev. 824ft./251m.; 🅿; ★ **IND**; **z** 46123; Ⓒ 6,248
Avondale; RMC Place; GRANT; ***174** F-10; ★ **MRN**; mail Marion **z** 46952; ● 500
Ayrshire; RMC Place; PIKE; ***175** Q-4; mail Winslow **z** 47598; ● 60
Azalia; RMC Place; BARTHOLOMEW; **175** N-10; ★ **COL**; mail Elizabethtown **z** 47232; ● 140

B

Babcock; RMC Place; PORTER; ***174** A-5; elev. 648ft./198m.; ★ **CHI**; mail Chesterton **z** 46304; rural
Bacon; RMC Place; MARION; ***174** J-9; ★ **IND**; mail Indianapolis **z** 46205, **z** 46220; pop. incl. with Indianapolis (Inc. Place)
Baileys Corner; RMC Place; JASPER; ***174** D-5; elev. 690ft./210m.; mail Rensselaer **z** 47978; ● 140
Bainbridge; MCD-Township; DUBOIS; ***175** Q-6; mail Jasper **z** 47546; Ⓟ 13,125; Ⓒ 14,950
Bainbridge; Inc. Place; PUTNAM; **174** J-6; elev. 929ft./283m.; 🅿; **z** 46105; Ⓟ 682; Ⓒ 743
Baker; MCD-Township; MORGAN; ***175** L-7; mail Gosport **z** 47433; Ⓟ 540; Ⓒ 747
Bakers Corner; RMC Place; HAMILTON; **174** I-9; ★ **IND**; mail Sheridan **z** 46069; ● 70
Bakertown; RMC Place; NOBLE; ***174** B-12; mail Albion **z** 46701; rural
Balbec; RMC Place; JAY; ***174** G-12; mail Pennville **z** 47369
Ball Lake; RMC Place; STEUBEN; ***174** B-13; mail Hamilton **z** 46742; ● 250
Bandon; RMC Place; PERRY; ***175** R-7; mail Branchville **z** 47514; ● 60
Banquo; RMC Place; HUNTINGTON; **174** F-11; mail La Fontaine **z** 46940; ● 50
Banta; RMC Place; JOHNSON, MORGAN; ***175** L-8; ★ **IND**; mail Bargersville **z** 46106; ● 50
Bar-Barry Heights; RMC Place; TIPPECANOE; ***174** G-6; ★ **LAF-**; mail West Lafayette **z** 47906; pop. incl. with West Lafayette (Inc. Place)
Barbee; RMC Place; KOSCIUSKO; ***174** C-10; mail Pierceton **z** 46562; ● 900
Bargersville; Inc. Place; JOHNSON; **175** L-9; elev. 819ft./250m.; 🅿; ★ **IND**; **z** 46106; Ⓟ 1,681; Ⓒ 2,120
Barkley; MCD-Township; JASPER; ***174** D-5; mail Rensselaer **z** 47978; Ⓟ 789; Ⓒ 836
Barnaby Acres; RMC Place; BARTHOLOMEW; ***175** M-9; ★ **COL**; mail Columbus **z** 47201; ● 60
Barnard; RMC Place; PUTNAM; **174** J-7; mail Roachdale **z** 46172; ● 30
Barr; MCD-Township; DAVIESS; ***175** P-5; mail Cannelburg **z** 47519, Montgomery **z** 47558; Ⓟ 3,396; Ⓒ 4,193
Barrick Corner; RMC Place; CLAY; ***175** M-5; mail Clay City **z** 47841; rural
BARTHOLOMEW; **175** M-9; Ⓟ 63,657; Ⓒ 71,435; ◆ 75,118
Bartlettsville; RMC Place; LAWRENCE; ***175** N-8; mail Bedford **z** 47421
Bartley; RMC Place; VIGO; ***175** K-4; ★ **T.H.**; mail Terre Haute **z** 47805; ● 70
Barton; MCD-Township; GIBSON; ***175** R-4; mail Oakland City **z** 47660; Ⓟ 1,650; Ⓒ 1,796
Bartonia; RMC Place; RANDOLPH; **174** I-14; mail Union City **z** 47390; ● 30
Bass Lake; CDP; STARKE; **174** C-7; mail Knox **z** 46534; summer pop. 4,000; Ⓒ 1,249
Bass Station; RMC Place; STARKE; **174** C-7; elev. 715ft./218m.; mail Knox **z** 46534; ● 50
Batesville; Inc. Place; RIPLEY, FRANKLIN; **175** M-12; 🅿 🄷; **z** 47006; Ⓟ 4,720; Ⓒ 6,033
Bath; RMC Place; FRANKLIN; ▲ Bath; **175** L-14; 🅿; **z** 47010; ● 100
Bath; MCD-Township; FRANKLIN; ***175** L-14; 🅿; **z** 47010; Ⓟ 405; Ⓒ 400
Battle Ground; Inc. Place; TIPPECANOE; **174** G-6; elev. 575ft./175m.; 🅿; ★ **LAF-**; **z** 47920; Ⓟ 806; Ⓒ 1,323
Baugh City; RMC Place; WARRICK; ***175** S-4; ★ **EV**; mail Chandler **z** 47610
Baugo; MCD-Township; ELKHART; ***174** A-9; ★ **ELK**; mail Elkhart **z** 46514; Ⓟ 6,640; Ⓒ 7,646
Bayfield; RMC Place; KOSCIUSKO; ***174** C-10; elev. 840ft./256m.; mail Pierceton **z** 46562; ● 75
Beacon Heights; RMC Place; FLOYD; ***175** Q-10; ★ **LOU**; mail New Albany **z** 47150; pop. incl. with New Albany (Inc. Place)
Beal; RMC Place; KNOX; ***175** P-3; mail Vincennes **z** 47591; ● 30
Beanblossom; RMC Place; BROWN; **175** M-8; mail Morgantown **z** 46160, Nashville **z** 47448; ● 200
Bean Blossom; MCD-Township; MONROE; ***175** M-7; ★ **BLMNG**; mail Ellettsville **z** 47429, Morgantown **z** 46160; Ⓟ 2,358; Ⓒ 2,740
Bear Branch; RMC Place; OHIO; ***175** O-13; mail Dillsboro **z** 47018; ● 50
Bearcreek; MCD-Township; JAY; ***174** G-13; mail Bryant **z** 47326; Ⓟ 1,228; Ⓒ 1,368
Beard; RMC Place; CLINTON; ***174** G-8; elev. 853ft./260m.; mail Frankfort **z** 46041
Beardstown; RMC Place; PULASKI; **174** D-7; mail Winamac **z** 46996; ● 50
Bear Lake; RMC Place; NOBLE; ***174** C-11; mail Albion **z** 46701; ● 300
Beattys Corner; RMC Place; LAPORTE; ***174** A-6; ★ **MICH**; mail Michigan City **z** 46360; rural
Beaver; MCD-Township; NEWTON; ***174** D-4; mail Morocco **z** 47963; Ⓟ 1,547; Ⓒ 1,667
Beaver; MCD-Township; PULASKI; ***174** D-6; mail Winamac **z** 46996; Ⓟ 379; Ⓒ 479
Beaver City; RMC Place; NEWTON; ***174** E-4; mail Brook **z** 47922
Beaver Dam (Beaver Dam Lake); RMC Place; KOSCIUSKO; **174** D-9; mail Claypool **z** 46510; summer pop. 400; ● 250
Beaver Dam Lake; KOSCIUSKO; see Beaver Dam (RMC Place)
Becks Grove; RMC Place; BROWN; ***175** N-9; mail Freetown **z** 47235; rural
Becks Mill; RMC Place; WASHINGTON; ***175** P-9; elev. 740ft./226m.; mail Salem **z** 47167
Bedford; Inc. Place; ⊡ LAWRENCE; **175** O-7; elev. 699ft./213m.; 🅿 🄷 ■; **z** 47421; Ⓟ 13,817; Ⓒ 13,768; ◆ 13,290
Beecamp; RMC Place; JEFFERSON; ***175** O-12; mail Madison **z** 47250; rural
Beech Brook; RMC Place; SHELBY; ***175** K-10; mail Shelbyville **z** 46176; ● 100
Beech Creek; MCD-Township; GREENE; ***175** M-6; mail Solsberry **z** 47459; Ⓟ 1,832; Ⓒ 2,365
Beech Grove; Inc. Place; MARION; **175** K-9; elev. 800ft./244m.; 🅿; ★ **IND**; **z** 46107; Ⓟ 13,383; Ⓒ 14,880
Beech Grove; RMC Place; MORGAN; ***175** L-8; 🄷; ★ **IND**; mail Martinsville **z** 46151; ● 60
Beechwood; RMC Place; CRAWFORD; ***175** R-8; mail Leavenworth **z** 47137
Bee Ridge; RMC Place; CLAY; ***175** K-5; mail Brazil **z** 47834; rural
Bellefountain; RMC Place; JAY; **174** G-14; mail Portland **z** 47371; ● 40
Belle Union; RMC Place; PUTNAM; **175** K-7; mail Cloverdale **z** 46120; ● 90
Belleview; RMC Place; JEFFERSON; ***175** O-12; mail Madison **z** 47250
Belleville; RMC Place; HENDRICKS; **175** K-7; ★ **IND**; mail Clayton **z** 46118; ● 400
Bellmore; RMC Place; PARKE; **174** J-5; elev. 739ft./225m.; 🅿; **z** 47830; ● 140
Bell Rohr Park; RMC Place; KOSCIUSKO; ***174** C-10; mail Leesburg **z** 46538; summer pop. 265; ● 100
Belmont; RMC Place; BROWN; **175** M-8; mail Nashville **z** 47448; ● 10
Belmont; RMC Place; HENRY; ***174** J-12; mail New Castle **z** 47362; pop. incl. with New Castle (Inc. Place)
Belshaw; RMC Place; LAKE; **174** C-4; mail Lowell **z** 46356; ● 40
Ben Davis; RMC Place; MARION; ***174** J-8; ★ **IND**; mail Indianapolis **z** 46241; pop. incl. with Indianapolis (Inc. Place)
Bengal; RMC Place; SHELBY; **175** L-10; elev. 741ft./226m.; mail Franklin **z** 46131; ● 30
Benham; RMC Place; RIPLEY; ***175** N-12; mail Versailles **z** 47042
Bennetts; MIAMI; see Bennetts Switch (RMC Place)
Bennetts Switch (Bennetts); RMC Place; MIAMI; **174** F-9; mail Kokomo **z** 46901; ● 90
Bennettsville; RMC Place; CLARK; ***175** Q-10; mail Memphis **z** 47143; rural
Bennington; RMC Place; SWITZERLAND; **175** O-13; elev. 891ft./272m.; 🅿; **z** 47011; ● 70
Benton; RMC Place; ELKHART; ▲ Benton; **174** B-10; elev. 833ft./254m.; mail Goshen **z** 46526-28; ● 150
Benton; MCD-Township; ELKHART; ***174** B-10; mail Goshen **z** 46526-28; Ⓟ 1,762; Ⓒ 2,342
Benton; MCD-Township; MONROE; ***175** M-8; mail Bloomington **z** 47401, **z** 47408; Ⓟ 3,116; Ⓒ 3,213
BENTON; **174** F-5; Ⓟ 9,441; Ⓒ 9,421; ◆ 8,620
Bentonville; RMC Place; FAYETTE; **174** J-12; elev. 1,053ft./321m.; 🅿; **z** 47322; ● 65
Benwood; RMC Place; CLAY; ***175** K-5; mail Brazil **z** 47834
Berlien; RMC Place; STEUBEN; ***174** A-13; elev. 1,033ft./315m.; mail Angola **z** 46703
Berne; Inc. Place; ADAMS; **174** F-13; elev. 848ft./258m.; 🅿; **z** 46711, **z** 46769; Ⓟ 3,559; Ⓒ 4,150
Berwick Manor; RMC Place; SHELBY; mail Shelbyville **z** 46176; pop. incl. with Shelbyville (Inc. Place)
Bethany (South Bethany); RMC Place; BARTHOLOMEW; **175** M-9; ★ **COL**; mail Columbus **z** 47201; ● 25
Bethany; Inc. Place; MORGAN; **175** L-8; elev. 648ft./198m.; ★ **IND**; mail Martinsville **z** 46151; Ⓟ 90; Ⓒ 94
Bethel; MCD-Township; POSEY; ***175** R-2; mail Griffin **z** 47616; Ⓟ 329; Ⓒ 327
Bethel; RMC Place; WAYNE; **174** I-14; mail Fountain City **z** 47341; ● 90
Bethel Village; RMC Place; BARTHOLOMEW; ***175** M-10; ★ **COL**; mail Columbus **z** 47201; ● 600
Bethlehem; MCD-Township; CASS; ***174** E-8; mail Logansport **z** 46947; Ⓟ 838; Ⓒ 867
Bethlehem; RMC Place; CLARK; ▲ Bethlehem; **175** P-11; 🅿; **z** 47104; ● 100
Bethlehem; MCD-Township; CLARK; ***175** P-11; 🅿; **z** 47104; Ⓟ 363; Ⓒ 330
Between-the-Lakes Park; RMC Place; KOSCIUSKO; ***174** C-10; elev. 840ft./256m.; mail Leesburg **z** 46538; ● 60

Entries in **UPPERCASE** are counties.
Entries in **bold** have populations of 2,500 or more.
Names in parentheses are alternate names.

Inc. Place	Incorporated Place
RMC Place	Rand McNally Designated Place
CDP	Census Designated Place
MCD	Minor Civil Division
⊡	County Seat
▲	Minor Civil Division
elev.	Elevation
🅿	Post Office
🄷	Hospital
🄲	College
■	Principal Business Center
★	Ranally Metro Area (RMA) Abbreviation
z	Zip Code(s)
Ⓟ	Previous Census Population
Ⓡ	Revised Census Population
Ⓐ	Annexation Population
●	Rand McNally Population Estimate
Ⓒ	Final Census Population
Ⓢ	Special Census Population
◆	Estimated Population

For additional definitions see Glossary, Volume 1, and Introduction, Volume 2.

Beverly Shores; Inc. Place; PORTER; 174 A-6; elev. 650ft./198m.; 🅿; ★ CHI; z 46301; Ⓟ 622; Ⓒ 708
Bicknell; Inc. Place; KNOX; 175 O-4; elev. 500ft./152m.; 🅿; z 47512; Ⓟ 3,357; Ⓒ 3,378
Big Bass Lake; RMC Place; PORTER; *174 B-5; ★ CHI; mail Crown Point z 46307
Big Creek; MCD-Township; WHITE; *174 F-6; mail Chalmers z 47929; Ⓟ 835; Ⓒ 856
Bigger; MCD-Township; JENNINGS; *175 N-11; mail North Vernon z 47265; Ⓟ 611; Ⓒ 688
Big Lake; RMC Place; NOBLE; *174 C-11; mail Albion z 46701, Columbia City z 46725; summer pop. 400; ● 100
Big Springs; RMC Place; BOONE; *174 I-8; mail Sheridan z 46069
Billingsville; RMC Place; UNION; *175 K-13; mail Liberty z 47353
Billtown; RMC Place; CLAY; *175 L-5; ★ T.H.; mail Brazil z 47834; ● 70
Billville; RMC Place; CLAY; *175 L-5; ★ T.H.; mail Brazil z 47834; ● 80
Bippus; RMC Place; HUNTINGTON; 174 E-11; elev. 849ft./259m.; 🅿; z 46713; ● 200
Birdseye; Inc. Place; DUBOIS; 175 Q-7; elev. 709ft./216m.; 🅿; z 47513; Ⓟ 472; Ⓒ 465
Birmingham; RMC Place; MIAMI; *174 E-9; mail Macy z 46951
Black; MCD-Township; POSEY; *175 S-2; mail Mount Vernon z 47620; Ⓟ 9,962; Ⓒ 10,288
BLACKFORD; 174 G-12; Ⓟ 14,067; Ⓒ 14,048; ◆ 12,955
Blackhawk; RMC Place; ALLEN; *174 D-13; ★ FTWA; mail Fort Wayne z 46815; pop. incl. with Fort Wayne (Inc. Place)
Blackhawk; RMC Place; VIGO; 175 M-4; mail Pimento z 47866; ● 80
Blackhawk Beach; RMC Place; PORTER; *174 B-5; ★ CHI; mail Valparaiso z 46383; ● 300
Blackhawk Forest; RMC Place; ALLEN; *174 D-13; ★ FTWA; mail Fort Wayne z 46815; pop. incl. with Fort Wayne (Inc. Place)
Blackman Lake; RMC Place; LAGRANGE; *174 B-12; mail Wolcottville z 46795; ● 80
Black Oak; RMC Place; LAKE; *174 A-4; ★ CHI; mail Gary z 46406; pop. incl. with Gary (Inc. Place)
Blaine; RMC Place; JAY; 174 G-13; mail Portland z 47371; ● 10
Blairsville; RMC Place; POSEY; 175 S-2; ★ EV; mail Wadesville z 47638; ● 250
Blanford; RMC Place; VERMILLION; 175 K-3; elev. 569ft./173m.; 🅿; z 47831; ● 300
Blocher; RMC Place; SCOTT; 175 O-11; elev. 676ft./206m.; 🅿; z 47138; ● 200
Bloomer; RMC Place; MADISON; *174 I-10; ★ AND; mail Anderson z 46011; rural
Bloomfield; Inc. Place; ⊡ GREENE; 175 N-6; elev. 600ft./183m.; 🅿; z 47424; Ⓟ 2,592; Ⓒ 2,542
Bloomfield; MCD-Township; LAGRANGE; *174 A-12; mail Lagrange z 46761; Ⓟ 4,737; Ⓒ 5,512
Bloomfield; RMC Place; SPENCER; *175 S-5; elev. 441ft./134m.; mail Chrisney z 47611; ● 40
Bloomingdale; Inc. Place; PARKE; 174 J-5; elev. 650ft./198m.; 🅿; z 47832; Ⓟ 341; Ⓒ 319
Blooming Grove; RMC Place; FRANKLIN; ▲ Blooming Grove; 175 L-13; mail Brookville z 47012; ● 75
Blooming Grove; MCD-Township; FRANKLIN; *175 L-13; mail Brookville z 47012; Ⓟ 924; Ⓒ 1,141
Bloomingport; RMC Place; RANDOLPH; 174 I-13; mail Lynn z 47355; ● 60
Bloomington; Inc. Place; ⊡ MONROE; 175 M-7; 🅿 🅷 🅲 38,247 ■; ★ BLMNG; z 47401-08; Ⓟ 60,633; Ⓒ 69,291; ◆ 78,719
Bloomington; MCD-Township; MONROE; *175 M-7; 🅿 🅲 38,247; ★ BLMNG; z 47401-08, z 98662; includes part of the City of Bloomington; Ⓟ 42,156; Ⓒ 41,032
Blountsville; Inc. Place; HENRY; 174 I-12; elev. 1,096ft./334m.; mail Losantville z 47354; Ⓟ 155; Ⓒ 166
Blue Creek; MCD-Township; ADAMS; *174 F-14; mail Monroe z 46772, Sunman z 47041; Ⓟ 873; Ⓒ 1,195
Blue Lake; RMC Place; WHITLEY; *174 C-12; mail Churubusco z 46723; summer pop. 600; ● 300
Blue Ridge; RMC Place; SHELBY; 175 L-11; mail Shelbyville z 46176; ● 250
Blue Ridge Estates; RMC Place; MONROE; *175 M-7; ★ BLMNG; mail Bloomington z 47408; pop. incl. with Bloomington (Inc. Place)
Blue River; MCD-Township; HANCOCK; *174 J-10; mail Greenfield z 46140; Ⓟ 1,033; Ⓒ 1,328
Blue River; MCD-Township; HARRISON; *175 Q-8; mail Depauw z 47115; Ⓟ 1,867; Ⓒ 1,923
Blue River; MCD-Township; HENRY; *174 I-12; mail Mooreland z 47360; Ⓟ 1,265; Ⓒ 1,179
Blue River; MCD-Township; JOHNSON; *175 L-9; ★ IND; mail Edinburgh z 46124; Ⓟ 5,115; Ⓒ 5,189
Bluff Creek; RMC Place; JOHNSON; *175 K-8; ★ IND; mail Bargersville z 46106; ● 60
Bluff Point; RMC Place; JAY; *174 G-13; mail Portland z 47371; ● 25
Bluffs; RMC Place; MORGAN; *175 K-8; ★ IND; mail Martinsville z 46151; ● 75
Bluffton; Inc. Place; ⊡ WELLS; 174 F-12; elev. 828ft./252m.; 🅿 🅷; z 46714; Ⓟ 9,020; Ⓒ 9,536
Bobtown; RMC Place; JACKSON; *175 N-9; mail Seymour z 47274; ● 70
Bogard; MCD-Township; DAVIESS; *175 O-5; mail Plainville z 47568, Washington z 47501; Ⓟ 1,068; Ⓒ 1,189
Boggstown; RMC Place; SHELBY; 175 K-10; elev. 752ft./229m.; 🅿; z 46110; ● 400
Bogle Corner; RMC Place; CLAY; *175 M-5; mail Jasonville z 47438
Bolivar; MCD-Township; BENTON; *174 G-5; mail Otterbein z 47970; Ⓟ 1,277; Ⓒ 1,310
Bonnell (Kennedy); RMC Place; DEARBORN; *175 M-13; mail Guilford z 47022, Lamar z 47550; rural
Bono; RMC Place; LAWRENCE; 175 O-8; elev. 662ft./202m.; mail Mitchell z 47446; ● 25
Bono; MCD-Township; LAWRENCE; *175 O-8; mail Mitchell z 47446; Ⓟ 668; Ⓒ 803
Boon; MCD-Township; WARRICK; *175 S-4; mail Boonville z 47601; Ⓟ 11,708; Ⓒ 12,844
Boone; MCD-Township; CASS; *174 E-7; mail Royal Center z 46978; Ⓟ 1,558; Ⓒ 1,531
Boone; MCD-Township; CRAWFORD; *175 R-8; mail Leavenworth z 47137; Ⓟ 153; Ⓒ 174
Boone; MCD-Township; DUBOIS; *175 Q-5; mail Jasper z 47546; Ⓟ 763; Ⓒ 795
Boone; MCD-Township; HARRISON; *175 S-9; mail Laconia z 47135; Ⓟ 1,161; Ⓒ 1,217
Boone; MCD-Township; MADISON; *174 G-10; mail Elwood z 46036; Ⓟ 681; Ⓒ 659
Boone; MCD-Township; PORTER; *174 C-5; ★ CHI; mail Hebron z 46341; Ⓟ 4,909; Ⓒ 5,884
BOONE; 174 I-7; Ⓟ 38,147; Ⓒ 46,107; ◆ 55,837
Boone Grove; RMC Place; PORTER; 174 B-5; elev. 719ft./219m.; 🅿; ★ CHI; z 46302; ● 175
Boonville; Inc. Place; ⊡ WARRICK; ▲ Boon; 175 S-4; elev. 400ft./122m.; 🅿 🅷; z 47601; Ⓟ 6,724; Ⓒ 6,834
Borden (New Providence); Inc. Place; CLARK; 175 Q-9; elev. 562ft./171m.; 🅿; z 47106; Ⓟ 270; Ⓒ 818
Boston; Inc. Place; WAYNE; ▲ Boston; 174 J-14; 🅿; z 47324; Ⓟ 159; Ⓒ 177
Boston; MCD-Township; WAYNE; *174 J-14; 🅿; z 47324; Ⓟ 917; Ⓒ 915
Boswell; Inc. Place; BENTON; 174 G-4; elev. 760ft./232m.; 🅿; z 47921; Ⓟ 767; Ⓒ 827
Boundary City; RMC Place; JAY; 174 G-13; mail Portland z 47371; ● 20
Bourbon; Inc. Place; MARSHALL; ▲ Bourbon; 174 C-9; 🅿; z 46504; Ⓟ 1,672; Ⓒ 1,691
Bourbon; MCD-Township; MARSHALL; *174 C-9; 🅿; z 46504; Ⓟ 2,976; Ⓒ 2,970
Bowers; RMC Place; MONTGOMERY; *174 H-6; mail Darlington z 47940
Bowerstown; RMC Place; HUNTINGTON; *174 E-11; mail Huntington z 46750; ● 50
Bowling Green; RMC Place; CLAY; 175 L-5; elev. 650ft./198m.; 🅿; z 47833; ● 300
Bowman; RMC Place; PIKE; *175 Q-4; mail Petersburg z 47567
Bowman Acres; RMC Place; HANCOCK; *174 J-10; ★ IND; mail Greenfield z 46140; pop. incl. with Greenfield (Inc. Place)
Boxley; RMC Place; HAMILTON; 174 H-9; ★ IND; mail Sheridan z 46069; ● 100
Boyleston; RMC Place; CLINTON; 174 H-8; mail Michigantown z 46057; ● 90
Bracken; RMC Place; HUNTINGTON; *174 D-11; mail Huntington z 46750
Bradford; RMC Place; HARRISON; 175 Q-9; elev. 837ft./255m.; 🅿; ★ LOU; z 47107; ● 150
Bradford Park; RMC Place; DELAWARE; *174 H-11; ★ MUN; mail Yorktown z 47396
Brairwood; RMC Place; STEUBEN; *174 A-13; mail Fremont z 46737; rural
Bramble; RMC Place; MARTIN; *175 O-6; mail Loogootee z 47553
Branchville; RMC Place; PERRY; 175 R-7; elev. 434ft./132m.; 🅿; z 47514; ● 70
Brandywine; MCD-Township; HANCOCK; *175 K-10; ★ IND; mail Greenfield z 46140; Ⓟ 1,646; Ⓒ 2,255
Brandywine; MCD-Township; SHELBY; *175 K-10; mail Fairland z 46126; Ⓟ 2,115; Ⓒ 2,111
Braytown; RMC Place; SWITZERLAND; *175 O-12; mail Vevay z 47043; rural
Brazil; Inc. Place; ⊡ CLAY; 175 L-5; elev. 659ft./201m.; 🅿 🅷; ★ T.H.; z 47834; Ⓟ 7,640; Ⓒ 8,188; Ⓡ 8,176
Brazil; MCD-Township; CLAY; *175 K-5; 🅿; z 47834; includes part of the City of Brazil; Ⓟ 8,216; Ⓒ 8,516; Ⓡ 8,504
Breezewood; RMC Place; GRANT; *174 F-10; ★ MRN; mail Marion z 46952; ● 120
Breezewood Park; RMC Place; DELAWARE; ★ MUN; mail Muncie z 47302; ● 200
Breezy Point; RMC Place; CARROLL; *174 F-6; mail Monticello z 47960; ● 60
Bremen; Inc. Place; MARSHALL; 174 B-9; elev. 854ft./260m.; 🅿 🅷; z 46506; Ⓟ 4,725; Ⓒ 4,486
Brems; RMC Place; STARKE; 174 C-7; mail Knox z 46534; ● 50
Brendan Wood; RMC Place; BOONE; *174 I-7; ★ IND; mail Lebanon z 46052; pop. incl. with Lebanon (Inc. Place)
Brendonwood; RMC Place; MARION; *174 J-9; ★ IND; mail Indianapolis z 46226; pop. incl. with Indianapolis (Inc. Place)
Brent Woods; RMC Place; SHELBY; *175 K-10; mail Shelbyville z 46176; pop. incl. with Shelbyville (Inc. Place)
Bretzville; RMC Place; DUBOIS; 175 R-6; mail Huntingburg z 47542; ● 50
Brewersville; RMC Place; JENNINGS; 175 N-11; mail North Vernon z 47265; ● 50
Brewington Woods; RMC Place; DELAWARE; *174 H-11; ★ MUN; mail Muncie z 47303-04; ● 400
Briarwood; RMC Place; MORGAN; *175 K-7; ★ IND; mail Monrovia z 46157; ● 150
Brice; RMC Place; JAY; *174 G-13; mail Portland z 47371; rural
Brick Chapel; RMC Place; PUTNAM; 175 K-6; mail Greencastle z 46135; ● 40
Bridgeport; RMC Place; MARION; *175 K-8; 🅿; ★ IND; z 46231; pop. incl. with Indianapolis (Inc. Place)
Bridgeton; RMC Place; PARKE; 175 K-5; elev. 560ft./171m.; 🅿; z 47836; ● 150
Brierwood Hills; RMC Place; ALLEN; *174 D-12; ★ FTWA; mail Fort Wayne z 46804; ● 400
Bright; CDP; DEARBORN; 175 M-14; ★ CIN; mail Lawrenceburg z 47025; Ⓟ 3,945; Ⓒ 5,405
Brighton; RMC Place; LAGRANGE; 174 A-12; elev. 942ft./287m.; mail Howe z 46746; ● 125
Brightwood; RMC Place; MARION; *174 J-9; ★ IND; mail Indianapolis z 46218; pop. incl. with Indianapolis (Inc. Place)
Brimfield; RMC Place; NOBLE; 174 B-12; elev. 951ft./290m.; 🅿; z 46794 & mail Kendallville z 46755; ● 150
Brinckley; RANDOLPH; see Shedville (RMC Place)
Bringhurst; RMC Place; CARROLL; 174 G-7; elev. 721ft./220m.; 🅿; z 46913; ● 125
Bristol; Inc. Place; ELKHART; 174 A-10; elev. 772ft./235m.; 🅿; ★ ELK; z 46507; Ⓟ 1,133; Ⓒ 1,382
Bristow; RMC Place; PERRY; 175 R-6; elev. 442ft./135m.; 🅿; z 47515; ● 120
Broadlands; RMC Place; VIGO; *175 K-4; ★ T.H.; mail Terre Haute z 47805; ● 200
Broad Ripple; RMC Place; MARION; *174 J-9; ★ IND; mail Indianapolis z 46220, z 46230; pop. incl. with Indianapolis (Inc. Place)
Broadview; RMC Place; GRANT; *174 F-10; ★ MRN; mail Marion z 46952; ● 100
Broadview; RMC Place; MONROE; *175 M-7; ★ BLMNG; mail Bloomington z 47403; ● 1,000
Bromer; RMC Place; ORANGE; *175 P-8; mail Orleans z 47452; rural
Brook; Inc. Place; NEWTON; 174 E-4; elev. 646ft./197m.; 🅿; z 47922; Ⓟ 899; Ⓒ 1,062
Brookfield; RMC Place; SHELBY; *175 K-9; ★ IND; mail Fairland z 46126; ● 40
Brook Haven; RMC Place; GRANT; *174 G-11; ★ MRN; mail Marion z 46952; ● 200
Brooklyn; Inc. Place; MORGAN; 175 K-8; elev. 650ft./198m.; 🅿; ★ IND; z 46111; Ⓟ 1,162; Ⓒ 1,545
Brookmoor; RMC Place; MORGAN; *175 K-8; ★ IND; mail Mooresville z 46158; pop. incl. with Mooresville (Inc. Place)
Brooksburg; Inc. Place; JEFFERSON; 175 O-12; elev. 473ft./144m.; mail Madison z 47250; Ⓟ 79; Ⓒ 74
Brookside Estates; RMC Place; ALLEN; *174 D-13; ★ FTWA; mail Fort Wayne z 46805; pop. incl. with Fort Wayne (Inc. Place)
Brookside Estates; RMC Place; VIGO; *175 L-4; ★ T.H.; mail Terre Haute z 47802; ● 90
Brookston; Inc. Place; WHITE; 174 F-6; 🅿; z 47923; Ⓟ 1,804; Ⓒ 1,717
Brookville; Inc. Place; ⊡ FRANKLIN; ▲ Brookville; 175 L-13; 🅿; z 47012; Ⓟ 2,529; Ⓒ 2,652
Brookville; MCD-Township; FRANKLIN; *175 L-13; 🅿; z 47012; Ⓟ 5,565; Ⓒ 5,800
Brookville Heights; RMC Place; HANCOCK; *175 K-10; ★ IND; mail New Palestine z 46163; ● 220
Broom Hill; RMC Place; CLARK; *175 Q-10; elev. 514ft./157m.; mail Borden z 47106; rural
Brown; MCD-Township; HANCOCK; *174 J-11; mail Shirley z 47384, Wilkinson z 46186; Ⓟ 2,573; Ⓒ 2,579
Brown; MCD-Township; HENDRICKS; *174 J-8; ★ IND; mail Brownsburg z 46112; Ⓟ 4,617; Ⓒ 8,142
Brown; MCD-Township; MONTGOMERY; *174 J-5; mail Crawfordsville z 47933; Ⓟ 1,660; Ⓒ 1,767
Brown; MCD-Township; MORGAN; *175 K-8; ★ IND; mail Mooresville z 46158; Ⓟ 10,049; Ⓒ 13,491
Brown; MCD-Township; RIPLEY; *175 N-12; mail Madison z 47250; Ⓟ 1,418; Ⓒ 1,499
Brown; MCD-Township; WASHINGTON; *175 P-8; mail Campbellsburg z 47108; Ⓟ 1,229; Ⓒ 1,219
BROWN; 175 M-8; Ⓟ 14,080; Ⓒ 14,957; ◆ 14,220
Brownsburg; Inc. Place; HENDRICKS; 174 J-8; elev. 884ft./269m.; 🅿; ★ IND; z 46112; Ⓟ 7,628; Ⓒ 14,520
Browns Corner (Toledo); RMC Place; HUNTINGTON; *174 E-11; mail Huntington z 46750; rural
Browns Crossing; RMC Place; MORGAN; *175 L-7; ★ IND; mail Martinsville z 46151; ● 200
Brownstown; RMC Place; CRAWFORD; *175 Q-7; elev. 661ft./201m.; mail English z 47118; rural
Brownstown; Inc. Place; ⊡ JACKSON; ▲ Brownstown; 175 O-9; 🅿; z 47220; Ⓟ 2,872; Ⓒ 2,978
Brownstown; MCD-Township; JACKSON; *175 O-9; 🅿; z 47220; Ⓟ 4,963; Ⓒ 5,301
Browns Valley; RMC Place; MONTGOMERY; 174 J-5; mail Crawfordsville z 47933; ● 90
Brownsville; RMC Place; UNION; ▲ Brownsville; 175 K-13; 🅿; z 47325; ● 250
Brownsville; MCD-Township; UNION; *175 K-13; 🅿; z 47325; Ⓟ 850; Ⓒ 857
Bruce Lake; RMC Place; FULTON; 174 D-8; mail Kewanna z 46939; summer pop. 250; ● 100
Bruceville; Inc. Place; KNOX; 175 O-4; elev. 513ft./156m.; 🅿; z 47516; Ⓟ 471; Ⓒ 469
Brummitt Acres; RMC Place; PORTER; *174 A-5; ★ CHI; mail Chesterton z 46304; ● 300
Brunswick; RMC Place; LAKE; 174 B-4; ★ CHI; mail Gary z 46406; ● 200
Brushy Prairie; RMC Place; LAGRANGE; 174 A-12; mail Lagrange z 46761; ● 30
Bryant; Inc. Place; JAY; 174 G-13; elev. 875ft./267m.; 🅿; z 47326; Ⓟ 273; Ⓒ 272
Bryantsburg; RMC Place; JEFFERSON; 175 O-12; mail Madison z 47250; ● 50
Bryantsville; RMC Place; LAWRENCE; *175 O-7; mail Mitchell z 47446; rural
Buck Creek; MCD-Township; HANCOCK; *174 J-10; ★ IND; mail Greenfield z 46140; Ⓟ 5,435; Ⓒ 6,659
Buck Creek; RMC Place; TIPPECANOE; 174 G-6; elev. 663ft./202m.; 🅿; ★ LAF-; z 47924; ● 250
Buckeye; RMC Place; HUNTINGTON; *174 F-12; mail Warren z 46792; rural
Buckskin; RMC Place; GIBSON; 175 R-4; elev. 414ft./126m.; 🅿; z 47647; ● 120
Bucktown; RMC Place; SULLIVAN; 175 N-4; mail Carlisle z 47838; ● 20
Bud; RMC Place; JOHNSON; *175 L-9; mail Franklin z 46131; rural
Buddha; RMC Place; LAWRENCE; 175 O-8; mail Bedford z 47421; ● 40
Buena Vista; RMC Place; FRANKLIN; 175 L-12; mail Laurel z 47024; ● 80
Buena Vista; GIBSON; see Giro (RMC Place)
Buffalo (French); RMC Place; OHIO; *175 N-14; mail Aurora z 47001
Buffalo; CDP; WHITE; 174 E-6; elev. 672ft./205m.; 🅿; z 47925; Ⓒ 672
Buffaloville; RMC Place; SPENCER; 175 S-5; elev. 452ft./138m.; 🅿; z 47550; ● 40
Buffington; RMC Place; LAKE; *174 A-4; ★ CHI; mail Gary z 46406; pop. incl. with Gary (Inc. Place)
Bufkin; RMC Place; POSEY; *175 S-2; mail Mount Vernon z 47620; ● 60
Bullocktown; RMC Place; WARRICK; *175 S-4; mail Boonville z 47601; ● 90
Bunker Hill; RMC Place; FAYETTE; *175 K-12; mail Connersville z 47331; ● 45
Bunker Hill; RMC Place; KNOX; *175 P-3; mail Vincennes z 47591; ● 500
Bunker Hill; Inc. Place; MIAMI; 174 F-9; elev. 800ft./244m.; 🅿; z 46914; Ⓟ 1,010; Ⓒ 987
Bunker Hill; RMC Place; WASHINGTON; *175 P-10; mail Salem z 47167; rural
Burdick; RMC Place; PORTER; *174 A-6; ★ CHI; mail Chesterton z 46304; ● 100
Burket; Inc. Place; KOSCIUSKO; 174 C-9; elev. 860ft./262m.; 🅿; z 46508; Ⓟ 200; Ⓒ 195
Burlington; Inc. Place; CARROLL; ▲ Burlington; 174 G-8; elev. 790ft./241m.; 🅿; z 46915; Ⓟ 568; Ⓒ 444; Ⓡ 457
Burlington; MCD-Township; CARROLL; *174 G-8; elev. 790ft./241m.; 🅿; z 46915; Ⓟ 1,686; Ⓒ 1,561
Burlington Beach; RMC Place; PORTER; 174 B-5; ★ CHI; mail Valparaiso z 46383; ● 900
Burnett; RMC Place; VIGO; *175 K-4; ★ T.H.; mail Terre Haute z 47805; ● 300
Burnettsville; Inc. Place; WHITE; 174 E-7; elev. 710ft./216m.; 🅿; z 47926; Ⓟ 401; Ⓒ 373
Burney; RMC Place; DECATUR; 175 M-11; elev. 824ft./251m.; 🅿; z 47240; ● 130
Burns City (Crane); RMC Place; MARTIN; 175 O-6; elev. 706ft./215m.; mail Crane z 47522, Loogootee z 47553
Burns Harbor; Inc. Place; PORTER; 174 A-5; elev. 630ft./192m.; 🅿; ★ CHI; z 46304; Ⓟ 788; Ⓒ 766
Burnsville; RMC Place; BARTHOLOMEW; 175 M-10; mail Columbus z 47201; ● 60
Burr Oak; RMC Place; MARSHALL; 174 C-8; elev. 775ft./236m.; 🅿; z 46511 & mail Albion z 46701; ● 100
Burr Oak; RMC Place; NOBLE; *174 C-11; 🅿; z 46511 & mail Albion z 46701; rural
Burrows; RMC Place; CARROLL; 174 F-7; elev. 695ft./212m.; 🅿; z 46916; ● 240
Busseron; RMC Place; KNOX; *175 O-4; mail Oaktown z 47561
Busseron; MCD-Township; KNOX; *175 O-4; mail Oaktown z 47561; Ⓟ 1,372; Ⓒ 1,385
Butler; Inc. Place; DE KALB; 174 B-13; elev. 870ft./265m.; 🅿; z 46721; Ⓟ 2,601; Ⓒ 2,725
Butler; MCD-Township; DE KALB; *174 C-12; 🅿; z 46721 & mail Laotto z 46763; Ⓟ 1,606; Ⓒ 1,805
Butler; MCD-Township; FRANKLIN; *175 L-13; mail Brookville z 47012; Ⓟ 992; Ⓒ 1,175
Butler; MCD-Township; MIAMI; *174 F-9; mail Peru z 46970; Ⓟ 791; Ⓒ 838
Butler Center; RMC Place; DE KALB; 174 C-13; mail Garrett z 46738; ● 35
Butlerville; RMC Place; JENNINGS; 175 N-11; elev. 814ft./248m.; 🅿; z 47223; ● 350
Byrneville; RMC Place; HARRISON; 175 Q-9; ★ LOU; mail Georgetown z 47122; ● 40
Byron; RMC Place; LAPORTE; *174 A-7; ★ MICH; mail La Porte z 46350

C

Caborn; RMC Place; POSEY; *175 S-2; ★ EV; mail Mount Vernon z 47620
Cadiz; Inc. Place; HENRY; 174 I-11; elev. 1,074ft./327m.; mail New Castle z 47362; Ⓟ 202; Ⓒ 161
Caesar Creek; MCD-Township; DEARBORN; *175 N-13; mail Dillsboro z 47018; Ⓟ 310; Ⓒ 286
Cain; MCD-Township; FOUNTAIN; *174 I-5; mail Hillsboro z 47949; Ⓟ 1,160; Ⓒ 1,090
Cairo; RMC Place; TIPPECANOE; *174 G-6; elev. 687ft./209m.; ★ LAF-; mail West Lafayette z 47906; rural
Cale; RMC Place; MARTIN; 175 O-6; mail Shoals z 47581; ● 35
California; MCD-Township; STARKE; *174 C-7; mail Knox z 46534; Ⓟ 2,077; Ⓒ 2,116
Calumet; MCD-Township; LAKE; *174 A-4; ★ CHI; mail Gary z 46408; Ⓟ 141,875; Ⓒ 127,800
Calvertville; RMC Place; GREENE; *175 N-6; mail Bloomfield z 47424; ● 25
Cambria; RMC Place; CLINTON; 174 G-7; mail Frankfort z 46041; ● 100
Cambridge City; Inc. Place; WAYNE; 174 J-12; elev. 937ft./286m.; 🅿; z 47327; Ⓟ 2,091; Ⓒ 2,121
Camby; RMC Place; MARION; *175 K-8; 🅿; ★ IND; z 46113; pop. incl. with Indianapolis (Inc. Place)
Camden; Inc. Place; CARROLL; 174 F-7; elev. 670ft./204m.; 🅿; z 46917; Ⓟ 607; Ⓒ 582
Cammack; RMC Place; DELAWARE; 174 H-11; ★ MUN; mail Muncie z 47304; ● 180
Campbell; MCD-Township; JENNINGS; *175 N-11; mail Butlerville z 47223; Ⓟ 1,790; Ⓒ 1,588
Campbell; MCD-Township; WARRICK; *175 S-4; mail Chandler z 47610; Ⓟ 620; Ⓒ 480
Campbellsburg; Inc. Place; WASHINGTON; 175 P-8; elev. 826ft./252m.; 🅿; z 47108; Ⓟ 606; Ⓒ 578
Campbelltown; RMC Place; PIKE; *175 Q-4; elev. 560ft./171m.; mail Winslow z 47598; ● 75
Canaan; RMC Place; JEFFERSON; 175 O-12; elev. 950ft./290m.; 🅿; z 47224; ● 80
Candleglo Village; RMC Place; SHELBY; *175 K-10; mail Shelbyville z 46176; ● 75
Candle Light Village; RMC Place; BARTHOLOMEW; *175 M-10; ★ COL; mail Columbus z 47203; pop. incl. with Columbus (Inc. Place)
Cannelburg; Inc. Place; DAVIESS; 175 P-5; elev. 426ft./130m.; 🅿; z 47519; Ⓟ 97; Ⓒ 140
Cannelton; Inc. Place; PERRY; 175 S-6; elev. 426ft./130m.; 🅿; z 47520; Ⓟ 1,786; Ⓒ 1,209
Canton; RMC Place; WASHINGTON; 175 P-9; mail Salem z 47167; ● 175
Cape Sandy; RMC Place; CRAWFORD; *175 R-8; mail Leavenworth z 47137; rural
Capilano by the Lake; RMC Place; TIPPECANOE; *174 G-6; ★ LAF-; mail West Lafayette z 47906; ● 200
Carbon; Inc. Place; CLAY; 175 K-5; 🅿; z 47837; Ⓟ 350; Ⓒ 334
Carbondale; RMC Place; WARREN; 174 G-4; mail Williamsport z 47993; ● 15
Cardonia; RMC Place; CLAY; 175 K-5; mail Brazil z 47834; ● 90
Carefree; RMC Place; CRAWFORD; 175 R-8; 🅿; z 47137; ● 25
Carlisle; Inc. Place; SULLIVAN; 175 N-4; elev. 500ft./152m.; 🅿; z 47838; Ⓟ 613; Ⓒ 2,660; Ⓡ 695
Carlos (Carlos City); RMC Place; RANDOLPH; 174 I-13; mail Lynn z 47355; ● 80
Carlos City; RANDOLPH; see Carlos (RMC Place)
Carmel; Inc. Place; HAMILTON; 174 I-9; elev. 829ft./253m.; 🅿 🅷; ★ IND; z 46032-33, z 46082; Ⓟ 25,380; Ⓒ 37,733; ◆ 64,711
Carp; RMC Place; OWEN; *175 L-6; elev. 723ft./220m.; mail Spencer z 47460
Carpenter; MCD-Township; JASPER; *174 E-5; mail Remington z 47977; Ⓟ 1,937; Ⓒ 2,096
Carpentersville; RMC Place; PUTNAM; 174 J-6; mail Roachdale z 46172; ● 40
Carr; MCD-Township; CLARK; *175 Q-10; mail Borden z 47106; Ⓟ 1,640; Ⓒ 2,263
Carr; MCD-Township; JACKSON; *175 O-8; mail Medora z 47260; Ⓟ 1,576; Ⓒ 1,384
Carriage Estates; RMC Place; BARTHOLOMEW; *175 M-10; ★ COL; mail Columbus z 47203; pop. incl. with Columbus (Inc. Place)
Carriage Estates; RMC Place; HANCOCK; *174 J-10; ★ IND; mail New Palestine z 46163; ● 100
CARROLL; 174 F-7; Ⓟ 18,809; Ⓒ 20,165; ◆ 19,695
Carrollton; RMC Place; CARROLL; *174 G-8; elev. 782ft./238m.; mail Bringhurst z 46913; ● 30
Carrollton; MCD-Township; CARROLL; *174 F-8; mail Flora z 46929; Ⓟ 593; Ⓒ 603
Carrollton (Finly, Reedville); RMC Place; HANCOCK; *175 K-10; elev. 835ft./255m.; ★ IND; mail Finly z 46129; ● 150
Carter; MCD-Township; SPENCER; *175 R-6; mail Dale z 47523; Ⓟ 3,032; Ⓒ 3,121
Cartersburg; RMC Place; HENDRICKS; *175 K-7; elev. 770ft./235m.; 🅿; ★ IND; z 46168; ● 225
Carthage; Inc. Place; RUSH; 175 K-11; elev. 886ft./270m.; 🅿; z 46115; Ⓟ 887; Ⓒ 928
Carwood; RMC Place; CLARK; *175 Q-10; mail Borden z 47106; rural
Cascade; RMC Place; MONROE; *175 M-7; ★ BLMNG; mail Bloomington z 47404; pop. incl. with Bloomington (Inc. Place)
Cass; MCD-Township; CLAY; *175 L-5; mail Poland z 47868; Ⓟ 310; Ⓒ 335
Cass; MCD-Township; DUBOIS; *175 R-5; mail Holland z 47541; Ⓟ 2,072; Ⓒ 2,185
Cass; MCD-Township; GREENE; *175 N-5; mail Newberry z 47449; Ⓟ 386; Ⓒ 392
Cass; MCD-Civil Township; LAPORTE; *174 B-6; mail Wanatah z 46390; Ⓟ 1,690; Ⓒ 1,677
Cass; MCD-Township; OHIO; *175 N-13; mail Rising Sun z 47040; Ⓟ 546; Ⓒ 649
Cass; MCD-Township; PULASKI; *174 D-6; mail Medaryville z 47957; Ⓟ 788; Ⓒ 1,013
Cass; RMC Place; SULLIVAN; ▲ Cass; 175 N-4; mail Dugger z 47848; ● 100
Cass; MCD-Township; SULLIVAN; *175 N-4; mail Dugger z 47848; Ⓟ 1,912; Ⓒ 1,932
Cass; MCD-Township; WHITE; *174 E-7; mail Monticello z 47960; Ⓟ 569; Ⓒ 590
CASS; 174 E-8; Ⓟ 38,413; Ⓒ 40,930; ◆ 38,365
Cassville; RMC Place; HOWARD; 174 F-9; ★ KOK; mail Kokomo z 46901; ● 120
Castleton; RMC Place; MARION; *174 J-9; elev. 810ft./247m.; 🅿; ★ IND; z 46250, z 46256; pop. incl. with Indianapolis (Inc. Place)
Cataract; RMC Place; OWEN; 175 L-6; mail Spencer z 47460; ● 50
Cates; RMC Place; FOUNTAIN; 174 I-4; elev. 640ft./195m.; 🅿; z 47952; ● 125
Catlin; RMC Place; PARKE; 175 K-5; mail Rockville z 47872; ● 100
Cato; RMC Place; PIKE; 175 Q-5; elev. 489ft./149m.; mail Winslow z 47598; ● 30
Cavanaugh; RMC Place; LAKE; *174 A-4; ★ CHI; mail Gary z 46406; pop. incl. with Gary (Inc. Place)
Cayuga; Inc. Place; VERMILLION; 174 I-4; elev. 511ft./156m.; 🅿; z 47928; Ⓟ 1,083; Ⓒ 1,109
Cedar; RMC Place; DE KALB; *174 C-12; mail Garrett z 46738; ● 25
Cedar Canyons; RMC Place; ALLEN; *174 C-13; ★ FTWA; mail Grabill z 46741; ● 200
Cedar Creek; MCD-Township; ALLEN; *174 C-13; ★ FTWA; mail Grabill z 46741; Ⓟ 6,688; Ⓒ 10,288
Cedar Creek; MCD-Township; LAKE; *174 C-4; ★ CHI; mail Lowell z 46356; Ⓟ 9,009; Ⓒ 10,649
Cedar Grove; Inc. Place; FRANKLIN; 175 L-13; elev. 593ft./181m.; 🅿; z 47016; Ⓟ 246; Ⓒ 185
Cedar Lake; Inc. Place; LAKE; 174 B-4; elev. 702ft./214m.; 🅿; ★ CHI; z 46303; Ⓟ 8,885; Ⓒ 9,279
Cedar Lake; RMC Place; WHITLEY; *174 C-11; mail Columbia City z 46725
Cedar Point; RMC Place; WHITE; *174 F-6; mail Monticello z 47960; ● 30
Cedar Shores; RMC Place; ALLEN; *174 C-13; ★ FTWA; mail Grabill z 46741, Leo z 46765; ● 100
Cedarville; RMC Place; ALLEN; *174 C-13; ★ FTWA; mail Grabill z 46741, Leo z 46765; pop. incl. with Leo-Cedarville (Inc. Place)
Celestine; RMC Place; DUBOIS; 175 Q-6; 🅿; z 47521; ● 250
Cemar Estates; RMC Place; VIGO; *175 K-4; ★ T.H.; mail Terre Haute z 47805; ● 250
Cementville; RMC Place; CLARK; *175 Q-10; elev. 466ft./142m.; ★ LOU; mail Clarksville z 47129, Jeffersonville z 47130; pop. incl. with Jeffersonville (Inc. Place)
Centenary; RMC Place; VERMILLION; *175 K-4; mail Clinton z 47842; ● 290
Centennial; RMC Place; ALLEN; *174 D-12; ★ FTWA; mail Fort Wayne z 46808, z 46825, z 46898; pop. incl. with Fort Wayne (Inc. Place)
Centennial; RMC Place; FOUNTAIN; *174 I-5; mail Kingman z 47952; ● 15
Center; MCD-Township; BENTON; *174 F-4; mail Fowler z 47944; Ⓟ 2,875; Ⓒ 2,854
Center; MCD-Township; BOONE; *174 I-7; ★ IND; mail Lebanon z 46052; Ⓟ 14,538; Ⓒ 17,102
Center; MCD-Township; CLINTON; *174 H-7; mail Frankfort z 46041; Ⓟ 15,845; Ⓒ 17,505
Center; MCD-Township; DEARBORN; *175 N-13; ★ CIN; mail Aurora z 47001; Ⓟ 5,182; Ⓒ 5,431
Center; MCD-Township; DELAWARE; *174 H-12; ★ MUN; mail Muncie z 47302; Ⓟ 74,656; Ⓒ 71,120
Center; MCD-Township; GIBSON; *175 Q-4; mail Francisco z 47649; Ⓟ 1,503; Ⓒ 1,478
Center; MCD-Township; GRANT; *174 G-11; ★ MRN; mail Marion z 46952; Ⓟ 25,894; Ⓒ 24,833
Center; MCD-Township; GREENE; *175 N-6; mail Bloomfield z 47424; Ⓟ 2,439; Ⓒ 3,109
Center; MCD-Township; HANCOCK; *174 J-10; ★ IND; mail Greenfield z 46140; Ⓟ 16,578; Ⓒ 20,096
Center; MCD-Township; HENDRICKS; *174 J-7; ★ IND; mail Danville z 46122; Ⓟ 7,359; Ⓒ 9,744
Center; RMC Place; HOWARD; 174 G-9; elev. 849ft./259m.; ★ KOK; mail Kokomo z 46902; ● 250
Center; MCD-Township; HOWARD; *174 G-9; ★ KOK; mail Kokomo z 46901-02; Ⓟ 47,354; Ⓒ 47,619
Center; RMC Place; JAY; *174 G-13; mail Portland z 47371; rural
Center; MCD-Township; JENNINGS; *175 N-11; mail North Vernon z 47265; Ⓟ 7,800; Ⓒ 8,593
Center; MCD-Township; LAPORTE; *174 A-6; ★ MICH; mail La Porte z 46350; Ⓟ 23,438; Ⓒ 24,405
Center; MCD-Township; LAKE; *174 B-4; ★ CHI; mail Crown Point z 46307; Ⓟ 24,369; Ⓒ 26,191
Center; MCD-Township; MARION; *174 J-9; ★ IND; mail Indianapolis z 46204; Ⓟ 182,140; Ⓒ 167,055
Center; MCD-Township; MARSHALL; *174 C-8; mail Plymouth z 46563; Ⓟ 12,501; Ⓒ 14,721
Center; MCD-Township; MARTIN; *175 P-6; mail Loogootee z 47553; Ⓟ 1,820; Ⓒ 1,734
Center; MCD-Township; PORTER; *174 B-5; ★ CHI; mail Valparaiso z 46383, z 46385; Ⓟ 32,603; Ⓒ 38,186
Center; MCD-Township; POSEY; *175 S-2; mail Wadesville z 47638; Ⓟ 1,166; Ⓒ 1,321
Center; MCD-Township; RIPLEY; *175 M-12; mail Osgood z 47037; Ⓟ 2,579; Ⓒ 2,677
Center; MCD-Township; RUSH; *174 J-11; mail Knightstown z 46148; Ⓟ 1,025; Ⓒ 768
Center; MCD-Township; STARKE; *174 C-7; mail Knox z 46534; Ⓟ 6,270; Ⓒ 6,271
Center; MCD-Township; UNION; *175 K-13; mail Liberty z 47353; Ⓟ 2,816; Ⓒ 2,880
Center; MCD-Township; VANDERBURGH; *175 S-3; ★ EV; mail Evansville z 47710-11; Ⓟ 27,185; Ⓒ 32,220
Center; RMC Place; WARRICK; *175 S-4; ★ EV; mail Boonville z 47601; ● 50
Center; MCD-Township; WAYNE; *174 J-13; ★ RICH; mail Centerville z 47330; Ⓟ 7,345; Ⓒ 7,331
Center Point; Inc. Place; CLAY; 175 L-5; elev. 637ft./194m.; 🅿; z 47840; Ⓟ 278; Ⓒ 292
Center Square; RMC Place; SWITZERLAND; 175 O-13; mail Vevay z 47043; ● 20
Centerton; RMC Place; MORGAN; 175 L-8; elev. 600ft./183m.; 🅿; ★ IND; z 46151; ● 200
Center Valley; RMC Place; HENDRICKS; *175 K-7; ★ IND; mail Mooresville z 46158; rural
Centerville; RMC Place; SPENCER; *175 S-5; mail Chrisney z 47611; rural
Centerville; Inc. Place; WAYNE; ▲ Center; 174 J-13; 🅿; ★ RICH; z 47330; Ⓟ 2,398; Ⓒ 2,427
Central; RMC Place; HARRISON; 175 S-9; elev. 700ft./213m.; 🅿; z 47110; ● 35
Central Barren; RMC Place; HARRISON; 175 Q-9; ★ LOU; mail New Salisbury z 47161; ● 120
Centre; MCD-Township; ST. JOSEPH; *174 A-8; ★ S.B.; mail South Bend z 46614; Ⓟ 13,031; Ⓒ 14,236
Centre East; RMC Place; MARION; *174 J-9; ★ IND; mail Indianapolis z 46229; pop. incl. with Indianapolis (Inc. Place)
Ceylon; RMC Place; ADAMS; 174 F-13; mail Geneva z 46740; ● 60
Chain O'Lakes; RMC Place; ST. JOSEPH; *174 A-8; ★ S.B.; mail South Bend z 46628; ● 400
Chalmers; Inc. Place; WHITE; 174 F-6; elev. 705ft./215m.; 🅿; z 47929; Ⓟ 525; Ⓒ 513
Chambersburg; RMC Place; ORANGE; 175 P-8; mail Paoli z 47454; ● 50
Champlin Meadows; RMC Place; MORGAN; *175 L-8; ★ IND; mail Martinsville z 46151; pop. incl. with Martinsville (Inc. Place)
Chandler; Inc. Place; WARRICK; 175 S-4; elev. 421ft./128m.; 🅿; ★ EV; z 47610; Ⓟ 3,099; Ⓒ 3,094
Chapel Creek; RMC Place; FLOYD; *175 Q-10; ★ LOU; mail New Albany z 47150; ● 400
Chapel Hill; RMC Place; MARION; *174 J-8; ★ IND; mail Indianapolis z 46214; pop. incl. with Indianapolis (Inc. Place)
Chapel Hill; RMC Place; MONROE; *175 N-8; mail Heltonville z 47436; ● 75
Charlestown; Inc. Place; CLARK; 175 Q-11; elev. 600ft./183m.; 🅿 🅷; ★ LOU; z 47111; Ⓟ 5,889; Ⓒ 5,993
Charlestown; MCD-Township; CLARK; *175 Q-11; 🅿; ★ LOU; z 47111; Ⓟ 9,933; Ⓒ 11,457
Charle Sumac Estates; RMC Place; MARION; *175 K-9; ★ IND; mail Indianapolis z 46259; pop. incl. with Indianapolis (Inc. Place)
Charlottesville; RMC Place; HANCOCK; 174 J-11; 🅿; z 46117; ● 450
Chase; RMC Place; BENTON; *174 G-4; mail Boswell z 47921; ● 20
Chelsea; RMC Place; JEFFERSON; 175 P-11; mail Lexington z 47138; ● 125
Cherokee Heights; RMC Place; FLOYD; *175 R-10; ★ LOU; mail New Albany z 47150; ● 200
Cherokee Terrace; RMC Place; CLARK; *175 R-10; ★ LOU; mail Jeffersonville z 47130; ● 200
Cherry Grove; RMC Place; MONTGOMERY; *174 I-6; mail Crawfordsville z 47933; rural
Chester; MCD-Township; WABASH; *174 D-10; mail North Manchester z 46962; Ⓟ 8,303; Ⓒ 8,044
Chester; RMC Place; WAYNE; 174 J-13; ★ RICH; mail Richmond z 47374; ● 50
Chester; MCD-Township; WELLS; *174 F-12; mail Poneto z 46781; Ⓟ 981; Ⓒ 1,002
Chesterfield; Inc. Place; MADISON; 174 I-11; elev. 908ft./277m.; 🅿; ★ AND; z 46017; Ⓟ 2,730; Ⓒ 2,969
Chesterton; RMC Place; HAMILTON; *174 J-9; ★ IND; mail Indianapolis z 46280; ● 600
Chesterton; Inc. Place; PORTER; 174 A-5; elev. 644ft./196m.; 🅿; ★ CHI; z 46304; Ⓟ 9,124; Ⓒ 10,488
Chesterville; RMC Place; DEARBORN; *175 N-13; ★ CIN; mail Moores Hill z 47032; ● 50
Chestnut Hill; RMC Place; PORTER; *174 A-5; ★ CHI; mail Chesterton z 46304; pop. incl. with Chesterton (Inc. Place)
Chestnut Ridge; RMC Place; JACKSON; *175 O-10; mail Seymour z 47274; rural
Chicago Avenue; RMC Place; LAKE; *174 A-4; ★ CHI; mail East Chicago z 46312; pop. incl. with East Chicago (Inc. Place)
Chili; RMC Place; MIAMI; 174 E-9; elev. 700ft./213m.; 🅿; z 46926; ● 150
China; RMC Place; JEFFERSON; *175 O-12; mail Madison z 47250
Chippewa; RMC Place; ST. JOSEPH; *174 A-8; ★ S.B.; mail South Bend z 46613-14, z 46680; pop. incl. with South Bend (Inc. Place)
Chrisney; Inc. Place; SPENCER; 175 S-5; elev. 440ft./134m.; 🅿; z 47611; Ⓟ 511; Ⓒ 544
Christiansburg; RMC Place; BROWN; *175 N-9; mail Columbus z 47201; rural
Churubusco; Inc. Place; WHITLEY; 174 C-12; elev. 900ft./274m.; 🅿; z 46723; Ⓟ 1,781; Ⓒ 1,666
Cicero; Inc. Place; HAMILTON; 174 I-9; elev. 838ft./255m.; 🅿; ★ IND; z 46034; Ⓟ 3,268; Ⓒ 4,303
Cicero; MCD-Township; TIPTON; *174 H-9; mail Atlanta z 46031; Ⓟ 8,060; Ⓒ 8,350
Cicero Heights; RMC Place; TIPTON; *174 H-9; mail Tipton z 46072; ● 150
Cincinnati; RMC Place; GREENE; 175 N-6; mail Bloomfield z 47424; ● 90
Circle City; RMC Place; MARION; ★ IND; mail Indianapolis z 46202, z 46204, z 46244; pop. incl. with Indianapolis (Inc. Place)
Circle Park; RMC Place; STEUBEN; *174 B-13; mail Hamilton z 46742; pop. incl. with Hamilton (Inc. Place)
Circleville; RMC Place; RUSH; 175 K-11; mail Rushville z 46173; ● 300
Clare; RMC Place; HAMILTON; *174 I-9; ★ IND; mail Noblesville z 46060; ● 100
Clark; MCD-Township; JOHNSON; *175 K-9; mail Greenwood z 46142; Ⓟ 1,632; Ⓒ 1,900
Clark; MCD-Township; MONTGOMERY; *174 J-6; mail Ladoga z 47954; Ⓟ 1,843; Ⓒ 1,898
Clark; MCD-Township; PERRY; *175 R-6; mail Bristow z 47515; Ⓟ 1,136; Ⓒ 1,250
CLARK; 175 Q-10; Ⓟ 87,777; Ⓒ 96,472; ◆ 107,308
Clarke; RMC Place; LAKE; ★ CHI; pop. incl. with Gary (Inc. Place)
Clarke Junction; RMC Place; LAKE; *174 A-4; ★ CHI; pop. incl. with Gary (Inc. Place)
Clarksburg; RMC Place; DECATUR; 175 L-12; elev. 1,065ft./325m.; 🅿; z 47225; ● 200
Clarks Hill; Inc. Place; TIPPECANOE; 174 H-7; elev. 826ft./252m.; 🅿; z 47930; Ⓟ 716; Ⓒ 680
Clarks Landing; RMC Place; STEUBEN; *174 A-13; mail Hamilton z 46742; ● 25
Clarksville; Inc. Place; CLARK; 175 R-10; elev. 450ft./137m.; 🅿 ■; ★ LOU; z 47129, z 47131; Ⓟ 19,833; Ⓒ 21,400; ◆ 22,521
Clarksville; RMC Place; HAMILTON; 174 I-10; mail Noblesville z 46060; ● 150
Clay; MCD-Township; BARTHOLOMEW; *175 M-10; ★ COL; mail Columbus z 47203; Ⓟ 2,421; Ⓒ 3,103
Clay; MCD-Township; CARROLL; *174 G-7; mail Delphi z 46923; Ⓟ 882; Ⓒ 1,079
Clay; MCD-Township; CASS; *174 E-8; mail Logansport z 46947; Ⓟ 2,878; Ⓒ 2,890
Clay; MCD-Township; DEARBORN; *175 N-13; ★ CIN; mail Dillsboro z 47018; Ⓟ 2,813; Ⓒ 3,051
Clay; MCD-Township; DECATUR; *175 M-11; mail Greensburg z 47240; Ⓟ 1,413; Ⓒ 1,266
Clay; MCD-Township; HAMILTON; *174 I-9; ★ IND; mail Carmel z 46032-33; Ⓟ 43,007; Ⓒ 64,709
Clay; MCD-Township; HENDRICKS; *175 K-7; mail Coatesville z 46121; Ⓟ 1,992; Ⓒ 2,211
Clay; MCD-Township; HOWARD; *174 G-8; ★ KOK; mail Kokomo z 46901; Ⓟ 3,707; Ⓒ 4,042
Clay; MCD-Township; KOSCIUSKO; *174 D-10; mail Claypool z 46510; Ⓟ 1,625; Ⓒ 1,582
Clay; MCD-Township; LAGRANGE; *174 A-11; mail Lagrange z 46761; Ⓟ 2,485; Ⓒ 2,888
Clay; MCD-Township; MIAMI; *174 F-9; mail Bunker Hill z 46914; Ⓟ 847; Ⓒ 933
Clay; MCD-Township; MORGAN; *175 L-8; ★ IND; mail Martinsville z 46151; Ⓟ 3,745; Ⓒ 4,178
Clay; MCD-Township; OWEN; *175 M-6; mail Spencer z 47460; Ⓟ 1,931; Ⓒ 2,553
Clay; MCD-Township; PIKE; *175 Q-4; mail Hazleton z 47640; Ⓟ 358; Ⓒ 340
Clay; MCD-Township; SPENCER; *175 S-6; mail Lamar z 47550; Ⓟ 1,467; Ⓒ 2,494
Clay; MCD-Township; ST. JOSEPH; *174 A-8; ★ S.B.; mail South Bend z 46637; Ⓟ 31,033; Ⓒ 39,145; Ⓡ 37,981
Clay; MCD-Township; WAYNE; *174 J-13; mail Greens Fork z 47345; Ⓟ 1,042; Ⓒ 1,023
CLAY; 175 L-5; Ⓟ 24,705; Ⓒ 26,556; Ⓡ 26,567; ◆ 26,253
Clay City; Inc. Place; CLAY; 175 M-5; elev. 587ft./179m.; 🅿; z 47841; Ⓟ 929; Ⓒ 1,019
Clay City; RMC Place; SPENCER; *175 S-6; mail Lamar z 47550; rural
Claypool; Inc. Place; KOSCIUSKO; 174 D-10; elev. 890ft./271m.; 🅿; z 46510; Ⓟ 411; Ⓒ 311
Claysville; RMC Place; WASHINGTON; *175 P-8; elev. 714ft./218m.; mail Campbellsburg z 47108; ● 20
Clayton; Inc. Place; HENDRICKS; 175 K-7; elev. 872ft./266m.; 🅿; ★ IND; z 46118; Ⓟ 610; Ⓒ 693
Clear Creek; MCD-Township; HUNTINGTON; *174 D-11; mail Huntington z 46750; Ⓟ 1,306; Ⓒ 1,742
Clear Creek; RMC Place; MONROE; 175 N-7; elev. 657ft./200m.; 🅿; ★ BLMNG; z 47426; ● 1,200
Clear Creek; MCD-Township; MONROE; *175 N-7; 🅿; ★ BLMNG; z 47426 & mail Bloomington z 47401; Ⓟ 3,883; Ⓒ 4,164
Clear Creek Estates; RMC Place; MONROE; *175 N-7; ★ BLMNG; mail Bloomington z 47403; ● 100
Clear Lake; Inc. Place; STEUBEN; ▲ Clear Lake; 174 A-13; mail Fremont z 46737; Ⓟ 272; summer pop. 800; Ⓒ 244
Clear Lake; MCD-Township; STEUBEN; *174 A-14; mail Fremont z 46737; Ⓟ 635; Ⓒ 687
Clear Spring; RMC Place; JACKSON; 175 N-8; mail Brownstown z 47220; ● 75
Clearspring; MCD-Township; LAGRANGE; *174 A-11; mail Topeka z 46571; Ⓟ 3,248; Ⓒ 4,005
Clermont; Inc. Place; MARION; 173 J-15; elev. 833ft./254m.; 🅿; ★ IND; z 46234; Ⓒ 1,477; Ⓡ 1,483
Clermont Heights; RMC Place; HENDRICKS; *174 J-8; ★ IND; mail Brownsburg z 46112; ● 600
Cleveland; MCD-Township; ELKHART; *174 A-9; ★ ELK; mail Elkhart z 46514; Ⓟ 7,843; Ⓒ 9,729
Cleveland; RMC Place; HANCOCK; *174 J-11; mail Greenfield z 46140; ● 30
Cleveland; MCD-Township; WHITLEY; *174 D-11; mail South Whitley z 46787; Ⓟ 3,215; Ⓒ 3,463
Clifford; Inc. Place; BARTHOLOMEW; 175 M-10; elev. 662ft./202m.; 🅿; z 47226; Ⓟ 308; Ⓒ 291
Clifton; RMC Place; UNION; *175 K-13; mail Liberty z 47353; rural
Clifty; MCD-Township; BARTHOLOMEW; *175 M-10; mail Columbus z 47203; Ⓟ 1,003; Ⓒ 1,200
Clifty Village; RMC Place; BARTHOLOMEW; *175 M-10; ★ COL; mail Columbus z 47203; ● 60
Clinton; MCD-Township; BOONE; *174 I-8; mail Lebanon z 46052; Ⓟ 786; Ⓒ 892
Clinton; MCD-Township; CASS; *174 F-8; mail Logansport z 46947; Ⓟ 1,014; Ⓒ 504
Clinton; MCD-Township; DECATUR; *175 L-11; mail Greensburg z 47240; Ⓟ 494; Ⓒ 473
Clinton; MCD-Township; ELKHART; *174 A-10; ★ ELK; mail Goshen z 46528; Ⓟ 3,735; Ⓒ 4,153
Clinton; MCD-Township; LAPORTE; *174 B-6; mail Union Mills z 46382; Ⓟ 1,034; Ⓒ 4,454; Ⓡ 1,359
Clinton; MCD-Township; PUTNAM; *174 J-6; mail Greencastle z 46135; Ⓟ 989; Ⓒ 1,459
Clinton; Inc. Place; VERMILLION; ▲ Clinton; 175 K-4; 🅿 🅷; z 47842; Ⓟ 5,040; Ⓒ 5,126
Clinton; MCD-Township; VERMILLION; *175 K-4; 🅿; z 47842; Ⓟ 9,250; Ⓒ 9,544
CLINTON; 174 H-7; Ⓟ 30,974; Ⓒ 33,866; ◆ 33,503
Clinton Falls; RMC Place; PUTNAM; 175 K-6; mail Greencastle z 46135; ● 100
Cloud Crest Hills; RMC Place; BROWN; mail Nashville z 47448; ● 75
Cloverdale; Inc. Place; PUTNAM; ▲ Cloverdale; 175 L-6; 🅿; z 46120; Ⓟ 1,681; Ⓒ 2,243
Cloverdale; MCD-Township; PUTNAM; *175 L-6; 🅿; z 46120; Ⓟ 3,079; Ⓒ 3,847
Cloverland; RMC Place; CLAY; 175 L-5; ★ T.H.; mail Brazil z 47834; ● 100
Clover Village; RMC Place; SHELBY; *175 K-10; mail Fairland z 46126; ● 200
Clunette; RMC Place; KOSCIUSKO; 174 C-9; mail Leesburg z 46538; ● 75
Clymers; RMC Place; CASS; 174 F-8; mail Logansport z 46947; ● 120
Coal Bluff; RMC Place; VIGO; *175 K-5; ★ T.H.; mail Rosedale z 47874; ● 125
Coal City; RMC Place; OWEN; 175 M-5; elev. 658ft./201m.; 🅿; z 47427; ● 270
Coal Creek; RMC Place; FOUNTAIN; 174 I-4; mail Covington z 47932; ● 10
Coal Creek; MCD-Township; MONTGOMERY; *174 H-5; mail New Richmond z 47967, Wingate z 47994; Ⓟ 1,461; Ⓒ 1,541
Coalmont; RMC Place; CLAY; 175 M-5; elev. 630ft./192m.; 🅿; z 47845; ● 275
Coatesville; Inc. Place; HENDRICKS; 175 K-7; elev. 873ft./266m.; 🅿; z 46121; Ⓟ 469; Ⓒ 516
Cobbler's Crossing; RMC Place; FLOYD; *175 Q-10; ★ LOU; mail New Albany z 47150; ● 300
Cochran; RMC Place; DEARBORN; *175 N-13; ★ CIN; mail Aurora z 47001; pop. incl. with Aurora (Inc. Place)
Coe; RMC Place; PIKE; *175 R-4; mail Winslow z 47598
Coesse; RMC Place; WHITLEY; 174 D-12; mail Columbia City z 46725; ● 100
Coffey; RMC Place; BROWN; mail Nashville z 47448; ● 60
Colburn; RMC Place; ST. JOSEPH; *174 B-8; ★ S.B.; mail Lakeville z 46536; ● 120
Colburn; RMC Place; TIPPECANOE; 174 G-7; elev. 662ft./202m.; 🅿; ★ LAF-; z 47905; ● 200
Cold Springs; RMC Place; DEARBORN; *175 N-13; ★ CIN; mail Moores Hill z 47032; rural
Cold Springs; RMC Place; STEUBEN; *174 A-13; mail Hamilton z 46742; ● 180
Colfax; Inc. Place; CLINTON; 174 H-7; elev. 845ft./258m.; 🅿; z 46035; Ⓟ 727; Ⓒ 768
Colfax; MCD-Township; NEWTON; *174 D-4; mail Lake Village z 46349; Ⓟ 197; Ⓒ 176
Collamer; RMC Place; WHITLEY; 174 D-10; mail South Whitley z 46787; ● 50
College Corner; RMC Place; JAY; *174 G-13; mail Portland z 47371
College Meadows; RMC Place; HAMILTON; *174 I-9; ★ IND; mail Indianapolis z 46280; ● 1,500
Collegeville; CDP; JASPER; 174 E-5; elev. 658ft./201m.; 🅿; z 47978; Ⓟ 993; Ⓒ 865
Collett; RMC Place; JAY; *174 G-13; mail Portland z 47371
Collins; RMC Place; WHITLEY; 174 C-12; mail Columbia City z 46725; ● 60
Coloma; RMC Place; PARKE; 174 J-4; mail Rockville z 47872; ● 80
Colonial Park; RMC Place; VIGO; *175 L-4; ★ T.H.; mail Terre Haute z 47802; ● 230
Colonial Village; RMC Place; HANCOCK; *174 I-10; ★ IND; mail Fortville z 46040; pop. incl. with Fortville (Inc. Place)
Columbia; MCD-Township; DUBOIS; *175 Q-6; mail Dubois z 47527; Ⓟ 952; Ⓒ 885
Columbia; RMC Place; FAYETTE; *175 K-12; mail Connersville z 47331; ● 40
Columbia; MCD-Township; FAYETTE; *175 K-12; mail Connersville z 47331; Ⓟ 1,128; Ⓒ 1,068
Columbia; MCD-Township; GIBSON; *175 Q-4; mail Oakland City z 47660; Ⓟ 4,244; Ⓒ 4,149
Columbia; MCD-Township; JENNINGS; *175 N-11; mail North Vernon z 47265; Ⓟ 813; Ⓒ 759
Columbia; MCD-Township; WHITLEY; *174 D-11; mail Columbia City z 46725; Ⓟ 8,134; Ⓒ 9,582
Columbia City; Inc. Place; ⊡ WHITLEY; 174 C-11; elev. 861ft./262m.; 🅿 🅷; z 46725; Ⓟ 5,706; Ⓒ 7,077
Columbus; Inc. Place; ⊡ BARTHOLOMEW; ▲ Columbus; 175 M-9; 🅿 🅷 ■; ★ COL; z 47201-03; Ⓟ 31,802; Ⓒ 39,059; ◆ 40,853
Columbus; MCD-Township; BARTHOLOMEW; *175 M-9; 🅿; ★ COL; z 47201-03; includes part of the City of Columbus; Ⓟ 37,466; Ⓒ 41,194
Commiskey; RMC Place; JENNINGS; 175 O-11; elev. 693ft./211m.; 🅿; z 47227; ● 100
Como; RMC Place; JAY; *174 G-13; mail Portland z 47371
Concord; RMC Place; DE KALB; ▲ Concord; *174 C-13; mail Auburn z 46706
Concord; MCD-Township; DE KALB; *174 C-13; mail Saint Joe z 46785; Ⓟ 1,166; Ⓒ 1,212
Concord; MCD-Township; ELKHART; *174 A-9; ★ ELK; mail Elkhart z 46517; Ⓟ 49,126; Ⓒ 55,377
Concord; RMC Place; TIPPECANOE; *174 H-6; mail Lafayette z 47905
Concordia Gardens; RMC Place; ALLEN; *174 D-13; ★ FTWA; mail Fort Wayne z 46825; pop. incl. with Fort Wayne (Inc. Place)
Connersville; Inc. Place; ⊡ FAYETTE; 175 K-13; elev. 835ft./255m.; 🅿 🅷; z 47331; Ⓟ 15,550; Ⓒ 15,411
Connersville; MCD-Township; FAYETTE; *175 K-12; 🅿; z 47331; includes part of the City of Connersville; Ⓟ 13,421; Ⓒ 13,163
Continental Camp; RMC Place; POSEY; *175 R-2; elev. 400ft./122m.; mail Griffin z 47616; rural
Converse; Inc. Place; MIAMI, GRANT; 174 F-10; elev. 832ft./254m.; 🅿; z 46919; Ⓟ 1,144; Ⓒ 1,137
Cook; RMC Place; LAKE; *174 B-4; ★ CHI; mail Cedar Lake z 46303; pop. incl. with Cedar Lake (Inc. Place)
Cook Acres; RMC Place; DELAWARE; *174 H-12; ★ MUN; mail Muncie z 47303; ● 150
Coolspring; MCD-Township; LAPORTE; *174 A-6; ★ MICH; mail Michigan City z 46360; Ⓟ 14,492; Ⓒ 14,910
Coolwood Acres; RMC Place; PORTER; *174 B-5; ★ CHI; mail Valparaiso z 46385; ● 100
Cope; RMC Place; MORGAN; *175 L-8; elev. 751ft./229m.; ★ IND; mail Martinsville z 46151
Copperfield; RMC Place; VANDERBURGH; *175 S-3; ★ EV; mail Evansville z 47711; ● 250
Cordry Lake; RMC Place; BROWN; *175 M-9; mail Nineveh z 46164; ● 350
Cornettsville; RMC Place; DAVIESS; 175 O-5; elev. 492ft./150m.; mail Plainville z 47568; ● 20
Correct; RMC Place; RIPLEY; *175 N-12; mail Versailles z 47042; rural
Cortland; RMC Place; JACKSON; 175 N-9; elev. 565ft./172m.; 🅿; z 47228; ● 175
Corunna; Inc. Place; DE KALB; 174 B-12; elev. 980ft./299m.; 🅿; z 46730; Ⓟ 241; Ⓒ 254
Cory; RMC Place; CLAY; 175 L-5; elev. 621ft./189m.; 🅿; z 47846; ● 135
Corydon; Inc. Place; ⊡ HARRISON; 175 R-9; elev. 549ft./167m.; 🅿 🅷; ★ LOU; z 47112; Ⓟ 2,661; Ⓒ 2,715
Corydon Junction; HARRISON; see New Salisbury (RMC Place)
Cosperville; RMC Place; NOBLE; *174 B-11; mail Wawaka z 46794; ● 60
Cottage Grove; RMC Place; UNION; *175 K-14; mail Liberty z 47353; ● 80
Cotton; MCD-Township; SWITZERLAND; *175 O-13; mail Vevay z 47043; Ⓟ 1,214; Ⓒ 1,476
Country Charm; RMC Place; TIPPECANOE; *174 G-6; ★ LAF-; mail Lafayette z 47905; pop. incl. with Lafayette (Inc. Place)
Country Club Gardens; RMC Place; ALLEN; *174 D-12; ★ FTWA; mail Fort Wayne z 46804; ● 900
Country Club Heights; Inc. Place; MADISON; 174 D-2; elev. 860ft./262m.; ★ AND; mail Anderson z 46011; Ⓟ 112; Ⓒ 91
Country Club Meadows; RMC Place; VANDERBURGH; *175 S-3; elev. 400ft./122m.; ★ EV; mail Evansville z 47710; pop. incl. with Evansville (Inc. Place)
Countryside Estates; RMC Place; ALLEN; *174 D-13; ★ FTWA; mail Fort Wayne z 46815; pop. incl. with Fort Wayne (Inc. Place)
Country Terrace; RMC Place; DELAWARE; *174 H-12; ★ MUN; mail Muncie z 47303; ● 300
Country Trace; RMC Place; VANDERBURGH; *175 S-3; ★ EV; mail Evansville z 47715; ● 100
Country View; RMC Place; TIPPECANOE; *174 G-6; ★ LAF-; mail Lafayette z 47905; ● 300
Country Village; RMC Place; DELAWARE; *174 H-11; elev. 920ft./280m.; ★ MUN; mail Muncie z 47303; ● 1,100
Courter; RMC Place; MIAMI; *174 E-9; mail Peru z 46970; ● 40
Coveyville; RMC Place; LAWRENCE; *175 N-7; ★ BLMNG; mail Bedford z 47421
Covington; Inc. Place; ⊡ FOUNTAIN; 174 H-4; elev. 563ft./172m.; 🅿; z 47932; Ⓟ 2,747; Ⓒ 2,565
Covington Dells; RMC Place; ALLEN; *174 D-12; ★ FTWA; mail Fort Wayne z 46804; ● 300
Cowan; RMC Place; DELAWARE; 174 I-12; ★ MUN; mail Muncie z 47302; ● 250
Coxton; RMC Place; LAWRENCE; *175 O-7; mail Bedford z 47421; rural
Coxville; RMC Place; PARKE; *175 K-4; mail Rosedale z 47874; ● 30
Craig; MCD-Township; SWITZERLAND; *175 O-13; mail Vevay z 47043; Ⓟ 695; Ⓒ 777
Craigville; RMC Place; WELLS; 174 E-13; elev. 850ft./259m.; 🅿; z 46731; ● 135
Crandall; Inc. Place; HARRISON; 175 R-9; elev. 659ft./201m.; 🅿; ★ LOU; z 47114; Ⓟ 147; Ⓒ 131
Crane; MARTIN; see Burns City (RMC Place)
Crane; Inc. Place; MARTIN; 175 O-6; elev. 614ft./187m.; 🅿; z 47522; Ⓟ 216; Ⓒ 203
CRAWFORD; 175 R-8; Ⓟ 9,914; Ⓒ 10,743; ◆ 10,499
Crawfordsville; Inc. Place; ⊡ MONTGOMERY; 174 I-6; elev. 769ft./234m.; 🅿 🅷 🅲 878 ■; z 47933-39; Ⓟ 13,584; Ⓒ 15,243; ◆ 15,356
Cree Lake; RMC Place; NOBLE; *174 B-12; mail Kendallville z 46755; ● 275
Crest Manor; RMC Place; ST. JOSEPH; *174 A-8; ★ S.B.; mail South Bend z 46614; pop. incl. with South Bend (Inc. Place)
Crestmoor; RMC Place; SHELBY; *175 L-10; elev. 790ft./241m.; mail Shelbyville z 46176; pop. incl. with Shelbyville (Inc. Place)
Creston; RMC Place; DELAWARE; *174 H-12; ★ MUN; mail Muncie z 47303; pop. incl. with Muncie (Inc. Place)
Creston; RMC Place; LAKE; 174 C-4; mail Lowell z 46356; ● 80
Crestview; RMC Place; FLOYD; *175 R-10; ★ LOU; mail New Albany z 47150; pop. incl. with New Albany (Inc. Place)
Crestwood; RMC Place; ALLEN; *174 D-12; elev. 800ft./244m.; ★ FTWA; mail Fort Wayne z 46825; pop. incl. with Fort Wayne (Inc. Place)
Crete; RMC Place; RANDOLPH; *174 I-14; mail Lynn z 47355; rural
Crisman; RMC Place; PORTER; *174 A-5; ★ CHI; pop. incl. with Portage (Inc. Place)
Critchfield; RMC Place; JOHNSON; *175 K-9; ★ IND; mail Greenwood z 46143; ● 350
Crocker; RMC Place; PORTER; *174 A-5; ★ CHI; mail Valparaiso z 46383; pop. incl. with Portage (Inc. Place)
Crompton Hill; RMC Place; VERMILLION; *175 K-4; mail Clinton z 47842; pop. incl. with Clinton (Inc. Place)
Cromwell; Inc. Place; NOBLE; 174 B-11; elev. 953ft./290m.; 🅿; z 46732; Ⓟ 520; Ⓒ 452
Crooked Lake; RMC Place; STEUBEN; 174 A-13; mail Angola z 46703; summer pop. 600; ● 300
Crooked Lake; RMC Place; WHITLEY; *174 C-11; mail Columbia City z 46725
Cross Plains; RMC Place; RIPLEY; 175 N-12; elev. 963ft./294m.; 🅿; z 47017; ● 150
Crothersville; Inc. Place; JACKSON; 175 O-10; elev. 563ft./172m.; 🅿; z 47229; Ⓟ 1,687; Ⓒ 1,570
Crown Center; RMC Place; MORGAN; 175 K-7; ★ IND; mail Monrovia z 46157; ● 30
Crown Colony; RMC Place; ALLEN; *174 D-13; ★ FTWA; mail Fort Wayne z 46816; pop. incl. with Fort Wayne (Inc. Place)
Crown Point; Inc. Place; ⊡ LAKE; 174 B-4; elev. 735ft./224m.; 🅿 🅷; ★ CHI; z 46307-08; Ⓟ 17,728; Ⓒ 19,806; ◆ 21,012
Crows Nest; Inc. Place; MARION; *174 J-9; ★ IND; mail Indianapolis z 46228; Ⓒ 96
Crump Estates; RMC Place; BARTHOLOMEW; *175 M-10; ★ COL; mail Columbus z 47203; pop. incl. with Columbus (Inc. Place)
Crumstown; RMC Place; ST. JOSEPH; 174 A-8; ★ S.B.; mail North Liberty z 46554; ● 120
Crystal; RMC Place; DUBOIS; 175 Q-6; elev. 501ft./153m.; mail Dubois z 47527; ● 100
Cuba; RMC Place; ALLEN; *174 C-13; mail Grabill z 46741; ● 40
Cuba; RMC Place; BARTHOLOMEW; *175 L-9; ★ COL; mail Edinburgh z 46124; pop. incl. with Edinburgh (Inc. Place)
Cuba; RMC Place; OWEN; 175 L-6; mail Spencer z 47460; ● 15
Culver; Inc. Place; MARSHALL; 174 C-8; elev. 754ft./230m.; 🅿; z 46511; Ⓟ 1,404; Ⓒ 1,539
Cumback; RMC Place; DAVIESS; *175 P-5; elev. 465ft./142m.; mail Washington z 47501; rural
Cumberland; Inc. Place; MARION, HANCOCK; *174 J-9; elev. 838ft./255m.; 🅿; ★ IND; z 46229; Ⓒ 5,500
Cunot; RMC Place; OWEN; 175 L-6; mail Cloverdale z 46120; ● 100
Curby; RMC Place; CRAWFORD; *175 R-8; mail English z 47118
Curry; MCD-Township; SULLIVAN; *175 M-4; mail Shelburn z 47879; Ⓟ 3,633; Ⓒ 3,769
Curryville; RMC Place; SULLIVAN; *175 M-4; mail Shelburn z 47879; ● 20
Curryville; RMC Place; WELLS; *174 E-13; mail Craigville z 46731
Curtis; RMC Place; LAKE; ★ CHI; pop. incl. with Gary (Inc. Place)
Curtisville; RMC Place; TIPTON; 174 H-10; mail Elwood z 46036; ● 150
Cutler; RMC Place; CARROLL; 174 G-7; elev. 745ft./227m.; 🅿; z 46920; ● 125
Cuzco; RMC Place; DUBOIS; 175 Q-6; mail French Lick z 47432; ● 50
Cyclone; RMC Place; CLINTON; 174 H-8; mail Frankfort z 46041; ● 20
Cynthiana; Inc. Place; POSEY; 175 R-3; elev. 441ft./134m.; 🅿; z 47612; Ⓟ 669; Ⓒ 693
Cypress; RMC Place; VANDERBURGH; *175 S-3; ★ EV; mail Evansville z 47712; rural

D

Dabney; RMC Place; RIPLEY; 175 N-12; mail Holton z 47023; ● 50
Daggett; RMC Place; OWEN; *175 M-5; mail Coal City z 47427; rural
Daisy Hill; RMC Place; WASHINGTON; *175 Q-9; mail Borden z 47106; rural
Dale; Inc. Place; SPENCER; 175 R-5; elev. 470ft./143m.; 🅿; z 47523; Ⓟ 1,553; Ⓒ 1,568
Daleville; Inc. Place; DELAWARE; 174 I-11; elev. 912ft./278m.; 🅿; ★ AND; z 47334; Ⓟ 1,681; Ⓒ 1,658
Dallas; MCD-Township; HUNTINGTON; *174 E-11; mail Andrews z 46702; Ⓟ 1,982; Ⓒ 2,243
Dallas Lake; RMC Place; LAGRANGE; *174 B-11; mail Wolcottville z 46795; summer pop. 500; ● 200
Dalton; RMC Place; WAYNE; ▲ Dalton; 174 I-12; mail Hagerstown z 47346; ● 40
Dalton; MCD-Township; WAYNE; *174 I-12; mail Hagerstown z 47346; Ⓟ 580; Ⓒ 588

Entries in **UPPERCASE** are counties.
Entries in **bold** have populations of 2,500 or more.
Names in parentheses are alternate names.
Inc. Place — Incorporated Place
RMC Place — Rand McNally Designated Place
CDP — Census Designated Place
MCD — Minor Civil Division

⊡ County Seat
▲ Minor Civil Division
elev. Elevation
🅿 Post Office
🅷 Hospital
🅲 College
■ Principal Business Center
★ Ranally Metro Area (RMA) Abbreviation
z Zip Code(s)

Ⓟ Previous Census Population
Ⓡ Revised Census Population
Ⓐ Annexation Population
● Rand McNally Population Estimate
Ⓒ Final Census Population
Ⓢ Special Census Population
◆ Estimated Population

For additional definitions see Glossary, Volume 1, and Introduction, Volume 2.

Dana; Inc. Place; VERMILLION; 174 J-4; elev. 640ft./195m.; 🅿; z 47847; Ⓟ 612; Ⓒ 662
Danville; Inc. Place; ⊡ HENDRICKS; 174 J-7; elev. 954ft./291m.; 🅿 🅷; ★ IND; z 46122; Ⓟ 4,345; Ⓒ 6,418
Darlington; Inc. Place; MONTGOMERY; 174 I-6; elev. 765ft./233m.; 🅿; z 47940; Ⓟ 740; Ⓒ 854
Darmstadt; Inc. Place; VANDERBURGH; 175 S-3; elev. 483ft./147m.; ★ EV; mail Evansville z 47711, z 47725; Ⓟ 1,346; Ⓒ 1,313
Darrough Chapel; RMC Place; HOWARD; *174 G-9; ★ KOK; mail Kokomo z 46901; ● 300
DAVIESS; 175 P-5; Ⓟ 27,533; Ⓒ 29,820; ◆ 30,110
Davis; MCD-Township; FOUNTAIN; *174 H-5; mail Attica z 47918; Ⓟ 527; Ⓒ 635
Davis; RMC Place; LAPORTE; *174 A-6; ★ MICH; mail Michigan City z 46360; pop. incl. with Michigan City (Inc. Place)
Davis; MCD-Township; STARKE; *174 B-7; mail Hamlet z 46532; Ⓟ 1,170; Ⓒ 1,142
Daylight; RMC Place; VANDERBURGH; 175 S-3; elev. 397ft./121m.; ★ EV; mail Evansville z 47711, z 47725; ● 200
Dayton; Inc. Place; TIPPECANOE; 174 G-6; elev. 673ft./205m.; 🅿; z 47941; Ⓟ 996; Ⓒ 1,120
Dayville; RMC Place; WARRICK; *175 S-4; elev. 392ft./119m.; mail Newburgh z 47630
Deacon; RMC Place; CASS; *174 F-8; mail Walton z 46994
DEARBORN; 175 M-13; Ⓟ 38,835; Ⓒ 46,109; Ⓡ 46,130; ◆ 50,252
De Camp Gardens; RMC Place; ELKHART; *174 A-10; elev. 745ft./227m.; ★ ELK; mail Elkhart z 46516; ● 150
Decatur; Inc. Place; ⊡ ADAMS; 174 E-13; elev. 807ft./246m.; 🅿 🅷; z 46733; Ⓟ 8,644; Ⓒ 9,528
Decatur; MCD-Township; MARION; *175 K-8; ★ IND; mail Indianapolis z 46221, z 46241; Ⓟ 21,092; Ⓒ 24,726
DECATUR; 175 L-11; Ⓟ 23,645; Ⓒ 24,555; ◆ 24,736
Decker; Inc. Place; KNOX; 175 P-3; elev. 502ft./153m.; 🅿; z 47524; Ⓟ 281; Ⓒ 283
Decker; MCD-Township; KNOX; *175 Q-3; 🅿; z 47524; does not include the Town of Decker; Ⓟ 251; Ⓒ 242
Deeds; MIAMI; see Deedsville (RMC Place)
Deedsville (Deeds); RMC Place; MIAMI; 174 E-9; elev. 834ft./254m.; 🅿; z 46921; ● 95
Deep River; RMC Place; LAKE; *174 B-5; ★ CHI; mail Hobart z 46342; pop. incl. with Merrillville (Inc. Place)
Deer Creek; RMC Place; CARROLL; 174 F-8; mail Camden z 46917; ● 160
Deer Creek; MCD-Township; CARROLL; *174 F-7; mail Camden z 46917, Delphi z 46923; Ⓟ 4,258; Ⓒ 4,768
Deer Creek; MCD-Township; CASS; *174 F-8; mail Galveston z 46932; Ⓟ 925; Ⓒ 972
Deer Creek; MCD-Township; MIAMI; *174 F-9; mail Miami z 46959; Ⓟ 1,656; Ⓒ 1,729
Deerfield; RMC Place; RANDOLPH; 174 H-13; mail Ridgeville z 47380; ● 50
Deerfield; RMC Place; VIGO; *175 L-4; ★ T.H.; mail Terre Haute z 47802; ● 200
Deers Mills; RMC Place; MONTGOMERY; *174 I-5; mail Waveland z 47989; rural
De Fries Landing; RMC Place; KOSCIUSKO; *174 B-10; mail Leesburg z 46538; ● 50
De Gonia; RMC Place; WARRICK; 175 S-5; mail Boonville z 47601; ● 40
DE KALB; 174 B-13; Ⓟ 35,324; Ⓒ 40,285; ◆ 42,021
Delaware; MCD-Township; DELAWARE; *174 H-12; ★ MUN; mail Albany z 47320; Ⓟ 3,781; Ⓒ 3,797
Delaware; MCD-Township; HAMILTON; *174 I-9; ★ IND; mail Noblesville z 46060; Ⓟ 10,524; Ⓒ 28,268
Delaware; RMC Place; RIPLEY; ▲ Delaware; 175 M-12; mail Osgood z 47037; ● 150
Delaware; MCD-Township; RIPLEY; *175 M-12; mail Osgood z 47037; Ⓟ 1,250; Ⓒ 1,298
DELAWARE; 174 H-12; Ⓟ 119,659; Ⓒ 118,769; ◆ 116,519
Delong; RMC Place; FULTON; 174 D-8; elev. 742ft./226m.; 🅿; z 46922; ● 140
Delp; RMC Place; TIPPECANOE; 174 G-6; ★ LAF-; mail Lafayette z 47905; ● 100
Delphi; Inc. Place; ⊡ CARROLL; 174 F-7; elev. 580ft./177m.; 🅿; z 46923; Ⓟ 2,531; Ⓒ 3,015
Deming; RMC Place; HAMILTON; *174 I-9; ★ IND; mail Cicero z 46034
Deming Woods; RMC Place; VIGO; *175 L-4; ★ T.H.; mail Terre Haute z 47803; pop. incl. with Terre Haute (Inc. Place)
Democrat; MCD-Township; CARROLL; *174 G-7; mail Cutler z 46920; Ⓟ 809; Ⓒ 881
Demotte; Inc. Place; JASPER; 174 C-5; elev. 688ft./210m.; 🅿; z 46310; Ⓟ 2,482; Ⓒ 3,234
Denham; RMC Place; PULASKI; 174 C-7; elev. 710ft./216m.; 🅿; z 46996; ● 150
Denmark; RMC Place; OWEN; *175 M-5; mail Coal City z 47427
Denver; Inc. Place; MIAMI; 174 E-9; elev. 709ft./216m.; 🅿; z 46926; Ⓟ 504; Ⓒ 541
Depauw; RMC Place; HARRISON; 175 Q-8; elev. 652ft./199m.; 🅿; z 47115; ● 120
Deputy; RMC Place; JEFFERSON; 175 O-11; elev. 611ft./186m.; 🅿; z 47230; ● 250
Derby; RMC Place; PERRY; 175 S-7; elev. 409ft./125m.; 🅿; z 47525; ● 100
Desoto; RMC Place; DELAWARE; 174 H-12; elev. 957ft./292m.; ★ MUN; mail Muncie z 47303; ● 180
Devonshire; RMC Place; MARION; *174 J-9; ★ IND; mail Indianapolis z 46220; pop. incl. with Indianapolis (Inc. Place)
Dewey; MCD-Civil Township; LAPORTE; *174 C-6; mail La Crosse z 46348; Ⓟ 1,179; Ⓒ 970
Diamond; RMC Place; PARKE; 175 K-5; mail Rosedale z 47874; ● 120
Diamond Lake; RMC Place; KOSCIUSKO; *174 D-9; mail Silver Lake z 46982; ● 50
Diamond Lake; RMC Place; NOBLE; *174 B-11; mail Wawaka z 46794; ● 100
Diamond Valley; RMC Place; VANDERBURGH; ★ EV; mail Evansville z 47710-11, z 47724; pop. incl. with Evansville (Inc. Place)
Dick Johnson; MCD-Township; CLAY; *175 K-5; mail Brazil z 47834; Ⓟ 1,147; Ⓒ 1,338
Dillman; RMC Place; WELLS; 174 F-11; mail Warren z 46792; ● 25
Dillsboro; Inc. Place; DEARBORN; 175 N-13; elev. 868ft./265m.; 🅿; ★ CIN; z 47018; Ⓟ 1,200; Ⓒ 1,436
Diplomat; RMC Place; ALLEN; *174 D-13; ★ FTWA; mail Fort Wayne z 46806, z 46816, z 46896; pop. incl. with Fort Wayne (Inc. Place)
Disko; RMC Place; FULTON, WABASH; 174 D-9; mail Silver Lake z 46982; ● 80
Dixon; RMC Place; ALLEN; 174 D-14; mail Convoy z 45832, Monroeville z 46773; total pop. including Dixon, OH...200; ● 100
Doans; RMC Place; GREENE; *175 N-6; mail Bloomfield z 47424
Dodd; RMC Place; PERRY; *175 S-7; mail Cannelton z 47520
Dodds Bridge; RMC Place; SULLIVAN; *175 M-3; mail Fairbanks z 47849; rural
Dogwood; RMC Place; HARRISON; 175 S-9; elev. 664ft./202m.; mail Laconia z 47135; ● 30
Dolan; RMC Place; MONROE; 175 M-7; ★ BLMNG; mail Bloomington z 47401, z 47408; ● 50
Domestic; RMC Place; WELLS; *174 F-13; mail Bluffton z 46714
Donaldson; RMC Place; MARSHALL; 174 B-8; elev. 784ft./239m.; 🅿; z 46513; ● 125
Dongola; RMC Place; GIBSON; *175 Q-4; mail Oakland City z 47660; rural
Doolittle Mills; RMC Place; PERRY; *175 R-7; mail English z 47118
Door Village; RMC Place; LAPORTE; *174 A-6; elev. 810ft./247m.; ★ MICH; mail La Porte z 46350; ● 150
Dover; RMC Place; BOONE; 174 I-7; mail Lebanon z 46052; ● 60
Dover; RMC Place; DEARBORN; ▲ Kelso; *175 M-13; ★ CIN; mail Guilford z 47022; ● 100
Dover Hill; RMC Place; MARTIN; 175 O-6; mail Shoals z 47581; ● 110
Dovers View; RMC Place; TIPTON; *174 H-9; mail Tipton z 46072; ● 200
Dowden Acres; RMC Place; VIGO; *175 L-4; ★ T.H.; mail Terre Haute z 47802; ● 150
Downeyville; RMC Place; DECATUR; *175 L-11; mail Saint Paul z 47272; ● 20
Downtown; RMC Place; DELAWARE; *174 H-12; ★ MUN; mail Muncie z 47305, z 47308; pop. incl. with Muncie (Inc. Place)
Downtown; RMC Place; LAKE; *174 A-4; ★ CHI; mail Gary z 46402; pop. incl. with Gary (Inc. Place)
Downtown; RMC Place; PORTER; ★ CHI; mail Valparaiso z 46383; pop. incl. with Valparaiso (Inc. Place)
Downtown; RMC Place; TIPPECANOE; *174 G-6; ★ LAF-; mail Lafayette z 47901-02; pop. incl. with Lafayette (Inc. Place)
Dresden; RMC Place; GREENE; mail Owensburg z 47453; rural
Dresser; VIGO; see Taylorville (RMC Place)
Drexel Gardens; RMC Place; MARION; *174 J-8; ★ IND; mail Indianapolis z 46241; pop. incl. with Indianapolis (Inc. Place)
Driftwood; MCD-Township; JACKSON; *175 O-9; mail Vallonia z 47281; Ⓟ 959; Ⓒ 836
Dublin; Inc. Place; WAYNE; 174 J-12; elev. 1,050ft./320m.; 🅿; z 47335; Ⓟ 805; Ⓒ 697
Dubois; RMC Place; DUBOIS; 175 Q-6; elev. 500ft./152m.; 🅿; z 47527; ● 600
DUBOIS; 175 Q-6; Ⓟ 36,616; Ⓒ 39,674; ◆ 41,349
Dubois Crossroads; RMC Place; DUBOIS; *175 Q-6; mail Dubois z 47527; ● 50
Duck Creek; MCD-Township; MADISON; *174 H-10; mail Elwood z 46036; Ⓟ 547; Ⓒ 542
Dudley; MCD-Township; HENRY; *174 J-12; mail Straughn z 47387; Ⓟ 1,300; Ⓒ 996
Dudleytown; RMC Place; JACKSON; 175 O-10; mail Seymour z 47274; ● 60
Duff; RMC Place; DUBOIS; *175 Q-5; mail Huntingburg z 47542; ● 50
Dugger; Inc. Place; SULLIVAN; 175 N-4; elev. 600ft./183m.; 🅿; z 47848; Ⓟ 936; Ⓒ 955
Dundee; RMC Place; MADISON; *174 H-10; ★ AND; mail Alexandria z 46001; ● 90
Dune Acres; Inc. Place; PORTER; 174 A-5; elev. 650ft./198m.; 🅿; ★ CHI; z 46304; Ⓟ 263; Ⓒ 213
Duneland Beach; RMC Place; LAPORTE; *174 A-6; ★ MICH; mail Michigan City z 46360; ● 450
Dunfee; RMC Place; ALLEN, WHITLEY; 174 D-12; ★ FTWA; mail Fort Wayne z 46814; ● 40
Dunkirk; RMC Place; CASS; *174 E-8; mail Logansport z 46947
Dunkirk; Inc. Place; JAY, BLACKFORD; 174 G-12; elev. 954ft./291m.; 🅿; z 47336; Ⓟ 2,739; Ⓒ 2,646
Dunlap; CDP; ELKHART; 174 A-10; ★ ELK; mail Elkhart z 46516-17; Ⓟ 5,705; Ⓒ 5,887
Dunlapsville; RMC Place; UNION; 175 K-13; mail Liberty z 47353; ● 45
Dunn; RMC Place; BENTON; *174 F-4; elev. 796ft./243m.; mail Fowler z 47944; rural
Dunnington; RMC Place; BENTON; 174 F-4; mail Fowler z 47944; ● 30
Dunns Bridge; RMC Place; JASPER; 174 C-6; mail Tefft z 46380; ● 70
Dunreith; Inc. Place; HENRY; 174 J-11; elev. 1,036ft./316m.; 🅿; z 47337; Ⓟ 205; Ⓒ 184
Dupont; Inc. Place; JEFFERSON; 175 O-11; elev. 783ft./239m.; 🅿; z 47231; Ⓟ 391; Ⓒ 392
Durbin; RMC Place; HAMILTON; *174 I-10; mail Noblesville z 46060
Dyer; Inc. Place; LAKE; 174 B-4; elev. 635ft./194m.; 🅿; ★ CHI; z 46311, z 46373; Ⓟ 10,923; Ⓒ 13,895

E

Eagle; MCD-Township; BOONE; *174 I-8; ★ IND; mail Zionsville z 46077; Ⓟ 9,864; Ⓒ 13,910
Eagle Creek; MCD-Township; LAKE; *174 C-4; mail Hebron z 46341; Ⓟ 1,431; Ⓒ 1,695
Eagle Creek; RMC Place; MARION; 🅿; ★ IND; z 46214, z 46253-54; pop. incl. with Indianapolis (Inc. Place)
Eagle Hollow; RMC Place; JEFFERSON; *175 O-12; mail Madison z 47250; rural
Eagletown; RMC Place; HAMILTON; 174 I-9; ★ IND; mail Westfield z 46074; ● 300
Eagle Village; RMC Place; BOONE; 174 I-8; ★ IND; mail Zionsville z 46077; ● 120
Eaglewood Estates; RMC Place; BOONE; *174 I-8; ★ IND; mail Zionsville z 46077; ● 100
Earle; RMC Place; VANDERBURGH; *175 S-3; elev. 449ft./137m.; ★ EV; mail Evansville z 47711; ● 50
Earlham; RMC Place; WAYNE; *174 J-13; ★ RICH; mail Richmond z 47374; pop. incl. with Richmond (Inc. Place)
Earl Park; Inc. Place; BENTON; 174 F-4; elev. 800ft./244m.; 🅿; z 47942; Ⓟ 443; Ⓒ 485
East Cedar Lake; RMC Place; LAKE; *174 B-4; elev. 700ft./213m.; ★ CHI; mail Cedar Lake z 46303; pop. incl. with Cedar Lake (Inc. Place)
East Chicago; Inc. Place; LAKE; 174 A-4; elev. 594ft./181m.; 🅿 🅷 ■; ★ CHI; z 46312; Ⓟ 33,892; Ⓒ 32,414; ◆ 31,212
East Clifford; RMC Place; BARTHOLOMEW; *175 M-10; mail Columbus z 47203; ● 120
East Columbus; RMC Place; BARTHOLOMEW; *175 M-10; ★ COL; mail Columbus z 47201; pop. incl. with Columbus (Inc. Place)
East Enterprise; RMC Place; SWITZERLAND; 175 O-13; elev. 880ft./268m.; 🅿; z 47019; ● 250
Eastern Heights; RMC Place; MONROE; *175 M-7; ★ BLMNG; mail Bloomington z 47401, z 47408; pop. incl. with Bloomington (Inc. Place)
East Gary; LAKE; see Lake Station (Inc. Place)
Eastgate; RMC Place; BARTHOLOMEW; *175 M-10; ★ COL; mail Columbus z 47203; pop. incl. with Columbus (Inc. Place)
Eastgate; RMC Place; CLARK; *175 Q-10; ★ LOU; mail Jeffersonville z 47130; pop. incl. with Jeffersonville (Inc. Place)
Eastgate; RMC Place; HANCOCK; *174 J-10; ★ IND; mail Fortville z 46040; ● 60
Eastgate; RMC Place; MARION; *174 J-9; ★ IND; mail Indianapolis z 46219; pop. incl. with Indianapolis (Inc. Place)
East Germantown (Pershing); Inc. Place; WAYNE; *174 J-13; mail Pershing z 47370; Ⓟ 372; Ⓒ 243
East Glenn; RMC Place; VIGO; *175 L-4; elev. 572ft./174m.; ★ T.H.; mail Terre Haute z 47803; ● 200
East Lake Estates; RMC Place; ELKHART; *174 A-9; ★ ELK; mail Elkhart z 46514; pop. incl. with Elkhart (Inc. Place)
Eastland Gardens; RMC Place; ALLEN; *174 D-13; ★ FTWA; mail Fort Wayne z 46816; pop. incl. with Fort Wayne (Inc. Place)
East Monticello; RMC Place; WHITE; *174 E-6; mail Monticello z 47960; ● 250
East Mount Carmel; RMC Place; GIBSON; *175 Q-2; mail Owensville z 47665
East Oolitic; RMC Place; LAWRENCE; *175 O-7; ★ BLMNG; mail Bedford z 47421; ● 225
Eastridge Manor; RMC Place; BARTHOLOMEW; *175 M-10; ★ COL; mail Columbus z 47203; pop. incl. with Columbus (Inc. Place)
East Shelburn; RMC Place; SULLIVAN; *175 M-4; mail Shelburn z 47879; ● 40
East Shoals; RMC Place; MARTIN; mail Shoals z 47581; pop. incl. with Shoals (Inc. Place)
East Union; RMC Place; TIPTON, HAMILTON; *174 H-9; mail Atlanta z 46031; rural
Eastwich; RMC Place; TIPPECANOE; *174 G-6; ★ LAF-; mail Lafayette z 47905; pop. incl. with Lafayette (Inc. Place)
Eastwood; RMC Place; MADISON; *174 I-11; ★ AND; mail Anderson z 46017; ● 600
Eaton; Inc. Place; DELAWARE; 174 H-12; elev. 914ft./279m.; 🅿; ★ MUN; z 47338; Ⓟ 1,614; Ⓒ 1,603
Echo Crest; RMC Place; HAMILTON; *174 I-9; ★ IND; mail Indianapolis z 46280
Eckerty; RMC Place; CRAWFORD; 175 Q-7; elev. 724ft./221m.; 🅿; z 47116; ● 150
Economy; Inc. Place; WAYNE; 174 I-13; elev. 1,146ft./349m.; 🅿; z 47339; Ⓟ 151; Ⓒ 200
Eddy; RMC Place; LAGRANGE; 174 B-11; mail Wolcottville z 46795; rural
Eden; RMC Place; HANCOCK; 174 J-10; mail Greenfield z 46140; ● 80
Eden; MCD-Township; LAGRANGE; *174 A-11; mail Topeka z 46571; Ⓟ 2,501; Ⓒ 3,459
Edgerton; RMC Place; ALLEN; 174 D-14; mail Woodburn z 46797; ● 100
Edgewater; RMC Place; PORTER; *174 B-5; ★ CHI; mail Valparaiso z 46383; ● 200
Edgewood; Inc. Place; MADISON; 174 I-10; elev. 860ft./262m.; ★ AND; mail Anderson z 46011; Ⓟ 2,057; Ⓒ 1,988
Edgewood; RMC Place; MARION; *175 K-9; ★ IND; mail Indianapolis z 46227; pop. incl. with Indianapolis (Inc. Place)
Edgewood Park; RMC Place; ALLEN; *174 D-12; ★ FTWA; mail Fort Wayne z 46818; ● 500
Edinburg; JOHNSON, BARTHOLOMEW, SHELBY; see Edinburgh (Inc. Place)
Edinburgh (Edinburg); Inc. Place; JOHNSON, BARTHOLOMEW, SHELBY; 175 L-9; elev. 670ft./204m.; 🅿; ★ COL; z 46124; Ⓟ 4,536; Ⓒ 4,505
Edison Park; RMC Place; ST. JOSEPH; *174 A-8; ★ S.B.; mail South Bend z 46615, z 46660; pop. incl. with South Bend (Inc. Place)
Edna Mills; RMC Place; CLINTON; 174 G-7; mail Rossville z 46065; ● 40
Edwardsport; Inc. Place; KNOX; 175 O-4; elev. 512ft./156m.; 🅿; z 47528; Ⓟ 380; Ⓒ 363
Edwardsville; RMC Place; FLOYD; 175 R-9; ★ LOU; mail New Albany z 47150; ● 600
Eel; MCD-Township; CASS; *174 E-8; mail Logansport z 46947; Ⓟ 17,746; Ⓒ 20,115
Eel River; MCD-Township; ALLEN; *174 C-12; ★ FTWA; mail Churubusco z 46723; Ⓟ 2,576; Ⓒ 3,004
Eel River; MCD-Township; HENDRICKS; *174 J-7; mail North Salem z 46165; Ⓟ 1,541; Ⓒ 1,713
Ege; RMC Place; NOBLE; 174 C-12; mail Laotto z 46763; ● 30
Ehrmandale; RMC Place; VIGO; *175 K-5; ★ T.H.; mail Terre Haute z 47805; rural
Ekin; RMC Place; HAMILTON, TIPTON; 174 H-9; ★ IND; mail Atlanta z 46031; ● 60
Elberfeld; Inc. Place; WARRICK; 175 R-4; elev. 445ft./136m.; 🅿; z 47613 & mail Buckskin z 47647; Ⓟ 635; Ⓒ 636
El Dorado; RMC Place; JOHNSON; *175 K-9; ★ IND; mail Greenwood z 46143; ● 400
Elizabeth; Inc. Place; HARRISON; 175 R-9; elev. 730ft./223m.; 🅿; z 47117; Ⓟ 153; Ⓒ 137
Elizabethtown; Inc. Place; BARTHOLOMEW; 175 M-10; elev. 644ft./196m.; 🅿; ★ COL; z 47232, z 47236; Ⓟ 495; Ⓒ 391
Elizaville; RMC Place; BOONE; 174 I-8; mail Lebanon z 46052; ● 80
Elkhart; Inc. Place; ELKHART; 174 A-9; 🅿 🅷 ■; ★ ELK; z 46514-17; Ⓟ 43,627; Ⓒ 51,874; ◆ 52,406
Elkhart; MCD-Township; ELKHART; *174 A-10; 🅿; ★ ELK; z 46514-17 & mail Goshen z 46526; Ⓟ 27,995; Ⓒ 33,986
Elkhart; MCD-Township; NOBLE; *174 B-11; elev. 748ft./228m.; mail Wawaka z 46794; Ⓟ 1,545; Ⓒ 1,910
ELKHART; 174 A-10; Ⓟ 156,198; Ⓒ 182,791; ◆ 196,497
Elkinsville; RMC Place; BROWN; *175 N-8; mail Nashville z 47448; rural
Elk Pointe; RMC Place; CLARK; *175 Q-10; ★ LOU; mail Jeffersonville z 47130; pop. incl. with Jeffersonville (Inc. Place)
Ellettsville; Inc. Place; MONROE; 175 M-7; elev. 722ft./220m.; 🅿; ★ BLMNG; z 47429; Ⓟ 3,275; Ⓒ 5,078
Ellis; RMC Place; GREENE; *175 N-5; mail Dugger z 47848
Elliston; RMC Place; GREENE; *175 N-6; mail Bloomfield z 47424; ● 40
Elmdale; RMC Place; MONTGOMERY; *174 H-5; mail Crawfordsville z 47933; ● 25
Elmhurst; RMC Place; MADISON; *174 I-10; ★ AND; mail Anderson z 46011; pop. incl. with Anderson (Inc. Place)
Elmira; RMC Place; LAGRANGE; *174 A-12; mail Lagrange z 46761; ● 80
Elmore; MCD-Township; DAVIESS; *175 O-5; mail Elnora z 47529; Ⓟ 1,305; Ⓒ 1,235
Elmwood; RMC Place; BOONE; *174 I-7; ★ IND; mail Lebanon z 46052; pop. incl. with Ulen (Inc. Place)
Elmwood; RMC Place; MIAMI; 🅷; mail Peru z 46970; pop. incl. with Peru (Inc. Place)
Elnora; Inc. Place; DAVIESS; 175 O-5; elev. 476ft./145m.; 🅿; z 47529; Ⓟ 679; Ⓒ 721
Elrod; RMC Place; RIPLEY; 175 N-12; mail Dillsboro z 47018; ● 60
Elston; RMC Place; TIPPECANOE; 174 C-2; ★ LAF-; mail Lafayette z 47905; ● 100
Elwood; Inc. Place; MADISON, TIPTON; 174 H-10; elev. 865ft./264m.; 🅿; ★ AND; z 46036; Ⓟ 9,494; Ⓒ 9,737
Elwren; RMC Place; MONROE; 175 N-7; ★ BLMNG; mail Bloomington z 47403; ● 30
Emerald Glen; RMC Place; MADISON; *174 I-11; ★ AND; mail Anderson z 46012; ● 180
Eminence; RMC Place; MORGAN; 175 L-7; elev. 782ft./238m.; 🅿; z 46125; ● 180
Emison; RMC Place; KNOX; 175 O-4; elev. 460ft./140m.; 🅿; z 47561; ● 60
Emma; RMC Place; LAGRANGE; 174 A-11; mail Topeka z 46571; ● 150
Emporia; RMC Place; MADISON; 174 I-11; ★ AND; mail Anderson z 46011, Markleville z 46056; ● 50
Enchanted Hills; RMC Place; KOSCIUSKO; *174 B-10; mail Cromwell z 46732; ● 600
Englewood; RMC Place; LAWRENCE; *175 O-7; mail Bedford z 47421; pop. incl. with Bedford (Inc. Place)
English; Inc. Place; ⊡ CRAWFORD; 175 Q-7; elev. 512ft./156m.; 🅿; z 47118; Ⓟ 614; Ⓒ 673
English Lake; RMC Place; STARKE; 174 C-6; elev. 675ft./206m.; mail North Judson z 46366; ● 30
Enochsburg; RMC Place; FRANKLIN, DECATUR; *175 L-12; mail Greensburg z 47240; ● 30
Enos; RMC Place; NEWTON; *174 D-4; mail Morocco z 47963
Enos Corner; RMC Place; PIKE; *175 R-4; mail Oakland City z 47660; ● 50
Enterprise; RMC Place; SPENCER; *175 T-5; elev. 375ft./114m.; mail Rockport z 47635
Epsom; RMC Place; DAVIESS; 175 O-5; elev. 523ft./159m.; mail Plainville z 47568; ● 30
Epworth Forest; RMC Place; KOSCIUSKO; *174 C-10; mail North Webster z 46555; summer pop. 300; ● 100
Erie; RMC Place; MIAMI; ▲ Erie; *174 E-9; mail Peru z 46970; ● 25
Erie; MCD-Township; MIAMI; *174 E-9; mail Peru z 46970; Ⓟ 451; Ⓒ 497
Ervin; MCD-Township; HOWARD; *174 G-8; mail Kokomo z 46901; Ⓟ 2,178; Ⓒ 2,331
Etna; MCD-Township; KOSCIUSKO; *174 C-9; mail Etna Green z 46524; Ⓟ 1,290; Ⓒ 1,521
Etna; RMC Place; WHITLEY; 174 C-11; mail Columbia City z 46725; ● 60
Etna Green; Inc. Place; KOSCIUSKO; 174 C-9; elev. 818ft./249m.; 🅿; z 46524; Ⓟ 578; Ⓒ 663
Etna-Troy; MCD-Township; WHITLEY; *174 C-11; mail Columbia City z 46725, Larwill z 46764; Ⓟ 1,564; Ⓒ 1,833
Eugene; RMC Place; VERMILLION; *174 I-4; elev. 506ft./154m.; mail Cayuga z 47928; ● 300
Eugene; MCD-Township; VERMILLION; *174 I-4; mail Cayuga z 47928; Ⓟ 2,138; Ⓒ 1,945
Eureka; RMC Place; LAWRENCE; *175 O-7; mail Bedford z 47421; rural
Eureka; RMC Place; SPENCER; 175 T-4; elev. 391ft./119m.; mail Rockport z 47635; ● 80
Evanston; RMC Place; SPENCER; *175 S-6; elev. 413ft./126m.; 🅿; z 47531; ● 50
Evansville; Inc. Place; ⊡ VANDERBURGH; 175 S-3; elev. 394ft./120m.; 🅿 🅷 🅲 12,829 ■; ★ EV; z 47701-06, z 47708, z 47710-16, z 47719-22, z 47724-25, z 47727-28, z 47730-37, z 47740, z 47744, z 47747, z 47750; Ⓟ 126,272; Ⓒ 121,582; ◆ 116,851
Evergreen Acres; RMC Place; CLARK; ★ LOU; mail Clarksville z 47129; pop. incl. with Clarksville (Inc. Place)
Everroad Park; RMC Place; BARTHOLOMEW; *175 M-10; elev. 635ft./194m.; ★ COL; mail Columbus z 47203; pop. incl. with Columbus (Inc. Place)
Everton; RMC Place; FAYETTE; 175 K-13; mail Connersville z 47331; ● 600
Ewing; RMC Place; JACKSON; *175 O-9; elev. 600ft./183m.; mail Brownstown z 47220; pop. incl. with Brownstown (Inc. Place)
Exchange; RMC Place; MORGAN; *175 L-8; elev. 679ft./207m.; ★ IND; mail Mooresville z 46158

F

Fair Acres; RMC Place; WASHINGTON; *175 P-9; mail Salem z 47167; pop. incl. with Salem (Inc. Place)
Fairbanks; RMC Place; SULLIVAN; ▲ Fairbanks; 175 M-3; 🅿; z 47849; ● 125
Fairbanks; MCD-Township; SULLIVAN; *175 M-3; 🅿; z 47849; Ⓟ 655; Ⓒ 728
Fairfax; RMC Place; MADISON; *174 I-11; ★ AND; mail Anderson z 46012; pop. incl. with Anderson (Inc. Place)
Fairfield; MCD-Township; DE KALB; *174 B-12; mail Corunna z 46730; Ⓟ 1,220; Ⓒ 1,319
Fairfield; MCD-Township; FRANKLIN; *175 L-13; mail Brookville z 47012; Ⓟ 276; Ⓒ 473
Fairfield; MCD-Township; TIPPECANOE; *174 G-6; ★ LAF-; mail Lafayette z 47905; Ⓟ 46,166; Ⓒ 49,970
Fairfield Center; RMC Place; DE KALB; ● 25
Fairland; CDP; SHELBY; 175 K-10; elev. 778ft./237m.; 🅿; z 46126; Ⓟ 1,348; Ⓒ 1,276
Fairlawn; RMC Place; BARTHOLOMEW; *175 M-10; ★ COL; mail Columbus z 47203; pop. incl. with Columbus (Inc. Place)
Fairmount; Inc. Place; GRANT; ▲ Fairmount; 174 G-11; 🅿; ★ MRN; z 46928; Ⓟ 3,130; Ⓒ 2,992
Fairmount; MCD-Township; GRANT; *174 G-11; 🅿; ★ MRN; z 46928; Ⓟ 4,571; Ⓒ 4,451
Fair Oaks; RMC Place; JASPER; 174 D-5; elev. 699ft./213m.; 🅿; z 47943; ● 145
Fairplay; MCD-Township; GREENE; *175 N-5; mail Bloomfield z 47424, Switz City z 47465; Ⓟ 643; Ⓒ 666
Fairview; RMC Place; FAYETTE; ▲ Fairview; 175 K-12; mail Connersville z 47331; ● 35
Fairview; MCD-Township; FAYETTE; *175 K-12; mail Connersville z 47331; Ⓟ 333; Ⓒ 298
Fairview; RMC Place; RANDOLPH; 174 H-12; mail Redkey z 47373; ● 100
Fairview; RMC Place; SWITZERLAND; *175 O-13; mail Bennington z 47011
Fairview Park; Inc. Place; VERMILLION; 175 K-4; elev. 508ft./155m.; mail Clinton z 47842; Ⓟ 1,446; Ⓒ 1,496
Fairwood Hills; RMC Place; MARION; *174 J-9; ★ IND; mail Indianapolis z 46256; pop. incl. with Indianapolis (Inc. Place)
Falcon Ridge; RMC Place; FLOYD; *175 R-10; ★ LOU; mail New Albany z 47150; pop. incl. with New Albany (Inc. Place)
Fall Creek; MCD-Township; HAMILTON; *174 I-9; ★ IND; mail Fishers z 46038; Ⓟ 4,415; Ⓒ 17,079
Fall Creek; MCD-Township; HENRY; *174 I-11; ★ AND; mail Middletown z 47356; Ⓟ 4,613; Ⓒ 4,811
Fall Creek; MCD-Township; MADISON; *174 I-10; ★ AND; mail Pendleton z 46064; Ⓟ 12,054; Ⓒ 13,363
Falmouth; RMC Place; RUSH, FAYETTE; 175 K-12; elev. 1,046ft./319m.; 🅿; z 46127; ● 100
Farlen; RMC Place; DAVIESS; *175 O-6; mail Odon z 47562; ● 50
Farmers; RMC Place; OWEN; *175 M-6; mail Freedom z 47431
Farmersburg; Inc. Place; SULLIVAN; 175 M-4; elev. 567ft./173m.; 🅿; z 47850; Ⓟ 1,159; Ⓒ 1,180
Farmers Retreat; RMC Place; DEARBORN; 175 N-13; elev. 878ft./268m.; mail Dillsboro z 47018; ● 60
Farmersville; RMC Place; POSEY; 175 S-2; elev. 419ft./128m.; mail Mount Vernon z 47620; ● 50
Farmland; Inc. Place; RANDOLPH; 174 H-13; elev. 1,039ft./317m.; 🅿; ★ MUN; z 47340; Ⓟ 1,412; Ⓒ 1,456
Farrabee; RMC Place; WASHINGTON; *175 P-9; mail Salem z 47167; rural
Farrville; RMC Place; GRANT; *174 F-11; mail Marion z 46952; rural
Fayette; RMC Place; BOONE; 174 J-8; mail Lebanon z 46052; ● 100
Fayette; MCD-Township; VIGO; *175 K-4; ★ T.H.; mail West Terre Haute z 47885; Ⓟ 2,787; Ⓒ 2,553
FAYETTE; 175 K-12; Ⓟ 26,015; Ⓒ 25,588; ◆ 23,906
Fayetteville; RMC Place; LAWRENCE; 175 O-7; mail Bedford z 47421; ● 60
Fenn Haven; RMC Place; PERRY; *175 S-6; mail Tell City z 47586; pop. incl. with Tell City (Inc. Place)
Ferdinand; Inc. Place; DUBOIS; ▲ Ferdinand; 175 R-6; elev. 541ft./165m.; 🅿; z 47532; Ⓟ 2,318; Ⓒ 2,277
Ferdinand; MCD-Township; DUBOIS; *175 R-6; 🅿; z 47532; Ⓟ 3,725; Ⓒ 3,622
Ferguson Hill; RMC Place; VIGO; 174 I-1; ★ T.H.; mail West Terre Haute z 47885; ● 160
Fewell Rhoades; RMC Place; MORGAN; *175 L-8; ★ IND; mail Martinsville z 46151; ● 200
Fiat; RMC Place; JAY; 174 F-12; mail Bryant z 47326; ● 30
Fickle; RMC Place; CLINTON; *174 H-7; mail Frankfort z 46041
Fields; RMC Place; MORGAN; *175 K-8; ★ IND; mail Mooresville z 46158; ● 100
Fifteenth Avenue; RMC Place; LAKE; *174 A-4; ★ CHI; mail Gary z 46407; pop. incl. with Gary (Inc. Place)
Fillmore; Inc. Place; PUTNAM; 175 K-6; 🅿; z 46128; Ⓟ 497; Ⓒ 545
Fincastle; RMC Place; PUTNAM; 174 J-6; mail Roachdale z 46172; ● 30
Finchland; RMC Place; FLOYD; *175 Q-10; ★ LOU; mail New Albany z 47150; pop. incl. with New Albany (Inc. Place)
Finley; MCD-Township; SCOTT; *175 P-10; mail Scottsburg z 47170; Ⓟ 1,123; Ⓒ 1,289
Finly; HANCOCK; see Carrollton (RMC Place)
Fishers; Inc. Place; HAMILTON; 174 I-9; elev. 824ft./251m.; 🅿; ★ IND; z 46037-38, z 46085; Ⓟ 7,508; Ⓒ 37,835; ◆ 80,191
Fishersburg; RMC Place; MADISON; 174 I-10; ★ AND; mail Lapel z 46051; ● 120
Fish Lake; RMC Place; LAGRANGE; *174 A-12; mail Lagrange z 46761; ● 200
Fish Lake; RMC Place; LAPORTE; 174 A-7; mail Walkerton z 46574; ● 1,300
Fiskville; RMC Place; MONTGOMERY; *174 I-6; mail Crawfordsville z 47933; pop. incl. with Crawfordsville (Inc. Place)
Five Points; RMC Place; ALLEN; *174 D-13; ★ FTWA; mail Woodburn z 46797; ● 40
Five Points; RMC Place; MARION; *175 K-9; ★ IND; mail Indianapolis z 46239; pop. incl. with Indianapolis (Inc. Place)
Five Points; RMC Place; MORGAN; 175 K-8; ★ IND; mail Mooresville z 46158; ● 125
Five Points; RMC Place; WHITLEY; *174 C-11; mail Columbia City z 46725; rural
Flat Rock; MCD-Township; BARTHOLOMEW; *175 M-10; mail Columbus z 47203; Ⓟ 1,468; Ⓒ 1,539
Flat Rock; RMC Place; SHELBY; 175 L-10; elev. 692ft./211m.; 🅿; z 47234; ● 250
Flat Rock Park; RMC Place; BARTHOLOMEW; *175 M-10; ★ COL; mail Columbus z 47203; pop. incl. with Columbus (Inc. Place)
Fleming; RMC Place; JACKSON; *175 N-10; mail Seymour z 47274
Fletcher Lake; RMC Place; FULTON; 174 E-8; mail Kewanna z 46939; ● 40
Flint; RMC Place; STEUBEN; 174 A-13; mail Angola z 46703; ● 90
Flintwood; RMC Place; BARTHOLOMEW; *175 K-10; mail Columbus z 47203
Flora; Inc. Place; CARROLL; 174 F-7; elev. 700ft./213m.; 🅿; z 46929; Ⓟ 2,179; Ⓒ 2,227
Flora; RMC Place; MIAMI; mail Peru z 46970; ● 115
Florence; RMC Place; SWITZERLAND; 175 O-13; elev. 464ft./141m.; 🅿; z 47020; ● 115
Florida; RMC Place; MADISON; 174 D-1; ★ AND; mail Anderson z 46011; ● 100
Florida; MCD-Township; PARKE; *175 K-4; mail Rosedale z 47874; Ⓟ 2,480; Ⓒ 2,500
Floyd; MCD-Township; PUTNAM; *175 K-6; mail Coatesville z 46121; Ⓟ 1,754; Ⓒ 3,173
FLOYD; 175 Q-9; Ⓟ 64,404; Ⓒ 70,823; ◆ 73,656
Floyds Knobs; RMC Place; FLOYD; 175 Q-10; elev. 796ft./243m.; 🅿; ★ LOU; z 47119; ● 800
Folsomville; RMC Place; WARRICK; 175 R-5; elev. 462ft./141m.; 🅿; z 47614; ● 50
Fontanet; RMC Place; VIGO; 175 K-5; elev. 542ft./165m.; 🅿; ★ T.H.; z 47851; ● 200
Foraker; RMC Place; ELKHART; 174 B-10; elev. 859ft./262m.; 🅿; z 46526; ● 80
Foresman; RMC Place; NEWTON; 174 E-4; mail Brook z 47922; ● 25
Forest; RMC Place; CLINTON; ▲ Forest; 174 G-8; 🅿; z 46039; ● 350
Forest; MCD-Township; CLINTON; *174 G-8; 🅿; z 46039; Ⓟ 890; Ⓒ 843
Forest Hill; RMC Place; DECATUR; 175 M-11; mail Greensburg z 47240; ● 100
Forest Hill; RMC Place; VANDERBURGH; *175 S-3; ★ EV; mail Evansville z 47711; pop. incl. with Evansville (Inc. Place)
Forest Park; RMC Place; BARTHOLOMEW; *175 M-10; ★ COL; mail Columbus z 47203; pop. incl. with Columbus (Inc. Place)
Forest Park; RMC Place; STEUBEN; *174 B-13; mail Hamilton z 46742; ● 90
Forest Park Heights; RMC Place; MONROE; *175 M-7; ★ BLMNG; mail Bloomington z 47404; ● 150
Forest Ridge; RMC Place; GRANT; *174 F-10; ★ MRN; mail Marion z 46952; ● 100
Forest Ridge Estates; RMC Place; ALLEN; *174 D-12; ★ FTWA; mail Fort Wayne z 46804; ● 300
Forrest Hills Estates; RMC Place; MADISON; *174 H-10; ★ AND; mail Elwood z 46036; ● 60
Fort Benjamin Harrison; RMC Place; MARION; *174 J-9; elev. 844ft./257m.; ★ IND; mail Indianapolis z 46216; pop. incl. with Indianapolis (Inc. Place)
Fort Branch; Inc. Place; GIBSON; 175 R-3; elev. 454ft./138m.; 🅿; z 47648; Ⓟ 2,447; Ⓒ 2,320
Fort Ritner; RMC Place; LAWRENCE; 175 O-8; elev. 521ft./159m.; 🅿; z 47430; ● 80
Fortville; Inc. Place; HANCOCK; 174 J-10; elev. 859ft./262m.; 🅿; ★ IND; z 46040; Ⓟ 2,690; Ⓒ 3,444
Fort Wayne; Inc. Place; ⊡ ALLEN; 174 D-13; elev. 767ft./234m.; 🅿 🅷 🅲 19,142 ■; ★ FTWA; z 46801-09, z 46814-16, z 46818-19, z 46825, z 46835, z 46845, z 46850-69, z 46885, z 46895-99; Ⓟ 172,971; Ⓒ 205,727; ◆ 213,506
Foster; RMC Place; WARREN; 174 H-4; mail Covington z 47932; ● 30
Fountain; RMC Place; FOUNTAIN; 174 H-4; mail Attica z 47918; ● 80
FOUNTAIN; 174 I-4; Ⓟ 17,808; Ⓒ 17,954; ◆ 16,791
Fountain City; Inc. Place; WAYNE; 174 I-13; elev. 1,114ft./340m.; 🅿; ★ RICH; z 47341; Ⓟ 766; Ⓒ 735
Fountain Park; RMC Place; JASPER; *174 E-5; mail Remington z 47977
Fountain Park; RMC Place; STEUBEN; *174 A-13; mail Hamilton z 46742; ● 100
Fountain Square; RMC Place; MARION; ★ IND; mail Indianapolis z 46203; pop. incl. with Indianapolis (Inc. Place)
Fountaintown; RMC Place; SHELBY; 175 K-10; 🅿; z 46130; ● 150
Fowler; Inc. Place; ⊡ BENTON; 174 F-4; elev. 826ft./252m.; 🅿; z 47944, z 47984, z 47986; Ⓟ 2,333; Ⓒ 2,415
Fowlerton; Inc. Place; GRANT; 174 G-11; 🅿; ★ MRN; z 46930; Ⓟ 306; Ⓒ 298
Fox Hill; RMC Place; MORGAN; *175 K-8; ★ IND; mail Camby z 46113; ● 300
Fox Lake; RMC Place; STEUBEN; *174 A-13; mail Angola z 46703; ● 250
Fox Ridge; RMC Place; PUTNAM; *175 K-6; mail Greencastle z 46135; pop. incl. with Greencastle (Inc. Place)
Francesville; Inc. Place; PULASKI; 174 D-6; elev. 680ft./207m.; 🅿; z 47946; Ⓟ 969; Ⓒ 905
Francisco; Inc. Place; GIBSON; 175 Q-4; elev. 441ft./134m.; 🅿; z 47649; Ⓟ 560; Ⓒ 543
Frankfort; Inc. Place; ⊡ CLINTON; 174 H-7; elev. 855ft./261m.; 🅿 🅷; z 46041, z 46058; Ⓟ 14,754; Ⓒ 16,662
Franklin; MCD-Township; DE KALB; *174 B-13; mail Butler z 46721; Ⓟ 1,087; Ⓒ 1,264
Franklin; MCD-Township; FLOYD; *175 R-10; mail New Albany z 47150; Ⓟ 1,307; Ⓒ 1,292
Franklin; MCD-Township; GRANT; *174 G-10; ★ MRN; mail Marion z 46952; Ⓟ 8,245; Ⓒ 8,108
Franklin; MCD-Township; HARRISON; *175 R-9; ★ LOU; mail Lanesville z 47136; Ⓟ 3,087; Ⓒ 3,642
Franklin; MCD-Township; HENDRICKS; *175 K-7; mail Stilesville z 46180; Ⓟ 1,135; Ⓒ 1,198
Franklin; MCD-Township; HENRY; *174 J-12; mail Lewisville z 47352; Ⓟ 1,219; Ⓒ 1,177
Franklin; Inc. Place; ⊡ JOHNSON; 175 L-9; elev. 721ft./220m.; 🅿 🅷 🅲 1,013; ★ IND; z 46131; Ⓟ 12,907; Ⓒ 19,463; ◆ 26,776
Franklin; MCD-Township; JOHNSON; *175 L-9; 🅿 🅲 1,013; ★ IND; z 46131; includes part of the City of Franklin; Ⓟ 13,774; Ⓒ 18,752
Franklin; MCD-Township; KOSCIUSKO; *174 D-9; mail Mentone z 46539; Ⓟ 985; Ⓒ 1,142
Franklin; MCD-Township; MARION; *175 K-9; ★ IND; mail Indianapolis z 46239; Ⓟ 21,458; Ⓒ 32,080
Franklin; MCD-Township; MONTGOMERY; *174 I-6; mail Darlington z 47940; Ⓟ 1,569; Ⓒ 1,906
Franklin; MCD-Township; OWEN; *175 M-6; mail Freedom z 47431; Ⓟ 1,003; Ⓒ 1,155
Franklin; MCD-Township; PULASKI; *174 D-7; mail Winamac z 46996; Ⓟ 637; Ⓒ 698
Franklin; MCD-Township; PUTNAM; *174 J-6; mail Roachdale z 46172; Ⓟ 1,495; Ⓒ 1,708
Franklin; MCD-Township; RANDOLPH; *174 H-13; mail Ridgeville z 47380; Ⓟ 1,343; Ⓒ 1,375
Franklin; MCD-Township; RIPLEY; *175 M-13; mail Milan z 47031; Ⓟ 3,053; Ⓒ 3,362
Franklin; MCD-Township; WASHINGTON; *175 P-9; mail Salem z 47167; Ⓟ 1,601; Ⓒ 2,006
Franklin; RMC Place; WAYNE; *174 I-12; mail Hagerstown z 47346
Franklin; MCD-Township; WAYNE; *174 I-14; mail Richmond z 47374; Ⓟ 1,306; Ⓒ 1,291
FRANKLIN; 175 L-13; Ⓟ 19,580; Ⓒ 22,151; ◆ 23,386
Frankton; Inc. Place; MADISON; 174 H-10; elev. 862ft./263m.; 🅿; ★ AND; z 46044; Ⓟ 1,736; Ⓒ 1,905
Fredericksburg; Inc. Place; WASHINGTON; 175 Q-8; elev. 617ft./188m.; 🅿; z 47120; Ⓟ 155; Ⓒ 92
Fredonia; RMC Place; CRAWFORD; 175 R-8; 🅿; z 47137; ● 40
Freedom; RMC Place; OWEN; 175 M-6; elev. 537ft./164m.; 🅿; z 47431; ● 160
Freeland Park; RMC Place; BENTON; 174 F-4; mail Fowler z 47944; ● 50
Freelandville; RMC Place; KNOX; 175 O-4; elev. 566ft./173m.; 🅿; z 47535; ● 630
Freeman; RMC Place; OWEN; *175 M-6; mail Spencer z 47460; rural
Freeport; RMC Place; SHELBY; *175 K-10; mail Morristown z 46161; ● 130
Freetown; RMC Place; JACKSON; 175 N-9; elev. 650ft./198m.; 🅿; z 47235, z 47249; ● 700
Fremont; Inc. Place; STEUBEN; ▲ Fremont; 174 A-13; 🅿; z 46737; Ⓟ 1,407; Ⓒ 1,696
Fremont; MCD-Township; STEUBEN; *174 A-13; 🅿; z 46737; Ⓟ 2,016; Ⓒ 2,467
French; MCD-Township; ADAMS; *174 F-13; mail Bluffton z 46714; Ⓟ 888; Ⓒ 1,019
French; OHIO; see Buffalo (RMC Place)
French Lake; RMC Place; VIGO; *175 L-4; mail Terre Haute z 47802; ● 70
French Lick; Inc. Place; ORANGE; ▲ French Lick; 175 P-7; 🅿; z 47432; Ⓟ 2,087; Ⓒ 1,941
French Lick; MCD-Township; ORANGE; *175 P-7; 🅿; z 47432; Ⓟ 4,902; Ⓒ 4,767
Frenchtown; RMC Place; HARRISON; 175 Q-8; mail Depauw z 47115; ● 30
Friendship; RMC Place; RIPLEY; 175 N-12; elev. 630ft./192m.; 🅿; z 47021; ● 100
Friendswood; RMC Place; HENDRICKS; *175 K-8; ★ IND; mail Camby z 46113; ● 120
Fritchton; RMC Place; KNOX; 175 P-4; mail Vincennes z 47591; ● 100
Fritz Terrace; RMC Place; MONROE; *175 M-7; ★ BLMNG; mail Bloomington z 47404; pop. incl. with Bloomington (Inc. Place)
Fruitdale; RMC Place; BROWN; *175 M-8; mail Morgantown z 46160; ● 80
Fugit; MCD-Township; DECATUR; *175 L-12; mail Greensburg z 47240; Ⓟ 1,639; Ⓒ 1,788
Fulda; RMC Place; SPENCER; 175 S-6; elev. 500ft./152m.; 🅿; z 47536 & mail Lamar z 47550; ● 130
Fulton; MCD-Township; FOUNTAIN; *174 I-4; mail Kingman z 47952; Ⓟ 725; Ⓒ 674
Fulton; Inc. Place; FULTON; 174 E-8; elev. 787ft./240m.; 🅿; z 46931; Ⓟ 371; Ⓒ 326
FULTON; 174 D-8; Ⓟ 18,840; Ⓒ 20,511; ◆ 20,151
Furnace; RMC Place; GREENE; *175 N-6; elev. 564ft./172m.; mail Bloomfield z 47424; rural
Furnessville; RMC Place; PORTER; *174 A-5; ★ CHI; mail Chesterton z 46304; ● 90

G

Gadsden; RMC Place; BOONE; 174 I-8; ★ IND; mail Lebanon z 46052; ● 30
Galena; CDP; FLOYD; 175 Q-10; 🅿; ★ LOU; z 47119; Ⓟ 1,231; Ⓒ 1,831
Galena; MCD-Township; LAPORTE; *174 A-7; mail Rolling Prairie z 46371; Ⓟ 1,543; Ⓒ 1,710
Galveston; Inc. Place; CASS; 174 F-9; elev. 814ft./248m.; 🅿; ★ KOK; z 46932; Ⓟ 1,609; Ⓒ 1,532
Gambill; RMC Place; SULLIVAN; *175 N-4; mail Dugger z 47848; rural
Gar Creek; RMC Place; ALLEN; *174 D-13; ★ FTWA; mail New Haven z 46774; ● 50
Garden Acres; RMC Place; MONROE; *175 M-7; ★ BLMNG; mail Bloomington z 47401, z 47403; ● 200
Garden City; RMC Place; BARTHOLOMEW; *175 M-9; ★ COL; mail Columbus z 47201; ● 200
Garden Park; RMC Place; BOONE; *174 I-7; mail Thorntown z 46071; ● 80
Garden Village; RMC Place; ELKHART; *174 A-10; ★ ELK; mail Elkhart z 46514; ● 4,000
Garfield; RMC Place; MARION; *174 J-9; ★ IND; mail Indianapolis z 46203; pop. incl. with Indianapolis (Inc. Place)
Garrett; Inc. Place; DE KALB; 174 B-13; elev. 880ft./268m.; 🅿; z 46738; Ⓟ 5,349; Ⓒ 5,803
Gary; Inc. Place; LAKE; 174 A-4; elev. 608ft./185m.; 🅿 🅷 🅲 4,819 ■; ★ CHI; z 46401-11; Ⓟ 116,646; Ⓒ 102,746; ◆ 99,455
Gasburg; RMC Place; MORGAN; *175 K-8; elev. 853ft./260m.; ★ IND; mail Mooresville z 46158; ● 50
Gas City; Inc. Place; GRANT; 174 G-11; elev. 853ft./260m.; 🅿; ★ MRN; z 46933; Ⓟ 6,296; Ⓒ 5,940
Gaston; Inc. Place; DELAWARE; 174 H-11; 🅿; z 47342; Ⓟ 979; Ⓒ 1,010
Gatchel; RMC Place; PERRY; *175 S-7; mail Tell City z 47586
Gatesville; RMC Place; BROWN; *175 M-9; elev. 650ft./198m.; mail Nineveh z 46164; rural
Gaynorsville; RMC Place; DECATUR; *175 M-11; elev. 880ft./268m.; mail Greensburg z 47240
Geetingsville; RMC Place; CLINTON; *174 G-7; mail Frankfort z 46041; ● 25
Gem; RMC Place; HANCOCK; *174 J-10; ★ IND; mail Greenfield z 46140
Geneva; Inc. Place; ADAMS; 174 F-13; elev. 846ft./258m.; 🅿; z 46740; Ⓟ 1,280; Ⓒ 1,368
Geneva; MCD-Township; JENNINGS; *175 N-10; mail Scipio z 47273; Ⓟ 5,040; Ⓒ 7,469
Geneva; RMC Place; SHELBY; 175 L-10; mail Flat Rock z 47234; ● 120
Gentry Estates; RMC Place; MONROE; *175 M-7; ★ BLMNG; mail Bloomington z 47401; pop. incl. with Bloomington (Inc. Place)
Gentryville; Inc. Place; SPENCER; 175 R-5; elev. 405ft./123m.; 🅿; z 47537; Ⓟ 277; Ⓒ 262
Georgetown; RMC Place; ALLEN; *174 C-13; mail Grabill z 46741
Georgetown; RMC Place; CASS; 174 F-7; mail Logansport z 46947; ● 50
Georgetown; Inc. Place; FLOYD; ▲ Georgetown; 175 R-9; 🅿; ★ LOU; z 47122; Ⓟ 2,092; Ⓒ 2,227
Georgetown; MCD-Township; FLOYD; *175 R-9; 🅿; ★ LOU; z 47122; Ⓟ 7,053; Ⓒ 8,337
Georgetown; RMC Place; RANDOLPH; *174 H-13; mail Farmland z 47340; rural
Georgetown; CDP-Census Area Only; ST. JOSEPH; *174 A-8; elev. 750ft./229m.; ★ S.B.; mail South Bend z 46637; Ⓟ 3,993; Ⓒ 4,497
Georgia; RMC Place; LAWRENCE; *175 P-7; mail Mitchell z 47446
Gerald; RMC Place; PERRY; *175 S-7; elev. 430ft./131m.; mail Cannelton z 47520; rural
German; MCD-Township; BARTHOLOMEW; *175 M-9; ★ COL; mail Columbus z 47203; Ⓟ 5,507; Ⓒ 7,062
German; MCD-Township; MARSHALL; *174 B-9; mail Bremen z 46506; Ⓟ 8,427; Ⓒ 8,584
German; MCD-Township; ST. JOSEPH; *174 A-8; ★ S.B.; mail South Bend z 46628; Ⓟ 7,222; Ⓒ 8,518
German; MCD-Township; VANDERBURGH; *175 S-3; ★ EV; mail Evansville z 47720; Ⓟ 7,063; Ⓒ 7,354
Germantown; RMC Place; DECATUR; *175 L-11; mail Saint Paul z 47272
Gessie; RMC Place; VERMILLION; 174 I-4; mail Perrysville z 47974; ● 80
Gibson; RMC Place; LAKE; *174 A-4; ★ CHI; pop. incl. with Hammond (Inc. Place)
Gibson; MCD-Township; WASHINGTON; *175 P-9; mail Scottsburg z 47170; Ⓟ 967; Ⓒ 1,207
GIBSON; 175 Q-3; Ⓟ 31,913; Ⓒ 32,500; ◆ 32,088
Gifford; RMC Place; JASPER; 174 D-5; mail Rensselaer z 47978; ● 45
Gilboa; MCD-Township; BENTON; *174 F-5; mail Fowler z 47944; Ⓟ 281; Ⓒ 241
Gilead; RMC Place; MIAMI; 174 D-9; mail Macy z 46951; ● 35
Gill; MCD-Township; SULLIVAN; *175 N-3; mail Merom z 47861; Ⓟ 959; Ⓒ 965
Gillam; MCD-Township; JASPER; *174 D-6; mail Wheatfield z 46392; Ⓟ 662; Ⓒ 723
Gilman; RMC Place; MADISON; 174 H-11; ★ AND; mail Alexandria z 46001; ● 20
Gilmer Park; RMC Place; ST. JOSEPH; 173 C-19; ★ S.B.; mail South Bend z 46624; ● 2,100
Gilmour; RMC Place; SULLIVAN, GREENE; *175 M-4; mail Jasonville z 47438
Gingrich; RMC Place; WHITE; *174 F-6; mail Monticello z 47960; ● 150
Gings; RMC Place; RUSH; *175 K-12; mail Rushville z 46173
Giro (Buena Vista); RMC Place; GIBSON; *175 P-4; mail Hazleton z 47640; ● 30
Glen Aire; RMC Place; VIGO; *175 L-4; ★ T.H.; mail Terre Haute z 47803; ● 200
Glendale; RMC Place; DAVIESS; 175 P-5; mail Montgomery z 47558; ● 40
Glendale Lake; RMC Place; GRANT; *174 G-10; ★ MRN; mail Marion z 46952; ● 200
Glen Eden; RMC Place; STEUBEN; *174 A-13; mail Angola z 46703; ● 125
Glenhall; RMC Place; TIPPECANOE; *174 G-5; mail Westpoint z 47992; ● 20
Glenns Valley; RMC Place; MARION; *175 K-8; ★ IND; mail Indianapolis z 46217; pop. incl. with Indianapolis (Inc. Place)
Glen Park; RMC Place; LAKE; *174 B-4; ★ CHI; mail Gary z 46409; pop. incl. with Gary (Inc. Place)
Glenview; RMC Place; BARTHOLOMEW; *175 M-10; mail Columbus z 47203; ● 75
Glenwood; Inc. Place; RUSH, FAYETTE; 175 K-12; elev. 1,082ft./330m.; 🅿; z 46133; Ⓟ 285; Ⓒ 318
Glenwood Acres; RMC Place; POSEY; mail Mount Vernon z 47620; ● 50
Glenwood Park; RMC Place; ALLEN; *174 D-13; ★ FTWA; mail Fort Wayne z 46815; pop. incl. with Fort Wayne (Inc. Place)
Glezen; RMC Place; PIKE; 175 Q-4; mail Petersburg z 47567; ● 100
Glyn Ellen; RMC Place; MADISON; *174 I-11; ★ AND; mail Anderson z 46012; pop. incl. with Anderson (Inc. Place)
Gnaw Bone; RMC Place; BROWN; 175 M-9; mail Nashville z 47448; ● 125
Goblesville; RMC Place; HUNTINGTON; 174 D-11; mail Huntington z 46750; ● 75
Goff; RMC Place; GRANT; ★ MRN; mail Marion z 46952; ● 150
Goff; RMC Place; LAKE; ★ CHI; pop. incl. with Gary (Inc. Place)
Golden Hill; RMC Place; WHITE; *174 F-6; mail Monticello z 47960; ● 40
Golden Lake; RMC Place; STEUBEN; *174 A-13; mail Pleasant Lake z 46779; ● 175
Goldsmith; RMC Place; TIPTON; 174 H-9; elev. 910ft./277m.; 🅿; z 46045; ● 225
Golfview Estates; RMC Place; CLARK; *175 Q-10; ★ LOU; mail Jeffersonville z 47130; pop. incl. with Jeffersonville (Inc. Place)
Goodland; Inc. Place; NEWTON; 174 E-4; elev. 721ft./220m.; 🅿; z 47948; Ⓟ 1,033; Ⓒ 1,096
Goose Lake; RMC Place; WHITLEY; *174 C-11; mail Columbia City z 46725; ● 120
Goshen; Inc. Place; ⊡ ELKHART; 174 A-10; elev. 799ft./244m.; 🅿 🅷 🅲 951 ■; ★ ELK; z 46526-28; Ⓟ 23,797; Ⓒ 29,383; ◆ 32,921
Goshen; RMC Place; SCOTT; *175 P-10; mail Scottsburg z 47170; rural
Gosport; Inc. Place; OWEN; 175 L-7; elev. 593ft./181m.; 🅿; z 47433; Ⓟ 764; Ⓒ 715
Gowdy; RMC Place; RUSH; *175 L-11; mail Rushville z 46173
Grabill; Inc. Place; ALLEN; 174 C-13; elev. 825ft./251m.; 🅿; ★ FTWA; z 46741; Ⓟ 751; Ⓒ 1,113
Grafton; RMC Place; POSEY; *175 S-2; mail Mount Vernon z 47620; rural
Graham; MCD-Township; JEFFERSON; *175 O-11; mail Deputy z 47230; Ⓟ 1,448; Ⓒ 1,666
Graham Valley; RMC Place; WARRICK; mail Boonville z 47601; ● 20
Graham Woods; RMC Place; PORTER; *174 A-5; ★ CHI; mail Chesterton z 46304; ● 200
Grammer; RMC Place; BARTHOLOMEW; 175 M-10; elev. 732ft./223m.; 🅿; z 47236 & mail Elizabethtown z 47232; ● 160
Grandview; RMC Place; MADISON; *174 I-10; ★ AND; mail Anderson z 46011; pop. incl. with Anderson (Inc. Place)
Grandview; RMC Place; MONROE; *175 M-7; ★ BLMNG; mail Bloomington z 47408; pop. incl. with Bloomington (Inc. Place)
Grandview; Inc. Place; SPENCER; 175 S-5; elev. 400ft./122m.; 🅿; z 47615; Ⓟ 761; Ⓒ 696
Grandview Lake; RMC Place; BARTHOLOMEW; *175 M-9; ★ COL; mail Columbus z 47201; ● 400
Grandview Village; RMC Place; FLOYD; ★ LOU; mail New Albany z 47150; ● 30
Granger; CDP; ST. JOSEPH; 174 A-9; elev. 800ft./244m.; 🅿; ★ S.B.; z 46530; Ⓟ 20,241; Ⓒ 28,284; ◆ 28,148
Grant; MCD-Township; BENTON; *174 G-4; mail Boswell z 47921; Ⓟ 1,118; Ⓒ 1,142
Grant; MCD-Township; DE KALB; *174 B-13; mail Waterloo z 46793; Ⓟ 2,801; Ⓒ 3,087
Grant; MCD-Township; GREENE; *175 N-5; mail Switz City z 47465; Ⓟ 704; Ⓒ 690
Grant; MCD-Township; NEWTON; *174 E-4; mail Goodland z 47948; Ⓟ 1,341; Ⓒ 1,293
GRANT; 174 G-11; Ⓟ 74,169; Ⓒ 73,403; ◆ 66,804
Grant City; RMC Place; HENRY; *174 J-11; mail Shirley z 47384; ● 100
Grantsburg; RMC Place; CRAWFORD; 175 R-7; elev. 609ft./186m.; 🅿; z 47123; ● 130
Granville; RMC Place; DELAWARE; *174 H-12; mail Eaton z 47338; ● 30
Grass; MCD-Township; SPENCER; *175 S-5; mail Chrisney z 47611; Ⓟ 1,456; Ⓒ 1,390
Grass Creek; RMC Place; FULTON; 174 E-8; 🅿; z 46935; ● 80
Grasselli; RMC Place; LAKE; ★ CHI; pop. incl. with East Chicago (Inc. Place)
Grassy Fork; MCD-Township; JACKSON; *175 O-9; mail Seymour z 47274; Ⓟ 732; Ⓒ 775
Gravel Beach; RMC Place; LAGRANGE; *174 B-12; mail Hudson z 46747, Wolcottville z 46795; ● 80
Gravelton; RMC Place; KOSCIUSKO, ELKHART; 174 B-10; mail Milford z 46542; ● 30
Grayford; RMC Place; JENNINGS; 175 N-11; mail North Vernon z 47265; ● 100
Graysville; RMC Place; SULLIVAN; 175 N-3; elev. 570ft./174m.; 🅿; z 47852; ● 135
Green; MCD-Township; GRANT; *174 G-10; mail Swayzee z 46986; Ⓟ 636; Ⓒ 576
Green; MCD-Township; HANCOCK; *174 J-10; mail Greenfield z 46140; Ⓟ 1,609; Ⓒ 1,622
Green; MCD-Township; MADISON; *174 I-10; ★ IND; mail Ingalls z 46048; Ⓟ 2,863; Ⓒ 3,561
Green; MCD-Township; MARSHALL; *174 C-8; mail Argos z 46501; Ⓟ 970; Ⓒ 1,092
Green; MCD-Township; MORGAN; *175 L-8; ★ IND; mail Martinsville z 46151; Ⓟ 2,419; Ⓒ 2,967
Green; MCD-Township; NOBLE; *174 C-12; mail Albion z 46701; Ⓟ 1,482; Ⓒ 1,769
Green; MCD-Township; RANDOLPH; *174 H-12; mail Farmland z 47340; Ⓟ 991; Ⓒ 1,098
Green; MCD-Township; WAYNE; *174 I-13; mail Williamsburg z 47393; Ⓟ 1,249; Ⓒ 1,261
Green Acres; RMC Place; LAKE; *174 B-4; ★ CHI; mail Merrillville z 46410; pop. incl. with Hobart (Inc. Place)
Greenbriar; RMC Place; PUTNAM; mail Greencastle z 46135; ● 200
Greenbriar Hills; RMC Place; VANDERBURGH; *175 S-3; ★ EV; mail Evansville z 47710; ● 300
Greenbrier; RMC Place; ORANGE; *175 Q-7; mail Paoli z 47454; rural
Greenbrier; RMC Place; WARRICK; *175 R-4; mail Boonville z 47601; ● 30
Greencastle; Inc. Place; ⊡ PUTNAM; 175 K-6; 🅿 🅷 🅲 2,326; z 46135; Ⓟ 8,984; Ⓒ 9,880
Greencastle; MCD-Township; PUTNAM; *175 K-6; 🅿 🅲 2,326; z 46135; Ⓟ 11,416; Ⓒ 12,491
Green Center; RMC Place; NOBLE; *174 C-12; mail Albion z 46701
Greendale; Inc. Place; DEARBORN; 175 M-14; elev. 528ft./161m.; 🅿; ★ CIN; z 47025; Ⓟ 3,881; Ⓒ 4,296
Greene; MCD-Township; JAY; *174 G-13; mail Portland z 47371; Ⓟ 982; Ⓒ 1,038
Greene; MCD-Township; PARKE; *174 J-5; mail Waveland z 47989; Ⓟ 416; Ⓒ 439
Greene; MCD-Township; ST. JOSEPH; *174 A-8; ★ S.B.; mail South Bend z 46614; Ⓟ 3,037; Ⓒ 3,040
GREENE; 175 N-6; Ⓟ 30,410; Ⓒ 33,157; ◆ 31,973
Greenfield; Inc. Place; ⊡ HANCOCK; 174 J-10; elev. 888ft./271m.; 🅿 🅷; ★ IND; z 46140; Ⓟ 11,657; Ⓒ 14,600
Greenfield; MCD-Township; LAGRANGE; *174 A-12; mail Howe z 46746; Ⓟ 1,135; Ⓒ 1,258
Greenfield; MCD-Township; ORANGE; *175 Q-7; mail English z 47118; Ⓟ 418; Ⓒ 559
Greenfield Estates; RMC Place; GRANT; *174 F-10; ★ MRN; mail Marion z 46952; ● 60
Greenfield Mills; RMC Place; LAGRANGE; *174 A-12; mail Howe z 46746; rural
Green Hill; RMC Place; WARREN; 174 G-5; mail Otterbein z 47970; ● 125
Greenleaf Manor; RMC Place; ELKHART; *174 A-9; ★ ELK; mail Elkhart z 46514; pop. incl. with Elkhart (Inc. Place)
Green Meadows; RMC Place; SHELBY; *175 K-10; ★ IND; mail Fairland z 46126; ● 100
Green Meadows; RMC Place; TIPPECANOE; *174 G-6; ★ LAF-; mail West Lafayette z 47906; ● 450
Green Oak; RMC Place; FULTON; *174 D-9; mail Rochester z 46975
Green River Estates; RMC Place; VANDERBURGH; *175 S-3; ★ EV; mail Evansville z 47711; ● 150
Greensboro; Inc. Place; HENRY; ▲ Greensboro; 174 J-11; 🅿; z 47344; Ⓟ 204; Ⓒ 174
Greensboro; MCD-Township; HENRY; *174 J-11; 🅿; z 47344 & mail New Castle z 47362; Ⓟ 1,483; Ⓒ 1,575
Greensburg; Inc. Place; ⊡ DECATUR; 175 L-11; elev. 970ft./296m.; 🅿 🅷; z 47240; Ⓟ 9,286; Ⓒ 10,260
Greensfork; MCD-Township; RANDOLPH; *174 I-14; mail Lynn z 47355; Ⓟ 1,219; Ⓒ 1,201
Greens Fork; Inc. Place; WAYNE; 174 J-13; elev. 1,000ft./305m.; 🅿; z 47345; Ⓟ 416; Ⓒ 371
Greentown; Inc. Place; HOWARD; 174 G-9; elev. 844ft./257m.; 🅿; ★ KOK; z 46936; Ⓟ 2,172; Ⓒ 2,546
Greenvalley Estates; RMC Place; FLOYD; *175 Q-10; ★ LOU; mail New Albany z 47150; pop. incl. with New Albany (Inc. Place)
Greenville; Inc. Place; FLOYD; ▲ Greenville; 175 Q-9; 🅿; ★ LOU; z 47124; Ⓟ 508; Ⓒ 591
Greenville; MCD-Township; FLOYD; *175 Q-9; 🅿; ★ LOU; z 47124; Ⓟ 5,190; Ⓒ 6,340
Greenwood; Inc. Place; JOHNSON; 175 K-9; elev. 800ft./244m.; 🅿 🅷 ■; ★ IND; z 46142-43; Ⓟ 26,265; Ⓒ 36,037; ◆ 47,651
Greenwood; RMC Place; LAGRANGE; *174 B-12; mail Wolcottville z 46795; ● 80
Greer; MCD-Township; WARRICK; *175 R-4; mail Elberfeld z 47613; Ⓟ 1,888; Ⓒ 1,881
Gregg; MCD-Township; MORGAN; *175 L-7; ★ IND; mail Martinsville z 46151; Ⓟ 2,530; Ⓒ 2,878
Greybrook Lake; RMC Place; OWEN; *175 L-6; mail Poland z 47868; ● 60
Griffin; Inc. Place; POSEY; 175 R-2; elev. 385ft./117m.; 🅿; z 47616; Ⓟ 171; Ⓒ 160
Griffith; Inc. Place; LAKE; 174 B-4; elev. 635ft./194m.; 🅿; ★ CHI; z 46319; Ⓟ 17,916; Ⓒ 17,334
Grissom AFB; CDP-Census Area Only; MIAMI, CASS; *174 F-9; mail Grissom Arb z 46971; Ⓒ 1,652
Groomsville; RMC Place; TIPTON; *174 G-8; mail Kempton z 46049; ● 25
Groveland; RMC Place; PUTNAM; 174 J-7; mail Bainbridge z 46105; ● 75
Grovertown; RMC Place; STARKE; 174 B-7; elev. 720ft./219m.; 🅿; z 46531; ● 150
Guilford; RMC Place; DEARBORN; 175 M-13; elev. 532ft./162m.; 🅿; z 47022; ● 100
Guilford; MCD-Township; HENDRICKS; *175 K-8; ★ IND; mail Plainfield z 46168; Ⓟ 19,468; Ⓒ 22,895
Guion; RMC Place; PARKE; 174 J-5; mail Rockville z 47872; ● 30
Gulivoire Park; CDP-Census Area Only; ST. JOSEPH; *174 A-8; elev. 825ft./251m.; ★ S.B.; mail South Bend z 46614, z 46624; Ⓟ 2,788; Ⓒ 2,974
Guthrie; RMC Place; LAWRENCE; 175 N-7; ★ BLMNG; mail Bedford z 47421; ● 25
Guthrie; MCD-Township; LAWRENCE; *175 O-8; mail Bedford z 47421; Ⓟ 1,358; Ⓒ 1,583
Guy; RMC Place; HOWARD; *174 G-9; ★ KOK; mail Greentown z 46936; ● 30
Gwynneville; RMC Place; SHELBY; 175 K-11; elev. 911ft./278m.; 🅿; z 46144; ● 250

H

Hacienda Village; RMC Place; ALLEN; *174 D-13; ★ FTWA; mail Fort Wayne z 46815; pop. incl. with Fort Wayne (Inc. Place)
Hackleman; RMC Place; GRANT; 174 G-10; mail Fairmount z 46928; ● 40
Haddon; MCD-Township; SULLIVAN; *175 N-4; mail Carlisle z 47838; Ⓟ 1,780; Ⓒ 3,977
Hadley; RMC Place; HENDRICKS; 175 K-7; mail Coatesville z 46121; ● 60
Hagerstown; Inc. Place; WAYNE; 174 J-12; elev. 1,008ft./307m.; 🅿; z 47346; Ⓟ 1,835; Ⓒ 1,768
Haglund; RMC Place; PORTER; ★ CHI; mail Chesterton z 46304; pop. incl. with Burns Harbor (Inc. Place)
Halbert; MCD-Township; MARTIN; *175 P-6; mail Shoals z 47581; Ⓟ 1,587; Ⓒ 1,721
Haleysbury; RMC Place; WASHINGTON; *175 O-9; mail Vallonia z 47281; rural
Hall; MCD-Township; DUBOIS; *175 Q-6; mail Jasper z 47546; Ⓟ 927; Ⓒ 1,109
Hall; RMC Place; MORGAN; 175 K-7; elev. 800ft./244m.; ★ IND; mail Monrovia z 46157; ● 100
Hamblen; MCD-Township; BROWN; *175 M-9; mail Nashville z 47448; Ⓟ 4,032; Ⓒ 4,591
Hamburg; RMC Place; CLARK; 175 Q-10; ★ LOU; mail Sellersburg z 47172; pop. incl. with Sellersburg (Inc. Place)
Hamburg; RMC Place; FRANKLIN; 175 L-12; mail Laurel z 47024; ● 100
Hamilton; RMC Place; CLINTON; *174 G-7; elev. 811ft./247m.; mail Mulberry z 46058

Entries in UPPERCASE are counties.
Entries in bold have populations of 2,500 or more.
Names in parentheses are alternate names.
Inc. Place — Incorporated Place
RMC Place — Rand McNally Designated Place
CDP — Census Designated Place
MCD — Minor Civil Division

⊡ County Seat
▲ Minor Civil Division
elev. Elevation
🅿 Post Office
🅷 Hospital
🅲 College
■ Principal Business Center
★ Ranally Metro Area (RMA) Abbreviation
z Zip Code(s)
Ⓟ Previous Census Population
Ⓡ Revised Census Population
Ⓐ Annexation Population
● Rand McNally Population Estimate
Ⓒ Final Census Population
Ⓢ Special Census Population
◆ Estimated Population

For additional definitions see Glossary, Volume 1, and Introduction, Volume 2.

Hamilton; MCD-Township; DELAWARE; ***174** H-12; ★ **MUN**; mail Muncie z 47303; Ⓟ 7,052; © 7,163
Hamilton; MCD-Township; JACKSON; ***175** N-9; mail Seymour z 47274; Ⓟ 1,680; © 1,615
Hamilton; RMC Place; MADISON; ***174** I-10; ★ **AND**; mail Anderson z 46011; ● 40
Hamilton; Inc. Place; STEUBEN, DE KALB; **174** B-13; elev. 900ft./274m.; 🅿; z 46742; Ⓟ 684; © 1,233
Hamilton; MCD-Township; SULLIVAN; ***175** N-4; mail Sullivan z 47882; Ⓟ 6,899; © 7,083
HAMILTON; **174** H-9; Ⓟ 108,936; © 182,740; ◆ 281,193
Hamilton Park; RMC Place; DELAWARE; ***174** H-12; ★ **MUN**; mail Muncie z 47303; ● 100
Hamilton Village; RMC Place; DELAWARE; ***174** H-12; elev. 930ft./283m.; ★ **MUN**; mail Muncie z 47303; ● 500
Hamlet; Inc. Place; STARKE; **174** B-7; elev. 695ft./212m.; 🅿; z 46532; Ⓟ 789; © 820
Hammond; Inc. Place; LAKE; **174** A-4; elev. 591ft./180m.; 🅿 🅷 🅲 9,303 ■; ★ **CHI**; z 46320-25, z 46327; Ⓟ 84,236; © 83,048; ◆ 79,917
Hammond; MCD-Township; SPENCER; ***175** S-6; mail Grandview z 47615; Ⓟ 1,667; © 1,607
Hamor Heights; RMC Place; BARTHOLOMEW; ***175** M-10; mail Columbus z 47203; ● 120
HANCOCK; **174** J-10; Ⓟ 45,527; © 55,391; ◆ 68,383
Hancock Chapel; RMC Place; HARRISON; ***175** Q-9; mail Depauw z 47115
Handy; RMC Place; MONROE; **175** N-7; ★ **BLMNG**; mail Bloomington z 47401; ● 125
Hanfield; RMC Place; GRANT; ***174** F-11; elev. 876ft./267m.; ★ **MRN**; mail Marion z 46952
Hanging Grove; MCD-Township; JASPER; ***174** E-6; mail Rensselaer z 47978; Ⓟ 230; © 236
Hanna; RMC Place; LAPORTE; ▲ Hanna; **174** B-6; 🅿; z 46340; ● 500
Hanna; MCD-Township; LAPORTE; ***174** B-6; 🅿; z 46340; Ⓟ 930; © 993
Hanover; Inc. Place; JEFFERSON; ▲ Hanover; **175** O-11; 🅿 🅲 1,000; z 47243; Ⓟ 3,610; © 2,834; Ⓡ 3,807
Hanover; MCD-Township; JEFFERSON; ***175** P-11; 🅿 🅲 1,000; z 47243; Ⓟ 4,898; © 5,409
Hanover; MCD-Township; LAKE; ***174** B-4; ★ **CHI**; mail Cedar Lake z 46303; Ⓟ 7,365; © 8,692
Hanover; MCD-Township; SHELBY; ***175** K-10; mail Morristown z 46161; Ⓟ 2,215; © 2,312
Hanover Beach; RMC Place; JEFFERSON; ***175** P-11; mail Hanover z 47243; ● 100
Happy Hollow Heights; RMC Place; TIPPECANOE; ***174** G-6; ★ **LAF-**; mail West Lafayette z 47906; pop. incl. with West Lafayette (Inc. Place)
Harbison; MCD-Township; DUBOIS; ***175** Q-6; mail Dubois z 47527, Jasper z 47546; Ⓟ 1,510; © 1,601
Harbor; RMC Place; LAKE; ***174** A-4; ★ **CHI**; mail East Chicago z 46312; pop. incl. with East Chicago (Inc. Place)
Hardinsburg; RMC Place; DEARBORN; ***175** M-14; ★ **CIN**; mail Lawrenceburg z 47025; ● 250
Hardinsburg; Inc. Place; WASHINGTON; **175** Q-8; elev. 700ft./213m.; 🅿; z 47125; Ⓟ 322; © 244
Hardscrabble; RMC Place; MADISON; ***174** I-10; ★ **IND**; mail Lapel z 46051; rural
Harlan; RMC Place; ALLEN; **174** C-13; elev. 794ft./242m.; 🅿; z 46743; ● 1,200
Harmony; Inc. Place; CLAY; **175** K-5; elev. 673ft./205m.; 🅿; z 47853; Ⓟ 645; © 589; Ⓡ 616
Harmony; MCD-Township; POSEY; ***175** R-2; mail New Harmony z 47631; Ⓟ 1,432; © 1,473
Harmony; MCD-Township; UNION; ***175** K-13; mail Connersville z 47331; Ⓟ 419; © 628
Harper; RMC Place; DECATUR; ***175** M-11; elev. 780ft./238m.; mail Westport z 47283; rural
Harris; MCD-Township; ST. JOSEPH; ***174** A-9; ★ **S.B.**; mail Granger z 46530; Ⓟ 11,543; © 19,873
Harrisburg; RMC Place; FAYETTE; **175** K-12; mail Connersville z 47331; ● 50
Harris City; RMC Place; DECATUR; ***175** M-11; mail Greensburg z 47240; rural
Harrison; MCD-Township; BARTHOLOMEW; ***175** M-9; ★ **COL**; mail Columbus z 47201; Ⓟ 2,769; © 3,453
Harrison; MCD-Township; BLACKFORD; ***174** G-12; mail Montpelier z 47359; Ⓟ 2,911; © 2,940
Harrison; MCD-Township; BOONE; ***174** I-7; mail Lebanon z 46052; Ⓟ 700; © 755
Harrison; MCD-Township; CASS; ***174** E-8; mail Lucerne z 46950; Ⓟ 809; © 805
Harrison; MCD-Township; CLAY; ***175** M-5; mail Clay City z 47841; Ⓟ 2,275; © 2,366
Harrison; MCD-Township; DAVIESS; ***175** P-5; mail Washington z 47501; Ⓟ 544; © 673
Harrison; DEARBORN; see West Harrison (Inc. Place)
Harrison; MCD-Township; DEARBORN; ***175** M-14; ★ **CIN**; mail West Harrison z 47060; Ⓟ 2,421; © 3,108
Harrison; MCD-Township; DELAWARE; ***174** H-11; ★ **MUN**; mail Muncie z 47304; Ⓟ 3,336; © 3,425
Harrison; MCD-Township; ELKHART; ***174** A-9; ★ **ELK**; mail Goshen z 46526; Ⓟ 2,693; © 2,885
Harrison; MCD-Township; FAYETTE; ***175** K-12; mail Connersville z 47331; Ⓟ 7,084; © 6,836
Harrison; MCD-Township; HARRISON; ***175** R-9; mail Corydon z 47112; Ⓟ 8,239; © 10,303
Harrison; MCD-Township; HENRY; ***174** I-11; mail Shirley z 47384; Ⓟ 1,379; © 1,485
Harrison; MCD-Township; HOWARD; ***174** G-9; ★ **KOK**; mail Kokomo z 46902; Ⓟ 6,960; © 8,498
Harrison; MCD-Township; KNOX; ***175** P-4; mail Monroe City z 47557; Ⓟ 1,911; © 1,966
Harrison; MCD-Township; KOSCIUSKO; ***174** C-9; mail Warsaw z 46580; Ⓟ 3,377; © 3,437
Harrison; MCD-Township; MIAMI; ***174** F-9; mail Amboy z 46911; Ⓟ 748; © 816
Harrison; MCD-Township; MORGAN; ***175** K-8; ★ **IND**; mail Martinsville z 46151; Ⓟ 1,538; © 1,601
Harrison; MCD-Township; OWEN; ***175** L-7; mail Gosport z 47433; Ⓟ 355; © 473
Harrison; MCD-Township; PULASKI; ***174** D-7; mail Kewanna z 46939; Ⓟ 650; © 657
Harrison; MCD-Township; SPENCER; ***175** R-6; mail Ferdinand z 47532; Ⓟ 2,286; © 2,036
Harrison; MCD-Township; UNION; ***175** K-14; mail Liberty z 47353; Ⓟ 481; © 406
Harrison; MCD-Township; VIGO; ***175** L-4; ★ **T.H.**; mail Terre Haute z 47807; Ⓟ 53,810; © 51,898
Harrison; MCD-Township; WAYNE; ***174** J-13; mail Cambridge City z 47327; Ⓟ 363; © 403
Harrison; MCD-Township; WELLS; ***174** F-12; mail Bluffton z 46714; Ⓟ 8,836; © 8,616
HARRISON; **175** R-9; Ⓟ 29,890; © 34,325; ◆ 36,881
Harrison Lake; RMC Place; BARTHOLOMEW; ***175** M-9; ★ **COL**; mail Columbus z 47201; ● 350
Harristown; RMC Place; WASHINGTON; ***175** P-9; mail Salem z 47167; ● 35
Harrisville; RMC Place; RANDOLPH; **174** H-13; mail Union City z 47390; ● 50
Harrodsburg; RMC Place; MONROE; **175** N-7; elev. 600ft./183m.; 🅿; ★ **BLMNG**; z 47434; ● 375
Hart; MCD-Township; WARRICK; ***175** R-4; mail Lynnville z 47619; Ⓟ 1,329; © 1,488
Hartford; MCD-Township; ADAMS; ***174** F-13; mail Geneva z 46740; Ⓟ 816; © 880
Hartford; RMC Place; OHIO; **175** N-13; mail Aurora z 47001; ● 40
Hartford City; Inc. Place; ⊡ BLACKFORD; **174** G-12; elev. 922ft./281m.; 🅿 🅷; ★ **MUN**; z 47348; Ⓟ 6,960; © 6,928
Hartford Place; RMC Place; BARTHOLOMEW; ***175** M-10; ★ **COL**; mail Columbus z 47203; pop. incl. with Columbus (Inc. Place)
Hartleyville; RMC Place; LAWRENCE; ***175** O-7; mail Bedford z 47421
Hartsdale; RMC Place; LAKE; ***174** B-4; ★ **CHI**; pop. incl. with Schererville (Inc. Place)
Hartsville; Inc. Place; BARTHOLOMEW; **175** M-10; elev. 761ft./232m.; 🅿; ★ **COL**; z 47244; Ⓟ 391; © 376
Hartzel; RMC Place; LAGRANGE; ***174** A-12; mail Wolcottville z 46795; summer pop. 400; ● 200
Harveysburg; RMC Place; FOUNTAIN; **174** I-4; mail Kingman z 47952; ● 30
Hashtown; RMC Place; GREENE; ***175** N-6; mail Bloomfield z 47424; ● 125
Haskell; RMC Place; LAPORTE; **174** B-6; mail Wanatah z 46390; ● 25
Haskell Heights; RMC Place; LAPORTE; ***174** B-6; mail Wanatah z 46390; ● 140
Hastings; RMC Place; KOSCIUSKO; ***174** B-9; elev. 837ft./255m.; mail Milford z 46542
Hatfield; RMC Place; SPENCER; **175** S-4; elev. 390ft./119m.; 🅿; z 47617; ● 700
Haubstadt; Inc. Place; GIBSON; **175** R-3; elev. 473ft./144m.; 🅿; ★ **EV**; z 47639; Ⓟ 1,455; © 1,529
Haw Creek; MCD-Township; BARTHOLOMEW; ***175** M-10; ★ **COL**; mail Hope z 47246; Ⓟ 3,914; © 4,015
Hawthorne Hills; RMC Place; LAKE; ***174** B-4; elev. 750ft./229m.; ★ **CHI**; mail Crown Point z 46307; ● 450
Hayden; RMC Place; JENNINGS; **175** N-10; elev. 618ft./188m.; 🅿; z 47245; ● 300
Haymond; FRANKLIN; see Saint Marys (RMC Place)
Haysville; RMC Place; DUBOIS; **175** Q-6; elev. 541ft./165m.; mail Jasper z 47546; ● 300
Hazelrigg; RMC Place; BOONE; ***174** I-7; mail Lebanon z 46052; ● 30
Hazelwood; RMC Place; ALLEN; ***174** D-13; ★ **FTWA**; mail Fort Wayne z 46805, z 46845, z 46895; pop. incl. with Fort Wayne (Inc. Place)
Hazelwood; RMC Place; HENDRICKS; **175** K-7; ★ **IND**; mail Clayton z 46118; ● 250
Hazelwood; RMC Place; SHELBY; mail Shelbyville z 46176; ● 130
Hazleton; Inc. Place; GIBSON; **175** Q-3; elev. 423ft./129m.; 🅿; z 47640; Ⓟ 357; © 288
Headlee; RMC Place; WHITE; **174** E-7; mail Monticello z 47960; ● 45
Heath; RMC Place; TIPPECANOE; **174** G-7; ★ **LAF-**
Heather Heights; RMC Place; BARTHOLOMEW; ***175** M-10; ★ **COL**; mail Columbus z 47203; pop. incl. with Columbus (Inc. Place)
Heaton Lake; RMC Place; ELKHART; ***174** A-10; ★ **ELK**; mail Elkhart z 46514; ● 200
Hebron; Inc. Place; PORTER; **174** C-5; elev. 703ft./214m.; 🅿; ★ **CHI**; z 46341; Ⓟ 3,183; © 3,596
Hedrick; RMC Place; WARREN; **174** H-4; elev. 709ft./216m.; mail Williamsport z 47993; ● 55
Heilman; RMC Place; WARRICK; ***175** R-5; elev. 484ft./148m.; mail Dale z 47523
Helmcrest; RMC Place; HANCOCK; ***174** I-10; ★ **IND**; mail Fortville z 46040; pop. incl. with Fortville (Inc. Place)
Helmer; RMC Place; STEUBEN; **174** B-12; elev. 986ft./301m.; 🅿; z 46747; ● 120
Helmsburg; RMC Place; BROWN; **175** M-8; elev. 669ft./204m.; 🅿; z 47435; ● 130
Helt; MCD-Township; VERMILLION; ***174** J-4; mail Dana z 47847; Ⓟ 2,691; © 2,651
Heltonville; RMC Place; LAWRENCE; **175** N-8; elev. 656ft./200m.; 🅿; z 47436; ● 500
Hemlock; RMC Place; HOWARD; **174** G-9; elev. 860ft./262m.; 🅿; ★ **KOK**; z 46937; ● 150
Hemlock Lakes; RMC Place; FOUNTAIN; ***174** I-5; mail Kingman z 47952; ● 20
Henderson; RMC Place; RUSH; **175** K-11; mail Rushville z 46173; ● 40
Hendricks; RMC Place; JOHNSON; ***175** K-9; ★ **IND**; mail Greenwood z 46142; ● 250
Hendricks; MCD-Township; SHELBY; ***175** L-10; mail Shelbyville z 46176; Ⓟ 1,219; © 1,314
HENDRICKS; **174** J-7; Ⓟ 75,717; © 104,093; ◆ 140,562
Hendricksville; RMC Place; GREENE; **175** M-7; mail Solsberry z 47459; ● 40
Henry; MCD-Township; FULTON; ***174** D-9; mail Akron z 46910; Ⓟ 2,615; © 2,827
Henry; MCD-Township; HENRY; ***174** J-12; mail New Castle z 47362; Ⓟ 23,814; © 23,859
HENRY; **174** I-11; Ⓟ 48,139; © 48,508; ◆ 45,950
Henryville; CDP; CLARK; **175** P-10; elev. 501ft./153m.; 🅿; z 47126; © 1,545
Hensley; MCD-Township; JOHNSON; ***175** L-9; mail Trafalgar z 46181; Ⓟ 2,500; © 3,002
Herbst; RMC Place; GRANT; **174** G-10; elev. 857ft./261m.; ★ **MRN**; mail Marion z 46952; ● 80
Heritage Hills; RMC Place; FLOYD; ***175** R-10; ★ **LOU**; mail New Albany z 47150; pop. incl. with New Albany (Inc. Place)
Heritage Lake; RMC Place; PUTNAM; ***175** K-7; mail Coatesville z 46121, Fillmore z 46128; ● 1,300
Herr; RMC Place; BOONE; ***174** I-8; mail Lebanon z 46052; rural
Hessen Cassel; RMC Place; ALLEN; ***174** D-13; ★ **FTWA**; mail Fort Wayne z 46819; ● 100
Hesston; RMC Place; LAPORTE; ***174** A-7; mail La Porte z 46350; ● 100
Hessville; RMC Place; LAKE; ***174** A-4; ★ **CHI**; mail Hammond z 46323; pop. incl. with Hammond (Inc. Place)
Heth; MCD-Township; HARRISON; ***175** S-9; mail Mauckport z 47142; Ⓟ 961; © 1,199
Heusler; RMC Place; POSEY; **175** S-3; ★ **EV**; mail Evansville z 47712; ● 150
Hibbard; RMC Place; MARSHALL; ***174** C-8; mail Culver z 46511; ● 50
Hibernia; RMC Place; CLARK; ***175** Q-11; elev. 721ft./220m.; mail Charlestown z 47111; ● 200
Hibernia; RMC Place; MONTGOMERY; ***174** I-5; mail Crawfordsville z 47933; rural
Hickory Grove; MCD-Township; BENTON; ***174** G-4; mail Ambia z 47917; Ⓟ 476; © 404
Hidden Lake Estates; RMC Place; CLARK; ***175** Q-10; ★ **LOU**; mail Jeffersonville z 47130; ● 200
Hidden Valley; CDP-Census Area Only; DEARBORN; ▲ Lawrenceburg; ***175** M-14; elev. 730ft./223m.; ★ **CIN**; mail Lawrenceburg z 47025; Ⓟ 2,116; © 4,417
Hideaway Lake; RMC Place; FOUNTAIN; ***174** I-4; mail Kingman z 47952; ● 350
Highbanks; RMC Place; KOSCIUSKO; ***174** C-10; mail North Webster z 46555; summer pop. 300; ● 100
High Lake; RMC Place; NOBLE; ***174** C-11; mail Albion z 46701; ● 150
Highland; MCD-Township; FRANKLIN; ***175** L-13; mail Brookville z 47012; Ⓟ 1,226; © 1,335
Highland; MCD-Township; GREENE; ***175** M-6; mail Bloomfield z 47424; Ⓟ 583; © 655
Highland (Highlands); Inc. Place; LAKE; **174** A-4; elev. 620ft./189m.; 🅿 ■; ★ **CHI**; z 46322 & mail Hillsdale z 47854; Ⓟ 23,696; © 23,546; ◆ 23,077
Highland; CDP; VANDERBURGH; **175** S-12; elev. 492ft./150m.; ★ **EV**; mail Evansville z 47710; Ⓟ 3,508; © 4,107
Highland; RMC Place; VERMILLION; ***174** J-4; mail Hillsdale z 47854
Highland; MCD-Township; VERMILLION; ***174** I-4; mail Perrysville z 47974; Ⓟ 1,672; © 1,655
Highland Meadows; RMC Place; GRANT; ★ **MRN**; mail Marion z 46952; ● 100
Highlands; LAKE; see Highland (Inc. Place)
Highland Village; RMC Place; MONROE; ***175** M-7; ★ **BLMNG**; mail Bloomington z 47401, z 47403
Highwoods; RMC Place; MARION; ***174** J-9; elev. 746ft./227m.; ★ **IND**; mail Indianapolis z 46208; pop. incl. with Indianapolis (Inc. Place)
Hildebrand Village; RMC Place; SHELBY; ***175** K-10; mail Shelbyville z 46176; pop. incl. with Shelbyville (Inc. Place)
Hillcrest; RMC Place; ALLEN; ***174** D-12; ★ **FTWA**; mail Fort Wayne z 46816; pop. incl. with Fort Wayne (Inc. Place)
Hillcrest; RMC Place; HARRISON; ***175** R-9; ★ **LOU**; mail Corydon z 47112; pop. incl. with Corydon (Inc. Place)
Hillcrest; RMC Place; MADISON; ***174** I-10; ★ **AND**; mail Anderson z 46012; pop. incl. with Anderson (Inc. Place)
Hillcrest; RMC Place; PORTER; ***174** B-5; ★ **CHI**; mail Valparaiso z 46383; ● 250
Hillendale; RMC Place; RIPLEY; ***175** M-12; mail Batesville z 47006; pop. incl. with Batesville (Inc. Place)
Hillham; RMC Place; DUBOIS; **175** Q-7; elev. 558ft./170m.; mail French Lick z 47432; ● 50
Hillisburg; RMC Place; CLINTON; **174** H-8; elev. 920ft./280m.; 🅿; z 46041; ● 180
Hills And Dales; RMC Place; DELAWARE; ***174** H-12; ★ **MUN**; mail Selma z 47383; ● 50
Hillsboro; Inc. Place; FOUNTAIN; **174** I-5; elev. 700ft./213m.; 🅿; z 47949; Ⓟ 499; © 489
Hillsboro; RMC Place; HENRY; **174** I-12; ★ **MUN**; mail New Castle z 47362; ● 140
Hillsdale; RMC Place; VANDERBURGH; **175** S-3; ★ **EV**; mail Evansville z 47711; ● 250
Hillsdale; RMC Place; VERMILLION; **174** J-4; elev. 586ft./179m.; 🅿; z 47854; ● 180
Hillview Estates; RMC Place; BARTHOLOMEW; ***175** N-9; mail Columbus z 47201; ● 50
Hindostan Falls; RMC Place; MARTIN; ***175** P-6; mail Shoals z 47581
Hindustan; RMC Place; MONROE; ***175** M-7; mail Bloomington z 47401, z 47408
Hitchcock; RMC Place; WASHINGTON; ***175** P-9; mail Salem z 47167
Hi-View; RMC Place; ST. JOSEPH; ***174** A-8; ★ **S.B.**; mail South Bend z 46624; pop. incl. with South Bend (Inc. Place)
Hoagland; RMC Place; ALLEN; **174** D-13; elev. 837ft./255m.; 🅿; ★ **FTWA**; z 46745; ● 675
Hobart; Inc. Place; LAKE; ▲ Hobart, Ross; **174** B-5; 🅿 🅷; ★ **CHI**; z 46342; Ⓟ 21,822; © 25,363; ◆ 26,028
Hobart; MCD-Township; LAKE; ***174** B-5; 🅿; ★ **CHI**; z 46342; Ⓟ 38,942; © 39,636
Hobbieville; RMC Place; GREENE; **175** N-7; mail Springville z 47462; ● 100
Hobbs; RMC Place; TIPTON; **174** H-9; elev. 868ft./265m.; 🅿; z 46047; ● 170
Hoffman Lake; RMC Place; KOSCIUSKO; ***174** C-9; mail Warsaw z 46580; ● 300
Hogan; MCD-Township; DEARBORN; ***175** N-13; mail Aurora z 47001; Ⓟ 936; © 1,138
Hogtown; RMC Place; CRAWFORD; ***175** Q-8; 🅿; z 47140; rural
Holaday Hills and Dales; RMC Place; HAMILTON; ***174** I-9; elev. 775ft./236m.; ★ **IND**; mail Carmel z 46032; ● 400
Holiday Lakes; RMC Place; DE KALB; ***174** C-12; elev. 544ft./166m.; mail Garrett z 46738; ● 250
Holiday Park; RMC Place; HOWARD; ***174** G-9; ★ **KOK**; mail Kokomo z 46902; ● 200
Holland; Inc. Place; DUBOIS; **175** R-5; 🅿; z 47541; Ⓟ 675; © 695
Hollandsburg; RMC Place; PARKE; **174** J-5; mail Rockville z 47872; ● 40
Hollybrook Lake; RMC Place; OWEN; ***175** L-7; mail Gosport z 47433; ● 40
Holton; Inc. Place; RIPLEY; **175** N-12; elev. 911ft./278m.; 🅿; z 47023; Ⓟ 451; © 407
Home Corner; RMC Place; GRANT; ***174** G-11; elev. 847ft./258m.; ★ **MRN**; mail Marion z 46952; pop. incl. with Marion (Inc. Place)
Homecroft; Inc. Place; MARION; ***175** K-9; ★ **IND**; mail Indianapolis z 46227; © 751
Home Place; RMC Place; HAMILTON; **174** J-9; ★ **IND**; mail Indianapolis z 46280; ● 1,300
Homer; RMC Place; RUSH; **175** K-11; elev. 908ft./277m.; 🅿; z 46146; ● 175
Homestead; RMC Place; DEARBORN; ***175** M-14; ★ **CIN**; mail Lawrenceburg z 47025; pop. incl. with Greendale (Inc. Place)
Honey Creek; RMC Place; HENRY; **174** I-11; ★ **AND**; mail Middletown z 47356; ● 120
Honey Creek; MCD-Township; HOWARD; ***174** G-8; ★ **KOK**; mail Russiaville z 46979; Ⓟ 1,724; © 1,966
Honey Creek; MCD-Township; VIGO; ***175** L-4; ★ **T.H.**; mail Terre Haute z 47802; Ⓟ 13,559; © 14,280
Honey Creek; MCD-Township; WHITE; ***174** E-6; mail Reynolds z 47980; Ⓟ 1,148; © 1,235
Honey Hills; RMC Place; VIGO; ***175** L-4; ★ **T.H.**; mail Terre Haute z 47802; ● 75
Honeyville; RMC Place; LAGRANGE; **174** A-11; mail Topeka z 46571; ● 100
Hoosier Acres; RMC Place; MONROE; ***175** M-7; ★ **BLMNG**; mail Bloomington z 47401; pop. incl. with Bloomington (Inc. Place)
Hoosier Highlands; RMC Place; PUTNAM; ***175** L-6; mail Poland z 47868; ● 100
Hoosierville; RMC Place; CLAY; ***175** L-5; mail Brazil z 47834; ● 40
Hoover; RMC Place; CASS; **174** E-9; mail Logansport z 46947; ● 40
Hope; Inc. Place; BARTHOLOMEW; **175** M-10; elev. 717ft./219m.; 🅿; ★ **COL**; z 47246; Ⓟ 2,171; © 2,140
Hopewell; RMC Place; DE KALB; ***174** C-13; elev. 850ft./259m.; mail Auburn z 46706; rural
Hopewell; RMC Place; JOHNSON; ***175** L-9; ★ **IND**; mail Franklin z 46131; rural
Horace; RMC Place; DECATUR; ***175** M-11; mail Greensburg z 47240; ● 30
Horseshoe Lake; RMC Place; LAPORTE; ***174** A-7; ★ **MICH**; mail La Porte z 46350; ● 50
Horton; HAMILTON; see Hortonville (RMC Place)
Hortonville (Horton); RMC Place; HAMILTON; **174** I-9; ★ **IND**; mail Sheridan z 46069; ● 200
Houston; RMC Place; JACKSON; **175** N-9; mail Freetown z 47235; ● 60
Hovey; RMC Place; POSEY; ***175** T-2; elev. 374ft./114m.; mail Mount Vernon z 47620
Howard; MCD-Township; HOWARD; ***174** G-9; ★ **KOK**; mail Kokomo z 46901; Ⓟ 2,694; © 2,866
Howard; RMC Place; PARKE; ***174** J-4; mail Kingman z 47952, Marshall z 47859; ● 50
Howard; MCD-Township; PARKE; ***174** J-5; mail Marshall z 47859; Ⓟ 244; © 324
Howard; MCD-Township; WASHINGTON; ***175** P-9; mail Salem z 47167; Ⓟ 1,084; © 1,375
HOWARD; **174** G-9; Ⓟ 80,827; © 84,964; ◆ 82,131
Howe; RMC Place; LAGRANGE; **174** A-11; elev. 882ft./269m.; 🅿; z 46746; ● 900
Howell; RMC Place; VANDERBURGH; ***175** S-3; ★ **EV**; mail Evansville z 47712; pop. incl. with Evansville (Inc. Place)
Howesville; RMC Place; CLAY; **175** M-5; mail Jasonville z 47438; ● 30
Hubbell; RMC Place; OWEN; ***175** M-5; mail Coal City z 47427; rural
Hubbells Corner; RMC Place; DEARBORN; ***175** M-13; mail Sunman z 47041; rural
Hudson; MCD-Township; LAPORTE; ***174** A-7; mail New Carlisle z 46552; Ⓟ 2,151; © 1,909
Hudson; Inc. Place; STEUBEN; **174** B-13; elev. 990ft./302m.; 🅿; z 46747; Ⓟ 438; © 596
Hudson Lake; RMC Place; LAPORTE; **174** A-7; mail New Carlisle z 46552; ● 1,300
Hudsonville; RMC Place; DAVIESS; ***175** P-5; mail Montgomery z 47558
Huff; MCD-Township; SPENCER; ***175** S-6; mail Grandview z 47615; Ⓟ 1,047; © 1,089
Huffman; RMC Place; SPENCER; ***175** S-6; mail Troy z 47588; rural
Hugo; RMC Place; ALLEN; ★ **FTWA**; pop. incl. with Fort Wayne (Inc. Place)
Hull Addition; RMC Place; TIPTON; ***174** H-9; mail Tipton z 46072; ● 100
Hunter Lake; RMC Place; ELKHART; ***174** A-10; ★ **ELK**; mail Middlebury z 46540; ● 55
Huntersville; RMC Place; FRANKLIN; ***175** M-12; mail Batesville z 47006; pop. incl. with Batesville (Inc. Place)
Huntertown; Inc. Place; ALLEN; **174** C-12; elev. 840ft./256m.; 🅿; ★ **FTWA**; z 46748; Ⓟ 1,330; © 1,771
Huntingburg; Inc. Place; DUBOIS; **175** R-6; 🅿 🅷; z 47542; Ⓟ 5,242; © 5,598
Huntington; Inc. Place; ⊡ HUNTINGTON; ▲ Huntington; **174** E-11; 🅿 🅷 🅲 1,084; z 46750; Ⓟ 16,389; © 17,450
Huntington; MCD-Township; HUNTINGTON; ***174** E-11; 🅿 🅲 1,084; z 46750; Ⓟ 20,236; © 21,262
HUNTINGTON; **174** E-11; Ⓟ 35,427; © 38,075; ◆ 37,353
Huntsville; RMC Place; MADISON; **174** I-10; ★ **AND**; mail Pendleton z 46064; ● 200
Huntsville; RMC Place; RANDOLPH; **174** I-13; mail Modoc z 47358; ● 60
Hurlburt; RMC Place; PORTER; ***174** B-5; ★ **CHI**; mail Hebron z 46341; rural
Huron; RMC Place; LAWRENCE; **175** O-7; elev. 560ft./171m.; 🅿; z 47437; ● 300
Hyde Park; RMC Place; DELAWARE; **174** G-3; ★ **MUN**; mail Muncie z 47302; ● 200
Hymera; Inc. Place; SULLIVAN; **175** M-4; elev. 524ft./160m.; 🅿; z 47855; Ⓟ 771; © 833

I

Idaho; RMC Place; VIGO; ***175** L-4; ★ **T.H.**; mail Terre Haute z 47802; pop. incl. with Terre Haute (Inc. Place)
Idaville; RMC Place; WHITE; **174** E-7; elev. 710ft./216m.; 🅿; z 47950; ● 500
Ijamsville; RMC Place; WABASH; **174** D-10; mail North Manchester z 46962; ● 70
Imperial Gardens; RMC Place; ALLEN; ***174** D-13; ★ **FTWA**; mail Fort Wayne z 46835; pop. incl. with Fort Wayne (Inc. Place)
Imperial Hills; RMC Place; JOHNSON; ***175** K-9; ★ **IND**; mail Indianapolis z 46227; pop. incl. with Greenwood (Inc. Place)
Independence; RMC Place; WARREN; **174** H-5; elev. 855ft./261m.; mail Attica z 47918; ● 120
Independence Hill; RMC Place; LAKE; ***174** B-4; ★ **CHI**; mail Merrillville z 46410; pop. incl. with Merrillville (Inc. Place)
Indiana Beach; RMC Place; WHITE; **174** E-6; mail Monticello z 47960; ● 80
Indiana Harbor; RMC Place; LAKE; ***174** A-4; ★ **CHI**; pop. incl. with East Chicago (Inc. Place)
Indiana Oaks; RMC Place; CLARK; ★ **LOU**; mail Sellersburg z 47172; ● 800
Indianapolis; Inc. Place; **STATE CAPITAL**; ⊡ MARION; **174** J-9; elev. 717ft./219m.; 🅿 🅷 🅲 40,951 ■; ★ **IND**; z 46201-09, z 46211, z 46214, z 46216-31, z 46234-37, z 46239-42, z 46244, z 46247, z 46249-51, z 46253-56, z 46259-60, z 46262, z 46266, z 46268, z 46274-75, z 46277-78, z 46280, z 46282-83, z 46285, z 46290-91, z 46295-96, z 46298; Ⓟ 731,327; © 781,870; Ⓡ 781,864; ◆ 811,560
Indianapolis Union Stockyards; RMC Place; MARION; ★ **IND**; pop. incl. with Indianapolis (Inc. Place)
Indian Creek; MCD-Township; LAWRENCE; ***175** O-7; mail Bedford z 47421; Ⓟ 2,528; © 2,662
Indian Creek; MCD-Township; MONROE; ***175** N-7; ★ **BLMNG**; mail Bloomington z 47403; Ⓟ 1,429; © 1,539
Indian Creek; MCD-Township; PULASKI; ***174** D-7; mail Star City z 46985; Ⓟ 632; © 756
Indian Heights; CDP; HOWARD; ***174** G-9; ★ **KOK**; mail Kokomo z 46902; Ⓟ 3,669; © 3,274
Indian Hills; RMC Place; BARTHOLOMEW; ***175** M-10; ★ **COL**; mail Columbus z 47203; pop. incl. with Columbus (Inc. Place)
Indian Lake; RMC Place; MARION; ***174** J-9; ★ **IND**; mail Corunna z 46730, Indianapolis z 46226; pop. incl. with Lawrence (Inc. Place)
Indianola; RMC Place; LAGRANGE; ***174** A-12; mail Wolcottville z 46795; ● 125
Indian Springs; RMC Place; MARTIN; **175** O-6; elev. 500ft./152m.; mail Shoals z 47581; ● 60
Indian Village; RMC Place; ALLEN; ***174** D-12; ★ **FTWA**; mail Fort Wayne z 46809; pop. incl. with Fort Wayne (Inc. Place)
Indian Village; RMC Place; NOBLE; ***174** B-11; mail Cromwell z 46732; ● 30
Indian Village; Inc. Place; ST. JOSEPH; ***174** A-8; elev. 725ft./221m.; ★ **S.B.**; mail South Bend z 46637; Ⓟ 142; © 144
Industry; RMC Place; DELAWARE; ★ **MUN**; mail Muncie z 47302; pop. incl. with Muncie (Inc. Place)
Ingalls; Inc. Place; MADISON; **174** I-10; elev. 869ft./265m.; 🅿; ★ **IND**; z 46048; Ⓟ 889; © 1,168
Ingle; VANDERBURGH; see Inglefield (RMC Place)
Inglefield (Ingle); RMC Place; VANDERBURGH; ***175** R-3; elev. 470ft./143m.; 🅿; ★ **EV**; z 47618
Innisdale; RMC Place; MADISON; ***174** H-10; ★ **AND**; mail Alexandria z 46001; ● 200
Inverness; RMC Place; STEUBEN; ***174** A-13; elev. 993ft./303m.; mail Angola z 46703; rural
Inwood; RMC Place; MARSHALL; **174** C-9; elev. 845ft./258m.; 🅿; z 46563; ● 100
Iona; RMC Place; KNOX; **175** P-4; mail Vincennes z 47591; ● 30
Ireland; RMC Place; DUBOIS; **175** Q-5; elev. 478ft./146m.; 🅿; z 47545; ● 450
Irondale; RMC Place; MADISON; ***174** I-11; ★ **AND**; mail Anderson z 46016; pop. incl. with Anderson (Inc. Place)
Ironton; RMC Place; MARTIN; ***175** P-6; mail Shoals z 47581; ● 25
Iroquois; MCD-Township; NEWTON; ***174** E-4; mail Brook z 47922; Ⓟ 1,341; © 1,428
Irvington; RMC Place; DELAWARE; ***174** H-12; ★ **MUN**; mail Indianapolis z 46219, Muncie z 47302; pop. incl. with Muncie (Inc. Place)
Island Park; RMC Place; KOSCIUSKO; ***174** C-10; mail Warsaw z 46580; ● 100
Island Park; RMC Place; STEUBEN; ***174** B-13; mail Hamilton z 46742; pop. incl. with Hamilton (Inc. Place)
Iva; RMC Place; PIKE; ***175** Q-5; mail Otwell z 47564
Ivanhoe; RMC Place; LAKE; ***174** A-4; ★ **CHI**; pop. incl. with Gary (Inc. Place)
Ivanhoe; RMC Place; MARION; ***174** J-9; ★ **IND**; mail Indianapolis z 46219; pop. incl. with Indianapolis (Inc. Place)
Ivy Hills; RMC Place; MARION; ***174** J-9; ★ **IND**; mail Indianapolis z 46250; pop. incl. with Indianapolis (Inc. Place)

J

Jackson; MCD-Township; ALLEN; ***174** D-14; mail Monroeville z 46773; Ⓟ 561; © 498
Jackson; MCD-Township; BARTHOLOMEW; ***175** N-9; mail Columbus z 47201, Seymour z 47274; Ⓟ 750; © 940
Jackson; MCD-Township; BLACKFORD; ***174** G-12; mail Hartford City z 47348; Ⓟ 1,394; © 1,424
Jackson; MCD-Township; BOONE; ***174** I-7; mail Jamestown z 46147; Ⓟ 2,526; © 2,677
Jackson; MCD-Township; BROWN; ***175** M-8; mail Nashville z 47448; Ⓟ 4,151; © 4,151
Jackson; MCD-Township; CARROLL; ***174** F-7; mail Camden z 46917; Ⓟ 1,285; © 1,262
Jackson; MCD-Township; CASS; ***174** F-8; ★ **KOK**; mail Galveston z 46932; Ⓟ 3,059; © 3,070
Jackson; MCD-Township; CLAY; ***175** L-5; mail Brazil z 47834; Ⓟ 2,126; © 2,602
Jackson; MCD-Township; CLINTON; ***174** H-7; mail Frankfort z 46041; Ⓟ 1,199; © 1,218
Jackson; MCD-Township; DE KALB; ***174** C-13; mail Auburn z 46706; Ⓟ 2,099; © 2,559
Jackson; MCD-Township; DEARBORN; ***175** M-13; mail Sunman z 47041; Ⓟ 1,184; © 1,419; Ⓡ 1,378
Jackson; MCD-Township; DECATUR; ***175** M-11; mail Westport z 47283; Ⓟ 1,000; © 1,040
Jackson; MCD-Township; DUBOIS; ***175** Q-6; mail Huntingburg z 47542; Ⓟ 1,919; © 2,070
Jackson; MCD-Township; ELKHART; ***174** B-10; ★ **ELK**; mail New Paris z 46553; Ⓟ 3,232; © 3,409
Jackson; MCD-Township; FAYETTE; ***175** K-13; mail Connersville z 47331; Ⓟ 1,387; © 1,525
Jackson; MCD-Township; FOUNTAIN; ***174** I-5; mail Hillsboro z 47949; Ⓟ 635; © 718
Jackson; MCD-Township; GREENE; ***175** N-6; mail Springville z 47462; Ⓟ 1,499; © 2,076
Jackson; MCD-Township; HAMILTON; ***174** H-9; ★ **IND**; mail Metamora z 47030; Ⓟ 8,446; © 9,919
Jackson; MCD-Township; HANCOCK; ***174** J-11; mail Greenfield z 46140; Ⓟ 1,762; © 1,793
Jackson; MCD-Township; HARRISON; ***175** R-9; ★ **LOU**; mail New Salisbury z 47161; Ⓟ 4,627; © 5,213
Jackson; MCD-Township; HOWARD; ***174** G-10; mail Greentown z 46936; Ⓟ 595; © 631
Jackson; MCD-Township; HUNTINGTON; ***174** D-11; mail Roanoke z 46783; Ⓟ 3,297; © 3,764
Jackson; MCD-Township; JACKSON; ***175** N-10; mail Seymour z 47274; Ⓟ 16,369; © 19,578
Jackson; MCD-Township; JAY; ***174** G-13; mail Bryant z 47326; Ⓟ 814; © 866
Jackson; MCD-Township; KOSCIUSKO; ***174** D-10; mail Claypool z 46510; Ⓟ 1,225; © 1,362
Jackson; MCD-Township; MADISON; ***174** H-10; ★ **AND**; mail Anderson z 46011; Ⓟ 1,910; © 1,889
Jackson; MCD-Township; MIAMI; ***174** F-10; mail Converse z 46919; Ⓟ 2,021; © 1,928
Jackson; MCD-Township; MORGAN; ***175** L-8; mail Martinsville z 46151; Ⓟ 3,057; © 3,089
Jackson; MCD-Township; NEWTON; ***174** D-4; mail Morocco z 47963; Ⓟ 480; © 439
Jackson; MCD-Township; ORANGE; ***175** Q-7; mail French Lick z 47432; Ⓟ 416; © 543
Jackson; MCD-Township; OWEN; ***175** L-6; mail Cloverdale z 46120; Ⓟ 1,103; © 1,981
Jackson; MCD-Township; PARKE; ***175** K-5; mail Rockville z 47872; Ⓟ 667; © 758
Jackson; MCD-Township; PORTER; ***174** A-6; ★ **CHI**; mail Chesterton z 46304; Ⓟ 3,473; © 4,592
Jackson; MCD-Township; PUTNAM; ***174** J-6; mail Roachdale z 46172; Ⓟ 798; © 933
Jackson; MCD-Township; RANDOLPH; ***174** H-14; mail Union City z 47390; Ⓟ 613; © 678
Jackson; MCD-Township; RIPLEY; ***175** M-12; mail Osgood z 47037; Ⓟ 956; © 980
Jackson; MCD-Township; RUSH; ***175** K-11; mail Rushville z 46173; Ⓟ 381; © 415
Jackson; MCD-Township; SHELBY; ***175** L-10; mail Shelbyville z 46176; Ⓟ 1,180; © 1,482
Jackson; MCD-Township; SPENCER; ***175** S-5; mail Gentryville z 47537; Ⓟ 824; © 868
Jackson; MCD-Township; STARKE; ***174** C-6; mail Knox z 46534; Ⓟ 482; © 526
Jackson; MCD-Township; STEUBEN; ***174** A-12; mail Angola z 46703; Ⓟ 1,425; © 1,783
Jackson; MCD-Township; SULLIVAN; ***175** M-4; mail Shelburn z 47879; Ⓟ 1,667; © 1,720
Jackson; MCD-Township; TIPPECANOE; ***174** H-5; mail Lafayette z 47905; Ⓟ 512; © 517
Jackson; MCD-Township; WASHINGTON; ***175** Q-9; mail Pekin z 47165; Ⓟ 1,247; © 2,037
Jackson; MCD-Township; WAYNE; ***174** J-12; mail Cambridge City z 47327; Ⓟ 4,803; © 4,626
Jackson; MCD-Township; WELLS; ***174** F-12; mail Van Buren z 46991; Ⓟ 824; © 871
Jackson; MCD-Township; WHITE; ***174** E-7; mail Burnettsville z 47926; Ⓟ 745; © 681
JACKSON; **175** N-9; Ⓟ 37,730; © 41,335; ◆ 42,005
Jacksonburg; RMC Place; WAYNE; **174** J-13; mail Cambridge City z 47327; ● 100
Jackson Hill; RMC Place; SULLIVAN; ***175** M-4; mail Shelburn z 47879; ● 60
Jacksons; RMC Place; TIPTON; mail Tipton z 46072; ● 50
Jalapa; RMC Place; GRANT; **174** F-10; ★ **MRN**; mail Marion z 46952; ● 90
Jamestown; Inc. Place; BOONE, HENDRICKS; **174** J-7; elev. 946ft./288m.; 🅿; z 46147; Ⓟ 764; © 886
Jamestown (Jimtown); RMC Place; ELKHART; **174** A-9; ★ **ELK**; mail Elkhart z 46517; ● 300
Jamestown; RMC Place; STEUBEN; **174** A-13; mail Fremont z 46737; summer pop. 900; ● 500
Jamestown; MCD-Township; STEUBEN; ***174** A-13; mail Angola z 46703; Ⓟ 3,018; © 3,389
Jasonville; Inc. Place; GREENE; **175** M-5; elev. 630ft./192m.; 🅿; z 47438; Ⓟ 2,200; © 2,490
Jasper; Inc. Place; ⊡ DUBOIS; **175** Q-6; elev. 472ft./144m.; 🅿 🅷 ■; z 47546-47, z 47549; Ⓟ 10,030; © 12,100; ◆ 13,057
JASPER; **174** D-5; Ⓟ 24,960; © 30,043; ◆ 32,908
JAY; **174** G-13; Ⓟ 21,512; © 21,806; ◆ 21,462
Jay City; RMC Place; JAY; ***174** F-14; mail Bryant z 47326; rural
Jefferson; MCD-Township; ADAMS; ***174** F-14; mail Berne z 46711; Ⓟ 848; © 947
Jefferson; MCD-Township; ALLEN; ***174** D-13; mail Monroeville z 46773, New Haven z 46774; Ⓟ 1,882; © 1,958
Jefferson; MCD-Township; BOONE; ***174** I-7; mail Lebanon z 46052; Ⓟ 969; © 1,295
Jefferson; MCD-Township; CARROLL; ***174** F-7; mail Monticello z 47960; Ⓟ 1,937; © 2,269
Jefferson; MCD-Township; CASS; ***174** E-7; mail Logansport z 46947; Ⓟ 1,432; © 1,562
Jefferson; RMC Place; CLINTON; ***174** H-7; mail Frankfort z 46041; ● 180
Jefferson; MCD-Township; DUBOIS; ***175** R-6; mail Birdseye z 47513; Ⓟ 1,538; © 1,638
Jefferson; MCD-Township; ELKHART; ***174** A-10; ★ **ELK**; mail Goshen z 46528; Ⓟ 4,604; © 6,545
Jefferson; MCD-Township; GRANT; ***174** G-11; ★ **MRN**; mail Upland z 46989; Ⓟ 5,230; © 5,850
Jefferson; MCD-Township; GREENE; ***175** M-5; mail Worthington z 47471; Ⓟ 1,964; © 2,036
Jefferson; MCD-Township; HENRY; ***174** I-11; mail Springport z 47386; Ⓟ 1,242; © 1,480
Jefferson; MCD-Township; HUNTINGTON; ***174** F-11; mail Warren z 46792; Ⓟ 834; © 805
Jefferson; MCD-Township; JAY; ***174** G-13; mail Portland z 47371; Ⓟ 859; © 802
Jefferson; MCD-Township; KOSCIUSKO; ***174** B-9; mail Nappanee z 46550; Ⓟ 1,201; © 1,648
Jefferson; MCD-Township; MIAMI; ***174** E-9; mail Peru z 46970; Ⓟ 2,630; © 2,730
Jefferson; MCD-Township; MORGAN; ***175** L-7; ★ **IND**; mail Martinsville z 46151; Ⓟ 2,867; © 3,281
Jefferson; MCD-Township; NEWTON; ***174** E-4; mail Kentland z 47951; Ⓟ 2,224; © 2,248
Jefferson; MCD-Township; NOBLE; ***174** B-12; mail Albion z 46701; Ⓟ 1,230; © 1,511
Jefferson; MCD-Township; OWEN; ***175** M-5; mail Coal City z 47427; Ⓟ 849; © 1,078
Jefferson; MCD-Township; PIKE; ***175** Q-5; mail Otwell z 47564; Ⓟ 1,626; © 1,773
Jefferson; MCD-Township; PULASKI; ***174** D-6; mail Winamac z 46996; Ⓟ 414; © 546
Jefferson; MCD-Township; PUTNAM; ***175** K-7; mail Cloverdale z 46120; Ⓟ 1,073; © 1,311
Jefferson; MCD-Township; SULLIVAN; ***175** N-4; mail Carlisle z 47838; Ⓟ 544; © 495
Jefferson; MCD-Township; SWITZERLAND; ***175** O-13; mail Vevay z 47043; Ⓟ 2,657; © 3,111
Jefferson; MCD-Township; TIPTON; ***174** H-9; mail Tipton z 46072; Ⓟ 1,501; © 1,486
Jefferson; MCD-Township; WASHINGTON; ***175** P-8; mail Campbellsburg z 47108; Ⓟ 944; © 841
Jefferson; MCD-Township; WAYNE; ***174** J-12; mail Hagerstown z 47346; Ⓟ 3,331; © 3,427
Jefferson; MCD-Township; WELLS; ***174** E-12; mail Ossian z 46777; Ⓟ 4,961; © 5,676
Jefferson; MCD-Township; WHITLEY; ***174** D-11; mail Columbia City z 46725; Ⓟ 1,855; © 2,060
JEFFERSON; **175** O-11; Ⓟ 29,797; © 31,705; ◆ 32,604
Jeffersonville; Inc. Place; ⊡ CLARK; ▲ Jeffersonville; **175** R-10; 🅿 🅷 ■; ★ **LOU**; z 47129-34, z 47144, z 47190, z 47199; Ⓟ 21,968; © 27,362; ◆ 30,668
Jeffersonville; MCD-Township; CLARK; ***175** Q-10; 🅿; ★ **LOU**; z 47129-34, z 47144, z 47190, z 47199; Ⓟ 53,449; © 56,695
Jennings; MCD-Township; CRAWFORD; ***175** R-8; mail Leavenworth z 47137; Ⓟ 1,235; © 1,386
Jennings; MCD-Township; FAYETTE; ***175** K-13; mail Connersville z 47331; Ⓟ 752; © 828
Jennings; MCD-Township; OWEN; ***175** L-6; mail Cloverdale z 46120; Ⓟ 706; © 839
Jennings; MCD-Township; SCOTT; ***175** O-10; mail Austin z 47102; Ⓟ 6,713; © 6,997
JENNINGS; **175** N-11; Ⓟ 23,661; © 27,554; ◆ 28,224
Jericho; RMC Place; SULLIVAN; ***175** N-4; elev. 540ft./165m.; mail Dugger z 47848; rural
Jerome; RMC Place; HOWARD; **174** G-10; mail Greentown z 46936; ● 100
Jessup; RMC Place; PARKE; **175** K-4; mail Rosedale z 47874; ● 40
Jewell Village; RMC Place; BARTHOLOMEW; **175** M-10; ★ **COL**; mail Columbus z 47201; ● 700
Jimtown; ELKHART; see Jamestown (RMC Place)
Jockey; RMC Place; WARRICK; ***175** R-5; mail Tennyson z 47637
Johnsburg; RMC Place; DUBOIS; ***175** R-6; mail Huntingburg z 47542; rural
Johnson; MCD-Township; CLINTON; ***174** H-8; mail Frankfort z 46041; Ⓟ 641; © 624
Johnson; MCD-Township; CRAWFORD; ***175** R-7; mail Eckerty z 47116; Ⓟ 526; © 556
Johnson; RMC Place; GIBSON; **175** R-2; mail Owensville z 47665; ● 75
Johnson; MCD-Township; GIBSON; ***175** R-3; ★ **EV**; mail Haubstadt z 47639; Ⓟ 3,099; © 3,462
Johnson; MCD-Township; KNOX; ***175** P-3; mail Vincennes z 47591; Ⓟ 1,449; © 1,486
Johnson; MCD-Township; LAGRANGE; ***174** A-12; mail Wolcottville z 46795; Ⓟ 2,880; © 3,304
Johnson; MCD-Township; LAPORTE; ***174** B-7; mail Walkerton z 46574; Ⓟ 229; © 221
Johnson; MCD-Township; RIPLEY; ***175** N-12; mail Versailles z 47042; Ⓟ 3,190; © 3,399
Johnson; MCD-Township; SCOTT; ***175** O-10; mail Scottsburg z 47170; Ⓟ 2,181; © 2,246
JOHNSON; **175** L-9; Ⓟ 88,109; © 115,209; ◆ 140,914
Johnsonville; RMC Place; WARREN; ***174** H-4; mail Williamsport z 47993
Johnstown; RMC Place; GREENE; ***175** M-5; mail Worthington z 47471; rural
Johnstown; RMC Place; KNOX; **175** O-4; mail Bicknell z 47512; ● 60
Jolietville; RMC Place; HAMILTON; **174** I-8; ★ **IND**; mail Sheridan z 46069; ● 225
Jonesboro; Inc. Place; GRANT; **174** G-11; elev. 859ft./262m.; 🅿; ★ **MRN**; z 46938; Ⓟ 2,073; © 1,887
Jonestown; RMC Place; VERMILLION; ***175** K-4; mail Bicknell z 47512, Clinton z 47842; ● 50
Jonesville; Inc. Place; BARTHOLOMEW; **175** N-10; elev. 595ft./181m.; 🅿; ★ **COL**; z 47247; Ⓟ 221; © 220
Joppa; RMC Place; HENDRICKS; ***175** K-8; ★ **IND**; mail Mooresville z 46158; rural
Jordan; MCD-Township; JASPER; ***174** E-5; mail Rensselaer z 47978; Ⓟ 297; © 345
Jordan; RMC Place; OWEN; **175** L-6; mail Poland z 47868; ● 75
Jordan; MCD-Township; WARREN; ***174** G-4; mail Williamsport z 47993; Ⓟ 313; © 254
Judah; RMC Place; LAWRENCE; ***175** N-7; ★ **BLMNG**; mail Bedford z 47421
Judson; RMC Place; HOWARD; ***174** G-8; mail Kokomo z 46901; rural
Judson; RMC Place; PARKE; ***174** J-5; elev. 607ft./185m.; 🅿; z 47872; ● 60
Judyville; RMC Place; WARREN; **174** G-4; mail Williamsport z 47993; ● 60
Julietta; RMC Place; MARION; ***174** J-9; ★ **IND**; mail Indianapolis z 46239; pop. incl. with Indianapolis (Inc. Place)

K

Kalorama Park; RMC Place; KOSCIUSKO; ***174** C-10; mail Leesburg z 46538; summer pop. 350; ● 200
Kankakee; MCD-Township; JASPER; ***174** C-6; mail Wheatfield z 46392; Ⓟ 853; © 945
Kankakee; MCD-Township; LAPORTE; ***174** A-7; ★ **MICH**; mail La Porte z 46350; Ⓟ 3,361; © 4,307
Kasson; RMC Place; VANDERBURGH; **175** S-3; ★ **EV**; mail Evansville z 47712; ● 150
Keener; MCD-Township; JASPER; ***174** C-5; mail Demotte z 46310; Ⓟ 6,495; © 8,826
Kellerville; RMC Place; DUBOIS; ***175** Q-6; mail Dubois z 47527
Kelso; MCD-Township; DEARBORN; ***175** M-13; ★ **CIN**; mail Guilford z 47022; Ⓟ 1,819; © 1,912; Ⓡ 1,974
Kempton; Inc. Place; TIPTON; **174** H-8; elev. 928ft./283m.; 🅿; z 46049; Ⓟ 362; © 380
Kendallville; Inc. Place; NOBLE; **174** B-12; elev. 976ft./297m.; 🅿 🅷; z 46755; Ⓟ 7,773; © 9,616
Kennard; Inc. Place; HENRY; **174** J-11; elev. 1,041ft./317m.; 🅿; z 47351; Ⓟ 382; © 455
Kennedy; DEARBORN; see Bonnell (RMC Place)
Kent; RMC Place; JEFFERSON; **175** O-11; mail Madison z 47250; ● 100
Kent; MCD-Township; WARREN; ***174** H-4; mail Covington z 47932; Ⓟ 467; © 421
Kentland; Inc. Place; ⊡ NEWTON; **174** E-4; elev. 676ft./206m.; 🅿; z 47951; Ⓟ 1,798; © 1,822
Kenwood; RMC Place; VIGO; ***175** L-4; ★ **T.H.**; mail West Terre Haute z 47885; ● 90
Kersey; RMC Place; JASPER; ***174** C-5; mail Demotte z 46310; ● 60
Kewanna; Inc. Place; FULTON; **174** D-8; elev. 774ft./236m.; 🅿; z 46935, z 46939; Ⓟ 542; © 614
Keyser; MCD-Township; DE KALB; ***174** B-12; mail Garrett z 46738; Ⓟ 6,459; © 7,090
Keystone; RMC Place; WELLS; **174** F-12; elev. 855ft./261m.; 🅿; z 46759; ● 150
Killbuck Terrace; RMC Place; MADISON; ***174** H-11; ★ **AND**; mail Anderson z 46012; ● 250
Kilmore; RMC Place; CLINTON; **174** G-7; elev. 839ft./256m.; mail Frankfort z 46041; ● 45
Kimberly Estates; RMC Place; TIPPECANOE; ***174** G-6; ★ **LAF-**; mail West Lafayette z 47906; ● 250
Kimmell; RMC Place; NOBLE; **174** B-11; elev. 914ft./279m.; 🅿; z 46760; ● 300
Kinder; RMC Place; JOHNSON; ***175** K-8; ★ **IND**; mail Bargersville z 46106; ● 50
Kingman; Inc. Place; FOUNTAIN; **174** I-4; elev. 705ft./215m.; 🅿; z 47952; Ⓟ 561; © 538
Kingsbury; Inc. Place; LAPORTE; **174** B-7; elev. 725ft./221m.; 🅿; z 46345; Ⓟ 258; © 229
Kingsford Heights; Inc. Place; LAPORTE; **174** B-7; elev. 725ft./221m.; 🅿; z 46346; Ⓟ 1,486; © 1,453
Kingsland; RMC Place; WELLS; **174** E-12; mail Ossian z 46777; ● 75
Kingston; RMC Place; DECATUR; ***175** L-12; mail Greensburg z 47240
Kingswood Terrace; RMC Place; VIGO; ***175** L-4; ★ **T.H.**; mail Terre Haute z 47802; ● 60
Kirkland; MCD-Township; ADAMS; ***174** E-13; mail Decatur z 46733; Ⓟ 845; © 885
Kirklin; Inc. Place; CLINTON; ▲ Kirklin; **174** H-8; 🅿; z 46050; Ⓟ 707; © 766
Kirklin; MCD-Township; CLINTON; ***174** H-8; 🅿; z 46050; Ⓟ 1,314; © 1,370
Kirkpatrick; RMC Place; MONTGOMERY; ***174** H-6; mail Linden z 47955
Kirksville; RMC Place; MONROE; ***175** N-7; mail Bloomington z 47401, z 47403
Kitchel (Kitchell); RMC Place; UNION; **175** K-14; mail Liberty z 47353; ● 25
Kitchell; UNION; see Kitchel (RMC Place)
Klemmes Corner; RMC Place; FRANKLIN; ***175** L-13; mail Brookville z 47012; rural
Klondike; RMC Place; TIPPECANOE; **174** F-5; ★ **LAF-**
Klondyke; RMC Place; VERMILLION; ***175** K-4; mail Clinton z 47842; ● 90
Knapp Lake; RMC Place; NOBLE; ***174** C-11; mail Cromwell z 46732; ● 300
Knight; MCD-Township; VANDERBURGH; ***175** S-3; ★ **EV**; mail Evansville z 47711, z 47714-15; Ⓟ 65,522; © 67,491
Knighthood Grove; RMC Place; SHELBY; ***175** K-10; elev. 770ft./235m.; mail Shelbyville z 46176; ● 30
Knighthood Village; RMC Place; SHELBY; ***175** K-10; mail Shelbyville z 46176; ● 100
Knightstown; Inc. Place; HENRY; **174** J-11; elev. 938ft./286m.; 🅿; z 46148; Ⓟ 2,048; © 2,148
Knightsville; Inc. Place; CLAY; **175** L-5; elev. 680ft./207m.; 🅿; z 47857; Ⓟ 740; © 624
Kniman; RMC Place; JASPER; **174** D-5; mail Wheatfield z 46392; ● 75
Knob Hill; RMC Place; VANDERBURGH; ***175** S-3; ★ **EV**; mail Evansville z 47711
Knox; MCD-Township; JAY; ***174** G-12; mail Portland z 47371; Ⓟ 474; © 510
Knox; Inc. Place; ⊡ STARKE; **174** C-7; elev. 702ft./214m.; 🅿 🅷; z 46534; Ⓟ 3,705; © 3,721
KNOX; **175** O-4; Ⓟ 39,884; © 39,256; ◆ 37,814
Kokomo; Inc. Place; ⊡ HOWARD; **174** G-9; elev. 810ft./247m.; 🅿 🅷 🅲 2,952 ■; ★ **KOK**; z 46901-04; Ⓟ 44,962; © 46,113; ◆ 44,378
Koleen; RMC Place; GREENE; **175** N-6; elev. 519ft./158m.; 🅿; z 47439; ● 60
Koontz Lake; CDP; STARKE, MARSHALL; **174** B-7; mail Walkerton z 46574; Ⓟ 1,615; © 1,554
KOSCIUSKO; **174** C-10; Ⓟ 65,294; © 74,057; ◆ 74,898
Kossuth; RMC Place; WASHINGTON; ***175** P-9; mail Salem z 47167
Kouts; Inc. Place; PORTER; **174** C-5; elev. 684ft./208m.; 🅿; z 46347; Ⓟ 1,603; © 1,698
Kramer; RMC Place; WARREN; **174** H-4; mail Attica z 47918; ● 90
Kreitsburg; RMC Place; LAKE; ***174** B-4; ★ **CHI**; mail Dyer z 46311; ● 45
Kriete Corner; RMC Place; JACKSON; ***175** O-10; mail Seymour z 47274; rural
Kurtz; RMC Place; JACKSON; **175** N-8; elev. 609ft./186m.; 🅿; z 47249; ● 125
Kyana; RMC Place; DUBOIS; **175** R-6; elev. 506ft./154m.; 🅿; z 47575; ● 30
Kyle; RMC Place; DEARBORN; ***175** M-13; mail Aurora z 47001; ● 40

L

Laconia; Inc. Place; HARRISON; **175** S-9; elev. 667ft./203m.; 🅿; z 47135; Ⓟ 75; © 29
La Crosse; Inc. Place; LAPORTE; **174** C-6; 🅿; z 46348; Ⓟ 677; © 561
Ladoga; Inc. Place; MONTGOMERY; **174** J-6; elev. 826ft./252m.; 🅿; z 47954; Ⓟ 1,124; © 1,047
Lafayette; MCD-Township; ALLEN; ***174** D-12; ★ **FTWA**; mail Roanoke z 46783; Ⓟ 2,530; © 2,707
Lafayette; MCD-Township; FLOYD; ***175** Q-10; ★ **LOU**; mail Floyds Knobs z 47119; Ⓟ 5,896; © 6,378
Lafayette; MCD-Township; MADISON; ***174** H-10; ★ **AND**; mail Anderson z 46011; Ⓟ 5,408; © 5,431
Lafayette; MCD-Township; OWEN; ***175** M-6; mail Spencer z 47460; Ⓟ 912; © 1,287
Lafayette; Inc. Place; ⊡ TIPPECANOE; **174** G-6; elev. 560ft./171m.; 🅿 🅷 ■; ★ **LAF-**; z 47901-07, z 47909, z 47996; Ⓟ 43,758; © 56,397; Ⓡ 56,629; ◆ 71,222
La Fontaine; Inc. Place; WABASH; **174** F-10; elev. 808ft./246m.; 🅿; z 46940; Ⓟ 909; © 900
Lagrange; Inc. Place; ⊡ LAGRANGE; **174** A-11; elev. 944ft./288m.; 🅿 🅷; z 46761; Ⓟ 2,382; © 2,919
LAGRANGE; **174** A-11; Ⓟ 29,477; © 34,909; ◆ 37,222
Lagro; Inc. Place; WABASH; ▲ Lagro; **174** E-10; 🅿; z 46941; Ⓟ 496; © 454
Lagro; MCD-Township; WABASH; ***174** E-10; 🅿; z 46941; Ⓟ 2,916; © 3,158
Lake; MCD-Township; ALLEN; ***174** D-12; mail Fort Wayne z 46818; Ⓟ 1,914; © 1,985
Lake; MCD-Township; KOSCIUSKO; ***174** D-10; mail Silver Lake z 46982; Ⓟ 1,566; © 1,716
Lake; MCD-Township; NEWTON; ***174** D-4; mail Lake Village z 46349; Ⓟ 2,208; © 2,465
LAKE; **174** C-4; Ⓟ 475,594; © 484,564; ◆ 485,174
Lake Bodona; RMC Place; MORGAN; ***175** K-8; ★ **IND**; mail Mooresville z 46158; ● 60
Lake Bruce; RMC Place; FULTON; **174** D-8; mail Kewanna z 46939; summer pop. 350; ● 150
Lake Cicott; RMC Place; CASS; **174** E-7; elev. 706ft./215m.; 🅿; z 46942; ● 100
Lake Dalecarlia; CDP; LAKE; ***174** C-4; ★ **CHI**; mail Lowell z 46356; Ⓟ 1,276; © 1,285
Lake Dilldear; RMC Place; DEARBORN; ***175** N-13; ★ **CIN**; mail Dillsboro z 47018; ● 60
Lake Edgewood; RMC Place; MORGAN; ***175** L-8; ★ **IND**; mail Martinsville z 46151; ● 350
Lake Eliza; RMC Place; PORTER; **174** B-5; ★ **CHI**; mail Valparaiso z 46385; ● 600
Lake Everett; RMC Place; ALLEN; ***174** C-12; mail Fort Wayne z 46818; ● 200
Lake Hart; RMC Place; MORGAN; ***175** K-8; elev. 750ft./229m.; ★ **IND**; mail Mooresville z 46158; Ⓟ 213
Lake Hills; RMC Place; LAKE; ***174** B-4; ★ **CHI**; mail Schererville z 46375; ● 200
Lake Holiday; RMC Place; LAKE; ***174** B-5; ★ **CHI**; mail Crown Point z 46307
Lake Holiday; RMC Place; MONTGOMERY; ***174** I-6; mail Crawfordsville z 47933; ● 750
Lake James; RMC Place; STEUBEN; **174** A-13; mail Angola z 46703; summer pop. 1,900; ● 800
Lake Latonka; RMC Place; MARSHALL; ***174** C-8; mail Culver z 46511, Plymouth z 46563; ● 150
Lake Lincoln; RMC Place; SPENCER; mail Lincoln City z 47552; ● 125
Lake Manitou; RMC Place; FULTON; ***174** D-9; mail Rochester z 46975; pop. incl. with Rochester (Inc. Place)
Lake Maxine; RMC Place; MORGAN; ***175** L-7; mail Quincy z 47456; ● 50
Lake McCoy; RMC Place; DECATUR; ***175** L-12; mail Greensburg z 47240; ● 200
Lake Mohee; RMC Place; BLACKFORD; ***174** G-11; ★ **MUN**; mail Hartford City z 47348; ● 75
Lake Noji; RMC Place; VIGO; ***175** L-4; mail Terre Haute z 47802; ● 50
Lake of the Woods; RMC Place; MARSHALL; ***174** B-8; mail Bremen z 46506; ● 700
Lake on the Green (New Bellsville); RMC Place; BROWN; ***175** M-9; mail Columbus z 47201
Lake Park; RMC Place; LAPORTE; ***174** A-7; mail New Carlisle z 46552; ● 150
Lake Santee; RMC Place; DECATUR; ***175** L-12; mail Greensburg z 47240; ● 200
Lake Shores; RMC Place; ALLEN; ***174** D-12; ★ **FTWA**; mail Fort Wayne z 46819; pop. incl. with Fort Wayne (Inc. Place)
Lakeside Park; RMC Place; KOSCIUSKO; ***174** C-10; mail Warsaw z 46580; pop. incl. with Warsaw (Inc. Place)
Lakes of the Four Seasons; CDP; LAKE, PORTER; ***174** B-5; ★ **CHI**; mail Crown Point z 46307; Ⓟ 6,556; © 7,291; Ⓡ 7,296
Lake Station (East Gary); Inc. Place; LAKE; **174** A-5; elev. 600ft./183m.; 🅿; ★ **CHI**; z 46405; Ⓟ 13,899; © 13,948
Lake Sullivan; RMC Place; SULLIVAN; ***175** M-4; mail Sullivan z 47882; ● 150
Laketon; RMC Place; WABASH; **174** D-10; elev. 760ft./232m.; 🅿; z 46943; ● 250
Lake View; RMC Place; FRANKLIN; ***175** L-12; mail Laurel z 47024; ● 80
Lakeview; RMC Place; LAGRANGE; ***174** B-12; mail Wolcottville z 46795; ● 60
Lake Village; CDP; NEWTON; ▲ Lake; **174** D-4; 🅿; z 46349; © 855
Lakeville; Inc. Place; ST. JOSEPH; **174** B-8; elev. 850ft./259m.; 🅿; ★ **S.B.**; z 46536; Ⓟ 655; © 567
Lake Wood; RMC Place; GRANT; ***174** F-11; ★ **MRN**; mail Marion z 46952; ● 80
Lakewood; RMC Place; VIGO; mail Terre Haute z 47802; ● 200
Lakewood; RMC Place; WHITE; ***174** F-6; mail Monticello z 47960; ● 80
Lakewood Hills; RMC Place; VANDERBURGH; ***175** S-3; ★ **EV**; mail Evansville z 47711; pop. incl. with Evansville (Inc. Place)
Lalimere (Wilhelm); RMC Place; LAPORTE; ***174** A-7; ★ **MICH**; mail La Porte z 46350; rural
Lamar; RMC Place; SPENCER; **175** S-6; elev. 412ft./126m.; 🅿; z 47550 & mail Fulda z 47536; ● 100
Lamb; RMC Place; SWITZERLAND; ***175** P-12; mail Vevay z 47043
Lamb Lake; RMC Place; JOHNSON; ***175** L-8; mail Trafalgar z 46181; ● 200
Lamong; RMC Place; HAMILTON; ***174** I-8; ★ **IND**; mail Sheridan z 46069; rural
Lancaster; RMC Place; HUNTINGTON; ▲ Lancaster; **174** F-11; mail Huntington z 46750; ● 100
Lancaster; MCD-Township; HUNTINGTON; ***174** E-11; mail Huntington z 46750; Ⓟ 1,058; © 1,225
Lancaster; RMC Place; JEFFERSON; ▲ Lancaster; ***175** O-11; mail Madison z 47250
Lancaster; MCD-Township; JEFFERSON; ***175** O-11; mail Madison z 47250; Ⓟ 1,534; © 1,608
Lancaster; MCD-Township; WELLS; ***174** E-12; mail Bluffton z 46714; Ⓟ 4,625; © 5,411
Lancaster Park; RMC Place; MONROE; ***175** M-7; ★ **BLMNG**; mail Bloomington z 47401, z 47403; ● 130
Landess; RMC Place; GRANT; **174** F-11; elev. 866ft./264m.; ★ **MRN**; mail Van Buren z 46991; ● 100
Lane; MCD-Township; WARRICK; ***175** R-5; mail Tennyson z 47637; Ⓟ 279; © 255
Lanesville; Inc. Place; HARRISON; **175** R-9; elev. 730ft./223m.; 🅿; ★ **LOU**; z 47136; Ⓟ 512; © 614
Lantana Estate; RMC Place; SHELBY; ***175** L-10; mail Shelbyville z 46176
Lantern Park; RMC Place; DELAWARE; ***174** H-11; ★ **MUN**; mail Muncie z 47304; ● 250
Laotto; RMC Place; NOBLE; **174** C-12; elev. 872ft./266m.; 🅿; z 46763; ● 250
La Paz; Inc. Place; MARSHALL; **174** B-8; elev. 879ft./268m.; 🅿; z 46537; Ⓟ 562; © 489
La Paz Junction; RMC Place; MARSHALL; ***174** B-8; mail Plymouth z 46563; rural
Lapel; Inc. Place; MADISON; **174** I-10; elev. 858ft./262m.; 🅿; ★ **AND**; z 46051; Ⓟ 1,742; © 1,855
LaPorte; Inc. Place; ⊡ LAPORTE; **174** A-7; elev. 807ft./246m.; 🅿 🅷 ■; ★ **MICH**; z 46350, z 46352; Ⓟ 21,507; © 21,621; ◆ 21,676
LAPORTE; **174** B-7; Ⓟ 107,066; © 110,106; ◆ 108,187
Lapping Park Estates; RMC Place; CLARK; ***175** Q-10; ★ **LOU**; mail Jeffersonville z 47130; pop. incl. with Clarksville (Inc. Place)
Larimer Hill; RMC Place; VIGO; ***175** L-4; ★ **T.H.**; mail West Terre Haute z 47885; ● 300
Larwill; Inc. Place; WHITLEY; **174** C-11; elev. 950ft./290m.; 🅿; z 46764; Ⓟ 219; © 282
Laud; RMC Place; WHITLEY; **174** D-11; mail Columbia City z 46725; ● 100
Laughery; MCD-Township; RIPLEY; ***175** M-12; mail Sunman z 47041; Ⓟ 4,441; © 4,581
Lauramie; MCD-Township; TIPPECANOE; ***174** H-6; mail Clarks Hill z 47930; Ⓟ 2,119; © 2,410
Laurel; Inc. Place; FRANKLIN; ▲ Laurel; **175** L-12; 🅿; z 47024; Ⓟ 544; © 579
Laurel; MCD-Township; FRANKLIN; ***175** L-12; 🅿; z 47024; Ⓟ 1,462; © 1,650
Lawrence; Inc. Place; MARION; ▲ Lawrence; **174** J-9; 🅿; ★ **IND**; z 46226 & mail Indianapolis z 46216, z 46256; Ⓟ 26,849; © 38,915; ◆ 43,883
Lawrence; MCD-Township; MARION; ***174** J-9; 🅿; ★ **IND**; z 46226 & mail Indianapolis z 46256; Ⓟ 94,548; © 111,961
LAWRENCE; **175** O-8; Ⓟ 42,836; © 45,922; ◆ 45,976
Lawrenceburg; Inc. Place; ⊡ DEARBORN; ▲ Lawrenceburg; **175** N-14; 🅿 🅷; ★ **CIN**; z 47025; Ⓟ 4,375; © 4,685
Lawrenceburg; MCD-Township; DEARBORN; ***175** M-14; 🅿; ★ **CIN**; z 47025; Ⓟ 9,923; © 10,434
Lawrenceport; RMC Place; LAWRENCE; **175** O-8; mail Mitchell z 47446; ● 100
Lawrenceville; RMC Place; DEARBORN; **175** M-13; elev. 962ft./293m.; mail Sunman z 47041; ● 70
Lawton; RMC Place; PULASKI; **174** D-7; elev. 714ft./218m.; mail Winamac z 46996; ● 30
Layton Mills; DECATUR; see Slabtown (RMC Place)
Leases Corner; RMC Place; CASS; ***174** E-8; mail Lucerne z 46950; rural

---

Entries in **UPPERCASE** are counties.
Entries in **bold** have populations of 2,500 or more.
Names in parentheses are alternate names.

Inc. Place	Incorporated Place
RMC Place	Rand McNally Designated Place
CDP	Census Designated Place
MCD	Minor Civil Division
⊡	County Seat
▲	Minor Civil Division
elev.	Elevation
🅿	Post Office
🅷	Hospital
🅲	College
■	Principal Business Center
★	Ranally Metro Area (RMA) Abbreviation
z	Zip Code(s)
Ⓟ	Previous Census Population
Ⓡ	Revised Census Population
Ⓐ	Annexation Population
●	Rand McNally Population Estimate
©	Final Census Population
Ⓢ	Special Census Population
◆	Estimated Population

For additional definitions see Glossary, Volume 1, and Introduction, Volume 2.

Leavenworth; Inc. Place; CRAWFORD; **175** R-8; elev. 668ft./204m.; 🅿; **z** 47137; ℗ 320; © 353
Lebanon; Inc. Place; ⊡ BOONE; **174** I-7; elev. 948ft./289m.; 🅿 🅷; ★ **IND**; **z** 46052; ℗ 12,059; © 14,222
Lee; RMC Place; WHITE; **174** E-6; mail Rensselaer **z** 47978; ● 25
Leesburg; Inc. Place; KOSCIUSKO; **174** C-10; elev. 850ft./259m.; 🅿; **z** 46538; ℗ 584; © 625
Leesville; RMC Place; LAWRENCE; **175** O-8; mail Bedford **z** 47421; ● 60
Leininger Acres; RMC Place; TIPTON; ***174** H-9; mail Tipton **z** 46072; ● 160
Leipsic; RMC Place; ORANGE; **175** P-8; elev. 725ft./221m.; mail Orleans **z** 47452; ● 50
Leisure; RMC Place; MADISON; **174** G-10; mail Elwood **z** 46036; ● 30
Leiters Ford; RMC Place; FULTON; **174** D-8; 🅿; **z** 46945; ● 200
Lena; RMC Place; PARKE, CLAY; **175** K-5; mail Brazil **z** 47834; ● 70
Leo; RMC Place; ALLEN; ***174** C-13; 🅿; ★ **FTWA**; **z** 46765; pop. incl. with Leo-Cedarville (Inc. Place)
Leo; ALLEN; see Leo-Cedarville (Inc. Place)
Leo-Cedarville (Leo); Inc. Place; ALLEN; **174** C-13; elev. 793ft./242m.; ★ **FTWA**; mail Grabill **z** 46741, Leo **z** 46765; © 2,782
Leopold; RMC Place; PERRY; ▲ Leopold; **175** S-7; elev. 725ft./221m.; 🅿; **z** 47551; ● 100
Leopold; MCD-Township; PERRY; ***175** S-7; 🅿; **z** 47551; ℗ 623; © 720
Leota; RMC Place; SCOTT; **175** P-10; elev. 613ft./187m.; mail Scottsburg **z** 47170; ● 40
Leroy; RMC Place; LAKE; **174** B-5; elev. 690ft./210m.; 🅿; ★ **CHI**; **z** 46355; ● 200
Letts; RMC Place; DECATUR; **175** M-11; mail Greensburg **z** 47240; ● 150
Letts Corner; RMC Place; DECATUR; ***175** M-11; elev. 895ft./273m.; mail Greensburg **z** 47240; ● 50
Lewis; MCD-Township; CLAY; ***175** M-5; mail Jasonville **z** 47438; ℗ 1,310; © 1,510
Lewis; RMC Place; VIGO; **175** M-4; elev. 617ft./188m.; 🅿; **z** 47858; ● 175
Lewisburg; RMC Place; CASS; ***174** F-8; mail Peru **z** 46970; ● 40
Lewis Creek; RMC Place; SHELBY; **175** L-10; mail Flat Rock **z** 47234; ● 30
Lewisville; Inc. Place; HENRY; **174** J-12; elev. 1,050ft./320m.; 🅿; **z** 47352; ℗ 437; © 395
Lewisville; RMC Place; MORGAN, OWEN; **175** L-7; mail Cloverdale **z** 46120; ● 25
Lex; CARROLL; see Lexington (RMC Place)
Lexington (Lex); RMC Place; CARROLL; ***174** G-7; mail Cutler **z** 46920
Lexington; RMC Place; SCOTT; ▲ Lexington; **175** P-11; 🅿; **z** 47138; ● 450
Lexington; MCD-Township; SCOTT; ***175** P-11; 🅿; **z** 47138; ℗ 2,803; © 3,268
Liber; RMC Place; JAY; ***174** G-13; mail Portland **z** 47371; ● 25
Liberty; MCD-Township; CARROLL; ***174** F-7; mail Camden **z** 46917; ℗ 487; © 444
Liberty; MCD-Township; CRAWFORD; ***175** Q-8; mail Marengo **z** 47140; ℗ 1,835; © 2,045
Liberty; MCD-Township; DELAWARE; ***174** H-12; ★ **MUN**; mail Selma **z** 47383; ℗ 4,917; © 4,919
Liberty; MCD-Township; FULTON; ***174** D-8; mail Fulton **z** 46931; ℗ 1,764; © 1,730
Liberty; MCD-Township; GRANT; ***174** G-10; mail Fairmount **z** 46928; ℗ 1,003; © 1,023
Liberty; MCD-Township; HENDRICKS; ***175** K-7; ★ **IND**; mail Clayton **z** 46118; ℗ 4,566; © 5,072
Liberty; MCD-Township; HENRY; ***174** J-12; mail New Castle **z** 47362; ℗ 1,504; © 1,441
Liberty; MCD-Township; HOWARD; ***174** G-9; ★ **KOK**; mail Kokomo **z** 46901; ℗ 4,387; © 5,032
Liberty; MCD-Township; PARKE; ***174** J-4; mail Kingman **z** 47952; ℗ 719; © 768
Liberty; MCD-Township; PORTER; ***174** A-5; ★ **CHI**; mail Valparaiso **z** 46383; ℗ 5,740; © 6,727
Liberty; MCD-Township; SHELBY; ***175** L-11; mail Waldron **z** 46182; ℗ 1,878; © 1,750
Liberty; MCD-Township; ST. JOSEPH; ***174** B-8; mail North Liberty **z** 46554; ℗ 3,011; © 3,053
Liberty; MCD-Township; TIPTON; ***174** G-9; ★ **KOK**; mail Sharpsville **z** 46068; ℗ 2,445; © 2,569
Liberty; Inc. Place; ⊡ UNION; **175** K-13; elev. 992ft./302m.; 🅿; **z** 47353; ℗ 2,051; © 2,061
Liberty; MCD-Township; UNION; ***175** K-13; 🅿; **z** 47353; does not include the Town of Liberty; ℗ 910; © 1,032
Liberty; MCD-Township; WABASH; ***174** F-10; mail La Fontaine **z** 46940; ℗ 2,398; © 2,527
Liberty; MCD-Township; WARREN; ***174** G-4; mail Attica **z** 47918; ℗ 680; © 850
Liberty; MCD-Township; WELLS; ***174** F-12; mail Liberty Center **z** 46766; ℗ 1,166; © 1,177
Liberty; MCD-Township; WHITE; ***174** E-6; mail Monticello **z** 47960; ℗ 1,777; © 2,225
Liberty Center; RMC Place; WELLS; ▲ Liberty; **174** F-12; 🅿; **z** 46766; ● 200
Liberty Hills; RMC Place; ALLEN; ***174** D-12; ★ **FTWA**; mail Fort Wayne **z** 46804; ● 900
Liberty Mills; RMC Place; WABASH; **174** D-10; elev. 781ft./238m.; 🅿; **z** 46946; ● 200
Liberty Park; RMC Place; LAKE; ***174** B-4; ★ **CHI**; mail Crown Point **z** 46307; ● 600
Libertyville; RMC Place; VIGO; **175** K-3; ★ **T.H.**; mail West Terre Haute **z** 47885; ● 80
Licking; MCD-Township; BLACKFORD; ***174** G-12; ★ **MUN**; mail Hartford City **z** 47348; ℗ 8,825; © 8,689
Liggett; RMC Place; VIGO; ***175** L-4; ★ **T.H.**; mail West Terre Haute **z** 47885; ● 80
Ligonier; Inc. Place; NOBLE; **174** B-11; elev. 880ft./268m.; 🅿; **z** 46767; ℗ 3,443; © 4,357
Lilly Dale; RMC Place; PERRY; ***175** S-7; elev. 451ft./137m.; mail Tell City **z** 47586
Lima; MCD-Township; LAGRANGE; ***174** A-11; mail Howe **z** 46746; ℗ 2,294; © 2,387
Limberlost Hills; RMC Place; VIGO; ***175** L-4; ★ **T.H.**; mail Terre Haute **z** 47803; ● 100
Limedale; RMC Place; PUTNAM; ***175** K-6; mail Greencastle **z** 46135; ● 50
Lincoln; RMC Place; CASS; **174** F-8; ★ **KOK**; mail Walton **z** 46994; ● 90
Lincoln; MCD-Township; HENDRICKS; ***174** J-8; ★ **IND**; mail Brownsburg **z** 46112; ℗ 14,008; © 18,967
Lincoln; MCD-Township; LAPORTE; ***174** A-7; mail Mill Creek **z** 46365; ℗ 1,862; © 1,835
Lincoln; MCD-Township; NEWTON; ***174** D-4; ★ **CHI**; mail Demotte **z** 46310; ℗ 3,591; © 4,268
Lincoln; MCD-Township; ST. JOSEPH; ***174** B-7; mail Walkerton **z** 46574; ℗ 2,782; © 3,053
Lincoln; MCD-Township; WHITE; ***174** E-7; mail Idaville **z** 47950; ℗ 673; © 635
Lincoln City; RMC Place; SPENCER; **175** R-5; elev. 437ft./133m.; 🅿; **z** 47552; ● 120
Lincoln Heights; RMC Place; CLARK; ***175** R-10; ★ **LOU**; mail Clarksville **z** 47129; pop. incl. with Clarksville (Inc. Place)
Lincoln Hills; RMC Place; PORTER; ***174** B-5; ★ **CHI**; mail Valparaiso **z** 46385; ● 250
Lincoln Park; RMC Place; CLARK; ***175** Q-10; ★ **LOU**; mail Clarksville **z** 47129; pop. incl. with Clarksville (Inc. Place)
Lincolnshire; RMC Place; ALLEN; ***174** D-12; ★ **FTWA**; mail Fort Wayne **z** 46807; pop. incl. with Fort Wayne (Inc. Place)
Lincolnshire; RMC Place; VIGO; ★ **T.H.**; mail Terre Haute **z** 47803; pop. incl. with Terre Haute (Inc. Place)
Lincoln Village; RMC Place; LAKE; ***174** B-4; ★ **CHI**; mail Merrillville **z** 46410; pop. incl. with Merrillville (Inc. Place)
Lincolnville; RMC Place; WABASH; **174** F-10; mail Wabash **z** 46992; ● 150
Lindbergh Estates; RMC Place; MADISON; ***174** I-11; ★ **AND**; mail Anderson **z** 46012; ● 150
Linden; Inc. Place; MONTGOMERY; **174** H-6; elev. 789ft./240m.; 🅿; **z** 47955; ℗ 718; © 700
Lindenwood; RMC Place; MARION; ***175** K-9; ★ **IND**; mail Indianapolis **z** 46227; pop. incl. with Indianapolis (Inc. Place)
Linkville; RMC Place; MARSHALL; **174** B-8; mail Plymouth **z** 46563; ● 30
Linn Grove; RMC Place; ADAMS; **174** F-13; elev. 828ft./252m.; 🅿; **z** 46711, **z** 46769; ● 200
Linnsburg; RMC Place; MONTGOMERY; ***174** I-6; mail Crawfordsville **z** 47933; ● 130
Linton; Inc. Place; GREENE; **175** N-5; elev. 526ft./160m.; 🅿 🅷; **z** 47441; ℗ 5,814; © 5,774
Linton; MCD-Township; VIGO; ***175** M-4; mail Terre Haute **z** 47802; ℗ 1,308; © 1,212
Linwood; RMC Place; MADISON; **174** H-10; ★ **AND**; mail Alexandria **z** 46001; ● 170
Linwood; RMC Place; MARION; ***174** J-9; ★ **IND**; mail Indianapolis **z** 46201; pop. incl. with Indianapolis (Inc. Place)
Lisbon; RMC Place; NOBLE; **174** B-12; mail Kendallville **z** 46755; ● 50
Little Acre; RMC Place; JACKSON; ***175** N-10; mail Seymour **z** 47274; ● 175
Little Cedar Lake; RMC Place; WHITLEY; ***174** C-11; mail Columbia City **z** 46725
Little Point; RMC Place; MORGAN; ***175** K-7; mail Stilesville **z** 46180, Stinesville **z** 47464; ● 50
Littles; RMC Place; PIKE; ***175** Q-4; mail Petersburg **z** 47567; rural
Little Saint Louis; RMC Place; HARRISON; ***175** R-8; mail Depauw **z** 47115; rural
Little York; Inc. Place; WASHINGTON; **175** P-10; elev. 563ft./172m.; 🅿; **z** 47139; ℗ 155; © 185
Liverpool; RMC Place; LAKE; ***174** B-4; ★ **CHI**; mail Lake Station **z** 46405; pop. incl. with Lake Station (Inc. Place)
Livonia; Inc. Place; WASHINGTON; **175** P-8; elev. 780ft./238m.; 🅿; **z** 47108; ℗ 136; © 112
Lizton; Inc. Place; HENDRICKS; **174** J-7; elev. 958ft./292m.; 🅿; **z** 46149; ℗ 410; © 372
Locke; RMC Place; ELKHART; ▲ Locke; **174** B-9; mail Nappanee **z** 46550; ● 80
Locke; MCD-Township; ELKHART; ***174** B-9; mail Nappanee **z** 46550; ℗ 3,881; © 4,200
Lockhart; MCD-Township; PIKE; ***175** R-5; mail Stendal **z** 47585; ℗ 724; © 690
Lockport; RMC Place; CARROLL; **174** F-7; mail Burnettsville **z** 47926; ● 20
Lodi; RMC Place; PARKE; **174** I-4; mail Kingman **z** 47952; ● 85
Logan; RMC Place; DEARBORN; ▲ Logan; ***175** M-13; ★ **CIN**; mail West Harrison **z** 47060
Logan; MCD-Township; DEARBORN; ***175** M-13; ★ **CIN**; mail West Harrison **z** 47060; ℗ 2,129; © 2,513
Logan; MCD-Township; FOUNTAIN; ***174** H-5; mail Attica **z** 47918; ℗ 4,064; © 3,968
Logan; MCD-Township; PIKE; ***175** Q-4; mail Petersburg **z** 47567; ℗ 379; © 335
Logansport; Inc. Place; ⊡ CASS; **174** E-8; elev. 640ft./195m.; 🅿 🅷 ■; **z** 46947; ℗ 16,812; © 19,684; ◆ 18,693
Lomax; RMC Place; STARKE; **174** C-6; mail San Pierre **z** 46374; ● 30
London; RMC Place; SHELBY; **175** K-10; ★ **IND**; mail Fairland **z** 46126; ● 100
London Heights; RMC Place; SHELBY; ***175** K-10; ★ **IND**; mail Fairland **z** 46126; ● 50
Long Acres; RMC Place; SHELBY; mail Shelbyville **z** 46176; ● 170
Long Beach; Inc. Place; LAPORTE; **174** A-6; elev. 620ft./189m.; 🅿; ★ **MICH**; **z** 46360; ℗ 2,044; © 1,559
Long Lake; RMC Place; STEUBEN; ***174** A-14; mail Fremont **z** 46737; ● 100
Long Lake; RMC Place; WABASH; ***174** D-10; mail North Manchester **z** 46962; ● 200
Long Lake Island; RMC Place; PORTER; ***174** B-5; ★ **CHI**; mail Valparaiso **z** 46383; ● 100
Loogootee; Inc. Place; MARTIN; **175** P-6; elev. 537ft./164m.; 🅿; **z** 47553; ℗ 2,884; © 2,741
Lookout; RMC Place; RIPLEY; ***175** M-12; mail Sunman **z** 47041; rural
Loon Lake; RMC Place; WHITLEY, NOBLE; ***174** C-11; mail Columbia City **z** 46725; ● 400
Lorane; RMC Place; WHITLEY; ***174** C-11; mail Columbia City **z** 46725
Loree; RMC Place; MIAMI; ***174** F-9; elev. 816ft./249m.; mail Bunker Hill **z** 46914; rural
Losantville; Inc. Place; RANDOLPH; **174** I-12; elev. 1,130ft./344m.; 🅿; **z** 47354; ℗ 253; © 280
Lost Creek; MCD-Township; VIGO; ***175** L-4; ★ **T.H.**; mail Terre Haute **z** 47803; ℗ 8,633; © 9,907
Lost River; MCD-Township; MARTIN; ***175** P-6; mail French Lick **z** 47432, Shoals **z** 47581; ℗ 449; © 532
Lottaville; RMC Place; LAKE; ***174** B-4; ★ **CHI**; mail Merrillville **z** 46410; pop. incl. with Merrillville (Inc. Place)
Lotus; RMC Place; UNION; ***175** K-13; mail Liberty **z** 47353
Lovett; RMC Place; JENNINGS; ▲ Lovett; **175** O-11; mail North Vernon **z** 47265; ● 65
Lovett; MCD-Township; JENNINGS; ***175** O-11; mail North Vernon **z** 47265; ℗ 768; © 982
Lowell; RMC Place; BARTHOLOMEW; ***175** M-9; ★ **COL**; mail Columbus **z** 47201; ● 400
Lowell; Inc. Place; LAKE; **174** C-4; elev. 684ft./208m.; 🅿; ★ **CHI**; **z** 46356; ℗ 6,430; © 7,505
Lower Sunset Park; RMC Place; CARROLL; ***174** F-6; mail Monticello **z** 47960; ● 120
Luce; MCD-Township; SPENCER; ***175** S-5; mail Richland **z** 47634; ℗ 2,862; © 2,694
Lucerne; RMC Place; CASS; **174** E-8; elev. 800ft./244m.; 🅿; **z** 46950; ● 130
Ludwig Park; RMC Place; ALLEN; ***174** D-12; ★ **FTWA**; mail Fort Wayne **z** 46825; pop. incl. with Fort Wayne (Inc. Place)
Lukens Lake; RMC Place; WABASH; ***174** D-9; mail Roann **z** 46974; ● 80
Luray; RMC Place; HENRY; ***174** I-12; ★ **MUN**; mail Springport **z** 47386; ● 25
Luther; RMC Place; WHITLEY, HUNTINGTON; ***174** D-11; mail South Whitley **z** 46787; rural
Lutheran Lake; RMC Place; BARTHOLOMEW; ***175** N-9; mail Columbus **z** 47201, Seymour **z** 47274; ● 250
Lydick; RMC Place; ST. JOSEPH; **174** A-8; ★ **S.B.**; mail South Bend **z** 46628; ● 800
Lyford; RMC Place; PARKE; **175** K-4; mail Rosedale **z** 47874; ● 400
Lynn; MCD-Township; POSEY; ***175** S-2; mail Mount Vernon **z** 47620; ℗ 991; © 945
Lynn; Inc. Place; RANDOLPH; **174** I-13; elev. 1,180ft./360m.; 🅿; **z** 47355; ℗ 1,183; © 1,143
Lynnhurst; RMC Place; MARION; ***174** J-8; ★ **IND**; mail Indianapolis **z** 46241; pop. incl. with Indianapolis (Inc. Place)
Lynnville (Lynnville Mine); Inc. Place; WARRICK; **175** R-4; elev. 497ft./151m.; 🅿; **z** 47619; ℗ 640; © 781
Lynnville Mine; WARRICK; see Lynnville (Inc. Place)
Lynwood Estates; RMC Place; MONROE; ***175** M-7; ★ **BLMNG**; mail Bloomington **z** 47404; ● 80
Lyons; Inc. Place; GREENE; **175** N-5; elev. 530ft./162m.; 🅿; **z** 47443; ℗ 753; © 748
Lyonsville; RMC Place; FAYETTE; ***175** K-13; mail Connersville **z** 47331; ● 40

M

Mace; RMC Place; MONTGOMERY; **174** I-6; mail Crawfordsville **z** 47933; ● 150
Mac-Fair-Mar; RMC Place; CASS; mail Logansport **z** 46947; ● 180
Mackey; Inc. Place; GIBSON; **175** R-4; elev. 439ft./134m.; 🅿; **z** 47654; ℗ 89; © 142
Macy; Inc. Place; MIAMI; **174** D-9; elev. 850ft./259m.; 🅿; **z** 46951; ℗ 218; © 248
Madison; MCD-Township; ALLEN; ***174** D-13; mail Monroeville **z** 46773; ℗ 1,615; © 1,796
Madison; MCD-Township; CARROLL; ***174** G-7; mail Delphi **z** 46923; ℗ 479; © 442
Madison; MCD-Township; CLINTON; ***174** G-7; mail Mulberry **z** 46058; ℗ 1,938; © 2,158
Madison; MCD-Township; DAVIESS; ***175** O-6; mail Odon **z** 47562; ℗ 2,609; © 2,793
Madison; MCD-Township; DUBOIS; ***175** Q-5; mail Jasper **z** 47546; ℗ 1,692; © 2,112
Madison; MCD-Township; JAY; ***174** G-14; mail Fort Recovery **z** 45846; ℗ 741; © 608
Madison; Inc. Place; ⊡ JEFFERSON; **175** O-12; elev. 497ft./151m.; 🅿 🅷 ■; **z** 47250; ℗ 12,006; © 12,004; ◆ 12,035
Madison; MCD-Township; JEFFERSON; ***175** O-12; 🅿; **z** 47250; ℗ 16,117; © 16,770
Madison; MCD-Township; MONTGOMERY; ***174** H-6; mail Crawfordsville **z** 47933; ℗ 1,274; © 1,253
Madison; MCD-Township; MORGAN; ***175** K-8; ★ **IND**; mail Mooresville **z** 46158; ℗ 5,408; © 7,391
Madison; MCD-Township; PIKE; ***175** Q-4; mail Petersburg **z** 47567; ℗ 443; © 406
Madison; MCD-Township; PUTNAM; ***175** K-6; mail Greencastle **z** 46135; ℗ 895; © 1,142
Madison; MCD-Township; ST. JOSEPH; ***174** B-9; mail South Bend **z** 46614; ℗ 1,798; © 1,770
Madison; MCD-Township; TIPTON; ***174** H-10; mail Tipton **z** 46072; ℗ 1,465; © 1,414
Madison; MCD-Township; WASHINGTON; ***175** P-8; mail Campbellsburg **z** 47108; ℗ 607; © 602
MADISON; **174** H-10; ℗ 130,669; © 133,358; ◆ 132,245
Magley; RMC Place; ADAMS; ***174** E-13; mail Decatur **z** 46733; ● 40
Magnet; RMC Place; PERRY; **175** S-7; elev. 500ft./152m.; 🅿; **z** 47520; ● 40
Mahalasville; RMC Place; MORGAN; ***175** L-8; ★ **IND**; mail Martinsville **z** 46151; ● 70
Mahon; RMC Place; HUNTINGTON; ***174** E-12; mail Huntington **z** 46750; ● 30
Majenica; RMC Place; HUNTINGTON; **174** E-11; mail Huntington **z** 46750; ● 75
Malden; RMC Place; PORTER; **174** B-5; mail Valparaiso **z** 46383; ● 120
Maltersville; RMC Place; DUBOIS; ***175** Q-6; mail Huntingburg **z** 47542; rural
Manchester; RMC Place; DEARBORN; ▲ Manchester; **175** M-13; mail Aurora **z** 47001; ● 120
Manchester; MCD-Township; DEARBORN; ***175** M-13; mail Aurora **z** 47001; ℗ 2,571; © 2,930
Manhattan; RMC Place; PUTNAM; **175** K-6; mail Greencastle **z** 46135; ● 50
Manilla; RMC Place; RUSH; **175** K-11; elev. 893ft./272m.; 🅿; **z** 46150 & mail Homer **z** 46146; ● 300
Manor Woods; RMC Place; ALLEN; ***174** D-12; ★ **FTWA**; mail Fort Wayne **z** 46804; ● 250
Mansfield; RMC Place; PARKE; **175** K-5; mail Rockville **z** 47872; ● 30
Manson; RMC Place; CLINTON; **174** H-7; mail Frankfort **z** 46041; ● 35
Manville; RMC Place; JEFFERSON; ***175** O-12; mail Madison **z** 47250; rural
Maple Lane; RMC Place; ST. JOSEPH; **173** B-20; ★ **S.B.**; mail South Bend **z** 46635; pop. incl. with South Bend (Inc. Place)
Maples; RMC Place; ALLEN; **174** D-13; elev. 797ft./243m.; mail Fort Wayne **z** 46816; ● 100
Mapleton; RMC Place; MARION; ***174** J-9; ★ **IND**; mail Indianapolis **z** 46208, **z** 46228; pop. incl. with Indianapolis (Inc. Place)
Maple Valley; RMC Place; HENRY; ***174** J-11; mail Wilkinson **z** 46186
Maplewood; RMC Place; HENDRICKS; **174** J-7; ★ **IND**; mail Danville **z** 46122; ● 50
Maplewood; RMC Place; VIGO; mail West Terre Haute **z** 47885; ● 30
Maplewood Park; RMC Place; ALLEN; ***174** D-13; ★ **FTWA**; mail Fort Wayne **z** 46815; pop. incl. with Fort Wayne (Inc. Place)
Marco; RMC Place; GREENE; **175** N-5; mail Lyons **z** 47443; ● 100
Marengo; Inc. Place; CRAWFORD; **175** Q-8; elev. 600ft./183m.; 🅿; **z** 47140; ℗ 856; © 829
Mariah Hill; RMC Place; SPENCER; **175** R-6; 🅿; **z** 47556; ● 500
Marietta; RMC Place; SHELBY; **175** L-10; mail Shelbyville **z** 46176; ● 200
Marineland Gardens; RMC Place; KOSCIUSKO; ***174** B-10; mail Syracuse **z** 46567; ● 150
Marion; MCD-Township; ALLEN; ***174** D-13; ★ **FTWA**; mail Hoagland **z** 46745; ℗ 3,529; © 3,655
Marion; MCD-Township; BOONE; ***174** I-8; mail Sheridan **z** 46069; ℗ 1,191; © 1,359
Marion; MCD-Township; DECATUR; ***175** M-11; mail Greensburg **z** 47240; ℗ 1,653; © 1,637
Marion; MCD-Township; DUBOIS; ***175** Q-6; mail Jasper **z** 47546; ℗ 1,646; © 1,529
Marion; Inc. Place; ⊡ GRANT; **174** F-11; elev. 815ft./248m.; 🅿 🅷 🅲 13,917 ■; ★ **MRN**; **z** 46952-53; ℗ 32,618; © 31,320; ◆ 27,849
Marion; MCD-Township; HENDRICKS; ***174** J-7; mail Danville **z** 46122; ℗ 1,273; © 1,398
Marion; MCD-Township; JASPER; ***174** E-5; mail Rensselaer **z** 47978; ℗ 6,913; © 7,227
Marion; MCD-Township; JENNINGS; ***175** O-10; mail Deputy **z** 47230; ℗ 972; © 1,058
Marion; MCD-Township; LAWRENCE; ***175** O-7; mail Mitchell **z** 47446; ℗ 8,983; © 9,491
Marion; MCD-Township; OWEN; ***175** M-5; mail Patricksburg **z** 47455; ℗ 798; © 1,004
Marion; MCD-Township; PIKE; ***175** Q-5; mail Velpen **z** 47590; ℗ 580; © 776
Marion; MCD-Township; PUTNAM; ***175** K-6; mail Fillmore **z** 46128; ℗ 1,844; © 1,980
Marion; RMC Place; SHELBY; ***175** K-10; elev. 786ft./240m.; mail Shelbyville **z** 46176; ● 150
Marion; MCD-Township; SHELBY; ***175** K-10; mail Shelbyville **z** 46176; ℗ 1,384; © 1,534
MARION; **174** J-8; ℗ 797,159; © 860,454; ◆ 894,532
Marion Heights; RMC Place; VIGO; **174** I-1; ★ **T.H.**; mail West Terre Haute **z** 47885; ● 220
Markland; RMC Place; SWITZERLAND; **175** O-13; mail Florence **z** 47020; ● 30
Markle; Inc. Place; HUNTINGTON, WELLS; **174** E-12; elev. 780ft./238m.; 🅿; **z** 46770; ℗ 1,208; © 1,102
Markleville; Inc. Place; MADISON; **174** I-11; 🅿; ★ **AND**; **z** 46056; ℗ 412; © 383
Marlin Hills; RMC Place; MONROE; ***175** M-7; ★ **BLMNG**; mail Bloomington **z** 47401, **z** 47408; ● 200
Marrs; MCD-Township; POSEY; ***175** S-2; ★ **EV**; mail Mount Vernon **z** 47620; ℗ 4,462; © 4,868
Marrs Center; RMC Place; POSEY; ***175** S-2; ★ **EV**; mail Mount Vernon **z** 47620; ● 100
Marshall; MCD-Township; LAWRENCE; ***175** N-7; ★ **BLMNG**; mail Bedford **z** 47421; ℗ 3,800; © 4,551
Marshall; Inc. Place; PARKE; **174** J-5; elev. 702ft./214m.; 🅿; **z** 47859; ℗ 379; © 360
MARSHALL; **174** B-8; ℗ 42,182; © 45,128; ◆ 46,238
Marshfield; RMC Place; WARREN; **174** H-4; elev. 692ft./211m.; 🅿; **z** 47993; ● 60
Mars Hill; RMC Place; MARION; ***175** K-8; ★ **IND**; mail Indianapolis **z** 46241; pop. incl. with Indianapolis (Inc. Place)
Marshtown; RMC Place; FULTON; ***174** E-8; elev. 789ft./240m.; mail Kewanna **z** 46939; ● 25
MARTIN; **175** P-6; ℗ 10,369; © 10,369; ◆ 9,785
Martin Heights; RMC Place; WASHINGTON; ***175** P-9; mail Salem **z** 47167; pop. incl. with Salem (Inc. Place)
Martinsburg; RMC Place; WASHINGTON; **175** Q-9; mail Pekin **z** 47165; ● 100
Martinsville; Inc. Place; ⊡ MORGAN; **175** L-8; elev. 607ft./185m.; 🅿 🅷; ★ **IND**; **z** 46151; ℗ 11,677; © 11,698
Martz; CLAY; see Middlebury (RMC Place)
Maryland; RMC Place; VIGO; **174** J-2; ★ **T.H.**; mail Terre Haute **z** 47802; ● 800
Marysville; RMC Place; CLARK; **175** P-11; elev. 712ft./217m.; 🅿; **z** 47141; ● 150
Marysville; RMC Place; PIKE; ***175** Q-4; mail Winslow **z** 47598; rural
Marywood; RMC Place; VIGO; **174** J-2; ★ **T.H.**; mail Terre Haute **z** 47802; ● 600
Matlock Heights; RMC Place; MONROE; ***175** M-7; ★ **BLMNG**; mail Bloomington **z** 47401, **z** 47408; pop. incl. with Bloomington (Inc. Place)
Matthews; Inc. Place; GRANT; **174** G-11; elev. 880ft./268m.; 🅿; ★ **MRN**; **z** 46957; ℗ 571; © 595
Mattix Corner; RMC Place; CLINTON; ***174** G-7; elev. 817ft./249m.; mail Frankfort **z** 46041; rural
Mauckport; Inc. Place; HARRISON; **175** S-8; elev. 423ft./129m.; 🅿; **z** 47142; ℗ 95; © 83
Maumee; MCD-Township; ALLEN; ***174** D-14; mail Woodburn **z** 46797; ℗ 2,459; © 2,619
Mauzy; RMC Place; RUSH; ***175** K-12; mail Rushville **z** 46173; rural
Max; RMC Place; BOONE; **174** I-7; ★ **IND**; mail Lebanon **z** 46052; ● 50
Maxinkuckee; RMC Place; MARSHALL; ***174** C-8; mail Culver **z** 46511
Maxville; RMC Place; RANDOLPH; ***174** H-13; mail Farmland **z** 47340
Maxwell; RMC Place; HANCOCK; **174** J-10; elev. 910ft./277m.; 🅿; ★ **IND**; **z** 46154; ● 200
Maxwell; RMC Place; MORGAN; ***175** L-7; ★ **IND**; mail Martinsville **z** 46151; ● 80
Mayfield; RMC Place; DELAWARE; ***174** H-12; ★ **MUN**; mail Muncie **z** 47303; pop. incl. with Muncie (Inc. Place)
Mays; RMC Place; RUSH; **174** J-11; elev. 1,010ft./308m.; 🅿; **z** 46155; ● 175
Maysville; RMC Place; DAVIESS; **175** P-5; mail Washington **z** 47501; ● 100
Maywood; RMC Place; MARION; ***175** K-8; ★ **IND**; mail Indianapolis **z** 46241; pop. incl. with Indianapolis (Inc. Place)
McCarty; RMC Place; JOHNSON; ***175** K-9; ★ **IND**; mail Greenwood **z** 46142; pop. incl. with Greenwood (Inc. Place)
McClellan; MCD-Township; NEWTON; ***174** D-4; mail Morocco **z** 47963; ℗ 237; © 228
Mc Col Place; RMC Place; WASHINGTON; ***175** P-9; mail Salem **z** 47167; pop. incl. with Salem (Inc. Place)
McCool; RMC Place; PORTER; ***174** A-5; ★ **CHI**; pop. incl. with Portage (Inc. Place)
McCordsville; Inc. Place; HANCOCK; **174** J-10; elev. 854ft./260m.; 🅿; ★ **IND**; **z** 46055; ℗ 684; © 1,134
McCoysburg; RMC Place; JASPER; **174** E-5; elev. 672ft./205m.; mail Rensselaer **z** 47978; ● 40
McCutchanville; RMC Place; VANDERBURGH; **175** S-3; ★ **EV**; mail Evansville **z** 47711, **z** 47725; ● 300
McDaniel; RMC Place; MORGAN; ***175** L-8; ★ **IND**; mail Martinsville **z** 46151; ● 70
McGrawsville; RMC Place; MIAMI; **174** F-9; mail Amboy **z** 46911; ● 70
McKinley; RMC Place; WASHINGTON; ***175** O-8; mail Campbellsburg **z** 47108
McNatts; RMC Place; WELLS; ***174** F-12; mail Montpelier **z** 47359; rural
Meadowbrook; RMC Place; ALLEN; ***174** D-13; ★ **FTWA**; mail New Haven **z** 46774; pop. incl. with New Haven (Inc. Place)
Meadowbrook; RMC Place; MADISON; ***174** I-10; ★ **AND**; pop. incl. with Anderson (Inc. Place)
Meadowbrook; RMC Place; TIPPECANOE; ***174** G-6; ★ **LAF-**; mail Lafayette **z** 47905; ● 250
Meadowood Estates; RMC Place; MADISON; ***174** H-10; ★ **AND**; mail Elwood **z** 46036; ● 30
Meadowview; RMC Place; CASS; mail Logansport **z** 46947; ● 225
Mead Village; RMC Place; BARTHOLOMEW; ★ **COL**; mail Columbus **z** 47201; pop. incl. with Columbus (Inc. Place)
Mecca; Inc. Place; PARKE; **175** K-4; elev. 500ft./152m.; 🅿; **z** 47860; ℗ 331; © 355
Mechanicsburg; RMC Place; BOONE; **174** H-7; mail Kirklin **z** 46050; ● 100
Mechanicsburg; RMC Place; DECATUR; ***175** L-12; mail New Point **z** 47263; rural
Mechanicsburg; RMC Place; HENRY; **174** I-11; ★ **AND**; mail Middletown **z** 47356; ● 150
Medaryville; Inc. Place; PULASKI; **174** D-6; elev. 686ft./209m.; 🅿; **z** 47957; ℗ 689; © 565
Medford; RMC Place; DELAWARE; **174** I-12; elev. 1,023ft./312m.; mail Muncie **z** 47302; ● 30
Medina; MCD-Township; WARREN; ***174** G-5; mail Otterbein **z** 47970; ℗ 371; © 452
Medora; Inc. Place; JACKSON; **175** O-9; elev. 526ft./160m.; 🅿; **z** 47260; ℗ 805; © 565
Meiks; RMC Place; SHELBY; ***175** K-10; mail Shelbyville **z** 46176; ● 200
Mellott; Inc. Place; FOUNTAIN; **174** H-5; elev. 700ft./213m.; 🅿; **z** 47958; ℗ 222; © 207
Melody Hill; CDP; VANDERBURGH; **175** S-13; ★ **EV**; mail Evansville **z** 47711; ℗ 2,932; © 3,066
Meltzer; RMC Place; SHELBY; ***175** L-11; mail Shelbyville **z** 46176; ● 75
Memphis; CDP-Census Area Only; CLARK; **175** Q-10; elev. 487ft./148m.; 🅿; ★ **LOU**; **z** 47143; © 400
Mentone; Inc. Place; KOSCIUSKO; **174** C-9; elev. 839ft./256m.; 🅿; **z** 46539; ℗ 912; © 898
Mentor; RMC Place; DUBOIS; ***175** Q-6; mail Birdseye **z** 47513
Meridian Hills; Inc. Place; MARION; ***174** J-9; ★ **IND**; mail Indianapolis **z** 46260; © 1,713
Merom; SULLIVAN; see Merom Station (RMC Place)
Merom; Inc. Place; SULLIVAN; **175** N-3; 🅿; **z** 47861; ℗ 257; © 294
Merom Station (Merom); RMC Place; SULLIVAN; ***175** N-3; elev. 550ft./168m.; mail Merom **z** 47861
Merriam; RMC Place; NOBLE; **174** C-11; mail Albion **z** 46701; ● 80
Merrillville; Inc. Place; LAKE; **174** B-4; elev. 661ft./201m.; 🅿 ■; ★ **CHI**; **z** 46410-11; ℗ 27,257; © 30,560; ◆ 32,406
Metamora; RMC Place; FRANKLIN; ▲ Metamora; **175** L-13; 🅿; **z** 47030; ● 450
Metamora; MCD-Township; FRANKLIN; ***175** L-13; 🅿; **z** 47030; ℗ 866; © 976
Metea; RMC Place; CASS; **174** E-8; mail Lucerne **z** 46950; ● 60
Metz; RMC Place; STEUBEN; **174** A-13; mail Angola **z** 46703; ● 90
Mexico; CDP; MIAMI; **174** E-9; elev. 700ft./213m.; 🅿; **z** 46958; ℗ 1,003; © 984
Miami; MCD-Township; CASS; ***174** E-8; mail Logansport **z** 46947; ℗ 1,158; © 1,305
Miami; RMC Place; MIAMI; **174** F-9; elev. 790ft./241m.; 🅿; **z** 46959; ● 325
MIAMI; **174** F-9; ℗ 36,897; © 36,082; ◆ 36,106
Miami Bend; RMC Place; CASS; ***174** E-8; mail Logansport **z** 46947; rural
Miami Trails Addition; RMC Place; ST. JOSEPH; ***174** A-8; elev. 840ft./256m.; ★ **S.B.**; mail South Bend **z** 46614; ● 350
Michaels; GRANT; see Michaelsville (RMC Place)
Michaelsville (Michaels); RMC Place; GRANT; ***174** G-10; elev. 850ft./259m.; ★ **MRN**; mail Marion **z** 46953; ● 80
Michiana Shores; Inc. Place; LAPORTE; **174** A-6; elev. 620ft./189m.; 🅿; ★ **MICH**; **z** 46360; ℗ 378; © 330
Michigan; MCD-Township; CLINTON; ***174** H-8; mail Michigantown **z** 46057; ℗ 1,566; © 1,684
Michigan; MCD-Township; LAPORTE; ***174** A-6; ★ **MICH**; mail Michigan City **z** 46360; ℗ 31,196; © 29,326
Michigan City; Inc. Place; LAPORTE; **174** A-6; elev. 600ft./183m.; 🅿 🅷 ■; ★ **MICH**; **z** 46360-61; ℗ 33,822; © 32,900; ◆ 32,332
Michigantown; Inc. Place; CLINTON; **174** H-8; elev. 873ft./266m.; 🅿; **z** 46057; ℗ 472; © 406
Mickleyville; RMC Place; MARION; ***174** J-8; ★ **IND**; mail Indianapolis **z** 46241; pop. incl. with Indianapolis (Inc. Place)
Middle; MCD-Township; HENDRICKS; ***174** J-7; ★ **IND**; mail Pittsboro **z** 46167; ℗ 3,466; © 4,657
Middleboro; RMC Place; WAYNE; **174** J-14; elev. 1,030ft./314m.; ★ **RICH**; mail Richmond **z** 47374; ● 50
Middlebury (Martz); RMC Place; CLAY; **175** M-5; mail Clay City **z** 47841; ● 100
Middlebury; Inc. Place; ELKHART; ▲ Middlebury; **174** A-10; 🅿; ★ **ELK**; **z** 46540; ℗ 2,004; © 2,956
Middlebury; MCD-Township; ELKHART; ***174** A-10; 🅿; ★ **ELK**; **z** 46540; ℗ 5,770; © 7,028
Middlefork; RMC Place; CLINTON; **174** G-8; mail Frankfort **z** 46041; ● 70
Middlefork; RMC Place; JEFFERSON; ***175** O-11; mail Dupont **z** 47231; rural
Middletons; HOWARD; see West Middleton (RMC Place)
Middletown; Inc. Place; HENRY; **174** I-11; elev. 965ft./294m.; 🅿; ★ **AND**; **z** 47356; ℗ 2,333; © 2,488
Middletown; RMC Place; SHELBY; ***175** L-11; mail Waldron **z** 46182; ● 100
Middletown Park; RMC Place; DELAWARE; **174** G-1; ★ **MUN**; mail Muncie **z** 47302; ● 850
Midland; RMC Place; GREENE; **175** N-5; elev. 650ft./198m.; 🅿; **z** 47445; ● 300
Midway; RMC Place; ELKHART; ***174** A-10; ★ **ELK**; mail Goshen **z** 46526
Midway; RMC Place; JEFFERSON; ***175** O-11; mail Madison **z** 47250; ● 30
Midway; RMC Place; SPENCER; **175** S-5; mail Boonville **z** 47601; ● 40
Midwest; RMC Place; PORTER; ★ **CHI**; pop. incl. with Portage (Inc. Place)
Mier; RMC Place; GRANT; **174** F-10; mail Converse **z** 46919; ● 100
Mifflin; RMC Place; CRAWFORD; ***175** R-7; elev. 512ft./156m.; mail English **z** 47118; rural
Milan; MCD-Township; ALLEN; ***174** D-13; ★ **FTWA**; mail New Haven **z** 46774; ℗ 3,165; © 3,503
Milan; Inc. Place; RIPLEY; **175** M-13; elev. 994ft./303m.; 🅿; **z** 47031; ℗ 1,529; © 1,816
Milan Center; RMC Place; ALLEN; ***174** D-13; ★ **FTWA**; mail New Haven **z** 46774; ● 40
Milford; RMC Place; DECATUR; **175** L-11; mail Greensburg **z** 47240; disincorporated june 4, 2007; ℗ 126; © 121
Milford; Inc. Place; KOSCIUSKO; **174** B-10; elev. 835ft./255m.; 🅿; **z** 46542; ℗ 1,388; © 1,550
Milford; MCD-Township; LAGRANGE; ***174** A-12; mail Wolcottville **z** 46795; ℗ 2,548; © 2,955
Milford Junction; RMC Place; KOSCIUSKO; ***174** B-10; mail Milford **z** 46542; ● 75
Mill; MCD-Township; GRANT; ***174** G-11; ★ **MRN**; mail Gas City **z** 46933; ℗ 11,522; © 11,271
Millcreek; MCD-Township; FOUNTAIN; ***174** I-4; mail Kingman **z** 47952; ℗ 1,450; © 1,610
Mill Creek; RMC Place; LAPORTE; ***174** A-7; elev. 700ft./213m.; 🅿; **z** 46365; ● 150
Milledgeville; RMC Place; BOONE; ***174** I-7; mail Lebanon **z** 46052
Miller; MCD-Township; DEARBORN; ***175** M-14; ★ **CIN**; mail Lawrenceburg **z** 47025; ℗ 4,761; © 8,605
Miller; RMC Place; LAKE; ***174** A-5; ★ **CHI**; mail Gary **z** 46403; pop. incl. with Gary (Inc. Place)
Millers; RMC Place; LAKE; ★ **CHI**; pop. incl. with Gary (Inc. Place)
Millersburg; Inc. Place; ELKHART; **174** B-10; elev. 880ft./268m.; 🅿; ★ **ELK**; **z** 46543; ℗ 854; © 868
Millersburg; RMC Place; HAMILTON; ***174** H-9; ★ **IND**; mail Arcadia **z** 46030; ● 35
Millersburg; RMC Place; ORANGE; ***175** P-8; elev. 722ft./220m.; mail Paoli **z** 47454
Millersville; RMC Place; MARION; ***174** J-9; ★ **IND**; mail Indianapolis **z** 46220; pop. incl. with Indianapolis (Inc. Place)
Millgrove; RMC Place; BLACKFORD; **174** G-12; mail Hartford City **z** 47348; ● 150
Millgrove; MCD-Township; STEUBEN; ***174** A-12; mail Orland **z** 46776; ℗ 1,326; © 1,639
Millhousen; Inc. Place; DECATUR; **175** M-11; elev. 900ft./274m.; 🅿; **z** 47261; ℗ 151; © 136
Milligan; RMC Place; PARKE; **174** J-5; mail Rockville **z** 47872; ● 35
Millport; RMC Place; WASHINGTON; ***175** O-9; mail Vallonia **z** 47281
Milltown; Inc. Place; CRAWFORD, HARRISON; **175** Q-8; elev. 562ft./171m.; 🅿; **z** 47145; ℗ 917; © 932
Millville; RMC Place; HENRY; **174** J-12; mail New Castle **z** 47362; ● 90
Milo; RMC Place; HUNTINGTON; ***174** F-11; mail Van Buren **z** 46991; rural
Milroy; MCD-Township; JASPER; ***174** E-5; elev. 937ft./286m.; mail Rensselaer **z** 47978; ℗ 227; © 275
Milroy; RMC Place; RUSH; **175** L-11; 🅿; **z** 46156; ● 850
Milton; MCD-Township; JEFFERSON; ***175** O-12; mail Madison **z** 47250; ℗ 879; © 864
Milton; RMC Place; OHIO; **175** N-13; mail Dillsboro **z** 47018; ● 20
Milton; Inc. Place; WAYNE; **174** J-12; elev. 929ft./283m.; 🅿; **z** 47357; ℗ 634; © 611
Mineral City; RMC Place; GREENE; ***175** N-6; mail Bloomfield **z** 47424; ● 25
Mineral Springs; RMC Place; KOSCIUSKO; ***174** C-10; mail Leesburg **z** 46538; ● 100
Mishawaka; Inc. Place; ST. JOSEPH; **174** A-9; elev. 720ft./219m.; 🅿 🅷 🅲 2,081 ■; ★ **S.B.**; **z** 46544-46; ℗ 42,608; © 46,557; ◆ 47,470
Mitchell; Inc. Place; LAWRENCE; **175** O-7; elev. 687ft./209m.; 🅿; **z** 47446; ℗ 4,669; © 4,567
Mitcheltree; MCD-Township; MARTIN; ***175** O-6; mail Shoals **z** 47581; ℗ 706; © 692
Mixersville (Mixerville); RMC Place; FRANKLIN; **175** L-14; mail Bath **z** 47010; ● 20
Mixerville; FRANKLIN; see Mixersville (RMC Place)
Moberly; RMC Place; HARRISON; ***175** R-8; mail Depauw **z** 47115
Modesto; RMC Place; MONROE; ***175** M-7; mail Bloomington **z** 47401, **z** 47408
Modoc; Inc. Place; RANDOLPH; **174** I-13; elev. 1,177ft./359m.; 🅿; **z** 47358; ℗ 218; © 225
Mohawk; RMC Place; HANCOCK; ***174** J-10; ★ **IND**; mail Greenfield **z** 46140; ● 190
Mongo; RMC Place; LAGRANGE; **174** A-12; elev. 910ft./277m.; 🅿; **z** 46771; ● 200
Monitor; RMC Place; TIPPECANOE; ***174** G-6; ★ **LAF-**; mail Lafayette **z** 47905
Monmouth; RMC Place; ADAMS; **174** E-13; mail Decatur **z** 46733; ● 60
Monon; Inc. Place; WHITE; ▲ Monon; **174** E-6; 🅿; **z** 47959; ℗ 1,585; © 1,733
Monon; MCD-Township; WHITE; ***174** E-6; 🅿; **z** 47959; ℗ 3,140; © 3,272
Monoquet; RMC Place; KOSCIUSKO; ***174** C-10; mail Warsaw **z** 46580; ● 90
Monroe; Inc. Place; ADAMS; **174** E-13; elev. 825ft./251m.; 🅿; **z** 46772; ℗ 788; © 734
Monroe; MCD-Township; ADAMS; ***174** F-13; 🅿; **z** 46772 & mail Berne **z** 46711; includes part of the Town of Monroe; ℗ 4,174; © 4,551
Monroe; MCD-Township; ALLEN; ***174** D-14; mail Monroeville **z** 46773; ℗ 1,969; © 1,963
Monroe; MCD-Township; CARROLL; ***174** G-7; mail Flora **z** 46929; ℗ 2,916; © 3,020
Monroe; MCD-Township; CLARK; ***175** P-10; mail Henryville **z** 47126; ℗ 3,917; © 4,688
Monroe; MCD-Township; DELAWARE; ***174** I-12; ★ **MUN**; mail Muncie **z** 47302; ℗ 3,458; © 3,636
Monroe; MCD-Township; GRANT; ***174** G-11; mail Marion **z** 46952; ℗ 1,448; © 1,601
Monroe; MCD-Township; HOWARD; ***174** G-8; ★ **KOK**; mail Russiaville **z** 46979; ℗ 1,397; © 1,387
Monroe; MCD-Township; JEFFERSON; ***175** O-11; mail Madison **z** 47250; ℗ 391; © 379
Monroe; MCD-Township; KOSCIUSKO; ***174** D-10; mail Warsaw **z** 46580; ℗ 1,088; © 1,166
Monroe; MCD-Township; MADISON; ***174** H-11; ★ **AND**; mail Alexandria **z** 46001; ℗ 10,057; © 10,233
Monroe; MCD-Township; MORGAN; ***175** K-7; ★ **IND**; mail Monrovia **z** 46157; ℗ 4,351; © 4,674
Monroe; MCD-Township; PIKE; ***175** R-4; mail Winslow **z** 47598; ℗ 733; © 715
Monroe; MCD-Township; PULASKI; ***174** D-7; mail Winamac **z** 46996; ℗ 3,802; © 4,015
Monroe; MCD-Township; PUTNAM; ***175** K-6; mail Greencastle **z** 46135; ℗ 1,393; © 1,455
Monroe; MCD-Township; RANDOLPH; ***174** H-12; ★ **MUN**; mail Farmland **z** 47340, Parker City **z** 47368; ℗ 3,602; © 3,819
Monroe; RMC Place; TIPPECANOE; **174** H-6; elev. 785ft./239m.; mail Lafayette **z** 47905; ● 40
Monroe; MCD-Township; WASHINGTON; ***175** O-9; mail Salem **z** 47167; ℗ 525; © 615
MONROE; **175** M-7; ℗ 108,978; © 120,563; ◆ 140,840
Monroe City; Inc. Place; KNOX; **175** P-4; elev. 520ft./158m.; 🅿; **z** 47557; ℗ 538; © 548
Monroe Manor; RMC Place; LAPORTE; ***174** A-7; ★ **MICH**; mail La Porte **z** 46350; pop. incl. with LaPorte (Inc. Place)
Monroeville; Inc. Place; ALLEN; **174** D-13; elev. 780ft./238m.; 🅿; **z** 46773; ℗ 1,232; © 1,236
Monrovia; Inc. Place; MORGAN; **175** K-7; elev. 808ft./246m.; 🅿; ★ **IND**; **z** 46157; © 628
Montclair; RMC Place; HENDRICKS; ***174** J-7; mail Lizton **z** 46149; ● 20
Monterey; Inc. Place; PULASKI; **174** D-7; elev. 723ft./220m.; 🅿; **z** 46960; ℗ 230; © 231
Monterey Village; RMC Place; HAMILTON; ***174** I-9; ★ **IND**; mail Noblesville **z** 46060; pop. incl. with Noblesville (Inc. Place)
Montezuma; Inc. Place; PARKE; **174** J-4; elev. 501ft./153m.; 🅿; **z** 47862; ℗ 1,134; © 1,179
Montgomery; Inc. Place; DAVIESS; **175** P-5; elev. 550ft./168m.; 🅿; **z** 47558; ℗ 351; © 368
Montgomery; MCD-Township; GIBSON; ***175** R-3; mail Owensville **z** 47665; ℗ 3,133; © 3,698
Montgomery; MCD-Township; JENNINGS; ***175** O-11; mail Deputy **z** 47230; ℗ 896; © 983
Montgomery; MCD-Township; OWEN; ***175** L-6; mail Spencer **z** 47460; ℗ 872; © 1,225
MONTGOMERY; **174** I-6; ℗ 34,436; © 37,629; ◆ 37,848
Monticello; Inc. Place; ⊡ WHITE; **174** F-6; elev. 682ft./208m.; 🅿 🅷; **z** 47960; ℗ 5,237; © 5,723
Montmorenci; RMC Place; TIPPECANOE; **174** G-5; elev. 697ft./212m.; 🅿; **z** 47962; ● 125
Montpelier; Inc. Place; BLACKFORD; **174** F-12; elev. 870ft./265m.; 🅿; **z** 47359; ℗ 1,880; © 1,929
Moonlight; RMC Place; STEUBEN; ***174** A-13; elev. 960ft./293m.; mail Pleasant Lake **z** 46779; ● 250
Moonville; RMC Place; MADISON; ***174** H-11; ★ **AND**; mail Alexandria **z** 46001; ● 50
Moore; RMC Place; DE KALB; ***174** B-13; mail Butler **z** 46721
Moorefield; RMC Place; MARION; ★ **IND**; pop. incl. with Indianapolis (Inc. Place)
Moorefield; RMC Place; SWITZERLAND; **175** O-12; mail Vevay **z** 47043; ● 50
Mooreland; Inc. Place; HENRY; **174** I-12; 🅿; **z** 47360; ℗ 465; © 393
Moores Hill; Inc. Place; DEARBORN; **175** N-13; elev. 994ft./303m.; 🅿; ★ **CIN**; **z** 47032; ℗ 649; © 635
Mooresville; Inc. Place; MORGAN; **175** K-8; elev. 721ft./220m.; 🅿 🅷; ★ **IND**; **z** 46158; ℗ 5,541; © 9,273
Moral; MCD-Township; SHELBY; ***175** K-10; ★ **IND**; mail Fairland **z** 46126; ℗ 4,567; © 4,712
Moran; RMC Place; CLINTON; **174** G-7; elev. 805ft./245m.; mail Frankfort **z** 46041; ● 75
Morgan; MCD-Township; HARRISON; ***175** Q-9; ★ **LOU**; mail Palmyra **z** 47164; ℗ 3,250; © 3,819
Morgan; MCD-Township; OWEN; ***175** L-6; mail Poland **z** 47868; ℗ 885; © 1,200
Morgan; MCD-Township; PORTER; ***174** B-6; mail Valparaiso **z** 46383; ℗ 2,102; © 2,658
MORGAN; **175** L-7; ℗ 55,920; © 66,689; ◆ 68,593
Morgan Park; RMC Place; PORTER; ***174** A-5; ★ **CHI**; mail Chesterton **z** 46304; pop. incl. with Chesterton (Inc. Place)
Morgantown; Inc. Place; MORGAN; **175** L-8; elev. 680ft./207m.; 🅿; **z** 46160; ℗ 978; © 964
Morningside; RMC Place; DELAWARE; ***174** H-12; ★ **MUN**; mail Muncie **z** 47303; pop. incl. with Muncie (Inc. Place)
Morocco; Inc. Place; NEWTON; **174** E-4; elev. 698ft./213m.; 🅿; **z** 47963; ℗ 1,044; © 1,127
Morris; RMC Place; RIPLEY; **175** M-12; elev. 986ft./301m.; 🅿; **z** 47033; ● 300
Morristown; Inc. Place; SHELBY; **175** K-10; elev. 830ft./253m.; 🅿; **z** 46161; ℗ 980; © 1,133
Morton; RMC Place; PUTNAM; **174** J-6; mail Greencastle **z** 46135; ● 100
Moscow; RMC Place; RUSH; **175** L-11; mail Milroy **z** 46156; ● 100
Mott Station; RMC Place; HARRISON; ***175** R-9; ★ **LOU**; mail New Salisbury **z** 47161; rural
Mound; MCD-Township; WARREN; ***174** H-4; mail Covington **z** 47932; ℗ 448; © 438
Mount Auburn; RMC Place; SHELBY; **175** L-10; elev. 819ft./250m.; mail Edinburgh **z** 46124; ● 45
Mount Auburn; Inc. Place; WAYNE; **174** J-12; elev. 995ft./303m.; mail Cambridge City **z** 47327; ℗ 138; © 75
Mount Ayr; Inc. Place; NEWTON; **174** D-4; 🅿; **z** 47964; ℗ 151; © 147
Mount Carmel; Inc. Place; FRANKLIN; **175** L-14; elev. 1,023ft./312m.; mail Brookville **z** 47012; ℗ 108; © 106
Mount Carmel; RMC Place; WASHINGTON; ***175** P-8; mail Campbellsburg **z** 47108; rural
Mount Comfort; RMC Place; HANCOCK; **174** J-10; ★ **IND**; mail Greenfield **z** 46140; ● 100
Mount Etna; Inc. Place; HUNTINGTON; **174** F-11; elev. 813ft./248m.; mail Huntington **z** 46750; ℗ 111; © 110
Mount Healthy; RMC Place; BARTHOLOMEW; ***175** N-9; mail Columbus **z** 47201
Mount Liberty; RMC Place; BROWN; ***175** M-9; mail Nashville **z** 47448; rural
Mount Meridian; RMC Place; PUTNAM; **175** K-6; mail Greencastle **z** 46135; ● 50
Mount Olympus; RMC Place; GIBSON; ***175** Q-4; elev. 524ft./160m.; mail Hazleton **z** 47640; ● 40
Mount Pisgah; RMC Place; LAGRANGE; ***174** A-12; mail Lagrange **z** 46761; rural
Mount Pleasant; RMC Place; DELAWARE; **174** I-12; mail Muncie **z** 47302; ● 70
Mount Pleasant; MCD-Township; DELAWARE; ***174** H-11; ★ **MUN**; mail Yorktown **z** 47396; ℗ 10,711; © 12,591
Mount Pleasant; RMC Place; JOHNSON; ***175** L-9; ★ **IND**; mail Franklin **z** 46131; rural
Mount Pleasant; RMC Place; MARTIN; ***175** P-6; mail Loogootee **z** 47553
Mount Pleasant; RMC Place; PERRY; ***175** R-7; elev. 789ft./240m.; 🅿; **z** 47520
Mount Sinai; RMC Place; DEARBORN; ***175** N-13; mail Moores Hill **z** 47032; ● 70
Mount Sterling; RMC Place; SWITZERLAND; **175** O-13; mail Vevay **z** 47043; ● 25
Mount Summit; Inc. Place; HENRY; **174** I-12; elev. 1,097ft./334m.; 🅿; ★ **MUN**; **z** 47361; ℗ 238; © 313
Mount Vernon; Inc. Place; ⊡ POSEY; **175** S-2; 🅿; **z** 47620; ℗ 7,217; © 7,478
Mount Vernon (Vernon); RMC Place; WABASH; ***174** F-10; mail La Fontaine **z** 46940; ● 40
Mount Zion; RMC Place; WELLS; **174** F-12; mail Warren **z** 46792; ● 30
Mud Center; RMC Place; VANDERBURGH; ***175** S-3; elev. 380ft./116m.; ★ **EV**; mail Evansville **z** 47712; pop. incl. with Evansville (Inc. Place)
Mudlavia Springs; RMC Place; WARREN; ***174** G-4; mail Attica **z** 47918; ● 20
Mulberry; Inc. Place; CLINTON; **174** G-7; elev. 770ft./235m.; 🅿; **z** 46058; ℗ 1,262; © 1,387
Mull; RMC Place; RANDOLPH; ***174** H-13; mail Winchester **z** 47394; rural
Muncie; Inc. Place; ⊡ DELAWARE; **174** H-12; elev. 950ft./290m.; 🅿 🅷 🅲 17,285 ■; ★ **MUN**; **z** 47302-08; ℗ 71,035; © 67,430; ◆ 65,581
Munster; Inc. Place; LAKE; **174** A-4; elev. 598ft./182m.; 🅿 🅷; ★ **CHI**; **z** 46321; ℗ 19,949; © 21,511; ◆ 21,582
Muren; RMC Place; PIKE; ***175** Q-4; mail Winslow **z** 47598
Murray; RMC Place; WELLS; **174** E-12; mail Bluffton **z** 46714; ● 110

N

Nabb; RMC Place; CLARK, SCOTT; **175** P-11; elev. 698ft./213m.; 🅿; **z** 47147; ● 150
Napoleon; Inc. Place; RIPLEY; **175** M-12; elev. 970ft./296m.; 🅿; **z** 47034; ℗ 238; © 238
Nappanee; Inc. Place; ELKHART, KOSCIUSKO; **174** B-9; elev. 878ft./268m.; 🅿; **z** 46550; ℗ 5,510; © 6,710
Nashville; Inc. Place; ⊡ BROWN; **175** M-8; elev. 629ft./192m.; 🅿; **z** 47448; ℗ 873; © 825
Navilleton; RMC Place; FLOYD; ***175** Q-9; 🅿; ★ **LOU**; **z** 47119
Nead; RMC Place; MIAMI; ***174** F-9; mail Peru **z** 46970; ● 30
Nebraska; RMC Place; JENNINGS; **175** N-11; elev. 861ft./262m.; 🅿; **z** 47223; ● 90
Needham; RMC Place; JOHNSON; **175** L-9; 🅿; ★ **IND**; **z** 46162; ● 80
Needham; MCD-Township; JOHNSON; ***175** L-9; elev. 729ft./222m.; 🅿; ★ **IND**; **z** 46162 & mail Franklin **z** 46131; ℗ 3,538; © 4,725
Needmore; RMC Place; BROWN; **175** M-8; mail Nashville **z** 47448; ● 30
Needmore; RMC Place; LAWRENCE; **175** N-7; ★ **BLMNG**; mail Bedford **z** 47421; ● 100
Negangards Corner; RMC Place; RIPLEY; ***175** M-13; mail Milan **z** 47031
Nevada; RMC Place; TIPTON; ***174** G-9; elev. 864ft./263m.; ★ **KOK**; mail Sharpsville **z** 46068
Nevada Mills; RMC Place; STEUBEN; **174** A-13; mail Angola **z** 46703; ● 50
Nevins; MCD-Township; VIGO; ***175** K-4; ★ **T.H.**; mail Fontanet **z** 47851, Terre Haute **z** 47805; ℗ 2,196; © 2,224
New Albany; Inc. Place; ⊡ FLOYD; ▲ New Albany; **175** R-10; 🅿 🅷 🅲 6,183 ■; ★ **LOU**; **z** 47150-51; ℗ 36,322; © 37,603; ◆ 38,012
New Albany; MCD-Township; FLOYD; ***175** Q-10; 🅿 🅲 6,183; ★ **LOU**; **z** 47150-51; ℗ 44,958; © 48,476
New Alsace; RMC Place; DEARBORN; **175** M-13; ★ **CIN**; mail Guilford **z** 47022; ● 150
New Amsterdam; Inc. Place; HARRISON; **175** S-8; elev. 450ft./137m.; mail Central **z** 47110; ℗ 30; © 1
Newark; RMC Place; GREENE; **175** M-6; mail Solsberry **z** 47459; ● 75
New Augusta; RMC Place; MARION; ***174** J-8; elev. 835ft./255m.; 🅿; ★ **IND**; **z** 46268, **z** 46278; pop. incl. with Indianapolis (Inc. Place)
New Bellsville; BROWN; see Lake on the Green (RMC Place)
Newbern; RMC Place; BARTHOLOMEW; **175** M-10; mail Columbus **z** 47201; ● 200
Newberry; Inc. Place; GREENE; **175** N-5; elev. 550ft./168m.; 🅿; **z** 47449; ℗ 207; © 206
New Bethel; MARION; see Wanamaker (RMC Place)
New Boston; RMC Place; HARRISON; ***175** S-9; mail Elizabeth **z** 47117
New Boston; RMC Place; SPENCER; **175** S-6; mail Evanston **z** 47531; ● 40
New Britton; RMC Place; HAMILTON; ***174** I-9; elev. 800ft./244m.; ★ **IND**; mail Fishers **z** 46038; ● 500
New Brunswick; RMC Place; BOONE; **174** J-7; mail Lebanon **z** 46052; ● 30
Newburgh; Inc. Place; WARRICK; **175** S-4; elev. 393ft./120m.; 🅿 🅲 6,492; ★ **EV**; **z** 47629-30; ℗ 2,880; © 3,088
New Burlington; RMC Place; DELAWARE; ***174** I-12; mail Muncie **z** 47302; ● 60
Newbury; MCD-Township; LAGRANGE; ***174** A-11; mail Shipshewana **z** 46565; ℗ 3,850; © 4,411
New Carlisle; Inc. Place; ST. JOSEPH; **174** A-7; elev. 778ft./237m.; 🅿; **z** 46552; ℗ 1,446; © 1,505
Newcastle; MCD-Township; FULTON; ***174** D-9; mail Rochester **z** 46975; ℗ 1,153; © 1,281
New Castle; Inc. Place; ⊡ HENRY; **174** J-12; elev. 1,055ft./322m.; 🅿 🅷 ■; **z** 47362; ℗ 17,753; © 17,780; ◆ 17,226
New Chicago; Inc. Place; LAKE; **174** B-5; elev. 630ft./192m.; 🅿; ★ **CHI**; **z** 46342; ℗ 2,066; © 2,063
New Columbus; RMC Place; MADISON; **174** I-11; ★ **AND**; mail Anderson **z** 46011, **z** 46013; ● 125
New Corydon; RMC Place; JAY; **174** F-14; mail Bryant **z** 47326; ● 100
New Durham; MCD-Civil Township; LAPORTE; ***174** A-6; ★ **MICH**; mail La Porte **z** 46350; ℗ 6,695; © 4,095; ® 7,190
New Elizabethtown; RMC Place; JACKSON; ***175** O-9; mail Seymour **z** 47274; rural
New Elliott; RMC Place; LAKE; **173** N-12; ★ **CHI**; mail Griffith **z** 46319; ● 800
New Fairfield; RMC Place; FRANKLIN; ***175** L-13; mail Brookville **z** 47012; ● 75
New Farmington; RMC Place; JACKSON; ***175** N-10; mail Seymour **z** 47274; ● 40
New Frankfort; RMC Place; SCOTT; **175** O-10; mail Scottsburg **z** 47170; ● 20
New Garden; MCD-Township; WAYNE; ***174** I-13; ★ **RICH**; mail Fountain City **z** 47341; ℗ 1,847; © 1,776
New Goshen; RMC Place; VIGO; **175** K-4; elev. 639ft./195m.; 🅿; ★ **T.H.**; **z** 47863; ● 500
New Harmony; Inc. Place; POSEY; **175** R-2; elev. 384ft./117m.; 🅿; **z** 47631; ℗ 846; © 916
New Haven; Inc. Place; ALLEN; **174** D-13; elev. 758ft./231m.; 🅿; ★ **FTWA**; **z** 46774; ℗ 9,320; © 12,406
Newland; RMC Place; JASPER; ***174** D-5; elev. 683ft./208m.; mail Rensselaer **z** 47978; ● 25
New Lebanon; RMC Place; SULLIVAN; **175** N-4; elev. 510ft./155m.; 🅿; **z** 47882; ● 120
New Lisbon; RMC Place; HENRY; **174** J-12; 🅿; **z** 47366; ● 200
New Lisbon; RMC Place; RANDOLPH; ***174** H-14; elev. 1,103ft./336m.; mail Union City **z** 47390; rural
New London; RMC Place; HOWARD; **174** G-8; ★ **KOK**; mail Russiaville **z** 46979; ● 200
New Marion; RMC Place; RIPLEY; **175** N-12; mail Holton **z** 47023; ● 120
New Market; RMC Place; CLARK; ***175** P-11; elev. 650ft./198m.; mail Marysville **z** 47141; rural
New Market; Inc. Place; MONTGOMERY; **174** I-6; elev. 800ft./244m.; 🅿; **z** 47965; ℗ 614; © 659
New Maysville; RMC Place; PUTNAM; **174** J-7; mail Roachdale **z** 46172; ● 60
New Middletown; Inc. Place; HARRISON; **175** R-9; elev. 700ft./213m.; 🅿; **z** 47160; ℗ 82; © 77
New Mount Pleasant; RMC Place; JAY; **174** G-13; elev. 1,033ft./315m.; mail Portland **z** 47371; ● 20
New Palestine; Inc. Place; HANCOCK; **175** K-10; elev. 827ft./252m.; 🅿; ★ **IND**; **z** 46163; ℗ 671; © 1,264
New Paris; CDP; ELKHART; **174** B-10; elev. 819ft./250m.; 🅿; ★ **ELK**; **z** 46553; ℗ 1,007; © 1,006
New Pekin (Pekin); Inc. Place; WASHINGTON; **175** Q-9; elev. 703ft./214m.; mail Pekin **z** 47165; ℗ 1,095; © 1,334
New Pennington; RMC Place; DECATUR; ***175** M-12; mail New Point **z** 47263; rural
New Philadelphia; RMC Place; WASHINGTON; **175** P-9; mail Salem **z** 47167; ● 60
New Pittsburg; RMC Place; RANDOLPH; **174** H-13; mail Union City **z** 47390; ● 35
New Point; Inc. Place; DECATUR; **175** M-12; elev. 990ft./302m.; 🅿; **z** 47263; ℗ 296; © 290
Newport; Inc. Place; ⊡ VERMILLION; **174** J-4; elev. 520ft./158m.; 🅿; **z** 47966; ℗ 627; © 578
New Providence; CLARK; see Borden (Inc. Place)
New Richmond; Inc. Place; MONTGOMERY; **174** H-6; elev. 782ft./238m.; 🅿; **z** 47967; ℗ 312; © 349
New Ross; Inc. Place; MONTGOMERY; **174** I-7; elev. 880ft./268m.; 🅿; **z** 47968; ℗ 331; © 334
New Salem; RMC Place; RUSH; **175** K-12; elev. 718ft./219m.; mail Rushville **z** 46173; ● 200
New Salisbury (Corydon Junction); RMC Place; HARRISON; **175** R-9; 🅿; ★ **LOU**; **z** 47161; ● 400
New Santa Fe; RMC Place; MIAMI; ***174** F-9; mail Peru **z** 46970; ● 35
Newton; MCD-Township; JASPER; ***174** D-5; mail Rensselaer **z** 47978; ℗ 658; © 733
NEWTON; **174** D-4; ℗ 13,551; © 14,566; ◆ 13,958
Newtonville; RMC Place; SPENCER; **175** S-6; elev. 438ft./134m.; mail Grandview **z** 47615; ● 90
Newtown; Inc. Place; FOUNTAIN; **174** H-5; elev. 711ft./217m.; 🅿; **z** 47969; ℗ 243; © 162
New Trenton; RMC Place; FRANKLIN; **175** M-13; elev. 613ft./187m.; 🅿; **z** 47035; ● 300
New Unionville (Unionville); RMC Place; MONROE; **175** M-8; 🅿; ★ **BLMNG**; **z** 47468 & mail Bloomington **z** 47408; ● 100
Newville; RMC Place; DE KALB; ▲ Newville; **174** B-13; elev. 821ft./250m.; mail Butler **z** 46721; ● 120
Newville; MCD-Township; DE KALB; ***174** C-14; mail Butler **z** 46721; ℗ 500; © 538
New Washington; CDP; CLARK; **175** P-11; elev. 721ft./220m.; 🅿; **z** 47162; © 547
New Waverly; RMC Place; CASS; **174** E-9; elev. 680ft./207m.; 🅿; **z** 46961; ● 150
New Whiteland; Inc. Place; JOHNSON; **175** K-9; 🅿; ★ **IND**; **z** 46184; ℗ 4,097; © 4,579
New Winchester; RMC Place; HENDRICKS; **174** J-7; elev. 950ft./290m.; mail Danville **z** 46122; ● 70
Nibbyville; RMC Place; ELKHART; ***174** A-10; ★ **ELK**; mail Bristol **z** 46507; rural
Niles; MCD-Township; DELAWARE; ***174** G-12; mail Eaton **z** 47338; ℗ 1,217; © 1,321
Nine Mile; RMC Place; ALLEN; **174** D-12; ★ **FTWA**; mail Fort Wayne **z** 46809; ● 60
Nineveh; RMC Place; JOHNSON; ▲ Nineveh; **175** L-9; 🅿; ★ **IND**; **z** 46164; ● 250
Nineveh; MCD-Township; JOHNSON; ***175** L-9; 🅿; ★ **IND**; **z** 46164; ℗ 3,278; © 3,975
Nisbet; RMC Place; VANDERBURGH; ***175** R-3; elev. 436ft./133m.; mail Haubstadt **z** 47639; rural
Noble; MCD-Township; CASS; ***174** E-8; mail Logansport **z** 46947; ℗ 1,942; © 1,962
Noble; MCD-Township; JAY; ***174** G-14; mail Portland **z** 47371; ℗ 688; © 690
Noble; MCD-Township; LAPORTE; ***174** B-6; mail Union Mills **z** 46382; ℗ 1,333; © 1,563
Noble; MCD-Township; NOBLE; ***174** C-11; mail Albion **z** 46701; ℗ 2,724; © 2,861
Noble; MCD-Township; RUSH; ***175** K-12; mail Rushville **z** 46173; ℗ 658; © 676
Noble; MCD-Township; SHELBY; ***175** L-10; mail Flat Rock **z** 47234; ℗ 1,469; © 1,438
Noble; MCD-Township; WABASH; ***174** E-10; mail Wabash **z** 46992; ℗ 16,066; © 15,580
NOBLE; **174** C-12; ℗ 37,877; © 46,275; ◆ 47,278
Noblesville; Inc. Place; ⊡ HAMILTON; ▲ Noblesville; **174** I-9; 🅿 🅷; ★ **IND**; **z** 46060-62 & mail Fishers **z** 46038; ℗ 17,655; © 28,590; ◆ 39,707
Noblesville; MCD-Township; HAMILTON; ***174** I-9; 🅿; ★ **IND**; **z** 46060-62; ℗ 24,247; © 34,534
Noblitt Falls; RMC Place; BARTHOLOMEW; ★ **COL**; mail Columbus **z** 47201; pop. incl. with Columbus (Inc. Place)
Nora; RMC Place; MARION; ***174** J-9; elev. 775ft./236m.; 🅿; ★ **IND**; **z** 46240, **z** 46260, **z** 46280, **z** 46290; pop. incl. with Indianapolis (Inc. Place)
Norland Park; RMC Place; DE KALB; mail Auburn **z** 46706; ● 150
Norma Jean; RMC Place; TIPPECANOE; ***174** G-6; ★ **LAF-**; mail Lafayette **z** 47905; pop. incl. with Lafayette (Inc. Place)
Normal; RMC Place; GRANT; ***174** G-10; mail Swayzee **z** 46986
Norman; RMC Place; JACKSON; **175** N-8; elev. 876ft./267m.; 🅿; **z** 47264; ● 100
Normanda; RMC Place; TIPTON; ***174** H-9; mail Tipton **z** 46072; ● 80
Norristown; RMC Place; SHELBY; **175** L-10; mail Flat Rock **z** 47234; ● 40
North; MCD-Township; LAKE; ***174** A-4; ★ **CHI**; mail East Chicago **z** 46312, Hammond **z** 46320, **z** 46323-24, Highland **z** 46322, Munster **z** 46321; ℗ 166,928; © 165,656
North; MCD-Township; MARSHALL; ***174** B-8; mail Plymouth **z** 46563; ℗ 4,088; © 4,028
North Anderson; RMC Place; MADISON; ***174** I-10; ★ **AND**; mail Anderson **z** 46012; pop. incl. with Anderson (Inc. Place)
Northaven; RMC Place; CLARK; ***175** R-10; ★ **LOU**; mail Jeffersonville **z** 47130; pop. incl. with Jeffersonville (Inc. Place)
North Bend; MCD-Township; STARKE; ***174** C-7; mail Knox **z** 46534; ℗ 1,214; © 1,294
Northcliff; RMC Place; BARTHOLOMEW; ***175** M-10; mail Columbus **z** 47203; ● 110
North Columbus; RMC Place; BARTHOLOMEW; ***175** M-10; ★ **COL**; mail Columbus **z** 47203; pop. incl. with Columbus (Inc. Place)
Northcrest; RMC Place; ALLEN; ***174** D-12; ★ **FTWA**; mail Fort Wayne **z** 46825; pop. incl. with Fort Wayne (Inc. Place)
North Crows Nest; Inc. Place; MARION; ***174** J-9; ★ **IND**; mail Indianapolis **z** 46228; © 42
North Delphi; RMC Place; CARROLL; ***174** F-7; mail Delphi **z** 46923
Northeast; MCD-Township; ORANGE; ***175** P-8; mail Orleans **z** 47452; ℗ 548; © 578
Northern Meadows; RMC Place; BOONE; ***174** I-8; ★ **IND**; mail Zionsville **z** 46077; pop. incl. with Zionsville (Inc. Place)

Entries in **UPPERCASE** are counties.
Entries in **bold** have populations of 2,500 or more.
Names in parentheses are alternate names.
Inc. Place — Incorporated Place
RMC Place — Rand McNally Designated Place
CDP — Census Designated Place
MCD — Minor Civil Division

⊡ County Seat
▲ Minor Civil Division
elev. Elevation
🅿 Post Office

🅷 Hospital
🅲 College
■ Principal Business Center
★ Ranally Metro Area (RMA) Abbreviation
z Zip Code(s)

℗ Previous Census Population
® Revised Census Population
Ⓐ Annexation Population
● Rand McNally Population Estimate
© Final Census Population
Ⓢ Special Census Population
◆ Estimated Population

For additional definitions see Glossary, Volume 1, and Introduction, Volume 2.

Northfield; RMC Place; BOONE; *174 I-8; elev. 906ft./276m.; mail Zionsville Z 46077; ● 40
Northfield Village; RMC Place; BOONE; *174 I-7; ★ IND; mail Lebanon Z 46052; pop. incl. with Lebanon (Inc. Place)
North Gate; RMC Place; BARTHOLOMEW; *175 M-9; ★ COL; mail Columbus Z 47201; ● 250
North Grove; RMC Place; MIAMI; 174 F-9; elev. 823ft./251m.; mail Amboy Z 46911; ● 120
North Hammond; RMC Place; LAKE; ★ CHI; pop. incl. with Hammond (Inc. Place)
North Hayden; RMC Place; LAKE; *174 C-4; elev. 698ft./213m.; mail Lowell Z 46356
North Highland; RMC Place; ALLEN; *174 D-12; ★ FTWA; mail Fort Wayne Z 46808; pop. incl. with Fort Wayne (Inc. Place)
North Judson; Inc. Place; STARKE; 174 C-6; elev. 700ft./213m.; 🄿; Z 46366; ℗ 1,582; © 1,675
North Liberty; Inc. Place; ST. JOSEPH; 174 B-8; elev. 733ft./223m.; 🄿; Z 46554; ℗ 1,366; © 1,402
North Madison; RMC Place; JEFFERSON; *175 O-12; mail Madison Z 47250; pop. incl. with Madison (Inc. Place)
North Manchester; Inc. Place; WABASH; 174 D-10; elev. 773ft./236m.; 🄿 🄲 1,056; Z 46962; ℗ 6,383; © 6,260
North Oaks; RMC Place; WELLS; *174 E-12; mail Bluffton Z 46714; ● 60
North Ogilville; RMC Place; BARTHOLOMEW; *175 M-9; ★ COL; mail Columbus Z 47201; ● 80
North Park; RMC Place; BARTHOLOMEW; *175 M-9; elev. 650ft./198m.; ★ COL; mail Evansville Z 47710, Taylorsville Z 47280
North Ridge Village; RMC Place; HAMILTON; *174 J-9; ★ IND; mail Indianapolis Z 46280; ● 900
North Salem; Inc. Place; HENDRICKS; 174 J-7; elev. 879ft./268m.; 🄿; Z 46165; ℗ 499; © 591
North Terre Haute; CDP; VIGO; 175 L-4; 🄿; ★ T.H.; Z 47805; ℗ 4,331; © 4,606
North Vernon; Inc. Place; JENNINGS; 175 N-11; elev. 733ft./223m.; 🄿 🄷; Z 47265; ℗ 5,311; © 6,515
North Webster; Inc. Place; KOSCIUSKO; 174 C-10; elev. 870ft./265m.; 🄿; Z 46555; ℗ 881; © 1,067
Northwest; MCD-Township; ORANGE; *175 P-7; mail West Baden Springs Z 47469; ℗ 359; © 345
Northwood; RMC Place; ALLEN; *174 D-13; elev. 808ft./246m.; ★ FTWA; mail Fort Wayne Z 46815, Z 46885; pop. incl. with Fort Wayne (Inc. Place)
Northwood; RMC Place; ELKHART; mail Nappanee Z 46550; pop. incl. with Nappanee (Inc. Place)
Northwood; RMC Place; LAGRANGE; *174 A-11; mail Lagrange Z 46761; pop. incl. with Lagrange (Inc. Place)
Northwood; RMC Place; VIGO; *175 K-4; ★ T.H.; mail Terre Haute Z 47805; ● 75
Northwood Hills; RMC Place; HAMILTON; *174 I-9; ★ IND; mail Carmel Z 46033; ● 600
North Wood Park; RMC Place; PORTER; *174 B-5; ★ CHI; mail Valparaiso Z 46383; ● 120
Norton; RMC Place; DUBOIS, ORANGE; *175 Q-7; mail French Lick Z 47432; rural
Nortonburg; RMC Place; BARTHOLOMEW; *175 M-10; mail Columbus Z 47203
Norway; CDP; WHITE; 174 E-6; mail Monticello Z 47960; © 437
Notre Dame; RMC Place; ST. JOSEPH; 173 B-20; elev. 734ft./224m.; 🄿 🄲 13,550; ★ S.B.; Z 46556; ● 11,000
Nottingham; RMC Place; WELLS; ▲ Nottingham; *174 F-12; mail Montpelier Z 47359
Nottingham; MCD-Township; WELLS; *174 F-12; mail Montpelier Z 47359; ℗ 1,086; © 1,065
Nulltown; RMC Place; FAYETTE; 175 K-12; mail Connersville Z 47331; ● 60
Numa; RMC Place; PARKE; 175 K-4; mail Rosedale Z 47874; ● 35
Nyesville; RMC Place; PARKE; *174 J-5; mail Rockville Z 47872; ● 30
Nyona Lake; RMC Place; FULTON; *174 D-9; mail Macy Z 46951; summer pop. 450; ● 250

O

Oak; PULASKI; see Thornhope (RMC Place)
Oakcrest; RMC Place; BARTHOLOMEW; *175 M-10; ★ COL; mail Columbus Z 47203; ● 150
Oakdale; RMC Place; MIAMI; *174 E-9; mail Peru Z 46970; pop. incl. with Peru (Inc. Place)
Oakford; RMC Place; HOWARD; 174 G-9; elev. 860ft./262m.; 🄿; ★ KOK; Z 46965; ● 225
Oak Forest; RMC Place; FRANKLIN; *175 L-13; elev. 970ft./296m.; mail Brookville Z 47012
Oak Grove; MCD-Township; BENTON; *174 G-4; mail Oxford Z 47971; ℗ 1,641; © 1,694
Oak Grove; RMC Place; STARKE; *174 C-7; mail Culver Z 46511; ● 25
Oak Grove; RMC Place; VIGO; *175 L-4; ★ T.H.; mail Terre Haute Z 47802; ● 120
Oak Hill; RMC Place; GIBSON; *175 R-4; elev. 486ft./148m.; mail Oakland City Z 47660; ● 50
Oakland City; Inc. Place; GIBSON; 175 Q-4; elev. 461ft./141m.; 🄿 🄷 🄲 2,018; Z 47660; ℗ 2,810; © 2,588
Oaklandon; RMC Place; MARION; *174 J-9; elev. 855ft./261m.; 🄿; ★ IND; Z 46235-36 & mail Indianapolis Z 46216; pop. incl. with Lawrence (Inc. Place)
Oaklawn Terrace; RMC Place; CLARK; *175 R-10; ★ LOU; mail Jeffersonville Z 47130; pop. incl. with Jeffersonville (Inc. Place)
Oak Park; CDP; CLARK; *175 R-10; ★ LOU; mail Jeffersonville Z 47130; ℗ 5,630; © 5,379
Oaktown; Inc. Place; KNOX; 175 O-4; elev. 469ft./143m.; 🄿; Z 47561; ℗ 655; © 633
Oakville; RMC Place; DELAWARE; 174 I-12; elev. 1,010ft./308m.; 🄿; ★ MUN; Z 47367; ● 225
Oakwood; RMC Place; STEUBEN; *174 B-13; mail Hamilton Z 46742; pop. incl. with Hamilton (Inc. Place)
Oakwood Park; RMC Place; KOSCIUSKO; *174 B-10; mail Syracuse Z 46567
Oakwood Shores; RMC Place; STEUBEN; *174 B-10; mail Hamilton Z 46742; ● 200
Oatsville; RMC Place; PIKE; *175 Q-4; mail Petersburg Z 47567; ● 60
Ober; RMC Place; STARKE; 174 C-7; 🄿; Z 46534; ● 100
Occident; RMC Place; RUSH; *175 K-11; mail Carthage Z 46115; rural
Ockley; RMC Place; CARROLL; 174 G-7; mail Delphi Z 46923; ● 80
Odell; RMC Place; TIPPECANOE; 174 H-5; mail Attica Z 47918; ● 30
Odon; Inc. Place; DAVIESS; 175 O-5; elev. 550ft./168m.; 🄿; Z 47562; ℗ 1,475; © 1,376
Ogden; RMC Place; HENRY; 174 J-11; mail Knightstown Z 46148; ● 120
Ogden Dunes; Inc. Place; PORTER; 174 A-5; elev. 610ft./186m.; 🄿; ★ CHI; Z 46368; ℗ 1,499; © 1,313
Ogilville; RMC Place; BARTHOLOMEW; *175 M-9; ★ COL; mail Columbus Z 47201
Ohio; MCD-Township; BARTHOLOMEW; *175 M-9; ★ COL; mail Columbus Z 47201; ℗ 1,557; © 1,632
Ohio; MCD-Township; CRAWFORD; *175 R-8; mail Leavenworth Z 47137; ℗ 568; © 689
Ohio; MCD-Township; SPENCER; *175 T-5; mail Rockport Z 47635; ℗ 4,849; © 5,092
Ohio; MCD-Township; WARRICK; *175 S-4; ★ EV; mail Chandler Z 47610; ℗ 24,933; © 31,002
OHIO; 175 N-13; ℗ 5,315; © 5,623; ◆ 5,594
Oil; MCD-Township; PERRY; *175 R-7; mail Saint Croix Z 47576; ℗ 1,639; © 2,032
Old Bargersville; RMC Place; JOHNSON; *175 L-9; ★ IND; mail Bargersville Z 46106; pop. incl. with Bargersville (Inc. Place)
Old Bath; RMC Place; FRANKLIN; *175 L-13; elev. 1,034ft./315m.; mail Brookville Z 47012; ● 70
Oldenburg; Inc. Place; FRANKLIN; 175 L-12; elev. 900ft./274m.; 🄿; Z 47036; ℗ 715; © 647
Old Milan; RMC Place; RIPLEY; *175 M-13; mail Milan Z 47031
Old Romney Heights; RMC Place; TIPPECANOE; *174 G-6; ★ LAF-; mail Bay Shore Z 49711, Lafayette Z 47905; ● 125
Old Tip Town; RMC Place; MARSHALL; *174 C-9; mail Tippecanoe Z 46570
Oldtown; RMC Place; DEARBORN; *175 N-14; ★ CIN; mail Lawrenceburg Z 47025; pop. incl. with Lawrenceburg (Inc. Place)
Olean; RMC Place; RIPLEY; *175 N-12; mail Versailles Z 47042
Olive; MCD-Township; ELKHART; *174 A-9; ★ ELK; mail Wakarusa Z 46573; ℗ 2,895; © 2,847
Olive; MCD-Township; ST. JOSEPH; *174 A-7; mail New Carlisle Z 46552; ℗ 3,573; © 3,914
Oliver; RMC Place; POSEY; *175 S-2; elev. 409ft./125m.; mail Mount Vernon Z 47620; ● 45
Oliver Lake; RMC Place; LAGRANGE; *174 A-11; mail Lagrange Z 46761, Wolcottville Z 46795; summer pop. 700; ● 200
Olive Street; RMC Place; ST. JOSEPH; *174 A-8; ★ S.B.; mail South Bend Z 46619, Z 46628; pop. incl. with South Bend (Inc. Place)
Omega; RMC Place; HAMILTON; 174 H-9; mail Arcadia Z 46030; ● 40
Ontario; RMC Place; LAGRANGE; 174 A-12; mail Howe Z 46746; ● 230
Onward; Inc. Place; CASS; 174 F-9; elev. 768ft./234m.; 🄿; Z 46967; ℗ 63; © 81
Oolitic; Inc. Place; LAWRENCE; 175 O-7; elev. 589ft./180m.; 🄿; ★ BLMNG; Z 47451; ℗ 1,424; © 1,152
Ora; RMC Place; STARKE, PULASKI; 174 C-7; elev. 725ft./221m.; 🄿; Z 46968; ● 200
Orange; RMC Place; FAYETTE; ▲ Orange; 175 K-12; mail Connersville Z 47331; ● 80
Orange; MCD-Township; FAYETTE; *175 K-12; mail Connersville Z 47331; ℗ 770; © 789
Orange; MCD-Township; NOBLE; *174 B-12; mail Rome City Z 46784; ℗ 3,703; © 3,917
Orange; MCD-Township; RUSH; *175 L-11; mail Rushville Z 46173; ℗ 811; © 844
ORANGE; 175 P-8; ℗ 18,409; © 19,306; ◆ 19,696
Orangeville; RMC Place; ORANGE; ▲ Orangeville; 175 P-7; mail Orleans Z 47452; ● 40
Orangeville; MCD-Township; ORANGE; *175 P-7; mail Huntingburg Z 47542, Orleans Z 47452; ℗ 559; © 613
Orchard Heights; RMC Place; TIPPECANOE; *174 G-6; ★ LAF-; mail Lafayette Z 47905; pop. incl. with Lafayette (Inc. Place)
Orchard Heights Addition; RMC Place; ST. JOSEPH; *174 A-8; elev. 841ft./256m.; ★ S.B.; mail South Bend Z 46614; ● 250
Orchard Park; RMC Place; HAMILTON; *174 I-9; ★ IND; mail Indianapolis Z 46280; ● 800
Oregon; MCD-Township; CLARK; *175 P-11; mail Marysville Z 47141; ℗ 1,212; © 1,540
Oregon; MCD-Township; STARKE; *174 B-7; mail Walkerton Z 46574; ℗ 3,144; © 3,074
Oregon Heights; RMC Place; LAKE; ★ CHI; mail Lake Station Z 46405; pop. incl. with Hobart (Inc. Place)
Orestes; Inc. Place; MADISON; 174 H-10; elev. 874ft./266m.; 🄿; ★ AND; Z 46063; ℗ 458; © 334
Oriole; RMC Place; PERRY; *175 R-7; mail Leopold Z 47551
Orland; Inc. Place; STEUBEN; 174 A-12; elev. 962ft./293m.; 🄿; Z 46776; ℗ 361; © 341
Orleans; Inc. Place; ORANGE; ▲ Orleans; 175 P-7; 🄿; Z 47452; ℗ 2,083; © 2,273
Orleans; MCD-Township; ORANGE; *175 P-8; 🄿; Z 47452; ℗ 3,202; © 3,508
Orleans Southwest; RMC Place; HOWARD; *174 G-9; ★ KOK; mail Kokomo Z 46902; ● 1,100
Ormas; RMC Place; NOBLE, WHITLEY; 174 C-11; mail Columbia City Z 46725; ● 30
Osborn; RMC Place; LAKE; *174 A-4; ★ CHI; pop. incl. with Hammond (Inc. Place)
Osborn Landing; RMC Place; KOSCIUSKO; *174 C-10; mail Warsaw Z 46580; ● 120
Osceola; Inc. Place; ST. JOSEPH; 174 A-9; elev. 740ft./226m.; 🄿; ★ S.B.; Z 46561; ℗ 1,999; © 1,859
Osgood; Inc. Place; RIPLEY; 175 M-12; elev. 990ft./302m.; 🄿; Z 47037; ℗ 1,688; © 1,669
Osolo; MCD-Township; ELKHART; *174 A-9; ★ ELK; mail Elkhart Z 46514; ℗ 22,452; © 26,369
Ossian; Inc. Place; WELLS; 174 E-12; elev. 830ft./253m.; 🄿; Z 46777; ℗ 2,428; © 2,943
Oswego; RMC Place; KOSCIUSKO; 174 C-10; mail Leesburg Z 46538; ● 150
Otis; RMC Place; LAPORTE; 174 A-6; elev. 748ft./228m.; 🄿; ★ MICH; Z 46391; ● 80
Otisco; RMC Place; CLARK; 175 P-11; elev. 670ft./204m.; 🄿; ★ LOU; Z 47163; ● 400
Otsego; MCD-Township; STEUBEN; *174 A-13; mail Hamilton Z 46742; ℗ 1,977; © 2,546
Otterbein; Inc. Place; BENTON, TIPPECANOE; 174 G-5; 🄿; Z 47970; ℗ 1,291; © 1,312
Otter Creek; MCD-Township; RIPLEY; *175 N-12; mail Holton Z 47023; ℗ 1,334; © 1,339
Otter Creek; MCD-Township; VIGO; *175 K-4; ★ T.H.; mail Terre Haute Z 47805; ℗ 8,792; © 9,059
Otter Lake; RMC Place; STEUBEN; *174 A-12; mail Angola Z 46703, Fremont Z 46737; summer pop. 250; ● 100
Otto; RMC Place; CLARK; *175 P-11; mail New Washington Z 47162
Otwell; RMC Place; PIKE; 175 Q-5; elev. 490ft./149m.; 🄿; Z 47564; ● 400
Owasco; RMC Place; CARROLL; 174 G-7; mail Rossville Z 46065; ● 45
Owen; MCD-Township; CLARK; *175 Q-11; mail Charlestown Z 47111; ℗ 646; © 865
Owen; MCD-Township; CLINTON; *174 G-7; mail Frankfort Z 46041, Rossville Z 46065; ℗ 838; © 923
Owen; MCD-Township; JACKSON; *175 O-8; mail Brownstown Z 47220; ℗ 1,525; © 1,625
Owen; MCD-Township; WARRICK; *175 R-5; mail Tennyson Z 47637; ℗ 628; © 619
OWEN; 175 M-6; ℗ 17,281; © 21,786; ◆ 22,332
Owensburg; RMC Place; GREENE; 175 O-6; 🄿; Z 47453; ● 400
Owensville; Inc. Place; GIBSON; 175 R-3; elev. 520ft./158m.; 🄿; Z 47665; ℗ 1,053; © 1,322
Oxford; Inc. Place; BENTON; 174 G-5; elev. 732ft./223m.; 🄿; Z 47971; ℗ 1,273; © 1,271

P

Packerton (Packertown); RMC Place; KOSCIUSKO; 174 D-10; mail Claypool Z 46510; ● 90
Packertown; KOSCIUSKO; see Packerton (RMC Place)
Paint Mill Lake; RMC Place; VIGO; *175 L-4; mail Terre Haute Z 47802; ● 250
Palestine; RMC Place; FRANKLIN; *175 L-13; mail Brookville Z 47012
Palestine; RMC Place; KOSCIUSKO; 174 C-9; mail Mentone Z 46539; ● 300
Palmer; RMC Place; LAKE; 174 B-5; ★ CHI; mail Crown Point Z 46307; pop. incl. with Winfield (Inc. Place)
Palmyra; Inc. Place; HARRISON; 175 Q-9; elev. 777ft./237m.; 🄿; ★ LOU; Z 47164; ℗ 621; © 633
Palmyra; MCD-Township; KNOX; *175 P-4; mail Vincennes Z 47591; ℗ 1,401; © 1,593
Panama; RMC Place; STEUBEN; *174 A-13; mail Angola Z 46703; ● 100
Paoli; Inc. Place; ⊡ ORANGE; ▲ Paoli; 175 P-7; elev. 615ft./187m.; 🄿 🄷; Z 47454; ℗ 3,542; © 3,844
Paoli; MCD-Township; ORANGE; *175 P-7; 🄿; Z 47454; ℗ 5,624; © 5,890
Papakeechie Lake; RMC Place; KOSCIUSKO; *174 B-10; mail Syracuse Z 46567; summer pop. 500
Paradise; RMC Place; WARRICK; *175 S-4; ★ EV; mail Newburgh Z 47630; ● 80
Paradise Lakes; RMC Place; MORGAN; *175 L-8; ★ IND; mail Martinsville Z 46151; ● 180
Paragon; Inc. Place; MORGAN; 175 L-7; elev. 580ft./177m.; 🄿; Z 46166; ℗ 515; © 663
Paris; RMC Place; JEFFERSON, JENNINGS; *175 O-11; mail Paris Crossing Z 47270; ● 50
Paris Crossing; RMC Place; JENNINGS; 175 O-11; elev. 623ft./190m.; 🄿; Z 47270; ● 100
Parish Grove; MCD-Township; BENTON; *174 F-4; mail Fowler Z 47944; ℗ 312; © 267
Park; RMC Place; GREENE; *175 N-6; mail Bloomfield Z 47424
PARKE; 174 J-5; ℗ 15,410; © 17,241; ◆ 17,210
Parker City; Inc. Place; RANDOLPH; 174 H-12; elev. 1,025ft./312m.; 🄿; ★ MUN; Z 47368; ℗ 1,323; © 1,416
Parkersburg; RMC Place; MONTGOMERY; 174 J-6; mail Ladoga Z 47954; ● 75
Parkers Settlement; RMC Place; POSEY; *175 S-3; ★ EV; mail Wadesville Z 47638; ● 125
Park Fletcher; RMC Place; MARION; *174 J-8; ★ IND; mail Indianapolis Z 46241-42; pop. incl. with Indianapolis (Inc. Place)
Park Forest Estates; RMC Place; BARTHOLOMEW; ★ COL; mail Columbus Z 47201; pop. incl. with Columbus (Inc. Place)
Park Ridge; RMC Place; MONROE; *175 M-7; ★ BLMNG; mail Bloomington Z 47401, Z 47408; pop. incl. with Bloomington (Inc. Place)
Park Ridge East; RMC Place; MONROE; *175 M-7; ★ BLMNG; mail Bloomington Z 47408; pop. incl. with Bloomington (Inc. Place)
Parkside; RMC Place; BARTHOLOMEW; *175 M-10; ★ COL; mail Columbus Z 47203; pop. incl. with Columbus (Inc. Place)
Parkview; RMC Place; VIGO; *175 L-4; ★ T.H.; mail Terre Haute Z 47805; pop. incl. with Terre Haute (Inc. Place)
Park View Heights; RMC Place; MIAMI; *174 F-9; mail Peru Z 46970; pop. incl. with Peru (Inc. Place)
Parkway Hills; RMC Place; ALLEN; *174 D-12; ★ FTWA; mail Fort Wayne Z 46804; ● 125
Parkwood; RMC Place; CLARK; *175 Q-10; ★ LOU; mail Clarksville Z 47129; pop. incl. with Jeffersonville (Inc. Place)
Parr; RMC Place; JASPER; 174 D-5; mail Rensselaer Z 47978; ● 150
Patoka; MCD-Township; CRAWFORD; *175 Q-7; mail Taswell Z 47175; ℗ 1,262; © 1,402
Patoka; MCD-Township; DUBOIS; *175 R-5; mail Huntingburg Z 47542; ℗ 6,747; © 7,178
Patoka; Inc. Place; GIBSON; 175 Q-3; elev. 410ft./125m.; 🄿; Z 47666; ℗ 704; © 749
Patoka; MCD-Township; GIBSON; *175 Q-3; 🄿; Z 47666 & mail Princeton Z 47670; ℗ 11,582; © 11,502
Patoka; MCD-Township; PIKE; *175 Q-4; mail Winslow Z 47598; ℗ 2,935; © 3,169
Patricksburg; RMC Place; OWEN; 175 M-6; elev. 774ft./236m.; 🄿; Z 47455; ● 275
Patriot; Inc. Place; SWITZERLAND; 175 O-14; 🄿; Z 47038; ℗ 190; © 202
Patronville; RMC Place; SPENCER; 175 T-5; mail Rockport Z 47635; ● 30
Patton; RMC Place; CARROLL; *174 F-6; mail Monticello Z 47960
Patton Hill; RMC Place; LAWRENCE; *175 O-7; ★ BLMNG; mail Bedford Z 47421; ● 40
Patton Lake; RMC Place; MORGAN; *175 L-7; ★ IND; mail Martinsville Z 46151; ● 250
Paw Paw; MCD-Township; WABASH; *174 E-10; mail Roann Z 46974; ℗ 1,612; © 1,583
Paxton; RMC Place; SULLIVAN; 175 N-4; elev. 500ft./152m.; 🄿; Z 47865; ● 300
Paynesville; RMC Place; JEFFERSON; *175 P-11; mail Hanover Z 47243; ● 60
Peabody; RMC Place; WHITLEY; 174 D-11; mail Columbia City Z 46725; ● 25
Pearsontown; RMC Place; ORANGE; *175 Q-8; mail Marengo Z 47140; ● 50
Peerless; RMC Place; LAWRENCE; *175 N-7; ★ BLMNG; mail Bedford Z 47421
Pekin; WASHINGTON; see New Pekin (Inc. Place)
Pelzer; RMC Place; WARRICK; 175 S-4; elev. 416ft./127m.; mail Boonville Z 47601; ● 60
Pence; RMC Place; WARREN; 174 G-4; 🄿; Z 47993; ● 85
Pendleton; Inc. Place; MADISON; 174 I-10; elev. 850ft./259m.; 🄿; ★ AND; Z 46064; ℗ 2,309; © 3,873
Penn; MCD-Township; JAY; *174 G-12; mail Pennville Z 47369; ℗ 1,236; © 1,308
Penn; MCD-Township; PARKE; *174 J-4; mail Bloomingdale Z 47832; ℗ 843; © 868
Penn; MCD-Township; ST. JOSEPH; *174 A-9; ★ S.B.; mail Mishawaka Z 46544, Osceola Z 46561; ℗ 59,879; © 64,322
Penn Meadows; RMC Place; ST. JOSEPH; *174 A-9; ★ S.B.; mail Mishawaka Z 46545; ● 1,000
Penn Park; RMC Place; STEUBEN; *174 B-13; mail Hamilton Z 46742; pop. incl. with Hamilton (Inc. Place)
Penntown; RMC Place; RIPLEY; 175 M-13; elev. 991ft./302m.; mail Sunman Z 47041; ● 120
Pennville; Inc. Place; JAY; 174 G-12; elev. 885ft./270m.; 🄿; Z 47369; ℗ 637; © 706
Pennville; RMC Place; WAYNE; 174 J-13; mail Cambridge City Z 47327; ● 100
Peoga; RMC Place; JOHNSON, BROWN; 175 L-9; mail Trafalgar Z 46181; ● 100
Peoria; RMC Place; FRANKLIN; *175 L-14; mail Oxford Z 45056; rural
Peoria; RMC Place; MIAMI; 174 F-9; mail Peru Z 46970; ● 50
Peppertown; RMC Place; FRANKLIN; 175 L-12; mail Metamora Z 47030; ● 20
Perkinsville; RMC Place; MADISON; 174 H-10; ★ AND; mail Anderson Z 46011; ● 100
Perry; MCD-Township; ALLEN; *174 C-12; ★ FTWA; mail Fort Wayne Z 46845, Huntertown Z 46748; ℗ 10,909; © 18,170
Perry; MCD-Township; BOONE; *174 I-8; mail Lebanon Z 46052; ℗ 1,162; © 1,166
Perry; MCD-Township; CLAY; *175 L-5; mail Cory Z 47846; ℗ 874; © 960
Perry; MCD-Township; CLINTON; *174 H-7; mail Colfax Z 46035; ℗ 1,396; © 1,466
Perry; MCD-Township; DELAWARE; *174 I-12; mail Muncie Z 47302; ℗ 1,377; © 1,528
Perry; MCD-Township; LAWRENCE; *175 N-7; mail Springville Z 47462; ℗ 1,726; © 1,893
Perry; MCD-Township; MARION; *175 K-9; ★ IND; mail Indianapolis Z 46227; ℗ 85,060; © 92,838
Perry; MCD-Township; MARTIN; *175 O-6; mail Loogootee Z 47553; ℗ 5,126; © 4,960
Perry; MCD-Township; MIAMI; *174 D-9; mail Denver Z 46926; ℗ 836; © 906
Perry; MCD-Township; MONROE; *175 N-7; ★ BLMNG; mail Bloomington Z 47401; ℗ 31,985; © 40,508
Perry; MCD-Township; NOBLE; *174 B-11; mail Ligonier Z 46767; ℗ 5,110; © 6,600
Perry; MCD-Township; TIPPECANOE; *174 G-6; ★ LAF-; mail Lafayette Z 47905; ℗ 2,990; © 5,322
Perry; MCD-Township; VANDERBURGH; *175 S-3; ★ EV; mail Evansville Z 47712; ℗ 20,615; © 23,687
Perry; MCD-Township; WAYNE; *174 I-13; mail Economy Z 47339; ℗ 700; © 763
PERRY; 175 S-7; ℗ 19,107; © 18,899; ◆ 19,237
Perry Manor; RMC Place; MARION; *175 K-9; ★ IND; mail Indianapolis Z 46227; pop. incl. with Indianapolis (Inc. Place)
Perrysburg; RMC Place; MIAMI; 174 E-9; mail Macy Z 46951; ● 50
Perrysville; Inc. Place; VERMILLION; 174 I-4; elev. 542ft./165m.; 🄿; Z 47974; ℗ 443; © 502
Pershing; RMC Place; FULTON; *174 D-8; mail Rochester Z 46975; rural
Pershing; MCD-Township; JACKSON; *175 N-9; mail Freetown Z 47235; ℗ 1,380; © 1,386
Pershing; WAYNE; see East Germantown (Inc. Place)
Perth; RMC Place; CLAY; 175 K-5; mail Carbon Z 47837; ● 45
Peru; Inc. Place; ⊡ MIAMI; 174 E-9; 🄿 🄷; Z 46970-71; ℗ 12,843; © 12,994
Peru; MCD-Township; MIAMI; *174 E-9; elev. 656ft./200m.; 🄿; Z 46970-71; includes part of the City of Peru; ℗ 12,730; © 12,666
Petersburg; Inc. Place; ⊡ PIKE; 175 Q-4; elev. 439ft./134m.; 🄿; Z 47567; ℗ 2,449; © 2,570
Peterson; RMC Place; ADAMS; *174 E-13; mail Decatur Z 46733; ● 20
Peters Switch; RMC Place; JACKSON; *175 N-10; elev. 580ft./177m.; mail Seymour Z 47274; rural
Petersville; RMC Place; BARTHOLOMEW; 175 M-10; ★ COL; mail Columbus Z 47203; ● 220
Petroleum; RMC Place; WELLS; 174 F-12; elev. 860ft./262m.; 🄿; Z 46778; ● 150
Pettit; RMC Place; TIPPECANOE; *174 G-7; ★ LAF-; mail Lafayette Z 47905
Pheasant Run; RMC Place; ALLEN; *174 D-12; ★ FTWA; mail Fort Wayne Z 46819; ● 1,200
Philadelphia; RMC Place; HANCOCK; 174 J-10; ★ IND; mail Greenfield Z 46140; ● 300
Philomath; RMC Place; UNION; 175 K-13; mail Brownsville Z 47325; ● 35
Phlox; RMC Place; HOWARD; 174 G-10; mail Greentown Z 46936; ● 120
Pickard; RMC Place; CLINTON; 174 H-8; mail Kirklin Z 46050; ● 60
Pierce; MCD-Township; WASHINGTON; *175 Q-9; mail Salem Z 47167; ℗ 1,948; © 2,505
Pierceton; Inc. Place; KOSCIUSKO; 174 C-10; elev. 928ft./283m.; 🄿; Z 46562; ℗ 1,030; © 695; ® 697
Pierceville; RMC Place; RIPLEY; *175 M-12; 🄿; Z 47039; ● 180
Pierson; MCD-Township; VIGO; *175 M-4; mail Terre Haute Z 47802; ℗ 1,339; © 1,269
Pigeon; MCD-Township; VANDERBURGH; *175 S-3; ★ EV; mail Evansville Z 47710-11, Z 47713, Z 47720; ℗ 37,856; © 33,682
Pigeon; MCD-Township; WARRICK; *175 R-5; mail Dale Z 47523; ℗ 927; © 850
Pike; RMC Place; BOONE; *174 I-7; mail Lebanon Z 46052
Pike; MCD-Township; JAY; *174 G-13; mail Portland Z 47371; ℗ 904; © 910
Pike; MCD-Township; MARION; *174 J-8; ★ IND; mail Indianapolis Z 46254; ℗ 45,204; © 71,465; ® 71,449
Pike; MCD-Township; OHIO; *175 N-13; mail Dillsboro Z 47018; ℗ 303; © 362
Pike; MCD-Township; WARREN; *174 H-4; mail West Lebanon Z 47991; ℗ 1,234; © 1,185
PIKE; 175 Q-4; ℗ 12,509; © 12,837; ◆ 12,459
Pikes Peak; RMC Place; BROWN; *175 M-9; mail Columbus Z 47201; ● 30
Pikeville; RMC Place; PIKE; *175 Q-5; mail Velpen Z 47590
Pilot Knob; RMC Place; CRAWFORD; *175 R-8; mail Marengo Z 47140, Milltown Z 47145; rural
Pimento; RMC Place; VIGO; 175 M-4; elev. 600ft./183m.; 🄿; Z 47866; ● 125
Pine; MCD-Township; BENTON; *174 F-5; mail Fowler Z 47944; ℗ 264; © 281
Pine; RMC Place; LAKE; *174 A-4; ★ CHI; pop. incl. with Gary (Inc. Place)
Pine; MCD-Township; PORTER; *174 A-6; ★ CHI; mail Michigan City Z 46360; ℗ 2,779; © 2,853
Pine; MCD-Township; WARREN; *174 G-4; mail Pine Village Z 47975; ℗ 446; © 436
Pine Grove Estates; RMC Place; RIPLEY; *175 M-12; mail Batesville Z 47006; pop. incl. with Batesville (Inc. Place)
Pine Junction; RMC Place; LAKE; ★ CHI; pop. incl. with Gary (Inc. Place)
Pine Lake; RMC Place; LAPORTE; *174 A-6; ★ MICH; mail La Porte Z 46350; ● 1,700
Pine Valley; RMC Place; ORANGE; *175 Q-8; mail Paoli Z 47454
Pine Village; Inc. Place; WARREN; 174 G-5; elev. 667ft./203m.; 🄿; Z 47975; ℗ 134; © 255
Pinhook; RMC Place; LAPORTE; 174 A-6; elev. 831ft./253m.; ★ MICH; mail La Porte Z 46350; ● 40
Pinhook; RMC Place; LAWRENCE; *175 O-8; mail Bedford Z 47421; rural
Pinola; RMC Place; LAPORTE; 174 A-6; elev. 843ft./257m.; ★ MICH; mail La Porte Z 46350; ● 50
Pipe Creek; MCD-Township; MADISON; *174 H-10; ★ AND; mail Elwood Z 46036; ℗ 13,795; © 13,762
Pipe Creek; MCD-Township; MIAMI; *174 F-9; mail Peru Z 46970; ℗ 8,074; © 6,677
Pittsboro; Inc. Place; HENDRICKS; 174 J-7; elev. 940ft./287m.; 🄿; ★ IND; Z 46167; ℗ 815; © 1,588
Pittsburg; RMC Place; CARROLL; 174 F-7; mail Delphi Z 46923; ● 300
Plain; MCD-Township; KOSCIUSKO; *174 C-10; mail Leesburg Z 46538, Warsaw Z 46580; ℗ 5,211; © 7,194; ® 7,192
Plainfield; Inc. Place; HENDRICKS; 175 K-8; 🄿; ★ IND; Z 46168; ℗ 10,433; © 18,396; ◆ 22,184
Plainville; Inc. Place; DAVIESS; 175 O-5; 🄿; Z 47568; ℗ 444; © 513
Plano; RMC Place; MORGAN; *175 L-7; mail Martinsville Z 46151
Plato; RMC Place; LAGRANGE; 174 A-12; mail Lagrange Z 46761; ● 20
Plattsburg; RMC Place; WASHINGTON; *175 O-9; mail Vallonia Z 47281
Pleasant; MCD-Township; ALLEN; *174 D-12; ★ FTWA; mail Fort Wayne Z 46819, Yoder Z 46798; ℗ 3,355; © 3,362
Pleasant; MCD-Township; GRANT; *174 F-10; ★ MRN; mail Marion Z 46952; ℗ 6,677; © 6,941
Pleasant; MCD-Township; JOHNSON; *175 K-9; ★ IND; mail Greenwood Z 46142; ℗ 28,094; © 39,901
Pleasant; MCD-Township; LAPORTE; *174 A-7; ★ MICH; mail La Porte Z 46350; ℗ 2,897; © 3,125
Pleasant; MCD-Township; PORTER; *174 C-6; mail Kouts Z 46347; ℗ 3,266; © 3,759
Pleasant; MCD-Township; STEUBEN; *174 A-13; mail Angola Z 46703; ℗ 10,874; © 13,312
Pleasant; RMC Place; SWITZERLAND; ▲ Pleasant; 175 O-12; mail Canaan Z 47224; ● 25
Pleasant; MCD-Township; SWITZERLAND; *175 O-13; mail Canaan Z 47224; ℗ 1,076; © 1,260
Pleasant; MCD-Township; WABASH; *174 D-10; mail North Manchester Z 46962; ℗ 2,469; © 2,576
Pleasant Gardens; RMC Place; PUTNAM; *175 K-6; mail Reelsville Z 46171; ● 100
Pleasant Lake; RMC Place; STEUBEN; 174 A-13; elev. 976ft./297m.; 🄿; Z 46779; ● 500
Pleasant Mills; RMC Place; ADAMS; 174 E-14; elev. 800ft./244m.; 🄿; Z 46780; ● 150
Pleasant Plain; RMC Place; HUNTINGTON; *174 F-11; mail Warren Z 46792
Pleasant Run; MCD-Township; LAWRENCE; *175 N-8; mail Heltonville Z 47436; ℗ 1,649; © 1,922
Pleasant Valley; RMC Place; ST. JOSEPH; *174 A-9; ★ S.B.; mail Osceola Z 46561; ● 400
Pleasant View; RMC Place; SHELBY; 175 K-9; ★ IND; mail Fairland Z 46126; ● 300
Pleasant View Village; RMC Place; BARTHOLOMEW; *175 L-9; ★ COL; mail Edinburgh Z 46124; ● 350
Pleasantville; RMC Place; SULLIVAN; 175 N-4; mail Carlisle Z 47838; ● 100
Pleasure Valley; RMC Place; SHELBY; *175 L-10; mail Waldron Z 46182; ● 40
Plevna; RMC Place; HOWARD; 174 G-9; elev. 852ft./260m.; ★ KOK; mail Kokomo Z 46901; ● 70
Plummer; RMC Place; GREENE; *175 N-6; mail Bloomfield Z 47424; ● 30
Plum Tree; RMC Place; HUNTINGTON; 174 F-12; mail Warren Z 46792; ● 25
Plymouth; Inc. Place; ⊡ MARSHALL; 174 C-8; elev. 799ft./244m.; 🄿 🄷; Z 46563; ℗ 8,303; © 9,840
Poe; RMC Place; ALLEN; 174 E-13; ★ FTWA; mail Fort Wayne Z 46819; ● 110
Point; MCD-Township; POSEY; *175 T-1; mail Mount Vernon Z 47620; ℗ 477; © 497
Point Commerce; RMC Place; GREENE; *175 M-6; mail Worthington Z 47471; rural
Point Idalawn; RMC Place; BROWN; *175 M-8; elev. 650ft./198m.; mail Unionville Z 47468; ● 50
Point Isabel; RMC Place; GRANT; 174 G-10; mail Fairmount Z 46928; ● 125
Poland; RMC Place; CLAY; 175 L-6; elev. 700ft./213m.; 🄿; Z 47868; ● 150
Polk; MCD-Township; HUNTINGTON; *174 E-11; mail Huntington Z 46750; ℗ 399; © 491
Polk; MCD-Township; MARSHALL; *174 B-8; mail Walkerton Z 46574; ℗ 2,497; © 2,784
Polk; MCD-Township; MONROE; *175 N-8; mail Heltonville Z 47436; ℗ 332; © 316
Polk; MCD-Township; WASHINGTON; *175 P-9; mail Pekin Z 47165; ℗ 1,863; © 2,394
Poneto; Inc. Place; WELLS; 174 F-12; elev. 852ft./260m.; 🄿; Z 46781; ℗ 236; © 240
Pontiac; RMC Place; CLAY; *175 K-5; mail Carbon Z 47837; rural
Pony Express; RMC Place; VANDERBURGH; ★ EV; mail Evansville Z 47710; pop. incl. with Evansville (Inc. Place)
Popcorn; RMC Place; LAWRENCE; *175 N-7; mail Springville Z 47462; rural
Portage; Inc. Place; PORTER; ▲ Portage; 174 A-5; elev. 643ft./196m.; 🄿; ★ CHI; Z 46368; ℗ 29,060; © 33,496; ◆ 36,864
Portage; MCD-Township; PORTER; *174 A-5; elev. 643ft./196m.; 🄿; ★ CHI; Z 46368; ℗ 40,929; © 43,956
Portage; MCD-Township; ST. JOSEPH; *174 A-8; ★ S.B.; mail South Bend Z 46619, Z 46628; ℗ 101,791; © 94,916; ® 96,080
Porter; Inc. Place; PORTER; 174 A-5; 🄿; ★ CHI; Z 46304; ℗ 3,118; © 4,972
Porter; MCD-Township; PORTER; *174 B-5; 🄿; ★ CHI; Z 46304 & mail Valparaiso Z 46383; does not include the Town of Porter; ℗ 7,300; © 8,459
PORTER; 174 B-5; ℗ 128,932; © 146,798; ◆ 160,712
Portersville; RMC Place; DUBOIS; 175 Q-5; mail Jasper Z 47546; ● 120
Portland; Inc. Place; ⊡ JAY; 174 G-13; elev. 908ft./277m.; 🄿 🄷; Z 47371; ℗ 6,483; © 6,437
Portland Mills; RMC Place; PARKE, PUTNAM; *175 K-5; mail Greencastle Z 46135
Posey; MCD-Township; CLAY; *175 L-5; ★ T.H.; mail Brazil Z 47834; ℗ 3,347; © 3,984
Posey; MCD-Township; FAYETTE; *174 J-12; mail Connersville Z 47331; ℗ 545; © 487
Posey; MCD-Township; FRANKLIN; *175 L-12; mail Laurel Z 47024; ℗ 930; © 1,030
Posey; MCD-Township; HARRISON; *175 R-9; mail Elizabeth Z 47117; ℗ 2,553; © 2,725
Posey; MCD-Township; RUSH; *175 K-11; mail Arlington Z 46104; ℗ 1,194; © 1,189
Posey; MCD-Township; SWITZERLAND; *175 O-14; mail Patriot Z 47038; ℗ 1,323; © 1,504
Posey; MCD-Township; WASHINGTON; *175 Q-8; mail Fredericksburg Z 47120, Hardinsburg Z 47125; ℗ 1,480; © 1,783
POSEY; 175 S-2; ℗ 25,968; © 27,061; ◆ 25,795
Poseyville; Inc. Place; POSEY; 175 R-2; elev. 434ft./132m.; 🄿; Z 47633; ℗ 1,089; © 1,187
Pottawattamie Park (Pottawattomie Park); Inc. Place; LAPORTE; *174 A-6; elev. 600ft./183m.; ★ MICH; mail Michigan City Z 46360; ℗ 281; © 300
Pottawattomie Park; LAPORTE; see Pottawattamie Park (Inc. Place)
Potters Hollow; RMC Place; TIPPECANOE; *174 G-6; ★ LAF-; mail Lafayette Z 47905; pop. incl. with Lafayette (Inc. Place)
Pottersville; RMC Place; OWEN; *175 M-6; mail Spencer Z 47460; rural
Powers; RMC Place; JAY; *174 H-13; elev. 988ft./301m.; mail Portland Z 47371
Prairie; MCD-Township; HENRY; *174 I-12; ★ MUN; mail New Castle Z 47362; ℗ 3,393; © 3,317
Prairie; MCD-Township; KOSCIUSKO; *174 C-9; mail Warsaw Z 46582; ℗ 1,279; © 1,590
Prairie; MCD-Civil Township; LAPORTE; *174 C-6; mail Hanna Z 46340; ℗ 224; © 181
Prairie; MCD-Township; TIPTON; *174 G-8; mail Kempton Z 46049; ℗ 1,125; © 1,213
Prairie; MCD-Township; WARREN; *174 G-4; mail Boswell Z 47921; ℗ 318; © 290
Prairie; MCD-Township; WHITE; *174 F-6; mail Brookston Z 47923; ℗ 2,950; © 3,191
Prairie City; RMC Place; CLAY; *175 L-5; mail Brazil Z 47834
Prairie Creek; RMC Place; VIGO; ▲ Prairie Creek; 175 M-4; 🄿; Z 47869; ● 250
Prairie Creek; MCD-Township; VIGO; *175 M-3; 🄿; Z 47869 & mail Terre Haute Z 47802; ℗ 1,299; © 1,220
Prairieton; RMC Place; VIGO; ▲ Prairieton; 175 L-4; 🄿; ★ T.H.; Z 47870; ● 175
Prairieton; MCD-Township; VIGO; *175 L-3; 🄿; ★ T.H.; Z 47870 & mail Terre Haute Z 47802; ℗ 1,277; © 1,300
Prairie Village; RMC Place; VIGO; *175 L-4; ★ T.H.; mail Terre Haute Z 47802; ● 250
Prather; RMC Place; MORGAN; *175 L-8; ★ IND; mail Martinsville Z 46151; ● 50
Preble; RMC Place; ADAMS; 174 E-13; elev. 815ft./248m.; 🄿; Z 46782; ● 140
Preble; MCD-Township; ADAMS; *174 E-13; 🄿; Z 46782 & mail Decatur Z 46733; ℗ 1,047; © 1,095
Prescott; RMC Place; SHELBY; *175 L-10; mail Shelbyville Z 46176
Presidential Village; RMC Place; ALLEN; *174 D-13; ★ FTWA; mail New Haven Z 46774; pop. incl. with New Haven (Inc. Place)
Pretty Lake; RMC Place; LAGRANGE; *174 A-12; mail Wolcottville Z 46795; ● 500
Pretty Lake; RMC Place; MARSHALL; *174 C-8; mail Plymouth Z 46563; ● 100
Prince's Lake; JOHNSON; see Princes Lakes (Inc. Place)
Princes Lakes (Prince's Lake); Inc. Place; JOHNSON; 175 L-9; elev. 850ft./259m.; ★ IND; mail Nineveh Z 46164; ℗ 1,055; © 1,506
Princeton; Inc. Place; ⊡ GIBSON; 175 Q-3; elev. 500ft./152m.; 🄿 🄷; Z 47670; ℗ 8,127; © 8,175
Princeton; MCD-Township; WHITE; *174 E-5; mail Wolcott Z 47995; ℗ 1,495; © 1,529
Progress; RMC Place; DELAWARE; 174 I-11; ★ AND; mail Muncie Z 47302; ● 40
Progress Acres; RMC Place; VIGO; *175 K-4; ★ T.H.; mail Terre Haute Z 47805; ● 50
Prospect; RMC Place; ORANGE; 175 P-7; mail West Baden Springs Z 47469; ● 100
Providence; RMC Place; JOHNSON; 175 L-9; mail Bargersville Z 46106; ● 75
Publico; RMC Place; FLOYD; ★ LOU; mail New Albany Z 47150; pop. incl. with New Albany (Inc. Place)
Puckett; RMC Place; GRANT; *174 G-11; ★ MRN; mail Marion Z 46953; rural
Pulaski; RMC Place; PULASKI; 174 D-7; mail Winamac Z 46996; ● 150
PULASKI; 174 D-7; ℗ 12,643; © 13,755; ◆ 13,684
Pumpkin Center; RMC Place; WASHINGTON; *175 P-9; mail Orleans Z 47452, Scottsburg Z 47170
Purcell; RMC Place; KNOX; *175 P-3; mail Vincennes Z 47591; rural
PUTNAM; 175 K-6; ℗ 30,315; © 36,019; ◆ 37,881
Putnamville; RMC Place; PUTNAM; 175 K-6; elev. 656ft./200m.; 🄿; Z 46170; ● 150
Pyrmont; RMC Place; CARROLL; 174 G-7; mail Delphi Z 46923; ● 220

Q

Queensville; RMC Place; JENNINGS; 175 N-11; mail North Vernon Z 47265; ● 100
Quercus Grove; RMC Place; SWITZERLAND; 175 O-13; mail Rising Sun Z 47040; ● 50
Quincy; RMC Place; OWEN; 175 L-7; elev. 759ft./231m.; 🄿; Z 47456; ● 150

R

Raber; RMC Place; WHITLEY; *174 D-11; mail Columbia City Z 46725; rural
Raccoon; MCD-Township; PARKE; *175 K-5; mail Rosedale Z 47874; ℗ 818; © 771
Raccoon; RMC Place; PUTNAM; 174 J-6; mail Roachdale Z 46172; ● 35
Radioville; RMC Place; PULASKI; *174 C-6; elev. 705ft./215m.; mail Medaryville Z 47957
Radley; RMC Place; GRANT; *174 G-10; mail Jonesboro Z 46938; rural
Radnor; RMC Place; CARROLL; 174 G-7; mail Delphi Z 46923; ● 75
Raglesville; RMC Place; DAVIESS; 175 O-6; mail Odon Z 47562; ● 90
Ragsdale; RMC Place; KNOX; 175 O-4; elev. 572ft./174m.; 🄿; Z 47573; ● 140
Railroad; MCD-Township; STARKE; *174 C-6; mail San Pierre Z 46374; ℗ 1,493; © 1,353
Rainbow; RMC Place; MARION; *174 J-8; ★ IND; mail Indianapolis Z 46222; pop. incl. with Indianapolis (Inc. Place)
Rainsville; RMC Place; WARREN; 174 G-4; mail Attica Z 47918; ● 50
Raleigh; RMC Place; RUSH; 174 J-12; mail Rushville Z 46173; ● 80
Ramsey; RMC Place; HARRISON; 175 Q-9; elev. 700ft./213m.; 🄿; ★ LOU; Z 47166; ● 200
Randolph; MCD-Township; OHIO; *175 N-13; mail Rising Sun Z 47040; ℗ 4,023; © 4,117
Randolph; MCD-Township; TIPPECANOE; *174 H-6; mail Romney Z 47981; ℗ 694; © 867
RANDOLPH; 174 H-13; ℗ 27,148; © 27,401; ◆ 25,106
Raub; RMC Place; BENTON; 174 F-4; elev. 730ft./223m.; mail Earl Park Z 47942; ● 100
Ravenswood; RMC Place; MARION; *174 J-9; ★ IND; mail Indianapolis Z 46240; pop. incl. with Indianapolis (Inc. Place)
Ravinamy; RMC Place; TIPPECANOE; *174 G-6; ★ LAF-; mail West Lafayette Z 47906; ● 150
Ray; MCD-Township; FRANKLIN; *175 L-12; mail Oldenburg Z 47036; ℗ 3,098; © 3,690
Ray; MCD-Township; MORGAN; *175 L-7; mail Paragon Z 46166; ℗ 1,255; © 1,701
Ray; RMC Place; STEUBEN; 174 A-13; mail Fremont Z 46737; total pop., including Ray, MI, 120; ● 60
Raymond; RMC Place; FRANKLIN; *175 L-14; mail Bath Z 47010
Rays Crossing; RMC Place; SHELBY; 175 K-11; mail Shelbyville Z 46176; ● 60
Raysville; RMC Place; HENRY; *174 J-11; mail Knightstown Z 46148; ● 150
Red Bank; RMC Place; VANDERBURGH; *175 S-3; ★ EV; mail Evansville Z 47712; pop. incl. with Evansville (Inc. Place)
Red Bush; RMC Place; WARRICK; *175 S-4; mail Newburgh Z 47630; rural
Redding; MCD-Township; JACKSON; *175 N-10; mail Seymour Z 47274; ℗ 3,758; © 4,002
Reddington; RMC Place; JACKSON; ▲ Redding; 175 N-10; mail Seymour Z 47274; ● 200
Red Hill; RMC Place; LAWRENCE; *175 N-7; mail Springville Z 47462; ● 100
Redkey; Inc. Place; JAY; 174 G-12; elev. 964ft./294m.; 🄿; Z 47373; ℗ 1,383; © 1,427
Redmon Park; RMC Place; KOSCIUSKO; *174 B-10; mail Syracuse Z 46567; summer pop. 300; ● 80
Reed; RMC Place; DELAWARE; *174 H-11; ★ MUN; mail Muncie Z 47304; ● 60
Reedville; HANCOCK; see Carrollton (RMC Place)
Reelsville; RMC Place; PUTNAM; 175 K-6; elev. 614ft./187m.; 🄿; Z 46171; ● 150
Reeve; MCD-Township; DAVIESS; *175 P-5; mail Loogootee Z 47553; ℗ 632; © 696
Rego; RMC Place; ORANGE; *175 Q-8; 🄿; Z 47125; rural
Reiffsburg; RMC Place; WELLS; 174 F-12; mail Bluffton Z 46714; ● 40
Remington; Inc. Place; JASPER; 174 E-5; elev. 718ft./219m.; 🄿; Z 47977; ℗ 1,247; © 1,323
Reno; RMC Place; HENDRICKS; *175 K-7; mail Coatesville Z 46121
Rensselaer; Inc. Place; ⊡ JASPER; 174 E-5; elev. 664ft./202m.; 🄿 🄷 🄲 1,031; Z 47978; ℗ 5,045; © 5,294
Reo; RMC Place; SPENCER; *175 T-5; mail Rockport Z 47635; ● 100
Republican; MCD-Township; JEFFERSON; *175 O-11; mail Madison Z 47250; ℗ 1,468; © 1,534
Reserve; MCD-Township; PARKE; *174 J-4; mail Montezuma Z 47862; ℗ 1,444; © 1,515
Retreat; RMC Place; JACKSON; *175 O-10; mail Crothersville Z 47229; ● 70
Rexville; RMC Place; RIPLEY; *175 N-12; mail Madison Z 47250; ● 30
Reynolds; Inc. Place; WHITE; 174 F-6; elev. 700ft./213m.; 🄿; Z 47980; ℗ 528; © 547
Riceville; RMC Place; CRAWFORD; *175 Q-7; mail Birdseye Z 47513; rural
Richey Park; RMC Place; WHITE; *174 F-6; mail Monticello Z 47960; ● 40
Rich Grove; MCD-Township; PULASKI; *174 D-6; mail Winamac Z 46996; ℗ 722; © 887
Richland; MCD-Township; BENTON; *174 F-4; mail Earl Park Z 47942; ℗ 679; © 709
Richland; MCD-Township; DE KALB; *174 B-12; mail Corunna Z 46730; ℗ 1,153; © 1,258
Richland; MCD-Township; FOUNTAIN; *174 H-5; mail Mellott Z 47958, Newtown Z 47969; ℗ 1,015; © 908
Richland; MCD-Township; FULTON; *174 D-8; mail Rochester Z 46975; ℗ 970; © 1,117
Richland; MCD-Township; GRANT; *174 F-10; mail Marion Z 46952; ℗ 946; © 951
Richland; MCD-Township; GREENE; *175 N-6; mail Bloomfield Z 47424; ℗ 4,904; © 5,008
Richland; MCD-Township; JAY; *174 G-12; mail Dunkirk Z 47336, Redkey Z 47373; ℗ 4,999; © 4,916
Richland; MCD-Township; MADISON; *174 H-11; ★ AND; mail Anderson Z 46011; ℗ 5,494; © 5,173
Richland; MCD-Township; MIAMI; *174 E-9; mail Peru Z 46970; ℗ 1,000; © 1,149
Richland; MCD-Township; MONROE; *175 M-7; ★ BLMNG; mail Ellettsville Z 47429; ℗ 10,156; © 12,349
Richland; RMC Place; RUSH; ▲ Richland; 175 L-12; mail Rushville Z 46173; ● 50
Richland; MCD-Township; RUSH; *175 L-12; mail Rushville Z 46173; ℗ 397; © 371
Richland; SPENCER; see Richland City (RMC Place)
Richland; MCD-Township; STEUBEN; *174 A-14; mail Hamilton Z 46742; ℗ 515; © 538
Richland; MCD-Township; WHITLEY; *174 C-11; mail Larwill Z 46764; ℗ 1,492; © 1,732
Richland City (Richland); RMC Place; SPENCER; 175 S-5; elev. 393ft./120m.; mail Richland Z 47634; ● 500
Richmond; Inc. Place; ⊡ WAYNE; 174 J-13; elev. 980ft./299m.; 🄿 🄷 🄲 3,494 ■; ★ RICH; Z 47374-75; ℗ 38,705; © 39,124; ◆ 37,278
Richvalley; RMC Place; WABASH; 174 E-10; mail Wabash Z 46992; ● 120
Riddle; RMC Place; CRAWFORD; *175 R-8; mail English Z 47118; rural
Ridgemede; RMC Place; MONROE; *175 M-7; ★ BLMNG; mail Bloomington Z 47401; pop. incl. with Bloomington (Inc. Place)
Ridgeport; RMC Place; GREENE; *175 N-6; mail Bloomfield Z 47424
Ridgeview Heights; RMC Place; ALLEN; *174 D-13; ★ FTWA; mail Fort Wayne Z 46806; ● 200
Ridgeville; Inc. Place; RANDOLPH; 174 H-13; elev. 1,000ft./305m.; 🄿; Z 47380; ℗ 808; © 843
Ridgeway; RMC Place; ALLEN; *174 D-12; ★ FTWA; mail Fort Wayne Z 46809; ● 120
Ridinger Lake; RMC Place; KOSCIUSKO; *174 C-10; mail Pierceton Z 46562; ● 100
Rigdon; RMC Place; GRANT, MADISON; 174 G-10; mail Elwood Z 46036; ● 60
Riley; Inc. Place; VIGO; ▲ Riley; 175 L-4; elev. 568ft./173m.; 🄿; Z 47871; ℗ 232; © 160
Riley; MCD-Township; VIGO; *175 L-4; 🄿; Z 47871 & mail Terre Haute Z 47802-03; ℗ 2,435; © 2,805
Rileysburg; RMC Place; VERMILLION; 174 I-3; elev. 648ft./198m.; mail Covington Z 47932; ● 35
Riley Village; RMC Place; SHELBY; *175 L-10; mail Shelbyville Z 46176; pop. incl. with Shelbyville (Inc. Place)
Ripley; MCD-Township; MONTGOMERY; *174 I-5; mail Crawfordsville Z 47933; ℗ 887; © 1,101
Ripley; RMC Place; PULASKI; *174 D-7; mail Winamac Z 46996; ● 30
Ripley; MCD-Township; RUSH; *174 J-11; mail Carthage Z 46115; ℗ 1,910; © 2,111
RIPLEY; 175 N-12; ℗ 24,616; © 26,523; ◆ 27,000
Rising Sun; Inc. Place; ⊡ OHIO; 175 N-14; elev. 519ft./158m.; 🄿; Z 47040; ℗ 2,311; © 2,470
Rivare; RMC Place; ADAMS; 174 E-14; mail Decatur Z 46733; ● 60
River City; RMC Place; VANDERBURGH; ★ EV; mail Evansville Z 47714, Z 47728; pop. incl. with Evansville (Inc. Place)
River Forest; Inc. Place; MADISON; *174 I-10; elev. 870ft./265m.; ★ AND; mail Anderson Z 46011; ℗ 16; © 28
Riverhaven; RMC Place; ALLEN; *174 D-13; ★ FTWA; mail Fort Wayne Z 46803; ● 600
River Ridge; RMC Place; TIPTON; mail Jeffersonville Z 47130; ● 100
Riverside; RMC Place; CLARK; *175 R-10; ★ LOU; mail Clarksville Z 47129, Jeffersonville Z 47130; ● 1,500
Riverside; RMC Place; FOUNTAIN; 174 H-5; mail Attica Z 47918; ● 75
Riverton; RMC Place; SULLIVAN; 175 N-3; mail Merom Z 47861; ● 25
Rivervale; RMC Place; LAWRENCE; *175 O-8; mail Mitchell Z 47446; rural
Riverview; RMC Place; SULLIVAN; 175 M-3; mail Fairbanks Z 47849; ● 50
Riverview Acres; RMC Place; BARTHOLOMEW; *175 M-10; ★ COL; mail Columbus Z 47203; pop. incl. with Columbus (Inc. Place)
Riverwood; RMC Place; HAMILTON; *174 I-9; ★ IND; mail Noblesville Z 46060; ● 500
Roachdale; Inc. Place; PUTNAM; 174 J-6; elev. 648ft./198m.; 🄿; Z 46172; ℗ 902; © 975
Roann; Inc. Place; WABASH; 174 E-10; 🄿; Z 46974; ℗ 447; © 400
Roanoke; Inc. Place; HUNTINGTON; 174 D-12; elev. 755ft./230m.; 🄿; Z 46783; ℗ 1,018; © 1,495
Robb; MCD-Township; POSEY; *175 R-2; mail Poseyville Z 47633; ℗ 2,009; © 2,074
Robertsdale; RMC Place; LAKE; *174 A-4; ★ CHI; mail Whiting Z 46394; pop. incl. with Hammond (Inc. Place)
Robinson; MCD-Township; POSEY; *175 S-2; ★ EV; mail Wadesville Z 47638; ℗ 3,863; © 3,976
Robinwood; RMC Place; VIGO; 174 I-2; ★ T.H.; mail Terre Haute Z 47803; ● 150
Roble Woods; RMC Place; PORTER; *174 B-5; ★ CHI; mail Valparaiso Z 46383; ● 150
Rob Roy; RMC Place; FOUNTAIN; 174 H-5; elev. 636ft./194m.; mail Attica Z 47918; ● 50
Roby; RMC Place; LAKE; *174 A-4; ★ CHI; pop. incl. with Hammond (Inc. Place)
Rochester; Inc. Place; ⊡ FULTON; ▲ Rochester; 174 D-8; 🄿 🄷; Z 46975; ℗ 5,969; © 6,414
Rochester; MCD-Township; FULTON; *174 D-8; 🄿; Z 46975; ℗ 9,110; © 9,992
Rock Creek; MCD-Township; BARTHOLOMEW; *175 M-10; mail Elizabethtown Z 47232; ℗ 1,261; © 1,313
Rock Creek; MCD-Township; CARROLL; *174 F-7; mail Delphi Z 46923; ℗ 409; © 442
Rock Creek; RMC Place; HUNTINGTON; ▲ Rock Creek; *174 E-12; mail Huntington Z 46750; rural
Rock Creek; MCD-Township; HUNTINGTON; *174 E-11; mail Huntington Z 46750; ℗ 1,471; © 1,417
Rockcreek; MCD-Township; WELLS; *174 E-12; mail Bluffton Z 46714; ℗ 1,541; © 1,670
Rockdale; RMC Place; FRANKLIN; *175 M-14; mail West Harrison Z 47060
Rockfield; RMC Place; CARROLL; 174 F-7; 🄿; Z 46977; ● 300
Rockford; RMC Place; JACKSON; 175 N-10; mail Seymour Z 47274; ● 400
Rockford; RMC Place; WELLS; 174 E-12; mail Bluffton Z 46714; ● 50
Rock Island; RMC Place; MARION; ★ IND
Rock Lake; RMC Place; FULTON, KOSCIUSKO; *174 D-9; mail Akron Z 46910; ● 60
Rocklane; RMC Place; JOHNSON; 175 K-9; mail Greenwood Z 46143; ● 120
Rockport; Inc. Place; ⊡ SPENCER; 175 T-5; elev. 445ft./136m.; 🄿; Z 47635; ℗ 2,315; © 2,160
Rockville; Inc. Place; ⊡ PARKE; 174 J-5; elev. 711ft./217m.; 🄿; Z 47872; ℗ 2,706; © 2,765
Rocky Ripple; Inc. Place; MARION; *174 J-9; ★ IND; mail Indianapolis Z 46208; © 712
Roland; RMC Place; ORANGE; *175 P-7; mail West Baden Springs Z 47469; rural
Roll; RMC Place; BLACKFORD; 174 F-12; mail Hartford City Z 47348; ● 100
Rolling Fields; RMC Place; CLARK; *175 R-10; ★ LOU; mail Jeffersonville Z 47130; pop. incl. with Jeffersonville (Inc. Place)
Rolling Hill Estates; RMC Place; LAKE; *174 B-4; ★ CHI; mail Schererville Z 46375; pop. incl. with Schererville (Inc. Place)
Rolling Hills; RMC Place; ALLEN; *174 D-12; ★ FTWA; mail Fort Wayne Z 46804; ● 300
Rolling Hills; RMC Place; CLARK; mail Charlestown Z 47111; ● 360
Rolling Hills; RMC Place; GRANT; *174 F-10; ★ MRN; mail Marion Z 46952; ● 150
Rolling Hills; RMC Place; TIPPECANOE; *174 G-6; ★ LAF-; mail Lafayette Z 47905; ● 450
Rolling Prairie; RMC Place; LAPORTE; 174 A-7; elev. 822ft./251m.; 🄿; ★ MICH; Z 46371; ● 500
Rolling Ridge; RMC Place; SHELBY; *175 K-10; mail Shelbyville Z 46176; pop. incl. with Shelbyville (Inc. Place)
Rome; RMC Place; PERRY; 175 S-7; elev. 410ft./125m.; 🄿; Z 47574; ● 40
Rome City; Inc. Place; NOBLE; 174 B-12; elev. 930ft./283m.; 🄿; Z 46784; ℗ 1,138; © 1,615
Romney; RMC Place; TIPPECANOE; 174 H-6; elev. 733ft./223m.; 🄿; Z 47981; ● 450
Romona; RMC Place; OWEN; *175 L-6; mail Spencer Z 47460; ● 50
Root; MCD-Township; ADAMS; *174 E-13; mail Decatur Z 46733; ℗ 3,922; © 4,433
Rose; RMC Place; VIGO; ★ T.H.; mail Terre Haute Z 47803; pop. incl. with Terre Haute (Inc. Place)
Roseburg; RMC Place; GRANT; *174 G-10; ★ MRN; mail Marion Z 46953; ● 50
Roseburg; RMC Place; UNION; *175 K-13; mail Liberty Z 47353
Rosedale; Inc. Place; PARKE; 175 K-4; elev. 542ft./165m.; 🄿; Z 47874; ℗ 783; © 750
Rosedale Hills; RMC Place; MARION; *175 K-9; ★ IND; mail Indianapolis Z 46227; pop. incl. with Indianapolis (Inc. Place)
Rose Hill Gardens; RMC Place; VIGO; *175 L-4; mail Terre Haute Z 47805; ● 55
Roseland; Inc. Place; ST. JOSEPH; 174 A-8; elev. 725ft./221m.; ★ S.B.; mail South Bend Z 46637; ℗ 706; © 1,809; ® 645
Roselawn; CDP; NEWTON; 174 D-4; 🄿; ★ CHI; Z 46372; © 3,933
Rosewood; RMC Place; HARRISON; *175 S-10; 🄿; Z 47117; rural
Ross; MCD-Township; CLINTON; *174 G-7; mail Rossville Z 46065; ℗ 2,217; © 2,743
Ross; RMC Place; LAKE; 174 B-4; ★ CHI; mail Gary Z 46408; ● 1,100
Ross; MCD-Township; LAKE; *174 B-4; ★ CHI; mail Merrillville Z 46410; ℗ 34,683; © 38,685
Rossburg; RMC Place; DECATUR; *175 L-12; mail New Point Z 47263; rural
Rosston; RMC Place; BOONE; 174 I-8; mail Zionsville Z 46077; ● 50
Rosstown; RMC Place; BARTHOLOMEW; *175 N-10; elev. 628ft./191m.; ★ COL; mail Columbus Z 47201; ● 75
Rossville; Inc. Place; CLINTON; 174 G-7; elev. 722ft./220m.; 🄿; Z 46065; ℗ 1,175; © 1,513
Roth Park; RMC Place; CARROLL; *174 F-6; mail Monticello Z 47960; ● 150
Round Grove; MCD-Township; WHITE; *174 F-5; mail Brookston Z 47923; ℗ 250; © 246
Round Lake; RMC Place; NOBLE; *174 B-12; mail Kendallville Z 46755; ● 30
Round Lake; RMC Place; WHITLEY; *174 C-11; mail Columbia City Z 46725
Royal Center (Royal Centre); Inc. Place; CASS; 174 E-7; elev. 730ft./223m.; 🄿; Z 46978; ℗ 859; © 832
Royal Centre; CASS; see Royal Center (Inc. Place)
Royal Oaks; RMC Place; ALLEN; *174 D-13; ★ FTWA; mail Fort Wayne Z 46815; pop. incl. with Fort Wayne (Inc. Place)
Royalton; RMC Place; BOONE; 174 J-8; ★ IND; mail Zionsville Z 46077; ● 50
Royal View; RMC Place; BARTHOLOMEW; *175 M-10; ★ COL; mail Columbus Z 47201
Royer Lake; RMC Place; LAGRANGE; *174 A-12; mail Lagrange Z 46761; ● 200
Royerton; RMC Place; DELAWARE; 174 H-12; ★ MUN; mail Muncie Z 47303; ● 900
Royerton Park; RMC Place; DELAWARE; *174 H-12; elev. 930ft./283m.; ★ MUN; mail Muncie Z 47303; ● 120
Rugby; RMC Place; BARTHOLOMEW; 175 M-10; ★ COL; mail Hope Z 47246; ● 50
Rural; RMC Place; RANDOLPH; *174 I-13; mail Winchester Z 47394; ● 30
RUSH; 175 K-11; ℗ 18,129; © 18,261; ◆ 17,341
Rushville; Inc. Place; ⊡ RUSH; ▲ Rushville; 175 K-11; 🄿 🄷; Z 46173 & mail Homer Z 46146; ℗ 5,533; © 5,995
Rushville; MCD-Township; RUSH; *175 K-11; 🄿; Z 46173 & mail Homer Z 46146; ℗ 7,996; © 8,264
Russell; MCD-Township; PUTNAM; *174 J-6; mail Roachdale Z 46172; ℗ 775; © 856
Russell Lake; RMC Place; BOONE; *174 I-8; ★ IND; mail Zionsville Z 46077; ● 150
Russellville; Inc. Place; PUTNAM; 174 J-5; elev. 831ft./253m.; 🄿; Z 46175; ℗ 336; © 340
Russels Point; RMC Place; STEUBEN; *174 A-13; mail Hamilton Z 46742; ● 35
Russiaville; Inc. Place; HOWARD; 174 G-8; elev. 850ft./259m.; 🄿; ★ KOK; Z 46979; ℗ 988; © 1,092
Rustic Hills; RMC Place; WARRICK; *175 S-4; elev. 459ft./140m.; ★ EV; mail Newburgh Z 47630; ● 140
Rutherford; MCD-Township; MARTIN; *175 P-6; mail Loogootee Z 47553; ℗ 681; © 730
Rutland; RMC Place; MARSHALL; *174 C-8; mail Plymouth Z 46563
Rykers Ridge; RMC Place; JEFFERSON; *175 O-12; mail Madison Z 47250; rural

S

Sagers Lake; RMC Place; PORTER; *174 B-5; ★ CHI; mail Valparaiso Z 46383; rural
Saint Anthony; RMC Place; DUBOIS; 175 R-6; elev. 560ft./171m.; 🄿; Z 47575; ● 400
Saint Bernice; RMC Place; VERMILLION; 175 K-3; elev. 594ft./181m.; 🄿; Z 47875; ● 800
Saint Croix; RMC Place; PERRY; 175 R-7; 🄿; Z 47576; ● 60
Saint Henry; RMC Place; DUBOIS; 175 R-6; mail Ferdinand Z 47532; ● 130
Saint James; RMC Place; GIBSON; *175 R-3; ★ EV; mail Haubstadt Z 47639; ● 100
Saint Joe; Inc. Place; DE KALB; 174 C-13; elev. 825ft./251m.; 🄿; Z 46785; ℗ 452; © 478
Saint John; Inc. Place; LAKE; ▲ St. John; 174 B-4; elev. 704ft./215m.; 🄿; ★ CHI; Z 46373; ℗ 4,921; © 8,382
St. John; MCD-Township; LAKE; *174 B-4; elev. 704ft./215m.; ★ CHI; mail Saint John Z 46373; ℗ 41,782; © 53,701
Saint Johns; RMC Place; DE KALB; *174 C-13; mail Garrett Z 46738
St. Joseph; MCD-Township; ALLEN; *174 D-13; ★ FTWA; mail Fort Wayne Z 46835; ℗ 61,167; © 68,276
Saint Joseph; RMC Place; VANDERBURGH; 175 S-3; elev. 547ft./167m.; ★ EV; mail Evansville Z 47720; ● 75
ST. JOSEPH; 174 B-8; ℗ 247,052; © 265,559; ◆ 264,319
Saint Leon; Inc. Place; DEARBORN; 175 M-13; elev. 1,016ft./310m.; 🄿; ★ CIN; Z 47012 & mail West Harrison Z 47060; ℗ 493; © 387; ® 458
Saint Louis; RMC Place; BARTHOLOMEW; *175 M-10; ★ COL; mail Hope Z 47246; ● 50
Saint Louis Crossing; RMC Place; BARTHOLOMEW; 175 M-10; mail Columbus Z 47201; ● 90
Saint Marks; RMC Place; DUBOIS; 175 R-6; mail Saint Anthony Z 47575; ● 100
Saint Marks; RMC Place; PERRY; *175 S-6; mail Tell City Z 47586; rural
Saint Mary-of-the-Woods; RMC Place; VIGO; 175 L-4; elev. 561ft./171m.; 🄿 🄲 1,668; ★ T.H.; Z 47876; ● 300
St. Marys; MCD-Township; ADAMS; *174 E-14; mail Decatur Z 46733; ℗ 1,213; © 1,264
Saint Marys; RMC Place; FLOYD; *175 Q-10; ★ LOU; mail Floyds Knobs Z 47119; rural
Saint Marys (Haymond); RMC Place; FRANKLIN; *175 L-13; mail Batesville Z 47006
Saint Marys (Saint Mary's College); RMC Place; ST. JOSEPH; *174 A-8; elev. 725ft./221m.; ★ S.B.; mail Fort Wayne Z 46808, Notre Dame Z 46556; ● 1,700
Saint Mary's College; ST. JOSEPH; see Saint Marys (RMC Place)
Saint Maurice; RMC Place; DECATUR; *175 L-12; mail Greensburg Z 47240; ● 30
Saint Meinrad; RMC Place; SPENCER; 175 R-6; 🄿; Z 47577; ● 500
Saint Omer; RMC Place; DECATUR; 175 L-11; mail Saint Paul Z 47272; ● 75
Saint Paul; Inc. Place; DECATUR, SHELBY; 175 L-11; elev. 858ft./262m.; 🄿; Z 47272; ℗ 1,032; © 1,022
Saint Peter; RMC Place; FRANKLIN; 175 L-13; mail Brookville Z 47012; ● 70

Entries in **UPPERCASE** are counties.
Entries in **bold** have populations of 2,500 or more.
Names in parentheses are alternate names.
Inc. Place — Incorporated Place
RMC Place — Rand McNally Designated Place
CDP — Census Designated Place
MCD — Minor Civil Division

⊡ County Seat
▲ Minor Civil Division
elev. Elevation
🄿 Post Office

🄷 Hospital
🄲 College
■ Principal Business Center
★ Ranally Metro Area (RMA) Abbreviation
Z Zip Code(s)

℗ Previous Census Population
® Revised Census Population
Ⓐ Annexation Population
● Rand McNally Population Estimate
© Final Census Population
Ⓢ Special Census Population
◆ Estimated Population

For additional definitions see Glossary, Volume 1, and Introduction, Volume 2.

Saint Philip; RMC Place; POSEY; **175** S-3; ★ **EV**; mail Mount Vernon **z** 47620; ● 500
Saint Thomas; RMC Place; KNOX; ***175** P-3; mail Vincennes **z** 47591; rural
Saint Wendel; RMC Place; POSEY, VANDERBURGH; **175** R-3; ★ **EV**; mail Evansville **z** 47712, **z** 47720; ● 500
Salamonia; Inc. Place; JAY; **174** G-14; elev. 970ft./296m.; 🅿; **z** 47381; Ⓟ 138; © 158
Salamonie; MCD-Township; HUNTINGTON; ***174** F-12; mail Warren **z** 46792; Ⓟ 2,404; © 2,529
Salem; RMC Place; ADAMS; ***174** F-14; mail Monroe **z** 46772
Salem; MCD-Township; DELAWARE; ***174** I-11; ★ **AND**; mail Daleville **z** 47334; Ⓟ 3,899; © 4,099
Salem; RMC Place; JAY; **174** H-14; mail Union City **z** 47390; ● 40
Salem; MCD-Township; PULASKI; ***174** D-6; mail Francesville **z** 47946; Ⓟ 1,429; © 1,500
Salem; MCD-Township; STEUBEN; ***174** A-12; mail Hudson **z** 46747; Ⓟ 1,848; © 2,182
Salem; Inc. Place; ⊡ WASHINGTON; **175** P-9; elev. 747ft./228m.; 🅿 🅷; **z** 47167; Ⓟ 5,619; © 6,172
Salem Center; RMC Place; STEUBEN; ▲ Salem; ***174** A-12; mail Hudson **z** 46747; ● 40
Salem Heights; RMC Place; LAPORTE; ***174** A-7; ★ **MICH**; mail La Porte **z** 46350; ● 90
Saline City; RMC Place; CLAY; **175** L-5; elev. 567ft./173m.; mail Centerpoint **z** 47840; ● 90
Saltcreek; MCD-Township; DECATUR; ***175** M-12; mail Greensburg **z** 47240; Ⓟ 1,187; © 1,174
Salt Creek; MCD-Township; FRANKLIN; ***175** L-12; mail Laurel **z** 47024; Ⓟ 868; © 943
Salt Creek; MCD-Township; JACKSON; ***175** N-8; mail Freetown **z** 47235; Ⓟ 309; © 309
Salt Creek; MCD-Township; MONROE; ***175** M-8; mail Bloomington **z** 47401; Ⓟ 1,316; © 1,443
Saltillo; Inc. Place; WASHINGTON; **175** P-8; elev. 801ft./244m.; mail Campbellsburg **z** 47108; Ⓟ 117; © 107
Saluda; RMC Place; JEFFERSON; ▲ Saluda; ***175** P-11; mail Hanover **z** 47243
Saluda; MCD-Township; JEFFERSON; ***175** P-11; mail Hanover **z** 47243; Ⓟ 1,305; © 1,358
Samaria; RMC Place; JOHNSON; **175** L-9; mail Trafalgar **z** 46181; ● 75
Sandborn; Inc. Place; KNOX; **175** O-5; elev. 470ft./143m.; 🅿; **z** 47578; Ⓟ 455; © 451
Sand Creek; MCD-Township; BARTHOLOMEW; ***175** N-10; ★ **COL**; mail Elizabethtown **z** 47232; Ⓟ 2,104; © 2,185
Sandcreek; MCD-Township; DECATUR; ***175** M-11; mail Westport **z** 47283; Ⓟ 3,040; © 3,061
Sand Creek; MCD-Township; JENNINGS; ***175** N-11; mail North Vernon **z** 47265; Ⓟ 714; © 818
Sandcut; RMC Place; VIGO; ***175** K-4; ★ **T.H.**; mail Terre Haute **z** 47805; ● 90
Sanders; RMC Place; MONROE; ***175** N-7; ★ **BLMNG**; mail Bloomington **z** 47401; ● 100
Sandford; RMC Place; VIGO; ***175** K-3; elev. 630ft./192m.; 🅿; ★ **T.H.**; **z** 47885; ● 180
Sand Ridge; RMC Place; SPENCER; ***175** S-5; mail Rockport **z** 47635; ● 45
Sandusky; RMC Place; DECATUR; **175** L-11; mail Greensburg **z** 47240; ● 60
Sandy Beach; RMC Place; CARROLL; ***174** F-6; mail Monticello **z** 47960; ● 90
Sandy Hook; RMC Place; BARTHOLOMEW; ★ **COL**; mail Columbus **z** 47201; pop. incl. with Columbus (Inc. Place)
Sandytown; RMC Place; VERMILLION; ***175** K-4; mail Clinton **z** 47842; ● 115
San Jacinto; RMC Place; JENNINGS; ***175** N-11; elev. 754ft./230m.; mail Butlerville **z** 47223
San Pierre; CDP; STARKE; **174** C-6; elev. 704ft./215m.; 🅿; **z** 46374; © 156
Santa Claus; Inc. Place; SPENCER; **175** S-6; elev. 519ft./158m.; 🅿; **z** 47579; Ⓟ 927; © 2,041
Santa Fe; RMC Place; MIAMI; **174** F-9; mail Peru **z** 46970; ● 100
Saratoga; Inc. Place; RANDOLPH; **174** H-13; elev. 1,050ft./320m.; 🅿; **z** 47382; Ⓟ 266; © 288
Sardinia; RMC Place; DECATUR; **175** M-11; mail Westport **z** 47283; ● 125
Saugany Lake; RMC Place; LAPORTE; ***174** A-7; mail Rolling Prairie **z** 46371; ● 500
Savah; RMC Place; POSEY; ***175** S-2; mail Mount Vernon **z** 47620
Scenic Heights; RMC Place; PERRY; mail Tell City **z** 47586; pop. incl. with Tell City (Inc. Place)
Scenic Hill; RMC Place; MARTIN; ***175** P-6; mail Loogootee **z** 47553; ● 40
Schaefer Lake; RMC Place; BARTHOLOMEW; ***175** M-10; ★ **COL**; mail Hope **z** 47246; ● 300
Schererville; Inc. Place; LAKE; **174** B-4; elev. 646ft./197m.; 🅿; ★ **CHI**; **z** 46375; Ⓟ 19,926; © 24,851; ◆ 25,690
Schneider; Inc. Place; LAKE; **174** C-4; elev. 636ft./194m.; 🅿; **z** 46376; Ⓟ 310; © 317
Schnellville; RMC Place; DUBOIS; **175** Q-6; elev. 650ft./198m.; 🅿; **z** 47580; ● 250
Scipio; MCD-Township; ALLEN; ***174** C-14; mail Antwerp **z** 45813; Ⓟ 414; © 414
Scipio; RMC Place; FRANKLIN; **175** L-14; mail Brookville **z** 47012; ● 30
Scipio; RMC Place; JENNINGS; **175** N-10; elev. 686ft./209m.; 🅿; **z** 47273; ● 95
Scipio; MCD-Township; LAPORTE; ***174** A-6; ★ **MICH**; mail La Porte **z** 46350; Ⓟ 3,490; © 4,269
Scircleville; RMC Place; CLINTON; **174** H-8; elev. 930ft./283m.; mail Frankfort **z** 46041; ● 140
Scotchtown; RMC Place; SULLIVAN; ***175** N-4; elev. 512ft./156m.; mail Dugger **z** 47848; ● 30
Scotland; RMC Place; GREENE; **175** O-6; elev. 612ft./187m.; 🅿; **z** 47457; ● 100
Scott; MCD-Township; KOSCIUSKO; ***174** B-9; mail Nappanee **z** 46550; Ⓟ 1,272; © 1,618
Scott; RMC Place; LAGRANGE; **174** A-11; mail Shipshewana **z** 46565; ● 60
Scott; MCD-Township; MONTGOMERY; ***174** J-6; mail Crawfordsville **z** 47933; Ⓟ 738; © 805
Scott; MCD-Township; STEUBEN; ***174** A-13; mail Angola **z** 46703; Ⓟ 865; © 1,123
Scott; MCD-Township; VANDERBURGH; ***175** R-3; ★ **EV**; mail Evansville **z** 47711; Ⓟ 4,731; © 5,445
SCOTT; **175** P-10; Ⓟ 20,991; © 22,960; ◆ 23,678
Scott City; RMC Place; SULLIVAN; **175** M-4; mail Shelburn **z** 47879; ● 15
Scottsburg; RMC Place; PIKE; ***175** R-5; elev. 443ft./135m.; mail Oakland City **z** 47660; rural
Scottsburg; Inc. Place; ⊡ SCOTT; **175** P-10; elev. 570ft./174m.; 🅿 🅷; **z** 47170; Ⓟ 5,334; © 6,040
Scottsville; RMC Place; FLOYD; ***175** Q-10; ★ **LOU**; mail Borden **z** 47106
Sedalia; RMC Place; CLINTON; **174** G-7; elev. 779ft./237m.; 🅿; **z** 46067; ● 130
Sedan; RMC Place; DE KALB; ***174** B-13; mail Waterloo **z** 46793
Seelyville; Inc. Place; VIGO; **175** L-4; elev. 588ft./179m.; 🅿; ★ **T.H.**; **z** 47878; Ⓟ 1,090; © 1,182
Sellersburg; Inc. Place; CLARK; **175** Q-10; elev. 476ft./145m.; 🅿; ★ **LOU**; **z** 47172; Ⓟ 5,745; © 6,071
Sellers Lake; RMC Place; KOSCIUSKO; ***174** D-10; mail Pierceton **z** 46562
Selma; Inc. Place; DELAWARE; **174** H-12; elev. 1,009ft./308m.; 🅿; ★ **MUN**; **z** 47383; Ⓟ 800; © 880
Selvin; RMC Place; WARRICK; **175** R-5; elev. 516ft./157m.; mail Dale **z** 47523; ● 50
Servia; RMC Place; WABASH; **174** D-10; elev. 812ft./247m.; 🅿; **z** 46980; ● 180
Sevastopol; RMC Place; KOSCIUSKO; **174** D-9; mail Claypool **z** 46510; ● 30
Seward; MCD-Township; KOSCIUSKO; ***174** D-9; mail Claypool **z** 46510; Ⓟ 2,039; © 2,462
Sexton; RMC Place; RUSH; **175** K-11; mail Rushville **z** 46173; ● 60
Seymour; Inc. Place; JACKSON; **175** N-10; elev. 605ft./184m.; 🅿 🅷; **z** 47274; Ⓟ 15,579; © 18,101
Shadeland; RMC Place; GRANT; ***174** F-11; ★ **MRN**; mail Marion **z** 46952; ● 100
Shadeland; Inc. Place; TIPPECANOE; **174** G-6; elev. 622ft./190m.; mail Lafayette **z** 47905; Ⓟ 1,674; © 1,682
Shady Hills; RMC Place; GRANT; ***174** F-10; ★ **MRN**; mail Marion **z** 46952; ● 300
Shady Lawn; RMC Place; LAKE; ***174** B-4; ★ **CHI**; mail Crown Point **z** 46307
Shady Nook; RMC Place; LAGRANGE; ***174** A-12; mail Wolcottville **z** 46795; ● 150
Shaffer Woods; RMC Place; DELAWARE; ***174** H-11; elev. 920ft./280m.; ★ **MUN**; mail Muncie **z** 47303; ● 40
Shamrock Lakes; Inc. Place; BLACKFORD; **174** G-11; elev. 900ft./274m.; ★ **MUN**; mail Hartford City **z** 47348; Ⓟ 207; © 168
Shannondale; RMC Place; MONTGOMERY; **174** I-7; mail Crawfordsville **z** 47933; ● 35
Sharon; RMC Place; CARROLL; ***174** F-8; mail Flora **z** 46929; ● 25
Sharpsville; Inc. Place; TIPTON; **174** G-9; elev. 881ft./269m.; 🅿; ★ **KOK**; **z** 46068; Ⓟ 769; © 618
Shawnee; MCD-Township; FOUNTAIN; ***174** H-4; mail Veedersburg **z** 47987; Ⓟ 585; © 616
Shawswick; MCD-Township; LAWRENCE; ***175** O-8; mail Bedford **z** 47421; Ⓟ 20,136; © 20,598
Shawville; RMC Place; VIGO; ***175** K-4; ★ **T.H.**; mail Terre Haute **z** 47805; ● 150
Sheddfield; RMC Place; LAKE; ★ **CHI**; mail Hammond **z** 46320; pop. incl. with Hammond (Inc. Place)
Shedville (Brinckley); RMC Place; RANDOLPH; ***174** H-13; mail Farmland **z** 47340; rural
Sheffield; MCD-Township; TIPPECANOE; ***174** G-6; mail Lafayette **z** 47905; Ⓟ 2,454; © 3,016
Shelburn; Inc. Place; SULLIVAN; **175** M-4; elev. 540ft./165m.; 🅿; **z** 47879; Ⓟ 1,147; © 1,268
Shelburne; RMC Place; MORGAN; ***175** L-8; ★ **IND**; mail Martinsville **z** 46151; ● 70
Shelby; MCD-Township; JEFFERSON; ***175** O-12; mail Madison **z** 47250; Ⓟ 827; © 1,052
Shelby; RMC Place; LAKE; **174** C-4; elev. 641ft./195m.; 🅿; ★ **CHI**; **z** 46377; ● 750
Shelby; MCD-Township; RIPLEY; ***175** N-12; mail Madison **z** 47250; Ⓟ 853; © 867
Shelby; MCD-Township; SHELBY; ***175** L-10; mail Shelbyville **z** 46176; Ⓟ 1,991; © 1,930
Shelby; MCD-Township; TIPPECANOE; ***174** G-5; mail West Lafayette **z** 47906; Ⓟ 1,974; © 2,078
SHELBY; **175** K-10; Ⓟ 40,307; © 43,445; ◆ 44,265
Shelbyville; Inc. Place; ⊡ SHELBY; **175** L-10; elev. 764ft./233m.; 🅿 🅷 ■; **z** 46176; Ⓟ 15,336; © 17,951; ◆ 19,160
Shepardsville; RMC Place; VIGO; ***175** K-4; elev. 503ft./153m.; 🅿; ★ **T.H.**; **z** 47880; ● 200
Sheridan; Inc. Place; HAMILTON; **174** I-8; elev. 949ft./289m.; 🅿; ★ **IND**; **z** 46069; Ⓟ 2,046; © 2,520
Sherwood Forest; RMC Place; MARION; ***174** J-9; ★ **IND**; mail Indianapolis **z** 46240; pop. incl. with Indianapolis (Inc. Place)
Shideler (Shidelers); RMC Place; DELAWARE; **174** H-12; ★ **MUN**; mail Eaton **z** 47338; ● 160
Shidelers; DELAWARE; see Shideler (RMC Place)
Shields; RMC Place; JACKSON; ***175** O-9; mail Seymour **z** 47274; rural
Shipshewana; Inc. Place; LAGRANGE; **174** A-11; elev. 900ft./274m.; 🅿; **z** 46565; Ⓟ 524; © 536
Shirkieville; RMC Place; VIGO; **175** K-3; ★ **T.H.**; mail West Terre Haute **z** 47885; ● 100
Shirley; Inc. Place; HANCOCK, HENRY; **174** J-11; elev. 1,029ft./314m.; 🅿; **z** 47384; Ⓟ 817; © 806
Shoals; Inc. Place; ⊡ MARTIN; **175** P-6; elev. 487ft./148m.; 🅿; **z** 47581; Ⓟ 853; © 807
Shoe Lake; RMC Place; KOSCIUSKO; ***174** C-10; mail Leesburg **z** 46538; ● 120
Shordon Estates; RMC Place; ALLEN; ***174** D-13; ★ **FTWA**; mail Fort Wayne **z** 46805; ● 350
Shoreland Hills; RMC Place; LAPORTE; ★ **MICH**; mail Michigan City **z** 46360; ● 500
Shorewood Forest; RMC Place; PORTER; ***174** B-5; ★ **CHI**; mail Valparaiso **z** 46383; ● 2,000
Shriner Lake; RMC Place; WHITLEY; ***174** C-11; mail Columbia City **z** 46725
Siberia; RMC Place; PERRY; **175** R-6; elev. 593ft./181m.; 🅿; **z** 47515; ● 50
Sidney; Inc. Place; KOSCIUSKO; **174** D-10; elev. 926ft./282m.; 🅿; **z** 46562; Ⓟ 167; © 168
Silver Creek; MCD-Township; CLARK; ***175** Q-10; ★ **LOU**; mail Sellersburg **z** 47172; Ⓟ 8,014; © 9,399
Silver Hills; RMC Place; FLOYD; ***175** R-10; ★ **LOU**; mail New Albany **z** 47150; pop. incl. with New Albany (Inc. Place)
Silver Lake; Inc. Place; KOSCIUSKO; **174** D-10; elev. 900ft./274m.; 🅿; **z** 46982; Ⓟ 528; © 546
Silver Lakes Estates; RMC Place; CLARK; ***175** Q-10; ★ **LOU**; mail Clarksville **z** 47129; pop. incl. with Clarksville (Inc. Place)
Silverville; RMC Place; LAWRENCE; ***175** O-7; mail Williams **z** 47470
Silverwood; RMC Place; FOUNTAIN; **174** I-4; elev. 523ft./159m.; mail Kingman **z** 47952; ● 50
Simonton Lake; CDP; ELKHART; **174** A-9; ★ **ELK**; mail Elkhart **z** 46514; Ⓟ 3,554; © 4,053
Sims; RMC Place; BARTHOLOMEW; ★ **COL**; mail Columbus **z** 47201; pop. incl. with Columbus (Inc. Place)
Sims; RMC Place; GRANT; ▲ Sims; ***174** G-10; 🅿; ★ **MRN**; **z** 46986; ● 250
Sims; MCD-Township; GRANT; ***174** G-10; 🅿; ★ **MRN**; **z** 46986 & mail Marion **z** 46952; Ⓟ 1,891; © 1,858
Sitka; RMC Place; WHITE; **174** E-7; mail Monticello **z** 47960; ● 20
Skelton; MCD-Township; WARRICK; ***175** S-5; mail Tennyson **z** 47637; Ⓟ 1,552; © 1,699
Skinner Lake; RMC Place; NOBLE; ***174** B-12; mail Albion **z** 46701; ● 250
Slabtown (Layton Mills); RMC Place; DECATUR; ***175** M-12; mail Greensburg **z** 47240; ● 30
Sleepy Hollow; RMC Place; SHELBY; ***175** L-10; mail Waldron **z** 46182; ● 40
Sleeth; RMC Place; CARROLL; ***174** F-7; mail Delphi **z** 46923; rural
Sloan; RMC Place; WARREN; ***174** H-4; elev. 713ft./217m.; mail Williamsport **z** 47993; rural
Smartsburg; RMC Place; MONTGOMERY; ***174** I-6; mail Crawfordsville **z** 47933; ● 100
Smedley; RMC Place; WASHINGTON; ***175** P-8; mail Campbellsburg **z** 47108; ● 50
Smith; MCD-Township; GREENE; ***175** M-5; mail Worthington **z** 47471; Ⓟ 401; © 344
Smith; MCD-Township; POSEY; ***175** R-3; mail Cynthiana **z** 47612; Ⓟ 1,277; © 1,292
Smith; MCD-Township; WHITLEY; ***174** C-12; mail Churubusco **z** 46723; Ⓟ 5,082; © 5,050
Smithfield; MCD-Township; DE KALB; ***174** B-13; mail Waterloo **z** 46793; Ⓟ 1,520; © 1,658
Smithfield; RMC Place; DELAWARE; **174** H-12; ★ **MUN**; mail Selma **z** 47383; ● 30
Smithland; RMC Place; SHELBY; ***175** L-10; mail Shelbyville **z** 46176; ● 75
Smithson; RMC Place; WHITE; ***174** F-6; mail Reynolds **z** 47980; rural
Smith Valley; RMC Place; JOHNSON; **175** K-8; ★ **IND**; mail Greenwood **z** 46142-43; ● 1,800
Smithville; RMC Place; MONROE; **175** N-7; elev. 761ft./232m.; 🅿; ★ **BLMNG**; **z** 47458; ● 200
Smyrna; RMC Place; DECATUR; ***175** M-12; mail Greensburg **z** 47240; rural
Smyrna; RMC Place; JEFFERSON; ▲ Smyrna; ***175** O-11; mail Madison **z** 47250; rural
Smyrna; MCD-Township; JEFFERSON; ***175** O-11; mail Madison **z** 47250; Ⓟ 930; © 1,065
Smythe; RMC Place; VANDERBURGH; ★ **EV**; pop. incl. with Evansville (Inc. Place)
Snow Hill; RMC Place; RANDOLPH; ***174** I-13; mail Winchester **z** 47394; ● 25
Solitude; RMC Place; POSEY; ***175** S-2; elev. 381ft./116m.; mail Mount Vernon **z** 47620
Solsberry; RMC Place; GREENE; **175** N-6; elev. 789ft./240m.; 🅿; **z** 47459; ● 200
Somerset; RMC Place; WABASH; **174** F-10; elev. 807ft./246m.; 🅿; **z** 46984; ● 250
Somerville; Inc. Place; GIBSON; **175** R-4; elev. 450ft./137m.; 🅿; **z** 47683; Ⓟ 223; © 312
South Bend; Inc. Place; ⊡ ST. JOSEPH; **174** A-8; 🅿 🅷 🅲 7,421 ■; ★ **S.B.**; **z** 46601, **z** 46613-17, **z** 46619, **z** 46624, **z** 46626, **z** 46628, **z** 46634-35, **z** 46637, **z** 46660, **z** 46680, **z** 46699; Ⓟ 105,511; © 107,789; ◆ 108,904
South Bethany; BARTHOLOMEW; see Bethany (RMC Place)
South Boston; RMC Place; WASHINGTON; **175** P-9; mail Salem **z** 47167; ● 75
South Calumet Avenue; RMC Place; LAKE; ***174** A-4; ★ **CHI**; mail Hammond **z** 46324; pop. incl. with Hammond (Inc. Place)
South Center; RMC Place; LAPORTE; **174** B-7; mail Hamlet **z** 46532; ● 150
Southeast; MCD-Township; ORANGE; ***175** Q-8; mail Marengo **z** 47140; Ⓟ 1,536; © 1,544
Southeast Grove; RMC Place; LAKE; ***174** C-4; elev. 727ft./222m.; mail Hebron **z** 46341; rural
Southeast Manor; RMC Place; SHELBY; ***175** K-10; ★ **IND**; mail Fairland **z** 46126; ● 50
South Edgewood; RMC Place; MADISON; ***174** I-10; ★ **AND**; mail Anderson **z** 46011; pop. incl. with Edgewood (Inc. Place)
Southern Estates; RMC Place; FLOYD; ***175** Q-10; ★ **LOU**; mail New Albany **z** 47150; ● 250
Southernview; RMC Place; TIPPECANOE; ***174** G-6; ★ **LAF-**; mail Lafayette **z** 47905; pop. incl. with Lafayette (Inc. Place)
South Gary; RMC Place; LAKE; ★ **CHI**; pop. incl. with Gary (Inc. Place)
South Gate; RMC Place; FRANKLIN; **175** L-13; mail West Harrison **z** 47060; ● 40
South Haven; CDP; PORTER; ***174** B-5; ★ **CHI**; mail Valparaiso **z** 46385; Ⓟ 6,112; © 5,619
South Lake; RMC Place; VIGO; ***175** L-4; ★ **T.H.**; mail West Terre Haute **z** 47885; ● 40
South Milford; RMC Place; LAGRANGE; **174** B-12; elev. 980ft./299m.; 🅿; **z** 46786; ● 200
South Mud Lake; RMC Place; FULTON; ***174** D-9; mail Macy **z** 46951; ● 50
South Park; RMC Place; KOSCIUSKO; ***174** B-10; mail Syracuse **z** 46567; summer pop. 100
South Peru; RMC Place; MIAMI; ***174** F-9; mail Peru **z** 46970; pop. incl. with Peru (Inc. Place)
Southport; Inc. Place; MARION; **175** K-9; elev. 760ft./232m.; 🅿; ★ **IND**; **z** 46217, **z** 46227, **z** 46237, **z** 46247; Ⓟ 1,969; © 1,852
Southport; RMC Place; OWEN; ***175** M-6; mail Spencer **z** 47460
South Raub; RMC Place; TIPPECANOE; ***174** H-6; ★ **LAF-**; mail Lafayette **z** 47905
South Salem; RMC Place; RANDOLPH; ***174** H-14; mail Union City **z** 47390; rural
South Wanatah; RMC Place; LAPORTE; ***174** B-6; mail Wanatah **z** 46390; ● 35
South Washington; RMC Place; DAVIESS; **175** P-5; mail Washington **z** 47501; ● 220
Southwest; RMC Place; ELKHART; **174** B-9; elev. 859ft./262m.; ★ **ELK**; mail Goshen **z** 46526; ● 50
South Whitley; Inc. Place; WHITLEY; **174** D-11; elev. 808ft./246m.; 🅿; **z** 46787; Ⓟ 1,482; © 1,782
Southwick; RMC Place; ALLEN; ***174** D-13; ★ **FTWA**; mail Fort Wayne **z** 46816; pop. incl. with Fort Wayne (Inc. Place)
Southwood; RMC Place; VIGO; **174** J-2; ★ **T.H.**; mail Terre Haute **z** 47802; ● 500
Spades; RMC Place; RIPLEY; ***175** M-13; mail Sunman **z** 47041; ● 90
Sparksville; RMC Place; JACKSON; **175** O-8; mail Medora **z** 47260; ● 50
Sparta; RMC Place; DEARBORN; ▲ Sparta; **175** N-13; ★ **CIN**; mail Moores Hill **z** 47032; ● 75
Sparta; MCD-Township; DEARBORN; ***175** N-13; ★ **CIN**; mail Moores Hill **z** 47032; Ⓟ 2,531; © 2,809
Sparta; MCD-Township; NOBLE; ***174** B-11; mail Cromwell **z** 46732, Kimmell **z** 46760; Ⓟ 2,497; © 3,111
Spartanburg; RMC Place; RANDOLPH; **174** I-14; mail Lynn **z** 47355; ● 110
Spearsville; RMC Place; BROWN; **175** M-9; mail Trafalgar **z** 46181; ● 40
Speed; RMC Place; CLARK; **175** Q-10; elev. 468ft./143m.; 🅿; ★ **LOU**; **z** 47172; ● 300
Speedway; Inc. Place; MARION; **174** J-8; 🅿; ★ **IND**; **z** 46224; Ⓟ 13,092; © 12,881
Speicherville; RMC Place; WABASH; **174** E-10; mail Wabash **z** 46992; ● 30
Spelterville; RMC Place; VIGO; **174** H-2; elev. 511ft./156m.; ★ **T.H.**; mail Terre Haute **z** 47805; ● 500
Spencer; MCD-Township; DE KALB; ***174** C-13; mail Spencerville **z** 46788; Ⓟ 923; © 1,057
Spencer; MCD-Township; HARRISON; ***175** R-8; mail Depauw **z** 47115; Ⓟ 1,687; © 1,694
Spencer; MCD-Township; JENNINGS; ***175** N-10; mail North Vernon **z** 47265; Ⓟ 1,980; © 2,073
Spencer; Inc. Place; ⊡ OWEN; **175** M-6; elev. 566ft./173m.; 🅿; **z** 47460; Ⓟ 2,609; © 2,508
SPENCER; **175** S-5; Ⓟ 19,490; © 20,391; ◆ 20,180
Spencerville; RMC Place; DE KALB; **174** C-13; elev. 817ft./249m.; 🅿; **z** 46788; ● 350
Spiceland; Inc. Place; HENRY; ▲ Spiceland; **174** J-11; elev. 1,050ft./320m.; 🅿; **z** 47385; Ⓟ 757; © 807
Spiceland; MCD-Township; HENRY; ***174** J-11; elev. 1,050ft./320m.; 🅿; **z** 47385; Ⓟ 2,270; © 2,200
Spice Valley; MCD-Township; LAWRENCE; ***175** O-7; mail Huron **z** 47437; Ⓟ 1,988; © 2,419
Spraytown; RMC Place; JACKSON; **175** N-9; mail Seymour **z** 47274; ● 50
Springersville; RMC Place; FAYETTE; ***175** K-13; mail Brownsville **z** 47325; ● 60
Springfield; MCD-Township; ALLEN; ***174** C-13; mail Grabill **z** 46741; Ⓟ 3,169; © 3,697
Springfield; MCD-Township; FRANKLIN; ***175** L-14; mail Brookville **z** 47012; Ⓟ 1,078; © 1,178
Springfield; MCD-Township; LAGRANGE; ***174** A-12; mail Lagrange **z** 46761; Ⓟ 1,188; © 1,284
Springfield; MCD-Township; LAPORTE; ***174** A-6; ★ **MICH**; mail Michigan City **z** 46360; Ⓟ 4,600; © 4,742
Springfield; RMC Place; POSEY; ***175** S-2; elev. 439ft./134m.; mail Mount Vernon **z** 47620, Wadesville **z** 47638
Spring Grove; Inc. Place; WAYNE; **174** J-13; elev. 950ft./290m.; ★ **RICH**; mail Richmond **z** 47374; Ⓟ 420; © 386
Spring Grove Heights; RMC Place; WAYNE; ***174** J-13; ★ **RICH**; mail Richmond **z** 47374; pop. incl. with Spring Grove (Inc. Place)
Spring Hill; MARION; see Spring Hills (Inc. Place)
Spring Hill Estates; RMC Place; VIGO; ***175** L-4; ★ **T.H.**; mail Terre Haute **z** 47802; ● 100
Spring Hills (Spring Hill); Inc. Place; MARION; ***174** J-8; ★ **IND**; mail Indianapolis **z** 46228; © 97
Spring Lake; Inc. Place; HANCOCK; **174** J-10; ★ **IND**; mail Greenfield **z** 46140; Ⓟ 216; © 262
Springport; Inc. Place; HENRY; **174** I-12; elev. 1,050ft./320m.; 🅿; ★ **MUN**; **z** 47386; Ⓟ 194; © 174
Springtown; RMC Place; HENDRICKS; mail Danville **z** 46122; ● 50
Springville; RMC Place; LAPORTE; ***174** A-6; elev. 769ft./234m.; ★ **MICH**; mail La Porte **z** 46350; ● 500
Springville; RMC Place; LAWRENCE; **175** N-7; elev. 700ft./213m.; 🅿; **z** 47462; ● 300
Springwood; RMC Place; VIGO; ***175** K-4; ★ **T.H.**; mail Terre Haute **z** 47805; ● 400
Spurgeon; Inc. Place; PIKE; **175** R-4; elev. 509ft./155m.; 🅿; **z** 47584; Ⓟ 149; © 227
Spurgeons Corner; RMC Place; BROWN; ***175** N-9; mail Freetown **z** 47235; rural
Stacer; RMC Place; VANDERBURGH; ***175** R-3; elev. 454ft./138m.; ★ **EV**; mail Haubstadt **z** 47639
Stafford; MCD-Township; DE KALB; ***174** B-14; mail Butler **z** 46721; Ⓟ 275; © 282
Stafford; MCD-Township; GREENE; ***175** N-5; mail Linton **z** 47441; Ⓟ 493; © 490
Stampers Creek; MCD-Township; ORANGE; ***175** P-8; mail Paoli **z** 47454; Ⓟ 845; © 959
Stanford; RMC Place; MONROE; **175** N-7; elev. 770ft./235m.; 🅿; ★ **BLMNG**; **z** 47463; ● 100
Star City; CDP; PULASKI; **174** D-7; elev. 719ft./219m.; 🅿; **z** 46985; © 377
STARKE; **174** C-7; Ⓟ 22,747; © 23,556; ◆ 23,407
Starlight; RMC Place; CLARK; ***175** Q-10; 🅿; **z** 47106
State Line; RMC Place; LAKE; ★ **CHI**; pop. incl. with Hammond (Inc. Place)
State Line; RMC Place; VIGO; ***175** L-3; ★ **T.H.**; mail West Terre Haute **z** 47885; rural
State Line (State Line City); Inc. Place; WARREN; **174** H-4; elev. 720ft./219m.; 🅿; **z** 47982; Ⓟ 182; © 141
State Line City; WARREN; see State Line (Inc. Place)
Staunton; Inc. Place; CLAY; **175** L-5; elev. 646ft./197m.; 🅿; ★ **T.H.**; **z** 47881; Ⓟ 592; © 550
Stavetown; RMC Place; FRANKLIN; ***175** L-13; mail Brookville **z** 47012; pop. incl. with Brookville (Inc. Place)
Stearleyville; RMC Place; CLAY; ***175** L-5; mail Brazil **z** 47834; rural
Steele; MCD-Township; DAVIESS; ***175** O-5; mail Washington **z** 47501; Ⓟ 895; © 930
Steen; MCD-Township; KNOX; ***175** P-4; mail Wheatland **z** 47597; Ⓟ 885; © 929
Steeplechase; RMC Place; CLARK; ***175** Q-10; ★ **LOU**; mail Jeffersonville **z** 47130; ● 120
Steinbarger Lake; RMC Place; NOBLE; ***174** B-11; mail Wawaka **z** 46794; ● 200
Stendal; RMC Place; PIKE; **175** R-5; elev. 626ft./191m.; 🅿; **z** 47585; ● 150
Sterling; MCD-Township; CRAWFORD; ***175** Q-7; mail English **z** 47118; Ⓟ 1,743; © 1,668
Steuben; MCD-Township; STEUBEN; ***174** A-13; mail Ashley **z** 46705, Pleasant Lake **z** 46779; Ⓟ 2,456; © 2,878
Steuben; MCD-Township; WARREN; ***174** H-4; mail Williamsport **z** 47993; Ⓟ 495; © 427
STEUBEN; **174** A-12; Ⓟ 27,446; © 33,214; ◆ 32,952
Steubenville; RMC Place; STEUBEN; ▲ Steuben; ***174** B-13; mail Ashley **z** 46705; ● 25
Stevenson; RMC Place; WARRICK; ***175** S-4; elev. 388ft./118m.; ★ **EV**; mail Chandler **z** 47610
Stewart; RMC Place; WARREN; ***174** G-4; elev. 711ft./217m.; mail Williamsport **z** 47993; rural
Stewartsville; RMC Place; POSEY; **175** R-2; elev. 470ft./143m.; mail Poseyville **z** 47633; ● 180
Stilesville; Inc. Place; HENDRICKS; **175** K-7; elev. 795ft./242m.; 🅿; **z** 46180; Ⓟ 298; © 261
Stillwell; RMC Place; LAPORTE; **174** B-7; elev. 732ft./223m.; ★ **MICH**; mail La Porte **z** 46350; ● 275
Stinesville; Inc. Place; MONROE; **175** M-7; elev. 650ft./198m.; 🅿; ★ **BLMNG**; **z** 47464; Ⓟ 204; © 194
Stockdale; RMC Place; MIAMI, WABASH; ***174** E-9; mail Roann **z** 46974
Stockton; MCD-Township; GREENE; ***175** N-5; mail Linton **z** 47441; Ⓟ 8,313; © 8,722
Stockton; RMC Place; LAKE; ★ **CHI**; pop. incl. with Gary (Inc. Place)
Stockwell; RMC Place; TIPPECANOE; **174** H-6; elev. 776ft./237m.; 🅿; **z** 47983; ● 500
Stone; RMC Place; RANDOLPH; ***174** H-13; mail Winchester **z** 47394; rural
Stonebluff; RMC Place; FOUNTAIN; **174** H-5; mail Veedersburg **z** 47987; ● 120
Stoneburner Landing; RMC Place; KOSCIUSKO; ***174** C-10; mail Warsaw **z** 46580; ● 30
Stonecrest; RMC Place; GRANT; ***174** G-11; ★ **MRN**; mail Marion **z** 46953; ● 300
Stone Head; RMC Place; BROWN; ***175** M-9; mail Nashville **z** 47448
Stones Crossing; RMC Place; JOHNSON; **175** K-9; ★ **IND**; mail Greenwood **z** 46143; ● 150
Stoney Creek; MCD-Township; HENRY; ***174** I-12; mail Mooreland **z** 47360; Ⓟ 815; © 818
Stoney Creek; MCD-Township; RANDOLPH; ***174** H-12; mail Parker City **z** 47368; Ⓟ 1,032; © 1,082
Stonington; RMC Place; LAWRENCE; ***175** O-8; mail Mitchell **z** 47446; rural
Stony Creek; MCD-Township; MADISON; ***174** I-10; ★ **AND**; mail Lapel **z** 46051; Ⓟ 3,588; © 3,632
Stony Lonesome; RMC Place; BARTHOLOMEW; ***175** M-9; ★ **COL**; mail Columbus **z** 47201; rural
Story; RMC Place; BROWN; ***175** N-8; mail Nashville **z** 47448
Stoutsburg; RMC Place; JASPER; ***174** C-5; mail Wheatfield **z** 46392; ● 150
Stratford Hills; RMC Place; VIGO; ***175** L-4; ★ **T.H.**; mail Terre Haute **z** 47802; pop. incl. with Terre Haute (Inc. Place)
Straughn; Inc. Place; HENRY; **174** J-12; elev. 1,075ft./328m.; 🅿; **z** 47387; Ⓟ 318; © 263
Strawtown; RMC Place; HAMILTON; **174** I-9; mail Noblesville **z** 46060; ● 120
Stringtown; RMC Place; BOONE; ***174** I-7; ★ **IND**; mail Lebanon **z** 46052; ● 50
Stringtown; RMC Place; HANCOCK; ***174** J-10; ★ **IND**; mail Greenfield **z** 46140; rural
Stringtown; RMC Place; VANDERBURGH; ***175** S-3; ★ **EV**; mail Evansville **z** 47711; pop. incl. with Evansville (Inc. Place)
Stroh; RMC Place; LAGRANGE; **174** A-12; elev. 940ft./287m.; 🅿; **z** 46789; ● 400
Sugar Creek; MCD-Township; BOONE; ***174** I-7; mail Thorntown **z** 46071; Ⓟ 2,231; © 2,268
Sugar Creek; MCD-Township; CLINTON; ***174** H-8; mail Kirklin **z** 46050; Ⓟ 485; © 486
Sugar Creek; MCD-Township; HANCOCK; ***174** J-10; ★ **IND**; mail New Palestine **z** 46163; Ⓟ 9,163; © 12,165
Sugar Creek; MCD-Township; MONTGOMERY; ***174** H-6; mail Crawfordsville **z** 47933; Ⓟ 372; © 426
Sugar Creek; MCD-Township; PARKE; ***174** J-5; mail Marshall **z** 47859; Ⓟ 300; © 349
Sugar Creek; RMC Place; SHELBY; ***175** K-10; ★ **IND**; mail Fairland **z** 46126; ● 160
Sugar Creek; MCD-Township; SHELBY; ***175** K-10; mail Boggstown **z** 46110; Ⓟ 958; © 1,055
Sugar Creek; MCD-Township; VIGO; ***175** L-4; ★ **T.H.**; mail West Terre Haute **z** 47885; Ⓟ 8,672; © 8,121
Sugar Ridge; MCD-Township; CLAY; ***175** L-5; mail Centerpoint **z** 47840; Ⓟ 955; © 999
Sullivan; Inc. Place; ⊡ SULLIVAN; **175** N-4; elev. 530ft./162m.; 🅿 🅷; **z** 47882; Ⓟ 4,663; © 4,617
SULLIVAN; **175** M-3; Ⓟ 18,993; © 21,751; ◆ 21,353
Sulphur; RMC Place; CRAWFORD; **175** R-7; elev. 715ft./218m.; 🅿; **z** 47118, **z** 47174; ● 100
Sulphur Springs; Inc. Place; HENRY; **174** I-11; elev. 1,060ft./323m.; 🅿; **z** 47388; Ⓟ 257; © 346
Suman; RMC Place; PORTER; ***174** B-6; elev. 740ft./226m.; ★ **CHI**; mail Valparaiso **z** 46383; rural
Sumava Resorts; RMC Place; NEWTON; **174** C-4; elev. 633ft./193m.; 🅿; **z** 46379; ● 300
Summit Grove; RMC Place; VERMILLION; ***175** K-4; mail Clinton **z** 47842; ● 35
Summit Ridge; RMC Place; ALLEN; ***174** D-13; ★ **FTWA**; mail Fort Wayne **z** 46815; pop. incl. with Fort Wayne (Inc. Place)
Summitville; Inc. Place; MADISON; **174** H-11; elev. 883ft./269m.; 🅿; ★ **AND**; **z** 46070; Ⓟ 1,010; © 1,090
Sundown Manor; RMC Place; MORGAN; ***175** K-8; ★ **IND**; mail Mooresville **z** 46158; pop. incl. with Mooresville (Inc. Place)
Sunman; Inc. Place; RIPLEY; **175** M-13; elev. 1,021ft./311m.; 🅿; **z** 47041; Ⓟ 623; © 805
Sunnybrook Acres; RMC Place; ALLEN; ***174** C-13; ★ **FTWA**; mail Fort Wayne **z** 46805; pop. incl. with Fort Wayne (Inc. Place)
Sunnymede; RMC Place; ALLEN; ***174** D-13; ★ **FTWA**; mail Fort Wayne **z** 46803; pop. incl. with New Haven (Inc. Place)
Sunnymede; RMC Place; WABASH; ***174** E-10; mail Wabash **z** 46992; pop. incl. with Wabash (Inc. Place)
Sunnymede Woods; RMC Place; ALLEN; ***174** D-13; ★ **FTWA**; mail Fort Wayne **z** 46803; pop. incl. with New Haven (Inc. Place)
Sunny Slopes; RMC Place; MONROE; ***175** M-7; elev. 780ft./238m.; ★ **BLMNG**; mail Bloomington **z** 47401; pop. incl. with Bloomington (Inc. Place)
Sunset Parkway; RMC Place; JACKSON; ***175** N-10; mail Seymour **z** 47274; pop. incl. with Seymour (Inc. Place)
Sunset Village; RMC Place; CLARK; ***175** Q-11; ★ **LOU**; mail Charlestown **z** 47111; ● 220
Sunshine Gardens; RMC Place; MARION; ***175** K-8; ★ **IND**; mail Indianapolis **z** 46217; pop. incl. with Indianapolis (Inc. Place)
Sunview; RMC Place; MADISON; ***174** I-10; ★ **IND**; mail Fortville **z** 46040; ● 40
Surprise; RMC Place; JACKSON; ***175** N-9; mail Seymour **z** 47274; ● 40
Swan; RMC Place; NOBLE; **174** C-12; mail Laotto **z** 46763; ● 55
Swan; MCD-Township; NOBLE; ***174** C-12; mail Laotto **z** 46763; Ⓟ 1,877; © 2,337
Swanington; RMC Place; BENTON; **174** F-4; mail Fowler **z** 47944; ● 60
Swayzee; Inc. Place; GRANT; **174** G-10; elev. 866ft./264m.; 🅿; ★ **MRN**; **z** 46986; Ⓟ 1,059; © 1,011
Sweetser; Inc. Place; GRANT; **174** F-10; elev. 850ft./259m.; 🅿; ★ **MRN**; **z** 46987; Ⓟ 924; © 906
Sweetwater Lake; RMC Place; BROWN; ***175** M-9; mail Nineveh **z** 46164; ● 450
Switz City; Inc. Place; GREENE; **175** N-5; elev. 523ft./159m.; 🅿; **z** 47465; Ⓟ 257; © 311
SWITZERLAND; **175** O-13; Ⓟ 7,738; © 9,065; ◆ 9,722
Sycamore; RMC Place; HOWARD; **174** G-10; mail Greentown **z** 46936; ● 90
Sycamore Hills; RMC Place; MADISON; ★ **AND**; mail Elwood **z** 46036; ● 50
Sycamore Hills; RMC Place; VIGO; ***175** L-4; ★ **T.H.**; mail Terre Haute **z** 47802; ● 40
Sycamore Park; RMC Place; VIGO; **174** I-1; ★ **T.H.**; mail West Terre Haute **z** 47885; ● 120
Sylvan Hills; RMC Place; GRANT; mail Marion **z** 46953; ● 100
Sylvania; RMC Place; PARKE; ***174** J-4; mail Bloomingdale **z** 47832
Sylvan Manor; RMC Place; PORTER; ***174** B-5; ★ **CHI**; mail Valparaiso **z** 46385; ● 300
Syndicate; RMC Place; VERMILLION; ***175** K-4; mail Clinton **z** 47842; ● 40
Syracuse; Inc. Place; KOSCIUSKO; **174** B-10; elev. 870ft./265m.; 🅿; **z** 46567; Ⓟ 2,729; © 3,038

T

Tab; RMC Place; WARREN; **174** G-4; mail Ambia **z** 47917; ● 60
Talbot; RMC Place; BENTON; **174** G-4; elev. 769ft./234m.; 🅿; **z** 47984; ● 40
Tall Timbers; RMC Place; GRANT; ***174** F-10; ★ **MRN**; mail Marion **z** 46952; ● 100
Talma; RMC Place; FULTON; **174** C-9; mail Rochester **z** 46975; ● 130
Tampico; RMC Place; JACKSON; **175** O-9; mail Brownstown **z** 47220, Crothersville **z** 47229; ● 60
Tangier; RMC Place; PARKE; **174** J-4; elev. 650ft./198m.; 🅿; **z** 47952; ● 30
Tarry Park; RMC Place; LAWRENCE; ***175** O-7; mail Bedford **z** 47421; rural
Taswell; RMC Place; CRAWFORD; **175** Q-7; elev. 730ft./223m.; 🅿; **z** 47175; ● 130
Taylor; MCD-Township; GREENE; ***175** N-6; mail Bloomfield **z** 47424; Ⓟ 1,086; © 1,124
Taylor; MCD-Township; HARRISON; ***175** S-9; mail Elizabeth **z** 47117; Ⓟ 576; © 718
Taylor; MCD-Township; HOWARD; ***174** G-9; ★ **KOK**; mail Kokomo **z** 46902; Ⓟ 8,877; © 9,536
Taylor; MCD-Township; OWEN; ***175** L-6; mail Spencer **z** 47460; Ⓟ 795; © 993
Taylorsville; CDP; BARTHOLOMEW; **175** M-9; elev. 650ft./198m.; 🅿; ★ **COL**; **z** 47280; Ⓟ 1,044; © 936
Taylorville (Dresser); RMC Place; VIGO; **174** I-1; ★ **T.H.**; mail West Terre Haute **z** 47885; ● 200
Tecumseh; RMC Place; TIPPECANOE; ***174** G-6; ★ **LAF-**; mail Lafayette **z** 47905; pop. incl. with Lafayette (Inc. Place)
Tecumseh; RMC Place; VIGO; ***175** K-4; ★ **T.H.**; mail West Terre Haute **z** 47885; ● 70
Teegarden; RMC Place; MARSHALL; **174** B-8; mail Walkerton **z** 46574; ● 160
Tee Lake; RMC Place; LAPORTE; ***174** A-7; mail La Porte **z** 46350; ● 60
Tefft; RMC Place; JASPER; **174** C-6; elev. 678ft./207m.; 🅿; **z** 46380; ● 100
Tell City; Inc. Place; ⊡ PERRY; **175** S-6; elev. 400ft./122m.; 🅿 🅷; **z** 47586; Ⓟ 8,088; © 7,845
Temple; RMC Place; CRAWFORD; ***175** Q-8; mail English **z** 47118
Templeton; RMC Place; BENTON; **174** G-5; elev. 702ft./214m.; 🅿; **z** 47986; ● 120
Tennyson; Inc. Place; WARRICK; **175** S-5; elev. 400ft./122m.; 🅿; **z** 47637; Ⓟ 267; © 290
Terhune; RMC Place; BOONE; **174** H-8; mail Sheridan **z** 46069; ● 90
Terrace Bay; RMC Place; CARROLL; ***174** F-6; mail Monticello **z** 47960; ● 60
Terrace Lake; RMC Place; BARTHOLOMEW; ★ **COL**; mail Columbus **z** 47201; pop. incl. with Columbus (Inc. Place)
Terra Vista; RMC Place; VIGO; ★ **T.H.**; mail Terre Haute **z** 47803; pop. incl. with Terre Haute (Inc. Place)
Terre Haute; Inc. Place; ⊡ VIGO; **175** L-4; elev. 507ft./155m.; 🅿 🅷 🅲 12,531 ■; ★ **T.H.**; **z** 47801-05, **z** 47807-09, **z** 47811-12; Ⓟ 55,439; © 59,614; ◆ 63,268
Terre Town; RMC Place; VIGO; ***175** L-4; ★ **T.H.**; mail Terre Haute **z** 47805; pop. incl. with Terre Haute (Inc. Place)
Tetersburg; RMC Place; TIPTON; **174** H-9; mail Tipton **z** 46072; ● 50
Texas; RMC Place; DEARBORN; ***175** N-13; ★ **CIN**; mail Aurora **z** 47001; pop. incl. with Aurora (Inc. Place)
Thayer; RMC Place; NEWTON; **174** C-4; elev. 645ft./197m.; 🅿; ★ **CHI**; **z** 46381; ● 400
The Hamlet; RMC Place; DELAWARE; ***174** H-11; elev. 920ft./280m.; ★ **MUN**; mail Muncie **z** 47303; ● 50
The Meadows; RMC Place; CLARK; ***175** Q-10; ★ **LOU**; mail Jeffersonville **z** 47130; pop. incl. with Jeffersonville (Inc. Place)
Thomas Lake; RMC Place; PUTNAM; ***175** K-5; mail Greencastle **z** 46135; ● 90
Thomaston; RMC Place; LAPORTE; **174** B-6; mail Wanatah **z** 46390; ● 20
Thorncreek; MCD-Township; WHITLEY; ***174** C-11; mail Columbia City **z** 46725; Ⓟ 3,299; © 3,925
Thornhope (Oak); RMC Place; PULASKI; **174** E-7; mail Star City **z** 46985; ● 150
Thorntown; Inc. Place; BOONE; **174** I-7; elev. 861ft./262m.; 🅿; **z** 46071; Ⓟ 1,506; © 1,562
Thurman; RMC Place; ALLEN; **173** E-20; ★ **FTWA**; mail New Haven **z** 46774; ● 40
Tilden; RMC Place; HENDRICKS; ***174** J-8; ★ **IND**; mail Brownsburg **z** 46112
Tillman; RMC Place; ALLEN; ***174** D-13; mail Monroeville **z** 46773; ● 30
Timbercrest; RMC Place; ALLEN; ***174** D-12; ★ **FTWA**; mail Fort Wayne **z** 46814; ● 100
Timbercrest; RMC Place; CASS; mail Logansport **z** 46947; ● 200
Timberhurst; RMC Place; LAGRANGE; ***174** B-12; mail Wolcottville **z** 46795; ● 50
Tiosa; RMC Place; FULTON; **174** C-9; mail Rochester **z** 46975; ● 150
Tippecanoe; MCD-Township; CARROLL; ***174** F-6; mail Delphi **z** 46923; Ⓟ 1,957; © 2,283
Tippecanoe; MCD-Township; KOSCIUSKO; ***174** C-10; mail North Webster **z** 46555; Ⓟ 6,197; © 6,493
Tippecanoe; RMC Place; MARSHALL; ▲ Tippecanoe; **174** C-9; 🅿; **z** 46570; ● 350
Tippecanoe; MCD-Township; MARSHALL; ***174** C-9; 🅿; **z** 46570; Ⓟ 1,188; © 1,256
Tippecanoe; MCD-Township; PULASKI; ***174** D-7; mail Monterey **z** 46960; Ⓟ 997; © 1,130
Tippecanoe; MCD-Township; TIPPECANOE; ***174** G-6; ★ **LAF-**; mail West Lafayette **z** 47906; Ⓟ 5,012; © 5,951; Ⓡ 5,937
TIPPECANOE; **174** H-6; Ⓟ 130,598; © 148,955; ◆ 177,953
Tipton; MCD-Township; CASS; ***174** F-8; elev. 873ft./266m.; mail Walton **z** 46994; Ⓟ 2,439; © 2,578
Tipton; Inc. Place; ⊡ TIPTON; **174** H-9; 🅿 🅷; **z** 46072; Ⓟ 4,751; © 5,251
TIPTON; **174** H-9; Ⓟ 16,119; © 16,577; ◆ 15,758
Tipton Park; RMC Place; BARTHOLOMEW; ★ **COL**; mail Columbus **z** 47201; pop. incl. with Columbus (Inc. Place)
Toad Hop; RMC Place; VIGO; **174** I-1; elev. 475ft./145m.; ★ **T.H.**; mail West Terre Haute **z** 47885; ● 140
Tobin; MCD-Township; PERRY; ***175** S-7; mail Cannelton **z** 47520, Rome **z** 47574; Ⓟ 684; © 709
Tobinsport; RMC Place; PERRY; ***175** T-7; elev. 408ft./124m.; 🅿; **z** 47520
Tocsin; RMC Place; WELLS; **174** E-13; elev. 834ft./254m.; mail Ossian **z** 46777; ● 120
Toledo; HUNTINGTON; see Browns Corner (RMC Place)
Tolleston; RMC Place; LAKE; ***174** A-4; ★ **CHI**; mail Gary **z** 46404; pop. incl. with Gary (Inc. Place)
Toll Gate Heights; RMC Place; WELLS; ***174** E-12; mail Bluffton **z** 46714; pop. incl. with Bluffton (Inc. Place)
Topeka; Inc. Place; LAGRANGE; **174** B-11; elev. 925ft./282m.; 🅿; **z** 46571; Ⓟ 912; © 1,159
Toto; RMC Place; STARKE; **174** C-7; mail Knox **z** 46534; ● 200
Townley; RMC Place; ALLEN; ***174** D-13; elev. 772ft./235m.; mail Monroeville **z** 46773; rural
Town of Pines; Inc. Place; PORTER; **174** A-6; elev. 610ft./186m.; ★ **CHI**; mail Michigan City **z** 46360; Ⓟ 789; © 798
Tracy; RMC Place; LAPORTE; **174** B-7; mail Hamlet **z** 46532; ● 200
Traders Point; RMC Place; MARION; ***174** J-8; ★ **IND**; mail Indianapolis **z** 46278; pop. incl. with Indianapolis (Inc. Place)
Trafalgar; Inc. Place; JOHNSON; **175** L-9; elev. 828ft./252m.; 🅿; ★ **IND**; **z** 46181; Ⓟ 531; © 798
Trail Creek; Inc. Place; LAPORTE; **174** A-6; elev. 630ft./192m.; 🅿; ★ **MICH**; **z** 46360; Ⓟ 2,463; © 2,296
Travisville; RMC Place; WELLS; **174** F-12; mail Bluffton **z** 46714; ● 30
Treaty; RMC Place; WABASH; **174** F-10; mail Wabash **z** 46992; ● 30
Tremont; RMC Place; PORTER; ***174** A-5; ★ **CHI**; mail Chesterton **z** 46304; ● 250
Trenton; RMC Place; BLACKFORD; **174** G-12; mail Hartford City **z** 47348; ● 35
Trevlac; RMC Place; BROWN; **175** M-8; mail Nashville **z** 47448; ● 150
Trier Ridge Park; RMC Place; ALLEN; ***174** D-13; ★ **FTWA**; mail Fort Wayne **z** 46816; pop. incl. with Fort Wayne (Inc. Place)
Tri-Lakes; CDP; WHITLEY; ***174** C-11; mail Columbia City **z** 46725; Ⓟ 3,299; © 3,925
Trinity; RMC Place; JAY; ***174** F-14; mail Bryant **z** 47326; rural
Trinity Springs; RMC Place; MARTIN; **175** O-6; mail Shoals **z** 47581; ● 60
Troy; MCD-Township; DE KALB; ***174** B-14; mail Butler **z** 46721; Ⓟ 302; © 322
Troy; MCD-Township; FOUNTAIN; ***174** H-4; mail Covington **z** 47932; Ⓟ 3,840; © 3,801
Troy; Inc. Place; PERRY; ▲ Troy; **175** S-6; elev. 440ft./134m.; 🅿; **z** 47588; Ⓟ 465; © 392
Troy; MCD-Township; PERRY; ***175** S-6; elev. 440ft./134m.; mail Tell City **z** 47586; Ⓟ 13,173; © 12,129
Tulip; RMC Place; GREENE; ***175** N-6; mail Bloomfield **z** 47424
Tunker; RMC Place; WHITLEY; ***174** D-11; mail South Whitley **z** 46787
Tunnel Hill; RMC Place; CRAWFORD; ***175** Q-7; mail English **z** 47118; rural
Tunnelton; RMC Place; LAWRENCE; **175** O-8; elev. 550ft./168m.; 🅿; **z** 47467; ● 120
Turkey Creek; MCD-Township; KOSCIUSKO; ***174** B-10; mail Syracuse **z** 46567; Ⓟ 7,695; © 9,032
Turkey Creek Meadows; RMC Place; LAKE; ***174** B-4; ★ **CHI**; mail Merrillville **z** 46410; pop. incl. with Merrillville (Inc. Place)
Turkey Track; RMC Place; MORGAN; ***175** L-7; elev. 800ft./244m.; mail Martinsville **z** 46151; rural
Turman; MCD-Township; SULLIVAN; ***175** M-3; mail Sullivan **z** 47882; Ⓟ 944; © 1,082
Turner; RMC Place; CLAY; **175** L-5; ★ **T.H.**; mail Brazil **z** 47834; ● 100
Twelve Mile; RMC Place; CASS; **174** E-8; 🅿; **z** 46988; ● 225
Twelve Points; RMC Place; VIGO; ***175** L-4; elev. 794ft./242m.; ★ **T.H.**; mail Terre Haute **z** 47804; pop. incl. with Terre Haute (Inc. Place)
Twin Brooks; RMC Place; MARION; ***175** K-9; ★ **IND**; mail Indianapolis **z** 46227; pop. incl. with Indianapolis (Inc. Place)
Twin Crest; RMC Place; BARTHOLOMEW; ***175** M-10; ★ **COL**; mail Columbus **z** 47203; ● 30
Twin Lakes; RMC Place; MARSHALL; **174** C-8; mail Plymouth **z** 46563; ● 200
Twin Oaks Lake; RMC Place; MORGAN; ***175** L-8; mail Morgantown **z** 46160; ● 60
Tyner; RMC Place; MARSHALL; **174** B-8; 🅿; **z** 46572; ● 250

U

Ulen; Inc. Place; BOONE; **174** I-8; ★ **IND**; mail Lebanon **z** 46052; Ⓟ 50; © 123
Underwood; RMC Place; CLARK, SCOTT; **175** P-10; elev. 623ft./190m.; 🅿; **z** 47177; ● 200
Underwood Meadows; RMC Place; MADISON; ★ **AND**; mail Elwood **z** 46036; ● 30
Union; MCD-Township; ADAMS; ***174** E-14; mail Decatur **z** 46733; Ⓟ 978; © 974
Union; MCD-Township; BENTON; ***174** F-4; mail Fowler **z** 47944; Ⓟ 294; © 278
Union; MCD-Township; BOONE; ***174** I-8; mail Sheridan **z** 46069; Ⓟ 1,707; © 2,014
Union; MCD-Township; CLARK; ***175** Q-10; ★ **LOU**; mail Memphis **z** 47143; Ⓟ 1,837; © 2,021
Union; MCD-Township; CLINTON; ***174** H-7; mail Frankfort **z** 46041; Ⓟ 905; © 1,019
Union; MCD-Township; CRAWFORD; ***175** R-7; mail Grantsburg **z** 47123; Ⓟ 863; © 838
Union; MCD-Township; DE KALB; ***174** B-13; mail Auburn **z** 46706; Ⓟ 10,404; © 12,716
Union; MCD-Township; DELAWARE; ***174** G-12; ★ **MUN**; mail Muncie **z** 47303; Ⓟ 3,054; © 3,004
Union; MCD-Township; ELKHART; ***174** B-9; mail Nappanee **z** 46550; Ⓟ 5,487; © 5,827
Union; MCD-Civil Township; FULTON; ***174** D-8; mail Kewanna **z** 46939; Ⓟ 1,355; © 1,457
Union; MCD-Township; GIBSON; ***175** R-3; mail Fort Branch **z** 47648; Ⓟ 4,031; © 3,954
Union; MCD-Township; HENDRICKS; ***174** J-7; mail Lizton **z** 46149; Ⓟ 1,586; © 1,777
Union; MCD-Township; HOWARD; ***174** G-10; mail Greentown **z** 46936; Ⓟ 954; © 1,056
Union; MCD-Township; HUNTINGTON; ***174** E-11; mail Huntington **z** 46750; Ⓟ 1,174; © 1,308
Union; MCD-Township; JASPER; ***174** D-5; mail Fair Oaks **z** 47943; Ⓟ 1,254; © 1,382
Union; MCD-Township; JOHNSON; ***175** L-9; mail Bargersville **z** 46106; Ⓟ 1,946; © 2,226
Union; MCD-Township; LAPORTE; ***174** B-7; mail Kingsford Heights **z** 46346; Ⓟ 2,505; © 2,484
Union; MCD-Township; MADISON; ***174** I-11; ★ **AND**; mail Anderson **z** 46011; Ⓟ 8,790; © 9,287
Union; MCD-Township; MARSHALL; ***174** C-8; mail Culver **z** 46511; Ⓟ 3,289; © 3,133
Union; MCD-Township; MIAMI; ***174** E-9; mail Denver **z** 46926; Ⓟ 813; © 892
Union; MCD-Township; MONTGOMERY; ***174** I-6; mail Crawfordsville **z** 47933; Ⓟ 21,663; © 23,837
Union; MCD-Township; OHIO; ***175** N-13; mail Aurora **z** 47001; Ⓟ 443; © 495
Union; MCD-Township; PARKE; ***174** J-5; mail Rockville **z** 47872; Ⓟ 1,169; © 1,569
Union; MCD-Township; PERRY; ***175** S-7; mail Cannelton **z** 47520; Ⓟ 512; © 523
Union; RMC Place; PIKE; **175** Q-4; mail Hazleton **z** 47640; ● 90
Union; MCD-Township; PORTER; ***174** B-5; ★ **CHI**; mail Hobart **z** 46342; Ⓟ 7,167; © 8,166
Union; MCD-Township; RANDOLPH; ***174** I-13; mail Losantville **z** 47354, Modoc **z** 47358; Ⓟ 2,201; © 2,278
Union; MCD-Township; RUSH; ***175** K-12; mail Rushville **z** 46173; Ⓟ 918; © 873
Union; MCD-Township; SHELBY; ***175** K-10; mail Shelbyville **z** 46176; Ⓟ 859; © 944
Union; MCD-Township; ST. JOSEPH; ***174** B-8; ★ **S.B.**; mail Lakeville **z** 46536; Ⓟ 3,355; © 3,289
Union; MCD-Township; TIPPECANOE; ***174** G-6; mail Lafayette **z** 47905; Ⓟ 1,674; © 1,682
Union; MCD-Township; UNION; ***175** K-14; mail West College Corner **z** 47003; Ⓟ 1,500; © 1,546
Union; MCD-Township; VANDERBURGH; ***175** T-3; mail Evansville **z** 47712; Ⓟ 392; © 392
Union; MCD-Township; WELLS; ***174** E-12; mail Ossian **z** 46777; Ⓟ 1,928; © 2,112
Union; MCD-Township; WHITE; ***174** E-6; mail Monticello **z** 47960; Ⓟ 9,265; © 10,436
Union; MCD-Township; WHITLEY; ***174** D-11; mail Columbia City **z** 46725; Ⓟ 1,898; © 1,941
UNION; **175** K-13; Ⓟ 6,976; © 7,349; ◆ 7,169
Union Center; RMC Place; LAPORTE; ***174** B-7; mail Hamlet **z** 46532; rural
Union City; Inc. Place; RANDOLPH; **174** H-14; elev. 1,114ft./340m.; 🅿; **z** 47390; Ⓟ 3,612; © 3,622
Uniondale; Inc. Place; WELLS; **174** E-12; elev. 817ft./249m.; 🅿; **z** 46791; Ⓟ 289; © 277
Union Mills; RMC Place; LAPORTE; **174** B-6; elev. 720ft./219m.; 🅿; **z** 46382; ● 400
Unionport; RMC Place; RANDOLPH; ***174** I-13; mail Farmland **z** 47340
Uniontown; RMC Place; JACKSON; **175** O-10; mail Crothersville **z** 47229; ● 60
Uniontown; RMC Place; PERRY; ***175** R-7; elev. 683ft./208m.; mail Bristow **z** 47515; rural
Unionville; RMC Place; MONROE; **175** M-8; elev. 878ft./268m.; 🅿; **z** 47468; ● 150
Unionville; MONROE; see New Unionville (RMC Place)
Universal; Inc. Place; VERMILLION; **175** K-4; elev. 550ft./168m.; 🅿; **z** 47884; Ⓟ 392; © 419
University Farms; RMC Place; TIPPECANOE; ***174** G-6; ★ **LAF-**; mail West Lafayette **z** 47906; pop. incl. with West Lafayette (Inc. Place)
University Heights; RMC Place; MARION; ***175** K-9; ★ **IND**; mail Indianapolis **z** 46227; pop. incl. with Indianapolis (Inc. Place)
Upland; Inc. Place; GRANT; **174** G-11; elev. 932ft./284m.; 🅿 🅲 1,807; ★ **MRN**; **z** 46989; Ⓟ 3,295; © 3,803
Upper Long Lake; RMC Place; NOBLE; ***174** B-11; mail Albion **z** 46701; ● 270
Upper Sunset Park; RMC Place; CARROLL; ***174** F-6; mail Monticello **z** 47960; ● 250
Upton; RMC Place; POSEY; ***175** S-2; mail Mount Vernon **z** 47620
Urbana; RMC Place; WABASH; **174** E-10; elev. 794ft./242m.; 🅿; **z** 46990; ● 350
Urbandale; RMC Place; HOWARD; ***174** G-9; ★ **KOK**; mail Kokomo **z** 46902; ● 150
Urmeyville; RMC Place; JOHNSON; ***175** L-9; ★ **IND**; mail Franklin **z** 46131
Utah; RMC Place; DEARBORN; ***175** N-13; mail Aurora **z** 47001; pop. incl. with Aurora (Inc. Place)
Utica; Inc. Place; CLARK; ▲ Utica; **175** Q-11; 🅿; ★ **LOU**; **z** 47130; Ⓟ 411; © 591
Utica; MCD-Township; CLARK; ***175** Q-11; 🅿; ★ **LOU**; **z** 47130; Ⓟ 3,124; © 3,085

V

Valeene; RMC Place; ORANGE; **175** Q-8; 🅿; **z** 47125; ● 130
Valentine; RMC Place; LAGRANGE; **174** A-12; mail Lagrange **z** 46761; ● 50
Valley Acres; RMC Place; GRANT; ***174** G-10; ★ **MRN**; mail Marion **z** 46953; ● 100
Valley Brook; RMC Place; WABASH; ***174** E-10; mail Wabash **z** 46992; pop. incl. with Wabash (Inc. Place)
Valley City; RMC Place; HARRISON; **175** S-8; mail Central **z** 47110; ● 35
Valley Mills; RMC Place; MARION; ***175** K-8; elev. 765ft./233m.; ★ **IND**; mail Indianapolis **z** 46241; pop. incl. with Indianapolis (Inc. Place)
Vallonia; RMC Place; JACKSON; **175** O-9; elev. 560ft./171m.; 🅿; **z** 47281; ● 500
Valparaiso; Inc. Place; ⊡ PORTER; **174** B-5; elev. 738ft./225m.; 🅿 🅷 🅲 3,871 ■; ★ **CHI**; **z** 46383-85; Ⓟ 24,414; © 27,428; ◆ 29,776
Van Bibber Lake; RMC Place; PUTNAM; ***175** K-6; mail Greencastle **z** 46135; ● 500
Van Blaricum; RMC Place; BARTHOLOMEW; ***175** M-10; ★ **COL**; mail Columbus **z** 47201; ● 175
Van Buren; MCD-Township; BROWN; ***175** N-9; mail Nashville **z** 47448; Ⓟ 1,419; © 1,782
Van Buren; MCD-Township; CLAY; ***175** K-5; mail Brazil **z** 47834; Ⓟ 3,411; © 3,144; Ⓡ 3,167
Van Buren; MCD-Township; DAVIESS; ***175** O-6; mail Odon **z** 47562; Ⓟ 1,589; © 1,960
Van Buren; MCD-Township; FOUNTAIN; ***174** I-4; mail Veedersburg **z** 47987; Ⓟ 3,081; © 3,121
Van Buren; Inc. Place; GRANT; ▲ Van Buren; **174** F-11; 🅿; **z** 46991; Ⓟ 934; © 935
Van Buren; MCD-Township; GRANT; ***174** F-11; 🅿; **z** 46991; Ⓟ 2,012; © 2,046
Van Buren; MCD-Township; KOSCIUSKO; ***174** B-10; mail Milford **z** 46542; Ⓟ 3,660; © 4,013
Van Buren; MCD-Township; LAGRANGE; ***174** A-11; mail Shipshewana **z** 46565; Ⓟ 2,611; © 3,446
Van Buren; MCD-Township; MADISON; ***174** G-11; ★ **AND**; mail Summitville **z** 46070; Ⓟ 1,902; © 2,020
Van Buren; MCD-Township; MONROE; ***175** M-7; ★ **BLMNG**; mail Bloomington **z** 47403; Ⓟ 10,470; © 11,434
Van Buren; MCD-Township; PULASKI; ***174** D-7; mail Star City **z** 46985; Ⓟ 951; © 1,005
Van Buren; MCD-Township; SHELBY; ***175** K-10; mail Shelbyville **z** 46176; Ⓟ 1,555; © 1,590
Van Buren Park; RMC Place; MONROE; ***175** M-7; ★ **BLMNG**; mail Bloomington **z** 47403; ● 700
Vandalia; RMC Place; OWEN; **175** M-6; mail Spencer **z** 47460; ● 35
VANDERBURGH; **175** R-3; Ⓟ 165,058; © 171,922; ◆ 176,130
Vanmeter Park; RMC Place; PULASKI; ***174** D-7; mail Winamac **z** 46996; ● 45
Vawter Park; RMC Place; KOSCIUSKO; ***174** B-10; mail Syracuse **z** 46567; seasonal pop. 200
Veale; MCD-Township; DAVIESS; ***175** P-5; mail Washington **z** 47501; Ⓟ 779; © 1,041
Veedersburg; Inc. Place; FOUNTAIN; **174** I-4; elev. 612ft./187m.; 🅿; **z** 47987; Ⓟ 2,192; © 2,299
Velpen; RMC Place; PIKE; **175** Q-5; elev. 489ft./149m.; 🅿; **z** 47590; ● 150
Vera Cruz; Inc. Place; WELLS; **174** F-13; elev. 825ft./251m.; mail Bluffton **z** 46714; Ⓟ 83; © 55
Vermillion; MCD-Township; VERMILLION; ***174** J-4; mail Newport **z** 47966; Ⓟ 1,022; © 993
VERMILLION; **174** J-4; Ⓟ 16,773; © 16,788; ◆ 16,180
Vermont; RMC Place; HOWARD; ***174** G-9; elev. 829ft./253m.; ★ **KOK**; mail Kokomo **z** 46901; rural
Verne; RMC Place; KNOX; ***175** P-4; mail Vincennes **z** 47591; ● 40
Vernon; MCD-Township; HANCOCK; ***174** J-10; ★ **IND**; mail Fortville **z** 46040; Ⓟ 5,728; © 6,894
Vernon; MCD-Township; JACKSON; ***175** O-10; mail Crothersville **z** 47229; Ⓟ 3,512; © 3,456
Vernon; Inc. Place; ⊡ JENNINGS; ▲ Vernon; **175** N-11; 🅿; **z** 47282; Ⓟ 370; © 330
Vernon; MCD-Township; JENNINGS; ***175** N-11; 🅿; **z** 47282; Ⓟ 2,277; © 2,543
Vernon; WABASH; see Mount Vernon (RMC Place)
Vernon; MCD-Township; WASHINGTON; ***175** P-8; mail Campbellsburg **z** 47108; Ⓟ 727; © 684
Versailles; Inc. Place; ⊡ RIPLEY; **175** N-12; elev. 968ft./295m.; 🅿; **z** 47042; Ⓟ 1,791; © 1,784
Vevay; Inc. Place; ⊡ SWITZERLAND; **175** O-13; elev. 489ft./149m.; 🅿; **z** 47043; Ⓟ 1,393; © 1,735
Vicksburg; RMC Place; GREENE; **175** N-5; mail Linton **z** 47441; ● 200
Victor; RMC Place; MONROE; ***175** N-7; mail Bloomington **z** 47403; rural
Vienna; RMC Place; SCOTT; ▲ Vienna; **175** P-10; mail Scottsburg **z** 47170; ● 120
Vienna; MCD-Township; SCOTT; ***175** P-10; mail Scottsburg **z** 47170; Ⓟ 8,171; © 9,160
Vigo; MCD-Township; KNOX; ***175** O-4; mail Bicknell **z** 47512; Ⓟ 4,666; © 4,798
Vigo; RMC Place; VIGO; **175** M-3
VIGO; **175** L-3; Ⓟ 106,107; © 105,848; ◆ 108,872
Vilas; RMC Place; OWEN; ***175** M-6; mail Spencer **z** 47460; rural
Vincennes; Inc. Place; ⊡ KNOX; ▲ Vincennes; **175** P-3; 🅿 🅷 🅲 9,399 ■; **z** 47591; Ⓟ 19,859; © 18,701; ◆ 18,417
Vincennes; MCD-Township; KNOX; ***175** P-3; 🅿 🅲 9,399; **z** 47591; Ⓟ 24,365; © 23,372
Virgie; RMC Place; JASPER; ***174** D-5; elev. 691ft./211m.; mail Rensselaer **z** 47978; ● 40
Vistula; RMC Place; ELKHART; ***174** A-10; ★ **ELK**; mail Bristol **z** 46507; ● 50
Volga; RMC Place; JEFFERSON; ***175** O-11; mail Madison **z** 47250; rural

W

Wabash; MCD-Township; ADAMS; ***174** F-13; mail Geneva **z** 46740; Ⓟ 5,394; © 5,854
Wabash; MCD-Township; FOUNTAIN; ***174** I-4; mail Covington **z** 47932; Ⓟ 726; © 813
Wabash; MCD-Township; GIBSON; ***175** R-2; mail Owensville **z** 47665; Ⓟ 55; © 44
Wabash; MCD-Township; JAY; ***174** G-14; mail Bryant **z** 47326; Ⓟ 541; © 628
Wabash; MCD-Township; PARKE; ***174** J-4; mail Rockville **z** 47872; Ⓟ 778; © 839
Wabash; MCD-Township; TIPPECANOE; ***174** G-6; ★ **LAF-**; mail West Lafayette **z** 47906; Ⓟ 49,348; © 51,261; Ⓡ 51,275
Wabash; Inc. Place; ⊡ WABASH; **174** E-10; elev. 700ft./213m.; 🅿 🅷; **z** 46992; Ⓟ 12,127; © 11,743
WABASH; **174** E-10; Ⓟ 35,069; © 34,960; ◆ 32,111
Wabash Shores; RMC Place; TIPPECANOE; ***174** G-6; ★ **LAF-**; mail West Lafayette **z** 47906; pop. incl. with West Lafayette (Inc. Place)
Wadena; RMC Place; BENTON; **174** F-4; mail Fowler **z** 47944; ● 35
Wadesville; RMC Place; POSEY; **175** R-2; elev. 475ft./145m.; 🅿; **z** 47638; ● 500
Wakarusa; Inc. Place; ELKHART; **174** B-9; elev. 847ft./258m.; 🅿; ★ **ELK**; **z** 46573; Ⓟ 1,667; © 1,618
Wakefield Village; RMC Place; NOBLE; ***174** B-12; mail Kendallville **z** 46755; ● 300
Wakeland; RMC Place; MORGAN; ***175** L-7; mail Paragon **z** 46166
Wake Robin Fields; RMC Place; PORTER; ***174** A-5; ★ **CHI**; mail Chesterton **z** 46304; ● 200
Walden; RMC Place; ALLEN; ***174** D-13; ★ **FTWA**; mail Fort Wayne **z** 46815; pop. incl. with Fort Wayne (Inc. Place)
Waldron; RMC Place; SHELBY; **175** L-10; elev. 824ft./251m.; 🅿; **z** 46182; ● 800
Waldron Lake; RMC Place; NOBLE; ***174** B-11; mail Wawaka **z** 46794; ● 100

Entries in **UPPERCASE** are counties.
Entries in **bold** have populations of 2,500 or more.
Names in parentheses are alternate names.

Inc. Place	Incorporated Place
RMC Place	Rand McNally Designated Place
CDP	Census Designated Place
MCD	Minor Civil Division
⊡	County Seat
▲	Minor Civil Division
elev.	Elevation
🅿	Post Office
🅷	Hospital
🅲	College
■	Principal Business Center
★	Ranally Metro Area (RMA) Abbreviation
z	Zip Code(s)
Ⓟ	Previous Census Population
Ⓡ	Revised Census Population
Ⓐ	Annexation Population
●	Rand McNally Population Estimate
©	Final Census Population
Ⓢ	Special Census Population
◆	Estimated Population

For additional definitions see Glossary, Volume 1, and Introduction, Volume 2.

Walesboro; RMC Place; BARTHOLOMEW; **175** M-10; ★ **COL**; mail Columbus **z** 47201; ● 125
Walford Manor; RMC Place; CLARK; ***175** R-10; ★ **LOU**; mail Jeffersonville **z** 47130; ● 200
Walker; MCD-Township; JASPER; ***174** D-5; mail Rensselaer **z** 47978; Ⓟ 2,098; Ⓒ 2,797
Walker; MCD-Township; RUSH; ***175** K-11; mail Rushville **z** 46173; Ⓟ 966; Ⓒ 916
Walker Park; RMC Place; KOSCIUSKO; ***174** C-10; mail Leesburg **z** 46538; summer pop. 200; ● 100
Walkerton; Inc. Place; ST. JOSEPH; **174** B-7; elev. 725ft./221m.; 🅿; **z** 46574; Ⓟ 2,061; Ⓒ 2,274
Walkerville; RMC Place; SHELBY; ***175** L-10; mail Shelbyville **z** 46176; pop. incl. with Shelbyville (Inc. Place)
Wallace; Inc. Place; FOUNTAIN; **174** I-5; 🅿; **z** 47988; Ⓟ 89; Ⓒ 100
Wall Lake; RMC Place; LAGRANGE, STEUBEN; ***174** A-12; mail Orland **z** 46776; summer pop. 500; ● 250
Walnut; RMC Place; MARSHALL; ▲ Walnut; ***174** C-8; mail Argos **z** 46501
Walnut; MCD-Township; MARSHALL; ***174** C-8; mail Argos **z** 46501; Ⓟ 2,660; Ⓒ 2,672
Walnut; MCD-Township; MONTGOMERY; ***174** I-6; mail Crawfordsville **z** 47933; Ⓟ 1,440; Ⓒ 1,474
Walnut Gardens; RMC Place; CARROLL; ***174** F-6; mail Monticello **z** 47960; ● 50
Walnut Grove; RMC Place; HAMILTON; ***174** H-9; mail Arcadia **z** 46030
Walnut Heights; RMC Place; LAWRENCE; mail Bedford **z** 47421; rural
Walnut Ridge; RMC Place; JENNINGS; ***175** N-11; mail North Vernon **z** 47265; ● 60
Walton; Inc. Place; CASS; **174** F-8; elev. 775ft./236m.; 🅿; ★ **KOK**; **z** 46994; Ⓟ 1,053; Ⓒ 1,069
Waltz; MCD-Township; WABASH; ***174** F-10; mail Wabash **z** 46992; Ⓟ 1,305; Ⓒ 1,492
Wanamaker (New Bethel); RMC Place; MARION; ***175** K-9; 🅿; ★ **IND**; **z** 46239; pop. incl. with Indianapolis (Inc. Place)
Wanatah; Inc. Place; LAPORTE; **174** B-6; elev. 725ft./221m.; 🅿; **z** 46390; Ⓟ 852; Ⓒ 1,013
Wansford; RMC Place; VANDERBURGH; ★ **EV**; pop. incl. with Evansville (Inc. Place)
Wantland Manor; RMC Place; MADISON; ***174** H-11; ★ **AND**; mail Anderson **z** 46012; ● 250
Ward; MCD-Township; RANDOLPH; ***174** H-13; mail Ridgeville **z** 47380; Ⓟ 1,244; Ⓒ 1,218
Warren; MCD-Township; CLINTON; ***174** G-8; mail Forest **z** 46039; Ⓟ 689; Ⓒ 634
Warren; Inc. Place; HUNTINGTON; **174** F-11; elev. 831ft./253m.; 🅿; **z** 46792; Ⓟ 1,185; Ⓒ 1,272
Warren; MCD-Township; HUNTINGTON; ***174** D-11; 🅿; **z** 46792 & mail Huntington **z** 46750; does not include the Town of Warren; Ⓟ 717; Ⓒ 730
Warren; MCD-Township; MARION; ***174** J-9; ★ **IND**; mail Indianapolis **z** 46219; Ⓟ 87,989; Ⓒ 93,941
Warren; MCD-Township; PUTNAM; ***175** K-6; mail Greencastle **z** 46135; Ⓟ 2,777; Ⓒ 2,788
Warren; MCD-Township; ST. JOSEPH; ***174** A-8; ★ **S.B.**; mail New Carlisle **z** 46552; Ⓟ 4,997; Ⓒ 6,430
Warren; MCD-Township; WARREN; ***174** G-5; mail Attica **z** 47918; Ⓟ 699; Ⓒ 754
WARREN; **174** G-4; Ⓟ 8,176; Ⓒ 8,419; ◆ 8,271
Warren Park; Inc. Place; MARION; ***174** J-9; ★ **IND**; mail Indianapolis **z** 46219; Ⓒ 1,656
Warrenton; RMC Place; GIBSON; **175** R-3; elev. 493ft./150m.; ★ **EV**; mail Haubstadt **z** 47639; ● 110
WARRICK; **175** R-4; Ⓟ 44,920; Ⓒ 52,383; ◆ 58,509
Warrington; RMC Place; HANCOCK; **174** J-11; mail Wilkinson **z** 46186; ● 50
Warsaw; Inc. Place; ⊡ KOSCIUSKO; **174** C-10; elev. 828ft./252m.; 🅿 🅷 ■; **z** 46580-82; Ⓟ 10,968; Ⓒ 12,415; ◆ 12,752
Washington; MCD-Township; ADAMS; ***174** E-13; mail Decatur **z** 46733; Ⓟ 10,097; Ⓒ 10,528
Washington; MCD-Township; ALLEN; ***174** D-12; ★ **FTWA**; mail Fort Wayne **z** 46818; Ⓟ 27,416; Ⓒ 33,105
Washington; MCD-Township; BLACKFORD; ***174** G-12; mail Hartford City **z** 47348; Ⓟ 937; Ⓒ 995
Washington; MCD-Township; BOONE; ***174** I-7; mail Thorntown **z** 46071; Ⓟ 1,095; Ⓒ 1,377
Washington; MCD-Township; BROWN; ***175** M-8; mail Nashville **z** 47448; Ⓟ 4,478; Ⓒ 4,433
Washington; MCD-Township; CARROLL; ***174** F-8; mail Logansport **z** 46947; Ⓟ 650; Ⓒ 647
Washington; MCD-Township; CASS; ***174** F-8; mail Logansport **z** 46947; Ⓟ 1,742; Ⓒ 1,642
Washington; MCD-Township; CLARK; ***175** P-11; mail New Washington **z** 47162; Ⓟ 1,534; Ⓒ 1,667
Washington; MCD-Township; CLAY; ***175** L-5; mail Bowling Green **z** 47833; Ⓟ 734; Ⓒ 802
Washington; MCD-Township; CLINTON; ***174** H-7; mail Frankfort **z** 46041; Ⓟ 1,051; Ⓒ 1,193
Washington; Inc. Place; ⊡ DAVIESS; ▲ Washington; **175** P-5; 🅿 🅷 ■; **z** 47501; Ⓟ 10,838; Ⓒ 11,380; ◆ 11,229
Washington; MCD-Township; DAVIESS; ***175** P-5; 🅿; **z** 47501; Ⓟ 14,716; Ⓒ 15,110
Washington; MCD-Township; DEARBORN; ***175** N-13; ★ **CIN**; mail Aurora **z** 47001; Ⓟ 1,387; Ⓒ 1,488
Washington; MCD-Township; DECATUR; ***175** L-11; mail Greensburg **z** 47240; Ⓟ 11,330; Ⓒ 12,206
Washington; MCD-Township; DELAWARE; ***174** G-11; mail Gaston **z** 47342; Ⓟ 2,201; Ⓒ 2,166
Washington; MCD-Township; ELKHART; ***174** A-10; ★ **ELK**; mail Bristol **z** 46507; Ⓟ 5,136; Ⓒ 7,019
Washington; MCD-Township; GIBSON; ***175** Q-4; mail Hazleton **z** 47640; Ⓟ 714; Ⓒ 703
Washington; MCD-Township; GRANT; ***174** F-11; ★ **MRN**; mail Marion **z** 46952; Ⓟ 4,094; Ⓒ 3,894
Washington; MCD-Township; GREENE; ***175** N-5; mail Lyons **z** 47443; Ⓟ 1,213; Ⓒ 1,256
Washington; MCD-Township; HAMILTON; ***174** I-9; ★ **IND**; mail Westfield **z** 46074; Ⓟ 9,272; Ⓒ 18,358
Washington; MCD-Township; HARRISON; ***175** R-8; mail Central **z** 47110; Ⓟ 392; Ⓒ 256
Washington; MCD-Township; HENDRICKS; ***174** J-8; ★ **IND**; mail Danville **z** 46122; Ⓟ 14,706; Ⓒ 26,319
Washington; MCD-Township; JACKSON; ***175** O-10; mail Seymour **z** 47274; Ⓟ 967; Ⓒ 1,068
Washington; MCD-Township; KNOX; ***175** O-4; mail Bruceville **z** 47516; Ⓟ 2,387; Ⓒ 2,320
Washington; MCD-Township; KOSCIUSKO; ***174** C-10; mail Pierceton **z** 46562; Ⓟ 3,128; Ⓒ 2,819; Ⓡ 2,821
Washington; MCD-Township; LAPORTE; ***174** B-7; mail La Porte **z** 46350; Ⓟ 926; Ⓒ 1,103
Washington; MCD-Township; MARION; ***174** J-9; ★ **IND**; mail Indianapolis **z** 46220, **z** 46260; Ⓟ 133,969; Ⓒ 132,927
Washington; MCD-Township; MIAMI; ***174** F-9; mail Peru **z** 46970; Ⓟ 3,603; Ⓒ 3,575
Washington; MCD-Township; MONROE; ***175** M-7; mail Bloomington **z** 47408; Ⓟ 1,777; Ⓒ 1,825
Washington; MCD-Township; MORGAN; ***175** L-8; ★ **IND**; mail Martinsville **z** 46151; Ⓟ 15,977; Ⓒ 17,978
Washington; MCD-Township; NEWTON; ***174** E-4; mail Brook **z** 47922; Ⓟ 385; Ⓒ 354
Washington; MCD-Township; NOBLE; ***174** C-11; mail Columbia City **z** 46725, Pierceton **z** 46562; Ⓟ 979; Ⓒ 1,182
Washington; MCD-Township; OWEN; ***175** M-6; mail Spencer **z** 47460; Ⓟ 5,570; Ⓒ 6,399
Washington; MCD-Township; PARKE; ***174** J-5; mail Marshall **z** 47859; Ⓟ 904; Ⓒ 1,142
Washington; MCD-Township; PIKE; ***175** Q-4; mail Petersburg **z** 47567; Ⓟ 4,731; Ⓒ 4,633
Washington; MCD-Township; PORTER; ***174** B-6; ★ **CHI**; mail Valparaiso **z** 46383; Ⓟ 3,113; Ⓒ 3,425
Washington; MCD-Township; PUTNAM; ***175** K-6; mail Reelsville **z** 46171; Ⓟ 2,027; Ⓒ 2,876
Washington; MCD-Township; RANDOLPH; ***174** I-13; mail Winchester **z** 47394; Ⓟ 2,325; Ⓒ 2,288
Washington; MCD-Township; RIPLEY; ***175** N-13; mail Versailles **z** 47042; Ⓟ 1,989; Ⓒ 2,196
Washington; MCD-Township; RUSH; ***174** J-12; mail Falmouth **z** 46127; Ⓟ 531; Ⓒ 471
Washington; MCD-Township; SHELBY; ***175** L-10; mail Flat Rock **z** 47234; Ⓟ 1,340; Ⓒ 1,330
Washington; MCD-Township; STARKE; ***174** C-7; mail Knox **z** 46534; Ⓟ 2,244; Ⓒ 2,793
Washington; MCD-Township; TIPPECANOE; ***174** G-6; ★ **LAF-**; mail Lafayette **z** 47905; Ⓟ 2,393; Ⓒ 2,473
Washington; MCD-Township; WARREN; ***174** H-4; mail Williamsport **z** 47993; Ⓟ 2,212; Ⓒ 2,351
Washington; MCD-Township; WASHINGTON; ***175** P-9; mail Salem **z** 47167; Ⓟ 9,495; Ⓒ 9,955
Washington; MCD-Township; WAYNE; ***174** J-13; mail Milton **z** 47357; Ⓟ 1,539; Ⓒ 1,579
Washington; MCD-Township; WHITLEY; ***174** D-11; mail Columbia City **z** 46725; Ⓟ 1,112; Ⓒ 1,121
WASHINGTON; **175** P-9; Ⓟ 23,717; Ⓒ 27,223; ◆ 27,862
Washington Center; RMC Place; WHITLEY; ***174** D-11; mail Columbia City **z** 46725
Washington Place; RMC Place; MARION; ***174** J-9; ★ **IND**; mail Indianapolis **z** 46219; pop. incl. with Indianapolis (Inc. Place)
Waterford; RMC Place; LAPORTE; **174** A-6; ★ **MICH**; mail Michigan City **z** 46360; ● 350
Waterford Mills; RMC Place; ELKHART; **174** B-10; elev. 812ft./247m.; ★ **ELK**; mail Goshen **z** 46526; ● 200
Waterloo; Inc. Place; DE KALB; **174** B-13; elev. 904ft./276m.; 🅿; **z** 46793; Ⓟ 2,040; Ⓒ 2,200
Waterloo; RMC Place; FAYETTE; ▲ Waterloo; ***175** K-13; mail Connersville **z** 47331
Waterloo; MCD-Township; FAYETTE; ***175** K-13; mail Connersville **z** 47331; Ⓟ 595; Ⓒ 594
Waterloo; RMC Place; JOHNSON; ***175** K-8; ★ **IND**; mail Bargersville **z** 46106; ● 50
Waterswolde; RMC Place; ALLEN; ***174** C-12; ★ **FTWA**; mail Fort Wayne **z** 46825; ● 300
Wathen Heights; RMC Place; CLARK; ***175** R-10; ★ **LOU**; mail Jeffersonville **z** 47130
Watson; RMC Place; CLARK; **175** Q-10; 🅿; ★ **LOU**; **z** 47130; ● 500
Waugh; RMC Place; BOONE; ***174** I-8; mail Whitestown **z** 46075
Wauhob Lake; RMC Place; PORTER; ***174** B-5; ★ **CHI**; mail Valparaiso **z** 46383; ● 150
Waveland; Inc. Place; MONTGOMERY; **174** J-5; elev. 760ft./232m.; 🅿; **z** 47989; Ⓟ 474; Ⓒ 416
Waverly; RMC Place; MORGAN; **175** K-8; ★ **IND**; mail Martinsville **z** 46151; ● 200
Waverly Woods; RMC Place; MORGAN; ***175** K-8; ★ **IND**; mail Martinsville **z** 46151; ● 120
Wawaka; RMC Place; NOBLE; **174** B-11; elev. 902ft./275m.; 🅿; **z** 46794; ● 200
Wawpecong; RMC Place; MIAMI; **174** F-9; mail Kokomo **z** 46901; ● 70
Waymansville; RMC Place; BARTHOLOMEW; **175** N-9; mail Columbus **z** 47201; ● 75
Wayne; MCD-Township; ALLEN; ***174** D-12; ★ **FTWA**; mail Fort Wayne **z** 46809; Ⓟ 116,005; Ⓒ 111,117
Wayne; MCD-Township; BARTHOLOMEW; ***175** N-9; ★ **COL**; mail Columbus **z** 47201; Ⓟ 3,437; Ⓒ 3,795
Wayne; MCD-Township; FULTON; ***174** D-8; mail Kewanna **z** 46939; Ⓟ 611; Ⓒ 606
Wayne; MCD-Township; HAMILTON; ***174** I-10; mail Noblesville **z** 46060; Ⓟ 2,071; Ⓒ 2,415
Wayne; MCD-Township; HENRY; ***174** J-11; mail Knightstown **z** 46148; Ⓟ 3,842; Ⓒ 4,170
Wayne; MCD-Township; HUNTINGTON; ***174** F-11; mail La Fontaine **z** 46940; Ⓟ 549; Ⓒ 559
Wayne; MCD-Township; JAY; ***174** G-13; mail Portland **z** 47371; Ⓟ 8,046; Ⓒ 8,162
Wayne; MCD-Township; KOSCIUSKO; ***174** C-10; mail Winona Lake **z** 46590; Ⓟ 22,456; Ⓒ 25,262
Wayne; MCD-Township; MARION; ***174** J-8; ★ **IND**; mail Indianapolis **z** 46224, **z** 46241; Ⓟ 125,699; Ⓒ 133,461; Ⓡ 133,477
Wayne; MCD-Township; MONTGOMERY; ***174** I-5; mail Waynetown **z** 47990; Ⓟ 1,529; Ⓒ 1,621
Wayne; MCD-Township; NOBLE; ***174** B-12; mail Kendallville **z** 46755; Ⓟ 8,636; Ⓒ 10,365
Wayne; MCD-Township; OWEN; ***175** L-7; mail Gosport **z** 47433; Ⓟ 1,502; Ⓒ 1,599
Wayne; MCD-Township; RANDOLPH; ***174** H-14; mail Union City **z** 47390; Ⓟ 4,780; Ⓒ 4,703
Wayne; MCD-Township; STARKE; ***174** C-6; mail North Judson **z** 46366; Ⓟ 4,653; Ⓒ 4,987
Wayne; MCD-Township; TIPPECANOE; ***174** G-5; mail Westpoint **z** 47992; Ⓟ 1,184; Ⓒ 1,306
Wayne; MCD-Township; WAYNE; ***174** J-14; ★ **RICH**; mail Richmond **z** 47374; Ⓟ 44,743; Ⓒ 43,742
WAYNE; **174** J-13; Ⓟ 71,951; Ⓒ 71,097; ◆ 66,812
Wayne Center; RMC Place; NOBLE; mail Kendallville **z** 46755; rural
Waynedale; RMC Place; ALLEN; ***174** D-12; ★ **FTWA**; mail Fort Wayne **z** 46804, **z** 46809, **z** 46819; pop. incl. with Fort Wayne (Inc. Place)
Waynesburg; RMC Place; DECATUR; **175** M-11; mail Hartsville **z** 47244; ● 35
Waynesville; RMC Place; BARTHOLOMEW; ▲ Wayne; **175** N-10; ★ **COL**; mail Columbus **z** 47201; ● 160
Waynetown; Inc. Place; MONTGOMERY; **174** I-5; elev. 750ft./229m.; 🅿; **z** 47990; Ⓟ 911; Ⓒ 909
Wea; MCD-Township; TIPPECANOE; ***174** G-6; ★ **LAF-**; mail Lafayette **z** 47905; Ⓟ 14,078; Ⓒ 22,102
Webster; MCD-Township; HARRISON; ***175** R-9; mail Corydon **z** 47112; Ⓟ 1,490; Ⓒ 1,616
Webster; RMC Place; WAYNE; ▲ Webster; **174** J-13; 🅿; ★ **RICH**; **z** 47392; ● 250
Webster; MCD-Township; WAYNE; ***174** J-13; 🅿; ★ **RICH**; **z** 47392; Ⓟ 1,321; Ⓒ 1,453
Wegan; RMC Place; JACKSON; ***175** O-9; mail Brownstown **z** 47220; rural
Weisburg; RMC Place; DEARBORN; ***175** M-13; mail Sunman **z** 47041; ● 75
Wellington Heights; RMC Place; SHELBY; ***175** L-10; mail Shelbyville **z** 46176; pop. incl. with Shelbyville (Inc. Place)
Wells; RMC Place; MIAMI; mail Peru **z** 46970; ● 365
WELLS; **174** F-12; Ⓟ 25,948; Ⓒ 27,600; ◆ 27,846
Wellsboro; RMC Place; LAPORTE; ***174** B-6; mail Union Mills **z** 46382; ● 225
Wellsburg; RMC Place; WELLS; ***174** F-12; elev. 850ft./259m.; mail Bluffton **z** 46714; rural
West; MCD-Township; MARSHALL; ***174** C-8; mail Plymouth **z** 46563; Ⓟ 3,586; Ⓒ 3,888
Westacres; RMC Place; DELAWARE, VIGO; ***174** H-12; ★ **MUN**; mail Muncie **z** 47304; ● 140
West Baden Springs; Inc. Place; ORANGE; **175** P-7; elev. 480ft./146m.; 🅿; **z** 47469; Ⓟ 675; Ⓒ 618
West Brook Downs; RMC Place; MONROE; ***175** M-7; ★ **BLMNG**; mail Bloomington **z** 47401, **z** 47404; ● 250
Westchester; RMC Place; ALLEN; ***174** D-12; ★ **FTWA**; mail Fort Wayne **z** 46816; pop. incl. with Fort Wayne (Inc. Place)
Westchester; RMC Place; JAY; ***174** G-13; mail Portland **z** 47371; rural
Westchester; MCD-Township; PORTER; ***174** A-5; ★ **CHI**; mail Chesterton **z** 46304; Ⓟ 15,551; Ⓒ 18,133
West College Corner; Inc. Place; UNION; **175** K-14; elev. 989ft./301m.; 🅿; **z** 47003; Ⓟ 686; Ⓒ 634
West Creek; MCD-Township; LAKE; ***174** C-4; mail Lowell **z** 46356; Ⓟ 4,223; Ⓒ 4,981
West Elwood; RMC Place; TIPTON; **174** H-10; ★ **KOK**; mail Elwood **z** 46036; ● 100
Western Acres; RMC Place; PORTER; ***174** A-5; ★ **CHI**; mail Chesterton **z** 46304; pop. incl. with Chesterton (Inc. Place)
Western Village; RMC Place; MADISON; ***174** I-10; ★ **AND**; mail Anderson **z** 46011; pop. incl. with Anderson (Inc. Place)
Westfield; Inc. Place; HAMILTON; **174** I-9; elev. 899ft./274m.; 🅿; ★ **IND**; **z** 46074; Ⓟ 3,304; Ⓒ 9,293; ◆ 13,572
Westfield; RMC Place; ST. JOSEPH; ***174** A-8; ★ **S.B.**; mail South Bend **z** 46619; ● 300
West Fork; RMC Place; CRAWFORD; ***175** R-7; mail English **z** 47118
West Franklin; RMC Place; POSEY; **175** S-3; ★ **EV**; mail Mount Vernon **z** 47620; ● 150
West Gary; RMC Place; LAKE; ★ **CHI**; pop. incl. with Gary (Inc. Place)
West Harrison (Harrison); Inc. Place; DEARBORN; **175** M-14; elev. 510ft./155m.; 🅿; ★ **CIN**; **z** 47060; Ⓟ 318; Ⓒ 284
West Haven; RMC Place; KOSCIUSKO; mail Warsaw **z** 46580; ● 250
West Hill; RMC Place; PORTER; ***174** B-5; ★ **CHI**; mail Valparaiso **z** 46385; ● 200
West Indianapolis; RMC Place; MARION; ***174** J-8; ★ **IND**; mail Indianapolis **z** 46221; pop. incl. with Indianapolis (Inc. Place)
West Lafayette; Inc. Place; TIPPECANOE; **174** G-6; elev. 600ft./183m.; 🅿 🅷 🅲 39,228; ★ **LAF-**; **z** 47906-07, **z** 47996 & mail Lafayette **z** 47901-05; Ⓟ 25,907; Ⓒ 28,778; ◆ 32,219
Westlawn; RMC Place; ALLEN; ***174** D-12; ★ **FTWA**; mail Fort Wayne **z** 46804; ● 700
West Lebanon; Inc. Place; WARREN; **174** H-4; elev. 714ft./218m.; 🅿; **z** 47991; Ⓟ 760; Ⓒ 793
West Liberty; RMC Place; HOWARD; ***174** G-10; mail Bryant **z** 47326, Greentown **z** 46936; ● 35
West Middleton (Middletons); RMC Place; HOWARD; **174** G-8; elev. 828ft./252m.; 🅿; ★ **KOK**; **z** 46995; ● 225
Westmoor; RMC Place; ALLEN; ***174** D-12; ★ **FTWA**; mail Fort Wayne **z** 46804; pop. incl. with Fort Wayne (Inc. Place)
West Newton; RMC Place; MARION; ***175** K-8; elev. 725ft./221m.; 🅿; ★ **IND**; **z** 46183; pop. incl. with Indianapolis (Inc. Place)
West Noblesville; RMC Place; HAMILTON; ***174** I-9; ★ **IND**; mail Noblesville **z** 46060; pop. incl. with Noblesville (Inc. Place)
West Peru; RMC Place; MIAMI; pop. incl. with Peru (Inc. Place)
West Petersburg; RMC Place; PIKE; ***175** Q-4; mail Petersburg **z** 47567; pop. incl. with Petersburg (Inc. Place)
Westphalia; RMC Place; KNOX; **175** O-5; elev. 470ft./143m.; 🅿; **z** 47596; ● 270
West Point; RMC Place; HOWARD; ***174** G-8; ★ **KOK**; mail Kokomo **z** 46901; ● 250
Westpoint; RMC Place; TIPPECANOE; **174** G-5; elev. 648ft./198m.; 🅿; **z** 47992; ● 250
West Point; MCD-Township; WHITE; ***174** F-5; mail Reynolds **z** 47980; Ⓟ 418; Ⓒ 371
Westport; Inc. Place; DECATUR; **175** M-11; elev. 806ft./246m.; 🅿; **z** 47283; Ⓟ 1,478; Ⓒ 1,515
Westside; RMC Place; DEARBORN; ***175** N-13; ★ **CIN**; mail Aurora **z** 47001; pop. incl. with Aurora (Inc. Place)
West Terre Haute; Inc. Place; VIGO; **175** L-4; elev. 470ft./143m.; 🅿; ★ **T.H.**; **z** 47885; Ⓟ 2,495; Ⓒ 2,330
Westville; Inc. Place; LAPORTE; **174** B-6; elev. 800ft./244m.; 🅿 🅲 3,724; ★ **MICH**; **z** 46391; Ⓟ 5,255; Ⓒ 2,116; Ⓡ 5,211
West Wabash; RMC Place; VANDERBURGH; ★ **EV**; mail Evansville **z** 47708, **z** 47712, **z** 47719; pop. incl. with Evansville (Inc. Place)
Westwood; RMC Place; HENRY; **174** J-11; mail New Castle **z** 47362; ● 150
Wheatfield; Inc. Place; JASPER; ▲ Wheatfield; **174** C-5; elev. 663ft./202m.; 🅿; **z** 46380, **z** 46392; Ⓟ 621; Ⓒ 772
Wheatfield; MCD-Township; JASPER; ***174** C-5; elev. 663ft./202m.; 🅿; **z** 46380, **z** 46392; Ⓟ 2,547; Ⓒ 3,622
Wheatland; Inc. Place; KNOX; **175** P-4; elev. 490ft./149m.; 🅿; **z** 47597; Ⓟ 439; Ⓒ 504
Wheatonville; RMC Place; WARRICK; ***175** R-4; elev. 432ft./132m.; ★ **EV**; mail Elberfeld **z** 47613
Wheeler; RMC Place; PORTER; **174** B-5; elev. 667ft./203m.; 🅿; ★ **CHI**; **z** 46393; ● 500
Wheeling; RMC Place; CARROLL; **174** F-8; mail Flora **z** 46929; ● 30
Wheeling; RMC Place; DELAWARE; ***174** G-11; mail Gaston **z** 47342; ● 100
Wheeling; RMC Place; GIBSON; **174** G-11; mail Francisco **z** 47649; ● 100
Whiskey Run; MCD-Township; CRAWFORD; ***175** Q-8; mail Milltown **z** 47145; Ⓟ 1,729; Ⓒ 1,985
Whitaker; RMC Place; MORGAN; ***175** L-7; mail Paragon **z** 46166
Whitcomb; RMC Place; FRANKLIN; **175** L-13; mail Brookville **z** 47012; ● 60
Whitcomb Heights; RMC Place; VIGO; **174** I-1; ★ **T.H.**; mail West Terre Haute **z** 47885; ● 300
WHITE; **174** F-6; Ⓟ 23,265; Ⓒ 25,267; ◆ 23,291
White Cloud; RMC Place; HARRISON; ***175** R-8; mail Corydon **z** 47112
Whitehall; RMC Place; OWEN; **175** M-7; mail Bloomington **z** 47401; ● 50
Whiteland; Inc. Place; JOHNSON; **175** K-9; elev. 800ft./244m.; 🅿; ★ **IND**; **z** 46184; Ⓟ 2,446; Ⓒ 3,958
Whiteoak; RMC Place; PIKE; ***175** Q-5; elev. 549ft./167m.; mail Winslow **z** 47598; rural
White Post; MCD-Township; PULASKI; ***174** D-6; mail Medaryville **z** 47957; Ⓟ 1,242; Ⓒ 1,069
White Ridge; RMC Place; GRANT; ***174** F-10; ★ **MRN**; mail Marion **z** 46952; ● 175
White River; MCD-Township; GIBSON; ***175** Q-3; mail Patoka **z** 47666; Ⓟ 1,902; Ⓒ 1,714
White River; MCD-Township; HAMILTON; ***174** H-9; mail Cicero **z** 46034; Ⓟ 2,450; Ⓒ 2,566
White River; MCD-Township; JOHNSON; ***175** K-9; ★ **IND**; mail Greenwood **z** 46142; Ⓟ 28,232; Ⓒ 35,539
White River; MCD-Township; RANDOLPH; ***174** H-13; mail Winchester **z** 47394; Ⓟ 7,798; Ⓒ 7,661
White Rose; RMC Place; GREENE; ***175** N-5; mail Linton **z** 47441; ● 60
Whitestown; Inc. Place; BOONE; **174** I-8; elev. 940ft./287m.; 🅿; ★ **IND**; **z** 46075; Ⓟ 476; Ⓒ 471
Whitesville; RMC Place; MONTGOMERY; **174** I-6; mail Crawfordsville **z** 47933; ● 60
Whitewater; MCD-Township; FRANKLIN; ***175** L-14; mail West Harrison **z** 47060; Ⓟ 1,890; Ⓒ 2,360
Whitewater; Inc. Place; WAYNE; **174** I-14; elev. 1,127ft./344m.; mail Richmond **z** 47374; Ⓟ 111; Ⓒ 78
Whitfield; RMC Place; MARTIN; **175** P-6; mail Loogootee **z** 47553; ● 100
Whiting; Inc. Place; LAKE; **174** A-4; elev. 585ft./178m.; 🅿 🅲 1,236; ★ **CHI**; **z** 46394; Ⓟ 5,155; Ⓒ 5,137
WHITLEY; **174** D-11; Ⓟ 27,651; Ⓒ 30,707; ◆ 32,758
Wickliffe; RMC Place; CRAWFORD; ***175** Q-7; mail Eckerty **z** 47116
Widner; MCD-Township; KNOX; ***175** O-4; mail Oaktown **z** 47561; Ⓟ 1,197; Ⓒ 1,165
Wilbur; RMC Place; MORGAN; ***175** L-7; ★ **IND**; mail Martinsville **z** 46151; ● 60
Wildcat; MCD-Township; TIPTON; ***174** G-10; mail Windfall **z** 46076; Ⓟ 1,523; Ⓒ 1,545
Wilders; RMC Place; LAPORTE; ***174** C-6; mail La Crosse **z** 46348
Wildwood; RMC Place; STEUBEN; ***174** A-12; mail Angola **z** 46703; summer pop. 250; ● 150
Wildwood Lake; RMC Place; ORANGE; ***175** Q-7; mail Paoli **z** 47454; ● 70
Wilfred; RMC Place; SULLIVAN; **175** M-4; mail Shelburn **z** 47879; ● 40
Wilhelm; LAPORTE; see Lalimere (RMC Place)
Wilkinson; Inc. Place; HANCOCK; **174** J-11; elev. 1,000ft./305m.; 🅿; **z** 46186; Ⓟ 446; Ⓒ 356
Williams; RMC Place; ADAMS; ***174** E-13; elev. 826ft./252m.; mail Decatur **z** 46733
Williams; RMC Place; LAWRENCE; **175** O-7; elev. 489ft./149m.; 🅿; **z** 47470; ● 250
Williamsburg; RMC Place; WAYNE; **174** I-13; elev. 1,060ft./323m.; 🅿; **z** 47393; ● 360
Williams Creek; Inc. Place; MARION; ***174** J-9; ★ **IND**; mail Indianapolis **z** 46240; Ⓒ 413
Williamsport; Inc. Place; ⊡ WARREN; **174** H-4; elev. 610ft./186m.; 🅿 🅷; **z** 47993; Ⓟ 1,798; Ⓒ 1,935
Williamstown; RMC Place; RUSH, DECATUR; ***175** L-11; mail Greensburg **z** 47240; ● 40
Willisville; RMC Place; PIKE; ***175** Q-4; elev. 467ft./142m.; mail Petersburg **z** 47567; rural
Willow Branch; RMC Place; HANCOCK; **174** J-10; elev. 936ft./285m.; 🅿; **z** 46186; ● 150
Willowbrook Estates; RMC Place; MORGAN; ***175** L-8; ★ **IND**; mail Martinsville **z** 46151; ● 125
Willow Creek; RMC Place; PORTER; ***174** A-5; ★ **CHI**; pop. incl. with Portage (Inc. Place)
Willow Valley; RMC Place; MARTIN; **175** P-7; mail Shoals **z** 47581; rural
Wills; MCD-Township; LAPORTE; ***174** A-7; mail Rolling Prairie **z** 46371; Ⓟ 1,291; Ⓒ 1,827
Wilmington; MCD-Township; DE KALB; ***174** B-13; mail Butler **z** 46721; Ⓟ 3,809; Ⓒ 4,118
Wilmington; RMC Place; DEARBORN; **175** N-13; mail Aurora **z** 47001; ● 150
Wilmot; RMC Place; NOBLE; **174** C-11; mail Pierceton **z** 46562; ● 60
Wilson; RMC Place; CLARK; ***175** Q-10; mail Borden **z** 47106
Wilson; RMC Place; PORTER; ***174** A-5; ★ **CHI**; pop. incl. with Portage (Inc. Place)
Wilson Corner; RMC Place; SHELBY; ***175** L-10; mail Shelbyville **z** 46176; rural
Wilson Lake; RMC Place; WHITLEY; ***174** C-11; mail Columbia City **z** 46725; ● 40
Winamac; Inc. Place; ⊡ PULASKI; **174** D-7; elev. 710ft./216m.; 🅿 🅷; **z** 46996; Ⓟ 2,262; Ⓒ 2,418
Winchester; Inc. Place; ⊡ RANDOLPH; **174** H-13; elev. 1,097ft./334m.; 🅿 🅷; **z** 47394; Ⓟ 5,095; Ⓒ 5,037
Windemere Lake; RMC Place; VIGO; ***175** L-3; ★ **T.H.**; mail West Terre Haute **z** 47885; ● 45
Windfall (Windfall City); Inc. Place; TIPTON; **174** G-9; elev. 866ft./264m.; 🅿; **z** 46076; Ⓟ 779; Ⓒ 712
Windfall City; TIPTON; see Windfall (Inc. Place)
Windom; RMC Place; MARTIN; ***175** P-6; mail Shoals **z** 47581; rural
Windsor; RMC Place; RANDOLPH; **174** H-12; mail Parker City **z** 47368; ● 110
Windsor Village; RMC Place; MARION; ***174** J-9; ★ **IND**; mail Indianapolis **z** 46219; pop. incl. with Indianapolis (Inc. Place)
Winfield; Inc. Place; LAKE; **174** B-5; ★ **CHI**; mail Crown Point **z** 46307; Ⓟ 645; Ⓒ 2,298; Ⓡ 2,028
Winfield; MCD-Township; LAKE; ***174** B-5; ★ **CHI**; mail Crown Point **z** 46307; Ⓟ 4,987; Ⓒ 6,878
Wingate; Inc. Place; MONTGOMERY; **174** H-5; elev. 769ft./234m.; 🅿; **z** 47994; Ⓟ 275; Ⓒ 299
Winona; RMC Place; STARKE; **174** C-7; mail Knox **z** 46534; summer pop. 400; ● 200
Winona Lake; Inc. Place; KOSCIUSKO; **174** C-10; 🅿 🅲 1,471; **z** 46590; Ⓟ 4,053; Ⓒ 3,987
Winslow; Inc. Place; PIKE; **175** Q-5; elev. 427ft./130m.; 🅿; **z** 47598; Ⓟ 875; Ⓒ 881
Winthrop; RMC Place; WARREN; ***174** G-5; mail Attica **z** 47918; ● 25
Wirt; RMC Place; JEFFERSON; **175** O-11; mail Madison **z** 47250; ● 25
Witmer Lake; RMC Place; LAGRANGE; ***174** B-11; mail Wolcottville **z** 46795; ● 450
Witmer Manor; RMC Place; LAGRANGE; ***174** B-11; mail Wolcottville **z** 46795; ● 300
Witts Station; RMC Place; UNION; ***175** K-14; mail Liberty **z** 47353; rural
Wolcott; Inc. Place; WHITE; **174** E-5; elev. 718ft./219m.; 🅿; **z** 47995; Ⓟ 886; Ⓒ 989
Wolcottville; Inc. Place; NOBLE, LAGRANGE; **174** B-12; elev. 934ft./285m.; 🅿; **z** 46795; Ⓟ 879; Ⓒ 933
Wolff; RMC Place; MORGAN; ***175** L-8; ★ **IND**; mail Martinsville **z** 46151; ● 60
Wolf Lake; RMC Place; LAKE; ★ **CHI**
Wolflake; RMC Place; NOBLE; **174** C-11; elev. 908ft./277m.; 🅿; **z** 46796; ● 250
Wonder Lake; RMC Place; VIGO; ***175** L-4; mail Terre Haute **z** 47802; ● 60
Wood; MCD-Township; CLARK; ***175** Q-10; mail Borden **z** 47106; Ⓟ 2,108; Ⓒ 2,462
Woodbridge; RMC Place; MONROE; ***175** M-7; 🅿; ★ **BLMNG**; **z** 47408 & mail Bloomington **z** 47407; pop. incl. with Bloomington (Inc. Place)
Woodburn; Inc. Place; ALLEN; **174** D-13; elev. 756ft./230m.; 🅿; **z** 46797; Ⓟ 1,321; Ⓒ 1,579
Woodbury; RMC Place; HANCOCK; **174** J-10; ★ **IND**; mail Mc Cordsville **z** 46055; ● 150
Woodcrest; RMC Place; MORGAN; ***175** L-8; ★ **IND**; mail Martinsville **z** 46151; ● 100
Woodgate; RMC Place; VIGO; ***175** L-4; ★ **T.H.**; mail Terre Haute **z** 47802; ● 300
Woodgate East; RMC Place; VIGO; ***175** L-4; ★ **T.H.**; mail Terre Haute **z** 47802; ● 250
Woodland; RMC Place; ST. JOSEPH; **174** A-9; mail South Bend **z** 46614; ● 60
Woodland Heights; RMC Place; GRANT; ***174** F-10; ★ **MRN**; mail Marion **z** 46952; ● 150
Woodland Hills; RMC Place; FLOYD; ***175** R-10; ★ **LOU**; mail New Albany **z** 47150; pop. incl. with New Albany (Inc. Place)
Woodland Hills; RMC Place; LAGRANGE; ***174** A-11; mail Lagrange **z** 46761; ● 75
Woodland Lake; RMC Place; BROWN; ***175** M-8; mail Morgantown **z** 46160; ● 150
Woodland Park; RMC Place; DELAWARE; **174** G-3; ★ **MUN**; mail Muncie **z** 47303; ● 200
Woodland Park; RMC Place; LAGRANGE; ***174** A-12; mail Wolcottville **z** 46795; ● 70
Woodlawn Heights; Inc. Place; MADISON; **174** D-2; elev. 850ft./259m.; ★ **AND**; mail Anderson **z** 46011; Ⓟ 109; Ⓒ 73
Woodridge; RMC Place; VIGO; **174** I-2; ★ **T.H.**; mail Terre Haute **z** 47803; pop. incl. with Terre Haute (Inc. Place)
Woodruff; RMC Place; LAGRANGE; **174** A-12; mail Wolcottville **z** 46795; ● 35
Woodruff Place; RMC Place; MARION; ***174** J-9; ★ **IND**; mail Indianapolis **z** 46201; pop. incl. with Indianapolis (Inc. Place)
Woodville; RMC Place; PORTER; ***174** A-5; ★ **CHI**; mail Chesterton **z** 46304
Woodville Hills; RMC Place; MONROE; mail Bloomington **z** 47401; ● 125
Wooster; RMC Place; KOSCIUSKO; **174** C-10; mail Pierceton **z** 46562; ● 35
Wooster; RMC Place; SCOTT; ***175** O-10; elev. 671ft./205m.; mail Lexington **z** 47138
Worth; MCD-Township; BOONE; ***174** I-8; ★ **IND**; mail Whitestown **z** 46075; Ⓟ 1,378; Ⓒ 1,292
Worthington; Inc. Place; GREENE; **175** N-6; 🅿; **z** 47471; Ⓟ 1,473; Ⓒ 1,481
Wright; MCD-Township; GREENE; ***175** M-5; mail Jasonville **z** 47438, Linton **z** 47441; Ⓟ 3,950; Ⓒ 4,224
Wrights Corner; RMC Place; DEARBORN; ***175** M-13; mail Aurora **z** 47001; ● 50
Wyandotte; RMC Place; CRAWFORD; ***175** R-8; mail Leavenworth **z** 47137; rural
Wyatt; RMC Place; ST. JOSEPH; **174** B-9; elev. 832ft./254m.; 🅿; **z** 46595; ● 400
Wynnedale; Inc. Place; MARION; ***174** J-8; ★ **IND**; mail Indianapolis **z** 46228; Ⓒ 275

Y

Yankeetown; RMC Place; WARRICK; **175** S-4; elev. 449ft./137m.; mail Newburgh **z** 47630; ● 250
Yeddo; RMC Place; FOUNTAIN; **174** I-4; mail Kingman **z** 47952; ● 110
Yellowbanks; RMC Place; KOSCIUSKO; ***174** C-10; mail North Webster **z** 46555; summer pop. 300; ● 100
Yellow Creek Lake; RMC Place; KOSCIUSKO; ***174** D-9; mail Claypool **z** 46510; summer pop. 300; ● 100
Yeoman; Inc. Place; CARROLL; **174** F-7; elev. 663ft./202m.; 🅿; **z** 47997; Ⓟ 131; Ⓒ 96
Yockey; RMC Place; LAWRENCE; ***175** O-7; mail Mitchell **z** 47446; rural
Yoder; RMC Place; ALLEN; **174** E-12; elev. 810ft./247m.; 🅿; ★ **FTWA**; **z** 46798; ● 250
York; MCD-Township; BENTON; ***174** F-4; mail Earl Park **z** 47942; Ⓟ 224; Ⓒ 241
York; MCD-Township; DEARBORN; ***175** M-13; mail Guilford **z** 47022; Ⓟ 868; Ⓒ 985
York; MCD-Township; ELKHART; ***174** A-10; ★ **ELK**; mail Bristol **z** 46507; Ⓟ 2,947; Ⓒ 3,429
York; MCD-Township; NOBLE; ***174** B-11; mail Albion **z** 46701; Ⓟ 1,011; Ⓒ 1,483
York; RMC Place; STEUBEN; ▲ York; ***174** A-14; mail Angola **z** 46703, Fremont **z** 46737; rural
York; MCD-Township; STEUBEN; ***174** A-13; mail Angola **z** 46703; Ⓟ 491; Ⓒ 670
York; MCD-Township; SWITZERLAND; ***175** O-13; mail Florence **z** 47020; Ⓟ 773; Ⓒ 937
Yorktown; Inc. Place; DELAWARE; **174** H-11; elev. 920ft./280m.; 🅿; ★ **MUN**; **z** 47396; Ⓟ 4,106; Ⓒ 4,785
Yorkville; RMC Place; DEARBORN; ***175** M-13; mail Guilford **z** 47022; ● 100
Young; RMC Place; MORGAN; ***175** K-8; ★ **IND**; mail Mooresville **z** 46158; ● 70
Young America; RMC Place; CASS; **174** F-8; elev. 760ft./232m.; 🅿; **z** 46998; ● 235
Youngs Corner; RMC Place; FRANKLIN; ***175** L-13; mail Brookville **z** 47012; rural
Youngs Creek; RMC Place; ORANGE; ***175** Q-7; elev. 591ft./180m.; mail Paoli **z** 47454
Youngstown; RMC Place; VIGO; **175** L-4; ★ **T.H.**; mail Terre Haute **z** 47802; ● 100
Youngstown Meadows; RMC Place; VIGO; ***175** L-4; ★ **T.H.**; mail Terre Haute **z** 47802; ● 350
Yountsville; RMC Place; MONTGOMERY; **174** I-6; mail Crawfordsville **z** 47933; ● 100

Z

Zanesville; Inc. Place; WELLS, ALLEN; **174** E-12; 🅿; ★ **FTWA**; **z** 46799; Ⓟ 673; Ⓒ 602
Zelma; RMC Place; LAWRENCE; ***175** N-8; mail Norman **z** 47264; rural
Zenas; RMC Place; JENNINGS; **175** N-11; mail Butlerville **z** 47223; ● 40
Zephyr; RMC Place; BARTHOLOMEW; ***175** M-10; ★ **COL**; mail Columbus **z** 47201; ● 150
Zionsville; Inc. Place; BOONE; **174** I-8; elev. 849ft./259m.; 🅿; ★ **IND**; **z** 46077; Ⓟ 5,281; Ⓒ 8,775
Zoar; RMC Place; PIKE, DUBOIS; ***175** R-5; mail Holland **z** 47541, Stendal **z** 47585; rural
Zulu; RMC Place; ALLEN; **174** D-13; mail Monroeville **z** 46773; ● 40

Entries in **UPPERCASE** are counties.
Entries in **bold** have populations of 2,500 or more.
Names in parentheses are alternate names.
Inc. Place — Incorporated Place
RMC Place — Rand McNally Designated Place
CDP — Census Designated Place
MCD — Minor Civil Division

⊡ County Seat
▲ Minor Civil Division
elev. Elevation
🅿 Post Office

🅷 Hospital
🅲 College
■ Principal Business Center
★ Ranally Metro Area (RMA) Abbreviation
z Zip Code(s)

Ⓟ Previous Census Population
Ⓡ Revised Census Population
Ⓐ Annexation Population
● Rand McNally Population Estimate
Ⓒ Final Census Population
Ⓢ Special Census Population
◆ Estimated Population

For additional definitions see Glossary, Volume 1, and Introduction, Volume 2.

IOWA

SD MN WI NE IL MO
Des Moines

Statistics

Total area (2000) — 56,272 square miles
Land area (2000) — 55,869 square miles
Water area (2000) — 403 square miles
Capital — Des Moines
Admitted as state — December, 1846

Maps

State maps can be found on pages 142-254 in Vol. 1

Ranally Metro Areas (RMAs) and Abbreviations

Ames, IA — AMES
Burlington, IA — BUR
Cedar Rapids, IA — CEDR
Clinton, IA-IL — CLNT
Davenport-Rock Island-Moline, IA-IL — D-RI-M
Des Moines, IA — DES
Dubuque, IA-WI-IL — DUB
Iowa City, IA — IACY
Omaha, NE-IA — OMA
Sioux City, IA-NE-SD — SXCY
Waterloo, IA — WATL

Principal Places

Place Name	Place Type	County	Population
Des Moines	Inc. Place	POLK	◆ 207,636
Cedar Rapids	Inc. Place	LINN	◆ 132,936
Davenport	Inc. Place	SCOTT	◆ 99,827
Sioux City	Inc. Place	WOODBURY	◆ 82,003
Iowa City	Inc. Place	JOHNSON	◆ 74,762
Waterloo	Inc. Place	BLACK HAWK	◆ 72,376
Ames	Inc. Place	STORY	◆ 59,548
Council Bluffs	Inc. Place	POTTAWATTAMIE	◆ 58,594
Dubuque	Inc. Place	DUBUQUE	◆ 55,684
West Des Moines	Inc. Place	POLK	◆ 54,465
Cedar Falls	Inc. Place	BLACK HAWK	◆ 38,132
Urbandale	Inc. Place	POLK	◆ 35,366
Ankeny	Inc. Place	POLK	◆ 35,084
Marion	Inc. Place	LINN	◆ 31,842
Bettendorf	Inc. Place	SCOTT	◆ 31,539
Mason City	Inc. Place	CERRO GORDO	◆ 27,254
Marshalltown	Inc. Place	MARSHALL	◆ 26,223
Clinton	Inc. Place	CLINTON	◆ 25,901
Burlington	Inc. Place	DES MOINES	◆ 25,613
Ottumwa	Inc. Place	WAPELLO	◆ 24,109
Fort Dodge	Inc. Place	WEBSTER	◆ 22,743
Muscatine	Inc. Place	MUSCATINE	◆ 22,482
Newton	Inc. Place	JASPER	© 15,579
Coralville	Inc. Place	JOHNSON	© 15,123
Indianola	Inc. Place	WARREN	© 12,998
Clive	Inc. Place	POLK	© 12,855
Boone	Inc. Place	BOONE	© 12,803
Fort Madison	Inc. Place	LEE	® 11,476
Keokuk	Inc. Place	LEE	© 11,427
Spencer	Inc. Place	CLAY	© 11,317
Oskaloosa	Inc. Place	MAHASKA	© 10,938
Altoona	Inc. Place	POLK	® 10,349
Carroll	Inc. Place	CARROLL	® 10,098
Storm Lake	Inc. Place	BUENA VISTA	© 10,076
Pella	Inc. Place	MARION	® 9,909
Fairfield	Inc. Place	JEFFERSON	® 9,602
Le Mars	Inc. Place	PLYMOUTH	© 9,237
Grinnell	Inc. Place	POWESHIEK	© 9,105
Waverly	Inc. Place	BREMER	© 8,968
Mount Pleasant	Inc. Place	HENRY	© 8,751
Johnston	Inc. Place	POLK	© 8,649
Webster City	Inc. Place	HAMILTON	© 8,176
Decorah	Inc. Place	WINNESHIEK	© 8,172
Clear Lake	Inc. Place	CERRO GORDO	© 8,161
Charles City	Inc. Place	FLOYD	© 7,812
Knoxville	Inc. Place	MARION	© 7,731
Perry	Inc. Place	DALLAS	© 7,633
Creston	Inc. Place	UNION	© 7,597
Denison	Inc. Place	CRAWFORD	© 7,339
Atlantic	Inc. Place	CASS	© 7,257
Washington	Inc. Place	WASHINGTON	© 7,047
Norwalk	Inc. Place	WARREN	© 6,884
Oelwein	Inc. Place	FAYETTE	© 6,692
Nevada	Inc. Place	STORY	© 6,658
Estherville	Inc. Place	EMMET	© 6,656
Hiawatha	Inc. Place	LINN	© 6,480
Red Oak	Inc. Place	MONTGOMERY	© 6,197
Maquoketa	Inc. Place	JACKSON	© 6,112
Independence	Inc. Place	BUCHANAN	© 6,014
Sioux Center	Inc. Place	SIOUX	© 6,002
Centerville	Inc. Place	APPANOOSE	© 5,924
Algona	Inc. Place	KOSSUTH	© 5,741
Clarinda	Inc. Place	PAGE	© 5,690
Orange City	Inc. Place	SIOUX	® 5,589
Shenandoah	Inc. Place	PAGE	© 5,546
Anamosa	Inc. Place	JONES	© 5,494
Cherokee	Inc. Place	CHEROKEE	© 5,369
North Liberty	Inc. Place	JOHNSON	© 5,367
Glenwood	Inc. Place	MILLS	© 5,358
Harlan	Inc. Place	SHELBY	© 5,282
Manchester	Inc. Place	DELAWARE	© 5,257
Iowa Falls	Inc. Place	HARDIN	© 5,193
Waukee	Inc. Place	DALLAS	© 5,126
Vinton	Inc. Place	BENTON	© 5,102
Grimes	Inc. Place	POLK	© 5,098
Pleasant Hill	Inc. Place	POLK	© 5,070
De Witt	Inc. Place	CLINTON	© 5,049

County Business Data

County	FIPS Code	County Seat	Land Area (Sq. Mi.)	Census Population			Wholesale Trade		Manufacturing, 2002			
				4/1/2000	4/1/1990	% Change 1990-2000	Sales, 2002 ($1,000)	% Change 1997-2002	Establish-ments	Total Employees	Value Added ($1,000)	Ranally Mfg. Units
Adair	001	Greenfield	569	8,243	8,409	-2.0	41,736	-49.8	6	(d)	(d)	...
Adams	003	Corning	424	4,482	4,866	-7.9	5,939	-67.9	...	(d)	(d)	...
Allamakee	005	Waukon	640	14,675	13,855	5.9	148,221	-6.3	28	1,630	121,556	64
Appanoose	007	Centerville	496	13,721	13,743	-0.2	13,012	-49.3	18	1,198	101,587	54
Audubon	009	Audubon	443	6,830	7,334	-6.9	63,262	-17.0	...	(d)	(d)	...
Benton	011	Vinton	716	25,308	22,429	12.8	(d)	(d)	31	807	83,516	44
Black Hawk	013	Waterloo	567	128,012	123,798	3.4	770,544	-19.1	157	12,878	2,058,977	1,089
Boone	015	Boone	571	26,224	25,186	4.1	261,667	68.6	35	(d)	(d)	...
Bremer	017	Waverly	438	23,325	22,813	2.2	(d)	(d)	37	1,609	116,611	62
Buchanan	019	Independence	571	21,093	20,844	1.2	264,367	18.7	34	1,358	107,784	57
Buena Vista	021	Storm Lake	575	20,411	19,965	2.2	226,105	-21.3	29	2,841	157,743	83
Butler	023	Allison	580	15,305	15,731	-2.7	164,554	3.8	...	(d)	(d)	...
Calhoun	025	Rockwell City	570	11,115	11,508	-3.4	164,909	-10.8	...	(d)	(d)	...
Carroll	027	Carroll	569	21,421	21,423	-0.0	937,841	164.5	35	1,428	141,510	75
Cass	029	Atlantic	564	14,684	15,128	-2.9	80,207	(d)	23	702	61,942	33
Cedar	031	Tipton	580	18,187	17,381	4.6	154,285	11.9	30	654	53,867	28
Cerro Gordo	033	Mason City	568	46,447	46,733	-0.6	503,127	2.8	55	3,760	396,710	210
Cherokee	035	Cherokee	577	13,035	14,098	-7.5	74,814	26.6	17	832	52,584	28
Chickasaw	037	New Hampton	505	13,095	13,295	-1.5	113,099	-36.9	33	1,073	110,052	58
Clarke	039	Osceola	431	9,133	8,287	10.2	18,520	(d)	14	1,056	92,841	49
Clay	041	Spencer	569	17,372	17,585	-1.2	269,840	9.3	29	1,294	118,943	63
Clayton	043	Elkader	779	18,678	19,054	-2.0	201,264	-25.4	32	1,022	49,493	26
Clinton	045	Clinton	695	50,149	51,040	-1.7	268,903	23.5	57	4,492	1,355,105	717
Crawford	047	Denison	714	16,942	16,775	1.0	175,541	-8.3	24	2,189	119,145	63
Dallas	049	Adel	586	40,750	29,755	37.0	1,080,462	(d)	39	2,149	144,083	76
Davis	051	Bloomfield	503	8,541	8,312	2.8	61,447	-1.9	...	(d)	(d)	...
Decatur	053	Leon	532	8,689	8,338	4.2	18,122	-73.5	...	(d)	(d)	...
Delaware	055	Manchester	578	18,404	18,035	2.0	178,308	-28.8	38	1,231	62,109	33
Des Moines	057	Burlington	416	42,351	42,614	-0.6	317,928	-15.4	65	(d)	(d)	...
Dickinson	059	Spirit Lake	381	16,424	14,909	10.2	229,142	30.2	31	2,127	357,127	189
Dubuque	061	Dubuque	608	89,143	86,403	3.2	1,108,401	19.6	144	8,872	1,222,906	647
Emmet	063	Estherville	396	11,027	11,569	-4.7	75,481	32.8	18	774	97,596	52
Fayette	065	West Union	731	22,008	21,843	0.8	298,800	(d)	35	1,059	111,571	59
Floyd	067	Charles City	501	16,900	17,058	-0.9	90,002	-19.8	17	954	74,793	40
Franklin	069	Hampton	582	10,704	11,364	-5.8	168,690	16.5	21	605	44,715	24
Fremont	071	Sidney	511	8,010	8,226	-2.6	50,464	-48.2	...	(d)	(d)	...
Greene	073	Jefferson	568	10,366	10,045	3.2	58,142	-50.2	14	517	33,182	18
Grundy	075	Grundy Center	503	12,369	12,029	2.8	(d)	(d)	...	(d)	(d)	...
Guthrie	077	Guthrie Center	591	11,353	10,935	3.8	84,861	20.2	...	(d)	(d)	...
Hamilton	079	Webster City	577	16,438	16,071	2.3	357,060	(d)	30	2,968	155,480	82
Hancock	081	Garner	571	12,100	12,638	-4.3	110,249	-38.7	31	1,034	82,413	44
Hardin	083	Eldora	569	18,812	19,094	-1.5	699,431	26.1	40	1,348	147,400	78
Harrison	085	Logan	697	15,666	14,730	6.4	(d)	(d)	...	(d)	(d)	...
Henry	087	Mount Pleasant	434	20,336	19,226	5.8	124,304	32.8	31	2,605	205,736	109
Howard	089	Cresco	473	9,932	9,809	1.3	79,961	-22.1	23	1,472	114,504	61
Humboldt	091	Dakota City	434	10,381	10,756	-3.5	163,206	-18.0	26	1,067	76,126	40
Ida	093	Ida Grove	432	7,837	8,365	-6.3	194,261	-8.0	11	854	89,777	47
Iowa	095	Marengo	586	15,671	14,630	7.1	56,768	-49.5	30	4,168	545,542	289
Jackson	097	Maquoketa	636	20,296	19,950	1.7	65,334	-11.3	43	1,042	74,432	39
Jasper	099	Newton	730	37,213	34,795	6.9	363,039	-22.0	49	4,874	474,860	251
Jefferson	101	Fairfield	435	16,181	16,310	-0.8	123,046	57.2	43	1,381	108,398	57
Johnson	103	Iowa City	614	111,006	96,119	15.5	446,909	(d)	75	4,605	3,032,308	1,604
Jones	105	Anamosa	575	20,221	19,444	4.0	(d)	(d)	29	635	77,878	41
Keokuk	107	Sigourney	579	11,400	11,624	-1.9	65,482	-27.9	...	(d)	(d)	...
Kossuth	109	Algona	973	17,163	18,591	-7.7	190,400	8.0	24	1,005	93,951	50
Lee	111	Fort Madison	517	38,052	38,687	-1.6	178,973	0.1	66	(d)	(d)	...
Linn	113	Cedar Rapids	717	191,701	168,767	13.6	2,437,660	4.9	234	18,044	2,938,626	1,555
Louisa	115	Wapello	402	12,183	11,592	5.1	86,056	21.4	11	(d)	(d)	...
Lucas	117	Chariton	431	9,422	9,070	3.9	19,115	-45.3	...	(d)	(d)	...
Lyon	119	Rock Rapids	588	11,763	11,952	-1.6	151,776	13.5	22	516	37,511	20
Madison	121	Winterset	561	14,019	12,483	12.3	(d)	(d)	...	(d)	(d)	...
Mahaska	123	Oskaloosa	571	22,335	21,522	3.8	220,553	14.4	28	822	100,621	53
Marion	125	Knoxville	554	32,052	30,001	6.8	124,112	25.8	47	7,515	876,110	464
Marshall	127	Marshalltown	572	39,311	38,276	2.7	242,017	6.4	47	5,398	1,058,620	560
Mills	129	Glenwood	437	14,547	13,202	10.2	(d)	(d)	...	(d)	(d)	...
Mitchell	131	Osage	469	10,874	10,928	-0.5	205,463	(d)	20	889	109,853	58
Monona	133	Onawa	693	10,020	10,034	-0.1	51,421	-41.7	...	(d)	(d)	...
Monroe	135	Albia	433	8,016	8,114	-1.2	21,610	3.6	...	(d)	(d)	...
Montgomery	137	Red Oak	424	11,771	12,076	-2.5	90,480	-40.2	12	831	64,180	34
Muscatine	139	Muscatine	439	41,722	39,907	4.5	292,858	10.9	73	(d)	(d)	...
O'Brien	141	Primghar	573	15,102	15,444	-2.2	259,556	29.1	28	1,071	66,736	35
Osceola	143	Sibley	399	7,003	7,267	-3.6	80,000	21.7	14	535	54,210	29
Page	145	Clarinda	535	16,976	16,870	0.6	84,605	-3.2	25	2,015	275,987	146
Palo Alto	147	Emmetsburg	564	10,147	10,669	-4.9	123,703	-24.9	21	544	51,556	27
Plymouth	149	Le Mars	864	24,849	23,388	6.2	(d)	(d)	30	(d)	(d)	...
Pocahontas	151	Pocahontas	578	8,662	9,525	-9.1	89,558	-54.6	18	549	38,806	21
Polk	153	Des Moines	569	374,601	327,140	14.5	8,267,367	(d)	399	17,294	2,286,551	1,210
Pottawattamie	155	Council Bluffs	954	87,704	82,628	6.1	772,779	(d)	65	4,717	498,198	264
Poweshiek	157	Montezuma	585	18,815	19,033	-1.1	82,362	-34.1	32	1,443	142,152	75
Ringgold	159	Mount Ayr	538	5,469	5,420	0.9	(d)	(d)	...	(d)	(d)	...
Sac	161	Sac City	576	11,529	12,324	-6.5	131,298	-9.1	...	(d)	(d)	...
Scott	163	Davenport	458	158,668	150,979	5.1	2,174,139	-35.4	201	12,169	2,086,645	1,104
Shelby	165	Harlan	591	13,173	13,230	-0.4	98,420	(d)	...	(d)	(d)	...
Sioux	167	Orange City	768	31,589	29,903	5.6	541,800	15.1	86	4,138	254,410	135
Story	169	Nevada	573	79,981	74,252	7.7	374,102	16.5	69	3,753	590,384	312
Tama	171	Toledo	721	18,103	17,419	3.9	185,394	-14.1	...	(d)	(d)	...
Taylor	173	Bedford	534	6,958	7,114	-2.2	20,682	-21.0	...	(d)	(d)	...
Union	175	Creston	424	12,309	12,750	-3.5	152,546	40.1	15	1,282	85,702	45
Van Buren	177	Keosauqua	485	7,809	7,676	1.7	14,049	-60.1	...	(d)	(d)	...
Wapello	179	Ottumwa	432	36,051	35,687	1.0	130,419	-7.2	32	4,112	710,036	376
Warren	181	Indianola	572	40,671	36,033	12.9	(d)	(d)	...	(d)	(d)	...
Washington	183	Washington	569	20,670	19,612	5.4	136,710	1.8	40	1,311	111,584	59

Entries in **UPPERCASE** are counties.
Entries in **bold** have populations of 2,500 or more.
Names in parentheses are alternate names.
Inc. Place — Incorporated Place
RMC Place — Rand McNally Designated Place
CDP — Census Designated Place
MCD — Minor Civil Division

⊡ County Seat
▲ Minor Civil Division
elev. Elevation
🅿 Post Office

🅷 Hospital
🅲 College
■ Principal Business Center
★ Ranally Metro Area (RMA) Abbreviation
z Zip Code(s)

℗ Previous Census Population
® Revised Census Population
Ⓐ Annexation Population
● Rand McNally Population Estimate
© Final Census Population
Ⓢ Special Census Population
◆ Estimated Population

For additional definitions see Glossary, Volume 1, and Introduction, Volume 2.

County	FIPS Code	County Seat	Land Area (Sq. Mi.)	Census Population			Wholesale Trade		Manufacturing, 2002			
				4/1/2000	4/1/1990	% Change 1990-2000	Sales, 2002 ($1,000)	% Change 1997-2002	Establish-ments	Total Employees	Value Added ($1,000)	Ranally Mfg. Units
Wayne	185	Corydon	526	6,730	7,067	-4.8	56,433	5.4	...	(d)	(d)	...
Webster	187	Fort Dodge	715	40,235	40,342	-0.3	811,895	14.3	52	2,154	613,126	324
Winnebago	189	Forest City	400	11,723	12,122	-3.3	109,644	(d)	18	4,696	415,690	220
Winneshiek	191	Decorah	690	21,310	20,847	2.2	109,018	-17.1	28	1,693	111,894	59
Woodbury	193	Sioux City	873	103,877	98,276	5.7	1,048,908	-14.2	108	(d)	(d)	...
Worth	195	Northwood	400	7,909	7,991	-1.0	69,948	-18.3	...	(d)	(d)	...
Wright	197	Clarion	581	14,334	14,269	0.5	91,457	(d)	30	1,161	205,079	109
The State			**55,869**	**2,926,324**	**2,776,755**	**5.4**	**33,546,948**	**-5.4**	**3,804**	**222,968**	**31,394,257**	**16,610**

(d) Data not available. Corresponding percentages or Ranally Manufacturing Units are estimates.
... Represents 0 or amount too minimal to be reported.

Index of Places and Counties

A

Abingdon; RMC Place; JEFFERSON; **177** K-14; mail Batavia z 52533; ● 80
Ackley; Inc. Place; HARDIN, FRANKLIN; **177** E-11; elev. 1,090ft./332m.; 🅿; z 50601; Ⓟ 1,696; Ⓒ 1,809
Ackworth; Inc. Place; WARREN; **176** J-10; elev. 900ft./274m.; 🅿; z 50001; Ⓟ 66; Ⓒ 85
Adair; Inc. Place; ADAIR, ADAIR; **176** I-7; elev. 1,466ft./447m.; 🅿; z 50002; Ⓟ 894; Ⓒ 839
ADAIR; **176** J-7; Ⓟ 8,409; Ⓒ 8,243; ◆ 7,415
ADAMS; **176** K-6; Ⓟ 4,866; Ⓒ 4,482; ◆ 3,936
Adaza; RMC Place; GREENE; ***176** G-7; mail Churdan z 50050
Adel; Inc. Place; ⊡ DALLAS; **176** I-8; elev. 930ft./283m.; 🅿; z 50003; Ⓟ 3,304; Ⓒ 3,435
Adelphi; RMC Place; POLK; ***176** I-10; elev. 850ft./259m.; mail Runnells z 50237; ● 30
Afton; Inc. Place; UNION; **176** K-8; elev. 1,201ft./366m.; 🅿; z 50830; Ⓟ 953; Ⓒ 917
Agency (Agency City); Inc. Place; WAPELLO; **177** K-14; elev. 810ft./247m.; 🅿; z 52530; Ⓟ 616; Ⓒ 622
Agency City; WAPELLO; see Agency (Inc. Place)
Ainsworth; Inc. Place; WASHINGTON; **177** J-16; elev. 700ft./213m.; 🅿; z 52201; Ⓟ 506; Ⓒ 524
Akron; Inc. Place; PLYMOUTH; **176** D-1; elev. 1,147ft./350m.; 🅿; z 51001; Ⓟ 1,450; Ⓒ 1,489
Aladdin; RMC Place; BLACK HAWK; ★ **WATL**; pop. incl. with Waterloo (Inc. Place)
Albaton; RMC Place; MONONA; ***176** G-2; elev. 1,071ft./326m.; mail Sloan z 51055; ● 30
Albert City; Inc. Place; BUENA VISTA; **176** D-6; elev. 1,320ft./402m.; 🅿; z 50510; Ⓟ 779; Ⓒ 709
Albia; Inc. Place; ⊡ MONROE; **177** K-12; elev. 969ft./295m.; 🅿 🅷; z 52531; Ⓟ 3,870; Ⓒ 3,706
Albion; Inc. Place; MARSHALL; **177** G-11; elev. 950ft./290m.; 🅿; z 50005; Ⓟ 585; Ⓒ 592
Alburnett; Inc. Place; LINN; **177** G-15; elev. 890ft./271m.; 🅿; z 52202; Ⓟ 456; Ⓒ 559
Alden; Inc. Place; HARDIN; **176** E-10; elev. 1,169ft./356m.; 🅿; z 50006 & mail Buckeye z 50043; Ⓟ 855; Ⓒ 904
Alexander; Inc. Place; FRANKLIN; **176** D-10; elev. 1,261ft./384m.; 🅿; z 50420; Ⓟ 170; Ⓒ 165
Algona; Inc. Place; ⊡ KOSSUTH; **176** C-8; elev. 1,200ft./366m.; 🅿 🅷; z 50511; Ⓟ 6,015; Ⓒ 5,741
ALLAMAKEE; **177** B-16; Ⓟ 13,855; Ⓒ 14,675; ◆ 14,332
Alleman; Inc. Place; POLK; **176** H-10; elev. 1,020ft./311m.; 🅿; z 50007; Ⓟ 340; Ⓒ 439
Allendorf; RMC Place; OSCEOLA; **176** B-4; elev. 1,598ft./487m.; 🅿; z 51354; ● 70
Allerton; Inc. Place; WAYNE; **176** M-10; elev. 1,100ft./335m.; 🅿; z 50008; Ⓟ 599; Ⓒ 559
Allison; Inc. Place; ⊡ BUTLER; **177** E-12; elev. 1,045ft./319m.; 🅿; z 50602; Ⓟ 1,000; Ⓒ 1,006
Alpha; RMC Place; FAYETTE; **177** D-14; elev. 1,040ft./317m.; 🅿; z 52171; ● 90
Alta; Inc. Place; BUENA VISTA; **176** E-5; elev. 1,514ft./461m.; 🅿; z 51002; Ⓟ 1,820; Ⓒ 1,865
Alta Vista; Inc. Place; CHICKASAW; **177** C-13; elev. 1,164ft./355m.; 🅿; z 50603; Ⓟ 246; Ⓒ 286
Alton; Inc. Place; SIOUX; **176** D-3; elev. 1,306ft./398m.; 🅿; z 51003; Ⓟ 1,063; Ⓒ 1,095
Altoona; Inc. Place; POLK; **176** I-10; elev. 952ft./290m.; 🅿; ★ **DES**; z 50009; Ⓟ 7,191; Ⓒ 10,345; Ⓡ 10,349
Alvord; Inc. Place; LYON; **176** B-2; elev. 1,330ft./405m.; 🅿; z 51230; Ⓟ 204; Ⓒ 187
Amana; RMC Place; IOWA; **177** H-15; elev. 715ft./218m.; 🅿; z 52203-04; ● 420
Amber; RMC Place; JONES; **177** G-17; mail Anamosa z 52205; ● 100
Amboy; RMC Place; JASPER; ***177** I-11; elev. 967ft./295m.; mail Newton z 50208; rural
Ames; Inc. Place; STORY; **176** G-10; elev. 921ft./281m.; 🅿 🅷 🅲 25,462 ■; ★ **AMES**; z 50010-14; Ⓟ 47,198; Ⓒ 50,731; ◆ 59,548
Amish (Joetown); RMC Place; JOHNSON; ***177** I-15; mail Kalona z 52247; ● 70
Amity; SCOTT; see Maysville (Inc. Place)
Anamosa; Inc. Place; ⊡ JONES; **177** G-16; elev. 829ft./253m.; 🅿 🅷; z 52205; Ⓟ 5,100; Ⓒ 5,494
Anderson; RMC Place; FREMONT; **176** L-4; mail Sidney z 51652; ● 50
Andover; Inc. Place; CLINTON; **177** G-20; elev. 730ft./223m.; 🅿; z 52701; Ⓟ 99; Ⓒ 87
Andrew; Inc. Place; JACKSON; **177** G-18; 🅿; z 52030; Ⓟ 319; Ⓒ 460
Anita; Inc. Place; CASS; **176** J-6; elev. 1,300ft./396m.; 🅿; z 50020; Ⓟ 1,068; Ⓒ 1,049
Ankeny; Inc. Place; POLK; **176** I-10; elev. 975ft./297m.; 🅿 🅲 518; ★ **DES**; z 50021, z 50023; Ⓟ 18,482; Ⓒ 27,117; ◆ 35,084
Anthon; Inc. Place; WOODBURY; **176** F-3; elev. 1,120ft./341m.; 🅿; z 51004; Ⓟ 638; Ⓒ 649
Aplington; Inc. Place; BUTLER; **177** E-12; elev. 967ft./295m.; 🅿; z 50604 & mail Austinville z 50608; Ⓟ 1,034; Ⓒ 1,054
APPANOOSE; **177** L-12; Ⓟ 13,743; Ⓒ 13,721; ◆ 12,443
Arcadia; Inc. Place; CARROLL; **176** G-5; elev. 1,386ft./422m.; 🅿; z 51430; Ⓟ 485; Ⓒ 443
Archer; Inc. Place; O'BRIEN; **176** C-3; elev. 1,474ft./449m.; 🅿; z 51231; Ⓟ 131; Ⓒ 126
Aredale; Inc. Place; BUTLER; **177** D-11; elev. 1,023ft./312m.; 🅿; z 50605; Ⓟ 88; Ⓒ 89
Argyle; RMC Place; LEE; **177** M-16; elev. 670ft./204m.; 🅿; z 52619 & mail Donnellson z 52625; ● 100
Arion; Inc. Place; CRAWFORD; **176** H-4; elev. 1,139ft./347m.; 🅿; z 51520; Ⓟ 148; Ⓒ 136
Arispe; Inc. Place; UNION; **176** L-8; 🅿; z 50831; Ⓟ 92; Ⓒ 89
Arlington; Inc. Place; FAYETTE; **177** D-15; elev. 1,130ft./344m.; 🅿; z 50606; Ⓟ 465; Ⓒ 490
Armstrong; Inc. Place; EMMET; **176** B-7; elev. 1,249ft./381m.; 🅿; z 50514; Ⓟ 1,025; Ⓒ 979
Arnolds Park; Inc. Place; DICKINSON; **176** B-5; elev. 1,402ft./427m.; 🅿; z 51331; Ⓟ 953; Ⓒ 1,162
Artesian; RMC Place; BREMER; ***177** E-13; mail Waverly z 50677
Arthur; Inc. Place; IDA; **176** F-4; elev. 1,287ft./392m.; 🅿; z 51431; Ⓟ 272; Ⓒ 245
Asbury; Inc. Place; DUBUQUE; **177** E-18; elev. 930ft./283m.; 🅿; ★ **DUB**; z 52002; Ⓟ 2,013; Ⓒ 2,450
Ashton; Inc. Place; OSCEOLA; **176** B-3; elev. 1,449ft./442m.; 🅿; z 51232; Ⓟ 462; Ⓒ 461
Aspinwall; Inc. Place; CRAWFORD; **176** H-5; elev. 1,381ft./421m.; 🅿; z 51432; Ⓟ 52; Ⓒ 58
Atalissa; Inc. Place; MUSCATINE; **177** I-17; elev. 660ft./201m.; 🅿; z 52720; Ⓟ 357; Ⓒ 283; Ⓡ 311
Athelstan; RMC Place; TAYLOR; **176** M-7; elev. 1,093ft./333m.; mail Blockton z 50836; disincorporated October 21, 2004; Ⓟ 31; Ⓒ 18
Atkins; Inc. Place; BENTON; **177** H-15; elev. 850ft./259m.; 🅿; z 52206; Ⓟ 637; Ⓒ 977
Atlantic; Inc. Place; ⊡ CASS; **176** J-5; elev. 1,215ft./370m.; 🅿 🅷; z 50022; Ⓟ 7,432; Ⓒ 7,257
Attica; RMC Place; MARION; **177** K-11; elev. 923ft./281m.; mail Knoxville z 50138; ● 80
Auburn; Inc. Place; SAC; **176** F-6; elev. 1,220ft./372m.; 🅿; z 51433; Ⓟ 283; Ⓒ 296
Audubon; Inc. Place; ⊡ AUDUBON; **176** I-6; elev. 1,373ft./418m.; 🅿 🅷; z 50025; Ⓟ 2,524; Ⓒ 2,382
AUDUBON; **176** I-5; Ⓟ 7,334; Ⓒ 6,830; ◆ 5,816
Augusta; RMC Place; DES MOINES; **177** L-17; mail Wever z 52658; ● 100
Aurelia; Inc. Place; CHEROKEE; **176** E-4; elev. 1,400ft./427m.; 🅿; z 51005; Ⓟ 1,034; Ⓒ 1,062
Aureola; RMC Place; FLOYD; ***177** D-12; mail Marble Rock z 50653; rural
Aurora; Inc. Place; BUCHANAN; **177** E-15; elev. 1,138ft./347m.; 🅿; z 50607 & mail Stanley z 50671; Ⓟ 196; Ⓒ 194
Austinville; RMC Place; BUTLER; **177** E-11; 🅿; z 50608; ● 100
Avery; RMC Place; MONROE; **177** K-12; elev. 1,003ft./306m.; mail Albia z 52531; ● 120
Avoca; Inc. Place; POTTAWATTAMIE; **176** J-4; elev. 1,138ft./347m.; 🅿; z 51521; Ⓟ 1,497; Ⓒ 1,610
Avon; RMC Place; POLK; ***176** I-10; ★ **DES**; mail Carlisle z 50047; ● 50
Avon Lake; RMC Place; POLK; ***176** I-10; ★ **DES**; mail Carlisle z 50047; ● 400
Ayrshire; Inc. Place; PALO ALTO; **176** C-6; elev. 1,315ft./401m.; 🅿; z 50515; Ⓟ 195; Ⓒ 202

B

Badger; Inc. Place; WEBSTER; **176** E-8; elev. 1,150ft./351m.; 🅿; z 50516; Ⓟ 569; Ⓒ 610
Bagley; Inc. Place; GUTHRIE; **176** H-7; elev. 1,106ft./337m.; 🅿; z 50026; Ⓟ 303; Ⓒ 354
Baldwin; Inc. Place; JACKSON; **177** G-18; elev. 740ft./226m.; 🅿; z 52207; Ⓟ 137; Ⓒ 127
Balltown; Inc. Place; DUBUQUE; **177** E-18; elev. 1,210ft./369m.; mail Sherrill z 52073; Ⓟ 64; Ⓒ 73
Bancroft; Inc. Place; KOSSUTH; **176** B-8; elev. 1,174ft./358m.; 🅿; z 50517; Ⓟ 857; Ⓒ 808
Bangor; RMC Place; MARSHALL; **177** G-11; mail Union z 50258; ● 30
Bankston; Inc. Place; DUBUQUE; **177** E-17; elev. 1,214ft./370m.; mail Epworth z 52045; Ⓟ 35; Ⓒ 27
Barnes City; Inc. Place; MAHASKA, POWESHIEK; **177** I-13; elev. 900ft./274m.; 🅿; z 50027; Ⓟ 221; Ⓒ 201
Barnum; Inc. Place; WEBSTER; **176** F-7; elev. 1,177ft./359m.; 🅿; z 50518; Ⓟ 174; Ⓒ 195
Bartlett; RMC Place; FREMONT; **176** L-3; elev. 946ft./288m.; 🅿; z 51654; ● 90
Bassett; Inc. Place; CHICKASAW; **177** C-13; elev. 1,023ft./312m.; mail Ionia z 50645; Ⓟ 74; Ⓒ 74
Batavia; Inc. Place; JEFFERSON; **177** K-14; 🅿; z 52533; Ⓟ 520; Ⓒ 500
Battle Creek; Inc. Place; IDA; **176** F-4; elev. 1,194ft./364m.; 🅿; z 51006; Ⓟ 818; Ⓒ 743
Baxter; Inc. Place; JASPER; **177** H-11; elev. 1,004ft./306m.; 🅿; z 50028; Ⓟ 938; Ⓒ 1,052
Bayard; Inc. Place; GUTHRIE; **176** H-7; elev. 1,135ft./346m.; 🅿; z 50029; Ⓟ 511; Ⓒ 536
Beacon; Inc. Place; MAHASKA; **177** J-12; elev. 761ft./232m.; 🅿; z 52534; Ⓟ 509; Ⓒ 518
Beaconsfield; Inc. Place; RINGGOLD; **176** L-8; elev. 1,212ft./369m.; 🅿; z 50074; Ⓟ 27; Ⓒ 11
Beaman; Inc. Place; GRUNDY; **177** G-12; elev. 1,000ft./305m.; 🅿; z 50609; Ⓟ 183; Ⓒ 210
Beaver; Inc. Place; BOONE; **176** G-8; elev. 1,024ft./312m.; 🅿; z 50031; Ⓟ 46; Ⓒ 53
Beaverdale; RMC Place; POLK; ***176** I-9; ★ **DES**; mail Des Moines z 50310; pop. incl. with Des Moines (Inc. Place)
Beckwith; RMC Place; JEFFERSON; ***177** K-15; mail Fairfield z 52556; ● 25
Bedford; Inc. Place; ⊡ TAYLOR; **176** M-6; elev. 1,100ft./335m.; 🅿; z 50833; Ⓟ 1,528; Ⓒ 1,620
Beebeetown; RMC Place; HARRISON; ***176** I-3; mail Logan z 51546
Beech; RMC Place; WARREN; **176** J-10; mail Pleasantville z 50225; ● 80
Bel Air Beach; RMC Place; BUENA VISTA; ***176** E-5; elev. 1,410ft./430m.; mail Storm Lake z 50588; ● 40
Belknap; RMC Place; DAVIS; **177** L-13; mail Bloomfield z 52537; ● 75
Bellefountain; RMC Place; MAHASKA; ***177** J-12; elev. 745ft./227m.; mail Leighton z 50143; ● 30
Belle Plaine; Inc. Place; BENTON; **177** H-14; elev. 844ft./257m.; 🅿; z 52208; Ⓟ 2,834; Ⓒ 2,878
Bellevue; Inc. Place; JACKSON; **177** F-19; elev. 622ft./190m.; 🅿; z 52031; Ⓟ 2,239; Ⓒ 2,350
Belmond; Inc. Place; WRIGHT; **176** D-10; elev. 1,190ft./363m.; 🅿 🅷; z 50421; Ⓟ 2,500; Ⓒ 2,560
Beloit; RMC Place; LYON; **176** B-1; mail Inwood z 51240; ● 70
Bennett; Inc. Place; CEDAR; **177** H-17; elev. 740ft./226m.; 🅿; z 52721; Ⓟ 395; Ⓒ 395
Benton; Inc. Place; RINGGOLD; **176** M-7; elev. 1,059ft./323m.; 🅿; z 50835; Ⓟ 39; Ⓒ 40
BENTON; **177** G-14; Ⓟ 22,429; Ⓒ 25,308; ◆ 26,035
Bentonsport; RMC Place; VAN BUREN; **177** M-15; mail Keosauqua z 52565; ● 40
Berkley; Inc. Place; BOONE; **176** H-8; elev. 973ft./297m.; mail Perry z 50220; Ⓟ 39; Ⓒ 24
Bernard; Inc. Place; DUBUQUE; **177** F-18; 🅿; z 52032; Ⓟ 123; Ⓒ 97
Bertram; Inc. Place; LINN; **177** M-20; elev. 730ft./223m.; ★ **CEDR**; mail Cedar Rapids z 52401; Ⓟ 201; Ⓒ 681; Ⓡ 263
Berwick; RMC Place; POLK; **177** A-20; elev. 850ft./259m.; 🅿; ★ **DES**; z 50032; ● 600
Bethelhem; RMC Place; WAYNE; ***177** L-11; mail Russell z 50238
Bettendorf; Inc. Place; SCOTT; **177** I-19; elev. 565ft./172m.; 🅿 ■; ★ **D-RI-M**; z 52722; Ⓟ 28,132; Ⓒ 31,275; Ⓡ 31,258; ◆ 31,539
Beverly; RMC Place; LINN; ★ **CEDR**; pop. incl. with Cedar Rapids (Inc. Place)
Bevington; Inc. Place; MADISON, WARREN; **176** J-9; elev. 840ft./256m.; 🅿; z 50033; Ⓟ 67; Ⓒ 58
Big Rock; RMC Place; SCOTT, CLINTON; **177** H-18; elev. 708ft./216m.; 🅿; z 52745; ● 70
Bingham; RMC Place; PAGE; ***176** M-4; mail Shenandoah z 51601
Birmingham; Inc. Place; VAN BUREN; **177** L-15; elev. 751ft./229m.; 🅿; z 52535; Ⓟ 386; Ⓒ 423
BLACK HAWK; **177** F-13; Ⓟ 123,798; Ⓒ 128,012; Ⓡ 128,013; ◆ 128,780
Bladensburg; RMC Place; WAPELLO; ***177** K-14; mail Ottumwa z 52501
Blairsburg; Inc. Place; HAMILTON; **176** F-9; elev. 1,229ft./375m.; 🅿; z 50034; Ⓟ 269; Ⓒ 235
Blairstown; Inc. Place; BENTON; **177** H-14; elev. 839ft./256m.; 🅿; z 52209; Ⓟ 672; Ⓒ 682
Blakesburg; Inc. Place; WAPELLO; **177** L-13; elev. 900ft./274m.; 🅿; z 52536; Ⓟ 333; Ⓒ 374
Blanchard; Inc. Place; PAGE; **176** M-5; elev. 984ft./300m.; 🅿; z 51630 & mail Northboro z 51647; Ⓟ 67; Ⓒ 61
Blencoe; Inc. Place; MONONA; **176** H-2; elev. 1,042ft./318m.; 🅿; z 51523; Ⓟ 250; Ⓒ 231
Blockton; Inc. Place; TAYLOR; **176** M-7; elev. 1,080ft./329m.; 🅿; z 50836; Ⓟ 213; Ⓒ 192
Bloomfield; Inc. Place; ⊡ DAVIS; **177** L-13; elev. 876ft./267m.; 🅿 🅷; z 52537; Ⓟ 2,580; Ⓒ 2,601
Blue Grass; Inc. Place; SCOTT; **177** I-18; elev. 780ft./238m.; 🅿; ★ **D-RI-M**; z 52726; Ⓟ 1,214; Ⓒ 1,169
Bluff Park; RMC Place; LEE; ***177** M-16; mail Montrose z 52639; pop. incl. with Montrose (Inc. Place)
Bluffs Yard; RMC Place; POTTAWATTAMIE; ★ **OMA**; pop. incl. with Council Bluffs (Inc. Place)
Bluffton; RMC Place; WINNESHIEK; **177** B-14; mail Decorah z 52101; ● 50
Bode; Inc. Place; HUMBOLDT; **176** D-8; elev. 1,155ft./352m.; 🅿; z 50519; Ⓟ 335; Ⓒ 327
Bolan; RMC Place; WORTH; ***177** B-11; mail Kensett z 50448
Bonair; RMC Place; HOWARD; ***177** B-14; mail Lime Springs z 52155
Bonaparte; Inc. Place; VAN BUREN; **177** M-15; elev. 600ft./183m.; 🅿; z 52620; Ⓟ 465; Ⓒ 458
Bondurant; Inc. Place; POLK; **176** I-10; 🅿; ★ **DES**; z 50035; Ⓟ 1,584; Ⓒ 1,846
Boone; Inc. Place; ⊡ BOONE; **176** G-9; elev. 960ft./293m.; 🅿 🅷; z 50036-37, z 50099; Ⓟ 12,392; Ⓒ 12,803
BOONE; **176** H-8; Ⓟ 25,186; Ⓒ 26,224; ◆ 26,136
Booneville; RMC Place; DALLAS; **176** I-9; elev. 854ft./260m.; 🅿; z 50038; ● 85
Botna; RMC Place; SHELBY; ***176** H-5; elev. 1,303ft./397m.; mail Manilla z 51454
Bouton; Inc. Place; DALLAS; **176** H-8; elev. 938ft./286m.; 🅿; z 50039; Ⓟ 149; Ⓒ 136
Boxholm; Inc. Place; BOONE; **176** G-8; elev. 1,145ft./349m.; 🅿; z 50040; Ⓟ 214; Ⓒ 215
Boyd; RMC Place; CHICKASAW; **177** C-14; mail New Hampton z 50659; ● 30
Boyden; Inc. Place; SIOUX; **176** C-3; elev. 1,420ft./433m.; 🅿; z 51234; Ⓟ 651; Ⓒ 672
Boyer; RMC Place; CRAWFORD; **176** G-5; mail Kiron z 51448; ● 30
Braddyville; Inc. Place; PAGE; **176** M-5; elev. 980ft./299m.; 🅿; z 51631; Ⓟ 219; Ⓒ 176
Bradford; RMC Place; FRANKLIN; **177** E-11; elev. 1,243ft./379m.; 🅿; z 50041; ● 130
Bradgate; Inc. Place; HUMBOLDT; **176** D-7; elev. 1,122ft./342m.; 🅿; z 50520; Ⓟ 124; Ⓒ 101
Brainard; RMC Place; FAYETTE; ***177** D-15; mail Elgin z 52141; rural
Brandon; Inc. Place; BUCHANAN; **177** F-14; elev. 836ft./255m.; 🅿; z 52210; Ⓟ 320; Ⓒ 311
Brayton; Inc. Place; AUDUBON; **176** I-6; elev. 1,220ft./372m.; 🅿; z 50042; Ⓟ 148; Ⓒ 145
Brazil; RMC Place; APPANOOSE; **177** L-12; mail Mystic z 52574; ● 90
Breda; Inc. Place; CARROLL; **176** G-6; elev. 1,365ft./416m.; 🅿; z 51436; Ⓟ 467; Ⓒ 477
Bremer; RMC Place; BREMER; **177** D-13; 🅿; z 50677; ● 30
BREMER; **177** E-13; Ⓟ 22,813; Ⓒ 23,325; ◆ 23,791
Bridgewater; Inc. Place; ADAIR; **176** K-6; elev. 1,220ft./372m.; 🅿; z 50837; Ⓟ 209; Ⓒ 178
Brighton; Inc. Place; WASHINGTON; **177** K-15; elev. 750ft./229m.; 🅿; z 52540; Ⓟ 684; Ⓒ 687
Bristow; Inc. Place; BUTLER; **177** D-12; elev. 1,030ft./314m.; 🅿; z 50611; Ⓟ 197; Ⓒ 202
Britt; Inc. Place; HANCOCK; **176** C-9; elev. 1,229ft./375m.; 🅿 🅷; z 50423; Ⓟ 2,133; Ⓒ 2,052
Bronson; Inc. Place; WOODBURY; **176** F-2; elev. 1,120ft./341m.; 🅿; z 51007; Ⓟ 209; Ⓒ 269
Brooklyn; Inc. Place; POWESHIEK; **177** I-13; elev. 859ft./262m.; 🅿; z 52211 & mail Guernsey z 52221; Ⓟ 1,439; Ⓒ 1,367
Brooks; RMC Place; ADAMS; **176** L-6; mail Corning z 50841; ● 60
Browns Station; RMC Place; CLINTON; ***177** G-19; elev. 688ft./210m.; mail Charlotte z 52731; rural
Brunsville; Inc. Place; PLYMOUTH; **176** D-2; elev. 1,280ft./390m.; 🅿; z 51008; Ⓟ 137; Ⓒ 146
Brushy; RMC Place; WEBSTER; ***176** F-8; mail Duncombe z 50532
Bryant; RMC Place; CLINTON; **177** H-19; elev. 800ft./244m.; 🅿; z 52727; ● 35
Bryantsburg; RMC Place; BUCHANAN; ***177** E-15; elev. 990ft./302m.; mail Hazleton z 50641; rural
Buchanan; RMC Place; CEDAR; **177** H-17; mail Tipton z 52772; ● 30
BUCHANAN; **177** E-14; Ⓟ 20,844; Ⓒ 21,093; ◆ 20,760
Buck Creek; RMC Place; BREMER; ***177** D-14; elev. 1,015ft./309m.; mail Sumner z 50674
Buckeye; Inc. Place; HARDIN; **176** F-10; elev. 1,154ft./352m.; 🅿; z 50006, z 50043; Ⓟ 105; Ⓒ 110
Buck Grove; Inc. Place; CRAWFORD; **176** H-4; elev. 1,302ft./397m.; mail Dow City z 51528; Ⓟ 20; Ⓒ 49
Buckingham; RMC Place; TAMA; **177** F-13; elev. 900ft./274m.; 🅿; z 50612; ● 40
BUENA VISTA; **176** D-5; Ⓟ 19,965; Ⓒ 20,411; ◆ 19,261
Buffalo; Inc. Place; SCOTT; **177** J-18; elev. 580ft./177m.; 🅿; ★ **D-RI-M**; z 52728; Ⓟ 1,260; Ⓒ 1,321
Buffalo Center; Inc. Place; WINNEBAGO; **176** B-9; elev. 1,196ft./365m.; 🅿; z 50424; Ⓟ 1,081; Ⓒ 963
Buffalo Heights; RMC Place; SCOTT; ***177** J-18; ★ **D-RI-M**; mail Buffalo z 52728; ● 150
Bunch; DAVIS; see Paris (RMC Place)
Burchinal; RMC Place; CERRO GORDO; **177** C-11; mail Rockwell z 50469; ● 40
Burlington; Inc. Place; ⊡ DES MOINES; **177** L-17; elev. 540ft./165m.; 🅿 🅷 ■; ★ **BUR**; z 52601; Ⓟ 27,208; Ⓒ 26,839; ◆ 25,613
Burnside; RMC Place; WEBSTER; **176** F-8; elev. 1,137ft./347m.; 🅿; z 50521; ● 130
Burr Oak; RMC Place; WINNESHIEK; **177** B-15; mail Decorah z 52101; ● 130
Burt; Inc. Place; KOSSUTH; **176** C-8; elev. 1,177ft./359m.; 🅿; z 50522; Ⓟ 575; Ⓒ 556
Bussey; Inc. Place; MARION; **177** K-12; elev. 840ft./256m.; 🅿; z 50044; Ⓟ 494; Ⓒ 450
BUTLER; **177** E-12; Ⓟ 15,731; Ⓒ 15,305; ◆ 14,453

C

Cairo; RMC Place; LOUISA; **177** K-16; mail Columbus Junction z 52738; ● 30
Calamus; Inc. Place; CLINTON; **177** H-18; elev. 700ft./213m.; 🅿; z 52729; Ⓟ 379; Ⓒ 394
Calhoun; RMC Place; HARRISON; ***176** I-3; mail Missouri Valley z 51555; rural
CALHOUN; **176** F-6; Ⓟ 11,508; Ⓒ 11,115; ◆ 9,575
California Junction; RMC Place; HARRISON; **176** I-2; elev. 1,006ft./307m.; mail Missouri Valley z 51555; ● 50
Callender; Inc. Place; WEBSTER; **176** F-8; elev. 1,150ft./351m.; 🅿; z 50523; Ⓟ 384; Ⓒ 424
Calmar; Inc. Place; WINNESHIEK; **177** C-15; elev. 1,258ft./383m.; 🅿; z 52132; Ⓟ 1,026; Ⓒ 1,058
Calumet; Inc. Place; O'BRIEN; **176** D-4; elev. 1,440ft./439m.; 🅿; z 51009; Ⓟ 160; Ⓒ 181
Camanche; Inc. Place; CLINTON; **177** H-20; elev. 600ft./183m.; 🅿; ★ **CLNT**; z 52730; Ⓟ 4,436; Ⓒ 4,215
Cambria; RMC Place; WAYNE; **176** L-10; elev. 1,090ft./332m.; mail Corydon z 50060; ● 50
Cambridge; Inc. Place; STORY; **176** H-10; elev. 871ft./265m.; 🅿; z 50046; Ⓟ 714; Ⓒ 819
Canby; RMC Place; ADAIR; ***176** J-7; mail Casey z 50048
Canton; RMC Place; JACKSON, JONES; **177** G-18; mail Monmouth z 52309; ● 40
Cantril; Inc. Place; VAN BUREN; **177** M-14; elev. 760ft./232m.; 🅿; z 52542 & mail Mount Sterling z 52573; Ⓟ 262; Ⓒ 257
Capital Heights; POLK; see Capitol Heights (RMC Place)
Capitol Heights (Capital Heights); RMC Place; POLK; **177** B-20; ★ **DES**; mail Des Moines z 50317; ● 900
Carbon; Inc. Place; ADAMS; **176** K-6; elev. 1,100ft./335m.; 🅿; z 50839; Ⓟ 60; Ⓒ 28
Carl; RMC Place; ADAMS; ***176** K-6; mail Corning z 50841
Carlisle; Inc. Place; WARREN, POLK; **176** J-10; elev. 800ft./244m.; 🅿; ★ **DES**; z 50047; Ⓟ 3,241; Ⓒ 3,497
Carmel; RMC Place; SIOUX; **176** C-2; mail Rock Valley z 51247; ● 70
Carnarvon; RMC Place; SAC; **176** F-5; elev. 1,260ft./384m.; 🅿; z 51450; ● 60
Carnes; RMC Place; SIOUX; ***176** D-2; mail Alton z 51003; rural
Carney; RMC Place; POLK; ***176** I-10; ★ **DES**; mail Ankeny z 50021; ● 160
Carnforth; RMC Place; POWESHIEK; ***177** I-13; mail Victor z 52347; rural
Carpenter; Inc. Place; MITCHELL; **177** B-11; elev. 1,190ft./363m.; 🅿; z 50426; Ⓟ 102; Ⓒ 130
Carroll; Inc. Place; ⊡ CARROLL; **176** G-6; elev. 1,261ft./384m.; 🅿 🅷; z 51401; Ⓟ 9,579; Ⓒ 10,106; Ⓡ 10,098
CARROLL; **176** G-6; Ⓟ 21,423; Ⓒ 21,421; ◆ 20,856
Carson; Inc. Place; POTTAWATTAMIE; **176** K-4; elev. 1,064ft./324m.; 🅿; z 51525; Ⓟ 705; Ⓒ 668
Carter Lake; Inc. Place; POTTAWATTAMIE; **176** J-3; elev. 981ft./299m.; 🅿; ★ **OMA**; z 51510; Ⓟ 3,200; Ⓒ 3,248
Cartersville; RMC Place; CERRO GORDO; ***177** D-11; mail Rockwell z 50469
Cascade; Inc. Place; DUBUQUE, JONES; **177** F-17; elev. 857ft./261m.; 🅿; z 52033; Ⓟ 1,812; Ⓒ 1,958
Casebeer; RMC Place; POLK; ***176** I-10; elev. 920ft./280m.; ★ **DES**; mail Altoona z 50009; rural
Casey; Inc. Place; GUTHRIE, ADAIR; **176** I-7; elev. 1,249ft./381m.; 🅿; z 50048; Ⓟ 441; Ⓒ 478
Casino Beach; RMC Place; BUENA VISTA; ***176** E-5; mail Storm Lake z 50588; ● 90
CASS; **176** J-6; Ⓟ 15,128; Ⓒ 14,684; ◆ 13,618
Castalia; Inc. Place; WINNESHIEK; **177** C-15; elev. 1,240ft./378m.; 🅿; z 52133; Ⓟ 177; Ⓒ 175
Castana; Inc. Place; MONONA; **176** G-3; elev. 1,166ft./355m.; 🅿; z 51010; Ⓟ 159; Ⓒ 178
Castle Hill; RMC Place; BLACK HAWK; ***177** E-13; ★ **WATL**; pop. incl. with Waterloo (Inc. Place)
Cedar; RMC Place; MAHASKA; **177** K-13; elev. 820ft./250m.; 🅿; z 52543; ● 120
CEDAR; **177** H-17; Ⓟ 17,381; Ⓒ 18,187; ◆ 17,698
Cedar Bluff; RMC Place; CEDAR; **177** H-16; mail Tipton z 52772; ● 60
Cedar Crest Woods; RMC Place; LINN; ***177** H-16; elev. 750ft./229m.; ★ **CEDR**; mail Cedar Rapids z 52401; ● 80
Cedar Falls; Inc. Place; BLACK HAWK; **177** E-13; elev. 900ft./274m.; 🅿 🅷 🅲 12,260 ■; ★ **WATL**; z 50613-14; Ⓟ 34,298; Ⓒ 36,145; ◆ 38,132
Cedar Falls Junction; RMC Place; BLACK HAWK; ***177** F-13; ★ **WATL**; pop. incl. with Waterloo (Inc. Place)
Cedar Hills; RMC Place; LINN; ***177** H-15; ★ **CEDR**; pop. incl. with Cedar Rapids (Inc. Place)
Cedar Rapids; Inc. Place; ⊡ LINN; **177** H-15; elev. 730ft./223m.; 🅿 🅷 🅲 6,445 ■; ★ **CEDR**; z 52401-11, z 52497-99; Ⓟ 108,751; Ⓒ 120,758; ◆ 132,936
Cedar Terrace; RMC Place; LINN; ***177** H-15; elev. 800ft./244m.; ★ **CEDR**; mail Cedar Rapids z 52401; pop. incl. with Cedar Rapids (Inc. Place)
Cedar Valley; RMC Place; CEDAR; **177** I-17; mail West Branch z 52358; ● 30
Cedar View; RMC Place; FLOYD; ***177** C-12; elev. 1,000ft./305m.; mail Charles City z 50616; ● 50
Centerdale; RMC Place; CEDAR; ***177** I-16; mail West Branch z 52358, West Liberty z 52776; rural
Center Grove; RMC Place; DUBUQUE; ***177** E-18; ★ **DUB**; mail Dubuque z 52001, z 52003; pop. incl. with Dubuque (Inc. Place)
Center Junction; Inc. Place; JONES; **177** G-17; elev. 900ft./274m.; 🅿; z 52212; Ⓟ 166; Ⓒ 131
Center Point; Inc. Place; LINN; **177** G-15; elev. 814ft./248m.; 🅿; ★ **CEDR**; z 52213; Ⓟ 1,693; Ⓒ 2,007
Centerville; Inc. Place; ⊡ APPANOOSE; **177** M-12; elev. 1,010ft./308m.; 🅿 🅷; z 52544; Ⓟ 5,936; Ⓒ 5,924
Centerville; RMC Place; BOONE; ***176** G-9; mail Boone z 50036; ● 30
Central; RMC Place; SCOTT; ***177** I-19; ★ **D-RI-M**; mail Davenport z 52801; pop. incl. with Davenport (Inc. Place)
Central City; Inc. Place; LINN; **177** G-16; elev. 850ft./259m.; 🅿; z 52214; Ⓟ 1,063; Ⓒ 1,157
Central College; RMC Place; MARION; ***177** J-12; mail Pella z 50219; pop. incl. with Pella (Inc. Place)
Central Heights (West Mason City); RMC Place; CERRO GORDO; ***177** C-11; elev. 1,180ft./360m.; mail Mason City z 50401; pop. incl. with Mason City (Inc. Place)
Centralia; Inc. Place; DUBUQUE; **177** F-18; elev. 1,120ft./341m.; mail Peosta z 52068; Ⓟ 123; Ⓒ 101
CERRO GORDO; **177** C-11; Ⓟ 46,733; Ⓒ 46,447; ◆ 43,243
Chapin; RMC Place; FRANKLIN; **177** D-11; elev. 1,165ft./355m.; 🅿; z 50427; ● 130
Chariton; Inc. Place; ⊡ LUCAS; **177** K-11; elev. 1,041ft./317m.; 🅿 🅷; z 50049; Ⓟ 4,616; Ⓒ 4,573
Charles City; Inc. Place; ⊡ FLOYD; **177** C-12; elev. 1,000ft./305m.; 🅿 🅷; z 50616 & mail Colwell z 50620; Ⓟ 7,878; Ⓒ 7,812
Charleston; RMC Place; LEE; **177** M-16; mail Argyle z 52619; ● 50
Charlotte; Inc. Place; CLINTON; **177** H-19; elev. 700ft./213m.; 🅿; z 52731; Ⓟ 359; Ⓒ 421
Charter Oak; Inc. Place; CRAWFORD; **176** G-4; elev. 1,264ft./385m.; 🅿; z 51439; Ⓟ 497; Ⓒ 530
Chatsworth; Inc. Place; SIOUX; **176** D-1; elev. 1,162ft./354m.; 🅿; z 51011; Ⓟ 103; Ⓒ 89
Chelsea; Inc. Place; TAMA; **177** H-13; elev. 792ft./241m.; 🅿; z 52215; Ⓟ 336; Ⓒ 287
Cherokee; Inc. Place; ⊡ CHEROKEE; **176** D-4; elev. 1,200ft./366m.; 🅿 🅷; z 51012; Ⓟ 6,026; Ⓒ 5,369
CHEROKEE; **176** E-3; Ⓟ 14,098; Ⓒ 13,035; ◆ 11,264
Chester; Inc. Place; HOWARD; **177** B-13; elev. 1,230ft./375m.; 🅿; z 52134; Ⓟ 158; Ⓒ 151
Chickasaw; RMC Place; CHICKASAW; **177** C-13; mail Ionia z 50645; ● 40
CHICKASAW; **177** C-13; Ⓟ 13,295; Ⓒ 13,095; ◆ 11,838
Chillicothe; Inc. Place; WAPELLO; **177** K-13; elev. 690ft./210m.; 🅿; z 52548; Ⓟ 119; Ⓒ 90
Church (Churchtown); RMC Place; ALLAMAKEE; ***177** B-16; mail Lansing z 52151
Churchtown; ALLAMAKEE; see Church (RMC Place)
Churchville; RMC Place; WARREN; **176** J-9; mail Norwalk z 50211; ● 50
Churdan; Inc. Place; GREENE; **176** G-7; elev. 1,110ft./338m.; 🅿; z 50050; Ⓟ 423; Ⓒ 418
Cincinnati; Inc. Place; APPANOOSE; **177** M-12; elev. 1,032ft./315m.; 🅿; z 52549; Ⓟ 363; Ⓒ 428
Clare; Inc. Place; WEBSTER; **176** E-7; elev. 1,216ft./371m.; 🅿; z 50524; Ⓟ 161; Ⓒ 190
Clarence; Inc. Place; CEDAR; **177** H-17; elev. 825ft./251m.; 🅿; z 52216; Ⓟ 936; Ⓒ 1,008
Clarinda; Inc. Place; ⊡ PAGE; **176** L-5; elev. 1,012ft./308m.; 🅿 🅷; z 51632; Ⓟ 5,104; Ⓒ 5,690
Clarion; Inc. Place; ⊡ WRIGHT; **176** E-9; elev. 1,166ft./355m.; 🅿 🅷; z 50525-26; Ⓟ 2,703; Ⓒ 2,968
Clarkdale; RMC Place; APPANOOSE; ***177** L-12; mail Centerville z 52544; ● 100
CLARKE; **176** K-9; Ⓟ 8,287; Ⓒ 9,133; ◆ 8,707
Clarksville; Inc. Place; BUTLER; **177** D-12; elev. 933ft./284m.; 🅿; z 50619; Ⓟ 1,382; Ⓒ 1,441
CLAY; **176** C-5; Ⓟ 17,585; Ⓒ 17,372; ◆ 16,380
Clayton; Inc. Place; CLAYTON; **177** D-17; elev. 656ft./200m.; mail Garnavillo z 52049; Ⓟ 41; Ⓒ 55
CLAYTON; **177** D-16; Ⓟ 19,054; Ⓒ 18,678; ◆ 17,261
Clayton Center; RMC Place; CLAYTON; **177** D-16; mail Elkader z 52043; ● 30
Clearfield; Inc. Place; TAYLOR, RINGGOLD; **176** L-7; elev. 1,253ft./382m.; 🅿; z 50840; Ⓟ 417; Ⓒ 371
Clear Lake; Inc. Place; CERRO GORDO; **176** C-10; elev. 1,236ft./377m.; 🅿; z 50428; Ⓟ 8,183; Ⓒ 8,161
Cleghorn; Inc. Place; CHEROKEE; **176** D-3; elev. 1,450ft./442m.; 🅿; z 51014; Ⓟ 275; Ⓒ 250
Clemons (Clemons Grove); Inc. Place; MARSHALL; **177** G-11; elev. 960ft./293m.; 🅿; z 50051; Ⓟ 173; Ⓒ 148
Clemons Grove; MARSHALL; see Clemons (Inc. Place)
Clermont; Inc. Place; FAYETTE; **177** C-15; elev. 847ft./258m.; 🅿; z 52135; Ⓟ 523; Ⓒ 716
Cleves; RMC Place; HARDIN; **177** F-11; mail Ackley z 50601; ● 20
Climbing Hill; RMC Place; WOODBURY; **176** F-2; elev. 1,140ft./347m.; 🅿; z 51015 & mail Hornick z 51026; ● 100
Clinton; Inc. Place; ⊡ CLINTON; **177** H-20; elev. 600ft./183m.; 🅿 🅷 🅲 847 ■; ★ **CLNT**; z 52732-34, z 52736, z 52771; Ⓟ 29,201; Ⓒ 27,772; ◆ 25,901
CLINTON; **177** H-19; Ⓟ 51,040; Ⓒ 50,149; ◆ 48,207
Clio; Inc. Place; WAYNE; **176** M-10; elev. 1,114ft./340m.; 🅿; z 50052; Ⓟ 103; Ⓒ 91
Clive; Inc. Place; POLK, DALLAS; **177** B-18; elev. 850ft./259m.; 🅿; ★ **DES**; z 50324-25; Ⓟ 7,462; Ⓒ 12,855
Cloverdale; RMC Place; OSCEOLA; ***176** B-4; mail Sibley z 51249
Cloverhills; RMC Place; POLK; ***176** I-9; ★ **DES**; mail West Des Moines z 50265; pop. incl. with West Des Moines (Inc. Place)
Clutier; Inc. Place; TAMA; **177** G-13; elev. 861ft./262m.; 🅿; z 52217; Ⓟ 219; Ⓒ 229
Coalville; CDP; WEBSTER; **176** F-8; mail Fort Dodge z 50501; Ⓒ 591
Coburg; Inc. Place; MONTGOMERY; **176** L-5; elev. 1,009ft./308m.; mail Red Oak z 51566; Ⓟ 58; Ⓒ 31
Coggon; Inc. Place; LINN; **177** F-16; elev. 916ft./279m.; 🅿; z 52218; Ⓟ 645; Ⓒ 745
Coin; Inc. Place; PAGE; **176** M-5; elev. 1,040ft./317m.; 🅿; z 51636; Ⓟ 278; Ⓒ 252
Colesburg; Inc. Place; DELAWARE; **177** E-17; elev. 1,150ft./351m.; 🅿; z 52035; Ⓟ 439; Ⓒ 412
Colfax; Inc. Place; JASPER; **177** I-11; elev. 792ft./241m.; 🅿; z 50054; Ⓟ 2,462; Ⓒ 2,223
College Springs; Inc. Place; PAGE; **176** M-5; elev. 1,150ft./351m.; 🅿; z 51637; Ⓟ 230; Ⓒ 246
Collins; Inc. Place; STORY; **176** H-10; elev. 1,005ft./306m.; 🅿; z 50055; Ⓟ 455; Ⓒ 499
Colo; Inc. Place; STORY; **176** G-10; elev. 1,043ft./318m.; 🅿; z 50056; Ⓟ 771; Ⓒ 868
Colonial Village; RMC Place; POLK; ★ **DES**; mail West Des Moines z 50266; pop. incl. with West Des Moines (Inc. Place)
Columbia; RMC Place; MARION; **177** K-11; elev. 952ft./290m.; 🅿; z 50057; ● 100
Columbus City; Inc. Place; LOUISA; **177** J-16; elev. 730ft./223m.; 🅿; z 52737 & mail Columbus Junction z 52738; Ⓟ 328; Ⓒ 376
Columbus Junction; Inc. Place; LOUISA; **177** J-16; elev. 590ft./180m.; 🅿; z 52738; Ⓟ 1,616; Ⓒ 1,900
Colwell; Inc. Place; FLOYD; **177** C-13; elev. 1,150ft./351m.; 🅿; z 50620; Ⓟ 94; Ⓒ 76
Commerce; RMC Place; POLK; ***176** I-9; ★ **DES**; mail West Des Moines z 50265; pop. incl. with West Des Moines (Inc. Place)
Cone; MUSCATINE; see Conesville (Inc. Place)
Conesville (Cone); Inc. Place; MUSCATINE; **177** J-16; elev. 610ft./186m.; 🅿; z 52739; Ⓟ 334; Ⓒ 424
Confidence; RMC Place; WAYNE; **177** L-11; mail Melrose z 52569; ● 25
Conger; RMC Place; WARREN; ***176** J-9; mail Saint Charles z 50240; ● 50
Conover; RMC Place; WINNESHIEK; ***177** C-15; mail Calmar z 52132
Conrad; Inc. Place; GRUNDY; **177** G-12; elev. 1,000ft./305m.; 🅿; z 50621; Ⓟ 964; Ⓒ 1,055
Conroy; RMC Place; IOWA; **177** I-14; elev. 880ft./268m.; 🅿; z 52220; ● 250
Conway; Inc. Place; TAYLOR; **176** L-7; elev. 1,140ft./347m.; mail Bedford z 50833; Ⓟ 57; Ⓒ 63
Cool; RMC Place; WARREN; ***176** K-10; mail Indianola z 50125; rural
Coon Rapids; Inc. Place; CARROLL, GUTHRIE; **176** H-6; elev. 1,200ft./366m.; 🅿; z 50058; Ⓟ 1,266; Ⓒ 1,305
Cooper; RMC Place; GREENE; **176** H-7; elev. 1,079ft./329m.; 🅿; z 50059; ● 35
Coppock; Inc. Place; HENRY, JEFFERSON, WASHINGTON; **177** K-15; elev. 620ft./189m.; mail Wayland z 52654; Ⓟ 50; Ⓒ 57
Coralville; Inc. Place; JOHNSON; **177** I-16; elev. 700ft./213m.; 🅿; ★ **IACY**; z 52241; Ⓟ 10,347; Ⓒ 15,123
Corley; RMC Place; SHELBY; **176** I-4; mail Harlan z 51537; ● 30
Cornelia; RMC Place; WRIGHT; **176** D-9; mail Clarion z 50525; ● 80
Cornell; RMC Place; CLAY; ***176** D-5; mail Sioux Rapids z 50585
Corning; Inc. Place; ⊡ ADAMS; **176** L-6; elev. 1,117ft./340m.; 🅿 🅷; z 50841; Ⓟ 1,806; Ⓒ 1,783
Correctionville; Inc. Place; WOODBURY; **176** F-3; elev. 1,122ft./342m.; 🅿; z 51016; Ⓟ 897; Ⓒ 851
Corwith; Inc. Place; HANCOCK; **176** D-9; elev. 1,174ft./358m.; 🅿; z 50430; Ⓟ 354; Ⓒ 350
Corydon; Inc. Place; ⊡ WAYNE; **176** L-10; elev. 1,093ft./333m.; 🅿 🅷; z 50060; Ⓟ 1,675; Ⓒ 1,591
Cosgrove; RMC Place; JOHNSON; ***177** I-15; elev. 805ft./245m.; mail Oxford z 52322; ● 30
Cotter; Inc. Place; LOUISA; **177** J-16; elev. 694ft./212m.; mail Columbus Junction z 52738; Ⓟ 53; Ⓒ 48
Cottonville; RMC Place; JACKSON; ***177** F-18; elev. 1,005ft./306m.; mail La Motte z 52054; rural
Coulter; Inc. Place; FRANKLIN; **176** E-10; elev. 1,239ft./378m.; 🅿; z 50431; Ⓟ 252; Ⓒ 262
Council Bluffs; Inc. Place; ⊡ POTTAWATTAMIE; **176** J-3; elev. 986ft./301m.; 🅿 🅷 ■; ★ **OMA**; z 51501-03 & mail Harlan z 51593; Ⓟ 54,315; Ⓒ 58,268; ◆ 58,594
Country Estate Acres; RMC Place; LINN; ***177** G-15; elev. 800ft./244m.; ★ **CEDR**; mail Cedar Rapids z 52401; ● 40
Country Rock Estates; RMC Place; LINN; ***177** G-15; elev. 769ft./234m.; ★ **CEDR**; mail Toddville z 52341; ● 60
Covington; RMC Place; LINN; **177** G-15; ★ **CEDR**; mail Palo z 52324; ● 200
Craig; Inc. Place; PLYMOUTH; **176** D-2; elev. 1,400ft./427m.; mail Le Mars z 51031; Ⓟ 116; Ⓒ 102
Crandic; RMC Place; LINN; ★ **CEDR**; pop. incl. with Cedar Rapids (Inc. Place)
Cranston; RMC Place; MUSCATINE; **177** J-17; elev. 660ft./201m.; mail Letts z 52754; ● 40
CRAWFORD; **176** G-5; Ⓟ 16,775; Ⓒ 16,942; ◆ 16,402
Crawfordsville; Inc. Place; WASHINGTON; **177** K-16; elev. 731ft./223m.; 🅿; z 52621; Ⓟ 265; Ⓒ 295
Crescent; Inc. Place; POTTAWATTAMIE; **176** J-3; elev. 1,010ft./308m.; 🅿; z 51526; Ⓟ 113; Ⓒ 537
Cresco; Inc. Place; ⊡ HOWARD; **177** B-14; elev. 1,300ft./396m.; 🅿 🅷; z 52136; Ⓟ 3,669; Ⓒ 3,905
Creston; Inc. Place; ⊡ UNION; **176** K-7; elev. 1,314ft./401m.; 🅿 🅷; z 50801; Ⓟ 7,911; Ⓒ 7,597
Crestview Acres; RMC Place; LINN; ***177** G-15; elev. 850ft./259m.; ★ **CEDR**; mail Cedar Rapids z 52401; ● 60
Crestwood; RMC Place; POLK; ***176** I-9; ★ **DES**; mail Des Moines z 50311; pop. incl. with Windsor Heights (Inc. Place)
Crestwood Acres; RMC Place; LINN; ***177** G-15; elev. 800ft./244m.; ★ **CEDR**; mail Cedar Rapids z 52401; pop. incl. with Cedar Rapids (Inc. Place)
Crocker; RMC Place; POLK; ***176** H-9; ★ **DES**; mail Polk City z 50226
Cromwell; Inc. Place; UNION; **176** K-7; elev. 1,253ft./382m.; 🅿; z 50842; Ⓟ 120; Ⓒ 120
Croton; RMC Place; LEE; **177** M-15; mail Farmington z 52626; ● 50
Crystal Lake; Inc. Place; HANCOCK; **176** C-9; elev. 1,258ft./383m.; 🅿; z 50432; Ⓟ 266; Ⓒ 285
Cumberland; Inc. Place; CASS; **176** J-6; elev. 1,316ft./401m.; 🅿; z 50843; Ⓟ 295; Ⓒ 281
Cumming; Inc. Place; WARREN; **176** J-9; elev. 980ft./299m.; 🅿; ★ **DES**; z 50061; Ⓟ 132; Ⓒ 162
Curlew; Inc. Place; PALO ALTO; **176** D-6; elev. 1,243ft./379m.; 🅿; z 50527; Ⓟ 56; Ⓒ 62
Cushing; Inc. Place; WOODBURY; **176** F-3; elev. 1,327ft./404m.; 🅿; z 51018; Ⓟ 220; Ⓒ 246
Cylinder; Inc. Place; PALO ALTO; **176** C-7; elev. 1,188ft./362m.; 🅿; z 50528; Ⓟ 112; Ⓒ 110

D

Dahlonega; RMC Place; WAPELLO; ***177** K-13; mail Ottumwa z 52501
Dakota City; Inc. Place; ⊡ HUMBOLDT; **176** E-8; elev. 1,064ft./324m.; 🅿; z 50529; Ⓟ 1,024; Ⓒ 911
Dallas; RMC Place; MARION; ***177** K-11; elev. 920ft./280m.; 🅿; z 50062 & mail Melcher z 50163
DALLAS; **176** I-8; Ⓟ 29,755; Ⓒ 40,750; ◆ 61,546
Dallas Center; Inc. Place; DALLAS; **176** I-9; elev. 1,072ft./327m.; 🅿; z 50063; Ⓟ 1,454; Ⓒ 1,595
Dalton; PLYMOUTH; see West Le Mars (RMC Place)
Dana; Inc. Place; GREENE; **176** G-8; elev. 1,123ft./342m.; 🅿; z 50064; Ⓟ 71; Ⓒ 84
Danbury; Inc. Place; WOODBURY; **176** G-3; elev. 1,162ft./354m.; 🅿; z 51019; Ⓟ 430; Ⓒ 384
Danville; Inc. Place; DES MOINES; **177** L-16; elev. 726ft./221m.; 🅿; z 52623; Ⓟ 926; Ⓒ 914
Darbyville; RMC Place; APPANOOSE; ***177** L-12; mail Centerville z 52544; ● 30
Davenport; Inc. Place; ⊡ SCOTT; **177** I-19; elev. 589ft./180m.; 🅿 🅷 🅲 28,993 ■; ★ **D-RI-M**; z 52801-09; Ⓟ 95,333; Ⓒ 98,359; ◆ 99,827
DAVIS; **177** L-13; Ⓟ 8,312; Ⓒ 8,541; ◆ 8,512
Davis City; Inc. Place; DECATUR; **176** M-9; elev. 914ft./279m.; 🅿; z 50065; Ⓟ 257; Ⓒ 275
Dawson; Inc. Place; DALLAS; **176** H-8; elev. 948ft./289m.; 🅿; z 50066; Ⓟ 174; Ⓒ 155
Dayton; Inc. Place; WEBSTER; **176** F-8; elev. 1,100ft./335m.; 🅿; z 50530; Ⓟ 818; Ⓒ 884
Daytonville; RMC Place; WASHINGTON; **177** J-15; mail Wellman z 52356; pop. incl. with Wellman (Inc. Place)
Dean; RMC Place; APPANOOSE; ***177** M-12; mail Moulton z 52572; rural
Decatur; DECATUR; see Decatur City (Inc. Place)
DECATUR; **176** L-9; Ⓟ 8,338; Ⓒ 8,689; ◆ 8,435
Decatur City (Decatur); Inc. Place; DECATUR; **176** M-9; elev. 1,137ft./347m.; mail Decatur z 50067; Ⓟ 177; Ⓒ 199
Decorah; Inc. Place; ⊡ WINNESHIEK; **177** B-15; elev. 904ft./276m.; 🅿 🅷 🅲 2,500; z 52101; Ⓟ 8,063; Ⓒ 8,172
Dedham; Inc. Place; CARROLL; **176** H-6; elev. 1,300ft./396m.; 🅿; z 51440; Ⓟ 264; Ⓒ 280
Deep River; Inc. Place; POWESHIEK; **177** I-13; elev. 900ft./274m.; 🅿; z 52222; Ⓟ 345; Ⓒ 288
Deer Lake Estates; RMC Place; LINN; ***177** G-16; elev. 800ft./244m.; ★ **CEDR**; mail Cedar Rapids z 52401; ● 60
Defiance; Inc. Place; SHELBY; **176** H-4; elev. 1,283ft./391m.; 🅿; z 51527; Ⓟ 312; Ⓒ 346
Delaware; Inc. Place; DELAWARE; **177** F-16; elev. 1,065ft./325m.; 🅿; z 52036, z 52057; Ⓟ 176; Ⓒ 188
DELAWARE; **177** E-16; Ⓟ 18,035; Ⓒ 18,404; ◆ 17,112
Delhi; Inc. Place; DELAWARE; **177** F-16; elev. 997ft./304m.; 🅿; z 52223; Ⓟ 485; Ⓒ 458
Delmar; Inc. Place; CLINTON; **177** G-18; elev. 800ft./244m.; 🅿; z 52037; Ⓟ 517; Ⓒ 514
Deloit; Inc. Place; CRAWFORD; **176** G-5; elev. 1,202ft./366m.; 🅿; z 51441; Ⓟ 296; Ⓒ 288
Delphos; Inc. Place; RINGGOLD; **176** M-7; elev. 1,133ft./345m.; 🅿; z 50860; Ⓟ 23; Ⓒ 25
Delta; Inc. Place; KEOKUK; **177** J-13; elev. 800ft./244m.; 🅿; z 52550; Ⓟ 409; Ⓒ 410
Denison; Inc. Place; ⊡ CRAWFORD; **176** G-4; elev. 1,280ft./390m.; 🅿 🅷; z 51442; Ⓟ 6,604; Ⓒ 7,339
Denmark; RMC Place; LEE; **177** L-16; 🅿; z 52624; ● 400
Denver; Inc. Place; BREMER; **177** E-13; elev. 950ft./290m.; 🅿; z 50622; Ⓟ 1,600; Ⓒ 1,627
Depew; RMC Place; PALO ALTO; ***176** C-7; mail Cylinder z 50528
Derby; Inc. Place; LUCAS; **176** L-10; elev. 1,060ft./323m.; 🅿; z 50068; Ⓟ 135; Ⓒ 131
Des Moines; Inc. Place; **STATE CAPITAL**; ⊡ POLK; **176** I-10; elev. 803ft./245m.; 🅿 🅷 🅲 9,221 ■; ★ **DES**; z 50301-25, z 50327-36, z 50339-40, z 50347, z 50359-64, z 50367-69, z 50380-81, z 50391-98, z 50936, z 50940, z 50947, z 50950, z 50980-81; Ⓟ 193,187; Ⓒ 198,682; ◆ 207,636
DES MOINES; **177** L-17; Ⓟ 42,614; Ⓒ 42,351; ◆ 40,344
De Soto; Inc. Place; DALLAS; **176** I-8; elev. 975ft./297m.; 🅿; z 50069; Ⓟ 1,033; Ⓒ 1,009
Dewar; RMC Place; BLACK HAWK; **177** E-14; elev. 897ft./273m.; 🅿; ★ **WATL**; z 50623; ● 250
Dewey; RMC Place; CASS; ***176** K-6; elev. 1,240ft./378m.; mail Massena z 50853; rural
De Witt; Inc. Place; CLINTON; **177** H-19; elev. 719ft./219m.; 🅿 🅷; z 52742; Ⓟ 4,514; Ⓒ 5,049
Dexter; Inc. Place; DALLAS; **176** I-8; elev. 1,150ft./351m.; 🅿; z 50070; Ⓟ 628; Ⓒ 689
Diagonal; Inc. Place; RINGGOLD; **176** L-7; elev. 1,094ft./333m.; 🅿; z 50845; Ⓟ 298; Ⓒ 312
Dickens; Inc. Place; CLAY; **176** C-5; elev. 1,340ft./408m.; 🅿; z 51333; Ⓟ 214; Ⓒ 202
DICKINSON; **176** B-5; Ⓟ 14,909; Ⓒ 16,424; ◆ 16,461
Dike; Inc. Place; GRUNDY; **177** F-12; elev. 950ft./290m.; 🅿; z 50624; Ⓟ 875; Ⓒ 944
Dillon; RMC Place; MARSHALL; **177** H-12; mail Marshalltown z 50158; ● 30
Dinsdale; RMC Place; TAMA; **177** F-13; mail Reinbeck z 50669; ● 40
Dixon; Inc. Place; SCOTT; **177** H-18; elev. 684ft./208m.; 🅿; z 52745; Ⓟ 202; Ⓒ 276
Dodge Park; RMC Place; POTTAWATTAMIE; ★ **OMA**; mail Council Bluffs z 51501; pop. incl. with Council Bluffs (Inc. Place)
Dodgeville; RMC Place; DES MOINES; ***177** L-17; mail Sperry z 52650
Dolliver; Inc. Place; EMMET; **176** B-7; elev. 1,287ft./392m.; 🅿; z 50531; Ⓟ 103; Ⓒ 77
Donahue; Inc. Place; SCOTT; **177** I-18; elev. 711ft./217m.; 🅿; z 52746; Ⓟ 316; Ⓒ 293
Donnan; RMC Place; FAYETTE; ***177** D-15; mail Fayette z 52142; rural
Donnellson; Inc. Place; LEE; **177** M-16; elev. 704ft./215m.; 🅿; z 52625 & mail Argyle z 52619; Ⓟ 940; Ⓒ 963
Doon; Inc. Place; LYON; **176** B-2; elev. 1,300ft./396m.; 🅿; z 51235; Ⓟ 476; Ⓒ 533
Dorchester; RMC Place; ALLAMAKEE; **177** B-16; elev. 760ft./232m.; 🅿; z 52140; ● 70
Douds; CDP; VAN BUREN; **177** L-14; elev. 600ft./183m.; 🅿; z 52551; Ⓒ 165
Dougherty; Inc. Place; CERRO GORDO; **177** D-11; elev. 1,099ft./335m.; 🅿; z 50433; Ⓟ 107; Ⓒ 80
Douglass; RMC Place; FAYETTE; ***177** C-15; elev. 970ft./296m.; mail West Union z 52175
Dow City; Inc. Place; CRAWFORD; **176** H-4; elev. 1,131ft./345m.; 🅿; z 51528; Ⓟ 439; Ⓒ 503
Downey; RMC Place; CEDAR; **177** I-16; mail West Branch z 52358; ● 100
Downtown; RMC Place; LINN; ★ **CEDR**; mail Cedar Rapids z 52401, z 52407; pop. incl. with Cedar Rapids (Inc. Place)
Dows; Inc. Place; WRIGHT, FRANKLIN; **176** E-10; elev. 1,150ft./351m.; 🅿; z 50071; Ⓟ 660; Ⓒ 675
Drakesville; Inc. Place; DAVIS; **177** L-13; elev. 858ft./262m.; 🅿; z 52552; Ⓟ 172; Ⓒ 185
Dubuque; Inc. Place; ⊡ DUBUQUE; **177** E-18; elev. 650ft./198m.; 🅿 🅷 🅲 4,372 ■; ★ **DUB**; z 52001-04, z 52099; Ⓟ 57,546; Ⓒ 57,686; ◆ 55,684
DUBUQUE; **177** F-17; Ⓟ 86,403; Ⓒ 89,143; Ⓡ 89,156; ◆ 91,225
Dubuque Junction; RMC Place; DUBUQUE; ★ **DUB**; pop. incl. with Dubuque (Inc. Place)
Dumont; Inc. Place; BUTLER; **177** E-11; elev. 978ft./298m.; 🅿; z 50625; Ⓟ 705; Ⓒ 676
Dunbar; RMC Place; MARSHALL; **177** H-12; mail Marshalltown z 50158; ● 50
Duncan; RMC Place; HANCOCK; **176** C-9; mail Britt z 50423; ● 80
Duncombe; Inc. Place; WEBSTER; **176** F-8; elev. 1,110ft./338m.; 🅿; z 50532; Ⓟ 488; Ⓒ 474
Dundee; Inc. Place; DELAWARE; **177** E-16; elev. 998ft./304m.; 🅿; z 52038; Ⓟ 174; Ⓒ 179
Dunkerton; Inc. Place; BLACK HAWK; **177** E-14; elev. 950ft./290m.; 🅿; z 50626; Ⓟ 746; Ⓒ 749; Ⓡ 750
Dunlap; Inc. Place; HARRISON; **176** H-4; elev. 1,158ft./353m.; 🅿; z 51529; Ⓟ 1,251; Ⓒ 1,139
Durango; Inc. Place; DUBUQUE; **177** E-18; elev. 644ft./196m.; 🅿; z 52039; Ⓟ 34; Ⓒ 24
Durant; Inc. Place; CEDAR, MUSCATINE, SCOTT; **177** I-18; elev. 700ft./213m.; 🅿; z 52747; Ⓟ 1,549; Ⓒ 1,677
Durham; RMC Place; MARION; ***177** J-12; mail Harvey z 50119; rural
Dutchman Landing; RMC Place; MARION; ***177** J-11; elev. 862ft./263m.; mail Pella z 50219; ● 50
Dutchtown; RMC Place; DELAWARE; ***177** E-16; mail Manchester z 52057; rural
Dyersville; Inc. Place; DUBUQUE, DELAWARE; **177** F-17; elev. 967ft./295m.; 🅿; z 52040; Ⓟ 3,703; Ⓒ 4,035
Dysart; Inc. Place; TAMA; **177** G-13; elev. 981ft./299m.; 🅿; z 52224; Ⓟ 1,230; Ⓒ 1,303

E

Eagle Center; RMC Place; BLACK HAWK; ***177** F-13; mail Waterloo z 50701
Eagle Grove; Inc. Place; WRIGHT; **176** E-9; elev. 1,115ft./340m.; 🅿; z 50533; Ⓟ 3,671; Ⓒ 3,712
Eagle Point; RMC Place; DUBUQUE; ***177** E-18; ★ **DUB**; mail Dubuque z 52001; pop. incl. with Dubuque (Inc. Place)
Earlham; Inc. Place; MADISON; **176** J-8; elev. 1,098ft./335m.; 🅿; z 50072; Ⓟ 1,157; Ⓒ 1,298
Earling; Inc. Place; SHELBY; **176** H-4; elev. 1,408ft./429m.; 🅿; z 51530; Ⓟ 466; Ⓒ 471
Earlville; Inc. Place; DELAWARE; **177** F-16; 🅿; z 52041; Ⓟ 822; Ⓒ 900
Early; Inc. Place; SAC; **176** F-5; elev. 1,331ft./406m.; 🅿; z 50535; Ⓟ 649; Ⓒ 605
East Amana; RMC Place; IOWA; **177** H-15; mail Amana z 52203; ● 60
East Des Moines; RMC Place; POLK; ***176** I-10; ★ **DES**; mail Des Moines z 50309; pop. incl. with Des Moines (Inc. Place)
East Fourteenth Street; RMC Place; POLK; ***176** I-10; ★ **DES**; mail Des Moines z 50316; pop. incl. with Des Moines (Inc. Place)
East Peru (Peru); Inc. Place; MADISON; **176** K-9; elev. 940ft./287m.; mail Peru z 50222; Ⓟ 132; Ⓒ 153
East Pleasant Plain; RMC Place; JEFFERSON; **177** K-15; mail Brighton z 52540
East Waterloo; RMC Place; BLACK HAWK; ★ **WATL**; pop. incl. with Waterloo (Inc. Place)
Eddyville; Inc. Place; WAPELLO, MAHASKA, MONROE; **177** K-13; elev. 670ft./204m.; 🅿; z 52553; Ⓟ 1,010; Ⓒ 1,064
Edenville; MARSHALL; see Rhodes (Inc. Place)
Edgewood; Inc. Place; CLAYTON, DELAWARE; **177** E-16; elev. 1,160ft./354m.; 🅿; z 52042 & mail Elkport z 52044; Ⓟ 776; Ⓒ 923
Edgewood Park; RMC Place; SCOTT; ★ **D-RI-M**; mail Bettendorf z 52722; pop. incl. with Bettendorf (Inc. Place)
Edna; RMC Place; LYON; **176** B-2; mail Rock Rapids z 51246; ● 20
Egralharve; RMC Place; DICKINSON; ***176** B-5; mail Spirit Lake z 51360; ● 50
Elberon; Inc. Place; TAMA; **177** G-13; elev. 900ft./274m.; 🅿; z 52225; Ⓟ 203; Ⓒ 245
Eldon; Inc. Place; WAPELLO; **177** L-14; elev. 630ft./192m.; 🅿; z 52554; Ⓟ 1,070; Ⓒ 998
Eldora; Inc. Place; ⊡ HARDIN; **177** F-11; elev. 1,088ft./332m.; 🅿 🅷; z 50627; Ⓟ 3,038; Ⓒ 3,035
Eldorado; RMC Place; FAYETTE; **177** C-15; elev. 924ft./282m.; 🅿; z 52175; ● 80
Eldridge; Inc. Place; SCOTT; **177** I-19; elev. 800ft./244m.; 🅿; ★ **D-RI-M**; z 52748; Ⓟ 3,378; Ⓒ 4,159
Elgin; Inc. Place; FAYETTE; **177** D-15; elev. 835ft./255m.; 🅿; z 52141; Ⓟ 637; Ⓒ 676
Elkader; Inc. Place; ⊡ CLAYTON; **177** D-16; elev. 745ft./227m.; 🅿 🅷; z 52043; Ⓟ 1,510; Ⓒ 1,465
Elkhart; Inc. Place; POLK; **176** H-10; 🅿; z 50073; Ⓟ 388; Ⓒ 362

Entries in **UPPERCASE** are counties.
Entries in **bold** have populations of 2,500 or more.
Names in parentheses are alternate names.
Inc. Place — Incorporated Place
RMC Place — Rand McNally Designated Place
CDP — Census Designated Place
MCD — Minor Civil Division

⊡ County Seat
▲ Minor Civil Division
elev. Elevation
🅿 Post Office
🅷 Hospital
🅲 College
■ Principal Business Center
★ Ranally Metro Area (RMA) Abbreviation
z Zip Code(s)
Ⓟ Previous Census Population
Ⓡ Revised Census Population
Ⓐ Annexation Population
● Rand McNally Population Estimate
Ⓒ Final Census Population
Ⓢ Special Census Population
◆ Estimated Population

For additional definitions see Glossary, Volume 1, and Introduction, Volume 2.

Elk Horn; Inc. Place; SHELBY; **176** I-5; elev. 1,363ft./415m.; [P]; z 51531; Ⓟ 672; Ⓒ 649
Elkport; Inc. Place; CLAYTON; **177** E-16; elev. 670ft./204m.; [P]; z 52044; Ⓟ 82; Ⓒ 88
Elk Run Heights; Inc. Place; BLACK HAWK; **177** F-14; elev. 860ft./262m.; [P]; ★ **WATL**; z 50707 & mail Waterloo z 50701; Ⓟ 1,088; Ⓒ 1,052
Elliott; Inc. Place; MONTGOMERY; **176** K-5; elev. 1,083ft./330m.; [P]; z 51532; Ⓟ 399; Ⓒ 402
Ellston; Inc. Place; RINGGOLD; **176** L-8; elev. 1,214ft./370m.; [P]; z 50074; Ⓟ 44; Ⓒ 57
Ellsworth; Inc. Place; HAMILTON; **176** F-10; elev. 1,082ft./330m.; [P]; z 50075; Ⓟ 451; Ⓒ 531
Elma; Inc. Place; HOWARD; **177** C-13; elev. 1,189ft./362m.; [P]; z 50628; Ⓟ 653; Ⓒ 598
Elon; RMC Place; ALLAMAKEE; ***177** B-16; mail Waterville z 52170; rural
Elrick Junction; RMC Place; LOUISA; ***177** K-17; elev. 555ft./169m.; mail Wapello z 52653; ● 30
Elvira; RMC Place; CLINTON; **177** H-19; mail Clinton z 52732; ● 60
Elwood; RMC Place; CLINTON; **177** G-18; elev. 740ft./226m.; [P]; z 52254; ● 100
Ely; Inc. Place; LINN; **177** H-16; elev. 726ft./221m.; [P]; ★ **CEDR**; z 52227; Ⓟ 517; Ⓒ 1,149
Emeline; RMC Place; JACKSON; ***177** G-18; mail Baldwin z 52207
Emerald Park; BUENA VISTA; see West Storm Lake (RMC Place)
Emerson; Inc. Place; MILLS; **176** K-4; elev. 1,056ft./322m.; [P]; z 51533; Ⓟ 476; Ⓒ 480
Emery; RMC Place; CERRO GORDO; ***177** C-11; elev. 1,170ft./357m.; mail Mason City z 50401
EMMET; **176** B-7; Ⓟ 11,569; Ⓒ 11,027; ◆ 10,256
Emmetsburg; Inc. Place; ⊡ PALO ALTO; **176** C-6; elev. 1,234ft./376m.; [P] [H]; z 50536; Ⓟ 3,940; Ⓒ 3,958; Ⓡ 3,904
Enterprise; RMC Place; POLK; ***176** I-10; elev. 1,003ft./306m.; mail Elkhart z 50073
Epworth; Inc. Place; DUBUQUE; **177** F-17; elev. 1,050ft./320m.; [P]; z 52045; Ⓟ 1,297; Ⓒ 1,428; Ⓡ 1,446
Essex; Inc. Place; PAGE; **176** L-4; elev. 1,000ft./305m.; [P]; z 51638; Ⓟ 916; Ⓒ 884
Estherville; Inc. Place; ⊡ EMMET; **176** B-6; elev. 1,298ft./396m.; [P] [H]; z 51334; Ⓟ 6,720; Ⓒ 6,656
Evans; RMC Place; MAHASKA; **177** J-12; mail Oskaloosa z 52577; ● 30
Evansdale; Inc. Place; BLACK HAWK; **177** F-14; elev. 840ft./256m.; [P]; ★ **WATL**; z 50707; Ⓟ 4,638; Ⓒ 4,526
Evanston; RMC Place; WEBSTER; ***176** F-8; mail Duncombe z 50532
Evergreen; RMC Place; SCOTT; ***177** I-18; elev. 700ft./213m.; ★ **D-RI-M**; mail Davenport z 52804; pop. incl. with Buffalo (Inc. Place)
Everlou Heights; RMC Place; LINN; ***177** H-15; elev. 850ft./259m.; ★ **CEDR**; mail Cedar Rapids z 52401; ● 60
Everly; Inc. Place; CLAY; **176** C-5; elev. 1,364ft./416m.; [P]; z 51338; Ⓟ 706; Ⓒ 647
Ewart; RMC Place; POWESHIEK; **177** I-13; mail Montezuma z 50171; ● 30
Exira; Inc. Place; AUDUBON; **176** I-6; elev. 1,225ft./373m.; [P]; z 50076; Ⓟ 955; Ⓒ 810
Exline; Inc. Place; APPANOOSE; **177** M-12; elev. 1,000ft./305m.; [P]; z 52555; Ⓟ 187; Ⓒ 191

F

Fairbank; Inc. Place; BUCHANAN, FAYETTE; **177** E-14; elev. 980ft./299m.; [P]; z 50629; Ⓟ 1,018; Ⓒ 1,041
Fairfax; Inc. Place; LINN; **177** H-15; elev. 768ft./234m.; [P]; ★ **CEDR**; z 52228; Ⓟ 780; Ⓒ 889
Fairfield; Inc. Place; ⊡ JEFFERSON; **177** K-15; elev. 778ft./237m.; [P] [H] [C] 712; z 52556-57; Ⓟ 9,768; Ⓒ 9,509; Ⓡ 9,602
Fair Ground; RMC Place; DUBUQUE; ***177** E-18; elev. 631ft./192m.; ★ **DUB**; mail Dubuque z 52002; pop. incl. with Dubuque (Inc. Place)
Fairmount Park; RMC Place; POTTAWATTAMIE; ★ **OMA**; mail Council Bluffs z 51503; pop. incl. with Council Bluffs (Inc. Place)
Fairport; RMC Place; MUSCATINE; **177** J-18; mail Muscatine z 52761; ● 300
Fairview; RMC Place; JONES; **177** G-16; mail Anamosa z 52205; ● 80
Farley; Inc. Place; DUBUQUE; **177** F-17; elev. 1,110ft./338m.; [P]; z 52046; Ⓟ 1,354; Ⓒ 1,334
Farlin; RMC Place; GREENE; **176** G-7; elev. 1,072ft./327m.; mail Jefferson z 50129; ● 70
Farmersburg; Inc. Place; CLAYTON; **177** D-16; elev. 910ft./277m.; [P]; z 52047; Ⓟ 291; Ⓒ 300
Farmington; Inc. Place; VAN BUREN; **177** M-15; elev. 569ft./173m.; [P]; z 52626; Ⓟ 655; Ⓒ 756
Farnhamville; Inc. Place; CALHOUN, WEBSTER; **176** F-7; elev. 1,140ft./347m.; [P]; z 50538; Ⓟ 414; Ⓒ 430
Farragut; Inc. Place; FREMONT; **176** M-4; elev. 963ft./294m.; [P]; z 51639; Ⓟ 498; Ⓒ 509
Farrar; RMC Place; POLK; ***176** H-10; mail Maxwell z 50161; ● 40
Farson; RMC Place; WAPELLO; **177** K-14; mail Hedrick z 52563; ● 40
Faulkner; RMC Place; FRANKLIN; **177** E-11; mail Ackley z 50601; ● 30
Fayette; Inc. Place; FAYETTE; **177** D-15; elev. 1,002ft./305m.; [P] [C] 5,671; z 52142; Ⓟ 1,317; Ⓒ 1,300; Ⓡ 1,351
FAYETTE; **177** D-14; Ⓟ 21,843; Ⓒ 22,008; ◆ 19,592
Fenton; Inc. Place; KOSSUTH; **176** C-7; elev. 1,241ft./378m.; [P]; z 50539; Ⓟ 346; Ⓒ 317
Ferguson; Inc. Place; MARSHALL; **177** H-12; elev. 911ft./278m.; [P]; z 50078; Ⓟ 166; Ⓒ 126
Fern; RMC Place; GRUNDY; **177** F-12; elev. 1,060ft./323m.; mail Parkersburg z 50665; ● 30
Fernald; RMC Place; STORY; **176** G-10; mail Nevada z 50201; ● 90
Fertile; Inc. Place; WORTH; **176** C-10; elev. 1,200ft./366m.; [P]; z 50434; Ⓟ 382; Ⓒ 360
Festina; RMC Place; WINNESHIEK; **177** C-15; elev. 900ft./274m.; [P]; z 52144; ● 150
Fillmore; RMC Place; DUBUQUE; ***177** F-18; mail Cascade z 52033
Finchford; RMC Place; BLACK HAWK; **177** E-13; mail Janesville z 50647; ● 130
Fiscus; RMC Place; AUDUBON; ***176** I-5; mail Audubon z 50025; rural
Five Points; RMC Place; DUBUQUE; ***177** E-18; mail Sherrill z 52073; rural
Flagler; RMC Place; MARION; **177** J-11; mail Knoxville z 50138; ● 50
Florenceville; RMC Place; HOWARD; **177** B-14; mail Cresco z 52136; ● 40
Floris; Inc. Place; DAVIS; **177** L-13; elev. 719ft./219m.; [P]; z 52560; Ⓟ 172; Ⓒ 153
Floyd; Inc. Place; FLOYD; **177** C-12; elev. 1,080ft./329m.; [P]; z 50435; Ⓟ 359; Ⓒ 361
FLOYD; **177** C-12; Ⓟ 17,058; Ⓒ 16,900; ◆ 15,937
Folletts; RMC Place; CLINTON; **177** H-19; ★ **CLNT**; mail Camanche z 52730; ● 100
Fonda; Inc. Place; POCAHONTAS; **176** E-6; elev. 1,230ft./375m.; [P]; z 50540; Ⓟ 731; Ⓒ 648
Fontanelle; Inc. Place; ADAIR; **176** J-7; elev. 1,340ft./408m.; [P]; z 50846; Ⓟ 712; Ⓒ 692
Forbush; RMC Place; APPANOOSE; ***177** L-12; mail Centerville z 52544; ● 40
Forest City; Inc. Place; ⊡ WINNEBAGO, HANCOCK; **176** B-10; elev. 1,249ft./381m.; [P] [C] 670; z 50436; Ⓟ 4,430; Ⓒ 4,362
Fort Atkinson; Inc. Place; WINNESHIEK; **177** C-14; elev. 1,019ft./311m.; [P]; z 52144; Ⓟ 367; Ⓒ 389
Fort Des Moines; RMC Place; POLK; ***176** I-10; ★ **DES**; pop. incl. with Des Moines (Inc. Place)
Fort Dodge; Inc. Place; ⊡ WEBSTER; **176** F-8; elev. 1,030ft./314m.; [P] [H] ■; z 50501; Ⓟ 25,894; Ⓒ 25,136; Ⓡ 26,309; ◆ 22,743
Fort Dodge Junction; RMC Place; WEBSTER; mail Fort Dodge z 50501; pop. incl. with Fort Dodge (Inc. Place)
Fort Madison; Inc. Place; ⊡ LEE; **177** M-17; elev. 536ft./163m.; [P] [H]; z 52627; Ⓟ 11,618; Ⓒ 10,715; Ⓡ 11,476
Fostoria; Inc. Place; CLAY; **176** C-5; elev. 1,450ft./442m.; [P]; z 51340; Ⓟ 205; Ⓒ 230
Four Corners; RMC Place; JEFFERSON; ***177** K-15; mail Lockridge z 52635; rural
Franklin; Inc. Place; LEE; **177** M-16; elev. 697ft./212m.; mail Donnellson z 52625; Ⓟ 152; Ⓒ 136
FRANKLIN; **176** E-10; Ⓟ 11,364; Ⓒ 10,704; ◆ 10,521
Frankville; RMC Place; WINNESHIEK; **177** C-15; mail Postville z 52162; ● 150
Fraser; Inc. Place; BOONE; **176** G-9; elev. 950ft./290m.; mail Boone z 50036; Ⓟ 120; Ⓒ 137
Fredericksburg; Inc. Place; CHICKASAW; **177** D-14; elev. 1,080ft./329m.; [P]; z 50630; Ⓟ 1,011; Ⓒ 984
Frederika; Inc. Place; BREMER; **177** D-13; elev. 1,030ft./314m.; [P]; z 50631; Ⓟ 188; Ⓒ 199
Fredonia; Inc. Place; LOUISA; **177** J-16; elev. 600ft./183m.; mail Columbus Junction z 52738; Ⓟ 201; Ⓒ 251
Freeman; RMC Place; CERRO GORDO; ***177** C-11; elev. 1,151ft./351m.; mail Mason City z 50401
Freeport; RMC Place; WINNESHIEK; **177** B-15; mail Decorah z 52101; ● 150
Fremont; Inc. Place; MAHASKA; **177** K-13; elev. 842ft./257m.; [P]; z 52561; Ⓟ 701; Ⓒ 704
FREMONT; **176** L-4; Ⓟ 8,226; Ⓒ 8,010; ◆ 7,434
Frenh Creek; RMC Place; ALLAMAKEE; ***177** B-16; elev. 1,072ft./327m.; mail Lansing z 52151; rural
Froelich; RMC Place; CLAYTON; ***177** C-16; mail Farmersburg z 52047
Fruitland; Inc. Place; MUSCATINE; **177** J-17; elev. 545ft./166m.; [P]; z 52749; Ⓟ 511; Ⓒ 703
Frytown; JOHNSON; see Williamstown (RMC Place)
Fulton; RMC Place; JACKSON; **177** G-18; mail Maquoketa z 52060; ● 30

G

Galesburg; RMC Place; JASPER; **177** I-12; mail Reasnor z 50232; ● 70
Galland; RMC Place; LEE; ***177** M-16; mail Montrose z 52639
Galt; Inc. Place; WRIGHT; **176** E-10; elev. 1,204ft./367m.; [P]; z 50101; Ⓟ 43; Ⓒ 30
Galva; Inc. Place; IDA; **176** F-4; elev. 1,300ft./396m.; [P]; z 51020; Ⓟ 398; Ⓒ 368
Garber; Inc. Place; CLAYTON; **177** D-16; elev. 660ft./201m.; [P]; z 52048; Ⓟ 118; Ⓒ 103
Garden City; RMC Place; HARDIN; **176** G-10; elev. 1,196ft./365m.; [P]; z 50102; ● 100
Garden Grove; Inc. Place; DECATUR; **176** L-10; elev. 1,100ft./335m.; [P]; z 50103; Ⓟ 229; Ⓒ 250
Gardiner; RMC Place; DALLAS; ***176** H-8; mail Bouton z 50039
Garnavillo; Inc. Place; CLAYTON; **177** D-17; elev. 1,030ft./314m.; [P]; z 52049; Ⓟ 727; Ⓒ 754
Garner; Inc. Place; ⊡ HANCOCK; **176** C-10; elev. 1,216ft./371m.; [P]; z 50438; Ⓟ 2,916; Ⓒ 2,922
Garrison; Inc. Place; BENTON; **177** G-14; elev. 868ft./265m.; [P]; z 52229; Ⓟ 320; Ⓒ 413
Garry Owen; RMC Place; JACKSON; ***177** F-18; elev. 1,050ft./320m.; mail Zwingle z 52079; rural
Garwin; Inc. Place; TAMA; **177** G-12; elev. 950ft./290m.; [P]; z 50632; Ⓟ 533; Ⓒ 565
Gaza; RMC Place; O'BRIEN; **176** C-4; mail Primghar z 51245; ● 40
Geneva; Inc. Place; FRANKLIN; **177** E-11; elev. 1,100ft./335m.; [P]; z 50633; Ⓟ 169; Ⓒ 171
George; Inc. Place; LYON; **176** B-3; elev. 1,370ft./418m.; [P]; z 51237; Ⓟ 1,066; Ⓒ 1,051
Georgetown; RMC Place; MONROE; ***177** K-12; mail Albia z 52531; rural
Germantown; RMC Place; O'BRIEN; **176** D-3; mail Paullina z 51046; ● 50
German Valley; RMC Place; KOSSUTH; ***176** B-8; mail Titonka z 50480; rural
Germanville; RMC Place; JEFFERSON; ***177** K-15; mail Brighton z 52540
Giard; RMC Place; CLAYTON; **177** C-16; mail Mc Gregor z 52157; ● 40
Gibson; Inc. Place; KEOKUK; **177** J-13; elev. 890ft./271m.; [P]; z 50104; Ⓟ 63; Ⓒ 92
Gifford; RMC Place; HARDIN; **177** F-11; elev. 956ft./291m.; [P]; z 50259; ● 100
Gilbert; Inc. Place; STORY; **176** G-9; elev. 980ft./299m.; [P]; ★ **AMES**; z 50105; Ⓟ 796; Ⓒ 987
Gilbertville; Inc. Place; BLACK HAWK; **177** F-14; elev. 850ft./259m.; [P]; ★ **WATL**; z 50634; Ⓟ 748; Ⓒ 767
Gillett Grove; Inc. Place; CLAY; **176** C-5; elev. 1,295ft./395m.; [P]; z 51341; Ⓟ 67; Ⓒ 55
Gilman; Inc. Place; MARSHALL; **177** H-12; elev. 1,037ft./316m.; [P]; z 50106; Ⓟ 586; Ⓒ 600
Gilmore City; Inc. Place; HUMBOLDT, POCAHONTAS; **176** E-7; elev. 1,228ft./374m.; [P]; z 50541; Ⓟ 560; Ⓒ 556
Gladbrook; Inc. Place; TAMA; **177** G-12; elev. 1,000ft./305m.; [P]; z 50635; Ⓟ 881; Ⓒ 1,015
Glasgow; RMC Place; JEFFERSON; **177** L-15; mail Fairfield z 52556; ● 30
Glendon; RMC Place; GUTHRIE; ***176** I-7; mail Menlo z 50164; rural
Glenwood; Inc. Place; ⊡ MILLS; **176** K-3; elev. 1,036ft./316m.; [P] [H]; z 51534; Ⓟ 4,571; Ⓒ 5,358
Glidden; Inc. Place; CARROLL; **176** G-6; elev. 1,226ft./374m.; [P]; z 51443; Ⓟ 1,099; Ⓒ 1,253
Goddard; RMC Place; JASPER; ***177** I-11; mail Colfax z 50054; rural
Goldfield; Inc. Place; WRIGHT; **176** E-9; elev. 1,115ft./340m.; [P]; z 50542; Ⓟ 710; Ⓒ 680
Goodell; Inc. Place; HANCOCK; **176** D-10; elev. 1,242ft./379m.; [P]; z 50439; Ⓟ 201; Ⓒ 174
Goose Lake; Inc. Place; CLINTON; **177** H-19; elev. 700ft./213m.; [P]; z 52750; Ⓟ 221; Ⓒ 232
Gowrie; Inc. Place; WEBSTER; **176** F-8; elev. 1,137ft./347m.; [P]; z 50543; Ⓟ 1,028; Ⓒ 1,038
Grace Hill; RMC Place; WASHINGTON; ***177** J-15; mail Washington z 52353
Graettinger; Inc. Place; PALO ALTO; **176** C-6; elev. 1,252ft./382m.; [P]; z 51342; Ⓟ 813; Ⓒ 900
Graf; Inc. Place; DUBUQUE; **177** E-18; mail Sherrill z 52073; Ⓟ 78; Ⓒ 73
Grafton; Inc. Place; WORTH; **177** B-11; elev. 1,225ft./373m.; [P]; z 50440; Ⓟ 282; Ⓒ 290
Grand Junction; Inc. Place; GREENE; **176** G-8; elev. 1,030ft./314m.; [P]; z 50107; Ⓟ 808; Ⓒ 964
Grand Mound; Inc. Place; CLINTON; **177** H-18; elev. 720ft./219m.; [P]; z 52751; Ⓟ 619; Ⓒ 676
Grand River; Inc. Place; DECATUR; **176** L-9; elev. 983ft./300m.; [P]; z 50108; Ⓟ 171; Ⓒ 225
Grandview; Inc. Place; LOUISA; **177** J-17; elev. 700ft./213m.; [P]; z 52752; Ⓟ 514; Ⓒ 600
Granger; Inc. Place; DALLAS; **176** H-9; elev. 880ft./268m.; [P]; z 50109; Ⓟ 624; Ⓒ 583
Granger Homesteads; RMC Place; DALLAS; **176** H-9; mail Granger z 50109; ● 240
Granite; RMC Place; LYON; ***176** B-1; mail Larchwood z 51241
Grant; Inc. Place; MONTGOMERY; **176** K-5; elev. 1,100ft./335m.; [P]; z 50847; Ⓟ 123; Ⓒ 102
Grant Wood; RMC Place; SCOTT; ★ **D-RI-M**; mail Bettendorf z 52722; pop. incl. with Bettendorf (Inc. Place)
Granville; Inc. Place; SIOUX; **176** D-3; elev. 1,450ft./442m.; [P]; z 51022; Ⓟ 298; Ⓒ 325
Gravity; Inc. Place; TAYLOR; **176** L-6; elev. 1,151ft./351m.; [P]; z 50848; Ⓟ 218; Ⓒ 218
Gray; Inc. Place; AUDUBON; **176** H-6; elev. 1,374ft./419m.; [P]; z 50110 & mail Audubon z 50025; Ⓟ 83; Ⓒ 82
Greeley; Inc. Place; DELAWARE; **177** E-16; elev. 1,150ft./351m.; [P]; z 52050; Ⓟ 263; Ⓒ 276
Green Acres; RMC Place; SCOTT; ***177** I-19; ★ **D-RI-M**; pop. incl. with Davenport (Inc. Place)
Green Castle; RMC Place; JASPER; **177** I-11; mail Colfax z 50054; ● 30
Greene; Inc. Place; BUTLER; **177** D-12; elev. 961ft./293m.; [P]; z 50636; Ⓟ 1,142; Ⓒ 1,099
GREENE; **176** G-7; Ⓟ 10,045; Ⓒ 10,366; ◆ 9,194
Greenfield; Inc. Place; ⊡ ADAIR; **176** J-7; elev. 1,375ft./419m.; [P] [H]; z 50849; Ⓟ 2,074; Ⓒ 2,129
Green Island; RMC Place; JACKSON; **177** G-19; elev. 600ft./183m.; [P]; z 52064; ● 50
Green Mountain; RMC Place; MARSHALL; **177** G-12; elev. 999ft./304m.; [P]; z 50632; ● 150
Greenville; Inc. Place; CLAY; **176** C-5; elev. 1,390ft./424m.; [P]; z 51343; Ⓟ 84; Ⓒ 93
Greenwood Acres; RMC Place; POLK; ***176** I-10; elev. 930ft./283m.; ★ **DES**; mail Ankeny z 50021; ● 80
Grimes; Inc. Place; POLK, DALLAS; **176** I-9; elev. 950ft./290m.; [P]; ★ **DES**; z 50111; Ⓟ 2,653; Ⓒ 5,098
Grinnell; Inc. Place; POWESHIEK; **177** I-12; elev. 1,016ft./310m.; [P] [H] [C] 1,556; z 50112; Ⓟ 8,902; Ⓒ 9,105
Griswold; Inc. Place; CASS; **176** K-5; elev. 1,106ft./337m.; [P]; z 51535; Ⓟ 1,049; Ⓒ 1,039
GRUNDY; **177** F-12; Ⓟ 12,029; Ⓒ 12,369; ◆ 11,814
Grundy Center; Inc. Place; ⊡ GRUNDY; **177** F-12; elev. 1,026ft./313m.; [P] [H]; z 50638; Ⓟ 2,491; Ⓒ 2,596
Gruver; Inc. Place; EMMET; **176** B-6; elev. 1,311ft./400m.; [P]; z 51334; Ⓟ 102; Ⓒ 106
Guernsey; Inc. Place; POWESHIEK; **177** I-13; elev. 810ft./247m.; [P]; z 52221; Ⓟ 70; Ⓒ 70
Gunder; RMC Place; CLAYTON; **177** D-16; mail Postville z 52162; ● 50
Guss; RMC Place; TAYLOR; ***176** L-6; mail Nodaway z 50857
GUTHRIE; **176** H-6; Ⓟ 10,935; Ⓒ 11,353; ◆ 10,776
Guthrie Center; Inc. Place; ⊡ GUTHRIE; **176** I-7; elev. 1,150ft./351m.; [P] [H]; z 50115; Ⓟ 1,614; Ⓒ 1,668
Guttenberg; Inc. Place; CLAYTON; **177** D-17; elev. 625ft./191m.; [P] [H]; z 52052; Ⓟ 2,257; Ⓒ 1,987

H

Halbur; Inc. Place; CARROLL; **176** G-6; elev. 1,377ft./420m.; [P]; z 51444 & mail Aspinwall z 51432; Ⓟ 215; Ⓒ 202; Ⓡ 213
Hale; RMC Place; JONES; **177** G-17; elev. 800ft./244m.; [P]; z 52362; ● 70
Hamburg; Inc. Place; FREMONT; **176** M-3; elev. 914ft./279m.; [P] [H]; z 51640; Ⓟ 1,248; Ⓒ 1,240
Hamill; LEE; see Mount Hamill (RMC Place)
Hamilton; Inc. Place; MARION; **177** K-12; elev. 900ft./274m.; [P]; z 50116; Ⓟ 115; Ⓒ 144
HAMILTON; **176** F-9; Ⓟ 16,071; Ⓒ 16,438; ◆ 14,961
Hamlin; RMC Place; AUDUBON; **176** I-6; elev. 1,266ft./386m.; [P]; z 50117; ● 70
Hampton; Inc. Place; ⊡ FRANKLIN; **177** E-11; elev. 1,145ft./349m.; [P] [H]; z 50441; Ⓟ 4,133; Ⓒ 4,218
Hancock; Inc. Place; POTTAWATTAMIE; **176** J-4; elev. 1,124ft./343m.; [P]; z 51536; Ⓟ 201; Ⓒ 207
HANCOCK; **176** C-9; Ⓟ 12,638; Ⓒ 12,100; ◆ 10,881
Hanford; RMC Place; CERRO GORDO; **177** C-11; mail Mason City z 50401; ● 30
Hanley; RMC Place; MADISON; **176** J-9; mail Saint Charles z 50240; ● 60
Hanlontown; Inc. Place; WORTH; **176** B-10; elev. 1,202ft./366m.; [P]; z 50444; Ⓟ 193; Ⓒ 229
Hanover; RMC Place; BUENA VISTA; ***176** E-4; mail Alta z 51002
Hansell; Inc. Place; FRANKLIN; **177** E-11; elev. 1,031ft./314m.; [P]; z 50441; Ⓟ 83; Ⓒ 96
Harcourt; Inc. Place; WEBSTER; **176** F-8; elev. 1,170ft./357m.; [P]; z 50544; Ⓟ 306; Ⓒ 340
HARDIN; **176** F-10; Ⓟ 19,094; Ⓒ 18,812; ◆ 17,015
Hardy; Inc. Place; HUMBOLDT; **176** D-8; elev. 1,135ft./346m.; [P]; z 50545; Ⓟ 47; Ⓒ 57
Harlan; Inc. Place; ⊡ SHELBY; **176** I-4; elev. 1,250ft./381m.; [P] [H]; z 51537, z 51593; Ⓟ 5,148; Ⓒ 5,282
Harper; Inc. Place; KEOKUK; **177** J-14; elev. 800ft./244m.; [P]; z 52231; Ⓟ 147; Ⓒ 134
Harpers Ferry; Inc. Place; ALLAMAKEE; **177** C-17; elev. 645ft./197m.; [P]; z 52146; Ⓟ 284; Ⓒ 330
Harris; Inc. Place; OSCEOLA; **176** B-4; elev. 1,550ft./472m.; [P]; z 51345; Ⓟ 170; Ⓒ 200
Harrisburg; RMC Place; VAN BUREN; ***177** L-15; elev. 744ft./227m.; mail Bonaparte z 52620; rural
HARRISON; **176** I-3; Ⓟ 14,730; Ⓒ 15,666; ◆ 15,009
Hartford; Inc. Place; WARREN; **176** J-10; elev. 815ft./248m.; [P]; z 50118; Ⓟ 768; Ⓒ 759
Hartley; Inc. Place; O'BRIEN; **176** C-4; elev. 1,458ft./444m.; [P]; z 51346; Ⓟ 1,632; Ⓒ 1,733
Hartwick; Inc. Place; POWESHIEK; **177** H-13; elev. 940ft./287m.; [P]; z 52232; Ⓟ 115; Ⓒ 83
Harvard; RMC Place; WAYNE; **177** M-11; mail Allerton z 50008, Corydon z 50060; ● 30
Harvey; Inc. Place; MARION; **177** J-12; elev. 720ft./219m.; [P]; z 50119; Ⓟ 235; Ⓒ 277
Haskins; RMC Place; WASHINGTON; **177** J-16; mail Ainsworth z 52201; ● 40
Hastings; Inc. Place; MILLS; **176** K-4; elev. 1,000ft./305m.; [P]; z 51540; Ⓟ 187; Ⓒ 214
Hauntown; RMC Place; CLINTON; ***177** G-20; mail Clinton z 52732; ● 30
Havelock; Inc. Place; POCAHONTAS; **176** D-6; elev. 1,231ft./375m.; [P]; z 50546; Ⓟ 217; Ⓒ 177
Haven; RMC Place; TAMA; ***177** H-13; mail Tama z 52339
Haverhill; Inc. Place; MARSHALL; **177** H-12; elev. 1,025ft./312m.; [P]; z 50120; Ⓟ 144; Ⓒ 170
Hawarden; Inc. Place; SIOUX; **176** C-1; elev. 1,183ft./361m.; [P] [H]; z 51023 & mail Chatsworth z 51011; Ⓟ 2,439; Ⓒ 2,478
Hawkeye; Inc. Place; FAYETTE; **177** D-14; elev. 1,174ft./358m.; [P]; z 52147; Ⓟ 460; Ⓒ 489
Hawleyville; RMC Place; PAGE; ***176** L-6; mail Clarinda z 51632
Hawthorne; RMC Place; MONTGOMERY; **176** K-4; mail Red Oak z 51566; ● 30
Hayesville; Inc. Place; KEOKUK; **177** J-14; elev. 800ft./244m.; [P]; z 52562; Ⓟ 62; Ⓒ 64
Hayfield; RMC Place; HANCOCK; **176** C-9; elev. 1,243ft./379m.; mail Garner z 50438; ● 50
Hazleton; Inc. Place; BUCHANAN; **177** E-15; elev. 996ft./304m.; [P]; z 50641; Ⓟ 733; Ⓒ 950
Hedrick; Inc. Place; KEOKUK; **177** K-13; elev. 823ft./251m.; [P]; z 52563; Ⓟ 810; Ⓒ 837
Henderson; Inc. Place; MILLS; **176** K-4; elev. 1,034ft./315m.; [P]; z 51541; Ⓟ 206; Ⓒ 171
HENRY; **177** K-16; Ⓟ 19,226; Ⓒ 20,336; ◆ 20,172
Hepburn; Inc. Place; PAGE; **176** L-5; elev. 1,023ft./312m.; mail Clarinda z 51632; Ⓟ 41; Ⓒ 39
Herndon; RMC Place; GUTHRIE; **176** H-7; elev. 1,058ft./322m.; mail Bagley z 50026, Jamaica z 50128; ● 40
Hesper; RMC Place; WINNESHIEK; **177** B-15; mail Decorah z 52101; ● 150
Heytmans Station; RMC Place; ALLAMAKEE; ***177** B-17; elev. 1,026ft./313m.; mail Lansing z 52151; rural
Hiawatha; Inc. Place; LINN; **177** G-15; elev. 840ft./256m.; [P]; ★ **CEDR**; z 52233; Ⓟ 4,986; Ⓒ 6,480
High Amana; RMC Place; IOWA; ***177** H-15; mail Amana z 52203; ● 120
Highland Center; RMC Place; WAPELLO; **177** K-13; elev. 777ft./237m.; mail Ottumwa z 52501; ● 40
Highland Park; RMC Place; POLK; ***176** I-10; ★ **DES**; mail Des Moines z 50313, z 50333; pop. incl. with Des Moines (Inc. Place)
Highlandville; RMC Place; WINNESHIEK; **177** B-15; elev. 1,136ft./346m.; [P]; z 52149; ● 40
High Point; RMC Place; DECATUR; ***176** L-10; mail Garden Grove z 50103; rural
Highview; RMC Place; HAMILTON; ***176** F-9; elev. 1,128ft./344m.; mail Webster City z 50595
Hills; Inc. Place; JOHNSON; **177** I-16; [P]; z 52235; Ⓟ 662; Ⓒ 679
Hillsboro; Inc. Place; HENRY; **177** L-15; [P]; z 52630; Ⓟ 151; Ⓒ 205
Hillsdale; RMC Place; MILLS; ***176** K-3; elev. 1,211ft./369m.; mail Glenwood z 51534; ● 40
Hilltop; RMC Place; BLACK HAWK; ***177** F-14; ★ **WATL**; pop. incl. with Waterloo (Inc. Place)
Hinton; Inc. Place; PLYMOUTH; **176** E-2; [P]; z 51024; Ⓟ 697; Ⓒ 808
Hiteman; RMC Place; MONROE; **177** K-12; [P]; z 52531; ● 100
Hobarton; RMC Place; KOSSUTH; ***176** C-8; mail Algona z 50511
Hocking; RMC Place; MONROE; ***177** L-12; elev. 930ft./283m.; mail Albia z 52531; rural
Holbrook; RMC Place; IOWA; ***177** I-15; mail Parnell z 52325
Holiday Lake; RMC Place; POWESHIEK; ***177** H-13; elev. 900ft./274m.; mail Brooklyn z 52211; ● 500
Holland; Inc. Place; GRUNDY; **177** F-12; [P]; z 50642; Ⓟ 215; Ⓒ 250
Holly Springs; RMC Place; WOODBURY; **176** F-2; elev. 1,078ft./329m.; mail Hornick z 51026; ● 50
Holmes; RMC Place; WRIGHT; ***176** E-9; mail Clarion z 50525
Holmes Morse; RMC Place; LINN; ***177** G-15; elev. 850ft./259m.; ★ **CEDR**; mail Cedar Rapids z 52401; ● 60
Holstein; Inc. Place; IDA; **176** F-4; elev. 1,437ft./438m.; [P]; z 51025; Ⓟ 1,449; Ⓒ 1,470
Holy Cross; Inc. Place; DUBUQUE; **177** E-17; [P]; z 52053; Ⓟ 304; Ⓒ 339
Homer; RMC Place; HAMILTON; ***176** F-9; mail Webster City z 50595; rural
Homestead; RMC Place; IOWA; **177** H-15; elev. 853ft./260m.; [P]; z 52236; ● 300
Honey Creek; RMC Place; POTTAWATTAMIE; ***176** J-3; [P]; z 51542; rural
Hopeville; RMC Place; CLARKE; **176** L-8; mail Murray z 50174; ● 30
Hopkinton; Inc. Place; DELAWARE; **177** F-17; elev. 898ft./274m.; [P]; z 52237; Ⓟ 695; Ⓒ 681
Hornick; Inc. Place; WOODBURY; **176** G-2; elev. 1,067ft./325m.; [P]; z 51026; Ⓟ 222; Ⓒ 253
Horton; RMC Place; BREMER; **177** D-13; mail Waverly z 50677; ● 50
Hospers; Inc. Place; SIOUX; **176** C-3; elev. 1,350ft./411m.; [P]; z 51238; Ⓟ 643; Ⓒ 672
Houghton; Inc. Place; LEE; **177** L-16; elev. 696ft./212m.; [P]; z 52631; Ⓟ 127; Ⓒ 130
HOWARD; **177** B-13; Ⓟ 9,809; Ⓒ 9,932; ◆ 9,356
Hubbard; Inc. Place; HARDIN; **176** F-10; elev. 1,097ft./334m.; [P]; z 50122; Ⓟ 814; Ⓒ 885
Hudson; Inc. Place; BLACK HAWK; **177** F-13; elev. 900ft./274m.; [P]; ★ **WATL**; z 50643; Ⓟ 2,037; Ⓒ 2,117
Hull; Inc. Place; SIOUX; **176** C-2; elev. 1,440ft./439m.; [P]; z 51239; Ⓟ 1,724; Ⓒ 1,960
Humboldt; Inc. Place; HUMBOLDT; **176** E-8; elev. 1,089ft./332m.; [P] [H]; z 50548; Ⓟ 4,438; Ⓒ 4,452
HUMBOLDT; **176** D-8; Ⓟ 10,756; Ⓒ 10,381; ◆ 9,162
Humeston; Inc. Place; WAYNE; **176** L-10; elev. 1,100ft./335m.; [P]; z 50123; Ⓟ 553; Ⓒ 543
Huntington; RMC Place; EMMET; **176** B-6; mail Estherville z 51334; ● 30
Hurstville; RMC Place; JACKSON; ***177** G-18; elev. 700ft./213m.; mail Maquoketa z 52060
Hustad; MITCHELL; see Mona (RMC Place)
Hutchins; RMC Place; HANCOCK; **176** C-9; mail Britt z 50423; ● 30
Huxley; Inc. Place; STORY; **176** H-10; elev. 1,039ft./317m.; [P]; ★ **AMES**; z 50124; Ⓟ 2,047; Ⓒ 2,316

I

Iconium; RMC Place; APPANOOSE; **177** L-12; elev. 993ft./303m.; mail Moravia z 52571; ● 40
IDA; **176** F-4; Ⓟ 8,365; Ⓒ 7,837; ◆ 6,728
Ida Grove; Inc. Place; ⊡ IDA; **176** F-4; elev. 1,236ft./377m.; [P] [H]; z 51445; Ⓟ 2,357; Ⓒ 2,350
Imogene; Inc. Place; FREMONT; **176** L-4; elev. 1,044ft./318m.; [P]; z 51645; Ⓟ 88; Ⓒ 66
Independence; Inc. Place; ⊡ BUCHANAN; **177** F-15; elev. 917ft./280m.; [P] [H]; z 50644; Ⓟ 5,972; Ⓒ 6,014
Indian Creek; RMC Place; LINN; ★ **CEDR**; mail Marion z 52302; pop. incl. with Marion (Inc. Place)
Indianola; Inc. Place; ⊡ WARREN; **176** J-10; elev. 970ft./296m.; [P] [C] 2,060; z 50125; Ⓟ 11,340; Ⓒ 12,998
Industry; RMC Place; WEBSTER; ***176** E-8; mail Fonda z 50540; rural
Inwood; Inc. Place; LYON; **176** B-1; elev. 1,460ft./445m.; [P]; z 51240; Ⓟ 824; Ⓒ 875
Ionia; Inc. Place; CHICKASAW; **177** C-13; elev. 1,144ft./349m.; [P]; z 50645; Ⓟ 304; Ⓒ 277
IOWA; **177** I-15; Ⓟ 14,630; Ⓒ 15,671; ◆ 15,473
Iowa Center; RMC Place; STORY; **176** H-10; mail Maxwell z 50161; ● 30
Iowa City; Inc. Place; ⊡ JOHNSON; **177** I-16; elev. 698ft./213m.; [P] [H] [C] 29,979 ■; ★ **IACY**; z 52240-46; Ⓟ 59,738; Ⓒ 62,220; Ⓡ 62,380; ◆ 74,762
Iowa Falls; Inc. Place; HARDIN; **177** E-11; elev. 1,107ft./337m.; [P] [H]; z 50126; Ⓟ 5,424; Ⓒ 5,193
Iowa State University; RMC Place; STORY; ★ **AMES**; mail Ames z 50010-13; pop. incl. with Ames (Inc. Place)
Ira; RMC Place; JASPER; **177** H-11; elev. 832ft./254m.; [P]; z 50127; ● 50
Ireton; Inc. Place; SIOUX; **176** D-2; elev. 1,400ft./427m.; [P]; z 51027; Ⓟ 597; Ⓒ 585
Ironhills; RMC Place; JACKSON; ***177** G-18; mail Maquoketa z 52060; rural
Irving; RMC Place; BENTON, TAMA; **177** H-13; mail Belle Plaine z 52208; ● 30
Irvington; RMC Place; KOSSUTH; **176** D-8; elev. 1,151ft./351m.; mail Lu Verne z 50560; ● 30
Irwin; Inc. Place; SHELBY; **176** H-5; elev. 1,264ft./385m.; [P]; z 51446; Ⓟ 394; Ⓒ 372
Ivy; RMC Place; POLK; ***176** I-10; ★ **DES**; mail Altoona z 50009; ● 25

J

JACKSON; **177** F-18; Ⓟ 19,950; Ⓒ 20,296; ◆ 19,683
Jackson Junction; Inc. Place; WINNESHIEK; **177** C-14; elev. 1,163ft./354m.; [P]; z 52171; Ⓟ 87; Ⓒ 60
Jacksonville; RMC Place; SHELBY; **176** I-5; elev. 1,274ft./388m.; mail Harlan z 51537; ● 50
Jamaica; Inc. Place; GUTHRIE; **176** H-8; elev. 1,048ft./319m.; [P]; z 50128; Ⓟ 232; Ⓒ 237
James; RMC Place; PLYMOUTH; **176** E-2; mail Sioux City z 51108; ● 50
Jamison; RMC Place; CLARKE; **176** K-9; mail New Virginia z 50210; ● 30
Janesville; Inc. Place; BREMER, BLACK HAWK; **177** E-13; elev. 900ft./274m.; [P]; z 50647; Ⓟ 822; Ⓒ 829
JASPER; **177** I-11; Ⓟ 34,795; Ⓒ 37,213; ◆ 35,937
Jefferson; Inc. Place; ⊡ GREENE; **176** G-7; elev. 1,078ft./329m.; [P] [H]; z 50129; Ⓟ 4,292; Ⓒ 4,626
JEFFERSON; **177** K-15; Ⓟ 16,310; Ⓒ 16,181; ◆ 15,482
Jerico; RMC Place; CHICKASAW; **177** C-14; mail New Hampton z 50659; ● 30
Jerome; RMC Place; APPANOOSE; **177** M-11; mail Centerville z 52544; ● 70
Jesup; Inc. Place; BUCHANAN; **177** F-14; elev. 980ft./299m.; [P]; z 50648; Ⓟ 2,121; Ⓒ 2,212
Jewell (Jewell Junction); Inc. Place; HAMILTON; **176** F-9; [P]; z 50130; Ⓟ 1,106; Ⓒ 1,239
Jewell Junction; HAMILTON; see Jewell (Inc. Place)
Joetown; JOHNSON; see Amish (RMC Place)
JOHNSON; **177** I-15; Ⓟ 96,119; Ⓒ 111,006; ◆ 139,675
Johnston; Inc. Place; POLK; **176** I-9; elev. 830ft./253m.; [P]; ★ **DES**; z 50131; Ⓟ 4,702; Ⓒ 8,649
Johnston Station; RMC Place; POLK; ★ **DES**; mail Johnston z 50131; pop. incl. with Johnston (Inc. Place)
Joice; Inc. Place; WORTH; **176** B-10; elev. 1,262ft./385m.; [P]; z 50446; Ⓟ 245; Ⓒ 231
Jolley; Inc. Place; CALHOUN; **176** F-6; elev. 1,230ft./375m.; [P]; z 50551; Ⓟ 68; Ⓒ 54
JONES; **177** G-17; Ⓟ 19,444; Ⓒ 20,221; ◆ 20,235
Jordan; RMC Place; BOONE; ***176** G-9; mail Boone z 50036
Julien; RMC Place; DUBUQUE; ***177** E-18; ★ **DUB**; mail Dubuque z 52001, z 52003
Juniata; RMC Place; BUENA VISTA; ***176** E-5; mail Storm Lake z 50588; rural

K

Kalo; RMC Place; WEBSTER; ***176** F-8; mail Otho z 50569; ● 30
Kalona; Inc. Place; WASHINGTON; **177** J-15; elev. 660ft./201m.; [P]; z 52247; Ⓟ 1,942; Ⓒ 2,293
Kamrar; Inc. Place; HAMILTON; **176** F-9; elev. 1,115ft./340m.; [P]; z 50132; Ⓟ 203; Ⓒ 229
Kanawha; Inc. Place; HANCOCK; **176** D-9; elev. 1,191ft./363m.; [P]; z 50447; Ⓟ 763; Ⓒ 739
Kellerton; Inc. Place; RINGGOLD; **176** M-8; elev. 1,193ft./364m.; [P]; z 50133; Ⓟ 314; Ⓒ 372
Kelley; Inc. Place; STORY; **176** H-9; elev. 1,040ft./317m.; [P]; ★ **AMES**; z 50134; Ⓟ 246; Ⓒ 300
Kellogg; Inc. Place; JASPER; **177** I-12; [P]; z 50135; Ⓟ 626; Ⓒ 606
Kendallville; RMC Place; WINNESHIEK; **177** B-14; mail Cresco z 52136; ● 40
Kensett; Inc. Place; WORTH; **177** B-11; elev. 1,225ft./373m.; [P]; z 50448; Ⓟ 298; Ⓒ 280
Kent; RMC Place; UNION; **176** L-7; elev. 1,191ft./363m.; [P]; z 50851; former incorporated place; disincorporated August 19, 2003; Ⓟ 65; Ⓒ 52
Keokuk; Inc. Place; LEE; **177** N-16; elev. 550ft./168m.; [P] [H]; z 52632; Ⓟ 12,451; Ⓒ 11,427
KEOKUK; **177** J-14; Ⓟ 11,624; Ⓒ 11,400; ◆ 10,565
Keomah Village; Inc. Place; MAHASKA; **177** J-13; mail Oskaloosa z 52577; Ⓟ 99; Ⓒ 97
Keosauqua; Inc. Place; ⊡ VAN BUREN; **177** M-15; elev. 600ft./183m.; [P] [H]; z 52565; Ⓟ 1,020; Ⓒ 1,066
Keota; Inc. Place; KEOKUK; **177** J-14; elev. 787ft./240m.; [P]; z 52248; Ⓟ 1,000; Ⓒ 1,025
Kesley; RMC Place; BUTLER; **177** E-12; elev. 995ft./303m.; [P]; z 50649; ● 100
Keswick; Inc. Place; KEOKUK; **177** J-14; elev. 870ft./265m.; [P]; z 50136; Ⓟ 284; Ⓒ 295
Keystone; Inc. Place; BENTON; **177** H-14; elev. 900ft./274m.; [P]; z 52249; Ⓟ 568; Ⓒ 687
Key West; RMC Place; DUBUQUE; ***177** F-18; ★ **DUB**; mail Dubuque z 52001, z 52003
Kilbourn; RMC Place; VAN BUREN; ***177** L-15; mail Birmingham z 52535; ● 30
Killduff; RMC Place; JASPER; **177** I-12; elev. 932ft./284m.; [P]; z 50137; ● 120
Kimballton; Inc. Place; AUDUBON; **176** I-5; elev. 1,200ft./366m.; [P]; z 51543; Ⓟ 289; Ⓒ 342
King (Saint Catherine); RMC Place; DUBUQUE; **177** F-18; mail Dubuque z 52003; ● 150
Kingsley; Inc. Place; PLYMOUTH; **176** E-3; elev. 1,255ft./383m.; [P]; z 51028; Ⓟ 1,129; Ⓒ 1,245
Kingston; RMC Place; DES MOINES; **177** L-17; mail Mediapolis z 52637; ● 120
Kinross; Inc. Place; KEOKUK; **177** J-14; elev. 758ft./231m.; [P]; z 52335; Ⓟ 89; Ⓒ 80
Kirkman; Inc. Place; SHELBY; **176** I-5; elev. 1,233ft./376m.; [P]; z 51447; Ⓟ 98; Ⓒ 76
Kirkville; Inc. Place; WAPELLO; **177** K-13; elev. 850ft./259m.; [P]; z 52566; Ⓟ 177; Ⓒ 214
Kiron; Inc. Place; CRAWFORD; **176** G-5; elev. 1,341ft./409m.; [P]; z 51448; Ⓟ 301; Ⓒ 273
Klemme; Inc. Place; HANCOCK; **176** D-10; elev. 1,227ft./374m.; [P]; z 50449; Ⓟ 587; Ⓒ 593
Klinger; RMC Place; BREMER; **177** E-14; mail Readlyn z 50668; ● 30
Knapp Garden; RMC Place; POLK; ***176** H-9; elev. 930ft./283m.; ★ **DES**; mail Granger z 50109; ● 50
Knierim; Inc. Place; CALHOUN; **176** F-7; elev. 1,175ft./358m.; [P]; z 50552; Ⓟ 71; Ⓒ 70
Knittel; RMC Place; BREMER; ***177** E-14; elev. 1,017ft./310m.; mail Readlyn z 50668; rural
Knoke; RMC Place; CALHOUN; **176** E-6; elev. 1,243ft./379m.; [P]; z 50575; ● 30
Knoxville; Inc. Place; ⊡ MARION; **177** J-11; elev. 900ft./274m.; [P] [H]; z 50138; Ⓟ 8,232; Ⓒ 7,731
Knoxville Estates; RMC Place; MARION; ***177** J-11; elev. 860ft./262m.; mail Knoxville z 50138; ● 100
Konigsmark; RMC Place; LINN; ***177** H-15; ★ **CEDR**; mail Cedar Rapids z 52401
Kossuth; RMC Place; DES MOINES; **177** K-17; mail Mediapolis z 52637; ● 100
KOSSUTH; **176** C-8; Ⓟ 18,591; Ⓒ 17,163; ◆ 15,161
Koszta; RMC Place; IOWA; ***177** H-14; mail Belle Plaine z 52208

L

Lacelle; RMC Place; CLARKE; ***176** L-9; elev. 1,105ft./337m.; mail Osceola z 50213
Lacey; RMC Place; MAHASKA; **177** J-13; mail New Sharon z 50207; ● 40
Lacona; Inc. Place; WARREN; **176** K-10; elev. 900ft./274m.; [P]; z 50139; Ⓟ 357; Ⓒ 360
Ladora; Inc. Place; IOWA; **177** H-14; elev. 772ft./235m.; [P]; z 52251; Ⓟ 308; Ⓒ 287
Lafayette; RMC Place; LINN; **177** G-15; mail Alburnett z 52202; ● 60
Lake Canyada; RMC Place; SCOTT; ***177** I-18; elev. 758ft./231m.; ★ **D-RI-M**; mail Davenport z 52804; ● 400
Lake City; Inc. Place; CALHOUN; **176** F-6; elev. 1,243ft./379m.; [P] [H]; z 51449; Ⓟ 1,841; Ⓒ 1,787; Ⓡ 1,827
Lake Mills; Inc. Place; WINNEBAGO; **176** B-10; [P]; z 50450; Ⓟ 2,143; Ⓒ 2,140
Lake Park; Inc. Place; DICKINSON; **176** B-5; elev. 1,480ft./451m.; [P]; z 51347; Ⓟ 996; Ⓒ 1,023
Lakeside; Inc. Place; BUENA VISTA; **176** E-5; elev. 1,407ft./429m.; [P]; z 50588; Ⓟ 522; Ⓒ 484
Lake View; Inc. Place; SAC; **176** F-5; elev. 1,245ft./379m.; [P]; z 51450; Ⓟ 1,303; Ⓒ 1,278
Lakewood; RMC Place; WARREN; ***176** J-9; ★ **DES**; mail Norwalk z 50211; pop. incl. with Norwalk (Inc. Place)
Lakonta (Truax); RMC Place; MAHASKA; ***177** K-12; mail Eddyville z 52553
Lakota; Inc. Place; KOSSUTH; **176** B-8; elev. 1,156ft./352m.; [P]; z 50451; Ⓟ 281; Ⓒ 255
Lambs Grove; Inc. Place; JASPER; **177** I-11; mail Newton z 50208; Ⓟ 212; Ⓒ 225
Lamoille; RMC Place; MARSHALL; **177** G-11; mail Marshalltown z 50158; ● 50
Lamoni; Inc. Place; DECATUR; **176** M-9; elev. 1,126ft./343m.; [P] [C] 2,563; z 50140; Ⓟ 2,319; Ⓒ 2,444
Lamont; Inc. Place; BUCHANAN; **177** E-15; elev. 1,047ft./319m.; [P]; z 50650; Ⓟ 471; Ⓒ 503
La Motte; Inc. Place; JACKSON; **177** F-18; elev. 915ft./279m.; [P]; z 52054; Ⓟ 219; Ⓒ 272
Lanesboro; Inc. Place; CARROLL; **176** G-6; elev. 1,149ft./350m.; [P]; z 51451; Ⓟ 182; Ⓒ 152
Langdon; RMC Place; CLAY; **176** C-5; mail Spencer z 51301; ● 70
Langworthy; RMC Place; JONES; **177** G-17; elev. 867ft./264m.; [P]; z 52252; ● 50
Lansing; Inc. Place; ALLAMAKEE; **177** B-16; elev. 654ft./199m.; [P]; z 52151; Ⓟ 1,007; Ⓒ 1,012
Lanyon; RMC Place; WEBSTER; **176** G-8; mail Harcourt z 50544; ● 60
La Porte City; Inc. Place; BLACK HAWK; **177** F-14; elev. 819ft./250m.; [P]; z 50651; Ⓟ 2,128; Ⓒ 2,275; Ⓡ 2,321
Larchwood; Inc. Place; LYON; **176** B-1; elev. 1,480ft./451m.; [P]; z 51241; Ⓟ 739; Ⓒ 788
Larrabee; Inc. Place; CHEROKEE; **176** D-4; elev. 1,360ft./415m.; [P]; z 51029; Ⓟ 175; Ⓒ 149
Latimer; Inc. Place; FRANKLIN; **176** E-10; elev. 1,247ft./380m.; [P]; z 50452; Ⓟ 430; Ⓒ 535
Laurel; Inc. Place; MARSHALL; **177** H-12; elev. 1,048ft./319m.; [P]; z 50141; Ⓟ 271; Ⓒ 266
Laurens; Inc. Place; POCAHONTAS; **176** D-6; elev. 1,300ft./396m.; [P]; z 50554; Ⓟ 1,550; Ⓒ 1,476
Lawler; Inc. Place; CHICKASAW; **177** C-14; elev. 1,084ft./330m.; [P]; z 52154; Ⓟ 517; Ⓒ 461
Lawn Hill; RMC Place; HARDIN; **177** F-11; mail New Providence z 50206; ● 30
Lawton; Inc. Place; WOODBURY; **176** E-2; elev. 1,179ft./359m.; [P]; z 51030; Ⓟ 482; Ⓒ 697
Leando; CDP; VAN BUREN; **177** L-14; mail Douds z 52551; Ⓒ 135
Lebanon; RMC Place; SIOUX; **176** C-2; mail Sioux Center z 51250; ● 40
Lebanon; RMC Place; VAN BUREN; ***177** M-14; mail Keosauqua z 52565
Le Claire; Inc. Place; SCOTT; **177** I-19; elev. 600ft./183m.; [P]; ★ **D-RI-M**; z 52753; Ⓟ 2,734; Ⓒ 2,847; Ⓡ 2,868
Ledyard; Inc. Place; KOSSUTH; **176** B-8; elev. 1,150ft./351m.; [P]; z 50556; Ⓟ 164; Ⓒ 147
LEE; **177** M-16; Ⓟ 38,687; Ⓒ 38,052; ◆ 35,014
Leeds; RMC Place; WOODBURY; ***176** E-1; ★ **SXCY**; mail Sioux City z 51108; pop. incl. with Sioux City (Inc. Place)
Le Grand; Inc. Place; MARSHALL; **177** G-12; elev. 920ft./280m.; [P]; z 50142; Ⓟ 854; Ⓒ 883
Lehigh; Inc. Place; WEBSTER; **176** F-8; [P]; z 50557; Ⓟ 536; Ⓒ 497
Leighton; Inc. Place; MAHASKA; **177** J-12; elev. 761ft./232m.; [P]; z 50143; Ⓟ 142; Ⓒ 153
Leland; Inc. Place; WINNEBAGO; **176** B-10; elev. 1,218ft./371m.; [P]; z 50453; Ⓟ 311; Ⓒ 258
Le Mars; Inc. Place; ⊡ PLYMOUTH; **176** D-2; elev. 1,231ft./375m.; [P] [H]; z 51031; Ⓟ 8,454; Ⓒ 9,237
Lenox; Inc. Place; TAYLOR, ADAMS; **176** L-7; elev. 1,295ft./395m.; [P]; z 50851; Ⓟ 1,303; Ⓒ 1,401
Leon; Inc. Place; ⊡ DECATUR; **176** M-9; elev. 1,110ft./338m.; [P] [H]; z 50144; Ⓟ 2,047; Ⓒ 1,983
Le Roy; Inc. Place; DECATUR; **176** L-10; elev. 1,110ft./338m.; mail Humeston z 50123; Ⓟ 34; Ⓒ 13
Lester; Inc. Place; LYON; **176** B-2; elev. 1,380ft./421m.; [P]; z 51242; Ⓟ 257; Ⓒ 251
Letts; Inc. Place; LOUISA; **177** J-17; elev. 650ft./198m.; [P]; z 52754; Ⓟ 390; Ⓒ 392
Lewis; Inc. Place; CASS; **176** J-5; elev. 1,200ft./366m.; [P]; z 51544; Ⓟ 433; Ⓒ 438
Liberty; RMC Place; CLARKE; **176** K-9; mail New Virginia z 50210; ● 30
Liberty Center; RMC Place; WARREN; **176** K-10; elev. 1,030ft./314m.; [P]; z 50145; ● 100
Libertyville; Inc. Place; JEFFERSON; **177** L-14; elev. 760ft./232m.; [P]; z 52567; Ⓟ 264; Ⓒ 325
Lidderdale; Inc. Place; CARROLL; **176** G-6; elev. 1,237ft./377m.; [P]; z 51452; Ⓟ 202; Ⓒ 186
Lime City; RMC Place; CEDAR; ***177** I-17; mail Wilton z 52778; rural
Lime Springs; Inc. Place; HOWARD; **177** B-13; elev. 1,245ft./379m.; [P]; z 52155; Ⓟ 438; Ⓒ 496
Linby; RMC Place; JEFFERSON; **177** K-14; mail Packwood z 52580; ● 30
Lincoln; Inc. Place; TAMA; **177** F-12; elev. 1,065ft./325m.; [P]; z 50652; Ⓟ 173; Ⓒ 182
Lincoln Center; RMC Place; ADAMS; ***176** K-6; elev. 1,213ft./370m.; mail Corning z 50841; rural
Lincolnway Village; RMC Place; LINN; ***177** H-15; ★ **CEDR**; pop. incl. with Cedar Rapids (Inc. Place)
Linden; Inc. Place; DALLAS; **176** I-8; elev. 1,120ft./341m.; [P]; z 50146; Ⓟ 201; Ⓒ 226
Lineville; Inc. Place; WAYNE; **176** M-10; elev. 1,093ft./333m.; [P]; z 50147; Ⓟ 289; Ⓒ 273
LINN; **177** G-15; Ⓟ 168,767; Ⓒ 191,701; ◆ 211,147
Linn Grove; Inc. Place; BUENA VISTA; **176** D-5; elev. 1,350ft./411m.; [P]; z 51033; Ⓟ 194; Ⓒ 211
Linwood; RMC Place; SCOTT; ***177** J-18; ★ **D-RI-M**; mail Davenport z 52805; pop. incl. with Buffalo (Inc. Place)
Lisbon; Inc. Place; LINN; **177** H-16; elev. 873ft./266m.; [P]; z 52253; Ⓟ 1,452; Ⓒ 1,898
Liscomb; Inc. Place; MARSHALL; **177** G-11; elev. 980ft./299m.; [P]; z 50148; Ⓟ 258; Ⓒ 272
Little Cedar; RMC Place; MITCHELL; **177** B-12; elev. 1,181ft./360m.; [P]; z 50454; ● 50
Littleport; RMC Place; CLAYTON; **177** D-16; elev. 708ft./216m.; [P]; z 52042; disincorporated August 9, 2004; Ⓟ 88; Ⓒ 26
Little Rock; Inc. Place; LYON; **176** B-3; elev. 1,477ft./450m.; [P]; z 51243; Ⓟ 493; Ⓒ 489
Little Sioux; Inc. Place; HARRISON; **176** H-2; elev. 1,033ft./315m.; [P]; z 51545; Ⓟ 205; Ⓒ 217
Littleton; RMC Place; BUCHANAN; **177** E-14; mail Jesup z 50648; ● 220
Little Turkey; RMC Place; CHICKASAW; **177** C-14; mail Lawler z 52154; ● 30
Livermore; Inc. Place; HUMBOLDT; **176** D-8; elev. 1,132ft./345m.; [P]; z 50558; Ⓟ 436; Ⓒ 431
Livingston; RMC Place; APPANOOSE; ***177** M-11; elev. 997ft./304m.; mail Cincinnati z 52549; rural
Lockridge; Inc. Place; JEFFERSON; **177** K-15; elev. 729ft./222m.; [P]; z 52635; Ⓟ 270; Ⓒ 275
Logan; Inc. Place; ⊡ HARRISON; **176** I-3; elev. 1,104ft./336m.; [P]; z 51546 & mail Magnolia z 51550; Ⓟ 1,401; Ⓒ 1,545
Logansport; RMC Place; BOONE; **176** G-9; mail Boone z 50036; ● 140
Lohrville; Inc. Place; CALHOUN; **176** F-7; elev. 1,148ft./350m.; [P]; z 51453; Ⓟ 453; Ⓒ 431
Lone Rock; Inc. Place; KOSSUTH; **176** C-8; elev. 1,210ft./369m.; [P]; z 50559; Ⓟ 185; Ⓒ 157
Lone Tree; Inc. Place; JOHNSON; **177** J-16; elev. 520ft./158m.; [P]; z 52755; Ⓟ 979; Ⓒ 1,151
Long Grove; Inc. Place; SCOTT; **177** I-19; elev. 780ft./238m.; [P]; z 52756; Ⓟ 605; Ⓒ 597
Lorah; RMC Place; CASS; ***176** J-6; elev. 1,222ft./372m.; mail Atlantic z 50022
Lorimor; Inc. Place; UNION; **176** K-8; elev. 1,230ft./375m.; [P]; z 50149; Ⓟ 377; Ⓒ 427
Loring; RMC Place; POLK; ***176** H-10; elev. 910ft./277m.; mail Maxwell z 50161; rural
Lost Nation; Inc. Place; CLINTON; **177** H-18; elev. 720ft./219m.; [P]; z 52254; Ⓟ 467; Ⓒ 497
Louisa; RMC Place; LINN; ***177** G-15; ★ **CEDR**; pop. incl. with Cedar Rapids (Inc. Place)
LOUISA; **177** K-16; Ⓟ 11,592; Ⓒ 12,183; ◆ 11,621
Lourdes; RMC Place; HOWARD; **177** B-13; mail Elma z 50628; ● 30
Loveland; RMC Place; POTTAWATTAMIE; **176** I-3; mail Missouri Valley z 51555; ● 75
Lovilia; Inc. Place; MONROE; **177** K-12; elev. 920ft./280m.; [P]; z 50150 & mail Columbia z 50057; Ⓟ 551; Ⓒ 583
Lovington; RMC Place; POLK; **177** A-19; ★ **DES**; mail Urbandale z 50322; ● 700
Lowden; Inc. Place; CEDAR; **177** H-18; elev. 720ft./219m.; [P]; z 52255; Ⓟ 726; Ⓒ 794
Lowell; RMC Place; HENRY; **177** L-16; [P]; z 52645; ● 100
Low Moor; Inc. Place; CLINTON; **177** H-19; elev. 650ft./198m.; [P]; ★ **CLNT**; z 52757; Ⓟ 280; Ⓒ 240
Luana; Inc. Place; CLAYTON; **177** C-16; elev. 1,132ft./345m.; [P]; z 52156; Ⓟ 190; Ⓒ 249
Lucas; Inc. Place; LUCAS; **176** K-10; elev. 895ft./273m.; [P]; z 50151; Ⓟ 224; Ⓒ 243
LUCAS; **176** K-10; Ⓟ 9,070; Ⓒ 9,422; ◆ 9,260
Lundstrom Heights; RMC Place; POLK; ***176** I-9; elev. 953ft./290m.; ★ **DES**; mail Ankeny z 50021; ● 130
Luther; Inc. Place; BOONE; **176** H-9; elev. 1,100ft./335m.; [P]; z 50152; Ⓟ 154; Ⓒ 158
Luther Manor; RMC Place; SCOTT; ★ **D-RI-M**; mail Bettendorf z 52722; pop. incl. with Bettendorf (Inc. Place)
Luton; RMC Place; WOODBURY; ***176** F-2; elev. 1,081ft./329m.; mail Salix z 51052
Lu Verne; Inc. Place; KOSSUTH, HUMBOLDT; **176** D-8; elev. 1,167ft./356m.; [P]; z 50560; Ⓟ 328; Ⓒ 299
Luxemburg; Inc. Place; DUBUQUE; **177** E-17; elev. 1,180ft./360m.; [P]; z 52056; Ⓟ 257; Ⓒ 246
Luzerne; Inc. Place; BENTON; **177** H-14; elev. 891ft./272m.; [P]; z 52257; Ⓟ 110; Ⓒ 105
Lyman; RMC Place; CASS; **176** K-5; mail Griswold z 51535; ● 100
Lynnville; Inc. Place; JASPER; **177** I-12; elev. 892ft./272m.; [P]; z 50153; Ⓟ 393; Ⓒ 366
LYON; **176** B-2; Ⓟ 11,952; Ⓒ 11,763; ◆ 10,875
Lyons; RMC Place; CLINTON; ***177** H-20; ★ **CLNT**; mail Clinton z 52732; pop. incl. with Clinton (Inc. Place)
Lyons; RMC Place; LINN; ***177** G-15; elev. 828ft./252m.; ★ **CEDR**; mail Marion z 52302; pop. incl. with Lyons (Inc. Place)
Lytton; Inc. Place; SAC, CALHOUN; **176** F-6; elev. 1,225ft./373m.; [P]; z 50561; Ⓟ 320; Ⓒ 305

M

Macedonia; Inc. Place; POTTAWATTAMIE; **176** K-4; elev. 1,112ft./339m.; [P]; z 51549; Ⓟ 262; Ⓒ 325
Macey (Macy); RMC Place; HARDIN; ***177** E-11; mail Ackley z 50601; rural
Macksburg; Inc. Place; MADISON; **176** K-8; elev. 1,240ft./378m.; [P]; z 50155; Ⓟ 110; Ⓒ 142
Macy; HARDIN; see Macey (RMC Place)
Madison; RMC Place; POTTAWATTAMIE; ★ **OMA**; mail Council Bluffs z 51503; pop. incl. with Council Bluffs (Inc. Place)
MADISON; **176** J-8; Ⓟ 12,483; Ⓒ 14,019; ◆ 15,539
Madrid; Inc. Place; BOONE; **176** H-9; elev. 1,010ft./308m.; [P]; z 50156; Ⓟ 2,395; Ⓒ 2,264; Ⓡ 2,418
Magnolia; Inc. Place; HARRISON; **176** I-3; elev. 1,300ft./396m.; [P]; z 51550; Ⓟ 204; Ⓒ 200
Maharishi Vedic City (Vedic City); Inc. Place; JEFFERSON; ***177** K-14; mail Fairfield z 52556; incorporated July 25, 2001; not reported in 2000 Census; ● 83
MAHASKA; **177** J-12; Ⓟ 21,522; Ⓒ 22,335; ◆ 22,184
Malcom; Inc. Place; POWESHIEK; **177** I-13; elev. 889ft./271m.; [P]; z 50157; Ⓟ 447; Ⓒ 352
Mallard; Inc. Place; PALO ALTO; **176** D-6; elev. 1,220ft./372m.; [P]; z 50562; Ⓟ 360; Ⓒ 298
Malone; RMC Place; CLINTON; **177** H-19; mail De Witt z 52742; ● 25
Maloy; Inc. Place; RINGGOLD; **176** M-7; elev. 1,120ft./341m.; [P]; z 50836; Ⓟ 36; Ⓒ 28
Malvern; Inc. Place; MILLS; **176** K-4; elev. 1,050ft./320m.; [P]; z 51551; Ⓟ 1,210; Ⓒ 1,256
Manawa; RMC Place; POTTAWATTAMIE; ***176** K-3; [P]; ★ **OMA**; z 51501; pop. incl. with Council Bluffs (Inc. Place)
Manchester; Inc. Place; ⊡ DELAWARE; **177** F-16; elev. 950ft./290m.; [P] [H]; z 52057; Ⓟ 5,137; Ⓒ 5,257
Manilla; Inc. Place; CRAWFORD; **176** H-5; elev. 1,317ft./401m.; [P]; z 51454; Ⓟ 898; Ⓒ 839
Manly; Inc. Place; WORTH; **177** B-11; elev. 1,198ft./365m.; [P]; z 50456; Ⓟ 1,349; Ⓒ 1,342
Manning; Inc. Place; CARROLL; **176** H-5; elev. 1,355ft./413m.; [P] [H]; z 51455; Ⓟ 1,484; Ⓒ 1,490
Manson; Inc. Place; CALHOUN; **176** E-7; elev. 1,234ft./376m.; [P]; z 50563; Ⓟ 1,844; Ⓒ 1,893
Maple Heights; RMC Place; FLOYD; ***177** C-12; elev. 1,000ft./305m.; mail Charles City z 50616; pop. incl. with Charles City (Inc. Place)
Maple Hill; RMC Place; EMMET; **176** B-7; elev. 1,285ft./392m.; mail Armstrong z 50514; ● 30
Maple River; RMC Place; CARROLL; **176** G-6; mail Carroll z 51401; ● 80
Mapleton; Inc. Place; MONONA; **176** G-3; elev. 1,157ft./353m.; [P]; z 51034; Ⓟ 1,294; Ⓒ 1,416; Ⓡ 1,322
Maquoketa; Inc. Place; ⊡ JACKSON; **177** G-18; elev. 700ft./213m.; [P] [H]; z 52060; Ⓟ 6,111; Ⓒ 6,112
Marathon; Inc. Place; BUENA VISTA; **176** D-6; elev. 1,390ft./424m.; [P]; z 50565; Ⓟ 320; Ⓒ 302
Marble Rock; Inc. Place; FLOYD; **177** D-12; elev. 1,018ft./310m.; [P]; z 50653; Ⓟ 361; Ⓒ 326
Marcus; Inc. Place; CHEROKEE; **176** D-3; elev. 1,460ft./445m.; [P]; z 51035; Ⓟ 1,171; Ⓒ 1,139
Marengo; Inc. Place; ⊡ IOWA; **177** H-14; elev. 735ft./224m.; [P] [H]; z 52301; Ⓟ 2,270; Ⓒ 2,535
Marietta; RMC Place; MARSHALL; **177** G-11; mail Marshalltown z 50158; ● 50
Marion; Inc. Place; LINN; **177** G-16; elev. 850ft./259m.; [P]; ★ **CEDR**; z 52302; Ⓟ 20,403; Ⓒ 26,294; ◆ 31,842
MARION; **177** J-11; Ⓟ 30,001; Ⓒ 32,052; Ⓡ 32,054; ◆ 31,723
Marion Junction; RMC Place; LINN; ★ **CEDR**; pop. incl. with Cedar Rapids (Inc. Place)
Mark; RMC Place; DAVIS; **177** M-13; mail Bloomfield z 52537; ● 30
Marne; Inc. Place; CASS; **176** J-5; elev. 1,200ft./366m.; [P]; z 51552; Ⓟ 149; Ⓒ 149
Marquette; Inc. Place; CLAYTON; **177** C-17; elev. 627ft./191m.; [P]; z 52158; Ⓟ 479; Ⓒ 421; Ⓡ 476
Marquisville; RMC Place; POLK; ***176** I-10; ★ **DES**; mail Des Moines z 50313
Marsh; RMC Place; LOUISA; ***177** K-16; elev. 735ft./224m.; mail Winfield z 52659; rural
MARSHALL; **177** G-11; Ⓟ 38,276; Ⓒ 39,311; ◆ 39,325
Marshalltown; Inc. Place; ⊡ MARSHALL; **177** G-12; elev. 938ft./286m.; [P] [H] ■; z 50158; Ⓟ 25,178; Ⓒ 26,009; ◆ 26,223
Martelle; Inc. Place; JONES; **177** G-16; [P]; z 52305; Ⓟ 290; Ⓒ 280
Martensdale; Inc. Place; WARREN; **176** J-9; elev. 830ft./253m.; [P]; z 50160; Ⓟ 491; Ⓒ 467
Martinsburg; Inc. Place; KEOKUK; **177** K-14; [P]; z 52568; Ⓟ 157; Ⓒ 126
Martinstown; RMC Place; APPANOOSE; ***177** M-12; elev. 1,026ft./313m.; mail Centerville z 52544
Marysville; Inc. Place; MARION; **177** K-12; elev. 740ft./226m.; mail Hamilton z 50116; Ⓟ 65; Ⓒ 54
Mason City; Inc. Place; ⊡ CERRO GORDO; **177** C-11; elev. 1,138ft./347m.; [P] [H] [C] 450 ■; z 50401-02 & mail Rock Falls z 50467; Ⓟ 29,040; Ⓒ 29,172; ◆ 27,254
Masonville; Inc. Place; DELAWARE; **177** F-16; elev. 1,002ft./305m.; [P]; z 50654; Ⓟ 129; Ⓒ 104
Massena; Inc. Place; CASS; **176** J-6; elev. 1,260ft./384m.; [P]; z 50853; Ⓟ 372; Ⓒ 414
Massey; RMC Place; DUBUQUE; ***177** F-18; mail Dubuque z 52001, z 52003; ● 120
Massillon; RMC Place; CEDAR; **177** H-18; mail Lowden z 52255; ● 50
Matlock; Inc. Place; SIOUX; **176** B-3; elev. 1,400ft./427m.; [P]; z 51244; Ⓟ 92; Ⓒ 83
Maurice; Inc. Place; SIOUX; **176** D-2; elev. 1,300ft./396m.; [P]; z 51036; Ⓟ 855; Ⓒ 254
Maxwell; Inc. Place; STORY; **176** H-10; elev. 885ft./270m.; [P]; z 50161; Ⓟ 788; Ⓒ 807
May City; RMC Place; OSCEOLA; **176** B-4; elev. 1,430ft./436m.; [P]; z 51354; ● 110
Maynard; Inc. Place; FAYETTE; **177** D-15; [P]; z 50655; Ⓟ 513; Ⓒ 500
Maysville (Amity); Inc. Place; SCOTT; **177** I-18; elev. 730ft./223m.; [P]; z 52773; Ⓟ 170; Ⓒ 163
McCallsburg; Inc. Place; STORY; **176** G-10; elev. 1,089ft./332m.; [P]; z 50154; Ⓟ 292; Ⓒ 318
McCausland; Inc. Place; SCOTT; **177** H-19; [P]; z 52758; Ⓟ 308; Ⓒ 299
McClelland; Inc. Place; POTTAWATTAMIE; **176** J-3; elev. 1,250ft./381m.; [P]; z 51548; Ⓟ 139; Ⓒ 129
McCoy; RMC Place; POLK; ★ **DES**
McGregor; Inc. Place; CLAYTON; **177** C-17; elev. 627ft./191m.; [P]; z 52157; Ⓟ 797; Ⓒ 871
McIntire; Inc. Place; MITCHELL; **177** B-13; elev. 1,280ft./390m.; [P]; z 50455; Ⓟ 147; Ⓒ 173
McNally; RMC Place; SIOUX; ***176** D-1; mail Ireton z 51027
Mechanicsville; Inc. Place; CEDAR; **177** H-17; elev. 900ft./274m.; [P]; z 52306; Ⓟ 1,012; Ⓒ 1,173
Mederville; RMC Place; CLAYTON; **177** D-16; mail Elkader z 52043; ● 30
Mediapolis; Inc. Place; DES MOINES; **177** K-17; elev. 770ft./235m.; [P]; z 52637; Ⓟ 1,637; Ⓒ 1,644
Medora; RMC Place; WARREN; **176** K-10; mail Indianola z 50125; ● 50
Melbourne; Inc. Place; MARSHALL; **177** H-11; elev. 1,045ft./319m.; [P]; z 50162; Ⓟ 669; Ⓒ 794
Melcher; RMC Place; MARION; [P]; z 50163; pop. incl. with Melcher-Dallas (Inc. Place)
Melcher; MARION; see Melcher-Dallas (Inc. Place)
Melcher-Dallas (Melcher); Inc. Place; MARION; **177** J-11; elev. 940ft./287m.; [P]; z 50062, z 50163; Ⓟ 1,302; Ⓒ 1,298
Melrose; Inc. Place; MONROE; **177** L-11; elev. 870ft./265m.; [P]; z 52569; Ⓟ 150; Ⓒ 130
Meltonville; RMC Place; WORTH; ***177** B-11; mail Saint Ansgar z 50472; rural
Melvin; Inc. Place; OSCEOLA; **176** B-4; elev. 1,585ft./483m.; [P]; z 51350; Ⓟ 250; Ⓒ 243
Menlo; Inc. Place; GUTHRIE; **176** I-7; elev. 1,265ft./386m.; [P]; z 50164; Ⓟ 356; Ⓒ 365
Meriden; Inc. Place; CHEROKEE; **176** D-4; elev. 1,420ft./433m.; [P]; z 51037; Ⓟ 193; Ⓒ 184
Meroa; MITCHELL; see Rock Creek (RMC Place)
Merrill; Inc. Place; PLYMOUTH; **176** E-2; elev. 1,200ft./366m.; [P]; z 51038; Ⓟ 729; Ⓒ 754
Meservey; Inc. Place; CERRO GORDO; **176** D-10; elev. 1,255ft./383m.; [P]; z 50457; Ⓟ 292; Ⓒ 252
Methodist Camp; RMC Place; DICKINSON; ***176** B-5; elev. 1,450ft./442m.; mail Spirit Lake z 51360; summer pop. 500; ● 90
Meyer; RMC Place; MITCHELL; **177** B-12; mail Mc Intire z 50455; ● 40
Middle; IOWA; see Middle Amana (RMC Place)
Middle Amana (Middle); RMC Place; IOWA; ***177** H-15; elev. 750ft./229m.; [P]; z 52307; ● 350
Middleburg; RMC Place; SIOUX; **176** C-2; mail Orange City z 51041; ● 30
Middle River; MADISON; see Webster (RMC Place)

Entries in **UPPERCASE** are counties.
Entries in **bold** have populations of 2,500 or more.
Names in parentheses are alternate names.

Inc. Place	Incorporated Place
RMC Place	Rand McNally Designated Place
CDP	Census Designated Place
MCD	Minor Civil Division
⊡	County Seat
▲	Minor Civil Division
elev.	Elevation
[P]	Post Office
[H]	Hospital
[C]	College
■	Principal Business Center
★	Ranally Metro Area (RMA) Abbreviation
z	Zip Code(s)
Ⓟ	Previous Census Population
Ⓡ	Revised Census Population
Ⓐ	Annexation Population
●	Rand McNally Population Estimate
Ⓒ	Final Census Population
Ⓢ	Special Census Population
◆	Estimated Population

For additional definitions see Glossary, Volume 1, and Introduction, Volume 2.

Middletown; Inc. Place; DES MOINES; **177** L-17; elev. 724ft./221m.; 🅿; ★ **BUR**; z 52638; Ⓟ 386; Ⓒ 535
Midway; RMC Place; LINN; **177** G-15; ★ **CEDR**; mail Marion z 52302; ● 150
Miles; Inc. Place; JACKSON; **177** G-19; elev. 780ft./238m.; 🅿; z 52064; Ⓟ 409; Ⓒ 462
Milford; Inc. Place; DICKINSON; **176** B-5; elev. 1,440ft./439m.; 🅿; z 51351; Ⓟ 2,170; Ⓒ 2,474
Miller; RMC Place; HANCOCK; **176** C-10; elev. 1,225ft./373m.; mail Garner z 50438; ● 40
Millerdale; RMC Place; BLACK HAWK; ★ **WATL**; pop. incl. with Waterloo (Inc. Place)
Millersburg; Inc. Place; IOWA; **177** I-14; elev. 870ft./265m.; 🅿; z 52308; Ⓟ 188; Ⓒ 184
Millerton; Inc. Place; WAYNE; **177** L-11; elev. 1,070ft./326m.; 🅿; z 50165; Ⓟ 44; Ⓒ 48
Millnerville; RMC Place; PLYMOUTH; ***176** E-1; mail Westfield z 51062; rural
MILLS; **176** K-4; Ⓟ 13,202; Ⓒ 14,547; ◆ 14,973
Millville; Inc. Place; CLAYTON; **177** E-17; elev. 628ft./191m.; mail Guttenberg z 52052; Ⓟ 20; Ⓒ 23
Milo; Inc. Place; WARREN; **176** J-10; elev. 970ft./296m.; 🅿; z 50166; Ⓟ 864; Ⓒ 839
Milton; Inc. Place; VAN BUREN; **177** M-14; elev. 780ft./238m.; 🅿; z 52570; Ⓟ 506; Ⓒ 550
Minburn; Inc. Place; DALLAS; **176** H-8; elev. 1,042ft./318m.; 🅿; z 50167; Ⓟ 346; Ⓒ 391
Minden; Inc. Place; POTTAWATTAMIE; **176** J-4; elev. 1,207ft./368m.; 🅿; z 51553; Ⓟ 498; Ⓒ 564
Mineola; RMC Place; MILLS; **176** K-3; elev. 1,025ft./312m.; 🅿; z 51554; ● 200
Mineral Ridge; BOONE; see Ridgeport (RMC Place)
Minerva; RMC Place; MARSHALL; ***177** G-11; mail Albion z 50005
Mingo; Inc. Place; JASPER; **177** H-11; elev. 827ft./252m.; 🅿; z 50168; Ⓟ 252; Ⓒ 269
Missouri Valley; Inc. Place; HARRISON; **176** I-3; elev. 1,019ft./311m.; 🅿 🅷; z 51555; Ⓟ 2,888; Ⓒ 2,992
Mitchell; Inc. Place; MITCHELL; **177** B-12; elev. 1,195ft./364m.; 🅿; z 50461; Ⓟ 170; Ⓒ 155
MITCHELL; **177** C-11; Ⓟ 10,928; Ⓒ 10,874; ◆ 10,546
Mitchellville; Inc. Place; POLK; **176** I-10; elev. 960ft./293m.; 🅿; ★ **DES**; z 50169; Ⓟ 1,670; Ⓒ 1,715; Ⓡ 2,037
Modale; Inc. Place; HARRISON; **176** I-2; elev. 1,013ft./309m.; 🅿; z 51556; Ⓟ 289; Ⓒ 303
Moingona; RMC Place; BOONE; **176** G-9; mail Boone z 50036; ● 100
Mona (Hustad); RMC Place; MITCHELL; **177** B-12; mail Saint Ansgar z 50472; ● 40
Mondamin; Inc. Place; HARRISON; **176** I-2; elev. 1,025ft./312m.; 🅿; z 51557; Ⓟ 403; Ⓒ 423
Moneta; RMC Place; O'BRIEN; **176** C-4; elev. 1,450ft./442m.; mail Hartley z 51346; Ⓟ 29
Monmouth; Inc. Place; JACKSON; **177** G-18; 🅿; z 52309; Ⓟ 169; Ⓒ 180
Monona; Inc. Place; CLAYTON; **177** C-16; elev. 1,200ft./366m.; 🅿; z 52159; Ⓟ 1,520; Ⓒ 1,550
MONONA; **176** G-3; Ⓟ 10,034; Ⓒ 10,020; ◆ 8,749
Monroe; Inc. Place; JASPER; **177** I-11; elev. 920ft./280m.; 🅿; z 50170; Ⓟ 1,739; Ⓒ 1,808
MONROE; **177** L-12; Ⓟ 8,114; Ⓒ 8,016; ◆ 7,372
Monteith; RMC Place; GUTHRIE; **176** I-7; elev. 1,037ft./316m.; mail Guthrie Center z 50115; ● 50
Monterey; RMC Place; DAVIS; **177** M-13; elev. 953ft./290m.; mail Bloomfield z 52537; ● 30
Montezuma; Inc. Place; ⊡ POWESHIEK; **177** I-13; elev. 948ft./289m.; 🅿; z 50171; Ⓟ 1,651; Ⓒ 1,440; Ⓡ 1,457
Montgomery; RMC Place; DICKINSON; **176** B-5; elev. 1,450ft./442m.; mail Spirit Lake z 51360; ● 80
MONTGOMERY; **176** K-5; Ⓟ 12,076; Ⓒ 11,771; ◆ 10,536
Monti; RMC Place; BUCHANAN; ***177** F-15; mail Coggon z 52218; rural
Monticello; Inc. Place; JONES; **177** G-17; elev. 800ft./244m.; 🅿; z 52310; Ⓟ 3,522; Ⓒ 3,607
Montour; Inc. Place; TAMA; **177** H-12; elev. 853ft./260m.; 🅿; z 50173; Ⓟ 312; Ⓒ 285
Montpelier; RMC Place; MUSCATINE; **177** J-18; elev. 604ft./184m.; 🅿; z 52759; ● 230
Montrose; Inc. Place; LEE; **177** M-16; elev. 530ft./162m.; 🅿; z 52639; Ⓟ 957; Ⓒ 957
Mooar; RMC Place; LEE; **177** N-16; mail Keokuk z 52632; ● 80
Moorhead; Inc. Place; MONONA; **176** H-3; elev. 1,200ft./366m.; 🅿; z 51558; Ⓟ 259; Ⓒ 232
Moorland; Inc. Place; WEBSTER; **176** F-8; elev. 1,150ft./351m.; 🅿; z 50566; Ⓟ 209; Ⓒ 197
Moran; RMC Place; DALLAS; **176** H-9; mail Woodward z 50276; ● 50
Moravia; Inc. Place; APPANOOSE; **177** L-12; elev. 999ft./304m.; 🅿; z 52571; Ⓟ 679; Ⓒ 713
Morley; Inc. Place; JONES; **177** G-17; 🅿; z 52312; Ⓟ 85; Ⓒ 88
Morningside; RMC Place; WOODBURY; ***176** F-1; ★ **SXCY**; mail Sioux City z 51106; pop. incl. with Sioux City (Inc. Place)
Morning Sun; Inc. Place; LOUISA; **177** K-17; elev. 750ft./229m.; 🅿; z 52640; Ⓟ 841; Ⓒ 872
Morrison; Inc. Place; GRUNDY; **177** F-12; elev. 950ft./290m.; 🅿; z 50657; Ⓟ 113; Ⓒ 97
Morse; RMC Place; JOHNSON; **177** H-16; mail Iowa City z 52240; ● 80
Morton Mills (Mortons Mill); RMC Place; MONTGOMERY; **176** K-5; mail Villisca z 50864; ● 25
Mortons Mill; MONTGOMERY; see Morton Mills (RMC Place)
Moscow; RMC Place; MUSCATINE; **177** I-17; elev. 650ft./198m.; 🅿; z 52760; ● 300
Moulton; Inc. Place; APPANOOSE; **177** M-12; elev. 991ft./302m.; 🅿; z 52572; Ⓟ 613; Ⓒ 658
Mount Auburn; Inc. Place; BENTON; **177** F-14; elev. 880ft./268m.; 🅿; z 52313; Ⓟ 134; Ⓒ 160
Mount Ayr; Inc. Place; ⊡ RINGGOLD; **176** M-8; elev. 1,217ft./371m.; 🅿 🅷; z 50854; Ⓟ 1,796; Ⓒ 1,822
Mount Carmel; RMC Place; CARROLL; **176** G-6; mail Carroll z 51401; ● 70
Mount Etna; RMC Place; ADAMS; **176** K-6; elev. 1,090ft./332m.; mail Corning z 50841; ● 30
Mount Hamill (Hamill); RMC Place; LEE; ***177** L-16; mail Donnellson z 52625; ● 30
Mount Joy; RMC Place; SCOTT; **177** I-19; ★ **D-RI-M**; mail Davenport z 52804; ● 400
Mount Pleasant; Inc. Place; ⊡ HENRY; **177** L-16; elev. 725ft./221m.; 🅿 🅷 🅲 839; z 52641; Ⓟ 8,027; Ⓒ 8,751
Mount Sterling; Inc. Place; VAN BUREN; **177** M-15; elev. 655ft./200m.; 🅿; z 52573; Ⓟ 53; Ⓒ 40
Mount Union; Inc. Place; HENRY; **177** K-16; elev. 727ft./222m.; 🅿; z 52644; Ⓟ 140; Ⓒ 132
Mount Vernon; Inc. Place; LINN; **177** H-16; elev. 843ft./257m.; 🅿 🅲 1,121; z 52314; Ⓟ 3,657; Ⓒ 3,390; Ⓡ 3,808
Mount Zion; RMC Place; VAN BUREN; **177** L-15; mail Keosauqua z 52565; ● 30
Moville; Inc. Place; WOODBURY; **176** E-2; elev. 1,180ft./360m.; 🅿; z 51039; Ⓟ 1,306; Ⓒ 1,583
Munterville; RMC Place; WAPELLO; ***177** K-13; mail Blakesburg z 52536
Murphy; RMC Place; BREMER; ***177** E-13; mail Waverly z 50677; ● 90
Murray; Inc. Place; CLARKE; **176** K-9; elev. 1,220ft./372m.; 🅿; z 50174; Ⓟ 731; Ⓒ 766
Muscatine; Inc. Place; ⊡ MUSCATINE; **177** J-17; elev. 550ft./168m.; 🅿 🅷 ■; z 52761; Ⓟ 22,881; Ⓒ 22,697; ◆ 22,482
MUSCATINE; **177** I-16; Ⓟ 39,907; Ⓒ 41,722; ◆ 42,076
Mystic; Inc. Place; APPANOOSE; **177** L-12; elev. 900ft./274m.; 🅿; z 52574; Ⓟ 545; Ⓒ 588

N

Nahant; RMC Place; SCOTT; ***177** I-18; ★ **D-RI-M**; pop. incl. with Davenport (Inc. Place)
Napier; RMC Place; BOONE; **176** H-9; mail Ames z 50010, z 50014; ● 50
Nashua; Inc. Place; CHICKASAW; **177** D-13; elev. 970ft./296m.; 🅿; z 50658; Ⓟ 1,476; Ⓒ 1,618
Nashville; RMC Place; JACKSON; **177** G-18; mail Maquoketa z 52060; ● 30
Nemaha; Inc. Place; SAC; **176** E-5; elev. 1,322ft./403m.; 🅿; z 50567; Ⓟ 112; Ⓒ 102
Neola; Inc. Place; POTTAWATTAMIE; **176** J-4; elev. 1,096ft./334m.; 🅿; z 51559; Ⓟ 894; Ⓒ 845
Neptune; RMC Place; PLYMOUTH; ***176** E-2; elev. 1,370ft./418m.; mail Hinton z 51024, Le Mars z 51031; ● 30
Nevada; Inc. Place; ⊡ STORY; **176** G-10; elev. 1,003ft./306m.; 🅿 🅷; z 50201; Ⓟ 6,009; Ⓒ 6,658
Nevinville; RMC Place; ADAMS; ***176** K-7; elev. 1,300ft./396m.; mail Creston z 50801
New Albin; Inc. Place; ALLAMAKEE; **177** B-16; elev. 655ft./200m.; 🅿; z 52160; Ⓟ 534; Ⓒ 527
New Boston; RMC Place; LEE; **177** M-16; mail Argyle z 52619; ● 60
Newburg; RMC Place; JASPER; **177** H-12; mail Grinnell z 50112; ● 120
Newell; Inc. Place; BUENA VISTA; **176** E-5; elev. 1,265ft./386m.; 🅿; z 50568; Ⓟ 1,089; Ⓒ 887
New Era; RMC Place; MUSCATINE; ***177** J-18; mail Muscatine z 52761; rural
Newhall; Inc. Place; BENTON; **177** H-14; elev. 899ft./274m.; 🅿; z 52315; Ⓟ 854; Ⓒ 886
New Hampton; Inc. Place; ⊡ CHICKASAW; **177** C-13; elev. 1,159ft./353m.; 🅿 🅷; z 50659, z 50661; Ⓟ 3,660; Ⓒ 3,692
New Hartford; Inc. Place; BUTLER; **177** E-12; elev. 900ft./274m.; 🅿; z 50660; Ⓟ 683; Ⓒ 659
New Haven; RMC Place; MITCHELL; **177** B-12; elev. 1,150ft./351m.; mail Osage z 50461; ● 75
Newkirk; RMC Place; SIOUX; **176** C-3; mail Hospers z 51238; ● 70
New Liberty; Inc. Place; SCOTT; **177** I-18; elev. 800ft./244m.; 🅿; z 52765; Ⓟ 139; Ⓒ 121
New London; Inc. Place; HENRY; **177** L-16; elev. 765ft./233m.; 🅿; z 52645; Ⓟ 1,922; Ⓒ 1,937
New Market; Inc. Place; TAYLOR; **176** M-6; elev. 1,198ft./365m.; 🅿; z 51646; Ⓟ 454; Ⓒ 456
New Providence; Inc. Place; HARDIN; **177** F-11; elev. 1,130ft./344m.; 🅿; z 50206; Ⓟ 240; Ⓒ 227
New Sharon; Inc. Place; MAHASKA; **177** J-12; elev. 870ft./265m.; 🅿; z 50207; Ⓟ 1,136; Ⓒ 1,301
Newton; Inc. Place; ⊡ JASPER; **177** I-11; elev. 950ft./290m.; 🅿 🅷; z 50208; Ⓟ 14,789; Ⓒ 15,579
New Vienna; Inc. Place; DUBUQUE; **177** E-17; elev. 1,010ft./308m.; 🅿; z 52065; Ⓟ 376; Ⓒ 400
New Virginia; Inc. Place; WARREN; **176** K-9; elev. 1,081ft./329m.; 🅿; z 50210; Ⓟ 433; Ⓒ 469
Nichols; Inc. Place; MUSCATINE; **177** J-16; elev. 637ft./194m.; 🅿; z 52766; Ⓟ 366; Ⓒ 374
Noble; RMC Place; WASHINGTON; **177** K-16; mail Mount Pleasant z 52641; ● 50
Nodaway; Inc. Place; ADAMS; **176** L-6; elev. 1,084ft./330m.; 🅿; z 50857; Ⓟ 153; Ⓒ 132
Nora Springs; Inc. Place; FLOYD, CERRO GORDO; **177** C-11; elev. 1,080ft./329m.; 🅿; z 50458; Ⓟ 1,505; Ⓒ 1,532
Nora Springs Junction; RMC Place; FLOYD; mail Nora Springs z 50458; pop. incl. with Nora Springs (Inc. Place)
Northboro; Inc. Place; PAGE; **176** M-5; elev. 1,051ft./320m.; 🅿; z 51647; Ⓟ 78; Ⓒ 60
North Branch; RMC Place; GUTHRIE; ***176** I-6; mail Adair z 50002; rural
North Buena Vista; Inc. Place; CLAYTON; **177** E-17; elev. 659ft./201m.; 🅿; z 52066; Ⓟ 145; Ⓒ 124
Northeast; RMC Place; LINN; ★ **CEDR**; mail Cedar Rapids z 52402; pop. incl. with Cedar Rapids (Inc. Place)
North English; Inc. Place; IOWA, KEOKUK; **177** I-14; elev. 815ft./248m.; 🅿; z 52316; Ⓟ 944; Ⓒ 991
North Liberty; Inc. Place; JOHNSON; **177** H-16; elev. 780ft./238m.; 🅿; ★ **IACY**; z 52317; Ⓟ 2,926; Ⓒ 5,367
North Side; RMC Place; WOODBURY; ***176** E-1; ★ **SXCY**; mail Sioux City z 51104; pop. incl. with Sioux City (Inc. Place)
North Wall Lake; RMC Place; SAC; ***176** F-5; mail Wall Lake z 51466; pop. incl. with Wall Lake (Inc. Place)
North Washington; Inc. Place; CHICKASAW; **177** C-13; elev. 1,150ft./351m.; 🅿; z 50659, z 50661; Ⓟ 107; Ⓒ 118
Northwest; RMC Place; LINN; ***177** D-15; mail Cedar Rapids z 52405
Northwest; RMC Place; SCOTT; ***177** I-19; ★ **D-RI-M**; mail Davenport z 52804; pop. incl. with Davenport (Inc. Place)
Northwood; Inc. Place; ⊡ WORTH; **177** B-11; elev. 1,236ft./377m.; 🅿; z 50459; Ⓟ 1,940; Ⓒ 2,050
Norwalk; Inc. Place; WARREN; **176** J-9; elev. 900ft./274m.; 🅿; ★ **DES**; z 50211; Ⓟ 5,726; Ⓒ 6,884
Norway; Inc. Place; BENTON; **177** H-15; elev. 796ft./243m.; 🅿; z 52318; Ⓟ 583; Ⓒ 601
Norwich; RMC Place; PAGE; **176** L-5; mail Shenandoah z 51601; ● 30
Norwood; RMC Place; LUCAS; **176** K-10; mail Lucas z 50151; ● 30
Norwoodville; RMC Place; POLK; **177** B-20; ★ **DES**; mail Des Moines z 50317; ● 1,200
Numa; Inc. Place; APPANOOSE; **177** M-11; elev. 1,037ft./316m.; 🅿; z 52544; Ⓟ 151; Ⓒ 109
Nyman; RMC Place; PAGE; ***176** L-5; mail Red Oak z 51566

O

Oakland; Inc. Place; POTTAWATTAMIE; **176** J-4; elev. 1,103ft./336m.; 🅿; z 51560; Ⓟ 1,496; Ⓒ 1,487
Oakland Acres; Inc. Place; JASPER; **177** I-12; 🅿; z 50112; Ⓟ 152; Ⓒ 166
Oakland Mills; RMC Place; HENRY; **177** L-16; mail Mount Pleasant z 52641; ● 50
Oakley; RMC Place; LUCAS; **176** K-10; mail Chariton z 50049; ● 30
Oak Valley; RMC Place; LINN; ***177** G-15; elev. 800ft./244m.; ★ **CEDR**; mail Cedar Rapids z 52401; ● 30
Oakville; Inc. Place; LOUISA; **177** K-17; elev. 543ft./166m.; 🅿; z 52646; Ⓟ 442; Ⓒ 439
Oakwood; RMC Place; FLOYD; ***177** D-12; mail Marble Rock z 50653; rural
Oasis; RMC Place; JOHNSON; ***177** I-16; elev. 804ft./245m.; mail West Branch z 52358; ● 30
O'BRIEN; **176** C-4; Ⓟ 15,444; Ⓒ 15,102; ◆ 13,674
Ocheyedan; Inc. Place; OSCEOLA; **176** B-4; elev. 1,555ft./474m.; 🅿; z 51354; Ⓟ 539; Ⓒ 536
Odebolt; Inc. Place; SAC; **176** F-5; elev. 1,377ft./420m.; 🅿; z 51458; Ⓟ 1,158; Ⓒ 1,153
Oelwein; Inc. Place; FAYETTE; **177** E-15; elev. 1,049ft./320m.; 🅿 🅷; z 50662; Ⓟ 6,493; Ⓒ 6,692
Ogden; Inc. Place; BOONE; **176** G-8; elev. 1,092ft./333m.; 🅿; z 50212; Ⓟ 1,909; Ⓒ 2,023
Okoboji; Inc. Place; DICKINSON; **176** B-5; elev. 1,450ft./442m.; 🅿; z 51355; Ⓟ 775; Ⓒ 820
Old Balltown; RMC Place; DUBUQUE; ***177** E-18; mail Sherrill z 52073
Olds; Inc. Place; HENRY; **177** K-16; elev. 737ft./225m.; 🅿; z 52647; Ⓟ 205; Ⓒ 249
Old Town; RMC Place; DICKINSON; ***176** B-5; mail Milford z 51351
Olin; Inc. Place; JONES; **177** G-17; elev. 760ft./232m.; 🅿; z 52320; Ⓟ 663; Ⓒ 716
Olivet; RMC Place; MAHASKA; ***177** J-12; mail Leighton z 50143; rural
Ollie; Inc. Place; KEOKUK; **177** K-14; elev. 789ft./240m.; 🅿; z 52576; Ⓟ 207; Ⓒ 224
Omaha Reservation; Indian Reservation; MONONA; Reservation extends into NE; Ⓒ 0
Onawa; Inc. Place; ⊡ MONONA; **176** G-2; elev. 1,052ft./321m.; 🅿 🅷; z 51040; Ⓟ 2,936; Ⓒ 3,091
Oneida; RMC Place; DELAWARE; **177** E-16; elev. 1,051ft./320m.; mail Manchester z 52057; ● 40
Onslow; Inc. Place; JONES; **177** G-17; elev. 920ft./280m.; 🅿; z 52321; Ⓟ 216; Ⓒ 223
Ontario; RMC Place; STORY; ***176** G-9; ★ **AMES**; mail Ames z 50010, z 50014; pop. incl. with Ames (Inc. Place)
Oralabor; RMC Place; POLK; ***176** I-10; ★ **DES**; mail Ankeny z 50021; ● 250
Oran; RMC Place; FAYETTE; **177** E-14; elev. 1,040ft./317m.; 🅿; z 50664; ● 150
Orange; RMC Place; BLACK HAWK; ***177** F-13; ★ **WATL**; mail Waterloo z 50701; pop. incl. with Waterloo (Inc. Place)
Orange City; Inc. Place; ⊡ SIOUX; **176** C-2; elev. 1,411ft./430m.; 🅿 🅷 🅲 1,342; z 51041; Ⓟ 4,940; Ⓒ 5,582; Ⓡ 5,589
Orchard; Inc. Place; MITCHELL; **177** C-12; elev. 1,100ft./335m.; 🅿; z 50460; Ⓟ 93; Ⓒ 88
Orient; Inc. Place; ADAIR; **176** K-7; elev. 1,346ft./410m.; 🅿; z 50858; Ⓟ 376; Ⓒ 402
Orilla; WARREN; see Orillia (RMC Place)
Orillia (Orilla); RMC Place; WARREN; ***176** I-9; ★ **DES**; mail Cumming z 50061; ● 50
Orleans; Inc. Place; DICKINSON; **176** B-5; elev. 1,413ft./431m.; mail Spirit Lake z 51360; Ⓟ 560; Ⓒ 583
Osage; Inc. Place; ⊡ MITCHELL; **177** B-12; elev. 1,172ft./357m.; 🅿 🅷; z 50461 & mail Little Cedar z 50454; Ⓟ 3,439; Ⓒ 3,451
Osborne; RMC Place; CLAYTON; ***177** D-16; mail Elkader z 52043
Osceola; Inc. Place; ⊡ CLARKE; **176** K-9; elev. 1,139ft./347m.; 🅿 🅷; z 50213; Ⓟ 4,164; Ⓒ 4,659
OSCEOLA; **176** B-4; Ⓟ 7,267; Ⓒ 7,003; ◆ 6,123
Osgood; RMC Place; PALO ALTO; ***176** C-6; mail Emmetsburg z 50536
Oskaloosa; Inc. Place; ⊡ MAHASKA; **177** J-12; elev. 845ft./258m.; 🅿 🅷 🅲 1,861; z 52577; Ⓟ 10,632; Ⓒ 10,938
Ossian; Inc. Place; WINNESHIEK; **177** C-15; elev. 1,266ft./386m.; 🅿; z 52161; Ⓟ 810; Ⓒ 853
Osterdock; Inc. Place; CLAYTON; **177** E-17; elev. 639ft./195m.; mail Colesburg z 52035; Ⓟ 49; Ⓒ 50
Otho; Inc. Place; WEBSTER; **176** F-8; elev. 1,120ft./341m.; 🅿; z 50569; Ⓟ 529; Ⓒ 571
Otley; RMC Place; MARION; **177** J-11; elev. 884ft./269m.; 🅿; z 50214; ● 300
Oto; Inc. Place; WOODBURY; **176** F-3; elev. 1,100ft./335m.; 🅿; z 51044; Ⓟ 118; Ⓒ 145
Otranto; RMC Place; MITCHELL; **177** B-11; mail Saint Ansgar z 50472; ● 25
Otter Creek; RMC Place; JACKSON; **177** F-18; mail Zwingle z 52079; ● 100
Otterville; RMC Place; BUCHANAN; **177** E-14; mail Independence z 50644; ● 50
Ottosen; Inc. Place; HUMBOLDT; **176** D-7; elev. 1,165ft./355m.; 🅿; z 50570; Ⓟ 72; Ⓒ 61
Ottumwa; Inc. Place; ⊡ WAPELLO; **177** K-13; elev. 650ft./198m.; 🅿 🅷 ■; z 52501; Ⓟ 24,488; Ⓒ 24,998; ◆ 24,109
Ottumwa Junction; RMC Place; WAPELLO; mail Ottumwa z 52501
Owasa; Inc. Place; HARDIN; **177** F-11; elev. 1,085ft./331m.; mail Iowa Falls z 50126; Ⓟ 37; Ⓒ 38
Oxford; Inc. Place; JOHNSON; **177** I-15; elev. 739ft./225m.; 🅿; z 52322; Ⓟ 663; Ⓒ 705
Oxford Junction; Inc. Place; JONES; **177** G-17; elev. 720ft./219m.; 🅿; z 52323; Ⓟ 581; Ⓒ 573
Oxford Mills; RMC Place; JONES; **177** H-17; mail Oxford Junction z 52323; ● 100
Oyens; Inc. Place; PLYMOUTH; **176** D-2; elev. 1,300ft./396m.; 🅿; z 51045; Ⓟ 113; Ⓒ 132

P

Pacific Junction; Inc. Place; MILLS; **176** K-3; elev. 961ft./293m.; 🅿; z 51561; Ⓟ 548; Ⓒ 507
Packard; RMC Place; BUTLER; ***177** D-12; elev. 953ft./290m.; mail Clarksville z 50619
Packwood; Inc. Place; JEFFERSON; **177** K-14; elev. 802ft./244m.; 🅿; z 52580; Ⓟ 208; Ⓒ 223
PAGE; **176** L-5; Ⓟ 16,870; Ⓒ 16,976; ◆ 15,509
Palmer; Inc. Place; POCAHONTAS; **176** E-7; elev. 1,246ft./380m.; 🅿; z 50571; Ⓟ 230; Ⓒ 214
Palm Grove; RMC Place; WEBSTER; ***176** F-8; elev. 1,165ft./355m.; mail Fort Dodge z 50501
Palmyra; RMC Place; WARREN; **176** J-10; mail Carlisle z 50047; ● 50
Palo; Inc. Place; LINN; **177** G-15; elev. 740ft./226m.; 🅿; ★ **CEDR**; z 52324; Ⓟ 514; Ⓒ 614
PALO ALTO; **176** D-6; Ⓟ 10,669; Ⓒ 10,147; ◆ 9,275
Panama; Inc. Place; SHELBY; **176** I-4; elev. 1,325ft./404m.; 🅿; z 51562 & mail Westphalia z 51578; Ⓟ 201; Ⓒ 212
Panora; Inc. Place; GUTHRIE; **176** I-7; elev. 1,071ft./326m.; 🅿; z 50216; Ⓟ 1,100; Ⓒ 1,175
Panorama Park; Inc. Place; SCOTT; ***177** I-19; elev. 650ft./198m.; ★ **D-RI-M**; mail Bettendorf z 52722; Ⓟ 127; Ⓒ 111; Ⓡ 131
Paralta; RMC Place; LINN; **177** G-16; mail Springville z 52336; ● 50
Paris (Bunch); RMC Place; DAVIS; **177** L-13; mail Drakesville z 52552; ● 40
Paris; RMC Place; LINN; **177** G-16; mail Central City z 52214; ● 60
Parkersburg; Inc. Place; BUTLER; **177** E-12; elev. 947ft./289m.; 🅿; z 50665; Ⓟ 1,804; Ⓒ 1,889
Park View; CDP; SCOTT; **177** I-19; mail Eldridge z 52748; Ⓟ 2,192; Ⓒ 2,169
Parnell; Inc. Place; IOWA; **177** I-14; elev. 860ft./262m.; 🅿; z 52325; Ⓟ 209; Ⓒ 220
Paton; Inc. Place; GREENE; **176** G-8; elev. 1,100ft./335m.; 🅿; z 50217; Ⓟ 255; Ⓒ 265
Patterson; Inc. Place; MADISON; **176** J-9; 🅿; z 50218; Ⓟ 128; Ⓒ 126
Paullina; Inc. Place; O'BRIEN; **176** D-4; elev. 1,400ft./427m.; 🅿; z 51046; Ⓟ 1,134; Ⓒ 1,124
Payne; RMC Place; FREMONT; ***176** M-3; elev. 921ft./281m.; mail Hamburg z 51640; rural
Pekin; RMC Place; JEFFERSON, KEOKUK; **177** K-14; mail Packwood z 52580; ● 30
Pella; Inc. Place; MARION; **177** J-12; elev. 878ft./268m.; 🅿 🅷 🅲 1,606; z 50219; Ⓟ 9,270; Ⓒ 9,832; Ⓡ 9,909
Peoria; RMC Place; MAHASKA; **177** J-12; mail Pella z 50219; ● 110
Peosta; Inc. Place; DUBUQUE; **177** F-18; elev. 1,040ft./317m.; 🅿; z 52068; Ⓟ 128; Ⓒ 651
Percival; RMC Place; FREMONT; **176** L-3; elev. 930ft./283m.; 🅿; z 51648; ● 110
Perkins; RMC Place; SIOUX; **176** C-2; mail Hull z 51239; ● 30
Perlee; RMC Place; JEFFERSON; ***177** K-15; mail Fairfield z 52556
Perry; Inc. Place; DALLAS; **176** H-8; elev. 998ft./304m.; 🅿 🅷; z 50220; Ⓟ 6,652; Ⓒ 7,633
Pershing; RMC Place; MARION; **177** J-11; 🅿; z 50138; ● 300
Persia; Inc. Place; HARRISON; **176** I-4; elev. 1,273ft./388m.; 🅿; z 51563; Ⓟ 312; Ⓒ 363
Peru; MADISON; see East Peru (Inc. Place)
Petersburg; RMC Place; DELAWARE; **177** E-17; mail Dyersville z 52040; ● 140
Peterson; Inc. Place; CLAY; **176** D-5; elev. 1,250ft./381m.; 🅿; z 51047; Ⓟ 390; Ⓒ 372
Petersville; RMC Place; CLINTON; ***177** H-19; mail Charlotte z 52731; rural
Pierceville; RMC Place; VAN BUREN; ***177** L-15; elev. 740ft./226m.; mail Keosauqua z 52565; rural
Pierson; Inc. Place; WOODBURY; **176** E-3; elev. 1,269ft./387m.; 🅿; z 51048; Ⓟ 341; Ⓒ 371
Pilot Grove; RMC Place; LEE; **177** L-16; elev. 643ft./196m.; 🅿; z 52648; ● 40
Pilot Mound; Inc. Place; BOONE; **176** G-8; 🅿; z 50223; Ⓟ 199; Ⓒ 214
Pinney; RMC Place; LINN; ★ **CEDR**; pop. incl. with Cedar Rapids (Inc. Place)
Pioneer; Inc. Place; HUMBOLDT; **176** E-7; elev. 1,190ft./363m.; mail Gilmore City z 50541; Ⓟ 46; Ⓒ 21
Piper; RMC Place; CALHOUN; ***176** F-7; mail Rockwell City z 50579
Pisgah; Inc. Place; HARRISON; **176** H-3; elev. 1,060ft./323m.; 🅿; z 51564; Ⓟ 268; Ⓒ 316
Pittsburg; RMC Place; VAN BUREN; ***177** L-14; mail Keosauqua z 52565
Pitzer; RMC Place; MADISON; ***176** J-8; mail Earlham z 50072
Plainfield; Inc. Place; BREMER; **177** D-13; elev. 942ft./287m.; 🅿; z 50666; Ⓟ 455; Ⓒ 438
Plainview; RMC Place; SCOTT; **177** I-18; elev. 700ft./213m.; mail Walcott z 52773; ● 50
Plano; Inc. Place; APPANOOSE; **177** L-11; elev. 1,030ft./314m.; 🅿; z 52581; Ⓟ 75; Ⓒ 58
Plaza Hills; RMC Place; POLK; ★ **DES**; mail Des Moines z 50311; pop. incl. with Windsor Heights (Inc. Place)
Pleasant Grove; RMC Place; DES MOINES; **177** L-17; mail New London z 52645; ● 40
Pleasant Hill (Youngstown); Inc. Place; POLK; **177** C-20; elev. 850ft./259m.; 🅿; ★ **DES**; z 50317, z 50327; Ⓟ 3,671; Ⓒ 5,070
Pleasanton; Inc. Place; DECATUR; **176** M-9; elev. 1,090ft./332m.; 🅿; z 50065; Ⓟ 58; Ⓒ 37
Pleasant Plain; Inc. Place; JEFFERSON; **177** K-15; elev. 750ft./229m.; mail Brighton z 52540; Ⓟ 128; Ⓒ 131
Pleasant Prairie; RMC Place; MUSCATINE; ***177** I-18; mail Muscatine z 52761
Pleasant Valley; RMC Place; SCOTT; **177** I-19; elev. 600ft./183m.; 🅿; ★ **D-RI-M**; z 52767; ● 700
Pleasantville; Inc. Place; MARION; **177** J-11; elev. 920ft./280m.; 🅿; z 50225; Ⓟ 1,536; Ⓒ 1,539; Ⓡ 1,537
Plover; Inc. Place; POCAHONTAS; **176** D-7; elev. 1,210ft./369m.; 🅿; z 50573; Ⓟ 101; Ⓒ 95
Plymouth; Inc. Place; CERRO GORDO; **177** C-11; elev. 1,128ft./344m.; 🅿; z 50464; Ⓟ 453; Ⓒ 429
PLYMOUTH; **176** E-2; Ⓟ 23,388; Ⓒ 24,849; ◆ 23,739
Pocahontas; Inc. Place; ⊡ POCAHONTAS; **176** E-6; elev. 1,227ft./374m.; 🅿 🅷; z 50574; Ⓟ 2,085; Ⓒ 1,970
POCAHONTAS; **176** E-6; Ⓟ 9,525; Ⓒ 8,662; ◆ 7,534
POLK; **176** I-10; Ⓟ 327,140; Ⓒ 374,601; Ⓡ 374,605; ◆ 431,720
Polk City; Inc. Place; POLK; **176** H-9; elev. 889ft./271m.; 🅿; ★ **DES**; z 50226; Ⓟ 1,908; Ⓒ 2,344
Pomeroy; Inc. Place; CALHOUN; **176** E-6; elev. 1,243ft./379m.; 🅿; z 50575; Ⓟ 762; Ⓒ 710
Pool Yard; RMC Place; POTTAWATTAMIE; ★ **OMA**; pop. incl. with Council Bluffs (Inc. Place)
Popejoy; Inc. Place; FRANKLIN; **176** E-10; elev. 1,155ft./352m.; 🅿; z 50227; Ⓟ 92; Ⓒ 78
Portland; RMC Place; CERRO GORDO; **177** C-11; mail Mason City z 50401; ● 40
Portsmouth; Inc. Place; SHELBY; **176** I-4; elev. 1,237ft./377m.; 🅿; z 51565; Ⓟ 209; Ⓒ 225
Postville; Inc. Place; ALLAMAKEE, CLAYTON; **177** C-16; elev. 1,191ft./363m.; 🅿; z 52162; Ⓟ 1,472; Ⓒ 2,273
POTTAWATTAMIE; **176** J-4; Ⓟ 82,628; Ⓒ 87,704; Ⓡ 87,803; ◆ 86,746
Powersville; RMC Place; FLOYD; ***177** D-12; mail Greene z 50636
POWESHIEK; **177** H-13; Ⓟ 19,033; Ⓒ 18,815; Ⓡ 18,832; ◆ 18,662
Prairieburg; Inc. Place; LINN; **177** G-16; elev. 1,004ft./306m.; 🅿; z 52219; Ⓟ 213; Ⓒ 175
Prairie City; Inc. Place; JASPER; **177** I-11; elev. 926ft./282m.; 🅿; z 50228; Ⓟ 1,360; Ⓒ 1,365
Prairie Grove; RMC Place; DES MOINES; ***177** L-17; ★ **BUR**; mail West Burlington z 52655
Prescott; Inc. Place; ADAMS; **176** K-7; elev. 1,153ft./351m.; 🅿; z 50859; Ⓟ 287; Ⓒ 266
Preston; Inc. Place; JACKSON; **177** G-19; elev. 660ft./201m.; 🅿; z 52069; Ⓟ 1,025; Ⓒ 949
Primghar; Inc. Place; ⊡ O'BRIEN; **176** C-4; elev. 1,520ft./463m.; 🅿 🅷; z 51245; Ⓟ 950; Ⓒ 891
Primrose; RMC Place; LEE; **177** M-16; mail Donnellson z 52625; ● 30
Princeton; Inc. Place; SCOTT; **177** I-19; elev. 600ft./183m.; 🅿; z 52768; Ⓟ 806; Ⓒ 946
Probstei; RMC Place; SCOTT; ***177** I-18; ★ **D-RI-M**; pop. incl. with Davenport (Inc. Place)
Prole; RMC Place; WARREN; **176** J-9; elev. 970ft./296m.; 🅿; z 50229; ● 50
Promise City; Inc. Place; WAYNE; **177** L-11; elev. 1,058ft./322m.; 🅿; z 52583; Ⓟ 132; Ⓒ 105
Prospect Hill; RMC Place; DES MOINES; ★ **BUR**; mail Burlington z 52601; pop. incl. with Burlington (Inc. Place)
Protivin; Inc. Place; HOWARD, CHICKASAW; **177** C-14; elev. 1,200ft./366m.; 🅿; z 52163; Ⓟ 305; Ⓒ 317
Pulaski; Inc. Place; DAVIS; **177** M-14; elev. 838ft./255m.; 🅿; z 52584; Ⓟ 221; Ⓒ 249

Q

Quarry; RMC Place; MARSHALL; **177** G-12; mail Marshalltown z 50158; ● 60
Quasqueton; Inc. Place; BUCHANAN; **177** F-15; elev. 920ft./280m.; 🅿; z 52326; Ⓟ 579; Ⓒ 574
Quimby; Inc. Place; CHEROKEE; **176** E-4; elev. 1,188ft./362m.; 🅿; z 51049; Ⓟ 334; Ⓒ 368

R

Radcliffe; Inc. Place; HARDIN; **176** F-10; elev. 1,189ft./362m.; 🅿; z 50230; Ⓟ 574; Ⓒ 607
Rake; Inc. Place; WINNEBAGO; **176** B-9; elev. 1,167ft./356m.; 🅿; z 50465; Ⓟ 238; Ⓒ 227
Ralston; Inc. Place; CARROLL, GREENE; **176** G-7; elev. 1,123ft./342m.; 🅿; z 51459; Ⓟ 119; Ⓒ 98
Randalia; Inc. Place; FAYETTE; **177** D-15; 🅿; z 52164; Ⓟ 88; Ⓒ 84
Randall; Inc. Place; HAMILTON; **176** G-10; elev. 1,018ft./310m.; 🅿; z 50231; Ⓟ 161; Ⓒ 148
Randolph; Inc. Place; FREMONT; **176** L-4; elev. 977ft./298m.; 🅿; z 51649; Ⓟ 243; Ⓒ 209
Rands; RMC Place; CALHOUN; ***176** F-7; mail Rockwell City z 50579; rural
Rathbun; Inc. Place; APPANOOSE; **177** L-12; elev. 900ft./274m.; 🅿; z 52544; Ⓟ 89; Ⓒ 88
Raymar; RMC Place; BLACK HAWK; ***177** F-14; ★ **WATL**; mail Evansdale z 50707, Waterloo z 50701; ● 80
Raymond; Inc. Place; BLACK HAWK; **177** F-14; elev. 900ft./274m.; 🅿; ★ **WATL**; z 50667; Ⓟ 619; Ⓒ 537
Readlyn; Inc. Place; BREMER; **177** E-14; elev. 1,030ft./314m.; 🅿; z 50668; Ⓟ 773; Ⓒ 786
Reasnor; Inc. Place; JASPER; **177** I-11; elev. 760ft./232m.; 🅿; z 50232; Ⓟ 191; Ⓒ 194
Redding; Inc. Place; RINGGOLD; **176** M-7; elev. 1,138ft./347m.; 🅿; z 50860; Ⓟ 119; Ⓒ 78
Redfield; Inc. Place; DALLAS; **176** I-8; elev. 1,000ft./305m.; 🅿; z 50233; Ⓟ 883; Ⓒ 833
Red Line; RMC Place; SHELBY; ***176** I-5; mail Kirkman z 51447; rural
Red Oak; Inc. Place; ⊡ MONTGOMERY; **176** K-5; elev. 1,077ft./328m.; 🅿 🅷; z 51566, z 51591; Ⓟ 6,264; Ⓒ 6,197
Red Rock Lakeview; RMC Place; MARION; ***177** J-11; elev. 848ft./258m.; mail Knoxville z 50138; ● 50
Reinbeck; Inc. Place; GRUNDY; **177** F-13; elev. 950ft./290m.; 🅿; z 50669 & mail Morrison z 50657; Ⓟ 1,605; Ⓒ 1,751
Rembrandt; Inc. Place; BUENA VISTA; **176** D-5; elev. 1,340ft./408m.; 🅿; z 50576; Ⓟ 229; Ⓒ 228
Remsen; Inc. Place; PLYMOUTH; **176** D-3; elev. 1,330ft./405m.; 🅿; z 51050; Ⓟ 1,513; Ⓒ 1,762
Renwick; Inc. Place; HUMBOLDT; **176** D-9; elev. 930ft./283m.; 🅿; z 50577; Ⓟ 287; Ⓒ 306
Rhodes (Edenville); Inc. Place; MARSHALL; **177** H-11; elev. 1,011ft./308m.; 🅿; z 50234; Ⓟ 272; Ⓒ 294
Riceville; Inc. Place; HOWARD, MITCHELL; **177** B-13; elev. 1,229ft./375m.; 🅿; z 50466; Ⓟ 827; Ⓒ 840
Richard (Richards); RMC Place; CALHOUN; **176** F-7; mail Rockwell City z 50579; ● 30
Richards; CALHOUN; see Richard (RMC Place)
Richland; Inc. Place; KEOKUK; **177** K-14; elev. 664ft./202m.; 🅿; z 52585; Ⓟ 522; Ⓒ 587
Richmond; RMC Place; WASHINGTON; **177** J-15; elev. 750ft./229m.; mail Kalona z 52247; ● 100
Rickardsville; Inc. Place; DUBUQUE; **177** E-18; elev. 1,000ft./305m.; mail Sherrill z 52073; Ⓟ 171; Ⓒ 191
Ricketts; Inc. Place; CRAWFORD; **176** G-4; elev. 1,366ft./416m.; 🅿; z 51460; Ⓟ 105; Ⓒ 144
Ridgeport (Mineral Ridge); RMC Place; BOONE; **176** G-9; mail Boone z 50036; ● 30
Ridgeview Park; RMC Place; SCOTT; ★ **D-RI-M**; pop. incl. with Davenport (Inc. Place)
Ridgeway; Inc. Place; WINNESHIEK; **177** B-14; elev. 1,211ft./369m.; 🅿; z 52165; Ⓟ 295; Ⓒ 293
Riggs; RMC Place; CLINTON; ***177** G-19; elev. 736ft./224m.; mail Charlotte z 52731; rural
Rinard; Inc. Place; CALHOUN; **176** F-7; elev. 1,160ft./354m.; 🅿; z 50538; Ⓟ 71; Ⓒ 72
RINGGOLD; **176** L-7; Ⓟ 5,420; Ⓒ 5,469; ◆ 5,077
Ringsted; Inc. Place; EMMET; **176** B-7; elev. 1,272ft./388m.; 🅿; z 50578; Ⓟ 481; Ⓒ 436
Rippey; Inc. Place; GREENE; **176** H-8; elev. 1,077ft./328m.; 🅿; z 50235; Ⓟ 275; Ⓒ 319
Rising Sun; RMC Place; POLK; ***176** I-10; ★ **DES**; mail Des Moines z 50317; ● 100
Ritter; RMC Place; O'BRIEN; ***176** B-3; mail Sheldon z 51201
Riverdale; Inc. Place; SCOTT; ***177** I-19; elev. 600ft./183m.; 🅿; ★ **D-RI-M**; z 52722; Ⓟ 433; Ⓒ 656; Ⓡ 653
River Heights; RMC Place; JOHNSON; ***177** I-16; ★ **IACY**; mail Iowa City z 52240; ● 580
River Junction; RMC Place; JOHNSON; ***177** I-16; mail Lone Tree z 52755; ● 40
Riverside; Inc. Place; WASHINGTON; **177** J-16; elev. 650ft./198m.; 🅿; z 52327; Ⓟ 824; Ⓒ 928
Riverside; RMC Place; WOODBURY; ***176** E-1; ★ **SXCY**; mail Sioux City z 51109; pop. incl. with Sioux City (Inc. Place)
River Sioux; RMC Place; HARRISON; **176** H-2; mail Little Sioux z 51545; ● 50
Riverton; Inc. Place; FREMONT; **176** M-4; elev. 922ft./281m.; 🅿; z 51650; Ⓟ 333; Ⓒ 304
Roberts; RMC Place; WEBSTER; ***176** F-8; elev. 1,129ft./344m.; mail Otho z 50569; rural
Robertson; RMC Place; HARDIN; ***177** F-11; mail Ackley z 50601
Robins; Inc. Place; LINN; **177** G-15; 🅿; ★ **CEDR**; z 52328 & mail Cedar Rapids z 52411; Ⓟ 875; Ⓒ 1,806
Robinson; RMC Place; DELAWARE; ***177** F-16; mail Ryan z 52330; ● 30
Rochester; RMC Place; CEDAR; **177** I-17; mail Tipton z 52772; ● 90
Rock Creek (Meroa); RMC Place; MITCHELL; ***177** C-12; mail Osage z 50461; ● 30
Rockdale; RMC Place; DUBUQUE; ***177** F-18; ★ **DUB**; mail Dubuque z 52001, z 52003; pop. incl. with Dubuque (Inc. Place)
Rock Falls; Inc. Place; CERRO GORDO; **177** C-11; 🅿; z 50467; Ⓟ 130; Ⓒ 170
Rockford; Inc. Place; FLOYD; **177** C-12; elev. 1,000ft./305m.; 🅿; z 50468; Ⓟ 863; Ⓒ 907
Rock Rapids; Inc. Place; ⊡ LYON; **176** B-2; elev. 1,350ft./411m.; 🅿 🅷; z 51246; Ⓟ 2,601; Ⓒ 2,573
Rock Valley; Inc. Place; SIOUX; **176** C-2; elev. 1,252ft./382m.; 🅿 🅷; z 51247; Ⓟ 2,540; Ⓒ 2,702
Rockwell; Inc. Place; CERRO GORDO; **177** D-11; elev. 1,138ft./347m.; 🅿; z 50469; Ⓟ 1,008; Ⓒ 989
Rockwell City; Inc. Place; ⊡ CALHOUN; **176** F-7; elev. 1,220ft./372m.; 🅿; z 50579; Ⓟ 1,981; Ⓒ 2,264; Ⓡ 2,224
Rodman; Inc. Place; PALO ALTO; **176** C-7; elev. 1,199ft./365m.; mail Mallard z 50562; Ⓟ 56; Ⓒ 56
Rodney; Inc. Place; MONONA; **176** G-3; elev. 1,122ft./342m.; 🅿; z 51051; Ⓟ 65; Ⓒ 74
Roelyn; RMC Place; WEBSTER; **176** F-7; elev. 1,160ft./354m.; mail Moorland z 50566; ● 30
Roland; Inc. Place; STORY; **176** G-10; elev. 1,020ft./311m.; 🅿; z 50236; Ⓟ 1,035; Ⓒ 1,324
Rolfe; Inc. Place; POCAHONTAS; **176** D-7; elev. 1,185ft./361m.; 🅿; z 50581; Ⓟ 721; Ⓒ 675
Rome; Inc. Place; HENRY; **177** L-15; elev. 628ft./191m.; 🅿; z 52642; Ⓟ 124; Ⓒ 113
Rose Hill; Inc. Place; MAHASKA; **177** J-13; elev. 800ft./244m.; 🅿; z 52586; Ⓟ 171; Ⓒ 205
Roselle; RMC Place; CARROLL; **176** G-6; mail Carroll z 51401; ● 60
Ross; RMC Place; AUDUBON; **176** H-6; mail Audubon z 50025; ● 60
Rosserdale; RMC Place; ADAIR; ***176** J-7; mail Menlo z 50164; rural
Rossie; Inc. Place; CLAY; **176** C-5; elev. 1,413ft./431m.; 🅿; z 51357; Ⓟ 68; Ⓒ 58
Rossville; RMC Place; ALLAMAKEE; **177** C-16; mail Monona z 52159, Waukon z 52172; ● 80
Rowan; Inc. Place; WRIGHT; **176** E-10; elev. 1,212ft./369m.; 🅿; z 50470; Ⓟ 189; Ⓒ 218
Rowley; Inc. Place; BUCHANAN; **177** F-15; 🅿; z 52329; Ⓟ 272; Ⓒ 290
Royal; Inc. Place; CLAY; **176** C-5; elev. 1,410ft./430m.; 🅿; z 51357; Ⓟ 466; Ⓒ 479
Rubio; RMC Place; WASHINGTON; **177** K-15; elev. 635ft./194m.; 🅿; z 52585; ● 60
Rudd; Inc. Place; FLOYD; **177** C-12; elev. 1,110ft./338m.; 🅿; z 50471; Ⓟ 429; Ⓒ 431
Runnells; Inc. Place; POLK; **176** I-10; elev. 780ft./238m.; 🅿; z 50237; Ⓟ 306; Ⓒ 352
Russell; Inc. Place; LUCAS; **177** L-11; elev. 1,030ft./314m.; 🅿; z 50238; Ⓟ 531; Ⓒ 559
Ruthven; Inc. Place; PALO ALTO; **176** C-6; elev. 1,431ft./436m.; 🅿; z 51358; Ⓟ 707; Ⓒ 711; Ⓡ 765
Rutland; Inc. Place; HUMBOLDT; **176** D-8; elev. 1,122ft./342m.; 🅿; z 50582; Ⓟ 149; Ⓒ 145
Ryan; Inc. Place; DELAWARE; **177** F-16; elev. 1,013ft./309m.; 🅿; z 52330; Ⓟ 382; Ⓒ 410

S

Sabula; Inc. Place; JACKSON; **177** G-20; elev. 602ft./183m.; 🅿; z 52070; Ⓟ 710; Ⓒ 670
SAC; **176** F-5; Ⓟ 12,324; Ⓒ 11,529; ◆ 9,913
Sac and Fox/Meskwaki Reservation; Indian Reservation; TAMA; mail Tama z 52339; Sac and Fox Indian Agency located in Tama; Ⓟ 509; Ⓒ 616
Sac City; Inc. Place; ⊡ SAC; **176** F-6; elev. 1,201ft./366m.; 🅿 🅷; z 50583; Ⓟ 2,492; Ⓒ 2,368
Sageville; Inc. Place; DUBUQUE; **177** E-18; elev. 616ft./188m.; ★ **DUB**; mail Dubuque z 52001; Ⓟ 288; Ⓒ 203
Saint Ansgar; Inc. Place; MITCHELL; **177** B-12; elev. 1,171ft./357m.; 🅿; z 50472 & mail Toeterville z 50481; Ⓟ 1,063; Ⓒ 1,031
Saint Anthony; Inc. Place; MARSHALL; **177** G-11; elev. 1,003ft./306m.; 🅿; z 50239; Ⓟ 112; Ⓒ 109
Saint Benedict; RMC Place; KOSSUTH; **176** C-8; mail Algona z 50511; ● 60
Saint Catherine; DUBUQUE; see King (RMC Place)
Saint Charles; Inc. Place; MADISON; **176** J-9; elev. 1,066ft./325m.; 🅿; z 50240; Ⓟ 537; Ⓒ 619
Saint Donatus; Inc. Place; JACKSON; **177** F-19; elev. 680ft./207m.; 🅿; z 52071; Ⓟ 145; Ⓒ 140
Saint Joseph; RMC Place; KOSSUTH; **176** D-8; mail Bode z 50519; ● 60
Saint Lucas; Inc. Place; FAYETTE; **177** C-14; elev. 1,060ft./323m.; 🅿; z 52166; Ⓟ 174; Ⓒ 178
Saint Marys; Inc. Place; WARREN; **176** J-9; elev. 1,033ft./315m.; 🅿; z 50241; Ⓟ 113; Ⓒ 134
Saint Olaf; Inc. Place; CLAYTON; **177** D-16; elev. 849ft./259m.; 🅿; z 52072; Ⓟ 111; Ⓒ 136
Saint Paul; Inc. Place; LEE; **177** L-16; elev. 700ft./213m.; 🅿; z 52657; Ⓟ 120; Ⓒ 118
Salem; Inc. Place; HENRY; **177** L-16; elev. 715ft./218m.; 🅿; z 52649; Ⓟ 453; Ⓒ 464
Salina; RMC Place; JEFFERSON; **177** K-15; mail Fairfield z 52556; ● 25
Salix; Inc. Place; WOODBURY; **176** F-2; elev. 1,083ft./330m.; 🅿; z 51052; Ⓟ 367; Ⓒ 370
Sanborn; Inc. Place; O'BRIEN; **176** C-4; elev. 1,550ft./472m.; 🅿; z 51248; Ⓟ 1,345; Ⓒ 1,353
Sand Prairie; LEE; see Vincennes (RMC Place)
Sand Springs; RMC Place; DELAWARE; **177** F-17; mail Hopkinton z 52237; ● 40
Sandusky; RMC Place; LEE; **177** N-16; mail Keokuk z 52632; ● 70
Sandyville; Inc. Place; WARREN; **176** J-10; elev. 942ft./287m.; mail Ackworth z 50001; Ⓟ 59; Ⓒ 61
Santiago; RMC Place; POLK; ***176** I-10; mail Mitchellville z 50169; ● 50
Saratoga; RMC Place; HOWARD; **177** B-13; elev. 1,250ft./381m.; 🅿; z 52155; ● 60
Saude; RMC Place; CHICKASAW; ***177** C-14; mail Lawler z 52154
Savannah; RMC Place; DAVIS; **177** M-13; mail Bloomfield z 52537; ● 30
Sawyer; RMC Place; LEE; ***177** M-16; mail Fort Madison z 52627
Saydel; RMC Place; POLK; **177** A-20; ★ **DES**; mail Des Moines z 50313; ● 3,500
Saylorville; CDP; POLK; **177** A-20; ★ **DES**; mail Des Moines z 50313; Ⓟ 2,709; Ⓒ 3,238
Scarville; Inc. Place; WINNEBAGO; **176** B-10; elev. 1,246ft./380m.; 🅿; z 50473; Ⓟ 92; Ⓒ 97
Schaller; Inc. Place; SAC; **176** E-5; elev. 1,439ft./439m.; 🅿; z 51053; Ⓟ 768; Ⓒ 779
Schleswig; Inc. Place; CRAWFORD; **176** G-4; elev. 1,497ft./456m.; 🅿; z 51461; Ⓟ 851; Ⓒ 833
Schley; RMC Place; HOWARD; **177** B-14; mail Cresco z 52136; ● 30
Sciola; RMC Place; MONTGOMERY; ***176** K-5; elev. 1,090ft./332m.; mail Villisca z 50864; rural
Scotch Grove; RMC Place; JONES; **177** G-17; elev. 900ft./274m.; 🅿; z 52310; ● 60
Scotch Ridge; RMC Place; WARREN; ***176** J-10; ★ **DES**; mail Carlisle z 50047
SCOTT; **177** I-19; Ⓟ 150,979; Ⓒ 158,668; Ⓡ 158,689; ◆ 160,853
Scranton; Inc. Place; GREENE; **176** G-7; elev. 1,185ft./361m.; 🅿; z 51462; Ⓟ 583; Ⓒ 604
Searsboro; Inc. Place; POWESHIEK; **177** I-12; elev. 817ft./249m.; 🅿; z 50242; Ⓟ 164; Ⓒ 155
Selma; RMC Place; VAN BUREN; **177** L-14; elev. 650ft./198m.; 🅿; z 52588; ● 80
Selser's; RMC Place; LINN; ***177** H-15; elev. 806ft./246m.; ★ **CEDR**; mail Fairfax z 52228; ● 90
Seneca; RMC Place; KOSSUTH; **176** B-7; mail Fenton z 50539; ● 30
Seney; RMC Place; PLYMOUTH; **176** D-2; mail Le Mars z 51031; ● 80
Sergeant Bluff; Inc. Place; WOODBURY; **176** F-2; elev. 1,092ft./333m.; 🅿; ★ **SXCY**; z 51054; Ⓟ 2,772; Ⓒ 3,321
Sewal; RMC Place; WAYNE; **177** M-11; elev. 1,100ft./335m.; 🅿; z 50060; ● 40
Sexton; RMC Place; KOSSUTH; **176** C-8; mail Algona z 50511, Wesley z 50483; ● 40
Seymour; Inc. Place; WAYNE; **177** M-11; elev. 1,068ft./326m.; 🅿; z 52590; Ⓟ 869; Ⓒ 810
Shaffton; RMC Place; CLINTON; ***177** H-19; ★ **CLNT**; mail Camanche z 52730; rural
Shambaugh; Inc. Place; PAGE; **176** M-5; elev. 983ft./300m.; 🅿; z 51651; Ⓟ 190; Ⓒ 188
Shannon City; Inc. Place; UNION, RINGGOLD; **176** L-8; elev. 1,144ft./349m.; 🅿; z 50861; Ⓟ 97; Ⓒ 70
Sharon Center; RMC Place; JOHNSON; **177** I-15; mail Iowa City z 52240; ● 120
Sharpsburg; Inc. Place; TAYLOR; **176** L-6; elev. 1,273ft./388m.; 🅿; z 50862; Ⓟ 116; Ⓒ 98
Shaver; RMC Place; LINN; ★ **CEDR**; pop. incl. with Cedar Rapids (Inc. Place)
Shawondasse; RMC Place; DUBUQUE; ***177** F-18; mail Dubuque z 52001, z 52003
Sheffield; Inc. Place; FRANKLIN; **177** D-11; elev. 1,079ft./329m.; 🅿; z 50475; Ⓟ 1,174; Ⓒ 930
Shelby; Inc. Place; SHELBY, POTTAWATTAMIE; **176** I-4; elev. 1,338ft./408m.; 🅿; z 51570; Ⓟ 637; Ⓒ 696
SHELBY; **176** I-4; Ⓟ 13,230; Ⓒ 13,173; Ⓡ 13,074; ◆ 12,170
Sheldahl; Inc. Place; STORY, BOONE, POLK; **176** H-9; elev. 1,020ft./311m.; 🅿; ★ **AMES**; z 50243; Ⓟ 315; Ⓒ 336
Sheldon; Inc. Place; O'BRIEN, SIOUX; **176** C-3; elev. 1,420ft./433m.; 🅿 🅷; z 51201; Ⓟ 4,937; Ⓒ 4,914
Shell Rock; Inc. Place; BUTLER; **177** E-13; elev. 903ft./275m.; 🅿; z 50670; Ⓟ 1,385; Ⓒ 1,298
Shellsburg; Inc. Place; BENTON; **177** G-15; elev. 774ft./236m.; 🅿; z 52332; Ⓟ 765; Ⓒ 938
Shenandoah; Inc. Place; PAGE, FREMONT; **176** L-4; elev. 981ft./299m.; 🅿 🅷; z 51601-03; Ⓟ 5,572; Ⓒ 5,546
Sheridan; RMC Place; POWESHIEK; ***177** H-13; mail Malcom z 50157; rural
Sherrill; Inc. Place; DUBUQUE; **177** E-18; elev. 980ft./299m.; 🅿; z 52073; Ⓟ 148; Ⓒ 186
Sherwood; RMC Place; CALHOUN; ***176** F-6; mail Rockwell City z 50579; rural
Shipley; RMC Place; STORY; ***176** H-10; mail Nevada z 50201
Shueyville; Inc. Place; JOHNSON; **177** H-15; elev. 791ft./241m.; ★ **CEDR**; mail Cedar Rapids z 52404; Ⓟ 223; Ⓒ 250
Siam; RMC Place; TAYLOR; ***176** M-6; mail Bedford z 50833
Sibley; Inc. Place; ⊡ OSCEOLA; **176** B-3; elev. 1,512ft./461m.; 🅿 🅷; z 51249; Ⓟ 2,815; Ⓒ 2,796
Sidney; Inc. Place; ⊡ FREMONT; **176** L-3; elev. 1,150ft./351m.; 🅿; z 51652; Ⓟ 1,253; Ⓒ 1,300
Sigourney; Inc. Place; ⊡ KEOKUK; **177** J-14; elev. 798ft./243m.; 🅿 🅷; z 52591; Ⓟ 2,111; Ⓒ 2,209
Silver City; Inc. Place; MILLS; **176** K-3; elev. 1,044ft./318m.; 🅿; z 51571; Ⓟ 252; Ⓒ 259
Sinclair; RMC Place; BUTLER; ***177** E-12; mail Parkersburg z 50665
SIOUX; **176** C-2; Ⓟ 29,903; Ⓒ 31,589; ◆ 31,669
Sioux Center; Inc. Place; SIOUX; **176** C-2; elev. 1,460ft./445m.; 🅿 🅷 🅲 1,266; z 51250; Ⓟ 5,074; Ⓒ 6,002
Sioux City; Inc. Place; ⊡ WOODBURY; **176** E-1; elev. 1,117ft./340m.; 🅿 🅷 🅲 2,918 ■; ★ **SXCY**; z 51101-06, z 51108-09, z 51111; Ⓟ 80,505; Ⓒ 85,013; ◆ 82,003
Sioux Rapids; Inc. Place; BUENA VISTA; **176** D-5; 🅿; z 50585; Ⓟ 761; Ⓒ 720
Sixmile; RMC Place; CLINTON; ***177** H-19; mail Clinton z 52732; rural
Slater; Inc. Place; STORY; **176** H-9; elev. 1,040ft./317m.; 🅿; ★ **AMES**; z 50244; Ⓟ 1,268; Ⓒ 1,306
Slifer; RMC Place; WEBSTER; **176** F-7; elev. 1,139ft./347m.; mail Gowrie z 50543; ● 30
Sloan; Inc. Place; WOODBURY; **176** F-2; elev. 1,072ft./327m.; 🅿; z 51055; Ⓟ 938; Ⓒ 1,032
Smithland; Inc. Place; WOODBURY; **176** G-3; elev. 1,090ft./332m.; 🅿; z 51056; Ⓟ 235; Ⓒ 221
Soldier; Inc. Place; MONONA; **176** H-3; elev. 1,180ft./360m.; 🅿; z 51572; Ⓟ 205; Ⓒ 207
Solon; Inc. Place; JOHNSON; **177** H-16; elev. 800ft./244m.; 🅿; ★ **IACY**; z 52333; Ⓟ 1,050; Ⓒ 1,177
Somers; Inc. Place; CALHOUN; **176** F-7; elev. 1,150ft./351m.; 🅿; z 50586; Ⓟ 161; Ⓒ 165
South Amana; RMC Place; IOWA; **177** H-14; elev. 770ft./235m.; 🅿; z 52334; ● 100
South Des Moines; RMC Place; POLK; ***176** I-10; ★ **DES**; mail Des Moines z 50315, z 50320-21; pop. incl. with Des Moines (Inc. Place)
South English; Inc. Place; KEOKUK; **177** J-14; elev. 840ft./256m.; 🅿; z 52335; Ⓟ 224; Ⓒ 213
South Muscatine; RMC Place; MUSCATINE; mail Muscatine z 52761; pop. incl. with Muscatine (Inc. Place)
South Ottumwa; RMC Place; WAPELLO; mail Ottumwa z 52501; pop. incl. with Ottumwa (Inc. Place)
Spaulding; RMC Place; UNION; ***176** K-7; mail Creston z 50801
Spencer; Inc. Place; ⊡ CLAY; **176** C-5; elev. 1,321ft./403m.; 🅿 🅷; z 51301 & mail Greenville z 51343; Ⓟ 11,066; Ⓒ 11,317
Sperry; RMC Place; DES MOINES; **177** L-17; elev. 750ft./229m.; 🅿; z 52650; ● 70
Spillville; Inc. Place; WINNESHIEK; **177** C-14; 🅿; z 52168; Ⓟ 387; Ⓒ 386
Spirit Lake; Inc. Place; ⊡ DICKINSON; **176** B-5; elev. 1,450ft./442m.; 🅿 🅷; z 51360; Ⓟ 3,871; Ⓒ 4,261
Spragueville; Inc. Place; JACKSON; **177** G-19; elev. 663ft./202m.; 🅿; z 52074; Ⓟ 118; Ⓒ 89
Springbrook; Inc. Place; JACKSON; **177** G-19; elev. 750ft./229m.; 🅿; z 52075; Ⓟ 116; Ⓒ 182
Springdale; RMC Place; CEDAR; **177** I-17; mail West Branch z 52358; ● 50
Springdale; RMC Place; WOODBURY; ***176** E-1; ★ **SXCY**; pop. incl. with Sioux City (Inc. Place)
Spring Green Estates; RMC Place; LINN; ***177** G-15; elev. 750ft./229m.; ★ **CEDR**; mail Cedar Rapids z 52411; ● 30
Spring Grove; RMC Place; DES MOINES; ***177** L-17; ★ **BUR**; mail Burlington z 52601; ● 100
Spring Hill; Inc. Place; WARREN; **176** J-9; elev. 820ft./250m.; 🅿; ★ **DES**; z 50125; Ⓟ 86; Ⓒ 92
Springville; Inc. Place; LINN; **177** G-16; elev. 845ft./258m.; 🅿; z 52336; Ⓟ 1,068; Ⓒ 1,091
Spruce Hills Village; RMC Place; SCOTT; ★ **D-RI-M**; mail Bettendorf z 52722; pop. incl. with Bettendorf (Inc. Place)
Stacyville; Inc. Place; MITCHELL; **177** B-12; elev. 1,203ft./367m.; 🅿; z 50476; Ⓟ 481; Ⓒ 469
Stanhope; Inc. Place; HAMILTON; **176** F-9; elev. 1,119ft./341m.; 🅿; z 50246; Ⓟ 447; Ⓒ 488
Stanley; Inc. Place; BUCHANAN, FAYETTE; **177** E-15; elev. 1,106ft./337m.; 🅿; z 50671; Ⓟ 116; Ⓒ 128
Stanton; Inc. Place; MONTGOMERY; **176** L-5; elev. 1,170ft./357m.; 🅿; z 51573; Ⓟ 692; Ⓒ 714
Stanwood; Inc. Place; CEDAR; **177** H-17; elev. 840ft./256m.; 🅿; z 52337; Ⓟ 646; Ⓒ 680
Stanzel; RMC Place; ADAIR; ***176** J-8; mail Greenfield z 50849; rural
State Center; Inc. Place; MARSHALL; **177** G-11; elev. 1,077ft./328m.; 🅿; z 50247; Ⓟ 1,248; Ⓒ 1,349
Steamboat Rock; Inc. Place; HARDIN; **177** F-11; elev. 983ft./300m.; 🅿; z 50672; Ⓟ 335; Ⓒ 336
Stennett; RMC Place; MONTGOMERY; ***176** K-5; mail Red Oak z 51566
Sterling; RMC Place; JACKSON; ***177** G-20; elev. 893ft./272m.; mail Sabula z 52070; rural
Stiles; RMC Place; DAVIS; ***177** M-13; mail Bloomfield z 52537; ● 20
Stilson; RMC Place; HANCOCK; ***176** C-9; mail Britt z 50423
Stockport; Inc. Place; VAN BUREN; **177** L-15; elev. 747ft./228m.; 🅿; z 52651; Ⓟ 260; Ⓒ 284
Stockton; Inc. Place; MUSCATINE; **177** I-18; elev. 717ft./219m.; 🅿; z 52769; Ⓟ 187; Ⓒ 182
Stone City; RMC Place; JONES; **177** G-16; mail Anamosa z 52205; ● 50
Storm Lake; Inc. Place; ⊡ BUENA VISTA; **176** E-5; elev. 1,435ft./437m.; 🅿 🅷 🅲 1,202; z 50588; Ⓟ 8,769; Ⓒ 10,076
STORY; **176** G-10; Ⓟ 74,252; Ⓒ 79,981; ◆ 93,217
Story City; Inc. Place; STORY; **176** G-10; elev. 999ft./304m.; 🅿; ★ **AMES**; z 50248; Ⓟ 2,959; Ⓒ 3,228
Stout; Inc. Place; GRUNDY; **177** E-12; elev. 1,020ft./311m.; 🅿; z 50673; Ⓟ 192; Ⓒ 217
Strahan; RMC Place; MILLS; **176** L-4; mail Hastings z 51540; ● 30
Stratford; Inc. Place; HAMILTON, WEBSTER; **176** F-9; elev. 1,116ft./340m.; 🅿; z 50249; Ⓟ 715; Ⓒ 746
Strawberry Point; Inc. Place; CLAYTON; **177** E-16; elev. 1,200ft./366m.; 🅿; z 52076; Ⓟ 1,357; Ⓒ 1,386
Stringtown; RMC Place; ADAMS; ***176** L-7; mail Lenox z 50851; rural
Struble; Inc. Place; PLYMOUTH; **176** D-2; elev. 1,260ft./384m.; mail Le Mars z 51031; Ⓟ 67; Ⓒ 85
Stuart; Inc. Place; GUTHRIE, ADAIR; **176** I-7; elev. 1,210ft./369m.; 🅿; z 50250; Ⓟ 1,522; Ⓒ 1,712
Suburban Heights; RMC Place; JEFFERSON; ***177** K-14; elev. 760ft./232m.; mail Fairfield z 52556; ● 200
Sully; Inc. Place; JASPER; **177** I-12; elev. 929ft./283m.; 🅿; z 50251; Ⓟ 841; Ⓒ 904
Sulphur Springs; RMC Place; BUENA VISTA; **176** E-5; mail Storm Lake z 50588; ● 40
Summerset; RMC Place; WARREN; **176** J-10; mail Indianola z 50125; ● 150
Summitville; RMC Place; LEE; **177** N-16; mail Keokuk z 52632; ● 50
Sumner; Inc. Place; BREMER, FAYETTE; **177** D-14; elev. 1,060ft./323m.; 🅿 🅷; z 50674; Ⓟ 2,078; Ⓒ 2,106
Sunbury; RMC Place; CEDAR; **177** I-18; mail Wilton z 52778; ● 50
Sunshine; RMC Place; APPANOOSE; ***177** M-12; mail Centerville z 52544
Superior; Inc. Place; DICKINSON; **176** B-6; elev. 1,501ft./458m.; 🅿; z 51363; Ⓟ 128; Ⓒ 142
Sutherland; Inc. Place; O'BRIEN; **176** D-4; elev. 1,450ft./442m.; 🅿; z 51058; Ⓟ 714; Ⓒ 707
Sutleff; JOHNSON; see Sutliff (RMC Place)
Sutliff (Sutleff); RMC Place; JOHNSON; ***177** H-16; elev. 700ft./213m.; mail Lisbon z 52253; ● 30
Swaledale; Inc. Place; CERRO GORDO; **176** D-10; elev. 1,149ft./350m.; 🅿; z 50477; Ⓟ 190; Ⓒ 174
Swan; Inc. Place; MARION; **176** J-10; 🅿; z 50252; Ⓟ 76; Ⓒ 121
Swea City; Inc. Place; KOSSUTH; **176** B-8; elev. 1,187ft./362m.; 🅿; z 50590; Ⓟ 634; Ⓒ 642
Swedesburg; RMC Place; HENRY; **177** K-16; 🅿; z 52652; ● 130
Sweetland Center; RMC Place; MUSCATINE; ***177** I-17; mail Muscatine z 52761
Swisher; Inc. Place; JOHNSON; **177** H-15; elev. 793ft./242m.; 🅿; ★ **CEDR**; z 52338; Ⓟ 645; Ⓒ 813

T

Tabor; Inc. Place; FREMONT, MILLS; **176** L-3; elev. 1,250ft./381m.; 🅿; z 51653; Ⓟ 957; Ⓒ 993
Taintor; RMC Place; MAHASKA; **177** J-12; elev. 884ft./269m.; 🅿; z 50207; ● 40
Talleyrand; RMC Place; KEOKUK; ***177** J-15; mail Keota z 52248; rural
Tama; Inc. Place; TAMA; **177** H-13; elev. 820ft./250m.; 🅿; z 52339; location of Sac and Fox Area Indian Agency; Ⓟ 2,697; Ⓒ 2,731
TAMA; **177** G-13; Ⓟ 17,419; Ⓒ 18,103; ◆ 17,434
Tara; RMC Place; WEBSTER; ***176** F-8; mail Fort Dodge z 50501
TAYLOR; **176** L-6; Ⓟ 7,114; Ⓒ 6,958; ◆ 6,083
Teeds Grove; RMC Place; CLINTON; **177** G-20; elev. 700ft./213m.; 🅿; z 52771; ● 100
Templar Park; RMC Place; DICKINSON; mail Spirit Lake z 51360; summer pop. 150
Templeton; Inc. Place; CARROLL; **176** H-6; elev. 1,431ft./436m.; 🅿; z 51463; Ⓟ 321; Ⓒ 334
Tenmile; RMC Place; CLINTON; **177** H-19; mail Bryant z 52727; ● 30
Tennant; Inc. Place; SHELBY; **176** I-4; elev. 1,382ft./421m.; 🅿; z 51537; Ⓟ 78; Ⓒ 73
Tenville; RMC Place; MONTGOMERY; ***176** K-5; elev. 1,060ft./323m.; mail Villisca z 50864
Terril; Inc. Place; DICKINSON; **176** B-6; elev. 1,415ft./431m.; 🅿; z 51364; Ⓟ 383; Ⓒ 404
Thayer; Inc. Place; UNION; **176** K-8; elev. 1,107ft./337m.; 🅿; z 50254; Ⓟ 79; Ⓒ 66
Thirty; RMC Place; APPANOOSE; ***177** M-12; elev. 1,022ft./312m.; mail Centerville z 52544; rural
Thompson; Inc. Place; WINNEBAGO; **176** B-9; elev. 1,259ft./384m.; 🅿; z 50478; Ⓟ 498; Ⓒ 596
Thor; Inc. Place; HUMBOLDT; **176** E-8; elev. 1,143ft./348m.; 🅿; z 50591; Ⓟ 205; Ⓒ 174
Thornburg; Inc. Place; KEOKUK; **177** J-13; elev. 880ft./268m.; 🅿; z 50255; Ⓟ 91; Ⓒ 84
Thornton; Inc. Place; CERRO GORDO; **176** D-10; elev. 1,191ft./363m.; 🅿; z 50479; Ⓟ 431; Ⓒ 422
Thorpe; RMC Place; DELAWARE; ***177** E-16; mail Manchester z 52057
Thurman; Inc. Place; FREMONT; **176** L-3; elev. 970ft./296m.; 🅿; z 51654; Ⓟ 239; Ⓒ 236
Ticonic; RMC Place; MONONA; ***176** G-3; elev. 1,086ft./331m.; mail Castana z 51010
Tiffin; Inc. Place; JOHNSON; **177** I-15; 🅿; ★ **IACY**; z 52340; Ⓟ 460; Ⓒ 975; Ⓡ 973
Timber Creek; RMC Place; LINN; ***177** G-15; elev. 785ft./239m.; ★ **CEDR**; mail Cedar Rapids z 52401; ● 30
Timberland Heights; RMC Place; STORY; ★ **AMES**; mail Ames z 50010, z 50014; pop. incl. with Ames (Inc. Place)
Tingley; Inc. Place; RINGGOLD; **176** L-8; elev. 1,251ft./381m.; 🅿; z 50863; Ⓟ 179; Ⓒ 171
Tipton; Inc. Place; ⊡ CEDAR; **177** H-17; elev. 820ft./250m.; 🅿; z 52772; Ⓟ 2,998; Ⓒ 3,155
Titonka; Inc. Place; KOSSUTH; **176** C-8; elev. 1,162ft./354m.; 🅿; z 50480; Ⓟ 612; Ⓒ 584
Toddville; RMC Place; LINN; **177** G-15; elev. 769ft./234m.; 🅿; ★ **CEDR**; z 52341; ● 200
Toeterville; RMC Place; MITCHELL; **177** B-12; elev. 1,200ft./366m.; 🅿; z 50481; ● 50
Toledo; Inc. Place; ⊡ TAMA; **177** H-13; elev. 850ft./259m.; 🅿; z 52342; Ⓟ 2,380; Ⓒ 2,539
Toolesboro; RMC Place; LOUISA; **177** K-17; mail Wapello z 52653; ● 40
Toronto; Inc. Place; CLINTON; **177** H-18; elev. 700ft./213m.; 🅿; z 52777; Ⓟ 132; Ⓒ 134
Tower Terrace; RMC Place; LINN; ***177** G-15; elev. 850ft./259m.; ★ **CEDR**; mail Hiawatha z 52233; pop. incl. with Hiawatha (Inc. Place)
Tracy; RMC Place; MARION; **177** J-12; elev. 730ft./223m.; 🅿; z 50256; ● 450
Traer; Inc. Place; TAMA; **177** G-13; elev. 913ft./278m.; 🅿; z 50675; Ⓟ 1,552; Ⓒ 1,594
Trenton; RMC Place; HENRY; **177** K-16; 🅿; z 52641; ● 120
Treynor; Inc. Place; POTTAWATTAMIE; **176** J-4; elev. 1,220ft./372m.; 🅿; z 51575; Ⓟ 897; Ⓒ 950
Triboji Beach; RMC Place; DICKINSON; ***176** B-5; mail Spirit Lake z 51360; summer pop. 500; ● 150
Tripoli; Inc. Place; BREMER; **177** D-14; elev. 1,017ft./310m.; 🅿; z 50676; Ⓟ 1,188; Ⓒ 1,310
Troy; RMC Place; DAVIS; **177** L-14; elev. 800ft./244m.; mail Bloomfield z 52537; ● 70
Troy Mills; RMC Place; LINN; **177** F-15; 🅿; z 52344; ● 200
Truax; MAHASKA; see Lakonta (RMC Place)
Truesdale; Inc. Place; BUENA VISTA; **176** E-5; elev. 1,359ft./414m.; 🅿; z 50592; Ⓟ 132; Ⓒ 91
Truro; Inc. Place; MADISON; **176** K-9; elev. 1,077ft./328m.; 🅿; z 50257; Ⓟ 391; Ⓒ 427
Turin; Inc. Place; MONONA; **176** G-3; elev. 1,054ft./321m.; 🅿; z 51040; Ⓟ 95; Ⓒ 75
Turkey River; RMC Place; CLAYTON; ***177** E-17; mail Guttenberg z 52052; rural

Entries in **UPPERCASE** are counties.
Entries in **bold** have populations of 2,500 or more.
Names in parentheses are alternate names.
Inc. Place — Incorporated Place
RMC Place — Rand McNally Designated Place
CDP — Census Designated Place
MCD — Minor Civil Division

⊡ County Seat
▲ Minor Civil Division
elev. Elevation
🅿 Post Office
🅷 Hospital
🅲 College
■ Principal Business Center
★ Ranally Metro Area (RMA) Abbreviation
z Zip Code(s)
Ⓟ Previous Census Population
Ⓡ Revised Census Population
Ⓐ Annexation Population
● Rand McNally Population Estimate
Ⓒ Final Census Population
Ⓢ Special Census Population
◆ Estimated Population

For additional definitions see Glossary, Volume 1, and Introduction, Volume 2.

Twin Knolls; RMC Place; LINN; ***177** G-15; elev. 835ft./255m.; ★ **CEDR**; mail Cedar Rapids **z** 52401; ● 30
Twin Lakes Estates; RMC Place; LINN; ***177** H-16; elev. 820ft./250m.; ★ **CEDR**; mail Cedar Rapids **z** 52401; ● 30
Twin View Heights; RMC Place; JOHNSON; ***177** H-16; ★ **IACY**; mail Solon **z** 52333; ● 350

U

Udell; Inc. Place; APPANOOSE; **177** L-12; elev. 980ft./299m.; 🅿; **z** 52593; Ⓟ 76; Ⓒ 58
Ulmer; RMC Place; SAC; **176** F-6; elev. 1,272ft./388m.; mail Lake View **z** 51450; ● 30
Underwood; Inc. Place; POTTAWATTAMIE; **176** J-3; elev. 1,072ft./327m.; 🅿; **z** 51576; Ⓟ 515; Ⓒ 688
Union; Inc. Place; HARDIN; **177** G-11; 🅿; **z** 50258 & mail Gifford **z** 50259; Ⓟ 448; Ⓒ 427
UNION; **176** L-7; Ⓟ 12,750; Ⓒ 12,309; ◆ 12,204
Union Center; RMC Place; PLYMOUTH; ***176** E-2; mail Le Mars **z** 51031; rural
Union Mills; RMC Place; MAHASKA; ***177** J-13; mail New Sharon **z** 50207; rural
Unionville; Inc. Place; APPANOOSE; **177** L-12; elev. 930ft./283m.; 🅿; **z** 52594; Ⓟ 133; Ⓒ 127
University Heights; Inc. Place; JOHNSON; **177** I-16; elev. 785ft./239m.; ★ **IACY**; mail Iowa City **z** 52246; Ⓟ 1,042; Ⓒ 987
University Park; Inc. Place; MAHASKA; **177** J-13; elev. 800ft./244m.; 🅿; **z** 52595; Ⓟ 604; Ⓒ 536
Urbana; Inc. Place; BENTON; **177** G-15; elev. 940ft./287m.; 🅿; **z** 52345; Ⓟ 595; Ⓒ 1,019
Urbandale; Inc. Place; POLK, DALLAS; **177** B-19; elev. 900ft./274m.; 🅿 🅲 700; ★ **DES**; **z** 50322-23, **z** 50391, **z** 50398; Ⓟ 23,500; Ⓒ 29,072; ◆ 35,366
Ute; Inc. Place; MONONA; **176** G-3; elev. 1,240ft./378m.; 🅿; **z** 51060; Ⓟ 395; Ⓒ 378
Utica; RMC Place; VAN BUREN; ***177** L-15; elev. 747ft./228m.; mail Stockport **z** 52651

V

Vail; Inc. Place; CRAWFORD; **176** G-5; elev. 1,257ft./383m.; 🅿; **z** 51465; Ⓟ 388; Ⓒ 452
Valeria; Inc. Place; JASPER; **176** I-10; mail Colfax **z** 50054; Ⓟ 69; Ⓒ 62
VAN BUREN; **177** L-14; Ⓟ 7,676; Ⓒ 7,809; ◆ 7,593
Van Cleve; RMC Place; MARSHALL; **177** H-11; mail Melbourne **z** 50162; ● 50
Vandalia; RMC Place; JASPER; **176** I-10; mail Prairie City **z** 50228; ● 60
Van Horne; Inc. Place; BENTON; **177** G-14; elev. 950ft./290m.; 🅿; **z** 52346; Ⓟ 695; Ⓒ 716
Van Meter; Inc. Place; DALLAS; **176** I-9; elev. 885ft./270m.; 🅿; **z** 50261; Ⓟ 751; Ⓒ 866
Van Wert; Inc. Place; DECATUR; **176** L-9; elev. 1,166ft./355m.; 🅿; **z** 50262; Ⓟ 249; Ⓒ 231
Varina; Inc. Place; POCAHONTAS; **176** E-6; elev. 1,258ft./383m.; 🅿; **z** 50593; Ⓟ 102; Ⓒ 90
Vedic City; JEFFERSON; see Maharishi Vedic City (Inc. Place)
Ventura; Inc. Place; CERRO GORDO; **176** C-10; elev. 1,256ft./383m.; 🅿; **z** 50482; Ⓟ 590; Ⓒ 670
Ventura Heights; RMC Place; CERRO GORDO; ***176** C-10; elev. 1,231ft./375m.; mail Ventura **z** 50482; ● 100
Vernon; RMC Place; VAN BUREN; **177** M-15; mail Keosauqua **z** 52565; ● 40
Vernon Springs; RMC Place; HOWARD; **177** B-14; mail Cresco **z** 52136; ● 40
Vernon View; RMC Place; LINN; ***177** H-16; ★ **CEDR**; mail Cedar Rapids **z** 52401; ● 120
Victor; Inc. Place; IOWA, POWESHIEK; **177** I-14; elev. 805ft./245m.; 🅿; **z** 52347; Ⓟ 966; Ⓒ 952
Villa Hermosa; RMC Place; LINN; ***177** H-15; elev. 850ft./259m.; ★ **CEDR**; mail Cedar Rapids **z** 52401; ● 50
Villisca; Inc. Place; MONTGOMERY; **176** L-5; elev. 1,050ft./320m.; 🅿; **z** 50864; Ⓟ 1,332; Ⓒ 1,344
Vincennes (Sand Prairie); RMC Place; LEE; ***177** N-16; mail Argyle **z** 52619; ● 40
Vincent; Inc. Place; WEBSTER; **176** E-8; elev. 1,130ft./344m.; 🅿; **z** 50594; Ⓟ 185; Ⓒ 158
Vining; Inc. Place; TAMA; **177** H-13; elev. 900ft./274m.; 🅿; **z** 52348; Ⓟ 78; Ⓒ 70
Vinton; Inc. Place; ⊡ BENTON; **177** G-14; elev. 800ft./244m.; 🅿 🅷; **z** 52349; Ⓟ 5,103; Ⓒ 5,102
Viola; RMC Place; LINN; **177** G-16; elev. 873ft./266m.; 🅿; **z** 52350; ● 120
Volga (Volga City); Inc. Place; CLAYTON; **177** D-16; elev. 796ft./243m.; 🅿; **z** 52077; Ⓟ 306; Ⓒ 247
Volga City; CLAYTON; see Volga (Inc. Place)
Volney; RMC Place; ALLAMAKEE; **177** C-16; mail Monona **z** 52159; ● 30
Voorhies; RMC Place; BLACK HAWK; **177** F-13; 🅿; **z** 50643; ● 60

W

Wadena; Inc. Place; FAYETTE; **177** D-15; elev. 880ft./268m.; 🅿; **z** 52169; Ⓟ 236; Ⓒ 243
Wahpeton; Inc. Place; DICKINSON; **176** B-5; elev. 1,400ft./427m.; mail Milford **z** 51351, Spirit Lake **z** 51360; Ⓟ 484; Ⓒ 462
Walcott; Inc. Place; SCOTT, MUSCATINE; **177** I-18; 🅿; ★ **D-RI-M**; **z** 52773; Ⓟ 1,356; Ⓒ 1,528
Wales; RMC Place; MONTGOMERY; **176** K-4; mail Emerson **z** 51533; ● 25
Walford; Inc. Place; BENTON, LINN; **177** H-15; elev. 800ft./244m.; 🅿; **z** 52351; Ⓟ 303; Ⓒ 1,224
Walker; Inc. Place; LINN; **177** F-15; elev. 882ft./269m.; 🅿; **z** 52352; Ⓟ 673; Ⓒ 750
Wallingford; Inc. Place; EMMET; **176** B-6; elev. 1,282ft./391m.; 🅿; **z** 51365; Ⓟ 196; Ⓒ 210
Wall Lake; Inc. Place; SAC; **176** F-5; elev. 1,231ft./375m.; 🅿; **z** 51466; Ⓟ 875; Ⓒ 841
Walnut; Inc. Place; POTTAWATTAMIE; **176** J-5; elev. 1,340ft./408m.; 🅿; **z** 51577; Ⓟ 857; Ⓒ 778; Ⓡ 877
Walnut City; RMC Place; APPANOOSE; ***177** L-12; mail Mystic **z** 52574; rural
Walnut Grove; RMC Place; SCOTT; ***177** J-18; ★ **D-RI-M**; pop. incl. with Davenport (Inc. Place)
Wapello; Inc. Place; ⊡ LOUISA; **177** K-17; elev. 580ft./177m.; 🅿; **z** 52653; Ⓟ 2,013; Ⓒ 2,124
WAPELLO; **177** K-13; Ⓟ 35,687; Ⓒ 36,051; ◆ 34,536
Ware; RMC Place; POCAHONTAS; ***176** D-6; mail Havelock **z** 50546
WARREN; **176** K-9; Ⓟ 36,033; Ⓒ 40,671; ◆ 45,334
Washburn; RMC Place; BLACK HAWK; **177** F-14; elev. 830ft./253m.; 🅿; ★ **WATL**; **z** 50702, **z** 50706; ● 1,400
Washington; Inc. Place; ⊡ WASHINGTON; **177** J-15; elev. 762ft./232m.; 🅿 🅷; **z** 52353; Ⓟ 7,074; Ⓒ 7,047
WASHINGTON; **177** J-15; Ⓟ 19,612; Ⓒ 20,670; ◆ 21,116
Washta; Inc. Place; CHEROKEE; **176** E-3; elev. 1,154ft./352m.; 🅿; **z** 51061; Ⓟ 284; Ⓒ 282
Waterloo; Inc. Place; ⊡ BLACK HAWK; **177** F-13; elev. 867ft./264m.; 🅿 🅷 🅲 426 ■; ★ **WATL**; **z** 50701-04, **z** 50706-07; Ⓟ 66,467; Ⓒ 68,747; ◆ 72,376
Waterville; Inc. Place; ALLAMAKEE; **177** C-16; elev. 900ft./274m.; 🅿; **z** 52170; Ⓟ 140; Ⓒ 145
Watkins; RMC Place; BENTON; **177** H-14; elev. 820ft./250m.; 🅿; **z** 52354; ● 130
Waubeek; RMC Place; LINN; **177** G-16; mail Central City **z** 52214; ● 100
Waucoma; Inc. Place; FAYETTE; **177** C-14; elev. 1,045ft./319m.; 🅿; **z** 52171; Ⓟ 277; Ⓒ 299
Waukee; Inc. Place; DALLAS; **176** I-9; elev. 1,030ft./314m.; 🅿; ★ **DES**; **z** 50263; Ⓟ 2,512; Ⓒ 5,126
Waukon; Inc. Place; ⊡ ALLAMAKEE; **177** B-16; elev. 1,260ft./384m.; 🅿 🅷; **z** 52172; Ⓟ 4,019; Ⓒ 4,131
Waukon Junction; RMC Place; ALLAMAKEE; **177** C-17; mail Harpers Ferry **z** 52146; ● 20
Waupeton; RMC Place; DUBUQUE; ***177** E-18; elev. 613ft./187m.; mail Sherrill **z** 52073
Waverly; Inc. Place; ⊡ BREMER; **177** E-13; elev. 919ft./280m.; 🅿 🅷 🅲 1,769; **z** 50677; Ⓟ 8,539; Ⓒ 8,968
Wayland; Inc. Place; HENRY; **177** K-15; elev. 745ft./227m.; 🅿; **z** 52654; Ⓟ 838; Ⓒ 945
WAYNE; **176** L-10; Ⓟ 7,067; Ⓒ 6,730; ◆ 5,987
Webb; Inc. Place; CLAY; **176** D-5; 🅿; **z** 51366; Ⓟ 167; Ⓒ 165
Webster; Inc. Place; KEOKUK; **177** J-14; elev. 860ft./262m.; 🅿; **z** 52355; Ⓟ 103; Ⓒ 110
Webster (Middle River); RMC Place; MADISON; ***176** J-8; mail Winterset **z** 50273; rural
WEBSTER; **176** E-8; Ⓟ 40,342; Ⓒ 40,235; ◆ 38,226
Webster City; Inc. Place; ⊡ HAMILTON; **176** F-9; elev. 1,050ft./320m.; 🅿 🅷; **z** 50595; Ⓟ 7,894; Ⓒ 8,176
Welch Avenue; RMC Place; STORY; ★ **AMES**; mail Ames **z** 50014; pop. incl. with Ames (Inc. Place)
Weldon; Inc. Place; DECATUR; **176** L-9; 🅿; **z** 50264; Ⓟ 151; Ⓒ 145
Wellman; Inc. Place; WASHINGTON; **177** J-15; elev. 633ft./193m.; 🅿; **z** 52356; Ⓟ 1,085; Ⓒ 1,393
Wellsburg; Inc. Place; GRUNDY; **177** F-12; elev. 1,068ft./326m.; 🅿; **z** 50680; Ⓟ 682; Ⓒ 716
Welton; Inc. Place; CLINTON; **177** H-19; 🅿; **z** 52774; Ⓟ 177; Ⓒ 159
Wesley; Inc. Place; KOSSUTH; **176** C-8; elev. 1,252ft./382m.; 🅿; **z** 50483; Ⓟ 444; Ⓒ 467
West Ackley; RMC Place; HARDIN; ***177** E-11; mail Ackley **z** 50601; pop. incl. with Ackley (Inc. Place)
West Amana; RMC Place; IOWA; **177** H-14; elev. 750ft./229m.; 🅿; **z** 52203; ● 140
West Bend; Inc. Place; PALO ALTO, KOSSUTH; **176** D-7; elev. 1,203ft./367m.; 🅿; **z** 50597; Ⓟ 862; Ⓒ 834
West Branch; Inc. Place; CEDAR; **177** I-16; elev. 710ft./216m.; 🅿; **z** 52358; Ⓟ 1,908; Ⓒ 2,188
West Broadway; RMC Place; POTTAWATTAMIE; ★ **OMA**; mail Council Bluffs **z** 51501; pop. incl. with Council Bluffs (Inc. Place)
West Burlington; Inc. Place; DES MOINES; **177** L-17; elev. 700ft./213m.; 🅿; ★ **BUR**; **z** 52655; Ⓟ 3,083; Ⓒ 3,161
West Chester; Inc. Place; WASHINGTON; **177** J-15; elev. 963ft./294m.; 🅿; **z** 52359; Ⓟ 178; Ⓒ 159
West Des Moines; Inc. Place; POLK, DALLAS; **176** I-9; elev. 850ft./259m.; 🅿 ■; ★ **DES**; **z** 50061, **z** 50265-66, **z** 50398 & mail Des Moines **z** 50391; Ⓟ 31,702; Ⓒ 46,403; ◆ 54,465
Western; RMC Place; LINN; ***177** H-15; mail Swisher **z** 52338; ● 150
Westfield; Inc. Place; PLYMOUTH; **176** D-1; elev. 1,128ft./344m.; 🅿; **z** 51062; Ⓟ 160; Ⓒ 189
Westgate; Inc. Place; FAYETTE; **177** D-14; elev. 1,093ft./333m.; 🅿; **z** 50681; Ⓟ 207; Ⓒ 234
West Grove; RMC Place; DAVIS; **177** M-13; elev. 942ft./287m.; 🅿; **z** 52537; ● 50
West Le Mars (Dalton); RMC Place; PLYMOUTH; **176** D-2; mail Le Mars **z** 51031; ● 30
West Liberty; Inc. Place; MUSCATINE; **177** I-17; elev. 675ft./206m.; 🅿; **z** 52776; Ⓟ 2,935; Ⓒ 3,332
West Mason City; CERRO GORDO; see Central Heights (RMC Place)
West Okoboji; Inc. Place; DICKINSON; **176** B-5; elev. 1,406ft./429m.; 🅿; **z** 51351; Ⓟ 263; Ⓒ 432
Weston; RMC Place; POTTAWATTAMIE; **176** J-3; mail Underwood **z** 51576; ● 60
Westphalia; Inc. Place; SHELBY; **176** I-4; elev. 1,402ft./427m.; 🅿; **z** 51578; Ⓟ 144; Ⓒ 160
West Point; Inc. Place; LEE; **177** M-16; elev. 740ft./226m.; 🅿; **z** 52656-57; Ⓟ 1,079; Ⓒ 980
West Post Estates; RMC Place; LINN; ***177** H-15; elev. 846ft./258m.; ★ **CEDR**; mail Cedar Rapids **z** 52404; ● 50
Westside; Inc. Place; CRAWFORD; **176** G-5; elev. 1,324ft./404m.; 🅿; **z** 51467; Ⓟ 348; Ⓒ 327
West Spencer; RMC Place; CLAY; ***176** C-5; mail Spencer **z** 51301; pop. incl. with Everly (Inc. Place)
West Storm Lake (Emerald Park); RMC Place; BUENA VISTA; mail Storm Lake **z** 50588; pop. incl. with Storm Lake (Inc. Place)
West Suburban; RMC Place; POLK; ★ **DES**; mail Clive **z** 50325; pop. incl. with Des Moines (Inc. Place)
West Union; Inc. Place; ⊡ FAYETTE; **177** D-15; elev. 1,107ft./337m.; 🅿 🅷; **z** 52175; Ⓟ 2,490; Ⓒ 2,549
Westwood; Inc. Place; HENRY; **177** L-16; mail Mount Pleasant **z** 52641; Ⓟ 104; Ⓒ 127
Wever; RMC Place; LEE; **177** M-17; elev. 560ft./171m.; 🅿; **z** 52658; ● 140
What Cheer; Inc. Place; KEOKUK; **177** J-13; elev. 800ft./244m.; 🅿; **z** 50268; Ⓟ 762; Ⓒ 678
Wheatland; Inc. Place; CLINTON; **177** H-18; elev. 700ft./213m.; 🅿; **z** 52777; Ⓟ 723; Ⓒ 772
White Oak; RMC Place; POLK; ***176** I-10; ★ **DES**; mail Elkhart **z** 50073; ● 60
Whiting; Inc. Place; MONONA; **176** G-2; elev. 1,060ft./323m.; 🅿; **z** 51063; Ⓟ 683; Ⓒ 707; Ⓡ 801
Whittemore; Inc. Place; KOSSUTH; **176** C-7; elev. 1,201ft./366m.; 🅿; **z** 50598; Ⓟ 535; Ⓒ 530
Whitten; Inc. Place; HARDIN; **177** F-11; elev. 1,040ft./317m.; 🅿; **z** 50269; Ⓟ 137; Ⓒ 160
Whittier; RMC Place; LINN; **177** G-16; elev. 900ft./274m.; 🅿; **z** 52336; ● 130
Wichita; RMC Place; GUTHRIE; ***176** I-7; mail Guthrie Center **z** 50115; rural
Wick; RMC Place; WARREN; **176** J-9; mail Saint Charles **z** 50240; ● 40
Wickham Spur; RMC Place; WOODBURY; ★ **SXCY**; mail Sioux City **z** 51101; pop. incl. with Sioux City (Inc. Place)
Wildwood; RMC Place; LINN; ***177** G-15; elev. 800ft./244m.; ★ **CEDR**; mail Toddville **z** 52341; ● 40
Wildwood Camp; RMC Place; SCOTT; ***177** H-19; elev. 612ft./187m.; mail Long Grove **z** 52756; ● 30
Willey; Inc. Place; CARROLL; **176** H-6; elev. 1,340ft./408m.; mail Carroll **z** 51401; Ⓟ 78; Ⓒ 103
William Penn College; RMC Place; MAHASKA; ***177** J-12; mail Oskaloosa **z** 52577; pop. incl. with Oskaloosa (Inc. Place)
Williams; Inc. Place; HAMILTON; **176** F-10; elev. 1,206ft./368m.; 🅿; **z** 50271; Ⓟ 368; Ⓒ 427
Williamsburg; Inc. Place; IOWA; **177** I-14; elev. 820ft./250m.; 🅿; **z** 52361; Ⓟ 2,174; Ⓒ 2,622
Williamson; RMC Place; ADAMS; ***176** K-7; mail Prescott **z** 50859; rural
Williamson; Inc. Place; LUCAS; **177** K-11; elev. 1,022ft./312m.; 🅿; **z** 50272; Ⓟ 166; Ⓒ 163
Williamstown (Frytown); RMC Place; JOHNSON; ***177** I-15; mail Kalona **z** 52247; ● 100
Wilton (Wilton Junction); Inc. Place; MUSCATINE, CEDAR; **177** I-17; elev. 702ft./214m.; 🅿; **z** 52778; Ⓟ 2,577; Ⓒ 2,829
Wilton Junction; MUSCATINE, CEDAR; see Wilton (Inc. Place)
Windham; RMC Place; JOHNSON; ***177** I-15; mail Oxford **z** 52322
Windsor Heights; Inc. Place; POLK; **177** B-18; elev. 850ft./259m.; 🅿; ★ **DES**; **z** 50311-12, **z** 50324 & mail Urbandale **z** 50322; Ⓟ 5,190; Ⓒ 4,805; Ⓡ 4,891
Winfield; Inc. Place; HENRY; **177** K-16; elev. 704ft./215m.; 🅿; **z** 52659; Ⓟ 1,051; Ⓒ 1,131
WINNEBAGO; **176** B-9; Ⓟ 12,122; Ⓒ 11,723; ◆ 10,645
Winnebago Heights; RMC Place; CERRO GORDO; ***177** C-11; elev. 1,115ft./340m.; mail Mason City **z** 50401; rural
Winnebago Reservation; Indian Reservation; WOODBURY; Reservation extends into NE; Ⓒ 0
WINNESHIEK; **177** C-14; Ⓟ 20,847; Ⓒ 21,310; ◆ 20,854
Winterset; Inc. Place; ⊡ MADISON; **176** J-8; elev. 1,100ft./335m.; 🅿 🅷; **z** 50273; Ⓟ 4,196; Ⓒ 4,768
Winthrop; Inc. Place; BUCHANAN; **177** F-15; elev. 1,038ft./316m.; 🅿; **z** 50682; Ⓟ 742; Ⓒ 772
Wiota; Inc. Place; CASS; **176** J-6; elev. 1,240ft./378m.; 🅿; **z** 50274; Ⓟ 160; Ⓒ 149
Wiscotta; RMC Place; DALLAS; **176** I-8; mail Redfield **z** 50233; ● 40
Woden; Inc. Place; HANCOCK; **176** C-9; elev. 1,233ft./376m.; 🅿; **z** 50484; Ⓟ 259; Ⓒ 243
Wood; RMC Place; CLAYTON; ***177** E-16; mail Edgewood **z** 52042
Woodbine; Inc. Place; HARRISON; **176** I-3; elev. 1,078ft./329m.; 🅿; **z** 51579; Ⓟ 1,500; Ⓒ 1,564
Woodburn; Inc. Place; CLARKE; **176** K-10; elev. 959ft./292m.; 🅿; **z** 50275; Ⓟ 240; Ⓒ 244
WOODBURY; **176** F-2; Ⓟ 98,276; Ⓒ 103,877; ◆ 100,093
Woodland; RMC Place; DECATUR; ***176** M-10; mail Garden Grove **z** 50103
Woodland; POLK; see Woodland Hills (RMC Place)
Woodland Hills (Woodland); RMC Place; POLK; ***176** I-10; elev. 916ft./279m.; ★ **DES**; mail Runnells **z** 50237; ● 80
Woodward; Inc. Place; DALLAS; **176** H-9; 🅿 🅷; **z** 50276; Ⓟ 1,197; Ⓒ 1,200
Woolstock; Inc. Place; WRIGHT; **176** E-9; elev. 1,090ft./332m.; 🅿; **z** 50599; Ⓟ 212; Ⓒ 204
WORTH; **177** B-11; Ⓟ 7,991; Ⓒ 7,909; ◆ 7,566
Worthington; Inc. Place; DUBUQUE; **177** F-17; 🅿; **z** 52078; Ⓟ 439; Ⓒ 381
Worthington Acres; RMC Place; LINN; ***177** H-15; ★ **CEDR**; pop. incl. with Cedar Rapids (Inc. Place)
Wright; RMC Place; MAHASKA; **177** K-13; mail Oskaloosa **z** 52577; ● 50
WRIGHT; **176** E-9; Ⓟ 14,269; Ⓒ 14,334; ◆ 12,618
Wyman; RMC Place; LOUISA; **177** K-16; mail Crawfordsville **z** 52621; ● 30
Wyoming; Inc. Place; JONES; **177** G-17; elev. 800ft./244m.; 🅿; **z** 52362; Ⓟ 659; Ⓒ 626

Y

Yale; Inc. Place; GUTHRIE; **176** H-7; elev. 1,120ft./341m.; 🅿; **z** 50277; Ⓟ 220; Ⓒ 287
Yarmouth; RMC Place; DES MOINES; **177** K-16; elev. 814ft./248m.; 🅿; **z** 52660; ● 120
Yetter; Inc. Place; CALHOUN; **176** F-6; elev. 1,216ft./371m.; 🅿; **z** 51433; Ⓟ 49; Ⓒ 36
Yorktown; Inc. Place; PAGE; **176** L-5; elev. 1,038ft./316m.; 🅿; **z** 51656; Ⓟ 100; Ⓒ 82
Youngstown; POLK; see Pleasant Hill (Inc. Place)

Z

Zaneta; RMC Place; GRUNDY; ***177** F-13; mail Hudson **z** 50643; rural
Zearing; Inc. Place; STORY; **177** G-11; elev. 1,060ft./323m.; 🅿; **z** 50278; Ⓟ 614; Ⓒ 617
Zion; RMC Place; ADAIR; ***176** K-8; mail Orient **z** 50858
Zook Spur; RMC Place; DALLAS; ***176** H-9; mail Madrid **z** 50156
Zwingle; Inc. Place; DUBUQUE, JACKSON; **177** F-18; elev. 902ft./275m.; 🅿; **z** 52079; Ⓟ 94; Ⓒ 100

KANSAS

NE
CO
Topeka
MO
OK

Statistics

Total area (2000) — 82,277 square miles
Land area (2000) — 81,815 square miles
Water area (2000) — 462 square miles
Capital — Topeka
Admitted as state — January, 1861

Maps

State maps can be found on pages 142-254 in Vol. 1

Ranally Metro Areas (RMAs) and Abbreviations

Hutchinson, KS — HUCH
Joplin, MO-KS — JOP
Kansas City, MO-KS — K.C.
Lawrence, KS — LAWR
Leavenworth, KS — LEAV
Manhattan, KS — MANH
St. Joseph, MO-KS — ST.JO
Salina, KS — SLN
Topeka, KS — TOP
Wichita, KS — WICH

Principal Places

Place Name	Place Type	County	Population
Wichita	Inc. Place	SEDGWICK	◆ 376,693
Overland Park	Inc. Place	JOHNSON	◆ 179,461
Kansas City	Inc. Place	WYANDOTTE	◆ 141,386
Olathe	Inc. Place	JOHNSON	◆ 124,151
Topeka	Inc. Place	SHAWNEE	◆ 123,802
Lawrence	Inc. Place	DOUGLAS	◆ 91,620
Shawnee	Inc. Place	JOHNSON	◆ 61,151
Manhattan	Inc. Place	RILEY	◆ 58,417
Lenexa	Inc. Place	JOHNSON	◆ 48,988
Salina	Inc. Place	SALINE	◆ 46,913
Hutchinson	Inc. Place	RENO	◆ 39,732
Leavenworth	Inc. Place	LEAVENWORTH	◆ 33,279
Leawood	Inc. Place	JOHNSON	◆ 32,755
Garden City	Inc. Place	FINNEY	◆ 31,351
Emporia	Inc. Place	LYON	◆ 27,957
Dodge City	Inc. Place	FORD	◆ 26,401
Prairie Village	Inc. Place	JOHNSON	◆ 20,905
Junction City	Inc. Place	GEARY	◆ 20,863
Liberal	Inc. Place	SEWARD	◆ 20,684
Hays	Inc. Place	ELLIS	◆ 20,442
Pittsburg	Inc. Place	CRAWFORD	◆ 19,893
Derby	Inc. Place	SEDGWICK	◆ 19,307
Newton	Inc. Place	HARVEY	© 17,190
Great Bend	Inc. Place	BARTON	◆ 15,404
McPherson	Inc. Place	MCPHERSON	© 13,770
Winfield	Inc. Place	COWLEY	© 12,206
El Dorado	Inc. Place	BUTLER	© 12,057
Arkansas City	Inc. Place	COWLEY	© 11,963
Ottawa	Inc. Place	FRANKLIN	© 11,921
Parsons	Inc. Place	LABETTE	◆ 11,127
Merriam	Inc. Place	JOHNSON	© 11,008
Atchison	Inc. Place	ATCHISON	© 10,232
Coffeyville	Inc. Place	MONTGOMERY	◆ 9,963
Independence	Inc. Place	MONTGOMERY	© 9,846
Mission	Inc. Place	JOHNSON	© 9,727
Chanute	Inc. Place	NEOSHO	© 9,411
Gardner	Inc. Place	JOHNSON	© 9,396
Lansing	Inc. Place	LEAVENWORTH	© 9,199
Wellington	Inc. Place	SUMNER	© 8,647
Haysville	Inc. Place	SEDGWICK	© 8,502
Augusta	Inc. Place	BUTLER	© 8,423
Fort Scott	Inc. Place	BOURBON	© 8,297
Fort Riley North	CDP-Census Area Only	RILEY	© 8,114
Roeland Park	Inc. Place	JOHNSON	® 7,210
Bonner Springs	Inc. Place	WYANDOTTE	© 6,768
Andover	Inc. Place	BUTLER	© 6,698
Pratt	Inc. Place	PRATT	© 6,570
Abilene	Inc. Place	DICKINSON	© 6,543
Iola	Inc. Place	ALLEN	© 6,302
Bellaire	Inc. Place	SEDGWICK	® 6,014
Ulysses	Inc. Place	GRANT	© 5,960
Park City	Inc. Place	SEDGWICK	© 5,814
Concordia	Inc. Place	CLOUD	© 5,714
Colby	Inc. Place	THOMAS	© 5,450
Mulvane	Inc. Place	SUMNER	© 5,155
Paola	Inc. Place	MIAMI	© 5,011

County Business Data

County	FIPS Code	County Seat	Land Area (Sq. Mi.)	Census Population			Wholesale Trade		Manufacturing, 2002			
				4/1/2000	4/1/1990	% Change 1990-2000	Sales, 2002 ($1,000)	% Change 1997-2002	Establish-ments	Total Employees	Value Added ($1,000)	Ranally Mfg. Units
Allen	001	Iola	503	14,385	14,638	-1.7	42,104	18.5	25	1,772	141,298	75
Anderson	003	Garnett	583	8,110	7,803	3.9	45,210	-6.6	...	(d)	(d)	...
Atchison	005	Atchison	432	16,774	16,932	-0.9	(d)	(d)	22	1,671	147,311	78
Barber	007	Medicine Lodge	1,134	5,307	5,874	-9.7	32,124	-10.1	...	(d)	(d)	...
Barton	009	Great Bend	894	28,205	29,382	-4.0	245,317	19.0	49	1,627	98,700	52
Bourbon	011	Fort Scott	637	15,379	14,966	2.8	334,183	43.3	29	1,161	74,726	40
Brown	013	Hiawatha	571	10,724	11,128	-3.6	60,601	-17.7	...	(d)	(d)	...
Butler	015	El Dorado	1,428	59,482	50,580	17.6	(d)	(d)	53	1,616	210,067	111
Chase	017	Cottonwood Falls	776	3,030	3,021	0.3	(d)	(d)	...	(d)	(d)	...
Chautauqua	019	Sedan	642	4,359	4,407	-1.1	(d)	(d)	...	(d)	(d)	...
Cherokee	021	Columbus	587	22,605	21,374	5.8	168,563	-19.9	37	1,738	142,969	76
Cheyenne	023	St. Francis	1,020	3,165	3,243	-2.4	39,766	-31.3	...	(d)	(d)	...
Clark	025	Ashland	975	2,390	2,418	-1.2	40,051	(d)	...	(d)	(d)	...
Clay	027	Clay Center	644	8,822	9,158	-3.7	27,648	-50.1	...	(d)	(d)	...
Cloud	029	Concordia	716	10,268	11,023	-6.8	93,100	-15.8	...	(d)	(d)	...
Coffey	031	Burlington	630	8,865	8,404	5.5	27,787	-27.8	...	(d)	(d)	...
Comanche	033	Coldwater	788	1,967	2,313	-15.0	(d)	(d)	...	(d)	(d)	...
Cowley	035	Winfield	1,126	36,291	36,915	-1.7	137,104	15.3	52	3,344	288,169	152
Crawford	037	Girard	593	38,242	35,568	7.5	313,422	80.8	73	3,252	282,258	149
Decatur	039	Oberlin	894	3,472	4,021	-13.7	23,603	-68.2	...	(d)	(d)	...
Dickinson	041	Abilene	848	19,344	18,958	2.0	217,235	-1.5	21	1,278	100,635	53
Doniphan	043	Troy	392	8,249	8,134	1.4	(d)	(d)	...	(d)	(d)	...
Douglas	045	Lawrence	457	99,962	81,798	22.2	346,393	39.2	86	3,612	524,692	278
Edwards	047	Kinsley	622	3,449	3,787	-8.9	48,898	-15.2	...	(d)	(d)	...
Elk	049	Howard	647	3,261	3,327	-2.0	(d)	(d)	...	(d)	(d)	...
Ellis	051	Hays	900	27,507	26,004	5.8	97,115	4.3	33	(d)	(d)	...
Ellsworth	053	Ellsworth	716	6,525	6,586	-0.9	(d)	(d)	...	(d)	(d)	...
Finney	055	Garden City	1,302	40,523	33,070	22.5	384,100	-22.5	32	3,627	269,342	143
Ford	057	Dodge City	1,098	32,458	27,463	18.2	338,389	-2.7	30	5,521	452,993	240
Franklin	059	Ottawa	574	24,784	21,994	12.7	101,277	-66.1	29	1,125	139,534	74
Geary	061	Junction City	385	27,947	30,453	-8.2	62,716	4.4	11	595	70,769	37
Gove	063	Gove	1,071	3,068	3,231	-5.0	(d)	(d)	...	(d)	(d)	...
Graham	065	Hill City	898	2,946	3,543	-16.9	13,013	-23.1	...	(d)	(d)	...
Grant	067	Ulysses	575	7,909	7,159	10.5	121,019	23.7	...	(d)	(d)	...
Gray	069	Cimarron	869	5,904	5,396	9.4	94,793	-25.0	...	(d)	(d)	...
Greeley	071	Tribune	778	1,534	1,774	-13.5	(d)	(d)	...	(d)	(d)	...
Greenwood	073	Eureka	1,140	7,673	7,847	-2.2	4,313	-30.9	...	(d)	(d)	...
Hamilton	075	Syracuse	996	2,670	2,388	11.8	34,728	-35.5	...	(d)	(d)	...
Harper	077	Anthony	801	6,536	7,124	-8.3	59,907	-22.0	...	(d)	(d)	...
Harvey	079	Newton	539	32,869	31,028	5.9	(d)	(d)	61	3,657	271,421	144
Haskell	081	Sublette	577	4,307	3,886	10.8	60,785	-34.2	...	(d)	(d)	...
Hodgeman	083	Jetmore	860	2,085	2,177	-4.2	(d)	(d)	...	(d)	(d)	...
Jackson	085	Holton	656	12,657	11,525	9.8	35,141	40.8	...	(d)	(d)	...
Jefferson	087	Oskaloosa	536	18,426	15,905	15.9	5,208	-46.0	...	(d)	(d)	...
Jewell	089	Mankato	909	3,791	4,251	-10.8	28,386	-43.4	...	(d)	(d)	...
Johnson	091	Olathe	477	451,086	355,054	27.0	19,688,243	-6.7	523	19,324	2,314,954	1,225
Kearny	093	Lakin	871	4,531	4,027	12.5	25,247	4.8	...	(d)	(d)	...
Kingman	095	Kingman	863	8,673	8,292	4.6	53,182	3.0	...	(d)	(d)	...
Kiowa	097	Greensburg	722	3,278	3,660	-10.4	44,790	48.3	...	(d)	(d)	...
Labette	099	Oswego	649	22,835	23,693	-3.6	107,505	31.5	35	2,165	146,474	77
Lane	101	Dighton	717	2,155	2,375	-9.3	30,153	-16.3	...	(d)	(d)	...
Leavenworth	103	Leavenworth	463	68,691	64,371	6.7	(d)	(d)	34	590	38,519	20
Lincoln	105	Lincoln	719	3,578	3,653	-2.1	15,758	-57.9	...	(d)	(d)	...
Linn	107	Mound City	599	9,570	8,254	15.9	(d)	(d)	...	(d)	(d)	...
Logan	109	Oakley	1,073	3,046	3,081	-1.1	44,876	46.6	...	(d)	(d)	...
Lyon	111	Emporia	851	35,935	34,732	3.5	(d)	(d)	39	(d)	(d)	...
Marion	115	Marion	943	13,361	12,888	3.7	63,656	-19.4	...	(d)	(d)	...
Marshall	117	Marysville	903	10,965	11,705	-6.3	72,430	-37.1	21	901	71,247	38
McPherson	113	McPherson	900	29,554	27,268	8.4	237,200	43.3	67	3,911	525,522	278
Meade	119	Meade	978	4,631	4,247	9.0	86,218	29.1	...	(d)	(d)	...
Miami	121	Paola	577	28,351	23,466	20.8	115,469	(d)	29	506	39,962	21
Mitchell	123	Beloit	700	6,932	7,203	-3.8	86,921	-34.9	...	(d)	(d)	...
Montgomery	125	Independence	645	36,252	38,816	-6.6	154,814	24.5	53	4,188	426,254	226
Morris	127	Council Grove	697	6,104	6,198	-1.5	4,508	-43.6	...	(d)	(d)	...
Morton	129	Elkhart	730	3,496	3,480	0.5	51,195	-35.1	...	(d)	(d)	...
Nemaha	131	Seneca	718	10,717	10,446	2.6	64,111	9.6	26	1,095	95,652	51
Neosho	133	Erie	572	16,997	17,035	-0.2	136,287	8.8	35	1,830	157,092	83
Ness	135	Ness City	1,075	3,454	4,033	-14.4	23,141	-41.3	...	(d)	(d)	...
Norton	137	Norton	878	5,953	5,947	0.1	111,849	69.1	...	(d)	(d)	...
Osage	139	Lyndon	704	16,712	15,248	9.6	33,660	-26.3	...	(d)	(d)	...
Osborne	141	Osborne	892	4,452	4,867	-8.5	39,054	-40.7	...	(d)	(d)	...
Ottawa	143	Minneapolis	721	6,163	5,634	9.4	25,792	-64.2	...	(d)	(d)	...
Pawnee	145	Larned	754	7,233	7,555	-4.3	82,550	91.5	...	(d)	(d)	...
Phillips	147	Phillipsburg	886	6,001	6,590	-8.9	(d)	(d)	...	(d)	(d)	...
Pottawatomie	149	Westmoreland	844	18,209	16,128	12.9	136,380	19.8	25	1,022	88,750	47
Pratt	151	Pratt	735	9,647	9,702	-0.6	207,360	-19.6	...	(d)	(d)	...
Rawlins	153	Atwood	1,070	2,966	3,404	-12.9	45,798	-2.6	...	(d)	(d)	...
Reno	155	Hutchinson	1,254	64,790	62,389	3.8	788,466	66.1	93	3,728	337,958	179
Republic	157	Belleville	716	5,835	6,482	-10.0	122,956	43.3	...	(d)	(d)	...
Rice	159	Lyons	727	10,761	10,610	1.4	50,634	6.3	...	(d)	(d)	...
Riley	161	Manhattan	610	62,843	67,139	-6.4	148,719	5.7	...	(d)	(d)	...
Rooks	163	Stockton	888	5,685	6,039	-5.9	65,079	20.9	...	(d)	(d)	...
Rush	165	La Crosse	718	3,551	3,842	-7.6	29,726	-49.4	...	(d)	(d)	...
Russell	167	Russell	885	7,370	7,835	-5.9	91,073	-16.2	...	(d)	(d)	...
Saline	169	Salina	720	53,597	49,301	8.7	905,144	7.6	85	(d)	(d)	...
Scott	171	Scott City	718	5,120	5,289	-3.2	58,398	-13.4	...	(d)	(d)	...
Sedgwick	173	Wichita	999	452,869	403,662	12.2	9,072,608	54.4	583	57,075	7,341,431	3,884
Seward	175	Liberal	640	22,510	18,743	20.1	(d)	(d)	10	(d)	(d)	...
Shawnee	177	Topeka	550	169,871	160,976	5.5	1,193,987	26.1	122	6,558	964,510	510
Sheridan	179	Hoxie	896	2,813	3,043	-7.6	48,651	-14.0	...	(d)	(d)	...
Sherman	181	Goodland	1,056	6,760	6,926	-2.4	86,492	-31.7	...	(d)	(d)	...
Smith	183	Smith Center	895	4,536	5,078	-10.7	53,274	-13.2	...	(d)	(d)	...
Stafford	185	St. John	792	4,789	5,365	-10.7	42,832	-25.0	...	(d)	(d)	...
Stanton	187	Johnson	680	2,406	2,333	3.1	48,390	-26.2	...	(d)	(d)	...
Stevens	189	Hugoton	728	5,463	5,048	8.2	91,503	-19.6	...	(d)	(d)	...
Sumner	191	Wellington	1,182	25,946	25,841	0.4	(d)	(d)	46	944	74,558	39
Thomas	193	Colby	1,075	8,180	8,258	-0.9	149,988	-27.8	...	(d)	(d)	...
Trego	195	WaKeeney	888	3,319	3,694	-10.2	19,969	-48.2	...	(d)	(d)	...
Wabaunsee	197	Alma	797	6,885	6,603	4.3	5,507	-18.4	...	(d)	(d)	...
Wallace	199	Sharon Springs	914	1,749	1,821	-4.0	40,131	(d)	...	(d)	(d)	...

Entries in **UPPERCASE** are counties.
Entries in **bold** have populations of 2,500 or more.
Names in parentheses are alternate names.
Inc. Place — Incorporated Place
RMC Place — Rand McNally Designated Place
CDP — Census Designated Place
MCD — Minor Civil Division

⊡ County Seat
▲ Minor Civil Division
elev. Elevation
🅿 Post Office

Ⓗ Hospital
Ⓒ College
■ Principal Business Center
★ Ranally Metro Area (RMA) Abbreviation
Z Zip Code(s)

Ⓟ Previous Census Population
® Revised Census Population
Ⓐ Annexation Population
● Rand McNally Population Estimate

© Final Census Population
Ⓢ Special Census Population
◆ Estimated Population

For additional definitions see Glossary, Volume 1, and Introduction, Volume 2.

County	FIPS Code	County Seat	Land Area (Sq. Mi.)	Census Population 4/1/2000	Census Population 4/1/1990	Census Population % Change 1990-2000	Wholesale Trade Sales, 2002 ($1,000)	Wholesale Trade % Change 1997-2002	Manufacturing, 2002 Establish-ments	Manufacturing, 2002 Total Employees	Manufacturing, 2002 Value Added ($1,000)	Manufacturing, 2002 Ranally Mfg. Units
Washington	201	Washington	898	6,483	7,073	-8.3	108,110	29.0	...	(d)	(d)	...
Wichita	203	Leoti	719	2,531	2,758	-8.2	36,985	16.7	...	(d)	(d)	...
Wilson	205	Fredonia	574	10,332	10,289	0.4	(d)	(d)	26	1,482	84,294	45
Woodson	207	Yates Center	501	3,788	4,116	-8.0	23,117	(d)	...	(d)	(d)	...
Wyandotte	209	Kansas City	151	157,882	161,993	-2.5	4,330,194	7.9	246	12,900	3,217,849	1,702
The State			**81,815**	**2,688,418**	**2,477,574**	**8.5**	**44,117,100**	**4.5**	**3,218**	**177,825**	**21,347,336**	**11,294**

(d) Data not available. Corresponding percentages or Ranally Manufacturing Units are estimates.
... Represents 0 or amount too minimal to be reported.

Index of Places and Counties

A

Abbyville; Inc. Place; RENO; 179 H-11; elev. 1,650ft./503m.; 🅿; z 67510; ℗ 140; © 128
Abilene; Inc. Place; ⊡ DICKINSON; 179 E-13; elev. 1,153ft./351m.; 🅿 🅷; z 67410; ℗ 6,242; © 6,543
Achilles; RMC Place; RAWLINS
Ada; RMC Place; OTTAWA; 179 D-11; elev. 1,301ft./397m.; 🅿; z 67467; ● 110
Adams; RMC Place; KINGMAN; 179 I-11; mail Spivey z 67142; ● 20
Adams Corner; RMC Place; RENO; *179 G-11; mail Nickerson z 67561; rural
Admire; Inc. Place; LYON; 179 F-16; elev. 1,230ft./375m.; 🅿; z 66830; ℗ 147; © 177
Aetna; RMC Place; BARBER; *178 J-9; mail Lake City z 67071; rural
Agenda; Inc. Place; REPUBLIC; 179 B-12; elev. 1,400ft./427m.; 🅿; z 66930; ℗ 81; © 81
Aggieville; RMC Place; RILEY; *179 D-14; ★ **MANH**; mail Manhattan z 66502; pop. incl. with Manhattan (Inc. Place)
Agra; Inc. Place; PHILLIPS; 178 B-8; elev. 1,855ft./565m.; 🅿; z 67621; ℗ 322; © 306
Agricola; RMC Place; COFFEY; *179 F-17; mail Waverly z 66871
Akron; RMC Place; COWLEY; *179 J-13; mail Winfield z 67156
Alamota; RMC Place; LANE; 178 F-6; elev. 2,650ft./808m.; 🅿; z 67839; ● 25
Albert; Inc. Place; BARTON; 178 F-9; elev. 1,915ft./584m.; 🅿; z 67511; ℗ 229; © 181
Alden; Inc. Place; RICE; 178 G-10; elev. 1,680ft./512m.; 🅿; z 67512; ℗ 182; © 168
Alexander; Inc. Place; RUSH; 178 F-7; elev. 2,070ft./631m.; 🅿; z 67513; ℗ 85; © 75
Aliceville; RMC Place; COFFEY; 179 G-17; mail Westphalia z 66093; ● 40
Allen; Inc. Place; LYON; 179 F-15; elev. 1,320ft./402m.; 🅿; z 66833; ℗ 191; © 211
ALLEN; 179 H-17; ℗ 14,638; © 14,385; ◆ 13,169
Alma; Inc. Place; ⊡ WABAUNSEE; 179 D-15; elev. 1,095ft./334m.; 🅿; z 66401, z 66501; ℗ 871; © 797
Almena; Inc. Place; NORTON; 178 B-7; elev. 2,155ft./657m.; 🅿; z 67622; ℗ 423; © 469
Altamont; Inc. Place; LABETTE; 179 J-18; elev. 910ft./277m.; 🅿; z 67330; ℗ 1,048; © 1,092
Alta Vista; Inc. Place; WABAUNSEE; 179 E-15; elev. 1,437ft./438m.; 🅿; z 66834; ℗ 477; © 442
Alton; Inc. Place; OSBORNE; 178 C-9; elev. 1,652ft./504m.; 🅿; z 67623; ℗ 115; © 117
Altoona; Inc. Place; WILSON; 179 I-17; elev. 828ft./252m.; 🅿; z 66710; ℗ 456; © 485
Americus; Inc. Place; LYON; 179 F-15; elev. 1,160ft./354m.; 🅿; z 66835; ℗ 891; © 938
Ames; RMC Place; CLOUD; 179 C-12; elev. 1,306ft./398m.; 🅿; z 66901; ● 40
Amy; RMC Place; LANE; *178 F-5; elev. 2,858ft./871m.; mail Healy z 67850
Andale; Inc. Place; SEDGWICK; 179 H-12; elev. 1,430ft./436m.; 🅿; z 67001; ℗ 566; © 766
ANDERSON; 179 G-17; ℗ 7,803; © 8,110; ◆ 7,880
Andover; Inc. Place; BUTLER; 179 H-13; elev. 1,350ft./411m.; 🅿; ★ **WICH**; z 67002; ℗ 4,047; © 6,698
Angelus; RMC Place; SHERIDAN; 178 D-5; mail Grinnell z 67738; ● 45
Angola; RMC Place; LABETTE; 179 J-17; elev. 980ft./299m.; mail Coffeyville z 67337; ● 50
Anna; BOURBON; see Pawnee Station (RMC Place)
Anness; RMC Place; SEDGWICK; *179 I-12; elev. 1,383ft./422m.; mail Milton z 67106; rural
Anson; RMC Place; SUMNER; 179 J-12; mail Wellington z 67152; ● 30
Antelope; RMC Place; MARION; *179 F-13; elev. 1,370ft./418m.; 🅿; z 66858
Anthony; Inc. Place; ⊡ HARPER; 179 J-11; elev. 1,320ft./402m.; 🅿 🅷; z 67003; ℗ 2,516; © 2,440
Antioch; RMC Place; MIAMI; *179 E-18; elev. 1,024ft./312m.; mail Spring Hill z 66083; rural
Antonino; RMC Place; ELLIS; 178 E-8; elev. 2,100ft./640m.; 🅿; z 67601; ● 50
Arcadia; Inc. Place; CRAWFORD; 179 H-19; elev. 822ft./251m.; 🅿; z 66711, z 66741; ℗ 338; © 391
Arcola; RMC Place; ELLSWORTH; *179 E-11; mail Brookville z 67425; rural
Argentine; RMC Place; WYANDOTTE; *179 D-19; ★ **K.C.**; mail Kansas City z 66106; pop. incl. with Kansas City (Inc. Place)
Argonia; Inc. Place; SUMNER; 179 J-12; elev. 1,250ft./381m.; 🅿; z 67004; ℗ 529; © 534
Arkansas City; Inc. Place; COWLEY; 179 J-13; elev. 1,120ft./341m.; 🅿 🅷; z 67005; ℗ 12,762; © 11,963
Arlington; Inc. Place; RENO; 179 H-11; elev. 1,600ft./488m.; 🅿; z 67514; ℗ 457; © 459
Arma; Inc. Place; CRAWFORD; 179 I-19; elev. 1,000ft./305m.; 🅿; z 66712; ℗ 1,542; © 1,529
Armourdale; RMC Place; WYANDOTTE; ★ **K.C.**; mail Kansas City z 66105; pop. incl. with Kansas City (Inc. Place)
Arnold; RMC Place; NESS; 178 F-6; elev. 2,550ft./777m.; 🅿; z 67515; ● 50
Arrington; RMC Place; ATCHISON; 179 C-17; mail Holton z 66436; ● 40
Arthur Heights; RMC Place; SEDGWICK; *179 H-13; ★ **WICH**; mail Wichita z 67220; pop. incl. with Bellaire (Inc. Place)
Arvonia; RMC Place; OSAGE; *179 F-16; mail Osage City z 66523; rural
Asherville; RMC Place; MITCHELL; 179 C-11; elev. 1,346ft./410m.; mail Beloit z 67420; ● 30
Ash Grove; RMC Place; LINCOLN; *178 D-10; mail Sylvan Grove z 67481
Ashland; Inc. Place; ⊡ CLARK; 178 J-7; elev. 1,979ft./603m.; 🅿; z 67831; ℗ 1,032; © 975
Ashland; RMC Place; RILEY; *179 D-14; 🅷; mail Manhattan z 66502; rural
Ashton; RMC Place; SUMNER; 179 J-13; elev. 1,217ft./371m.; mail Geuda Springs z 67051; ● 25
Assaria; Inc. Place; SALINE; 179 F-12; elev. 1,282ft./391m.; 🅿; z 67416; ℗ 387; © 438
Atchison; Inc. Place; ⊡ ATCHISON; 179 C-18; elev. 810ft./247m.; 🅿 🅷 🅲 1,507; z 66002; ℗ 10,656; © 10,232
ATCHISON; 179 C-17; ℗ 16,932; © 16,774; ◆ 16,255
Athens; RMC Place; WOODSON; mail Piqua z 66761
Athol; Inc. Place; SMITH; 178 B-9; elev. 1,785ft./544m.; 🅿; z 66932; ℗ 86; © 51
Atlanta; Inc. Place; COWLEY; 179 I-14; elev. 1,433ft./437m.; 🅿; z 67008; ℗ 232; © 255
Attica; Inc. Place; HARPER; 179 J-11; elev. 1,453ft./443m.; 🅿; z 67009; ℗ 716; © 636
Atwood; Inc. Place; ⊡ RAWLINS; 178 B-4; elev. 2,860ft./872m.; 🅿 🅷; z 67730; ℗ 1,388; © 1,279
Aubry; RMC Place; JOHNSON; 179 E-19; ★ **K.C.**; mail Stilwell z 66085; ● 100
Auburn; Inc. Place; SHAWNEE; 179 E-16; elev. 1,080ft./329m.; 🅿; z 66402; ℗ 908; © 1,121
Augusta; Inc. Place; BUTLER; 179 I-14; elev. 1,233ft./376m.; 🅿 🅷; ★ **WICH**; z 67010; ℗ 7,876; © 8,423
Aulne; RMC Place; MARION; 179 G-13; elev. 1,403ft./428m.; mail Marion z 66861; ● 50
Aurora; Inc. Place; CLOUD; 179 C-12; elev. 1,476ft./450m.; 🅿; z 67417; ℗ 101; © 79
Aurora Park; RMC Place; SEDGWICK; ★ **WICH**; mail Wichita z 67220; pop. incl. with Bellaire (Inc. Place)
Axtell; Inc. Place; MARSHALL; 179 B-15; elev. 1,368ft./417m.; 🅿; z 66403; ℗ 432; © 445

B

Baileyville; RMC Place; NEMAHA; 179 B-15; elev. 1,300ft./396m.; 🅿; z 66404; ● 200
Bala; RMC Place; RILEY; 179 D-14; mail Riley z 66531; ● 30
Baldwin City; Inc. Place; DOUGLAS; 179 E-18; elev. 1,050ft./320m.; 🅿 🅲 3,932; z 66006; ℗ 2,961; © 3,400
Balta; RMC Place; RUSSELL
Bancroft; RMC Place; NEMAHA; *179 C-16; mail Goff z 66428
BARBER; 178 J-9; ℗ 5,874; © 5,307; ◆ 4,631
Barclay; RMC Place; OSAGE; *179 F-16; elev. 1,183ft./361m.; mail Osage City z 66523
Barker; RMC Place; WYANDOTTE; ★ **K.C.**; mail Kansas City z 66104; pop. incl. with Kansas City (Inc. Place)
Barnard; Inc. Place; LINCOLN; 179 D-11; elev. 1,315ft./401m.; 🅿; z 67418; ℗ 129; © 123
Barnes; Inc. Place; WASHINGTON; 179 B-14; elev. 1,331ft./406m.; 🅿; z 66933; ℗ 167; © 152
Bartlett; Inc. Place; LABETTE; 179 J-18; elev. 890ft./271m.; 🅿; z 67332; ℗ 107; © 124
BARTON; 178 F-9; ℗ 29,382; © 28,205; ◆ 27,614
Basehor; Inc. Place; LEAVENWORTH; 179 D-18; elev. 984ft./300m.; 🅿; ★ **K.C.**; z 66007, z 66012; ℗ 1,591; © 2,238
Bassett; Inc. Place; ALLEN; *179 H-17; elev. 980ft./299m.; mail Iola z 66749; ℗ 20; © 22
Bavaria; RMC Place; SALINE; 179 E-12; elev. 1,276ft./389m.; 🅿; z 67401; ● 90
Baxter Springs; Inc. Place; CHEROKEE; 179 J-19; elev. 840ft./256m.; 🅿; z 66713; ℗ 4,351; © 4,602
Bayard; RMC Place; ALLEN; *179 G-18; mail Kincaid z 66039
Bazaar (Bazar); RMC Place; CHASE; 179 G-15; mail Cottonwood Falls z 66845; ● 25
Bazar; CHASE; see Bazaar (RMC Place)
Bazine; Inc. Place; NESS; 178 F-7; elev. 2,140ft./652m.; 🅿; z 67516; ℗ 373; © 311
Beagle; RMC Place; MIAMI; 179 F-18; mail Osawatomie z 66064; ● 70
Beardsley; RMC Place; RAWLINS; *178 B-3; mail Atwood z 67730
Beattie; Inc. Place; MARSHALL; 179 B-15; elev. 1,300ft./396m.; 🅿; z 66406; ℗ 221; © 277
Beaumont; RMC Place; BUTLER; 179 I-15; elev. 1,600ft./488m.; 🅿; z 67012; ● 200
Beaver; RMC Place; BARTON; 178 F-9; elev. 1,920ft./585m.; 🅿; z 67525; ● 40
Beech; RMC Place; SEDGWICK; *179 H-13; ★ **WICH**; mail Wichita z 67207; rural
Beeler; RMC Place; NESS; 178 F-6; elev. 2,500ft./762m.; 🅿; z 67518; ● 45
Bel Aire; SEDGWICK; see Bellaire (Inc. Place)
Bellaire (Bel Aire); Inc. Place; SEDGWICK; 178 K-9; ★ **WICH**; mail Wichita z 67220, z 67226; ℗ 3,695; © 5,836; ® 6,014
Bellaire; RMC Place; SMITH; *178 B-9; elev. 1,800ft./549m.; 🅿; z 66952
Belle Plaine; Inc. Place; SUMNER; 179 I-13; elev. 1,220ft./372m.; 🅿; ★ **WICH**; z 67013; ℗ 1,649; © 1,708
Belleville; Inc. Place; ⊡ REPUBLIC; 179 B-12; elev. 1,550ft./472m.; 🅿 🅷; z 66935; ℗ 2,517; © 2,239
Belmont; RMC Place; KINGMAN; 179 I-11; elev. 1,580ft./482m.; 🅿; z 67068; ● 35
Beloit; Inc. Place; ⊡ MITCHELL; 179 C-11; elev. 1,386ft./422m.; 🅿 🅷; z 67420; ℗ 4,066; © 4,019
Belpre; Inc. Place; EDWARDS; 178 H-8; elev. 2,090ft./637m.; 🅿; z 67519; ℗ 116; © 104
Belvidere; RMC Place; KIOWA; 178 I-8; elev. 1,845ft./562m.; 🅿; z 67028; ● 25
Belvue; Inc. Place; POTTAWATOMIE; 179 D-15; elev. 960ft./293m.; 🅿; z 66407; ℗ 207; © 228
Bendena; RMC Place; DONIPHAN; 179 B-18; elev. 1,113ft./339m.; 🅿; z 66008; ● 200
Benedict; Inc. Place; WILSON; 179 I-17; elev. 900ft./274m.; 🅿; z 66714; ℗ 84; © 103
Bennington; Inc. Place; OTTAWA; 179 D-12; elev. 1,221ft./372m.; 🅿; z 67422; ℗ 568; © 623
Bentley; Inc. Place; SEDGWICK; 179 H-12; elev. 1,385ft./422m.; 🅿; z 67016; ℗ 360; © 368
Benton; Inc. Place; BUTLER; 179 H-13; elev. 1,370ft./418m.; 🅿; z 67017; ℗ 669; © 827
Bern; Inc. Place; NEMAHA; 179 B-16; elev. 1,281ft./390m.; 🅿; z 66408; ℗ 190; © 204
Berryton; RMC Place; SHAWNEE; 179 E-17; elev. 1,000ft./305m.; 🅿; ★ **TOP**; z 66409; ● 400
Berwick; RMC Place; NEMAHA; *179 B-16; elev. 1,366ft./416m.; mail Sabetha z 66534
Beulah; RMC Place; CRAWFORD; 179 I-19; mail Girard z 66743; ● 60
Beverly; Inc. Place; LINCOLN; 179 E-11; elev. 1,322ft./403m.; 🅿; z 67423; ℗ 131; © 199
Big Bow; RMC Place; STANTON; 178 I-2; elev. 3,174ft./967m.; mail Johnson z 67855; ● 95
Big Springs; RMC Place; DOUGLAS; 179 D-17; mail Lecompton z 66050; ● 75
Bird City; Inc. Place; CHEYENNE; 178 B-3; elev. 3,460ft./1,055m.; 🅿; z 67731; ℗ 467; © 482
Birmingham; RMC Place; JACKSON; *179 C-16; mail Holton z 66436
Bismarck Grove; RMC Place; DOUGLAS; ★ **LAWR**; mail Lawrence z 66044; pop. incl. with Lawrence (Inc. Place)
Bison; Inc. Place; RUSH; 178 F-8; elev. 2,011ft./613m.; 🅿; z 67520; ℗ 252; © 235
Black Wolf; RMC Place; ELLSWORTH; *178 E-10; elev. 1,568ft./478m.; mail Wilson z 67490; rural
Blaine; RMC Place; POTTAWATOMIE; 179 C-15; elev. 1,507ft./459m.; 🅿; z 66549; ● 80
Blair; RMC Place; DONIPHAN; 179 B-18; ★ **ST.JO**; mail Wathena z 66090; ● 40
Blakeman; RMC Place; RAWLINS; *178 B-4; mail Atwood z 67730
Bloom; RMC Place; FORD; 178 I-6; elev. 2,584ft./788m.; 🅿; z 67865; ● 75
Bloomington; RMC Place; BUTLER; *179 I-14; mail Augusta z 67010; rural
Bloomington; RMC Place; OSBORNE; 178 C-9; elev. 1,590ft./485m.; mail Osborne z 67473; ● 60
Blue Hills; RMC Place; RILEY; *179 D-14; ★ **MANH**; mail Manhattan z 66502; pop. incl. with Manhattan (Inc. Place)
Blue Mound; Inc. Place; LINN; 179 G-18; elev. 1,030ft./314m.; 🅿; z 66010; ℗ 251; © 277
Blue Rapids; Inc. Place; MARSHALL; 179 B-14; elev. 1,158ft./353m.; 🅿; z 66411; ℗ 1,131; © 1,088
Blue Valley; RMC Place; JOHNSON; *179 E-19; ★ **K.C.**; mail Overland Park z 66213, z 66225; pop. incl. with Overland Park (Inc. Place)
Bluff City; Inc. Place; HARPER; 179 J-11; elev. 1,230ft./375m.; 🅿; z 67018; ℗ 69; © 80
Bogue; Inc. Place; GRAHAM; 178 C-7; elev. 1,203ft./367m.; 🅿; z 67625; ℗ 150; © 179
Boicourt; RMC Place; LINN; 179 G-19; elev. 800ft./244m.; mail Pleasanton z 66075; ● 30
Bolton; RMC Place; MONTGOMERY; 179 J-16; mail Independence z 67301; ● 40
Bonita; RMC Place; JOHNSON; *179 E-19; elev. 1,102ft./336m.; ★ **K.C.**; mail Olathe z 66061
Bonner Springs; Inc. Place; WYANDOTTE, JOHNSON; 179 D-18; elev. 801ft./244m.; 🅿; ★ **K.C.**; z 66012; ℗ 6,413; © 6,768
Bonnie Brae; RMC Place; SEDGWICK; *179 I-13; ★ **WICH**; mail Wichita z 67207; pop. incl. with Wichita (Inc. Place)
Bonnie Ridge; RMC Place; SALINE; mail Salina z 67401; ● 300
BOURBON; 179 H-18; ℗ 14,966; © 15,379; ◆ 14,673
Boyle; RMC Place; JEFFERSON; 179 C-17; elev. 1,144ft./349m.; mail Valley Falls z 66088; ● 30
Bradford; RMC Place; WABAUNSEE; *179 E-16; mail Eskridge z 66423; rural
Brainerd; RMC Place; BUTLER; 179 H-13; mail Whitewater z 67154; ● 70
Brantford; RMC Place; WASHINGTON; elev. 1,456ft./444m.; mail Clyde z 66938
Brazilton; RMC Place; CRAWFORD; 179 I-18; elev. 1,013ft./309m.; mail Girard z 66743; ● 80
Bremen; RMC Place; MARSHALL; 179 B-14; elev. 1,320ft./402m.; 🅿; z 66412; ● 80
Brenham; RMC Place; KIOWA; *178 I-8; mail Haviland z 67059; rural
Brenner Heights; RMC Place; WYANDOTTE; ★ **K.C.**; mail Kansas City z 66104; pop. incl. with Kansas City (Inc. Place)
Brewster; Inc. Place; THOMAS; 178 C-3; elev. 3,428ft./1,045m.; 🅿; z 67732; ℗ 296; © 285
Bridgeport; RMC Place; SALINE; 179 F-12; elev. 1,302ft./397m.; mail Assaria z 67416; ● 75
Bronson; Inc. Place; BOURBON; 179 H-18; elev. 1,070ft./326m.; 🅿; z 66716; ℗ 343; © 346
Brookhaven Estates; RMC Place; SEDGWICK; *179 H-13; ★ **WICH**; mail Wichita z 67230; ● 75
Brookridge; RMC Place; JOHNSON; *179 E-19; elev. 900ft./274m.; ★ **K.C.**; mail Overland Park z 66212, z 66282; pop. incl. with Overland Park (Inc. Place)
Brookville; Inc. Place; SALINE; 179 E-11; elev. 1,369ft./417m.; 🅿; z 67425; ℗ 226; © 259
BROWN; 179 B-17; ℗ 11,128; © 10,724; ◆ 9,882
Brownell; Inc. Place; NESS; 178 F-7; elev. 2,400ft./732m.; 🅿; z 67521; ℗ 44; © 48
Browns; KINGMAN; see Browns Spur (RMC Place)
Browns Spur (Browns); RMC Place; KINGMAN; *179 I-11; mail Kingman z 67068; rural
Buckeye; RMC Place; DICKINSON; *179 D-13; elev. 1,294ft./394m.; mail Abilene z 67410; rural
Bucklin; Inc. Place; FORD; 178 I-7; elev. 2,412ft./735m.; 🅿; z 67834; ℗ 710; © 725
Bucyrus; RMC Place; MIAMI; 179 E-19; elev. 1,090ft./332m.; 🅿; z 66013; ● 140
Buffalo; Inc. Place; WILSON; 179 H-17; elev. 902ft./275m.; 🅿; z 66717; ℗ 293; © 284
Buffalo Park; GOVE; see Park (Inc. Place)
Buhler; Inc. Place; RENO; 179 G-12; elev. 1,480ft./451m.; 🅿; z 67522; ℗ 1,277; © 1,358
Bunker Hill; Inc. Place; RUSSELL; 178 E-9; elev. 1,860ft./567m.; 🅿; z 67626; ℗ 111; © 101
Burden; Inc. Place; COWLEY; 179 J-14; elev. 1,383ft./422m.; 🅿; z 67019; ℗ 518; © 564
Burdett; Inc. Place; PAWNEE; 178 G-7; elev. 2,133ft./650m.; 🅿; z 67523; ℗ 248; © 256
Burdick; RMC Place; MORRIS; 179 F-14; elev. 1,456ft./444m.; 🅿; z 66838; ● 75
Burlingame; Inc. Place; OSAGE; 179 E-16; elev. 1,055ft./322m.; 🅿; z 66413; ℗ 1,074; © 1,017
Burlington; Inc. Place; ⊡ COFFEY; 179 G-16; elev. 1,037ft./316m.; 🅿 🅷; z 66839; ℗ 2,735; © 2,790
Burns; Inc. Place; MARION; 179 G-14; elev. 1,504ft./458m.; 🅿; z 66840; ℗ 226; © 268
Burr Oak; Inc. Place; JEWELL; 178 B-10; elev. 1,664ft./507m.; 🅿; z 66936; ℗ 278; © 265
Burrton; Inc. Place; HARVEY; 179 H-12; elev. 1,450ft./442m.; 🅿; z 67020; ℗ 866; © 932
Busby; RMC Place; ELK; *179 I-16; mail Longton z 67352; rural
Bush City; RMC Place; ANDERSON; *179 G-18; elev. 1,031ft./314m.; mail Garnett z 66032
Bushong; Inc. Place; LYON; 179 F-15; elev. 1,383ft./422m.; 🅿; z 66833; ℗ 57; © 55
Bushton; Inc. Place; RICE; 178 F-10; elev. 1,770ft./539m.; 🅿; z 67427; ℗ 341; © 314
BUTLER; 179 H-14; ℗ 50,580; © 59,482; ® 59,484; ◆ 63,553
Buxton; RMC Place; WILSON; *179 I-16; mail Fredonia z 66736; rural
Byers; Inc. Place; PRATT; 178 H-9; elev. 2,006ft./611m.; 🅿; z 67021; ℗ 46; © 50

C

Cadmus; RMC Place; LINN; *179 F-18; elev. 881ft./269m.; mail Fontana z 66026
Cairo; RMC Place; PRATT; 178 I-10; mail Cunningham z 67035; ● 20
Caldwell; Inc. Place; SUMNER; 179 K-12; elev. 1,149ft./350m.; 🅿 🅷; z 67022; ℗ 1,351; © 1,284
Calista; RMC Place; KINGMAN; *178 I-10; elev. 1,590ft./485m.; mail Cunningham z 67035
Callahan; RMC Place; SEDGWICK; ★ **WICH**; mail Wichita z 67209; pop. incl. with Wichita (Inc. Place)
Calvert; RMC Place; NORTON; 178 B-7; mail Almena z 67622; ● 25
Cambridge; Inc. Place; COWLEY; 179 J-14; elev. 1,252ft./382m.; 🅿; z 67023; ℗ 74; © 103
Camp Fifty; CRAWFORD; see Polk (RMC Place)
Camp Forsyth; RMC Place; GEARY; *179 D-14; mail Fort Riley z 66442; ℗ 1,967
Camp Naish; RMC Place; WYANDOTTE; *179 D-18; ★ **K.C.**; mail Kansas City z 66111; pop. incl. with Bonner Springs (Inc. Place)
Campus; RMC Place; GOVE; *178 D-5; mail Oakley z 67748; rural
Canada; RMC Place; MARION; 179 F-13; elev. 1,364ft./416m.; mail Marion z 66861; ● 75
Caney; Inc. Place; MONTGOMERY; 179 J-16; elev. 770ft./235m.; 🅿; z 67333; ℗ 2,062; © 2,092
Canton; Inc. Place; MCPHERSON; 179 F-12; elev. 1,590ft./485m.; 🅿; z 67428; ℗ 794; © 829
Capaldo; RMC Place; CRAWFORD; 179 I-19; mail Pittsburg z 66762; pop. incl. with Frontenac (Inc. Place)
Carbondale; Inc. Place; OSAGE; 179 E-17; elev. 1,087ft./331m.; 🅿; z 66414; ℗ 1,526; © 1,478
Carlton; Inc. Place; DICKINSON; 179 E-13; elev. 1,320ft./402m.; 🅿; z 67448; ℗ 39; © 38
Carlyle; RMC Place; ALLEN; 179 G-17; elev. 1,000ft./305m.; 🅿; z 66749; ● 100
Carneiro; RMC Place; ELLSWORTH; *179 E-11; mail Brookville z 67425
Carona; RMC Place; CHEROKEE; 179 J-19; elev. 914ft./279m.; 🅿; z 66773; ● 60
Cassoday; Inc. Place; BUTLER; 179 G-14; elev. 1,460ft./445m.; 🅿; z 66842 & mail Matfield Green z 66862; ℗ 95; © 130
Castleton; RMC Place; RENO; 179 H-11; mail Hutchinson z 67501; ● 25
Catharine; RMC Place; ELLIS; 178 E-8; elev. 2,010ft./613m.; 🅿; z 67627; ● 105
Cato; RMC Place; CRAWFORD; *179 H-19; mail Arcadia z 66711; rural
Cave (Cooperville); RMC Place; STEVENS; *178 I-3; mail Moscow z 67952; rural
Cawker City; Inc. Place; MITCHELL; 178 C-10; elev. 1,500ft./457m.; 🅿; z 67430; ℗ 588; © 521
Cedar (Corliss); RMC Place; JOHNSON; *179 D-18; mail De Soto z 66018; pop. incl. with De Soto (Inc. Place)
Cedar; Inc. Place; SMITH; 178 C-9; elev. 1,631ft./497m.; 🅿; z 67628; ℗ 25; © 26
Cedar Bluffs; RMC Place; DECATUR; 178 B-5; mail Oberlin z 67749; ● 35
Cedar Point; Inc. Place; CHASE; 179 G-14; elev. 1,250ft./381m.; 🅿; z 66843; ℗ 39; © 53
Cedar Vale; Inc. Place; CHAUTAUQUA; 179 J-15; elev. 949ft./289m.; 🅿 🅷; z 67024; ℗ 760; © 723
Centerview; RMC Place; EDWARDS; *178 H-8; mail Lewis z 67552; rural
Centerville; RMC Place; LINN; 179 G-18; elev. 915ft./279m.; 🅿; z 66014; ● 100
Centralia; Inc. Place; NEMAHA; 179 B-15; elev. 1,260ft./384m.; 🅿; z 66415; ℗ 452; © 534
Centropolis; RMC Place; FRANKLIN; 179 E-17; elev. 971ft./296m.; 🅿; z 66067; ● 170
Chanute; Inc. Place; NEOSHO; 179 H-17; elev. 943ft./287m.; 🅿 🅷; z 66720; ℗ 9,488; © 9,411
Chapman; Inc. Place; DICKINSON; 179 E-13; elev. 1,113ft./339m.; 🅿; z 67431; ℗ 1,264; © 1,241
Charleston; RMC Place; GRAY; 178 H-5; elev. 2,712ft./827m.; mail Ingalls z 67853; ● 25
Chase; Inc. Place; RICE; 178 G-10; elev. 1,718ft./524m.; 🅿; z 67524; ℗ 577; © 490
CHASE; 179 G-14; ℗ 3,021; © 3,030; ◆ 2,618
Chautauqua; Inc. Place; CHAUTAUQUA; 179 K-16; elev. 903ft./275m.; 🅿; z 67334; ℗ 132; © 113
CHAUTAUQUA; 179 J-15; ℗ 4,407; © 4,359; ◆ 3,650
Cheney; Inc. Place; SEDGWICK; 179 I-12; elev. 1,380ft./421m.; 🅿; z 67025; ℗ 1,560; © 1,783
Cherokee; Inc. Place; CRAWFORD; 179 I-19; elev. 949ft./289m.; 🅿; z 66724; ℗ 651; © 722
CHEROKEE; 179 J-18; ℗ 21,374; © 22,605; ◆ 21,096
Cherryvale; Inc. Place; MONTGOMERY; 179 J-17; elev. 850ft./259m.; 🅿; z 67335; ℗ 2,464; © 2,386
Chetopa; Inc. Place; LABETTE; 179 J-18; elev. 824ft./251m.; 🅿; z 67336; ℗ 1,357; © 1,281
CHEYENNE; 178 B-2; ℗ 3,243; © 3,165; ◆ 2,656
Chicopee; RMC Place; CRAWFORD; *179 I-19; elev. 921ft./281m.; mail Pittsburg z 66762; ● 250
Child's Acres; RMC Place; SEDGWICK; *179 H-12; ★ **WICH**; mail Maize z 67101; ● 500
Chiles; RMC Place; MIAMI; *179 E-19; elev. 1,096ft./334m.; mail Paola z 66071
Chisholm; RMC Place; SEDGWICK; *179 I-13; ★ **WICH**; mail Wichita z 67213, z 67217; pop. incl. with Wichita (Inc. Place)
Cicero; RMC Place; SUMNER; *179 J-13; mail Wellington z 67152; rural
Cimarron; Inc. Place; ⊡ GRAY; 178 H-5; elev. 2,627ft./801m.; 🅿; z 67835; ℗ 1,626; © 1,934
Circleville; Inc. Place; JACKSON; 179 C-16; elev. 1,103ft./336m.; 🅿; z 66416; ℗ 153; © 185
Civic Center; RMC Place; WYANDOTTE; *179 D-19; ★ **K.C.**; mail Kansas City z 66101, z 66115, z 66117; pop. incl. with Kansas City (Inc. Place)
Claflin; Inc. Place; BARTON; 178 F-10; elev. 1,810ft./552m.; 🅿; z 67525; ℗ 678; © 705
Clare; RMC Place; JOHNSON; 179 E-18; elev. 1,028ft./313m.; ★ **K.C.**; mail Olathe z 66061; ● 40
CLARK; 178 J-6; ℗ 2,418; © 2,390; ◆ 1,971
Claudell; RMC Place; SMITH; *178 C-9; elev. 1,660ft./506m.; mail Kensington z 66951
CLAY; 179 D-13; ℗ 9,158; © 8,822; ◆ 8,859
Clay Center; Inc. Place; ⊡ CLAY; 179 C-13; elev. 1,201ft./366m.; 🅿 🅷; z 67432; ℗ 4,613; © 4,564
Clayton; Inc. Place; NORTON, DECATUR; 178 B-6; elev. 2,420ft./738m.; 🅿; z 67629; ℗ 91; © 66
Clearfield; RMC Place; DOUGLAS; *179 E-18; elev. 999ft./304m.; mail Eudora z 66025; rural
Clearview City (Sunflower); RMC Place; JOHNSON; *179 E-18; elev. 930ft./283m.; 🅿; z 66019; pop. incl. with De Soto (Inc. Place)
Clearwater; Inc. Place; SEDGWICK; 179 I-12; elev. 1,274ft./388m.; 🅿; z 67026; ℗ 1,875; © 2,178
Clements; RMC Place; CHASE; *179 G-14; elev. 1,230ft./375m.; 🅿; z 66843
Cleveland; RMC Place; KINGMAN; *179 I-11; mail Kingman z 67068; rural
Clifton; Inc. Place; WASHINGTON, CLAY; 179 C-13; elev. 1,302ft./397m.; 🅿; z 66937; ℗ 561; © 557
Climax; Inc. Place; GREENWOOD; 179 H-15; elev. 1,028ft./313m.; 🅿; z 67137; ℗ 57; © 64
Clinton; RMC Place; DOUGLAS; 179 E-17; elev. 946ft./288m.; mail Lawrence z 66049; ● 40
Clonmel; RMC Place; SEDGWICK; *179 I-12; elev. 1,372ft./418m.; mail Viola z 67149
CLOUD; 179 C-11; ℗ 11,023; © 10,268; ◆ 9,241
Cloverdale; RMC Place; CHAUTAUQUA; *179 J-15; mail Cedar Vale z 67024; rural
Clyde; Inc. Place; CLOUD; 179 C-12; elev. 1,300ft./396m.; 🅿; z 66938 & mail Agenda z 66930; ℗ 793; © 740
Coalvale; RMC Place; CRAWFORD; *179 I-19; elev. 860ft./262m.; mail Arcadia z 66711; rural
Coats; Inc. Place; PRATT; 178 I-9; elev. 1,980ft./604m.; 🅿; z 67028; ℗ 127; © 112
Codell; RMC Place; ROOKS; 178 D-8; elev. 1,985ft./605m.; 🅿; z 67663; ● 75
COFFEY; 179 G-16; ℗ 8,404; © 8,865; ◆ 8,132
Coffeyville; Inc. Place; MONTGOMERY; 179 J-17; elev. 736ft./224m.; 🅿 🅷 ■; z 67337; ℗ 12,917; © 11,021; ® 11,060; ◆ 9,963
Colby; Inc. Place; ⊡ THOMAS; 178 C-4; elev. 3,160ft./963m.; 🅿 🅷; z 67701; ℗ 5,396; © 5,450
Coldwater; Inc. Place; ⊡ COMANCHE; 178 J-8; elev. 2,112ft./644m.; 🅿 🅷; z 67029; ℗ 939; © 792
Collyer; Inc. Place; TREGO; 178 D-6; elev. 2,578ft./786m.; 🅿; z 67631; ℗ 144; © 133
Colony; Inc. Place; ANDERSON; 179 G-17; elev. 1,120ft./341m.; 🅿; z 66015; ℗ 447; © 397
Columbus; Inc. Place; ⊡ CHEROKEE; 179 J-19; elev. 904ft./276m.; 🅿 🅷; z 66725; ℗ 3,268; © 3,396
Colwich; Inc. Place; SEDGWICK; 179 H-12; elev. 1,380ft./421m.; 🅿; z 67030; ℗ 1,091; © 1,229
COMANCHE; 178 J-8; ℗ 2,313; © 1,967; ◆ 1,911
Concordia; Inc. Place; ⊡ CLOUD; 179 C-12; elev. 1,369ft./417m.; 🅿 🅷; z 66901; ℗ 6,167; © 5,714
Conway; RMC Place; MCPHERSON; *179 F-12; elev. 1,540ft./469m.; 🅿; z 67460
Conway Springs; Inc. Place; SUMNER; 179 I-12; elev. 1,366ft./416m.; 🅿; z 67031; ℗ 1,384; © 1,322
Coolidge; Inc. Place; HAMILTON; 178 G-1; elev. 3,360ft./1,024m.; 🅿; z 67836; ℗ 90; © 86
Cooperville; STEVENS; see Cave (RMC Place)
Copeland; Inc. Place; GRAY; 178 I-5; elev. 2,821ft./860m.; 🅿; z 67837; ℗ 290; © 339
Corbin; RMC Place; MONTGOMERY; *179 J-17; mail Cherryvale z 67335; rural
Corbin; RMC Place; SUMNER; 179 J-12; elev. 1,155ft./352m.; mail Caldwell z 67022; ● 100
Corliss; JOHNSON; see Cedar (RMC Place)
Corning; Inc. Place; NEMAHA; 179 B-16; elev. 1,350ft./411m.; 🅿; z 66417; ℗ 142; © 170
Corporate Hills; RMC Place; SEDGWICK; ★ **WICH**; mail Wichita z 67207, z 67278; pop. incl. with Wichita (Inc. Place)
Corwin; RMC Place; HARPER; 178 J-10; mail Hazelton z 67061; ● 25
Cottonwood Falls; Inc. Place; ⊡ CHASE; 179 F-15; elev. 1,491ft./454m.; 🅿; z 66845; ℗ 889; © 966
Council Grove; Inc. Place; ⊡ MORRIS; 179 F-15; elev. 1,233ft./376m.; 🅿 🅷; z 66846, z 66873; ℗ 2,228; © 2,321
Countryside; RMC Place; JOHNSON; 196 J-2; elev. 1,000ft./305m.; 🅿; ★ **K.C.**; z 66202; former incorporated place; disincorporated January 1, 2003; ℗ 312; © 295
County Acres; RMC Place; SEDGWICK; *179 H-12; ★ **WICH**; mail Wichita z 67212; pop. incl. with Wichita (Inc. Place)
Courtland; Inc. Place; REPUBLIC; 179 B-11; elev. 1,499ft./457m.; 🅿; z 66939; ℗ 343; © 334
Covert; RMC Place; OSBORNE; *178 D-9; elev. 1,761ft./537m.; mail Natoma z 67651; rural
COWLEY; 179 J-14; ℗ 36,915; © 36,291; ◆ 34,099
Cow Town; RMC Place; SEDGWICK; *179 I-13; ★ **WICH**; mail Wichita z 67203; pop. incl. with Wichita (Inc. Place)
Coyville; Inc. Place; WILSON; 179 H-16; elev. 876ft./267m.; 🅿; z 66736; ℗ 78; © 71
Craig; RMC Place; JOHNSON; *179 D-19; elev. 838ft./255m.; ★ **K.C.**; mail Lenexa z 66215; pop. incl. with Lenexa (Inc. Place)
CRAWFORD; 179 I-18; ℗ 35,568; © 38,242; ◆ 38,718
Crestline; RMC Place; CHEROKEE; 179 J-19; elev. 870ft./265m.; 🅿; z 66728; ● 110
Croweburg; RMC Place; CRAWFORD; 179 I-19; mail Mulberry z 66756; ● 75
Cruppers Corner; RMC Place; RENO; *179 H-11; elev. 1,538ft./469m.; mail Hutchinson z 67501; rural
Crystal Springs; RMC Place; HARPER; *179 J-11; elev. 1,440ft./439m.; mail Harper z 67058; ● 30
Cuba; Inc. Place; REPUBLIC; 179 B-12; elev. 1,590ft./485m.; 🅿; z 66940; ℗ 242; © 231
Cullen Village; RMC Place; SHAWNEE; *179 E-16; elev. 1,057ft./322m.; ★ **TOP**; mail Topeka z 66619
Cullison; Inc. Place; PRATT; 178 I-9; elev. 2,040ft./622m.; 🅿; z 67124; ℗ 120; © 98
Culver; Inc. Place; OTTAWA; 179 E-12; elev. 1,260ft./384m.; 🅿; z 67484; ℗ 162; © 164
Cummings; RMC Place; ATCHISON; 179 C-17; elev. 1,000ft./305m.; 🅿; z 66016; ● 70
Cunningham; Inc. Place; KINGMAN; 178 I-10; elev. 1,705ft./520m.; 🅿; z 67035; ℗ 535; © 514
Curranville; RMC Place; CRAWFORD; *179 I-19; mail Mulberry z 66756; rural

D

Dalton; RMC Place; SUMNER; *179 J-13; mail Wellington z 67152
Damar; Inc. Place; ROOKS; 178 D-7; elev. 2,106ft./642m.; 🅿; z 67632; ℗ 112; © 155
Danville; Inc. Place; HARPER; 179 J-11; elev. 1,346ft./410m.; 🅿; z 67036; ℗ 56; © 59
Dartmouth; RMC Place; BARTON; *178 F-9; mail Great Bend z 67530; rural
Dearing; Inc. Place; MONTGOMERY; 179 J-17; elev. 760ft./232m.; 🅿; z 67340; ℗ 428; © 415; ® 409
DECATUR; 178 B-5; ℗ 4,021; © 3,472; ◆ 2,781
Deerfield; Inc. Place; KEARNY; 178 H-4; elev. 2,947ft./898m.; 🅿; z 67838; ℗ 677; © 884
Deerhead; RMC Place; BARBER; *178 J-9; elev. 1,951ft./595m.; mail Lake City z 67071; rural
De Graff; RMC Place; BUTLER; *179 H-14; mail Burns z 66840
Delano; RMC Place; SEDGWICK; ★ **WICH**; mail Wichita z 67209, z 67275; pop. incl. with Wichita (Inc. Place)
Delavan; RMC Place; MORRIS; 179 F-14; elev. 1,500ft./457m.; 🅿; z 67449; ● 25
Delia; Inc. Place; JACKSON; 179 D-16; elev. 972ft./296m.; 🅿; z 66418; ℗ 172; © 179
Dellvale; RMC Place; NORTON; *178 B-6; mail Norton z 67654; rural
Delphos; Inc. Place; OTTAWA; 179 D-12; elev. 1,300ft./396m.; 🅿; z 67436; ℗ 494; © 469
Denison; Inc. Place; JACKSON; 179 C-17; elev. 1,050ft./320m.; 🅿; z 66419; ℗ 225; © 231
Denmark; RMC Place; LINCOLN; *178 D-10; mail Lincoln z 67455
Dennis; RMC Place; LABETTE; 179 I-17; elev. 923ft./281m.; 🅿; z 67341; ● 150
Densmore; RMC Place; NORTON; 178 C-7; elev. 2,100ft./640m.; 🅿; z 67645; ● 35
Denton; Inc. Place; DONIPHAN; 179 B-17; elev. 1,078ft./329m.; 🅿; z 66017; ℗ 166; © 186
Dentonia; RMC Place; JEWELL; *178 B-10; mail Esbon z 66941; rural
Derby; Inc. Place; SEDGWICK; 179 I-13; elev. 1,300ft./396m.; 🅿; ★ **WICH**; z 67037; ℗ 14,699; © 17,807; ◆ 19,307
Dermot; RMC Place; MORTON; mail Rolla z 67954; rural
De Soto; Inc. Place; JOHNSON; 179 D-18; elev. 842ft./257m.; 🅿; z 66018-19; ℗ 2,291; © 4,561
Detroit; RMC Place; DICKINSON; 179 E-13; mail Abilene z 67410; ● 60
Devon; RMC Place; BOURBON; 179 H-19; elev. 867ft./264m.; mail Fort Scott z 66701; ● 30
Dexter; Inc. Place; COWLEY; 179 J-14; elev. 1,208ft./368m.; 🅿; z 67038; ℗ 320; © 364
Diamond Springs; RMC Place; MORRIS; *179 F-14; mail Burdick z 66838
DICKINSON; 179 E-13; ℗ 18,958; © 19,344; ◆ 18,885
Dighton; Inc. Place; ⊡ LANE; 178 F-5; elev. 2,765ft./843m.; 🅿 🅷; z 67839; ℗ 1,361; © 1,261
Dillwyn; RMC Place; STAFFORD; *178 H-9; mail Macksville z 67557; rural
Dispatch; RMC Place; SMITH; *178 C-10; elev. 1,548ft./472m.; mail Cawker City z 67430; rural
Dodge City; Inc. Place; ⊡ FORD; 178 H-6; elev. 2,530ft./771m.; 🅿 🅷 ■; z 67801, z 67843; ℗ 21,129; © 25,176; ◆ 26,401
Doniphan; RMC Place; DONIPHAN; *179 B-18; mail Atchison z 66002
DONIPHAN; 179 B-17; ℗ 8,134; © 8,249; ◆ 7,789
Dorrance; Inc. Place; RUSSELL; 178 E-10; elev. 1,730ft./527m.; 🅿; z 67634; ℗ 195; © 205
DOUGLAS; 179 E-17; ℗ 81,798; © 99,962; ◆ 115,356
Douglass; Inc. Place; BUTLER; 179 I-13; elev. 1,205ft./367m.; 🅿; z 67039; ℗ 1,722; © 1,813
Dover; RMC Place; SHAWNEE; 179 E-16; elev. 1,010ft./308m.; 🅿; z 66420; ● 140
Downs; Inc. Place; OSBORNE; 178 C-10; elev. 1,484ft./452m.; 🅿; z 67437; ℗ 1,119; © 1,038
Downtown; RMC Place; SEDGWICK; *179 I-13; ★ **WICH**; mail Wichita z 67201-03; pop. incl. with Wichita (Inc. Place)
Downtown; RMC Place; SHAWNEE; ★ **TOP**; mail Topeka z 66601, z 66603; pop. incl. with Topeka (Inc. Place)
Dresden; Inc. Place; DECATUR; 178 C-5; elev. 2,731ft./832m.; 🅿; z 67635; ℗ 73; © 51
Drury; RMC Place; SUMNER; *179 K-12; elev. 1,092ft./333m.; mail Caldwell z 67022; ● 75
Dubuque; RMC Place; BARTON; *178 E-10; elev. 1,888ft./575m.; mail Dorrance z 67634; rural
Duluth; RMC Place; POTTAWATOMIE; 179 C-15; elev. 1,250ft./381m.; 🅿; z 66521; ● 25
Dunavant; RMC Place; JEFFERSON; *179 C-17; mail Valley Falls z 66088
Dundee; RMC Place; BARTON; 178 G-9; 🅿; z 67530; ● 60
Dunkirk; RMC Place; CRAWFORD; *179 I-19; mail Pittsburg z 66762; rural
Dunlap; Inc. Place; MORRIS; 179 F-15; elev. 1,186ft./361m.; 🅿; z 66846; ℗ 65; © 81
Duquoin; RMC Place; HARPER; *179 I-11; elev. 1,582ft./482m.; mail Harper z 67058
Durham; Inc. Place; MARION; 179 F-13; elev. 1,396ft./426m.; 🅿; z 67438; ℗ 119; © 114
Dwight; Inc. Place; MORRIS; 179 E-14; elev. 1,500ft./457m.; 🅿; z 66849; ℗ 365; © 330

E

Earlton; Inc. Place; NEOSHO; 179 I-17; elev. 960ft./293m.; mail Chanute z 66720; ℗ 69; © 80
East Bank; RMC Place; ALLEN; *179 H-17; mail Iola z 66749; pop. incl. with Iola (Inc. Place)
Eastborough; Inc. Place; SEDGWICK; 178 M-9; elev. 1,370ft./418m.; 🅿; ★ **WICH**; z 67206-08; ℗ 896; © 826
East Forbes; RMC Place; SHAWNEE; mail Topeka z 66620; rural
Easton; Inc. Place; LEAVENWORTH; 179 C-18; elev. 903ft./275m.; 🅿; z 66020; ℗ 405; © 362
Eastshore; RMC Place; MARION; *179 F-13; mail Marion z 66861; ● 200
Edgerton; Inc. Place; JOHNSON; 179 E-18; elev. 990ft./302m.; 🅿; z 66021; ℗ 1,244; © 1,440
Edmond; Inc. Place; NORTON; 178 C-7; elev. 2,200ft./671m.; 🅿; z 67645; ℗ 37; © 47
Edna; Inc. Place; LABETTE; 179 J-18; elev. 979ft./298m.; 🅿; z 67342; ℗ 438; © 423
Edson; RMC Place; SHERMAN; 178 C-3; elev. 3,563ft./1,086m.; 🅿; z 67733; ● 40
EDWARDS; 178 H-8; ℗ 3,787; © 3,449; ◆ 3,016
Edwardsville; Inc. Place; WYANDOTTE; 179 D-19; elev. 795ft./242m.; 🅿; ★ **K.C.**; z 66111, z 66113; ℗ 3,979; © 4,146
Effingham; Inc. Place; ATCHISON; 179 C-17; elev. 1,138ft./347m.; 🅿; z 66023; ℗ 540; © 588
Elbing; Inc. Place; BUTLER; 179 G-13; elev. 1,440ft./439m.; 🅿; z 67041; ℗ 184; © 218
El Dorado; Inc. Place; ⊡ BUTLER; 179 H-14; elev. 1,291ft./393m.; 🅿 🅷; z 67042; ℗ 11,504; © 12,057
Elgin; Inc. Place; CHAUTAUQUA; 179 K-15; elev. 784ft./239m.; mail Sedan z 67361; ℗ 118; © 82
ELK; 179 I-15; ℗ 3,327; © 3,261; ◆ 2,986
Elk City; Inc. Place; MONTGOMERY; 179 J-16; elev. 835ft./255m.; 🅿; z 67344; ℗ 334; © 305
Elk Falls; Inc. Place; ELK; 179 I-15; elev. 938ft./286m.; 🅿; z 67345; ℗ 122; © 112
Elkhart; Inc. Place; ⊡ MORTON; 178 J-2; elev. 3,624ft./1,105m.; 🅿 🅷; z 67950; ℗ 2,318; © 2,233
Ellinwood; Inc. Place; BARTON; 178 G-10; elev. 1,790ft./546m.; 🅿 🅷; z 67526; ℗ 2,329; © 2,164
Ellis; Inc. Place; ELLIS; 178 E-7; elev. 2,117ft./645m.; 🅿; z 67637; ℗ 1,814; © 1,873
ELLIS; 178 D-8; ℗ 26,004; © 27,507; ◆ 27,477
Ellsworth; Inc. Place; ⊡ ELLSWORTH; 178 E-10; elev. 1,540ft./469m.; 🅿 🅷; z 67439; ℗ 2,294; © 2,965
ELLSWORTH; 179 E-11; ℗ 6,586; © 6,525; ◆ 6,276
Elmdale; Inc. Place; CHASE; 179 F-14; elev. 1,200ft./366m.; 🅿; z 66850; ℗ 83; © 50
Elmhurst; RMC Place; JOHNSON; *179 D-19; ★ **K.C.**; mail Overland Park z 66204; pop. incl. with Overland Park (Inc. Place)
Elmo; RMC Place; DICKINSON; 179 F-13; mail Hope z 67451; ● 30
Elmont; RMC Place; SHAWNEE; 179 D-16; ★ **TOP**; mail Topeka z 66618; ● 100
Elsmore; Inc. Place; ALLEN; 179 H-18; elev. 1,050ft./320m.; 🅿; z 66732; ℗ 91; © 73
Elwood; Inc. Place; DONIPHAN; 179 B-18; elev. 813ft./248m.; 🅿; ★ **ST.JO**; z 66024; ℗ 1,079; © 1,145
Elyria; RMC Place; MCPHERSON; 179 G-12; elev. 1,485ft./453m.; mail McPherson z 67460; ● 75
Emmeram; RMC Place; ELLIS; *178 E-8; elev. 2,002ft./610m.; mail Victoria z 67671; rural
Emmett; Inc. Place; POTTAWATOMIE; 179 D-16; elev. 1,030ft./314m.; 🅿; z 66422; ℗ 165; © 277
Empire; CHEROKEE; see Empire City (RMC Place)
Empire City (Empire); RMC Place; CHEROKEE; ★ **JOP**; mail Galena z 66739; pop. incl. with Galena (Inc. Place)
Empire Junction; RMC Place; CHEROKEE; ★ **JOP**; mail Galena z 66739; pop. incl. with Galena (Inc. Place)
Emporia; Inc. Place; ⊡ LYON; 179 F-15; elev. 1,150ft./351m.; 🅿 🅷 🅲 6,473 ■; z 66801; ℗ 25,512; © 26,760; ◆ 27,957
Englevale; RMC Place; CRAWFORD; 179 I-19; mail Mulberry z 66756; ● 25
Englewood; Inc. Place; CLARK; 178 K-6; elev. 1,970ft./600m.; 🅿; z 67840; ℗ 96; © 109
Ensign; Inc. Place; GRAY; 178 I-6; elev. 2,719ft./829m.; 🅿; z 67841; ℗ 192; © 203
Enterprise; Inc. Place; DICKINSON; 179 E-13; elev. 1,137ft./347m.; 🅿; z 67441; ℗ 865; © 836
Erie; Inc. Place; ⊡ NEOSHO; 179 I-18; elev. 893ft./272m.; 🅿; z 66733; ℗ 1,276; © 1,211
Esbon; Inc. Place; JEWELL; 178 B-10; elev. 1,848ft./563m.; 🅿; z 66941; ℗ 167; © 148
Eskridge; Inc. Place; WABAUNSEE; 179 E-16; elev. 1,420ft./433m.; 🅿; z 66423; ℗ 518; © 589
Eudora; Inc. Place; DOUGLAS; 179 E-18; elev. 813ft./248m.; 🅿; z 66025; ℗ 3,006; © 4,307
Eureka; Inc. Place; ⊡ GREENWOOD; 179 H-15; elev. 1,084ft./330m.; 🅿 🅷; z 67045; ℗ 2,974; © 2,914
Eureka City Lake; RMC Place; GREENWOOD; *179 H-15; mail Eureka z 67045; ● 100
Everest; Inc. Place; BROWN; 179 B-17; elev. 1,150ft./351m.; 🅿; z 66424; ℗ 310; © 314
Ewell; RMC Place; SUMNER; *179 J-12; mail Conway Springs z 67031; rural

F

Fairfax; RMC Place; WYANDOTTE; *179 D-19; ★ **K.C.**; mail Kansas City z 66115; pop. incl. with Kansas City (Inc. Place)
Fairmount; RMC Place; LEAVENWORTH; 179 D-18; ★ **K.C.**; mail Leavenworth z 66048; ● 100
Fairport; RMC Place; RUSSELL; *178 D-9; elev. 1,679ft./512m.; mail Russell z 67665
Fairview; Inc. Place; BROWN; 179 B-16; elev. 1,220ft./372m.; 🅿; z 66425; ℗ 306; © 271
Fairway; Inc. Place; JOHNSON; 196 J-3; elev. 900ft./274m.; 🅿; ★ **K.C.**; z 66205; ℗ 4,173; © 3,952
Fall; LEAVENWORTH; see Fall Leaf (RMC Place)
Fall Leaf (Fall); RMC Place; LEAVENWORTH; *179 D-18; mail Linwood z 66052; rural
Fall River; Inc. Place; GREENWOOD; 179 I-16; elev. 933ft./284m.; 🅿; z 67047; ℗ 113; © 156
Falun; RMC Place; SALINE; 179 F-12; elev. 1,352ft./412m.; 🅿; z 67442; ● 95
Fanning; RMC Place; DONIPHAN; *179 B-18; mail Troy z 66087; ● 70
Farlington; RMC Place; CRAWFORD; 179 I-19; elev. 989ft./301m.; 🅿; z 66734; ● 75
Farlinville; RMC Place; LINN; *179 G-19; mail Centerville z 66014
Farmington; RMC Place; ATCHISON; *179 C-17; elev. 1,027ft./313m.; mail Effingham z 66023; ● 25
Faulkner; RMC Place; CHEROKEE; 179 J-18; mail Chetopa z 67336; ● 30
Fellsburg; RMC Place; EDWARDS; 178 H-8; elev. 2,100ft./640m.; mail Lewis z 67552; ● 20
FINNEY; 178 G-4; ℗ 33,070; © 40,523; ◆ 40,807
Fleming; RMC Place; CRAWFORD; *179 I-19; mail Pittsburg z 66762; rural
Floral; RMC Place; COWLEY; 179 J-14; elev. 1,228ft./374m.; mail Winfield z 67156; ● 40
Florence; Inc. Place; MARION; 179 G-14; elev. 1,270ft./387m.; 🅿; z 66851; ℗ 636; © 671
Flush; RMC Place; POTTAWATOMIE; *179 D-15; mail Saint George z 66535; rural
Fontana; Inc. Place; MIAMI; 179 F-19; elev. 890ft./271m.; 🅿; z 66026; ℗ 131; © 149
Ford; Inc. Place; FORD; 178 I-7; elev. 2,406ft./733m.; 🅿; z 67842; ℗ 247; © 314
FORD; 178 I-6; ℗ 27,463; © 32,458; ◆ 33,565
Forest Hills; RMC Place; SEDGWICK; *179 I-13; ★ **WICH**; mail Wichita z 67206; pop. incl. with Wichita (Inc. Place)
Forest Lake; RMC Place; WYANDOTTE; ★ **K.C.**; mail Edwardsville z 66113; pop. incl. with Edwardsville (Inc. Place)
Forest Lake; WYANDOTTE; see Lake of the Forest (RMC Place)
Formoso; Inc. Place; JEWELL; 179 B-11; elev. 1,527ft./465m.; 🅿; z 66942; ℗ 128; © 129
Fort Dodge; RMC Place; FORD; ● 450
Fort Riley-Camp Whiteside; CDP-Census Area Only; GEARY; *179 D-14; mail Fort Riley z 66442; ℗ 112; © 103
Fort Riley North; CDP-Census Area Only; RILEY, GEARY; *179 D-14; mail Fort Riley z 66442; ℗ 12,848; © 8,114
Fort Scott; Inc. Place; ⊡ BOURBON; 179 H-19; elev. 846ft./258m.; 🅿 🅷; z 66701; ℗ 8,362; © 8,297
Fostoria; RMC Place; OSAGE; 179 E-16; mail Burlingame z 66413; ● 35
Fostoria; RMC Place; POTTAWATOMIE; 179 C-15; elev. 1,458ft./444m.; 🅿; z 66426; ● 70
Four Corners; RMC Place; OSAGE; *179 E-17; elev. 1,099ft./335m.; mail Scranton z 66537; ● 50
Fowler; Inc. Place; MEADE; 178 I-6; elev. 2,481ft./756m.; 🅿; z 67844; ℗ 571; © 567
Fox Town; RMC Place; CRAWFORD; *179 I-19; mail Mulberry z 66756; ● 35
Frankfort; Inc. Place; MARSHALL; 179 B-15; elev. 1,150ft./351m.; 🅿; z 66427; ℗ 927; © 855
Franklin; RMC Place; CRAWFORD; 179 I-19; elev. 970ft./296m.; 🅿; z 66735; ● 350
FRANKLIN; 179 F-17; ℗ 21,994; © 24,784; ◆ 26,516
Frederick; Inc. Place; RICE; 178 F-10; elev. 1,762ft./537m.; mail Geneseo z 67444; ℗ 18; © 11
Fredonia; Inc. Place; ⊡ WILSON; 179 I-16; elev. 893ft./272m.; 🅿 🅷; z 66736; ℗ 2,599; © 2,600
Freemount; RMC Place; MCPHERSON; *179 F-12; mail Lindsborg z 67456; rural
Freeport; Inc. Place; HARPER; 179 J-11; elev. 1,335ft./407m.; 🅿; z 67049; ℗ 8; © 6
Friend; RMC Place; FINNEY; 178 G-4; elev. 2,911ft./887m.; 🅿; z 67871; ● 30
Frontenac; Inc. Place; CRAWFORD; 179 I-19; elev. 950ft./290m.; 🅿; z 66763; ℗ 2,588; © 2,996
Fulton; Inc. Place; BOURBON; 179 G-19; elev. 850ft./259m.; 🅿; z 66738; ℗ 191; © 184
Furley; RMC Place; SEDGWICK; 179 H-13; mail Valley Center z 67147; ● 100

G

Galatia; Inc. Place; BARTON; 178 F-9; elev. 2,000ft./610m.; 🅿; z 67565; ℗ 47; © 61
Galena; Inc. Place; CHEROKEE; 179 J-19; elev. 941ft./287m.; 🅿; ★ **JOP**; z 66739; ℗ 3,308; © 3,287
Galesburg; Inc. Place; NEOSHO; 179 I-17; elev. 980ft./299m.; 🅿; z 66740; ℗ 160; © 150
Galva; Inc. Place; MCPHERSON; 179 F-12; elev. 1,546ft./471m.; 🅿; z 67443; ℗ 651; © 701
Garden City; Inc. Place; ⊡ FINNEY; 178 H-4; elev. 2,839ft./865m.; 🅿 🅷 ■; z 67846, z 67868; ℗ 24,097; © 28,451; ◆ 31,351
Garden Plain; Inc. Place; SEDGWICK; 179 I-12; elev. 1,450ft./442m.; 🅿; z 67050; ℗ 731; © 797
Gardner; Inc. Place; JOHNSON; 179 E-18; elev. 1,050ft./320m.; 🅿 🅷; ★ **K.C.**; z 66030 & mail New Century z 66031; ℗ 3,191; © 9,396
Gardner Lake; RMC Place; JOHNSON; *179 E-18; ★ **K.C.**; mail Gardner z 66030; pop. incl. with Gardner (Inc. Place)
Garfield; Inc. Place; PAWNEE; 178 G-8; elev. 2,075ft./632m.; 🅿; z 67529; ℗ 236; © 198
Garland; RMC Place; BOURBON; 179 H-19; elev. 880ft./268m.; 🅿; z 66741; ● 100
Garnett; Inc. Place; ⊡ ANDERSON; 179 G-18; elev. 1,049ft./320m.; 🅿 🅷; z 66032; ℗ 3,210; © 3,368
Gas; Inc. Place; ALLEN; 179 H-17; elev. 1,020ft./311m.; 🅿; z 66742; ℗ 505; © 556
Gaylord; Inc. Place; SMITH; 178 C-9; elev. 1,592ft./485m.; 🅿; z 67638; ℗ 173; © 145
GEARY; 179 E-14; ℗ 30,453; © 27,947; ◆ 30,448
Gem; Inc. Place; THOMAS; 178 C-4; elev. 3,050ft./930m.; 🅿; z 67734; ℗ 104; © 96
Geneseo; Inc. Place; RICE; 179 F-11; elev. 1,750ft./533m.; 🅿; z 67444; ℗ 382; © 272
Gerlane; RMC Place; BARBER; *178 J-10; mail Medicine Lodge z 67104
Geuda Springs; Inc. Place; SUMNER, COWLEY; 179 J-13; elev. 1,120ft./341m.; 🅿; z 67051; ℗ 219; © 212
Girard; Inc. Place; ⊡ CRAWFORD; 179 I-19; elev. 986ft./301m.; 🅿 🅷; z 66743; ℗ 2,794; © 2,773
Glade; Inc. Place; PHILLIPS; 178 B-8; elev. 1,811ft./552m.; 🅿; z 67639; ℗ 101; © 114
Glasco; Inc. Place; CLOUD; 179 C-11; elev. 1,320ft./402m.; 🅿; z 67445; ℗ 556; © 536
Glendale; RMC Place; SALINE; 179 E-11; mail Brookville z 67425; ● 35
Glen Elder; Inc. Place; MITCHELL; 178 C-10; elev. 1,424ft./434m.; 🅿; z 67446; ℗ 448; © 439
Glen Park; RMC Place; WYANDOTTE; ★ **K.C.**; mail Kansas City z 66102; pop. incl. with Kansas City (Inc. Place)
Glenville; RMC Place; SEDGWICK; *179 I-13; ★ **WICH**; mail Wichita z 67217; pop. incl. with Wichita (Inc. Place)
Globe; RMC Place; DOUGLAS; *179 E-17; mail Baldwin City z 66006; rural
Goddard; Inc. Place; SEDGWICK; 179 I-12; elev. 1,465ft./447m.; 🅿; ★ **WICH**; z 67052; ℗ 1,804; © 2,037
Goessel; Inc. Place; MARION; 179 G-13; elev. 1,533ft./467m.; 🅿; z 67053; ℗ 506; © 565
Goff; Inc. Place; NEMAHA; 179 B-16; elev. 1,250ft./381m.; 🅿; z 66428 & mail Corning z 66417; ℗ 156; © 181
Golden Belt Spur; RMC Place; SALINE; ★ **SLN**; mail Salina z 67401; pop. incl. with Salina (Inc. Place)
Goodland; Inc. Place; ⊡ SHERMAN; 178 C-2; elev. 3,683ft./1,123m.; 🅿 🅷; z 67735; ℗ 4,983; © 4,948

Entries in **UPPERCASE** are counties.
Entries in **bold** have populations of 2,500 or more.
Names in parentheses are alternate names.
Inc. Place — Incorporated Place
RMC Place — Rand McNally Designated Place
CDP — Census Designated Place
MCD — Minor Civil Division

⊡ County Seat
▲ Minor Civil Division
elev. Elevation
🅿 Post Office
🅷 Hospital
🅲 College
■ Principal Business Center
★ Ranally Metro Area (RMA) Abbreviation
z Zip Code(s)
℗ Previous Census Population
® Revised Census Population
Ⓐ Annexation Population
● Rand McNally Population Estimate
© Final Census Population
Ⓢ Special Census Population
◆ Estimated Population

For additional definitions see Glossary, Volume 1, and Introduction, Volume 2.

Goodrich; RMC Place; LINN; **179** G-18; mail Parker z 66072; ● 40
Gordon; RMC Place; BUTLER; ***179** I-13; mail Augusta z 67010; rural
Gorham; Inc. Place; RUSSELL; **178** E-9; elev. 1,914ft./583m.; [P]; z 67640; Ⓟ 284; Ⓒ 360
Gove (Gove City); Inc. Place; ⊡ GOVE; **178** E-5; elev. 2,634ft./803m.; [P]; z 67736; Ⓟ 103; Ⓒ 105
GOVE; **178** E-5; Ⓟ 3,231; Ⓒ 3,068; ◆ 2,470
Gove City; GOVE; see Gove (Inc. Place)
GRAHAM; **178** D-6; Ⓟ 3,543; Ⓒ 2,946; ◆ 2,521
Grainfield; Inc. Place; GOVE; **178** D-5; elev. 2,800ft./853m.; [P]; z 67737; Ⓟ 357; Ⓒ 327
Granada; RMC Place; NEMAHA; ***179** B-16; mail Wetmore z 66550
Grand Summit; RMC Place; COWLEY; ***179** I-15; mail Cambridge z 67023; rural
Grandview; RMC Place; WYANDOTTE; ***179** D-18; ★ **K.C.**; mail Bonner Springs z 66012; pop. incl. with Bonner Springs (Inc. Place)
Grandview Plaza; Inc. Place; GEARY; **179** D-14; elev. 1,160ft./354m.; mail Junction City z 66441; Ⓟ 1,233; Ⓒ 1,184
GRANT; **178** I-3; Ⓟ 7,159; Ⓒ 7,909; ◆ 7,482
Grantville; RMC Place; JEFFERSON; **179** D-17; elev. 870ft./265m.; [P]; z 66429; ● 165
GRAY; **178** H-5; Ⓟ 5,396; Ⓒ 5,904; ◆ 5,407
Great Bend; Inc. Place; ⊡ BARTON; **178** F-9; elev. 1,849ft./564m.; [P] [H] ■; z 67530; Ⓟ 15,427; Ⓒ 15,345; ◆ 15,404
Greeley; Inc. Place; ANDERSON; **179** F-18; elev. 890ft./271m.; [P]; z 66033; Ⓟ 339; Ⓒ 327
GREELEY; **178** F-2; Ⓟ 1,774; Ⓒ 1,534; ◆ 1,303
Green; Inc. Place; CLAY; **179** C-13; elev. 1,383ft./422m.; [P]; z 67447; Ⓟ 150; Ⓒ 147
Greenbush; RMC Place; CRAWFORD; ***179** I-18; elev. 984ft./300m.; mail Girard z 66743; rural
Greenleaf; Inc. Place; WASHINGTON; **179** B-13; elev. 1,417ft./432m.; [P]; z 66943; Ⓟ 353; Ⓒ 357
Greensburg; Inc. Place; ⊡ KIOWA; **178** I-8; elev. 2,230ft./680m.; [P] [H]; z 67054; Ⓟ 1,792; Ⓒ 1,574
Greenwich; RMC Place; SEDGWICK; **178** K-10; elev. 1,400ft./427m.; [P]; z 67055; ● 80
Greenwich Heights; RMC Place; SEDGWICK; ***179** I-13; ★ **WICH**; mail Wichita z 67207; ● 960
GREENWOOD; **179** H-15; Ⓟ 7,847; Ⓒ 7,673; ◆ 7,023
Grenola; Inc. Place; ELK; **179** J-15; elev. 1,117ft./340m.; [P]; z 67346; Ⓟ 256; Ⓒ 231
Gretna; RMC Place; PHILLIPS; ***178** B-8; mail Phillipsburg z 67661
Gridley; Inc. Place; COFFEY; **179** G-16; elev. 1,140ft./347m.; [P]; z 66852; Ⓟ 356; Ⓒ 372
Grigston; RMC Place; SCOTT; ***178** F-5; mail Scott City z 67871
Grinnell; Inc. Place; GOVE; **178** D-5; elev. 2,939ft./896m.; [P]; z 67738; Ⓟ 348; Ⓒ 329
Gross; RMC Place; CRAWFORD; **179** I-19; mail Arcadia z 66711; ● 50
Grove; RMC Place; SHAWNEE; ***179** D-16; elev. 937ft./286m.; mail Silver Lake z 66539; rural
Groveland; RMC Place; MCPHERSON; ***179** G-12; mail Inman z 67546
Gypsum; Inc. Place; SALINE; **179** E-12; elev. 1,229ft./375m.; [P]; z 67448; Ⓟ 365; Ⓒ 414

H

Hackney; RMC Place; COWLEY; **179** J-13; elev. 1,151ft./351m.; mail Winfield z 67156; ● 25
Haddam; Inc. Place; WASHINGTON; **179** B-13; elev. 1,400ft./427m.; [P]; z 66944; Ⓟ 195; Ⓒ 169
Haggard; RMC Place; GRAY; ***178** I-5; elev. 2,776ft./846m.; mail Cimarron z 67835; rural
Hale; RMC Place; CHAUTAUQUA; ***179** J-16; mail Elk City z 67344; rural
Half Mound; RMC Place; JEFFERSON; ***179** C-17; elev. 967ft./295m.; mail Valley Falls z 66088
Halford; RMC Place; THOMAS; ***178** C-4; mail Colby z 67701; rural
Hallowell; RMC Place; CHEROKEE; **179** J-18; elev. 850ft./259m.; [P]; z 66725; ● 200
Halls Summit; RMC Place; COFFEY; ***179** F-17; mail Waverly z 66871
Halstead; Inc. Place; HARVEY; **179** H-12; elev. 1,395ft./425m.; [P] [H]; z 67056; Ⓟ 2,015; Ⓒ 1,873
Hamilton; Inc. Place; GREENWOOD; **179** H-15; elev. 1,098ft./335m.; [P]; z 66853; Ⓟ 301; Ⓒ 334
HAMILTON; **178** G-2; Ⓟ 2,388; Ⓒ 2,670; ◆ 2,680
Hamlin; Inc. Place; BROWN; **179** B-17; elev. 991ft./302m.; mail Hiawatha z 66434; Ⓟ 50; Ⓒ 53
Hammond; RMC Place; BOURBON; ***179** H-19; mail Fort Scott z 66701
Hanover; Inc. Place; WASHINGTON; **179** B-14; elev. 1,231ft./375m.; [P] [H]; z 66945; Ⓟ 696; Ⓒ 653
Hanston; Inc. Place; HODGEMAN; **178** G-7; elev. 2,160ft./658m.; [P]; z 67849; Ⓟ 326; Ⓒ 259
Harding; RMC Place; BOURBON; **179** G-19; elev. 850ft./259m.; mail Mapleton z 66754
Hardtner; Inc. Place; BARBER; **178** K-10; elev. 1,450ft./442m.; [P]; z 67057; Ⓟ 198; Ⓒ 199
Harlan; RMC Place; SMITH; **178** C-9; elev. 1,576ft./480m.; [P]; z 66967; ● 25
Harper; Inc. Place; HARPER; **179** J-11; elev. 1,421ft./433m.; [P] [H]; z 67058; Ⓟ 1,735; Ⓒ 1,567
HARPER; **179** J-11; Ⓟ 7,124; Ⓒ 6,536; ◆ 5,729
Harris; RMC Place; ANDERSON; **179** G-17; elev. 1,000ft./305m.; mail Garnett z 66032; disincorporated April 6, 2001; Ⓟ 39; Ⓒ 53
Hartford; Inc. Place; LYON; **179** G-16; elev. 1,080ft./329m.; [P]; z 66854; Ⓟ 541; Ⓒ 500
HARVEY; **179** G-12; Ⓟ 31,028; Ⓒ 32,869; ◆ 33,610
Harveyville; Inc. Place; WABAUNSEE; **179** E-16; elev. 1,121ft./342m.; [P]; z 66431; Ⓟ 267; Ⓒ 267
HASKELL; **178** I-4; Ⓟ 3,886; Ⓒ 4,307; ◆ 3,905
Havana; Inc. Place; MONTGOMERY; **179** J-16; elev. 760ft./232m.; [P]; z 67347; Ⓟ 121; Ⓒ 86
Haven; Inc. Place; RENO; **179** H-12; elev. 1,480ft./451m.; [P]; z 67543; Ⓟ 1,198; Ⓒ 1,175
Havensville; Inc. Place; POTTAWATOMIE; **179** C-16; elev. 1,200ft./366m.; [P]; z 66432; Ⓟ 135; Ⓒ 146
Haverhill; RMC Place; BUTLER; **179** I-14; elev. 1,327ft./404m.; mail Augusta z 67010; ● 50
Haviland; Inc. Place; KIOWA; **178** I-8; elev. 2,150ft./655m.; [P]; z 67059; Ⓟ 624; Ⓒ 612
Hays; Inc. Place; ⊡ ELLIS; **178** E-8; elev. 1,997ft./609m.; [P] [H] [C] 9,122 ■; z 67601, z 67667; Ⓟ 17,767; Ⓒ 20,013; ◆ 20,442
Haysville; Inc. Place; SEDGWICK; **179** I-13; elev. 1,260ft./384m.; [P]; ★ **WICH**; z 67060; Ⓟ 8,364; Ⓒ 8,502
Hazelton; Inc. Place; BARBER; **178** J-10; elev. 1,340ft./408m.; [P]; z 67061; Ⓟ 128; Ⓒ 144
Healy; RMC Place; LANE; **178** F-5; elev. 2,854ft./870m.; [P]; z 67850; ● 300
Hedville; RMC Place; SALINE; **179** E-12; elev. 1,271ft./387m.; mail Salina z 67401; ● 50
Heizer; RMC Place; BARTON; **178** F-9; [P]; z 67530; ● 125
Hepler; Inc. Place; CRAWFORD; **179** H-18; elev. 1,000ft./305m.; [P]; z 66746; Ⓟ 150; Ⓒ 154
Herington; Inc. Place; DICKINSON, MORRIS; **179** F-14; elev. 1,333ft./406m.; [P] [H]; z 67449; Ⓟ 2,685; Ⓒ 2,563
Heritage Hills; RMC Place; ATCHISON; ***179** C-18; mail Atchison z 66002; ● 80
Herkimer; RMC Place; MARSHALL; **179** B-14; elev. 1,250ft./381m.; [P]; z 66508; ● 50
Herndon; Inc. Place; RAWLINS; **178** B-4; elev. 2,680ft./817m.; [P]; z 67739; Ⓟ 170; Ⓒ 149
Hesper; RMC Place; DOUGLAS; ***179** E-18; elev. 921ft./281m.; mail Eudora z 66025; rural
Hessdale; RMC Place; WABAUNSEE; ***179** E-15; elev. 1,198ft./365m.; mail Alma z 66401
Hesston; Inc. Place; HARVEY; **179** G-12; elev. 1,476ft./450m.; [P]; z 67062; Ⓟ 3,012; Ⓒ 3,509
Hewins; RMC Place; CHAUTAUQUA; **179** J-15; elev. 885ft./270m.; mail Cedar Vale z 67024; ● 40
Hiattville; RMC Place; BOURBON; **179** H-19; elev. 990ft./302m.; [P]; z 66701; ● 60
Hiawatha; Inc. Place; ⊡ BROWN; **179** B-17; elev. 1,136ft./346m.; [P] [H]; z 66434; Ⓟ 3,603; Ⓒ 3,417
Hickok; RMC Place; GRANT; **178** I-3; mail Ulysses z 67880; ● 80
Hickory Acres; RMC Place; JEFFERSON; ***179** D-17; mail Meriden z 66512; ● 100
Hidden Lakes; RMC Place; SEDGWICK; ★ **WICH**; mail Wichita z 67212; pop. incl. with Wichita (Inc. Place)
Highland; Inc. Place; DONIPHAN; **179** B-17; elev. 1,051ft./320m.; [P]; z 66035; Ⓟ 942; Ⓒ 976
Highland Park; RMC Place; SHAWNEE; ***179** D-17; ★ **TOP**; mail Topeka z 66605; pop. incl. with Topeka (Inc. Place)
Hill City; Inc. Place; ⊡ GRAHAM; **178** C-7; elev. 2,134ft./650m.; [P] [H]; z 67642; Ⓟ 1,835; Ⓒ 1,604
Hillsboro; Inc. Place; MARION; **179** F-13; elev. 1,454ft./443m.; [P] [H] [C] 603; z 67063; Ⓟ 2,704; Ⓒ 2,854
Hillsdale; RMC Place; MIAMI; **179** E-19; elev. 907ft./276m.; [P]; z 66036; ● 250
Hillside; RMC Place; SEDGWICK; ★ **WICH**; mail Wichita z 67208; pop. incl. with Wichita (Inc. Place)
Hill Top; RMC Place; GREENWOOD; ***179** G-16; mail Madison z 66860; rural
Hitschmann; RMC Place; BARTON; **178** F-10; mail Claflin z 67525; ● 20
HODGEMAN; **178** G-6; Ⓟ 2,177; Ⓒ 2,085; ◆ 1,809
Hoge; RMC Place; LEAVENWORTH; ***179** D-18; elev. 854ft./260m.; ★ **K.C.**; mail Tonganoxie z 66086; rural
Hoisington; Inc. Place; BARTON; **178** F-9; elev. 1,850ft./564m.; [P] [H]; z 67544; Ⓟ 3,182; Ⓒ 2,975
Holcomb; Inc. Place; FINNEY; **178** H-4; elev. 2,885ft./879m.; [P]; z 67851; Ⓟ 1,400; Ⓒ 2,026
Holland; RMC Place; DICKINSON; ***179** E-13; mail Abilene z 67410
Hollenberg; Inc. Place; WASHINGTON; **179** B-13; elev. 1,300ft./396m.; [P]; z 66946; Ⓟ 28; Ⓒ 31
Holliday; RMC Place; JOHNSON; ***179** D-19; ★ **K.C.**; mail Shawnee z 66218; pop. incl. with Shawnee (Inc. Place)
Hollis; RMC Place; CLOUD; ***179** C-12; mail Concordia z 66901
Holton; Inc. Place; ⊡ JACKSON; **179** C-16; elev. 1,095ft./334m.; [P] [H]; z 66436; Ⓟ 3,196; Ⓒ 3,353
Holyrood; Inc. Place; ELLSWORTH; **178** F-10; elev. 1,800ft./549m.; [P]; z 67450; Ⓟ 492; Ⓒ 464
Home (Home City); RMC Place; MARSHALL; **179** B-14; elev. 1,341ft./409m.; [P]; z 66438; ● 200
Home City; MARSHALL; see Home (RMC Place)
Homewood; RMC Place; FRANKLIN; **179** F-17; mail Williamsburg z 66095; ● 30
Hope; Inc. Place; DICKINSON; **179** E-13; elev. 1,400ft./427m.; [P]; z 67451; Ⓟ 404; Ⓒ 372
Hopewell; RMC Place; PRATT; ***178** H-9; mail Macksville z 67557
Horace; Inc. Place; GREELEY; **178** F-2; elev. 3,640ft./1,109m.; mail Tribune z 67879; Ⓟ 168; Ⓒ 143
Horton; Inc. Place; BROWN; **179** B-17; elev. 1,082ft./330m.; [P] [H]; z 66439; location of Indian Agency; Ⓟ 1,885; Ⓒ 1,967
Howard; Inc. Place; ⊡ ELK; **179** I-15; elev. 1,030ft./314m.; [P]; z 67349; Ⓟ 815; Ⓒ 808
Hoxie; Inc. Place; ⊡ SHERIDAN; **178** C-5; elev. 2,655ft./809m.; [P] [H]; z 67740; Ⓟ 1,342; Ⓒ 1,244
Hoyt; Inc. Place; JACKSON; **179** D-16; elev. 1,170ft./357m.; [P]; z 66440; Ⓟ 489; Ⓒ 571
Hudson; Inc. Place; STAFFORD; **178** G-9; elev. 1,870ft./570m.; [P]; z 67545; Ⓟ 159; Ⓒ 133
Hugoton; Inc. Place; ⊡ STEVENS; **178** J-3; elev. 3,100ft./945m.; [P] [H]; z 67951; Ⓟ 3,179; Ⓒ 3,708
Humboldt; Inc. Place; ALLEN; **179** H-17; elev. 980ft./299m.; [P]; z 66748; Ⓟ 2,178; Ⓒ 1,999
Hunnewell; Inc. Place; SUMNER; **179** K-13; elev. 1,110ft./338m.; [P]; z 67140; Ⓟ 87; Ⓒ 83
Hunter; Inc. Place; MITCHELL; **178** D-10; elev. 1,600ft./488m.; [P]; z 67452; Ⓟ 116; Ⓒ 77
Huron; Inc. Place; ATCHISON; **179** B-17; elev. 1,160ft./354m.; [P]; z 66041; Ⓟ 75; Ⓒ 87
Huscher; RMC Place; CLOUD; ***179** C-12; elev. 1,459ft./445m.; mail Concordia z 66901
Hutchinson; Inc. Place; ⊡ RENO; **179** G-11; elev. 1,538ft./469m.; [P] [H] ■; ★ **HUCH**; z 67501-02, z 67504-05; Ⓟ 39,308; Ⓒ 40,787; ◆ 39,732

I

Idana; RMC Place; CLAY; **179** C-13; elev. 1,270ft./387m.; mail Clay Center z 67432; ● 70
Imes; RMC Place; FRANKLIN; ***179** F-18; mail Rantoul z 66079
Independence; Inc. Place; ⊡ MONTGOMERY; **179** J-17; elev. 826ft./252m.; [P] [H]; z 67301; Ⓟ 9,942; Ⓒ 9,846
Indian Creek; RMC Place; JOHNSON; ***179** E-19; ★ **K.C.**; mail Overland Park z 66207; pop. incl. with Overland Park (Inc. Place)
Indian Ridge; RMC Place; JEFFERSON; ***179** D-17; mail Meriden z 66512; ● 50
Indian Valley; RMC Place; SHAWNEE; ***179** D-17; ★ **TOP**; mail Topeka z 66608; ● 370
Indian Village; RMC Place; MONTGOMERY; ***179** J-17; elev. 864ft./263m.; mail Coffeyville z 67337; ● 140
Industry; RMC Place; CLAY, DICKINSON; ***179** D-13; [P]; z 67410
Ingalls; Inc. Place; GRAY; **178** H-5; elev. 2,700ft./823m.; [P]; z 67853; Ⓟ 301; Ⓒ 328
Inman; Inc. Place; MCPHERSON; **179** G-12; elev. 1,527ft./465m.; [P]; z 67546; Ⓟ 1,035; Ⓒ 1,142; Ⓡ 1,222
Iola; Inc. Place; ⊡ ALLEN; **179** H-17; elev. 960ft./293m.; [P] [H]; z 66749; Ⓟ 6,351; Ⓒ 6,302
Ionia; RMC Place; JEWELL; **178** C-10; elev. 1,140ft./347m.; [P]; z 66949; ● 80
Iowa Point; RMC Place; DONIPHAN; **179** B-17; elev. 858ft./262m.; mail Highland z 66035; ● 35
Iowa Reservation; Indian Reservation; BROWN, DONIPHAN; Reservation extends into NE; mail White Cloud z 66094; Ⓟ 93; Ⓒ 146
Isabel; Inc. Place; BARBER; **178** I-10; elev. 1,820ft./555m.; [P]; z 67065; Ⓟ 104; Ⓒ 108
Iuka; Inc. Place; PRATT; **178** H-9; elev. 1,950ft./594m.; [P]; z 67066; Ⓟ 197; Ⓒ 185

J

JACKSON; **179** C-16; Ⓟ 11,525; Ⓒ 12,657; ◆ 13,288
Jacobs Creek Landing; RMC Place; COFFEY; ***179** G-16; mail Hartford z 66854; summer pop. 150; ● 50
Jamestown; Inc. Place; CLOUD; **179** C-11; elev. 1,411ft./430m.; [P]; z 66948; Ⓟ 325; Ⓒ 399
Jarbalo; RMC Place; LEAVENWORTH; **179** D-18; mail Leavenworth z 66048; ● 100
Jayhawk; RMC Place; DOUGLAS; ***179** A-17; mail Lawrence z 66046
Jefferson; RMC Place; MONTGOMERY; **179** J-17; mail Independence z 67301; ● 50
JEFFERSON; **179** D-17; Ⓟ 15,905; Ⓒ 18,426; ◆ 18,366
Jennings; Inc. Place; DECATUR; **178** B-6; elev. 2,541ft./774m.; [P]; z 67643; Ⓟ 188; Ⓒ 146
Jetmore; Inc. Place; ⊡ HODGEMAN; **178** G-7; elev. 2,307ft./703m.; [P] [H]; z 67854; Ⓟ 850; Ⓒ 903
Jewell; Inc. Place; JEWELL; **179** C-11; elev. 1,550ft./472m.; [P]; z 66949; Ⓟ 529; Ⓒ 483
JEWELL; **179** B-11; Ⓟ 4,251; Ⓒ 3,791; ◆ 3,082
Jingo; RMC Place; MIAMI; ***179** F-19; mail Lacygne z 66040; rural
Johnson (Johnson City); Inc. Place; ⊡ STANTON; **178** I-2; elev. 3,335ft./1,017m.; [P] [H]; z 67855; Ⓟ 1,348; Ⓒ 1,528
JOHNSON; **179** E-18; Ⓟ 355,054; Ⓒ 451,086; Ⓡ 451,479; ◆ 543,067
Johnson City; STANTON; see Johnson (Inc. Place)
Junction City; Inc. Place; ⊡ GEARY; **179** D-14; elev. 1,107ft./337m.; [P] [H] ■; z 66441-42; Ⓟ 20,604; Ⓒ 18,886; ◆ 20,863
Juniata; RMC Place; LINCOLN; ***179** E-11; mail Beverly z 67423; rural

K

Kackley; RMC Place; REPUBLIC; **179** B-11; elev. 1,509ft./460m.; mail Jamestown z 66948; ● 25
Kalvesta; RMC Place; FINNEY; **178** G-6; elev. 2,668ft./813m.; [P]; z 67835; ● 40
Kanona; RMC Place; DECATUR; ***178** B-5; mail Oberlin z 67749; rural
Kanopolis; Inc. Place; ELLSWORTH; **179** E-11; elev. 1,574ft./480m.; [P]; z 67454; Ⓟ 605; Ⓒ 543
Kanorado; Inc. Place; SHERMAN; **178** C-2; elev. 3,908ft./1,191m.; [P]; z 67741; Ⓟ 276; Ⓒ 248
Kansas City; Inc. Place; ⊡ WYANDOTTE; **179** D-19; elev. 744ft./227m.; [P] [H] [C] 2,840 ■; ★ **K.C.**; z 66101-06, z 66109-13, z 66115, z 66117-19, z 66160; Ⓟ 149,800; Ⓒ 146,866; ◆ 141,386
Kansas City Stock Yards; RMC Place; WYANDOTTE; ★ **K.C.**; pop. incl. with Kansas City (Inc. Place)
Kansas State University; RMC Place; RILEY; ★ **MANH**; mail Manhattan z 66506; pop. incl. with Manhattan (Inc. Place)
Kanwaka; RMC Place; DOUGLAS; ***179** D-17; ★ **LAWR**; mail Lawrence z 66049; rural
KEARNY; **178** G-3; Ⓟ 4,027; Ⓒ 4,531; ◆ 3,923
Keats; RMC Place; RILEY; **179** D-14; elev. 1,138ft./347m.; mail Manhattan z 66503; ● 170
Kechi; Inc. Place; SEDGWICK; **179** H-13; elev. 1,380ft./421m.; [P]; ★ **WICH**; z 67067; Ⓟ 517; Ⓒ 1,038
Keene; RMC Place; WABAUNSEE; ***179** E-16; elev. 1,152ft./351m.; mail Eskridge z 66423; rural
Kellogg; RMC Place; COWLEY; ***179** J-13; elev. 1,177ft./359m.; mail Winfield z 67156; rural
Kelly; RMC Place; NEMAHA; **179** B-16; elev. 1,200ft./366m.; [P]; z 66538; ● 40
Kelso; RMC Place; MORRIS; ***179** E-14; mail Council Grove z 66846; rural
Kendall; RMC Place; HAMILTON; **178** H-2; elev. 3,136ft./956m.; [P]; z 67857; ● 250
Kennekuk; RMC Place; ATCHISON; ***179** B-17; elev. 1,105ft./337m.; mail Horton z 66439; ● 25
Kenneth; RMC Place; JOHNSON; ***179** E-19; ★ **K.C.**; mail Overland Park z 66223; pop. incl. with Overland Park (Inc. Place)
Kensington; Inc. Place; SMITH; **178** B-9; elev. 1,775ft./541m.; [P]; z 66951; Ⓟ 553; Ⓒ 529
Kickapoo; RMC Place; LEAVENWORTH; ***179** C-18; mail Leavenworth z 66048; ● 200
Kickapoo (KS) Reservation; Indian Reservation; BROWN, ATCHISON, JACKSON; mail Horton z 66439; Ⓟ 461; Ⓒ 4,419
Kickapoo (KS)/Sac and Fox joint use area; BROWN; Indian Reservation; Ⓒ 0
Kimball; RMC Place; NEOSHO; ***179** H-18; mail Erie z 66733
Kimeo; RMC Place; WASHINGTON; ***179** C-13; elev. 1,444ft./440m.; mail Greenleaf z 66943; rural
Kincaid; Inc. Place; ANDERSON; **179** G-18; elev. 1,045ft./319m.; [P]; z 66039; Ⓟ 170; Ⓒ 178
Kingman; Inc. Place; ⊡ KINGMAN; **179** I-11; elev. 1,510ft./460m.; [P] [H]; z 67068; Ⓟ 3,196; Ⓒ 3,387
KINGMAN; **179** I-11; Ⓟ 8,292; Ⓒ 8,673; ◆ 7,612
Kingsdown; RMC Place; FORD; **178** I-7; elev. 2,512ft./766m.; [P]; z 67842 & mail Minneola z 67865; ● 200
Kinsley; Inc. Place; ⊡ EDWARDS; **178** H-8; elev. 2,168ft./661m.; [P]; z 67547; Ⓟ 1,875; Ⓒ 1,658
Kiowa; Inc. Place; BARBER; **178** K-10; elev. 1,360ft./415m.; [P] [H]; z 67070; Ⓟ 1,160; Ⓒ 1,055
KIOWA; **178** I-8; Ⓟ 3,660; Ⓒ 3,278; ◆ 2,894
Kipp; RMC Place; SALINE; **179** E-12; mail Salina z 67401; ● 80
Kirkwood; RMC Place; CRAWFORD; ***179** I-19; mail Pittsburg z 66762
Kiro; RMC Place; SHAWNEE; ***179** D-16; elev. 902ft./275m.; mail Silver Lake z 66539
Kirwin; Inc. Place; PHILLIPS; **178** B-8; elev. 1,696ft./517m.; [P]; z 67644; Ⓟ 269; Ⓒ 229
Kismet; Inc. Place; SEWARD; **178** J-5; elev. 2,775ft./846m.; [P]; z 67859; Ⓟ 421; Ⓒ 484

L

Labette; Inc. Place; LABETTE; **179** J-18; elev. 860ft./262m.; mail Oswego z 67356; Ⓟ 74; Ⓒ 68
LABETTE; **179** J-18; Ⓟ 23,693; Ⓒ 22,835; ◆ 21,918
La Crosse; Inc. Place; ⊡ RUSH; **178** F-8; elev. 2,060ft./628m.; [P] [H]; z 67548 & mail Liebenthal z 67553; Ⓟ 1,427; Ⓒ 1,376
La Cygne; Inc. Place; LINN; **179** F-19; elev. 828ft./252m.; [P]; z 66040; Ⓟ 1,066; Ⓒ 1,115
Lafontaine; RMC Place; WILSON; **179** I-16; elev. 920ft./280m.; [P]; z 66736; ● 100
La Harpe; Inc. Place; ALLEN; **179** H-18; elev. 1,040ft./317m.; [P]; z 66751; Ⓟ 650; Ⓒ 706
Lake Chaparral; RMC Place; LINN; ***179** G-19; mail Mound City z 66056; ● 80
Lake City; RMC Place; BARBER; **178** J-9; elev. 1,619ft./493m.; [P]; z 67071; ● 50
Lake Dabanawa; RMC Place; JEFFERSON; ***179** D-18; mail Mc Louth z 66054
Lake Kahola; RMC Place; CHASE, MORRIS; mail Council Grove z 66846; summer pop. 500; rural
Lakeland Estates; RMC Place; WILSON; ***179** I-16; mail Fall River z 67047; ● 300
Lake of the Forest (Forest Lake); RMC Place; WYANDOTTE; ***179** D-19; elev. 800ft./244m.; [P]; ★ **K.C.**; z 66012; pop. incl. with Bonner Springs (Inc. Place)
Lake Quivira; Inc. Place; JOHNSON, WYANDOTTE; **196** J-1; elev. 850ft./259m.; [P]; ★ **K.C.**; z 66217 & mail Kansas City z 66106; Ⓟ 983; Ⓒ 932
Lake Shore; ELLSWORTH; see Yankee Run (RMC Place)
Lake Shore; RMC Place; JEFFERSON; ***179** D-17; mail Ozawkie z 66070; ● 70
Lakeshore; RMC Place; SHAWNEE; ***179** D-17; ★ **TOP**; mail Topeka z 66605; pop. incl. with Topeka (Inc. Place)
Lakeside Acres Addition; RMC Place; SEDGWICK; mail Wichita z 67208; ● 40
Lakeside Village; RMC Place; JEFFERSON; ***179** D-17; mail Ozawkie z 66070; ● 145
Lake View; RMC Place; DOUGLAS; ***179** D-17; elev. 832ft./254m.; ★ **LAWR**; mail Lawrence z 66049; rural
Lakeview Heights; RMC Place; BUTLER; ***179** I-13; elev. 1,300ft./396m.; ★ **WICH**; mail Wichita z 67230; pop. incl. with Andover (Inc. Place)
Lake Wabaunsee; RMC Place; WABAUNSEE; ***179** E-15; mail Alma z 66401; ● 250
Lakewood Hills; RMC Place; JEFFERSON; ***179** D-17; mail Ozawkie z 66070; pop. incl. with Homewood (Inc. Place)
Lakin; Inc. Place; ⊡ KEARNY; **178** H-3; elev. 3,001ft./915m.; [P] [H]; z 67860; Ⓟ 2,060; Ⓒ 2,316
Lamar; RMC Place; OTTAWA
Lamont; RMC Place; GREENWOOD; **179** G-16; elev. 1,125ft./343m.; [P]; z 66855; ● 45
Lancaster; Inc. Place; ATCHISON; **179** C-17; elev. 1,150ft./351m.; [P]; z 66041; Ⓟ 299; Ⓒ 291
Lane; Inc. Place; FRANKLIN; **179** F-18; elev. 880ft./268m.; [P]; z 66042; Ⓟ 247; Ⓒ 256
LANE; **178** F-5; Ⓟ 2,375; Ⓒ 2,155; ◆ 1,714
Langdon; RMC Place; CRAWFORD; ***179** I-19; mail Pittsburg z 66762; ● 250
Langdon; Inc. Place; RENO; **178** H-10; elev. 1,690ft./515m.; [P]; z 67583; Ⓟ 62; Ⓒ 72
Langley; RMC Place; ELLSWORTH; ***179** F-11; mail Marquette z 67464
Lansing; Inc. Place; LEAVENWORTH; **179** D-18; elev. 835ft./255m.; [P]; ★ **LEAV**; z 66043; Ⓟ 7,120; Ⓒ 9,199
Larkinburg; RMC Place; JACKSON, ATCHISON; **179** C-17; mail Holton z 66436; ● 30
Larned; Inc. Place; ⊡ PAWNEE; **178** G-8; elev. 2,004ft./611m.; [P] [H]; z 67550; Ⓟ 4,490; Ⓒ 4,236
Latham; Inc. Place; BUTLER; **179** I-14; elev. 1,455ft./443m.; [P]; z 67072; Ⓟ 160; Ⓒ 164
Latimer; Inc. Place; MORRIS; **179** E-14; elev. 1,413ft./431m.; [P]; z 67449; Ⓟ 20; Ⓒ 21
Lawrence; Inc. Place; ⊡ DOUGLAS; **179** E-18; elev. 850ft./259m.; [P] [H] [C] 30,526 ■; ★ **LAWR**; z 66044-47, z 66049; Ⓟ 65,608; Ⓒ 80,098; ◆ 91,620
Lawton; RMC Place; CHEROKEE; **179** J-19; elev. 900ft./274m.; [P]; z 66781; ● 90
Leavenworth; Inc. Place; ⊡ LEAVENWORTH; **179** C-18; elev. 800ft./244m.; [P] [H] [C] 1,844 ■; ★ **LEAV**; z 66043, z 66048; Ⓟ 38,495; Ⓒ 35,420; ◆ 33,279
LEAVENWORTH; **179** D-18; Ⓟ 64,371; Ⓒ 68,691; ◆ 73,163
Leawalk; RMC Place; CHEROKEE; ***179** I-19; mail Weir z 66781; rural
Leawood; Inc. Place; JOHNSON; **179** E-19; elev. 950ft./290m.; [P]; ★ **K.C.**; z 66206, z 66209, z 66211, z 66224 & mail Overland Park z 66207; Ⓟ 19,693; Ⓒ 27,656; ◆ 32,755
Lebanon; Inc. Place; SMITH; **178** B-10; elev. 1,821ft./555m.; [P]; z 66952; Ⓟ 364; Ⓒ 303
Lebo; Inc. Place; COFFEY; **179** F-16; elev. 1,157ft./353m.; [P]; z 66856; Ⓟ 835; Ⓒ 961
Lecompton; Inc. Place; DOUGLAS; **179** D-17; elev. 879ft./268m.; [P]; z 66050; Ⓟ 619; Ⓒ 608
Lehigh; Inc. Place; MARION; **179** F-13; elev. 1,529ft./466m.; [P]; z 67073; Ⓟ 180; Ⓒ 215
Le Loup; RMC Place; FRANKLIN; **179** E-18; elev. 952ft./290m.; mail Wellsville z 66092; ● 50
Lenape; RMC Place; LEAVENWORTH; ***179** D-18; elev. 789ft./240m.; mail Linwood z 66052; ● 40
Lenexa; Inc. Place; JOHNSON; **179** D-19; elev. 1,050ft./320m.; [P] [H] ■; ★ **K.C.**; z 66062, z 66210, z 66214-17, z 66219-20, z 66227, z 66285-86 & mail Overland Park z 66213, z 66251; Ⓟ 34,034; Ⓒ 40,238; ◆ 48,988
Lenora; Inc. Place; NORTON; **178** C-6; elev. 2,275ft./693m.; [P]; z 67645; Ⓟ 329; Ⓒ 306
Leon; Inc. Place; BUTLER; **179** I-14; elev. 1,350ft./411m.; [P]; z 67074; Ⓟ 707; Ⓒ 645; Ⓡ 647
Leona; Inc. Place; DONIPHAN; **179** B-17; elev. 950ft./290m.; [P]; z 66532; Ⓟ 39; Ⓒ 88
Leonardville; Inc. Place; RILEY; **179** C-14; elev. 1,380ft./421m.; [P]; z 66449; Ⓟ 374; Ⓒ 398
Leoti; Inc. Place; ⊡ WICHITA; **178** F-3; elev. 3,305ft./1,007m.; [P] [H]; z 67861; Ⓟ 1,738; Ⓒ 1,598
Leoville; RMC Place; DECATUR; **178** C-5; elev. 2,541ft./774m.; mail Selden z 67757; ● 50
Lerado; RMC Place; RENO; ***178** H-10; elev. 1,670ft./509m.; mail Turon z 67583; rural
LeRoy; Inc. Place; COFFEY; **179** G-17; elev. 1,007ft./307m.; [P]; z 66857; Ⓟ 568; Ⓒ 593
Levant; RMC Place; THOMAS; **178** C-3; elev. 3,311ft./1,009m.; [P]; z 67743; ● 120
Lewis; Inc. Place; EDWARDS; **178** H-8; elev. 2,142ft./653m.; [P]; z 67552; Ⓟ 451; Ⓒ 486
Liberal; Inc. Place; ⊡ SEWARD; **178** J-4; elev. 2,836ft./864m.; [P] [H] ■; z 67901, z 67905; Ⓟ 16,573; Ⓒ 19,666; ◆ 20,684
Liberty; Inc. Place; MONTGOMERY; **179** J-17; elev. 750ft./229m.; [P]; z 67351; Ⓟ 140; Ⓒ 95
Liebenthal; Inc. Place; RUSH; **178** F-8; elev. 1,976ft./602m.; [P]; z 67553; Ⓟ 112; Ⓒ 111
Lillis; RMC Place; MARSHALL; ***179** C-15; elev. 1,243ft./379m.; mail Frankfort z 66427, Vermillion z 66544
Lincoln (Lincoln Center); Inc. Place; ⊡ LINCOLN; **179** D-11; elev. 1,418ft./432m.; [P] [H]; z 67455; Ⓟ 1,381; Ⓒ 1,349
LINCOLN; **179** D-11; Ⓟ 3,653; Ⓒ 3,578; ◆ 3,305
Lincoln Center; LINCOLN; see Lincoln (Inc. Place)
Lincolnville; Inc. Place; MARION; **179** F-14; elev. 1,420ft./433m.; [P]; z 66858; Ⓟ 197; Ⓒ 225
Lindsborg; Inc. Place; MCPHERSON; **179** F-12; elev. 1,333ft./406m.; [P] [H] [C] 554; z 67456; Ⓟ 3,076; Ⓒ 3,321
Linn; Inc. Place; WASHINGTON; **179** B-13; elev. 1,460ft./445m.; [P]; z 66953; Ⓟ 472; Ⓒ 425
LINN; **179** G-18; Ⓟ 8,254; Ⓒ 9,570; ◆ 9,420
Linn Valley; Inc. Place; LINN; ***179** F-19; [P]; z 66040; Ⓒ 562
Linn Valley Lakes; RMC Place; LINN; ***179** F-19; elev. 940ft./287m.; mail Lacygne z 66040; pop. incl. with Linn Valley (Inc. Place)
Linwood; Inc. Place; LEAVENWORTH; **179** D-18; elev. 800ft./244m.; [P]; z 66052; Ⓟ 409; Ⓒ 374
Little River; Inc. Place; RICE; **179** F-11; elev. 1,600ft./488m.; [P]; z 67457; Ⓟ 496; Ⓒ 536
Logan; Inc. Place; PHILLIPS; **178** C-7; elev. 1,950ft./594m.; [P]; z 67646; Ⓟ 633; Ⓒ 603
LOGAN; **178** E-3; Ⓟ 3,081; Ⓒ 3,046; ◆ 2,550
Lone Elm; Inc. Place; ANDERSON; **179** G-18; elev. 1,100ft./335m.; mail Kincaid z 66039; Ⓟ 32; Ⓒ 27
Lone Star; RMC Place; CRAWFORD; ***179** I-19; mail Pittsburg z 66762; ● 270
Lone Star; RMC Place; DOUGLAS; ***179** E-17; mail Lawrence z 66046
Longford; Inc. Place; CLAY; **179** D-13; elev. 1,350ft./411m.; [P]; z 67458; Ⓟ 68; Ⓒ 94
Long Island; Inc. Place; PHILLIPS; **178** B-7; elev. 2,071ft./631m.; [P]; z 67647; Ⓟ 170; Ⓒ 155
Longton; Inc. Place; ELK; **179** I-16; elev. 918ft./280m.; [P]; z 67352; Ⓟ 389; Ⓒ 394
Loretta; RMC Place; RUSH; **178** F-8; elev. 2,001ft./610m.; mail Bison z 67520; ● 30
Lorraine; Inc. Place; ELLSWORTH; **178** F-10; elev. 1,781ft./543m.; [P]; z 67459; Ⓟ 147; Ⓒ 136
Lost Springs; Inc. Place; MARION; **179** F-14; elev. 1,490ft./454m.; [P]; z 66859; Ⓟ 106; Ⓒ 71
Louisburg; Inc. Place; MIAMI; **179** F-19; elev. 1,080ft./329m.; [P]; z 66053; Ⓟ 1,964; Ⓒ 2,576
Louisville; Inc. Place; POTTAWATOMIE; **179** D-15; elev. 1,000ft./305m.; [P]; z 66547; Ⓟ 215; Ⓒ 209
Lovewell; RMC Place; JEWELL; **179** B-11; mail Formoso z 66942; ● 25
Lowell; RMC Place; CHEROKEE; **179** J-19; ★ **JOP**; mail Baxter Springs z 66713, Galena z 66739; ● 200
Lowemont; RMC Place; LEAVENWORTH; ***179** C-18; mail Easton z 66020
Lucas; Inc. Place; RUSSELL; **178** D-10; elev. 1,493ft./455m.; [P]; z 67648; Ⓟ 452; Ⓒ 436
Ludell; RMC Place; RAWLINS; **178** B-4; elev. 2,770ft./844m.; [P]; z 67744; ● 100
Luray; Inc. Place; RUSSELL; **178** D-9; elev. 1,570ft./479m.; [P]; z 67649; Ⓟ 261; Ⓒ 203
Lydia; RMC Place; WICHITA; ***178** G-3; elev. 3,256ft./992m.; mail Leoti z 67861; rural
Lyle; RMC Place; DECATUR; ***178** B-6; elev. 2,407ft./734m.; mail Norcatur z 67653; rural
Lyndon; Inc. Place; ⊡ OSAGE; **179** F-17; elev. 1,115ft./340m.; [P]; z 66451; Ⓟ 964; Ⓒ 1,038
LYON; **179** G-15; Ⓟ 34,732; Ⓒ 35,935; ◆ 36,103
Lyons; Inc. Place; ⊡ RICE; **179** G-11; elev. 1,700ft./518m.; [P] [H]; z 67554; Ⓟ 3,688; Ⓒ 3,732

M

Macksville; Inc. Place; STAFFORD; **178** H-9; elev. 2,030ft./619m.; [P]; z 67557; Ⓟ 488; Ⓒ 514
Macyville; RMC Place; CLOUD; ***179** C-11; mail Concordia z 66901; rural
Madison; Inc. Place; GREENWOOD; **179** G-16; elev. 1,070ft./326m.; [P]; z 66855, z 66860; Ⓟ 845; Ⓒ 857
Mahaska; Inc. Place; WASHINGTON; **179** B-13; elev. 1,600ft./488m.; [P]; z 66955; Ⓟ 98; Ⓒ 107
Maize; Inc. Place; SEDGWICK; **179** H-12; elev. 1,350ft./411m.; [P]; ★ **WICH**; z 67101; Ⓟ 1,520; Ⓒ 1,868
Manchester; Inc. Place; DICKINSON; **179** D-13; elev. 1,295ft./395m.; [P]; z 67410; Ⓟ 80; Ⓒ 102
Manhattan; Inc. Place; ⊡ RILEY, POTTAWATOMIE; **179** D-14; elev. 1,040ft./317m.; [P] [H] [C] 23,519 ■; ★ **MANH**; z 66502-03, z 66505-06; Ⓟ 37,737; Ⓒ 44,831; Ⓡ 45,007; ◆ 58,417
Mankato; Inc. Place; ⊡ JEWELL; **178** B-10; elev. 1,776ft./541m.; [P] [H]; z 66956; Ⓟ 1,037; Ⓒ 976
Manning; RMC Place; SCOTT; ***178** F-5; elev. 2,919ft./890m.; mail Scott City z 67871
Manter; Inc. Place; STANTON; **178** I-2; elev. 3,490ft./1,064m.; [P]; z 67862; Ⓟ 186; Ⓒ 178
Maple City; RMC Place; COWLEY; **179** J-14; elev. 1,345ft./410m.; [P]; z 67102; ● 20
Maple Hill; Inc. Place; WABAUNSEE; **179** D-16; elev. 960ft./293m.; [P]; z 66507; Ⓟ 406; Ⓒ 469
Mapleton; Inc. Place; BOURBON; **179** G-19; elev. 878ft./268m.; [P]; z 66754; Ⓟ 96; Ⓒ 98
Marienthal; RMC Place; WICHITA; **178** F-3; elev. 3,210ft./978m.; [P]; z 67863; ● 100
Marietta; RMC Place; MARSHALL; ***179** B-14; elev. 1,176ft./358m.; mail Oketo z 66518
Marion; Inc. Place; ⊡ MARION; **179** G-13; elev. 1,307ft./398m.; [P] [H]; z 66861; Ⓟ 1,906; Ⓒ 2,110
MARION; **179** G-13; Ⓟ 12,888; Ⓒ 13,361; ◆ 11,834
Marion County Lake; RMC Place; MARION; ***179** G-13; mail Marion z 66861; ● 800
Marmaton; RMC Place; BOURBON; ***179** H-19; mail Fort Scott z 66701; rural
Marquette; Inc. Place; MCPHERSON; **179** F-11; elev. 1,390ft./424m.; [P]; z 67464; Ⓟ 593; Ⓒ 542; Ⓡ 593
MARSHALL; **179** B-14; Ⓟ 11,705; Ⓒ 10,965; ◆ 10,113
Marysville; Inc. Place; ⊡ MARSHALL; **179** B-14; elev. 1,202ft./366m.; [P] [H]; z 66508; Ⓟ 3,359; Ⓒ 3,271
Matfield Green; Inc. Place; CHASE; ***179** G-14; elev. 1,400ft./427m.; [P]; z 66862; Ⓟ 33; Ⓒ 60
May Day; RMC Place; RILEY; **179** C-14; elev. 1,226ft./374m.; rural
Mayetta; Inc. Place; JACKSON; **179** C-16; elev. 1,200ft./366m.; [P]; z 66509; Ⓟ 267; Ⓒ 312
Mayfield; Inc. Place; SUMNER; **179** J-12; elev. 1,281ft./390m.; [P]; z 67103; Ⓟ 110; Ⓒ 113
McCracken; Inc. Place; RUSH; **178** F-7; elev. 2,141ft./653m.; [P]; z 67556; Ⓟ 231; Ⓒ 211
McCune; Inc. Place; CRAWFORD; **179** I-18; elev. 912ft./278m.; [P]; z 66753; Ⓟ 462; Ⓒ 426
McDonald; Inc. Place; RAWLINS; **178** B-3; elev. 3,368ft./1,027m.; [P]; z 67745; Ⓟ 184; Ⓒ 159
McFarland; Inc. Place; WABAUNSEE; **179** D-15; elev. 1,020ft./311m.; [P]; z 66501; Ⓟ 224; Ⓒ 271
McLouth; Inc. Place; JEFFERSON; **179** D-18; elev. 1,188ft./362m.; [P]; z 66054; Ⓟ 719; Ⓒ 868
McPherson; Inc. Place; ⊡ MCPHERSON; **179** F-12; elev. 1,504ft./458m.; [P] [H] [C] 829; z 67460; Ⓟ 12,422; Ⓒ 13,770
MCPHERSON; **179** F-11; Ⓟ 27,268; Ⓒ 29,554; ◆ 29,207
Meade; Inc. Place; ⊡ MEADE; **178** J-5; elev. 2,497ft./761m.; [P] [H]; z 67864; Ⓟ 1,526; Ⓒ 1,672
MEADE; **178** J-6; Ⓟ 4,247; Ⓒ 4,631; ◆ 4,219
Meadowview; RMC Place; SEDGWICK; ***179** I-12; ★ **WICH**; mail Wichita z 67212; pop. incl. with Wichita (Inc. Place)
Mecca Acres; RMC Place; BUTLER; ***179** I-13; ★ **WICH**; mail Wichita z 67230; ● 285
Medicine Lodge; Inc. Place; ⊡ BARBER; **178** J-10; elev. 1,510ft./460m.; [P] [H]; z 67104 & mail Lake City z 67071; Ⓟ 2,453; Ⓒ 2,193
Medina; RMC Place; JEFFERSON; ***179** D-17; mail Perry z 66073; rural
Medora; RMC Place; RENO; **179** G-11; elev. 1,482ft./452m.; [P]; z 67502; ● 50
Melrose; RMC Place; CHEROKEE; **179** J-19; mail Chetopa z 67336, Columbus z 66725, Treece z 66778; ● 50
Melvern; Inc. Place; OSAGE; **179** F-17; elev. 1,012ft./308m.; [P]; z 66510; Ⓟ 423; Ⓒ 429
Menlo; Inc. Place; THOMAS; **178** C-5; elev. 2,950ft./899m.; [P]; z 67753; Ⓟ 50; Ⓒ 57
Mentor; RMC Place; SALINE; **179** E-12; elev. 1,273ft./388m.; [P]; z 67416 & mail Salina z 67401; ● 100
Mercier; RMC Place; BROWN; **179** B-17; elev. 1,170ft./357m.; mail Horton z 66439; ● 25
Meriden; Inc. Place; JEFFERSON; **179** D-17; elev. 980ft./299m.; [P]; z 66512; Ⓟ 622; Ⓒ 706
Merriam; Inc. Place; JOHNSON; **196** J-2; elev. 1,000ft./305m.; [P]; ★ **K.C.**; z 66202-04; Ⓟ 11,821; Ⓒ 11,008
MIAMI; **179** F-18; Ⓟ 23,466; Ⓒ 28,351; ◆ 32,046
Michigan; OSAGE; see Michigan Valley (RMC Place)
Michigan Valley (Michigan); RMC Place; OSAGE; **179** E-17; mail Quenemo z 66528; ● 150
Midland; RMC Place; DOUGLAS; ***179** D-18; ★ **LAWR**; mail Lawrence z 66044; rural
Midland; RMC Place; SEDGWICK; ***179** I-13; ★ **WICH**; mail Wichita z 67216; pop. incl. with Wichita (Inc. Place)
Midland Park; RMC Place; SEDGWICK; ***179** I-13; ★ **WICH**; mail Wichita z 67216; ● 1,350
Midway; RMC Place; KINGMAN; ***179** I-11; mail Murdock z 67111
Midway; RMC Place; RAWLINS; ***178** B-4; mail Herndon z 67739; rural
Milan; Inc. Place; SUMNER; **179** J-12; elev. 1,221ft./372m.; [P]; z 67105; Ⓟ 109; Ⓒ 137
Milberger; RMC Place; RUSSELL; **178** E-9; elev. 1,859ft./567m.; mail Russell z 67665; ● 25
Mildred; Inc. Place; ALLEN; **179** G-18; elev. 1,064ft./324m.; mail Kincaid z 66039; Ⓟ 46; Ⓒ 36
Milford; Inc. Place; GEARY; **179** D-14; elev. 1,194ft./364m.; [P]; z 66514; Ⓟ 384; Ⓒ 502
Millbrook; RMC Place; SEDGWICK; ★ **WICH**; mail Wichita z 67212; pop. incl. with Wichita (Inc. Place)
Miller; RMC Place; LYON; **179** F-16; mail Reading z 66868; ● 50
Milton; RMC Place; SUMNER; **179** I-12; elev. 1,473ft./449m.; [P]; z 67106; ● 110
Miltonvale; Inc. Place; CLOUD; **179** C-12; elev. 1,373ft./418m.; [P]; z 67466; Ⓟ 484; Ⓒ 523
Mineola; CLARK; see Minneola (Inc. Place)
Mingo; RMC Place; THOMAS; **178** D-4; mail Colby z 67701; ● 40
Minneapolis; Inc. Place; ⊡ OTTAWA; **179** D-12; elev. 1,253ft./382m.; [P] [H]; z 67467; Ⓟ 1,983; Ⓒ 2,046
Minneola (Mineola); Inc. Place; CLARK; **178** I-6; elev. 2,548ft./777m.; [P] [H]; z 67865; Ⓟ 705; Ⓒ 717
Mission; Inc. Place; JOHNSON; **196** J-2; elev. 1,000ft./305m.; [P]; ★ **K.C.**; z 66201-02, z 66205, z 66222; Ⓟ 9,504; Ⓒ 9,727
Mission Hills; Inc. Place; JOHNSON; **196** J-3; elev. 900ft./274m.; [P]; ★ **K.C.**; z 66208; Ⓟ 3,446; Ⓒ 3,593
Mission Woods; Inc. Place; JOHNSON; **179** D-19; elev. 900ft./274m.; [P]; ★ **K.C.**; z 66205; Ⓟ 182; Ⓒ 165
Mitchell; RMC Place; RICE; ***179** F-11; elev. 1,738ft./530m.; mail Lyons z 67554
MITCHELL; **179** D-11; Ⓟ 7,203; Ⓒ 6,932; ◆ 6,212
Modoc; RMC Place; SCOTT; **178** F-4; elev. 3,137ft./956m.; [P]; z 67863; ● 35
Moline; Inc. Place; ELK; **179** I-15; elev. 1,055ft./322m.; [P]; z 67353; Ⓟ 473; Ⓒ 457
Monmouth; RMC Place; CRAWFORD; ***179** I-18; mail Mc Cune z 66753
Monrovia; RMC Place; ATCHISON; ***179** C-17; elev. 1,037ft./316m.; mail Effingham z 66023; ● 25
Montana; RMC Place; LABETTE; **179** J-18; mail Oswego z 67356; ● 55
Montara; RMC Place; SHAWNEE; ***179** E-16; ★ **TOP**; mail Topeka z 66619; ● 570
Montezuma; Inc. Place; GRAY; **178** I-5; elev. 2,780ft./847m.; [P]; z 67867; Ⓟ 838; Ⓒ 966
MONTGOMERY; **179** I-16; Ⓟ 38,816; Ⓒ 36,252; Ⓡ 36,254; ◆ 34,579
Monticello; RMC Place; JOHNSON; ***179** D-19; elev. 1,010ft./308m.; ★ **K.C.**; mail Shawnee z 66218, z 66286; pop. incl. with Shawnee (Inc. Place)
Mont Ida; RMC Place; ANDERSON; **179** G-17; mail Welda z 66091; ● 50
Montrose; RMC Place; JEWELL; ***179** B-11; mail Mankato z 66956
Monument; RMC Place; LOGAN; **178** D-4; elev. 3,173ft./967m.; [P]; z 67747, z 67764; ● 75
Moolight; RMC Place; DICKINSON; ***179** E-13; mail Chapman z 67431; rural
Moran; Inc. Place; ALLEN; **179** H-18; elev. 1,100ft./335m.; [P]; z 66755; Ⓟ 551; Ⓒ 562
Moray; RMC Place; DONIPHAN; ***179** B-18; elev. 1,044ft./318m.; mail Troy z 66087
Morehead; RMC Place; LABETTE, NEOSHO; **179** I-17; mail Thayer z 66776; ● 50
Morganville; Inc. Place; CLAY; **179** C-13; elev. 1,230ft./375m.; [P]; z 67468; Ⓟ 181; Ⓒ 198
Morland; Inc. Place; GRAHAM; **178** C-6; elev. 2,302ft./702m.; [P]; z 67650; Ⓟ 234; Ⓒ 164
Morrill; Inc. Place; BROWN; **179** B-16; elev. 1,091ft./333m.; [P]; z 66515; Ⓟ 299; Ⓒ 277
MORRIS; **179** E-14; Ⓟ 6,198; Ⓒ 6,104; ◆ 6,006
Morrowville; Inc. Place; WASHINGTON; **179** B-13; elev. 1,350ft./411m.; [P]; z 66958; Ⓟ 173; Ⓒ 168
Morse; RMC Place; JOHNSON; ***179** E-19; elev. 1,085ft./331m.; ★ **K.C.**; mail Olathe z 66061; pop. incl. with Overland Park (Inc. Place)
MORTON; **178** J-2; Ⓟ 3,480; Ⓒ 3,496; ◆ 2,865
Moscow; Inc. Place; STEVENS; **178** J-3; elev. 3,050ft./930m.; [P]; z 67952; Ⓟ 252; Ⓒ 247
Mound City; Inc. Place; ⊡ LINN; **179** G-19; elev. 870ft./265m.; [P]; z 66056; Ⓟ 789; Ⓒ 821
Moundridge; Inc. Place; MCPHERSON; **179** G-12; elev. 1,475ft./450m.; [P] [H]; z 67107; Ⓟ 1,531; Ⓒ 1,593
Mound Valley; Inc. Place; LABETTE; **179** J-17; elev. 824ft./251m.; [P]; z 67354; Ⓟ 405; Ⓒ 418
Mount Hope; Inc. Place; SEDGWICK; **179** H-12; elev. 1,440ft./439m.; [P]; z 67108; Ⓟ 805; Ⓒ 830
Mount Vernon; RMC Place; KINGMAN; ***179** H-11; mail Cheney z 67025; rural
Mulberry; Inc. Place; CRAWFORD; **179** I-19; elev. 920ft./280m.; [P]; z 66756; Ⓟ 555; Ⓒ 577
Mullinville; Inc. Place; KIOWA; **178** I-8; elev. 2,330ft./710m.; [P]; z 67109; Ⓟ 289; Ⓒ 279
Mulvane; Inc. Place; SUMNER, SEDGWICK; **179** I-13; elev. 1,250ft./381m.; [P]; ★ **WICH**; z 67110; Ⓟ 4,674; Ⓒ 5,155
Muncie; RMC Place; WYANDOTTE; ***179** D-19; ★ **K.C.**; mail Kansas City z 66111; pop. incl. with Kansas City (Inc. Place)
Munden; Inc. Place; REPUBLIC; **179** B-12; elev. 1,630ft./497m.; [P]; z 66959; Ⓟ 143; Ⓒ 122
Munger; RMC Place; SEDGWICK; ***179** H-13; ★ **WICH**; mail Wichita z 67208; pop. incl. with Wichita (Inc. Place)
Munjor; RMC Place; ELLIS; **178** E-8; mail Hays z 67601; ● 400
Murdock; RMC Place; KINGMAN; **179** I-11; elev. 1,470ft./448m.; [P]; z 67111; ● 75
Muscotah; Inc. Place; ATCHISON; **179** C-17; elev. 964ft./294m.; [P]; z 66058; Ⓟ 194; Ⓒ 200

N

Narka; Inc. Place; REPUBLIC; **179** B-12; elev. 1,590ft./485m.; [P]; z 66960; Ⓟ 113; Ⓒ 93
Nashville; Inc. Place; KINGMAN; **178** I-10; elev. 1,740ft./530m.; [P]; z 67112; Ⓟ 118; Ⓒ 111
Natoma; Inc. Place; OSBORNE; **178** D-9; elev. 1,840ft./561m.; [P]; z 67651; Ⓟ 392; Ⓒ 367
Navarre; RMC Place; DICKINSON; **179** E-13; elev. 1,350ft./411m.; [P]; z 67451; ● 75
Neal; RMC Place; GREENWOOD; **179** H-16; elev. 960ft./293m.; [P]; z 66863; ● 65
Nekoma; RMC Place; RUSH; **178** F-8; elev. 2,036ft./621m.; [P]; z 67559; ● 80
NEMAHA; **179** B-16; Ⓟ 10,446; Ⓒ 10,717; ◆ 10,100
Neodesha; Inc. Place; WILSON; **179** I-17; elev. 819ft./250m.; [P] [H]; z 66757; Ⓟ 2,837; Ⓒ 2,848
NEOSHO; **179** I-17; Ⓟ 17,035; Ⓒ 16,997; ◆ 16,294
Neosho Falls; Inc. Place; WOODSON; **179** H-17; elev. 975ft./297m.; [P]; z 66758; Ⓟ 157; Ⓒ 179
Neosho Rapids; Inc. Place; LYON; **179** F-16; elev. 1,090ft./332m.; [P]; z 66864; Ⓟ 235; Ⓒ 274
NESS; **178** F-7; Ⓟ 4,033; Ⓒ 3,454; ◆ 2,968
Ness City; Inc. Place; ⊡ NESS; **178** F-7; elev. 2,251ft./686m.; [P] [H]; z 67560; Ⓟ 1,724; Ⓒ 1,534
Netawaka; Inc. Place; JACKSON; **179** C-16; elev. 1,140ft./347m.; [P]; z 66516; Ⓟ 167; Ⓒ 170
Neuchatel; RMC Place; NEMAHA; ***179** C-15; mail Onaga z 66521; rural
Neutral; RMC Place; CHEROKEE; ***179** J-19; elev. 860ft./262m.; mail Columbus z 66725
New Albany; Inc. Place; WILSON; **179** I-16; elev. 894ft./272m.; [P]; z 66759; Ⓟ 60; Ⓒ 73
New Almelo; RMC Place; NORTON; **178** C-6; elev. 2,300ft./701m.; [P]; z 67645; ● 50
Newbury; RMC Place; WABAUNSEE; ***179** D-15; mail Paxico z 66526; ● 35
New Cambria; Inc. Place; SALINE; **179** E-12; elev. 1,196ft./365m.; [P]; z 67470; Ⓟ 152; Ⓒ 150
New Gottland; RMC Place; MCPHERSON; ***179** F-12; elev. 1,528ft./466m.; mail McPherson z 67460; ● 35
New Lancaster; RMC Place; MIAMI; **179** F-19; elev. 956ft./291m.; mail Lacygne z 66040; ● 25
Newman; RMC Place; JEFFERSON; **179** D-17; mail Perry z 66073; ● 40
New Salem; RMC Place; COWLEY; **179** J-14; elev. 1,247ft./380m.; mail Winfield z 67156; ● 80
New Strawn (Strawn); Inc. Place; COFFEY; **179** G-16; elev. 1,100ft./335m.; [P]; z 66839; Ⓟ 428; Ⓒ 425
Newton; Inc. Place; ⊡ HARVEY; **179** G-13; elev. 1,448ft./441m.; [P] [H]; z 67114, z 67117; Ⓟ 16,700; Ⓒ 17,190
Nickerson; Inc. Place; RENO; **179** G-11; elev. 1,593ft./486m.; [P]; z 67561; Ⓟ 1,137; Ⓒ 1,194
Nicodemus; RMC Place; GRAHAM; **178** C-7; mail Bogue z 67625; ● 60
Niles; RMC Place; OTTAWA; **179** E-12; mail Solomon z 67480; ● 40
Niotaze; Inc. Place; CHAUTAUQUA; **179** J-16; elev. 760ft./232m.; [P]; z 67355; Ⓟ 99; Ⓒ 122
Norcatur; Inc. Place; DECATUR; **178** B-6; elev. 2,610ft./796m.; [P]; z 67653; Ⓟ 198; Ⓒ 169
Northbranch; RMC Place; JEWELL; **178** B-10; mail Burr Oak z 66936; ● 25
Northern Hills; RMC Place; SHAWNEE; ***179** D-17; ★ **TOP**; mail Topeka z 66608; ● 470
North Newton; Inc. Place; HARVEY; **179** G-13; elev. 1,452ft./443m.; [P] [C] 539; z 67117; Ⓟ 1,262; Ⓒ 1,522
North Osage City; RMC Place; OSAGE; mail Osage City z 66523; pop. incl. with Osage City (Inc. Place)
North Topeka; RMC Place; SHAWNEE; ***179** D-17; ★ **TOP**; mail Topeka z 66608, z 66675; pop. incl. with Topeka (Inc. Place)
North Wichita; RMC Place; SEDGWICK; ***179** H-13; ★ **WICH**; mail Wichita z 67204; pop. incl. with Wichita (Inc. Place)
Norton; Inc. Place; ⊡ NORTON; **178** B-7; elev. 2,339ft./713m.; [P] [H]; z 67654; Ⓟ 3,017; Ⓒ 3,012
NORTON; **178** B-6; Ⓟ 5,947; Ⓒ 5,953; ◆ 5,163
Nortonville; Inc. Place; JEFFERSON; **179** C-17; elev. 1,163ft./354m.; [P]; z 66060; Ⓟ 643; Ⓒ 620
Norway; RMC Place; REPUBLIC; **179** B-12; elev. 1,410ft./430m.; [P]; z 66961; ● 40
Norwich; Inc. Place; KINGMAN; **179** I-11; elev. 1,500ft./457m.; [P]; z 67118; Ⓟ 455; Ⓒ 551

O

Oak Hill; Inc. Place; CLAY; **179** D-13; elev. 1,260ft./384m.; [P]; z 67432; Ⓟ 13; Ⓒ 35
Oakland; RMC Place; SHAWNEE; ***179** D-17; ★ **TOP**; mail Topeka z 66616; pop. incl. with Topeka (Inc. Place)
Oaklawn; RMC Place; SEDGWICK; **178** N-9; ★ **WICH**; mail Wichita z 67216; ● 3,000
Oaklawn-Sunview; CDP-Census Area Only; SEDGWICK; ***179** I-13; elev. 1,266ft./386m.; ★ **WICH**; mail Wichita z 67216; Ⓟ 3,240; Ⓒ 3,135
Oakley; Inc. Place; ⊡ LOGAN, THOMAS; **178** D-4; elev. 3,029ft./923m.; [P] [H]; z 67748; Ⓟ 2,045; Ⓒ 2,173
Oak Valley; RMC Place; ELK; **179** I-16; elev. 868ft./265m.; mail Longton z 67352; ● 25
Oatville; RMC Place; SEDGWICK; ***179** I-13; ★ **WICH**; mail Haysville z 67060, Wichita z 67215; ● 300
Oberlin; Inc. Place; ⊡ DECATUR; **178** B-5; elev. 2,562ft./781m.; [P] [H]; z 67749; Ⓟ 2,197; Ⓒ 1,994
Ocheltree; RMC Place; JOHNSON; **179** E-19; elev. 1,079ft./329m.; ★ **K.C.**; mail Spring Hill z 66083; ● 100
Odense; RMC Place; NEOSHO; ***179** H-18; mail Savonburg z 66772; rural
Odin; RMC Place; BARTON; **178** F-10; elev. 1,839ft./561m.; [P]; z 67525; ● 110
Offerle; Inc. Place; EDWARDS; **178** H-7; elev. 2,270ft./692m.; [P]; z 67563; Ⓟ 228; Ⓒ 220
Ogallah; RMC Place; TREGO; **178** E-7; elev. 2,360ft./719m.; [P]; z 67656; ● 90
Ogden; Inc. Place; RILEY; **179** D-14; elev. 1,048ft./319m.; [P]; z 66517; Ⓟ 1,494; Ⓒ 1,762
Oketo; Inc. Place; MARSHALL; **179** B-14; elev. 1,178ft./359m.; [P]; z 66518; Ⓟ 116; Ⓒ 87
Olathe; Inc. Place; ⊡ JOHNSON; **179** E-19; elev. 1,037ft./316m.; [P] [H] [C] 1,823 ■; ★ **K.C.**; z 66051, z 66061-63; Ⓟ 63,352; Ⓒ 92,962; ◆ 124,151
Olathe East; RMC Place; JOHNSON; ★ **K.C.**; mail Olathe z 66062-63; pop. incl. with Olathe (Inc. Place)
Olivet; Inc. Place; OSAGE; **179** F-16; elev. 1,150ft./351m.; mail Lebo z 66856; Ⓟ 59; Ⓒ 64
Olmitz; Inc. Place; BARTON; **178** F-9; elev. 2,010ft./613m.; [P]; z 67564; Ⓟ 130; Ⓒ 138
Olpe; Inc. Place; LYON; **179** G-15; elev. 1,200ft./366m.; [P]; z 66865; Ⓟ 431; Ⓒ 504
Olsburg; Inc. Place; POTTAWATOMIE; **179** C-14; elev. 1,420ft./433m.; [P]; z 66520; Ⓟ 192; Ⓒ 192
Onaga; Inc. Place; POTTAWATOMIE; **179** C-15; elev. 1,150ft./351m.; [P] [H]; z 66521; Ⓟ 761; Ⓒ 704
Oneida; Inc. Place; NEMAHA; **179** B-16; elev. 1,213ft./370m.; [P]; z 66522; Ⓟ 79; Ⓒ 70
Opolis; RMC Place; CRAWFORD; **179** I-19; elev. 920ft./280m.; [P]; z 66760; total pop. including 30 in Missouri...160; ● 130
Orchard Park; RMC Place; LABETTE; ***179** I-18; mail Parsons z 67357; pop. incl. with Parsons (Inc. Place)
Oronoque; RMC Place; NORTON; ***178** B-6; mail Norton z 67654; rural
OSAGE; **179** F-16; Ⓟ 15,248; Ⓒ 16,712; ◆ 15,979
Osage City; Inc. Place; OSAGE; **179** F-16; elev. 1,085ft./331m.; [P]; z 66523; Ⓟ 2,689; Ⓒ 3,034
Osawatomie; Inc. Place; MIAMI; **179** F-18; elev. 865ft./264m.; [P] [H]; z 66064; Ⓟ 4,590; Ⓒ 4,645
Osborne; Inc. Place; ⊡ OSBORNE; **178** C-9; elev. 1,554ft./474m.; [P] [H]; z 67473; Ⓟ 1,778; Ⓒ 1,607
OSBORNE; **178** C-9; Ⓟ 4,867; Ⓒ 4,452; ◆ 3,689
Oskaloosa; Inc. Place; ⊡ JEFFERSON; **179** D-17; elev. 1,123ft./342m.; [P]; z 66066; Ⓟ 1,074; Ⓒ 1,165
Ost (Saint Joe); RMC Place; RENO; ***179** H-12; mail Mount Hope z 67108
Oswego; Inc. Place; ⊡ LABETTE; **179** J-18; elev. 907ft./276m.; [P]; z 67356; Ⓟ 1,870; Ⓒ 2,046
Otego; RMC Place; JEWELL; ***178** B-10; elev. 1,795ft./547m.; mail Burr Oak z 66936; rural
Otis; Inc. Place; RUSH; **178** F-9; elev. 2,037ft./621m.; [P]; z 67565; Ⓟ 385; Ⓒ 325
Ottawa; Inc. Place; ⊡ FRANKLIN; **179** F-18; elev. 901ft./275m.; [P] [H] [C] 2,915; z 66067; Ⓟ 10,667; Ⓒ 11,921
OTTAWA; **179** D-12; Ⓟ 5,634; Ⓒ 6,163; ◆ 6,021
Ottumwa; RMC Place; COFFEY; ***179** G-16; mail Burlington z 66839
Overbrook; Inc. Place; OSAGE; **179** E-17; elev. 1,200ft./366m.; [P]; z 66524; Ⓟ 920; Ⓒ 947
Overland Park; Inc. Place; JOHNSON; **179** D-19; elev. 950ft./290m.; [P] [H] ■; ★ **K.C.**; z 66062, z 66085, z 66201-04, z 66206-07, z 66209-15, z 66221, z 66223-25, z 66251, z 66282-83 & mail Prairie Village z 66208; Ⓟ 111,790; Ⓒ 149,080; ◆ 179,461
Oxford; Inc. Place; SUMNER; **179** J-13; elev. 1,180ft./360m.; [P]; z 67119; Ⓟ 1,143; Ⓒ 1,173
Ozawkie; Inc. Place; JEFFERSON; **179** D-17; elev. 900ft./274m.; [P]; z 66070; Ⓟ 403; Ⓒ 552

P

Packers; RMC Place; WYANDOTTE; ***179** D-19; ★ **K.C.**; mail Kansas City z 66109; pop. incl. with Kansas City (Inc. Place)
Padonia; RMC Place; BROWN; ***179** B-17; elev. 939ft./286m.; mail Hiawatha z 66434; ● 25
Page City; RMC Place; LOGAN; **178** D-4; elev. 3,232ft./985m.; mail Winona z 67764; ● 40
Palco; Inc. Place; ROOKS; **178** D-7; elev. 2,250ft./686m.; [P]; z 67657; Ⓟ 295; Ⓒ 248
Palermo; RMC Place; DONIPHAN; ***179** B-18; ★ **ST.JO**; mail Wathena z 66090; rural
Palmer; Inc. Place; WASHINGTON; **179** C-13; elev. 1,320ft./402m.; [P]; z 66962; Ⓟ 121; Ⓒ 108
Paola; Inc. Place; ⊡ MIAMI; **179** F-19; elev. 900ft./274m.; [P] [H]; z 66071; Ⓟ 4,698; Ⓒ 5,011
Paradise; Inc. Place; RUSSELL; **178** D-9; elev. 1,695ft./517m.; [P]; z 67658; Ⓟ 66; Ⓒ 64
Park (Buffalo Park); Inc. Place; GOVE; **178** D-5; elev. 2,750ft./838m.; [P]; z 67751; Ⓟ 150; Ⓒ 151
Park City; Inc. Place; SEDGWICK; **179** H-13; [P]; ★ **WICH**; z 67147, z 67204, z 67219; Ⓟ 5,054; Ⓒ 5,814
Park East; RMC Place; SEDGWICK; ***179** I-13; ★ **WICH**; mail Wichita z 67208; pop. incl. with Wichita (Inc. Place)
Parker; Inc. Place; LINN; **179** F-18; elev. 1,000ft./305m.; [P]; z 66072; Ⓟ 256; Ⓒ 281
Parkerfield; Inc. Place; COWLEY; [P]; z 67005; incorporated March 16, 2004; not reported in 2000 Census; ● 300
Parkerville; Inc. Place; MORRIS; **179** E-14; elev. 1,350ft./411m.; mail Council Grove z 66846; Ⓟ 28; Ⓒ 73
Parsons; Inc. Place; LABETTE; **179** I-18; elev. 907ft./276m.; [P] [H] ■; z 67357; Ⓟ 11,924; Ⓒ 11,514; ◆ 11,127
Partridge; Inc. Place; RENO; **179** H-11; elev. 1,611ft./491m.; [P]; z 67566; Ⓟ 213; Ⓒ 259
Patterson; RMC Place; HARVEY; ***179** H-12; mail Burrton z 67020; rural
Pauline; RMC Place; SHAWNEE; ***179** E-17; [P]; ★ **TOP**; z 66619
PAWNEE; **178** G-7; Ⓟ 7,555; Ⓒ 7,233; ◆ 6,223
Pawnee Rock; Inc. Place; BARTON; **178** G-9; elev. 1,950ft./594m.; [P]; z 67567; Ⓟ 367; Ⓒ 356
Pawnee Station (Anna); RMC Place; BOURBON; ***179** H-19; mail Fort Scott z 66701
Paxico; Inc. Place; WABAUNSEE; **179** D-15; elev. 990ft./302m.; [P]; z 66526; Ⓟ 174; Ⓒ 211
Peabody; Inc. Place; MARION; **179** G-13; elev. 1,361ft./415m.; [P]; z 66866; Ⓟ 1,349; Ⓒ 1,384
Pearl; RMC Place; DICKINSON; ***179** E-13; mail Chapman z 67431; rural
Peck; RMC Place; SUMNER, SEDGWICK; **179** I-13; elev. 1,252ft./382m.; [P]; z 67120; ● 110
Peck Addition; RMC Place; SHAWNEE; ***179** D-17; ★ **TOP**; mail Topeka z 66605; ● 1,520
Penalosa; Inc. Place; KINGMAN; **178** H-10; elev. 1,725ft./526m.; [P]; z 67035; Ⓟ 21; Ⓒ 27
Pence; RMC Place; SCOTT; ***178** F-4; elev. 3,135ft./956m.; mail Scott City z 67871; rural
Pendennis; RMC Place; LANE; ***178** F-5; mail Dighton z 67839; rural
Penokee; RMC Place; GRAHAM; **178** C-6; elev. 2,250ft./686m.; [P]; z 67659; ● 150
Peoria; RMC Place; FRANKLIN; **179** F-18; mail Ottawa z 66067, Rantoul z 66079; ● 40
Perry; Inc. Place; JEFFERSON; **179** D-17; elev. 850ft./259m.; [P]; z 66073; Ⓟ 881; Ⓒ 901
Perth; RMC Place; SUMNER; **179** J-12; mail Wellington z 67152; ● 50
Peru; Inc. Place; CHAUTAUQUA; **179** J-16; elev. 784ft./239m.; [P]; z 67360; Ⓟ 206; Ⓒ 183
Petrolia; RMC Place; ALLEN; **179** H-17; [P]; z 66720; ● 85
Pfeifer; RMC Place; ELLIS; **178** E-8; elev. 1,870ft./570m.; [P]; z 67660; ● 80
PHILLIPS; **178** B-8; Ⓟ 6,590; Ⓒ 6,001; ◆ 5,324
Phillipsburg; Inc. Place; ⊡ PHILLIPS; **178** B-8; elev. 1,951ft./595m.; [P] [H]; z 67661; Ⓟ 2,828; Ⓒ 2,668
Pickrell Corner; RMC Place; BUTLER; **179** I-14; elev. 1,352ft./412m.; mail Augusta z 67010; ● 40
Piedmont; RMC Place; GREENWOOD; **179** I-15; elev. 1,200ft./366m.; [P]; z 67122; ● 250
Pierceville; RMC Place; FINNEY; **178** H-5; elev. 2,760ft./841m.; [P]; z 67868; ● 100

Entries in **UPPERCASE** are counties.
Entries in **bold** have populations of 2,500 or more.
Names in parentheses are alternate names.

Inc. Place	Incorporated Place
RMC Place	Rand McNally Designated Place
CDP	Census Designated Place
MCD	Minor Civil Division
⊡	County Seat
▲	Minor Civil Division
elev.	Elevation
[P]	Post Office
[H]	Hospital
[C]	College
■	Principal Business Center
★	Ranally Metro Area (RMA) Abbreviation
z	Zip Code(s)
Ⓟ	Previous Census Population
Ⓡ	Revised Census Population
Ⓐ	Annexation Population
●	Rand McNally Population Estimate
Ⓒ	Final Census Population
Ⓢ	Special Census Population
◆	Estimated Population

For additional definitions see Glossary, Volume 1, and Introduction, Volume 2.

Pilsen; RMC Place; MARION; 179 F-13; elev. 1,434ft./437m.; mail Marion z 66861; ● 200
Piper; RMC Place; WYANDOTTE; *179 D-18; elev. 964ft./294m.; ★ **K.C.**; mail Kansas City z 66109; pop. incl. with Kansas City (Inc. Place)
Piqua; RMC Place; WOODSON; 179 H-17; elev. 1,030ft./314m.; [P]; z 66761; ● 125
Pittsburg; Inc. Place; CRAWFORD; 179 I-19; elev. 944ft./288m.; [P] [H] [C] 6,859 ■; z 66762-63; Ⓟ 17,775; © 19,243; ◆ 19,893
Plains (Plains City); Inc. Place; MEADE; 178 J-5; elev. 2,760ft./841m.; [P]; z 67869; Ⓟ 957; © 1,163
Plains City; MEADE; see Plains (Inc. Place)
Plainville; Inc. Place; ROOKS; 178 D-8; elev. 2,143ft./653m.; [P] [H]; z 67663; Ⓟ 2,173; © 2,029
Pleasant Grove; RMC Place; DOUGLAS; *179 E-18; elev. 1,086ft./331m.; mail Lawrence z 66046
Pleasanton; Inc. Place; LINN; 179 G-19; elev. 861ft./262m.; [P]; z 66075; Ⓟ 1,231; © 1,387
Plevna; Inc. Place; RENO; 178 H-10; elev. 1,700ft./518m.; [P]; z 67568; Ⓟ 117; © 99
Plymell; RMC Place; FINNEY; *178 H-4; elev. 2,878ft./877m.; mail Garden City z 67846; rural
Plymouth; RMC Place; LYON; 179 F-15; mail Emporia z 66801; ● 50
Polk (Camp Fifty); RMC Place; CRAWFORD; *179 I-19; mail Arma z 66712; rural
Pomona; Inc. Place; FRANKLIN; 179 F-17; elev. 950ft./290m.; [P]; z 66076; Ⓟ 835; © 923
Portis; Inc. Place; OSBORNE; 178 C-9; elev. 1,542ft./470m.; [P]; z 67474; Ⓟ 129; © 123
Portland; RMC Place; SUMNER; *179 J-13; elev. 1,189ft./362m.; mail South Haven z 67140
POTTAWATOMIE; 179 C-15; Ⓟ 16,128; © 18,209; ◆ 20,381
Potter; RMC Place; ATCHISON; 179 C-18; elev. 933ft./284m.; [P]; z 66002; ● 100
Potwin; Inc. Place; BUTLER; 179 H-13; elev. 1,350ft./411m.; [P]; z 67123; Ⓟ 448; © 457
Powhattan; Inc. Place; BROWN; 179 B-17; elev. 1,203ft./367m.; [P]; z 66527; Ⓟ 111; © 91
Prairie Band Potawatomi Reservation; JACKSON; Indian Reservation; © 1,238
Prairie View; Inc. Place; PHILLIPS; 178 B-7; elev. 2,175ft./663m.; [P]; z 67664; Ⓟ 111; © 141
Prairie Village; Inc. Place; JOHNSON; 179 D-19; elev. 1,050ft./320m.; [P]; ★ **K.C.**; z 66202, z 66204, z 66206-08; Ⓟ 23,186; © 22,072; ◆ 20,905
Pratt; Inc. Place; ⊡ PRATT; 178 I-9; elev. 1,891ft./576m.; [P] [H]; z 67124; Ⓟ 6,687; © 6,570
PRATT; 178 H-9; Ⓟ 9,702; © 9,647; ◆ 9,311
Prescott; Inc. Place; LINN; 179 G-19; elev. 889ft./271m.; [P]; z 66767; Ⓟ 301; © 280
Preston; Inc. Place; PRATT; 178 H-10; elev. 1,840ft./561m.; [P]; z 67583; Ⓟ 177; © 164
Pretty Prairie; Inc. Place; RENO; 179 H-11; elev. 1,576ft./480m.; [P]; z 67570; Ⓟ 601; © 615
Princeton; Inc. Place; FRANKLIN; 179 F-18; elev. 970ft./296m.; [P]; z 66078; Ⓟ 275; © 317
Prospect; RMC Place; BUTLER; *179 H-14; mail El Dorado z 67042; ● 500
Prospect Park; RMC Place; SEDGWICK; *179 I-12; ★ **WICH**; mail Wichita z 67215; ● 250
Protection; Inc. Place; COMANCHE; 178 J-7; elev. 1,845ft./562m.; [P]; z 67127; Ⓟ 625; © 558
Purcell; RMC Place; DONIPHAN; *179 B-17; elev. 1,159ft./353m.; mail Lancaster z 66041

Q

Quenemo; Inc. Place; OSAGE; 179 F-17; elev. 941ft./287m.; [P]; z 66528; Ⓟ 369; © 468
Quincy; RMC Place; GREENWOOD; *179 H-16; mail Virgil z 66870
Quindaro; RMC Place; WYANDOTTE; ★ **K.C.**; pop. incl. with Kansas City (Inc. Place)
Quinter; Inc. Place; GOVE; 178 D-6; elev. 2,664ft./812m.; [P] [H]; z 67752; Ⓟ 945; © 961

R

Radium; Inc. Place; STAFFORD; 178 G-9; elev. 1,951ft./595m.; [P]; z 67550; Ⓟ 47; © 40
Radley; RMC Place; CRAWFORD; *179 I-19; elev. 970ft./296m.; [P]; z 66762; ● 200
Rago; RMC Place; KINGMAN; 179 I-11; elev. 1,440ft./439m.; [P]; z 67142; ● 30
Ramona; Inc. Place; MARION; 179 F-13; elev. 1,433ft./437m.; [P]; z 67475; Ⓟ 106; © 94
Randall; Inc. Place; JEWELL; 179 C-11; elev. 1,457ft./444m.; [P]; z 66963; Ⓟ 96; © 90
Randolph; Inc. Place; RILEY; 179 C-14; elev. 1,250ft./381m.; [P]; z 66554; Ⓟ 129; © 175
Ransom; Inc. Place; NESS; 178 F-6; elev. 2,515ft./767m.; [P] [H]; z 67572; Ⓟ 386; © 338
Rantoul; Inc. Place; FRANKLIN; 179 F-18; elev. 892ft./272m.; [P]; z 66079; Ⓟ 200; © 241
RAWLINS; 178 B-3; Ⓟ 3,404; © 2,966; ◆ 2,529
Raymond; Inc. Place; RICE; 178 G-10; elev. 1,726ft./526m.; [P]; z 67573; Ⓟ 125; © 95
Reading; Inc. Place; LYON; 179 F-16; elev. 1,080ft./329m.; [P]; z 66868; Ⓟ 264; © 247
Reager; RMC Place; NORTON; *178 B-6; mail Norton z 67654; rural
Redel; RMC Place; JOHNSON; *179 E-19; ★ **K.C.**; mail Stilwell z 66085; rural
Redfield; Inc. Place; BOURBON; 179 H-19; elev. 853ft./260m.; [P]; z 66769; Ⓟ 143; © 140
Red Onion; RMC Place; CRAWFORD; *179 I-19; mail Mulberry z 66756; rural
Redwing; RMC Place; BARTON; 178 F-9; elev. 1,811ft./552m.; mail Hoisington z 67544; ● 20
Reece; RMC Place; GREENWOOD; 179 H-15; mail Eureka z 67045; ● 140
Renco; LEAVENWORTH; see Reno (RMC Place)
Reno (Renco); RMC Place; LEAVENWORTH; *179 D-18; mail Tonganoxie z 66086; ● 60
RENO; 179 H-11; Ⓟ 62,389; © 64,790; ◆ 62,331
Republic; Inc. Place; REPUBLIC; 179 B-11; elev. 1,500ft./457m.; [P]; z 66964; Ⓟ 177; © 161
REPUBLIC; 179 B-12; Ⓟ 6,482; © 5,835; ◆ 4,741
Reserve; Inc. Place; BROWN; 179 A-17; elev. 908ft./277m.; [P]; z 66434; Ⓟ 108; © 100
Rexford; Inc. Place; THOMAS; 178 C-5; elev. 2,955ft./901m.; [P]; z 67753; Ⓟ 171; © 157
Rice; RMC Place; CLOUD; *179 C-12; elev. 1,336ft./407m.; [P]; z 66901
RICE; 178 F-10; Ⓟ 10,610; © 10,761; ◆ 9,685
Richfield; Inc. Place; MORTON; 178 J-2; [P]; z 67953; Ⓟ 50; © 48
Richland; RMC Place; SHAWNEE; *179 E-17; mail Berryton z 66409; rural
Richmond; Inc. Place; FRANKLIN; 179 F-18; elev. 1,030ft./314m.; [P]; z 66080; Ⓟ 528; © 510
Richter; RMC Place; FRANKLIN; 179 F-17; mail Ottawa z 66067; ● 20
Riley; Inc. Place; RILEY; 179 D-14; elev. 1,300ft./396m.; [P]; z 66531; Ⓟ 804; © 886
RILEY; 179 D-14; Ⓟ 67,139; © 62,843; Ⓡ 62,852; ◆ 69,097
Ringer; RMC Place; SEDGWICK; ★ **WICH**; mail Wichita z 67212; pop. incl. with Wichita (Inc. Place)
Ringo; RMC Place; CRAWFORD; *179 I-19; mail Girard z 66743; ● 50
River City; RMC Place; SEDGWICK; ★ **WICH**; mail Wichita z 67216; pop. incl. with Wichita (Inc. Place)
Riverdale; RMC Place; SUMNER; 179 I-13; elev. 1,321ft./403m.; mail Wellington z 67152; ● 60
Riverside; RMC Place; SEDGWICK; *179 I-13; ★ **WICH**; mail Wichita z 67203; pop. incl. with Wichita (Inc. Place)
Riverton; RMC Place; CHEROKEE; 179 J-19; elev. 833ft./254m.; [P]; ★ **JOP**; z 66770; ● 600
Riverview; RMC Place; SEDGWICK; *179 H-13; ★ **WICH**; mail Wichita z 67204; pop. incl. with Wichita (Inc. Place)
Robinson; Inc. Place; BROWN; 179 B-17; elev. 955ft./291m.; [P]; z 66532; Ⓟ 268; © 216
Rock; RMC Place; COWLEY; 179 I-13; elev. 1,170ft./357m.; [P]; z 67131; ● 80
Rock Creek; RMC Place; JEFFERSON; 179 D-17; mail Meriden z 66512; ● 50
Rocky Ford; RMC Place; RILEY; *179 D-14; elev. 1,086ft./331m.; ★ **MANH**; mail Manhattan z 66502
Roeland Park; Inc. Place; JOHNSON; 196 J-3; elev. 950ft./290m.; [P]; ★ **K.C.**; z 66202, z 66205; Ⓟ 7,706; © 6,817; Ⓡ 7,210
Rolla; Inc. Place; MORTON; 178 J-2; elev. 3,648ft./1,112m.; [P]; z 67954; Ⓟ 387; © 482
Rolling Hills; RMC Place; SEDGWICK; *179 I-12; ★ **WICH**; mail Wichita z 67212; pop. incl. with Wichita (Inc. Place)
Rome; RMC Place; SUMNER; *179 J-13; elev. 1,220ft./372m.; mail Wellington z 67152
ROOKS; 178 D-8; Ⓟ 6,039; © 5,685; ◆ 5,023
Roper; RMC Place; WILSON; *179 I-17; mail Benedict z 66714
Rosalia; RMC Place; BUTLER; 179 H-14; elev. 1,520ft./463m.; [P]; z 67132; ● 150
Rose; RMC Place; WOODSON; *179 H-17; mail Yates Center z 66783
Rosedale; RMC Place; WYANDOTTE; *179 D-19; [P]; ★ **K.C.**; z 66103; pop. incl. with Kansas City (Inc. Place)
Rose Hill; Inc. Place; BUTLER; 179 I-13; elev. 1,330ft./405m.; [P]; ★ **WICH**; z 67133; Ⓟ 2,399; © 3,432
Roseland; Inc. Place; CHEROKEE; *179 J-19; elev. 920ft./280m.; mail Scammon z 66773; Ⓟ 98; © 101
Rosewood; RMC Place; LABETTE; mail Parsons z 67357; pop. incl. with Parsons (Inc. Place)
Rossville; Inc. Place; SHAWNEE; 179 D-16; elev. 930ft./283m.; [P]; z 66533; Ⓟ 1,052; © 1,014
Roxbury; RMC Place; MCPHERSON; 179 F-12; elev. 1,350ft./411m.; [P]; z 67476; ● 100
Rozel; Inc. Place; PAWNEE; 178 G-8; elev. 2,075ft./632m.; [P]; z 67574; Ⓟ 187; © 182
Ruleton; RMC Place; SHERMAN; 178 C-2; mail Goodland z 67735; ● 30
Runnymede; RMC Place; HARPER; *179 J-11; mail Harper z 67058; rural
RUSH; 178 F-8; Ⓟ 3,842; © 3,551; ◆ 3,141
Rush Center; Inc. Place; RUSH; 178 F-8; elev. 2,000ft./610m.; [P]; z 67575; Ⓟ 177; © 176
Russell; Inc. Place; ⊡ RUSSELL; 178 E-9; elev. 1,826ft./557m.; [P] [H]; z 67665; Ⓟ 4,781; © 4,696
RUSSELL; 178 D-9; Ⓟ 7,835; © 7,370; ◆ 6,710
Russell Springs; Inc. Place; LOGAN; 178 E-3; elev. 2,964ft./903m.; [P]; z 67764; Ⓟ 29; © 32

S

Sabetha; Inc. Place; NEMAHA, BROWN; 179 B-16; elev. 1,318ft./402m.; [P] [H]; z 66534; Ⓟ 2,341; © 2,589
Sac and Fox Reservation; Indian Reservation; BROWN; Reservation extends into NE; mail Hiawatha z 66434; Ⓟ 22; © 86
Saffordville; RMC Place; CHASE; *179 F-15; elev. 1,146ft./349m.; mail Emporia z 66801; rural
Saint Benedict; RMC Place; NEMAHA; 179 B-15; mail Seneca z 66538; ● 70
Saint Clere; RMC Place; POTTAWATOMIE; *179 C-15; mail Emmett z 66422
Saint Francis; Inc. Place; ⊡ CHEYENNE; 178 B-2; elev. 3,356ft./1,023m.; [P] [H]; z 67756; Ⓟ 1,495; © 1,497
Saint George; Inc. Place; POTTAWATOMIE; 179 D-15; elev. 1,005ft./306m.; [P]; z 66535; Ⓟ 397; © 434
Saint Joe; RENO; see Ost (RMC Place)
Saint John; Inc. Place; ⊡ STAFFORD; 178 H-9; elev. 1,909ft./582m.; [P]; z 67576; Ⓟ 1,357; © 1,318
Saint Joseph; RMC Place; CLOUD; 179 C-12; elev. 1,373ft./418m.; mail Clyde z 66938; ● 55
Saint Leo; RMC Place; KINGMAN; 178 I-10; elev. 1,760ft./536m.; mail Nashville z 67112; ● 25
Saint Mark; RMC Place; SEDGWICK; 179 H-12; ★ **WICH**; mail Colwich z 67030; ● 100
Saint Marys; Inc. Place; POTTAWATOMIE, WABAUNSEE; 179 D-16; elev. 960ft./293m.; [P]; z 66536; Ⓟ 1,791; © 2,198
Saint Marys; RMC Place; SEDGWICK; *179 H-12; elev. 1,510ft./460m.; mail Garden Plain z 67050; rural
Saint Pats; RMC Place; ATCHISON; *179 C-18; mail Atchison z 66002; rural
Saint Paul; Inc. Place; NEOSHO; 179 I-18; elev. 897ft./273m.; [P]; z 66771; Ⓟ 687; © 646
Saint Peter; RMC Place; GRAHAM; 178 D-6; mail Morland z 67650; ● 30
Salina; Inc. Place; ⊡ SALINE; 179 E-12; elev. 1,220ft./372m.; [P] [H] [C] 1,673 ■; ★ **SLN**; z 67401-02; Ⓟ 42,303; © 45,679; ◆ 46,913
SALINE; 179 E-11; Ⓟ 49,301; © 53,597; ◆ 54,885
Sand Spring; RMC Place; DICKINSON; *179 E-13; mail Abilene z 67410; rural
Sanford; RMC Place; PAWNEE; *178 G-8; mail Larned z 67550; rural
Sarcoxie; RMC Place; LEAVENWORTH; *179 D-18; mail Linwood z 66052; ● 125
Satanta; Inc. Place; HASKELL; 178 I-4; elev. 2,960ft./902m.; [P] [H]; z 67870; Ⓟ 1,073; © 1,239
Saunders; RMC Place; STANTON; *178 I-1; elev. 3,665ft./1,117m.; mail Manter z 67862; rural
Savonburg; Inc. Place; ALLEN; 179 H-18; elev. 1,053ft./321m.; [P]; z 66772; Ⓟ 93; © 91
Sawyer; Inc. Place; PRATT; 178 I-9; elev. 1,900ft./579m.; [P]; z 67134; Ⓟ 183; © 124
Saxman; RMC Place; RICE; 179 G-11; mail Sterling z 67579; ● 25
Scammon; Inc. Place; CHEROKEE; 179 J-19; elev. 900ft./274m.; [P]; z 66773; Ⓟ 466; © 496
Scandia; Inc. Place; REPUBLIC; 179 B-12; elev. 1,440ft./439m.; [P]; z 66966; Ⓟ 421; © 436
Schoenchen; Inc. Place; ELLIS; 178 E-8; elev. 1,930ft./588m.; [P]; z 67667; Ⓟ 128; © 214
Schulte; RMC Place; SEDGWICK; 179 I-12; mail Wichita z 67215; ● 50
Scipio; RMC Place; ANDERSON; *179 F-18; elev. 1,026ft./313m.; mail Garnett z 66032
SCOTT; 178 F-4; Ⓟ 5,289; © 5,120; ◆ 4,523
Scott City; Inc. Place; ⊡ SCOTT; 178 F-4; elev. 2,978ft./908m.; [P] [H]; z 67871; Ⓟ 3,785; © 3,855
Scottsville; Inc. Place; MITCHELL; 179 C-11; elev. 1,560ft./475m.; [P]; z 67420; Ⓟ 26; © 21
Scranton; Inc. Place; OSAGE; 179 E-16; elev. 1,123ft./342m.; [P]; z 66537; Ⓟ 674; © 724
Sedan; Inc. Place; ⊡ CHAUTAUQUA; 179 J-16; elev. 862ft./263m.; [P] [H]; z 67361; Ⓟ 1,306; © 1,342
Sedgwick; Inc. Place; HARVEY, SEDGWICK; 179 H-12; elev. 1,379ft./420m.; [P]; z 67135; Ⓟ 1,438; © 1,537
SEDGWICK; 179 I-12; Ⓟ 403,662; © 452,869; ◆ 484,101
Seguin; RMC Place; SHERIDAN; 178 C-5; mail Hoxie z 67740; ● 25
Selden; Inc. Place; SHERIDAN; 178 C-5; elev. 2,838ft./865m.; [P]; z 67757; Ⓟ 248; © 201
Selkirk; RMC Place; WICHITA; 178 F-3; elev. 3,440ft./1,049m.; mail Leoti z 67861; ● 35
Selma; RMC Place; ANDERSON; *179 G-18; mail Kincaid z 66039
Seneca; Inc. Place; ⊡ NEMAHA; 179 B-16; elev. 1,131ft./345m.; [P] [H]; z 66538; Ⓟ 2,027; © 2,122
Severance; Inc. Place; DONIPHAN; 179 B-17; elev. 912ft./278m.; [P]; z 66087; Ⓟ 98; © 108
Severy; Inc. Place; GREENWOOD; 179 I-15; elev. 1,107ft./337m.; [P]; z 67137; Ⓟ 357; © 359
Seward; Inc. Place; STAFFORD; 178 G-9; elev. 1,910ft./582m.; [P]; z 67576; Ⓟ 71; © 63
SEWARD; 178 J-4; Ⓟ 18,743; © 22,510; ◆ 23,333
Shady Bend; RMC Place; LINCOLN; *179 D-11; mail Lincoln z 67455
Shady Brook; RMC Place; DICKINSON; *179 E-13; mail Herington z 67449; rural
Shaffer; RMC Place; RUSH; *178 F-8; mail Rush Center z 67575; rural
Shallow Water; RMC Place; SCOTT; 178 F-4; elev. 2,949ft./899m.; mail Scott City z 67871; ● 40
Sharon; Inc. Place; BARBER; 178 J-10; elev. 1,440ft./439m.; [P]; z 67138; Ⓟ 256; © 210
Sharon Springs; Inc. Place; ⊡ WALLACE; 178 E-2; elev. 3,471ft./1,058m.; [P]; z 67758; Ⓟ 872; © 835
Sharpe; RMC Place; COFFEY; *179 G-17; elev. 1,152ft./351m.; mail Waverly z 66871
Shaw; RMC Place; NEOSHO; *179 I-18; mail Erie z 66733
Shawnee; Inc. Place; JOHNSON; 179 D-19; elev. 1,050ft./320m.; [P]; ★ **K.C.**; z 66203, z 66214, z 66216-20, z 66226-27, z 66286; Ⓟ 37,993; © 47,996; ◆ 61,151
SHAWNEE; 179 E-16; Ⓟ 160,976; © 169,871; ◆ 174,156
Shawnee Mission; RMC Place; JOHNSON; *179 D-19; elev. 1,000ft./305m.; [P] [H]; ★ **K.C.**; z 66201-27, z 66250-51, z 66276, z 66282-83, z 66285-86; pop. incl. with Merriam (Inc. Place)
SHERIDAN; 178 D-5; Ⓟ 3,043; © 2,813; ◆ 2,443
Sherman (Sherman City); RMC Place; CHEROKEE; 179 J-18; mail Oswego z 67356; ● 50
SHERMAN; 178 C-2; Ⓟ 6,926; © 6,760; ◆ 6,073
Sherman City; CHEROKEE; see Sherman (RMC Place)
Sherwin; RMC Place; CHEROKEE; 179 J-19; mail Columbus z 66725; ● 40
Sherwood Estates; RMC Place; SHAWNEE; *179 D-16; mail Topeka z 66604; ● 500
Shields; RMC Place; LANE; 178 F-5; elev. 2,783ft./848m.; [P]; z 67839; ● 30
Sibleyville; RMC Place; DOUGLAS; *179 E-18; ★ **LAWR**; mail Lawrence z 66044; rural
Silverdale; RMC Place; COWLEY; 179 J-14; elev. 1,086ft./331m.; mail Arkansas City z 67005; ● 50
Silver Lake; Inc. Place; SHAWNEE; 179 D-16; elev. 911ft./278m.; [P]; ★ **TOP**; z 66539; Ⓟ 1,390; © 1,358
Simpson; Inc. Place; MITCHELL, CLOUD; 179 C-11; elev. 1,337ft./408m.; [P]; z 67478; Ⓟ 107; © 114
Sitka; RMC Place; CLARK; *178 J-7; mail Ashland z 67831
Skiddy; RMC Place; MORRIS; *179 E-14; mail White City z 66872
Skidmore; RMC Place; CHEROKEE; *179 J-19; mail Scammon z 66773; ● 25
SMITH; 178 B-9; Ⓟ 5,078; © 4,536; ◆ 3,815
Smith Center; Inc. Place; ⊡ SMITH; 178 B-9; elev. 1,804ft./550m.; [P] [H]; z 66967; Ⓟ 2,016; © 1,931
Smolan; Inc. Place; SALINE; 179 E-12; elev. 1,280ft./390m.; [P]; z 67456; Ⓟ 195; © 218
Soldier; Inc. Place; JACKSON; 179 C-16; elev. 1,200ft./366m.; [P]; z 66540; Ⓟ 135; © 122
Solomon; Inc. Place; DICKINSON; 179 E-13; elev. 1,218ft./371m.; [P]; z 67480; Ⓟ 939; © 1,072
Somerset; RMC Place; MIAMI; 179 F-19; mail Paola z 66071; ● 40
South Dodge; RMC Place; FORD; *178 H-6; mail Dodge City z 67801; pop. incl. with Dodge City (Inc. Place)
Southeast; RMC Place; SEDGWICK; *179 I-13; ★ **WICH**; mail Wichita z 67218; pop. incl. with Wichita (Inc. Place)
South Haven; Inc. Place; SUMNER; 179 J-13; elev. 1,121ft./342m.; [P]; z 67140; Ⓟ 420; © 390
South Hoisington; RMC Place; BARTON; *178 F-9; mail Hoisington z 67544; rural
South Hutchinson; Inc. Place; RENO; 179 H-11; elev. 1,530ft./466m.; [P]; ★ **HUCH**; z 67505; Ⓟ 2,444; © 2,539
South Mound; RMC Place; NEOSHO; *179 I-18; mail Parsons z 67357
South Radley; RMC Place; CRAWFORD; 179 I-19; mail Pittsburg z 66762; ● 50
South Seneca Gardens; RMC Place; SEDGWICK; *179 I-13; ★ **WICH**; mail Wichita z 67217; pop. incl. with Wichita (Inc. Place)
Sparks; RMC Place; DONIPHAN; 179 B-18; mail Highland z 66035; ● 50
Spearville; Inc. Place; FORD; 178 H-7; elev. 2,450ft./747m.; [P]; z 67876; Ⓟ 716; © 813
Speed; Inc. Place; PHILLIPS; 178 B-8; elev. 1,850ft./564m.; mail Phillipsburg z 67661; Ⓟ 64; © 44
Spivey; Inc. Place; KINGMAN; 179 I-11; elev. 1,500ft./457m.; [P]; z 67142; Ⓟ 88; © 80
Springdale; RMC Place; LEAVENWORTH; 179 D-18; mail Easton z 66020; ● 30
Springdale; RMC Place; SEDGWICK; *179 I-13; ★ **WICH**; mail Wichita z 67230; ● 250
Spring Grove; RMC Place; CHEROKEE; ★ **JOP**; mail Galena z 66739; pop. incl. with Galena (Inc. Place)
Spring Hill; Inc. Place; JOHNSON, MIAMI; 179 E-19; elev. 1,050ft./320m.; [P]; ★ **K.C.**; z 66083; Ⓟ 2,191; © 2,727
Stafford; Inc. Place; STAFFORD; 178 H-10; elev. 1,858ft./566m.; [P] [H]; z 67578; Ⓟ 1,344; © 1,161
STAFFORD; 178 H-9; Ⓟ 5,365; © 4,789; ◆ 4,369
Stanley; RMC Place; JOHNSON; 179 E-19; elev. 1,000ft./305m.; [P]; ★ **K.C.**; z 66221, z 66223-24 & mail Overland Park z 66283; pop. incl. with Overland Park (Inc. Place)
Stanton; RMC Place; MIAMI; *179 F-18; mail Osawatomie z 66064
STANTON; 178 I-2; Ⓟ 2,333; © 2,406; ◆ 2,052
Stark; Inc. Place; NEOSHO; 179 H-18; elev. 1,060ft./323m.; [P]; z 66775; Ⓟ 79; © 106
State House; RMC Place; SHAWNEE; *179 D-17; ★ **TOP**; mail Topeka z 66612; pop. incl. with Topeka (Inc. Place)
Sterling; Inc. Place; RICE; 179 G-11; elev. 1,640ft./500m.; [P] [C] 550; z 67579; Ⓟ 2,115; © 2,642
STEVENS; 178 J-3; Ⓟ 5,048; © 5,463; ◆ 4,804
Stilwell; RMC Place; JOHNSON; 179 E-19; elev. 1,050ft./320m.; [P]; ★ **K.C.**; z 66085; ● 250
Stippville; RMC Place; CHEROKEE; 179 J-19; mail Columbus z 66725; ● 30
Stockton; Inc. Place; ⊡ ROOKS; 178 C-8; elev. 1,792ft./546m.; [P]; z 67669; Ⓟ 1,507; © 1,558
Stony Point; RMC Place; WYANDOTTE; *179 D-19; ★ **K.C.**; mail Kansas City z 66111; pop. incl. with Kansas City (Inc. Place)
Strauss; RMC Place; LABETTE; *179 I-18; mail Mc Cune z 66753
Strawn; COFFEY; see New Strawn (Inc. Place)
Strong City; Inc. Place; CHASE; 179 F-15; elev. 1,182ft./360m.; [P]; z 66869; Ⓟ 617; © 584
Studley; RMC Place; SHERIDAN; 178 C-6; elev. 2,381ft./726m.; [P]; z 67740; ● 50
Stull; RMC Place; DOUGLAS; 179 E-17; mail Lecompton z 66050; ● 45
Stuttgart; RMC Place; PHILLIPS; 178 B-8; elev. 1,986ft./605m.; [P]; z 67661; ● 75
Sublette; Inc. Place; ⊡ HASKELL; 178 I-4; elev. 2,918ft./889m.; [P]; z 67877; Ⓟ 1,378; © 1,592
Suburban Heights; RMC Place; MONTGOMERY; mail Independence z 67301; pop. incl. with Independence (Inc. Place)
Sugar Valley; RMC Place; LINN; *179 G-19; mail Mound City z 66056; ● 110
Summerfield; Inc. Place; MARSHALL; 179 A-15; elev. 1,510ft./460m.; [P]; z 66541; Ⓟ 169; © 211
Summit; RMC Place; MARSHALL
SUMNER; 179 J-12; Ⓟ 25,841; © 25,946; ◆ 23,163
Sun City; Inc. Place; BARBER; 178 I-9; elev. 1,676ft./511m.; [P]; z 67143; Ⓟ 88; © 81
Sunflower; JOHNSON; see Clearview City (RMC Place)
Sunnydale; RMC Place; SEDGWICK; *179 H-13; elev. 1,415ft./431m.; ★ **WICH**; mail Valley Center z 67147; ● 80
Sunset Lakes; RMC Place; RENO; *178 H-10; mail Sylvia z 67581; rural
Sunset Park; RMC Place; SEDGWICK; *179 I-13; ★ **WICH**; mail Haysville z 67060; pop. incl. with Haysville (Inc. Place)
Suppesville; RMC Place; SUMNER; 179 I-12; mail Milton z 67106; ● 75
Susank; Inc. Place; BARTON; 178 F-9; elev. 1,970ft./600m.; [P]; z 67544; Ⓟ 61; © 57
Sutphen; RMC Place; DICKINSON; *179 D-13; mail Chapman z 67431; rural
Sycamore; RMC Place; MONTGOMERY; 179 J-17; elev. 840ft./256m.; [P]; z 67363; ● 200
Sylvan Grove; Inc. Place; LINCOLN; 178 E-10; elev. 1,445ft./440m.; [P]; z 67481; Ⓟ 321; © 324
Sylvia; Inc. Place; RENO; 178 H-10; elev. 1,738ft./530m.; [P]; z 67581; Ⓟ 308; © 297
Syracuse; Inc. Place; ⊡ HAMILTON; 178 H-2; elev. 3,233ft./985m.; [P] [H]; z 67878; Ⓟ 1,606; © 1,824

T

Talmage; RMC Place; DICKINSON; 179 D-13; elev. 1,212ft./369m.; [P]; z 67482; ● 120
Talmo; RMC Place; REPUBLIC; 179 B-12; mail Belleville z 66935; ● 50
Tampa; Inc. Place; MARION; 179 F-13; elev. 1,424ft./434m.; [P]; z 67483; Ⓟ 113; © 144
Tanglewood Lake; RMC Place; LINN; *179 G-19; mail Lacygne z 66040; ● 200
Tasco; RMC Place; SHERIDAN; *178 C-6; mail Hoxie z 67740
Tecumseh; RMC Place; SHAWNEE; 179 M-17; elev. 900ft./274m.; [P]; ★ **TOP**; z 66542; ● 650
Terra Heights; RMC Place; SHAWNEE; *179 E-17; ★ **TOP**; mail Topeka z 66609; pop. incl. with Topeka (Inc. Place)
Tescott; Inc. Place; OTTAWA; 179 E-11; elev. 1,294ft./394m.; [P]; z 67484; Ⓟ 317; © 339
Thayer; Inc. Place; NEOSHO; 179 I-17; elev. 1,033ft./315m.; [P]; z 66776; Ⓟ 435; © 500
The Dell; RMC Place; SEDGWICK; *179 I-12; ★ **WICH**; mail Wichita z 67209; pop. incl. with Wichita (Inc. Place)
THOMAS; 178 D-3; Ⓟ 8,258; © 8,180; ◆ 7,141
Thompsonville; RMC Place; JEFFERSON; *179 D-17; mail Perry z 66073; rural
Thrall; RMC Place; GREENWOOD; *179 G-15; elev. 1,371ft./418m.; mail Eureka z 67045
Timken; Inc. Place; RUSH; 178 F-8; elev. 1,963ft./598m.; [P]; z 67575; Ⓟ 87; © 83
Tipton; Inc. Place; MITCHELL; 178 D-10; elev. 1,604ft./489m.; [P]; z 67485; Ⓟ 267; © 243
Toledo; RMC Place; CHASE; *179 F-15; mail Emporia z 66801; rural
Tonganoxie; Inc. Place; LEAVENWORTH; 179 D-18; elev. 853ft./260m.; [P]; z 66086; Ⓟ 2,347; © 2,728
Topeka; Inc. Place; **STATE CAPITAL**; ⊡ SHAWNEE; 179 D-17; elev. 951ft./290m.; [P] [H] [C] 7,153 ■; ★ **TOP**; z 66601, z 66603-12, z 66614-22, z 66624-26, z 66628-29, z 66636, z 66647, z 66667, z 66675, z 66683, z 66699; Ⓟ 119,883; © 122,377; ◆ 123,802
Toronto; Inc. Place; WOODSON; 179 H-16; elev. 950ft./290m.; [P]; z 66777; Ⓟ 317; © 312
Towanda; Inc. Place; BUTLER; 179 H-13; elev. 1,255ft./383m.; [P]; z 67144; Ⓟ 1,289; © 1,338
Trading Post; RMC Place; LINN; *179 G-19; mail Pleasanton z 66075
Traer; RMC Place; DECATUR; 178 B-5; mail Oberlin z 67749; ● 25
Travel Air; RMC Place; SEDGWICK; *179 I-13; ★ **WICH**; mail Wichita z 67206; pop. incl. with Wichita (Inc. Place)
Treece; Inc. Place; CHEROKEE; 179 J-19; elev. 840ft./256m.; [P]; z 66778; Ⓟ 172; © 149
TREGO; 178 E-6; Ⓟ 3,694; © 3,319; ◆ 2,813
Trego Center; RMC Place; TREGO; *178 E-7; elev. 2,382ft./726m.; mail Wakeeney z 67672; rural
Tribune; Inc. Place; ⊡ GREELEY; 178 F-2; elev. 3,616ft./1,102m.; [P] [H]; z 67879; Ⓟ 918; © 835
Trousdale; RMC Place; EDWARDS; *178 H-8; mail Haviland z 67059
Troy; Inc. Place; ⊡ DONIPHAN; 179 B-18; elev. 1,099ft./335m.; [P]; z 66087; Ⓟ 1,073; © 1,054
Turck; RMC Place; CHEROKEE; *179 J-19; mail Columbus z 66725; ● 50
Turner; RMC Place; WYANDOTTE; *179 D-19; ★ **K.C.**; mail Kansas City z 66106; pop. incl. with Kansas City (Inc. Place)
Turon; Inc. Place; RENO; 178 H-10; elev. 1,760ft./536m.; [P]; z 67583; Ⓟ 393; © 436
Tyro; Inc. Place; MONTGOMERY; 179 J-16; elev. 891ft./272m.; [P]; z 67364; Ⓟ 243; © 226

U

Udall; Inc. Place; COWLEY; 179 I-13; elev. 1,267ft./386m.; [P]; z 67146; Ⓟ 824; © 794
Ulysses; Inc. Place; ⊡ GRANT; 178 I-3; elev. 3,057ft./932m.; [P] [H]; z 67880; Ⓟ 5,474; © 5,960
Union Stock Yards; RMC Place; SEDGWICK; *179 H-13; ★ **WICH**; mail Wichita z 67219; pop. incl. with Wichita (Inc. Place)
Uniontown; Inc. Place; BOURBON; 179 H-18; elev. 890ft./271m.; [P]; z 66779; Ⓟ 290; © 288
Upland; RMC Place; DICKINSON; 179 D-13; elev. 1,261ft./384m.; mail Chapman z 67431; ● 25
Urbana; RMC Place; NEOSHO; 179 I-17; elev. 955ft./291m.; mail Chanute z 66720; ● 30
Utica; Inc. Place; NESS; 178 F-6; elev. 2,615ft./797m.; [P]; z 67584; Ⓟ 208; © 223

V

Valeda; RMC Place; LABETTE; 179 J-17; mail Coffeyville z 67337; ● 70
Valencia; RMC Place; SHAWNEE; *179 D-16; ★ **TOP**; mail Topeka z 66604; ● 80
Valley Center; Inc. Place; SEDGWICK; 179 H-13; elev. 1,350ft./411m.; [P]; ★ **WICH**; z 67147; Ⓟ 3,624; © 4,883
Valley Falls; Inc. Place; JEFFERSON; 179 C-17; elev. 950ft./290m.; [P]; z 66088; Ⓟ 1,253; © 1,254
Varner; RMC Place; KINGMAN; *179 H-11; mail Kingman z 67068
Vassar; RMC Place; OSAGE; 179 F-17; elev. 1,103ft./336m.; [P]; z 66543; ● 150
Venango; RMC Place; ELLSWORTH; 179 F-11; mail Marquette z 67464; ● 100
Verdi; RMC Place; OTTAWA; *179 E-12; elev. 1,199ft./365m.; mail Solomon z 67480
Vermillion; Inc. Place; MARSHALL; 179 B-15; elev. 1,200ft./366m.; [P]; z 66544; Ⓟ 113; © 107
Vernon; RMC Place; WOODSON; *179 H-17; mail Yates Center z 66783
Vesper; RMC Place; LINCOLN; 178 D-10; mail Lincoln z 67455; ● 25
Victoria; Inc. Place; ELLIS; 178 E-8; elev. 1,910ft./582m.; [P]; z 67671; Ⓟ 1,157; © 1,208
Vilas; RMC Place; WILSON; *179 I-17; mail Chanute z 66720
Vine Creek; RMC Place; OTTAWA; *179 D-12; mail Longford z 67458; rural
Vining; Inc. Place; CLAY, WASHINGTON; 179 C-13; elev. 1,280ft./390m.; mail Clifton z 66937; Ⓟ 55; © 58
Vinland; RMC Place; DOUGLAS; 179 E-18; elev. 884ft./269m.; mail Baldwin City z 66006; ● 30
Viola; Inc. Place; SEDGWICK; 179 I-12; elev. 1,330ft./405m.; [P]; z 67149; Ⓟ 185; © 211
Virgil; Inc. Place; GREENWOOD; 179 H-16; elev. 979ft./298m.; [P]; z 66870; Ⓟ 91; © 113
Vliets; RMC Place; MARSHALL; 179 B-15; elev. 1,198ft./365m.; [P]; z 66544; ● 35
Voda; RMC Place; TREGO; *178 D-6; mail Collyer z 67631

W

Wabaunsee; RMC Place; WABAUNSEE; 179 D-15; mail Wamego z 66547; ● 110
WABAUNSEE; 179 E-15; Ⓟ 6,603; © 6,885; ◆ 7,074
Waco; RMC Place; SEDGWICK; *179 I-13; ★ **WICH**; mail Haysville z 67060
Wagon Wheel Ranch; RMC Place; BUTLER; mail Augusta z 67010; ● 200
Wagstaff; RMC Place; MIAMI; 179 E-19; elev. 1,056ft./322m.; mail Paola z 66071; ● 25
Wakarusa; RMC Place; SHAWNEE; 179 E-16; elev. 955ft./291m.; [P]; ★ **TOP**; z 66546; ● 300
WaKeeney; Inc. Place; ⊡ TREGO; 178 D-7; elev. 2,465ft./751m.; [P] [H]; z 67672; Ⓟ 2,161; © 1,924
Wakefield; Inc. Place; CLAY; 179 D-13; elev. 1,148ft./350m.; [P]; z 67487; Ⓟ 900; © 838
Waldo; Inc. Place; RUSSELL; 178 D-9; elev. 1,711ft./522m.; [P]; z 67673; Ⓟ 57; © 48
Waldron; Inc. Place; HARPER; 179 K-11; elev. 1,246ft./380m.; [P]; z 67150; Ⓟ 19; © 17
Walker; RMC Place; ELLIS; 178 E-9; elev. 1,942ft./592m.; [P]; z 67674; ● 60
Wallace; Inc. Place; WALLACE; 178 E-2; elev. 3,311ft./1,009m.; [P]; z 67761; Ⓟ 75; © 67
WALLACE; 178 E-2; Ⓟ 1,821; © 1,749; ◆ 1,338
Walnut; Inc. Place; CRAWFORD; 179 I-18; elev. 925ft./282m.; [P]; z 66780; Ⓟ 214; © 221
Walton; Inc. Place; HARVEY; 179 G-13; elev. 1,537ft./468m.; [P]; z 67151; Ⓟ 226; © 284
Wamego; Inc. Place; POTTAWATOMIE; 179 D-15; elev. 990ft./302m.; [P] [H]; z 66547; Ⓟ 3,706; © 4,246
Washington; Inc. Place; ⊡ WASHINGTON; 179 B-13; elev. 1,335ft./407m.; [P] [H]; z 66968; Ⓟ 1,304; © 1,223
WASHINGTON; 179 B-13; Ⓟ 7,073; © 6,483; ◆ 5,626
Waterloo; RMC Place; KINGMAN; 179 I-11; mail Murdock z 67111; ● 30
Waterville; Inc. Place; MARSHALL; 179 B-14; elev. 1,176ft./358m.; [P]; z 66548; Ⓟ 601; © 681
Wathena; Inc. Place; DONIPHAN; 179 B-18; elev. 823ft./251m.; [P]; ★ **ST.JO**; z 66090; Ⓟ 1,160; © 1,348
Watson; RMC Place; SHAWNEE; *179 D-17; elev. 1,070ft./326m.; ★ **TOP**; mail Tecumseh z 66542; ● 30
Wauneta; RMC Place; CHAUTAUQUA; *179 J-15; elev. 959ft./292m.; mail Cedar Vale z 67024
Waverly; Inc. Place; COFFEY; 179 F-17; elev. 1,131ft./345m.; [P]; z 66871; Ⓟ 618; © 589
Wayne; RMC Place; REPUBLIC; *179 B-12; mail Clyde z 66938
Wayside; RMC Place; MONTGOMERY; 179 J-16; elev. 877ft./267m.; mail Independence z 67301; ● 65
Wea; RMC Place; MIAMI; *179 E-19; elev. 1,077ft./328m.; mail Bucyrus z 66013; rural
Webber; Inc. Place; JEWELL; 179 B-11; elev. 1,670ft./509m.; [P]; z 66970; Ⓟ 39; © 37
Webster; RMC Place; ROOKS; *178 C-8; mail Stockton z 67669; rural
Wego-Waco; RMC Place; SEDGWICK; *179 I-13; ★ **WICH**; mail Haysville z 67060; ● 110
Weir; Inc. Place; CHEROKEE; 179 J-19; elev. 920ft./280m.; [P]; z 66781; Ⓟ 730; © 780
Welborn; RMC Place; WYANDOTTE; *179 D-19; ★ **K.C.**; mail Kansas City z 66104; pop. incl. with Kansas City (Inc. Place)
Welda; RMC Place; ANDERSON; 179 G-18; elev. 1,100ft./335m.; [P]; z 66091; ● 120
Wellington; Inc. Place; ⊡ SUMNER; 179 J-13; elev. 1,223ft./373m.; [P] [H]; z 67152; Ⓟ 8,411; © 8,647
Wells; RMC Place; OTTAWA; 179 D-12; elev. 1,372ft./418m.; [P]; z 67467; ● 40
Wellsford; RMC Place; KIOWA; 178 I-9; elev. 2,116ft./645m.; mail Haviland z 67059; ● 25
Wellsville; Inc. Place; FRANKLIN; 179 E-18; elev. 1,039ft./317m.; [P]; z 66092; Ⓟ 1,563; © 1,606
Weskan; RMC Place; WALLACE; 178 E-2; elev. 3,846ft./1,172m.; [P]; z 67762; ● 300
Westboro; RMC Place; SHAWNEE; ★ **TOP**; mail Topeka z 66604; pop. incl. with Topeka (Inc. Place)
West Coffeyville; RMC Place; MONTGOMERY; *179 J-17; mail Coffeyville z 67337; pop. incl. with Coffeyville (Inc. Place)
Westfall; RMC Place; LINCOLN; 179 E-11; elev. 1,420ft./433m.; [P]; z 67455; ● 40
Westlink Village; RMC Place; SEDGWICK; *179 H-12; ★ **WICH**; mail Wichita z 67212; pop. incl. with Wichita (Inc. Place)
West Mineral; Inc. Place; CHEROKEE; 179 J-19; elev. 900ft./274m.; [P]; z 66782; Ⓟ 226; © 243
Westmoreland; Inc. Place; ⊡ POTTAWATOMIE; 179 C-15; elev. 1,168ft./356m.; [P] [H]; z 66426, z 66549; Ⓟ 541; © 631
Westphalia; Inc. Place; ANDERSON; 179 G-17; elev. 1,100ft./335m.; [P]; z 66093; Ⓟ 152; © 165
Westport; RMC Place; SEDGWICK; ★ **WICH**; mail Wichita z 67217; pop. incl. with Wichita (Inc. Place)
West Shore; RMC Place; JEFFERSON; *179 D-17; mail Meriden z 66512; ● 25
Westwood; Inc. Place; JOHNSON; 196 J-3; elev. 900ft./274m.; [P]; ★ **K.C.**; z 66205; Ⓟ 1,772; © 1,533
Westwood Hills; Inc. Place; JOHNSON; 196 J-3; elev. 900ft./274m.; [P]; ★ **K.C.**; z 66205; Ⓟ 383; © 378
Wetmore; Inc. Place; NEMAHA; 179 C-16; elev. 1,150ft./351m.; [P]; z 66550; Ⓟ 284; © 362
Wheaton; Inc. Place; POTTAWATOMIE; 179 C-15; elev. 1,500ft./457m.; [P]; z 66521; Ⓟ 106; © 92
Wheatridge Addition; RMC Place; SEDGWICK; ★ **WICH**; mail Wichita z 67212; pop. incl. with Wichita (Inc. Place)
Wheeler; RMC Place; CHEYENNE; 178 B-2; elev. 3,482ft./1,061m.; [P]; z 67756; ● 50
White Church; RMC Place; WYANDOTTE; ★ **K.C.**; mail Kansas City z 66109; pop. incl. with Kansas City (Inc. Place)
White City; Inc. Place; MORRIS; 179 E-14; elev. 1,470ft./448m.; [P]; z 66872; Ⓟ 533; © 518
White Cloud; Inc. Place; DONIPHAN; 179 A-17; elev. 888ft./271m.; [P]; z 66094; Ⓟ 255; © 239
Whitewater; Inc. Place; BUTLER; 179 H-13; elev. 1,370ft./418m.; [P]; z 67154; Ⓟ 683; © 653
Whiting; Inc. Place; JACKSON; 179 C-17; elev. 1,113ft./339m.; [P]; z 66552; Ⓟ 213; © 206
Wichita; Inc. Place; ⊡ SEDGWICK; 179 I-13; elev. 1,305ft./398m.; [P] [H] [C] 19,596 ■; ★ **WICH**; z 67201-21, z 67223, z 67226-28, z 67230, z 67232, z 67235, z 67260, z 67275-78; Ⓟ 304,011; © 344,284; Ⓡ 346,753; ◆ 376,693
WICHITA; 178 F-3; Ⓟ 2,758; © 2,531; ◆ 2,134
Wichita State University; RMC Place; SEDGWICK; ★ **WICH**; mail Wichita z 67208, z 67260; pop. incl. with Wichita (Inc. Place)
Wilburton; RMC Place; MORTON; *178 J-2; mail Elkhart z 67950
Wilder (Wilder Junction); RMC Place; JOHNSON; *179 D-18; ★ **K.C.**; mail Shawnee z 66226; pop. incl. with Shawnee (Inc. Place)
Wilder Junction; JOHNSON; see Wilder (RMC Place)
Willard; Inc. Place; SHAWNEE, WABAUNSEE; 179 D-16; elev. 920ft./280m.; mail Topeka z 66604; Ⓟ 110; © 86
Williamsburg; Inc. Place; FRANKLIN; 179 F-17; elev. 1,138ft./347m.; [P]; z 66095; Ⓟ 261; © 351
Williamstown; RMC Place; JEFFERSON; 179 D-17; mail Perry z 66073; ● 75
Willis; Inc. Place; BROWN; 179 B-17; elev. 1,150ft./351m.; [P]; z 66434; Ⓟ 86; © 69
Willowbrook; Inc. Place; RENO; 179 G-11; elev. 1,560ft./475m.; ★ **HUCH**; mail Hutchinson z 67501; Ⓟ 95; © 36; Ⓡ 88
Willowdale; RMC Place; KINGMAN; 178 I-10; mail Spivey z 67142; ● 20
Wilmore; Inc. Place; COMANCHE; 178 J-8; elev. 2,022ft./616m.; [P]; z 67155; Ⓟ 78; © 57
Wilmot; RMC Place; COWLEY; 179 I-14; mail Winfield z 67156; ● 30
Wilroads Gardens; RMC Place; FORD; 178 H-6; mail Dodge City z 67801; ● 400
Wilsey; Inc. Place; MORRIS; 179 F-14; elev. 1,505ft./459m.; [P]; z 66873; Ⓟ 149; © 191
Wilson; Inc. Place; ELLSWORTH; 178 E-10; elev. 1,689ft./515m.; [P]; z 67490; Ⓟ 834; © 799
WILSON; 179 I-16; Ⓟ 10,289; © 10,332; ◆ 9,954
Winchester; Inc. Place; JEFFERSON; 179 C-17; elev. 1,170ft./357m.; [P] [H]; z 66097; Ⓟ 613; © 579
Windom; Inc. Place; MCPHERSON; 179 F-11; elev. 1,650ft./503m.; [P]; z 67491; Ⓟ 136; © 137
Windsor Park; RMC Place; SEDGWICK; ★ **WICH**; mail Wichita z 67207; ● 140
Windthorst; RMC Place; FORD; 178 H-7; mail Spearville z 67876; ● 15
Winfield; Inc. Place; ⊡ COWLEY; 179 J-14; elev. 1,127ft./344m.; [P] [H] [C] 1,557; z 67156; Ⓟ 11,931; © 12,206
Winifred; RMC Place; MARSHALL; 179 B-15; elev. 1,200ft./366m.; mail Frankfort z 66427; ● 25
Winona; Inc. Place; LOGAN; 178 D-3; elev. 3,329ft./1,015m.; [P]; z 67747, z 67764; Ⓟ 194; © 228
Winway; RMC Place; LABETTE; mail Parsons z 67357; pop. incl. with Parsons (Inc. Place)
Wolcott; RMC Place; WYANDOTTE; *179 D-19; ★ **K.C.**; mail Kansas City z 66109; pop. incl. with Kansas City (Inc. Place)
Womer; RMC Place; SMITH; *178 B-9; elev. 1,933ft./589m.; mail Lebanon z 66952; rural
Wonsevu; RMC Place; CHASE; *179 G-14; elev. 1,354ft./413m.; mail Burns z 66840; rural
Woodbine; Inc. Place; DICKINSON; 179 E-13; elev. 1,250ft./381m.; [P]; z 67492; Ⓟ 186; © 207
Woodlawn; RMC Place; NEMAHA; *179 B-16; elev. 1,270ft./387m.; mail Sabetha z 66534; rural
Woodruff; RMC Place; PHILLIPS; 178 B-8; elev. 2,003ft./611m.; mail Phillipsburg z 67661; ● 25
Woods; RMC Place; STEVENS; *178 J-3; mail Hugoton z 67951; rural
WOODSON; 179 H-16; Ⓟ 4,116; © 3,788; ◆ 3,165
Woodston; Inc. Place; ROOKS; 178 C-8; elev. 1,712ft./522m.; [P]; z 67675; Ⓟ 121; © 116
Worden; RMC Place; DOUGLAS; *179 E-17; elev. 1,093ft./333m.; mail Baldwin City z 66006
Wright; RMC Place; FORD; 178 H-7; elev. 2,550ft./777m.; [P]; z 67882; ● 200
WYANDOTTE; 179 D-18; Ⓟ 161,993; © 157,882; ◆ 150,234
Wyandotte West; RMC Place; WYANDOTTE; *179 D-19; ★ **K.C.**; mail Kansas City z 66111-12; pop. incl. with Kansas City (Inc. Place)

X

Xenia; RMC Place; BOURBON; 179 G-18; elev. 1,047ft./319m.; mail Bronson z 66716; ● 25

Y

Yaggy; RMC Place; RENO; *179 G-11; ★ **HUCH**; mail Hutchinson z 67501; ● 55
Yale; RMC Place; CRAWFORD; *179 I-19; mail Pittsburg z 66762; ● 50
Yankee Run (Lake Shore); RMC Place; ELLSWORTH; *179 F-11; mail Kanopolis z 67454
Yates Center; Inc. Place; ⊡ WOODSON; 179 H-17; elev. 1,136ft./346m.; [P]; z 66783; Ⓟ 1,815; © 1,599
Yocemento; RMC Place; ELLIS; *178 E-8; elev. 2,051ft./625m.; mail Hays z 67601; rural
Yoder; RMC Place; RENO; 179 H-11; elev. 1,539ft./469m.; [P]; z 67585; ● 250

Z

Zarah; RMC Place; JOHNSON; *179 D-19; ★ **K.C.**; mail Shawnee z 66218; pop. incl. with Shawnee (Inc. Place)
Zeandale; RMC Place; RILEY; 179 D-15; elev. 1,010ft./308m.; mail Manhattan z 66502; ● 50
Zenda; Inc. Place; KINGMAN; 178 I-10; elev. 1,663ft./507m.; [P]; z 67159; Ⓟ 96; © 123
Zenith; RMC Place; STAFFORD; *178 H-10; mail Stafford z 67578
Zook; RMC Place; PAWNEE; *178 G-8; elev. 2,045ft./623m.; mail Larned z 67550
Zurich; Inc. Place; ROOKS; 178 D-8; elev. 2,214ft./675m.; [P]; z 67663; Ⓟ 151; © 126

KENTUCKY

IL IN OH WV MO VA TN NC
Frankfort

Statistics

Total area (2000) — 40,409 square miles
Land area (2000) — 39,728 square miles
Water area (2000) — 681 square miles
Capital — Frankfort
Admitted as state — June, 1792

Maps

State maps can be found on pages 142-254 in Vol. 1

Ranally Metro Areas (RMAs) and Abbreviations

Bowling Green, KY — BOWLG
Cincinnati, OH-KY-IN — CIN
Clarksville, TN-KY — CLRKV
Evansville, IN-KY — EV
Hopkinsville, KY — HPKNV
Huntington, WV-KY-OH — HNTG
Lexington, KY — LEX
Louisville, KY-IN — LOU
Owensboro, KY — OWNS
Paducah, KY-IL — PAD
Portsmouth, OH-KY — PTSM

Principal Places

Place Name	Place Type	County	Population
Louisville	Inc. Place	JEFFERSON	◆ 572,800
Lexington	Inc. Place	FAYETTE	◆ 297,867
Bowling Green	Inc. Place	WARREN	◆ 59,834
Owensboro	Inc. Place	DAVIESS	◆ 52,889
Covington	Inc. Place	KENTON	◆ 45,301
Hopkinsville	Inc. Place	CHRISTIAN	◆ 44,452
Richmond	Inc. Place	MADISON	◆ 33,739
Florence	Inc. Place	BOONE	◆ 29,353
Jeffersontown	Inc. Place	JEFFERSON	◆ 28,193
Henderson	Inc. Place	HENDERSON	◆ 27,985
Frankfort	Inc. Place	FRANKLIN	◆ 27,855
Nicholasville	Inc. Place	JESSAMINE	◆ 26,677
Paducah	Inc. Place	MCCRACKEN	◆ 25,643
Elizabethtown	Inc. Place	HARDIN	◆ 25,291
Georgetown	Inc. Place	SCOTT	◆ 24,858
Radcliff	Inc. Place	HARDIN	◆ 23,651
Ashland	Inc. Place	BOYD	◆ 20,686
Madisonville	Inc. Place	HOPKINS	◆ 18,661
Fern Creek	CDP	JEFFERSON	© 17,870
Okolona	CDP	JEFFERSON	© 17,807
Independence	Inc. Place	KENTON	◆ 17,158
Saint Matthews	Inc. Place	JEFFERSON	◆ 16,831
Winchester	Inc. Place	CLARK	© 16,724
Erlanger	Inc. Place	KENTON	© 16,676
Newport	Inc. Place	CAMPBELL	◆ 16,564
Fort Thomas	Inc. Place	CAMPBELL	© 16,495
Danville	Inc. Place	BOYLE	◆ 15,492
Murray	Inc. Place	CALLOWAY	◆ 15,448
Highview	CDP	JEFFERSON	© 15,161
Shively	Inc. Place	JEFFERSON	© 15,157
Fort Campbell North	CDP-Census Area Only	CHRISTIAN	© 14,338
Glasgow	Inc. Place	BARREN	◆ 14,203
Somerset	Inc. Place	PULASKI	◆ 12,553
Fort Knox	CDP-Census Area Only	HARDIN	© 12,377
Burlington	CDP	BOONE	© 10,779
Campbellsville	Inc. Place	TAYLOR	© 10,498
Bardstown	Inc. Place	NELSON	© 10,374
Lyndon	Inc. Place	JEFFERSON	Ⓐ 10,167
Shelbyville	Inc. Place	SHELBY	© 10,085
Middlesboro	Inc. Place	BELL	◆ 9,862
Berea	Inc. Place	MADISON	© 9,851
Mayfield	Inc. Place	GRAVES	◆ 9,662
Edgewood	Inc. Place	KENTON	© 9,400
Paris	Inc. Place	BOURBON	© 9,183
Saint Dennis	CDP	JEFFERSON	© 9,177
Maysville	Inc. Place	MASON	◆ 9,153
Lawrenceburg	Inc. Place	ANDERSON	© 9,014
Mount Washington	Inc. Place	BULLITT	© 8,485
Shepherdsville	Inc. Place	BULLITT	Ⓡ 8,367
Alexandria	Inc. Place	CAMPBELL	© 8,286
Elsmere	Inc. Place	KENTON	© 8,139
Fort Mitchell	Inc. Place	KENTON	© 8,089
Harrodsburg	Inc. Place	MERCER	© 8,014
Franklin	Inc. Place	SIMPSON	© 7,996
Villa Hills	Inc. Place	KENTON	© 7,948
Corbin	Inc. Place	WHITLEY	◆ 7,791
Oakbrook	CDP-Census Area Only	BOONE	© 7,726
Fairdale	CDP	JEFFERSON	© 7,658
Flatwoods	Inc. Place	GREENUP	© 7,605
Morehead	Inc. Place	ROWAN	Ⓡ 7,593
Versailles	Inc. Place	WOODFORD	© 7,511
Buechel	CDP	JEFFERSON	© 7,272
Russellville	Inc. Place	LOGAN	© 7,149
Hillview	Inc. Place	BULLITT	© 7,037
Oak Grove	Inc. Place	CHRISTIAN	Ⓡ 6,951
Taylor Mill	Inc. Place	KENTON	© 6,913
Highland Heights	Inc. Place	CAMPBELL	© 6,554
Princeton	Inc. Place	CALDWELL	© 6,536
Bellevue	Inc. Place	CAMPBELL	© 6,480
Cynthiana	Inc. Place	HARRISON	© 6,258
Leitchfield	Inc. Place	GRAYSON	© 6,139
Pikeville	Inc. Place	PIKE	◆ 6,069
Monticello	Inc. Place	WAYNE	© 5,981
Dayton	Inc. Place	CAMPBELL	© 5,966
Wilmore	Inc. Place	JESSAMINE	© 5,905
Central City	Inc. Place	MUHLENBERG	© 5,893
Mount Sterling	Inc. Place	MONTGOMERY	© 5,876
Middletown	Inc. Place	JEFFERSON	Ⓡ 5,801
Lebanon	Inc. Place	MARION	© 5,718
London	Inc. Place	LAUREL	© 5,692
Fort Wright	Inc. Place	KENTON	© 5,681
La Grange	Inc. Place	OLDHAM	© 5,676
Douglass Hills	Inc. Place	JEFFERSON	Ⓡ 5,576
Williamsburg	Inc. Place	WHITLEY	© 5,143

County Business Data

County	FIPS Code	County Seat	Land Area (Sq. Mi.)	Census Population 4/1/2000	Census Population 4/1/1990	Census Population % Change 1990-2000	Wholesale Trade Sales, 1997 ($1,000)	Wholesale Trade % Change 1992-97	Manufacturing, 1997 Establish-ments	Manufacturing, 1997 Total Employees	Manufacturing, 1997 Value Added ($1,000)	Manufacturing, 1997 Ranally Mfg. Units
Adair	001	Columbia	407	17,244	15,360	12.3	29,385	-13.5	20	533	18,826	11
Allen	003	Scottsville	346	17,800	14,628	21.7	15,328	-16.4	12	1,858	110,617	63
Anderson	005	Lawrenceburg	203	19,111	14,571	31.2	(d)	(d)	20	(d)	(d)	...
Ballard	007	Wickliffe	251	8,286	7,902	4.9	28,697	-6.3	12	(d)	(d)	...
Barren	009	Glasgow	491	38,033	34,001	11.9	97,615	-2.5	55	5,672	325,717	186
Bath	011	Owingsville	279	11,085	9,692	14.4	(d)	(d)	...	(d)	(d)	...
Bell	013	Pineville	361	30,060	31,506	-4.6	88,889	-0.1	22	858	50,564	29
Boone	015	Burlington	246	85,991	57,589	49.3	1,005,020	123.2	134	9,050	880,419	503
Bourbon	017	Paris	291	19,360	19,236	0.6	(d)	(d)	19	(d)	(d)	...
Boyd	019	Catlettsburg	160	49,752	51,150	-2.7	515,254	36.3	42	4,395	668,204	382
Boyle	021	Danville	182	27,697	25,641	8.0	196,989	93.2	33	4,604	370,541	212
Bracken	023	Brooksville	203	8,279	7,766	6.6	18,235	31.1	...	(d)	(d)	...
Breathitt	025	Jackson	495	16,100	15,703	2.5	40,073	36.0	...	(d)	(d)	...
Breckinridge	027	Hardinsburg	572	18,648	16,312	14.3	(d)	(d)	...	(d)	(d)	...
Bullitt	029	Shepherdsville	299	61,236	47,567	28.7	92,833	54.3	49	2,959	172,024	98
Butler	031	Morgantown	428	13,010	11,245	15.7	13,925	16.3	15	1,886	228,665	131
Caldwell	033	Princeton	347	13,060	13,232	-1.3	27,183	149.0	19	659	49,438	28
Calloway	035	Murray	386	34,177	30,735	11.2	(d)	(d)	28	2,983	519,845	297
Campbell	037	Alexandria	152	88,616	83,866	5.7	230,131	-71.6	83	3,043	400,229	229
Carlisle	039	Bardwell	192	5,351	5,238	2.2	21,993	47.0	...	(d)	(d)	...
Carroll	041	Carrollton	130	10,155	9,292	9.3	63,415	-52.3	18	2,378	634,872	362
Carter	043	Grayson	411	26,889	24,340	10.5	(d)	(d)	18	612	29,421	17
Casey	045	Liberty	446	15,447	14,211	8.7	18,167	49.0	27	946	34,533	20
Christian	047	Hopkinsville	721	72,265	68,941	4.8	682,474	65.4	56	4,469	332,176	190
Clark	049	Winchester	254	33,144	29,496	12.4	(d)	(d)	46	3,635	252,353	144
Clay	051	Manchester	471	24,556	21,746	12.9	13,422	-27.5	...	(d)	(d)	...
Clinton	053	Albany	197	9,634	9,135	5.5	12,830	-44.8	15	671	24,217	14
Crittenden	055	Marion	362	9,384	9,196	2.0	(d)	(d)	...	(d)	(d)	...
Cumberland	057	Burkesville	306	7,147	6,784	5.4	(d)	(d)	...	(d)	(d)	...
Daviess	059	Owensboro	462	91,545	87,189	5.0	872,936	-6.8	114	8,011	1,106,787	632
Edmonson	061	Brownsville	303	11,644	10,357	12.4	(d)	(d)	...	(d)	(d)	...
Elliott	063	Sandy Hook	234	6,748	6,455	4.5	(d)	(d)	...	(d)	(d)	...
Estill	065	Irvine	254	15,307	14,614	4.7	(d)	(d)	...	(d)	(d)	...
Fayette	067	Lexington	285	260,512	225,366	15.6	4,181,465	31.0	283	17,403	2,147,695	1,226
Fleming	069	Flemingsburg	351	13,792	12,292	12.2	58,177	15.2	19	650	22,304	13
Floyd	071	Prestonsburg	394	42,441	43,586	-2.6	312,632	30.2	...	(d)	(d)	...
Franklin	073	Frankfort	210	47,687	43,781	8.9	(d)	(d)	40	3,435	302,002	172
Fulton	075	Hickman	209	7,752	8,271	-6.3	(d)	(d)	14	1,087	80,526	46
Gallatin	077	Warsaw	99	7,870	5,393	45.9	(d)	(d)	...	(d)	(d)	...
Garrard	079	Lancaster	231	14,792	11,579	27.7	(d)	(d)	...	(d)	(d)	...
Grant	081	Williamstown	260	22,384	15,737	42.2	(d)	(d)	16	(d)	(d)	...
Graves	083	Mayfield	556	37,028	33,550	10.4	201,753	46.4	50	3,053	208,769	119
Grayson	085	Leitchfield	504	24,053	21,050	14.3	(d)	(d)	31	2,462	107,878	62
Green	087	Greensburg	289	11,518	10,371	11.1	6,661	-32.4	...	(d)	(d)	...
Greenup	089	Greenup	346	36,891	36,742	0.4	(d)	(d)	13	600	48,522	28
Hancock	091	Hawesville	189	8,392	7,864	6.7	(d)	(d)	13	1,862	222,810	127
Hardin	093	Elizabethtown	628	94,174	89,240	5.5	134,659	-7.7	68	7,162	734,376	419
Harlan	095	Harlan	467	33,202	36,574	-9.2	108,943	15.0	...	(d)	(d)	...
Harrison	097	Cynthiana	310	17,983	16,248	10.7	(d)	(d)	19	1,730	196,360	112
Hart	099	Munfordville	416	17,445	14,890	17.2	(d)	(d)	10	(d)	(d)	...
Henderson	101	Henderson	440	44,829	43,044	4.1	728,360	118.3	78	6,862	912,163	521
Henry	103	New Castle	289	15,060	12,823	17.4	114,425	38.4	8	555	72,980	42
Hickman	105	Clinton	244	5,262	5,566	-5.5	40,428	58.3	...	(d)	(d)	...
Hopkins	107	Madisonville	551	46,519	46,126	0.9	189,964	-19.3	55	2,606	245,189	140
Jackson	109	McKee	346	13,495	11,955	12.9	(d)	(d)	13	1,940	5,372	3
Jefferson	111	Louisville	385	693,604	664,937	4.3	15,932,870	21.8	873	56,948	15,278,704	8,723
Jessamine	113	Nicholasville	173	39,041	30,508	28.0	513,676	222.4	67	2,379	327,000	187
Johnson	115	Paintsville	262	23,445	23,248	0.8	60,136	-39.4	...	(d)	(d)	...
Kenton	117	Independence	162	151,464	142,031	6.6	1,370,272	0.2	161	6,810	860,506	491
Knott	119	Hindman	352	17,649	17,906	-1.4	3,558	224.3	...	(d)	(d)	...
Knox	121	Barbourville	388	31,795	29,676	7.1	52,371	17.1	17	877	67,932	39
Larue	123	Hodgenville	263	13,373	11,679	14.5	3,427	-66.9	12	641	11,354	6
Laurel	125	London	436	52,715	43,438	21.4	520,185	26.0	44	2,595	130,592	75
Lawrence	127	Louisa	419	15,569	13,998	11.2	(d)	(d)	...	(d)	(d)	...
Lee	129	Beattyville	210	7,916	7,422	6.7	16,298	-61.0	...	(d)	(d)	...
Leslie	131	Hyden	404	12,401	13,642	-9.1	(d)	(d)	...	(d)	(d)	...
Letcher	133	Whitesburg	339	25,277	27,000	-6.4	111,309	28.2	...	(d)	(d)	...
Lewis	135	Vanceburg	484	14,092	13,029	8.2	5,567	-0.2	15	804	66,977	38
Lincoln	137	Stanford	336	23,361	20,045	16.5	12,098	-15.6	18	737	20,156	12
Livingston	139	Smithland	316	9,804	9,062	8.2	4,432	-28.7	...	(d)	(d)	...
Logan	141	Russellville	556	26,573	24,416	8.8	79,844	32.0	41	4,650	394,462	225
Lyon	143	Eddyville	216	8,080	6,624	22.0	42,654	110.9	...	(d)	(d)	...
Madison	151	Richmond	441	70,872	57,508	23.2	285,704	124.0	68	5,460	543,471	310
Magoffin	153	Salyersville	309	13,332	13,077	1.9	45,179	776.8	...	(d)	(d)	...
Marion	155	Lebanon	346	18,212	16,499	10.4	40,254	5.0	22	1,554	87,164	50
Marshall	157	Benton	305	30,125	27,205	10.7	124,184	58.9	35	2,881	747,050	427
Martin	159	Inez	231	12,578	12,526	0.4	73,894	344.8	...	(d)	(d)	...
Mason	161	Maysville	241	16,800	16,666	0.8	93,665	-63.9	19	3,167	200,430	114
McCracken	145	Paducah	251	65,514	62,879	4.2	1,556,988	29.2	58	4,081	543,237	310
McCreary	147	Whitley City	428	17,080	15,603	9.5	976	-90.6	16	(d)	(d)	...
McLean	149	Calhoun	254	9,938	9,628	3.2	52,473	70.0	...	(d)	(d)	...
Meade	163	Brandenburg	309	26,349	24,170	9.0	59,047	161.3	...	(d)	(d)	...
Menifee	165	Frenchburg	204	6,556	5,092	28.8	(d)	(d)	...	(d)	(d)	...
Mercer	167	Harrodsburg	251	20,817	19,148	8.7	23,732	-33.1	16	3,053	272,356	156
Metcalfe	169	Edmonton	291	10,037	8,963	12.0	11,772	11.1	13	1,829	107,918	62
Monroe	171	Tompkinsville	331	11,756	11,401	3.1	(d)	(d)	32	1,966	80,535	46
Montgomery	173	Mount Sterling	199	22,554	19,561	15.3	126,671	-16.5	32	2,124	99,524	57
Morgan	175	West Liberty	381	13,948	11,648	19.7	(d)	(d)	...	(d)	(d)	...
Muhlenberg	177	Greenville	475	31,839	31,318	1.7	(d)	(d)	36	1,399	78,485	45
Nelson	179	Bardstown	423	37,477	29,710	26.1	133,317	45.2	56	3,616	528,578	302

Entries in **UPPERCASE** are counties.
Entries in **bold** have populations of 2,500 or more.
Names in parentheses are alternate names.
Inc. Place — Incorporated Place
RMC Place — Rand McNally Designated Place
CDP — Census Designated Place
MCD — Minor Civil Division

⊡ County Seat
▲ Minor Civil Division
elev. Elevation
🅿 Post Office

Ⓗ Hospital
Ⓒ College
■ Principal Business Center
★ Ranally Metro Area (RMA) Abbreviation
z Zip Code(s)

Ⓟ Previous Census Population
Ⓡ Revised Census Population
Ⓐ Annexation Population
● Rand McNally Population Estimate
© Final Census Population
Ⓢ Special Census Population
◆ Estimated Population

For additional definitions see Glossary, Volume 1, and Introduction, Volume 2.

County	FIPS Code	County Seat	Land Area (Sq. Mi.)	Census Population			Wholesale Trade		Manufacturing, 1997			
				4/1/2000	4/1/1990	% Change 1990-2000	Sales, 1997 ($1,000)	% Change 1992-97	Establish-ments	Total Employees	Value Added ($1,000)	Ranally Mfg. Units
Nicholas	181	Carlisle	197	6,813	6,725	1.3	(d)	(d)	5	(d)	(d)	...
Ohio	183	Hartford	594	22,916	21,105	8.6	45,417	28.5	27	2,010	107,308	61
Oldham	185	La Grange	189	46,178	33,263	38.8	272,579	270.4	41	1,004	101,366	58
Owen	187	Owenton	352	10,547	9,035	16.7	2,963	-58.7	...	(d)	(d)	...
Owsley	189	Booneville	198	4,858	5,036	-3.5	(d)	(d)	...	(d)	(d)	...
Pendleton	191	Falmouth	281	14,390	12,036	19.6	(d)	(d)	12	(d)	(d)	...
Perry	193	Hazard	342	29,390	30,283	-2.9	233,746	26.0	9	614	43,325	25
Pike	195	Pikeville	788	68,736	72,583	-5.3	318,419	17.2	26	587	27,905	16
Powell	197	Stanton	180	13,237	11,686	13.3	23,235	229.9	16	1,185	138,233	79
Pulaski	199	Somerset	662	56,217	49,489	13.6	318,356	8.6	84	4,564	322,649	184
Robertson	201	Mount Olivet	100	2,266	2,124	6.7	(d)	(d)	...	(d)	(d)	...
Rockcastle	203	Mount Vernon	318	16,582	14,803	12.0	11,355	-34.2	11	(d)	(d)	...
Rowan	205	Morehead	281	22,094	20,353	8.6	61,202	1.8	13	647	86,221	49
Russell	207	Jamestown	254	16,315	14,716	10.9	83,226	119.0	24	2,098	220,286	126
Scott	209	Georgetown	285	33,061	23,867	38.5	319,491	43.2	45	(d)	(d)	...
Shelby	211	Shelbyville	384	33,337	24,824	34.3	140,389	15.7	42	4,095	392,327	224
Simpson	213	Franklin	236	16,405	15,145	8.3	130,625	8.1	34	3,390	235,679	135
Spencer	215	Taylorsville	186	11,766	6,801	73.0	(d)	(d)	...	(d)	(d)	...
Taylor	217	Campbellsville	270	22,927	21,146	8.4	37,101	1.3	38	4,088	293,348	167
Todd	219	Elkton	376	11,971	10,940	9.4	54,066	-17.7	19	1,299	51,790	30
Trigg	221	Cadiz	443	12,597	10,361	21.6	18,276	74.4	19	1,083	73,058	42
Trimble	223	Bedford	149	8,125	6,090	33.4	(d)	(d)	...	(d)	(d)	...
Union	225	Morganfield	345	15,637	16,557	-5.6	66,766	42.0	18	1,214	102,599	59
Warren	227	Bowling Green	545	92,522	76,673	20.7	1,367,411	-38.4	104	(d)	(d)	...
Washington	229	Springfield	301	10,916	10,441	4.5	(d)	(d)	13	1,049	56,362	32
Wayne	231	Monticello	459	19,923	17,468	14.1	15,204	-21.1	33	1,877	78,227	45
Webster	233	Dixon	335	14,120	13,955	1.2	(d)	(d)	19	798	48,032	27
Whitley	235	Williamsburg	440	35,865	33,326	7.6	(d)	(d)	33	1,927	106,005	61
Wolfe	237	Campton	223	7,065	6,503	8.6	3,864	-34.6	...	(d)	(d)	...
Woodford	239	Versailles	191	23,208	19,955	16.3	(d)	(d)	22	(d)	(d)	...
The State			**39,728**	**4,041,769**	**3,685,296**	**9.7**	**35,042,505**	**11.0**	**3,945**	**251,729**	**34,447,545**	**19,673**

(d) Data not available. Corresponding percentages or Ranally Manufacturing Units are estimates.
... Represents 0 or amount too minimal to be reported.

Index of Places and Counties

A

Aaron; RMC Place; CLINTON; 180 M-10; elev. 1,090ft./332m.; 🅿; z 42602; ● 70
Abbey of Our Lady of Gethsemani; NELSON; see Trappist (RMC Place)
Abbott; RMC Place; TRIMBLE; *180 F-10; mail Bedford z 40006; rural
Abegall; RMC Place; ROBERTSON; *181 F-14; mail Germantown z 41044; rural
Aberdeen; RMC Place; BUTLER; 180 K-5; elev. 592ft./180m.; 🅿; z 42201; ● 200
Absher; RMC Place; ADAIR; *180 L-10; elev. 906ft./276m.; mail Columbia z 42728; rural
Access; RMC Place; ELLIOTT; *181 G-17; mail Olive Hill z 41164; rural
Acorn; RMC Place; PULASKI; *181 L-13; elev. 1,175ft./358m.; 🅿; z 42501; ● 15
Acorn Village; RMC Place; HENDERSON; *180 I-3; ★ EV; mail Henderson z 42420; pop. incl. with Henderson (Inc. Place)
Acton; RMC Place; TAYLOR; 180 K-10; elev. 729ft./222m.; mail Campbellsville z 42718; ● 125
Acup; RMC Place; PERRY; mail Jeff z 41751; rural
Adaburg; RMC Place; OHIO; *180 J-5; elev. 588ft./179m.; mail Hartford z 42347
Adair; RMC Place; HANCOCK; *180 H-5; mail Hawesville z 42348; rural
ADAIR; 180 L-10; Ⓟ 15,360; Ⓒ 17,244; ◆ 17,843
Adairville; Inc. Place; LOGAN; 180 N-5; elev. 558ft./170m.; 🅿; z 42202; Ⓟ 906; Ⓒ 920
Adams; RMC Place; LAWRENCE; *181 H-18; elev. 648ft./198m.; 🅿; z 41201 & mail Louisa z 41230; rural
Adamson; RMC Place; LETCHER; *181 K-18; mail Burdine z 41517
Add; RMC Place; MARTIN; *181 H-18; mail Inez z 41224; rural
Addison; RMC Place; BRECKINRIDGE; *180 I-6; elev. 404ft./123m.; mail Hardinsburg z 40143; ● 50
Adele (Insko); RMC Place; MORGAN; *181 I-16; elev. 1,007ft./307m.; mail Hazel Green z 41332; ● 75
Adeline; RMC Place; LAWRENCE; *181 G-18; mail Catlettsburg z 41129; rural
Aden; RMC Place; CARTER; *181 G-17; mail Grahn z 41142; rural
Adolphus; RMC Place; ALLEN; 180 N-7; elev. 750ft./229m.; 🅿; z 42120; ● 150
Aetnaville; RMC Place; OHIO; *180 J-5; mail Reynolds Station z 42368; rural
Aflex; RMC Place; PIKE; *181 I-19; elev. 766ft./233m.; 🅿; z 41514; ● 250
Ages (Ages-Brookside); RMC Place; HARLAN; 181 M-16; mail Ages Brookside z 40801; ● 500
Ages-Brookside; HARLAN; see Ages (RMC Place)
Airport Gardens; RMC Place; PERRY; 181 K-17; mail Hazard z 41701; ● 700
Airview Estates; RMC Place; HARDIN; *180 I-8; mail Elizabethtown z 42701; ● 300
Akers; RMC Place; HARLAN; pop. incl. with Cumberland (Inc. Place)
Akersville; RMC Place; MONROE; *180 N-8; mail Fountain Run z 42133
Albany; Inc. Place; ⊡ CLINTON; 180 M-10; elev. 962ft./293m.; 🅿 🅷; z 42602; Ⓟ 2,062; Ⓒ 2,220
Alberta; RMC Place; HARRISON; *181 G-12; elev. 996ft./304m.; mail Sadieville z 40370; rural
Alcalde; RMC Place; PULASKI; *181 L-12; elev. 850ft./259m.; 🅿; z 42501; ● 35
Alcorn; RMC Place; JACKSON; *181 J-14; mail Mc Kee z 40447; rural
Alexandria; Inc. Place; ⊡ CAMPBELL; 181 D-13; elev. 823ft./251m.; 🅿; ★ CIN; z 41001; Ⓟ 5,592; Ⓒ 8,286
Alhambra; RMC Place; ROBERTSON; *181 F-14; mail Mayslick z 41055; rural
Aliceton; RMC Place; BOYLE; *181 J-11; mail Gravel Switch z 40328; rural
Allais; RMC Place; PERRY; *181 K-17; mail Hazard z 41701; pop. incl. with Hazard (Inc. Place)
Allegre; RMC Place; TODD; 180 L-4; elev. 644ft./196m.; 🅿; z 42220; ● 100
Allen; FLOYD; see Allen City (Inc. Place)
ALLEN; 180 N-7; Ⓟ 14,628; Ⓒ 17,800; ◆ 19,141
Allen City (Allen); Inc. Place; FLOYD; 181 J-18; elev. 650ft./198m.; mail Allen z 41601; Ⓟ 229; Ⓒ 150
Allendale; RMC Place; GREEN; *180 K-9; mail Summersville z 42782; rural
Allen Springs; RMC Place; ALLEN; *180 M-7; mail Alvaton z 42122; rural
Allensville; RMC Place; TODD; 180 M-4; elev. 581ft./177m.; 🅿; z 42204; disincorporated since 2000 Census; Ⓟ 218; Ⓒ 189
Allock; RMC Place; PERRY; *181 K-17; elev. 1,200ft./366m.; 🅿; z 41773; ● 45
Almo; RMC Place; CALLOWAY; 180 G-4; elev. 428ft./130m.; 🅿; z 42020; ● 100
Almo Heights; RMC Place; CALLOWAY; *180 G-4; elev. 520ft./158m.; mail Almo z 42020; ● 150
Alonzo; RMC Place; ALLEN; *180 M-6; elev. 592ft./180m.; mail Adolphus z 42120; ● 25
Alpha; RMC Place; CLINTON; 181 M-11; elev. 1,055ft./322m.; 🅿; z 42603; ● 25
Alphoretta (Dinwood); RMC Place; FLOYD; *181 J-18; mail Drift z 41619; ● 150
Alpine; RMC Place; PULASKI; 181 M-12; elev. 1,102ft./336m.; mail Burnside z 42519; ● 50
Alton; RMC Place; ANDERSON; 181 H-11; mail Lawrenceburg z 40342; ● 300
Alton Station; RMC Place; ANDERSON; 181 H-11; mail Lawrenceburg z 40342; ● 450
Altro; RMC Place; BREATHITT; 181 K-16; elev. 790ft./241m.; 🅿; z 41339; ● 35
Alumbaugh; RMC Place; ESTILL; *181 J-14; mail Irvine z 40336; rural
Alum Springs; RMC Place; BOYLE; *181 J-11; mail Junction City z 40440; ● 50
Alva; RMC Place; HARLAN; *181 M-16; 🅿; z 40863; rural
Alvaton; RMC Place; WARREN; 180 M-6; elev. 656ft./200m.; 🅿; z 42122; ● 80
Amandaville; RMC Place; CUMBERLAND; *180 M-10
Amba; RMC Place; FLOYD; *181 J-18; mail Harold z 41635
Amburgey; RMC Place; KNOTT; *181 K-17; elev. 1,007ft./307m.; 🅿; z 41773; ● 125
Ammie; RMC Place; CLAY; *181 K-15; mail Manchester z 40962; rural
Ammons; RMC Place; BRECKINRIDGE; *180 H-6; elev. 422ft./129m.; mail Stephensport z 40170; rural
Amos; RMC Place; ALLEN; 180 N-7; elev. 839ft./256m.; mail Holland z 42153; ● 50
Anchorage; Inc. Place; JEFFERSON; 180 G-9; elev. 700ft./213m.; 🅿; ★ LOU; z 40223 & mail Louisville z 40245; Ⓟ 2,082; Ⓒ 2,264; Ⓡ 2,328
Anco; RMC Place; KNOTT; 181 K-17; elev. 1,197ft./365m.; 🅿; z 41759; ● 360
ANDERSON; 181 H-11; Ⓟ 14,571; Ⓒ 19,111; ◆ 22,054
Andyville; RMC Place; MEADE; *180 H-6; elev. 714ft./218m.; mail Payneville z 40157
Anna; RMC Place; WARREN; *180 L-6; elev. 539ft./164m.; ★ BOWLG
Anneta; RMC Place; GRAYSON; *180 K-7; elev. 763ft./233m.; mail Leitchfield z 42754; rural
Annville; RMC Place; JACKSON; 181 K-14; elev. 1,094ft./333m.; 🅿; z 40402; disincorporated December 15, 2000; Ⓟ 470; Ⓒ 589
Ano; RMC Place; PULASKI; *181 L-13; elev. 1,106ft./337m.; mail Somerset z 42501; rural
Ansel; RMC Place; PULASKI; *181 K-12; mail Science Hill z 42553; rural
Anthoston; RMC Place; HENDERSON; 180 I-3; mail Henderson z 42420; ● 250
Antioch; RMC Place; HARRISON; *181 F-13; mail Berry z 41003; rural
Antioch Shores; RMC Place; PULASKI; *181 L-12; mail Burnside z 42519; ● 125
Anton; RMC Place; HOPKINS; 180 K-3; elev. 410ft./125m.; mail Madisonville z 42431; ● 200
Apex; RMC Place; CHRISTIAN; *180 L-3; mail White Plains z 42464; rural
Aqua Shores; RMC Place; SHELBY; *180 G-10; mail Shelbyville z 40065; ● 150
Arat; RMC Place; CUMBERLAND; *180 M-9; elev. 700ft./213m.; mail Burkesville z 42717; rural
Arch; RMC Place; HARDIN; *180 I-7; mail Cecilia z 42724; rural
Argillite; RMC Place; GREENUP; 181 F-18; elev. 549ft./167m.; 🅿; ★ HNTG; z 41121; ● 50
Argo; RMC Place; PIKE; *181 J-20; elev. 889ft./271m.; 🅿; z 41568
Argyle; RMC Place; CASEY; *181 K-11; elev. 1,208ft./368m.; mail Bethelridge z 42516
Arista; RMC Place; TAYLOR; *180 K-10; mail Campbellsville z 42718; rural
Arjay; RMC Place; BELL; 181 M-15; elev. 1,027ft./313m.; 🅿; z 40902; ● 600
Arkansas; RMC Place; FLOYD; *181 J-18; mail Martin z 41649; rural
Arkansas Creek; RMC Place; FLOYD; *181 J-18; mail Martin z 41649; rural
Arkle; RMC Place; KNOX; *181 M-14; mail Gray z 40734; rural
Arlington; Inc. Place; CARLISLE; 180 F-2; elev. 347ft./106m.; 🅿; z 42021; Ⓟ 449; Ⓒ 395
Arlington; RMC Place; MADISON; *181 I-13; mail Richmond z 40475; pop. incl. with Richmond (Inc. Place)
Arlington Heights; RMC Place; FRANKLIN; mail Frankfort z 40601; pop. incl. with Frankfort (Inc. Place)
Armstrong Hill; RMC Place; CARTER; *181 G-16; mail Olive Hill z 41164; rural
Arnett; RMC Place; OWSLEY; *181 K-15; elev. 834ft./254m.; mail Booneville z 41314; rural
Arnold; RMC Place; OHIO; *180 K-5; elev. 492ft./150m.; mail Horse Branch z 42349; rural
Arnold Ridge Estates; RMC Place; FRANKLIN; *181 G-11; mail Frankfort z 40601; pop. incl. with Frankfort (Inc. Place)
Arrington Corner; RMC Place; HANCOCK; *180 I-5; mail Hawesville z 42348; rural
Artemus; RMC Place; KNOX; 181 M-14; elev. 1,016ft./310m.; 🅿; z 40903; ● 800
Arthurmable; RMC Place; MAGOFFIN; *181 J-17; mail Salyersville z 41465; rural
Artville; RMC Place; MENIFEE; *181 H-16; mail Wellington z 40387; rural
Arvel; RMC Place; LEE; *181 J-14; elev. 1,204ft./367m.; mail Mc Kee z 40447; rural
Ary; RMC Place; PERRY; 181 K-17; elev. 873ft./266m.; 🅿; z 41712; ● 60
Ashbyburg; RMC Place; HOPKINS; 180 J-3; elev. 388ft./118m.; mail Slaughters z 42456; ● 40
Ashcamp; RMC Place; PIKE; 181 K-19; elev. 1,064ft./324m.; 🅿; z 41512; ● 150
Asher; RMC Place; LESLIE; 181 L-16; elev. 971ft./296m.; 🅿; z 40803; ● 100
Ashers Fork; RMC Place; CLAY; *181 L-15; mail Manchester z 40962; rural
Ashland; Inc. Place; BOYD; 181 F-18; elev. 558ft./170m.; 🅿 🅷 ■; ★ HNTG; z 41101-02, z 41105, z 41114; Ⓟ 23,622; Ⓒ 21,981; ◆ 20,686
Ashland Park; RMC Place; FAYETTE; *181 H-12; ★ LEX; mail Lexington z 40502; pop. incl. with Lexington (Inc. Place)
Ashlock; RMC Place; CUMBERLAND; *180 N-9; mail Burkesville z 42717; ● 40
Ashville; RMC Place; JEFFERSON; *180 H-9; elev. 690ft./210m.; ★ LOU; mail Louisville z 40291; became part of Louisville/Jefferson County Metro Jan. 6, 2003
Askin; RMC Place; BRECKINRIDGE, OHIO; *180 J-6; mail Fordsville z 42343; rural
Atchison; RMC Place; TAYLOR; *180 K-10; elev. 876ft./267m.; mail Campbellsville z 42718; rural
Athens; RMC Place; FAYETTE; *181 H-13; ★ LEX; mail Lexington z 40509, z 40515; pop. incl. with Lexington (Inc. Place)
Athertonville; RMC Place; LARUE; 180 J-9; mail Hodgenville z 42748; ● 75
Athol; RMC Place; LEE; 181 J-15; elev. 745ft./227m.; 🅿; z 41307; ● 75
Atkinstown; RMC Place; JACKSON; *181 K-14; mail Gray Hawk z 40434, Mc Kee z 40447; rural
Atoka; RMC Place; BOYLE; *181 J-11; mail Danville z 40422; rural
Atwood; RMC Place; KENTON; *181 E-12; elev. 890ft./271m.; ★ CIN; mail Morning View z 41063; rural
Auburn; Inc. Place; LOGAN; 180 M-5; elev. 642ft./196m.; 🅿; z 42206; Ⓟ 1,273; Ⓒ 1,444
Audobon Acres; RMC Place; DAVIESS; *180 I-4; ★ OWNS; mail Owensboro z 42301; pop. incl. with Owensboro (Inc. Place)
Audubon Park; Inc. Place; JEFFERSON; 180 C-7; elev. 510ft./155m.; ★ LOU; mail Louisville z 40213; Ⓟ 1,520; Ⓒ 1,545
Augusta; Inc. Place; BRACKEN; 181 E-14; elev. 510ft./155m.; 🅿; z 41002; Ⓟ 1,336; Ⓒ 1,204
Ault; RMC Place; ELLIOTT; *181 G-16; elev. 1,133ft./345m.; mail Olive Hill z 41164; rural
Aurora; RMC Place; MARSHALL; 180 M-1; elev. 463ft./141m.; mail Hardin z 42048; ● 200
Austerlitz; RMC Place; BOURBON; *181 H-13; mail Paris z 40361; rural
Austin; RMC Place; BARREN; 180 M-7; elev. 779ft./237m.; 🅿; z 42123; ● 150
Auxier; RMC Place; FLOYD; 181 I-18; elev. 629ft./192m.; 🅿; z 41602; ● 900
Avawam; RMC Place; PERRY; 181 K-16; elev. 966ft./294m.; 🅿; z 41713; ● 250
Avoca; RMC Place; JEFFERSON; *180 G-9; ★ LOU; mail Louisville z 40223; became part of Louisville/Jefferson County Metro Jan. 6, 2003
Avon; RMC Place; FAYETTE; *181 H-13; elev. 944ft./288m.; ★ LEX; mail Lexington z 40516; pop. incl. with Lexington (Inc. Place)
Avondale; RMC Place; MCCRACKEN; *180 E-3; ★ PAD; mail Paducah z 42001; pop. incl. with Paducah (Inc. Place)
Axtel; RMC Place; BRECKINRIDGE; 180 J-6; elev. 606ft./185m.; mail Hardinsburg z 40143; ● 60
Azalea Hills; RMC Place; HENDERSON; *180 I-3; mail Henderson z 42420; ● 65

B

Bachelors Rest; RMC Place; PENDLETON; *181 F-13; mail Falmouth z 41040; rural
Backusburg; RMC Place; CALLOWAY; *180 G-4; mail Kirksey z 42054; rural
Bagdad; RMC Place; SHELBY; 181 G-11; elev. 912ft./278m.; 🅿; z 40003; ● 220
Bailey Creek; RMC Place; HARLAN; *181 M-17; 🅿; z 40828; ● 125
Baileys; KNOX; see Bailey Switch (RMC Place)
Baileys Switch; KNOX; see Bailey Switch (RMC Place)
Bailey Switch (Baileys, Baileys Switch); RMC Place; KNOX; *181 M-14; elev. 978ft./298m.; 🅿; z 40906; rural
Bainbridge; RMC Place; CHRISTIAN; *180 L-2; elev. 510ft./155m.; mail Cerulean z 42215; rural
Baizetown; RMC Place; OHIO; 180 K-5; elev. 619ft./189m.; mail Horse Branch z 42349; ● 25
Baker Branch; RMC Place; JOHNSON; *181 I-18; mail Tutor Key z 41263; rural
Baker Fork; LESLIE; see Causey (RMC Place)
Bakerton; RMC Place; CUMBERLAND; 180 M-10; elev. 595ft./181m.; 🅿; z 42717; ● 35
Bald Hill; RMC Place; FLEMING; *181 G-15; mail Flemingsburg z 41041; rural
Baldrock; RMC Place; LAUREL; *181 L-13; mail London z 40744; rural
Baldwin; RMC Place; MADISON; *181 I-13; mail Richmond z 40475
Ballard; RMC Place; ANDERSON; *181 I-11; elev. 890ft./271m.; mail Lawrenceburg z 40342; rural
BALLARD; 180 E-2; Ⓟ 7,902; Ⓒ 8,286; ◆ 8,232
Ballardsville; RMC Place; OLDHAM; 180 G-10; 🅿; ★ LOU; z 40014; ● 200
Balltown; RMC Place; NELSON; 180 I-9; elev. 634ft./193m.; mail New Haven z 40051; ● 80
Balltown; RMC Place; WHITLEY; *181 M-13; mail Williamsburg z 40769; pop. incl. with Williamsburg (Inc. Place)
Balmoral; RMC Place; HENDERSON; *180 I-3; ★ EV; mail Henderson z 42420; pop. incl. with Henderson (Inc. Place)
Baltimore; RMC Place; GRAVES; *180 G-3; mail Mayfield z 42066; rural
Bancroft; Inc. Place; JEFFERSON; *180 G-9; elev. 629ft./192m.; ★ LOU; mail Louisville z 40222; Ⓟ 582; Ⓒ 536
Bancroft; RMC Place; MUHLENBERG; *180 L-4; mail Greenville z 42345
Bandana; RMC Place; BALLARD; 180 E-2; elev. 354ft./108m.; 🅿; z 42022; ● 300
Bandy; PULASKI; see Randy (RMC Place)
Bank Lick; RMC Place; KENTON; *181 E-12; ★ CIN; mail Walton z 41094; rural
Banner; RMC Place; FLOYD; 181 J-18; elev. 656ft./200m.; 🅿; z 41603; ● 100
Baptist; RMC Place; WOLFE; *181 I-16; mail Campton z 41301; rural
Barbourmeade; Inc. Place; JEFFERSON; 180 A-9; elev. 629ft./192m.; ★ LOU; mail Louisville z 40222; Ⓟ 1,402; Ⓒ 1,260
Barbourville; Inc. Place; ⊡ KNOX; 181 M-14; elev. 986ft./301m.; 🅿 🅷 🅲 1,429; z 40906; Ⓟ 3,658; Ⓒ 3,589
Barcreek; RMC Place; CLAY; *181 K-15; mail Oneida z 40972; rural
Bardo; RMC Place; HARLAN; *181 M-16; mail Harlan z 40831; ● 150
Bardstown; Inc. Place; ⊡ NELSON; 180 I-9; elev. 647ft./197m.; 🅿 🅷; z 40004; Ⓟ 6,801; Ⓒ 10,374
Bardstown Junction; RMC Place; BULLITT; *180 H-9; ★ LOU; mail Shepherdsville z 40165
Bardwell; Inc. Place; ⊡ CARLISLE; 180 F-2; elev. 359ft./109m.; 🅿; z 42023; Ⓟ 819; Ⓒ 799
Barefoot; RMC Place; NICHOLAS; *181 G-13; mail Carlisle z 40311; rural
Bark Camp; RMC Place; WHITLEY; *181 M-13; mail Corbin z 40701; rural
Barlow; Inc. Place; BALLARD; 180 E-2; elev. 378ft./115m.; 🅿; z 42024; Ⓟ 706; Ⓒ 715
Barnesburg; RMC Place; PULASKI; *181 L-12; mail Somerset z 42501; rural
Barnes Store; CALDWELL; see Fryer (RMC Place)
Barnetts Creek; RMC Place; JOHNSON; *181 I-17; elev. 664ft./202m.; 🅿; z 41256; rural
Barnrock; RMC Place; JOHNSON; *181 H-17; mail Flatgap z 41219; rural
Barnsley; RMC Place; HOPKINS; *180 K-3; elev. 483ft./147m.; mail Madisonville z 42431; ● 200
Barnyard; RMC Place; KNOX; *181 M-15; elev. 1,010ft./308m.; mail Flat Lick z 40935; rural
Barrallton; RMC Place; BULLITT; *180 H-8; ★ LOU; mail Shepherdsville z 40165; rural
BARREN; 180 L-8; Ⓟ 34,001; Ⓒ 38,033; ◆ 41,867
Barren River; RMC Place; WARREN; *180 L-6; ★ BOWLG; mail Bowling Green z 42101; rural
Barrier; RMC Place; WAYNE; 181 M-12; 🅿; z 42633; ● 75
Barr Street; RMC Place; FAYETTE; *181 H-12; ★ LEX; mail Lexington z 40507, z 40588, z 40591; pop. incl. with Lexington (Inc. Place)
Barterville; RMC Place; NICHOLAS; *181 G-14; mail Carlisle z 40311; rural
Barthell; RMC Place; MCCREARY; *181 M-12; mail Stearns z 42647; rural
Barwick; RMC Place; BREATHITT; *181 K-16; mail Jackson z 41339; rural
Bascom; RMC Place; ELLIOTT; *181 H-17; elev. 765ft./233m.; mail Sandy Hook z 41171; rural
Baskett; RMC Place; HENDERSON; 180 I-3; elev. 389ft./119m.; 🅿; z 42402; ● 300
Bass; RMC Place; TAYLOR; *180 K-10; mail Elk Horn z 42733; rural
Bath; RMC Place; KNOTT; *181 K-17; mail Mallie z 41836; rural
BATH; 181 G-14; Ⓟ 9,692; Ⓒ 11,085; ◆ 11,358
Battle; RMC Place; WASHINGTON; *181 I-11; mail Mackville z 40040; rural
Battle Run; RMC Place; FLEMING; *181 G-14; elev. 638ft./194m.; mail Ewing z 41039; rural
Battletown; RMC Place; MEADE; 180 H-7; elev. 664ft./202m.; 🅿; z 40104; ● 150
Baughman; RMC Place; KNOX; *181 M-15; elev. 998ft./304m.; 🅿; z 40906; ● 50
Baughman Heights; RMC Place; BOYLE; *181 J-11; mail Danville z 40422; pop. incl. with Danville (Inc. Place)
Baxter; RMC Place; HARLAN; 181 M-16; elev. 1,174ft./358m.; 🅿; z 40806; ● 800
Baxter; RMC Place; JEFFERSON; *180 G-8; ★ LOU; mail Louisville z 40204; became part of Louisville/Jefferson County Metro Jan. 6, 2003
Bayfork; RMC Place; WARREN; *180 M-7; mail Alvaton z 42122; rural
Bayou; RMC Place; LIVINGSTON; *180 D-4; mail Smithland z 42081
Bays; RMC Place; BREATHITT; 181 J-16; elev. 883ft./269m.; 🅿; z 41310; ● 25
Bays Branch; RMC Place; FLOYD; *181 I-18; mail East Point z 41216; rural
Bealers Knob; RMC Place; MCLEAN; *180 J-4; mail Rumsey z 42371; rural
Beals; RMC Place; HENDERSON; *180 I-3; elev. 381ft./116m.; mail Reed z 42451; ● 75
Bear Branch; RMC Place; LESLIE; 181 L-15; elev. 865ft./264m.; 🅿; z 41714; ● 80
Beartown; RMC Place; ELLIOTT; *181 G-16; mail Olive Hill z 41164; rural
Bearville; RMC Place; KNOTT; *181 K-17; elev. 1,034ft./315m.; 🅿; z 41740; rural
Bear Wallow; RMC Place; BARREN, HART; *180 L-8; mail Cave City z 42127; ● 30
Beattyville; Inc. Place; ⊡ LEE; 181 J-15; elev. 666ft./203m.; 🅿; z 41311; Ⓟ 1,131; Ⓒ 1,193
Beaumont; RMC Place; METCALFE; 180 M-9; elev. 1,052ft./321m.; 🅿; z 42124; ● 100
Beaumont Park; RMC Place; FAYETTE; *181 H-12; ★ LEX; mail Lexington z 40504; pop. incl. with Lexington (Inc. Place)
Beauty; RMC Place; MARTIN; 181 I-19; elev. 636ft./194m.; 🅿; z 41203; ● 600
Beaver; RMC Place; FLOYD; 181 K-18; elev. 1,002ft./305m.; 🅿; z 41604; ● 200
Beaver Bottom (Cedarville); RMC Place; PIKE; 181 K-19; elev. 770ft./235m.; mail Elkhorn City z 41522; disincorporated since 2000 Census; pop. incl. with Cedarville (RMC Place); Ⓟ 65; Ⓒ 52
Beaver Dam; Inc. Place; OHIO; 180 K-5; elev. 414ft./126m.; 🅿; z 42320; Ⓟ 2,904; Ⓒ 3,033
Beaver Junction; RMC Place; FLOYD; *181 J-18; pop. incl. with Allen City (Inc. Place)
Beaverlick; RMC Place; BOONE; *181 E-12; ★ CIN; mail Union z 41091, Walton z 41094; ● 75
Becknerville; RMC Place; CLARK; *181 H-13; mail Winchester z 40391
Beckton; RMC Place; BARREN; *180 L-7; elev. 743ft./226m.; mail Glasgow z 42141; rural
Beda; RMC Place; OHIO; *180 J-5; mail Hartford z 42347
Bedford; Inc. Place; ⊡ TRIMBLE; 180 F-10; elev. 895ft./273m.; 🅿; z 40006; Ⓟ 761; Ⓒ 677
Beech; RMC Place; BREATHITT; *181 K-16; mail Jackson z 41339; rural
Beech Bottom; RMC Place; CASEY; *181 K-11; mail Liberty z 42539; rural
Beechburg; RMC Place; FLEMING; *181 F-15; elev. 899ft./274m.; mail Wallingford z 41093; rural
Beech Creek; RMC Place; MUHLENBERG; 180 K-4; elev. 476ft./145m.; 🅿; z 42321; ● 250
Beech Grove; RMC Place; BULLITT; *180 H-8; ★ LOU; mail Lebanon Junction z 40150, Shepherdsville z 40165; rural
Beech Grove; RMC Place; CARTER; *181 G-17; ★ HNTG; mail Grayson z 41143; ● 30
Beech Grove; RMC Place; MCLEAN; 180 J-3; elev. 398ft./121m.; 🅿; z 42322; ● 250
Beechland; RMC Place; LOGAN; *180 L-5; elev. 480ft./146m.; mail Lewisburg z 42256; rural
Beechmont; RMC Place; JEFFERSON; *180 H-8; ★ LOU; mail Louisville z 40214; pop. incl. with Louisville (Inc. Place)
Beechmont; RMC Place; MUHLENBERG; 180 K-4; elev. 481ft./147m.; 🅿; z 42323; ● 600
Beechville; RMC Place; METCALFE; *180 L-9; elev. 687ft./209m.; mail Edmonton z 42129; rural
Beechwood; RMC Place; OWEN; *181 G-12; elev. 922ft./281m.; mail Owenton z 40359
Beechwood Village; Inc. Place; JEFFERSON; 180 B-8; elev. 524ft./160m.; ★ LOU; mail Louisville z 40207; Ⓟ 1,263; Ⓒ 1,173
Beechy; RMC Place; GREENUP; *181 F-17; mail South Shore z 41175; rural
Beefhide; RMC Place; LETCHER; *181 K-18; mail Jenkins z 41537; rural
Beelerton; RMC Place; HICKMAN; *180 G-2; elev. 393ft./120m.; mail Fulton z 42041; rural
Bee Lick; RMC Place; LINCOLN, PULASKI, ROCKCASTLE; *181 K-12; mail Crab Orchard z 40419; rural
Bee Spring; RMC Place; EDMONSON; 180 K-7; elev. 696ft./212m.; 🅿; z 42207; ● 150
Beetle; RMC Place; CARTER; *181 G-17; mail Grayson z 41143; rural
Bel-Air; RMC Place; CLARK; *181 H-13; ★ LEX; mail Winchester z 40391; pop. incl. with Winchester (Inc. Place)
Belcher; RMC Place; PIKE; 181 K-19; elev. 756ft./230m.; 🅿; z 41513; ● 150
Belcourt; RMC Place; WEBSTER; *180 J-3; mail Slaughters z 42456; rural
Belcraft; RMC Place; LETCHER; *181 L-18; mail Whitesburg z 41858; ● 150
Belfry; RMC Place; PIKE; 181 J-19; elev. 709ft./216m.; 🅿; z 41514; ● 600
Belknap; RMC Place; WOLFE; *181 I-16; rural
Belknap Beach; RMC Place; OLDHAM; *180 G-9; ★ LOU; mail Prospect z 40059; ● 200
BELL; 181 M-15; Ⓟ 31,506; Ⓒ 30,060; ◆ 28,529
Bell City; RMC Place; ELLIOTT; *181 H-17; mail Sandy Hook z 41171; pop. incl. with Sandy Hook (Inc. Place)
Bell City; RMC Place; GRAVES; *180 G-4; elev. 439ft./134m.; mail Farmington z 42040; rural
Bellefonte; Inc. Place; GREENUP; 181 E-19; elev. 671ft./205m.; ★ HNTG; mail Ashland z 41101; Ⓟ 838; Ⓒ 837
Bellemeade; Inc. Place; JEFFERSON; 180 B-9; elev. 602ft./183m.; ★ LOU; mail Louisville z 40222; Ⓟ 927; Ⓒ 871
Bellepoint; RMC Place; FRANKLIN; *181 G-11; mail Frankfort z 40601; pop. incl. with Frankfort (Inc. Place)
Belleview; RMC Place; BOONE; 181 D-11; mail Burlington z 41005; ● 180
Bellevue; Inc. Place; CAMPBELL; 181 A-17; elev. 549ft./167m.; 🅿; ★ CIN; z 41073-74; Ⓟ 6,997; Ⓒ 6,480
Bellewood; Inc. Place; JEFFERSON; *180 G-9; elev. 550ft./168m.; ★ LOU; mail Louisville z 40207; Ⓟ 329; Ⓒ 300
Bell Farm; RMC Place; MCCREARY; *181 N-12; mail Stearns z 42647; rural
Bells Run; RMC Place; OHIO; *180 J-5; mail Whitesville z 42378
Belltown; RMC Place; MARION; *180 J-10; mail Lebanon z 40033; rural
Bellview; RMC Place; FRANKLIN; *181 G-11; mail Frankfort z 40601; pop. incl. with Frankfort (Inc. Place)
Belmont; RMC Place; BULLITT; 180 I-8; mail Lebanon Junction z 40150; ● 100
Belmont; RMC Place; HARRISON; *181 G-13; mail Cynthiana z 41031; pop. incl. with Cynthiana (Inc. Place)
Belton; RMC Place; MUHLENBERG; 180 L-4; 🅿; z 42324; ● 250
Ben Bow; RMC Place; LAWRENCE; *181 H-18; mail Louisa z 41230; rural
Bengal; RMC Place; TAYLOR; *180 K-9; elev. 716ft./218m.; mail Campbellsville z 42718
Benham; Inc. Place; HARLAN; 181 L-17; 🅿; z 40807; Ⓟ 717; Ⓒ 599
Benito; RMC Place; HARLAN; *181 M-17; mail Lejunior z 40849
Bennettstown; RMC Place; CHRISTIAN; 180 M-2; mail Herndon z 42236; ● 35
Benson; RMC Place; FRANKLIN; *181 G-11; mail Frankfort z 40601; rural
Bent; RMC Place; PULASKI; *181 L-13; mail Somerset z 42501; rural
Benton; Inc. Place; ⊡ MARSHALL; 180 F-4; elev. 508ft./155m.; 🅿 🅷; z 42025; Ⓟ 3,899; Ⓒ 4,197
Bentwoods; RMC Place; FRANKLIN; *181 H-11; mail Frankfort z 40601; ● 75
Berea; Inc. Place; MADISON; 181 J-13; elev. 1,034ft./315m.; 🅿 🅷 🅲 1,576; z 40403-04; Ⓟ 9,126; Ⓒ 9,851
Berea College; RMC Place; MADISON; mail Berea z 40404; pop. incl. with Berea (Inc. Place)
Berkeley; CARLISLE; see Berkley (RMC Place)
Berkley (Berkeley, Burkley); RMC Place; CARLISLE; 180 F-2; mail Arlington z 42021; ● 125
Berlin; RMC Place; BRACKEN; 181 E-13; elev. 971ft./296m.; mail Foster z 41043; ● 45
Bernice; RMC Place; CLAY; *181 K-15; elev. 884ft./269m.; mail Fall Rock z 40932; rural
Bernstadt; RMC Place; LAUREL; *181 L-13; mail London z 40741
Berry; Inc. Place; HARRISON; 181 F-13; elev. 676ft./206m.; 🅿; z 41003; Ⓟ 240; Ⓒ 310
Berrytown; RMC Place; JEFFERSON; *180 G-9; ★ LOU; mail Louisville z 40223; became part of Louisville/Jefferson County Metro Jan. 6, 2003
Bethanna; RMC Place; MAGOFFIN; *181 I-17; elev. 858ft./262m.; 🅿; z 41465; rural
Bethany; RMC Place; WOLFE; 181 J-16; elev. 822ft./251m.; 🅿; z 41313; ● 65
Bethel; RMC Place; BATH; 181 G-14; elev. 942ft./287m.; 🅿; z 40374; ● 200
Bethel; RMC Place; JESSAMINE; ★ LEX; mail Nicholasville z 40356; rural
Bethelridge; RMC Place; CASEY; 181 K-12; elev. 1,129ft./344m.; 🅿; z 42516; ● 30
Bethesda; RMC Place; WAYNE; *181 M-11; 🅿; z 42633; rural
Bethlehem; RMC Place; HENRY; 181 G-11; elev. 835ft./255m.; 🅿; z 40007; ● 260
Betsey; RMC Place; WAYNE; *181 M-12; elev. 953ft./290m.; 🅿; z 42633; rural
Betsy Layne; RMC Place; FLOYD; 181 J-18; elev. 665ft./203m.; 🅿; z 41605; ● 450
Beulah; RMC Place; HICKMAN; *180 F-3; elev. 419ft./128m.; mail Fancy Farm z 42039; ● 50
Beulah; RMC Place; HOPKINS; 180 F-3; mail Dawson Springs z 42408; ● 50
Beulah Heights; RMC Place; MCCREARY; 181 M-13; elev. 1,305ft./398m.; mail Whitley City z 42653; ● 50
Beverly; RMC Place; BELL; 181 L-15; elev. 1,275ft./389m.; 🅿; z 40913; ● 30
Beverly Hills; RMC Place; BOYLE; *181 J-11; mail Danville z 40422; pop. incl. with Danville (Inc. Place)
Bevier; RMC Place; MUHLENBERG; *180 K-4; elev. 421ft./128m.; mail Drakesboro z 42337; rural
Bevinsville; FLOYD; see Jacks Creek (RMC Place)
Bewleyville; RMC Place; BRECKINRIDGE; 180 I-7; elev. 711ft./217m.; mail Irvington z 40146; ● 100
Biddle; RMC Place; SCOTT; *181 G-12; elev. 870ft./265m.; mail Georgetown z 40324; rural
Big Bear Creek; RMC Place; MARSHALL; *180 M-1; mail Benton z 42025; summer pop. 250; ● 150
Big Bone; RMC Place; BOONE; *181 E-11; mail Union z 41091; rural
Big Branch; RMC Place; PIKE; *181 K-19; mail Elkhorn City z 41522; ● 50
Big Clifty; RMC Place; GRAYSON; 180 J-7; elev. 752ft./229m.; 🅿; z 42712; ● 300
Big Creek; RMC Place; CLAY; 181 L-15; elev. 857ft./261m.; 🅿; z 40914; ● 300
Big Eddy; RMC Place; FRANKLIN; 181 B-12; mail Frankfort z 40601; ● 150
Big Fork; RMC Place; LESLIE; *181 L-16; mail Yeaddiss z 41777; rural
Biggs; RMC Place; PIKE; *181 J-19; elev. 802ft./244m.; 🅿; z 41524; rural
Bighill; RMC Place; MADISON; 181 J-13; elev. 813ft./248m.; 🅿; z 40405; ● 200
Big Laurel; RMC Place; HARLAN; 181 L-16; elev. 1,319ft./402m.; 🅿; z 40808; ● 120
Big Rock; RMC Place; LESLIE; *181 L-17; elev. 1,337ft./408m.; 🅿; z 41777; rural
Big Sandy Junction; RMC Place; BOYD; *181 F-18; ★ HNTG; mail Catlettsburg z 41129; pop. incl. with Catlettsburg (Inc. Place)
Big Spring; RMC Place; BRECKINRIDGE, HARDIN, MEADE; 180 I-7; elev. 700ft./213m.; 🅿; z 40175; ● 90
Bigstone; RMC Place; ELLIOTT; *181 H-17; mail Sandy Hook z 41171; rural
Big Woods; RMC Place; MENIFEE; *181 H-16; mail Wellington z 40387; rural
Bimble; RMC Place; KNOX; 181 M-15; elev. 1,068ft./326m.; 🅿; z 40915; ● 200
Birdie; RMC Place; ANDERSON; *181 H-11; elev. 896ft./273m.; mail Lawrenceburg z 40342; rural
Birdsville; RMC Place; LIVINGSTON; *180 E-4; mail Smithland z 42081
Birk City; RMC Place; DAVIESS; *180 I-3; ★ OWNS; mail Owensboro z 42301; ● 75
Birmingham; RMC Place; MARSHALL; *180 L-1; mail Gilbertsville z 42044; ● 75
Bishop; RMC Place; FAYETTE; ★ LEX; pop. incl. with Lexington (Inc. Place)
Black Bottom; RMC Place; HARLAN; *181 M-17; mail Evarts z 40828; ● 150
Blackey; Inc. Place; LETCHER; 181 L-17; elev. 993ft./303m.; 🅿; z 41804; Ⓟ 207; Ⓒ 153
Blackford; RMC Place; WEBSTER; 180 J-1; elev. 368ft./112m.; 🅿; z 42403; ● 100
Black Gnat; RMC Place; GREEN, TAYLOR; 180 K-9; mail Campbellsville z 42718; ● 50
Black Gold; RMC Place; EDMONSON; *180 K-6; mail Sweeden z 42285; rural
Black Jack; RMC Place; SIMPSON; *180 M-6; mail Franklin z 42134; ● 80
Blackjack; RMC Place; SIMPSON; *180 M-6; elev. 697ft./212m.; mail Franklin z 42134; rural
Blackmont (Hulen); RMC Place; BELL; 181 M-16; elev. 1,090ft./332m.; mail Hulen z 40845; ● 300
Black Mountain; RMC Place; HARLAN; *181 M-17; mail Kenvir z 40847
Black Rock; RMC Place; GRAYSON; *180 J-6; elev. 738ft./225m.; mail Leitchfield z 42754; ● 30
Black Snake; RMC Place; BELL; 181 M-16; elev. 1,127ft./344m.; mail Hulen z 40845; ● 200
Blackwater; RMC Place; LAUREL; *181 L-14; elev. 1,181ft./360m.; mail London z 40744; rural
Bladeston; RMC Place; BRACKEN; *181 E-14; elev. 862ft./263m.; mail Brooksville z 41004; rural
Blaine; Inc. Place; LAWRENCE; 181 H-18; elev. 655ft./200m.; 🅿; z 41124; Ⓟ 271; Ⓒ 245
Blair; RMC Place; HARLAN; *181 L-17; elev. 1,467ft./447m.; mail Cumberland z 40823; ● 100
Blairs Mill; MORGAN; see Blairs Mills (RMC Place)
Blairs Mills (Blairs Mill); RMC Place; MORGAN; *181 H-16; elev. 1,164ft./355m.; mail West Liberty z 41472; rural
Blair Town; RMC Place; PIKE; *181 J-18; mail Pikeville z 41501; ● 200
Blanche; RMC Place; BELL; *181 M-15; mail Arjay z 40902
Blanchet; RMC Place; GRANT; *181 F-12; elev. 938ft./286m.; 🅿; z 41010; rural
Blandville; Inc. Place; BALLARD; 180 F-2; elev. 467ft./142m.; 🅿; z 42087; Ⓟ 95; Ⓒ 99
Blaze; RMC Place; MORGAN; *181 H-16; elev. 928ft./283m.; 🅿; z 41472; rural
Bledsoe; RMC Place; HARLAN; 181 L-16; elev. 1,432ft./436m.; 🅿; z 40810; ● 50
Blevins; RMC Place; LAWRENCE; *181 H-17; mail Blaine z 41124; rural
Blincoe; RMC Place; WASHINGTON; mail Loretto z 40037; rural
Blood; RMC Place; CALLOWAY; *180 N-1; mail Murray z 42071; rural
Bloomfield; Inc. Place; NELSON; 180 I-10; elev. 657ft./200m.; 🅿; z 40008; Ⓟ 845; Ⓒ 855
Bloomingdale; RMC Place; CLARK; *181 I-13; elev. 612ft./187m.; mail Winchester z 40391; rural
Bloomington; RMC Place; GRAYSON; *180 J-7; mail Leitchfield z 42754; pop. incl. with Leitchfield (Inc. Place)
Bloomington; RMC Place; MAGOFFIN; *181 I-17; mail Salyersville z 41465; rural
Bloss; RMC Place; ROCKCASTLE; *181 K-13; mail Mount Vernon z 40456; rural
Blowing Spring; RMC Place; GREEN; *180 K-9; mail Greensburg z 42743; rural
Bluebank; RMC Place; FLEMING; *181 G-15; mail Flemingsburg z 41041; rural
Blue Diamond; RMC Place; PERRY; *181 K-16; elev. 988ft./301m.; 🅿; z 41719; rural
Blue Grass; RMC Place; FAYETTE; ★ LEX; mail Lexington z 40503, z 40523-24; pop. incl. with Lexington (Inc. Place)
Bluegrass Estates; RMC Place; BOYLE; *181 J-11; mail Danville z 40422; pop. incl. with Danville (Inc. Place)
Blue Heron; RMC Place; MCCREARY; *181 N-12; mail Stearns z 42647; rural
Bluehole; RMC Place; CLAY; *181 L-15; elev. 861ft./262m.; 🅿; z 40962
Blue John; RMC Place; PULASKI; *181 M-12; mail Burnside z 42519; rural
Blue Level; RMC Place; WARREN; *180 L-6; elev. 757ft./231m.; ★ BOWLG; mail Rockfield z 42274; rural
Blue Licks Spring; RMC Place; NICHOLAS, ROBERTSON; *181 F-14; mail Carlisle z 40311
Blue Moon; RMC Place; FLOYD; *181 J-18; mail Printer z 41655; rural
Blue Ridge Manor; Inc. Place; JEFFERSON; 180 B-9; elev. 695ft./212m.; ★ LOU; mail Louisville z 40223; Ⓟ 565; Ⓒ 623
Blue River; RMC Place; FLOYD; 181 J-18; elev. 675ft./206m.; 🅿; z 41607; ● 30
Blue Spring; RMC Place; TRIGG; *180 M-1; mail Cadiz z 42211; ● 50
Bluestone; RMC Place; ROWAN; *181 H-15; mail Morehead z 40351; rural
Blue Water Estates; RMC Place; TRIGG; *180 M-1; mail Cadiz z 42211; ● 50
Bluff Boom; RMC Place; GREEN; *180 K-9; mail Greensburg z 42743; rural
Bluff City; RMC Place; HENDERSON; *180 I-3; mail Henderson z 42420; ● 70
Board Tree; RMC Place; PIKE; 181 J-20; mail Freeburn z 41528; ● 50
Boatwright; RMC Place; CALLOWAY; *180 N-1; mail Murray z 42071; rural
Boaz; RMC Place; GRAVES; 180 F-3; elev. 395ft./120m.; 🅿; z 42027; ● 20
Bobs Creek; RMC Place; HARLAN; *181 M-16; mail Cawood z 40815; ● 125
Bobs Fork; RMC Place; LESLIE; *181 L-16; mail Bear Branch z 41714; ● 175
Bobtown; RMC Place; MADISON; *181 J-13; mail Berea z 40403; rural
Bohon; RMC Place; MERCER; 181 I-11; mail Harrodsburg z 40330; ● 30
Boiling Spring; RMC Place; WARREN; *180 L-7; ★ BOWLG; mail Bowling Green z 42101; rural
Boldman; RMC Place; FLOYD, PIKE; 181 J-18; mail Pikeville z 41501; ● 130
Boles; RMC Place; MONROE; *180 N-9; mail Tompkinsville z 42167; ● 30
Boltsfork; RMC Place; BOYD; *181 G-18; mail Rush z 41168
Bolyn; RMC Place; KNOTT; *181 J-17; mail Garrett z 41630; rural
Bon; RMC Place; WHITLEY; *181 M-13; elev. 979ft./298m.; mail Williamsburg z 40769; rural
Bon Air Hills; RMC Place; FRANKLIN; *181 G-11; mail Frankfort z 40601; ● 100
Bonanza; RMC Place; FLOYD; *181 I-18; mail Prestonsburg z 41653; ● 40
Bonayer; BARREN; see Bon Ayr (RMC Place)
Bon Ayr (Bonayer); RMC Place; BARREN; *180 L-7; mail Park City z 42160; ● 60
Bond; RMC Place; JACKSON; 181 K-14; elev. 1,024ft./312m.; 🅿; z 40402; ● 90
Bondurant; RMC Place; FULTON; *180 G-1; mail Hickman z 42050; rural
Bondville; RMC Place; MERCER; *181 I-11; elev. 779ft./237m.; 🅿; z 40372
Boneyville; RMC Place; LINCOLN; *181 J-12; mail Stanford z 40484; ● 50
Bon Haven; RMC Place; CLARK; *181 H-13; ★ LEX; mail Winchester z 40391; pop. incl. with Winchester (Inc. Place)
Bonnie Brae; RMC Place; SHELBY; *180 G-10; mail Shelbyville z 40065; ● 50
Bonnieville; Inc. Place; HART; 180 K-8; elev. 645ft./197m.; 🅿; z 42713, z 42765; Ⓟ 300; Ⓒ 354
Bonnyman; RMC Place; PERRY; *181 K-16; elev. 917ft./280m.; 🅿; z 41719; ● 300
Booker; RMC Place; WASHINGTON; *180 I-10; mail Springfield z 40069; rural
Boone; RMC Place; ROCKCASTLE; *181 J-13; elev. 1,051ft./320m.; mail Berea z 40403
BOONE; 181 D-11; Ⓟ 57,589; Ⓒ 85,991; ◆ 116,242
Boone Aire (The Crossings); RMC Place; BOONE; *181 D-12; ★ CIN; mail Florence z 41042; ● 1,000
Boone Heights; RMC Place; KNOX; 181 M-14; mail Barbourville z 40906; pop. incl. with Barbourville (Inc. Place)
Boonesboro; MADISON; see Boonesborough (RMC Place)
Boonesborough; RMC Place; CLARK, MADISON; *181 I-13; mail Richmond z 40475
Boonesborough (Boonesboro); RMC Place; MADISON; *181 I-13; mail Richmond z 40475
Booneville; Inc. Place; ⊡ OWSLEY; 181 J-15; elev. 708ft./216m.; 🅿; z 41314; Ⓟ 232; Ⓒ 111
Boons Camp; RMC Place; JOHNSON; 181 I-18; elev. 624ft./190m.; 🅿; z 41204; ● 125
Bordley; RMC Place; UNION; *180 J-2; mail Clay z 42404; rural
Boreing; RMC Place; LAUREL; *181 L-14; mail Lily z 40740; ● 60
Borowick Farms; RMC Place; OLDHAM; *180 G-9; ★ LOU; mail La Grange z 40031; ● 250
Bosco (Hueysville); RMC Place; FLOYD; 181 J-18; elev. 695ft./212m.; mail Hueysville z 41640; ● 200
Boston; RMC Place; BUTLER; *180 L-5; mail Lewisburg z 42256; rural
Boston; RMC Place; NELSON; 180 I-9; elev. 454ft./138m.; 🅿; z 40107; ● 300
Boston; RMC Place; PENDLETON; 181 E-13; elev. 553ft./169m.; mail Butler z 41006; ● 80
Botland; RMC Place; NELSON; *180 I-9; mail Bardstown z 40004; ● 120
Botto; RMC Place; CLAY; *181 L-15; mail Goose Rock z 40944; ● 150
BOURBON; 181 H-13; Ⓟ 19,236; Ⓒ 19,360; ◆ 19,740
Bourbon Downs; RMC Place; NELSON; *180 I-9; mail Bardstown z 40004; pop. incl. with Bardstown (Inc. Place)
Bourbon Furnace; RMC Place; BATH; *181 H-15; mail Owingsville z 40360; rural
Bourne; RMC Place; GARRARD; *181 I-12; elev. 928ft./283m.; mail Lancaster z 40444; rural
Bow; RMC Place; CUMBERLAND; 180 M-10; elev. 575ft./175m.; 🅿; z 42717; ● 25
Bowen; RMC Place; POWELL; 181 I-15; elev. 683ft./208m.; 🅿; z 40380; ● 35
Bowling Green; Inc. Place; ⊡ WARREN; 180 L-6; elev. 496ft./151m.; 🅿 🅷 🅲 18,664 ■; ★ BOWLG; z 42101-04 & mail Drake z 42128; Ⓟ 40,641; Ⓒ 49,296; Ⓡ 49,278; ◆ 59,834
Boyce; RMC Place; WARREN; *180 M-6; elev. 646ft./197m.; mail Alvaton z 42122; rural
Boyd; RMC Place; HARRISON; *181 F-13; mail Berry z 41003; ● 50
BOYD; 181 G-18; Ⓟ 51,150; Ⓒ 49,752; ◆ 47,696
Boyds Crossing; RMC Place; GREEN; *180 K-9; mail Summersville z 42782; rural
Boydsville; RMC Place; GRAVES; *180 G-4; mail Sedalia z 42079; rural
Boydtown; RMC Place; SCOTT; *181 G-12; mail Georgetown z 40324; rural
BOYLE; 181 J-11; Ⓟ 25,641; Ⓒ 27,697; ◆ 28,894
Bracht; RMC Place; KENTON; *181 E-12; elev. 931ft./284m.; ★ CIN; mail Crittenden z 41030
BRACKEN; 181 E-13; Ⓟ 7,766; Ⓒ 8,279; ◆ 8,471
Bracktown; RMC Place; FAYETTE; *181 H-12; ★ LEX; mail Lexington z 40510; pop. incl. with Lexington (Inc. Place)
Bradford; RMC Place; BRACKEN; *181 E-13; mail Foster z 41043; rural
Bradfordsville; Inc. Place; MARION; 180 J-10; elev. 682ft./208m.; 🅿; z 40009; Ⓟ 199; Ⓒ 304
Bradley; RMC Place; MAGOFFIN; *181 I-17; mail Salyersville z 41465; rural
Bradshaw; RMC Place; JACKSON; *181 J-14; mail Gray Hawk z 40434; rural
Brady; RMC Place; ROWAN; *181 G-16; mail Morehead z 40351; pop. incl. with Morehead (Inc. Place)
Brainard; RMC Place; FLOYD; *181 I-17; mail Salyersville z 41465
Bramlett; RMC Place; GREEN; *180 L-9; mail Greensburg z 42743; rural
Brandenburg; Inc. Place; ⊡ MEADE; 180 H-7; elev. 553ft./169m.; 🅿; z 40108; Ⓟ 1,857; Ⓒ 2,049
Brandenburg Station; RMC Place; MEADE; *180 H-7; mail Brandenburg z 40108; ● 50
Brandy; RMC Place; ROWAN; *181 H-16; mail Morehead z 40351; rural
Brandykeg; RMC Place; FLOYD; *181 I-18; mail Prestonsburg z 41653; rural
Brannon (Providence); RMC Place; JESSAMINE; ★ LEX; mail Lexington z 40503
Brassfield; RMC Place; MADISON; *181 J-13; elev. 947ft./289m.; mail Waco z 40385; rural
Braxton; RMC Place; MERCER; *181 I-11; elev. 884ft./269m.; mail Harrodsburg z 40330; rural
Breadens Creek; RMC Place; HARLAN; *181 M-17; mail Closplint z 40927; rural
BREATHITT; 181 J-16; Ⓟ 15,703; Ⓒ 16,100; ◆ 15,522
Breckinridge; RMC Place; HARRISON; *181 F-13; mail Cynthiana z 41031
BRECKINRIDGE; 180 I-6; Ⓟ 16,312; Ⓒ 18,648; ◆ 19,043
Breckinridge Center; CDP-Census Area Only; UNION; *180 I-2; mail Morganfield z 42437; Ⓟ 2,375; Ⓒ 1,874
Breeding; RMC Place; ADAIR; 180 L-9; elev. 1,000ft./305m.; 🅿; z 42715 & mail Glens Fork z 42741; ● 60
Bremen; Inc. Place; MUHLENBERG; 180 K-4; elev. 460ft./140m.; 🅿; z 42325; Ⓟ 267; Ⓒ 365
Brentsville; RMC Place; BOURBON; *181 G-13; mail Paris z 40361
Brentwood; RMC Place; HOPKINS; *180 K-3; mail Madisonville z 42431; pop. incl. with Madisonville (Inc. Place)
Brewers; RMC Place; MARSHALL; 180 F-4; mail Benton z 42025; ● 125

Entries in **UPPERCASE** are counties.
Entries in **bold** have populations of 2,500 or more.
Names in parentheses are alternate names.
Inc. Place — Incorporated Place
RMC Place — Rand McNally Designated Place
CDP — Census Designated Place
MCD — Minor Civil Division

⊡ County Seat
▲ Minor Civil Division
elev. Elevation
🅿 Post Office
🅷 Hospital
🅲 College
■ Principal Business Center
★ Ranally Metro Area (RMA) Abbreviation
z Zip Code(s)
Ⓟ Previous Census Population
Ⓡ Revised Census Population
Ⓐ Annexation Population
● Rand McNally Population Estimate
Ⓒ Final Census Population
Ⓢ Special Census Population
◆ Estimated Population

For additional definitions see Glossary, Volume 1, and Introduction, Volume 2.

Briartown; RMC Place; WASHINGTON; ***180** I-10; mail Springfield **z** 40069
Briarwood; Inc. Place; JEFFERSON; **180** B-9; elev. 630ft./192m.; ★ **LOU**; mail Louisville **z** 40222; Ⓟ 658; © 554
Briarwood Manor; RMC Place; WARREN; ***180** L-6; ★ **BOWLG**; mail Bowling Green **z** 42103; pop. incl. with Bowling Green (Inc. Place)
Bridgeport; RMC Place; FRANKLIN; **181** H-11; mail Frankfort **z** 40601; ● 200
Bridge Street; RMC Place; MCCRACKEN; ***180** E-4; ★ **PAD**; mail Paducah **z** 42003; pop. incl. with Paducah (Inc. Place)
Bridgeville; RMC Place; BRACKEN; ***181** F-14; mail Brooksville **z** 41004; rural
Briensburg; RMC Place; MARSHALL; **180** F-4; mail Benton **z** 42025; ● 250
Brighton; RMC Place; FAYETTE; ***181** H-13; elev. 1,047ft./319m.; ★ **LEX**; mail Lexington **z** 40505; pop. incl. with Lexington (Inc. Place)
Brightshade; RMC Place; CLAY; ***181** L-15; elev. 936ft./285m.; 🅿; **z** 40962; rural
Brinegar; RMC Place; CARTER; ***181** G-16; mail Olive Hill **z** 41164; ● 25
Brinkley; RMC Place; KNOTT; **181** K-17; elev. 1,092ft./333m.; 🅿; **z** 41822; ● 125
Bristow; RMC Place; WARREN; ***180** L-6; elev. 540ft./165m.; ★ **BOWLG**; mail Bowling Green **z** 42101; ● 90
Britmart; RMC Place; TODD; ***180** M-3; mail Elkton **z** 42220; rural
Broadbent Subdivision; RMC Place; TRIGG; ***180** M-2; mail Cadiz **z** 42211; ● 180
Broad Bottom; RMC Place; PIKE; ***181** J-18; elev. 669ft./204m.; 🅿; **z** 41501; rural
Broad Fields; RMC Place; JEFFERSON; **180** B-8; elev. 534ft./163m.; ★ **LOU**; mail Louisville **z** 40207; former incorporated place; became part of St. Matthews July 1, 2000; pop. incl. with Saint Matthews (Inc. Place); Ⓟ 273; © 250
Broad Ford; RMC Place; GRAYSON; ***180** K-7; mail Clarkson **z** 42726
Broadview Manor; RMC Place; FRANKLIN; ***181** H-11; mail Frankfort **z** 40601; ● 100
Broadway; RMC Place; EDMONSON; ***180** K-7; mail Bee Spring **z** 42207; rural
Broadwell; RMC Place; HARRISON; ***181** G-13; mail Cynthiana **z** 41031
Brodhead; Inc. Place; ROCKCASTLE; **181** K-13; elev. 940ft./287m.; 🅿; **z** 40409; Ⓟ 1,140; © 1,193
Broeck Pointe; Inc. Place; JEFFERSON; ***180** G-9; ★ **LOU**; mail Louisville **z** 40201; Ⓟ 325; © 294
Bromley; Inc. Place; KENTON; **181** B-16; elev. 491ft./150m.; 🅿; ★ **CIN**; **z** 41016-17; Ⓟ 1,137; © 838
Bromley; RMC Place; OWEN; ***181** F-11; elev. 914ft./279m.; mail Sparta **z** 41086; rural
Bromo; RMC Place; ROCKCASTLE; mail Mount Vernon **z** 40456; rural
Bronston; RMC Place; PULASKI; **181** L-12; elev. 818ft./249m.; 🅿; **z** 42518; ● 400
Brookhaven; RMC Place; FAYETTE; ***181** H-12; ★ **LEX**; mail Lexington **z** 40503; pop. incl. with Lexington (Inc. Place)
Brooklyn; RMC Place; BUTLER; ***180** K-6; elev. 425ft./130m.; 🅿; **z** 42261; ● 40
Brooks; CDP; BULLITT; **180** H-8; elev. 515ft./157m.; 🅿; ★ **LOU**; **z** 40109; Ⓟ 2,464; © 2,678
Brookside; RMC Place; HARLAN; ***181** M-16; mail Ages Brookside **z** 40801; ● 200
Brooksville; Inc. Place; ⊡ BRACKEN; **181** E-14; elev. 954ft./291m.; 🅿; **z** 41004; Ⓟ 670; © 589
Broughtentown; RMC Place; LINCOLN; **181** K-12; elev. 1,287ft./392m.; mail Crab Orchard **z** 40419; ● 50
Browder; RMC Place; MUHLENBERG; **180** K-4; elev. 423ft./129m.; 🅿; **z** 42326; ● 300
Browning; RMC Place; WARREN; ***180** L-6; elev. 548ft./167m.; 🅿; **z** 42274; rural
Browning Corner; RMC Place; PENDLETON; ***181** F-13; mail Falmouth **z** 41040; rural
Brownsboro; RMC Place; OLDHAM; **180** G-9; ★ **LOU**; mail Crestwood **z** 40014; ● 100
Brownsboro Farm; Inc. Place; JEFFERSON; **180** A-9; elev. 629ft./192m.; ★ **LOU**; mail Louisville **z** 40222; Ⓟ 670; © 676
Brownsboro Village; Inc. Place; JEFFERSON; **180** B-8; elev. 550ft./168m.; ★ **LOU**; mail Louisville **z** 40207; Ⓟ 361; © 318
Browns Crossroads; RMC Place; CLINTON; ***180** M-10; 🅿; **z** 42602; ● 80
Browns Fork; RMC Place; PERRY; ***181** K-16; elev. 907ft./276m.; 🅿; **z** 41701; ● 30
Browns Grove; RMC Place; CALLOWAY, GRAVES; ***180** G-4; mail Murray **z** 42071; rural
Browns Valley; RMC Place; DAVIESS; ***180** J-4; mail Utica **z** 42376; ● 50
Brownsville; Inc. Place; ⊡ EDMONSON; **180** K-7; elev. 537ft./164m.; 🅿; **z** 42210; Ⓟ 897; © 921
Brownsville; RMC Place; FULTON; ***180** G-1; mail Hickman **z** 42050; rural
Brownwood Manor; RMC Place; DAVIESS; ***180** I-4; ★ **OWNS**; mail Owensboro **z** 42303; ● 165
Bruin; RMC Place; ELLIOTT; **181** G-17; elev. 700ft./213m.; 🅿; **z** 41171; ● 60
Brushart; RMC Place; GREENUP; ***181** F-17; mail Greenup **z** 41144; rural
Brush Grove; RMC Place; WASHINGTON; ***180** I-10; mail Mackville **z** 40040
Brutus; RMC Place; CLAY; ***181** K-15; elev. 896ft./273m.; mail Oneida **z** 40972; rural
Bryan; RMC Place; RUSSELL; ***180** M-10; 🅿; **z** 42629; rural
Bryants Store; RMC Place; KNOX; ***181** M-14; elev. 971ft./296m.; 🅿; **z** 40921; ● 40
Bryantsville; RMC Place; GARRARD; **181** I-12; elev. 953ft./290m.; 🅿; **z** 40410; ● 130
Buchanan; RMC Place; LAWRENCE; **181** G-18; mail Catlettsburg **z** 41129; ● 50
Buckettown; MADISON; see Buggytown (RMC Place)
Buckeye; RMC Place; GARRARD; ***181** I-12; elev. 959ft./292m.; mail Lancaster **z** 40444
Buck Grove; RMC Place; MEADE; ***180** I-7; mail Ekron **z** 40117; rural
Buckhorn; Inc. Place; PERRY; **181** K-16; elev. 769ft./234m.; 🅿; **z** 41721; Ⓟ 168; © 144
Buckingham; RMC Place; FLOYD; ***181** K-18; elev. 876ft./267m.; 🅿; **z** 41636; ● 50
Buckner; CDP; OLDHAM; **180** G-9; elev. 831ft./253m.; 🅿; ★ **LOU**; **z** 40010; © 4,000
Buechel; CDP; JEFFERSON; ***180** G-9; elev. 500ft./152m.; 🅿; ★ **LOU**; **z** 40218 & mail Louisville **z** 40228, **z** 40261; former CDP; became part of Louisville/Jefferson County Metro Jan. 6, 2003; Ⓟ 7,081; © 7,272
Buel; RMC Place; MCLEAN; ***180** J-4; elev. 446ft./136m.; mail Calhoun **z** 42327
Buena Vista; RMC Place; GARRARD; ***181** I-12; elev. 860ft./262m.; mail Lancaster **z** 40444
Buena Vista; RMC Place; HARRISON; ***181** F-13; elev. 888ft./271m.; mail Cynthiana **z** 41031; rural
Buena Vista; RMC Place; LEWIS; ***181** F-16; mail Vanceburg **z** 41179; ● 125
Buena Vista; RMC Place; MARSHALL; ***180** L-1; mail Gilbertsville **z** 42044; ● 30
Buffalo; RMC Place; LARUE; **180** J-9; elev. 759ft./231m.; 🅿; **z** 42716; ● 400
Buffalo; RMC Place; TRIGG; ***180** L-2; mail Cadiz **z** 42211; rural
Buffalo Creek; JOHNSON; see Meally (RMC Place)
Buford; RMC Place; OHIO; **180** J-4; elev. 477ft./145m.; mail Utica **z** 42376; ● 75
Bug; RMC Place; CLINTON; ***180** N-10; mail Albany **z** 42602; rural
Buggytown (Buckettown); RMC Place; MADISON; ***181** J-13; mail Richmond **z** 40475; rural
Bugtussle; RMC Place; MONROE; ***180** N-8; mail Gamaliel **z** 42140; rural
Bulan; RMC Place; PERRY; **181** K-17; elev. 904ft./276m.; 🅿; **z** 41722; ● 600
Bull Creek; RMC Place; FLOYD; ***181** I-18; mail Prestonsburg **z** 41653; rural
BULLITT; **180** H-9; Ⓟ 47,567; © 61,236; ◆ 75,457
Bullittsville; RMC Place; BOONE; ***181** D-12; ★ **CIN**; mail Burlington **z** 41005; ● 250
Burdick; RMC Place; TAYLOR; ***180** K-10; elev. 844ft./257m.; mail Campbellsville **z** 42718; rural
Burdine; RMC Place; LETCHER; ***181** K-18; elev. 1,456ft./444m.; 🅿; **z** 41517; pop. incl. with Jenkins (Inc. Place)
Burfield; RMC Place; WAYNE; ***181** M-11; mail Monticello **z** 42633; rural
Burgin; Inc. Place; MERCER; **181** I-11; elev. 893ft./272m.; 🅿; **z** 40310; Ⓟ 1,009; © 874
Burke; RMC Place; ELLIOTT; ***181** H-17; elev. 787ft./240m.; 🅿; **z** 41171; rural
Burkes Spring; RMC Place; MARION; ***180** J-10; mail Loretto **z** 40037; rural
Burkesville; Inc. Place; ⊡ CUMBERLAND; **180** M-10; elev. 582ft./177m.; 🅿 🅷; **z** 42717; Ⓟ 1,815; © 1,756
Burkhart; RMC Place; WOLFE; **181** I-16; elev. 1,020ft./311m.; 🅿; **z** 41301; ● 30
Burk Hollow; RMC Place; WHITLEY; ***181** N-14; mail Williamsburg **z** 40769; ● 75
Burkley; CARLISLE; see Berkley (RMC Place)
Burkshire Terrace; RMC Place; JEFFERSON; ***180** H-8; ★ **LOU**; mail Louisville **z** 40214; became part of Louisville/Jefferson County Metro Jan. 6, 2003
Burlington; CDP; ⊡ BOONE; **181** D-12; elev. 833ft./254m.; 🅿; ★ **CIN**; **z** 41005; Ⓟ 6,070; © 10,779
Burna; RMC Place; LIVINGSTON; **180** D-4; elev. 554ft./169m.; 🅿; **z** 42028; ● 300
Burnaugh; RMC Place; BOYD; **181** G-18; ★ **HNTG**; mail Catlettsburg **z** 41129; ● 175
Burnetta; RMC Place; PULASKI; ***181** L-11; elev. 1,050ft./320m.; mail Nancy **z** 42544; rural
Burning Fork; RMC Place; MAGOFFIN; ***181** I-17; elev. 901ft./275m.; 🅿; **z** 41465; ● 50
Burning Fork; RMC Place; PIKE; ***181** J-19; mail Pikeville **z** 41501; rural
Burning Springs; RMC Place; CLAY; **181** K-15; elev. 908ft./277m.; mail Manchester **z** 40962; ● 100
Burnside; Inc. Place; PULASKI; **181** L-12; elev. 864ft./263m.; 🅿; **z** 42519; Ⓟ 695; © 637
Burnwell (Stringtown); RMC Place; PIKE; ***181** J-20; elev. 679ft./207m.; 🅿; **z** 41514; ● 200
Burr; RMC Place; ROCKCASTLE; ***181** K-13; mail Mount Vernon **z** 40456; ● 85
Burton; RMC Place; FLOYD; **181** K-18; mail Bypro **z** 41612; ● 70
Burtonville; RMC Place; LEWIS; **181** F-15; mail Tollesboro **z** 41189; ● 60
Bush; RMC Place; LAUREL; **181** L-14; elev. 1,214ft./370m.; 🅿; **z** 40724; ● 15
Bushtown; RMC Place; MERCER; ***181** I-11; elev. 878ft./268m.; mail Harrodsburg **z** 40330; rural
Buskirk; MORGAN; see Salem (RMC Place)
Buskirk; RMC Place; PIKE; **181** J-20; mail Mc Carr **z** 41544; ● 150
Busseyville; RMC Place; LAWRENCE; ***181** H-18; mail Louisa **z** 41230; ● 40
Busy; RMC Place; PERRY; ***181** K-16; elev. 829ft./253m.; 🅿; **z** 41723; ● 100
Butler; RMC Place; FRANKLIN; ***181** G-11; mail Frankfort **z** 40601; pop. incl. with Frankfort (Inc. Place)
Butler; Inc. Place; PENDLETON; **181** E-13; elev. 540ft./165m.; 🅿; **z** 41006; Ⓟ 625; © 613
BUTLER; **180** K-6; Ⓟ 11,245; © 13,010; ◆ 12,871
Butterfly; RMC Place; PERRY; ***181** K-16; elev. 837ft./255m.; 🅿; **z** 41719; rural
Buttimer Hill; RMC Place; FRANKLIN; ***181** G-11; mail Frankfort **z** 40601; pop. incl. with Frankfort (Inc. Place)
Buttonsberry; RMC Place; MCLEAN; ***180** J-4; mail Island **z** 42350; ● 90
Bybee; RMC Place; MADISON; **181** I-14; elev. 910ft./277m.; 🅿; **z** 40385; ● 150
Bypro (Wheelwright); RMC Place; FLOYD; ***181** K-18; elev. 945ft./288m.; 🅿; **z** 41612; rural

C

Cabell; RMC Place; WAYNE; ***181** M-11; mail Monticello **z** 42633; ● 50
Cabot; RMC Place; HANCOCK; ***180** I-5; mail Fordsville **z** 42343; rural
Caddo; RMC Place; PENDLETON; ***181** E-13; elev. 910ft./277m.; mail Falmouth **z** 41040
Cadentown; RMC Place; FAYETTE; ***181** H-13; ★ **LEX**; mail Lexington **z** 40505; pop. incl. with Lexington (Inc. Place)
Cadiz; Inc. Place; ⊡ TRIGG; **180** M-2; elev. 423ft./129m.; 🅿 🅷; **z** 42211; Ⓟ 2,148; © 2,373
Cains Store; RMC Place; PULASKI; ***181** L-11; elev. 1,138ft./347m.; 🅿; **z** 42544; rural
Cairo; RMC Place; HENDERSON; **180** I-2; mail Henderson **z** 42420; ● 150
CALDWELL; **180** K-1; Ⓟ 13,232; © 13,060; ◆ 12,698
Caldwell Manor; RMC Place; BOYLE; ***181** J-11; mail Danville **z** 40422; pop. incl. with Danville (Inc. Place)
Caleast; RMC Place; MADISON; ***181** I-13; mail Richmond **z** 40475; rural
Caledonia; RMC Place; TRIGG; ***180** M-2; mail Cadiz **z** 42211, Gracey **z** 42232; rural
Calf Creek; RMC Place; MARTIN; ***181** H-19; mail Inez **z** 41224; ● 120
Calhoun; Inc. Place; ⊡ MCLEAN; **180** J-4; elev. 384ft./117m.; 🅿 🅷; **z** 42327; Ⓟ 854; © 836
California; Inc. Place; CAMPBELL; **181** E-13; elev. 494ft./151m.; 🅿; ★ **CIN**; **z** 41007; Ⓟ 130; © 86
Calla; RMC Place; ESTILL; mail Irvine **z** 40336; rural
Callaway; RMC Place; BELL; **181** M-15; elev. 1,200ft./366m.; 🅿; **z** 40977; ● 300
Calloway; RMC Place; ROCKCASTLE; ***181** K-13; mail Mount Vernon **z** 40456; ● 100
CALLOWAY; **180** N-1; Ⓟ 30,735; © 34,177; ◆ 36,161
Calvary; RMC Place; MARION; **180** J-10; 🅿; **z** 40033; ● 60
Calvert; MARSHALL; see Calvert City (Inc. Place)
Calvert City (Calvert); Inc. Place; MARSHALL; **180** E-4; elev. 353ft./108m.; 🅿; **z** 42029; Ⓟ 2,531; © 2,701
Calvin; RMC Place; BELL; **181** M-15; elev. 1,050ft./320m.; 🅿; **z** 40813; ● 150
Camargo; Inc. Place; MONTGOMERY; **181** H-14; mail Mount Sterling **z** 40353; Ⓟ 1,022; © 923
Cambridge; Inc. Place; JEFFERSON; **180** C-8; elev. 589ft./180m.; ★ **LOU**; mail Louisville **z** 40220; Ⓟ 193; © 192
Cambridge Shores; RMC Place; MARSHALL; ***180** L-1; mail Gilbertsville **z** 42044; ● 250
CAMPBELL; **181** E-13; Ⓟ 83,866; © 88,616; ◆ 86,133
Campbellsburg; Inc. Place; HENRY; **180** F-10; elev. 901ft./275m.; 🅿; **z** 40011; Ⓟ 604; © 705
Campbellsville; Inc. Place; ⊡ TAYLOR; **180** K-10; elev. 813ft./248m.; 🅿 🅷 🅲 2,310; **z** 42718-19; Ⓟ 9,577; © 10,498
Camp Dick Robinson; RMC Place; GARRARD; ***181** I-12; mail Lancaster **z** 40444; rural
Camp Dix; RMC Place; LEWIS; **181** F-16; elev. 636ft./194m.; 🅿; **z** 41179; ● 30
Camp Grounds; RMC Place; LAUREL, KNOX; ***181** L-14; mail Corbin **z** 40701; ● 200
Camp Kennedy; RMC Place; GARRARD; **181** I-12; mail Lancaster **z** 40444; ● 30
Camp Nelson; RMC Place; JESSAMINE; **181** I-12; elev. 860ft./262m.; ★ **LEX**; mail Lancaster **z** 40444; ● 40
Camp Nelson; RMC Place; JESSAMINE; ***181** I-12; ★ **LEX**; mail Nicholasville **z** 40356; rural
Camp Pleasant; RMC Place; FRANKLIN; ***181** G-11; mail Frankfort **z** 40601; rural
Camp Springs; RMC Place; CAMPBELL; ***181** D-13; ★ **CIN**; mail Melbourne **z** 41059; ● 400
Camp Taylor; RMC Place; JEFFERSON; ***180** G-8; ★ **LOU**; mail Louisville **z** 40213; pop. incl. with Louisville (Inc. Place)
Campton; Inc. Place; ⊡ WOLFE; **181** I-15; elev. 975ft./297m.; 🅿; **z** 41301 & mail Slade **z** 40376; Ⓟ 484; © 424
Canada; RMC Place; PIKE; **181** J-19; elev. 838ft./255m.; 🅿; **z** 41519; ● 400
Canby; RMC Place; OWEN; ***181** F-12; mail Corinth **z** 41010; rural
Cane Creek; RMC Place; LAUREL; ***181** L-14; mail London **z** 40744; rural
Cane Valley; RMC Place; ADAIR; **180** L-10; elev. 847ft./258m.; 🅿; **z** 42720; ● 150
Caney; RMC Place; MORGAN; **181** I-16; elev. 866ft./264m.; 🅿; **z** 41472; ● 100
Caneyville; Inc. Place; GRAYSON; **180** K-6; elev. 470ft./143m.; 🅿; **z** 42721; Ⓟ 549; © 627
Canmer; RMC Place; HART; **180** K-8; elev. 645ft./197m.; 🅿; **z** 42722; ● 140
Cannel City; RMC Place; MORGAN; **181** I-16; elev. 887ft./270m.; 🅿; **z** 41408; ● 250
Cannon; RMC Place; KNOX; **181** M-14; elev. 990ft./302m.; 🅿; **z** 40923; ● 150
Cannonsburg; RMC Place; BOYD; **181** G-18; ★ **HNTG**; mail Ashland **z** 41102, **z** 41105; ● 700
Canoe; RMC Place; BREATHITT; ***181** J-16; elev. 726ft./221m.; 🅿; **z** 41339; rural
Canton; RMC Place; TRIGG; **180** M-1; elev. 382ft./116m.; 🅿; **z** 42211; ● 75
Canton Heights Estates; RMC Place; TRIGG; ***180** M-1; mail Cadiz **z** 42211; ● 50
Canyon Falls; RMC Place; LEE; ***181** J-15; mail Beattyville **z** 41311; rural
Capital Estates; RMC Place; FRANKLIN; ***181** G-11; mail Frankfort **z** 40601; ● 30
Capito; RMC Place; BELL; ***181** N-15; mail Middlesboro **z** 40965; rural
Carbondale; RMC Place; HOPKINS; ***180** K-2; mail Dawson Springs **z** 42408; rural
Carbon Glow; RMC Place; LETCHER; ***181** K-17; mail Letcher **z** 41832; ● 30
Carcassonne; RMC Place; LETCHER; ***181** K-17; elev. 640ft./195m.; 🅿; **z** 41804; rural
Cardinal Hill; RMC Place; NELSON; ***180** I-9; mail Bardstown **z** 40004; ● 90
Cardinal Hills; RMC Place; FRANKLIN; ***181** G-11; mail Frankfort **z** 40601; pop. incl. with Frankfort (Inc. Place)
Cardinal Valley; RMC Place; FAYETTE; ***181** H-12; ★ **LEX**; mail Lexington **z** 40503; pop. incl. with Lexington (Inc. Place)
Cardwell; RMC Place; WASHINGTON; ***181** I-11; elev. 847ft./258m.; mail Harrodsburg **z** 40330; rural
Carlisle; Inc. Place; ⊡ NICHOLAS; **181** G-14; elev. 879ft./268m.; 🅿 🅷; **z** 40311 & mail Moorefield **z** 40350; Ⓟ 1,639; © 1,917
CARLISLE; **180** F-2; Ⓟ 5,238; © 5,351; ◆ 4,919
Carntown; RMC Place; PENDLETON; ***181** E-13; mail Butler **z** 41006; rural
Carpenter; RMC Place; WHITLEY; ***181** M-14; elev. 995ft./303m.; mail Barbourville **z** 40906; rural
Carr Creek; RMC Place; KNOTT; ***181** K-17; mail Redfox **z** 41847; rural
Carrie; RMC Place; KNOTT; **181** K-17; elev. 990ft./302m.; 🅿; **z** 41725; ● 80
CARROLL; **180** E-10; Ⓟ 9,292; © 10,155; ◆ 10,630
Carrollton; Inc. Place; ⊡ CARROLL; **180** F-10; elev. 469ft./143m.; 🅿 🅷; **z** 41008 & mail Ghent **z** 41045; Ⓟ 3,715; © 3,846
Carrsville; Inc. Place; LIVINGSTON; **180** D-4; elev. 361ft./110m.; 🅿; **z** 42081; Ⓟ 98; © 64
Carter; RMC Place; CARTER; **181** F-17; elev. 674ft./205m.; 🅿; **z** 41128; ● 50
CARTER; **181** G-17; Ⓟ 24,340; © 26,889; ◆ 27,160
Cartertown; ALLEN; see Walnut Grove (RMC Place)
Carthage; RMC Place; CAMPBELL; ***181** D-13; ★ **CIN**; mail California **z** 41007; rural
Cartwright; RMC Place; CLINTON; **180** M-10; mail Albany **z** 42602; ● 40
Carver; RMC Place; MAGOFFIN; ***181** J-17; elev. 916ft./279m.; 🅿; **z** 41465; rural
Cary; RMC Place; BELL; ***181** M-15; 🅿; **z** 40977; rural
Cary Ridge; CUMBERLAND; see Hickory Grove (RMC Place)
CASEY; **181** K-11; Ⓟ 14,211; © 15,447; ◆ 16,090
Casey Creek; RMC Place; ADAIR; **180** K-10; 🅿; **z** 42728; ● 50
Caseyville; RMC Place; UNION; **180** J-1; mail Sturgis **z** 42459; ● 40
Cash; RMC Place; HART; ***180** J-8; elev. 641ft./195m.; mail Upton **z** 42784; rural
Casky; RMC Place; CHRISTIAN; ***180** M-3; elev. 608ft./185m.; ★ **HPKNV**; mail Hopkinsville **z** 42240; pop. incl. with Hopkinsville (Inc. Place)
Castner; RMC Place; JEFFERSON; ***180** G-9; ★ **LOU**; pop. incl. with Louisville (Inc. Place)
Catalpa; RMC Place; LAWRENCE; ***181** G-18; mail Catlettsburg **z** 41129; ● 75
Catawba; RMC Place; PENDLETON; ***181** E-13; elev. 590ft./180m.; mail Falmouth **z** 41040; rural
Cat Creek; RMC Place; POWELL; ***181** I-15; mail Stanton **z** 40380; ● 50
Catlettsburg; Inc. Place; ⊡ BOYD; **181** F-18; elev. 555ft./169m.; 🅿; ★ **HNTG**; **z** 41129; Ⓟ 2,231; © 1,960
Causey (Baker Fork); RMC Place; LESLIE; ***181** L-16; mail Yeaddiss **z** 41777
Cave City; Inc. Place; BARREN; **180** L-8; elev. 636ft./194m.; 🅿; **z** 42127; Ⓟ 1,953; © 1,880
Cavehill; RMC Place; WARREN; ***180** L-5; mail Rockfield **z** 42274; rural
Cave Ridge; RMC Place; METCALFE; ***180** L-9; mail Edmonton **z** 42129; rural
Cave Spring; RMC Place; LOGAN; ***180** M-4; mail Olmstead **z** 42265, Russellville **z** 42276; rural
Cawood; RMC Place; HARLAN; **181** M-16; elev. 1,253ft./382m.; 🅿; **z** 40815; ● 850
Cayce; RMC Place; FULTON; **180** G-2; mail Fulton **z** 42041; ● 160
Cecil; RMC Place; MCCRACKEN; **180** E-3; ★ **PAD**; mail Paducah **z** 42001; ● 125
Cecilia; RMC Place; HARDIN; **180** J-8; elev. 709ft./216m.; 🅿; **z** 42724; ● 750
Cedar Bluff; RMC Place; CALDWELL; ***180** L-2; elev. 512ft./156m.; mail Princeton **z** 42445; ● 20
Cedar Brook; RMC Place; HARRISON; ***181** G-13; mail Cynthiana **z** 41031; rural
Cedar Flats; RMC Place; METCALFE; ***180** L-9; mail Edmonton **z** 42129; rural
Cedar Grove; RMC Place; TODD; ***180** L-4; elev. 812ft./247m.; mail Elkton **z** 42220; rural
Cedar Hill Heights; RMC Place; PULASKI; ***181** L-12; mail Bronston **z** 42518; ● 190
Cedar Run Creek; RMC Place; FRANKLIN; ***181** H-11; mail Frankfort **z** 40601; ● 200
Cedar Spring; RMC Place; EDMONSON; ***180** L-7; mail Brownsville **z** 42210, Park City **z** 42160; ● 45
Cedar Springs; RMC Place; ALLEN; ***180** M-7; mail Scottsville **z** 42164; rural
Cedarville; PIKE; see Beaver Bottom (RMC Place)
Cedarville; RMC Place; ROCKCASTLE; ***181** K-13; mail Mount Vernon **z** 40456; rural
Center; RMC Place; METCALFE; **180** L-9; elev. 806ft./246m.; 🅿; **z** 42214; ● 125
Centerfield; RMC Place; OLDHAM; ***180** G-9; ★ **LOU**; mail Crestwood **z** 40014; ● 300
Center Point; RMC Place; MONROE; ***180** M-9; mail Tompkinsville **z** 42167; rural
Center Ridge; RMC Place; CALLOWAY; ***180** N-1; mail Murray **z** 42071; ● 120
Centertown; Inc. Place; OHIO; **180** K-4; elev. 424ft./129m.; 🅿; **z** 42328; Ⓟ 383; © 416
Centerview; RMC Place; BRECKINRIDGE; ***180** J-7; elev. 824ft./251m.; mail Hudson **z** 40145; rural
Centerville (Centreville); RMC Place; BOURBON; **181** G-13; mail Georgetown **z** 40324, Paris **z** 40361; ● 120
Central Avenue; RMC Place; MCCRACKEN; ***180** E-3; ★ **PAD**; mail Paducah **z** 42001; pop. incl. with Paducah (Inc. Place)
Central City; Inc. Place; MUHLENBERG; **180** K-4; elev. 415ft./126m.; 🅿; **z** 42330; Ⓟ 4,979; © 5,893
Central Covington; RMC Place; KENTON; ★ **CIN**; pop. incl. with Covington (Inc. Place)
Centreville; BOURBON; see Centerville (RMC Place)
Ceralvo; RMC Place; OHIO; ***180** K-4; mail Rockport **z** 42369; rural
Cerulean; RMC Place; TRIGG; **180** L-2; elev. 513ft./156m.; 🅿; **z** 42215; ● 200
Chad; RMC Place; HARLAN; ***181** L-17; elev. 1,396ft./426m.; 🅿; **z** 40823; rural
Chalybeate; RMC Place; EDMONSON; **180** L-7; mail Smiths Grove **z** 42171; ● 50
Chambers; RMC Place; HANCOCK; ***180** I-5; mail Hawesville **z** 42348; rural
Chance; RMC Place; ADAIR; ***180** L-10; elev. 1,042ft./318m.; mail Columbia **z** 42728; rural
Chandlers Chapel; RMC Place; LOGAN; ***180** L-5; elev. 633ft./193m.; mail Auburn **z** 42206; ● 75
Chandlerville; RMC Place; JOHNSON; ***181** H-18; elev. 801ft./244m.; mail Stambaugh **z** 41257; rural
Chapel Hill; RMC Place; ALLEN; **180** M-7; elev. 751ft./229m.; mail Adolphus **z** 42120; ● 50
Chaplin; RMC Place; NELSON; **180** I-10; elev. 797ft./243m.; 🅿; **z** 40012; ● 500
Chapman; RMC Place; LAWRENCE; ***181** H-18; elev. 588ft./179m.; mail Louisa **z** 41230; ● 45
Chappell; RMC Place; LESLIE; **181** L-16; elev. 1,056ft./322m.; 🅿; **z** 40816; ● 50
Charleston; RMC Place; HOPKINS; **180** K-2; mail Dawson Springs **z** 42408; ● 200
Charleswood; RMC Place; JEFFERSON; ***180** H-9; ★ **LOU**; mail Louisville **z** 40229; became part of Louisville/Jefferson County Metro Jan. 6, 2003
Charley; RMC Place; LAWRENCE; ***181** H-18; mail Louisa **z** 41230; ● 20
Charters; RMC Place; LEWIS; ***181** F-16; mail Vanceburg **z** 41179
Chatham; RMC Place; BRACKEN; **181** E-14; elev. 939ft./286m.; mail Augusta **z** 41002; ● 40
Chavies; RMC Place; PERRY; **181** K-16; elev. 805ft./245m.; 🅿; **z** 41727; ● 170
Chenault; RMC Place; BRECKINRIDGE; ***180** H-6; elev. 420ft./128m.; mail Stephensport **z** 40170; rural
Chenoa; RMC Place; BELL; ***181** N-14; elev. 1,440ft./439m.; 🅿; **z** 40977; rural
Chenowee; RMC Place; BREATHITT; ***181** J-16; mail Jackson **z** 41339; rural
Cherokee; RMC Place; JEFFERSON; ***180** G-9; ★ **LOU**; mail Louisville **z** 40205, **z** 40255; pop. incl. with Louisville (Inc. Place)
Cherokee; RMC Place; LAWRENCE; ***181** H-18; elev. 644ft./196m.; mail Webbville **z** 41180; rural
Cherry; RMC Place; CALLOWAY; ***180** N-1; mail Murray **z** 42071; rural
Cherrywood Village; RMC Place; JEFFERSON; **180** B-8; elev. 534ft./163m.; ★ **LOU**; mail Louisville **z** 40207; former incorporated place; became part of St. Matthews September 1, 2000; pop. incl. with Saint Matthews (Inc. Place); Ⓟ 340; © 327
Chesnutburg; CLAY; see Chestnutburg (RMC Place)
Chestnutburg (Chesnutburg); RMC Place; CLAY; ***181** K-15; elev. 818ft./249m.; 🅿; **z** 40962; rural
Chestnut Gap; RMC Place; OWSLEY; ***181** J-15; elev. 945ft./288m.; mail Booneville **z** 41314; rural
Chestnut Grove; RMC Place; SHELBY; **180** G-10; mail Shelbyville **z** 40065; ● 60
Chevrolet; RMC Place; HARLAN; ***181** M-16; elev. 1,400ft./427m.; 🅿; **z** 40831; ● 150
Chevy Chase; RMC Place; FAYETTE; ***181** H-12; ★ **LEX**; mail Lexington **z** 40502; pop. incl. with Lexington (Inc. Place)
Chicken Bristle; RMC Place; LINCOLN; ***181** J-11; mail Stanford **z** 40484; ● 25
Chilesburg; RMC Place; FAYETTE; ***181** H-13; elev. 1,014ft./309m.; ★ **LEX**; mail Lexington **z** 40509; pop. incl. with Lexington (Inc. Place)
Chloe; RMC Place; PIKE; **181** J-19; mail Pikeville **z** 41501; ● 150
Choateville; RMC Place; FRANKLIN; **181** A-11; mail Frankfort **z** 40601; ● 200
CHRISTIAN; **180** L-3; Ⓟ 68,941; © 72,265; Ⓡ 72,309; ◆ 107,752
Christianburg; RMC Place; SHELBY; ***180** G-10; elev. 904ft./276m.; mail Shelbyville **z** 40065; ● 90
Christine; RMC Place; ADAIR; ***180** L-10; mail Columbia **z** 42728; rural
Christopher; RMC Place; PERRY; ***181** K-17; mail Hazard **z** 41701; ● 75
Church Hill; RMC Place; CHRISTIAN; ***180** M-2; elev. 549ft./167m.; mail Hopkinsville **z** 42240; rural
Cinda; RMC Place; LESLIE; **181** L-16; elev. 978ft./298m.; 🅿; **z** 41776; ● 60
Cinderella Estates; RMC Place; JEFFERSON; ***180** H-9; ★ **LOU**; mail Louisville **z** 40229; became part of Louisville/Jefferson County Metro Jan. 6, 2003
Cisco; RMC Place; MAGOFFIN; ***181** I-17; elev. 900ft./274m.; 🅿; **z** 41465; ● 15
Cisselville; RMC Place; WASHINGTON; ***180** I-10; mail Springfield **z** 40069; rural
Clabber Bottom; RMC Place; SCOTT; ***181** G-12; ★ **LEX**; mail Georgetown **z** 40324; ● 25
Clare; RMC Place; ALLEN; ***180** M-6; mail Franklin **z** 42134; rural
Clarence; RMC Place; PULASKI; ***181** K-12; mail Eubank **z** 42567; rural
Clark; RMC Place; SHELBY, JEFFERSON; ***180** G-9; mail Fisherville **z** 40023; ● 60
CLARK; **181** H-13; Ⓟ 29,496; © 33,144; ◆ 36,158
Clark Hill; RMC Place; CARTER; **181** G-16; mail Olive Hill **z** 41164; ● 300
Clarksburg; RMC Place; LEWIS; ***181** F-16; elev. 548ft./167m.; mail Vanceburg **z** 41179
Clarkson; Inc. Place; GRAYSON; **180** J-7; elev. 731ft./223m.; 🅿; **z** 42726; Ⓟ 611; © 794
Clark Street; RMC Place; MCCRACKEN; ***180** E-3; ★ **PAD**; mail Paducah **z** 42001; pop. incl. with Paducah (Inc. Place)
Claryville; CDP; CAMPBELL; ***181** E-13; elev. 736ft./224m.; ★ **CIN**; mail Alexandria **z** 41001; Ⓟ 2,038; © 2,588
Claxton; RMC Place; CALDWELL; ***180** L-2; mail Dawson Springs **z** 42408; rural
Clay; Inc. Place; WEBSTER; **180** J-2; elev. 379ft./116m.; 🅿; **z** 42404; Ⓟ 1,173; © 1,179
CLAY; **181** K-15; Ⓟ 21,746; © 24,556; ◆ 23,512
Clay City; Inc. Place; POWELL; **181** I-14; elev. 621ft./189m.; 🅿; **z** 40312; Ⓟ 1,258; © 1,303
Clayhole; RMC Place; BREATHITT; ***181** J-16; elev. 789ft./240m.; 🅿; **z** 41317; ● 30
Clay Lick; RMC Place; MENIFEE; ***181** H-15; mail Jeffersonville **z** 40337; rural
Claymour; RMC Place; TODD; ***180** M-4; elev. 678ft./207m.; mail Elkton **z** 42220
Claypool; RMC Place; WARREN; ***180** M-7; elev. 599ft./183m.; mail Bowling Green **z** 42103; rural
Claysville; RMC Place; HARRISON; **181** F-13; elev. 582ft./177m.; mail Cynthiana **z** 41031; ● 50
Clay Village; RMC Place; SHELBY; ***180** G-10; elev. 908ft./277m.; mail Shelbyville **z** 40065; ● 140
Clear Creek Junction; RMC Place; FLOYD
Clear Creek Springs; RMC Place; BELL; ***181** M-15; 🅿; **z** 40977; ● 120
Clearfield; RMC Place; ROWAN; **181** H-16; elev. 716ft./218m.; 🅿; **z** 40313; ● 1,300
Cleaton; RMC Place; MUHLENBERG; **180** K-4; elev. 422ft./129m.; 🅿; **z** 42332; ● 500
Clementsville; RMC Place; CASEY; **180** K-10; elev. 771ft./235m.; 🅿; **z** 42539; ● 75
Clemons; RMC Place; PERRY; ***181** K-16; elev. 928ft./283m.; mail Bonnyman **z** 41719; ● 150
Cleopatra; RMC Place; MCLEAN; ***180** J-3; mail Calhoun **z** 42327; rural
Clermont; RMC Place; BULLITT; **180** I-9; elev. 478ft./146m.; 🅿; ★ **LOU**; **z** 40110; ● 250
Cliff; RMC Place; FLOYD; ***181** I-18; mail Prestonsburg **z** 41653; pop. incl. with Prestonsburg (Inc. Place)
Clifford; RMC Place; LAWRENCE; **181** H-19; elev. 583ft./178m.; 🅿; **z** 41230; ● 40
Clifton; RMC Place; WOODFORD; **181** H-11; mail Versailles **z** 40383; ● 200
Cliftons; RMC Place; JEFFERSON; ★ **LOU**; became part of Louisville/Jefferson County Metro Jan. 6, 2003
Clifty; RMC Place; TODD; **180** L-4; elev. 813ft./248m.; 🅿; **z** 42216; ● 275
Climax; RMC Place; ROCKCASTLE; ***181** J-13; elev. 1,254ft./382m.; 🅿; **z** 40456; ● 40
Clinton; Inc. Place; ⊡ HICKMAN; **180** G-2; elev. 354ft./108m.; 🅿; **z** 42031; Ⓟ 1,547; © 1,415
CLINTON; **181** M-11; Ⓟ 9,135; © 9,634; ◆ 9,637
Clintonville; RMC Place; BOURBON; ***181** H-13; mail Paris **z** 40361; ● 80
Clio; RMC Place; WHITLEY; ***181** M-13; elev. 1,048ft./319m.; mail Williamsburg **z** 40769; rural
Closplint; RMC Place; HARLAN; **181** M-17; elev. 1,550ft./472m.; 🅿; **z** 40927; ● 150
Clover Bottom; RMC Place; JACKSON; ***181** J-13; elev. 1,471ft./448m.; 🅿; **z** 40447; rural
Cloverdale; RMC Place; FRANKLIN; ***181** H-11; mail Frankfort **z** 40601; pop. incl. with Frankfort (Inc. Place)
Clover-Darby; RMC Place; HARLAN; ***181** M-17; mail Closplint **z** 40927; ● 30
Cloverport; Inc. Place; BRECKINRIDGE; **180** I-6; elev. 411ft./125m.; 🅿; **z** 40111; Ⓟ 1,207; © 1,256
Clovertown; RMC Place; HARLAN; ***181** M-16; mail Harlan **z** 40831; ● 200
Cloyds Landing; RMC Place; CUMBERLAND; ***180** M-9; mail Burkesville **z** 42717; rural
Clutts; RMC Place; HARLAN; ***181** L-17; mail Cumberland **z** 40823; pop. incl. with Cumberland (Inc. Place)
Clyffeside; RMC Place; BOYD; ★ **HNTG**; pop. incl. with Ashland (Inc. Place)
Coakley; RMC Place; GREEN; ***180** K-9; mail Greensburg **z** 42743; rural
Coalgood; HARLAN; see Mary Helen (RMC Place)
Coal Run; PIKE; see Coal Run Village (Inc. Place)
Coal Run Village (Coal Run); Inc. Place; PIKE; **181** J-19; elev. 678ft./207m.; mail Pikeville **z** 41501; Ⓟ 262; © 577
Coalton; RMC Place; BOYD; ***181** G-18; elev. 616ft./188m.; ★ **HNTG**; mail Rush **z** 41168; ● 125
Cobb; RMC Place; CALDWELL; **180** L-2; mail Princeton **z** 42445; ● 30
Cobhill; RMC Place; ESTILL; ***181** I-14; elev. 1,228ft./374m.; 🅿; **z** 40336; ● 40
Coburg; RMC Place; ADAIR; ***180** K-10; mail Greensburg **z** 42743
Codyville; RMC Place; BRECKINRIDGE; ***180** I-6; elev. 714ft./218m.; mail Hardinsburg **z** 40143; pop. incl. with Hardinsburg (Inc. Place)
Cofer; RMC Place; METCALFE; ***180** L-9; mail Edmonton **z** 42129; rural
Colby; RMC Place; CLARK; ***181** H-13; elev. 1,030ft./314m.; mail Winchester **z** 40391; ● 30
Colby Hills; RMC Place; CLARK; ***181** H-13; ★ **LEX**; mail Winchester **z** 40391; ● 75
Coldiron; RMC Place; HARLAN; ***181** M-16; elev. 1,117ft./340m.; 🅿; **z** 40819; ● 200
Cold Spring; Inc. Place; CAMPBELL; **181** C-17; elev. 859ft./262m.; 🅿; ★ **CIN**; **z** 41076; Ⓟ 2,880; © 3,806
Cold Spring-Highland Heights; RMC Place; CAMPBELL; ***181** D-12; ★ **CIN**; mail Newport **z** 41076; pop. incl. with Highland Heights (Inc. Place)
Coldstream; Inc. Place; JEFFERSON; **180** A-10; ★ **LOU**; mail Louisville **z** 40202; Ⓟ 862; © 956
Coldwater; RMC Place; CALLOWAY; **180** G-4; elev. 343ft./105m.; mail Murray **z** 42071; ● 125
Coleman; RMC Place; PIKE; ***181** J-20; mail Phelps **z** 41553
Colemansville; RMC Place; HARRISON; **181** F-13; mail Berry **z** 41003; ● 40
Colesburg; RMC Place; HARDIN; **180** I-8; elev. 447ft./136m.; mail Lebanon Junction **z** 40150; ● 90
Coletown; RMC Place; FAYETTE; ***181** H-12; ★ **LEX**; mail Lexington **z** 40515; pop. incl. with Lexington (Inc. Place)
Colfax; RMC Place; FLEMING; ***181** G-15; mail Hillsboro **z** 41049; rural
College Farm; RMC Place; PIKE; ***181** J-19; mail Pikeville **z** 41501; rural
College Heights; RMC Place; WARREN; ***180** L-6; ★ **BOWLG**; mail Bowling Green **z** 42101; pop. incl. with Bowling Green (Inc. Place)
College Hill; RMC Place; MADISON; ***181** I-14; elev. 894ft./272m.; 🅿; **z** 40385
College Park; RMC Place; FRANKLIN; ***181** G-11; mail Frankfort **z** 40601; pop. incl. with Frankfort (Inc. Place)
Collins; RMC Place; PIKE; ***181** J-19; mail Pikeville **z** 41501; ● 100
Collista; RMC Place; JOHNSON; ***181** I-18; mail Hagerhill **z** 41222; rural
Colmar; RMC Place; BELL; ***181** N-15; mail Middlesboro **z** 40965; ● 80
Colonial Terrace; RMC Place; JEFFERSON; **180** B-9; ★ **LOU**; mail Louisville **z** 40222; became part of Louisville/Jefferson County Metro Jan. 6, 2003; pop. incl. with Louisville (Inc. Place)
Colony; RMC Place; FRANKLIN; ***181** G-11; mail Frankfort **z** 40601; pop. incl. with Frankfort (Inc. Place)
Colson; RMC Place; LETCHER; ***181** K-18; elev. 1,163ft./354m.; mail Whitesburg **z** 41858
Columbia; Inc. Place; ⊡ ADAIR; **180** L-10; elev. 752ft./229m.; 🅿 🅷 🅲 1,792; **z** 42728 & mail Knifley **z** 42753; Ⓟ 3,845; © 4,014
Columbus; Inc. Place; HICKMAN; **180** F-2; elev. 463ft./141m.; 🅿; **z** 42032; Ⓟ 252; © 229
Colville; RMC Place; HARRISON; ***181** G-13; elev. 888ft./271m.; mail Cynthiana **z** 41031
Combs; RMC Place; PERRY; **181** K-16; elev. 839ft./256m.; 🅿; **z** 41729; ● 900
Comer; RMC Place; MCLEAN; ***180** J-3; mail Calhoun **z** 42327
Concord; RMC Place; FLEMING; ***181** G-15; elev. 858ft./262m.; mail Flemingsburg **z** 41041; rural
Concord; Inc. Place; LEWIS; **181** E-15; elev. 526ft./160m.; 🅿; **z** 41179; Ⓟ 65; © 28
Concord; RMC Place; PENDLETON; ***181** E-13; mail Falmouth **z** 41040; rural
Concordia; RMC Place; MEADE; ***180** H-6; elev. 428ft./130m.; mail Payneville **z** 40157; ● 40
Conder; RMC Place; PIKE; ***181** I-19; mail Belfry **z** 41514; rural
Confederate; RMC Place; LYON; ***180** L-1; elev. 588ft./179m.; mail Eddyville **z** 42038; rural
Confederate Estates; RMC Place; OLDHAM; ***180** G-9; ★ **LOU**; mail Pewee Valley **z** 40056; ● 500
Confluence; RMC Place; LESLIE; **181** K-16; elev. 805ft./245m.; 🅿; **z** 41749; ● 20
Congleton; RMC Place; LEE; ***181** J-15; mail Beattyville **z** 41311; rural
Congleton; RMC Place; MCLEAN; ***180** J-3; mail Calhoun **z** 42327; rural
Conley; RMC Place; MAGOFFIN; ***181** I-17; elev. 918ft./280m.; 🅿; **z** 41465; rural
Connersville; RMC Place; HARRISON; **181** G-13; mail Cynthiana **z** 41031; ● 35
Conoloway; RMC Place; GRAYSON; ***180** K-7; mail Clarkson **z** 42726; ● 50
Consolation; RMC Place; SHELBY; ***181** G-11; mail Bagdad **z** 40003; rural
Constance; RMC Place; BOONE; **181** D-12; elev. 488ft./149m.; ★ **CIN**; mail Hebron **z** 41048; ● 100
Constantine; RMC Place; BRECKINRIDGE; **180** J-7; elev. 813ft./248m.; 🅿; **z** 40140; ● 40
Conway; RMC Place; ROCKCASTLE; **181** J-13; elev. 975ft./297m.; 🅿; **z** 40456; ● 50
Cooktown; RMC Place; BARREN; ***180** M-8; mail Austin **z** 42123; rural
Coolbrook; RMC Place; FRANKLIN; ***181** H-11; mail Frankfort **z** 40601; ● 250
Cool Springs; RMC Place; OHIO; **180** K-5; mail Beaver Dam **z** 42320; ● 50
Cooper; RMC Place; WAYNE; ***181** M-11; mail Monticello **z** 42633; rural
Co-Operative; RMC Place; MCCREARY; **181** M-12; elev. 900ft./274m.; mail Stearns **z** 42647; ● 180
Cooperstown; RMC Place; LOGAN; ***180** L-5; mail Lewisburg **z** 42256, Russellville **z** 42276; rural
Coopersville; RMC Place; WAYNE; **181** M-12; elev. 861ft./262m.; 🅿; **z** 42633; ● 80
Copebranch; RMC Place; BREATHITT; ***181** J-15; elev. 690ft./210m.; mail Jackson **z** 41339; rural
Copland (Saldee); RMC Place; BREATHITT; ***181** J-16; elev. 765ft./233m.; mail Jackson **z** 41339; rural
Copperfield; RMC Place; JEFFERSON; ***180** G-9; ★ **LOU**; mail Louisville **z** 40223; became part of Louisville/Jefferson County Metro Jan. 6, 2003
Coral Hill; RMC Place; BARREN; ***180** L-8; elev. 849ft./259m.; mail Glasgow **z** 42141; rural
Coral Ridge; RMC Place; JEFFERSON; **180** E-7; ★ **LOU**; mail Fairdale **z** 40118; became part of Louisville/Jefferson County Metro Jan. 6, 2003
Corbin; Inc. Place; WHITLEY, KNOX; **181** L-14; elev. 1,080ft./329m.; 🅿 🅷 ■; **z** 40701-02; Ⓟ 7,419; © 7,742; ◆ 7,791
Cordell; RMC Place; LAWRENCE; ***181** H-18; mail Blaine **z** 41124; rural
Cordia; RMC Place; KNOTT; ***181** K-17; mail Hazard **z** 41701; rural
Cordova; RMC Place; GRANT; ***181** F-12; elev. 734ft./224m.; mail Corinth **z** 41010
Corey; RMC Place; CARTER; ***181** G-17; mail Grahn **z** 41142; rural
Corinth; Inc. Place; GRANT, HARRISON, SCOTT; **181** F-12; elev. 1,001ft./305m.; 🅿; **z** 41010; Ⓟ 137; © 181
Corinth; RMC Place; LOGAN; ***180** M-5; mail Russellville **z** 42276
Cork; RMC Place; METCALFE; ***180** L-9; elev. 956ft./291m.; mail Edmonton **z** 42129; rural
Corn Creek; RMC Place; TRIMBLE; ***180** F-9; mail Bedford **z** 40006; rural
Corners; RMC Place; BRECKINRIDGE; ***180** I-7; elev. 616ft./188m.; mail Irvington **z** 40146; rural
Cornette; RMC Place; LAUREL; ***181** K-14; mail East Bernstadt **z** 40729; rural
Cornettsville; RMC Place; PERRY; **181** L-17; elev. 953ft./290m.; 🅿; **z** 41731; ● 90
Cornishville; RMC Place; MERCER; **181** I-11; elev. 733ft./223m.; 🅿; **z** 40330; ● 90
Corydon; Inc. Place; HENDERSON; **180** I-2; elev. 458ft./140m.; 🅿; **z** 42406; Ⓟ 790; © 744
Costelow; RMC Place; LOGAN; ***180** L-5; mail Russellville **z** 42276; rural
Cote; RMC Place; HARLAN; mail Evarts **z** 40828; rural
Cottageville; RMC Place; LEWIS; ***181** F-15; mail Vanceburg **z** 41179; rural
Cottle; RMC Place; MORGAN; ***181** I-16; elev. 1,022ft./312m.; 🅿; **z** 41472
Cottonburg; RMC Place; MADISON; ***181** I-12; elev. 969ft./295m.; mail Richmond **z** 40475; rural
Country Club Estates; RMC Place; MADISON; ***181** I-13; mail Richmond **z** 40475; pop. incl. with Huntsville (Inc. Place)
Country Club Heights; RMC Place; FRANKLIN; ***181** G-11; mail Frankfort **z** 40601; pop. incl. with Frankfort (Inc. Place)
Country Club Heights; RMC Place; MASON; ***181** F-15; mail Maysville **z** 41056; pop. incl. with Maysville (Inc. Place)
Country Lane Estates; RMC Place; FRANKLIN; ***181** G-11; mail Frankfort **z** 40601; ● 250
Country Manor; RMC Place; SHELBY; ***180** G-10; mail Shelbyville **z** 40065; ● 200
Countryside; RMC Place; OLDHAM; ***180** G-9; ★ **LOU**; mail Prospect **z** 40059; ● 300
Country Village; RMC Place; OLDHAM; ***180** G-9; ★ **LOU**; mail Crestwood **z** 40014; ● 200
Counts Crossroads; RMC Place; CARTER; ***181** G-17; mail Olive Hill **z** 41164; ● 150
Covedale; RMC Place; LEWIS; ***181** F-15; elev. 927ft./283m.; mail Vanceburg **z** 41179; rural
Covington; Inc. Place; KENTON; **181** D-12; elev. 531ft./162m.; 🅿 🅷 ■; ★ **CIN**; **z** 41011-12, **z** 41014-19 & mail Independence **z** 41051; Ⓟ 43,264; © 43,370; ◆ 45,301
Cowan; RMC Place; FLEMING; **181** G-14; mail Ewing **z** 41039; ● 150
Cow Creek; RMC Place; ESTILL; ***181** I-14; mail Ravenna **z** 40472; rural
Cowcreek; RMC Place; OWSLEY; ***181** J-15; mail Booneville **z** 41314; rural
Cox Bend; RMC Place; PULASKI; ***181** L-12; mail Burnside **z** 42519; ● 300
Coxs Creek; RMC Place; NELSON; **180** I-9; elev. 700ft./213m.; 🅿; **z** 40013; ● 50
Coxton; RMC Place; HARLAN; ***181** M-16; elev. 1,224ft./373m.; mail Harlan **z** 40831; ● 200
Crab Orchard; Inc. Place; LINCOLN; **181** J-12; elev. 952ft./290m.; 🅿; **z** 40419; Ⓟ 825; © 842
Cracker; RMC Place; FLOYD; ***181** J-18; mail Martin **z** 41649; rural
Crailhope; RMC Place; GREEN; ***180** L-9; mail Center **z** 42214; rural
Craintown; RMC Place; FLEMING; ***181** G-15; mail Flemingsburg **z** 41041; rural
Crane Nest; RMC Place; KNOX; ***181** L-14; elev. 1,012ft./308m.; 🅿; **z** 40906; rural
Cranks; RMC Place; HARLAN; **181** M-17; elev. 1,447ft./441m.; 🅿; **z** 40820; ● 120
Cranston; RMC Place; ROWAN; ***181** G-16; elev. 769ft./234m.; mail Morehead **z** 40351; rural
Crawford; RMC Place; PERRY; ***181** K-16; mail Bonnyman **z** 41719; rural
Crayne; RMC Place; CRITTENDEN; **180** K-1; elev. 642ft./196m.; 🅿; **z** 42033; ● 150
Craynor; RMC Place; FLOYD; **181** J-18; elev. 1,000ft./305m.; 🅿; **z** 41635; ● 85
Creal; RMC Place; GREEN; ***180** K-9; mail Mount Sherman **z** 42764; rural
Creech; HARLAN; see Twila (RMC Place)
Creekmore; RMC Place; MCCREARY; ***181** N-13; mail Strunk **z** 42649; rural
Creekside; Inc. Place; JEFFERSON; ***180** G-9; ★ **LOU**; mail Louisville **z** 40222; Ⓟ 323; © 336
Creekville; RMC Place; CLAY; ***181** L-15; mail Manchester **z** 40962; rural
Creelsboro; RMC Place; RUSSELL; ***180** M-10; elev. 613ft./187m.; 🅿; **z** 42629; rural
Crenshaw; RMC Place; SPENCER; ***180** H-9; elev. 609ft./186m.; mail Taylorsville **z** 40071; rural
Crescent Hill; RMC Place; JEFFERSON; ***180** G-9; ★ **LOU**; mail Louisville **z** 40206; pop. incl. with Louisville (Inc. Place)
Crescent Park; RMC Place; KENTON; **181** C-15; 🅿; ★ **CIN**; **z** 41017; pop. incl. with Fort Mitchell (Inc. Place); Ⓟ 364
Crescent Springs; Inc. Place; KENTON; **181** B-15; elev. 742ft./226m.; 🅿; ★ **CIN**; **z** 41017; Ⓟ 2,179; © 3,931
Cressmont; RMC Place; LEE; ***181** J-15; mail Beattyville **z** 41311; rural
Crest; RMC Place; HARDIN; ***180** I-8; mail Elizabethtown **z** 42701; rural
Crestmoor; RMC Place; WARREN; ***180** L-6; ★ **BOWLG**; mail Bowling Green **z** 42101; pop. incl. with Bowling Green (Inc. Place)
Creston; RMC Place; CASEY; ***181** K-11; elev. 1,065ft./325m.; mail Liberty **z** 42539; rural
Crestview; Inc. Place; CAMPBELL; **181** C-18; elev. 848ft./258m.; ★ **CIN**; mail Newport **z** 41076; Ⓟ 356; © 471
Crestview Hills; Inc. Place; KENTON; **181** C-15; elev. 880ft./268m.; 🅿 🅲 1,400; ★ **CIN**; **z** 41017; Ⓟ 2,546; © 2,889
Crestwood; RMC Place; FAYETTE; ***181** H-12; ★ **LEX**; mail Lexington **z** 40503; pop. incl. with Lexington (Inc. Place)
Crestwood; RMC Place; FRANKLIN; ***181** F-11; mail Frankfort **z** 40601
Crestwood; Inc. Place; OLDHAM; **180** G-9; elev. 798ft./243m.; 🅿; ★ **LOU**; **z** 40014; includes Park Lake annexed May 1, 2006; Ⓟ 1,435; © 1,999; Ⓐ 2,536
Creswell; RMC Place; CALDWELL; ***180** K-1; mail Fredonia **z** 42411; rural
Crider; RMC Place; CALDWELL; **180** K-1; mail Princeton **z** 42445; ● 60
Crittenden; Inc. Place; GRANT; **181** E-12; elev. 918ft./280m.; 🅿; ★ **CIN**; **z** 41030; Ⓟ 731; © 2,401
CRITTENDEN; **180** J-1; Ⓟ 9,196; © 9,384; ◆ 9,069
Crix; RMC Place; ROWAN; ***181** H-16; mail Clearfield **z** 40313; rural
Croakes; RMC Place; WASHINGTON; ***180** I-10; mail Springfield **z** 40069; rural
Crockett; RMC Place; MORGAN; **181** H-17; elev. 871ft./265m.; 🅿; **z** 41413; ● 40
Crocus; RMC Place; ADAIR; ***180** L-10; mail Columbia **z** 42728; rural
Crofton; Inc. Place; CHRISTIAN; **180** L-3; elev. 608ft./185m.; 🅿; **z** 42217; Ⓟ 699; © 838; Ⓡ 871
Croley; RMC Place; HICKMAN; ***180** G-2; mail Clinton **z** 42031; rural
Cromona (Haymond); RMC Place; LETCHER; **181** K-18; elev. 1,304ft./397m.; 🅿; **z** 41810; ● 400
Cromwell; RMC Place; OHIO; **180** K-5; elev. 461ft./141m.; 🅿; **z** 42333; ● 240
Cropper; RMC Place; SHELBY; **180** G-10; elev. 900ft./274m.; 🅿; **z** 40057; ● 150
Crossgate; Inc. Place; JEFFERSON; ***180** G-9; elev. 550ft./168m.; ★ **LOU**; mail Louisville **z** 40222; Ⓟ 261; © 251
Cross Keys; RMC Place; SHELBY; ***180** G-10; mail Shelbyville **z** 40065; ● 100
Crossland; RMC Place; CALLOWAY; **180** G-4; mail Hazel **z** 42049; ● 50
Crown; RMC Place; LETCHER; **181** K-18; elev. 1,279ft./390m.; 🅿; **z** 41858; ● 50
Crowtown; RMC Place; CALDWELL; ***180** L-1; elev. 566ft./173m.; mail Princeton **z** 42445; pop. incl. with Princeton (Inc. Place)
Crummies; RMC Place; HARLAN; ***181** M-17; elev. 1,419ft./433m.; 🅿; **z** 40815; ● 50
Crutchfield; RMC Place; FULTON; **180** G-2; elev. 368ft./112m.; 🅿; **z** 42041; ● 110
Crystal; RMC Place; ESTILL; **181** J-14; elev. 620ft./189m.; 🅿; **z** 40336; ● 20
Crystal Lake; RMC Place; OLDHAM; ***180** G-10; ★ **LOU**; mail La Grange **z** 40031; ● 200
Cuba; RMC Place; GRAVES; **180** G-3; mail Mayfield **z** 42066; ● 125
Cubage; RMC Place; BELL; ***181** M-16; elev. 1,161ft./354m.; mail Miracle **z** 40856; rural
Cub Run; RMC Place; HART; **180** K-7; elev. 706ft./215m.; 🅿; **z** 42729; ● 125
Culver; RMC Place; ELLIOTT; **181** H-17; elev. 740ft./226m.; 🅿; **z** 41171; ● 30
Culvertown; RMC Place; NELSON; ***180** I-9; elev. 651ft./198m.; mail New Haven **z** 40051; rural
Cumberland; Inc. Place; HARLAN; **181** L-17; elev. 1,440ft./439m.; 🅿; **z** 40823; Ⓟ 3,112; © 2,611
CUMBERLAND; **180** M-9; Ⓟ 6,784; © 7,147; ◆ 6,650
Cumberland City; RMC Place; CLINTON; ***181** M-11; elev. 1,053ft./321m.; mail Albany **z** 42602; rural
Cumberland Falls; MCCREARY; see Parkers Lake (RMC Place)
Cumberlane Estates; RMC Place; TAYLOR; ***180** K-10; mail Campbellsville **z** 42718; pop. incl. with Campbellsville (Inc. Place)
Cumminsville; RMC Place; BRACKEN; ***181** E-14; mail Brooksville **z** 41004; rural
Cundiff; RMC Place; ADAIR; ***180** L-10; elev. 976ft./297m.; 🅿; **z** 42728
Cunningham; RMC Place; CARLISLE; **180** F-3; elev. 398ft./121m.; 🅿; **z** 42035; ● 400
Cupio; RMC Place; BULLITT; ***180** H-8; ★ **LOU**; mail West Point **z** 40177; rural
Curdsville; RMC Place; DAVIESS; **180** I-3; elev. 392ft./119m.; 🅿; **z** 42334; ● 150
Curdsville; RMC Place; MERCER; ***181** I-12; mail Harrodsburg **z** 40330; rural
Curt; RMC Place; BREATHITT; ***181** J-16; mail Jackson **z** 41339; rural
Custer; RMC Place; BRECKINRIDGE; **180** I-7; elev. 824ft./251m.; 🅿; **z** 40115; ● 125
Cutshin; RMC Place; LESLIE; **181** L-16; elev. 1,012ft./308m.; 🅿; **z** 41776; ● 100
Cutuno; RMC Place; MAGOFFIN; ***181** I-16; elev. 1,000ft./305m.; 🅿; **z** 41465; rural
Cuzick; RMC Place; MADISON; ***181** I-12; mail Richmond **z** 40475; rural
Cyclone; RMC Place; MONROE; ***180** M-9; mail Summer Shade **z** 42166; rural
Cynthiana; Inc. Place; ⊡ HARRISON; **181** G-13; elev. 723ft./220m.; 🅿 🅷; **z** 41031; Ⓟ 6,497; © 6,258

D

Dabney; RMC Place; PULASKI; ***181** K-12; elev. 1,059ft./323m.; mail Somerset **z** 42501; rural
Dabolt; RMC Place; JACKSON; ***181** K-14; elev. 1,342ft./409m.; 🅿; **z** 40402; ● 25
Dahl; RMC Place; PULASKI; ***181** K-13; mail Somerset **z** 42501; rural
Daisy; RMC Place; PERRY; **181** L-17; elev. 952ft./290m.; 🅿; **z** 41731; ● 200
Dal; RMC Place; WHITLEY; ***181** M-14; mail Williamsburg **z** 40769; rural
Dalesburg; RMC Place; BREATHITT; ***181** K-15; mail Booneville **z** 41314; rural
Dalesburg; RMC Place; FLEMING; ***181** F-15; mail Flemingsburg **z** 41041; rural
Dalton; RMC Place; HOPKINS; ***180** K-2; mail Princeton **z** 42445; rural
Dan; RMC Place; MENIFEE; ***181** H-16; mail Wellington **z** 40387; rural
Dan; RMC Place; OHIO; ***180** J-5; mail Horse Branch **z** 42349; rural
Dana; RMC Place; FLOYD; ***181** J-18; elev. 758ft./231m.; 🅿; **z** 41615; ● 50
Danby; RMC Place; LOGAN; ***180** M-5; mail Russellville **z** 42276; ● 50
Daniel Boone; RMC Place; HOPKINS; ***180** K-3; mail Nortonville **z** 42442; rural
Daniels Creek; JOHNSON; see Odds (RMC Place)
Danleytown; RMC Place; GREENUP; ***181** F-18; ★ **HNTG**; mail Greenup **z** 41144; ● 100
Dant; RMC Place; MARION; ***180** J-9; mail Loretto **z** 40037; rural
Danville; Inc. Place; ⊡ BOYLE; **181** J-11; elev. 989ft./301m.; 🅿 🅷 🅲 1,145 ■; **z** 40422-23; Ⓟ 12,559; © 15,477; ◆ 15,492
Darfork; RMC Place; PERRY; ***181** K-17; elev. 865ft./264m.; mail Hazard **z** 41701; ● 100
Dartmont; RMC Place; HARLAN; mail Evarts **z** 40828; ● 175
Davella; RMC Place; MARTIN; ***181** I-18; elev. 690ft./210m.; 🅿; **z** 41214
David; RMC Place; FLOYD; **181** J-17; elev. 718ft./219m.; 🅿; **z** 41616; ● 300
DAVIESS; **180** J-4; Ⓟ 87,189; © 91,545; ◆ 93,280
Davis; RMC Place; SCOTT; ***181** G-12; elev. 886ft./270m.; mail Sadieville **z** 40370
Davisburg; RMC Place; BELL; ***181** M-15; 🅿; **z** 40977; rural
Davis Crossroads; RMC Place; BUTLER; ***180** L-5; elev. 634ft./193m.; mail Lewisburg **z** 42256; rural
Davison Station; RMC Place; OHIO; ***180** J-5; mail Olaton **z** 42361; rural
Davisport; RMC Place; MARTIN; ***181** I-18; elev. 699ft./213m.; 🅿; **z** 41262; rural
Davistown; RMC Place; GARRARD; ***181** I-12; mail Lancaster **z** 40444; ● 40
Davistown; RMC Place; WOODFORD; ***181** H-12; ★ **LEX**; mail Midway **z** 40347; ● 40
Dawson Springs; Inc. Place; HOPKINS; **180** K-2; elev. 414ft./126m.; 🅿; **z** 42408; Ⓟ 3,129; © 2,980
Day; RMC Place; LETCHER; ***181** L-18; elev. 1,266ft./386m.; mail Whitesburg **z** 41858
Dayhoit; HARLAN; see Wilhoit (RMC Place)
Daylight; RMC Place; HOPKINS; ***180** K-2; mail Dawson Springs **z** 42408; rural
Daysboro; RMC Place; WOLFE; ***181** I-16; elev. 928ft./283m.; mail Hazel Green **z** 41332; rural
Daysville; RMC Place; TODD; **180** M-4; mail Russellville **z** 42276; ● 75
Dayton; Inc. Place; CAMPBELL; **181** A-17; elev. 520ft./158m.; 🅿; ★ **CIN**; **z** 41073-74; Ⓟ 6,576; © 5,966
Deane; RMC Place; LETCHER; **181** K-18; elev. 1,262ft./385m.; 🅿; **z** 41812; ● 80
Deatsville; RMC Place; NELSON; **180** I-9; elev. 687ft./209m.; 🅿; **z** 40013; ● 80
Debord; RMC Place; MARTIN; **181** I-19; elev. 671ft./205m.; 🅿; **z** 41214; ● 30
Decker; RMC Place; BUTLER; ***180** K-6; elev. 758ft./231m.; mail Caneyville **z** 42721; rural
DeCoursey; RMC Place; KENTON; ***181** D-12; ★ **CIN**; mail Covington **z** 41011, Latonia **z** 41015; pop. incl. with Taylor Mill (Inc. Place)
Decoy; RMC Place; KNOTT; **181** J-17; elev. 1,059ft./323m.; 🅿; **z** 41339; ● 20
Dee Acres; RMC Place; DAVIESS; ***180** I-5; mail Philpot **z** 42366; ● 100
Deep Springs; RMC Place; FAYETTE; ***181** H-12; ★ **LEX**; mail Lexington **z** 40505; pop. incl. with Lexington (Inc. Place)
Deepwood; RMC Place; CHRISTIAN; ***180** M-3; ★ **HPKNV**; mail Hopkinsville **z** 42240; pop. incl. with Hopkinsville (Inc. Place)
Deer Lick; RMC Place; LOGAN; ***180** L-4; mail Lewisburg **z** 42256; ● 35
Defeated Creek; RMC Place; LETCHER; ***181** L-17; mail Linefork **z** 41833; rural
Defiance; RMC Place; PERRY; ***181** K-17; mail Scuddy **z** 41760
Defoe; RMC Place; HENRY; **181** G-11; elev. 867ft./264m.; 🅿; **z** 40057; ● 50
Defries; RMC Place; HART; ***180** K-9; mail Canmer **z** 42722; rural
Dehart; RMC Place; MORGAN; ***181** H-16; elev. 867ft./264m.; mail West Liberty **z** 41472; rural
Dekoven; RMC Place; UNION; **180** J-1; mail Sturgis **z** 42459; ● 125
Delafield; RMC Place; WARREN; ***180** L-6; ★ **BOWLG**; mail Bowling Green **z** 42101; pop. incl. with Bowling Green (Inc. Place)
Delaplain; RMC Place; SCOTT; ***181** G-12; mail Georgetown **z** 40324; pop. incl. with Georgetown (Inc. Place)
Delaware; RMC Place; DAVIESS; ***180** I-3; elev. 392ft./119m.; mail Owensboro **z** 42301; ● 30
Delia; RMC Place; GRANT; ***181** F-12; mail Williamstown **z** 41097; rural
Delmer; RMC Place; PULASKI; ***181** L-12; mail Nancy **z** 42544; rural
Delphia; RMC Place; PERRY; **181** L-17; elev. 1,495ft./456m.; 🅿; **z** 41735; ● 100
Delta; RMC Place; WAYNE; ***181** M-12; elev. 1,000ft./305m.; 🅿; **z** 42633; rural
Delville; RMC Place; HENRY; ***180** F-10; mail Campbellsburg **z** 40011; rural
Delvinta; RMC Place; LEE; ***181** J-15; mail Beattyville **z** 41311; rural
Dema; RMC Place; FLOYD, KNOTT; ***181** J-18; elev. 740ft./226m.; 🅿; **z** 41859; ● 75
Democrat; RMC Place; LETCHER; ***181** K-18; elev. 1,330ft./405m.; 🅿; **z** 41858; ● 50
Demossville; RMC Place; PENDLETON; **181** E-13; elev. 521ft./159m.; 🅿; **z** 41033; ● 60
Demplytown; RMC Place; OLDHAM; ***180** G-9; ★ **LOU**; mail Crestwood **z** 40014; rural
Denney; RMC Place; WAYNE; ***181** M-12; mail Monticello **z** 42633; rural
Dennis; RMC Place; LOGAN; ***180** M-5; mail Auburn **z** 42206, Russellville **z** 42276
Denniston; RMC Place; MENIFEE; **181** I-15; elev. 1,105ft./337m.; 🅿; **z** 40316; ● 75
Denton; RMC Place; CARTER; **181** G-17; elev. 628ft./191m.; 🅿; **z** 41132; ● 30
Denver; RMC Place; JOHNSON; ***181** I-18; elev. 624ft./190m.; 🅿; **z** 41222; ● 40
Depoy; RMC Place; MUHLENBERG; **180** K-4; elev. 498ft./152m.; mail Greenville **z** 42345; ● 70
Derby Hills; RMC Place; WOODFORD; ***181** H-12; ★ **LEX**; mail Versailles **z** 40383; ● 90
Dermont; RMC Place; DAVIESS; **180** B-3; elev. 481ft./147m.; ★ **OWNS**; mail Owensboro **z** 42303; ● 75
Desda; RMC Place; CLINTON; ***180** M-10; mail Albany **z** 42602; rural
Devon; RMC Place; BOONE; **181** D-12; ★ **CIN**; mail Florence **z** 41042; ● 50
Devondale; RMC Place; JEFFERSON; ***180** G-9; elev. 601ft./183m.; ★ **LOU**; mail Louisville **z** 40222; pop. incl. with Graymoor-Devondale (Inc. Place)
Dewdrop; RMC Place; ELLIOTT; ***181** H-17; mail Sandy Hook **z** 41171; rural
Dewitt; RMC Place; KNOX; ***181** M-15; 🅿; **z** 40930; ● 50
Dexter; RMC Place; CALLOWAY; **180** F-4; elev. 412ft./126m.; 🅿; **z** 42036; ● 350
Dexterville; RMC Place; BUTLER; ***180** K-5; mail Morgantown **z** 42261; rural
Diablock; RMC Place; PERRY; **181** K-17; mail Hazard **z** 41701; ● 200
Diamond; RMC Place; WEBSTER; **180** J-2; mail Clay **z** 42404, Providence **z** 42450; ● 150
Dice; RMC Place; PERRY; **181** K-16; elev. 938ft./286m.; 🅿; **z** 41736; ● 20
Dietz Acres; RMC Place; HARDIN; ***180** I-5; mail Fort Knox **z** 40121
Dillon; RMC Place; HARLAN; ***181** M-16; mail Putney **z** 40865
Dimple; RMC Place; BUTLER; ***180** L-5; elev. 504ft./154m.; mail Morgantown **z** 42261; rural
Dingus; RMC Place; MORGAN; ***181** H-17; elev. 855ft./261m.; 🅿; **z** 41472; ● 10
Dinwood; FLOYD; see Alphoretta (RMC Place)
Dione; RMC Place; HARLAN; ***181** L-17; mail Cumberland **z** 40823; ● 90
Dishman Springs; RMC Place; KNOX; ***181** M-14; mail Barbourville **z** 40906; rural
Disputanta; RMC Place; ROCKCASTLE; ***181** J-13; elev. 1,044ft./318m.; 🅿; **z** 40456; ● 35
Dix Fork; RMC Place; PIKE; mail Sidney **z** 41564; rural
Dixie; RMC Place; HENDERSON; **180** I-2; elev. 458ft./140m.; mail Corydon **z** 42406; ● 100
Dixie; RMC Place; KENTON; ***181** D-12; ★ **CIN**; mail Ft Mitchell **z** 41017; pop. incl. with Lakeside Park (Inc. Place)
Dixie Bend; RMC Place; PULASKI; ***181** L-12; mail Tateville **z** 42558; ● 200
Dixie Plantation; RMC Place; FAYETTE; ***181** H-12; ★ **LEX**; mail Lexington **z** 40505; pop. incl. with Lexington (Inc. Place)
Dixon; Inc. Place; ⊡ WEBSTER; **180** J-2; elev. 538ft./164m.; 🅿; **z** 42409; Ⓟ 552; © 632
Dix River Estates; RMC Place; LINCOLN; ***181** J-12; mail Stanford **z** 40484; ● 200
Dixville; RMC Place; MERCER; ***181** I-11; elev. 929ft./283m.; mail Harrodsburg **z** 40330; rural
Dizney; RMC Place; HARLAN; **181** M-17; elev. 1,800ft./549m.; 🅿; **z** 40828; ● 250
Dobson; RMC Place; JOHNSON; ***181** I-17; rural
Dock; RMC Place; FLOYD; ***181** J-18; mail Prestonsburg **z** 41653; rural
Doddy; RMC Place; ALLEN; mail Scottsville **z** 42164; rural
Doe Creek; RMC Place; ESTILL; mail Irvine **z** 40336; rural
Doe Valley Estates; RMC Place; MEADE; ***180** H-7; mail Brandenburg **z** 40108; ● 600
Dogtown; RMC Place; MARSHALL; ***180** F-4; mail Benton **z** 42025; rural
Dog Walk; RMC Place; LINCOLN; ***181** K-12; elev. 1,277ft./389m.; mail Brodhead **z** 40409, Crab Orchard **z** 40419
Dogwalk; RMC Place; OHIO; ***180** K-6; mail Caneyville **z** 42721; rural
Dogwood; RMC Place; GRAVES; ***180** F-4; mail Hickory **z** 42051; rural
Donaldson; RMC Place; TRIGG; ***180** M-1; elev. 390ft./119m.; mail Cadiz **z** 42211; ● 30
Donansburg; RMC Place; GREEN; ***180** K-9; mail Greensburg **z** 42743; ● 25
Donerail; RMC Place; FAYETTE; ***181** H-12; elev. 886ft./270m.; ★ **LEX**; mail Lexington **z** 40511; pop. incl. with Lexington (Inc. Place)
Dongola; RMC Place; LETCHER; ***181** L-18; elev. 1,148ft./350m.; 🅿; **z** 41858
Dorton; RMC Place; PIKE; **181** K-18; elev. 1,017ft./310m.; 🅿; **z** 41520; ● 250
Dorton Branch; RMC Place; BELL; ***181** M-15; elev. 1,012ft./308m.; 🅿; **z** 40977; ● 200
Do Stop; RMC Place; GRAYSON; ***180** J-6; elev. 494ft./151m.; mail Caneyville **z** 42721; ● 30
Dot; RMC Place; LOGAN; ***180** M-4; elev. 530ft./162m.; mail Adairville **z** 42202; rural
Douglas; RMC Place; PIKE; ***181** K-19; mail Pikeville **z** 41501, Robinson Creek **z** 41560; ● 75
Douglass Hills; Inc. Place; JEFFERSON; **180** B-9; elev. 700ft./213m.; ★ **LOU**; mail Louisville **z** 40243; Ⓟ 5,549; © 5,718; Ⓡ 5,576
Dover; Inc. Place; MASON; **181** E-14; elev. 514ft./157m.; 🅿; **z** 41034; Ⓟ 297; © 316
Downtown; RMC Place; JEFFERSON; ***180** G-8; ★ **LOU**; mail Louisville **z** 40201, **z** 40203; pop. incl. with Louisville (Inc. Place)
Downtown; RMC Place; WARREN; mail Bowling Green **z** 42101; pop. incl. with Bowling Green (Inc. Place)
Doylesville; RMC Place; MADISON; ***181** I-13; mail Richmond **z** 40475; rural
Dozier Heights; RMC Place; HOPKINS; ***180** K-3; mail Madisonville **z** 42431; pop. incl. with Madisonville (Inc. Place)
Draffenville; RMC Place; MARSHALL; **180** F-4; mail Benton **z** 42025; ● 300
Draffin; RMC Place; PIKE; ***181** K-19; elev. 729ft./222m.; 🅿; **z** 41522; ● 175
Drake; RMC Place; WARREN; ***180** M-6; elev. 587ft./179m.; 🅿; **z** 42128; ● 40
Drakesboro; Inc. Place; MUHLENBERG; **180** K-4; elev. 429ft./131m.; 🅿; **z** 42337; Ⓟ 565; © 627
Draper; RMC Place; HARLAN; ***181** M-16; mail Evarts **z** 40828; pop. incl. with Evarts (Inc. Place)
Drennon Springs; RMC Place; HENRY; ***181** F-11; mail Campbellsburg **z** 40011; rural
Dressen; RMC Place; HARLAN; ***181** M-16; mail Harlan **z** 40831
Dreyfus; RMC Place; MADISON; **181** J-13; elev. 1,000ft./305m.; 🅿; **z** 40385; ● 150
Drift; RMC Place; FLOYD; **181** J-18; elev. 691ft./211m.; 🅿; **z** 41619; ● 300
Dripping Spring; RMC Place; EDMONSON; ***180** L-7; mail Smiths Grove **z** 42171; rural
Drip Rock; RMC Place; ESTILL; ***181** J-14; mail Irvine **z** 40336; rural
Druid Hills; Inc. Place; JEFFERSON; ***180** G-9; elev. 554ft./169m.; ★ **LOU**; mail Louisville **z** 40207; Ⓟ 305; © 318
Drum; RMC Place; PULASKI; ***181** L-12; mail Somerset **z** 42501; rural
Dry Creek; RMC Place; KNOTT; ***181** K-18; elev. 1,200ft./366m.; 🅿; **z** 41862; rural
Dry Fork; RMC Place; BARREN; ***180** M-8; elev. 807ft./246m.; mail Etoile **z** 42131, Glasgow **z** 42141; rural
Dry Fork; RMC Place; PIKE; ***181** K-19; mail Rockhouse **z** 41561; ● 100

Entries in **UPPERCASE** are counties.
Entries in **bold** have populations of 2,500 or more.
Names in parentheses are alternate names.
Inc. Place — Incorporated Place
RMC Place — Rand McNally Designated Place
CDP — Census Designated Place
MCD — Minor Civil Division

⊡ County Seat
▲ Minor Civil Division
elev. Elevation
🅿 Post Office

🅷 Hospital
🅲 College
■ Principal Business Center
★ Ranally Metro Area (RMA) Abbreviation
z Zip Code(s)

Ⓟ Previous Census Population
Ⓡ Revised Census Population
Ⓐ Annexation Population
● Rand McNally Population Estimate
© Final Census Population
Ⓢ Special Census Population
◆ Estimated Population

For additional definitions see Glossary, Volume 1, and Introduction, Volume 2.

Dryhill; RMC Place; LESLIE; *181 K-16; elev. 843ft./257m.; 🅿; z 41749; rural
Dry Ridge; Inc. Place; GRANT; 181 E-12; elev. 958ft./292m.; 🅿; z 41035; Ⓟ 1,601; Ⓒ 1,995
Dublin; RMC Place; GRAVES; 180 F-3; elev. 500ft./152m.; mail Fancy Farm z 42039; ● 50
Dubre; RMC Place; CUMBERLAND; 180 M-9; elev. 648ft./198m.; 🅿; z 42731; ● 60
Duckers; RMC Place; WOODFORD; *181 H-11; elev. 814ft./248m.; ★ LEX; mail Midway z 40347
Duckrun; RMC Place; WHITLEY; *181 M-13; mail Williamsburg z 40769; rural
Duco; RMC Place; MAGOFFIN; *181 J-17; elev. 950ft./290m.; 🅿; z 41465; rural
Duff; RMC Place; GRAYSON; *180 J-6; elev. 651ft./198m.; mail Leitchfield z 42754; rural
Duganville; RMC Place; MERCER; *181 I-11; mail Harrodsburg z 40330; rural
Dukedom; RMC Place; GRAVES; 180 G-3; mail Water Valley z 42085; total pop., including Dukedom, TN, 130; ● 50
Dukes; RMC Place; HANCOCK; *180 I-5; mail Hawesville z 42348
Dulaney; RMC Place; CALDWELL; *180 L-1; mail Princeton z 42445; rural
Duluth; RMC Place; MADISON; *181 J-13; mail Berea z 40403; rural
Dunbar; RMC Place; BUTLER; 180 K-5; elev. 466ft./142m.; 🅿; z 42219; ● 75
Duncan; RMC Place; CASEY; *181 K-12; elev. 1,330ft./405m.; mail Kings Mountain z 40442; rural
Duncan; RMC Place; MERCER; *181 I-11; elev. 841ft./256m.; mail Harrodsburg z 40330
Dundee; RMC Place; OHIO; 180 J-5; elev. 420ft./128m.; 🅿; z 42338; ● 150
Dunham; RMC Place; LETCHER; *181 K-18; mail Jenkins z 41537; pop. incl. with Jenkins (Inc. Place)
Dunlap; RMC Place; PIKE; *181 J-20; mail Fedscreek z 41524; rural
Dunleary; RMC Place; PIKE; *181 K-19; mail Elkhorn City z 41522; rural
Dunmor; RMC Place; MUHLENBERG; 180 L-4; elev. 589ft./180m.; 🅿; z 42339; ● 200
Dunnville; RMC Place; CASEY; 181 K-11; elev. 742ft./226m.; 🅿; z 42528; ● 225
Dunraven; RMC Place; PERRY; *181 K-16; mail Krypton z 41754; rural
Durbin; RMC Place; BOYD; *181 G-18; ★ HNTG; mail Catlettsburg z 41129; rural
Durbintown; RMC Place; HARRISON; *181 F-13; mail Berry z 41003; rural
Duval; RMC Place; SCOTT; *181 G-12; mail Georgetown z 40324; rural
Dwale; RMC Place; FLOYD; 181 J-18; elev. 645ft./197m.; 🅿; z 41621; ● 180
Dwarf; RMC Place; PERRY; 181 K-17; elev. 908ft./277m.; 🅿; z 41739; ● 100
Dycusburg; Inc. Place; CRITTENDEN; 180 K-1; elev. 342ft./104m.; 🅿; z 42037; Ⓟ 47; Ⓒ 39
Dyer; RMC Place; BRECKINRIDGE; 180 I-7; mail Custer z 40115; ● 125
Dykes; RMC Place; PULASKI; *181 L-13; mail Somerset z 42501; rural

E

Eadsville; RMC Place; WAYNE; *181 M-11; mail Monticello z 42633; rural
Eagle Creek; RMC Place; OWEN; *180 F-10; mail Worthville z 41098; private resort; summer pop. 300; ● 75
Eagle Hill; RMC Place; OWEN; *181 E-11; mail Glencoe z 41046; rural
Eagle Station; RMC Place; CARROLL; *181 F-11; mail Sanders z 41083; rural
Earlington; Inc. Place; HOPKINS; 180 K-3; elev. 422ft./129m.; 🅿; z 42410; Ⓟ 1,833; Ⓒ 1,649
East Bernstadt; CDP; LAUREL; 181 K-14; elev. 1,182ft./360m.; 🅿; z 40729; Ⓒ 774
Easterday; RMC Place; CARROLL; *180 F-10; mail Carrollton z 41008; rural
Eastern; RMC Place; FLOYD; *181 J-18; elev. 800ft./244m.; 🅿; z 41622; ● 150
East Fork; RMC Place; METCALFE; *180 L-9; mail Edmonton z 42129; rural
East Hickman; RMC Place; JESSAMINE; *181 I-12; ★ LEX; mail Nicholasville z 40356; pop. incl. with Lexington (Inc. Place)
East Jenkins; RMC Place; LETCHER; *181 K-18; mail Jenkins z 41537; pop. incl. with Jenkins (Inc. Place)
Eastland; RMC Place; NELSON; *180 I-9; mail Bardstown z 40004; ● 200
Eastland Park; RMC Place; FAYETTE; *181 H-12; ★ LEX; mail Lexington z 40505; pop. incl. with Lexington (Inc. Place)
Eastland Park; RMC Place; WARREN; *180 L-6; ★ BOWLG; mail Bowling Green z 42104; pop. incl. with Bowling Green (Inc. Place)
East McDowell; RMC Place; FLOYD; *181 J-18; elev. 782ft./238m.; 🅿; z 41647; rural
Easton; RMC Place; HANCOCK; *180 I-5; elev. 563ft./172m.; mail Fordsville z 42343; rural
East Pineville; RMC Place; BELL; *181 M-15; 🅿; z 40977; ● 200
East Point; RMC Place; JOHNSON; *181 I-18; elev. 624ft./190m.; 🅿; z 41216; ● 200
East Union; RMC Place; NICHOLAS; *181 G-14; mail Carlisle z 40311
Eastview; RMC Place; HARDIN; 180 J-7; elev. 863ft./263m.; 🅿; z 42732; ● 60
Eastwood; RMC Place; JEFFERSON; *180 G-9; elev. 659ft./201m.; 🅿; ★ LOU; z 40018; became part of Louisville/Jefferson County Metro Jan. 6, 2003
Ebenezer; RMC Place; MERCER; *181 I-11; elev. 830ft./253m.; mail Salvisa z 40372
Ebenezer; RMC Place; MONROE; mail Tompkinsville z 42167; rural
Ebenezer; RMC Place; MUHLENBERG; *180 K-4; mail Drakesboro z 42337; ● 90
Echo; RMC Place; METCALFE; *180 L-8; mail Knob Lick z 42154; rural
Echols; RMC Place; OHIO; 180 K-4; elev. 321ft./98m.; mail Beaver Dam z 42320; ● 50
Echo Point; RMC Place; PULASKI; *181 M-12; mail Bronston z 42518; ● 80
Echo Valley; RMC Place; OLDHAM; *180 G-9; ★ LOU; mail La Grange z 40031; ● 150
Eddyville; Inc. Place; ⊡ LYON; 180 L-1; elev. 496ft./151m.; 🅿; z 42038; Ⓟ 1,889; Ⓒ 2,350
Eddyville Shores; RMC Place; LYON; *180 L-1; mail Eddyville z 42038; ● 75
Edenton; RMC Place; MADISON; *181 I-12; mail Richmond z 40475; rural
Edgewater; RMC Place; PIKE; *181 K-19; elev. 1,395ft./425m.; mail Hellier z 41534; rural
Edgewood; RMC Place; FRANKLIN; *181 H-11; mail Frankfort z 40601; ● 200
Edgewood; RMC Place; JEFFERSON; *180 H-8; ★ LOU; mail Louisville z 40213; pop. incl. with Louisville (Inc. Place)
Edgewood; Inc. Place; KENTON; 181 C-15; elev. 870ft./265m.; 🅿; ★ CIN; z 41017-18; Ⓟ 8,143; Ⓒ 9,400
Edgewood; RMC Place; NELSON; *180 I-9; mail Bardstown z 40004; pop. incl. with Bardstown (Inc. Place)
EDMONSON; 180 K-7; Ⓟ 10,357; Ⓒ 11,644; ◆ 12,020
Edmonton; Inc. Place; ⊡ METCALFE; 180 L-9; elev. 843ft./257m.; 🅿; z 42129; Ⓟ 1,477; Ⓒ 1,586
Edna; RMC Place; MAGOFFIN; *181 I-17; elev. 822ft./251m.; 🅿; z 41465; ● 10
Edwards; RMC Place; LOGAN; *180 L-4; elev. 555ft./169m.; mail Lewisburg z 42256; ● 25
Eglon; RMC Place; JACKSON; *181 J-14; mail Mc Kee z 40447; rural
Egypt; RMC Place; JACKSON; 181 K-14; elev. 1,137ft./347m.; mail Tyner z 40486; ● 30
Eighty Eight; RMC Place; BARREN; 180 M-8; elev. 805ft./245m.; 🅿; z 42130; ● 75
Ekron; Inc. Place; MEADE; 180 H-7; elev. 680ft./207m.; 🅿; z 40117; Ⓟ 110; Ⓒ 170
Elamton; RMC Place; MORGAN; *181 H-17; elev. 835ft./255m.; 🅿; z 41472; rural
Elba; RMC Place; MCLEAN; 180 J-3; mail Calhoun z 42327; ● 30
Elcomb; RMC Place; HARLAN; *181 M-16; elev. 1,203ft./367m.; mail Harlan z 40831; ● 200
Eldridge; RMC Place; ELLIOTT; *181 H-17; mail Isonville z 41149; rural
Eli; RMC Place; RUSSELL; 181 L-11; mail Russell Springs z 42642; ● 100
Elihu; RMC Place; PULASKI; 181 L-12; elev. 832ft./254m.; 🅿; z 42501; ● 100
Elizabeth Station; RMC Place; BOURBON; *181 G-13; mail Paris z 40361
Elizabethtown; Inc. Place; ⊡ HARDIN; 180 I-8; elev. 731ft./223m.; 🅿 🅷 ■; z 42701-02; Ⓟ 18,167; Ⓒ 22,542; ◆ 25,291
Elizaville; RMC Place; FLEMING; 181 G-14; elev. 909ft./277m.; 🅿; z 41037; ● 200
Elkatawa; RMC Place; BREATHITT; 181 J-16; elev. 756ft./230m.; 🅿; z 41339; ● 50
Elk Creek; RMC Place; SPENCER; 180 H-10; mail Fisherville z 40023; ● 20
Elkfork; RMC Place; MORGAN; 181 H-17; elev. 826ft./252m.; 🅿; z 41421; ● 15
Elk Horn; RMC Place; TAYLOR; 180 K-10; elev. 747ft./228m.; 🅿; z 42733; ● 50
Elkhorn City; Inc. Place; PIKE; 181 K-19; elev. 802ft./244m.; 🅿; z 41522; Ⓟ 1,035; Ⓒ 1,060
Elk Lake Shores; RMC Place; OWEN; *181 F-11; mail Owenton z 40359; ● 300
Elkton; Inc. Place; ⊡ TODD; 180 M-4; elev. 631ft./192m.; 🅿; z 42220 & mail Sharon Grove z 42280; Ⓟ 1,789; Ⓒ 1,984
Ella; RMC Place; ADAIR; 180 L-10; mail Columbia z 42728; rural
Ellington; RMC Place; CUMBERLAND; *180 M-9; mail Burkesville z 42717; rural
ELLIOTT; 181 H-17; Ⓟ 6,455; Ⓒ 6,748; ◆ 7,171
Elliottville; RMC Place; ROWAN; 181 G-16; elev. 1,022ft./312m.; 🅿; z 40317; ● 40
Ellisburg; RMC Place; CASEY; *181 J-11; mail Hustonville z 40437; rural
Elliston; RMC Place; GRANT; *181 E-11; elev. 588ft./179m.; mail Dry Ridge z 41035; rural
Elliston; RMC Place; MADISON; *181 I-13; mail Richmond z 40475; ● 50
Ellisville; RMC Place; NICHOLAS; *181 G-14; mail Carlisle z 40311; rural
Ellmitch; RMC Place; OHIO; *180 J-5; mail Fordsville z 42343; rural
Ellwood; RMC Place; PIKE; *181 K-18; mail Jonancy z 41538; ● 75
Elmburg; RMC Place; SHELBY; 180 G-10; elev. 880ft./268m.; mail Pleasureville z 40057; ● 75
Elmer Davis Lake; RMC Place; OWEN; *181 F-11; mail Owenton z 40359; ● 30
Elmrock; RMC Place; KNOTT; *181 J-17; elev. 990ft./302m.; 🅿; z 41640; rural
Elmville; RMC Place; FRANKLIN; *181 G-11; mail Frankfort z 40601; rural
Elna; RMC Place; MORGAN, JOHNSON; *181 H-17; elev. 842ft./257m.; 🅿; z 41219; rural
Elsie; RMC Place; MAGOFFIN; 181 I-17; elev. 832ft./254m.; 🅿; z 41465; ● 25
Elsinore; RMC Place; FRANKLIN; *181 G-11; elev. 672ft./205m.; mail Frankfort z 40601
Elsmere; Inc. Place; KENTON; 181 D-12; elev. 889ft./271m.; 🅿; ★ CIN; z 41018; Ⓟ 6,847; Ⓒ 8,139
Elswick; RMC Place; PIKE; *181 K-18; mail Jonancy z 41538; rural
Elva; RMC Place; MARSHALL; *180 F-4; mail Symsonia z 42082; rural
Elys; RMC Place; KNOX; *181 M-15; 🅿; z 40939; rural
Emanuel; RMC Place; KNOX; *181 M-14; mail Gray z 40734; rural
Emerson; RMC Place; LEWIS; 181 G-16; elev. 797ft./243m.; 🅿; z 41135; ● 25
Eminence; Inc. Place; HENRY; 180 G-10; elev. 939ft./286m.; 🅿; ★ LOU; z 40019; Ⓟ 2,055; Ⓒ 2,231
Emlyn; RMC Place; WHITLEY; 181 M-14; elev. 971ft./296m.; 🅿; z 40730; ● 350
Emma; RMC Place; FLOYD; *181 J-18; elev. 645ft./197m.; 🅿; z 41653; ● 120
Emmalena; RMC Place; KNOTT; 181 K-17; elev. 985ft./300m.; 🅿; z 41740; ● 100
Empire; RMC Place; CHRISTIAN; *180 L-3; elev. 512ft./156m.; mail Crofton z 42217, Nortonville z 42442
Endicott; RMC Place; FLOYD; *181 I-18; elev. 701ft./214m.; 🅿; z 41653; ● 50
End of Line; RMC Place; FLOYD; *181 K-18; mail Weeksbury z 41667; rural
Engle; RMC Place; PERRY; *181 K-16; elev. 867ft./264m.; mail Chavies z 41727; rural
English; RMC Place; CARROLL; 180 F-10; mail Carrollton z 41008; ● 150
Ennis; RMC Place; MUHLENBERG; *180 K-4; elev. 458ft./140m.; mail Drakesboro z 42337; rural
Enon (Walnut Grove); RMC Place; CALDWELL; *180 K-1; mail Fredonia z 42411; rural
Ensor; RMC Place; DAVIESS; *180 I-4; elev. 477ft./145m.; ★ OWNS; mail Philpot z 42366
Enterprise; RMC Place; CARTER; *181 G-16; elev. 844ft./257m.; mail Olive Hill z 41164; rural
Eolia; RMC Place; LETCHER; 181 L-18; elev. 1,684ft./513m.; 🅿; z 40826; ● 300
Epleys; RMC Place; LOGAN; 180 M-5; elev. 680ft./207m.; mail Russellville z 42276; ● 75
Epperson; RMC Place; MCCRACKEN; *180 E-4; ★ PAD; mail Paducah z 42003; ● 150
Epson; RMC Place; MAGOFFIN; *181 I-16; mail Salyersville z 41465; rural
Epworth; RMC Place; LEWIS; *181 F-15; elev. 827ft./252m.; mail Tollesboro z 41189
Equality (Kronos); RMC Place; OHIO; *180 K-4; mail Centertown z 42328; rural
Eriline; RMC Place; CLAY; *181 K-15; elev. 1,200ft./366m.; 🅿; z 40931 & mail Manchester z 40962; rural
Erlanger; Inc. Place; KENTON; 181 D-12; elev. 903ft./275m.; 🅿; ★ CIN; z 41017-18; Ⓟ 15,979; Ⓒ 16,676
Ermine; RMC Place; LETCHER; 181 L-18; elev. 1,172ft./357m.; 🅿; z 41815; ● 300
Erose; RMC Place; KNOX; *181 L-15; mail Flat Lick z 40935; rural
Essie; RMC Place; LESLIE; *181 L-16; elev. 1,879ft./573m.; 🅿; z 40827; ● 60
Estesburg; RMC Place; PULASKI; *181 K-12; elev. 1,128ft./344m.; mail Waynesburg z 40489; rural
Estill; RMC Place; FLOYD; *181 J-18; elev. 707ft./215m.; 🅿; z 41666; ● 300
ESTILL; 181 I-14; Ⓟ 14,614; Ⓒ 15,307; ◆ 14,889
Esto; RMC Place; RUSSELL; *180 L-10; mail Russell Springs z 42642; rural
Ethridge; RMC Place; GALLATIN; *181 E-11; elev. 488ft./149m.; mail Warsaw z 41095
Etna; RMC Place; PULASKI; *181 K-12; mail Eubank z 42567; rural
Etoile; RMC Place; BARREN; *180 M-8; elev. 724ft./221m.; 🅿; z 42131; ● 50
Etterwood; RMC Place; SCOTT; *181 G-12; ★ LEX; mail Georgetown z 40324; ● 175
Etty; RMC Place; PIKE; 181 K-18; elev. 1,252ft./382m.; 🅿; z 41572; ● 100
Eubank; Inc. Place; PULASKI, LINCOLN; 181 K-12; elev. 1,202ft./366m.; 🅿; z 42567; Ⓟ 354; Ⓒ 358
Eunice; RMC Place; ADAIR; *180 L-10; mail Columbia z 42728; rural
Evanston; RMC Place; BREATHITT; *181 J-17; mail Jackson z 41339
Evarts; Inc. Place; HARLAN; 181 M-17; elev. 1,299ft./396m.; 🅿; z 40828; Ⓟ 1,063; Ⓒ 1,101
Eveleigh; RMC Place; GRAYSON; *180 J-6; mail Leitchfield z 42754; rural
Ever; RMC Place; MAGOFFIN; *181 I-17; 🅿; z 41465; rural
Everett; RMC Place; LOGAN, TODD; *180 L-4; mail Lewisburg z 42256; rural
Evergreen; RMC Place; FRANKLIN; *181 H-11; elev. 853ft./260m.; mail Frankfort z 40601; ● 80
Eversole; RMC Place; OWSLEY; *181 J-15; mail Booneville z 41314; rural
Ewing; Inc. Place; FLEMING; 181 F-14; elev. 907ft./276m.; 🅿; z 41039; Ⓟ 268; Ⓒ 278
Ewingford; RMC Place; TRIMBLE; *180 F-10; mail Bedford z 40006; rural
Ewington; RMC Place; MONTGOMERY; *181 H-14; mail Mount Sterling z 40353; rural
Exie; RMC Place; GREEN; *180 L-9; mail Greensburg z 42743
Ezel; RMC Place; MORGAN; 181 I-16; elev. 948ft./289m.; 🅿; z 41425; ● 300

F

Faber; RMC Place; WHITLEY; *181 M-14; mail Corbin z 40701; ● 50
Fagan; RMC Place; MENIFEE; *181 I-15; mail Frenchburg z 40322; rural
Fairbanks; RMC Place; GRAVES; *180 G-4; elev. 553ft./169m.; mail Sedalia z 42079
Fairbanks; RMC Place; OWEN; *181 F-12; elev. 917ft./280m.; mail Owenton z 40359; rural
Fairdale; CDP; JEFFERSON; *180 H-8; elev. 475ft./145m.; 🅿; ★ LOU; z 40118; former CDP; became part of Louisville/Jefferson County Metro Jan. 6, 2003; Ⓟ 6,563; Ⓒ 7,658
Fairdealing; RMC Place; MARSHALL; 180 M-1; mail Benton z 42025; ● 100
Fairfield; RMC Place; BRECKINRIDGE; *180 J-7; elev. 758ft./231m.; mail Harned z 40144; rural
Fairfield; Inc. Place; NELSON; 180 H-10; elev. 721ft./220m.; 🅿; z 40020; Ⓟ 142; Ⓒ 72
Fairland; RMC Place; CLINTON; *180 M-10; mail Albany z 42602; rural
Fairmeade; RMC Place; JEFFERSON; *180 G-9; elev. 520ft./158m.; ★ LOU; mail Louisville z 40207; former incorporated place; became part of St. Matthews September 1, 2000; pop. incl. with Saint Matthews (Inc. Place); Ⓟ 280; Ⓒ 264
Fairmont; RMC Place; JEFFERSON; *180 H-9; ★ LOU; mail Louisville z 40291; became part of Louisville/Jefferson County Metro Jan. 6, 2003
Fairmont; RMC Place; WEBSTER; *180 J-2; mail Clay z 42404; rural
Fairplay; RMC Place; ADAIR; 180 L-10; elev. 984ft./300m.; 🅿; z 42728; ● 20
Fairview; RMC Place; ANDERSON; *180 I-10; mail Lawrenceburg z 40342; rural
Fairview; RMC Place; BOYD; *181 F-18; ★ HNTG; mail Ashland z 41101
Fairview; RMC Place; CHRISTIAN, TODD; 180 M-3; elev. 628ft./191m.; 🅿; z 42221; ● 300
Fairview; RMC Place; EDMONSON; *180 L-7; mail Brownsville z 42210; rural
Fairview (Oakwood); RMC Place; FLEMING; 181 F-14; mail Ewing z 41039; ● 40
Fairview; Inc. Place; KENTON; *181 D-12; ★ CIN; mail Latonia z 41015; Ⓟ 119; Ⓒ 156
Fairview; RMC Place; LYON; *180 L-1; mail Eddyville z 42038; pop. incl. with Eddyville (Inc. Place)
Fairview; RMC Place; WHITLEY; *181 N-14; mail Williamsburg z 40769; ● 175
Fairview Heights; RMC Place; FRANKLIN; *181 G-11; mail Frankfort z 40601; pop. incl. with Frankfort (Inc. Place)
Fairview Hill; RMC Place; CARTER; *181 G-17; ★ HNTG; mail Hitchins z 41146
Fairway; RMC Place; FAYETTE; *181 H-12; ★ LEX; mail Lexington z 40502; pop. incl. with Lexington (Inc. Place)
Falcon; RMC Place; MAGOFFIN; 181 I-17; elev. 960ft./293m.; 🅿; z 41426; ● 120
Fall Rock; RMC Place; CLAY; 181 K-15; elev. 1,022ft./312m.; 🅿; z 40932; ● 90
Fallsburg; RMC Place; LAWRENCE; 181 G-18; elev. 568ft./173m.; 🅿; z 41230; ● 125
Falls of Rough; RMC Place; BRECKINRIDGE, GRAYSON; 180 J-6; elev. 452ft./138m.; 🅿; z 40119; ● 75
Falmouth; Inc. Place; ⊡ PENDLETON; 181 E-13; elev. 558ft./170m.; 🅿; z 41040; Ⓟ 2,378; Ⓒ 2,058
Fancy Farm; RMC Place; GRAVES; 180 F-3; elev. 410ft./125m.; 🅿; z 42039; ● 300
Fannin; RMC Place; ELLIOTT; *181 H-17; elev. 707ft./215m.; mail Sandy Hook z 41171; ● 20
Fariston; RMC Place; LAUREL; *181 L-14; mail London z 40744; ● 100
Farler; RMC Place; PERRY; *181 L-17; elev. 1,092ft./333m.; 🅿; z 41774; rural
Farmdale; RMC Place; FRANKLIN; *181 H-11; mail Frankfort z 40601; ● 300
Farmers; RMC Place; ROWAN; 181 H-15; elev. 672ft./205m.; 🅿; z 40319 & mail Morehead z 40351; ● 275
Farmers Mill; RMC Place; HARLAN; *181 M-16; mail Harlan z 40831; rural
Farmersville; RMC Place; CALDWELL; 180 K-1; mail Princeton z 42445; ● 40
Farmington; RMC Place; GRAVES; 180 G-4; elev. 553ft./169m.; 🅿; z 42040; ● 150
Farraday; RMC Place; LETCHER; *181 K-18; mail Thornton z 41855; ● 50
Farristown; RMC Place; MADISON; *181 J-13; elev. 959ft./292m.; mail Berea z 40403
Faubush; RMC Place; PULASKI; 181 L-11; elev. 1,150ft./351m.; 🅿; z 42544; ● 80
Faulconer; RMC Place; BOYLE; *181 I-11; elev. 892ft./272m.; mail Danville z 40422; rural
Faxon; RMC Place; CALLOWAY; *180 M-1; elev. 516ft./157m.; mail Murray z 42071; rural
Faye; RMC Place; ELLIOTT; *181 H-17; elev. 753ft./230m.; mail Sandy Hook z 41171; rural
FAYETTE; 181 H-13; Ⓟ 225,366; Ⓒ 260,512; ◆ 293,121
Faywood; RMC Place; WOODFORD; 181 H-12; elev. 824ft./251m.; mail Versailles z 40383; ● 100
Fearisville; RMC Place; LEWIS; *181 F-15; elev. 585ft./178m.; mail Vanceburg z 41179; rural
Fearsville; RMC Place; CHRISTIAN; 180 L-3; mail Hopkinsville z 42240; ● 60
Feathersburg; RMC Place; ADAIR, TAYLOR; *180 K-10; elev. 1,037ft./316m.; mail Elk Horn z 42733; rural
Fedscreek; RMC Place; PIKE; 181 J-20; elev. 824ft./251m.; 🅿; z 41524; ● 175
Feds Creek Spur Junction; RMC Place; PIKE; *181 J-20
Feliciana; RMC Place; GRAVES; *180 G-3; mail Water Valley z 42085; rural
Felty; RMC Place; CLAY; *181 K-15; mail Manchester z 40962; rural
Fentress Lookout; RMC Place; GRAYSON; *180 J-6; mail Falls of Rough z 40119; ● 85
Fenwick; RMC Place; FAYETTE; *181 H-13; elev. 936ft./285m.; ★ LEX; mail Lexington z 40516; pop. incl. with Lexington (Inc. Place)
Ferguson; RMC Place; LOGAN; *180 M-4; mail Olmstead z 42265, Russellville z 42276; rural
Ferguson; Inc. Place; PULASKI; 181 L-12; elev. 896ft./273m.; 🅿; z 42533; Ⓟ 934; Ⓒ 881
Ferguson Creek; RMC Place; PIKE; *181 J-19; mail Pikeville z 41501; pop. incl. with Pikeville (Inc. Place)
Fern Creek; CDP; JEFFERSON; *180 H-9; elev. 710ft./216m.; 🅿; ★ LOU; z 40291; former CDP; became part of Louisville/Jefferson County Metro Jan. 6, 2003; Ⓟ 16,406; Ⓒ 17,870
Ferndale; RMC Place; BELL; 181 M-15; mail Pineville z 40977; ● 200
Fernleaf; RMC Place; MASON; *181 F-14; elev. 944ft./288m.; mail Dover z 41034; rural
Ferrells Creek; RMC Place; PIKE; *181 K-19; mail Belcher z 41513; rural
Fiddle Bow; RMC Place; HOPKINS; *180 K-2; mail Dawson Springs z 42408; rural
Fielden; RMC Place; ELLIOTT; *181 H-17; elev. 713ft./217m.; mail Sandy Hook z 41171; rural
Fillmore; RMC Place; LEE; *181 J-15; elev. 816ft./249m.; 🅿; z 41311; ● 40
Fincastle; Inc. Place; JEFFERSON; 180 A-10; elev. 700ft./213m.; ★ LOU; mail Louisville z 40222; Ⓟ 838; Ⓒ 825
Finchville; RMC Place; SHELBY; 180 H-10; elev. 748ft./228m.; 🅿; z 40022; ● 200
Finley; RMC Place; TAYLOR; 180 J-10; elev. 1,014ft./309m.; 🅿; z 42718; ● 20
Finley Addition; RMC Place; HENDERSON; *180 I-2; ★ EV; mail Henderson z 42420; ● 200
Finney; RMC Place; BARREN; *180 M-7; mail Glasgow z 42141
Fipaco; RMC Place; JEFFERSON; ★ LOU; pop. incl. with Louisville (Inc. Place)
Firebrick; RMC Place; LEWIS; 181 E-17; elev. 546ft./166m.; 🅿; z 41174; ● 350
Firmantown; RMC Place; WOODFORD; *181 H-12; ★ LEX; mail Versailles z 40383; ● 25
Fisherville; RMC Place; JEFFERSON; 180 G-9; elev. 559ft./170m.; 🅿; ★ LOU; z 40023; became part of Louisville/Jefferson County Metro Jan. 6, 2003
Fishtrap; RMC Place; PIKE; *181 J-19; elev. 708ft./216m.; 🅿; z 41557; rural
Fiskburg; RMC Place; KENTON; *181 E-12; elev. 885ft./270m.; ★ CIN; mail De Mossville z 41033; ● 60
Fisty; RMC Place; KNOTT; 181 K-17; elev. 923ft./281m.; 🅿; z 41743; ● 125
Fitch; RMC Place; CARTER; *181 G-16; mail Olive Hill z 41164; rural
Fitchburg; RMC Place; ESTILL; *181 I-14; mail Ravenna z 40472; rural
Five Forks; RMC Place; LAWRENCE; *181 H-18; mail Louisa z 41230; rural
Fivemile; RMC Place; BREATHITT; *181 J-16; mail Jackson z 41339; rural
Fixer; RMC Place; LEE; *181 I-15; mail Zoe z 41397; rural
Flag Fork; RMC Place; FRANKLIN; *181 G-11; mail Frankfort z 40601; rural
Flagg Spring (Flag Spring); RMC Place; CAMPBELL; *181 E-13; ★ CIN; mail California z 41007; rural
Flag Spring; CAMPBELL; see Flagg Spring (RMC Place)
Flaherty; RMC Place; MEADE; 180 I-7; elev. 793ft./242m.; 🅿; z 40175; ● 250
Flat; RMC Place; WOLFE; *181 J-15; elev. 867ft./264m.; 🅿; z 41301; rural
Flat Fork; RMC Place; MAGOFFIN; *181 I-17; elev. 957ft./292m.; 🅿; z 41465; ● 25
Flatgap; RMC Place; JOHNSON; 181 H-17; elev. 815ft./248m.; 🅿; z 41219; ● 100
Flat Lick; RMC Place; KNOX; 181 M-15; elev. 1,037ft./316m.; 🅿; z 40935; ● 700
Flat Rock; RMC Place; CALDWELL; *180 K-1; mail Fredonia z 42411; rural
Flat Rock; RMC Place; MCCREARY; *181 M-12; mail Whitley City z 42653
Flat Rock; RMC Place; ROCKCASTLE; *181 K-13; mail Orlando z 40460; rural
Flat Rock; RMC Place; SIMPSON; *180 N-6; elev. 689ft./210m.; mail Woodburn z 42170; rural
Flatwoods; Inc. Place; GREENUP; 181 F-18; elev. 689ft./210m.; 🅿; ★ HNTG; z 41139; Ⓟ 7,799; Ⓒ 7,605
Fleming; RMC Place; LETCHER; *181 K-18; elev. 1,289ft./393m.; 🅿; z 41840; pop. incl. with Fleming-Neon (Inc. Place)
FLEMING; 181 G-14; Ⓟ 12,292; Ⓒ 13,792; ◆ 14,920
Fleming-Neon; Inc. Place; LETCHER; 181 K-18; 🅿; z 41840; Ⓟ 759; Ⓒ 840
Flemingsburg; Inc. Place; ⊡ FLEMING; 181 F-15; elev. 823ft./251m.; 🅿 🅷; z 41041; Ⓟ 3,071; Ⓒ 3,010
Flemingsburg Junction (Johnson Junction); RMC Place; FLEMING; *181 F-14; mail Flemingsburg z 41041; rural
Flener; RMC Place; BUTLER; *180 K-5; mail Morgantown z 42261; rural
Flingsville; RMC Place; GRANT; *181 E-12; elev. 911ft./278m.; ★ CIN; mail Crittenden z 41030; ● 20
Flint Springs; RMC Place; OHIO; *180 K-5; mail Horse Branch z 42349; rural
Flintville; RMC Place; BREATHITT; *181 J-16; mail Lost Creek z 41348; ● 50
Flippin; RMC Place; MONROE; 180 M-8; elev. 834ft./254m.; mail Tompkinsville z 42167; ● 35
Floral; RMC Place; HANCOCK; *180 I-5; mail Hawesville z 42348; rural
Florence; Inc. Place; BOONE; 181 D-12; elev. 923ft./281m.; 🅿 🅷 🅲 543 ■; ★ CIN; z 41022, z 41042; Ⓟ 18,624; Ⓒ 23,551; ◆ 29,353
Florress; RMC Place; MORGAN; *181 I-17; mail West Liberty z 41472; rural
Flournoy; RMC Place; UNION; *180 I-2; mail Morganfield z 42437; ● 25
Floyd; RMC Place; PULASKI; *181 K-12; mail Eubank z 42567; rural
FLOYD; 181 J-18; Ⓟ 43,586; Ⓒ 42,441; ◆ 41,790
Floydsburg; RMC Place; OLDHAM; *180 G-9; ★ LOU; mail Crestwood z 40014; ● 100
Fogertown; RMC Place; CLAY; *181 K-14; elev. 1,076ft./328m.; 🅿; z 40962; rural
Folsom; RMC Place; GRANT; 181 E-11; mail Dry Ridge z 41035; ● 40
Folsomdale; RMC Place; GRAVES; 180 F-3; mail Hickory z 42051; ● 150
Fonde; RMC Place; BELL; 181 N-14; elev. 1,850ft./564m.; 🅿; z 40940; ● 75
Fonthill; RMC Place; RUSSELL; *181 L-11; elev. 932ft./284m.; mail Russell Springs z 42642; rural
Foraker; RMC Place; MAGOFFIN; 181 I-17; elev. 899ft./274m.; 🅿; z 41465; ● 40
Ford; RMC Place; CLARK; 181 I-13; elev. 622ft./190m.; 🅿; z 40391 & mail Winchester z 40392; ● 140
Fords Branch; RMC Place; PIKE; 181 J-19; elev. 800ft./244m.; 🅿; z 41526; ● 200
Fordsville; Inc. Place; OHIO; 180 J-5; elev. 499ft./152m.; 🅿; z 42343; Ⓟ 522; Ⓒ 531
Forest Grove; RMC Place; CLARK; 181 H-13; mail Winchester z 40391; ● 125
Forest Hills; Inc. Place; JEFFERSON; 180 C-9; elev. 661ft./201m.; ★ LOU; mail Louisville z 40299; Ⓟ 454; Ⓒ 494
Forest Hills; RMC Place; MCCRACKEN; *180 E-3; ★ PAD; mail Paducah z 42003; pop. incl. with Paducah (Inc. Place)
Forest Hills (Road Fork); RMC Place; PIKE; 181 J-19; elev. 810ft./247m.; 🅿; z 41527; ● 300
Forest Hills; RMC Place; TAYLOR; *180 K-10; mail Campbellsville z 42718; pop. incl. with Campbellsville (Inc. Place)
Forks of Elkhorn; RMC Place; FRANKLIN; *181 G-11; mail Frankfort z 40601; ● 150
Forkton; RMC Place; MONROE; *180 M-8; mail Tompkinsville z 42167; rural
Forrest Park; RMC Place; CLARK; *181 H-13; ★ LEX; mail Winchester z 40391; pop. incl. with Winchester (Inc. Place)
Fort Campbell North; CDP-Census Area Only; CHRISTIAN; *180 N-3; ★ CLRKV; mail Fort Campbell z 42223; Ⓟ 18,861; Ⓒ 14,338
Fort Garrett; RMC Place; WOODFORD; *181 H-12; elev. 878ft./268m.; mail Versailles z 40383; ● 30
Fort Knox; CDP-Census Area Only; HARDIN, MEADE; *180 I-8; 🅿; z 40121; Ⓟ 21,495; Ⓒ 12,377
Fort Mitchell; Inc. Place; KENTON; 181 D-12; elev. 800ft./244m.; 🅿; ★ CIN; z 41017 & mail Covington z 41011, Independence z 41051; Ⓟ 7,438; Ⓒ 8,089
Fort Spring; RMC Place; FAYETTE; *181 H-12; elev. 853ft./260m.; ★ LEX; mail Lexington z 40510, z 40513; pop. incl. with Lexington (Inc. Place)
Fort Thomas; Inc. Place; CAMPBELL; 181 D-12; elev. 840ft./256m.; 🅿 🅷; ★ CIN; z 41071, z 41075; Ⓟ 16,032; Ⓒ 16,495
Fort Wright; Inc. Place; KENTON; 181 B-16; elev. 844ft./257m.; ★ CIN; mail Covington z 41011, Ft Mitchell z 41017; Ⓟ 6,570; Ⓒ 5,681
Foster; RMC Place; BRACKEN; 181 E-13; elev. 527ft./161m.; 🅿; z 41043; ● 65
Fount; RMC Place; KNOX; *181 L-15
Fountain Run; Inc. Place; MONROE; 180 M-8; elev. 775ft./236m.; 🅿; z 42133; Ⓟ 259; Ⓒ 236
Fourmile; RMC Place; BELL; 181 M-15; elev. 1,014ft./309m.; 🅿; z 40939; ● 450
Four Oaks; RMC Place; PENDLETON; 181 F-13; elev. 635ft./194m.; mail Falmouth z 41040; ● 140
Fourseam; RMC Place; PERRY; *181 K-17; mail Hazard z 41701; rural
Fox; RMC Place; ESTILL; *181 I-14; mail Irvine z 40336; rural
Fox Chase; Inc. Place; BULLITT; *180 H-9; ★ LOU; mail Shepherdsville z 40165; Ⓟ 528; Ⓒ 476
Fox Creek; RMC Place; ANDERSON; *181 H-11; mail Lawrenceburg z 40342; ● 75
Foxport; RMC Place; FLEMING; 181 F-15; mail Wallingford z 41093; ● 50
Foxtown; RMC Place; JACKSON; *181 J-14; elev. 1,064ft./324m.; 🅿; z 40447; rural
Frakes; RMC Place; BELL; 181 N-14; elev. 1,432ft./436m.; 🅿; z 40940; ● 125
Frances; RMC Place; CRITTENDEN; 180 K-1; mail Marion z 42064; ● 50
Francisville; RMC Place; BOONE; *181 D-12; ★ CIN; mail Hebron z 41048; ● 50
Frankfort; Inc. Place; STATE CAPITAL; ⊡ FRANKLIN; 181 G-11; elev. 510ft./155m.; 🅿 🅷 🅲 2,500 ■; z 40601-04, z 40618-22; Ⓟ 25,968; Ⓒ 27,741; ◆ 27,855
Franklin; Inc. Place; ⊡ SIMPSON; 180 M-6; elev. 720ft./219m.; 🅿 🅷; z 42134-35; Ⓟ 7,607; Ⓒ 7,996
FRANKLIN; 181 G-11; Ⓟ 43,781; Ⓒ 47,687; ◆ 48,087
Franklin Cross Roads; RMC Place; HARDIN; 180 J-7; elev. 715ft./218m.; mail Cecilia z 42724; ● 60
Franklinton; RMC Place; HENRY; *181 F-11; elev. 868ft./265m.; 🅿; z 40057; ● 100
Frazer; RMC Place; WAYNE; 181 L-12; elev. 904ft./276m.; 🅿; z 42633; ● 35
Fraziertown; RMC Place; OLDHAM; *180 G-9; ★ LOU; mail Pewee Valley z 40056; ● 50
Fredericktown; RMC Place; WASHINGTON; 180 I-10; mail Springfield z 40069; ● 150
Fredonia; Inc. Place; CALDWELL; 180 K-1; elev. 402ft./123m.; 🅿; z 42411; Ⓟ 490; Ⓒ 420
Fredville; RMC Place; MAGOFFIN; *181 J-17; elev. 1,200ft./366m.; 🅿; z 41465; rural
Freeburn; RMC Place; PIKE; 181 J-20; elev. 746ft./227m.; 🅿; z 41528; ● 500
Freedom; RMC Place; BARREN; *180 M-8; mail Mount Hermon z 42157; rural
Freedom; RMC Place; RUSSELL; *180 M-10; elev. 1,034ft./315m.; mail Jamestown z 42629; rural
Freemont (Fremont); RMC Place; MCCRACKEN; *180 F-3; ★ PAD; mail Paducah z 42001, z 42003; rural
Free Union; RMC Place; WEBSTER; *180 J-2; mail Dixon z 42409; rural
Fremont; MCCRACKEN; see Freemont (RMC Place)
Frenchburg; Inc. Place; ⊡ MENIFEE; 181 H-15; elev. 864ft./263m.; 🅿; z 40322; Ⓟ 625; Ⓒ 551
Fresh Meadows; RMC Place; HARLAN; *181 M-16; mail Dayhoit z 40824; ● 50
Friendly Hills; RMC Place; JEFFERSON; ★ LOU; mail Louisville z 40219; pop. incl. with Louisville (Inc. Place)
Frisby; RMC Place; WAYNE; *181 M-11; 🅿; z 42633; rural
Fritz; RMC Place; MAGOFFIN; *181 I-17; elev. 871ft./265m.; 🅿; z 41465; rural
Frogtown; RMC Place; MARION; *180 J-10; mail Lebanon z 40033; rural
Frogue; RMC Place; CUMBERLAND; *180 N-10; mail Burkesville z 42717; rural
Frontier Village; RMC Place; HENDERSON; *180 I-3; ★ EV; mail Henderson z 42420; pop. incl. with Henderson (Inc. Place)
Frozen Creek; RMC Place; BREATHITT; *181 J-16; elev. 738ft./225m.; 🅿; z 41339; rural
Fruit Hill; RMC Place; CHRISTIAN; *180 L-3; elev. 642ft./196m.; mail Crofton z 42217; rural
Fry; RMC Place; GREEN; *180 L-9; mail Greensburg z 42743; rural
Fryer (Barnes Store); RMC Place; CALDWELL; *180 K-2; elev. 380ft./116m.; mail Princeton z 42445; rural
Fuget; RMC Place; JOHNSON; *181 I-17; elev. 846ft./258m.; 🅿; z 41219; rural
Fulgham; RMC Place; HICKMAN; 180 G-3; elev. 475ft./145m.; mail Clinton z 42031; ● 60
Fulton; Inc. Place; FULTON; 180 G-2; elev. 380ft./116m.; 🅿 🅷; z 42041; Ⓟ 3,078; Ⓒ 2,775
FULTON; 180 G-1; Ⓟ 8,271; Ⓒ 7,752; ◆ 6,623
Fultz; RMC Place; CARTER; *181 G-17; elev. 610ft./186m.; 🅿; z 41143; rural
Funston; RMC Place; MCCREARY; *181 M-13; mail Parkers Lake z 42634; rural
Furnace; RMC Place; ESTILL, POWELL; *181 I-14; elev. 1,245ft./379m.; mail Ravenna z 40472, Stanton z 40380
Fusonia; RMC Place; PERRY; *181 K-17; mail Viper z 41774; rural
Future City; RMC Place; MCCRACKEN; 180 E-3; elev. 375ft./114m.; mail Kevil z 42053; ● 200

G

Gabbard; RMC Place; OWSLEY; *181 K-15; mail Ricetown z 41364; rural
Gabe; RMC Place; GREEN; *180 K-9; elev. 763ft./233m.; mail Greensburg z 42743; rural
Gadberry; RMC Place; ADAIR; *180 L-10; mail Columbia z 42728; rural
Gaffey Heights; RMC Place; HARDIN; *180 I-8; mail Fort Knox z 40121
Gage; RMC Place; BALLARD; 180 E-3; elev. 473ft./144m.; mail La Center z 42056; ● 40
Gainesville; RMC Place; ALLEN; *180 M-7; elev. 544ft./166m.; mail Scottsville z 42164; rural
Gainesway; RMC Place; FAYETTE; *181 H-12; ★ LEX; mail Lexington z 40502; pop. incl. with Lexington (Inc. Place)
Galilee; GARRARD; see White Oak (RMC Place)
GALLATIN; 181 E-11; Ⓟ 5,393; Ⓒ 7,870; ◆ 8,015
Gallup; RMC Place; LAWRENCE; *181 H-18; mail Louisa z 41230; ● 20
Galveston; RMC Place; FLOYD; *181 J-18; elev. 1,600ft./488m.; 🅿; z 41635; ● 200
Gamaliel; Inc. Place; MONROE; 180 N-8; elev. 688ft./210m.; 🅿; z 42140; Ⓟ 462; Ⓒ 439
Gano (Lejunior); RMC Place; HARLAN; 181 M-17; elev. 1,395ft./425m.; mail Lejunior z 40849; ● 300
Gapcreek; RMC Place; WAYNE; *181 M-11; mail Alpha z 42603; rural
Gap in Knob; RMC Place; BULLITT; 180 H-8; ★ LOU; mail Shepherdsville z 40165; ● 180
Gapville; RMC Place; MAGOFFIN; *181 J-17; elev. 937ft./286m.; 🅿; z 41465; ● 20
Gardenside; RMC Place; FAYETTE; *181 H-12; ★ LEX; mail Lexington z 40504, z 40533, z 40544; pop. incl. with Lexington (Inc. Place)
Garden Springs; RMC Place; FAYETTE; *181 H-12; ★ LEX; mail Lexington z 40504; pop. incl. with Lexington (Inc. Place)
Garden Village; RMC Place; PIKE; 181 J-19; mail Pikeville z 41501; ● 100
Gardnersville; RMC Place; PENDLETON; 181 E-12; elev. 882ft./269m.; mail De Mossville z 41033; ● 50
Garfield; RMC Place; BRECKINRIDGE; 180 I-6; elev. 809ft./247m.; 🅿; z 40115, z 40140; ● 150
Garlin; RMC Place; ADAIR; *180 L-10; mail Columbia z 42728; rural
Garner; RMC Place; BOYD; *181 G-18; elev. 642ft./196m.; mail Rush z 41168; rural
Garner; RMC Place; KNOTT; 181 K-17; elev. 1,095ft./334m.; 🅿; z 41817; ● 150
Garrard; RMC Place; CLAY; 181 L-15; elev. 858ft./262m.; 🅿; z 40941; ● 65
GARRARD; 181 J-12; Ⓟ 11,579; Ⓒ 14,792; ◆ 17,461
Garrett; RMC Place; FLOYD; 181 J-18; elev. 699ft./213m.; 🅿; z 41630; ● 500
Garrett; RMC Place; MEADE; 180 I-7; elev. 684ft./208m.; mail Ekron z 40117; ● 150
Garrettsburg; RMC Place; CHRISTIAN; *180 M-3; elev. 536ft./163m.; mail Herndon z 42236; rural
Garrison; RMC Place; LEWIS; 181 F-16; elev. 535ft./163m.; 🅿; z 41141; ● 600
Garvin Ridge; RMC Place; CARTER; *181 G-16; mail Olive Hill z 41164; ● 150
Gascon; RMC Place; METCALFE; *180 L-9; elev. 1,007ft./307m.; mail Edmonton z 42129
Gaskill; RMC Place; LETCHER; *181 K-18; mail Jenkins z 41537; pop. incl. with Jenkins (Inc. Place)
Gasper; RMC Place; LOGAN; *180 L-5; mail Auburn z 42206
Gates; RMC Place; ROWAN; *181 G-16; mail Morehead z 40351; ● 50
Gatewood; RMC Place; DAVIESS; *180 I-5; mail Hawesville z 42348; rural
Gatliff; RMC Place; WHITLEY; 181 M-14; elev. 1,007ft./307m.; mail Williamsburg z 40769; ● 60
Gatun; RMC Place; HARLAN; *181 M-16; mail Baxter z 40806; rural
Gausdale; RMC Place; WHITLEY; *181 M-14; elev. 958ft./292m.; 🅿; z 40906; rural
Gaybourn; RMC Place; WOODFORD; *181 H-12; ★ LEX; mail Versailles z 40383; ● 140
Gays Creek; RMC Place; PERRY; 181 K-16; elev. 807ft./246m.; 🅿; z 41745; ● 80
Geddes; RMC Place; SIMPSON; *180 N-6; elev. 750ft./229m.; mail Franklin z 42134; rural
Geneva; RMC Place; HENDERSON; 180 I-2; elev. 389ft./119m.; mail Corydon z 42406; ● 150
Geneva; RMC Place; LINCOLN; *181 J-12; mail Hustonville z 40437; ● 100
Gentrys Mill; RMC Place; ADAIR; *180 L-10; mail Columbia z 42728; rural
Georgetown; RMC Place; HARLAN; *181 M-17; mail Holmes Mill z 40843; ● 125
Georgetown; Inc. Place; ⊡ SCOTT; 181 G-12; elev. 871ft./265m.; 🅿 🅷 🅲 1,910; ★ LEX; z 40324; Ⓟ 11,414; Ⓒ 18,080; ◆ 24,858
Germantown; Inc. Place; BRACKEN, MASON; 181 F-14; elev. 978ft./298m.; 🅿; z 41044; Ⓟ 213; Ⓒ 190
Germantown; RMC Place; JEFFERSON; *180 G-8; ★ LOU; mail Louisville z 40217; pop. incl. with Louisville (Inc. Place)
Gertrude; RMC Place; BRACKEN; *181 E-14; elev. 917ft./280m.; mail Brooksville z 41004; rural
Gesling; RMC Place; CARTER; *181 F-17; mail Carter z 41128; rural
Gest; RMC Place; HENRY; 181 G-11; mail Pleasureville z 40057; ● 50
Gethsemane; RMC Place; NELSON; *180 J-9; mail New Haven z 40051; rural
Ghent; Inc. Place; CARROLL; 181 E-11; elev. 495ft./151m.; 🅿; z 41045; Ⓟ 365; Ⓒ 371
Gibbs; RMC Place; KNOX; *181 L-14; mail Barbourville z 40906; rural
Gibson; FLOYD; see Minnie (RMC Place)
Gifford; RMC Place; MAGOFFIN; *181 I-17; elev. 840ft./256m.; 🅿; z 41465; rural
Gilbertsville; RMC Place; MARSHALL; 180 E-4; 🅿; z 42044; ● 800
Gillem Branch; RMC Place; JOHNSON; *181 H-17; mail Flatgap z 41219; rural
Gilley; RMC Place; LETCHER; 181 L-17; elev. 1,592ft./485m.; mail Gordon z 41819; ● 50
Gillmore; RMC Place; WOLFE; *181 I-16; elev. 978ft./298m.; 🅿; z 41301; rural
Gilpin; RMC Place; CASEY; 181 K-11; mail Liberty z 42539; ● 50
Gilreath; RMC Place; MCCREARY; *181 M-13; mail Pine Knot z 42635; rural
Gilstrap; RMC Place; BUTLER; *180 K-5; mail Horse Branch z 42349, Morgantown z 42261; rural
Gimlet; RMC Place; ELLIOTT; *181 G-17; mail Olive Hill z 41164; rural
Girdler; RMC Place; KNOX; 181 L-14; 🅿; z 40943; ● 250
Girkin; RMC Place; WARREN; *180 L-6; ★ BOWLG; mail Bowling Green z 42101; rural
Gishton; RMC Place; MUHLENBERG; *180 K-4; mail Bremen z 42325; ● 75
Glasgow; Inc. Place; ⊡ BARREN; 180 L-8; elev. 790ft./241m.; 🅿 🅷 ■; z 42141-42 & mail Lucas z 42156; Ⓟ 12,351; Ⓒ 13,019; ◆ 14,203
Gleanings; RMC Place; LARUE; *180 J-9; mail New Hope z 40052
Glenarm; RMC Place; OLDHAM; *180 G-9; ★ LOU; mail Crestwood z 40014; rural
Glencoe; Inc. Place; GALLATIN; 181 E-11; elev. 544ft./166m.; 🅿; z 41046; Ⓟ 257; Ⓒ 251
Glendale; RMC Place; HARDIN; 180 J-8; elev. 709ft./216m.; 🅿; z 42701, z 42740; ● 350
Glendale Junction; RMC Place; HARDIN; *180 J-8; mail Glendale z 42740; ● 15
Glen Dean; RMC Place; BRECKINRIDGE; 180 J-6; elev. 466ft./142m.; 🅿; z 40119; ● 50
Glengary; RMC Place; JEFFERSON; *180 H-8; ★ LOU; mail Fairdale z 40118; became part of Louisville/Jefferson County Metro Jan. 6, 2003
Glensboro; RMC Place; ANDERSON; 181 H-11; elev. 621ft./189m.; mail Lawrenceburg z 40342; ● 130
Glens Fork; RMC Place; ADAIR; 180 L-10; elev. 802ft./244m.; 🅿; z 42728, z 42741; ● 100
Glen Springs; RMC Place; LEWIS; *181 F-15; elev. 663ft./202m.; mail Vanceburg z 41179; rural
Glenview; Inc. Place; JEFFERSON; 180 A-8; elev. 438ft./134m.; 🅿; ★ LOU; z 40025; Ⓟ 653; Ⓒ 558
Glenview; RMC Place; SHELBY; *180 G-10; mail Shelbyville z 40065; ● 50
Glenview Hills; Inc. Place; JEFFERSON; 180 A-8; ★ LOU; mail Louisville z 40222; Ⓟ 353; Ⓒ 337
Glenview Manor; Inc. Place; JEFFERSON; *180 G-9; elev. 568ft./173m.; ★ LOU; mail Louisville z 40222; Ⓟ 197; Ⓒ 191
Glenville; RMC Place; MCLEAN; 180 J-4; elev. 441ft./134m.; mail Utica z 42376; ● 20
Glenwood; RMC Place; LAWRENCE; *181 G-18; mail Louisa z 41230; rural
Glo; RMC Place; FLOYD; *181 J-18; mail Wayland z 41666; ● 150
Globe; RMC Place; CARTER; 181 G-16; mail Olive Hill z 41164; ● 250
Glomawr; RMC Place; PERRY; *181 K-17; mail Hazard z 41701; ● 50
Goddard; RMC Place; FLEMING; *181 G-15; mail Wallingford z 41093
Goering; RMC Place; HANCOCK; *180 I-5; mail Hawesville z 42348; rural
Goffs Corner; RMC Place; CLARK; *181 H-14; mail Winchester z 40391; rural
Goforth; RMC Place; PENDLETON; *181 F-12; mail Falmouth z 41040; rural
Goins; RMC Place; WHITLEY; *181 M-14; elev. 1,023ft./312m.; mail Siler z 40763; rural
Goldbug; RMC Place; WHITLEY; 181 M-13; mail Williamsburg z 40769; ● 100
Gold City; RMC Place; SIMPSON; *180 M-6; elev. 722ft./220m.; mail Franklin z 42134
Golden Ash; RMC Place; HARLAN; *181 M-16; mail Harlan z 40831
Golden Pond; RMC Place; TRIGG; *180 M-1; elev. 414ft./126m.; 🅿; z 42211; rural
Golo; RMC Place; GRAVES; *180 F-4; mail Kirksey z 42054
Goochtown; RMC Place; PULASKI; *181 K-12; mail Eubank z 42567; rural
Goodluck; RMC Place; METCALFE; *180 M-9; mail Edmonton z 42129; rural
Goodnight; RMC Place; BARREN; *180 L-8; mail Cave City z 42127; ● 40
Goodwater; RMC Place; PULASKI; *181 L-13; mail Somerset z 42501; rural
Goody; RMC Place; PIKE; *181 I-19; elev. 665ft./203m.; 🅿; z 41514; ● 200
Goose Creek; Inc. Place; JEFFERSON; *180 G-9; elev. 440ft./134m.; ★ LOU; mail Louisville z 40222; Ⓟ 321; Ⓒ 272
Goose Rock; RMC Place; CLAY; 181 L-15; elev. 874ft./266m.; 🅿; z 40944; ● 200
Gordon; RMC Place; LETCHER; 181 L-17; elev. 1,309ft./399m.; 🅿; z 41819; ● 100
Gordon Ford; RMC Place; MORGAN; *181 I-16; mail West Liberty z 41472; rural
Gordonsville; RMC Place; LOGAN; *180 M-4; mail Russellville z 42276; ● 40
Goshen; Inc. Place; OLDHAM; 180 G-9; elev. 700ft./213m.; 🅿; ★ LOU; z 40026; Ⓟ 903; Ⓒ 907
Gotts; RMC Place; WARREN; *180 L-7; mail Bowling Green z 42103; rural
Grab; RMC Place; GREEN; *180 K-9; mail Greensburg z 42743; rural
Grace; RMC Place; CLAY; *181 K-14; elev. 940ft./287m.; 🅿; z 40962; rural
Gracey; RMC Place; CHRISTIAN; 180 M-2; elev. 510ft./155m.; 🅿; z 42232; ● 300
Gradyville; RMC Place; ADAIR; 180 L-9; elev. 712ft./217m.; 🅿; z 42742; ● 75
Graefenburg; RMC Place; SHELBY; *181 H-11; mail Frankfort z 40601; ● 100
Graham; RMC Place; MUHLENBERG; 180 K-3; elev. 466ft./142m.; 🅿; z 42344; ● 700
Graham Hill; RMC Place; HENDERSON; *180 I-3; ★ EV; mail Henderson z 42420; ● 100
Grahamville; RMC Place; MCCRACKEN; 180 E-3; elev. 379ft./116m.; ★ PAD; mail West Paducah z 42086; ● 200
Grahn; RMC Place; CARTER; 181 G-17; elev. 718ft./219m.; 🅿; z 41142; ● 550
Gra-Mor; RMC Place; NELSON; *180 I-9; mail Bardstown z 40004; ● 70
Grancer; RMC Place; BUTLER; *180 K-6; elev. 438ft./134m.; mail Welchs Creek z 42287; rural
Grand Rivers; Inc. Place; LIVINGSTON; 180 L-1; elev. 451ft./137m.; 🅿; z 42045; Ⓟ 351; Ⓒ 343
Grandview; RMC Place; MONROE; *180 M-9; mail Tompkinsville z 42167; pop. incl. with Tompkinsville (Inc. Place)
Grandview Heights; RMC Place; FRANKLIN; *181 G-11; mail Frankfort z 40601; pop. incl. with Frankfort (Inc. Place)
Grange City; RMC Place; FLEMING; 181 G-15; mail Hillsboro z 41049; ● 75
Grangertown; RMC Place; UNION; 180 J-1; mail Sturgis z 42459; ● 100
GRANT; 181 F-12; Ⓟ 15,737; Ⓒ 22,384; ◆ 25,710
Grants Lick; RMC Place; CAMPBELL; 181 E-13; elev. 638ft./194m.; ★ CIN; mail Alexandria z 41001; ● 100
Grant Wood Hills; RMC Place; HENDERSON; *180 I-3; ★ EV; mail Henderson z 42420; ● 160
Grapevine; RMC Place; HOPKINS; *180 K-3; elev. 517ft./158m.; mail Madisonville z 42431; ● 200
Grassy Creek; RMC Place; MORGAN; *181 I-16; elev. 789ft./240m.; 🅿; z 41352 & mail Hazel Green z 41332
Grassy Lick; RMC Place; MONTGOMERY; *181 H-14; elev. 891ft./272m.; mail Mount Sterling z 40353; rural
Gratz; Inc. Place; OWEN; 181 F-11; elev. 484ft./148m.; 🅿; z 40359; Ⓟ 65; Ⓒ 89
Gravel Switch; RMC Place; MARION; 181 J-11; elev. 910ft./277m.; 🅿; z 40328; ● 75
Graveltown; BUTLER; see Harreldsville (RMC Place)
GRAVES; 180 F-3; Ⓟ 33,550; Ⓒ 37,028; ◆ 37,634
Gray (Grays); RMC Place; KNOX; 181 L-14; elev. 1,102ft./336m.; 🅿; z 40734; ● 750
Gray Hawk; RMC Place; JACKSON; 181 K-14; elev. 1,268ft./386m.; 🅿; z 40434; ● 100
Graymoor; RMC Place; JEFFERSON; *180 G-9; ★ LOU; mail Louisville z 40222; pop. incl. with Graymoor-Devondale (Inc. Place)
Graymoor-Devondale; Inc. Place; JEFFERSON; 180 B-9; elev. 564ft./172m.; ★ LOU; mail Louisville z 40222; Ⓟ 2,911; Ⓒ 2,925
Grays; KNOX; see Gray (RMC Place)
Grays Branch; RMC Place; GREENUP; 181 E-17; mail Greenup z 41144; ● 125
Grays Knob; RMC Place; HARLAN; 181 M-16; elev. 1,208ft./368m.; 🅿; z 40829; ● 300
Grayson; Inc. Place; ⊡ CARTER; 181 G-17; elev. 608ft./185m.; 🅿 🅲 542; ★ HNTG; z 41143; Ⓟ 3,510; Ⓒ 3,877
GRAYSON; 180 J-7; Ⓟ 21,050; Ⓒ 24,053; ◆ 25,293
Grayson Springs; RMC Place; GRAYSON; *180 J-7; elev. 573ft./175m.; mail Clarkson z 42726
Graysville; RMC Place; BRECKINRIDGE; *180 I-7; mail Irvington z 40146; rural
Greasy Creek; RMC Place; PIKE; *181 K-19; mail Shelbiana z 41562; ● 450
Great Crossing; RMC Place; SCOTT; *181 G-12; mail Georgetown z 40324; ● 100
Greear; RMC Place; MORGAN; *181 I-16; mail West Liberty z 41472; rural
Green; RMC Place; ELLIOTT; *181 H-17; mail Olive Hill z 41164; rural
GREEN; 180 K-9; Ⓟ 10,371; Ⓒ 11,518; ◆ 11,509
Green Acres; RMC Place; BOYLE; mail Danville z 40422; pop. incl. with Danville (Inc. Place)
Green Acres; RMC Place; FAYETTE; *181 H-12; ★ LEX; mail Lexington z 40511; pop. incl. with Lexington (Inc. Place)
Greenbriar; RMC Place; DAVIESS; *180 I-4; ★ OWNS; mail Owensboro z 42303; ● 400
Greenbriar; RMC Place; MARION; *180 J-10; mail Lebanon z 40033; rural
Greenbriar; RMC Place; OLDHAM; *180 G-9; ★ LOU; mail La Grange z 40031; ● 75
Greenbrier; RMC Place; LINCOLN; *181 K-12; mail Waynesburg z 40489; rural
Greencastle; RMC Place; WARREN; *180 L-6; elev. 424ft./129m.; rural
Greendale; RMC Place; FAYETTE; *181 H-12; ★ LEX; mail Lexington z 40511; pop. incl. with Lexington (Inc. Place)
Green Fields Estates; RMC Place; CLARK; *181 H-13; ★ LEX; mail Winchester z 40391; ● 300
Green Grove; RMC Place; CUMBERLAND; *180 M-10; mail Burkesville z 42717; rural
Green Hall; RMC Place; OWSLEY, JACKSON; 181 K-14; elev. 984ft./300m.; 🅿; z 41314; rural
Green Hill; RMC Place; JACKSON; *181 K-14; mail Annville z 40402; rural
Greenhill; RMC Place; WARREN; *180 M-7; elev. 584ft./178m.; mail Bowling Green z 42103; rural
Green Hills; RMC Place; ADAIR; *180 L-10; mail Columbia z 42728; ● 70
Greenland Park; RMC Place; SHELBY; *180 G-10; mail Shelbyville z 40065; ● 250
Greenmount; RMC Place; LAUREL; *181 K-14; mail London z 40741; rural
Greenough; RMC Place; PIKE
Green Road; RMC Place; KNOX; *181 L-14; elev. 944ft./288m.; 🅿; z 40946; ● 125
Greensburg; Inc. Place; ⊡ GREEN; 180 K-9; elev. 632ft./193m.; 🅿 🅷; z 42743; Ⓟ 1,990; Ⓒ 2,396
Green Spring; Inc. Place; JEFFERSON; 180 A-9; elev. 559ft./170m.; ★ LOU; mail Louisville z 40222; Ⓟ 768; Ⓒ 759
Greenup; Inc. Place; ⊡ GREENUP; 181 F-18; elev. 536ft./163m.; 🅿; ★ HNTG; z 41144; Ⓟ 1,158; Ⓒ 1,198
GREENUP; 181 F-17; Ⓟ 36,742; Ⓒ 36,891; ◆ 37,232
Greenview; RMC Place; BOONE; *181 D-12; ★ CIN; mail Florence z 41042; ● 300
Greenville; Inc. Place; ⊡ MUHLENBERG; 180 K-4; elev. 538ft./164m.; 🅿 🅷; z 42345; Ⓟ 4,689; Ⓒ 4,398
Greenwood; RMC Place; MCCREARY; 181 M-12; 🅿; z 42634; ● 95
Greenwood; RMC Place; PENDLETON; *181 E-13; mail Butler z 41006; rural
Greenwood; RMC Place; WARREN; *180 L-6; ★ BOWLG; mail Bowling Green z 42104; pop. incl. with Bowling Green (Inc. Place)
Gregory; RMC Place; WAYNE; *181 M-12; elev. 952ft./290m.; 🅿; z 42633; rural
Gregoryville; RMC Place; CARTER; *181 G-17; mail Grayson z 41143; ● 50
Gresham; RMC Place; GREEN; *180 K-9; mail Greensburg z 42743
Grethel; RMC Place; FLOYD; 181 J-18; elev. 707ft./215m.; 🅿; z 41631; ● 100
Grider; RMC Place; CUMBERLAND; 180 M-9; mail Burkesville z 42717; ● 50
Griderville; RMC Place; BARREN; *180 L-8; mail Cave City z 42127; ● 30
Griffin; RMC Place; WAYNE; *181 M-12; mail Monticello z 42633; rural
Griffith; RMC Place; DAVIESS; *180 I-4; elev. 836ft./255m.; ★ OWNS; mail Owensboro z 42301; rural
Griffytown; RMC Place; JEFFERSON; *180 G-9; ★ LOU; mail Louisville z 40243; became part of Louisville/Jefferson County Metro Jan. 6, 2003
Grigsby; RMC Place; PERRY; *181 K-17; mail Bulan z 41722; rural
Grove Center; RMC Place; UNION; 180 J-1; mail Morganfield z 42437; ● 70
Grundy; RMC Place; PULASKI; *181 L-12; mail Somerset z 42501; rural
Guage; RMC Place; BREATHITT; *181 J-16; elev. 800ft./244m.; 🅿; z 41339; rural
Gubser Mill (Gubser Mills); RMC Place; CAMPBELL; *181 E-13; ★ CIN; mail California z 41007; rural
Gubser Mills; CAMPBELL; see Gubser Mill (RMC Place)
Guerrant; RMC Place; BREATHITT; *181 J-16; elev. 800ft./244m.; 🅿; z 41339; ● 50
Guffie; RMC Place; MCLEAN; *180 J-4; elev. 433ft./132m.; mail Calhoun z 42327
Gulfco; RMC Place; BOYD; ★ HNTG; pop. incl. with Ashland (Inc. Place)
Gullett; RMC Place; MAGOFFIN; *181 I-17; mail Salyersville z 41465; rural
Gulnare; RMC Place; PIKE; *181 J-19; elev. 694ft./212m.; 🅿; z 41501
Gulston; HARLAN; see Pansy (RMC Place)
Gum Sulphur; RMC Place; ROCKCASTLE; *181 K-12; mail Crab Orchard z 40419
Gum Tree; RMC Place; MONROE; *180 M-8; mail Tompkinsville z 42167; ● 25
Gunlock; RMC Place; MAGOFFIN; 181 J-17; elev. 989ft./301m.; 🅿; z 41632; ● 20
Guston; RMC Place; MEADE; 180 I-7; elev. 698ft./213m.; 🅿; z 40142; ● 200
Guthrie; Inc. Place; TODD; 180 N-4; elev. 548ft./167m.; 🅿; z 42234; Ⓟ 1,504; Ⓒ 1,469
Guy; RMC Place; WARREN; *180 L-6; elev. 508ft./155m.; mail Bowling Green z 42101; rural
Gwinn Island; RMC Place; BOYLE; *181 I-11; mail Danville z 40422; ● 50
Gypsy; RMC Place; MAGOFFIN; *181 I-17; elev. 933ft./284m.; 🅿; z 41464; rural

H

Habit; RMC Place; DAVIESS; 180 I-4; elev. 560ft./171m.; mail Philpot z 42366; ● 100
Haddix; RMC Place; BREATHITT; 181 J-16; elev. 760ft./232m.; 🅿; z 41339; ● 150
Hadensville; RMC Place; TODD; *180 N-4; elev. 559ft./170m.; mail Guthrie z 42234; rural
Hadley; RMC Place; WARREN; 180 L-6; elev. 680ft./207m.; 🅿; z 42101; ● 25
Hager; RMC Place; MAGOFFIN; *181 I-16; elev. 844ft./257m.; 🅿; z 41465; rural
Hagerhill; RMC Place; JOHNSON; 181 I-18; elev. 622ft./190m.; 🅿; z 41222; ● 150
Hail; RMC Place; PULASKI; *181 L-12; mail Somerset z 42501; rural
Halcom; RMC Place; ELLIOTT; *181 H-17; mail Sandy Hook z 41171; rural
Haldeman; RMC Place; ROWAN; 181 G-16; elev. 943ft./287m.; 🅿; z 40351; ● 250
Halfway; RMC Place; ALLEN; 180 M-7; elev. 770ft./235m.; 🅿; z 42164; ● 35
Halifax; RMC Place; ALLEN; *180 M-7; elev. 734ft./224m.; mail Scottsville z 42164; rural
Hall; RMC Place; JESSAMINE; *181 I-12; ★ LEX; mail Nicholasville z 40356; ● 100
Hall; RMC Place; KNOTT; *181 K-18; 🅿; z 41840 & mail Kite z 41828; rural
Hallie; RMC Place; LETCHER; *181 L-17; elev. 1,011ft./308m.; 🅿; z 41821; ● 40
Halls Gap; RMC Place; LINCOLN; 181 J-12; mail Waynesburg z 40489; ● 90
Halls Store; RMC Place; LOGAN; *180 M-5; elev. 631ft./192m.; mail Russellville z 42276; rural
Halo; RMC Place; FLOYD; 181 K-18; elev. 1,187ft./362m.; 🅿; z 41606; ● 150
Hamlin; RMC Place; CALLOWAY; 180 N-1; elev. 384ft./117m.; 🅿; z 42076; ● 175
Hammackville; TODD; see Zion (RMC Place)
Hammond; RMC Place; JOHNSON; *181 I-18; mail Paintsville z 41240; rural
Hammonville; RMC Place; HART; 180 K-8; mail Magnolia z 42757; ● 30
Hampton; RMC Place; LIVINGSTON; 180 D-4; elev. 518ft./158m.; 🅿; z 42047; ● 100
Hampton Manor; RMC Place; CLARK; *181 H-13; ★ LEX; mail Winchester z 40391; pop. incl. with Winchester (Inc. Place)
HANCOCK; 180 I-5; Ⓟ 7,864; Ⓒ 8,392; ◆ 8,545
Handshoe; RMC Place; KNOTT; *181 J-17; mail Hueysville z 41640; rural
Hanly; RMC Place; JESSAMINE; *181 I-12; ★ LEX; mail Nicholasville z 40356
Hannah; RMC Place; LAWRENCE; *181 H-17; mail Blaine z 41124; rural
Hansford; RMC Place; ROCKCASTLE; *181 K-13; mail Mount Vernon z 40456; rural
Hanson; Inc. Place; HOPKINS; 180 J-3; elev. 433ft./132m.; 🅿; z 42413; Ⓟ 450; Ⓒ 625
Happy; RMC Place; PERRY; *181 K-17; elev. 920ft./280m.; 🅿; z 41746; ● 100
Happy Acre; RMC Place; RUSSELL; *181 L-11; mail Russell Springs z 42642; ● 70
Happy Landing; RMC Place; MADISON; *181 J-13; mail Berea z 40403; rural
Harcrow; RMC Place; HARLAN; *181 M-17; pop. incl. with Evarts (Inc. Place)
Hardburly; RMC Place; PERRY; *181 K-17; elev. 1,058ft./322m.; 🅿; z 41747; ● 350
Hardin; Inc. Place; MARSHALL; 180 M-1; elev. 418ft./127m.; 🅿; z 42048; Ⓟ 595; Ⓒ 564
HARDIN; 180 J-7; Ⓟ 89,240; Ⓒ 94,174; ◆ 98,861
Hardinsburg; Inc. Place; ⊡ BRECKINRIDGE; 180 I-6; elev. 714ft./218m.; 🅿 🅷; z 40143; Ⓟ 1,906; Ⓒ 2,345
Hardin Springs; RMC Place; HARDIN; *180 J-7
Hardmoney; RMC Place; MCCRACKEN; *180 F-4; ★ PAD; mail Paducah z 42003; rural
Hardshell; RMC Place; BREATHITT; 181 J-16; elev. 787ft./240m.; 🅿; z 41348; ● 15
Hardwick; RMC Place; WAYNE; *181 M-12; mail Monticello z 42633; rural
Hardy; RMC Place; PIKE; 181 J-20; elev. 740ft./226m.; 🅿; z 41531 & mail Ransom z 41558; ● 650
Hardyville; RMC Place; HART; 180 K-8; elev. 690ft./210m.; 🅿; z 42746; ● 250
Hare; RMC Place; LAUREL; *181 K-13; mail East Bernstadt z 40729; rural
Hargett; RMC Place; ESTILL; *181 I-14; mail Irvine z 40336; rural
Harlan; Inc. Place; ⊡ HARLAN; 181 M-16; elev. 1,197ft./365m.; 🅿 🅷 ■; z 40831, z 40840; Ⓟ 2,686; Ⓒ 2,081; ◆ 1,815
HARLAN; 181 L-17; Ⓟ 36,574; Ⓒ 33,202; ◆ 30,795
Harlan Crossroads; RMC Place; MONROE; *180 N-8; elev. 872ft./266m.; mail Tompkinsville z 42167; ● 35
Harlan Gas; RMC Place; HARLAN; *181 M-16; mail Harlan z 40831; ● 50
Harmony; RMC Place; OWEN; *181 G-12; elev. 726ft./221m.; mail Owenton z 40359; rural
Harmony Lake Estates; RMC Place; OLDHAM; *180 G-9; ★ LOU; mail Prospect z 40059; ● 750
Harmony Village; RMC Place; OLDHAM; *180 G-9; ★ LOU; mail Prospect z 40059; ● 125
Harned; RMC Place; BRECKINRIDGE; 180 I-6; elev. 755ft./230m.; 🅿; z 40144; ● 140
Harold; RMC Place; FLOYD; 181 J-18; elev. 664ft./202m.; 🅿; z 41635; ● 400
Harper; RMC Place; MAGOFFIN; *181 I-16; elev. 843ft./257m.; 🅿; z 41465; rural
Harreldsville (Graveltown); RMC Place; BUTLER; *180 L-5; elev. 622ft./190m.; mail Lewisburg z 42256; rural
Harrington Mill Estates; RMC Place; SHELBY; *180 G-10; mail Shelbyville z 40065; ● 50
Harris; RMC Place; LEWIS; *181 G-16; mail Vanceburg z 41179; rural
Harris Grove; RMC Place; CALLOWAY; *180 G-4; mail Murray z 42071; rural
HARRISON; 181 F-12; Ⓟ 16,248; Ⓒ 17,983; ◆ 18,782
Harrisonville; RMC Place; SHELBY; 181 H-11; elev. 889ft./271m.; mail Waddy z 40076; ● 75
Harrodsburg; Inc. Place; ⊡ MERCER; 181 I-11; elev. 886ft./270m.; 🅿 🅷; z 40330; Ⓟ 7,335; Ⓒ 8,014
Harrods Creek; RMC Place; JEFFERSON; 180 A-8; elev. 452ft./138m.; 🅿; ★ LOU; z 40027; became part of Louisville/Jefferson County Metro Jan. 6, 2003
Harrods Hills; RMC Place; FAYETTE; *181 H-12; ★ LEX; mail Lexington z 40513; pop. incl. with Lexington (Inc. Place)
Hart; RMC Place; LAUREL; mail London z 40741; rural
HART; 180 K-8; Ⓟ 14,890; Ⓒ 17,445; ◆ 18,461
Hartford; Inc. Place; ⊡ OHIO; 180 J-5; elev. 428ft./130m.; 🅿 🅷; z 42347; Ⓟ 2,532; Ⓒ 2,571
Hartley; RMC Place; PIKE; *181 K-18; mail Virgie z 41572; rural
Harvey (Harvy); RMC Place; MARSHALL; *180 F-4; mail Benton z 42025; rural
Harveyton; RMC Place; PERRY; *181 K-16; mail Bonnyman z 41719; rural
Harvy; MARSHALL; see Harvey (RMC Place)
Haselton; LEWIS; see Heselton (RMC Place)
Haskingsville; RMC Place; GREEN; *180 K-9; mail Greensburg z 42743; rural
Hatcher; RMC Place; TAYLOR; 180 K-10; mail Campbellsville z 42718; ● 60
Hatfield; RMC Place; PIKE; *181 I-19; 🅿; z 41514; rural
Hatton; RMC Place; SHELBY; *181 G-11; elev. 693ft./211m.; 🅿; z 40601; ● 40
Hawesville; Inc. Place; ⊡ HANCOCK; 180 I-5; elev. 531ft./162m.; 🅿; z 42348; Ⓟ 998; Ⓒ 971
Hawkeegan Point; RMC Place; FRANKLIN; mail Frankfort z 40601; ● 50
Hayes; RMC Place; PENDLETON; *181 F-13; mail Falmouth z 41040; rural
Haymond; LETCHER; see Cromona (RMC Place)
Haynesville; RMC Place; OHIO; *180 I-5; elev. 476ft./145m.; mail Reynolds Station z 42368; rural
Hays; RMC Place; WARREN; 180 L-7; elev. 672ft./205m.; mail Smiths Grove z 42171; ● 30
Hays Crossing; RMC Place; ROWAN; *181 G-16; mail Morehead z 40351; ● 200
Hayward; RMC Place; CARTER; *181 G-16; mail Olive Hill z 41164, Soldier z 41173; rural
Haywood; RMC Place; BARREN; *180 L-8; mail Glasgow z 42141
Hazard; Inc. Place; ⊡ PERRY; 181 K-17; elev. 867ft./264m.; 🅿 🅷; z 41701-02; Ⓟ 5,416; Ⓒ 4,806; Ⓡ 4,861
Hazel; Inc. Place; CALLOWAY; 180 G-4; elev. 561ft./171m.; 🅿; z 42049; Ⓟ 460; Ⓒ 440
Hazel Green; RMC Place; WOLFE; 181 I-16; elev. 937ft./286m.; 🅿; z 41332; ● 300
Hazel Patch; RMC Place; LAUREL; *181 K-13; mail East Bernstadt z 40729; rural
Head of Grassy; RMC Place; LEWIS; *181 G-16; elev. 716ft./218m.; 🅿; z 41135; rural
Headquarters; RMC Place; NICHOLAS; *181 G-14; mail Carlisle z 40311
Hearin; RMC Place; WEBSTER; *180 J-2; mail Clay z 42404; rural
Heath; RMC Place; MCCRACKEN; 180 E-3; ★ PAD; mail West Paducah z 42086; ● 125
Hebbardsville; RMC Place; HENDERSON; 180 I-3; elev. 423ft./129m.; mail Henderson z 42420; ● 125

Entries in **UPPERCASE** are counties.
Entries in **bold** have populations of 2,500 or more.
Names in parentheses are alternate names.
Inc. Place — Incorporated Place
RMC Place — Rand McNally Designated Place
CDP — Census Designated Place
MCD — Minor Civil Division

⊡ County Seat
▲ Minor Civil Division
elev. Elevation
🅿 Post Office

🅷 Hospital
🅲 College
■ Principal Business Center
★ Ranally Metro Area (RMA) Abbreviation
z Zip Code(s)

Ⓟ Previous Census Population
Ⓡ Revised Census Population
Ⓐ Annexation Population
● Rand McNally Population Estimate
Ⓒ Final Census Population
Ⓢ Special Census Population
◆ Estimated Population

For additional definitions see Glossary, Volume 1, and Introduction, Volume 2.

Hebron; RMC Place; BOONE; **181** D-12; elev. 875ft./267m.; 🅿; ★ **CIN**; z 41048; ● 3,500

Hebron Estates; Inc. Place; BULLITT; ***180** H-9; ★ **LOU**; mail Shepherdsville z 40165; Ⓟ 930; © 1,104

Hecla; RMC Place; HOPKINS; ***180** K-3; mail Earlington z 42410; ● 100

Hector; RMC Place; CLAY; ***181** L-15; elev. 956ft./291m.; mail Manchester z 40962; rural

Hedgeville; RMC Place; BOYLE; ***181** J-12; mail Lancaster z 40444; rural

Heekin; RMC Place; GRANT; ***181** F-12; mail Williamstown z 41097; rural

Heenon; RMC Place; PIKE; ***181** I-19; mail Pikeville z 41501; rural

Heflin; RMC Place; OHIO; ***180** J-4; mail Hartford z 42347

Hegira; RMC Place; CUMBERLAND; ***180** M-10; elev. 1,053ft./321m.; mail Burkesville z 42717; rural

Heidelberg; RMC Place; LEE; **181** J-15; elev. 688ft./210m.; 🅿; z 41333; ● 300

Heidrick; RMC Place; KNOX; **181** M-14; elev. 983ft./300m.; 🅿; z 40949; ● 700

Heiner; RMC Place; PERRY; ***181** K-17; mail Bulan z 41722; ● 80

Helechawa; RMC Place; WOLFE; **181** I-16; elev. 957ft./292m.; 🅿; z 41332; ● 25

Helena; RMC Place; MASON; **181** F-15; mail Mayslick z 41055; ● 50

Hellier; RMC Place; PIKE; **181** K-19; elev. 1,128ft./344m.; 🅿; z 41534; ● 400

Helton; RMC Place; LESLIE; **181** L-16; elev. 1,226ft./374m.; 🅿; z 40840 & mail Harlan z 40831; ● 30

Hemphill (Jackhorn); RMC Place; LETCHER; **181** K-18; elev. 1,377ft./420m.; mail Jackhorn z 41825; ● 500

Hemp Ridge; RMC Place; SHELBY; ***180** H-10; mail Waddy z 40076; rural

Henderson; Inc. Place; ⊡ HENDERSON; **180** I-3; elev. 409ft./125m.; 🅿 🅷 ■; ★ **EV**; z 42419-20; Ⓟ 25,945; © 27,373; ◆ 27,985

HENDERSON; **180** I-2; Ⓟ 43,044; © 44,829; ◆ 44,921

Hendricks; RMC Place; MAGOFFIN; **181** I-17; elev. 881ft./269m.; 🅿; z 41465; ● 60

Hendron; CDP; MCCRACKEN; ***180** E-3; elev. 366ft./112m.; ★ **PAD**; mail Paducah z 42001; Ⓟ 3,712; © 4,239

Henrietta; RMC Place; JOHNSON; ***181** I-18; mail Paintsville z 41240; rural

HENRY; **181** G-11; Ⓟ 12,823; © 15,060; ◆ 15,518

Henry Clay; RMC Place; FAYETTE; ***181** H-12; ★ **LEX**; mail Lexington z 40502, z 40522; pop. incl. with Lexington (Inc. Place)

Henry Clay; RMC Place; PIKE; ***181** K-19; mail Lookout z 41542

Henryville; RMC Place; NICHOLAS; ***181** G-14; mail Carlisle z 40311; ● 75

Henshaw; RMC Place; UNION; **180** J-1; 🅿; z 42437; ● 100

Hensley; RMC Place; BRECKINRIDGE; ***180** I-6; elev. 833ft./254m.; mail Irvington z 40146; rural

Hensley; RMC Place; CLAY; ***181** K-15; mail Manchester z 40962; rural

Herbert; RMC Place; OHIO; ***180** I-5; elev. 529ft./161m.; mail Reynolds Station z 42368; rural

Herd; RMC Place; JACKSON; **181** K-14; elev. 1,103ft./336m.; 🅿; z 40486; ● 15

Heritage Creek (Minor Lane Heights); Inc. Place; JEFFERSON; **180** D-7; elev. 460ft./140m.; ★ **LOU**; mail Louisville z 40219; Ⓟ 1,675; © 1,435

Heritage Village; RMC Place; TAYLOR; ***180** K-10; mail Campbellsville z 42718; pop. incl. with Campbellsville (Inc. Place)

Hermitage Hills; RMC Place; FAYETTE; ***181** H-12; ★ **LEX**; mail Lexington z 40505; pop. incl. with Lexington (Inc. Place)

Hermon; RMC Place; TODD; ***180** M-4; mail Guthrie z 42234; rural

Herndon; RMC Place; CHRISTIAN; **180** M-2; elev. 500ft./152m.; 🅿; z 42236; ● 150

Herron Hill; RMC Place; LEWIS; ***181** F-15; mail Tollesboro z 41189; rural

Heselton (Haselton); RMC Place; LEWIS; ***181** F-16; mail Vanceburg z 41179; rural

Hesler; RMC Place; OWEN; **181** F-11; elev. 944ft./288m.; mail Owenton z 40359; ● 60

Hestand; RMC Place; MONROE; **180** N-9; elev. 896ft./273m.; 🅿; z 42151; ● 25

Hi Acres; RMC Place; FAYETTE; ***181** H-12; ★ **LEX**; mail Lexington z 40505; pop. incl. with Lexington (Inc. Place)

Hickman; Inc. Place; ⊡ FULTON; **180** G-1; elev. 310ft./94m.; 🅿; z 42050; Ⓟ 2,689; © 2,560

HICKMAN; **180** G-2; Ⓟ 5,566; © 5,262; ◆ 4,860

Hickory; RMC Place; GRAVES; **180** F-3; elev. 426ft./130m.; 🅿; z 42051; ● 150

Hickory Flat; RMC Place; SIMPSON; ***180** M-6; elev. 709ft./216m.; mail Franklin z 42134; rural

Hickory Grove (Cary Ridge); RMC Place; CUMBERLAND; mail Burkesville z 42717; rural

Hickory Grove; RMC Place; MCCREARY; ***181** N-12; elev. 1,300ft./396m.; mail Revelo z 42638; rural

Hickory Hill; Inc. Place; JEFFERSON; ***180** G-9; ★ **LOU**; mail Louisville z 40222; Ⓟ 152; © 144

Hickory Hills; RMC Place; FRANKLIN; ***181** G-11; mail Frankfort z 40601; pop. incl. with Frankfort (Inc. Place)

Hidalgo; RMC Place; WAYNE; ***181** M-11; mail Monticello z 42633; rural

Hide-A-Way Hills; RMC Place; OWEN; ***181** F-11; mail Owenton z 40359; ● 50

High Bridge; RMC Place; JESSAMINE; **181** I-12; elev. 798ft./243m.; ★ **LEX**; mail Wilmore z 40390; ● 150

High Falls; RMC Place; WOLFE; ***181** I-15; mail Campton z 41301; rural

Highgrove; RMC Place; NELSON; ***180** H-9; 🅿; z 40013

High Knob; RMC Place; JACKSON; ***181** K-14; mail Annville z 40402; rural

Highland; RMC Place; LINCOLN; ***181** K-12; mail Stanford z 40484, Waynesburg z 40489; ● 60

Highland; RMC Place; SIMPSON; ***180** M-6; mail Franklin z 42134; rural

Highland Heights; Inc. Place; CAMPBELL; **181** C-17; elev. 852ft./260m.; 🅿 🅲 14,617; ★ **CIN**; z 41076 & mail Newport z 41099; Ⓟ 4,223; © 6,554

Highland Park; RMC Place; JEFFERSON; ***180** G-8; ★ **LOU**; mail Louisville z 40209; pop. incl. with Louisville (Inc. Place)

Highland Park; RMC Place; WHITLEY; ***181** M-13; mail Williamsburg z 40769; pop. incl. with Williamsburg (Inc. Place)

Highlands; RMC Place; FAYETTE; ***181** H-12; ★ **LEX**; mail Lexington z 40511; pop. incl. with Lexington (Inc. Place)

Highlands; RMC Place; JEFFERSON; ***180** G-8; ★ **LOU**; mail Louisville z 40206; pop. incl. with Louisville (Inc. Place)

High Plains; RMC Place; BRECKINRIDGE; ***180** I-7; mail Vine Grove z 40175; rural

High Point; RMC Place; MCCRACKEN; ***180** E-3; elev. 335ft./102m.; ★ **PAD**; mail West Paducah z 42086; ● 100

Highsplint; RMC Place; HARLAN; ***181** M-17; mail Evarts z 40828; ● 20

Hightop; RMC Place; LAUREL; ***181** L-13; mail London z 40744; rural

Highview; CDP; JEFFERSON; ***180** H-9; ★ **LOU**; mail Louisville z 40219, z 40228; former CDP; became part of Louisville/Jefferson County Metro Jan. 6, 2003; Ⓟ 14,814; © 15,161

Highview; RMC Place; OHIO; ***180** K-5; mail Beaver Dam z 42320; ● 15

Highway; RMC Place; CLINTON; ***180** M-10; 🅿; z 42602; rural

Hignite; RMC Place; BELL; mail Middlesboro z 40965; rural

Hi Hat; RMC Place; FLOYD; **181** K-18; elev. 815ft./248m.; 🅿; z 41636; ● 200

Hikes Point; RMC Place; JEFFERSON; ***180** G-9; ★ **LOU**; mail Louisville z 40220, z 40250; pop. incl. with Louisville (Inc. Place)

Hilda; RMC Place; ROWAN; ***181** G-15; mail Morehead z 40351

Hillcrest; RMC Place; MADISON; **181** I-13; mail Richmond z 40475; ● 300

Hillendale; RMC Place; GALLATIN; ***181** E-11; mail Warsaw z 41095; summer pop. 100; ● 20

Hill-N-Dale; RMC Place; SHELBY; ***180** G-10; mail Shelbyville z 40065; ● 50

Hill Ridge; RMC Place; JEFFERSON; ***180** G-9; ★ **LOU**; mail Louisville z 40299; became part of Louisville/Jefferson County Metro Jan. 6, 2003

Hills and Dales; Inc. Place; JEFFERSON; ***180** G-9; ★ **LOU**; mail Louisville z 40222; Ⓟ 154; © 153

Hillsboro; RMC Place; FLEMING; **181** G-15; elev. 868ft./265m.; 🅿; z 41049; ● 150

Hillsdale; RMC Place; SIMPSON; ***180** M-6; mail Franklin z 42134; rural

Hillside; RMC Place; MUHLENBERG; ***180** K-4; elev. 469ft./143m.; mail Central City z 42330; ● 70

Hill Top; RMC Place; FLEMING; ***181** G-14; elev. 894ft./272m.; mail Ewing z 41039; ● 50

Hilltop; RMC Place; GRANT; ***181** F-12; mail Williamstown z 41097; pop. incl. with Williamstown (Inc. Place)

Hilltop; RMC Place; LOGAN; ***180** N-5; mail Adairville z 42202; rural

Hill Top; RMC Place; MCCREARY; ***181** M-12; elev. 1,253ft./382m.; mail Stearns z 42647; rural

Hillview; Inc. Place; BULLITT; **180** H-9; elev. 550ft./168m.; 🅿; ★ **LOU**; z 40129 & mail Louisville z 40229; Ⓟ 6,119; © 7,037

Hillview; RMC Place; EDMONSON; ***180** K-7; elev. 600ft./183m.; mail Bee Spring z 42207; rural

Hima; RMC Place; CLAY; **181** L-15; elev. 900ft./274m.; 🅿; z 40951; ● 250

Himyar; RMC Place; KNOX; **181** M-15; elev. 1,029ft./314m.; 🅿; z 40906; ● 100

Hinda Heights; RMC Place; FAYETTE; ***181** H-12; ★ **LEX**; mail Lexington z 40502; pop. incl. with Lexington (Inc. Place)

Hindman; Inc. Place; ⊡ KNOTT; **181** K-17; elev. 1,031ft./314m.; 🅿; z 41822; Ⓟ 798; © 787

Hinkle; RMC Place; KNOX; ***181** M-15; elev. 1,011ft./308m.; 🅿; z 40953; ● 70

Hinkleville; RMC Place; BALLARD; ***180** E-2; mail La Center z 42056; rural

Hinton; RMC Place; HARRISON, SCOTT; ***181** F-12; mail Corinth z 41010; ● 50

Hinton Hills; RMC Place; BRECKINRIDGE; ***180** J-6; mail Hardinsburg z 40143; ● 400

Hippo; RMC Place; FLOYD; ***181** J-18; elev. 729ft./222m.; 🅿; z 41653; ● 150

Hiram; RMC Place; HARLAN; **181** L-17; 🅿; z 40823; ● 100

Hisel (Hisle); RMC Place; JACKSON; ***181** J-14; elev. 1,433ft./437m.; mail Mc Kee z 40447; rural

Hiseville; RMC Place; BARREN; **180** L-8; elev. 762ft./232m.; 🅿; z 42152; former incorporated place; disincorporated November 2, 2004; Ⓟ 220; © 224

Hisle; JACKSON; see Hisel (RMC Place)

Hislope; RMC Place; PULASKI; ***181** L-12; elev. 965ft./294m.; mail Nancy z 42544; rural

Hitchins; RMC Place; CARTER; **181** G-17; elev. 665ft./203m.; 🅿; ★ **HNTG**; z 41146; ● 350

Hite; RMC Place; FLOYD; ***181** J-18; elev. 654ft./199m.; 🅿; z 41649; rural

Hitesville; RMC Place; UNION; ***180** I-2; mail Morganfield z 42437; rural

Hobson; RMC Place; TAYLOR; ***180** K-10; mail Campbellsville z 42718

Hode; RMC Place; MARTIN; ***181** I-19; elev. 620ft./189m.; 🅿; z 41267; ● 100

Hodgenville; Inc. Place; ⊡ LARUE; **180** J-8; elev. 730ft./223m.; 🅿; z 42748; Ⓟ 2,721; © 2,874

Hogue; RMC Place; PULASKI; ***181** L-12; elev. 782ft./238m.; mail Science Hill z 42553; rural

Holbrook; RMC Place; GRANT; ***181** F-12; mail Williamstown z 41097; rural

Holiday Hills; RMC Place; FAYETTE; ***181** H-12; ★ **LEX**; mail Lexington z 40504; pop. incl. with Lexington (Inc. Place)

Holifield; RMC Place; GRAVES; ***180** G-3; mail Wingo z 42088; rural

Holland; RMC Place; ALLEN; **180** M-7; elev. 803ft./245m.; 🅿; z 42153; ● 75

Holliday; RMC Place; MORGAN; ***181** I-16; elev. 899ft./274m.; mail West Liberty z 41472; rural

Hollonville; RMC Place; WOLFE; ***181** I-16; mail Campton z 41301; rural

Holloway Hills; RMC Place; HENDERSON; ***180** I-3; ★ **EV**; mail Henderson z 42420; ● 45

Hollow Bill; RMC Place; LOGAN; ***180** L-4; mail Lewisburg z 42256; rural

Hollow Creek; Inc. Place; JEFFERSON; **180** D-8; ★ **LOU**; mail Louisville z 40228; Ⓟ 991; © 815

Hollybush; RMC Place; KNOTT; ***181** K-18; elev. 872ft./266m.; 🅿; z 41844; ● 75

Hollyhill; RMC Place; MCCREARY; ***181** N-13; elev. 1,178ft./359m.; mail Pine Knot z 42635; rural

Hollyvilla; Inc. Place; JEFFERSON; **180** H-8; elev. 500ft./152m.; ★ **LOU**; mail Fairdale z 40118; Ⓟ 649; © 481

Holmes Mill; RMC Place; HARLAN; **181** M-17; elev. 1,698ft./518m.; 🅿; z 40843; ● 75

Holt; RMC Place; MUHLENBERG; ***180** K-4; mail Cleaton z 42332

Holy Cross; RMC Place; MARION; **180** J-9; elev. 698ft./213m.; mail Loretto z 40037; ● 70

Homer; RMC Place; LOGAN; ***180** L-5; elev. 525ft./160m.; mail Russellville z 42276; ● 35

Homestead; RMC Place; WOODFORD; ***181** H-12; ★ **LEX**; mail Versailles z 40383; ● 30

Honaker; RMC Place; FLOYD; ***181** J-18; elev. 692ft./211m.; 🅿; z 41603; ● 100

Honeybee; RMC Place; MCCREARY; ***181** M-13; elev. 1,255ft./383m.; 🅿; z 42634; rural

Honey Fork; RMC Place; PIKE; ***181** K-19; mail Belcher z 41513; rural

Honey Grove; RMC Place; CHRISTIAN; ***180** M-3; mail Hopkinsville z 42240; rural

Honeysuckle Estates; RMC Place; ANDERSON; ***181** H-11; mail Lawrenceburg z 40342; ● 60

Hooktown; RMC Place; NICHOLAS; ***181** G-13; elev. 795ft./242m.; mail Cynthiana z 41031

Hootentown; RMC Place; CLARK; ***181** I-13; mail Winchester z 40391

Hope; RMC Place; MONTGOMERY; **181** H-15; elev. 800ft./244m.; 🅿; z 40334; ● 90

Hopeful Heights; RMC Place; BOONE; ***181** D-12; ★ **CIN**; mail Florence z 41042; pop. incl. with Florence (Inc. Place)

Hopewell; RMC Place; GREENUP; ***181** F-17; mail Greenup z 41144; rural

Hopewell; RMC Place; JEFFERSON; ***180** H-9; elev. 716ft./218m.; ★ **LOU**; mail Louisville z 40299; became part of Louisville/Jefferson County Metro Jan. 6, 2003

HOPKINS; **180** K-2; Ⓟ 46,126; © 46,519; ◆ 45,798

Hopkinsville; Inc. Place; ⊡ CHRISTIAN; **180** M-3; elev. 548ft./167m.; 🅿 🅷 ■; ★ **HPKNV**; z 42240-41; Ⓟ 29,809; © 30,089; Ⓡ 30,064; ◆ 44,452

Hopson; RMC Place; CALDWELL; ***180** L-2; elev. 539ft./164m.; mail Princeton z 42445; rural

Horntown; RMC Place; RUSSELL; ***181** L-11; elev. 1,054ft./321m.; mail Russell Springs z 42642; ● 100

Horse Branch; RMC Place; OHIO; **180** J-5; elev. 444ft./135m.; 🅿; z 42349; ● 200

Horse Cave; Inc. Place; HART; **180** L-8; 🅿 🅷; z 42749; Ⓟ 2,284; © 2,252

Horton; RMC Place; OHIO; ***180** J-5; mail Beaver Dam z 42320; rural

Hoskinston; RMC Place; LESLIE; **181** L-16; elev. 917ft./280m.; 🅿; z 40844; ● 150

Hot Spot (Premium); RMC Place; LETCHER; **181** L-17; elev. 1,054ft./321m.; mail Premium z 41845; ● 150

Houston; RMC Place; BREATHITT; ***181** J-15; mail Booneville z 41314; rural

Houston Acres; Inc. Place; JEFFERSON; **180** C-9; elev. 550ft./168m.; ★ **LOU**; mail Louisville z 40220; Ⓟ 496; © 491

Hovious Ridge; RMC Place; ADAIR; ***180** K-10; mail Columbia z 42728; rural

Howard Mills; RMC Place; MONTGOMERY; ***181** H-14; mail Hope z 40334; ● 50

Howardstown; RMC Place; NELSON; **180** J-9; elev. 507ft./155m.; 🅿; z 40051; ● 100

Howel; RMC Place; CHRISTIAN; ***180** M-3; mail Oak Grove z 42262

Howe Valley; RMC Place; HARDIN; ***180** I-7; elev. 682ft./208m.; mail Cecilia z 42724; ● 70

Hubble; RMC Place; LINCOLN; ***181** J-12; elev. 967ft./295m.; mail Lancaster z 40444; ● 40

Hubbs; RMC Place; KNOX; ***181** M-14; mail Bryants Store z 40921; rural

Huddy; RMC Place; PIKE; **181** J-19; elev. 829ft./253m.; 🅿; z 41535; ● 450

Hudgins; RMC Place; GREEN; ***180** K-9; elev. 716ft./218m.; mail Summersville z 42782; rural

Hudson; RMC Place; BRECKINRIDGE; **180** J-7; elev. 783ft./239m.; 🅿; z 40145; ● 50

Hueys Corners; RMC Place; BOONE; ***181** D-12; ★ **CIN**; mail Union z 41091; rural

Hueysville; FLOYD; see Bosco (RMC Place)

Huff; RMC Place; EDMONSON; **180** K-6; elev. 528ft./161m.; 🅿; z 42210; ● 40

Hulen; BELL; see Blackmont (RMC Place)

Humble; RMC Place; RUSSELL; ***181** L-11; elev. 1,045ft./319m.; mail Russell Springs z 42642; rural

Hummel; RMC Place; ROCKCASTLE; ***181** K-13; mail Wildie z 40492; rural

Hunnewell; RMC Place; GREENUP; ***181** F-18; ★ **HNTG**; mail Argillite z 41121; rural

Hunt; RMC Place; CLARK; ***181** I-13; elev. 770ft./235m.; mail Winchester z 40391

Hunter; RMC Place; FLOYD; **181** J-18; elev. 670ft./204m.; 🅿; z 41655; ● 150

Hunter Hill; RMC Place; JEFFERSON; ***180** H-8; ★ **LOU**; mail Louisville z 40258; became part of Louisville/Jefferson County Metro Jan. 6, 2003

Hunters Hollow; Inc. Place; BULLITT; ***180** H-9; ★ **LOU**; mail Louisville z 40229; Ⓟ 286; © 372

Hunters Trace; RMC Place; JEFFERSON; ***180** H-8; ★ **LOU**; mail Louisville z 40216; became part of Louisville/Jefferson County Metro Jan. 6, 2003

Huntersville; RMC Place; CLINTON; ***180** N-10; mail Albany z 42602; rural

Hunter Town; RMC Place; WOODFORD; ***181** H-12; ★ **LEX**; mail Versailles z 40383; ● 30

Hunting Creek; RMC Place; CHRISTIAN; ***180** M-3; ★ **HPKNV**; mail Hopkinsville z 42240; pop. incl. with Hopkinsville (Inc. Place)

Huntington Woods; RMC Place; FRANKLIN; ***181** H-11; mail Frankfort z 40601; ● 60

Huntsville; RMC Place; BUTLER; **180** L-5; elev. 548ft./167m.; 🅿; z 42261; ● 100

Hurley; RMC Place; JACKSON; ***181** K-14; elev. 999ft./304m.; mail Mc Kee z 40447; rural

Hurricane Hills; RMC Place; NELSON; ***180** I-9; mail Boston z 40107; ● 75

Hurstbourne; Inc. Place; JEFFERSON; **180** B-9; ★ **LOU**; mail Louisville z 40222; Ⓟ 4,420; © 3,884

Hurstbourne Acres; Inc. Place; JEFFERSON; **180** C-9; elev. 651ft./198m.; ★ **LOU**; mail Louisville z 40220; Ⓟ 1,072; © 1,504

Hustonville; Inc. Place; LINCOLN; **181** J-11; elev. 974ft./297m.; 🅿; z 40437; Ⓟ 313; © 347

Hutch; RMC Place; BELL; ***181** N-15; mail Middlesboro z 40965; ● 75

Hutchison; RMC Place; BOURBON; ***181** H-13; elev. 902ft./275m.; mail Paris z 40361

Hyattsville; RMC Place; GARRARD; ***181** J-12; elev. 1,035ft./315m.; mail Lancaster z 40444

Hyden; Inc. Place; ⊡ LESLIE; **181** L-16; elev. 836ft./255m.; 🅿 🅷; z 41749, z 41762; Ⓟ 375; © 204

Hydro; RMC Place; WARREN; ***180** L-7; elev. 658ft./201m.; mail Smiths Grove z 42171; rural

I

Iberia; RMC Place; GRAYSON; ***180** K-7; elev. 663ft./202m.; mail Clarkson z 42726; rural

Ibex; RMC Place; ELLIOTT; ***181** G-17; mail Olive Hill z 41164; rural

Ice; RMC Place; LETCHER; ***181** L-18; mail Whitesburg z 41858; rural

Ida; RMC Place; CLINTON; ***180** M-10; elev. 921ft./281m.; mail Albany z 42602; rural

Ida May; RMC Place; LEE; ***181** J-15; mail Beattyville z 41311; rural

Idle Hour; RMC Place; FAYETTE; ***181** H-12; ★ **LEX**; mail Lexington z 40502; pop. incl. with Lexington (Inc. Place)

Idlewild; RMC Place; BOONE; ***181** D-11; elev. 662ft./202m.; ★ **CIN**; mail Burlington z 41005; ● 600

Ilsley; RMC Place; HOPKINS; ***180** K-2; mail Dawson Springs z 42408; ● 150

Independence; Inc. Place; ⊡ KENTON; **181** D-12; elev. 903ft./275m.; 🅿; ★ **CIN**; z 41051; Ⓟ 10,444; © 14,982; ◆ 17,158

Index; RMC Place; MORGAN; ***181** I-16; elev. 778ft./237m.; 🅿; z 41472; pop. incl. with West Liberty (Inc. Place)

Indian Fields; RMC Place; CLARK; ***181** H-14; elev. 745ft./227m.; mail Winchester z 40391; rural

Indian Hills; RMC Place; CARROLL; **180** F-10; mail Carrollton z 41008; ● 80

Indian Hills; RMC Place; CHRISTIAN; ***180** M-3; ★ **HPKNV**; mail Hopkinsville z 42240; pop. incl. with Hopkinsville (Inc. Place)

Indian Hills; RMC Place; FRANKLIN; ***181** G-11; mail Frankfort z 40601; pop. incl. with Frankfort (Inc. Place)

Indian Hills; RMC Place; HARDIN; ***180** I-8; elev. 800ft./244m.; mail Elizabethtown z 42701; pop. incl. with Elizabethtown (Inc. Place)

Indian Hills; Inc. Place; JEFFERSON; **180** B-8; ★ **LOU**; mail Louisville z 40207; Ⓟ 1,074; © 2,882; Ⓡ 2,887

Indian Hills; RMC Place; RUSSELL; **181** L-11; mail Russell Springs z 42642; ● 200

Indian Hills; RMC Place; SCOTT; ***181** G-12; ★ **LEX**; mail Georgetown z 40324; pop. incl. with Georgetown (Inc. Place)

Indian Hills; RMC Place; WARREN; ***180** L-6; ★ **BOWLG**; mail Bowling Green z 42103; pop. incl. with Bowling Green (Inc. Place)

Indian Hills Cherokee Section; RMC Place; JEFFERSON; ***180** G-9; elev. 587ft./179m.; ★ **LOU**; mail Louisville z 40207; pop. incl. with Indian Hills (Inc. Place); Ⓟ 1,005

Indian Lake; RMC Place; HANCOCK; ***180** I-5; mail Hawesville z 42348; rural

Inez; Inc. Place; ⊡ MARTIN; **181** I-19; elev. 636ft./194m.; 🅿; z 41224; Ⓟ 511; © 466

Ingle; RMC Place; PULASKI; ***181** L-11; elev. 1,077ft./328m.; 🅿; z 42544; ● 20

Ingleside; RMC Place; BALLARD; ***180** E-3; mail Kevil z 42053; ● 50

Ingram; RMC Place; BELL; **181** M-15; elev. 1,040ft./317m.; 🅿; z 40955; ● 250

Insco; RMC Place; LOGAN; ***180** L-5; elev. 631ft./192m.; mail Russellville z 42276; rural

Insko; MORGAN; see Adele (RMC Place)

Inverness Estates; RMC Place; FRANKLIN; ***181** H-11; mail Frankfort z 40601; pop. incl. with Frankfort (Inc. Place)

Iron Hill; RMC Place; CARTER; ***181** F-17; elev. 656ft./200m.; mail Grayson z 41143; rural

Iron Hill; RMC Place; LYON; ***180** L-1; mail Kuttawa z 42055; summer pop. 200

Ironville; RMC Place; BOYD; **181** E-19; ★ **HNTG**; mail Ashland z 41101-02; ● 600

Ironworks Estates; RMC Place; SCOTT; ***181** G-12; ★ **LEX**; mail Georgetown z 40324; ● 225

Iroquois; RMC Place; JEFFERSON; ***180** H-8; ★ **LOU**; mail Louisville z 40209, z 40214; pop. incl. with Louisville (Inc. Place)

Iroquois Heights; RMC Place; JEFFERSON; ***180** H-8; ★ **LOU**; mail Louisville z 40214; became part of Louisville/Jefferson County Metro Jan. 6, 2003

Irvine; Inc. Place; ⊡ ESTILL; **181** I-14; elev. 685ft./209m.; 🅿 🅷; z 40336 & mail Ravenna z 40472; Ⓟ 2,836; © 2,843

Irvington; Inc. Place; BRECKINRIDGE; **180** I-7; elev. 620ft./189m.; 🅿; z 40146; Ⓟ 1,180; © 1,257

Irvins Store; RMC Place; RUSSELL; ***181** L-11; mail Russell Springs z 42642; rural

Island; Inc. Place; MCLEAN; **180** J-4; elev. 430ft./131m.; 🅿; z 42350; Ⓟ 446; © 435

Island City; RMC Place; OWSLEY; **181** K-15; elev. 838ft./255m.; 🅿; z 41338; ● 25

Isom; RMC Place; LETCHER; **181** K-17; elev. 1,106ft./337m.; 🅿; z 41824; ● 150

Isonville; RMC Place; ELLIOTT; **181** H-17; elev. 690ft./210m.; 🅿; z 41149; ● 100

Iuka; RMC Place; LIVINGSTON; ***180** L-1; elev. 343ft./105m.; 🅿; z 42045; rural

Ivel; RMC Place; FLOYD; ***181** J-18; elev. 654ft./199m.; 🅿; z 41642; ● 150

Ivis; RMC Place; KNOTT; ***181** K-17; mail Hindman z 41822; rural

Ivor; RMC Place; PENDLETON; ***181** E-13; mail California z 41007; rural

Ivy Grove; RMC Place; BELL; ***181** M-15; 🅿; z 40939; rural

Ivyton; RMC Place; MAGOFFIN; **181** I-17; elev. 954ft./291m.; 🅿; z 41465; ● 30

J

Jabez; RMC Place; RUSSELL; ***181** L-11; elev. 1,058ft./322m.; 🅿; z 42544

Jackhorn; LETCHER; see Hemphill (RMC Place)

Jacks Creek (Bevinsville); RMC Place; FLOYD; **181** K-18; elev. 897ft./273m.; mail Bevinsville z 41606; ● 150

Jackson; Inc. Place; ⊡ BREATHITT; **181** J-16; elev. 787ft./240m.; 🅿 🅷; z 41307, z 41339; Ⓟ 2,466; © 2,490

JACKSON; **181** K-14; Ⓟ 11,955; © 13,495; ◆ 13,580

Jacksonville; RMC Place; BOURBON; ***181** G-13; mail Paris z 40361; rural

Jacksonville; RMC Place; SHELBY; **181** G-11; elev. 911ft./278m.; mail Bagdad z 40003; ● 40

Jackstown; RMC Place; BOURBON; ***181** G-14; mail Carlisle z 40311

Jacktown; RMC Place; CASEY; ***181** J-11; mail Bradfordsville z 40009; rural

Jacobs; RMC Place; CARTER; **181** G-16; elev. 838ft./255m.; mail Olive Hill z 41164; ● 25

Jamboree; RMC Place; PIKE; **181** J-20; elev. 911ft./278m.; 🅿; z 41553; ● 100

Jamestown; Inc. Place; ⊡ RUSSELL; **181** L-11; elev. 1,024ft./312m.; 🅿; z 42629; Ⓟ 1,641; © 1,624

Jarvis; RMC Place; KNOX; ***181** L-14; elev. 992ft./302m.; 🅿; z 40906; rural

Jason; RMC Place; LESLIE; ***181** K-16; mail Bear Branch z 41714; ● 40

Jasper Bend; RMC Place; PULASKI; ***181** L-13; mail Burnside z 42519; ● 200

Jax; RMC Place; KNOTT; ***181** K-18

Jeff; RMC Place; PERRY; **181** K-17; elev. 890ft./271m.; 🅿; z 41751; ● 400

JEFFERSON (Louisville/Jefferson County Metro); **180** H-9; Ⓟ 664,937; © 693,604; ◆ 718,766

Jeffersontown; Inc. Place; JEFFERSON; **180** G-9; elev. 711ft./217m.; 🅿; ★ **LOU**; z 40269, z 40299 & mail Louisville z 40229; Ⓟ 23,221; © 26,633; ◆ 28,193

Jeffersonville; Inc. Place; MONTGOMERY; **181** H-14; elev. 842ft./257m.; 🅿; z 40337; Ⓟ 1,854; © 1,804

Jeffrey; RMC Place; MONROE; ***180** M-8; elev. 757ft./231m.; mail Mount Hermon z 42157; rural

Jellico; RMC Place; WHITLEY; ***181** N-14; urban area on KY side of KY-TN border, adjacent to city of Jellico, TN; mail Williamsburg z 40769; ● 200

Jellico Creek; RMC Place; WHITLEY; ***181** M-13; elev. 1,163ft./354m.; mail Williamsburg z 40769; ● 50

Jenkins; Inc. Place; LETCHER; **181** K-18; elev. 1,526ft./465m.; 🅿 🅷; z 41537; Ⓟ 2,751; © 2,401

Jenkinsville; RMC Place; WASHINGTON; ***181** I-11; elev. 787ft./240m.; mail Mackville z 40040; rural

Jenson; RMC Place; BELL; ***181** M-15; elev. 1,029ft./314m.; 🅿; z 40977; rural

Jeptha; RMC Place; MORGAN; ***181** H-17; mail West Liberty z 41472; rural

Jeremiah; RMC Place; LETCHER; **181** K-17; elev. 1,065ft./325m.; 🅿; z 41826; ● 200

Jericho; RMC Place; HENRY; ***180** G-10; ★ **LOU**; mail Smithfield z 40068; rural

Jericho; RMC Place; LARUE; ***180** J-9; mail Hodgenville z 42748; rural

Jerico; RMC Place; LOGAN; ***180** L-4; elev. 417ft./127m.; mail Lewisburg z 42256; rural

JESSAMINE; **181** I-12; Ⓟ 30,508; © 39,041; ◆ 47,169

Jessietown; RMC Place; MARION; ***180** J-10; elev. 631ft./192m.; mail Lebanon z 40033; rural

Jetson; RMC Place; BUTLER; **180** K-6; elev. 640ft./195m.; 🅿; z 42252; ● 25

Jett; RMC Place; FRANKLIN; **181** B-13; mail Frankfort z 40601; ● 180

Jetts Creek; RMC Place; BREATHITT; ***181** J-15; mail Booneville z 41314; rural

Jewell City; RMC Place; HOPKINS; ***180** J-3; mail Slaughters z 42456; ● 20

Jimtown; RMC Place; FAYETTE; ***181** G-13; elev. 973ft./297m.; ★ **LEX**; mail Lexington z 40505; pop. incl. with Lexington (Inc. Place)

Jimtown; RMC Place; WASHINGTON; ***180** J-10; mail Springfield z 40069; ● 60

Jinks; RMC Place; ESTILL; ***181** J-14; elev. 684ft./208m.; 🅿; z 40336; rural

Job; RMC Place; MARTIN; **181** H-19; elev. 618ft./188m.; 🅿; z 41224; ● 100

Jock; RMC Place; EDMONSON; ***180** K-7; mail Bee Spring z 42207; rural

Johnetta; RMC Place; ROCKCASTLE; ***181** K-13; elev. 970ft./296m.; 🅿; z 40460; rural

Johns Creek; RMC Place; JOHNSON; ***181** I-18; mail Van Lear z 41265; ● 75

JOHNSON; **181** H-17; Ⓟ 23,248; © 23,445; ◆ 23,949

Johnson Junction; FLEMING; see Flemingsburg Junction (RMC Place)

Johnsontown; RMC Place; JEFFERSON; ***180** H-8; elev. 450ft./137m.; ★ **LOU**; mail Louisville z 40272; became part of Louisville/Jefferson County Metro Jan. 6, 2003

Johnsport; RMC Place; TAYLOR; ***180** K-10; mail Campbellsville z 42718; pop. incl. with Campbellsville (Inc. Place)

Johns Run; RMC Place; CARTER; ***181** G-17; elev. 618ft./188m.; 🅿; z 41143; rural

Johnsville; RMC Place; BRACKEN; ***181** E-13; elev. 879ft./268m.; mail Foster z 41043

Jonancy; RMC Place; PIKE; **181** K-18; elev. 888ft./271m.; 🅿; z 41538; ● 125

Jonesville; RMC Place; GRANT, OWEN; **181** F-11; elev. 914ft./279m.; 🅿; z 41052; ● 150

Jonesville; RMC Place; HART; **180** K-8; mail Magnolia z 42757; ● 35

Joppa; RMC Place; ADAIR; ***180** L-10; mail Columbia z 42728; rural

Jordan; RMC Place; FULTON; **180** G-2; mail Hickman z 42050; ● 20

Josephine; RMC Place; SCOTT; ***181** G-12; mail Sadieville z 40370; rural

Joy; RMC Place; LIVINGSTON; **180** D-4; elev. 428ft./130m.; mail Hampton z 42047

Judio; RMC Place; CUMBERLAND; ***180** M-9; mail Burkesville z 42717; rural

Judson; RMC Place; GARRARD; ***181** I-12; mail Lancaster z 40444; rural

Judy; RMC Place; MONTGOMERY; ***181** H-14; elev. 1,008ft./307m.; mail Hope z 40334

Judyville; RMC Place; BOURBON; mail Carlisle z 40311; ● 150

Julien; RMC Place; CHRISTIAN; ***180** M-2; elev. 492ft./150m.; mail Gracey z 42232, Hopkinsville z 42240; rural

Julip; RMC Place; WHITLEY; ***181** M-14; elev. 1,090ft./332m.; mail Williamsburg z 40769; rural

Jumbo; RMC Place; LINCOLN; ***181** J-12; elev. 992ft./302m.; mail Stanford z 40484; rural

Junction City; Inc. Place; BOYLE, LINCOLN; **181** J-11; elev. 986ft./301m.; 🅿; z 40440; Ⓟ 1,983; © 2,184

Juniper Hill; RMC Place; FRANKLIN; ***181** G-11; mail Frankfort z 40601; pop. incl. with Frankfort (Inc. Place)

Justell; RMC Place; FLOYD; ***181** J-18; mail Betsy Layne z 41605

Justice; RMC Place; LOGAN; ***180** M-4; elev. 699ft./213m.; mail Lewisburg z 42256; rural

Justiceville; RMC Place; PIKE; ***181** J-19; mail Pikeville z 41501; ● 150

K

Kaler; RMC Place; GRAVES; ***180** F-4; mail Hickory z 42051; rural

Kaliopi; RMC Place; LESLIE; ***181** K-16; elev. 890ft./271m.; 🅿; z 41749; rural

Kansas; RMC Place; GRAVES; ***180** F-3; mail Melber z 42069

Karlus; RMC Place; RUSSELL; ***181** L-11; mail Jamestown z 42629; rural

Katharyn; RMC Place; BULLITT; ***180** H-8; ★ **LOU**; mail West Point z 40177; rural

Kavanaugh; RMC Place; BOYD; ***181** G-18; ★ **HNTG**; mail Catlettsburg z 41129; rural

Kayjay; RMC Place; KNOX; **181** M-14; 🅿; z 40906; ● 100

Keaton; RMC Place; JOHNSON; **181** H-17; elev. 746ft./227m.; 🅿; z 41226; ● 70

Keavy; RMC Place; LAUREL; **181** L-13; elev. 1,268ft./386m.; 🅿; z 40701, z 40737; ● 125

Keefer; RMC Place; GRANT; ***181** F-12; mail Corinth z 41010; rural

Keene; RMC Place; JESSAMINE; **181** H-12; elev. 911ft./278m.; 🅿; ★ **LEX**; z 40339; ● 300

Keeneland; RMC Place; JEFFERSON; ***180** G-9; elev. 650ft./198m.; ★ **LOU**; mail Louisville z 40223; former incorporated place; became part of Lyndon November 27, 2000; pop. incl. with Lyndon (Inc. Place); Ⓟ 393; © 383

Kehoe; RMC Place; GREENUP; ***181** F-17; elev. 625ft./191m.; mail Garrison z 41141; rural

Keith; RMC Place; HARLAN; ***181** M-16; elev. 1,186ft./361m.; 🅿; z 40806; ● 100

Kelat; RMC Place; HARRISON; **181** F-13; elev. 967ft./295m.; mail Berry z 41003; ● 85

Kellacey; RMC Place; MORGAN; ***181** H-16; mail West Liberty z 41472; rural

Kelly; RMC Place; CHRISTIAN; **180** L-3; elev. 691ft./211m.; ★ **HPKNV**; mail Hopkinsville z 42240; ● 100

Kellyville; RMC Place; ADAIR; ***180** K-10; mail Columbia z 42728; rural

Keltner; RMC Place; ADAIR; ***180** L-9; elev. 971ft./296m.; ● 65

Ken Acres; RMC Place; SHELBY; ***180** H-10; mail Shelbyville z 40065; ● 175

Kenawood; RMC Place; FAYETTE; ***181** H-12; ★ **LEX**; mail Lexington z 40505; pop. incl. with Lexington (Inc. Place)

Kendall Springs; RMC Place; BATH; ***181** H-15; mail Owingsville z 40360; rural

Kennianna; RMC Place; CALLOWAY; rural

Keno; RMC Place; PULASKI; ***181** M-12; mail Tateville z 42558; rural

Kensee; RMC Place; WHITLEY; ***181** N-14; mail Williamsburg z 40769; ● 30

Kenshores; RMC Place; CALLOWAY; ***180** N-1; rural

Kentenia; RMC Place; HARLAN; ***181** M-16; mail Wallins Creek z 40873; ● 225

Kenton; RMC Place; KENTON; **181** E-12; elev. 535ft./163m.; 🅿; ★ **CIN**; z 41053; ● 175

KENTON; **181** E-12; Ⓟ 142,031; © 151,464; ◆ 158,873

Kenton Hills; RMC Place; KENTON; ***181** D-12; ★ **CIN**; mail Covington z 41011; pop. incl. with Covington (Inc. Place)

Kentontown; RMC Place; ROBERTSON; ***181** F-13; mail Mount Olivet z 41064

Kenton Vale; Inc. Place; KENTON; **181** B-16; elev. 750ft./229m.; ★ **CIN**; mail Latonia z 41015; Ⓟ 358; © 156

Kentucky Heights; RMC Place; LEWIS; ***181** F-17; mail Quincy z 41166; ● 100

Kenvir; RMC Place; HARLAN; **181** M-17; elev. 1,600ft./488m.; 🅿; z 40847; ● 900

Kenwood; RMC Place; JEFFERSON; ***180** H-8; ★ **LOU**; mail Louisville z 40214; pop. incl. with Louisville (Inc. Place)

Kerby Knob; RMC Place; JACKSON; **181** J-14; elev. 1,488ft./454m.; 🅿; z 40447; ● 15

Kernie; RMC Place; MAGOFFIN; ***181** I-17; mail Salyersville z 41465; rural

Kessinger; RMC Place; HART; **180** K-8; elev. 967ft./295m.; mail Munfordville z 42765; ● 125

Keswick; RMC Place; WHITLEY; ***181** N-14; mail Williamsburg z 40769; rural

Kettle; RMC Place; CUMBERLAND; **180** M-10; elev. 994ft./303m.; 🅿; z 42717; ● 50

Kettlecamp; RMC Place; PIKE; ***181** K-19; mail Elkhorn City z 41522; ● 100

Kettle Island; RMC Place; BELL; ***181** M-15; elev. 1,200ft./366m.; 🅿; z 40958; ● 400

Kevil; Inc. Place; BALLARD; **180** E-3; elev. 412ft./126m.; 🅿; z 42053; Ⓟ 337; © 574

Keysburg; RMC Place; LOGAN; **180** N-4; elev. 561ft./171m.; mail Allensville z 42204; ● 50

Keyser Heights; RMC Place; PIKE; ***181** J-18; mail Pikeville z 41501; ● 120

Kidder; RMC Place; WAYNE; ***181** M-12; mail Bronston z 42518; rural

Kidds Crossing; RMC Place; WAYNE; ***181** M-12; elev. 887ft./270m.; mail Monticello z 42633; rural

Kidds Store; RMC Place; CASEY; ***181** K-11; elev. 881ft./269m.; mail Hustonville z 40437; rural

Kiddville; RMC Place; CLARK; ***181** H-14; mail Mount Sterling z 40353; rural

Kildav; RMC Place; HARLAN; ***181** M-17; mail Evarts z 40828; ● 125

Kilgore; RMC Place; CARTER; ***181** G-18; ★ **HNTG**; mail Rush z 41168; ● 60

Kimbrell; RMC Place; ESTILL; ***181** I-14; mail Irvine z 40336; rural

Kimper; RMC Place; PIKE; **181** J-19; elev. 897ft./273m.; 🅿; z 41539; ● 75

Kinchloes Bluff; RMC Place; MUHLENBERG; mail Central City z 42330; rural

Kingbee; RMC Place; PULASKI; ***181** L-12; elev. 1,090ft./332m.; mail Bethelridge z 42516; rural

Kings Creek; RMC Place; LETCHER; ***181** L-17; elev. 1,251ft./381m.; mail Whitesburg z 41858

Kings Forest; RMC Place; BULLITT; ***180** H-8; ★ **LOU**; mail Shepherdsville z 40165; ● 300

Kingsley; Inc. Place; JEFFERSON; **180** C-8; elev. 544ft./166m.; ★ **LOU**; mail Louisville z 40205; Ⓟ 399; © 428

Kings Mountain; RMC Place; LINCOLN; **181** K-12; elev. 1,170ft./357m.; 🅿; z 40442; ● 125

Kingston; RMC Place; FAYETTE; ***181** H-12; mail Lexington z 40505; pop. incl. with Lexington (Inc. Place)

Kingston; RMC Place; MADISON; **181** J-13; mail Berea z 40403; ● 130

Kingswood; RMC Place; BRECKINRIDGE; **180** I-6; mail Harned z 40144; ● 200

Kinniconick; RMC Place; LEWIS; ***181** F-16; elev. 686ft./209m.; mail Vanceburg z 41179

Kino; RMC Place; BARREN; ***180** L-8; elev. 799ft./244m.; mail Glasgow z 42141; rural

Kirbyton; RMC Place; CARLISLE; **180** F-3; elev. 370ft./113m.; mail Bardwell z 42023; ● 70

Kirk; RMC Place; BRECKINRIDGE; ***180** I-6; mail Hardinsburg z 40143; ● 35

Kirkmansville; RMC Place; TODD; **180** L-4; mail Elkton z 42220; ● 50

Kirksey; RMC Place; CALLOWAY; **180** G-4; elev. 550ft./168m.; 🅿; z 42054; ● 150

Kirksville; RMC Place; MADISON; **181** J-13; elev. 994ft./303m.; mail Richmond z 40475; ● 250

Kirkwood; RMC Place; MERCER; ***181** I-11; elev. 853ft./260m.; mail Salvisa z 40372

Kirkwood Springs; RMC Place; HOPKINS; ***180** K-2; mail Dawson Springs z 42408; rural

Kite; RMC Place; KNOTT; **181** K-18; elev. 879ft./268m.; 🅿; z 41828 & mail Dema z 41859; ● 150

Kitts; RMC Place; HARLAN; ***181** M-16; elev. 1,212ft./369m.; mail Harlan z 40831; ● 300

Knifley; RMC Place; ADAIR; **180** K-10; elev. 736ft./224m.; 🅿; z 42753; ● 75

Knob Lick; RMC Place; METCALFE; **180** L-8; elev. 755ft./230m.; 🅿; z 42154; ● 40

KNOTT; **181** K-17; Ⓟ 17,906; © 17,649; ◆ 17,030

Knottsville; RMC Place; DAVIESS; **180** I-5; 🅿; z 42366; ● 400

Knowlton; RMC Place; POWELL; ***181** I-14; mail Stanton z 40380; rural

KNOX; **181** L-15; Ⓟ 29,676; © 31,795; ◆ 32,666

Knoxfork; RMC Place; KNOX; ***181** L-14; mail Barbourville z 40906; rural

Knoxville; RMC Place; PENDLETON; **181** E-12; elev. 922ft./281m.; mail Williamstown z 41097; ● 75

Kodak; RMC Place; PERRY; ***181** K-17; mail Vicco z 41773; ● 150

Kona; RMC Place; LETCHER; **181** K-18; elev. 1,258ft./383m.; 🅿; z 41858; ● 200

Korea; RMC Place; MENIFEE; ***181** H-16; elev. 1,155ft./352m.; mail Wellington z 40387

Kragon; RMC Place; BREATHITT; ***181** J-16; mail Jackson z 41339; rural

Kronos; OHIO; see Equality (RMC Place)

Krypton; RMC Place; PERRY; **181** K-16; elev. 806ft./246m.; 🅿; z 41754; ● 120

Kuttawa; Inc. Place; LYON; **180** L-1; elev. 466ft./142m.; 🅿; z 42055; Ⓟ 535; © 596

Kyrock; RMC Place; EDMONSON; ***180** K-7; 🅿; z 42285; rural

L

Labascus; RMC Place; CASEY; ***181** K-11; elev. 829ft./253m.; mail Liberty z 42539; rural

La Center; Inc. Place; BALLARD; **180** E-2; elev. 374ft./114m.; 🅿; z 42056; Ⓟ 1,040; © 1,038

Lacey; RMC Place; MAGOFFIN; ***181** I-17; mail Salyersville z 41465; rural

Lacie; RMC Place; HENRY; ***180** F-10; elev. 885ft./270m.; mail Turners Station z 40075; rural

Lackey; RMC Place; FLOYD; **181** J-18; elev. 708ft./216m.; 🅿; z 41643; ● 250

Lacon; RMC Place; GRAYSON; ***180** J-7; mail Clarkson z 42726; rural

Laden; RMC Place; HARLAN; ***181** L-17; mail Putney z 40865; rural

La Fayette; Inc. Place; CHRISTIAN; **180** N-2; elev. 550ft./168m.; 🅿; z 42254; Ⓟ 106; © 193; Ⓡ 195

La Grange; Inc. Place; ⊡ OLDHAM; **180** G-10; elev. 867ft./264m.; 🅿 🅷; ★ **LOU**; z 40031-32; Ⓟ 3,853; © 5,676

Lair; RMC Place; HARRISON; **181** G-13; mail Cynthiana z 41031; ● 80

Lake; RMC Place; LAUREL; ***181** L-14; mail London z 40744; rural

Lake Carnico; RMC Place; NICHOLAS; ***181** G-14; mail Carlisle z 40311; ● 100

Lake City; RMC Place; LIVINGSTON; **180** L-1; elev. 419ft./128m.; mail Grand Rivers z 42045; summer pop. 600; ● 300

Lake Dreamland; RMC Place; JEFFERSON; ***180** G-8; ★ **LOU**; mail Louisville z 40216; became part of Louisville/Jefferson County Metro Jan. 6, 2003

Lake Louisvilla; RMC Place; JEFFERSON, OLDHAM; ***180** G-9; elev. 628ft./191m.; ★ **LOU**; mail Crestwood z 40014; became part of Louisville/Jefferson County Metro Jan. 6, 2003

Lakeside Park; Inc. Place; KENTON; **181** C-16; elev. 879ft./268m.; 🅿; ★ **CIN**; z 41017; Ⓟ 3,131; © 2,869

Lakeview; RMC Place; KENTON; ***181** D-12; ★ **CIN**; mail Covington z 41011; pop. incl. with Fort Wright (Inc. Place)

Lakeview Heights; Inc. Place; ROWAN; ***181** H-15; mail Morehead z 40351; Ⓟ 252; © 251

Lakeview-Mount Tabor; RMC Place; FAYETTE; ***181** H-12; ★ **LEX**; mail Lexington z 40502; pop. incl. with Lexington (Inc. Place)

Lakeview-Woodspoint; RMC Place; FAYETTE; ***181** H-12; ★ **LEX**; mail Lexington z 40509; pop. incl. with Lexington (Inc. Place)

Lakeville; RMC Place; MAGOFFIN; ***181** I-17; mail Salyersville z 41465; ● 30

Lakeway Shore; RMC Place; CALLOWAY; ***180** N-1; mail Murray z 42071; ● 100

Lakewood Acres; RMC Place; FAYETTE; ***181** H-12; ★ **LEX**; mail Lexington z 40502; pop. incl. with Lexington (Inc. Place)

Lamasco; RMC Place; LYON; **180** L-1; mail Eddyville z 42038; ● 100

Lamb; RMC Place; MONROE; **180** M-8; elev. 918ft./280m.; 🅿; z 42141; ● 50

Lambric; RMC Place; BREATHITT; **181** J-17; elev. 732ft./223m.; 🅿; z 41339; ● 20

Lamero; RMC Place; ROCKCASTLE; **181** K-13; elev. 926ft./282m.; mail Livingston z 40445; ● 20

Lamont; RMC Place; MCCRACKEN; ***180** E-3; elev. 398ft./121m.; mail Kevil z 42053; rural

Lamont; RMC Place; PERRY; ***181** K-16; mail Chavies z 41727

Lancaster; Inc. Place; ⊡ GARRARD; **181** J-12; elev. 1,032ft./315m.; 🅿 🅷; z 40444, z 40446; Ⓟ 3,421; © 3,734

Lancelot Estates; RMC Place; SCOTT; ***181** G-12; ★ **LEX**; mail Georgetown z 40324; ● 350

Lancer; RMC Place; FLOYD; ***181** I-18; mail Prestonsburg z 41653; pop. incl. with Prestonsburg (Inc. Place)

Landsaw; RMC Place; WOLFE; ***181** I-16; mail Campton z 41301; rural

Langdon Place; Inc. Place; JEFFERSON; ***180** G-9; ★ **LOU**; mail Louisville z 40222; Ⓟ 874; © 974

Langley; RMC Place; FLOYD; **181** J-18; elev. 661ft./201m.; 🅿; z 41645; ● 400

Langnau; RMC Place; LAUREL; ***181** K-14; mail London z 40741; rural

Lanhamtown; RMC Place; CASEY; ***181** K-11; mail Liberty z 42539; rural

Lansdowne; RMC Place; FAYETTE; ***181** H-12; ★ **LEX**; mail Lexington z 40502; pop. incl. with Lexington (Inc. Place)

Larkslane; RMC Place; KNOTT; ***181** K-18; elev. 898ft./274m.; 🅿; z 41817; ● 75

LARUE; **180** J-8; Ⓟ 11,679; © 13,373; ◆ 13,671

Latonia; RMC Place; KENTON; ***181** D-12; 🅿; ★ **CIN**; z 41015; pop. incl. with Covington (Inc. Place)

Latonia Lakes; RMC Place; KENTON; ***181** D-12; elev. 883ft./269m.; 🅿; ★ **CIN**; z 41015; disincorporated December 16, 2006; Ⓟ 410; © 325

Laura; RMC Place; MARTIN; ***181** I-19; elev. 800ft./244m.; 🅿; z 41250; rural

LAUREL; **181** L-14; Ⓟ 43,438; © 52,715; ◆ 58,058

Laurel Creek; RMC Place; CLAY; ***181** K-15; mail Manchester z 40962; rural

Laurel Fork; RMC Place; BELL; ***181** M-15; 🅿; z 40940; rural

Laurel Ridge; RMC Place; EDMONSON; ***180** K-7; elev. 600ft./183m.; mail Mammoth Cave z 42259; rural

Lawhorn Hill; RMC Place; CASEY; ***181** K-11; mail Liberty z 42539; rural

LAWRENCE; **181** H-18; Ⓟ 13,998; © 15,569; ◆ 16,322

Lawrenceburg; Inc. Place; ⊡ ANDERSON; **181** H-11; elev. 791ft./241m.; 🅿; z 40342; Ⓟ 5,911; © 9,014

Lawrenceville; RMC Place; GRANT; ***181** F-12; elev. 906ft./276m.; mail Corinth z 41010, Williamstown z 41097; rural

Lawson; RMC Place; BREATHITT; ***181** J-16; mail Jackson z 41339; ● 60

Lawton; RMC Place; CARTER; ***181** G-16; elev. 790ft./241m.; 🅿; z 41164

Layman; RMC Place; HARLAN; ***181** M-16; mail Coldiron z 40819; ● 30

Leafdale; RMC Place; LARUE; ***180** J-9; mail Hodgenville z 42748; rural

Leander; RMC Place; JOHNSON; **181** I-17; elev. 646ft./197m.; 🅿; z 41222; ● 30

Leatha; RMC Place; MAGOFFIN; ***181** I-17; mail Salyersville z 41465; rural

Leatherwood; RMC Place; PERRY; **181** L-17; elev. 1,734ft./529m.; 🅿; z 41731; ● 140

Lebanon; Inc. Place; ⊡ MARION; **180** J-10; elev. 797ft./243m.; 🅿 🅷; z 40033; Ⓟ 5,695; © 5,718

Lebanon Junction; Inc. Place; BULLITT; **180** I-8; elev. 454ft./138m.; 🅿; z 40150; Ⓟ 1,741; © 1,801

Leburn; RMC Place; KNOTT; **181** K-17; elev. 1,048ft./319m.; 🅿; z 41831; ● 250

Leckieville; RMC Place; PIKE; ***181** I-19; mail Belfry z 41514

Lecta; RMC Place; BARREN; **180** L-8; mail Glasgow z 42141; ● 80

Ledbetter; CDP; LIVINGSTON; **180** E-4; elev. 350ft./107m.; 🅿; ★ **PAD**; z 42058; Ⓟ 1,694; © 1,700

Ledocio; RMC Place; LAWRENCE; ***181** H-18; mail Louisa z 41230; rural

LEE; **181** J-15; Ⓟ 7,422; © 7,916; ◆ 7,286

Lee City; RMC Place; WOLFE; **181** I-16; elev. 962ft./293m.; 🅿; z 41301; ● 100

Leeco; RMC Place; LEE; **181** I-15; elev. 1,296ft./395m.; 🅿; z 41301; rural

Leesburg; RMC Place; HARRISON; **181** G-13; mail Cynthiana z 41031; ● 75

Lees Lick; RMC Place; HARRISON; ***181** G-13; mail Cynthiana z 41031; rural

LeGrande; RMC Place; HART; ***180** L-8; mail Horse Cave z 42749; rural

Leighton; RMC Place; ESTILL; ***181** J-14; mail Irvine z 40336; rural

Leitchfield; Inc. Place; ⊡ GRAYSON; **180** J-7; elev. 750ft./229m.; 🅿 🅷; z 42754-55 & mail Clarkson z 42726; Ⓟ 4,965; © 6,139

Leitchfield Crossing; RMC Place; HART; ***180** K-8; mail Munfordville z 42765; pop. incl. with Munfordville (Inc. Place)

Lejunior; HARLAN; see Gano (RMC Place)

Lemon; RMC Place; MCLEAN; ***180** J-3; mail Calhoun z 42327; rural

Lenarue; RMC Place; HARLAN; ***181** M-16; mail Coalgood z 40818; ● 150

Lennut; RMC Place; PERRY; mail Combs z 41729

Lenore; RMC Place; NELSON; ***180** H-9; elev. 538ft./164m.; 🅿; z 40013; rural

Lenox; RMC Place; MORGAN; **181** H-16; elev. 794ft./242m.; 🅿; z 41472; ● 20

Lenoxburg; RMC Place; BRACKEN, PENDLETON; **181** E-13; mail Falmouth z 41040, Foster z 41043; ● 40

Leon; RMC Place; CARTER; ***181** G-17; elev. 607ft./185m.; mail Grayson z 41143; rural

Lerose; RMC Place; OWSLEY; **181** J-15; elev. 737ft./225m.; ● 100

Lesbas; RMC Place; LAUREL; ***181** L-14; mail London z 40744; rural

Leslie; RMC Place; CUMBERLAND; ***180** M-9; mail Burkesville z 42717; rural

LESLIE; **181** L-16; Ⓟ 13,642; © 12,401; ◆ 11,596

Letcher; RMC Place; LETCHER; **181** L-17; elev. 1,014ft./309m.; 🅿; z 41832; ● 150

LETCHER; **181** L-17; Ⓟ 27,000; © 25,277; ◆ 23,594

Levee; RMC Place; MONTGOMERY; ***181** H-14; mail Jeffersonville z 40337

Level Green; RMC Place; ROCKCASTLE; ***181** K-13; elev. 1,030ft./314m.; mail Mount Vernon z 40456

Levi; RMC Place; OWSLEY; ***181** J-15; elev. 833ft./254m.; mail Booneville z 41314

Levias; RMC Place; CRITTENDEN; ***180** K-1; elev. 471ft./144m.; mail Marion z 42064; rural

LEWIS; **181** F-16; Ⓟ 13,029; © 14,092; ◆ 13,792

Lewisburg; Inc. Place; LOGAN; **180** L-4; elev. 483ft./147m.; 🅿; z 42256; Ⓟ 772; © 903

Lewisburg; RMC Place; MASON; **181** F-15; elev. 756ft./230m.; mail Maysville z 41056; ● 125

Lewisport; Inc. Place; HANCOCK; **180** H-5; elev. 394ft./120m.; 🅿; z 42351; Ⓟ 1,778; © 1,639

Lexington (Lexington-Fayette); Inc. Place; ⊡ FAYETTE; **181** H-12; elev. 983ft./300m.; 🅿 🅷 🅲 27,499 ■; ★ **LEX**; z 40502-17, z 40522-24, z 40526, z 40533, z 40536, z 40544, z 40546, z 40550, z 40555, z 40574-83, z 40588, z 40591, z 40598; the governments of Lexington and Fayette county are united as Lexington-Fayette Urban County.; Ⓟ 225,366; © 260,512; ◆ 297,867

Lexington-Fayette; FAYETTE; see Lexington (Inc. Place)

Liberty; Inc. Place; ⊡ CASEY; **181** K-11; elev. 816ft./249m.; 🅿; z 42539; Ⓟ 1,937; © 1,850

Liberty; WEBSTER; see Stanhope (RMC Place)

Liberty; RMC Place; WHITLEY; ***181** M-13; mail Williamsburg z 40769; ● 75

Liberty Heights; RMC Place; FAYETTE; ***181** H-12; ★ **LEX**; mail Lexington z 40505; pop. incl. with Lexington (Inc. Place)

Liberty Heights; RMC Place; NICHOLAS; ***181** G-14; mail Carlisle z 40311, Lexington z 40555; pop. incl. with Carlisle (Inc. Place)

Liberty Road; RMC Place; FAYETTE; mail Lexington z 40505, z 40555; pop. incl. with Lexington (Inc. Place)

Liberty Road; RMC Place; MORGAN; ***181** I-16; mail West Liberty z 41472; pop. incl. with West Liberty (Inc. Place)

Lick Branch; RMC Place; MORGAN; ***181** H-16; mail West Liberty z 41472; rural

Lickburg; RMC Place; MAGOFFIN; ***181** I-17; elev. 855ft./261m.; 🅿; z 41465; ● 50

Lick Creek; RMC Place; PIKE; ***181** K-19; elev. 811ft./247m.; 🅿; z 41540; ● 180

Lick Fork; RMC Place; ROWAN; ***181** H-16; mail Clearfield z 40313; rural

Licking River; RMC Place; MORGAN; ***181** H-16; mail West Liberty z 41472; rural

Lickskillet; RMC Place; LOGAN; ***180** M-4; elev. 529ft./161m.; mail Olmstead z 42265; rural

Lickskillet; RMC Place; MEADE; ***180** H-7; mail Vine Grove z 40175; rural

Lida; RMC Place; LAUREL; ***181** L-14; mail London z 40744

Liggett; RMC Place; HARLAN; **181** M-16; mail Harlan z 40831; ● 180

Ligon; RMC Place; FLOYD; ***181** K-18; elev. 1,400ft./427m.; 🅿; z 41604; rural

Liletown; RMC Place; GREEN; ***180** L-9; mail Greensburg z 42743; rural

Lily; RMC Place; LAUREL; **181** L-14; elev. 1,131ft./345m.; 🅿; z 40740; ● 500

Limaburg; RMC Place; BOONE; **181** C-13; ★ **CIN**; mail Burlington z 41005; ● 200

Limestone; RMC Place; CARTER; ***181** G-16; elev. 784ft./239m.; mail Olive Hill z 41164; rural

Limestone Springs; RMC Place; BULLITT; ***180** I-9; ★ **LOU**; mail Shepherdsville z 40165; rural

Limeville; RMC Place; GREENUP; ***181** E-17; elev. 536ft./163m.; ★ **PTSM**; mail South Shore z 41175; rural

Lincoln; RMC Place; CLAY; ***181** L-15; mail Manchester z 40962; rural

LINCOLN; **181** K-12; Ⓟ 20,045; © 23,361; ◆ 25,270

Lincolnshire; Inc. Place; JEFFERSON; ***180** G-9; elev. 580ft./177m.; ★ **LOU**; mail Louisville z 40220; Ⓟ 125; © 154

Lindseyville; RMC Place; EDMONSON; **180** K-7; elev. 699ft./213m.; 🅿; z 42210; ● 200

Linefork; RMC Place; LETCHER; **181** L-17; elev. 1,164ft./355m.; 🅿; z 41833; ● 125

Linton; RMC Place; TRIGG; **180** M-1; mail Cadiz z 42211; ● 40

Linwood; RMC Place; GRAYSON; ***180** K-7; mail Clarkson z 42726; ● 60

Linwood; RMC Place; HART; **180** K-8; mail Magnolia z 42757; ● 50

Lionilli; RMC Place; PIKE; ***181** K-18; mail Jenkins z 41537; rural

Lisletown; RMC Place; CLARK; ***181** I-13; mail Winchester z 40391

Lisman; RMC Place; WEBSTER; ***180** J-2; elev. 410ft./125m.; mail Clay z 42404; ● 50

Litsey; RMC Place; WASHINGTON; ***180** I-10; mail Springfield z 40069; rural

Littcarr; RMC Place; KNOTT; **181** K-17; elev. 1,036ft./316m.; 🅿; z 41834; ● 75

Little; RMC Place; BREATHITT; **181** J-16; elev. 771ft./235m.; 🅿; z 41339; ● 40

Little Barren; RMC Place; GREEN; ***180** L-9; mail Greensburg z 42743; rural

Little Bear Creek; RMC Place; MARSHALL; ***180** L-1; mail Gilbertsville z 42044; ● 100

Little Creek; RMC Place; BELL; ***181** M-15; mail Arjay z 40902; rural

Little Cypress; RMC Place; MARSHALL; ***180** E-4; elev. 349ft./106m.; mail Calvert City z 42029; rural

Little Dixie; RMC Place; PIKE; ***181** J-19; mail Pikeville z 41501; rural

Little Georgetown; RMC Place; FAYETTE; ***181** H-12; ★ **LEX**; mail Lexington z 40513; pop. incl. with Lexington (Inc. Place)

Little Hickman; RMC Place; JESSAMINE; ***181** I-12; mail Nicholasville z 40356

Little Mount; RMC Place; SPENCER; **180** H-10; elev. 758ft./231m.; mail Taylorsville z 40071; ● 60

Little Needmore; RMC Place; BOYLE; ***181** J-12; mail Danville z 40422; rural

Little Rock; RMC Place; BOURBON; **181** G-14; mail Carlisle z 40311; ● 75

Little Sandy; RMC Place; ELLIOTT; **181** H-16; elev. 774ft./236m.; 🅿; z 41171; ● 50

Little Tar Springs; RMC Place; HANCOCK; ***180** I-5; mail Hawesville z 42348; rural

Little Texas; RMC Place; FAYETTE; ***181** H-12; ★ **LEX**; mail Lexington z 40513; pop. incl. with Lexington (Inc. Place)

Littleton; RMC Place; CLAY; **181** L-15; mail Manchester z 40962; ● 275

Littrell; RMC Place; CUMBERLAND; ***180** M-9; elev. 1,069ft./326m.; mail Burkesville z 42717; rural

Livermore; Inc. Place; MCLEAN; **180** J-4; elev. 408ft./124m.; 🅿; z 42352; Ⓟ 1,534; © 1,482

Livia; RMC Place; DAVIESS, MCLEAN; **180** J-4; mail Calhoun z 42327; ● 15

Livingston; Inc. Place; ROCKCASTLE; **181** K-13; elev. 889ft./271m.; 🅿; z 40445; Ⓟ 241; © 228

LIVINGSTON; **180** D-4; Ⓟ 9,062; © 9,804; ◆ 9,483

Lloyd; RMC Place; GREENUP; **181** F-17; elev. 547ft./167m.; 🅿; z 41144; ● 900

Load; RMC Place; GREENUP; ***181** F-17; elev. 568ft./173m.; 🅿; z 41144

Lockards Creek; RMC Place; CLAY; ***181** L-15; mail Garrard z 40941; ● 125

Lockport; RMC Place; HENRY; **181** F-11; elev. 474ft./144m.; 🅿; z 40036; ● 100

Lockwood Estates; RMC Place; OLDHAM; ***180** G-9; ★ **LOU**; mail Crestwood z 40014; ● 65

Locust; RMC Place; CARROLL; ***180** E-10; 🅿; z 40045 & mail Carrollton z 41008; rural

Locust Grove; RMC Place; CLARK; ***181** H-13; elev. 949ft./289m.; mail Winchester z 40391; rural

Locust Grove; RMC Place; PENDLETON; ***181** F-12; elev. 930ft./283m.; mail Falmouth z 41040

Locust Hill; RMC Place; BRECKINRIDGE; ***180** I-6; elev. 612ft./187m.; 🅿; z 40144; rural

Lodiburg; RMC Place; BRECKINRIDGE; ***180** I-6; elev. 520ft./158m.; 🅿; z 40146; rural

LOGAN; **180** L-5; Ⓟ 24,416; © 26,573; ◆ 27,137

Logana; RMC Place; JESSAMINE; ***181** I-12; elev. 880ft./268m.; ★ **LEX**; mail Nicholasville z 40356

Logansport; RMC Place; BUTLER; ***180** K-5; elev. 489ft./149m.; 🅿; z 42261; rural

Logantown; RMC Place; LINCOLN; ***181** J-12; elev. 957ft./292m.; mail Stanford z 40484; rural

Log Lick; RMC Place; CLARK; ***181** I-14; mail Winchester z 40391; rural

Log Mountain; RMC Place; BELL; 🅿; z 40977; rural

Logville; RMC Place; MAGOFFIN; ***181** I-17; elev. 870ft./265m.; 🅿; z 41465; rural

Lola; RMC Place; LIVINGSTON; **180** D-4; elev. 399ft./122m.; 🅿; z 42078; ● 200

Lombard; RMC Place; POWELL; ***181** I-15; mail Stanton z 40380

London; Inc. Place; ⊡ LAUREL; **181** L-14; elev. 1,255ft./383m.; 🅿 🅷; z 40741-45; Ⓟ 5,757; © 5,692

Lone; RMC Place; LEE; ***181** J-15; elev. 752ft./229m.; 🅿; z 41347; ● 50

Lone Oak; Inc. Place; MCCRACKEN; **180** E-3; elev. 474ft./144m.; ★ **PAD**; mail Paducah z 42001, z 42003; Ⓟ 465; © 454

Lone Star; RMC Place; HART; ***180** K-8; elev. 891ft./272m.; mail Bonnieville z 42713; rural

Lone Way Acres; RMC Place; TAYLOR; ***180** K-10; mail Campbellsville z 42718; ● 150

Long Fork; RMC Place; PIKE; ***181** K-18; mail Virgie z 41572; rural

Longlick; RMC Place; SCOTT; ***181** G-12; mail Stamping Ground z 40379; rural

Long Ridge; RMC Place; OWEN; ***181** F-11; elev. 936ft./285m.; mail Owenton z 40359

Long Run; RMC Place; JEFFERSON; ***180** G-9; ★ **LOU**; mail Louisville z 40245; became part of Louisville/Jefferson County Metro Jan. 6, 2003

Long View; RMC Place; HARDIN; **180** I-8; mail Elizabethtown z 42701; pop. incl. with Radcliff (Inc. Place)

Longview Estates; RMC Place; BOYLE; ***181** J-12; mail Danville z 40422; ● 150

Lookout; RMC Place; PIKE; **181** K-19; elev. 978ft./298m.; 🅿; z 41542; ● 350

Lookout Heights; RMC Place; KENTON; ***181** D-12; ★ **CIN**; mail Covington z 41011; pop. incl. with Fort Wright (Inc. Place)

Loradale; RMC Place; FAYETTE; ***181** G-13; elev. 955ft./291m.; ★ **LEX**; mail Lexington z 40505; pop. incl. with Lexington (Inc. Place)

Loretto; Inc. Place; MARION; **180** J-9; elev. 744ft./227m.; 🅿; z 40037; Ⓟ 820; © 623

Lost Creek; RMC Place; BREATHITT; **181** J-16; elev. 775ft./236m.; 🅿; z 41348; ● 40

Lot; RMC Place; WHITLEY; ***181** N-14; mail Williamsburg z 40769; ● 100

Lothair; RMC Place; PERRY; ***181** K-17; mail Hazard z 41701; pop. incl. with Hazard (Inc. Place)

Lotus; RMC Place; BULLITT; ***180** I-9; ★ **LOU**; mail Coxs Creek z 40013; rural

Louden; RMC Place; WHITLEY; ***181** M-14; mail Williamsburg z 40769; rural

Louellen; RMC Place; HARLAN; ***181** L-17; elev. 1,500ft./457m.; 🅿; z 40828

Louisa; Inc. Place; ⊡ LAWRENCE; **181** H-18; elev. 590ft./180m.; 🅿 🅷; z 41201, z 41230; Ⓟ 1,990; © 2,018

Louisville (Louisville-Jefferson County, Louisville/Jefferson County Metro); Inc. Place; ⊡ JEFFERSON; **180** G-8; elev. 462ft./141m.; 🅿 🅷 🅲 35,221 ■; ★ **LOU**; z 40201-25, z 40228-29, z 40231-33, z 40241-43, z 40245, z 40250-53, z 40255-59, z 40261, z 40266, z 40268-70, z 40272, z 40280-83, z 40285, z 40287, z 40289-99 & mail Crestwood z 40014, Eastwood z 40018, Fairdale z 40118, Fisherville z 40023, Harrods Creek z 40027, Hillview z 40129; Louisville and Jefferson county governments merged Jan. 6, 2003; Ⓟ 269,063; © 256,231; ◆ 572,800

Louisville-Jefferson County; JEFFERSON; see Louisville (Inc. Place)

Louisville/Jefferson County Metro; JEFFERSON; see Louisville (Inc. Place)

LOUISVILLE/JEFFERSON COUNTY METRO see Jefferson (County)

Lovelaceville; RMC Place; BALLARD; **180** F-3; elev. 400ft./122m.; 🅿; z 42060; ● 250

Lovely; RMC Place; MARTIN; **181** I-19; elev. 625ft./191m.; 🅿; z 41231; ● 700

Lowell; RMC Place; GARRARD; ***181** J-13; mail Paint Lick z 40461; rural

Lower Kings Addition; RMC Place; GREENUP; ***181** E-17; ★ **PTSM**; mail South Shore z 41175; ● 150

Lower Pompey; RMC Place; PIKE; mail Pikeville z 41501; rural

Lowes; RMC Place; GRAVES; **180** F-3; elev. 473ft./144m.; 🅿; z 42061; ● 200

Lowmansville; RMC Place; LAWRENCE, JOHNSON; **181** H-18; elev. 643ft./196m.; 🅿; z 41232; ● 50

Loyall; Inc. Place; HARLAN; **181** M-16; elev. 1,165ft./355m.; 🅿; z 40854; Ⓟ 1,100; © 766

Lucas; RMC Place; BARREN; **180** M-7; elev. 762ft./232m.; 🅿; z 42156; ● 120

Lucastown; RMC Place; LETCHER; ***181** K-18; mail Thornton z 41855; rural

Lucky Fork; RMC Place; OWSLEY; ***181** K-15; mail Ricetown z 41364; rural

Lucky Stop; RMC Place; MONTGOMERY; ***181** H-14; mail Jeffersonville z 40337; pop. incl. with Jeffersonville (Inc. Place)

Ludlow; Inc. Place; KENTON; **181** D-12; elev. 520ft./158m.; 🅿; ★ **CIN**; z 41016; Ⓟ 4,736; © 4,409

Luner; RMC Place; ROCKCASTLE; ***181** K-13; elev. 882ft./269m.; mail Mount Vernon z 40456; rural

Lusby's Mill; RMC Place; OWEN; **181** F-12; mail Owenton z 40359; ● 50

Luzerne; RMC Place; MUHLENBERG; ***180** K-4; mail Greenville z 42345; ● 200

Lykins; RMC Place; MAGOFFIN; ***181** I-16; mail Salyersville z 41465; rural

Lynch; Inc. Place; HARLAN; **181** L-17; elev. 1,740ft./530m.; 🅿; z 40855; Ⓟ 1,166; © 900

Lyndale; RMC Place; CLARK; ***181** H-13; mail Winchester z 40391; ● 450

Lyndon; Inc. Place; JEFFERSON; **180** B-9; elev. 558ft./170m.; 🅿; ★ **LOU**; z 40222, z 40241-42, z 40252; includes Keeneland annexed November 27, 2000 and Whipps Millgate annexed July 1, 2001; Ⓟ 8,037; © 9,369; Ⓐ 10,167

Lynn; RMC Place; GREENUP; ***181** F-17; elev. 574ft./175m.; mail Greenup z 41144

Lynn City; RMC Place; MUHLENBERG; ***180** K-4; elev. 458ft./140m.; mail Sacramento z 42372; rural

Lynn Grove; RMC Place; CALLOWAY; **180** G-4; elev. 569ft./173m.; mail Murray z 42071; ● 250

Lynnview; Inc. Place; JEFFERSON; **180** C-7; elev. 475ft./145m.; ★ **LOU**; mail Louisville z 40213; Ⓟ 1,017; © 965

Lynnville; RMC Place; GRAVES; **180** G-3; elev. 755ft./230m.; 🅿; z 42063; ● 120

LYON; **180** L-1; Ⓟ 6,624; © 8,080; ◆ 8,093

Lyonia; HANCOCK; see Roseville (RMC Place)

Entries in **UPPERCASE** are counties.
Entries in **bold** have populations of 2,500 or more.
Names in parentheses are alternate names.

Inc. Place	Incorporated Place
RMC Place	Rand McNally Designated Place
CDP	Census Designated Place
MCD	Minor Civil Division

⊡	County Seat
▲	Minor Civil Division
elev.	Elevation
🅿	Post Office
🅷	Hospital
🅲	College
■	Principal Business Center
★	Ranally Metro Area (RMA) Abbreviation
z	Zip Code(s)
Ⓟ	Previous Census Population
Ⓡ	Revised Census Population
Ⓐ	Annexation Population
●	Rand McNally Population Estimate
©	Final Census Population
Ⓢ	Special Census Population
◆	Estimated Population

For additional definitions see Glossary, Volume 1, and Introduction, Volume 2.

Lyons; RMC Place; LARUE; **180** J-9; elev. 487ft./148m.; mail New Haven Z 40051; ● 60
Lytten; RMC Place; ELLIOTT; ***181** H-16; elev. 1,098ft./335m.; 🅿; Z 41171

M

Mac; RMC Place; TAYLOR; ***180** K-9; elev. 837ft./255m.; mail Campbellsville Z 42718; rural
Macedonia; RMC Place; CHRISTIAN; ***180** L-2; mail Crofton Z 42217
Macedonia; RMC Place; JACKSON; ***181** J-14; mail Mc Kee Z 40447; rural
Maceo; RMC Place; DAVIESS; **180** I-4; elev. 558ft./170m.; 🅿; Z 42355; ● 500
Mackville; Inc. Place; WASHINGTON; **181** I-11; elev. 917ft./280m.; 🅿; Z 40040; Ⓟ 200; Ⓒ 206
MADISON; **181** I-13; Ⓟ 57,508; Ⓒ 70,872; ◆ 84,596
Madison Hills; RMC Place; MADISON; ***181** I-13; mail Richmond Z 40475; pop. incl. with Richmond (Inc. Place)
Madisonville; Inc. Place; ⊡ HOPKINS; **180** K-3; elev. 470ft./143m.; 🅿 🅷 ■; Z 42431; Ⓟ 16,203; Ⓒ 19,307; ◆ 18,661
Madrid; RMC Place; BRECKINRIDGE; **180** J-6; elev. 773ft./236m.; mail Leitchfield Z 42754; ● 50
Magan; RMC Place; OHIO; ***180** J-5; elev. 589ft./180m.; mail Fordsville Z 42343; rural
Maggard; RMC Place; MAGOFFIN; ***181** I-17; elev. 863ft./263m.; 🅿; Z 41465; ● 50
Magnolia; RMC Place; LARUE; **180** J-8; elev. 865ft./264m.; 🅿; Z 42757; ● 800
Magoffin; RMC Place; MAGOFFIN; ***181** I-17; mail Salyersville Z 41465; rural
MAGOFFIN; **181** J-17; Ⓟ 13,077; Ⓒ 13,332; ◆ 13,180
Majestic; RMC Place; PIKE; **181** J-20; elev. 935ft./285m.; 🅿; Z 41547; ● 400
Major; RMC Place; OWSLEY; ***181** K-15; elev. 767ft./234m.; mail Booneville Z 41314; rural
Malaga; RMC Place; WOLFE; ***181** I-16; mail Campton Z 41301; rural
Mallard Point; RMC Place; SCOTT; ***181** G-12; mail Georgetown Z 40324; ● 300
Mallie; RMC Place; KNOTT; **181** K-17; elev. 1,198ft./365m.; 🅿; Z 41836; ● 50
Malone; RMC Place; MORGAN; **181** I-16; elev. 792ft./241m.; 🅿; Z 41451; ● 100
Maloneton; RMC Place; GREENUP; **181** E-17; elev. 545ft./166m.; mail South Shore Z 41175; ● 200
Manchester; Inc. Place; ⊡ CLAY; **181** L-15; elev. 870ft./265m.; 🅿 🅷; Z 40962; Ⓟ 1,634; Ⓒ 1,738
Mangum; RMC Place; PULASKI; ***181** L-11; elev. 1,122ft./342m.; mail Bethelridge Z 42516; rural
Manila; RMC Place; JOHNSON; ***181** I-17; elev. 1,000ft./305m.; 🅿; Z 41238; ● 15
Manitou; RMC Place; HOPKINS; **180** K-2; elev. 405ft./123m.; 🅿; Z 42436; ● 150
Mannington; RMC Place; CHRISTIAN; **180** L-3; mail Crofton Z 42217; ● 125
Mannsville; RMC Place; TAYLOR; **180** K-10; elev. 733ft./223m.; 🅿; Z 42758; ● 150
Manor Creek; Inc. Place; JEFFERSON; ***180** G-9; ★ **LOU**; mail Louisville Z 40222; Ⓟ 179; Ⓒ 221
Manse; RMC Place; GARRARD; ***181** J-13; mail Paint Lick Z 40461; rural
Manton; RMC Place; FLOYD; **181** J-18; elev. 712ft./217m.; mail Martin Z 41649; ● 200
Manton; RMC Place; WASHINGTON; ***180** I-9; elev. 530ft./162m.; mail Loretto Z 40037; rural
Maple Grove; RMC Place; TRIGG; ***180** M-1; mail Cadiz Z 42211; rural
Maple Mount; DAVIESS; see Saint Joseph (RMC Place)
Maplesville; RMC Place; LAUREL; ***181** L-14; mail London Z 40741; rural
Marcellus; RMC Place; GARRARD; ***181** I-12; mail Lancaster Z 40444; rural
Marcum; RMC Place; CLAY; ***181** L-15; elev. 910ft./277m.; 🅿; Z 40962
Marcus; RMC Place; PENDLETON; ***181** F-12; mail Berry Z 41003; rural
Mare Creek; FLOYD; see Stanville (RMC Place)
Maretburg; RMC Place; ROCKCASTLE; ***181** K-13; mail Mount Vernon Z 40456; rural
Mariba; RMC Place; MENIFEE; **181** H-15; elev. 1,174ft./358m.; 🅿; Z 40322; ● 60
Marion; Inc. Place; ⊡ CRITTENDEN; **180** K-1; elev. 594ft./181m.; 🅿 🅷; Z 42064; Ⓟ 3,320; Ⓒ 3,196
MARION; **180** J-10; Ⓟ 16,499; Ⓒ 18,212; ◆ 18,866
Mark; RMC Place; PULASKI; ***181** L-12; mail Somerset Z 42501; rural
Marksbury; RMC Place; GARRARD; ***181** J-12; mail Lancaster Z 40444; rural
Marlowe; RMC Place; LETCHER; ***181** L-18; mail Whitesburg Z 41858; ● 200
Marrowbone; RMC Place; CUMBERLAND; **180** M-9; elev. 631ft./192m.; 🅿; Z 42759; ● 120
Marrowbone (Regina); RMC Place; PIKE; **181** K-19; elev. 719ft./219m.; mail Regina Z 41559; ● 400
Marshall; RMC Place; MARSHALL; ***180** L-1; mail Gilbertsville Z 42044; summer pop. 200; ● 100
Marshall; RMC Place; MASON; ***181** F-15; elev. 787ft./240m.; mail Maysville Z 41056
MARSHALL; **180** F-4; Ⓟ 27,205; Ⓒ 30,125; ◆ 31,310
Marshallville; RMC Place; MAGOFFIN; ***181** I-17; elev. 983ft./300m.; 🅿; Z 41465; ● 65
Marshes Siding; RMC Place; MCCREARY; **181** M-12; elev. 1,320ft./402m.; 🅿; Z 42631; ● 700
Martha; RMC Place; LAWRENCE; **181** H-17; elev. 687ft./209m.; 🅿; Z 41159; ● 20
Martin; Inc. Place; FLOYD; **181** J-18; elev. 662ft./202m.; 🅿 🅷; Z 41649; Ⓟ 694; Ⓒ 633
MARTIN; **181** I-19; Ⓟ 12,526; Ⓒ 12,578; ◆ 11,333
Martinsville; RMC Place; WARREN; ***180** M-7; elev. 623ft./190m.; mail Oakland Z 42159; rural
Mary; RMC Place; WOLFE; ***181** I-15; elev. 846ft./258m.; 🅿; Z 41301; rural
Mary Alice; RMC Place; HARLAN; **181** M-16; elev. 1,308ft./399m.; 🅿; Z 40964; ● 350
Marydell; RMC Place; LAUREL; ***181** L-14; elev. 1,183ft./361m.; 🅿; Z 40741; ● 30
Mary Helen (Coalgood, Merna); RMC Place; HARLAN; **181** M-16; mail Coalgood Z 40818; ● 160
Maryhill Estates; Inc. Place; JEFFERSON; ***180** G-9; elev. 500ft./152m.; ★ **LOU**; mail Louisville Z 40207; Ⓟ 177; Ⓒ 175
Mashfork; RMC Place; MAGOFFIN; ***181** I-17; elev. 949ft./289m.; 🅿; Z 41465; rural
Mason; RMC Place; GRANT; **181** F-12; 🅿; Z 41054; ● 90
Mason; RMC Place; MAGOFFIN; ***181** I-17; elev. 890ft./271m.; mail Salyersville Z 41465; ● 45
MASON; **181** F-15; Ⓟ 16,666; Ⓒ 16,800; ◆ 17,303
Masonic Home; RMC Place; JEFFERSON; ***180** G-9; 🅿; ★ **LOU**; Z 40041; pop. incl. with Louisville (Inc. Place)
Masonville; CDP; DAVIESS; **180** I-4; elev. 424ft./129m.; ★ **OWNS**; mail Utica Z 42376; Ⓟ 1,119; Ⓒ 1,075
Massac; CDP; MCCRACKEN; ***180** E-3; elev. 479ft./146m.; ★ **PAD**; mail Paducah Z 42001; Ⓟ 3,733; Ⓒ 3,888
Matanzas; RMC Place; OHIO; ***180** J-4; elev. 416ft./127m.; mail Centertown Z 42328
Matlock; RMC Place; WARREN; ***180** M-6; elev. 626ft./191m.; mail Bowling Green Z 42104; rural
Matthew; RMC Place; MORGAN; ***181** I-17; elev. 852ft./260m.; 🅿; Z 41472; rural
Mattingly; RMC Place; BRECKINRIDGE; ***180** I-6; mail Cloverport Z 40111; rural
Mattoon; RMC Place; CRITTENDEN; ***180** K-1; mail Marion Z 42064
Mattoxtown; RMC Place; FAYETTE; ***181** H-12; ★ **LEX**; mail Lexington Z 40505; pop. incl. with Lexington (Inc. Place)
Maud; RMC Place; WASHINGTON; **180** I-10; elev. 558ft./170m.; 🅿; Z 40069; ● 40
Maulden; RMC Place; JACKSON; ***181** K-14; elev. 1,028ft./313m.; 🅿; Z 40486; rural
Mavity; RMC Place; BOYD; ***181** G-18; elev. 617ft./188m.; mail Catlettsburg Z 41129; ● 75
Maxine; RMC Place; LARUE; ***180** J-8; elev. 821ft./250m.; mail Sonora Z 42776; rural
Maxon; MCCRACKEN; see West Paducah (RMC Place)
Maxwell; RMC Place; OHIO, DAVIESS; ***180** J-4; mail Utica Z 42376; rural
Mayfield; Inc. Place; ⊡ GRAVES; **180** F-3; elev. 492ft./150m.; 🅿 🅷 🅲 1,172 ■; Z 42066; Ⓟ 9,935; Ⓒ 10,349; ◆ 9,662
Mayflower; RMC Place; PIKE; ***181** J-19; mail Pikeville Z 41501; rural
Mayking; RMC Place; LETCHER; **181** L-18; elev. 1,214ft./370m.; 🅿; Z 41837; ● 600
Maynard; RMC Place; ALLEN; ***180** M-7; mail Scottsville Z 42164; rural
Mayo; RMC Place; MERCER; ***181** I-11; mail Harrodsburg Z 40330
Mayo Village; RMC Place; PIKE; ***181** J-19; mail Pikeville Z 41501; pop. incl. with Pikeville (Inc. Place)
Mays Lick; RMC Place; MASON; **181** F-14; elev. 898ft./274m.; 🅿; Z 41055; ● 350
Maysville; Inc. Place; ⊡ MASON; **181** F-15; elev. 514ft./157m.; 🅿 🅷 ■; Z 41056; Ⓟ 7,169; Ⓒ 8,993; ◆ 9,153
Maytown; RMC Place; MORGAN; ***181** I-16; elev. 938ft./286m.; 🅿; Z 41301 & mail West Liberty Z 41472
Maywood; RMC Place; LINCOLN; ***181** J-12; elev. 1,017ft./310m.; mail Stanford Z 40484; rural
Mazie; RMC Place; LAWRENCE; **181** H-17; elev. 735ft./224m.; 🅿; Z 41160; ● 30
McAfee; RMC Place; MERCER; **181** I-11; mail Harrodsburg Z 40330; ● 50
McAndrews; RMC Place; PIKE; **181** J-19; elev. 833ft./254m.; 🅿; Z 41543; ● 450
McBrayer; RMC Place; ANDERSON; ***181** H-11; elev. 833ft./254m.; mail Lawrenceburg Z 40342
McCarr; RMC Place; PIKE; ***181** J-20; elev. 700ft./213m.; 🅿; Z 41544; ● 200
McClure; RMC Place; MARTIN; ***181** I-19; mail Pilgrim Z 41250; rural
McCombs; RMC Place; PIKE; ***181** I-18; elev. 677ft./206m.; 🅿; Z 41501; ● 15
MCCRACKEN; **180** E-3; Ⓟ 62,879; Ⓒ 65,514; ◆ 64,640
McCreary; RMC Place; GARRARD; ***181** J-12; elev. 971ft./296m.; mail Lancaster Z 40444
MCCREARY; **181** N-12; Ⓟ 15,603; Ⓒ 17,080; ◆ 17,250
McDaniels; RMC Place; BRECKINRIDGE; **180** J-6; elev. 650ft./198m.; 🅿; Z 40152; ● 200
McDowell; RMC Place; FLOYD; **181** J-18; elev. 705ft./215m.; 🅿 🅷; Z 41647; ● 400
McGowan; RMC Place; CALDWELL; ***180** L-2; mail Princeton Z 42445; rural
McHenry; Inc. Place; OHIO; **180** K-5; elev. 426ft./130m.; 🅿; Z 42354; Ⓟ 414; Ⓒ 417
McKee; Inc. Place; ⊡ JACKSON; **181** J-14; elev. 1,030ft./314m.; 🅿; Z 40447; Ⓟ 870; Ⓒ 878
McKinney; RMC Place; LINCOLN; **181** J-12; elev. 1,012ft./308m.; 🅿; Z 40448; ● 275
McKinneysburg; RMC Place; PENDLETON; ***181** F-13; mail Falmouth Z 41040; rural
MCLEAN; **180** J-3; Ⓟ 9,628; Ⓒ 9,938; ◆ 9,666
McQuady; RMC Place; BRECKINRIDGE; **180** I-6; elev. 676ft./206m.; 🅿; Z 40153; ● 75
McRoberts; CDP; LETCHER; **181** K-18; elev. 1,423ft./434m.; 🅿; Z 41835; Ⓟ 1,101; Ⓒ 921
McVeigh; RMC Place; PIKE; **181** J-19; elev. 1,012ft./308m.; 🅿; Z 41555; ● 250
McVille; RMC Place; BOONE; **181** D-11; mail Burlington Z 41005; ● 85
McWhorter; RMC Place; LAUREL; ***181** K-14; mail London Z 40741; rural
MEADE; **180** H-7; Ⓟ 24,170; Ⓒ 26,349; ◆ 26,458
Meador; RMC Place; ALLEN; ***180** M-7; elev. 658ft./201m.; mail Scottsville Z 42164; rural
Meadowbrook; RMC Place; CLARK; ***181** H-13; ★ **LEX**; mail Winchester Z 40391; pop. incl. with Winchester (Inc. Place)
Meadowbrook; RMC Place; SHELBY; ***180** G-10; mail Shelbyville Z 40065; ● 550
Meadowbrook Farm; Inc. Place; JEFFERSON; ***180** G-9; ★ **LOU**; mail Louisville Z 40223; Ⓟ 163; Ⓒ 146
Meadow Creek; RMC Place; WHITLEY; ***181** M-14; 🅿; Z 40759; rural
Meadowrun; RMC Place; SHELBY; ***180** G-10; mail Shelbyville Z 40065; ● 250
Meadows; RMC Place; FAYETTE; ***181** H-12; ★ **LEX**; mail Lexington Z 40505; pop. incl. with Lexington (Inc. Place)
Meadows; RMC Place; FRANKLIN; ***181** H-11; mail Frankfort Z 40601; pop. incl. with Frankfort (Inc. Place)
Meadowthorpe; RMC Place; FAYETTE; ***181** H-12; ★ **LEX**; mail Lexington Z 40511; pop. incl. with Lexington (Inc. Place)
Meadow Vale; Inc. Place; JEFFERSON; **180** A-9; elev. 645ft./197m.; ★ **LOU**; mail Louisville Z 40222; Ⓟ 798; Ⓒ 765
Meadowview Estates; Inc. Place; JEFFERSON; **180** C-8; elev. 530ft./162m.; ★ **LOU**; mail Amlin Z 43002, Louisville Z 40220; Ⓟ 259; Ⓒ 422
Meads; RMC Place; BOYD; ***181** F-18; ★ **HNTG**; mail Ashland Z 41101; rural
Meally (Buffalo Creek); RMC Place; JOHNSON; ***181** I-18; elev. 649ft./198m.; 🅿; Z 41234; ● 200
Means; RMC Place; MENIFEE; **181** H-15; elev. 836ft./255m.; 🅿; Z 40346; ● 150
Medora; RMC Place; JEFFERSON; ***180** H-8; elev. 450ft./137m.; ★ **LOU**; mail Louisville Z 40272; became part of Louisville/Jefferson County Metro Jan. 6, 2003
Meece; RMC Place; PULASKI; ***181** L-12; mail Somerset Z 42501; rural
Meeting Creek; RMC Place; HARDIN; ***180** J-7; 🅿; Z 42732; rural
Melber; RMC Place; MCCRACKEN, GRAVES; **180** F-3; elev. 365ft./111m.; 🅿; Z 42069; ● 300
Melbourne; Inc. Place; CAMPBELL; **181** D-13; elev. 503ft./153m.; 🅿; ★ **CIN**; Z 41059; Ⓟ 660; Ⓒ 457
Meldrum; RMC Place; BELL; **181** N-15; mail Middlesboro Z 40965; ● 150
Mell; RMC Place; GREEN; ***180** L-9; elev. 1,024ft./312m.; mail Greensburg Z 42743; rural
Melody Lake; RMC Place; NELSON; ***180** J-9; mail New Haven Z 40051; ● 100
Melvin; RMC Place; FLOYD; **181** K-18; elev. 996ft./304m.; 🅿; Z 41650; ● 250
Memphis Junction; RMC Place; WARREN; **180** C-3; elev. 555ft./169m.; ★ **BOWLG**; mail Bowling Green Z 42101; ● 250
MENIFEE; **181** H-15; Ⓟ 5,092; Ⓒ 6,556; ◆ 6,682
Mentor; Inc. Place; CAMPBELL; **181** E-13; elev. 531ft./162m.; 🅿; ★ **CIN**; Z 41007; Ⓟ 169; Ⓒ 181
MERCER; **181** I-11; Ⓟ 19,148; Ⓒ 20,817; ◆ 21,931
Meredith; RMC Place; GRAYSON; ***180** K-7; mail Leitchfield Z 42754
Merewood; RMC Place; WOODFORD; ***181** H-12; ★ **LEX**; mail Versailles Z 40383; pop. incl. with Versailles (Inc. Place)
Meridian; RMC Place; PENDLETON; ***181** E-13; elev. 550ft./168m.; mail Butler Z 41006; rural
Merna; HARLAN; see Mary Helen (RMC Place)
Merrick Place; RMC Place; FAYETTE; ***181** H-12; ★ **LEX**; mail Lexington Z 40502; pop. incl. with Lexington (Inc. Place)
Merrimac; RMC Place; TAYLOR; ***180** K-10; mail Bradfordsville Z 40009; rural
Merrittstown; RMC Place; CHRISTIAN; ***180** M-2; ★ **HPKNV**; mail Hopkinsville Z 42240; ● 50
Merry Oaks; RMC Place; BARREN; **180** L-7; mail Smiths Grove Z 42171; ● 50
Mershons; RMC Place; LAUREL; ***181** K-14; elev. 1,062ft./324m.; mail East Bernstadt Z 40729; rural
Meshack; RMC Place; MONROE; ***180** M-9; elev. 561ft./171m.; mail Tompkinsville Z 42167; rural
Meta; RMC Place; PIKE; **181** J-19; elev. 745ft./227m.; 🅿; Z 41501; ● 250
METCALFE; **180** L-9; Ⓟ 8,963; Ⓒ 10,037; ◆ 10,375
Mexico; RMC Place; CRITTENDEN; **180** K-1; mail Marion Z 42064; ● 30
Midas; RMC Place; FLOYD; ***181** J-18; mail Hueysville Z 41640; rural
Middleburg; RMC Place; CASEY; **181** K-11; elev. 840ft./256m.; 🅿; Z 42541; ● 200
Middlesboro (Middlesborough); Inc. Place; BELL; **181** N-15; elev. 1,138ft./347m.; 🅿 🅷 ■; Z 40965; Ⓟ 11,328; Ⓒ 10,384; ◆ 9,862
Middlesborough; BELL; see Middlesboro (Inc. Place)
Middleton; RMC Place; SIMPSON; **180** M-5; elev. 645ft./197m.; mail Franklin Z 42134; ● 60
Middleton Heights; RMC Place; SHELBY; ***180** G-10; mail Shelbyville Z 40065
Middletown; Inc. Place; JEFFERSON; **180** G-9; elev. 721ft./220m.; 🅿; ★ **LOU**; Z 40243, Z 40253; Ⓟ 5,016; Ⓒ 5,744; Ⓡ 5,801
Middletown; RMC Place; MADISON; ***181** J-13; elev. 982ft./299m.; mail Berea Z 40403; pop. incl. with Berea (Inc. Place)
Midland; RMC Place; BATH; **181** H-15; elev. 688ft./210m.; mail Salt Lick Z 40371; ● 175
Midland; RMC Place; MUHLENBERG; ***180** K-4; elev. 475ft./145m.; mail Bremen Z 42325; ● 90
Midway (Tobacco); RMC Place; CALLOWAY; **180** G-4; mail Hazel Z 42049; ● 45
Midway; RMC Place; CRITTENDEN; ***180** K-1; elev. 523ft./159m.; mail Marion Z 42064; rural
Midway; RMC Place; MEADE; **180** H-7; mail Guston Z 40142; ● 60
Midway; Inc. Place; WOODFORD; **181** H-12; elev. 789ft./240m.; 🅿 🅲 1,321; ★ **LEX**; Z 40347; Ⓟ 1,290; Ⓒ 1,620
Milburn; RMC Place; CARLISLE; **180** F-2; elev. 460ft./140m.; 🅿; Z 42070; ● 250
Mildred; RMC Place; JACKSON; ***181** K-14; mail Mc Kee Z 40447; rural
Milford; RMC Place; BRACKEN; **181** F-13; elev. 613ft./187m.; 🅿; Z 41061; ● 90
Millard; RMC Place; PIKE; ***181** J-19; mail Shelbiana Z 41562; ● 60
Mill Creek; RMC Place; MASON; ***181** F-15; mail Mayslick Z 41055; rural
Milledgeville; RMC Place; LINCOLN; ***181** J-11; mail Hustonville Z 40437; ● 50
Miller; RMC Place; FULTON; ***180** G-1; mail Hickman Z 42050; rural
Miller; RMC Place; NICHOLAS; ***181** G-14; mail Carlisle Z 40311; rural
Millersburg; Inc. Place; BOURBON; **181** G-13; elev. 803ft./245m.; 🅿; Z 40348; Ⓟ 937; Ⓒ 842
Millers Creek; RMC Place; ESTILL; ***181** J-14; mail Ravenna Z 40472; rural
Millerstown; RMC Place; GRAYSON; **180** J-7; elev. 589ft./180m.; 🅿; Z 42726; ● 40
Million; RMC Place; MADISON; ***181** I-13; mail Richmond Z 40475
Mill Pond; RMC Place; CLAY; ***181** K-15; mail Manchester Z 40962; rural
Millport; RMC Place; MUHLENBERG; ***180** K-3; elev. 409ft./125m.; mail Sacramento Z 42372; ● 50
Mills; RMC Place; KNOX; ***181** L-15; elev. 1,096ft./334m.; 🅿; Z 40935; ● 40
Millseat; RMC Place; BOYD; ***181** F-18; ★ **HNTG**; mail Ashland Z 41101
Mill Springs; RMC Place; WAYNE; **181** M-11; elev. 844ft./257m.; 🅿; Z 42633; ● 50
Millstone; RMC Place; LETCHER; **181** K-18; elev. 1,230ft./375m.; 🅿; Z 41838; ● 300
Milltown; RMC Place; ADAIR; **180** L-9; elev. 681ft./208m.; 🅿; Z 42728; ● 25
Milltown; RMC Place; NICHOLAS; ***181** G-14; mail Moorefield Z 40350; rural
Millville; RMC Place; WOODFORD; **181** H-11; mail Frankfort Z 40601; ● 200
Millwood; RMC Place; GRAYSON; **180** J-6; elev. 673ft./205m.; 🅿; Z 42762; ● 200
Milner; RMC Place; WOODFORD; ***181** H-11; elev. 860ft./262m.; mail Versailles Z 40383; ● 45
Milo; RMC Place; MARTIN; ***181** H-18; elev. 635ft./194m.; 🅿; Z 41262; rural
Milton; Inc. Place; TRIMBLE; **180** E-10; elev. 468ft./143m.; 🅿; Z 40045; Ⓟ 563; Ⓒ 525
Mima; RMC Place; MORGAN; ***181** H-17; elev. 794ft./242m.; 🅿; Z 41472; ● 40
Minerva; RMC Place; MASON; **181** E-14; elev. 958ft./292m.; 🅿; Z 41062; ● 70
Minnie (Gibson); RMC Place; FLOYD; ***181** J-18; elev. 691ft./211m.; 🅿; Z 41651; ● 150
Minor Lane Heights; JEFFERSON; see Heritage Creek (Inc. Place)
Minorsville; RMC Place; SCOTT; **181** G-12; mail Stamping Ground Z 40379; ● 50
Mintonville; RMC Place; CASEY; ***181** L-11; elev. 1,190ft./363m.; mail Bethelridge Z 42516, Liberty Z 42539
Miracle; RMC Place; BELL; ***181** M-15; elev. 1,064ft./324m.; 🅿; Z 40856; ● 30
Mistletoe; RMC Place; OWSLEY; ***181** K-15; elev. 858ft./262m.; 🅿; Z 41351; ● 30
Mitchell Hill; RMC Place; HOPKINS; ***180** K-3; mail Madisonville Z 42431; pop. incl. with Madisonville (Inc. Place)
Mitchellsburg; RMC Place; BOYLE; **181** J-11; elev. 990ft./302m.; 🅿; Z 40452; ● 350
Mize; RMC Place; MORGAN; **181** I-16; elev. 832ft./254m.; 🅿; Z 41352; ● 10
Moberly; RMC Place; MADISON; ***181** I-13; mail Richmond Z 40475; ● 90
Mockingbird Valley; Inc. Place; JEFFERSON; ***180** G-9; elev. 482ft./147m.; ★ **LOU**; mail Louisville Z 40207; Ⓟ 177; Ⓒ 190
Moct; RMC Place; BREATHITT; ***181** J-16; mail Vancleve Z 41385; rural
Modoc; RMC Place; CUMBERLAND; ***180** M-10; mail Burkesville Z 42717; rural
Molus; RMC Place; HARLAN; **181** M-16; 🅿; Z 40819; ● 130
Monford; RMC Place; BUTLER; ***180** K-5; mail Jetson Z 42252; rural
Monica; RMC Place; LEE; ***181** J-15; mail Primrose Z 41362; rural
Monica Gardens; RMC Place; SHELBY; ***180** G-10; mail Shelbyville Z 40065; ● 65
Monitor; RMC Place; TRIMBLE; ***180** F-10; elev. 924ft./282m.; mail Bedford Z 40006; rural
Monkeys Eyebrow; RMC Place; BALLARD; ***180** E-2; mail La Center Z 42056; rural
Monroe; RMC Place; HART; **180** K-8; mail Hardyville Z 42746; ● 50
MONROE; **180** M-9; Ⓟ 11,401; Ⓒ 11,756; ◆ 11,407
Montclair; RMC Place; FAYETTE; ***181** H-12; ★ **LEX**; mail Lexington Z 40502; pop. incl. with Lexington (Inc. Place)
Montclair; RMC Place; SHELBY; ***180** G-10; elev. 773ft./236m.; mail Simpsonville Z 40067; ● 140
Monterey; Inc. Place; OWEN; **181** G-11; elev. 487ft./148m.; mail Owenton Z 40359; Ⓟ 164; Ⓒ 167
Montgomery; RMC Place; TRIGG; ***180** M-2; mail Cadiz Z 42211; pop. incl. with Cadiz (Inc. Place)
MONTGOMERY; **181** H-14; Ⓟ 19,561; Ⓒ 22,554; ◆ 25,856
Montgomerys Mill; RMC Place; GREEN; mail Greensburg Z 42743; rural
Monticello; Inc. Place; ⊡ WAYNE; **181** M-11; elev. 923ft./281m.; 🅿 🅷; Z 42633; Ⓟ 5,357; Ⓒ 5,981
Monticello Estates; RMC Place; FAYETTE; ***181** H-12; ★ **LEX**; mail Lexington Z 40503; pop. incl. with Lexington (Inc. Place)
Montpelier; RMC Place; ADAIR; ***180** L-10; elev. 870ft./265m.; 🅿; Z 42728; rural
Montrose; RMC Place; FAYETTE; ***181** H-13; ★ **LEX**; mail Lexington Z 40516; pop. incl. with Lexington (Inc. Place)
Montrose Park; RMC Place; FRANKLIN; ***181** G-11; mail Frankfort Z 40601; pop. incl. with Frankfort (Inc. Place)
Mooleyville; RMC Place; BRECKINRIDGE; **180** H-6; elev. 585ft./178m.; 🅿; Z 40143; ● 30
Moon; RMC Place; MORGAN; **181** H-17; 🅿; Z 41472; ● 10
Moon Lake Estates; RMC Place; SCOTT; ***181** G-12; mail Georgetown Z 40324; ● 300
Moorefield; RMC Place; NICHOLAS; **181** G-14; elev. 987ft./301m.; 🅿; Z 40350; ● 125
Moore Hill; RMC Place; KNOX; ***181** L-14; mail Corbin Z 40701; ● 300
Moores Creek; RMC Place; JACKSON; ***181** K-14; elev. 1,049ft./320m.; 🅿; Z 40402; rural
Moores Ferry; RMC Place; BATH; ***181** G-15; mail Salt Lick Z 40371; rural
Moore Spring (Subtle); RMC Place; METCALFE; ***180** M-9; elev. 1,036ft./316m.; mail Edmonton Z 42129; rural
Mooresville; RMC Place; WASHINGTON; **180** I-10; mail Springfield Z 40069; ● 45
Moorland; Inc. Place; JEFFERSON; **180** B-9; elev. 648ft./198m.; ★ **LOU**; mail Louisville Z 40223; Ⓟ 467; Ⓒ 464
Moorman; RMC Place; MUHLENBERG; **180** K-4; elev. 421ft./128m.; mail Central City Z 42330; ● 175
Moranburg; RMC Place; MASON; ***181** E-14; mail Maysville Z 41056
Morehead; Inc. Place; ⊡ ROWAN; **181** G-16; elev. 748ft./228m.; 🅿 🅷 🅲 9,025; Z 40351; Ⓟ 8,357; Ⓒ 5,914; Ⓡ 7,593
Moreland; RMC Place; LINCOLN; **181** J-11; elev. 1,089ft./332m.; mail Hustonville Z 40437; ● 150
Morgan; RMC Place; PENDLETON; **181** F-13; elev. 639ft./195m.; mail Falmouth Z 41040; ● 30
MORGAN; **181** H-16; Ⓟ 11,648; Ⓒ 13,948; ◆ 14,200
Morganfield; Inc. Place; ⊡ UNION; **180** I-1; elev. 437ft./133m.; 🅿 🅷; Z 42437; Ⓟ 3,776; Ⓒ 3,494
Morgantown; Inc. Place; ⊡ BUTLER; **180** K-5; elev. 573ft./175m.; 🅿; Z 42261 & mail Welchs Creek Z 42287; Ⓟ 2,284; Ⓒ 2,544
Morning Glory; RMC Place; NICHOLAS; ***181** G-13; elev. 777ft./237m.; mail Cynthiana Z 41031; rural
Morning View; RMC Place; KENTON; **181** E-12; elev. 545ft./166m.; 🅿; ★ **CIN**; Z 41063; ● 100
Morrill; RMC Place; JACKSON, ROCKCASTLE; **181** J-13; elev. 1,373ft./418m.; 🅿; Z 40447; ● 100
Morris Fork; RMC Place; BREATHITT; ***181** K-15; elev. 802ft./244m.; 🅿; Z 41314; rural
Mortiner Station; RMC Place; LOGAN; ***180** M-5; mail Adairville Z 42202; ● 10
Morton; HOPKINS; see Mortons Gap (Inc. Place)
Mortons Gap (Morton); Inc. Place; HOPKINS; **180** K-3; elev. 444ft./135m.; 🅿; Z 42440; Ⓟ 987; Ⓒ 952
Mortonsville; RMC Place; WOODFORD; **181** H-12; elev. 780ft./238m.; mail Versailles Z 40383; ● 90
Moscow; RMC Place; HICKMAN; **180** G-2; mail Clinton Z 42031; ● 45
Moseleyville; RMC Place; DAVIESS; **180** J-4; elev. 391ft./119m.; mail Owensboro Z 42301; ● 200
Mossy Bottom; RMC Place; PIKE; ***181** J-18; mail Pikeville Z 41501; rural
Motley; RMC Place; WARREN; ***180** M-7; mail Bowling Green Z 42103; rural
Mount Aerial; RMC Place; ALLEN; ***180** M-6; mail Scottsville Z 42164; rural
Mountain Ash; RMC Place; WHITLEY; **181** N-14; mail Williamsburg Z 40769; ● 200
Mountain Top; RMC Place; CARTER; ***181** G-17; mail Olive Hill Z 41164; rural
Mountain Valley; RMC Place; BREATHITT; ***181** J-16; mail Vancleve Z 41385; rural
Mount Auburn; RMC Place; PENDLETON; ***181** E-13; elev. 905ft./276m.; mail Butler Z 41006; rural
Mount Carmel; RMC Place; FLEMING; **181** F-15; mail Flemingsburg Z 41041; ● 100
Mount Carmel; RMC Place; HOPKINS; ***180** L-3; mail White Plains Z 42464; rural
Mount Eden; RMC Place; SPENCER, SHELBY; **180** H-10; elev. 841ft./256m.; 🅿; Z 40046; ● 200
Mount Gilead; RMC Place; GREEN; ***180** L-10; mail Greensburg Z 42743; rural
Mount Gilead; RMC Place; MONROE; ***180** M-8; mail Tompkinsville Z 42167; rural
Mount Hermon; RMC Place; MONROE; **180** M-8; elev. 989ft./301m.; 🅿; Z 42157; ● 40
Mount Lebanon; RMC Place; JESSAMINE; ***181** I-12; mail Nicholasville Z 40356; rural
Mount Olive; RMC Place; CASEY; ***181** K-11; elev. 1,289ft./393m.; mail Liberty Z 42539; rural
Mount Olive; RMC Place; LEE; ***181** J-15; mail Beattyville Z 41311; rural
Mount Olivet; Inc. Place; ⊡ ROBERTSON; **181** F-14; elev. 958ft./292m.; 🅿; Z 41064; Ⓟ 384; Ⓒ 289
Mount Pisgah; RMC Place; WAYNE; ***181** N-11; 🅿; Z 42633; rural
Mount Pleasant; RMC Place; OHIO; ***180** K-5; mail Cromwell Z 42333; rural
Mount Pleasant; RMC Place; TRIMBLE; ***180** F-9; elev. 859ft./262m.; mail Bedford Z 40006; rural
Mount Salem; RMC Place; LINCOLN; ***181** K-11; elev. 945ft./288m.; mail Hustonville Z 40437; rural
Mount Sherman; RMC Place; LARUE; **180** J-9; elev. 896ft./273m.; 🅿; Z 42764; ● 250
Mount Sterling; Inc. Place; ⊡ MONTGOMERY; **181** H-14; elev. 1,027ft./313m.; 🅿 🅷; Z 40353; Ⓟ 5,362; Ⓒ 5,876
Mount Tabor; RMC Place; LARUE; ***180** J-9; mail Buffalo Z 42716; rural
Mount Tabor; RMC Place; TODD; ***180** L-4; mail Elkton Z 42220; rural
Mount Union; RMC Place; ALLEN; ***180** N-7; mail Adolphus Z 42120, Scottsville Z 42164; rural
Mount Vernon; Inc. Place; ⊡ ROCKCASTLE; **181** K-13; elev. 1,156ft./352m.; 🅿 🅷; Z 40456; Ⓟ 2,654; Ⓒ 2,592
Mount Vernon; RMC Place; SCOTT; ★ **LEX**; mail Georgetown Z 40324; pop. incl. with Georgetown (Inc. Place)
Mount Victor; RMC Place; WARREN; ***180** L-6; ★ **BOWLG**; mail Bowling Green Z 42104; ● 150
Mount Victory; RMC Place; PULASKI; ***181** L-13; elev. 1,184ft./361m.; mail Somerset Z 42501
Mount Washington; Inc. Place; BULLITT; **180** H-9; elev. 688ft./210m.; 🅿; ★ **LOU**; Z 40047; Ⓟ 5,226; Ⓒ 8,485
Mount Zion; RMC Place; ALLEN; ***180** N-7; elev. 812ft./247m.; mail Scottsville Z 42164; ● 45
Mount Zion; RMC Place; GRANT; ***181** E-12; elev. 925ft./282m.; ★ **CIN**; mail Dry Ridge Z 41035; rural
Mount Zion; RMC Place; PULASKI; ***181** K-12; mail Science Hill Z 42553; rural
Mousie; RMC Place; KNOTT; **181** J-18; elev. 785ft./239m.; 🅿; Z 41839; ● 400
Moutardier; RMC Place; GRAYSON; ***180** K-7; mail Leitchfield Z 42754; rural
Mouthcard; RMC Place; PIKE; **181** K-19; elev. 837ft./255m.; 🅿; Z 41548; ● 150
Moxley; RMC Place; OWEN; ***181** F-11; mail Perry Park Z 40363; rural
Mozelle; RMC Place; LESLIE; **181** L-16; elev. 1,400ft./427m.; 🅿; Z 40858; ● 150
Mud Camp; RMC Place; CUMBERLAND; ***180** M-9; mail Burkesville Z 42717; rural
Muddy Ford; RMC Place; SCOTT; ***181** G-12; mail Georgetown Z 40324; rural
Mud Lick; RMC Place; MONROE; ***180** M-8; elev. 992ft./302m.; mail Tompkinsville Z 42167
MUHLENBERG; **180** L-4; Ⓟ 31,318; Ⓒ 31,839; ◆ 31,005
Muir; RMC Place; FAYETTE; ***181** H-13; elev. 938ft./286m.; ★ **LEX**; mail Lexington Z 40516; pop. incl. with Lexington (Inc. Place)
Mulberry; RMC Place; SHELBY; ***180** G-10; mail Shelbyville Z 40065; rural
Muldraugh; Inc. Place; MEADE, HARDIN; **180** H-8; elev. 720ft./219m.; 🅿; Z 40155; Ⓟ 1,376; Ⓒ 1,298
Mulfordtown; RMC Place; UNION; ***180** J-1; mail Sturgis Z 42459
Mullikin Junction; RMC Place; LIVINGSTON; ***180** E-4; mail Burna Z 42028; rural
Mullins; RMC Place; ROCKCASTLE; ***181** K-13; mail Mount Vernon Z 40456; rural
Mummie; RMC Place; JACKSON; ***181** K-14; elev. 990ft./302m.; mail Tyner Z 40486; rural
Munfordville; Inc. Place; ⊡ HART; **180** K-8; elev. 612ft./187m.; 🅿; Z 42765; Ⓟ 1,556; Ⓒ 1,563
Murl; RMC Place; WAYNE; ***181** M-11; elev. 1,043ft./318m.; mail Monticello Z 42633; rural
Murphyfork; RMC Place; MORGAN; ***181** I-16; mail Hazel Green Z 41332; rural
Murphysville; RMC Place; MASON; ***181** F-14; mail Maysville Z 41056; rural
Murray; Inc. Place; ⊡ CALLOWAY; **180** G-4; elev. 515ft./157m.; 🅿 🅷 🅲 10,304 ■; Z 42071; Ⓟ 14,439; Ⓒ 14,950; ◆ 15,448
Murray Hill; Inc. Place; JEFFERSON; **180** A-9; ★ **LOU**; mail Louisville Z 40222; Ⓟ 619; Ⓒ 616
Muses Mills; RMC Place; FLEMING; **181** G-15; elev. 714ft./218m.; 🅿; Z 41065; ● 80
Music; RMC Place; CARTER; ***181** G-18; mail Rush Z 41168; rural
Myers; RMC Place; NICHOLAS; **181** G-14; elev. 640ft./195m.; mail Carlisle Z 40311; ● 50
Myra; RMC Place; PIKE; **181** K-18; elev. 986ft./301m.; 🅿; Z 41549; ● 100
Mystic; RMC Place; BRECKINRIDGE; ***180** I-6; mail Irvington Z 40146; rural

N

Nada; RMC Place; POWELL; ***181** I-15; mail Stanton Z 40380; ● 100
Nancy; RMC Place; PULASKI; **181** L-12; elev. 1,084ft./330m.; 🅿; Z 42544; ● 400
Naomi; RMC Place; PULASKI; ***181** L-11; 🅿; Z 42544; rural
Napfor; RMC Place; PERRY; ***181** K-16; 🅿; Z 41754; rural
Naples; RMC Place; GREENUP; ***181** F-18; elev. 551ft./168m.; ★ **HNTG**; mail Ashland Z 41101-02, Z 41105; ● 30
Napoleon; RMC Place; GALLATIN; **181** E-11; elev. 853ft./260m.; 🅿; Z 41095 & mail Glencoe Z 41046; ● 50
Narco; RMC Place; FAYETTE; ★ **LEX**; pop. incl. with Lexington (Inc. Place)
Narrows; RMC Place; OHIO; ***180** J-5; elev. 550ft./168m.; 🅿; Z 42347; ● 40
Narvel; RMC Place; CLINTON; ***181** M-11; mail Albany Z 42602; rural
Nashtown; RMC Place; LEWIS; ***181** F-15; mail Tollesboro Z 41189; rural
Natlee; RMC Place; OWEN; ***181** F-12; mail Corinth Z 41010; rural
Natural Bridge; RMC Place; POWELL; **181** I-15; mail Slade Z 40376; summer pop. 200; ● 10
Nazareth; RMC Place; NELSON; **180** I-9; elev. 749ft./228m.; 🅿; Z 40048; ● 400
Neafus; RMC Place; BUTLER, GRAYSON; ***180** K-6; elev. 631ft./192m.; 🅿; Z 42721; ● 20
Neave; RMC Place; BRACKEN; ***181** F-13; mail Falmouth Z 41040; rural
Nebo; Inc. Place; HOPKINS; **180** K-2; elev. 382ft./116m.; 🅿; Z 42441; Ⓟ 227; Ⓒ 220
Nebo; RMC Place; MUHLENBERG; ***180** K-4; elev. 592ft./180m.; mail Greenville Z 42345; rural
Ned; RMC Place; BREATHITT; ***181** K-16; elev. 1,000ft./305m.; 🅿; Z 41348 & mail Clayhole Z 41317; rural
Needmore; RMC Place; BOYLE; ***181** J-11; elev. 958ft./292m.; mail Danville Z 40422; rural
Needmore; RMC Place; BUTLER; ***180** L-5; elev. 500ft./152m.; mail Morgantown Z 42261; rural
Needmore; RMC Place; CALDWELL; ***180** K-2; mail Princeton Z 42445; rural
Nelse; RMC Place; PIKE; ***181** J-19; elev. 806ft./246m.; 🅿; Z 41501; ● 50
Nelson; RMC Place; MUHLENBERG; ***180** K-4; elev. 418ft./127m.; mail Central City Z 42330; ● 75
NELSON; **180** I-9; Ⓟ 29,710; Ⓒ 37,477; ◆ 43,469
Nelsonville; RMC Place; NELSON; ***180** I-9; elev. 473ft./144m.; mail Boston Z 40107; rural
Neon; RMC Place; LETCHER; ***181** K-18; 🅿; Z 41840; pop. incl. with Fleming-Neon (Inc. Place)
Neon Junction; RMC Place; LETCHER; ***181** K-18; mail Neon Z 41840; ● 20
Neosheo; RMC Place; SIMPSON; ***180** M-5; mail Franklin Z 42134; rural
Nepton; RMC Place; FLEMING; ***181** F-14; mail Ewing Z 41039; ● 100
Nerinx; RMC Place; MARION; **180** J-9; elev. 704ft./215m.; 🅿; Z 40049; ● 300
Nero; RMC Place; JOHNSON; ***181** I-18; mail Van Lear Z 41265
Netty; RMC Place; MAGOFFIN; ***181** I-16; mail Salyersville Z 41465; rural
Nevada; RMC Place; MERCER; ***181** I-11; elev. 821ft./250m.; mail Harrodsburg Z 40330
Nevelsville; RMC Place; MCCREARY; ***181** M-12; mail Whitley City Z 42653; rural
Nevin; RMC Place; ANDERSON; ***181** H-11; mail Lawrenceburg Z 40342; rural
Nevisdale; RMC Place; WHITLEY; **181** M-14; elev. 972ft./296m.; 🅿; Z 40769; ● 200
New; RMC Place; OWEN; ***181** G-11; elev. 675ft./206m.; mail Owenton Z 40359; rural
New Allen; RMC Place; FLOYD; ***181** J-18; mail Allen Z 41601; ● 150
Newburg; CDP; JEFFERSON; ***180** H-9; ★ **LOU**; mail Louisville Z 40213, Z 40218-19; former CDP; became part of Louisville/Jefferson County Metro Jan. 6, 2003; Ⓟ 21,647; Ⓒ 20,636; ◆ 0
Newby; RMC Place; MADISON; ***181** I-13; mail Richmond Z 40475
New Camp; RMC Place; PIKE; ***181** I-19; mail South Williamson Z 41503; ● 200
New Castle; Inc. Place; ⊡ HENRY; **180** F-10; elev. 844ft./257m.; 🅿; Z 40050; Ⓟ 893; Ⓒ 919
New Columbus; RMC Place; OWEN; **181** F-12; elev. 869ft./265m.; mail Corinth Z 41010; ● 75
Newcombe; RMC Place; ELLIOTT; ***181** H-17; mail Isonville Z 41149; rural
New Concord; RMC Place; CALLOWAY; **180** N-1; elev. 423ft./129m.; 🅿; Z 42076; ● 100
New Cypress; RMC Place; HICKMAN; ***180** F-2; elev. 377ft./115m.; mail Clinton Z 42031; rural
New Cypress; RMC Place; MUHLENBERG; ***180** K-4; mail Greenville Z 42345; rural
Newfound; RMC Place; CLAY; ***181** K-15; mail Oneida Z 40972; rural
Newfoundland; RMC Place; ELLIOTT; ***181** H-17; elev. 802ft./244m.; 🅿; Z 41171
Newgarden; RMC Place; HARDIN; ***180** I-8; mail Fort Knox Z 40121
New Haven; Inc. Place; NELSON; **180** J-9; elev. 472ft./144m.; 🅿; Z 40051; Ⓟ 796; Ⓒ 849
New Hope; RMC Place; NELSON; **180** J-9; elev. 518ft./158m.; 🅿; Z 40052; ● 200
New Liberty; RMC Place; OWEN; **181** F-11; elev. 894ft./272m.; 🅿; Z 40355; ● 115
Newman; RMC Place; DAVIESS; **180** I-3; ★ **OWNS**; mail Owensboro Z 42301; ● 100
New Market; RMC Place; MARION; **180** J-10; mail Lebanon Z 40033; ● 50
Newport; Inc. Place; CAMPBELL; **181** D-12; elev. 489ft./149m.; 🅿 ■; ★ **CIN**; Z 41071-76, Z 41099; Ⓟ 18,871; Ⓒ 17,048; ◆ 16,564
New Providence; RMC Place; CALLOWAY; ***180** N-1; mail Hazel Z 42049; ● 60
New Roe; RMC Place; ALLEN; ***180** N-6; elev. 711ft./217m.; mail Adolphus Z 42120, Franklin Z 42134; rural
New Salem; RMC Place; CRITTENDEN; **180** K-1; mail Marion Z 42064; rural
New Salem; RMC Place; LINCOLN; ***181** K-11; elev. 900ft./274m.; mail Hustonville Z 40437, Marion Z 42064; rural
Newstead; RMC Place; CHRISTIAN; ***180** M-2; elev. 528ft./161m.; mail Hopkinsville Z 42240; rural
Newt; RMC Place; GREEN; ***180** L-9; mail Greensburg Z 42743; rural
Newtown; RMC Place; SCOTT; **181** G-12; elev. 861ft./262m.; mail Georgetown Z 40324; ● 60
New Zion; RMC Place; JACKSON; ***181** J-14; elev. 1,235ft./376m.; 🅿; Z 40447; rural
New Zion; RMC Place; SCOTT, FAYETTE; **181** G-12; mail Georgetown Z 40324, Lexington Z 40511; ● 120
Niagara; RMC Place; HENDERSON; ***180** I-3; elev. 479ft./146m.; mail Henderson Z 42420
NICHOLAS; **181** G-14; Ⓟ 6,725; Ⓒ 6,813; ◆ 6,718
Nicholasville; Inc. Place; ⊡ JESSAMINE; **181** I-12; elev. 966ft./294m.; 🅿; ★ **LEX**; Z 40340, Z 40356; Ⓟ 13,603; Ⓒ 19,680; ◆ 26,677
Nichols; RMC Place; BULLITT; ★ **LOU**; mail West Point Z 40177; rural
Nichols; RMC Place; HICKMAN; ***180** G-3; mail Clinton Z 42031; rural
Nicholson; RMC Place; KENTON; ***181** E-12; elev. 930ft./283m.; ★ **CIN**; mail Independence Z 41051; ● 500
Nickell; RMC Place; MORGAN; ***181** I-16; mail Hazel Green Z 41332; rural
Nigh Siding; RMC Place; PIKE; ***181** J-19; mail Fedscreek Z 41524; rural
Nina; RMC Place; GARRARD; ***181** J-12; mail Lancaster Z 40444; rural
Nineteen; RMC Place; OHIO; ***180** K-5; elev. 470ft./143m.; mail Beaver Dam Z 42320; rural
Ninevah; RMC Place; ANDERSON; ***181** H-11; mail Lawrenceburg Z 40342
Nippa; RMC Place; JOHNSON; **181** I-18; elev. 628ft./191m.; 🅿; Z 41240; ● 125
Noble; RMC Place; BREATHITT; ***181** J-17; elev. 820ft./250m.; mail Clayhole Z 41317; rural
Nobob; RMC Place; BARREN; ***180** M-8; mail Summer Shade Z 42166
No Creek; RMC Place; OHIO; ***180** J-4; mail Hartford Z 42347; rural
Noctor; RMC Place; BREATHITT; **181** J-16; elev. 1,000ft./305m.; 🅿; Z 41339; ● 40
Node; RMC Place; METCALFE; ***180** L-9; mail Center Z 42214; rural
Noetown; RMC Place; BELL; ***181** N-15; mail Middlesboro Z 40965; pop. incl. with Middlesboro (Inc. Place)
Nolansburg; RMC Place; HARLAN; ***181** L-17; mail Totz Z 40870; ● 75
Nolin; RMC Place; HARDIN; ***180** J-8; mail Sonora Z 42776; ● 40
Nolin Lake Estates; RMC Place; GRAYSON; ***180** K-7; elev. 600ft./183m.; mail Clarkson Z 42726; ● 200
Nonesuch; RMC Place; WOODFORD; ***181** I-11; elev. 813ft./248m.; mail Versailles Z 40383; ● 75
Nonnel; RMC Place; MUHLENBERG; ***180** K-4; mail Drakesboro Z 42337; ● 80
Nora; RMC Place; CLINTON; ***181** M-11; elev. 1,056ft./322m.; mail Albany Z 42602; rural
Norbourne Estates; Inc. Place; JEFFERSON; **180** B-8; elev. 532ft./162m.; ★ **LOU**; mail Louisville Z 40207; Ⓟ 461; Ⓒ 461
Norfleet; RMC Place; PULASKI; ***181** L-11; elev. 1,088ft./332m.; mail Nancy Z 42544; rural
Normal; RMC Place; BOYD; ***181** F-18; ★ **HNTG**; mail Ashland Z 41101; pop. incl. with Ashland (Inc. Place)
Normandy; RMC Place; SPENCER; ***180** H-10; mail Taylorsville Z 40071; ● 25
North Corbin; CDP; LAUREL, KNOX; **181** L-14; mail Corbin Z 40701; Ⓟ 1,601; Ⓒ 1,662
Northfield; Inc. Place; JEFFERSON; **180** B-8; elev. 586ft./179m.; ★ **LOU**; mail Louisville Z 40222; Ⓟ 898; Ⓒ 970
North Irvine; RMC Place; ESTILL; ***181** I-14; mail Irvine Z 40336; ● 100
North Lexington; RMC Place; FAYETTE; ★ **LEX**; pop. incl. with Lexington (Inc. Place)
North Mayfield; RMC Place; GRAVES; pop. incl. with Mayfield (Inc. Place)
North Middletown; Inc. Place; BOURBON; **181** H-14; elev. 916ft./279m.; 🅿; Z 40357; Ⓟ 602; Ⓒ 562
Northtown; RMC Place; HART; ***180** K-8; mail Horse Cave Z 42749; rural
Norton Branch; RMC Place; CARTER; ***181** G-18; ★ **HNTG**; mail Rush Z 41168; rural
Nortonville; Inc. Place; HOPKINS; **180** K-3; elev. 407ft./124m.; 🅿; Z 42442; Ⓟ 1,209; Ⓒ 1,264
Norwood; Inc. Place; JEFFERSON; **180** B-9; elev. 550ft./168m.; ★ **LOU**; mail Louisville Z 40222; Ⓟ 372; Ⓒ 395
Norwood; RMC Place; PULASKI; ***181** L-12; mail Science Hill Z 42553; ● 30
Nuckols; RMC Place; MCLEAN; **180** J-4; elev. 409ft./125m.; mail Livermore Z 42352; ● 60
Nugent Cross Roads; RMC Place; WOODFORD; ***181** H-12; elev. 861ft./262m.; ★ **LEX**; mail Versailles Z 40383
Nugym; RMC Place; BELL; mail Arjay Z 40902; rural
Number One; RMC Place; WAYNE; ***181** M-11; 🅿; Z 42633; rural

O

Oakbrook; CDP-Census Area Only; BOONE; ***181** D-12; elev. 878ft./268m.; ★ **CIN**; mail Florence Z 41042; Ⓟ 4,113; Ⓒ 7,726
Oakdale; RMC Place; BREATHITT; ***181** J-15; mail Jackson Z 41339; rural
Oakdale; RMC Place; JEFFERSON; ***180** G-8; ★ **LOU**; mail Louisville Z 40215; pop. incl. with Louisville (Inc. Place)
Oakdale; RMC Place; MCCRACKEN; **180** E-4; ★ **PAD**; mail Paducah Z 42001, Z 42003; ● 1,900
Oak Forest (Roary); RMC Place; ALLEN; ***180** M-7; mail Scottsville Z 42164; rural
Oak Grove; Inc. Place; CHRISTIAN; **180** N-3; elev. 541ft./165m.; 🅿; ★ **CLRKV**; Z 42262; Ⓟ 2,863; Ⓒ 7,064; Ⓡ 6,951
Oak Grove; RMC Place; OHIO; ***180** K-5; mail Cromwell Z 42333; rural
Oak Hill; RMC Place; HOPKINS; ***180** K-3; mail Nortonville Z 42442; ● 100
Oak Hill; RMC Place; PULASKI; ***181** L-12; mail Somerset Z 42501; rural
Oakland; Inc. Place; WARREN; **180** L-7; elev. 579ft./176m.; 🅿; ★ **BOWLG**; Z 42159; Ⓟ 202; Ⓒ 260
Oaklawn Estates; RMC Place; JOHNSON; ***181** I-18; mail Hagerhill Z 41222; ● 30
Oak Level; RMC Place; MARSHALL; ***180** F-4; elev. 496ft./151m.; mail Benton Z 42025
Oakley; RMC Place; LAUREL; ***181** K-14; mail East Bernstadt Z 40729; rural
Oak Ridge; RMC Place; EDMONSON; ***180** K-7; mail Bee Spring Z 42207; rural
Oak Ridge; RMC Place; KENTON; ***181** D-12; ★ **CIN**; mail Independence Z 41051; pop. incl. with Independence (Inc. Place)
Oaks; RMC Place; BELL; ***181** M-15; mail Miracle Z 40856; rural
Oaks; RMC Place; MCCRACKEN; ***180** F-4; ★ **PAD**; mail Paducah Z 42003
Oaks; RMC Place; OHIO; ***180** J-5; mail Fordsville Z 42343; rural
Oak Street; RMC Place; JEFFERSON; ***180** G-8; ★ **LOU**; pop. incl. with Louisville (Inc. Place)
Oakton; RMC Place; HICKMAN; **180** G-2; elev. 374ft./114m.; mail Clinton Z 42031; ● 125
Oakville; RMC Place; LOGAN; ***180** M-5; elev. 591ft./180m.; 🅿; Z 42276; ● 80
Oakwood; RMC Place; FAYETTE; ***181** H-12; ★ **LEX**; mail Lexington Z 40511; pop. incl. with Lexington (Inc. Place)
Oakwood; FLEMING; see Fairview (RMC Place)
O'Bannon; RMC Place; JEFFERSON; ***180** G-9; ★ **LOU**; mail Louisville Z 40223; became part of Louisville/Jefferson County Metro Jan. 6, 2003
Odds (Daniels Creek); RMC Place; JOHNSON; ***181** I-18; mail Van Lear Z 41265; ● 60
Oddville; RMC Place; HARRISON; ***181** F-13; elev. 831ft./253m.; mail Cynthiana Z 41031
Odessa; RMC Place; BATH; ***181** G-15; mail Owingsville Z 40360; rural
Offutt; RMC Place; JOHNSON; ***181** I-18; elev. 639ft./195m.; 🅿; Z 41240; ● 65
Ogle; RMC Place; CLAY; ***181** L-15; elev. 1,002ft./305m.; 🅿; Z 40962; rural
OHIO; **180** J-5; Ⓟ 21,105; Ⓒ 22,916; ◆ 23,620
Oil City; RMC Place; BARREN; ***180** L-8; elev. 650ft./198m.; mail Glasgow Z 42141; rural
Oil Springs; RMC Place; JOHNSON; **181** I-17; elev. 843ft./257m.; 🅿; Z 41238; ● 150
Oil Valley; RMC Place; WAYNE; ***181** M-11; 🅿; Z 42633; rural
Okolona; CDP; JEFFERSON; ***180** H-9; elev. 470ft./143m.; 🅿; ★ **LOU**; Z 40219, Z 40229, Z 40259; former CDP; became part of Louisville/Jefferson County Metro Jan. 6, 2003; Ⓟ 18,902; Ⓒ 17,807
Olaton; RMC Place; OHIO; ***180** J-5; elev. 500ft./152m.; 🅿; Z 42361; ● 35
Olcott; RMC Place; BELL; ***181** M-15; mail Pineville Z 40977; rural
Old Brownsboro Place; Inc. Place; JEFFERSON; ***180** G-9; ★ **LOU**; mail Louisville Z 40222; Ⓟ 348; Ⓒ 384
Old Christianburg; RMC Place; SHELBY; ***180** G-10; elev. 870ft./265m.; mail Bagdad Z 40003; rural
Old Flat Lick; RMC Place; KNOX; ***181** M-15; mail Flat Lick Z 40935
OLDHAM; **180** G-10; Ⓟ 33,263; Ⓒ 46,178; Ⓡ 46,618; ◆ 58,120
Oldham Acres; RMC Place; OLDHAM; ***180** G-9; ★ **LOU**; mail Prospect Z 40059; ● 175
Old Landing; RMC Place; LEE; ***181** J-15; elev. 646ft./197m.; 🅿; Z 41311; rural
Old Olga; RMC Place; RUSSELL; ***180** M-10; elev. 981ft./299m.; mail Jamestown Z 42629; rural
Old Pine Grove; RMC Place; CLARK; ***181** H-13; ★ **LEX**; mail Winchester Z 40391
Old Stephensburg; RMC Place; HARDIN; ***180** J-7; mail Cecilia Z 42724
Old Taylor Place; RMC Place; OLDHAM; ***180** G-9; ★ **LOU**; mail Goshen Z 40026; ● 250
Oldtown; RMC Place; GREENUP; **181** F-17; elev. 561ft./171m.; 🅿; Z 41144; ● 60
Old Volney; RMC Place; LOGAN; ***180** M-4; elev. 605ft./184m.; mail Olmstead Z 42265; rural
Olga; RMC Place; RUSSELL; ***180** L-10; elev. 981ft./299m.; mail Jamestown Z 42629; rural
Olin; RMC Place; JACKSON; ***181** K-14; mail Mc Kee Z 40447; rural
Olive; RMC Place; MARSHALL; **180** M-1; mail Benton Z 42025, Hardin Z 42048; ● 100
Olive Branch; RMC Place; FLEMING; ***181** G-14; mail Flemingsburg Z 41041; rural
Olive Branch; RMC Place; SHELBY; ***180** H-10; mail Shelbyville Z 40065; rural
Olive Hill; Inc. Place; CARTER; **181** G-16; elev. 760ft./232m.; 🅿; Z 41164; Ⓟ 1,809; Ⓒ 1,813
Ollie; RMC Place; EDMONSON; ***180** K-7; elev. 831ft./253m.; 🅿; Z 42259; rural
Olmstead; RMC Place; LOGAN; **180** M-4; elev. 578ft./176m.; 🅿; Z 42265; ● 125
Olney; RMC Place; HOPKINS; ***180** K-2; mail Dawson Springs Z 42408; rural
Olympia; RMC Place; BATH; **181** H-15; elev. 773ft./236m.; 🅿; Z 40358; ● 125
Olympia Springs; RMC Place; BATH; ***181** H-15; mail Olympia Z 40358
Omaha; RMC Place; KNOTT; ***181** K-18; elev. 1,202ft./366m.; mail Pine Top Z 41843
Oneida; RMC Place; CLAY; **181** K-15; elev. 827ft./252m.; 🅿; Z 40972; ● 300
Oneonta; RMC Place; CAMPBELL; ***181** D-13; ★ **CIN**; mail California Z 41007
Ono; RMC Place; RUSSELL; ***181** L-11; elev. 971ft./296m.; mail Russell Springs Z 42642; rural
Onton; RMC Place; WEBSTER; **180** J-3; elev. 461ft./141m.; mail Sebree Z 42455; ● 100
Open Gates; RMC Place; FAYETTE; ***181** H-12; ★ **LEX**; mail Lexington Z 40503; pop. incl. with Lexington (Inc. Place)
Ophir; RMC Place; MORGAN; ***181** H-17; elev. 700ft./213m.; 🅿; Z 41459; ● 20
Orangeburg; RMC Place; MASON; ***181** F-15; elev. 761ft./232m.; mail Maysville Z 41056; ● 75
Orchard Grass Hills; Inc. Place; OLDHAM; ***180** G-9; ★ **LOU**; mail Crestwood Z 40014; Ⓟ 1,058; Ⓒ 1,031; Ⓡ 1,326
Ordinary; RMC Place; ELLIOTT; ***181** H-16; mail Sandy Hook Z 41171; rural
Oregon; RMC Place; MERCER; ***181** I-11; elev. 523ft./159m.; mail Salvisa Z 40372; rural
Orkney; RMC Place; FLOYD; ***181** J-18; elev. 718ft./219m.; 🅿; Z 41647; rural
Orlando; RMC Place; ROCKCASTLE; ***181** K-13; elev. 925ft./282m.; 🅿; Z 40460; ● 100
Orr; RMC Place; LAWRENCE; ***181** H-17; mail Webbville Z 41180; rural
Ortiz; RMC Place; WEBSTER; ***180** J-2; mail Sebree Z 42455; rural
Orville; RMC Place; HENRY; ***181** G-11; elev. 554ft./169m.; mail Pleasureville Z 40057
Osborn; RMC Place; FLOYD; ***181** J-18; mail Harold Z 41635; rural
Oscaloosa; RMC Place; LETCHER; ***181** L-18; elev. 1,143ft./348m.; 🅿; Z 41858; rural
Oscar; RMC Place; BALLARD; **180** E-2; mail La Center Z 42056; ● 50
Otia; RMC Place; MONROE; ***180** M-9; mail Tompkinsville Z 42167; rural
Ottawa; RMC Place; ROCKCASTLE; ***181** K-12; elev. 1,183ft./361m.; mail Brodhead Z 40409; rural
Ottenheim; RMC Place; LINCOLN; ***181** K-12; mail Waynesburg Z 40489; rural
Otter Pond; RMC Place; CALDWELL; ***180** L-2; mail Princeton Z 42445; rural
Oven Fork; RMC Place; LETCHER; **181** L-18; elev. 1,623ft./495m.; 🅿; Z 40823; ● 170
Overlook; RMC Place; LYON; elev. 450ft./137m.; mail Eddyville Z 42038; pop. incl. with Eddyville (Inc. Place)
Ovesen Heights; RMC Place; LARUE; ***180** J-8; mail Hodgenville Z 42748; ● 125
OWEN; **181** F-11; Ⓟ 9,035; Ⓒ 10,547; ◆ 11,616
Owensboro; Inc. Place; ⊡ DAVIESS; **180** I-4; elev. 401ft./122m.; 🅿 🅷 🅲 1,534 ■; ★ **OWNS**; Z 42301-04; Ⓟ 53,549; Ⓒ 54,067; ◆ 52,889
Owensboro East; RMC Place; DAVIESS; ★ **OWNS**; mail Owensboro Z 42303; pop. incl. with Owensboro (Inc. Place)
Owensboro West; RMC Place; DAVIESS; ★ **OWNS**; mail Owensboro Z 42301; pop. incl. with Owensboro (Inc. Place)
Owenton; Inc. Place; ⊡ OWEN; **181** F-11; elev. 960ft./293m.; 🅿 🅷; Z 40359; Ⓟ 1,306; Ⓒ 1,387
Owingsville; Inc. Place; ⊡ BATH; **181** H-15; elev. 1,000ft./305m.; 🅿; Z 40360 & mail Preston Z 40366; Ⓟ 1,491; Ⓒ 1,488
Owsley; RMC Place; PIKE; ***181** J-18; mail Pikeville Z 41501; rural
OWSLEY; **181** J-15; Ⓟ 5,036; Ⓒ 4,858; ◆ 4,485
Oxford; RMC Place; SCOTT; ***181** G-12; elev. 965ft./294m.; mail Georgetown Z 40324
Ozark; RMC Place; ADAIR; ***180** L-10; mail Columbia Z 42728; rural

P

Pactolus; RMC Place; CARTER; ***181** G-17; ★ **HNTG**; mail Grayson Z 41143; ● 30
Paddock Place; RMC Place; WOODFORD; ***181** H-12; ★ **LEX**; mail Versailles Z 40383; ● 225
Paducah; Inc. Place; ⊡ MCCRACKEN; **180** E-3; elev. 339ft./103m.; 🅿 🅷 ■; ★ **PAD**; Z 42001-03; Ⓟ 27,256; Ⓒ 26,307; ◆ 25,643
Paint Lick; RMC Place; GARRARD; **181** J-13; elev. 902ft./275m.; 🅿; Z 40461; ● 150
Paintsville; Inc. Place; ⊡ JOHNSON; **181** I-18; elev. 632ft./193m.; 🅿 🅷; Z 41240; Ⓟ 4,354; Ⓒ 4,132
Palestine; RMC Place; BOONE; ***181** E-12; ★ **CIN**; mail Union Z 41091; ● 250
Palma; RMC Place; MARSHALL; **180** F-4; elev. 461ft./141m.; mail Benton Z 42025; ● 100
Palmer; RMC Place; ESTILL; ***181** I-14; mail Irvine Z 40336
Panama; RMC Place; MORGAN; ***181** I-16; mail West Liberty Z 41472; rural
Panco; RMC Place; CLAY; ***181** K-15; mail Oneida Z 40972; rural
Panola; RMC Place; MADISON; ***181** J-14; elev. 791ft./241m.; mail Waco Z 40385; rural
Panorama Shores; RMC Place; CALLOWAY; mail Murray Z 42071; rural
Pansy (Gulston); RMC Place; HARLAN; **181** M-16; elev. 1,336ft./407m.; mail Gulston Z 40830; ● 350
Panther; RMC Place; DAVIESS; ***180** J-4; mail Utica Z 42376; ● 125
Paragon Park; RMC Place; HENDERSON; ***180** I-2; mail Henderson Z 42420; pop. incl. with Henderson (Inc. Place)
Paris; Inc. Place; ⊡ BOURBON; **181** G-13; elev. 845ft./258m.; 🅿 🅷; Z 40361-62; Ⓟ 8,730; Ⓒ 9,183
Park City; Inc. Place; BARREN; **180** L-7; elev. 650ft./198m.; 🅿; Z 42160; Ⓟ 549; Ⓒ 517
Parkdale; RMC Place; HARLAN; pop. incl. with Evarts (Inc. Place)
Parkers Lake (Cumberland Falls); RMC Place; MCCREARY; **181** M-12; elev. 1,245ft./379m.; 🅿; Z 42634; ● 55
Park Hills; RMC Place; FAYETTE; ***181** H-12; ★ **LEX**; mail Lexington Z 40502; pop. incl. with Lexington (Inc. Place)
Park Hills; Inc. Place; KENTON; **181** B-16; elev. 830ft./253m.; 🅿; ★ **CIN**; Z 41011; Ⓟ 3,321; Ⓒ 2,977
Park Hills; RMC Place; ROWAN; ***181** G-15; mail Morehead Z 40351; ● 70
Park Lake; RMC Place; OLDHAM; ***180** G-9; ★ **LOU**; mail Wallingford Z 41093; former incorporated place; became part of Crestwood May 1, 2006; pop. incl. with Crestwood (Inc. Place); Ⓟ 263; Ⓒ 537
Parkland; RMC Place; JEFFERSON; ***180** G-8; ★ **LOU**; mail Louisville Z 40211; pop. incl. with Louisville (Inc. Place)
Parkside; RMC Place; JEFFERSON; ***180** G-9; ★ **LOU**; pop. incl. with Saint Matthews (Inc. Place)
Parksville; RMC Place; BOYLE; **181** J-11; elev. 1,077ft./328m.; 🅿; Z 40464; ● 400
Parkview Shores Number 1; RMC Place; ALLEN; mail Scottsville Z 42164; ● 20
Parkview Shores Number 2; RMC Place; ALLEN; ***180** M-7; mail Scottsville Z 42164; ● 300
Parkway Village; Inc. Place; JEFFERSON; **180** C-7; elev. 500ft./152m.; ★ **LOU**; mail Louisville Z 40207; Ⓟ 707; Ⓒ 715
Parmleysville; RMC Place; WAYNE; ***181** M-12; elev. 895ft./273m.; mail Monticello Z 42633; rural
Parnell; RMC Place; WAYNE; ***181** M-11; 🅿; Z 42633; rural
Parrot; RMC Place; JACKSON; ***181** K-14; elev. 1,280ft./390m.; 🅿; Z 40447; ● 30
Partridge; RMC Place; LETCHER; **181** L-17; elev. 1,543ft./470m.; 🅿; Z 40862; ● 50
Partridge Run; RMC Place; HENDERSON; ***180** I-3; ★ **EV**; mail Henderson Z 42420; pop. incl. with Henderson (Inc. Place)
Pascal; RMC Place; HART; ***180** K-8; elev. 722ft./220m.; mail Hardyville Z 42746; rural
Patesville; RMC Place; HANCOCK; ***180** I-5; mail Hawesville Z 42348
Pathfork; RMC Place; HARLAN; **181** M-16; elev. 1,240ft./378m.; 🅿; Z 40863; ● 400
Patrick; RMC Place; LAWRENCE; ***181** H-18; mail Louisa Z 41230; rural
Patsey; RMC Place; ESTILL; ***181** I-15; elev. 1,210ft./369m.; 🅿; Z 40380; rural
Pauley; RMC Place; PIKE; ***181** J-19; mail Pikeville Z 41501; pop. incl. with Pikeville (Inc. Place)
Paw Paw; RMC Place; PIKE; **181** J-20; elev. 1,110ft./338m.; 🅿; Z 41553; ● 75
Paxton; RMC Place; BREATHITT; ***181** I-16; mail Vancleve Z 41385; rural
Payne Gap; RMC Place; LETCHER; **181** K-18; elev. 1,672ft./510m.; 🅿; Z 41537; ● 300
Paynes Depot; RMC Place; SCOTT; ***181** H-12; ★ **LEX**; mail Georgetown Z 40324; ● 45
Payneville; RMC Place; MEADE; **180** H-7; elev. 816ft./249m.; 🅿; Z 40157; ● 150
Payton; RMC Place; MORGAN; ***181** I-16; mail Hazel Green Z 41332; rural
Peabody; RMC Place; CLAY; ***181** L-15; elev. 844ft./257m.; 🅿; Z 40914; rural
Peach Grove; RMC Place; PENDLETON; **181** E-13; elev. 871ft./265m.; mail Butler Z 41006; ● 100
Peach Orchard; RMC Place; LAWRENCE; ***181** H-18; mail Louisa Z 41230; rural
Peak; RMC Place; SCOTT; ***181** H-12; ★ **LEX**; mail Georgetown Z 40324; ● 150
Peaks Mill; RMC Place; FRANKLIN; ***181** G-11; elev. 521ft./159m.; mail Frankfort Z 40601; ● 100
Pea Ridge; SCOTT; see Sand Lick (RMC Place)
Pea Ridge; RMC Place; TODD; ***180** M-4; elev. 766ft./233m.; mail Elkton Z 42220; rural
Pearl; RMC Place; WHITLEY; ***181** N-14; mail Frakes Z 40940; rural
Pearman; RMC Place; GRAYSON; ***180** K-7; mail Clarkson Z 42726; rural
Peasticks; RMC Place; BATH; ***181** H-15; mail Owingsville Z 40360; rural
Pebble; RMC Place; BATH; ***181** G-15; mail Owingsville Z 40360; rural
Pebworth; RMC Place; OWSLEY; ***181** J-15; elev. 899ft./274m.; 🅿; Z 41314
Peden Mill; RMC Place; SIMPSON; ***180** M-6; mail Franklin Z 42134; rural
Peedee; RMC Place; CHRISTIAN; **180** M-2; mail Herndon Z 42236; ● 30
Pelfrey; RMC Place; ROWAN; ***181** H-16; mail Clearfield Z 40313; rural
Pellville; RMC Place; HANCOCK; **180** I-5; elev. 536ft./163m.; 🅿; Z 42364; ● 120
Pellyton; RMC Place; ADAIR; ***180** K-10; mail Columbia Z 42728
Pembroke; Inc. Place; CHRISTIAN; **180** M-3; elev. 582ft./177m.; 🅿; Z 42266; Ⓟ 640; Ⓒ 797; Ⓡ 819
Pence; RMC Place; WOLFE; ***181** J-16; mail Bethany Z 41313; rural
Pendleton; RMC Place; HENRY; **180** F-10; elev. 834ft./254m.; 🅿; Z 40055; ● 80
PENDLETON; **181** F-13; mail Falmouth Z 41040; Ⓟ 12,036; Ⓒ 14,390; ◆ 14,908
Penile; RMC Place; JEFFERSON; ***180** H-8; ★ **LOU**; mail Louisville Z 40272; became part of Louisville/Jefferson County Metro Jan. 6, 2003
Penny; RMC Place; CALLOWAY; ***180** G-4; elev. 557ft./170m.; mail Murray Z 42071; rural
Penny; RMC Place; PIKE; ***181** K-19; mail Pikeville Z 41501; rural
Penrod; RMC Place; MUHLENBERG; **180** L-4; elev. 432ft./132m.; 🅿; Z 42339; ● 70
Peonia; RMC Place; GRAYSON; **180** K-7; elev. 778ft./237m.; 🅿; Z 42726; ● 40
Peoples; RMC Place; JACKSON; **181** K-14; elev. 976ft./297m.; 🅿; Z 40447; ● 20
PERRY; **181** K-17; Ⓟ 30,283; Ⓒ 29,390; Ⓡ 29,422; ◆ 28,857
Perry Park; RMC Place; OWEN; **181** F-11; elev. 453ft./138m.; 🅿; Z 40363; ● 160
Perryville; Inc. Place; BOYLE; **181** J-11; elev. 851ft./259m.; 🅿; Z 40468; Ⓟ 815; Ⓒ 763
Persimmon Grove; RMC Place; CAMPBELL; ***181** E-13; ★ **CIN**; mail Alexandria Z 41001, California Z 41007; ● 100
Persimon; RMC Place; MONROE; ***180** M-9; mail Tompkinsville Z 42167; rural
Petersburg; RMC Place; BOONE; **181** D-11; elev. 510ft./155m.; 🅿; Z 41080; ● 400
Petersville; RMC Place; LEWIS; **181** F-15; mail Vanceburg Z 41179; ● 20
Petra; RMC Place; BRACKEN; ***181** F-13; mail Brooksville Z 41004; rural
Petrie; RMC Place; HANCOCK; ***180** H-5; mail Hawesville Z 42348; rural
Petroleum; RMC Place; ALLEN; **180** M-7; elev. 614ft./187m.; mail Adolphus Z 42120; ● 50
Petros; RMC Place; WARREN; ***180** M-6; elev. 600ft./183m.; mail Rockfield Z 42274; rural
Pettit; RMC Place; DAVIESS; ***180** I-4; ★ **OWNS**; mail Owensboro Z 42301; ● 100
Pewee Valley; Inc. Place; OLDHAM; **180** A-10; elev. 710ft./216m.; 🅿; ★ **LOU**; Z 40056; Ⓟ 1,283; Ⓒ 1,436
Peytona; RMC Place; SHELBY; ***181** H-11; elev. 922ft./281m.; mail Shelbyville Z 40065; rural
Peyton Creek; RMC Place; PIKE; mail Pikeville Z 41501; rural
Peytonsburg; RMC Place; CUMBERLAND; **180** N-9; elev. 1,018ft./310m.; 🅿; Z 42717; ● 60
Peytons Store; RMC Place; CASEY; ***181** J-11; elev. 860ft./262m.; mail Hustonville Z 40437; rural
Peytontown; RMC Place; MADISON; ***181** J-13; mail Richmond Z 40475; rural
Phelps; CDP; PIKE; **181** J-20; 🅿; Z 41553; Ⓟ 1,298; Ⓒ 1,053
Phillipsburg; RMC Place; MARION; ***180** J-10; mail Campbellsville Z 42718
Philpot; RMC Place; DAVIESS; **180** I-4; elev. 430ft./131m.; 🅿; ★ **OWNS**; Z 42366; ● 400
Phyllis; RMC Place; PIKE; **181** J-19; elev. 879ft./268m.; 🅿; Z 41554; ● 350
Pickett; RMC Place; ADAIR; ***180** L-9; elev. 681ft./208m.; rural
Pickway; RMC Place; FAYETTE; ***181** H-12; ★ **LEX**; mail Lexington Z 40503; pop. incl. with Lexington (Inc. Place)
Pierce; RMC Place; GREEN; ***180** K-9; elev. 803ft./245m.; mail Greensburg Z 42743
Pig; RMC Place; EDMONSON; ***180** L-7; mail Smiths Grove Z 42171; rural
Pigeon; RMC Place; PIKE; ***181** J-19; mail Pikeville Z 41501; rural
Pigeonroost; RMC Place; CLAY; ***181** L-15; mail Manchester Z 40962; ● 100
PIKE; **181** J-19; Ⓟ 72,583; Ⓒ 68,736; ◆ 62,466
Pike View; RMC Place; HART; **180** K-8; elev. 825ft./251m.; mail Magnolia Z 42757; ● 20
Pikeville; Inc. Place; ⊡ PIKE; **181** J-19; elev. 685ft./209m.; 🅿 🅷 🅲 1,098 ■; Z 41501-02 & mail Varney Z 41571; Ⓟ 6,324; Ⓒ 6,295; Ⓡ 6,390; ◆ 6,069
Pilgrim; RMC Place; MARTIN; **181** I-19; elev. 617ft./188m.; 🅿; Z 41250; ● 150
Pilot Oak; RMC Place; GRAVES; **180** G-3; elev. 531ft./162m.; mail Water Valley Z 42085; ● 100
Pilot View; RMC Place; CLARK; ***181** H-14; elev. 1,049ft./320m.; mail Winchester Z 40391

Pinchem; RMC Place; CLARK; ***181** H-13; mail Winchester z 40391; rural
Pinchem; RMC Place; TODD; ***180** M-4; elev. 598ft./182m.; mail Guthrie z 42234; rural
Pinckard; RMC Place; WOODFORD; **181** H-12; elev. 824ft./251m.; mail Versailles z 40383; ● 30
Pinckneyville; RMC Place; LIVINGSTON; ***180** K-1; mail Salem z 42078; ● 20
Pine Bluffs; RMC Place; CALLOWAY; rural
Pine Grove; RMC Place; CLARK; ***181** H-13; elev. 950ft./290m.; mail Winchester z 40391
Pine Grove; RMC Place; LAUREL; ***181** L-14; mail Lily z 40740; rural
Pine Hill; RMC Place; ROCKCASTLE; **181** K-13; mail Mount Vernon z 40456; ● 40
Pine Knob; RMC Place; GRAYSON; ***180** J-6; elev. 522ft./159m.; mail Caneyville z 42721; ● 35
Pine Knot; CDP; MCCREARY; **181** N-13; elev. 1,420ft./433m.; 🄿; z 42635; Ⓟ 1,549; © 1,680
Pine Meadows; RMC Place; FAYETTE; ***181** H-12; ★ **LEX**; mail Lexington z 40504; pop. incl. with Lexington (Inc. Place)
Pine Mountain; RMC Place; HARLAN; ***181** L-17; 🄿; z 40810; rural
Piner; RMC Place; KENTON; ***181** E-12; elev. 910ft./277m.; ★ **CIN**; mail Morning View z 41063
Pine Ridge; RMC Place; WOLFE; **181** I-15; elev. 1,256ft./383m.; 🄿; z 41360; ● 125
Pine Top; RMC Place; KNOTT; **181** K-18; elev. 1,120ft./341m.; 🄿; z 41843; ● 100
Pineville; Inc. Place; ⊡ BELL; **181** M-15; elev. 1,015ft./309m.; 🄿 🄷; z 40977; Ⓟ 2,198; © 2,093
Piney Fork; RMC Place; CRITTENDEN; ***180** K-1; elev. 540ft./165m.; mail Marion z 42064; rural
Piney Grove; RMC Place; PULASKI; ***181** L-12; mail Somerset z 42501; rural
Pink; RMC Place; JESSAMINE; ***181** I-12; mail Nicholasville z 40356
Pinnacle; RMC Place; LEE; ***181** J-14; mail Beattyville z 41311; rural
Pinson; RMC Place; PIKE; mail Mc Andrews z 41543
Pinsonfork; RMC Place; PIKE; ***181** J-19; elev. 912ft./278m.; 🄿; z 41555; ● 250
Pioneer; RMC Place; BOONE; ***181** D-12; ★ **CIN**; mail Burlington z 41005; ● 500
Pioneer Village; Inc. Place; BULLITT; **180** H-9; elev. 500ft./152m.; ★ **LOU**; mail Shepherdsville z 40165; Ⓟ 1,130; © 2,555
Pippa Passes; Inc. Place; KNOTT; **181** K-18; elev. 1,002ft./305m.; 🄿 🄲 613; z 41844 & mail Raven z 41861; Ⓟ 195; © 297
Piqua; RMC Place; ROBERTSON; ***181** F-14; mail Mount Olivet z 41064
Pisgah; RMC Place; WOODFORD; ***181** H-12; elev. 868ft./265m.; ★ **LEX**; mail Versailles z 40383
Piso; RMC Place; PIKE; ***181** J-19; elev. 799ft./244m.; 🄿; z 41501; rural
Pitts; RMC Place; ESTILL; ***181** I-14; elev. 1,261ft./384m.; mail Ravenna z 40472; rural
Pittsburg; RMC Place; LAUREL; **181** L-14; elev. 1,153ft./351m.; 🄿; z 40755; ● 600
Plainview; RMC Place; JEFFERSON; ***180** G-9; ★ **LOU**; mail Louisville z 40224; became part of Louisville/Jefferson County Metro Jan. 6, 2003
Plank; RMC Place; CLAY; **181** L-15; elev. 926ft./282m.; 🄿; z 40962; ● 20
Plano; RMC Place; WARREN; ***180** M-6; elev. 614ft./187m.; mail Bowling Green z 42104; ● 250
Plantation; Inc. Place; JEFFERSON; **180** B-9; elev. 636ft./194m.; ★ **LOU**; mail Louisville z 40222; Ⓟ 830; © 902
Plato; RMC Place; PULASKI; ***181** K-13; mail Somerset z 42501; rural
Pleasant Grove Hill; RMC Place; CHRISTIAN; ***180** L-3; ★ **HPKNV**; mail Hopkinsville z 42240; ● 40
Pleasant Hill; RMC Place; BUTLER; ***180** K-5; mail Rochester z 42273; rural
Pleasant Hill; MERCER; see Shakertown (RMC Place)
Pleasant Hill; RMC Place; PENDLETON; ***181** E-13; mail Butler z 41006; rural
Pleasant Home; RMC Place; OWEN; ***181** F-11; elev. 883ft./269m.; mail Owenton z 40359; ● 20
Pleasant Ridge; RMC Place; DAVIESS, OHIO; **180** J-4; mail Utica z 42376; ● 200
Pleasant Valley; RMC Place; NICHOLAS; ***181** G-14; mail Ewing z 41039; rural
Pleasant Valley; RMC Place; PIKE; ***181** J-19; mail Pikeville z 41501; pop. incl. with Pikeville (Inc. Place)
Pleasant View; RMC Place; WHITLEY; **181** M-14; elev. 1,007ft./307m.; mail Williamsburg z 40769; ● 500
Pleasure Ridge Park; CDP; JEFFERSON; ***180** H-8; elev. 454ft./138m.; 🄿; ★ **LOU**; z 40258, z 40268, z 40281-83 & mail Louisville z 40216; former CDP; became part of Louisville/Jefferson County Metro Jan. 6, 2003; Ⓟ 25,131; © 25,776; ◆ 0
Pleasureville; RMC Place; FLEMING; ***181** F-15; elev. 838ft./255m.; mail Wallingford z 41093; ● 40
Pleasureville (Port Royal); Inc. Place; HENRY, SHELBY; **180** G-10; elev. 898ft./274m.; 🄿; z 40057; Ⓟ 761; © 869
Plum; RMC Place; BOURBON; ***181** G-14; mail Paris z 40361; rural
Plummers Landing; RMC Place; FLEMING; **181** G-15; elev. 673ft./205m.; 🄿; z 41081; ● 30
Plummers Mill; RMC Place; FLEMING; ***181** G-15; elev. 668ft./204m.; mail Plummers Landing z 41081, Wallingford z 41093
Plum Springs; Inc. Place; WARREN; **180** L-6; elev. 536ft./163m.; 🄿; ★ **BOWLG**; z 42101; Ⓟ 361; © 447
Plumville; RMC Place; MASON; **181** F-15; elev. 909ft./277m.; mail Maysville z 41056; ● 150
Plymouth Village; RMC Place; JEFFERSON; ***180** G-9; elev. 534ft./163m.; ★ **LOU**; mail Louisville z 40207; former incorporated place; became part of St. Matthews July 1, 2000; pop. incl. with Saint Matthews (Inc. Place); Ⓟ 162; © 201
Poindexter; RMC Place; HARRISON; ***181** F-13; elev. 718ft./219m.; mail Cynthiana z 41031; rural
Pointer; RMC Place; PULASKI; ***181** L-11; elev. 1,097ft./334m.; 🄿; z 42544; rural
Point Leavell; RMC Place; GARRARD; ***181** J-12; elev. 917ft./280m.; mail Lancaster z 40444, Paint Lick z 40461; rural
Point Pleasant; RMC Place; TAYLOR; ***180** K-10; mail Campbellsville z 42718; rural
Polksville; RMC Place; BATH; **181** H-15; mail Salt Lick z 40371; ● 60
Polkville; RMC Place; WARREN; ***180** L-7; elev. 568ft./173m.; mail Oakland z 42159; rural
Polly; RMC Place; LETCHER; ***181** K-18; mail Whitesburg z 41858; rural
Pomeroyton; RMC Place; MENIFEE; **181** I-15; elev. 991ft./302m.; 🄿; z 40387; ● 75
Pomp; RMC Place; MORGAN; ***181** H-16; mail West Liberty z 41472; rural
Ponderosa; RMC Place; GRAYSON; ***180** K-7; mail Clarkson z 42726; ● 70
Pondsville; RMC Place; WARREN; ***180** L-7; mail Smiths Grove z 42171; rural
Pongo; RMC Place; ROCKCASTLE; ***181** K-13; mail Mount Vernon z 40456; rural
Poole; RMC Place; WEBSTER, HENDERSON; **180** J-2; elev. 498ft./152m.; 🄿; z 42444; ● 400
Poortown; RMC Place; JESSAMINE; ★ **LEX**; mail Nicholasville z 40356; rural
Pope; RMC Place; ALLEN; ***180** M-6; elev. 732ft./223m.; mail Scottsville z 42164; rural
Poplar; RMC Place; CARTER; ***181** F-17; elev. 756ft./230m.; mail Carter z 41128; rural
Poplar Corner; RMC Place; MARION; ***180** J-10; mail Lebanon z 40033; rural
Poplar Flat; RMC Place; LEWIS; ***181** F-15; elev. 696ft./212m.; mail Tollesboro z 41189; rural
Poplar Grove; RMC Place; FLEMING; ***181** F-15; mail Flemingsburg z 41041; rural
Poplar Grove; RMC Place; MCLEAN; ***180** J-3; mail Sacramento z 42372; rural
Poplar Grove; RMC Place; OWEN; ***181** F-11; mail Glencoe z 41046; rural
Poplar Highlands; RMC Place; GREENUP; ***181** F-18; ★ **HNTG**; mail Russell z 41169; ● 450
Poplar Hills; Inc. Place; JEFFERSON; **180** C-8; ★ **LOU**; mail Louisville z 40213; Ⓟ 377; © 396
Poplar Plains; RMC Place; FLEMING; **181** G-15; mail Flemingsburg z 41041; ● 120
Poplarville; RMC Place; PULASKI; ***181** L-13; elev. 1,040ft./317m.; 🄿; z 42501; rural
Porter; RMC Place; SCOTT; ***181** G-12; mail Sadieville z 40370; rural
Portland; RMC Place; ADAIR; ***180** L-9; rural
Portland; RMC Place; JEFFERSON; ***180** G-8; ★ **LOU**; mail Louisville z 40212; pop. incl. with Louisville (Inc. Place)
Portland; RMC Place; PENDLETON; ***181** E-12; elev. 876ft./267m.; mail De Mossville z 41033; rural
Port Royal; RMC Place; HENRY; **180** F-10; elev. 841ft./256m.; 🄿; z 40058; ● 130
Port Royal; HENRY, SHELBY; see Pleasureville (Inc. Place)
Portsmouth; RMC Place; BREATHITT; ***181** J-16; mail Jackson z 41339; rural
Possum Trot; RMC Place; MARSHALL; ***180** E-4; mail Calvert City z 42029; ● 150
Potters; RMC Place; LAWRENCE; ***181** G-18; mail Louisa z 41230; rural
Potters Fork; RMC Place; LETCHER; ***181** K-18; mail Cromona z 41810, Jenkins z 41537; ● 150
Pottsville; RMC Place; GRAVES; **180** F-3; elev. 453ft./138m.; mail Hickory z 42051; ● 20
Pottsville; RMC Place; WASHINGTON; ***181** J-11; mail Springfield z 40069
Powderly; Inc. Place; MUHLENBERG; **180** K-4; elev. 438ft./134m.; 🄿; z 42367; Ⓟ 748; © 846
POWELL; **181** I-14; Ⓟ 11,686; © 13,237; ◆ 14,002
Powells Creek; RMC Place; PIKE; ***181** J-19; mail Pikeville z 41501; rural
Powersburg; RMC Place; WAYNE; ***181** M-11; 🄿; z 42633; rural
Powersville; RMC Place; BRACKEN; **181** F-14; elev. 963ft./294m.; mail Brooksville z 41004; ● 60
Prairie Village; RMC Place; JEFFERSON; ***180** H-8; ★ **LOU**; mail Louisville z 40272; became part of Louisville/Jefferson County Metro Jan. 6, 2003
Prater; RMC Place; CARTER; ***181** G-17; mail Olive Hill z 41164; rural
Pratt; RMC Place; WEBSTER; ***180** J-3; mail Sebree z 42455; rural
Preachersville; RMC Place; LINCOLN; **181** J-12; mail Crab Orchard z 40419; ● 30
Premium; LETCHER; see Hot Spot (RMC Place)
Prentiss; RMC Place; OHIO; ***180** K-5; elev. 427ft./130m.; mail Beaver Dam z 42320; ● 45
Presidential; RMC Place; NELSON; ***180** I-9; mail Bardstown z 40004; ● 280
Press; RMC Place; BREATHITT; ***181** J-16; mail Jackson z 41339; rural
Preston; RMC Place; BATH; **181** H-15; elev. 755ft./230m.; 🄿; z 40366; ● 150
Preston Estates; RMC Place; JOHNSON; ***181** I-18; mail Paintsville z 41240; ● 30
Prestonia; RMC Place; JEFFERSON; ***180** G-8; ★ **LOU**; mail Louisville z 40213; pop. incl. with Louisville (Inc. Place)
Prestonsburg; Inc. Place; ⊡ FLOYD; **181** I-18; elev. 642ft./196m.; 🄿 🄷; z 41653; Ⓟ 3,558; © 3,612
Prestonville; Inc. Place; CARROLL; **180** F-10; elev. 459ft./140m.; mail Carrollton z 41008; Ⓟ 205; © 164
Price; RMC Place; FLOYD; ***181** J-18; elev. 762ft./232m.; 🄿; z 41636; ● 150
Prices Mill; RMC Place; SIMPSON; **180** N-5; elev. 577ft./176m.; mail Franklin z 42134; ● 40
Pricetown; RMC Place; CASEY; ***181** K-11; mail Liberty z 42539
Pricetown; RMC Place; FAYETTE; ***181** H-13; ★ **LEX**; mail Lexington z 40509; pop. incl. with Lexington (Inc. Place)
Priceville; RMC Place; HART; **180** K-8; elev. 621ft./189m.; mail Munfordville z 42765; ● 50
Pride; RMC Place; UNION; **180** J-2; elev. 395ft./120m.; mail Clay z 42404, Morganfield z 42437; ● 75
Primrose; RMC Place; LEE; ***181** J-15; elev. 826ft./252m.; 🄿; z 41362; ● 30
Princess; RMC Place; BOYD; **181** G-18; elev. 603ft./184m.; ★ **HNTG**; mail Ashland z 41101-02; ● 200
Princeton; Inc. Place; ⊡ CALDWELL; **180** L-1; elev. 489ft./149m.; 🄿 🄷; z 42445; Ⓟ 6,940; © 6,536
Printer; RMC Place; FLOYD; ***181** J-18; elev. 669ft./204m.; 🄿; z 41655; ● 120
Pritchardsville; RMC Place; BARREN; **180** L-8; mail Glasgow z 42141; ● 90
Privett; RMC Place; JACKSON; ***181** K-14; elev. 1,292ft./394m.; mail Tyner z 40486; rural
Proctor; RMC Place; LEE; ***181** J-15; mail Beattyville z 41311; rural
Prospect; Inc. Place; JEFFERSON; **180** G-9; elev. 483ft./147m.; 🄿; ★ **LOU**; z 40059; Ⓟ 2,788; © 4,657
Prosperity; RMC Place; EDMONSON; ***180** K-7; mail Bee Spring z 42207; rural
Providence; JESSAMINE; see Brannon (RMC Place)
Providence; RMC Place; KNOX; ***181** M-14; mail Barbourville z 40906; ● 200
Providence; RMC Place; SIMPSON; **180** N-5; elev. 736ft./224m.; mail Franklin z 42134; ● 30
Providence; RMC Place; TRIMBLE; ***180** F-10; elev. 850ft./259m.; mail Campbellsburg z 40011; rural
Providence; Inc. Place; WEBSTER; **180** K-2; elev. 374ft./114m.; 🄿; z 42450; Ⓟ 4,123; © 3,611
Provo; RMC Place; BUTLER; ***180** K-5; elev. 468ft./143m.; 🄿; z 42261; ● 40
Pruden; RMC Place; BELL; **181** N-14; 🄿; z 37851; ● 150
Pryorsburg; RMC Place; GRAVES; **180** G-3; mail Mayfield z 42066; ● 250
Pryse; RMC Place; ESTILL; ***181** J-14; elev. 640ft./195m.; 🄿; z 40336; ● 30
Public; RMC Place; PULASKI; ***181** K-13; 🄿; z 42501; rural
Pueblo; RMC Place; WAYNE; ***181** M-12; elev. 837ft./255m.; 🄿; z 42633; rural
Pulaski; RMC Place; PULASKI; **181** K-12; elev. 1,123ft./342m.; 🄿; z 42567; ● 100
PULASKI; **181** L-12; Ⓟ 49,489; © 56,217; ◆ 60,755
Pumpkin Center; RMC Place; CALDWELL; **180** L-2; elev. 485ft./148m.; mail Princeton z 42445; pop. incl. with Princeton (Inc. Place)
Puncheon; RMC Place; KNOTT; ***181** K-18; elev. 984ft./300m.; mail Kite z 41828; rural
Purdy; RMC Place; ADAIR; ***180** L-10; elev. 1,018ft./310m.; mail Columbia z 42728; rural
Putney; RMC Place; HARLAN; **181** M-16; elev. 1,248ft./380m.; 🄿; z 40865; ● 250
Pyles; RMC Place; LIVINGSTON; ***180** E-4; ★ **PAD**; mail Ledbetter z 42058; ● 500
Pyramid; RMC Place; FLOYD; ***181** J-18; elev. 728ft./222m.; mail Prestonsburg z 41653; rural

Q

Quail; RMC Place; ROCKCASTLE; ***181** K-12; elev. 1,126ft./343m.; mail Brodhead z 40409; rural
Quality; RMC Place; BUTLER; **180** L-5; elev. 503ft./153m.; 🄿; z 42256; ● 50
Quicksand; RMC Place; BREATHITT; **181** J-16; elev. 800ft./244m.; 🄿; z 41339; ● 150
Quincy; RMC Place; LEWIS; **181** F-17; elev. 544ft./166m.; 🄿; z 41166; ● 350
Quinton; RMC Place; PULASKI; ***181** L-12; mail Bronston z 42518

R

Rabbit Hash; RMC Place; BOONE; ***181** D-11; elev. 474ft./144m.; 🄿; z 41005
Rabbit Ridge; RMC Place; HOPKINS; ***180** K-2; elev. 497ft./151m.; mail Nebo z 42441; ● 100
Raccoon; RMC Place; PIKE; **181** J-19; elev. 877ft./267m.; 🄿; z 41557; ● 400
Raceland; Inc. Place; GREENUP; **181** F-18; elev. 546ft./166m.; 🄿; ★ **HNTG**; z 41169; Ⓟ 2,256; © 2,355
Radcliff; RMC Place; FAYETTE; ***181** H-14; mail Lexington z 40505
Radcliff; Inc. Place; HARDIN; **180** I-8; elev. 767ft./234m.; 🄿 🄷; z 40159-60; Ⓟ 19,772; © 21,961; ◆ 23,651
Ragland; RMC Place; MCCRACKEN; ***180** E-3; mail Kevil z 42053
Railton; RMC Place; BARREN; ***180** L-7; elev. 751ft./229m.; mail Smiths Grove z 42171; rural
Randolph; RMC Place; METCALFE; ***180** L-8; elev. 945ft./288m.; mail Edmonton z 42129
Randy (Bandy); RMC Place; PULASKI; ***181** K-12; mail Eubank z 42567; rural
Ransom; RMC Place; PIKE; ***181** J-20; 🄿; z 41558 & mail Hardy z 41531; ● 175
Rapids; RMC Place; SIMPSON; ***180** N-6; mail Franklin z 42134; rural
Raven; RMC Place; KNOTT; **181** J-18; elev. 1,000ft./305m.; 🄿; z 41861; ● 75
Ravenna; Inc. Place; ESTILL; **181** I-14; elev. 643ft./196m.; 🄿; z 40472; Ⓟ 804; © 693
Raymond; RMC Place; BRECKINRIDGE; ***180** H-6; 🄿; z 40176; rural
Raywick; Inc. Place; MARION; **180** J-9; elev. 609ft./186m.; 🄿; z 40060; Ⓟ 157; © 144
Ready; RMC Place; GRAYSON; ***180** K-6; elev. 559ft./170m.; mail Caneyville z 42721
Rectorville; RMC Place; MASON; **181** F-15; mail Maysville z 41056; ● 150
Redbud; RMC Place; HARLAN; ***181** M-17; 🄿; z 40828; ● 150
Redbush; RMC Place; JOHNSON; **181** H-17; 🄿; z 41219; ● 60
Red Cross; RMC Place; BARREN; ***180** L-7; elev. 784ft./239m.; mail Park City z 42160; rural
Redfox; RMC Place; KNOTT; **181** K-17; elev. 1,110ft./338m.; 🄿; z 41847; ● 150
Red Hill; RMC Place; ALLEN; ***180** M-7; elev. 722ft./220m.; mail Scottsville z 42164; rural
Red Hill; RMC Place; DAVIESS; ***180** J-4; elev. 466ft./142m.; mail Utica z 42376; rural
Redhouse; RMC Place; MADISON; ***181** I-13; mail Richmond z 40475
Red Lick; RMC Place; METCALFE; ***180** L-9; mail Edmonton z 42129; rural
Red River; RMC Place; LOGAN; ***180** M-5; mail Adairville z 42202; rural
Redwine; RMC Place; MORGAN; ***181** H-16; mail Wrigley z 41477; rural
Reed; RMC Place; HENDERSON; **180** I-3; elev. 378ft./115m.; 🄿; z 42451 & mail Stanley z 42375; ● 100
Reeds Crossing; RMC Place; MADISON; **181** I-13; elev. 944ft./288m.; mail Richmond z 40475; ● 150
Reedville; RMC Place; CARTER; ***181** G-17; mail Grayson z 41143; rural
Reedyville; RMC Place; BUTLER; ***180** K-6; elev. 508ft./155m.; mail Roundhill z 42275; rural
Regina; PIKE; see Marrowbone (RMC Place)
Region; RMC Place; BUTLER; ***180** K-6; mail Roundhill z 42275; rural
Reidland; CDP; MCCRACKEN; **180** E-4; ★ **PAD**; mail Paducah z 42001, z 42003; Ⓟ 4,054; © 4,353
Reid Village; RMC Place; MONTGOMERY; **181** H-14; elev. 1,043ft./318m.; mail Mount Sterling z 40353; ● 150
Relief; RMC Place; MORGAN; ***181** H-17; 🄿; z 41472; rural
Rella; RMC Place; BELL; ***181** M-15; mail Arjay z 40902
Renaker; RMC Place; HARRISON; ***181** F-13; elev. 832ft./254m.; mail Berry z 41003; ● 25
Render; RMC Place; OHIO; ***180** K-4; mail Beaver Dam z 42320; rural
Renfro Valley; RMC Place; ROCKCASTLE; **181** K-13; elev. 948ft./289m.; 🄿; z 40473; pop. incl. with Mount Vernon (Inc. Place)
Renfrow; RMC Place; OHIO; ***180** K-5; elev. 683ft./208m.; mail Horse Branch z 42349; rural
Repton; RMC Place; CRITTENDEN; ***180** K-1; elev. 483ft./147m.; mail Marion z 42064; ● 15
Reservoir; RMC Place; JEFFERSON; ★ **LOU**; pop. incl. with Louisville (Inc. Place)
Revelo; RMC Place; MCCREARY; **181** M-12; elev. 1,336ft./407m.; 🄿; z 42638; ● 700
Rex; RMC Place; HART; ***180** K-8; elev. 701ft./214m.; mail Hardyville z 42746; rural
Rexville; RMC Place; MORGAN; ***181** I-16; mail Hazel Green z 41332; rural
Reynolds Station; RMC Place; OHIO; **180** J-5; elev. 449ft./137m.; 🄿; z 42368; ● 100
Reynoldsville; RMC Place; BATH; ***181** G-14; mail Owingsville z 40360, Sharpsburg z 40374; rural
Rhea; RMC Place; HARLAN; ***181** M-16; mail Baxter z 40806; rural
Rheber; RMC Place; CASEY; ***181** K-11; mail Dunnville z 42528, Liberty z 42539; ● 30
Rhoda; RMC Place; EDMONSON; **180** L-7; mail Brownsville z 42210; ● 100
Rhodelia; RMC Place; MEADE; **180** H-6; elev. 645ft./197m.; 🄿; z 40161; ● 20
Ribolt; RMC Place; LEWIS; **181** F-15; elev. 697ft./212m.; mail Tollesboro z 41189; ● 80
Rice Station; RMC Place; ESTILL; ***181** I-14; mail Irvine z 40336; rural
Ricetown; RMC Place; OWSLEY; ***181** K-15; elev. 815ft./248m.; 🄿; z 41364; ● 30
Riceville; RMC Place; FULTON; ***180** G-2; mail Fulton z 42041; pop. incl. with Fulton (Inc. Place)
Riceville; RMC Place; JOHNSON; ***181** I-17; elev. 696ft./212m.; mail Paintsville z 41240
Richardson; RMC Place; LAWRENCE; ***181** H-18; elev. 600ft./183m.; 🄿; z 41230; ● 50
Richardsville; RMC Place; WARREN; **180** L-6; elev. 672ft./205m.; 🄿; z 42101; ● 300
Richelieu; RMC Place; LOGAN, BUTLER; ***180** L-5; mail Auburn z 42206
Richland; RMC Place; HOPKINS; **180** K-2; mail Madisonville z 42431; ● 75
Richlawn; Inc. Place; JEFFERSON; **180** B-8; elev. 550ft./168m.; ★ **LOU**; mail Louisville z 40207; Ⓟ 435; © 454
Richmond; Inc. Place; ⊡ MADISON; **181** I-13; elev. 975ft./297m.; 🄿 🄷 🄲 15,763 ■; z 40475-76; Ⓟ 21,155; © 27,152; ◆ 33,739
Rich Pond; RMC Place; WARREN; **180** M-6; mail Bowling Green z 42104; ● 300
Richwood; RMC Place; BOONE; ***181** E-12; ★ **CIN**; mail Verona z 41092, Walton z 41094
Ridgeview Estates; RMC Place; FRANKLIN; ***181** F-11; mail Frankfort z 40601
Ridgeview Heights; RMC Place; KENTON; ***181** D-12; elev. 782ft./238m.; ★ **CIN**; mail Independence z 41051; pop. incl. with Independence (Inc. Place)
Ridgeway; RMC Place; HARLAN; ***181** M-17; mail Lejunior z 40849; ● 25
Riley; RMC Place; MARION; ***180** J-10; mail Gravel Switch z 40328; rural
Rileyville; RMC Place; HARLAN; ***181** M-17; mail Closplint z 40927; ● 10
Riney; HARDIN; see Rineyville (RMC Place)
Rineyville (Riney); RMC Place; HARDIN; **180** I-8; elev. 776ft./237m.; 🄿; z 40162; ● 400
Ringgold; RMC Place; PULASKI; ***181** L-12; mail Somerset z 42503; rural
Ringos Mills; RMC Place; FLEMING; **181** G-15; mail Hillsboro z 41049; ● 45
Rio Vista; RMC Place; HARLAN; ***181** M-16; mail Loyall z 40854
Risner; RMC Place; FLOYD; ***181** J-18; 🄿; z 41649; rural
Ritchie; RMC Place; KNOTT; ***181** K-17; mail Hazard z 41701; rural
Ritner; RMC Place; WAYNE; ***181** M-12; elev. 827ft./252m.; 🄿; z 42633; rural
Rivals; RMC Place; SPENCER; ***180** H-10; elev. 567ft./173m.; mail Taylorsville z 40071; rural
River; RMC Place; JOHNSON; ***181** I-18; 🄿; z 41254; ● 75
River Bluff; Inc. Place; OLDHAM; ***180** G-9; ★ **LOU**; mail Prospect z 40059; Ⓟ 452; © 402
Riverfront; RMC Place; JEFFERSON; ***180** G-8; ★ **LOU**; mail Louisville z 40270; pop. incl. with Louisville (Inc. Place)
River Oaks; RMC Place; HART; ***180** K-8; mail Munfordville z 42765; ● 50
River Park; RMC Place; FAYETTE; ***181** H-12; ★ **LEX**; mail Lexington z 40502; pop. incl. with Lexington (Inc. Place)
River Ridge; RMC Place; HARLAN; ***181** M-17; mail Evarts z 40828; ● 125
Riverside; RMC Place; WARREN; ***180** L-6; elev. 579ft./176m.; rural
Riverside Gardens; RMC Place; JEFFERSON; ***180** G-8; ★ **LOU**; mail Louisville z 40216; became part of Louisville/Jefferson County Metro Jan. 6, 2003
Riverview; RMC Place; MCCRACKEN; ***180** E-4; ★ **PAD**; mail Paducah z 42003; ● 150
Riverview Estates; RMC Place; MERCER; ***181** I-11; mail Harrodsburg z 40330
Riverway; RMC Place; JEFFERSON; ★ **LOU**; pop. incl. with Louisville (Inc. Place)
Riverwood; Inc. Place; JEFFERSON; **180** A-8; ★ **LOU**; mail Louisville z 40207; Ⓟ 506; © 469
Road Fork; PIKE; see Forest Hills (RMC Place)
Road Junction; RMC Place; PIKE; ***181** K-19; mail Elkhorn City z 41522; rural
Roaring Spring; RMC Place; TRIGG; ***180** M-2; mail Cadiz z 42211; rural
Roark; RMC Place; LESLIE; **181** L-16; elev. 988ft./301m.; 🄿; z 40979; ● 75
Roary; ALLEN; see Oak Forest (RMC Place)
Robards; Inc. Place; HENDERSON; **180** I-3; elev. 415ft./126m.; 🄿; z 42452; Ⓟ 526; © 564
ROBERTSON; **181** F-14; Ⓟ 2,124; © 2,266; ◆ 2,021
Robinson; RMC Place; HARRISON; ***181** F-13; elev. 670ft./204m.; mail Cynthiana z 41031; rural
Robinson Creek; RMC Place; PIKE; **181** K-19; 🄿; z 41560; ● 400
Robinsville; RMC Place; MADISON; ***181** I-13; mail Richmond z 40475; ● 90
Robinswood; RMC Place; JEFFERSON; ***180** G-9; elev. 553ft./169m.; ★ **LOU**; mail Louisville z 40207; pop. incl. with Indian Hills (Inc. Place); Ⓟ 250
Robinwood Estates; RMC Place; FAYETTE; ***181** H-12; ★ **LEX**; mail Lexington z 40503; pop. incl. with Lexington (Inc. Place)
Rob Roy; RMC Place; OHIO; ***180** K-5; mail Beaver Dam z 42320, Cromwell z 42333; rural
Rochester; Inc. Place; BUTLER; **180** K-5; elev. 450ft./137m.; 🄿; z 42273; Ⓟ 191; © 186
Rockbridge; RMC Place; MONROE; ***180** M-9; mail Tompkinsville z 42167; rural
Rockcastle; RMC Place; TRIGG; ***180** M-1; mail Cadiz z 42211; ● 20
ROCKCASTLE; **181** K-13; Ⓟ 14,803; © 16,582; ◆ 16,671
Rockdale; RMC Place; BOYD; ***181** F-18; ★ **HNTG**; mail Ashland z 41101-02; ● 500
Rockdale; RMC Place; OWEN; ***181** G-12; mail Owenton z 40359; rural
Rockfield; RMC Place; WARREN; **180** M-6; elev. 591ft./180m.; 🄿; ★ **BOWLG**; z 42274; ● 70
Rock Haven; RMC Place; MEADE; ***180** H-7; mail Vine Grove z 40175; rural
Rockholds; RMC Place; WHITLEY; **181** M-14; elev. 986ft./301m.; 🄿; z 40759; ● 300
Rockhouse; RMC Place; PIKE; **181** K-19; elev. 1,200ft./366m.; 🄿; z 41561; ● 200
Rockland; RMC Place; WARREN; ***180** L-6; mail Bowling Green z 42101; rural
Rockport; Inc. Place; OHIO; **180** K-4; elev. 410ft./125m.; 🄿; z 42369; Ⓟ 385; © 334
Rock Springs; RMC Place; HENDERSON; ***180** I-2; mail Corydon z 42406; rural
Rockybranch; RMC Place; WAYNE; ***181** M-12; elev. 1,016ft./310m.; 🄿; z 42633; ● 15
Rocky Hill; RMC Place; BARREN; ***180** L-7; mail Glasgow z 42141; rural
Rocky Hill; RMC Place; EDMONSON; **180** L-7; elev. 625ft./191m.; 🄿; z 42163; ● 160
Rodburn; RMC Place; ROWAN; ***181** G-16; mail Morehead z 40351; pop. incl. with Morehead (Inc. Place)
Roff; RMC Place; BRECKINRIDGE; ***180** J-6; elev. 689ft./210m.; mail Westview z 40178
Rogers; RMC Place; WOLFE; **181** I-15; elev. 1,220ft./372m.; 🄿; z 41365; ● 100
Rogers Chapel; RMC Place; POWELL; ***181** I-15; mail Stanton z 40380; rural
Rogers Gap; RMC Place; SCOTT; ***181** G-12; mail Georgetown z 40324; ● 25
Rolling Acres; RMC Place; FRANKLIN; ***181** G-11; mail Frankfort z 40601; pop. incl. with Frankfort (Inc. Place)
Rolling Fields; Inc. Place; JEFFERSON; **180** B-8; elev. 554ft./169m.; ★ **LOU**; mail Louisville z 40207; Ⓟ 593; © 648
Rolling Hills; Inc. Place; JEFFERSON; **180** A-9; ★ **LOU**; mail Louisville z 40222; Ⓟ 1,135; © 907
Rollington; RMC Place; OLDHAM; ***180** G-9; ★ **LOU**; mail Pewee Valley z 40056; pop. incl. with Pewee Valley (Inc. Place)
Rome; RMC Place; DAVIESS; **180** C-2; ★ **OWNS**; mail Owensboro z 42301; ● 150
Romine; RMC Place; TAYLOR; ***180** K-10; mail Campbellsville z 42718; rural
Rookwood; RMC Place; FAYETTE; ***181** H-12; ★ **LEX**; mail Lexington z 40505; pop. incl. with Lexington (Inc. Place)
Rooster Run; RMC Place; NELSON; mail Coxs Creek z 40013
Roscoe; RMC Place; ELLIOTT; ***181** H-17; mail Sandy Hook z 41171; ● 30
Rose Crossroads; RMC Place; RUSSELL; ***180** L-10; mail Jamestown z 42629; rural
Rosefork; RMC Place; WOLFE; ***181** I-16; mail Campton z 41301; rural
Rose Hill; RMC Place; CARTER; ***181** G-16; mail Olive Hill z 41164; rural
Rose Hill; RMC Place; MERCER; ***181** I-11; mail Harrodsburg z 40330
Rose Terrace; RMC Place; HARDIN; ***180** I-8; mail Fort Knox z 40121
Rosetta; RMC Place; BRECKINRIDGE; ***180** I-7; elev. 554ft./169m.; mail Irvington z 40146; rural
Roseville; RMC Place; BARREN; ***180** M-8; elev. 740ft./226m.; mail Glasgow z 42141
Roseville (Lyonia); RMC Place; HANCOCK; ***180** I-5; elev. 518ft./158m.; mail Reynolds Station z 42368
Rosewood; RMC Place; MUHLENBERG; ***180** L-4; elev. 602ft./183m.; mail Greenville z 42345
Rosine; RMC Place; OHIO; **180** J-5; elev. 564ft./172m.; 🄿; z 42370; ● 200
Ross; RMC Place; CAMPBELL; ***181** D-13; ★ **CIN**; mail Melbourne z 41059; ● 150
Rossland; RMC Place; KNOX; ***181** L-14; mail Gray z 40734; ● 60
Rosslyn; RMC Place; POWELL; ***181** I-14; elev. 670ft./204m.; 🄿; z 40380
Rosspoint; RMC Place; HARLAN; ***181** M-16; mail Baxter z 40806; ● 200
Rothwell; RMC Place; MENIFEE; ***181** H-15; mail Frenchburg z 40322; rural
Roundhill; RMC Place; EDMONSON; ***180** K-6; elev. 454ft./138m.; 🄿; z 42275
Round Hill; RMC Place; MADISON; **181** J-13; mail Richmond z 40475; ● 120
Roundstone; RMC Place; ROCKCASTLE; ***181** J-13; mail Mount Vernon z 40456; rural
Rouse; RMC Place; KENTON; ***181** D-12; 🄿; ★ **CIN**; z 41014; pop. incl. with Covington (Inc. Place)
Rousseau; RMC Place; BREATHITT; **181** J-16; elev. 783ft./239m.; 🄿; z 41366; ● 110
Routt; RMC Place; JEFFERSON; ***180** H-9; ★ **LOU**; mail Louisville z 40299; became part of Louisville/Jefferson County Metro Jan. 6, 2003
ROWAN; **181** H-16; Ⓟ 20,353; © 22,094; ◆ 22,727
Rowdy; PERRY; see Stacy (RMC Place)
Rowena; RMC Place; RUSSELL; ***180** M-10; 🄿; z 42629; rural
Rowland; RMC Place; LINCOLN; **181** J-12; mail Stanford z 40484; ● 75
Rowletts; RMC Place; HART; **180** K-8; elev. 663ft./202m.; 🄿; z 42765; ● 300
Roxana; RMC Place; LETCHER; **181** L-17; elev. 1,043ft./318m.; 🄿; z 41848; ● 150
Royalton; RMC Place; MAGOFFIN; **181** I-17; elev. 890ft./271m.; 🄿; z 41464; ● 200
Royrader; RMC Place; JACKSON; ***181** K-14; elev. 1,036ft./316m.; mail Annville z 40402; rural
Royville; RMC Place; RUSSELL; **180** L-10; elev. 1,072ft./327m.; mail Russell Springs z 42642; ● 55
Ruckerville; RMC Place; CLARK; ***181** H-14; elev. 823ft./251m.; mail Winchester z 40391
Ruddels Mills; RMC Place; BOURBON; **181** G-13; mail Cynthiana z 41031, Paris z 40361; ● 200
Ruin; RMC Place; ELLIOTT; ***181** H-16; mail Sandy Hook z 41171; rural
Rumsey; RMC Place; MCLEAN; **180** J-4; 🄿; z 42371; ● 200
Rural; RMC Place; PIKE; ***181** I-19; mail Belfry z 41514; rural
Rush; RMC Place; BOYD; **181** G-18; elev. 646ft./197m.; 🄿; z 41168; ● 200
Russell; Inc. Place; GREENUP; **181** F-18; elev. 560ft./171m.; 🄿; ★ **HNTG**; z 41169; Ⓟ 4,014; © 3,645
RUSSELL; **180** M-10; Ⓟ 14,716; © 16,315; ◆ 17,136
Russell Heights; RMC Place; GREENUP; ***181** F-18; ★ **HNTG**; mail Russell z 41169; pop. incl. with Russell (Inc. Place)
Russell Springs; Inc. Place; RUSSELL; **180** L-10; elev. 1,090ft./332m.; 🄿 🄷; z 42642; Ⓟ 2,363; © 2,399
Russellville; Inc. Place; ⊡ LOGAN; **180** M-5; elev. 595ft./181m.; 🄿 🄷; z 42276; Ⓟ 7,454; © 7,149
Ruth; RMC Place; PULASKI; ***181** L-12; elev. 831ft./253m.; 🄿; z 42501; rural
Rutherford; RMC Place; HARLAN; ***181** M-17; mail Closplint z 40927; ● 65
Rutland; RMC Place; HARRISON; ***181** F-12; mail Cynthiana z 41031; rural
Ryan; RMC Place; FLEMING; ***181** G-15; mail Wallingford z 41093; rural
Ryland; RMC Place; KENTON; **181** D-12; ★ **CIN**; mail Latonia z 41015; ● 200
Ryland Heights; Inc. Place; KENTON; ***181** D-12; 🄿; ★ **CIN**; z 41015; Ⓟ 279; © 799

S

Sacramento; Inc. Place; MCLEAN; **180** K-3; elev. 497ft./151m.; 🄿; z 42372; Ⓟ 563; © 517
Sadieville; Inc. Place; SCOTT; **181** G-12; elev. 858ft./262m.; 🄿; z 40370; Ⓟ 255; © 263
Sadler; RMC Place; GRAYSON; ***180** K-6; elev. 708ft./216m.; mail Leitchfield z 42754; rural
Saint Catharine; RMC Place; WASHINGTON; **180** I-10; elev. 784ft./239m.; 🄿 🄲 618; z 40061; ● 500
Saint Charles; Inc. Place; HOPKINS; **180** K-3; elev. 433ft./132m.; 🄿; z 42453; Ⓟ 316; © 309
Saint Dennis; RMC Place; JEFFERSON; **180** C-5; ★ **LOU**; mail Louisville z 40216; became part of Louisville/Jefferson County Metro Jan. 6, 2003
Saint Dennis; CDP; JEFFERSON; ***180** G-8; elev. 450ft./137m.; ★ **LOU**; mail Louisville z 40216; former CDP; became part of Louisville/Jefferson County Metro Jan. 6, 2003; Ⓟ 10,326; © 9,177
Saint Elmo; RMC Place; CHRISTIAN; ***180** M-3; mail Pembroke z 42266; rural
Saint Francis; RMC Place; MARION; **180** J-9; elev. 701ft./214m.; 🄿; z 40062; ● 80
Saint Helens; RMC Place; LEE; **181** J-15; elev. 744ft./227m.; 🄿; z 41368; ● 100
Saint John; RMC Place; HARDIN; ***180** I-8; mail Elizabethtown z 42701; ● 200
Saint Johns; RMC Place; MCCRACKEN; ***180** F-3; ★ **PAD**; mail Paducah z 42001; rural
Saint Joseph (Maple Mount); RMC Place; DAVIESS; **180** I-3; elev. 420ft./128m.; 🄿; z 42301 & mail Maple Mount z 42356; ● 50
Saint Joseph; RMC Place; MARION; ***180** J-9; elev. 626ft./191m.; mail Raywick z 40060; rural
Saint Mary; RMC Place; MARION; **180** J-10; elev. 762ft./232m.; 🄿; z 40063; ● 150
Saint Matthews; Inc. Place; JEFFERSON; **180** G-9; elev. 554ft./169m.; 🄿 ■; ★ **LOU**; z 40207, z 40257 & mail Louisville z 40206, z 40222; includes Broad Fields, Plymouth Village annexed July 1, 2000 and Cherrywood Village, Fairmeade, Springlee annexed September 1, 2000; Ⓟ 15,800; © 15,852; Ⓐ 17,320; ◆ 16,831
Saint Paul; RMC Place; GRAYSON; ***180** J-7; mail Leitchfield z 42754; ● 75
Saint Paul; RMC Place; LEWIS; **181** E-17; 🄿; z 41166; ● 80
Saint Regis Park; Inc. Place; JEFFERSON; **180** C-9; elev. 570ft./174m.; ★ **LOU**; mail Louisville z 40220; Ⓟ 1,756; © 1,520
Saint Vincent; RMC Place; UNION; ***180** I-2; mail Morganfield z 42437; rural
Saldee; BREATHITT; see Copland (RMC Place)
Salem; Inc. Place; LIVINGSTON; **180** K-1; elev. 448ft./137m.; 🄿 🄷; z 42078; Ⓟ 770; © 769
Salem (Buskirk, Shawnee); RMC Place; MORGAN; ***181** I-16; elev. 857ft./261m.; mail Hazel Green z 41332; ● 50
Salem; RMC Place; RUSSELL; ***181** L-11; elev. 983ft./300m.; mail Russell Springs z 42642; rural
Salleeton; RMC Place; MARION; ***180** J-10; mail Lebanon z 40033; rural
Salmon; SIMPSON; see Salmons (RMC Place)
Salmons (Salmon); RMC Place; SIMPSON; **180** M-6; mail Franklin z 42134; ● 40
Saloma; RMC Place; TAYLOR; **180** K-9; elev. 880ft./268m.; mail Campbellsville z 42718; ● 40
Salt Gum; RMC Place; KNOX; **181** L-15; elev. 1,057ft./322m.; 🄿; z 40935; ● 20
Salt Lick; Inc. Place; BATH; **181** H-15; elev. 669ft./204m.; 🄿; z 40371; Ⓟ 342; © 342
Salt River; RMC Place; BULLITT; ***180** H-8; ★ **LOU**; mail Shepherdsville z 40165; pop. incl. with Shepherdsville (Inc. Place)
Salt Well; RMC Place; NICHOLAS; ***181** G-14; mail Carlisle z 40311; rural
Salvisa; RMC Place; MERCER; **181** I-11; elev. 823ft./251m.; 🄿; z 40372; ● 250
Salyersville; Inc. Place; ⊡ MAGOFFIN; **181** I-17; elev. 854ft./260m.; 🄿; z 41465; Ⓟ 1,917; © 1,604
Sample; RMC Place; BRECKINRIDGE; **180** I-6; elev. 423ft./129m.; 🄿; z 40143; ● 70
Samuels; RMC Place; NELSON; **180** I-9; elev. 677ft./206m.; 🄿; z 40013; ● 60
Sandefur Crossing; RMC Place; OHIO; ***180** K-5; mail Beaver Dam z 42320; rural
Sanders; Inc. Place; CARROLL; **181** F-11; elev. 486ft./148m.; 🄿; z 41083; Ⓟ 231; © 246
Sandgap; RMC Place; JACKSON; **181** J-14; elev. 1,490ft./454m.; 🄿; z 40481; ● 300
Sand Hill; RMC Place; ESTILL; ***181** I-14; mail Irvine z 40336; rural
Sand Hill; RMC Place; HARLAN; ***181** L-17; mail Cumberland z 40823
Sand Hill; RMC Place; WARREN; ***180** L-6; elev. 723ft./220m.; ★ **BOWLG**; mail Bowling Green z 42101; rural
Sand Lick (Pea Ridge); RMC Place; SCOTT; ***181** G-12; mail Stamping Ground z 40379; rural
Sand Springs; RMC Place; JACKSON; ***181** J-14; mail Mc Kee z 40447; rural
Sand Springs; RMC Place; ROCKCASTLE; ***181** K-13; elev. 967ft./295m.; mail Mount Vernon z 40456; rural
Sandy; RMC Place; MUHLENBERG; ***180** K-3; mail Bremen z 42325; rural
Sandy Hook; Inc. Place; ⊡ ELLIOTT; **181** H-17; elev. 723ft./220m.; 🄿; z 41171; Ⓟ 548; © 678
Sano; RMC Place; RUSSELL; ***180** L-10; elev. 1,021ft./311m.; mail Columbia z 42728; rural
Sarah; RMC Place; ELLIOTT; ***181** H-17; mail Sandy Hook z 41171; rural
Saratoga; RMC Place; LYON; ***180** L-1; elev. 390ft./119m.; mail Princeton z 42445; rural
Sardis; Inc. Place; MASON; **181** F-14; elev. 945ft./288m.; 🄿; z 41056; Ⓟ 171; © 149
Sassafras; RMC Place; KNOTT; **181** K-17; elev. 947ft./289m.; 🄿; z 41759; ● 950
Sassafras Ridge; RMC Place; FULTON; ***180** G-1; mail Hickman z 42050; rural
Sasser; RMC Place; LAUREL; ***181** L-14; elev. 1,209ft./369m.; 🄿; z 40741 & mail London z 40744; rural
Saul; RMC Place; PERRY; **181** K-16; elev. 1,053ft./321m.; 🄿; z 40981; ● 30
Savage; RMC Place; CLINTON; ***181** M-11; mail Albany z 42602; rural
Savage Branch; RMC Place; BOYD; ***181** G-18; ★ **HNTG**; mail Catlettsburg z 41129; rural
Savoy; RMC Place; WHITLEY; **181** M-13; mail Williamsburg z 40769; pop. incl. with Williamsburg (Inc. Place)
Savoyard; RMC Place; METCALFE; ***180** L-8; mail Horse Cave z 42749
Sawyer; RMC Place; MCCREARY; ***181** M-13; elev. 1,159ft./353m.; 🄿; z 42634; ● 10
Saxton; RMC Place; WHITLEY; **181** N-14; mail Williamsburg z 40769; ● 120
Saylor; RMC Place; LESLIE; ***181** M-16; mail Helton z 40840; rural
Scale; RMC Place; MARSHALL; ***180** F-4; elev. 469ft./143m.; mail Benton z 42025; ● 50
Scalf; RMC Place; KNOX; **181** M-15; elev. 1,054ft./321m.; 🄿; z 40982; ● 30
Schley; RMC Place; LOGAN; ***180** M-5; mail Adairville z 42202; rural
Schochoh; RMC Place; LOGAN; **180** M-5; elev. 637ft./194m.; mail Adairville z 42202; ● 60
Schultztown; RMC Place; OHIO; ***180** K-5; mail Beaver Dam z 42320; rural
Schweizer; RMC Place; SIMPSON; ***180** N-5; mail Franklin z 42134; rural
Science Hill; Inc. Place; PULASKI; **181** K-12; elev. 1,117ft./340m.; 🄿; z 42553; Ⓟ 628; © 634
Scot; RMC Place; HARLAN; pop. incl. with Cumberland (Inc. Place)
SCOTT; **181** G-12; Ⓟ 23,867; © 33,061; ◆ 45,431
Scottown; RMC Place; OHIO; ***180** K-4; mail Beaver Dam z 42320; ● 25
Scottsburg; RMC Place; CALDWELL; ***180** L-2; elev. 521ft./159m.; mail Princeton z 42445; rural
Scotts Station; RMC Place; SHELBY; ***180** G-10; elev. 750ft./229m.; mail Shelbyville z 40065; rural
Scottsville; Inc. Place; ⊡ ALLEN; **180** M-7; elev. 760ft./232m.; 🄿 🄷; z 42164; Ⓟ 4,278; © 4,327
Scoville; RMC Place; OWSLEY; ***181** J-15; mail Booneville z 41314; rural
Scranton; RMC Place; MENIFEE; ***181** H-15; elev. 734ft./224m.; 🄿; z 40322; rural
Scuddy; RMC Place; PERRY; ***181** K-17; elev. 923ft./281m.; 🄿; z 41760; ● 150
Seatonville; RMC Place; JEFFERSON; ***180** H-9; ★ **LOU**; mail Louisville z 40299; became part of Louisville/Jefferson County Metro Jan. 6, 2003
Seaville; RMC Place; WASHINGTON; ***181** I-11; elev. 866ft./264m.; mail Willisburg z 40078; rural
Sebastians Branch; RMC Place; BREATHITT; ***181** J-16; elev. 704ft./215m.; 🄿; z 41314; ● 30
Sebree; Inc. Place; WEBSTER; **180** J-3; elev. 404ft./123m.; 🄿; z 42455; Ⓟ 1,510; © 1,558
Seco; RMC Place; LETCHER; ***181** K-18; elev. 1,309ft./399m.; 🄿; z 41849; ● 175
Sedalia; RMC Place; GRAVES; **180** G-3; elev. 506ft./154m.; 🄿; z 42079; ● 300
Segal; RMC Place; EDMONSON; ***180** K-6; elev. 617ft./188m.; mail Brownsville z 42210; rural
Seitz; RMC Place; MAGOFFIN; ***181** I-17; elev. 884ft./269m.; 🄿; z 41465; rural
Select; RMC Place; OHIO; ***180** K-5; mail Cromwell z 42333; rural
Seminary; RMC Place; CLINTON; ***180** M-10; elev. 1,023ft./312m.; 🄿; z 42602; rural
Seminary Village; RMC Place; JEFFERSON; ***180** G-9; elev. 560ft./171m.; ★ **LOU**; mail Louisville z 40207; pop. incl. with Louisville (Inc. Place)
Semiway; RMC Place; MCLEAN; ***180** J-4; elev. 397ft./121m.; mail Rumsey z 42371; rural
Seneca Gardens; Inc. Place; JEFFERSON; **180** C-8; elev. 555ft./169m.; ★ **LOU**; mail Louisville z 40205; Ⓟ 684; © 699
Senterville; RMC Place; PIKE; ***181** K-19; elev. 802ft./244m.; 🄿; z 41522; ● 100
Se Ree; RMC Place; BRECKINRIDGE; **180** I-6; elev. 700ft./213m.; 🄿; z 40144; ● 100
Sergent; RMC Place; LETCHER; ***181** L-18; elev. 1,217ft./371m.; mail Whitesburg z 41858; ● 250
Settle; RMC Place; ALLEN; ***180** M-7; mail Scottsville z 42164
Settlers Point; RMC Place; OLDHAM; ***180** G-9; ★ **LOU**; mail Prospect z 40059; ● 200
Seventy Six; RMC Place; CLINTON; ***180** M-10; 🄿; z 42602; rural
Sewell; RMC Place; BREATHITT; ***181** J-16; mail Vancleve z 41385; rural
Sewellton; RMC Place; RUSSELL; ***180** L-10; elev. 1,031ft./314m.; 🄿; z 42629; rural
Sextons Creek; RMC Place; CLAY; **181** K-15; elev. 815ft./248m.; 🄿; z 40983; ● 30
Seymour; RMC Place; HART; ***180** L-8; elev. 700ft./213m.; mail Horse Cave z 42749; rural
Shadeland; RMC Place; FAYETTE; ***181** H-12; ★ **LEX**; mail Lexington z 40502; pop. incl. with Lexington (Inc. Place)
Shady Grove; RMC Place; CRITTENDEN; **180** K-2; elev. 427ft./130m.; mail Marion z 42064; ● 35
Shady Grove; RMC Place; MCCRACKEN; ***180** F-4; ★ **PAD**; mail Paducah z 42003; ● 120
Shady Grove; RMC Place; METCALFE; ***180** L-9; mail Center z 42214
Shady Nook; RMC Place; HARRISON; ***181** G-13; elev. 851ft./259m.; mail Cynthiana z 41031; rural
Shafter; RMC Place; PULASKI; ***181** L-12; mail Somerset z 42501; rural
Shakertown (Pleasant Hill); RMC Place; MERCER; ***181** I-12; mail Harrodsburg z 40330; rural
Sha Lawn Village; RMC Place; TAYLOR; ***180** K-9; mail Campbellsville z 42718; ● 50
Shannon; RMC Place; MASON; ***181** F-14; elev. 909ft./277m.; mail Mayslick z 41055
Sharer; RMC Place; BUTLER; ***180** L-5; elev. 620ft./189m.; rural
Sharkey; RMC Place; FLEMING, ROWAN; ***181** G-15; mail Hillsboro z 41049, Morehead z 40351
Sharon; RMC Place; BRACKEN; ***181** E-14; mail Augusta z 41002; rural
Sharondale; RMC Place; PIKE; ***181** J-19; mail Belfry z 41514
Sharon Grove; RMC Place; TODD; **180** M-4; elev. 646ft./197m.; 🄿; z 42280; ● 175
Sharpe; RMC Place; MARSHALL; **180** F-4; elev. 407ft./124m.; mail Benton z 42025, Calvert City z 42029; ● 300
Sharpsburg; Inc. Place; BATH; **181** G-14; elev. 1,014ft./309m.; 🄿; z 40374; Ⓟ 315; © 295
Sharpsville; RMC Place; WASHINGTON; ***181** I-11; mail Harrodsburg z 40330; rural
Shawhan; RMC Place; BOURBON; **181** G-13; mail Cynthiana z 41031, Paris z 40361; ● 140
Shawnee; RMC Place; JEFFERSON; ***180** G-8; ★ **LOU**; mail Louisville z 40212; pop. incl. with Louisville (Inc. Place)
Shawnee; MORGAN; see Salem (RMC Place)
Shawnee Estates; RMC Place; WARREN; ***180** L-6; ★ **BOWLG**; mail Bowling Green z 42104; pop. incl. with Bowling Green (Inc. Place)
Shearer Valley; RMC Place; WAYNE; ***181** M-11; mail Monticello z 42633; rural
Shelbiana (Shelby); RMC Place; PIKE; **181** J-19; elev. 598ft./182m.; 🄿; z 41562; ● 350
Shelby; RMC Place; JEFFERSON; ***180** G-9; ★ **LOU**; mail Louisville z 40217; pop. incl. with Louisville (Inc. Place)
Shelby; PIKE; see Shelbiana (RMC Place)
SHELBY; **180** G-10; Ⓟ 24,824; © 33,337; ◆ 42,085
Shelby City; RMC Place; BOYLE; ***181** J-11; elev. 995ft./303m.; mail Danville z 40422; pop. incl. with Junction City (Inc. Place)
Shelby Gap; RMC Place; PIKE; **181** K-19; elev. 1,384ft./422m.; 🄿; z 41563; rural
Shelbyville; Inc. Place; ⊡ SHELBY; **180** G-10; elev. 791ft./241m.; 🄿 🄷; z 40065-66; Ⓟ 6,238; © 10,085
Shepherdsville; Inc. Place; ⊡ BULLITT; **180** H-8; elev. 449ft./137m.; 🄿; ★ **LOU**; z 40165; Ⓟ 4,805; © 8,334; Ⓡ 8,367
Shepola; RMC Place; PULASKI; ***181** L-12; mail Nancy z 42544; rural
Sherburne; RMC Place; FLEMING; **181** G-14; mail Flemingsburg z 41041; ● 60
Sheridan; RMC Place; CRITTENDEN; **180** K-1; mail Marion z 42064; ● 40
Sherman; RMC Place; GRANT; **181** E-12; elev. 933ft./284m.; ★ **CIN**; mail Dry Ridge z 41035; ● 50
Sherwood Shores; RMC Place; MARSHALL; ***180** L-1; mail Gilbertsville z 42044; ● 200
Shetland; RMC Place; WOODFORD; ***181** H-12; ★ **LEX**; mail Versailles z 40383; ● 100
Shields; RMC Place; HARLAN; ***181** M-17; mail Lejunior z 40849; ● 300
Shiloh; RMC Place; CALLOWAY; ***180** M-1; elev. 504ft./154m.; mail Murray z 42071
Shipley; RMC Place; CLINTON; ***180** N-10; mail Albany z 42602; rural
Shively; Inc. Place; JEFFERSON; **180** G-8; elev. 455ft./139m.; 🄿; ★ **LOU**; z 40216, z 40256; Ⓟ 15,535; © 15,157
Shopville; RMC Place; PULASKI; ***181** L-12; elev. 879ft./268m.; mail Somerset z 42501
Shore Acres; RMC Place; WOODFORD; ***181** H-11; mail Frankfort z 40601; ● 40
Short Creek; RMC Place; GRAYSON; **180** J-6; elev. 592ft./180m.; mail Caneyville z 42721; ● 45
Short Town; RMC Place; HARLAN; ***181** M-17; mail Evarts z 40828; ● 100
Shoulderblade; RMC Place; BREATHITT; ***181** J-16; elev. 756ft./230m.; mail Jackson z 41339
Shreve; RMC Place; OHIO; ***180** J-6; mail Fordsville z 42343; rural
Shrewsbury; RMC Place; GRAYSON; **180** K-6; elev. 660ft./201m.; mail Caneyville z 42721; ● 50
Sibert; RMC Place; CLAY; **181** L-15; mail Manchester z 40962; ● 150
Sidell; RMC Place; CLAY; ***181** K-15; mail Manchester z 40962; ● 100
Sideview; RMC Place; MONTGOMERY; ***181** H-14; elev. 902ft./275m.; mail Mount Sterling z 40353
Sideway; RMC Place; ELLIOTT; ***181** G-16; mail Olive Hill z 41164; rural
Sidney; RMC Place; PIKE; **181** J-19; elev. 752ft./229m.; 🄿; z 41564; ● 200
Siler; RMC Place; KNOX; **181** L-14; mail Corbin z 40701; ● 300
Siler; RMC Place; WHITLEY; ***181** M-14; elev. 988ft./301m.; 🄿; z 40763; ● 60
Silerville; RMC Place; MCCREARY; ***181** N-13; mail Strunk z 42649; rural
Silica; RMC Place; CARTER; ***181** G-16; mail Olive Hill z 41164; rural
Siloam; RMC Place; GREENUP; **181** E-17; ★ **PTSM**; mail South Shore z 41175; ● 175
Silver City; RMC Place; BUTLER; ***180** L-5; mail Morgantown z 42261; rural
Silver Creek; RMC Place; MADISON; ***181** J-13; mail Berea z 40403; rural
Silver Grove (Stevens); Inc. Place; CAMPBELL; **181** D-13; elev. 494ft./151m.; 🄿; ★ **CIN**; z 41085; Ⓟ 1,102; © 1,215
Silverhill; RMC Place; MORGAN; ***181** I-17; elev. 934ft./285m.; 🄿; z 41472; ● 15
Silver Lake Farm; RMC Place; FRANKLIN; ***181** G-11; mail Frankfort z 40601; pop. incl. with Frankfort (Inc. Place)
Simmons; RMC Place; OHIO; ***180** K-5; mail Mc Henry z 42354; rural
Simpson; RMC Place; BREATHITT; ***181** I-16; mail Campton z 41301; rural
SIMPSON; **180** M-6; Ⓟ 15,145; © 16,405; ◆ 17,099
Simpsonville; Inc. Place; SHELBY; **180** G-10; elev. 815ft./248m.; 🄿; z 40067; Ⓟ 907; © 1,281
Sims Fork; RMC Place; BELL; ***181** M-15; mail Arjay z 40902; rural
Sinai; RMC Place; ANDERSON; ***181** H-11; elev. 791ft./241m.; mail Lawrenceburg z 40342; rural
Sinking Fork; RMC Place; CHRISTIAN; ***180** L-2; mail Hopkinsville z 42240; rural
Sirocco; RMC Place; MEADE; ***180** H-7; mail Brandenburg z 40108; rural
Sitka; RMC Place; JOHNSON; **181** I-18; elev. 684ft./208m.; 🄿; z 41255; ● 150
Sizerock; RMC Place; LESLIE; **181** K-16; elev. 1,087ft./331m.; 🄿; z 41762; ● 40
Skillman; RMC Place; HANCOCK; ***180** I-5; elev. 417ft./127m.; mail Hawesville z 42348; rural
Skinnersburg; RMC Place; SCOTT; ***181** G-12; mail Stamping Ground z 40379; rural
Skycrest; RMC Place; FAYETTE; ***181** H-12; ★ **LEX**; mail Lexington z 40504; pop. incl. with Lexington (Inc. Place)
Skylight; RMC Place; OLDHAM; **180** F-9; ★ **LOU**; mail Goshen z 40026; ● 90
Skyline; RMC Place; LETCHER; ***181** L-17; elev. 1,067ft./325m.; 🄿; z 41821; rural
Slade; RMC Place; POWELL; **181** I-15; elev. 709ft./216m.; 🄿; z 40376; ● 80
Slat; RMC Place; WAYNE; ***181** M-11; 🄿; z 42633; rural
Slate Lick; RMC Place; MADISON; ***181** J-13; mail Berea z 40403; rural
Slater; RMC Place; BALLARD; ***180** E-2; elev. 468ft./143m.; mail Wickliffe z 42087; rural
Slate Valley; RMC Place; BATH; ***181** G-15; elev. 707ft./215m.; mail Owingsville z 40360
Slaughters; Inc. Place; WEBSTER; **180** J-3; elev. 452ft./138m.; 🄿; z 42456; Ⓟ 235; © 238
Slavans; RMC Place; MCCREARY; ***181** M-12; elev. 872ft./266m.; mail Whitley City z 42653; rural
Slemp; RMC Place; PERRY; **181** L-17; elev. 1,045ft./319m.; 🄿; z 41763; ● 50
Slickford; RMC Place; WAYNE; ***181** M-11; elev. 879ft./268m.; mail Monticello z 42633; rural
Slick Rock; RMC Place; BARREN; ***180** L-8; mail Glasgow z 42141; rural
Sligo; RMC Place; HENRY; **180** F-10; mail Pendleton z 40055; ● 60
Sloans Valley; RMC Place; PULASKI; **181** L-12; elev. 854ft./260m.; 🄿; z 42519; ● 200
Smilax; RMC Place; LESLIE; **181** L-16; elev. 926ft./282m.; 🄿; z 41764; ● 100
Smile; RMC Place; ROWAN; ***181** G-15; elev. 872ft./266m.; mail Morehead z 40351; rural
Smith; RMC Place; HARLAN; **181** M-16; elev. 1,367ft./417m.; 🄿; z 40831; ● 150
Smithfield; Inc. Place; HENRY; **180** G-10; elev. 891ft./272m.; 🄿; ★ **LOU**; z 40068; Ⓟ 115; © 102
Smithland; Inc. Place; ⊡ LIVINGSTON; **180** E-4; elev. 344ft./105m.; 🄿; z 42081; Ⓟ 384; © 401
Smith Mills; RMC Place; HENDERSON; **180** I-2; elev. 440ft./134m.; 🄿; z 42457; ● 450
Smiths Creek; RMC Place; CARTER; ***181** F-16; elev. 884ft./269m.; 🄿; z 41128 & mail Olive Hill z 41164; rural
Smiths Grove; Inc. Place; WARREN; **180** L-7; elev. 632ft./193m.; 🄿; ★ **BOWLG**; z 42171; Ⓟ 703; © 784
Smith Town; RMC Place; MCCREARY; ***181** M-12; mail Stearns z 42647; ● 175
Smithview; RMC Place; GRAYSON; ***180** J-6; mail Caneyville z 42721; ● 35
Smithwood; RMC Place; CALLOWAY; ***180** N-1; mail New Concord z 42076; ● 150
Smoky Valley; RMC Place; CARTER; ***181** G-16; mail Olive Hill z 41164; rural
Smyrna; RMC Place; JEFFERSON; ***180** H-9; ★ **LOU**; mail Louisville z 40219; became part of Louisville/Jefferson County Metro Jan. 6, 2003
Snell; RMC Place; PULASKI; ***181** L-13; mail Somerset z 42501; rural
Snow; RMC Place; CLINTON; ***180** M-10; elev. 980ft./299m.; 🄿; z 42602; rural
Snow Hill; RMC Place; SHELBY; ***180** G-10; mail Shelbyville z 40065; pop. incl. with Shelbyville (Inc. Place)
Soft Shell; RMC Place; KNOTT; **181** K-17; elev. 1,150ft./351m.; 🄿; z 41831; ● 30
Soldier; RMC Place; CARTER; **181** G-16; elev. 985ft./300m.; 🄿; z 41173; ● 200
Somerset; Inc. Place; ⊡ PULASKI; **181** L-12; elev. 975ft./297m.; 🄿 🄷 ■; z 42501-03 & mail West Somerset z 42564; Ⓟ 10,733; © 11,352; ◆ 12,553
Sonora; Inc. Place; HARDIN; **180** J-8; elev. 768ft./234m.; 🄿; z 42776; Ⓟ 295; © 350
Sorgho; RMC Place; DAVIESS; **180** I-4; elev. 390ft./119m.; ★ **OWNS**; mail Owensboro z 42301; ● 160
South; RMC Place; GRAYSON; **180** K-6; elev. 621ft./189m.; mail Leitchfield z 42754; ● 25
South Buffalo; RMC Place; LARUE; ***180** J-8; mail Buffalo z 42716; ● 180
South Campbellsville; RMC Place; TAYLOR; ***180** K-10; mail Campbellsville z 42718
South Carrollton; Inc. Place; MUHLENBERG; **180** K-4; elev. 458ft./140m.; 🄿; z 42374; Ⓟ 202; © 184
Southdown; RMC Place; LETCHER; ***181** K-18; mail Ermine z 41815; rural
South Elkhorn; RMC Place; FAYETTE; ***181** H-12; ★ **LEX**; mail Lexington z 40503; pop. incl. with Lexington (Inc. Place)
Southern Hills; RMC Place; MADISON; ***181** I-13; mail Richmond z 40475; pop. incl. with Richmond (Inc. Place)
South Fork; RMC Place; LINCOLN; ***181** K-12; elev. 968ft./295m.; mail Hustonville z 40437; rural
Southfork; RMC Place; OWSLEY; ***181** K-15; mail Booneville z 41314; rural
Southgate; Inc. Place; CAMPBELL; **181** B-17; elev. 625ft./191m.; 🄿; ★ **CIN**; z 41071; Ⓟ 3,266; © 3,472
South Higginsport; RMC Place; BRACKEN; ***181** E-14; mail Augusta z 41002; rural
South Highlands; RMC Place; GRAVES; ***180** G-3; mail Mayfield z 42066; ● 200
South Hill; RMC Place; BUTLER; ***180** L-5; mail Morgantown z 42261
South Irvine; RMC Place; ESTILL; **181** I-14; mail Irvine z 40336; ● 400
Southland; RMC Place; FAYETTE; ***181** H-12; ★ **LEX**; mail Lexington z 40503; pop. incl. with Lexington (Inc. Place)
South Marshall; RMC Place; MARSHALL; ***180** F-4; mail Benton z 42025; rural
South Park; RMC Place; JEFFERSON; **180** E-7; ★ **LOU**; mail Fairdale z 40118; became part of Louisville/Jefferson County Metro Jan. 6, 2003
South Park View; Inc. Place; JEFFERSON; **180** E-7; ★ **LOU**; mail Louisville z 40219; Ⓟ 214; © 196
Southport; RMC Place; FAYETTE; ***181** H-12; ★ **LEX**; mail Lexington z 40503; pop. incl. with Lexington (Inc. Place)
South Portsmouth; RMC Place; GREENUP; **181** E-17; elev. 540ft./165m.; 🄿; ★ **PTSM**; z 41174; ● 900
South Ripley; RMC Place; MASON; ***181** E-14; elev. 579ft./176m.; mail Dover z 41034; rural
South Shore (Taylor); Inc. Place; GREENUP; **181** E-17; elev. 546ft./166m.; 🄿; ★ **PTSM**; z 41175; Ⓟ 1,318; © 1,226
South Shores; RMC Place; SHELBY; ***180** G-10; mail Shelbyville z 40065; ● 60
South Union; RMC Place; LOGAN; **180** M-5; elev. 608ft./185m.; 🄿; z 42283; ● 75
Southville; RMC Place; SHELBY; ***180** H-10; elev. 809ft./247m.; mail Shelbyville z 40065
South Wallins; CDP; HARLAN; ***181** M-16; elev. 1,150ft./351m.; mail Wallins Creek z 40873; Ⓟ 1,022; © 996
South Williamson; RMC Place; PIKE; **181** I-19; 🄿 🄷; z 41503; ● 1,000
Southwire; RMC Place; HANCOCK; mail Hawesville z 42348; rural
Spa; RMC Place; LOGAN; **180** L-4; elev. 490ft./149m.; mail Lewisburg z 42256
Spann; RMC Place; WAYNE; ***181** M-11; mail Monticello z 42633; ● 100
Sparksville; RMC Place; ADAIR; **180** L-9; elev. 1,093ft./333m.; mail Columbia z 42728; ● 50
Sparta; Inc. Place; GALLATIN, OWEN; **181** E-11; elev. 503ft./153m.; 🄿; z 41086; Ⓟ 133; © 230
Spears; RMC Place; JESSAMINE; ***181** I-13; ★ **LEX**; mail Lexington z 40502
Speck; RMC Place; ADAIR, TAYLOR; ***180** K-10; mail Columbia z 42728; rural
Speedwell; RMC Place; MADISON; ***181** J-13; mail Richmond z 40475
Speight; RMC Place; PIKE; **181** K-18; elev. 1,113ft./339m.; 🄿; z 41572; ● 100
Spence; RMC Place; CAMPBELL; ***181** D-12; 🄿; ★ **CIN**; z 41071; pop. incl. with Newport (Inc. Place)
Spencer; RMC Place; MONTGOMERY; ***181** H-14; mail Mount Sterling z 40353; rural
SPENCER; **180** H-10; Ⓟ 6,801; © 11,766; ◆ 18,189
Spider; RMC Place; KNOTT; ***181** K-17; mail Pine Top z 41843; rural
Spindletop; RMC Place; SCOTT; ***181** H-12; elev. 897ft./273m.; ★ **LEX**; mail Georgetown z 40324; ● 300
Spiro; RMC Place; ROCKCASTLE; ***181** K-13; elev. 1,116ft./340m.; mail Mount Vernon z 40456; rural
Spottsville; RMC Place; HENDERSON; **180** I-3; elev. 374ft./114m.; 🄿; z 42458; ● 350
Spring Creek; RMC Place; CLAY; ***181** L-15; elev. 931ft./284m.; mail Manchester z 40962; rural
Springfield; Inc. Place; ⊡ WASHINGTON; **180** I-10; elev. 773ft./236m.; 🄿; z 40069; Ⓟ 2,875; © 2,634
Spring Grove; RMC Place; UNION; **180** I-1; elev. 416ft./127m.; mail Morganfield z 42437; ● 60
Spring Hill; RMC Place; HICKMAN; ***180** F-2; mail Clinton z 42031
Springhill; RMC Place; NELSON; ***180** I-9; mail Bardstown z 40004; pop. incl. with Bardstown (Inc. Place)
Springhill; RMC Place; WARREN; ***180** L-6; ★ **BOWLG**; mail Bowling Green z 42101; pop. incl. with Bowling Green (Inc. Place)
Spring Hill Estates; RMC Place; FRANKLIN; ***181** G-11; mail Frankfort z 40601; ● 300
Springlake; RMC Place; KENTON; ***181** D-12; ★ **CIN**; mail Latonia z 41015; rural
Springlee; RMC Place; JEFFERSON; **180** B-8; elev. 532ft./162m.; ★ **LOU**; mail Louisville z 40207; former incorporated place; became part of St. Matthews September 1, 2000; pop. incl. with Saint Matthews (Inc. Place); Ⓟ 451; © 426
Spring Lick; RMC Place; GRAYSON; **180** J-6; elev. 460ft./140m.; 🄿; z 42721; ● 40
Spring Mill; Inc. Place; JEFFERSON; **180** D-8; ★ **LOU**; mail Louisville z 40228; Ⓟ 342; © 380
Spring Station; RMC Place; WOODFORD; ***181** H-12; elev. 815ft./248m.; ★ **LEX**; mail Midway z 40347; rural
Spring Valley; Inc. Place; JEFFERSON; **180** A-9; ★ **LOU**; mail Louisville z 40222; Ⓟ 400; © 668
Sprout; RMC Place; NICHOLAS; ***181** G-14; elev. 745ft./227m.; mail Moorefield z 40350; rural
Spruce Pine; RMC Place; LESLIE; ***181** L-16; mail Warbranch z 40874; ● 40
Sprule; RMC Place; KNOX; ***181** L-14; elev. 968ft./295m.; mail Barbourville z 40906; rural
Spurlington; RMC Place; TAYLOR; ***180** K-10; elev. 1,007ft./307m.; mail Campbellsville z 42718; rural
Spurlock; RMC Place; CLAY; ***181** K-15; elev. 812ft./247m.; mail Oneida z 40972; rural
Squib; RMC Place; PULASKI; ***181** L-13; mail Somerset z 42501; rural
Squiresville; RMC Place; OWEN; ***181** F-11; mail Owenton z 40359; rural
Stab; RMC Place; PULASKI; **181** L-13; 🄿; z 42501; ● 20
Stacy (Rowdy); RMC Place; PERRY; **181** K-16; elev. 825ft./251m.; mail Rowdy z 41367; ● 70
Stacy Fork; RMC Place; MORGAN; ***181** I-16; elev. 822ft./251m.; 🄿; z 41472; rural
Staffordsburg; RMC Place; KENTON; ***181** E-12; elev. 876ft./267m.; ★ **CIN**; mail Independence z 41051; rural
Staffordsville; RMC Place; JOHNSON; **181** I-18; elev. 628ft./191m.; 🄿; z 41256; ● 200
Stambaugh; RMC Place; JOHNSON; ***181** I-18; elev. 672ft./205m.; 🄿; z 41257; rural
Stamping Ground; Inc. Place; SCOTT; **181** G-12; elev. 785ft./239m.; 🄿; z 40379; Ⓟ 698; © 566
Stanfill; RMC Place; HARLAN; ***181** M-16; mail Harlan z 40831; ● 80
Stanford; Inc. Place; ⊡ LINCOLN; **181** J-12; elev. 946ft./288m.; 🄿 🄷; z 40484; Ⓟ 2,686; © 3,430
Stanhope (Liberty); RMC Place; WEBSTER; ***180** J-2; mail Dixon z 42409
Stanley; RMC Place; DAVIESS; **180** I-4; elev. 388ft./118m.; 🄿; ★ **OWNS**; z 42375; ● 300

Entries in **UPPERCASE** are counties.
Entries in **bold** have populations of 2,500 or more.
Names in parentheses are alternate names.

Inc. Place	Incorporated Place
RMC Place	Rand McNally Designated Place
CDP	Census Designated Place
MCD	Minor Civil Division
⊡	County Seat
▲	Minor Civil Division
elev.	Elevation
🄿	Post Office
🄷	Hospital
🄲	College
■	Principal Business Center
★	Ranally Metro Area (RMA) Abbreviation
z	Zip Code(s)
Ⓟ	Previous Census Population
Ⓡ	Revised Census Population
Ⓐ	Annexation Population
●	Rand McNally Population Estimate
©	Final Census Population
Ⓢ	Special Census Population
◆	Estimated Population

For additional definitions see Glossary, Volume 1, and Introduction, Volume 2.

Stanton; Inc. Place; ⊡ POWELL; 181 I-14; elev. 662ft./202m.; 🅿; z 40380; Ⓟ 2,795; © 3,029
Stanville (Mare Creek); RMC Place; FLOYD; 181 J-18; elev. 653ft./199m.; 🅿; z 41659; ● 125
Stark; RMC Place; ELLIOTT; *181 G-17; elev. 1,109ft./338m.; 🅿; z 41164; ● 15
Star Mills; RMC Place; HARDIN; *180 J-8; mail Glendale z 42740; rural
Stateland; RMC Place; MADISON; *181 I-13; mail Richmond z 40475; pop. incl. with Richmond (Inc. Place)
State Line; RMC Place; FULTON; 180 G-2; mail Hickman z 42050; ● 10
Static; RMC Place; CLINTON; *180 N-10; 🅿; z 42602
Station Camp; RMC Place; ESTILL; *181 J-14; mail Irvine z 40336; rural
Stay; RMC Place; OWSLEY; *181 J-15; mail Ricetown z 41364; rural
Stearns; CDP; MCCREARY; 181 M-12; 🅿; z 42647 & mail Revelo z 42638; Ⓟ 1,550; © 1,586
Steele; RMC Place; PIKE; *181 J-20; elev. 1,144ft./349m.; 🅿; z 41566; rural
Steff; RMC Place; GRAYSON; 180 J-6; elev. 446ft./136m.; mail Caneyville z 42721; ● 10
Stella; RMC Place; CALLOWAY; 180 G-4; mail Murray z 42071; ● 100
Stella; RMC Place; MAGOFFIN; *181 I-17; elev. 861ft./262m.; 🅿; z 41465; rural
Stephens; RMC Place; ELLIOTT; 181 H-17; elev. 686ft./209m.; 🅿; z 41171; ● 15
Stephensburg; RMC Place; HARDIN; 180 J-7; elev. 687ft./209m.; 🅿; z 42724; ● 150
Stephensport; RMC Place; BRECKINRIDGE; 180 I-6; elev. 423ft./129m.; 🅿; z 40170; ● 200
Stepstone; RMC Place; MONTGOMERY; *181 H-14; mail Owingsville z 40360; rural
Steubenville; RMC Place; WAYNE; 181 M-11; elev. 899ft./274m.; 🅿; z 42633; ● 150
Stevens; CAMPBELL; see Silver Grove (Inc. Place)
Stewart; RMC Place; MERCER; *181 I-11; elev. 942ft./287m.; mail Harrodsburg z 40330, Perryville z 40468; rural
Stewartsville; RMC Place; GRANT; *181 F-12; elev. 909ft./277m.; mail Williamstown z 41097; rural
Stiles; RMC Place; NELSON; *180 J-9; elev. 535ft./163m.; mail New Haven z 40051; rural
Stillwater; RMC Place; WOLFE; *181 I-16; mail Campton z 41301; rural
Stinnett; RMC Place; LESLIE; 181 L-16; elev. 901ft./275m.; 🅿; z 40868; ● 125
Stinnettsville; RMC Place; BRECKINRIDGE; *180 I-7; elev. 810ft./247m.; mail Irvington z 40146; rural
Stinson; RMC Place; CARTER; *181 G-17; ★ **HNTG**; mail Grayson z 41143; rural
Stockholm; RMC Place; EDMONSON; *180 K-7; mail Mammoth Cave z 42259; rural
Stone; RMC Place; PIKE; *181 J-19; elev. 782ft./238m.; 🅿; z 41567; ● 300
Stonegate; RMC Place; WOODFORD; *181 H-12; ★ **LEX**; mail Versailles z 40383; ● 300
Stone Hedge Estates; RMC Place; SCOTT; *181 G-12; mail Georgetown z 40324; ● 250
Stonestreet; RMC Place; JEFFERSON; *180 H-8; elev. 460ft./140m.; ★ **LOU**; mail Louisville z 40272; became part of Louisville/Jefferson County Metro Jan. 6, 2003
Stonewall; RMC Place; BRACKEN; *181 F-14; elev. 921ft./281m.; mail Brooksville z 41004
Stonewall; RMC Place; SCOTT; *181 F-12; mail Sadieville z 40370; rural
Stonewall Estates; RMC Place; FAYETTE; *181 H-12; ★ **LEX**; mail Lexington z 40503; pop. incl. with Lexington (Inc. Place)
Stonewall Estates; RMC Place; FRANKLIN; *181 G-11; mail Frankfort z 40601; ● 150
Stoney Fork; RMC Place; BELL; 181 M-15; elev. 1,097ft./334m.; 🅿; z 40988; ● 125
Stoney Point; RMC Place; BRACKEN; *181 E-14; mail Dover z 41034; rural
Stony Fork Junction; RMC Place; BELL; mail Middlesboro z 40965; pop. incl. with Middlesboro (Inc. Place)
Stony Point; RMC Place; BOURBON; *181 H-13; elev. 946ft./288m.; mail Paris z 40361; ● 30
Stop; RMC Place; WAYNE; 🅿; z 42633; rural
Stopover; RMC Place; PIKE; *181 J-20; elev. 1,099ft./335m.; 🅿; z 41568; ● 200
Stormking; RMC Place; PERRY; mail Hazard z 41701; rural
Stovall; RMC Place; BARREN; *180 L-7; mail Park City z 42160; rural
Straight Creek; RMC Place; BELL; 181 M-15; elev. 1,016ft./310m.; mail Pineville z 40977; ● 50
Strait Creek; RMC Place; CARTER; *181 G-17; mail Denton z 41132; rural
Strathmoor Gardens; RMC Place; JEFFERSON; *180 G-9; elev. 530ft./162m.; ★ **LOU**; mail Louisville z 40205; pop. incl. with Strathmoor Village (Inc. Place)
Strathmoor Manor; Inc. Place; JEFFERSON; *180 G-9; elev. 530ft./162m.; ★ **LOU**; mail Louisville z 40205; Ⓟ 391; © 333
Strathmoor Village; Inc. Place; JEFFERSON; 180 C-8; elev. 530ft./162m.; ★ **LOU**; mail Louisville z 40205; Ⓟ 361; © 625
Straw; RMC Place; EDMONSON; *180 K-7; elev. 810ft./247m.; mail Mammoth Cave z 42259; rural
Strawberry; RMC Place; JEFFERSON; ★ **LOU**; pop. incl. with Louisville (Inc. Place)
Stricklett; RMC Place; LEWIS; *181 F-16; mail Vanceburg z 41179; rural
Stringtown; RMC Place; ANDERSON; *181 H-11; mail Lawrenceburg z 40342; ● 250
Stringtown; RMC Place; BOONE; 181 B-14; ★ **CIN**; mail Hebron z 41048; ● 40
Stringtown; RMC Place; FLEMING; *181 G-15; mail Hillsboro z 41049; rural
Stringtown; RMC Place; GRANT; *181 F-12; elev. 917ft./280m.; mail Berry z 41003; rural
Stringtown; RMC Place; LAWRENCE; *181 G-18; mail Louisa z 41230; ● 50
Stringtown; RMC Place; MADISON; *181 I-13; mail Richmond z 40475; rural
Stringtown; RMC Place; MAGOFFIN; *181 I-17; mail Salyersville z 41465; rural
Stringtown; RMC Place; MCLEAN; *180 J-3; mail Sacramento z 42372; rural
Stringtown; RMC Place; MERCER; *181 I-11; mail Harrodsburg z 40330
Stringtown; RMC Place; MUHLENBERG; *180 K-3; elev. 410ft./125m.; mail Sacramento z 42372; rural
Stringtown; PIKE; see Burnwell (RMC Place)
Strunk; RMC Place; MCCREARY; 181 N-13; elev. 1,426ft./435m.; 🅿; z 42649; ● 70
Stubblefield; RMC Place; GRAVES; *180 G-3; mail Wingo z 42088; rural
Sturgeon; RMC Place; OWSLEY; *181 K-15; mail Booneville z 41314; rural
Sturgis; Inc. Place; UNION; 180 J-1; elev. 370ft./113m.; 🅿; z 42459; Ⓟ 2,184; © 2,030; Ⓡ 2,056
Sublett; RMC Place; MAGOFFIN; *181 I-17; elev. 882ft./269m.; 🅿; z 41465
Sublimity City; RMC Place; LAUREL; 181 L-14; mail London z 40744; ● 800
Subtle; METCALFE; see Moore Spring (RMC Place)
Sudith; RMC Place; MENIFEE; *181 H-15; elev. 750ft./229m.; 🅿; z 40371
Sugar Creek; RMC Place; GALLATIN; 181 E-11; mail Warsaw z 41095; ● 25
Sugar Grove; RMC Place; BUTLER; *180 L-5; mail Morgantown z 42261
Sugar Hill; RMC Place; PULASKI; *181 L-12; mail Somerset z 42501; rural
Sugartit; RMC Place; BOONE; 181 D-12; elev. 796ft./243m.; ★ **CIN**; mail Florence z 41042
Sullivan; RMC Place; UNION; 180 J-1; elev. 377ft./115m.; 🅿; z 42460; ● 300
Sulphur; RMC Place; HENRY; 180 F-10; elev. 691ft./211m.; 🅿; z 40055, z 40070; ● 220
Sulphur Lick; RMC Place; MONROE; *180 M-8; mail Summer Shade z 42166, Tompkinsville z 42167; rural
Sulphur Springs; RMC Place; OHIO; 180 J-5; mail Hartford z 42347; ● 30
Sulphur Well; RMC Place; JESSAMINE; *181 I-12; mail Nicholasville z 40356
Sulphur Well; RMC Place; METCALFE; 180 L-9; elev. 612ft./187m.; 🅿; z 42129; ● 50
Summer Shade; RMC Place; METCALFE; 180 M-8; elev. 877ft./267m.; 🅿; z 42166 & mail Eighty Eight z 42130; ● 300
Summersville; RMC Place; GREEN; 180 K-9; elev. 820ft./250m.; 🅿; z 42782; ● 150
Summit (Summitt); RMC Place; BOYD; 181 F-18; ★ **HNTG**; mail Ashland z 41101-02, z 41105; ● 900
Summit; RMC Place; HARDIN; 180 J-7; elev. 852ft./260m.; 🅿; z 42732; ● 150
Summit Hills Heights; RMC Place; KENTON; *181 D-12; ★ **CIN**; mail Ft Mitchell z 41017; pop. incl. with Edgewood (Inc. Place)
Summitt; BOYD; see Summit (RMC Place)
Sumpter; RMC Place; WAYNE; *181 M-11; mail Monticello z 42633; rural
Sunfish; RMC Place; EDMONSON; 180 K-6; elev. 522ft./159m.; 🅿; z 42210; ● 30
Sunny Acres; RMC Place; KENTON; *181 D-12; ★ **CIN**; mail Latonia z 41015; pop. incl. with Taylor Mill (Inc. Place)
Sunnybrook; RMC Place; WAYNE; *181 N-11; elev. 939ft./286m.; 🅿; z 42633; rural
Sunny Corner; RMC Place; HANCOCK; *180 I-5; mail Hawesville z 42348; rural
Sunnydale; RMC Place; OHIO; *180 J-5; elev. 426ft./130m.; mail Hartford z 42347; rural
Sunnyside; RMC Place; WARREN; *180 L-7; elev. 559ft./170m.; ★ **BOWLG**; mail Bowling Green z 42101; rural
Sunrise; RMC Place; HARRISON; 181 F-13; elev. 819ft./250m.; mail Cynthiana z 41031; ● 45
Sunset; RMC Place; FLEMING; *181 G-15; mail Hillsboro z 41049; rural
Sunshine; RMC Place; GREENUP; *181 E-17; elev. 556ft./169m.; ★ **PTSM**; mail South Shore z 41175; ● 250
Sunshine; RMC Place; HARLAN; 181 M-16; mail Harlan z 40831; ● 350
Susie; RMC Place; WAYNE; *181 M-11; elev. 1,041ft./317m.; 🅿; z 42633; rural
Sussex Estates; RMC Place; JESSAMINE; *181 I-12; ★ **LEX**; mail Nicholasville z 40356; ● 50
Suterville; RMC Place; SCOTT; *181 G-12; mail Stamping Ground z 40379; rural
Sutherland; RMC Place; DAVIESS; *180 J-4; elev. 400ft./122m.; mail Utica z 42376; rural
Sutton; RMC Place; PIKE; *181 J-19; mail Flemingsburg z 41041, Shelbiana z 41562; ● 75
Suwanee; RMC Place; LYON; *180 L-1; mail Kuttawa z 42055; ● 100
Swallowfield; RMC Place; FRANKLIN; *181 G-11; mail Frankfort z 40601; ● 90
Swamp Branch; RMC Place; JOHNSON; 181 I-17; elev. 667ft./203m.; 🅿; z 41240; ● 10
Swampton; RMC Place; MAGOFFIN; *181 I-17; elev. 908ft./277m.; 🅿; z 41465
Swanee Shores; RMC Place; GRANT; *181 F-12; mail Williamstown z 41097; ● 30
Swan Lake; RMC Place; KNOX; *181 M-14; mail Barbourville z 40906; rural
Swanpond; RMC Place; KNOX; *181 M-14; 🅿; z 40906; rural
Sweeden; RMC Place; EDMONSON; 180 K-7; elev. 772ft./235m.; 🅿; z 42285; ● 125
Sweeneyville; RMC Place; TAYLOR; *180 K-9; elev. 788ft./240m.; mail Campbellsville z 42718; rural
Sweet Owen; RMC Place; OWEN; *181 F-11; mail Owenton z 40359; rural
Switzer; RMC Place; FRANKLIN; *181 G-11; mail Frankfort z 40601; ● 150
Sycamore; Inc. Place; JEFFERSON; *180 G-9; ★ **LOU**; mail Louisville z 40223; Ⓟ 70; © 159
Sycamore Estates; RMC Place; WOODFORD; *181 H-12; ★ **LEX**; mail Versailles z 40383; ● 650
Sylvandell; RMC Place; HARRISON; *181 F-13; mail Cynthiana z 41031; rural
Sylvania; RMC Place; JEFFERSON; *180 H-8; ★ **LOU**; mail Louisville z 40258; became part of Louisville/Jefferson County Metro Jan. 6, 2003
Symbol; RMC Place; LAUREL; *181 K-13; 🅿; z 40729; rural
Symsonia; RMC Place; GRAVES; 180 F-4; elev. 400ft./122m.; 🅿; z 42082; ● 500

T

Tabernacle; RMC Place; TODD; *180 M-4; mail Elkton z 42220; rural
Tablow; RMC Place; MERCER, WASHINGTON; *181 I-11; mail Harrodsburg z 40330; rural
Tacky Town; RMC Place; HARLAN; *181 M-16; mail Stoney Fork z 40988; ● 50
Taffy; RMC Place; OHIO; *180 J-5; elev. 492ft./150m.; mail Hartford z 42347; rural
Taft; RMC Place; OWSLEY; *181 K-15; mail Booneville z 41314; rural
Talbert; RMC Place; BREATHITT; 181 J-16; elev. 793ft./242m.; 🅿; z 41339; ● 75
Talcum; RMC Place; KNOTT; 181 K-17; elev. 895ft./273m.; 🅿; z 41722; ● 300
Tallega; RMC Place; LEE; 181 J-15; elev. 733ft./223m.; 🅿; z 41311; ● 30
Talmage; RMC Place; MERCER; *181 I-11; elev. 821ft./250m.; mail Harrodsburg z 40330
Tanbark; RMC Place; CUMBERLAND; *180 M-10; mail Burkesville z 42717; rural
Tanglewood; RMC Place; FRANKLIN; *181 H-11; mail Frankfort z 40601; pop. incl. with Frankfort (Inc. Place)
Tanksley; RMC Place; CLAY; *181 K-15; elev. 820ft./250m.; 🅿; z 40962; rural
Tanner; RMC Place; LARUE; *180 J-8; elev. 819ft./250m.; mail Hodgenville z 42748; rural
Tar Fork; RMC Place; BRECKINRIDGE; *180 I-6; mail Cloverport z 40111; rural
Tar Hill; RMC Place; GRAYSON; *180 J-7; elev. 712ft./217m.; mail Leitchfield z 42754; rural
Tarryon Number 1; RMC Place; LYON; *180 L-1; mail Kuttawa z 42055; summer pop. 100
Tates Creek Estates; RMC Place; JESSAMINE; *181 I-12; ★ **LEX**; mail Nicholasville z 40356; ● 750
Tateville; RMC Place; PULASKI; 181 L-12; elev. 872ft./266m.; 🅿; z 42558; ● 500
Tatham Springs; RMC Place; WASHINGTON; *180 I-10; mail Willisburg z 40078; rural
Tattersail Trails Estates; RMC Place; WHITLEY; *181 M-13; mail Corbin z 40701; ● 300
Tatumsville; RMC Place; MARSHALL; *180 F-4; mail Gilbertsville z 42044; rural
Taulbee; RMC Place; BREATHITT; *181 J-16; mail Vancleve z 41385; rural
Taylor; GREENUP; see South Shore (Inc. Place)
TAYLOR; 180 K-10; Ⓟ 21,146; © 22,927; ◆ 23,968
Taylor Mill; Inc. Place; KENTON; 181 C-17; elev. 890ft./271m.; 🅿; ★ **CIN**; z 41015; Ⓟ 5,530; © 6,913
Taylor Mines; RMC Place; OHIO; *180 K-5; mail Beaver Dam z 42320; rural
Taylorsport; RMC Place; BOONE; 181 A-13; ★ **CIN**; mail Hebron z 41048; ● 100
Taylors Store; RMC Place; CALLOWAY; *180 G-4; mail Hazel z 42049; ● 15
Taylorsville; Inc. Place; ⊡ SPENCER; 180 H-10; elev. 490ft./149m.; 🅿; z 40071; Ⓟ 774; © 1,009
Teaberry; RMC Place; FLOYD; 181 J-18; elev. 838ft./255m.; 🅿; z 41660; ● 100
Tedders; RMC Place; KNOX; *181 L-14; elev. 1,049ft./320m.; 🅿; z 40906; rural
Teddy; RMC Place; CASEY; *181 L-11; mail Liberty z 42539; rural
Teetersville; RMC Place; HARLAN; *181 M-16; mail Harlan z 40831; ● 150
Teges; RMC Place; CLAY; *181 K-15; elev. 773ft./236m.; mail Oneida z 40972; rural
Temperance; RMC Place; SIMPSON; *180 M-6; mail Franklin z 42134; rural
Temple Hill; RMC Place; BARREN; 180 M-8; elev. 803ft./245m.; mail Glasgow z 42141; ● 75
Ten Broeck; Inc. Place; JEFFERSON; *180 G-9; ★ **LOU**; mail Louisville z 40222; Ⓟ 128; © 129
Ten Spot; RMC Place; HARLAN; mail Evarts z 40828
Teresita; RMC Place; OWEN; *181 G-11; mail Owenton z 40359; rural
Terrapin; RMC Place; MERCER; *181 I-11; elev. 897ft./273m.; mail Harrodsburg z 40330
Terryville; RMC Place; LAWRENCE; *181 H-17; mail Martha z 41159; rural
Texas; RMC Place; WASHINGTON; 180 J-10; elev. 897ft./273m.; mail Springfield z 40069; ● 60
Texola; RMC Place; ESTILL; *181 J-14; mail Irvine z 40336; ● 20
Thealka; RMC Place; JOHNSON; 181 I-18; elev. 800ft./244m.; 🅿; z 41240; ● 400
The Colony; RMC Place; FAYETTE; *181 H-12; ★ **LEX**; mail Lexington z 40504; pop. incl. with Lexington (Inc. Place)
The Colony; RMC Place; WOODFORD; *181 H-12; ★ **LEX**; mail Versailles z 40383; ● 220
The Crossings; BOONE; see Boone Aire (RMC Place)
Thelma; RMC Place; JOHNSON; *181 I-18; elev. 626ft./191m.; 🅿; z 41260; ● 250
The Moors; RMC Place; MARSHALL; *180 L-1; mail Gilbertsville z 42044; ● 300
The Ridge; RMC Place; ELLIOTT; *181 H-16; mail Sandy Hook z 41171; rural
Thistleton Heights; RMC Place; FRANKLIN; *181 H-11; mail Frankfort z 40601; pop. incl. with Frankfort (Inc. Place)
Thixton; RMC Place; JEFFERSON; *180 H-9; ★ **LOU**; mail Louisville z 40291; became part of Louisville/Jefferson County Metro Jan. 6, 2003
Thomas; RMC Place; FLOYD; *181 I-18; mail Prestonsburg z 41653; rural
Thompsonville; RMC Place; WASHINGTON; *180 I-10; mail Springfield z 40069; rural
Thorn Hill; RMC Place; FRANKLIN; *181 G-11; mail Frankfort z 40601; pop. incl. with Frankfort (Inc. Place)
Thornhill; Inc. Place; JEFFERSON; *180 G-9; ★ **LOU**; mail Louisville z 40222; Ⓟ 146; © 175
Thornton; RMC Place; LETCHER; *181 K-18; elev. 1,600ft./488m.; 🅿; z 41855; ● 200
Thorobred East Subdivision Number 2; RMC Place; DAVIESS; *180 I-4; ★ **OWNS**; mail Owensboro z 42301; ● 350
Thousandsticks; RMC Place; LESLIE; 181 K-16; elev. 966ft./294m.; 🅿; z 41766; ● 70
Threeforks; RMC Place; MARTIN; *181 I-19; elev. 649ft./198m.; 🅿; z 41224; ● 75
Three Forks; RMC Place; WARREN; *180 L-7; mail Oakland z 42159; rural
Threelinks; RMC Place; JACKSON, ROCKCASTLE; *181 J-13; mail Mount Vernon z 40456; rural
Three Mile; RMC Place; GREENUP; *181 F-18; ★ **HNTG**; mail Greenup z 41144; rural
Three Point; RMC Place; HARLAN; *181 M-16; 🅿; z 40815; ● 100
Three Springs; RMC Place; HART; 180 L-8; mail Hardyville z 42746; ● 30
Three Springs; RMC Place; WARREN; *180 M-6; ★ **BOWLG**; mail Bowling Green z 42104; ● 80
Thruston; RMC Place; DAVIESS; 180 I-4; elev. 405ft./123m.; ★ **OWNS**; mail Owensboro z 42301; ● 150
Thurlow; RMC Place; GREEN; *180 K-9; mail Greensburg z 42743
Tierra Linda; RMC Place; FRANKLIN; *181 G-11; mail Frankfort z 40601; pop. incl. with Frankfort (Inc. Place)
Tierra Linda III; RMC Place; FRANKLIN; *181 G-11; mail Frankfort z 40601; pop. incl. with Frankfort (Inc. Place)
Tilden; RMC Place; WEBSTER; 180 J-2; mail Dixon z 42409; ● 40
Tilford; RMC Place; BUTLER; *180 K-6; elev. 569ft./173m.; mail Caneyville z 42721
Tiline; RMC Place; LIVINGSTON; 180 E-5; elev. 375ft./114m.; 🅿; z 42083; ● 75
Tilton; RMC Place; FLEMING; 181 G-15; mail Flemingsburg z 41041; ● 50
Timber Lake; RMC Place; PULASKI; mail Bronston z 42518; ● 65
Timberwood Lake Shores; RMC Place; OWEN; *181 F-12; mail Corinth z 41010; ● 60
Timsley (Tinsley); RMC Place; BELL; 181 M-15; elev. 1,004ft./306m.; mail Pineville z 40977; ● 100
Tina; RMC Place; KNOTT; *181 K-17; elev. 1,058ft./322m.; 🅿; z 41740; rural
Tinsley; BELL; see Timsley (RMC Place)
Tiny Town; RMC Place; TODD; 180 N-4; 🅿; z 42234; pop. incl. with Guthrie (Inc. Place)
Tiptop; RMC Place; MAGOFFIN; *181 J-17; mail Salyersville z 41465; rural
Titan Siding; RMC Place; PIKE; *181 J-19; pop. incl. with Pikeville (Inc. Place)
Tobacco; CALLOWAY; see Midway (RMC Place)
TODD; 180 M-4; Ⓟ 10,940; © 11,971; ◆ 12,104
Todds Point; RMC Place; SHELBY; *180 G-10; mail Shelbyville z 40065
Toddville; RMC Place; GARRARD; *181 I-12; mail Lancaster z 40444; rural
Toler; RMC Place; PIKE; *181 J-19; elev. 673ft./205m.; 🅿; z 41514; ● 400
Toliver; RMC Place; WOLFE; *181 I-16; mail Hazel Green z 41332; rural
Tollesboro; RMC Place; LEWIS; 181 F-15; elev. 816ft./249m.; 🅿; z 41189; ● 600
Tolliver Town; RMC Place; LETCHER; *181 K-18; mail Cromona z 41810; ● 50
Tolu; RMC Place; CRITTENDEN; 180 J-1; elev. 373ft./114m.; 🅿; z 42084; ● 150
Tomahawk; RMC Place; MARTIN; 181 I-18; elev. 671ft./205m.; 🅿; z 41262; ● 150
Tompkinsville; Inc. Place; ⊡ MONROE; 180 M-9; elev. 923ft./281m.; 🅿 🄷; z 42167; Ⓟ 2,861; © 2,660
Tonieville; RMC Place; LARUE; *180 J-8; mail Hodgenville z 42748; ● 20
Toonerville; RMC Place; PIKE; *181 K-20; mail Mouthcard z 41548; rural
Topmost; RMC Place; KNOTT; 181 K-18; elev. 826ft./252m.; 🅿; z 41862; ● 200
Topton; RMC Place; LAUREL; mail London z 40741; rural
Torrent; RMC Place; WOLFE; *181 I-15; elev. 945ft./288m.; mail Campton z 41301; rural
Totz; RMC Place; HARLAN; 181 L-17; elev. 1,328ft./405m.; 🅿; z 40870; ● 250
Toulouse; RMC Place; LESLIE; *181 K-16; mail Busy z 41723; rural
Touristville; RMC Place; WAYNE; *181 M-12; elev. 896ft./273m.; 🅿; z 42633
Tousey; RMC Place; GRAYSON; *180 J-6; mail Falls of Rough z 40119; rural
Town and Country; RMC Place; DAVIESS; *180 I-4; ★ **OWNS**; mail Owensboro z 42301; ● 200
Town and Country; RMC Place; LOGAN; *180 M-5; mail Russellville z 42276; ● 90
Tracy; RMC Place; BARREN; *180 M-8; elev. 853ft./260m.; mail Fountain Run z 42133; rural
Trailwood Lakes; RMC Place; SHELBY; *181 G-11; mail Bagdad z 40003; rural
Tram; RMC Place; FLOYD; 181 J-18; elev. 651ft./198m.; 🅿; z 41663; ● 125
Trammel; RMC Place; ALLEN; *180 M-6; elev. 738ft./225m.; mail Scottsville z 42164; rural
Trapp; RMC Place; CLARK; 181 I-14; elev. 807ft./246m.; mail Winchester z 40391; ● 30
Trappist (Abbey of Our Lady of Gethsemani); RMC Place; NELSON; *180 J-9; elev. 571ft./174m.; 🅿; z 40051; rural
Travellers Rest; RMC Place; OWSLEY; *181 J-15; mail Booneville z 41314; ● 60
Treasure Island; RMC Place; JEFFERSON; *180 H-9; ★ **LOU**; mail Louisville z 40229; became part of Louisville/Jefferson County Metro Jan. 6, 2003
Tremont; RMC Place; HARLAN; *181 M-16; mail Wallins Creek z 40873; ● 150
Trent; RMC Place; WOLFE; *181 I-16; mail Campton z 41301
Trenton; Inc. Place; TODD; 180 M-3; elev. 596ft./182m.; 🅿; z 42286; Ⓟ 378; © 419
Tress Shop; RMC Place; TODD; *180 M-4; elev. 681ft./208m.; mail Elkton z 42220
Tribbey; RMC Place; PERRY; *181 K-17; elev. 974ft./297m.; 🅿; z 41722; rural
Tribune; RMC Place; CRITTENDEN; *180 K-1; elev. 433ft./132m.; mail Marion z 42064; rural
Tri City; RMC Place; GRAVES; 180 G-4; elev. 523ft./159m.; mail Farmington z 42040; ● 110
TRIGG; 180 M-2; Ⓟ 10,361; © 12,597; ◆ 13,684
Trigg Furnace; RMC Place; TRIGG; *180 M-1; mail Cadiz z 42211; rural
Trimble; RMC Place; PULASKI; *181 L-12; elev. 921ft./281m.; 🅿; z 42544; rural
TRIMBLE; 180 F-10; Ⓟ 6,090; © 8,125; ◆ 9,026
Trinity; RMC Place; LEWIS; *181 E-15; elev. 563ft./172m.; 🅿; z 41179; ● 40
Trisler; RMC Place; OHIO; *180 J-5; mail Fordsville z 42343; rural
Trosper; RMC Place; KNOX; 181 M-15; elev. 1,007ft./307m.; 🅿; z 40995; ● 120
Troublesome; RMC Place; PERRY; *181 K-17; mail Ary z 41712; rural
Troy; RMC Place; WOODFORD; *181 I-12; mail Versailles z 40383
Tuckertown; RMC Place; WARREN; *180 L-7; ★ **BOWLG**; mail Oakland z 42159; rural
Tuggleville; RMC Place; BELL; *181 M-16; elev. 1,130ft./344m.; mail Hulen z 40845
Tunnel Hill; RMC Place; HARDIN; *180 I-8; elev. 800ft./244m.; mail Elizabethtown z 42701; ● 200
Turkey; RMC Place; BREATHITT; *181 J-15; elev. 709ft./216m.; 🅿; z 41314; rural
Turkey Creek; RMC Place; PIKE; *181 I-19; elev. 652ft./199m.; 🅿; z 41514; ● 500
Turkey Foot; RMC Place; SCOTT; *181 G-12; elev. 829ft./253m.; mail Sadieville z 40370; rural
Turkeytown; RMC Place; LINCOLN; *181 K-12; elev. 942ft./287m.; mail Crab Orchard z 40419; rural
Turners Station; RMC Place; HENRY; *180 F-10; elev. 747ft./228m.; 🅿; z 40075; ● 50
Turnersville; RMC Place; LINCOLN; *181 J-12; elev. 935ft./285m.; mail Stanford z 40484; rural
Turnertown; RMC Place; BUTLER; *180 L-5; mail Lewisburg z 42256; rural
Turnertown; RMC Place; SIMPSON; *180 M-5; mail Franklin z 42134; rural
Tutor Key; RMC Place; JOHNSON; *181 I-18; elev. 605ft./184m.; 🅿; z 41263; ● 120
Tuttle; RMC Place; LAUREL; *181 L-14; elev. 1,174ft./358m.; 🅿; z 40741 & mail London z 40744; rural
Tway; RMC Place; HARLAN; *181 M-16; mail Harlan z 40831; pop. incl. with Harlan (Inc. Place)
Twentysix; RMC Place; MORGAN; *181 H-16; mail West Liberty z 41472; rural
Twila (Creech); RMC Place; HARLAN; *181 M-16; mail Wallins Creek z 40873; rural
Twin Lakes; RMC Place; BOONE; *181 E-12; ★ **CIN**; mail Union z 41091; ● 150
Twin Oaks; RMC Place; FAYETTE; *181 H-12; ★ **LEX**; mail Lexington z 40503; pop. incl. with Lexington (Inc. Place)
Two Creeks; RMC Place; FRANKLIN; *181 G-11; mail Frankfort z 40601; ● 150
Tyewhoppety; RMC Place; TODD; *180 L-4; mail Clifty z 42216; rural
Tyner; RMC Place; JACKSON; 181 K-14; elev. 1,182ft./360m.; 🅿; z 40486; ● 100
Typo; RMC Place; PERRY; *181 K-16; elev. 842ft./257m.; 🅿; z 41701; ● 60
Tyrone; RMC Place; ANDERSON; 181 H-11; elev. 523ft./159m.; mail Lawrenceburg z 40342; ● 100

U

Ula; RMC Place; PULASKI; *181 L-13; mail Somerset z 42501; rural
Ulvah; RMC Place; LETCHER; 181 L-17; elev. 962ft./293m.; 🅿; z 41731; ● 75
Ulysses; RMC Place; LAWRENCE; 181 H-18; elev. 595ft./181m.; 🅿; z 41264; ● 30
Union; Inc. Place; BOONE; 181 D-12; elev. 831ft./253m.; 🅿; ★ **CIN**; z 41091; Ⓟ 1,001; © 2,893
UNION; 180 J-2; Ⓟ 16,557; © 15,637; ◆ 14,836
Union City; RMC Place; MADISON; *181 I-13; mail Richmond z 40475; ● 90
Union Hall; RMC Place; ESTILL; *181 I-14; mail Ravenna z 40472; rural
Union Mills; RMC Place; JESSAMINE; *181 I-12; elev. 881ft./269m.; ★ **LEX**; mail Nicholasville z 40356
Union Ridge; RMC Place; MUHLENBERG; *180 L-4; rural
Union Star; RMC Place; BRECKINRIDGE; 180 H-6; elev. 744ft./227m.; 🅿; z 40171; ● 50
Uniontown; Inc. Place; UNION; 180 I-1; elev. 360ft./110m.; 🅿; z 42461; Ⓟ 1,008; © 1,064
University Estates; RMC Place; HARDIN; *180 J-8; mail Elizabethtown z 42701; ● 400
University Heights; RMC Place; CHRISTIAN; *180 M-3; ★ **HPKNV**; mail Hopkinsville z 42240; pop. incl. with Hopkinsville (Inc. Place)
Uno; RMC Place; HART; 180 K-8; mail Horse Cave z 42749; ● 25
Upchurch; RMC Place; CLINTON; *180 M-10; mail Albany z 42602; rural
Upper Kings Addition; RMC Place; GREENUP; *181 E-17; ★ **PTSM**; mail South Shore z 41175; ● 350
Upper Tygart; RMC Place; CARTER; *181 G-16; elev. 845ft./258m.; 🅿; z 41164
Upton; Inc. Place; HARDIN, LARUE; 180 J-8; elev. 744ft./227m.; 🅿; z 42784; Ⓟ 719; © 654
Urban; RMC Place; CLAY; *181 L-14; elev. 886ft./270m.; 🅿; z 40962; rural
Utica; RMC Place; DAVIESS; 180 J-4; elev. 416ft./127m.; 🅿; z 42376; ● 300
Utility; RMC Place; HANCOCK; *180 I-5; mail Hawesville z 42348
Uttingertown; RMC Place; FAYETTE; *181 H-13; ★ **LEX**; mail Lexington z 40516; pop. incl. with Lexington (Inc. Place)

V

Vada; RMC Place; LEE; *181 J-15; elev. 3,876ft./1,181m.; 🅿; z 41311; rural
Valeria; RMC Place; WOLFE; *181 I-15; elev. 1,031ft./314m.; 🅿; z 41301; rural
Valley Downs; RMC Place; JEFFERSON; *180 H-8; elev. 450ft./137m.; ★ **LOU**; mail Louisville z 40272; became part of Louisville/Jefferson County Metro Jan. 6, 2003
Valley Gardens; RMC Place; JEFFERSON; *180 H-8; ★ **LOU**; mail Louisville z 40258; became part of Louisville/Jefferson County Metro Jan. 6, 2003
Valley Hill; RMC Place; WASHINGTON; *180 I-10; mail Springfield z 40069; rural
Valley Oak; RMC Place; PULASKI; *181 K-12; mail Somerset z 42501; rural
Valley Station; CDP; JEFFERSON; *180 H-8; 🅿; ★ **LOU**; z 40272 & mail Louisville z 40258, z 40270; former CDP; became part of Louisville/Jefferson County Metro Jan. 6, 2003; Ⓟ 22,840; © 22,946; ◆ 0
Valley View; RMC Place; BRACKEN; *181 E-14; mail Augusta z 41002; ● 50
Valley View; RMC Place; MADISON; 181 I-13; elev. 568ft./173m.; mail Richmond z 40475; ● 150
Valley Village; RMC Place; JEFFERSON; *180 H-8; ★ **LOU**; mail Louisville z 40272; became part of Louisville/Jefferson County Metro Jan. 6, 2003
Van; RMC Place; LETCHER; *181 L-18; elev. 1,232ft./376m.; 🅿; z 41858; rural
Vanarsdell; RMC Place; MERCER; *181 I-11; mail Harrodsburg z 40330; rural
Vanceburg; Inc. Place; ⊡ LEWIS; 181 F-16; elev. 525ft./160m.; 🅿; z 41179 & mail Emerson z 41135; Ⓟ 1,713; © 1,731
Vancleve; RMC Place; BREATHITT; 181 J-16; elev. 732ft./223m.; 🅿; z 41385; ● 80
Vanderburg; RMC Place; WEBSTER; *180 J-2; elev. 584ft./178m.; mail Dixon z 42409; rural
Vandetta; RMC Place; HOPKINS; *180 J-3; elev. 396ft./121m.; mail Hanson z 42413; rural
Vanhook; RMC Place; PULASKI; *181 K-13; mail Somerset z 42501; rural
Van Lear; RMC Place; JOHNSON; 181 I-18; elev. 624ft./190m.; 🅿; z 41265; ● 1,050
Van Lear Junction; JOHNSON; see West Van Lear (RMC Place)
Van Voorhis Manor; RMC Place; MEADE; *180 I-8; mail Fort Knox z 40121
Vanzant; RMC Place; BRECKINRIDGE; *180 J-6; elev. 684ft./208m.; 🅿; z 40119; rural
Varilla; RMC Place; BELL; *181 M-15; mail Calvin z 40813; ● 90
Varney; RMC Place; PIKE; *181 J-19; elev. 907ft./276m.; 🅿; z 41571; ● 50
Veech; RMC Place; SHELBY; *180 H-10; mail Finchville z 40022; rural
Venters; RMC Place; PIKE; *181 K-19; mail Elkhorn City z 41522; ● 50
Verda; RMC Place; HARLAN; 181 M-16; mail Evarts z 40828; ● 800
Verna Hills; RMC Place; CLARK; *181 H-13; ★ **LEX**; mail Winchester z 40391; ● 300
Verne; RMC Place; WHITLEY; *181 M-14; mail Williamsburg z 40769; rural
Vernon; RMC Place; MONROE; *180 N-9; elev. 554ft./169m.; mail Hestand z 42151; rural
Verona; RMC Place; BOONE; 181 E-12; elev. 857ft./261m.; 🅿; ★ **CIN**; z 41092; ● 600
Versailles; Inc. Place; ⊡ WOODFORD; 181 H-12; elev. 897ft./273m.; 🅿 🄷; ★ **LEX**; z 40383-84, z 40390; Ⓟ 7,269; © 7,511
Vertrees; RMC Place; HARDIN; *180 I-7; elev. 634ft./193m.; 🅿; z 42724
Vest; RMC Place; KNOTT; 181 K-17; elev. 1,045ft./319m.; 🅿; z 41772; ● 100
Vester; RMC Place; ADAIR; *180 L-10; elev. 957ft./292m.; mail Columbia z 42728
Vicco; Inc. Place; PERRY; 181 K-17; elev. 949ft./289m.; 🅿; z 41773; Ⓟ 244; © 318
Victory; RMC Place; LAUREL; *181 K-14; elev. 1,194ft./364m.; 🅿; z 40729
Viley; RMC Place; FAYETTE; *181 H-12; elev. 870ft./265m.; ★ **LEX**; pop. incl. with Lexington (Inc. Place)
Village Center; RMC Place; HARLAN; mail Harlan z 40831; pop. incl. with Harlan (Inc. Place)
Villa Hills; Inc. Place; KENTON; 181 B-15; 🅿; ★ **CIN**; z 41017; Ⓟ 7,739; © 7,948
Vincent; RMC Place; OWSLEY; 181 J-15; elev. 1,008ft./307m.; 🅿; z 41386; ● 30
Vine Grove; Inc. Place; HARDIN; 180 I-8; elev. 682ft./208m.; 🅿; z 40175; Ⓟ 3,586; © 4,169
Vineyard; RMC Place; JESSAMINE; *181 I-12; ★ **LEX**; mail Nicholasville z 40356; ● 50
Viola; RMC Place; GRAVES; *180 F-3; mail Hickory z 42051; ● 50
Viper; RMC Place; PERRY; 181 K-17; elev. 905ft./276m.; 🅿; z 41774; ● 100
Virden; RMC Place; POWELL; *181 I-14; mail Clay City z 40312; ● 75
Virgie; RMC Place; PIKE; 181 K-18; elev. 837ft./255m.; 🅿; z 41572; ● 300
Visalia; RMC Place; KENTON; 181 E-12; ★ **CIN**; mail Latonia z 41015, Morning View z 41063; disincorporated November, 2006; Ⓟ 190; © 111
Volga; RMC Place; JOHNSON; 181 I-18; elev. 669ft./204m.; 🅿; z 41219; ● 50
Vortex; RMC Place; WOLFE; *181 I-15; mail Campton z 41301; rural

W

Wabaco; RMC Place; PERRY; *181 K-17; mail Hazard z 41701; ● 150
Wabash; RMC Place; HART; *180 K-8; elev. 680ft./207m.; mail Bonnieville z 42713; rural
Wabd; RMC Place; ROCKCASTLE; *181 K-13; elev. 1,121ft./342m.; mail Mount Vernon z 40456; rural
Waco; RMC Place; MADISON; 181 I-13; elev. 827ft./252m.; 🅿; z 40385; ● 200
Waddy; RMC Place; SHELBY; 180 H-10; elev. 899ft./274m.; 🅿; z 40076; ● 220
Wadesboro; RMC Place; CALLOWAY; *180 F-4; mail Hardin z 42048; rural
Wagersville; RMC Place; ESTILL; *181 J-14; mail Irvine z 40336; rural
Wago; RMC Place; CLINTON; *180 M-10; mail Albany z 42602; rural
Wait; RMC Place; WAYNE; *181 M-11; mail Alpha z 42603; rural
Wakefield; RMC Place; SPENCER; 180 H-10; elev. 715ft./218m.; mail Taylorsville z 40071; ● 30
Walden; RMC Place; WHITLEY; *181 M-13; elev. 1,176ft./358m.; mail Corbin z 40701; rural
Waldo; RMC Place; MAGOFFIN; *181 J-17; elev. 965ft./294m.; 🅿; z 41632
Wales; RMC Place; PIKE; *181 K-18; mail Virgie z 41572; rural
Walker; RMC Place; KNOX; 181 M-15; elev. 1,003ft./306m.; 🅿; z 40997; ● 75
Walkertown; RMC Place; PERRY; *181 K-17; 🅿; z 41701; pop. incl. with Hazard (Inc. Place)
Wallaceton; RMC Place; MADISON; *181 J-13; elev. 884ft./269m.; mail Paint Lick z 40461; ● 30
Wallingford; RMC Place; FLEMING; 181 G-15; elev. 795ft./242m.; 🅿; z 41093; ● 100
Wallins Creek; Inc. Place; HARLAN; 181 M-16; elev. 1,134ft./346m.; 🅿; z 40873; Ⓟ 261; © 257
Wallonia; RMC Place; TRIGG; 180 L-2; mail Cadiz z 42211; ● 60
Wallsend; RMC Place; BELL; *181 M-15; 🅿; z 40977; pop. incl. with Pineville (Inc. Place)
Walltown; RMC Place; CASEY; *181 K-12; mail Waynesburg z 40489; rural
Walnut Grove (Cartertown); RMC Place; ALLEN; *180 N-7; mail Adolphus z 42120; rural
Walnut Grove; CALDWELL; see Enon (RMC Place)
Walnut Grove; RMC Place; MARSHALL; *180 F-4; mail Benton z 42025; rural
Walnut Grove; RMC Place; PULASKI; 181 K-13; elev. 1,068ft./326m.; 🅿; z 42501; ● 10
Walsh; RMC Place; GREENUP; *181 E-17; mail South Shore z 41175; rural
Waltersville; RMC Place; POWELL; *181 I-14; mail Clay City z 40312; pop. incl. with Clay City (Inc. Place)
Walton; Inc. Place; BOONE, KENTON; 181 E-12; elev. 930ft./283m.; 🅿; ★ **CIN**; z 41094; Ⓟ 2,034; © 2,450
Waltz; RMC Place; ROWAN; *181 G-16; elev. 862ft./263m.; mail Morehead z 40351; rural
Wanamaker; RMC Place; WEBSTER; *180 J-2; elev. 435ft./133m.; mail Sebree z 42455; rural
Waneta; RMC Place; JACKSON; 181 J-14; elev. 1,076ft./328m.; 🅿; z 40488; ● 75
Warbranch; RMC Place; LESLIE; *181 L-16; elev. 1,251ft./381m.; 🅿; z 40874; ● 50
Warco; RMC Place; FLOYD; *181 J-18; mail Langley z 41645; rural
War Creek; RMC Place; BREATHITT; *181 J-16; mail Jackson z 41339; rural
Warfield; Inc. Place; MARTIN; 181 I-19; elev. 627ft./191m.; 🅿; z 41267; Ⓟ 364; © 284
Warnock; RMC Place; GREENUP; *181 F-17; mail Greenup z 41144; rural
Warren; RMC Place; KNOX; *181 M-14; mail Barbourville z 40906; ● 100
WARREN; 180 L-7; Ⓟ 76,673; © 92,522; ◆ 108,648
Warsaw; Inc. Place; ⊡ GALLATIN; 181 E-11; elev. 495ft./151m.; 🅿; z 41095; Ⓟ 1,202; © 1,811
Washington; RMC Place; MASON; *181 F-14; elev. 547ft./167m.; 🅿; z 41096; pop. incl. with Maysville (Inc. Place)
WASHINGTON; 180 I-10; Ⓟ 10,441; © 10,916; ◆ 11,812
Wasioto; RMC Place; BELL; *181 M-15; mail Pineville z 40977; rural
Watauga; RMC Place; CLINTON; *181 M-11; mail Albany z 42602; rural
Watch; RMC Place; KNOX; *181 L-14; mail Corbin z 40701; ● 75
Waterford; RMC Place; SPENCER; 180 H-9; mail Taylorsville z 40071; ● 90
Watergap; RMC Place; FLOYD; *181 J-18; elev. 644ft./196m.; mail Prestonsburg z 41653
Waterloo; RMC Place; BOONE; *181 D-11; mail Burlington z 41005; rural
Water Valley; Inc. Place; GRAVES; 180 G-3; elev. 387ft./118m.; 🅿; z 42085; Ⓟ 321; © 316
Waterview; RMC Place; CUMBERLAND; 180 M-9; elev. 571ft./174m.; 🅿; z 42717; ● 40
Watkinsville; RMC Place; SCOTT; *181 G-12; elev. 765ft./233m.; mail Stamping Ground z 40379; rural
Watterson Park; Inc. Place; JEFFERSON; 180 C-8; ★ **LOU**; mail Louisville z 40213, z 40218; Ⓟ 1,542; © 953
Watts; RMC Place; BREATHITT; *181 J-16; mail Lost Creek z 41348; rural
Waverly; Inc. Place; UNION; 180 I-2; elev. 407ft./124m.; 🅿; z 42462; Ⓟ 345; © 297
Waverly Hills; RMC Place; JEFFERSON; *180 H-8; ★ **LOU**; mail Louisville z 40272; became part of Louisville/Jefferson County Metro Jan. 6, 2003
Wax; RMC Place; GRAYSON; *180 K-7; elev. 612ft./187m.; 🅿; z 42726; rural
Wayland; Inc. Place; FLOYD; 181 J-18; elev. 714ft./218m.; 🅿; z 41666; Ⓟ 359; © 298
WAYNE; 181 M-11; Ⓟ 17,468; © 19,923; ◆ 20,801
Waynesburg; RMC Place; LINCOLN; 181 K-12; elev. 1,252ft./382m.; 🅿; z 40489; ● 200
Weaverton; RMC Place; HENDERSON; *180 I-3; elev. 391ft./119m.; ★ **EV**; mail Henderson z 42420; pop. incl. with Henderson (Inc. Place)
Webbs; RMC Place; GREEN; *180 K-9; elev. 708ft./216m.; mail Greensburg z 42743; rural
Webbs Cross Roads; RMC Place; RUSSELL; 181 L-11; elev. 1,043ft./318m.; 🅿; z 42642; ● 50
Webbville; RMC Place; LAWRENCE; 181 G-17; elev. 649ft./198m.; 🅿; z 41180; ● 80
Weberstown; RMC Place; HANCOCK; *180 I-5; mail Pellville z 42364; rural
Webster; RMC Place; BRECKINRIDGE; 180 I-6; elev. 580ft./177m.; 🅿; z 40176; ● 120
WEBSTER; 180 J-2; Ⓟ 13,955; © 14,120; ◆ 13,775
Wedonia; RMC Place; MASON; 181 F-15; mail Mayslick z 41055; ● 10
Weeksbury; RMC Place; FLOYD; 181 K-18; elev. 1,094ft./333m.; 🅿; z 41667; ● 800
Weir; RMC Place; MUHLENBERG; 180 L-4; elev. 629ft./192m.; mail Greenville z 42345; ● 70
Welborn; RMC Place; PULASKI; *181 K-12; mail Somerset z 42501; rural
Welchs Creek; RMC Place; BUTLER; 180 K-6; elev. 593ft./181m.; 🅿; z 42287; ● 65
Welcome; RMC Place; BUTLER; *180 K-5; mail Morgantown z 42261; rural
Weldon; RMC Place; MEADE; *180 H-7; mail Brandenburg z 40108; rural
Wellhope; RMC Place; ROCKCASTLE; *181 K-13; mail Mount Vernon z 40456; rural
Wellington; Inc. Place; JEFFERSON; 180 C-8; elev. 512ft./156m.; ★ **LOU**; mail Louisville z 40205; Ⓟ 593; © 561
Wellington; RMC Place; MENIFEE; 181 I-15; elev. 1,202ft./366m.; 🅿; z 40387; ● 50
Wellington Place; RMC Place; NELSON; *180 I-9; mail Bardstown z 40004; pop. incl. with Bardstown (Inc. Place)
Wells; RMC Place; MUHLENBERG; *180 L-4; mail Central City z 42330; rural
Wellsburg; RMC Place; BRACKEN; *181 E-14; mail Foster z 41043; rural
Wells Landing; RMC Place; BOYLE; *181 I-11; mail Danville z 40422; ● 75
Wendover; RMC Place; LESLIE; *181 L-16; elev. 1,000ft./305m.; 🅿; z 41775; ● 50
Wentz; RMC Place; PERRY; *181 L-17; mail Cornettsville z 41731; rural
Wesco; RMC Place; HOPKINS; 180 K-3; mail Madisonville z 42431; ● 250
Wesleyan Park; RMC Place; CLARK; *181 H-13; ★ **LEX**; mail Winchester z 40391; pop. incl. with Winchester (Inc. Place)
Wesleyville; RMC Place; CARTER; *181 G-16; elev. 752ft./229m.; mail Olive Hill z 41164; rural
Westbend; RMC Place; POWELL; 181 I-14; elev. 729ft./222m.; 🅿; z 40312; ● 300
West Brook; RMC Place; CHRISTIAN; *180 M-3; ★ **HPKNV**; mail Hopkinsville z 42240; rural
West Buechel; Inc. Place; JEFFERSON; 180 C-8; elev. 469ft./143m.; ★ **LOU**; mail Louisville z 40218; Ⓟ 1,587; © 1,301
West Clifty; RMC Place; GRAYSON; *180 J-7; mail Leitchfield z 42754; rural
West Danville; RMC Place; BOYLE; *181 J-11; mail Danville z 40422; pop. incl. with Danville (Inc. Place)
Western; RMC Place; FULTON; mail Hickman z 42050; rural
West Fairview; RMC Place; BOYD; *181 F-18; ★ **HNTG**; mail Ashland z 41101
West Frankfort; RMC Place; FRANKLIN; pop. incl. with Frankfort (Inc. Place)
West Future City; RMC Place; MCCRACKEN; *180 E-3; mail Kevil z 42053
West Garrett; RMC Place; FLOYD; *181 J-18; mail Garrett z 41630; ● 200
Westgate; RMC Place; FRANKLIN; *181 H-11; mail Frankfort z 40601; pop. incl. with Frankfort (Inc. Place)
West Irvine; RMC Place; ESTILL; 181 I-14; elev. 662ft./202m.; 🅿; z 40336; ● 500
West Liberty; Inc. Place; ⊡ MORGAN; 181 H-16; elev. 830ft./253m.; 🅿 🄷; z 41472 & mail Wrigley z 41477; Ⓟ 1,887; © 3,277
West Louisville; RMC Place; DAVIESS; 180 I-3; 🅿; z 42377; ● 100
Weston; RMC Place; NICHOLAS; *181 G-14; mail Carlisle z 40311; rural
West Paducah (Maxon); RMC Place; MCCRACKEN; 180 E-3; elev. 363ft./111m.; 🅿; ★ **PAD**; z 42086; ● 100
Westplains; RMC Place; GRAVES; *180 F-3; mail Hickory z 42051; rural
West Point; Inc. Place; HARDIN; 180 H-8; elev. 438ft./134m.; 🅿; z 40177; Ⓟ 1,216; © 1,100
Westport; RMC Place; OLDHAM; 180 F-9; elev. 486ft./148m.; 🅿; z 40077; ● 300
West Prestonsburg; RMC Place; FLOYD; *181 I-18; pop. incl. with Prestonsburg (Inc. Place)
West Russell; RMC Place; GREENUP; *181 F-18; ★ **HNTG**; mail Russell z 41169; pop. incl. with Flatwoods (Inc. Place)
Westside Station; RMC Place; FRANKLIN; mail Frankfort z 40604; pop. incl. with Frankfort (Inc. Place)
West Somerset; RMC Place; PULASKI; *181 L-12; 🅿; z 42564 & mail Somerset z 42503
West Van Lear (Van Lear Junction); RMC Place; JOHNSON; 181 I-18; elev. 623ft./190m.; 🅿; z 41268; ● 600
Westview; RMC Place; BRECKINRIDGE; *180 I-6; elev. 747ft./228m.; 🅿; z 40178; ● 40
Westwood; CDP; BOYD; 181 F-18; elev. 600ft./183m.; 🅿; ★ **HNTG**; z 41101; Ⓟ 5,300; © 4,888
Westwood; Inc. Place; JEFFERSON; 180 B-9; elev. 630ft./192m.; ★ **LOU**; mail Louisville z 40222; Ⓟ 734; © 612
Westwood Park; RMC Place; FRANKLIN; *181 H-11; mail Frankfort z 40601; pop. incl. with Frankfort (Inc. Place)
Wheatcroft; Inc. Place; WEBSTER; 180 J-2; elev. 372ft./113m.; 🅿; z 42463; Ⓟ 206; © 173
Wheatley; RMC Place; OWEN; 181 F-11; elev. 904ft./276m.; 🅿; z 40359; ● 50
Wheel; RMC Place; GRAVES; *180 F-3; mail Lowes z 42061; rural
Wheeler; RMC Place; KNOX; *181 M-14; elev. 1,140ft./347m.; mail Barbourville z 40906
Wheelersburg; RMC Place; MAGOFFIN; 181 I-17; elev. 856ft./261m.; mail Salyersville z 41465; ● 60
Wheelwright; FLOYD; see Bypro (RMC Place)
Wheelwright; Inc. Place; FLOYD; 181 K-18; elev. 1,102ft./336m.; 🅿; z 41669; Ⓟ 721; © 1,042
Whick; RMC Place; BREATHITT; *181 J-16; elev. 777ft./237m.; 🅿; z 41390; ● 75
Whipps Millgate; RMC Place; JEFFERSON; *180 G-9; elev. 648ft./198m.; ★ **LOU**; mail Louisville z 40223; former incorporated place; became part of Lyndon July 1, 2001; pop. incl. with Lyndon (Inc. Place); Ⓟ 454; © 415
Whitaker; RMC Place; FLOYD; *181 I-18; mail East Point z 41216; rural
Whitaker; RMC Place; LETCHER; *181 K-18; mail Seco z 41849; ● 150
Whitco; RMC Place; LETCHER; *181 L-18; mail Whitesburg z 41858; ● 200
White City; RMC Place; HOPKINS; mail White Plains z 42464; rural
White City; RMC Place; LARUE; 180 J-9; 🅿; z 42748; ● 50
White Hall; RMC Place; MADISON; *181 I-13; mail Richmond z 40475
Whitehouse; RMC Place; JOHNSON; *181 I-18; elev. 606ft./185m.; 🅿; z 41240; ● 150
White Lily; RMC Place; PULASKI; *181 L-12; mail Somerset z 42501; rural
White Mills; RMC Place; HARDIN; 180 J-7; elev. 656ft./200m.; 🅿; z 42788; ● 150
White Oak (Galilee); RMC Place; GARRARD; *181 I-12; mail Lancaster z 40444; rural
White Oak; RMC Place; MORGAN; 181 I-16; elev. 797ft./243m.; 🅿; z 41472; ● 75
White Oak Junction; RMC Place; MCCREARY; *181 M-12; mail Stearns z 42647; ● 20
White Plains; RMC Place; ALLEN; *180 M-7; mail Scottsville z 42164; pop. incl. with Scottsville (Inc. Place)
White Plains; Inc. Place; HOPKINS; 180 K-3; elev. 412ft./126m.; 🅿; z 42464; Ⓟ 598; © 800
Whitepost; RMC Place; PIKE; *181 I-19; mail Belfry z 41514; rural
White Run; RMC Place; OHIO; *180 J-5; elev. 435ft./133m.; mail Horse Branch z 42349; rural
Whitesburg; Inc. Place; ⊡ LETCHER; 181 L-18; elev. 1,164ft./355m.; 🅿 🄷; z 41858; Ⓟ 1,636; © 1,600
White Sulphur; RMC Place; CALDWELL; *180 L-1; elev. 507ft./155m.; mail Fredonia z 42411; rural
White Sulphur; RMC Place; SCOTT; *181 G-12; mail Georgetown z 40324
Whitesville; Inc. Place; DAVIESS; 180 I-5; elev. 495ft./151m.; 🅿; z 42378; Ⓟ 682; © 632
White Tower; RMC Place; KENTON; *181 E-12; ★ **CIN**; mail Independence z 41051; pop. incl. with Independence (Inc. Place)
White Villa; RMC Place; KENTON; *181 E-12; ★ **CIN**; mail Morning View z 41063; ● 80
Whitewood; RMC Place; GREEN; *180 K-9; mail Campbellsville z 42718, Greensburg z 42743; rural
Whitfield; RMC Place; BULLITT; *180 H-9; ★ **LOU**; mail Mount Washington z 40047; rural
Whitley; MCCREARY; see Whitley City (CDP)
WHITLEY; 181 M-13; Ⓟ 33,326; © 35,865; ◆ 38,758
Whitley City (Whitley); CDP; ⊡ MCCREARY; 181 M-12; elev. 1,357ft./414m.; 🅿; z 42653; Ⓟ 1,133; © 1,111
Wiborg; RMC Place; MCCREARY; *181 M-12; elev. 1,354ft./413m.; mail Whitley City z 42653
Wickliffe; Inc. Place; ⊡ BALLARD; 180 E-2; elev. 330ft./101m.; 🅿; z 42087; Ⓟ 851; © 794
Wicks Well; RMC Place; HOPKINS; *180 K-3; mail Madisonville z 42431; ● 75
Widecreek; RMC Place; BREATHITT; *181 J-15; elev. 783ft./239m.; 🅿; z 41311; ● 20
Wilbur; RMC Place; LAWRENCE; *181 H-18; mail Blaine z 41124; rural
Wild Cat; RMC Place; CLAY; *181 K-15; elev. 798ft./243m.; 🅿; z 40962; rural
Wilder; Inc. Place; CAMPBELL; 181 B-17; elev. 532ft./162m.; 🅿; ★ **CIN**; z 41071, z 41076; Ⓟ 691; © 2,624
Wilderness Road; RMC Place; EDMONSON; *180 K-7; mail Mammoth Cave z 42259; rural
Wildie; RMC Place; ROCKCASTLE; 181 K-13; elev. 929ft./283m.; 🅿; z 40492; ● 150
Wildwood; Inc. Place; JEFFERSON; *180 G-9; elev. 654ft./199m.; ★ **LOU**; mail Louisville z 40223; Ⓟ 266; © 247
Wilhoit (Dayhoit); RMC Place; HARLAN; *181 M-16; elev. 1,160ft./354m.; mail Dayhoit z 40824; ● 250
Wilhurst; RMC Place; BREATHITT; *181 J-16; mail Vancleve z 41385; rural
Willailla; RMC Place; ROCKCASTLE; *181 K-12; elev. 1,098ft./335m.; mail Brodhead z 40409; rural
Willard; RMC Place; CARTER; 181 G-17; elev. 700ft./213m.; 🅿; z 41181; ● 150
Williams; RMC Place; MORGAN; *181 I-17; mail West Liberty z 41472; rural
Williamsburg; Inc. Place; ⊡ WHITLEY; 181 M-13; elev. 951ft./290m.; 🅿 🄲 1,884; z 40769; Ⓟ 5,493; © 5,143
Williamsport; RMC Place; JOHNSON; 181 I-18; elev. 664ft./202m.; 🅿; z 41271; ● 200
Williamstown; Inc. Place; ⊡ GRANT; 181 F-12; elev. 974ft./297m.; 🅿 🄷; z 41097; Ⓟ 3,023; © 3,227
Willisburg; Inc. Place; WASHINGTON; 180 I-10; elev. 857ft./261m.; 🅿; z 40078; Ⓟ 223; © 304
Willow; RMC Place; BRACKEN; *181 F-13; elev. 976ft./297m.; mail Brooksville z 41004; rural
Willow; RMC Place; LEE; *181 J-15; mail Beattyville z 41311; rural
Willowcrest; RMC Place; FRANKLIN; *181 H-11; mail Frankfort z 40601; ● 300
Willow Grove; RMC Place; BRACKEN; *181 E-13; mail Foster z 41043; rural
Willow Shade; RMC Place; METCALFE; *180 M-9; elev. 699ft./213m.; 🅿; z 42166; ● 20
Willowtown; RMC Place; TAYLOR; *180 J-9; mail Campbellsville z 42718; rural
Willow Tree; RMC Place; ESTILL; *181 I-14; mail Ravenna z 40472; rural
Wilmore; Inc. Place; JESSAMINE; 181 I-12; elev. 926ft./282m.; 🅿 🄲 2,882; ★ **LEX**; z 40390; Ⓟ 4,215; © 5,905
Wilson; RMC Place; HENDERSON; *180 I-2; mail Corydon z 42406; rural
Wilsonville; RMC Place; BOYLE; *181 J-11; mail Danville z 40422; ● 60
Wilsonville; RMC Place; SPENCER; *180 H-9; 🅿; z 40023; ● 50
Wilstacy; RMC Place; BREATHITT; *181 J-16; mail Jackson z 41339; rural
Wilton; RMC Place; KNOX; *181 M-14; mail Woodbine z 40771
Winburn Estates; RMC Place; FAYETTE; *181 H-12; ★ **LEX**; mail Lexington z 40511; pop. incl. with Lexington (Inc. Place)
Winchester; Inc. Place; ⊡ CLARK; 181 H-13; elev. 972ft./296m.; 🅿 🄷; ★ **LEX**; z 40391-92; Ⓟ 15,799; © 16,724
Wind Cave; RMC Place; JACKSON; *181 J-14; elev. 1,006ft./307m.; 🅿; z 40447; ● 10
Winding Falls; RMC Place; JEFFERSON; 180 B-8; ★ **LOU**; mail Louisville z 40207; pop. incl. with Indian Hills (Inc. Place); Ⓟ 657
Windsor; RMC Place; CASEY; 181 L-11; elev. 1,154ft./352m.; 🅿; z 42565; ● 50
Windy; RMC Place; WAYNE; 181 M-11; elev. 1,035ft./315m.; 🅿; z 42633; ● 75
Windy Hill; RMC Place; OHIO; *180 K-5; mail Horse Branch z 42349; rural
Windy Hills; Inc. Place; JEFFERSON; 180 B-8; elev. 550ft./168m.; ★ **LOU**; mail Louisville z 40207; Ⓟ 2,452; © 2,480
Windyville; RMC Place; EDMONSON; *180 K-6; mail Brownsville z 42210; ● 60
Wingo; Inc. Place; GRAVES; 180 G-3; elev. 469ft./143m.; 🅿; z 42088; Ⓟ 568; © 581
Winifred; RMC Place; JOHNSON; *181 H-18; elev. 835ft./255m.; mail Flatgap z 41219; rural
Winlow Park; RMC Place; CRITTENDEN; *180 K-1; mail Marion z 42064; rural
Winston; RMC Place; ESTILL; 181 I-14; elev. 888ft./271m.; 🅿; z 40495; ● 120
Winston Park; RMC Place; KENTON; *181 D-12; ★ **CIN**; mail Latonia z 41015; pop. incl. with Taylor Mill (Inc. Place)
Winwright; RMC Place; PIKE; *181 K-19; elev. 713ft./217m.; mail Pikeville z 41501; rural
Wiscoal; RMC Place; KNOTT; *181 K-17; mail Sassafras z 41759
Wisconsin; RMC Place; KNOTT; mail Sassafras z 41759; rural
Wisdom; RMC Place; METCALFE; *180 L-8; elev. 940ft./287m.; mail Edmonton z 42129; rural
Wisemantown; RMC Place; ESTILL; *181 I-14; elev. 661ft./201m.; mail Irvine z 40336; ● 80
Wises Landing; RMC Place; TRIMBLE; *180 F-9; mail Bedford z 40006; ● 50
Wiswell; RMC Place; CALLOWAY; *180 G-4; mail Murray z 42071; rural
Wittensville; RMC Place; JOHNSON; 181 I-18; elev. 629ft./192m.; 🅿; z 41274; ● 200
Witt Springs; RMC Place; ESTILL; *181 I-14; mail Irvine z 40336; rural
Wofford; RMC Place; WHITLEY; 181 M-14; mail Williamsburg z 40769; ● 200
Wolf; RMC Place; CARTER; *181 G-17; elev. 913ft./278m.; 🅿; z 41164; rural
Wolf Coal; RMC Place; BREATHITT; *181 K-16; elev. 770ft./235m.; 🅿; z 41339; rural
Wolf Creek; RMC Place; MEADE; 180 H-6; mail Battletown z 40104; ● 80
WOLFE; 181 I-15; Ⓟ 6,503; © 7,065; ◆ 7,060
Wolfpit; RMC Place; PIKE; *181 K-19; mail Elkhorn City z 41522; ● 180
Wolverine; RMC Place; BREATHITT; *181 J-16; elev. 726ft./221m.; 🅿; z 41339; ● 40
Wonder; RMC Place; FLOYD; *181 J-18; mail Prestonsburg z 41653; rural
Wonnie; RMC Place; MAGOFFIN; *181 I-17; elev. 819ft./250m.; 🅿; z 41465
Woodbine; RMC Place; WHITLEY; 181 M-14; elev. 1,106ft./337m.; 🅿; z 40701, z 40771; ● 500
Woodburn; Inc. Place; WARREN; 180 M-6; elev. 638ft./194m.; 🅿; z 42170; Ⓟ 343; © 323
Woodbury; Inc. Place; BUTLER; 180 K-6; elev. 465ft./142m.; 🅿; z 42288; Ⓟ 117; © 87
WOODFORD; 181 H-11; Ⓟ 19,955; © 23,208; ◆ 24,209
Woodford Village; RMC Place; WOODFORD; *181 H-12; ★ **LEX**; mail Versailles z 40383; pop. incl. with Versailles (Inc. Place)
Woodlake; RMC Place; FRANKLIN; *181 G-11; elev. 752ft./229m.; mail Frankfort z 40601; ● 40
Woodland Estates; RMC Place; JOHNSON; *181 I-18; mail Paintsville z 41240; ● 30
Woodland Hills; Inc. Place; JEFFERSON; 180 B-10; elev. 730ft./223m.; ★ **LOU**; mail Louisville z 40243; Ⓟ 714; © 657
Woodland Park; RMC Place; PERRY; *181 K-17; mail Hazard z 41701; pop. incl. with Hazard (Inc. Place)
Woodlands; RMC Place; FRANKLIN; *181 G-11; mail Frankfort z 40601; pop. incl. with Frankfort (Inc. Place)
Woodlawn; Inc. Place; CAMPBELL; 181 B-17; elev. 625ft./191m.; ★ **CIN**; mail Newport z 41071; Ⓟ 308; © 268
Woodlawn; RMC Place; NELSON; *180 I-10; mail Bardstown z 40004; ● 100
Woodlawn-Oakdale; CDP-Census Area Only; MCCRACKEN; *180 E-4; ★ **PAD**; mail Paducah z 42003; Ⓟ 4,954; © 4,937
Woodlawn Park; RMC Place; ANDERSON; *181 H-11; mail Lawrenceburg z 40342; ● 50
Woodlawn Park; Inc. Place; JEFFERSON; 180 B-8; elev. 553ft./169m.; ★ **LOU**; mail Louisville z 40207; Ⓟ 1,099; © 1,033
Woodman; RMC Place; PIKE; *181 J-20; elev. 793ft./242m.; 🅿; z 41568; ● 100
Woods; RMC Place; FLOYD; *181 J-18; 🅿; z 40828 & mail Prestonsburg z 41653
Woodsbend; RMC Place; MORGAN; *181 I-16; mail West Liberty z 41472; ● 30
Woodson Bend; RMC Place; PULASKI; *181 L-12; mail Bronston z 42518; summer pop. 800; ● 100
Woodsonville; RMC Place; HART; *180 K-8; mail Munfordville z 42765; ● 75
Woodstock; RMC Place; PULASKI; *181 K-12; elev. 1,070ft./326m.; mail Somerset z 42501
Woodville; RMC Place; MCCRACKEN; *180 E-3; mail West Paducah z 42086; ● 25
Wooleyville; RMC Place; TAYLOR; *180 K-10; mail Campbellsville z 42718; rural
Woollum; RMC Place; KNOX; 181 L-15; elev. 902ft./275m.; 🅿; z 40906; ● 20
Wooton; RMC Place; LESLIE; 181 K-16; elev. 873ft./266m.; 🅿; z 41776; ● 200
Worthington; Inc. Place; GREENUP; 181 F-18; elev. 550ft./168m.; 🅿; ★ **HNTG**; z 41183; Ⓟ 1,751; © 1,673
Worthington Hills; Inc. Place; JEFFERSON; 180 A-10; ★ **LOU**; mail Louisville z 40223; Ⓟ 973; © 1,594
Worthville; Inc. Place; CARROLL; 181 F-11; elev. 486ft./148m.; 🅿; z 41098; Ⓟ 191; © 215
Wray Gap; RMC Place; WAYNE; *181 M-11; mail Monticello z 42633; rural
Wrights; RMC Place; TAYLOR; *180 K-9; mail Campbellsville z 42718; rural
Wrightsburg; RMC Place; MCLEAN; *180 J-3; mail Calhoun z 42327; rural
Wrigley; RMC Place; MORGAN; 181 H-16; elev. 816ft./249m.; 🅿; z 41477; ● 100
Wurtland; Inc. Place; GREENUP; 181 F-18; elev. 551ft./168m.; 🅿; ★ **HNTG**; z 41144; Ⓟ 1,221; © 1,049
Wyett; RMC Place; ELLIOTT; *181 H-16; mail Sandy Hook z 41171; rural
Wyman; RMC Place; MCLEAN; *180 J-3; mail Calhoun z 42327; rural

Y

Yaden; RMC Place; WHITLEY; *181 M-14; elev. 944ft./288m.; mail Williamsburg z 40769; rural
Yancey; RMC Place; HARLAN; *181 M-16; mail Harlan z 40831; ● 100
Yatesville; RMC Place; LAWRENCE; *181 H-18; mail Louisa z 41230; rural
Yeaddiss; RMC Place; LESLIE; 181 L-16; elev. 1,111ft./339m.; 🅿; z 41777; ● 50
Yeager; RMC Place; PIKE; *181 K-19; mail Pikeville z 41501; ● 90
Yeaman; RMC Place; GRAYSON; *180 J-6; elev. 659ft./201m.; mail Fordsville z 42343, Olaton z 42361
Yellow Rock; RMC Place; LEE; *181 J-15; elev. 666ft./203m.; 🅿; z 41311; ● 35
Yelvington; RMC Place; DAVIESS; 180 I-4; mail Maceo z 42355; ● 175
Yerkes; RMC Place; PERRY; 181 K-16; elev. 825ft./251m.; 🅿; z 41778; ● 140
Yesse; RMC Place; ALLEN; *180 M-7; elev. 708ft./216m.; mail Scottsville z 42164; rural
Yocum; RMC Place; MORGAN; *181 H-16; elev. 900ft./274m.; 🅿; z 41472; ● 20
York; RMC Place; GREENUP; *181 F-17; elev. 710ft./216m.; mail South Shore z 41175; rural
Yosemite; RMC Place; CASEY; 181 K-11; elev. 836ft./255m.; 🅿; z 42566; ● 250
Younger Creek; RMC Place; HARDIN; 180 I-8; mail Elizabethtown z 42701; ● 150
Youngs Creek; RMC Place; WHITLEY; *181 M-13; mail Corbin z 40701; rural
Yuma; RMC Place; TAYLOR; *180 K-10; elev. 728ft./222m.; mail Elk Horn z 42733; rural

Z

Zachariah; RMC Place; LEE, WOLFE; 181 I-15; elev. 1,239ft./378m.; 🅿; z 41301; rural
Zag; RMC Place; MORGAN; *181 H-16; mail West Liberty z 41472; rural
Zandale; RMC Place; FAYETTE; *181 H-12; ★ **LEX**; mail Lexington z 40503; pop. incl. with Lexington (Inc. Place)
Zebulon; RMC Place; PIKE; 181 J-19; mail Pikeville z 41501; ● 200
Zelda; RMC Place; LAWRENCE; *181 G-18; mail Catlettsburg z 41129; rural
Zion; GRANT; see Zion Station (RMC Place)
Zion; RMC Place; HENDERSON; 180 I-3; elev. 424ft./129m.; mail Henderson z 42420; ● 350
Zion (Hammackville); RMC Place; TODD; *180 M-3; elev. 559ft./170m.; mail Guthrie z 42234
Zion Hill; RMC Place; SCOTT; *181 H-12; ★ **LEX**; mail Midway z 40347; ● 120
Zion Station (Zion); RMC Place; GRANT; *181 E-12; elev. 623ft./190m.; mail Dry Ridge z 41035; rural
Zoe; RMC Place; LEE; 181 I-15; elev. 1,207ft./368m.; 🅿; z 41397; ● 40

Entries in **UPPERCASE** are counties.
Entries in **bold** have populations of 2,500 or more.
Names in parentheses are alternate names.
Inc. Place — Incorporated Place
RMC Place — Rand McNally Designated Place
CDP — Census Designated Place
MCD — Minor Civil Division

⊡ County Seat
▲ Minor Civil Division
elev. Elevation
🅿 Post Office

🄷 Hospital
🄲 College
■ Principal Business Center
★ Ranally Metro Area (RMA) Abbreviation
z Zip Code(s)

Ⓟ Previous Census Population
Ⓡ Revised Census Population
Ⓐ Annexation Population
● Rand McNally Population Estimate
© Final Census Population
Ⓢ Special Census Population
◆ Estimated Population

For additional definitions see Glossary, Volume 1, and Introduction, Volume 2.

LOUISIANA

Statistics

Total area (2000) — 51,840 square miles
Land area (2000) — 43,562 square miles
Water area (2000) — 8,278 square miles
Capital — Baton Rouge
Admitted as state — April, 1812

Maps

State maps can be found on pages 142-254 in Vol. 1

Ranally Metro Areas (RMAs) and Abbreviations

Alexandria, LA — ALEX
Baton Rouge, LA — B.R.
Houma-Thibodaux, LA — HOMA-
Lafayette, LA — LAF
Lake Charles, LA — LKCH
Monroe, LA — MONR
Natchez, MS-LA — NCHZ
New Orleans, LA — N.O.
Shreveport, LA-TX — SHRE
Vicksburg, MS-LA — VICK

Principal Places

Place Name	Place Type	Parish	Population
New Orleans	Inc. Place	ORLEANS	◆ 268,724
Baton Rouge	Inc. Place	EAST BATON ROUGE	◆ 239,580
Shreveport	Inc. Place	CADDO	◆ 186,137
Metairie	CDP	JEFFERSON	◆ 130,008
Lafayette	Inc. Place	LAFAYETTE	◆ 109,094
Kenner	Inc. Place	JEFFERSON	◆ 70,549
Lake Charles	Inc. Place	CALCASIEU	◆ 70,061
Bossier City	Inc. Place	BOSSIER	◆ 64,543
Monroe	Inc. Place	OUACHITA	◆ 53,736
Alexandria	Inc. Place	RAPIDES	◆ 47,000
New Iberia	Inc. Place	IBERIA	◆ 32,312
Marrero	CDP	JEFFERSON	◆ 32,177
Houma	Inc. Place	TERREBONNE	◆ 31,910
Laplace	CDP	ST. JOHN THE BAPTIST	◆ 30,451
Slidell	Inc. Place	ST. TAMMANY	◆ 24,559
Opelousas	Inc. Place	ST. LANDRY	◆ 23,774
Terrytown	CDP	JEFFERSON	◆ 22,627
Ruston	Inc. Place	LINCOLN	◆ 21,525
Hammond	Inc. Place	TANGIPAHOA	◆ 20,665
Harvey	CDP	JEFFERSON	◆ 19,772
Chalmette	CDP	ST. BERNARD	◆ 19,359
Sulphur	Inc. Place	CALCASIEU	◆ 19,245
Gretna	Inc. Place	JEFFERSON	◆ 18,571
Natchitoches	Inc. Place	NATCHITOCHES	© 17,865
Shenandoah	CDP-Census Area Only	EAST BATON ROUGE	© 17,070
Bayou Cane	CDP-Census Area Only	TERREBONNE	© 17,046
Estelle	CDP	JEFFERSON	© 15,880
River Ridge	CDP	JEFFERSON	© 14,588
Thibodaux	Inc. Place	LAFOURCHE	◆ 14,351
Crowley	Inc. Place	ACADIA	® 14,228
Pineville	Inc. Place	RAPIDES	© 13,829
Baker	Inc. Place	EAST BATON ROUGE	© 13,793
Bogalusa	Inc. Place	WASHINGTON	© 13,365
Woodmere	CDP-Census Area Only	JEFFERSON	© 13,058
Minden	Inc. Place	WEBSTER	© 13,027
Bastrop	Inc. Place	MOREHOUSE	© 12,988
West Monroe	Inc. Place	OUACHITA	◆ 12,852
Abbeville	Inc. Place	VERMILION	© 11,887
Jefferson	CDP	JEFFERSON	© 11,843
Luling	CDP	ST. CHARLES	© 11,512
Eunice	Inc. Place	ST. LANDRY	© 11,499
Timberlane	CDP-Census Area Only	JEFFERSON	© 11,405
Morgan City	Inc. Place	ST. MARY	◆ 11,293
Zachary	Inc. Place	EAST BATON ROUGE	© 11,275
Destrehan	CDP	ST. CHARLES	© 11,260
Fort Polk South	CDP-Census Area Only	VERNON	© 11,000
Jennings	Inc. Place	JEFFERSON DAVIS	© 10,986
Westwego	Inc. Place	JEFFERSON	© 10,763
Moss Bluff	CDP	CALCASIEU	© 10,535
Mandeville	Inc. Place	ST. TAMMANY	© 10,489
Merrydale	CDP-Census Area Only	EAST BATON ROUGE	© 10,427
Raceland	CDP	LAFOURCHE	© 10,224
Meraux	CDP	ST. BERNARD	© 10,192
Harahan	Inc. Place	JEFFERSON	© 9,885
Belle Chasse	CDP	PLAQUEMINES	© 9,848
Claiborne	CDP	OUACHITA	© 9,830
DeRidder	Inc. Place	BEAUREGARD	© 9,808
Waggaman	CDP	JEFFERSON	© 9,435
Tallulah	Inc. Place	MADISON	© 9,189
Reserve	CDP	ST. JOHN THE BAPTIST	© 9,111
Gardere	CDP	EAST BATON ROUGE	© 8,992
Denham Springs	Inc. Place	LIVINGSTON	© 8,757
Ville Platte	Inc. Place	EVANGELINE	® 8,596
Violet	CDP	ST. BERNARD	© 8,555
Rayne	Inc. Place	ACADIA	© 8,552
Covington	Inc. Place	ST. TAMMANY	© 8,483
Franklin	Inc. Place	ST. MARY	© 8,354
Bridge City	CDP	JEFFERSON	© 8,323
Gonzales	Inc. Place	ASCENSION	© 8,156
Oakdale	Inc. Place	ALLEN	© 8,137
Arabi	CDP	ST. BERNARD	© 8,093
Oak Hills Place	CDP	EAST BATON ROUGE	© 7,996
Scott	Inc. Place	LAFAYETTE	© 7,870
Brownsville-Bawcomville	CDP-Census Area Only	OUACHITA	© 7,616
Donaldsonville	Inc. Place	ASCENSION	© 7,605
Lacombe	CDP	ST. TAMMANY	© 7,518
Galliano	CDP	LAFOURCHE	© 7,356
Larose	CDP	LAFOURCHE	© 7,306
Breaux Bridge	Inc. Place	ST. MARTIN	© 7,281
Prien	CDP	CALCASIEU	© 7,215
Plaquemine	Inc. Place	IBERVILLE	© 7,064
Village Saint George	CDP	EAST BATON ROUGE	© 6,993
Saint Martinville	Inc. Place	ST. MARTIN	© 6,989
Leesville	Inc. Place	VERNON	© 6,753
Saint Rose	CDP	ST. CHARLES	© 6,540
Eden Isle	CDP-Census Area Only	ST. TAMMANY	© 6,261
Carencro	Inc. Place	LAFAYETTE	© 6,120
Jeanerette	Inc. Place	IBERIA	© 5,997
Red Chute	CDP	BOSSIER	© 5,984
Schriever	CDP	TERREBONNE	© 5,880
Broussard	Inc. Place	LAFAYETTE	© 5,874
Winnfield	Inc. Place	WINN	© 5,749
Cut Off	CDP	LAFOURCHE	© 5,635
Old Jefferson	CDP	EAST BATON ROUGE	© 5,631
Mansfield	Inc. Place	DE SOTO	© 5,582
Marksville	Inc. Place	AVOYELLES	© 5,537
Saint Gabriel	Inc. Place	IBERVILLE	© 5,514
Avondale	CDP	JEFFERSON	© 5,441
Springhill	Inc. Place	WEBSTER	© 5,439
Winnsboro	Inc. Place	FRANKLIN	© 5,344
Port Allen	Inc. Place	WEST BATON ROUGE	© 5,278
Brownfields	CDP-Census Area Only	EAST BATON ROUGE	© 5,222
Ponchatoula	Inc. Place	TANGIPAHOA	© 5,180
Kaplan	Inc. Place	VERMILION	© 5,177
Patterson	Inc. Place	ST. MARY	© 5,130
Lake Providence	Inc. Place	EAST CARROLL	© 5,104

Parish Business Data

Parish	FIPS Code	Parish Seat	Land Area (Sq. Mi.)	Census Population			Wholesale Trade		Manufacturing, 2002			
				4/1/2000	4/1/1990	% Change 1990-2000	Sales, 2002 ($1,000)	% Change 1997-2002	Establish-ments	Total Employees	Value Added ($1,000)	Ranally Mfg. Units
Acadia	001	Crowley	655	58,861	55,882	5.3	(d)	(d)	52	1,941	114,248	60
Allen	003	Oberlin	764	25,440	21,226	19.9	23,063	-38.8	...	(d)	(d)	...
Ascension	005	Donaldsonville	292	76,627	58,214	31.6	354,422	12.8	94	5,505	2,489,897	1,317
Assumption	007	Napoleonville	339	23,388	22,753	2.8	(d)	(d)	...	(d)	(d)	...
Avoyelles	009	Marksville	832	41,481	39,159	5.9	(d)	(d)	19	708	41,885	22
Beauregard	011	DeRidder	1,160	32,986	30,083	9.6	(d)	(d)	20	988	257,975	136
Bienville	013	Arcadia	811	15,752	15,979	-1.4	115,998	-38.6	12	1,064	107,073	57
Bossier	015	Benton	839	98,310	86,088	14.2	(d)	(d)	80	(d)	(d)	...
Caddo	017	Shreveport	882	252,161	248,253	1.6	(d)	(d)	218	(d)	(d)	...
Calcasieu	019	Lake Charles	1,071	183,577	168,134	9.2	(d)	(d)	137	9,626	2,892,830	1,531
Caldwell	021	Columbia	529	10,560	9,810	7.6	(d)	(d)	...	(d)	(d)	...
Cameron	023	Cameron	1,313	9,991	9,260	7.9	(d)	(d)	...	(d)	(d)	...
Catahoula	025	Harrisonburg	704	10,920	11,065	-1.3	(d)	(d)	...	(d)	(d)	...
Claiborne	027	Homer	755	16,851	17,405	-3.2	82,098	-32.5	...	(d)	(d)	...
Concordia	029	Vidalia	696	20,247	20,828	-2.8	(d)	(d)	...	(d)	(d)	...
De Soto	031	Mansfield	877	25,494	25,346	0.6	(d)	(d)	15	(d)	(d)	
East Baton Rouge	033	Baton Rouge	455	412,852	380,105	8.6	4,838,465	20.8	346	11,523	3,819,231	2,021
East Carroll	035	Lake Providence	421	9,421	9,709	-3.0	(d)	(d)	...	(d)	(d)	...
East Feliciana	037	Clinton	453	21,360	19,211	11.2	(d)	(d)	...	(d)	(d)	...
Evangeline	039	Ville Platte	664	35,434	33,274	6.5	(d)	(d)	17	(d)	(d)	...
Franklin	041	Winnsboro	624	21,263	22,387	-5.0	(d)	(d)	...	(d)	(d)	...
Grant	043	Colfax	645	18,698	17,526	6.7	(d)	(d)	...	(d)	(d)	...
Iberia	045	New Iberia	575	73,266	68,297	7.3	343,569	-4.3	97	3,861	413,576	219
Iberville	047	Plaquemine	619	33,320	31,049	7.3	102,967	14.8	33	3,823	1,023,866	542
Jackson	049	Jonesboro	570	15,397	15,705	-2.0	(d)	(d)	...	(d)	(d)	...
Jefferson	051	Gretna	307	455,466	448,306	1.6	6,442,790	-35.8	399	15,508	1,069,557	566
Jefferson Davis	053	Jennings	652	31,435	30,722	2.3	380,249	40.5	...	(d)	(d)	...
Lafayette	055	Lafayette	270	190,503	164,762	15.6	2,545,328	-2.9	251	6,444	555,167	294
Lafourche	057	Thibodaux	1,085	89,974	85,860	4.8	663,618	102.0	57	2,090	206,449	109
La Salle	059	Jena	624	14,282	13,662	4.5	(d)	(d)	...	(d)	(d)	...
Lincoln	061	Ruston	471	42,509	41,745	1.8	(d)	(d)	34	(d)	(d)	...
Livingston	063	Livingston	648	91,814	70,526	30.2	163,871	17.0	59	1,553	129,572	69
Madison	065	Tallulah	624	13,728	12,463	10.2	(d)	(d)	...	(d)	(d)	...
Morehouse	067	Bastrop	794	31,021	31,938	-2.9	47,127	2.9	14	1,050	189,688	100
Natchitoches	069	Natchitoches	1,255	39,080	36,689	6.5	88,230	-3.0	22	2,540	373,916	198
Orleans	071	New Orleans	181	484,674	496,938	-2.5	2,792,080	13.9	225	8,584	1,221,934	646
Ouachita	073	Monroe	611	147,250	142,191	3.6	(d)	(d)	149	7,365	819,734	434
Plaquemines	075	Pointe a la Hache	845	26,757	25,575	4.6	424,523	-49.3	42	1,963	469,399	248
Pointe Coupee	077	New Roads	557	22,763	22,540	1.0	70,173	(d)	...	(d)	(d)	...
Rapides	079	Alexandria	1,323	126,337	131,556	-4.0	(d)	(d)	70	3,083	824,894	436
Red River	081	Coushatta	389	9,622	9,387	2.5	(d)	(d)	...	(d)	(d)	...
Richland	083	Rayville	558	20,981	20,629	1.7	163,161	1.7	17	(d)	(d)	...
Sabine	085	Many	865	23,459	22,646	3.6	(d)	(d)	18	792	80,734	43
St. Bernard	087	Chalmette	465	67,229	66,631	0.9	(d)	(d)	58	2,101	394,835	209
St. Charles	089	Hahnville	284	48,072	42,437	13.3	2,223,674	-15.4	38	4,894	3,175,388	1,680
St. Helena	091	Greensburg	408	10,525	9,874	6.6	(d)	(d)	...	(d)	(d)	...
St. James	093	Convent	246	21,216	20,879	1.6	(d)	(d)	26	2,402	697,207	369
St. John The Baptist	095	Edgard	219	43,044	39,996	7.6	(d)	(d)	24	2,175	1,006,079	532
St. Landry	097	Opelousas	929	87,700	80,331	9.2	448,341	8.0	48	1,669	211,720	112
St. Martin	099	St. Martinville	740	48,583	43,978	10.5	114,617	-1.6	47	718	67,359	36
St. Mary	101	Franklin	613	53,500	58,086	-7.9	484,162	-31.3	90	5,225	464,225	246
St. Tammany	103	Covington	854	191,268	144,508	32.4	6,428,544	-2.7	127	2,130	195,878	104
Tangipahoa	105	Amite	790	100,588	85,709	17.4	373,886	-48.5	81	3,032	264,994	140
Tensas	107	St. Joseph	602	6,618	7,103	-6.8	55,146	9.2	...	(d)	(d)	...
Terrebonne	109	Houma	1,255	104,503	96,982	7.8	670,803	-15.1	125	4,401	357,385	189
Union	111	Farmerville	878	22,803	20,690	10.2	(d)	(d)	13	1,787	64,785	34
Vermilion	113	Abbeville	1,174	53,807	50,055	7.5	(d)	(d)	39	1,712	164,798	87
Vernon	115	Leesville	1,328	52,531	61,961	-15.2	(d)	(d)	...	(d)	(d)	...
Washington	117	Franklinton	670	43,926	43,185	1.7	(d)	(d)	36	1,367	250,639	133
Webster	119	Minden	595	41,831	41,989	-0.4	181,173	(d)	39	2,104	151,385	80
West Baton Rouge	121	Port Allen	191	21,601	19,419	11.2	415,772	-6.4	39	2,313	474,395	251
West Carroll	123	Oak Grove	359	12,314	12,093	1.8	(d)	(d)	...	(d)	(d)	...
West Feliciana	125	St. Francisville	406	15,111	12,915	17.0	(d)	(d)	6	(d)	(d)	...
Winn	127	Winnfield	950	16,894	16,269	3.8	(d)	(d)	17	948	52,577	28
The State			**43,562**	**4,468,976**	**4,219,973**	**5.9**	**47,192,153**	**0.5**	**3,524**	**150,401**	**28,404,879**	**15,028**

(d) Data not available. Corresponding percentages or Ranally Manufacturing Units are estimates.
... Represents 0 or amount too minimal to be reported.

Index of Places and Parishes

Entries in **UPPERCASE** are parishes.
Entries in **bold** have populations of 2,500 or more.
Names in parentheses are alternate names.
Inc. Place — Incorporated Place
RMC Place — Rand McNally Designated Place
CDP — Census Designated Place
MCD — Minor Civil Division

⊡ Parish Seat
▲ Minor Civil Division
elev. Elevation
🅿 Post Office

🄷 Hospital
🄲 College
■ Principal Business Center
★ Ranally Metro Area (RMA) Abbreviation
z Zip Code(s)

℗ Previous Census Population
® Revised Census Population
Ⓐ Annexation Population
● Rand McNally Population Estimate
© Final Census Population
Ⓢ Special Census Population
◆ Estimated Population

For additional definitions see Glossary, Volume 1, and Introduction, Volume 2.

Albania; RMC Place; ST. MARY; mail Jeanerette z 70544; rural
Albany; Inc. Place; LIVINGSTON; 182 G-8; elev. 41ft./12m.; 🅿; z 70711; Ⓟ 645; Ⓒ 865
Alberta; RMC Place; BIENVILLE; *182 C-3; elev. 196ft./60m.; mail Castor z 71016; rural
Alco; RMC Place; VERNON; *182 E-3; elev. 320ft./98m.; mail Leesville z 71446; rural
Alden Bridge; RMC Place; BOSSIER; *182 B-2; elev. 222ft./68m.; mail Benton z 71006; rural
Alexandria; Inc. Place; ⊡ RAPIDES; 182 E-4; elev. 82ft./25m.; 🅿 🅷 🅲 2,720 ■; ★ ALEX; z 71301-03, z 71306-07, z 71309, z 71315; Ⓟ 49,188; Ⓒ 46,342; ◆ 47,000
Alfalfa; RMC Place; RAPIDES; *182 E-4; ★ ALEX; mail Boyce z 71409; rural
Alfords; RMC Place; WEST BATON ROUGE; *182 G-7; mail Port Allen z 70767; rural
Algiers; RMC Place; ORLEANS; *182 H-9; ★ N.O.; mail New Orleans z 70114; pop. incl. with New Orleans (Inc. Place)
Alice B; RMC Place; ST. MARY; *182 I-6; elev. 9ft./3m.; mail Franklin z 70538; ● 40
Alice C; RMC Place; ST. MARY; mail Franklin z 70538; rural
Allemand; RMC Place; TERREBONNE; *182 I-8; ★ HOMA-; mail Houma z 70360; ● 260
Allen; RMC Place; NATCHITOCHES; *182 D-3; elev. 172ft./52m.; mail Robeline z 71469; ● 100
ALLEN; 182 G-3; Ⓟ 21,226; Ⓒ 25,440; ◆ 25,573
Allendale; RMC Place; WEST BATON ROUGE; *182 G-7; ★ B.R.; mail Port Allen z 70767; rural
Alliance; RMC Place; PLAQUEMINES; *182 I-9; mail Belle Chasse z 70037; rural
Allon; RMC Place; POINTE COUPEE; *182 G-6; mail New Roads z 70760; ● 50
Alluvial City (Yscloskey); RMC Place; ST. BERNARD; 182 I-10; elev. 4ft./1m.; mail Saint Bernard z 70085; ● 520
Almadane; RMC Place; VERNON; *182 F-2; mail Evans z 70639; rural
Aloha; RMC Place; GRANT; *182 E-4; elev. 101ft./31m.; mail Colfax z 71417; rural
Aloysia; RMC Place; IBERVILLE; mail White Castle z 70788; ● 30
Alsen; RMC Place; EAST BATON ROUGE; *182 G-7; ★ B.R.; mail Baton Rouge z 70807; ● 290
Alto; RMC Place; RICHLAND; 182 C-6; elev. 75ft./23m.; 🅿; z 71269; ● 160
Alton; RMC Place; ST. TAMMANY; 182 H-10; elev. 28ft./9m.; ★ N.O.; mail Slidell z 70460; ● 380
Ama; CDP; ST. CHARLES; *182 H-9; elev. 10ft./3m.; 🅿; ★ N.O.; z 70031; Ⓒ 1,285
Amelia; CDP; ST. MARY; 182 I-7; elev. 5ft./2m.; 🅿; z 70340; Ⓟ 2,447; Ⓒ 2,423

Amite (Amite City); Inc. Place; ⊡ TANGIPAHOA; 182 G-8; 🅿 🅷; z 70422; Ⓟ 4,236; Ⓒ 4,110
Amite City; TANGIPAHOA; see Amite (Inc. Place)
Anacoco; Inc. Place; VERNON; 182 E-3; elev. 338ft./103m.; 🅿; z 71403; Ⓟ 823; Ⓒ 866
Anandale; RMC Place; RAPIDES; 182 E-4; ★ ALEX; mail Alexandria z 71301; pop. incl. with Alexandria (Inc. Place)
Andrew; RMC Place; VERMILION; *182 H-5; mail Kaplan z 70548; ● 60
Andrew Guillot Subdivision; RMC Place; LAFOURCHE; *182 I-8; ★ HOMA-; mail Thibodaux z 70301; ● 200
Angelina; RMC Place; ST. JOHN THE BAPTIST; *182 H-8; elev. 12ft./4m.; mail Mount Airy z 70076
Angie; Inc. Place; WASHINGTON; 182 F-10; elev. 142ft./43m.; 🅿; z 70426, z 70467; Ⓟ 235; Ⓒ 240
Annadale; RMC Place; IBERVILLE; *182 H-7; mail White Castle z 70788; rural
Ansley; RMC Place; JACKSON; *182 C-4; mail Ruston z 71270; rural
Antioch; RMC Place; CLAIBORNE; *182 B-3; elev. 309ft./94m.; mail Homer z 71040
Antioch; RMC Place; LINCOLN; *182 B-4; mail Simsboro z 71275; rural
Antonia; RMC Place; GRANT; *182 E-4; elev. 186ft./57m.; mail Pollock z 71467; rural
Antonio; RMC Place; WEST BATON ROUGE; *182 G-7; ★ B.R.; mail Port Allen z 70767; ● 30
Antrim; RMC Place; BOSSIER; *182 A-2; elev. 279ft./85m.; mail Plain Dealing z 71064; rural
Arabi; CDP; ST. BERNARD; 182 H-9; elev. 5ft./2m.; 🅿; ★ N.O.; z 70032; Ⓟ 8,787; Ⓒ 8,093
Ararat; RMC Place; CALCASIEU; *182 H-3; elev. 21ft./6m.; ★ LKCH; mail Lake Charles z 70601
Arbroth; RMC Place; WEST BATON ROUGE; *182 G-7; ● 30
Arcadia; Inc. Place; ⊡ BIENVILLE; 182 B-3; elev. 360ft./110m.; 🅿; z 71001; Ⓟ 3,079; Ⓒ 3,041
Archibald; RMC Place; RICHLAND; 182 C-6; elev. 74ft./23m.; 🅿; z 71218; ● 230
Archie; RMC Place; CATAHOULA; *182 E-5; elev. 67ft./20m.; mail Jonesville z 71343; rural
Arcola; RMC Place; TANGIPAHOA; *182 F-8; mail Roseland z 70456; ● 170
Ardoyne; RMC Place; TERREBONNE; *182 I-8; ★ HOMA-; mail Houma z 70360; rural
Argo; RMC Place; CATAHOULA; *182 E-5; mail Jonesville z 71343; rural
Argyle; RMC Place; TERREBONNE; *182 I-8; ★ HOMA-; mail Houma z 70360; pop. incl. with Houma (Inc. Place)
Arizona; RMC Place; CLAIBORNE; *182 B-3; elev. 282ft./86m.; mail Homer z 71040; rural
Arklatex; RMC Place; CADDO; ★ SHRE; mail Mooringsport z 71060; pop. incl. with Mooringsport (Inc. Place)
Arlington; RMC Place; EAST BATON ROUGE; *182 G-7; ★ B.R.; mail Baton Rouge z 70808; pop. incl. with Baton Rouge (Inc. Place)
Armistead; RMC Place; RED RIVER; *182 D-2; elev. 131ft./40m.; mail Coushatta z 71019
Arnaudville; Inc. Place; ST. LANDRY, ST. MARTIN; 182 G-5; elev. 29ft./9m.; 🅿; ★ LAF; z 70512; Ⓟ 1,444; Ⓒ 1,398
ASCENSION; 182 H-7; Ⓟ 58,214; Ⓒ 76,627; ◆ 101,629
Ashland; Inc. Place; NATCHITOCHES; 182 C-3; elev. 238ft./73m.; 🅿; z 71002; Ⓟ 289; Ⓒ 291
Ashland; RMC Place; TENSAS; *182 D-6; mail Saint Joseph z 71366; rural
Ashland; RMC Place; TERREBONNE; *182 I-8; ★ HOMA-; mail Houma z 70360; ● 150
Ashley; RMC Place; MADISON; *182 C-7; mail Tallulah z 71282; rural
Ashton; RMC Place; ST. MARY; *182 I-6; elev. 5ft./2m.; mail Franklin z 70538; rural
ASSUMPTION; 182 I-7; Ⓟ 22,753; Ⓒ 23,388; ◆ 22,656
Athens; Inc. Place; CLAIBORNE; 182 B-3; elev. 299ft./91m.; 🅿; z 71003; Ⓟ 278; Ⓒ 262
Atlanta; Inc. Place; WINN; 182 D-4; elev. 200ft./61m.; 🅿; z 71404; Ⓟ 118; Ⓒ 150
Attakapas Canal; ASSUMPTION; see Attakapas Landing (RMC Place)
Attakapas Landing (Attakapas Canal); RMC Place; ASSUMPTION; *182 I-7; elev. 8ft./2m.; mail Napoleonville z 70390; rural
Audubon; RMC Place; EAST BATON ROUGE; *182 G-7; ★ B.R.; mail Baton Rouge z 70806, z 70896; pop. incl. with Baton Rouge (Inc. Place)
Audubon Terrace; RMC Place; EAST BATON ROUGE; *182 G-7; ★ B.R.; mail Baton Rouge z 70808; ● 210
Augusta; RMC Place; IBERVILLE; *182 H-7; ● 30
Augusta; RMC Place; PLAQUEMINES; *182 I-9; ★ N.O.; mail Belle Chasse z 70037
Aurora Gardens; RMC Place; ORLEANS; ★ N.O.; pop. incl. with New Orleans (Inc. Place)
Avalon; RMC Place; ST. MARY; *182 I-7; elev. 11ft./3m.; mail Patterson z 70392; rural
Avery Island; RMC Place; IBERIA; 182 I-5; elev. 50ft./15m.; 🅿; z 70513; ● 350
Avondale; CDP; JEFFERSON; 182 E-12; 🅿; ★ N.O.; z 70094; Ⓟ 5,813; Ⓒ 5,441
Avondale; RMC Place; TENSAS; *182 D-7; mail Saint Joseph z 71366; rural
AVOYELLES; 182 E-5; Ⓟ 39,159; Ⓒ 41,481; ◆ 41,656
Aycock; RMC Place; CLAIBORNE; *182 B-3; elev. 357ft./109m.; mail Arcadia z 71001, Homer z 71040; rural
Azucena; RMC Place; TENSAS; *182 D-6; mail Waterproof z 71375; rural

B

Bagdad; RMC Place; GRANT; *182 E-4; mail Colfax z 71417; rural
Bains; RMC Place; WEST FELICIANA; 182 F-7; elev. 188ft./57m.; 🅿; z 70775; ● 60
Baker; Inc. Place; EAST BATON ROUGE; 182 G-7; 🅿; ★ B.R.; z 70704, z 70714; Ⓟ 13,233; Ⓒ 13,793
Baldwin; Inc. Place; ST. MARY; 182 I-6; 🅿; z 70514; Ⓟ 2,379; Ⓒ 2,497
Ball; Inc. Place; RAPIDES; 182 E-4; elev. 141ft./43m.; 🅿; ★ ALEX; z 71405 & mail Pineville z 71360; Ⓟ 3,305; Ⓒ 3,681
Bancroft; RMC Place; BEAUREGARD; *182 G-2; elev. 95ft./29m.; mail Merryville z 70653; rural
Bankers; RMC Place; ST. MARTIN; *182 H-6; mail Saint Martinville z 70582; rural
Banks; RMC Place; EAST BATON ROUGE; ★ B.R.; mail Baton Rouge z 70807; pop. incl. with Baton Rouge (Inc. Place)
Banks Springs; RMC Place; CALDWELL; *182 C-5; mail Columbia z 71418; ● 150
Baptist; RMC Place; TANGIPAHOA; *182 G-8; elev. 41ft./12m.; mail Hammond z 70403; ● 200
Barataria; CDP; JEFFERSON; 182 I-9; 🅿; ★ N.O.; z 70036; Ⓟ 1,160; Ⓒ 1,333
Barber Spur (The Y); RMC Place; EVANGELINE; *182 G-4; elev. 68ft./21m.; mail Ville Platte z 70586; rural
Barcelona; RMC Place; TENSAS; *182 D-6; mail Waterproof z 71375; rural
Bardel; RMC Place; RICHLAND; *182 B-6; mail Rayville z 71269; rural
Barnet Springs; RMC Place; LINCOLN; *182 B-4; mail Ruston z 71270; pop. incl. with Ruston (Inc. Place)
Barnsdall; RMC Place; JEFFERSON DAVIS; *182 G-4; mail Elton z 70532; ● 30
Barron; RMC Place; RAPIDES; *182 E-5; mail Deville z 71328; rural
Barton; RMC Place; ASCENSION; *182 H-7; mail Donaldsonville z 70346; ● 30
Basile; Inc. Place; EVANGELINE, ACADIA; 182 G-4; elev. 46ft./14m.; 🅿; z 70515; Ⓟ 1,808; Ⓒ 1,660; Ⓡ 2,431
Baskin; Inc. Place; FRANKLIN; 182 C-6; 🅿; z 71219; Ⓟ 243; Ⓒ 188
Baskinton; RMC Place; FRANKLIN; *182 C-6; mail Baskin z 71219
Bastrop; Inc. Place; ⊡ MOREHOUSE; 182 B-5; elev. 126ft./38m.; 🅿 🅷; z 71220-21; Ⓟ 13,916; Ⓒ 12,988
Batchelor; RMC Place; POINTE COUPEE; 182 F-6; elev. 45ft./14m.; 🅿; z 70715; ● 150
Baton Rouge; Inc. Place; STATE CAPITAL; ⊡ EAST BATON ROUGE; 182 G-7; 🅿 🅷 🅲 35,259 ■; ★ B.R.; z 70801-23, z 70825-27, z 70831, z 70833, z 70835-37, z 70873-74, z 70879, z 70884, z 70891-96, z 70898; Ⓟ 219,531; Ⓒ 227,818; ◆ 239,580
Baton Rouge Junction; RMC Place; EAST BATON ROUGE; elev. 19ft./6m.; ★ B.R.; pop. incl. with Baton Rouge (Inc. Place)
Batree (Baytree); RMC Place; ST. JAMES; *182 H-8; mail Vacherie z 70090; rural
Bawcomville; RMC Place; OUACHITA; 182 C-5; ★ MONR; mail West Monroe z 71292; ● 2,300
Bayou Barbary; RMC Place; LIVINGSTON; *182 H-8; mail Livingston z 70754; rural
Bayou Blue (Savoie); RMC Place; LAFOURCHE, TERREBONNE; *182 I-8; ★ HOMA-; mail Houma z 70360; ● 2,800
Bayou Boeuf; LAFOURCHE; see Kraemer (RMC Place)
Bayou Cane; CDP-Census Area Only; TERREBONNE; 182 I-8; ★ HOMA-; mail Gray z 70359; Ⓟ 15,876; Ⓒ 17,046
Bayou Chicot; RMC Place; EVANGELINE; 182 F-5; elev. 127ft./39m.; mail Ville Platte z 70586; ● 150
Bayou Crab; RMC Place; ASSUMPTION; *182 I-7; elev. 4ft./1m.; mail Napoleonville z 70390; rural
Bayou Current; RMC Place; ST. LANDRY; *182 F-6; mail Melville z 71353
Bayou Gauche; CDP; ST. CHARLES; *182 I-9; mail Des Allemands z 70030; Ⓒ 1,770
Bayou Goula; RMC Place; IBERVILLE; 182 H-7; 🅿; z 70788; ● 650
Bayou Pigeon; IBERVILLE; see Pigeon (RMC Place)
Bayou Sale; RMC Place; ST. MARY; *182 I-6; mail Franklin z 70538; rural
Bayou Sorrel; RMC Place; IBERVILLE; 182 H-7; mail Plaquemine z 70764; ● 420
Bayou Vista; CDP; ST. MARY; 182 I-7; mail Morgan City z 70380; Ⓟ 4,733; Ⓒ 4,351
Baytree; ST. JAMES; see Batree (RMC Place)
Baywood; RMC Place; EAST BATON ROUGE; *182 G-8; mail Greenwell Springs z 70739; ● 100
Beach Grove; RMC Place; UNION; *182 A-4; mail Spearsville z 71277; ● 30
Beachview; RMC Place; JEFFERSON; ★ N.O.; mail Kenner z 70062; pop. incl. with Kenner (Inc. Place)
Bear Creek; RMC Place; BIENVILLE; *182 C-3; mail Bienville z 71008; ● 30
Bear Skin; RMC Place; WEST CARROLL; *182 B-6; mail Pioneer z 71266; rural
Beattieville; TERREBONNE; see Gray (CDP)
BEAUREGARD; 182 G-2; Ⓟ 30,083; Ⓒ 32,986; ◆ 34,716
Beaver; RMC Place; EVANGELINE; *182 F-4; elev. 99ft./30m.; mail Oakdale z 71463; rural
Bee Bayou; RMC Place; RICHLAND; *182 B-6; mail Rayville z 71269; rural
Beech Springs; RMC Place; JACKSON; *182 C-4; mail Quitman z 71268; rural
Beekman; RMC Place; MOREHOUSE; 182 A-5; mail Bastrop z 71220; ● 200
Beggs; RMC Place; ST. LANDRY; *182 G-5; mail Bunkie z 71322
Bel; RMC Place; ALLEN; *182 G-3; elev. 70ft./21m.; mail Reeves z 70658; rural
Belah; RMC Place; LA SALLE; *182 D-5; mail Trout z 71371; ● 100
Belair; RMC Place; PLAQUEMINES; *182 I-9; elev. 4ft./1m.; mail Braithwaite z 70040; ● 120
Belair Cove; RMC Place; EVANGELINE; *182 G-5; mail Ville Platte z 70586; ● 50
Belcher; Inc. Place; CADDO; 182 B-2; elev. 180ft./55m.; 🅿; z 71004; Ⓟ 249; Ⓒ 272
Belfield; RMC Place; CALCASIEU; *182 H-3; mail Lake Charles z 70611; rural
Bell City; RMC Place; CALCASIEU; 182 H-3; elev. 8ft./2m.; 🅿; z 70630; ● 350
Belle Amie; RMC Place; LAFOURCHE; *182 J-9; mail Cut Off z 70345; ● 60
Belle Chasse; CDP; PLAQUEMINES; 182 I-9; elev. 5ft./2m.; 🅿; ★ N.O.; z 70037, z 70093; Ⓟ 8,512; Ⓒ 9,848
Belledeau (New Belledeau); RMC Place; AVOYELLES; *182 F-5; mail Hessmer z 71341; ● 300
Belle Place; RMC Place; IBERIA; *182 H-6; ★ LAF; mail Loreauville z 70552; rural
Belle Point; RMC Place; ST. JOHN THE BAPTIST; mail Reserve z 70084
Belle River; RMC Place; ASSUMPTION; *182 I-7; mail Pierre Part z 70339; ● 250
Belle Rose; CDP; ASSUMPTION; 182 H-7; elev. 21ft./6m.; 🅿; z 70341; Ⓒ 1,944
Belle Terre; RMC Place; ASSUMPTION; *182 H-7; elev. 17ft./5m.; mail Donaldsonville z 70346; rural
Belle Terre; RMC Place; IBERVILLE; *182 H-7; ★ B.R.; mail Plaquemine z 70764; ● 100
Belleview; RMC Place; ST. LANDRY; mail Opelousas z 70570; rural
Bellevue; RMC Place; BOSSIER; 182 B-2; elev. 286ft./87m.; ★ SHRE; mail Haughton z 71037; ● 70
Bellevue; RMC Place; CALDWELL; *182 C-5; elev. 64ft./20m.; mail Columbia z 71418; rural
Bellfontaine; RMC Place; EAST BATON ROUGE; ★ B.R.; mail Baton Rouge z 70815; pop. incl. with Baton Rouge (Inc. Place)
Bell Helene; RMC Place; ASCENSION; *182 H-7; mail Geismar z 70734; rural
Bellwood; RMC Place; NATCHITOCHES; *182 E-3; elev. 144ft./44m.; mail Provencal z 71468
Belmont; RMC Place; SABINE; 182 D-2; elev. 339ft./103m.; 🅿; z 71406; ● 140
Belmont; RMC Place; ST. JAMES; *182 H-8; elev. 17ft./5m.; mail Hester z 70743
Belmont; RMC Place; WEST BATON ROUGE; *182 G-7; ★ B.R.; mail Port Allen z 70767; rural
Benson; RMC Place; DE SOTO; 182 D-2; mail Converse z 71419; ● 130
Bentley; RMC Place; GRANT; 182 E-4; elev. 215ft./66m.; 🅿; z 71407; ● 300
Benton; Inc. Place; ⊡ BOSSIER; 182 B-2; elev. 215ft./66m.; 🅿; ★ SHRE; z 71006; Ⓟ 2,047; Ⓒ 2,035
Bermuda; RMC Place; NATCHITOCHES; *182 D-3; mail Natchez z 71456; ● 30
Bernard Terrace; RMC Place; EAST BATON ROUGE; ★ B.R.; pop. incl. with Baton Rouge (Inc. Place)
Bernice; Inc. Place; UNION; 182 B-4; 🅿 🅷; z 71222; Ⓟ 1,543; Ⓒ 1,809
Bertie; RMC Place; ASSUMPTION; *182 I-7; elev. 15ft./5m.; mail Napoleonville z 70390; ● 30
Bertrand; RMC Place; LAFAYETTE; ★ LAF; mail Lafayette z 70596; pop. incl. with Lafayette (Inc. Place)
Bertrandville; RMC Place; ASSUMPTION; *182 H-7; mail Napoleonville z 70390; ● 150
Bertrandville; RMC Place; PLAQUEMINES; 182 I-9; elev. 8ft./2m.; ★ N.O.; mail Braithwaite z 70040; ● 100
Berwick; Inc. Place; ST. MARY; 182 I-7; 🅿; z 70342; Ⓟ 4,375; Ⓒ 4,418
Bethany; RMC Place; CADDO; 182 C-1; see also Bethany, TX; elev. 330ft./101m.; 🅿; ★ SHRE; z 71007; ● 150
Bienville; Inc. Place; BIENVILLE; 182 C-3; elev. 238ft./73m.; 🅿; z 71008; Ⓟ 316; Ⓒ 262
BIENVILLE; 182 C-3; Ⓟ 15,979; Ⓒ 15,752; ◆ 14,788
Big Bend; RMC Place; AVOYELLES; 182 F-6; elev. 50ft./15m.; mail Moreauville z 71355; ● 60
Big Branch; RMC Place; ST. TAMMANY; *182 H-9; ★ N.O.; mail Lacombe z 70445; rural
Big Cane; RMC Place; ST. LANDRY; *182 F-5; elev. 40ft./12m.; mail Morrow z 71356; ● 50
Big Creek; RMC Place; FRANKLIN; *182 C-6; mail Baskin z 71219; rural
Big Island; RMC Place; RAPIDES; *182 E-5; mail Deville z 71328; ● 200
Big Woods; RMC Place; CALCASIEU; *182 H-2; elev. 30ft./9m.; mail Vinton z 70668; ● 150
Bijou; RAPIDES; see Echo (RMC Place)
Billeaud; RMC Place; LAFAYETTE; *182 H-5; ★ LAF; mail Broussard z 70518; pop. incl. with Broussard (Inc. Place)
Bird; RMC Place; EAST BATON ROUGE; *182 G-7; ★ B.R.; pop. incl. with Baton Rouge (Inc. Place)
Bissonnet; RMC Place; JEFFERSON; ★ N.O.; mail Metairie z 70003
Bivens; RMC Place; BEAUREGARD; *182 G-2; mail Merryville z 70653; rural
Blackburn; RMC Place; CLAIBORNE; *182 B-3; mail Haynesville z 71038
Black Hawk; RMC Place; CONCORDIA; *182 F-6; elev. 54ft./16m.; mail Vidalia z 71373; rural
Blade; RMC Place; LA SALLE; *182 D-5; mail Jena z 71342; rural
Blanchard; Inc. Place; CADDO; *182 B-1; elev. 220ft./67m.; 🅿; ★ SHRE; z 71009 & mail Shreveport z 71107; Ⓟ 1,175; Ⓒ 2,050
Blanche; RMC Place; RAPIDES; *182 F-4; elev. 153ft./47m.; mail Glenmora z 71433; rural
Blanks; RMC Place; POINTE COUPEE; *182 G-6; elev. 25ft./8m.; 🅿; z 70756; ● 100
Blankston; RMC Place; CALDWELL; *182 C-5; elev. 66ft./20m.; mail Monroe z 71202; rural
Blond; RMC Place; ST. TAMMANY; *182 G-9; elev. 135ft./41m.; mail Covington z 70435; rural
Bluff Creek; RMC Place; EAST FELICIANA; *182 G-8; elev. 132ft./40m.; mail Clinton z 70722; rural
Bob Acres; RMC Place; IBERIA; *182 H-5; mail New Iberia z 70560; rural
Bodcau; RMC Place; BOSSIER; *182 B-2; elev. 208ft./63m.; ★ SHRE; mail Haughton z 71037; rural
Bodoc; RMC Place; AVOYELLES; *182 F-5; elev. 43ft./13m.; mail Plaucheville z 71362; ● 30
Bogalusa; Inc. Place; WASHINGTON; 182 F-10; elev. 100ft./30m.; 🅿 🅷; z 70427, z 70429; Ⓟ 14,280; Ⓒ 13,365
Bohemia; RMC Place; PLAQUEMINES; 182 I-10; mail Pointe a la Hache z 70082; ● 40
Boise Southern; RMC Place; BEAUREGARD; pop. incl. with DeRidder (Inc. Place)
Bolden; RMC Place; ST. LANDRY; *182 G-5; mail Palmetto z 71358; ● 40
Boleyn; RMC Place; SABINE; mail Marthaville z 71450; rural
Bolinger; RMC Place; BOSSIER; 182 A-2; mail Plain Dealing z 71064; ● 200
Bolivar; RMC Place; TANGIPAHOA; *182 F-9; mail Kentwood z 70444; ● 200
Bonaire; RMC Place; EAST BATON ROUGE; *182 G-7; ★ B.R.; mail Baton Rouge z 70808; ● 320
Bond; RMC Place; ALLEN; *182 G-4; mail Oakdale z 71463; rural
Bonfouca; RMC Place; ST. TAMMANY; *182 H-10; ★ N.O.; mail Slidell z 70458; ● 600
Bonita; Inc. Place; MOREHOUSE; 182 A-6; elev. 105ft./32m.; 🅿; z 71223; Ⓟ 265; Ⓒ 335
Bonnabel Place; RMC Place; JEFFERSON; *182 H-9; ★ N.O.
Bon Secour; RMC Place; ST. JAMES; *182 H-8; mail Saint James z 70086; rural
Book; RMC Place; CATAHOULA; *182 E-6; mail Jonesville z 71343; rural
Boone's Corner; RMC Place; CAMERON; *182 H-3; mail Lake Charles z 70607; ● 30
Boothville; RMC Place; PLAQUEMINES; 182 J-11; elev. 5ft./2m.; 🅿; z 70038; ● 900
Boothville-Venice; CDP-Census Area Only; PLAQUEMINES; *182 J-11; elev. 5ft./2m.; mail Boothville z 70038; Ⓟ 2,743; Ⓒ 2,220
Bordelonville; RMC Place; AVOYELLES; 182 F-5; 🅿; z 71320; ● 400
Borgne Mouth; RMC Place; ST. BERNARD; ★ N.O.; mail Violet z 70092
Borodino; RMC Place; AVOYELLES; 182 F-5; mail Moreauville z 71355; ● 240
Bosco; RMC Place; OUACHITA; 182 C-5; mail Monroe z 71201; ● 50
BOSSIER; 182 B-2; Ⓟ 86,088; Ⓒ 98,310; ◆ 110,765
Bossier City; Inc. Place; BOSSIER; 182 B-2; elev. 174ft./53m.; 🅿 🅷 ■; ★ SHRE; z 71111-13, z 71171-72; Ⓟ 52,721; Ⓒ 56,461; Ⓡ 56,466; ◆ 64,543
Boston; RMC Place; VERMILION; *182 I-5; elev. 7ft./2m.; mail Erath z 70533; rural
Boudreaux; RMC Place; IBERIA; *182 I-6; ★ LAF; mail New Iberia z 70560; ● 300
Boudreaux (Grand Caillou); RMC Place; TERREBONNE; *182 J-8; ★ HOMA-; mail Houma z 70360; ● 1,500
Boudreaux Canal; RMC Place; TERREBONNE; *182 J-8; ★ HOMA-; mail Chauvin z 70344; rural
Bourg; RMC Place; TERREBONNE; 182 I-8; elev. 7ft./2m.; 🅿; ★ HOMA-; z 70343; ● 2,160
Boutte; CDP; ST. CHARLES; *182 I-9; elev. 5ft./2m.; 🅿; ★ N.O.; z 70039; Ⓟ 2,702; Ⓒ 2,181
Boyce; Inc. Place; RAPIDES; 182 E-4; elev. 84ft./26m.; 🅿; z 71409; Ⓟ 1,361; Ⓒ 1,190
Braithwaite; RMC Place; PLAQUEMINES; *182 I-10; elev. 4ft./1m.; 🅿; ★ N.O.; z 70040; ● 40
Branch; RMC Place; ACADIA; 182 H-5; elev. 40ft./12m.; 🅿; z 70516; ● 250
Breard; RMC Place; OUACHITA; *182 B-5; ★ MONR; pop. incl. with Monroe (Inc. Place)
Breaux Bridge; Inc. Place; ST. MARTIN; 182 H-5; elev. 15ft./5m.; 🅿 🅷; ★ LAF; z 70517; Ⓟ 6,515; Ⓒ 7,281
Breezy Hill; RMC Place; GRANT; *182 D-4; elev. 180ft./55m.; mail Pollock z 71467; rural
Brewtons Mill; RMC Place; WINN; *182 C-4; mail Goldonna z 71031
Brice; BIENVILLE; see Bryceland (Inc. Place)
Bridge City; CDP; JEFFERSON; 182 E-12; elev. 5ft./2m.; 🅿; ★ N.O.; z 70094; Ⓟ 8,327; Ⓒ 8,323
Bridgedale; RMC Place; JEFFERSON; ★ N.O.
Brignac; RMC Place; ASCENSION; *182 H-8; elev. 15ft./5m.; ★ B.R.; mail Gonzales z 70737; rural
Bristol; RMC Place; ST. LANDRY; *182 G-5; ★ LAF; mail Sunset z 70584; ● 50
Brittany; RMC Place; ASCENSION; *182 H-8; elev. 6ft./2m.; 🅿; ★ B.R.; z 70718; ● 230
Broadacres; RMC Place; CADDO; ★ SHRE; pop. incl. with Shreveport (Inc. Place)
Broadmoor; RMC Place; EAST BATON ROUGE; *182 G-7; ★ B.R.; pop. incl. with Baton Rouge (Inc. Place)
Broadmoor; RMC Place; ORLEANS; *182 H-9; ★ N.O.; mail New Orleans z 70125; pop. incl. with New Orleans (Inc. Place)
Broadmoor; RMC Place; TERREBONNE; *182 I-8; ★ HOMA-; mail Houma z 70360
Brooks; RMC Place; POINTE COUPEE; *182 G-6; mail New Roads z 70760; rural
Brookstown; RMC Place; EAST BATON ROUGE; *182 G-7; ★ B.R.; pop. incl. with Baton Rouge (Inc. Place)
Brookwood; RMC Place; CADDO; ★ SHRE; mail Woodworth z 71485; pop. incl. with Shreveport (Inc. Place)
Brouillette; RMC Place; AVOYELLES; *182 E-5; elev. 57ft./17m.; mail Marksville z 71351; ● 200
Broussard; Inc. Place; LAFAYETTE; 182 H-5; 🅿; ★ LAF; z 70518; Ⓟ 3,213; Ⓒ 5,874
Brown; RMC Place; BIENVILLE; *182 C-3; elev. 285ft./87m.; mail Castor z 71016; rural
Brownell; RMC Place; FRANKLIN; *182 C-6; mail Winnsboro z 71295; rural
Brownfields; CDP-Census Area Only; EAST BATON ROUGE; *182 G-7; elev. 55ft./17m.; ★ B.R.; mail Baton Rouge z 70811; Ⓟ 5,229; Ⓒ 5,222
Brown Heights; RMC Place; EAST BATON ROUGE; *182 G-7; ★ B.R.; mail Baker z 70714; ● 950
Brownlee; RMC Place; BOSSIER; *182 B-2; elev. 173ft./53m.; ★ SHRE; mail Bossier City z 71111; pop. incl. with Bossier City (Inc. Place)
Brownsville (Brownville); RMC Place; OUACHITA; 182 B-5; ★ MONR; mail West Monroe z 71291-92; ● 1,750
Brownsville-Bawcomville; CDP-Census Area Only; OUACHITA; *182 B-5; ★ MONR; mail West Monroe z 71291; Ⓟ 7,397; Ⓒ 7,616
Brownville; RMC Place; CALDWELL; mail Columbia z 71418; ● 200
Brownville; OUACHITA; see Brownsville (RMC Place)
Brule (Brule Labadieville); RMC Place; ASSUMPTION; *182 I-7; elev. 11ft./3m.; mail Labadieville z 70372; rural
Brule; RMC Place; LAFOURCHE; *182 I-8; ★ HOMA-; mail Thibodaux z 70301; rural
Brule Labadieville; ASSUMPTION; see Brule (RMC Place)
Bruly La Croix; RMC Place; IBERVILLE; *182 H-7; mail White Castle z 70788; rural
Bruly McCall; RMC Place; ASCENSION, IBERVILLE; *182 H-7; mail Donaldsonville z 70346; ● 50
Bruly Saint Martin; RMC Place; ASSUMPTION; *182 H-7; mail Belle Rose z 70341; ● 250
Brusle Saint Vincent (Saint Vincent); RMC Place; ASSUMPTION; *182 H-7; mail Napoleonville z 70390; ● 50
Brusly; Inc. Place; WEST BATON ROUGE; 182 G-7; elev. 25ft./8m.; 🅿; ★ B.R.; z 70719; Ⓟ 1,824; Ⓒ 2,020
Bryant; RMC Place; IBERIA; ★ LAF; mail New Iberia z 70560; pop. incl. with New Iberia (Inc. Place)
Bryceland (Brice); Inc. Place; BIENVILLE; 182 B-3; elev. 264ft./80m.; 🅿; z 71008; Ⓟ 103; Ⓒ 114
Buckeye; RMC Place; RAPIDES; 182 E-5; elev. 73ft./22m.; 🅿; z 71328; ● 100
Buckner; RMC Place; RICHLAND; *182 C-5; mail Rayville z 71269; rural
Bucktown; RMC Place; JEFFERSON; *182 H-9; ★ N.O.
Bueche; RMC Place; WEST BATON ROUGE; *182 G-7; elev. 25ft./8m.; 🅿; z 70729; ● 200
Buhler; RMC Place; CALCASIEU; *182 H-2; mail Sulphur z 70663; rural
Bull Run; RMC Place; TERREBONNE; *182 I-8; ★ HOMA-; mail Schriever z 70395; rural
Bunkie; Inc. Place; AVOYELLES; 182 F-5; elev. 65ft./20m.; 🅿 🅷; z 71322; Ⓟ 5,044; Ⓒ 4,662
Buras; RMC Place; PLAQUEMINES; 182 J-11; elev. 2ft./1m.; 🅿; z 70041; ● 1,480
Buras-Triumph; CDP-Census Area Only; PLAQUEMINES; *182 J-11; mail Buras z 70041; Ⓟ 3,702; Ⓒ 3,358
Burkplace; RMC Place; BIENVILLE; *182 C-3; mail Castor z 71016; rural
Burnley Pines; RMC Place; CADDO; ★ SHRE; pop. incl. with Shreveport (Inc. Place)
Burr Ferry; RMC Place; VERNON; 182 F-2; mail Anacoco z 71403, Leesville z 71446; ● 120
Burroughs; RMC Place; CALDWELL; *182 C-5; mail Columbia z 71418; rural
Burrwood; RMC Place; PLAQUEMINES; mail Venice z 70091; rural
Burton Lane; RMC Place; ST. JAMES; *182 H-8; mail Saint James z 70086; ● 170
Bush; RMC Place; ST. TAMMANY; 182 G-10; elev. 85ft./26m.; 🅿; z 70431; ● 300
Bushes; RMC Place; FRANKLIN; *182 C-6; mail Winnsboro z 71295; rural
Bywater; RMC Place; ORLEANS; *182 H-9; ★ N.O.; mail New Orleans z 70117, z 70177; pop. incl. with New Orleans (Inc. Place)

C

Caddo; RMC Place; CADDO; mail Oil City z 71061; pop. incl. with Oil City (Inc. Place)
CADDO; 182 B-1; Ⓟ 248,253; Ⓒ 252,161; ◆ 249,830
Cade; RMC Place; ST. MARTIN; 182 H-5; elev. 31ft./9m.; 🅿; ★ LAF; z 70519; ● 550
Cadeville; RMC Place; OUACHITA; *182 C-5; elev. 167ft./51m.; ★ MONR; mail Eros z 71238; rural
Caernarvon (Caernovan); RMC Place; ST. BERNARD; *182 I-10; ★ N.O.; mail Braithwaite z 70040; ● 210
Caernovan; ST. BERNARD; see Caernarvon (RMC Place)
Caffery; RMC Place; ST. MARY; *182 I-6; elev. 10ft./3m.; mail Franklin z 70538; rural
Calcasieu; RMC Place; ALLEN; *182 F-4; mail Glenmora z 71433; rural
Calcasieu; RMC Place; RAPIDES; *182 F-4; elev. 166ft./51m.; mail Glenmora z 71433; ● 150
CALCASIEU; 182 H-2; Ⓟ 168,134; Ⓒ 183,577; ◆ 183,010
CALDWELL; 182 C-5; Ⓟ 9,810; Ⓒ 10,560; ◆ 10,158
Calhoun; RMC Place; OUACHITA; 182 B-5; elev. 162ft./49m.; 🅿; z 71225; ● 400
Calumet; RMC Place; ST. MARY; *182 I-7; mail Patterson z 70392
Calvin; Inc. Place; WINN; 182 D-4; elev. 160ft./49m.; 🅿; z 71410; Ⓟ 207; Ⓒ 236
Camelia Gardens; RMC Place; RAPIDES; ★ ALEX; mail Alexandria z 71301; pop. incl. with Alexandria (Inc. Place)
Cameron; CDP; ⊡ CAMERON; 182 I-3; elev. 5ft./2m.; 🅿 🅷; z 70631; Ⓟ 2,041; Ⓒ 1,965
CAMERON; 182 I-3; Ⓟ 9,260; Ⓒ 9,991; ◆ 6,830
Camperdown; RMC Place; ST. MARY; *182 I-6; mail Franklin z 70538; rural
Camp Livinston; GRANT; see Simms (RMC Place)
Campti; Inc. Place; NATCHITOCHES; 182 D-3; 🅿; z 71411; Ⓟ 929; Ⓒ 1,057
Cancienne; RMC Place; ASSUMPTION; *182 I-7; elev. 10ft./3m.; mail Napoleonville z 70390; rural
Canebrake; RMC Place; CONCORDIA; *182 D-6; mail Ferriday z 71334; rural
Caney; RMC Place; VERNON; *182 F-2; mail Leesville z 71446; rural
Cankton; Inc. Place; ST. LANDRY; 182 H-5; elev. 45ft./14m.; 🅿; ★ LAF; z 70584; Ⓟ 323; Ⓒ 362
Cannonburg; RMC Place; IBERVILLE; *182 H-7; mail White Castle z 70788; ● 30
Capital Heights; RMC Place; EAST BATON ROUGE; ★ B.R.; pop. incl. with Baton Rouge (Inc. Place)
Capitan; RMC Place; LAFAYETTE; *182 H-5; ★ LAF; mail Youngsville z 70592; rural
Capitol; RMC Place; EAST BATON ROUGE; *182 G-7; ★ B.R.; mail Baton Rouge z 70804; pop. incl. with Baton Rouge (Inc. Place)
Caplis; RMC Place; BOSSIER; *182 C-2; elev. 156ft./48m.; mail Bossier City z 71111; rural
Carencro; Inc. Place; LAFAYETTE; 182 H-5; elev. 40ft./12m.; 🅿; ★ LAF; z 70520; Ⓟ 5,429; Ⓒ 6,120
Carlisle; RMC Place; PLAQUEMINES; 182 I-10; elev. 3ft./1m.; 🅿; z 70040; ● 50
Carlton; RMC Place; OUACHITA; *182 B-5; mail Calhoun z 71225; rural
Carlyss; CDP; CALCASIEU; *182 H-2; ★ LKCH; mail Sulphur z 70665; Ⓟ 3,305; Ⓒ 4,049
Carmel; RMC Place; DE SOTO; 182 C-2; mail Mansfield z 71052; ● 70
Caroline; RMC Place; IBERIA; *182 H-6; ★ LAF; mail Loreauville z 70552; ● 40
Carrollton; RMC Place; ORLEANS; *182 H-9; ★ N.O.; mail New Orleans z 70118, z 70178, z 70185; pop. incl. with New Orleans (Inc. Place)
Carrolwood; RMC Place; ST. JOHN THE BAPTIST; *182 H-8; ★ N.O.; mail La Place z 70068
Carterville; RMC Place; BOSSIER; *182 A-2; elev. 245ft./75m.; mail Plain Dealing z 71064
Carthage Bluff Landing; RMC Place; LIVINGSTON; *182 H-8; mail Springfield z 70462; ● 30
Cartwright; RMC Place; JACKSON; *182 B-4; mail Choudrant z 71227; rural
Carville; RMC Place; IBERVILLE; 182 H-7; elev. 21ft./6m.; 🅿; z 70721; pop. incl. with Saint Gabriel (Inc. Place)
Caspiana; RMC Place; CADDO; 182 C-2; elev. 152ft./46m.; 🅿; z 71115; ● 60
Castle Village; RMC Place; RAPIDES; ★ ALEX; mail Alexandria z 71301; ● 350
Castlewood; RMC Place; EAST BATON ROUGE; *182 G-7; ★ B.R.; pop. incl. with Baton Rouge (Inc. Place)
Castor; Inc. Place; BIENVILLE; 182 C-3; elev. 165ft./50m.; 🅿; z 71016; Ⓟ 196; Ⓒ 209
Catahoula; RMC Place; ST. MARTIN; 182 H-6; elev. 10ft./3m.; mail Saint Martinville z 70582; ● 700
CATAHOULA; 182 D-5; Ⓟ 11,065; Ⓒ 10,920; ◆ 10,453
Catherine; RMC Place; IBERVILLE; *182 H-7; rural
Catuna; RMC Place; DE SOTO; *182 D-2; elev. 280ft./85m.; mail Mansfield z 71052; rural
Cavett; RMC Place; CADDO; *182 B-2; mail Belcher z 71004; rural
Cecelia; ST. MARTIN; see Cecilia (CDP)
Cecile; RMC Place; CADDO; *182 C-2; elev. 153ft./47m.; mail Shreveport z 71105; rural
Cecilia (Cecelia); CDP; ST. MARTIN; 182 H-6; elev. 25ft./8m.; 🅿; ★ LAF; z 70521; Ⓟ 1,374; Ⓒ 1,505
Cedar Crest; RMC Place; EAST BATON ROUGE; ★ B.R.; mail Baton Rouge z 70816
Cedar Glen; RMC Place; EAST BATON ROUGE; ★ B.R.; mail Baton Rouge z 70811
Cedar Grove; RMC Place; ASSUMPTION; *182 I-7; mail Labadieville z 70372; rural
Cedar Grove; RMC Place; CADDO; *182 B-2; ★ SHRE; mail Shreveport z 71106; pop. incl. with Shreveport (Inc. Place)
Cedar Grove; RMC Place; PLAQUEMINES; *182 I-9; elev. 6ft./2m.; ★ N.O.; mail Belle Chasse z 70037; ● 220
Cedar Grove Plantation; IBERVILLE; see Soniat (RMC Place)
Cedarton; RMC Place; LINCOLN; *182 B-4; mail Choudrant z 71227; rural
Centenary; RMC Place; CADDO; *182 B-2; ★ SHRE; mail Shreveport z 71104, z 71134; pop. incl. with Shreveport (Inc. Place)
Center Point; RMC Place; AVOYELLES; 182 E-5; elev. 89ft./27m.; 🅿; z 71323; ● 140
Centerville; RMC Place; EVANGELINE; *182 F-5; elev. 53ft./16m.; mail Saint Landry z 71367; rural
Centerville; RMC Place; ST. MARY; 182 I-6; elev. 113ft./34m.; 🅿; z 70522; ● 700
Central; RMC Place; EAST BATON ROUGE; *182 G-7; elev. 66ft./20m.; 🅿; ★ B.R.; z 70837 & mail Baton Rouge z 70818; ● 950
Central; RMC Place; ST. JAMES; *182 H-8; elev. 21ft./6m.; mail Convent z 70723; rural
Central; RMC Place; TERREBONNE; *182 I-8; ★ HOMA-; mail Houma z 70360; rural
Chacahoula; RMC Place; TERREBONNE; 182 I-8; mail Schriever z 70395; ● 150
Chackbay; CDP; LAFOURCHE; *182 I-8; elev. 6ft./2m.; mail Thibodaux z 70301; Ⓟ 2,276; Ⓒ 4,018
Chakley; RMC Place; CALCASIEU; *182 H-3; mail Bell City z 70630; rural
Chalmette; CDP; ⊡ ST. BERNARD; 182 H-10; elev. 5ft./2m.; 🅿 🅷; ★ N.O.; z 70043-44; Ⓟ 31,860; Ⓒ 32,069; ◆ 19,359
Chalmette Vista; RMC Place; ST. BERNARD; *182 H-9; ★ N.O.; mail Chalmette z 70043
Chamale Cove; RMC Place; ST. TAMMANY; ★ N.O.; mail Slidell z 70460
Chamberlin; RMC Place; WEST BATON ROUGE; *182 G-7; mail Port Allen z 70767; ● 50
Chambers; RMC Place; RAPIDES; 182 F-4; elev. 74ft./23m.; ★ ALEX; mail Lecompte z 71346; ● 200
Chandler Park; RMC Place; RAPIDES; ★ ALEX; mail Alexandria z 71301; pop. incl. with Alexandria (Inc. Place)
Charenton; CDP; ST. MARY; 182 I-6; elev. 15ft./5m.; 🅿; z 70523; Ⓟ 1,584; Ⓒ 1,944
Charles Park; RMC Place; RAPIDES; ★ ALEX; mail Alexandria z 71301; pop. incl. with Alexandria (Inc. Place)
Charlieville; RICHLAND; see Gilleyville (RMC Place)
Charlotte; RMC Place; IBERIA; *182 H-5; elev. 10ft./3m.; ★ LAF; mail New Iberia z 70560; rural
Chase; RMC Place; FRANKLIN; 182 C-6; elev. 75ft./23m.; 🅿; z 71324; ● 170
Chataignier; Inc. Place; EVANGELINE; 182 G-5; elev. 55ft./17m.; 🅿; z 70524; Ⓟ 281; Ⓒ 383
Chatham; Inc. Place; JACKSON; 182 C-4; elev. 196ft./60m.; 🅿; z 71226; Ⓟ 617; Ⓒ 623
Chatman Town; RMC Place; ST. JAMES; *182 H-8; elev. 20ft./6m.; mail Vacherie z 70090; rural
Chauvin; CDP; TERREBONNE; 182 J-8; elev. 5ft./2m.; 🅿; ★ HOMA-; z 70344; Ⓟ 3,375; Ⓒ 3,229
Chef Menteur; RMC Place; ORLEANS; *182 H-10; ★ N.O.; mail New Orleans z 70126, z 70186; pop. incl. with New Orleans (Inc. Place)
Chegby; RMC Place; LAFOURCHE; *182 I-8
Chenal; POINTE COUPEE; see Rougon (RMC Place)
Cheneyville; Inc. Place; RAPIDES; 182 F-5; elev. 63ft./19m.; 🅿; z 71325; Ⓟ 1,005; Ⓒ 901
Cheniere; RMC Place; OUACHITA; *182 B-5; ★ MONR; mail West Monroe z 71291-92
Cherokee Court; RMC Place; JEFFERSON; ★ N.O.; mail New Orleans z 70123
Cherokee Village; RMC Place; RAPIDES; ★ ALEX; mail Alexandria z 71301; pop. incl. with Alexandria (Inc. Place)
Cherry Grove; RMC Place; ALLEN; *182 G-3; mail Dry Creek z 70637; rural
Chesbrough; RMC Place; TANGIPAHOA; *182 F-8; mail Kentwood z 70444; ● 250
Chester; RMC Place; WINN; *182 C-5; mail Grayson z 71435; rural
Chestnut; RMC Place; NATCHITOCHES; 182 C-3; 🅿; z 71070; ● 40
Chickama; RMC Place; RAPIDES; mail Lecompte z 71346; rural
Chickasaw; RMC Place; WEST CARROLL; *182 A-7; mail Oak Grove z 71263; rural
China; RMC Place; JEFFERSON DAVIS; *182 G-4; mail Elton z 70532; rural
Chinchuba; RMC Place; ST. TAMMANY; *182 G-9; ★ N.O.; mail Mandeville z 70448, z 70471
Chipola; RMC Place; ST. HELENA; *182 F-8; mail Greensburg z 70441; rural
Chitimacha Reservation; Indian Reservation; ST. MARY; mail Charenton z 70523; Ⓟ 1,300; Ⓒ 409
Chloe; RMC Place; CALCASIEU; *182 H-3; elev. 15ft./5m.; ★ LKCH; mail Iowa z 70647; rural
Choctaw; RMC Place; IBERVILLE; *182 H-7; mail Port Allen z 70767
Choctaw; RMC Place; LAFOURCHE; *182 I-8; mail Thibodaux z 70301; ● 600
Chopin; RMC Place; NATCHITOCHES; *182 E-4; elev. 100ft./30m.; 🅿; z 71447; ● 100
Choudrant; Inc. Place; LINCOLN; 182 B-4; elev. 188ft./57m.; 🅿; z 71227; Ⓟ 557; Ⓒ 582
Choupique; RMC Place; CALCASIEU; *182 H-2; mail Sulphur z 70665; rural
Choupique; RMC Place; LAFOURCHE; *182 I-8; mail Thibodaux z 70301; ● 450
Choupique; RMC Place; ST. MARY; *182 I-6; elev. 8ft./2m.; mail Franklin z 70538; rural
Chula; RMC Place; ASSUMPTION; *182 I-7; elev. 19ft./6m.; mail Labadieville z 70372
Church Point; Inc. Place; ACADIA; 182 G-5; elev. 48ft./15m.; 🅿 🅷; z 70525; Ⓟ 4,677; Ⓒ 4,756
Church Spur; RMC Place; ASSUMPTION; *182 H-7; elev. 20ft./6m.; mail Napoleonville z 70390; rural
Cinclare; RMC Place; WEST BATON ROUGE; *182 G-7; ★ B.R.; mail Port Allen z 70767; rural
Cindy Park; RMC Place; ST. BERNARD; ★ N.O.; mail Meraux z 70075
City Price; PLAQUEMINES; see Fosters Canal (RMC Place)
Claiborne; CDP; OUACHITA; *182 B-5; ★ MONR; mail West Monroe z 71291; Ⓟ 8,300; Ⓒ 9,830
Claiborne; RMC Place; ST. TAMMANY; *182 G-9; ★ N.O.; mail Covington z 70433; ● 200
CLAIBORNE; 182 B-3; Ⓟ 17,405; Ⓒ 16,851; ◆ 15,976
Claibourne Gardens; RMC Place; JEFFERSON; *182 I-9; ★ N.O.; mail Westwego z 70094; ● 700
Clare; RMC Place; SABINE; *182 E-2; elev. 219ft./67m.; mail Florien z 71429, Many z 71449; rural
Clarence; Inc. Place; NATCHITOCHES; 182 D-3; elev. 118ft./36m.; 🅿; z 71414; Ⓟ 577; Ⓒ 516
Clarks; Inc. Place; CALDWELL; 182 D-5; elev. 133ft./41m.; 🅿; z 71415; Ⓟ 650; Ⓒ 1,071
Clay; RMC Place; JACKSON; 182 C-4; elev. 206ft./63m.; mail Ruston z 71270; ● 120
Clayton; Inc. Place; CONCORDIA; 182 D-6; elev. 61ft./19m.; 🅿; ★ NCHZ; z 71326; Ⓟ 917; Ⓒ 858
Clayton Junction; RMC Place; CONCORDIA; ★ NCHZ; mail Clayton z 71326; pop. incl. with Clayton (Inc. Place)
Clearwater; RMC Place; EVANGELINE; *182 F-4; elev. 114ft./35m.; mail Cheneyville z 71325; ● 30
Clifton; RMC Place; RAPIDES; *182 E-3; 🅿; z 71447 & mail Mora z 71455; ● 130
Clifton; RMC Place; WASHINGTON; *182 F-9; elev. 196ft./60m.; mail Franklinton z 70438
Clinton; Inc. Place; ⊡ EAST FELICIANA; 182 F-7; elev. 209ft./64m.; 🅿; z 70722; Ⓟ 1,904; Ⓒ 1,998
Clio; RMC Place; LIVINGSTON; *182 H-8; elev. 12ft./4m.; mail Maurepas z 70449; rural
Clotilda; RMC Place; LAFOURCHE; *182 I-8; mail Raceland z 70394; ● 70
Cloutierville; RMC Place; NATCHITOCHES; 182 E-3; elev. 107ft./33m.; 🅿; z 71416; ● 230
Clovelly Farms; RMC Place; LAFOURCHE; *182 I-9; mail Cut Off z 70345; ● 50
Coburn; RMC Place; SABINE; *182 E-3; mail Florien z 71429; rural
Cocodrie; RMC Place; TERREBONNE; *182 J-8; mail Chauvin z 70344; ● 100
Cocoville (Hydropolis); RMC Place; AVOYELLES; *182 F-5; mail Mansura z 71350; rural
Coker; RMC Place; DE SOTO; *182 D-2; mail Mansfield z 71052; rural
Coleman; RMC Place; MADISON; *182 C-7; elev. 90ft./27m.; mail Tallulah z 71282; rural
Coleman Town; RMC Place; ST. HELENA; *182 F-8; mail Greensburg z 70441; ● 50
Colfax; Inc. Place; ⊡ GRANT; 182 E-4; elev. 100ft./30m.; 🅿; z 71417; Ⓟ 1,696; Ⓒ 1,659
Colgrade; RMC Place; WINN; *182 D-4; elev. 121ft./37m.; mail Winnfield z 71483; ● 50
College Hills; RMC Place; EAST BATON ROUGE; *182 G-7; ★ B.R.; pop. incl. with Baton Rouge (Inc. Place)
College Town; RMC Place; EAST BATON ROUGE; *182 G-7; ★ B.R.; pop. incl. with Baton Rouge (Inc. Place)
Collinsburg; RMC Place; BOSSIER; *182 A-2; elev. 268ft./82m.; mail Plain Dealing z 71064; rural
Collinston; Inc. Place; MOREHOUSE; 182 B-6; elev. 82ft./25m.; 🅿; z 71229; Ⓟ 375; Ⓒ 327
Colonial Heights; RMC Place; CADDO; *182 B-1; mail Shreveport z 71109; ● 100
Colquitt; RMC Place; CLAIBORNE; *182 A-3; mail Haynesville z 71038; rural
Columbia; Inc. Place; ⊡ CALDWELL; 182 C-5; elev. 66ft./20m.; 🅿 🅷; z 71418; Ⓟ 386; Ⓒ 477
Columbia (Columbia Plantation); RMC Place; ST. JOHN THE BAPTIST; *182 H-8; elev. 10ft./3m.; mail Edgard z 70049; rural
Columbia Heights; RMC Place; CALDWELL; *182 C-5; mail Columbia z 71418; ● 350
Columbia Plantation; ST. JOHN THE BAPTIST; see Columbia (RMC Place)
Commerce Park; RMC Place; EAST BATON ROUGE; ★ B.R.; mail Baton Rouge z 70809-10, z 70884; pop. incl. with Baton Rouge (Inc. Place)
Como; RMC Place; FRANKLIN; *182 C-6; mail Winnsboro z 71295; rural
Concession; RMC Place; PLAQUEMINES; *182 I-9; elev. 4ft./1m.; ★ N.O.; mail Belle Chasse z 70037
Concord; RMC Place; WEST CARROLL; *182 A-6; mail Oak Grove z 71263; rural
CONCORDIA; 182 E-6; Ⓟ 20,828; Ⓒ 20,247; ◆ 18,634
Constance Beach; RMC Place; CAMERON; *182 I-2; elev. 10ft./3m.; mail Cameron z 70631; ● 100
Consuella; RMC Place; TENSAS; *182 D-6; mail Waterproof z 71375; rural
Contreras; RMC Place; ST. BERNARD; *182 I-10; ★ N.O.; mail Saint Bernard z 70085; rural
Convent; RMC Place; ⊡ ST. JAMES; 182 H-8; 🅿; z 70723; ● 500
Converse; Inc. Place; SABINE; 182 D-2; 🅿; z 71419; Ⓟ 436; Ⓒ 400
Conway; RMC Place; UNION; *182 A-4; mail Marion z 71260; rural
Coon; RMC Place; POINTE COUPEE; *182 F-6; elev. 35ft./11m.; mail Batchelor z 70715; rural
Cooper Road (North Shreveport); RMC Place; CADDO; *182 B-2; elev. 181ft./55m.; ★ SHRE; mail Shreveport z 71107; pop. incl. with Shreveport (Inc. Place)
Coopers; RMC Place; VERNON; *182 F-3; elev. 217ft./66m.; mail Leesville z 71446; rural
Copenhagen; RMC Place; CALDWELL; *182 D-5; mail Columbia z 71418; rural
Cora; RMC Place; VERNON; *182 F-3; mail Hineston z 71438; rural
Corbin; RMC Place; LIVINGSTON; *182 G-8; ★ B.R.; mail Walker z 70785; pop. incl. with Walker (Inc. Place)
Corey; RMC Place; CALDWELL; *182 C-5; elev. 70ft./21m.; mail Monroe z 71201-02; rural
Corinth; RMC Place; LINCOLN; *182 B-4; mail Dubach z 71235; rural
Corleyville; RMC Place; SABINE; *182 E-2; mail Florien z 71429; rural
Cornerview; RMC Place; ASCENSION; *182 H-7; ★ B.R.; mail Gonzales z 70737; rural
Cornor; RMC Place; WEST FELICIANA; *182 F-7; elev. 272ft./83m.; mail Woodville z 39669; rural
Cossinade; RMC Place; VERMILION; *182 H-5; mail Kaplan z 70548; rural
Coteau Holmes; RMC Place; ST. MARTIN; *182 H-6; mail Saint Martinville z 70582; ● 140
Coteau Rodaire; RMC Place; ST. MARTIN; *182 G-5; ★ LAF; mail Arnaudville z 70512; ● 50
Cotton Plant; RMC Place; CALDWELL; *182 C-5; mail Grayson z 71435; ● 30
Cottonport; Inc. Place; AVOYELLES; 182 F-5; elev. 56ft./17m.; 🅿; z 71327; Ⓟ 2,600; Ⓒ 2,316
Cotton Valley; Inc. Place; WEBSTER; 182 B-2; elev. 220ft./67m.; 🅿; z 71018; Ⓟ 1,130; Ⓒ 1,189
Couchwood; RMC Place; WEBSTER; 182 B-2; mail Cotton Valley z 71018; ● 140
Coulon Plantation; RMC Place; LAFOURCHE; *182 I-8; ★ HOMA-; mail Thibodaux z 70301; rural
Country Club Subdivision; RMC Place; LAFOURCHE; *182 I-8; ★ HOMA-; mail Thibodaux z 70301; ● 800
Courtableau; RMC Place; ST. LANDRY; 182 G-6; mail Port Barre z 70577; ● 65
Coushatta; Inc. Place; ⊡ RED RIVER; 182 D-3; elev. 145ft./44m.; 🅿 🅷; z 71019; Ⓟ 1,845; Ⓒ 2,299
Coushatta Reservation; Indian Reservation; ALLEN; Ⓒ 25
Covington; Inc. Place; ⊡ ST. TAMMANY; 182 G-9; 🅿 🅷; ★ N.O.; z 70433-35; Ⓟ 7,691; Ⓒ 8,483
Covington Country Club Estates; RMC Place; ST. TAMMANY; *182 G-9; ★ N.O.; mail Covington z 70433; ● 1,200
Cow Island; RMC Place; VERMILION; *182 I-5; 🅿; z 70510; ● 70
Cravens; RMC Place; VERNON; 182 F-3; elev. 234ft./71m.; mail Pitkin z 70656; ● 150
Creedmoor; RMC Place; ST. BERNARD; ★ N.O.; mail Saint Bernard z 70085
Creola; Inc. Place; GRANT; incorporated October 7, 2000; not reported in 2000 Census; ● 100
Creole; RMC Place; CAMERON; 182 I-3; elev. 6ft./2m.; 🅿; z 70632; ● 250
Crescent; RMC Place; IBERVILLE; *182 H-7; ★ B.R.; mail Plaquemine z 70764; rural
Crescent; RMC Place; TERREBONNE; *182 I-8; ★ HOMA-; mail Houma z 70360; ● 180
Creston; RMC Place; NATCHITOCHES; 182 D-3; elev. 163ft./50m.; 🅿; z 71070; ● 70
Crew Lake; RMC Place; RICHLAND; 182 B-5; mail Rayville z 71269; ● 140
Crews; RMC Place; WINN; *182 D-3; mail Montgomery z 71454; rural
Crichton; RMC Place; RED RIVER; *182 C-2; mail Coushatta z 71019; rural
Crimea; RMC Place; TENSAS; *182 D-7; mail Saint Joseph z 71366; rural
Cross-Road; RMC Place; CALDWELL; *182 C-5; mail Grayson z 71435; ● 50
Crossroads; RMC Place; LINCOLN; *182 B-4; mail Dubach z 71235; rural
Cross Roads; RMC Place; RED RIVER; 182 C-2; elev. 237ft./72m.; mail Coushatta z 71019; ● 50
Crowley; Inc. Place; ⊡ ACADIA; 182 H-4; 🅿 🅷; ★ LAF; z 70526-27; Ⓟ 13,983; Ⓒ 14,225; Ⓡ 14,228
Crown Point; RMC Place; JEFFERSON; 182 I-9; ★ N.O.; mail Marrero z 70072; ● 980
Crowville; RMC Place; FRANKLIN; 182 C-6; elev. 85ft./26m.; 🅿; z 71230; ● 250
Crozier; RMC Place; TERREBONNE; *182 I-8; ★ HOMA-; mail Houma z 70360; ● 1,250
Cullen; Inc. Place; WEBSTER; 182 A-2; elev. 240ft./73m.; 🅿; z 71021; Ⓟ 1,642; Ⓒ 1,296
Curry; RMC Place; WINN; *182 D-4; elev. 94ft./29m.; mail Winnfield z 71483; ● 30
Curtis; RMC Place; BOSSIER; *182 B-2; mail Bossier City z 71112; pop. incl. with Bossier City (Inc. Place)
Cut Off; CDP; LAFOURCHE; 182 I-9; elev. 5ft./2m.; 🅿 🅷; z 70345; Ⓟ 5,325; Ⓒ 5,635
Cutoff; RMC Place; ORLEANS; *182 H-9; ★ N.O.; pop. incl. with New Orleans (Inc. Place)
Cut Off Junction; RMC Place; CADDO; *182 B-2; ★ SHRE; pop. incl. with Shreveport (Inc. Place)
Cypremort (Louisa); RMC Place; ST. MARY; *182 I-6; mail Franklin z 70538
Cypress; RMC Place; NATCHITOCHES; 182 E-3; elev. 101ft./31m.; 🅿; z 71457; ● 150
Cypress; RMC Place; OUACHITA; *182 C-5; mail West Monroe z 71291; rural
Cypress Gardens; RMC Place; ST. BERNARD; *182 H-10; ★ N.O.; mail Meraux z 70075; ● 680
Cypress Gardens; RMC Place; TERREBONNE; *182 I-8; ★ HOMA-; mail Houma z 70360
Cypress Island; RMC Place; ST. MARTIN; *182 H-6; ★ LAF; mail Saint Martinville z 70582; ● 100

D

Daigleville; RMC Place; TERREBONNE; ★ HOMA-; mail Houma z 70360; pop. incl. with Houma (Inc. Place)
Dalcour; RMC Place; PLAQUEMINES; 182 I-9; mail Braithwaite z 70040; ● 140
Danville; RMC Place; BIENVILLE; *182 C-4; mail Bienville z 71008; ● 80
D'Arbonne; RMC Place; UNION; *182 B-4; elev. 108ft./33m.; mail Choudrant z 71227; rural
Darlington; RMC Place; ST. HELENA; *182 F-8; elev. 262ft./80m.; mail Greensburg z 70441
Darnell; RMC Place; WEST CARROLL; 182 B-6; elev. 100ft./30m.; mail Pioneer z 71266; ● 100
Darrow; RMC Place; ASCENSION; 182 H-7; elev. 21ft./6m.; 🅿; z 70725; ● 460
Daspit; RMC Place; IBERIA; *182 H-6; ★ LAF; mail New Iberia z 70560; rural
Davant; RMC Place; PLAQUEMINES; 182 I-10; 🅿; z 70082 & mail Braithwaite z 70040; ● 120
Dean; RMC Place; UNION; *182 A-5; mail Marion z 71260; rural
De Broeck Landing; RMC Place; CADDO; *182 C-2; ★ SHRE; mail Shreveport z 71106; rural
Deerford; RMC Place; EAST BATON ROUGE; *182 G-7; elev. 90ft./27m.; ★ B.R.; mail Zachary z 70791; ● 30
Deer Park; RMC Place; CONCORDIA; *182 E-6; mail Vidalia z 71373; rural
Dehlco; RMC Place; RICHLAND; *182 C-6; mail Rayville z 71269; rural
Delacroix; RMC Place; ST. BERNARD; 182 I-10; mail Saint Bernard z 70085; ● 450
Delacroix; RMC Place; ST. MARTIN; *182 H-6; mail Saint Martinville z 70582; rural
Del Bueno Park; RMC Place; ST. BERNARD; ★ N.O.; mail Meraux z 70075
Delcambre; Inc. Place; VERMILION, IBERIA; 182 H-5; 🅿; z 70528; Ⓟ 1,978; Ⓒ 2,168
Delhi; Inc. Place; RICHLAND; 182 B-6; 🅿 🅷; z 71232; Ⓟ 3,169; Ⓒ 3,066
Delmont Place; RMC Place; EAST BATON ROUGE; *182 G-7; ★ B.R.; pop. incl. with Baton Rouge (Inc. Place)
Delphine Place; RMC Place; EAST BATON ROUGE; ★ B.R.; pop. incl. with Baton Rouge (Inc. Place)
Delta (Delta Point); Inc. Place; MADISON; *182 C-7; 🅿; ★ VICK; z 71233; Ⓟ 234; Ⓒ 239
Delta Farms; RMC Place; LAFOURCHE; *182 I-9; mail Lockport z 70374; ● 100
Delta Point; MADISON; see Delta (Inc. Place)
Denham Springs; Inc. Place; LIVINGSTON; 182 G-7; elev. 50ft./15m.; 🅿; ★ B.R.; z 70706, z 70726-27; Ⓟ 8,381; Ⓒ 8,757
Denhart; RMC Place; TENSAS; *182 D-7; mail Saint Joseph z 71366; rural
Dennis Mills; RMC Place; ST. HELENA; *182 G-8; elev. 96ft./29m.; 🅿; z 70726; rural
Denson; RMC Place; LIVINGSTON; *182 H-8; elev. 8ft./2m.; mail Maurepas z 70449; ● 150
Dent Terrace; RMC Place; EAST BATON ROUGE; *182 G-7; ★ B.R.; mail Baton Rouge z 70808; pop. incl. with Baton Rouge (Inc. Place)
DeQuincy; Inc. Place; CALCASIEU; 182 G-2; elev. 65ft./20m.; 🅿 🅷; z 70633; Ⓟ 3,474; Ⓒ 3,398
DeRidder; Inc. Place; ⊡ BEAUREGARD, VERNON; 182 F-3; 🅿 🅷; z 70634; Ⓟ 9,868; Ⓒ 9,808
Derry; RMC Place; NATCHITOCHES; 182 E-3; 🅿; z 71416; ● 30
Des Allemands; CDP; ST. CHARLES, LAFOURCHE; 182 I-8; 🅿; z 70030; Ⓟ 2,504; Ⓒ 2,500
De Selle; RMC Place; RAPIDES; *182 E-4; ★ ALEX; mail Alexandria z 71301; pop. incl. with Alexandria (Inc. Place)
Deshotels; ST. LANDRY; see Faubourg (RMC Place)
DE SOTO; 182 C-2; Ⓟ 25,346; Ⓒ 25,494; ◆ 26,514
Dess; RMC Place; SABINE; *182 E-2; mail Florien z 71429; rural
Destrehan; CDP; ST. CHARLES; *182 H-9; elev. 10ft./3m.; 🅿; ★ N.O.; z 70047; Ⓟ 8,031; Ⓒ 11,260
Devalls; RMC Place; WEST BATON ROUGE; *182 G-7; mail Port Allen z 70767; rural
Deville; CDP; RAPIDES; 182 E-5; elev. 85ft./26m.; 🅿; z 71328; Ⓟ 1,113; Ⓒ 1,007
Dewdrop; RMC Place; MOREHOUSE; *182 B-5; mail Bastrop z 71220; rural
Diamond; RMC Place; PLAQUEMINES; *182 I-10; mail Port Sulphur z 70083; ● 180
Dido; RMC Place; VERNON; *182 F-3; mail Pitkin z 70656; rural
Dixie; RMC Place; CADDO; 182 B-2; elev. 180ft./55m.; 🅿; z 71107; ● 100
Dixie Acres; RMC Place; OUACHITA; ★ MONR; mail Sterlington z 71280; ● 30
Dixie Gardens; RMC Place; CADDO; *182 B-2; ★ SHRE; mail Shreveport z 71105; ● 500
Dixie Inn; Inc. Place; WEBSTER; 182 B-3; elev. 160ft./49m.; mail Minden z 71055; Ⓟ 347; Ⓒ 352
Dodson; Inc. Place; WINN; 182 C-4; elev. 232ft./71m.; 🅿; z 71422; Ⓟ 350; Ⓒ 357
Donaldsonville; Inc. Place; ⊡ ASCENSION; 182 H-7; elev. 29ft./9m.; 🅿 🅷; z 70346; Ⓟ 7,949; Ⓒ 7,605
Donner; RMC Place; TERREBONNE; 182 I-7; elev. 5ft./2m.; 🅿; z 70352; ● 260
Dorcyville; RMC Place; IBERVILLE; *182 H-7; ● 350
Dossman; RMC Place; EVANGELINE; *182 F-5; mail Saint Landry z 71367; ● 30
Douglas; RMC Place; LINCOLN; *182 B-4; elev. 289ft./88m.; mail Choudrant z 71227; rural
Downsville; Inc. Place; UNION, LINCOLN; 182 B-4; elev. 253ft./77m.; 🅿; z 71234; Ⓟ 101; Ⓒ 118
Downtown; RMC Place; CADDO; ★ SHRE; mail Shreveport z 71101, z 71120, z 71161-66; pop. incl. with Shreveport (Inc. Place)
Downtown; RMC Place; EAST BATON ROUGE; ★ B.R.; mail Baton Rouge z 70821; pop. incl. with Baton Rouge (Inc. Place)
Downtown; RMC Place; OUACHITA; *182 B-5; ★ MONR; mail Monroe z 71201, z 71210; pop. incl. with Monroe (Inc. Place)
Downtown; RMC Place; RAPIDES; *182 E-4; ★ ALEX; mail Alexandria z 71309; pop. incl. with Alexandria (Inc. Place)
Downtown; RMC Place; ST. MARY; *182 I-7; mail Morgan City z 70380
Doyle; RMC Place; LIVINGSTON; *182 G-8; ★ B.R.; mail Livingston z 70754; pop. incl. with Livingston (Inc. Place)
Doyline; Inc. Place; WEBSTER; 182 B-2; 🅿; z 71023; Ⓟ 884; Ⓒ 841
Drew; RMC Place; CALCASIEU; *182 H-3; ★ LKCH; mail Lake Charles z 70602, z 70605, z 70607, West Monroe z 71291; pop. incl. with Lake Charles (Inc. Place)
Drew; RMC Place; OUACHITA; *182 B-5; ★ MONR; mail Lake Charles z 70607, West Monroe z 71291; rural
Drusilla; RMC Place; EAST BATON ROUGE; ★ B.R.; mail Baton Rouge z 70809; pop. incl. with Baton Rouge (Inc. Place)
Dry Creek; RMC Place; BEAUREGARD; 182 G-3; elev. 105ft./32m.; 🅿; z 70637; ● 300
Dry Prong; Inc. Place; GRANT; 182 E-4; elev. 196ft./60m.; 🅿; z 71423; Ⓟ 380; Ⓒ 421
Dubach; Inc. Place; LINCOLN; 182 B-4; elev. 142ft./43m.; 🅿; z 71235; Ⓟ 843; Ⓒ 800
Dubberly; Inc. Place; WEBSTER; 182 B-3; elev. 256ft./78m.; 🅿; z 71024; Ⓟ 253; Ⓒ 290
Duchein Place; RMC Place; EAST BATON ROUGE; ★ B.R.; pop. incl. with Baton Rouge (Inc. Place)
Duckroost; RMC Place; ASCENSION; *182 H-8; elev. 9ft./3m.; ★ B.R.; mail Saint Amant z 70774; ● 100
Dufresne; RMC Place; ST. CHARLES; *182 H-9; ★ N.O.; mail Luling z 70070; rural
Dukedale; RMC Place; BOSSIER; *182 B-2; ★ SHRE; mail Benton z 71006; rural
Dulac; CDP; TERREBONNE; 182 J-8; elev. 3ft./1m.; 🅿; ★ HOMA-; z 70353; Ⓟ 3,273; Ⓒ 2,458
Dunbarton; RMC Place; CONCORDIA; *182 D-6; mail Ferriday z 71334; rural
Dunn (Dunns); RMC Place; RICHLAND; 182 B-6; elev. 85ft./26m.; mail Delhi z 71232; ● 180
Dunns; RICHLAND; see Dunn (RMC Place)
Duplessis; RMC Place; ASCENSION; 182 H-7; elev. 17ft./5m.; 🅿; ★ B.R.; z 70728; ● 350
Dupont; RMC Place; AVOYELLES; *182 F-5; elev. 40ft./12m.; 🅿; z 71329; ● 200
Dupont; IBERVILLE; see Plaquemine Southwest (RMC Place)
Dupont; RMC Place; POINTE COUPEE; *182 G-6; mail Ventress z 70783; rural
Duralde; RMC Place; EVANGELINE; *182 G-4; mail Eunice z 70535, Mamou z 70554; ● 30
Duson; Inc. Place; LAFAYETTE, ACADIA; 182 H-5; elev. 30ft./9m.; 🅿; ★ LAF; z 70529; Ⓟ 1,465; Ⓒ 1,672
Dutch Town; RMC Place; ASCENSION; *182 H-7; ★ B.R.; mail Geismar z 70734; rural
Dykesville; RMC Place; CLAIBORNE; *182 A-3; mail Haynesville z 71038; rural

Entries in **UPPERCASE** are parishes.
Entries in **bold** have populations of 2,500 or more.
Names in parentheses are alternate names.

Inc. Place	Incorporated Place
RMC Place	Rand McNally Designated Place
CDP	Census Designated Place
MCD	Minor Civil Division

⊡	Parish Seat
▲	Minor Civil Division
elev.	Elevation
🅿	Post Office
🅷	Hospital
🅲	College
■	Principal Business Center
★	Ranally Metro Area (RMA) Abbreviation
z	Zip Code(s)
Ⓟ	Previous Census Population
Ⓡ	Revised Census Population
Ⓐ	Annexation Population
●	Rand McNally Population Estimate
Ⓒ	Final Census Population
Ⓢ	Special Census Population
◆	Estimated Population

For additional definitions see Glossary, Volume 1, and Introduction, Volume 2.

E

Easleyville; RMC Place; ST. HELENA; *182 F-8; elev. 246ft./75m.; mail Greensburg z 70441; rural
East Bank; JEFFERSON; see River Ridge (CDP)
EAST BATON ROUGE; 182 G-7; Ⓟ 380,105; © 412,852; ◆ 429,583
EAST CARROLL; 182 B-7; Ⓟ 9,709; © 9,421; ◆ 8,202
EAST FELICIANA; 182 F-7; Ⓟ 19,211; © 21,360; ◆ 20,449
East Hammond; RMC Place; TANGIPAHOA; *182 G-8; mail Hammond z 70401, z 70403
East Hodge; Inc. Place; JACKSON; *182 C-4; elev. 200ft./61m.; mail Hodge z 71247; Ⓟ 421; © 366
East Natchitoches; RMC Place; NATCHITOCHES; mail Natchitoches z 71457; pop. incl. with Natchitoches (Inc. Place)
Easton; RMC Place; EVANGELINE; 182 G-4; mail Ville Platte z 70586; ● 170
East Point; RMC Place; RED RIVER; 182 C-2; 🅿; z 71019; ● 90
East Side; RMC Place; CALCASIEU; *182 H-3; ★ LKCH; mail Lake Charles z 70615-16; pop. incl. with Lake Charles (Inc. Place)
Eastside Columbia; RMC Place; CALDWELL; *182 C-5; mail Columbia z 71418; ● 150
Eastwood; CDP; BOSSIER; *182 B-2; elev. 239ft./73m.; ★ SHRE; mail Haughton z 71037; Ⓟ 2,987; © 3,374
Ebenezer; RMC Place; ACADIA; *182 H-5; mail Crowley z 70526; ● 30
Echo (Bijou); RMC Place; RAPIDES; 182 F-5; elev. 62ft./19m.; 🅿; z 71330; ● 300
Eden; RMC Place; LA SALLE; *182 D-5; elev. 166ft./51m.; mail Trout z 71371; rural
Eden Isle; CDP-Census Area Only; ST. TAMMANY; *182 H-10; ★ N.O.; mail Slidell z 70458; Ⓟ 3,768; © 6,261
Eden Park; RMC Place; EAST BATON ROUGE; *182 G-7; ★ B.R.; pop. incl. with Baton Rouge (Inc. Place)
Edgard; CDP; ⊡ ST. JOHN THE BAPTIST; 182 H-8; elev. 10ft./3m.; 🅿; z 70049; Ⓟ 2,753; © 2,637
Edgefield; Inc. Place; RED RIVER; 182 C-3; elev. 180ft./55m.; mail Coushatta z 71019; Ⓟ 207; © 190
Edge Lake; RMC Place; ORLEANS; ★ N.O.; pop. incl. with New Orleans (Inc. Place)
Edgerly; RMC Place; CALCASIEU; 182 H-2; mail Vinton z 70668; ● 400
Edith; RMC Place; BEAUREGARD; *182 G-3; mail Ragley z 70657; rural
Edna; RMC Place; JEFFERSON DAVIS; *182 G-3; elev. 37ft./11m.; mail Kinder z 70648
Effie; RMC Place; AVOYELLES; 182 E-5; elev. 85ft./26m.; 🅿; z 71331; ● 200
Egan; RMC Place; ACADIA; 182 H-4; elev. 25ft./8m.; 🅿; z 70531; ● 540
Elam; RMC Place; FRANKLIN; *182 D-6; mail Wisner z 71378; ● 140
Elba; RMC Place; ST. LANDRY; *182 G-6; elev. 38ft./12m.; mail Melville z 71353; rural
Eliza; RMC Place; WEST BATON ROUGE; *182 H-7; ★ B.R.; mail Plaquemine z 70764; ● 150
Elizabeth; Inc. Place; ALLEN; 182 F-4; elev. 140ft./43m.; 🅿; z 70638; Ⓟ 414; © 574
Elkhorn; RMC Place; CONCORDIA; *182 D-6; mail Ferriday z 71334; ● 30
Ellendale; RMC Place; TERREBONNE; *182 I-8; ★ HOMA-; mail Houma z 70360; rural
Ellis; RMC Place; ACADIA; *182 H-4; mail Crowley z 70526; rural
Ellsworth; RMC Place; TERREBONNE; *182 I-8; elev. 11ft./3m.; ★ HOMA-; mail Houma z 70360; ● 230
Elmer (Greenwood Plantation); RMC Place; LAFOURCHE; *182 I-8; mail Thibodaux z 70301; rural
Elmer; RMC Place; RAPIDES; *182 F-4; elev. 180ft./55m.; 🅿; z 71424; ● 100
Elmfield; RMC Place; ASSUMPTION; *182 H-7; elev. 14ft./4m.; mail Napoleonville z 70390; ● 30
Elm Grove; RMC Place; BOSSIER; 182 C-2; elev. 150ft./46m.; 🅿; z 71051; ● 230
Elm Hall; RMC Place; ASSUMPTION; *182 H-7; elev. 13ft./4m.; mail Napoleonville z 70390; ● 30
Elm Hall Junction; RMC Place; ASSUMPTION; *182 I-7; elev. 12ft./4m.; mail Napoleonville z 70390; rural
Elm Park; RMC Place; WEST FELICIANA; *182 F-7; mail Saint Francisville z 70775; rural
Elmwood; RMC Place; JEFFERSON; 🅿; ★ N.O.; z 70123 & mail New Orleans z 70181, z 70183
Elmwood; CDP; JEFFERSON; *182 H-9; 🅿; ★ N.O.; z 70123 & mail New Orleans z 70181, z 70183; © 4,270
Elton; Inc. Place; JEFFERSON DAVIS; 182 G-4; elev. 50ft./15m.; 🅿; z 70532; Ⓟ 1,277; © 1,261
Empire; CDP; PLAQUEMINES; 182 J-10; elev. 4ft./1m.; 🅿; z 70050; Ⓟ 2,654; © 2,211
Encalade; RMC Place; PLAQUEMINES; *182 I-10; mail Port Sulphur z 70083
Energy Center; RMC Place; LAFAYETTE; ★ LAF; mail Lafayette z 70598; pop. incl. with Lafayette (Inc. Place)
Englewood; RMC Place; MADISON; *182 C-7; mail Tallulah z 71282; rural
English Turn; RMC Place; PLAQUEMINES; *182 I-10; ★ N.O.; mail Braithwaite z 70040; ● 120
Enoka; RMC Place; MADISON; *182 B-7; mail Tallulah z 71282; rural
Enola; RMC Place; ASSUMPTION; *182 H-7; elev. 13ft./4m.; mail Napoleonville z 70390; rural
Enon; RMC Place; WASHINGTON; *182 G-9; mail Franklinton z 70438; ● 100
Enterprise; RMC Place; CATAHOULA; 182 D-5; elev. 60ft./18m.; 🅿; z 71425; ● 130
Enterprise; RMC Place; IBERIA; ★ LAF; mail Jeanerette z 70544; pop. incl. with Jeanerette (Inc. Place)
Eola; RMC Place; AVOYELLES; *182 F-5; elev. 55ft./17m.; 🅿; z 71322; ● 40
Epps; Inc. Place; WEST CARROLL; 182 B-6; elev. 100ft./30m.; 🅿; z 71237; Ⓟ 541; © 1,153
Erath; Inc. Place; VERMILION; 182 H-5; elev. 9ft./3m.; 🅿; z 70533; Ⓟ 2,428; © 2,187
Eros; Inc. Place; JACKSON; 182 C-4; elev. 192ft./59m.; 🅿; z 71238; Ⓟ 177; © 202
Erwinville; RMC Place; WEST BATON ROUGE; 182 G-7; 🅿; z 70729; ● 600
Essen Heights; RMC Place; EAST BATON ROUGE; *182 G-7; ★ B.R.; mail Baton Rouge z 70808; ● 280
Estelle; CDP; JEFFERSON; *182 I-9; ★ N.O.; mail Marrero z 70072; Ⓟ 14,091; © 15,880
Esther; RMC Place; VERMILION; *182 I-5; elev. 5ft./2m.; mail Abbeville z 70510
Estherwood; Inc. Place; ACADIA; 182 H-4; elev. 15ft./5m.; 🅿; z 70534; Ⓟ 745; © 807
Esto; RMC Place; SABINE; *182 E-2; mail Many z 71449; rural
Estopinal; ST. BERNARD; see Kenilworth (RMC Place)
Ethel; RMC Place; EAST FELICIANA; 182 F-7; elev. 165ft./50m.; 🅿; z 70730; ● 300
Eunice; Inc. Place; ST. LANDRY, ACADIA; 182 G-4; elev. 49ft./15m.; 🅿 🅷; z 70535; Ⓟ 11,162; © 11,499
Eureka; RMC Place; OUACHITA; *182 B-5; mail Downsville z 71234; rural
Eva; RMC Place; CONCORDIA; 182 E-6; elev. 54ft./16m.; mail Monterey z 71354
Evangeline; RMC Place; ACADIA; 182 H-4; elev. 30ft./9m.; 🅿; z 70537; ● 340
EVANGELINE; 182 G-4; Ⓟ 33,274; © 35,434; ◆ 36,187
Evans; RMC Place; VERNON; 182 F-2; elev. 129ft./39m.; 🅿; z 70639; ● 250
Evelyn; RMC Place; DE SOTO; 182 D-2; elev. 129ft./39m.; mail Coushatta z 71019, Mansfield z 71052; ● 50
Evergreen; Inc. Place; AVOYELLES; 182 F-5; elev. 65ft./20m.; 🅿; z 71333; Ⓟ 283; © 314
Evergreen; RMC Place; UNION; *182 B-4; mail Bernice z 71222; rural
Evergreen; RMC Place; WEBSTER; *182 B-3; elev. 300ft./91m.; mail Minden z 71055; rural
Extension; RMC Place; FRANKLIN; 182 D-6; elev. 65ft./20m.; 🅿; z 71243; ● 100

F

Fairbanks; RMC Place; OUACHITA; 182 B-5; elev. 85ft./26m.; 🅿; ★ MONR; z 71240; ● 280
Fairfield; RMC Place; GRANT; *182 E-4; mail Dry Prong z 71423; rural
Fairlane; RMC Place; TERREBONNE; ★ HOMA-; mail Houma z 70360
Fairmont; RMC Place; GRANT; *182 E-4; mail Colfax z 71417; rural
Fairview; RMC Place; CONCORDIA; *182 E-6; elev. 58ft./18m.; mail Vidalia z 71373; rural
Farmer Spur; RMC Place; LINCOLN; mail Ruston z 71270; pop. incl. with Vienna (Inc. Place)
Farmerville; Inc. Place; ⊡ UNION; 182 B-4; elev. 113ft./34m.; 🅿 🅷; z 71241; Ⓟ 3,334; © 3,808
Faubourg (Deshotels); RMC Place; ST. LANDRY; *182 G-5; mail Washington z 70589; rural
Felixville; RMC Place; EAST FELICIANA; *182 F-8; elev. 320ft./98m.; mail Clinton z 70722; ● 50
Fellowship; RMC Place; LA SALLE; *182 D-5; mail Trout z 71371; ● 120
Fenris; RMC Place; EVANGELINE; *182 G-4; mail Mamou z 70554; rural
Fenton; Inc. Place; JEFFERSON DAVIS; 182 G-3; elev. 34ft./10m.; 🅿; z 70640; Ⓟ 265; © 380
Ferriday; Inc. Place; CONCORDIA; 182 D-6; elev. 63ft./19m.; 🅿 🅷; ★ NCHZ; z 71334; Ⓟ 4,111; © 3,723
Ferry Lake; RMC Place; CADDO; *182 B-1; elev. 192ft./59m.; mail Oil City z 71061; ● 170
Fields; RMC Place; BEAUREGARD; 182 G-2; elev. 103ft./31m.; 🅿; z 70653; ● 40
Fifth Ward; RMC Place; AVOYELLES; *182 F-5; mail Marksville z 71351; ● 150
Fillmore; RMC Place; BOSSIER; *182 B-2; ★ SHRE; mail Haughton z 71037
Fisher; Inc. Place; SABINE; 182 E-2; elev. 336ft./102m.; 🅿; z 71426; Ⓟ 277; © 268
Fishville; RMC Place; GRANT; *182 E-5; mail Pollock z 71467
Fiske; RMC Place; WEST CARROLL; *182 A-6; mail Oak Grove z 71263; ● 50
Five Forks; RMC Place; WINN; *182 D-4; mail Winnfield z 71483; ● 50
Flat Creek; RMC Place; WINN; *182 D-4; elev. 200ft./61m.; mail Tullos z 71479; rural
Flatwoods; RMC Place; RAPIDES; 182 E-3; elev. 300ft./91m.; 🅿; z 71427; ● 200
Flora (Weaver); RMC Place; NATCHITOCHES; 182 D-3; elev. 114ft./35m.; 🅿; z 71428; ● 130
Florence; RMC Place; ST. MARY; *182 I-6; mail Franklin z 70538; rural
Florien; Inc. Place; SABINE; 182 E-2; elev. 253ft./77m.; 🅿; z 71429; Ⓟ 626; © 692
Florrissant; RMC Place; ST. BERNARD; ★ N.O.; mail Saint Bernard z 70085; ● 100
Flournoy; RMC Place; CADDO; 182 B-1; ★ SHRE; mail Shreveport z 71109; pop. incl. with Shreveport (Inc. Place)
Floyd; RMC Place; WEST CARROLL; *182 B-6; mail Pioneer z 71266; ● 80
Fluker; RMC Place; TANGIPAHOA; 182 F-8; elev. 151ft./46m.; 🅿; z 70436; ● 300
Foley; RMC Place; ALLEN; *182 G-4; elev. 88ft./27m.; mail Oakdale z 71463; rural
Foley; RMC Place; ASSUMPTION; *182 I-7; elev. 12ft./4m.; mail Napoleonville z 70390; ● 60
Folsom; Inc. Place; ST. TAMMANY; 182 G-9; elev. 150ft./46m.; 🅿; z 70437; Ⓟ 469; © 525
Fondale; RMC Place; OUACHITA; *182 C-5; mail Monroe z 71201; rural
Forbing; RMC Place; CADDO; 182 C-2; 🅿; ★ SHRE; z 71106; pop. incl. with Shreveport (Inc. Place)
Fordoche; Inc. Place; POINTE COUPEE; 182 G-6; 🅿; z 70732; Ⓟ 869; © 933
Foreman; RMC Place; EAST BATON ROUGE; *182 G-7; elev. 24ft./7m.; ★ B.R.; mail Baton Rouge z 70815; rural
Forest; Inc. Place; WEST CARROLL; 182 B-6; elev. 125ft./38m.; 🅿; z 71242; Ⓟ 263; © 275
Forest Glen; RMC Place; ST. TAMMANY; *182 H-9; ★ N.O.; mail Lacombe z 70445; ● 600
Forest Hill; Inc. Place; RAPIDES; 182 F-4; elev. 167ft./51m.; 🅿; z 71430; Ⓟ 408; © 456
Forest Oaks; RMC Place; EAST BATON ROUGE; 182 B-14; ★ B.R.; mail Baton Rouge z 70815; pop. incl. with Baton Rouge (Inc. Place)
Forest Park; RMC Place; OUACHITA; *182 B-5; ★ MONR; mail West Monroe z 71291; ● 1,450
Forked Island; RMC Place; VERMILION; 182 I-5; elev. 3ft./1m.; mail Abbeville z 70510; ● 300
Forksville; RMC Place; OUACHITA; *182 B-5; elev. 150ft./46m.; mail Calhoun z 71225; rural
Fort De Russy; RMC Place; AVOYELLES; *182 F-5; mail Marksville z 71351; rural
Fort Jesup; RMC Place; SABINE; 182 D-2; elev. 368ft./112m.; mail Many z 71449; ● 200
Fort Necessity; RMC Place; FRANKLIN; 182 C-6; elev. 67ft./20m.; 🅿; z 71243; ● 190
Fort Polk North; CDP-Census Area Only; VERNON; *182 F-3; mail Fort Polk z 71459; Ⓟ 3,819; © 3,279
Fort Polk South; CDP-Census Area Only; VERNON; *182 F-3; mail Fort Polk z 71459; Ⓟ 10,911; © 11,000
Fosters; RMC Place; BOSSIER; *182 B-2; ★ SHRE; mail Bossier City z 71111; pop. incl. with Bossier City (Inc. Place)
Fosters Canal (City Price); RMC Place; PLAQUEMINES; *182 I-10; elev. 3ft./1m.; mail Port Sulphur z 70083; ● 100
Foules; RMC Place; CATAHOULA; *182 D-6; mail Clayton z 71326; rural
Fourborge; RMC Place; EVANGELINE; mail Ville Platte z 70586; rural
Four Corners; RMC Place; ST. MARY; *182 I-6; mail Franklin z 70538; ● 70
Four Forks; RMC Place; CADDO; *182 C-1; mail Keatchie z 71046; rural
Four Forks; RMC Place; RICHLAND; *182 C-6; mail Mangham z 71259; rural
Fowler; RMC Place; OUACHITA; *182 B-5; ★ MONR; mail Fairbanks z 71240
Francis Place; RMC Place; ST. BERNARD; *182 H-10; ★ N.O.; mail Meraux z 70075, Violet z 70092; ● 990
Franklin; Inc. Place; ⊡ ST. MARY; 182 I-6; 🅿 🅷; z 70538; Ⓟ 9,004; © 8,354
FRANKLIN; 182 C-6; Ⓟ 22,387; © 21,263; ◆ 19,925
Franklinton; Inc. Place; ⊡ WASHINGTON; 182 F-9; elev. 155ft./47m.; 🅿 🅷; z 70438; Ⓟ 4,007; © 3,657
Fred; RMC Place; EAST BATON ROUGE; *182 G-7; ★ B.R.; mail Zachary z 70791; pop. incl. with Zachary (Inc. Place)
Freetown; RMC Place; ASSUMPTION; *182 H-7; elev. 22ft./7m.; mail Napoleonville z 70390; rural
Freetown; RMC Place; ST. MARY; *182 I-6; mail Franklin z 70538; rural
French Settlement; Inc. Place; LIVINGSTON; 182 H-8; elev. 14ft./4m.; 🅿; ★ B.R.; z 70733; Ⓟ 829; © 945
Frenier; RMC Place; ST. JOHN THE BAPTIST; *182 H-9; ★ N.O.; mail La Place z 70068
Frey; RMC Place; ACADIA; *182 G-4; mail Eunice z 70535; rural
Friendship; RMC Place; BIENVILLE; 182 C-3; mail Bienville z 71008; ● 60
Friendship; RMC Place; LIVINGSTON; *182 G-8; ★ B.R.; mail Walker z 70785; rural
Frierson; RMC Place; DE SOTO; 182 C-2; 🅿; z 71027; ● 400
Frisco; RMC Place; POINTE COUPEE; *182 G-6; elev. 25ft./8m.; mail Livonia z 70755; ● 190
Frogmore; RMC Place; CONCORDIA; 182 E-6; elev. 61ft./19m.; 🅿; z 71334; ● 80
Frost; RMC Place; LIVINGSTON; *182 G-8; elev. 21ft./6m.; mail Livingston z 70754
Frost Town; RMC Place; OUACHITA; *182 B-4; mail Downsville z 71234; rural
Fryeburg; RMC Place; BIENVILLE; *182 C-3; elev. 255ft./78m.; mail Heflin z 71039; ● 130
Fullerton; RMC Place; VERNON; 182 F-3; elev. 226ft./69m.; 🅿; z 70656; ● 60
Fulton; RMC Place; BEAUREGARD; *182 G-3; elev. 80ft./24m.; mail Ragley z 70657; rural
Funston; RMC Place; DE SOTO; *182 C-1; elev. 215ft./66m.; mail Logansport z 71049; ● 100

G

Gaars Mill; RMC Place; WINN; *182 C-4; mail Dodson z 71422; rural
Gahagan; RMC Place; RED RIVER; *182 C-2; elev. 138ft./42m.; mail Coushatta z 71019; rural
Galbraith; RMC Place; NATCHITOCHES; *182 E-4; mail Lena z 71447
Galion; RMC Place; MOREHOUSE; *182 B-6; elev. 99ft./30m.; mail Bonita z 71223; rural
Galliano; CDP; LAFOURCHE; 182 J-9; 🅿; z 70354; Ⓟ 4,294; © 7,356
Galva; RMC Place; ST. JOHN THE BAPTIST; *182 H-9; ★ N.O.; mail Akers z 70421; rural
Galvez; RMC Place; ASCENSION; *182 H-8; 🅿; ★ B.R.; z 70769
Gandy; RMC Place; SABINE; *182 E-2; mail Florien z 71429; rural
Gansville; RMC Place; WINN; *182 C-4; elev. 199ft./61m.; mail Dodson z 71422
Garden City; RMC Place; ST. MARY; 182 I-6; elev. 10ft./3m.; 🅿; z 70540; ● 300
Gardere; CDP; EAST BATON ROUGE; *182 H-7; elev. 24ft./7m.; ★ B.R.; mail Baton Rouge z 70810; Ⓟ 7,209; © 8,992
Gardner; RMC Place; RAPIDES; 182 E-4; elev. 182ft./55m.; 🅿; z 71409, z 71431; ● 150
Garland; RMC Place; ST. LANDRY; *182 G-5; mail Bunkie z 71322; ● 50
Garyville; CDP; ST. JOHN THE BAPTIST; 182 H-8; elev. 15ft./5m.; 🅿; z 70051 & mail Mount Airy z 70076; Ⓟ 3,181; © 2,775
Gassoway; RMC Place; EAST CARROLL; *182 A-7; elev. 113ft./34m.; mail Lake Providence z 71254; rural
Gateway; RMC Place; EAST BATON ROUGE; ★ B.R.; mail Baton Rouge z 70835; pop. incl. with Baton Rouge (Inc. Place)
Gayles; RMC Place; CADDO; *182 C-2; elev. 156ft./48m.; mail Shreveport z 71105
Gaytime; RMC Place; BEAUREGARD; *182 G-3; mail Ragley z 70657; rural
Ged; RMC Place; CALCASIEU; *182 H-2; mail Vinton z 70668; ● 70
Geismar; RMC Place; ASCENSION; 182 H-7; elev. 24ft./7m.; 🅿; z 70734; ● 200
Gentilly Terrace; RMC Place; ORLEANS; ★ N.O.; pop. incl. with New Orleans (Inc. Place)
Gentilly Woods; RMC Place; ORLEANS; ★ N.O.; pop. incl. with New Orleans (Inc. Place)
Georgetown; Inc. Place; GRANT; 182 D-4; elev. 96ft./29m.; 🅿; z 71432; Ⓟ 273; © 301
Georgetown; RMC Place; ORLEANS; ★ N.O.; pop. incl. with New Orleans (Inc. Place)
Georgeville; RMC Place; ST. HELENA; *182 G-8; mail Independence z 70443; rural
Georgia; RMC Place; ASSUMPTION; *182 I-7; mail Napoleonville z 70390; rural
Getty Camp; RMC Place; PLAQUEMINES; mail Venice z 70091; ● 100
Gheens; RMC Place; LAFOURCHE; *182 I-8; elev. 5ft./2m.; 🅿; z 70355; ● 180
Gibbstown; RMC Place; CAMERON; *182 H-3; mail Bell City z 70630
Gibsland; Inc. Place; BIENVILLE; 182 B-3; elev. 294ft./90m.; 🅿; z 71028; Ⓟ 1,224; © 1,119
Gibson; RMC Place; TERREBONNE; 182 I-7; elev. 5ft./2m.; 🅿; z 70356 & mail Donner z 70352; ● 500
Giddens; BIENVILLE; see Woodardville (RMC Place)
Gilark; RMC Place; WEBSTER; 182 B-3; mail Minden z 71055; ● 100
Gilbert; Inc. Place; FRANKLIN; 182 C-6; 🅿; z 71336; Ⓟ 704; © 561
Gilleyville (Charlieville); RMC Place; RICHLAND; *182 C-5; mail Rayville z 71269; rural
Gilliam; Inc. Place; CADDO; 182 B-2; elev. 190ft./58m.; 🅿; z 71029; Ⓟ 202; © 178
Gillis; RMC Place; CALCASIEU; 182 G-3; elev. 26ft./8m.; mail Lake Charles z 70611; ● 150
Girard; RMC Place; RICHLAND; *182 B-6; 🅿; z 71269; ● 180
Glade; RMC Place; CATAHOULA; *182 E-6; elev. 50ft./15m.; mail Jonesville z 71343; ● 30
Glencoe; RMC Place; ST. MARY; 182 I-6; mail Franklin z 70538; ● 100
Glen Dale; RMC Place; ST. JOHN THE BAPTIST; *182 H-8; ★ N.O.; mail Edgard z 70049; rural
Glenmora; Inc. Place; RAPIDES; 182 F-4; elev. 136ft./41m.; 🅿; z 71433; Ⓟ 1,686; © 1,558
Glenwild; RMC Place; ST. MARY; *182 I-7; mail Berwick z 70342; pop. incl. with Berwick (Inc. Place)
Glenwood; RMC Place; ASSUMPTION; *182 H-7; mail Napoleonville z 70390; rural
Gloria; RMC Place; PLAQUEMINES; *182 I-9; elev. 5ft./2m.; mail Belle Chasse z 70037; rural
Gloster; RMC Place; DE SOTO; 182 C-2; elev. 241ft./73m.; 🅿; z 71030; ● 250
Glynn; RMC Place; POINTE COUPEE; *182 G-7; elev. 35ft./11m.; 🅿; z 70736; ● 80
Godchaux; RMC Place; LAFOURCHE; mail Raceland z 70394
Godchaux Community; RMC Place; ST. JOHN THE BAPTIST; mail La Place z 70068
Godchaux Mill; RMC Place; LAFOURCHE
Goff; RICHLAND; see Start (RMC Place)
Gold Dust; RMC Place; AVOYELLES; *182 F-5; mail Bunkie z 71322; ● 30
Golden Meadow; Inc. Place; LAFOURCHE; 182 J-9; elev. 2ft./1m.; 🅿; z 70357; Ⓟ 2,049; © 2,193
Golden Star Plantation; RMC Place; ST. JOHN THE BAPTIST; *182 H-8; mail Vacherie z 70090; rural
Goldman; RMC Place; TENSAS; *182 D-7; mail Waterproof z 71375; rural
Goldonna; Inc. Place; NATCHITOCHES; 182 D-3; elev. 144ft./44m.; 🅿; z 71031; Ⓟ 417; © 457
Goldridge; RMC Place; IBERVILLE; *182 H-7; mail White Castle z 70788; rural
Gonzales; Inc. Place; ASCENSION; 182 H-8; elev. 10ft./3m.; 🅿 🅷; ★ B.R.; z 70707, z 70737; Ⓟ 7,003; © 8,156
Goodbee; RMC Place; ST. TAMMANY; *182 G-9; mail Covington z 70433, z 70435
Good Hope; RMC Place; ST. CHARLES; *182 H-9; ★ N.O.; mail Norco z 70079
Good Pine; RMC Place; LA SALLE; 182 D-5; mail Jena z 71342; ● 700
Goodwill; RMC Place; WEST CARROLL; 182 B-6; mail Oak Grove z 71263; ● 200
Goodwood; RMC Place; EAST BATON ROUGE; *182 G-7; ★ B.R.; pop. incl. with Baton Rouge (Inc. Place)
Goodwood; RMC Place; ST. LANDRY; *182 G-6; mail Melville z 71353; rural
Goosport; RMC Place; CALCASIEU; *182 H-3; elev. 18ft./5m.; ★ LKCH; pop. incl. with Lake Charles (Inc. Place)
Gordon; RMC Place; CLAIBORNE; *182 A-3; elev. 273ft./83m.; mail Haynesville z 71038; rural
Gorhamtown; WINN; see Joyce (RMC Place)
Gorum; RMC Place; NATCHITOCHES; 182 E-3; elev. 130ft./40m.; 🅿; z 71434; ● 150
Goudeau; RMC Place; AVOYELLES; 182 F-5; elev. 74ft./23m.; 🅿; z 71333 & mail Morrow z 71356; ● 130
Gouldsboro; RMC Place; JEFFERSON; *182 H-9; ★ N.O.; mail Gretna z 70053; pop. incl. with Gretna (Inc. Place)
Gowen; RMC Place; WEST CARROLL; *182 B-6; mail Pioneer z 71266; rural
Grambling; Inc. Place; LINCOLN; 182 B-4; elev. 305ft./93m.; 🅿 🅲 5,065; z 71245; Ⓟ 5,512; © 4,693
Gramercy; Inc. Place; ST. JAMES; 182 H-8; elev. 15ft./5m.; 🅿; z 70052; Ⓟ 2,412; © 3,066; Ⓡ 3,047
Grand Bayou; RMC Place; RED RIVER; 182 C-2; mail Mansfield z 71052; ● 50
Grandbois; RMC Place; LAFOURCHE; *182 I-8; elev. 5ft./2m.; mail Bourg z 70343; ● 250
Grand Caillou; TERREBONNE; see Boudreaux (RMC Place)
Grand Cane; Inc. Place; DE SOTO; 182 C-2; elev. 302ft./92m.; 🅿; z 71032; Ⓟ 233; © 191
Grand Chenier; RMC Place; CAMERON; 182 I-3; elev. 5ft./2m.; 🅿; z 70643; ● 500
Grand Coteau; Inc. Place; ST. LANDRY; 182 G-5; elev. 53ft./16m.; 🅿; ★ LAF; z 70541; Ⓟ 1,118; © 1,040
Grand Ecore; RMC Place; NATCHITOCHES; 182 D-3; elev. 130ft./40m.; mail Natchitoches z 71457; ● 450
Grand Isle; Inc. Place; JEFFERSON; 182 J-9; elev. 5ft./2m.; 🅿; z 70358; Ⓟ 1,455; © 1,541
Grand Lake; RMC Place; CAMERON; 182 H-3; elev. 12ft./4m.; mail Lake Charles z 70607; ● 300
Grand Point; RMC Place; ST. JAMES; *182 H-8; mail Paulina z 70763; ● 300
Grand Prairie; RMC Place; ST. LANDRY; *182 G-5; mail Washington z 70589; ● 30
Grand River; RMC Place; IBERVILLE; *182 H-6; mail Plaquemine z 70764; rural
Grangeville; RMC Place; ST. HELENA; 182 G-8; mail Amite z 70422; ● 70
Grant; RMC Place; ALLEN; 182 F-3; elev. 120ft./37m.; 🅿; z 70644; ● 100
GRANT; 182 E-4; Ⓟ 17,526; © 18,698; ◆ 19,690
Gray (Beattieville); CDP; TERREBONNE; 182 I-8; elev. 15ft./5m.; 🅿; ★ HOMA-; z 70359; Ⓟ 4,260; © 4,958
Gray Point; RMC Place; EVANGELINE; *182 G-4; mail Ville Platte z 70586; rural
Grayson; Inc. Place; CALDWELL; 182 C-5; elev. 163ft./50m.; 🅿; z 71435; Ⓟ 529; © 531
Greenacres; RMC Place; BOSSIER; ★ SHRE; pop. incl. with Bossier City (Inc. Place)
Green Acres; RMC Place; CONCORDIA; *182 E-6; ★ NCHZ; mail Vidalia z 71373; ● 350
Green Acres; RMC Place; EAST BATON ROUGE; *182 G-7; ★ B.R.; mail Baton Rouge z 70811; ● 250
Green Acres; RMC Place; ST. CHARLES; *182 I-9; mail Des Allemands z 70030; ● 280
Green Gables; RMC Place; RAPIDES; *182 E-5; ★ ALEX; mail Pineville z 71360; ● 200
Greenlaw; RMC Place; TANGIPAHOA; *182 F-8; mail Kentwood z 70444; ● 100
Green Lawn; RMC Place; JEFFERSON; ★ N.O.; mail Kenner z 70065; pop. incl. with Kenner (Inc. Place)
Green Lawn Terrace; RMC Place; JEFFERSON; ★ N.O.; mail Kenner z 70062, z 70065; pop. incl. with Kenner (Inc. Place)
Greensburg; Inc. Place; ⊡ ST. HELENA; 182 F-8; elev. 223ft./68m.; 🅿 🅷; z 70441; Ⓟ 583; © 631
Greens Ditch; RMC Place; ORLEANS; *182 H-10; elev. 4ft./1m.; ★ N.O.; pop. incl. with New Orleans (Inc. Place)
Greenwell Springs; RMC Place; EAST BATON ROUGE; 182 G-7; elev. 65ft./20m.; 🅿 🅷; ★ B.R.; z 70739; ● 200
Greenwich Village; RMC Place; CALCASIEU; ★ LKCH; pop. incl. with Lake Charles (Inc. Place)
Greenwood; Inc. Place; CADDO; 182 C-1; elev. 244ft./74m.; 🅿; ★ SHRE; z 71033; Ⓟ 2,092; © 2,458
Greenwood; RMC Place; ST. MARY; *182 I-7; elev. 5ft./2m.; mail Morgan City z 70380
Greenwood; RMC Place; TERREBONNE; *182 I-8; ★ HOMA-; mail Gibson z 70356; rural
Greenwood Park; RMC Place; CADDO; mail Shreveport z 71108; ● 400
Greenwood Plantation; LAFOURCHE; see Elmer (RMC Place)
Greinwich Terrace; RMC Place; CALCASIEU; ★ LKCH; pop. incl. with Lake Charles (Inc. Place)
Greinwich Village; RMC Place; CALCASIEU; *182 H-3; ★ LKCH; pop. incl. with Lake Charles (Inc. Place)
Gretna; Inc. Place; ⊡ JEFFERSON; 182 I-9; elev. 5ft./2m.; 🅿 🅷 ■; ★ N.O.; z 70053-54, z 70056; Ⓟ 17,208; © 17,423; ◆ 18,571
Gretna Green; RMC Place; TENSAS; *182 D-6; mail Waterproof z 71375; rural
Grosse Tete; Inc. Place; IBERVILLE; 182 G-6; elev. 11ft./3m.; 🅿; z 70740; Ⓟ 541; © 670
Gueydan; Inc. Place; VERMILION; 182 H-4; 🅿; z 70542; Ⓟ 1,611; © 1,598
Gulf Outport; RMC Place; ORLEANS; ★ N.O.; mail New Orleans z 70146; pop. incl. with New Orleans (Inc. Place)
Gullett; RMC Place; TANGIPAHOA; *182 G-8; mail Amite z 70422; ● 400
Gum Ridge; RMC Place; MOREHOUSE; *182 B-6; mail Oak Ridge z 71264; rural
Gurley; RMC Place; EAST FELICIANA; *182 F-7; elev. 210ft./64m.; mail Ethel z 70730; rural

H

Haas; RMC Place; AVOYELLES; *182 F-5; mail Bunkie z 71322; rural
Haaswood; RMC Place; ST. TAMMANY; *182 H-10; elev. 27ft./8m.; ★ N.O.; mail Pearl River z 70452; ● 120
Hackberry; CDP; CAMERON; 182 H-2; elev. 6ft./2m.; 🅿; z 70645; Ⓟ 1,664; © 1,699
Hacketts Corner; RMC Place; CAMERON; *182 H-3; mail Bell City z 70630; rural
Hackley; RMC Place; WASHINGTON; *182 F-9; elev. 349ft./106m.; mail Franklinton z 70438
Hagewood; RMC Place; NATCHITOCHES; 182 D-3; mail Natchitoches z 71457; ● 150
Hahnville; CDP; ⊡ ST. CHARLES; 182 H-9; 🅿; ★ N.O.; z 70057; Ⓟ 2,599; © 2,792
Haile; RMC Place; UNION; 182 B-5; elev. 106ft./32m.; mail Marion z 71260; ● 130
Haire; VERMILION; see Wright (RMC Place)
Half Way; RMC Place; ASSUMPTION; *182 H-7; mail Donaldsonville z 70346; rural
Hall Summit; Inc. Place; RED RIVER; 182 C-3; elev. 223ft./68m.; 🅿; z 71034; Ⓟ 227; © 264
Hamburg; RMC Place; AVOYELLES; 182 F-5; elev. 50ft./15m.; 🅿; z 71339; ● 280
Hammet; RMC Place; CONCORDIA; mail Vidalia z 71373; ● 200
Hammond; Inc. Place; TANGIPAHOA; 182 G-8; elev. 47ft./14m.; 🅿 🅷 🅲 15,118 ■; z 70401-04; Ⓟ 15,871; © 17,639; ◆ 20,665
Hanna; RMC Place; RED RIVER; 182 D-3; elev. 131ft./40m.; 🅿; z 71019; ● 100
Hanson City; RMC Place; JEFFERSON; ★ N.O.; mail Kenner z 70062; pop. incl. with Kenner (Inc. Place)
Happy Jack; RMC Place; PLAQUEMINES; 182 I-10; elev. 3ft./1m.; mail Port Sulphur z 70083; ● 200
Harahan; Inc. Place; JEFFERSON; 182 H-9; elev. 5ft./2m.; 🅿; ★ N.O.; z 70123; Ⓟ 9,927; © 9,885
Hardwood; RMC Place; WEST FELICIANA; 182 F-7; elev. 140ft./43m.; 🅿; z 70775; ● 500
Hargis; RMC Place; GRANT; *182 D-4; elev. 217ft./66m.; mail Montgomery z 71454; rural
Hargrove; RMC Place; CALCASIEU; *182 G-2; mail DeQuincy z 70633; ● 200
Harlem; RMC Place; PLAQUEMINES; *182 I-10; rural
Harlem; RMC Place; VERMILION; mail Abbeville z 70510; pop. incl. with Abbeville (Inc. Place)
Harmon; RMC Place; RED RIVER; *182 C-2; elev. 139ft./42m.; 🅿; z 71019; ● 70
Harrisonburg; Inc. Place; ⊡ CATAHOULA; 182 D-6; elev. 80ft./24m.; 🅿; z 71340; Ⓟ 453; © 746
Harvey; CDP; JEFFERSON; 182 E-13; 🅿; ★ N.O.; z 70058-59; Ⓟ 21,222; © 22,226; ◆ 19,772
Hatcher; SABINE; see Union Springs (RMC Place)
Hatfield; RMC Place; WINN; *182 D-4; elev. 135ft./41m.; pop. incl. with Winnfield (Inc. Place)
Hathaway; RMC Place; JEFFERSON DAVIS; *182 H-4; elev. 28ft./9m.; mail Jennings z 70546
Haughton; Inc. Place; BOSSIER; 182 B-2; elev. 237ft./72m.; 🅿; ★ SHRE; z 71037; Ⓟ 1,664; © 2,792
Hawthorne; RMC Place; VERNON; *182 E-3; mail Leesville z 71446; ● 30
Hayes; RMC Place; CALCASIEU; 182 H-3; elev. 11ft./3m.; 🅿; z 70646; ● 880
Haynesville; Inc. Place; CLAIBORNE; 182 A-3; elev. 360ft./110m.; 🅿; z 71038; Ⓟ 2,854; © 2,679
Hazelwood; RMC Place; ST. LANDRY; *182 G-5; mail Port Barre z 70577; ● 100
Head of Island; RMC Place; LIVINGSTON; 182 H-8; mail Maurepas z 70449, Springfield z 70462; ● 250
Hearn Island; RMC Place; CALDWELL; *182 C-5; mail Columbia z 71418; ● 80
Hebert; RMC Place; CALDWELL; *182 C-5; elev. 60ft./18m.; mail Columbia z 71418; ● 200
Hebron; RMC Place; CLAIBORNE; *182 A-4; mail Bernice z 71222, Sikes z 71473; rural
Hecker; RMC Place; CALCASIEU; *182 G-3; mail Iowa z 70647; rural
Heflin; Inc. Place; WEBSTER; 182 B-3; elev. 272ft./83m.; 🅿; z 71039; Ⓟ 253; © 245
Helena; RMC Place; TENSAS; *182 D-6; elev. 69ft./21m.; mail Saint Joseph z 71366, Waterproof z 71375; rural
Henderson; Inc. Place; ST. MARTIN; 182 H-6; elev. 10ft./3m.; 🅿; ★ LAF; z 70517; Ⓟ 1,543; © 1,531
Henfer Park; RMC Place; JEFFERSON; ★ N.O.; mail New Orleans z 70123
Henry; RMC Place; VERMILION; 182 I-5; mail Erath z 70533; ● 350
Hermitage; RMC Place; POINTE COUPEE; 182 G-7; mail Jarreau z 70749; ● 250
Hessmer; Inc. Place; AVOYELLES; 182 F-5; elev. 78ft./24m.; 🅿; z 71341; Ⓟ 578; © 642
Hester; RMC Place; ST. JAMES; *182 H-8; elev. 15ft./5m.; 🅿; z 70743; rural
Hewes; RMC Place; POINTE COUPEE; mail Oscar z 70762
Hickory; RMC Place; AVOYELLES; *182 F-5; mail Cottonport z 71327; rural
Hickory; RMC Place; ST. TAMMANY; *182 G-10; elev. 45ft./14m.; mail Pearl River z 70452; ● 140
Hickory Grove; RMC Place; RAPIDES; *182 E-5; mail Deville z 71328; ● 100
Hickory Valley; RMC Place; WINN; *182 D-4; mail Sikes z 71473; rural
Hicks; RMC Place; VERNON; 182 F-3; elev. 292ft./89m.; 🅿; z 71446; ● 50
Hico; RMC Place; LINCOLN; 182 B-4; elev. 263ft./80m.; mail Dubach z 71235; ● 100
Higginbotham; RMC Place; ACADIA; *182 H-5; elev. 45ft./14m.; mail Church Point z 70525; rural
Highland; RMC Place; TENSAS; *182 D-6; mail Waterproof z 71375; rural
Highland Acres; RMC Place; JEFFERSON; ★ N.O.; mail New Orleans z 70123
Highland Heights; RMC Place; EAST BATON ROUGE; ★ B.R.; mail Baton Rouge z 70808; pop. incl. with Baton Rouge (Inc. Place)
Highland Park; RMC Place; OUACHITA; ★ MONR; mail West Monroe z 71291; pop. incl. with West Monroe (Inc. Place)
Highland Park; RMC Place; TERREBONNE; *182 I-8; ★ HOMA-; mail Houma z 70360; ● 210
High Point; LA SALLE; see Whitehall (RMC Place)
Highway Park; RMC Place; JEFFERSON; ★ N.O.; mail Kenner z 70065; pop. incl. with Kenner (Inc. Place)
Hi-Land; RMC Place; ST. BERNARD; *182 I-10; ★ N.O.; mail Violet z 70092
Hill; RMC Place; WINN; *182 C-4; mail Sikes z 71473; rural
Hillaryville (Marchandville); RMC Place; ASCENSION; *182 H-7; mail Darrow z 70725; ● 350
Hillsdale; RMC Place; ST. HELENA; *182 G-8; elev. 157ft./48m.; 🅿; z 70422; rural
Hilltop; RMC Place; JACKSON; *182 C-4; mail Quitman z 71268; rural
Hilly; RMC Place; LINCOLN; *182 B-4; mail Dubach z 71235; ● 30
Hineston; RMC Place; RAPIDES; 182 F-4; elev. 202ft./62m.; 🅿; z 71438; ● 350
Hinkle; RMC Place; BOSSIER; *182 B-2; ★ SHRE; pop. incl. with Bossier City (Inc. Place)
Hobart; RMC Place; ASCENSION; *182 H-7; elev. 20ft./6m.; ★ B.R.; mail Prairieville z 70769; rural
Hodge; Inc. Place; JACKSON; 182 C-4; elev. 191ft./58m.; 🅿; z 71247; Ⓟ 562; © 492
Hohen Solms; RMC Place; ASCENSION; *182 H-7; mail White Castle z 70788; ● 180
Holden; RMC Place; LIVINGSTON; *182 G-8; elev. 38ft./12m.; 🅿; z 70744; ● 350
Holiday Park; RMC Place; LAFAYETTE; 5 mi. S of Lafayette; ★ LAF; mail Lafayette z 70502; ● 1,000
Holloway; RMC Place; RAPIDES; *182 E-5; elev. 78ft./24m.; mail Deville z 71328; ● 70
Holly; RMC Place; DE SOTO; *182 C-2; elev. 189ft./58m.; mail Grand Cane z 71032; rural
Holly Beach; RMC Place; CAMERON; 182 I-2; mail Cameron z 70631; ● 140
Hollybrook; RMC Place; EAST CARROLL; *182 B-7; elev. 98ft./30m.; mail Lake Providence z 71254; rural
Holly Grove; RMC Place; FRANKLIN; *182 D-6; mail Wisner z 71378; rural
Holly Ridge; RMC Place; RICHLAND; 182 B-6; 🅿; z 71269; ● 50
Holly Ridge; RMC Place; TENSAS; *182 D-6; elev. 62ft./19m.; mail Saint Joseph z 71366; rural
Hollywood; RMC Place; CALCASIEU; *182 H-3; ★ LKCH; mail Sulphur z 70663; pop. incl. with Sulphur (Inc. Place)
Hollywood; RMC Place; EAST BATON ROUGE; ★ B.R.; pop. incl. with Baton Rouge (Inc. Place)
Hollywood; RMC Place; TERREBONNE; *182 I-8; ★ HOMA-; mail Houma z 70360; ● 160
Hollywood; RMC Place; WEST FELICIANA; *182 F-6; mail Saint Francisville z 70775; rural
Hollywood Yard; RMC Place; CADDO; ★ SHRE; pop. incl. with Shreveport (Inc. Place)
Holmwood; RMC Place; CALCASIEU; *182 H-3; elev. 16ft./5m.; mail Iowa z 70647
Holton; RMC Place; TANGIPAHOA; *182 G-9; mail Amite z 70422; rural
Holum; RMC Place; CALDWELL; *182 D-5; elev. 182ft./55m.; mail Grayson z 71435; ● 50
Home Place; RMC Place; PLAQUEMINES; *182 J-10; elev. 1ft./0m.; mail Port Sulphur z 70083
Homer; Inc. Place; ⊡ CLAIBORNE; 182 B-3; elev. 281ft./86m.; 🅿 🅷; z 71040; Ⓟ 4,152; © 3,788
Hoods Mill; RMC Place; JACKSON; *182 C-4; mail Chatham z 71226; rural
Hopedale; RMC Place; ST. BERNARD; *182 I-10; mail Saint Bernard z 70085; ● 310
Hope Villa; RMC Place; ASCENSION; *182 H-7; ★ B.R.; mail Baton Rouge z 70808; ● 200
Hornbeck; Inc. Place; VERNON; 182 E-2; elev. 360ft./110m.; 🅿; z 71439; Ⓟ 427; © 435
Horse Bluff Landing; RMC Place; LIVINGSTON; *182 G-8; elev. 10ft./3m.; mail Springfield z 70462; rural
Hosston; Inc. Place; CADDO; 182 A-1; elev. 220ft./67m.; 🅿; z 71043; Ⓟ 417; © 387
Hotwells; RMC Place; RAPIDES; 182 E-4; mail Boyce z 71409; ● 150
Houltonville; RMC Place; ST. TAMMANY; *182 G-9; ★ N.O.; mail Madisonville z 70447; ● 180
Houma; Inc. Place; ⊡ TERREBONNE; 182 I-8; 🅿 🅷 ■; ★ HOMA-; z 70360-61, z 70363-64; Ⓟ 30,495; © 32,393; ◆ 31,910
Howard; RMC Place; RED RIVER; *182 C-2; elev. 144ft./44m.; mail Shreveport z 71105; rural
Hubertville; RMC Place; IBERIA; *182 I-6; ★ LAF; mail Jeanerette z 70544; pop. incl. with Jeanerette (Inc. Place)
Hudson; RMC Place; WINN; *182 C-4; elev. 136ft./41m.; mail Dodson z 71422
Hughes (Swindleville); RMC Place; BOSSIER; *182 B-2; mail Benton z 71006; ● 110
Humphreys; RMC Place; TERREBONNE; *182 I-8; ★ HOMA-; mail Gibson z 70356
Hundley; RMC Place; ACADIA; *182 G-5; mail Eunice z 70535; rural
Hunter; RMC Place; DE SOTO; *182 D-2; elev. 267ft./81m.; mail Logansport z 71049, Mansfield z 71052; ● 50
Huntington; RMC Place; CADDO; ★ SHRE; mail Shreveport z 71129, z 71149; pop. incl. with Shreveport (Inc. Place)
Huron; RMC Place; ST. MARTIN; *182 H-6; ★ LAF; mail Arnaudville z 70512; ● 100
Hurricane; RMC Place; CLAIBORNE; *182 B-3; elev. 416ft./127m.; mail Athens z 71003; rural
Husser; RMC Place; TANGIPAHOA; 182 G-9; elev. 49ft./15m.; 🅿; z 70442; ● 70
Hutton; RMC Place; VERNON; *182 E-3; mail Leesville z 71446; ● 30
Hyde; RMC Place; AVOYELLES; mail Simmesport z 71369; pop. incl. with Simmesport (Inc. Place)
Hydropolis; AVOYELLES; see Cocoville (RMC Place)
Hymel (Saint Amelia); RMC Place; ST. JAMES; *182 H-8; mail Vacherie z 70090; rural

I

IBERIA; 182 H-6; Ⓟ 68,297; © 73,266; ◆ 73,281
Iberville; RMC Place; IBERVILLE; *182 H-7; elev. 20ft./6m.; 🅿; ★ B.R.; z 70776; pop. incl. with Saint Gabriel (Inc. Place)
IBERVILLE; 182 H-6; Ⓟ 31,049; © 33,320; ◆ 31,725
Ida; Inc. Place; CADDO; 182 A-1; elev. 286ft./87m.; 🅿; z 71044; Ⓟ 250; © 258
Idlewild; RMC Place; ST. MARY; *182 I-7; mail Patterson z 70392; rural
Idlewild; RMC Place; TERREBONNE; *182 I-8; ★ HOMA-; mail Houma z 70364; ● 470
Ikes; RMC Place; BEAUREGARD; *182 F-3; mail DeRidder z 70634; rural
Independence; Inc. Place; TANGIPAHOA; 182 G-8; elev. 93ft./28m.; 🅿 🅷; z 70443; Ⓟ 1,632; © 1,724
Indian Bayou; RMC Place; VERMILION; 182 H-5; mail Rayne z 70578; ● 80
Indian Mound; RMC Place; EAST BATON ROUGE; *182 G-7; ★ B.R.; mail Greenwell Springs z 70739; ● 150
Indian Village; RMC Place; ALLEN; 182 G-3; mail Kinder z 70648; ● 320
Indian Village; RMC Place; OUACHITA; *182 B-4; mail Calhoun z 71225; rural
Ingleside; RMC Place; ASSUMPTION; *182 I-7; elev. 19ft./6m.; mail Napoleonville z 70390; rural
Innis; RMC Place; POINTE COUPEE; *182 F-6; elev. 45ft./14m.; 🅿; z 70747; ● 250
Inniswold; CDP; EAST BATON ROUGE; 182 C-13; ★ B.R.; mail Baton Rouge z 70809; Ⓟ 3,474; © 4,944
International Trade Mart; RMC Place; ORLEANS; *182 H-9; ★ N.O.; mail New Orleans z 70130; pop. incl. with New Orleans (Inc. Place)
Intracoastal City; RMC Place; VERMILION; 182 I-5; elev. 4ft./1m.; mail Abbeville z 70510; ● 180
Iota; Inc. Place; ACADIA; 182 H-4; elev. 30ft./9m.; 🅿; z 70543; Ⓟ 1,256; © 1,376
Iowa; Inc. Place; CALCASIEU; 182 H-3; elev. 25ft./8m.; 🅿; ★ LKCH; z 70647; Ⓟ 2,588; © 2,663
Irish Bend; RMC Place; ST. MARY; *182 I-6; mail Franklin z 70538; ● 130
Irma; RMC Place; NATCHITOCHES; *182 D-3; elev. 114ft./35m.; mail Natchitoches z 71457; rural
Ironton; RMC Place; PLAQUEMINES; 182 I-10; mail Port Sulphur z 70083; ● 230
Isabel; RMC Place; WASHINGTON; *182 G-9; mail Bogalusa z 70427; rural
Isle Labbe; RMC Place; ST. MARTIN; *182 H-6; mail Saint Martinville z 70582; rural
Istrouma; RMC Place; EAST BATON ROUGE; *182 G-7; ★ B.R.; mail Baton Rouge z 70805, z 70892; pop. incl. with Baton Rouge (Inc. Place)
Ivan; RMC Place; BOSSIER; *182 B-2; mail Benton z 71006

J

Jack; RMC Place; ST. HELENA; *182 G-8; mail Greensburg z 70441; rural
Jackson; Inc. Place; EAST FELICIANA; 182 F-7; elev. 180ft./55m.; 🅿 🅷; z 70748; Ⓟ 3,891; © 4,130
JACKSON; 182 C-4; Ⓟ 15,705; © 15,397; ◆ 14,719
Jackson Road; RMC Place; EAST FELICIANA; *182 G-7; mail Jackson z 70748; rural
Jacoby; RMC Place; POINTE COUPEE; *182 F-6; elev. 43ft./13m.; mail Lettsworth z 70753; rural
Jamestown; Inc. Place; BIENVILLE; 182 C-3; elev. 227ft./69m.; 🅿; z 71045; Ⓟ 148; © 149
Janie; RMC Place; NATCHITOCHES; *182 E-3; mail Lena z 71447; rural
Jarreau; RMC Place; POINTE COUPEE; 182 G-6; elev. 30ft./9m.; 🅿; z 70749; ● 520
Jay (Valentine); RMC Place; LAFOURCHE; *182 I-8; mail Lockport z 70374; ● 100
Jeanerette; Inc. Place; IBERIA; 182 I-6; elev. 15ft./5m.; 🅿; ★ LAF; z 70544; Ⓟ 6,205; © 5,997
Jean Lafitte; Inc. Place; JEFFERSON; *182 I-9; elev. 1ft./0m.; ★ N.O.; mail Lafitte z 70067; Ⓟ 1,469; © 2,137
Jefferson; CDP; JEFFERSON; 182 E-12; elev. 5ft./2m.; 🅿 🅷; ★ N.O.; z 70121 & mail New Orleans z 70181; Ⓟ 14,521; © 11,843
Jefferson; RMC Place; LAFAYETTE; *182 H-5; ★ LAF; mail Lafayette z 70501-02; pop. incl. with Lafayette (Inc. Place)
JEFFERSON; 182 I-9; Ⓟ 448,306; © 455,466; ◆ 405,214
JEFFERSON DAVIS; 182 H-3; Ⓟ 30,722; © 31,435; ◆ 30,753
Jefferson Island; RMC Place; IBERIA; *182 H-5; mail New Iberia z 70560
Jefferson Terrace; RMC Place; EAST BATON ROUGE; *182 G-7; ★ B.R.; mail Baton Rouge z 70808; ● 2,200
Jena; Inc. Place; ⊡ LA SALLE; 182 D-5; elev. 157ft./48m.; 🅿 🅷; z 71342; Ⓟ 2,626; © 2,971
Jennings; Inc. Place; ⊡ JEFFERSON DAVIS; 182 H-4; elev. 22ft./7m.; 🅿 🅷; z 70546; Ⓟ 11,305; © 10,986
Jesuit Bend; RMC Place; PLAQUEMINES; *182 I-9; mail Belle Chasse z 70037
Jewella; RMC Place; CADDO; *182 B-2; ★ SHRE; mail Shreveport z 71109; pop. incl. with Shreveport (Inc. Place)
Jigger; RMC Place; FRANKLIN; 182 C-6; elev. 65ft./20m.; 🅿; z 71249; ● 180
Johnson; RMC Place; ST. JOHN THE BAPTIST; *182 H-8; elev. 14ft./4m.; mail Edgard z 70049; rural
Johnson; RMC Place; ST. MARY; *182 I-6; elev. 9ft./3m.; mail Franklin z 70538; rural
Johnson Ridge; RMC Place; TERREBONNE; *182 I-8; ★ HOMA-; mail Thibodaux z 70301; ● 320
Johnson's Bayou; RMC Place; CAMERON; 182 I-2; mail Cameron z 70631; ● 150
Johnson Street; RMC Place; JEFFERSON; *182 H-9; ★ N.O.; mail Metairie z 70001, z 70004; pop. incl. with New Orleans (Inc. Place)
Jones; RMC Place; MOREHOUSE; 182 A-6; elev. 105ft./32m.; 🅿; z 71250; ● 300
Jonesboro; Inc. Place; ⊡ JACKSON; 182 C-4; elev. 215ft./66m.; 🅿 🅷; z 71251; Ⓟ 4,305; © 3,914
Jonesburg; RMC Place; RICHLAND; *182 B-6; elev. 85ft./26m.; mail Rayville z 71269; rural
Jones Park; RMC Place; JEFFERSON; ★ N.O.; mail Kenner z 70065; pop. incl. with Kenner (Inc. Place)
Jonesville; Inc. Place; CATAHOULA; 182 D-6; elev. 59ft./18m.; 🅿; z 71343 & mail Wildsville z 71377; Ⓟ 2,720; © 2,469
Jordan Hill; RMC Place; WINN; *182 D-4; elev. 125ft./38m.; mail Winnfield z 71483; ● 300
Joyce (Gorhamtown); RMC Place; WINN; 182 D-4; elev. 128ft./39m.; 🅿; z 71440; ● 470
Judice; RMC Place; LAFAYETTE; *182 H-5; ★ LAF; mail Lafayette z 70506; rural
Junction; RMC Place; BEAUREGARD; *182 F-2; elev. 101ft./31m.; mail Merryville z 70653; ● 50
Junction City; Inc. Place; UNION, CLAIBORNE; 182 A-4; see also Junction City, AR; 🅿; z 71256, z 71749; Ⓟ 749; © 652

K

Kadesh; RMC Place; GRANT; *182 D-3; mail Montgomery z 71454; rural
Kahns; RMC Place; WEST BATON ROUGE; *182 G-7; ★ B.R.; mail Port Allen z 70767; ● 100
Kaplan; Inc. Place; VERMILION; 182 H-5; elev. 15ft./5m.; 🅿 🅷; z 70548; Ⓟ 4,535; © 5,177
Kateland; RMC Place; GRANT; *182 E-4; mail Colfax z 71417; rural
Katy; RMC Place; ST. MARY; *182 I-6; elev. 10ft./3m.; mail Franklin z 70538; rural
Keachi; DE SOTO; see Keatchie (Inc. Place)
Keatchie (Keachi); Inc. Place; DE SOTO; 182 C-1; elev. 336ft./102m.; 🅿; z 71046; Ⓟ 277; © 323
Kedron; RMC Place; ST. HELENA; *182 G-8; mail Amite z 70422; rural
Keithville; RMC Place; CADDO; 182 C-2; elev. 198ft./60m.; 🅿; ★ SHRE; z 71047; ● 300
Kelly; RMC Place; CALDWELL; 182 D-5; elev. 119ft./36m.; 🅿; z 71441; ● 200
Kellys; RMC Place; JACKSON; *182 B-4; mail Ruston z 71270
Kendale; RMC Place; JEFFERSON; ★ N.O.; mail Kenner z 70062; ● 400
Kendrick's Ferry; RMC Place; FRANKLIN; *182 D-6; mail Gilbert z 71336; rural
Kenilworth (Estopinal); RMC Place; ST. BERNARD; *182 I-10; elev. 5ft./2m.; ★ N.O.; mail Saint Bernard z 70085; ● 360
Kenmore; RMC Place; POINTE COUPEE; *182 G-6; mail Maringouin z 70757; rural
Kennedy Heights; RMC Place; JEFFERSON; *182 I-9; ★ N.O.; mail Westwego z 70094; ● 1,800
Kenner; Inc. Place; JEFFERSON; 182 H-9; elev. 5ft./2m.; 🅿 🅷 🅲 350 ■; ★ N.O.; z 70062-65, z 70097; Ⓟ 72,033; © 70,517; ◆ 70,549
Kenner Junction; RMC Place; JEFFERSON; ★ N.O.; mail Kenner z 70062; pop. incl. with Kenner (Inc. Place)
Kentwood; Inc. Place; TANGIPAHOA; 182 F-8; elev. 220ft./67m.; 🅿; z 70444; Ⓟ 2,468; © 2,205
Kernan; RMC Place; BEAUREGARD; *182 G-3; mail Ragley z 70657; rural
Kickapoo; RMC Place; DE SOTO; *182 C-2; elev. 325ft./99m.; mail Gloster z 71030; ● 150
Kilbourne; Inc. Place; WEST CARROLL; 182 A-7; elev. 125ft./38m.; 🅿; z 71253; Ⓟ 409; © 436
Killian; Inc. Place; LIVINGSTON; 182 G-8; elev. 14ft./4m.; mail Springfield z 70462; Ⓟ 721; © 1,053
Killona; CDP; ST. CHARLES; *182 H-8; elev. 10ft./3m.; 🅿; ★ N.O.; z 70057; © 797
Kinder; Inc. Place; ALLEN; 182 G-3; elev. 49ft./15m.; 🅿 🅷; z 70648; Ⓟ 2,246; © 2,148
King Hill; RMC Place; NATCHITOCHES; *182 D-3; elev. 163ft./50m.; mail Coushatta z 71019; rural
Kingston; RMC Place; DE SOTO; *182 C-2; elev. 204ft./62m.; mail Grand Cane z 71032; rural
Kingsville; RMC Place; RAPIDES; *182 E-4; ★ ALEX; mail Pineville z 71360; pop. incl. with Pineville (Inc. Place)
Kipling; RMC Place; BEAUREGARD; *182 G-3; mail DeRidder z 70634; rural
Kiroli Woods; RMC Place; OUACHITA; *182 B-5; ★ MONR; mail West Monroe z 71291; ● 460
Kisatchie; RMC Place; NATCHITOCHES; 182 E-3; elev. 286ft./87m.; mail Provencal z 71468; ● 80
Kleinpeter; RMC Place; EAST BATON ROUGE; *182 G-7; ★ B.R.; mail Baton Rouge z 70808; rural
Klondyke; RMC Place; TERREBONNE; *182 I-8; ★ HOMA-; mail Bourg z 70343; ● 400
Klotzville; RMC Place; ASSUMPTION; *182 H-7; mail Belle Rose z 70341; ● 400
Knight; RMC Place; VERNON; *182 F-2; mail Evans z 70639; rural
Kolin; RMC Place; RAPIDES; 182 E-5; elev. 120ft./37m.; 🅿; ★ ALEX; z 71360; ● 50
Kolter; RMC Place; DE SOTO; *182 C-1; mail Keatchie z 71046; pop. incl. with Keatchie (Inc. Place)
Koran; RMC Place; BOSSIER; *182 C-2; mail Haughton z 71037; rural
Kraemer (Bayou Boeuf); RMC Place; LAFOURCHE; 182 I-8; elev. 4ft./1m.; 🅿; z 70371; ● 500
Krotz Springs; Inc. Place; ST. LANDRY; 182 G-6; elev. 26ft./8m.; 🅿; z 70750; Ⓟ 1,285; © 1,219
Kurthwood; RMC Place; VERNON; 182 E-3; elev. 340ft./104m.; 🅿; z 71443; ● 70

L

Laark; RMC Place; MOREHOUSE; *182 A-6; mail Jones z 71250; rural
Labadieville; CDP; ASSUMPTION; 182 I-7; elev. 15ft./5m.; 🅿; z 70372; Ⓟ 1,821; © 1,811
Labarre; RMC Place; POINTE COUPEE; *182 G-6; elev. 35ft./11m.; 🅿; z 70759; ● 140
Lacamp; RMC Place; VERNON; 182 F-3; elev. 253ft./77m.; 🅿; z 71438; ● 100
Lacassine; RMC Place; JEFFERSON DAVIS; *182 H-3; elev. 20ft./6m.; 🅿; z 70650; ● 450
Lachute; RMC Place; CADDO; *182 C-2; elev. 146ft./45m.; mail Shreveport z 71115; rural
Lacombe; CDP; ST. TAMMANY; 182 H-10; elev. 10ft./3m.; 🅿; ★ N.O.; z 70445; Ⓟ 6,523; © 7,518
Lacour; RMC Place; POINTE COUPEE; *182 F-6; mail Batchelor z 70715; rural
Lafayette; Inc. Place; ⊡ LAFAYETTE; 182 H-5; elev. 41ft./12m.; 🅿 🅷 🅲 16,302 ■; ★ LAF; z 70500-09, z 70593, z 70595-96, z 70598; Ⓟ 94,421; © 110,257; ◆ 109,094
LAFAYETTE; 182 H-5; Ⓟ 164,762; © 190,503; ◆ 206,778
Lafayette Square; RMC Place; ORLEANS; *182 H-9; ★ N.O.; mail New Orleans z 70130, z 70176, z 70190; pop. incl. with New Orleans (Inc. Place)
Lafayette Woods; RMC Place; TERREBONNE; *182 I-8; elev. 7ft./2m.; ★ HOMA-; mail Houma z 70360; ● 320
Lafitte; CDP; JEFFERSON; 182 I-9; elev. 1ft./0m.; 🅿; ★ N.O.; z 70067; Ⓟ 1,507; © 1,576
Lafourche; RMC Place; LAFOURCHE; *182 I-8; elev. 13ft./4m.; mail Thibodaux z 70301; ● 600
LAFOURCHE; 182 I-8; Ⓟ 85,860; © 89,974; ◆ 90,331
Lagan; RMC Place; ST. JAMES; *182 H-8; mail Saint James z 70086; rural
Lagonda; RMC Place; ST. MARY; *182 I-7; mail Morgan City z 70380
Lake; RMC Place; ASCENSION; *182 H-8; elev. 13ft./4m.; ★ B.R.; mail Prairieville z 70769; rural
Lake Arthur; Inc. Place; JEFFERSON DAVIS; 182 H-4; elev. 5ft./2m.; 🅿; z 70549; Ⓟ 3,194; © 3,007
Lake Bruin; RMC Place; TENSAS; *182 D-7; mail Newellton z 71357, Saint Joseph z 71366; rural
Lake Catherine; RMC Place; ORLEANS; *182 H-10; ★ N.O.; pop. incl. with New Orleans (Inc. Place)
Lake Charles; Inc. Place; ⊡ CALCASIEU; 182 H-3; elev. 20ft./6m.; 🅿 🅷 🅲 8,992 ■; ★ LKCH; z 70601-02, z 70605-07, z 70609, z 70611-12, z 70615-16, z 70629; Ⓟ 70,580; © 71,757; ◆ 70,061
Lake Charles Northeast; RMC Place; CALCASIEU; ★ LKCH; pop. incl. with Lake Charles (Inc. Place)
Lake End; RMC Place; RED RIVER; *182 D-3; elev. 127ft./39m.; mail Coushatta z 71019
Lake Forest; RMC Place; ORLEANS; ★ N.O.; mail New Orleans z 70127, z 70187; pop. incl. with New Orleans (Inc. Place)
Lake Hermitage; PLAQUEMINES; see Lake Judge Perez (RMC Place)
Lake Judge Perez (Lake Hermitage); RMC Place; PLAQUEMINES; *182 I-10; mail Port Sulphur z 70083; ● 200
Lakeland; RMC Place; POINTE COUPEE; 182 G-6; elev. 35ft./11m.; 🅿; z 70752; ● 300
Lake Providence; Inc. Place; ⊡ EAST CARROLL; 182 B-7; elev. 106ft./32m.; 🅿 🅷; z 71254; Ⓟ 5,380; © 5,104
Lakeshore; RMC Place; OUACHITA; 182 B-5; ★ MONR; mail Monroe z 71203; ● 1,400
Lakeshore East; RMC Place; ORLEANS; ★ N.O.; pop. incl. with New Orleans (Inc. Place)
Lakeshore West; RMC Place; ORLEANS; ★ N.O.; pop. incl. with New Orleans (Inc. Place)
Lakeside; RMC Place; CAMERON; *182 H-4; mail Gueydan z 70542; rural
Lakeside; RMC Place; RAPIDES; *182 E-4; ★ ALEX; mail Pineville z 71360; ● 900
Lakeview; RMC Place; CADDO; 182 A-8; elev. 199ft./61m.; ★ SHRE; mail Shreveport z 71107; ● 1,200
Lakeview; RMC Place; NATCHITOCHES; *182 E-3; mail Natchez z 71456; rural
Lakeview; RMC Place; ORLEANS; *182 H-9; ★ N.O.; mail New Orleans z 70124, z 70184; pop. incl. with New Orleans (Inc. Place)
Lake Vista; RMC Place; ORLEANS; ★ N.O.; pop. incl. with New Orleans (Inc. Place)
Lakewood East; RMC Place; ORLEANS; ★ N.O.; pop. incl. with New Orleans (Inc. Place)
Lamar; RMC Place; FRANKLIN; *182 C-6; mail Delhi z 71232
Lamourie; RMC Place; RAPIDES; *182 F-4; ★ ALEX; mail Lecompte z 71346; ● 30
Lampman; RMC Place; VERMILION; mail Abbeville z 70510; pop. incl. with Abbeville (Inc. Place)
Landay Gautreaux Subdivision; RMC Place; TERREBONNE; *182 I-8; ★ HOMA-; mail Thibodaux z 70301; ● 180
Lapine; RMC Place; OUACHITA; *182 C-5; ★ MONR; mail West Monroe z 71291-92; rural
Laplace; CDP; ST. JOHN THE BAPTIST; 182 H-8; elev. 13ft./4m.; 🅿 🅷; ★ N.O.; z 70068-69; Ⓟ 24,194; © 27,684; ◆ 30,451
Laran; RMC Place; UNION; *182 A-4; elev. 166ft./51m.; mail Strong z 71765; rural
La Reussite; RMC Place; PLAQUEMINES; *182 I-9; mail Belle Chasse z 70037; rural
Larose; CDP; LAFOURCHE; 182 I-9; elev. 8ft./2m.; 🅿; z 70345, z 70373-74; Ⓟ 5,772; © 7,306
La Rosen; RMC Place; CADDO; *182 C-2; ★ SHRE; mail Shreveport z 71118; pop. incl. with Shreveport (Inc. Place)
Larto; RMC Place; CATAHOULA; 182 E-5; elev. 52ft./16m.; 🅿; z 71343; ● 120
LA SALLE; 182 D-5; Ⓟ 13,662; © 14,282; ◆ 13,996
Latanier; RMC Place; RAPIDES; *182 E-5; elev. 69ft./21m.; ★ ALEX; mail Lecompte z 71346; ● 50
Lauderdale; RMC Place; ALLEN; *182 G-4; mail Kinder z 70648; ● 30
Laurel Grove; RMC Place; LAFOURCHE; *182 I-8; mail Thibodaux z 70301; rural
Laurel Hill; RMC Place; WEST FELICIANA; 182 F-7; mail Woodville z 39669; ● 50
Laurel Lea; RMC Place; EAST BATON ROUGE; ★ B.R.; mail Baton Rouge z 70808; pop. incl. with Baton Rouge (Inc. Place)
Laurel Ridge; RMC Place; IBERVILLE; *182 H-7; elev. 19ft./6m.; mail White Castle z 70788; rural
Laurel Valley Plantation; RMC Place; LAFOURCHE; *182 I-8; mail Thibodaux z 70301; rural
Lawhon; RMC Place; BIENVILLE; *182 C-3; mail Jamestown z 71045, Ringgold z 71068; rural
Lawtell; RMC Place; ST. LANDRY; 182 G-5; elev. 60ft./18m.; 🅿; z 70550; ● 1,000
Lazy Acres; RMC Place; TERREBONNE; *182 I-8; ★ HOMA-; mail Houma z 70360; ● 160
Leander; RMC Place; VERNON; *182 F-4; elev. 220ft./67m.; 🅿; z 71438; ● 120
Lebeau; RMC Place; ST. LANDRY; 182 G-5; elev. 30ft./9m.; 🅿; z 71345; ● 200
Le Blanc; RMC Place; ALLEN; 182 G-3; elev. 40ft./12m.; 🅿; z 70651; ● 200
Le Bleu; RMC Place; CALCASIEU; *182 H-3; elev. 19ft./6m.; ★ LKCH; mail Lake Charles z 70615; ● 200
Lecompte; Inc. Place; RAPIDES; 182 F-4; elev. 74ft./23m.; 🅿; ★ ALEX; z 71346; Ⓟ 1,592; © 1,366
Lee Bayou; RMC Place; CATAHOULA; *182 D-6; mail Clayton z 71326; rural
Lee Heights; RMC Place; RAPIDES; *182 E-4; elev. 160ft./49m.; ★ ALEX; mail Pineville z 71360; ● 1,000

Entries in **UPPERCASE** are parishes.
Entries in **bold** have populations of 2,500 or more.
Names in parentheses are alternate names.

Inc. Place	Incorporated Place
RMC Place	Rand McNally Designated Place
CDP	Census Designated Place
MCD	Minor Civil Division

⊡ Parish Seat
▲ Minor Civil Division
elev. Elevation
🅿 Post Office
🅷 Hospital
🅲 College
■ Principal Business Center
★ Ranally Metro Area (RMA) Abbreviation
z Zip Code(s)
Ⓟ Previous Census Population
Ⓡ Revised Census Population
Ⓐ Annexation Population
● Rand McNally Population Estimate
© Final Census Population
Ⓢ Special Census Population
◆ Estimated Population

For additional definitions see Glossary, Volume 1, and Introduction, Volume 2.

Lees Creek; RMC Place; WASHINGTON; ***182** G-10; mail Bogalusa **z** 70427; ● 350
Lees Landing; RMC Place; TANGIPAHOA; **182** G-9; mail Ponchatoula **z** 70454; ● 150
Leesville; Inc. Place; ⊡ VERNON; **182** F-3; elev. 254ft./77m.; 🅿 🅷; **z** 71446, **z** 71459, **z** 71496; Ⓟ 7,638; Ⓒ 6,753
Leeville; RMC Place; LAFOURCHE; **182** J-9; mail Golden Meadow **z** 70357; ● 200
Legonier; RMC Place; POINTE COUPEE; **182** F-6; mail Lettsworth **z** 70753; ● 230
Leighton; RMC Place; LAFOURCHE; ***182** I-8; ★ **HOMA-**; mail Thibodaux **z** 70301; rural
Leland; RMC Place; CATAHOULA; ***182** D-6; mail Sicily Island **z** 71368; ● 50
Leleux; RMC Place; IBERIA; ***182** H-5; elev. 7ft./2m.; ★ **LAF**; mail New Iberia **z** 70560; rural
Lelieux; RMC Place; VERMILION; ***182** H-5; mail Kaplan **z** 70548; rural
Lemannville; RMC Place; ASCENSION; ***182** H-8; elev. 21ft./6m.; mail Donaldsonville **z** 70346; ● 260
Le Moyen; RMC Place; ST. LANDRY; **182** F-5; elev. 40ft./12m.; 🅿; **z** 71356; ● 200
Lena; RMC Place; RAPIDES; **182** E-4; elev. 132ft./40m.; 🅿; **z** 71447; ● 350
Leonville; Inc. Place; ST. LANDRY; **182** G-5; elev. 25ft./8m.; 🅿; ★ **LAF**; **z** 70551; Ⓟ 825; Ⓒ 1,007
Leroy; RMC Place; VERMILION; ***182** H-5; mail Maurice **z** 70555; ● 150
Leton; RMC Place; WEBSTER; ***182** B-3; elev. 231ft./70m.; mail Shongaloo **z** 71072
Lettsworth; RMC Place; POINTE COUPEE; **182** F-6; elev. 44ft./13m.; 🅿; **z** 70753; ● 200
Levert (Saint John); RMC Place; ST. MARTIN; ***182** H-6; mail Saint Martinville **z** 70582; ● 100
Levins; RMC Place; CONCORDIA; ★ **NCHZ**; mail Ferriday **z** 71334; ● 450
Lewisburg; RMC Place; ST. LANDRY; **182** G-5; mail Church Point **z** 70525; ● 260
Lewisburg; RMC Place; ST. TAMMANY; ***182** G-9; ★ **N.O.**; mail Mandeville **z** 70448; ● 180
Lewiston; RMC Place; TANGIPAHOA; ***182** F-9; mail Kentwood **z** 70444; ● 100
Lewistown; RMC Place; LAFOURCHE; ***182** I-8; mail Raceland **z** 70394; ● 500
Liberty; RMC Place; OUACHITA; ***182** B-5; mail Calhoun **z** 71225; ● 100
Liberty Hill; RMC Place; BIENVILLE; **182** C-3; elev. 299ft./91m.; mail Bienville **z** 71008; ● 50
Libuse; RMC Place; RAPIDES; ***182** E-5; elev. 169ft./52m.; 🅿; ★ **ALEX**; **z** 71348; ● 800
Liddieville; RMC Place; FRANKLIN; **182** C-6; mail Winnsboro **z** 71295; ● 50
Lillie; Inc. Place; UNION; **182** A-4; elev. 114ft./35m.; 🅿; **z** 71256; Ⓟ 145; Ⓒ 139
Lincecum; RMC Place; GRANT; ***182** D-4; mail Pollock **z** 71467; rural
LINCOLN; **182** B-4; Ⓟ 41,745; Ⓒ 42,509; ◆ 42,437
Linda Lee; RMC Place; LIVINGSTON; ★ **B.R.**; mail Denham Springs **z** 70706; ● 200
Lindsay; RMC Place; EAST FELICIANA; **182** G-7; mail Jackson **z** 70748; ● 20
Link; RMC Place; ACADIA; ***182** H-5; mail Branch **z** 70516; rural
Linton; RMC Place; BOSSIER; ***182** B-2; elev. 236ft./72m.; mail Benton **z** 71006; rural
Linville; RMC Place; UNION; **182** B-5; elev. 180ft./55m.; 🅿; **z** 71260; ● 150
Linwood; PLAQUEMINES; see Woodlawn (RMC Place)
Linwood; RMC Place; ST. MARY; ***182** I-6; elev. 15ft./5m.; mail Baldwin **z** 70514; ● 100
Linwood Park; RMC Place; CADDO; ★ **SHRE**; pop. incl. with Shreveport (Inc. Place)
Lions; RMC Place; ST. JOHN THE BAPTIST; ***182** H-8; mail La Place **z** 70068, Reserve **z** 70084; ● 120
Lisbon; Inc. Place; CLAIBORNE; **182** B-4; elev. 344ft./105m.; 🅿; **z** 71048; Ⓟ 160; Ⓒ 162
Lismore; RMC Place; CONCORDIA; ***182** E-6; elev. 55ft./17m.; mail Jonesville **z** 71343; rural
Litroe; RMC Place; UNION; ***182** A-5; elev. 99ft./30m.; mail Marion **z** 71260; rural
Little Caillou; RMC Place; TERREBONNE; ★ **HOMA-**; mail Chauvin **z** 70344
Little Creek; RMC Place; LA SALLE; **182** D-5; elev. 127ft./39m.; mail Trout **z** 71371; ● 130
Little Prairie; RMC Place; ASCENSION; ***182** H-7; elev. 22ft./7m.; ★ **B.R.**; mail Prairieville **z** 70769; rural
Little Texas; RMC Place; ASSUMPTION; ***182** I-7; elev. 9ft./3m.; mail Napoleonville **z** 70390; rural
Little Woods; RMC Place; ORLEANS; ***182** H-10; ★ **N.O.**; pop. incl. with New Orleans (Inc. Place)
Live Oak; RMC Place; PLAQUEMINES; ***182** I-9; elev. 6ft./2m.; mail Belle Chasse **z** 70037; rural
Live Oak Hills; RMC Place; ST. TAMMANY; ***182** G-9; mail Madisonville **z** 70447; ● 250
Live Oak Manor; RMC Place; JEFFERSON; **182** E-11; ★ **N.O.**; mail Westwego **z** 70094; ● 1,900
Live Oaks; RMC Place; ORLEANS; ★ **N.O.**; pop. incl. with New Orleans (Inc. Place)
Liverpool; RMC Place; ST. HELENA; ***182** F-8; mail Greensburg **z** 70441; rural
Livingston; Inc. Place; ⊡ LIVINGSTON; **182** G-8; elev. 40ft./12m.; 🅿; ★ **B.R.**; **z** 70754; Ⓟ 999; Ⓒ 1,342
LIVINGSTON; **182** G-8; Ⓟ 70,526; Ⓒ 91,814; ◆ 119,105
Livonia; Inc. Place; POINTE COUPEE; **182** G-6; elev. 10ft./3m.; 🅿; **z** 70755; Ⓟ 970; Ⓒ 1,339
Lobdell; RMC Place; WEST BATON ROUGE; ***182** G-7; ★ **B.R.**; mail Port Allen **z** 70767; rural
Lockhart; RMC Place; UNION; ***182** A-4; mail Spearsville **z** 71277; ● 30
Lockport; LAFOURCHE; see Rita (RMC Place)
Lockport; Inc. Place; LAFOURCHE; **182** I-8; elev. 5ft./2m.; 🅿; **z** 70374; Ⓟ 2,503; Ⓒ 2,624
Lockport Heights; RMC Place; LAFOURCHE; ***182** I-8; mail Lockport **z** 70374; ● 570
Locust Ridge; RMC Place; TENSAS; ***182** D-7; elev. 67ft./20m.; mail Saint Joseph **z** 71366; rural
Logansport; Inc. Place; DE SOTO; **182** D-1; elev. 204ft./62m.; 🅿; **z** 71049 & mail Longstreet **z** 71050; Ⓟ 1,390; Ⓒ 1,630
Log Cabin; RMC Place; MOREHOUSE; **182** B-5; mail Bastrop **z** 71220; ● 300
Logtown; RMC Place; OUACHITA; ***182** C-5; elev. 73ft./22m.; mail Monroe **z** 71202; rural
Lone Pine; RMC Place; EVANGELINE; ***182** F-5; mail Saint Landry **z** 71367
Lone Star; RMC Place; IBERVILLE; ***182** H-7; elev. 7ft./2m.; mail White Castle **z** 70788; rural
Lone Star; RMC Place; ST. CHARLES; ***182** H-9; ★ **N.O.**; mail Luling **z** 70070; Ⓟ 1,367
Longbridge; RMC Place; AVOYELLES; ***182** F-5; mail Cottonport **z** 71327; ● 280
Long Bridge; RMC Place; LAFAYETTE; ***182** H-5; ★ **LAF**; mail Lafayette **z** 70501; ● 300
Longlake; RMC Place; CALDWELL; ***182** C-5; mail Columbia **z** 71418; rural
Longleaf; RMC Place; RAPIDES; **182** F-4; elev. 114ft./35m.; 🅿; **z** 71448; ● 300
Long Straw; RMC Place; JACKSON; ***182** B-4; mail Choudrant **z** 71227; rural
Longstreet; Inc. Place; DE SOTO; **182** C-1; elev. 330ft./101m.; 🅿; **z** 71050; Ⓟ 189; Ⓒ 163
Longview; RMC Place; FRANKLIN; ***182** C-6; mail Winnsboro **z** 71295; rural
Longville; RMC Place; BEAUREGARD; **182** G-3; elev. 134ft./41m.; 🅿; **z** 70652; ● 300
Longwood; RMC Place; CADDO; ***182** B-1; elev. 278ft./85m.; ★ **SHRE**; mail Mooringsport **z** 71060; ● 30
Longwood; RMC Place; EAST BATON ROUGE; ***182** H-7; ★ **B.R.**; mail Sunshine **z** 70780; rural
Loranger; RMC Place; TANGIPAHOA; **182** G-9; elev. 112ft./34m.; 🅿; **z** 70446; ● 670
Loreauville; Inc. Place; IBERIA; **182** H-6; elev. 20ft./6m.; 🅿; ★ **LAF**; **z** 70552; Ⓟ 860; Ⓒ 938
Lorelein; RMC Place; FRANKLIN; ***182** C-6; mail Gilbert **z** 71336; rural
Lottie; RMC Place; POINTE COUPEE; **182** G-6; elev. 25ft./8m.; 🅿; **z** 70756; ● 450
Lotus; RMC Place; NATCHITOCHES; ***182** E-3; mail Provencal **z** 71468; rural
Louisa; ST. MARY; see Cypremort (RMC Place)
Louisville; RMC Place; OUACHITA; ***182** B-5; ★ **MONR**; mail Monroe **z** 71207; pop. incl. with Monroe (Inc. Place)
Lower Bonne Idee; RMC Place; MOREHOUSE; mail Oak Ridge **z** 71264; rural
Lower Texas; RMC Place; ASSUMPTION; ***182** I-7; elev. 7ft./2m.; mail Napoleonville **z** 70390; rural
Lower Vacherie; ST. JAMES; see South Vacherie (CDP-Census Area Only)
Loyds; RMC Place; RAPIDES; ***182** F-5; mail Cheneyville **z** 71325; rural
Lozes; RMC Place; IBERIA; ***182** H-5; ★ **LAF**; mail New Iberia **z** 70560; rural
Lucas; RMC Place; CADDO; ***182** C-2; elev. 162ft./49m.; ★ **SHRE**; mail Shreveport **z** 71105; rural
Lucky; Inc. Place; BIENVILLE; **182** C-3; elev. 271ft./83m.; mail Bienville **z** 71008; Ⓟ 342; Ⓒ 355
Lucy; RMC Place; ST. JOHN THE BAPTIST; ***182** H-8; elev. 14ft./4m.; ★ **N.O.**; mail Edgard **z** 70049; ● 420
Ludington; RMC Place; BEAUREGARD; ***182** F-3; mail DeRidder **z** 70634; pop. incl. with DeRidder (Inc. Place)
Ludvine; RMC Place; LAFOURCHE; ***182** I-9; mail Lockport **z** 70374; rural
Lukeville; RMC Place; WEST BATON ROUGE; ***182** G-7; ★ **B.R.**; mail Brusly **z** 70719; ● 200
Lula; RMC Place; DE SOTO; ***182** D-2; mail Mansfield **z** 71052; rural
Luling; CDP; ST. CHARLES; **182** H-9; elev. 10ft./3m.; 🅿 🅷; ★ **N.O.**; **z** 70070; Ⓟ 2,803; Ⓒ 11,512
Luna; RMC Place; OUACHITA; ***182** C-5; elev. 206ft./63m.; mail West Monroe **z** 71291-92; ● 50
Lunita; RMC Place; CALCASIEU; **182** G-2; elev. 40ft./12m.; mail Starks **z** 70661; ● 50
Lutcher; Inc. Place; ST. JAMES; **182** H-8; 🅿 🅷; **z** 70071; Ⓟ 3,907; Ⓒ 3,735
Lydia; CDP; IBERIA; **182** I-6; elev. 10ft./3m.; 🅿; ★ **LAF**; **z** 70569; Ⓟ 1,136; Ⓒ 1,079
Lyle; RMC Place; ALLEN; ***182** G-4; mail Kinder **z** 70648; rural
Lynbrook; RMC Place; CADDO; ★ **SHRE**; mail Shreveport **z** 71106, **z** 71136; pop. incl. with Shreveport (Inc. Place)
Lyons Point; RMC Place; ACADIA; ***182** H-4; elev. 14ft./4m.; mail Crowley **z** 70526; ● 40

M

Madewood; RMC Place; ASSUMPTION; ***182** H-7; mail Napoleonville **z** 70390; rural
MADISON; **182** C-7; Ⓟ 12,463; Ⓒ 13,728; ◆ 11,530
Madisonville; Inc. Place; ST. TAMMANY; **182** G-9; 🅿; ★ **N.O.**; **z** 70447; Ⓟ 659; Ⓒ 677
Magda; RMC Place; RAPIDES; ***182** F-5; mail Alexandria **z** 71301, **z** 71303; rural
Magnolia; RMC Place; ASSUMPTION; ***182** H-7; mail Belle Rose **z** 70341; rural
Magnolia; RMC Place; EAST BATON ROUGE; ***182** G-7; elev. 47ft./14m.; ★ **B.R.**; mail Greenwell Springs **z** 70739; ● 50
Magnolia; RMC Place; LIVINGSTON; ***182** G-8; mail Holden **z** 70744; rural
Magnolia; RMC Place; NATCHITOCHES; ***182** E-3; mail Natchez **z** 71456; rural
Magnolia; RMC Place; PLAQUEMINES; ***182** I-10; elev. 5ft./2m.; mail Port Sulphur **z** 70083; rural
Magnolia; RMC Place; TERREBONNE; ***182** I-8; ★ **HOMA-**; mail Houma **z** 70360; ● 70
Magnolia Park; RMC Place; GRANT; ***182** E-4; mail Colfax **z** 71417; ● 70
Magnolia Woods; RMC Place; EAST BATON ROUGE; ***182** G-7; ★ **B.R.**; mail Baton Rouge **z** 70808; pop. incl. with Baton Rouge (Inc. Place)
Maitland; RMC Place; CATAHOULA; ***182** D-6; mail Clayton **z** 71326; ● 30
Major; RMC Place; POINTE COUPEE; ***182** G-6; mail New Roads **z** 70760; pop. incl. with New Roads (Inc. Place)
Mallard Junction; RMC Place; CALCASIEU; ***182** H-3; elev. 15ft./5m.; ★ **LKCH**; mail Iowa **z** 70647; rural
Mamou; Inc. Place; EVANGELINE; **182** G-4; elev. 60ft./18m.; 🅿 🅷; **z** 70554; Ⓟ 3,483; Ⓒ 3,566
Manchac; TANGIPAHOA; see Akers (RMC Place)
Manchester; RMC Place; CALCASIEU; ***182** H-3; elev. 25ft./8m.; ★ **LKCH**; mail Iowa **z** 70647; ● 50
Mandalay; RMC Place; TERREBONNE; ***182** I-8; ★ **HOMA-**; mail Houma **z** 70360; rural
Mandeville; Inc. Place; ST. TAMMANY; **182** G-9; 🅿; ★ **N.O.**; **z** 70448, **z** 70470-71; Ⓟ 7,083; Ⓒ 10,489
Mangham; Inc. Place; RICHLAND; **182** C-6; elev. 74ft./23m.; 🅿; **z** 71259; Ⓟ 598; Ⓒ 595
Manifest; RMC Place; CATAHOULA; **182** D-5; elev. 80ft./24m.; mail Jonesville **z** 71343; ● 120
Mansfield; Inc. Place; ⊡ DE SOTO; **182** C-2; elev. 330ft./101m.; 🅿 🅷; **z** 71052; Ⓟ 5,389; Ⓒ 5,582
Mansford; RMC Place; MADISON; ***182** B-7; mail Tallulah **z** 71282; rural
Mansura; Inc. Place; AVOYELLES; **182** F-5; elev. 77ft./23m.; 🅿; **z** 71350; Ⓟ 1,601; Ⓒ 1,573
Many; Inc. Place; ⊡ SABINE; **182** E-2; elev. 321ft./98m.; 🅿 🅷; **z** 71449; Ⓟ 3,112; Ⓒ 2,889
Maplewood; RMC Place; CALCASIEU; ***182** H-3; ★ **LKCH**; mail Sulphur **z** 70663; pop. incl. with Sulphur (Inc. Place)
Marcel; RMC Place; IBERIA; ***182** H-6; elev. 6ft./2m.; ★ **LAF**; mail New Iberia **z** 70560; rural
Marchandville; ASCENSION; see Hillaryville (RMC Place)
Marco; RMC Place; NATCHITOCHES; ***182** E-4; elev. 103ft./31m.; mail Lena **z** 71447; rural
Maringouin; Inc. Place; IBERVILLE; **182** G-6; elev. 23ft./7m.; 🅿; **z** 70757; Ⓟ 1,149; Ⓒ 1,262
Marion; Inc. Place; UNION; **182** A-5; elev. 202ft./62m.; 🅿; **z** 71260; Ⓟ 775; Ⓒ 806
Marksville; Inc. Place; ⊡ AVOYELLES; **182** F-5; elev. 82ft./25m.; 🅿 🅷; **z** 71351; Ⓟ 5,526; Ⓒ 5,537
Marrero; CDP; JEFFERSON; **182** E-13; elev. 5ft./2m.; 🅿 🅷; ★ **N.O.**; **z** 70072-73; Ⓟ 36,671; Ⓒ 36,165; ◆ 32,177
Marsalis; RMC Place; CLAIBORNE; ***182** B-3; mail Athens **z** 71003
Mars Hill; RMC Place; WINN; ***182** D-4; mail Atlanta **z** 71404; rural
Marthaville; RMC Place; NATCHITOCHES; **182** D-2; 🅿; **z** 71450; ● 330
Martin; Inc. Place; RED RIVER; **182** C-3; elev. 247ft./75m.; mail Coushatta **z** 71019; Ⓟ 545; Ⓒ 625
Martin Park; RMC Place; RAPIDES; ★ **ALEX**; mail Alexandria **z** 71301; pop. incl. with Alexandria (Inc. Place)
Mason; RMC Place; FRANKLIN; ***182** C-5; mail Winnsboro **z** 71295; rural
Mathews; CDP; LAFOURCHE; ***182** I-8; elev. 11ft./3m.; 🅿; **z** 70375; Ⓟ 3,009; Ⓒ 2,003
Maurepas; RMC Place; LIVINGSTON; **182** H-8; elev. 13ft./4m.; 🅿; **z** 70449; ● 150
Maurice; Inc. Place; VERMILION; **182** H-5; elev. 23ft./7m.; 🅿; ★ **LAF**; **z** 70555 & mail Lafayette **z** 70503; Ⓟ 432; Ⓒ 642
Maxie; RMC Place; ACADIA; **182** H-4; mail Crowley **z** 70526; ● 100
Mayflower; RMC Place; TENSAS; ***182** D-6; mail Saint Joseph **z** 71366; rural
Mayna; RMC Place; CATAHOULA; **182** E-6; mail Jonesville **z** 71343; ● 100
McBride; RMC Place; TERREBONNE; ***182** I-8; ★ **HOMA-**; mail Houma **z** 70360; rural
McCall; RMC Place; ASCENSION; ***182** H-7; elev. 18ft./5m.; mail Donaldsonville **z** 70346; ● 50
McClane City; RMC Place; ST. TAMMANY; ***182** H-10; mail Slidell **z** 70458
McClendon; RMC Place; WASHINGTON; mail Franklinton **z** 70438; rural
McCrea; RMC Place; POINTE COUPEE; ***182** F-6; mail Batchelor **z** 70715; rural
McDade; RMC Place; BOSSIER; ***182** C-2; elev. 152ft./46m.; mail Elm Grove **z** 71051; rural
McDonoghville; RMC Place; JEFFERSON; ***182** H-9; ★ **N.O.**; mail Gretna **z** 70053; pop. incl. with Gretna (Inc. Place)
McGinty; RMC Place; MOREHOUSE; ***182** A-6; elev. 108ft./33m.; mail Jones **z** 71250; rural
McIlhenny; RMC Place; IBERIA; mail Avery Island **z** 70513
McIntyre; RMC Place; WEBSTER; ***182** B-3; elev. 211ft./64m.; mail Minden **z** 71055; ● 70
McKneeley; RMC Place; POINTE COUPEE; ***182** G-6; mail Fordoche **z** 70732; rural
McLeod; RMC Place; LAFOURCHE; ***182** I-8; mail Lockport **z** 70374; rural
McManus; RMC Place; EAST FELICIANA; **182** F-7; elev. 187ft./57m.; mail Jackson **z** 70748; ● 300
McNary; Inc. Place; RAPIDES; **182** F-4; elev. 108ft./33m.; mail Glenmora **z** 71433; Ⓟ 248; Ⓒ 211
McNeely; RMC Place; GRANT; ***182** E-4; mail Colfax **z** 71417; rural
McNeese University; RMC Place; CALCASIEU; ***182** H-3; ★ **LKCH**; mail Lake Charles **z** 70609; pop. incl. with Lake Charles (Inc. Place)
Meadowbrook; RMC Place; JEFFERSON; ***182** I-9; ★ **N.O.**; mail Gretna **z** 70056; ● 600
Meadow Lea; RMC Place; EAST BATON ROUGE; ★ **B.R.**; pop. incl. with Baton Rouge (Inc. Place)
Meadow Park Heights; RMC Place; CADDO; ★ **SHRE**; mail Shreveport **z** 71108; ● 300
Meadowview Park; RMC Place; BOSSIER; ★ **SHRE**; pop. incl. with Bossier City (Inc. Place)
Meaux; RMC Place; VERMILION; ***182** H-5; elev. 18ft./5m.; 🅿; ★ **LAF**; **z** 70510
Mechanicsville; RMC Place; TERREBONNE; ★ **HOMA-**; mail Houma **z** 70360; pop. incl. with Houma (Inc. Place)
Meeker; RMC Place; RAPIDES; ***182** F-4; mail Lecompte **z** 71346; rural
Melder; RMC Place; RAPIDES; **182** F-4; elev. 174ft./53m.; 🅿; **z** 71433; ● 70
Melia; RMC Place; ORLEANS; ★ **N.O.**; pop. incl. with New Orleans (Inc. Place)
Melrose; RMC Place; NATCHITOCHES; **182** E-3; elev. 109ft./33m.; 🅿; **z** 71452; ● 150
Melville; Inc. Place; ST. LANDRY; **182** G-6; elev. 125ft./38m.; 🅿; **z** 71353; Ⓟ 1,562; Ⓒ 1,376
Meraux; CDP; ST. BERNARD; **182** H-10; elev. 5ft./2m.; 🅿; ★ **N.O.**; **z** 70075; Ⓟ 8,849; Ⓒ 10,192
Mermentau; Inc. Place; ACADIA; **182** H-4; elev. 10ft./3m.; 🅿; **z** 70556; Ⓟ 760; Ⓒ 721
Mer Rouge; Inc. Place; MOREHOUSE; **182** B-6; elev. 90ft./27m.; 🅿; **z** 71261; Ⓟ 586; Ⓒ 721
Merrydale; CDP-Census Area Only; EAST BATON ROUGE; ***182** G-7; elev. 55ft./17m.; ★ **B.R.**; mail Baton Rouge **z** 70812; Ⓟ 10,395; Ⓒ 10,427
Merryville; Inc. Place; BEAUREGARD; **182** G-2; elev. 82ft./25m.; 🅿; **z** 70653; Ⓟ 1,235; Ⓒ 1,126
Messick; RMC Place; NATCHITOCHES; ***182** D-3; elev. 176ft./54m.; mail Coushatta **z** 71019; rural
Metairie; CDP; JEFFERSON; **182** H-9; elev. 5ft./2m.; 🅿 🅷; ★ **N.O.**; **z** 70001-06, **z** 70009-11, **z** 70033, **z** 70055, **z** 70060; Ⓟ 149,428; Ⓒ 146,136; ◆ 130,008
Methvin; RMC Place; RED RIVER; ***182** C-3; mail Coushatta **z** 71019; rural
Metropolis; RMC Place; FRANKLIN; ***182** D-6; mail Wisner **z** 71378; ● 30
Michoud; RMC Place; ORLEANS; ***182** H-10; ★ **N.O.**; mail New Orleans **z** 70129, **z** 70189; pop. incl. with New Orleans (Inc. Place)
Mid City; RMC Place; ORLEANS; ***182** H-9; ★ **N.O.**; mail New Orleans **z** 70119, **z** 70179; pop. incl. with New Orleans (Inc. Place)
Midland; RMC Place; ACADIA; **182** H-4; elev. 15ft./5m.; 🅿; **z** 70559; ● 310
Midway; RMC Place; BOSSIER; ***182** B-2; elev. 237ft./72m.; mail Benton **z** 71006; rural
Midway; CDP; LA SALLE; ***182** D-5; mail Jena **z** 71342; Ⓟ 1,586; Ⓒ 1,505
Midway; RMC Place; RAPIDES; ***182** F-4; elev. 162ft./49m.; mail Forest Hill **z** 71430; rural
Midway; RMC Place; ST. MARY; ***182** I-6; elev. 7ft./2m.; mail Franklin **z** 70538; rural
Midway; RMC Place; WEBSTER; ***182** A-2; elev. 262ft./80m.; mail Sarepta **z** 71071; ● 150
Milldale; RMC Place; EAST BATON ROUGE; ***182** G-7; elev. 111ft./34m.; ★ **B.R.**; mail Zachary **z** 70791; ● 50
Millerton; RMC Place; CLAIBORNE; ***182** A-3; mail Haynesville **z** 71038; rural
Millerville; RMC Place; ACADIA; ***182** H-4; mail Iota **z** 70543; rural
Millerville; RMC Place; EAST BATON ROUGE; ***182** G-7; elev. 40ft./12m.; ★ **B.R.**; mail Baton Rouge **z** 70815; ● 200
Millikin; RMC Place; EAST CARROLL; ***182** A-7; elev. 10ft./3m.; mail Lake Providence **z** 71254; rural
Milly Plantation; RMC Place; IBERVILLE; ***182** H-7; ★ **B.R.**; mail Plaquemine **z** 70764; rural
Milneburg; RMC Place; ORLEANS; ★ **N.O.**; pop. incl. with New Orleans (Inc. Place)
Milton; RMC Place; LAFAYETTE; **182** H-5; elev. 20ft./6m.; 🅿; ★ **LAF**; **z** 70558; ● 750
Mimosa Park; RMC Place; ST. CHARLES; ***182** I-9; ★ **N.O.**; mail Luling **z** 70070; Ⓟ 4,516
Minden; Inc. Place; ⊡ WEBSTER; **182** B-3; elev. 259ft./79m.; 🅿 🅷; **z** 71055, **z** 71058; Ⓟ 13,661; Ⓒ 13,027
Mineral Springs; RMC Place; LINCOLN; ***182** B-4; mail Dubach **z** 71235; ● 50
Mineral Springs; RMC Place; OUACHITA; ***182** B-5; mail Calhoun **z** 71225; ● 80
Minerva; RMC Place; TERREBONNE; ★ **HOMA-**; mail Houma **z** 70360
Minorca; RMC Place; CONCORDIA; ***182** E-6; ★ **NCHZ**; mail Ferriday **z** 71334; rural
Mira; RMC Place; CADDO; **182** A-1; elev. 240ft./73m.; 🅿; **z** 71044; ● 100
Mire; RMC Place; ACADIA; ***182** H-5; mail Rayne **z** 70578; ● 130
Mitchell; RMC Place; SABINE; **182** D-2; elev. 330ft./101m.; 🅿; **z** 71419; ● 100
Mittie; RMC Place; ALLEN; **182** G-3; elev. 90ft./27m.; 🅿; **z** 70654; ● 120
Mix; RMC Place; POINTE COUPEE; **182** G-6; mail New Roads **z** 70760; ● 200
Modeste; RMC Place; ASCENSION; ***182** H-7; elev. 25ft./8m.; 🅿; **z** 70346; ● 270
Moncla; RMC Place; AVOYELLES; ***182** E-5; mail Marksville **z** 71351; rural
Monette Ferry; RMC Place; NATCHITOCHES; ***182** E-4; mail Lena **z** 71447; rural
Monroe; Inc. Place; ⊡ OUACHITA; **182** B-5; elev. 74ft./23m.; 🅿 🅷 🅲 8,571 ■; ★ **MONR**; **z** 71201-03, **z** 71207, **z** 71209-13, **z** 71217; Ⓟ 54,909; Ⓒ 53,107; ◆ 53,736
Montegut; CDP; TERREBONNE; **182** J-8; elev. 5ft./2m.; 🅿; ★ **HOMA-**; **z** 70377; Ⓟ 1,784; Ⓒ 1,803
Monterey; RMC Place; CONCORDIA; **182** E-6; elev. 55ft./17m.; 🅿; **z** 71354; ● 250
Montgomery; Inc. Place; GRANT; **182** D-3; elev. 165ft./50m.; 🅿; **z** 71454; Ⓟ 645; Ⓒ 787
Monticello; CDP; EAST BATON ROUGE; ***182** G-7; elev. 50ft./15m.; ★ **B.R.**; mail Baton Rouge **z** 70815; Ⓟ 4,710; Ⓒ 4,763
Monticello; RMC Place; EAST CARROLL; ***182** B-6; mail Lake Providence **z** 71254
Montpelier; Inc. Place; ST. HELENA; **182** G-8; elev. 140ft./43m.; 🅿; **z** 70422; Ⓟ 247; Ⓒ 214
Montrose; RMC Place; NATCHITOCHES; ***182** E-3; elev. 102ft./31m.; mail Melrose **z** 71452, Natchitoches **z** 71457; rural
Montz; CDP; ST. CHARLES; ***182** H-8; 🅿; ★ **N.O.**; **z** 70068; Ⓒ 1,120
Mooringsport; Inc. Place; CADDO; **182** B-1; elev. 200ft./61m.; 🅿; ★ **SHRE**; **z** 71060; Ⓟ 873; Ⓒ 833
Mora; RMC Place; NATCHITOCHES; **182** E-3; elev. 277ft./84m.; 🅿; **z** 71455; ● 150
Morbihan; RMC Place; IBERIA; ***182** H-6; ★ **LAF**; mail New Iberia **z** 70560; ● 500
Moreauville; Inc. Place; AVOYELLES; **182** F-5; elev. 55ft./17m.; 🅿; **z** 71355; Ⓟ 919; Ⓒ 922
MOREHOUSE; **182** B-5; Ⓟ 31,938; Ⓒ 31,021; ◆ 27,664
Moreland; RMC Place; RAPIDES; ***182** E-4; ★ **ALEX**; mail Alexandria **z** 71301; rural
Morgan City; Inc. Place; ST. MARY; **182** I-7; elev. 5ft./2m.; 🅿 🅷 ■; **z** 70380-81; Ⓟ 14,531; Ⓒ 12,703; ◆ 11,293
Morganza; Inc. Place; POINTE COUPEE; **182** G-6; elev. 38ft./12m.; 🅿; **z** 70759; Ⓟ 759; Ⓒ 659
Morningside; RMC Place; CADDO; ***182** B-2; ★ **SHRE**; mail Shreveport **z** 71108, **z** 71148; pop. incl. with Shreveport (Inc. Place)
Morrisonville; RMC Place; IBERVILLE; ***182** H-7; ★ **B.R.**; mail Plaquemine **z** 70764; ● 100
Morrow (Morrows); RMC Place; ST. LANDRY; **182** F-5; elev. 45ft./14m.; 🅿; **z** 71356; ● 530
Morrows; ST. LANDRY; see Morrow (RMC Place)
Morse; Inc. Place; ACADIA; **182** H-4; elev. 15ft./5m.; 🅿; **z** 70559; Ⓟ 782; Ⓒ 759
Morvant; RMC Place; LAFOURCHE; ***182** I-8; elev. 14ft./4m.; ★ **HOMA-**; mail Thibodaux **z** 70301; rural
Morville; RMC Place; CONCORDIA; ***182** E-6; mail Vidalia **z** 71373; rural
Moss Bluff; CDP; CALCASIEU; **182** H-3; elev. 21ft./6m.; 🅿; ★ **LKCH**; **z** 70611 & mail Lake Charles **z** 70612; Ⓟ 8,039; Ⓒ 10,535
Moss Lake; RMC Place; CALCASIEU; ***182** H-2; ★ **LKCH**; mail Sulphur **z** 70665; ● 150
Mossville; RMC Place; CALCASIEU; ***182** H-3; elev. 18ft./5m.; ★ **LKCH**; mail Sulphur **z** 70663; ● 1,000
Mot; RMC Place; BOSSIER; ***182** A-2; elev. 243ft./74m.; mail Plain Dealing **z** 71064; rural
Mound; Inc. Place; MADISON; **182** C-7; elev. 90ft./27m.; 🅿; **z** 71282; Ⓟ 16; Ⓒ 12
Mount Airy; RMC Place; ST. JOHN THE BAPTIST; ***182** H-8; elev. 10ft./3m.; 🅿; **z** 70076 & mail Garyville **z** 70051; ● 540
Mount Carmel; RMC Place; SABINE; ***182** E-2; mail Florien **z** 71429; rural
Mount Hermon; RMC Place; WASHINGTON; **182** F-9; elev. 320ft./98m.; 🅿; **z** 70450; ● 300
Mount Lebanon; Inc. Place; BIENVILLE; ***182** B-3; elev. 336ft./102m.; mail Gibsland **z** 71028; Ⓟ 102; Ⓒ 73
Mount Moriah; RMC Place; JACKSON; ***182** C-4; elev. 235ft./72m.; mail Chatham **z** 71226; ● 80
Mount Olive; RMC Place; BIENVILLE; ***182** C-4; mail Quitman **z** 71268; rural
Mount Sinai; RMC Place; CLAIBORNE; mail Haynesville **z** 71038; rural
Mount Union; RMC Place; UNION; ***182** A-4; mail Spearsville **z** 71277; ● 30
Mount Zion; RMC Place; LINCOLN; ***182** B-4; mail Dubach **z** 71235; rural
Mount Zion; RMC Place; WINN; ***182** D-4; mail Montgomery **z** 71454; rural
Mowata; RMC Place; ACADIA; ***182** G-4; mail Eunice **z** 70535; rural
Mudville; RMC Place; GRANT; ***182** D-4; mail Georgetown **z** 71432; rural
Mulberry; RMC Place; TERREBONNE; ***182** I-8; ★ **HOMA-**; mail Houma **z** 70360; rural
Mulvey; RMC Place; VERMILION; ***182** H-4; mail Kaplan **z** 70548; rural
Musson; RMC Place; IBERVILLE; ***182** G-6; mail Maringouin **z** 70757; ● 30
Myrtle Grove; RMC Place; IBERVILLE; ★ **B.R.**; mail Plaquemine **z** 70764
Myrtle Grove; RMC Place; PLAQUEMINES; **182** I-10; elev. 2ft./1m.; mail Port Sulphur **z** 70083; ● 40

N

Naborton; RMC Place; DE SOTO; ***182** C-2; mail Mansfield **z** 71052; ● 50
Nairn; RMC Place; PLAQUEMINES; **182** J-10; mail Buras **z** 70041; ● 1,000
Naomi; RMC Place; PLAQUEMINES; ***182** I-9; elev. 6ft./2m.; mail Belle Chasse **z** 70037
Napoleonville; Inc. Place; ⊡ ASSUMPTION; **182** H-7; elev. 15ft./5m.; 🅿; **z** 70390; Ⓟ 802; Ⓒ 686
Napoleonville Junction; RMC Place; LAFOURCHE; ★ **HOMA-**; mail Thibodaux **z** 70301; pop. incl. with Thibodaux (Inc. Place)
Naquin; RMC Place; LAFOURCHE; ***182** I-8; ★ **HOMA-**; mail Thibodaux **z** 70301; rural
Natalbany; CDP; TANGIPAHOA; ***182** G-8; elev. 50ft./15m.; 🅿; **z** 70451; Ⓟ 1,289; Ⓒ 1,739
Natchez; Inc. Place; NATCHITOCHES; **182** D-3; 🅿; **z** 71456; Ⓟ 434; Ⓒ 583
Natchitoches; Inc. Place; ⊡ NATCHITOCHES; **182** D-3; 🅿 🅷 🅲 9,431; **z** 71457-58, **z** 71497; Ⓟ 16,609; Ⓒ 17,865
NATCHITOCHES; **182** E-3; Ⓟ 36,689; Ⓒ 39,080; ◆ 39,415
Neal Landing; RMC Place; LIVINGSTON; ***182** G-8; elev. 5ft./2m.; mail Springfield **z** 70462; ● 30
Nebo; RMC Place; LA SALLE; **182** E-5; mail Jena **z** 71342; ● 150
Negreet; RMC Place; SABINE; **182** E-2; elev. 187ft./57m.; 🅿; **z** 71460; ● 150
Nelson; BIENVILLE; see Taylor (RMC Place)
Nesser; RMC Place; EAST BATON ROUGE; ***182** G-7; ★ **B.R.**; mail Baton Rouge **z** 70815; pop. incl. with Baton Rouge (Inc. Place)
New Belledeau; AVOYELLES; see Belledeau (RMC Place)
Newellton; Inc. Place; TENSAS; **182** C-7; elev. 79ft./24m.; 🅿; **z** 71357; Ⓟ 1,576; Ⓒ 1,482
New Era; RMC Place; CONCORDIA; ***182** E-6; mail Acme **z** 71316, Monterey **z** 71354; rural
New Flanders; RMC Place; LAFAYETTE; ***182** H-5; ★ **LAF**; mail Youngsville **z** 70592; ● 50
Newhope; RMC Place; WEST CARROLL; ***182** B-6; mail Pioneer **z** 71266; rural
New Iberia; Inc. Place; ⊡ IBERIA; **182** H-6; elev. 20ft./6m.; 🅿 🅷 ■; ★ **LAF**; **z** 70560, **z** 70562-63; Ⓟ 31,828; Ⓒ 32,623; ◆ 32,312
New Light; RMC Place; RICHLAND; ***182** C-6; elev. 76ft./23m.; mail Mangham **z** 71259; rural
Newlight; RMC Place; TENSAS; ***182** C-6; mail Newellton **z** 71357
New Llano; Inc. Place; VERNON; **182** F-3; elev. 218ft./66m.; 🅿; **z** 71461; Ⓟ 2,660; Ⓒ 2,415
New Orleans; Inc. Place; ⊡ ORLEANS; **182** H-9; 🅿 🅷 🅲 39,943 ■; ★ **N.O.**; **z** 70112-19, **z** 70121-31, **z** 70139-43, **z** 70145-46, **z** 70148-54, **z** 70156-67, **z** 70170, **z** 70172, **z** 70174-79, **z** 70181-87, **z** 70189-90, **z** 70195; Ⓟ 496,938; Ⓒ 484,674; ◆ 268,724
New Roads; Inc. Place; ⊡ POINTE COUPEE; **182** G-6; elev. 32ft./10m.; 🅿 🅷; **z** 70760; Ⓟ 5,303; Ⓒ 4,966
New Rockdale; RMC Place; DE SOTO; ***182** C-2; mail Mansfield **z** 71052; rural
New Sarpy; CDP; ST. CHARLES; ***182** H-9; 🅿; ★ **N.O.**; **z** 70078; Ⓟ 2,946; Ⓒ 1,568
Newton; RMC Place; CALCASIEU; ***182** H-3; elev. 27ft./8m.; ★ **LKCH**; mail Lake Charles **z** 70601
New Verda; RMC Place; GRANT; ***182** D-4; elev. 157ft./48m.; mail Atlanta **z** 71404, Montgomery **z** 71454; ● 100
Nibletts Bluff; RMC Place; CALCASIEU; ***182** H-2; mail Vinton **z** 70668; ● 50
Nicholas; RMC Place; IBERIA; ***182** H-6; elev. 10ft./3m.; ★ **LAF**; mail New Iberia **z** 70560; rural
Nicholls University; RMC Place; LAFOURCHE; ***182** I-8; ★ **HOMA-**; mail Thibodaux **z** 70301; pop. incl. with Thibodaux (Inc. Place)
Nickel; RMC Place; LA SALLE; ***182** D-5; mail Olla **z** 71465; ● 30
Ninock; RMC Place; BOSSIER; ***182** C-2; mail Elm Grove **z** 71051; rural
Noble; Inc. Place; SABINE; **182** D-2; elev. 281ft./86m.; 🅿; **z** 71462; Ⓟ 225; Ⓒ 259
Noles Landing; RMC Place; WEBSTER; ***182** B-3; mail Sibley **z** 71073; rural
Norah; RMC Place; LAFOURCHE; ***182** I-8; mail Lockport **z** 70374; rural
Norco; CDP; ST. CHARLES; **182** H-9; elev. 10ft./3m.; 🅿; ★ **N.O.**; **z** 70079; Ⓟ 3,385; Ⓒ 3,579
Normandy Park; RMC Place; JEFFERSON; 1 mi. NW of Westwego; ★ **N.O.**; mail Westwego **z** 70094; ● 1,150
Norris Springs; RMC Place; CATAHOULA; ***182** D-6; mail Sicily Island **z** 71368; rural
North 18th Street; RMC Place; OUACHITA; ★ **MONR**; mail Monroe **z** 71201; pop. incl. with Monroe (Inc. Place)
Northeast Louisiana University; RMC Place; OUACHITA; ***182** B-5; ★ **MONR**; mail Monroe **z** 71209; pop. incl. with Monroe (Inc. Place)
North Highlands; RMC Place; CADDO; ***182** B-2; ★ **SHRE**; pop. incl. with Shreveport (Inc. Place)
North Highlands; RMC Place; EAST BATON ROUGE; ***182** G-7; ★ **B.R.**; pop. incl. with Baton Rouge (Inc. Place)
North Hodge; Inc. Place; JACKSON; ***182** C-4; elev. 200ft./61m.; mail Hodge **z** 71247; Ⓟ 477; Ⓒ 436
North Island; RMC Place; CAMERON; ***182** I-4; mail Grand Chenier **z** 70643; rural
North Kenner; RMC Place; JEFFERSON; ★ **N.O.**; mail Kenner **z** 70065; pop. incl. with Kenner (Inc. Place)
North Merrydale; RMC Place; EAST BATON ROUGE; **182** A-13; ★ **B.R.**; mail Baton Rouge **z** 70812; ● 4,000
North Monroe; RMC Place; OUACHITA; ***182** B-5; ★ **MONR**; mail Monroe **z** 71201; pop. incl. with Monroe (Inc. Place)
North Plaquemine; RMC Place; IBERVILLE; ★ **B.R.**; mail Plaquemine **z** 70764; pop. incl. with Plaquemine (Inc. Place)
North Shore; RMC Place; ST. TAMMANY; ***182** H-10; ★ **N.O.**; mail Slidell **z** 70458; ● 980
North Shore Beach; RMC Place; ST. TAMMANY; ***182** H-10; ★ **N.O.**; mail Slidell **z** 70458; ● 620
North Shreveport; CADDO; see Cooper Road (RMC Place)
Northside; RMC Place; OUACHITA; mail Monroe **z** 71207; pop. incl. with Monroe (Inc. Place)
North Slidell; RMC Place; ST. TAMMANY; ***182** H-10; ★ **N.O.**; mail Slidell **z** 70458
North Vacherie (Vacherie); CDP-Census Area Only; ST. JAMES; **182** H-8; elev. 15ft./5m.; mail Vacherie **z** 70090; Ⓟ 2,354; Ⓒ 2,411
Norton Corner (Norton Shop); RMC Place; CLAIBORNE; ***182** A-3; mail Haynesville **z** 71038; rural
Norton Shop; CLAIBORNE; see Norton Corner (RMC Place)
Norwood; Inc. Place; EAST FELICIANA; **182** F-7; elev. 320ft./98m.; 🅿; **z** 70761; Ⓟ 317; Ⓒ 337
Notleyville; RMC Place; ST. LANDRY; ***182** G-5; mail Port Barre **z** 70577; rural
Notnac; RMC Place; TENSAS; ***182** C-7; elev. 80ft./24m.; mail Newellton **z** 71357; rural
Numa; RMC Place; IBERIA; ***182** H-5; elev. 10ft./3m.; ★ **LAF**; mail New Iberia **z** 70560; rural
Nunez; RMC Place; VERMILION; ***182** H-5; mail Kaplan **z** 70548; ● 150

O

Oakdale; Inc. Place; ALLEN; **182** F-4; elev. 117ft./36m.; 🅿 🅷; **z** 71463; Ⓟ 6,832; Ⓒ 8,137
Oak Forest; RMC Place; TERREBONNE; ***182** I-7; mail Gibson **z** 70356; rural
Oak Grove; RMC Place; ASCENSION; ***182** H-7; elev. 25ft./8m.; ★ **B.R.**; mail Prairieville **z** 70769; rural
Oak Grove; RMC Place; CAMERON; ***182** I-3; mail Creole **z** 70632, Grand Chenier **z** 70643; ● 100
Oak Grove; RMC Place; GRANT; ***182** E-4; mail Colfax **z** 71417; rural
Oak Grove; RMC Place; LINCOLN; ***182** B-4; mail Simsboro **z** 71275; rural
Oak Grove; RMC Place; SABINE; ***182** D-2; elev. 304ft./93m.; mail Converse **z** 71419; rural
Oak Grove; Inc. Place; ⊡ WEST CARROLL; **182** B-6; elev. 120ft./37m.; 🅿 🅷; **z** 71263; Ⓟ 2,126; Ⓒ 2,174
Oak Hills Place; CDP; EAST BATON ROUGE; ***182** G-7; elev. 40ft./12m.; ★ **B.R.**; mail Baton Rouge **z** 70808; Ⓟ 5,479; Ⓒ 7,996
Oakland; RMC Place; BOSSIER; ***182** B-2; mail Haughton **z** 71037; rural
Oakland; RMC Place; UNION; ***182** A-5; elev. 256ft./78m.; mail Marion **z** 71260
Oaklawn; RMC Place; ST. MARY; ***182** I-6; mail Franklin **z** 70538; rural
Oaklawn; RMC Place; ST. TAMMANY; ***182** H-10; ★ **N.O.**; mail Lacombe **z** 70445; ● 490
Oakley; RMC Place; ASSUMPTION; ***182** I-7; mail Napoleonville **z** 70390; rural
Oak Manor; RMC Place; EAST BATON ROUGE; **182** B-14; ★ **B.R.**; mail Baton Rouge **z** 70815; pop. incl. with Baton Rouge (Inc. Place)
Oaknolia; RMC Place; EAST FELICIANA; ***182** G-7; elev. 147ft./45m.; mail Slaughter **z** 70777; rural
Oak Ridge; Inc. Place; MOREHOUSE; **182** B-6; elev. 92ft./28m.; 🅿; **z** 71264; Ⓟ 174; Ⓒ 142
Oak Ridge Park; RMC Place; JEFFERSON; ★ **N.O.**
Oaks; RMC Place; CLAIBORNE; ***182** A-3; mail Haynesville **z** 71038; rural
Oakshire Manor; RMC Place; TERREBONNE; ***182** I-8; ★ **HOMA-**; mail Houma **z** 70364; ● 550
Oakville; RMC Place; PLAQUEMINES; ***182** I-9; ★ **N.O.**; mail Belle Chasse **z** 70037; ● 240
Oberlin; Inc. Place; ⊡ ALLEN; **182** G-4; elev. 75ft./23m.; 🅿; **z** 70655; Ⓟ 1,808; Ⓒ 1,853
Ogden Park; RMC Place; EAST BATON ROUGE; ★ **B.R.**; pop. incl. with Baton Rouge (Inc. Place)
Oil Center; RMC Place; LAFAYETTE; ***182** H-5; ★ **LAF**; mail Lafayette **z** 70501, **z** 70505; pop. incl. with Lafayette (Inc. Place)
Oil City; Inc. Place; CADDO; **182** B-1; 🅿; **z** 71061; Ⓟ 1,282; Ⓒ 1,219
Okaloosa; RMC Place; OUACHITA; ***182** C-5; elev. 232ft./71m.; ★ **MONR**; mail Eros **z** 71238; rural
Old Athens; RMC Place; CLAIBORNE; ***182** B-3; elev. 470ft./143m.; mail Athens **z** 71003; rural
Oldfield; RMC Place; LIVINGSTON; ***182** G-8; mail Walker **z** 70785; rural
Old Hammond; RMC Place; EAST BATON ROUGE; ★ **B.R.**; mail Baton Rouge **z** 70815-19; pop. incl. with Baton Rouge (Inc. Place)
Old Jefferson; CDP; EAST BATON ROUGE; ***182** G-7; elev. 30ft./9m.; ★ **B.R.**; mail Baton Rouge **z** 70816; Ⓟ 4,531; Ⓒ 5,631
Old Lafitte; RMC Place; JEFFERSON; ★ **N.O.**; mail Lafitte **z** 70067
Old Shongaloo; RMC Place; WEBSTER; ***182** A-3; elev. 293ft./89m.; mail Shongaloo **z** 71072; rural
Olinkraft; RMC Place; OUACHITA; ***182** B-5; ★ **MONR**; mail West Monroe **z** 71292
Olive Branch; RMC Place; EAST FELICIANA; ***182** G-7; mail Slaughter **z** 70777; rural
Oliver; RMC Place; TANGIPAHOA; mail Hammond **z** 70401; pop. incl. with Hammond (Inc. Place)
Olivier; RMC Place; IBERIA; ***182** H-6; elev. 24ft./7m.; ★ **LAF**; mail New Iberia **z** 70560
Olla; Inc. Place; LA SALLE; **182** D-5; elev. 155ft./47m.; 🅿 🅷; **z** 71465; Ⓟ 1,410; Ⓒ 1,417
Ollie; RMC Place; PLAQUEMINES; ***182** I-9; elev. 5ft./2m.; mail Belle Chasse **z** 70037; rural
Omega; RMC Place; MADISON; ***182** B-7; elev. 91ft./28m.; mail Sondheimer **z** 71276; rural
Opelousas; Inc. Place; ⊡ ST. LANDRY; **182** G-5; elev. 70ft./21m.; 🅿 🅷 ■; **z** 70570-71; Ⓟ 18,151; Ⓒ 22,860; ◆ 23,774
Orange Grove Plantation; RMC Place; LAFOURCHE; ***182** I-8; mail Thibodaux **z** 70301; rural
Oretta; RMC Place; BEAUREGARD; **182** G-2; mail DeQuincy **z** 70633, Singer **z** 70660; ● 50
ORLEANS; **182** H-9; Ⓟ 496,938; Ⓒ 484,674; ◆ 268,724
Oscar; RMC Place; POINTE COUPEE; **182** G-6; elev. 35ft./11m.; 🅿; **z** 70762; ● 200
Osceola; RMC Place; TENSAS; ***182** D-7; mail Saint Joseph **z** 71366; rural
Ossun; RMC Place; LAFAYETTE; ***182** H-5; ★ **LAF**; mail Scott **z** 70583; rural
Ostrica; RMC Place; PLAQUEMINES; ***182** J-10; mail Buras **z** 70041; ● 80
Otis; RMC Place; RAPIDES; ***182** E-4; elev. 235ft./72m.; 🅿; **z** 71466; ● 100
OUACHITA; **182** C-5; Ⓟ 142,191; Ⓒ 147,250; ◆ 148,905
Ouachita City; RMC Place; UNION; ***182** B-5; mail Sterlington **z** 71280; rural
Oubre; RMC Place; IBERIA; ***182** H-6; ★ **LAF**; mail Loreauville **z** 70552; pop. incl. with Loreauville (Inc. Place)
Oxford; RMC Place; DE SOTO; **182** D-2; mail Mansfield **z** 71052; ● 100
Oxford; RMC Place; ST. MARY; ***182** I-6; elev. 14ft./4m.; mail Franklin **z** 70538; rural

P

Pace; RMC Place; WEBSTER; ***182** B-3; mail Minden **z** 71055; rural
Packton; RMC Place; WINN; ***182** D-4; elev. 151ft./46m.; mail Winnfield **z** 71483; rural
Paincourtville; CDP; ASSUMPTION; **182** H-7; elev. 20ft./6m.; 🅿; **z** 70391; Ⓟ 1,550; Ⓒ 884
Palmetto; Inc. Place; ST. LANDRY; **182** G-5; elev. 37ft./11m.; 🅿; **z** 71358; Ⓟ 229; Ⓒ 188
Palo Alto; RMC Place; ASCENSION; ***182** H-7; elev. 2ft./1m.; mail Donaldsonville **z** 70346; rural
Panchoville; RMC Place; JEFFERSON DAVIS; ***182** G-4; mail Jennings **z** 70546; rural
Panola; RMC Place; EAST CARROLL; ***182** A-7; mail Ferriday **z** 71334, Lake Providence **z** 71254; rural
Paradis; CDP; ST. CHARLES; **182** I-9; elev. 2ft./1m.; 🅿; **z** 70080; Ⓒ 1,252
Paradise; RMC Place; RAPIDES; ***182** E-4; ★ **ALEX**; mail Pineville **z** 71360; ● 500
Paradise Manor; RMC Place; JEFFERSON; ★ **N.O.**; mail New Orleans **z** 70123
Parhams; RMC Place; CATAHOULA; ***182** E-6; mail Jonesville **z** 71343; rural
Park Manor; RMC Place; JEFFERSON; ***182** H-9; ★ **N.O.**; mail Metairie **z** 70003
Parks; Inc. Place; ST. MARTIN; **182** H-6; elev. 25ft./8m.; 🅿; ★ **LAF**; **z** 70582; Ⓟ 400; Ⓒ 533
Parkside Manor; RMC Place; JEFFERSON; ★ **N.O.**; mail New Orleans **z** 70123
Park Timbers; RMC Place; ORLEANS; ★ **N.O.**; pop. incl. with New Orleans (Inc. Place)
Park Vista; RMC Place; ST. LANDRY; mail Opelousas **z** 70570; pop. incl. with Opelousas (Inc. Place)
Patoutville; RMC Place; IBERIA; ***182** I-6; elev. 9ft./3m.; ★ **LAF**; mail Jeanerette **z** 70544; ● 150
Patterson; Inc. Place; ST. MARY; **182** I-7; elev. 12ft./4m.; 🅿; **z** 70392; Ⓟ 4,736; Ⓒ 5,130
Paulina; RMC Place; ST. JAMES; ***182** H-8; elev. 15ft./5m.; 🅿; **z** 70763; ● 800
Pearl River; Inc. Place; ST. TAMMANY; **182** G-10; 🅿; ★ **N.O.**; **z** 70452; Ⓟ 1,507; Ⓒ 1,839
Peason; RMC Place; SABINE; ***182** E-3; elev. 354ft./108m.; mail Florien **z** 71429; rural
Pecan Grove; RMC Place; JEFFERSON; ***182** H-9; ★ **N.O.**; mail Westwego **z** 70094; ● 1,050
Pecaniere; RMC Place; ST. LANDRY; ***182** G-5; elev. 24ft./7m.; mail Arnaudville **z** 70512; ● 50
Pecan Island; RMC Place; VERMILION; **182** I-4; mail Kaplan **z** 70548; ● 400
Pecan Place; RMC Place; IBERVILLE; ***182** H-7; ★ **B.R.**; mail Plaquemine **z** 70764; ● 60
Peck; RMC Place; CATAHOULA; ***182** D-6; mail Sicily Island **z** 71368; rural
Pelican; RMC Place; DE SOTO; **182** D-2; elev. 317ft./97m.; 🅿; **z** 71063; ● 200
Percle; RMC Place; ASSUMPTION; ***182** I-7; mail Napoleonville **z** 70390; rural
Perkins; RMC Place; CALCASIEU; ***182** G-2; mail DeQuincy **z** 70633; rural
Perry; RMC Place; VERMILION; **182** H-5; elev. 10ft./3m.; 🅿; **z** 70575; ● 200
Perryville; RMC Place; OUACHITA; **182** B-5; ★ **MONR**; mail Bastrop **z** 71220; ● 90
Phoenix; RMC Place; PLAQUEMINES; **182** I-10; ● 500
Pickering; RMC Place; VERNON; ***182** F-3; mail Leesville **z** 71446; ● 50
Pierre Part (Pierre Pass); CDP; ASSUMPTION; **182** H-7; elev. 5ft./2m.; 🅿; **z** 70339; Ⓟ 3,053; Ⓒ 3,239
Pierre Part Settlement; RMC Place; ASSUMPTION; ***182** H-7; mail Pierre Part **z** 70339; ● 580
Pierre Pass; ASSUMPTION; see Pierre Part (CDP)
Pigeon (Bayou Pigeon); RMC Place; IBERVILLE; ***182** H-7; elev. 42ft./13m.; mail Plaquemine **z** 70764; ● 600
Pilottown; RMC Place; PLAQUEMINES; **182** J-11; 🅿; **z** 70081; ● 170
Pine; RMC Place; WASHINGTON; **182** F-9; elev. 348ft./106m.; mail Franklinton **z** 70438; ● 120
Pine Coupee; RMC Place; RAPIDES; ***182** E-3; mail Flatwoods **z** 71427, Lena **z** 71447; rural
Pine Grove; RMC Place; OUACHITA; ***182** B-5; ★ **MONR**; mail Monroe **z** 71201
Pine Grove; RMC Place; ST. HELENA; **182** G-8; elev. 170ft./52m.; 🅿; **z** 70453; ● 280
Pine Island; RMC Place; JEFFERSON DAVIS; ***182** H-4; elev. 41ft./12m.; mail Jennings **z** 70546
Pine Oak Terrace; RMC Place; CADDO; ★ **SHRE**; mail Shreveport **z** 71108; pop. incl. with Shreveport (Inc. Place)
Pine Prairie; Inc. Place; EVANGELINE; **182** F-4; elev. 123ft./37m.; 🅿; **z** 70576; Ⓟ 713; Ⓒ 1,087
Pine Village; RMC Place; ORLEANS; ★ **N.O.**; pop. incl. with New Orleans (Inc. Place)
Pineville; Inc. Place; RAPIDES; **182** E-4; elev. 123ft./37m.; 🅿 🅷 🅲 987; ★ **ALEX**; **z** 71359-61, **z** 71405; Ⓟ 12,255; Ⓒ 13,829
Pioneer; Inc. Place; WEST CARROLL; **182** B-6; elev. 100ft./30m.; 🅿; **z** 71266; Ⓟ 116; Ⓒ 171
Pitkin; RMC Place; VERNON; **182** F-3; 🅿; **z** 70656; ● 700
Pitreville; RMC Place; ACADIA, ST. LANDRY; ***182** G-5; elev. 57ft./17m.; mail Church Point **z** 70525; rural
Plain Dealing; Inc. Place; BOSSIER; **182** A-2; elev. 265ft./81m.; 🅿; **z** 71064; Ⓟ 1,074; Ⓒ 1,071; Ⓡ 1,089
Plains; RMC Place; EAST BATON ROUGE; ***182** G-7; ★ **B.R.**; mail Zachary **z** 70791; pop. incl. with Zachary (Inc. Place)
Plainview; RMC Place; WASHINGTON; ***182** G-9; mail Bogalusa **z** 70427; rural
Plaisance; RMC Place; ST. LANDRY; ***182** G-5; mail Opelousas **z** 70570; ● 50
Plantation Acres; RMC Place; RAPIDES; ★ **ALEX**; mail Alexandria **z** 71301; pop. incl. with Alexandria (Inc. Place)
Plantation Park; RMC Place; BOSSIER; ★ **SHRE**; pop. incl. with Bossier City (Inc. Place)
Plantation Station; RMC Place; BOSSIER; ★ **SHRE**; mail Bossier City **z** 71112; pop. incl. with Bossier City (Inc. Place)
Plaquemine; Inc. Place; ⊡ IBERVILLE; **182** H-7; 🅿 🅷; ★ **B.R.**; **z** 70764-65; Ⓟ 7,186; Ⓒ 7,064
PLAQUEMINES; **182** I-10; Ⓟ 25,575; Ⓒ 26,757; ◆ 21,411
Plaquemine Southwest (Dupont); RMC Place; IBERVILLE; ***182** H-7; ★ **B.R.**; mail Plaquemine **z** 70764; pop. incl. with Plaquemine (Inc. Place)
Plattenville; RMC Place; ASSUMPTION; **182** H-7; elev. 20ft./6m.; 🅿; **z** 70393; ● 390
Plaucheville; Inc. Place; AVOYELLES; **182** F-5; elev. 45ft./14m.; 🅿; **z** 71362; Ⓟ 187; Ⓒ 281
Pleasant Hill; RMC Place; BIENVILLE; ***182** B-3; mail Gibsland **z** 71028; rural
Pleasant Hill; Inc. Place; SABINE; **182** D-2; 🅿; **z** 71065; Ⓟ 824; Ⓒ 786
Pleasant Hills; RMC Place; EAST BATON ROUGE; ***182** G-7; ★ **B.R.**; mail Baton Rouge **z** 70811; ● 300
Pleasant Valley; RMC Place; OUACHITA; ***182** B-4; mail Downsville **z** 71234; ● 140
Plettenberg; RMC Place; WEST FELICIANA; ***182** F-6; mail Saint Francisville **z** 70775; rural
Point; RMC Place; UNION; ***182** B-5; elev. 165ft./50m.; mail Downsville **z** 71234; ● 70
Point Au Chien; RMC Place; TERREBONNE; ***182** J-8; ★ **HOMA-**; mail Montegut **z** 70377; rural
Point Blue; RMC Place; EVANGELINE; **182** G-5; mail Ville Platte **z** 70586; ● 140
Pointe a la Hache; RMC Place; ⊡ PLAQUEMINES; **182** I-10; elev. 6ft./2m.; 🅿; **z** 70082; ● 700
Pointe Aux Chenes; RMC Place; TERREBONNE; ***182** J-8; ★ **HOMA-**; mail Montegut **z** 70377; ● 200
Pointe Coupee; RMC Place; POINTE COUPEE; ***182** G-6; mail New Roads **z** 70760; rural
POINTE COUPEE; **182** G-6; Ⓟ 22,540; Ⓒ 22,763; ◆ 22,161
Point Pleasant; RMC Place; MOREHOUSE; ***182** B-5; mail Bastrop **z** 71220; ● 150
Poland; RMC Place; RAPIDES; ***182** F-5; elev. 68ft./21m.; mail Alexandria **z** 71301; rural
Pollard Estates; RMC Place; EAST BATON ROUGE; ★ **B.R.**; pop. incl. with Baton Rouge (Inc. Place)
Pollock; Inc. Place; GRANT; **182** E-4; elev. 129ft./39m.; 🅿; **z** 71405, **z** 71467; Ⓟ 330; Ⓒ 376
Ponchatoula; Inc. Place; TANGIPAHOA; **182** G-9; elev. 27ft./8m.; 🅿; **z** 70454; Ⓟ 5,425; Ⓒ 5,180
Ponchatoula Beach; RMC Place; TANGIPAHOA; mail Ponchatoula **z** 70454; rural
Pontchartrain Beach; RMC Place; ORLEANS; ★ **N.O.**; mail New Orleans **z** 70122; pop. incl. with New Orleans (Inc. Place)
Pontchartrain Shores; RMC Place; ORLEANS; ★ **N.O.**; mail New Orleans **z** 70122; pop. incl. with New Orleans (Inc. Place)
Poole; RMC Place; BOSSIER; ***182** C-2; mail Elm Grove **z** 71051; rural
Poplar Grove; RMC Place; WEST BATON ROUGE; **182** A-12; ★ **B.R.**; mail Port Allen **z** 70767; ● 200
Portage; RMC Place; ST. LANDRY, ST. MARTIN; ***182** G-6; ★ **LAF**; mail Arnaudville **z** 70512; rural
Port Allen; Inc. Place; ⊡ WEST BATON ROUGE; **182** G-7; elev. 25ft./8m.; 🅿; ★ **B.R.**; **z** 70767; Ⓟ 6,277; Ⓒ 5,278
Port Barre; Inc. Place; ST. LANDRY; **182** G-5; elev. 25ft./8m.; 🅿; **z** 70577; Ⓟ 2,144; Ⓒ 2,287
Port Barrow; RMC Place; ASCENSION; mail Donaldsonville **z** 70346; pop. incl. with Donaldsonville (Inc. Place)
Port Eads; RMC Place; PLAQUEMINES; mail Venice **z** 70091; rural
Porters Curve; RMC Place; WASHINGTON; ***182** F-9; mail Mount Hermon **z** 70450; ● 40
Porterville; RMC Place; WEBSTER; ***182** A-2; elev. 270ft./82m.; mail Sarepta **z** 71071; ● 100
Port Fourchon; RMC Place; LAFOURCHE; **182** J-9; mail Golden Meadow **z** 70357; ● 150
Port Gardner; EAST BATON ROUGE; see Port Hudson (RMC Place)
Port Hickey; RMC Place; EAST BATON ROUGE; ***182** G-7; elev. 90ft./27m.; mail Zachary **z** 70791; rural
Port Hudson (Port Gardner); RMC Place; EAST BATON ROUGE; ***182** G-7; ★ **B.R.**; mail Zachary **z** 70791; ● 300
Port Manchac; RMC Place; TANGIPAHOA; ***182** H-9; mail Akers **z** 70421; ● 300
Port of West Saint Mary; RMC Place; ST. MARY; ***182** I-6; mail Franklin **z** 70538; ● 50
Port Sulphur; CDP; PLAQUEMINES; **182** J-10; elev. 3ft./1m.; 🅿; **z** 70083; Ⓟ 3,523; Ⓒ 3,115
Port Vincent; Inc. Place; LIVINGSTON; **182** H-8; elev. 15ft./5m.; 🅿; ★ **B.R.**; **z** 70726; Ⓟ 446; Ⓒ 463
Potash; RMC Place; PLAQUEMINES; ***182** I-10; mail Port Sulphur **z** 70083
Pot Cove; RMC Place; ST. LANDRY; mail Ville Platte **z** 70586; rural
Poufette; RMC Place; IBERIA; ***182** H-5; elev. 7ft./2m.; mail New Iberia **z** 70560; rural
Powhatan; Inc. Place; NATCHITOCHES; **182** D-3; elev. 127ft./39m.; 🅿; **z** 71066; Ⓟ 147; Ⓒ 141
Poydras; CDP; ST. BERNARD; ***182** I-10; ★ **N.O.**; mail Saint Bernard **z** 70085; Ⓟ 4,029; Ⓒ 3,886
Poydras Junction; RMC Place; ST. BERNARD; ★ **N.O.**
Prairieland; RMC Place; CALCASIEU; ***182** H-3; ★ **LKCH**; mail Lake Charles **z** 70611; rural
Prairie Ronde; RMC Place; ST. LANDRY; ***182** G-5; elev. 66ft./20m.; mail Opelousas **z** 70570; ● 30
Prairieville; RMC Place; ASCENSION; **182** H-7; elev. 22ft./7m.; 🅿; ★ **B.R.**; **z** 70769; ● 510
Pratt; RMC Place; BIENVILLE; ***182** B-3; mail Gibsland **z** 71028; rural
Presque Isle; RMC Place; TERREBONNE; ***182** I-8; ★ **HOMA-**; mail Houma **z** 70363; ● 550
Pride; RMC Place; EAST BATON ROUGE; ***182** G-7; elev. 103ft./31m.; 🅿; **z** 70770; ● 150
Prien; CDP; CALCASIEU; ***182** H-3; ★ **LKCH**; mail Lake Charles **z** 70605; Ⓟ 6,448; Ⓒ 7,215
Princeton; RMC Place; BOSSIER; ***182** B-2; elev. 280ft./85m.; 🅿; ★ **SHRE**; **z** 71067; ● 350
Promised Land; RMC Place; PLAQUEMINES; ***182** I-9; mail Braithwaite **z** 70040; rural
Prospect; RMC Place; GRANT; ***182** E-4; mail Bentley **z** 71407, Dry Prong **z** 71423; ● 50
Prospect; RMC Place; ST. CHARLES; ★ **N.O.**; mail New Sarpy **z** 70078
Provencal; Inc. Place; NATCHITOCHES; **182** D-3; elev. 210ft./64m.; 🅿; **z** 71468; Ⓟ 538; Ⓒ 708
Providence; RMC Place; JEFFERSON; ★ **N.O.**; mail Kenner **z** 70062; ● 350
Puckett; RMC Place; EAST BATON ROUGE; ***182** G-7; elev. 73ft./22m.; ★ **B.R.**; mail Zachary **z** 70791; rural
Pumpkin Center; RMC Place; TANGIPAHOA; ***182** G-8; mail Hammond **z** 70403; ● 300
Punkin Center; RMC Place; JACKSON; ***182** C-4; mail Quitman **z** 71268; rural

Q

Quaid; RMC Place; CATAHOULA; ***182** D-6; mail Jonesville **z** 71343; rural
Quebec; RMC Place; MADISON; ***182** C-7; mail Tallulah **z** 71282; rural
Queensborough; RMC Place; CADDO; ★ **SHRE**; pop. incl. with Shreveport (Inc. Place)
Quimby; RMC Place; MADISON; ***182** C-7; mail Tallulah **z** 71282; rural
Quitman; Inc. Place; JACKSON; **182** C-4; elev. 200ft./61m.; 🅿; **z** 71268; Ⓟ 162; Ⓒ 168

R

Raceland; CDP; LAFOURCHE; **182** I-8; elev. 14ft./4m.; 🅿 🅷; **z** 70394; Ⓟ 5,564; Ⓒ 10,224
Ragley; RMC Place; BEAUREGARD; **182** G-3; elev. 84ft./26m.; 🅿; **z** 70657; ● 100
Ramah; RMC Place; IBERVILLE; **182** G-6; elev. 16ft./5m.; 🅿; **z** 70757
Rambin; RMC Place; DE SOTO; ***182** D-2; mail Pelican **z** 71063; rural
Ramsay; RMC Place; ST. TAMMANY; ***182** G-9; elev. 40ft./12m.; ★ **N.O.**; mail Covington **z** 70435; rural
Randolph; RMC Place; UNION; ***182** A-4; mail Lillie **z** 71256; ● 50
Rapides; RMC Place; RAPIDES; ***182** E-4; ★ **ALEX**; mail Boyce **z** 71409
RAPIDES; **182** F-4; Ⓟ 131,556; Ⓒ 126,337; ◆ 129,042
Ratliff; RMC Place; ASSUMPTION; ***182** H-7; mail Napoleonville **z** 70390; rural
Rattan; RMC Place; SABINE; ***182** E-2; mail Florien **z** 71429, Many **z** 71449; rural
Raymond; RMC Place; JEFFERSON DAVIS; ***182** H-4; mail Elton **z** 70532; rural
Rayne; Inc. Place; ACADIA; **182** H-5; elev. 32ft./10m.; 🅿; ★ **LAF**; **z** 70578; Ⓟ 8,502; Ⓒ 8,552
Rayville; Inc. Place; ⊡ RICHLAND; **182** B-6; elev. 81ft./25m.; 🅿 🅷; **z** 71269; Ⓟ 4,411; Ⓒ 4,234
Readheimer (Readhimer); RMC Place; NATCHITOCHES; ***182** C-3; mail Saline **z** 71070
Readhimer; NATCHITOCHES; see Readheimer (RMC Place)
Reaves; ALLEN; see Reeves (Inc. Place)
Recovery; RMC Place; ORLEANS; ★ **N.O.**; pop. incl. with New Orleans (Inc. Place)
Red Chute; CDP; BOSSIER; ***182** B-2; elev. 215ft./66m.; ★ **SHRE**; mail Haughton **z** 71037; Ⓟ 5,431; Ⓒ 5,984
Reddell; RMC Place; EVANGELINE; **182** G-4; elev. 65ft./20m.; 🅿; **z** 70580; ● 600
Red Gum; RMC Place; CONCORDIA; ***182** D-6; ★ **NCHZ**; mail Clayton **z** 71326, Ferriday **z** 71334; ● 30
Redich; RMC Place; ACADIA; ***182** G-4; mail Eunice **z** 70535; rural
Redland; RMC Place; BOSSIER; ***182** A-2; mail Plain Dealing **z** 71064; rural
Redland; RMC Place; EVANGELINE; ***182** G-4; mail Mamou **z** 70554; rural
Red Oaks; RMC Place; EAST BATON ROUGE; **182** B-14; ★ **B.R.**; mail Baton Rouge **z** 70815; pop. incl. with Baton Rouge (Inc. Place)
RED RIVER; **182** C-3; Ⓟ 9,387; Ⓒ 9,622; ◆ 9,102
Redwing; RMC Place; WEST CARROLL; ***182** B-6; mail Oak Grove **z** 71263; rural
Reeves (Reaves); Inc. Place; ALLEN; **182** G-3; elev. 45ft./14m.; 🅿; **z** 70658; Ⓟ 188; Ⓒ 209
Regency Park; RMC Place; ORLEANS; ★ **N.O.**; pop. incl. with New Orleans (Inc. Place)
Reggio; RMC Place; ST. BERNARD; **182** I-10; mail Saint Bernard **z** 70085; ● 160
Reids; RMC Place; ALLEN; ***182** F-3; mail Pitkin **z** 70656; rural
Reisor; RMC Place; CADDO; ***182** C-2; ★ **SHRE**; pop. incl. with Shreveport (Inc. Place)
Remy (The Bend); RMC Place; ST. JAMES; ***182** H-8; mail Paulina **z** 70763; ● 250
Reserve; CDP; ST. JOHN THE BAPTIST; **182** H-8; elev. 15ft./5m.; 🅿; **z** 70084; Ⓟ 8,847; Ⓒ 9,111
Rhinehart; RMC Place; CATAHOULA; **182** D-5; elev. 63ft./19m.; 🅿; **z** 71363; ● 130
Rhymes; RMC Place; RICHLAND; ***182** C-5; elev. 75ft./23m.; mail Rayville **z** 71269; rural
Riceville; RMC Place; VERMILION; ***182** H-4; mail Gueydan **z** 70542; ● 50
Richard; RMC Place; ACADIA; ***182** G-5; elev. 45ft./14m.; mail Church Point **z** 70525; ● 180
Richardson; RMC Place; WASHINGTON; ***182** F-9; mail Franklinton **z** 70438; ● 70
Richland; RICHLAND; see Warden (RMC Place)
Richland; RMC Place; TENSAS; ***182** D-6; mail Waterproof **z** 71375; rural
RICHLAND; **182** C-6; Ⓟ 20,629; Ⓒ 20,981; ◆ 20,350
Richmond; Inc. Place; MADISON; ***182** C-7; elev. 80ft./24m.; mail Tallulah **z** 71282; Ⓟ 447; Ⓒ 499
Richohoc; RMC Place; ST. MARY; ***182** I-7; mail Franklin **z** 70538; rural
Richwood; Inc. Place; OUACHITA; **182** C-5; 🅿; ★ **MONR**; **z** 71202 & mail Monroe **z** 71201; Ⓟ 1,253; Ⓒ 2,115
Rideau Settlement; RMC Place; ST. LANDRY; ***182** G-5; mail Palmetto **z** 71358; ● 80
Ridge; RMC Place; LAFAYETTE; ***182** H-5; elev. 29ft./9m.; ★ **LAF**; mail Rayne **z** 70578
Ridgecrest; Inc. Place; CONCORDIA; **182** E-6; 🅿; ★ **NCHZ**; **z** 71334; Ⓟ 804; Ⓒ 801
Ridgewood; RMC Place; EAST BATON ROUGE; ***182** G-7; ★ **B.R.**; mail Greenwell Springs **z** 70739; ● 210
Rienzi Plantation; RMC Place; LAFOURCHE; ***182** I-8; elev. 8ft./2m.; mail Thibodaux **z** 70301; pop. incl. with Thibodaux (Inc. Place)
Rigolets; RMC Place; ORLEANS; ***182** H-10; ★ **N.O.**; pop. incl. with New Orleans (Inc. Place)
Ringgold; Inc. Place; BIENVILLE; **182** C-3; elev. 270ft./82m.; 🅿; **z** 71068; Ⓟ 1,856; Ⓒ 1,660
Rio; RMC Place; WASHINGTON; ***182** G-10; mail Bogalusa **z** 70427; rural
Risinger Woods; RMC Place; CADDO; mail Shreveport **z** 71107; ● 150
Rita (Lockport); RMC Place; LAFOURCHE; ***182** I-8; mail Lockport **z** 70374
Riverlands; RMC Place; ST. JOHN THE BAPTIST; ★ **N.O.**; mail La Place **z** 70068
River Ridge (East Bank); CDP; JEFFERSON; **182** E-11; elev. 5ft./2m.; 🅿; ★ **N.O.**; **z** 70123; Ⓟ 14,800; Ⓒ 14,588

Entries in **UPPERCASE** are parishes.
Entries in **bold** have populations of 2,500 or more.
Names in parentheses are alternate names.

Inc. Place	Incorporated Place
RMC Place	Rand McNally Designated Place
CDP	Census Designated Place
MCD	Minor Civil Division
⊡	Parish Seat
▲	Minor Civil Division
elev.	Elevation
🅿	Post Office
🅷	Hospital
🅲	College
■	Principal Business Center
★	Ranally Metro Area (RMA) Abbreviation
z	Zip Code(s)
Ⓟ	Previous Census Population
Ⓡ	Revised Census Population
Ⓐ	Annexation Population
●	Rand McNally Population Estimate
Ⓒ	Final Census Population
Ⓢ	Special Census Population
◆	Estimated Population

For additional definitions see Glossary, Volume 1, and Introduction, Volume 2.

Riverton; RMC Place; CALDWELL; **182** C-5; mail Columbia **z** 71418; ● 80
Riverwood; RMC Place; ST. TAMMANY; ***182** G-9; ★ **N.O.**; mail Covington **z** 70433; ● 400
Roanoke; RMC Place; JEFFERSON DAVIS; ***182** H-4; elev. 28ft./9m.; 🅿; **z** 70581; ● 630
Robeline; Inc. Place; NATCHITOCHES; **182** D-3; elev. 160ft./49m.; 🅿; **z** 71469; Ⓟ 149; © 183
Robert; RMC Place; TANGIPAHOA; **182** G-9; elev. 31ft./9m.; 🅿; **z** 70455; ● 400
Roberts Cove; RMC Place; ACADIA; ***182** H-5; mail Rayne **z** 70578; ● 50
Robin; RMC Place; ST. LANDRY; ***182** G-5; mail Arnaudville **z** 70512; rural
Robson; RMC Place; CADDO; ***182** C-2; elev. 155ft./47m.; mail Shreveport **z** 71105; rural
Rock (Rock Quarry); RMC Place; RAPIDES; ***182** E-4; elev. 104ft./32m.; mail Colfax **z** 71417, Lena **z** 71447; ● 50
Rock Hill; RMC Place; GRANT; ***182** E-4; elev. 124ft./38m.; mail Colfax **z** 71417, Dry Prong **z** 71423
Rock Quarry; RAPIDES; see Rock (RMC Place)
Rocky Branch; RMC Place; UNION; **182** B-5; elev. 163ft./50m.; mail Farmerville **z** 71241; ● 200
Rocky Mount; RMC Place; BOSSIER; **182** B-2; elev. 405ft./123m.; mail Plain Dealing **z** 71064; ● 100
Rodessa; Inc. Place; CADDO; **182** A-1; elev. 261ft./80m.; 🅿; **z** 71069; Ⓟ 294; © 307
Rogers; RMC Place; LA SALLE; ***182** E-5; elev. 89ft./27m.; mail Jena **z** 71342; rural
Rogillioville; RMC Place; WEST FELICIANA; ***182** F-7; mail Jackson **z** 70748; rural
Romeville; RMC Place; ST. JAMES; ***182** H-8; mail Convent **z** 70723; ● 200
Roosevelt; RMC Place; EAST CARROLL; ***182** B-7; mail Sondheimer **z** 71276; rural
Rosa; RMC Place; ST. LANDRY; ***182** G-5; 🅿; **z** 71345; ● 50
Rosedale; RMC Place; ASSUMPTION; ***182** I-7; mail Napoleonville **z** 70390; rural
Rosedale; Inc. Place; IBERVILLE; **182** G-6; elev. 20ft./6m.; 🅿; **z** 70772; Ⓟ 807; © 753
Rosefield; RMC Place; CATAHOULA; ***182** D-5; elev. 293ft./89m.; mail Grayson **z** 71435, Olla **z** 71465; ● 30
Roseland; Inc. Place; TANGIPAHOA; **182** G-8; elev. 132ft./40m.; 🅿; **z** 70456; Ⓟ 1,093; © 1,162
Rosepine; Inc. Place; VERNON; **182** F-3; elev. 221ft./67m.; 🅿; **z** 70659; Ⓟ 1,135; © 1,390
Rougon (Chenal); RMC Place; POINTE COUPEE; ***182** G-7; elev. 35ft./11m.; 🅿; **z** 70773; ● 250
Rousseau; RMC Place; LAFOURCHE; ***182** I-8; elev. 9ft./3m.; mail Raceland **z** 70394; rural
Roxana; RMC Place; RAPIDES; ***182** F-5; mail Alexandria **z** 71301, **z** 71303; rural
Roy; RMC Place; BIENVILLE; **182** C-3; mail Castor **z** 71016; ● 80
Ruby; RMC Place; RAPIDES; ***182** F-5; elev. 98ft./30m.; 🅿; **z** 71365; ● 60
Rum Center; RMC Place; UNION; ***182** A-4; mail Lillie **z** 71256; ● 50
Ruple; RMC Place; CLAIBORNE; ***182** B-3; mail Haynesville **z** 71038; rural
Rural Park; RMC Place; JEFFERSON; ★ **N.O.**; mail New Orleans **z** 70123
Ruston; Inc. Place; ⊡ LINCOLN; **182** B-4; elev. 319ft./97m.; 🅿 🅷 🅲 11,232 ■; **z** 71270, **z** 71272-73; Ⓟ 20,027; © 20,546; ◆ 21,525
Ruth; RMC Place; ST. MARTIN; ***182** H-6; ★ **LAF**; mail Breaux Bridge **z** 70517; rural
Rynella; RMC Place; IBERIA; ***182** H-6; elev. 5ft./2m.; mail New Iberia **z** 70560; rural

S

SABINE; **182** E-2; Ⓟ 22,646; © 23,459; ◆ 23,633
Sadie; RMC Place; UNION; ***182** A-5; elev. 158ft./48m.; mail Marion **z** 71260; rural
Sadou; RMC Place; LAFAYETTE; ***182** H-5; ★ **LAF**; mail Duson **z** 70529; rural
Sailes; RMC Place; BIENVILLE; ***182** C-3; elev. 255ft./78m.; mail Gibsland **z** 71028; rural
Saint Amant; RMC Place; ASCENSION; **182** H-8; elev. 5ft./2m.; 🅿; ★ **B.R.**; **z** 70774; ● 300
Saint Amelia; ST. JAMES; see Hymel (RMC Place)
Saint Bernard; RMC Place; ST. BERNARD; **182** I-10; elev. 5ft./2m.; 🅿; ★ **N.O.**; **z** 70085; ● 830
ST. BERNARD; **182** I-10; Ⓟ 66,631; © 67,229; ◆ 40,591
Saint Bernard Grove; RMC Place; ST. BERNARD; ***182** H-10; ★ **N.O.**; mail Meraux **z** 70075; ● 810
Saint Charles; RMC Place; LAFOURCHE; ***182** I-8; mail Raceland **z** 70394, Thibodaux **z** 70301; ● 100
ST. CHARLES; **182** I-9; Ⓟ 42,437; © 48,072; ◆ 51,778
Saint Clair; RMC Place; PLAQUEMINES; ***182** I-9; elev. 10ft./3m.; ★ **N.O.**; mail Braithwaite **z** 70040
Saint Claude Heights; RMC Place; ST. BERNARD; ***182** H-9; ★ **N.O.**; mail Arabi **z** 70032
Saint Elmo; RMC Place; ASCENSION; ***182** H-7; elev. 20ft./6m.; mail Darrow **z** 70725; ● 60
Saint Francisville; Inc. Place; ⊡ WEST FELICIANA; **182** F-7; elev. 115ft./35m.; 🅿 🅷; **z** 70775; Ⓟ 1,700; © 1,712
Saint Gabriel; Inc. Place; IBERVILLE; **182** H-7; 🅿; ★ **B.R.**; **z** 70776; Ⓟ 3,771; © 5,514
Saint Genevieve; RMC Place; CONCORDIA; ***182** E-6; elev. 56ft./17m.; mail Vidalia **z** 71373; rural
ST. HELENA; **182** G-8; Ⓟ 9,874; © 10,525; ◆ 10,351
Saint James; RMC Place; ST. JAMES; **182** H-8; elev. 17ft./5m.; 🅿; **z** 70086; ● 310
ST. JAMES; **182** I-8; Ⓟ 20,879; © 21,216; Ⓡ 21,195; ◆ 21,479
Saint Joe; RMC Place; ST. TAMMANY; ***182** G-10; elev. 30ft./9m.; ★ **N.O.**; mail Pearl River **z** 70452; ● 150
Saint John; ST. MARTIN; see Levert (RMC Place)
ST. JOHN THE BAPTIST; **182** H-8; Ⓟ 39,996; © 43,044; ◆ 47,348
Saint Joseph; Inc. Place; ⊡ TENSAS; **182** D-7; 🅿; **z** 71366; Ⓟ 1,517; © 1,340
Saint Landry; RMC Place; EVANGELINE; **182** F-5; elev. 49ft./15m.; 🅿; **z** 71367; ● 450
ST. LANDRY; **182** G-5; Ⓟ 80,331; © 87,700; ◆ 90,331
ST. MARTIN; **182** H-6; Ⓟ 43,978; © 48,583; ◆ 52,132
Saint Martinville; Inc. Place; ⊡ ST. MARTIN; **182** H-6; elev. 19ft./6m.; 🅿; **z** 70582; Ⓟ 7,137; © 6,989
ST. MARY; **182** I-6; Ⓟ 58,086; © 53,500; ◆ 50,229
Saint Maurice; RMC Place; WINN; **182** D-3; elev. 179ft./55m.; 🅿; **z** 71471; ● 180
Saint Rosalie; RMC Place; PLAQUEMINES; ***182** I-10; elev. 4ft./1m.; mail Belle Chasse **z** 70037; rural
Saint Rose; CDP; ST. CHARLES; ***182** H-9; 🅿; ★ **N.O.**; **z** 70087; Ⓟ 6,259; © 6,540
Saint Tammany; RMC Place; ST. TAMMANY; ***182** G-10; mail Lacombe **z** 70445; ● 180
ST. TAMMANY; **182** G-9; Ⓟ 144,508; © 191,268; ◆ 217,065
Saint Thomas; RMC Place; ASSUMPTION; ***182** I-7; mail Napoleonville **z** 70390; rural
Saint Vincent; ASSUMPTION; see Brusle Saint Vincent (RMC Place)
Saline; Inc. Place; BIENVILLE; **182** C-3; elev. 183ft./56m.; 🅿; **z** 71070; Ⓟ 272; © 296
Samstown; RMC Place; IBERVILLE; ***182** H-7; elev. 6ft./2m.; mail White Castle **z** 70788; rural
Samtown; RMC Place; RAPIDES; **182** E-4; ★ **ALEX**; mail Alexandria **z** 71301; pop. incl. with Alexandria (Inc. Place)
Sandel; RMC Place; SABINE; ***182** E-2; mail Florien **z** 71429; rural
Sandy Hill; RMC Place; VERNON; **182** F-3; mail Leesville **z** 71446; ● 300
Sardis; RMC Place; SABINE; ***182** D-2; mail Converse **z** 71419; rural
Sardis; RMC Place; WINN; ***182** D-4; mail Winnfield **z** 71483; rural
Sarepta; Inc. Place; WEBSTER; **182** A-2; elev. 254ft./77m.; 🅿; **z** 71071; Ⓟ 886; © 925
Satsuma; RMC Place; LIVINGSTON; ***182** G-8; elev. 44ft./13m.; ★ **B.R.**; mail Livingston **z** 70754; ● 100
Savoie; LAFOURCHE, TERREBONNE; see Bayou Blue (RMC Place)
Savoy; RMC Place; ST. LANDRY; ***182** G-5; elev. 53ft./16m.; mail Eunice **z** 70535; rural
Scarsdale; RMC Place; PLAQUEMINES; ***182** I-9; elev. 4ft./1m.; mail Braithwaite **z** 70040; ● 50
Schriever; CDP; TERREBONNE; **182** I-8; elev. 14ft./4m.; 🅿; ★ **HOMA-**; **z** 70395; Ⓟ 4,958; © 5,880
Scotland; EAST BATON ROUGE; see Scotlandville (RMC Place)
Scotlandville (Scotland); RMC Place; EAST BATON ROUGE; **182** G-7; elev. 60ft./18m.; 🅿; ★ **B.R.**; **z** 70807, **z** 70811 & mail Baton Rouge **z** 70874; pop. incl. with Baton Rouge (Inc. Place)
Scott; Inc. Place; LAFAYETTE; **182** H-5; elev. 35ft./11m.; 🅿; ★ **LAF**; **z** 70583; Ⓟ 4,912; © 7,870
Seabrook; RMC Place; ORLEANS; ★ **N.O.**; pop. incl. with New Orleans (Inc. Place)
Searcy; RMC Place; LA SALLE; ***182** D-5; mail Trout **z** 71371; ● 30
Sebastapol; RMC Place; ST. BERNARD; ***182** I-10; mail Saint Bernard **z** 70085
Sellers; RMC Place; ST. CHARLES; ***182** H-9; ★ **N.O.**; mail Norco **z** 70079
Selma; RMC Place; GRANT; ***182** D-4; elev. 79ft./24m.; mail Georgetown **z** 71432; rural
Sentell; RMC Place; CADDO; ***182** B-2; elev. 177ft./54m.; ★ **SHRE**; mail Shreveport **z** 71107; rural
Serena; RMC Place; CATAHOULA; mail Jonesville **z** 71343
Seymourville; RMC Place; IBERVILLE; **182** H-7; ★ **B.R.**; mail Plaquemine **z** 70764; ● 3,000
Shadyside; RMC Place; ST. MARY; ***182** I-7; mail Franklin **z** 70538; rural
Shamrock (Shamrock Mill); RMC Place; NATCHITOCHES; ***182** D-3; mail Robeline **z** 71469; rural
Shamrock Mill; NATCHITOCHES; see Shamrock (RMC Place)
Sharon; RMC Place; CLAIBORNE; ***182** B-4; elev. 297ft./91m.; mail Dubach **z** 71235, Homer **z** 71040; ● 70
Sharon Hills; RMC Place; EAST BATON ROUGE; ***182** G-7; ★ **B.R.**; mail Baton Rouge **z** 70811; ● 900
Sharp; RMC Place; RAPIDES; ***182** E-4; mail Lena **z** 71447; rural
Shaw; RMC Place; CONCORDIA; ***182** E-6; mail Vidalia **z** 71373; rural
Shelburn; RMC Place; EAST CARROLL; ***182** A-7; mail Lake Providence **z** 71254; ● 110
Shelton; RMC Place; MOREHOUSE; ***182** B-5; mail Bastrop **z** 71220; ● 250
Shenandoah; CDP-Census Area Only; EAST BATON ROUGE; ***182** G-7; elev. 40ft./12m.; ★ **B.R.**; mail Baton Rouge **z** 70816; Ⓟ 13,429; © 17,070
Sherburne; RMC Place; POINTE COUPEE; ***182** G-6; elev. 26ft./8m.; mail Krotz Springs **z** 70750; rural
Sheridan; RMC Place; WASHINGTON; ***182** F-9; 🅿; **z** 70438; rural
Sherwood; RMC Place; CATAHOULA; ***182** D-5; mail Grayson **z** 71435; rural
Sherwood Forest; RMC Place; EAST BATON ROUGE; ★ **B.R.**; pop. incl. with Baton Rouge (Inc. Place)
Shiloh; RMC Place; TANGIPAHOA; ***182** G-8; mail Amite **z** 70422; rural
Shiloh; RMC Place; UNION; ***182** B-4; elev. 244ft./74m.; mail Bernice **z** 71222; rural
Shongaloo; Inc. Place; WEBSTER; **182** A-3; elev. 260ft./79m.; 🅿; **z** 71072; Ⓟ 161; © 162
Shreveport; Inc. Place; ⊡ CADDO, BOSSIER; **182** B-2; 🅿 🅷 🅲 5,040 ■; ★ **SHRE**; **z** 71101-09, **z** 71115, **z** 71118-20, **z** 71129-30, **z** 71133-38, **z** 71148-54, **z** 71156, **z** 71161-66 & mail Barksdale AFB **z** 71110; Ⓟ 198,525; © 200,145; ◆ 186,137
Shrewsbury; RMC Place; JEFFERSON; ***182** H-9; ★ **N.O.**; mail New Orleans **z** 70121
Shuteston; RMC Place; ST. LANDRY; ***182** G-5; elev. 54ft./16m.; mail Opelousas **z** 70570; ● 30
Sibley; RMC Place; LINCOLN; ***182** B-4; elev. 244ft./74m.; mail Choudrant **z** 71227
Sibley; Inc. Place; WEBSTER; **182** B-3; 🅿; **z** 71073; Ⓟ 997; © 1,098
Sicard; RMC Place; OUACHITA; ***182** B-5; elev. 83ft./25m.; ★ **MONR**; mail Monroe **z** 71201
Sicily Island; Inc. Place; CATAHOULA; **182** D-6; elev. 35ft./11m.; 🅿; **z** 71368; Ⓟ 421; © 453
Siegle; RMC Place; OUACHITA; ***182** B-5; ★ **MONR**; mail West Monroe **z** 71291-92; ● 1,600
Sieper; RMC Place; RAPIDES; **182** E-4; elev. 180ft./55m.; 🅿; **z** 71472; ● 100
Sikes; Inc. Place; WINN; **182** C-4; elev. 154ft./47m.; 🅿; **z** 71473; Ⓟ 120; © 120
Sikes Ferry; RMC Place; WEBSTER; ***182** A-3; mail Shongaloo **z** 71072; rural
Silverwood; RMC Place; JEFFERSON DAVIS; ***182** H-4; mail Jennings **z** 70546; ● 60
Simmesport; Inc. Place; AVOYELLES; **182** F-6; elev. 43ft./13m.; 🅿; **z** 71369; Ⓟ 2,092; © 2,239
Simms (Camp Livinston); RMC Place; GRANT; ***182** E-4; elev. 186ft./57m.; mail Pollock **z** 71467; rural
Simpson; Inc. Place; VERNON; **182** E-3; elev. 300ft./91m.; 🅿; **z** 71474; Ⓟ 536; © 583
Simsboro; Inc. Place; LINCOLN; **182** B-4; elev. 348ft./106m.; 🅿; **z** 71275; Ⓟ 634; © 684
Singer; RMC Place; BEAUREGARD; **182** G-2; elev. 146ft./45m.; 🅿; **z** 70660; ● 200
Siracusaville; RMC Place; ST. MARY; ***182** I-7; elev. 5ft./2m.; mail Morgan City **z** 70380; ● 500
Slacks; RMC Place; IBERVILLE; ***182** G-6; mail Maringouin **z** 70757; rural
Slagle; RMC Place; VERNON; **182** E-3; elev. 280ft./85m.; 🅿; **z** 71475; ● 200
Slaughter; Inc. Place; EAST FELICIANA; **182** G-7; elev. 133ft./41m.; 🅿; ★ **B.R.**; **z** 70777; Ⓟ 827; © 1,011
Slidell; Inc. Place; ST. TAMMANY; **182** H-10; elev. 9ft./3m.; 🅿 🅷 🅲 6,000 ■; ★ **N.O.**; **z** 70458-61, **z** 70469; Ⓟ 24,124; © 25,695; ◆ 24,559
Sligo; RMC Place; BOSSIER; ***182** B-2; mail Bossier City **z** 71112, Haughton **z** 71037; rural
Smiley Heights; RMC Place; EAST BATON ROUGE; ***182** G-7; elev. 55ft./17m.; ★ **B.R.**; pop. incl. with Baton Rouge (Inc. Place)
Smithfield; RMC Place; WEST BATON ROUGE; ***182** G-7; elev. 32ft./10m.; mail Port Allen **z** 70767; ● 250
Smith Ridge; RMC Place; TERREBONNE; ***182** J-8; ★ **HOMA-**; mail Chauvin **z** 70344; ● 320
Smithville; RMC Place; RAPIDES; ***182** E-4; ★ **ALEX**; pop. incl. with Pineville (Inc. Place)
Smoke Bend; RMC Place; ASCENSION; ***182** H-7; mail Donaldsonville **z** 70346; ● 350
Socola; RMC Place; PLAQUEMINES; ***182** I-10; mail Port Sulphur **z** 70083
Soileau; RMC Place; ALLEN; ***182** G-4; mail Oberlin **z** 70655; rural
Somerset; RMC Place; TENSAS; ***182** C-7; mail Newellton **z** 71357; rural
Sondheimer; RMC Place; EAST CARROLL; **182** B-7; elev. 85ft./26m.; 🅿; **z** 71276; ● 200
Soniat (Cedar Grove Plantation); RMC Place; IBERVILLE; ***182** H-7; mail White Castle **z** 70788; ● 170
Sorrell; RMC Place; ST. MARY; **182** I-6; mail Jeanerette **z** 70544; ● 230
Sorrento; Inc. Place; ASCENSION; **182** H-8; elev. 7ft./2m.; 🅿; ★ **B.R.**; **z** 70778; Ⓟ 1,119; © 1,227
South Acres (Sulphur South); RMC Place; CALCASIEU; ***182** H-2; ★ **LKCH**; mail Sulphur **z** 70665; pop. incl. with Sulphur (Inc. Place)
South Bend; RMC Place; ST. MARY; ***182** I-6; mail Franklin **z** 70538; rural
Southdown; RMC Place; TERREBONNE; ***182** I-8; ★ **HOMA-**; mail Houma **z** 70360; ● 420
Southeast; RMC Place; EAST BATON ROUGE; ***182** G-7; ★ **B.R.**; mail Baton Rouge **z** 70808, **z** 70898; pop. incl. with Baton Rouge (Inc. Place)
Southern Hills; RMC Place; CADDO; ★ **SHRE**; mail Shreveport **z** 71108; pop. incl. with Shreveport (Inc. Place)
Southfield; RMC Place; CADDO; ***182** B-2; ★ **SHRE**; mail Shreveport **z** 71105, **z** 71135; pop. incl. with Shreveport (Inc. Place)
South Highlands; RMC Place; CADDO; ★ **SHRE**; pop. incl. with Shreveport (Inc. Place)
South Kenner; RMC Place; JEFFERSON; ***182** H-9; ★ **N.O.**; mail Westwego **z** 70094; ● 150
South Lafourche; RMC Place; LAFOURCHE; ***182** J-9; mail Golden Meadow **z** 70357
Southland Park; RMC Place; CADDO; ★ **SHRE**; pop. incl. with Shreveport (Inc. Place)
South Mansfield; Inc. Place; DE SOTO; **182** D-2; elev. 390ft./119m.; mail Mansfield **z** 71052; Ⓟ 407; © 352
South Park; RMC Place; CADDO; ***182** C-2; ★ **SHRE**; mail Shreveport **z** 71118, **z** 71138; pop. incl. with Shreveport (Inc. Place)
South Park; RMC Place; RAPIDES; ***182** E-4; ★ **ALEX**; mail Alexandria **z** 71301, **z** 71307; pop. incl. with Alexandria (Inc. Place)
South Pass; RMC Place; PLAQUEMINES; mail Venice **z** 70091; rural
South Point; RMC Place; ORLEANS; ***182** H-10; ★ **N.O.**; pop. incl. with New Orleans (Inc. Place)
Southport; RMC Place; JEFFERSON; ***182** H-9; ★ **N.O.**; mail New Orleans **z** 70121
South Sherwood; RMC Place; EAST BATON ROUGE; ***182** G-7; ★ **B.R.**; mail Baton Rouge **z** 70816; pop. incl. with Baton Rouge (Inc. Place)
South Vacherie (Lower Vacherie); CDP-Census Area Only; ST. JAMES; ***182** H-8; mail Vacherie **z** 70090; Ⓟ 3,462; © 3,543
Southwestern University; RMC Place; LAFAYETTE; ***182** H-5; ★ **LAF**; mail Lafayette **z** 70504; pop. incl. with Lafayette (Inc. Place)
Spaulding; RMC Place; CALDWELL; ***182** D-5; mail Kelly **z** 71441; ● 30
Spearsville; Inc. Place; UNION; **182** A-4; elev. 180ft./55m.; 🅿; **z** 71277; Ⓟ 132; © 155
Spencer; RMC Place; UNION; **182** B-5; elev. 120ft./37m.; 🅿; **z** 71280; ● 100
Spillman; RMC Place; WEST FELICIANA; ***182** F-7; elev. 260ft./79m.; mail Jackson **z** 70748; rural
Splane Place; RMC Place; OUACHITA; ★ **MONR**; mail West Monroe **z** 71291; pop. incl. with West Monroe (Inc. Place)
Spokane; RMC Place; CONCORDIA; ***182** D-6; elev. 65ft./20m.; mail Ferriday **z** 71334; ● 30
Spring Creek; RMC Place; TANGIPAHOA; ***182** F-8; mail Kentwood **z** 70444; ● 150
Springfield; Inc. Place; LIVINGSTON; **182** G-8; elev. 16ft./5m.; 🅿; **z** 70462; Ⓟ 439; © 395
Spring Hill; RMC Place; JACKSON; ***182** C-4; mail Jonesboro **z** 71251; rural
Springhill; RMC Place; WASHINGTON; ***182** F-9; mail Franklinton **z** 70438; rural
Springhill; Inc. Place; WEBSTER; **182** A-2; elev. 280ft./85m.; 🅿 🅷; **z** 71075; Ⓟ 5,668; © 5,439
Spring Ridge; RMC Place; CADDO; ***182** C-1; mail Keithville **z** 71047
Spring Ridge; RMC Place; SABINE; ***182** D-2; mail Pleasant Hill **z** 71065; rural
Springville; RMC Place; LIVINGSTON; ***182** G-8; elev. 30ft./9m.; mail Livingston **z** 70754; rural
Springville; RMC Place; RED RIVER; ***182** D-3; mail Coushatta **z** 71019; ● 840
Standard; RMC Place; LA SALLE; ***182** D-5; elev. 172ft./52m.; mail Olla **z** 71465; ● 150
Standard Heights; RMC Place; EAST BATON ROUGE; ★ **B.R.**; pop. incl. with Baton Rouge (Inc. Place)
Stanley; Inc. Place; DE SOTO; **182** D-1; elev. 200ft./61m.; mail Logansport **z** 71049; Ⓟ 131; © 145
Stanton; RMC Place; ORLEANS; ***182** H-10; ★ **N.O.**; pop. incl. with New Orleans (Inc. Place)
Star; RMC Place; PLAQUEMINES; ***182** I-9; mail Belle Chasse **z** 70037; rural
Starhill; RMC Place; WEST FELICIANA; ***182** G-7; mail Jackson **z** 70748; rural
Staring; RMC Place; EAST BATON ROUGE; ★ **B.R.**; mail Baton Rouge **z** 70801; pop. incl. with Baton Rouge (Inc. Place)
Starks; RMC Place; CALCASIEU; **182** H-2; elev. 33ft./10m.; 🅿; **z** 70661; ● 950
Start (Goff); RMC Place; RICHLAND; **182** B-6; elev. 75ft./23m.; 🅿; **z** 71279; ● 420
State Line; RMC Place; WASHINGTON; ***182** F-9; mail Franklinton **z** 70438; rural
Stella; RMC Place; PLAQUEMINES; ***182** I-9; elev. 9ft./3m.; mail Braithwaite **z** 70040
Stephensville; RMC Place; ST. MARTIN; ***182** I-7; mail Morgan City **z** 70380; ● 500
Sterlington; Inc. Place; OUACHITA; **182** B-5; elev. 80ft./24m.; 🅿 🅷; ★ **MONR**; **z** 71280; Ⓟ 1,140; © 1,276
Stevensdale; RMC Place; EAST BATON ROUGE; ***182** G-7; ★ **B.R.**; mail Baton Rouge **z** 70815; pop. incl. with Baton Rouge (Inc. Place)
Stevenson; RMC Place; MOREHOUSE; ***182** A-5; mail Bastrop **z** 71220; rural
Stonewall; Inc. Place; DE SOTO; **182** C-2; elev. 220ft./67m.; 🅿; **z** 71078; Ⓟ 1,266; © 1,668
Stoney Point; RMC Place; WASHINGTON; ***182** F-9; mail Franklinton **z** 70438; rural
Sugarcreek; RMC Place; CLAIBORNE; ***182** B-3; elev. 317ft./97m.; mail Arcadia **z** 71001; rural
Sugartown; RMC Place; BEAUREGARD; **182** F-3; elev. 172ft./52m.; 🅿; **z** 70662; ● 150
Sulphur; Inc. Place; CALCASIEU; **182** H-2; elev. 15ft./5m.; 🅿 🅷; ★ **LKCH**; **z** 70663-65; Ⓟ 20,125; © 20,512; ◆ 19,245
Sulphur South; CALCASIEU; see South Acres (RMC Place)
Summerfield; RMC Place; CLAIBORNE; **182** A-4; elev. 237ft./72m.; 🅿; **z** 71079; ● 180
Summerfield; RMC Place; GRANT; ***182** E-4; mail Colfax **z** 71417; rural
Summer Grove; RMC Place; CADDO; ***182** C-2; ★ **SHRE**; mail Shreveport **z** 71108, **z** 71118; pop. incl. with Shreveport (Inc. Place)
Summer Grove Estates; RMC Place; CADDO; ★ **SHRE**; pop. incl. with Shreveport (Inc. Place)
Summerville; RMC Place; LA SALLE; ***182** D-5; mail Olla **z** 71465; ● 150
Sun; Inc. Place; ST. TAMMANY; **182** G-10; elev. 80ft./24m.; 🅿; **z** 70463; Ⓟ 429; © 471
Sunnybrook; RMC Place; EAST BATON ROUGE; **182** A-13; ★ **B.R.**; mail Baton Rouge **z** 70814; ● 800
Sunny Hill; RMC Place; WASHINGTON; ***182** F-9; mail Franklinton **z** 70438; ● 50
Sunrise; RMC Place; PLAQUEMINES; ***182** J-10; mail Empire **z** 70050; ● 100
Sunrise; RMC Place; WEST BATON ROUGE; **182** B-12; ★ **B.R.**; mail Port Allen **z** 70767; ● 400
Sunset; Inc. Place; ST. LANDRY; **182** G-5; elev. 5ft./2m.; 🅿; ★ **LAF**; **z** 70584; Ⓟ 2,201; © 2,352
Sunshine; RMC Place; IBERVILLE; ***182** H-7; elev. 200ft./61m.; 🅿; ★ **B.R.**; **z** 70780; pop. incl. with Saint Gabriel (Inc. Place)
Sun Spur; RMC Place; RICHLAND; ***182** B-6; mail Delhi **z** 71232; rural
Supreme; CDP; ASSUMPTION; ***182** I-7; mail Napoleonville **z** 70390; Ⓟ 1,020; © 1,119
Susan Park; RMC Place; JEFFERSON; ***182** I-9; ★ **N.O.**; mail Kenner **z** 70062
Swampers; RMC Place; FRANKLIN; ***182** C-6; mail Winnsboro **z** 71295; rural
Swartz; CDP; OUACHITA; **182** B-5; elev. 94ft./29m.; 🅿; ★ **MONR**; **z** 71281; Ⓟ 3,698; © 4,247
Sweet Lake; RMC Place; CAMERON; ***182** H-3; elev. 34ft./10m.; mail Bell City **z** 70630, Lake Charles **z** 70605; ● 100
Swindleville; BOSSIER; see Hughes (RMC Place)
Swords; RMC Place; ST. LANDRY; ***182** G-5; mail Church Point **z** 70525; rural

T

Taconey; RMC Place; CONCORDIA; ***182** E-6; ★ **NCHZ**; mail Vidalia **z** 71373; ● 300
Taft; CDP; ST. CHARLES; ***182** H-8; ★ **N.O.**; mail Hahnville **z** 70057; © 0
Talisheek; RMC Place; ST. TAMMANY; **182** G-10; elev. 59ft./18m.; 🅿; **z** 70464; ● 400
Talla Bena; RMC Place; MADISON; **182** B-7; mail Sondheimer **z** 71276; ● 50
Tall Timbers; RMC Place; ORLEANS; ★ **N.O.**; pop. incl. with New Orleans (Inc. Place)
Tallulah; Inc. Place; ⊡ MADISON; **182** C-7; elev. 87ft./27m.; 🅿 🅷; **z** 71282, **z** 71284; Ⓟ 8,526; © 9,189
Tangipahoa; Inc. Place; TANGIPAHOA; **182** F-8; elev. 179ft./55m.; 🅿; **z** 70465; Ⓟ 569; © 747
TANGIPAHOA; **182** G-8; Ⓟ 85,709; © 100,588; ◆ 118,979
Tanglewood; RMC Place; EAST BATON ROUGE; ***182** G-7; ★ **B.R.**; mail Baton Rouge **z** 70811; ● 950
Tanglewood; RMC Place; RAPIDES; ★ **ALEX**; mail Alexandria **z** 71301; ● 600
Tannehill; RMC Place; WINN; ***182** D-4; elev. 136ft./41m.; mail Dodson **z** 71422
Tate Cove; RMC Place; EVANGELINE; ***182** G-5; elev. 79ft./24m.; mail Ville Platte **z** 70586; ● 80
Taylor (Nelson); RMC Place; BIENVILLE; ***182** B-3; elev. 226ft./69m.; 🅿; **z** 71080; ● 50
Taylortown; RMC Place; BOSSIER; ***182** C-2; mail Elm Grove **z** 71051
Taylortown; RMC Place; UNION; ***182** A-4; mail Spearsville **z** 71277; ● 50
Tchefuncte Club Estates; RMC Place; ST. TAMMANY; ***182** G-9; ★ **N.O.**; mail Covington **z** 70433; ● 1,000
Temple; RMC Place; VERNON; ***182** E-3; elev. 281ft./86m.; 🅿; **z** 71474; rural
Tendal; RMC Place; MADISON; ***182** C-7; mail Tallulah **z** 71282; ● 50
TENSAS; **182** C-6; Ⓟ 7,103; © 6,618; ◆ 5,480
TERREBONNE; **182** I-7; Ⓟ 96,982; © 104,503; ◆ 105,714
Terry; RMC Place; WEST CARROLL; **182** A-7; elev. 110ft./34m.; 🅿; **z** 71263; ● 150
Terrytown; CDP; JEFFERSON; **182** E-14; 🅿; ★ **N.O.**; **z** 70056 & mail Gretna **z** 70053; Ⓟ 23,787; © 25,430; ◆ 22,627
The Bend; ST. JAMES; see Remy (RMC Place)
Theriot; RMC Place; TERREBONNE; **182** J-8; elev. 5ft./2m.; 🅿; **z** 70397; ● 200
The Rock; RMC Place; GRANT; ***182** E-4; mail Colfax **z** 71417; ● 150
The Y; EVANGELINE; see Barber Spur (RMC Place)
Thibodaux; Inc. Place; ⊡ LAFOURCHE; **182** I-8; elev. 15ft./5m.; 🅿 🅷 🅲 6,814 ■; ★ **HOMA-**; **z** 70301-02, **z** 70310; Ⓟ 14,035; © 14,431; ◆ 14,351
Thomas; RMC Place; WASHINGTON; ***182** F-9; mail Franklinton **z** 70438; ● 60
Thomastown; RMC Place; MADISON; ***182** C-7; elev. 90ft./27m.; mail Tallulah **z** 71282; rural
Thornwell; RMC Place; JEFFERSON DAVIS; **182** H-4; mail Lake Arthur **z** 70549; ● 190
Three Oaks; RMC Place; ST. BERNARD; ★ **N.O.**; mail Arabi **z** 70032
Three Rivers Heights; RMC Place; ST. TAMMANY; ***182** G-9; ★ **N.O.**; mail Madisonville **z** 70447; ● 150
Tickfaw; Inc. Place; TANGIPAHOA; **182** G-8; elev. 64ft./20m.; 🅿; **z** 70466; Ⓟ 565; © 617
Tidewater; RMC Place; PLAQUEMINES; ***182** J-11; mail Venice **z** 70091; ● 50
Tigerville; RMC Place; ST. JOHN THE BAPTIST; ***182** H-8; mail Edgard **z** 70049; ● 480
Timberlane; CDP-Census Area Only; JEFFERSON; ***182** I-9; ★ **N.O.**; mail Gretna **z** 70056; Ⓟ 12,614; © 11,405
Timber Trails; RMC Place; RAPIDES; ***182** E-4; elev. 154ft./47m.; ★ **ALEX**; mail Alexandria **z** 71301, Pineville **z** 71360; ● 400
Tioga; RMC Place; RAPIDES; **182** E-4; elev. 151ft./46m.; 🅿; ★ **ALEX**; **z** 71477; ● 1,300
Toca; RMC Place; ST. BERNARD; ***182** I-10; elev. 5ft./2m.; ★ **N.O.**; mail Saint Bernard **z** 70085; ● 310
Toomey; RMC Place; CALCASIEU; ***182** H-2; mail Vinton **z** 70668; ● 50
Topsy; RMC Place; JEFFERSON DAVIS; ***182** G-3; elev. 25ft./8m.; mail Lake Charles **z** 70611; ● 100
Torbert; RMC Place; POINTE COUPEE; ***182** G-6; elev. 23ft./7m.; 🅿; **z** 70762; ● 160
Toro; RMC Place; SABINE; ***182** E-2; mail Florien **z** 71429
Torras; RMC Place; POINTE COUPEE; ***182** F-6; mail Lettsworth **z** 70753; ● 50
Tower Park; RMC Place; VERNON; ***182** F-3; mail Leesville **z** 71446; pop. incl. with Leesville (Inc. Place)
Town and Country; RMC Place; OUACHITA; ***182** B-5; ★ **MONR**; mail Monroe **z** 71201; ● 1,300
Transylvania; RMC Place; EAST CARROLL; **182** B-7; elev. 100ft./30m.; 🅿; **z** 71286; ● 180
Trees; RMC Place; CADDO; **182** B-1; elev. 222ft./68m.; 🅿; **z** 71082; ● 160
Tremont; RMC Place; LINCOLN; ***182** B-4; elev. 116ft./35m.; mail Choudrant **z** 71227; rural
Trenton; RMC Place; DE SOTO; ***182** D-2; mail Mansfield **z** 71052; rural
Trinity; RMC Place; CATAHOULA; ***182** D-6; mail Jonesville **z** 71343; ● 130
Trinity; RMC Place; IBERVILLE; mail Rosedale **z** 70772; pop. incl. with Rosedale (Inc. Place)
Triumph; RMC Place; PLAQUEMINES; **182** J-11; elev. 10ft./3m.; mail Buras **z** 70041; ● 1,080
Tropical Bend; RMC Place; PLAQUEMINES; ***182** J-10; mail Empire **z** 70050; ● 150
Trout; RMC Place; LA SALLE; **182** D-5; elev. 200ft./61m.; 🅿; **z** 71371; ● 200
Troy; RMC Place; TENSAS; ***182** D-6; mail Waterproof **z** 71375; rural
Truxno; RMC Place; UNION; ***182** A-4; mail Marion **z** 71260; ● 100
Tullos; Inc. Place; LA SALLE, WINN; **182** D-5; elev. 143ft./44m.; 🅿; **z** 71479; Ⓟ 427; © 419
Tunica; RMC Place; WEST FELICIANA; **182** F-6; elev. 200ft./61m.; 🅿; **z** 70782; ● 230
Tunica-Biloxi Reservation; Indian Reservation; AVOYELLES; © 89
Turkey Creek; Inc. Place; EVANGELINE; **182** F-4; elev. 130ft./40m.; 🅿; **z** 70585; Ⓟ 283; © 356
Turnerville; RMC Place; IBERVILLE; ★ **B.R.**; mail Plaquemine **z** 70764; pop. incl. with Plaquemine (Inc. Place)
Turps; RMC Place; BEAUREGARD; ***182** G-3; mail Ragley **z** 70657; rural
Twin Oaks; RMC Place; MOREHOUSE; ***182** A-6; mail Bonita **z** 71223; rural

U

Uncle Sam; RMC Place; ST. JAMES; ***182** H-8; elev. 20ft./6m.; 🅿; **z** 70792; rural
Uneedus; RMC Place; TANGIPAHOA; ***182** G-9; mail Folsom **z** 70437, Loranger **z** 70446; rural
Union; RMC Place; ST. JAMES; ***182** H-8; mail Convent **z** 70723; ● 300
UNION; **182** A-4; Ⓟ 20,690; © 22,803; ◆ 22,437
Union Church; RMC Place; BIENVILLE; ***182** C-4; mail Quitman **z** 71268; rural
Union Hill; RMC Place; RAPIDES; ***182** F-4; elev. 198ft./60m.; mail Glenmora **z** 71433; rural
Union Hill; RMC Place; WINN; ***182** D-4; mail Montgomery **z** 71454, Winnfield **z** 71483; ● 50
Union Landing; RMC Place; LIVINGSTON; ***182** H-8; elev. 5ft./2m.; mail Livingston **z** 70754; rural
Union Springs (Hatcher); RMC Place; SABINE; ***182** D-2; mail Converse **z** 71419; rural
Unionville; RMC Place; LINCOLN; ***182** B-4; elev. 229ft./70m.; mail Dubach **z** 71235; rural
University Gardens; RMC Place; EAST BATON ROUGE; ★ **B.R.**; pop. incl. with Baton Rouge (Inc. Place)
University Hills; RMC Place; EAST BATON ROUGE; ★ **B.R.**; pop. incl. with Baton Rouge (Inc. Place)
University Place; RMC Place; CALCASIEU; ***182** H-3; ★ **LKCH**; pop. incl. with Lake Charles (Inc. Place)
Upland; RMC Place; MOREHOUSE; ***182** B-5; mail Bastrop **z** 71220; rural
Upstream; RMC Place; JEFFERSON; ★ **N.O.**; mail New Orleans **z** 70123
Uptown; RMC Place; ORLEANS; ★ **N.O.**; mail New Orleans **z** 70115, **z** 70175; pop. incl. with New Orleans (Inc. Place)
Urania; Inc. Place; LA SALLE; **182** D-5; elev. 92ft./28m.; 🅿; **z** 71480; Ⓟ 782; © 700
Utility; RMC Place; CATAHOULA; ***182** E-5; elev. 56ft./17m.; mail Jonesville **z** 71343; rural

V

Vacherie; ST. JAMES; see North Vacherie (CDP-Census Area Only)
Valentine; LAFOURCHE; see Jay (RMC Place)
Valmar; RMC Place; ST. BERNARD; ★ **N.O.**; mail Meraux **z** 70075
Valverda; RMC Place; POINTE COUPEE; ***182** G-6; mail Maringouin **z** 70757; ● 100
Vanceville; RMC Place; BOSSIER; ***182** B-2; ★ **SHRE**; mail Bossier City **z** 71111; rural
Varnado; Inc. Place; WASHINGTON; **182** F-10; elev. 120ft./37m.; 🅿; **z** 70467; Ⓟ 236; © 342
Vatican; RMC Place; LAFAYETTE; ***182** H-5; ★ **LAF**; mail Carencro **z** 70520; rural
Vaughn; RMC Place; MOREHOUSE; ***182** A-5; mail Bastrop **z** 71220; rural
Velma; RMC Place; TANGIPAHOA; ***182** G-8; mail Amite **z** 70422; ● 50
Venice; RMC Place; PLAQUEMINES; **182** J-11; 🅿; **z** 70091; ● 500
Ventress; RMC Place; POINTE COUPEE; ***182** G-6; elev. 25ft./8m.; 🅿; **z** 70783; ● 420
Verda; RMC Place; GRANT; **182** D-4; elev. 157ft./48m.; 🅿; **z** 71454; ● 150
Verdun; RMC Place; LIVINGSTON; ***182** H-8; elev. 20ft./6m.; mail Livingston **z** 70754; rural
Verdunville; RMC Place; ST. MARY; ***182** I-7; mail Franklin **z** 70538; ● 350
VERMILION; **182** I-4; Ⓟ 50,055; © 53,807; ◆ 55,814
Vernon; RMC Place; JACKSON; **182** C-4; elev. 271ft./83m.; mail Ruston **z** 71270; ● 30
VERNON; **182** F-3; Ⓟ 61,961; © 52,531; ◆ 45,528
Verret; RMC Place; ST. BERNARD; ***182** I-10; elev. 6ft./2m.; ★ **N.O.**; mail Saint Bernard **z** 70085; ● 230
Verrett; RMC Place; CALCASIEU; ***182** H-3; mail Iowa **z** 70647; rural
Vick; RMC Place; AVOYELLES; ***182** E-5; elev. 60ft./18m.; 🅿; **z** 71331; ● 50
Vidalia; Inc. Place; ⊡ CONCORDIA; **182** E-6; elev. 65ft./20m.; 🅿; ★ **NCHZ**; **z** 71373; Ⓟ 4,953; © 4,543
Vidrine; RMC Place; EVANGELINE; **182** G-4; elev. 71ft./22m.; mail Ville Platte **z** 70586; ● 150
Vienna; Inc. Place; LINCOLN; **182** B-4; elev. 269ft./82m.; mail Ruston **z** 71270; Ⓟ 404; © 424
Vieux Carre; RMC Place; ORLEANS; ***182** H-9; ★ **N.O.**; mail New Orleans **z** 70112, **z** 70172; pop. incl. with New Orleans (Inc. Place)
Villa De Rey; RMC Place; EAST BATON ROUGE; ★ **B.R.**; pop. incl. with Baton Rouge (Inc. Place)
Village East; RMC Place; TERREBONNE; ***182** I-8; ★ **HOMA-**; mail Houma **z** 70360; ● 950
Village Saint George; CDP; EAST BATON ROUGE; ***182** G-7; ★ **B.R.**; mail Baton Rouge **z** 70808; Ⓟ 6,242; © 6,993
Ville Platte; Inc. Place; ⊡ EVANGELINE; **182** G-5; elev. 75ft./23m.; 🅿 🅷; **z** 70586; Ⓟ 9,037; © 8,145; Ⓡ 8,596
Vincent Landing; RMC Place; CALCASIEU; ***182** H-2; ★ **LKCH**; mail Sulphur **z** 70665; ● 100
Vincent Park; RMC Place; ST. BERNARD; ★ **N.O.**; mail Meraux **z** 70075
Vinton; Inc. Place; CALCASIEU; **182** H-2; elev. 19ft./6m.; 🅿; **z** 70668; Ⓟ 3,154; © 3,338
Violet; CDP; ST. BERNARD; ***182** I-10; elev. 5ft./2m.; 🅿; ★ **N.O.**; **z** 70092; Ⓟ 8,574; © 8,555
Vivian; Inc. Place; CADDO; **182** A-1; elev. 240ft./73m.; 🅿 🅷; **z** 71082; Ⓟ 4,156; © 4,031
Vixen; RMC Place; CALDWELL; ***182** C-5; mail Columbia **z** 71418; ● 30
Voorhies; RMC Place; AVOYELLES; ***182** F-5; mail Moreauville **z** 71355; rural
Vowells Mill; RMC Place; NATCHITOCHES; ***182** E-3; elev. 225ft./69m.; mail Robeline **z** 71469; ● 30

W

Wadesboro; RMC Place; TANGIPAHOA; ***182** G-8; mail Ponchatoula **z** 70454; ● 50
Waggaman; CDP; JEFFERSON; **182** E-11; ★ **N.O.**; mail Westwego **z** 70094; Ⓟ 9,405; © 9,435
Wakefield; RMC Place; WEST FELICIANA; **182** F-7; elev. 220ft./67m.; 🅿; **z** 70784; ● 110
Waldheim; RMC Place; ST. TAMMANY; ***182** G-9; mail Covington **z** 70435; rural
Walker; RMC Place; JACKSON; ***182** C-4; mail Jonesboro **z** 71251; rural
Walker; Inc. Place; LIVINGSTON; **182** G-8; elev. 46ft./14m.; 🅿; ★ **B.R.**; **z** 70785; Ⓟ 3,727; © 4,801
Wallace; CDP; ST. JOHN THE BAPTIST; ***182** H-8; mail Edgard **z** 70049; © 570
Wallace Ridge; RMC Place; CATAHOULA; ***182** D-6; elev. 63ft./19m.; mail Jonesville **z** 71343
Walls; RMC Place; WEST BATON ROUGE; ***182** G-7; mail Port Allen **z** 70767; rural
Walters; RMC Place; CATAHOULA; **182** E-5; elev. 62ft./19m.; mail Jonesville **z** 71343; ● 50
Ward; RMC Place; ALLEN; ***182** G-4; mail Oakdale **z** 71463; rural
Warden (Richland); RMC Place; RICHLAND; **182** B-6; elev. 90ft./27m.; 🅿; **z** 71232; ● 90
Wardview; RMC Place; BOSSIER; ***182** A-2; elev. 203ft./62m.; mail Plain Dealing **z** 71064; rural
Wardville; RMC Place; MOREHOUSE; ***182** A-5; mail Bastrop **z** 71220; rural
Wardville; RMC Place; RAPIDES; **182** E-4; ★ **ALEX**; mail Pineville **z** 71360; ● 1,200
Warnerton; RMC Place; WASHINGTON; ***182** F-9; elev. 203ft./62m.; mail Franklinton **z** 70438
Warsaw Landing; RMC Place; LIVINGSTON; ***182** G-8; mail Springfield **z** 70462; ● 50
Washington; Inc. Place; ST. LANDRY; **182** G-5; elev. 63ft./19m.; 🅿; **z** 70589; Ⓟ 1,253; © 1,082
WASHINGTON; **182** F-9; Ⓟ 43,185; © 43,926; ◆ 46,615
Waterloo; RMC Place; POINTE COUPEE; ***182** G-7; elev. 35ft./11m.; mail Ventress **z** 70783; ● 100
Waterproof; Inc. Place; TENSAS; **182** D-7; elev. 83ft./25m.; 🅿; **z** 71375; Ⓟ 1,080; © 834
Waterproof; RMC Place; TERREBONNE; ***182** I-8; ★ **HOMA-**; mail Houma **z** 70360; rural
Watson; RMC Place; LIVINGSTON; **182** G-7; elev. 68ft./21m.; 🅿; ★ **B.R.**; **z** 70786; ● 600
Waverly; RMC Place; MADISON; ***182** C-6; 🅿; **z** 71232
Waxia; RMC Place; ST. LANDRY; ***182** G-5; elev. 35ft./11m.; mail Washington **z** 70589; ● 30
Weaver; NATCHITOCHES; see Flora (RMC Place)
Weber City; RMC Place; ASCENSION; ***182** H-8; ★ **B.R.**; mail Gonzales **z** 70737; ● 150
WEBSTER; **182** B-2; Ⓟ 41,989; © 41,831; ◆ 40,464
Weil; RMC Place; RAPIDES; ***182** E-4; ★ **ALEX**; mail Alexandria **z** 71301, **z** 71303; rural
Weiss; RMC Place; LIVINGSTON; ***182** G-8; ★ **B.R.**; mail Walker **z** 70785; rural
Welcome; RMC Place; ST. JAMES; **182** H-8; elev. 17ft./5m.; mail Saint James **z** 70086; ● 450
Weldon; RMC Place; CLAIBORNE; ***182** B-4; elev. 178ft./54m.; mail Bernice **z** 71222; ● 80
Welsh; Inc. Place; JEFFERSON DAVIS; **182** H-4; 🅿 🅷; **z** 70591; Ⓟ 3,299; © 3,380
Wemple; RMC Place; DE SOTO; ***182** D-2; elev. 172ft./52m.; mail Mansfield **z** 71052; rural
Werner Park; RMC Place; CADDO; ★ **SHRE**; pop. incl. with Shreveport (Inc. Place)
WEST BATON ROUGE; **182** G-7; Ⓟ 19,419; © 21,601; ◆ 23,319
WEST CARROLL; **182** B-6; Ⓟ 12,093; © 12,314; ◆ 11,232
Westdale; RMC Place; EAST BATON ROUGE; ★ **B.R.**; pop. incl. with Baton Rouge (Inc. Place)
Westdale; RMC Place; RED RIVER; ***182** C-2; elev. 138ft./42m.; mail Shreveport **z** 71105; rural
West End; RMC Place; ORLEANS; ★ **N.O.**; pop. incl. with New Orleans (Inc. Place)
Western Hills; RMC Place; CADDO; ★ **SHRE**; pop. incl. with Shreveport (Inc. Place)
Western Kraft; RMC Place; NATCHITOCHES; mail Campti **z** 71411; rural
WEST FELICIANA; **182** F-6; Ⓟ 12,915; © 15,111; ◆ 14,886
West Ferriday; CDP-Census Area Only; CONCORDIA; ***182** D-6; ★ **NCHZ**; mail Ferriday **z** 71334; Ⓟ 1,632; © 1,541
Westfield; RMC Place; ASSUMPTION; ***182** H-7; mail Napoleonville **z** 70390; rural
Westgate; RMC Place; JEFFERSON; ***182** H-9; ★ **N.O.**
Westlake; Inc. Place; CALCASIEU; **182** H-3; 🅿; ★ **LKCH**; **z** 70669; Ⓟ 5,007; © 4,668
Westminster; CDP; EAST BATON ROUGE; **182** C-13; ★ **B.R.**; mail Baton Rouge **z** 70809; Ⓟ 2,582; © 2,515
West Monroe; Inc. Place; OUACHITA; **182** B-5; elev. 88ft./27m.; 🅿 🅷 ■; ★ **MONR**; **z** 71291-92, **z** 71294; Ⓟ 14,096; © 13,250; ◆ 12,852
Weston; RMC Place; JACKSON; ***182** C-4; elev. 283ft./86m.; mail Jonesboro **z** 71251; ● 50
Westover; RMC Place; WEST BATON ROUGE; ***182** G-7; ★ **B.R.**; mail Port Allen **z** 70767; ● 50
West Pointe a la Hache; RMC Place; PLAQUEMINES; ***182** I-10; elev. 3ft./1m.; mail Port Sulphur **z** 70083; ● 100
Westport; RMC Place; RAPIDES; ***182** F-4; mail Pitkin **z** 70656
Westside; RMC Place; RAPIDES; ★ **ALEX**; mail Alexandria **z** 71301, **z** 71315; pop. incl. with Alexandria (Inc. Place)
West Slidell; RMC Place; ST. TAMMANY; ***182** H-10; ★ **N.O.**; mail Slidell **z** 70460; pop. incl. with Slidell (Inc. Place)
Westwego; Inc. Place; JEFFERSON; **182** I-9; elev. 5ft./2m.; 🅿; ★ **N.O.**; **z** 70094, **z** 70096; Ⓟ 11,218; © 10,763
Weyanoke; RMC Place; WEST FELICIANA; **182** F-6; elev. 154ft./47m.; 🅿; **z** 70787; ● 150
Wheeling; RMC Place; WINN; ***182** D-4; elev. 232ft./71m.; mail Montgomery **z** 71454; rural
White; RMC Place; LAFOURCHE; ***182** I-8; ★ **HOMA-**; mail Thibodaux **z** 70301; rural
White Castle; Inc. Place; IBERVILLE; **182** H-7; 🅿; **z** 70788; Ⓟ 2,102; © 1,946
Whitehall (High Point); RMC Place; LA SALLE; ***182** D-5; elev. 95ft./29m.; mail Jena **z** 71342; ● 90
Whitehall; RMC Place; LIVINGSTON; ***182** H-8; elev. 14ft./4m.; mail Maurepas **z** 70449; ● 50
White Hall; RMC Place; ST. JAMES; ***182** H-8; mail Convent **z** 70723
White Hills; RMC Place; EAST BATON ROUGE; ***182** G-7; ★ **B.R.**; mail Baker **z** 70714; ● 630
White Sulphur Springs; RMC Place; LA SALLE; ***182** E-5; elev. 95ft./29m.; mail Trout **z** 71371; ● 30
Whiteville; RMC Place; ST. LANDRY; ***182** F-5; elev. 45ft./14m.; mail Bunkie **z** 71322; ● 30
Whittington; RMC Place; RAPIDES; ***182** F-5; mail Alexandria **z** 71301; rural
Wickland Terrace; RMC Place; EAST BATON ROUGE; **182** B-14; ★ **B.R.**; mail Baton Rouge **z** 70816; pop. incl. with Baton Rouge (Inc. Place)
Wickliffe; RMC Place; POINTE COUPEE; ***182** G-7; mail Ventress **z** 70783; rural
Wildsville; RMC Place; CONCORDIA; ***182** D-6; elev. 57ft./17m.; 🅿; **z** 71377; ● 500
Wildwood; RMC Place; ASSUMPTION; ***182** I-7; elev. 12ft./4m.; mail Napoleonville **z** 70390; rural
Wildwood; RMC Place; EAST BATON ROUGE; ***182** G-7; ★ **B.R.**; mail Baton Rouge **z** 70808; pop. incl. with Baton Rouge (Inc. Place)
Willhite; RMC Place; UNION; ***182** B-5; elev. 138ft./42m.; mail Downsville **z** 71234; rural
Williams; RMC Place; RED RIVER; ***182** C-2; elev. 145ft./44m.; mail Shreveport **z** 71105; rural
Williana; RMC Place; GRANT; ***182** D-4; mail Dry Prong **z** 71423; ● 50
Willowdale; RMC Place; JEFFERSON; ***182** H-9; ★ **N.O.**
Willow Glen; RMC Place; RAPIDES; **182** E-4; ★ **ALEX**; mail Alexandria **z** 71301-02; ● 500
Wills Point; RMC Place; PLAQUEMINES; ***182** I-9; elev. 6ft./2m.; mail Braithwaite **z** 70040; ● 100
Wilmer; RMC Place; TANGIPAHOA; ***182** F-9; elev. 203ft./62m.; mail Kentwood **z** 70444; ● 100
Wilshire Park; RMC Place; RAPIDES; ★ **ALEX**; mail Alexandria **z** 71301, **z** 71303; ● 550
Wilson; Inc. Place; EAST FELICIANA; **182** F-7; elev. 256ft./78m.; 🅿; **z** 70789; Ⓟ 707; © 668
Wilsona; RMC Place; TENSAS; ***182** D-7; mail Saint Joseph **z** 71366; rural
Wilson Place; RMC Place; EAST BATON ROUGE; ★ **B.R.**; pop. incl. with Baton Rouge (Inc. Place)
Wilson Point; RMC Place; RAPIDES; ***182** F-5; mail Alexandria **z** 71301; rural
Wilton Subdivision; RMC Place; CADDO; mail Shreveport **z** 71107; ● 200
Windsor Place; RMC Place; EAST BATON ROUGE; ★ **B.R.**; pop. incl. with Baton Rouge (Inc. Place)
WINN; **182** D-4; Ⓟ 16,269; © 16,894; ◆ 15,160
Winnfield; Inc. Place; ⊡ WINN; **182** D-4; elev. 143ft./44m.; 🅿 🅷; **z** 71483 & mail Saint Maurice **z** 71471; Ⓟ 6,138; © 5,749
Winnsboro; Inc. Place; ⊡ FRANKLIN; **182** C-6; elev. 70ft./21m.; 🅿 🅷; **z** 71295; Ⓟ 5,755; © 5,344
Winter Gardens; RMC Place; CADDO; ★ **SHRE**; pop. incl. with Shreveport (Inc. Place)
Wisner; Inc. Place; FRANKLIN; **182** D-6; 🅿; **z** 71378; Ⓟ 1,153; © 1,140
Womack; RMC Place; JACKSON; ***182** C-4; elev. 181ft./55m.; mail Chatham **z** 71226; rural
Womack; RMC Place; RED RIVER; ***182** C-3; elev. 174ft./53m.; mail Ringgold **z** 71068; rural
Woodardville (Giddens); RMC Place; BIENVILLE; ***182** C-3; mail Ringgold **z** 71068; rural
Woodhaven; RMC Place; TANGIPAHOA; ***182** G-8; elev. 50ft./15m.; mail Tickfaw **z** 70466; ● 300
Wood Lake; RMC Place; ST. BERNARD; ***182** I-10; mail Saint Bernard **z** 70085; ● 30
Woodland; RMC Place; EAST FELICIANA; **182** F-7; rural
Woodland; RMC Place; PLAQUEMINES; ***182** I-10; elev. 6ft./2m.; mail Port Sulphur **z** 70083; rural
Woodland Estates; RMC Place; ORLEANS; ★ **N.O.**; pop. incl. with New Orleans (Inc. Place)
Woodlawn; RMC Place; ASSUMPTION; ***182** I-7; mail Napoleonville **z** 70390; rural
Woodlawn; RMC Place; EAST BATON ROUGE; ★ **B.R.**; mail Baton Rouge **z** 70816-17, **z** 70879
Woodlawn; RMC Place; JEFFERSON DAVIS; **182** H-3; elev. 28ft./9m.; mail Iowa **z** 70647; ● 250
Woodlawn (Linwood); RMC Place; PLAQUEMINES; ***182** I-9; mail Braithwaite **z** 70040; rural
Woodlawn; RMC Place; TERREBONNE; ***182** I-8; ★ **HOMA-**; mail Houma **z** 70360; pop. incl. with Houma (Inc. Place)
Woodmere; CDP-Census Area Only; JEFFERSON; ***182** I-9; ★ **N.O.**; © 13,058
Woodside; RMC Place; AVOYELLES, ST. LANDRY; ***182** F-6; mail Melville **z** 71353; rural
Woodville; RMC Place; LINCOLN; ***182** B-4; mail Ruston **z** 71270; rural
Woodworth; Inc. Place; RAPIDES; **182** F-4; 🅿; ★ **ALEX**; **z** 71485; Ⓟ 754; © 1,080
Wright (Haire); RMC Place; VERMILION; ***182** H-4; mail Kaplan **z** 70548; rural
Wyandotte; RMC Place; ST. MARY; **182** I-7; mail Morgan City **z** 70380; pop. incl. with Morgan City (Inc. Place)
Wyatt; RMC Place; JACKSON; ***182** C-4; elev. 184ft./56m.; mail Jonesboro **z** 71251

Y

Yellow Pine; RMC Place; WEBSTER; ***182** B-3; elev. 198ft./60m.; mail Sibley **z** 71073; rural
Youngsville; Inc. Place; LAFAYETTE; **182** H-5; elev. 25ft./8m.; 🅿; ★ **LAF**; **z** 70592; Ⓟ 1,195; © 3,992
Yscloskey; ST. BERNARD; see Alluvial City (RMC Place)

Z

Zachary; Inc. Place; EAST BATON ROUGE; **182** G-7; 🅿 🅷; ★ **B.R.**; **z** 70791; Ⓟ 9,036; © 11,275
Zebedee; RMC Place; RICHLAND; mail Rayville **z** 71269; rural
Zenoria; RMC Place; LA SALLE; ***182** D-5; mail Trout **z** 71371; ● 30
Zion; RMC Place; GRANT; ***182** D-4; elev. 134ft./41m.; mail Georgetown **z** 71432; rural
Zion City; RMC Place; EAST BATON ROUGE; ***182** G-7; ★ **B.R.**; mail Baton Rouge **z** 70811; pop. incl. with Baton Rouge (Inc. Place)
Zwolle; Inc. Place; SABINE; **182** D-2; elev. 148ft./45m.; 🅿; **z** 71486; Ⓟ 1,779; © 1,783
Zylks; RMC Place; CADDO; **182** A-1; elev. 211ft./64m.; mail Rodessa **z** 71069; ● 60

MAINE

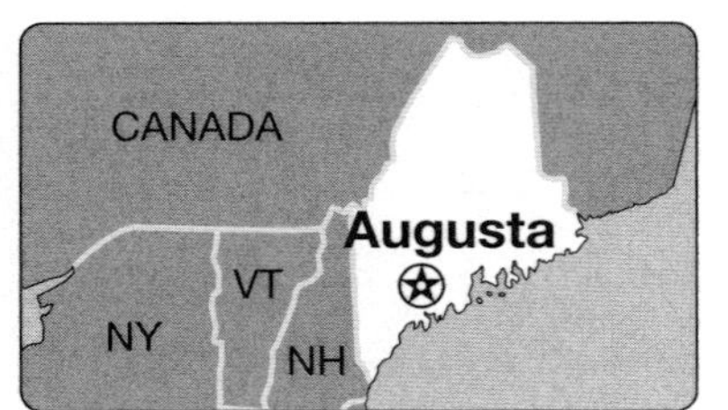

Statistics

Total area (2000) — 35,385 square miles
Land area (2000) — 30,862 square miles
Water area (2000) — 4,523 square miles
Capital — Augusta
Admitted as state — March, 1820

Maps

State maps can be found on pages 142-254 in Vol. 1
County Subdivision maps can be found on pages 255-271 in Vol. 1

Ranally Metro Areas (RMAs) and Abbreviations

Augusta, ME — AUG
Bangor, ME — BANG
Brunswick-Bath, ME — BR-BA
Lewiston-Auburn, ME — LEW-
Portland, ME — POR
Portsmouth-Dover-Rochester, NH-ME — PTSM-
Waterville, ME — WATRVL

Principal Places

Place Name	Place Type	County	Population
Portland	Inc. Place	CUMBERLAND	◆ 62,982
Lewiston	Inc. Place	ANDROSCOGGIN	◆ 34,356
Bangor	Inc. Place	PENOBSCOT	◆ 31,643
South Portland	Inc. Place	CUMBERLAND	◆ 23,090
Auburn	Inc. Place	ANDROSCOGGIN	◆ 23,029
Brunswick	MCD-Town	CUMBERLAND	◆ 21,179
Sanford	MCD-Town	YORK	◆ 19,316
Biddeford	Inc. Place	YORK	◆ 19,236
Scarborough	MCD-Town	CUMBERLAND	◆ 18,143
Augusta	Inc. Place	KENNEBEC	◆ 17,502
Saco	Inc. Place	YORK	© 16,822
Westbrook	Inc. Place	CUMBERLAND	◆ 16,495
Windham	MCD-Town	CUMBERLAND	◆ 15,747
York	MCD-Town	YORK	◆ 15,651
Waterville	Inc. Place	KENNEBEC	◆ 15,353
Brunswick	CDP	CUMBERLAND	◆ 15,165
Gorham	MCD-Town	CUMBERLAND	◆ 14,913
Falmouth	MCD-Town	CUMBERLAND	◆ 10,958
Kennebunk	MCD-Town	YORK	© 10,476
Sanford	CDP	YORK	© 10,133
Kittery	MCD-Town	YORK	◆ 9,968
Standish	MCD-Town	CUMBERLAND	◆ 9,689
Old Orchard Beach	MCD-Town	YORK	◆ 9,683
Wells	MCD-Town	YORK	© 9,400
Brewer	Inc. Place	PENOBSCOT	◆ 9,290
Orono	MCD-Town	PENOBSCOT	◆ 9,224
Topsham	MCD-Town	SAGADAHOC	© 9,100
Lisbon	MCD-Town	ANDROSCOGGIN	◆ 8,958
Presque Isle	Inc. Place	AROOSTOOK	◆ 8,877
Old Orchard Beach	CDP	YORK	© 8,856
Cape Elizabeth	RMC Place	CUMBERLAND	● 8,854
Skowhegan	MCD-Town	SOMERSET	© 8,824
Cape Elizabeth	MCD-Town	CUMBERLAND	◆ 8,799
Bath	Inc. Place	SAGADAHOC	◆ 8,533
Old Town	Inc. Place	PENOBSCOT	◆ 8,399
Caribou	Inc. Place	AROOSTOOK	© 8,312
Orono	CDP	PENOBSCOT	© 8,253
Yarmouth	MCD-Town	CUMBERLAND	◆ 8,084
Freeport	MCD-Town	CUMBERLAND	◆ 8,072
Winslow	CDP	KENNEBEC	© 7,743
Winslow	MCD-Town	KENNEBEC	© 7,743
Cumberland	MCD-Town	CUMBERLAND	◆ 7,637
Buxton	MCD-Town	YORK	◆ 7,624
Falmouth	RMC Place	CUMBERLAND	● 7,610
Rockland	Inc. Place	KNOX	© 7,609
Farmington	MCD-Town	FRANKLIN	© 7,410
Gray	MCD-Town	CUMBERLAND	◆ 7,211
South Berwick	MCD-Town	YORK	◆ 6,875
Hampden	MCD-Town	PENOBSCOT	◆ 6,806
Skowhegan	CDP	SOMERSET	© 6,696
Berwick	MCD-Town	YORK	◆ 6,635
Fairfield	MCD-Town	SOMERSET	© 6,573
Houlton	MCD-Town	AROOSTOOK	© 6,476
Rumford	MCD-Town	OXFORD	© 6,472
Ellsworth	Inc. Place	HANCOCK	© 6,456
Belfast	Inc. Place	WALDO	© 6,381
Topsham	CDP	SAGADAHOC	© 6,271
Winthrop	MCD-Town	KENNEBEC	© 6,232
Waterboro	MCD-Town	YORK	© 6,214
Gardiner	Inc. Place	KENNEBEC	© 6,198
Eliot	MCD-Town	YORK	◆ 5,960
Oakland	MCD-Town	KENNEBEC	© 5,959
Turner	MCD-Town	ANDROSCOGGIN	◆ 5,532
Houlton	CDP	AROOSTOOK	© 5,270
Camden	MCD-Town	KNOX	© 5,254
Poland	MCD-Town	ANDROSCOGGIN	◆ 5,250
Harpswell	MCD-Town	CUMBERLAND	© 5,239
Lincoln	MCD-Town	PENOBSCOT	© 5,221
Millinocket	MCD-Town	PENOBSCOT	© 5,203
Millinocket	CDP	PENOBSCOT	© 5,190
Hermon	MCD-Town	PENOBSCOT	◆ 5,103
Lebanon	MCD-Town	YORK	© 5,083

County Business Data

County	FIPS Code	County Seat	Land Area (Sq. Mi.)	Census Population			Wholesale Trade		Manufacturing, 2002			
				4/1/2000	4/1/1990	% Change 1990-2000	Sales, 2002 ($1,000)	% Change 1997-2002	Establish-ments	Total Employees	Value Added ($1,000)	Ranally Mfg. Units
Androscoggin	001	Auburn	470	103,793	105,259	-1.4	451,541	62.6	169	7,115	864,123	457
Aroostook	003	Houlton	6,672	73,938	86,936	-15.0	239,166	13.3	102	3,724	512,782	271
Cumberland	005	Portland	836	265,612	243,135	9.2	5,807,142	58.1	415	12,149	1,178,933	624
Franklin	007	Farmington	1,698	29,467	29,008	1.6	42,496	58.5	46	2,163	318,752	169
Hancock	009	Ellsworth	1,588	51,791	46,948	10.3	196,905	42.0	104	2,345	313,966	166
Kennebec	011	Augusta	868	117,114	115,904	1.0	1,136,056	38.2	127	3,180	271,535	144
Knox	013	Rockland	366	39,618	36,310	9.1	177,099	3.1	88	1,331	139,024	74
Lincoln	015	Wiscasset	456	33,616	30,357	10.7	72,284	8.7	79	849	51,663	27
Oxford	017	South Paris	2,078	54,755	52,602	4.1	208,012	70.3	90	3,429	559,970	296
Penobscot	019	Bangor	3,396	144,919	146,601	-1.1	1,001,721	6.8	173	6,082	416,544	220
Piscataquis	021	Dover Foxcroft	3,966	17,235	18,653	-7.6	(d)	(d)	28	1,519	89,694	47
Sagadahoc	023	Bath	254	35,214	33,535	5.0	61,692	-21.6	35	(d)	(d)	...
Somerset	025	Skowhegan	3,926	50,888	49,767	2.3	(d)	(d)	77	3,724	549,200	291
Waldo	027	Belfast	730	36,280	33,018	9.9	(d)	(d)	46	1,270	86,562	46
Washington	029	Machias	2,568	33,941	35,308	-3.9	57,127	(d)	44	1,460	182,247	96
York	031	Alfred	991	186,742	164,587	13.5	592,649	35.1	257	(d)	(d)	...
The State			**30,862**	**1,274,923**	**1,227,928**	**3.8**	**10,371,084**	**42.0**	**1,880**	**67,738**	**7,122,274**	**3,768**

(d) Data not available. Corresponding percentages or Ranally Manufacturing Units are estimates.
... Represents 0 or amount too minimal to be reported.

Administrative Divisions

Towns and Plantations: Although all Maine counties have towns or plantations, they may not cover the entire area of each county. Although legally incorporated, towns and plantations are not treated as incorporated places by the U.S. Census because the population often is scattered among several localities and rural areas rather than being concentrated in a single place. Only towns and plantations with an active government recognized by the U.S. Census of Governments are printed in this index.

Unincorporated County Subdivisions: Gores and Unorganized Townships do not possess governmental and taxing powers, and they are not listed in this index.

Index of Places and Counties

A

Abbot; PISCATAQUIS; see Abbot Village (RMC Place)
Abbot; MCD-Town; PISCATAQUIS; ***183** C-5; 🅿; **z** 04406; Ⓟ 677; © 630
Abbotts Mill; RMC Place; OXFORD; ▲ Rumford; ***183** F-2; mail Bryant Pond **z** 04219; rural
Abbot Village (Abbot); RMC Place; PISCATAQUIS; ▲ Abbot; **183** C-5; elev. 458ft./140m.; mail Abbot **z** 04406; ● 150
Acton; RMC Place; YORK; ▲ Acton; **183** I-1; 🅿; **z** 04001; ● 40
Acton; MCD-Town; YORK; ***183** I-1; 🅿; **z** 04001; Ⓟ 1,727; © 2,145
Addison; RMC Place; WASHINGTON; ▲ Addison; **183** E-9; elev. 17ft./5m.; 🅿; **z** 04606; ● 250
Addison; MCD-Town; WASHINGTON; ***183** F-9; 🅿; **z** 04606; Ⓟ 1,114; © 1,209
Admiralty Village; RMC Place; YORK; ▲ Kittery; ***183** J-2; ★ **PTSM-**; mail Kittery **z** 03904
Agamenticus Village; RMC Place; YORK; ▲ York; ***183** J-2; ★ **PTSM-**; mail Cape Neddick **z** 03902; ● 25
Albion; RMC Place; KENNEBEC; ▲ Albion; **183** E-5; 🅿; **z** 04910; ● 225
Albion; MCD-Town; KENNEBEC; ***183** F-5; 🅿; **z** 04910; Ⓟ 1,736; © 1,946
Alexander; RMC Place; WASHINGTON; ▲ Alexander; **183** D-9; elev. 423ft./129m.; 🅿; **z** 04694; ● 50
Alexander; MCD-Town; WASHINGTON; ***183** D-9; 🅿; **z** 04694 & mail Calais **z** 04619; Ⓟ 478; © 514
Alfred; RMC Place; ⊡ YORK; ▲ Alfred; **183** I-2; elev. 266ft./81m.; 🅿; **z** 04002; ● 600
Alfred; MCD-Town; YORK; ***183** I-2; 🅿; **z** 04002; Ⓟ 2,238; © 2,497
Alfred Mills; RMC Place; YORK; ▲ Alfred; ***183** I-2; mail Alfred **z** 04002; ● 150
Allagash; RMC Place; AROOSTOOK; ▲ Allagash; **183** A-12; 🅿; **z** 04774; ● 100
Allagash; MCD-Town; AROOSTOOK; ***183** A-12; 🅿; **z** 04774; Ⓟ 359; © 277
Allens; OXFORD; see West Bethel (RMC Place)
Allens Mills; RMC Place; FRANKLIN; ▲ Industry; **183** E-3; elev. 564ft./172m.; mail Farmington **z** 04938; ● 200
Alna; RMC Place; LINCOLN; ▲ Alna; **183** G-4; 🅿; **z** 04535; ● 130
Alna; MCD-Town; LINCOLN; ***183** G-4; 🅿; **z** 04535; Ⓟ 571; © 675
Alna Center; RMC Place; LINCOLN; ▲ Alna; ***183** G-4; elev. 159ft./48m.; mail Alna **z** 04535; rural
Alton; RMC Place; PENOBSCOT; ▲ Alton; ***183** D-6; 🅿; **z** 04468; rural
Alton; MCD-Town; PENOBSCOT; ***183** D-6; 🅿; **z** 04468; Ⓟ 771; © 816
Amherst; RMC Place; HANCOCK; ▲ Amherst; **183** D-7; elev. 301ft./92m.; 🅿; **z** 04605; ● 130
Amherst; MCD-Town; HANCOCK; ***183** D-7; 🅿; **z** 04605; Ⓟ 226; © 230
Amity; MCD-Town; AROOSTOOK; ***183** A-8; 🅿; **z** 04471; Ⓟ 186; © 199
Andover; RMC Place; OXFORD; ▲ Andover; **183** E-2; elev. 723ft./220m.; 🅿; **z** 04216; ● 600
Andover; MCD-Town; OXFORD; ***183** E-2; 🅿; **z** 04216; Ⓟ 953; © 864
ANDROSCOGGIN; **183** G-3; Ⓟ 105,259; © 103,793; ◆ 104,816
Anson; CDP; SOMERSET; ▲ Anson; **183** E-4; 🅿; **z** 04911; © 818
Anson; MCD-Town; SOMERSET; ***183** E-4; 🅿; **z** 04911; Ⓟ 2,382; © 2,583
Appleton; RMC Place; KNOX; ▲ Appleton; ***183** F-5; 🅿; **z** 04862; ● 125
Appleton; MCD-Town; KNOX; ***183** F-5; 🅿; **z** 04862; Ⓟ 1,069; © 1,271
Areys Corners; RMC Place; PENOBSCOT; ▲ Hampden; ***183** E-6; ★ **BANG**; mail Hampden **z** 04444; rural
Argyle; RMC Place; PENOBSCOT; ▲ Argyle; ***183** D-7; mail Old Town **z** 04468; rural
AROOSTOOK; **183** B-12; Ⓟ 86,936; © 73,938; ◆ 69,772
Aroostook Farm; RMC Place; AROOSTOOK; mail Presque Isle **z** 04769; pop. incl. with Presque Isle (Inc. Place)
Arrowsic; RMC Place; SAGADAHOC; ▲ Arrowsic; ***183** H-4; 🅿; ★ **BR-BA**; **z** 04530; rural
Arrowsic; MCD-Town; SAGADAHOC; ***183** H-4; 🅿; ★ **BR-BA**; **z** 04530; Ⓟ 498; © 477
Arundel; RMC Place; YORK; ▲ Kennebunk; ***183** I-2; 🅿; **z** 04046; ● 150
Arundel; MCD-Town; YORK; ***183** I-2; 🅿; **z** 04046; Ⓟ 2,669; © 3,571
Ashdale; RMC Place; SAGADAHOC; ▲ Phippsburg; ***183** H-4; elev. 52ft./16m.; ★ **BR-BA**; mail Sebasco Estates **z** 04565; rural
Ashland; RMC Place; AROOSTOOK; ▲ Ashland; **183** B-13; elev. 572ft./174m.; 🅿; **z** 04732 & mail Clayton Lake **z** 04737; ● 750
Ashland; MCD-Town; AROOSTOOK; ***183** B-13; 🅿; **z** 04732 & mail Clayton Lake **z** 04737; Ⓟ 1,542; © 1,474
Ash Point; RMC Place; KNOX; ▲ Owls Head; ***183** G-6; mail Owls Head **z** 04854; rural
Ashville; RMC Place; HANCOCK; ▲ Sullivan, Gouldsboro; ***183** F-8; mail Gouldsboro **z** 04607; ● 100
Athens; RMC Place; SOMERSET; ▲ Athens; **183** D-4; elev. 344ft./105m.; 🅿; **z** 04912; ● 275
Athens; MCD-Town; SOMERSET; ***183** D-4; 🅿; **z** 04912; Ⓟ 897; © 847
Atkinson; MCD-Town; PISCATAQUIS; ***183** C-6; 🅿; **z** 04426; Ⓟ 332; © 323
Atkinson Corner; RMC Place; PISCATAQUIS; ▲ Atkinson; ***183** C-6; mail Dover Foxcroft **z** 04426; ● 25
Atkinson Mills; RMC Place; PISCATAQUIS; ▲ Atkinson; ***183** C-6; mail Dover Foxcroft **z** 04426; rural
Atlantic; RMC Place; HANCOCK; ▲ Swans Island; **183** G-7; mail Swans Island **z** 04685; ● 60
Auburn; Inc. Place; ⊡ ANDROSCOGGIN; **183** G-3; elev. 188ft./57m.; 🅿 ■; ★ **LEW-**; **z** 04210-12; Ⓟ 24,309; © 23,203; ◆ 23,029
Auburn Plains; RMC Place; ANDROSCOGGIN; ***183** G-3; ★ **LEW-**; mail Auburn **z** 04210; pop. incl. with Auburn (Inc. Place)
Augusta; Inc. Place; **STATE CAPITAL**; ⊡ KENNEBEC; **183** F-4; elev. 153ft./47m.; 🅿 🅷 🅲 5,257 ■; ★ **AUG**; **z** 04330, **z** 04332-33, **z** 04336, **z** 04338; Ⓟ 21,325; © 18,560; ◆ 17,502
Aurora; RMC Place; HANCOCK; ▲ Aurora; **183** D-7; 🅿; **z** 04408; ● 60
Aurora; MCD-Town; HANCOCK; ***183** D-7; 🅿; **z** 04408; Ⓟ 82; © 121
Avon; RMC Place; FRANKLIN; ▲ Avon; ***183** E-3; 🅿; **z** 04966; rural
Avon; MCD-Town; FRANKLIN; ***183** E-3; 🅿; **z** 04966; Ⓟ 559; © 504

B

Back Narrows; RMC Place; LINCOLN; ▲ Boothbay; ***183** H-4; mail Boothbay **z** 04537; ● 90
Bailey Corner; RMC Place; KENNEBEC; ▲ Pittston; ***183** G-4; ★ **AUG**; mail Gardiner **z** 04345; rural
Bailey Island; RMC Place; CUMBERLAND; ▲ Harpswell; **183** H-3; 🅿; ★ **BR-BA**; **z** 04003; ● 650
Baileyville; WASHINGTON; see Woodland (CDP)
Baileyville; MCD-Town; WASHINGTON; ***183** C-9; 🅿; **z** 04694; Ⓟ 2,031; © 1,686
Baker Corner; RMC Place; CUMBERLAND; ▲ Windham; ***183** H-2; ★ **POR**; mail Windham **z** 04062; rural
Balch Pond; RMC Place; YORK; ▲ Newfield; ***183** H-1; mail East Wakefield **z** 03830; summer pop. 250
Bald Head; RMC Place; YORK; ▲ York; ***183** J-2; ★ **PTSM-**; mail Cape Neddick **z** 03902; ● 75
Bald Mountain; RMC Place; FRANKLIN; ▲ Rangeley; ***183** D-2; mail Rangeley **z** 04970; summer pop. 300
Baldwin; MCD-Town; CUMBERLAND; ***183** H-2; mail East Baldwin **z** 04024; Ⓟ 1,219; © 1,290
Bancroft; RMC Place; AROOSTOOK; ▲ Bancroft; **183** B-8; elev. 340ft./104m.; 🅿; **z** 04497; ● 30
Bancroft; MCD-Town; AROOSTOOK; ***183** B-8; 🅿; **z** 04497; Ⓟ 66; © 61
Bangor; Inc. Place; ⊡ PENOBSCOT; **183** E-6; elev. 158ft./48m.; 🅿 🅷 🅲 1,900 ■; ★ **BANG**; **z** 04401-02; Ⓟ 33,181; © 31,473; ◆ 31,643
Bar Harbor; CDP; HANCOCK; ▲ Bar Harbor; **183** F-8; 🅿 🅷; **z** 04609; Ⓟ 2,768; © 2,680
Bar Harbor; MCD-Town; HANCOCK; ***183** F-8; 🅿; **z** 04609; Ⓟ 4,443; © 4,820
Baring; RMC Place; WASHINGTON; ▲ Baring; **183** D-10; mail Baileyville **z** 04694; ● 125
Baring; MCD-Plantation; WASHINGTON; ***183** D-10; mail Baileyville **z** 04694, Calais **z** 04619; Ⓟ 275; © 273
Bar Mills; RMC Place; YORK; ▲ Buxton, Hollis; **183** H-2; elev. 156ft./48m.; 🅿; ★ **POR**; **z** 04004; ● 275
Barretts; RMC Place; AROOSTOOK; ***183** B-14; mail Caribou **z** 04736; pop. incl. with Caribou (Inc. Place)
Bartlett Mills; RMC Place; YORK; ▲ Arundel, Kennebunk; ***183** I-2; mail Kennebunk **z** 04043
Basin Mills; RMC Place; PENOBSCOT; ▲ Orono; ***183** D-7; ★ **BANG**; mail Orono **z** 04473
Bass Harbor; RMC Place; HANCOCK; ▲ Tremont; **183** F-7; 🅿; **z** 04653; ● 500
Batchelders Crossing; RMC Place; KENNEBEC; ▲ Litchfield; ***183** G-4; ★ **AUG**; mail Litchfield **z** 04350; rural
Bates; OXFORD; see West Paris (RMC Place)
Bath; Inc. Place; ⊡ SAGADAHOC; **183** H-4; elev. 79ft./24m.; 🅿 🅷; ★ **BR-BA**; **z** 04530; Ⓟ 9,799; © 9,266; ◆ 8,533
Bay Point; RMC Place; SAGADAHOC; ▲ Georgetown; ***183** H-4; elev. 45ft./14m.; ★ **BR-BA**; mail Georgetown **z** 04548; summer pop. 100
Bayside; RMC Place; HANCOCK; ▲ Trenton; ***183** F-7; elev. 61ft./19m.; mail Ellsworth **z** 04605; rural
Bayside; RMC Place; WALDO; ▲ Northport; ***183** F-6; mail Lincolnville **z** 04849; summer pop. 400; ● 150
Bayview; RMC Place; YORK; ***183** I-2; mail Saco **z** 04072; pop. incl. with Saco (Inc. Place)
Bayville; RMC Place; LINCOLN; ▲ Boothbay Harbor; ***183** H-4; summer pop. 120; ● 30
Beals; RMC Place; WASHINGTON; ▲ Beals; **183** F-9; 🅿; **z** 04611; ● 400
Beals; MCD-Town; WASHINGTON; ***183** F-9; 🅿; **z** 04611; Ⓟ 667; © 618
Beans Corner; RMC Place; FRANKLIN; ▲ Jay; ***183** E-3; mail Dryden **z** 04225
Beaver Cove; MCD-Town; PISCATAQUIS; ***183** B-5; 🅿; **z** 04441; Ⓟ 104; © 91
Beaver Dam; RMC Place; YORK; mail North Berwick **z** 03906; rural
Beddington; RMC Place; WASHINGTON; **183** D-8; mail Cherryfield **z** 04622; rural
Beddington; MCD-Town; WASHINGTON; ***183** E-8; 🅿; **z** 04622; Ⓟ 43; © 29
Beech Hill Pond; RMC Place; HANCOCK; ***183** E-7; mail Ellsworth **z** 04605; summer pop. 500
Beech Ridge; RMC Place; YORK; ▲ York; ***183** J-2; ★ **PTSM-**; mail York **z** 03909; rural
Belfast; Inc. Place; ⊡ WALDO; **183** F-6; elev. 103ft./31m.; 🅿 🅷; **z** 04915; Ⓟ 6,355; © 6,381
Belgrade; RMC Place; KENNEBEC; ▲ Belgrade; **183** F-4; 🅿; **z** 04917; ● 200
Belgrade; MCD-Town; KENNEBEC; ***183** F-4; 🅿; **z** 04917; Ⓟ 2,375; © 2,978
Belgrade Lakes; RMC Place; KENNEBEC; ▲ Rome, Belgrade; **183** F-4; 🅿; **z** 04918; summer pop. 800; ● 300
Belmont; MCD-Town; WALDO; ***183** F-5; 🅿; **z** 04952; Ⓟ 652; © 821
Belmont Corner; RMC Place; WALDO; ▲ Belmont; **183** F-5; elev. 402ft./123m.; mail Morrill **z** 04952; ● 25
Benedicta; RMC Place; AROOSTOOK; **183** A-7; elev. 619ft./189m.; 🅿; **z** 04733; ● 60
Benton; RMC Place; KENNEBEC; ▲ Benton; **183** E-4; 🅿; ★ **WATRVL**; **z** 04901; ● 120
Benton; MCD-Town; KENNEBEC; ***183** E-5; 🅿; ★ **WATRVL**; **z** 04901; Ⓟ 2,312; © 2,557
Benton Falls; RMC Place; KENNEBEC; ▲ Benton; ***183** E-4; ★ **WATRVL**; mail Waterville **z** 04901; ● 75
Benton Station; RMC Place; KENNEBEC; ▲ Benton; ***183** E-4; ★ **WATRVL**; mail Waterville **z** 04901; ● 450
Bernard; RMC Place; HANCOCK; ▲ Tremont; **183** J-11; 🅿; **z** 04612; ● 200
Berry Mills; RMC Place; FRANKLIN; ▲ Carthage; ***183** E-2; mail Dixfield **z** 04224; ● 50
Berwick; CDP; YORK; ▲ Berwick; **183** J-1; elev. 182ft./55m.; 🅿; ★ **PTSM-**; **z** 03901; © 1,993
Berwick; MCD-Town; YORK; ***183** I-1; 🅿; ★ **PTSM-**; **z** 03901; Ⓟ 5,995; © 6,353; ◆ 6,635
Bethel; RMC Place; OXFORD; ▲ Bethel; **183** F-2; 🅿; **z** 04217 & mail West Bethel **z** 04286; ● 1,200
Bethel; MCD-Town; OXFORD; ***183** F-2; 🅿; **z** 04217 & mail West Bethel **z** 04286; Ⓟ 2,329; © 2,411
Biddeford (Biddeford-Saco); Inc. Place; YORK; **183** I-2; elev. 75ft./23m.; 🅿 🅷 🅲 3,379 ■; **z** 04005, **z** 04007; Ⓟ 20,710; © 20,942; ◆ 19,236
Biddeford Pool; RMC Place; YORK; ***183** I-3; elev. 20ft./6m.; 🅿; **z** 04006
Biddeford-Saco; YORK; see Biddeford (Inc. Place)
Bigelow; RMC Place; FRANKLIN; ▲ Carrabassett Valley; ***183** D-3; mail Kingfield **z** 04947; ● 15
Big Lake Campground; RMC Place; WASHINGTON; ▲ North Washington; ***183** C-9; mail Princeton **z** 04668; summer pop. 100
Bingham; CDP; SOMERSET; ▲ Bingham; **183** D-4; elev. 371ft./113m.; 🅿; **z** 04920; Ⓟ 1,071; © 856
Bingham; MCD-Town; SOMERSET; ***183** D-4; 🅿; **z** 04920; Ⓟ 1,230; © 989
Birch Harbor; RMC Place; HANCOCK; ▲ Gouldsboro; ***183** F-8; 🅿; **z** 04613; ● 150
Birch Island; RMC Place; CUMBERLAND; ▲ Harpswell; ***183** H-3; 🅿; ★ **BR-BA**; **z** 04011; summer pop. 80
Birch Point; RMC Place; AROOSTOOK; ▲ Island Falls; ***183** D-13; mail Island Falls **z** 04747; summer pop. 150
Blackstrap; RMC Place; CUMBERLAND; ▲ Falmouth; ***183** H-3; elev. 404ft./123m.; ★ **POR**; mail Falmouth **z** 04105
Blaine; RMC Place; AROOSTOOK; ▲ Blaine; **183** C-14; 🅿; **z** 04734; ● 500
Blaine; MCD-Town; AROOSTOOK; ***183** C-14; 🅿; **z** 04734; Ⓟ 784; © 806
Blaisdell Corners; RMC Place; YORK; ▲ Lebanon; **183** I-1; elev. 250ft./76m.; mail Lebanon **z** 04027; ● 200
Blake Corner; RMC Place; ANDROSCOGGIN; ▲ Lisbon; ***183** G-3; ★ **LEW-**; mail Lisbon **z** 04250; rural
Blanchard; RMC Place; PISCATAQUIS; ▲ Blanchard; ***183** C-4; elev. 581ft./177m.; mail Abbot **z** 04406
Blanchard Corner; RMC Place; WASHINGTON; ▲ Charlotte; ***183** D-10; mail Pembroke **z** 04666; rural
Blue Hill; RMC Place; HANCOCK; ▲ Blue Hill; **183** F-7; 🅿 🅷; **z** 04614; ● 800
Blue Hill; MCD-Town; HANCOCK; ***183** F-7; 🅿; **z** 04614; Ⓟ 1,941; © 2,390
Blue Hill Falls; RMC Place; HANCOCK; ▲ Blue Hill; **183** F-7; ● 100
Blue Point; RMC Place; CUMBERLAND; ▲ Scarborough; ***183** I-3; ★ **POR**; mail Scarborough **z** 04074; ● 500
Bolsters Mills; RMC Place; CUMBERLAND, OXFORD; ▲ Harrison, Otisfield; **183** G-2; mail Harrison **z** 04040; ● 90
Bonny Eagle; RMC Place; YORK; ▲ Hollis; ***183** H-2; elev. 234ft./71m.; ★ **POR**; mail Buxton **z** 04093; rural
Boothbay; RMC Place; LINCOLN; ▲ Boothbay; **183** H-4; elev. 127ft./39m.; 🅿; **z** 04537, **z** 04549; ● 450
Boothbay; MCD-Town; LINCOLN; ***183** H-4; 🅿; **z** 04537, **z** 04549; Ⓟ 2,648; © 2,960
Boothbay Harbor; CDP; LINCOLN; ▲ Boothbay Harbor; **183** H-4; 🅿 🅷; **z** 04538, **z** 04570; Ⓟ 1,267; © 1,237
Boothbay Harbor; MCD-Town; LINCOLN; ***183** H-4; 🅿; **z** 04538, **z** 04570; Ⓟ 2,347; © 2,334
Boothbay Park; RMC Place; YORK; ***183** I-2; mail Saco **z** 04072; pop. incl. with Saco (Inc. Place)
Bowdoin; SAGADAHOC; see Bowdoin Center (RMC Place)
Bowdoin; SAGADAHOC; see West Bowdoin (RMC Place)
Bowdoin; MCD-Town; SAGADAHOC; ***183** G-3; 🅿; **z** 04287 & mail Bowdoinham **z** 04008; Ⓟ 2,207; © 2,727
Bowdoin Center (Bowdoin); RMC Place; SAGADAHOC; ▲ Bowdoin; ***183** G-3; mail Bowdoinham **z** 04008; ● 65
Bowdoinham; RMC Place; SAGADAHOC; ▲ Bowdoinham; **183** G-4; 🅿; **z** 04008; ● 400
Bowdoinham; MCD-Town; SAGADAHOC; ***183** G-4; 🅿; **z** 04008; Ⓟ 2,192; © 2,612
Bowerbank; RMC Place; PISCATAQUIS; ▲ Northeast Piscataquis; ● 70
Bowerbank; MCD-Town; PISCATAQUIS; ***183** C-5; 🅿; **z** 04426; Ⓟ 72; © 123
Boyd Lake; RMC Place; PISCATAQUIS; ▲ Southeast Piscataquis; ***183** C-6; mail Milo **z** 04463; ● 25
Bradburys; RMC Place; AROOSTOOK; ▲ Fort Kent; ***183** A-13; mail Fort Kent **z** 04743; ● 90
Bradford; RMC Place; PENOBSCOT; ▲ Bradford; **183** D-6; elev. 235ft./72m.; 🅿; **z** 04410; ● 80
Bradford; MCD-Town; PENOBSCOT; ***183** D-6; 🅿; **z** 04410; Ⓟ 1,103; © 1,186
Bradford Center; RMC Place; PENOBSCOT; ▲ Bradford; ***183** D-6; mail Bradford **z** 04410; ● 70
Bradley; RMC Place; PENOBSCOT; ▲ Bradley; ***183** D-7; 🅿; **z** 04411; ● 650
Bradley; MCD-Town; PENOBSCOT; ***183** D-7; 🅿; **z** 04411; Ⓟ 1,136; © 1,242
Bremen (Medomak); RMC Place; LINCOLN; ▲ Bremen; **183** G-5; 🅿; **z** 04551; ● 100
Bremen; MCD-Town; LINCOLN; ***183** G-5; 🅿; **z** 04551; Ⓟ 674; © 782
Brewer (Brewer Junction); Inc. Place; PENOBSCOT; **183** E-6; elev. 40ft./12m.; 🅿; ★ **BANG**; **z** 04412; Ⓟ 9,021; © 8,987; ◆ 9,290
Brewer Junction; PENOBSCOT; see Brewer (Inc. Place)
Brewer Lake; RMC Place; PENOBSCOT; ▲ Orrington; ***183** E-6; ★ **BANG**; mail Orrington **z** 04474; summer pop. 300
Bridgewater; RMC Place; AROOSTOOK; ▲ Bridgewater; **183** C-14; elev. 428ft./130m.; 🅿; **z** 04735; ● 325
Bridgewater; MCD-Town; AROOSTOOK; ***183** C-14; 🅿; **z** 04735; Ⓟ 647; © 612
Bridgton; CDP; CUMBERLAND; ▲ Bridgton; **183** G-2; elev. 494ft./151m.; 🅿 🅷; **z** 04009; Ⓟ 2,195; © 2,359
Bridgton; MCD-Town; CUMBERLAND; ***183** G-2; 🅿; **z** 04009; Ⓟ 4,307; © 4,883
Briggs Corner; RMC Place; YORK; ▲ Kittery; ***183** J-2; ★ **PTSM-**; mail Kittery Point **z** 03905; rural
Brighton; RMC Place; SOMERSET; ▲ Brighton; **183** D-4; elev. 890ft./271m.; mail Athens **z** 04912; ● 40
Brighton; MCD-Plantation; SOMERSET; ***183** D-4; mail Athens **z** 04912; Ⓟ 94; © 86
Bristol; RMC Place; LINCOLN; ▲ Bristol; **183** G-5; elev. 73ft./22m.; 🅿; **z** 04539; ● 300
Bristol; MCD-Town; LINCOLN; ***183** G-5; 🅿; **z** 04539; Ⓟ 2,326; © 2,644
Brixham; RMC Place; YORK; ▲ York; ***183** J-2; ★ **PTSM-**; mail York **z** 03909; rural
Brixham Lower Corners; RMC Place; YORK; ▲ York; ***183** J-2; ★ **PTSM-**; mail York **z** 03909; rural
Broad Cove; RMC Place; LINCOLN; ▲ Bremen; ***183** G-5; mail Waldoboro **z** 04572
Brookhaven; RMC Place; CUMBERLAND; ▲ Windham; ***183** H-2; ★ **POR**; mail Windham **z** 04062; pop. incl. with Crossville (Inc. Place)
Brooklin; RMC Place; HANCOCK; ▲ Brooklin; **183** F-7; elev. 125ft./38m.; 🅿; **z** 04616; ● 225
Brooklin; MCD-Town; HANCOCK; ***183** F-7; 🅿; **z** 04616; Ⓟ 785; © 841
Brooks; RMC Place; WALDO; ▲ Brooks; **183** E-5; elev. 387ft./118m.; 🅿; **z** 04921; ● 400
Brooks; MCD-Town; WALDO; ***183** E-5; 🅿; **z** 04921; Ⓟ 900; © 1,022
Brooksville; RMC Place; HANCOCK; ▲ Brooksville; ***183** F-7; 🅿; **z** 04617; ● 30
Brooksville; HANCOCK; see South Brooksville (RMC Place)
Brooksville; MCD-Town; HANCOCK; ***183** F-6; 🅿; **z** 04617 & mail Harborside **z** 04642; Ⓟ 760; © 911
Brookton; RMC Place; WASHINGTON; **183** B-9; elev. 439ft./134m.; 🅿; **z** 04413; ● 170
Brown Corner; RMC Place; AROOSTOOK; ▲ Limestone; ***183** B-14; elev. 616ft./188m.; mail Limestone **z** 04750; pop. incl. with Caribou (Inc. Place)
Brown Corner; RMC Place; WALDO; ▲ Prospect; ***183** E-6; elev. 322ft./98m.; mail Lincolnville **z** 04849; rural
Brownfield; RMC Place; OXFORD; ▲ Brownfield; ***183** G-1; elev. 424ft./129m.; 🅿; **z** 04010; ● 200
Brownfield; MCD-Town; OXFORD; ***183** G-1; 🅿; **z** 04010; Ⓟ 1,034; © 1,251
Brownville; RMC Place; PISCATAQUIS; ▲ Brownville; **183** C-6; 🅿; **z** 04414, **z** 04481; ● 350
Brownville; MCD-Town; PISCATAQUIS; ***183** C-6; 🅿; **z** 04414, **z** 04481; Ⓟ 1,506; © 1,259
Brownville Junction; RMC Place; PISCATAQUIS; ▲ Brownville; **183** C-6; elev. 391ft./119m.; 🅿; **z** 04415; ● 800
Brunswick; CDP; CUMBERLAND; ▲ Brunswick; **183** H-3; elev. 67ft./20m.; 🅿 🅷 🅲 1,734; ★ **BR-BA**; **z** 04011; Ⓟ 14,683; © 14,816; ◆ 15,165
Brunswick; MCD-Town; CUMBERLAND; ***183** H-3; 🅿 🅲 1,734 ■; ★ **BR-BA**; **z** 04011; Ⓟ 20,906; © 21,172; ◆ 21,179
Brunswick Station; CDP-Census Area Only; CUMBERLAND; ***183** H-4; ★ **BR-BA**; mail Brunswick **z** 04011; Ⓟ 1,829; © 1,511
Bryant Pond (Bryants Pond); RMC Place; OXFORD; ▲ Woodstock; **183** F-2; 🅿; **z** 04219; ● 500
Bryants Corner; RMC Place; WALDO; ***183** F-6; mail Belfast **z** 04915; pop. incl. with Belfast (Inc. Place)
Bryants Pond; OXFORD; see Bryant Pond (RMC Place)
Buckfield; RMC Place; OXFORD; ▲ Buckfield; **183** F-3; 🅿; **z** 04220; ● 400
Buckfield; MCD-Town; OXFORD; ***183** F-3; 🅿; **z** 04220; Ⓟ 1,566; © 1,723
Bucks Harbor; RMC Place; WASHINGTON; ▲ Machiasport; **183** E-10; 🅿; **z** 04655; ● 120
Bucksport; CDP; HANCOCK; ▲ Bucksport; **183** E-6; elev. 43ft./13m.; 🅿; **z** 04416; Ⓟ 2,989; © 2,970
Bucksport; MCD-Town; HANCOCK; ***183** E-6; 🅿; **z** 04416; Ⓟ 4,825; © 4,908

Entries in **UPPERCASE** are counties.
Entries in **bold** have populations of 2,500 or more.
Names in parentheses are alternate names.

Inc. Place	Incorporated Place
RMC Place	Rand McNally Designated Place
CDP	Census Designated Place
MCD	Minor Civil Division
⊡	County Seat
▲	Minor Civil Division
elev.	Elevation
🅿	Post Office
🅷	Hospital
🅲	College
■	Principal Business Center
★	Ranally Metro Area (RMA) Abbreviation
z	Zip Code(s)
Ⓟ	Previous Census Population
Ⓡ	Revised Census Population
Ⓐ	Annexation Population
●	Rand McNally Population Estimate
©	Final Census Population
Ⓢ	Special Census Population
◆	Estimated Population

For additional definitions see Glossary, Volume 1, and Introduction, Volume 2.

Bucksport Center; RMC Place; HANCOCK; ▲ Bucksport; *183 E-6; elev. 140ft./43m.; mail Bucksport z 04416

Bunganuc Landing; RMC Place; CUMBERLAND; ▲ Brunswick; *183 H-3; ★ **BR-BA**; mail Brunswick z 04011; rural

Bunkers Harbor; RMC Place; HANCOCK; ▲ Gouldsboro; *183 F-8; mail Birch Harbor z 04613; ● 40

Burkettville; RMC Place; KNOX; ▲ Appleton; *183 F-5; elev. 277ft./84m.; mail Union z 04862; ● 60

Burlington; RMC Place; PENOBSCOT; ▲ Burlington; 183 C-7; 🅿; z 04417; ● 140

Burlington; MCD-Town; PENOBSCOT; *183 C-7; 🅿; z 04417; Ⓟ 360; Ⓒ 351

Burnham (Burnham Junction); RMC Place; WALDO; ▲ Burnham; 183 E-5; elev. 161ft./49m.; 🅿; z 04922; ● 200

Burnham; MCD-Town; WALDO; *183 E-5; 🅿; z 04922; Ⓟ 961; Ⓒ 1,142

Burnham Junction; WALDO; see Burnham (RMC Place)

Burnt Meadow Pond; RMC Place; OXFORD; ▲ Brownfield; mail Hiram z 04041; summer pop. 100

Bustins Island; RMC Place; CUMBERLAND; ▲ Freeport; *183 H-3; elev. 130ft./40m.; 🅿; ★ **POR**; z 04013; summer pop. 300; ● 40

Buxton; RMC Place; YORK; ▲ Buxton; *183 H-2; elev. 186ft./57m.; 🅿; ★ **POR**; z 04093; rural

Buxton; YORK; see Buxton Center (RMC Place)

Buxton; MCD-Town; YORK; *183 H-2; 🅿; ★ **POR**; z 04093; Ⓟ 6,494; Ⓒ 7,452; ◆ 7,624

Buxton Center (Buxton); RMC Place; YORK; ▲ Buxton; *183 H-2; elev. 202ft./62m.; 🅿; ★ **POR**; z 04093; ● 100

Byron; RMC Place; OXFORD; ▲ Byron; 183 E-2; 🅿; z 04275; ● 75

Byron; MCD-Town; OXFORD; *183 E-2; 🅿; z 04275; Ⓟ 111; Ⓒ 121

C

Calais; Inc. Place; WASHINGTON; 183 C-10; elev. 19ft./6m.; 🅿 🅷; z 04619; Ⓟ 3,963; Ⓒ 3,447

Caldwell Corner; RMC Place; OXFORD; ▲ Oxford; *183 G-2; elev. 550ft./168m.; mail Oxford z 04270; rural

Cambridge; RMC Place; SOMERSET; ▲ Cambridge; 183 D-5; elev. 356ft./109m.; 🅿; z 04923; ● 125

Cambridge; MCD-Town; SOMERSET; *183 D-5; 🅿; z 04923; Ⓟ 490; Ⓒ 492

Camden; CDP; KNOX; ▲ Camden; 183 G-6; elev. 33ft./10m.; 🅿; z 04843, z 04847; Ⓟ 4,022; Ⓒ 3,934

Camden; MCD-Town; KNOX; *183 F-6; 🅿; z 04843, z 04847; Ⓟ 5,060; Ⓒ 5,254

Camp Ellis; RMC Place; YORK; *183 I-2; mail Saco z 04072; pop. incl. with Saco (Inc. Place)

Canaan; RMC Place; SOMERSET; ▲ Canaan; 183 E-4; elev. 236ft./72m.; 🅿; z 04924; ● 400

Canaan; MCD-Town; SOMERSET; *183 E-5; 🅿; z 04924; Ⓟ 1,636; Ⓒ 2,017

Canton; RMC Place; OXFORD; ▲ Canton; 183 F-3; 🅿; z 04221; ● 400

Canton; MCD-Town; OXFORD; *183 F-3; 🅿; z 04221; Ⓟ 951; Ⓒ 1,121

Canton Point; RMC Place; OXFORD; ▲ Canton; *183 F-3; mail Canton z 04221

Cape Cottage; RMC Place; CUMBERLAND; ▲ Cape Elizabeth; *183 H-3; 🅿; ★ **POR**; z 04107

Cape Elizabeth; RMC Place; CUMBERLAND; ▲ Cape Elizabeth; 183 I-3; 🅿; ★ **POR**; z 04107; ● 8,854

Cape Elizabeth; MCD-Town; CUMBERLAND; *183 I-3; 🅿; ★ **POR**; z 04107; Ⓟ 8,854; Ⓒ 9,068; ◆ 8,799

Cape Neddick; CDP; YORK; ▲ York; *183 J-2; elev. 27ft./8m.; 🅿; ★ **PTSM-**; z 03902; Ⓟ 2,193; Ⓒ 2,997

Cape Porpoise; RMC Place; YORK; ▲ Kennebunkport; 183 I-2; 🅿; z 04014; ● 500

Capitol Island; RMC Place; LINCOLN; ▲ Southport; *183 H-4; 🅿; z 04538; summer pop. 150

Caratunk; RMC Place; SOMERSET; ▲ Caratunk; 183 C-3; elev. 549ft./167m.; 🅿; z 04925; ● 70

Caratunk; MCD-Plantation; SOMERSET; *183 C-4; 🅿; z 04925; Ⓟ 98; Ⓒ 108

Cardville; RMC Place; PENOBSCOT; ▲ Greenbush; ● 150

Caribou; Inc. Place; AROOSTOOK; 183 B-14; elev. 442ft./135m.; 🅿 🅷; z 04736; Ⓟ 9,415; Ⓒ 8,312

Caribou Road; RMC Place; AROOSTOOK; *183 B-14; elev. 436ft./133m.; mail Presque Isle z 04769; pop. incl. with Presque Isle (Inc. Place)

Carmel; RMC Place; PENOBSCOT; ▲ Carmel; 183 E-6; 🅿; z 04419; ● 550

Carmel; MCD-Town; PENOBSCOT; *183 E-6; 🅿; z 04419; Ⓟ 1,906; Ⓒ 2,416

Carrabassett (Carrabassett Valley); RMC Place; FRANKLIN; ▲ Carrabassett Valley; 183 D-3; mail Kingfield z 04947; ● 225

Carrabassett Valley; FRANKLIN; see Carrabassett (RMC Place)

Carrabassett Valley; MCD-Town; FRANKLIN; *183 D-3; 🅿; z 04947; Ⓟ 325; Ⓒ 399

Carroll; RMC Place; PENOBSCOT; ▲ Carroll; *183 C-8; elev. 839ft./256m.; mail Springfield z 04487; rural

Carroll; MCD-Plantation; PENOBSCOT; *183 C-8; mail Springfield z 04487; Ⓟ 185; Ⓒ 144

Carson; RMC Place; AROOSTOOK; ▲ Woodland; *183 B-14; elev. 574ft./175m.; mail Washburn z 04786

Carthage; RMC Place; FRANKLIN; ▲ Carthage; *183 E-2; elev. 457ft./139m.; 🅿; z 04224

Carthage; MCD-Town; FRANKLIN; *183 E-2; 🅿; z 04224; Ⓟ 458; Ⓒ 520

Cary; RMC Place; AROOSTOOK; ▲ Cary; *183 D-14; mail Orient z 04471

Cary; MCD-Plantation; AROOSTOOK; *183 D-14; mail Orient z 04471; Ⓟ 235; Ⓒ 217

Carys Mills; RMC Place; AROOSTOOK; ▲ Houlton; *183 C-14; mail Houlton z 04730

Casco; RMC Place; CUMBERLAND; ▲ Casco; 183 G-2; 🅿; ★ **POR**; z 04015; ● 450

Casco; MCD-Town; CUMBERLAND; *183 G-2; 🅿; ★ **POR**; z 04015; Ⓟ 3,018; Ⓒ 3,469; ◆ 3,718

Cash Corner; RMC Place; CUMBERLAND; *183 H-3; ★ **POR**; mail South Portland z 04106; pop. incl. with South Portland (Inc. Place)

Castine; RMC Place; HANCOCK; ▲ Castine; 183 F-6; 🅿 🅲 834; z 04420-21; ● 800

Castine; MCD-Town; HANCOCK; *183 F-6; 🅿 🅲 834; z 04420-21; Ⓟ 1,161; Ⓒ 1,343

Castle Hill; MCD-Town; AROOSTOOK; *183 B-13; 🅿; z 04757; Ⓟ 449; Ⓒ 454

Caswell; MCD-Town; AROOSTOOK; *183 B-14; 🅿; z 04750; Ⓟ 408; Ⓒ 326

Caswell Plantation; RMC Place; AROOSTOOK; ▲ Caswell; *183 B-14; mail Limestone z 04750; ● 50

Cathance; RMC Place; SAGADAHOC; ▲ Topsham; *183 G-4; elev. 72ft./22m.; ★ **BR-BA**; mail Topsham z 04086; rural

Center Lebanon; RMC Place; YORK; ▲ Lebanon; *183 I-1; mail Lebanon z 04027

Center Lovell; RMC Place; OXFORD; ▲ Lovell; 183 G-1; elev. 532ft./162m.; 🅿; z 04016; ● 200

Center Minot; RMC Place; ANDROSCOGGIN; ▲ Minot; *183 G-3; elev. 527ft./161m.; ★ **LEW-**; mail Minot z 04258; rural

Center Montville (Montville); RMC Place; WALDO; ▲ Montville; *183 F-5; elev. 508ft./155m.; mail Freedom z 04941; ● 40

Center Vassalboro; RMC Place; KENNEBEC; ▲ Vassalboro; *183 F-4; elev. 260ft./79m.; ★ **AUG**; mail Vassalboro z 04989; ● 60

Centerville; RMC Place; WASHINGTON; *183 E-9; elev. 103ft./31m.; 🅿; z 04623; rural

Chamberlain; RMC Place; LINCOLN; ▲ Bristol; *183 H-5; elev. 25ft./8m.; 🅿; z 04541; ● 125

Chapman; RMC Place; AROOSTOOK; ▲ Chapman; *183 B-14; elev. 551ft./168m.; 🅿; z 04757; ● 60

Chapman; MCD-Town; AROOSTOOK; *183 B-14; 🅿; z 04757; Ⓟ 422; Ⓒ 465

Charles Chase Corner; RMC Place; YORK; *183 I-2; mail Wells z 04090; ● 200

Charleston; RMC Place; PENOBSCOT; ▲ Charleston; 183 D-6; elev. 471ft./144m.; 🅿; z 04422; ● 275

Charleston; MCD-Town; PENOBSCOT; *183 D-6; 🅿; z 04422; Ⓟ 1,187; Ⓒ 1,397

Charlotte; MCD-Town; WASHINGTON; *183 D-10; 🅿; z 04666; Ⓟ 271; Ⓒ 324

Chases Pond; RMC Place; YORK; ▲ York; *183 J-2; ★ **PTSM-**; mail York z 03909; rural

Chebeague Island; RMC Place; CUMBERLAND; ▲ Cumberland; 183 H-3; 🅿; ★ **POR**; z 04017; summer pop. 1,200; ● 400

Chelsea; RMC Place; KENNEBEC; ▲ Chelsea; *183 F-4; 🅿; ★ **AUG**; z 04330; ● 200

Chelsea; MCD-Town; KENNEBEC; *183 F-4; 🅿; ★ **AUG**; z 04330 & mail Gardiner z 04345; Ⓟ 2,497; Ⓒ 2,559

Cherryfield; RMC Place; WASHINGTON; ▲ Cherryfield; 183 E-8; elev. 54ft./16m.; 🅿; z 04622; ● 350

Cherryfield; MCD-Town; WASHINGTON; *183 E-8; 🅿; z 04622; Ⓟ 1,183; Ⓒ 1,157

Chester; RMC Place; PENOBSCOT; ▲ Chester; 183 C-7; 🅿; z 04457; ● 100

Chester; MCD-Town; PENOBSCOT; *183 C-7; 🅿; z 04457; Ⓟ 442; Ⓒ 525

Chesterville; RMC Place; FRANKLIN; ▲ Chesterville; 183 E-3; elev. 360ft./110m.; 🅿; z 04938; ● 110

Chesterville; MCD-Town; FRANKLIN; *183 E-3; 🅿; z 04938; Ⓟ 1,012; Ⓒ 1,170

Chesuncook; RMC Place; PISCATAQUIS; *183 C-12; mail Greenville z 04441

Chicopee; RMC Place; YORK; ▲ Buxton; *183 H-2; ★ **POR**; mail Buxton z 04093; rural

China (China Village); RMC Place; KENNEBEC; ▲ China; 183 F-5; elev. 203ft./62m.; 🅿; z 04358 & mail China Village z 04926; ● 450

China; MCD-Town; KENNEBEC; *183 F-5; 🅿; z 04358 & mail China Village z 04926; Ⓟ 3,713; Ⓒ 4,106

China Village; KENNEBEC; see China (RMC Place)

Chisholm; CDP; FRANKLIN; ▲ Jay; 183 F-3; elev. 362ft./110m.; mail Jay z 04239; Ⓟ 1,653; Ⓒ 1,399

Christmas Cove; RMC Place; LINCOLN; ▲ South Bristol; *183 H-4; mail South Bristol z 04568; ● 60

Cider Hill; RMC Place; YORK; ▲ York; *183 J-2; ★ **PTSM-**; mail York z 03909; ● 140

City Point; RMC Place; WALDO; *183 F-6; mail Belfast z 04915; pop. incl. with Belfast (Inc. Place)

Clark Island; RMC Place; KNOX; ▲ St. George; 183 G-5; mail Spruce Head z 04859; ● 120

Clarks Mills; RMC Place; YORK; ▲ Hollis, Dayton; *183 I-2; ★ **POR**; mail Hollis Center z 04042; ● 90

Clay Hill; RMC Place; YORK; ▲ York; *183 J-2; ★ **PTSM-**; mail Cape Neddick z 03902; rural

Clayton Lake; RMC Place; AROOSTOOK; 183 B-12; elev. 1,041ft./317m.; 🅿; z 04737; ● 20

Cleveland; RMC Place; AROOSTOOK; ▲ Madawaska; *183 A-13; mail Saint Agatha z 04772; ● 20

Cliff Island; RMC Place; CUMBERLAND; *183 H-3; elev. 40ft./12m.; 🅿; ★ **POR**; z 04019; pop. incl. with Portland (Inc. Place)

Clifton; RMC Place; PENOBSCOT; ▲ Clifton; 183 E-7; 🅿; z 04428; ● 150

Clifton; MCD-Town; PENOBSCOT; *183 E-7; 🅿; z 04428; Ⓟ 607; Ⓒ 743

Clifton Corners; RMC Place; PENOBSCOT; *183 E-7; mail Eddington z 04428; ● 50

Clinton; CDP; KENNEBEC; ▲ Clinton; 183 E-5; elev. 124ft./38m.; 🅿; z 04927; Ⓟ 1,485; Ⓒ 1,305

Clinton; MCD-Town; KENNEBEC; *183 E-5; elev. 124ft./38m.; 🅿; z 04927; Ⓟ 3,332; Ⓒ 3,340

Cobbs Bridge; RMC Place; CUMBERLAND; ▲ New Gloucester; *183 G-3; elev. 131ft./40m.; mail New Gloucester z 04260; rural

Coburn Gore; RMC Place; FRANKLIN; 183 C-2; 🅿; z 04936; ● 15

Codyville; RMC Place; WASHINGTON; ▲ Codyville; *183 B-9; mail Topsfield z 04490; rural

Codyville; MCD-Plantation; WASHINGTON; *183 B-9; mail Topsfield z 04490; Ⓟ 35; Ⓒ 19

Colby; RMC Place; AROOSTOOK; ▲ Woodland; *183 B-14; elev. 635ft./194m.; mail Caribou z 04736; ● 120

Colby College; RMC Place; KENNEBEC; *183 E-4; ★ **WATRVL**; mail Waterville z 04901; pop. incl. with Waterville (Inc. Place)

Cold Brook; RMC Place; PENOBSCOT; ▲ Hermon; *183 E-6; ★ **BANG**; mail Bangor z 04401; rural

Coles Corner; RMC Place; WALDO; ▲ Winterport; *183 E-6; ★ **BANG**; mail Winterport z 04496; rural

Columbia; MCD-Town; WASHINGTON; *183 E-9; 🅿; z 04623; Ⓟ 437; Ⓒ 459

Columbia Falls; RMC Place; WASHINGTON; ▲ Columbia Falls; 183 E-9; 🅿; z 04623; ● 250

Columbia Falls; MCD-Town; WASHINGTON; *183 E-9; 🅿; z 04623; Ⓟ 552; Ⓒ 599

Comments; CUMBERLAND; see East Baldwin Mattocks Station (RMC Place)

Concord; RMC Place; SOMERSET; ▲ Central Somerset; *183 D-4; mail Bingham z 04920; rural

Concordville; RMC Place; YORK; *183 J-2; elev. 72ft./22m.; ★ **PTSM-**; mail York Beach z 03910

Convene; RMC Place; CUMBERLAND; ▲ Sebago; *183 H-2; mail Sebago z 04029; rural

Cook Mills; RMC Place; CUMBERLAND; ▲ Casco; *183 G-2; ★ **POR**; mail Casco z 04015; ● 120

Cooks Corner; RMC Place; CUMBERLAND; ▲ Brunswick; *183 H-4; ★ **BR-BA**; mail Brunswick z 04011; ● 500

Cooks Corner; RMC Place; WALDO; ▲ Troy; *183 E-5; mail Troy z 04987; rural

Cooper; RMC Place; WASHINGTON; ▲ Cooper; *183 D-9; 🅿; z 04657; rural

Cooper; MCD-Town; WASHINGTON; *183 D-9; 🅿; z 04657; Ⓟ 124; Ⓒ 145

Coopers Corner (Lower Village); RMC Place; YORK; ▲ Kennebunk; *183 I-2; mail Kennebunk z 04043; ● 150

Coopers Mills; RMC Place; LINCOLN; ▲ Whitefield; 183 F-4; 🅿; z 04341; ● 250

Coplin; MCD-Plantation; FRANKLIN; *183 D-2; mail Rangeley z 04970, Stratton z 04982; Ⓟ 120; Ⓒ 135

Corea; RMC Place; HANCOCK; ▲ Gouldsboro; 183 F-8; 🅿; z 04624; ● 300

Corinna; RMC Place; PENOBSCOT; ▲ Corinna; 183 D-5; 🅿; z 04928; ● 1,100

Corinna; MCD-Town; PENOBSCOT; *183 D-5; 🅿; z 04928; Ⓟ 2,196; Ⓒ 2,145

Corinna Center; RMC Place; PENOBSCOT; ▲ Corinna; *183 D-5; mail Corinna z 04928; rural

Corinth; PENOBSCOT; see East Corinth (RMC Place)

Corinth; MCD-Town; PENOBSCOT; *183 D-6; 🅿; z 04427; Ⓟ 2,177; Ⓒ 2,511

Cornish; RMC Place; CUMBERLAND; ▲ Baldwin; *183 H-2; mail West Baldwin z 04091; rural

Cornish; RMC Place; YORK; ▲ Cornish; 183 H-2; elev. 353ft./108m.; 🅿; z 04020; ● 600

Cornish; MCD-Town; YORK; *183 H-1; 🅿; z 04020; Ⓟ 1,178; Ⓒ 1,269

Cornville; RMC Place; SOMERSET; ▲ Cornville; *183 D-4; elev. 460ft./140m.; 🅿; z 04976

Cornville; MCD-Town; SOMERSET; *183 D-4; 🅿; z 04976; Ⓟ 1,008; Ⓒ 1,208

Costigan; RMC Place; PENOBSCOT; ▲ Milford; 183 D-7; elev. 115ft./35m.; 🅿; ★ **BANG**; z 04418; ● 60

Cote Corner; RMC Place; AROOSTOOK; ▲ Limestone; *183 B-14; elev. 683ft./208m.; mail Limestone z 04750; rural

Country Living; RMC Place; YORK; ▲ Sanford; mail Sanford z 04073; ● 70

Cousins Island; RMC Place; CUMBERLAND; ▲ Yarmouth; *183 H-3; ★ **POR**; mail Yarmouth z 04096; summer pop. 400; ● 100

Coventry North; RMC Place; YORK; ▲ Limington; *183 H-2; ★ **POR**; mail Limerick z 04048; ● 175

Crams Corner; RMC Place; YORK; ▲ Eliot; *183 J-1; ★ **PTSM-**; mail Eliot z 03903

Cranberry Isles; RMC Place; HANCOCK; ▲ Cranberry Isles; 183 I-12; 🅿; z 04625; ● 90

Cranberry Isles; MCD-Town; HANCOCK; *183 F-8; 🅿; z 04625; Ⓟ 189; Ⓒ 128

Cranes Corners; RMC Place; HANCOCK; ▲ Orland; *183 E-6; mail Orland z 04472; rural

Crawford; MCD-Town; WASHINGTON; *183 D-9; mail Baileyville z 04694, Calais z 04619; Ⓟ 89; Ⓒ 108

Crescent Beach; RMC Place; KNOX; ▲ Owls Head; *183 G-6; mail Owls Head z 04854; ● 125

Crescent Lake (Webb Mills); RMC Place; CUMBERLAND; ▲ Casco; 183 G-2; ★ **POR**; mail Casco z 04015; ● 200

Crockett Corner; RMC Place; CUMBERLAND; ▲ North Yarmouth; *183 H-3; elev. 115ft./35m.; ★ **POR**; mail Cumberland Center z 04021; rural

Crossman Corner; RMC Place; ANDROSCOGGIN; ▲ Durham; *183 G-3; elev. 166ft./51m.; mail Lisbon Falls z 04252; rural

Crouseville; RMC Place; AROOSTOOK; ▲ Washburn; 183 B-14; elev. 455ft./139m.; 🅿; z 04738; ● 175

Crystal; RMC Place; AROOSTOOK; ▲ Crystal; 183 A-7; elev. 511ft./156m.; 🅿; z 04747; ● 25

Crystal; MCD-Town; AROOSTOOK; *183 D-13; 🅿; z 04747; Ⓟ 303; Ⓒ 285

Cumberland; MCD-Town; CUMBERLAND; *183 H-3; 🅿; ★ **POR**; z 04021; Ⓟ 5,836; Ⓒ 7,159; ◆ 7,637

CUMBERLAND; 183 G-2; Ⓟ 243,135; Ⓒ 265,612; ◆ 275,321

Cumberland Center; CDP; CUMBERLAND; ▲ Cumberland; 183 H-3; 🅿; ★ **POR**; z 04021; Ⓟ 1,890; Ⓒ 2,596

Cumberland Foreside; RMC Place; CUMBERLAND; ▲ Cumberland; *183 H-3; elev. 75ft./23m.; 🅿; ★ **POR**; z 04110; ● 575

Cumberland Mills; RMC Place; CUMBERLAND; *183 H-3; ★ **POR**; mail Westbrook z 04092; pop. incl. with Westbrook (Inc. Place)

Cundys Harbor; RMC Place; CUMBERLAND; ▲ Harpswell; *183 H-4; 🅿; ★ **BR-BA**; z 04011; summer pop. 350; ● 175

Curtis Corner; RMC Place; ANDROSCOGGIN; ▲ Leeds; *183 F-3; mail Leeds z 04263

Cushing; RMC Place; KNOX; ▲ Cushing; 183 G-5; elev. 41ft./12m.; 🅿; z 04563; ● 50

Cushing; MCD-Town; KNOX; *183 G-5; 🅿; z 04563; Ⓟ 988; Ⓒ 1,322

Cushing Island; RMC Place; CUMBERLAND; *183 H-3; 🅿; ★ **POR**; z 04109; pop. incl. with Portland (Inc. Place)

Cutler; RMC Place; WASHINGTON; ▲ Cutler; 183 E-10; elev. 20ft./6m.; 🅿; z 04626; ● 200

Cutler; MCD-Town; WASHINGTON; *183 E-10; 🅿; z 04626; Ⓟ 779; Ⓒ 623

Cutts Island; RMC Place; YORK; ▲ Kittery; *183 J-2; elev. 34ft./10m.; ★ **PTSM-**; mail Kittery Point z 03905; rural

Cyr; MCD-Plantation; AROOSTOOK; *183 A-14; mail Van Buren z 04785; Ⓟ 142; Ⓒ 117

D

Daigle; RMC Place; AROOSTOOK; ▲ New Canada; *183 A-13; mail Fort Kent z 04743; ● 40

Dallas; MCD-Plantation; FRANKLIN; *183 D-2; mail Rangeley z 04970; Ⓟ 161; Ⓒ 250

Damariscotta; RMC Place; LINCOLN; ▲ Damariscotta; 183 G-5; elev. 69ft./21m.; 🅿 🅷; z 04543; ● 1,100

Damariscotta; MCD-Town; LINCOLN; *183 G-5; 🅿; z 04543; Ⓟ 1,811; Ⓒ 2,041

Damariscotta Mills; RMC Place; LINCOLN; ▲ Nobleboro; *183 G-5; mail Newcastle z 04553; ● 200

Damariscotta-Newcastle; CDP-Census Area Only; LINCOLN; ▲ Newcastle, Damariscotta; *183 G-5; mail Damariscotta z 04543; Ⓟ 1,567; Ⓒ 1,751

Damascus; RMC Place; PENOBSCOT; ▲ Carmel; *183 E-6; elev. 204ft./62m.; mail Carmel z 04419; rural

Danforth; RMC Place; WASHINGTON; ▲ Danforth; 183 B-8; 🅿; z 04424; ● 500

Danforth; MCD-Town; WASHINGTON; *183 B-8; 🅿; z 04424; Ⓟ 710; Ⓒ 629

Danville (Danville Junction); RMC Place; ANDROSCOGGIN; *183 G-3; elev. 207ft./63m.; 🅿; ★ **LEW-**; z 04223; pop. incl. with Auburn (Inc. Place)

Danville Junction; ANDROSCOGGIN; see Danville (RMC Place)

Dark Harbor; RMC Place; WALDO; ▲ Islesboro; *183 F-6; mail Islesboro z 04848; ● 100

Davenport Cove; RMC Place; AROOSTOOK; ▲ Weston; *183 B-8; mail Danforth z 04424; summer pop. 150; ● 30

Davis Island; RMC Place; LINCOLN; ▲ Edgecomb; *183 G-4; mail Edgecomb z 04556; ● 30

Days Ferry; RMC Place; SAGADAHOC; ▲ Woolwich; *183 G-4; ★ **BR-BA**; mail Woolwich z 04579; ● 70

Dayton; MCD-Town; YORK; *183 I-2; 🅿; z 04005; Ⓟ 1,197; Ⓒ 1,805

Deblois; RMC Place; WASHINGTON; ▲ Deblois; 183 E-8; elev. 204ft./62m.; 🅿; z 04622; ● 30

Deblois; MCD-Town; WASHINGTON; *183 E-8; 🅿; z 04622; Ⓟ 73; Ⓒ 49

Dedham; RMC Place; HANCOCK; ▲ Dedham; 183 E-7; elev. 136ft./41m.; 🅿; z 04429; ● 125

Dedham; MCD-Town; HANCOCK; *183 E-7; 🅿; z 04429; Ⓟ 1,229; Ⓒ 1,422

Deep Cut; RMC Place; CUMBERLAND; ▲ Brunswick; *183 G-3; ★ **BR-BA**; mail Brunswick z 04011; rural

Deering; RMC Place; AROOSTOOK; mail Presque Isle z 04769; pop. incl. with Presque Isle (Inc. Place)

Deering; RMC Place; CUMBERLAND; *183 H-3; ★ **POR**; mail Portland z 04103; pop. incl. with Portland (Inc. Place)

Deering Junction; RMC Place; CUMBERLAND; *183 H-3; ★ **POR**; pop. incl. with Portland (Inc. Place)

Deer Isle; RMC Place; HANCOCK; ▲ Deer Isle; 183 F-7; 🅿; z 04627; ● 400

Deer Isle; MCD-Town; HANCOCK; *183 F-6; 🅿; z 04627; Ⓟ 1,829; Ⓒ 1,876

Delano Park; RMC Place; CUMBERLAND; ▲ Cape Elizabeth; *183 H-3; ★ **POR**; mail South Portland z 04106

Denmark; RMC Place; OXFORD; ▲ Denmark; 183 G-2; 🅿; z 04022; ● 125

Denmark; MCD-Town; OXFORD; *183 G-2; 🅿; z 04022; Ⓟ 855; Ⓒ 1,004

Dennistown; MCD-Plantation; SOMERSET; *183 B-3; 🅿; z 04945; Ⓟ 32; Ⓒ 30

Dennysville; RMC Place; WASHINGTON; ▲ Dennysville; 183 D-10; elev. 57ft./17m.; 🅿; z 04628; ● 150

Dennysville; MCD-Town; WASHINGTON; *183 D-10; 🅿; z 04628; Ⓟ 355; Ⓒ 319

Derby; RMC Place; PISCATAQUIS; ▲ Milo; *183 C-6; elev. 306ft./93m.; 🅿; z 04463

Detroit; RMC Place; SOMERSET; ▲ Detroit; 183 E-5; elev. 207ft./63m.; 🅿; z 04929; ● 175

Detroit; MCD-Town; SOMERSET; *183 E-5; 🅿; z 04929; Ⓟ 751; Ⓒ 816

Dexter; CDP; PENOBSCOT; ▲ Dexter; 183 D-5; 🅿; z 04930; Ⓟ 2,650; Ⓒ 2,201

Dexter; MCD-Town; PENOBSCOT; *183 D-5; 🅿; z 04930; Ⓟ 4,419; Ⓒ 3,890

Dickey; RMC Place; AROOSTOOK; ▲ Allagash; *183 A-12; elev. 629ft./192m.; mail Saint Francis z 04774

Dickvale; RMC Place; OXFORD; ▲ Peru; *183 F-2; elev. 510ft./155m.; mail Peru z 04290; ● 40

Dirigo Corner; RMC Place; KENNEBEC; ▲ China; *183 F-5; mail South China z 04358; rural

Dixfield; CDP; OXFORD; ▲ Dixfield; 183 E-2; elev. 417ft./127m.; 🅿; z 04224; Ⓟ 1,300; Ⓒ 1,137

Dixfield; MCD-Town; OXFORD; *183 E-3; 🅿; z 04224; Ⓟ 2,574; Ⓒ 2,514

Dixfield Center; RMC Place; OXFORD; ▲ Dixfield; *183 E-3; elev. 813ft./248m.; mail Dixfield z 04224

Dixmont; RMC Place; PENOBSCOT; ▲ Dixmont; 183 E-5; elev. 543ft./166m.; 🅿; z 04932; ● 80

Dixmont; MCD-Town; PENOBSCOT; *183 E-5; 🅿; z 04932; Ⓟ 1,007; Ⓒ 1,065

Dixmont Center; RMC Place; PENOBSCOT; ▲ Dixmont; *183 E-5; elev. 462ft./141m.; mail Dixmont z 04932

Dog Corner; RMC Place; CUMBERLAND; ▲ Gorham; *183 H-2; ★ **POR**; mail Gorham z 04038; rural

Dog Island Corner; RMC Place; WALDO; *183 F-6; elev. 150ft./46m.; mail Belfast z 04915; pop. incl. with Belfast (Inc. Place)

Dogtown; RMC Place; SOMERSET; ▲ Palmyra, Detroit; *183 E-5; mail Pittsfield z 04967; rural

Dog Town; RMC Place; WASHINGTON; ▲ East Machias; *183 E-10; mail East Machias z 04630; ● 40

Dorman; RMC Place; WASHINGTON; ▲ Harrington; *183 E-8; elev. 107ft./33m.; mail Harrington z 04643

Douglas Hill; RMC Place; CUMBERLAND; ▲ Sebago; *183 H-2; mail Sebago z 04029; ● 50

Dover-Foxcroft; CDP; ⊡ PISCATAQUIS; ▲ Dover-Foxcroft; 183 C-5; elev. 356ft./109m.; 🅿 🅷; z 04426; Ⓟ 3,077; Ⓒ 2,592

Dover-Foxcroft; MCD-Town; PISCATAQUIS; *183 C-5; 🅿; z 04426; Ⓟ 4,657; Ⓒ 4,211

Dover South Mills; RMC Place; PISCATAQUIS; ▲ Dover-Foxcroft; *183 D-5; mail Dover Foxcroft z 04426

Dow; RMC Place; AROOSTOOK; *183 B-14; pop. incl. with Caribou (Inc. Place)

Downtown; RMC Place; CUMBERLAND; *183 H-3; ★ **POR**; mail Portland z 04101, z 04112; pop. incl. with Portland (Inc. Place)

Drake Corner; RMC Place; WALDO; ▲ Lincolnville; *183 F-6; elev. 180ft./55m.; mail Lincolnville z 04849; rural

Drakes Island; RMC Place; YORK; ▲ Wells; *183 I-2; elev. 12ft./4m.; mail Wells z 04090; summer pop. 300; ● 100

Dresden; LINCOLN; see Dresden Mills (RMC Place)

Dresden; MCD-Town; LINCOLN; *183 G-4; 🅿; z 04342; Ⓟ 1,332; Ⓒ 1,625

Dresden Mills (Dresden); RMC Place; LINCOLN; ▲ Dresden; 183 G-4; mail Dresden z 04342; ● 140

Drew; MCD-Plantation; PENOBSCOT; *183 B-8; mail Wytopitlock z 04497; Ⓟ 43; Ⓒ 57

Dryden; RMC Place; FRANKLIN; ▲ Wilton; *183 E-3; 🅿; z 04225; ● 450

Dry Mills; RMC Place; CUMBERLAND; ▲ Gray; 183 G-3; elev. 301ft./92m.; ★ **POR**; mail Gray z 04039; ● 350

Duck Pond Center; CUMBERLAND; see Highland Lake (RMC Place)

Ducktrap; RMC Place; WALDO; ▲ Lincolnville; *183 F-6; mail Lincolnville z 04849; ● 110

Dunkertown; RMC Place; OXFORD; ▲ Otisfield; *183 G-2; elev. 450ft./137m.; mail Oxford z 04270; rural

Dunns Corner; RMC Place; KENNEBEC; ▲ Mount Vernon; *183 F-4; mail Mount Vernon z 04352

Dunstan; CUMBERLAND; see West Scarborough (RMC Place)

Durgintown; RMC Place; OXFORD; ▲ Hiram; *183 H-1; mail Hiram z 04041; rural

Durham; ANDROSCOGGIN; see South West Bend (RMC Place)

Durham; MCD-Town; ANDROSCOGGIN; *183 G-3; 🅿; z 04222; Ⓟ 2,842; Ⓒ 3,381

Dyer Brook; RMC Place; AROOSTOOK; ▲ Dyer Brook; 183 C-13; elev. 642ft./196m.; 🅿; z 04747; ● 60

Dyer Brook; MCD-Town; AROOSTOOK; *183 C-13; 🅿; z 04747; Ⓟ 243; Ⓒ 199

Dyer Cove; RMC Place; CUMBERLAND; ▲ Harpswell; *183 H-4; ★ **BR-BA**; mail Brunswick z 04011; summer pop. 100; ● 10

E

Eagle Lake; RMC Place; AROOSTOOK; ▲ Eagle Lake; 183 B-13; elev. 603ft./184m.; 🅿; z 04739; ● 600

Eagle Lake; MCD-Town; AROOSTOOK; *183 B-13; 🅿; z 04739; Ⓟ 942; Ⓒ 815

East Andover; RMC Place; OXFORD; ▲ Andover; 183 E-2; elev. 684ft./208m.; 🅿; z 04226; ● 150

East Auburn; RMC Place; ANDROSCOGGIN; *183 G-3; ★ **LEW-**; mail Auburn z 04210; pop. incl. with Auburn (Inc. Place)

East Baldwin; CUMBERLAND; see East Baldwin Mattocks Station (RMC Place)

East Baldwin Mattocks Station (Comments, East Baldwin, Mattocks); RMC Place; CUMBERLAND; ▲ Baldwin; *183 H-2; mail East Baldwin z 04024; ● 200

East Benton; RMC Place; KENNEBEC; ▲ Benton; *183 E-5; ★ **WATRVL**; mail Albion z 04910

East Bethel; RMC Place; OXFORD; ▲ Bethel; *183 F-2; elev. 640ft./195m.; mail Bethel z 04217

East Blue Hill; RMC Place; HANCOCK; ▲ Blue Hill; 183 F-7; 🅿; z 04629; ● 150

East Boothbay; RMC Place; LINCOLN; ▲ Boothbay; *183 H-4; elev. 1ft./0m.; 🅿; z 04544; ● 450

Eastbrook; RMC Place; HANCOCK; ▲ Eastbrook; 183 E-7; elev. 172ft./52m.; 🅿; z 04634; ● 125

Eastbrook; MCD-Town; HANCOCK; *183 E-8; 🅿; z 04634; Ⓟ 289; Ⓒ 370

East Brownfield; RMC Place; OXFORD; *183 G-1; mail Brownfield z 04010; ● 75

East Buckfield; RMC Place; OXFORD; ▲ Buckfield; *183 F-3; elev. 464ft./141m.; mail Buckfield z 04220; rural

East Corinth (Corinth); RMC Place; PENOBSCOT; ▲ Corinth; 183 D-6; elev. 306ft./93m.; mail Corinth z 04427; ● 400

East Deering; RMC Place; CUMBERLAND; *183 H-3; ★ **POR**; mail Portland z 04103; pop. incl. with Portland (Inc. Place)

East Denmark; RMC Place; OXFORD; ▲ Denmark; *183 G-2; elev. 699ft./213m.; mail Denmark z 04022

East Dixfield; RMC Place; FRANKLIN, OXFORD; ▲ Dixfield, Wilton; 183 E-3; 🅿; z 04227; ● 120

East Dixmont; RMC Place; PENOBSCOT; ▲ Dixmont; *183 E-6; elev. 508ft./155m.; mail Dixmont z 04932; ● 60

East Dover; RMC Place; PISCATAQUIS; ▲ Dover-Foxcroft; *183 C-5; mail Dover Foxcroft z 04426

East Eddington; RMC Place; PENOBSCOT; ▲ Eddington; 183 E-7; elev. 194ft./59m.; ★ **BANG**; mail Eddington z 04428; ● 250

East Edgecomb; RMC Place; LINCOLN; ▲ Edgecomb; *183 G-4; elev. 81ft./25m.; mail Edgecomb z 04556; rural

East Eliot; RMC Place; YORK; ▲ Eliot; *183 J-2; ★ **PTSM-**; mail Eliot z 03903; rural

East End; RMC Place; CUMBERLAND; *183 H-3; ★ **POR**; mail Portland z 04101; pop. incl. with Portland (Inc. Place)

East Exeter; RMC Place; PENOBSCOT; ▲ Exeter; *183 D-6; mail Corinth z 04427

East Franklin; RMC Place; HANCOCK; ▲ Franklin; *183 E-8; elev. 52ft./16m.; mail Franklin z 04634

East Friendship; RMC Place; KNOX; ▲ Friendship; *183 G-5; mail Friendship z 04547

East Fryeburg; RMC Place; OXFORD; ▲ Fryeburg; *183 G-1; elev. 488ft./149m.; mail Fryeburg z 04037

East Hampden; RMC Place; PENOBSCOT; ▲ Hampden; 183 J-6; ★ **BANG**; mail Hampden z 04444; ● 1,200

East Harpswell; RMC Place; CUMBERLAND; ▲ Harpswell; *183 H-4; ★ **BR-BA**; mail Brunswick z 04011; rural

East Hebron; RMC Place; ANDROSCOGGIN, OXFORD; ▲ Hebron, Turner; *183 F-3; elev. 550ft./168m.; ★ **LEW-**; mail Hebron z 04238; rural

East Hiram; RMC Place; OXFORD; ▲ Hiram; 183 H-2; mail Hiram z 04041; ● 250

East Holden; RMC Place; PENOBSCOT; ▲ Holden; 183 E-7; 🅿; ★ **BANG**; z 04429; ● 175

East Knox; RMC Place; WALDO; ▲ Knox; *183 F-5; elev. 715ft./218m.; mail Thorndike z 04986; rural

East Lamoine; RMC Place; HANCOCK; ▲ Lamoine; 183 F-7; mail Ellsworth z 04605; ● 50

East Lebanon; YORK; see Lebanon (RMC Place)

East Limington; RMC Place; YORK; ▲ Limington; *183 H-2; elev. 236ft./72m.; ★ **POR**; mail Limington z 04049; ● 40

East Livermore; RMC Place; ANDROSCOGGIN; ▲ Livermore Falls; 183 F-3; elev. 336ft./102m.; 🅿; z 04228; ● 60

East Lowell; RMC Place; PENOBSCOT; ▲ Lowell; *183 C-7; elev. 231ft./70m.; mail West Enfield z 04493; ● 40

East Lyndon; RMC Place; AROOSTOOK; *183 B-14; mail Caribou z 04736; pop. incl. with Caribou (Inc. Place)

East Machias; RMC Place; WASHINGTON; ▲ East Machias; 183 E-10; elev. 43ft./13m.; 🅿; z 04630; ● 300

East Machias; MCD-Town; WASHINGTON; *183 E-9; 🅿; z 04630; Ⓟ 1,218; Ⓒ 1,298

East Madison; RMC Place; SOMERSET; ▲ Madison; *183 D-4; mail Madison z 04950; ● 130

East Millinocket; CDP; PENOBSCOT; ▲ East Millinocket; 183 B-7; 🅿; z 04430; Ⓟ 2,075; Ⓒ 1,701

East Millinocket; MCD-Town; PENOBSCOT; *183 B-7; 🅿; z 04430; Ⓟ 2,166; Ⓒ 1,828

East Monmouth; RMC Place; KENNEBEC; ▲ Monmouth; *183 F-3; ★ **AUG**; mail Monmouth z 04259; ● 45

East Newport; RMC Place; PENOBSCOT; ▲ Newport; 183 E-5; 🅿; z 04933; ● 120

East New Portland; RMC Place; SOMERSET; ▲ New Portland; *183 D-3; mail New Portland z 04961; ● 60

East Northport; RMC Place; WALDO; ▲ Northport; *183 F-6; mail Lincolnville z 04849; ● 50

Easton; RMC Place; AROOSTOOK; ▲ Easton; 183 B-14; 🅿; z 04740; ● 300

Easton; MCD-Town; AROOSTOOK; *183 B-14; 🅿; z 04740; Ⓟ 1,291; Ⓒ 1,249

Easton Center; RMC Place; AROOSTOOK; ▲ Easton; *183 B-14; mail Easton z 04740; ● 30

Easton Station; RMC Place; AROOSTOOK; ▲ Easton; *183 B-14; mail Easton z 04740; ● 25

East Orland; RMC Place; HANCOCK; ▲ Orland; *183 E-7; 🅿; z 04431; ● 100

East Orrington; RMC Place; PENOBSCOT; ▲ Orrington; *183 E-6; elev. 105ft./32m.; ★ **BANG**; mail Orrington z 04474; ● 400

East Otisfield; RMC Place; OXFORD; ▲ Otisfield; *183 G-2; mail Oxford z 04270; rural

East Palermo; RMC Place; WALDO; ▲ Palermo; *183 F-5; elev. 508ft./155m.; mail Palermo z 04354; rural

East Parsonfield; YORK; see East Parsonsfield (RMC Place)

East Parsonsfield (East Parsonfield); RMC Place; YORK; ▲ Parsonsfield; *183 H-1; 🅿; z 04028; ● 180

East Peru; RMC Place; OXFORD; ▲ Peru; 183 F-3; mail Peru z 04290; ● 100

East Pittston; RMC Place; KENNEBEC; ▲ Pittston; *183 G-4; elev. 111ft./34m.; ★ **AUG**; mail Gardiner z 04345; ● 90

East Poland (Empire Road); RMC Place; ANDROSCOGGIN; ▲ Minot, Poland; *183 G-3; 🅿; ★ **LEW-**; z 04230; ● 130

Eastport; Inc. Place; WASHINGTON; 183 D-10; elev. 60ft./18m.; 🅿; z 04631; Ⓟ 1,965; Ⓒ 1,640

East Raymond; RMC Place; CUMBERLAND; ▲ Raymond; *183 G-2; elev. 540ft./165m.; ★ **POR**; mail Raymond z 04071; ● 100

East Sebago (Sebago); RMC Place; CUMBERLAND; ▲ Sebago; 183 H-2; elev. 290ft./88m.; 🅿; z 04029; ● 325

East Stoneham (Stoneham); RMC Place; OXFORD; ▲ Stoneham; *183 F-2; elev. 627ft./191m.; mail Stoneham z 04231; ● 150

East Sullivan; RMC Place; HANCOCK; ▲ Sullivan; *183 F-8; elev. 43ft./13m.; mail Gouldsboro z 04607; ● 80

East Sumner; RMC Place; OXFORD; ▲ Sumner; 183 F-3; mail Buckfield z 04220; ● 100

East Surry; RMC Place; HANCOCK; ▲ Surry; *183 F-7; mail Ellsworth z 04605; rural

East Thorndike; RMC Place; WALDO; ▲ Thorndike; *183 E-5; elev. 525ft./160m.; mail Thorndike z 04986; rural

East Troy; RMC Place; WALDO; ▲ Troy; *183 E-5; mail Troy z 04987; rural

East Union; RMC Place; KNOX; ▲ Union; *183 G-5; elev. 281ft./86m.; mail Union z 04862; ● 100

East Vassalboro; RMC Place; KENNEBEC; ▲ Vassalboro; 183 F-4; 🅿; ★ **AUG**; z 04935; ● 300

East Warren; RMC Place; KNOX; *183 G-5; elev. 214ft./65m.; mail Warren z 04864; rural

East Waterboro; RMC Place; YORK; ▲ Waterboro; 183 I-2; 🅿; z 04030; ● 250

East Waterford; RMC Place; OXFORD; ▲ Waterford; *183 F-2; elev. 481ft./147m.; mail Waterford z 04088; ● 35

East Wilton; RMC Place; FRANKLIN; ▲ Wilton; 183 E-3; elev. 416ft./127m.; 🅿; z 04234; ● 350

East Winn; RMC Place; PENOBSCOT; ▲ Winn; *183 C-7; elev. 309ft./94m.; mail Lee z 04455

East Winthrop; RMC Place; KENNEBEC; ▲ Winthrop; *183 F-4; elev. 174ft./53m.; 🅿; ★ **AUG**; z 04343; ● 250

Eaton; RMC Place; WASHINGTON; ▲ Danforth; 183 B-9; mail Danforth z 04424; ● 40

Eddington; RMC Place; PENOBSCOT; ▲ Eddington; *183 E-6; elev. 146ft./45m.; 🅿; ★ **BANG**; z 04428; ● 200

Eddington; MCD-Town; PENOBSCOT; *183 E-7; 🅿; ★ **BANG**; z 04428; Ⓟ 1,947; Ⓒ 2,052; ◆ 2,245

Eden; RMC Place; HANCOCK; ▲ Bar Harbor; 183 G-12; mail Salsbury Cove z 04672; ● 75

Edes Falls; RMC Place; CUMBERLAND; ▲ Naples; *183 G-2; mail Naples z 04055; rural

Edgecomb; RMC Place; LINCOLN; ▲ Edgecomb; 183 G-4; 🅿; z 04556; ● 110

Edgecomb; MCD-Town; LINCOLN; *183 G-4; 🅿; z 04556; Ⓟ 993; Ⓒ 1,090

Edinburg; MCD-Town; PENOBSCOT; *183 C-6; 🅿; z 04448; Ⓟ 107; Ⓒ 98

Edmunds; RMC Place; WASHINGTON; *183 D-10; mail Dennysville z 04628

Eggemoggin; RMC Place; HANCOCK; ▲ Deer Isle; *183 F-6; elev. 46ft./14m.; mail Little Deer Isle z 04650; summer pop. 100

Egypt; RMC Place; HANCOCK; ▲ Franklin; *183 E-7; mail Ellsworth z 04605; rural

Eight Corners; RMC Place; CUMBERLAND; ▲ Scarborough; *183 H-3; ★ **POR**; mail Scarborough z 04074; ● 80

Eliot; RMC Place; YORK; ▲ Eliot; 183 J-1; 🅿; ★ **PTSM-**; z 03903; ● 90

Eliot; MCD-Town; YORK; *183 J-2; 🅿; ★ **PTSM-**; z 03903; Ⓟ 5,329; Ⓒ 5,954; ◆ 5,960

Ellingwood Corner; RMC Place; WALDO; ▲ Winterport; *183 E-6; ★ **BANG**; mail Winterport z 04496

Ellis Pond; RMC Place; OXFORD; ▲ Roxbury, Byron; *183 E-2; mail Roxbury z 04275; summer pop. 300; ● 100

Ellsworth; Inc. Place; ⊡ HANCOCK; 183 E-7; elev. 100ft./30m.; 🅿 🅷; z 04605; Ⓟ 5,975; Ⓒ 6,456

Ellsworth Falls; RMC Place; HANCOCK; *183 E-7; elev. 122ft./37m.; mail Ellsworth z 04605; pop. incl. with Ellsworth (Inc. Place)

Elmore (Harts Neck); RMC Place; KNOX; *183 G-5; mail Tenants Harbor z 04860; ● 50

Elms; RMC Place; YORK; ▲ Wells; *183 I-2; mail Wells z 04090; ● 150

Elmwood; RMC Place; CUMBERLAND; ▲ Standish; *183 H-2; ★ **POR**; mail Standish z 04084; rural

Embden; RMC Place; SOMERSET; ▲ Embden; *183 D-4; 🅿; z 04958 & mail Solon z 04979; rural

Embden; MCD-Town; SOMERSET; *183 D-4; 🅿; z 04958; Ⓟ 659; Ⓒ 881

Embden Pond; RMC Place; SOMERSET; ▲ Embden; *183 D-4; mail North Anson z 04958; summer pop. 400

Emerson Corner; RMC Place; SOMERSET; ▲ Pittsfield; *183 E-5; mail Pittsfield z 04967; rural

Emery Mills; RMC Place; YORK; ▲ Shapleigh; 183 I-1; elev. 494ft./151m.; mail Shapleigh z 04076; ● 200

Emerys Bridge; RMC Place; YORK; ▲ South Berwick; *183 J-2; ★ **PTSM-**; mail South Berwick z 03908; rural

Emerys Corner; RMC Place; YORK; ▲ Limerick; *183 H-2; elev. 593ft./181m.; mail Limerick z 04048; rural

Emory Corner; RMC Place; YORK; ▲ Buxton; *183 H-2; ★ **POR**; mail Bar Mills z 04004

Empire Road; ANDROSCOGGIN; see East Poland (RMC Place)

Enfield; RMC Place; PENOBSCOT; ▲ Enfield; 183 C-7; elev. 211ft./64m.; 🅿; z 04493; ● 350

Enfield; MCD-Town; PENOBSCOT; *183 C-7; 🅿; z 04493; Ⓟ 1,476; Ⓒ 1,616

English; RMC Place; AROOSTOOK; mail Presque Isle z 04769; pop. incl. with Presque Isle (Inc. Place)

Epping; RMC Place; WASHINGTON; *183 E-9; mail Columbia Falls z 04623; rural

Estcourt Station; RMC Place; AROOSTOOK; 183 A-12; elev. 708ft./216m.; 🅿; z 04741 & mail Fort Kent z 04743, Standish z 04084; ● 25

Estes Lake; RMC Place; YORK; ▲ Sanford; *183 I-2; mail Sanford z 04073; ● 100

Etna; RMC Place; PENOBSCOT; ▲ Etna; 183 E-6; elev. 234ft./71m.; 🅿; z 04434; ● 140

Etna; MCD-Town; PENOBSCOT; *183 E-5; 🅿; z 04434; Ⓟ 977; Ⓒ 1,012

Etna Center; RMC Place; PENOBSCOT; ▲ Etna; *183 E-6; mail Etna z 04434; rural

Eugley Corner; RMC Place; LINCOLN; ▲ Waldoboro; *183 G-5; mail Waldoboro z 04572; rural

Eustis; RMC Place; FRANKLIN; ▲ Eustis; 183 C-2; elev. 1,172ft./357m.; 🅿; z 04936; ● 75

Eustis; MCD-Town; FRANKLIN; *183 C-2; 🅿; z 04936; Ⓟ 616; Ⓒ 685

Exeter; PENOBSCOT; see Exeter Corners (RMC Place)

Exeter; MCD-Town; PENOBSCOT; *183 D-5; 🅿; z 04435; Ⓟ 937; Ⓒ 997

Exeter Center; RMC Place; PENOBSCOT; ▲ Exeter; *183 D-5; elev. 310ft./94m.; mail Exeter z 04435; rural

Exeter Corners (Exeter); RMC Place; PENOBSCOT; ▲ Exeter; 183 D-5; mail Exeter z 04435; ● 80

Exeter Mills; RMC Place; PENOBSCOT; ▲ Exeter; *183 D-6; mail Corinth z 04427

F

Fairbanks; RMC Place; FRANKLIN; ▲ Farmington; 183 E-3; elev. 403ft./123m.; mail Farmington z 04938; ● 180

Fairfield; CDP; SOMERSET; ▲ Fairfield; 183 E-4; elev. 142ft./43m.; 🅿; ★ **WATRVL**; z 04937; Ⓟ 2,794; Ⓒ 2,569

Fairfield; MCD-Town; SOMERSET; *183 E-4; 🅿; ★ **WATRVL**; z 04937; Ⓟ 6,718; Ⓒ 6,573

Fairfield Center; RMC Place; SOMERSET; ▲ Fairfield; *183 E-4; elev. 205ft./62m.; ★ **WATRVL**; mail Fairfield z 04937; ● 150

Fairmount; RMC Place; AROOSTOOK; ▲ Fort Fairfield; *183 B-14; elev. 654ft./199m.; mail Fort Fairfield z 04742; rural

Falmouth; RMC Place; CUMBERLAND; ▲ Falmouth; 183 H-3; 🅿; ★ **POR**; z 04105; ● 7,610

Falmouth; MCD-Town; CUMBERLAND; *183 H-3; 🅿; ★ **POR**; z 04105; Ⓟ 7,610; Ⓒ 10,310; ◆ 10,958

Falmouth Foreside; CDP; CUMBERLAND; ▲ Falmouth; 183 H-10; ★ **POR**; mail Falmouth z 04105; Ⓟ 1,708; Ⓒ 1,964

Farmingdale; CDP; KENNEBEC; ▲ Farmingdale; 183 F-4; 🅿; ★ **AUG**; z 04344; Ⓟ 2,070; Ⓒ 1,935

Farmingdale; MCD-Town; KENNEBEC; *183 F-4; 🅿; ★ **AUG**; z 04344 & mail Hallowell z 04347; Ⓟ 2,918; Ⓒ 2,804

Farmington; CDP; ⊡ FRANKLIN; ▲ Farmington; 183 E-3; elev. 425ft./130m.; 🅿 🅷 🅲 2,267; z 04938; Ⓟ 4,197; Ⓒ 4,098

Farmington; MCD-Town; FRANKLIN; *183 E-3; 🅿 🅲 2,267; z 04938; Ⓟ 7,436; Ⓒ 7,410

Farmington Falls; RMC Place; FRANKLIN; ▲ Farmington, Chesterville; 183 E-3; 🅿; z 04940; ● 300

Farwells Corner; RMC Place; WALDO; ▲ Unity; *183 E-5; elev. 367ft./112m.; mail Unity z 04988; rural

Fayette; RMC Place; KENNEBEC; ▲ Fayette; 183 F-3; elev. 320ft./98m.; 🅿; z 04349; ● 100

Fayette; MCD-Town; KENNEBEC; *183 F-3; 🅿; z 04349; Ⓟ 855; Ⓒ 1,040

Fayette Corner; RMC Place; KENNEBEC; ▲ Fayette; *183 F-3; mail Kents Hill z 04349; rural

Felch Corner; RMC Place; YORK; ▲ Limerick; *183 H-2; elev. 538ft./164m.; mail Limerick z 04048

Ferry Beach; RMC Place; YORK; *183 I-2; mail Saco z 04072; pop. incl. with Saco (Inc. Place)

Fish Street; RMC Place; OXFORD; ▲ Fryeburg; *183 G-1; mail Fryeburg z 04037; rural

Five Corners; RMC Place; ANDROSCOGGIN; ▲ Poland, Mechanic Falls; *183 G-2; elev. 320ft./98m.; ★ **LEW-**; mail Mechanic Falls z 04256; ● 40

Five Corners; RMC Place; YORK; ▲ North Berwick; *183 I-2; mail North Berwick z 03906; ● 130

Five Islands; RMC Place; SAGADAHOC; ▲ Georgetown; *183 H-4; elev. 27ft./8m.; ★ **BR-BA**; mail Georgetown z 04548; ● 250

Five Mile Corners; RMC Place; HANCOCK; ▲ Orland; *183 E-6; mail East Orland z 04431; rural

Fletchers Landing; RMC Place; HANCOCK; *183 E-7; mail Ellsworth z 04605; ● 150

Forest City; RMC Place; WASHINGTON; 183 B-9; mail Brookton z 04413; ● 45

Fort Fairfield; CDP; AROOSTOOK; ▲ Fort Fairfield; 183 B-14; 🅿; z 04742; Ⓟ 1,729; Ⓒ 1,600

Fort Fairfield; MCD-Town; AROOSTOOK; *183 B-14; 🅿; z 04742; Ⓟ 3,998; Ⓒ 3,579

Fort Kent; CDP; AROOSTOOK; ▲ Fort Kent; 183 A-13; elev. 530ft./162m.; 🅿 🅷 🅲 1,339; z 04743 & mail Estcourt Station z 04741, Standish z 04084; Ⓟ 2,123; Ⓒ 1,978

Fort Kent; MCD-Town; AROOSTOOK; *183 A-13; 🅿 🅲 1,339; z 04743 & mail Estcourt Station z 04741; Ⓟ 4,268; Ⓒ 4,233

Fort Kent Mills; RMC Place; AROOSTOOK; ▲ Fort Kent; *183 A-13; 🅿; z 04744; ● 150

Fort Kent Village; RMC Place; AROOSTOOK; ▲ Fort Kent; *183 A-13; mail Fort Kent z 04743

Fortunes Rocks; RMC Place; YORK; *183 I-2; mail Biddeford z 04005

Fosters Corner; RMC Place; CUMBERLAND; ▲ Windham; *183 H-2; ★ **POR**; mail Windham z 04062; ● 75

Fosters Corner; RMC Place; WALDO; ▲ Knox; *183 F-5; elev. 599ft./183m.; mail Brooks z 04921; rural

Four Corners; RMC Place; AROOSTOOK; ▲ Limestone; *183 B-14; elev. 537ft./164m.; mail Limestone z 04750; rural

Four Corners; RMC Place; YORK; ▲ Kennebunk; *183 I-2; elev. 28ft./9m.; mail Kennebunk z 04043; ● 150

Fournier; RMC Place; AROOSTOOK; ▲ Madawaska; *183 A-13; elev. 511ft./156m.; mail Madawaska z 04756; rural

Frankfort; RMC Place; WALDO; ▲ Frankfort; 183 E-6; 🅿; z 04438; ● 180

Frankfort; MCD-Town; WALDO; *183 E-6; 🅿; z 04438; Ⓟ 1,020; Ⓒ 1,041

Franklin; RMC Place; HANCOCK; ▲ Franklin; 183 E-8; 🅿; z 04634; ● 300

Franklin; MCD-Town; HANCOCK; *183 E-8; 🅿; z 04634; Ⓟ 1,141; Ⓒ 1,370

FRANKLIN; 183 D-2; Ⓟ 29,008; Ⓒ 29,467; ◆ 29,758

Franklin Road; RMC Place; HANCOCK; ▲ Hancock; *183 E-7; mail Ellsworth z 04605; rural

Freedom; RMC Place; WALDO; ▲ Freedom; 183 E-5; 🅿; z 04941; ● 150

Freedom; MCD-Town; WALDO; *183 F-5; 🅿; z 04941; Ⓟ 593; Ⓒ 645

Freeport; CDP; CUMBERLAND; ▲ Freeport; 183 H-3; elev. 130ft./40m.; 🅿; ★ **POR**; z 04032-34; Ⓟ 1,829; Ⓒ 1,813

Freeport; MCD-Town; CUMBERLAND; *183 H-3; elev. 130ft./40m.; 🅿; ★ **POR**; z 04032-34; Ⓟ 6,905; Ⓒ 7,800; ◆ 8,072

Frenchboro; RMC Place; HANCOCK; ▲ Frenchboro; 183 G-7; 🅿; z 04635; ● 40

Frenchboro; MCD-Town; HANCOCK; *183 G-8; 🅿; z 04635; Ⓟ 44; Ⓒ 38

Frenchville; RMC Place; AROOSTOOK; ▲ Ashland; *183 B-13; 🅿; z 04745 & mail Ashland z 04732; ● 140

Frenchville; RMC Place; AROOSTOOK; ▲ Frenchville; 183 A-13; 🅿; z 04745; ● 475

Frenchville; AROOSTOOK; see Upper Frenchville (RMC Place)

Frenchville; MCD-Town; AROOSTOOK; *183 A-13; 🅿; z 04745; Ⓟ 1,338; Ⓒ 1,225

Friendship; RMC Place; KNOX; ▲ Friendship; 183 G-5; 🅿; z 04547; ● 600

Friendship; MCD-Town; KNOX; *183 G-5; 🅿; z 04547; Ⓟ 1,099; Ⓒ 1,204

Frye; RMC Place; OXFORD; ▲ Roxbury; 183 E-2; elev. 576ft./176m.; mail Roxbury z 04275; ● 60

Fryeburg; CDP; OXFORD; ▲ Fryeburg; 183 G-1; elev. 430ft./131m.; 🅿; z 04037; Ⓟ 1,580; Ⓒ 1,549

Fryeburg; MCD-Town; OXFORD; *183 G-1; 🅿; z 04037; Ⓟ 2,968; Ⓒ 3,083

Fryeburg Center; RMC Place; OXFORD; ▲ Fryeburg; *183 G-1; elev. 438ft./134m.; mail Fryeburg z 04037

Fryeburg Harbor; RMC Place; OXFORD; ▲ Fryeburg; mail Fryeburg z 04037; rural

Frye Island; RMC Place; CUMBERLAND; ▲ Raymond; *183 H-2; 🅿; ★ **POR**; z 04071; disincorporated March 8, 2000; summer pop. 150

Frye Island; MCD-Town; CUMBERLAND; *183 H-2; 🅿; ★ **POR**; z 04071; Ⓒ 0

G

Gardiner; Inc. Place; KENNEBEC; 183 F-4; elev. 122ft./37m.; 🅿; ★ **AUG**; z 04345; Ⓟ 6,746; Ⓒ 6,198

Garfield; MCD-Plantation; AROOSTOOK; *183 B-13; mail Ashland z 04732; Ⓟ 102; Ⓒ 86

Garland; RMC Place; PENOBSCOT; ▲ Garland; 183 D-5; 🅿; z 04939; ● 150

Garland; MCD-Town; PENOBSCOT; *183 D-5; 🅿; z 04939; Ⓟ 1,064; Ⓒ 990

Georgetown; RMC Place; SAGADAHOC; ▲ Georgetown; 183 H-4; 🅿; ★ **BR-BA**; z 04548; ● 150

Georgetown; MCD-Town; SAGADAHOC; *183 H-4; 🅿; ★ **BR-BA**; z 04548; Ⓟ 914; Ⓒ 1,020

Gerrishville; RMC Place; HANCOCK; ▲ Winter Harbor; *183 F-8; mail Winter Harbor z 04693; ● 15

Ghent; RMC Place; WALDO; ▲ Searsmont; *183 F-5; mail Searsmont z 04973; rural

Gilbertville; RMC Place; OXFORD; ▲ Canton; *183 F-3; mail Canton z 04221

Gilead; RMC Place; OXFORD; ▲ Gilead; 183 F-1; 🅿; z 04217; ● 50

Gilead; MCD-Town; OXFORD; *183 F-1; 🅿; z 04217; Ⓟ 204; Ⓒ 156

Glantz Corner; RMC Place; CUMBERLAND; ▲ Windham; *183 H-2; ★ **POR**; mail Windham z 04062; rural

Glenburn; PENOBSCOT; see Glenburn Center (RMC Place)

Glenburn; MCD-Town; PENOBSCOT; *183 D-6; 🅿; ★ **BANG**; z 04401; Ⓟ 3,198; Ⓒ 3,964; ◆ 4,509

Glenburn Center (Glenburn); RMC Place; PENOBSCOT; ▲ Glenburn; 183 D-6; elev. 182ft./55m.; ★ **BANG**; mail Bangor z 04401; ● 60

Glen Cove; RMC Place; KNOX; ▲ Rockport; *183 G-6; 🅿; z 04846; ● 225

Glendon; RMC Place; LINCOLN; ▲ Nobleboro; *183 G-5; mail Waldoboro z 04572; rural

Glenmere; RMC Place; KNOX; ▲ St. George; *183 G-5; mail Tenants Harbor z 04860; rural

Glenwood; MCD-Plantation; AROOSTOOK; *183 A-8; mail Wytopitlock z 04497; Ⓟ 8; Ⓒ 0

Goodings; RMC Place; AROOSTOOK; mail Presque Isle z 04769; pop. incl. with Presque Isle (Inc. Place)

Good Will-Hinckley School; RMC Place; SOMERSET; ▲ Fairfield; *183 E-4; ★ **WATRVL**; mail Hinckley z 04944

Goodwins Mills; RMC Place; YORK; ▲ Lyman, Dayton; 183 I-2; mail Biddeford z 04005; ● 50

Goose Rocks Beach; RMC Place; YORK; ▲ Kennebunkport; *183 I-2; mail Kennebunkport z 04046; summer pop. 400; ● 100

Gorham; CDP; CUMBERLAND; ▲ Gorham; 183 H-2; elev. 212ft./65m.; 🅿; ★ **POR**; z 04038; Ⓟ 3,618; Ⓒ 4,164

Gorham; MCD-Town; CUMBERLAND; *183 H-2; 🅿; ★ **POR**; z 04038; Ⓟ 11,856; Ⓒ 14,141; ◆ 14,913

Gotts Island; RMC Place; HANCOCK; ▲ Tremont; mail Bass Harbor z 04653; summer pop. 80

Gould Corner; RMC Place; YORK; ▲ Eliot; *183 J-1; ★ **PTSM-**; mail Eliot z 03903; rural

Gould Landing; RMC Place; PENOBSCOT; ▲ Orono; *183 D-6; elev. 137ft./42m.; ★ **BANG**; mail Bangor z 04401; ● 30

Gouldsboro; RMC Place; HANCOCK; ▲ Gouldsboro; 183 F-8; 🅿; z 04607; ● 200

Gouldsboro; MCD-Town; HANCOCK; *183 F-8; 🅿; z 04607; Ⓟ 1,986; Ⓒ 1,941

Grand Beach; RMC Place; CUMBERLAND; ▲ Scarborough; *183 I-3; ★ **POR**; mail Scarborough z 04074; summer pop. 300; ● 100

Grand Isle; RMC Place; AROOSTOOK; ▲ Grand Isle; 183 A-14; 🅿; z 04746; ● 375

Grand Isle; MCD-Town; AROOSTOOK; *183 A-14; 🅿; z 04746; Ⓟ 558; Ⓒ 518

Grand Lake Stream; RMC Place; WASHINGTON; ▲ Grand Lake Stream; 183 C-9; elev. 303ft./92m.; 🅿; z 04637; ● 140

Grand Lake Stream; MCD-Plantation; WASHINGTON; *183 C-9; 🅿; z 04637; Ⓟ 174; Ⓒ 150

Granite Hill; RMC Place; KENNEBEC; ★ **AUG**; mail Hallowell z 04347; pop. incl. with Hallowell (Inc. Place)

Grass Corner; RMC Place; AROOSTOOK; ▲ Limestone; *183 B-14; elev. 722ft./220m.; mail Limestone z 04750; rural

Gray; RMC Place; CUMBERLAND; ▲ Gray; 183 H-3; elev. 301ft./92m.; 🅿; ★ **POR**; z 04039; ● 1,100

Gray; MCD-Town; CUMBERLAND; *183 H-3; 🅿; ★ **POR**; z 04039; Ⓟ 5,904; Ⓒ 6,820; ◆ 7,211

Grays Corner; RMC Place; HANCOCK; ▲ Sedgwick; *183 F-7; elev. 127ft./39m.; mail Sedgwick z 04676; rural

Great Diamond Island; RMC Place; CUMBERLAND; *183 H-3; 🅿; ★ **POR**; z 04109; pop. incl. with Portland (Inc. Place)

Great East Lake; RMC Place; YORK; ▲ Acton; *183 I-1; mail Acton z 04001; summer pop. 400

Great Falls; RMC Place; ANDROSCOGGIN; *183 G-3; ★ **LEW-**; mail Auburn z 04210, z 04212; pop. incl. with Auburn (Inc. Place)

Great Pond; RMC Place; HANCOCK; ▲ Great Pond; 183 D-7; 🅿; z 04408; ● 50

Great Pond; MCD-Town; HANCOCK; *183 D-7; 🅿; z 04408; Ⓟ 59; Ⓒ 47

Great Works; RMC Place; PENOBSCOT; *183 D-7; ★ **BANG**; mail Old Town z 04468; pop. incl. with Old Town (Inc. Place)

Great Works; RMC Place; YORK; ▲ South Berwick; *183 J-1; ★ **PTSM-**; mail South Berwick z 03908

Greeleys Landing; RMC Place; PISCATAQUIS; ▲ Dover-Foxcroft; *183 C-5; mail Dover Foxcroft z 04426

Green Acre; RMC Place; YORK; *183 J-1; ★ **PTSM-**; mail Eliot z 03903

Greenbush; RMC Place; PENOBSCOT; ▲ Greenbush; 183 D-7; 🅿; z 04418; ● 80

Greenbush; MCD-Town; PENOBSCOT; *183 D-7; 🅿; z 04418 & mail Vancouver z 98662; Ⓟ 1,309; Ⓒ 1,421

Greene; RMC Place; ANDROSCOGGIN; ▲ Greene; 183 G-3; elev. 316ft./96m.; 🅿; ★ **LEW-**; z 04236; ● 500

Greene; MCD-Town; ANDROSCOGGIN; *183 G-3; 🅿; ★ **LEW-**; z 04236; Ⓟ 3,661; Ⓒ 4,076; ◆ 4,494

Greenfield; RMC Place; PENOBSCOT; ▲ East Central Penobscot; 183 D-7; elev. 411ft./125m.; ● 40

Green Lake; RMC Place; HANCOCK; ▲ Dedham; *183 E-7; elev. 178ft./54m.; mail Holden z 04429

Greens Corner; RMC Place; WALDO; ▲ Troy; *183 E-5; elev. 313ft./95m.; mail Unity z 04988; rural

Greenville; CDP; PISCATAQUIS; ▲ Greenville; 183 B-4; 🅿; z 04441, z 04485 & mail Greenville Junction z 04442; Ⓟ 1,601; Ⓒ 1,319

Greenville; PISCATAQUIS; see Greenville Junction (RMC Place)

Greenville; MCD-Town; PISCATAQUIS; *183 B-4; 🅿; z 04441, z 04485; Ⓟ 1,884; Ⓒ 1,623

Greenville Junction (Greenville); RMC Place; PISCATAQUIS; ▲ Greenville; 183 B-4; elev. 1,059ft./323m.; 🅿; z 04442 & mail Greenville z 04441, Shirley Mills z 04485; ● 450

Greenwood; RMC Place; OXFORD; ▲ Greenwood; *183 F-2; elev. 687ft./209m.; 🅿; z 04255 & mail West Paris z 04289

Greenwood; OXFORD; see Locke Mills (RMC Place)

Greenwood; MCD-Town; OXFORD; *183 F-2; 🅿; z 04255 & mail West Paris z 04289; Ⓟ 689; Ⓒ 802

Grimes Mill; RMC Place; AROOSTOOK; *183 B-14; mail Caribou z 04736; pop. incl. with Caribou (Inc. Place)

Grindstone; RMC Place; PENOBSCOT; 183 B-7; mail Medway z 04460; ● 50

Grindstone Neck; RMC Place; HANCOCK; ▲ Winter Harbor; *183 F-8; mail Winter Harbor z 04693; summer pop. 200

Grove; RMC Place; WASHINGTON; ▲ Cooper; 183 D-9; elev. 407ft./124m.; mail Meddybemps z 04657; ● 40

Groveville; RMC Place; YORK; ▲ Buxton; *183 H-2; elev. 251ft./77m.; ★ **POR**; mail Buxton z 04093; ● 180

Growstown; RMC Place; CUMBERLAND; ▲ Brunswick; *183 H-3; ★ **BR-BA**; mail Brunswick z 04011; rural

Guerette; RMC Place; AROOSTOOK; 183 A-13; elev. 591ft./180m.; mail Stockholm z 04783; ● 45

Entries in **UPPERCASE** are counties.
Entries in **bold** have populations of 2,500 or more.
Names in parentheses are alternate names.

Inc. Place	Incorporated Place
RMC Place	Rand McNally Designated Place
CDP	Census Designated Place
MCD	Minor Civil Division
⊡	County Seat
▲	Minor Civil Division
elev.	Elevation
🅿	Post Office
🅷	Hospital
🅲	College
■	Principal Business Center
★	Ranally Metro Area (RMA) Abbreviation
z	Zip Code(s)
Ⓟ	Previous Census Population
Ⓡ	Revised Census Population
Ⓐ	Annexation Population
●	Rand McNally Population Estimate
Ⓒ	Final Census Population
Ⓢ	Special Census Population
◆	Estimated Population

For additional definitions see Glossary, Volume 1, and Introduction, Volume 2.

Guilford; CDP; PISCATAQUIS; ▲ Guilford; 183 C-5; 🅿; z 04443; Ⓒ 945
Guilford; MCD-Town; PISCATAQUIS; *183 C-5; 🅿; z 04443; Ⓟ 1,710; Ⓒ 1,531
Guillemette; RMC Place; YORK; ▲ Sanford; mail Sanford z 04073; ● 300

H

Hackett Mills; RMC Place; ANDROSCOGGIN; ▲ Poland, Minot; *183 G-3; ★ LEW-; mail Minot z 04258
Haines Corner; RMC Place; ANDROSCOGGIN; ▲ Livermore Falls; *183 F-3; mail East Livermore z 04228; rural
Haines Landing; FRANKLIN; see Mooselookmeguntic (RMC Place)
Halldale; RMC Place; WALDO; ▲ Montville; *183 F-5; mail Freedom z 04941; ● 35
Hallowell; Inc. Place; KENNEBEC; 183 F-4; elev. 200ft./61m.; 🅿; ★ AUG; z 04347; Ⓟ 2,534; Ⓒ 2,467
Hall Quarry; RMC Place; HANCOCK; ▲ Mount Desert; 183 H-12; mail Mount Desert z 04660; ● 100
Hamilton Station; RMC Place; HANCOCK; ▲ Bar Harbor; *183 F-7; mail Salsbury Cove z 04672; ● 30
Hamlin; RMC Place; AROOSTOOK; ▲ Hamlin; *183 B-14; elev. 537ft./164m.; 🅿; z 04785; ● 90
Hamlin; MCD-Town; AROOSTOOK; *183 A-14; 🅿; z 04785; Ⓟ 204; Ⓒ 257
Hammond; MCD-Town; AROOSTOOK; *183 C-14; 🅿; z 04730; Ⓟ 93; Ⓒ 98
Hampden; CDP; PENOBSCOT; ▲ Hampden; 183 E-6; 🅿; ★ BANG; z 04444; Ⓟ 3,895; Ⓒ 4,126
Hampden; MCD-Town; PENOBSCOT; *183 E-6; 🅿; ★ BANG; z 04444; Ⓟ 5,974; Ⓒ 6,327; ◆ 6,806
Hampden Center; RMC Place; PENOBSCOT; ▲ Hampden; *183 E-6; ★ BANG; mail Hampden z 04444; rural
Hampden Highlands; RMC Place; PENOBSCOT; ▲ Hampden; 183 E-6; elev. 162ft./49m.; ★ BANG; mail Hampden z 04444; ● 800
Hancock; RMC Place; HANCOCK; ▲ Hancock; 183 E-8; 🅿; z 04640; ● 400
Hancock; MCD-Town; HANCOCK; *183 E-7; 🅿; z 04640; Ⓟ 1,757; Ⓒ 2,147
HANCOCK; 183 D-7; Ⓟ 46,948; Ⓒ 51,791; ◆ 52,919
Hancock Point; RMC Place; HANCOCK; ▲ Hancock; 183 F-8; mail Hancock z 04640; ● 40
Hanover; RMC Place; OXFORD; ▲ Hanover; 183 F-2; elev. 635ft./194m.; 🅿; z 04237; ● 175
Hanover; MCD-Town; OXFORD; *183 F-2; 🅿; z 04237; Ⓟ 272; Ⓒ 251
Harborside; RMC Place; HANCOCK; ▲ Brooksville; 183 F-6; elev. 85ft./26m.; 🅿; z 04642; ● 100
Harding; RMC Place; CUMBERLAND; ▲ Brunswick; *183 G-4; ★ BR-BA; mail Brunswick z 04011; rural
Harfords Point; RMC Place; PISCATAQUIS; *183 B-4; mail Greenville Junction z 04442; summer pop. 200
Harmon Beach; RMC Place; CUMBERLAND; ▲ Standish; *183 H-2; ★ POR; mail Standish z 04084; summer pop. 150; ● 40
Harmony; RMC Place; SOMERSET; ▲ Harmony; 183 D-4; elev. 316ft./96m.; 🅿; z 04942; ● 275
Harmony; MCD-Town; SOMERSET; *183 D-4; 🅿; z 04942; Ⓟ 838; Ⓒ 954
Harpswell; CUMBERLAND; see South Harpswell (RMC Place)
Harpswell; MCD-Town; CUMBERLAND; *183 H-3; 🅿; ★ BR-BA; z 04079; Ⓟ 5,012; Ⓒ 5,239
Harpswell Center; RMC Place; CUMBERLAND; ▲ Harpswell; *183 H-3; ★ BR-BA; mail Harpswell z 04079; rural
Harrington; RMC Place; WASHINGTON; ▲ Harrington; 183 E-9; 🅿; z 04643; ● 300
Harrington; MCD-Town; WASHINGTON; *183 E-9; 🅿; z 04643; Ⓟ 893; Ⓒ 882
Harrington Corner; RMC Place; LINCOLN; ▲ Nobleboro; *183 G-5; mail Nobleboro z 04555
Harrison; RMC Place; CUMBERLAND; ▲ Harrison; 183 G-2; 🅿; z 04040; ● 600
Harrison; MCD-Town; CUMBERLAND; *183 G-2; 🅿; z 04040; Ⓟ 1,951; Ⓒ 2,315
Hartford; RMC Place; OXFORD; ▲ Hartford; 183 F-3; elev. 460ft./140m.; 🅿; z 04220 & mail Canton z 04221; ● 60
Hartford; MCD-Town; OXFORD; *183 F-3; 🅿; z 04220 & mail Canton z 04221; Ⓟ 722; Ⓒ 963
Hartland; CDP; SOMERSET; ▲ Hartland; 183 D-5; elev. 258ft./79m.; 🅿; z 04943; Ⓟ 1,038; Ⓒ 872
Hartland; MCD-Town; SOMERSET; *183 D-4; 🅿; z 04943; Ⓟ 1,806; Ⓒ 1,816
Harts Neck; KNOX; see Elmore (RMC Place)
Haskell Corner; RMC Place; ANDROSCOGGIN; *183 G-3; ★ LEW-; mail Auburn z 04210; pop. incl. with Auburn (Inc. Place)
Hatchs Corner; RMC Place; LINCOLN; ▲ Dresden; *183 G-4; mail Dresden z 04342
Haven; RMC Place; HANCOCK; ▲ Brooklin; *183 F-7; elev. 78ft./24m.; mail Brooklin z 04616; ● 175
Hayden Corner; RMC Place; KENNEBEC; ▲ Winslow; *183 E-4; ★ WATRVL; mail Waterville z 04901; ● 50
Hayford Corner; RMC Place; WALDO; *183 F-6; pop. incl. with Belfast (Inc. Place)
Haynesville; RMC Place; AROOSTOOK; ▲ Haynesville; 183 A-8; 🅿; z 04497; ● 70
Haynesville; MCD-Town; AROOSTOOK; *183 A-8; 🅿; z 04497; Ⓟ 243; Ⓒ 122
Head of the Tide; RMC Place; WALDO; *183 F-6; mail Belfast z 04915; pop. incl. with Belfast (Inc. Place)
Head Tide; RMC Place; LINCOLN; ▲ Alna; *183 G-4; elev. 34ft./10m.; mail Alna z 04535; ● 75
Hebron; RMC Place; OXFORD; ▲ Hebron; 183 G-2; elev. 576ft./176m.; 🅿; z 04238; ● 300
Hebron; MCD-Town; OXFORD; *183 G-3; 🅿; z 04238; Ⓟ 878; Ⓒ 1,053
Hermon; RMC Place; PENOBSCOT; ▲ Hermon; *183 E-6; elev. 178ft./54m.; 🅿; ★ BANG; z 04401; ● 200
Hermon; MCD-Town; PENOBSCOT; *183 E-6; 🅿; ★ BANG; z 04401; Ⓟ 3,755; Ⓒ 4,437; ◆ 5,103
Hermon Center; RMC Place; PENOBSCOT; ▲ Hermon; *183 E-6; elev. 137ft./42m.; ★ BANG; mail Bangor z 04401; ● 100
Hermon Pond; RMC Place; PENOBSCOT; ▲ Hermon; *183 E-6; ★ BANG; mail Bangor z 04401; rural
Heron Island; RMC Place; LINCOLN; ▲ South Bristol; *183 H-4; mail South Bristol z 04568; summer pop. 150; ● 20
Herricks; RMC Place; HANCOCK; ▲ Brooksville; *183 F-6; mail Brooksville z 04617; ● 10
Hersey; MCD-Town; AROOSTOOK; *183 C-13; 🅿; z 04780 & mail Patten z 04765; Ⓟ 69; Ⓒ 63
Higgins Beach; RMC Place; CUMBERLAND; ▲ Scarborough; *183 I-3; ★ POR; mail Scarborough z 04074; summer pop. 500; ● 200
Higginsville; RMC Place; PENOBSCOT; ▲ Kenduskeag; *183 D-6; ★ BANG; mail Kenduskeag z 04450; rural
Highland; MCD-Plantation; SOMERSET; *183 D-3; mail New Portland z 04961; Ⓟ 38; Ⓒ 52
Highland Lake (Duck Pond Center); RMC Place; CUMBERLAND; *183 H-3; ★ POR; mail Westbrook z 04092; pop. incl. with Westbrook (Inc. Place)
Highpine; RMC Place; YORK; ▲ Wells; *183 I-2; mail Wells z 04090; rural
Hills Beach; RMC Place; YORK; *183 I-2; mail Biddeford z 04005; pop. incl. with Biddeford (Inc. Place)
Hillside; RMC Place; CUMBERLAND; ▲ Sebago; *183 G-2; elev. 144ft./44m.; mail Sebago z 04029; rural
Hinckley; RMC Place; SOMERSET; ▲ Fairfield; 183 E-4; elev. 135ft./41m.; 🅿; ★ WATRVL; z 04944; ● 120
Hiram; RMC Place; OXFORD; ▲ Hiram; 183 H-2; elev. 369ft./112m.; 🅿; z 04041; ● 350
Hiram; MCD-Town; OXFORD; *183 H-1; 🅿; z 04041; Ⓟ 1,260; Ⓒ 1,423
Hodgdon; RMC Place; AROOSTOOK; ▲ Hodgdon; 183 D-14; 🅿; z 04730; ● 350
Hodgdon; MCD-Town; AROOSTOOK; *183 C-14; 🅿; z 04730; Ⓟ 1,257; Ⓒ 1,240
Hodgdon Corners; RMC Place; AROOSTOOK; ▲ Hodgdon; *183 D-14; mail Houlton z 04730
Holden (Holden Center); RMC Place; PENOBSCOT; ▲ Holden; 183 E-6; 🅿; ★ BANG; z 04429; ● 125
Holden; MCD-Town; PENOBSCOT; *183 E-7; 🅿; ★ BANG; z 04429; Ⓟ 2,952; Ⓒ 2,827; ◆ 2,960
Holden Center; PENOBSCOT; see Holden (RMC Place)
Hollis; MCD-Town; YORK; *183 H-2; ★ POR; mail Hollis Center z 04042; Ⓟ 3,573; Ⓒ 4,114; ◆ 4,308
Hollis Center; RMC Place; YORK; ▲ Hollis; 183 H-2; elev. 180ft./55m.; 🅿; ★ POR; z 04042; ● 250
Holmes Bay; RMC Place; WASHINGTON; ▲ Machiasport; *183 E-10; mail Whiting z 04691; rural
Holmes Mill; RMC Place; WALDO; *183 F-6; elev. 122ft./37m.; mail Belfast z 04915; pop. incl. with Belfast (Inc. Place)
Hope; RMC Place; KNOX; ▲ Hope; 183 F-5; elev. 349ft./106m.; 🅿; z 04847; ● 100
Hope; MCD-Town; KNOX; *183 F-5; 🅿; z 04847; Ⓟ 1,017; Ⓒ 1,310
Houghton; RMC Place; OXFORD; ▲ Byron; *183 E-2; mail Roxbury z 04275; rural
Houlton; CDP; ⊡ AROOSTOOK; ▲ Houlton; 183 C-14; elev. 366ft./112m.; 🅿 🅷; z 04730, z 04761; Ⓟ 5,627; Ⓒ 5,270
Houlton; MCD-Town; AROOSTOOK; *183 C-14; 🅿; z 04730, z 04761; Ⓟ 6,613; Ⓒ 6,476
Howes Corner; RMC Place; ANDROSCOGGIN; ▲ Turner; *183 F-3; ★ LEW-; mail Turner z 04282; rural
Howland; CDP; PENOBSCOT; ▲ Howland; 183 C-7; 🅿; z 04448; Ⓟ 1,304; Ⓒ 1,210
Howland; MCD-Town; PENOBSCOT; *183 C-6; 🅿; z 04448; Ⓟ 1,435; Ⓒ 1,362
Hoyttown; RMC Place; WASHINGTON; ▲ Machias; *183 E-9; mail Machias z 04654; ● 50
Hudson; RMC Place; PENOBSCOT; ▲ Hudson; 183 D-6; 🅿; z 04449; ● 150
Hudson; MCD-Town; PENOBSCOT; *183 D-6; 🅿; z 04449; Ⓟ 1,048; Ⓒ 1,393
Hulls Cove; RMC Place; HANCOCK; ▲ Bar Harbor; 183 F-8; 🅿; z 04644; ● 250
Hunts Corner; RMC Place; OXFORD; ▲ South Oxford; *183 F-2; elev. 1,049ft./320m.; mail Bethel z 04217; rural
Hutchins Corner; RMC Place; PISCATAQUIS; ▲ Wellington; *183 D-4; elev. 762ft./232m.; mail Harmony z 04942; rural

I

Indian Point; RMC Place; HANCOCK; ▲ Bar Harbor; *183 F-7; elev. 117ft./36m.; mail Mount Desert z 04660; rural
Indian River; RMC Place; WASHINGTON; ▲ Addison; 183 E-9; mail Addison z 04606; ● 40
Industrial; RMC Place; AROOSTOOK; mail Presque Isle z 04769; pop. incl. with Presque Isle (Inc. Place)
Industry; MCD-Town; FRANKLIN; *183 E-3; 🅿; z 04938; Ⓟ 685; Ⓒ 790
Ingall's Hill; RMC Place; CUMBERLAND; ▲ Bridgton; *183 G-2; mail Bridgton z 04009; rural
Intervale; RMC Place; CUMBERLAND; ▲ New Gloucester; *183 G-3; elev. 119ft./36m.; mail New Gloucester z 04260; rural
Ireland Corner; RMC Place; CUMBERLAND; ▲ Windham; *183 H-3; ★ POR; mail Windham z 04062; rural
Irish Settlement; RMC Place; WASHINGTON; *183 B-8; mail Danforth z 04424; rural
Island Falls; RMC Place; AROOSTOOK; ▲ Island Falls; 183 A-7; 🅿; z 04747; ● 600
Island Falls; MCD-Town; AROOSTOOK; *183 D-13; 🅿; z 04747; Ⓟ 897; Ⓒ 793
Isle au Haut; RMC Place; KNOX; ▲ Isle Au Haut; 183 G-7; 🅿; z 04645; summer pop. 250; ● 75
Isle Au Haut; MCD-Town; KNOX; *183 G-7; 🅿; z 04645; Ⓟ 46; Ⓒ 79
Isle of Springs; RMC Place; LINCOLN; ▲ Boothbay Harbor; *183 H-4; 🅿; z 04549; summer pop. 150; rural
Islesboro; RMC Place; WALDO; ▲ Islesboro; 183 F-6; elev. 42ft./13m.; 🅿; z 04848; ● 140
Islesboro; MCD-Town; WALDO; *183 F-6; 🅿; z 04848; Ⓟ 579; Ⓒ 603
Islesford; RMC Place; HANCOCK; ▲ Cranberry Isles; 183 I-13; 🅿; z 04646; summer pop. 300; ● 80

J

Jackman; RMC Place; SOMERSET; ▲ Jackman; 183 B-3; elev. 1,172ft./357m.; 🅿; z 04945; ● 800
Jackman; MCD-Town; SOMERSET; *183 B-3; 🅿; z 04945; Ⓟ 920; Ⓒ 718
Jackson; RMC Place; WALDO; ▲ Jackson; 183 E-5; elev. 198ft./60m.; 🅿; z 04921; ● 100
Jackson; MCD-Town; WALDO; *183 E-5; 🅿; z 04921; Ⓟ 415; Ⓒ 506
Jackson Corner; RMC Place; PISCATAQUIS; ▲ Sangerville; *183 D-5; mail Sangerville z 04479; rural
Jackson Corners; RMC Place; WALDO; ▲ Jackson; *183 F-5; elev. 477ft./145m.; mail Brooks z 04921; rural
Jacksonville; RMC Place; WASHINGTON; ▲ East Machias; 183 E-9; elev. 47ft./14m.; mail East Machias z 04630; ● 150
Jay; RMC Place; FRANKLIN; ▲ Jay; 183 F-3; elev. 374ft./114m.; 🅿; z 04239 & mail North Jay z 04262; ● 600
Jay; MCD-Town; FRANKLIN; *183 E-3; 🅿; z 04239 & mail North Jay z 04262; Ⓟ 5,080; Ⓒ 4,985
Jefferson; RMC Place; LINCOLN; ▲ Jefferson; 183 G-5; 🅿; z 04348; ● 275
Jefferson; MCD-Town; LINCOLN; *183 G-5; 🅿; z 04348; Ⓟ 2,111; Ⓒ 2,388
Jemtland; RMC Place; AROOSTOOK; ▲ New Sweden; *183 B-14; mail Stockholm z 04783; ● 40
Jewett; RMC Place; YORK; ▲ South Berwick; *183 J-2; ★ PTSM-; mail South Berwick z 03908; rural
Jonesboro; RMC Place; WASHINGTON; ▲ Jonesboro; 183 E-9; 🅿; z 04648; ● 220
Jonesboro; MCD-Town; WASHINGTON; *183 E-9; 🅿; z 04648; Ⓟ 585; Ⓒ 594
Jonesport; RMC Place; WASHINGTON; ▲ Jonesport; 183 E-9; elev. 19ft./6m.; 🅿; z 04649; ● 1,100
Jonesport; MCD-Town; WASHINGTON; *183 E-9; 🅿; z 04649; Ⓟ 1,525; Ⓒ 1,408
Jordan Mills; RMC Place; PENOBSCOT; ▲ Mattawamkeag; *183 B-7; mail Mattawamkeag z 04459; rural

K

Kalers Corner; RMC Place; LINCOLN; ▲ Waldoboro; *183 G-5; mail Waldoboro z 04572
Keegan; RMC Place; AROOSTOOK; ▲ Van Buren; 183 A-14; elev. 452ft./138m.; mail Van Buren z 04785; ● 200
Keenes Corner; RMC Place; ANDROSCOGGIN; ▲ Leeds; *183 F-3; mail Leeds z 04263; rural
Kendalls Corner; RMC Place; WALDO; ▲ Waldo; *183 F-6; mail Belfast z 04915; rural
Kenduskeag; RMC Place; PENOBSCOT; ▲ Kenduskeag; 183 D-6; elev. 127ft./39m.; 🅿; ★ BANG; z 04450; ● 350
Kenduskeag; MCD-Town; PENOBSCOT; *183 D-6; 🅿; ★ BANG; z 04450; Ⓟ 1,234; Ⓒ 1,171; ◆ 1,209
Kennard Corner; RMC Place; YORK; *183 J-1; ★ PTSM-; mail Eliot z 03903
Kennebago Lake Camps; RMC Place; FRANKLIN; *183 D-2; mail Rangeley z 04970
Kennebec; RMC Place; WASHINGTON; ▲ Machias; *183 E-9; elev. 25ft./8m.; mail Machias z 04654; ● 40
KENNEBEC; 183 F-4; Ⓟ 115,904; Ⓒ 117,114; ◆ 119,613
Kennebunk; CDP; YORK; ▲ Kennebunk; 183 I-2; 🅿; z 04043; Ⓟ 4,206; Ⓒ 4,804
Kennebunk; MCD-Town; YORK; *183 I-2; 🅿; z 04043; Ⓟ 8,004; Ⓒ 10,476
Kennebunk Beach; RMC Place; YORK; ▲ Kennebunk; *183 I-2; mail Kennebunk z 04043; summer pop. 350; ● 150
Kennebunk Landing; RMC Place; YORK; ▲ Kennebunk, Arundel; *183 I-2; mail Kennebunk z 04043; ● 200
Kennebunk Pond; RMC Place; YORK; ▲ Lyman; *183 I-2; mail Alfred z 04002; summer pop. 200
Kennebunkport; CDP; YORK; ▲ Kennebunkport; 183 I-2; 🅿; z 04046; Ⓟ 1,100; Ⓒ 1,376
Kennebunkport; MCD-Town; YORK; *183 I-2; 🅿; z 04046; Ⓟ 3,356; Ⓒ 3,720
Kents Hill; RMC Place; KENNEBEC; ▲ Readfield; 183 F-3; 🅿; z 04349; ● 200
Kezar Falls (Parsonfield); RMC Place; OXFORD, YORK; ▲ Porter, Parsonsfield; 183 H-1; 🅿; z 04047; ● 900
Kingfield; RMC Place; FRANKLIN; ▲ Kingfield; 183 D-3; elev. 560ft./171m.; 🅿; z 04947; ● 850
Kingfield; MCD-Town; FRANKLIN; *183 D-3; 🅿; z 04947; Ⓟ 1,114; Ⓒ 1,103
Kingman; RMC Place; PENOBSCOT; 183 B-8; elev. 341ft./104m.; 🅿; z 04451; ● 140
Kingsbury; RMC Place; PISCATAQUIS; ▲ Kingsbury; *183 D-4; mail Harmony z 04942; ● 10
Kingsbury; MCD-Plantation; PISCATAQUIS; *183 C-4; mail Harmony z 04942; Ⓟ 13; Ⓒ 9
Kinney Shores; RMC Place; YORK; *183 I-2; mail Saco z 04072; pop. incl. with Saco (Inc. Place)
Kittery; CDP; YORK; ▲ Kittery; 183 J-2; elev. 22ft./7m.; 🅿; ★ PTSM-; z 03904; Ⓟ 5,151; Ⓒ 4,884
Kittery; MCD-Town; YORK; *183 J-2; 🅿; ★ PTSM-; z 03904; Ⓟ 9,372; Ⓒ 9,543; ◆ 9,968
Kittery Foreside; RMC Place; YORK; ▲ Kittery; *183 J-2; ★ PTSM-; mail Kittery z 03904
Kittery Point; CDP; YORK; ▲ Kittery; 183 J-2; 🅿; ★ PTSM-; z 03905; Ⓟ 1,093; Ⓒ 1,135
Knights Landing; RMC Place; PISCATAQUIS; ▲ Brownville, Lake View; 183 C-6; mail Brownville z 04414; summer pop. 100; ● 20
Knightville; RMC Place; CUMBERLAND; *183 H-3; ★ POR; mail South Portland z 04106; pop. incl. with South Portland (Inc. Place)
Knowles Corner; RMC Place; AROOSTOOK; ▲ Moro; *183 C-13; elev. 1,069ft./326m.; mail Smyrna Mills z 04780; rural
Knox; MCD-Town; WALDO; *183 F-5; 🅿; z 04986; Ⓟ 681; Ⓒ 747
KNOX; 183 F-5; Ⓟ 36,310; Ⓒ 39,618; ◆ 40,328
Knox Center; RMC Place; WALDO; ▲ Knox; *183 F-5; mail Thorndike z 04986; rural
Knox Corner; RMC Place; WALDO; ▲ Knox; *183 E-5; elev. 615ft./187m.; mail Thorndike z 04986
Knox Station; RMC Place; WALDO; ▲ Thorndike, Knox; *183 E-5; elev. 410ft./125m.; mail Thorndike z 04986; rural
Kokadjo; RMC Place; PISCATAQUIS; 183 B-5; elev. 1,227ft./374m.; mail Greenville z 04441; ● 10

L

Lagrange; RMC Place; PENOBSCOT; ▲ Lagrange; 183 C-6; elev. 314ft./96m.; 🅿; z 04453; ● 120
Lagrange; MCD-Town; PENOBSCOT; *183 C-6; 🅿; z 04453; Ⓟ 557; Ⓒ 747
Lake Arrowhead; CDP-Census Area Only; YORK; *183 H-2; Ⓒ 2,264
Lake Arrowhead Estates; RMC Place; YORK; ▲ Waterboro; *183 H-2; mail North Waterboro z 04061; ● 200
Lake City; RMC Place; KNOX; ▲ Camden; *183 F-6; mail Camden z 04843; summer pop. 125; ● 15
Lake Moxie; RMC Place; SOMERSET; ▲ The Forks; *183 C-4; mail West Forks z 04985
Lake View; RMC Place; PISCATAQUIS; ▲ Lake View; *183 C-6; mail Milo z 04463; summer pop. 100; ● 35
Lake View; MCD-Plantation; PISCATAQUIS; *183 C-6; mail Milo z 04463; Ⓟ 23; Ⓒ 43
Lakeville; MCD-Town; PENOBSCOT; *183 C-8; 🅿; z 04487; Ⓟ 45; Ⓒ 63
Lakewood; RMC Place; SOMERSET; ▲ Madison; 183 E-4; mail Madison z 04950; ● 80
Lambert Lake; RMC Place; WASHINGTON; 183 B-9; elev. 450ft./137m.; 🅿; z 04454; ● 130
Lambs Corner; RMC Place; KENNEBEC; ▲ Winslow; *183 F-4; ★ WATRVL; mail Waterville z 04901; rural
Lamoine; MCD-Town; HANCOCK; *183 F-7; 🅿; z 04605; Ⓟ 1,311; Ⓒ 1,495
Lamoine Beach; RMC Place; HANCOCK; ▲ Lamoine; *183 F-7; mail Ellsworth z 04605; ● 60
Lamoine Corner; RMC Place; HANCOCK; ▲ Lamoine; *183 F-7; elev. 89ft./27m.; mail Ellsworth z 04605; ● 90
Land of Nod; RMC Place; CUMBERLAND; ▲ Windham; *183 H-2; ★ POR; mail Windham z 04062; rural
Larone; RMC Place; SOMERSET; ▲ Fairfield; *183 E-4; ★ WATRVL; mail Fairfield z 04937; rural
Larrabee; RMC Place; WASHINGTON; ▲ Machiasport; *183 E-10; mail Machiasport z 04655
Lawry; RMC Place; KNOX; ▲ Friendship; *183 G-5; mail Friendship z 04547; ● 125
Lebanon (East Lebanon); RMC Place; YORK; ▲ Lebanon; 183 I-1; 🅿; z 04027; ● 90
Lebanon; MCD-Town; YORK; *183 I-1; 🅿; z 04027; Ⓟ 4,263; Ⓒ 5,083
Lee; RMC Place; PENOBSCOT; ▲ Lee; 183 C-7; elev. 408ft./124m.; 🅿; z 04455; ● 250
Lee; MCD-Town; PENOBSCOT; *183 C-7; 🅿; z 04455; Ⓟ 832; Ⓒ 845
Leeds; RMC Place; ANDROSCOGGIN; ▲ Leeds; *183 F-3; 🅿; z 04263; ● 80
Leeds; MCD-Town; ANDROSCOGGIN; *183 F-3; 🅿; z 04263; Ⓟ 1,669; Ⓒ 2,001
Leeds Junction; RMC Place; ANDROSCOGGIN; ▲ Wales; *183 G-3; elev. 271ft./83m.; ★ LEW-; mail Leeds z 04263; ● 75
Levant; RMC Place; PENOBSCOT; ▲ Levant; 183 D-6; 🅿; z 04456; ● 250
Levant; MCD-Town; PENOBSCOT; *183 D-6; 🅿; z 04456; Ⓟ 1,627; Ⓒ 2,171
Lewiston; Inc. Place; ANDROSCOGGIN; 183 G-3; elev. 121ft./37m.; 🅿 🅷 🅲 1,744 ■; ★ LEW-; z 04240-41, z 04243; Ⓟ 39,757; Ⓒ 35,690; ◆ 34,356
Lewiston Junction; RMC Place; ANDROSCOGGIN; *183 G-3; ★ LEW-; mail Auburn z 04210; pop. incl. with Auburn (Inc. Place)
Lewiston Lower; RMC Place; ANDROSCOGGIN; ★ LEW-; pop. incl. with Lewiston (Inc. Place)
Lewiston Upper; RMC Place; ANDROSCOGGIN; ★ LEW-; pop. incl. with Lewiston (Inc. Place)
Libby Hill; RMC Place; KENNEBEC; *183 G-4; elev. 379ft./116m.; ★ AUG; mail Gardiner z 04345; pop. incl. with Gardiner (Inc. Place)
Liberty; RMC Place; WALDO; ▲ Liberty; 183 F-5; 🅿; z 04949; ● 180
Liberty; MCD-Town; WALDO; *183 F-5; 🅿; z 04949; Ⓟ 790; Ⓒ 927
Lille; RMC Place; AROOSTOOK; ▲ Grand Isle; *183 A-14; elev. 488ft./149m.; 🅿; z 04746; ● 100
Lily Bay; RMC Place; PISCATAQUIS; *183 B-5; mail Greenville z 04441; summer pop. 150; ● 25
Limerick; RMC Place; YORK; ▲ Limerick; 183 H-2; 🅿; z 04048; ● 400
Limerick; MCD-Town; YORK; *183 H-2; 🅿; z 04048; Ⓟ 1,688; Ⓒ 2,240
Limerick Mills; RMC Place; YORK; ▲ Limerick; *183 H-2; mail Limerick z 04048; ● 150
Limestone; CDP; AROOSTOOK; ▲ Limestone; 183 B-14; elev. 521ft./159m.; 🅿; z 04750-51; Ⓟ 1,245; Ⓒ 1,453
Limestone; MCD-Town; AROOSTOOK; *183 B-14; 🅿; z 04750-51; Ⓟ 7,587; Ⓒ 2,361
Limington; RMC Place; YORK; ▲ Limington; 183 H-2; elev. 474ft./144m.; 🅿; ★ POR; z 04049; ● 220
Limington; MCD-Town; YORK; *183 H-2; 🅿; ★ POR; z 04049; Ⓟ 2,796; Ⓒ 3,403; ◆ 3,741
Lincoln; MCD-Plantation; OXFORD; *183 D-1; mail Errol z 03579; Ⓟ 38; Ⓒ 46
Lincoln; CDP; PENOBSCOT; ▲ Lincoln; 183 C-7; elev. 180ft./55m.; 🅿 🅷; z 04457; Ⓟ 3,399; Ⓒ 2,933
Lincoln; MCD-Town; PENOBSCOT; *183 C-7; elev. 180ft./55m.; 🅿; z 04457; Ⓟ 5,587; Ⓒ 5,221
LINCOLN; 183 G-4; Ⓟ 30,357; Ⓒ 33,616; ◆ 34,500
Lincoln Center; RMC Place; PENOBSCOT; ▲ Lincoln; *183 C-7; elev. 180ft./55m.; 🅿; z 04457; ● 250
Lincoln Mills; RMC Place; PENOBSCOT; ▲ Corinna; *183 D-5; mail Corinna z 04928; rural
Lincolnville (Lincolnville Beach); RMC Place; WALDO; ▲ Lincolnville; 183 F-6; 🅿; z 04849; ● 300
Lincolnville; MCD-Town; WALDO; *183 F-6; 🅿; z 04849; Ⓟ 1,809; Ⓒ 2,042
Lincolnville Beach; WALDO; see Lincolnville (RMC Place)
Lincolnville Center; RMC Place; WALDO; ▲ Lincolnville; *183 F-6; 🅿; z 04850; ● 150
Linekin; RMC Place; LINCOLN; ▲ Boothbay; *183 H-4; elev. 83ft./25m.; mail East Boothbay z 04544; ● 80
Linneus; RMC Place; AROOSTOOK; ▲ Linneus; 183 A-8; elev. 645ft./197m.; 🅿; z 04730; ● 100
Linneus; MCD-Town; AROOSTOOK; *183 C-14; 🅿; z 04730; Ⓟ 810; Ⓒ 892
Lisbon; RMC Place; ANDROSCOGGIN; ▲ Lisbon; 183 G-3; elev. 184ft./56m.; 🅿; ★ LEW-; z 04250, z 04252; ● 1,400
Lisbon; MCD-Town; ANDROSCOGGIN; *183 G-3; 🅿; ★ LEW-; z 04250, z 04252; Ⓟ 9,457; Ⓒ 9,077; ◆ 8,958
Lisbon Center; RMC Place; ANDROSCOGGIN; ▲ Lisbon; *183 G-3; ★ LEW-; mail Lisbon Falls z 04252; ● 600
Lisbon Falls; CDP; ANDROSCOGGIN; ▲ Lisbon; 183 G-3; 🅿; ★ LEW-; z 04252; Ⓟ 4,674; Ⓒ 4,420
Litchfield; KENNEBEC; see Purgatory (RMC Place)
Litchfield; MCD-Town; KENNEBEC; *183 G-4; 🅿; ★ AUG; z 04350; Ⓟ 2,650; Ⓒ 3,110
Litchfield Corners; RMC Place; KENNEBEC; ▲ Litchfield; 183 G-3; elev. 140ft./43m.; ★ AUG; mail Litchfield z 04350; ● 200
Litchfield Plains; RMC Place; KENNEBEC; ▲ Litchfield; *183 G-4; ★ AUG; mail Litchfield z 04350; rural
Little Deer Isle; RMC Place; HANCOCK; ▲ Deer Isle; 183 F-6; 🅿; z 04650; ● 150
Little Diamond Island; RMC Place; CUMBERLAND; *183 H-3; 🅿; ★ POR; z 04109; pop. incl. with Portland (Inc. Place)
Little Falls; RMC Place; CUMBERLAND; ▲ Gorham; *183 H-2; ★ POR; mail Gorham z 04038
Little Falls-South Windham; CDP-Census Area Only; CUMBERLAND; ▲ Windham, Gorham; *183 H-2; ★ POR; mail South Windham z 04082; Ⓟ 1,715; Ⓒ 1,792
Littlefield Corner; RMC Place; ANDROSCOGGIN; *183 G-3; ★ LEW-; mail Auburn z 04210; pop. incl. with Auburn (Inc. Place)
Littlejohn Island; RMC Place; CUMBERLAND; ▲ Yarmouth; *183 H-3; ★ POR; mail Yarmouth z 04096; summer pop. 100; ● 10
Little Machias; RMC Place; WASHINGTON; ▲ Cutler; *183 E-10; mail Cutler z 04626; rural
Littleton; RMC Place; AROOSTOOK; ▲ Littleton; 183 C-14; elev. 466ft./142m.; 🅿; z 04730; ● 200
Littleton; MCD-Town; AROOSTOOK; *183 C-14; 🅿; z 04730; Ⓟ 956; Ⓒ 955
Livermore; RMC Place; ANDROSCOGGIN; ▲ Livermore; 183 F-3; elev. 412ft./126m.; 🅿; z 04253; ● 200
Livermore; MCD-Town; ANDROSCOGGIN; *183 F-3; 🅿; z 04253; Ⓟ 1,950; Ⓒ 2,106
Livermore Falls; CDP; ANDROSCOGGIN; ▲ Livermore Falls; 183 F-3; 🅿; z 04254; Ⓟ 1,935; Ⓒ 1,626
Livermore Falls; MCD-Town; ANDROSCOGGIN; *183 F-3; 🅿; z 04254; Ⓟ 3,455; Ⓒ 3,227
Locke Mills (Greenwood, Lockes Mills); RMC Place; OXFORD; ▲ Greenwood; 183 F-2; elev. 753ft./230m.; mail Greenwood z 04255; ● 200
Lockes Mills; OXFORD; see Locke Mills (RMC Place)
Long Beach; RMC Place; CUMBERLAND; ▲ Sebago; *183 H-2; mail Standish z 04084; summer pop. 400; ● 100
Long Beach; RMC Place; YORK; ▲ York; *183 J-2; ★ PTSM-; mail York Beach z 03910; summer pop. 2,500; ● 800
Long Cove; RMC Place; KNOX; ▲ St. George; *183 G-5; ● 120
Long Island; RMC Place; CUMBERLAND; ▲ Long Island; *183 H-3; 🅿; ★ POR; z 04050; ● 200
Long Island; MCD-Town; CUMBERLAND; *183 H-3; elev. 40ft./12m.; 🅿; ★ POR; z 04050; Ⓟ 201; Ⓒ 202; ◆ 196
Long Pond; RMC Place; SOMERSET; *183 B-3; mail Jackman z 04945; rural
Lookout; RMC Place; KNOX; ▲ Isle Au Haut; *183 G-7; mail Isle au Haut z 04645; summer pop. 100
Loring AFB; CDP-Census Area Only; AROOSTOOK; *183 B-14; Ⓒ 225
Lovell; RMC Place; OXFORD; ▲ Lovell; 183 G-1; elev. 407ft./124m.; 🅿; z 04051; ● 225
Lovell; MCD-Town; OXFORD; *183 G-1; 🅿; z 04051; Ⓟ 888; Ⓒ 974
Lowell; RMC Place; PENOBSCOT; ▲ Lowell; *183 C-7; 🅿; z 04493; ● 35
Lowell; MCD-Town; PENOBSCOT; *183 C-7; 🅿; z 04493; Ⓟ 267; Ⓒ 291
Lower Dennysville; RMC Place; WASHINGTON; ▲ Dennysville; *183 D-10; mail Dennysville z 04628; rural
Lower Village; YORK; see Coopers Corner (RMC Place)
Lubec; RMC Place; WASHINGTON; ▲ Lubec; 183 D-10; 🅿; z 04652; ● 800
Lubec; MCD-Town; WASHINGTON; *183 D-10; 🅿; z 04652; Ⓟ 1,853; Ⓒ 1,652
Lucerne-in-Maine; RMC Place; HANCOCK; ▲ Dedham; *183 E-7; elev. 254ft./77m.; mail Holden z 04429; summer pop. 100
Ludlow; RMC Place; AROOSTOOK; ▲ Ludlow; 183 C-14; 🅿; z 04730; ● 40
Ludlow; MCD-Town; AROOSTOOK; *183 C-14; 🅿; z 04730; Ⓟ 430; Ⓒ 402
Lyman; MCD-Town; YORK; *183 I-2; 🅿; z 04002 & mail Biddeford z 04005; Ⓟ 3,390; Ⓒ 3,795
Lynchville; RMC Place; OXFORD; *183 F-2; mail Stoneham z 04231

M

Machias; CDP; ⊡ WASHINGTON; ▲ Machias; 183 E-9; elev. 70ft./21m.; 🅿 🅷 🅲 1,259; z 04654, z 04686; Ⓟ 1,773; Ⓒ 1,376
Machias; MCD-Town; WASHINGTON; *183 E-9; 🅿 🅲 1,259; z 04654, z 04686; Ⓟ 2,569; Ⓒ 2,353
Machiasport; RMC Place; WASHINGTON; ▲ Machiasport; 183 E-9; 🅿; z 04655; ● 250
Machiasport; MCD-Town; WASHINGTON; *183 E-10; 🅿; z 04655; Ⓟ 1,166; Ⓒ 1,160
Mackworth Island; RMC Place; CUMBERLAND; ▲ Falmouth; *183 H-3; ★ POR; mail Falmouth z 04105
Mackworth Point; RMC Place; CUMBERLAND; ▲ Falmouth; *183 H-3; ★ POR; mail Falmouth z 04105
MacMahan; RMC Place; SAGADAHOC; ▲ Georgetown; *183 H-4; 🅿; ★ BR-BA; z 04548; summer pop. 100
Macwahoc; RMC Place; AROOSTOOK; ▲ Macwahoc; 183 B-7; mail Kingman z 04451; ● 90
Macwahoc; MCD-Plantation; AROOSTOOK; *183 B-8; mail Kingman z 04451; Ⓟ 114; Ⓒ 98
Madawaska; CDP; AROOSTOOK; ▲ Madawaska; 183 A-13; elev. 413ft./126m.; 🅿; z 04756; Ⓟ 3,653; Ⓒ 3,326
Madawaska; RMC Place; AROOSTOOK; *183 B-14; 🅿; z 04756 & mail Caribou z 04736
Madawaska; MCD-Town; AROOSTOOK; *183 A-13; 🅿; z 04756; Ⓟ 4,803; Ⓒ 4,534
Madawaska Lake; RMC Place; AROOSTOOK; *183 B-13; mail Stockholm z 04783; summer pop. 200; ● 100
Madison; CDP; SOMERSET; ▲ Madison; 183 E-4; elev. 297ft./91m.; 🅿; z 04950; Ⓟ 2,956; Ⓒ 2,733
Madison; MCD-Town; SOMERSET; *183 E-4; 🅿; z 04950; Ⓟ 4,725; Ⓒ 4,523
Madrid; RMC Place; FRANKLIN; ▲ Madrid; *183 D-2; elev. 856ft./261m.; mail Phillips z 04966
Magalloway; MCD-Plantation; OXFORD; *183 D-1; mail Errol z 03579; Ⓟ 45; Ⓒ 37
Maine; RMC Place; AROOSTOOK; *183 B-14; mail Caribou z 04736; pop. incl. with Caribou (Inc. Place)
Mainstream; RMC Place; SOMERSET; ▲ Harmony; *183 D-5; mail Harmony z 04942; ● 60
Manchester; RMC Place; KENNEBEC; ▲ Manchester; 183 F-4; 🅿; ★ AUG; z 04351; ● 650
Manchester; MCD-Town; KENNEBEC; *183 F-4; 🅿; ★ AUG; z 04351; Ⓟ 2,099; Ⓒ 2,465
Manset; RMC Place; HANCOCK; ▲ Southwest Harbor; 183 I-12; mail Southwest Harbor z 04679; ● 200
Maple Grove; RMC Place; AROOSTOOK; ▲ Fort Fairfield; *183 B-14; elev. 622ft./190m.; mail Fort Fairfield z 04742
Mapleton; RMC Place; AROOSTOOK; ▲ Mapleton; 183 B-14; elev. 548ft./167m.; 🅿; z 04757; ● 500
Mapleton; MCD-Town; AROOSTOOK; *183 B-14; 🅿; z 04757; Ⓟ 1,853; Ⓒ 1,889
Maplewood; RMC Place; YORK; ▲ Parsonsfield, Newfield; 183 H-1; elev. 676ft./206m.; mail Parsonsfield z 04047, West Newfield z 04095; ● 30
Mariaville; RMC Place; HANCOCK; ▲ Mariaville; *183 E-7; elev. 231ft./70m.; 🅿; z 04605; rural
Mariaville; MCD-Town; HANCOCK; *183 E-7; 🅿; z 04605; Ⓟ 270; Ⓒ 414
Marion; RMC Place; WASHINGTON; *183 D-10; mail Dennysville z 04628; rural
Marlboro; RMC Place; HANCOCK; ▲ Lamoine; *183 F-7; mail Ellsworth z 04605; ● 50
Marrtown; RMC Place; SAGADAHOC; ▲ Georgetown; *183 H-4; ★ BR-BA; mail Georgetown z 04548
Marshfield; RMC Place; WASHINGTON; ▲ Marshfield; *183 E-9; elev. 33ft./10m.; 🅿; z 04654; ● 100
Marshfield; MCD-Town; WASHINGTON; *183 E-9; 🅿; z 04654; Ⓟ 461; Ⓒ 494
Mars Hill; RMC Place; AROOSTOOK; ▲ Mars Hill; 183 C-14; elev. 435ft./133m.; 🅿; z 04758; ● 1,200
Mars Hill; MCD-Town; AROOSTOOK; *183 B-14; 🅿; z 04758; Ⓟ 1,760; Ⓒ 1,480
Mars Hill-Blaine; CDP-Census Area Only; AROOSTOOK; ▲ Blaine, Mars Hill; *183 C-14; mail Mars Hill z 04758; Ⓟ 1,717; Ⓒ 1,428
Marshville; RMC Place; WASHINGTON; ▲ Harrington; *183 E-9; mail Harrington z 04643
Marston Corner; RMC Place; ANDROSCOGGIN; *183 G-3; ★ LEW-; mail Auburn z 04210; pop. incl. with Auburn (Inc. Place)
Martin; RMC Place; KNOX; ▲ Friendship; *183 G-5; mail Friendship z 04547
Martinsville; RMC Place; KNOX; ▲ St. George; 183 G-5; mail Tenants Harbor z 04860; ● 100
Masardis; RMC Place; AROOSTOOK; ▲ Masardis; *183 C-13; elev. 580ft./177m.; 🅿; z 04732; ● 75
Masardis; MCD-Town; AROOSTOOK; *183 C-13; 🅿; z 04732; Ⓟ 305; Ⓒ 255
Mason Bay; RMC Place; WASHINGTON; ▲ Jonesport; *183 E-9; elev. 102ft./31m.; mail Jonesport z 04649; rural
Mast Landing; RMC Place; CUMBERLAND; ▲ Freeport; *183 H-3; elev. 15ft./5m.; ★ POR; mail Freeport z 04032; ● 60
Matinicus; RMC Place; KNOX; ▲ Matinicus Isle; 183 H-6; 🅿; z 04851; summer pop. 150; ● 50
Matinicus Isle; MCD-Plantation; KNOX; *183 H-6; mail Matinicus z 04851; Ⓟ 67; Ⓒ 51
Mattawamkeag; RMC Place; PENOBSCOT; ▲ Mattawamkeag; 183 B-7; elev. 217ft./66m.; 🅿; z 04459; ● 650
Mattawamkeag; MCD-Town; PENOBSCOT; *183 B-7; 🅿; z 04459; Ⓟ 830; Ⓒ 825
Mattocks; CUMBERLAND; see East Baldwin Mattocks Station (RMC Place)
Maxfield; MCD-Town; PENOBSCOT; *183 C-6; 🅿; z 04453; Ⓟ 86; Ⓒ 87
Mayberry Hill; RMC Place; CUMBERLAND; ▲ Casco; *183 G-2; ★ POR; mail Casco z 04015; rural
Maysville (Maysville Center); RMC Place; AROOSTOOK; *183 B-14; mail Presque Isle z 04769; pop. incl. with Presque Isle (Inc. Place)
Maysville Center; AROOSTOOK; see Maysville (RMC Place)
Mayville; RMC Place; OXFORD; ▲ Bethel; *183 F-2; mail Bethel z 04217; ● 75
McFarlands Corner; RMC Place; WALDO; ▲ Montville; *183 F-5; elev. 528ft./161m.; mail Freedom z 04941
McGraw; RMC Place; AROOSTOOK; *183 B-13; mail Caribou z 04736; pop. incl. with Caribou (Inc. Place)
McShea; RMC Place; AROOSTOOK; ▲ Fort Fairfield; *183 B-14; mail Fort Fairfield z 04742; rural
Mechanic Falls; CDP; ANDROSCOGGIN; ▲ Mechanic Falls; 183 G-2; elev. 304ft./93m.; 🅿; ★ LEW-; z 04256; Ⓟ 2,388; Ⓒ 2,450
Mechanic Falls; MCD-Town; ANDROSCOGGIN; *183 G-2; 🅿; ★ LEW-; z 04256; Ⓟ 2,919; Ⓒ 3,138; ◆ 3,304
Meddybemps; RMC Place; WASHINGTON; ▲ Meddybemps; 183 D-10; elev. 174ft./53m.; 🅿; z 04657; ● 70
Meddybemps; MCD-Town; WASHINGTON; *183 D-10; 🅿; z 04657; Ⓟ 133; Ⓒ 150
Medford; RMC Place; PISCATAQUIS; ▲ Medford; *183 C-6; 🅿; z 04463 & mail Lagrange z 04453; rural
Medford; MCD-Town; PISCATAQUIS; *183 C-6; 🅿; z 04463 & mail Lagrange z 04453; Ⓟ 194; Ⓒ 231
Medford Center; RMC Place; PISCATAQUIS; ▲ Medford; *183 C-6; elev. 288ft./88m.; mail Lagrange z 04453; ● 20
Medomak; LINCOLN; see Bremen (RMC Place)
Medway; RMC Place; PENOBSCOT; ▲ Medway; 183 B-7; elev. 296ft./90m.; 🅿; z 04460; ● 900
Medway; MCD-Town; PENOBSCOT; *183 B-7; 🅿; z 04460; Ⓟ 1,922; Ⓒ 1,489
Melvin Heights; RMC Place; KNOX; ▲ Camden; *183 G-6; elev. 330ft./101m.; mail Camden z 04843; rural
Mercer; RMC Place; SOMERSET; ▲ Mercer; *183 E-4; 🅿; z 04957; ● 90
Mercer; MCD-Town; SOMERSET; *183 E-4; 🅿; z 04957; Ⓟ 593; Ⓒ 647
Merepoint; RMC Place; CUMBERLAND; ▲ Brunswick; *183 H-3; 🅿; ★ BR-BA; z 04011; summer pop. 100; ● 25
Merrill; MCD-Town; AROOSTOOK; *183 C-13; 🅿; z 04780; Ⓟ 296; Ⓒ 249
Mexico; CDP; OXFORD; ▲ Mexico; 183 E-2; 🅿; z 04257; Ⓟ 2,302; Ⓒ 1,946
Mexico; MCD-Town; OXFORD; *183 E-2; 🅿; z 04257; Ⓟ 3,344; Ⓒ 2,959
Middle Dam; RMC Place; OXFORD; *183 E-1; elev. 1,463ft./446m.; mail Andover z 04216; ● 10
Middle Intervale; RMC Place; OXFORD; ▲ Bethel; *183 F-2; mail Bethel z 04217; rural
Milbridge; RMC Place; WASHINGTON; ▲ Milbridge; 183 E-8; elev. 21ft./6m.; 🅿; z 04658; ● 600
Milbridge; MCD-Town; WASHINGTON; *183 F-8; 🅿; z 04658; Ⓟ 1,305; Ⓒ 1,279
Milford; CDP; PENOBSCOT; ▲ Milford; 183 D-7; 🅿; ★ BANG; z 04461; Ⓟ 2,228; Ⓒ 2,197
Milford; MCD-Town; PENOBSCOT; *183 D-7; 🅿; ★ BANG; z 04461; Ⓟ 2,884; Ⓒ 2,950; ◆ 3,161
Milliken Mills; RMC Place; YORK; ▲ Old Orchard Beach; *183 I-2; ★ POR; mail Old Orchard Beach z 04064
Millinocket; CDP; PENOBSCOT; ▲ Millinocket; 183 B-6; elev. 358ft./109m.; 🅿 🅷; z 04462; Ⓟ 6,922; Ⓒ 5,190
Millinocket; MCD-Town; PENOBSCOT; *183 B-6; 🅿; z 04462; Ⓟ 6,956; Ⓒ 5,203
Milltown; RMC Place; WASHINGTON; *183 C-10; mail Calais z 04619; pop. incl. with Calais (Inc. Place)
Milltown Junction; RMC Place; WASHINGTON; pop. incl. with Calais (Inc. Place)
Milo; CDP; PISCATAQUIS; ▲ Milo; 183 C-6; 🅿; z 04463; Ⓟ 2,129; Ⓒ 1,898
Milo; MCD-Town; PISCATAQUIS; *183 C-6; 🅿; z 04463; Ⓟ 2,600; Ⓒ 2,383
Milton; RMC Place; OXFORD; *183 F-2; mail Bryant Pond z 04219; rural
Minot; RMC Place; ANDROSCOGGIN; ▲ Minot; *183 G-3; elev. 2,631ft./802m.; 🅿; ★ LEW-; z 04258; ● 300
Minot; MCD-Town; ANDROSCOGGIN; *183 G-3; 🅿; ★ LEW-; z 04258; Ⓟ 1,664; Ⓒ 2,248
Minturn; RMC Place; HANCOCK; ▲ Swans Island; 183 G-7; 🅿; z 04685; ● 90
Molunkus; RMC Place; AROOSTOOK; 183 B-7; elev. 450ft./137m.; mail Kingman z 04451; ● 35
Monarda; RMC Place; AROOSTOOK; *183 A-7; elev. 567ft./173m.; mail Sherman z 04776
Monhegan; RMC Place; LINCOLN; ▲ Monhegan; 183 H-5; 🅿; z 04852; ● 75
Monhegan; MCD-Plantation; LINCOLN; *183 H-5; 🅿; z 04852; Ⓟ 88; Ⓒ 75
Monmouth; RMC Place; KENNEBEC; ▲ Monmouth; 183 F-3; elev. 270ft./82m.; 🅿; ★ AUG; z 04259; ● 600
Monmouth; MCD-Town; KENNEBEC; *183 F-3; 🅿; ★ AUG; z 04259; Ⓟ 3,353; Ⓒ 3,785
Monroe; RMC Place; WALDO; ▲ Monroe; 183 E-6; 🅿; z 04951; ● 140
Monroe; MCD-Town; WALDO; *183 E-6; 🅿; z 04951; Ⓟ 802; Ⓒ 882
Monroe Center; RMC Place; WALDO; ▲ Monroe; *183 E-6; mail Monroe z 04951; rural
Monson; RMC Place; PISCATAQUIS; ▲ Monson; 183 C-5; 🅿; z 04464; ● 500
Monson; MCD-Town; PISCATAQUIS; *183 C-5; 🅿; z 04464; Ⓟ 744; Ⓒ 666
Monticello; RMC Place; AROOSTOOK; ▲ Monticello; 183 C-14; elev. 392ft./119m.; 🅿; z 04760; ● 400
Monticello; MCD-Town; AROOSTOOK; *183 C-14; 🅿; z 04760; Ⓟ 872; Ⓒ 790
Montsweag; RMC Place; SAGADAHOC; ▲ Woolwich; *183 G-4; elev. 64ft./20m.; ★ BR-BA; mail Woolwich z 04579; ● 200
Montville; WALDO; see Center Montville (RMC Place)
Montville; MCD-Town; WALDO; *183 F-5; 🅿; z 04941; Ⓟ 877; Ⓒ 1,002
Moody; RMC Place; YORK; ▲ Wells; *183 J-2; 🅿; z 04054; ● 500
Moody Beach; RMC Place; YORK; ▲ Wells; *183 J-2; mail Moody z 04054, Wells z 04090; summer pop. 3,000; ● 500
Moody Point; RMC Place; YORK; *183 J-2; mail Wells z 04090; summer pop. 1,500; ● 400
Moosehead; RMC Place; PISCATAQUIS; 183 B-4; elev. 1,028ft./313m.; mail Greenville Junction z 04442; ● 15
Mooselookmeguntic (Haines Landing); RMC Place; FRANKLIN; ▲ Rangeley; *183 D-2; mail Oquossoc z 04964; summer pop. 100
Moose River; RMC Place; SOMERSET; ▲ Moose River; 183 B-3; elev. 1,187ft./362m.; 🅿; z 04945; ● 200
Moose River; MCD-Town; SOMERSET; *183 B-3; 🅿; z 04945; Ⓟ 233; Ⓒ 219
Morgan Beach; RMC Place; PENOBSCOT; ▲ Enfield; *183 C-7; mail West Enfield z 04493; summer pop. 200
Moro; MCD-Plantation; AROOSTOOK; *183 C-13; mail Smyrna Mills z 04780; Ⓟ 38; Ⓒ 63
Morrill; RMC Place; WALDO; ▲ Morrill; 183 F-5; elev. 238ft./73m.; 🅿; z 04952; ● 150
Morrill; MCD-Town; WALDO; *183 F-5; 🅿; z 04952; Ⓟ 644; Ⓒ 774
Morris Corner; RMC Place; AROOSTOOK; ▲ Limestone; *183 B-14; elev. 666ft./203m.; mail Limestone z 04750; rural
Morrison Corner; RMC Place; KENNEBEC; ▲ Clinton; *183 E-4; mail Clinton z 04927; rural
Morse Corners; RMC Place; PENOBSCOT; ▲ Corinna; *183 D-5; mail Corinna z 04928; ● 20
Moscow; RMC Place; SOMERSET; ▲ Moscow; 183 D-4; 🅿; z 04920; ● 400
Moscow; MCD-Town; SOMERSET; *183 D-4; 🅿; z 04920; Ⓟ 608; Ⓒ 577
Mountainview; RMC Place; FRANKLIN; ▲ Rangeley; *183 D-2; mail Oquossoc z 04964; ● 30
Mount Chase; MCD-Town; PENOBSCOT; *183 C-13; 🅿; z 04765; Ⓟ 254; Ⓒ 247
Mount Desert; HANCOCK; see Somesville (RMC Place)
Mount Desert; MCD-Town; HANCOCK; *183 F-7; 🅿; z 04660; Ⓟ 1,899; Ⓒ 2,109
Mount Pisgah; RMC Place; LINCOLN; ▲ Boothbay Harbor; *183 H-4; mail Boothbay Harbor z 04538
Mount Vernon; RMC Place; KENNEBEC; ▲ Mount Vernon; 183 F-3; elev. 339ft./103m.; 🅿; z 04352; ● 200
Mount Vernon; MCD-Town; KENNEBEC; *183 F-4; 🅿; z 04352; Ⓟ 1,362; Ⓒ 1,524
Mousam Lake; RMC Place; YORK; ▲ Shapleigh, Acton; *183 I-1; mail Acton z 04001, Shapleigh z 04076; summer pop. 600
Murphys Corner; RMC Place; SAGADAHOC; ▲ Woolwich; *183 G-4; ★ BR-BA; mail Woolwich z 04579; ● 60
Muscongus; RMC Place; LINCOLN; ▲ Bristol, Bremen; *183 G-5; mail Bremen z 04551; ● 30

N

Naples; RMC Place; CUMBERLAND; ▲ Naples; 183 G-2; 🅿; z 04055; ● 600
Naples; MCD-Town; CUMBERLAND; *183 G-2; 🅿; z 04055; Ⓟ 2,860; Ⓒ 3,274
Nashville; MCD-Plantation; AROOSTOOK; *183 B-13; mail Ashland z 04732; Ⓟ 43; Ⓒ 55
Naskeag; RMC Place; HANCOCK; ▲ Brooklin; *183 F-7; elev. 114ft./35m.; mail Brooklin z 04616
Nequasset; RMC Place; SAGADAHOC; ▲ Woolwich; *183 G-4; ★ BR-BA; mail Woolwich z 04579; rural
Newagen; RMC Place; LINCOLN; ▲ Southport; 183 H-4; 🅿; z 04576; summer pop. 300; ● 125
New Auburn; RMC Place; ANDROSCOGGIN; *183 G-3; ★ LEW-; mail Auburn z 04210; pop. incl. with Auburn (Inc. Place)
Newburgh; PENOBSCOT; see Newburgh Village (RMC Place)
Newburgh; MCD-Town; PENOBSCOT; *183 E-6; 🅿; z 04444; Ⓟ 1,317; Ⓒ 1,394
Newburgh Center; RMC Place; PENOBSCOT; ▲ Newburgh; *183 E-6; mail Hampden z 04444; rural
Newburgh Village (Newburgh); RMC Place; PENOBSCOT; ▲ Newburgh; 183 E-6; mail Hampden z 04444; ● 120
New Canada; MCD-Town; AROOSTOOK; *183 A-13; 🅿; z 04743; Ⓟ 253; Ⓒ 306
Newcastle; RMC Place; LINCOLN; ▲ Newcastle; 183 G-4; elev. 91ft./28m.; 🅿; z 04553; ● 600
Newcastle; MCD-Town; LINCOLN; *183 G-4; 🅿; z 04553; Ⓟ 1,538; Ⓒ 1,748
Newfield; RMC Place; YORK; ▲ Newfield; 183 H-1; elev. 406ft./124m.; 🅿; z 04056; ● 225
Newfield; MCD-Town; YORK; *183 H-1; 🅿; z 04056; Ⓟ 1,042; Ⓒ 1,328
New Gloucester; RMC Place; CUMBERLAND; ▲ New Gloucester; *183 G-3; 🅿; z 04260; ● 300
New Gloucester; MCD-Town; CUMBERLAND; *183 G-3; 🅿; z 04260; Ⓟ 3,916; Ⓒ 4,803
Newhall; RMC Place; CUMBERLAND; ▲ Windham; *183 H-2; elev. 211ft./64m.; ★ POR; mail Windham z 04062; ● 150
New Harbor; RMC Place; LINCOLN; ▲ Bristol; 183 H-5; 🅿; z 04554, z 04558; ● 500
New Limerick; RMC Place; AROOSTOOK; ▲ New Limerick; *183 C-14; 🅿; z 04761; ● 120
New Limerick; MCD-Town; AROOSTOOK; *183 C-14; 🅿; z 04761; Ⓟ 524; Ⓒ 523
New Meadows; RMC Place; SAGADAHOC; ▲ West Bath; *183 H-4; ★ BR-BA; mail Bath z 04530; rural
Newport (Newport Junction); CDP; PENOBSCOT; ▲ Newport; 183 D-5; elev. 202ft./62m.; 🅿; z 04953; Ⓟ 1,843; Ⓒ 1,754
Newport; MCD-Town; PENOBSCOT; *183 D-5; 🅿; z 04953; Ⓟ 3,036; Ⓒ 3,017
Newport Junction; PENOBSCOT; see Newport (CDP)
New Portland; RMC Place; SOMERSET; ▲ New Portland; 183 D-3; 🅿; z 04954, z 04961; ● 200
New Portland; MCD-Town; SOMERSET; *183 D-3; 🅿; z 04954, z 04961; Ⓟ 789; Ⓒ 785
Newry; RMC Place; OXFORD; ▲ Newry, Bethel, Hanover; 183 F-2; elev. 642ft./196m.; 🅿; z 04261; ● 150
Newry; MCD-Town; OXFORD; *183 E-2; 🅿; z 04261; Ⓟ 316; Ⓒ 344
New Sharon; RMC Place; FRANKLIN; ▲ New Sharon; 183 E-3; elev. 369ft./112m.; 🅿; z 04955; ● 300
New Sharon; MCD-Town; FRANKLIN; *183 E-3; 🅿; z 04955; Ⓟ 1,175; Ⓒ 1,297
New Sweden; RMC Place; AROOSTOOK; ▲ New Sweden; 183 B-14; elev. 866ft./264m.; 🅿; z 04762; ● 60
New Sweden; MCD-Town; AROOSTOOK; *183 B-14; 🅿; z 04762; Ⓟ 715; Ⓒ 621
Newtown; RMC Place; YORK; *183 I-2; mail Biddeford z 04005; pop. incl. with Biddeford (Inc. Place)
New Vineyard; RMC Place; FRANKLIN; ▲ New Vineyard; 183 E-3; 🅿; z 04956; ● 220
New Vineyard; MCD-Town; FRANKLIN; *183 E-3; 🅿; z 04956; Ⓟ 661; Ⓒ 725
Nickerson Lake; RMC Place; AROOSTOOK; ▲ New Limerick, Linneus; *183 C-14; mail Houlton z 04730, New Limerick z 04761; summer pop. 200; ● 40
Nobleboro; RMC Place; LINCOLN; ▲ Nobleboro; 183 G-5; elev. 168ft./51m.; 🅿; z 04555; ● 150
Nobleboro; MCD-Town; LINCOLN; *183 G-5; 🅿; z 04555; Ⓟ 1,455; Ⓒ 1,626
Nobles Corner; RMC Place; OXFORD; ▲ Norway; *183 F-2; mail Norway z 04268; rural
Norcross; RMC Place; PENOBSCOT; ▲ North Penobscot; *183 B-6; mail Millinocket z 04462; rural
Norridgewock; CDP; SOMERSET; ▲ Norridgewock; 183 E-4; elev. 204ft./62m.; 🅿; z 04957; Ⓟ 1,496; Ⓒ 1,557
Norridgewock; MCD-Town; SOMERSET; *183 E-4; 🅿; z 04957; Ⓟ 3,105; Ⓒ 3,294
North Alfred; RMC Place; YORK; ▲ Alfred; *183 I-2; elev. 376ft./115m.; mail Alfred z 04002
North Amity; RMC Place; AROOSTOOK; ▲ Amity; *183 A-8; elev. 611ft./186m.; mail Orient z 04471
North Anson; RMC Place; SOMERSET; ▲ Anson; 183 D-4; elev. 296ft./90m.; 🅿; z 04958; ● 750
North Appleton; RMC Place; KNOX; ▲ Appleton; *183 F-5; mail Union z 04862; rural
North Auburn; RMC Place; ANDROSCOGGIN; *183 G-3; ★ LEW-; mail Auburn z 04210; pop. incl. with Auburn (Inc. Place)
North Augusta; RMC Place; KENNEBEC; *183 F-4; ★ AUG; mail Augusta z 04330; pop. incl. with Augusta (Inc. Place)
North Baldwin; RMC Place; CUMBERLAND; ▲ Baldwin; *183 H-2; elev. 513ft./156m.; mail East Baldwin z 04024; rural
North Bancroft; RMC Place; AROOSTOOK; ▲ Bancroft; *183 A-8; mail Danforth z 04424; rural
North Bangor; RMC Place; PENOBSCOT; *183 D-6; elev. 146ft./45m.; ★ BANG; mail Bangor z 04401; pop. incl. with Bangor (Inc. Place)
North Bath; RMC Place; SAGADAHOC; *183 G-4; ★ BR-BA; mail Bath z 04530; pop. incl. with Bath (Inc. Place)
North Belgrade; RMC Place; KENNEBEC; ▲ Belgrade; *183 F-4; mail Belgrade z 04917
North Berwick; CDP; YORK; ▲ North Berwick; 183 I-2; elev. 147ft./45m.; 🅿; z 03906; Ⓟ 1,568; Ⓒ 1,580
North Berwick; MCD-Town; YORK; *183 I-2; 🅿; z 03906; Ⓟ 3,793; Ⓒ 4,293
North Blue Hill; RMC Place; HANCOCK; ▲ Blue Hill; *183 F-7; mail Blue Hill z 04614
North Bradford; RMC Place; PENOBSCOT; ▲ Bradford; 183 D-6; elev. 474ft./144m.; mail Bradford z 04410; ● 50
North Brewer; RMC Place; PENOBSCOT; *183 E-6; ★ BANG; mail Brewer z 04412; pop. incl. with Brewer (Inc. Place)
North Bridgton; RMC Place; CUMBERLAND; ▲ Bridgton; 183 G-2; 🅿; z 04057; ● 500
North Brooklin; RMC Place; HANCOCK; ▲ Brooklin; *183 F-7; mail Brooklin z 04616
North Brooksville; RMC Place; HANCOCK; ▲ Brooksville; *183 F-6; mail Brooksville z 04617; ● 60
North Buckfield; RMC Place; OXFORD; ▲ Buckfield; *183 F-2; mail Buckfield z 04220; ● 50
North Bucksport; RMC Place; HANCOCK; ▲ Bucksport; *183 E-6; mail Bucksport z 04416; rural
North Castine; RMC Place; HANCOCK; ▲ Castine; *183 F-6; mail Castine z 04421
North Chesterville; RMC Place; FRANKLIN; ▲ Chesterville; *183 E-3; mail Farmington z 04938; ● 70
North Cushing; RMC Place; KNOX; ▲ Cushing; *183 G-5; mail Cushing z 04563; rural
North Cutler; RMC Place; WASHINGTON; ▲ Cutler; *183 E-10; elev. 60ft./18m.; mail East Machias z 04630
North Deering; RMC Place; CUMBERLAND; *183 H-3; ★ POR; mail Portland z 04103; pop. incl. with Portland (Inc. Place)
North Deer Isle; RMC Place; HANCOCK; ▲ Deer Isle; *183 F-7; mail Deer Isle z 04627; ● 50
North Dexter; RMC Place; PENOBSCOT, PISCATAQUIS; ▲ Dexter; *183 D-5; mail Dexter z 04930; rural
North Dixmont; RMC Place; PENOBSCOT; ▲ Dixmont; *183 E-5; mail Dixmont z 04932; ● 70
North East Carry; RMC Place; PISCATAQUIS; *183 A-4; elev. 1,033ft./315m.; mail Rockwood z 04478
Northeast Harbor; RMC Place; HANCOCK; ▲ Mount Desert; 183 F-8; 🅿; z 04662; summer pop. 2,500; ● 650
North Edgecomb; RMC Place; LINCOLN; ▲ Edgecomb; *183 G-4; elev. 163ft./50m.; mail Edgecomb z 04556; ● 80
North Ellsworth; RMC Place; HANCOCK; *183 E-7; elev. 410ft./125m.; mail Ellsworth z 04605; pop. incl. with Ellsworth (Inc. Place)
Northern Maine Junction; RMC Place; PENOBSCOT; ▲ Hermon; *183 E-6; ★ BANG; mail Bangor z 04401; ● 120
North Fairfield; RMC Place; SOMERSET; ▲ Fairfield; *183 E-4; elev. 168ft./51m.; ★ WATRVL; mail Fairfield z 04937; rural
North Falmouth; RMC Place; CUMBERLAND; ▲ Falmouth; *183 H-3; elev. 362ft./110m.; ★ POR; mail Falmouth z 04105
Northfield; RMC Place; WASHINGTON; ▲ Northfield; *183 D-9; elev. 265ft./81m.; 🅿; z 04654; rural
Northfield; MCD-Town; WASHINGTON; *183 E-9; mail Machias z 04654; Ⓟ 99; Ⓒ 131
North Fryeburg; RMC Place; OXFORD; ▲ Fryeburg; 183 G-1; 🅿; z 04037; ● 70
North Gorham; RMC Place; CUMBERLAND; ▲ Gorham; *183 H-2; ★ POR; ● 175
North Gray; RMC Place; CUMBERLAND; ▲ Gray; *183 G-3; elev. 199ft./61m.; ★ POR; mail Gray z 04039; rural
North Guilford; RMC Place; PISCATAQUIS; ▲ Guilford; *183 C-5; elev. 514ft./157m.; mail Guilford z 04443
North Harpswell; RMC Place; CUMBERLAND; ▲ Harpswell; *183 H-3; ★ BR-BA; mail Harpswell z 04079; rural
North Haven; RMC Place; KNOX; ▲ North Haven; 183 G-6; elev. 20ft./6m.; 🅿; z 04853; summer pop. 1,000; ● 275
North Haven; MCD-Town; KNOX; *183 G-6; 🅿; z 04853; Ⓟ 332; Ⓒ 381
North Hermon; RMC Place; PENOBSCOT; ▲ Hermon; *183 D-6; ★ BANG; mail Bangor z 04401; ● 40
North Hollis; RMC Place; YORK; ▲ Hollis; *183 H-2; ★ POR; mail Hollis Center z 04042; rural
North Islesboro; RMC Place; WALDO; ▲ Islesboro; *183 F-6; mail Islesboro z 04848
North Jay; RMC Place; FRANKLIN; ▲ Jay; 183 E-3; elev. 373ft./114m.; 🅿; z 04262; ● 200
North Jefferson; RMC Place; LINCOLN; ▲ Jefferson; *183 G-5; mail Jefferson z 04348; rural
North Lamoine; RMC Place; HANCOCK; ▲ Lamoine; *183 F-7; mail Ellsworth z 04605
North Lebanon; RMC Place; YORK; ▲ Lebanon; *183 I-1; elev. 401ft./122m.; mail Lebanon z 04027; ● 60
North Leeds; RMC Place; ANDROSCOGGIN; ▲ Leeds; 183 F-3; elev. 285ft./87m.; mail Leeds z 04263; ● 20
North Limington; RMC Place; YORK; ▲ Limington; *183 H-2; elev. 284ft./87m.; ★ POR; mail Limington z 04049; ● 30
North Lincoln; RMC Place; PENOBSCOT; ▲ Lincoln; *183 C-7; elev. 210ft./64m.; mail Lincoln z 04457; rural
North Livermore; RMC Place; ANDROSCOGGIN; ▲ Livermore; *183 F-3; elev. 501ft./153m.; mail Livermore Falls z 04254; ● 25
North Lovell; RMC Place; OXFORD; ▲ Lovell; *183 F-1; elev. 439ft./134m.; mail Lovell z 04051
North Lubec; RMC Place; WASHINGTON; ▲ Lubec; *183 D-10; mail Lubec z 04652; ● 100

Entries in **UPPERCASE** are counties.
Entries in **bold** have populations of 2,500 or more.
Names in parentheses are alternate names.

Inc. Place	Incorporated Place
RMC Place	Rand McNally Designated Place
CDP	Census Designated Place
MCD	Minor Civil Division
⊡	County Seat
▲	Minor Civil Division
elev.	Elevation
🅿	Post Office
🅷	Hospital
🅲	College
■	Principal Business Center
★	Ranally Metro Area (RMA) Abbreviation
z	Zip Code(s)
Ⓟ	Previous Census Population
Ⓡ	Revised Census Population
Ⓐ	Annexation Population
●	Rand McNally Population Estimate
Ⓒ	Final Census Population
Ⓢ	Special Census Population
◆	Estimated Population

For additional definitions see Glossary, Volume 1, and Introduction, Volume 2.

North Lyndon; RMC Place; AROOSTOOK; *183 B-14; elev. 686ft./209m.; mail Caribou z 04736; pop. incl. with Caribou (Inc. Place)
North Monmouth; RMC Place; KENNEBEC; ▲ Monmouth; 183 F-3; 🅿; ★ AUG; z 04265; ● 200
North Monroe; RMC Place; WALDO; ▲ Monroe, Jackson; *183 E-6; elev. 394ft./120m.; mail Monroe z 04951; rural
North Newcastle; RMC Place; LINCOLN; ▲ Newcastle; *183 G-4; elev. 89ft./27m.; mail Newcastle z 04553
North New Portland; RMC Place; SOMERSET; ▲ New Portland; 183 D-3; 🅿; z 04954, z 04961; ● 225
North Newry; RMC Place; OXFORD; ▲ Newry; *183 E-1; mail Newry z 04261; ● 30
North Norway; RMC Place; OXFORD; ▲ Norway; *183 F-2; elev. 752ft./229m.; mail Norway z 04268; rural
North Orrington; RMC Place; PENOBSCOT; ▲ Orrington; *183 E-6; ★ BANG; mail Orrington z 04474; ● 600
North Palermo; RMC Place; WALDO; ▲ Palermo; *183 F-5; elev. 732ft./223m.; mail Palermo z 04354
North Paris; RMC Place; OXFORD; ▲ West Paris; *183 F-2; mail West Paris z 04289; ● 70
North Parsonsfield; RMC Place; YORK; ▲ Parsonsfield; 183 H-1; mail Parsonsfield z 04047; ● 50
North Penobscot; RMC Place; HANCOCK; ▲ Penobscot; *183 F-7; mail Penobscot z 04476
North Perry; RMC Place; WASHINGTON; ▲ Perry; *183 D-10; mail Perry z 04667; ● 50
North Pittston; RMC Place; KENNEBEC; ▲ Pittston; *183 F-4; elev. 295ft./90m.; ★ AUG; mail Gardiner z 04345; rural
Northport; RMC Place; WALDO; ▲ Northport; 183 F-6; 🅿; z 04849; ● 90
Northport; MCD-Town; WALDO; *183 F-6; 🅿; z 04849 & mail Belfast z 04915; Ⓟ 1,201; Ⓒ 1,331
North Pownal; RMC Place; CUMBERLAND; ▲ Pownal; *183 G-3; elev. 268ft./82m.; mail Pownal z 04069; ● 65
North Raymond; RMC Place; CUMBERLAND; ▲ Raymond; *183 G-2; ★ POR; mail Raymond z 04071; ● 100
North Scarborough; RMC Place; CUMBERLAND; ▲ Scarborough; *183 H-2; ★ POR; mail Scarborough z 04074; ● 100
North Searsmont; RMC Place; WALDO; ▲ Searsmont; *183 F-5; elev. 238ft./73m.; mail Searsmont z 04973
North Searsport; RMC Place; WALDO; ▲ Searsport; *183 E-6; elev. 394ft./120m.; mail Searsport z 04974; ● 125
North Sebago; RMC Place; CUMBERLAND; ▲ Sebago; 183 H-2; mail Sebago z 04029; ● 275
North Sedgwick; RMC Place; HANCOCK; ▲ Sedgwick; *183 F-7; mail Sedgwick z 04676
North Shapleigh; RMC Place; YORK; ▲ Shapleigh; 183 H-1; 🅿; z 04076; ● 125
North Sidney; RMC Place; KENNEBEC; ▲ Sidney; *183 F-4; mail Augusta z 04330; rural
North Sullivan (Sullivan); RMC Place; HANCOCK; ▲ Sullivan; *183 E-8; 🅿; z 04664; ● 225
North Turner; RMC Place; ANDROSCOGGIN; ▲ Turner; 183 F-3; 🅿; ★ LEW-; z 04266; ● 350
North Vassalboro; RMC Place; KENNEBEC; ▲ Vassalboro; 183 F-4; 🅿; ★ AUG; z 04962; ● 900
North Wade; RMC Place; AROOSTOOK; ▲ Wade; *183 B-13; mail Washburn z 04786
North Waldoboro; RMC Place; LINCOLN; ▲ Waldoboro; 183 G-5; elev. 243ft./74m.; mail Waldoboro z 04572; ● 175
North Waterboro; RMC Place; YORK; ▲ Waterboro; 183 H-2; elev. 358ft./109m.; 🅿; z 04061; ● 200
North Waterford; RMC Place; OXFORD; ▲ Waterford; 183 F-2; elev. 544ft./166m.; 🅿; z 04267; ● 300
North Wayne; RMC Place; KENNEBEC; ▲ Wayne; *183 F-3; mail Wayne z 04284
Northwest Bethel; RMC Place; OXFORD; ▲ Bethel; *183 F-1; mail Bethel z 04217; rural
North Whitefield; RMC Place; LINCOLN; ▲ Whitefield; 183 G-4; elev. 219ft./67m.; mail Whitefield z 04353; ● 60
North Windham (Windham); CDP; CUMBERLAND; ▲ Windham; 183 H-2; ★ POR; mail South Windham z 04082, Windham z 04062; Ⓟ 4,077; Ⓒ 4,568
North Windsor; RMC Place; KENNEBEC; ▲ Windsor; *183 F-4; elev. 288ft./88m.; mail Windsor z 04363; rural
North Woodstock; RMC Place; OXFORD; ▲ Woodstock; *183 F-2; elev. 731ft./223m.; mail Bryant Pond z 04219
North Yarmouth; CUMBERLAND; see Walnut Hill (RMC Place)
North Yarmouth; MCD-Town; CUMBERLAND; *183 H-3; 🅿; ★ POR; z 04097 & mail Cumberland Center z 04021; Ⓟ 2,429; Ⓒ 3,210; ◆ 3,512
Norway; CDP; OXFORD; ▲ Norway; 183 G-2; elev. 383ft./117m.; 🅿 🅷; z 04268; Ⓟ 3,023; Ⓒ 2,623
Norway; MCD-Town; OXFORD; *183 F-2; 🅿; z 04268; Ⓟ 4,754; Ⓒ 4,611
Norway Center; RMC Place; OXFORD; ▲ Norway; *183 F-2; elev. 550ft./168m.; mail Norway z 04268
Norway Lake; RMC Place; OXFORD; ▲ Norway; *183 F-2; mail Norway z 04268; ● 150
Notre Dame; RMC Place; AROOSTOOK; *183 A-14; mail Grand Isle z 04746; rural
Number Four; RMC Place; OXFORD; ▲ Lovell; *183 G-1; elev. 469ft./143m.; mail Lovell z 04051; rural

O

Oakdale; RMC Place; CUMBERLAND; *183 H-3; ★ POR; mail Portland z 04101-03; pop. incl. with Portland (Inc. Place)
Oakfield; RMC Place; AROOSTOOK; ▲ Oakfield; *183 C-14; elev. 565ft./172m.; 🅿; z 04763; ● 500
Oakfield; MCD-Town; AROOSTOOK; *183 C-14; 🅿; z 04763; Ⓟ 846; Ⓒ 732
Oak Hill; RMC Place; ANDROSCOGGIN; ▲ Poland; *183 G-2; ★ LEW-; mail Poland z 04274; rural
Oak Hill; RMC Place; CUMBERLAND; ▲ Scarborough; 183 I-3; ★ POR; mail Scarborough z 04074; ● 700
Oakland; CDP; KENNEBEC; ▲ Oakland; 183 E-4; elev. 238ft./73m.; 🅿; ★ WATRVL; z 04963; Ⓟ 3,510; Ⓒ 2,758
Oakland; MCD-Town; KENNEBEC; *183 E-4; 🅿; ★ WATRVL; z 04963; Ⓟ 5,595; Ⓒ 5,959
Oak Point; RMC Place; HANCOCK; ▲ Trenton; *183 F-7; elev. 89ft./27m.; mail Ellsworth z 04605; rural
Oak Ridge; RMC Place; YORK; *183 I-2; mail Biddeford z 04005; pop. incl. with Biddeford (Inc. Place)
Oaks Pond; RMC Place; SOMERSET; ▲ Canaan; *183 E-4; ★ WATRVL; mail Skowhegan z 04976; summer pop. 200
Oak Terrace; RMC Place; YORK; ▲ Kittery; *183 J-2; ★ PTSM-; mail Kittery z 03904
Ocean Park; RMC Place; YORK; ▲ Old Orchard Beach; *183 I-2; 🅿; ★ POR; z 04063
Ocean Point; RMC Place; LINCOLN; ▲ Boothbay; *183 H-4; mail East Boothbay z 04544; summer pop. 400; ● 100
Oceanview Harbor; RMC Place; CUMBERLAND; ▲ Scarborough; *183 I-3; ★ POR; mail Scarborough z 04074; ● 150
Oceanville; RMC Place; HANCOCK; ▲ Stonington; 183 G-7; mail Stonington z 04681; ● 70
Ogontz; RMC Place; SOMERSET; *183 A-4; mail Rockwood z 04478
Ogunquit; RMC Place; YORK; ▲ Ogunquit; 183 J-2; 🅿; z 03907; summer pop. 5,000; ● 974
Ogunquit; MCD-Town; YORK; *183 J-2; 🅿; z 03907; Ⓟ 974; Ⓒ 1,226
Olamon; RMC Place; PENOBSCOT; ▲ Greenbush; 183 D-7; elev. 154ft./47m.; 🅿; z 04418; ● 220
Olde Mill Brook; RMC Place; CUMBERLAND; ▲ Scarborough; *183 I-3; ★ POR; mail Scarborough z 04074; ● 300
Old Orchard Beach; CDP; YORK; ▲ Old Orchard Beach; 183 I-2; 🅿; ★ POR; z 04064; Ⓟ 7,789; summer pop. 12,000; Ⓒ 8,856
Old Orchard Beach; MCD-Town; YORK; *183 I-2; 🅿; ★ POR; z 04064; Ⓟ 7,789; Ⓒ 8,856; ◆ 9,683
Old Town; Inc. Place; PENOBSCOT; 183 D-7; elev. 108ft./33m.; 🅿; ★ BANG; z 04468; Ⓟ 8,317; Ⓒ 8,130; ◆ 8,399
Onawa; RMC Place; PISCATAQUIS; *183 C-5; elev. 633ft./193m.; mail Guilford z 04443; rural
Oquossoc; RMC Place; FRANKLIN; ▲ Rangeley; 183 D-2; 🅿; z 04964; ● 150
Orffs Corner; RMC Place; LINCOLN; ▲ Waldoboro; *183 G-5; mail Waldoboro z 04572; rural
Orient; RMC Place; AROOSTOOK; ▲ Orient; 183 A-8; 🅿; z 04471; ● 30
Orient; MCD-Town; AROOSTOOK; *183 A-8; 🅿; z 04471; Ⓟ 157; Ⓒ 145
Orland; RMC Place; HANCOCK; ▲ Orland; 183 E-6; 🅿; z 04472; ● 300
Orland; MCD-Town; HANCOCK; *183 E-7; 🅿; z 04472; Ⓟ 1,805; Ⓒ 2,134
Orono; CDP; PENOBSCOT; ▲ Orono; 183 D-7; elev. 132ft./40m.; 🅿 🅲 11,797; ★ BANG; z 04469, z 04473; Ⓟ 9,789; Ⓒ 8,253
Orono; MCD-Town; PENOBSCOT; *183 D-6; 🅿 🅲 11,797; ★ BANG; z 04469, z 04473; Ⓟ 10,573; Ⓒ 9,112; ◆ 9,224
Orrington; RMC Place; PENOBSCOT; ▲ Orrington; 183 E-6; 🅿; ★ BANG; z 04474; ● 400
Orrington; MCD-Town; PENOBSCOT; *183 E-6; 🅿; ★ BANG; z 04474; Ⓟ 3,309; Ⓒ 3,526; ◆ 3,876
Orrington Center; RMC Place; PENOBSCOT; ▲ Orrington; *183 E-6; elev. 133ft./41m.; ★ BANG; mail Orrington z 04474
Orrs Island; RMC Place; CUMBERLAND; ▲ Harpswell; *183 H-3; elev. 54ft./16m.; 🅿; ★ BR-BA; z 04066; ● 600
Osborn; MCD-Town; HANCOCK; *183 E-8; 🅿; z 04605; Ⓟ 72; Ⓒ 69
Otis; RMC Place; HANCOCK; ▲ Otis; *183 E-7; elev. 295ft./90m.; 🅿; z 04605; ● 50
Otis; MCD-Town; HANCOCK; *183 E-7; 🅿; z 04605; Ⓟ 355; Ⓒ 543
Otisfield; OXFORD; see Spurrs Corner (RMC Place)
Otisfield; MCD-Town; OXFORD; *183 G-2; 🅿; z 04270; Ⓟ 1,136; Ⓒ 1,560
Otter Creek; RMC Place; HANCOCK; ▲ Mount Desert; 183 H-13; 🅿; z 04660; ● 250
Owls Head; RMC Place; KNOX; ▲ Owls Head; 183 G-6; 🅿; z 04854; ● 350
Owls Head; MCD-Town; KNOX; *183 G-6; 🅿; z 04854; Ⓟ 1,574; Ⓒ 1,601
Oxbow; RMC Place; AROOSTOOK; ▲ Oxbow; *183 C-13; 🅿; z 04764; ● 25
Oxbow; MCD-Plantation; AROOSTOOK; *183 C-13; 🅿; z 04764; Ⓟ 69; Ⓒ 56
Oxford; CDP; OXFORD; ▲ Oxford; 183 G-2; 🅿; z 04270; Ⓟ 1,284; Ⓒ 1,300
Oxford; MCD-Town; OXFORD; *183 G-2; 🅿; z 04270; Ⓟ 3,705; Ⓒ 3,960
OXFORD; 183 F-2; Ⓟ 52,602; Ⓒ 54,755; ◆ 56,762

P

Paine Corner; RMC Place; OXFORD; ▲ Oxford; *183 G-2; elev. 614ft./187m.; mail South Paris z 04281; rural
Paines Corner; RMC Place; KENNEBEC; ▲ Winslow; *183 F-4; ★ WATRVL; mail Waterville z 04901; rural
Palermo; RMC Place; WALDO, KENNEBEC; ▲ China, Palermo; 183 F-5; elev. 366ft./112m.; 🅿; z 04354; ● 120
Palermo; MCD-Town; WALDO; *183 F-5; 🅿; z 04354; Ⓟ 1,021; Ⓒ 1,220
Palmyra; RMC Place; SOMERSET; ▲ Palmyra; 183 D-5; elev. 310ft./94m.; 🅿; z 04965; ● 160
Palmyra; MCD-Town; SOMERSET; *183 D-5; 🅿; z 04965; Ⓟ 1,867; Ⓒ 1,953
Paris; RMC Place; OXFORD; ▲ Paris; *183 F-2; 🅿; z 04271; ● 300
Paris; MCD-Town; OXFORD; *183 F-2; 🅿; z 04271; Ⓟ 4,492; Ⓒ 4,793
Parker Head; RMC Place; SAGADAHOC; ▲ Phippsburg; *183 H-4; mail Phippsburg z 04562; summer pop. 250; ● 80
Parkhurst; RMC Place; AROOSTOOK; *183 B-14; elev. 443ft./135m.; mail Presque Isle z 04769; pop. incl. with Presque Isle (Inc. Place)
Parkman; RMC Place; PISCATAQUIS; ▲ Parkman; 183 D-5; elev. 576ft./176m.; 🅿; z 04443; ● 80
Parkman; MCD-Town; PISCATAQUIS; *183 D-5; 🅿; z 04443; Ⓟ 790; Ⓒ 811
Parsonfield; OXFORD, YORK; see Kezar Falls (RMC Place)
Parsonsfield; RMC Place; YORK; ▲ Parsonsfield; *183 H-1; 🅿; z 04047; ● 35
Parsonsfield; MCD-Town; YORK; *183 H-1; 🅿; z 04047 & mail East Parsonsfield z 04028; Ⓟ 1,472; Ⓒ 1,584
Passadumkeag; RMC Place; PENOBSCOT; ▲ Passadumkeag; 183 C-7; elev. 143ft./44m.; 🅿; z 04475; ● 150
Passadumkeag; MCD-Town; PENOBSCOT; *183 C-7; 🅿; z 04475; Ⓟ 428; Ⓒ 441
Passamaquoddy Indian Township Reservation; Indian Reservation; WASHINGTON; mail Princeton z 04668; Ⓒ 676
Passamaquoddy Pleasant Point Indian Reservation (Pleasant Point Reservation); Indian Reservation; WASHINGTON; mail Perry z 04667; Ⓟ 549; Ⓒ 640
Patten; RMC Place; PENOBSCOT; ▲ Patten; 183 A-7; elev. 546ft./166m.; 🅿; z 04765; ● 1,000
Patten; MCD-Town; PENOBSCOT; *183 D-13; 🅿; z 04765; Ⓟ 1,256; Ⓒ 1,111
Pauls; RMC Place; AROOSTOOK; *183 B-14; mail Caribou z 04736; pop. incl. with Caribou (Inc. Place)
Peaks Island; RMC Place; CUMBERLAND; *183 H-3; 🅿; ★ POR; z 04108; pop. incl. with Portland (Inc. Place)
Pea Ridge; RMC Place; PENOBSCOT; ▲ Chester; *183 C-7; mail Lincoln z 04457
Pejepscot (Pejepscot Mills); RMC Place; SAGADAHOC; ▲ Topsham; *183 G-3; 🅿; ★ BR-BA; z 04086; ● 175
Pejepscot Mills; SAGADAHOC; see Pejepscot (RMC Place)
Pelton Hill; RMC Place; KENNEBEC; *183 F-4; ★ AUG; mail Augusta z 04330; pop. incl. with Augusta (Inc. Place)
Pemaquid; RMC Place; LINCOLN; ▲ Bristol; *183 H-5; elev. 76ft./23m.; 🅿; z 04558; ● 125
Pemaquid Beach; RMC Place; LINCOLN; ▲ Bristol; *183 H-5; mail New Harbor z 04554; summer pop. 350; ● 125
Pemaquid Harbor; RMC Place; LINCOLN; ▲ Bristol; *183 H-5; mail Pemaquid z 04558; ● 30
Pemaquid Point; RMC Place; LINCOLN; ▲ Bristol; *183 H-5; mail New Harbor z 04554; summer pop. 300; ● 100
Pembroke; RMC Place; WASHINGTON; ▲ Pembroke; 183 D-10; elev. 19ft./6m.; 🅿; z 04666; ● 275
Pembroke; MCD-Town; WASHINGTON; *183 D-10; 🅿; z 04666; Ⓟ 852; Ⓒ 879
Penley's Corner; RMC Place; ANDROSCOGGIN; *183 G-3; ★ LEW-; mail Auburn z 04210; pop. incl. with Auburn (Inc. Place)
Penobscot; RMC Place; HANCOCK; ▲ Penobscot; 183 F-6; elev. 54ft./16m.; 🅿; z 04476; ● 100
Penobscot; MCD-Town; HANCOCK; *183 F-6; 🅿; z 04476; Ⓟ 1,131; Ⓒ 1,344
PENOBSCOT; 183 B-7; Ⓟ 146,601; Ⓒ 144,919; ◆ 151,193
Penobscot Reservation; Indian Reservation; PENOBSCOT, AROOSTOOK; mail Old Town z 04468; Ⓟ 458; Ⓒ 562; ◆ 579
Perham; RMC Place; AROOSTOOK; ▲ Perham; 183 B-13; elev. 630ft./192m.; 🅿; z 04766; ● 150
Perham; MCD-Town; AROOSTOOK; *183 B-13; 🅿; z 04766; Ⓟ 395; Ⓒ 434
Perry; RMC Place; AROOSTOOK; mail Presque Isle z 04769; pop. incl. with Presque Isle (Inc. Place)
Perry; RMC Place; WASHINGTON; ▲ Perry; 183 D-10; 🅿; z 04667; ● 90
Perry; MCD-Town; WASHINGTON; *183 D-10; 🅿; z 04667; Ⓟ 758; Ⓒ 847
Perrys Corner; RMC Place; YORK; ▲ Limerick; *183 H-1; mail Limerick z 04048; rural
Peru; RMC Place; OXFORD; ▲ Peru; *183 F-2; 🅿; z 04290; ● 75
Peru; MCD-Town; OXFORD; *183 F-2; 🅿; z 04290; Ⓟ 1,541; Ⓒ 1,515
Peter Dana Point; RMC Place; WASHINGTON; *183 C-9; mail Princeton z 04668; ● 100
Phair; RMC Place; AROOSTOOK; *183 B-14; elev. 583ft./178m.; mail Presque Isle z 04769; pop. incl. with Presque Isle (Inc. Place)
Phillips; RMC Place; FRANKLIN; ▲ Phillips; 183 E-3; elev. 571ft./174m.; 🅿; z 04966; ● 750
Phillips; MCD-Town; FRANKLIN; *183 D-3; 🅿; z 04966; Ⓟ 1,148; Ⓒ 990
Phippsburg; RMC Place; SAGADAHOC; ▲ Phippsburg; 183 H-4; elev. 49ft./15m.; 🅿; z 04562; ● 150
Phippsburg; MCD-Town; SAGADAHOC; *183 H-4; 🅿; ★ BR-BA; z 04562; Ⓟ 1,815; Ⓒ 2,106
Pigeon Hill; RMC Place; WASHINGTON; ▲ Steuben; *183 F-8; mail Milbridge z 04658; rural
Pike Corner; RMC Place; CUMBERLAND; ▲ Casco; *183 G-2; elev. 451ft./137m.; ★ POR; mail Casco z 04015
Pine Cliff; RMC Place; LINCOLN; ▲ Southport; *183 H-4; mail Southport z 04576
Pine Hill; RMC Place; YORK; ▲ York; *183 J-2; ★ PTSM-; mail Cape Neddick z 03902; ● 200
Pine Park; RMC Place; YORK; ▲ Old Orchard Beach; *183 I-2; ★ POR; mail Old Orchard Beach z 04064
Pine Point; RMC Place; CUMBERLAND; ▲ Scarborough; 183 I-3; 🅿; ★ POR; z 04074; summer pop. 500; ● 200
Pinkhams Cove; RMC Place; KENNEBEC; ▲ Belgrade; *183 F-4; mail Belgrade z 04917; summer pop. 125; ● 50
PISCATAQUIS; 183 B-5; Ⓟ 18,653; Ⓒ 17,235; ◆ 17,023
Pishon Ferry; RMC Place; KENNEBEC; ▲ Clinton; *183 E-4; mail Hinckley z 04944; ● 60
Pittsfield; CDP; SOMERSET; ▲ Pittsfield; 183 E-5; elev. 223ft./68m.; 🅿 🅷; z 04967; Ⓟ 3,222; Ⓒ 3,217
Pittsfield; MCD-Town; SOMERSET; *183 E-5; 🅿; z 04967; Ⓟ 4,190; Ⓒ 4,214
Pittston; RMC Place; KENNEBEC; ▲ Pittston; 183 G-4; 🅿; ★ AUG; z 04345; ● 150
Pittston; MCD-Town; KENNEBEC; *183 G-4; ★ AUG; mail Gardiner z 04345; Ⓟ 2,444; Ⓒ 2,548
Pittston Farm; RMC Place; SOMERSET; *183 A-4; elev. 1,102ft./336m.; mail Rockwood z 04478
Plaisted; RMC Place; AROOSTOOK; ▲ Eagle Lake; *183 A-13; mail Eagle Lake z 04739; ● 120
Pleasant Beach; RMC Place; KNOX; ▲ South Thomaston; *183 G-5; mail South Thomaston z 04858
Pleasantdale; RMC Place; CUMBERLAND; *183 H-3; ★ POR; mail South Portland z 04106; pop. incl. with South Portland (Inc. Place)
Pleasant Hill; RMC Place; CUMBERLAND; ▲ Freeport; *183 H-3; ★ POR; mail Freeport z 04032; rural
Pleasant Hill; RMC Place; CUMBERLAND; ▲ Freeport; *183 I-3; elev. 130ft./40m.; ★ POR; mail Falmouth z 04105
Pleasant Hill; RMC Place; CUMBERLAND; ▲ Scarborough; 183 H-9; ★ POR; mail Scarborough z 04074; ● 900
Pleasant Lake; RMC Place; WASHINGTON; ▲ Alexander; *183 D-9; mail Baileyville z 04694; ● 100
Pleasant Point; RMC Place; KNOX; ▲ Cushing; *183 G-5; 🅿; z 04667 & mail Cushing z 04563
Pleasant Point Reservation; WASHINGTON; see Passamaquoddy Pleasant Point Indian Reservation (Indian Reservation)
Pleasant Pond; RMC Place; SOMERSET; ▲ Caratunk; 183 C-4; mail Caratunk z 04925; summer pop. 100; ● 15
Pleasant Ridge; RMC Place; SOMERSET; ▲ Pleasant Ridge; *183 D-4; mail Bingham z 04920; rural
Pleasant Ridge; MCD-Plantation; SOMERSET; *183 D-3; mail Bingham z 04920; Ⓟ 91; Ⓒ 83
Plummer Island; RMC Place; CUMBERLAND; ▲ Scarborough; *183 I-3; ★ POR; mail Scarborough z 04074; ● 40
Plymouth; RMC Place; PENOBSCOT; ▲ Plymouth; 183 E-5; 🅿; z 04969; ● 200
Plymouth; MCD-Town; PENOBSCOT; *183 E-5; 🅿; z 04969; Ⓟ 1,152; Ⓒ 1,257
Poland; RMC Place; ANDROSCOGGIN; ▲ Poland; 183 G-2; 🅿; ★ LEW-; z 04274; ● 350
Poland; MCD-Town; ANDROSCOGGIN; *183 G-2; 🅿; ★ LEW-; z 04274; Ⓟ 4,342; Ⓒ 4,866; ◆ 5,250
Poland Spring (South Poland); RMC Place; ANDROSCOGGIN; ▲ Poland; *183 G-3; 🅿; ★ LEW-; z 04274; ● 200
Pond Cove; RMC Place; CUMBERLAND; ▲ Cape Elizabeth; *183 I-3; 🅿; ★ POR; z 04107
Poors Mills; RMC Place; WALDO; mail Belfast z 04915; pop. incl. with Belfast (Inc. Place)
Popham Beach; RMC Place; SAGADAHOC; ▲ Phippsburg; 183 H-4; ★ BR-BA; mail Phippsburg z 04562; summer pop. 200; ● 40
Portage; RMC Place; AROOSTOOK; ▲ Portage Lake; 183 B-13; elev. 641ft./195m.; 🅿; z 04768; ● 350
Portage Lake; MCD-Town; AROOSTOOK; *183 B-13; 🅿; z 04768; Ⓟ 455; Ⓒ 390
Port Clyde; RMC Place; KNOX; ▲ St. George; 183 G-5; elev. 65ft./20m.; 🅿; z 04855; ● 600
Porter; RMC Place; OXFORD; ▲ Porter; 183 H-1; elev. 411ft./125m.; 🅿; z 04068; ● 200
Porter; MCD-Town; OXFORD; *183 H-1; 🅿; z 04068; Ⓟ 1,301; Ⓒ 1,438
Porterfield; RMC Place; OXFORD; ▲ Porter; *183 H-1; mail Parsonsfield z 04047; rural
Porter Landing; RMC Place; CUMBERLAND; ▲ Freeport; *183 H-3; elev. 130ft./40m.; ★ POR; mail Freeport z 04032; ● 100
Portland; Inc. Place; ⊡ CUMBERLAND; 183 H-3; elev. 70ft./21m.; 🅿 🅷 🅲 10,873 ■; ★ POR; z 04101-10, z 04112, z 04116, z 04122-24; Ⓟ 64,358; Ⓒ 64,249; ◆ 62,982
Pownal; CUMBERLAND; see West Pownal (RMC Place)
Pownal; MCD-Town; CUMBERLAND; *183 H-3; 🅿; z 04069; Ⓟ 1,262; Ⓒ 1,491
Pownal Center; RMC Place; CUMBERLAND; ▲ Pownal; *183 H-3; mail Pownal z 04069; ● 50
Pratt Corner; RMC Place; OXFORD; ▲ Oxford; *183 G-2; elev. 588ft./179m.; mail South Paris z 04281; rural
Prentiss; RMC Place; PENOBSCOT; ▲ Prentiss; *183 B-8; elev. 622ft./190m.; mail Springfield z 04487; rural
Presque Isle; Inc. Place; AROOSTOOK; 183 B-14; elev. 446ft./136m.; 🅿 🅷 🅲 1,655 ■; z 04769; Ⓟ 10,550; Ⓒ 9,511; ◆ 8,877
Prides Corner; RMC Place; CUMBERLAND; *183 H-3; elev. 128ft./39m.; ★ POR; mail Westbrook z 04092; pop. incl. with Westbrook (Inc. Place)
Princeton; RMC Place; WASHINGTON; ▲ Princeton; 183 C-9; elev. 211ft./64m.; 🅿; z 04668; ● 750
Princeton; MCD-Town; WASHINGTON; *183 C-9; 🅿; z 04668; Ⓟ 973; Ⓒ 892
Promised Land; RMC Place; ANDROSCOGGIN; ▲ Poland; *183 G-2; ★ LEW-; mail Poland z 04274; rural
Prospect; RMC Place; WALDO; ▲ Prospect; 183 E-6; 🅿; z 04981; ● 100
Prospect; MCD-Town; WALDO; *183 E-6; 🅿; z 04981; Ⓟ 542; Ⓒ 642
Prospect Ferry; RMC Place; WALDO; ▲ Prospect; *183 E-6; mail Stockton Springs z 04981
Prospect Harbor; RMC Place; HANCOCK; ▲ Gouldsboro; 183 F-8; 🅿; z 04669; ● 400
Prouts Neck; RMC Place; CUMBERLAND; ▲ Scarborough; 183 I-3; ★ POR; mail Scarborough z 04074; summer pop. 300; ● 50
Pulpit Harbor; RMC Place; KNOX; ▲ North Haven; 183 G-6; mail North Haven z 04853; ● 20
Pumpkin Valley; RMC Place; CUMBERLAND; ▲ Bridgton; *183 G-2; elev. 517ft./158m.; mail Bridgton z 04009; rural
Purgatory (Litchfield); RMC Place; KENNEBEC; ▲ Litchfield; 183 F-4; ★ AUG; mail Litchfield z 04350; ● 300

Q

Quimby (Winterville); RMC Place; AROOSTOOK; ▲ Winterville; *183 B-13; 🅿; z 04739; ● 80
Quoddy; RMC Place; WASHINGTON; *183 D-10; mail Eastport z 04631; pop. incl. with Eastport (Inc. Place)

R

Randolph; CDP; KENNEBEC; ▲ Randolph; 183 F-4; 🅿; ★ AUG; z 04346; Ⓟ 1,949; Ⓒ 1,911
Randolph; MCD-Town; KENNEBEC; *183 F-4; 🅿; ★ AUG; z 04346; Ⓟ 1,949; Ⓒ 1,911
Rangeley; RMC Place; FRANKLIN; ▲ Rangeley; 183 D-2; elev. 1,545ft./471m.; 🅿; z 04970; ● 700
Rangeley; MCD-Plantation; FRANKLIN; *183 D-2; 🅿; z 04970; Ⓟ 103; Ⓒ 123
Rangeley; MCD-Town; FRANKLIN; *183 D-2; 🅿; z 04970; Ⓟ 1,063; Ⓒ 1,052
Raymond; RMC Place; CUMBERLAND; ▲ Raymond; 183 H-2; 🅿; ★ POR; z 04071; ● 600
Raymond; MCD-Town; CUMBERLAND; *183 G-2; 🅿; ★ POR; z 04071; Ⓟ 3,311; Ⓒ 4,299; ◆ 4,536
Rayville; RMC Place; OXFORD; ▲ Otisfield; *183 G-2; mail Oxford z 04270; ● 50
Razorville; RMC Place; KNOX; ▲ Washington; *183 F-5; elev. 332ft./101m.; mail Washington z 04574; ● 25
Reach; RMC Place; HANCOCK; ▲ Deer Isle; *183 F-7; mail Deer Isle z 04627; rural
Readfield; RMC Place; KENNEBEC; ▲ Readfield; 183 F-3; 🅿; z 04355; ● 400
Readfield; MCD-Town; KENNEBEC; *183 F-4; 🅿; z 04355; Ⓟ 2,033; Ⓒ 2,360
Readfield Depot; RMC Place; KENNEBEC; ▲ Readfield; *183 F-4; elev. 300ft./91m.; mail Readfield z 04355; ● 60
Red Beach; RMC Place; WASHINGTON; *183 D-10; elev. 108ft./33m.; mail Calais z 04619; pop. incl. with Calais (Inc. Place)
Redding; RMC Place; OXFORD; ▲ Sumner; *183 F-2; mail Sumner z 04292; rural
Red Rock Corner; RMC Place; HANCOCK; ▲ Bar Harbor; *183 F-7; mail Salsbury Cove z 04672; ● 25
Reed; MCD-Plantation; AROOSTOOK; *183 B-8; mail Wytopitlock z 04497; Ⓟ 296; Ⓒ 207
Reeds; RMC Place; FRANKLIN; ▲ Madrid; *183 D-2; elev. 900ft./274m.; mail Phillips z 04966; rural
Remick Corners; RMC Place; YORK; ▲ Kittery; *183 J-2; ★ PTSM-; mail Kittery z 03904
Reynolds Corner; RMC Place; WALDO; ▲ Burnham; *183 E-5; mail Burnham z 04922; rural
Richmond; CDP; SAGADAHOC; ▲ Richmond; 183 G-4; elev. 31ft./9m.; 🅿; ★ AUG; z 04357; Ⓟ 1,775; Ⓒ 1,864
Richmond; MCD-Town; SAGADAHOC; *183 G-4; 🅿; ★ AUG; z 04357; Ⓟ 3,072; Ⓒ 3,298
Richmond Corner; RMC Place; SAGADAHOC; ▲ Richmond; *183 G-4; ★ AUG; mail Richmond z 04357; rural
Richmond Mill; RMC Place; KENNEBEC; ▲ Fayette; *183 F-3; mail Wayne z 04284; rural
Richville; RMC Place; CUMBERLAND; ▲ Standish; *183 H-2; ★ POR; mail Standish z 04084; rural
Ridge; RMC Place; WASHINGTON; ▲ Lubec; *183 D-10; mail Lubec z 04652; ● 75
Ridlonville; RMC Place; OXFORD; ▲ Mexico; *183 E-2; mail Mexico z 04257
Riley; RMC Place; FRANKLIN; ▲ Jay; *183 F-3; mail Jay z 04239; ● 100
Ripley; RMC Place; SOMERSET; ▲ Ripley; 183 D-5; 🅿; z 04930; ● 110
Ripley; MCD-Town; SOMERSET; *183 D-5; 🅿; z 04930; Ⓟ 445; Ⓒ 452
Ripley; RMC Place; WASHINGTON; ▲ Harrington; *183 E-9; mail Harrington z 04643; ● 30
Riverside; RMC Place; KENNEBEC; ▲ Vassalboro; *183 F-4; ★ AUG; mail Augusta z 04330; ● 90
Riverton; RMC Place; CUMBERLAND; *183 H-3; ★ POR; mail Portland z 04103; pop. incl. with Portland (Inc. Place)
Riverview; RMC Place; AROOSTOOK; mail Presque Isle z 04769; pop. incl. with Presque Isle (Inc. Place)
Robbinston; RMC Place; WASHINGTON; ▲ Robbinston; 183 D-10; 🅿; z 04671; ● 200
Robbinston; MCD-Town; WASHINGTON; *183 D-10; 🅿; z 04671; Ⓟ 495; Ⓒ 525
Roberts; RMC Place; AROOSTOOK; *183 B-14; mail Caribou z 04736; pop. incl. with Caribou (Inc. Place)
Roberts Corner; RMC Place; YORK; ▲ Buxton; *183 H-2; ★ POR; mail Buxton z 04093; rural
Robinhood; RMC Place; SAGADAHOC; ▲ Georgetown; *183 H-4; ★ BR-BA; mail Georgetown z 04548; ● 30
Robinson (Robinsons); RMC Place; AROOSTOOK; ▲ Blaine; *183 C-14; mail Mars Hill z 04758; ● 75
Robinson Corner; RMC Place; ANDROSCOGGIN; ▲ Sabattus; *183 G-3; ★ LEW-; mail Lewiston z 04240; ● 60
Robinsons; AROOSTOOK; see Robinson (RMC Place)
Robyville; RMC Place; PENOBSCOT; ▲ Corinth; *183 D-6; mail Kenduskeag z 04450; rural
Rockland; Inc. Place; ⊡ KNOX; 183 G-6; elev. 35ft./11m.; 🅿; z 04841; Ⓟ 7,972; Ⓒ 7,609
Rockport; RMC Place; KNOX; ▲ Rockport; 183 G-6; elev. 66ft./20m.; 🅿 🅷; z 04856; ● 1,200
Rockport; MCD-Town; KNOX; *183 G-6; 🅿; z 04856; Ⓟ 2,854; Ⓒ 3,209
Rockville; RMC Place; KNOX; ▲ Rockport; *183 G-5; elev. 222ft./68m.; mail Rockport z 04856; ● 100
Rockwood; RMC Place; SOMERSET; 183 B-4; elev. 1,050ft./320m.; 🅿; z 04478; ● 300
Rogers Corners; RMC Place; WALDO; ▲ Troy; *183 E-5; mail Troy z 04987; rural
Rome; RMC Place; KENNEBEC; ▲ Rome; 183 E-4; elev. 311ft./95m.; 🅿; z 04963 & mail Norridgewock z 04957; ● 200
Rome; MCD-Town; KENNEBEC; *183 E-4; 🅿; z 04963 & mail Norridgewock z 04957; Ⓟ 758; Ⓒ 980
Rome Corner; RMC Place; KENNEBEC; ▲ Rome; *183 E-4; mail Norridgewock z 04957; rural
Roque Bluffs; RMC Place; WASHINGTON; ▲ Roque Bluffs; 183 E-9; 🅿; z 04654; ● 100
Roque Bluffs; MCD-Town; WASHINGTON; *183 E-9; 🅿; z 04654; Ⓟ 234; Ⓒ 264
Rosemont; RMC Place; CUMBERLAND; *183 H-3; ★ POR; mail Portland z 04103; pop. incl. with Portland (Inc. Place)
Ross Corner; RMC Place; YORK; ▲ Waterboro, Shapleigh; *183 I-2; elev. 450ft./137m.; mail Waterboro z 04087
Round Pond; RMC Place; LINCOLN; ▲ Bristol; 183 G-5; 🅿; z 04564; ● 400
Rowe Corner; RMC Place; ANDROSCOGGIN; *183 G-3; ★ LEW-; mail Auburn z 04210; pop. incl. with Auburn (Inc. Place)
Roxbury; RMC Place; OXFORD; ▲ Roxbury; 183 E-2; 🅿; z 04275; ● 180
Roxbury; MCD-Town; OXFORD; *183 E-2; 🅿; z 04275; Ⓟ 437; Ⓒ 384
Rumford; CDP; OXFORD; ▲ Rumford; 183 E-2; 🅿 🅷; z 04276; Ⓟ 5,419; Ⓒ 4,795
Rumford; MCD-Town; OXFORD; *183 E-2; 🅿; z 04276; Ⓟ 7,078; Ⓒ 6,472
Rumford Center; RMC Place; OXFORD; ▲ Rumford; *183 F-2; 🅿; z 04276; ● 90
Rumford Corner; RMC Place; OXFORD; ▲ Rumford; *183 F-2; elev. 645ft./197m.; mail Bryant Pond z 04219
Rumford Point; RMC Place; OXFORD; ▲ Rumford; *183 F-2; elev. 636ft./194m.; 🅿; z 04276; ● 125

S

Sabattus; RMC Place; ANDROSCOGGIN; ▲ Sabattus; 183 G-3; 🅿; ★ LEW-; z 04280; ● 1,300
Sabattus; MCD-Town; ANDROSCOGGIN; *183 G-3; 🅿; ★ LEW-; z 04280; Ⓟ 3,696; Ⓒ 4,486; ◆ 4,702
Sabbathday Lake; RMC Place; CUMBERLAND; ▲ New Gloucester; *183 G-3; mail New Gloucester z 04260; ● 200
Saco; Inc. Place; YORK; 183 I-2; elev. 60ft./18m.; 🅿; z 04072; Ⓟ 15,181; Ⓒ 16,822
SAGADAHOC; 183 G-4; Ⓟ 33,535; Ⓒ 35,214; ◆ 35,961
Saint Agatha; RMC Place; AROOSTOOK; ▲ St. Agatha; 183 A-13; 🅿; z 04772; ● 500
St. Agatha; MCD-Town; AROOSTOOK; *183 A-13; mail Saint Agatha z 04772; Ⓟ 919; Ⓒ 802
Saint Albans; RMC Place; SOMERSET; ▲ St. Albans; 183 D-5; 🅿; z 04971; ● 250
St. Albans; MCD-Town; SOMERSET; *183 D-5; mail Saint Albans z 04971; Ⓟ 1,724; Ⓒ 1,836
Saint David; RMC Place; AROOSTOOK; ▲ Madawaska; *183 A-13; elev. 516ft./157m.; 🅿; z 04773; ● 75
Saint Francis; RMC Place; AROOSTOOK; ▲ St. Francis; 183 A-13; elev. 597ft./182m.; 🅿; z 04774; ● 300
St. Francis; MCD-Town; AROOSTOOK; *183 A-13; mail Saint Francis z 04774; Ⓟ 683; Ⓒ 577
Saint George; RMC Place; KNOX; ▲ St. George; 183 G-5; elev. 113ft./34m.; 🅿; z 04860; ● 275
St. George; MCD-Town; KNOX; *183 H-5; Ⓟ 2,261; Ⓒ 2,580
Saint John; RMC Place; AROOSTOOK; ▲ Saint John; 183 A-13; mail Fort Kent z 04743; ● 125
Saint John; MCD-Plantation; AROOSTOOK; *183 A-13; mail Fort Kent z 04743; Ⓟ 274; Ⓒ 282
Salem; RMC Place; FRANKLIN; 183 D-3; mail Strong z 04983; ● 50
Salmon Falls; RMC Place; YORK; ▲ Hollis, Buxton; *183 I-2; elev. 144ft./44m.; ★ POR; mail Bar Mills z 04004; ● 100
Salsbury Cove; RMC Place; HANCOCK; ▲ Bar Harbor; 183 G-12; 🅿; z 04672; ● 250
Sanderson Corners; RMC Place; KENNEBEC; ▲ Fayette; *183 F-3; elev. 445ft./136m.; mail Kents Hill z 04349; rural
Sandhill Corner; RMC Place; LINCOLN; ▲ Somerville; *183 F-5; elev. 293ft./89m.; mail Coopers Mills z 04341; rural
Sandy Beach; RMC Place; PENOBSCOT; ▲ Glenburn; *183 D-6; ★ BANG; mail Bangor z 04401; ● 20
Sandy Creek; RMC Place; CUMBERLAND; ▲ Bridgton; *183 G-2; mail Bridgton z 04009; ● 100
Sandy Point; RMC Place; WALDO; ▲ Stockton Springs; *183 F-6; elev. 95ft./29m.; 🅿; z 04972; ● 150
Sandy River; MCD-Plantation; FRANKLIN; *183 D-2; mail Rangeley z 04970; Ⓟ 64; Ⓒ 93
Sandy River Beach; RMC Place; WASHINGTON; ▲ Jonesport; *183 E-9; mail Jonesport z 04649; ● 40
Sanford; CDP; YORK; ▲ Sanford; 183 I-2; 🅿 🅷; z 04073; Ⓟ 10,296; Ⓒ 10,133
Sanford; MCD-Town; YORK; *183 I-2; 🅿; z 04073; Ⓟ 20,463; Ⓒ 20,806; ◆ 19,316
Sangerville; RMC Place; PISCATAQUIS; ▲ Sangerville; 183 C-5; elev. 518ft./158m.; 🅿; z 04479; ● 650
Sangerville; MCD-Town; PISCATAQUIS; *183 D-5; 🅿; z 04479; Ⓟ 1,398; Ⓒ 1,270
Saponac; RMC Place; PENOBSCOT; ▲ East Central Penobscot; *183 C-7; mail Burlington z 04417; ● 15
Sargentville; RMC Place; HANCOCK; ▲ Sedgwick; *183 F-7; elev. 128ft./39m.; 🅿; z 04673; ● 130
Saunders; RMC Place; AROOSTOOK; mail Presque Isle z 04769; pop. incl. with Presque Isle (Inc. Place)
Scarborough; CDP; CUMBERLAND; ▲ Scarborough; 183 H-3; elev. 17ft./5m.; 🅿; ★ POR; z 04070, z 04074; Ⓟ 2,586; Ⓒ 3,867
Scarborough; MCD-Town; CUMBERLAND; *183 I-3; 🅿; ★ POR; z 04070, z 04074; Ⓟ 12,518; Ⓒ 16,970; ◆ 18,143
Schoodic Lake; RMC Place; WASHINGTON; ▲ Columbia, North Washington; *183 E-8; mail Columbia Falls z 04623; summer pop. 250
Scituate; RMC Place; YORK; ▲ York; *183 J-2; ★ PTSM-; mail York z 03909; rural
Scotland; RMC Place; CUMBERLAND; ▲ Windham; *183 H-3; ★ POR; mail Windham z 04062; rural
Scotland; RMC Place; YORK; ▲ York; *183 J-2; ★ PTSM-; mail York z 03909
Scott; RMC Place; AROOSTOOK; *183 C-14; mail Presque Isle z 04769
Scribners Mill; RMC Place; CUMBERLAND; ▲ Harrison; *183 G-2; mail Harrison z 04040; rural
Seabury; RMC Place; YORK; ▲ York; *183 J-2; elev. 20ft./6m.; ★ PTSM-; mail York z 03909
Seal Cove; RMC Place; HANCOCK; ▲ Tremont; 183 F-7; 🅿; z 04674; ● 100
Seal Harbor; RMC Place; HANCOCK; ▲ Mount Desert; 183 I-13; 🅿; z 04675; summer pop. 1,000; ● 250
Searsmont; RMC Place; WALDO; ▲ Searsmont; 183 F-5; elev. 227ft./69m.; 🅿; z 04973; ● 175
Searsmont; MCD-Town; WALDO; *183 F-5; 🅿; z 04973; Ⓟ 938; Ⓒ 1,174
Searsport; CDP; WALDO; ▲ Searsport; 183 F-6; elev. 60ft./18m.; 🅿; z 04974; Ⓟ 1,151; Ⓒ 1,102
Searsport; MCD-Town; WALDO; *183 F-6; 🅿; z 04974; Ⓟ 2,603; Ⓒ 2,641
Seawall; RMC Place; HANCOCK; ▲ Southwest Harbor; 183 J-12; mail Southwest Harbor z 04679; ● 50
Sebago; CUMBERLAND; see East Sebago (RMC Place)
Sebago; CUMBERLAND; see Sebago Center (RMC Place)
Sebago; MCD-Town; CUMBERLAND; *183 H-2; 🅿; z 04029; Ⓟ 1,259; Ⓒ 1,433
Sebago Center (Sebago); RMC Place; CUMBERLAND; ▲ Sebago; *183 H-2; mail Sebago z 04029; rural
Sebago Lake; RMC Place; CUMBERLAND; ▲ Standish; 183 H-2; elev. 284ft./87m.; 🅿; ★ POR; z 04084; ● 600
Sebasco; RMC Place; SAGADAHOC; ▲ Phippsburg; *183 H-4; mail Sebasco Estates z 04565; ● 150
Sebasco Estates; RMC Place; SAGADAHOC; ▲ Phippsburg; 183 H-4; 🅿; z 04565; ● 200
Sebec; RMC Place; PISCATAQUIS; ▲ Sebec; 183 C-5; elev. 358ft./109m.; 🅿; z 04426, z 04481; ● 100
Sebec; MCD-Town; PISCATAQUIS; *183 C-6; 🅿; z 04426, z 04481; Ⓟ 554; Ⓒ 612
Sebec Corners; RMC Place; PISCATAQUIS; ▲ Sebec; *183 C-6; elev. 444ft./135m.; mail Dover Foxcroft z 04426; rural
Sebec Lake; RMC Place; PISCATAQUIS; ▲ Willimantic; 183 C-5; elev. 338ft./103m.; 🅿; z 04443; summer pop. 75; ● 5
Seboeis; RMC Place; PENOBSCOT; ▲ Seboeis; 183 C-6; mail Howland z 04448; ● 30
Seboeis; MCD-Plantation; PENOBSCOT; *183 C-6; mail Howland z 04448; Ⓟ 40; Ⓒ 41
Seboomook; RMC Place; SOMERSET; *183 A-4; mail Rockwood z 04478
Sedgwick; RMC Place; HANCOCK; ▲ Sedgwick; 183 F-7; 🅿; z 04676; ● 150
Sedgwick; MCD-Town; HANCOCK; *183 F-7; 🅿; z 04676; Ⓟ 905; Ⓒ 1,102
Shady Nook; RMC Place; YORK; ▲ Newfield; *183 H-1; elev. 687ft./209m.; mail East Wakefield z 03830; rural
Shaker Village; RMC Place; CUMBERLAND; ▲ New Gloucester; *183 G-3; mail New Gloucester z 04260; ● 20
Shapleigh; RMC Place; YORK; ▲ Shapleigh; 183 I-1; 🅿; z 04076; ● 175
Shapleigh; MCD-Town; YORK; *183 I-1; 🅿; z 04076; Ⓟ 1,911; Ⓒ 2,326
Shaw Mills; RMC Place; CUMBERLAND; ▲ Standish, Gorham; *183 H-2; ★ POR; mail Standish z 04084; rural
Shawmut; RMC Place; SOMERSET; ▲ Fairfield; *183 E-4; 🅿; ★ WATRVL; z 04975; ● 175
Sheepscot; RMC Place; LINCOLN; ▲ Newcastle; *183 G-4; mail Wiscasset z 04578; ● 90
Sheridan; RMC Place; AROOSTOOK; ▲ Ashland; *183 B-13; 🅿; z 04775; ● 145
Sherman; RMC Place; AROOSTOOK; ▲ Sherman; *183 A-7; elev. 522ft./159m.; 🅿; z 04776; ● 100
Sherman; MCD-Town; AROOSTOOK; *183 A-7; 🅿; z 04776; Ⓟ 1,027; Ⓒ 937
Sherman Mills; RMC Place; AROOSTOOK; ▲ Sherman; 183 A-7; 🅿; z 04776; ● 450
Shermans Corner; RMC Place; WALDO; ▲ Liberty; *183 I-5; mail Liberty z 04949; pop. incl. with Belfast (Inc. Place)
Shermans Corner; RMC Place; WALDO; *183 F-6; mail Belfast z 04915
Sherman Station; RMC Place; PENOBSCOT; ▲ Stacyville; 183 A-7; elev. 485ft./148m.; 🅿; z 04777; ● 325
Shin Pond; RMC Place; PENOBSCOT; ▲ Mount Chase; *183 C-13; elev. 788ft./240m.; mail Patten z 04765; summer pop. 250
Shirley; MCD-Town; PISCATAQUIS; *183 C-4; mail Shirley Mills z 04485; Ⓟ 271; Ⓒ 183
Shirley Mills; RMC Place; PISCATAQUIS; ▲ Shirley; 183 C-4; elev. 1,043ft./318m.; 🅿; z 04485; ● 150
Shy Corner; RMC Place; ANDROSCOGGIN; ▲ Livermore Falls; *183 F-3; mail Livermore Falls z 04254
Sibley Pond; RMC Place; SOMERSET; ▲ Canaan, Pittsfield; *183 E-5; mail Canaan z 04924, Pittsfield z 04967; summer pop. 200
Sidney; RMC Place; KENNEBEC; ▲ Sidney; *183 F-4; 🅿; z 04330
Sidney; MCD-Town; KENNEBEC; *183 F-4; 🅿; z 04330; Ⓟ 2,593; Ⓒ 3,514
Sidney Center; RMC Place; KENNEBEC; ▲ Sidney; *183 F-4; mail Augusta z 04330; ● 40
Sidney Center; RMC Place; KENNEBEC; *183 F-4; mail Augusta z 04330; ● 30
Silver Ridge; RMC Place; AROOSTOOK; *183 A-7; 🅿; z 04776; rural
Simonton Corners; RMC Place; KNOX; ▲ Rockport; *183 G-6; mail Rockport z 04856; rural
Simpson Corners; RMC Place; PENOBSCOT; ▲ Dixmont; *183 E-6; elev. 459ft./140m.; mail Dixmont z 04932; rural
Sinclair; RMC Place; AROOSTOOK; *183 A-13; elev. 593ft./181m.; 🅿; z 04779; ● 380
Skillings Corner; RMC Place; ANDROSCOGGIN; ▲ Turner; *183 G-3; ★ LEW-; mail Turner z 04282; rural
Skowhegan; CDP; ⊡ SOMERSET; ▲ Skowhegan; 183 E-4; elev. 175ft./53m.; 🅿 🅷; ★ WATRVL; z 04976; Ⓟ 6,990; Ⓒ 6,696
Skowhegan; MCD-Town; SOMERSET; *183 E-4; 🅿; ★ WATRVL; z 04976; Ⓟ 8,725; Ⓒ 8,824
Slab City; RMC Place; OXFORD; ▲ Lovell; *183 F-1; mail Lovell z 04051
Slab City; RMC Place; WALDO; ▲ Lincolnville; *183 F-6; mail Lincolnville z 04849; rural
Small Point; RMC Place; SAGADAHOC; ▲ Phippsburg; *183 H-4; elev. 37ft./11m.; ★ BR-BA; ● 30
Small Point Beach; RMC Place; SAGADAHOC; *183 H-4; summer pop. 100
Smithfield; RMC Place; SOMERSET; ▲ Smithfield; 183 E-4; 🅿; z 04978; ● 225
Smithfield; MCD-Town; SOMERSET; *183 E-4; 🅿; z 04978; Ⓟ 865; Ⓒ 930
Smithville; RMC Place; WASHINGTON; ▲ Steuben; *183 E-8; mail Steuben z 04680
Smyrna; MCD-Town; AROOSTOOK; *183 C-14; mail Smyrna Mills z 04780; Ⓟ 378; Ⓒ 415
Smyrna Center; RMC Place; AROOSTOOK; ▲ Smyrna; *183 C-14; mail Smyrna Mills z 04780; rural
Smyrna Mills; RMC Place; AROOSTOOK; ▲ Merrill, Smyrna; 183 C-13; elev. 579ft./176m.; 🅿; z 04780; ● 250
Soldier Pond; RMC Place; AROOSTOOK; ▲ Wallagrass; *183 A-13; elev. 590ft./180m.; mail Wallagrass z 04781; ● 200
Solon; RMC Place; SOMERSET; ▲ Solon; 183 D-4; elev. 405ft./123m.; 🅿; z 04979; ● 450
Solon; MCD-Town; SOMERSET; *183 D-4; 🅿; z 04979; Ⓟ 916; Ⓒ 940
SOMERSET; 183 C-3; Ⓟ 49,767; Ⓒ 50,888; ◆ 51,575
Somerville; RMC Place; LINCOLN; ▲ Somerville; *183 F-5; elev. 232ft./71m.; 🅿; z 04348; ● 50
Somerville; MCD-Town; LINCOLN; *183 F-5; 🅿; z 04348; Ⓟ 458; Ⓒ 509
Somesville (Mount Desert); RMC Place; HANCOCK; *183 F-7; mail Mount Desert z 04660; ● 250
Sorrento; RMC Place; HANCOCK; ▲ Sorrento; *183 F-8; 🅿; z 04677; summer pop. 500; ● 190
Sorrento; MCD-Town; HANCOCK; *183 F-8; 🅿; z 04677; Ⓟ 295; Ⓒ 290
Sound; RMC Place; HANCOCK; ▲ Mount Desert; *183 F-7; mail Mount Desert z 04660; rural
South Acton; RMC Place; YORK; ▲ Acton; *183 I-1; mail Acton z 04001; rural
South Addison; RMC Place; WASHINGTON; ▲ Addison; 183 F-9; mail Addison z 04606; ● 100
South Andover; RMC Place; OXFORD; ▲ Andover; *183 E-2; elev. 672ft./205m.; mail Andover z 04216; rural
South Arm; RMC Place; OXFORD; 183 E-1; mail Andover z 04216; ● 15
South Berwick; RMC Place; YORK; ▲ South Berwick; 183 J-1; elev. 102ft./31m.; 🅿; ★ PTSM-; z 03908; ● 3,000
South Berwick; MCD-Town; YORK; *183 J-2; 🅿; ★ PTSM-; z 03908; Ⓟ 5,877; Ⓒ 6,671; ◆ 6,875
South Blue Hill; RMC Place; HANCOCK; ▲ Blue Hill; *183 F-7; ● 150
South Brewer; RMC Place; PENOBSCOT; *183 E-6; ★ BANG; mail Brewer z 04412; pop. incl. with Brewer (Inc. Place)
South Bridgton; RMC Place; CUMBERLAND; ▲ Bridgton; *183 G-2; mail Bridgton z 04009; ● 60
South Bristol; RMC Place; LINCOLN; ▲ South Bristol; 183 H-4; elev. 36ft./11m.; 🅿; z 04568; ● 500
South Bristol; MCD-Town; LINCOLN; *183 H-4; 🅿; z 04568; Ⓟ 825; Ⓒ 897
South Brooksville (Brooksville); RMC Place; HANCOCK; ▲ Brooksville; 183 F-7; mail Brooksville z 04617, Harborside z 04642; ● 120
South Buxton; RMC Place; YORK; ▲ Buxton; *183 H-2; ★ POR; mail Gorham z 04038; rural
South Casco; RMC Place; CUMBERLAND; ▲ Casco; *183 G-2; 🅿; ★ POR; z 04077; ● 300
South China; RMC Place; KENNEBEC; ▲ China; 183 F-4; elev. 223ft./68m.; 🅿; z 04358; ● 500
South Corinth; RMC Place; PENOBSCOT; ▲ Corinth; *183 D-6; mail Corinth z 04427
South Deer Isle; RMC Place; HANCOCK; ▲ Deer Isle; *183 G-7; mail Stonington z 04681; ● 30
South Dover; RMC Place; PISCATAQUIS; ▲ Dover-Foxcroft; *183 C-5; elev. 528ft./161m.; mail Dover Foxcroft z 04426
South Durham; RMC Place; ANDROSCOGGIN; ▲ Durham; *183 G-3; elev. 292ft./89m.; mail Durham z 04222
South Eliot; CDP; YORK; ▲ Eliot; 183 J-1; ★ PTSM-; mail Eliot z 03903; Ⓟ 3,112; Ⓒ 3,445
South Exeter; RMC Place; PENOBSCOT; ▲ Exeter; *183 D-5; elev. 372ft./113m.; mail Exeter z 04435; rural
South Freeport; RMC Place; CUMBERLAND; ▲ Freeport; *183 H-3; elev. 130ft./40m.; 🅿; ★ POR; z 04013, z 04078; summer pop. 600; ● 400
South Gardiner; RMC Place; KENNEBEC; *183 G-4; elev. 50ft./15m.; 🅿; ★ AUG; z 04359; pop. incl. with Gardiner (Inc. Place)
South Gorham; RMC Place; CUMBERLAND; ▲ Gorham; *183 H-2; ★ POR; mail Gorham z 04038; rural
South Gouldsboro; RMC Place; HANCOCK; ▲ Gouldsboro; 183 G-14; 🅿; z 04607; ● 175
South Gray; RMC Place; CUMBERLAND; ▲ Gray; *183 H-3; ★ POR; mail Gray z 04039
South Hancock; RMC Place; HANCOCK; ▲ Hancock; *183 F-8; elev. 73ft./22m.; mail Ellsworth z 04605
South Harpswell (Harpswell); RMC Place; CUMBERLAND; ▲ Harpswell; 183 H-3; 🅿; ★ BR-BA; z 04079; ● 225
South Hiram; RMC Place; OXFORD; ▲ Hiram; *183 H-1; elev. 383ft./117m.; mail Hiram z 04041; ● 200
South Hollis; RMC Place; YORK; ▲ Hollis; *183 I-2; ★ POR; mail Hollis Center z 04042; rural
South Hope; RMC Place; KNOX; ▲ Hope; *183 G-5; mail Hope z 04847; ● 80
South Jefferson; RMC Place; LINCOLN; ▲ Jefferson; *183 G-4; elev. 199ft./61m.; mail Newcastle z 04553; rural
South Lagrange; RMC Place; PENOBSCOT; ▲ Lagrange; 183 D-6; elev. 192ft./59m.; mail Lagrange z 04453; ● 60
South Lebanon; RMC Place; YORK; ▲ Lebanon; 183 I-1; mail Lebanon z 04027; ● 225
South Levant; RMC Place; PENOBSCOT; ▲ Levant; *183 D-6; mail Levant z 04456; rural
South Lewiston; RMC Place; ANDROSCOGGIN; *183 G-3; elev. 189ft./58m.; ★ LEW-; mail Lewiston z 04240; pop. incl. with Lewiston (Inc. Place)
South Liberty; RMC Place; WALDO; ▲ Liberty; *183 F-5; mail Liberty z 04949
South Limington; RMC Place; YORK; ▲ Limington; *183 H-2; elev. 309ft./94m.; ★ POR; mail Limington z 04049
South Lincoln; RMC Place; PENOBSCOT; ▲ Lincoln; 183 C-7; elev. 180ft./55m.; mail Lincoln z 04457; ● 180
South Livermore; RMC Place; ANDROSCOGGIN; ▲ Livermore; *183 F-3; mail Livermore Falls z 04254; rural
South Lubec; RMC Place; WASHINGTON; ▲ Lubec; 183 D-10; elev. 28ft./9m.; mail Lubec z 04652; ● 120
South Monmouth; RMC Place; KENNEBEC; ▲ Monmouth; *183 G-3; elev. 215ft./66m.; ★ AUG; mail Monmouth z 04259; ● 50
South Montville; RMC Place; WALDO; ▲ Montville; *183 F-5; mail Liberty z 04949; ● 70
South Newcastle; RMC Place; LINCOLN; ▲ Newcastle, Edgecomb; *183 G-4; mail Newcastle z 04553; rural
South Orland; RMC Place; HANCOCK; ▲ Orland; *183 F-6; mail Orland z 04472; rural
South Orrington; RMC Place; PENOBSCOT; ▲ Orrington; 183 E-6; ★ BANG; mail Orrington z 04474; ● 300
South Paris; CDP; ⊡ OXFORD; ▲ Paris; 183 F-2; elev. 416ft./127m.; 🅿; z 04281; Ⓟ 2,320; Ⓒ 2,237
South Parsonsfield; RMC Place; YORK; ▲ Parsonsfield; *183 H-1; elev. 555ft./169m.; mail Parsonsfield z 04047; rural
South Penobscot; RMC Place; HANCOCK; ▲ Penobscot; *183 F-6; mail Penobscot z 04476; ● 120
South Poland; ANDROSCOGGIN; see Poland Spring (RMC Place)
Southport; RMC Place; LINCOLN; ▲ Southport; *183 H-4; 🅿; z 04576; ● 150
Southport; MCD-Town; LINCOLN; *183 H-4; 🅿; z 04576; Ⓟ 645; Ⓒ 684
South Portland; Inc. Place; CUMBERLAND; 183 H-3; elev. 26ft./8m.; 🅿 🅷 ■; ★ POR; z 04106, z 04116; Ⓟ 23,163; Ⓒ 23,324; ◆ 23,090
South Portland Heights; RMC Place; CUMBERLAND; *183 H-3; ★ POR; mail South Portland z 04106; pop. incl. with South Portland (Inc. Place)
South Princeton; RMC Place; WASHINGTON; ▲ Princeton; *183 C-9; elev. 356ft./109m.; mail Princeton z 04668; rural
South Rangeley; RMC Place; FRANKLIN; ▲ Rangeley; *183 D-2; mail Oquossoc z 04964
South Rumford; RMC Place; OXFORD; ▲ Rumford; *183 E-2; mail Rumford z 04276; ● 150
South Sanford; CDP; YORK; ▲ Sanford; 183 I-2; elev. 283ft./86m.; mail Sanford z 04073; Ⓟ 3,929; Ⓒ 4,173
South Sebec; RMC Place; PISCATAQUIS; *183 C-6; elev. 301ft./92m.; mail Sebec z 04481; rural
South Side; RMC Place; YORK; ▲ York; *183 J-2; ★ PTSM-; mail York z 03909; rural
South Springfield; RMC Place; PENOBSCOT; ▲ Springfield; *183 C-8; mail Springfield z 04487; ● 20
South Strong; RMC Place; FRANKLIN; ▲ Strong; *183 E-3; mail Strong z 04983; rural
South Surry; RMC Place; HANCOCK; ▲ Surry; *183 F-7; mail Surry z 04684; summer pop. 200
South Thomaston; RMC Place; KNOX; ▲ South Thomaston; *183 G-5; 🅿; z 04858; ● 350
South Thomaston; MCD-Town; KNOX; *183 G-5; 🅿; z 04858; Ⓟ 1,227; Ⓒ 1,416
South Trescott; RMC Place; WASHINGTON; *183 E-10; mail Lubec z 04652
South Union; RMC Place; KNOX; ▲ Union; *183 G-5; elev. 96ft./29m.; mail Warren z 04864; ● 100
South Vassalboro; RMC Place; KENNEBEC; ▲ Vassalboro; *183 F-4; ★ AUG; mail Vassalboro z 04989; rural
South Waldoboro; RMC Place; LINCOLN; ▲ Waldoboro; *183 G-5; mail Waldoboro z 04572
South Warren; RMC Place; KNOX; *183 G-5; mail Warren z 04864
South Waterford; RMC Place; OXFORD; ▲ Waterford; 183 G-2; elev. 458ft./140m.; mail Waterford z 04088; ● 175
South West Bend (Durham); RMC Place; ANDROSCOGGIN; ▲ Durham; *183 G-3; mail Durham z 04222; ● 70
Southwest Harbor; RMC Place; HANCOCK; ▲ Southwest Harbor; 183 F-7; elev. 468ft./143m.; 🅿; z 04679; ● 1,200
Southwest Harbor; MCD-Town; HANCOCK; *183 F-7; 🅿; z 04679; Ⓟ 1,952; Ⓒ 1,966
South Windham; RMC Place; CUMBERLAND; ▲ Gorham, Windham; 183 H-2; elev. 154ft./47m.; 🅿; ★ POR; z 04082; ● 400
South Windsor; RMC Place; KENNEBEC; ▲ Windsor; *183 F-4; mail Windsor z 04363; ● 75
South Woodstock; RMC Place; OXFORD; ▲ Woodstock; 183 F-2; elev. 598ft./182m.; mail West Paris z 04289; ● 65
South Woodville; RMC Place; PENOBSCOT; ▲ Woodville; *183 B-7; elev. 479ft./146m.; mail Lincoln z 04457; rural
Spears Corner; RMC Place; KENNEBEC; ▲ West Gardiner; *183 G-4; elev. 190ft./58m.; ★ AUG; mail Gardiner z 04345
Spooners Mill; RMC Place; PENOBSCOT; ▲ Dexter; *183 D-5; mail Dexter z 04930; rural
Spragueville; RMC Place; AROOSTOOK; *183 B-14; mail Presque Isle z 04769; pop. incl. with Presque Isle (Inc. Place)
Springfield; RMC Place; PENOBSCOT; ▲ Springfield; 183 C-8; elev. 555ft./169m.; 🅿; z 04487; ● 120
Springfield; MCD-Town; PENOBSCOT; *183 C-8; 🅿; z 04487; Ⓟ 406; Ⓒ 379
Springvale; CDP; YORK; ▲ Sanford; 183 I-2; 🅿; z 04083; Ⓟ 3,542; Ⓒ 3,488
Spruce Head; RMC Place; KNOX; ▲ South Thomaston; 183 G-5; elev. 36ft./11m.; 🅿; z 04859; ● 220
Spruce Head Island; RMC Place; KNOX; ▲ South Thomaston; *183 G-5; mail Spruce Head z 04859; ● 150
Spruce Point; RMC Place; LINCOLN; ▲ Boothbay Harbor; *183 H-4; mail Boothbay Harbor z 04538; summer pop. 150; ● 20
Spruce Shores; RMC Place; LINCOLN; ▲ Boothbay; *183 H-4; mail East Boothbay z 04544; rural
Spurrs Corner (Otisfield); RMC Place; OXFORD; ▲ Otisfield; *183 G-2; elev. 482ft./147m.; mail Oxford z 04270; ● 50
Squapan; RMC Place; AROOSTOOK; ▲ Masardis, Ashland; *183 B-13; mail Ashland z 04732; ● 20
Square Pond; RMC Place; YORK; ▲ Acton, Shapleigh; *183 I-1; mail Acton z 04001, Shapleigh z 04076; summer pop. 300
Squirrel Island; RMC Place; LINCOLN; ▲ Southport; *183 H-4; 🅿; z 04570; summer pop. 350
Stacyville; RMC Place; PENOBSCOT; ▲ Stacyville; 183 A-7; elev. 517ft./158m.; 🅿; z 04777; ● 35
Stacyville; MCD-Town; PENOBSCOT; *183 A-7; 🅿; z 04777; Ⓟ 480; Ⓒ 405
Standish; RMC Place; CUMBERLAND; ▲ Standish; 183 H-2; elev. 433ft./132m.; 🅿 🅲 1,015; ★ POR; z 04084; ● 500
Standish; MCD-Town; CUMBERLAND; *183 H-2; 🅿 🅲 1,015; ★ POR; z 04084; Ⓟ 7,678; Ⓒ 9,285; ◆ 9,689
Stanwood Park; RMC Place; CUMBERLAND; *183 H-3; ★ POR; mail South Portland z 04106; pop. incl. with South Portland (Inc. Place)
Starboard; RMC Place; WASHINGTON; ▲ Machiasport; 183 E-10; mail Machiasport z 04655; ● 50
Starks; RMC Place; SOMERSET; ▲ Starks; 183 E-3; 🅿; z 04911; ● 135
Starks; MCD-Town; SOMERSET; *183 E-4; 🅿; z 04911; Ⓟ 508; Ⓒ 578
State Road; RMC Place; AROOSTOOK; ▲ Mapleton; *183 B-14; mail Mapleton z 04757; rural
Stebbins; RMC Place; AROOSTOOK; ▲ Fort Fairfield; *183 B-14; mail Fort Fairfield z 04742; rural

Entries in **UPPERCASE** are counties.
Entries in **bold** have populations of 2,500 or more.
Names in parentheses are alternate names.

Inc. Place	Incorporated Place
RMC Place	Rand McNally Designated Place
CDP	Census Designated Place
MCD	Minor Civil Division

⊡	County Seat
▲	Minor Civil Division
elev.	Elevation
🅿	Post Office
🅷	Hospital
🅲	College
■	Principal Business Center
★	Ranally Metro Area (RMA) Abbreviation
z	Zip Code(s)
Ⓟ	Previous Census Population
Ⓡ	Revised Census Population
Ⓐ	Annexation Population
●	Rand McNally Population Estimate
Ⓒ	Final Census Population
Ⓢ	Special Census Population
◆	Estimated Population

For additional definitions see Glossary, Volume 1, and Introduction, Volume 2.

Steep Falls; RMC Place; CUMBERLAND; ▲ Standish; **183** H-2; 🅿; ★ **POR**; z 04085; ● 400
Stetson; RMC Place; PENOBSCOT; ▲ Stetson; **183** D-5; elev. 225ft./69m.; 🅿; z 04488; ● 150
Stetson; MCD-Town; PENOBSCOT; ***183** D-6; 🅿; z 04488; Ⓟ 847; © 981
Steuben; RMC Place; WASHINGTON; ▲ Steuben; **183** F-8; 🅿; z 04680; ● 150
Steuben; MCD-Town; WASHINGTON; ***183** F-8; 🅿; z 04680; Ⓟ 1,084; © 1,126
Stevens Corner; RMC Place; YORK; ▲ Newfield; ***183** H-1; elev. 735ft./224m.; mail East Wakefield z 03830; rural
Stevensville; RMC Place; AROOSTOOK; ▲ Fort Fairfield; ***183** B-14; mail Fort Fairfield z 04742; rural
Stickney Corner; RMC Place; KNOX; ▲ Washington; ***183** F-5; elev. 309ft./94m.; mail Washington z 04574; ● 65
Stillwater; RMC Place; PENOBSCOT; ***183** D-6; elev. 133ft./41m.; 🅿; ★ **BANG**; z 04489; pop. incl. with Old Town (Inc. Place)
Stockholm; RMC Place; AROOSTOOK; ▲ Stockholm; ***183** B-14; elev. 554ft./169m.; 🅿; z 04783; ● 180
Stockholm; MCD-Town; AROOSTOOK; ***183** A-14; 🅿; z 04783; Ⓟ 286; © 271
Stockton Springs; RMC Place; WALDO; ▲ Stockton Springs; **183** F-6; 🅿; z 04981; ● 325
Stockton Springs; MCD-Town; WALDO; ***183** F-6; 🅿; z 04981; Ⓟ 1,383; © 1,481
Stoneham; OXFORD; see East Stoneham (RMC Place)
Stoneham; MCD-Town; OXFORD; ***183** F-1; 🅿; z 04231; Ⓟ 224; © 255
Stonington; RMC Place; HANCOCK; ▲ Stonington; **183** G-7; 🅿; z 04645, z 04681; ● 800
Stonington; MCD-Town; HANCOCK; ***183** G-7; 🅿; z 04645, z 04681; Ⓟ 1,252; © 1,152
Stover Corner; RMC Place; HANCOCK; ▲ Brooksville; ***183** F-6; elev. 40ft./12m.; mail Brooksville z 04617; rural
Stow; RMC Place; OXFORD; ▲ Stow; ***183** G-1; elev. 434ft./132m.; 🅿; z 04037
Stow; MCD-Town; OXFORD; ***183** G-1; 🅿; z 04037; Ⓟ 283; © 288
Stratton; RMC Place; FRANKLIN; ▲ Eustis; **183** C-2; 🅿; z 04982; ● 400
Strickland; RMC Place; ANDROSCOGGIN; ▲ Livermore Falls; ***183** F-3; mail Leeds z 04263; rural
Strong; RMC Place; FRANKLIN; ▲ Strong; **183** E-3; elev. 501ft./153m.; 🅿; z 04983; ● 700
Strong; MCD-Town; FRANKLIN; ***183** E-3; 🅿; z 04983; Ⓟ 1,217; © 1,259
Stroudwater; RMC Place; CUMBERLAND; ***183** H-3; ★ **POR**; mail Portland z 04102; pop. incl. with Portland (Inc. Place)
Sugar Hill; RMC Place; AROOSTOOK; ▲ Bridgewater; ***183** C-14; mail Bridgewater z 04735; rural
Sullivan; RMC Place; HANCOCK; ▲ Sullivan; **183** E-8; elev. 81ft./25m.; 🅿; z 04664; ● 175
Sullivan; HANCOCK; see North Sullivan (RMC Place)
Sullivan; MCD-Town; HANCOCK; ***183** F-2; 🅿; z 04664; Ⓟ 1,118; © 1,185
Summerhaven; RMC Place; KENNEBEC; ***183** F-4; ★ **AUG**; mail Augusta z 04330; pop. incl. with Augusta (Inc. Place)
Sumner; RMC Place; OXFORD; **183** F-2; mail Sumner z 04292; rural
Sumner; MCD-Town; OXFORD; ***183** F-2; 🅿; z 04292 & mail Buckfield z 04220; Ⓟ 761; © 854
Sunset; RMC Place; HANCOCK; ▲ Deer Isle; ***183** G-6; elev. 91ft./28m.; 🅿; z 04683; summer pop. 500; ● 150
Sunset Park; RMC Place; CUMBERLAND; ***183** H-3; ★ **POR**; mail South Portland z 04106; pop. incl. with South Portland (Inc. Place)
Sunshine; RMC Place; HANCOCK; ▲ Deer Isle; **183** G-7; elev. 109ft./33m.; mail Deer Isle z 04627; ● 60
Surfside; RMC Place; YORK; ▲ Old Orchard Beach; ***183** I-3; ★ **POR**; mail Old Orchard Beach z 04064
Surry; RMC Place; HANCOCK; ▲ Surry; **183** F-7; 🅿; z 04629, z 04684; ● 225
Surry; MCD-Town; HANCOCK; ***183** F-7; 🅿; z 04629, z 04684; Ⓟ 1,004; © 1,361
Sutton Island; RMC Place; HANCOCK; ▲ Cranberry Isles; ***183** F-8; mail Northeast Harbor z 04662; summer pop. 70
Swan Pond; RMC Place; YORK; ▲ Lyman; ***183** I-2; mail Alfred z 04002; summer pop. 125
Swans Island; RMC Place; HANCOCK; ▲ Swans Island; ***183** G-7; 🅿; z 04685; ● 150
Swans Island; MCD-Town; HANCOCK; ***183** G-7; 🅿; z 04685; Ⓟ 348; © 327
Swanville; RMC Place; WALDO; ▲ Swanville; **183** F-6; elev. 210ft./64m.; 🅿; z 04915; ● 150
Swanville; MCD-Town; WALDO; ***183** F-6; 🅿; z 04915; Ⓟ 1,130; © 1,357
Sweden; RMC Place; AROOSTOOK; ▲ New Sweden; ***183** B-14; elev. 717ft./219m.; mail New Sweden z 04762; ● 75
Sweden; MCD-Town; OXFORD; ***183** G-2; 🅿; z 04040; Ⓟ 222; © 324

T

Tacoma; RMC Place; KENNEBEC; ▲ Monmouth, Litchfield; ***183** G-3; elev. 186ft./57m.; ★ **AUG**; mail Litchfield z 04350; ● 150
Tainter Corner; RMC Place; FRANKLIN; ▲ Carthage; ***183** E-3; elev. 867ft./264m.; mail Dixfield z 04224; rural
Tallwood; RMC Place; KENNEBEC; ▲ Winthrop; ***183** F-4; ★ **AUG**; mail Readfield z 04355; rural
Talmadge; MCD-Town; WASHINGTON; ***183** C-9; 🅿; z 04492; Ⓟ 62; © 70
Tatnic; RMC Place; YORK; ▲ Wells; ***183** J-2; mail Wells z 04090; rural
Tattle Corner; RMC Place; YORK; ***183** I-2; mail Biddeford z 04005; pop. incl. with Biddeford (Inc. Place)
Tea Kettle Corner; RMC Place; YORK; ***183** I-2; mail Biddeford z 04005; pop. incl. with Biddeford (Inc. Place)
Temple; RMC Place; FRANKLIN; ▲ Temple; **183** E-3; 🅿; z 04984; ● 225
Temple; MCD-Town; FRANKLIN; ***183** E-3; 🅿; z 04984; Ⓟ 560; © 572
Temple Heights; RMC Place; WALDO; ▲ Northport; ***183** F-6; mail Lincolnville z 04849; ● 100
Tenants Harbor; RMC Place; KNOX; ▲ St. George; **183** G-5; 🅿; z 04859-60; ● 400
The Forks; RMC Place; SOMERSET; ***183** C-4; mail West Forks z 04985; ● 10
The Forks; MCD-Plantation; SOMERSET; ***183** C-4; mail West Forks z 04985; Ⓟ 30; © 35
The Highlands; RMC Place; PISCATAQUIS; ▲ Greenville; ***183** B-4; mail Greenville z 04441; ● 100
The Kingdom; RMC Place; WALDO; ▲ Montville; ***183** F-5; elev. 307ft./94m.; mail Freedom z 04941; rural
Thomaston; CDP; KNOX; ▲ Thomaston; **183** G-5; 🅿; z 04861; Ⓟ 2,445; © 2,714
Thomaston; MCD-Town; KNOX; ***183** G-5; 🅿; z 04861; Ⓟ 3,306; © 3,748
Thompson Point; RMC Place; CUMBERLAND; mail Naples z 04055; summer pop. 500
Thorndike; RMC Place; WALDO; ▲ Thorndike; **183** E-5; elev. 275ft./84m.; 🅿; z 04986; ● 140
Thorndike; MCD-Town; WALDO; ***183** E-5; 🅿; z 04986; Ⓟ 702; © 712
Thornton Heights; RMC Place; CUMBERLAND; ***183** H-3; ★ **POR**; mail South Portland z 04106; pop. incl. with South Portland (Inc. Place)
Tibbettstown; RMC Place; WASHINGTON; ▲ Columbia Falls; ***183** E-9; mail Columbia Falls z 04623; rural
Tobeys Corner; RMC Place; YORK; ***183** J-1; ★ **PTSM-**; mail Eliot z 03903
Topsfield; RMC Place; WASHINGTON; ▲ Topsfield; **183** C-9; 🅿; z 04490; ● 125
Topsfield; MCD-Town; WASHINGTON; ***183** B-9; 🅿; z 04490; Ⓟ 235; © 225
Topsham; CDP; SAGADAHOC; ▲ Topsham; **183** G-3; 🅿; ★ **BR-BA**; z 04086; Ⓟ 6,147; © 6,271
Topsham; MCD-Town; SAGADAHOC; ***183** G-4; 🅿; ★ **BR-BA**; z 04086; Ⓟ 8,746; © 9,100
Tory Hill; RMC Place; YORK; ▲ Buxton; ***183** H-2; elev. 249ft./76m.; ★ **POR**; mail Buxton z 04093; rural
Toulouse Corner; RMC Place; SOMERSET; ▲ Fairfield; ***183** E-4; ★ **WATRVL**; mail Fairfield z 04937; rural
Town Farm Hill; RMC Place; CUMBERLAND; ▲ Harrison; ***183** G-2; mail Harrison z 04040; rural
Town Hill; RMC Place; HANCOCK; ▲ Bar Harbor; **183** G-12; elev. 182ft./55m.; mail Bar Harbor z 04609; ● 60
Tracy Corners; RMC Place; WASHINGTON; ▲ Addison; ***183** E-9; elev. 117ft./36m.; mail Addison z 04606; rural
Trainor Corner; RMC Place; LINCOLN; ▲ Whitefield; ***183** F-4; elev. 237ft./72m.; mail Gardiner z 04345; rural
Trap Corner; RMC Place; OXFORD; ▲ West Paris; ***183** F-2; elev. 475ft./145m.; mail West Paris z 04289; ● 50
Trefethen; RMC Place; CUMBERLAND; ***183** H-3; ★ **POR**; mail Peaks Island z 04108; pop. incl. with Portland (Inc. Place)
Tremont; RMC Place; HANCOCK; ▲ Tremont; ***183** F-7; mail Ellsworth z 04605; ● 80
Tremont; MCD-Town; HANCOCK; ***183** F-7; mail Bass Harbor z 04653; Ⓟ 1,324; © 1,529
Trenton; RMC Place; HANCOCK; ▲ Trenton; **183** F-7; elev. 62ft./19m.; 🅿; z 04605; ● 170
Trenton; MCD-Town; HANCOCK; ***183** F-7; 🅿; z 04605; Ⓟ 1,060; © 1,370
Trevett; RMC Place; LINCOLN; ▲ Boothbay; ***183** H-4; 🅿; z 04571; ● 150
Troutdale; RMC Place; SOMERSET; ▲ The Forks; ***183** C-4; mail West Forks z 04985
Troy; RMC Place; WALDO; ▲ Troy; **183** E-5; elev. 472ft./144m.; 🅿; z 04987; ● 60
Troy; MCD-Town; WALDO; ***183** E-5; 🅿; z 04987; Ⓟ 802; © 963
Troy Center; RMC Place; WALDO; ▲ Troy; ***183** E-5; elev. 360ft./110m.; mail Troy z 04987
Turbats Creek; RMC Place; YORK; ▲ Kennebunkport; ***183** I-2; elev. 42ft./13m.; mail Kennebunkport z 04046; ● 75
Turner; RMC Place; ANDROSCOGGIN; ▲ Turner; **183** F-3; elev. 303ft./92m.; 🅿; ★ **LEW-**; z 04282; ● 500
Turner; MCD-Town; ANDROSCOGGIN; ***183** F-3; 🅿; ★ **LEW-**; z 04282; Ⓟ 4,315; © 4,972; ◆ 5,532
Turner Center; RMC Place; ANDROSCOGGIN; ▲ Turner; ***183** F-3; elev. 297ft./91m.; ★ **LEW-**; ● 150
Turners Corner; RMC Place; LINCOLN; ▲ Bremen; ***183** G-5; mail Waldoboro z 04572; rural
Twelve Corners; RMC Place; KENNEBEC; ▲ Fayette; ***183** F-3; elev. 415ft./126m.; mail Livermore Falls z 04254; rural
Two Trails; RMC Place; CUMBERLAND; ▲ Standish; ***183** H-2; ★ **POR**; mail Standish z 04084; rural

U

Union; RMC Place; KNOX; ▲ Union; **183** G-5; elev. 97ft./30m.; 🅿; z 04862; ● 600
Union; MCD-Town; KNOX; ***183** G-5; 🅿; z 04862; Ⓟ 1,989; © 2,209
Unionville; RMC Place; WASHINGTON; ▲ Steuben; ***183** E-8; mail Cherryfield z 04622; ● 60
Unity; CDP; WALDO; ▲ Unity; **183** E-5; 🅿 🅲 556; z 04988; © 486
Unity; MCD-Town; WALDO; ***183** E-5; 🅿 🅲 556; z 04988; Ⓟ 1,817; © 1,889
University Bookstore; RMC Place; PENOBSCOT; ***183** D-7; ★ **BANG**; mail Orono z 04473
Upper Abbot; RMC Place; PISCATAQUIS; ▲ Abbot; ***183** C-5; mail Abbot z 04406
Upper Frenchville (Frenchville); RMC Place; AROOSTOOK; ▲ Frenchville; ***183** A-13; 🅿; z 04745; ● 350
Upper Gloucester; RMC Place; CUMBERLAND; ▲ New Gloucester; **183** G-3; elev. 388ft./118m.; mail New Gloucester z 04260; ● 300
Upton; RMC Place; OXFORD; ▲ Upton; **183** E-1; elev. 1,722ft./525m.; 🅿; z 04261; ● 50
Upton; MCD-Town; OXFORD; ***183** E-1; 🅿; z 04261; Ⓟ 70; © 62

V

Van Buren; CDP; AROOSTOOK; ▲ Van Buren; **183** A-14; 🅿; z 04785; Ⓟ 2,759; © 2,369
Van Buren; MCD-Town; AROOSTOOK; ***183** A-14; 🅿; z 04785; Ⓟ 3,045; © 2,631
Vanceboro; RMC Place; WASHINGTON; ▲ Vanceboro; **183** B-9; elev. 392ft./119m.; 🅿; z 04491; ● 190
Vanceboro; MCD-Town; WASHINGTON; ***183** B-9; 🅿; z 04491; Ⓟ 201; © 147
Vassalboro; RMC Place; KENNEBEC; ▲ Vassalboro; **183** F-4; 🅿; ★ **AUG**; z 04989; ● 200
Vassalboro; MCD-Town; KENNEBEC; ***183** F-4; 🅿; ★ **AUG**; z 04989; Ⓟ 3,769; © 4,047
Veazie; RMC Place; PENOBSCOT; ▲ Veazie; **183** D-6; 🅿; ★ **BANG**; z 04401; ● 1,633
Veazie; MCD-Town; PENOBSCOT; ***183** D-6; 🅿; ★ **BANG**; z 04401; Ⓟ 1,633; © 1,744; ◆ 1,916
Verona; RMC Place; HANCOCK; ▲ Verona; ***183** E-6; mail Bucksport z 04416; ● 250
Verona; MCD-Town; HANCOCK; ***183** E-6; mail Bucksport z 04416; Ⓟ 515; © 533
Verona Park; RMC Place; HANCOCK; ▲ Verona; ***183** E-6; mail Bucksport z 04416; rural
Vienna; RMC Place; KENNEBEC; ▲ Vienna; **183** E-3; elev. 396ft./121m.; 🅿; z 04360; ● 70
Vienna; MCD-Town; KENNEBEC; ***183** E-3; 🅿; z 04360; Ⓟ 417; © 527
Vinalhaven; RMC Place; KNOX; ▲ Vinalhaven; **183** G-6; 🅿; z 04863; ● 800
Vinalhaven; MCD-Town; KNOX; ***183** G-6; 🅿; z 04863; Ⓟ 1,072; © 1,235
Virginia; RMC Place; OXFORD; ▲ Rumford; ***183** E-2; mail Rumford z 04276

W

Wade; MCD-Town; AROOSTOOK; ***183** B-13; 🅿; z 04786; Ⓟ 243; © 250
Waite; RMC Place; WASHINGTON; ▲ Waite; **183** C-9; elev. 367ft./112m.; 🅿; z 04492; ● 35
Waite; MCD-Town; WASHINGTON; ***183** C-9; 🅿; z 04492; Ⓟ 119; © 105
Waldo; RMC Place; WALDO; ▲ Waldo; ***183** F-6; elev. 261ft./80m.; 🅿; z 04915; ● 75
Waldo; MCD-Town; WALDO; ***183** F-6; 🅿; z 04915; Ⓟ 626; © 733
WALDO; **183** E-5; Ⓟ 33,018; © 36,280; ◆ 38,242
Waldoboro; CDP; LINCOLN; ▲ Waldoboro; **183** G-5; 🅿; z 04572; Ⓟ 1,420; © 1,291
Waldoboro; MCD-Town; LINCOLN; ***183** G-5; 🅿; z 04572; Ⓟ 4,601; © 4,916
Wales; MCD-Town; ANDROSCOGGIN; ***183** G-3; 🅿; ★ **LEW-**; z 04280; Ⓟ 1,223; © 1,322; ◆ 1,377
Wales Center; RMC Place; ANDROSCOGGIN; ***183** G-3; ★ **LEW-**; mail Sabattus z 04280; rural
Wales Corner; RMC Place; ANDROSCOGGIN; ▲ Wales; ***183** G-3; elev. 432ft./132m.; ★ **LEW-**; mail Sabattus z 04280; ● 30
Wallagrass; RMC Place; AROOSTOOK; ▲ Wallagrass; ***183** A-13; 🅿; z 04781; ● 50
Wallagrass; MCD-Town; AROOSTOOK; ***183** A-13; 🅿; z 04781; Ⓟ 582; © 561
Walnut Hill (North Yarmouth); RMC Place; CUMBERLAND; ▲ North Yarmouth; ***183** H-3; elev. 202ft./62m.; ★ **POR**; mail North Yarmouth z 04097; ● 250
Walpole; RMC Place; LINCOLN; ▲ South Bristol; ***183** G-4; elev. 157ft./48m.; 🅿; z 04573; ● 50
Waltham; RMC Place; HANCOCK; ▲ Waltham; **183** E-7; elev. 342ft./104m.; 🅿; z 04605; ● 75
Waltham; MCD-Town; HANCOCK; ***183** E-7; mail Ellsworth z 04605; Ⓟ 276; © 306
Wards Cove; RMC Place; CUMBERLAND; ▲ Standish; ***183** H-2; elev. 275ft./84m.; ★ **POR**; summer pop. 300; ● 75
Wardtown; RMC Place; CUMBERLAND; ▲ Freeport; ***183** G-3; elev. 130ft./40m.; ★ **POR**; mail Freeport z 04032; rural
Warren (Warren Station); RMC Place; KNOX; ▲ Warren; ***183** G-5; 🅿; z 04864; ● 400
Warren; MCD-Town; KNOX; ***183** G-5; 🅿; z 04864; Ⓟ 3,192; © 3,794
Warren Station; KNOX; see Warren (RMC Place)
Washburn; RMC Place; AROOSTOOK; ▲ Washburn; **183** B-13; elev. 483ft./147m.; 🅿; z 04786; ● 1,200
Washburn; MCD-Town; AROOSTOOK; ***183** B-14; 🅿; z 04786; Ⓟ 1,880; © 1,627
Washington; RMC Place; KNOX; ▲ Washington; **183** F-5; 🅿; z 04574; ● 240
Washington; MCD-Town; KNOX; ***183** F-5; 🅿; z 04574; Ⓟ 1,185; © 1,345
WASHINGTON; **183** D-9; Ⓟ 35,308; © 33,941; ◆ 32,457
Waterboro; RMC Place; YORK; ▲ Waterboro; **183** I-2; 🅿; z 04087; ● 750
Waterboro; MCD-Town; YORK; ***183** I-2; 🅿; z 04087; Ⓟ 4,510; © 6,214
Waterboro Center; RMC Place; YORK; ▲ Waterboro; ***183** I-2; elev. 328ft./100m.; mail Waterboro z 04087; ● 300
Waterford; OXFORD; see Waterford Flat (RMC Place)
Waterford; MCD-Town; OXFORD; ***183** G-2; 🅿; z 04088; Ⓟ 1,299; © 1,455
Waterford Flat (Waterford); RMC Place; OXFORD; ▲ Waterford; **183** G-2; mail Waterford z 04088; ● 120
Waterman Beach; RMC Place; KNOX; ▲ South Thomaston; ***183** G-5; mail South Thomaston z 04858; summer pop. 100
Water Street; RMC Place; KENNEBEC; ***183** F-4; ★ **AUG**; mail Augusta z 04330, z 04338; pop. incl. with Augusta (Inc. Place)
Waterville; Inc. Place; KENNEBEC; **183** E-4; elev. 113ft./34m.; 🅿 🅷 🅲 2,822 ■; ★ **WATRVL**; z 04901, z 04903; Ⓟ 17,173; © 15,605; ◆ 15,353
Waverly; RMC Place; SOMERSET; ▲ Pittsfield; ***183** E-5; mail Pittsfield z 04967
Wayne; RMC Place; KENNEBEC; ▲ Wayne; **183** F-3; 🅿; z 04284; ● 250
Wayne; MCD-Town; KENNEBEC; ***183** F-3; 🅿; z 04284; Ⓟ 1,029; © 1,112
Webb Hill; RMC Place; PENOBSCOT; ▲ Mattawamkeag; ***183** B-7; mail Mattawamkeag z 04459; ● 25
Webb Mills; CUMBERLAND; see Crescent Lake (RMC Place)
Webster; RMC Place; PENOBSCOT; ▲ Orono; ***183** D-7; ★ **BANG**; mail Orono z 04473
Webster; MCD-Plantation; PENOBSCOT; ***183** B-8; mail Springfield z 04487; Ⓟ 95; © 82
Webster Corner; RMC Place; ANDROSCOGGIN; ▲ Sabattus; ***183** G-3; ★ **LEW-**; mail Lisbon z 04250
Weeks Mills; RMC Place; KENNEBEC; ▲ China; ***183** F-4; elev. 221ft./67m.; 🅿; z 04358; ● 300
Welchville; RMC Place; OXFORD; ▲ Oxford; ***183** G-2; mail Oxford z 04270; ● 120
Weld; RMC Place; FRANKLIN; ▲ Weld; **183** E-2; elev. 767ft./234m.; 🅿; z 04285; summer pop. 800; ● 200
Weld; MCD-Town; FRANKLIN; ***183** E-2; 🅿; z 04285; Ⓟ 430; © 402
Wellington; RMC Place; PISCATAQUIS; ▲ Wellington; **183** D-4; elev. 571ft./174m.; 🅿; z 04942; ● 45
Wellington; MCD-Town; PISCATAQUIS; ***183** D-5; 🅿; z 04942; Ⓟ 270; © 258
Wells (Wells Beach); RMC Place; YORK; ▲ Wells; **183** I-2; 🅿; z 04090; ● 1,200
Wells; MCD-Town; YORK; ***183** I-2; 🅿; z 04090; Ⓟ 7,778; © 9,400
Wells Beach; RMC Place; YORK; ▲ Wells; **183** I-2; mail Wells z 04090; summer pop. 4,000; ● 500
Wells Beach; YORK; see Wells (RMC Place)
Wells Branch; RMC Place; YORK; ▲ Wells; ***183** I-2; elev. 201ft./61m.; mail Wells z 04090; rural
Wesley; RMC Place; WASHINGTON; ▲ Wesley; **183** D-9; elev. 447ft./136m.; 🅿; z 04686; ● 50
Wesley; MCD-Town; WASHINGTON; ***183** D-9; 🅿; z 04686; Ⓟ 146; © 114
West Appleton; RMC Place; KNOX; ▲ Appleton; ***183** F-5; elev. 315ft./96m.; mail Union z 04862; rural
West Athens; RMC Place; SOMERSET; ▲ Amherst; ***183** D-4; mail Athens z 04912; ● 100
West Auburn; RMC Place; ANDROSCOGGIN; ***183** G-3; ★ **LEW-**; mail Auburn z 04210; pop. incl. with Auburn (Inc. Place)
West Baldwin; RMC Place; CUMBERLAND; ▲ Baldwin; **183** H-2; 🅿; z 04091; ● 150
West Bath; MCD-Town; SAGADAHOC; ***183** H-4; 🅿; ★ **BR-BA**; z 04530; Ⓟ 1,716; © 1,798
West Bethel (Allens); RMC Place; OXFORD; ▲ Bethel; **183** F-1; elev. 680ft./207m.; 🅿; z 04286 & mail Bethel z 04217; ● 175
West Boothbay Harbor; RMC Place; LINCOLN; ▲ Boothbay Harbor; ***183** H-4; elev. 27ft./8m.; 🅿; z 04575; ● 500
West Bowdoin (Bowdoin); RMC Place; SAGADAHOC; ▲ Bowdoin; ***183** G-3; mail Bowdoin z 04287; ● 10
West Bridgton; RMC Place; CUMBERLAND; ▲ Bridgton; ***183** G-1; elev. 302ft./92m.; mail Bridgton z 04009; rural
Westbrook; Inc. Place; CUMBERLAND; **183** H-3; elev. 65ft./20m.; 🅿 🅷; ★ **POR**; z 04092, z 04098; Ⓟ 16,121; © 16,142; ◆ 16,495
West Brooklin; RMC Place; HANCOCK; ▲ Brooklin; ***183** F-7; elev. 119ft./36m.; mail Brooklin z 04616; ● 125
West Brooksville; RMC Place; HANCOCK; ▲ Brooksville; ***183** F-6; mail Brooksville z 04617; ● 100
West Buxton; RMC Place; YORK; ▲ Hollis, Buxton; **183** H-2; elev. 176ft./54m.; ★ **POR**; mail Buxton z 04093; ● 300
West Charleston; RMC Place; PENOBSCOT; ▲ Charleston; ***183** D-6; elev. 418ft./127m.; mail Charleston z 04422
West Corinth; RMC Place; PENOBSCOT; ▲ Corinth; ***183** D-6; elev. 333ft./101m.; mail Corinth z 04427
West Cumberland; RMC Place; CUMBERLAND; ▲ Cumberland; ***183** H-3; ★ **POR**; mail Cumberland Center z 04021; ● 800
West Denmark; RMC Place; OXFORD; ▲ Denmark; ***183** G-1; elev. 379ft./116m.; mail Denmark z 04022; rural
West Durham; RMC Place; ANDROSCOGGIN; ▲ Durham; ***183** G-3; elev. 226ft./69m.; mail Pownal z 04069
West Ellsworth; RMC Place; HANCOCK; ***183** E-7; mail Ellsworth z 04605; pop. incl. with Ellsworth (Inc. Place)
West End; RMC Place; CUMBERLAND; ***183** H-3; ★ **POR**; mail Portland z 04102; pop. incl. with Portland (Inc. Place)
West Enfield; RMC Place; PENOBSCOT; ▲ Enfield; **183** C-7; 🅿; z 04493; ● 600
West Falmouth Corner; RMC Place; CUMBERLAND; ▲ Falmouth; ***183** H-3; ★ **POR**; mail Falmouth z 04105
West Farmington; RMC Place; FRANKLIN; ▲ Farmington; ***183** E-3; elev. 388ft./118m.; 🅿; z 04992; ● 400
Westfield; RMC Place; AROOSTOOK; ▲ Westfield; ***183** B-14; 🅿; z 04787; ● 200
Westfield; MCD-Town; AROOSTOOK; ***183** C-14; 🅿; z 04787; Ⓟ 589; © 559
West Forks; RMC Place; SOMERSET; ▲ West Forks, The Forks; **183** C-3; 🅿; z 04985; ● 30
West Forks; MCD-Plantation; SOMERSET; ***183** C-3; 🅿; z 04985; Ⓟ 63; © 47
West Franklin; RMC Place; HANCOCK; ▲ Franklin; ***183** E-7; mail Franklin z 04634; ● 125
West Fryeburg; RMC Place; OXFORD; ▲ Fryeburg; ***183** G-1; elev. 401ft./122m.; mail Fryeburg z 04037; rural
West Gardiner; MCD-Town; KENNEBEC; ***183** F-4; 🅿; ★ **AUG**; z 04345; Ⓟ 2,531; © 2,902
West Georgetown; RMC Place; SAGADAHOC; ▲ Georgetown; ***183** H-4; elev. 33ft./10m.; ★ **BR-BA**; mail Georgetown z 04548; ● 30
West Gorham; RMC Place; CUMBERLAND; ▲ Gorham; ***183** H-2; ★ **POR**; mail Gorham z 04038; ● 50
West Gouldsboro; RMC Place; HANCOCK; ▲ Gouldsboro; ***183** F-8; mail Gouldsboro z 04607; ● 100
West Gray; RMC Place; CUMBERLAND; ▲ Gray; ***183** H-3; ★ **POR**; mail Gray z 04039
West Hampden; RMC Place; PENOBSCOT; ▲ Hampden; ***183** E-6; ★ **BANG**; mail Hampden z 04444; rural
West Harpswell; RMC Place; CUMBERLAND; ▲ Harpswell; ***183** H-3; ★ **BR-BA**; mail Harpswell z 04079; ● 135
West Harrington; RMC Place; WASHINGTON; ▲ Harrington; ***183** E-8; mail Harrington z 04643; ● 25
West Hollis; RMC Place; YORK; ▲ Hollis; ***183** H-2; elev. 393ft./120m.; ★ **POR**; mail Hollis Center z 04042; rural
West Jonesport; RMC Place; WASHINGTON; ▲ Jonesport; ***183** E-9; mail Jonesport z 04649
West Kennebunk; CDP; YORK; ▲ Kennebunk; **183** I-2; elev. 143ft./44m.; 🅿; z 04094; © 809
West Lebanon; RMC Place; YORK; ▲ Lebanon; ***183** I-1; elev. 547ft./167m.; mail Lebanon z 04027; ● 100
West Leeds; RMC Place; ANDROSCOGGIN; ▲ Leeds; ***183** F-3; elev. 281ft./86m.; mail Leeds z 04263
West Levant; RMC Place; PENOBSCOT; ▲ Levant; ***183** D-6; elev. 281ft./86m.; mail Levant z 04456
West Lubec; RMC Place; WASHINGTON; ▲ Lubec; ***183** E-10; mail Lubec z 04652
Westmanland; MCD-Town; AROOSTOOK; ***183** B-13; 🅿; z 04783; Ⓟ 72; © 71
West Mills; RMC Place; FRANKLIN; ▲ Industry; **183** E-3; elev. 512ft./156m.; mail Farmington z 04938; ● 100
West Minot; RMC Place; ANDROSCOGGIN; ▲ Minot; **183** G-3; elev. 334ft./102m.; 🅿; ★ **LEW-**; z 04288; ● 125
West Mount Vernon; RMC Place; KENNEBEC; ▲ Mount Vernon; ***183** F-3; mail Mount Vernon z 04352; ● 70
West Newfield; RMC Place; YORK; ▲ Newfield; **183** H-1; elev. 552ft./168m.; 🅿; z 04095; ● 100
West Old Town; RMC Place; PENOBSCOT; ***183** D-6; elev. 127ft./39m.; ★ **BANG**; mail Old Town z 04468; pop. incl. with Old Town (Inc. Place)
Weston; RMC Place; AROOSTOOK; ▲ Weston; **183** B-8; elev. 717ft./219m.; 🅿; z 04424; ● 90
Weston; MCD-Town; AROOSTOOK; ***183** B-8; 🅿; z 04424; Ⓟ 207; © 203
West Palmyra; RMC Place; SOMERSET; ▲ Palmyra; ***183** D-5; mail Palmyra z 04965; rural
West Paris (Bates); RMC Place; OXFORD; ▲ West Paris; **183** F-2; elev. 486ft./148m.; 🅿; z 04289; ● 550
West Paris; MCD-Town; OXFORD; ***183** F-2; 🅿; z 04289; Ⓟ 1,514; © 1,722
West Pembroke; RMC Place; WASHINGTON; ▲ Pembroke; ***183** D-10; mail Pembroke z 04666; ● 200
West Penobscot; RMC Place; HANCOCK; ▲ Penobscot; ***183** F-6; elev. 57ft./17m.; mail Penobscot z 04476; rural
West Peru; RMC Place; OXFORD; ▲ Peru; ● 120
West Point; RMC Place; SAGADAHOC; ▲ Phippsburg; ***183** H-4; ★ **BR-BA**; mail Sebasco Estates z 04565; summer pop. 150; ● 60
West Poland; RMC Place; ANDROSCOGGIN; ▲ Poland; **183** G-2; 🅿; ★ **LEW-**; z 04291; ● 325
Westport; RMC Place; LINCOLN; ▲ Westport; ***183** H-4; mail Wiscasset z 04578; ● 50
Westport; MCD-Town; LINCOLN; ***183** H-4; mail Wiscasset z 04578; Ⓟ 663; © 745
West Pownal (Pownal); RMC Place; CUMBERLAND; ▲ Pownal; **183** H-3; mail Pownal z 04069; ● 60
West Princeton; RMC Place; WASHINGTON; ▲ Princeton; ***183** C-9; elev. 252ft./77m.; mail Princeton z 04668
West Ripley; RMC Place; SOMERSET; ▲ Ripley; ***183** D-5; elev. 686ft./209m.; mail Dexter z 04930; rural
West Rockport; RMC Place; KNOX; ▲ Rockport; **183** G-5; elev. 207ft./63m.; 🅿; z 04865; ● 250
West Scarborough (Dunstan); RMC Place; CUMBERLAND; ▲ Scarborough; **183** I-2; 🅿; ★ **POR**; z 04070; ● 900
West Seboois; RMC Place; PENOBSCOT; ▲ Seboeis; ***183** B-6; mail Millinocket z 04462
West Sidney; RMC Place; KENNEBEC; ▲ Sidney; ***183** F-4; mail Augusta z 04330; rural
West Southport; RMC Place; LINCOLN; ▲ Southport; ***183** H-4; elev. 81ft./25m.; 🅿; z 04576; ● 200
West Stonington; RMC Place; HANCOCK; ▲ Stonington; ***183** G-6; mail Stonington z 04681; ● 50
West Sullivan; RMC Place; HANCOCK; ▲ Sullivan; ***183** E-8; mail Sullivan z 04664; ● 100
West Sumner; RMC Place; OXFORD; ▲ Sumner; **183** F-2; mail Buckfield z 04220, Sumner z 04292; ● 25
West Tremont; RMC Place; HANCOCK; ▲ Tremont; **183** F-7; 🅿; z 04612; ● 80
West Trenton; RMC Place; HANCOCK; ▲ Trenton; ***183** F-7; elev. 73ft./22m.; mail Ellsworth z 04605
West Waldoboro; RMC Place; LINCOLN; ▲ Waldoboro; ***183** G-5; mail Waldoboro z 04572; ● 130
West Washington; RMC Place; KNOX; ▲ Washington; ***183** F-5; elev. 346ft./105m.; mail Washington z 04574; rural
West Winterport; RMC Place; WALDO; ▲ Winterport; ***183** E-6; elev. 167ft./51m.; ★ **BANG**; mail Winterport z 04496
Wheelock; RMC Place; AROOSTOOK; ▲ Saint John; ***183** A-13; mail Fort Kent z 04743; rural
Whitefield; RMC Place; LINCOLN; ▲ Whitefield; **183** G-4; 🅿; z 04353; ● 100
Whitefield; MCD-Town; LINCOLN; ***183** G-4; 🅿; z 04353; Ⓟ 1,931; © 2,273
White Oak Corner; RMC Place; KNOX; ▲ Warren; ***183** G-5; mail Warren z 04864; rural
White Rock; RMC Place; CUMBERLAND; ▲ Gorham; ***183** H-2; ★ **POR**; mail Gorham z 04038; rural
White School Corner; RMC Place; SOMERSET; ▲ Madison; ***183** E-4; mail Madison z 04950; rural
Whites Corner; RMC Place; CUMBERLAND; ▲ New Gloucester; ***183** G-3; mail New Gloucester z 04260; ● 80
Whiting; RMC Place; WASHINGTON; ▲ Whiting; **183** E-10; elev. 37ft./11m.; 🅿; z 04691; ● 110
Whiting; MCD-Town; WASHINGTON; ***183** E-10; 🅿; z 04691; Ⓟ 407; © 430
Whitlocks Mill; RMC Place; WASHINGTON; ***183** C-10; mail Calais z 04619; pop. incl. with Calais (Inc. Place)
Whitney Corner; RMC Place; KNOX; ▲ Warren; ***183** G-5; mail Warren z 04864; rural
Whitneyville; RMC Place; WASHINGTON; ▲ Whitneyville; **183** E-9; 🅿; z 04654; ● 150
Whitneyville; MCD-Town; WASHINGTON; ***183** E-9; 🅿; z 04654; Ⓟ 241; © 262
Wildes District; RMC Place; YORK; ▲ Kennebunkport; ***183** I-2; mail Kennebunkport z 04046; ● 150
Wildwood Park; RMC Place; CUMBERLAND; ▲ Cumberland; ***183** H-3; ★ **POR**; mail Cumberland Foreside z 04110
Wiley Corners; RMC Place; KNOX; ▲ Thomaston; ***183** G-5; mail Thomaston z 04861; rural
Williams; RMC Place; AROOSTOOK; pop. incl. with Caribou (Inc. Place)
Willimantic; RMC Place; PISCATAQUIS; ▲ Willimantic; **183** C-5; 🅿; z 04443; ● 40
Willimantic; MCD-Town; PISCATAQUIS; ***183** C-5; 🅿; z 04443; Ⓟ 170; © 135
Wilson Corner; RMC Place; HANCOCK; ***183** E-7; elev. 430ft./131m.; mail Ellsworth z 04605; pop. incl. with Ellsworth (Inc. Place)
Wilsons Mills; RMC Place; OXFORD; ▲ Lincoln; **183** D-1; elev. 1,292ft./394m.; mail Errol z 03579; ● 30
Wilton; CDP; FRANKLIN; ▲ Wilton; **183** E-3; elev. 642ft./196m.; 🅿; z 04294; Ⓟ 2,453; © 2,290
Wilton; MCD-Town; FRANKLIN; ***183** E-3; 🅿; z 04294; Ⓟ 4,242; © 4,123
Windemere; RMC Place; WALDO; ▲ Unity; ***183** E-5; mail Unity z 04988; summer pop. 150; ● 50
Windham; CUMBERLAND; see North Windham (CDP)
Windham; MCD-Town; CUMBERLAND; ***183** H-2; 🅿; ★ **POR**; z 04062, z 04082; Ⓟ 13,020; © 14,904; ◆ 15,747
Windham Center; RMC Place; CUMBERLAND; ▲ Windham; ***183** H-2; ★ **POR**; mail Windham z 04062; ● 125
Windham Hill; RMC Place; CUMBERLAND; ▲ Windham; ***183** H-2; ★ **POR**; mail Windham z 04062; ● 100
Windsor; RMC Place; KENNEBEC; ▲ Windsor; **183** F-4; elev. 297ft./91m.; 🅿; z 04363; ● 120
Windsor; MCD-Town; KENNEBEC; ***183** F-4; 🅿; z 04363; Ⓟ 1,895; © 2,204
Winn; RMC Place; PENOBSCOT; ▲ Winn; **183** B-7; 🅿; z 04495; ● 200
Winn; MCD-Town; PENOBSCOT; ***183** B-7; 🅿; z 04495; Ⓟ 479; © 420
Winnecook; RMC Place; WALDO; ▲ Burnham; ***183** E-5; elev. 185ft./56m.; mail Burnham z 04922; rural
Winnegance; RMC Place; SAGADAHOC; ▲ Phippsburg; ***183** H-4; elev. 48ft./15m.; mail Phippsburg z 04562; ● 40
Winslow; CDP; KENNEBEC; ▲ Winslow; **183** E-4; 🅿; ★ **WATRVL**; z 04901; Ⓟ 5,436; © 7,743
Winslow; MCD-Town; KENNEBEC; ***183** F-4; 🅿; ★ **WATRVL**; z 04901; Ⓟ 7,997; © 7,743
Winslows Mills; RMC Place; LINCOLN; ▲ Waldoboro; ***183** G-5; mail Waldoboro z 04572; ● 100
Winter Harbor; RMC Place; HANCOCK; ▲ Winter Harbor; **183** F-8; elev. 11ft./3m.; 🅿; z 04693; ● 900
Winter Harbor; MCD-Town; HANCOCK; ***183** F-8; 🅿; z 04693; Ⓟ 1,157; © 988
Winterport; CDP; WALDO; ▲ Winterport; **183** E-6; 🅿; ★ **BANG**; z 04496; Ⓟ 1,274; © 1,307
Winterport; MCD-Town; WALDO; ***183** E-6; 🅿; ★ **BANG**; z 04496; Ⓟ 3,175; © 3,602; ◆ 3,352
Winterville; RMC Place; AROOSTOOK; ▲ Winterville; **183** B-13; ● 30
Winterville; AROOSTOOK; see Quimby (RMC Place)
Winterville; MCD-Plantation; AROOSTOOK; ***183** B-13; mail Eagle Lake z 04739; Ⓟ 217; © 196
Winthrop; CDP; KENNEBEC; ▲ Winthrop; **183** F-3; elev. 225ft./69m.; 🅿; ★ **AUG**; z 04364; Ⓟ 2,819; © 2,893
Winthrop; MCD-Town; KENNEBEC; ***183** F-4; 🅿; ★ **AUG**; z 04364; Ⓟ 5,968; © 6,232
Winthrop Center; RMC Place; KENNEBEC; ▲ Winthrop; ***183** F-4; ★ **AUG**; mail Winthrop z 04364; rural
Wiscasset; CDP; ⊡ LINCOLN; ▲ Wiscasset; **183** G-4; 🅿; ★ **BR-BA**; z 04578; Ⓟ 1,233; © 1,203
Wiscasset; MCD-Town; LINCOLN; ***183** G-4; 🅿; ★ **BR-BA**; z 04578; Ⓟ 3,339; © 3,603
Wonsqueak Harbor; RMC Place; HANCOCK; ▲ Gouldsboro; ***183** F-8; mail Birch Harbor z 04613; ● 30
Woodfords; RMC Place; CUMBERLAND; ***183** H-3; ★ **POR**; mail Portland z 04101, z 04103; pop. incl. with Portland (Inc. Place)
Woodland; MCD-Town; AROOSTOOK; ***183** B-14; 🅿; z 04736; Ⓟ 1,402; © 1,403
Woodland (Baileyville); CDP; WASHINGTON; ▲ Baileyville; **183** C-9; mail Baileyville z 04694; Ⓟ 1,287; © 1,044
Woodland Junction; RMC Place; WASHINGTON; ▲ Baileyville; ***183** C-9; mail Baileyville z 04694; ● 75
Woodmans Mills; RMC Place; WALDO; ▲ Searsmont; ***183** F-5; elev. 271ft./83m.; mail Searsmont z 04973; rural
Woodstock; MCD-Town; OXFORD; ***183** F-2; mail Bryant Pond z 04219; Ⓟ 1,194; © 1,307
Woodville; MCD-Town; PENOBSCOT; ***183** B-7; 🅿; z 04457; Ⓟ 215; © 286
Woolwich; RMC Place; SAGADAHOC; ▲ Woolwich; **183** G-4; 🅿; ★ **BR-BA**; z 04579; ● 600
Woolwich; MCD-Town; SAGADAHOC; ***183** G-4; 🅿; ★ **BR-BA**; z 04579; Ⓟ 2,570; © 2,810
Worthley Pond; RMC Place; OXFORD; ▲ Peru; ***183** F-3; mail Peru z 04290; summer pop. 400; ● 200
Wyman; RMC Place; WASHINGTON; ▲ Milbridge; ***183** F-8; elev. 24ft./7m.; mail Milbridge z 04658
Wytopitlock; RMC Place; AROOSTOOK; ▲ Reed; **183** B-8; elev. 349ft./106m.; 🅿; z 04497; ● 150

Y

Yarmouth; CDP; CUMBERLAND; ▲ Yarmouth; **183** H-3; 🅿; ★ **POR**; z 04096; Ⓟ 3,338; © 3,560
Yarmouth; MCD-Town; CUMBERLAND; ***183** H-3; 🅿; ★ **POR**; z 04096; Ⓟ 7,862; © 8,360; ◆ 8,084
York; YORK; see York Village (RMC Place)
York; MCD-Town; YORK; ***183** J-2; 🅿; ★ **PTSM-**; z 03909; Ⓟ 9,818; © 12,854; ◆ 15,651
YORK; **183** I-1; Ⓟ 164,587; © 186,742; ◆ 198,288
York Beach; RMC Place; YORK; ▲ York; **183** J-2; 🅿; ★ **PTSM-**; z 03910; summer pop. 3,000; ● 900
York Cliffs; RMC Place; YORK; ▲ York; ***183** J-2; ★ **PTSM-**; mail Cape Neddick z 03902; ● 100
York Corner; RMC Place; YORK; ▲ York; ***183** J-2; ★ **PTSM-**; mail York Harbor z 03911; ● 100
York Harbor; CDP; YORK; ▲ York; **183** J-2; 🅿; ★ **PTSM-**; z 03911 & mail York z 03909, York Beach z 03910; Ⓟ 2,555; © 3,321
York Heights; RMC Place; YORK; ▲ York; ***183** J-2; ★ **PTSM-**; mail York z 03909; ● 150
York Village (York); RMC Place; YORK; ▲ York; ***183** J-2; 🅷; ★ **PTSM-**; mail York z 03909; ● 1,000
Youngs Corner; RMC Place; ANDROSCOGGIN; ***183** G-3; ★ **LEW-**; mail Auburn z 04210; pop. incl. with Auburn (Inc. Place)
Youngtown; RMC Place; WALDO; ▲ Lincolnville; ***183** F-6; elev. 267ft./81m.; mail Lincolnville Center z 04850

MARYLAND

Statistics

Total area (2000) — 12,407 square miles
Land area (2000) — 9,774 square miles
Water area (2000) — 2,633 square miles
Capital — Annapolis
One of the Thirteen Original States

Maps

State maps can be found on pages 142-254 in Vol. 1

Ranally Metro Areas (RMAs) and Abbreviations

Annapolis, MD — ANPLS
Baltimore, MD-PA — BAL
Cumberland, MD-WV — CUMB
Hagerstown, MD-PA-WV — HAG
Philadelphia-Trenton-Wilmington, PA-NJ-DE-MD — PHIL-
Salisbury, MD-DE — SLSB
Washington, DC-MD-VA — WASH

Principal Places

Place Name	Place Type	County	Population
Baltimore	Independent City		◆ 649,405
Wheaton	RMC Place	MONTGOMERY	● 134,800
Columbia	CDP	HOWARD	◆ 94,166
Silver Spring	CDP	MONTGOMERY	◆ 81,297
Dundalk	CDP	BALTIMORE	◆ 65,409
Frederick	Inc. Place	FREDERICK	◆ 64,095
Ellicott City	CDP	HOWARD	◆ 62,804
Gaithersburg	Inc. Place	MONTGOMERY	◆ 62,324
Wheaton-Glenmont	CDP-Census Area Only	MONTGOMERY	◆ 61,275
Germantown	CDP	MONTGOMERY	◆ 58,856
Bethesda	CDP	MONTGOMERY	◆ 58,710
Towson	CDP	BALTIMORE	◆ 54,374
Bowie	Inc. Place	PRINCE GEORGE'S	◆ 53,711
Aspen Hill	CDP	MONTGOMERY	◆ 53,348
Rockville	Inc. Place	MONTGOMERY	◆ 51,673
Potomac	CDP	MONTGOMERY	◆ 47,597
Bel Air South	CDP-Census Area Only	HARFORD	◆ 43,074
Catonsville	CDP	BALTIMORE	◆ 41,801
Glen Burnie	CDP	ANNE ARUNDEL	◆ 41,153
Essex	CDP	BALTIMORE	◆ 41,019
North Bethesda	CDP-Census Area Only	MONTGOMERY	◆ 41,012
Hagerstown	Inc. Place	WASHINGTON	◆ 40,921
Montgomery Village	CDP	MONTGOMERY	◆ 40,411
Annapolis	Inc. Place	ANNE ARUNDEL	◆ 39,114
Saint Charles	CDP	CHARLES	◆ 38,876
Woodlawn	CDP	BALTIMORE	◆ 37,875
Severn	CDP	ANNE ARUNDEL	◆ 37,085
Oxon Hill-Glassmanor	CDP-Census Area Only	PRINCE GEORGE'S	◆ 35,452
Chillum	CDP	PRINCE GEORGE'S	◆ 34,353
Suitland-Silver Hill	CDP-Census Area Only	PRINCE GEORGE'S	◆ 33,612
Olney	CDP	MONTGOMERY	◆ 33,392
Parkville	CDP	BALTIMORE	◆ 32,672
Randallstown	CDP	BALTIMORE	◆ 32,415
Pikesville	CDP	BALTIMORE	◆ 30,570
South Gate	CDP-Census Area Only	ANNE ARUNDEL	◆ 30,318
Severna Park	CDP	ANNE ARUNDEL	◆ 30,144
Perry Hall	CDP	BALTIMORE	◆ 30,138
Carney	CDP	BALTIMORE	◆ 29,672
Salisbury	Inc. Place	WICOMICO	◆ 29,575
Eldersburg	CDP	CARROLL	◆ 28,601
Bel Air North	CDP-Census Area Only	HARFORD	◆ 27,981
Milford Mill	CDP-Census Area Only	BALTIMORE	◆ 27,850
Suitland	RMC Place	PRINCE GEORGE'S	● 26,750
Lochearn	CDP	BALTIMORE	◆ 26,523
Clinton	CDP	PRINCE GEORGE'S	◆ 26,139
Waldorf	CDP	CHARLES	◆ 25,987
Edgewood	CDP	HARFORD	◆ 25,361
Middle River	CDP	BALTIMORE	◆ 25,156
Arnold	CDP	ANNE ARUNDEL	◆ 24,766
Elkridge	CDP	HOWARD	◆ 24,539
North Potomac	CDP	MONTGOMERY	◆ 24,477
Fort Washington	CDP	PRINCE GEORGE'S	◆ 23,922
Reisterstown	CDP	BALTIMORE	◆ 23,548
College Park	Inc. Place	PRINCE GEORGE'S	◆ 23,279
Fairland	CDP	MONTGOMERY	◆ 23,087
Greater Landover	CDP-Census Area Only	PRINCE GEORGE'S	◆ 22,968
North Laurel	CDP-Census Area Only	HOWARD	◆ 22,795
White Oak	CDP	MONTGOMERY	◆ 22,272
Odenton	CDP	ANNE ARUNDEL	◆ 21,713
Laurel	Inc. Place	PRINCE GEORGE'S	◆ 21,387
Crofton	CDP	ANNE ARUNDEL	◆ 21,241
Owings Mills	CDP	BALTIMORE	◆ 21,199
Arbutus	CDP	BALTIMORE	◆ 20,664
South Laurel	CDP-Census Area Only	PRINCE GEORGE'S	◆ 20,541
Greenbelt	Inc. Place	PRINCE GEORGE'S	◆ 20,290
Colesville	CDP	MONTGOMERY	© 19,810
Cumberland	Inc. Place	ALLEGANY	◆ 19,424
Cockeysville	CDP	BALTIMORE	© 19,388
Rosedale	CDP	BALTIMORE	© 19,199
Greater Upper Marlboro	CDP-Census Area Only	PRINCE GEORGE'S	© 18,720
Lanham-Seabrook	CDP-Census Area Only	PRINCE GEORGE'S	© 18,190
Camp Springs	CDP	PRINCE GEORGE'S	© 17,968
Green Haven	CDP	ANNE ARUNDEL	© 17,415
Takoma Park	Inc. Place	MONTGOMERY	© 17,299
Redland	CDP	MONTGOMERY	© 16,998
Westminster	Inc. Place	CARROLL	© 16,731
Hillcrest Heights	CDP	PRINCE GEORGE'S	© 16,359
Langley Park	CDP	PRINCE GEORGE'S	© 16,214
Ferndale	CDP	ANNE ARUNDEL	© 16,056
Lutherville-Timonium	CDP-Census Area Only	BALTIMORE	© 15,814
Lansdowne-Baltimore Highlands	CDP-Census Area Only	BALTIMORE	© 15,724
Beltsville	CDP	PRINCE GEORGE'S	© 15,690
Adelphi	CDP	PRINCE GEORGE'S	© 14,998
East Riverdale	CDP	PRINCE GEORGE'S	© 14,961
Hyattsville	Inc. Place	PRINCE GEORGE'S	© 14,733
Parole	CDP	ANNE ARUNDEL	© 14,031
Aberdeen	Inc. Place	HARFORD	© 13,842
Easton	Inc. Place	TALBOT	◆ 13,790
Ballenger Creek	CDP-Census Area Only	FREDERICK	© 13,518
Lake Shore	CDP	ANNE ARUNDEL	© 13,065
Savage-Guilford	CDP-Census Area Only	HOWARD	© 12,918
Forestville	CDP	PRINCE GEORGE'S	® 12,712
Riviera Beach	CDP	ANNE ARUNDEL	© 12,695
Calverton	CDP	PRINCE GEORGE'S	© 12,610
Glenn Dale	CDP	PRINCE GEORGE'S	© 12,609
New Carrollton	Inc. Place	PRINCE GEORGE'S	© 12,589
Linganore-Bartonsville	CDP-Census Area Only	FREDERICK	© 12,529
Rosaryville	CDP	PRINCE GEORGE'S	© 12,322
Green Valley	CDP	FREDERICK	© 12,262
Overlea	CDP	BALTIMORE	© 12,148
Pasadena	CDP	ANNE ARUNDEL	© 12,093
Elkton	Inc. Place	CECIL	© 11,893
Rossville	CDP	BALTIMORE	© 11,515
Chesapeake Ranch Estates-Drum Point	CDP-Census Area Only	CALVERT	© 11,503
Damascus	CDP	MONTGOMERY	© 11,430
Mays Chapel	CDP-Census Area Only	BALTIMORE	© 11,427
Joppatowne	CDP	HARFORD	© 11,391
Havre de Grace	Inc. Place	HARFORD	© 11,331
Walker Mill	CDP-Census Area Only	PRINCE GEORGE'S	© 11,104
Lexington Park	CDP	ST. MARY'S	© 11,021
Kettering	CDP	PRINCE GEORGE'S	© 11,008
Cambridge	Inc. Place	DORCHESTER	® 10,976
Brooklyn Park	CDP	ANNE ARUNDEL	© 10,938
Friendly	CDP	PRINCE GEORGE'S	© 10,938
Coral Hills	CDP	PRINCE GEORGE'S	© 10,720
Bel Air	Inc. Place	HARFORD	◆ 10,538
Ocean Pines	CDP	WORCESTER	© 10,496
Germantown Park	RMC Place	MONTGOMERY	● 10,400
Halfway	CDP	WASHINGTON	© 10,065
Kemp Mill	CDP-Census Area Only	MONTGOMERY	© 9,956
Fort Meade	CDP-Census Area Only	ANNE ARUNDEL	© 9,882
Mitchellville	CDP-Census Area Only	PRINCE GEORGE'S	© 9,611
Chevy Chase	CDP-Census Area Only	MONTGOMERY	© 9,381
California	CDP	ST. MARY'S	® 9,300
Edgemere	CDP	BALTIMORE	© 9,248
The Lakes	RMC Place	BALTIMORE	● 9,000
North Kensington	CDP	MONTGOMERY	© 8,940
Glassmanor	RMC Place	PRINCE GEORGE'S	● 8,800
Pinefield	RMC Place	CHARLES	● 8,800
Lansdowne	RMC Place	BALTIMORE	● 8,700
Lake Arbor	CDP-Census Area Only	PRINCE GEORGE'S	© 8,533
Mount Rainier	Inc. Place	PRINCE GEORGE'S	© 8,498
White Marsh	CDP	BALTIMORE	© 8,485
Fallston	CDP	HARFORD	© 8,427
Largo	CDP	PRINCE GEORGE'S	© 8,408
Woodmoor	RMC Place	BALTIMORE	● 8,400
Cape Saint Claire	CDP	ANNE ARUNDEL	© 8,022
Savage	RMC Place	HOWARD	● 8,000
Seabrook	RMC Place	PRINCE GEORGE'S	● 8,000
Garrison	CDP	BALTIMORE	© 7,969
Andrews AFB	CDP-Census Area Only	PRINCE GEORGE'S	© 7,925
South Kensington	CDP-Census Area Only	MONTGOMERY	© 7,887
Frostburg	Inc. Place	ALLEGANY	© 7,873
Jessup	CDP	ANNE ARUNDEL	© 7,865
Cloverly	CDP	MONTGOMERY	© 7,835
Marlton	CDP	PRINCE GEORGE'S	© 7,798
Temple Hills	CDP	PRINCE GEORGE'S	© 7,792
Bladensburg	Inc. Place	PRINCE GEORGE'S	© 7,661
Londontowne	CDP	ANNE ARUNDEL	© 7,595
Rossmoor	CDP-Census Area Only	MONTGOMERY	© 7,569
Linthicum	CDP	ANNE ARUNDEL	© 7,539
Travilah	CDP	MONTGOMERY	© 7,442
Accokeek	CDP	PRINCE GEORGE'S	© 7,349
Forest Glen	CDP	MONTGOMERY	© 7,344
Bennsville	CDP	CHARLES	© 7,325
Burtonsville	CDP	MONTGOMERY	© 7,305
Ocean City	Inc. Place	WORCESTER	© 7,173
Pleasant Fields	RMC Place	MONTGOMERY	● 7,100
Palmer Park	RMC Place	PRINCE GEORGE'S	℗ 7,019
Edgewater Village	RMC Place	HARFORD	● 7,000
Westview Park	RMC Place	BALTIMORE	● 7,000
Maryland City	CDP	ANNE ARUNDEL	© 6,814
Baltimore Highlands	RMC Place	BALTIMORE	● 6,700
Lynne Acres	RMC Place	BALTIMORE	● 6,700
Rockdale	RMC Place	BALTIMORE	● 6,700
La Plata	Inc. Place	CHARLES	© 6,551
Cheverly	Inc. Place	PRINCE GEORGE'S	© 6,433
Mount Airy	Inc. Place	CARROLL	© 6,425
Darnestown	CDP	MONTGOMERY	© 6,378
Glenarden	Inc. Place	PRINCE GEORGE'S	© 6,318
Bowleys Quarters	CDP	BALTIMORE	© 6,314
Riverdale Park	Inc. Place	PRINCE GEORGE'S	® 6,311
Woodlawn	CDP	PRINCE GEORGE'S	© 6,251
Fox Chapel	RMC Place	MONTGOMERY	● 6,200
Randolph Hills	RMC Place	MONTGOMERY	● 6,150
Riverside	CDP-Census Area Only	HARFORD	© 6,128
Woodmore	CDP	PRINCE GEORGE'S	© 6,077
Marlow Heights	CDP	PRINCE GEORGE'S	© 6,059
New Hampshire Estates	RMC Place	MONTGOMERY	● 6,050
Harford Square	RMC Place	HARFORD	● 6,000
Hillcrest Terrace	RMC Place	PRINCE GEORGE'S	● 6,000
Whiskey Bottom	RMC Place	HOWARD	● 6,000
District Heights	Inc. Place	PRINCE GEORGE'S	® 5,953
Cresaptown-Bel Air	CDP-Census Area Only	ALLEGANY	© 5,884
Stevensville	CDP	QUEEN ANNE'S	© 5,880
Edmonson Heights	RMC Place	BALTIMORE	● 5,800
Manor Woods	RMC Place	MONTGOMERY	● 5,800
Powder Mill Village	RMC Place	PRINCE GEORGE'S	● 5,800
Belvedere Heights	RMC Place	ANNE ARUNDEL	● 5,600
Ellicott Mills	RMC Place	BALTIMORE	● 5,600
Strathmore At Bel Pre	RMC Place	MONTGOMERY	● 5,600
Thurmont	Inc. Place	FREDERICK	© 5,588
Shady Side	CDP	ANNE ARUNDEL	© 5,559
Goddard	CDP-Census Area Only	PRINCE GEORGE'S	© 5,554
Birchwood City	RMC Place	PRINCE GEORGE'S	● 5,500
Quince Orchard	RMC Place	MONTGOMERY	● 5,500
Presidential Park	RMC Place	PRINCE GEORGE'S	● 5,400
Pumphrey	CDP	ANNE ARUNDEL	© 5,317
Barnaby Village	RMC Place	PRINCE GEORGE'S	● 5,300
Emory Grove	RMC Place	MONTGOMERY	● 5,300
Lanham	RMC Place	PRINCE GEORGE'S	● 5,200
Walkersville	Inc. Place	FREDERICK	© 5,192
Poolesville	Inc. Place	MONTGOMERY	© 5,151
Taneytown	Inc. Place	CARROLL	© 5,128
Hampstead	Inc. Place	CARROLL	© 5,060
Hampton	CDP	BALTIMORE	© 5,004
Fort Foote Village	RMC Place	PRINCE GEORGE'S	● 5,000

County and Independent City Business Data

County	FIPS Code	County Seat	Land Area (Sq. Mi.)	Census Population			Wholesale Trade		Manufacturing, 2002			
				4/1/2000	4/1/1990	% Change 1990-2000	Sales, 2002 ($1,000)	% Change 1997-2002	Establish-ments	Total Employees	Value Added ($1,000)	Ranally Mfg. Units
Allegany	001	Cumberland	425	74,930	74,946	-0.0	(d)	(d)	59	3,422	432,450	229
Anne Arundel	003	Annapolis	416	489,656	427,239	14.6	11,140,063	26.2	342	14,949	1,919,110	1,015
Baltimore	005	Towson	599	754,292	692,134	9.0	8,697,131	29.7	556	26,874	4,154,684	2,198
Calvert	009	Prince Frederick	215	74,563	51,372	45.1	(d)	(d)	46	703	73,020	39
Caroline	011	Denton	320	29,772	27,035	10.1	141,364	-13.4	35	1,693	152,977	81
Carroll	013	Westminster	449	150,897	123,372	22.3	490,347	67.4	153	3,953	475,107	251
Cecil	015	Elkton	348	85,951	71,347	20.5	(d)	(d)	59	4,285	438,953	232
Charles	017	La Plata	461	120,546	101,154	19.2	(d)	(d)	63	1,243	78,129	41
Dorchester	019	Cambridge	558	30,674	30,236	1.4	(d)	(d)	55	2,696	278,869	148
Frederick	021	Frederick	663	195,277	150,208	30.0	(d)	(d)	201	8,190	1,764,746	934
Garrett	023	Oakland	648	29,846	28,138	6.1	(d)	(d)	62	904	57,026	30
Harford	025	Bel Air	440	218,590	182,132	20.0	1,320,444	28.9	164	6,620	787,936	417
Howard	027	Ellicott City	252	247,842	187,328	32.3	9,089,992	-3.2	249	8,074	884,629	468
Kent	029	Chestertown	279	19,197	17,842	7.6	(d)	(d)	34	1,023	139,627	74
Montgomery	031	Rockville	496	873,341	757,027	15.4	7,116,773	-19.1	506	14,735	1,469,808	778
Prince George's	033	Upper Marlboro	485	801,515	729,268	9.9	10,488,336	15.8	382	11,952	1,124,263	595
Queen Anne's	035	Centreville	372	40,563	33,953	19.5	335,017	60.3	48	926	66,639	35
St. Mary's	037	Leonardtown	361	86,211	75,974	13.5	(d)	(d)	...	(d)	(d)	...
Somerset	039	Princess Anne	327	24,747	23,440	5.6	(d)	(d)	...	(d)	(d)	...
Talbot	041	Easton	269	33,812	30,549	10.7	(d)	(d)	51	2,696	468,498	248
Washington	043	Hagerstown	458	131,923	121,393	8.7	1,278,754	38.6	149	8,822	1,139,530	603
Wicomico	045	Salisbury	377	84,644	74,339	13.9	548,598	9.3	94	(d)	(d)	...
Worcester	047	Snow Hill	473	46,543	35,028	32.9	(d)	(d)	45	1,565	116,971	62
Independent City												
Baltimore	510		81	651,154	736,014	-11.5	6,047,618	-2.0	591	21,042	2,807,410	1,485
The State			**9,774**	**5,296,486**	**4,781,468**	**10.8**	**60,679,602**	**10.5**	**3,999**	**151,294**	**19,265,920**	**10,193**

(d) Data not available. Corresponding percentages or Ranally Manufacturing Units are estimates.
... Represents 0 or amount too minimal to be reported.

Index of Places and Counties

A

Abell; RMC Place; ST. MARY'S; **185** J-13; elev. 16ft./5m.; 🅿; ★ **WASH**; z 20606; ● 160
Aberdeen; Inc. Place; HARFORD; **185** B-15; elev. 83ft./25m.; 🅿; z 21001; ℗ 13,087; © 13,842
Aberdeen Proving Ground; CDP-Census Area Only; HARFORD; ***185** B-16; 🅿; z 21005, z 21010; ℗ 5,267; © 3,116
Abingdon; RMC Place; HARFORD; **185** C-15; elev. 140ft./43m.; 🅿; ★ **BAL**; z 21009; ● 2,000
Academy Heights; RMC Place; BALTIMORE; ***185** D-13; ★ **BAL**; mail Catonsville z 21228
Academy Junction; RMC Place; ANNE ARUNDEL; ***185** E-13; ★ **BAL**; mail Odenton z 21113; ● 380
Accident; Inc. Place; GARRETT; **184** B-1; elev. 2,415ft./736m.; 🅿; z 21520; ℗ 349; © 353
Accokeek; CDP; PRINCE GEORGE'S; **185** G-12; elev. 190ft./58m.; 🅿; ★ **WASH**; z 20607; ℗ 4,477; © 7,349
Accokeek Acres; RMC Place; PRINCE GEORGE'S; ***185** G-12; ★ **WASH**; mail Accokeek z 20607
Accokeek Groves; RMC Place; PRINCE GEORGE'S; ***185** G-12; ★ **WASH**; mail Accokeek z 20607
Acco Park; RMC Place; PRINCE GEORGE'S; ★ **WASH**; mail Accokeek z 20607
Adams Heights; RMC Place; HARFORD; ***185** B-15; elev. 280ft./85m.; mail Aberdeen z 21001; ● 100
Adamstown; RMC Place; FREDERICK; **184** C-10; elev. 303ft./92m.; 🅿; ★ **WASH**; z 21710; ● 400
Adams Woods; RMC Place; PRINCE GEORGE'S; mail Hyattsville z 20783
Adelina; RMC Place; CALVERT; **185** H-13; ★ **WASH**; mail Prince Frederick z 20678; ● 150
Adelphi; CDP; PRINCE GEORGE'S; **249** D-7; elev. 174ft./53m.; 🅿 🅲 33,096; ★ **WASH**; z 20783 & mail Hyattsville z 20787; ℗ 13,524; © 14,998
Adelphi Hills; RMC Place; PRINCE GEORGE'S; ***185** F-12; ★ **WASH**; mail Hyattsville z 20783
Adelphi Manor; RMC Place; PRINCE GEORGE'S; ***185** E-12; ★ **WASH**; mail Hyattsville z 20783
Ady; RMC Place; HARFORD; ***185** B-15; elev. 473ft./144m.; ★ **BAL**; mail Street z 21154; rural
Aero Acres; RMC Place; BALTIMORE; ***185** C-14; ★ **BAL**; mail Middle River z 21220
Aikin; RMC Place; CECIL; ***185** B-16; elev. 114ft./35m.; mail Perryville z 21903; pop. incl. with Perryville (Inc. Place)
Airey (Aireys); RMC Place; DORCHESTER; **185** H-16; mail Cambridge z 21613; ● 30
Aireys; DORCHESTER; see Airey (RMC Place)
Albantown; RMC Place; BALTIMORE; ***185** B-13; elev. 784ft./239m.; ★ **BAL**; mail Hampstead z 21074; ● 70
Albeth Heights; RMC Place; HOWARD; ***185** C-12; elev. 467ft./142m.; ★ **BAL**; mail Woodstock z 21163; ● 140
Aldino; RMC Place; HARFORD; ***185** B-15; elev. 391ft./119m.; mail Aberdeen z 21001; ● 50
Alesia; RMC Place; CARROLL; **185** A-12; ★ **BAL**; mail Manchester z 21102; ● 230
Algonquin; CDP; DORCHESTER; ***185** H-16; © 1,361
Allanwood; RMC Place; MONTGOMERY; ***185** E-12; ★ **WASH**; mail Silver Spring z 20906; ● 1,500
Allegany; ALLEGANY; see Zihlman (RMC Place)
ALLEGANY; **184** B-5; ℗ 74,946; © 74,930; ◆ 72,158
Allegany Grove; RMC Place; ALLEGANY; ***184** A-4; ★ **CUMB**; mail Cumberland z 21502
Allen; RMC Place; WICOMICO; **185** I-18; elev. 20ft./6m.; 🅿; z 21810; ● 520
Allenford; RMC Place; HOWARD; ***185** C-12; ★ **BAL**; mail Ellicott City z 21042
Allens Fresh; RMC Place; CHARLES; **185** I-12; mail Faulkner z 20632; ● 100
Allenwood; RMC Place; WICOMICO; ***185** I-18; ★ **SLSB**; mail Salisbury z 21801; ● 170
Allenwood Acres; RMC Place; PRINCE GEORGE'S; ***185** F-12; ★ **WASH**; mail Temple Hills z 20748; ● 1,400
Allview; RMC Place; HOWARD; ★ **BAL**; mail Columbia z 21045
Allview Estates; RMC Place; HOWARD; ★ **BAL**; mail Columbia z 21046
Alpha; RMC Place; HOWARD; **185** C-12; ★ **BAL**; mail Marriottsville z 21104; ● 100
Alpine Beach; RMC Place; ANNE ARUNDEL; ***185** D-14; ★ **BAL**; mail Pasadena z 21122
Altamont; RMC Place; GARRETT; ***184** C-2; mail Swanton z 21561
Alta Vista; RMC Place; MONTGOMERY; ***185** E-11; ★ **WASH**; mail Bethesda z 20817
Alta Vista Gardens; RMC Place; MONTGOMERY; ***185** E-11; ★ **WASH**; mail Bethesda z 20814
Alta Vista Terrace; RMC Place; MONTGOMERY; ***185** E-11; ★ **WASH**; mail Bethesda z 20814
Amberly; RMC Place; ANNE ARUNDEL; ***185** E-14; ★ **ANPLS**; mail Annapolis z 21401; ● 450

Entries in **UPPERCASE** are counties.
Entries in **bold** have populations of 2,500 or more.
Names in parentheses are alternate names.

Inc. Place	Incorporated Place
RMC Place	Rand McNally Designated Place
CDP	Census Designated Place
MCD	Minor Civil Division
⊡	County Seat
▲	Minor Civil Division
elev.	Elevation
🅿	Post Office
🅷	Hospital
🅲	College
■	Principal Business Center
★	Ranally Metro Area (RMA) Abbreviation
z	Zip Code(s)
℗	Previous Census Population
®	Revised Census Population
Ⓐ	Annexation Population
●	Rand McNally Population Estimate
©	Final Census Population
Ⓢ	Special Census Population
◆	Estimated Population

For additional definitions see Glossary, Volume 1, and Introduction, Volume 2.

Amberly of Kings Court; RMC Place; BALTIMORE; ***185** C-14; ★ **BAL**; mail Rosedale z 21237; ● 1,870
Amber Meadows; RMC Place; PRINCE GEORGE'S; ★ **WASH**; mail Bowie z 20716; pop. incl. with Bowie (Inc. Place)
Amcelle; RMC Place; ALLEGANY; ***184** B-4; ★ **CUMB**; mail Cumberland z 21502
Amcelle Acres; RMC Place; ALLEGANY; ***184** B-3; ★ **CUMB**; mail Cumberland z 21502; ● 770
American Cities; RMC Place; HOWARD; ***185** D-12; ★ **BAL**; mail Columbia z 21044
American Corner (American Corners); RMC Place; CAROLINE; ***185** F-17; mail Federalsburg z 21632
American Corners; CAROLINE; see American Corner (RMC Place)
Ammendale; RMC Place; PRINCE GEORGE'S; ***185** E-12; elev. 140ft./43m.; ★ **WASH**; mail Beltsville z 20705
Anchorage; RMC Place; ANNE ARUNDEL; ★ **ANPLS**; mail Annapolis z 21403
Ancient Oak; RMC Place; MONTGOMERY; ***185** E-11; ★ **WASH**; mail Gaithersburg z 20878; ● 400
Ancient Oak North; RMC Place; MONTGOMERY; ***184** D-10; ★ **WASH**; mail Gaithersburg z 20878; ● 550
Andersontown; RMC Place; CAROLINE; **185** F-17; mail Denton z 21629; ● 30
Andora; RMC Place; CECIL; ***185** A-17; elev. 352ft./107m.; ★ **PHIL-**; mail Elkton z 21921; ● 30
Andover Estates; RMC Place; ST. MARY'S; ***185** J-14; mail Valley Lee z 20692; ● 100
Andrew Hills; RMC Place; PRINCE GEORGE'S; ***185** F-12; ★ **WASH**; mail Temple Hills z 20748; ● 1,200
Andrews; RMC Place; DORCHESTER; **185** I-16; elev. 3ft./1m.; mail Crapo z 21626; ● 130
Andrews AFB; CDP-Census Area Only; PRINCE GEORGE'S; ***185** F-12; 🅿; ★ **WASH**; z 20762; Ⓟ 10,228; Ⓒ 7,925
Andrews Estates; RMC Place; PRINCE GEORGE'S; ***185** F-12; ★ **WASH**; mail Suitland z 20746; ● 1,440
Andrews Manor; RMC Place; PRINCE GEORGE'S; ***185** F-12; elev. 270ft./82m.; ★ **WASH**; mail Suitland z 20746; ● 2,050
Annapolis; Inc. Place; **STATE CAPITAL**; ⊡ ANNE ARUNDEL; **185** E-14; elev. 57ft./17m.; 🅿 🅷 🅲 5,030 ■; ★ **ANPLS**; z 21401-05, z 21409, z 21411-12; Ⓟ 33,187; Ⓒ 35,838; ◆ 39,114
Annapolis Junction; RMC Place; HOWARD, ANNE ARUNDEL; **185** E-13; elev. 180ft./55m.; 🅿; ★ **BAL**; z 20701; ● 800
Annapolis Rock; RMC Place; HOWARD; ***185** D-11; elev. 530ft./162m.; ★ **WASH**; mail Woodbine z 21797; rural
ANNE ARUNDEL; **185** E-13; Ⓟ 427,239; Ⓒ 489,656; ◆ 517,714
Anneslie; RMC Place; BALTIMORE; ***185** C-13; ★ **BAL**; mail Baltimore z 21212
Anthony; RMC Place; CAROLINE; ***185** F-17; elev. 41ft./12m.; mail Denton z 21629; rural
Antietam; RMC Place; WASHINGTON; **184** C-8; ★ **HAG**; mail Sharpsburg z 21782; ● 50
Apple Green; RMC Place; CALVERT; ***185** G-13; ★ **WASH**; mail Dunkirk z 20754; ● 160
Apple Grove; RMC Place; PRINCE GEORGE'S; ***185** F-12; ★ **WASH**; mail Fort Washington z 20744; ● 2,000
Appleton; RMC Place; CECIL; ***185** A-17; elev. 335ft./102m.; ★ **PHIL-**; mail Elkton z 21921; ● 30
Appleton Acres; RMC Place; CECIL; **185** A-17; ★ **PHIL-**; mail Elkton z 21921; ● 200
Appliance Park East; RMC Place; BALTIMORE (Independent City); ★ **BAL**; mail Columbia z 21045; pop. incl. with Baltimore (Independent City)
Appolds; RMC Place; FREDERICK; ***184** B-10; mail Rocky Ridge z 21778; rural
Aquasco; RMC Place; PRINCE GEORGE'S; **185** H-13; elev. 160ft./49m.; 🅿; ★ **WASH**; z 20608; ● 180
Aragona Village; RMC Place; PRINCE GEORGE'S; ***185** G-12; ★ **WASH**; mail Fort Washington z 20744; ● 630
Arbutus; CDP; BALTIMORE; **184** K-3; 🅿; ★ **BAL**; z 21227; Ⓟ 19,750; Ⓒ 20,116; ◆ 20,664
Arcadia; BALTIMORE; see Upperco (RMC Place)
Arden-on-the-Severn; CDP; ANNE ARUNDEL; **185** E-14; ★ **WASH**; mail Crownsville z 21032; Ⓟ 2,427; Ⓒ 1,971
Ardmore; RMC Place; PRINCE GEORGE'S; **249** F-9; ★ **WASH**; mail Hyattsville z 20785; pop. incl. with Glenarden (Inc. Place)
Ardwick; RMC Place; PRINCE GEORGE'S; ***185** F-12; ★ **WASH**; mail Hyattsville z 20785
Argonne Hills; RMC Place; ANNE ARUNDEL; ★ **BAL**; mail Fort George G Meade z 20755
Argyle Park; RMC Place; MONTGOMERY; ***185** E-12; ★ **WASH**; mail Silver Spring z 20901
Arlington; RMC Place; BALTIMORE (Independent City); ***185** C-13; 🅿; ★ **BAL**; z 21215; pop. incl. with Baltimore (Independent City)
Armagh; RMC Place; BALTIMORE; ***185** C-13; ★ **BAL**; mail Towson z 21204
Arnold; CDP; ANNE ARUNDEL; **185** E-14; elev. 120ft./37m.; 🅿; ★ **BAL**; z 21012; Ⓟ 20,261; Ⓒ 23,422; ◆ 24,766
Arnold Heights; RMC Place; PRINCE GEORGE'S; ***185** F-12; elev. 289ft./88m.; ★ **WASH**; mail Suitland z 20746
Arnoldtown; RMC Place; FREDERICK; ***184** C-9; ★ **WASH**; mail Jefferson z 21755; rural
Arrowhead; RMC Place; HOWARD; ★ **BAL**; mail Columbia z 21046
Arrow Head; RMC Place; MONTGOMERY; ***185** D-11; ★ **WASH**; mail Gaithersburg z 20879
Arrowood; RMC Place; MONTGOMERY; ***185** E-11; ★ **WASH**; mail Bethesda z 20817
Arundel Gardens; RMC Place; ANNE ARUNDEL; **184** L-5; ★ **BAL**; mail Brooklyn z 21225; ● 1,250
Arundel Hills; RMC Place; ANNE ARUNDEL; ***185** D-13; ★ **BAL**; mail Linthicum Heights z 21090
Arundel on the Bay; RMC Place; ANNE ARUNDEL; **185** F-14; ★ **ANPLS**; mail Annapolis z 21403; ● 1,100
Arundel View; RMC Place; ANNE ARUNDEL; ***185** E-13; ★ **BAL**; mail Gambrills z 21054
Arundel Village; RMC Place; ANNE ARUNDEL; **184** L-5; ★ **BAL**; mail Brooklyn z 21225; ● 2,700
Asbury Methodist Home; RMC Place; MONTGOMERY; ***185** A-11; mail Gaithersburg z 20877
Ashburton; RMC Place; MONTGOMERY; ***185** E-11; ★ **WASH**; mail Bethesda z 20817
Asher Glade; RMC Place; GARRETT; ***184** A-1; elev. 1,941ft./592m.; mail Friendsville z 21531; rural
Ashland; RMC Place; BALTIMORE; ***185** B-13; ★ **BAL**; mail Cockeysville z 21030
Ashton; RMC Place; MONTGOMERY; **185** D-12; elev. 499ft./152m.; 🅿; ★ **WASH**; z 20861; ● 1,500
Ashton Pond; RMC Place; MONTGOMERY; ***185** D-12; ★ **WASH**; mail Ashton z 20861
Ashton-Sandy Springs; CDP-Census Area Only; MONTGOMERY; ***185** D-12; ★ **WASH**; mail Ashton z 20861, Sandy Spring z 20860; Ⓟ 3,092; Ⓒ 3,437
Asleigh; RMC Place; MONTGOMERY; ***185** E-11; ★ **WASH**; mail Bethesda z 20817; ● 370
Aspen Hill; CDP; MONTGOMERY; **185** E-11; 🅿; ★ **WASH**; z 20906, z 20916 & mail Rockville z 20853; Ⓟ 45,494; Ⓒ 50,228; ◆ 53,348
Aspen Hill Park; RMC Place; MONTGOMERY; ***185** E-11; ★ **WASH**; mail Rockville z 20853
Aspen Knolls; RMC Place; MONTGOMERY; ***185** E-11; ★ **WASH**; mail Rockville z 20853
Athol; RMC Place; WICOMICO; **185** H-17; mail Mardela Springs z 21837; ● 50
Atholton; RMC Place; HOWARD; ★ **BAL**; mail Columbia z 21045
Atholton Manor; RMC Place; HOWARD; ★ **BAL**; mail Columbia z 21045
Augusta; RMC Place; WASHINGTON; ***184** C-9; ★ **WASH**; mail Knoxville z 21758; rural
Aurora Hills; RMC Place; ANNE ARUNDEL; ***185** E-13; elev. 100ft./30m.; ★ **BAL**; mail Millersville z 21108; ● 340
Auth Village; RMC Place; PRINCE GEORGE'S; ***185** F-12; ★ **WASH**; mail Suitland z 20746
Autrey Park; RMC Place; MONTGOMERY; ★ **WASH**; mail Rockville z 20850; pop. incl. with Rockville (Inc. Place)
Autumn Hill; RMC Place; HOWARD; ***185** D-13; elev. 400ft./122m.; ★ **BAL**; mail Ellicott City z 21043; ● 200
Avalon; RMC Place; TALBOT; ***185** G-15; elev. 10ft./3m.; mail Tilghman z 21671; ● 300
Avalon Shores; RMC Place; ANNE ARUNDEL; ***185** F-14; ★ **WASH**; mail Shady Side z 20764
Avenue; RMC Place; ST. MARY'S; **185** I-13; elev. 15ft./5m.; 🅿; ★ **WASH**; z 20609; ● 450
Avilton; RMC Place; GARRETT; ***184** A-3; elev. 2,653ft./809m.; mail Lonaconing z 21539
Avondale Grove; RMC Place; PRINCE GEORGE'S; ***185** E-12; ★ **WASH**; mail Hyattsville z 20782; ● 1,950
Ayrlawn; RMC Place; MONTGOMERY; ***185** E-11; ★ **WASH**; mail Bethesda z 20814

B

Back Bay Beach; RMC Place; ANNE ARUNDEL; ***185** E-14; ★ **ANPLS**; mail West River z 20778
Back River Highlands; RMC Place; BALTIMORE; ***185** C-14; ★ **BAL**; mail Essex z 21221
Baden; RMC Place; PRINCE GEORGE'S; **185** G-13; ★ **WASH**; mail Brandywine z 20613; ● 270
Bakersville; RMC Place; WASHINGTON; ***184** B-8; ★ **HAG**; mail Boonsboro z 21713; ● 50
Bald Eagle; RMC Place; PRINCE GEORGE'S; ***185** G-13; elev. 142ft./43m.; ★ **WASH**; mail Brandywine z 20613; ● 50
Baldwin; RMC Place; BALTIMORE; **185** B-14; elev. 380ft./116m.; 🅿; ★ **BAL**; z 21013; ● 420
Baldwin Hill; RMC Place; ANNE ARUNDEL; ***185** E-13; ★ **BAL**; mail Millersville z 21108; ● 340
Baldwin Hills South; RMC Place; ANNE ARUNDEL; ***185** E-13; elev. 100ft./30m.; ★ **WASH**; mail Crownsville z 21032; ● 90
Ballard; RMC Place; PRINCE GEORGE'S; ***185** G-12; ★ **WASH**; mail Clinton z 20735
Ballard Gardens; RMC Place; BALTIMORE; ***185** C-15; ★ **BAL**; mail Middle River z 21220
Ballenger Creek; CDP-Census Area Only; FREDERICK; ***184** C-10; elev. 287ft./87m.; ★ **WASH**; mail Frederick z 21701; Ⓟ 5,546; Ⓒ 13,518
Baltimore; Independent City; **185** C-13; elev. 32ft./10m.; 🅿 🅷 🅲 86,429 ■; ★ **BAL**; z 21201-31, z 21233-37, z 21239-41, z 21244, z 21250-52, z 21260, z 21263-65, z 21270, z 21273-75, z 21278-90, z 21297-98 & mail Elkridge z 21075; Ⓟ 736,014; Ⓒ 651,154; ◆ 649,405
BALTIMORE; **185** C-13; Ⓟ 692,134; Ⓒ 754,292; ◆ 791,853
Baltimore Corner; RMC Place; CAROLINE; ***185** E-17; mail Henderson z 21640; rural
Baltimore Highlands; RMC Place; BALTIMORE; **184** K-4; ★ **BAL**; mail Halethorpe z 21227; ● 6,700
Banks O'Dee; RMC Place; CHARLES; ***185** I-12; mail Newburg z 20664; ● 70
Bannockburn; RMC Place; MONTGOMERY; ***185** E-11; ★ **WASH**; mail Bethesda z 20814
Bannockburn Estates; RMC Place; MONTGOMERY; ***185** E-11; ★ **WASH**; mail Bethesda z 20817
Bannockburn Heights; RMC Place; MONTGOMERY; ***185** E-11; ★ **WASH**; mail Bethesda z 20817
Bantry; RMC Place; TALBOT; ***185** F-16; elev. 13ft./4m.; mail Easton z 21601; rural
Barclay (Merrickton); Inc. Place; QUEEN ANNE'S; **185** D-17; elev. 69ft./21m.; 🅿; z 21607; Ⓟ 170; Ⓒ 143
Barefoot Acres; RMC Place; ST. MARY'S; ***185** I-14; mail California z 20619; ● 50
Bar Harbor; RMC Place; ANNE ARUNDEL; ***185** D-14; ★ **BAL**; mail Pasadena z 21122
Bark Hill; RMC Place; CARROLL; ***185** B-11; mail Union Bridge z 21791; ● 300
Barksdale; RMC Place; CECIL; ***185** A-17; elev. 209ft./64m.; ★ **PHIL-**; mail Elkton z 21921; rural
Barnaby Manor; RMC Place; PRINCE GEORGE'S; ***185** F-12; ★ **WASH**; mail Fort Washington z 20744
Barnaby Run Estates; RMC Place; PRINCE GEORGE'S; ***185** F-12; ★ **WASH**; mail Oxon Hill z 20745
Barnaby Village; RMC Place; PRINCE GEORGE'S; **249** H-7; ★ **WASH**; mail Oxon Hill z 20745; ● 5,300
Bar Neck; RMC Place; TALBOT; ***185** G-15; mail Tilghman z 21671; rural
Barnes Corner; RMC Place; CECIL; ***185** A-16; elev. 409ft./125m.; ★ **PHIL-**; mail Colora z 21917, Rising Sun z 21911; ● 180
Barnesville; Inc. Place; MONTGOMERY; **184** D-10; elev. 548ft./167m.; 🅿; ★ **WASH**; z 20838; Ⓟ 170; Ⓒ 161
Barrelville; RMC Place; ALLEGANY; **184** A-4; elev. 1,000ft./305m.; ★ **CUMB**; mail Mount Savage z 21545; ● 300
Barstow; RMC Place; CALVERT; **185** H-13; elev. 160ft./49m.; 🅿; ★ **WASH**; z 20610; ● 200
Bartholow; FREDERICK; see Bartholows (RMC Place)
Bartholows (Bartholow); RMC Place; FREDERICK; ***185** C-11; ★ **WASH**; mail Mount Airy z 21771
Barton; Inc. Place; ALLEGANY; **184** B-3; elev. 1,251ft./381m.; 🅿; ★ **CUMB**; z 21521; Ⓟ 530; Ⓒ 478
Bartonsville; RMC Place; FREDERICK; **184** C-10; ★ **WASH**; mail Frederick z 21701; ● 1,650
Battery Park; RMC Place; MONTGOMERY; ***185** E-11; ★ **WASH**; mail Bethesda z 20814
Battle Grove; RMC Place; BALTIMORE; ***185** D-14; ★ **BAL**; mail Dundalk z 21222
Bayberry; RMC Place; ANNE ARUNDEL; ***185** E-14; ★ **BAL**; mail Arnold z 21012; ● 3,500
Bay City; RMC Place; QUEEN ANNE'S; ***185** E-15; elev. 18ft./5m.; ★ **ANPLS**; mail Stevensville z 21666
Bay Highlands; RMC Place; ANNE ARUNDEL; ***185** F-14; ★ **ANPLS**; mail Annapolis z 21403; ● 320
Baynesville; RMC Place; BALTIMORE; ***185** C-14; ★ **BAL**; mail Towson z 21204
Bay Ridge; RMC Place; ANNE ARUNDEL; **185** F-14; ★ **ANPLS**; mail Annapolis z 21403; ● 2,200
Bayshore Estates; RMC Place; WORCESTER; mail Ocean City z 21842; pop. incl. with Ocean City (Inc. Place)
Bayside Beach; RMC Place; ANNE ARUNDEL; **185** D-14; ★ **BAL**; mail Pasadena z 21122; ● 950
Bay View; RMC Place; BALTIMORE (Independent City); ***185** C-14; ★ **BAL**; mail Baltimore z 21224; pop. incl. with Baltimore (Independent City)
Bay View; RMC Place; CECIL; **185** A-16; elev. 385ft./117m.; ★ **PHIL-**; mail North East z 21901; ● 300
Bay View Estates; RMC Place; CECIL; ***185** C-16; mail Earleville z 21919; ● 60
Beachville; RMC Place; ST. MARY'S; **185** J-14; mail Saint Inigoes z 20684; ● 300
Beachwood Forest; RMC Place; ANNE ARUNDEL; ***185** E-14; ★ **BAL**; mail Pasadena z 21122
Beachwood Grove; RMC Place; ANNE ARUNDEL; ***185** E-14; ★ **BAL**; mail Pasadena z 21122
Beachwood on the Burley; RMC Place; ANNE ARUNDEL; ***185** E-14; ★ **ANPLS**; mail Annapolis z 21401; ● 60
Beacon Heights; RMC Place; PRINCE GEORGE'S; ***185** E-12; ★ **WASH**; mail Riverdale z 20737; ● 2,100
Beacon Hill; RMC Place; ANNE ARUNDEL; ***185** E-14; ★ **BAL**; mail Annapolis z 21401; ● 90
Beale Manor; RMC Place; ANNE ARUNDEL; ***185** F-14; ★ **ANPLS**; mail Annapolis z 21403
Beall Estates; RMC Place; PRINCE GEORGE'S; ***185** F-13; ★ **WASH**; mail Bowie z 20716; ● 1,300
Beallsville; RMC Place; MONTGOMERY; **184** D-10; elev. 521ft./159m.; 🅿; ★ **WASH**; z 20839; ● 400
Beantown; RMC Place; CHARLES; ***185** G-12; ★ **WASH**; mail Waldorf z 20601
Bear Creek Junction; RMC Place; BALTIMORE; ***185** D-14; ★ **BAL**; mail Dundalk z 21222
Beaufort Park; RMC Place; HOWARD; ***185** D-12; ★ **WASH**; mail Fulton z 20759; ● 370
Beauty Beach; RMC Place; ANNE ARUNDEL; ***185** D-14; ★ **BAL**; mail Glen Burnie z 21061
Beauvue; RMC Place; ST. MARY'S; ***185** I-13; ★ **WASH**; mail Leonardtown z 20650; rural
Beaver Creek; RMC Place; WASHINGTON; **184** B-9; ★ **HAG**; mail Hagerstown z 21740; ● 350
Beaver Dam; RMC Place; WORCESTER; **185** K-18; elev. 18ft./5m.; mail Pocomoke City z 21851; ● 50
Beaver Dam Estates; RMC Place; PRINCE GEORGE'S; ***185** F-12; ★ **WASH**; mail Hyattsville z 20785; ● 1,200
Beaver Heights; RMC Place; PRINCE GEORGE'S; ***185** F-12; ★ **WASH**; mail Capitol Heights z 20743; ● 450
Beckleysville; RMC Place; BALTIMORE; ***185** B-13; ★ **BAL**; mail Hampstead z 21074; rural
Bedford; RMC Place; PRINCE GEORGE'S; ***185** E-12; ★ **WASH**; mail Laurel z 20708; ● 1,150
Bedfordshire; RMC Place; MONTGOMERY; ***185** E-11; ★ **WASH**; mail Potomac z 20854
Bedsworth; SOMERSET; see Mariners (RMC Place)
Bel Air; RMC Place; ALLEGANY; ***184** B-3; elev. 800ft./244m.; ★ **CUMB**; mail Cumberland z 21502; ● 1,250
Bel Air; Inc. Place; ⊡ HARFORD; **185** B-15; elev. 380ft./116m.; 🅿 ■; ★ **BAL**; z 21014-15; Ⓟ 8,860; Ⓒ 10,080; Ⓡ 9,722; ◆ 10,538
Belair; RMC Place; PRINCE GEORGE'S; ★ **WASH**; mail Bowie z 20715; pop. incl. with Bowie (Inc. Place)
Bel Air Acres; RMC Place; CHARLES; ***185** G-12; ★ **WASH**; mail Waldorf z 20601
Bel Air Acres; RMC Place; HARFORD; ***185** B-15; ★ **BAL**; mail Bel Air z 21014; ● 800
Belair Buckingham; RMC Place; PRINCE GEORGE'S; ★ **WASH**; mail Bowie z 20715; pop. incl. with Bowie (Inc. Place)
Belair Chapel Forge; RMC Place; PRINCE GEORGE'S; ★ **WASH**; mail Bowie z 20715; pop. incl. with Bowie (Inc. Place)
Belair Foxhill; RMC Place; PRINCE GEORGE'S; ★ **WASH**; mail Bowie z 20715; pop. incl. with Bowie (Inc. Place)
Belair Heather Hills; RMC Place; PRINCE GEORGE'S; ★ **WASH**; mail Bowie z 20715; pop. incl. with Bowie (Inc. Place)
Belair Idlewild; RMC Place; PRINCE GEORGE'S; ★ **WASH**; mail Bowie z 20715; pop. incl. with Bowie (Inc. Place)
Belair Kenilworth; RMC Place; PRINCE GEORGE'S; ★ **WASH**; mail Bowie z 20715; pop. incl. with Bowie (Inc. Place)
Belair Longridge; RMC Place; PRINCE GEORGE'S; ★ **WASH**; mail Bowie z 20715; pop. incl. with Bowie (Inc. Place)
Bel Air North; CDP-Census Area Only; HARFORD; ***185** B-15; ★ **BAL**; mail Forest Hill z 21050; Ⓟ 14,880; Ⓒ 25,798; Ⓡ 26,156; ◆ 27,981
Belair Overbrook; RMC Place; PRINCE GEORGE'S; ★ **WASH**; mail Bowie z 20715; pop. incl. with Bowie (Inc. Place)
Belair Rockledge; RMC Place; PRINCE GEORGE'S; ★ **WASH**; mail Bowie z 20715; pop. incl. with Bowie (Inc. Place)
Belair Somerset; RMC Place; PRINCE GEORGE'S; ★ **WASH**; mail Bowie z 20715; pop. incl. with Bowie (Inc. Place)
Bel Air South; CDP-Census Area Only; HARFORD; ***185** B-15; ★ **BAL**; mail Bel Air z 21015; Ⓟ 26,421; Ⓒ 39,711; ◆ 43,074
Belair Tulip Grove; RMC Place; PRINCE GEORGE'S; ★ **WASH**; mail Bowie z 20715; pop. incl. with Bowie (Inc. Place)
Belair White Hall; RMC Place; PRINCE GEORGE'S; ★ **WASH**; mail Bowie z 20715; pop. incl. with Bowie (Inc. Place)
Belair Yorktown; RMC Place; PRINCE GEORGE'S; ★ **WASH**; mail Bowie z 20715; pop. incl. with Bowie (Inc. Place)
Bel Alton (Cox); RMC Place; CHARLES; **185** H-12; elev. 173ft./53m.; 🅿; z 20611; ● 1,000
Belcamp; HARFORD; see Riverside (CDP-Census Area Only)
Belhaven; RMC Place; ANNE ARUNDEL; **184** N-6; ★ **BAL**; mail Pasadena z 21122; ● 500
Belleair Estates; RMC Place; PRINCE GEORGE'S; ***185** G-12; ★ **WASH**; mail Fort Washington z 20744
Belle Farm Estates; RMC Place; BALTIMORE; ***185** C-13; ★ **BAL**; mail Pikesville z 21208; ● 3,300
Bellefonte; RMC Place; PRINCE GEORGE'S; ***185** F-12; ★ **WASH**; mail Clinton z 20735; ● 900
Belle Grove; RMC Place; ALLEGANY; ***184** A-6; mail Little Orleans z 21766; rural
Bellemead; RMC Place; PRINCE GEORGE'S; ***185** F-12; ★ **WASH**; mail Hyattsville z 20784; ● 1,000
Belleview Estates; RMC Place; ANNE ARUNDEL; ***185** E-14; ★ **BAL**; mail Severna Park z 21146
Bellevue; RMC Place; TALBOT; **185** G-15; mail Royal Oak z 21662; ● 330
Bellevue Estates; RMC Place; PRINCE GEORGE'S; ***185** G-12; ★ **WASH**; mail Accokeek z 20607
Bells Mill Village; RMC Place; MONTGOMERY; ***185** E-11; ★ **WASH**; mail Potomac z 20854
Belltown; RMC Place; BALTIMORE; **184** F-1; ★ **BAL**
Belmar; RMC Place; BALTIMORE; ***185** C-14; ★ **BAL**; mail Baltimore z 21206; pop. incl. with Baltimore (Independent City)
Bel Pre Estates; RMC Place; MONTGOMERY; ***185** E-11; ★ **WASH**; mail Silver Spring z 20906
Bel Pre Park; RMC Place; MONTGOMERY; ***185** E-11; ★ **WASH**; mail Silver Spring z 20906
Bel Pre Woods; RMC Place; MONTGOMERY; ***185** E-11; ★ **WASH**; mail Rockville z 20853
Beltsville; CDP; PRINCE GEORGE'S; **185** E-12; elev. 128ft./39m.; 🅿; ★ **WASH**; z 20704-05; Ⓟ 14,476; Ⓒ 15,690
Beltsville Heights; RMC Place; PRINCE GEORGE'S; ***185** E-12; ★ **WASH**; mail Beltsville z 20705
Belvedere Heights; RMC Place; ANNE ARUNDEL; **185** E-14; ★ **BAL**; mail Arnold z 21012; ● 5,600
Bembe Beach; RMC Place; ANNE ARUNDEL; **185** M-20; ★ **ANPLS**; mail Annapolis z 21403; pop. incl. with Annapolis (Inc. Place)
Benedict; RMC Place; CHARLES; **185** H-13; elev. 9ft./3m.; 🅿; ★ **WASH**; z 20612; ● 600
Benevola; RMC Place; WASHINGTON; ***184** B-9; ★ **HAG**; mail Boonsboro z 21713
Bennsville; CDP; CHARLES; ***185** G-12; ★ **WASH**; mail Waldorf z 20603; Ⓒ 7,325
Ben Oaks; RMC Place; ANNE ARUNDEL; ***185** E-13; elev. 100ft./30m.; ★ **BAL**; mail Severna Park z 21146
Benson; RMC Place; HARFORD; ***185** B-14; elev. 434ft./132m.; 🅿; ★ **BAL**; z 21018
Bentley Springs; RMC Place; BALTIMORE; **185** A-13; elev. 502ft./153m.; 🅿; ★ **BAL**; z 21120; ● 130
Bentons Pleasure; RMC Place; QUEEN ANNE'S; ***185** E-15; ★ **ANPLS**; mail Chester z 21619; ● 180
Berkley; RMC Place; HARFORD; ***185** A-15; elev. 348ft./106m.; ★ **BAL**; mail Darlington z 21034; ● 100
Berkshire; RMC Place; PRINCE GEORGE'S; ***185** F-12; ★ **WASH**; mail Suitland z 20746
Berlin; Inc. Place; WORCESTER; **185** I-20; elev. 45ft./14m.; 🅿 🅷; z 21811; Ⓟ 2,616; Ⓒ 3,491
Berrett; RMC Place; CARROLL; ***185** C-12; ★ **BAL**; mail Sykesville z 21784; ● 260
Berry; RMC Place; CHARLES; ***185** G-12; ★ **WASH**; mail Waldorf z 20603
Berrywood; RMC Place; ANNE ARUNDEL; ***185** E-14; elev. 20ft./6m.; ★ **BAL**; mail Severna Park z 21146; ● 1,200
Berwyn; RMC Place; PRINCE GEORGE'S; ***185** E-12; ★ **WASH**; mail College Park z 20740; pop. incl. with College Park (Inc. Place)
Berwyn Heights; Inc. Place; PRINCE GEORGE'S; **249** D-8; elev. 100ft./30m.; 🅿; ★ **WASH**; z 20740; Ⓟ 2,952; Ⓒ 2,942
Bestgate; RMC Place; ANNE ARUNDEL; ***185** E-14; ★ **ANPLS**; mail Annapolis z 21401
Bethany Manor; RMC Place; HOWARD; ***185** D-12; ★ **BAL**; mail Ellicott City z 21042; ● 500
Bethel; RMC Place; CARROLL; ***185** B-12; ★ **BAL**; mail Finksburg z 21048; rural
Bethel; RMC Place; CECIL; ***185** B-17; ★ **PHIL-**; mail Chesapeake City z 21915; rural
Bethel; RMC Place; FREDERICK; ***184** B-10; ★ **WASH**; mail Frederick z 21702; ● 330
Bethel (Bethelham); RMC Place; GARRETT; ***184** C-2; mail Oakland z 21550; rural
Bethelham; GARRETT; see Bethel (RMC Place)
Bethesda; CDP; MONTGOMERY; **185** E-11; elev. 305ft./93m.; 🅿 🅷; ★ **WASH**; z 20810-11, z 20813-17, z 20824-25, z 20827, z 20889, z 20892, z 20894; Ⓟ 62,936; Ⓒ 55,277; ◆ 58,710
Bethgate; RMC Place; HOWARD; ***185** C-12; ★ **BAL**; mail Ellicott City z 21043
Bethlehem; RMC Place; CAROLINE; **185** G-16; elev. 48ft./15m.; 🅿; z 21609; ● 150
Betterton; Inc. Place; KENT; **185** C-16; elev. 327ft./100m.; 🅿; z 21610; Ⓟ 360; Ⓒ 376
Beulah; RMC Place; DORCHESTER; ***185** G-17; mail Hurlock z 21643; rural
Beverly Beach; RMC Place; ANNE ARUNDEL; **185** F-14; ★ **ANPLS**; mail Edgewater z 21037, Mayo z 21106; ● 170
Beverly Estate; RMC Place; ST. MARY'S; ***185** I-13; elev. 100ft./30m.; ★ **WASH**; mail Mechanicsville z 20659; ● 100
Beverly Farms; RMC Place; MONTGOMERY; ***185** E-11; ★ **WASH**; mail Potomac z 20854
Beverly Knolls; RMC Place; CALVERT; ***185** G-13; elev. 100ft./30m.; ★ **WASH**; mail Huntingtown z 20639; ● 30
Biertown; RMC Place; ALLEGANY; ***184** B-3; elev. 751ft./229m.; ★ **CUMB**; mail Rawlings z 21557; rural
Big Pines; RMC Place; MONTGOMERY; ***185** E-11; ★ **WASH**; mail Rockville z 20850; ● 500
Big Pool; RMC Place; WASHINGTON; **184** B-7; elev. 435ft./133m.; 🅿; z 21711; ● 300
Big Spring; RMC Place; WASHINGTON; **184** B-8; elev. 440ft./134m.; 🅿; ★ **HAG**; z 21722; ● 30
Bigwoods; RMC Place; KENT; ***185** D-16; elev. 71ft./22m.; mail Worton z 21678; ● 120
Billingsley Forest; RMC Place; CHARLES; ***185** G-12; ★ **WASH**; mail Bryans Road z 20616; ● 400
Birchwood City; RMC Place; PRINCE GEORGE'S; ***185** F-12; ★ **WASH**; mail Oxon Hill z 20745; ● 5,500
Birchwood Gardens; RMC Place; PRINCE GEORGE'S; ***185** E-12; ★ **WASH**; mail Laurel z 20708
Birdlawn; RMC Place; PRINCE GEORGE'S; ***185** G-12; ★ **WASH**; mail Fort Washington z 20744
Bird River Beach; RMC Place; BALTIMORE; ***185** C-14; ★ **BAL**; mail Middle River z 21220; ● 220
Birdsville; RMC Place; ANNE ARUNDEL; **185** F-14; ★ **WASH**; mail Harwood z 20776; ● 250
Birmingham Estates; RMC Place; PRINCE GEORGE'S; ***185** E-12; ★ **WASH**; mail Beltsville z 20705
Birmingham Terrace; RMC Place; PRINCE GEORGE'S; ***185** E-12; ★ **WASH**; mail Beltsville z 20705
Bishop; RMC Place; WORCESTER; **185** H-20; elev. 44ft./13m.; mail Bishopville z 21813; ● 40
Bishops Head; RMC Place; DORCHESTER; **185** I-16; elev. 3ft./1m.; mail Toddville z 21672; ● 200
Bishopville; RMC Place; WORCESTER; **185** H-20; elev. 14ft./4m.; 🅿; z 21813; ● 280
Bitter Sweet; RMC Place; ANNE ARUNDEL; ***185** E-14; ★ **ANPLS**; mail Annapolis z 21403; ● 340
Bittinger; RMC Place; GARRETT; **184** B-2; elev. 2,673ft./815m.; 🅿; z 21522; ● 70
Bivalve; RMC Place; WICOMICO; **185** I-17; 🅿; z 21814; ● 350
Black Horse; RMC Place; HARFORD; **185** B-14; ★ **BAL**; mail White Hall z 21161; ● 130
Blackrock Estates; RMC Place; MONTGOMERY; ***184** D-10; elev. 400ft./122m.; ★ **WASH**; mail Germantown z 20874; ● 110
Blacks Corner; RMC Place; CARROLL; ***185** A-11; mail Westminster z 21157; ● 120
Blackwater; RMC Place; DORCHESTER; ***185** I-16; mail Church Creek z 21622; rural
Bladensburg; Inc. Place; PRINCE GEORGE'S; **249** F-8; elev. 45ft./14m.; 🅿; ★ **WASH**; z 20710; Ⓟ 8,064; Ⓒ 7,661
Bladenwoods; RMC Place; PRINCE GEORGE'S; ★ **WASH**; mail Bladensburg z 20710; pop. incl. with Bladensburg (Inc. Place)
Blair; RMC Place; MONTGOMERY; ***185** E-12; elev. 250ft./76m.; ★ **WASH**; mail Silver Spring z 20910
Blenheim; RMC Place; BALTIMORE; ***185** B-14; ★ **BAL**; mail Phoenix z 21131; ● 220
Bloomfield; RMC Place; FREDERICK; ***184** B-10; ★ **WASH**; mail Frederick z 21702; rural
Bloomfield; RMC Place; TALBOT; ***185** F-16; elev. 16ft./5m.; mail Easton z 21601; rural
Blooming Rose; RMC Place; GARRETT; ***184** A-1; elev. 2,000ft./610m.; mail Friendsville z 21531; rural
Bloomington; RMC Place; GARRETT; **184** B-2; elev. 1,049ft./320m.; 🅿; z 21523; ● 350
Bloomsbury; RMC Place; BALTIMORE; ***185** D-13; ★ **BAL**; mail Catonsville z 21228
Blossom Hills; RMC Place; ANNE ARUNDEL; ***185** D-14; ★ **BAL**; mail Pasadena z 21122; ● 680
Blueball; RMC Place; CECIL; ***185** A-16; elev. 374ft./114m.; ★ **PHIL-**; mail Elkton z 21921; rural
Blueberry Hills; RMC Place; MONTGOMERY; ★ **WASH**; mail Derwood z 20855
Blue Hill; RMC Place; WASHINGTON; ***184** A-6; mail Hancock z 21750; pop. incl. with Hancock (Inc. Place)
Blue Mount; RMC Place; BALTIMORE; ***185** B-13; ★ **BAL**; mail Monkton z 21111; rural
Blue Mountain; RMC Place; FREDERICK; ***184** B-10; mail Thurmont z 21788; ● 100
Blue Mountain; RMC Place; WASHINGTON; ***184** A-9; ★ **HAG**; mail Smithsburg z 21783; ● 100
Blue Ridge Manor; RMC Place; MONTGOMERY; ***185** E-11; ★ **WASH**; mail Silver Spring z 20902
Blue Ridge View; RMC Place; CARROLL; ***185** B-12; ★ **BAL**; mail Westminster z 21157; rural
Blythedale; RMC Place; CECIL; ***185** B-16; mail Perryville z 21903; ● 150
Bolivar Heights; RMC Place; FREDERICK; ***184** C-9; elev. 515ft./157m.; ★ **WASH**; mail Middletown z 21769; ● 100
Bolton; RMC Place; CHARLES; ***185** G-12; ★ **WASH**; mail Waldorf z 20603; ● 30
Bond Mill Park; RMC Place; PRINCE GEORGE'S; ***185** E-12; ★ **WASH**; mail Laurel z 20707; ● 1,000
Bonds; RMC Place; PRINCE GEORGE'S; ***185** G-11; elev. 50ft./15m.; ★ **WASH**; mail Accokeek z 20607; rural
Bon Haven; RMC Place; ANNE ARUNDEL; ***185** E-14; ★ **ANPLS**; mail Annapolis z 21401
Bonnie Acres; RMC Place; HOWARD; ***185** D-13; ★ **BAL**; mail Ellicott City z 21043; ● 150
Bonnie Brae; RMC Place; CARROLL; ***185** C-12; ★ **BAL**; mail Sykesville z 21784; ● 1,250
Bonnie Brook; RMC Place; DORCHESTER; ***185** H-16; mail Cambridge z 21613; ● 250
Bonnie Knob; RMC Place; FREDERICK; mail Woodsboro z 21798; pop. incl. with Woodsboro (Inc. Place)
Bonnie Ridge; RMC Place; BALTIMORE; ***185** C-13; ★ **BAL**; mail Baltimore z 21209; ● 2,500
Boonsboro; RMC Place; CAROLINE; **185** E-17; 🅿; z 21713
Boonsboro; Inc. Place; WASHINGTON; **184** B-9; elev. 591ft./180m.; 🅿; ★ **HAG**; z 21713; Ⓟ 2,445; Ⓒ 2,803
Borden Shaft; RMC Place; ALLEGANY; ***184** B-3; elev. 794ft./242m.; ★ **CUMB**; mail Frostburg z 21532; ● 100
Boring; RMC Place; BALTIMORE; **185** B-13; elev. 680ft./207m.; 🅿; ★ **BAL**; z 21020; ● 300
Boulevard Heights; RMC Place; PRINCE GEORGE'S; ***185** F-12; elev. 235ft./72m.; ★ **WASH**; mail Capitol Heights z 20743; ● 1,750
Boulevard Park on the Magothy; RMC Place; ANNE ARUNDEL; ***185** E-14; ★ **BAL**; mail Pasadena z 21122
Bowens; RMC Place; CALVERT; **185** H-13; elev. 151ft./46m.; ★ **WASH**; mail Prince Frederick z 20678; ● 50
Bowie; Inc. Place; PRINCE GEORGE'S; **185** E-13; elev. 150ft./46m.; 🅿 🅲 5,292; ★ **WASH**; z 20715-21; Ⓟ 37,589; Ⓒ 50,269; ◆ 53,711
Bowleys Quarters; CDP; BALTIMORE; ***185** C-14; ★ **BAL**; mail Middle River z 21220; Ⓟ 5,595; Ⓒ 6,314
Bowling Green (Roberts); RMC Place; ALLEGANY; **184** B-4; ★ **CUMB**; mail Cumberland z 21502; ● 1,800
Bowlings Alley; RMC Place; CHARLES; ***185** H-12; mail Charlotte Hall z 20622; ● 30
Boxhill North; RMC Place; HARFORD; ***185** B-15; ★ **BAL**; mail Abingdon z 21009; ● 3,700
Boxiron; RMC Place; WORCESTER; **185** J-19; elev. 16ft./5m.; mail Girdletree z 21829; ● 110
Boxwood Village; RMC Place; PRINCE GEORGE'S; ***185** E-12; ★ **WASH**; mail Greenbelt z 20770; pop. incl. with Greenbelt (Inc. Place)
Boyd; MONTGOMERY; see Boyds (RMC Place)
Boyds (Boyd); RMC Place; MONTGOMERY; **184** D-10; elev. 422ft./129m.; 🅿; ★ **WASH**; z 20841; ● 900
Boyer Mill Heights; RMC Place; FREDERICK; ***184** C-10; ★ **WASH**; mail New Midway z 21775
Bozman; RMC Place; TALBOT; **185** G-15; 🅿; z 21612; ● 440
Bradbury Heights; RMC Place; PRINCE GEORGE'S; ***185** F-12; ★ **WASH**; mail Capitol Heights z 20743; ● 1,550
Bradbury Park; RMC Place; PRINCE GEORGE'S; ***185** F-12; elev. 293ft./89m.; ★ **WASH**; mail Suitland z 20746
Braddock; RMC Place; FREDERICK; ***184** C-10; elev. 516ft./157m.; ★ **WASH**; mail Frederick z 21702; ● 550
Braddock Estates; RMC Place; ALLEGANY; ***184** A-3; ★ **CUMB**; mail Frostburg z 21532; pop. incl. with Frostburg (Inc. Place)
Braddock Heights; CDP; FREDERICK; **184** C-9; elev. 900ft./274m.; 🅿; ★ **WASH**; z 21714; Ⓟ 4,778; Ⓒ 4,627
Bradley Farms; RMC Place; MONTGOMERY; ***185** E-11; ★ **WASH**; mail Potomac z 20854
Bradley Hills; RMC Place; MONTGOMERY; ***185** E-11; ★ **WASH**; mail Bethesda z 20817
Bradley Hills Grove; RMC Place; MONTGOMERY; ***185** E-11; ★ **WASH**; mail Bethesda z 20817
Bradley Woods; RMC Place; MONTGOMERY; ***185** E-11; ★ **WASH**; mail Bethesda z 20817
Bradshaw; RMC Place; BALTIMORE; **185** C-14; elev. 41ft./12m.; 🅿; ★ **BAL**; z 21087; ● 500
Brady; RMC Place; ALLEGANY; ***184** B-4; ★ **CUMB**; mail Cumberland z 21502
Braebrook Village (Goddard Space Village); RMC Place; PRINCE GEORGE'S; ***185** E-12; ★ **WASH**; mail Greenbelt z 20770; ● 670
Bramblewood; RMC Place; HARFORD; ***185** B-15; elev. 400ft./122m.; ★ **BAL**; mail Churchville z 21028; ● 80
Branchville; RMC Place; PRINCE GEORGE'S; ***185** E-12; ★ **WASH**; mail College Park z 20740; pop. incl. with College Park (Inc. Place)
Brandwine Farms; RMC Place; HARFORD; ***185** B-14; ★ **BAL**; mail Fallston z 21047
Brandywine; CDP; PRINCE GEORGE'S; **185** G-12; elev. 234ft./71m.; 🅿; ★ **WASH**; z 20613; Ⓟ 1,406; Ⓒ 1,410
Brandywine Country; RMC Place; PRINCE GEORGE'S; ***185** G-13; ★ **WASH**; mail Upper Marlboro z 20772; ● 2,300
Brandywine Heights; RMC Place; PRINCE GEORGE'S; ***185** G-12; ★ **WASH**; mail Brandywine z 20613
Breathedsville; RMC Place; WASHINGTON; ***184** B-9; ★ **HAG**; mail Hagerstown z 21740; ● 150
Breezewood Farms; RMC Place; HOWARD; ***185** C-12; ★ **BAL**; mail Woodstock z 21163; ● 50
Breezy Point (Breezy Point Beach); RMC Place; CALVERT; **185** G-14; ★ **WASH**; mail Chesapeake Beach z 20732; ● 230
Breezy Point Beach; RMC Place; BALTIMORE; ***185** D-14; ★ **BAL**; mail Essex z 21221; ● 350
Breezy Point Beach; CALVERT; see Breezy Point (RMC Place)
Brentwood; Inc. Place; PRINCE GEORGE'S; **249** F-8; elev. 40ft./12m.; 🅿; ★ **WASH**; z 20722; Ⓟ 3,005; Ⓒ 2,844
Breton Beach; RMC Place; ST. MARY'S; ***185** J-13; ★ **WASH**; mail Leonardtown z 20650; ● 220
Briarcrest Heights; RMC Place; FREDERICK; ***184** C-9; ★ **WASH**; mail Jefferson z 21755; ● 650
Briarwood; RMC Place; CHARLES; ***185** G-12; ★ **WASH**; mail Waldorf z 20601
Briarwood; RMC Place; PRINCE GEORGE'S; ***185** E-12; ★ **WASH**; mail Laurel z 20708
Briddletown; RMC Place; WORCESTER; ***185** I-20; mail Berlin z 21811; ● 30
Bridgeport; RMC Place; FREDERICK; ***185** A-11; mail Taneytown z 21787; rural
Bridgeport; RMC Place; WASHINGTON; **185** M-14; ★ **HAG**; mail Hagerstown z 21742; ● 860
Bridgetown; RMC Place; CAROLINE; **185** E-17; mail Goldsboro z 21636, Henderson z 21640; ● 80
Bright Oaks; RMC Place; HARFORD; ***185** B-15; ★ **BAL**; mail Bel Air z 21015; ● 3,200
Brighton; RMC Place; BALTIMORE; **184** H-3; ★ **BAL**; mail Windsor Mill z 21244; pop. incl. with Baltimore (Independent City)
Brighton; RMC Place; MONTGOMERY; **185** D-12; ★ **WASH**; mail Brookeville z 20833; ● 110
Brightview Woods; RMC Place; ANNE ARUNDEL; ***185** E-13; ★ **BAL**; mail Millersville z 21108
Brightwood Acres; RMC Place; WASHINGTON; **185** N-14; ★ **HAG**; mail Hagerstown z 21740
Brink; RMC Place; MONTGOMERY; ***185** D-11; elev. 626ft./191m.; ★ **WASH**; mail Germantown z 20876; rural
Brinkleigh; RMC Place; HOWARD; ***185** C-12; ★ **BAL**; mail Ellicott City z 21042
Brinkleigh Manor; RMC Place; HOWARD; ***185** D-12; ★ **BAL**; mail Ellicott City z 21042; ● 2,500
Brinkley Manor; RMC Place; PRINCE GEORGE'S; ***185** F-12; ★ **WASH**; mail Temple Hills z 20748; ● 1,400
Brinklow; RMC Place; MONTGOMERY; **185** D-12; elev. 459ft./140m.; 🅿; ★ **WASH**; z 20862; ● 300
Bristol; RMC Place; ANNE ARUNDEL; **185** F-13; ★ **WASH**; mail Lothian z 20711; ● 30
Broad Creek; RMC Place; HARFORD; ***185** A-15; ★ **BAL**; mail Whiteford z 21160
Broadfording; RMC Place; WASHINGTON; ***184** A-8; elev. 400ft./122m.; ★ **HAG**; mail Clear Spring z 21722; ● 50
Broadmoor; RMC Place; BALTIMORE; ***185** B-13; ★ **BAL**; mail Cockeysville z 21030; ● 200
Broad Run; RMC Place; FREDERICK; ***184** C-9; ★ **WASH**; mail Jefferson z 21755
Broadview; RMC Place; HARFORD; ***185** B-15; elev. 300ft./91m.; ★ **BAL**; mail Aberdeen Proving Ground z 21005; ● 150
Broadview; RMC Place; PRINCE GEORGE'S; ***185** F-12; ★ **WASH**; mail Temple Hills z 20748
Broadview Acres; RMC Place; FREDERICK; ***184** C-10; ★ **WASH**; mail Frederick z 21701; ● 140
Broadwater Estates; RMC Place; PRINCE GEORGE'S; ***185** G-12; ★ **WASH**; mail Fort Washington z 20744; ● 180
Broadwater Point; RMC Place; ANNE ARUNDEL; ***185** F-14; ★ **WASH**; mail Churchton z 20733
Broadwood Manor; RMC Place; MONTGOMERY; ***185** E-11; ★ **WASH**; mail Rockville z 20851; pop. incl. with Rockville (Inc. Place)
Brock Bridge; RMC Place; PRINCE GEORGE'S; ★ **WASH**; mail Laurel z 20708
Brock Hall; RMC Place; PRINCE GEORGE'S; ***185** F-13; ★ **WASH**; mail Upper Marlboro z 20774
Brock Hall Estates; RMC Place; PRINCE GEORGE'S; ***185** F-13; ★ **WASH**; mail Upper Marlboro z 20774
Brock Hall Gardens; RMC Place; PRINCE GEORGE'S; ***185** F-13; ★ **WASH**; mail Upper Marlboro z 20774
Brock Hall Manor; RMC Place; PRINCE GEORGE'S; ***185** F-13; ★ **WASH**; mail Upper Marlboro z 20774
Brookdale; RMC Place; MONTGOMERY; ***185** E-11; ★ **WASH**; mail Chevy Chase z 20815
Brookdale Heights; RMC Place; WICOMICO; ***185** I-18; ★ **SLSB**; mail Salisbury z 21804; ● 250
Brooke-Jane Manor; RMC Place; PRINCE GEORGE'S; ***185** G-12; ★ **WASH**; mail Clinton z 20735
Brooke Manor; RMC Place; PRINCE GEORGE'S; ***185** F-12; ★ **WASH**; mail Oxon Hill z 20745; ● 2,150
Brookemanor Estates; RMC Place; MONTGOMERY; ***185** D-11; ★ **WASH**; mail Rockville z 20853; ● 2,550
Brookeville; Inc. Place; MONTGOMERY; **185** D-11; elev. 400ft./122m.; 🅿; ★ **WASH**; z 20833; Ⓟ 54; Ⓒ 120
Brook Hill; RMC Place; FREDERICK; ***184** B-10; ★ **WASH**; mail Frederick z 21702; ● 330
Brooklandville; RMC Place; BALTIMORE; **184** G-4; elev. 300ft./91m.; 🅿; ★ **BAL**; z 21022; ● 1,700
Brooklyn; RMC Place; BALTIMORE (Independent City); ***185** D-13; 🅿; ★ **BAL**; z 21225 & mail Curtis Bay z 21226; pop. incl. with Baltimore (Independent City)
Brooklyn Park; CDP; ANNE ARUNDEL; **184** K-5; 🅿; ★ **BAL**; z 21225; Ⓟ 10,987; Ⓒ 10,938
Brookmead; RMC Place; MONTGOMERY; ***184** E-10; ★ **WASH**; mail Germantown z 20874; ● 260
Brookmead North; RMC Place; MONTGOMERY; ***184** E-10; ★ **WASH**; mail Germantown z 20874; ● 140
Brookmont; CDP; MONTGOMERY; **249** E-5; ★ **WASH**; mail Bethesda z 20816; Ⓒ 3,202
Brookside Forest; RMC Place; MONTGOMERY; ***185** E-12; ★ **WASH**; mail Silver Spring z 20901
Brookside Manor; RMC Place; PRINCE GEORGE'S; ***185** E-12; ★ **WASH**; mail Hyattsville z 20782
Brookview; Inc. Place; DORCHESTER; **185** H-17; elev. 24ft./7m.; mail Rhodesdale z 21659; Ⓟ 64; Ⓒ 65
Brookville Knolls; RMC Place; MONTGOMERY; ***185** D-11; ★ **WASH**; mail Brookeville z 20833
Brookwood; RMC Place; PRINCE GEORGE'S; **249** I-10; ★ **WASH**; mail Upper Marlboro z 20772; ● 2,200
Brookwood Estates; RMC Place; CHARLES; ***185** G-12; ★ **WASH**; mail White Plains z 20695
Broomes Island; RMC Place; CALVERT; **185** I-14; elev. 15ft./5m.; 🅿; z 20615; ● 550
Browns Corner; RMC Place; QUEEN ANNE'S; mail Centreville z 21617
Brownsville; RMC Place; QUEEN ANNE'S; **185** E-16; mail Centreville z 21617; ● 100
Brownsville; RMC Place; WASHINGTON; **184** C-9; elev. 533ft./162m.; 🅿; ★ **WASH**; z 21715; ● 210
Browns Woods Villa; RMC Place; ANNE ARUNDEL; **185** L-20; ★ **ANPLS**; mail Annapolis z 21401; ● 400
Bruceville; RMC Place; CARROLL; ***185** B-11; mail Keymar z 21757; ● 270
Bruceville; RMC Place; TALBOT; **185** G-16; mail Trappe z 21673; ● 60
Brunswick; Inc. Place; FREDERICK; **184** C-9; elev. 247ft./75m.; 🅿; ★ **WASH**; z 21716, z 21758; Ⓟ 5,117; Ⓒ 4,894
Bryans Road; CDP; CHARLES; **185** G-11; elev. 180ft./55m.; 🅿; ★ **WASH**; z 20616; Ⓟ 3,809; Ⓒ 4,912
Bryantown; RMC Place; CHARLES; **185** H-12; elev. 140ft./43m.; 🅿; ★ **WASH**; z 20617; ● 1,000
Bryantown; RMC Place; QUEEN ANNE'S; ***185** F-15; ★ **ANPLS**; mail Queenstown z 21658
Bryant Square; RMC Place; HOWARD; ***185** D-12; ★ **BAL**; mail Columbia z 21044
Bryant Woods; RMC Place; HOWARD; ***185** D-12; ★ **BAL**; mail Columbia z 21044
Buckeystown; RMC Place; FREDERICK; **184** C-10; elev. 260ft./79m.; 🅿; ★ **WASH**; z 21717; ● 350
Buckingham Terrace; RMC Place; MONTGOMERY; ***185** E-12; ★ **WASH**
Buckingham View; RMC Place; CARROLL; ***185** B-12; ★ **BAL**; mail Westminster z 21157; ● 400
Buck Lodge; RMC Place; PRINCE GEORGE'S; ***185** E-12; ★ **WASH**; mail Hyattsville z 20783; ● 1,100
Bucktown; RMC Place; DORCHESTER; **185** H-16; elev. 5ft./2m.; mail Cambridge z 21613; ● 30
Budds Creek; RMC Place; ST. MARY'S; ***185** I-12; ★ **WASH**; mail Mechanicsville z 20659
Buena Vista; RMC Place; CALVERT; ***185** H-13; ★ **WASH**; mail Prince Frederick z 20678; ● 30
Buena Vista (Glenwood Park); RMC Place; PRINCE GEORGE'S; ***185** E-13; elev. 120ft./37m.; ★ **WASH**; mail Lanham z 20706; ● 310
Buffalo Run; RMC Place; GARRETT; mail Friendsville z 21531; rural
Burgundy Estates; RMC Place; MONTGOMERY; ★ **WASH**; mail Rockville z 20851; pop. incl. with Rockville (Inc. Place)
Burgundy Knolls; RMC Place; MONTGOMERY; ★ **WASH**; mail Rockville z 20850; pop. incl. with Rockville (Inc. Place)
Burgundy Village; RMC Place; MONTGOMERY; ★ **WASH**; mail Rockville z 20850; pop. incl. with Rockville (Inc. Place)
Burkittsville; Inc. Place; FREDERICK; **184** C-9; elev. 560ft./171m.; 🅿; ★ **WASH**; z 21718; Ⓟ 194; Ⓒ 171
Burning Tree Estates; RMC Place; MONTGOMERY; ***185** E-11; ★ **WASH**; mail Bethesda z 20817; ● 1,050
Burning Tree Manor; RMC Place; MONTGOMERY; ***185** E-11; ★ **WASH**; mail Bethesda z 20817
Burns Corner; RMC Place; HARFORD; ***185** B-15; mail Aberdeen z 21001; pop. incl. with Aberdeen (Inc. Place)
Burnt Mills; RMC Place; MONTGOMERY; ***185** E-12; ★ **WASH**; mail Silver Spring z 20901
Burnt Mills Hills; RMC Place; MONTGOMERY; ***185** E-12; ★ **WASH**; mail Silver Spring z 20901; ● 1,100
Burnt Mills Knolls; RMC Place; MONTGOMERY; ***185** E-12; ★ **WASH**; mail Silver Spring z 20901; ● 750
Burnt Mills Manor; RMC Place; MONTGOMERY; ***185** E-12; ★ **WASH**; mail Silver Spring z 20901; ● 750
Burnt Mills Village; RMC Place; MONTGOMERY; ***185** E-12; elev. 309ft./94m.; ★ **WASH**; mail Silver Spring z 20901
Burrisville; RMC Place; QUEEN ANNE'S; **185** E-16; mail Centreville z 21617; ● 100
Burrsville; RMC Place; CAROLINE; **185** F-17; mail Denton z 21629; ● 130
Burtner; RMC Place; WASHINGTON; ***184** B-9; ★ **HAG**; mail Boonsboro z 21713; rural
Burtonsville; CDP; MONTGOMERY; **185** E-12; elev. 486ft./148m.; 🅿; ★ **WASH**; z 20866; Ⓟ 5,853; Ⓒ 7,305
Bush (Bush River); RMC Place; HARFORD; **185** C-15; ★ **BAL**; mail Abingdon z 21009; ● 50
Bush River; HARFORD; see Bush (RMC Place)
Bushs Corner; RMC Place; HARFORD; ***185** A-14; elev. 539ft./164m.; ★ **BAL**; mail Pylesville z 21132; rural
Bushwood; RMC Place; ST. MARY'S; **185** I-13; elev. 137ft./42m.; 🅿; ★ **WASH**; z 20618; ● 400
Butler; RMC Place; BALTIMORE; **185** B-13; 🅿; ★ **BAL**; z 21023; ● 350
Butlertown; RMC Place; KENT; **185** D-16; mail Worton z 21678; ● 160
Buttercup Estates; RMC Place; HOWARD; ***185** C-12; ★ **BAL**; mail West Friendship z 21794; ● 110
Buttonwood Beach; RMC Place; CECIL; ***185** C-16; mail Earleville z 21919; summer pop. 1,000; ● 200
Byforde; RMC Place; MONTGOMERY; ***185** E-11; ★ **WASH**; mail Kensington z 20895
Bynum (Bynum Hills); RMC Place; HARFORD; ***185** B-15; ★ **BAL**; mail Forest Hill z 21050; ● 1,200
Bynum Hills; HARFORD; see Bynum (RMC Place)
Bynum Ridge; RMC Place; HARFORD; ***185** B-15; ★ **BAL**; mail Forest Hill z 21050; ● 2,700
Byrdtown; RMC Place; SOMERSET; **185** K-17; mail Crisfield z 21817; ● 110

C

Cabin Creek; RMC Place; DORCHESTER; ***185** G-17; mail Hurlock z 21643; rural
Cabin John; CDP; MONTGOMERY; **249** E-4; elev. 153ft./47m.; 🅿; ★ **WASH**; z 20818; Ⓒ 1,734
Cabin John Park; RMC Place; MONTGOMERY; ***185** E-11; ★ **WASH**; mail Cabin John z 20818
Cactus Hill; RMC Place; PRINCE GEORGE'S; ***185** G-11; ★ **WASH**; mail Accokeek z 20607; ● 30
Cadillac Homes; RMC Place; ANNE ARUNDEL; ***185** D-14; ★ **BAL**; mail Glen Burnie z 21060
California; CDP; ST. MARY'S; **185** I-14; elev. 116ft./35m.; 🅿; z 20619; Ⓟ 7,626; Ⓒ 9,307; Ⓡ 9,300
Callaway; RMC Place; ST. MARY'S; **185** J-14; 🅿; z 20620; ● 470
Caltor Manor; RMC Place; PRINCE GEORGE'S; ***185** G-12; ★ **WASH**; mail Fort Washington z 20744; ● 1,650
Calvary; RMC Place; HARFORD; ***185** B-15; elev. 305ft./93m.; ★ **BAL**; mail Churchville z 21028; ● 80
Calvert; RMC Place; BALTIMORE (Independent City); ***185** D-13; ★ **BAL**; mail Baltimore z 21202; pop. incl. with Baltimore (Independent City)
Calvert; RMC Place; CECIL; **185** A-16; ★ **PHIL-**; mail North East z 21901; ● 150
CALVERT; **185** G-13; Ⓟ 51,372; Ⓒ 74,563; ◆ 87,009
Calvert Beach; RMC Place; CALVERT; **185** H-14; mail Saint Leonard z 20685; ● 600
Calvert Beach-Long Beach; CDP-Census Area Only; CALVERT; ***185** H-14; mail Saint Leonard z 20685; Ⓟ 1,728; Ⓒ 2,487
Calvert Manor; RMC Place; PRINCE GEORGE'S; ***185** G-12; ★ **WASH**; mail Accokeek z 20607; ● 250
Calverton; CDP; PRINCE GEORGE'S, MONTGOMERY; **185** E-12; 🅿; ★ **WASH**; z 20705 & mail Silver Spring z 20904; Ⓟ 12,046; Ⓒ 12,610
Cambria; RMC Place; BALTIMORE; ***185** B-14; ★ **BAL**; mail Phoenix z 21131; ● 220
Cambridge; Inc. Place; ⊡ DORCHESTER; **185** H-16; elev. 14ft./4m.; 🅿 🅷; z 21613; Ⓟ 11,514; Ⓒ 10,911; Ⓡ 10,976
Cambridge Estates; RMC Place; PRINCE GEORGE'S; ***185** F-12; ★ **WASH**; mail Clinton z 20735
Camden; RMC Place; BALTIMORE (Independent City); ***185** D-13; ★ **BAL**; mail Baltimore z 21230; pop. incl. with Baltimore (Independent City)
Camden; RMC Place; WICOMICO; ★ **SLSB**; mail Allen z 21810; pop. incl. with Salisbury (Inc. Place)
Camelback Village; RMC Place; MONTGOMERY; ***185** D-11; ★ **WASH**; mail Olney z 20832
Camelot; RMC Place; HARFORD; ***185** B-15; ★ **BAL**; mail Bel Air z 21015; ● 2,400
Camelot; RMC Place; PRINCE GEORGE'S; ***185** E-13; ★ **WASH**; mail Glenn Dale z 20769
Cameron Heights; RMC Place; MONTGOMERY; ***185** E-12; ★ **WASH**
Camotop; RMC Place; MONTGOMERY; ***185** E-11; ★ **WASH**; mail Potomac z 20854
Campbell (Campbelltown); RMC Place; WORCESTER; ***185** H-20; elev. 25ft./8m.; mail Bishopville z 21813; rural
Campbelltown; WORCESTER; see Campbell (RMC Place)
Camp Leonard; RMC Place; CALVERT; ***185** I-14; elev. 95ft./29m.; mail Saint Leonard z 20685; ● 80
Camp Springs; CDP; PRINCE GEORGE'S; **249** I-8; 🅿; ★ **WASH**; z 20746, z 20748; Ⓟ 16,392; Ⓒ 17,968
Camp Springs Forest; RMC Place; PRINCE GEORGE'S; ***185** F-12; ★ **WASH**; mail Temple Hills z 20748
Campus Hills; RMC Place; BALTIMORE; ***185** C-14; ★ **BAL**; mail Towson z 21286
Canal; RMC Place; CECIL; mail Port Deposit z 21904; rural
Candlewood Park; RMC Place; MONTGOMERY; ***185** D-11; ★ **WASH**; mail Derwood z 20855
Cannon Acres; RMC Place; DORCHESTER; ***185** H-16; mail Cambridge z 21613; ● 100
Canton; RMC Place; BALTIMORE (Independent City); **184** J-4; ★ **BAL**; mail Baltimore z 21224; pop. incl. with Baltimore (Independent City)
Cape Anne; RMC Place; ANNE ARUNDEL; ***185** F-14; ★ **WASH**; mail Churchton z 20733
Cape Arthur; RMC Place; ANNE ARUNDEL; ***185** E-14; ★ **BAL**; mail Severna Park z 21146
Cape Estate; RMC Place; ANNE ARUNDEL; ***185** K-14; mail Arnold z 21012
Cape Isle of Wight; RMC Place; WORCESTER; **185** I-20; mail Ocean City z 21842; ● 750
Cape Loch Haven; RMC Place; ANNE ARUNDEL; ***185** F-14; ★ **ANPLS**; mail Edgewater z 21037; ● 950
Cape May Beach; RMC Place; BALTIMORE; ***185** C-14; ★ **BAL**; mail Essex z 21221
Cape Saint Claire; CDP; ANNE ARUNDEL; **185** E-14; 🅿; ★ **BAL**; z 21401; Ⓟ 7,878; Ⓒ 8,022
Cape Saint John; RMC Place; ANNE ARUNDEL; ***185** E-14; ★ **ANPLS**; mail Annapolis z 21401
Capital Estates; RMC Place; CHARLES; ***185** H-12; ★ **WASH**; mail White Plains z 20695
Capitola; RMC Place; WICOMICO; ***185** I-17; elev. 2ft./1m.; mail Tyaskin z 21865; rural
Capitol Heights; Inc. Place; PRINCE GEORGE'S; **185** F-12; elev. 109ft./33m.; 🅿; ★ **WASH**; z 20731, z 20743, z 20790-91, z 20799 & mail District Heights z 20753; Ⓟ 3,633; Ⓒ 4,138
Capitol Hills; RMC Place; ANNE ARUNDEL; ***185** D-13; ★ **BAL**; mail Glen Burnie z 21061
Capitol View Park; RMC Place; MONTGOMERY; ***185** E-11; ★ **WASH**; mail Silver Spring z 20910; ● 1,650
Capri Estate; RMC Place; ANNE ARUNDEL; ***185** K-14; mail Arnold z 21012
Captains Hill; RMC Place; WORCESTER; ***185** I-20; mail Ocean City z 21842; ● 320
Carderock Springs; RMC Place; MONTGOMERY; ***185** E-11; ★ **WASH**; mail Bethesda z 20817; ● 2,100
Cardiff; RMC Place; HARFORD; **185** A-15; elev. 460ft./140m.; 🅿; ★ **BAL**; z 21160; ● 300
Carea; RMC Place; HARFORD; ***185** A-14; elev. 625ft./191m.; ★ **BAL**; mail White Hall z 21161
Careytown; RMC Place; WORCESTER; ***185** H-19; elev. 36ft./11m.; mail Whaleyville z 21872; rural
Carleton East; RMC Place; PRINCE GEORGE'S; ***185** E-12; ★ **WASH**; mail Lanham z 20706; ● 3,200
Carlos; RMC Place; ALLEGANY; ***184** B-3; ★ **CUMB**; mail Frostburg z 21532; ● 150
Carlos; ALLEGANY; see National (RMC Place)
Carlson Spring; RMC Place; PRINCE GEORGE'S; ***185** F-12; ★ **WASH**; mail District Heights z 20747
Carmichael; RMC Place; QUEEN ANNE'S; **185** F-16; ★ **ANPLS**; mail Queenstown z 21658; ● 30
Carmody Hills; RMC Place; PRINCE GEORGE'S; ***185** F-12; ★ **WASH**; mail Capitol Heights z 20743; ● 1,550
Carmody Hills-Pepper Mill Village; CDP-Census Area Only; PRINCE GEORGE'S; ***185** F-12; ★ **WASH**; mail Capitol Heights z 20743; Ⓟ 4,815; Ⓒ 4,801
Carney; CDP; BALTIMORE; **184** G-7; ★ **BAL**; mail Parkville z 21234; Ⓟ 25,578; Ⓒ 28,264; ◆ 29,672
Carney Grove; RMC Place; BALTIMORE; ***185** C-14; ★ **BAL**; mail Parkville z 21234
Carney Heights; RMC Place; BALTIMORE; ***185** C-14; ★ **BAL**; mail Parkville z 21234
Carole Highlands; RMC Place; PRINCE GEORGE'S; ***185** E-12; ★ **WASH**; mail Hyattsville z 20782, Silver Spring z 20910; ● 2,850
CAROLINE; **185** F-17; Ⓟ 27,035; Ⓒ 29,772; ◆ 33,952
Carpenter Beach; CALVERT; see Plum Point (RMC Place)
Carpenter Point; RMC Place; CECIL; ***185** B-16; ★ **PHIL-**; mail Perryville z 21903; ● 400
Carroll; RMC Place; BALTIMORE (Independent City); ***185** D-13; 🅿; ★ **BAL**; z 21229; pop. incl. with Baltimore (Independent City)
CARROLL; **185** B-11; Ⓟ 123,372; Ⓒ 150,897; ◆ 167,143
Carroll County Trails; RMC Place; CARROLL; ***185** B-12; ★ **BAL**; mail Finksburg z 21048; ● 570
Carroll Heights; RMC Place; WASHINGTON; ★ **HAG**; mail Hagerstown z 21740; pop. incl. with Hagerstown (Inc. Place)

Entries in **UPPERCASE** are counties.
Entries in **bold** have populations of 2,500 or more.
Names in parentheses are alternate names.
Inc. Place — Incorporated Place
RMC Place — Rand McNally Designated Place
CDP — Census Designated Place
MCD — Minor Civil Division

⊡ County Seat
▲ Minor Civil Division
elev. Elevation
🅿 Post Office

🅷 Hospital
🅲 College
■ Principal Business Center
★ Ranally Metro Area (RMA) Abbreviation
z Zip Code(s)

Ⓟ Previous Census Population
Ⓡ Revised Census Population
Ⓐ Annexation Population
● Rand McNally Population Estimate
Ⓒ Final Census Population
Ⓢ Special Census Population
◆ Estimated Population

For additional definitions see Glossary, Volume 1, and Introduction, Volume 2.

Carroll Highlands; RMC Place; CARROLL; 185 C-12; ★ BAL; mail Sykesville z 21784; ● 2,000
Carroll Island; RMC Place; BALTIMORE; *185 C-14; ★ BAL; mail Middle River z 21220; ● 600
Carroll Knolls; RMC Place; MONTGOMERY; *185 E-11; ★ WASH; mail Silver Spring z 20910
Carroll Manor; RMC Place; MONTGOMERY; *185 E-12; ★ WASH; mail Takoma Park z 20912; pop. incl. with Takoma Park (Inc. Place)
Carrollton; RMC Place; CARROLL; *185 B-12; elev. 700ft./213m.; ★ BAL; mail Sykesville z 21784, Westminster z 21157
Carrollton; PRINCE GEORGE'S; see New Carrollton (Inc. Place)
Carrollton Manor; RMC Place; ANNE ARUNDEL; *185 E-14; ★ BAL; mail Severna Park z 21146
Carrollwood; RMC Place; BALTIMORE; *185 C-14; ★ BAL; mail Middle River z 21220
Carrollwood Estate; RMC Place; CARROLL; *185 C-11; ★ BAL; mail Mount Airy z 21771; ● 450
Carsins Run; RMC Place; HARFORD; 185 B-15; ★ BAL; mail Aberdeen z 21001; ● 100
Carsondale; RMC Place; PRINCE GEORGE'S; *185 F-12; ★ WASH; mail Lanham z 20706; ● 870
Carter Hill; RMC Place; MONTGOMERY; ★ WASH; mail Rockville z 20850; pop. incl. with Rockville (Inc. Place)
Carvel Beach; RMC Place; ANNE ARUNDEL; *185 D-14; ★ BAL; mail Curtis Bay z 21226
Carver Heights; RMC Place; ST. MARY'S; mail Lexington Park z 20653
Cascade; RMC Place; WASHINGTON; 184 A-10; elev. 1,360ft./415m.; 🅿; ★ HAG; z 21719; ● 1,000
Cashell Estates; RMC Place; MONTGOMERY; *185 D-11; ★ WASH; mail Derwood z 20855; ● 1,200
Casselman; RMC Place; GARRETT; *184 A-2; mail Grantsville z 21536; rural
Castle Hill Estates; RMC Place; WORCESTER; *185 J-19; elev. 28ft./9m.; mail Snow Hill z 21863; ● 50
Castle Marina; RMC Place; QUEEN ANNE'S; *185 E-15; ★ ANPLS; mail Chester z 21619; ● 220
Castleton; RMC Place; HARFORD; 185 A-15; ★ BAL; mail Darlington z 21034; ● 200
Catchpenny; RMC Place; WICOMICO; *185 I-18; mail Quantico z 21856; rural
Catoctin; FREDERICK; see Lander (RMC Place)
Catoctin Furnace; RMC Place; FREDERICK; *184 B-10; ★ WASH; mail Thurmont z 21788; ● 150
Catoctin View; RMC Place; FREDERICK; *185 C-11; ★ WASH; mail Mount Airy z 21771; ● 110
Catonsville; CDP; BALTIMORE; 184 J-2; elev. 478ft./146m.; 🅿 🄷; ★ BAL; z 21228 & mail Baltimore z 21250; Ⓟ 35,233; © 39,820; ◆ 41,801
Catonsville Heights; RMC Place; BALTIMORE; *185 D-13; ★ BAL; mail Catonsville z 21228
Catonsville Manor; RMC Place; BALTIMORE; 184 J-2; ★ BAL; mail Gwynn Oak z 21207; ● 2,600
Cavalier Country; RMC Place; CALVERT; *185 G-13; ★ WASH; mail Dunkirk z 20754; ● 400
Cavetown; CDP; WASHINGTON; 184 A-9; elev. 716ft./218m.; 🅿; ★ HAG; z 21720; © 1,486
Cayots (Cayots Corner); RMC Place; CECIL; *185 B-17; elev. 84ft./26m.; ★ PHIL-; mail Chesapeake City z 21915; rural
Cayots Corner; CECIL; see Cayots (RMC Place)
Cearfoss; RMC Place; WASHINGTON; 185 L-13; elev. 508ft./155m.; ★ HAG; mail Hagerstown z 21740; ● 300
CECIL; 185 B-17; Ⓟ 71,347; © 85,951; ◆ 100,008
Cecilton; Inc. Place; CECIL; 185 C-17; elev. 79ft./24m.; 🅿; z 21913; Ⓟ 489; © 474
Cedar Acres; RMC Place; HOWARD; *185 D-12; ★ BAL; mail Columbia z 21044
Cedar Beach; RMC Place; BALTIMORE; 185 D-14; ★ BAL; mail Essex z 21221; ● 500
Cedar Grove; RMC Place; MONTGOMERY; 185 D-11; ★ WASH; mail Germantown z 20876; ● 500
Cedar Grove Beach; RMC Place; DORCHESTER; *185 H-16; elev. 25ft./8m.; mail East New Market z 21631; ● 150
Cedar Hall; RMC Place; WORCESTER; *185 K-18; mail Pocomoke City z 21851; ● 50
Cedar Haven; RMC Place; PRINCE GEORGE'S; *185 H-13; ★ WASH; mail Aquasco z 20608; ● 100
Cedar Heights; RMC Place; PRINCE GEORGE'S; 249 F-8; ★ WASH; mail Capitol Heights z 20743; ● 1,150
Cedar Hill; RMC Place; CECIL; *185 A-17; elev. 360ft./110m.; ★ PHIL-; mail Elkton z 21921; rural
Cedarhurst; RMC Place; ANNE ARUNDEL; *185 F-14; ★ WASH; mail Shady Side z 20764
Cedarhurst (Lamotte); RMC Place; CARROLL; *185 B-12; ★ BAL; mail Finksburg z 21048; rural
Cedarhurst Acres; RMC Place; WICOMICO; *185 I-18; ★ SLSB; mail Hebron z 21830; ● 300
Cedarhurst-on-the-Bay; RMC Place; ANNE ARUNDEL; *185 F-14; ★ WASH; mail Shady Side z 20764
Cedar Lawn; RMC Place; WASHINGTON; 185 M-13; ★ HAG; mail Hagerstown z 21740; ● 400
Cedarmere; RMC Place; BALTIMORE; *185 C-13; ★ BAL; mail Owings Mills z 21117
Cedar Park; RMC Place; ANNE ARUNDEL; ★ ANPLS; mail Annapolis z 21401; pop. incl. with Annapolis (Inc. Place)
Cedar Ridge; RMC Place; ANNE ARUNDEL; ★ ANPLS; pop. incl. with Annapolis (Inc. Place)
Cedar Spring; RMC Place; HARFORD; *185 B-15; ★ BAL; mail Bel Air z 21015
Cedartown; RMC Place; WORCESTER; *185 J-19; mail Snow Hill z 21863
Cedarville; RMC Place; PRINCE GEORGE'S; 185 G-13; ★ WASH; mail Brandywine z 20613; ● 300
Centenial Village; RMC Place; WICOMICO; *185 I-18; elev. 40ft./12m.; ★ SLSB; mail Salisbury z 21801; ● 200
Centennial; RMC Place; HOWARD; *185 D-12; ★ BAL; mail Ellicott City z 21042
Centennial Estates; RMC Place; HOWARD; *185 D-12; ★ BAL; mail Ellicott City z 21042; ● 1,000
Center Court; RMC Place; MONTGOMERY; *185 D-11; ★ WASH; mail Gaithersburg z 20879
Centerville; RMC Place; FREDERICK; *184 C-10; ★ WASH; mail Ijamsville z 21754; ● 30
Centreville; Inc. Place; ⊡ QUEEN ANNE'S; 185 E-16; elev. 63ft./19m.; 🅿; z 21617; Ⓟ 2,097; © 1,970
Ceresville; RMC Place; FREDERICK; 184 C-10; ★ WASH; mail Frederick z 21701; ● 70
Chadwick Manor; RMC Place; BALTIMORE; *185 C-13; ★ BAL; mail Windsor Mill z 21244; ● 4,800
Chalfone Manor; RMC Place; BALTIMORE; *185 D-13; ★ BAL; mail Catonsville z 21228
Chalk Point; RMC Place; ANNE ARUNDEL; *185 F-14; ★ WASH; mail West River z 20778
Champ (Saint Peters Creek); RMC Place; SOMERSET; 185 J-17; mail Princess Anne z 21853; ● 100
Chance (Rock Creek); CDP; SOMERSET; 185 J-17; elev. 3ft./1m.; 🅿; z 21821; © 377
Chaney; RMC Place; CALVERT; *185 G-13; ★ WASH; mail Dunkirk z 20754
Chaneyville; RMC Place; CALVERT; 185 G-13; elev. 118ft./36m.; ★ WASH; mail Owings z 20736; ● 90
Chaneyville Farm Estates; RMC Place; CALVERT; *185 G-13; ★ WASH; mail Owings z 20736; ● 150
Chapel; RMC Place; HARFORD; *185 B-15; elev. 300ft./91m.; mail Aberdeen z 21001; ● 30
Chapel; RMC Place; TALBOT; *185 F-16; mail Easton z 21601; ● 50
Chapel Gate; RMC Place; ANNE ARUNDEL; *185 E-13; ★ BAL; mail Odenton z 21113
Chapel Hill; RMC Place; PRINCE GEORGE'S; *185 G-12; ★ WASH; mail Fort Washington z 20744
Chapel Hill Estates; RMC Place; CALVERT; *185 H-14; ★ WASH; mail Barstow z 20610; ● 80
Chapel Oaks; RMC Place; PRINCE GEORGE'S; *185 F-12; ★ WASH; mail Capitol Heights z 20743; ● 2,650
Chapelview; RMC Place; HOWARD; *185 D-13; ★ BAL; mail Ellicott City z 21043
Chaptico; RMC Place; ST. MARY'S; 185 I-13; elev. 8ft./2m.; 🅿; ★ WASH; z 20621; ● 850
CHARLES; 185 H-11; Ⓟ 101,154; © 120,546; ◆ 140,400
Charles Manor; RMC Place; HARFORD; *185 C-14; ★ BAL; mail Fallston z 21047
Charlesmont; RMC Place; BALTIMORE; *185 D-14; ★ BAL; mail Dundalk z 21222
Charlestown; RMC Place; ALLEGANY; *184 B-3; ★ CUMB; mail Lonaconing z 21539; pop. incl. with Lonaconing (Inc. Place)
Charlestown; Inc. Place; CECIL; 185 B-16; elev. 42ft./13m.; 🅿; ★ PHIL-; z 21914; Ⓟ 578; © 1,019
Charlestown Manor Beach; RMC Place; CECIL; *185 B-16; ★ PHIL-; mail North East z 21901; pop. incl. with Charlestown (Inc. Place)
Charlesville; RMC Place; FREDERICK; *184 B-10; ★ WASH; mail Frederick z 21702; ● 160
Charlotte Hall; CDP; ST. MARY'S, CHARLES; 185 H-13; 🅿; ★ WASH; z 20622; Ⓟ 1,992; © 1,214
Charlton; RMC Place; WASHINGTON; *184 B-8; ★ HAG; mail Clear Spring z 21722; ● 30
Char-Nor Manor; RMC Place; QUEEN ANNE'S; *185 D-16; elev. 20ft./6m.; mail Chestertown z 21620; ● 30
Charred Oak Estates; RMC Place; MONTGOMERY; *185 E-11; ★ WASH; mail Bethesda z 20817
Chartley; RMC Place; BALTIMORE; *185 C-12; ★ BAL; mail Reisterstown z 21136
Chartridge; RMC Place; ANNE ARUNDEL; *185 E-14; ★ BAL; mail Severna Park z 21146
Chartwell; RMC Place; ANNE ARUNDEL; *185 E-14; ★ BAL; mail Severna Park z 21146
Chase; RMC Place; BALTIMORE; 185 C-15; elev. 20ft./6m.; 🅿; ★ BAL; z 21027; ● 920
Chateau Valley; RMC Place; HOWARD; *185 D-12; ★ BAL; mail Ellicott City z 21042; ● 1,900
Chatham; RMC Place; PRINCE GEORGE'S; *185 E-12; ★ WASH; mail Hyattsville z 20783
Chattolanee; RMC Place; BALTIMORE; *185 C-13; ★ BAL; mail Owings Mills z 21117
Chelsea Beach; RMC Place; ANNE ARUNDEL; 185 E-14; ★ BAL; mail Pasadena z 21122; ● 3,300
Chelsea Woods; RMC Place; PRINCE GEORGE'S; ★ WASH; mail Greenbelt z 20770; pop. incl. with Greenbelt (Inc. Place)
Cheltenham; RMC Place; PRINCE GEORGE'S; 185 G-12; elev. 238ft./73m.; 🅿; ★ WASH; z 20588, z 20623; ● 950
Cheltenham Forest; RMC Place; PRINCE GEORGE'S; *185 G-12; ★ WASH; mail Clinton z 20735; ● 980
Chelten Park; RMC Place; PRINCE GEORGE'S; *185 G-12; ★ WASH; mail Clinton z 20735
Cherry Hill; RMC Place; CECIL; 185 A-17; ★ PHIL-; mail Elkton z 21921; ● 500
Cherry Hill; RMC Place; HARFORD; *185 A-14; ★ BAL; mail Street z 21154; rural
Cherry Hill; RMC Place; PRINCE GEORGE'S; *185 E-12; ★ WASH; mail College Park z 20740; pop. incl. with College Park (Inc. Place)
Cherrywalk; RMC Place; WICOMICO; *185 I-17; mail Hebron z 21830; rural
Chesaco Park; RMC Place; BALTIMORE; 184 J-7; elev. 38ft./12m.; ★ BAL; mail Rosedale z 21237; ● 450
Chesapeake Beach; Inc. Place; CALVERT; 185 G-14; elev. 20ft./6m.; 🅿; ★ WASH; z 20732; Ⓟ 2,403; © 3,180
Chesapeake City; Inc. Place; CECIL; 185 B-17; elev. 20ft./6m.; 🅿; ★ PHIL-; z 21915; Ⓟ 735; © 787
Chesapeake Estates; RMC Place; QUEEN ANNE'S; *185 F-15; ★ ANPLS; mail Stevensville z 21666; ● 290
Chesapeake Haven; RMC Place; CECIL; *185 C-16; elev. 43ft./13m.; mail Earleville z 21919; ● 250
Chesapeake Heights; RMC Place; WICOMICO; 185 I-18; ★ SLSB; mail Salisbury z 21804; ● 550
Chesapeake Isle; RMC Place; CECIL; *185 C-16; ★ PHIL-; mail North East z 21901; ● 520
Chesapeake Landing; RMC Place; KENT; *185 D-16; elev. 44ft./13m.; mail Chestertown z 21620; ● 200
Chesapeake Ranch Estates; RMC Place; CALVERT; *185 I-14; mail Lusby z 20657; ● 3,800
Chesapeake Ranch Estates-Drum Point; CDP-Census Area Only; CALVERT; *185 I-14; © 11,503
Chesapeake Terrace; RMC Place; BALTIMORE; *185 D-14; ★ BAL; mail Dundalk z 21222
Cheshaven; RMC Place; CECIL; *185 C-16; mail Earleville z 21919; ● 150
Chester; CDP; QUEEN ANNE'S; 185 E-15; elev. 16ft./5m.; 🅿; ★ ANPLS; z 21619; © 3,723
Chesterfield; RMC Place; ANNE ARUNDEL; *185 E-13; ★ WASH; mail Crownsville z 21032; ● 100
Chesterfield Gardens; RMC Place; ANNE ARUNDEL; *185 D-14; ★ BAL; mail Pasadena z 21122; ● 710
Chester Harbor; RMC Place; QUEEN ANNE'S; *185 D-16; elev. 23ft./7m.; mail Chestertown z 21620
Chester River Beach; RMC Place; QUEEN ANNE'S; *185 E-15; ★ ANPLS; mail Grasonville z 21638
Chestertown; Inc. Place; ⊡ KENT; 185 D-16; elev. 22ft./7m.; 🅿 🄷 🄲 1,307; z 21620, z 21690; Ⓟ 4,005; © 4,746
Chesterville; RMC Place; KENT; 185 D-17; elev. 55ft./17m.; mail Millington z 21651; ● 100
Chesterville Forest; RMC Place; KENT; *185 D-17; mail Millington z 21651; ● 200
Chestnut Grove; RMC Place; FREDERICK; *184 C-10; elev. 619ft./189m.; ★ WASH; mail Frederick z 21701; rural
Chestnut Grove; RMC Place; WASHINGTON; *184 C-9; ★ WASH; mail Keedysville z 21756; ● 40
Chestnut Hill; RMC Place; BALTIMORE; *185 C-13; ★ BAL; mail Towson z 21286
Chestnut Hill; RMC Place; HARFORD; *185 B-15; elev. 408ft./124m.; ★ BAL; mail Forest Hill z 21050; ● 80
Chestnut Hill; RMC Place; HOWARD; *185 D-13; ★ BAL; mail Ellicott City z 21043
Chestnut Hill Estates; RMC Place; HOWARD; *185 D-13; ★ BAL; mail Ellicott City z 21043
Chestnut Hills; RMC Place; PRINCE GEORGE'S; *185 E-12; ★ WASH; mail Beltsville z 20705
Chestnut Ridge; RMC Place; BALTIMORE; 184 E-1; ★ BAL; mail Owings Mills z 21117; ● 230
Chestnut Ridge; RMC Place; PRINCE GEORGE'S; *185 E-12; ★ WASH; mail Riverdale z 20737
Cheverly; Inc. Place; PRINCE GEORGE'S; 249 F-8; elev. 100ft./30m.; 🅿 🄷; ★ WASH; z 20784-85 & mail Hyattsville z 20781; Ⓟ 6,023; © 6,433
Cheverly Manor; RMC Place; PRINCE GEORGE'S; ★ WASH; mail Hyattsville z 20785; ● 300
Chevy Chase; Inc. Place; MONTGOMERY; *185 E-11; 🅿; ★ WASH; z 20815, z 20825 & mail Bethesda z 20813; Ⓟ 2,675; © 2,726
Chevy Chase; CDP-Census Area Only; MONTGOMERY; 249 E-5; elev. 350ft./107m.; 🅿; ★ WASH; z 20815, z 20825 & mail Bethesda z 20813; Ⓟ 8,559; © 9,381
Chevy Chase Lake; RMC Place; MONTGOMERY; *185 E-11; ★ WASH; mail Chevy Chase z 20815
Chevy Chase Manor; RMC Place; MONTGOMERY; *185 E-11; ★ WASH; mail Chevy Chase z 20815
Chevy Chase Section Five; Inc. Place; MONTGOMERY; *185 E-11; ★ WASH; mail Chevy Chase z 20815; Ⓟ 632; © 641
Chevy Chase Section Three; Inc. Place; MONTGOMERY; *185 E-11; ★ WASH; mail Chevy Chase z 20815; Ⓟ 2,078; © 773
Chevy Chase Terrace; RMC Place; MONTGOMERY; *185 E-11; ★ WASH; mail Chevy Chase z 20815
Chevy Chase View; Inc. Place; MONTGOMERY; 249 D-5; ★ WASH; mail Kensington z 20895; © 863
Chevy Chase Village; Inc. Place; MONTGOMERY; *185 E-11; ★ WASH; mail Chevy Chase z 20815; Ⓟ 749; © 2,043
Chewsville; CDP; WASHINGTON; 184 A-9; elev. 636ft./194m.; 🅿; ★ HAG; z 21721; © 293
Chicamuxen; RMC Place; CHARLES; 185 H-11; ★ WASH; mail Indian Head z 20640; ● 100
Childs; RMC Place; CECIL; 185 A-17; elev. 139ft./42m.; 🅿; ★ PHIL-; z 21916; ● 370
Chillum; CDP; PRINCE GEORGE'S; 249 E-7; 🅿; ★ WASH; z 20782 & mail Silver Spring z 20910; Ⓟ 31,309; © 34,252; ◆ 34,353
Chillum Estates; RMC Place; PRINCE GEORGE'S; *185 E-12; ★ WASH; mail Hyattsville z 20783
Chillum Heights; RMC Place; PRINCE GEORGE'S; *185 E-12; ★ WASH; mail Hyattsville z 20783; ● 1,800
Chillum Manor; RMC Place; PRINCE GEORGE'S; *185 E-12; ★ WASH; mail Hyattsville z 20783
Chingville; RMC Place; ST. MARY'S; *185 J-14; elev. 110ft./34m.; ★ WASH; mail Callaway z 20620, Leonardtown z 20650; ● 220
Choptank; RMC Place; CAROLINE; 185 G-16; mail Preston z 21655; ● 100
Christs Rock; RMC Place; DORCHESTER; 185 H-16; mail Cambridge z 21613; ● 120
Church Creek; Inc. Place; DORCHESTER; 185 H-16; elev. 6ft./2m.; 🅿; z 21622; Ⓟ 113; © 85
Church Hill; RMC Place; FREDERICK; *184 C-10; ★ WASH; mail Myersville z 21773; rural
Church Hill; Inc. Place; QUEEN ANNE'S; 185 D-16; elev. 247ft./75m.; 🅿; z 21623, z 21656; Ⓟ 481; © 530
Churchill Town Sector; RMC Place; MONTGOMERY; *184 D-10; ★ WASH; mail Germantown z 20874; ● 3,800
Churchton; RMC Place; ANNE ARUNDEL; *185 F-14; 🅿; ★ WASH; z 20733
Churchville; RMC Place; HARFORD; 185 B-15; 🅿; ★ BAL; z 21028; ● 600
Cinnamon Ridge; RMC Place; PRINCE GEORGE'S; *185 F-12; ★ WASH; mail Upper Marlboro z 20774
Cissel Farms; RMC Place; HOWARD; *185 D-12; ★ WASH; mail Highland z 20777; ● 150
Claggettsville; RMC Place; MONTGOMERY; 185 C-11; ★ WASH; mail Damascus z 20872; ● 400
Claiborne; RMC Place; TALBOT; 185 F-15; elev. 8ft./2m.; 🅿; z 21624; ● 170
Clara; RMC Place; WICOMICO; *185 I-17; elev. 2ft./1m.; mail Tyaskin z 21865; rural
Claremont; RMC Place; BALTIMORE (Independent City); *185 D-13; ★ BAL; mail Baltimore z 21223; pop. incl. with Baltimore (Independent City)
Clarksburg; CDP; MONTGOMERY; 184 D-10; elev. 658ft./201m.; 🅿; ★ WASH; z 20871; © 1,834
Clarks Landing; RMC Place; ST. MARY'S; *185 I-14; ★ WASH; mail Hollywood z 20636; ● 160
Clarksville; RMC Place; HOWARD; 185 D-12; elev. 483ft./147m.; 🅿; ★ WASH; z 21029; ● 830
Clarksville Ridge; RMC Place; HOWARD; *185 D-12; ★ WASH; mail Clarksville z 21029; ● 200
Clarysville; RMC Place; ALLEGANY; 184 A-3; ★ CUMB; mail Frostburg z 21532; ● 70
Clayburn Hills; HOWARD; see Ridge Lake (RMC Place)
Clayton Manor; RMC Place; HARFORD; *185 C-15; ★ BAL; mail Joppa z 21085
Clearfield; RMC Place; CARROLL; *185 B-12; ★ BAL; mail Westminster z 21157
Clear Spring; Inc. Place; WASHINGTON; 184 A-8; elev. 580ft./177m.; 🅿; ★ HAG; z 21722; Ⓟ 415; © 455
Clearview; RMC Place; HARFORD; *185 C-15; ★ BAL; mail Edgewood z 21040
Clearview Manor; RMC Place; PRINCE GEORGE'S; *185 F-12; ★ WASH; mail Oxon Hill z 20745
Clearview Village; RMC Place; ANNE ARUNDEL; *185 D-14; ★ BAL; mail Pasadena z 21122
Clearwater Beach; RMC Place; ANNE ARUNDEL; *185 D-14; ★ BAL; mail Curtis Bay z 21226
Cleaview; RMC Place; CARROLL; ★ BAL; mail Hampstead z 21074; pop. incl. with Hampstead (Inc. Place)
Clements; RMC Place; ST. MARY'S; 185 I-13; elev. 20ft./6m.; 🅿; ★ WASH; z 20624; ● 270
Clemsonville; RMC Place; FREDERICK; *185 B-11; elev. 509ft./155m.; mail Union Bridge z 21791; ● 30
Clifford; RMC Place; BALTIMORE (Independent City); *185 D-13; ★ BAL; mail Baltimore z 21230; pop. incl. with Baltimore (Independent City)
Cliffs City; RMC Place; KENT; 185 D-16; mail Chestertown z 21620; ● 60
Clifton; RMC Place; FREDERICK; *184 C-10; 🅿; ★ WASH; z 21213 & mail Frederick z 21702
Clifton-East End; RMC Place; BALTIMORE (Independent City); *185 C-14; ★ BAL; mail Baltimore z 21205, z 21213; pop. incl. with Baltimore (Independent City)
Clifton on the Potomac; RMC Place; CHARLES; *185 I-12; mail Newburg z 20664; ● 580
Clifton Park; RMC Place; MONTGOMERY; *185 E-12; ★ WASH; mail Silver Spring z 20901
Clinton (Sorrattsville); CDP; PRINCE GEORGE'S; 185 G-12; elev. 248ft./76m.; 🅿 🄷; ★ WASH; z 20735; Ⓟ 19,987; © 26,064; ◆ 26,139
Clinton Acres; RMC Place; PRINCE GEORGE'S; *185 G-12; ★ WASH; mail Brandywine z 20613; ● 600
Clinton Estates; RMC Place; PRINCE GEORGE'S; *185 F-12; ★ WASH; mail Clinton z 20735
Clinton Gardens; RMC Place; PRINCE GEORGE'S; *185 G-12; ★ WASH; mail Clinton z 20735
Clinton Grove; RMC Place; PRINCE GEORGE'S; *185 G-12; ★ WASH; mail Clinton z 20735
Clinton Hills; RMC Place; PRINCE GEORGE'S; *185 G-12; ★ WASH; mail Clinton z 20735; ● 950
Clinton Park; RMC Place; PRINCE GEORGE'S; *185 G-12; ★ WASH; mail Clinton z 20735
Clinton Vista; RMC Place; PRINCE GEORGE'S; *185 G-12; ★ WASH; mail Clinton z 20735
Clinton Woods; RMC Place; PRINCE GEORGE'S; *185 G-12; ★ WASH; mail Clinton z 20735; ● 3,900
Clopper; RMC Place; MONTGOMERY; 249 A-3; ★ WASH; mail Gaithersburg z 20878; ● 1,000
Cloverfields; RMC Place; QUEEN ANNE'S; *185 E-15; ★ ANPLS; mail Stevensville z 21666
Clover Hill; CDP; FREDERICK; *184 C-10; ★ WASH; mail Frederick z 21702; Ⓟ 2,823; © 3,260
Cloverlea; RMC Place; ANNE ARUNDEL; *185 F-14; ★ ANPLS; mail Mayo z 21106; ● 230
Cloverly; CDP; MONTGOMERY; *185 E-12; ★ WASH; mail Silver Spring z 20904, Spencerville z 20868; Ⓟ 7,904; © 7,835
Club of Stedwick; RMC Place; MONTGOMERY; *185 D-11; ★ WASH; mail Gaithersburg z 20879
Clubside; RMC Place; MONTGOMERY; *185 D-11; ★ WASH; mail Gaithersburg z 20879
Clydesdale Acres; RMC Place; CARROLL; *185 B-12; ★ BAL; mail Finksburg z 21048, Reisterstown z 21136; ● 100
Cobb Island; RMC Place; CHARLES; 185 I-12; elev. 15ft./5m.; 🅿; z 20625; ● 900
Cockeysville; CDP; BALTIMORE; 185 B-13; elev. 260ft./79m.; 🅿; ★ BAL; z 21030 & mail Hunt Valley z 21031, z 21065; Ⓟ 18,668; © 19,388
Cohasset; RMC Place; MONTGOMERY; *185 E-11; ★ WASH; mail Bethesda z 20814
Cohill Estates; RMC Place; WASHINGTON; *184 A-6; mail Hancock z 21750; rural
Cokesburg; SOMERSET; see Cokesbury (RMC Place)
Cokesbury; RMC Place; CECIL; *185 B-16; elev. 325ft./99m.; mail Port Deposit z 21904; ● 100
Cokesbury (Cokesburg); RMC Place; SOMERSET; 185 J-18; mail Pocomoke City z 21851; ● 110
Colbourne; RMC Place; WORCESTER; 185 I-19; rural
Cold Spring Estates; RMC Place; MONTGOMERY; *185 E-11; ★ WASH; mail Potomac z 20854
Coleman; RMC Place; KENT; 185 C-16; elev. 84ft./26m.; mail Worton z 21678; ● 130
Coles Corner; RMC Place; PRINCE GEORGE'S; *185 F-12; elev. 250ft./76m.; ★ WASH; mail Clinton z 20735; ● 80
Colesville; CDP; MONTGOMERY; 185 E-12; 🅿; ★ WASH; z 20904-05, z 20914; Ⓟ 18,819; © 19,810
Colesville Farm Estates; RMC Place; MONTGOMERY; *185 E-12; ★ WASH; mail Silver Spring z 20904; ● 950
Colesville Gardens; RMC Place; MONTGOMERY; *185 E-12; ★ WASH; mail Silver Spring z 20904
Colesville Manor; RMC Place; MONTGOMERY; *185 E-12; ★ WASH; mail Silver Spring z 20904
Colesville Park; RMC Place; MONTGOMERY; *185 E-12; ★ WASH; mail Silver Spring z 20904; ● 950
College Estates; RMC Place; FREDERICK; ★ WASH; mail Frederick z 21702; pop. incl. with Frederick (Inc. Place)
College Gardens; RMC Place; MONTGOMERY; ★ WASH; mail Rockville z 20850; pop. incl. with Rockville (Inc. Place)
College Heights Estates; RMC Place; PRINCE GEORGE'S; *185 G-12; ★ WASH; mail Hyattsville z 20783; ● 710
College Park; Inc. Place; PRINCE GEORGE'S; 185 E-12; elev. 190ft./58m.; 🅿 🄲 35,102; ★ WASH; z 20740-42; Ⓟ 21,927; © 24,657; ◆ 23,279
College Park Woods; RMC Place; PRINCE GEORGE'S; *185 E-12; ★ WASH; mail College Park z 20740; pop. incl. with College Park (Inc. Place)
College View; RMC Place; MONTGOMERY; *185 E-11; ★ WASH; mail Silver Spring z 20902; ● 2,900
Colmar Manor; Inc. Place; PRINCE GEORGE'S; 249 F-8; elev. 30ft./9m.; 🅿; ★ WASH; z 20722; Ⓟ 1,249; © 1,257
Colonial Acres; RMC Place; CECIL; *185 B-17; ★ PHIL-; mail Elkton z 21921; ● 110
Colonial Acres; RMC Place; HARFORD; *185 B-15; ★ BAL; mail Bel Air z 21014
Colonial Gardens; RMC Place; BALTIMORE; *185 D-13; ★ BAL; mail Catonsville z 21228
Colonial Park; RMC Place; BALTIMORE; 185 N-14; ★ BAL; mail Gwynn Oak z 21207; ● 600
Colonial Park; RMC Place; WASHINGTON; *184 B-9; ★ HAG; mail Hagerstown z 21740
Colonial Village; RMC Place; BALTIMORE; *185 C-13; ★ BAL; mail Pikesville z 21208; pop. incl. with Baltimore (Independent City)
Colony Heights; RMC Place; ALLEGANY; ★ CUMB; mail Cumberland z 21502
Colony Ridge; RMC Place; ANNE ARUNDEL; *185 E-13; ★ BAL; mail Odenton z 21113
Colora; RMC Place; CECIL; 185 A-16; elev. 279ft./85m.; 🅿; ★ PHIL-; z 21917; ● 120
Coltons Point; RMC Place; ST. MARY'S; 185 J-13; 🅿; ★ WASH; z 20626; ● 500
Columbia; CDP; HOWARD; 185 D-12; elev. 402ft./123m.; 🅿 🄷; ★ BAL; z 20588, z 21044-46; Ⓟ 75,883; © 88,254; ◆ 94,166
Columbia Beach; RMC Place; ANNE ARUNDEL; *185 F-14; ★ WASH; mail Shady Side z 20764
Columbia Hills; RMC Place; HOWARD; *185 D-12; ★ BAL; mail Ellicott City z 21043
Columbia Park; RMC Place; PRINCE GEORGE'S; 249 F-9; ★ WASH; mail Hyattsville z 20785; ● 1,000
Compton; RMC Place; ST. MARY'S; 185 I-13; elev. 22ft./7m.; 🅿; ★ WASH; z 20627; ● 250
Comus; RMC Place; MONTGOMERY; *184 D-10; elev. 592ft./180m.; ★ WASH; mail Dickerson z 20842
Concord; RMC Place; CAROLINE; *185 F-17; mail Federalsburg z 21632; rural
Congressional Forest Estates (Congressional Manor); RMC Place; MONTGOMERY; *185 E-11; ★ WASH; mail Bethesda z 20817
Congressional Manor; MONTGOMERY; see Congressional Forest Estates (RMC Place)
Connecticut Avenue Estates; RMC Place; MONTGOMERY; *185 E-11; ★ WASH; mail Silver Spring z 20902
Connecticut Avenue Hills; RMC Place; MONTGOMERY; *185 E-11; ★ WASH; mail Silver Spring z 20902
Connecticut Avenue Park; RMC Place; MONTGOMERY; *185 E-11; ★ WASH; mail Silver Spring z 20906
Connecticut Gardens; RMC Place; MONTGOMERY; *185 E-11; ★ WASH; mail Silver Spring z 20902
Conowingo (Kilby Corner); RMC Place; CECIL; 185 A-15; elev. 294ft./90m.; 🅿; ★ PHIL-; z 21918; ● 150
Conowingo Village; RMC Place; HARFORD; *185 A-15; ★ BAL; mail Darlington z 21034; ● 80
Contee; RMC Place; PRINCE GEORGE'S; *185 E-12; ★ WASH; mail Laurel z 20708
Cooksville; RMC Place; HOWARD; 185 C-12; elev. 580ft./177m.; 🅿; ★ WASH; z 21723; ● 500
Cool Hollow Estates; RMC Place; WASHINGTON; *184 B-9; elev. 500ft./152m.; ★ HAG; mail Hagerstown z 21740; ● 100
Cooperstown; RMC Place; BALTIMORE; *185 B-13; ★ BAL; mail Butler z 21023; rural
Coopstown; RMC Place; HARFORD; *185 B-14; ★ BAL; mail Forest Hill z 21050; ● 350
Copenhaver; RMC Place; MONTGOMERY; *185 E-11; ★ WASH; mail Potomac z 20854; ● 4,200
Copperville; RMC Place; CARROLL; *185 B-11; mail Mount Airy z 21771, Taneytown z 21787; rural
Copperville; RMC Place; TALBOT; *185 F-15; mail Easton z 21601; ● 30
Coral Hills; CDP; PRINCE GEORGE'S; 249 G-8; ★ WASH; mail Capitol Heights z 20743; Ⓟ 11,032; © 10,720
Corbett; RMC Place; BALTIMORE; *185 B-13; ★ BAL; mail Monkton z 21111; ● 100
Corbett; RMC Place; WASHINGTON; ★ HAG; mail Hagerstown z 21740; pop. incl. with Hagerstown (Inc. Place)
Cordova; CDP; TALBOT; 185 F-16; elev. 60ft./18m.; 🅿; z 21625; © 592
Cornersville; RMC Place; DORCHESTER; 185 G-15; mail Cambridge z 21613; ● 100
Cornfield Harbor; RMC Place; ST. MARY'S; *185 K-15; mail Scotland z 20687; rural
Corriganville (Kreigbaum); RMC Place; ALLEGANY; 184 A-4; elev. 740ft./226m.; 🅿; ★ CUMB; z 21524; ● 930
Costen; RMC Place; SOMERSET; *185 J-18; mail Pocomoke City z 21851; ● 50
Cottage City; Inc. Place; PRINCE GEORGE'S; 249 F-8; elev. 30ft./9m.; 🅿; ★ WASH; z 20722; Ⓟ 1,236; © 1,136
Country Club Acres; RMC Place; GARRETT; *184 C-1; mail Oakland z 21550; pop. incl. with Oakland (Inc. Place)
Country Club Estate; RMC Place; ANNE ARUNDEL; *185 D-14; ★ BAL; mail Glen Burnie z 21060
Country Club Manor; RMC Place; ANNE ARUNDEL; *185 D-14; ★ BAL; mail Glen Burnie z 21060
Country Club Park; RMC Place; BALTIMORE; *185 C-13; ★ BAL; mail Lutherville Timonium z 21093
Country Club Village; RMC Place; MONTGOMERY; ★ WASH; mail Bethesda z 20814
Country Place; RMC Place; MONTGOMERY; *185 E-12; ★ WASH; mail Burtonsville z 20866
Country Road Estates; RMC Place; CALVERT; *185 G-13; ★ WASH; mail Dunkirk z 20754; ● 250
Courthouse; RMC Place; MONTGOMERY; ★ WASH; mail Rockville z 20850; pop. incl. with Rockville (Inc. Place)
Courtleigh; RMC Place; BALTIMORE; *185 C-13; ★ BAL; mail Randallstown z 21133
Cove; RMC Place; GARRETT; *184 A-1; elev. 2,318ft./707m.; mail Accident z 21520; ● 30
Coventry; RMC Place; BALTIMORE; *185 C-14; ★ BAL; mail Parkville z 21234
Cove Point; RMC Place; CALVERT; 185 I-14; mail Lusby z 20657; ● 1,200
Cowentown; RMC Place; CECIL; *185 A-17; ★ PHIL-; mail Elkton z 21921; ● 30
Cox; CHARLES; see Bel Alton (RMC Place)
Coxby Estates; RMC Place; ANNE ARUNDEL; *185 F-14; ★ ANPLS; mail Edgewater z 21037
Cox Creek Acres; RMC Place; QUEEN ANNE'S; *185 F-15; ★ ANPLS; mail Chester z 21619; ● 60
Coxs Corner; RMC Place; WICOMICO; *185 I-17; mail Tyaskin z 21865
Crabtree; RMC Place; GARRETT; mail Swanton z 21561; rural
Craigtown; RMC Place; CECIL; 185 B-16; mail Port Deposit z 21904; ● 200
Cranberry; RMC Place; CARROLL; 185 B-12; ★ BAL; mail Westminster z 21157; ● 200
Crapo; RMC Place; DORCHESTER; 185 I-16; elev. 3ft./1m.; 🅿; z 21626; ● 130
Creagerstown; RMC Place; FREDERICK; 184 B-10; mail Thurmont z 21788; ● 150
Crellin; RMC Place; GARRETT; 184 C-1; elev. 2,395ft./730m.; 🅿; z 21550; ● 200
Cremona; RMC Place; ST. MARY'S; *185 H-13; ★ WASH; mail Mechanicsville z 20659; ● 50
Cresaptown; RMC Place; ALLEGANY; 184 B-4; ★ CUMB; ● 1,850
Cresaptown; ALLEGANY; see Cresaptown-Bel Air (CDP-Census Area Only)
Cresaptown-Bel Air (Cresaptown); CDP-Census Area Only; ALLEGANY; 184 B-4; elev. 775ft./236m.; ★ CUMB; mail Cumberland z 21502, z 21505; Ⓟ 4,586; © 5,884
Crescendo; RMC Place; TALBOT; *185 F-15; mail Wittman z 21676; rural
Cresthaven; RMC Place; MONTGOMERY; *185 E-12; ★ WASH; mail Silver Spring z 20903; ● 1,120
Crestleigh; RMC Place; HOWARD; *185 D-12; ★ BAL; mail Ellicott City z 21042
Crestview; RMC Place; MONTGOMERY; *185 E-11; ★ WASH; mail Bethesda z 20814
Crestview Manor; RMC Place; PRINCE GEORGE'S; *185 G-12; elev. 200ft./61m.; ★ WASH; mail Clinton z 20735; ● 1,950
Crestwood; RMC Place; ANNE ARUNDEL; *185 D-13; ★ BAL; mail Linthicum Heights z 21090; ● 1,250
Crestwood; RMC Place; WICOMICO; 185 I-18; ★ SLSB; mail Salisbury z 21804; ● 200
Crestwood Acres; RMC Place; HARFORD; *185 C-15; ★ BAL; mail Edgewood z 21040
Creswell; RMC Place; HARFORD; *185 B-15; elev. 250ft./76m.; ★ BAL; mail Bel Air z 21015; ● 100
Crisfield; Inc. Place; SOMERSET; 185 K-17; elev. 4ft./1m.; 🅿 🄷; z 21817; Ⓟ 2,880; © 2,723
Crisp; RMC Place; BALTIMORE (Independent City); *185 D-14; ★ BAL; mail Brooklyn z 21225; pop. incl. with Baltimore (Independent City)
Criswood Manor; RMC Place; HOWARD; *185 D-12; ★ WASH; mail Clarksville z 21029; ● 100
Crocheron; RMC Place; DORCHESTER; 185 J-16; elev. 3ft./1m.; 🅿; z 21627; ● 120
Crofton; CDP; ANNE ARUNDEL; 185 E-13; elev. 100ft./30m.; 🅿; ★ BAL; z 21114; Ⓟ 12,781; © 20,091; ◆ 21,241
Crofton Meadows; RMC Place; ANNE ARUNDEL; *185 E-13; ★ BAL; mail Crofton z 21114
Crofton Mews; RMC Place; ANNE ARUNDEL; ★ BAL; mail Crofton z 21114
Cromwood; RMC Place; BALTIMORE; *185 C-14; ★ BAL; mail Parkville z 21234
Crooked Oak Estate; RMC Place; WICOMICO; *185 I-18; elev. 40ft./12m.; ★ SLSB; mail Hebron z 21830; rural
Croom; RMC Place; PRINCE GEORGE'S; 185 G-13; ★ WASH; mail Upper Marlboro z 20772; ● 120
Crosby; RMC Place; KENT; 185 E-15; mail Rock Hall z 21661; ● 50
Crowder; RMC Place; HOWARD; *185 D-13; ★ BAL; mail Ellicott City z 21043
Crownsville; CDP; ANNE ARUNDEL; 185 E-14; elev. 140ft./43m.; 🅿 🄷; ★ WASH; z 21032; Ⓟ 1,514; © 1,670
Croydon Park; RMC Place; MONTGOMERY; *185 E-11; ★ WASH; mail Rockville z 20850; pop. incl. with Rockville (Inc. Place)
Crumpton; RMC Place; QUEEN ANNE'S; 185 D-17; elev. 18ft./5m.; 🅿; z 21628; ● 550
Crystal Beach; RMC Place; CECIL; 185 C-16; mail Earleville z 21919; ● 250
Cub Hill; RMC Place; BALTIMORE; *185 C-14; ★ BAL; mail Parkville z 21234
Cuckhold Creek; RMC Place; CHARLES; *185 I-12; mail Newburg z 20664; ● 50
Cumberland; Inc. Place; ⊡ ALLEGANY; 184 A-4; elev. 688ft./210m.; 🅿 🄷 ■; ★ CUMB; z 21501-05; Ⓟ 23,706; © 21,518; ◆ 19,424
Curtis Bay; RMC Place; BALTIMORE (Independent City); *185 D-14; 🅿; ★ BAL; z 21226; pop. incl. with Baltimore (Independent City)
Cypress Creek; RMC Place; ANNE ARUNDEL; *185 E-14; ★ BAL; mail Severna Park z 21146

D

Dailsville; RMC Place; DORCHESTER; *185 H-16; mail Cambridge z 21613; ● 30
Daisy; RMC Place; HOWARD; *185 D-11; elev. 553ft./169m.; ★ WASH; mail Woodbine z 21797; ● 70
Dalton; RMC Place; HOWARD; *185 D-12; ★ BAL; mail Columbia z 21045
Damascus; CDP; MONTGOMERY; 185 D-11; elev. 828ft./252m.; 🅿; ★ WASH; z 20872; Ⓟ 9,817; © 11,430
Dameron; RMC Place; ST. MARY'S; 185 J-15; elev. 91ft./28m.; 🅿; z 20628; ● 350
Dames Quarter; CDP; SOMERSET; 185 J-17; elev. 4ft./1m.; 🅿; z 21821; © 188
Dam Number 4; RMC Place; WASHINGTON; *184 B-8; ★ HAG; mail Sharpsburg z 21782; ● 50
Daniel; RMC Place; CARROLL; 185 C-11; elev. 773ft./236m.; ★ BAL; mail Woodbine z 21797; ● 100
Daniels Park; RMC Place; PRINCE GEORGE'S; *185 E-12; ★ WASH; mail College Park z 20740; pop. incl. with College Park (Inc. Place)
Danville; RMC Place; ALLEGANY; 184 B-3; ★ CUMB; mail Rawlings z 21557; ● 270
Danwood; RMC Place; WICOMICO; *185 H-18; ★ SLSB; mail Salisbury z 21804; ● 80
Darcy Manor; RMC Place; PRINCE GEORGE'S; *185 F-12; elev. 250ft./76m.; ★ WASH; mail Suitland z 20746; ● 1,700
Dares Beach; RMC Place; CALVERT; 185 H-14; 🅿; ★ WASH; z 20678; ● 500
Dargan; RMC Place; WASHINGTON; 184 C-8; ★ WASH; mail Sharpsburg z 21782; ● 100
Darleigh Manor; RMC Place; BALTIMORE; *185 C-14; ★ BAL; mail Nottingham z 21236
Darlington; RMC Place; HARFORD; 185 B-15; elev. 330ft./101m.; 🅿; ★ BAL; z 21034; ● 800
Darnestown; CDP; MONTGOMERY; 184 E-10; elev. 449ft./137m.; 🅿; ★ WASH; z 20874, z 20878; © 6,378
Darryl Gardens; RMC Place; BALTIMORE; *185 C-14; ★ BAL; mail White Marsh z 21162; ● 850
Davidsonville; RMC Place; ANNE ARUNDEL; 185 F-13; elev. 182ft./55m.; 🅿; ★ WASH; z 21035; ● 780
Dawson; RMC Place; ALLEGANY; 184 B-3; ★ CUMB; mail Keyser z 26726; ● 120
Dawsonville; RMC Place; MONTGOMERY; 184 D-10; ★ WASH; mail Boyds z 20841; ● 120
Day; RMC Place; CARROLL; *185 C-11; elev. 767ft./234m.; ★ BAL; mail Woodbine z 21797; ● 30
Daysville; RMC Place; FREDERICK; *184 B-10; ★ WASH; mail Walkersville z 21793; ● 100
Dayton; RMC Place; HOWARD; 185 D-12; elev. 600ft./183m.; 🅿; ★ WASH; z 21036; ● 800
Deale; CDP; ANNE ARUNDEL; 185 F-14; elev. 9ft./3m.; 🅿; ★ WASH; z 20751; Ⓟ 4,151; © 4,796
Deale Beach; RMC Place; ANNE ARUNDEL; *185 F-14; ★ WASH; mail Deale z 20751
Deal Island; CDP; SOMERSET; 185 J-17; elev. 8ft./2m.; 🅿; z 21821; © 578
Deanwood Park; RMC Place; PRINCE GEORGE'S; *185 F-12; ★ WASH; mail Capitol Heights z 20743
Decatur Heights; RMC Place; PRINCE GEORGE'S; ★ WASH; mail Bladensburg z 20710; pop. incl. with Bladensburg (Inc. Place)
Deep Creek; RMC Place; ANNE ARUNDEL; *185 E-13; ★ BAL; mail Arnold z 21012
Deep Creek Lake; RMC Place; GARRETT; *184 B-1; mail Mc Henry z 21541, Oakland z 21550, Swanton z 21561; ● 110
Deep Landing Estates; RMC Place; CALVERT; *185 H-13; ★ WASH; mail Huntingtown z 20639; ● 80
Deerfield (Lantz); RMC Place; FREDERICK; *184 A-10; elev. 1,000ft./305m.; mail Sabillasville z 21780; pop. incl. with Walkersville (Inc. Place)
Deerfield; RMC Place; HARFORD; *185 A-15; ★ BAL; mail Darlington z 21034; ● 100
Deerfield (Smithfield); RMC Place; MONTGOMERY; *185 E-11; ★ WASH; mail Bethesda z 20817; ● 650
Deerfield Run (Village Square North); RMC Place; PRINCE GEORGE'S; *185 E-12; ★ WASH; mail Laurel z 20708; ● 2,250
Deer Harbour; RMC Place; WICOMICO; *185 I-18; ★ SLSB; mail Salisbury z 21804; ● 250
Deer Park; Inc. Place; GARRETT; 184 C-1; elev. 2,500ft./762m.; 🅿; z 21550; Ⓟ 419; © 405
Deer Park; RMC Place; MONTGOMERY; *185 E-12; ★ WASH; mail Gaithersburg z 20877
Deer Park; RMC Place; PRINCE GEORGE'S; ★ WASH; mail Temple Hills z 20748
Deer Park Estates; RMC Place; CARROLL; *185 B-12; ★ BAL; mail Finksburg z 21048
Deer Park Heights; RMC Place; PRINCE GEORGE'S; *185 F-12; ★ WASH; mail Temple Hills z 20748
Deers Head; RMC Place; WICOMICO; *185 I-18; ★ SLSB; mail Salisbury z 21801; pop. incl. with Salisbury (Inc. Place)
Defense Heights; RMC Place; BALTIMORE; *185 C-14; ★ BAL; mail Dundalk z 21222
Defense Heights; RMC Place; PRINCE GEORGE'S; 249 E-9; ★ WASH; mail Hyattsville z 20784; ● 2,250
Delight; RMC Place; BALTIMORE; *185 C-13; ★ BAL; mail Owings Mills z 21117
Delmar; Inc. Place; WICOMICO; 185 H-18; elev. 55ft./17m.; 🅿; ★ SLSB; z 21875; Ⓟ 1,430; © 1,859
Delmont; RMC Place; ANNE ARUNDEL; *185 D-13; ★ BAL; mail Severn z 21144; ● 170
Den Lee Acres; RMC Place; PRINCE GEORGE'S; *185 G-12; ★ WASH; mail Clinton z 20735
Dennings; RMC Place; CARROLL; *185 B-11; ★ BAL; mail New Windsor z 21776; rural
Dennis Grove Apartments; RMC Place; PRINCE GEORGE'S; ★ WASH; mail Oxon Hill z 20745
Denton; Inc. Place; ⊡ CAROLINE; 185 F-17; elev. 40ft./12m.; 🅿; z 21629; Ⓟ 2,977; © 2,960
Dentsville; RMC Place; CHARLES; 185 H-12; 🅿; z 20646; ● 50
Derwood; RMC Place; MONTGOMERY; 249 B-4; elev. 477ft./145m.; 🅿; ★ WASH; z 20855; ● 2,000
Detmold; RMC Place; ALLEGANY; *184 B-3; ★ CUMB; mail Lonaconing z 21539; rural
Detour; RMC Place; CARROLL; 185 B-11; elev. 363ft./111m.; 🅿; z 21757; ● 520
Devonshire Forest; RMC Place; BALTIMORE; *185 C-13; ★ BAL; mail Lutherville Timonium z 21093
Diamond Farms; RMC Place; MONTGOMERY; ★ WASH; mail Gaithersburg z 20878; pop. incl. with Gaithersburg (Inc. Place)
Dickerson; RMC Place; MONTGOMERY; 184 D-10; elev. 356ft./109m.; 🅿; ★ WASH; z 20842; ● 1,000
Discovery-Spring Garden; CDP-Census Area Only; FREDERICK; *184 C-10; ★ WASH; mail Walkersville z 21793; Ⓟ 2,443; © 2,152
District Heights; Inc. Place; PRINCE GEORGE'S; 185 F-12; 🅿; ★ WASH; z 20747, z 20753; Ⓟ 6,704; © 5,958; Ⓡ 5,953
Dodge Park; RMC Place; PRINCE GEORGE'S; *185 F-12; ★ WASH; mail Hyattsville z 20785; Ⓟ 4,842
Dogwood Flats; RMC Place; ALLEGANY; *184 B-3; ★ CUMB; mail Barton z 21521; ● 200
Dogwood Hills; RMC Place; BALTIMORE; *185 C-14; ★ BAL; mail Towson z 21286
Dominion; RMC Place; QUEEN ANNE'S; 185 F-15; ★ ANPLS; mail Chester z 21619; ● 470
Doncaster; RMC Place; CHARLES; 185 H-11; elev. 141ft./43m.; mail Indian Head z 20640, Ironsides z 20643, Nanjemoy z 20662; ● 200
Doncaster; RMC Place; TALBOT; *185 F-16; elev. 12ft./4m.; mail Easton z 21601; ● 40
Doncaster Village; RMC Place; BALTIMORE; *185 C-14; ★ BAL; mail Parkville z 21234; ● 3,250
Donleigh; RMC Place; HOWARD; *185 D-12; ★ BAL; mail Columbia z 21046
Donnybrook; RMC Place; BALTIMORE; *185 C-14; ★ BAL; mail Towson z 21204
Dorceytown; RMC Place; CARROLL; *185 C-11; ★ WASH; mail Mount Airy z 21771; ● 50
DORCHESTER; 185 H-16; Ⓟ 30,236; © 30,674; ◆ 32,804
Dorchester Estates (Suburban Estates); RMC Place; PRINCE GEORGE'S; *185 F-12; ★ WASH; mail Clinton z 20735; ● 2,300
Dorrs Corner; RMC Place; ANNE ARUNDEL; 185 E-13; ★ BAL; mail Millersville z 21108; ● 170
Dorsey; RMC Place; ANNE ARUNDEL, HOWARD; 184 M-2; ★ BAL; mail Elkridge z 21075; ● 1,350
Dorsey Crossroads; RMC Place; CARROLL; *185 C-12; elev. 718ft./219m.; ★ BAL; mail Sykesville z 21784; rural
Dorseys Regard; RMC Place; MONTGOMERY; *185 D-11; ★ WASH; mail Gaithersburg z 20879
Doub; FREDERICK; see Doubs (RMC Place)
Doubs (Doub); RMC Place; FREDERICK; 184 C-10; 🅿; ★ WASH; z 21710; ● 160
Dowell; RMC Place; CALVERT; 185 I-14; elev. 20ft./6m.; 🅿; z 20629; ● 300
Downsville; RMC Place; WASHINGTON; 184 B-8; ★ HAG; mail Williamsport z 21795; ● 380
Drayden; RMC Place; ST. MARY'S; 185 J-14; elev. 80ft./24m.; 🅿; z 20630; ● 110
Dresden Green; RMC Place; PRINCE GEORGE'S; ★ WASH; mail Lanham z 20706
Drexel Woods; RMC Place; BALTIMORE; *185 D-13; ★ BAL; mail Catonsville z 21228
Druid; RMC Place; BALTIMORE (Independent City); *185 C-13; 🅿; ★ BAL; z 21217; pop. incl. with Baltimore (Independent City)
Drumcliff; RMC Place; ST. MARY'S; *185 I-14; ★ WASH; mail Hollywood z 20636; ● 110
Drumeldra Hills; RMC Place; MONTGOMERY; *185 E-12; ★ WASH; mail Silver Spring z 20904
Drum Point; RMC Place; CALVERT; 185 I-14; mail Lusby z 20657; ● 1,600
Drury; RMC Place; ANNE ARUNDEL; 185 F-13; ★ WASH; mail Lothian z 20711; ● 300
Drybranch; RMC Place; HARFORD; *185 A-14; ★ BAL; mail White Hall z 21161
Dry Run; RMC Place; WASHINGTON; *184 A-8; elev. 600ft./183m.; ★ HAG; mail Clear Spring z 21722; rural
Dublin; RMC Place; HARFORD; 185 A-15; ★ BAL; mail Darlington z 21034, Street z 21154; ● 500
Dufief; RMC Place; MONTGOMERY; *185 E-11; ★ WASH; mail Gaithersburg z 20878; ● 4,500
Dulaney Village; RMC Place; BALTIMORE; *185 C-13; ★ BAL; mail Towson z 21204
Dulls Corner; RMC Place; ANNE ARUNDEL; *185 E-14; elev. 54ft./16m.; ★ ANPLS; mail Annapolis z 21401; rural
Dumbarton; RMC Place; BALTIMORE; *185 C-13; ★ BAL; mail Pikesville z 21208
Dumbarton Heights; RMC Place; BALTIMORE; *185 C-13; ★ BAL; mail Pikesville z 21208
Dunbrook; RMC Place; ANNE ARUNDEL; *185 D-14; ★ BAL; mail Pasadena z 21122
Dundalk; CDP; BALTIMORE; 185 D-14; 🅿; ★ BAL; z 21222; Ⓟ 65,800; © 62,306; ◆ 65,409
Dundalk-Sparrows Point; RMC Place; BALTIMORE; *185 D-14; ★ BAL; mail Dundalk z 21222, Sparrows Point z 21219
Dundee Village; RMC Place; BALTIMORE; *185 C-14; ★ BAL; mail Middle River z 21220; ● 500
Dunkirk; CDP; CALVERT; 185 G-13; elev. 152ft./46m.; 🅿; ★ WASH; z 20754; © 2,363
Dunlaney Village; RMC Place; BALTIMORE; *185 B-13; ★ BAL; mail Lutherville Timonium z 21093
Dunloggin; RMC Place; HOWARD; *185 D-12; ★ BAL; mail Ellicott City z 21042
Dunwood; RMC Place; HARFORD; *185 B-14; ★ BAL; mail Joppa z 21085
Dupont Heights; RMC Place; PRINCE GEORGE'S; *185 F-12; ★ WASH; mail Suitland z 20746
Dynard; RMC Place; ST. MARY'S; 185 I-13; elev. 100ft./30m.; ★ WASH; mail Chaptico z 20621, Clements z 20624; ● 50

E

Eagle Harbor; Inc. Place; PRINCE GEORGE'S; 185 H-13; elev. 20ft./6m.; ★ WASH; mail Aquasco z 20608; Ⓟ 38; © 55
Eakles Mills; RMC Place; WASHINGTON; *184 C-9; elev. 470ft./143m.; ★ WASH; mail Keedysville z 21756; ● 100
Earleigh Heights; RMC Place; ANNE ARUNDEL; *185 E-14; ★ BAL; mail Severna Park z 21146
Earleville; RMC Place; CECIL; 185 C-17; elev. 85ft./26m.; 🅿; z 21919; ● 500
Earlton; RMC Place; HARFORD; *185 B-16; elev. 400ft./122m.; mail Havre de Grace z 21078; ● 200
East Columbia Park; RMC Place; PRINCE GEORGE'S; *185 F-12; ★ WASH; mail Hyattsville z 20785; ● 1,050
Eastfield; RMC Place; BALTIMORE; *185 D-14; ★ BAL; mail Dundalk z 21222
East Fort Foote Village; RMC Place; PRINCE GEORGE'S; *185 G-12; ★ WASH; mail Fort Washington z 20744
East Meadow; RMC Place; PRINCE GEORGE'S; *185 F-12; ★ WASH; mail Oxon Hill z 20745
East New Market; Inc. Place; DORCHESTER; 185 G-17; elev. 43ft./13m.; 🅿 🄷; z 21631; Ⓟ 153; © 167
Easton; Inc. Place; ⊡ TALBOT; 185 F-16; elev. 38ft./12m.; 🅿 🄷 ■; z 21601; Ⓟ 9,372; © 11,708; ◆ 13,790
Easton Point; RMC Place; TALBOT; *185 F-16; elev. 17ft./5m.; mail Easton z 21601; ● 60
Eastover Knolls; RMC Place; PRINCE GEORGE'S; *185 F-12; ★ WASH; mail Oxon Hill z 20745
East Park Village; RMC Place; ANNE ARUNDEL; *185 D-14; ★ BAL; mail Glen Burnie z 21061
Eastpines; RMC Place; PRINCE GEORGE'S; 249 E-8; ★ WASH; mail Riverdale z 20737; ● 1,250
Eastpoint; RMC Place; BALTIMORE; *185 D-14; ★ BAL; mail Dundalk z 21222
East Riverdale; CDP; PRINCE GEORGE'S; *185 E-12; ★ WASH; mail Riverdale z 20737; Ⓟ 14,187; © 14,961
East Springbrook; RMC Place; MONTGOMERY; *185 E-12; ★ WASH; mail Silver Spring z 20904; ● 2,050
Eastview; RMC Place; CARROLL; *185 B-12; ★ BAL; mail Finksburg z 21048; ● 60
Eastview; RMC Place; FREDERICK; 185 M-15; ★ WASH; mail Frederick z 21702; ● 330
Eastview Estates; RMC Place; CARROLL; *185 B-12; ★ BAL; mail Finksburg z 21048; ● 370
Eckhart; ALLEGANY; see Eckhart Mines (RMC Place)
Eckhart Mines (Eckhart); RMC Place; ALLEGANY; 184 A-3; elev. 1,688ft./515m.; 🅿; ★ CUMB; z 21528; ● 1,500
Eden; CDP; SOMERSET; 185 I-18; elev. 31ft./9m.; 🅿; z 21822; © 793
Eder; RMC Place; CECIL; *185 B-17; ★ PHIL-; mail Elkton z 21921; rural
Edesville; RMC Place; KENT; 185 D-15; mail Rock Hall z 21661; ● 160
Edgemere; CDP; BALTIMORE; 185 D-14; 🅿; ★ BAL; z 21219 & mail Essex z 21221; Ⓟ 9,226; © 9,248
Edgemont; RMC Place; FREDERICK; *184 C-10; elev. 724ft./221m.; ★ WASH; mail Frederick z 21702
Edgemont; RMC Place; WASHINGTON; *184 A-9; elev. 960ft./293m.; ★ HAG; mail Smithsburg z 21783; ● 140
Edgemoor; RMC Place; MONTGOMERY; *185 E-11; ★ WASH; mail Bethesda z 20814
Edgewater; RMC Place; ANNE ARUNDEL; 185 N-19; elev. 40ft./12m.; 🅿; ★ ANPLS; z 21037; ● 1,400
Edgewater Beach; RMC Place; ANNE ARUNDEL; *185 E-14; ★ ANPLS; mail Edgewater z 21037
Edgewater Village; RMC Place; HARFORD; *185 C-15; ★ BAL; mail Edgewood z 21040; ● 7,000
Edgewood; RMC Place; FREDERICK; *184 C-10; elev. 765ft./233m.; ★ WASH; mail Frederick z 21702; ● 160
Edgewood; CDP; HARFORD; 185 C-15; elev. 38ft./12m.; 🅿; ★ BAL; z 21040; Ⓟ 23,903; © 23,378; ◆ 25,361
Edgewood; RMC Place; MONTGOMERY; *185 E-11; ★ WASH; mail Bethesda z 20814
Edgewood Heights; HARFORD; see Edgewood Meadows (RMC Place)
Edgewood Meadows (Edgewood Heights); RMC Place; HARFORD; *185 C-15; ★ BAL; mail Edgewood z 21040; ● 3,500
Edmondson Heights; BALTIMORE; see Edmonson Heights (RMC Place)
Edmondson Ridge; RMC Place; BALTIMORE; *185 C-13; ★ BAL; mail Catonsville z 21228
Edmonson Heights (Edmondson Heights); RMC Place; BALTIMORE; *185 C-13; ★ BAL; mail Gwynn Oak z 21207; ● 5,800
Edmonston; Inc. Place; PRINCE GEORGE'S; 249 E-8; elev. 40ft./12m.; ★ WASH; mail Hyattsville z 20781; Ⓟ 851; © 959; Ⓡ 1,338
Ednor; RMC Place; MONTGOMERY; *185 D-12; ★ WASH; mail Silver Spring z 20905
Ednor Acres; RMC Place; MONTGOMERY; *185 D-12; ★ WASH; mail Silver Spring z 20904
Elberon; RMC Place; MONTGOMERY; *185 E-11; ★ WASH; mail Potomac z 20854
Elder Hill; RMC Place; GARRETT; *184 A-1; mail Friendsville z 21531; rural
Eldersburg; CDP; CARROLL; 185 C-12; 🅿; ★ BAL; z 21784; Ⓟ 9,720; © 27,741; ◆ 28,601
Eldorado; Inc. Place; DORCHESTER; 185 H-17; elev. 9ft./3m.; mail Rhodesdale z 21659; Ⓟ 49; © 60
Elioak; RMC Place; HOWARD; 185 D-12; elev. 432ft./132m.; ★ BAL; mail Columbia z 21044; ● 290
Elk Mills; RMC Place; CECIL; 185 A-17; elev. 140ft./43m.; 🅿; ★ PHIL-; z 21920; ● 700
Elkmore; RMC Place; CECIL; *185 B-17; ★ PHIL-; mail Elkton z 21921; ● 400
Elk Neck; RMC Place; CECIL; 185 B-16; elev. 186ft./57m.; ★ PHIL-; mail North East z 21901; ● 130
Elk Ranch Park; RMC Place; CECIL; *185 B-17; ★ PHIL-; mail Elkton z 21921; ● 100
Elkridge; CDP; HOWARD; 185 D-13; elev. 200ft./61m.; 🅿; ★ BAL; z 21075; Ⓟ 12,953; © 22,042; ◆ 24,539
Elkton; Inc. Place; ⊡ CECIL; 185 B-17; elev. 30ft./9m.; 🅿 🄷; ★ PHIL-; z 21921-22; Ⓟ 9,073; © 11,893
Elkton Heights; RMC Place; CECIL; *185 B-17; ★ PHIL-; mail Elkton z 21921; pop. incl. with Elkton (Inc. Place)
Elktonia; RMC Place; ANNE ARUNDEL; *185 E-14; ★ ANPLS; mail Annapolis z 21401; rural
Elkton Landing; RMC Place; CECIL; *185 B-17; ★ PHIL-; mail Elkton z 21921; pop. incl. with Elkton (Inc. Place)
Elkwood Estates; RMC Place; CECIL; *185 B-17; ★ PHIL-; mail Elkton z 21921; pop. incl. with Elkton (Inc. Place)
Ellerslie; RMC Place; ALLEGANY; 184 A-4; elev. 733ft./223m.; 🅿; ★ CUMB; z 21529; ● 1,400
Ellerton; RMC Place; FREDERICK; *184 B-9; mail Myersville z 21773
Ellicott City; CDP; ⊡ HOWARD; 185 D-13; 🅿 🄷; ★ BAL; z 21041-43; Ⓟ 41,396; © 56,397; ◆ 62,804
Ellicott Mills; RMC Place; BALTIMORE; *185 C-13; ★ BAL; mail Catonsville z 21228; ● 5,600
Ellicott Mills; RMC Place; HOWARD; *185 D-17; mail Ellicott City z 21041, z 21043
Elliott; RMC Place; DORCHESTER; 185 I-16; elev. 3ft./1m.; mail Vienna z 21869; ● 200
Ellwood (Elwood); RMC Place; DORCHESTER; 185 G-17; mail Hurlock z 21643; ● 130
Elmwood; RMC Place; BALTIMORE; 184 H-6; ★ BAL; mail Baltimore z 21206; ● 1,650
Elvaton; ANNE ARUNDEL; see Elvaton Acres (RMC Place)
Elvaton Acres (Elvaton); RMC Place; ANNE ARUNDEL; *185 D-14; ★ BAL; mail Millersville z 21108

Entries in **UPPERCASE** are counties.
Entries in **bold** have populations of 2,500 or more.
Names in parentheses are alternate names.
Inc. Place — Incorporated Place
RMC Place — Rand McNally Designated Place
CDP — Census Designated Place
MCD — Minor Civil Division

⊡ County Seat
▲ Minor Civil Division
elev. Elevation
🅿 Post Office
🄷 Hospital
🄲 College
■ Principal Business Center
★ Ranally Metro Area (RMA) Abbreviation
z Zip Code(s)
Ⓟ Previous Census Population
Ⓡ Revised Census Population
Ⓐ Annexation Population
● Rand McNally Population Estimate
© Final Census Population
Ⓢ Special Census Population
◆ Estimated Population

For additional definitions see Glossary, Volume 1, and Introduction, Volume 2.

Elvatone Town; RMC Place; ANNE ARUNDEL; *185 E-13; ★ BAL; mail Glen Burnie z 21061

Elwood; DORCHESTER; see Ellwood (RMC Place)

Emmitsburg; Inc. Place; FREDERICK; 184 A-10; elev. 449ft./137m.; [P] [H] [C] 2,186; z 21727; Ⓟ 1,688; © 2,290

Emmorton; RMC Place; HARFORD; 185 B-15; ★ BAL; mail Abingdon z 21009, Bel Air z 21014; ● 1,400

Emory Grove; RMC Place; BALTIMORE; *185 B-13; ★ BAL; mail Glyndon z 21071

Emory Grove; RMC Place; MONTGOMERY; 249 A-4; ★ WASH; mail Gaithersburg z 20877; ● 5,300

Emory Hills; RMC Place; CARROLL; *185 B-12; ★ BAL; mail Finksburg z 21048, Reisterstown z 21136; ● 130

Engle Mill; RMC Place; GARRETT; *184 A-2; elev. 2,130ft./649m.; mail Accident z 21520; rural

Englewood; RMC Place; PRINCE GEORGE'S; *185 F-12; ★ WASH; mail Hyattsville z 20785; pop. incl. with Cheverly (Inc. Place)

English Consul; RMC Place; BALTIMORE; *185 D-13; ★ BAL

English Manor; RMC Place; MONTGOMERY; *185 E-11; ★ WASH; mail Rockville z 20853

English Village; RMC Place; MONTGOMERY; *185 E-11; ★ WASH; mail Bethesda z 20814

Enterprise Estates; RMC Place; PRINCE GEORGE'S; *185 F-13; ★ WASH; mail Bowie z 20721; ● 1,800

Epping Forest; RMC Place; ANNE ARUNDEL; *185 E-14; ★ ANPLS; mail Annapolis z 21401

Ernstville; RMC Place; WASHINGTON; *184 B-7; mail Big Pool z 21711; ● 60

Essex; CDP; BALTIMORE; 185 C-14; elev. 40ft./12m.; [P]; ★ BAL; z 21221; Ⓟ 40,872; © 39,078; ◆ 41,019

Estonian Estates; RMC Place; PRINCE GEORGE'S; *185 F-12; ★ WASH; mail Upper Marlboro z 20772; ● 740

Etchison; RMC Place; MONTGOMERY; 185 D-11; ★ WASH; mail Gaithersburg z 20882; ● 200

Eudowood; RMC Place; BALTIMORE; *185 C-14; elev. 400ft./122m.; [P]; ★ BAL; z 21204 & mail Towson z 21286

Eutaw Forest; RMC Place; CHARLES; *185 G-12; ★ WASH; mail Waldorf z 20603; ● 400

Evanston; RMC Place; PRINCE GEORGE'S; *185 F-12; ★ WASH; mail District Heights z 20747

Evergreen Estates; RMC Place; ANNE ARUNDEL; *185 E-14; ★ BAL; mail Severna Park z 21146

Evergreen Hills; RMC Place; CARROLL; *185 B-12; ★ BAL; mail Finksburg z 21048; ● 200

Evergreen Overlook; RMC Place; PRINCE GEORGE'S; *185 F-12; ★ WASH; mail Oxon Hill z 20745

Evergreen Park; RMC Place; BALTIMORE; 185 D-14; ★ BAL; mail Essex z 21221; ● 70

Evergreen Valley Estates; RMC Place; HOWARD; *185 D-12; ★ BAL; mail Ellicott City z 21042; ● 200

Everlea; RMC Place; CAROLINE; *185 G-16; elev. 38ft./12m.; mail Preston z 21655; ● 50

Evitts Creek; RMC Place; ALLEGANY; *184 B-4; mail Cumberland z 21502; rural

Ewell; RMC Place; SOMERSET; 185 K-16; elev. 3ft./1m.; [P]; z 21824; ● 250

Ewingtown; QUEEN ANNE'S; see Ewingville (RMC Place)

Ewingville (Ewingtown); RMC Place; QUEEN ANNE'S; *185 D-16; mail Chestertown z 21620; ● 120

F

Fahrney Keedy Memorial Home; RMC Place; WASHINGTON; *184 B-9; elev. 500ft./152m.; ★ HAG; mail Boonsboro z 21713; ● 180

Fairbank; RMC Place; TALBOT; *185 G-15; elev. 5ft./2m.; mail Tilghman z 21671

Fairfield; RMC Place; BALTIMORE (Independent City); *185 D-14; ★ BAL; mail Curtis Bay z 21226; pop. incl. with Baltimore (Independent City)

Fairfield; RMC Place; CARROLL; *185 B-12; ★ BAL; mail Westminster z 21157

Fairfield Knolls (Waterford); RMC Place; PRINCE GEORGE'S; *185 F-12; ★ WASH; mail District Heights z 20747; ● 1,500

Fairgreen; RMC Place; PRINCE GEORGE'S; *185 G-13; ★ WASH; mail Upper Marlboro z 20772

Fairgreen Acres; RMC Place; WASHINGTON; ★ HAG; mail Hagerstown z 21740

Fair Haven; RMC Place; ANNE ARUNDEL; 185 G-14; ★ WASH; mail Dunkirk z 20754; ● 500

Fairhaven on the Bay; RMC Place; ANNE ARUNDEL; *185 G-14; ★ WASH; mail Dunkirk z 20754

Fair Hill; RMC Place; CECIL; 185 A-17; elev. 384ft./117m.; ★ PHIL-; mail Elkton z 21921; ● 100

Fairidge; RMC Place; MONTGOMERY; *185 D-11; elev. 400ft./122m.; ★ WASH; mail Gaithersburg z 20879; ● 1,900

Fairknoll; RMC Place; MONTGOMERY; *185 E-12; ★ WASH; mail Silver Spring z 20905; ● 2,300

Fairland; CDP; MONTGOMERY; 185 E-12; ★ WASH; mail Silver Spring z 20904; Ⓟ 19,828; © 21,738; ◆ 23,087

Fairland Acres; RMC Place; MONTGOMERY; *185 E-12; ★ WASH; mail Burtonsville z 20866

Fairland Heights; RMC Place; MONTGOMERY; *185 E-12; ★ WASH; mail Silver Spring z 20904

Fairlee; RMC Place; KENT; 185 D-15; elev. 79ft./24m.; mail Chestertown z 21620; ● 250

Fairmont; RMC Place; HARFORD; *185 B-15; ★ BAL; mail Bel Air z 21014

Fairmont Heights; PRINCE GEORGE'S; see Fairmount Heights (Inc. Place)

Fairmount; CDP; SOMERSET; 185 J-17; elev. 2ft./1m.; [P]; z 21867 & mail Westover z 21871; © 537

Fairmount Heights (Fairmont Heights); Inc. Place; PRINCE GEORGE'S; 249 F-8; elev. 100ft./30m.; [P]; ★ WASH; z 20743; Ⓟ 1,238; © 1,508

Fairplay; RMC Place; WASHINGTON; 184 B-8; elev. 460ft./140m.; [P]; ★ HAG; z 21733; ● 440

Fairview; RMC Place; ANNE ARUNDEL; 184 M-6; ★ WASH; mail Laurel z 20707; ● 680

Fairview; RMC Place; ANNE ARUNDEL; *185 D-14; ★ BAL; mail Pasadena z 21122; ● 230

Fairview; RMC Place; WASHINGTON; 184 A-8; ★ HAG; mail Clear Spring z 21722; pop. incl. with Hancock (Inc. Place)

Fairview Estates; RMC Place; MONTGOMERY; *185 E-12; ★ WASH; mail Silver Spring z 20904

Fairway; RMC Place; HARFORD; *185 B-15; ★ BAL; mail Bel Air z 21015; ● 500

Fairway Hills; RMC Place; MONTGOMERY; *185 E-11; ★ WASH; mail Glen Echo z 20812

Fairway Island; RMC Place; MONTGOMERY; *185 D-11; ★ WASH; mail Gaithersburg z 20879

Fallsmont; RMC Place; HARFORD; *185 B-14; ★ BAL; mail Fallston z 21047

Falls Orchard; RMC Place; MONTGOMERY; *185 E-11; ★ WASH; pop. incl. with Rockville (Inc. Place)

Fallston; CDP; HARFORD; 185 B-14; elev. 456ft./139m.; [P] [H]; ★ BAL; z 21047; Ⓟ 5,730; © 8,427

Family Estates; RMC Place; PRINCE GEORGE'S; *185 F-12; ★ WASH; mail Capitol Heights z 20743

Farmington; RMC Place; CECIL; 185 A-16; elev. 417ft./127m.; ★ PHIL-; mail Rising Sun z 21911; ● 180

Farmington; RMC Place; MONTGOMERY; *185 E-11; ★ WASH; mail Chevy Chase z 20815

Farmsbrook; RMC Place; FREDERICK; *184 C-10; ★ WASH; mail Frederick z 21702; ● 160

Faulkner; RMC Place; CHARLES; 185 H-12; elev. 158ft./48m.; [P]; z 20632; ● 450

Faulkner Ridge; RMC Place; HOWARD; *185 D-12; ★ BAL; mail Columbia z 21044

Fawsett Farms; RMC Place; MONTGOMERY; *185 E-11; ★ WASH; mail Potomac z 20854

Feagaville; RMC Place; FREDERICK; 185 N-16; ★ WASH; mail Frederick z 21702; ● 220

Federal Hill; RMC Place; HARFORD; *185 B-14; ★ BAL; mail Jarrettsville z 21084; ● 100

Federalsburg; Inc. Place; CAROLINE; 185 G-17; elev. 20ft./6m.; [P]; z 21632; Ⓟ 2,365; © 2,620

Felicity Cove; RMC Place; ANNE ARUNDEL; *185 F-14; ★ WASH; mail Shady Side z 20764

Fellowship Forest; RMC Place; BALTIMORE; *185 C-14; ★ BAL; mail Towson z 21204

Fells Point; RMC Place; BALTIMORE (Independent City); 184 J-5; ★ BAL; pop. incl. with Baltimore (Independent City)

Ferdinand Heights; RMC Place; ANNE ARUNDEL; *185 D-14; ★ BAL; mail Glen Burnie z 21061

Ferguson; RMC Place; CALVERT; *185 G-13; elev. 100ft./30m.; ★ WASH; mail Huntingtown z 20639; rural

Ferndale; CDP; ANNE ARUNDEL; 184 M-4; ★ BAL; mail Glen Burnie z 21060; Ⓟ 16,355; © 16,056

Fernglen Manor; RMC Place; ANNE ARUNDEL; *185 D-13; ★ BAL; mail Glen Burnie z 21061; ● 860

Fernwood; RMC Place; MONTGOMERY; *185 E-11; ★ WASH; mail Bethesda z 20817

Fernwood; RMC Place; PRINCE GEORGE'S; *185 F-12; ★ WASH; mail Capitol Heights z 20743; ● 900

Fernwood; RMC Place; PRINCE GEORGE'S; *185 E-12; ★ WASH; mail Riverdale z 20737

Ferry Landing Woods; RMC Place; CALVERT; *185 G-13; elev. 60ft./18m.; ★ WASH; mail Dunkirk z 20754; rural

Fiddlersburg; RMC Place; WASHINGTON; 185 M-14; ★ HAG; mail Hagerstown z 21742; ● 180

Figgs Landing; RMC Place; WORCESTER; *185 J-19; mail Snow Hill z 21863; rural

Finksburg; RMC Place; CARROLL; 185 B-12; elev. 569ft./173m.; [P]; ★ BAL; z 21048; ● 1,000

Finzel; RMC Place; GARRETT; *184 A-3; mail Frostburg z 21532

Fishing Creek; RMC Place; DORCHESTER; 185 I-15; [P]; z 21634; ● 700

Fleishman Village; RMC Place; PRINCE GEORGE'S; *185 F-12; ★ WASH; mail Suitland z 20746; ● 3,900

Flickersville; RMC Place; WASHINGTON; *184 C-9; ★ WASH; mail Keedysville z 21756; rural

Flintstone; RMC Place; ALLEGANY; 184 A-5; elev. 829ft./253m.; [P]; z 21530; ● 500

Flohrville; RMC Place; CARROLL; 185 C-12; ★ BAL; mail Sykesville z 21784; ● 800

Florence; RMC Place; HOWARD; 185 C-11; elev. 620ft./189m.; ★ WASH; mail Woodbine z 21797; ● 100

Flower Valley; RMC Place; MONTGOMERY; *185 E-11; ★ WASH; mail Rockville z 20853; ● 2,000

Flower Valley Estates; RMC Place; MONTGOMERY; *185 E-11; ★ WASH; mail Rockville z 20853

Fontana Village; RMC Place; BALTIMORE; *185 C-14; ★ BAL; mail Rosedale z 21237; ● 1,900

Font Hill; RMC Place; HOWARD; 185 D-13; ★ BAL; mail Ellicott City z 21042; ● 890

Font Hill Manor; RMC Place; HOWARD; 185 D-12; ★ BAL; mail Ellicott City z 21042; ● 2,500

Forest Estates; RMC Place; MONTGOMERY; *185 E-12; ★ WASH; mail Silver Spring z 20910

Forest Glen; CDP; MONTGOMERY; *185 E-11; ★ WASH; mail Silver Spring z 20910; © 7,344

Forest Greens; RMC Place; HARFORD; *185 C-15; mail Aberdeen z 21001; ● 450

Forest Heights; Inc. Place; PRINCE GEORGE'S; 185 F-12; elev. 150ft./46m.; [P]; ★ WASH; z 20745; Ⓟ 2,859; © 2,585

Forest Hill; RMC Place; HARFORD; 185 B-14; elev. 546ft./166m.; [P]; ★ BAL; z 21050; ● 900

Forest Knolls; RMC Place; MONTGOMERY; *185 E-12; ★ WASH; mail Silver Spring z 20901; ● 1,600

Forest Knolls; RMC Place; PRINCE GEORGE'S; *185 G-12; ★ WASH; mail Fort Washington z 20744; ● 1,450

Forest Lake (Lake Forest); RMC Place; HARFORD; *185 B-14; ★ BAL; mail Forest Hill z 21050; ● 1,650

Forest Lawn; RMC Place; HARFORD; *185 B-15; ★ BAL; mail Bel Air z 21014; ● 2,200

Forest Manor; RMC Place; PRINCE GEORGE'S; *185 F-12; ★ WASH; mail District Heights z 20747; ● 2,450

Forest Oaks; RMC Place; CARROLL; *185 C-12; ★ BAL; mail Sykesville z 21784

Forest Park; RMC Place; PRINCE GEORGE'S; *185 E-12; ★ WASH; mail Beltsville z 20705

Forest Villa; RMC Place; ANNE ARUNDEL; *185 E-14; ★ ANPLS; pop. incl. with Annapolis (Inc. Place)

Forestville; CDP; PRINCE GEORGE'S; 185 F-12; [P]; ★ WASH; z 20747 & mail District Heights z 20753; Ⓟ 16,731; © 12,707; Ⓡ 12,712

Forestville Estates; RMC Place; PRINCE GEORGE'S; *185 F-12; ★ WASH; mail District Heights z 20747; ● 140

Forge Acres; RMC Place; BALTIMORE; *185 C-14; ★ BAL; mail Perry Hall z 21128; ● 980

Forge Heights; RMC Place; BALTIMORE; *185 C-14; ★ BAL; mail Perry Hall z 21128

Fork; RMC Place; BALTIMORE; 185 B-14; elev. 434ft./132m.; [P]; ★ BAL; z 21051; ● 500

Forrest Hall; RMC Place; ST. MARY'S; *185 I-13; elev. 154ft./47m.; ★ WASH; mail Mechanicsville z 20659; rural

Fort Foote Estates; RMC Place; PRINCE GEORGE'S; ★ WASH; mail District Heights z 20747

Fort Foote Village; RMC Place; PRINCE GEORGE'S; 249 I-7; ★ WASH; mail Fort Washington z 20744; ● 5,000

Fort Howard; RMC Place; BALTIMORE; 185 D-14; [P] [H]; ★ BAL; z 21052; ● 890

Fort Meade; CDP-Census Area Only; ANNE ARUNDEL; *185 E-13; [P]; ★ BAL; z 20755; Ⓟ 12,509; © 9,882

Fort Ritchie; CDP-Census Area Only; WASHINGTON; *184 A-9; [P]; ★ HAG; z 21719; Ⓟ 1,249; © 276

Fort Sumner; RMC Place; MONTGOMERY; *185 E-11; ★ WASH; mail Bethesda z 20816; ● 740

Fort Washington; CDP; PRINCE GEORGE'S; *185 G-12; [P] [H]; ★ WASH; z 20744, z 20749 & mail Oxon Hill z 20750; Ⓟ 24,032; © 23,845; ◆ 23,922

Fort Washington Estates; RMC Place; PRINCE GEORGE'S; *185 G-12; ★ WASH; mail Fort Washington z 20744; ● 870

Fort Washington Forest; RMC Place; PRINCE GEORGE'S; 185 G-12; ★ WASH; mail Fort Washington z 20744; ● 1,200

Foundry Siding; RMC Place; ALLEGANY; ★ CUMB; mail Westernport z 21562; pop. incl. with Westernport (Inc. Place)

Fountaindale; RMC Place; FREDERICK; *184 C-9; ★ WASH; mail Middletown z 21769

Fountain Green; RMC Place; HARFORD; 185 B-15; elev. 330ft./101m.; ★ BAL; mail Bel Air z 21015; ● 1,400

Fountain Green Heights; RMC Place; HARFORD; *185 B-15; ★ BAL; mail Bel Air z 21015

Fountain Head; RMC Place; WASHINGTON; 184 A-8; ★ HAG; mail Hagerstown z 21742; ● 1,350

Fountainhead-Orchard Hills; CDP-Census Area Only; WASHINGTON; *184 A-9; ★ HAG; © 3,844

Fountain Mills; RMC Place; FREDERICK; *185 C-11; ★ WASH; mail Ijamsville z 21754

Fountain Rock; RMC Place; FREDERICK; *184 B-10; ★ WASH; mail Walkersville z 21793

Fountain Valley; RMC Place; CARROLL; *185 B-12; ★ BAL; mail Westminster z 21157; rural

Four Locks; RMC Place; WASHINGTON; *184 B-7; mail Clear Spring z 21722; rural

Four Seasons Estates; RMC Place; ANNE ARUNDEL; *185 E-13; ★ BAL; mail Odenton z 21113; ● 2,800

Four Winds; RMC Place; BALTIMORE; *185 C-13; ★ BAL; mail Towson z 21204

Fowblesburg; RMC Place; BALTIMORE; 185 B-12; ★ BAL; mail Upperco z 21155; ● 250

Fowlers Concord; RMC Place; PRINCE GEORGE'S; *185 F-12; ★ WASH; mail District Heights z 20747

Fox Chapel; RMC Place; MONTGOMERY; *185 D-11; ★ WASH; mail Germantown z 20876; ● 6,200

Fox Chapel North; RMC Place; MONTGOMERY; *185 D-11; ★ WASH; mail Germantown z 20876

Fox Chase; RMC Place; ANNE ARUNDEL; *185 D-13; ★ BAL; mail Glen Burnie z 21061

Foxhall; RMC Place; MONTGOMERY; *185 E-11; ★ WASH; mail Silver Spring z 20906

Foxhall Estates; RMC Place; ANNE ARUNDEL; *185 F-13; ★ WASH; mail Davidsonville z 21035; ● 200

Fox Hills; RMC Place; MONTGOMERY; *185 E-11; ★ WASH; mail Potomac z 20854

Fox Hills West; RMC Place; MONTGOMERY; *185 E-11; ★ WASH; mail Potomac z 20854; pop. incl. with Rockville (Inc. Place)

Foxley Manor; RMC Place; KENT; *185 D-16; mail Chestertown z 21620; pop. incl. with Chestertown (Inc. Place)

Fox Rest; RMC Place; PRINCE GEORGE'S; *185 E-12; ★ WASH; mail Laurel z 20708

Fox Rest South; RMC Place; PRINCE GEORGE'S; *185 E-12; ★ WASH; mail Laurel z 20708; ● 2,400

Foxridge; RMC Place; HARFORD; *185 B-15; mail Havre de Grace z 21078, Randallstown z 21133; ● 150

Fox Run Estates; RMC Place; PRINCE GEORGE'S; *185 G-12; ★ WASH; mail Clinton z 20735

Foxville; RMC Place; FREDERICK; *184 B-9; elev. 1,452ft./443m.; mail Sabillasville z 21780; rural

Franklin (Gannon); RMC Place; ALLEGANY; *184 B-3; ★ CUMB; mail Westernport z 21562; ● 130

Franklin; RMC Place; BALTIMORE (Independent City); *185 D-13; [P]; ★ BAL; z 21223; pop. incl. with Baltimore (Independent City)

Franklin Heights; RMC Place; WORCESTER; *185 I-20; elev. 40ft./12m.; mail Berlin z 21811; pop. incl. with Berlin (Inc. Place)

Franklin Manor Beach; RMC Place; ANNE ARUNDEL; *185 F-14; ★ WASH; mail Churchton z 20733

Franklin Manor on-the-Bay; RMC Place; ANNE ARUNDEL; *185 F-14; ★ WASH; mail Churchton z 20733

Franklin Park; RMC Place; MONTGOMERY; *185 E-11; ★ WASH; mail Rockville z 20852; ● 1,500

Franklin Square; RMC Place; PRINCE GEORGE'S; *185 G-12; ★ WASH; mail Fort Washington z 20744

Franklinville; RMC Place; BALTIMORE, HARFORD; *185 C-14; ★ BAL; mail Kingsville z 21087; ● 320

Franklinville; RMC Place; FREDERICK; mail Thurmont z 21788; pop. incl. with Thurmont (Inc. Place)

Frederick; Inc. Place; ⊡ FREDERICK; 184 C-10; elev. 290ft./88m.; [P] [H] [C] 2,248 ■; ★ WASH; z 21701-05, z 21709; Ⓟ 40,148; © 52,767; ◆ 64,095

FREDERICK; 184 B-10; Ⓟ 150,208; © 195,277; ◆ 228,130

Frederick Junction; RMC Place; FREDERICK; *184 C-10; elev. 268ft./82m.; ★ WASH; mail Frederick z 21701; rural

Fredericktown (Georgetown); RMC Place; CECIL; *185 C-17; elev. 60ft./18m.; mail Georgetown z 21930; ● 250

Frederick Village; RMC Place; BALTIMORE; *185 D-13; ★ BAL; mail Catonsville z 21228

Freedom; RMC Place; CARROLL; *185 C-12; elev. 600ft./183m.; ★ BAL; mail Sykesville z 21784

Freedom Forest; RMC Place; CARROLL; *185 C-12; ★ BAL; mail Sykesville z 21784

Freeland; RMC Place; BALTIMORE; 185 A-13; elev. 664ft./202m.; [P]; ★ BAL; z 21053; ● 600

Frenchtown; RMC Place; CECIL; *185 B-16; mail Perryville z 21903; pop. incl. with Perryville (Inc. Place)

Frenchtown; RMC Place; SOMERSET; *185 J-17; mail Westover z 21871; ● 30

Frenchtown-Rumbly; CDP-Census Area Only; SOMERSET; *185 J-17; © 96

Friendly; CDP; PRINCE GEORGE'S; 249 J-7; ★ WASH; mail Fort Washington z 20744; Ⓟ 9,028; © 10,938

Friendly Farms; RMC Place; PRINCE GEORGE'S; *185 G-12; ★ WASH; mail Fort Washington z 20744

Friends Creek; RMC Place; FREDERICK; *184 A-10; mail Emmitsburg z 21727; rural

Friendship; RMC Place; ANNE ARUNDEL; 185 G-14; elev. 140ft./43m.; [P]; ★ WASH; z 20758; ● 170

Friendship; RMC Place; FREDERICK; ★ WASH; mail Union Bridge z 21791

Friendship; RMC Place; WORCESTER; *185 I-20; elev. 32ft./10m.; mail Berlin z 21811; rural

Friendship Heights; RMC Place; MONTGOMERY; *185 E-11; ★ WASH; mail Bethesda z 20813

Friendship Park; RMC Place; WASHINGTON; *184 B-8; elev. 580ft./177m.; ★ HAG; mail Hagerstown z 21740; ● 1,100

Friendship Village; CDP-Census Area Only; MONTGOMERY; *185 E-11; ★ WASH; © 4,512

Friendsville; Inc. Place; GARRETT; 184 A-1; elev. 1,497ft./456m.; [P]; z 21531; Ⓟ 577; © 539

Frizzelburg; RMC Place; CARROLL; 185 B-11; mail Westminster z 21158; ● 280

Frostburg; Inc. Place; ALLEGANY; 184 A-3; elev. 2,075ft./632m.; [P] [C] 4,910; ★ CUMB; z 21532; Ⓟ 8,075; © 7,873

Frostown; RMC Place; FREDERICK; *184 B-9; ★ WASH; mail Middletown z 21769; rural

Fruitland; Inc. Place; WICOMICO; 185 I-18; elev. 39ft./12m.; [P]; ★ SLSB; z 21826; Ⓟ 3,511; © 3,774

Fullerton; RMC Place; BALTIMORE; 184 J-4; ★ BAL; mail Nottingham z 21236; ● 2,400

Fulton; RMC Place; BALTIMORE (Independent City); *185 C-13; ★ BAL; mail Baltimore z 21217; pop. incl. with Baltimore (Independent City)

Fulton; RMC Place; HOWARD; 185 D-12; elev. 453ft./138m.; [P]; ★ WASH; z 20759; ● 1,150

Funkstown; Inc. Place; WASHINGTON; 184 B-9; [P]; ★ HAG; z 21734; Ⓟ 1,136; © 983

Furnace; RMC Place; WORCESTER; *185 J-19; elev. 28ft./9m.; mail Snow Hill z 21863; rural

Furnace Branch; RMC Place; ANNE ARUNDEL; *185 D-13; ★ BAL; mail Glen Burnie z 21061

G

Gaither; RMC Place; CARROLL; 185 C-12; [P]; ★ BAL; z 21784; ● 300

Gaithersburg; Inc. Place; MONTGOMERY; 185 D-11; elev. 508ft./155m.; [P] ■; ★ WASH; z 20877-79, z 20882-86, z 20898-99; Ⓟ 39,542; © 52,613; ◆ 62,324

Galena; Inc. Place; KENT; 185 C-17; elev. 83ft./25m.; [P]; z 21635; Ⓟ 324; © 428

Galestown; Inc. Place; DORCHESTER; 185 H-18; elev. 10ft./3m.; mail Seaford z 19973; Ⓟ 123; © 101

Galesville; RMC Place; ANNE ARUNDEL; 185 F-14; elev. 20ft./6m.; [P]; ★ WASH; z 20765; ● 1,000

Gallant Green; RMC Place; CHARLES; *185 H-13; ★ WASH; mail Waldorf z 20601; ● 50

Gamber; RMC Place; CARROLL; 185 C-12; elev. 648ft./198m.; ★ BAL; mail Finksburg z 21048, Sykesville z 21784; ● 250

Gambrills; RMC Place; ANNE ARUNDEL; 185 E-13; elev. 160ft./49m.; [P]; ★ BAL; z 21054; ● 1,500

Gannon; ALLEGANY; see Franklin (RMC Place)

Gapland; RMC Place; WASHINGTON; 184 C-9; elev. 620ft./189m.; [P]; ★ WASH; z 21779; ● 240

Garfield; RMC Place; FREDERICK; *184 B-9; mail Smithsburg z 21783; rural

Garland; RMC Place; ANNE ARUNDEL; 184 M-4; ★ BAL; mail Glen Burnie z 21061; ● 1,800

GARRETT; 184 B-2; Ⓟ 28,138; © 29,846; ◆ 29,703

Garrett Forest; RMC Place; MONTGOMERY; ★ WASH; mail Silver Spring z 20906

Garrett Park; Inc. Place; MONTGOMERY; 185 E-11; elev. 314ft./96m.; [P]; ★ WASH; z 20896; Ⓟ 884; © 917

Garrett Park Estates; RMC Place; MONTGOMERY; *185 E-11; ★ WASH; mail Kensington z 20895; ● 2,500

Garretts Mill; RMC Place; WASHINGTON; *184 C-9; elev. 400ft./122m.; ★ WASH; mail Knoxville z 21758; rural

Garrison; CDP; BALTIMORE; 184 G-2; elev. 460ft./140m.; [P]; ★ BAL; z 21117; Ⓟ 5,045; © 7,969

Gatts Corner; RMC Place; ANNE ARUNDEL; *185 F-14; ★ ANPLS; mail Mayo z 21106

Gayfields; RMC Place; MONTGOMERY; *185 E-12; ★ WASH; mail Silver Spring z 20906

Gemmills; BALTIMORE; see Vernon (RMC Place)

George Island Landing; RMC Place; WORCESTER; *185 K-19; mail Stockton z 21864; rural

Georgetown; RMC Place; ANNE ARUNDEL; *185 D-13; ★ BAL; mail Jessup z 20794; rural

Georgetown; CECIL; see Fredericktown (RMC Place)

Georgetown; RMC Place; KENT; *185 C-17; [P]; z 21930; ● 100

Georgetown; RMC Place; KENT; 185 C-17; elev. 43ft./13m.; mail Chestertown z 21620; ● 100

Georgetown Estates; RMC Place; MONTGOMERY; *185 E-11; ★ WASH; mail Rockville z 20852

Georgetown Village; RMC Place; MONTGOMERY; *185 E-11; ★ WASH; mail Glen Echo z 20812

Georgian Forest; RMC Place; MONTGOMERY; *185 E-11; ★ WASH; mail Silver Spring z 20902; ● 410

Germantown; RMC Place; ANNE ARUNDEL; *185 F-14; ★ ANPLS

Germantown; CDP; MONTGOMERY; 185 D-11; elev. 428ft./130m.; [P]; ★ WASH; z 20874-76; Ⓟ 41,145; © 55,419; ◆ 58,856

Germantown; RMC Place; WORCESTER; *185 I-20; mail Berlin z 21811

Germantown Estates; RMC Place; MONTGOMERY; *184 D-10; ★ WASH; mail Germantown z 20874; ● 1,350

Germantown Park; RMC Place; MONTGOMERY; *185 D-11; ★ WASH; mail Germantown z 20874; ● 10,400

Germantown View; RMC Place; MONTGOMERY; *185 D-11; ★ WASH; mail Germantown z 20874

Gibson; HARFORD; see Gibson Manor (RMC Place)

Gibson Island; RMC Place; ANNE ARUNDEL; 185 E-14; elev. 20ft./6m.; [P]; ★ BAL; z 21056; ● 400

Gibson Manor (Gibson); RMC Place; HARFORD; *185 B-15; ★ BAL; mail Bel Air z 21015; ● 200

Gilmore (Tannery); RMC Place; ALLEGANY; *184 B-3; ★ CUMB; mail Frostburg z 21532; ● 250

Gilpin; RMC Place; ALLEGANY; *184 A-5; elev. 777ft./237m.; mail Flintstone z 21530; ● 30

Gingerville Manor Estates; RMC Place; ANNE ARUNDEL; 185 N-18; ★ ANPLS; mail Edgewater z 21037

Girdletree; CDP; WORCESTER; 185 J-19; elev. 34ft./10m.; [P]; z 21829; © 117

Gist; RMC Place; CARROLL; *185 C-12; ★ BAL; mail Sykesville z 21784; ● 50

Glade Towne; RMC Place; FREDERICK; *184 B-10; ★ WASH; mail Walkersville z 21793; pop. incl. with Walkersville (Inc. Place)

Gladstone Acres; RMC Place; HARFORD; *185 A-15; ★ BAL; mail Darlington z 21034; ● 50

Glassmanor; RMC Place; PRINCE GEORGE'S; 249 H-7; ★ WASH; mail Oxon Hill z 20745; ● 8,800

Glazewood Manor; RMC Place; PRINCE GEORGE'S; ★ WASH; mail Takoma Park z 20912; pop. incl. with Takoma Park (Inc. Place)

Glebe Heights; RMC Place; ANNE ARUNDEL; *185 F-14; ★ ANPLS; mail Edgewater z 21037; ● 380

Glebe Villa; RMC Place; TALBOT; *185 F-16; elev. 16ft./5m.; mail Easton z 21601; ● 50

Glen; MONTGOMERY; see The Glen (RMC Place)

Glenallen; RMC Place; MONTGOMERY; *185 E-12; ★ WASH; mail Silver Spring z 20902

Glenarden; Inc. Place; PRINCE GEORGE'S; 185 F-12; elev. 110ft./34m.; [P]; ★ WASH; z 20706, z 20774; Ⓟ 5,025; © 6,318

Glen Arm; RMC Place; BALTIMORE; 185 C-14; elev. 323ft./98m.; [P]; ★ BAL; z 21057; ● 730

Glen Brook; RMC Place; HOWARD; *185 D-12; ★ BAL; mail Ellicott City z 21042

Glenbrook Knolls; RMC Place; MONTGOMERY; *185 E-11; ★ WASH; mail Bethesda z 20814

Glenbrook Village; RMC Place; MONTGOMERY; *185 E-11; ★ WASH; mail Bethesda z 20814

Glen Burnie; CDP; ANNE ARUNDEL; 185 D-13; [P] [H]; ★ BAL; z 21060-62; Ⓟ 37,305; © 38,922; ◆ 41,153

Glen Burnie Park; RMC Place; ANNE ARUNDEL; *185 D-13; ★ BAL; mail Glen Burnie z 21061; ● 3,000

Glencoe; RMC Place; BALTIMORE; 185 B-13; [P]; ★ BAL; z 21152; ● 220

Glencoe; RMC Place; KENT; *185 C-16; mail Kennedyville z 21645; ● 70

Glen Cove; RMC Place; MONTGOMERY; *185 E-11; ★ WASH; mail Bethesda z 20816

Glendale; RMC Place; BALTIMORE; *185 C-14; ★ BAL; mail Towson z 21204

Glendale; RMC Place; WICOMICO; ★ SLSB; mail Salisbury z 21801; pop. incl. with Salisbury (Inc. Place)

Glen Echo; Inc. Place; MONTGOMERY; 249 E-5; elev. 153ft./47m.; [P]; ★ WASH; z 20812; Ⓟ 234; © 242

Glen Echo Heights; RMC Place; MONTGOMERY; *185 E-11; ★ WASH; mail Bethesda z 20816; ● 2,100

Glenelg; RMC Place; HOWARD; 185 D-12; elev. 580ft./177m.; [P]; ★ WASH; z 21737; ● 1,000

Glen Ellen; RMC Place; BALTIMORE; *185 C-14; ★ BAL; mail Towson z 21286

Glen Elyn; RMC Place; HARFORD; *185 B-14; ★ BAL; mail Fallston z 21047; ● 980

Glen Farms; RMC Place; CECIL; *185 A-17; ★ PHIL-; mail Elkton z 21921; ● 850

Glen Gardens; RMC Place; ANNE ARUNDEL; *185 D-13; ★ BAL; mail Glen Burnie z 21060

Glen Haven; RMC Place; MONTGOMERY; *185 E-12; ★ WASH

Glen Hills (North Glen Hills); RMC Place; MONTGOMERY; 249 C-3; ★ WASH; mail Rockville z 20850; ● 1,400

Glen Isle; RMC Place; ANNE ARUNDEL; *185 E-14; ★ ANPLS; mail Annapolis z 21401

Glen Kyle; RMC Place; CECIL; *185 A-17; ★ PHIL-; mail Newark z 19711

Glenmar; RMC Place; BALTIMORE; *185 C-14; ★ BAL; mail Middle River z 21220

Glenmar; RMC Place; HOWARD; *185 D-13; ★ BAL; mail Ellicott City z 21043

Glenmar Manor; BALTIMORE; see Maple Crest (RMC Place)

Glen Mar Park; RMC Place; MONTGOMERY; *185 E-11; ★ WASH; mail Bethesda z 20814

Glen Mary Heights; RMC Place; CECIL; ★ PHIL-; mail Elkton z 21921; pop. incl. with Elkton (Inc. Place)

Glenmont; RMC Place; BALTIMORE; *185 C-14; ★ BAL; mail Baltimore z 21239

Glenmont; RMC Place; MONTGOMERY; *185 E-11; ★ WASH; mail Silver Spring z 20902, z 20906

Glenmont Park; RMC Place; MONTGOMERY; *185 E-11; ★ WASH; mail Silver Spring z 20906

Glenmore; RMC Place; ANNE ARUNDEL; *185 D-13; ★ BAL; mail Glen Burnie z 21061; ● 1,500

Glen Morris; RMC Place; BALTIMORE; *185 B-12; ★ BAL; mail Reisterstown z 21136

Glenn Dale; CDP; PRINCE GEORGE'S; 185 E-13; elev. 46ft./14m.; [P]; ★ WASH; z 20769; Ⓟ 9,689; © 12,609

Glenn Dale Heights; RMC Place; PRINCE GEORGE'S; *185 E-13; ★ WASH; mail Glenn Dale z 20769

Glenn Heights; RMC Place; HARFORD; *185 B-16; mail Havre de Grace z 21078; ● 200

Glen Oaks; RMC Place; MONTGOMERY; ★ WASH; mail Potomac z 20854

Glenora Hills; RMC Place; MONTGOMERY; *185 E-11; ★ WASH; mail Rockville z 20850; pop. incl. with Rockville (Inc. Place)

Glen Park; RMC Place; MONTGOMERY; *185 E-11; ★ WASH; mail Potomac z 20854

Glen Ridge; RMC Place; PRINCE GEORGE'S; *185 E-12; ★ WASH; mail Hyattsville z 20784

Glenside Park; RMC Place; BALTIMORE; *185 C-14; ★ BAL; mail Parkville z 21234

Glenville; RMC Place; HARFORD; *185 B-15; elev. 184ft./56m.; mail Churchville z 21028, Darlington z 21034, Havre de Grace z 21078; ● 150

Glen Westover; RMC Place; CECIL; *185 A-17; ★ PHIL-; mail Newark z 19711

Glen Willows; RMC Place; PRINCE GEORGE'S; *185 F-12; ★ WASH; mail Capitol Heights z 20743

Glenwood; RMC Place; HARFORD; *185 B-15; ★ BAL; mail Bel Air z 21014; ● 3,700

Glenwood; RMC Place; HOWARD; 185 D-12; elev. 540ft./165m.; [P]; ★ WASH; z 21738; ● 200

Glenwood Estates; RMC Place; HOWARD; *185 D-12; ★ WASH; mail Glenwood z 21738; ● 110

Glenwood Park; PRINCE GEORGE'S; see Buena Vista (RMC Place)

Glover Acres; RMC Place; CARROLL; *185 B-12; ★ BAL; mail Westminster z 21157

Glymont; RMC Place; CHARLES; *185 G-11; ★ WASH; mail Indian Head z 20640; pop. incl. with Indian Head (Inc. Place)

Glyndon; RMC Place; BALTIMORE; 185 B-13; elev. 619ft./189m.; [P]; ★ BAL; z 21071 & mail Reisterstown z 21136; ● 900

Gnegy Church; RMC Place; GARRETT; 184 C-1; rural

Goddard; CDP-Census Area Only; PRINCE GEORGE'S; *185 E-12; ★ WASH; mail Greenbelt z 20770; Ⓟ 4,576; © 5,554

Goddard Space Village; PRINCE GEORGE'S; see Braebrook Village (RMC Place)

Golden Beach; CDP; ST. MARY'S; 185 H-13; ★ WASH; mail Mechanicsville z 20659; Ⓟ 2,944; © 2,665; Ⓡ 2,669

Golden Hill; RMC Place; DORCHESTER; 185 I-15; mail Church Creek z 21622; ● 40

Golden Ring; RMC Place; BALTIMORE; *185 C-14; ★ BAL; mail Rosedale z 21237

Goldsboro; Inc. Place; CAROLINE; 185 E-17; elev. 60ft./18m.; [P]; z 21636; Ⓟ 185; © 216

Golf Club Shores; RMC Place; WORCESTER; *185 I-20; mail Berlin z 21811; ● 340

Golts; RMC Place; KENT; 185 C-17; elev. 78ft./24m.; [P]; z 21635; ● 150

Good Acres; RMC Place; WASHINGTON; ★ HAG; mail Hagerstown z 21740

Good Hope; RMC Place; MONTGOMERY; *185 E-12; elev. 487ft./148m.; ★ WASH; mail Silver Spring z 20905

Goodwill; RMC Place; WORCESTER; 185 J-19; elev. 32ft./10m.; mail Pocomoke City z 21851; ● 50

Gorman; RMC Place; GARRETT; 184 C-1; mail Gormania z 26720; ● 150

Gortner; RMC Place; GARRETT; 184 C-1; elev. 2,427ft./740m.; mail Oakland z 21550; ● 230

Goshen; RMC Place; MONTGOMERY; 185 D-11; ★ WASH; mail Gaithersburg z 20879; ● 530

Goshen Estates; RMC Place; MONTGOMERY; *185 D-11; ★ WASH; mail Gaithersburg z 20879; ● 500

Gotts; RMC Place; ANNE ARUNDEL; *185 E-14; ★ BAL; mail Crownsville z 21032

Govans; RMC Place; BALTIMORE (Independent City); *185 C-13; [P]; ★ BAL; z 21212; pop. incl. with Baltimore (Independent City)

Governors Run; RMC Place; CALVERT; 185 H-14; mail Port Republic z 20676; ● 30

Graceham; RMC Place; FREDERICK; 184 B-10; [P]; z 21788; ● 120

Graceton; RMC Place; HARFORD; *185 A-14; ★ BAL; mail Whiteford z 21160; ● 50

Grahamtown; RMC Place; ALLEGANY; *184 A-3; ★ CUMB; mail Frostburg z 21532; ● 900

Granby Woods; RMC Place; MONTGOMERY; *185 D-11; ★ WASH; mail Derwood z 20855; ● 550

Grand Bel Manor; RMC Place; MONTGOMERY; *185 E-11; ★ WASH; mail Silver Spring z 20906

Grandview; RMC Place; CARROLL; *185 C-12; ★ BAL; mail Sykesville z 21784; ● 320

Granite; RMC Place; BALTIMORE; 185 C-12; [P]; ★ BAL; z 21163; ● 950

Grantsville; Inc. Place; GARRETT; 184 A-2; elev. 2,300ft./701m.; [P]; z 21536; Ⓟ 505; © 619

Grasonville; CDP; QUEEN ANNE'S; 185 E-15; elev. 2,300ft./701m.; [P]; ★ ANPLS; z 21638; Ⓟ 2,439; © 2,193

Gratitude; RMC Place; KENT; *185 D-15; mail Rock Hall z 21661

Gray Haven; RMC Place; BALTIMORE; *185 D-14; ★ BAL; mail Dundalk z 21222

Gray Manor; RMC Place; BALTIMORE; *185 D-14; ★ BAL; mail Dundalk z 21222

Gray Rock; RMC Place; HOWARD; ★ BAL; mail Ellicott City z 21042

Graystone; RMC Place; BALTIMORE; *185 B-13; elev. 361ft./110m.; ★ BAL; mail White Hall z 21161; ● 50

Grayton; RMC Place; CHARLES; *185 H-11; mail Nanjemoy z 20662; rural

Greater Capitol Heights (Hillside); RMC Place; PRINCE GEORGE'S; *185 F-12; ★ WASH; mail Capitol Heights z 20743; ● 4,150

Greater Landover; CDP-Census Area Only; PRINCE GEORGE'S; *185 F-12; ★ WASH; © 22,900; ◆ 22,968

Greater Upper Marlboro; CDP-Census Area Only; PRINCE GEORGE'S; *185 F-13; elev. 160ft./49m.; ★ WASH; mail Upper Marlboro z 20772, z 20774; Ⓟ 11,528; © 18,720

Great Falls; RMC Place; MONTGOMERY; 249 E-3; ★ WASH

Great Mills; RMC Place; ST. MARY'S; 185 J-14; elev. 14ft./4m.; [P]; z 20634; ● 700

Green Acres; RMC Place; HARFORD; *185 C-15; ★ BAL; mail Joppa z 21085; ● 150

Green Acres; RMC Place; MONTGOMERY; *185 E-11; ★ WASH; mail Bethesda z 20817

Greenbelt; Inc. Place; PRINCE GEORGE'S; 185 E-12; elev. 180ft./55m.; [P]; ★ WASH; z 20768, z 20770-71; Ⓟ 21,096; © 21,456; ◆ 20,290

Greenberry Hills; RMC Place; WASHINGTON; 185 N-13; ★ HAG; mail Hagerstown z 21740; ● 1,400

Greenbriar; RMC Place; WASHINGTON; *184 B-9; elev. 668ft./204m.; ★ HAG; mail Boonsboro z 21713; rural

Greenbrier; RMC Place; CECIL; *185 B-17; elev. 40ft./12m.; ★ PHIL-; mail Chesapeake City z 21915; rural

Greenbrier; RMC Place; PRINCE GEORGE'S; ★ WASH; mail Greenbelt z 20770; pop. incl. with Greenbelt (Inc. Place)

Greendale Estates; RMC Place; HARFORD; *185 B-14; ★ BAL; mail Fallston z 21047; ● 400

Greenfield; RMC Place; PRINCE GEORGE'S; *185 G-12; ★ WASH; mail Clinton z 20735

Greenfield Mills; RMC Place; FREDERICK; *184 D-10; ★ WASH; mail Adamstown z 21710; rural

Green Glade; RMC Place; GARRETT; *184 B-2; mail Swanton z 21561; summer pop. 200; ● 50

Green Haven; CDP; ANNE ARUNDEL; 185 D-14; ★ BAL; mail Pasadena z 21122; Ⓟ 14,416; © 17,415

Green Hill; RMC Place; WICOMICO; 185 I-17; mail Quantico z 21856; ● 70

Green Hill Acres; RMC Place; WASHINGTON; *184 B-9; ★ HAG; mail Hagerstown z 21742; ● 220

Green Meadows; RMC Place; CALVERT; *185 G-13; elev. 100ft./30m.; ★ WASH; mail Huntingtown z 20639; ● 30

Green Meadows; RMC Place; CHARLES; *185 G-11; ★ WASH; mail Indian Head z 20640

Green Meadows; RMC Place; PRINCE GEORGE'S; *185 E-12; ★ WASH; mail Hyattsville z 20782; ● 3,450

Greenmount; RMC Place; CARROLL; *185 B-12; [P]; ★ BAL; z 21074

Green Ridge; RMC Place; ALLEGANY; *184 B-5; mail Flintstone z 21530

Green Ridge; RMC Place; BALTIMORE; *185 C-13; ★ BAL; mail Lutherville Timonium z 21093

Greenridge; RMC Place; HARFORD; *185 B-15; ★ BAL; mail Bel Air z 21015; ● 1,300

Greensboro; Inc. Place; CAROLINE; 185 E-17; elev. 20ft./6m.; [P]; z 21639; Ⓟ 1,441; © 1,632

Greensburg; RMC Place; WASHINGTON; *184 A-9; ★ HAG; mail Smithsburg z 21783; ● 370

Green Spring Hills; RMC Place; HARFORD; *185 C-15; ★ BAL; mail Joppa z 21085; ● 260

Greentop Manor; RMC Place; BALTIMORE; *185 B-13; ★ BAL; mail Cockeysville z 21030; ● 3,000

Greentree; RMC Place; ANNE ARUNDEL; *185 D-13; ★ BAL; mail Glen Burnie z 21061

Greentree; RMC Place; MONTGOMERY; *185 D-11; ★ WASH; mail Gaithersburg z 20879

Green Tree Manor; RMC Place; MONTGOMERY; *185 E-11; ★ WASH; mail Bethesda z 20817

Greenvale Village; RMC Place; WASHINGTON; *184 B-9; elev. 676ft./206m.; ★ HAG; mail Smithsburg z 21783; ● 200

Green Valley; CDP; FREDERICK; *184 C-10; ★ WASH; mail Mount Airy z 21771; Ⓟ 9,424; © 12,262

Greenview Knolls; RMC Place; ST. MARY'S; *185 I-14; mail Great Mills z 20634; ● 370

Greenwich Forest; RMC Place; MONTGOMERY; *185 E-11; ★ WASH; mail Bethesda z 20814

Greenwood Acres; RMC Place; ANNE ARUNDEL; *185 E-14; ★ ANPLS; mail Annapolis z 21401

Greenwood Farms; RMC Place; HOWARD; *185 D-12; elev. 500ft./152m.; ★ WASH; mail Highland z 20777; ● 150

Greenwood Forest; RMC Place; PRINCE GEORGE'S; *185 E-12; ★ WASH; mail Lanham z 20706

Gregg Neck; RMC Place; KENT; *185 C-17; mail Galena z 21635; ● 200

Greystone Manor; RMC Place; WASHINGTON; ★ HAG; mail Hagerstown z 21740; pop. incl. with Hagerstown (Inc. Place)

Griffith Park; RMC Place; MONTGOMERY; *185 D-11; elev. 587ft./179m.; ★ WASH; mail Gaithersburg z 20877; ● 50

Grimesville; RMC Place; BALTIMORE; *185 A-13; ★ BAL; mail Freeland z 21053; ● 120

Grove; RMC Place; CAROLINE; *185 G-17; mail Preston z 21655; rural

Grove Hill; RMC Place; FREDERICK; *184 C-10; ★ WASH; mail Frederick z 21702; pop. incl. with Frederick (Inc. Place)

Guilford; RMC Place; HOWARD; 185 D-12; ★ BAL; mail Jessup z 20794; ● 1,000

Guilford Manor; RMC Place; ANNE ARUNDEL; *185 D-13; ★ BAL; mail Brooklyn z 21225; ● 900

Gum Springs; RMC Place; MONTGOMERY; *185 E-12; ★ WASH; mail Spencerville z 20868

Gum Springs Farm; RMC Place; MONTGOMERY; *185 E-12; ★ WASH; mail Spencerville z 20868

Gunners Lake Village; RMC Place; MONTGOMERY; *185 D-11; ★ WASH; mail Germantown z 20874

Gunpowder; RMC Place; BALTIMORE; *185 C-14; ★ BAL; mail Kingsville z 21087; rural

Gunpowder Estates; RMC Place; BALTIMORE; ★ BAL; mail Perry Hall z 21128

Guys; RMC Place; QUEEN ANNE'S; *185 F-15; elev. 14ft./4m.; ★ ANPLS; mail Queenstown z 21658; ● 50

Gwenlee Estates; RMC Place; HOWARD; *185 D-12; ★ WASH; mail Glenwood z 21738; ● 170

Gwynn; RMC Place; HOWARD; *185 D-12; ★ BAL; mail Ellicott City z 21042

Gwynn Acres; RMC Place; HOWARD; *185 D-12; ★ BAL; mail Ellicott City z 21042

Gwynnbrook; RMC Place; BALTIMORE; *185 C-13; ★ BAL; mail Owings Mills z 21117

Gwynn Oak; RMC Place; BALTIMORE (Independent City); *185 C-13; [P]; ★ BAL; z 21207 & mail Windsor Mill z 21244; pop. incl. with Baltimore (Independent City)

H

Hack Point; RMC Place; CECIL; 185 C-17; mail Earleville z 21919; summer pop. 1,500; ● 500

Hacks Point Acre; RMC Place; CECIL; *185 B-17; mail Earleville z 21919; ● 250

Hagerstown; Inc. Place; ⊡ WASHINGTON; 184 A-8; elev. 552ft./168m.; [P] [H] ■; ★ HAG; z 21740-42, z 21746-49; Ⓟ 35,445; © 36,687; ◆ 40,921

Halethorpe; RMC Place; BALTIMORE; *185 D-13; elev. 100ft./30m.; [P]; ★ BAL; z 21227 & mail Elkridge z 21075

Halfway; CDP; WASHINGTON; 184 B-8; ★ HAG; mail Hagerstown z 21740; Ⓟ 8,873; © 10,065

Halfway Manor; RMC Place; WASHINGTON; *184 B-8; ★ HAG; mail Hagerstown z 21740

Hallett Heights; RMC Place; WORCESTER; *185 J-19; mail Snow Hill z 21863; ● 110

Halley Estates; RMC Place; CHARLES; *185 H-12; ★ WASH; mail White Plains z 20695

Hallmark Estates; RMC Place; CALVERT; *185 G-13; elev. 100ft./30m.; ★ WASH; mail Huntingtown z 20639; rural

Hallmark Woods; RMC Place; ANNE ARUNDEL; *185 E-13; elev. 100ft./30m.; ★ BAL; mail Gambrills z 21054

Halpine Village; RMC Place; MONTGOMERY; *185 E-11; ★ WASH; mail Rockville z 20852; ● 2,200

Hambleton Estates; RMC Place; ANNE ARUNDEL; ★ ANPLS; mail Riva z 21140

Hamilton; RMC Place; BALTIMORE (Independent City); *185 C-14; elev. 335ft./102m.; ★ BAL; mail Baltimore z 21214; pop. incl. with Baltimore (Independent City)

Hamilton Park; RMC Place; WASHINGTON; ★ HAG; mail Hagerstown z 21740; pop. incl. with Hagerstown (Inc. Place)

Hamlet North; RMC Place; MONTGOMERY; *185 D-11; ★ WASH; mail Derwood z 20855

Hammond; RMC Place; HOWARD; *185 D-12; ★ WASH; mail Laurel z 20723

Hammondell Heights; RMC Place; ANNE ARUNDEL; *185 E-13; ★ WASH; mail Millersville z 21108; ● 60

Hampden; RMC Place; BALTIMORE (Independent City); 184 I-4; ★ BAL; mail Baltimore z 21210-11; pop. incl. with Baltimore (Independent City)

Hampshire Knolls; RMC Place; PRINCE GEORGE'S; *185 E-12; ★ WASH; mail Hyattsville z 20783

Hampstead; Inc. Place; CARROLL, BALTIMORE; 185 B-12; elev. 914ft./279m.; [P]; ★ BAL; z 21074; Ⓟ 2,608; © 5,060

Hampton; CDP; BALTIMORE; 184 F-4; ★ BAL; mail Towson z 21286; Ⓟ 4,926; © 5,004

Hampton Gardens; RMC Place; BALTIMORE; ★ BAL; mail Towson z 21286

Hampton Park; RMC Place; PRINCE GEORGE'S; ★ WASH; mail Capitol Heights z 20791; pop. incl. with Capitol Heights (Inc. Place)

Hance Point; RMC Place; CECIL; *185 B-16; ★ PHIL-; mail North East z 21901; ● 130

Hancock; Inc. Place; WASHINGTON; 184 A-6; elev. 448ft./137m.; [P]; z 21750; Ⓟ 1,926; © 1,725

Hanesville; RMC Place; KENT; 185 D-16; mail Worton z 21678; ● 30

Hanover; RMC Place; HOWARD; 184 L-1; elev. 200ft./61m.; [P]; ★ BAL; z 21076 & mail Elkridge z 21075; ● 210

Hanson Valley View; RMC Place; PRINCE GEORGE'S; *185 F-12; ★ WASH; mail Temple Hills z 20748

Hansonville; RMC Place; FREDERICK; *184 B-10; ★ WASH; mail Frederick z 21702; rural

Harbor View; RMC Place; ANNE ARUNDEL; *185 F-14; ★ ANPLS; mail Edgewater z 21037; ● 290

Harbor View; RMC Place; QUEEN ANNE'S; *185 E-15; ★ ANPLS; mail Chester z 21619; ● 900

Hardesty Estates; RMC Place; ANNE ARUNDEL; *185 F-13; ★ WASH; mail Davidsonville z 21035; ● 250

Harewood; RMC Place; BALTIMORE; *185 C-15; ★ BAL; mail Middle River z 21220; ● 1,150

Harewood Park; RMC Place; BALTIMORE; 185 C-14; ★ BAL; mail Middle River z 21220; ● 1,100

HARFORD; 185 B-14; Ⓟ 182,132; © 218,590; ◆ 237,097

Harford Estates; RMC Place; HARFORD; *185 B-14; ★ BAL; mail Forest Hill z 21050; ● 3,000

Harford Farms; RMC Place; BALTIMORE; *185 C-14; ★ BAL; mail Parkville z 21234; ● 1,650

Harford Furnace; RMC Place; HARFORD; *185 B-15; ★ BAL; mail Bel Air z 21015; ● 300

Harford Hills; RMC Place; BALTIMORE; *185 C-14; ★ BAL; mail Parkville z 21234

Harford Park; RMC Place; BALTIMORE; *185 C-14; ★ BAL; mail Parkville z 21234

Harford Square; RMC Place; HARFORD; *185 C-15; ★ BAL; mail Edgewood z 21040; ● 6,000

Harman; ANNE ARUNDEL; see Harmans (RMC Place)

Harmans (Harman); RMC Place; ANNE ARUNDEL; 184 M-2; elev. 120ft./37m.; [P]; ★ BAL; z 21077 & mail Hanover z 21076; ● 400

Harmony; RMC Place; CAROLINE; 185 F-17; elev. 49ft./15m.; mail Preston z 21655; ● 150

Harmony; RMC Place; FREDERICK; *184 B-9; ★ WASH; mail Myersville z 21773; ● 110

Harmony Grove; RMC Place; FREDERICK; *184 C-10; elev. 315ft./96m.; ★ WASH; mail Frederick z 21701; ● 60

Harmony Hall; RMC Place; PRINCE GEORGE'S; 249 J-7; ★ WASH; mail Fort Washington z 20744; ● 90

Harmony Hills; RMC Place; MONTGOMERY; *185 E-11; ★ WASH; mail Silver Spring z 20906

Harness Woods; RMC Place; ANNE ARUNDEL; *185 F-14; ★ ANPLS; mail Annapolis z 21403; pop. incl. with Annapolis (Inc. Place)

Harney; RMC Place; CARROLL; 185 A-11; mail Taneytown z 21787; ● 240

Harpers Choice; RMC Place; HOWARD; ★ BAL; mail Columbia z 21044

Harpers Corner; RMC Place; ST. MARY'S; ★ WASH; mail Mechanicsville z 20659; rural

Harpers Mill; RMC Place; ANNE ARUNDEL; *185 E-13; ★ BAL; mail Millersville z 21108

Harris Heights; RMC Place; ANNE ARUNDEL; *185 D-13; ★ BAL; mail Glen Burnie z 21061

Harrison Ferry; RMC Place; DORCHESTER; *185 G-17; elev. 24ft./7m.; mail Hurlock z 21643; rural

Harrisonville; RMC Place; BALTIMORE; 184 G-1; ★ BAL; mail Randallstown z 21133; ● 270

Harrisville; RMC Place; CARROLL; *185 C-11; ★ WASH; mail Mount Airy z 21771; ● 50

Harrisville; RMC Place; CECIL; *185 A-16; elev. 371ft./113m.; ★ PHIL-; mail Colora z 21917, Rising Sun z 21911; ● 150

Harundale; RMC Place; ANNE ARUNDEL; *185 D-13; ★ BAL; mail Glen Burnie z 21060

Harvest Hills; RMC Place; HARFORD; *185 B-14; ★ BAL; mail Fallston z 21047

Harwood; RMC Place; ANNE ARUNDEL; 185 F-13; elev. 160ft./49m.; [P]; ★ WASH; z 20776; ● 450

Har Wood; RMC Place; HOWARD; ★ BAL; mail Elkridge z 21075

Harwood Estates; RMC Place; PRINCE GEORGE'S; *185 F-12; ★ WASH; mail Temple Hills z 20748

Harwood Park; RMC Place; HOWARD; *185 D-13; ★ BAL; mail Elkridge z 21075

Havenwood Hills; RMC Place; WASHINGTON; *184 B-9; elev. 700ft./213m.; ★ HAG; mail Smithsburg z 21783; ● 200

Haverhill; RMC Place; BALTIMORE; *185 C-14; ★ BAL; mail Parkville z 21234

Havre de Grace; Inc. Place; HARFORD; 185 B-16; [P] [H]; z 21078; Ⓟ 8,952; © 11,331

Havre de Grace Heights; RMC Place; HARFORD; *185 B-16; mail Havre de Grace z 21078; ● 330

Hawbottom; RMC Place; FREDERICK; *184 B-9; ★ WASH; mail Middletown z 21769; rural

Hawkeye; RMC Place; DORCHESTER; *185 H-17; mail East New Market z 21631; rural

Hayes Landing; RMC Place; WORCESTER; *185 I-20; elev. 5ft./2m.; mail Berlin z 21811; ● 80

Hazelhurst; RMC Place; GARRETT; *184 B-2; mail Swanton z 21561; summer pop. 200; ● 70

Hazelmoor; RMC Place; CECIL; *185 C-16; mail Earleville z 21919; ● 180

Head of the Creek; RMC Place; WICOMICO; *185 I-17; mail Quantico z 21856; ● 100

Hearn Bailey Farm; RMC Place; WICOMICO; *185 I-18; ★ SLSB; mail Salisbury z 21801; ● 500

Heather Heights; RMC Place; CARROLL; *185 C-12; ★ BAL; mail Sykesville z 21784

Heather Hill Apartments; RMC Place; PRINCE GEORGE'S; *185 F-12; ★ WASH; mail Temple Hills z 20748

Hebbville; RMC Place; BALTIMORE; 184 I-2; ★ BAL; mail Windsor Mill z 21244; ● 2,500

Hebron; Inc. Place; WICOMICO; 185 H-18; elev. 43ft./13m.; [P]; ★ SLSB; z 21830; Ⓟ 665; © 807

Helen; RMC Place; ST. MARY'S; 185 I-13; elev. 129ft./39m.; [P]; ★ WASH; z 20635; ● 70

Helen Estates; RMC Place; ST. MARY'S; *185 I-13; ★ WASH; mail Helen z 20635, Mechanicsville z 20659; ● 180

Henderson; Inc. Place; CAROLINE; 185 E-17; elev. 56ft./17m.; [P]; z 21640; Ⓟ 66; © 118

Herald Harbor; CDP; ANNE ARUNDEL; 185 E-14; ★ WASH; mail Crownsville z 21032; Ⓟ 1,707; © 2,313

Herald Square; RMC Place; BALTIMORE; *185 C-13; ★ BAL; mail Windsor Mill z 21244

Hereford; RMC Place; BALTIMORE; 185 B-13; [P]; ★ BAL; z 21111; ● 700

Heritage Harbor; RMC Place; ANNE ARUNDEL; *185 E-14; ★ ANPLS; mail Annapolis z 21401

Heritage Hills; RMC Place; ANNE ARUNDEL; *185 D-13; ★ BAL; mail Glen Burnie z 21061; ● 3,300

Heritage Walk; RMC Place; MONTGOMERY; *185 E-11; ★ WASH; mail Rockville z 20852

Hermanville; RMC Place; ST. MARY'S; *185 J-14; mail Lexington Park z 20653; ● 300

Hermitage Park; RMC Place; MONTGOMERY; *185 E-11; ★ WASH; mail Silver Spring z 20906

Hernwood Heights; RMC Place; BALTIMORE; 184 H-1; ★ BAL; mail Randallstown z 21133; ● 960

Herrington Manor; RMC Place; GARRETT; *184 B-1; mail Oakland z 21550; ● 30

Hickman; RMC Place; CAROLINE; *185 F-17; elev. 54ft./16m.; mail Denton z 21629; ● 70

Hickory; RMC Place; HARFORD; 185 B-15; ★ BAL; mail Bel Air z 21014; ● 610

Hickory Hills; RMC Place; HARFORD; ★ BAL; mail Bel Air z 21014

Hickory Ridge; RMC Place; HOWARD; ★ BAL; mail Columbia z 21044

Hickory Ridge; RMC Place; QUEEN ANNE'S; *185 E-16; elev. 19ft./6m.; ★ ANPLS; mail Queenstown z 21658; ● 150

Hicksburg; RMC Place; DORCHESTER; *185 H-16; mail East New Market z 21631; ● 30

Hicksville; RMC Place; WASHINGTON; *184 A-8; elev. 500ft./152m.; ★ HAG; mail Clear Spring z 21722; ● 50

Hidden Point; RMC Place; ANNE ARUNDEL; 185 M-20; ★ ANPLS; mail Annapolis z 21401; ● 70

High Bridge; RMC Place; PRINCE GEORGE'S; *185 E-13; ★ WASH; mail Bowie z 20720

High Bridge Estates; RMC Place; PRINCE GEORGE'S; *185 E-13; ★ WASH; mail Bowie z 20720

Highfield; RMC Place; CARROLL; ★ BAL; mail Hampstead z 21074; pop. incl. with Hampstead (Inc. Place)

Highfield; RMC Place; MONTGOMERY; *185 D-11; ★ WASH; mail Gaithersburg z 20879

Highfield; RMC Place; WASHINGTON; 184 A-10; elev. 1,392ft./424m.; [P]; ★ HAG; z 21719; ● 210

Highfield-Cascade; CDP-Census Area Only; WASHINGTON; *184 A-10; ★ HAG; © 1,141

Highland; RMC Place; FREDERICK; *184 B-9; mail Myersville z 21773; rural

Highland; RMC Place; HOWARD; 185 D-12; [P]; ★ WASH; z 20777; ● 1,700

Highland Acres; RMC Place; HOWARD; *185 D-12; elev. 500ft./152m.; ★ WASH; mail Highland z 20777; ● 30

Highland Beach; Inc. Place; ANNE ARUNDEL; 185 F-14; ★ ANPLS; mail Annapolis z 21403; Ⓟ 102; © 109

Highland Park; RMC Place; PRINCE GEORGE'S; *185 F-12; ★ WASH; mail Capitol Heights z 20743; ● 2,300

Highland Park; RMC Place; WORCESTER; *185 I-20; elev. 15ft./5m.; mail Berlin z 21811; ● 50

Highlands; RMC Place; MONTGOMERY; *185 E-11; ★ WASH; mail Potomac z 20854

Highlands of Olney; RMC Place; MONTGOMERY; *185 D-11; ★ WASH; mail Olney z 20832

Highland Stone; RMC Place; MONTGOMERY; *185 E-11; ★ WASH; mail Potomac z 20854

Highlandtown; RMC Place; BALTIMORE (Independent City); *185 D-14; [P]; ★ BAL; z 21224; pop. incl. with Baltimore (Independent City)

Entries in **UPPERCASE** are counties.
Entries in **bold** have populations of 2,500 or more.
Names in parentheses are alternate names.

Inc. Place	Incorporated Place
RMC Place	Rand McNally Designated Place
CDP	Census Designated Place
MCD	Minor Civil Division
⊡	County Seat
▲	Minor Civil Division
elev.	Elevation
[P]	Post Office
[H]	Hospital
[C]	College
■	Principal Business Center
★	Ranally Metro Area (RMA) Abbreviation
z	Zip Code(s)
Ⓟ	Previous Census Population
Ⓡ	Revised Census Population
Ⓐ	Annexation Population
●	Rand McNally Population Estimate
©	Final Census Population
Ⓢ	Special Census Population
◆	Estimated Population

For additional definitions see Glossary, Volume 1, and Introduction, Volume 2.

High Point; RMC Place; ANNE ARUNDEL; 184 M-6; ★ BAL; mail Pasadena z 21122; ● 3,700
High Point; RMC Place; MONTGOMERY; *185 E-11; ★ WASH; mail Bethesda z 20814
Highpoint Heights; RMC Place; PRINCE GEORGE'S; *185 E-12; ★ WASH; mail Beltsville z 20705
High Point Manor; RMC Place; HARFORD; *185 B-14; ★ BAL; mail Forest Hill z 21050; ● 610
High Ridge; RMC Place; HOWARD; 249 B-9; ★ WASH; mail Laurel z 20723; ● 2,500
High Ridge Park; RMC Place; HOWARD; *185 E-12; ★ WASH; mail Laurel z 20723
High View; RMC Place; FREDERICK; *185 C-11; ★ WASH; mail Mount Airy z 21771
High-View Estates; RMC Place; CARROLL; *185 C-11; ★ BAL; mail Hampstead z 21074; ● 160
Highview Estates; RMC Place; HOWARD; *185 D-12; ★ BAL; mail Ellicott City z 21042
Highview on the Bay; RMC Place; ANNE ARUNDEL; *185 G-14; ★ WASH; mail Tracys Landing z 20779; ● 100
Hillandale; CDP; MONTGOMERY, PRINCE GEORGE'S; *185 E-12; ★ WASH; mail Silver Spring z 20903; Ⓟ 10,318; © 3,054
Hillandale Forest; RMC Place; MONTGOMERY; *185 E-12; 3 mi. NE of Silver Spring; ★ WASH; mail Silver Spring z 20907; ● 1,400
Hillandale Heights; RMC Place; MONTGOMERY; *185 E-12; ★ WASH; mail Silver Spring z 20903; ● 1,500
Hillcrest; RMC Place; ANNE ARUNDEL; *185 D-13; ★ BAL; mail Brooklyn z 21225; ● 830
Hill Crest; RMC Place; MONTGOMERY; ★ WASH; mail Takoma Park z 20912
Hillcrest; RMC Place; PRINCE GEORGE'S; *185 F-12; ★ WASH; mail Temple Hills z 20748; ● 2,500
Hillcrest Estates; RMC Place; PRINCE GEORGE'S; *185 F-12; ★ WASH; mail Temple Hills z 20748; ● 2,600
Hillcrest Heights; RMC Place; HOWARD; 249 A-9; ★ WASH; mail Laurel z 20723; ● 380
Hillcrest Heights; CDP; PRINCE GEORGE'S; 185 F-12; 🅿; ★ WASH; z 20748 & mail Suitland z 20746; Ⓟ 17,136; © 16,359
Hillcrest Terrace; RMC Place; PRINCE GEORGE'S; *185 F-12; ★ WASH; mail Temple Hills z 20748; ● 6,000
Hillmead; RMC Place; MONTGOMERY; *185 E-11; ★ WASH; mail Bethesda z 20817
Hillmeade; RMC Place; PRINCE GEORGE'S; *185 E-13; ★ WASH; mail Glenn Dale z 20769
Hillmeade Manor; RMC Place; PRINCE GEORGE'S; *185 E-13; ★ WASH; mail Glenn Dale z 20769
Hillsboro; Inc. Place; CAROLINE; 185 F-17; elev. 47ft./14m.; 🅿; z 21641; Ⓟ 164; © 163
Hillsborough; RMC Place; PRINCE GEORGE'S; *185 E-12; ★ WASH; mail Laurel z 20707; ● 200
Hillside; RMC Place; CARROLL; *185 B-12; ★ BAL; mail Westminster z 21157; ● 280
Hillside; PRINCE GEORGE'S; see Greater Capitol Heights (RMC Place)
Hillsmere Estates; RMC Place; ANNE ARUNDEL; *185 F-14; ★ ANPLS; mail Annapolis z 21403
Hillsmere Shores; CDP; ANNE ARUNDEL; 185 F-14; ★ ANPLS; mail Annapolis z 21403; Ⓟ 3,321; © 2,977
Hills Point; RMC Place; DORCHESTER; *185 G-15; mail Cambridge z 21613; ● 40
Hill Top; RMC Place; CHARLES; 185 H-11; mail La Plata z 20646; ● 50
Hillwood Manor; RMC Place; PRINCE GEORGE'S; *185 E-12; ★ WASH; mail Hyattsville z 20783
Hobbs; RMC Place; CAROLINE; 185 F-17; mail Denton z 21629; ● 60
Hoffman; RMC Place; ALLEGANY; *184 A-3; ★ CUMB; mail Frostburg z 21532; ● 60
Holabird; RMC Place; BALTIMORE (Independent City); *185 D-14; ★ BAL; mail Baltimore z 21224; pop. incl. with Baltimore (Independent City)
Holbrook; RMC Place; BALTIMORE; *185 C-12; ★ BAL; mail Randallstown z 21133; ● 200
Holiday Acres; RMC Place; WASHINGTON; *184 A-9; elev. 676ft./206m.; ★ HAG; mail Smithsburg z 21783; ● 360
Holiday Beach; RMC Place; CALVERT; *185 G-14; ★ WASH; mail Chesapeake Beach z 20732; ● 50
Holiday Hills; RMC Place; HOWARD; ★ BAL; mail Columbia z 21044
Holiday Park; RMC Place; MONTGOMERY; *185 E-11; ★ WASH; mail Silver Spring z 20906
Holland Cliff Shores; RMC Place; CALVERT; *185 G-13; ★ WASH; mail Huntingtown z 20639; ● 400
Holland Heights; RMC Place; WICOMICO; *185 I-18; ★ SLSB; mail Salisbury z 21801; ● 50
Hollaway Estates; RMC Place; PRINCE GEORGE'S; *185 G-13; ★ WASH; mail Upper Marlboro z 20772
Hollinsworth Manor; RMC Place; CECIL; ★ PHIL-; mail Elkton z 21921; pop. incl. with Elkton (Inc. Place)
Holly Beach; RMC Place; BALTIMORE; *185 D-14; ★ BAL; mail Essex z 21221; ● 80
Holly Gaf Acres; RMC Place; ST. MARY'S; *185 I-14; ★ WASH; mail Hollywood z 20636; ● 350
Holly Hall Terrace; RMC Place; CECIL; *185 B-17; ★ PHIL-; mail Elkton z 21921; ● 500
Holly Hill Harbor; RMC Place; ANNE ARUNDEL; *185 F-14; ★ ANPLS; mail Edgewater z 21037; ● 950
Holly Lake Estates; RMC Place; WICOMICO; *185 H-18; ★ SLSB; mail Salisbury z 21804; ● 120
Holly Spring; RMC Place; PRINCE GEORGE'S; *185 F-12; ★ WASH; mail District Heights z 20747
Holly Tree; RMC Place; CHARLES; *185 G-12; ★ WASH; mail Waldorf z 20601
Hollywood; RMC Place; PRINCE GEORGE'S; *185 E-12; ★ WASH; mail College Park z 20740; pop. incl. with College Park (Inc. Place)
Hollywood; RMC Place; ST. MARY'S; 185 I-14; elev. 132ft./40m.; 🅿; ★ WASH; z 20636; ● 1,000
Hollywood Beach; RMC Place; CECIL; *185 B-17; ★ PHIL-; mail Chesapeake City z 21915; ● 60
Hollywood Estates; RMC Place; PRINCE GEORGE'S; ★ WASH; mail College Park z 20740; pop. incl. with College Park (Inc. Place)
Hollywood Park; RMC Place; MONTGOMERY; *185 E-12; ★ WASH; mail Silver Spring z 20904
Hollywood Shores; RMC Place; ST. MARY'S; *185 I-14; ★ WASH; mail Hollywood z 20636; ● 650
Holmehurst; RMC Place; PRINCE GEORGE'S; *185 E-13; ★ WASH; mail Bowie z 20720; ● 450
Home Acres; RMC Place; PRINCE GEORGE'S; *185 E-12; ★ WASH; mail Beltsville z 20705
Homecrest; RMC Place; MONTGOMERY; *185 E-11; ★ WASH; mail Silver Spring z 20906
Homestead Estates; RMC Place; MONTGOMERY; *185 E-12; ★ WASH; mail Silver Spring z 20904
Homewood (Lower Homewood); RMC Place; ALLEGANY; *184 A-4; ★ CUMB; mail Cumberland z 21502
Homewood; RMC Place; ANNE ARUNDEL; ★ ANPLS; pop. incl. with Annapolis (Inc. Place)
Homewood; RMC Place; MONTGOMERY; *185 E-11; ★ WASH; mail Kensington z 20895; ● 830
Honey Cove Estates; RMC Place; CALVERT; *185 H-14; elev. 100ft./30m.; ★ WASH; mail Prince Frederick z 20678; rural
Honga; RMC Place; DORCHESTER; 185 I-15; mail Church Creek z 21622; ● 100
Hood's Mill; RMC Place; CARROLL, HOWARD; *185 C-12; elev. 439ft./134m.; ★ BAL; mail Cooksville z 21723; ● 100
Hoopersville; RMC Place; DORCHESTER; 185 I-15; elev. 2ft./1m.; mail Fishing Creek z 21634; ● 250
Hope Hill; RMC Place; FREDERICK; *184 C-10; ★ WASH; mail Frederick z 21701; rural
Hopewell; RMC Place; SOMERSET; *185 K-17; mail Crisfield z 21817
Hopkins Mead; RMC Place; HOWARD; *185 D-12; ★ WASH; mail Clarksville z 21029; ● 200
Horizon Run; RMC Place; MONTGOMERY; mail Gaithersburg z 20877
Houcksville; RMC Place; CARROLL; *185 B-12; ★ BAL; mail Hampstead z 21074; ● 300
HOWARD; 185 D-12; Ⓟ 187,328; © 247,842; ◆ 275,960
Howard Heights; RMC Place; HOWARD; *185 D-12; ★ BAL; mail Ellicott City z 21042
Howardville; RMC Place; BALTIMORE; *185 C-13; ★ BAL; mail Pikesville z 21208
Hoyes; RMC Place; GARRETT; *184 B-1; elev. 2,566ft./782m.; mail Friendsville z 21531
Hudson; RMC Place; DORCHESTER; 185 H-15; mail Cambridge z 21613; ● 250
Hughesville; CDP; CHARLES; 185 H-13; elev. 179ft./55m.; 🅿; ★ WASH; z 20637; Ⓟ 1,319; © 1,537
Hungerford Towne; RMC Place; MONTGOMERY; *185 E-11; ★ WASH; mail Rockville z 20852; pop. incl. with Rockville (Inc. Place)
Hunt Club Estates; RMC Place; CHARLES; *185 G-12; ★ WASH; mail Waldorf z 20601
Hunt Club Estates; RMC Place; HOWARD; ★ BAL; mail Elkridge z 21075
Hunt Crest Estates; RMC Place; BALTIMORE; *185 C-14; ★ BAL; mail Towson z 21286; ● 1,400
Hunters Harbor; RMC Place; ANNE ARUNDEL; *185 E-14; ★ BAL; mail Pasadena z 21122; ● 2,800
Hunters Hill; RMC Place; BALTIMORE; *185 C-13; ★ BAL; mail Lutherville Timonium z 21093
Hunters Ridge; RMC Place; CALVERT; *185 H-13; ★ WASH; mail Barstow z 20610; ● 50
Huntersville; RMC Place; ST. MARY'S; *185 H-13; ★ WASH; mail Mechanicsville z 20659; rural
Hunting Hills; RMC Place; CALVERT; *185 H-13; ★ WASH; mail Huntingtown z 20639; ● 150
Hunting Lodge; RMC Place; BALTIMORE; *185 C-14; ★ BAL; mail Parkville z 21234
Hunting Park; RMC Place; WICOMICO; *185 I-18; ★ SLSB; mail Salisbury z 21801; ● 290
Huntington Terrace; RMC Place; MONTGOMERY; *185 E-11; ★ WASH; mail Bethesda z 20814
Huntingtown; CDP; CALVERT; 185 G-13; elev. 180ft./55m.; 🅿; ★ WASH; z 20639; © 2,436
Huntsmoor; RMC Place; BALTIMORE; ★ BAL; mail Halethorpe z 21227
Huntsville; RMC Place; PRINCE GEORGE'S; *185 F-12; ★ WASH; mail Hyattsville z 20785
Hunt Valley; RMC Place; BALTIMORE; *185 B-13; elev. 320ft./98m.; 🅿; ★ BAL; z 21030-31, z 21065
Hurlock; Inc. Place; DORCHESTER; 185 G-17; elev. 40ft./12m.; 🅿; z 21643; Ⓟ 1,706; © 1,874
Hurry; RMC Place; ST. MARY'S; *185 I-13; ★ WASH; mail Chaptico z 20621; ● 50
Hutton; RMC Place; GARRETT; 184 C-1; 🅿; z 21550; ● 110
Huyett; RMC Place; WASHINGTON; 184 A-8; ★ HAG; mail Hagerstown z 21740; ● 100
Hyattstown; RMC Place; MONTGOMERY; 184 D-10; 🅿; ★ WASH; z 20871; ● 120
Hyattsville; Inc. Place; PRINCE GEORGE'S; 185 E-12; elev. 59ft./18m.; 🅿; ★ WASH; z 20781-85, z 20787-88; Ⓟ 13,864; © 14,733
Hyde; BALTIMORE; see Hydes (RMC Place)
Hyde Park; RMC Place; BALTIMORE; *185 D-14; ★ BAL; mail Essex z 21221
Hyde Park; RMC Place; WICOMICO; *185 I-18; ★ SLSB; mail Salisbury z 21801; pop. incl. with Salisbury (Inc. Place)
Hydes (Hyde); RMC Place; BALTIMORE; 185 B-14; elev. 335ft./102m.; 🅿; ★ BAL; z 21082; ● 250
Hynesboro; RMC Place; PRINCE GEORGE'S; *185 E-12; ★ WASH; mail Lanham z 20706
Hynson; RMC Place; CAROLINE; *185 G-17; mail Federalsburg z 21632; rural

I

Idlewild; RMC Place; ANNE ARUNDEL; ★ WASH; mail Shady Side z 20764
Idlewylde; RMC Place; BALTIMORE; *185 C-14; ★ BAL; mail Towson z 21204
Ijamsville; RMC Place; FREDERICK; 184 C-10; elev. 351ft./107m.; 🅿; ★ WASH; z 21754; ● 400
Ilchester; RMC Place; HOWARD; 184 K-1; elev. 109ft./33m.; 🅿; ★ BAL; z 21043; ● 890
Imperial Gardens; RMC Place; BALTIMORE; *185 C-13; ★ BAL; mail Randallstown z 21133
Indian Acres; RMC Place; CECIL; *185 C-17; elev. 80ft./24m.; mail Earleville z 21919; ● 80
Indian Creek Estates; RMC Place; ST. MARY'S; *185 H-13; ★ WASH; mail Charlotte Hall z 20622; ● 100
Indian Head; Inc. Place; CHARLES; 185 H-11; elev. 38ft./12m.; 🅿; ★ WASH; z 20640; Ⓟ 3,531; © 3,422
Indian Head Junction; CHARLES; see White Plains (RMC Place)
Indian Head Manor; RMC Place; CHARLES; *185 G-11; ★ WASH; mail Bryans Road z 20616; ● 1,150
Indian Queen Estates; RMC Place; PRINCE GEORGE'S; *185 G-12; ★ WASH; mail Fort Washington z 20744; ● 2,000
Indian River Estates; RMC Place; ST. MARY'S; *185 H-13; ★ WASH; mail Mechanicsville z 20659
Indian Springs; RMC Place; FREDERICK; *184 C-10; ★ WASH; mail Frederick z 21702; ● 220
Indian Springs; RMC Place; WASHINGTON; 184 A-7; elev. 545ft./166m.; mail Big Pool z 21711; ● 50
Indiantown; RMC Place; WORCESTER; *185 J-19; elev. 120ft./37m.; mail Snow Hill z 21863; rural
Ingleside; RMC Place; QUEEN ANNE'S; 185 E-17; elev. 62ft./19m.; 🅿; z 21644; ● 350
Inverness; RMC Place; BALTIMORE; *185 D-14; ★ BAL; mail Dundalk z 21222
Inverness Forest; RMC Place; MONTGOMERY; *185 E-11; ★ WASH; mail Potomac z 20854
Inverness Woods; RMC Place; MONTGOMERY; *185 E-11; ★ WASH; mail Potomac z 20854
Iron Hill; RMC Place; CECIL; *185 A-17; ★ PHIL-; mail Newark z 19711; rural
Ironshire; RMC Place; WORCESTER; *185 I-20; mail Berlin z 21811
Ironsides; RMC Place; CHARLES; 185 H-11; elev. 125ft./38m.; 🅿; z 20643; ● 180
Isabella Park; RMC Place; PRINCE GEORGE'S; *185 E-12; ★ WASH; mail Hyattsville z 20783
Island Creek; RMC Place; CALVERT; 185 H-14; mail Saint Leonard z 20685; ● 100
Island View Beach; RMC Place; BALTIMORE; *185 D-14; ★ BAL; mail Essex z 21221; ● 80
Issue; RMC Place; CHARLES; 185 I-12; elev. 15ft./5m.; 🅿; z 20645; ● 430
Ivy Hills; RMC Place; HOWARD; *185 D-13; ★ BAL; mail Ellicott City z 21043
Ivytown; RMC Place; TALBOT; *185 G-16; elev. 66ft./20m.; mail Easton z 21601; rural

J

Jackson; RMC Place; CECIL; *185 B-16; ★ PHIL-; mail Perryville z 21903; ● 100
Jacksonville; RMC Place; BALTIMORE; 185 B-14; 🅿; ★ BAL; z 21131; ● 600
Jacksonville; RMC Place; SOMERSET; mail Crisfield z 21817; ● 300
Jacktown; RMC Place; DORCHESTER; *185 H-16; elev. 20ft./6m.; mail Cambridge z 21613; ● 650
Jacobsville; RMC Place; ANNE ARUNDEL; *185 D-14; ★ BAL; mail Pasadena z 21122
James; RMC Place; DORCHESTER; *185 H-15; mail Cambridge z 21613; rural
Jamestown; SOMERSET; see Manokin (RMC Place)
Jarrettsville; CDP; HARFORD; 185 B-14; elev. 641ft./195m.; 🅿; ★ BAL; z 21084; Ⓟ 2,148; © 2,756
Jefferson; RMC Place; FREDERICK; 184 C-9; elev. 583ft./178m.; 🅿; ★ WASH; z 21755; ● 300
Jefferson Heights; RMC Place; PRINCE GEORGE'S; *185 F-12; ★ WASH; mail Capitol Heights z 20743
Jefferson Heights; RMC Place; WASHINGTON; 185 M-14; elev. 600ft./183m.; ★ HAG; mail Hagerstown z 21742; ● 800
Jenkins Corner; RMC Place; PRINCE GEORGE'S; *185 F-12; elev. 244ft./74m.; ★ WASH; mail Clinton z 20735; ● 350
Jennings; RMC Place; GARRETT; *184 A-2; 🅿; z 21536; ● 150
Jersey Heights; RMC Place; WICOMICO; *185 I-18; ★ SLSB; mail Salisbury z 21801
Jerusalem; RMC Place; BALTIMORE; *185 C-14; ★ BAL; mail Kingsville z 21087; rural
Jerusalem; RMC Place; FREDERICK; *184 B-9; mail Myersville z 21773; rural
Jerusalem; RMC Place; MONTGOMERY; *184 D-10; ★ WASH; mail Poolesville z 20837; ● 100
Jessup; CDP; ANNE ARUNDEL, HOWARD; 184 M-2; elev. 180ft./55m.; 🅿 🅷; ★ BAL; z 20794; Ⓟ 6,537; © 7,865
Jesterville; RMC Place; WICOMICO; *185 I-17; mail Bivalve z 21814; ● 230
Jewell; RMC Place; ANNE ARUNDEL; *185 G-13; elev. 152ft./46m.; ★ WASH; mail Dunkirk z 20754; rural
Jimtown; RMC Place; FREDERICK; *184 B-10; elev. 400ft./122m.; mail Thurmont z 21788; rural
Johnsontown; RMC Place; KENT; *185 D-16; mail Chestertown z 21620; ● 30
Johnsville; RMC Place; CARROLL; 185 C-12; ★ BAL; mail Sykesville z 21784; ● 1,200
Johnsville; RMC Place; FREDERICK; 185 B-11; elev. 586ft./179m.; mail Union Bridge z 21791; ● 550
Jones; RMC Place; ANNE ARUNDEL; *185 E-14; elev. 62ft./19m.; ★ BAL; mail Severna Park z 21146
Jonestown; RMC Place; CAROLINE; 185 G-17; mail Preston z 21655; ● 250
Joppa; RMC Place; HARFORD; 🅿; ★ BAL; z 21085
Joppa Heights; RMC Place; BALTIMORE; *185 C-14; ★ BAL; mail Parkville z 21234
Joppatowne; CDP; HARFORD; 185 C-15; elev. 70ft./21m.; ★ BAL; mail Joppa z 21085; Ⓟ 11,084; © 11,391
Joppa View; RMC Place; BALTIMORE; *185 C-14; ★ BAL; mail Perry Hall z 21128
Josenhans Corner; RMC Place; BALTIMORE; *185 C-14; ★ BAL; mail Essex z 21221
Joyce Acres; RMC Place; ANNE ARUNDEL; *185 E-14; ★ BAL; mail Arnold z 21012

K

Kalma Ridge; RMC Place; ANNE ARUNDEL; *185 E-14; elev. 100ft./30m.; ★ ANPLS; mail Crownsville z 21032
Kalmia; RMC Place; HARFORD; *185 B-15; elev. 414ft./126m.; ★ BAL; mail Bel Air z 21015; ● 80
Kalmia Farms; RMC Place; HOWARD; *185 D-12; elev. 528ft./161m.; ★ WASH; mail Dayton z 21036; ● 250
Kalten Acres; RMC Place; CARROLL; *185 B-12; ★ BAL; mail Westminster z 21158; ● 210
Kastle Estates; RMC Place; PRINCE GEORGE'S; *185 G-12; ★ WASH; mail Clinton z 20735
Kaywood; RMC Place; WICOMICO; *185 I-18; elev. 15ft./5m.; ★ SLSB; mail Salisbury z 21804; ● 100
Kaywood Gardens; RMC Place; PRINCE GEORGE'S; *185 F-12; ★ WASH; mail Mount Rainier z 20712; pop. incl. with Mount Rainier (Inc. Place)
Keedysville; Inc. Place; WASHINGTON; 184 B-9; elev. 404ft./123m.; 🅿; ★ WASH; z 21756; Ⓟ 464; © 482
Keeler Glade; RMC Place; GARRETT; *184 A-1; elev. 2,296ft./700m.; mail Friendsville z 21531; rural
Keifer; RMC Place; ALLEGANY; *184 B-5; elev. 537ft./164m.; mail Paw Paw z 25434; rural
Kemp Mill; CDP-Census Area Only; MONTGOMERY; *185 E-12; ★ WASH; © 9,956
Kemp Mill Estates; RMC Place; MONTGOMERY; 249 C-6; ★ WASH; mail Silver Spring z 20902; ● 3,050
Kemp Mill Farms; RMC Place; MONTGOMERY; *185 E-12; ★ WASH; mail Silver Spring z 20902; ● 1,350
Kempsfield; RMC Place; CARROLL; *185 B-12; elev. 800ft./244m.; ★ BAL; mail Hampstead z 21074; ● 30
Kempton; RMC Place; GARRETT; *184 D-1; elev. 2,850ft./869m.; mail Thomas z 26292; ● 50
Kemptown; RMC Place; FREDERICK; *185 C-11; ★ WASH; mail Monrovia z 21770
Ken Gar; RMC Place; MONTGOMERY; *185 E-11; ★ WASH; mail Kensington z 20895
Kennedyville; RMC Place; KENT; 185 C-16; elev. 60ft./18m.; 🅿; z 21645; ● 200
Kensington; Inc. Place; MONTGOMERY; 185 E-11; elev. 306ft./93m.; 🅿; ★ WASH; z 20891, z 20895; Ⓟ 1,713; © 1,873
Kensington Estates; RMC Place; MONTGOMERY; *185 E-11; ★ WASH; mail Kensington z 20895
Kensington Heights; RMC Place; MONTGOMERY; *185 E-11; ★ WASH; mail Silver Spring z 20902; ● 2,100
Kensington View; RMC Place; MONTGOMERY; *185 E-11; ★ WASH; mail Kensington z 20895
KENT; 185 C-16; Ⓟ 17,842; © 19,197; ◆ 20,047
Kent Acres; RMC Place; KENT; *185 D-16; elev. 60ft./18m.; mail Chestertown z 21620; rural
Kent Island Estates; RMC Place; QUEEN ANNE'S; *185 F-15; ★ ANPLS; mail Stevensville z 21666; ● 1,100
Kentland; RMC Place; PRINCE GEORGE'S; *185 F-12; ★ WASH; mail Hyattsville z 20785; ● 1,950
Kentmore Park; RMC Place; KENT; 185 C-16; mail Kennedyville z 21645; ● 250
Kentmorr; RMC Place; QUEEN ANNE'S; *185 F-15; ★ ANPLS; mail Stevensville z 21666; ● 350
Kent Narrows; QUEEN ANNE'S; see Narrows (RMC Place)
Kent Narrows; CDP-Census Area Only; QUEEN ANNE'S; *185 E-15; ★ ANPLS; © 567
Kent Village; RMC Place; PRINCE GEORGE'S; 249 F-9; elev. 100ft./30m.; ★ WASH; mail Hyattsville z 20785; ● 2,700
Kenwood; RMC Place; BALTIMORE; 184 I-7; elev. 337ft./103m.; ★ BAL; mail Nottingham z 21236; ● 2,500
Kenwood; RMC Place; MONTGOMERY; *185 E-11; ★ WASH; mail Chevy Chase z 20815
Kenwood Beach; RMC Place; CALVERT; *185 H-14; mail Port Republic z 20676; ● 200
Kerby Hills; RMC Place; PRINCE GEORGE'S; *185 F-12; ★ WASH; mail Fort Washington z 20744
Kettering; CDP; PRINCE GEORGE'S; 185 F-13; 🅿; ★ WASH; z 20774 & mail Upper Marlboro z 20775; Ⓟ 9,901; © 11,008
Kettering Estate Park; RMC Place; PRINCE GEORGE'S; *185 F-13; ★ WASH; mail Upper Marlboro z 20774
Keymar; RMC Place; CARROLL; 185 B-11; elev. 451ft./137m.; 🅿; z 21757; ● 520
Keysers Ridge; RMC Place; GARRETT; 184 A-2; elev. 2,880ft./878m.; mail Grantsville z 21536; ● 30
Keystone Manor; RMC Place; PRINCE GEORGE'S; *185 F-12; ★ WASH; mail District Heights z 20747
Keysville; RMC Place; CARROLL; *185 B-11; elev. 485ft./148m.; mail Keymar z 21757; ● 100
Kidmore Lane; PRINCE GEORGE'S; see Lanham Woods (RMC Place)
Kilbirnie Estates; RMC Place; WICOMICO; *185 I-19; ★ SLSB; mail Salisbury z 21804; ● 160
Kilbourn Estates; RMC Place; PRINCE GEORGE'S; *185 F-12; ★ WASH; mail Temple Hills z 20748; ● 1,100
Kilby Corner; CECIL; see Conowingo (RMC Place)
Kilmarock; RMC Place; MONTGOMERY; *185 E-12; ★ WASH; mail Takoma Park z 20912
Kimberly Gardens; RMC Place; PRINCE GEORGE'S; *185 E-12; ★ WASH; mail Laurel z 20708
Kings Contrivance; RMC Place; HOWARD; *185 D-12; ★ BAL; mail Columbia z 21045
Kings County; RMC Place; BALTIMORE; *185 C-14; ★ BAL; mail Kingsville z 21087; ● 200
Kings Creek Estate; RMC Place; PRINCE GEORGE'S; *185 F-13; ★ WASH; mail Upper Marlboro z 20774
Kingsford; RMC Place; PRINCE GEORGE'S; *185 F-13; ★ WASH; mail Bowie z 20721; ● 2,150
Kings Grove; RMC Place; ALLEGANY; ★ CUMB; mail Ellerslie z 21529
Kings Manor (Kings Manor South); RMC Place; CHARLES; *185 H-12; ★ WASH; mail White Plains z 20695
Kings Manor South; CHARLES; see Kings Manor (RMC Place)
Kings Park; RMC Place; BALTIMORE; *185 C-12; ★ BAL; mail Baltimore z 21233; ● 3,000
Kings Ransom; RMC Place; ANNE ARUNDEL; *185 E-13; ★ BAL; mail Odenton z 21113
Kings Ridge; RMC Place; BALTIMORE; *185 C-14; ★ BAL; mail Parkville z 21234
Kingston; RMC Place; SOMERSET; 185 J-18; elev. 9ft./3m.; mail Westover z 21871; ● 50
Kingston Manor; RMC Place; PRINCE GEORGE'S; *185 F-12; ★ WASH; mail Upper Marlboro z 20772; ● 370
Kingstown; CDP; QUEEN ANNE'S; 185 D-16; mail Chestertown z 21620; Ⓟ 1,660; © 1,644
Kingsville; CDP; BALTIMORE; 185 C-14; elev. 272ft./83m.; 🅿; ★ BAL; z 21087; Ⓟ 3,550; © 4,214
Kingwood Common; RMC Place; BALTIMORE; *185 C-13; ★ BAL; mail Windsor Mill z 21244
Kirkham; RMC Place; TALBOT; *185 G-16; mail Easton z 21601; rural
Kirkwood; RMC Place; PRINCE GEORGE'S; *185 E-12; ★ WASH; mail Hyattsville z 20782; pop. incl. with Hyattsville (Inc. Place)
Kitzmiller; Inc. Place; GARRETT; 184 C-2; elev. 1,600ft./488m.; 🅿; z 21538; Ⓟ 275; © 302
Klee Mill Terrace; RMC Place; CARROLL; *185 C-12; elev. 660ft./201m.; ★ BAL; mail Sykesville z 21784; ● 150
Klej Grange; RMC Place; WORCESTER; *185 J-19; mail Pocomoke City z 21851; ● 50
Klondike (Lord); RMC Place; ALLEGANY; *184 B-3; ★ CUMB; mail Frostburg z 21532; ● 120
Knettishall; RMC Place; BALTIMORE; *185 C-14; ★ BAL; mail Towson z 21204
Knollview; RMC Place; HOWARD; *185 D-13; ★ BAL; mail Ellicott City z 21043
Knollwood; RMC Place; BALTIMORE; *185 C-14; ★ BAL; mail Towson z 21204
Knollwood; RMC Place; PRINCE GEORGE'S; 249 D-7; ★ WASH; mail Hyattsville z 20783; ● 1,250
Knoxville; RMC Place; FREDERICK; 184 C-9; elev. 297ft./91m.; 🅿; ★ WASH; z 21758; ● 340
Kreigbaum; ALLEGANY; see Corriganville (RMC Place)

L

Ladiesburg; RMC Place; FREDERICK; 185 B-11; elev. 472ft./144m.; 🅿; z 21759; ● 230
Lake Arbor; CDP-Census Area Only; PRINCE GEORGE'S; *185 F-12; ★ WASH; © 8,533
Lake Forest; HARFORD; see Forest Lake (RMC Place)
Lakeland; RMC Place; ANNE ARUNDEL; *185 E-14; ★ WASH; mail Severna Park z 21146
Lakeland; RMC Place; PRINCE GEORGE'S; ★ WASH; mail College Park z 20740; pop. incl. with College Park (Inc. Place)
Lake Linganore; RMC Place; FREDERICK; *184 C-10; ★ WASH; mail New Market z 21774; ● 1,300
Lake Normandy Estates; RMC Place; MONTGOMERY; *185 E-11; ★ WASH; mail Potomac z 20854
Lake Roland; RMC Place; BALTIMORE; ★ BAL; mail Baltimore z 21209
Lake Shore; CDP; ANNE ARUNDEL; 185 E-14; 🅿; ★ BAL; z 21122-23; Ⓟ 13,269; © 13,065
Lakeside Manor; RMC Place; WICOMICO; *185 I-18; ★ SLSB; mail Salisbury z 21801; ● 150
Lakeside Park; RMC Place; CECIL; *185 B-16; elev. 150ft./46m.; ★ PHIL-; mail North East z 21901; ● 300
Lakeside Park; RMC Place; WASHINGTON; *184 B-8; ★ HAG; mail Hagerstown z 21740; ● 600
Lakeside Terrace; RMC Place; MONTGOMERY; *185 E-11; ★ WASH; mail Bethesda z 20817; ● 2,350
Lakeside Vista; RMC Place; HARFORD; *185 B-15; ★ BAL; mail Joppa z 21085; ● 450
Lakesville; RMC Place; DORCHESTER; 185 I-16; mail Church Creek z 21622; ● 30
Lakeview; RMC Place; HOWARD; *185 D-12; ★ WASH; mail Laurel z 20723; ● 750
Lakeview; RMC Place; MONTGOMERY; ★ WASH; mail Bethesda z 20817
Lakewood; RMC Place; WICOMICO; *185 I-18; ★ SLSB; mail Salisbury z 21804; pop. incl. with Salisbury (Inc. Place)
Lakewood at Tanterra; MONTGOMERY; see Tanterra (RMC Place)
Lakewood Estates; RMC Place; CALVERT; *185 G-13; ★ WASH; mail Dunkirk z 20754; ● 300
Lakewood Estates; RMC Place; MONTGOMERY; *185 E-11; ★ WASH; mail Rockville z 20850
Lamotte; CARROLL; see Cedarhurst (RMC Place)
Lancaster; RMC Place; CHARLES; *185 G-12; ★ WASH; mail Waldorf z 20603
Lander (Catoctin); RMC Place; FREDERICK; 184 B-10; ★ WASH; mail Brunswick z 21716; ● 110
Land-O-Lakes; RMC Place; ST. MARY'S; *185 I-14; ★ WASH; mail Hollywood z 20636; ● 300
Landon Woods; RMC Place; MONTGOMERY; *185 E-11; ★ WASH; mail Bethesda z 20817
Landover; RMC Place; PRINCE GEORGE'S; 249 F-9; elev. 100ft./30m.; 🅿; ★ WASH; z 20785; ● 640
Landover Estates; RMC Place; PRINCE GEORGE'S; *185 F-12; ★ WASH; mail Hyattsville z 20784; ● 2,800
Landover Hills; Inc. Place; PRINCE GEORGE'S; 249 E-9; elev. 100ft./30m.; 🅿; ★ WASH; z 20784; Ⓟ 2,074; © 1,534
Landover Knolls; RMC Place; PRINCE GEORGE'S; *185 F-12; ★ WASH; mail Hyattsville z 20785; ● 910
Landover Park; RMC Place; PRINCE GEORGE'S; *185 F-12; ★ WASH; mail Hyattsville z 20785; pop. incl. with Cheverly (Inc. Place)
Lane Beach; RMC Place; ST. MARY'S; *185 J-14; mail Leonardtown z 20650; ● 110
Lanedon; RMC Place; ST. MARY'S; *185 J-14; elev. 17ft./5m.; ★ WASH; mail Leonardtown z 20650; ● 100
Langford; RMC Place; KENT; *185 D-16; elev. 68ft./21m.; mail Chestertown z 21620; rural
Langford Estates; RMC Place; KENT; *185 D-15; elev. 19ft./6m.; mail Chestertown z 21620; ● 100
Langley Park; CDP; PRINCE GEORGE'S, MONTGOMERY; 249 E-7; 🅿; ★ WASH; z 20787 & mail Hyattsville z 20783, Silver Spring z 20903; Ⓟ 17,474; © 16,214
Lanham; RMC Place; PRINCE GEORGE'S; 249 E-9; 🅿 🅷 🅲 655; ★ WASH; z 20703, z 20706 & mail Hyattsville z 20784; ● 5,200
Lanham Heights; RMC Place; PRINCE GEORGE'S; *185 E-12; ★ WASH; mail Lanham z 20706; pop. incl. with Hyattsville (Inc. Place)
Lanham-Seabrook; CDP-Census Area Only; PRINCE GEORGE'S; *185 E-12; 🅿; ★ WASH; z 20703, z 20706; Ⓟ 16,792; © 18,190
Lanham Woods (Kidmore Lane); RMC Place; PRINCE GEORGE'S; *185 E-12; ★ WASH; mail Lanham z 20706
Lansdowne; RMC Place; BALTIMORE; 184 K-4; elev. 100ft./30m.; 🅿; ★ BAL; z 21227; ● 8,700
Lansdowne-Baltimore Highlands; CDP-Census Area Only; BALTIMORE; *185 D-13; ★ BAL; mail Halethorpe z 21227; Ⓟ 15,509; © 15,724
Lantz; FREDERICK; see Deerfield (RMC Place)
Lapidum; RMC Place; HARFORD; *185 B-16; elev. 17ft./5m.; mail Havre de Grace z 21078; ● 100
La Plata; Inc. Place; ⊡ CHARLES; 185 H-12; elev. 193ft./59m.; 🅿 🅷; ★ WASH; z 20646; Ⓟ 5,841; © 6,551
Lappans; RMC Place; WASHINGTON; 184 B-8; ★ HAG; mail Fairplay z 21733; ● 30
Larchmont Knolls; RMC Place; MONTGOMERY; *185 E-11; ★ WASH; mail Kensington z 20895; ● 230
Largo; CDP; PRINCE GEORGE'S; 249 F-10; 🅿; ★ WASH; z 20774, z 20792; Ⓟ 9,475; © 8,408
Largo/Kettering; RMC Place; PRINCE GEORGE'S; *185 F-13; ★ WASH; mail Upper Marlboro z 20775
Largo Knolls; RMC Place; PRINCE GEORGE'S; *185 F-13; ★ WASH; mail Upper Marlboro z 20774
Laurel; Inc. Place; PRINCE GEORGE'S; 185 E-12; elev. 160ft./49m.; 🅿 🅷 🅲 1,095 ■; ★ WASH; z 20707-09, z 20723-26; Ⓟ 19,438; © 19,960; ◆ 21,387
Laurel Acres; RMC Place; ANNE ARUNDEL; *185 E-14; ★ BAL; mail Pasadena z 21122; ● 1,100
Laurel Brook; RMC Place; HARFORD; *185 B-14; ★ BAL; mail Fallston z 21047
Laureldale; RMC Place; BALTIMORE; *185 C-14; ★ BAL; mail Parkville z 21234
Laurel Grove; RMC Place; ST. MARY'S; *185 I-13; ★ WASH; mail Mechanicsville z 20659; ● 110
Laurel Pines; RMC Place; PRINCE GEORGE'S; *185 E-12; ★ WASH; mail Laurel z 20708
Laurel Walk; PRINCE GEORGE'S; see Villages of Montpelier (RMC Place)
Laurel Wood; RMC Place; PRINCE GEORGE'S; *185 E-12; ★ WASH; mail Laurel z 20708
La Vale; CDP; ALLEGANY; 184 A-4; 🅿; ★ CUMB; z 21502, z 21504; Ⓟ 4,694; © 4,613
Lawndale Acres; RMC Place; CARROLL; *185 B-12; ★ BAL; mail Finksburg z 21048; ● 350
Lawsonia; RMC Place; SOMERSET; 185 K-17; mail Crisfield z 21817; Ⓟ 1,326
Layhill; RMC Place; MONTGOMERY; 185 E-12; ★ WASH; mail Silver Spring z 20906; ● 1,600
Layhill Gardens; RMC Place; MONTGOMERY; ★ WASH; mail Silver Spring z 20906
Layhill South; MONTGOMERY; see South Layhill (RMC Place)
Layhill Village; RMC Place; MONTGOMERY; *185 E-11; ★ WASH; mail Silver Spring z 20906
Laytonia; RMC Place; MONTGOMERY; *185 D-11; ★ WASH; mail Gaithersburg z 20877
Laytonsville; Inc. Place; MONTGOMERY; 185 D-11; elev. 609ft./186m.; 🅿; ★ WASH; z 20879, z 20882; Ⓟ 248; © 277
Leeds; RMC Place; CECIL; *185 A-17; elev. 200ft./61m.; ★ PHIL-; mail Elkton z 21921; ● 30
Lees Woods; RMC Place; HARFORD; *185 B-15; ★ BAL; mail Bel Air z 21014; ● 610
Legion Avenue; RMC Place; ANNE ARUNDEL; ★ ANPLS; mail Annapolis z 21401; pop. incl. with Annapolis (Inc. Place)
Le Gore; RMC Place; FREDERICK; 184 B-10; mail Keymar z 21757; ● 110
Leisure World; MONTGOMERY; see Rossmoor (CDP-Census Area Only)
Leitersburg; CDP; WASHINGTON; 184 A-9; ★ HAG; mail Hagerstown z 21742; © 523
Leon; RMC Place; ANNE ARUNDEL; *185 F-13; ★ WASH; mail Lothian z 20711; ● 30
Leonardtown; Inc. Place; ⊡ ST. MARY'S; 185 I-13; elev. 87ft./27m.; 🅿 🅷; ★ WASH; z 20650; Ⓟ 1,475; © 1,896
Leslie; RMC Place; CECIL; *185 B-16; ★ PHIL-; mail North East z 21901; ● 100
Level; RMC Place; HARFORD; 185 B-15; mail Havre de Grace z 21078; ● 400
Lewis Corner; RMC Place; WORCESTER; *185 I-20; elev. 10ft./3m.; mail Berlin z 21811; rural
Lewisdale; RMC Place; PRINCE GEORGE'S; 249 E-7; ★ WASH; mail Hyattsville z 20782; ● 3,100
Lewis Heights; RMC Place; PRINCE GEORGE'S; *185 E-12; ★ WASH; mail Hyattsville z 20783
Lewis Spring Manor; RMC Place; PRINCE GEORGE'S; ★ WASH; mail Clinton z 20735
Lewistown; RMC Place; FREDERICK; 184 B-10; elev. 402ft./123m.; 🅿; ★ WASH; z 21701; ● 270
Lewistown; RMC Place; TALBOT; *185 F-16; mail Cordova z 21625; ● 80
Lexington Park; CDP; ST. MARY'S; 185 I-14; elev. 101ft./31m.; 🅿; z 20653; Ⓟ 9,943; © 11,021
Lexington Run; RMC Place; CARROLL; *185 C-12; elev. 600ft./183m.; ★ BAL; mail Sykesville z 21784; pop. incl. with Sykesville (Inc. Place)
Liberty Grove; RMC Place; CECIL; 185 A-16; elev. 173ft./53m.; ★ PHIL-; mail Conowingo z 21918; ● 90
Liberty Manor; RMC Place; BALTIMORE; 184 H-1; ★ BAL; mail Windsor Mill z 21244; ● 920
Libertytown; RMC Place; FREDERICK; 185 B-11; elev. 524ft./160m.; 🅿; ★ WASH; z 21762; ● 750
Libertytown; RMC Place; WORCESTER; *185 I-19; mail Berlin z 21811
Lime Kiln; RMC Place; FREDERICK; *184 C-10; ★ WASH; mail Frederick z 21701
Linchester; RMC Place; CAROLINE; *185 G-17; mail Preston z 21655; ● 30
Lincoln Avenue; RMC Place; WASHINGTON; ★ HAG; mail Hagerstown z 21740
Lincoln Heights; RMC Place; WICOMICO; ★ SLSB; mail Salisbury z 21801
Lincoln Manor; RMC Place; CARROLL; *185 B-12; ★ BAL; mail Manchester z 21102; ● 200
Lincoln Park; RMC Place; MONTGOMERY; ★ WASH; mail Rockville z 20850; pop. incl. with Rockville (Inc. Place)
Lindamoor on the Severn; RMC Place; ANNE ARUNDEL; *185 E-14; ★ ANPLS; mail Annapolis z 21401
Linden; RMC Place; MONTGOMERY; *185 E-12; ★ WASH; mail Silver Spring z 20907
Linden Chapel Hills; RMC Place; HOWARD; *185 D-12; elev. 500ft./152m.; ★ WASH; mail Dayton z 21036; ● 300
Lineboro; RMC Place; CARROLL; 185 A-12; elev. 678ft./207m.; 🅿; ★ BAL; z 21088, z 21102; ● 350
Linganore-Bartonsville; CDP-Census Area Only; FREDERICK; *184 C-10; elev. 400ft./122m.; ★ WASH; mail Frederick z 21701; Ⓟ 4,079; © 12,529
Linhigh; RMC Place; BALTIMORE; 184 H-7; ★ BAL; mail Nottingham z 21236; ● 2,100
Linkwood; RMC Place; DORCHESTER; 185 H-16; elev. 22ft./7m.; 🅿; z 21835; ● 240
Linsey Acres; RMC Place; PRINCE GEORGE'S; *185 F-12; ★ WASH; mail Temple Hills z 20748
Linsted on the Severn; RMC Place; ANNE ARUNDEL; *185 E-14; ★ BAL; mail Severna Park z 21146
Linthicum; CDP; ANNE ARUNDEL; 184 L-4; elev. 161ft./49m.; 🅿; ★ BAL; z 21090; Ⓟ 7,547; © 7,539
Linthicum Heights; RMC Place; ANNE ARUNDEL; *185 D-13; 🅿; ★ BAL; z 21090; ● 3,100
Linthicum Hills; RMC Place; ANNE ARUNDEL; *185 D-13; ★ BAL; mail Linthicum Heights z 21090
Linthicum Oaks; RMC Place; ANNE ARUNDEL; *185 D-13; ★ BAL; mail Linthicum Heights z 21090; ● 2,750
Linton Springs; RMC Place; CARROLL; *185 C-12; elev. 600ft./183m.; ★ BAL; mail Sykesville z 21784; ● 50
Linwood; RMC Place; CARROLL; 185 B-11; elev. 417ft./127m.; 🅿; z 21791; ● 130
Linwood; RMC Place; HOWARD; ★ BAL; mail Ellicott City z 21043
Linwood Village; RMC Place; ANNE ARUNDEL; *185 E-14; ★ BAL; mail Pasadena z 21122; ● 2,200
Lipins Corner; RMC Place; ANNE ARUNDEL; 184 N-4; ★ BAL; mail Pasadena z 21122; ● 80
Lisbon; RMC Place; HOWARD; 185 C-11; elev. 592ft./180m.; 🅿; ★ WASH; z 21765; ● 1,150
Little Orleans; RMC Place; ALLEGANY; 184 B-6; 🅿; z 21766; ● 200
Little Washington; RMC Place; PRINCE GEORGE'S; *185 F-12; ★ WASH; mail District Heights z 20747; ● 310
Livingston Grove; RMC Place; PRINCE GEORGE'S; *185 G-12; ★ WASH; mail Accokeek z 20607
Llandaff; RMC Place; TALBOT; *185 G-16; elev. 27ft./8m.; mail Easton z 21601; ● 30
Lloyds; RMC Place; DORCHESTER; 185 H-15; elev. 5ft./2m.; mail Cambridge z 21613; ● 30
Loartown; ALLEGANY; see Loarville (RMC Place)
Loarville (Loartown); RMC Place; ALLEGANY; *184 B-3; elev. 2,100ft./640m.; ★ CUMB; mail Frostburg z 21532; ● 140
Lochearn; CDP; BALTIMORE; 184 I-2; ★ BAL; mail Gwynn Oak z 21207, Pikesville z 21208; Ⓟ 25,240; © 25,269; ◆ 26,523
Loch Haven; RMC Place; BALTIMORE; *185 C-14; ★ BAL; mail Parkville z 21234
Loch Hill; RMC Place; BALTIMORE; *185 C-14; ★ BAL; mail Baltimore z 21212
Loch Lynn Heights; Inc. Place; GARRETT; 184 C-1; elev. 2,438ft./743m.; mail Oakland z 21550; Ⓟ 461; © 469
Loch Raven; RMC Place; BALTIMORE; *185 C-14; 🅿; ★ BAL; z 21204, z 21284, z 21286 & mail Parkville z 21234
Loch Raven Heights; RMC Place; BALTIMORE; *185 C-14; ★ BAL; mail Parkville z 21234
Loch Raven Village; RMC Place; BALTIMORE; *185 C-14; 🅿; ★ BAL; z 21234, z 21286
Locust Grove; RMC Place; ALLEGANY; 185 C-16; ★ CUMB; mail Cumberland z 21502; ● 30
Locust Grove; RMC Place; KENT; *185 C-16; mail Kennedyville z 21645; ● 30
Locust Grove; RMC Place; WASHINGTON; *184 C-9; elev. 566ft./173m.; ★ WASH; mail Rohrersville z 21779; ● 100
Locust Grove Beach; RMC Place; CALVERT; *185 G-14; elev. 9ft./3m.; ★ WASH; mail Chesapeake Beach z 20732; ● 50
Locust Grove Station; RMC Place; FREDERICK; *184 B-10; ★ WASH; mail Thurmont z 21788; ● 100
Locust Hill Estates; RMC Place; MONTGOMERY; *185 E-11; ★ WASH; mail Bethesda z 20814
Locust Point; RMC Place; BALTIMORE (Independent City); pop. incl. with Baltimore (Independent City)
Locust Valley; RMC Place; FREDERICK; *184 C-9; elev. 708ft./216m.; ★ WASH; mail Middletown z 21769; rural
Lodge Forest; RMC Place; BALTIMORE; ★ BAL; mail Dundalk z 21222
Lonaconing; Inc. Place; ALLEGANY; 184 B-3; elev. 1,461ft./445m.; 🅿; ★ CUMB; z 21539; Ⓟ 1,122; © 1,205
Londontown (Woodland Beach); RMC Place; ANNE ARUNDEL; 185 F-14; ★ ANPLS; mail Edgewater z 21037; ● 4,000
Londontowne; CDP; ANNE ARUNDEL; *185 F-14; ★ ANPLS; mail Edgewater z 21037; Ⓟ 6,992; © 7,595
London Woods; RMC Place; PRINCE GEORGE'S; *185 F-12; ★ WASH; mail Capitol Heights z 20743; ● 110
Lone Oak; RMC Place; MONTGOMERY; *185 E-11; ★ WASH; mail Bethesda z 20814
Long; RMC Place; ALLEGANY; ★ CUMB; mail Cumberland z 21502
Long Bar Harbor; RMC Place; HARFORD; *185 C-15; ★ BAL; mail Abingdon z 21009; ● 750
Long Beach; RMC Place; CALVERT; 185 H-14; mail Saint Leonard z 20685; ● 1,100
Long Corner; RMC Place; HOWARD; *185 C-11; elev. 813ft./248m.; ★ WASH; mail Mount Airy z 21771; ● 90
Longfellow; RMC Place; HOWARD; *185 D-12; ★ BAL; mail Ellicott City z 21043
Longfield Estates; RMC Place; PRINCE GEORGE'S; *185 F-12; ★ WASH; mail District Heights z 20747
Long Green; RMC Place; BALTIMORE; 185 B-14; elev. 500ft./152m.; 🅿; ★ BAL; z 21092; ● 500
Long Meadow; RMC Place; CARROLL; *185 C-12; ★ BAL; mail Sykesville z 21784
Long Meadow Estates; RMC Place; MONTGOMERY; ★ WASH; mail Bethesda z 20814
Long Meadow West; RMC Place; BALTIMORE; *185 C-13; ★ BAL; mail Pikesville z 21208; ● 2,700
Long Point; RMC Place; ANNE ARUNDEL; *185 E-14; ★ BAL; mail Pasadena z 21122
Long Reach; RMC Place; HOWARD; ★ BAL; mail Columbia z 21045
Longridge; RMC Place; WORCESTER; 185 I-18; rural
Longview Beach; RMC Place; ST. MARY'S; *185 I-13; ★ WASH; mail Bushwood z 20618, Chaptico z 20621; summer pop. 400; ● 300
Longwood; RMC Place; MONTGOMERY; *185 E-11; ★ WASH; mail Bethesda z 20817
Longwoods; RMC Place; TALBOT; 185 F-16; elev. 51ft./16m.; mail Easton z 21601; ● 50
Lord; ALLEGANY; see Klondike (RMC Place)
Lord Calvert Estates; RMC Place; CALVERT; *185 G-13; ★ WASH; mail Owings z 20736; ● 80
Lord Cecil Woods; RMC Place; CALVERT; *185 H-14; elev. 60ft./18m.; ★ WASH; mail Huntingtown z 20639; ● 30
Loreley; RMC Place; BALTIMORE; *185 C-14; ★ BAL; mail White Marsh z 21162
Loretta Heights; RMC Place; ANNE ARUNDEL; *185 E-14; ★ ANPLS; mail Annapolis z 21401
Lothian; RMC Place; ANNE ARUNDEL; 185 F-13; elev. 180ft./55m.; 🅿; ★ WASH; z 20711; ● 300
Louisville; RMC Place; CARROLL; 185 C-12; elev. 605ft./184m.; ★ BAL; mail Finksburg z 21048, Sykesville z 21784; ● 200
Lou Mar Estates; RMC Place; HARFORD; *185 B-15; ★ BAL; mail Abingdon z 21009; ● 200
Love Point; RMC Place; QUEEN ANNE'S; 185 E-15; ★ ANPLS; mail Stevensville z 21666; ● 290
Loveville; RMC Place; ST. MARY'S; 185 I-13; elev. 150ft./46m.; 🅿; ★ WASH; z 20656; ● 640
Lower Homewood; ALLEGANY; see Homewood (RMC Place)
Lower Magothy Beach; RMC Place; ANNE ARUNDEL; *185 E-14; elev. 20ft./6m.; ★ BAL; mail Severna Park z 21146
Lower Marlboro; RMC Place; CALVERT; 185 G-13; elev. 30ft./9m.; ★ WASH; mail Owings z 20736; ● 170
Lucas Heights; RMC Place; ALLEGANY; *184 A-4; ★ CUMB; mail Cumberland z 21502; ● 250
Luke; Inc. Place; ALLEGANY; 184 B-3; elev. 1,000ft./305m.; 🅿; ★ CUMB; z 21540; Ⓟ 184; © 80
Lusby; CDP; CALVERT; 185 I-14; elev. 100ft./30m.; 🅿; z 20657; © 1,666
Lusby Crossroads; RMC Place; ANNE ARUNDEL; *185 E-14; ★ ANPLS; mail Annapolis z 21401; ● 60
Lute; RMC Place; MONTGOMERY; *185 E-12; ★ WASH; mail Silver Spring z 20906
Lutherville; RMC Place; BALTIMORE; *185 C-13; 🅿; ★ BAL; z 21093-94
Lutherville-Timonium; CDP-Census Area Only; BALTIMORE; 185 C-13; elev. 304ft./93m.; 🅿; ★ BAL; z 21093-94; Ⓟ 16,442; © 15,814
Lutz Hill; RMC Place; BALTIMORE; *185 C-14; ★ BAL; mail Rosedale z 21237; ● 4,200
Luxmanor; RMC Place; MONTGOMERY; 249 C-5; elev. 396ft./121m.; ★ WASH; mail Rockville z 20852; ● 2,500
Lynch; RMC Place; KENT; 185 C-16; elev. 70ft./21m.; 🅿; z 21678; ● 200
Lynch Point; RMC Place; BALTIMORE; *185 D-14; ★ BAL; mail Dundalk z 21222
Lynnbrook; RMC Place; ANNE ARUNDEL; *185 D-13; ★ BAL; mail Brooklyn z 21225
Lynnbrook; RMC Place; CHARLES; *185 G-12; ★ WASH; mail Waldorf z 20601
Lynne Acres; RMC Place; BALTIMORE; 184 H-2; ★ BAL; mail Windsor Mill z 21244; ● 6,700
Lyons Creek; RMC Place; ANNE ARUNDEL; *185 F-13; ★ WASH; mail Lothian z 20711; ● 620
Lyons Creek; RMC Place; CALVERT; 185 G-13; ★ WASH; mail Dunkirk z 20754; ● 50
Lyons Homes; RMC Place; BALTIMORE; *185 D-14; ★ BAL; mail Dundalk z 21222

M

Mac Alpine; HOWARD; see McAlpine (RMC Place)
Mac Donald Farms; RMC Place; CALVERT; *185 G-13; ★ WASH; mail Owings z 20736; ● 80
Maceys Corner; RMC Place; ANNE ARUNDEL; *185 E-14; ★ BAL; mail Severna Park z 21146
Mackall; RMC Place; CALVERT; *185 I-14; elev. 95ft./29m.; mail Saint Leonard z 20685; ● 30
Maddox; RMC Place; ST. MARY'S; 185 I-13; elev. 37ft./11m.; 🅿; ★ WASH; z 20621; ● 230
Madison; RMC Place; DORCHESTER; 185 H-15; elev. 6ft./2m.; 🅿; z 21648 & mail Woolford z 21677; ● 160
Madonna; RMC Place; HARFORD; 185 B-14; ★ BAL; mail Jarrettsville z 21084; ● 200
Madonna Manor; RMC Place; HARFORD; *185 B-14; ★ BAL; mail Jarrettsville z 21084; ● 200
Magnolia; RMC Place; HARFORD; *185 C-15; elev. 60ft./18m.; ★ BAL; mail Joppa z 21085
Magnolia Springs; RMC Place; PRINCE GEORGE'S; *185 E-12; ★ WASH; mail Hyattsville z 20784
Magothy Beach; RMC Place; ANNE ARUNDEL; *185 E-14; elev. 20ft./6m.; ★ BAL; mail Pasadena z 21122
Magothy Park Beach; RMC Place; ANNE ARUNDEL; *185 E-14; ★ BAL; mail Pasadena z 21122
Mago Vista; ANNE ARUNDEL; see Mago Vista Beach (RMC Place)
Mago Vista Beach (Mago Vista); RMC Place; ANNE ARUNDEL; *185 E-14; ★ BAL; mail Arnold z 21012; ● 2,100
Magruder Landing; RMC Place; PRINCE GEORGE'S; *185 G-13; ★ WASH; mail Brandywine z 20613; rural
Main Street; RMC Place; WICOMICO; ★ SLSB; mail Salisbury z 21801; pop. incl. with Salisbury (Inc. Place)
Malcolm; RMC Place; CHARLES; 185 G-13; ★ WASH; mail Waldorf z 20601; ● 50
Malvern; RMC Place; BALTIMORE; *185 C-13; ★ BAL; mail Towson z 21204
Manchester; Inc. Place; CARROLL; 185 A-12; elev. 1,000ft./305m.; 🅿; ★ BAL; z 21088, z 21102; Ⓟ 2,810; © 3,329
Manchester Estates; RMC Place; PRINCE GEORGE'S; *185 F-12; ★ WASH; mail Suitland z 20746
Manhattan Woods; RMC Place; ANNE ARUNDEL; *185 E-14; ★ BAL; mail Severna Park z 21146
Manokin (Jamestown); RMC Place; SOMERSET; 185 J-17; elev. 8ft./2m.; 🅿; z 21836; ● 250
Manokin; RMC Place; WICOMICO; *185 I-18; ★ SLSB; mail Salisbury z 21801; ● 350
Manor; RMC Place; BALTIMORE; *185 B-14; ★ BAL; mail Monkton z 21111
Manor Lake; RMC Place; MONTGOMERY; *185 E-11; ★ WASH; mail Rockville z 20853; ● 2,400
Manor Park; RMC Place; MONTGOMERY; *185 E-11; ★ WASH; mail Rockville z 20853; ● 2,400
Manor View; RMC Place; BALTIMORE; *185 C-14; ★ BAL; mail Glen Arm z 21057
Manor Woods; RMC Place; MONTGOMERY; *185 E-11; ★ WASH; mail Rockville z 20853; ● 5,800
Maple Crest (Glenmar Manor); RMC Place; BALTIMORE; *185 C-14; ★ BAL; mail Middle River z 21220
Maplecrest; RMC Place; CARROLL; *185 B-12; ★ BAL; mail Westminster z 21157
Maple Plains; RMC Place; WICOMICO; *185 I-18; ★ SLSB; mail Salisbury z 21804; ● 390
Mapleside; RMC Place; ALLEGANY; ★ CUMB; mail Cumberland z 21502; pop. incl. with Cumberland (Inc. Place)
Maple View; RMC Place; CARROLL; *185 B-12; ★ BAL; mail Westminster z 21157; rural
Mapleville; RMC Place; WASHINGTON; *184 B-9; ★ HAG; mail Boonsboro z 21713; ● 190
Maplewood; RMC Place; HOWARD; *185 C-12; ★ BAL; mail Ellicott City z 21042; ● 1,100
Maplewood; RMC Place; MONTGOMERY; *185 E-11; ★ WASH; mail Bethesda z 20814
Maplewood; RMC Place; PRINCE GEORGE'S; *185 G-12; ★ WASH; mail Fort Washington z 20744; ● 1,050
Marbury; RMC Place; CHARLES; 185 H-11; elev. 80ft./24m.; 🅿; ★ WASH; z 20658; Ⓟ 1,244
Mardela Springs; Inc. Place; WICOMICO; 185 H-17; 🅿; z 21837; Ⓟ 360; © 364
Margate; RMC Place; ANNE ARUNDEL; 184 M-5; ★ BAL; mail Glen Burnie z 21060; ● 1,500
Mariners (Bedsworth); RMC Place; SOMERSET; *185 K-17; mail Crisfield z 21817; rural
Marion (Marion Station); RMC Place; SOMERSET; 185 K-17; elev. 8ft./2m.; 🅿; z 21838; ● 1,050
Marion Station; SOMERSET; see Marion (RMC Place)
Market Center; RMC Place; BALTIMORE (Independent City); ★ BAL; mail Baltimore z 21201; pop. incl. with Baltimore (Independent City)
Marlboro; PRINCE GEORGE'S; see Upper Marlboro (Inc. Place)
Marley; RMC Place; ANNE ARUNDEL; 184 M-5; ★ BAL; mail Glen Burnie z 21060; ● 1,500
Marley Heights; RMC Place; ANNE ARUNDEL; *185 D-14; ★ BAL; mail Glen Burnie z 21061
Marling Farms; RMC Place; QUEEN ANNE'S; *185 F-15; ★ ANPLS; mail Chester z 21619; ● 640
Marlow Heights; CDP; PRINCE GEORGE'S; *185 F-12; 🅿; ★ WASH; z 20748 & mail Suitland z 20746; Ⓟ 5,885; © 6,059
Marlton; CDP; PRINCE GEORGE'S; 185 F-13; ★ WASH; mail Upper Marlboro z 20772; Ⓟ 5,523; © 7,798
Marlywood; RMC Place; BALTIMORE; *185 C-13; ★ BAL; mail Towson z 21286
Marriottsville; RMC Place; HOWARD; 185 C-12; elev. 292ft./89m.; 🅿; ★ BAL; z 21104; ● 110
Mars Estates; RMC Place; BALTIMORE; *185 C-14; ★ BAL; mail Essex z 21221
Marshall Hall; RMC Place; CHARLES; 185 G-11; ★ WASH; mail Bryans Road z 20616; ● 230
Marshalls Corner; RMC Place; CHARLES; *185 H-12; ★ WASH; mail La Plata z 20646, Pomfret z 20675; ● 40
Marston; RMC Place; CARROLL; 185 B-11; elev. 658ft./201m.; mail New Windsor z 21776; ● 50
Martingham; RMC Place; TALBOT; *185 F-15; elev. 10ft./3m.; mail Saint Michaels z 21663; ● 50
Martins Additions; Inc. Place; MONTGOMERY; *185 E-11; ★ WASH; mail Chevy Chase z 20815; Ⓟ 846; © 875
Martinsburg; RMC Place; MONTGOMERY; *184 D-10; elev. 399ft./122m.; ★ WASH; mail Dickerson z 20842
Martins Woods; RMC Place; PRINCE GEORGE'S; *185 E-12; ★ WASH; mail Lanham z 20706; pop. incl. with New Carrollton (Inc. Place)
Marwood; RMC Place; ANNE ARUNDEL; *185 D-14; ★ BAL; mail Glen Burnie z 21061
Marydel; Inc. Place; CAROLINE; 185 D-17; elev. 60ft./18m.; 🅿; z 21649; Ⓟ 143; © 147
Maryland City; CDP; ANNE ARUNDEL; 185 E-13; 🅿; ★ WASH; z 20724; Ⓟ 6,813; © 6,814
Maryland Line; RMC Place; BALTIMORE; 185 A-13; elev. 860ft./262m.; 🅿; ★ BAL; z 21105; ● 400
Maryland Park; RMC Place; PRINCE GEORGE'S; *185 F-12; ★ WASH; mail Capitol Heights z 20743; ● 1,300
Maryland Point; RMC Place; CHARLES; *185 I-11; mail Nanjemoy z 20662; rural
Marymount; RMC Place; MONTGOMERY; *185 E-11; ★ WASH; mail Bethesda z 20814
Maryvale; RMC Place; MONTGOMERY; *185 E-11; ★ WASH; mail Rockville z 20850; pop. incl. with Rockville (Inc. Place)
Marywood; RMC Place; HARFORD; *185 B-15; ★ BAL; mail Bel Air z 21014; ● 3,800
Masons Beach; RMC Place; ANNE ARUNDEL; *185 G-14; ★ WASH; mail Deale z 20751
Mason Springs; RMC Place; CHARLES; 185 H-11; ★ WASH; mail Indian Head z 20640; ● 30
Masonville; RMC Place; BALTIMORE (Independent City); pop. incl. with Baltimore (Independent City)

Entries in **UPPERCASE** are counties.
Entries in **bold** have populations of 2,500 or more.
Names in parentheses are alternate names.

Inc. Place	Incorporated Place
RMC Place	Rand McNally Designated Place
CDP	Census Designated Place
MCD	Minor Civil Division

⊡ County Seat
▲ Minor Civil Division
elev. Elevation
🅿 Post Office
🅷 Hospital
🅲 College
■ Principal Business Center
★ Ranally Metro Area (RMA) Abbreviation
z Zip Code(s)
Ⓟ Previous Census Population
Ⓡ Revised Census Population
Ⓐ Annexation Population
● Rand McNally Population Estimate
© Final Census Population
Ⓢ Special Census Population
◆ Estimated Population

For additional definitions see Glossary, Volume 1, and Introduction, Volume 2.

Massey; RMC Place; KENT; **185** C-17; elev. 73ft./22m.; 🅿; **z** 21650; ● 150
Matapeake Estates; RMC Place; QUEEN ANNE'S; ***185** E-15; elev. 8ft./2m.; ★ **ANPLS**; mail Stevensville **z** 21666
Mattapex; RMC Place; QUEEN ANNE'S; ***185** F-15; ★ **ANPLS**; mail Stevensville **z** 21666; rural
Mattapony; RMC Place; PRINCE GEORGE'S; ★ **WASH**; mail Bladensburg **z** 20710; pop. incl. with Bladensburg (Inc. Place)
Mattawoman; CHARLES; see Pinefield (RMC Place)
Matthews; RMC Place; TALBOT; **185** F-16; elev. 53ft./16m.; mail Easton **z** 21601; ● 30
Maugansville; CDP; WASHINGTON; **184** A-8; elev. 620ft./189m.; 🅿; ★ **HAG**; **z** 21767; © 2,295
Mayberry; RMC Place; CARROLL; ***185** B-11; mail Westminster **z** 21158; ● 140
Maydale; RMC Place; MONTGOMERY; ***185** E-12; ★ **WASH**; mail Spencerville **z** 20868
Mayfield; RMC Place; ANNE ARUNDEL; ***185** E-13; ★ **BAL**; mail Odenton **z** 21113
Mayfield; RMC Place; HOWARD; ***185** D-12; ★ **BAL**; mail Ellicott City **z** 21043; ● 110
Mayo; CDP; ANNE ARUNDEL; **185** F-14; 🅿; ★ **ANPLS**; **z** 21106; ℗ 2,537; © 3,153
Mays Chapel; CDP-Census Area Only; BALTIMORE; **184** F-3; ★ **BAL**; mail Lutherville Timonium **z** 21093; ℗ 10,132; © 11,427
Mays Chapel Village; RMC Place; BALTIMORE; ***185** C-13; ★ **BAL**; mail Lutherville Timonium **z** 21093; ● 2,200
McAlpine (Mac Alpine); RMC Place; HOWARD; **184** K-1; ★ **BAL**; mail Ellicott City **z** 21042; ● 4,400
McCahill Estates; RMC Place; PRINCE GEORGE'S; ***185** E-12; ★ **WASH**; mail Laurel **z** 20707; ● 560
McCanns Corner; RMC Place; HARFORD; ***185** B-15; elev. 414ft./126m.; ★ **BAL**; mail Street **z** 21154; ● 250
McComas Beach; RMC Place; GARRETT; ***184** B-1; mail Oakland **z** 21550; ● 60
McCoole; RMC Place; ALLEGANY; **184** C-3; 🅿; ★ **CUMB**; **z** 21562 & mail Keyser **z** 26726; ● 350
McDaniel; RMC Place; TALBOT; **185** F-15; elev. 16ft./5m.; 🅿; **z** 21647; ● 170
Mc Daniel City; RMC Place; CHARLES; ***185** G-12; ★ **WASH**; mail Waldorf **z** 20603
McDonogh (McDonogh School); RMC Place; BALTIMORE; ***185** C-13; ★ **BAL**; mail Pikesville **z** 21208
Mcdonogh Manor; RMC Place; BALTIMORE; ***185** C-13; ★ **BAL**; mail Randallstown **z** 21133
McDonogh School; BALTIMORE; see McDonogh (RMC Place)
McHenry; RMC Place; GARRETT; **184** B-1; elev. 2,479ft./756m.; 🅿; **z** 21541; summer pop. 1,500; ● 1,000
McKaig; RMC Place; FREDERICK; ***184** C-10; elev. 538ft./164m.; ★ **WASH**; mail Frederick **z** 21701; ● 110
McKay Beach; RMC Place; ST. MARY'S; ***185** J-14; mail Leonardtown **z** 20650; ● 350
Mc Kendree; RMC Place; MONTGOMERY; ***185** D-11; ★ **WASH**; mail Gaithersburg **z** 20879
McKenney Hills; RMC Place; MONTGOMERY; ***185** E-11; ★ **WASH**; mail Silver Spring **z** 20910
McKinleyville; RMC Place; KENT; ***185** E-15; mail Rock Hall **z** 21661; rural
McKinstrys Mill; RMC Place; CARROLL; ***185** B-11; mail Union Bridge **z** 21791; ● 130
Meadowbrook; RMC Place; PRINCE GEORGE'S; ★ **WASH**; mail Bowie **z** 20715; pop. incl. with Bowie (Inc. Place)
Meadowbrook Estates; RMC Place; MONTGOMERY; ***185** D-11; ★ **WASH**; mail Germantown **z** 20876; ● 1,050
Meadowcliff; RMC Place; BALTIMORE; ***185** C-14; ★ **BAL**; mail Glen Arm **z** 21057
Meadowland; RMC Place; BALTIMORE; **184** F-4; ★ **BAL**; mail Lutherville Timonium **z** 21093; ● 2,700
Meadowood; RMC Place; ANNE ARUNDEL; ***185** F-13; ★ **WASH**; mail Davidsonville **z** 21035; ● 150
Meadowood; RMC Place; MONTGOMERY; **249** C-7; ★ **WASH**; mail Silver Spring **z** 20904; ● 1,100
Meadowvale Manor; RMC Place; HARFORD; ***185** B-16; mail Havre de Grace **z** 21078; pop. incl. with Havre de Grace (Inc. Place)
Meadowview Park; RMC Place; CECIL; ***185** G-17; mail Elkton **z** 21921
Mechanicsville; RMC Place; ST. MARY'S; **185** H-13; elev. 165ft./50m.; 🅿; ★ **WASH**; **z** 20659; ● 1,000
Mechanic Valley; RMC Place; CECIL; ***185** B-17; elev. 100ft./30m.; ★ **PHIL-**; mail North East **z** 21901; ● 30
Medford; RMC Place; CARROLL; ***185** B-11; elev. 531ft./162m.; ★ **BAL**; mail New Windsor **z** 21776; rural
Melitota; RMC Place; KENT; **185** D-16; elev. 48ft./15m.; mail Chestertown **z** 21620; ● 70
Mellwood Hills; RMC Place; PRINCE GEORGE'S; ***185** F-12; ★ **WASH**; mail Upper Marlboro **z** 20772; ● 370
Melody Acres; RMC Place; ST. MARY'S; ***185** H-13; ★ **WASH**; mail Charlotte Hall **z** 20622
Melrose; RMC Place; CARROLL; **185** A-12; ★ **BAL**; mail Manchester **z** 21102; ● 200
Melson; RMC Place; WICOMICO; ***185** H-19; elev. 65ft./20m.; ★ **SLSB**; mail Delmar **z** 21875
Merchants; RMC Place; BALTIMORE (Independent City); ***185** D-13; ★ **BAL**; mail Baltimore **z** 21201; pop. incl. with Baltimore (Independent City)
Merrickton; QUEEN ANNE'S; see Barclay (Inc. Place)
Merrimack Park; RMC Place; MONTGOMERY; ***185** E-11; ★ **WASH**; mail Bethesda **z** 20817
Merritt Heights; RMC Place; WICOMICO; ***185** I-18; ★ **SLSB**; mail Salisbury **z** 21804; ● 280
Merrymount; RMC Place; BALTIMORE; ***185** A-13; ★ **BAL**; mail Windsor Mill **z** 21244
Michigan Park Hills; RMC Place; PRINCE GEORGE'S; ***185** E-12; ★ **WASH**; mail Hyattsville **z** 20782
Middleborough; RMC Place; BALTIMORE; ***185** C-14; ★ **BAL**; mail Essex **z** 21221
Middlebrook; RMC Place; MONTGOMERY; ***185** D-11; ★ **WASH**; mail Germantown **z** 20876; ● 2,600
Middleburg; RMC Place; CARROLL; **185** B-11; elev. 496ft./151m.; 🅿; **z** 21757; ● 310
Middlepoint; RMC Place; FREDERICK; ***184** B-9; mail Myersville **z** 21773; ● 30
Middle River; CDP; BALTIMORE; **185** C-14; elev. 30ft./9m.; 🅿; ★ **BAL**; **z** 21220; ℗ 24,616; © 23,958; ◆ 25,156
Middlesex; RMC Place; BALTIMORE; ***185** C-14; ★ **BAL**; mail Essex **z** 21221
Middleton Valley; RMC Place; PRINCE GEORGE'S; ***185** F-12; ★ **WASH**; mail Temple Hills **z** 20748; ● 1,200
Middletown; RMC Place; BALTIMORE; **185** A-13; ★ **BAL**; mail Freeland **z** 21053; ● 100
Middletown; Inc. Place; FREDERICK; **184** C-9; elev. 547ft./167m.; 🅿; ★ **WASH**; **z** 21769; ℗ 1,834; © 2,668
Middletown Heights; RMC Place; FREDERICK; ***184** C-9; ★ **WASH**; mail Middletown **z** 21769; ● 50
Midland; Inc. Place; ALLEGANY; **184** B-3; elev. 1,694ft./516m.; 🅿; ★ **CUMB**; **z** 21542; ℗ 574; © 473
Midlothian; RMC Place; ALLEGANY; **184** B-3; elev. 2,000ft./610m.; 🅿; ★ **CUMB**; **z** 21543; ● 450
Milford; RMC Place; BALTIMORE; **184** H-2; ★ **BAL**; mail Gwynn Oak **z** 21207; ● 690
Milford Mill; CDP-Census Area Only; BALTIMORE; ***185** C-13; ★ **BAL**; mail Windsor Mill **z** 21244; ℗ 22,547; © 26,527; ◆ 27,850
Milford Park; RMC Place; BALTIMORE; ***185** C-13; ★ **BAL**; mail Owings Mills **z** 21117; ● 3,200
Milford Ridge; RMC Place; BALTIMORE; ***185** C-13; ★ **BAL**; mail Windsor Mill **z** 21244; ● 2,450
Millbrook; RMC Place; PRINCE GEORGE'S; ★ **WASH**; mail Laurel **z** 20707; pop. incl. with Laurel (Inc. Place)
Mill Creek South; RMC Place; MONTGOMERY; ***185** D-11; ★ **WASH**; mail Derwood **z** 20855
Mill Creek Towne; RMC Place; MONTGOMERY; ***185** D-11; ★ **WASH**; mail Laurel **z** 20707; ● 4,600
Mill Creek Towne East; RMC Place; MONTGOMERY; ***185** D-11; ★ **WASH**; mail Derwood **z** 20855
Miller; RMC Place; ALLEGANY; ***184** B-3; ★ **CUMB**; mail Frostburg **z** 21532; ● 150
Millers; RMC Place; CARROLL; **185** A-12; elev. 820ft./250m.; 🅿; ★ **BAL**; **z** 21102; ● 180
Millers Island; BALTIMORE; see Swan Point (RMC Place)
Millersville; RMC Place; ANNE ARUNDEL; **185** E-13; elev. 120ft./37m.; 🅿; ★ **BAL**; **z** 21108, **z** 21122; ● 950
Mill Green; RMC Place; HARFORD; ***185** A-15; ★ **BAL**; mail Street **z** 21154; rural
Millington; Inc. Place; KENT, QUEEN ANNE'S; **185** D-17; elev. 27ft./8m.; 🅿; **z** 21651; ℗ 409; © 416
Mill Point; RMC Place; ST. MARY'S; ***185** I-12; ★ **WASH**; mail Chaptico **z** 20621
Mill Point Shores; RMC Place; ST. MARY'S; ***185** I-12; ★ **WASH**; mail Chaptico **z** 20621; ● 350
Millrace; RMC Place; ANNE ARUNDEL; ***185** E-13; ★ **BAL**; mail Millersville **z** 21108
Mill Run; RMC Place; ALLEGANY; ***184** B-3; elev. 1,300ft./396m.; ★ **CUMB**; mail Westernport **z** 21562; ● 50
Mills Choice; RMC Place; MONTGOMERY; ***185** D-11; ★ **WASH**; mail Gaithersburg **z** 20879
Millville; RMC Place; WORCESTER; ***185** I-19; elev. 35ft./11m.; mail Snow Hill **z** 21863; rural
Millwood; RMC Place; PRINCE GEORGE'S; **249** G-9; ★ **WASH**; mail Capitol Heights **z** 20743; ● 1,100
Millwood Towne; RMC Place; PRINCE GEORGE'S; ***185** F-12; ★ **WASH**; mail Capitol Heights **z** 20743
Mimosa Cove; RMC Place; ANNE ARUNDEL; ***185** F-14; ★ **WASH**; mail Deale **z** 20751
Minefield; RMC Place; HARFORD; ***185** A-14; ★ **BAL**; mail Street **z** 21154; ● 50
Mitchell Manor; RMC Place; GARRETT; ***184** C-1; mail Oakland **z** 21550; ● 100
Mitchellville; RMC Place; PRINCE GEORGE'S; ***185** F-13; elev. 114ft./35m.; 🅿; ★ **WASH**; **z** 20716-17, **z** 20721
Mitchellville; CDP-Census Area Only; PRINCE GEORGE'S; ***185** F-13; elev. 100ft./30m.; ★ **WASH**; mail Lanham **z** 20706; ℗ 12,593; © 9,611
Monie; RMC Place; SOMERSET; **185** J-17; mail Princess Anne **z** 21853; ● 110
Monkton; RMC Place; BALTIMORE; **185** B-13; elev. 400ft./122m.; 🅿; ★ **BAL**; **z** 21111; ● 800
Monrovia; RMC Place; FREDERICK; ***185** C-11; elev. 431ft./131m.; 🅿; ★ **WASH**; **z** 21770
Montego; RMC Place; WORCESTER; mail Ocean City **z** 21842; pop. incl. with Ocean City (Inc. Place)
Montel; RMC Place; ALLEGANY; ***184** B-3; elev. 1,700ft./518m.; ★ **CUMB**; mail Cumberland **z** 21502; rural
Montevideo; RMC Place; ANNE ARUNDEL; **184** M-2; elev. 158ft./48m.; ★ **BAL**; mail Hanover **z** 21076; ● 230
Montevideo; RMC Place; HOWARD; ***185** D-13; ★ **BAL**; mail Jessup **z** 20794
MONTGOMERY; **185** D-11; ℗ 757,027; © 873,341; ◆ 927,547
Montgomery Knolls; RMC Place; HOWARD; ***185** D-13; ★ **BAL**; mail Ellicott City **z** 21043
Montgomery Square; RMC Place; MONTGOMERY; ***185** E-11; ★ **WASH**; mail Potomac **z** 20854; ● 1,050
Montgomery Village; CDP; MONTGOMERY; **185** D-11; 🅿; ★ **WASH**; **z** 20877, **z** 20879, **z** 20886; ℗ 32,315; © 38,051; ◆ 40,411
Montgomery White Oak; RMC Place; MONTGOMERY; ***185** E-12; ★ **WASH**; mail Silver Spring **z** 20904
Montpelier; RMC Place; PRINCE GEORGE'S; **249** C-10; 🅿; ★ **WASH**; **z** 20708-09; ● 3,600
Montpelier Woods; RMC Place; PRINCE GEORGE'S; ***185** E-12; ★ **WASH**; mail Laurel **z** 20708
Montrose; RMC Place; MONTGOMERY; **249** C-5; ★ **WASH**; mail Rockville **z** 20852; pop. incl. with Rockville (Inc. Place)
Monumental; RMC Place; BALTIMORE; ***185** D-13; ★ **BAL**; mail Halethorpe **z** 21227
Mooresfield; RMC Place; HOWARD; ***185** D-12; ★ **WASH**; mail Fulton **z** 20759; ● 370
Morantown; RMC Place; ALLEGANY; ***184** A-3; elev. 1,492ft./455m.; ★ **CUMB**; mail Frostburg **z** 21532; ● 100
Morgan; RMC Place; CARROLL; ***185** C-12; elev. 468ft./143m.; ★ **BAL**; mail Woodbine **z** 21797; rural
Morgantown; RMC Place; CHARLES; **185** I-12; mail Newburg **z** 20664; ● 200
Morganza; RMC Place; ST. MARY'S; **185** I-13; elev. 100ft./30m.; 🅿; ★ **WASH**; **z** 20660; ● 150
Morningside; Inc. Place; PRINCE GEORGE'S; **185** F-12; elev. 250ft./76m.; ★ **WASH**; mail Suitland **z** 20746; ℗ 930; © 1,295
Moscow; RMC Place; ALLEGANY; **184** B-3; elev. 1,316ft./401m.; ★ **CUMB**; mail Barton **z** 21521; ● 230
Motters; RMC Place; FREDERICK; **184** A-10
Mount Aetna; CDP; WASHINGTON; **184** B-9; ★ **HAG**; mail Hagerstown **z** 21740; ℗ 3,608; © 838
Mountain; RMC Place; HARFORD; ***185** C-15; ★ **BAL**; mail Joppa **z** 21085; ● 60
Mountaindale; RMC Place; FREDERICK; ***184** B-10; ★ **WASH**; mail Thurmont **z** 21788; ● 200
Mountain Lake Park; Inc. Place; GARRETT; **184** C-1; 🅿; **z** 21550; ℗ 1,938; © 2,248
Mountain View; RMC Place; CARROLL; ***185** B-12; elev. 2,400ft./732m.; ★ **BAL**; mail Westminster **z** 21157; ● 100
Mountain View Estates; RMC Place; MONTGOMERY; ***185** E-11; ★ **WASH**; mail Gaithersburg **z** 20878; ● 600
Mountain Wood; RMC Place; ANNE ARUNDEL; ***185** E-14; ★ **BAL**; mail Pasadena **z** 21122
Mount Airy; Inc. Place; CARROLL, FREDERICK; **185** C-11; elev. 764ft./233m.; 🅿; ★ **WASH**; **z** 21771; ℗ 3,730; © 6,425
Mount Briar; RMC Place; WASHINGTON; ***184** C-9; ★ **WASH**; mail Keedysville **z** 21756; ● 40
Mount Carmel; RMC Place; ANNE ARUNDEL; ***185** E-14; ★ **BAL**; mail Pasadena **z** 21122; rural
Mount Clare; RMC Place; BALTIMORE (Independent City); ***185** D-13; ★ **BAL**; mail Baltimore **z** 21223; pop. incl. with Baltimore (Independent City)
Mount De Sales; RMC Place; BALTIMORE; ***185** D-13; ★ **BAL**; mail Catonsville **z** 21228
Mount Harmony; RMC Place; CALVERT; ***185** G-14; elev. 186ft./57m.; ★ **WASH**; mail Owings **z** 20736
Mount Hebron; RMC Place; HOWARD; **185** C-12; ★ **BAL**; mail Ellicott City **z** 21042; ● 2,000
Mount Hermon; RMC Place; WICOMICO; ***185** I-18; ★ **SLSB**; mail Salisbury **z** 21804; ● 30
Mount Hope; RMC Place; BALTIMORE (Independent City); ★ **BAL**; mail Baltimore **z** 21215; pop. incl. with Baltimore (Independent City)
Mount Lena; CDP; WASHINGTON; **184** B-9; ★ **HAG**; mail Boonsboro **z** 21713; © 501
Mount Pleasant; RMC Place; FREDERICK; **184** C-10; elev. 475ft./145m.; ★ **WASH**; mail Frederick **z** 21701; ● 330
Mount Pleasant; RMC Place; WASHINGTON; ***184** B-9; ★ **HAG**; mail Boonsboro **z** 21713
Mount Pleasant; RMC Place; WICOMICO; ***185** I-19; mail Willards **z** 21874; rural
Mount Pleasant Beach; RMC Place; ANNE ARUNDEL; **184** M-6; ★ **BAL**; mail Pasadena **z** 21122; ● 2,100
Mount Pleasant Landing; RMC Place; TALBOT; ***185** F-15; elev. 10ft./3m.; mail Saint Michaels **z** 21663; rural
Mount Rainier; Inc. Place; PRINCE GEORGE'S; **249** E-7; elev. 100ft./30m.; 🅿; ★ **WASH**; **z** 20712; ℗ 7,954; © 8,498
Mount Savage; RMC Place; ALLEGANY; **184** A-3; elev. 1,178ft./359m.; 🅿; ★ **CUMB**; **z** 21545; ● 1,300
Mount Vernon; CDP; SOMERSET; **185** J-17; mail Princess Anne **z** 21853; © 761
Mount Victoria; RMC Place; CHARLES; **185** I-12; elev. 140ft./43m.; 🅿; **z** 20661; ● 150
Mountview; RMC Place; HOWARD; ***185** C-12; ★ **BAL**; mail Marriottsville **z** 21104; rural
Mountville; RMC Place; FREDERICK; ***184** C-9; ★ **WASH**; mail Frederick **z** 21701
Mount Washington; RMC Place; BALTIMORE (Independent City); ***185** C-13; 🅿; ★ **BAL**; **z** 21209; pop. incl. with Baltimore (Independent City)
Mount Westley; RMC Place; WORCESTER; ***185** J-19; mail Snow Hill **z** 21863; rural
Mount Wilson; RMC Place; BALTIMORE; ***185** C-13; elev. 560ft./171m.; ★ **BAL**; mail Pikesville **z** 21208
Mount Winans; RMC Place; BALTIMORE (Independent City); ★ **BAL**; pop. incl. with Baltimore (Independent City)
Mount Zion; RMC Place; CAROLINE; **185** E-17; elev. 70ft./21m.; mail Marydel **z** 21649; ● 80
Mount Zoar; RMC Place; CECIL; ***185** A-15; ★ **PHIL-**; mail Conowingo **z** 21918; ● 170
Mousetown; RMC Place; WASHINGTON; ***184** B-9; ★ **HAG**; mail Boonsboro **z** 21713; rural
Muirkirk; RMC Place; PRINCE GEORGE'S; **249** C-9; ★ **WASH**; mail Beltsville **z** 20705; ● 650
Mulberry Hills; RMC Place; ANNE ARUNDEL; ***185** E-14; ★ **ANPLS**; mail Annapolis **z** 21401; ● 250
Murray Hills; RMC Place; PRINCE GEORGE'S; ***185** F-12; ★ **WASH**; mail Oxon Hill **z** 20745; ● 600
Myersdale; RMC Place; WASHINGTON; ***184** A-6; mail Hancock **z** 21750
Myersville; Inc. Place; FREDERICK; **184** B-9; elev. 669ft./204m.; 🅿; **z** 21773; ℗ 464; © 1,382

N

Nanjemoy; RMC Place; CHARLES; **185** H-11; elev. 82ft./25m.; 🅿; **z** 20662; ● 240
Nanticoke; RMC Place; WICOMICO; **185** I-17; 🅿; **z** 21840; ● 580
Narrows (Kent Narrows); RMC Place; QUEEN ANNE'S; ***185** E-15; ★ **ANPLS**; mail Grasonville **z** 21638
Narrows Park; RMC Place; ALLEGANY; ★ **CUMB**; mail Cumberland **z** 21502
National (Carlos); RMC Place; ALLEGANY; ***184** B-3; ★ **CUMB**; mail Frostburg **z** 21532; ● 100
Naval Academy (United States Naval Academy); CDP-Census Area Only; ANNE ARUNDEL; ***185** E-14; elev. 40ft./12m.; 🅿; ★ **ANPLS**; **z** 21402; ℗ 5,420; © 4,264
Naylor; RMC Place; PRINCE GEORGE'S; mail Upper Marlboro **z** 20772
Neavitt; RMC Place; TALBOT; **185** G-15; elev. 6ft./2m.; 🅿; **z** 21652; ● 300
Needwood Estates; RMC Place; MONTGOMERY; ***185** D-11; ★ **WASH**; mail Derwood **z** 20855; ● 1,850
Neeld Estates; RMC Place; CALVERT; ***185** G-14; ★ **WASH**; mail Huntingtown **z** 20639; ● 250
Neelsville; RMC Place; MONTGOMERY; ***185** D-11; ★ **WASH**; mail Germantown **z** 20876; ● 200
Neilwood; RMC Place; MONTGOMERY; ***185** E-11; ★ **WASH**; mail Rockville **z** 20852
New Addition; RMC Place; FREDERICK; ***184** C-9; ★ **WASH**; mail Knoxville **z** 21758; ● 110
Newark (Queponco); CDP; WORCESTER; **185** I-19; elev. 35ft./11m.; 🅿; **z** 21841; © 339
New Birmingham Manor; RMC Place; MONTGOMERY; ***185** E-12; ★ **WASH**; mail Burtonsville **z** 20866
Newburg; RMC Place; CHARLES; **185** I-12; elev. 139ft./42m.; 🅿; **z** 20664; ● 720
New Carrollton (Carrollton); Inc. Place; PRINCE GEORGE'S; **185** E-12; elev. 100ft./30m.; 🅿; ★ **WASH**; **z** 20784; ℗ 12,002; © 12,589
Newcomb; RMC Place; TALBOT; **185** G-15; elev. 9ft./3m.; 🅿; **z** 21653; ● 250
New Germany; RMC Place; GARRETT; **184** A-2; mail Grantsville **z** 21536; summer pop. 150; ● 30
New Hampshire Estates; RMC Place; MONTGOMERY, PRINCE GEORGE'S; ***185** E-12; ★ **WASH**; mail Hyattsville **z** 20783, Silver Spring **z** 20903; ● 6,050
New Hampshire Gardens; RMC Place; PRINCE GEORGE'S; ***185** E-12; ★ **WASH**; mail Takoma Park **z** 20912; pop. incl. with Takoma Park (Inc. Place)
Newhope; RMC Place; WICOMICO; ***185** I-19; mail Willards **z** 21874; rural
New London; RMC Place; FREDERICK; **185** C-11; elev. 423ft./129m.; ★ **WASH**; mail Mount Airy **z** 21771; ● 170
New Mark Commons; RMC Place; MONTGOMERY; ***185** E-11; ★ **WASH**; mail Rockville **z** 20850; pop. incl. with Rockville (Inc. Place)
New Market; Inc. Place; FREDERICK; **184** C-10; elev. 551ft./168m.; 🅿; ★ **WASH**; **z** 21774; ℗ 328; © 427
New Market; RMC Place; ST. MARY'S; ***185** H-13; ★ **WASH**; mail Charlotte Hall **z** 20622
New Market View; RMC Place; FREDERICK; ***185** C-11; ★ **WASH**; mail Mount Airy **z** 21771
New Midway; RMC Place; FREDERICK; **184** B-10; elev. 468ft./143m.; 🅿; **z** 21775; ● 380
New Orchard Estates; RMC Place; PRINCE GEORGE'S; ***185** F-12; ★ **WASH**; mail Upper Marlboro **z** 20774; ● 1,900
Newport; RMC Place; CHARLES; **185** I-12; elev. 14ft./4m.; mail Charlotte Hall **z** 20622; ● 80
Newport Hills; RMC Place; MONTGOMERY; ***185** E-11; ★ **WASH**; mail Kensington **z** 20895
New Road Landing; RMC Place; WICOMICO; ***185** I-17; elev. 1ft./0m.; mail Tyaskin **z** 21865; rural
Newton; RMC Place; CAROLINE; ***185** G-17; mail Preston **z** 21655; ● 100
Newton Village; RMC Place; PRINCE GEORGE'S; ***185** F-12; ★ **WASH**; mail Hyattsville **z** 20781; ● 1,100
Newtown; RMC Place; CHARLES; **185** H-12; ★ **WASH**; mail La Plata **z** 20646; ● 330
Newtown; RMC Place; KENT; **185** C-16; mail Worton **z** 21678; ● 80
Newtown; RMC Place; TALBOT; ***185** F-16; elev. 45ft./14m.; mail Cordova **z** 21625; ● 180
New Valley; RMC Place; CECIL; ***185** A-16; elev. 200ft./61m.; ★ **PHIL-**; mail Conowingo **z** 21918; rural
New Windsor; Inc. Place; CARROLL; **185** B-11; elev. 452ft./138m.; 🅿; **z** 21776; ℗ 757; © 1,303
Nikep (Pekin); RMC Place; ALLEGANY; **184** B-3; elev. 1,394ft./425m.; ★ **CUMB**; mail Lonaconing **z** 21539; ● 270
Nob Hill; RMC Place; HOWARD; ***185** D-12; ★ **BAL**; mail Ellicott City **z** 21042
Nob Hill; RMC Place; MONTGOMERY; ***185** E-12; ★ **WASH**; mail Silver Spring **z** 20903
Nomira Heights; RMC Place; CECIL; ★ **PHIL-**; mail Elkton **z** 21921; pop. incl. with Elkton (Inc. Place)
Norbeck; RMC Place; MONTGOMERY; ***185** E-11; elev. 499ft./152m.; ★ **WASH**; mail Silver Spring **z** 20906
Normandy Heights; RMC Place; HOWARD; ★ **BAL**; mail Ellicott City **z** 21043
Normans; RMC Place; QUEEN ANNE'S; **185** F-15; ★ **ANPLS**; mail Stevensville **z** 21666; ● 100
Norris Corner; RMC Place; HARFORD; ***185** B-15; elev. 191ft./58m.; ★ **BAL**; mail Abingdon **z** 21009; ● 200
Norrisville; RMC Place; HARFORD; **185** A-14; elev. 740ft./226m.; ★ **BAL**; mail White Hall **z** 21161; ● 250
Northampton; RMC Place; BALTIMORE; ***185** C-13; ★ **BAL**; mail Lutherville Timonium **z** 21093
Northampton; RMC Place; PRINCE GEORGE'S; ***185** F-12; ★ **WASH**; mail Upper Marlboro **z** 20774; ● 1,350
North Barnaby; RMC Place; PRINCE GEORGE'S; ***185** F-12; elev. 271ft./83m.; ★ **WASH**; mail Oxon Hill **z** 20745
North Beach; Inc. Place; CALVERT; **185** G-14; elev. 20ft./6m.; 🅿; ★ **WASH**; **z** 20714; ℗ 1,173; © 1,880
North Beach Park; RMC Place; ANNE ARUNDEL; ***185** G-14; ★ **WASH**; mail North Beach **z** 20714
North Bend Estates; RMC Place; TALBOT; ***185** F-16; elev. 12ft./4m.; mail Easton **z** 21601; ● 30
North Bethesda; CDP-Census Area Only; MONTGOMERY; ***185** E-11; 🅿; ★ **WASH**; **z** 20852 & mail Bethesda **z** 20814, Kensington **z** 20895, Rockville **z** 20851; ℗ 29,656; © 38,610; ◆ 41,012
North Branch; RMC Place; ALLEGANY; ***184** B-4; elev. 641ft./195m.; mail Cumberland **z** 21502
North Brentwood; Inc. Place; PRINCE GEORGE'S; ***185** F-12; elev. 30ft./9m.; 🅿; ★ **WASH**; **z** 20722; ℗ 512; © 469
North Chevy Chase; Inc. Place; MONTGOMERY; ***185** E-11; ★ **WASH**; mail Chevy Chase **z** 20815; © 465
North Deale; RMC Place; ANNE ARUNDEL; ***185** F-14; ★ **WASH**; mail Deale **z** 20751
North East; Inc. Place; CECIL; **185** B-16; elev. 10ft./3m.; 🅿; ★ **PHIL-**; **z** 21901 & mail Port Deposit **z** 21904; ℗ 1,913; © 2,733
Northeast Heights; RMC Place; CECIL; ***185** B-16; ★ **PHIL-**; mail North East **z** 21901; ● 190
North Easton; RMC Place; TALBOT; ***185** F-16; elev. 60ft./18m.; mail Easton **z** 21601; ● 150
North End Harbor; RMC Place; CECIL; ***185** B-16; elev. 50ft./15m.; ★ **PHIL-**; mail North East **z** 21901; ● 200
North Englewood; RMC Place; PRINCE GEORGE'S; 🅿; ★ **WASH**; **z** 20785
Northern; RMC Place; WASHINGTON; ★ **HAG**; mail Hagerstown **z** 21740, **z** 21742; pop. incl. with Hagerstown (Inc. Place)
North Forestville; RMC Place; PRINCE GEORGE'S; ***185** F-12; ★ **WASH**; mail District Heights **z** 20747
North Fort Foote Village; RMC Place; PRINCE GEORGE'S; ***185** G-12; ★ **WASH**; mail Fort Washington **z** 20744
North Glade; RMC Place; GARRETT; ***184** B-2; elev. 2,503ft./763m.; mail Swanton **z** 21561; ● 60
North Glen Hills; MONTGOMERY; see Glen Hills (RMC Place)
North Indian Head Estates; RMC Place; CHARLES; ***185** G-11; ★ **WASH**; mail Bryans Road **z** 20616; ● 1,350
North Junction; RMC Place; WASHINGTON; ★ **HAG**; mail Hagerstown **z** 21740; pop. incl. with Hagerstown (Inc. Place)
North Kensington; CDP; MONTGOMERY; ***185** E-11; ★ **WASH**; mail Silver Spring **z** 20902; ℗ 8,607; © 8,940
North Laurel; CDP-Census Area Only; HOWARD; ***185** D-12; ★ **WASH**; mail Sykesville **z** 21784; ℗ 15,008; © 20,468; ◆ 22,795
North Laurel Park; RMC Place; HOWARD; ***185** D-12; ★ **WASH**; mail Laurel **z** 20723
North Linthicum; RMC Place; ANNE ARUNDEL; ***185** D-13; ★ **BAL**; mail Linthicum Heights **z** 21090; ● 2,900
North Ocean City; RMC Place; WORCESTER; ***185** I-20; elev. 10ft./3m.; mail Ocean City **z** 21842; pop. incl. with Ocean City (Inc. Place)
North Point; RMC Place; BALTIMORE; ***185** D-14; ★ **BAL**; mail Dundalk **z** 21222
North Point Village; RMC Place; BALTIMORE; ***185** D-14; ★ **BAL**; mail Dundalk **z** 21222
North Potomac; CDP; MONTGOMERY; **249** C-2; 🅿; ★ **WASH**; **z** 20878; ℗ 18,456; © 23,044; ◆ 24,477
North Potomac Vista; RMC Place; PRINCE GEORGE'S; ***185** F-12; ★ **WASH**; mail Oxon Hill **z** 20745
Northridge; RMC Place; HARFORD; ***185** B-15; elev. 200ft./61m.; ★ **BAL**; mail Bel Air **z** 21015; ● 100
Northridge Manor; RMC Place; WASHINGTON; ***184** A-9; elev. 665ft./203m.; ★ **HAG**; mail Hagerstown **z** 21740; ● 150
North Roblee Acres; RMC Place; PRINCE GEORGE'S; ***185** F-13; ★ **WASH**; mail Upper Marlboro **z** 20772; ● 1,350
North Sherwood Forest; RMC Place; MONTGOMERY; ***185** E-12; ★ **WASH**; mail Silver Spring **z** 20904; ● 1,600
Northshire; RMC Place; BALTIMORE; ***185** D-14; ★ **BAL**; mail Dundalk **z** 21222
North Shore; RMC Place; ANNE ARUNDEL; ***185** E-14; elev. 40ft./12m.; ★ **BAL**; mail Pasadena **z** 21122; ● 700
North Springbrook; RMC Place; MONTGOMERY; ***185** E-12; ★ **WASH**; mail Silver Spring **z** 20904; ● 1,100
North Wellham; RMC Place; ANNE ARUNDEL; ***185** D-13; ★ **BAL**; mail Glen Burnie **z** 21061
Northwest Park; RMC Place; MONTGOMERY, PRINCE GEORGE'S; ***185** E-12; ★ **WASH**; mail Silver Spring **z** 20903; ● 2,800
Northwest Park; RMC Place; MONTGOMERY; ***185** E-11; ★ **WASH**; mail Bethesda **z** 20814
Northwood; RMC Place; BALTIMORE (Independent City); ***185** C-14; 🅿; ★ **BAL**; **z** 21239; pop. incl. with Baltimore (Independent City)
Northwood Park; RMC Place; MONTGOMERY; ***185** E-12; ★ **WASH**; mail Silver Spring **z** 20901
Northwood Village; RMC Place; MONTGOMERY; ***185** E-12; ★ **WASH**; mail Silver Spring **z** 20901; ● 1,200
Norwood (Norwood Corner); RMC Place; MONTGOMERY; **249** B-6; ★ **WASH**; mail Silver Spring **z** 20906; ● 250
Norwood Corner; MONTGOMERY; see Norwood (RMC Place)
Norwood Estates; RMC Place; MONTGOMERY; ***185** E-12; ★ **WASH**; mail Silver Spring **z** 20905; ● 350
Notch Cliff; RMC Place; BALTIMORE; ***185** C-14; ★ **BAL**; mail Glen Arm **z** 21057
Nottingham; RMC Place; BALTIMORE; ***185** C-14; 🅿; ★ **BAL**; **z** 21236; ● 240
Nottingham Woods; RMC Place; BALTIMORE; ***185** C-14; ★ **BAL**; mail Nottingham **z** 21236

O

Oak Acres; RMC Place; FREDERICK; ***184** C-10; ★ **WASH**; mail Frederick **z** 21701; ● 1,150
Oak Court; RMC Place; ANNE ARUNDEL; ***185** E-14; ★ **ANPLS**; mail Annapolis **z** 21401
Oakcrest; RMC Place; PRINCE GEORGE'S; **249** B-9; ★ **WASH**; mail Laurel **z** 20707; pop. incl. with Laurel (Inc. Place)
Oakcrest Towers; RMC Place; PRINCE GEORGE'S; ***185** F-12; ★ **WASH**; mail Capitol Heights **z** 20743
Oakdale; RMC Place; MONTGOMERY; ***185** D-11; ★ **WASH**; mail Rockville **z** 20853
Oakdale Manor; RMC Place; CARROLL; ***185** B-12; elev. 860ft./262m.; ★ **BAL**; mail Hampstead **z** 21074; ● 60
Oak Estates; RMC Place; CHARLES; ***185** H-13; ★ **WASH**; mail Charlotte Hall **z** 20622; ● 360
Oak Forest; RMC Place; BALTIMORE; ***185** D-13; ★ **BAL**; mail Catonsville **z** 21228
Oak Hollow; RMC Place; ANNE ARUNDEL; ***185** E-14; ★ **BAL**; mail Pasadena **z** 21122; ● 3,400
Oakhurst; RMC Place; MONTGOMERY; ***185** E-12; ★ **WASH**; mail Burtonsville **z** 20866
Oakington; RMC Place; HARFORD; ***185** B-16; mail Havre de Grace **z** 21078; ● 100
Oakland; RMC Place; BALTIMORE; ***185** A-13; ★ **BAL**; mail Freeland **z** 21053; ● 30
Oakland; RMC Place; CARROLL; **185** C-12; ★ **BAL**; mail Sykesville **z** 21784; ℗ 2,078
Oakland; Inc. Place; ⊡ GARRETT; **184** C-1; elev. 2,384ft./727m.; 🅿 🅷; **z** 21550; ℗ 1,741; © 1,930
Oakland; RMC Place; PRINCE GEORGE'S; **249** G-8; ★ **WASH**; mail District Heights **z** 20747; ● 2,500
Oakland Acres; RMC Place; CHARLES; ***185** H-13; ★ **WASH**; mail Charlotte Hall **z** 20622; ● 510
Oakland Mills; RMC Place; HOWARD; ***185** D-12; ★ **BAL**; mail Columbia **z** 21045
Oakland Park; RMC Place; BALTIMORE; ***185** C-13; ★ **BAL**; mail Randallstown **z** 21133
Oaklands; RMC Place; TALBOT; ***185** G-16; elev. 6ft./2m.; mail Easton **z** 21601; ● 70
Oakland Terrace; RMC Place; MONTGOMERY; ***185** E-11; ★ **WASH**; mail Kensington **z** 20895; ● 1,300
Oaklawn; RMC Place; PRINCE GEORGE'S; **249** I-8; ★ **WASH**; mail Fort Washington **z** 20744; ● 1,600
Oakleigh; RMC Place; BALTIMORE; ***185** C-14; ★ **BAL**; mail Parkville **z** 21234; ● 110
Oakleigh Forest; RMC Place; ANNE ARUNDEL; ***185** E-14; ★ **BAL**; mail Severna Park **z** 21146
Oakleigh Manor; RMC Place; BALTIMORE; ***185** C-14; ★ **BAL**; mail Parkville **z** 21234
Oakley; RMC Place; ST. MARY'S; **185** I-13; ★ **WASH**; mail Avenue **z** 20609; ● 50
Oaklyn Manor; RMC Place; HARFORD; ***185** C-15; ★ **BAL**; mail Joppa **z** 21085
Oakmont; RMC Place; MONTGOMERY; **249** D-5; ★ **WASH**; mail Bethesda **z** 20814
Oak Orchard; RMC Place; PRINCE GEORGE'S; ***185** G-12; ★ **WASH**; mail Clinton **z** 20735
Oak Park; RMC Place; BALTIMORE; ***185** D-13; ★ **BAL**; mail Halethorpe **z** 21227
Oak Park; RMC Place; GARRETT; **184** C-1; mail Oakland **z** 21550; ● 30
Oak Ridge; RMC Place; WASHINGTON; **185** N-13; ★ **HAG**; mail Hagerstown **z** 21740; ● 580
Oak Springs; RMC Place; MONTGOMERY; ***185** E-12; ★ **WASH**; mail Spencerville **z** 20868
Oak Summit; RMC Place; BALTIMORE; ***185** C-14; ★ **BAL**; mail Parkville **z** 21234
Oaksville; RMC Place; SOMERSET; ***185** J-18; mail Princess Anne **z** 21853; ● 80
Oak View; RMC Place; MONTGOMERY; **249** D-7; elev. 251ft./77m.; ★ **WASH**; mail Silver Spring **z** 20903; ● 3,400
Oakville; RMC Place; ST. MARY'S; ***185** I-13; elev. 143ft./44m.; ★ **WASH**; mail Mechanicsville **z** 20659
Oakwood; RMC Place; CECIL; ***185** A-15; elev. 368ft./112m.; ★ **PHIL-**; mail Conowingo **z** 21918
Oakwood Knolls; RMC Place; MONTGOMERY; ***185** E-11; ★ **WASH**; mail Bethesda **z** 20817
Ocean City; Inc. Place; WORCESTER; **185** I-20; elev. 8ft./2m.; 🅿; **z** 21842-43; ℗ 5,146; © 7,173
Ocean City Harbor; RMC Place; WORCESTER; ***185** I-20; mail Ocean City **z** 21842; ● 210
Ocean Pines; CDP; WORCESTER; **185** I-20; 🅿; **z** 21811; ℗ 4,251; © 10,496
Odenton; CDP; ANNE ARUNDEL; **185** E-13; 🅿; ★ **BAL**; **z** 21113; ℗ 12,833; © 20,534; ◆ 21,713
Odenton Gardens; RMC Place; ANNE ARUNDEL; ***185** E-13; ★ **BAL**; mail Odenton **z** 21113
Odenton Heights; RMC Place; ANNE ARUNDEL; ***185** E-13; ★ **BAL**; mail Odenton **z** 21113
Odenton Park; RMC Place; ANNE ARUNDEL; ***185** E-13; ★ **BAL**; mail Odenton **z** 21113; ● 1,450
Odyssey; RMC Place; CALVERT; ***185** G-13; ★ **WASH**; mail Owings **z** 20736; ● 80
Oella; RMC Place; BALTIMORE; ***185** D-13; 🅿; ★ **BAL**; **z** 21043 & mail Catonsville **z** 21228
Old Country Estates; RMC Place; ANNE ARUNDEL; ***185** E-14; ★ **BAL**; mail Severna Park **z** 21146
Olde Colonial Woods; RMC Place; MONTGOMERY; ***185** D-11; ★ **WASH**; mail Olney **z** 20832
Olde Fort Village; RMC Place; PRINCE GEORGE'S; ★ **WASH**; mail Fort Washington **z** 20744
Olde Towne Village; RMC Place; PRINCE GEORGE'S; ★ **WASH**; mail District Heights **z** 20747; pop. incl. with District Heights (Inc. Place)
Old Farm; RMC Place; MONTGOMERY; ***185** E-11; ★ **WASH**; mail Rockville **z** 20852; ● 3,450
Old Field; RMC Place; CALVERT; ***185** G-14; elev. 100ft./30m.; ★ **WASH**; mail Huntingtown **z** 20639; rural
Old Field; RMC Place; DORCHESTER; ***185** H-16; mail Church Creek **z** 21622; rural
Oldfield; RMC Place; FREDERICK; ***185** B-11; ★ **WASH**; mail Union Bridge **z** 21791; ● 90
Old Field; RMC Place; MONTGOMERY; ***185** E-11; ★ **WASH**; mail Potomac **z** 20854
Old Fort Hills; RMC Place; PRINCE GEORGE'S; ***185** G-12; ★ **WASH**; mail Fort Washington **z** 20744
Old Glory Beach; RMC Place; ANNE ARUNDEL; ***185** D-14; ★ **BAL**; mail Glen Burnie **z** 21060; ● 500
Old Salem Village; RMC Place; MONTGOMERY; ***185** E-12; ★ **WASH**; mail Silver Spring **z** 20904; ● 530
Old Severna Park; RMC Place; ANNE ARUNDEL; ***185** E-14; ★ **BAL**; mail Severna Park **z** 21146
Oldtown; RMC Place; ALLEGANY; **184** B-5; elev. 600ft./183m.; 🅿; **z** 21555; ● 600
Olive; RMC Place; FREDERICK; ***184** C-9; elev. 445ft./136m.; ★ **WASH**; mail Knoxville **z** 21758; rural
Oliver Beach; RMC Place; BALTIMORE; ***185** C-15; ★ **BAL**; mail Middle River **z** 21220; ● 600
Olivet; RMC Place; CALVERT; **185** I-14; mail Lusby **z** 20657; ● 500
Olivet Hill; RMC Place; KENT; ***185** C-17; mail Galena **z** 21635; ● 60
Olney; CDP; MONTGOMERY; **185** D-11; 🅿 🅷; ★ **WASH**; **z** 20830, **z** 20832 & mail Rockville **z** 20853; ℗ 23,019; © 31,438; ◆ 33,392
Olney Mills; RMC Place; MONTGOMERY; ***185** D-11; ★ **WASH**; mail Olney **z** 20832
Olney Square; RMC Place; MONTGOMERY; ***185** D-11; ★ **WASH**; mail Olney **z** 20832
Orangeville; RMC Place; BALTIMORE (Independent City); ★ **BAL**; mail Baltimore **z** 21224; pop. incl. with Baltimore (Independent City)
Oraville; RMC Place; ST. MARY'S; **185** I-13; ★ **WASH**; mail Mechanicsville **z** 20659; ● 50
Orchard Beach; RMC Place; ANNE ARUNDEL; **184** M-6; 🅿; ★ **BAL**; **z** 21226; ● 2,200
Orchard Hills; RMC Place; BALTIMORE; ***185** C-13; ★ **BAL**; mail Lutherville Timonium **z** 21093
Orchard Hills; RMC Place; WASHINGTON; **185** L-14; ★ **HAG**; mail Hagerstown **z** 21742; ● 1,250
Oregon; RMC Place; BALTIMORE; ***185** B-13; ★ **BAL**; mail Cockeysville **z** 21030; rural
Oriole; RMC Place; SOMERSET; **185** J-17; elev. 4ft./1m.; mail Princess Anne **z** 21853; ● 100
Otter Point; RMC Place; HARFORD; ***185** C-15; ★ **BAL**; mail Abingdon **z** 21009; ● 200
Overlea; CDP; BALTIMORE; **184** H-6; elev. 200ft./61m.; ★ **BAL**; mail Baltimore **z** 21206; ℗ 12,137; © 12,148
Owen Brown; RMC Place; HOWARD; ***185** D-12; ★ **BAL**; mail Columbia **z** 21045
Owensville; ANNE ARUNDEL; see West River (RMC Place)
Owings; CDP; CALVERT; **185** G-14; elev. 100ft./30m.; 🅿; ★ **WASH**; **z** 20736; © 1,325
Owings Beach; RMC Place; ANNE ARUNDEL; ***185** F-14; ★ **WASH**; mail Deale **z** 20751
Owings Mills; CDP; BALTIMORE; **184** G-2; elev. 496ft./151m.; 🅿; ★ **BAL**; **z** 21117; ℗ 9,474; © 20,193; ◆ 21,199
Owings Wood; RMC Place; CALVERT; ***185** G-14; ★ **WASH**; mail North Beach **z** 20714
Oxford; Inc. Place; TALBOT; **185** G-15; elev. 10ft./3m.; 🅿; **z** 21654; ℗ 699; © 771
Oxon Hill; RMC Place; PRINCE GEORGE'S; **185** F-12; elev. 200ft./61m.; ★ **WASH**; ● 4,200
Oxon Hill-Glassmanor; CDP-Census Area Only; PRINCE GEORGE'S; **185** F-12; ★ **WASH**; mail Oxon Hill **z** 20745, **z** 20750; ℗ 35,794; © 35,355; ◆ 35,452
Oxon Hill Village; RMC Place; PRINCE GEORGE'S; ***185** F-12; ★ **WASH**; mail Oxon Hill **z** 20745
Oxon Run Hills; RMC Place; PRINCE GEORGE'S; ***185** F-12; ★ **WASH**; mail Temple Hills **z** 20748
Oyster Harbor; RMC Place; ANNE ARUNDEL; ***185** F-14; ★ **ANPLS**; mail Annapolis **z** 21401

P

Padonia; RMC Place; BALTIMORE; ***185** C-13; ★ **BAL**; mail Cockeysville **z** 21030
Pagetts Corner; RMC Place; PRINCE GEORGE'S; ***185** F-12; elev. 269ft./82m.; ★ **WASH**; mail Temple Hills **z** 20748
Paint Branch Estates; RMC Place; MONTGOMERY; ***185** E-12; ★ **WASH**; mail Silver Spring **z** 20904; ● 1,100
Paint Branch Farm; RMC Place; MONTGOMERY; ***185** E-12; ★ **WASH**; mail Silver Spring **z** 20904
Palmer Park; RMC Place; PRINCE GEORGE'S; **249** F-9; elev. 100ft./30m.; ★ **WASH**; mail Hyattsville **z** 20785; ℗ 7,019
Palmers Corner; RMC Place; PRINCE GEORGE'S; ***185** F-12; elev. 255ft./78m.; ★ **WASH**; mail Fort Washington **z** 20744
Palmetto; RMC Place; SOMERSET; ***185** J-18; mail Princess Anne **z** 21853; rural
Paradise; RMC Place; BALTIMORE; ***185** D-13; ★ **BAL**; mail Catonsville **z** 21228
Paradise Beach; RMC Place; ANNE ARUNDEL; **184** N-8; ★ **BAL**; mail Pasadena **z** 21122; ● 350
Paramount; RMC Place; WASHINGTON; **185** L-14; ★ **HAG**; mail Hagerstown **z** 21742; ● 1,450
Paramount-Long Meadow; CDP-Census Area Only; WASHINGTON; ***184** A-9; ★ **HAG**; © 2,722
Paramount Manor; RMC Place; WASHINGTON; ***184** A-9; ★ **HAG**; mail Hagerstown **z** 21740
Paris; RMC Place; CALVERT; ***185** G-14; ★ **WASH**; mail Owings **z** 20736; ● 110
Parkers Creek; RMC Place; CALVERT; ***185** H-14; mail Saint Leonard **z** 20685; rural
Parkertown; RMC Place; WORCESTER; ***185** I-20; elev. 19ft./6m.; mail Berlin **z** 21811; rural
Parker Wharf; RMC Place; CALVERT; ***185** I-14; mail Saint Leonard **z** 20685; ● 300
Park Hall; RMC Place; ST. MARY'S; **185** J-14; elev. 105ft./32m.; 🅿; **z** 20667; ● 700
Park Hall; RMC Place; WASHINGTON; ***184** C-9; ★ **WASH**; mail Boonsboro **z** 21713; rural
Parkhead; RMC Place; WASHINGTON; ***184** A-7; mail Big Pool **z** 21711; ● 40
Parkhurst Manor; RMC Place; WICOMICO; ***185** I-18; ★ **SLSB**; mail Salisbury **z** 21804; ● 200
Parkland; RMC Place; PRINCE GEORGE'S; ***185** F-12; ★ **WASH**; mail Suitland **z** 20746
Parkland Apartments; RMC Place; PRINCE GEORGE'S; ★ **WASH**; mail Suitland **z** 20746
Parkland Terrace; RMC Place; PRINCE GEORGE'S; ***185** F-12; ★ **WASH**; mail Suitland **z** 20746
Park Mills; RMC Place; FREDERICK; ***184** C-10; elev. 296ft./90m.; ★ **WASH**; mail Adamstown **z** 21710; ● 50
Park Overlook; RMC Place; MONTGOMERY; ***185** D-11; ★ **WASH**; mail Derwood **z** 20855
Parkridge; RMC Place; MONTGOMERY; ***185** D-11; elev. 400ft./122m.; ★ **WASH**; mail Gaithersburg **z** 20878; ● 400
Parkside; RMC Place; MONTGOMERY; ***185** E-11; ★ **WASH**; mail Bethesda **z** 20814; ● 4,650
Parkside Estates; RMC Place; MONTGOMERY; ***185** D-11; ★ **WASH**; mail Derwood **z** 20855; ● 1,500
Parkton; RMC Place; BALTIMORE; **185** B-13; elev. 420ft./128m.; 🅿; ★ **BAL**; **z** 21120; ● 500
Parktowne; RMC Place; BALTIMORE; ***185** C-14; ★ **BAL**; mail Parkville **z** 21234
Parkview; RMC Place; PRINCE GEORGE'S; ★ **WASH**; mail Clinton **z** 20735
Parkville; CDP; BALTIMORE; **185** C-14; elev. 300ft./91m.; 🅿; ★ **BAL**; **z** 21234; ℗ 31,617; © 31,118; ◆ 32,672
Park West; RMC Place; ANNE ARUNDEL; ***185** D-13; ★ **BAL**; mail Glen Burnie **z** 21061; ● 4,300
Parkwood; RMC Place; MONTGOMERY; ***185** E-11; ★ **WASH**; mail Bethesda **z** 20814; ● 3,600
Parole; CDP; ANNE ARUNDEL; **185** M-19; ★ **ANPLS**; mail Annapolis **z** 21401; ℗ 10,054; © 14,031
Parran; RMC Place; CALVERT; ***185** G-14; elev. 128ft./39m.; ★ **WASH**; mail Huntingtown **z** 20639; rural
Parrans Woods; RMC Place; CALVERT; ***185** G-14; elev. 100ft./30m.; ★ **WASH**; mail Huntingtown **z** 20639; rural
Parsonsburg; RMC Place; WICOMICO; **185** I-19; elev. 81ft./25m.; 🅿; ★ **SLSB**; **z** 21849; ● 680
Partridge Place; RMC Place; MONTGOMERY; ***185** D-11; ★ **WASH**; mail Gaithersburg **z** 20879
Pasadena; CDP; ANNE ARUNDEL; **185** E-14; 🅿; ★ **BAL**; **z** 21122-23; ℗ 10,012; © 12,093
Patapsco; RMC Place; CARROLL; **185** B-12; elev. 499ft./152m.; 🅿; ★ **BAL**; **z** 21048; ● 200
Patterson; RMC Place; BALTIMORE (Independent City); ***185** D-14; ★ **BAL**; mail Baltimore **z** 21231; pop. incl. with Baltimore (Independent City)
Patuxent; RMC Place; ANNE ARUNDEL; ***185** E-13; elev. 83ft./25m.; ★ **BAL**; mail Odenton **z** 21113; ● 130
Patuxent Beach; RMC Place; ST. MARY'S; ***185** I-14; elev. 107ft./33m.; ★ **WASH**; mail California **z** 20619; ● 1,200
Patuxent Manor; RMC Place; ANNE ARUNDEL; ***185** F-13; ★ **WASH**; mail Davidsonville **z** 21035; ● 450
Patuxent Palisades; RMC Place; CALVERT; ***185** G-13; ★ **WASH**; mail Dunkirk **z** 20754; ● 30
Patuxent Park; RMC Place; ST. MARY'S; ***185** I-14; elev. 93ft./28m.; mail Lexington Park **z** 20653; ● 1,150
Patuxent River; RMC Place; ST. MARY'S; elev. 118ft./36m.; 🅿 🅷; **z** 20670
Peach Orchard Heights; RMC Place; MONTGOMERY; ***185** E-12; ★ **WASH**; mail Spencerville **z** 20868; ● 750
Peachwood; RMC Place; MONTGOMERY; ***185** E-12; ★ **WASH**; mail Silver Spring **z** 20905; ● 210
Peacock Corners; RMC Place; KENT; ***185** D-17; mail Millington **z** 21651; ● 30
Pearl; RMC Place; FREDERICK; ***184** C-10; ★ **WASH**; mail Frederick **z** 21701; rural
Pectonville; RMC Place; WASHINGTON; ***184** A-7; mail Big Pool **z** 21711; ● 70
Pekin; ALLEGANY; see Nikep (RMC Place)
Pendennis Mount; RMC Place; ANNE ARUNDEL; **185** L-20; ★ **ANPLS**; mail Annapolis **z** 21401; ● 350
Pen Mar; RMC Place; WASHINGTON; **184** A-9; ★ **HAG**; mail Cascade **z** 21719; ● 210
Penn Mary Junction; RMC Place; BALTIMORE (Independent City); ***185** D-14; ★ **BAL**; mail Baltimore **z** 21224; pop. incl. with Baltimore (Independent City)
Pepper Mill Village; RMC Place; PRINCE GEORGE'S; ***185** F-12; ★ **WASH**; mail Capitol Heights **z** 20743; ● 2,450
Perry Hall; CDP; BALTIMORE; **185** C-14; elev. 200ft./61m.; 🅿; ★ **BAL**; **z** 21128; ℗ 22,723; © 28,705; ◆ 30,138
Perry Hall Estates; RMC Place; BALTIMORE; ***185** C-15; ★ **BAL**; mail Nottingham **z** 21236
Perry Hall Manor; RMC Place; BALTIMORE; ***185** C-14; ★ **BAL**; mail Perry Hall **z** 21128
Perry Hall Village; RMC Place; BALTIMORE; ***185** C-14; ★ **BAL**; mail Perry Hall **z** 21128
Perryman; CDP; HARFORD; **185** B-15; elev. 42ft./13m.; 🅿; **z** 21130; ℗ 2,160; © 2,461
Perry Point; RMC Place; CECIL; ***185** B-16; elev. 40ft./12m.; 🅿 🅷; **z** 21902; ● 500
Perrys Corner; RMC Place; QUEEN ANNE'S; ★ **ANPLS**; mail Grasonville **z** 21638
Perry View; RMC Place; BALTIMORE; ***185** C-14; ★ **BAL**; mail Perry Hall **z** 21128
Perryville; Inc. Place; CECIL; **185** B-16; elev. 40ft./12m.; 🅿; **z** 21903; ℗ 2,456; © 3,672
Perrywood Estates; RMC Place; MONTGOMERY; ***185** E-12; elev. 485ft./148m.; ★ **WASH**; mail Burtonsville **z** 20866
Perry Wright (Woodland Village); RMC Place; CHARLES; ***185** H-11; ★ **WASH**; mail Indian Head **z** 20640; pop. incl. with Indian Head (Inc. Place)
Petersburg; RMC Place; DORCHESTER; ***185** G-17; mail Hurlock **z** 21643; ● 100
Petersville; RMC Place; FREDERICK; ***184** C-9; elev. 517ft./158m.; ★ **WASH**; mail Knoxville **z** 21758; ● 330
Pfeiffer Corners; RMC Place; HOWARD; ***185** D-13; ★ **BAL**; mail Columbia **z** 21045
Pheasant Run; RMC Place; PRINCE GEORGE'S; ***185** E-12; ★ **WASH**; mail Laurel **z** 20708
Phoenix; RMC Place; BALTIMORE; **185** B-13; elev. 300ft./91m.; 🅿; ★ **BAL**; **z** 21131; ● 600
Picketts Corner; RMC Place; CARROLL; ***185** C-11; elev. 833ft./254m.; ★ **BAL**; mail Woodbine **z** 21797; ● 50
Pike; RMC Place; MONTGOMERY; ★ **WASH**; mail Rockville **z** 20847, **z** 20852; pop. incl. with Rockville (Inc. Place)
Pikesville; CDP; BALTIMORE; **185** C-13; 🅿; ★ **BAL**; **z** 21208, **z** 21282 & mail Baltimore **z** 21209; ℗ 24,815; © 29,123; ◆ 30,570
Pilot Town; RMC Place; CECIL; ***185** A-15; ★ **PHIL-**; mail Conowingo **z** 21918; ● 150
Pindell; RMC Place; ANNE ARUNDEL; ***185** F-13; ★ **WASH**; mail Lothian **z** 20711; ● 30
Pineburg; WASHINGTON; see Pinesburg (RMC Place)
Pine Cliff; RMC Place; FREDERICK; ★ **WASH**; mail Frederick **z** 21701
Pinecrest; RMC Place; PRINCE GEORGE'S; ★ **WASH**; mail Takoma Park **z** 20912; pop. incl. with Takoma Park (Inc. Place)
Pinedale; RMC Place; BALTIMORE; ***185** C-14; ★ **BAL**; mail Perry Hall **z** 21128
Pinefield (Mattawoman); RMC Place; CHARLES; **185** G-12; ★ **WASH**; mail Waldorf **z** 20601; ● 8,800
Pine Grove; RMC Place; WICOMICO; ***185** I-18; ★ **SLSB**; mail Salisbury **z** 21804; ● 130
Pine Grove Village; RMC Place; ANNE ARUNDEL; ***185** D-14; ★ **BAL**; mail Pasadena **z** 21122
Pine Hill; RMC Place; ST. MARY'S; ***185** I-14; elev. 20ft./6m.; mail Lexington Park **z** 20653; ● 80
Pine Hill Estates; RMC Place; CHARLES; ***185** G-12; ★ **WASH**; mail Waldorf **z** 20601
Pinehurst Estates; RMC Place; PRINCE GEORGE'S; ***185** G-12; ★ **WASH**; mail Fort Washington **z** 20744; ● 1,250
Pinehurst on the Bay; RMC Place; ANNE ARUNDEL; **185** E-14; ★ **BAL**; mail Pasadena **z** 21122; ● 570
Pine Knoll; RMC Place; CARROLL; ***185** B-12; ★ **BAL**; mail Westminster **z** 21157
Pine Knoll Terrace; RMC Place; WICOMICO; ***185** H-18; ★ **SLSB**; mail Salisbury **z** 21804; ● 350
Pineleigh; RMC Place; BALTIMORE; ***185** C-14; ★ **BAL**; mail Towson **z** 21286
Pine Orchard Meadows; RMC Place; HOWARD; ***185** D-12; ★ **BAL**; mail Ellicott City **z** 21042; ● 690
Pine Ridge; RMC Place; BALTIMORE; ***185** C-14; ★ **BAL**; mail Parkville **z** 21234
Pinesburg (Pineburg); RMC Place; WASHINGTON; **184** B-8; elev. 501ft./153m.; ★ **HAG**; mail Williamsport **z** 21795; ● 250
Pines on the Severn; RMC Place; ANNE ARUNDEL; ***185** E-14; ★ **BAL**; mail Arnold **z** 21012
Pinewiff Beach; RMC Place; ANNE ARUNDEL; ***185** F-14; ★ **ANPLS**; mail Edgewater **z** 21037
Pinewood Hill; RMC Place; PRINCE GEORGE'S; ***185** G-12; ★ **WASH**; mail Fort Washington **z** 20744
Piney Glen Farms; RMC Place; MONTGOMERY; **249** C-3; ★ **WASH**; mail Potomac **z** 20854; ● 470
Piney Grove; RMC Place; ALLEGANY; ***184** A-6; elev. 957ft./292m.; mail Flintstone **z** 21530
Piney Point; RMC Place; ST. MARY'S; **185** J-14; elev. 9ft./3m.; 🅿; **z** 20674; ● 1,500
Pinto; RMC Place; ALLEGANY; **184** B-3; elev. 720ft./219m.; 🅿; ★ **CUMB**; **z** 21556; ● 300
Pioneer City; RMC Place; ANNE ARUNDEL; ***185** E-13; ★ **BAL**; mail Severn **z** 21144
Piscataway; RMC Place; PRINCE GEORGE'S; ***185** G-12; ★ **WASH**; mail Accokeek **z** 20607
Piscataway Bay; RMC Place; PRINCE GEORGE'S; ***185** G-12; ★ **WASH**; mail Fort Washington **z** 20744
Piscataway Estates; RMC Place; PRINCE GEORGE'S; ***185** G-12; ★ **WASH**; mail Fort Washington **z** 20744; ● 930
Piscataway Hills; RMC Place; PRINCE GEORGE'S; ***185** G-12; ★ **WASH**; mail Fort Washington **z** 20744
Pisgah; RMC Place; CHARLES; **185** H-11; elev. 125ft./38m.; 🅿; ★ **WASH**; **z** 20640; ● 300
Pittsville; Inc. Place; WICOMICO; **185** I-19; 🅿; **z** 21850 & mail Powellville **z** 21852; ℗ 602; © 1,182
Plainfield; RMC Place; WICOMICO; ***185** I-18; ★ **SLSB**; mail Salisbury **z** 21804; ● 150
Plane Number Four; RMC Place; FREDERICK; ***185** C-11; ★ **WASH**; mail Mount Airy **z** 21771; ● 60
Pleasant Fields; RMC Place; MONTGOMERY; ***185** D-11; ★ **WASH**; mail Germantown **z** 20874; ● 7,100
Pleasant Grove; RMC Place; BALTIMORE; ***185** B-13; ★ **BAL**; mail Reisterstown **z** 21136; rural
Pleasant Grove; RMC Place; FREDERICK; ***185** C-11; ★ **WASH**; mail Mount Airy **z** 21771
Pleasant Hill; RMC Place; BALTIMORE; ***185** C-13; ★ **BAL**; mail Owings Mills **z** 21117
Pleasant Hill; RMC Place; CECIL; **185** A-17; ★ **PHIL-**; mail Elkton **z** 21921; ● 250
Pleasant Hills; CDP; HARFORD; **185** B-14; ★ **BAL**; mail Kingsville **z** 21087; ℗ 2,591; © 2,851
Pleasant Ridge; RMC Place; CARROLL; ***185** C-11; ★ **BAL**; mail Woodbine **z** 21797; ● 400
Pleasant Springs; RMC Place; PRINCE GEORGE'S; ***185** G-12; ★ **WASH**; mail Brandywine **z** 20613; ● 330
Pleasant Valley; RMC Place; ALLEGANY; ***184** A-4; ★ **CUMB**; mail Flintstone **z** 21530; rural
Pleasant Valley; RMC Place; CARROLL; ***185** B-12; ★ **BAL**; mail Westminster **z** 21158; ● 60
Pleasant Valley; RMC Place; WASHINGTON; ***184** B-9; elev. 1,532ft./467m.; ★ **HAG**; mail Smithsburg **z** 21783; ● 30
Pleasant View; RMC Place; FREDERICK; ***184** D-10; ★ **WASH**; mail Adamstown **z** 21710
Pleasant View; RMC Place; HOWARD; ***185** D-13; ★ **BAL**; mail Ellicott City **z** 21043; ● 220
Pleasantville; RMC Place; ANNE ARUNDEL; ***185** D-13; ★ **BAL**; mail Glen Burnie **z** 21061; ● 1,400
Pleasant Walk; RMC Place; FREDERICK; ***184** B-9; elev. 1,046ft./319m.; mail Myersville **z** 21773; rural
Plumgar; RMC Place; MONTGOMERY; ***185** D-11; ★ **WASH**; mail Germantown **z** 20876; ● 3,800
Plum Point (Carpenter Beach); RMC Place; CALVERT; **185** G-14; ★ **WASH**; mail Huntingtown **z** 20639; ● 200
Pocomoke; WORCESTER; see Pocomoke City (Inc. Place)
Pocomoke City (Pocomoke); Inc. Place; WORCESTER; **185** K-18; elev. 22ft./7m.; 🅿; **z** 21851; ℗ 3,922; © 4,098
Pointer Ridge; RMC Place; PRINCE GEORGE'S; ***185** E-13; ★ **WASH**; mail Bowie **z** 20716
Point Lookout; RMC Place; ST. MARY'S; **185** K-15; mail Scotland **z** 20687; ● 70
Point of Rocks; RMC Place; FREDERICK; **184** D-9; elev. 233ft./71m.; 🅿; ★ **WASH**; **z** 21777; ● 1,200
Point of Rocks Estates; RMC Place; FREDERICK; ***184** D-9; ★ **WASH**; mail Point of Rocks **z** 21777
Point Pleasant; RMC Place; ANNE ARUNDEL; **184** M-4; ★ **BAL**; mail Glen Burnie **z** 21060; ● 1,000
Pomfret; RMC Place; CHARLES; **185** H-12; elev. 193ft./59m.; 🅿; ★ **WASH**; **z** 20675; ● 620
Pomona; RMC Place; KENT; **185** D-16; mail Chestertown **z** 21620; ● 60
Pomonkey; RMC Place; CHARLES; **185** G-11; elev. 161ft./49m.; ★ **WASH**; mail Indian Head **z** 20640, La Plata **z** 20646; ● 500
Ponder Cove; RMC Place; ANNE ARUNDEL; ***185** F-14; ★ **ANPLS**; mail Edgewater **z** 21037
Pondsville; RMC Place; WASHINGTON; ***184** B-9; ★ **HAG**; mail Smithsburg **z** 21783; ● 130
Pooks Hill; RMC Place; MONTGOMERY; ***185** E-11; ★ **WASH**; mail Bethesda **z** 20814
Poole; RMC Place; HARFORD; ***185** A-15; ★ **BAL**; mail Darlington **z** 21034, Street **z** 21154; ● 50
Poolesville; Inc. Place; MONTGOMERY; **184** D-10; elev. 400ft./122m.; 🅿; ★ **WASH**; **z** 20837; ℗ 3,796; © 5,151
Popes Creek; RMC Place; CHARLES; **185** I-12; elev. 11ft./3m.; mail Newburg **z** 20664; ● 80
Poplar Grove; RMC Place; HARFORD; ***185** B-15; ★ **BAL**; mail Street **z** 21154; ● 550
Poplar Hill; RMC Place; PRINCE GEORGE'S; ***185** G-13; ★ **WASH**; mail Brandywine **z** 20613; rural
Poplar Hill Estates; RMC Place; PRINCE GEORGE'S; ***185** G-12; ★ **WASH**; mail Clinton **z** 20735; ● 320

Entries in **UPPERCASE** are counties.
Entries in **bold** have populations of 2,500 or more.
Names in parentheses are alternate names.

Inc. Place	Incorporated Place
RMC Place	Rand McNally Designated Place
CDP	Census Designated Place
MCD	Minor Civil Division

⊡ County Seat
▲ Minor Civil Division
elev. Elevation
🅿 Post Office
🅷 Hospital
🅲 College
■ Principal Business Center
★ Ranally Metro Area (RMA) Abbreviation
z Zip Code(s)
℗ Previous Census Population
® Revised Census Population
Ⓐ Annexation Population
● Rand McNally Population Estimate
© Final Census Population
Ⓢ Special Census Population
◆ Estimated Population

For additional definitions see Glossary, Volume 1, and Introduction, Volume 2.

Poplar Knob; RMC Place; FREDERICK; *184 B-10; elev. 511ft./156m.; mail Thurmont z 21788; ● 100
Poplar Springs; RMC Place; HOWARD; 185 C-11; elev. 730ft./223m.; ★ WASH; mail Mount Airy z 21771; ● 220
Port Covington; RMC Place; BALTIMORE (Independent City); *185 D-13; ★ BAL; mail Baltimore z 21230; pop. incl. with Baltimore (Independent City)
Port Deposit; Inc. Place; CECIL; 185 B-16; elev. 20ft./6m.; 🅿; z 21904; Ⓟ 685; Ⓒ 676
Porters Park; RMC Place; BALTIMORE; *185 D-14; elev. 14ft./4m.; ★ BAL; mail Essex z 21221; rural
Porterstown; RMC Place; WASHINGTON; *184 C-9; ★ WASH; mail Keedysville z 21756; rural
Port Herman (Port Herman Beach); RMC Place; CECIL; 185 B-17; ★ PHIL-; mail Chesapeake City z 21915; ● 270
Port Herman Beach; CECIL; see Port Herman (RMC Place)
Port Republic; RMC Place; CALVERT; 185 H-14; elev. 150ft./46m.; 🅿; z 20676; ● 200
Port Tobacco (Port Tobacco Village); Inc. Place; CHARLES; 185 H-12; elev. 16ft./5m.; 🅿; ★ WASH; z 20677; Ⓟ 36; Ⓒ 15
Port Tobacco Riviera; RMC Place; CHARLES; *185 H-12; ★ WASH; mail Port Tobacco z 20677; ● 230
Port Tobacco Village; CHARLES; see Port Tobacco (Inc. Place)
Potomac; CDP; MONTGOMERY; 185 E-11; 🅿; ★ WASH; z 20854, z 20859 & mail Rockville z 20851; Ⓟ 45,634; Ⓒ 44,822; ◆ 47,597
Potomac Commons; RMC Place; MONTGOMERY; *185 E-11; ★ WASH; mail Potomac z 20854
Potomac Falls Estates; RMC Place; MONTGOMERY; *185 E-11; ★ WASH; mail Potomac z 20854
Potomac Green; RMC Place; MONTGOMERY; ★ WASH; mail Potomac z 20854
Potomac Heights; CDP; CHARLES; 185 G-11; elev. 70ft./21m.; ★ WASH; mail Indian Head z 20640; Ⓟ 1,524; Ⓒ 1,154
Potomac Heights; RMC Place; WASHINGTON; ★ HAG; mail Hagerstown z 21740; pop. incl. with Hagerstown (Inc. Place)
Potomac Hills; RMC Place; MONTGOMERY; *185 E-11; ★ WASH; mail Potomac z 20854
Potomac Park; RMC Place; ALLEGANY; 184 B-4; ★ CUMB; mail Cumberland z 21502; ● 1,600
Potomac Ranch; RMC Place; MONTGOMERY; *185 E-11; ★ WASH; mail Potomac z 20854
Potomac Shores; RMC Place; CHARLES; *185 H-12; ★ WASH; mail Port Tobacco z 20677; ● 50
Potomac Shores; RMC Place; ST. MARY'S; *185 J-14; mail Leonardtown z 20650; ● 220
Potomac View; RMC Place; CHARLES; *185 I-12; mail Newburg z 20664; ● 120
Potomac View Estates; RMC Place; MONTGOMERY; *185 E-11; ★ WASH; mail Potomac z 20854
Potomac Village; RMC Place; MONTGOMERY; *185 E-11; ★ WASH; mail Potomac z 20854
Potomac Vista; RMC Place; PRINCE GEORGE'S; *185 F-12; ★ WASH; mail Oxon Hill z 20745; ● 830
Potomac Woods; RMC Place; MONTGOMERY; *185 E-11; ★ WASH; mail Potomac z 20854; pop. incl. with Rockville (Inc. Place)
Pot Spring; RMC Place; BALTIMORE; *185 C-14; ★ BAL; mail Lutherville Timonium z 21093
Powder Mill Estates; RMC Place; PRINCE GEORGE'S; *185 E-12; ★ WASH; mail Hyattsville z 20783
Powder Mill Village; RMC Place; PRINCE GEORGE'S; *185 E-12; ★ WASH; mail Beltsville z 20705; ● 5,800
Powellville; RMC Place; WICOMICO; 185 I-19; elev. 40ft./12m.; 🅿; z 21852; ● 170
Powhatan Beach; RMC Place; ANNE ARUNDEL; *185 D-14; ★ BAL; mail Pasadena z 21122
Powhattan Mill; RMC Place; BALTIMORE; 184 I-3; ★ BAL; mail Gwynn Oak z 21207; ● 2,300
Prathertown; RMC Place; MONTGOMERY; *185 D-11; ★ WASH; mail Gaithersburg z 20879; ● 3,200
Presidential Park; RMC Place; PRINCE GEORGE'S; *185 E-12; ★ WASH; mail Hyattsville z 20783; ● 5,400
Presidential Towers; RMC Place; PRINCE GEORGE'S; *185 E-12; ★ WASH; mail Hyattsville z 20783
Presley Manor; RMC Place; PRINCE GEORGE'S; *185 E-12; ★ WASH; mail Hyattsville z 20784; ● 700
Preston; Inc. Place; CAROLINE; 185 G-17; elev. 53ft./16m.; 🅿; z 21655; Ⓟ 437; Ⓒ 566
Preston Manor; RMC Place; HARFORD; *185 B-15; ★ BAL; mail Abingdon z 21009; ● 100
Price; RMC Place; QUEEN ANNE'S; 185 E-16; 🅿; z 21656; ● 180
Priceville; RMC Place; BALTIMORE; *185 B-13; ★ BAL; mail Sparks Glencoe z 21152; rural
Primrose Acres; RMC Place; ANNE ARUNDEL; *185 E-14; ★ ANPLS; pop. incl. with Annapolis (Inc. Place)
Prince Frederick; CDP; ⊡ CALVERT; 185 H-14; elev. 147ft./45m.; 🅿 🅷; ★ WASH; z 20678; Ⓟ 1,885; Ⓒ 1,432
PRINCE GEORGE'S; 185 G-13; Ⓟ 729,268; Ⓒ 801,515; ◆ 803,893
Princess Anne; Inc. Place; ⊡ SOMERSET; 185 J-18; elev. 18ft./5m.; 🅿 🅲 4,130; z 21853; Ⓟ 1,666; Ⓒ 2,313
Princeton; RMC Place; PRINCE GEORGE'S; ★ WASH; mail Suitland z 20746
Principio; CECIL; see Principio Furnace (RMC Place)
Principio Furnace (Principio); RMC Place; CECIL; 185 B-16; ★ PHIL-; mail Perryville z 21903; ● 130
Prophecy; RMC Place; PRINCE GEORGE'S; *185 F-12; ★ WASH; mail Fort Washington z 20744
Prospect Knolls; RMC Place; PRINCE GEORGE'S; *185 E-13; ★ WASH; mail Bowie z 20720
Prospect Walk; RMC Place; HOWARD; ★ BAL; mail Columbia z 21044
Providence; RMC Place; BALTIMORE; 184 F-6; ★ BAL; mail Towson z 21286; ● 1,400
Providence; RMC Place; CECIL; *185 A-17; ★ PHIL-; mail Elkton z 21921; rural
Public Landing; RMC Place; WORCESTER; 185 J-19; elev. 4ft./1m.; mail Snow Hill z 21863; ● 230
Pumphrey; CDP; ANNE ARUNDEL; 184 L-4; ★ BAL; mail Brooklyn z 21225; Ⓟ 5,483; Ⓒ 5,317
Puncheon Landing; RMC Place; SOMERSET; *185 J-18; elev. 20ft./6m.; mail Pocomoke City z 21851; ● 30
Putnam; RMC Place; HARFORD; 185 B-14; elev. 553ft./169m.; ★ BAL; mail Forest Hill z 21050; ● 300
Putty Hill; RMC Place; BALTIMORE; *185 C-14; ★ BAL; mail Nottingham z 21236
Pylesville; RMC Place; HARFORD; 185 A-15; elev. 358ft./109m.; 🅿; ★ BAL; z 21132; ● 350

Q

Quail Ridge; RMC Place; HOWARD; *185 D-13; ★ BAL; mail Elkridge z 21075
Quail Run; RMC Place; MONTGOMERY; *185 E-11; elev. 400ft./122m.; ★ WASH; mail Gaithersburg z 20879; ● 500
Quaint Acres; RMC Place; MONTGOMERY; *185 E-12; ★ WASH; mail Silver Spring z 20904
Quaker Neck Landing; RMC Place; KENT; 185 D-16; mail Chestertown z 21620; ● 30
Quantico; RMC Place; WICOMICO; 185 I-17; elev. 20ft./6m.; 🅿; z 21856; ● 300
Queen Anne; Inc. Place; QUEEN ANNE'S, TALBOT; 185 F-16; 🅿; z 21657; Ⓟ 250; Ⓒ 176
Queen Anne Colony; RMC Place; QUEEN ANNE'S; *185 F-15; ★ ANPLS; mail Stevensville z 21666; ● 250
QUEEN ANNE'S; 185 E-16; Ⓟ 33,953; Ⓒ 40,563; ◆ 47,874
Queen Anne's Estate; RMC Place; QUEEN ANNE'S; *185 F-15; elev. 10ft./3m.; ★ ANPLS; mail Queenstown z 21658; ● 200
Queen Anne Woods; RMC Place; QUEEN ANNE'S; *185 F-15; elev. 12ft./4m.; ★ ANPLS; mail Queenstown z 21658; ● 90
Queens Chapel Manor; RMC Place; PRINCE GEORGE'S; ★ WASH; mail Hyattsville z 20782; pop. incl. with Hyattsville (Inc. Place)
Queenstown; RMC Place; PRINCE GEORGE'S; *185 E-12; ★ WASH; mail Mount Rainier z 20712; pop. incl. with Mount Rainier (Inc. Place)
Queenstown; Inc. Place; QUEEN ANNE'S; 185 E-16; elev. 20ft./6m.; 🅿; ★ ANPLS; z 21658; Ⓟ 453; Ⓒ 617
Queenswood; RMC Place; PRINCE GEORGE'S; *185 F-12; ★ WASH; mail Upper Marlboro z 20772; ● 440
Queponco; WORCESTER; see Newark (CDP)
Quince Orchard; RMC Place; MONTGOMERY; 185 E-11; ★ WASH; mail Gaithersburg z 20878; ● 5,500
Quincy Manor; RMC Place; PRINCE GEORGE'S; *185 F-12; ★ WASH; mail Hyattsville z 20784; ● 2,000

R

Radiant Valley; RMC Place; PRINCE GEORGE'S; *185 F-12; ★ WASH; mail Hyattsville z 20784; ● 720
Ramblewood Village; RMC Place; PRINCE GEORGE'S; *185 F-12; ★ WASH; mail Clinton z 20735
Ramgate; RMC Place; PRINCE GEORGE'S; *185 G-12; ★ WASH; mail Fort Washington z 20744
Ranchleigh; RMC Place; BALTIMORE (Independent City); ★ BAL; mail Baltimore z 21209
Randalia; RMC Place; CECIL; *185 B-17; ★ PHIL-; mail Chesapeake City z 21915; ● 60
Randallstown; CDP; BALTIMORE; 185 C-13; 🅿 🅷; ★ BAL; z 21133; Ⓟ 26,277; Ⓒ 30,870; ◆ 32,415
Randle Cliff Beach; RMC Place; CALVERT; *185 G-14; ★ WASH; mail Chesapeake Beach z 20732; ● 350
Randolph Farms; RMC Place; MONTGOMERY; *185 E-11; ★ WASH; mail Rockville z 20852
Randolph Hills; RMC Place; MONTGOMERY; 249 C-5; elev. 270ft./82m.; ★ WASH; mail Rockville z 20852; ● 6,150
Random Heights; RMC Place; CARROLL; *185 B-12; elev. 900ft./274m.; ★ BAL; mail Westminster z 21157; rural
Rasin; RMC Place; BALTIMORE (Independent City); pop. incl. with Baltimore (Independent City)
Raspeburg; RMC Place; BALTIMORE (Independent City); *185 C-14; 🅿; ★ BAL; z 21206; pop. incl. with Baltimore (Independent City)
Rawlings; RMC Place; ALLEGANY; 184 B-3; elev. 745ft./227m.; 🅿; ★ CUMB; z 21557; ● 850
Rawlings Heights; RMC Place; ALLEGANY; ★ CUMB; mail Rawlings z 21557
Raynor Heights; RMC Place; ANNE ARUNDEL; *185 D-13; ★ BAL; mail Linthicum Heights z 21090
Rayville; RMC Place; BALTIMORE; 185 A-13; ★ BAL; mail Parkton z 21120; ● 100
Red Coat Woods; RMC Place; MONTGOMERY; *185 E-11; ★ WASH; mail Potomac z 20854
Reddings Corner; RMC Place; KENT; *185 C-16; elev. 90ft./27m.; mail Worton z 21678; rural
Redford Estates; RMC Place; PRINCE GEORGE'S; *185 F-12; ★ WASH; mail Fort Washington z 20744
Redgate; RMC Place; ST. MARY'S; *185 I-14; elev. 100ft./30m.; ★ WASH; mail Leonardtown z 20650; ● 50
Red Hill; RMC Place; ALLEGANY; *184 A-3; elev. 1,228ft./374m.; ★ CUMB; mail Frostburg z 21532; rural
Red Hill; RMC Place; CHARLES; *185 H-11; ★ WASH; mail Indian Head z 20640; ● 330
Redhouse; RMC Place; GARRETT; 184 C-1; elev. 2,557ft./779m.; mail Oakland z 21550; ● 30
Redland; CDP; MONTGOMERY; 249 A-4; ★ WASH; mail Derwood z 20855; Ⓟ 16,145; Ⓒ 16,998
Red Point; RMC Place; CECIL; *185 B-16; ★ PHIL-; mail North East z 21901; ● 150
Reeder Development; RMC Place; FREDERICK; ★ WASH; mail Frederick z 21701; pop. incl. with Frederick (Inc. Place)
Reese; RMC Place; CARROLL; *185 B-12; ★ BAL; mail Westminster z 21157; ● 100
Reese Manor; RMC Place; CARROLL; *185 B-12; ★ BAL; mail Finksburg z 21048; ● 200
Regal Estates; RMC Place; CALVERT; *185 G-13; ★ WASH; mail Dunkirk z 20754; ● 250
Regency Estates; RMC Place; MONTGOMERY; *185 E-11; ★ WASH; mail Rockville z 20852
Regent Park; RMC Place; MONTGOMERY; ★ WASH; mail Potomac z 20854
Regent Square; RMC Place; MONTGOMERY; ★ WASH; mail Rockville z 20850; pop. incl. with Rockville (Inc. Place)
Rehobeth; RMC Place; SOMERSET; 185 K-18; elev. 8ft./2m.; 🅿; z 21857; ● 50
Reid; RMC Place; WASHINGTON; *184 A-9; ★ HAG; mail Hagerstown z 21742; ● 50
Reids Grove; RMC Place; DORCHESTER; 185 H-17; mail Rhodesdale z 21659; ● 50
Reisterstown; CDP; BALTIMORE; 185 C-12; elev. 720ft./219m.; 🅿; ★ BAL; z 21136 & mail Glyndon z 21071; Ⓟ 19,314; Ⓒ 22,438; ◆ 23,548
Relay; RMC Place; BALTIMORE; *185 D-13; ★ BAL; mail Halethorpe z 21227
Reliance; RMC Place; DORCHESTER; 185 G-18; mail Seaford z 19973; total pop., including Reliance, DE: 60; ● 30
Rest Haven; RMC Place; ANNE ARUNDEL; *185 F-14; ★ WASH; mail Deale z 20751
Revell; RMC Place; ANNE ARUNDEL; *185 E-14; ★ BAL; mail Arnold z 21012; ● 40
Revere Park; RMC Place; BALTIMORE; *185 C-14; ★ BAL; mail Parkville z 21234
Reynolds; RMC Place; ALLEGANY; *184 B-3; ★ CUMB; mail Lonaconing z 21539; rural
Rhodesdale; RMC Place; DORCHESTER; 185 H-17; elev. 41ft./12m.; 🅿; z 21659; ● 50
Rhodes Point; RMC Place; SOMERSET; 185 K-16; mail Ewell z 21824; ● 150
Riawakin Acres; RMC Place; WICOMICO; *185 I-18; ★ SLSB; mail Hebron z 21830; ● 150
Richards Oak; RMC Place; CECIL; *185 A-16; ★ PHIL-; mail Colora z 21917, Rising Sun z 21911; ● 80
Ricmar; RMC Place; WICOMICO; *185 I-18; ★ SLSB; mail Salisbury z 21804; ● 350
Riderwood; RMC Place; BALTIMORE; *185 C-13; elev. 280ft./85m.; 🅿; ★ BAL; z 21139
Riderwood Hills; RMC Place; BALTIMORE; *185 C-13; ★ BAL; mail Riderwood z 21139
Ridge; RMC Place; ST. MARY'S; 185 J-15; elev. 50ft./15m.; 🅿; z 20680; ● 450
Ridge Lake (Clayburn Hills); RMC Place; HOWARD; *185 D-12; ★ BAL; mail Ellicott City z 21042; ● 1,000
Ridgeleigh; RMC Place; BALTIMORE; *185 C-14; ★ BAL; mail Parkville z 21234
Ridgely; Inc. Place; CAROLINE; 185 E-17; elev. 70ft./21m.; 🅿; z 21660; Ⓟ 1,034; Ⓒ 1,352
Ridgeview; RMC Place; ANNE ARUNDEL; *185 D-13; ★ BAL; mail Harmans z 21077
Ridgeville; RMC Place; FREDERICK; *185 C-11; ★ WASH; mail Mount Airy z 21771; pop. incl. with Mount Airy (Inc. Place)
Ridgeway; RMC Place; ANNE ARUNDEL; 185 E-13; ★ BAL; mail Severn z 21144; ● 500
Ridgeway Estates; RMC Place; PRINCE GEORGE'S; *185 F-12; ★ WASH; mail Capitol Heights z 20743; ● 960
Ridgley Park; RMC Place; CARROLL; *185 C-12; ★ BAL; mail Sykesville z 21784
Riding Woods; RMC Place; ANNE ARUNDEL; *185 E-14; ★ BAL; mail Pasadena z 21122
Riggins Corner; RMC Place; DORCHESTER; *185 I-15; mail Church Creek z 21622; rural
Ringgold; RMC Place; WASHINGTON; 184 A-9; elev. 767ft./234m.; ★ HAG; mail Hagerstown z 21740; ● 160
Rio Vista; RMC Place; TALBOT; *185 F-15; elev. 7ft./2m.; mail Saint Michaels z 21663; ● 500
Ripley; RMC Place; CHARLES; *185 H-11; mail La Plata z 20646; ● 110
Ripplewood; RMC Place; BALTIMORE; *185 C-13; ★ BAL; mail Windsor Mill z 21244
Rippling Ridge; RMC Place; ANNE ARUNDEL; 184 L-4; ★ BAL; mail Glen Burnie z 21061; ● 2,100
Rising Sun; Inc. Place; CECIL; 185 A-16; elev. 388ft./118m.; 🅿; ★ PHIL-; z 21911; Ⓟ 1,263; Ⓒ 1,702
Rison; RMC Place; CHARLES; 185 H-11; 🅿; ★ WASH; z 20658 & mail Indian Head z 20640; ● 450
Ritchie; RMC Place; PRINCE GEORGE'S; *185 F-12; ★ WASH; mail District Heights z 20747
Ritchie Heights; RMC Place; PRINCE GEORGE'S; *185 F-12; ★ WASH; mail District Heights z 20747; ● 1,050
Ritchie Manor; RMC Place; PRINCE GEORGE'S; *185 F-12; ★ WASH; mail District Heights z 20747
Riva; CDP; ANNE ARUNDEL; 185 E-14; elev. 40ft./12m.; 🅿; ★ ANPLS; z 21140; Ⓟ 3,438; Ⓒ 3,966
Rivendell; RMC Place; ANNE ARUNDEL; *185 E-14; ★ BAL; mail Severna Park z 21146
River Bend; RMC Place; PRINCE GEORGE'S; *185 G-12; ★ WASH; mail Fort Washington z 20744
River Bend Estates; RMC Place; PRINCE GEORGE'S; *185 G-12; ★ WASH; mail Fort Washington z 20744; ● 1,000
River Club Estates; RMC Place; ANNE ARUNDEL; *185 F-14; ★ ANPLS; mail Edgewater z 21037
Riverdale; RMC Place; ANNE ARUNDEL; *185 E-14; ★ BAL; mail Severna Park z 21146
Riverdale; PRINCE GEORGE'S; see Riverdale Park (Inc. Place)
Riverdale Heights; RMC Place; PRINCE GEORGE'S; *185 E-12; ★ WASH; mail Riverdale z 20737; ● 3,600
Riverdale Hills; RMC Place; PRINCE GEORGE'S; *185 E-12; ★ WASH; mail Riverdale z 20737
Riverdale Park (Riverdale); Inc. Place; PRINCE GEORGE'S; 249 E-8; elev. 50ft./15m.; ★ WASH; mail Riverdale z 20737-38; Ⓟ 5,185; Ⓒ 6,690; Ⓡ 6,311
River Falls; RMC Place; MONTGOMERY; *185 E-11; ★ WASH; mail Potomac z 20854
River Forest; RMC Place; PRINCE GEORGE'S; *185 G-12; ★ WASH; mail Fort Washington z 20744
River Isle Estate; RMC Place; WICOMICO; *185 I-18; elev. 8ft./2m.; ★ SLSB; mail Salisbury z 21801; ● 50
River Meadows; RMC Place; HOWARD; ★ BAL; mail Columbia z 21045
River Ridge Estates; RMC Place; PRINCE GEORGE'S; *185 F-12; ★ WASH; mail Oxon Hill z 20745; ● 1,600
Riverside; RMC Place; CHARLES; *185 I-11; mail Nanjemoy z 20662; rural
Riverside (Belcamp); CDP-Census Area Only; HARFORD; 185 B-15; ★ BAL; mail Belcamp z 21017; Ⓒ 6,128
River Springs; RMC Place; ST. MARY'S; *185 J-13; ★ WASH; mail Avenue z 20609; ● 50
Riverton; RMC Place; WICOMICO; *185 H-17; mail Mardela Springs z 21837; ● 50
Riverview Manor; RMC Place; ANNE ARUNDEL; *185 E-14; ★ ANPLS; mail Annapolis z 21401
Riverview Village; RMC Place; CHARLES; *185 G-11; ★ WASH; mail Indian Head z 20640
Riverwood; RMC Place; ANNE ARUNDEL; *185 F-13; ★ WASH; mail Davidsonville z 21035; ● 400
Riviera Beach; CDP; ANNE ARUNDEL; 185 D-14; 🅿; ★ BAL; z 21122-23 & mail Curtis Bay z 21226; Ⓟ 11,376; Ⓒ 12,695
Riviera Isle; RMC Place; ANNE ARUNDEL; *185 D-14; ★ BAL; mail Pasadena z 21122
Robbins; RMC Place; DORCHESTER; *185 I-16; mail Crapo z 21626; ● 100
Roberts; ALLEGANY; see Bowling Green (RMC Place)
Roberts; RMC Place; QUEEN ANNE'S; 185 D-17; elev. 75ft./23m.; mail Church Hill z 21623; ● 50
Roberts Glen; RMC Place; MONTGOMERY; *185 E-11; ★ WASH; mail Potomac z 20854
Robinson; RMC Place; ANNE ARUNDEL; *185 E-14; elev. 48ft./15m.; ★ BAL; mail Severna Park z 21146
Robinwood; CDP-Census Area Only; WASHINGTON; *184 B-9; ★ HAG; mail Hagerstown z 21742; Ⓒ 4,731
Roblee Acres; RMC Place; PRINCE GEORGE'S; *185 F-13; ★ WASH; mail Upper Marlboro z 20772
Rockawalkin Village; RMC Place; WICOMICO; *185 I-18; ★ SLSB; mail Salisbury z 21801; ● 230
Rockaway Beach; RMC Place; BALTIMORE; *185 C-14; ★ BAL; mail Essex z 21221
Rock Creek; SOMERSET; see Chance (CDP)
Rock Creek Forest; RMC Place; MONTGOMERY; *185 E-11; ★ WASH; mail Chevy Chase z 20815
Rock Creek Gardens; RMC Place; MONTGOMERY; *185 E-12; ★ WASH; mail Chevy Chase z 20815
Rock Creek Highlands; RMC Place; MONTGOMERY; *185 E-11; ★ WASH; mail Kensington z 20895; ● 1,000
Rock Creek Hills; RMC Place; MONTGOMERY; *185 E-11; ★ WASH; mail Kensington z 20895; ● 1,700
Rock Creek Manor; RMC Place; MONTGOMERY; *185 E-11; ★ WASH; mail Rockville z 20853
Rock Creek Palisades; RMC Place; MONTGOMERY; *185 E-11; ★ WASH; mail Kensington z 20895
Rock Creek Village; RMC Place; MONTGOMERY; *185 E-11; ★ WASH; mail Rockville z 20853
Rockcrest; RMC Place; MONTGOMERY; *185 E-11; ★ WASH; mail Rockville z 20851; pop. incl. with Rockville (Inc. Place)
Rockdale; RMC Place; BALTIMORE; 184 H-2; ★ BAL; mail Windsor Mill z 21244; ● 6,700
Rock Hall; RMC Place; FREDERICK; *184 D-9; ★ WASH; mail Tuscarora z 21790; rural
Rock Hall; Inc. Place; KENT; 185 D-15; elev. 25ft./8m.; 🅿; z 21661; Ⓟ 1,584; Ⓒ 1,396
Rock Hill Beach; RMC Place; ANNE ARUNDEL; 184 M-7; ★ BAL; mail Pasadena z 21122; ● 1,350
Rockland; RMC Place; HOWARD; *185 C-13; ★ BAL; mail Ellicott City z 21043
Rockland; RMC Place; MONTGOMERY; *185 E-11; ★ WASH; mail Rockville z 20850; pop. incl. with Rockville (Inc. Place)
Rockland Run; RMC Place; BALTIMORE; *185 C-13; ★ BAL; mail Baltimore z 21209
Rock Point; RMC Place; CHARLES; 185 I-12; elev. 15ft./5m.; 🅿; z 20682; ● 280
Rock Run; RMC Place; HARFORD; *185 B-16; mail Havre de Grace z 21078; ● 150
Rocks; RMC Place; HARFORD; *185 B-14; elev. 307ft./94m.; ★ BAL; mail Street z 21154; rural
Rockshire; RMC Place; MONTGOMERY; ★ WASH; mail Rockville z 20850; pop. incl. with Rockville (Inc. Place)
Rockshire Square; RMC Place; MONTGOMERY; *185 E-11; ★ WASH; mail Rockville z 20850; pop. incl. with Rockville (Inc. Place)
Rockshire Village; RMC Place; MONTGOMERY; *185 E-11; ★ WASH; mail Rockville z 20850; pop. incl. with Rockville (Inc. Place)
Rockview Beach; RMC Place; ANNE ARUNDEL; *185 D-14; ★ BAL; mail Pasadena z 21122; ● 600
Rockville; Inc. Place; ⊡ MONTGOMERY; 185 E-11; elev. 451ft./137m.; 🅿 🅷 ■; ★ WASH; z 20847-55, z 20857, z 20859; Ⓟ 44,835; Ⓒ 47,388; ◆ 51,673
Rockville Estates; RMC Place; MONTGOMERY; *185 E-11; ★ WASH; mail Rockville z 20850; pop. incl. with Rockville (Inc. Place)
Rockwell; RMC Place; BALTIMORE; ★ BAL; mail Catonsville z 21228
Rocky Gorge Estates; RMC Place; PRINCE GEORGE'S; *185 E-12; ★ WASH; mail Laurel z 20707
Rocky Ridge; RMC Place; FREDERICK; 184 B-10; elev. 415ft./126m.; 🅿; z 21778; ● 900
Rocky Springs; RMC Place; FREDERICK; *184 C-10; elev. 411ft./125m.; ★ WASH; mail Frederick z 21702; ● 160
Rodgers Forge; RMC Place; BALTIMORE; *185 C-13; ★ BAL; mail Towson z 21204
Rodo Beach; RMC Place; ST. MARY'S; *185 J-15; elev. 6ft./2m.; mail Scotland z 20687; rural
Rogers Heights; RMC Place; PRINCE GEORGE'S; *185 E-12; ★ WASH; mail Hyattsville z 20781; ● 3,500
Rohrersville; CDP; WASHINGTON; *184 C-9; elev. 624ft./190m.; 🅿; ★ WASH; z 21779; Ⓒ 170
Rohrersville Station (Trego); RMC Place; WASHINGTON; 184 C-9; ★ WASH; mail Keedysville z 21756; ● 300
Roland Park; RMC Place; BALTIMORE (Independent City); *185 C-13; 🅿; ★ BAL; z 21210 & mail Baltimore z 21211; pop. incl. with Baltimore (Independent City)
Rolling Acres; RMC Place; PRINCE GEORGE'S; *185 G-12; elev. 200ft./61m.; ★ WASH; mail Cheltenham z 20623; ● 890
Rolling Acres; RMC Place; ST. MARY'S; *185 H-13; ★ WASH; mail Charlotte Hall z 20622
Rolling Green; RMC Place; HARFORD; *185 B-15; ★ BAL; mail Churchville z 21028; ● 200
Rolling Hills; RMC Place; ANNE ARUNDEL; *185 E-14; ★ ANPLS; mail Annapolis z 21401
Rolling Hills; RMC Place; CARROLL; *185 C-12; ★ BAL; mail Sykesville z 21784; ● 300
Rolling Knolls; RMC Place; ANNE ARUNDEL; *185 E-14; ★ ANPLS; mail Annapolis z 21401; ● 1,150
Rolling Ridge; RMC Place; CARROLL; *185 B-12; ★ BAL; mail Westminster z 21157; ● 100
Rolling Ridge; RMC Place; HOWARD; *185 C-13; ★ BAL; mail Ellicott City z 21043
Rolling Ridge; RMC Place; PRINCE GEORGE'S; *185 F-12; ★ WASH; mail Capitol Heights z 20743
Rolling Terrace; RMC Place; MONTGOMERY; *185 E-12; ★ WASH; mail Takoma Park z 20912; ● 2,500
Rolling Terrace Estates; RMC Place; MONTGOMERY; *185 E-12; ★ WASH; mail Takoma Park z 20912; ● 1,600
Rollingwood; RMC Place; MONTGOMERY; *185 E-11; ★ WASH; mail Chevy Chase z 20815; pop. incl. with Martins Additions (Inc. Place)
Rollins Park; RMC Place; MONTGOMERY; *185 E-11; ★ WASH; mail Rockville z 20852; pop. incl. with Rockville (Inc. Place)
Rolphs; RMC Place; QUEEN ANNE'S; *185 D-16; mail Chestertown z 21620; rural
Romancoke; RMC Place; QUEEN ANNE'S; 185 F-15; ★ ANPLS; mail Stevensville z 21666; ● 470
Rosaryville; CDP; PRINCE GEORGE'S; *185 F-13; elev. 200ft./61m.; ★ WASH; mail Upper Marlboro z 20772; Ⓟ 8,976; Ⓒ 12,322
Rosaryville Estates; RMC Place; PRINCE GEORGE'S; 185 G-13; ★ WASH; mail Upper Marlboro z 20772; ● 1,250
Rosecroft; RMC Place; PRINCE GEORGE'S; *185 F-12; ★ WASH; mail Temple Hills z 20748
Rosecroft Park; RMC Place; PRINCE GEORGE'S; *185 F-12; ★ WASH; mail Fort Washington z 20744; ● 1,550
Rosedale; CDP; BALTIMORE; 185 C-14; elev. 100ft./30m.; 🅿; ★ BAL; z 21237; Ⓟ 18,703; Ⓒ 19,199
Rosedale Estates; RMC Place; PRINCE GEORGE'S; *185 F-12; ★ WASH; mail Fort Washington z 20744; ● 3,500
Rosedale Park; RMC Place; MONTGOMERY; *185 E-11; ★ WASH; mail Chevy Chase z 20815
Rose Haven; RMC Place; ANNE ARUNDEL; 185 G-14; 🅿; ★ WASH; z 20714; ● 550
Rose Hill Estates; RMC Place; MONTGOMERY; *185 E-11; ★ WASH; mail Bethesda z 20817; ● 1,900
Rosemary Hills; RMC Place; MONTGOMERY; *185 E-12; ★ WASH; mail Silver Spring z 20910
Rosemont; RMC Place; BALTIMORE; *185 D-13; ★ BAL; mail Brooklyn z 21225
Rosemont; Inc. Place; FREDERICK; 184 C-9; elev. 500ft./152m.; ★ WASH; mail Knoxville z 21758; Ⓟ 256; Ⓒ 273; Ⓡ 284
Rosemont; RMC Place; MONTGOMERY; *185 D-11; ★ WASH; mail Gaithersburg z 20877; ● 820
Rose Valley Estates; RMC Place; PRINCE GEORGE'S; *185 G-12; ★ WASH; mail Fort Washington z 20744; ● 1,650
Rossmoor (Leisure World, Rossmoor Leisure); CDP-Census Area Only; MONTGOMERY; 249 B-6; elev. 450ft./137m.; ★ WASH; mail Silver Spring z 20906, z 20908; Ⓟ 6,182; Ⓒ 7,569
Rossmoor Leisure; MONTGOMERY; see Rossmoor (CDP-Census Area Only)
Rossville; CDP; BALTIMORE; 184 I-7; ★ BAL; mail Rosedale z 21237; Ⓟ 9,492; Ⓒ 11,515
Round Acres; RMC Place; HARFORD; *185 B-14; ★ BAL; mail Fallston z 21047; ● 500
Round Bay; RMC Place; ANNE ARUNDEL; *185 E-14; ★ BAL; mail Severna Park z 21146
Round Hill; RMC Place; FREDERICK; *184 C-9; ★ WASH; mail Frederick z 21702
Roundtop; RMC Place; WASHINGTON; *184 A-6; elev. 700ft./213m.; mail Hancock z 21750; rural
Rover Mill Estates; RMC Place; HOWARD; *185 D-12; ★ WASH; mail West Friendship z 21794; ● 220
Rowlandsville; RMC Place; CECIL; *185 A-16; ★ PHIL-; mail Conowingo z 21918; ● 90
Roxboro; RMC Place; MONTGOMERY; *185 E-11; ★ WASH; mail Rockville z 20850; pop. incl. with Rockville (Inc. Place)
Royal Beach; RMC Place; ANNE ARUNDEL; *185 E-14; ★ BAL; mail Pasadena z 21122; ● 100
Royal Oak; RMC Place; TALBOT; 185 G-15; 🅿; z 21662; ● 550
Royal Oak; RMC Place; WICOMICO; 185 I-17; elev. 6ft./2m.; mail Quantico z 21856; ● 50
Rugby Hall; RMC Place; ANNE ARUNDEL; *185 E-14; ★ BAL; mail Arnold z 21012; ● 700
Ruhl; RMC Place; BALTIMORE; *185 A-13; ★ BAL; mail Freeland z 21053; ● 30
Rumbley; RMC Place; SOMERSET; 185 J-17; mail Westover z 21871; ● 200
Rumsey Island; RMC Place; HARFORD; *185 C-15; ★ BAL; mail Joppa z 21085
Running Brook; RMC Place; HOWARD; ★ BAL; mail Columbia z 21044
Rustic Acres; RMC Place; WICOMICO; *185 I-18; ★ SLSB; mail Salisbury z 21804; ● 230
Rusty Acres; RMC Place; MONTGOMERY; *185 E-12; ★ WASH; mail Burtonsville z 20866
Ruthsburg; RMC Place; QUEEN ANNE'S; 185 E-16; elev. 67ft./20m.; mail Centreville z 21617; ● 30
Rutledge; RMC Place; HARFORD; *185 B-14; ★ BAL; mail Fallston z 21047; ● 250
Ruxton; RMC Place; BALTIMORE; *185 C-13; 🅿; ★ BAL; z 21204 & mail Towson z 21286
Ryceville; RMC Place; CHARLES; *185 H-12; mail Mechanicsville z 20659; rural

S

Sabillasville; RMC Place; FREDERICK; 184 A-10; elev. 1,108ft./338m.; 🅿; z 21780; ● 1,100
Sackertown; RMC Place; SOMERSET; *185 K-17; mail Crisfield z 21817; rural
Saint Andrews Estates; RMC Place; ST. MARY'S; *185 I-14; elev. 117ft./36m.; ★ WASH; mail California z 20619; ● 1,100
Saint Anthony's; RMC Place; FREDERICK; *184 A-10; mail Emmitsburg z 21727; ● 30
Saint Aubins Heights; RMC Place; TALBOT; *185 F-16; mail Easton z 21601; pop. incl. with Easton (Inc. Place)
Saint Augustine; RMC Place; CECIL; *185 B-17; ★ PHIL-; mail Chesapeake City z 21915
Saint Charles; CDP; CHARLES; 185 H-12; 🅿; ★ WASH; z 20602-04 & mail Waldorf z 20601; Ⓟ 28,717; Ⓒ 33,379; ◆ 38,876
Saint Clement Shores; RMC Place; ST. MARY'S; 185 I-13; ★ WASH; mail Leonardtown z 20650; ● 400
Saint Denis; RMC Place; BALTIMORE; *185 D-13; ★ BAL; mail Halethorpe z 21227
Saint George Island; RMC Place; ST. MARY'S; 185 J-14; mail Piney Point z 20674; ● 250
Saint Georges; RMC Place; BALTIMORE; *185 C-13; elev. 625ft./191m.; ★ BAL; mail Glyndon z 21071
Saint George's Park; RMC Place; ST. MARY'S; mail Tall Timbers z 20690; rural
Saint Helena; RMC Place; BALTIMORE; *185 D-14; ★ BAL; mail Dundalk z 21222
Saint Inigoes; RMC Place; ST. MARY'S; 185 J-14; elev. 81ft./25m.; 🅿; z 20684; ● 500
Saint James; CDP; WASHINGTON; 184 B-8; elev. 480ft./146m.; 🅿; ★ HAG; z 21781; Ⓒ 1,657
Saint James; RMC Place; WORCESTER; *185 K-18; mail Pocomoke City z 21851; ● 50
Saint Jeromes; RMC Place; ST. MARY'S; mail Dameron z 20628; rural
Saint Johns Manor; RMC Place; HOWARD; ★ BAL; mail Ellicott City z 21042
Saint Johns Village; RMC Place; HOWARD; ★ BAL; mail Ellicott City z 21042
Saint Leonard; CDP; CALVERT; 185 H-14; elev. 115ft./35m.; 🅿; z 20685; Ⓒ 536
Saint Leonard Shores; RMC Place; CALVERT; *185 H-14; elev. 100ft./30m.; mail Saint Leonard z 20685; ● 30
Saint Margarets; RMC Place; ANNE ARUNDEL; 185 L-20; elev. 95ft./29m.; ★ ANPLS; mail Annapolis z 21401; ● 350
Saint Margarets Farm; RMC Place; ANNE ARUNDEL; *185 E-14; ★ ANPLS; mail Annapolis z 21401; ● 150
Saint Mark's; FREDERICK; see Slabtown (RMC Place)
Saint Martin (Saint Martins); RMC Place; WORCESTER; *185 I-20; mail Berlin z 21811
Saint Martins; WORCESTER; see Saint Martin (RMC Place)
ST. MARY'S; 185 I-13; Ⓟ 75,974; Ⓒ 86,211; Ⓡ 86,232; ◆ 103,381
Saint Marys City; RMC Place; ST. MARY'S; 185 J-14; elev. 36ft./11m.; 🅿 🅲 1,957; z 20686; ● 3,300
Saint Michaels; Inc. Place; TALBOT; 185 F-15; 🅿; z 21663 & mail Claiborne z 21624, McDaniel z 21647; Ⓟ 1,301; Ⓒ 1,193
SaintPauls Church; RMC Place; WASHINGTON; *184 A-8; elev. 507ft./155m.; ★ HAG; mail Clear Spring z 21722; ● 50
Saint Peters Creek; SOMERSET; see Champ (RMC Place)
Saint Stephen; RMC Place; SOMERSET; *185 J-17; mail Princess Anne z 21853; ● 40
Salem; RMC Place; DORCHESTER; 185 H-17; mail Vienna z 21869; ● 60
Salisbury; Inc. Place; ⊡ WICOMICO; 185 I-18; elev. 33ft./10m.; 🅿 🅷 🅲 7,383 ■; ★ SLSB; z 21801-04; Ⓟ 20,592; Ⓒ 23,743; ◆ 29,575
Samples Manor; RMC Place; WASHINGTON; *184 C-9; elev. 609ft./186m.; ★ WASH; mail Sharpsburg z 21782; ● 50
Sams Creek; RMC Place; CARROLL, FREDERICK; *185 B-11; mail New Windsor z 21776; ● 40
Sanders Park; RMC Place; ANNE ARUNDEL; 184 M-6; ★ BAL; mail Pasadena z 21122; ● 450
Sandgates; RMC Place; ST. MARY'S; 185 I-13; ★ WASH; mail Mechanicsville z 20659; ● 450
San Domingo; RMC Place; WICOMICO; *185 H-18; mail Mardela Springs z 21837; ● 50
Sand Spring; RMC Place; GARRETT; *184 A-1; mail Friendsville z 21531; rural
Sandy Acres; RMC Place; DORCHESTER; *185 H-16; mail Cambridge z 21613; ● 150
Sandy Bottom; RMC Place; KENT; *185 D-15; mail Chestertown z 21620
Sandy Hook; RMC Place; WASHINGTON; 184 C-9; ★ WASH; mail Knoxville z 21758; ● 120
Sandymount; CARROLL; see Sandyville (RMC Place)
Sandy Spring; RMC Place; MONTGOMERY; 185 D-12; elev. 484ft./148m.; 🅿; ★ WASH; z 20860; ● 1,200
Sandy Spring Estates; RMC Place; PRINCE GEORGE'S; *185 E-12; ★ WASH; mail Laurel z 20707; ● 820
Sandy Spring Meadows; RMC Place; MONTGOMERY; *185 D-11; ★ WASH; mail Sandy Spring z 20860
Sandyville (Sandymount); RMC Place; CARROLL; 185 B-12; ★ BAL; mail Finksburg z 21048; ● 650
Sang Run; RMC Place; GARRETT; 184 B-1; elev. 2,014ft./614m.; 🅿; z 21541; ● 180
San Mar; CDP; WASHINGTON; *184 B-9; ★ HAG; mail Boonsboro z 21713; Ⓒ 515
Sansbury Park; RMC Place; PRINCE GEORGE'S; *185 F-12; ★ WASH; mail District Heights z 20747; ● 1,150
Santa Fe Acres; RMC Place; WICOMICO; *185 I-18; ★ SLSB; mail Salisbury z 21801; ● 230
Sassafras; RMC Place; KENT; 185 C-17; mail Galena z 21635; ● 70
Satyr Hill; RMC Place; BALTIMORE; *185 C-14; ★ BAL; mail Parkville z 21234
Saunders Point; RMC Place; ANNE ARUNDEL; *185 F-14; ★ ANPLS; mail Edgewater z 21037; ● 190
Savage (Savage Factory); RMC Place; HOWARD; 185 D-13; elev. 200ft./61m.; 🅿; ★ BAL; z 20763; ● 8,000
Savage Factory; HOWARD; see Savage (RMC Place)
Savage-Guilford; CDP-Census Area Only; HOWARD; *185 D-13; ★ BAL; mail Jessup z 20794, Savage z 20763; Ⓟ 9,669; Ⓒ 12,918
Scaggsville; RMC Place; HOWARD; 185 D-12; 🅿; ★ WASH; z 20723; ● 270
Scarboro; RMC Place; HARFORD; *185 A-15; elev. 445ft./136m.; ★ BAL; mail Street z 21154; ● 150
Scarboro; RMC Place; WORCESTER; *185 J-19; mail Snow Hill z 21863; rural
Schnaders Shores; RMC Place; ANNE ARUNDEL; *185 D-14; ★ BAL; mail Pasadena z 21122
Schultz; RMC Place; PRINCE GEORGE'S; *185 G-12; ★ WASH; mail Clinton z 20735
Scientists Cliffs; RMC Place; CALVERT; 185 H-14; mail Port Republic z 20676; ● 750
Scotland; RMC Place; MONTGOMERY; *185 E-11; ★ WASH; mail Potomac z 20854
Scotland; RMC Place; ST. MARY'S; 185 J-15; elev. 16ft./5m.; 🅿; z 20687; ● 350
Scotland Beach; RMC Place; ST. MARY'S; *185 K-15; mail Scotland z 20687; ● 110
Seabrook; RMC Place; PRINCE GEORGE'S; 249 E-9; elev. 149ft./45m.; 🅿; ★ WASH; z 20706 & mail Lanham z 20703; ● 8,000
Seabrook Acres; RMC Place; PRINCE GEORGE'S; *185 E-12; ★ WASH; mail Lanham z 20706
Seabrook Park Estates; RMC Place; PRINCE GEORGE'S; ★ WASH; mail Lanham z 20706
Seat Pleasant; Inc. Place; PRINCE GEORGE'S; 185 F-12; 🅿; ★ WASH; z 20743; Ⓟ 5,359; Ⓒ 4,885
Sebring; RMC Place; HOWARD; ★ BAL; mail Columbia z 21045
Secretary; Inc. Place; DORCHESTER; 185 G-16; elev. 20ft./6m.; 🅿; z 21664; Ⓟ 528; Ⓒ 503
Security; RMC Place; WASHINGTON; 185 M-14; ★ HAG; mail Hagerstown z 21742; ● 270
Security Junction; RMC Place; WASHINGTON; ★ HAG
Selassie Villa; RMC Place; ANNE ARUNDEL; *185 F-14; ★ WASH; mail Shady Side z 20764
Selby-on-the-Bay; CDP-Census Area Only; ANNE ARUNDEL; 185 F-14; ★ ANPLS; mail Edgewater z 21037; Ⓟ 3,101; Ⓒ 3,674
Selbysport; RMC Place; GARRETT; 184 A-1; elev. 1,484ft./452m.; mail Friendsville z 21531; ● 50
Sellman; RMC Place; MONTGOMERY; *184 D-10; ★ WASH; mail Barnesville z 20838; rural
Seneca; RMC Place; MONTGOMERY; *184 E-10; elev. 206ft./63m.; ★ WASH; mail Poolesville z 20837
Seneca Park; RMC Place; MONTGOMERY; *185 D-11; ★ WASH; mail Germantown z 20876
Sequioa; RMC Place; MONTGOMERY; *185 E-12; ★ WASH; mail Spencerville z 20868; ● 2,400
Severn; CDP; ANNE ARUNDEL; 185 D-13; elev. 180ft./55m.; 🅿; ★ BAL; z 21144; Ⓟ 24,499; Ⓒ 35,076; ◆ 37,085
Severna Forest; RMC Place; ANNE ARUNDEL; ★ BAL; mail Severna Park z 21146
Severna Park; CDP; ANNE ARUNDEL; 185 E-14; elev. 40ft./12m.; 🅿; ★ BAL; z 21146; Ⓟ 25,879; Ⓒ 28,507; ◆ 30,144
Severn Grove; RMC Place; ANNE ARUNDEL; *185 E-14; ★ ANPLS; mail Annapolis z 21401
Severn Heights; RMC Place; ANNE ARUNDEL; *185 E-14; ★ BAL; mail Severna Park z 21146
Severnside; RMC Place; ANNE ARUNDEL; *185 E-14; ★ ANPLS; mail Annapolis z 21401; rural
Sewell; RMC Place; HARFORD; *185 C-15; ★ BAL; mail Abingdon z 21009; rural
Sewells Orchard; RMC Place; HOWARD; *185 D-13; ★ BAL; mail Columbia z 21045
Shad Point; RMC Place; WICOMICO; *185 I-18; ★ SLSB; mail Salisbury z 21801; ● 390
Shady Bower; RMC Place; WASHINGTON; *184 A-8; elev. 500ft./152m.; ★ HAG; mail Clear Spring z 21722; ● 50
Shady Dale; RMC Place; ST. MARY'S; *185 H-13; ★ WASH; mail Mechanicsville z 20659; ● 110
Shady Oaks; RMC Place; ANNE ARUNDEL; *185 F-14; ★ WASH; mail West River z 20778
Shady Side; CDP; ANNE ARUNDEL; 185 F-14; elev. 8ft./2m.; 🅿; ★ WASH; z 20764; Ⓟ 4,107; Ⓒ 5,559
Shallmar; RMC Place; GARRETT; 184 C-2; 🅿; z 21538; ● 150
Shane; RMC Place; BALTIMORE; *185 A-14; ★ BAL; mail White Hall z 21161
Sharewood Acres; RMC Place; HOWARD; *185 D-13; ★ BAL; mail Jessup z 20794
Sharonville; RMC Place; ANNE ARUNDEL; *185 D-14; ★ BAL; mail Pasadena z 21122
Sharon Woods; RMC Place; MONTGOMERY; *185 D-11; ★ WASH; mail Gaithersburg z 20879
Sharperville; RMC Place; PRINCE GEORGE'S; *185 G-12; ★ WASH; mail Waldorf z 20601; ● 50
Sharpsburg; Inc. Place; WASHINGTON; 184 C-8; elev. 413ft./126m.; 🅿; ★ HAG; z 21782; Ⓟ 659; Ⓒ 691
Sharpstown; RMC Place; KENT; *185 D-15; mail Rock Hall z 21661; rural
Sharptown; Inc. Place; WICOMICO; 185 H-18; elev. 20ft./6m.; 🅿; z 21861; Ⓟ 609; Ⓒ 649
Shavox; RMC Place; WICOMICO; *185 I-19; ★ SLSB; mail Salisbury z 21804; ● 50
Shawsville; RMC Place; HARFORD; 185 B-14; ★ BAL; mail White Hall z 21161; ● 80
Shawsville Acres; RMC Place; HARFORD; *185 B-14; ★ BAL; mail White Hall z 21161; ● 200
Shelltown; RMC Place; SOMERSET; 185 K-18; mail Marion Station z 21838; ● 100
Shervettes Corner; RMC Place; CARROLL; *185 C-12; ★ BAL; mail Sykesville z 21784
Sherwood; RMC Place; TALBOT; 185 G-15; elev. 11ft./3m.; 🅿; z 21665; ● 250
Sherwood Forest; RMC Place; ANNE ARUNDEL; 185 E-14; 🅿; ★ ANPLS; z 21405; ● 630
Sherwood Forest; RMC Place; MONTGOMERY; *185 E-12; ★ WASH; mail Silver Spring z 20904; ● 2,700
Sherwood Forest; RMC Place; PRINCE GEORGE'S; *185 F-12; elev. 100ft./30m.; ★ WASH; mail Upper Marlboro z 20772; ● 900
Sherwood Manor; RMC Place; PRINCE GEORGE'S; *185 E-13; ★ WASH; mail Bowie z 20715; ● 350
Sherwood Manor; RMC Place; WICOMICO; *185 I-18; ★ SLSB; mail Salisbury z 21804; ● 280
Shetland Hills; RMC Place; BALTIMORE; *185 C-13; ★ BAL; mail Lutherville Timonium z 21093
Shiloh; RMC Place; CARROLL; *185 B-12; elev. 800ft./244m.; ★ BAL; mail Hampstead z 21074; rural
Shiloh; RMC Place; CHARLES; 185 I-12; mail Newburg z 20664; ● 130
Shiloh; RMC Place; DORCHESTER; *185 H-17; elev. 47ft./14m.; mail Hurlock z 21643; rural
Shipley; RMC Place; ANNE ARUNDEL; *185 D-13; ★ BAL; mail Linthicum Heights z 21090
Shookstown; RMC Place; FREDERICK; 185 M-16; ★ WASH; mail Frederick z 21702; ● 550
Shore Acres; RMC Place; ANNE ARUNDEL; *185 E-14; ★ BAL; mail Arnold z 21012; ● 1,150
Shoreham Beach; RMC Place; ANNE ARUNDEL; *185 F-14; ★ ANPLS; mail Edgewater z 21037; ● 370
Shoreland; RMC Place; ANNE ARUNDEL; *185 D-14; ★ BAL; mail Glen Burnie z 21061
Shorewood Estates; RMC Place; KENT; *185 C-17; elev. 50ft./15m.; mail Galena z 21635; ● 150
Showell; RMC Place; WORCESTER; 185 I-20; elev. 25ft./8m.; 🅿; z 21862; ● 400
Sierra Manor; RMC Place; WICOMICO; *185 I-19; ★ SLSB; mail Salisbury z 21804; ● 250
Silesia; RMC Place; PRINCE GEORGE'S; 185 G-12; ★ WASH; mail Fort Washington z 20744; ● 240
Sillery Bay; RMC Place; ANNE ARUNDEL; *185 E-14; ★ BAL; mail Pasadena z 21122
Siloam; RMC Place; WICOMICO; *185 I-18; mail Eden z 21822, Salisbury z 21801; rural
Silver Gate Village; RMC Place; BALTIMORE; *185 C-14; ★ BAL; mail Nottingham z 21236
Silver Hill; RMC Place; PRINCE GEORGE'S; 249 H-8; ★ WASH; mail Suitland z 20746; ● 1,850
Silver Hill Park; RMC Place; PRINCE GEORGE'S; *185 F-12; ★ WASH; mail Suitland z 20746
Silver Meadow; RMC Place; BALTIMORE; *185 C-14; ★ BAL; mail Perry Hall z 21128; ● 3,600
Silver Rock; RMC Place; MONTGOMERY; *185 E-11; ★ WASH; mail Rockville z 20850; pop. incl. with Rockville (Inc. Place)
Silver Run; RMC Place; CARROLL; 185 A-11; mail Westminster z 21158; ● 180
Silver Sands; RMC Place; ANNE ARUNDEL; 184 M-5; ★ BAL; mail Glen Burnie z 21060; ● 350
Silver Spring; CDP; MONTGOMERY; 185 E-12; 🅿 🅷 🅲 1,115; ★ WASH; z 20901-08, z 20910-16, z 20918, z 20993, z 20997; Ⓟ 76,046; Ⓒ 76,540; ◆ 81,297
Silver Valley; RMC Place; PRINCE GEORGE'S; *185 F-12; ★ WASH; mail Suitland z 20746
Simpsonville; RMC Place; HOWARD; *185 D-12; elev. 380ft./116m.; 🅿; ★ BAL; z 21150
Sinepuxent; RMC Place; WORCESTER; *185 I-20; mail Berlin z 21811; rural
Singer Heights; RMC Place; CARROLL; *185 B-12; elev. 881ft./269m.; ★ BAL; mail Hampstead z 21074; ● 30
Singerly; RMC Place; CECIL; *185 A-17; ★ PHIL-; mail Childs z 21916; ● 50
Skidmore; RMC Place; ANNE ARUNDEL; 185 E-14; ★ ANPLS; mail Annapolis z 21401; ● 450
Skipton; RMC Place; TALBOT; *185 F-16; mail Cordova z 21625; ● 80
Skyline; RMC Place; PRINCE GEORGE'S; *185 F-12; ★ WASH; mail Suitland z 20746; ● 900
Skyline Additions; RMC Place; PRINCE GEORGE'S; *185 F-12; ★ WASH; mail Suitland z 20746; pop. incl. with Morningside (Inc. Place)
Sky Valley; RMC Place; GARRETT; *184 B-2; mail Swanton z 21561; summer pop. 350
Slabtown; RMC Place; ALLEGANY; *184 A-3; ★ CUMB; mail Mount Savage z 21545
Slabtown (Saint Mark's); RMC Place; FREDERICK; *184 C-9; elev. 500ft./152m.; ★ WASH; mail Knoxville z 21758; rural
Sligo Park Knolls; RMC Place; MONTGOMERY; *185 E-12; ★ WASH; mail Silver Spring z 20901
Smallwood; RMC Place; CARROLL; *185 B-12; ★ BAL; mail Westminster z 21157; ● 250
Smithfield; MONTGOMERY; see Deerfield (RMC Place)
Smith Island; CDP-Census Area Only; SOMERSET; *185 K-16; Ⓒ 364
Smithsburg; Inc. Place; WASHINGTON; 184 A-9; elev. 800ft./244m.; 🅿; ★ HAG; z 21783; Ⓟ 1,221; Ⓒ 2,146
Smithville; RMC Place; CAROLINE; 185 F-17; mail Federalsburg z 21632; ● 50
Smithville; RMC Place; DORCHESTER; 185 H-15; mail Taylors Island z 21669; ● 100
Smithville; RMC Place; KENT; *185 C-16; elev. 80ft./24m.; mail Worton z 21678; ● 30
Smoketown; RMC Place; WASHINGTON; ★ HAG; mail Boonsboro z 21713
Smoky; RMC Place; CALVERT; *185 G-13; elev. 100ft./30m.; ★ WASH; mail Huntingtown z 20639; ● 30
Smugglers Cove; RMC Place; ANNE ARUNDEL; *185 E-14; ★ BAL; mail Severna Park z 21146
Snowden Manor; RMC Place; CARROLL; *185 B-12; ★ BAL; mail Westminster z 21157; ● 200
Snowden Oaks; RMC Place; PRINCE GEORGE'S; *185 E-12; elev. 200ft./61m.; ★ WASH; mail Laurel z 20708; ● 730
Snow Hill; Inc. Place; ⊡ WORCESTER; 185 J-19; elev. 21ft./6m.; 🅿; z 21863; Ⓟ 2,217; Ⓒ 2,409
Snow Hill Manor; RMC Place; PRINCE GEORGE'S; *185 E-12; ★ WASH; mail Laurel z 20708
Snug Harbor; RMC Place; ANNE ARUNDEL; *185 F-14; ★ WASH; mail Shady Side z 20764
Snug Harbor; RMC Place; WORCESTER; *185 I-20; mail Berlin z 21811; ● 30
Snydersburg; RMC Place; CARROLL; *185 B-12; ★ BAL; mail Hampstead z 21074, Westminster z 21157; ● 130
Society Hill; RMC Place; ST. MARY'S; *185 I-13; ★ WASH; mail Leonardtown z 20650; ● 450
Sollers Homes; RMC Place; BALTIMORE; *185 D-14; ★ BAL; mail Dundalk z 21222
Sollers Point; RMC Place; BALTIMORE; *185 D-14; ★ BAL; mail Dundalk z 21222
Solley Heights; RMC Place; ANNE ARUNDEL; *185 D-14; ★ BAL; mail Glen Burnie z 21060
Solomons; CDP; CALVERT; 185 I-14; elev. 10ft./3m.; 🅿; z 20688; Ⓒ 1,536
Somerset; Inc. Place; MONTGOMERY; 249 E-5; elev. 300ft./91m.; ★ WASH; mail Chevy Chase z 20815; Ⓟ 993; Ⓒ 1,124
SOMERSET; 185 J-18; Ⓟ 23,440; Ⓒ 24,747; ◆ 26,953
Sonoma; RMC Place; MONTGOMERY; *185 E-11; ★ WASH; mail Bethesda z 20814
Sorrattsville; PRINCE GEORGE'S; see Clinton (CDP)
South; RMC Place; BALTIMORE (Independent City); *185 D-13; ★ BAL; mail Baltimore z 21230; pop. incl. with Baltimore (Independent City)
Southampton; RMC Place; ST. MARY'S; *185 I-14; mail Lexington Park z 20653; ● 1,200
South Cheverly Forest; RMC Place; PRINCE GEORGE'S; ★ WASH; mail Hyattsville z 20784
South Cumberland; RMC Place; ALLEGANY; *184 B-4; ★ CUMB; mail Cumberland z 21502; pop. incl. with Cumberland (Inc. Place)
Southdown Shores; RMC Place; ANNE ARUNDEL; *185 F-14; ★ ANPLS; mail Edgewater z 21037; ● 800
Southeast; RMC Place; BALTIMORE (Independent City); *185 D-14; ★ BAL; mail Baltimore z 21281; pop. incl. with Baltimore (Independent City)
Southern Garden Apartments; RMC Place; PRINCE GEORGE'S; ★ WASH; mail Washington z 20032
South Fort Foote Village; RMC Place; PRINCE GEORGE'S; *185 G-12; ★ WASH; mail Fort Washington z 20744
South Gate; CDP-Census Area Only; ANNE ARUNDEL; 185 D-13; ★ BAL; mail Glen Burnie z 21061, Millersville z 21108; Ⓟ 27,564; Ⓒ 28,672; ◆ 30,318
South Haven; RMC Place; ANNE ARUNDEL; *185 E-14; ★ ANPLS; mail Annapolis z 21401
South Kensington; CDP-Census Area Only; MONTGOMERY; *185 E-11; ★ WASH; mail Kensington z 20895; Ⓟ 8,777; Ⓒ 7,887
Southland Hills; RMC Place; BALTIMORE; *185 C-13; ★ BAL; mail Towson z 21204
South Laurel; CDP-Census Area Only; PRINCE GEORGE'S; *185 E-12; ★ WASH; mail Laurel z 20708; Ⓟ 18,591; Ⓒ 20,479; ◆ 20,541
South Lawn; RMC Place; PRINCE GEORGE'S; *185 F-12; ★ WASH; mail Oxon Hill z 20745
South Layhill (Layhill South); RMC Place; MONTGOMERY; *185 E-12; ★ WASH; mail Silver Spring z 20906
South Ocean Pines; RMC Place; WORCESTER; *185 I-20; elev. 5ft./2m.; mail Berlin z 21811; ● 50
South Piscataway; RMC Place; PRINCE GEORGE'S; *185 G-12; ★ WASH; mail Waldorf z 20601; ● 300
South River Park; RMC Place; ANNE ARUNDEL; 185 F-14; ★ ANPLS; mail Edgewater z 21037; ● 550
South Salisbury; RMC Place; WICOMICO; ★ SLSB; mail Salisbury z 21801; pop. incl. with Salisbury (Inc. Place)
South Tantallon; RMC Place; PRINCE GEORGE'S; *185 G-12; ★ WASH; mail Fort Washington z 20744
Southview; RMC Place; PRINCE GEORGE'S; 1 mi. N of Glassmanor; ★ WASH; mail Oxon Hill z 20745
South Woodside Park; RMC Place; MONTGOMERY; *185 E-12; ★ WASH; mail Silver Spring z 20910
Sparks (Sparks Glencoe); RMC Place; BALTIMORE; *185 B-13; elev. 400ft./122m.; 🅿; ★ BAL; z 21152; ● 670
Sparks Glencoe; BALTIMORE; see Sparks (RMC Place)
Sparrows Point; RMC Place; BALTIMORE; *185 D-14; elev. 40ft./12m.; 🅿; ★ BAL; z 21219
Spaulding Heights; RMC Place; PRINCE GEORGE'S; *185 F-12; elev. 250ft./76m.; ★ WASH; mail District Heights z 20747; ● 380
Spence; RMC Place; WORCESTER; *185 J-19; elev. 25ft./8m.; mail Snow Hill z 21863
Spencerville; RMC Place; MONTGOMERY; 185 E-12; elev. 500ft./152m.; 🅿; ★ WASH; z 20868; ● 2,850
Spickler; RMC Place; WASHINGTON; *184 A-8; elev. 500ft./152m.; ★ HAG; mail Clear Spring z 21722; ● 50
Spielman; RMC Place; WASHINGTON; *184 B-8; ★ HAG; mail Fairplay z 21733; ● 50
Spoolsville; RMC Place; FREDERICK; *184 C-9; elev. 421ft./128m.; ★ WASH; mail Middletown z 21769; rural
Springbrook; RMC Place; BALTIMORE; *185 C-13; ★ BAL; mail Randallstown z 21133
Springbrook; RMC Place; MONTGOMERY; 249 C-7; ★ WASH; mail Silver Spring z 20904; ● 1,100
Springbrook Forest; RMC Place; MONTGOMERY; *185 E-12; ★ WASH; mail Silver Spring z 20902; ● 1,000
Springbrook Manor; RMC Place; MONTGOMERY; *185 E-12; ★ WASH; mail Silver Spring z 20904
Springbrook Village; RMC Place; MONTGOMERY; *185 E-12; ★ WASH; mail Silver Spring z 20904
Springdale; RMC Place; BALTIMORE; *185 B-13; ★ BAL; mail Cockeysville z 21030; ● 3,850
Springdale; CDP-Census Area Only; PRINCE GEORGE'S; *185 F-12; 🅿; ★ WASH; z 20774 & mail Lanham z 20706; Ⓒ 2,645
Springdale Gardens; RMC Place; PRINCE GEORGE'S; *185 F-12; ★ WASH; mail Lanham z 20706; ● 2,200
Springfield; RMC Place; MONTGOMERY; *185 E-11; ★ WASH; mail Bethesda z 20814
Spring Gap; RMC Place; ALLEGANY; 184 B-4; 🅿; z 21560; ● 450
Spring Garden Estates; RMC Place; FREDERICK; *184 B-10; ★ WASH; mail Walkersville z 21793; ● 2,300
Spring Grove; RMC Place; PRINCE GEORGE'S; *185 G-12; elev. 150ft./46m.; ★ WASH; mail Accokeek z 20607; ● 60
Spring Grove; RMC Place; WICOMICO; *185 H-17; mail Mardela Springs z 21837; ● 50
Spring Hill Acres; RMC Place; WICOMICO; *185 I-18; elev. 38ft./12m.; ★ SLSB; mail Salisbury z 21801; ● 220
Springhill Lake; RMC Place; PRINCE GEORGE'S; *185 E-12; ★ WASH; mail Greenbelt z 20770; pop. incl. with Greenbelt (Inc. Place)
Springlake; RMC Place; MONTGOMERY; *185 E-11; ★ WASH; mail Bethesda z 20817
Spring Meadow; RMC Place; HARFORD; *185 B-14; ★ BAL; mail Jarrettsville z 21084; ● 200
Spring Mills; RMC Place; CARROLL; *185 B-12; ★ BAL; mail Westminster z 21157; rural
Spring Valley; RMC Place; WASHINGTON; ★ HAG; mail Hagerstown z 21740
Squires Woods; RMC Place; PRINCE GEORGE'S; *185 F-12; ★ WASH; mail Fort Washington z 20744
Stablersville; RMC Place; BALTIMORE; *185 A-13; ★ BAL; mail White Hall z 21161; rural
Stafford; RMC Place; HARFORD; *185 B-15; ★ BAL; mail Havre de Grace z 21078; rural
Stanbrook; RMC Place; BALTIMORE; *185 D-14; ★ BAL; mail Dundalk z 21222
Stansbury Estates; RMC Place; BALTIMORE; *185 C-14; ★ BAL; mail Middle River z 21220
Stansbury Manor; RMC Place; BALTIMORE; *185 C-14; ★ BAL; mail Middle River z 21220
Staples Corners; RMC Place; ANNE ARUNDEL; *185 E-13; elev. 158ft./48m.; ★ BAL; mail Gambrills z 21054
Starkey Corner (Starkeys Corner); RMC Place; QUEEN ANNE'S; *185 D-16; mail Church Hill z 21623

Entries in **UPPERCASE** are counties.
Entries in **bold** have populations of 2,500 or more.
Names in parentheses are alternate names.
Inc. Place — Incorporated Place
RMC Place — Rand McNally Designated Place
CDP — Census Designated Place
MCD — Minor Civil Division
⊡ County Seat
▲ Minor Civil Division
elev. Elevation
🅿 Post Office
🅷 Hospital
🅲 College
■ Principal Business Center
★ Ranally Metro Area (RMA) Abbreviation
z Zip Code(s)
Ⓟ Previous Census Population
Ⓡ Revised Census Population
Ⓐ Annexation Population
● Rand McNally Population Estimate
Ⓒ Final Census Population
Ⓢ Special Census Population
◆ Estimated Population

For additional definitions see Glossary, Volume 1, and Introduction, Volume 2.

Starkeys Corner; QUEEN ANNE'S; see Starkey Corner (RMC Place)
Starr; RMC Place; QUEEN ANNE'S; 185 E-16; elev. 79ft./24m.; mail Centreville z 21617; ● 30
Stemmer's Run; RMC Place; BALTIMORE; *185 C-14; ★ BAL; mail Middle River z 21220
Stepney; RMC Place; HARFORD; 185 B-15; ★ BAL; mail Aberdeen z 21001; ● 350
Steuart Level; RMC Place; ANNE ARUNDEL; *185 F-14; ★ ANPLS; mail Edgewater z 21037
Stevenson; RMC Place; BALTIMORE; 184 G-3; elev. 320ft./98m.; 🅿 🅲 3,123; ★ BAL; z 21153; ● 750
Stevensville; CDP; QUEEN ANNE'S; 185 E-15; elev. 18ft./5m.; 🅿; ★ ANPLS; z 21666; Ⓟ 1,862; Ⓒ 5,880
Stevensville South; RMC Place; QUEEN ANNE'S; *185 E-15; elev. 9ft./3m.; ★ ANPLS; mail Stevensville z 21666; Ⓟ 1,751
Stewartown; RMC Place; MONTGOMERY; *185 D-11; elev. 446ft./136m.; ★ WASH; mail Gaithersburg z 20879; ● 3,850
Stillmeadows; RMC Place; ANNE ARUNDEL; *185 E-13; ★ BAL; mail Severn z 21144
Still Pond; RMC Place; KENT; 185 C-16; elev. 60ft./18m.; 🅿; z 21667; ● 400
Stockton; CDP; WORCESTER; 185 K-19; elev. 34ft./10m.; 🅿; z 21864; Ⓒ 143
Stonecrest Hill; RMC Place; HOWARD; 184 K-1; elev. 400ft./122m.; ★ BAL; mail Ellicott City z 21043; ● 1,250
Stonegate; RMC Place; MONTGOMERY; *185 E-12; ★ WASH; mail Silver Spring z 20905; pop. incl. with Blacksburg (Inc. Place)
Stone Haven; RMC Place; ANNE ARUNDEL; *185 D-14; ★ BAL; mail Glen Burnie z 21060; ● 250
Stoneleigh; RMC Place; BALTIMORE; *185 C-13; ★ BAL; mail Baltimore z 21212
Stoneybrook Estates; RMC Place; MONTGOMERY; ★ WASH; mail Silver Spring z 20906
Stony Beach; RMC Place; ANNE ARUNDEL; *185 D-14; ★ BAL; mail Curtis Bay z 21226
Stony Run; RMC Place; ANNE ARUNDEL; *185 D-13; ★ BAL; mail Hanover z 21076; ● 110
Stratford; RMC Place; BALTIMORE; *185 C-13; ★ BAL; mail Lutherville Timonium z 21093
Strathmore At Bel Pre; RMC Place; MONTGOMERY; *185 E-11; ★ WASH; mail Silver Spring z 20906; ● 5,600
Strathmore Estates; RMC Place; MONTGOMERY; *185 E-11; ★ WASH; mail Silver Spring z 20906
Stratton Woods; RMC Place; MONTGOMERY; *185 E-11; ★ WASH; mail Bethesda z 20817
Strawberry Hills Estates; RMC Place; CHARLES; *185 G-11; ★ WASH; mail Bryans Road z 20616; ● 600
Strawbridge Estates; RMC Place; CARROLL; *185 C-12; ★ BAL; mail Sykesville z 21784; ● 1,350
Strawleigh; RMC Place; FREDERICK; *184 C-9; ★ WASH; mail Frederick z 21702
Street; RMC Place; HARFORD; 185 A-14; elev. 520ft./158m.; 🅿; ★ BAL; z 21154; ● 900
Stronghold; RMC Place; FREDERICK; *184 D-10; ★ WASH; mail Dickerson z 20842; rural
Suburban Acres; RMC Place; WICOMICO; *185 I-18; ★ SLSB; mail Salisbury z 21804; ● 390
Suburban Estates; PRINCE GEORGE'S; see Dorchester Estates (RMC Place)
Suburbia; RMC Place; ANNE ARUNDEL; *185 D-14; ★ BAL; mail Glen Burnie z 21060
Sudbrook Park; RMC Place; BALTIMORE; *185 C-13; ★ BAL; mail Baltimore z 21202; ● 2,700
Sudlersville; Inc. Place; QUEEN ANNE'S; 185 D-17; elev. 67ft./20m.; 🅿; z 21668; Ⓟ 428; Ⓒ 391
Sugarland; RMC Place; MONTGOMERY; *184 E-10; ★ WASH; mail Poolesville z 20837; rural
Sugarloaf Estates; RMC Place; FREDERICK; *184 C-10; ★ WASH; mail Adamstown z 21710; ● 170
Suitland; RMC Place; PRINCE GEORGE'S; 185 F-12; elev. 290ft./88m.; 🅿; ★ WASH; z 20746, z 20752; ● 26,750
Suitland-Silver Hill; CDP-Census Area Only; PRINCE GEORGE'S; *185 F-12; ★ WASH; mail Suitland z 20746; Ⓟ 35,111; Ⓒ 33,515; ◆ 33,612
Sullivan Heights; RMC Place; CARROLL; *185 B-12; ★ BAL; mail Westminster z 21157; ● 500
Summerhill; RMC Place; MONTGOMERY; ★ WASH; mail Poolesville z 20837; pop. incl. with Poolesville (Inc. Place)
Summerhill Trailer Park; RMC Place; ANNE ARUNDEL; *185 C-14; ★ BAL; mail Crownsville z 21032; pop. incl. with Baltimore (Independent City)
Summit Farms; RMC Place; BALTIMORE; *185 C-14; ★ BAL; mail Rosedale z 21237
Summit Park; RMC Place; BALTIMORE; *185 C-13; ★ BAL; mail Baltimore z 21209; ● 2,900
Sumner; RMC Place; MONTGOMERY; *185 E-11; ★ WASH; mail Bethesda z 20816
Sunair; RMC Place; WICOMICO; ★ SLSB; mail Salisbury z 21801; pop. incl. with Salisbury (Inc. Place)
Sunderland; RMC Place; CALVERT; 185 G-14; elev. 140ft./43m.; 🅿; ★ WASH; z 20689; ● 600
Sunny Acres; RMC Place; PRINCE GEORGE'S; *185 F-12; ★ WASH; mail District Heights z 20747
Sunnybrook; RMC Place; BALTIMORE; 185 B-14; ★ BAL; mail Phoenix z 21131; ● 980
Sunnybrook Hills; RMC Place; BALTIMORE; *185 B-14; ★ BAL; mail Phoenix z 21131
Sunny Isle of Kent; RMC Place; QUEEN ANNE'S; *185 F-15; ★ ANPLS; mail Stevensville z 21666; ● 230
Sunrise; RMC Place; PRINCE GEORGE'S; *185 F-12; ★ WASH; mail Fort Washington z 20744
Sunrise Beach; RMC Place; ANNE ARUNDEL; *185 E-14; ★ WASH; mail Crownsville z 21032
Sunset Acres; RMC Place; WASHINGTON; *184 A-9; ★ HAG; mail Hagerstown z 21740
Sunset Beach; RMC Place; ANNE ARUNDEL; *185 D-14; ★ BAL; mail Pasadena z 21122; ● 1,150
Sunset Heights; RMC Place; WICOMICO; *185 I-18; ★ SLSB; mail Salisbury z 21801
Sunset Hills; RMC Place; FREDERICK; *184 C-10; ★ WASH; mail Frederick z 21702
Sunset Knoll; RMC Place; ANNE ARUNDEL; ★ BAL; mail Pasadena z 21122
Sunshine; RMC Place; MONTGOMERY; 185 D-11; ★ WASH; mail Brookeville z 20833; ● 100
Sunshine Acres; RMC Place; CALVERT; *185 G-13; ★ WASH; mail Huntingtown z 20639; ● 80
Sun Valley; RMC Place; ANNE ARUNDEL; *185 D-14; ★ BAL; mail Glen Burnie z 21060
Surratt Gardens; RMC Place; PRINCE GEORGE'S; *185 G-12; ★ WASH; mail Clinton z 20735
Susquehanna Hills; RMC Place; HARFORD; *185 B-16; mail Havre de Grace z 21078; ● 230
Sussex Square; RMC Place; ANNE ARUNDEL; *185 D-13; ★ BAL; mail Millersville z 21108
Sutton Acres; RMC Place; CHARLES; *185 H-12; ★ WASH; mail Port Tobacco z 20677; ● 50
Swallow Falls; RMC Place; GARRETT; *184 B-1; mail Oakland z 21550; ● 30
Swan Creek; RMC Place; HARFORD; *185 B-16; mail Havre de Grace z 21078; pop. incl. with Aberdeen (Inc. Place)
Swan Point (Millers Island); RMC Place; BALTIMORE; 185 D-14; 🅿; ★ BAL; z 20645 & mail Sparrows Point z 21219; ● 280
Swanton; RMC Place; GARRETT; 184 C-2; elev. 2,296ft./700m.; 🅿; z 21561; ● 300
Sweet Air Manor; RMC Place; BALTIMORE; 185 B-14; elev. 619ft./189m.; ★ BAL; mail Baldwin z 21013; ● 450
Sweetser Heights; RMC Place; ANNE ARUNDEL; *185 D-13; ★ BAL; mail Linthicum Heights z 21090
Sycamore Acres; RMC Place; MONTGOMERY; *185 E-11; ★ WASH; mail Rockville z 20853
Sycamore Heights; RMC Place; WASHINGTON; *184 B-9; ★ HAG; mail Hagerstown z 21742; ● 250
Sykesville; Inc. Place; CARROLL; 185 C-12; elev. 541ft./165m.; 🅿 🅷; ★ BAL; z 21784; Ⓟ 2,303; Ⓒ 4,197
Sylmar; RMC Place; CECIL; *185 A-16; elev. 489ft./149m.; ★ PHIL-; mail Rising Sun z 21911; ● 130
Sylvan Grove; RMC Place; WASHINGTON; *184 A-8; elev. 500ft./152m.; ★ HAG; mail Hagerstown z 21740; ● 220
Sylvan View; RMC Place; ANNE ARUNDEL; *185 E-14; ★ BAL; mail Pasadena z 21122

T

Table Rock; RMC Place; GARRETT; *184 C-1; elev. 3,073ft./937m.; mail Gormania z 26720; rural
Takoma Park; Inc. Place; MONTGOMERY; 249 E-7; 🅿 🅷 🅲 1,092; ★ WASH; z 20901, z 20912-13 & mail Silver Spring z 20903; Ⓟ 16,700; Ⓒ 17,299
TALBOT; 185 F-16; Ⓟ 30,549; Ⓒ 33,812; ◆ 36,305
Tall Timbers; RMC Place; ST. MARY'S; 185 J-14; elev. 10ft./3m.; 🅿; z 20690; ● 400
Tammany Manor; RMC Place; WASHINGTON; *184 B-8; elev. 500ft./152m.; ★ HAG; mail Williamsport z 21795; ● 940
Tanager Forest; RMC Place; ANNE ARUNDEL; *185 E-13; ★ WASH; mail Millersville z 21108; ● 250
Taneytown; Inc. Place; CARROLL; 185 A-11; elev. 524ft./160m.; 🅿; z 21787; Ⓟ 3,695; Ⓒ 5,128
Tanglewood; RMC Place; ANNE ARUNDEL; *185 E-14; ★ ANPLS; mail Annapolis z 21401; ● 60
Tanglewood; RMC Place; CALVERT; *185 H-14; elev. 100ft./30m.; ★ WASH; mail Huntingtown z 20639; rural
Tannery; ALLEGANY; see Gilmore (RMC Place)
Tantallon; RMC Place; PRINCE GEORGE'S; *185 G-12; ★ WASH; mail Fort Washington z 20744; ● 4,400
Tantallon North; RMC Place; PRINCE GEORGE'S; *185 G-12; ★ WASH; mail Fort Washington z 20744; ● 1,970
Tantallon on the Potomac; RMC Place; PRINCE GEORGE'S; *185 G-12; ★ WASH; mail Fort Washington z 20744
Tantallon Square; RMC Place; PRINCE GEORGE'S; *185 G-12; ★ WASH; mail Fort Washington z 20744
Tanterra (Lakewood at Tanterra); RMC Place; MONTGOMERY; *185 D-11; ★ WASH; mail Brookeville z 20833
Tanyard; RMC Place; CAROLINE; *185 G-16; mail Preston z 21655
Tarquin Village; RMC Place; PRINCE GEORGE'S; *185 F-12; ★ WASH; mail Clinton z 20735; ● 680
Taylor Mill Village; RMC Place; WICOMICO; *185 I-18; ★ SLSB; mail Salisbury z 21801
Taylors Island; RMC Place; DORCHESTER; 185 H-15; elev. 3ft./1m.; 🅿; z 21669; ● 400
Taylorsville; RMC Place; CARROLL; 185 C-11; elev. 803ft./245m.; ★ BAL; mail Mount Airy z 21771, New Windsor z 21776, Westminster z 21157; ● 150
Taylorville; RMC Place; WORCESTER; 185 I-20; mail Berlin z 21811; ● 30
Temple Heights; RMC Place; PRINCE GEORGE'S; *185 F-12; ★ WASH; mail Temple Hills z 20748; ● 2,900
Temple Hills; CDP; PRINCE GEORGE'S; 249 H-8; 🅿; ★ WASH; z 20748, z 20757 & mail Andrews Air Force Base z 20762, Suitland z 20752; Ⓟ 6,865; Ⓒ 7,792
Temple Hills Park; RMC Place; PRINCE GEORGE'S; *185 F-12; ★ WASH; mail Temple Hills z 20748; ● 2,700
Templeton Estates; RMC Place; PRINCE GEORGE'S; *185 E-12; ★ WASH; mail Riverdale z 20737
Templeton Manor; RMC Place; PRINCE GEORGE'S; *185 E-12; ★ WASH; mail Riverdale z 20737; ● 2,540
Templeville; Inc. Place; CAROLINE, QUEEN ANNE'S; 185 D-17; elev. 74ft./23m.; 🅿; z 21670; Ⓟ 66; Ⓒ 80
Temple Woods; RMC Place; PRINCE GEORGE'S; *185 G-12; ★ WASH; mail Fort Washington z 20744
Terrace Gardens; RMC Place; ANNE ARUNDEL; *185 E-14; ★ BAL; mail Arnold z 21012
Terrace View Estates; RMC Place; ANNE ARUNDEL; *185 D-13; ★ BAL; mail Brooklyn z 21225
Texas; RMC Place; BALTIMORE; *185 C-13; elev. 330ft./101m.; ★ BAL; mail Cockeysville z 21030
Thayerville; RMC Place; GARRETT; *184 B-1; elev. 2,500ft./762m.; mail Oakland z 21550; ● 50
The Colony; RMC Place; MONTGOMERY; *184 D-10; ★ WASH; mail Germantown z 20874
The Crest of Wickford; MONTGOMERY; see Wickford (RMC Place)
The Downs; RMC Place; ANNE ARUNDEL; *185 E-14; ★ ANPLS; mail Annapolis z 21401; ● 90
The Glen (Glen); RMC Place; MONTGOMERY; *185 E-11; ★ WASH; mail Potomac z 20854
The Hamlet; RMC Place; MONTGOMERY; *185 E-11; ★ WASH; mail Chevy Chase z 20815
The Highlands; RMC Place; ANNE ARUNDEL; *185 D-13; ★ BAL; mail Glen Burnie z 21061
The Lakes; RMC Place; BALTIMORE; *185 B-13; ★ BAL; mail Cockeysville z 21030; ● 9,000
The Meadows; RMC Place; CALVERT; *185 G-13; ★ WASH; mail Owings z 20736; ● 100
The Oaks; RMC Place; CALVERT; *185 H-13; ★ WASH; mail Huntingtown z 20639; ● 180
The Oaks; RMC Place; HOWARD; ★ BAL; mail Ellicott City z 21043
Theodore; RMC Place; CECIL; *185 A-16; elev. 414ft./126m.; ★ PHIL-; mail Rising Sun z 21911; ● 70
The Orchards; RMC Place; HOWARD; *185 C-12; ★ BAL; mail Ellicott City z 21043
The Pines; RMC Place; PRINCE GEORGE'S; *185 F-12; ★ WASH; mail Upper Marlboro z 20774
The Points; RMC Place; MONTGOMERY; *185 D-11; ★ WASH; mail Gaithersburg z 20879
Thomas; RMC Place; DORCHESTER; *185 H-15; mail Cambridge z 21613
Thomas Choice; RMC Place; MONTGOMERY; *185 D-11; ★ WASH; mail Gaithersburg z 20879
Thomas Run; RMC Place; HARFORD; *185 B-15; elev. 202ft./62m.; ★ BAL; mail Bel Air z 21015; ● 100
Thomas Town; RMC Place; CAROLINE; *185 F-17; mail Denton z 21629; ● 50
Thompson Corner; RMC Place; ST. MARY'S; *185 H-13; ★ WASH; mail Mechanicsville z 20659; rural
Thompsontown; RMC Place; DORCHESTER; *185 H-17; mail East New Market z 21631; ● 100
Thomson Estates; RMC Place; CECIL; *185 B-17; ★ PHIL-; mail Elkton z 21921; ● 900
Thornleigh; RMC Place; BALTIMORE; *185 C-13; ★ BAL; mail Riderwood z 21139
Thornwood Knoll; RMC Place; PRINCE GEORGE'S; *185 G-12; ★ WASH; mail Fort Washington z 20744
Thorwood Park; RMC Place; BALTIMORE; *185 C-14; ★ BAL; mail Parkville z 21234
Thrift; RMC Place; PRINCE GEORGE'S; *185 G-12; elev. 200ft./61m.; ★ WASH; mail Clinton z 20735; ● 30
Thunder Hill; RMC Place; HOWARD; *185 D-12; ★ BAL; mail Columbia z 21045
Thurmont; Inc. Place; FREDERICK; 184 B-10; elev. 523ft./159m.; 🅿; z 21788; Ⓟ 3,398; Ⓒ 5,588
Thurston; RMC Place; FREDERICK; *184 D-10; ★ WASH; mail Dickerson z 20842; rural
Tilden Woods; RMC Place; MONTGOMERY; *185 E-11; ★ WASH; mail Rockville z 20852; ● 900
Tilghman; RMC Place; TALBOT; 185 G-15; elev. 8ft./2m.; 🅿; z 21671; ● 1,000
Tilghman Island; CDP-Census Area Only; TALBOT; *185 G-15; Ⓒ 854
Tilghmanton; RMC Place; WASHINGTON; 184 B-8; ★ HAG; mail Boonsboro z 21713; ● 170
Timber Grove; RMC Place; BALTIMORE; *185 C-13; ★ BAL; mail Owings Mills z 21117
Timber Ridge; RMC Place; ANNE ARUNDEL; *185 J-13; mail Hanover z 21076
Timber Ridge; RMC Place; CARROLL; *185 B-12; ★ BAL; mail Westminster z 21157
Timberview; RMC Place; HOWARD; *185 D-13; ★ BAL; mail Elkridge z 21075
Timonium; RMC Place; BALTIMORE; *185 C-13; 🅿; ★ BAL; z 21093-94
Tintop Hill; RMC Place; ST. MARY'S; *185 I-13; ★ WASH; mail Leonardtown z 20650; ● 110
Tippett; RMC Place; PRINCE GEORGE'S; *185 G-12; elev. 247ft./75m.; ★ WASH; mail Clinton z 20735; ● 30
Tobytown; RMC Place; MONTGOMERY; *184 E-10; elev. 300ft./91m.; ★ WASH; mail Potomac z 20854; ● 210
Todd Village; RMC Place; CARROLL; *185 B-12; ★ BAL; mail Finksburg z 21048; ● 300
Toddville; RMC Place; DORCHESTER; 185 I-16; elev. 2ft./1m.; 🅿; z 21672; ● 250
Tolchester Beach; RMC Place; KENT; 185 D-15; mail Chestertown z 21620; ● 150
Tollgate; RMC Place; BALTIMORE; ★ BAL; mail Owings Mills z 21117
Tompkinsville; RMC Place; CHARLES; 185 I-12; mail Newburg z 20664; ● 150
Tonytank; RMC Place; WICOMICO; *185 I-18; ★ SLSB; mail Salisbury z 21801; ● 160
Tower Acres; RMC Place; HOWARD; *185 D-12; ★ WASH; mail Laurel z 20723
Tower Garden on the Bay; RMC Place; QUEEN ANNE'S; *185 F-15; ★ ANPLS; mail Stevensville z 21666; ● 700
Town Creek; RMC Place; ALLEGANY; *184 B-5; mail Paw Paw z 25434; rural
Town Creek Estates; RMC Place; ST. MARY'S; *185 I-14; mail California z 20619; ● 790
Town Creek Manor; RMC Place; ST. MARY'S; *185 I-14; ★ WASH; mail Lexington Park z 20653; ● 980
Town Crest; RMC Place; MONTGOMERY; *185 D-12; ★ WASH; mail Derwood z 20855
Towne and Country North; RMC Place; BALTIMORE; *185 C-13; ★ BAL; mail Cockeysville z 21030; pop. incl. with Baltimore (Independent City)
Towne Center; RMC Place; PRINCE GEORGE'S; *185 E-12; ★ WASH; mail Laurel z 20708
Town Point; RMC Place; CECIL; *185 B-17; ★ PHIL-; mail Chesapeake City z 21915; ● 30
Townshend; RMC Place; PRINCE GEORGE'S; *185 G-12; ★ WASH; mail Brandywine z 20613; ● 300
Towson; CDP; ⊡ BALTIMORE; 185 C-13; elev. 465ft./142m.; 🅿 🅷 🅲 2,310; ★ BAL; z 21204, z 21252, z 21284-86; Ⓟ 49,445; Ⓒ 51,793; ◆ 54,374
Towson Estates; RMC Place; BALTIMORE; *185 C-14; ★ BAL; mail Towson z 21204
Towson Park; RMC Place; BALTIMORE; *185 C-13; ★ BAL; mail Towson z 21286
Tracys Landing; RMC Place; ANNE ARUNDEL; 185 F-14; elev. 100ft./30m.; 🅿; ★ WASH; z 20779; ● 440
Trappe; RMC Place; ST. MARY'S; mail Dameron z 20628; rural
Trappe; Inc. Place; TALBOT; 185 G-16; elev. 56ft./17m.; 🅿; z 21673; Ⓟ 974; Ⓒ 1,146
Trappe; RMC Place; WORCESTER; *185 I-20; mail Berlin z 21811; rural
Trappe Station; RMC Place; TALBOT; *185 G-16; mail Oxford z 21654; rural
Travilah; CDP; MONTGOMERY; *185 E-11; elev. 356ft./109m.; ★ WASH; mail Rockville z 20850; Ⓒ 7,442
Treetops; RMC Place; ANNE ARUNDEL; *185 E-14; ★ BAL; mail Pasadena z 21122
Trego; WASHINGTON; see Rohrersville Station (RMC Place)
Trengall Acres; RMC Place; WASHINGTON; *184 A-9; ★ HAG; mail Hagerstown z 21740
Trent Hall; RMC Place; ST. MARY'S; *185 H-13; ★ WASH; mail Mechanicsville z 20659; rural
Trenton; RMC Place; BALTIMORE; *185 B-13; ★ BAL; mail Upperco z 21155; ● 120
Trescher Heights; RMC Place; ALLEGANY; *184 B-4; ★ CUMB; mail Cumberland z 21502; ● 150
Triple Lakes; RMC Place; ALLEGANY; *184 B-3; ★ CUMB; mail Cumberland z 21502; ● 270
Troutville; RMC Place; FREDERICK; *184 B-10; mail Woodsboro z 21798; rural
Truman Heights; RMC Place; PRINCE GEORGE'S; *185 F-12; ★ WASH; mail Temple Hills z 20748
Truxton Heights; RMC Place; ANNE ARUNDEL; *185 E-14; ★ ANPLS; pop. incl. with Annapolis (Inc. Place)
Tuckahoe Springs; RMC Place; CAROLINE; *185 F-17; elev. 20ft./6m.; mail Denton z 21629; ● 50
Tulip Hill; RMC Place; FREDERICK; *184 C-10; ★ WASH; mail Frederick z 21702; ● 380
Tulip Hill; RMC Place; MONTGOMERY; *185 E-11; ★ WASH; mail Bethesda z 20816
Tunis Mills; RMC Place; TALBOT; 185 F-15; mail Easton z 21601; ● 70
Turkey Neck; RMC Place; GARRETT; *184 B-1; mail Swanton z 21561; summer pop. 200
Turkey Point; RMC Place; ANNE ARUNDEL; *185 F-14; ★ ANPLS; mail Edgewater z 21037; ● 260
Turkey Point; RMC Place; BALTIMORE; *185 D-14; ★ BAL; mail Essex z 21221
Turnbull Estates; RMC Place; ANNE ARUNDEL; *185 F-14; ★ ANPLS; mail Edgewater z 21037
Turners Station; RMC Place; BALTIMORE; *185 D-14; ★ BAL; mail Dundalk z 21222
Tuscarora; RMC Place; FREDERICK; 184 D-10; elev. 280ft./85m.; 🅿; ★ WASH; z 21790; ● 150
Tuxedo; RMC Place; PRINCE GEORGE'S; *185 F-12; ★ WASH; mail Hyattsville z 20781, z 20785; pop. incl. with Cheverly (Inc. Place)
Tuxedo Colony; RMC Place; PRINCE GEORGE'S; *185 F-12; ★ WASH; mail Hyattsville z 20785
Twinbrook; RMC Place; MONTGOMERY; *185 E-11; ★ WASH; mail Rockville z 20848, z 20851; pop. incl. with Rockville (Inc. Place)
Twinbrook Estates; RMC Place; CHARLES; *185 G-12; ★ WASH; mail Waldorf z 20603; ● 110
Twin Brook Forest; RMC Place; MONTGOMERY; *185 E-11; ★ WASH; mail Rockville z 20851; pop. incl. with Rockville (Inc. Place)
Twinbrook Park; RMC Place; MONTGOMERY; ★ WASH; mail Rockville z 20851; pop. incl. with Rockville (Inc. Place)
Twin Harbors; RMC Place; ANNE ARUNDEL; *185 E-14; ★ BAL; mail Arnold z 21012; ● 1,800
Twin River Beach; BALTIMORE; see West Twin River Beach (RMC Place)
Two Johns Estates; RMC Place; CAROLINE; *185 F-17; elev. 20ft./6m.; mail Preston z 21655; ● 50
Tyaskin; RMC Place; WICOMICO; 185 I-17; elev. 20ft./6m.; 🅿; z 21865; ● 350
Tydings on the Bay; RMC Place; ANNE ARUNDEL; *185 E-14; ★ BAL; mail Annapolis z 21401; ● 90
Tyler Heights; RMC Place; ANNE ARUNDEL; *185 E-14; ★ ANPLS; pop. incl. with Annapolis (Inc. Place)
Tylerton; RMC Place; SOMERSET; 185 K-16; elev. 3ft./1m.; 🅿; z 21866; ● 150
Tyrone; RMC Place; CARROLL; *185 B-11; mail Westminster z 21158; ● 60

U

Ulmsted Acres; RMC Place; ANNE ARUNDEL; *185 E-14; ★ BAL; mail Arnold z 21012
Ulmsted Estate; RMC Place; ANNE ARUNDEL; *185 E-14; ★ BAL; mail Arnold z 21012
Ulmsted Gardens; RMC Place; ANNE ARUNDEL; *185 E-16; mail Arnold z 21012
Ulmsted Point; RMC Place; ANNE ARUNDEL; *185 E-14; ★ BAL; mail Arnold z 21012
Union Bridge; Inc. Place; CARROLL; 185 B-11; elev. 402ft./123m.; 🅿; z 21791; Ⓟ 910; Ⓒ 989
Union Corner; RMC Place; CAROLINE; mail Goldsboro z 21636; rural
Union Mills; RMC Place; CARROLL; 185 A-12; mail Westminster z 21158; ● 150
Uniontown; RMC Place; CARROLL; 185 B-11; elev. 450ft./137m.; mail Westminster z 21158; ● 350
Unionville; RMC Place; FREDERICK; 185 C-11; 🅿; ★ WASH; z 21792 & mail Union Bridge z 21791; ● 220
Unionville; RMC Place; TALBOT; 185 F-16; mail Easton z 21601; ● 80
Unionville; RMC Place; WORCESTER; 185 K-18; mail Pocomoke City z 21851; ● 230
United States Naval Academy; ANNE ARUNDEL; see Naval Academy (CDP-Census Area Only)
Unity; RMC Place; MONTGOMERY; 185 D-11; ★ WASH; mail Brookeville z 20833; ● 80
University City; RMC Place; PRINCE GEORGE'S; *185 E-12; ★ WASH; mail Hyattsville z 20783
University Gardens; RMC Place; PRINCE GEORGE'S; *185 E-12; ★ WASH; mail Hyattsville z 20782; ● 2,850
University Hills; RMC Place; PRINCE GEORGE'S; *185 E-12; ★ WASH; mail Hyattsville z 20783; ● 1,650
University Park; Inc. Place; PRINCE GEORGE'S; 249 E-8; 🅿; ★ WASH; z 20782 & mail Hyattsville z 20784; Ⓟ 2,243; Ⓒ 2,318
Upperco (Arcadia); RMC Place; BALTIMORE; 185 B-12; elev. 800ft./244m.; 🅿; ★ BAL; z 21155; ● 700
Upper Crossroads; RMC Place; HARFORD; 185 B-14; elev. 582ft./177m.; ★ BAL; mail Fallston z 21047; ● 300
Upper Fairmount; RMC Place; SOMERSET; 185 J-17; elev. 6ft./2m.; 🅿; z 21867; ● 450
Upper Falls; RMC Place; BALTIMORE; 185 C-14; elev. 242ft./74m.; 🅿; ★ BAL; z 21156; ● 450
Upper Ferry; RMC Place; WICOMICO; *185 I-18; mail Salisbury z 21801; rural
Upper Hill; RMC Place; SOMERSET; 185 J-17; elev. 6ft./2m.; mail Upper Fairmount z 21867; ● 190
Upper Homewood; RMC Place; ALLEGANY; ★ CUMB; mail Cumberland z 21502
Upper Marlboro (Marlboro); Inc. Place; ⊡ PRINCE GEORGE'S; 185 F-13; elev. 39ft./12m.; 🅿; ★ WASH; z 20772-75, z 20792; Ⓟ 745; Ⓒ 648
Urbana; RMC Place; FREDERICK; 184 C-10; elev. 468ft./143m.; 🅿; ★ WASH; z 21704 & mail Frederick z 21701; ● 330
Utica (Utica Mills); RMC Place; FREDERICK; *184 B-10; ★ WASH; mail Thurmont z 21788; ● 70
Utica Mills; FREDERICK; see Utica (RMC Place)

V

Vale; RMC Place; HARFORD; *185 B-14; ★ BAL; mail Bel Air z 21015; ● 300
Vale Summit; RMC Place; ALLEGANY; 184 B-3; ★ CUMB; mail Frostburg z 21532; ● 200
Valley Crest; RMC Place; BALTIMORE; *185 C-13; ★ BAL; mail Lutherville Timonium z 21093
Valley Lee; RMC Place; ST. MARY'S; 185 J-14; elev. 20ft./6m.; 🅿; z 20692; ● 500
Valley Mede; RMC Place; HOWARD; 184 J-1; ★ BAL; mail Ellicott City z 21042; ● 4,700
Valley Stream Estates; RMC Place; MONTGOMERY; *185 E-12; elev. 463ft./141m.; ★ WASH; mail Burtonsville z 20866
Valley View; RMC Place; HOWARD; ★ BAL; mail Ellicott City z 21043
Valley View; RMC Place; PRINCE GEORGE'S; *185 G-12; ★ WASH; mail Fort Washington z 20744
Valleywood; RMC Place; BALTIMORE; *185 C-13; ★ BAL; mail Lutherville Timonium z 21093; ● 3,500
Valleywood; RMC Place; WICOMICO; *185 I-18; ★ SLSB; mail Salisbury z 21801; pop. incl. with Salisbury (Inc. Place)
Van Bibber; RMC Place; HARFORD; 185 C-15; elev. 26ft./8m.; ★ BAL; mail Edgewood z 21040; ● 1,000
Van Bibber Manor; RMC Place; HARFORD; *185 C-15; ★ BAL; mail Edgewood z 21040
Van Lear Manor; RMC Place; WASHINGTON; 185 N-13; ★ HAG; mail Williamsport z 21795; ● 1,050
Vansville; RMC Place; PRINCE GEORGE'S; *185 E-12; elev. 186ft./57m.; ★ WASH; mail Beltsville z 20705
Venice on the Bay; RMC Place; ANNE ARUNDEL; 184 M-7; ★ BAL; mail Pasadena z 21122; ● 300
Venton; RMC Place; SOMERSET; 185 J-17; mail Princess Anne z 21853; ● 150
Vernon (Gemmills); RMC Place; BALTIMORE; *185 B-13; elev. 609ft./186m.; ★ BAL; mail White Hall z 21161; rural
Victor Haven; RMC Place; ANNE ARUNDEL; *185 E-14; ★ ANPLS; pop. incl. with Annapolis (Inc. Place)
Victory Villa; RMC Place; BALTIMORE; *185 C-14; ★ BAL; mail Middle River z 21220
Vienna; Inc. Place; DORCHESTER; 185 H-17; elev. 13ft./4m.; 🅿; z 21869; Ⓟ 264; Ⓒ 280
Viers Mill Village; RMC Place; MONTGOMERY; *185 E-11; elev. 366ft./112m.; ★ WASH; mail Silver Spring z 20906
View More Acres; RMC Place; FREDERICK; *184 C-10; ★ WASH; mail Frederick z 21701; ● 160
Villa Cresta; RMC Place; BALTIMORE; *185 C-14; ★ BAL; mail Parkville z 21234
Village of Vanderway; RMC Place; BALTIMORE; *185 C-14; ★ BAL; mail Parkville z 21234; ● 2,350
Villages of Montpelier (Laurel Walk); RMC Place; PRINCE GEORGE'S; *185 E-12; ★ WASH; mail Laurel z 20708; ● 1,700
Village Square North; PRINCE GEORGE'S; see Deerfield Run (RMC Place)
Villa Heights; RMC Place; PRINCE GEORGE'S; *185 F-12; ★ WASH; mail Hyattsville z 20784
Villa Monticello; RMC Place; HOWARD; *185 C-12; ★ WASH; mail Cooksville z 21723; ● 110
Villa Nova; RMC Place; BALTIMORE; 184 H-2; elev. 395ft./120m.; ★ BAL; mail Gwynn Oak z 21207; ● 940
Villa Toscano; RMC Place; ANNE ARUNDEL; *185 D-14; ★ BAL; mail Pasadena z 21122; ● 470
Villa Verdi; RMC Place; ANNE ARUNDEL; *185 E-13; ★ BAL; mail Gambrills z 21054
Vindex; RMC Place; GARRETT; *184 C-2; elev. 1,700ft./518m.; mail Kitzmiller z 21538; ● 50
Virginia Avenue; RMC Place; ALLEGANY; ★ CUMB; pop. incl. with Cumberland (Inc. Place)

W

Waggaman Heights; RMC Place; PRINCE GEORGE'S; *185 F-12; ★ WASH; mail Temple Hills z 20748; ● 760
Wagners Point; RMC Place; BALTIMORE (Independent City); pop. incl. with Baltimore (Independent City)
Wakefield; RMC Place; BALTIMORE; *185 C-14; ★ BAL; mail Lutherville Timonium z 21093; pop. incl. with Baltimore (Independent City)
Wakefield; RMC Place; CARROLL; *185 B-11; elev. 490ft./149m.; mail New Windsor z 21776; ● 200
Wakefield Meadows; RMC Place; HARFORD; *185 B-15; ★ BAL; mail Bel Air z 21014; ● 1,900
Walbrook; RMC Place; BALTIMORE (Independent City); *185 C-13; ★ BAL; mail Baltimore z 21216; pop. incl. with Baltimore (Independent City)
Waldon Woods; RMC Place; PRINCE GEORGE'S; *185 G-12; ★ WASH; mail Clinton z 20735; ● 2,250
Waldorf; CDP; CHARLES; 185 G-12; elev. 215ft./66m.; 🅿; ★ WASH; z 20601-04; Ⓟ 15,058; Ⓒ 22,312; ◆ 25,987
Walker Hill; RMC Place; PRINCE GEORGE'S; *185 E-12; ★ WASH; mail Laurel z 20707; ● 1,000
Walker Mill; CDP-Census Area Only; PRINCE GEORGE'S; *185 F-12; ★ WASH; mail Capitol Heights z 20743, District Heights z 20747; Ⓟ 10,920; Ⓒ 11,104
Walker Mill Estates; RMC Place; PRINCE GEORGE'S; *185 F-12; ★ WASH; mail Capitol Heights z 20743
Walkersville; Inc. Place; FREDERICK; 184 B-10; elev. 320ft./98m.; 🅿; ★ WASH; z 21793; Ⓟ 4,145; Ⓒ 5,192
Wallington Estates; RMC Place; PRINCE GEORGE'S; *185 F-12; ★ WASH; mail District Heights z 20747; ● 4,900
Wallville; RMC Place; CALVERT; *185 I-14; elev. 102ft./31m.; mail Saint Leonard z 20685
Walnut Hill; RMC Place; MONTGOMERY; *185 D-11; elev. 500ft./152m.; ★ WASH; mail Gaithersburg z 20877; ● 820
Walnut Ridge; RMC Place; CARROLL; ★ BAL; mail Westminster z 21157
Walnut Woods; RMC Place; MONTGOMERY; *185 E-11; ★ WASH; mail Rockville z 20852
Walston; RMC Place; WICOMICO; 185 I-18; ★ SLSB; mail Parsonsburg z 21849, Salisbury z 21804; ● 50
Walter Heights; RMC Place; PRINCE GEORGE'S; *185 F-12; ★ WASH; mail Temple Hills z 20748
Wango; RMC Place; WICOMICO; *185 I-19; mail Salisbury z 21804; rural
Warburton Oaks; RMC Place; PRINCE GEORGE'S; *185 G-12; ★ WASH; mail Fort Washington z 20744
Wardour; RMC Place; ANNE ARUNDEL; *185 E-14; ★ ANPLS; pop. incl. with Annapolis (Inc. Place)
Wards Chapel; RMC Place; BALTIMORE; 185 C-12; ★ BAL; mail Randallstown z 21133; ● 270
Warfield Estates; RMC Place; HOWARD; *185 D-12; ★ WASH; mail Glenwood z 21738; ● 110
Warfieldsburg; RMC Place; CARROLL; *185 B-12; ★ BAL; mail Westminster z 21157
Warington Hills; RMC Place; CHARLES; *185 H-11; ★ WASH; mail Indian Head z 20640; pop. incl. with Indian Head (Inc. Place)
Warlinda; RMC Place; CHARLES; *185 H-12; ★ WASH; mail La Plata z 20646; ● 320
Warren; RMC Place; BALTIMORE; *185 B-13; ★ BAL; mail Cockeysville z 21030
Warwick; RMC Place; CECIL; 185 C-17; elev. 72ft./22m.; 🅿; z 21912; ● 850
WASHINGTON; 184 A-7; Ⓟ 121,393; Ⓒ 131,923; ◆ 147,821
Washington Grove; Inc. Place; MONTGOMERY; 185 D-11; 🅿; ★ WASH; z 20880; Ⓟ 434; Ⓒ 515
Waterbury; RMC Place; ANNE ARUNDEL; *185 E-13; ★ WASH; mail Crownsville z 21032; ● 150
Waterford; PRINCE GEORGE'S; see Fairfield Knolls (RMC Place)
Waterloo; RMC Place; HOWARD; *185 D-13; ★ BAL; mail Elkridge z 21075
Wateroak Point; RMC Place; ANNE ARUNDEL; *185 D-14; ★ BAL; mail Pasadena z 21122; ● 300
Watersville; RMC Place; CARROLL; *185 C-11; elev. 582ft./177m.; ★ WASH; mail Mount Airy z 21771; ● 30
Waterview; RMC Place; WICOMICO; *185 I-17; mail Nanticoke z 21840
Watkins Glen; RMC Place; MONTGOMERY; *185 E-11; ★ WASH; mail Potomac z 20854
Waverly; RMC Place; BALTIMORE (Independent City); *185 C-13; ★ BAL; mail Baltimore z 21218; pop. incl. with Baltimore (Independent City)
Wayside; RMC Place; CHARLES; *185 I-12; mail Newburg z 20664; ● 50
Waysons Corner; RMC Place; ANNE ARUNDEL; *185 F-13; elev. 63ft./19m.; ★ WASH; mail Lothian z 20711; ● 100
Webster; HARFORD; see Webster Village (RMC Place)
Webster Village (Webster); RMC Place; HARFORD; 185 B-15; mail Havre de Grace z 21078; ● 380
Weems Creek; RMC Place; ANNE ARUNDEL; *185 E-14; ★ ANPLS; mail Annapolis z 21401
Weisburg; BALTIMORE; see Wiseburg (RMC Place)
Welcome; RMC Place; CHARLES; 185 H-11; elev. 136ft./41m.; 🅿; z 20693; ● 600
Wellington Estates; RMC Place; HOWARD; *185 D-12; ★ WASH; mail Laurel z 20707; ● 280
Wenona; RMC Place; SOMERSET; 185 J-16; elev. 6ft./2m.; 🅿; z 21821; ● 390
Wesley; RMC Place; DORCHESTER; *185 I-16; mail Crapo z 21626; ● 250
Wesmond; RMC Place; MONTGOMERY; *184 D-10; ★ WASH; mail Poolesville z 20837; pop. incl. with Poolesville (Inc. Place)
West Annapolis; RMC Place; ANNE ARUNDEL; *185 E-14; ★ ANPLS; pop. incl. with Annapolis (Inc. Place)
West Baltimore; RMC Place; BALTIMORE (Independent City); *185 D-13; ★ BAL; mail Halethorpe z 21227; pop. incl. with Baltimore (Independent City)
West Beach; RMC Place; CALVERT; *185 G-14; ★ WASH; mail Chesapeake Beach z 20732; pop. incl. with Chesapeake Beach (Inc. Place)
West Bethesda; RMC Place; MONTGOMERY; *185 E-11; elev. 350ft./107m.; 🅿; ★ WASH; z 20817 & mail Bethesda z 20827
Westboro; RMC Place; MONTGOMERY; *185 E-11; ★ WASH; mail Bethesda z 20814
West Bowie; RMC Place; PRINCE GEORGE'S; *185 E-13; ★ WASH; mail Bowie z 20719; pop. incl. with Bowie (Inc. Place)
Westbury Acres; RMC Place; WICOMICO; *185 I-18; elev. 10ft./3m.; ★ SLSB; mail Salisbury z 21801; ● 50
Westchester; RMC Place; BALTIMORE; *185 D-13; ★ BAL; mail Catonsville z 21228
Westchester; RMC Place; MONTGOMERY; *185 E-11; ★ WASH; mail Silver Spring z 20902
Westchester Estates; RMC Place; PRINCE GEORGE'S; *185 F-12; ★ WASH; mail Temple Hills z 20748
Westchester Park; RMC Place; PRINCE GEORGE'S; ★ WASH; mail College Park z 20740; pop. incl. with College Park (Inc. Place)
West Denton; RMC Place; CAROLINE; 185 F-17; mail Denton z 21629; ● 150
West Edmondale; RMC Place; BALTIMORE; 184 J-3; ★ BAL; mail Baltimore z 21229; ● 3,450
West Elkridge; RMC Place; HOWARD; *185 D-13; ★ BAL; mail Elkridge z 21075
West End; RMC Place; ANNE ARUNDEL; *185 E-14; elev. 79ft./24m.; ★ ANPLS; mail Annapolis z 21401; pop. incl. with Annapolis (Inc. Place)
West End Park; RMC Place; MONTGOMERY; *185 E-11; ★ WASH; mail Rockville z 20850; pop. incl. with Rockville (Inc. Place)
Westerlea; RMC Place; BALTIMORE; *185 D-13; ★ BAL; mail Catonsville z 21228
Westernport; Inc. Place; ALLEGANY; 184 B-3; elev. 1,000ft./305m.; 🅿; ★ CUMB; z 21540, z 21562; Ⓟ 2,454; Ⓒ 2,104
Western Shores Estates; RMC Place; CALVERT; *185 H-14; mail Port Republic z 20676; ● 440
West Friendship; RMC Place; HOWARD; 185 C-12; elev. 480ft./146m.; 🅿; ★ BAL; z 21794; ● 1,200
Westgate; RMC Place; MONTGOMERY; *185 E-11; ★ WASH; mail Bethesda z 20816
West Gate Woods; RMC Place; PRINCE GEORGE'S; ★ WASH; mail Lanham z 20706
West Hills; RMC Place; BALTIMORE; *185 C-13; ★ BAL; mail Gwynn Oak z 21207
West Hills; RMC Place; FREDERICK; *184 C-10; ★ WASH; mail Frederick z 21702
West Hyattsville; RMC Place; PRINCE GEORGE'S; *185 E-12; 🅿; ★ WASH; z 20782 & mail Hyattsville z 20788; pop. incl. with Hyattsville (Inc. Place)
Westlake; RMC Place; WICOMICO; *185 I-18; ★ SLSB; mail Salisbury z 21801; ● 230
West Lanham Estates; RMC Place; PRINCE GEORGE'S; *185 E-12; ★ WASH; mail Hyattsville z 20784; ● 430
West Lanham Hills; RMC Place; PRINCE GEORGE'S; *185 E-12; ★ WASH; mail Hyattsville z 20784; ● 1,700
West Laurel; CDP-Census Area Only; PRINCE GEORGE'S; *185 E-12; elev. 398ft./121m.; ★ WASH; mail Laurel z 20707; Ⓟ 4,151; Ⓒ 4,083
West Laurel Acres; RMC Place; PRINCE GEORGE'S; *185 E-12; ★ WASH; mail Laurel z 20707; ● 550
West Liberty; RMC Place; BALTIMORE; *185 A-14; ★ BAL; mail White Hall z 21161; ● 50
West Magothy Manor; RMC Place; ANNE ARUNDEL; *185 E-14; ★ BAL; mail Arnold z 21012
Westminster; Inc. Place; ⊡ CARROLL; 185 B-12; elev. 717ft./219m.; 🅿 🅷 🅲 3,879; ★ BAL; z 21157-58; Ⓟ 13,068; Ⓒ 16,731
Westminster; RMC Place; MONTGOMERY; *185 E-11; ★ WASH; mail Rockville z 20852
Westminster South; RMC Place; CARROLL; *185 B-12; ★ BAL; mail Westminster z 21157; Ⓟ 4,284
Westmore; RMC Place; MONTGOMERY; *185 E-11; ★ WASH; mail Rockville z 20850; pop. incl. with Rockville (Inc. Place)
Westmoreland Hills; RMC Place; MONTGOMERY; *185 E-11; ★ WASH; mail Bethesda z 20816
West Nottingham; RMC Place; CECIL; *185 A-16; ★ PHIL-; mail Colora z 21917; ● 30
West Ocean City; CDP; WORCESTER; 185 I-20; elev. 12ft./4m.; mail Ocean City z 21842; Ⓟ 1,928; Ⓒ 3,311
Westover; RMC Place; SOMERSET; 185 J-18; elev. 15ft./5m.; 🅿; z 21871, z 21890; ● 800
Westowne; RMC Place; BALTIMORE; *185 D-13; ★ BAL; mail Baltimore z 21229
Westphalia Estates; RMC Place; PRINCE GEORGE'S; *185 F-12; ★ WASH; mail Upper Marlboro z 20772; ● 550
Westphalia Woods; RMC Place; PRINCE GEORGE'S; *185 F-12; ★ WASH; mail Upper Marlboro z 20774; ● 850
West Pocomoke; CDP-Census Area Only; SOMERSET; *185 J-18; Ⓒ 498
Westport; RMC Place; BALTIMORE (Independent City); ★ BAL; pop. incl. with Baltimore (Independent City)
West River (Owensville); RMC Place; ANNE ARUNDEL; *185 F-14; elev. 184ft./56m.; 🅿; ★ WASH; z 20778
West Severna Park; RMC Place; ANNE ARUNDEL; *185 E-14; ★ BAL; mail Severna Park z 21146
West Shady Side; RMC Place; ANNE ARUNDEL; *185 F-14; ★ WASH; mail Shady Side z 20764
West Twin River Beach (Twin River Beach); RMC Place; BALTIMORE; *185 C-15; ★ BAL; mail Middle River z 21220; ● 850
Westview; RMC Place; WICOMICO; *185 I-18; ★ SLSB; mail Salisbury z 21801; ● 100
Westview Park; RMC Place; BALTIMORE; *185 C-13; ★ BAL; mail Catonsville z 21228; ● 7,000
West View Shores; RMC Place; CECIL; *185 C-16; mail Earleville z 21919; ● 250
West Vindex; RMC Place; GARRETT; *184 C-2; mail Kitzmiller z 21538; ● 50
Westwood; RMC Place; PRINCE GEORGE'S; *185 G-13; elev. 186ft./57m.; ★ WASH; mail Brandywine z 20613
Westwood Estates; RMC Place; CHARLES; *185 G-12; ★ WASH; mail Waldorf z 20601
Westwood Estates; RMC Place; PRINCE GEORGE'S; *185 G-12; ★ WASH; mail Cheltenham z 20623; ● 560
Wetipquin; RMC Place; WICOMICO; 185 I-17; mail Quantico z 21856; ● 80
Weverton; RMC Place; WASHINGTON; 184 C-9; ★ WASH; mail Knoxville z 21758; ● 140
Wexford; RMC Place; ANNE ARUNDEL; *185 E-14; elev. 100ft./30m.; ★ BAL; mail Arnold z 21012; ● 930
Whaleysville; WORCESTER; see Whaleyville (CDP)
Whaleyville (Whaleysville); CDP; WORCESTER; 185 I-19; elev. 32ft./10m.; 🅿; z 21872; Ⓒ 124
Wheaton; RMC Place; MONTGOMERY; 185 E-11; elev. 469ft./143m.; 🅿; ★ WASH; z 20902, z 20915 & mail Silver Spring z 20906; ● 134,800
Wheaton Crest; RMC Place; MONTGOMERY; *185 E-11; ★ WASH; mail Silver Spring z 20902
Wheaton Forest; RMC Place; MONTGOMERY; *185 E-12; ★ WASH; mail Silver Spring z 20902
Wheaton-Glenmont; CDP-Census Area Only; MONTGOMERY; *185 E-11; ★ WASH; mail Silver Spring z 20902; Ⓟ 53,720; Ⓒ 57,694; ◆ 61,275
Wheaton Hills; RMC Place; MONTGOMERY; *185 E-11; elev. 365ft./111m.; ★ WASH; mail Silver Spring z 20902
Wheaton Woods; RMC Place; MONTGOMERY; *185 E-11; ★ WASH; mail Rockville z 20853
Whetstone; RMC Place; MONTGOMERY; *185 D-11; ★ WASH; mail Gaithersburg z 20879
Whipporwill Estates; RMC Place; ANNE ARUNDEL; *185 E-14; ★ BAL; mail Pasadena z 21122
Whiskey Bottom; RMC Place; HOWARD; *185 E-12; ★ WASH; mail Laurel z 20723; ● 6,000
Whiteburg (Whitesburg); RMC Place; WORCESTER; *185 J-18; mail Snow Hill z 21863; rural
White Crystal Beach; RMC Place; CECIL; *185 C-16; mail Earleville z 21919; summer pop. 300; ● 130
Whitefield Knolls; RMC Place; PRINCE GEORGE'S; ★ WASH; mail Lanham z 20706
Whitefield Woods; RMC Place; PRINCE GEORGE'S; ★ WASH; mail Lanham z 20706
White Flint Park; RMC Place; MONTGOMERY; ★ WASH; mail Kensington z 20895
Whiteford; RMC Place; HARFORD; 185 A-15; elev. 540ft./165m.; 🅿; ★ BAL; z 21160; ● 750
White Hall; RMC Place; BALTIMORE; 185 B-13; elev. 360ft./110m.; 🅿; ★ BAL; z 21161; ● 700
Whitehall; RMC Place; PRINCE GEORGE'S; *185 G-12; ★ WASH; mail Accokeek z 20607; ● 300
Whitehall Beach; RMC Place; ANNE ARUNDEL; *185 E-14; ★ ANPLS; mail Annapolis z 21401; ● 200
Whitehall Manor; RMC Place; MONTGOMERY; *185 E-11; ★ WASH; mail Bethesda z 20814
Whitehaven; RMC Place; WICOMICO; 185 I-17; elev. 3ft./1m.; mail Quantico z 21856; ● 80
Whitehouse; RMC Place; BALTIMORE; 185 B-13; ★ BAL; mail Upperco z 21155
Whitehouse Heights; RMC Place; PRINCE GEORGE'S; *185 F-12; ★ WASH; mail Hyattsville z 20785
White Landing; RMC Place; PRINCE GEORGE'S; *185 G-13; ★ WASH; mail Brandywine z 20613; rural
Whiteleysburg; RMC Place; CAROLINE; *185 E-17; mail Greensboro z 21639
White Marsh; CDP; BALTIMORE; 185 C-14; elev. 30ft./9m.; 🅿; ★ BAL; z 21162; Ⓟ 8,183; Ⓒ 8,485
White Oak; CDP; MONTGOMERY; 249 C-7; ★ WASH; mail Silver Spring z 20901, z 20903-04; Ⓒ 20,973; ◆ 22,272
White Oak Manor; RMC Place; PRINCE GEORGE'S; *185 E-12; ★ WASH; mail Silver Spring z 20904; ● 1,600
White Oak Park; RMC Place; MONTGOMERY; *185 E-12; ★ WASH; mail Silver Spring z 20904
White Oak Tower; RMC Place; MONTGOMERY; *185 E-12; ★ WASH; mail Silver Spring z 20904
White Plains (Indian Head Junction); RMC Place; CHARLES; 185 H-12; elev. 194ft./59m.; 🅿; ★ WASH; z 20695; Ⓟ 3,560
White Point Beach; RMC Place; ST. MARY'S; 185 J-13; ★ WASH; mail Leonardtown z 20650; ● 450
White Rock; RMC Place; FREDERICK; *184 B-10; ★ WASH; mail Frederick z 21702; ● 400
White Sands; RMC Place; CALVERT; *185 H-14; elev. 100ft./30m.; mail Lusby z 20657; ● 1,400
Whitesburg; WORCESTER; see Whiteburg (RMC Place)
Whiton; RMC Place; WICOMICO, WORCESTER; 185 I-19; mail Snow Hill z 21863; ● 60
Wickford (The Crest of Wickford); RMC Place; MONTGOMERY; 249 C-5; elev. 342ft./104m.; ★ WASH; mail Rockville z 20852; ● 900
Wicomico; RMC Place; CHARLES; *185 I-12; elev. 155ft./47m.; mail Charlotte Hall z 20622; ● 50
WICOMICO; 185 I-18; Ⓟ 74,339; Ⓒ 84,644; ◆ 96,779
Wicomico Beach; RMC Place; CHARLES; *185 I-12; mail Newburg z 20664; ● 120
Widgeon; RMC Place; SOMERSET; 185 I-17; mail Princess Anne z 21853
Wilburn Estates; RMC Place; PRINCE GEORGE'S; mail Capitol Heights z 20743
Wilde Lake; RMC Place; HOWARD; ★ BAL; mail Columbia z 21044
Wildercroft; RMC Place; PRINCE GEORGE'S; *185 E-12; ★ WASH; mail Riverdale z 20737; ● 990
Wilderness; RMC Place; ST. MARY'S; *185 J-14; elev. 100ft./30m.; ★ WASH; mail Leonardtown z 20650; rural
Wildewood; RMC Place; ST. MARY'S; mail California z 20619
Wild Rose Shores; RMC Place; ANNE ARUNDEL; 185 N-19; ★ ANPLS; mail Annapolis z 21403; ● 300
Wild Wood Beach; RMC Place; BALTIMORE; *185 D-14; ★ BAL; mail Essex z 21221; ● 200
Wildwood Estates; RMC Place; PRINCE GEORGE'S; *185 G-12; ★ WASH; mail Clinton z 20735
Wildwood Hills; RMC Place; MONTGOMERY; *185 E-11; ★ WASH; mail Bethesda z 20817; ● 930
Wildwood Manor; RMC Place; MONTGOMERY; *185 E-11; ★ WASH; mail Bethesda z 20817
Wildwoods; RMC Place; BALTIMORE; *185 C-13; ★ BAL; mail Randallstown z 21133
Wilelinor Estates; RMC Place; ANNE ARUNDEL; *185 E-14; ★ ANPLS; mail Edgewater z 21037; ● 200
Willards; Inc. Place; WICOMICO; 185 I-19; elev. 40ft./12m.; 🅿; z 21874; Ⓟ 708; Ⓒ 938
Willerburn Acres; RMC Place; MONTGOMERY; *185 E-11; ★ WASH; mail Potomac z 20854
Williamsburg; RMC Place; DORCHESTER; 185 G-17; elev. 38ft./12m.; mail Hurlock z 21643; ● 100
Williamsburg Estates; RMC Place; PRINCE GEORGE'S; *185 G-12; ★ WASH; mail Upper Marlboro z 20772; ● 1,250
Williamsburg Gardens; RMC Place; MONTGOMERY; *185 E-11; ★ WASH; mail Potomac z 20854
Williamsburg Village; RMC Place; MONTGOMERY; *185 D-11; ★ WASH; mail Olney z 20832; ● 3,700
Williamsbury; RMC Place; BALTIMORE; *185 C-13; ★ BAL; mail Pikesville z 21208; ● 2,250
Williamsport; Inc. Place; WASHINGTON; 184 B-8; elev. 400ft./122m.; 🅿; ★ HAG; z 21795; Ⓟ 2,103; Ⓒ 1,868
Williams Wharf; RMC Place; CALVERT; *185 H-14; mail Saint Leonard z 20685; rural
Williston; RMC Place; CAROLINE; 185 F-17; mail Denton z 21629; ● 110
Willoughby Beach; RMC Place; HARFORD; ★ BAL; mail Edgewood z 21040
Willow Beach Colony (Willows); RMC Place; CALVERT; 185 G-14; ★ WASH; mail Chesapeake Beach z 20732; ● 230
Willowbrook; RMC Place; MONTGOMERY; ★ WASH; mail Potomac z 20854
Willowbrook; RMC Place; PRINCE GEORGE'S; *185 E-12; ★ WASH; mail Hyattsville z 20783
Willow Grove; RMC Place; WORCESTER; *185 J-19; elev. 10ft./3m.; mail Pocomoke City z 21851; rural
Willow Lake; RMC Place; PRINCE GEORGE'S; *185 E-12; ★ BAL; mail Laurel z 20708
Willows; CALVERT; see Willow Beach Colony (RMC Place)
Wilson; RMC Place; WASHINGTON; 184 A-8; ★ HAG; mail Clear Spring z 21722; ● 50
Wilson-Conococheague; CDP-Census Area Only; WASHINGTON; *184 A-8; ★ HAG; Ⓒ 1,885
Wilson Hills; RMC Place; MONTGOMERY; *185 E-12; ★ WASH; mail Silver Spring z 20906
Wilson Point; RMC Place; BALTIMORE; *185 C-14; ★ BAL; mail Middle River z 21220
Wiltondale; RMC Place; BALTIMORE; *185 C-13; ★ BAL; mail Towson z 21204
Wilton Farm Acres; RMC Place; HOWARD; 184 I-1; ★ BAL; mail Ellicott City z 21043; ● 1,900
Winchester on the Severn; RMC Place; ANNE ARUNDEL; 185 L-19; ★ ANPLS; mail Annapolis z 21401; ● 700
Winchester Park; RMC Place; CARROLL; *185 B-12; ★ BAL; mail Westminster z 21157
Windbrook; RMC Place; PRINCE GEORGE'S; *185 G-12; ★ WASH; mail Clinton z 20735; ● 1,300
Windham Manor; RMC Place; MONTGOMERY; *185 E-12; ★ WASH; mail Silver Spring z 20904
Windham Manor; RMC Place; WICOMICO; *185 I-18; ★ SLSB; mail Salisbury z 21804; ● 290
Winding Brook Village; RMC Place; CECIL; *185 A-17; ★ PHIL-; mail Elkton z 21921; ● 700
Windmere Acres; RMC Place; HOWARD; *185 B-12; ★ BAL; mail Savage z 20763
Windsor; RMC Place; BALTIMORE; *185 C-13; ★ BAL; mail Windsor Mill z 21244
Windsor Estates; RMC Place; FREDERICK; *184 C-10; ★ WASH; mail Buckeystown z 21717; ● 80
Windsor Terrace; RMC Place; BALTIMORE; *185 C-13; ★ BAL; mail Gwynn Oak z 21207; ● 610
Winfield; RMC Place; CARROLL; 185 C-11; elev. 788ft./240m.; ★ BAL; mail Westminster z 21157; ● 200
Winfield; RMC Place; HOWARD; ★ BAL; mail Columbia z 21044
Winfield Heights; RMC Place; CARROLL; *185 C-11; ★ BAL; mail Westminster z 21157; ● 500
Wingate; RMC Place; DORCHESTER; 185 I-16; elev. 2ft./1m.; 🅿; z 21675; ● 230
Wingates Point; RMC Place; DORCHESTER; mail Wingate z 21675
Winsor Hills; RMC Place; MONTGOMERY; *185 E-11; ★ WASH; mail Potomac z 20854
Winterest; RMC Place; MONTGOMERY; *185 E-11; ★ WASH; mail Potomac z 20854
Wiseburg (Weisburg); RMC Place; BALTIMORE; *185 B-13; ★ BAL; mail White Hall z 21161
Wisperren Oaks; RMC Place; FREDERICK; *185 B-11; ★ WASH; mail Frederick z 21701; ● 200
Wittman; RMC Place; TALBOT; 185 F-15; elev. 10ft./3m.; 🅿; z 21676; ● 600
Wolf Hill; RMC Place; CARROLL; *185 B-12; elev. 803ft./245m.; ★ BAL; mail Hampstead z 21074; ● 30
Wolfsville; RMC Place; FREDERICK; 184 B-9; elev. 1,044ft./318m.; mail Myersville z 21773, Smithsburg z 21783; ● 150
Wolverton Park; RMC Place; PRINCE GEORGE'S; *185 F-12; ★ WASH; mail Clinton z 20735
Woodacres; RMC Place; MONTGOMERY; *185 E-11; ★ WASH; mail Bethesda z 20816
Woodberry Forest; RMC Place; PRINCE GEORGE'S; *185 F-12; ★ WASH; mail Temple Hills z 20748
Woodbine; RMC Place; CARROLL, HOWARD; 185 C-11; elev. 494ft./151m.; 🅿; ★ BAL; z 21797; ● 500
Woodbrook; RMC Place; BALTIMORE; *185 C-13; ★ BAL; mail Baltimore z 21212
Woodburn; RMC Place; MONTGOMERY; *185 E-11; ★ WASH; mail Bethesda z 20817
Wood Creek; RMC Place; HOWARD; ★ BAL; mail Columbia z 21045
Woodcroft; RMC Place; BALTIMORE; *185 C-14; ★ BAL; mail Parkville z 21234
Woodensburg; RMC Place; BALTIMORE; 185 B-12; ★ BAL; mail Reisterstown z 21136; ● 150
Woodfield; RMC Place; MONTGOMERY; *185 D-11; ★ WASH; mail Gaithersburg z 20882
Woodford; RMC Place; HOWARD; ★ BAL; mail Columbia z 21044
Woodhaven; RMC Place; MONTGOMERY; *185 E-11; ★ WASH; mail Bethesda z 20817
Woodhaven Park; RMC Place; CHARLES; *185 H-12; ★ WASH; mail La Plata z 20646; ● 120
Woodland; RMC Place; ALLEGANY; 184 B-3; ★ CUMB; mail Frostburg z 21532; ● 80
Woodland; RMC Place; TALBOT; *185 F-16; elev. 69ft./21m.; mail Easton z 21601; pop. incl. with Easton (Inc. Place)
Woodland Acres; RMC Place; ST. MARY'S; *185 I-14; mail California z 20619
Woodland Beach; ANNE ARUNDEL; see Londontown (RMC Place)
Woodland Point; RMC Place; CHARLES; *185 I-12; mail Newburg z 20664; ● 30
Woodlands; RMC Place; BALTIMORE; *185 C-13; ★ BAL; mail Randallstown z 21133
Woodland Village; CHARLES; see Perry Wright (RMC Place)
Woodlane; RMC Place; PRINCE GEORGE'S; *185 F-12; ★ WASH; mail Temple Hills z 20748; ● 700
Woodlark; RMC Place; PRINCE GEORGE'S; *185 E-12; ★ WASH; mail Hyattsville z 20784; ● 3,200
Woodlawn; CDP; BALTIMORE; 185 C-13; 🅿; ★ BAL; z 21207; Ⓟ 32,907; Ⓒ 36,079; ◆ 37,875
Woodlawn; RMC Place; CECIL; 185 B-16; mail Port Deposit z 21904; ● 150
Woodlawn; CDP; PRINCE GEORGE'S; *185 E-12; ★ WASH; mail Hyattsville z 20784; Ⓟ 5,329; Ⓒ 6,251
Woodlawn Heights; RMC Place; ANNE ARUNDEL; 184 L-4; ★ BAL; mail Glen Burnie z 21061; ● 2,400

Entries in **UPPERCASE** are counties.
Entries in **bold** have populations of 2,500 or more.
Names in parentheses are alternate names.
Inc. Place — Incorporated Place
RMC Place — Rand McNally Designated Place
CDP — Census Designated Place
MCD — Minor Civil Division

⊡ County Seat
▲ Minor Civil Division
elev. Elevation
🅿 Post Office
🅷 Hospital
🅲 College
■ Principal Business Center
★ Ranally Metro Area (RMA) Abbreviation
z Zip Code(s)
Ⓟ Previous Census Population
Ⓡ Revised Census Population
Ⓐ Annexation Population
● Rand McNally Population Estimate
Ⓒ Final Census Population
Ⓢ Special Census Population
◆ Estimated Population

For additional definitions see Glossary, Volume 1, and Introduction, Volume 2.

Woodley Gardens; RMC Place; MONTGOMERY; ***185** E-11; ★ **WASH**; pop. incl. with Rockville (Inc. Place)
Woodmont; RMC Place; MONTGOMERY; ***185** E-11; ★ **WASH**; mail Chevy Chase **z** 20815
Woodmoor; RMC Place; BALTIMORE; **184** H-2; ★ **BAL**; mail Gwynn Oak **z** 21207; ● 8,400
Woodmoor; RMC Place; MONTGOMERY; ***185** E-12; elev. 300ft./91m.; ★ **WASH**; mail Silver Spring **z** 20901, **z** 20918
Woodmoor; RMC Place; WASHINGTON; ***184** B-8; ★ **HAG**; mail Hagerstown **z** 21740; ● 700
Woodmore; CDP; PRINCE GEORGE'S; ***185** F-13; elev. 120ft./37m.; ★ **WASH**; mail Bowie **z** 20716; Ⓟ 2,874; Ⓒ 6,077
Wood Point; RMC Place; WASHINGTON; **185** M-13; ★ **HAG**; mail Hagerstown **z** 21740; pop. incl. with Hagerstown (Inc. Place)
Woodsboro; Inc. Place; FREDERICK; **184** B-10; elev. 400ft./122m.; 🅿; **z** 21798; Ⓟ 513; Ⓒ 846
Woods Corner; RMC Place; PRINCE GEORGE'S; ***185** F-12; elev. 250ft./76m.; ★ **WASH**; mail Temple Hills **z** 20748; rural
Woodside; RMC Place; MONTGOMERY; ***185** E-12; elev. 373ft./114m.; ★ **WASH**; mail Silver Spring **z** 20901
Woodside Park; RMC Place; MONTGOMERY; ***185** E-12; ★ **WASH**; mail Silver Spring **z** 20901
Woodstock; RMC Place; HOWARD; **185** C-12; elev. 400ft./122m.; 🅿; ★ **BAL**; **z** 21104, **z** 21163; ● 850
Woodville; RMC Place; FREDERICK; ***185** C-11; ★ **WASH**; mail Mount Airy **z** 21771
Woolford; RMC Place; DORCHESTER; **185** H-15; 🅿; **z** 21677 & mail Madison **z** 21648; ● 290
WORCESTER; **185** I-19; Ⓟ 35,028; Ⓒ 46,543; ◆ 49,642
Worthington; RMC Place; BALTIMORE; **185** C-13; mail Owings Mills **z** 21117; ● 90
Worthington; RMC Place; HOWARD; **184** K-1; ★ **BAL**; mail Ellicott City **z** 21043; ● 2,350
Worthington Heights; RMC Place; HARFORD; ***185** B-15; ★ **BAL**; mail Bel Air **z** 21014; ● 3,200
Worton; RMC Place; KENT; **185** D-16; elev. 79ft./24m.; 🅿; **z** 21678; ● 500
Wrights Crossing; RMC Place; ALLEGANY; ***184** A-3; ★ **CUMB**; mail Frostburg **z** 21532; ● 100
Wye Mills; RMC Place; TALBOT; **185** F-16; elev. 22ft./7m.; 🅿; **z** 21679; ● 400
Wye River Farms; RMC Place; QUEEN ANNE'S; ***185** E-15; elev. 18ft./5m.; ★ **ANPLS**; mail Queenstown **z** 21658; ● 50
Wyngate; RMC Place; MONTGOMERY; ***185** E-11; ★ **WASH**; mail Bethesda **z** 20814
Wynne Wood; RMC Place; BALTIMORE; ***185** D-13; ★ **BAL**; mail Halethorpe **z** 21227

Y

Yarrowsburg; RMC Place; WASHINGTON; ***184** C-9; ★ **WASH**; mail Knoxville **z** 21758; ● 200
Yellow Springs; RMC Place; FREDERICK; **184** B-10; elev. 607ft./185m.; ★ **WASH**; mail Frederick **z** 21702; ● 450
Yorkshire Knolls; RMC Place; PRINCE GEORGE'S; ***185** F-12; ★ **WASH**; mail Capitol Heights **z** 20743; ● 800

Z

Zihlman (Allegany); RMC Place; ALLEGANY; ***184** A-3; ★ **CUMB**; mail Frostburg **z** 21532; ● 400
Zion; RMC Place; CECIL; ***185** A-16; ★ **PHIL-**; mail North East **z** 21901; ● 250
Zittlestown; RMC Place; WASHINGTON; ***184** B-9; ★ **HAG**; mail Boonsboro **z** 21713; rural

MASSACHUSETTS

Statistics

Total area (2000) — 10,555 square miles
Land area (2000) — 7,840 square miles
Water area (2000) — 2,715 square miles
Capital — Boston
One of Thirteen Original States

Maps

State maps can be found on pages 142-254 in Vol. 1
County Subdivision maps can be found on pages 255-271 in Vol. 1

Ranally Metro Areas (RMAs) and Abbreviations

Barnstable, MA — BARN
Boston, MA-NH — BOS
Fall River, MA-RI — F.R.
New Bedford, MA — N.BED
Pittsfield, MA — PTSF
Providence-Warwick, RI-MA — PROV-
Springfield, MA — SPRG
Worcester, MA-CT — WORC

Principal Places

Place Name	Place Type	County	Population
Boston	Inc. Place	SUFFOLK	◆ 640,242
Worcester	Inc. Place	WORCESTER	◆ 172,480
Springfield	Inc. Place	HAMPDEN	◆ 150,970
Lowell	Inc. Place	MIDDLESEX	◆ 108,112
Cambridge	Inc. Place	MIDDLESEX	◆ 105,225
Brockton	Inc. Place	PLYMOUTH	◆ 94,221
Lynn	Inc. Place	ESSEX	◆ 89,737
Quincy	Inc. Place	NORFOLK	◆ 89,734
Fall River	Inc. Place	BRISTOL	◆ 89,253
New Bedford	Inc. Place	BRISTOL	◆ 88,951
Newton	Inc. Place	MIDDLESEX	◆ 86,587
Somerville	Inc. Place	MIDDLESEX	◆ 78,019
Lawrence	Inc. Place	ESSEX	◆ 72,739
Framingham	CDP	MIDDLESEX	◆ 67,378
Framingham	MCD-Town	MIDDLESEX	◆ 67,378
Haverhill	Inc. Place	ESSEX	◆ 61,480
Waltham	Inc. Place	MIDDLESEX	◆ 60,706
Malden	Inc. Place	MIDDLESEX	◆ 58,774
Revere	Inc. Place	SUFFOLK	◆ 57,980
Taunton	Inc. Place	BRISTOL	◆ 57,321
Brookline	CDP	NORFOLK	◆ 56,161
Brookline	MCD-Town	NORFOLK	◆ 56,161
Plymouth	MCD-Town	PLYMOUTH	◆ 56,113
Chicopee	Inc. Place	HAMPDEN	◆ 54,378
Weymouth	CDP	NORFOLK	◆ 54,144
Weymouth	MCD-Town	NORFOLK	◆ 54,144
Medford	Inc. Place	MIDDLESEX	◆ 53,812
Peabody	Inc. Place	ESSEX	◆ 48,082
Methuen	Inc. Place	ESSEX	◆ 44,829
Barnstable	Inc. Place	BARNSTABLE	◆ 44,721
Attleboro	Inc. Place	BRISTOL	◆ 43,681
Chelsea	Inc. Place	SUFFOLK	◆ 41,427
Leominster	Inc. Place	WORCESTER	◆ 41,075
Pittsfield	Inc. Place	BERKSHIRE	◆ 40,983
Salem	Inc. Place	ESSEX	◆ 40,944
Arlington	CDP	MIDDLESEX	◆ 40,709
Arlington	MCD-Town	MIDDLESEX	◆ 40,709
Westfield	Inc. Place	HAMPDEN	◆ 40,373
Holyoke	Inc. Place	HAMPDEN	◆ 39,483
Billerica	MCD-Town	MIDDLESEX	◆ 39,372
Everett	Inc. Place	MIDDLESEX	◆ 39,348
Beverly	Inc. Place	ESSEX	◆ 39,245
Marlborough	Inc. Place	MIDDLESEX	◆ 37,998
Fitchburg	Inc. Place	WORCESTER	◆ 37,254
Woburn	Inc. Place	MIDDLESEX	◆ 36,787
Shrewsbury	MCD-Town	WORCESTER	◆ 35,178
Amherst	MCD-Town	HAMPSHIRE	◆ 34,951
Braintree	MCD-Town	NORFOLK	◆ 34,288
Chelmsford	RMC Place	MIDDLESEX	● 34,200
Chelmsford	MCD-Town	MIDDLESEX	◆ 34,196
Braintree	CDP	NORFOLK	◆ 33,943
Watertown	Inc. Place	MIDDLESEX	◆ 32,783
Natick	MCD-Town	MIDDLESEX	◆ 32,656
Natick	RMC Place	MIDDLESEX	● 32,200
Shrewsbury	RMC Place	WORCESTER	● 31,600
Andover	MCD-Town	ESSEX	◆ 31,352
Dartmouth	MCD-Town	BRISTOL	◆ 31,296
Falmouth	MCD-Town	BARNSTABLE	◆ 31,172
Lexington	CDP	MIDDLESEX	◆ 31,023
Lexington	MCD-Town	MIDDLESEX	◆ 31,023
Randolph	CDP	NORFOLK	◆ 30,816
Randolph	MCD-Town	NORFOLK	◆ 30,816
Franklin	Inc. Place	NORFOLK	◆ 30,600
Gloucester	Inc. Place	ESSEX	◆ 30,039
Dracut	MCD-Town	MIDDLESEX	◆ 29,624
Tewksbury	MCD-Town	MIDDLESEX	◆ 29,192
Needham	CDP	NORFOLK	◆ 29,150
Needham	MCD-Town	NORFOLK	◆ 29,150
Northampton	Inc. Place	HAMPSHIRE	◆ 28,708
Norwood	CDP	NORFOLK	◆ 28,588
Norwood	MCD-Town	NORFOLK	◆ 28,588
Agawam	Inc. Place	HAMPDEN	◆ 28,389
West Springfield	Inc. Place	HAMPDEN	◆ 28,041
North Attleborough	MCD-Town	BRISTOL	◆ 27,933
West Springfield	CDP-Census Area Only	HAMPDEN	© 27,899
Milford	MCD-Town	WORCESTER	◆ 27,626
Stoughton	MCD-Town	NORFOLK	◆ 27,573
North Andover	MCD-Town	ESSEX	◆ 27,341
Stoughton	RMC Place	NORFOLK	® 26,777
Wellesley	CDP	NORFOLK	◆ 26,696
Wellesley	MCD-Town	NORFOLK	◆ 26,696
Bridgewater	MCD-Town	PLYMOUTH	◆ 26,612
Melrose	Inc. Place	MIDDLESEX	◆ 26,587
Saugus	CDP	ESSEX	◆ 26,527
Saugus	MCD-Town	ESSEX	◆ 26,527
Milton	CDP	NORFOLK	◆ 25,673
Milton	MCD-Town	NORFOLK	◆ 25,673
Marshfield	MCD-Town	PLYMOUTH	◆ 25,629
Dracut	RMC Place	MIDDLESEX	● 25,594
Danvers	CDP	ESSEX	◆ 25,592
Danvers	MCD-Town	ESSEX	◆ 25,592
Milford	CDP	WORCESTER	◆ 24,974
Wakefield	CDP	MIDDLESEX	◆ 24,973
Wakefield	MCD-Town	MIDDLESEX	◆ 24,973
Mansfield	MCD-Town	BRISTOL	◆ 24,294
Belmont	CDP	MIDDLESEX	◆ 23,983
Belmont	MCD-Town	MIDDLESEX	◆ 23,983
Yarmouth	MCD-Town	BARNSTABLE	◆ 23,901
Dedham	CDP	NORFOLK	◆ 23,626
Dedham	MCD-Town	NORFOLK	◆ 23,626
Reading	CDP	MIDDLESEX	◆ 23,594
Reading	MCD-Town	MIDDLESEX	◆ 23,594
Walpole	MCD-Town	NORFOLK	◆ 23,240
Burlington	CDP	MIDDLESEX	◆ 23,025
Burlington	MCD-Town	MIDDLESEX	◆ 23,025
Easton	MCD-Town	BRISTOL	◆ 22,853
North Andover	RMC Place	ESSEX	● 22,792
Westford	MCD-Town	MIDDLESEX	◆ 22,406
Wilmington	CDP	MIDDLESEX	◆ 22,365
Wilmington	MCD-Town	MIDDLESEX	◆ 22,365
Acton	MCD-Town	MIDDLESEX	◆ 21,827
Ludlow	MCD-Town	HAMPDEN	◆ 21,768
Stoneham	CDP	MIDDLESEX	◆ 21,613
Stoneham	MCD-Town	MIDDLESEX	◆ 21,613
Canton	MCD-Town	NORFOLK	◆ 21,447
Wareham	MCD-Town	PLYMOUTH	◆ 21,399
Winchester	CDP	MIDDLESEX	◆ 21,307
Winchester	MCD-Town	MIDDLESEX	◆ 21,307
Middleborough	MCD-Town	PLYMOUTH	◆ 21,098
Hingham	MCD-Town	PLYMOUTH	◆ 20,560
Gardner	Inc. Place	WORCESTER	◆ 20,403
Winthrop	MCD-Town	SUFFOLK	◆ 20,023
Marblehead	CDP	ESSEX	◆ 19,943
Marblehead	MCD-Town	ESSEX	◆ 19,943
Sandwich	MCD-Town	BARNSTABLE	◆ 19,722
Norton	MCD-Town	BRISTOL	◆ 19,568
Westborough	MCD-Town	WORCESTER	◆ 19,458
Hudson	MCD-Town	MIDDLESEX	◆ 18,927
Ludlow	RMC Place	HAMPDEN	● 18,820
Bourne	MCD-Town	BARNSTABLE	© 18,721
Canton	RMC Place	NORFOLK	● 18,530
Winthrop	CDP	SUFFOLK	© 18,303
Scituate	MCD-Town	PLYMOUTH	◆ 18,252
Somerset	MCD-Town	BRISTOL	◆ 18,245
Somerset	CDP	BRISTOL	© 18,234
Sudbury	MCD-Town	MIDDLESEX	◆ 18,039
Pembroke	MCD-Town	PLYMOUTH	◆ 17,960
Rockland	MCD-Town	PLYMOUTH	◆ 17,939
Sharon	MCD-Town	NORFOLK	◆ 17,693
Greenfield	MCD-Town	FRANKLIN	◆ 17,444
Newburyport	Inc. Place	ESSEX	◆ 17,245
South Hadley	MCD-Town	HAMPSHIRE	◆ 17,243
Amherst Center	CDP-Census Area Only	HAMPSHIRE	© 17,050
Grafton	MCD-Town	WORCESTER	◆ 16,994
North Attleborough Center	CDP-Census Area Only	BRISTOL	© 16,796
Concord	MCD-Town	MIDDLESEX	◆ 16,775
Foxborough	MCD-Town	NORFOLK	◆ 16,579
Amesbury	MCD-Town	ESSEX	◆ 16,498
Easthampton	Inc. Place	HAMPSHIRE	◆ 16,249
Southbridge	MCD-Town	WORCESTER	◆ 16,198
Fairhaven	RMC Place	BRISTOL	● 16,132
Rockland	RMC Place	PLYMOUTH	● 16,123
Holden	MCD-Town	WORCESTER	◆ 16,116
Amherst	RMC Place	HAMPSHIRE	● 16,100
Auburn	MCD-Town	WORCESTER	◆ 16,056
Ashland	MCD-Town	MIDDLESEX	◆ 15,897
Bellingham	MCD-Town	NORFOLK	◆ 15,782
Webster	MCD-Town	WORCESTER	◆ 15,781
Fairhaven	MCD-Town	BRISTOL	◆ 15,762
Swansea	MCD-Town	BRISTOL	◆ 15,686
Longmeadow	CDP	HAMPDEN	© 15,633
Longmeadow	MCD-Town	HAMPDEN	◆ 15,595
Dennis	MCD-Town	BARNSTABLE	◆ 15,238
Abington	MCD-Town	PLYMOUTH	◆ 15,083
Auburn	RMC Place	WORCESTER	● 15,005
North Reading	MCD-Town	MIDDLESEX	◆ 14,896
Northborough	MCD-Town	WORCESTER	◆ 14,766
East Longmeadow	MCD-Town	HAMPDEN	◆ 14,675
Swampscott	MCD-Town	ESSEX	◆ 14,674
Abington	CDP	PLYMOUTH	© 14,605
Westwood	MCD-Town	NORFOLK	◆ 14,600
Hopkinton	MCD-Town	MIDDLESEX	◆ 14,527
Swampscott	CDP	ESSEX	© 14,412
Hudson	CDP	MIDDLESEX	© 14,388
Westport	MCD-Town	BRISTOL	◆ 14,327
Holliston	MCD-Town	MIDDLESEX	◆ 14,125
East Bridgewater	MCD-Town	PLYMOUTH	◆ 14,046
Whitman	MCD-Town	PLYMOUTH	◆ 14,027
Duxbury	MCD-Town	PLYMOUTH	◆ 13,957
Wayland	MCD-Town	MIDDLESEX	◆ 13,857
Mashpee	MCD-Town	BARNSTABLE	◆ 13,824
Belchertown	MCD-Town	HAMPSHIRE	◆ 13,775
Wilbraham	MCD-Town	HAMPDEN	◆ 13,764
Greenfield	CDP	FRANKLIN	© 13,716
Clinton	MCD-Town	WORCESTER	◆ 13,549
Hanover	MCD-Town	PLYMOUTH	◆ 13,494
East Longmeadow	RMC Place	HAMPDEN	● 13,367
Whitman	RMC Place	PLYMOUTH	● 13,240
Northbridge	MCD-Town	WORCESTER	◆ 13,210
Ipswich	MCD-Town	ESSEX	◆ 13,179
Oxford	MCD-Town	WORCESTER	◆ 13,144
Seekonk	MCD-Town	BRISTOL	◆ 13,118
Kingston	MCD-Town	PLYMOUTH	◆ 13,098
Millbury	MCD-Town	WORCESTER	◆ 13,053
Seekonk	RMC Place	BRISTOL	● 13,046
Bedford	RMC Place	MIDDLESEX	● 12,996
Holliston	RMC Place	MIDDLESEX	● 12,926
Southbridge	CDP	WORCESTER	© 12,878
Medway	MCD-Town	NORFOLK	◆ 12,868
North Adams	Inc. Place	BERKSHIRE	◆ 12,817
Raynham	MCD-Town	BRISTOL	◆ 12,792
Bedford	MCD-Town	MIDDLESEX	◆ 12,762
Palmer	MCD-Town	HAMPDEN	◆ 12,702
Charlton	MCD-Town	WORCESTER	◆ 12,622
Medfield	MCD-Town	NORFOLK	◆ 12,475
Amesbury	CDP	ESSEX	© 12,327
Weston	MCD-Town	MIDDLESEX	◆ 12,250
Tyngsborough	MCD-Town	MIDDLESEX	◆ 12,075
Ashland	RMC Place	MIDDLESEX	● 12,066
North Reading	RMC Place	MIDDLESEX	● 12,002
North Attleboro	RMC Place	BRISTOL	● 11,900
Harwich	MCD-Town	BARNSTABLE	◆ 11,695
South Yarmouth	CDP	BARNSTABLE	© 11,603
Webster	CDP	WORCESTER	© 11,600
Lynnfield	CDP	ESSEX	© 11,542
Hull	MCD-Town	PLYMOUTH	◆ 11,464
Uxbridge	MCD-Town	WORCESTER	◆ 11,455
Lynnfield	MCD-Town	ESSEX	◆ 11,444
Pepperell	MCD-Town	MIDDLESEX	◆ 11,380
Athol	MCD-Town	WORCESTER	© 11,299
Carver	MCD-Town	PLYMOUTH	◆ 11,299
Lakeville	MCD-Town	PLYMOUTH	◆ 11,263
Spencer	MCD-Town	WORCESTER	◆ 11,193
Hull	CDP	PLYMOUTH	© 11,050
Tewksbury	RMC Place	MIDDLESEX	● 11,000
Wrentham	MCD-Town	NORFOLK	◆ 10,941
Holbrook	MCD-Town	NORFOLK	◆ 10,861
Dudley	MCD-Town	WORCESTER	◆ 10,826
Rehoboth	MCD-Town	BRISTOL	◆ 10,803
Norfolk	MCD-Town	NORFOLK	◆ 10,790
Holbrook	CDP	NORFOLK	© 10,785
Maynard	CDP	MIDDLESEX	© 10,433
Leicester	MCD-Town	WORCESTER	◆ 10,425
Maynard	MCD-Town	MIDDLESEX	◆ 10,313
Winchendon	MCD-Town	WORCESTER	◆ 10,214
Weston	RMC Place	MIDDLESEX	● 10,200
Acushnet	MCD-Town	BRISTOL	◆ 10,087
Groton	MCD-Town	MIDDLESEX	◆ 9,994
Ware	MCD-Town	HAMPSHIRE	◆ 9,902
Southborough	MCD-Town	WORCESTER	◆ 9,862
South Dartmouth	RMC Place	BRISTOL	● 9,800
Norwell	MCD-Town	PLYMOUTH	◆ 9,753
Hanson	MCD-Town	PLYMOUTH	◆ 9,701
Brewster	MCD-Town	BARNSTABLE	◆ 9,560
Nantucket	MCD-Town	NANTUCKET	© 9,520
Lunenburg	MCD-Town	WORCESTER	◆ 9,450
Townsend	MCD-Town	MIDDLESEX	◆ 9,369
Sutton	MCD-Town	WORCESTER	◆ 9,177
Blackstone	MCD-Town	WORCESTER	◆ 9,006
Southwick	MCD-Town	HAMPDEN	◆ 8,991
Monson	MCD-Town	HAMPDEN	◆ 8,531
Freetown	MCD-Town	BRISTOL	◆ 8,487
Montague	MCD-Town	FRANKLIN	® 8,468
Hamilton	MCD-Town	ESSEX	◆ 8,433
Littleton	MCD-Town	MIDDLESEX	◆ 8,432
Williamstown	MCD-Town	BERKSHIRE	© 8,424
Athol	CDP	WORCESTER	© 8,370
Middleton	MCD-Town	ESSEX	◆ 8,295
Salisbury	MCD-Town	ESSEX	◆ 8,260
Lincoln	MCD-Town	MIDDLESEX	◆ 8,243
West Boylston	MCD-Town	WORCESTER	◆ 8,099
Plainville	MCD-Town	NORFOLK	◆ 8,052
Boxford	MCD-Town	ESSEX	◆ 8,047
Halifax	MCD-Town	PLYMOUTH	◆ 8,036
Millis	MCD-Town	NORFOLK	◆ 7,950
Shirley	MCD-Town	MIDDLESEX	◆ 7,910
Adams	MCD-Town	BERKSHIRE	◆ 7,906
Andover	CDP	ESSEX	© 7,900
Clinton	CDP	WORCESTER	© 7,884
Sturbridge	MCD-Town	WORCESTER	◆ 7,880
Plymouth	CDP	PLYMOUTH	© 7,658
Rockport	MCD-Town	ESSEX	◆ 7,654
Georgetown	MCD-Town	ESSEX	◆ 7,597
Great Barrington	MCD-Town	BERKSHIRE	© 7,527
Orange	MCD-Town	FRANKLIN	© 7,518
Sterling	MCD-Town	WORCESTER	◆ 7,449
Ayer	MCD-Town	MIDDLESEX	◆ 7,397
Douglas	MCD-Town	WORCESTER	◆ 7,329
Rutland	MCD-Town	WORCESTER	◆ 7,328
Mansfield Center	CDP-Census Area Only	BRISTOL	© 7,320
Cohasset	MCD-Town	NORFOLK	◆ 7,319
Westminster	MCD-Town	WORCESTER	◆ 7,176
Dalton	RMC Place	BERKSHIRE	◆ 7,155
Newbury	MCD-Town	ESSEX	◆ 7,036
Pinehurst	CDP	MIDDLESEX	© 6,941
Middleborough Center	CDP-Census Area Only	PLYMOUTH	© 6,913
Templeton	MCD-Town	WORCESTER	◆ 6,894
Lancaster	MCD-Town	WORCESTER	◆ 6,879
Plainville	RMC Place	NORFOLK	● 6,871
Billerica	RMC Place	MIDDLESEX	● 6,850
Cochituate	CDP	MIDDLESEX	© 6,768
Medfield	CDP	NORFOLK	© 6,670
Bridgewater	CDP	PLYMOUTH	© 6,664
East Falmouth	CDP	BARNSTABLE	© 6,615
West Bridgewater	MCD-Town	PLYMOUTH	◆ 6,514
Westwood	RMC Place	NORFOLK	● 6,500
Dighton	MCD-Town	BRISTOL	◆ 6,493
West Yarmouth	CDP	BARNSTABLE	© 6,460
Granby	MCD-Town	HAMPSHIRE	◆ 6,352
Whitinsville	CDP	WORCESTER	© 6,340
Groveland	MCD-Town	ESSEX	◆ 6,336
Merrimac	MCD-Town	ESSEX	◆ 6,282
Dalton	MCD-Town	BERKSHIRE	◆ 6,264
Mattapoisett	MCD-Town	PLYMOUTH	◆ 6,263
Northborough	CDP	WORCESTER	© 6,257
Chatham	MCD-Town	BARNSTABLE	◆ 6,229
Stow	MCD-Town	MIDDLESEX	◆ 6,220
Ware	CDP	HAMPSHIRE	© 6,174
Topsfield	MCD-Town	ESSEX	◆ 6,118
Berkley	MCD-Town	BRISTOL	◆ 6,090
Hopedale	MCD-Town	WORCESTER	◆ 6,077
Spencer	CDP	WORCESTER	© 6,032
North Amherst	CDP	HAMPSHIRE	© 6,019
Cohasset	RMC Place	NORFOLK	● 6,000
Upton	MCD-Town	WORCESTER	◆ 5,955
Mendon	MCD-Town	WORCESTER	◆ 5,947
Sharon	CDP	NORFOLK	© 5,941
Orleans	MCD-Town	BARNSTABLE	◆ 5,911
Oxford	CDP	WORCESTER	© 5,899
Walpole	CDP	NORFOLK	© 5,867
Adams	CDP	BERKSHIRE	© 5,784
Southampton	MCD-Town	HAMPSHIRE	◆ 5,768
Dover	MCD-Town	NORFOLK	◆ 5,709
Harvard	MCD-Town	WORCESTER	◆ 5,700
West Concord	CDP	MIDDLESEX	© 5,632
Rowley	MCD-Town	ESSEX	◆ 5,613
Rockport	CDP	ESSEX	© 5,606
Lee	MCD-Town	BERKSHIRE	◆ 5,585
Middleboro	RMC Place	PLYMOUTH	● 5,580
Ashburnham	MCD-Town	WORCESTER	◆ 5,558
Foxborough	CDP-Census Area Only	NORFOLK	© 5,509
North Billerica	RMC Place	MIDDLESEX	● 5,500
South Hadley	RMC Place	HAMPSHIRE	● 5,500
Bliss Corner	CDP	BRISTOL	© 5,466
Yarmouth Port	CDP	BARNSTABLE	© 5,395
Kingston	CDP	PLYMOUTH	© 5,380
Eastham	MCD-Town	BARNSTABLE	◆ 5,370
Hingham	CDP	PLYMOUTH	© 5,352
Hampden	MCD-Town	HAMPDEN	◆ 5,318
Barre	MCD-Town	WORCESTER	◆ 5,304
Manchester	RMC Place	ESSEX	● 5,286
Boxborough	MCD-Town	MIDDLESEX	◆ 5,257
Manchester-by-the-Sea	MCD-Town	ESSEX	◆ 5,215
West Acton	RMC Place	MIDDLESEX	● 5,200
Marion	MCD-Town	PLYMOUTH	◆ 5,128
Mansfield	RMC Place	BRISTOL	● 5,100
Ocean Bluff-Brant Rock	CDP-Census Area Only	PLYMOUTH	© 5,100
South Hadley Falls	RMC Place	HAMPSHIRE	● 5,100
Scituate	CDP	PLYMOUTH	© 5,069
North Scituate	CDP	PLYMOUTH	© 5,065
South Amherst	CDP	HAMPSHIRE	© 5,039
Blackstone	RMC Place	WORCESTER	● 5,000
Millbury	RMC Place	WORCESTER	● 5,000

Entries in **UPPERCASE** are counties.
Entries in **bold** have populations of 2,500 or more.
Names in parentheses are alternate names.
Inc. Place — Incorporated Place
RMC Place — Rand McNally Designated Place
CDP — Census Designated Place
MCD — Minor Civil Division

⊡ County Seat
▲ Minor Civil Division
elev. Elevation
▣ Post Office

H Hospital
C College
■ Principal Business Center
★ Ranally Metro Area (RMA) Abbreviation
z Zip Code(s)

Ⓟ Previous Census Population
® Revised Census Population
Ⓐ Annexation Population
● Rand McNally Population Estimate
© Final Census Population
Ⓢ Special Census Population
◆ Estimated Population

For additional definitions see Glossary, Volume 1, and Introduction, Volume 2.

County Business Data

County	FIPS Code	County Seat	Land Area (Sq. Mi.)	Census Population			Wholesale Trade		Manufacturing, 2002			
				4/1/2000	4/1/1990	% Change 1990-2000	Sales, 2002 ($1,000)	% Change 1997-2002	Establish-ments	Total Employees	Value Added ($1,000)	Ranally Mfg. Units
Barnstable	001	Barnstable	396	222,230	186,605	19.1	(d)	(d)	221	2,478	262,445	139
Berkshire	003	Pittsfield	931	134,953	139,352	-3.2	1,549,814	(d)	203	7,249	694,785	368
Bristol	005	Taunton	556	534,678	506,325	5.6	14,394,030	24.2	883	41,278	3,994,700	2,113
Dukes	007	Edgartown	104	14,987	11,639	28.8	(d)	(d)	...	(d)	(d)	...
Essex	009	Salem	501	723,419	670,080	8.0	11,235,768	21.2	1,134	55,183	8,128,805	4,301
Franklin	011	Greenfield	702	71,535	70,092	2.1	(d)	(d)	120	5,035	619,289	328
Hampden	013	Springfield	618	456,228	456,310	-0.0	5,103,910	13.9	748	28,386	2,902,052	1,535
Hampshire	015	Northampton	529	152,251	146,568	3.9	(d)	(d)	188	4,812	436,199	231
Middlesex	017	Cambridge	823	1,465,396	1,398,468	4.8	39,147,055	15.5	2,189	90,711	13,764,714	7,282
Nantucket	019	Nantucket	48	9,520	6,012	58.3	29,274	(d)	...	(d)	(d)	...
Norfolk	021	Dedham	400	650,308	616,087	5.6	18,197,692	-17.1	813	32,586	4,177,358	2,210
Plymouth	023	Plymouth	661	472,822	435,276	8.6	5,591,985	-3.1	620	13,261	1,280,522	677
Suffolk	025	Boston	59	689,807	663,906	3.9	15,426,399	41.1	468	17,893	2,361,083	1,249
Worcester	027	Worcester	1,513	750,963	709,705	5.8	13,411,687	11.4	1,243	50,060	5,870,004	3,106
The State			**7,840**	**6,349,097**	**6,016,425**	**5.5**	**127,129,789**	**12.7**	**8,859**	**349,184**	**44,508,791**	**23,548**

(d) Data not available. Corresponding percentages or Ranally Manufacturing Units are estimates.
... Represents 0 or amount too minimal to be reported.

Administrative Divisions

Towns: All Massachusetts counties are divided into towns. Although legally incorporated, towns are not treated as incorporated places by the U.S. Census because the population often is scattered among several localities and rural areas rather than being concentrated in a single place. Only towns with an active government recognized by the U.S. Census of Governments are printed in this index.

Cities: Incorporated cities do not form part of the towns which adjoin or surround them.

Index of Places and Counties

A

Aberdeen; RMC Place; SUFFOLK; ***187** E-14; elev. 100ft./30m.; ★ **BOS**; mail Brighton z 02135; pop. incl. with Boston (Inc. Place)
Abington; CDP; PLYMOUTH; ▲ Abington; **187** G-15; elev. 108ft./33m.; 🅿; ★ **BOS**; z 02351; Ⓟ 13,817; Ⓒ 14,605
Abington; MCD-Town; PLYMOUTH; ***187** G-15; 🅿; ★ **BOS**; z 02351; Ⓟ 13,817; Ⓒ 14,605; ◆ 15,083
Acapesket; RMC Place; BARNSTABLE; ▲ Falmouth; ***187** K-17; elev. 8ft./2m.; mail East Falmouth z 02536
Accord; RMC Place; PLYMOUTH; ▲ Hingham; ***187** F-15; elev. 150ft./46m.; 🅿; ★ **BOS**; z 02018 & mail Hingham z 02043
Acoaxet; RMC Place; BRISTOL; ▲ Westport; **187** L-14; ★ **F.R.**; mail Adamsville z 02801; ● 220
Acton; RMC Place; MIDDLESEX; ▲ Acton; **187** D-12; elev. 250ft./76m.; 🅿; ★ **BOS**; z 01718-20; ● 2,300
Acton; MCD-Town; MIDDLESEX; ***187** D-12; elev. 250ft./76m.; 🅿; ★ **BOS**; z 01718-20; Ⓟ 17,872; Ⓒ 20,331; ◆ 21,827
Acton Center; RMC Place; MIDDLESEX; ▲ Acton; ***187** N-20; elev. 250ft./76m.; ★ **BOS**; mail Acton z 01720
Acushnet; RMC Place; BRISTOL, BRISTOL; ▲ Acushnet; **187** J-15; ★ **N.BED**; ● 3,220
Acushnet; MCD-Town; BRISTOL; ***187** J-15; 🅿; ★ **N.BED**; z 02743, z 02745; Ⓟ 9,554; Ⓒ 10,161; ◆ 10,087
Acushnet Center; CDP-Census Area Only; BRISTOL; ▲ Acushnet; **187** J-15; ★ **N.BED**; mail Acushnet z 02743, New Bedford z 02745; Ⓟ 3,170; Ⓒ 3,171
Adams; CDP; BERKSHIRE; ▲ Adams; **186** C-2; 🅿; ★ **PTSF**; z 01220; Ⓟ 6,356; Ⓒ 5,784
Adams; MCD-Town; BERKSHIRE; ***186** C-2; 🅿; ★ **PTSF**; z 01220; Ⓟ 9,445; Ⓒ 8,809; ◆ 7,906
Adamsdale; RMC Place; BRISTOL; ▲ North Attleborough; ***187** H-12; elev. 105ft./32m.; ★ **PROV-**; mail North Attleboro z 02760
Adams Shore; RMC Place; NORFOLK; **186** M-8; elev. 10ft./3m.; ★ **BOS**; mail Quincy z 02169; pop. incl. with Quincy (Inc. Place)
Adamsville; RMC Place; FRANKLIN; ▲ Colrain; ***186** C-5; elev. 660ft./201m.; mail Colrain z 01340
Agawam; Inc. Place; HAMPDEN; **186** G-5; elev. 90ft./27m.; 🅿; ★ **SPRG**; z 01001; Ⓟ 27,323; Ⓒ 28,144; ◆ 28,389
Agawam; PLYMOUTH; see East Wareham (RMC Place)
Agawam Beach; RMC Place; PLYMOUTH; ▲ Wareham; ***187** J-16; ★ **BOS**; mail Wareham z 02571; ● 250
Aldenville; RMC Place; HAMPDEN; **187** L-12; elev. 220ft./67m.; ★ **SPRG**; mail Chicopee z 01013; pop. incl. with Chicopee (Inc. Place)
Alford; RMC Place; BERKSHIRE; ▲ Alford; **186** F-1; elev. 839ft./256m.; 🅿; z 01266 & mail Great Barrington z 01230; ● 160
Alford; MCD-Town; BERKSHIRE; ***186** F-1; 🅿; z 01266 & mail Great Barrington z 01230; Ⓟ 418; Ⓒ 399
Allendale; RMC Place; BERKSHIRE; ***186** D-2; ★ **PTSF**; mail Pittsfield z 01201; pop. incl. with Pittsfield (Inc. Place)
Allerton; RMC Place; PLYMOUTH; ▲ Hull; **186** L-10; elev. 8ft./2m.; ★ **BOS**; mail Hull z 02045
Allston; RMC Place; SUFFOLK; ***187** E-14; elev. 15ft./5m.; 🅿; ★ **BOS**; z 02134; pop. incl. with Boston (Inc. Place)
Amesbury; CDP; ESSEX; ▲ Amesbury; **187** A-15; 🅿; ★ **BOS**; z 01913; Ⓟ 12,109; Ⓒ 12,327
Amesbury; MCD-Town; ESSEX; ***187** A-15; 🅿; ★ **BOS**; z 01913; Ⓟ 14,997; Ⓒ 16,450; ◆ 16,498
Amesbury Center; RMC Place; ESSEX; ▲ Amesbury; ***187** N-20; ★ **BOS**; mail Amesbury z 01913
Amherst; RMC Place; HAMPSHIRE; ▲ Amherst; **186** E-6; elev. 320ft./98m.; 🅿 🅷 🅲 28,641; ★ **SPRG**; z 01002-04, z 01059; Ⓟ 17,824; ● 16,100
Amherst; MCD-Town; HAMPSHIRE; ***186** E-6; 🅿 🅲 28,641; ★ **SPRG**; z 01002-04, z 01059; Ⓟ 35,228; Ⓒ 34,874; ◆ 34,951
Amherst Center; CDP-Census Area Only; HAMPSHIRE; ***186** E-6; ★ **SPRG**; Ⓒ 17,050
Amostown; RMC Place; HAMPDEN; ▲ West Springfield; ***186** G-5; ★ **SPRG**; mail West Springfield z 01089
Amrita; RMC Place; BARNSTABLE; ▲ Bourne; ***187** J-17; mail Cataumet z 02534
Andover; CDP; ESSEX; ▲ Andover; **187** C-14; 🅿 🅷 🅲 629; ★ **BOS**; z 01810, z 01812, z 01899, z 05501, z 05544; Ⓟ 8,242; Ⓒ 7,900
Andover; MCD-Town; ESSEX; ***187** C-14; 🅿 🅲 629; ★ **BOS**; z 01810, z 01812, z 01899, z 05501, z 05544; Ⓟ 29,151; Ⓒ 31,247; ◆ 31,352
Annisquam; RMC Place; ESSEX; ***187** C-16; elev. 65ft./20m.; ★ **BOS**; mail Gloucester z 01930; pop. incl. with Gloucester (Inc. Place)
Antassawamock (Antassawamock Beach); RMC Place; PLYMOUTH; ▲ Mattapoisett; ***187** K-16; ★ **N.BED**; mail Mattapoisett z 02739; ● 30
Antassawamock Beach; PLYMOUTH; see Antassawamock (RMC Place)
Apponagansett Village; RMC Place; BRISTOL; ▲ Dartmouth; ***187** N-20; ★ **N.BED**; mail South Dartmouth z 02748
Aquinnah (Gay Head); MCD-Town; DUKES; ***187** M-16; 🅿; z 02535; Ⓟ 201; Ⓒ 344
Arlington; CDP; MIDDLESEX; ▲ Arlington; **187** E-14; elev. 46ft./14m.; 🅿 🅷; ★ **BOS**; z 02474, z 02476 & mail Arlington Heights z 02475; Ⓟ 44,630; Ⓒ 42,389; ◆ 40,709
Arlington; MCD-Town; MIDDLESEX; ***187** E-14; 🅿; ★ **BOS**; z 02474, z 02476 & mail Arlington Heights z 02475; Ⓟ 44,630; Ⓒ 42,389; ◆ 40,709
Arlington Heights; RMC Place; MIDDLESEX; ▲ Arlington; ***187** E-13; elev. 350ft./107m.; 🅿; ★ **BOS**; z 02475
Armory; RMC Place; HAMPDEN; ***187** N-20; ★ **SPRG**; mail Springfield z 01101; pop. incl. with Springfield (Inc. Place)
Arnoldsville; BERKSHIRE; see Arnoldville (RMC Place)
Arnoldville (Arnoldsville); RMC Place; BERKSHIRE; ▲ Adams; ***186** C-2; ★ **PTSF**; mail Adams z 01220
Asbury Grove; RMC Place; ESSEX; ▲ Hamilton; ***187** C-15; ★ **BOS**; mail South Hamilton z 01982
Ashburnham (Ashburnham Center); RMC Place; WORCESTER; ▲ Ashburnham; **186** C-9; elev. 1,028ft./313m.; 🅿 🅷; ★ **BOS**; z 01430; ● 1,500
Ashburnham; MCD-Town; WORCESTER; ***186** C-9; 🅿; ★ **BOS**; z 01430; Ⓟ 5,433; Ⓒ 5,546; ◆ 5,558
Ashburnham Center; WORCESTER; see Ashburnham (RMC Place)
Ashby; RMC Place; MIDDLESEX; ▲ Ashby; **186** C-10; elev. 904ft./276m.; 🅿; ★ **BOS**; z 01431; ● 700
Ashby; MCD-Town; MIDDLESEX; ***186** C-10; 🅿; ★ **BOS**; z 01431; Ⓟ 2,717; Ⓒ 2,845; ◆ 2,860
Ashcroft; RMC Place; NORFOLK; ***187** F-14; elev. 140ft./43m.; ★ **BOS**; mail Dedham z 02026
Ashdod; RMC Place; PLYMOUTH; ▲ Duxbury; ***187** G-16; elev. 80ft./24m.; ★ **BOS**; mail Duxbury z 02332; rural
Ashfield; RMC Place; FRANKLIN; ▲ Ashfield; **186** D-4; elev. 1,244ft./379m.; 🅿; z 01330; ● 1,050
Ashfield; MCD-Town; FRANKLIN; ***186** D-4; 🅿; z 01330; Ⓟ 1,715; Ⓒ 1,800
Ashland; RMC Place; MIDDLESEX; ▲ Ashland; **187** F-12; elev. 188ft./57m.; 🅿; ★ **BOS**; z 01721; ● 12,066
Ashland; MCD-Town; MIDDLESEX; ***187** F-12; 🅿; ★ **BOS**; z 01721; Ⓟ 12,066; Ⓒ 14,674; ◆ 15,897
Ashley Falls; RMC Place; BERKSHIRE; ▲ Sheffield; **186** G-1; elev. 675ft./206m.; 🅿; z 01222; ● 850
Ashley Heights; RMC Place; BRISTOL; ▲ Freetown; **187** I-15; elev. 80ft./24m.; ★ **N.BED**; mail East Freetown z 02717; ● 110
Ashmont; RMC Place; SUFFOLK; ***187** F-14; ★ **BOS**; mail Boston z 02124; pop. incl. with Boston (Inc. Place)
Assinippi; RMC Place; PLYMOUTH; ▲ Norwell, Hanover; **187** G-15; elev. 149ft./45m.; ★ **BOS**; mail Hanover z 02339; ● 1,400
Assonet; RMC Place; BRISTOL; ▲ Freetown; **187** I-14; elev. 10ft./3m.; 🅿; ★ **N.BED**; z 02702; ● 1,300
Assonet Bay Shores; RMC Place; BRISTOL; ▲ Freetown; ***187** I-14; elev. 30ft./9m.; ★ **N.BED**; mail Assonet z 02702
Assumption College; RMC Place; WORCESTER; ***186** F-10; ★ **WORC**; mail Worcester z 01609; pop. incl. with Worcester (Inc. Place)
Astor; RMC Place; SUFFOLK; ***187** E-14; ★ **BOS**; mail Boston z 02123; pop. incl. with Boston (Inc. Place)
Athol; CDP; WORCESTER; ▲ Athol; **186** C-8; 🅿 🅷; z 01331 & mail Royalston z 01368; Ⓟ 8,732; Ⓒ 8,370
Athol; MCD-Town; WORCESTER; ***186** C-8; 🅿; z 01331 & mail Royalston z 01368; Ⓟ 11,451; Ⓒ 11,299
Athol Junction; RMC Place; HAMPDEN; ***186** G-6; elev. 220ft./67m.; ★ **SPRG**; mail Springfield z 01101; pop. incl. with Springfield (Inc. Place)
Atlantic; RMC Place; NORFOLK; ***187** F-14; elev. 10ft./3m.; ★ **BOS**; mail Quincy z 02169; pop. incl. with Quincy (Inc. Place)
Attleboro; Inc. Place; BRISTOL; **187** H-13; elev. 138ft./42m.; 🅿 🅷 ■; ★ **PROV-**; z 02703; Ⓟ 38,383; Ⓒ 42,068; ◆ 43,681
Attleboro Falls; RMC Place; BRISTOL; ▲ North Attleborough; ***187** H-13; elev. 150ft./46m.; 🅿; ★ **PROV-**; z 02763
Auburn; RMC Place; WORCESTER; ▲ Auburn; **186** F-10; elev. 603ft./184m.; 🅿; ★ **WORC**; z 01501; ● 15,005
Auburn; MCD-Town; WORCESTER; ***186** F-10; 🅿; ★ **WORC**; z 01501; Ⓟ 15,005; Ⓒ 15,901; ◆ 16,056
Auburndale; RMC Place; MIDDLESEX; ***187** E-13; elev. 75ft./23m.; 🅿; ★ **BOS**; z 02466; pop. incl. with Newton (Inc. Place)
Avon; RMC Place; NORFOLK; ▲ Avon; **187** G-14; elev. 219ft./67m.; 🅿; ★ **BOS**; z 02322; ● 4,558
Avon; MCD-Town; NORFOLK; ***187** G-14; 🅿; ★ **BOS**; z 02322; Ⓟ 4,558; Ⓒ 4,443; ◆ 4,397
Ayer; CDP; MIDDLESEX; ▲ Ayer; **187** D-11; 🅿 🅷; ★ **BOS**; z 01432, z 01434; Ⓟ 2,889; Ⓒ 2,960
Ayer; MCD-Town; MIDDLESEX; ***187** C-11; 🅿; ★ **BOS**; z 01432, z 01434; Ⓟ 6,871; Ⓒ 7,287; ◆ 7,397
Ayers Village; RMC Place; ESSEX; ***187** B-14; elev. 187ft./57m.; ★ **BOS**; mail Haverhill z 01830; pop. incl. with Haverhill (Inc. Place)

B

Babson Park; RMC Place; NORFOLK; ▲ Wellesley; ***187** F-13; elev. 150ft./46m.; 🅿 🅲 3,359; ★ **BOS**; z 02457
Back Bay Annex; RMC Place; SUFFOLK; ***187** E-14; ★ **BOS**; mail Boston z 02115, z 02117; pop. incl. with Boston (Inc. Place)
Bakers Grove; RMC Place; WORCESTER; ▲ Westminster; ***186** D-9; elev. 900ft./274m.; ★ **BOS**; mail Westminster z 01473; ● 70
Bakers Island; RMC Place; ESSEX; ***187** D-16; ★ **BOS**; mail Salem z 01970
Baldwinville; CDP; WORCESTER; ▲ Templeton; **186** C-8; elev. 867ft./264m.; 🅿; ★ **BOS**; z 01436; Ⓟ 1,795; Ⓒ 1,852
Ballardvale; RMC Place; ESSEX; ▲ Andover; **187** C-14; elev. 80ft./24m.; ★ **BOS**; mail Andover z 01810; ● 1,400
Bancroft; RMC Place; HAMPSHIRE; ▲ Middlefield; ***186** E-3; elev. 520ft./158m.; mail Middlefield z 01243
Baptist Corner; RMC Place; FRANKLIN; ▲ Ashfield; ***186** D-4; elev. 1,088ft./332m.; mail Shelburne Falls z 01370; rural
Barber; RMC Place; WORCESTER; ***187** N-20; ★ **WORC**; pop. incl. with Worcester (Inc. Place)
Barkerville; RMC Place; BERKSHIRE; ***186** E-1; elev. 1,174ft./358m.; ★ **PTSF**; mail Pittsfield z 01201; pop. incl. with Pittsfield (Inc. Place)
Barnstable (Barnstable Town); Inc. Place; ⊡ BARNSTABLE; **187** J-19; elev. 37ft./11m.; 🅿; ★ **BARN**; z 02630 & mail Centerville z 02634, West Barnstable z 02668; Ⓟ 40,949; Ⓒ 47,821; ◆ 44,721
BARNSTABLE; **187** J-17; Ⓟ 186,605; Ⓒ 222,230; ◆ 216,949
Barnstable Town; BARNSTABLE; see Barnstable (Inc. Place)
Barre; CDP; WORCESTER; ▲ Barre; **186** E-8; elev. 886ft./270m.; 🅿; ★ **WORC**; z 01005; Ⓟ 1,094; Ⓒ 1,150
Barre; MCD-Town; WORCESTER; ***186** D-8; 🅿; ★ **WORC**; z 01005; Ⓟ 4,546; Ⓒ 5,113; ◆ 5,304
Barre Plains; RMC Place; WORCESTER; ▲ Barre; **186** E-8; elev. 589ft./180m.; ★ **WORC**; mail Barre z 01005; ● 400
Barrowsville; RMC Place; BRISTOL; ▲ Norton; **187** H-13; elev. 90ft./27m.; ★ **BOS**; mail Norton z 02766; ● 250
Bass Point; RMC Place; ESSEX; ▲ Nahant; ***187** N-20; ★ **BOS**; mail Nahant z 01908
Bass River; RMC Place; BARNSTABLE; ▲ Yarmouth; ***187** J-19; elev. 10ft./3m.; 🅿; ★ **BARN**; z 02664
Bass Rocks; RMC Place; ESSEX; ***187** C-17; elev. 40ft./12m.; ★ **BOS**; mail Gloucester z 01930; pop. incl. with Gloucester (Inc. Place)
Bay State; HAMPSHIRE; see Bay State Village (RMC Place)
Bay State Village (Bay State); RMC Place; HAMPSHIRE; ***186** E-5; elev. 220ft./67m.; 🅿; ★ **SPRG**; z 01062; pop. incl. with Northampton (Inc. Place)
Bayview; RMC Place; BRISTOL; ▲ Dartmouth; **187** K-15; elev. 30ft./9m.; ★ **N.BED**; mail South Dartmouth z 02748; ● 200
Bayview; RMC Place; ESSEX; ***187** C-16; elev. 60ft./18m.; ★ **BOS**; mail Gloucester z 01930; pop. incl. with Gloucester (Inc. Place)
Beach; RMC Place; SUFFOLK; ***187** E-14; elev. 30ft./9m.; ★ **BOS**; mail Revere z 02151; pop. incl. with Revere (Inc. Place)
Beach Bluff; RMC Place; ESSEX; ▲ Swampscott; ***187** D-15; ★ **BOS**; mail Swampscott z 01907
Beachmont; RMC Place; SUFFOLK; ***187** E-15; elev. 100ft./30m.; ★ **BOS**; mail Revere z 02151; pop. incl. with Revere (Inc. Place)
Beach Point; RMC Place; BARNSTABLE; ▲ Truro; **187** G-20; mail North Truro z 02652; summer pop. 150; ● 50
Beachwood; RMC Place; BERKSHIRE; ▲ Stockbridge; ***186** E-1; elev. 950ft./290m.; ★ **PTSF**; mail Stockbridge z 01262; summer pop. 200
Beacon Hill; RMC Place; SUFFOLK; ***187** E-14; ★ **BOS**; mail Boston z 02108; pop. incl. with Boston (Inc. Place)
Beaver Brook; RMC Place; MIDDLESEX; ***187** N-20; ★ **BOS**; mail Waltham z 02452; pop. incl. with Waltham (Inc. Place)
Beaver Brook; RMC Place; WORCESTER; ***186** F-10; elev. 484ft./148m.; ★ **WORC**; mail Worcester z 01602; pop. incl. with Worcester (Inc. Place)
Beaverdam; RMC Place; MIDDLESEX; ▲ Natick; ***187** F-12; ★ **BOS**; mail Natick z 01760
Becket; RMC Place; BERKSHIRE; ▲ Becket; **186** E-3; elev. 1,200ft./366m.; 🅿; z 01223; ● 600
Becket; MCD-Town; BERKSHIRE; ***186** F-3; 🅿; z 01223; Ⓟ 1,481; Ⓒ 1,755
Becket Center; RMC Place; BERKSHIRE; ▲ Becket; **186** F-3; elev. 1,580ft./482m.; mail Chester z 01011; ● 80
Bedford; RMC Place; MIDDLESEX; ▲ Bedford; **187** D-13; elev. 135ft./41m.; 🅿 🅷; ★ **BOS**; z 01730-31; ● 12,996
Bedford; MCD-Town; MIDDLESEX; ***187** D-13; 🅿; ★ **BOS**; z 01730-31; Ⓟ 12,996; Ⓒ 12,595; ◆ 12,762
Bedford Springs; RMC Place; MIDDLESEX; ▲ Bedford; ***187** D-13; elev. 220ft./67m.; ★ **BOS**; mail Bedford z 01730
Beechwood; RMC Place; NORFOLK; ▲ Cohasset; **187** F-16; elev. 60ft./18m.; ★ **BOS**; mail Cohasset z 02025; ● 500
Belcher Square; RMC Place; BERKSHIRE; ▲ Great Barrington; ***186** F-1; elev. 715ft./218m.; mail Great Barrington z 01230
Belchertown; CDP; HAMPSHIRE; ▲ Belchertown; **186** F-7; elev. 613ft./187m.; 🅿; ★ **SPRG**; z 01007; Ⓟ 2,339; Ⓒ 2,626
Belchertown; MCD-Town; HAMPSHIRE; ***186** F-7; 🅿; ★ **SPRG**; z 01007; Ⓟ 10,579; Ⓒ 12,968; ◆ 13,775
Bellevue; RMC Place; SUFFOLK; ***187** F-14; elev. 125ft./38m.; ★ **BOS**; pop. incl. with Boston (Inc. Place)
Bellingham; CDP; NORFOLK; ▲ Bellingham; **187** G-12; 🅿; ★ **BOS**; z 02019; Ⓟ 4,535; Ⓒ 4,497
Bellingham; MCD-Town; NORFOLK; ***187** G-12; 🅿; ★ **BOS**; z 02019; Ⓟ 14,877; Ⓒ 15,314; ◆ 15,782
Bell Rock; RMC Place; MIDDLESEX; ***187** N-20; ★ **BOS**; mail Malden z 02148; pop. incl. with Malden (Inc. Place)
Belmont; CDP; MIDDLESEX; ▲ Belmont; **187** E-13; elev. 44ft./13m.; 🅿 🅷; ★ **BOS**; z 02478 & mail Waverley z 02479; Ⓟ 24,720; Ⓒ 24,194; ◆ 23,983
Belmont; MCD-Town; MIDDLESEX; ***187** E-13; 🅿; ★ **BOS**; z 02478 & mail Waverley z 02479; Ⓟ 24,720; Ⓒ 24,194; ◆ 23,983
Belvidere; RMC Place; MIDDLESEX; ***187** C-13; elev. 200ft./61m.; ★ **BOS**; mail Lowell z 01852; pop. incl. with Lowell (Inc. Place)
Bennetts Corner; RMC Place; PLYMOUTH; ▲ West Bridgewater; ***187** H-14; elev. 70ft./21m.; ★ **BOS**; mail West Bridgewater z 02379
Berkley; RMC Place; BRISTOL; ▲ Berkley; **187** I-14; elev. 80ft./24m.; 🅿; ★ **BOS**; z 02779; ● 200
Berkley; MCD-Town; BRISTOL; ***187** I-14; 🅿; ★ **BOS**; z 02779; Ⓟ 4,237; Ⓒ 5,749; ◆ 6,090
Berkshire; RMC Place; BERKSHIRE; ▲ Lanesborough; **186** D-2; elev. 965ft./294m.; 🅿; ★ **PTSF**; z 01224 & mail Lanesboro z 01237; ● 200
BERKSHIRE; **186** E-2; Ⓟ 139,352; Ⓒ 134,953; ◆ 127,184
Berkshire Heights; RMC Place; BERKSHIRE; ▲ Great Barrington; ***186** F-1; elev. 800ft./244m.; mail Great Barrington z 01230
Berlin; RMC Place; WORCESTER; ▲ Berlin; **187** E-11; elev. 300ft./91m.; 🅿; ★ **BOS**; z 01503; ● 700
Berlin; MCD-Town; WORCESTER; ***187** E-11; 🅿; ★ **BOS**; z 01503; Ⓟ 2,293; Ⓒ 2,380; ◆ 2,534
Bernardston; RMC Place; FRANKLIN; ▲ Bernardston; **186** C-6; elev. 360ft./110m.; 🅿; z 01337; ● 900
Bernardston; MCD-Town; FRANKLIN; ***186** B-6; 🅿; z 01337; Ⓟ 2,048; Ⓒ 2,155
Beverly; Inc. Place; ESSEX; **187** D-15; elev. 26ft./8m.; 🅿 🅷 🅲 4,404 ■; ★ **BOS**; z 01915; Ⓟ 38,195; Ⓒ 39,862; ◆ 39,245
Beverly Cove; RMC Place; ESSEX; ***187** D-15; elev. 30ft./9m.; ★ **BOS**; mail Beverly z 01915; pop. incl. with Beverly (Inc. Place)
Beverly Farms; RMC Place; ESSEX; ***187** C-16; elev. 40ft./12m.; ★ **BOS**; mail Beverly z 01915; pop. incl. with Beverly (Inc. Place)
Beverly Junction; RMC Place; ESSEX; ***187** N-20; ★ **BOS**; mail Beverly z 01915; pop. incl. with Beverly (Inc. Place)
Billerica (Billerica Center); RMC Place; MIDDLESEX; ▲ Billerica; **187** C-13; elev. 250ft./76m.; 🅿; ★ **BOS**; z 01821-22 & mail North Billerica z 01862; ● 6,850
Billerica; MCD-Town; MIDDLESEX; ***187** C-13; 🅿; ★ **BOS**; z 01821-22 & mail North Billerica z 01862; Ⓟ 37,609; Ⓒ 38,981; ◆ 39,372
Billerica Center; MIDDLESEX; see Billerica (RMC Place)
Birch Island; RMC Place; WORCESTER; ▲ Webster; ***186** G-10; ★ **WORC**; mail Webster z 01570
Birds Hill; RMC Place; NORFOLK; ***187** F-13; elev. 150ft./46m.; ★ **BOS**; mail Needham z 02492
Blackinton; RMC Place; BERKSHIRE; ***186** B-2; elev. 623ft./190m.; mail North Adams z 01247; pop. incl. with North Adams (Inc. Place)
Black Rock; RMC Place; NORFOLK; ▲ Cohasset; ***187** F-16; elev. 40ft./12m.; ★ **BOS**; mail Cohasset z 02025
Blackstone; RMC Place; WORCESTER; ▲ Blackstone; **187** H-12; elev. 186ft./57m.; 🅿; ★ **BOS**; z 01504; ● 5,000
Blackstone; MCD-Town; WORCESTER; ***187** H-11; 🅿; ★ **BOS**; z 01504; Ⓟ 8,023; Ⓒ 8,804; ◆ 9,006
Blandford; RMC Place; HAMPDEN; ▲ Blandford; **186** F-3; elev. 1,452ft./443m.; 🅿; z 01008; ● 950
Blandford; MCD-Town; HAMPDEN; ***186** F-3; 🅿; z 01008; Ⓟ 1,187; Ⓒ 1,214
Bleachery; RMC Place; MIDDLESEX; ***187** C-13; ★ **BOS**; mail Lowell z 01852; pop. incl. with Lowell (Inc. Place)
Bliss Corner; CDP; BRISTOL; ▲ Dartmouth; ***187** K-15; elev. 68ft./21m.; ★ **N.BED**; mail South Dartmouth z 02748; Ⓟ 4,908; Ⓒ 5,466
Blissville; RMC Place; FRANKLIN; ▲ Orange; ***186** C-7; elev. 640ft./195m.; mail Orange z 01364; rural
Bloomingdale; RMC Place; WORCESTER; ***186** F-10; elev. 600ft./183m.; ★ **WORC**; mail Worcester z 01604; pop. incl. with Worcester (Inc. Place)
Blue Hills; RMC Place; NORFOLK; ▲ Milton; ***187** F-14; elev. 61ft./19m.; ★ **BOS**; mail Milton z 02186
Bolton; RMC Place; WORCESTER; ▲ Bolton; **187** D-11; elev. 387ft./118m.; 🅿; ★ **BOS**; z 01740; ● 550
Bolton; MCD-Town; WORCESTER; ***187** D-11; 🅿; ★ **BOS**; z 01740; Ⓟ 3,134; Ⓒ 4,148; ◆ 4,685
Bondsville; CDP; HAMPDEN, HAMPSHIRE; ▲ Belchertown, Palmer; **186** F-7; elev. 380ft./116m.; 🅿; ★ **SPRG**; z 01009; Ⓟ 1,992; Ⓒ 1,876
Boston; Inc. Place; **STATE CAPITAL**; ⊡ SUFFOLK; **187** E-14; elev. 20ft./6m.; 🅿 🅷 🅲 111,723 ■; ★ **BOS**; z 02108-37, z 02163, z 02196, z 02199, z 02201, z 02203-06, z 02210-12, z 02215, z 02217, z 02222, z 02228, z 02241, z 02266, z 02283-84, z 02293, z 02295, z 02297-98 & mail Chestnut Hill z 02467, North Waltham z 02455; Ⓟ 574,283; Ⓒ 589,141; ◆ 640,242
Boston College; RMC Place; MIDDLESEX; ***187** E-14; elev. 200ft./61m.; 🅿; ★ **BOS**; z 02467; pop. incl. with Newton (Inc. Place)
Boston University; RMC Place; SUFFOLK; ***187** E-14; ★ **BOS**; mail Boston z 02215; pop. incl. with Boston (Inc. Place)
Bourne; CDP; BARNSTABLE; ▲ Bourne; **187** J-17; 🅿; z 02532 & mail Monument Beach z 02553, Pocasset z 02559; Ⓟ 1,284; Ⓒ 1,443
Bourne; MCD-Town; BARNSTABLE; ***187** J-17; 🅿 🅲 1,045; z 02532 & mail Pocasset z 02559; Ⓟ 16,064; Ⓒ 18,721
Bournedale; RMC Place; BARNSTABLE; ▲ Bourne; **187** I-17; elev. 10ft./3m.; mail Buzzards Bay z 02532; ● 150
Boxboro (Boxborough); RMC Place; MIDDLESEX; ▲ Boxborough; **187** D-12; 🅿; ★ **BOS**; z 01719; ● 500
Boxborough; MIDDLESEX; see Boxboro (RMC Place)
Boxborough; MCD-Town; MIDDLESEX; ***187** D-12; 🅿; ★ **BOS**; z 01719; Ⓟ 3,343; Ⓒ 4,868; ◆ 5,257
Boxford; CDP; ESSEX; ▲ Boxford; **187** C-15; elev. 95ft./29m.; 🅿; ★ **BOS**; z 01921; Ⓟ 2,072; Ⓒ 2,340
Boxford; MCD-Town; ESSEX; ***187** C-14; 🅿; ★ **BOS**; z 01921; Ⓟ 6,266; Ⓒ 7,921; ◆ 8,047
Boylston; WORCESTER; see Boylston Center (RMC Place)
Boylston; MCD-Town; WORCESTER; ***186** E-10; 🅿; ★ **WORC**; z 01505; Ⓟ 3,517; Ⓒ 4,008; ◆ 4,158
Boylston Center (Boylston); RMC Place; WORCESTER; ▲ Boylston; **186** E-10; ★ **WORC**; mail Boylston z 01505; ● 950
Bradford; RMC Place; ESSEX; ***187** B-14; elev. 59ft./18m.; 🅿; ★ **BOS**; z 01835; pop. incl. with Haverhill (Inc. Place)
Bradstreet; RMC Place; HAMPSHIRE; ▲ Hatfield; **186** E-5; elev. 130ft./40m.; ★ **SPRG**; mail Hatfield z 01038; ● 200
Braintree; CDP; NORFOLK; ▲ Braintree; **187** F-14; elev. 90ft./27m.; 🅿 🅷; ★ **BOS**; z 02184-85; Ⓟ 33,836; Ⓒ 33,698; ◆ 33,943
Braintree; MCD-Town; NORFOLK; ***187** F-14; 🅿 ■; ★ **BOS**; z 02184-85; Ⓟ 33,836; Ⓒ 33,828; ◆ 34,288
Braintree Highlands; RMC Place; NORFOLK; ▲ Braintree; ***187** F-14; elev. 160ft./49m.; ★ **BOS**; mail Braintree z 02184
Braleys; RMC Place; BRISTOL; ▲ Freetown; **187** J-15; elev. 120ft./37m.; ★ **N.BED**; mail East Freetown z 02717; ● 350
Bramanville; RMC Place; WORCESTER; ▲ Millbury; ***186** F-10; elev. 450ft./137m.; ★ **WORC**; mail Millbury z 01527
Brant Rock; RMC Place; PLYMOUTH; ▲ Marshfield; **187** G-17; elev. 10ft./3m.; 🅿; ★ **BOS**; z 02020; ● 1,800
Brayton Point; RMC Place; BRISTOL; ▲ Somerset; **187** F-18; elev. 20ft./6m.; ★ **F.R.**; mail Somerset z 02725
Brewster; CDP; BARNSTABLE; ▲ Brewster; **187** J-20; elev. 39ft./12m.; 🅿; ★ **BARN**; z 02631; Ⓟ 1,818; Ⓒ 2,212
Brewster; MCD-Town; BARNSTABLE; ***187** J-20; 🅿; ★ **BARN**; z 02631; Ⓟ 8,440; Ⓒ 10,094; ◆ 9,560
Briarwood Beach; RMC Place; PLYMOUTH; ▲ Wareham; ***187** J-16; elev. 10ft./3m.; ★ **BOS**; mail Wareham z 02571; ● 200
Bridgewater; CDP; PLYMOUTH; ▲ Bridgewater; **187** H-15; elev. 104ft./32m.; 🅿 🅷 🅲 9,655; ★ **BOS**; z 02324-25; Ⓟ 7,242; Ⓒ 6,664
Bridgewater; MCD-Town; PLYMOUTH; ***187** H-15; 🅿 🅲 9,655; ★ **BOS**; z 02324-25; Ⓟ 21,249; Ⓒ 25,185; ◆ 26,612
Brier; RMC Place; BERKSHIRE; ▲ Savoy; ***186** C-3; elev. 1,709ft./521m.; mail Savoy z 01256; ● 50
Brier Neck; RMC Place; ESSEX; ***187** N-20; ★ **BOS**; mail Gloucester z 01930; pop. incl. with Gloucester (Inc. Place)
Brigadoon Village; RMC Place; ESSEX; ▲ Middleton; ***187** C-14; elev. 100ft./30m.; ★ **BOS**; mail Middleton z 01949
Briggs Corner; RMC Place; BRISTOL; elev. 142ft./43m.; mail Attleboro z 02703; pop. incl. with Attleboro (Inc. Place)
Briggsville; RMC Place; BERKSHIRE; ▲ Clarksburg; ***186** B-3; elev. 957ft./292m.; mail North Adams z 01247
Brighton; RMC Place; SUFFOLK; **186** K-6; elev. 90ft./27m.; 🅿; ★ **BOS**; z 02135; pop. incl. with Boston (Inc. Place)
Brightside; RMC Place; HAMPDEN; ***186** G-5; elev. 80ft./24m.; ★ **SPRG**; mail Holyoke z 01040; pop. incl. with Holyoke (Inc. Place)
Brightwood; RMC Place; HAMPDEN; **187** M-11; elev. 60ft./18m.; ★ **SPRG**; mail Springfield z 01107; pop. incl. with Springfield (Inc. Place)
Brimfield; RMC Place; HAMPDEN; ▲ Brimfield; **186** G-8; elev. 668ft./204m.; 🅿; z 01010; ● 800
Brimfield; MCD-Town; HAMPDEN; ***186** G-8; 🅿; z 01010; Ⓟ 3,001; Ⓒ 3,339
BRISTOL; **187** I-13; Ⓟ 506,325; Ⓒ 534,678; ◆ 538,261
Brittan Square; RMC Place; WORCESTER; ***186** F-10; elev. 600ft./183m.; ★ **WORC**; mail Worcester z 01605; pop. incl. with Worcester (Inc. Place)
Broadway; RMC Place; MIDDLESEX; ***187** N-20; ★ **BOS**; mail Malden z 02148; pop. incl. with Malden (Inc. Place)
Brockton; Inc. Place; PLYMOUTH; **187** G-14; elev. 112ft./34m.; 🅿 🅷 ■; ★ **BOS**; z 02301-05; Ⓟ 92,788; Ⓒ 94,304; ◆ 94,221
Brookfield; RMC Place; WORCESTER; ▲ Brookfield; **186** F-8; elev. 714ft./218m.; 🅿; ★ **WORC**; z 01506; ● 1,200
Brookfield; MCD-Town; WORCESTER; ***186** F-8; 🅿; ★ **WORC**; z 01506; Ⓟ 2,968; Ⓒ 3,051; ◆ 3,029
Brookline; CDP; NORFOLK; ▲ Brookline; **187** E-14; 🅿 🅷 🅲 2,782; ★ **BOS**; z 02445-46 & mail Brookline Village z 02447, Chestnut Hill z 02467; Ⓟ 54,718; Ⓒ 57,107; ◆ 56,161
Brookline; MCD-Town; NORFOLK; ***187** E-14; 🅿 🅲 2,782 ■; ★ **BOS**; z 02445-46 & mail Brookline Village z 02447, Chestnut Hill z 02467; Ⓟ 54,718; Ⓒ 57,107; ◆ 56,161
Brookline Hill; RMC Place; NORFOLK; ***187** E-14; elev. 120ft./37m.; ★ **BOS**; mail Brookline z 02445
Brookline Village; RMC Place; NORFOLK; ▲ Brookline; ***187** E-14; elev. 30ft./9m.; 🅿; ★ **BOS**; z 02447
Brooks Place; RMC Place; PLYMOUTH; ▲ West Bridgewater; ***187** G-14; elev. 114ft./35m.; ★ **BOS**; mail West Bridgewater z 02379; ● 500
Brookville; RMC Place; NORFOLK; ▲ Holbrook; ***187** G-14; elev. 166ft./51m.; ★ **BOS**; mail Holbrook z 02343
Brownell Corner; RMC Place; BRISTOL; ▲ Westport; ***187** K-14; elev. 204ft./62m.; ★ **F.R.**; mail Westport z 02790; ● 50
Browns Point; RMC Place; ESSEX; ▲ Salisbury; ***187** A-15; ★ **BOS**; mail Newburyport z 01950
Brush Hollow; RMC Place; HAMPSHIRE; ▲ Middlefield; ***186** E-3; mail Middlefield z 01243; rural
Brushwood; RMC Place; NORFOLK; ***187** G-12; elev. 250ft./76m.; ★ **BOS**; mail Franklin z 02038; pop. incl. with Franklin (Inc. Place)
Bryantville; RMC Place; PLYMOUTH; ▲ Hanson, Pembroke; **187** G-15; elev. 80ft./24m.; 🅿; ★ **BOS**; z 02327; ● 1,800
Buckland; RMC Place; FRANKLIN; ▲ Buckland; **186** C-4; elev. 690ft./210m.; 🅿; z 01338; ● 200
Buckland; MCD-Town; FRANKLIN; ***186** C-4; 🅿; z 01338; Ⓟ 1,928; Ⓒ 1,991
Buckland Four Corners; RMC Place; FRANKLIN; ▲ Buckland; ***186** C-4; mail Buckland z 01338; rural
Buena Vista Shores; RMC Place; PLYMOUTH; ▲ Lakeville; **187** I-15; elev. 100ft./30m.; ★ **BOS**; mail Middleboro z 02346; ● 700
Buffington Corner; RMC Place; BRISTOL; ▲ Somerset; **187** D-18; ★ **N.BED**; mail Somerset z 02726
Bullardville; RMC Place; WORCESTER; ▲ Winchendon; ***186** B-8; elev. 860ft./262m.; ★ **BOS**; mail Winchendon z 01475; ● 120
Burlington; CDP; MIDDLESEX; ▲ Burlington; **187** D-13; elev. 218ft./66m.; 🅿 🅷; ★ **BOS**; z 01803, z 01805; Ⓟ 23,302; Ⓒ 22,876; ◆ 23,025
Burlington; MCD-Town; MIDDLESEX; ***187** D-13; 🅿 ■; ★ **BOS**; z 01803, z 01805; Ⓟ 23,302; Ⓒ 22,876; ◆ 23,025
Burncoat; RMC Place; WORCESTER; ***186** E-10; elev. 680ft./207m.; ★ **WORC**; mail Worcester z 01606; pop. incl. with Worcester (Inc. Place)
Buzzards Bay; CDP; BARNSTABLE; ▲ Bourne; **187** J-17; elev. 10ft./3m.; 🅿 🅲 1,045; z 02532, z 02542; Ⓟ 3,250; Ⓒ 3,549
Byfield; RMC Place; ESSEX; ▲ Newbury; **187** B-15; elev. 66ft./20m.; 🅿; ★ **BOS**; z 01922; ● 1,300

C

Cabot; RMC Place; MIDDLESEX; ***187** N-20; ★ **BOS**; mail Newton z 02458; pop. incl. with Newton (Inc. Place)
Cambridge; Inc. Place; ⊡ MIDDLESEX; **187** E-14; elev. 40ft./12m.; 🅿 🅷 🅲 42,944 ■; ★ **BOS**; z 02138-42, z 02163, z 02238; Ⓟ 95,802; Ⓒ 101,355; ◆ 105,225
Campello; RMC Place; PLYMOUTH; ***187** G-14; elev. 110ft./34m.; ★ **BOS**; mail Brockton z 02303-04; pop. incl. with Brockton (Inc. Place)
Campground Landing; RMC Place; BARNSTABLE; ▲ Eastham; ***187** I-20; elev. 30ft./9m.; ★ **BARN**; mail North Eastham z 02651
Camp Grounds; RMC Place; WORCESTER; ▲ Sterling; ***187** N-20; ★ **WORC**; mail Sterling z 01564
Canterbury Estates; RMC Place; BARNSTABLE; ▲ Sandwich; ***187** J-18; ★ **BARN**; mail Sandwich z 02563; ● 300
Canton; RMC Place; NORFOLK; ▲ Canton; **187** G-14; elev. 100ft./30m.; 🅿 🅷; ★ **BOS**; z 02021; ● 18,530
Canton; MCD-Town; NORFOLK; ***187** F-14; 🅿; ★ **BOS**; z 02021; Ⓟ 18,530; Ⓒ 20,775; ◆ 21,447
Canton Junction; RMC Place; NORFOLK; ▲ Canton; ***187** G-14; elev. 108ft./33m.; ★ **BOS**; mail Canton z 02021
Carletonville (Carltonville); RMC Place; ESSEX; ***187** N-20; ★ **BOS**; mail Salem z 01970; pop. incl. with Salem (Inc. Place)
Carlisle; RMC Place; MIDDLESEX; ▲ Carlisle; **187** D-13; elev. 205ft./62m.; 🅿; ★ **BOS**; z 01741; ● 800
Carlisle; MCD-Town; MIDDLESEX; ***187** D-12; 🅿; ★ **BOS**; z 01741; Ⓟ 4,333; Ⓒ 4,717; ◆ 4,765
Carltonville; ESSEX; see Carletonville (RMC Place)
Carver; RMC Place; PLYMOUTH; ▲ Carver; **187** I-16; elev. 92ft./28m.; 🅿; ★ **BOS**; z 02330 & mail North Carver z 02355, South Carver z 02366; ● 1,500
Carver; MCD-Town; PLYMOUTH; ***187** I-16; 🅿; ★ **BOS**; z 02330 & mail North Carver z 02355, South Carver z 02366; Ⓟ 10,590; Ⓒ 11,163; ◆ 11,299
Castle Hill; RMC Place; ESSEX; ***187** N-20; ★ **BOS**; mail Salem z 01970; pop. incl. with Salem (Inc. Place)
Cataumet; RMC Place; BARNSTABLE; ▲ Bourne; **187** J-17; elev. 45ft./14m.; 🅿; z 02534; ● 1,500
Cathedral; RMC Place; SUFFOLK; ***187** E-14; ★ **BOS**; mail Boston z 02118; pop. incl. with Boston (Inc. Place)
Cayenne; RMC Place; HAMPDEN; ▲ West Springfield; ***186** G-5; ★ **SPRG**; mail West Springfield z 01089
Cedar Bushes; RMC Place; PLYMOUTH; ▲ Plymouth; ***187** I-17; elev. 40ft./12m.; ★ **BOS**; mail Manomet z 02345
Cedar Crest; RMC Place; PLYMOUTH; ▲ Marshfield; ***187** G-16; ★ **BOS**; mail Green Harbor z 02041; ● 700
Cedarville; RMC Place; PLYMOUTH; ▲ Plymouth; **187** I-17; elev. 49ft./15m.; ★ **BOS**; mail Plymouth z 02360; summer pop. 600; ● 450
Center; RMC Place; MIDDLESEX; ***187** N-20; ★ **BOS**; mail Woburn z 01801; pop. incl. with Woburn (Inc. Place)
Centerville; RMC Place; BARNSTABLE; ***187** J-18; elev. 40ft./12m.; 🅿; ★ **BARN**; z 02632, z 02634, z 02636; pop. incl. with Barnstable (Inc. Place)
Centerville; RMC Place; ESSEX; ***187** C-15; elev. 62ft./19m.; ★ **BOS**; mail Beverly z 01915; pop. incl. with Beverly (Inc. Place)
Central Village; RMC Place; BRISTOL; ▲ Westport; **187** K-14; elev. 174ft./53m.; ★ **F.R.**; mail Westport z 02790; ● 400
Centralville; RMC Place; MIDDLESEX; ***187** C-13; elev. 106ft./32m.; ★ **BOS**; mail Lowell z 01850; pop. incl. with Lowell (Inc. Place)
Chadwick Square; RMC Place; WORCESTER; ***186** F-10; elev. 630ft./192m.; ★ **WORC**; mail Worcester z 01605; pop. incl. with Worcester (Inc. Place)
Chaffin; WORCESTER; see Chaffinville (RMC Place)
Chaffinville (Chaffin); RMC Place; WORCESTER; ▲ Holden; **186** E-10; ★ **WORC**; mail Holden z 01520; ● 4,000
Chandler Hill; RMC Place; WORCESTER; ***186** F-10; elev. 550ft./168m.; ★ **WORC**; mail Worcester z 01609; pop. incl. with Worcester (Inc. Place)
Chappaquiddick Island; RMC Place; DUKES; ▲ Edgartown; ***187** N-20; mail Edgartown z 02539; summer pop. 450
Chappaquoit; RMC Place; BARNSTABLE; ▲ Falmouth; ***187** K-17; elev. 46ft./14m.; mail West Falmouth z 02574; ● 80
Charlemont; RMC Place; FRANKLIN; ▲ Charlemont; **186** C-4; elev. 584ft./178m.; 🅿; z 01339, z 01346 & mail Drury z 01343; ● 800
Charlemont; MCD-Town; FRANKLIN; ***186** C-4; 🅿; z 01339, z 01346 & mail Drury z 01343; Ⓟ 1,249; Ⓒ 1,358
Charles River Grove; RMC Place; NORFOLK; ▲ Bellingham; ***187** G-12; elev. 260ft./79m.; ★ **BOS**; mail Bellingham z 02019
Charles Street; RMC Place; SUFFOLK; ***187** E-14; ★ **BOS**; mail Boston z 02114; pop. incl. with Boston (Inc. Place)
Charlestown; RMC Place; SUFFOLK; ***187** E-14; elev. 80ft./24m.; 🅿; ★ **BOS**; z 02129; pop. incl. with Boston (Inc. Place)
Charlton (Charlton Center); RMC Place; WORCESTER; ▲ Charlton; **186** G-9; elev. 895ft./273m.; 🅿; ★ **WORC**; z 01507; ● 550
Charlton; MCD-Town; WORCESTER; ***186** G-9; 🅿; ★ **WORC**; z 01507; Ⓟ 9,576; Ⓒ 11,263; ◆ 12,622
Charlton Center; WORCESTER; see Charlton (RMC Place)
Charlton City; RMC Place; WORCESTER; ▲ Charlton; **186** G-9; elev. 701ft./214m.; 🅿; ★ **WORC**; z 01508; ● 1,400
Charlton Depot; RMC Place; WORCESTER; ▲ Charlton; **186** F-9; elev. 901ft./275m.; 🅿; ★ **WORC**; z 01509; ● 400
Chartley; RMC Place; BRISTOL; ▲ Norton; **187** H-13; elev. 100ft./30m.; 🅿; ★ **BOS**; z 02712; ● 750
Chaseville; RMC Place; WORCESTER; ▲ Dudley; ***186** G-9; elev. 560ft./171m.; ★ **WORC**; mail Dudley z 01571
Chatham; CDP; BARNSTABLE; ▲ Chatham; **187** J-20; elev. 46ft./14m.; 🅿; ★ **BARN**; z 02633; Ⓟ 1,916; Ⓒ 1,667
Chatham; MCD-Town; BARNSTABLE; ***187** J-20; 🅿; ★ **BARN**; z 02633; Ⓟ 6,579; Ⓒ 6,625; ◆ 6,229
Chelmsford; RMC Place; MIDDLESEX; ▲ Chelmsford, Tyngsborough, Westford; **187** C-13; 🅿; ★ **BOS**; z 01824; Ⓟ 32,383; ● 34,200
Chelmsford; MCD-Town; MIDDLESEX; ***187** C-12; 🅿 ■; ★ **BOS**; z 01824; Ⓟ 32,383; Ⓒ 33,858; Ⓡ 33,613; ◆ 34,196
Chelsea; Inc. Place; SUFFOLK; **187** E-14; elev. 10ft./3m.; 🅿 🅷 ■; ★ **BOS**; z 02150 & mail Boston z 02204; Ⓟ 28,710; Ⓒ 35,080; ◆ 41,427
Cherry Brook; RMC Place; MIDDLESEX; ▲ Weston; ***187** N-20; ★ **BOS**; mail Weston z 02493
Cherry Valley; RMC Place; WORCESTER; ▲ Leicester; **186** F-10; elev. 708ft./216m.; 🅿; ★ **WORC**; z 01611; ● 1,200
Cheshire (Cheshire Center); RMC Place; BERKSHIRE; ▲ Cheshire; **186** C-2; elev. 963ft./294m.; 🅿; ★ **PTSF**; z 01225; ● 1,200
Cheshire; MCD-Town; BERKSHIRE; ***186** C-2; 🅿; ★ **PTSF**; z 01225; Ⓟ 3,479; Ⓒ 3,401; ◆ 3,096
Cheshire Center; BERKSHIRE; see Cheshire (RMC Place)
Cheshire Harbor; RMC Place; BERKSHIRE; ▲ Cheshire; **186** C-2; elev. 920ft./280m.; ★ **PTSF**; mail Adams z 01220; ● 60
Chester; RMC Place; HAMPDEN; ▲ Chester; **186** F-3; elev. 601ft./183m.; 🅿; z 01011; ● 800
Chester; MCD-Town; HAMPDEN; ***186** E-3; 🅿; z 01011; Ⓟ 1,280; Ⓒ 1,308
Chester Center; RMC Place; HAMPDEN; ▲ Chester; ***186** F-4; elev. 1,237ft./377m.; mail Chester z 01011; rural
Chesterfield; RMC Place; HAMPSHIRE; ▲ Chesterfield; **186** E-4; elev. 1,427ft./435m.; 🅿; z 01012; ● 700
Chesterfield; MCD-Town; HAMPSHIRE; ***186** E-4; 🅿; z 01012; Ⓟ 1,048; Ⓒ 1,201
Chestnut Hill; RMC Place; MIDDLESEX; ***187** E-14; elev. 200ft./61m.; 🅿; ★ **BOS**; z 02467; pop. incl. with Newton (Inc. Place)
Chicopee; Inc. Place; HAMPDEN; **186** G-5; elev. 100ft./30m.; 🅿 🅷 🅲 1,177 ■; ★ **SPRG**; z 01013-14, z 01020-22; Ⓟ 56,632; Ⓒ 54,653; ◆ 54,378
Chicopee Center; RMC Place; HAMPDEN; ***186** F-6; ★ **SPRG**; mail Chicopee z 01020; pop. incl. with Chicopee (Inc. Place)
Chicopee Falls; RMC Place; HAMPDEN; **187** L-12; elev. 180ft./55m.; ★ **SPRG**; pop. incl. with Chicopee (Inc. Place)
Chilmark; RMC Place; DUKES; ▲ Chilmark; **187** M-16; elev. 91ft./28m.; 🅿; z 02535 & mail Menemsha z 02552; ● 200
Chilmark; MCD-Town; DUKES; ***187** M-16; 🅿; z 02535 & mail Menemsha z 02552; Ⓟ 650; Ⓒ 843
Chiltonville; RMC Place; PLYMOUTH; ▲ Plymouth; ***187** H-17; elev. 57ft./17m.; ★ **BOS**; mail Plymouth z 02360; ● 65
Churchill Landing; RMC Place; PLYMOUTH; ▲ Plymouth; ***187** I-17; ★ **BOS**; mail Manomet z 02345
Churchill Shores; RMC Place; PLYMOUTH; ▲ Lakeville; ***187** I-15; elev. 80ft./24m.; ★ **BOS**; mail Middleboro z 02346; ● 70
City Mills; RMC Place; NORFOLK; ▲ Norfolk; **187** G-13; elev. 225ft./69m.; ★ **BOS**; mail Norfolk z 02056; ● 250
City Point; RMC Place; SUFFOLK; ***187** E-14; elev. 25ft./8m.; ★ **BOS**; mail Boston z 02127; pop. incl. with Boston (Inc. Place)
Clarendon Hills; RMC Place; SUFFOLK; ***187** F-14; elev. 50ft./15m.; ★ **BOS**; mail Roslindale z 02131; pop. incl. with Boston (Inc. Place)
Clarksburg; MCD-Town; BERKSHIRE; ***186** B-3; 🅿; z 01247; Ⓟ 1,745; Ⓒ 1,686
Clayton; RMC Place; BERKSHIRE; ▲ New Marlborough; ***186** G-1; elev. 690ft./210m.; mail Canaan z 06018
Cleghorn; WORCESTER; see Clinton (RMC Place)
Clematis Brook; RMC Place; MIDDLESEX; ***187** N-20; ★ **BOS**; mail Waltham z 02453; pop. incl. with Waltham (Inc. Place)

Entries in **UPPERCASE** are counties.
Entries in **bold** have populations of 2,500 or more.
Names in parentheses are alternate names.

Inc. Place	Incorporated Place
RMC Place	Rand McNally Designated Place
CDP	Census Designated Place
MCD	Minor Civil Division
⊡	County Seat
▲	Minor Civil Division
elev.	Elevation
🅿	Post Office
🅷	Hospital
🅲	College
■	Principal Business Center
★	Ranally Metro Area (RMA) Abbreviation
z	Zip Code(s)
Ⓟ	Previous Census Population
Ⓡ	Revised Census Population
Ⓐ	Annexation Population
●	Rand McNally Population Estimate
Ⓒ	Final Census Population
Ⓢ	Special Census Population
◆	Estimated Population

For additional definitions see Glossary, Volume 1, and Introduction, Volume 2.

Clevelandtown; RMC Place; DUKES; ▲ Edgartown; ***187** L-17; elev. 37ft./11m.; mail Edgartown **z** 02539
Clicquot; RMC Place; NORFOLK; ▲ Millis; ***187** F-13; elev. 190ft./58m.; ★ **BOS**; mail Millis **z** 02054
Clifford; RMC Place; BRISTOL; ▲ Dartmouth; ***187** J-15; elev. 131ft./40m.; ★ **N.BED**; mail New Bedford **z** 02745; pop. incl. with New Bedford (Inc. Place)
Clifton; RMC Place; ESSEX; **186** I-10; elev. 20ft./6m.; ★ **BOS**; mail Marblehead **z** 01945
Cliftondale; RMC Place; ESSEX; ▲ Saugus; **186** J-8; elev. 194ft./59m.; ★ **BOS**; mail Saugus **z** 01906
Clinton; CDP; WORCESTER; ▲ Clinton; **187** E-11; elev. 366ft./112m.; 🄿 🄷; ★ **WORC**; **z** 01510; Ⓟ 7,943; © 7,884
Clinton (Cleghorn); RMC Place; WORCESTER; ***187** E-11; ★ **WORC**; mail Fitchburg **z** 01420
Clinton; MCD-Town; WORCESTER; ***187** E-11; 🄿; ★ **WORC**; **z** 01510; Ⓟ 13,222; © 13,435; ◆ 13,549
Cobbs Village; RMC Place; BARNSTABLE; ***187** J-19; elev. 10ft./3m.; ★ **BARN**; pop. incl. with Barnstable (Inc. Place)
Coburnville; RMC Place; MIDDLESEX; ▲ Framingham; ***187** F-12; ★ **BOS**; mail Framingham **z** 01702
Cochesett; RMC Place; PLYMOUTH; ▲ West Bridgewater; **187** H-14; elev. 93ft./28m.; ★ **BOS**; mail West Bridgewater **z** 02379; ● 300
Cochituate; CDP; MIDDLESEX; ▲ Wayland, Natick; **187** E-12; elev. 172ft./52m.; ★ **BOS**; mail Wayland **z** 01778; Ⓟ 6,046; © 6,768
Cohasset; RMC Place; NORFOLK; ▲ Cohasset; **187** F-16; elev. 50ft./15m.; 🄿; ★ **BOS**; **z** 02025; ● 6,000
Cohasset; MCD-Town; NORFOLK; ***187** F-16; 🄿; ★ **BOS**; **z** 02025; Ⓟ 7,075; © 7,261; ◆ 7,319
Coldbrook Springs; RMC Place; WORCESTER; ▲ Oakham; ***186** E-9; ★ **WORC**; mail Oakham **z** 01068; rural
Cold Spring; RMC Place; BERKSHIRE; ▲ Otis; ***186** G-3; elev. 1,110ft./338m.; mail Otis **z** 01253; rural
Cole Corner; RMC Place; PLYMOUTH; ▲ Hingham; ***187** F-15; ★ **BOS**; mail Hingham **z** 02043
College Hill; RMC Place; WORCESTER; **187** C-19; elev. 600ft./183m.; ★ **WORC**; mail Worcester **z** 01610; pop. incl. with Worcester (Inc. Place)
Collinsville; RMC Place; MIDDLESEX; ▲ Dracut; ***187** C-12; elev. 144ft./44m.; ★ **BOS**; mail Dracut **z** 01826
Colonial Park; RMC Place; WORCESTER; ▲ Webster; ***186** H-10; elev. 500ft./152m.; ★ **WORC**; mail Webster **z** 01570
Colonial Station; RMC Place; HAMPDEN; ***187** N-20; ★ **SPRG**; mail Springfield **z** 01103; pop. incl. with Springfield (Inc. Place)
Colrain; RMC Place; FRANKLIN; ▲ Colrain; **186** C-5; elev. 633ft./193m.; 🄿; **z** 01340; ● 500
Colrain; MCD-Town; FRANKLIN; ***186** C-5; 🄿; **z** 01340; Ⓟ 1,757; © 1,813
Coltsville; RMC Place; BERKSHIRE; ***186** D-2; elev. 998ft./304m.; ★ **PTSF**; mail Pittsfield **z** 01201; pop. incl. with Pittsfield (Inc. Place)
Columbus Park; RMC Place; WORCESTER; ***186** F-10; elev. 600ft./183m.; ★ **WORC**; mail Worcester **z** 01603; pop. incl. with Worcester (Inc. Place)
Cominsville; RMC Place; WORCESTER; ▲ Oxford; **187** D-18; elev. 650ft./198m.; ★ **WORC**; mail Rochdale **z** 01542
Concord; RMC Place; MIDDLESEX; ▲ Concord; **187** D-13; elev. 141ft./43m.; 🄿 🄷; ★ **BOS**; **z** 01742; ● 4,700
Concord; MCD-Town; MIDDLESEX; ***187** D-12; 🄿; ★ **BOS**; **z** 01742; Ⓟ 17,076; © 16,993; ◆ 16,775
Congamond; RMC Place; HAMPDEN; ▲ Southwick; **186** H-4; elev. 230ft./70m.; ★ **SPRG**; mail Southwick **z** 01077; ● 900
Conway; RMC Place; FRANKLIN; ▲ Conway; **186** D-5; elev. 620ft./189m.; 🄿; **z** 01341; ● 800
Conway; MCD-Town; FRANKLIN; ***186** D-5; 🄿; **z** 01341; Ⓟ 1,529; © 1,809
Cooks Brook Beach; RMC Place; BARNSTABLE; ▲ Eastham; ***187** I-20; ★ **BARN**; mail North Eastham **z** 02651
Cooleyville; RMC Place; FRANKLIN; ▲ New Salem; ***186** D-7; elev. 638ft./194m.; mail New Salem **z** 01355; rural
Coolidge Corner; RMC Place; NORFOLK; ▲ Brookline; ***187** E-14; ★ **BOS**; mail Brookline **z** 02445
Cordaville; CDP; WORCESTER; ▲ Southborough; **187** F-12; elev. 250ft./76m.; ★ **BOS**; mail Southborough **z** 01772; Ⓟ 1,530; © 2,515
Cotley; RMC Place; BRISTOL; ***187** N-20; ★ **BOS**; mail Taunton **z** 02780; pop. incl. with Taunton (Inc. Place)
Cottage Hill; RMC Place; SUFFOLK; ▲ Winthrop; ***187** E-15; elev. 102ft./31m.; ★ **BOS**; mail Winthrop **z** 02152
Cottage Park; RMC Place; SUFFOLK; ▲ Winthrop; ***187** E-15; elev. 20ft./6m.; ★ **BOS**; mail Winthrop **z** 02152
Cotuit; RMC Place; BARNSTABLE; ***187** K-18; elev. 38ft./12m.; 🄿; ★ **BARN**; **z** 02635; pop. incl. with Barnstable (Inc. Place)
Country View Estates; RMC Place; NORFOLK; ***187** G-12; elev. 200ft./61m.; ★ **BOS**; mail Franklin **z** 02038; pop. incl. with Franklin (Inc. Place)
Court Park; RMC Place; SUFFOLK; ▲ Winthrop; ***187** E-15; elev. 20ft./6m.; ★ **BOS**; mail Winthrop **z** 02152
Coury Heights; RMC Place; BRISTOL; ▲ Acushnet; **187** E-20; elev. 80ft./24m.; ★ **N.BED**; mail Acushnet **z** 02743
Cow Yard; RMC Place; BRISTOL; ▲ Dartmouth; ***187** K-15; elev. 10ft./3m.; ★ **N.BED**; mail South Dartmouth **z** 02748; rural
Craigville; RMC Place; BARNSTABLE; ***187** K-18; elev. 30ft./9m.; ★ **BARN**; mail Centerville **z** 02636; pop. incl. with Barnstable (Inc. Place)
Craigville Beach; RMC Place; BARNSTABLE; ***187** K-18; elev. 7ft./2m.; ★ **BARN**; mail Centerville **z** 02636; pop. incl. with Barnstable (Inc. Place)
Crescent Beach; RMC Place; PLYMOUTH; ▲ Mattapoisett; ***187** J-16; elev. 10ft./3m.; ★ **N.BED**; mail Mattapoisett **z** 02739
Crescent Beach; RMC Place; SUFFOLK; ***187** E-15; elev. 9ft./3m.; ★ **BOS**; mail Revere **z** 02151; pop. incl. with Revere (Inc. Place)
Crescent Mills; RMC Place; HAMPDEN; ▲ Russell; ***186** F-4; elev. 350ft./107m.; ★ **SPRG**; mail Huntington **z** 01050
Crooks Corner; RMC Place; NORFOLK; ▲ Bellingham; ***187** H-12; elev. 192ft./59m.; ★ **BOS**; mail Bellingham **z** 02019
Cummaquid; RMC Place; BARNSTABLE; ***187** J-19; elev. 40ft./12m.; 🄿; ★ **BARN**; **z** 02637; pop. incl. with Barnstable (Inc. Place)
Cummington; RMC Place; HAMPSHIRE; ▲ Cummington; **186** D-4; elev. 1,010ft./308m.; 🄿; **z** 01026; ● 300
Cummington; MCD-Town; HAMPSHIRE; ***186** D-4; 🄿; **z** 01026; Ⓟ 785; © 978
Cushman; RMC Place; HAMPSHIRE; ▲ Amherst; **186** E-6; elev. 305ft./93m.; 🄿; ★ **SPRG**; **z** 01002; ● 400
Cuttyhunk; RMC Place; DUKES; ▲ Gosnold; **187** L-15; elev. 50ft./15m.; 🄿; **z** 02713; summer pop. 200; ● 70

D

Dalton; RMC Place; BERKSHIRE; ▲ Dalton; **186** D-2; elev. 1,199ft./365m.; 🄿; ★ **PTSF**; **z** 01226-27; ● 7,155
Dalton; MCD-Town; BERKSHIRE; ***186** D-2; 🄿; ★ **PTSF**; **z** 01226-27; Ⓟ 7,155; © 6,892; ◆ 6,264
Danvers; CDP; ESSEX; ▲ Danvers; **187** C-15; elev. 48ft./15m.; 🄿 🄷; ★ **BOS**; **z** 01923; Ⓟ 24,174; © 25,212; ◆ 25,592
Danvers; MCD-Town; ESSEX; ***187** C-15; 🄿 ■; ★ **BOS**; **z** 01923; Ⓟ 24,174; © 25,212; ◆ 25,592
Danvers Center; RMC Place; ESSEX; ▲ Danvers; ***187** C-15; ★ **BOS**; mail Danvers **z** 01923
Danversport; RMC Place; ESSEX; ▲ Danvers; ***187** D-15; elev. 20ft./6m.; ★ **BOS**; mail Danvers **z** 01923
Dartmouth; BRISTOL; see Russells Mills (RMC Place)
Dartmouth; MCD-Town; BRISTOL; ***187** K-15; 🄿 🄲 8,756; ★ **N.BED**; **z** 02714, **z** 02747-48; Ⓟ 27,244; © 30,666; ◆ 31,296
Davisville; RMC Place; BARNSTABLE; ▲ Falmouth; ***187** K-17; elev. 10ft./3m.; mail East Falmouth **z** 02536
Dawson; RMC Place; WORCESTER; ▲ Holden; ***186** E-10; ★ **WORC**; mail Holden **z** 01520; ● 150
Dedham; CDP; ⊡ NORFOLK; ▲ Dedham; **187** F-14; elev. 120ft./37m.; 🄿; ★ **BOS**; **z** 02026-27; Ⓟ 23,782; © 23,464; ◆ 23,626
Dedham; MCD-Town; NORFOLK; ***187** F-13; 🄿 ■; ★ **BOS**; **z** 02026-27; Ⓟ 23,782; © 23,464; ◆ 23,626
Deerfield; RMC Place; FRANKLIN; ▲ Deerfield; **186** D-5; elev. 150ft./46m.; 🄿; **z** 01342; ● 700
Deerfield; MCD-Town; FRANKLIN; ***186** D-5; 🄿; **z** 01342; Ⓟ 5,018; © 4,750
Deer Island; RMC Place; SUFFOLK; ***187** N-20; ★ **BOS**; mail Winthrop **z** 02152; pop. incl. with Boston (Inc. Place)
Dennis; CDP; BARNSTABLE; ▲ Dennis; **187** J-19; elev. 24ft./7m.; 🄿; ★ **BARN**; **z** 02638; Ⓟ 2,633; © 2,798
Dennis; MCD-Town; BARNSTABLE; ***187** J-19; 🄿; ★ **BARN**; **z** 02638; Ⓟ 13,864; © 15,973; ◆ 15,238
Dennis Port; CDP; BARNSTABLE; ▲ Dennis; **187** J-20; elev. 13ft./4m.; 🄿; ★ **BARN**; **z** 02639; Ⓟ 2,775; summer pop. 15,000; © 3,612
Devenscrest; RMC Place; MIDDLESEX; ▲ Ayer; ***187** D-11; elev. 300ft./91m.; ★ **BOS**; mail Ayer **z** 01432
Devereux; RMC Place; ESSEX; ▲ Marblehead; ***187** N-20; ★ **BOS**; mail Marblehead **z** 01945
Dighton; RMC Place; BRISTOL; ▲ Dighton; **187** I-14; elev. 19ft./6m.; 🄿; ★ **BOS**; **z** 02715; ● 1,100
Dighton; MCD-Town; BRISTOL; ***187** I-14; 🄿; ★ **BOS**; **z** 02715; Ⓟ 5,631; © 6,175; ◆ 6,493
Dodge; RMC Place; WORCESTER; ▲ Charlton; **186** G-9; elev. 680ft./207m.; ★ **WORC**; mail Charlton **z** 01507; ● 200
Dorchester Center; RMC Place; SUFFOLK; **186** M-7; elev. 120ft./37m.; 🄿; ★ **BOS**; **z** 02124 & mail Boston **z** 02121-22, **z** 02125; pop. incl. with Boston (Inc. Place)
Dorothy Manor; RMC Place; WORCESTER; ▲ Millbury; ***186** F-10; elev. 420ft./128m.; ★ **WORC**; mail Millbury **z** 01527
Dorothy Pond; RMC Place; WORCESTER; ▲ Millbury; **186** F-10; elev. 450ft./137m.; ★ **WORC**; mail Millbury **z** 01527; ● 1,700
Douglas; RMC Place; WORCESTER; ▲ Douglas; **186** G-10; elev. 582ft./177m.; 🄿; ★ **WORC**; **z** 01516; ● 400
Douglas; MCD-Town; WORCESTER; ***186** G-10; 🄿; ★ **WORC**; **z** 01516; Ⓟ 5,438; © 7,045; ◆ 7,329
Dover; CDP; NORFOLK; ▲ Dover; **187** F-13; elev. 150ft./46m.; 🄿; ★ **BOS**; **z** 02030; Ⓟ 2,163; © 2,216
Dover; MCD-Town; NORFOLK; ***187** F-13; 🄿; ★ **BOS**; **z** 02030; Ⓟ 4,915; © 5,558; ◆ 5,709
Downtown; RMC Place; MIDDLESEX; ***187** N-20; ★ **BOS**; mail Lowell **z** 01852; pop. incl. with Lowell (Inc. Place)
Dracut; RMC Place; MIDDLESEX; ▲ Dracut; **187** C-13; elev. 156ft./48m.; 🄿; ★ **BOS**; **z** 01826; ● 25,594
Dracut; MCD-Town; MIDDLESEX; ***187** C-13; 🄿; ★ **BOS**; **z** 01826; Ⓟ 25,594; © 28,562; ◆ 29,624
Drury; RMC Place; BERKSHIRE; ▲ Florida; **186** C-3; elev. 1,596ft./486m.; 🄿; **z** 01343; ● 150
Dry Pond; RMC Place; NORFOLK; ▲ Stoughton; ***187** N-20; ★ **BOS**; mail Stoughton **z** 02072
Dudley (Merino Village); RMC Place; WORCESTER; ▲ Dudley; **186** G-9; elev. 670ft./204m.; 🄿 🄲 1,466; ★ **WORC**; **z** 01571; ● 3,700
Dudley; MCD-Town; WORCESTER; ***186** G-9; 🄿 🄲 1,466; ★ **WORC**; **z** 01571; Ⓟ 9,540; © 10,036; ◆ 10,826
Dudley Hill; RMC Place; WORCESTER; ▲ Dudley; ***186** H-9; 🄿; ★ **WORC**; **z** 01570; rural
Dudleyville; RMC Place; FRANKLIN; ▲ Leverett; ***186** D-6; mail Shutesbury **z** 01072; rural
DUKES; **187** L-17; Ⓟ 11,639; © 14,987; ◆ 15,573
Dunstable; RMC Place; MIDDLESEX; ▲ Dunstable; **187** C-12; elev. 224ft./68m.; 🄿; ★ **BOS**; **z** 01827; ● 900
Dunstable; MCD-Town; MIDDLESEX; ***187** C-11; 🄿; ★ **BOS**; **z** 01827; Ⓟ 2,236; © 2,829; ◆ 2,998
Duxbury; CDP; PLYMOUTH; ▲ Duxbury; **187** G-16; elev. 36ft./11m.; 🄿; ★ **BOS**; **z** 02331-32; Ⓟ 1,637; © 1,426
Duxbury; MCD-Town; PLYMOUTH; ***187** H-16; 🄿; ★ **BOS**; **z** 02331-32; Ⓟ 13,895; © 14,248; ◆ 13,957
Dwight; RMC Place; HAMPSHIRE; ▲ Belchertown; **186** E-6; elev. 286ft./87m.; ★ **SPRG**; mail Belchertown **z** 01007; ● 200

E

Eagleville; RMC Place; FRANKLIN; ▲ Orange; ***186** C-7; mail Orange **z** 01364; ● 50
East Acton; RMC Place; MIDDLESEX; ▲ Acton; **187** D-12; elev. 140ft./43m.; ★ **BOS**; mail Acton **z** 01720; ● 950
East Arlington; RMC Place; MIDDLESEX; ▲ Arlington; **186** J-6; elev. 14ft./4m.; 🄿; ★ **BOS**; **z** 02474 & mail Arlington **z** 02476
East Billerica; RMC Place; MIDDLESEX; ▲ Billerica; **187** C-13; elev. 110ft./34m.; ★ **BOS**; mail Billerica **z** 01821; ● 3,850
East Blackstone; RMC Place; WORCESTER; ▲ Blackstone; ***187** G-12; elev. 202ft./62m.; ★ **BOS**; mail Blackstone **z** 01504
East Boston; RMC Place; SUFFOLK; **186** K-8; elev. 11ft./3m.; 🄿; ★ **BOS**; **z** 02128, **z** 02228; pop. incl. with Boston (Inc. Place)
East Boxford; RMC Place; ESSEX; ▲ Boxford; ***187** B-15; elev. 103ft./31m.; ★ **BOS**; mail Boxford **z** 01921
East Braintree; RMC Place; NORFOLK; ▲ Braintree; **186** N-8; elev. 70ft./21m.; ★ **BOS**; mail Braintree **z** 02184
East Brewster; RMC Place; BARNSTABLE; ▲ Brewster; **187** I-20; elev. 60ft./18m.; ★ **BARN**; mail Brewster **z** 02631; ● 800
East Bridgewater; RMC Place; PLYMOUTH; ▲ East Bridgewater; **187** H-15; 🄿; ★ **BOS**; **z** 02333 & mail Bridgewater **z** 02324, Elmwood **z** 02337; ● 3,400
East Bridgewater; MCD-Town; PLYMOUTH; ***187** H-15; 🄿; ★ **BOS**; **z** 02333 & mail Bridgewater **z** 02324, Elmwood **z** 02337; Ⓟ 11,104; © 12,974; ◆ 14,046
East Brimfield; RMC Place; HAMPDEN; ▲ Brimfield; **186** G-8; elev. 673ft./205m.; mail Brimfield **z** 01010; ● 150
East Brookfield; CDP; WORCESTER; ▲ Brookfield; **186** F-9; elev. 620ft./189m.; 🄿; ★ **WORC**; **z** 01515; Ⓟ 1,396; © 1,410
East Brookfield; MCD-Town; WORCESTER; ***186** F-9; 🄿; ★ **WORC**; **z** 01515; Ⓟ 2,033; © 2,097; ◆ 2,067
East Cambridge; RMC Place; MIDDLESEX; ***187** E-14; elev. 15ft./5m.; 🄿; ★ **BOS**; **z** 02141; pop. incl. with Cambridge (Inc. Place)
East Carver; RMC Place; PLYMOUTH; ▲ Plymouth, Carver; ***187** H-16; elev. 135ft./41m.; ★ **BOS**; mail North Carver **z** 02355
East Charlemont; RMC Place; FRANKLIN; ▲ Charlemont; **186** C-4; elev. 500ft./152m.; mail Shelburne Falls **z** 01370; ● 200
East Chelmsford; RMC Place; MIDDLESEX; ▲ Chelmsford; ***187** C-13; ★ **BOS**; mail Chelmsford **z** 01824
East Dedham; RMC Place; NORFOLK; ▲ Dedham; ***187** F-14; elev. 110ft./34m.; ★ **BOS**; mail Dedham **z** 02026
East Deerfield; RMC Place; FRANKLIN; ▲ Deerfield; ***186** C-6; elev. 202ft./62m.; mail Deerfield **z** 01342
East Dennis; CDP; BARNSTABLE; ▲ Dennis; **187** J-19; elev. 31ft./9m.; 🄿; ★ **BARN**; **z** 02641; Ⓟ 2,584; © 3,299
East Douglas; CDP; WORCESTER; ▲ Douglas; **186** G-10; elev. 456ft./139m.; 🄿; ★ **WORC**; **z** 01516; Ⓟ 1,945; © 2,319
East Fairhaven; RMC Place; BRISTOL; ▲ Fairhaven; ***187** J-15; elev. 40ft./12m.; ★ **N.BED**; mail Fairhaven **z** 02719
East Falmouth; CDP; BARNSTABLE; ▲ Falmouth; **187** K-17; elev. 37ft./11m.; 🄿; **z** 02536; Ⓟ 5,577; © 6,615
East Forest Park; RMC Place; HAMPDEN; ***186** G-6; ★ **SPRG**; mail Springfield **z** 01108; pop. incl. with Springfield (Inc. Place)
East Foxboro; RMC Place; NORFOLK; ▲ Foxborough; **187** G-13; elev. 201ft./61m.; ★ **BOS**; mail Foxboro **z** 02035; ● 1,000
East Freetown; RMC Place; BRISTOL; ▲ Freetown; **187** J-15; elev. 75ft./23m.; 🄿; ★ **N.BED**; **z** 02717; ● 850
East Gloucester; RMC Place; ESSEX; ***187** C-17; elev. 50ft./15m.; ★ **BOS**; mail Gloucester **z** 01930; pop. incl. with Gloucester (Inc. Place)
East Greenfield; RMC Place; FRANKLIN; ▲ Greenfield; ***186** C-6; elev. 167ft./51m.; mail Greenfield **z** 01301
Eastham; RMC Place; BARNSTABLE; ▲ Eastham; **187** I-20; elev. 48ft./15m.; 🄿; ★ **BARN**; **z** 02642; ● 1,250
Eastham; MCD-Town; BARNSTABLE; ***187** I-20; 🄿; ★ **BARN**; **z** 02642; Ⓟ 4,462; © 5,453; ◆ 5,370
Easthampton; Inc. Place; HAMPSHIRE; **186** F-5; elev. 170ft./52m.; 🄿; ★ **SPRG**; **z** 01027; Ⓟ 15,537; © 15,994; ◆ 16,249
East Harwich; CDP; BARNSTABLE; ▲ Harwich; **187** J-20; elev. 69ft./21m.; 🄿; ★ **BARN**; **z** 02645; Ⓟ 3,828; © 4,744
East Holliston; RMC Place; MIDDLESEX; ▲ Holliston; **186** N-2; elev. 193ft./59m.; ★ **BOS**; mail Holliston **z** 01746
East Junction; RMC Place; BRISTOL; ***187** I-13; elev. 100ft./30m.; ★ **PROV-**; mail Attleboro **z** 02703; pop. incl. with Attleboro (Inc. Place)
East Lee; RMC Place; BERKSHIRE; ▲ Lee; ***186** E-2; elev. 963ft./294m.; ★ **PTSF**; mail Lee **z** 01238
East Leverett; RMC Place; FRANKLIN; ▲ Leverett; **186** D-6; elev. 416ft./127m.; mail Leverett **z** 01054; ● 170
East Longmeadow; RMC Place; HAMPDEN; ▲ East Longmeadow; **186** G-6; elev. 226ft./69m.; 🄿; ★ **SPRG**; **z** 01028, **z** 01116; ● 13,367
East Longmeadow; MCD-Town; HAMPDEN; ***186** G-6; 🄿; ★ **SPRG**; **z** 01028, **z** 01116; Ⓟ 13,367; © 14,100; ◆ 14,675
East Lynn; RMC Place; ESSEX; **186** I-9; elev. 34ft./10m.; 🄿; ★ **BOS**; **z** 01904; pop. incl. with Lynn (Inc. Place)
East Mansfield; RMC Place; BRISTOL; ▲ Mansfield; **187** H-14; elev. 139ft./42m.; 🄿; ★ **BOS**; **z** 02031; ● 350
East Marion; RMC Place; PLYMOUTH; ▲ Marion; **187** J-16; elev. 40ft./12m.; ★ **N.BED**; mail Marion **z** 02738; ● 370
East Middleboro; RMC Place; PLYMOUTH; ▲ Middleborough; ***187** N-20; ★ **BOS**; mail Middleboro **z** 02346; ● 250
East Millbury; RMC Place; WORCESTER; ▲ Millbury; **186** F-10; elev. 430ft./131m.; ★ **WORC**; mail Millbury **z** 01527; ● 1,000
East Milton; RMC Place; NORFOLK; ▲ Milton; ***187** F-14; elev. 50ft./15m.; ★ **BOS**; mail Milton **z** 02186
East Natick; RMC Place; MIDDLESEX; ▲ Natick; ***187** E-13; ★ **BOS**; mail Natick **z** 01760
East Northfield; RMC Place; FRANKLIN; ▲ Northfield; ***186** B-6; elev. 450ft./137m.; mail Northfield **z** 01360
Easton (Easton Center); RMC Place; BRISTOL; ▲ Easton; **187** G-14; 🄿; ★ **BOS**; **z** 02334 & mail North Easton **z** 02356-57, South Easton **z** 02375; ● 530
Easton; MCD-Town; BRISTOL; ***187** H-14; 🄿 🄲 2,386; ★ **BOS**; **z** 02334 & mail North Easton **z** 02356-57, South Easton **z** 02375; Ⓟ 19,807; © 22,299; ◆ 22,853
Easton Center; BRISTOL; see Easton (RMC Place)
Eastondale; RMC Place; BRISTOL; ▲ Easton; **187** G-14; elev. 120ft./37m.; ★ **BOS**; mail South Easton **z** 02375; ● 750
East Orleans; RMC Place; BARNSTABLE; ▲ Orleans; **187** I-20; elev. 39ft./12m.; 🄿; ★ **BARN**; **z** 02643; ● 1,200
East Otis; RMC Place; BERKSHIRE; ▲ Otis; **186** F-3; elev. 1,470ft./448m.; 🄿; **z** 01029; ● 200
East Pembroke; RMC Place; PLYMOUTH; ▲ Pembroke; ***187** G-16; elev. 44ft./13m.; ★ **BOS**; mail Pembroke **z** 02359
East Pepperell (Pepperell); CDP; MIDDLESEX; ▲ Pepperell; **187** C-11; elev. 210ft./64m.; ★ **BOS**; mail Pepperell **z** 01463; Ⓟ 2,296; © 2,034
East Princeton; RMC Place; WORCESTER; ▲ Princeton; **186** D-10; elev. 713ft./217m.; 🄿; ★ **WORC**; **z** 01517 & mail Princeton **z** 01541; ● 200
East Sandwich; CDP; BARNSTABLE; ▲ Sandwich; **187** J-18; elev. 20ft./6m.; 🄿; ★ **BARN**; **z** 02537; Ⓟ 3,171; © 3,720
East Saugus; RMC Place; ESSEX; ▲ Saugus; ***187** N-20; ★ **BOS**; mail Saugus **z** 01906
East Somerville; RMC Place; MIDDLESEX; ***187** E-14; elev. 25ft./8m.; ★ **BOS**; mail Somerville **z** 02143, **z** 02145; pop. incl. with Somerville (Inc. Place)
East Springfield; RMC Place; HAMPDEN; **187** L-12; elev. 220ft./67m.; ★ **SPRG**; mail Springfield **z** 01101; pop. incl. with Springfield (Inc. Place)
East Sudbury; MIDDLESEX; see East Sudbury Station (RMC Place)
East Sudbury Station (East Sudbury); RMC Place; MIDDLESEX; ▲ Sudbury; **187** E-12; ★ **BOS**; mail Sudbury **z** 01776; ● 800
East Swansea; RMC Place; BRISTOL; ▲ Swansea; **187** J-14; ★ **F.R.**; mail Swansea **z** 02777; pop. incl. with Fall River (Inc. Place)
East Taunton; RMC Place; BRISTOL; ***187** I-14; elev. 15ft./5m.; 🄿; ★ **BOS**; **z** 02718; pop. incl. with Taunton (Inc. Place)
East Templeton; RMC Place; WORCESTER; ▲ Templeton; **186** C-9; elev. 1,061ft./323m.; 🄿; ★ **BOS**; **z** 01438 & mail Attleboro Falls **z** 02763, North Attleboro **z** 02760-61, Plainville **z** 02762; ● 1,350
East Village; RMC Place; WORCESTER; ▲ Webster; ***186** G-10; elev. 478ft./146m.; ★ **WORC**; mail Webster **z** 01570
Eastville; RMC Place; DUKES; ▲ Oak Bluffs; ***187** L-17; mail Oak Bluffs **z** 02557
East Walpole; RMC Place; NORFOLK; ▲ Walpole; **187** G-13; elev. 120ft./37m.; 🄿; ★ **BOS**; **z** 02032; ● 3,800
East Wareham (Agawam); RMC Place; PLYMOUTH; ▲ Wareham; **187** J-16; elev. 20ft./6m.; 🄿; ★ **BOS**; **z** 02538 & mail Onset **z** 02558; ● 1,500
East Watertown; RMC Place; MIDDLESEX; ***187** E-14; elev. 50ft./15m.; 🄿; ★ **BOS**; **z** 02472; pop. incl. with Watertown (Inc. Place)
East Weymouth; RMC Place; NORFOLK; ▲ Weymouth; **186** N-9; elev. 50ft./15m.; 🄿; ★ **BOS**; **z** 02189
East Windsor; RMC Place; BERKSHIRE; ▲ Windsor; **186** D-3; elev. 1,388ft./423m.; mail Windsor **z** 01270; ● 100
Eddyville; RMC Place; PLYMOUTH; ▲ Middleborough; ***187** H-15; elev. 90ft./27m.; ★ **BOS**; mail Middleboro **z** 02346; ● 110
Edgartown; RMC Place; ⊡ DUKES; ▲ Edgartown; **187** L-17; elev. 17ft./5m.; 🄿; **z** 02539; ● 1,500
Edgartown; MCD-Town; DUKES; ***187** L-17; 🄿; **z** 02539; Ⓟ 3,062; © 3,779
Edgemere; RMC Place; WORCESTER; ▲ Shrewsbury; **187** C-20; elev. 380ft./116m.; ★ **WORC**; mail Shrewsbury **z** 01545
Edgeworth; RMC Place; MIDDLESEX; ***187** E-14; elev. 20ft./6m.; ★ **BOS**; mail Malden **z** 02148; pop. incl. with Malden (Inc. Place)
Egleston Square; RMC Place; SUFFOLK; ***187** N-20; ★ **BOS**; mail Boston **z** 02116; pop. incl. with Boston (Inc. Place)
Egremont; MCD-Town; BERKSHIRE; ***186** F-1; 🄿; **z** 01230 & mail North Egremont **z** 01252; Ⓟ 1,229; © 1,345
Egypt; RMC Place; PLYMOUTH; ▲ Scituate; **187** F-16; elev. 27ft./8m.; ★ **BOS**; mail Scituate **z** 02066; ● 900
Ellisville; RMC Place; PLYMOUTH; ▲ Plymouth; **187** I-17; elev. 26ft./8m.; ★ **BOS**; mail Plymouth **z** 02360; ● 120
Elmdale; RMC Place; WORCESTER; ▲ Uxbridge; ***187** G-11; ★ **WORC**; mail Uxbridge **z** 01569; ● 150
Elm Grove; RMC Place; FRANKLIN; ▲ Colrain; ***186** B-5; elev. 721ft./220m.; mail Colrain **z** 01340
Elm Square; RMC Place; PLYMOUTH; ▲ West Bridgewater; ***187** H-14; elev. 67ft./20m.; ★ **BOS**; mail West Bridgewater **z** 02379
Elmwood; RMC Place; HAMPDEN; **187** K-11; elev. 250ft./76m.; ★ **SPRG**; mail Holyoke **z** 01040; pop. incl. with Holyoke (Inc. Place)
Elmwood; RMC Place; PLYMOUTH; ▲ East Bridgewater; **187** H-15; elev. 70ft./21m.; 🄿; ★ **BOS**; **z** 02337; ● 500
Endicott; RMC Place; NORFOLK; ▲ Dedham; **186** N-6; elev. 110ft./34m.; ★ **BOS**; mail Dedham **z** 02026
Englewood; RMC Place; BARNSTABLE; ▲ Yarmouth; ***187** J-19; elev. 10ft./3m.; ★ **BARN**; mail West Yarmouth **z** 02673
Erving; RMC Place; FRANKLIN; ▲ Erving; **186** C-7; elev. 475ft./145m.; 🄿; **z** 01344; ● 420
Erving; MCD-Town; FRANKLIN; ***186** C-6; 🄿; **z** 01344; Ⓟ 1,372; © 1,467
Essex; CDP; ESSEX; ▲ Essex; **187** C-16; elev. 26ft./8m.; 🄿; ★ **BOS**; **z** 01929; Ⓟ 1,507; © 1,426
Essex; MCD-Town; ESSEX; ***187** C-16; 🄿; ★ **BOS**; **z** 01929; Ⓟ 3,260; © 3,267; ◆ 3,272
Essex; RMC Place; SUFFOLK; ***187** E-14; ★ **BOS**; mail Boston **z** 02112; pop. incl. with Boston (Inc. Place)
ESSEX; **187** C-14; Ⓟ 670,080; © 723,419; ◆ 727,299
Essex Falls; RMC Place; ESSEX; ▲ Essex; ***187** C-16; elev. 60ft./18m.; ★ **BOS**; mail Essex **z** 01929
Everett; Inc. Place; MIDDLESEX; **187** E-14; elev. 10ft./3m.; 🄿; ★ **BOS**; **z** 02149; Ⓟ 35,701; © 38,037; ◆ 39,348

F

Factory Hollow; RMC Place; HAMPSHIRE; ▲ Amherst; ***186** E-6; elev. 250ft./76m.; ★ **SPRG**; mail Amherst **z** 01002
Fairhaven; RMC Place; BRISTOL; ▲ Fairhaven; **187** K-15; elev. 15ft./5m.; 🄿; ★ **N.BED**; **z** 02719; ● 16,132
Fairhaven; MCD-Town; BRISTOL; ***187** K-15; 🄿; ★ **N.BED**; **z** 02719; Ⓟ 16,132; © 16,159; ◆ 15,762
Fairlawn (Turnpike); RMC Place; WORCESTER; ▲ Shrewsbury; ***186** F-10; elev. 400ft./122m.; ★ **WORC**; mail Shrewsbury **z** 01545
Fairmount; RMC Place; SUFFOLK; ***187** F-14; elev. 150ft./46m.; ★ **BOS**; mail Hyde Park **z** 02136; pop. incl. with Boston (Inc. Place)
Fairview; RMC Place; HAMPDEN; **187** K-12; elev. 240ft./73m.; ★ **SPRG**; mail Chicopee **z** 01020; pop. incl. with Chicopee (Inc. Place)
Fall River; Inc. Place; BRISTOL; **187** J-14; elev. 200ft./61m.; 🄿 🄷 ■; ★ **F.R.**; **z** 02720-24 & mail Somerset **z** 02725-26; Ⓟ 92,703; © 91,938; ◆ 89,253
Falmouth; CDP; BARNSTABLE; ▲ Falmouth; **187** K-17; elev. 10ft./3m.; 🄿 🄷 🄲 1,200; **z** 02540-41, **z** 02543; Ⓟ 4,047; © 4,115
Falmouth; MCD-Town; BARNSTABLE; ***187** K-17; 🄿 🄲 1,200; **z** 02540-41, **z** 02543; Ⓟ 27,960; © 32,660; ◆ 31,172
Falmouth Cliffs; RMC Place; BARNSTABLE; ▲ Falmouth; ***187** K-17; mail West Falmouth **z** 02574
Falmouth Heights; RMC Place; BARNSTABLE; ▲ Falmouth; ***187** K-17; elev. 12ft./4m.; mail Falmouth **z** 02540
Farley; RMC Place; FRANKLIN; ▲ Erving; **186** C-6; elev. 425ft./130m.; mail Erving **z** 01344; ● 50
Farmersville (South Sandwich); RMC Place; BARNSTABLE; ▲ Sandwich; ***187** J-18; ★ **BARN**; mail Sandwich **z** 02563; rural
Farm Hill; RMC Place; MIDDLESEX; ▲ Stoneham; ***187** N-20; ★ **BOS**; mail Stoneham **z** 02180
Farnams; RMC Place; BERKSHIRE; ▲ Cheshire; ***186** D-2; elev. 1,052ft./321m.; ★ **PTSF**; mail Cheshire **z** 01225; rural
Farnumsville; RMC Place; WORCESTER; ▲ Grafton; ***187** F-11; elev. 305ft./93m.; ★ **WORC**; mail South Grafton **z** 01560
Faulkner; RMC Place; MIDDLESEX; ***187** D-14; elev. 13ft./4m.; ★ **BOS**; mail Malden **z** 02148; pop. incl. with Malden (Inc. Place)
Fayville; RMC Place; WORCESTER; ▲ Southborough; **187** F-12; elev. 310ft./94m.; 🄿; ★ **BOS**; **z** 01745; ● 1,000
Federal; RMC Place; WORCESTER; ***186** F-10; ★ **WORC**; mail Worcester **z** 01601; pop. incl. with Worcester (Inc. Place)
Feeding Hills; RMC Place; HAMPDEN; **186** G-5; elev. 218ft./66m.; 🄿; ★ **SPRG**; **z** 01030; pop. incl. with Agawam (Inc. Place)
Felchville; RMC Place; MIDDLESEX; ▲ Natick; **186** L-3; elev. 185ft./56m.; ★ **BOS**; mail Natick **z** 01760
Fellsway; RMC Place; MIDDLESEX; ***187** N-20; ★ **BOS**; mail Medford **z** 02155; pop. incl. with Medford (Inc. Place)
Fentonville; RMC Place; HAMPDEN; ▲ Brimfield; ***186** G-7; elev. 377ft./115m.; mail Palmer **z** 01069; ● 50
Fields Corner; RMC Place; SUFFOLK; ***187** E-14; elev. 70ft./21m.; ★ **BOS**; mail Boston **z** 02122; pop. incl. with Boston (Inc. Place)
Fieldston; RMC Place; PLYMOUTH; ▲ Marshfield; ***187** G-16; elev. 20ft./6m.; ★ **BOS**; mail Ocean Bluff **z** 02065
Findlen; RMC Place; NORFOLK; ▲ Dedham; ***187** N-20; ★ **BOS**; mail Dedham **z** 02026
First Cliff; RMC Place; PLYMOUTH; ▲ Scituate; ***187** F-16; elev. 20ft./6m.; ★ **BOS**; mail Scituate **z** 02066
Fisherville (South Grafton); RMC Place; WORCESTER; ▲ Grafton; **187** F-11; ★ **WORC**; mail South Grafton **z** 01560; ● 2,750
Fiskdale; CDP; WORCESTER; ▲ Sturbridge; **186** G-8; elev. 636ft./194m.; 🄿; ★ **WORC**; **z** 01518, **z** 01521; Ⓟ 2,189; © 2,156
Fitchburg; Inc. Place; WORCESTER; **186** C-10; elev. 482ft./147m.; 🄿 🄲 5,508 ■; ★ **BOS**; **z** 01420; Ⓟ 41,194; © 39,102; ◆ 37,254
Five Corners; RMC Place; BRISTOL; ▲ Easton; **187** H-14; elev. 125ft./38m.; ★ **BOS**; mail North Easton **z** 02356, South Easton **z** 02375; ● 110
Flint; RMC Place; BRISTOL; **187** F-18; ★ **F.R.**; mail Fall River **z** 02723; pop. incl. with Fall River (Inc. Place)
Flints Corner; RMC Place; MIDDLESEX; ▲ Tyngsborough; ***187** C-12; ★ **BOS**; mail Tyngsboro **z** 01879; ● 40
Florence; RMC Place; HAMPSHIRE; ***186** E-5; elev. 280ft./85m.; 🄿; ★ **SPRG**; **z** 01062; pop. incl. with Northampton (Inc. Place)
Florida; RMC Place; BERKSHIRE; ▲ Florida; **186** C-3; elev. 1,895ft./578m.; 🄿; **z** 01247; ● 50
Florida; MCD-Town; BERKSHIRE; ***186** C-3; 🄿; **z** 01247; Ⓟ 742; © 676
Fore River; RMC Place; NORFOLK; ***187** N-20; ★ **BOS**; mail Quincy **z** 02169; pop. incl. with Quincy (Inc. Place)
Forestdale; CDP; BARNSTABLE; ▲ Sandwich; **187** J-17; elev. 145ft./44m.; 🄿; ★ **BARN**; **z** 02644; Ⓟ 2,833; © 3,992
Forest Hills; RMC Place; SUFFOLK; ***187** F-14; elev. 75ft./23m.; ★ **BOS**; mail Jamaica Plain **z** 02130; pop. incl. with Boston (Inc. Place)
Forest Lake (Forest Lake Junction); RMC Place; HAMPDEN; ▲ Palmer; ***186** F-7; ★ **SPRG**; mail Palmer **z** 01069; rural
Forest Lake Junction; HAMPDEN; see Forest Lake (RMC Place)
Forest Park; RMC Place; HAMPDEN; **187** M-12; elev. 185ft./56m.; ★ **SPRG**; mail Springfield **z** 01108; pop. incl. with Springfield (Inc. Place)
Forest Park; RMC Place; NORFOLK; ▲ Bellingham; ***187** G-12; elev. 260ft./79m.; ★ **BOS**; mail Bellingham **z** 02019; pop. incl. with Norfolk (Independent City)
Forest River; RMC Place; ESSEX; ***187** N-20; ★ **BOS**; mail Salem **z** 01970; pop. incl. with Salem (Inc. Place)
Forge Village; RMC Place; MIDDLESEX; ▲ Westford; **187** C-12; elev. 204ft./62m.; ★ **BOS**; mail Westford **z** 01886; ● 850
Fort Bellingham; RMC Place; NORFOLK; ▲ Bellingham; ***187** N-20; ★ **BOS**; mail Bellingham **z** 02019
Fort Devens; CDP-Census Area Only; WORCESTER, MIDDLESEX; ▲ Shirley, Ayer, Harvard; ***187** D-11; ★ **BOS**; mail Ayer **z** 01432; Ⓟ 8,973; © 1,017
Fort Point; RMC Place; SUFFOLK; ***187** N-20; ★ **BOS**; mail Boston **z** 02205; pop. incl. with Boston (Inc. Place)
Foundry Village; RMC Place; FRANKLIN; ▲ Colrain; ***186** C-5; elev. 554ft./169m.; mail Colrain **z** 01340; ● 120
Foxboro; RMC Place; NORFOLK; ▲ Foxborough; **187** G-13; ★ **BOS**; ● 4,220
Foxborough; CDP-Census Area Only; NORFOLK; ▲ Foxborough; **187** G-13; elev. 280ft./85m.; 🄿; ★ **BOS**; **z** 02035; Ⓟ 5,706; © 5,509
Foxborough; MCD-Town; NORFOLK; ***187** G-13; 🄿; ★ **BOS**; **z** 02035; Ⓟ 14,637; © 16,246; ◆ 16,579
Foxvale; RMC Place; NORFOLK; ▲ Foxborough; **187** G-13; elev. 205ft./62m.; ★ **BOS**; mail Foxboro **z** 02035; ● 500
Framingham; CDP; MIDDLESEX; ▲ Framingham, Natick; **187** F-12; elev. 165ft./50m.; 🄿 🄷 🄲 5,861; ★ **BOS**; **z** 01701-05; Ⓟ 64,989; © 66,910; ◆ 67,378
Framingham; MCD-Town; MIDDLESEX; ***187** E-12; 🄿 🄲 5,861 ■; ★ **BOS**; **z** 01701-05; Ⓟ 64,989; © 66,910; ◆ 67,378
Framingham Center (Framingham Centre); RMC Place; MIDDLESEX; ▲ Framingham; **186** L-2; elev. 200ft./61m.; ★ **BOS**; mail Framingham **z** 01703
Framingham Centre; MIDDLESEX; see Framingham Center (RMC Place)
Franklin; Inc. Place; NORFOLK; **187** G-12; elev. 300ft./91m.; 🄿 🄲 1,256; ★ **BOS**; **z** 02038; Ⓟ 22,095; © 29,560; ◆ 30,600
FRANKLIN; **186** D-5; Ⓟ 70,092; © 71,535; ◆ 70,442
Franklin Park; RMC Place; SUFFOLK; ***186** E-3; elev. 100ft./30m.; mail Revere **z** 02151; pop. incl. with Revere (Inc. Place)
Freetown; MCD-Town; BRISTOL; ***187** J-14; ★ **N.BED**; mail Assonet **z** 02702; Ⓟ 8,522; © 8,472; ◆ 8,487
Fresh Pond; RMC Place; MIDDLESEX; ***187** N-20; ★ **BOS**; mail Cambridge **z** 02138; pop. incl. with Cambridge (Inc. Place)
Freshwater Cove; RMC Place; ESSEX; ***187** C-16; ★ **BOS**; mail Gloucester **z** 01930; pop. incl. with Gloucester (Inc. Place)
Fuller Shores; RMC Place; PLYMOUTH; ▲ Lakeville; ***187** I-15; elev. 65ft./20m.; ★ **BOS**; mail Middleboro **z** 02346; ● 30
Furnace (Old Furnace); RMC Place; WORCESTER; ▲ Hardwick; ***186** E-8; mail Gilbertville **z** 01031
Furnace Village; RMC Place; BRISTOL; ▲ Easton; ***187** N-20; ★ **BOS**; mail Easton **z** 02334

G

Gardner; Inc. Place; WORCESTER; **186** C-9; elev. 1,100ft./335m.; 🄿 🄷; ★ **BOS**; **z** 01440 & mail Westminster **z** 01441; Ⓟ 20,125; © 20,770; ◆ 20,403
Gay Head; RMC Place; DUKES; ▲ Aquinnah; **187** M-16; elev. 166ft./51m.; 🄿; **z** 02535; ● 130
Gay Head; DUKES; see Aquinnah (MCD-Town)
Georgetown; RMC Place; ESSEX; ▲ Georgetown; **187** B-15; elev. 79ft./24m.; 🄿 🄷; ★ **BOS**; **z** 01833; ● 2,200
Georgetown; MCD-Town; ESSEX; ***187** B-15; 🄿; ★ **BOS**; **z** 01833; Ⓟ 6,384; © 7,377; ◆ 7,597
Germantown; RMC Place; NORFOLK; ***187** F-15; elev. 10ft./3m.; ★ **BOS**; mail Quincy **z** 02169; pop. incl. with Quincy (Inc. Place)
Gilbertville; RMC Place; WORCESTER; ▲ Hardwick; **186** E-8; elev. 548ft./167m.; 🄿; **z** 01031; ● 1,050
Gill; RMC Place; FRANKLIN; ▲ Gill; **186** C-6; 🄿; **z** 01354, **z** 01376; ● 150
Gill; MCD-Town; FRANKLIN; ***186** C-6; 🄿; **z** 01354, **z** 01376; Ⓟ 1,583; © 1,363
Gillett Corner; RMC Place; HAMPDEN; ▲ Southwick; ***186** H-4; elev. 273ft./83m.; ★ **SPRG**; mail Southwick **z** 01077
Gill Station; RMC Place; FRANKLIN; ▲ Northfield; ***186** C-6; mail Northfield **z** 01360; rural
Gleasondale; RMC Place; MIDDLESEX; ▲ Hudson; **187** E-12; ★ **BOS**; mail Stow **z** 01775; ● 250
Glendale; RMC Place; BERKSHIRE; ▲ Stockbridge; **186** F-1; elev. 880ft./268m.; 🄿; ★ **PTSF**; **z** 01229; ● 400
Glen Echo; RMC Place; NORFOLK; ▲ Stoughton; ***187** G-14; ★ **BOS**; mail Stoughton **z** 02072
Glen Grove; RMC Place; WORCESTER; ▲ Charlton; **186** G-9; elev. 822ft./251m.; ★ **WORC**; mail Charlton City **z** 01508; ● 270
Glen Grove Annex; RMC Place; WORCESTER; ▲ Charlton; ***186** G-9; elev. 81ft./25m.; ★ **WORC**; mail Charlton City **z** 01508; ● 350
Glenridge; RMC Place; NORFOLK; ▲ Dover; **186** M-3; elev. 250ft./76m.; ★ **BOS**; mail Dover **z** 02030; ● 350
Gloucester; Inc. Place; ESSEX; **187** C-16; elev. 50ft./15m.; 🄿 ■; ★ **BOS**; **z** 01930-31; Ⓟ 28,716; © 30,273; ◆ 30,039
Goodrichville; RMC Place; WORCESTER; ▲ Lunenburg; ***187** C-11; ★ **BOS**; mail Lunenburg **z** 01462; ● 100
Goshen; RMC Place; HAMPSHIRE; ▲ Goshen; **186** D-4; elev. 1,450ft./442m.; 🄿; **z** 01032; ● 600
Goshen; MCD-Town; HAMPSHIRE; ***186** D-4; 🄿; **z** 01032; Ⓟ 830; © 921
Gosnold; MCD-Town; DUKES; ***187** L-16; mail Cuttyhunk **z** 02713; Ⓟ 98; © 86
Goss Heights; RMC Place; HAMPSHIRE; ▲ Huntington; **186** F-4; elev. 550ft./168m.; ★ **SPRG**; mail Huntington **z** 01050; ● 100
Goulding Village; RMC Place; WORCESTER; ▲ Phillipston; ***186** D-8; mail Athol **z** 01331
Grafton (Grafton Center); RMC Place; WORCESTER; ▲ Grafton; **187** F-11; elev. 425ft./130m.; 🄿; ★ **WORC**; **z** 01519; ● 1,650
Grafton; MCD-Town; WORCESTER; ***187** F-11; 🄿; ★ **WORC**; **z** 01519; Ⓟ 13,035; © 14,894; ◆ 16,994
Grafton Center; WORCESTER; see Grafton (RMC Place)
Granby; CDP; HAMPSHIRE; ▲ Granby; **186** F-6; elev. 330ft./101m.; 🄿; ★ **SPRG**; **z** 01033; Ⓟ 1,327; © 1,344
Granby; MCD-Town; HAMPSHIRE; ***186** F-6; 🄿; ★ **SPRG**; **z** 01033; Ⓟ 5,565; © 6,132; ◆ 6,352
Graniteville; RMC Place; MIDDLESEX; ▲ Westford; **187** C-12; elev. 217ft./66m.; ★ **BOS**; mail Westford **z** 01886; ● 1,200
Granville; RMC Place; HAMPDEN; ▲ Granville; **186** G-4; elev. 685ft./209m.; 🄿; **z** 01034; ● 450
Granville; MCD-Town; HAMPDEN; ***186** G-4; 🄿; **z** 01034; Ⓟ 1,403; © 1,521
Granville Center; RMC Place; HAMPDEN; ▲ Granville; ***186** G-4; elev. 1,043ft./318m.; mail Granville **z** 01034
Gray Gables; RMC Place; BARNSTABLE; ▲ Bourne; **187** J-17; elev. 10ft./3m.; mail Buzzards Bay **z** 02532; ● 600
Great Barrington; CDP; BERKSHIRE; ▲ Great Barrington; **186** F-1; elev. 721ft./220m.; 🄿 🄷 🄲 370; **z** 01230; Ⓟ 2,810; © 2,459
Great Barrington; MCD-Town; BERKSHIRE; ***186** F-1; 🄿 🄲 370; **z** 01230; Ⓟ 7,725; © 7,527
Great Brook Valley; RMC Place; WORCESTER; **187** A-20; elev. 453ft./138m.; ★ **WORC**; mail Worcester **z** 01605; pop. incl. with Worcester (Inc. Place)
Greenbush; RMC Place; PLYMOUTH; ▲ Scituate; ***187** F-16; elev. 54ft./16m.; 🄿; ★ **BOS**; **z** 02040
Greendale; RMC Place; WORCESTER; **187** A-19; elev. 650ft./198m.; ★ **WORC**; mail Worcester **z** 01606; pop. incl. with Worcester (Inc. Place)
Greenfield; CDP; ⊡ FRANKLIN; ▲ Greenfield; **186** C-5; elev. 250ft./76m.; 🄿 🄷; **z** 01301-02; Ⓟ 14,016; © 13,716
Greenfield; MCD-Town; FRANKLIN; ***186** C-5; 🄿 ■; **z** 01301-02; Ⓟ 18,666; © 18,168; ◆ 17,444
Greenfield Center; RMC Place; FRANKLIN; ▲ Greenfield; ***187** N-20; mail Greenfield **z** 01301
Green Harbor; RMC Place; PLYMOUTH; ▲ Marshfield; **187** G-17; elev. 10ft./3m.; 🄿; ★ **BOS**; **z** 02041; ● 1,500
Green Harbor-Cedar Crest; CDP-Census Area Only; PLYMOUTH; ***187** G-16; ★ **BOS**; mail Green Harbor **z** 02041; Ⓟ 2,205; © 2,397
Greenlodge; RMC Place; NORFOLK; ▲ Dedham; ***187** F-14; elev. 140ft./43m.; ★ **BOS**; mail Dedham **z** 02026
Green Ridge Park; RMC Place; BERKSHIRE; ▲ Dalton; ***186** D-2; elev. 1,050ft./320m.; ★ **PTSF**; mail Dalton **z** 01226
Greenview Estates; RMC Place; NORFOLK; ▲ Foxborough; ***187** H-13; ★ **BOS**; mail Foxboro **z** 02035; ● 450
Greenville; RMC Place; WORCESTER; ▲ Leicester; ***186** F-9; elev. 792ft./241m.; ★ **WORC**; mail Rochdale **z** 01542
Greenwood; RMC Place; MIDDLESEX; ▲ Wakefield; **186** I-7; elev. 150ft./46m.; ★ **BOS**; mail Wakefield **z** 01880
Greylock; RMC Place; BERKSHIRE; ***186** B-2; elev. 650ft./198m.; mail North Adams **z** 01247; pop. incl. with North Adams (Inc. Place)
Griswoldville; RMC Place; FRANKLIN; ▲ Colrain; **186** C-5; elev. 503ft./153m.; mail Colrain **z** 01340; ● 380
Grosvenor Corner; RMC Place; ESSEX; ***187** B-14; ★ **BOS**; mail Methuen **z** 01844; pop. incl. with Methuen (Inc. Place)
Groton; CDP; MIDDLESEX; ▲ Groton; **187** C-11; elev. 320ft./98m.; 🄿; ★ **BOS**; **z** 01450, **z** 01470-71; Ⓟ 1,044; © 1,113
Groton; MCD-Town; MIDDLESEX; ***187** C-11; 🄿; ★ **BOS**; **z** 01450, **z** 01470-71; Ⓟ 7,511; © 9,547; ◆ 9,994
Grove Hall; RMC Place; SUFFOLK; ***187** E-14; elev. 90ft./27m.; 🄿; ★ **BOS**; **z** 02121; pop. incl. with Boston (Inc. Place)
Groveland; RMC Place; ESSEX; ▲ Groveland; **187** B-14; elev. 48ft./15m.; 🄿; ★ **BOS**; **z** 01834; ● 3,800
Groveland; MCD-Town; ESSEX; ***187** B-14; 🄿; ★ **BOS**; **z** 01834; Ⓟ 5,214; © 6,038; ◆ 6,336

H

Hadley; RMC Place; HAMPSHIRE; ▲ Hadley; **186** E-5; elev. 129ft./39m.; 🄿; ★ **SPRG**; **z** 01035; ● 970
Hadley; MCD-Town; HAMPSHIRE; ***186** E-6; 🄿; ★ **SPRG**; **z** 01035; Ⓟ 4,231; © 4,793; ◆ 4,881
Halfway Pond; RMC Place; PLYMOUTH; ▲ Plymouth; ***187** I-17; ★ **BOS**; mail Plymouth **z** 02360; ● 120
Halifax; RMC Place; PLYMOUTH; ▲ Halifax; **187** H-15; elev. 90ft./27m.; 🄿; ★ **BOS**; **z** 02338; ● 980
Halifax; MCD-Town; PLYMOUTH; ***187** H-15; 🄿; ★ **BOS**; **z** 02338; Ⓟ 6,526; © 7,500; ◆ 8,036
Halifax Beach; RMC Place; PLYMOUTH; ▲ Halifax; ***187** H-15; elev. 60ft./18m.; ★ **BOS**; mail Halifax **z** 02338
Hamilton; RMC Place; ESSEX; ▲ Hamilton; **187** C-15; 🄿; ★ **BOS**; **z** 01936 & mail South Hamilton **z** 01982; ● 1,000
Hamilton; MCD-Town; ESSEX; ***187** C-15; 🄿 🄲 2,212; ★ **BOS**; **z** 01936 & mail South Hamilton **z** 01982; Ⓟ 7,280; © 8,315; ◆ 8,433
Hamilton; RMC Place; WORCESTER; ***186** F-10; elev. 500ft./152m.; ★ **WORC**; mail Worcester **z** 01604; pop. incl. with Worcester (Inc. Place)
Hamilton Beach; RMC Place; PLYMOUTH; ▲ Wareham; ***187** J-16; elev. 10ft./3m.; ★ **BOS**; mail Wareham **z** 02571
Hampden; RMC Place; HAMPDEN; ▲ Hampden; **186** G-6; elev. 290ft./88m.; 🄿; ★ **SPRG**; **z** 01036; ● 900
Hampden; MCD-Town; HAMPDEN; ***186** G-6; 🄿; ★ **SPRG**; **z** 01036; Ⓟ 4,709; © 5,171; ◆ 5,318
HAMPDEN; **186** G-7; Ⓟ 456,310; © 456,228; ◆ 452,661
HAMPSHIRE; **186** E-4; Ⓟ 146,568; © 152,251; ◆ 152,496
Hampton Mills; RMC Place; HAMPSHIRE; ***187** N-20; ★ **SPRG**; mail Easthampton **z** 01027; pop. incl. with Easthampton (Inc. Place)
Hancock; RMC Place; BERKSHIRE; ▲ Hancock; **186** D-1; elev. 1,058ft./322m.; 🄿; **z** 01237; ● 200
Hancock; MCD-Town; BERKSHIRE; ***186** D-1; 🄿; **z** 01237; Ⓟ 628; © 721
Hancock Village; NORFOLK; see Westbrook Village (RMC Place)
Hanover; RMC Place; PLYMOUTH; ▲ Hanover; **187** G-16; elev. 60ft./18m.; 🄿; ★ **BOS**; **z** 02339-40; ● 2,500
Hanover; MCD-Town; PLYMOUTH; ***187** G-15; 🄿; ★ **BOS**; **z** 02339-40; Ⓟ 11,912; © 13,164; ◆ 13,494
Hanover Center; RMC Place; PLYMOUTH; ▲ Hanover; **187** G-15; elev. 114ft./35m.; ★ **BOS**; mail Hanover **z** 02339; ● 1,000
Hanover Street; RMC Place; SUFFOLK; ***187** E-14; ★ **BOS**; mail Boston **z** 02113; pop. incl. with Boston (Inc. Place)
Hanson; CDP; PLYMOUTH; ▲ Hanson; **187** G-15; elev. 90ft./27m.; 🄿; ★ **BOS**; **z** 02341 & mail Monponsett **z** 02350; Ⓟ 2,188; © 2,044
Hanson; MCD-Town; PLYMOUTH; ***187** G-15; 🄿; ★ **BOS**; **z** 02341 & mail Monponsett **z** 02350; Ⓟ 9,028; © 9,495; ◆ 9,701
Happy Hills; RMC Place; NORFOLK; ▲ Bellingham; ***187** G-12; elev. 290ft./88m.; ★ **BOS**; mail Bellingham **z** 02019
Harbor Beach; RMC Place; PLYMOUTH; ▲ Mattapoisett; ***187** J-16; elev. 10ft./3m.; ★ **N.BED**; mail Mattapoisett **z** 02739; ● 50
Harbor View; RMC Place; BRISTOL; ▲ Fairhaven; ***187** K-15; ★ **N.BED**; mail Fairhaven **z** 02719
Harding; RMC Place; NORFOLK; ▲ Medfield; **187** F-13; elev. 165ft./50m.; ★ **BOS**; mail Medfield **z** 02052; ● 850
Hardwick (Hardwick Center); RMC Place; WORCESTER; ▲ Hardwick; **186** E-8; elev. 880ft./268m.; 🄿; **z** 01037; ● 530
Hardwick; MCD-Town; WORCESTER; ***186** E-8; 🄿; **z** 01037; Ⓟ 2,385; © 2,622
Hardwick Center; WORCESTER; see Hardwick (RMC Place)
Harrisville; RMC Place; WORCESTER; ▲ Winchendon; ***186** B-8; ★ **BOS**; mail Winchendon **z** 01475; ● 30
Harrubs Corner; RMC Place; PLYMOUTH; ▲ Plympton; ***187** H-16; ★ **BOS**; mail Plympton **z** 02367
Harthaven; RMC Place; DUKES; ▲ Oak Bluffs; ***187** L-17; elev. 10ft./3m.; mail Oak Bluffs **z** 02557
Hartsville; RMC Place; BERKSHIRE; ▲ New Marlborough; **186** G-2; elev. 921ft./281m.; mail Great Barrington **z** 01230; ● 125
Harvard; RMC Place; WORCESTER; ▲ Harvard; **187** D-11; elev. 421ft./128m.; 🄿; ★ **BOS**; **z** 01451; ● 1,200
Harvard; MCD-Town; WORCESTER; ***187** D-11; 🄿; ★ **BOS**; **z** 01451; Ⓟ 12,329; © 5,981; ◆ 5,700
Harvard Square; RMC Place; MIDDLESEX; ***187** E-14; 🄿; ★ **BOS**; **z** 02238 & mail Cambridge **z** 02138; pop. incl. with Cambridge (Inc. Place)
Harwich; RMC Place; BARNSTABLE; **187** J-20; ★ **BARN**; ● 2,000
Harwich; MCD-Town; BARNSTABLE; ***187** J-20; 🄿; ★ **BARN**; **z** 02645; Ⓟ 10,275; © 12,386; ◆ 11,695
Harwich Center; CDP-Census Area Only; BARNSTABLE; ▲ Harwich; **187** J-20; elev. 55ft./17m.; ★ **BARN**; mail Harwich **z** 02645; Ⓟ 1,668; © 1,832
Harwich Port; CDP; BARNSTABLE; ▲ Harwich; **187** J-20; elev. 12ft./4m.; 🄿; ★ **BARN**; **z** 02646; Ⓟ 1,742; © 1,809
Hassanamisco Reservation; Indian Reservation; WORCESTER; ***187** N-20; State Reservation; © 2
Hastings; RMC Place; MIDDLESEX; ▲ Weston; ***187** E-13; elev. 180ft./55m.; ★ **BOS**; mail Weston **z** 02493
Hatchville; RMC Place; BARNSTABLE; ▲ Falmouth; **187** K-17; elev. 92ft./28m.; 🄿; **z** 02536; ● 330
Hatfield; CDP; HAMPSHIRE; ▲ Hatfield; **186** E-5; elev. 129ft./39m.; 🄿; ★ **SPRG**; **z** 01038; Ⓟ 1,234; © 1,298
Hatfield; HAMPSHIRE; see West Hatfield (RMC Place)
Hatfield; MCD-Town; HAMPSHIRE; ***186** E-5; 🄿; ★ **SPRG**; **z** 01038; Ⓟ 3,184; © 3,249; ◆ 3,281
Hathorne; RMC Place; ESSEX; **187** C-15; mail Danvers **z** 01923; ● 230
Haverhill; Inc. Place; ESSEX; **187** B-14; elev. 27ft./8m.; 🄿 🄷 ■; ★ **BOS**; **z** 01830-33, **z** 01835; Ⓟ 51,418; © 58,969; ◆ 61,480
Hawley; RMC Place; FRANKLIN; ▲ Hawley; **186** C-4; elev. 1,752ft./534m.; 🄿; **z** 01339; ● 60
Hawley; MCD-Town; FRANKLIN; ***186** C-4; 🄿; **z** 01339; Ⓟ 317; © 336
Hayden Row; RMC Place; MIDDLESEX; ▲ Hopkinton; ***187** F-12; ★ **BOS**; mail Hopkinton **z** 01748; ● 200
Haydenville; RMC Place; HAMPSHIRE; ▲ Williamsburg; **186** E-5; elev. 450ft./137m.; 🄿; ★ **SPRG**; **z** 01039; ● 550
Head of Westport; RMC Place; BRISTOL; ▲ Westport; **187** K-14; elev. 15ft./5m.; ★ **F.R.**; mail Westport **z** 02790; ● 650
Heath; RMC Place; FRANKLIN; ▲ Heath; **186** C-4; elev. 1,680ft./512m.; 🄿; **z** 01346; ● 150
Heath; MCD-Town; FRANKLIN; ***186** C-4; 🄿; **z** 01346; Ⓟ 716; © 805
Heaven Heights; RMC Place; BRISTOL; ▲ Freetown; **187** I-15; elev. 70ft./21m.; ★ **N.BED**; mail East Freetown **z** 02717; ● 330
Hebronville; RMC Place; BRISTOL; ***187** N-20; ★ **PROV-**; mail Attleboro **z** 02703; pop. incl. with Attleboro (Inc. Place)
Hemlocks; RMC Place; PLYMOUTH; ▲ Lakeville; ***187** I-15; elev. 80ft./24m.; ★ **BOS**; mail Middleboro **z** 02346; ● 80
Hickory Hills Lake; RMC Place; WORCESTER; ▲ Lunenburg; ***186** C-10; ★ **BOS**; mail Lunenburg **z** 01462; ● 700
Highland; RMC Place; HAMPDEN; ***186** G-6; ★ **SPRG**; mail Springfield **z** 01109, **z** 01119, **z** 01129; pop. incl. with Springfield (Inc. Place)
Highland; RMC Place; SUFFOLK; ***187** F-14; elev. 150ft./46m.; ★ **BOS**; pop. incl. with Boston (Inc. Place)
Highland Lake; RMC Place; NORFOLK; ▲ Norfolk; **187** G-13; elev. 180ft./55m.; ★ **BOS**; mail Norfolk **z** 02056; ● 200
Highland Park; RMC Place; HAMPDEN; ***187** N-20; ★ **SPRG**; mail Holyoke **z** 01040; pop. incl. with Holyoke (Inc. Place)
Highlands; RMC Place; HAMPDEN; **187** K-11; elev. 260ft./79m.; ★ **SPRG**; mail Holyoke **z** 01040; pop. incl. with Holyoke (Inc. Place)
Highlands; RMC Place; MIDDLESEX; ***187** C-13; elev. 170ft./52m.; ★ **BOS**; mail Lowell **z** 01851; pop. incl. with Lowell (Inc. Place)
High Rock Woods; RMC Place; NORFOLK; ▲ Needham; ***187** F-13; ★ **BOS**; mail Needham **z** 02492
Hillcrest Acres; RMC Place; BRISTOL; ▲ Westport; ***187** N-20; ★ **F.R.**; mail Westport **z** 02790; ● 50
Hilltop Acres; RMC Place; PLYMOUTH; ▲ Lakeville; ***187** I-15; elev. 70ft./21m.; ★ **BOS**; mail Middleboro **z** 02346; ● 50
Hingham; CDP; PLYMOUTH; ▲ Hingham; **187** F-15; 🄿; ★ **BOS**; **z** 02018, **z** 02043-44; Ⓟ 5,454; © 5,352
Hingham; MCD-Town; PLYMOUTH; ***187** F-15; 🄿; ★ **BOS**; **z** 02018, **z** 02043-44; Ⓟ 19,821; © 19,882; ◆ 20,560
Hingham Center; RMC Place; PLYMOUTH; ▲ Hingham; **186** N-10; ★ **BOS**; mail Hingham **z** 02043
Hinsdale; RMC Place; BERKSHIRE; ▲ Hinsdale; **186** D-2; elev. 1,442ft./440m.; 🄿; ★ **PTSF**; **z** 01235; ● 1,050
Hinsdale; MCD-Town; BERKSHIRE; ***186** D-2; 🄿; ★ **PTSF**; **z** 01235; Ⓟ 1,959; © 1,872; ◆ 1,693
Hinsdale Estates; RMC Place; NORFOLK; ▲ Bellingham; ***187** N-20; ★ **BOS**; mail Bellingham **z** 02019
Hixville; RMC Place; BRISTOL; ▲ Dartmouth; **187** J-14; ★ **N.BED**; mail North Dartmouth **z** 02747; ● 150
Hodges Village; RMC Place; WORCESTER; ▲ Oxford; **186** G-9; ★ **WORC**; mail Oxford **z** 01540; ● 100
Holbrook; CDP; NORFOLK; ▲ Holbrook; **187** G-15; elev. 212ft./65m.; 🄿; ★ **BOS**; **z** 02343; Ⓟ 11,041; © 10,785
Holbrook; MCD-Town; NORFOLK; ***187** G-14; 🄿; ★ **BOS**; **z** 02343; Ⓟ 11,041; © 10,785; ◆ 10,861
Holden (Holden Center); RMC Place; WORCESTER; ▲ Holden; **186** E-10; elev. 860ft./262m.; 🄿; ★ **WORC**; **z** 01520; ● 4,200
Holden; MCD-Town; WORCESTER; ***186** E-10; 🄿; ★ **WORC**; **z** 01520; Ⓟ 14,628; © 15,621; ◆ 16,116
Holden Center; WORCESTER; see Holden (RMC Place)
Holland; CDP; HAMPDEN; ▲ Holland; **186** G-8; elev. 743ft./226m.; 🄿; ★ **WORC**; **z** 01521; Ⓟ 1,331; © 1,444
Holland; MCD-Town; HAMPDEN; ***186** G-8; 🄿; ★ **WORC**; **z** 01521; Ⓟ 2,185; © 2,407; ◆ 2,457
Holliston; RMC Place; MIDDLESEX; ▲ Holliston; **187** F-12; elev. 188ft./57m.; 🄿; ★ **BOS**; **z** 01746; ● 12,926
Holliston; MCD-Town; MIDDLESEX; ***187** F-12; 🄿; ★ **BOS**; **z** 01746; Ⓟ 12,926; © 13,801; ◆ 14,125
Hollywood; PLYMOUTH; see Holly Woods (RMC Place)
Holly Woods (Hollywood); RMC Place; PLYMOUTH; ▲ Mattapoisett; **187** J-16; elev. 10ft./3m.; ★ **N.BED**; mail Mattapoisett **z** 02739; ● 70

Entries in **UPPERCASE** are counties.
Entries in **bold** have populations of 2,500 or more.
Names in parentheses are alternate names.

Inc. Place	Incorporated Place
RMC Place	Rand McNally Designated Place
CDP	Census Designated Place
MCD	Minor Civil Division
⊡	County Seat
▲	Minor Civil Division
elev.	Elevation
🄿	Post Office
🄷	Hospital
🄲	College
■	Principal Business Center
★	Ranally Metro Area (RMA) Abbreviation
z	Zip Code(s)
Ⓟ	Previous Census Population
Ⓡ	Revised Census Population
Ⓐ	Annexation Population
●	Rand McNally Population Estimate
©	Final Census Population
Ⓢ	Special Census Population
◆	Estimated Population

For additional definitions see Glossary, Volume 1, and Introduction, Volume 2.

Holyoke; Inc. Place; HAMPDEN; 186 F-5; elev. 270ft./82m.; 🅿 🅷 ■; ★ SPRG; z 01040-41; ℗ 43,704; © 39,838; ◆ 39,483
Hoosac Tunnel; RMC Place; BERKSHIRE; ▲ Florida; *186 C-3; elev. 750ft./229m.; mail Rowe z 01367
Hopedale; CDP; WORCESTER; ▲ Hopedale; 187 G-11; 🅿; ★ BOS; z 01747; ℗ 3,961; © 4,158
Hopedale; MCD-Town; WORCESTER; *187 G-11; 🅿; ★ BOS; z 01747; ℗ 5,666; © 5,907; ◆ 6,077
Hopkinton; CDP; MIDDLESEX; ▲ Hopkinton; 187 F-12; elev. 410ft./125m.; 🅿; ★ BOS; z 01748; ℗ 2,305; © 2,628
Hopkinton; MCD-Town; MIDDLESEX; *187 F-11; 🅿; ★ BOS; z 01748; ℗ 9,191; © 13,346; ◆ 14,527
Horseneck Beach; RMC Place; BRISTOL; ▲ Westport; *187 L-14; ★ F.R.; mail Westport z 02790
Hortonville; RMC Place; BRISTOL; ▲ Swansea; 187 I-13; elev. 70ft./21m.; ★ F.R.; mail Swansea z 02777; ● 260
Houghs Neck; RMC Place; NORFOLK; 186 M-9; elev. 26ft./8m.; ★ BOS; mail Quincy z 02169; pop. incl. with Quincy (Inc. Place)
Houghtonville; RMC Place; BERKSHIRE; ▲ Clarksburg; *186 B-3; elev. 1,071ft./326m.; mail North Adams z 01247
Housatonic; CDP; BERKSHIRE; ▲ Great Barrington; 186 F-1; elev. 744ft./227m.; 🅿; z 01236; ℗ 1,184; © 1,335
Hovey Corner; RMC Place; MIDDLESEX; mail Pepperell z 01463; ● 300
Howe; RMC Place; ESSEX; ▲ Middleton; *187 C-15; elev. 100ft./30m.; ★ BOS; mail Middleton z 01949
Hubbardston; RMC Place; WORCESTER; ▲ Hubbardston; 186 D-9; elev. 993ft./303m.; 🅿; z 01452; ● 800
Hubbardston; MCD-Town; WORCESTER; *186 D-9; 🅿; z 01452; ℗ 2,797; © 3,909
Huckleberry Corner; RMC Place; PLYMOUTH; ▲ Carver; *187 I-16; elev. 83ft./25m.; ★ BOS; mail West Wareham z 02576
Huckleberry Shores (Huckleyberry Shores); RMC Place; PLYMOUTH; ▲ Lakeville; *187 I-15; ★ BOS; mail Middleboro z 02346; rural
Huckleyberry Shores; PLYMOUTH; see Huckleberry Shores (RMC Place)
Hudson; CDP; MIDDLESEX; ▲ Hudson; 187 E-11; elev. 263ft./80m.; 🅿; ★ BOS; z 01749; ℗ 14,267; © 14,388
Hudson; MCD-Town; MIDDLESEX; *187 E-11; 🅿; ★ BOS; z 01749; ℗ 17,233; © 18,113; ◆ 18,927
Hull; CDP; PLYMOUTH; ▲ Hull; 187 E-15; elev. 50ft./15m.; 🅿; ★ BOS; z 02045; ℗ 10,466; © 11,050
Hull; MCD-Town; PLYMOUTH; *187 E-15; 🅿; ★ BOS; z 02045; ℗ 10,466; © 11,050; ◆ 11,464
Humarock; RMC Place; PLYMOUTH; ▲ Scituate; 187 G-16; elev. 20ft./6m.; 🅿; ★ BOS; z 02047; ● 500
Huntington; RMC Place; HAMPSHIRE; ▲ Huntington; 186 F-4; elev. 382ft./116m.; 🅿; ★ SPRG; z 01050; ● 1,200
Huntington; MCD-Town; HAMPSHIRE; *186 F-4; 🅿; ★ SPRG; z 01050; ℗ 1,987; © 2,174; ◆ 2,210
Hyannis; RMC Place; BARNSTABLE; 187 J-19; elev. 19ft./6m.; 🅿 🅷; ★ BARN; z 02601; pop. incl. with Barnstable (Inc. Place)
Hyannis Park; RMC Place; BARNSTABLE; *187 J-19; elev. 10ft./3m.; ★ BARN; mail Hyannis z 02601
Hyannis Port; RMC Place; BARNSTABLE; 187 K-19; elev. 40ft./12m.; 🅿; ★ BARN; z 02647; pop. incl. with Barnstable (Inc. Place)
Hyde Park; RMC Place; SUFFOLK; 186 M-6; 🅿; ★ BOS; z 02136-37; pop. incl. with Boston (Inc. Place)
Hydeville; RMC Place; WORCESTER; ▲ Winchendon; *186 C-8; ★ BOS; mail Winchendon z 01475; ● 90

I

Idlewell; RMC Place; NORFOLK; ▲ Weymouth; *187 F-15; elev. 25ft./8m.; ★ BOS; mail Weymouth z 02188
Idlewood; RMC Place; BRISTOL; ▲ Dartmouth; 187 F-20; elev. 50ft./15m.; ★ N.BED; mail North Dartmouth z 02747
Indian Orchard; RMC Place; HAMPDEN; 187 L-13; elev. 220ft./67m.; 🅿; ★ SPRG; z 01151; pop. incl. with Springfield (Inc. Place)
Indian Shore; RMC Place; PLYMOUTH; ▲ Lakeville; *187 I-15; elev. 58ft./18m.; ★ BOS; mail Middleboro z 02346; rural
Ingleside; RMC Place; HAMPDEN; *186 F-5; elev. 120ft./37m.; ★ SPRG; mail Holyoke z 01040; pop. incl. with Holyoke (Inc. Place)
Inman Square; RMC Place; MIDDLESEX; *187 E-14; elev. 20ft./6m.; ★ BOS; mail Cambridge z 02139; pop. incl. with Cambridge (Inc. Place)
Interlaken; RMC Place; BERKSHIRE; ▲ Stockbridge; 186 E-1; elev. 900ft./274m.; ★ PTSF; mail West Stockbridge z 01266; ● 300
Ipswich; CDP; ESSEX; ▲ Ipswich; 187 C-15; elev. 50ft./15m.; 🅿; ★ BOS; z 01938; ℗ 4,132; © 4,161
Ipswich; MCD-Town; ESSEX; *187 B-15; 🅿; ★ BOS; z 01938; ℗ 11,873; © 12,987; ◆ 13,179
Ironstone (South Uxbridge); RMC Place; WORCESTER; ▲ Uxbridge; *187 H-11; ★ WORC; mail Uxbridge z 01569; rural
Island Creek; RMC Place; PLYMOUTH; ▲ Duxbury; 187 H-16; elev. 75ft./23m.; ★ BOS; mail Duxbury z 02332; ● 160
Islington; RMC Place; NORFOLK; ▲ Westwood; 187 F-13; elev. 103ft./31m.; ★ BOS; mail Westwood z 02090; ● 4,800

J

Jamaica Plain; RMC Place; SUFFOLK; *187 E-14; elev. 150ft./46m.; 🅿; ★ BOS; z 02130; pop. incl. with Boston (Inc. Place)
Jamesville; RMC Place; WORCESTER; 187 C-18; elev. 600ft./183m.; ★ WORC; pop. incl. with Worcester (Inc. Place)
Jefferson; RMC Place; WORCESTER; ▲ Holden; 186 E-10; elev. 802ft./244m.; 🅿; ★ WORC; z 01522; ● 1,000
Jefferson Shores; RMC Place; PLYMOUTH; ▲ Wareham; *187 J-17; ★ BOS; mail Buzzards Bay z 02532; ● 375
Jeffries Point; RMC Place; SUFFOLK; *187 E-14; elev. 50ft./15m.; ★ BOS; mail Boston z 02128; pop. incl. with Boston (Inc. Place)
John Fitzgerald Kennedy; RMC Place; SUFFOLK; *187 E-14; ★ BOS; mail Boston z 02114, z 02203; pop. incl. with Boston (Inc. Place)
Joppa; RMC Place; ESSEX; *187 B-15; elev. 20ft./6m.; ★ BOS; mail Newburyport z 01950; pop. incl. with Newburyport (Inc. Place)

K

Katama; RMC Place; DUKES; ▲ Edgartown; 187 M-17; elev. 17ft./5m.; mail Edgartown z 02539; ● 400
Kearney Square; RMC Place; MIDDLESEX; *187 C-11; ★ BOS; mail Lowell z 01852
Kelly Corner (Kelly's Corner); RMC Place; MIDDLESEX; ▲ Acton; *187 D-12; ★ BOS; mail Acton z 01720
Kelly's Corner; MIDDLESEX; see Kelly Corner (RMC Place)
Kendal Green; RMC Place; MIDDLESEX; ▲ Weston; *187 E-13; elev. 100ft./30m.; ★ BOS; mail Weston z 02493
Kendall Square; RMC Place; MIDDLESEX; *187 E-14; elev. 10ft./3m.; ★ BOS; mail Cambridge z 02142; pop. incl. with Cambridge (Inc. Place)
Kenmore; RMC Place; SUFFOLK; *187 E-14; ★ BOS; mail Boston z 02215; pop. incl. with Boston (Inc. Place)
Kent Park; RMC Place; PLYMOUTH; ▲ Marshfield; 187 G-16; elev. 10ft./3m.; ★ BOS; mail Marshfield z 02050; ● 550
Kenwood; RMC Place; MIDDLESEX; ▲ Dracut; *187 C-13; elev. 70ft./21m.; ★ BOS; mail Dracut z 01826
Kingsbury Beach; RMC Place; BARNSTABLE; ▲ Eastham; *187 I-20; elev. 20ft./6m.; ★ BARN; mail Eastham z 02642
Kings Forest; RMC Place; ESSEX; ▲ Boxford; *187 B-15; elev. 150ft./46m.; ★ BOS; mail Boxford z 01921
Kingston; CDP; PLYMOUTH; ▲ Kingston; 187 H-16; elev. 62ft./19m.; 🅿; ★ BOS; z 02364; ℗ 4,774; © 5,380
Kingston; MCD-Town; PLYMOUTH; *187 H-16; 🅿; ★ BOS; z 02364; ℗ 9,045; © 11,780; ◆ 13,098
Kinsman Corner (Kinsmans Corner); RMC Place; ESSEX; ▲ Topsfield; *187 C-15; ★ BOS; mail Topsfield z 01983
Kinsmans Corner; ESSEX; see Kinsman Corner (RMC Place)
Knightville; RMC Place; HAMPSHIRE; ▲ Huntington; *186 F-4; elev. 490ft./149m.; ★ SPRG; mail Huntington z 01050
Knollmere; RMC Place; BRISTOL; ▲ Fairhaven; *187 K-15; elev. 10ft./3m.; ★ N.BED; mail Fairhaven z 02719
Konkapot; RMC Place; BERKSHIRE; ▲ New Marlborough; *186 G-2; elev. 714ft./218m.; mail Southfield z 01259; rural

L

Lagoon Heights; RMC Place; DUKES; ▲ Oak Bluffs; *187 L-17; elev. 30ft./9m.; mail Oak Bluffs z 02557
Lake Attitash; RMC Place; ESSEX; ▲ Amesbury; *187 N-20; ★ BOS; mail Amesbury z 01913
Lake Forest Park; RMC Place; MIDDLESEX; ▲ Natick; *187 E-13; elev. 190ft./58m.; ★ BOS; mail Natick z 01760
Lake Hiawatha; RMC Place; NORFOLK; ▲ Bellingham; *187 N-20; ★ BOS; mail Bellingham z 02019
Lake Mattawa; RMC Place; FRANKLIN; ▲ Orange; 186 C-7; mail Orange z 01364; summer pop. 350; ● 150
Lake Pleasant; RMC Place; FRANKLIN; ▲ Montague; 186 D-6; elev. 300ft./91m.; 🅿; z 01347; ● 300
Lakeside; RMC Place; BRISTOL; ▲ Westport; *187 J-14; elev. 200ft./61m.; ★ F.R.; mail Westport z 02790; ● 600
Lakeside; RMC Place; PLYMOUTH; ▲ Middleborough; *187 I-15; elev. 60ft./18m.; ★ BOS; mail Middleboro z 02346
Lakeview; RMC Place; MIDDLESEX; *187 E-13; elev. 250ft./76m.; ★ BOS; mail Waltham z 02451; pop. incl. with Waltham (Inc. Place)
Lake View; RMC Place; WORCESTER; 187 B-20; elev. 400ft./122m.; ★ WORC; mail Worcester z 01604; pop. incl. with Worcester (Inc. Place)
Lakeview Heights; RMC Place; PLYMOUTH; ▲ Lakeville; *187 I-15; elev. 70ft./21m.; ★ BOS; mail East Freetown z 02717; ● 75
Lakeview Terrace; RMC Place; BERKSHIRE; *186 D-2; ★ PTSF; mail Pittsfield z 01201; pop. incl. with Pittsfield (Inc. Place)
Lakeville; RMC Place; PLYMOUTH; ▲ Lakeville; ★ BOS; ● 150
Lakeville; MCD-Town; PLYMOUTH; *187 I-15; 🅿; ★ BOS; z 02347-48; ℗ 7,785; © 9,821; ◆ 11,263
Lakewood; RMC Place; BERKSHIRE; *186 D-2; elev. 1,000ft./305m.; ★ PTSF; mail Pittsfield z 01201; pop. incl. with Pittsfield (Inc. Place)
Lakewood Hills; RMC Place; BARNSTABLE; ▲ Sandwich; *187 J-18; ★ BARN; mail East Sandwich z 02537; ● 1,200
Lakewood Park; RMC Place; WORCESTER; ▲ Westminster; *186 D-10; elev. 890ft./271m.; ★ BOS; mail Westminster z 01473; ● 250
Lambs Grove; RMC Place; WORCESTER; ▲ Spencer; *186 F-9; elev. 917ft./280m.; ★ WORC; mail Spencer z 01562; ● 150
Lancaster (Lancaster Center); RMC Place; WORCESTER; ▲ Lancaster; 187 D-11; elev. 300ft./91m.; 🅿; ★ BOS; z 01523; ● 900
Lancaster; MCD-Town; WORCESTER; *187 D-11; 🅿 🅲 572; ★ BOS; z 01523; ℗ 6,661; © 7,380; ® 6,382; ◆ 6,879
Lancaster Center; WORCESTER; see Lancaster (RMC Place)
Lanesboro; BERKSHIRE; see Lanesborough (RMC Place)
Lanesborough (Lanesboro); RMC Place; BERKSHIRE; ▲ Lanesborough; 186 D-2; ★ PTSF; mail Berkshire z 01224, Lanesboro z 01237; ● 1,000
Lanesborough; MCD-Town; BERKSHIRE; *186 D-2; ★ PTSF; mail Lanesboro z 01237; ℗ 3,032; © 2,990; ◆ 2,679
Lanesville; RMC Place; ESSEX; *187 C-16; elev. 69ft./21m.; ★ BOS; mail Gloucester z 01930; pop. incl. with Gloucester (Inc. Place)
Lane Village; RMC Place; WORCESTER; ▲ Ashburnham; 186 C-9; elev. 1,140ft./347m.; ★ BOS; mail Ashburnham z 01430; ● 130
Larrywaug; RMC Place; BERKSHIRE; ▲ Stockbridge; *186 E-1; elev. 850ft./259m.; ★ PTSF; mail Stockbridge z 01262; rural
Laurel Park; RMC Place; HAMPSHIRE; *186 E-5; elev. 200ft./61m.; ★ SPRG; mail Northampton z 01060; pop. incl. with Northampton (Inc. Place)
Lawrence; Inc. Place; ESSEX; 187 B-14; elev. 50ft./15m.; 🅿 🅷 ■; ★ BOS; z 01840-43; ℗ 70,207; © 72,043; ◆ 72,739
Le Count Hollow; RMC Place; BARNSTABLE; ▲ Wellfleet; *187 H-20; elev. 20ft./6m.; mail South Wellfleet z 02663; rural
Lee; CDP; BERKSHIRE; ▲ Lee; 186 E-2; elev. 1,000ft./305m.; 🅿; ★ PTSF; z 01238, z 01264; ℗ 2,020; © 2,021
Lee; MCD-Town; BERKSHIRE; *186 E-2; 🅿; ★ PTSF; z 01238, z 01264; ℗ 5,849; © 5,985; ◆ 5,585
Leeds; RMC Place; HAMPSHIRE; *186 E-5; elev. 380ft./116m.; 🅿; ★ SPRG; z 01053; pop. incl. with Northampton (Inc. Place)
Leicester (Leicester Center); RMC Place; WORCESTER; ▲ Leicester; 186 F-9; elev. 1,009ft./308m.; 🅿; ★ WORC; z 01524 & mail Cherry Valley z 01611, Rochdale z 01542; ● 3,200
Leicester; MCD-Town; WORCESTER; *186 F-9; 🅿; ★ WORC; z 01524; ℗ 10,191; © 10,471; ◆ 10,425
Leicester Center; WORCESTER; see Leicester (RMC Place)
Leino Park; RMC Place; WORCESTER; ▲ Westminster; 186 D-9; elev. 890ft./271m.; ★ BOS; mail Westminster z 01473; ● 230
Lenox; CDP; BERKSHIRE; ▲ Lenox; 186 E-1; 🅿; ★ PTSF; z 01240; ℗ 1,687; © 1,667
Lenox; MCD-Town; BERKSHIRE; *186 E-1; 🅿; ★ PTSF; z 01240; ℗ 5,069; © 5,077; ◆ 4,633
Lenox Dale; RMC Place; BERKSHIRE; ▲ Lenox; 186 E-2; elev. 970ft./296m.; 🅿; ★ PTSF; z 01242; ● 600
Leominster; Inc. Place; WORCESTER; 186 D-10; elev. 400ft./122m.; 🅿 🅷 ■; ★ BOS; z 01453; ℗ 38,145; © 41,303; ◆ 41,075
Leverett; RMC Place; FRANKLIN; ▲ Leverett; 186 D-6; 🅿; z 01054; ● 500
Leverett; MCD-Town; FRANKLIN; *186 D-6; 🅿; z 01054; ℗ 1,785; © 1,663; ® 1,698
Lexington; CDP; MIDDLESEX; ▲ Lexington; 187 D-13; elev. 210ft./64m.; 🅿; ★ BOS; z 02420-21; ℗ 28,974; © 30,355; ◆ 31,023
Lexington; MCD-Town; MIDDLESEX; *187 D-13; 🅿; ★ BOS; z 02420-21; ℗ 28,974; © 30,355; ◆ 31,023
Leyden; MCD-Town; FRANKLIN; *186 B-5; 🅿; z 01301, z 01337; ℗ 662; © 772
Liberty Heights; RMC Place; HAMPDEN; *186 G-5; ★ SPRG; mail Springfield z 01104; pop. incl. with Springfield (Inc. Place)
Liberty Plain; RMC Place; PLYMOUTH; ▲ Hingham; *187 F-15; elev. 140ft./43m.; ★ BOS; mail Hingham z 02043
Lincoln; RMC Place; MIDDLESEX; ▲ Lincoln; 187 E-13; elev. 258ft./79m.; 🅿; ★ BOS; z 01773; ● 2,850
Lincoln; MCD-Town; MIDDLESEX; *187 D-13; 🅿; ★ BOS; z 01773; ℗ 7,666; © 8,056; ◆ 8,243
Lincoln Square; RMC Place; WORCESTER; *186 F-10; ★ WORC; mail Worcester z 01601; pop. incl. with Worcester (Inc. Place)
Linden; RMC Place; MIDDLESEX; *187 D-14; elev. 15ft./5m.; ★ BOS; mail Malden z 02148; pop. incl. with Malden (Inc. Place)
Lindenwood; RMC Place; MIDDLESEX; ▲ Stoneham; *187 D-14; elev. 100ft./30m.; ★ BOS; mail Stoneham z 02180
Linwood (Whitins); RMC Place; WORCESTER; ▲ Uxbridge, Northbridge; 187 G-11; elev. 278ft./85m.; 🅿; ★ WORC; z 01525; ● 750
Lithia; RMC Place; HAMPSHIRE; ▲ Goshen; 186 D-4; elev. 1,179ft./359m.; mail Goshen z 01032; ● 100
Little Acres; RMC Place; PLYMOUTH; ▲ Pembroke; *187 N-20; ★ BOS; mail Bryantville z 02327
Little Harbor Beach; RMC Place; PLYMOUTH; ▲ Wareham; *187 J-16; ★ BOS; mail Wareham z 02571; ● 150
Little Nahant; RMC Place; ESSEX; ▲ Nahant; 186 J-9; elev. 70ft./21m.; ★ BOS; mail Nahant z 01908
Little Neck; RMC Place; BRISTOL; ▲ Swansea; *187 N-20; ★ F.R.; mail Swansea z 02777; ● 200
Little Neck; RMC Place; ESSEX; ▲ Ipswich; 187 B-16; elev. 80ft./24m.; ★ BOS; mail Ipswich z 01938; summer pop. 500; ● 50
Little River; RMC Place; HAMPDEN; *186 G-5; elev. 150ft./46m.; ★ SPRG; mail Westfield z 01085; pop. incl. with Westfield (Inc. Place)
Littleton; MIDDLESEX; see Littleton Common (CDP)
Littleton; MCD-Town; MIDDLESEX; *187 D-12; 🅿; ★ BOS; z 01460; ℗ 7,051; © 8,184; ◆ 8,432
Littleton Common (Littleton); CDP; MIDDLESEX; ▲ Littleton; 187 D-12; elev. 229ft./70m.; ★ BOS; mail Littleton z 01460; ℗ 2,867; © 2,816
Lobsterville; RMC Place; DUKES; ▲ Aquinnah; *187 M-16; elev. 10ft./3m.; mail Chilmark z 02535; ● 50
Lockerville; RMC Place; MIDDLESEX; ▲ Natick; *187 N-20; ★ BOS; mail Natick z 01760
Locks Village (Lock Village); RMC Place; FRANKLIN; ▲ Shutesbury; 186 D-6; elev. 840ft./256m.; mail Shutesbury z 01072; ● 200
Lock Village; FRANKLIN; see Locks Village (RMC Place)
Long Beach; RMC Place; ESSEX; ▲ Rockport; *187 C-17; ★ BOS; mail Rockport z 01966; summer pop. 300
Long Hill Acres; RMC Place; PLYMOUTH; ▲ Pembroke; *187 N-20; ★ BOS; mail Pembroke z 02359
Longmeadow; CDP; HAMPDEN; ▲ Longmeadow; 186 G-5; elev. 160ft./49m.; 🅿 🅲 1,479; ★ SPRG; z 01106, z 01116; ℗ 15,467; © 15,633
Longmeadow; MCD-Town; HAMPDEN; *186 G-6; 🅿 🅲 1,479; ★ SPRG; z 01106, z 01116; ℗ 15,467; © 15,633; ◆ 15,595
Long Plain; RMC Place; BRISTOL; ▲ Acushnet; 187 J-15; elev. 70ft./21m.; ★ N.BED; mail Acushnet z 02743; ● 300
Long Pond Park; RMC Place; MIDDLESEX; ▲ Dracut; *187 B-12; ★ BOS; mail Dracut z 01826
Long Pond Village; RMC Place; PLYMOUTH; ▲ Plymouth; *187 I-17; ★ BOS; mail Plymouth z 02360; ● 250
Longwood; NORFOLK; see Longwood Station (RMC Place)
Longwood Station (Longwood); RMC Place; NORFOLK; ▲ Brookline; *187 E-14; elev. 30ft./9m.; ★ BOS; mail Brookline z 02445
Loudville; RMC Place; HAMPSHIRE; *186 F-5; elev. 335ft./102m.; ★ SPRG; mail Easthampton z 01027
Lovell Corners; RMC Place; NORFOLK; ▲ Weymouth; 186 N-9; elev. 95ft./29m.; ★ BOS; mail Weymouth z 02188
Lowell; Inc. Place; MIDDLESEX; 187 C-13; elev. 102ft./31m.; 🅿 🅷 🅲 11,208 ■; ★ BOS; z 01850-54; ℗ 103,439; © 105,167; ◆ 108,112
Lower Mills; RMC Place; SUFFOLK; *187 F-14; elev. 50ft./15m.; ★ BOS; mail Mattapan z 02126; pop. incl. with Boston (Inc. Place)
Lower Village; RMC Place; MIDDLESEX; ▲ Stow; *187 D-12; elev. 230ft./70m.; ★ BOS; mail Stow z 01775
Ludlow; RMC Place; HAMPDEN; ▲ Ludlow; 186 G-6; elev. 240ft./73m.; 🅿; ★ SPRG; z 01056; ● 18,820
Ludlow; MCD-Town; HAMPDEN; *186 F-6; 🅿; ★ SPRG; z 01056; ℗ 18,820; © 21,209; ◆ 21,768
Ludlow; RMC Place; WORCESTER; 187 C-18; elev. 550ft./168m.; 🅷; ★ WORC; mail Worcester z 01603; pop. incl. with Worcester (Inc. Place)
Ludlow Center; RMC Place; HAMPDEN; ▲ Ludlow; *186 F-6; elev. 270ft./82m.; ★ SPRG; mail Ludlow z 01056
Lunenburg; CDP; WORCESTER; ▲ Lunenburg; 186 C-10; elev. 510ft./155m.; 🅿; ★ BOS; z 01462; ℗ 1,694; © 1,695
Lunenburg; MCD-Town; WORCESTER; *186 C-10; 🅿; ★ BOS; z 01462; ℗ 9,117; © 9,401; ◆ 9,450
Lynn; Inc. Place; ESSEX; 187 D-15; elev. 30ft./9m.; 🅿 🅷 ■; ★ BOS; z 01901-05, z 01910; ℗ 81,245; © 89,050; ◆ 89,737
Lynnfield (Lynnfield Centre); CDP; ESSEX; ▲ Lynnfield; 187 D-14; elev. 98ft./30m.; 🅿; ★ BOS; z 01940; ℗ 11,274; © 11,542
Lynnfield; MCD-Town; ESSEX; *187 D-14; 🅿; ★ BOS; z 01940; ℗ 11,274; © 11,542; ◆ 11,444
Lynnfield Centre; ESSEX; see Lynnfield (CDP)
Lynnhurst; RMC Place; ESSEX; ▲ Saugus; *187 D-15; elev. 100ft./30m.; ★ BOS; mail Saugus z 01906
Lyonsville; RMC Place; FRANKLIN; ▲ Colrain; 186 C-5; elev. 580ft./177m.; mail Colrain z 01340; ● 654

M

Madaket (Maddaket); RMC Place; NANTUCKET; ▲ Nantucket; 187 M-19; elev. 15ft./5m.; mail Nantucket z 02554; summer pop. 500; ● 350
Maddaket; NANTUCKET; see Madaket (RMC Place)
Magnolia; RMC Place; ESSEX; *187 C-16; elev. 50ft./15m.; ★ BOS; mail Gloucester z 01930
Mahkeenac Heights; RMC Place; BERKSHIRE; ▲ Stockbridge; *186 E-1; elev. 1,000ft./305m.; ★ PTSF; mail Stockbridge z 01262; ● 500
Main Street Station; RMC Place; WORCESTER; *187 N-20; ★ WORC; mail Worcester z 01601; pop. incl. with Worcester (Inc. Place)
Malden; Inc. Place; MIDDLESEX; 187 D-14; elev. 13ft./4m.; 🅿 🅷 ■; ★ BOS; z 02148; ℗ 53,884; © 56,340; ◆ 58,774
Manchaug; RMC Place; WORCESTER; ▲ Sutton; 186 G-10; elev. 420ft./128m.; 🅿; ★ WORC; z 01526; ● 800
Manchester (Manchester by-the-Sea); RMC Place; ESSEX; ▲ Manchester-by-the-Sea; 187 C-16; elev. 30ft./9m.; 🅿; ★ BOS; z 01944; ● 5,286
Manchester; ESSEX; see Manchester-by-the-Sea (MCD-Town)
Manchester by-the-Sea; ESSEX; see Manchester (RMC Place)
Manchester-by-the-Sea (Manchester); MCD-Town; ESSEX; *187 C-16; 🅿; ★ BOS; z 01944; ℗ 5,286; © 5,228; ◆ 5,215
Manleys Corner; RMC Place; PLYMOUTH; ▲ West Bridgewater; *187 G-14; elev. 124ft./38m.; ★ BOS; mail West Bridgewater z 02379; ● 150
Manomet; RMC Place; PLYMOUTH; ▲ Plymouth; 187 H-17; elev. 40ft./12m.; 🅿; ★ BOS; z 02345; ● 1,600
Manomet Beach; RMC Place; PLYMOUTH; ▲ Plymouth; *187 I-17; elev. 50ft./15m.; ★ BOS; mail Manomet z 02345
Manomet Bluffs; RMC Place; PLYMOUTH; ▲ Plymouth; *187 H-17; elev. 60ft./18m.; ★ BOS; mail Manomet z 02345
Mansfield; RMC Place; BRISTOL; ▲ Mansfield; 187 H-13; ★ BOS; ● 5,100
Mansfield; MCD-Town; BRISTOL; *187 H-13; 🅿; ★ BOS; z 02048 & mail East Mansfield z 02031; ℗ 16,568; © 22,414; ◆ 24,294
Mansfield Center; CDP-Census Area Only; BRISTOL; ▲ Mansfield; 187 H-13; elev. 160ft./49m.; ★ BOS; mail East Mansfield z 02031, Mansfield z 02048; ℗ 7,170; © 7,320
Maple Grove; RMC Place; BERKSHIRE; ▲ Adams; *186 C-2; elev. 840ft./256m.; ★ PTSF; mail Adams z 01220
Maple Park; RMC Place; ESSEX; *187 B-14; ★ BOS; mail Methuen z 01844; pop. incl. with Methuen (Inc. Place)
Maplewood; RMC Place; MIDDLESEX; *187 D-14; elev. 100ft./30m.; ★ BOS; mail Malden z 02148; pop. incl. with Malden (Inc. Place)
Maplewood; RMC Place; WORCESTER; ▲ Grafton; 187 C-20; elev. 379ft./116m.; ★ WORC; mail North Grafton z 01536
Mara Vista; RMC Place; BARNSTABLE; ▲ Falmouth; *187 K-17; elev. 7ft./2m.; mail East Falmouth z 02536
Marblehead; CDP; ESSEX; ▲ Marblehead; 187 D-15; elev. 65ft./20m.; 🅿; ★ BOS; z 01945; ℗ 19,971; © 20,377; ◆ 19,943
Marblehead; MCD-Town; ESSEX; *187 D-15; 🅿; ★ BOS; z 01945; ℗ 19,971; © 20,377; ◆ 19,943
Marblehead Neck; RMC Place; ESSEX; ▲ Marblehead; *187 D-15; elev. 65ft./20m.; ★ BOS; mail Marblehead z 01945
Marion; RMC Place; PLYMOUTH, PLYMOUTH; ▲ Marion; 187 J-16; ★ N.BED; ● 1,400
Marion; MCD-Town; PLYMOUTH; *187 J-16; 🅿; ★ N.BED; z 02738; ℗ 4,496; © 5,123; ◆ 5,128
Marion Center; CDP-Census Area Only; PLYMOUTH; ▲ Marion; 187 J-16; elev. 20ft./6m.; ★ N.BED; mail Marion z 02738; ℗ 1,426; © 1,202
Marlboro; RMC Place; ESSEX; ▲ Georgetown; 187 B-15; elev. 90ft./27m.; 🅷; ★ BOS; mail Georgetown z 01833; ● 220
Marlboro; MIDDLESEX; see Marlborough (Inc. Place)
Marlborough (Marlboro); Inc. Place; MIDDLESEX; 187 E-11; elev. 450ft./137m.; 🅿 ■; ★ BOS; z 01752; ℗ 31,813; © 36,255; ◆ 37,998
Marshfield; CDP; PLYMOUTH; ▲ Marshfield; 187 G-16; elev. 17ft./5m.; 🅿; ★ BOS; z 02050, z 02065 & mail Brant Rock z 02020, Green Harbor z 02041, Humarock z 02047, Marshfield Hills z 02051, North Marshfield z 02059; ℗ 4,002; © 4,246
Marshfield; MCD-Town; PLYMOUTH; *187 G-16; 🅿; ★ BOS; z 02050, z 02065 & mail Brant Rock z 02020, Green Harbor z 02041, Humarock z 02047, Marshfield Hills z 02051, North Marshfield z 02059; ℗ 21,531; © 24,324; ◆ 25,629
Marshfield Center; RMC Place; PLYMOUTH; ▲ Marshfield; *187 G-16; elev. 100ft./30m.; ★ BOS; mail Marshfield z 02050; ● 200
Marshfield Hills; CDP; PLYMOUTH; ▲ Marshfield; 187 G-16; elev. 155ft./47m.; 🅿; ★ BOS; z 02051; ℗ 2,201; © 2,369
Marstons Mills; RMC Place; BARNSTABLE; *187 J-18; elev. 36ft./11m.; 🅿; ★ BARN; z 02648; pop. incl. with Barnstable (Inc. Place)
Mashnee Island; RMC Place; BARNSTABLE; ▲ Bourne; *187 J-17; mail Buzzards Bay z 02532; ● 950
Mashpee (Mashpee Center); RMC Place; BARNSTABLE; ▲ Mashpee; 187 J-18; elev. 55ft./17m.; 🅿; ★ BARN; z 02649; ● 800
Mashpee; MCD-Town; BARNSTABLE; *187 K-17; 🅿; ★ BARN; z 02649; ℗ 7,884; © 12,946; ◆ 13,824
Mashpee Center; BARNSTABLE; see Mashpee (RMC Place)
Mashpee Neck; CDP-Census Area Only; BARNSTABLE; *187 K-18; ★ BARN; © 901
Masons Corner; RMC Place; BRISTOL; ▲ Freetown; *187 J-15; elev. 79ft./24m.; ★ N.BED; mail East Freetown z 02717; ● 50
Matfield; RMC Place; PLYMOUTH; ▲ West Bridgewater; 187 H-15; elev. 104ft./32m.; ★ BOS; mail West Bridgewater z 02379; ● 700
Mathies Manor; RMC Place; HAMPDEN; *186 F-6; elev. 240ft./73m.; ★ SPRG; pop. incl. with Chicopee (Inc. Place)
Mattapan; RMC Place; SUFFOLK; *187 F-14; elev. 50ft./15m.; 🅿; ★ BOS; z 02126; pop. incl. with Boston (Inc. Place)
Mattapoisett; RMC Place; PLYMOUTH; 187 J-16; ★ N.BED; ● 1,660
Mattapoisett; MCD-Town; PLYMOUTH; *187 J-16; 🅿; ★ N.BED; z 02739; ℗ 5,850; © 6,268; ◆ 6,263
Mattapoisett Center; CDP-Census Area Only; PLYMOUTH; ▲ Mattapoisett; 187 J-16; ★ N.BED; mail Mattapoisett z 02739; ℗ 2,949; © 2,966
Mayflower Heights; RMC Place; BARNSTABLE; *187 G-19; elev. 20ft./6m.; mail Provincetown z 02657
Maynard; CDP; MIDDLESEX; ▲ Maynard; 187 D-12; elev. 186ft./57m.; 🅿; ★ BOS; z 01754; ℗ 10,325; © 10,433
Maynard; MCD-Town; MIDDLESEX; *187 E-12; 🅿; ★ BOS; z 01754; ℗ 10,325; © 10,433; ◆ 10,313
Mayo Beach; RMC Place; BARNSTABLE; ▲ Wellfleet; *187 H-20; elev. 40ft./12m.; mail Wellfleet z 02667
Medfield; CDP; NORFOLK; ▲ Medfield; 187 F-13; elev. 178ft./54m.; 🅿 🅷; ★ BOS; z 02052; ℗ 5,985; © 6,670
Medfield; MCD-Town; NORFOLK; *187 F-13; 🅿; ★ BOS; z 02052; ℗ 10,531; © 12,273; ◆ 12,475
Medford; Inc. Place; MIDDLESEX; 187 E-14; elev. 14ft./4m.; 🅿 🅷 🅲 9,682 ■; ★ BOS; z 02153, z 02155 & mail West Medford z 02156; ℗ 57,407; © 55,765; ◆ 53,812
Medway; RMC Place; NORFOLK; ▲ Medway; 187 G-12; elev. 200ft./61m.; 🅿; ★ BOS; z 02053; ● 4,000
Medway; MCD-Town; NORFOLK; *187 G-12; 🅿; ★ BOS; z 02053; ℗ 9,931; © 12,448; ◆ 12,868
Meeting House Hill; RMC Place; SUFFOLK; *187 E-14; elev. 80ft./24m.; ★ BOS; mail Boston z 02122; pop. incl. with Boston (Inc. Place)
Megansett; RMC Place; BARNSTABLE; ▲ Falmouth; *187 J-17; elev. 40ft./12m.; mail North Falmouth z 02556
Melrose; Inc. Place; MIDDLESEX; 187 D-14; elev. 133ft./41m.; 🅿 🅷; ★ BOS; z 02176; ℗ 28,150; © 27,134; ◆ 26,587
Melrose Highlands; RMC Place; MIDDLESEX; 186 I-7; elev. 150ft./46m.; ★ BOS; pop. incl. with Melrose (Inc. Place)
Menauhant; RMC Place; BARNSTABLE; ▲ Falmouth; *187 K-17; elev. 10ft./3m.; mail East Falmouth z 02536
Mendon; RMC Place; WORCESTER; ▲ Mendon; 187 G-11; elev. 330ft./101m.; 🅿; ★ BOS; z 01756; ● 1,000
Mendon; MCD-Town; WORCESTER; *187 G-11; 🅿; ★ BOS; z 01756; ℗ 4,010; © 5,286; ® 5,302; ◆ 5,947
Menemsha; RMC Place; DUKES; ▲ Chilmark; 187 M-16; elev. 30ft./9m.; 🅿; z 02552; ● 250
Merino Village; WORCESTER; see Dudley (RMC Place)
Merrick; RMC Place; HAMPDEN; ▲ West Springfield; *186 G-5; elev. 100ft./30m.; ★ SPRG; mail West Springfield z 01089
Merrimac; RMC Place; ESSEX; ▲ Merrimac; 187 A-14; elev. 107ft./33m.; 🅿; ★ BOS; z 01860; ● 2,200
Merrimac; MCD-Town; ESSEX; *187 A-14; 🅿; ★ BOS; z 01860; ℗ 5,166; © 6,138; ◆ 6,282
Merrimack College; RMC Place; ESSEX; ▲ North Andover; *187 C-14; ★ BOS; mail North Andover z 01845
Merrimacport; RMC Place; ESSEX; ▲ Merrimac; 187 A-15; elev. 100ft./30m.; ★ BOS; mail Merrimac z 01860; ● 250
Merrymount; RMC Place; NORFOLK; *187 F-15; elev. 32ft./10m.; ★ BOS; mail Quincy z 02169; pop. incl. with Quincy (Inc. Place)
Methuen; Inc. Place; ESSEX; 187 B-13; elev. 115ft./35m.; 🅿 🅷 ■; ★ BOS; z 01844; ℗ 39,990; © 43,789; ◆ 44,829
Middleboro; RMC Place; PLYMOUTH; ▲ Middleborough; 187 I-15; ★ BOS; ● 5,580
Middleborough; MCD-Town; PLYMOUTH; *187 I-15; 🅿; ★ BOS; z 02344, z 02348-49 & mail Middleboro z 02346; ℗ 17,867; © 19,941; ◆ 21,098
Middleborough Center; CDP-Census Area Only; PLYMOUTH; ▲ Middleborough; 187 I-15; elev. 100ft./30m.; 🅷; ★ BOS; mail Lakeville z 02348, Middleboro z 02344, z 02346, z 02349; ℗ 6,837; © 6,913
Middlefield; RMC Place; HAMPSHIRE; ▲ Middlefield; 186 E-3; elev. 1,677ft./511m.; 🅿; z 01243; ● 350
Middlefield; MCD-Town; HAMPSHIRE; *186 E-3; 🅿; z 01243; ℗ 392; © 542
Middlesex; RMC Place; MIDDLESEX; *187 C-13; ★ BOS; pop. incl. with Lowell (Inc. Place)
MIDDLESEX; 187 D-12; ℗ 1,398,468; © 1,465,396; ® 1,466,394; ◆ 1,485,991
Middleton; RMC Place; ESSEX; ▲ Middleton; 187 C-14; elev. 94ft./29m.; 🅿; ★ BOS; z 01949; ● 4,921
Middleton; MCD-Town; ESSEX; *187 C-14; 🅿; ★ BOS; z 01949; ℗ 4,921; © 7,744; ◆ 8,295
Midland; RMC Place; NORFOLK; ▲ Bellingham; *187 G-12; elev. 250ft./76m.; ★ BOS; mail Bellingham z 02019
Mile Oak Center; RMC Place; HAMPDEN; ▲ Wilbraham; 186 G-6; ★ SPRG; mail Wilbraham z 01095; ● 2,050
Milford; CDP; WORCESTER; ▲ Milford; 187 G-12; 🅿 🅷; ★ BOS; z 01757; ℗ 23,339; © 24,230; ◆ 24,974
Milford; MCD-Town; WORCESTER; *187 G-11; 🅿 ■; ★ BOS; z 01757; ℗ 25,355; © 26,799; ® 26,720; ◆ 27,626
Millbrook; RMC Place; PLYMOUTH; ▲ Duxbury; *187 G-16; elev. 19ft./6m.; ★ BOS; mail Duxbury z 02332
Millbury; RMC Place; WORCESTER; ▲ Millbury; 186 F-10; elev. 417ft./127m.; 🅿; ★ WORC; z 01527, z 01586; ● 5,000
Millbury; MCD-Town; WORCESTER; *186 F-10; 🅿; ★ WORC; z 01527, z 01586; ℗ 12,228; © 12,784; ◆ 13,053
Millers Falls; CDP; FRANKLIN; ▲ Erving, Montague; 186 C-6; elev. 300ft./91m.; 🅿; z 01349; ℗ 1,084; © 1,072
Millerville; RMC Place; WORCESTER; ▲ Blackstone; *187 H-12; ★ BOS; mail Blackstone z 01504
Millis; RMC Place; NORFOLK; ▲ Millis; 187 F-12; elev. 163ft./50m.; 🅿; ★ BOS; z 02054; ● 3,800
Millis; MCD-Town; NORFOLK; *187 G-12; 🅿; ★ BOS; z 02054; ℗ 7,613; © 7,902; ◆ 7,950
Millis-Clicquot; CDP-Census Area Only; NORFOLK; ▲ Millis; *187 G-12; ★ BOS; mail Millis z 02054; ℗ 4,081; © 4,607
Mill River; RMC Place; BERKSHIRE; ▲ New Marlborough; 186 G-2; elev. 829ft./253m.; 🅿; z 01244; ● 400
Mill River; RMC Place; FRANKLIN; ▲ Deerfield; *186 D-5; mail South Deerfield z 01373; rural
Mill Valley; RMC Place; HAMPSHIRE; ▲ Amherst; *186 E-6; ★ SPRG; mail Amherst z 01002
Millville; RMC Place; WORCESTER; ▲ Millville; 187 H-11; elev. 230ft./70m.; 🅿; ★ BOS; z 01529; ● 2,236
Millville; MCD-Town; WORCESTER; *187 H-11; 🅿; ★ BOS; z 01529; ℗ 2,236; © 2,724; ◆ 2,950
Millville Center; RMC Place; WORCESTER; ▲ Millville; *187 N-20; ★ BOS; mail Millville z 01529
Milton; CDP; NORFOLK; ▲ Milton; 187 F-14; 🅿 🅷 🅲 3,073; ★ BOS; z 02186; ℗ 25,725; © 26,062; ◆ 25,673
Milton; MCD-Town; NORFOLK; *187 F-14; 🅿 🅲 3,073; ★ BOS; z 02186; ℗ 25,725; © 26,062; ◆ 25,673
Milton Center; RMC Place; NORFOLK; ▲ Milton; 186 M-7; ★ BOS; mail Milton z 02186
Milton Village; RMC Place; NORFOLK; ▲ Milton; 186 M-7; elev. 50ft./15m.; 🅿; ★ BOS; z 02187
Minot; RMC Place; PLYMOUTH; ▲ Scituate; 187 F-16; elev. 15ft./5m.; 🅿; ★ BOS; z 02055; ● 900
Miramar; RMC Place; PLYMOUTH; ▲ Duxbury; *187 H-16; ★ BOS; mail Duxbury z 02332; rural
Mirror Lake; RMC Place; NORFOLK; ▲ Wrentham, Norfolk; *187 G-13; ★ BOS; mail Wrentham z 02093; ● 500
Mishaum Point; RMC Place; BRISTOL; ▲ Dartmouth; *187 K-15; ★ N.BED; mail South Dartmouth z 02748; ● 25
Mission Hill; RMC Place; SUFFOLK; *187 E-14; elev. 30ft./9m.; 🅿; ★ BOS; z 02120; pop. incl. with Boston (Inc. Place)
Mittineague; RMC Place; HAMPDEN; ▲ West Springfield; *186 G-5; ★ SPRG; mail West Springfield z 01089
Monomoscoy Island; CDP-Census Area Only; BARNSTABLE; *187 K-17; ★ BARN; © 152
Monomoy; RMC Place; NANTUCKET; ▲ Nantucket; 187 M-20; elev. 24ft./7m.; mail Nantucket z 02554; ● 250
Monponsett; RMC Place; PLYMOUTH; ▲ Hanson, Halifax; 187 H-15; elev. 60ft./18m.; 🅿; ★ BOS; z 02350; ● 730
Monroe; MCD-Town; FRANKLIN; *186 B-3; 🅿; z 01350; ℗ 115; © 93
Monroe Bridge; RMC Place; FRANKLIN; ▲ Monroe; 186 B-3; elev. 1,106ft./337m.; 🅿; z 01350; ● 90
Monson; RMC Place; HAMPDEN; ▲ Monson; ★ SPRG; ● 900
Monson; MCD-Town; HAMPDEN; *186 G-7; 🅿; ★ SPRG; z 01057; ℗ 7,776; © 8,359; ◆ 8,531
Monson Center; CDP-Census Area Only; HAMPDEN; ▲ Monson; 186 G-7; elev. 407ft./124m.; ★ SPRG; mail Monson z 01057; ℗ 2,102; © 2,103
Montague; RMC Place; FRANKLIN; ▲ Montague; 186 D-6; elev. 235ft./72m.; 🅿; z 01351; ● 830
Montague; MCD-Town; FRANKLIN; *186 D-6; 🅿; z 01351; ℗ 8,316; © 8,489; ® 8,468
Montague City; RMC Place; FRANKLIN; ▲ Montague; *186 C-6; elev. 160ft./49m.; mail Turners Falls z 01376
Montclair; RMC Place; NORFOLK; *187 F-14; elev. 20ft./6m.; ★ BOS; mail Quincy z 02171; pop. incl. with Quincy (Inc. Place)
Montello; RMC Place; PLYMOUTH; *187 G-14; elev. 130ft./40m.; ★ BOS; mail Brockton z 02303, z 02305; pop. incl. with Brockton (Inc. Place)
Monterey; RMC Place; BERKSHIRE; ▲ Monterey; 186 F-2; elev. 1,244ft./379m.; 🅿; z 01245; ● 600
Monterey; MCD-Town; BERKSHIRE; *186 F-2; 🅿; z 01245; ℗ 805; © 934
Montgomery; RMC Place; HAMPDEN; ▲ Montgomery; 186 F-4; elev. 1,049ft./320m.; 🅿; ★ SPRG; z 01050, z 01085; ● 325
Montgomery; MCD-Town; HAMPDEN; *186 F-4; 🅿; ★ SPRG; z 01050, z 01085; ℗ 759; © 654; ◆ 668
Montserrat; RMC Place; ESSEX; *187 C-15; elev. 56ft./17m.; ★ BOS; mail Beverly z 01915; pop. incl. with Beverly (Inc. Place)
Montvale; RMC Place; MIDDLESEX; *187 D-14; elev. 70ft./21m.; ★ BOS; mail Woburn z 01801; pop. incl. with Woburn (Inc. Place)
Montville; RMC Place; BERKSHIRE; ▲ Sandisfield; 186 G-2; elev. 1,165ft./355m.; mail Sandisfield z 01255; ● 90
Monument Beach; CDP; BARNSTABLE; ▲ Bourne; 187 J-17; elev. 20ft./6m.; 🅿; z 02553; ℗ 1,842; summer pop. 3,000; © 2,438
Moores Corner; RMC Place; FRANKLIN; ▲ Leverett; 186 D-6; elev. 650ft./198m.; mail Leverett z 01054; ● 100
Moores Corners; RMC Place; WORCESTER; ▲ Sterling; *186 D-10; ★ WORC; mail Sterling z 01564; ● 100
Morningdale; RMC Place; WORCESTER; ▲ Boylston; 186 E-10; elev. 479ft./146m.; ★ WORC; mail Boylston z 01505; ● 1,150
Morrills; RMC Place; NORFOLK; ▲ Norwood; *187 N-20; ★ BOS; mail Norwood z 02062
Morseville; RMC Place; MIDDLESEX; ▲ Natick; 186 M-3; elev. 172ft./52m.; ★ BOS; mail Natick z 01760
Mount Auburn; RMC Place; MIDDLESEX; *187 E-14; elev. 44ft./13m.; ★ BOS; mail Watertown z 02472; pop. incl. with Watertown (Inc. Place)
Mount Bowdoin; RMC Place; SUFFOLK; *187 E-14; elev. 100ft./30m.; ★ BOS; mail Boston z 02121; pop. incl. with Boston (Inc. Place)
Mount Hermon; RMC Place; FRANKLIN; ▲ Northfield; 186 C-6; 🅿; z 01354; ● 650
Mount Pleasant; RMC Place; BRISTOL; *187 N-20; ★ N.BED; mail New Bedford z 02745; pop. incl. with New Bedford (Inc. Place)
Mount Saint James; RMC Place; WORCESTER; *186 F-10; ★ WORC; mail Worcester z 01610; pop. incl. with Worcester (Inc. Place)
Mount Tom; RMC Place; HAMPSHIRE; *186 F-5; elev. 125ft./38m.; 🅿; ★ SPRG; z 01027; pop. incl. with Easthampton (Inc. Place)
Mount Washington; RMC Place; BERKSHIRE; ▲ Mount Washington; 186 G-1; 🅿; z 01258 & mail Copake Falls z 12517; rural
Mount Washington; MCD-Town; BERKSHIRE; *186 G-1; 🅿; z 01258 & mail Copake Falls z 12517; ℗ 135; © 130
Myricks; RMC Place; BRISTOL; ▲ Berkley; 187 I-14; elev. 64ft./20m.; ★ BOS; mail Assonet z 02702, Berkley z 02779; ● 60
Mystic Grove; RMC Place; WORCESTER; ▲ Charlton; 186 F-9; elev. 780ft./238m.; ★ WORC; mail Charlton z 01507; ● 150
Mystic Wharf; RMC Place; SUFFOLK; *187 N-20; ★ BOS; mail Boston z 02109; pop. incl. with Boston (Inc. Place)

N

Nabnasset; RMC Place; MIDDLESEX; ▲ Westford; 187 C-12; elev. 181ft./55m.; ★ BOS; mail Westford z 01886; ● 3,600
Nahant; CDP; ESSEX; ▲ Nahant; 187 E-15; elev. 50ft./15m.; 🅿; ★ BOS; z 01908; ℗ 3,828; © 3,632
Nahant; MCD-Town; ESSEX; *187 E-15; 🅿; ★ BOS; z 01908; ℗ 3,828; © 3,632; ◆ 3,528
Nameloc Heights; RMC Place; PLYMOUTH; ▲ Plymouth; *187 I-17; elev. 110ft./34m.; ★ BOS; mail Plymouth z 02360; ● 100
Nantasket Beach; RMC Place; PLYMOUTH; ▲ Hull; *187 F-15; ★ BOS; mail Hull z 02045
Nantucket; CDP; ⊡ NANTUCKET; ▲ Nantucket; 187 M-20; elev. 30ft./9m.; 🅿 🅷; z 02554, z 02564, z 02584; ℗ 3,069; © 3,830
Nantucket; MCD-Town; NANTUCKET; *187 M-19; 🅿; z 02554, z 02564, z 02584; ℗ 6,012; © 9,520
NANTUCKET; 187 M-20; ℗ 6,012; © 9,520; ◆ 11,539
Nashaquitsa; RMC Place; DUKES; ▲ Chilmark; 187 M-16; elev. 56ft./17m.; mail Chilmark z 02535; ● 150
Natick; RMC Place; MIDDLESEX; ▲ Natick; 187 F-12; elev. 180ft./55m.; 🅿; ★ BOS; z 01760; ℗ 30,510; ● 32,200
Natick; MCD-Town; MIDDLESEX; *187 F-12; 🅿 ■; ★ BOS; z 01760; ℗ 30,510; © 32,170; ◆ 32,656
Natick Development Center; RMC Place; MIDDLESEX; *187 N-20; ★ BOS; mail Natick z 01760
Nauset Heights; RMC Place; BARNSTABLE; ▲ Orleans; *187 I-20; elev. 40ft./12m.; ★ BARN; mail East Orleans z 02643, Orleans z 02653; ● 500
Needham; CDP; NORFOLK; ▲ Needham; 187 F-13; elev. 162ft./49m.; 🅿 🅷; ★ BOS; z 02492, z 02494; ℗ 27,557; © 28,911; ◆ 29,150
Needham; MCD-Town; NORFOLK; *187 F-13; 🅿 ■; ★ BOS; z 02492, z 02494; ℗ 27,557; © 28,911; ◆ 29,150
Needham Heights; RMC Place; NORFOLK; ▲ Needham; 186 L-5; elev. 190ft./58m.; 🅿; ★ BOS; z 02494
Needham Junction; RMC Place; NORFOLK; *187 F-13; elev. 170ft./52m.; ★ BOS; mail Needham z 02492
Nelsons Grove; RMC Place; PLYMOUTH; ▲ Lakeville; *187 I-15; elev. 57ft./17m.; ★ BOS; mail Middleboro z 02346
Nelsons Shores; RMC Place; PLYMOUTH; ▲ Lakeville; *187 I-15; elev. 60ft./18m.; ★ BOS; mail Middleboro z 02346; ● 30
Neponset; RMC Place; SUFFOLK; *187 F-14; elev. 25ft./8m.; ★ BOS; mail Boston z 02122; pop. incl. with Boston (Inc. Place)
New Ashford; RMC Place; BERKSHIRE; ▲ New Ashford; 186 C-2; elev. 1,256ft./383m.; 🅿; z 01237; ● 80
New Ashford; MCD-Town; BERKSHIRE; *186 C-2; 🅿; z 01237; ℗ 192; © 247
New Bedford; Inc. Place; BRISTOL; 187 K-15; elev. 50ft./15m.; 🅿 ■; ★ N.BED; z 02740-46; ℗ 99,922; © 93,768; ◆ 88,951
New Boston; RMC Place; BERKSHIRE; ▲ Sandisfield; 186 G-3; elev. 826ft./252m.; mail Sandisfield z 01255; ● 110
New Braintree; RMC Place; WORCESTER; ▲ New Braintree; 186 E-8; elev. 945ft./288m.; 🅿; z 01531; ● 500
New Braintree; MCD-Town; WORCESTER; *186 E-8; 🅿; z 01531; ℗ 881; © 927
Newbury; RMC Place; ESSEX; ▲ Newbury; 187 B-15; 🅿; ★ BOS; z 01922, z 01951; pop. incl. with Newburyport (Inc. Place)
Newbury; MCD-Town; ESSEX; *187 B-15; 🅿; ★ BOS; z 01922, z 01951 & mail Newburyport z 01950; ℗ 5,623; © 6,717; ◆ 7,036
Newburyport; Inc. Place; ESSEX; 187 B-15; elev. 37ft./11m.; 🅿 🅷; ★ BOS; z 01950-51; ℗ 16,317; © 17,189; ◆ 17,245
New Lenox; RMC Place; BERKSHIRE; ▲ Lenox; 186 E-2; elev. 965ft./294m.; ★ PTSF; mail Lenox z 01240; ● 800
New Marlboro; BERKSHIRE; see New Marlborough (RMC Place)
New Marlborough (New Marlboro); RMC Place; BERKSHIRE; ▲ New Marlborough; 186 G-2; 🅿; z 01230; ● 185
New Marlborough; MCD-Town; BERKSHIRE; *186 G-2; 🅿; z 01230; ℗ 1,240; © 1,494
New Salem; RMC Place; FRANKLIN; ▲ New Salem; 186 D-7; elev. 1,048ft./319m.; 🅿; z 01355 & mail Orange z 01364; ● 450
New Salem; MCD-Town; FRANKLIN; *186 D-7; 🅿; z 01355 & mail Orange z 01364; ℗ 802; © 929
New Seabury; CDP-Census Area Only; BARNSTABLE; ▲ Mashpee; 187 K-18; ★ BARN; mail Mashpee z 02649; © 815
Newton; Inc. Place; MIDDLESEX; 187 E-13; elev. 100ft./30m.; 🅿 🅷 🅲 18,541 ■; ★ BOS; z 02458-62, z 02464-65, z 02495 & mail Auburndale z 02466, Chestnut Hill z 02467, New Town z 02456, Waban z 02468; ℗ 82,585; © 83,829; ◆ 86,587
Newton Center; RMC Place; MIDDLESEX; 186 L-5; elev. 150ft./46m.; 🅿; ★ BOS; z 02459; pop. incl. with Newton (Inc. Place)
Newton Highlands; RMC Place; MIDDLESEX; 186 L-5; elev. 130ft./40m.; 🅿; ★ BOS; z 02461; pop. incl. with Newton (Inc. Place)
Newton Lower Falls; RMC Place; MIDDLESEX; 186 L-4; elev. 70ft./21m.; 🅿; ★ BOS; z 02462; pop. incl. with Newton (Inc. Place)
Newton Upper Falls; RMC Place; MIDDLESEX; *187 E-13; elev. 190ft./58m.; 🅿; ★ BOS; z 02464; pop. incl. with Newton (Inc. Place)
Newtonville; RMC Place; MIDDLESEX; *187 E-13; elev. 50ft./15m.; 🅿; ★ BOS; z 02458, z 02460, z 02462; pop. incl. with Newton (Inc. Place)
New Town; RMC Place; MIDDLESEX; *187 N-20; 🅿; ★ BOS; z 02456; pop. incl. with Newton (Inc. Place)
New Village; RMC Place; WORCESTER; ▲ Northbridge; *187 G-11; elev. 367ft./112m.; ★ WORC; mail Whitinsville z 01588
Nipmuck Pond; RMC Place; WORCESTER; 187 G-11; ★ BOS
Nobscot; RMC Place; MIDDLESEX; ▲ Framingham; *187 E-12; ★ BOS; mail Framingham z 01701
Nobska Beach; RMC Place; PLYMOUTH; ▲ Wareham; *187 J-16; ★ BOS; mail Wareham z 02571
Nonantum; RMC Place; MIDDLESEX; *187 E-13; elev. 50ft./15m.; 🅿; ★ BOS; z 02495; pop. incl. with Newton (Inc. Place)
Nonquitt; RMC Place; BRISTOL; ▲ Dartmouth; 187 K-15; elev. 50ft./15m.; 🅿; ★ N.BED; z 02748; ● 200
Norfolk; RMC Place; NORFOLK; ▲ Norfolk; 187 G-13; elev. 212ft./65m.; 🅿 🅷; ★ BOS; z 02056; ● 550
Norfolk; MCD-Town; NORFOLK; *187 G-13; 🅿; ★ BOS; z 02056; ℗ 9,270; © 10,460; ◆ 10,790
NORFOLK; 187 F-13; ℗ 616,087; © 650,308; ◆ 655,121
North; RMC Place; BRISTOL; *187 J-15; ★ N.BED; mail New Bedford z 02746; pop. incl. with New Bedford (Inc. Place)
North Abington; RMC Place; PLYMOUTH; ▲ Abington; *187 G-15; elev. 138ft./42m.; ★ BOS; mail Abington z 02351
North Acton; RMC Place; MIDDLESEX; ▲ Acton; 187 D-12; elev. 171ft./52m.; ★ BOS; mail Acton z 01720; ● 900
North Adams; Inc. Place; BERKSHIRE; 186 B-2; elev. 707ft./215m.; 🅿 🅷 🅲 1,805 ■; z 01247; ℗ 16,797; © 14,681; ◆ 12,817
North Agawam; RMC Place; HAMPDEN; *186 G-5; ★ SPRG; mail Feeding Hills z 01030; pop. incl. with Agawam (Inc. Place)
North Amherst; CDP; HAMPSHIRE; ▲ Amherst; 186 E-6; elev. 187ft./57m.; 🅿; ★ SPRG; z 01059; ℗ 6,239; © 6,019
Northampton; Inc. Place; ⊡ HAMPSHIRE; 186 E-5; elev. 140ft./43m.; 🅿 🅷 🅲 3,092 ■; ★ SPRG; z 01060-63; ℗ 29,289; © 28,978; ◆ 28,708
North Andover; RMC Place; ESSEX; ▲ North Andover; 187 B-14; elev. 75ft./23m.; 🅿 🅲 2,300; ★ BOS; z 01845; ● 22,792
North Andover; MCD-Town; ESSEX; *187 C-14; 🅿 🅲 2,300; ★ BOS; z 01845; ℗ 22,792; © 27,202; ◆ 27,341
North Andover Center; RMC Place; ESSEX; ▲ North Andover; *187 C-14; elev. 220ft./67m.; ★ BOS; mail North Andover z 01845
North Ashburnham; RMC Place; WORCESTER; ▲ Ashburnham; 186 C-9; elev. 1,129ft./344m.; ★ BOS; mail Ashburnham z 01430; ● 800
North Attleboro; RMC Place; BRISTOL; ▲ North Attleborough; 187 H-13; ★ PROV-; ● 11,900
North Attleborough; MCD-Town; BRISTOL; *187 H-13; ★ PROV-; mail North Attleboro z 02760; ℗ 25,038; © 27,143; ◆ 27,933
North Attleborough Center; CDP-Census Area Only; BRISTOL; ▲ North Attleborough; 187 H-13; elev. 200ft./61m.; ★ PROV-; mail Attleboro Falls z 02763, North Attleboro z 02760-61, Plainville z 02762; ℗ 16,178; © 16,796
North Bellingham; RMC Place; NORFOLK; ▲ Bellingham; *187 G-12; elev. 206ft./63m.; ★ BOS; mail Bellingham z 02019
North Beverly; RMC Place; ESSEX; *187 C-15; elev. 66ft./20m.; ★ BOS; mail Beverly z 01915; pop. incl. with Beverly (Inc. Place)
North Billerica; RMC Place; MIDDLESEX; ▲ Billerica; 187 C-13; elev. 127ft./39m.; 🅿; ★ BOS; z 01862; ● 5,500
North Blandford; RMC Place; HAMPDEN; ▲ Blandford; *186 F-3; elev. 1,170ft./357m.; mail Blandford z 01008
Northboro; WORCESTER; see Northborough (CDP)
Northborough (Northboro, Northborough Center); CDP; WORCESTER; ▲ Northborough; 187 E-11; elev. 300ft./91m.; 🅿; ★ WORC; z 01532; ℗ 5,761; © 6,257
Northborough; MCD-Town; WORCESTER; *187 E-11; 🅿; ★ WORC; z 01532; ℗ 11,929; © 14,013; ◆ 14,766
Northborough Center; WORCESTER; see Northborough (CDP)
Northbridge (Northbridge Compact); RMC Place; WORCESTER; ▲ Northbridge; 187 G-11; elev. 300ft./91m.; 🅿; ★ WORC; z 01534; ● 3,600
Northbridge; MCD-Town; WORCESTER; *187 G-11; 🅿; ★ WORC; z 01534; ℗ 13,371; © 13,182; ◆ 13,210
Northbridge Center; RMC Place; WORCESTER; ▲ Northbridge; 187 G-11; elev. 550ft./168m.; ★ WORC; mail Whitinsville z 01588; ● 220
Northbridge Compact; WORCESTER; see Northbridge (RMC Place)
North Brighton; RMC Place; SUFFOLK; *187 E-14; elev. 20ft./6m.; ★ BOS; mail Brighton z 02135; pop. incl. with Boston (Inc. Place)
North Brookfield; CDP; WORCESTER; ▲ North Brookfield; 186 F-8; elev. 915ft./279m.; 🅿; ★ WORC; z 01535; ℗ 2,635; © 2,527
North Brookfield; MCD-Town; WORCESTER; *186 F-8; 🅿; ★ WORC; z 01535; ℗ 4,708; © 4,683; ◆ 4,538
North Cambridge; RMC Place; MIDDLESEX; *187 E-14; elev. 10ft./3m.; 🅿; ★ BOS; z 02140 & mail Cambridge z 02138; pop. incl. with Cambridge (Inc. Place)
North Carver; RMC Place; PLYMOUTH; ▲ Carver; 187 H-16; elev. 99ft./30m.; 🅿; ★ BOS; z 02355; ● 600
North Chatham; RMC Place; BARNSTABLE; ▲ Chatham; 187 J-20; elev. 52ft./16m.; 🅿; ★ BARN; z 02650; ● 950
North Chelmsford; RMC Place; MIDDLESEX; ▲ Chelmsford; *187 C-12; elev. 150ft./46m.; 🅿; ★ BOS; z 01863
North Chester; RMC Place; HAMPDEN; ▲ Chester; *186 E-4; elev. 687ft./209m.; mail Huntington z 01050
North Chicopee; RMC Place; HAMPDEN; *186 F-5; elev. 110ft./34m.; ★ SPRG; pop. incl. with Chicopee (Inc. Place)
North Cohasset; RMC Place; NORFOLK; ▲ Cohasset; 187 F-15; elev. 60ft./18m.; ★ BOS; mail Cohasset z 02025; ● 500
North Dartmouth; RMC Place; BRISTOL; ▲ Dartmouth; *187 K-15; elev. 153ft./47m.; 🅿 🅲 8,756; ★ N.BED; z 02747
North Dighton; RMC Place; BRISTOL; ▲ Dighton; 187 I-14; elev. 16ft./5m.; 🅿; ★ BOS; z 02764; ● 1,250
North Duxbury; RMC Place; PLYMOUTH; ▲ Duxbury; *187 G-16; elev. 69ft./21m.; ★ BOS; mail Duxbury z 02332
North Eastham; CDP; BARNSTABLE; ▲ Eastham; 187 I-20; elev. 60ft./18m.; 🅿; ★ BARN; z 02651; ℗ 1,570; © 1,915
North Easton; RMC Place; BRISTOL; ▲ Easton; 187 G-14; elev. 150ft./46m.; 🅿; ★ BOS; z 02356-57; ● 4,500
North Egremont; RMC Place; BERKSHIRE; ▲ Egremont; 186 F-1; elev. 766ft./233m.; 🅿; z 01230, z 01252; ● 300

Entries in **UPPERCASE** are counties.
Entries in **bold** have populations of 2,500 or more.
Names in parentheses are alternate names.

Inc. Place	Incorporated Place
RMC Place	Rand McNally Designated Place
CDP	Census Designated Place
MCD	Minor Civil Division

⊡	County Seat
▲	Minor Civil Division
elev.	Elevation
🅿	Post Office
🅷	Hospital
🅲	College
■	Principal Business Center
★	Ranally Metro Area (RMA) Abbreviation
z	Zip Code(s)
℗	Previous Census Population
®	Revised Census Population
Ⓐ	Annexation Population
●	Rand McNally Population Estimate
©	Final Census Population
Ⓢ	Special Census Population
◆	Estimated Population

For additional definitions see Glossary, Volume 1, and Introduction, Volume 2.

Northey Point; RMC Place; ESSEX; *187 N-20; ★ **BOS**; mail Salem z 01970; pop. incl. with Salem (Inc. Place)
North Fairhaven; RMC Place; BRISTOL; ▲ Fairhaven; *187 J-15; ★ **N.BED**; mail Fairhaven z 02719
North Falmouth; CDP; BARNSTABLE; ▲ Falmouth; **187** J-17; elev. 20ft./6m.; 🅿; z 02556, z 02565; Ⓟ 2,625; Ⓒ 3,355
North Farms; RMC Place; HAMPSHIRE; *186 E-5; elev. 390ft./119m.; ★ **SPRG**; mail Florence z 01062; pop. incl. with Northampton (Inc. Place)
Northfield; CDP; FRANKLIN; ▲ Northfield; **186** B-6; elev. 300ft./91m.; 🅿; z 01360 & mail Gill z 01354; Ⓟ 1,322; Ⓒ 1,141
Northfield; MCD-Town; FRANKLIN; *186 C-6; 🅿; z 01360 & mail Gill z 01354; Ⓟ 2,838; Ⓒ 2,951
North Grafton; RMC Place; WORCESTER; ▲ Grafton; **186** F-10; elev. 358ft./109m.; 🅿; ★ **WORC**; z 01536; ● 3,150
North Hadley; RMC Place; HAMPSHIRE; ▲ Hadley; **186** E-5; elev. 142ft./43m.; ★ **SPRG**; mail Hadley z 01035; ● 350
North Hancock; RMC Place; BERKSHIRE; ▲ Hancock; *186 C-1; elev. 1,194ft./364m.; mail Williamstown z 01267; rural
North Hanover; RMC Place; PLYMOUTH; ▲ Hanover; **187** G-15; elev. 110ft./34m.; ★ **BOS**; mail Hanover z 02339; ● 980
North Harwich; RMC Place; BARNSTABLE; ▲ Harwich; **187** J-20; elev. 38ft./12m.; ★ **BARN**; mail Harwich z 02645; ● 500
North Hatfield; RMC Place; HAMPSHIRE; ▲ Hatfield; **186** E-5; elev. 170ft./52m.; 🅿; ★ **SPRG**; z 01066; ● 470
North Lakeville; CDP-Census Area Only; PLYMOUTH; ▲ Lakeville; **187** I-15; elev. 90ft./27m.; ★ **BOS**; mail Lakeville z 02347-48; Ⓟ 2,048; Ⓒ 2,233
North Lancaster; WORCESTER; see North Village (RMC Place)
North Leominster; RMC Place; WORCESTER; *186 D-10; elev. 429ft./131m.; ★ **BOS**; mail Leominster z 01453; pop. incl. with Leominster (Inc. Place)
North Leverett; RMC Place; FRANKLIN; ▲ Leverett; **186** D-6; elev. 484ft./148m.; mail Leverett z 01054; ● 200
North Littleton; RMC Place; MIDDLESEX; ▲ Littleton; *187 N-20; ★ **BOS**; mail Littleton z 01460; ● 450
North Marshfield; RMC Place; PLYMOUTH; ▲ Marshfield; **187** G-16; elev. 120ft./37m.; 🅿; ★ **BOS**; z 02059; ● 450
North Middleboro; RMC Place; PLYMOUTH; ▲ Middleborough; **187** H-15; elev. 50ft./15m.; ★ **BOS**; mail Middleboro z 02346; ● 250
North Milford; RMC Place; WORCESTER; ▲ Milford; *187 F-11; elev. 470ft./143m.; ★ **BOS**; mail Milford z 01757
North Natick; RMC Place; MIDDLESEX; ▲ Natick; *187 E-12; elev. 200ft./61m.; ★ **BOS**; mail Natick z 01760
North New Salem; RMC Place; FRANKLIN; ▲ New Salem; **186** D-7; elev. 580ft./177m.; mail Orange z 01364; ● 50
North Orange; RMC Place; FRANKLIN; ▲ Orange; **186** C-7; elev. 840ft./256m.; mail Orange z 01364; ● 80
North Otis; RMC Place; BERKSHIRE; ▲ Otis; *186 F-2; elev. 1,356ft./413m.; mail Otis z 01253
North Oxford; RMC Place; WORCESTER; ▲ Oxford; **186** G-10; elev. 535ft./163m.; 🅿; ★ **WORC**; z 01537; ● 1,200
North Pembroke; CDP; PLYMOUTH; ▲ Pembroke; **187** G-16; elev. 35ft./11m.; 🅿; ★ **BOS**; z 02358; Ⓟ 2,485; Ⓒ 2,913
North Pepperell; RMC Place; MIDDLESEX; ▲ Pepperell; *187 B-11; elev. 230ft./70m.; ★ **BOS**; mail Pepperell z 01463; rural
North Plymouth; CDP; PLYMOUTH; ▲ Plymouth; *187 H-16; elev. 58ft./18m.; ★ **BOS**; mail Plymouth z 02360; Ⓟ 3,450; Ⓒ 3,593
North Plympton; RMC Place; PLYMOUTH; ▲ Plympton; *187 H-16; elev. 62ft./19m.; ★ **BOS**; mail Kingston z 02364
North Quincy; RMC Place; NORFOLK; **186** M-8; elev. 10ft./3m.; 🅿; ★ **BOS**; z 02171; pop. incl. with Quincy (Inc. Place)
North Randolph; RMC Place; NORFOLK; ▲ Randolph; *187 F-14; elev. 200ft./61m.; ★ **BOS**; mail Randolph z 02368
North Reading; RMC Place; MIDDLESEX; ▲ North Reading; **187** C-14; elev. 100ft./30m.; 🅿; ★ **BOS**; z 01864, z 01889; ● 12,002
North Reading; MCD-Town; MIDDLESEX; *187 C-14; 🅿; ★ **BOS**; z 01864, z 01889; Ⓟ 12,002; Ⓒ 13,837; ◆ 14,896
North Rehoboth; RMC Place; BRISTOL; ▲ Rehoboth; *187 I-13; elev. 130ft./40m.; ★ **PROV-**; mail Rehoboth z 02769
North Rutland; RMC Place; WORCESTER; ▲ Rutland; *186 E-9; elev. 876ft./267m.; ★ **WORC**; mail Rutland z 01543
North Salem; RMC Place; ESSEX; *187 D-15; elev. 50ft./15m.; ★ **BOS**; mail Salem z 01970; pop. incl. with Salem (Inc. Place)
North Saugus; RMC Place; ESSEX; ▲ Saugus; **186** I-8; elev. 50ft./15m.; ★ **BOS**; mail Saugus z 01906
North Scituate; CDP; PLYMOUTH; ▲ Scituate; **187** F-16; 🅿; ★ **BOS**; z 02060; Ⓟ 4,891; Ⓒ 5,065
North Seekonk; CDP-Census Area Only; BRISTOL; ▲ Seekonk; *187 I-13; elev. 82ft./25m.; ★ **PROV-**; mail Seekonk z 02771; Ⓟ 2,635; Ⓒ 2,598
North Somerville; RMC Place; MIDDLESEX; *187 N-20; ★ **BOS**; mail Somerville z 02143; pop. incl. with Somerville (Inc. Place)
North Stoughton; RMC Place; NORFOLK; ▲ Stoughton; *187 G-14; elev. 249ft./76m.; ★ **BOS**; mail Stoughton z 02072
North Sudbury; RMC Place; MIDDLESEX; ▲ Sudbury; **187** E-12; elev. 130ft./40m.; ★ **BOS**; mail Sudbury z 01776; ● 2,600
North Swansea; RMC Place; BRISTOL; ▲ Swansea; **187** J-13; elev. 58ft./18m.; ★ **F.R.**; mail Swansea z 02777; ● 900
North Tewksbury; RMC Place; MIDDLESEX; ▲ Tewksbury; **187** C-13; elev. 246ft./75m.; ★ **BOS**; mail Tewksbury z 01876; ● 1,200
North Tisbury; RMC Place; DUKES; ▲ West Tisbury; **187** L-16; elev. 60ft./18m.; mail Vineyard Haven z 02568; ● 200
North Truro; RMC Place; BARNSTABLE; ▲ Truro; **187** G-20; elev. 20ft./6m.; 🅿; z 02652; ● 950
North Uxbridge; RMC Place; WORCESTER; ▲ Uxbridge; **187** G-11; elev. 260ft./79m.; 🅿; ★ **WORC**; z 01538; ● 1,800
North Village (North Lancaster); RMC Place; WORCESTER; *186 G-10; ★ **WORC**; mail Webster z 01570
North Waltham; RMC Place; MIDDLESEX; *187 F-13; elev. 100ft./30m.; 🅿; ★ **BOS**; z 02451-52, z 02455
Northwest Harwich; CDP-Census Area Only; BARNSTABLE; *187 J-20; elev. 10ft./3m.; ★ **BARN**; mail Harwich z 02645; Ⓟ 3,037; Ⓒ 4,001
North Westport (Westport); CDP-Census Area Only; BRISTOL; ▲ Westport; **187** J-14; ★ **F.R.**; mail Westport z 02790; Ⓟ 4,697; Ⓒ 4,533
North Weymouth; RMC Place; NORFOLK; ▲ Weymouth; **186** M-9; elev. 39ft./12m.; 🅿; ★ **BOS**; z 02191
North Wilmington; RMC Place; MIDDLESEX; ▲ Wilmington; *187 C-14; elev. 100ft./30m.; ★ **BOS**; mail Wilmington z 01887
North Woburn; RMC Place; MIDDLESEX; **186** H-6; elev. 107ft./33m.; ★ **BOS**; mail Woburn z 01801; pop. incl. with Woburn (Inc. Place)
North Worcester; RMC Place; WORCESTER; *186 E-10; elev. 700ft./213m.; ★ **WORC**; mail Worcester z 01606; pop. incl. with Worcester (Inc. Place)
Norton; RMC Place; BRISTOL; ▲ Wareham; **187** H-13; ★ **BOS**; ● 2,200
Norton; MCD-Town; BRISTOL; *187 H-14; 🅿 🅲 1,561; ★ **BOS**; z 02766 & mail Chartley z 02712; Ⓟ 14,265; Ⓒ 18,036; ◆ 19,568
Norton Center; CDP-Census Area Only; BRISTOL; ▲ Norton; **187** H-13; elev. 105ft./32m.; 🅲 1,561; ★ **BOS**; mail Chartley z 02712, Norton z 02766; Ⓟ 1,899; Ⓒ 2,618
Norton Grove; RMC Place; BRISTOL; ▲ Norton; **187** H-13; elev. 104ft./32m.; ★ **BOS**; mail Norton z 02766; ● 2,100
Norwell; RMC Place; PLYMOUTH; ▲ Norwell; **187** G-16; elev. 81ft./25m.; 🅿; ★ **BOS**; z 02061 & mail Accord z 02018; ● 1,200
Norwell; MCD-Town; PLYMOUTH; *187 F-16; 🅿; ★ **BOS**; z 02061 & mail Accord z 02018; Ⓟ 9,279; Ⓒ 9,765; ◆ 9,753
Norwich Bridge; RMC Place; HAMPSHIRE; ▲ Huntington; *186 F-4; ★ **SPRG**; mail Huntington z 01050; ● 100
Norwood; CDP; NORFOLK; ▲ Norwood; **187** F-13; elev. 146ft./45m.; 🅿 🅷; ★ **BOS**; z 02062; Ⓟ 28,700; Ⓒ 28,587; ◆ 28,588
Norwood; MCD-Town; NORFOLK; *187 F-13; 🅿 ■; ★ **BOS**; z 02062; Ⓟ 28,700; Ⓒ 28,587; ◆ 28,588
Norwood Central; RMC Place; NORFOLK; ▲ Norwood; *187 N-20; ★ **BOS**; mail Norwood z 02062
Nutting Lake; RMC Place; MIDDLESEX; ▲ Billerica; **187** D-13; elev. 190ft./58m.; 🅿; ★ **BOS**; z 01865; ● 3,200

O

Oak Bluffs; RMC Place; DUKES; ▲ Oak Bluffs; **187** L-17; elev. 30ft./9m.; 🅿 🅷; z 02557 & mail Vineyard Haven z 02568; summer pop. 3,500; ● 2,000
Oak Bluffs; MCD-Town; DUKES; *187 L-17; 🅿; z 02557 & mail Vineyard Haven z 02568; Ⓟ 2,804; Ⓒ 3,713
Oakdale; RMC Place; HAMPDEN; **187** K-11; elev. 270ft./82m.; ★ **SPRG**; mail Holyoke z 01040; pop. incl. with Holyoke (Inc. Place)
Oakdale; RMC Place; NORFOLK; ▲ Dedham; **186** M-6; elev. 110ft./34m.; ★ **BOS**; mail Dedham z 02026
Oakdale; RMC Place; WORCESTER; ▲ West Boylston; **186** E-10; elev. 420ft./128m.; ★ **WORC**; mail West Boylston z 01583; ● 600
Oak Grove; RMC Place; MIDDLESEX; *187 D-14; elev. 45ft./14m.; ★ **BOS**; mail Malden z 02148; pop. incl. with Malden (Inc. Place)
Oakham; RMC Place; WORCESTER; ▲ Oakham; **186** E-9; elev. 1,050ft./320m.; 🅿; ★ **WORC**; z 01068; ● 600
Oakham; MCD-Town; WORCESTER; *186 E-9; 🅿; ★ **WORC**; z 01068; Ⓟ 1,503; Ⓒ 1,673; ◆ 1,716
Oak Island; RMC Place; SUFFOLK; **186** J-8; elev. 15ft./5m.; ★ **BOS**; mail Revere z 02151; pop. incl. with Revere (Inc. Place)
Oakland Vale; RMC Place; ESSEX; ▲ Saugus; *187 D-14; elev. 58ft./18m.; ★ **BOS**; mail Saugus z 01906
O'Briens Corner; RMC Place; HAMPDEN; *186 G-5; ★ **SPRG**; mail Feeding Hills z 01030; pop. incl. with Agawam (Inc. Place)
Ocean Bluff; RMC Place; PLYMOUTH; ▲ Marshfield; **187** G-17; elev. 25ft./8m.; 🅿; ★ **BOS**; z 02065; ● 2,500
Ocean Bluff-Brant Rock; CDP-Census Area Only; PLYMOUTH; ▲ Marshfield; *187 G-16; ★ **BOS**; mail Brant Rock z 02020, Marshfield z 02050; Ⓟ 4,541; Ⓒ 5,100
Ocean Grove; CDP; BRISTOL; ▲ Swansea; **187** J-13; elev. 30ft./9m.; ★ **F.R.**; mail Swansea z 02777; Ⓟ 3,169; Ⓒ 3,012
Ocean Heights; RMC Place; DUKES; ▲ Edgartown; *187 L-17; elev. 15ft./5m.; mail Edgartown z 02539
Old City; RMC Place; MIDDLESEX; ▲ Townsend; *186 C-10; elev. 510ft./155m.; ★ **BOS**; mail West Townsend z 01474
Old Common; RMC Place; WORCESTER; *186 F-10; elev. 635ft./194m.; ★ **WORC**; mail Millbury z 01527; rural
Old Furnace; WORCESTER; see Furnace (RMC Place)
Oldham Pines; RMC Place; PLYMOUTH; ▲ Pembroke; *187 G-16; elev. 70ft./21m.; ★ **BOS**; mail Pembroke z 02359; ● 300
Oldham Village; RMC Place; PLYMOUTH; ▲ Pembroke; **187** G-16; elev. 65ft./20m.; ★ **BOS**; mail Pembroke z 02359; ● 900
Old Hill; RMC Place; HAMPDEN; *186 G-6; ★ **SPRG**; mail Springfield z 01109; pop. incl. with Springfield (Inc. Place)
Old Silver Beach; RMC Place; BARNSTABLE; ▲ Falmouth; *187 K-17; elev. 21ft./6m.; mail North Falmouth z 02556
Old Sturbridge Village; RMC Place; WORCESTER; ▲ Sturbridge; *186 G-8; ★ **WORC**; mail Sturbridge z 01566; ● 150
Old Town House; RMC Place; ESSEX; ▲ Andover; *187 N-20; ★ **BOS**; mail Andover z 01810
Onset; CDP; PLYMOUTH; ▲ Wareham; **187** J-17; elev. 30ft./9m.; 🅿; ★ **BOS**; z 02558; Ⓟ 1,461; Ⓒ 1,292
Orange; CDP; FRANKLIN; ▲ Orange; **186** C-7; elev. 510ft./155m.; 🅿; z 01364, z 01378 & mail New Salem z 01355; Ⓟ 3,791; Ⓒ 3,945
Orange; MCD-Town; FRANKLIN; *186 C-7; 🅿; z 01364, z 01378 & mail New Salem z 01355; Ⓟ 7,312; Ⓒ 7,518
Orchard Street; RMC Place; BRISTOL; *187 N-20; ★ **N.BED**; mail New Bedford z 02740; pop. incl. with New Bedford (Inc. Place)
Orient Heights; RMC Place; SUFFOLK; *187 E-15; elev. 12ft./4m.; ★ **BOS**; mail Boston z 02128; pop. incl. with Boston (Inc. Place)
Orleans; CDP; BARNSTABLE; ▲ Orleans; **187** I-20; elev. 60ft./18m.; 🅿; ★ **BARN**; z 02653; Ⓟ 1,699; Ⓒ 1,716
Orleans; MCD-Town; BARNSTABLE; *187 I-20; 🅿; ★ **BARN**; z 02653; Ⓟ 5,838; Ⓒ 6,341; ◆ 5,911
Osceola; RMC Place; BERKSHIRE; ▲ Richmond; *187 N-20; ★ **PTSF**; mail Richmond z 01254; rural
Osterville; RMC Place; BARNSTABLE; *187 K-18; elev. 32ft./10m.; 🅿; ★ **BARN**; z 02655; pop. incl. with Barnstable (Inc. Place)
Otis (Otis Center); RMC Place; BERKSHIRE; ▲ Otis; **186** F-3; elev. 1,220ft./372m.; 🅿; z 01253; ● 650
Otis; MCD-Town; BERKSHIRE; *186 F-3; 🅿; z 01253; Ⓟ 1,073; Ⓒ 1,365
Otis Center; BERKSHIRE; see Otis (RMC Place)
Otter River; RMC Place; WORCESTER; ▲ Templeton; **186** C-9; elev. 900ft./274m.; ★ **BOS**; mail Baldwinville z 01436; ● 630
Overbrook; RMC Place; NORFOLK; ▲ Wellesley; *187 E-13; elev. 125ft./38m.; ★ **BOS**; mail Wellesley z 02482
Oxford; RMC Place; BRISTOL; ▲ Fairhaven; *187 J-15; ★ **N.BED**; mail Fairhaven z 02719
Oxford; CDP; WORCESTER; ▲ Oxford; **186** G-10; elev. 508ft./155m.; 🅿; ★ **WORC**; z 01540; Ⓟ 5,969; Ⓒ 5,899
Oxford; MCD-Town; WORCESTER; *186 G-10; 🅿; ★ **WORC**; z 01540; Ⓟ 12,588; Ⓒ 13,352; ◆ 13,144
Oyster Harbors; RMC Place; BARNSTABLE; *187 K-18; elev. 32ft./10m.; ★ **BARN**; mail Osterville z 02655; pop. incl. with Barnstable (Inc. Place)

P

Packard Heights; RMC Place; FRANKLIN; ▲ Orange; **186** C-7; elev. 610ft./186m.; mail Athol z 01331; summer pop. 150; ● 50
Padanaram; BRISTOL; see South Dartmouth (RMC Place)
Pages Beach; RMC Place; WORCESTER; ▲ Ashburnham; *187 N-20; ★ **BOS**; mail Ashburnham z 01430; ● 270
Painting Island; RMC Place; PLYMOUTH; ▲ Marion; *187 J-16; ★ **N.BED**; mail Marion z 02738; ● 130
Pakachoag; RMC Place; WORCESTER; ▲ Auburn; **187** C-19; elev. 650ft./198m.; ★ **WORC**; mail Auburn z 01501
Palmer; CDP; HAMPDEN; ▲ Palmer; **186** G-7; elev. 330ft./101m.; 🅿 🅷; ★ **SPRG**; z 01069; Ⓟ 4,069; Ⓒ 3,900
Palmer; MCD-Town; HAMPDEN; *186 F-7; 🅿; ★ **SPRG**; z 01069; Ⓟ 12,054; Ⓒ 12,497; ◆ 12,702
Park Street; RMC Place; MIDDLESEX; *187 N-20; ★ **BOS**; mail Medford z 02155; pop. incl. with Medford (Inc. Place)
Parkwood Beach; RMC Place; PLYMOUTH; ▲ Wareham; **187** J-16; elev. 22ft./7m.; ★ **BOS**; mail Wareham z 02571; ● 250
Patuisset; RMC Place; BARNSTABLE; ▲ Bourne; *187 J-17; elev. 10ft./3m.; mail Pocasset z 02559
Pawtucketville; RMC Place; MIDDLESEX; *187 C-13; elev. 150ft./46m.; ★ **BOS**; mail Lowell z 01854; pop. incl. with Lowell (Inc. Place)
Paxton; RMC Place; WORCESTER; ▲ Paxton; **186** E-9; elev. 1,158ft./353m.; 🅿 🅲 1,200; ★ **WORC**; z 01612; ● 1,600
Paxton; MCD-Town; WORCESTER; *186 E-9; 🅿 🅲 1,200; ★ **WORC**; z 01612; Ⓟ 4,047; Ⓒ 4,386; ◆ 4,351
Payson Park; RMC Place; MIDDLESEX; *187 E-14; elev. 100ft./30m.; ★ **BOS**; mail Watertown z 02472
Peabody; Inc. Place; ESSEX; **187** D-15; elev. 17ft./5m.; 🅿 🅷 ■; ★ **BOS**; z 01960-61; Ⓟ 47,039; Ⓒ 48,129; ◆ 48,082
Pearl Hill; RMC Place; WORCESTER; *186 C-10; ★ **BOS**; mail Fitchburg z 01420; pop. incl. with Fitchburg (Inc. Place)
Pelham; RMC Place; HAMPSHIRE; ▲ Pelham; **186** E-6; elev. 1,146ft./349m.; 🅿; z 01002; ● 500
Pelham; MCD-Town; HAMPSHIRE; *186 E-6; 🅿; z 01002; Ⓟ 1,373; Ⓒ 1,403
Pembroke (Pembroke Center); RMC Place; PLYMOUTH; ▲ Pembroke; **187** G-16; elev. 70ft./21m.; 🅿 🅷; ★ **BOS**; z 02359 & mail Bryantville z 02327, North Pembroke z 02358; ● 2,100
Pembroke; MCD-Town; PLYMOUTH; *187 G-16; 🅿; ★ **BOS**; z 02359 & mail Bryantville z 02327, North Pembroke z 02358; Ⓟ 14,544; Ⓒ 16,927; ◆ 17,960
Pembroke Center; PLYMOUTH; see Pembroke (RMC Place)
Pembroke Heights; RMC Place; PLYMOUTH; ▲ Pembroke; *187 N-20; ★ **BOS**; mail North Pembroke z 02358, Pembroke z 02359
Pepperell; CDP; MIDDLESEX; ▲ Pepperell; **187** C-11; 🅿; ★ **BOS**; z 01463; Ⓟ 2,350; Ⓒ 2,517
Pepperell; MIDDLESEX; see East Pepperell (CDP)
Pepperell; MCD-Town; MIDDLESEX; *187 C-11; 🅿; ★ **BOS**; z 01463; Ⓟ 10,098; Ⓒ 11,142; ◆ 11,380
Perry Manor; RMC Place; HAMPDEN; *186 F-6; elev. 250ft./76m.; ★ **SPRG**; pop. incl. with Chicopee (Inc. Place)
Perryville; RMC Place; BRISTOL; ▲ Rehoboth; *187 I-13; elev. 85ft./26m.; ★ **PROV-**; mail Rehoboth z 02769; rural
Perryville; RMC Place; WORCESTER; ▲ Dudley; *186 H-9; ★ **WORC**; mail Webster z 01570
Peru; RMC Place; BERKSHIRE; ▲ Peru; **186** D-3; elev. 2,064ft./629m.; 🅿; z 01235; ● 400
Peru; MCD-Town; BERKSHIRE; *186 D-3; 🅿; z 01235; Ⓟ 779; Ⓒ 821
Petersham; RMC Place; WORCESTER; ▲ Petersham; **186** D-8; elev. 1,080ft./329m.; 🅿; z 01366; ● 700
Petersham; MCD-Town; WORCESTER; *186 D-7; 🅿; z 01366; Ⓟ 1,131; Ⓒ 1,180
Phelps Mills; RMC Place; ESSEX; *187 N-20; ★ **BOS**; mail Peabody z 01960; pop. incl. with Peabody (Inc. Place)
Phillips Beach; RMC Place; ESSEX; ▲ Swampscott; *187 D-15; ★ **BOS**; mail Swampscott z 01907
Phillipston; RMC Place; WORCESTER; ▲ Phillipston; **186** D-8; elev. 1,166ft./355m.; 🅿; z 01331; ● 200
Phillipston; MCD-Town; WORCESTER; *186 C-8; 🅿; z 01331; Ⓟ 1,485; Ⓒ 1,621
Phillipston Four Corners; RMC Place; WORCESTER; ▲ Phillipston; **186** C-8; elev. 1,040ft./317m.; mail Athol z 01331; ● 50
Piety Corner; RMC Place; MIDDLESEX; *187 E-13; elev. 87ft./27m.; ★ **BOS**; mail Waltham z 02451; pop. incl. with Waltham (Inc. Place)
Pigeon Cove; RMC Place; ESSEX; ▲ Rockport; **187** C-17; elev. 101ft./31m.; ★ **BOS**; mail Rockport z 01966; ● 1,800
Pilgrim Heights; RMC Place; BARNSTABLE; ▲ Truro; *187 G-20; elev. 60ft./18m.; mail North Truro z 02652
Pilgrim Village; RMC Place; NORFOLK; ▲ Bellingham; *187 N-20; ★ **BOS**; mail Bellingham z 02019
Pilot Grove Hill; RMC Place; MIDDLESEX; ▲ Stow; *187 D-12; ★ **BOS**; mail Stow z 01775
Pine Bluffs; RMC Place; PLYMOUTH; ▲ Lakeville; *187 I-15; elev. 90ft./27m.; ★ **BOS**; mail Middleboro z 02346; ● 25
Pinefield; RMC Place; ESSEX; ▲ Ipswich; *187 B-15; elev. 130ft./40m.; ★ **BOS**; mail Ipswich z 01938; ● 550
Pine Grove; RMC Place; HAMPSHIRE; *186 E-5; elev. 259ft./79m.; ★ **SPRG**; mail Florence z 01062; pop. incl. with Northampton (Inc. Place)
Pine Hill Acres; RMC Place; BRISTOL; ▲ Dartmouth; *187 J-15; ★ **N.BED**; mail New Bedford z 02745; pop. incl. with New Bedford (Inc. Place)
Pinehurst; CDP; MIDDLESEX; ▲ Billerica; **187** D-13; elev. 104ft./32m.; 🅿; ★ **BOS**; z 01866; Ⓟ 6,614; Ⓒ 6,941
Pinehurst Beach; RMC Place; PLYMOUTH; ▲ Wareham; *187 J-16; elev. 10ft./3m.; ★ **BOS**; mail Wareham z 02571
Pine Island; RMC Place; ESSEX; ▲ Newbury; *187 B-15; ★ **BOS**; mail Newbury z 01951; ● 75
Pine Island Lake; RMC Place; HAMPSHIRE; ▲ Westhampton; *186 E-4; mail Easthampton z 01027; summer pop. 300; ● 75
Pine Lake; RMC Place; MIDDLESEX; ▲ Sudbury; **187** E-12; elev. 207ft./63m.; ★ **BOS**; mail Sudbury z 01776; ● 750
Pine Point; RMC Place; HAMPDEN; **187** M-12; elev. 210ft./64m.; ★ **SPRG**; mail Springfield z 01101; pop. incl. with Springfield (Inc. Place)
Pine Rest; RMC Place; MIDDLESEX; ▲ Sudbury; **187** E-12; elev. 172ft./52m.; ★ **BOS**; mail Sudbury z 01776; ● 750
Piney Point Beach; RMC Place; PLYMOUTH; ▲ Marion; *187 J-16; ★ **N.BED**; mail Marion z 02738; ● 250
Pingryville; RMC Place; MIDDLESEX; ▲ Littleton, Ayer; *187 D-11; elev. 250ft./76m.; ★ **BOS**; mail Littleton z 01460; rural
Pittsfield; Inc. Place; ⊡ BERKSHIRE; **186** D-2; elev. 1,039ft./317m.; 🅿 🅷 ■; ★ **PTSF**; z 01201-03; Ⓟ 48,622; Ⓒ 45,793; ◆ 40,983
Plainfield; RMC Place; HAMPSHIRE; ▲ Plainfield; **186** D-4; elev. 1,720ft./524m.; 🅿; z 01070; ● 150
Plainfield; MCD-Town; HAMPSHIRE; *186 D-4; 🅿; z 01070; Ⓟ 571; Ⓒ 589
Plainville; RMC Place; HAMPSHIRE; ▲ Hadley; *186 E-6; elev. 166ft./51m.; ★ **SPRG**; mail Amherst z 01002; ● 130
Plainville; RMC Place; NORFOLK; ▲ Plainville; **187** H-13; elev. 250ft./76m.; 🅿; ★ **BOS**; z 02762; ● 6,871
Plainville; MCD-Town; NORFOLK; *187 H-13; 🅿; ★ **BOS**; z 02762; Ⓟ 6,871; Ⓒ 7,683; ◆ 8,052
Pleasant Lake; RMC Place; BARNSTABLE; ▲ Harwich; **187** J-20; elev. 50ft./15m.; ★ **BARN**; mail Harwich z 02645; ● 450
Plimptonville; RMC Place; NORFOLK; ▲ Walpole; *187 G-13; elev. 150ft./46m.; ★ **BOS**; mail Walpole z 02081
Plumbush; RMC Place; ESSEX; ▲ Newbury; *187 B-15; ★ **BOS**; mail Newbury z 01951; ● 80
Plum Island; RMC Place; ESSEX; *187 B-16; elev. 10ft./3m.; ★ **BOS**; mail Newbury z 01951, Newburyport z 01950; pop. incl. with Newburyport (Inc. Place)
Plummer Corner; RMC Place; WORCESTER; ▲ Northbridge; *187 G-11; elev. 325ft./99m.; ★ **WORC**; mail Whitinsville z 01588
Plymouth; CDP; ⊡ PLYMOUTH; ▲ Plymouth; **187** H-16; elev. 50ft./15m.; 🅿 🅷; ★ **BOS**; z 02360-62 & mail Manomet z 02345, White Horse Beach z 02381; Ⓟ 7,258; Ⓒ 7,658
Plymouth; MCD-Town; PLYMOUTH; *187 I-17; 🅿; ★ **BOS**; z 02360-62 & mail Manomet z 02345, White Horse Beach z 02381; Ⓟ 45,608; Ⓒ 51,701; ◆ 56,113
PLYMOUTH; **187** H-15; Ⓟ 435,276; Ⓒ 472,822; ◆ 483,521
Plympton; RMC Place; PLYMOUTH; ▲ Plympton; **187** H-16; elev. 105ft./32m.; 🅿; ★ **BOS**; z 02367; ● 500
Plympton; MCD-Town; PLYMOUTH; *187 H-16; 🅿; ★ **BOS**; z 02367; Ⓟ 2,384; Ⓒ 2,637; ◆ 2,701
Pocasset; CDP; BARNSTABLE; ▲ Bourne; **187** J-17; elev. 40ft./12m.; 🅿 🅷; z 02559; Ⓟ 2,756; Ⓒ 2,671
Pocomo; RMC Place; NANTUCKET; ▲ Nantucket; *187 M-20; elev. 25ft./8m.; mail Nantucket z 02554; summer pop. 100; ● 30
Podunk; RMC Place; WORCESTER; ▲ East Brookfield; *187 N-20; ★ **WORC**; mail East Brookfield z 01515; ● 250
Point Independence; RMC Place; PLYMOUTH; ▲ Wareham; **187** J-17; elev. 30ft./9m.; ★ **BOS**; mail Buzzards Bay z 02532; ● 870
Point of Pines; RMC Place; SUFFOLK; *187 E-15; elev. 20ft./6m.; ★ **BOS**; mail Revere z 02151; pop. incl. with Revere (Inc. Place)
Point Pleasant; RMC Place; WORCESTER; ▲ Webster; *187 N-20; ★ **WORC**; mail Webster z 01570
Point Shirley; RMC Place; SUFFOLK; ▲ Winthrop; *187 E-15; elev. 20ft./6m.; ★ **BOS**; mail Winthrop z 02152
Polpis; RMC Place; NANTUCKET; ▲ Nantucket; **187** M-20; elev. 10ft./3m.; mail Nantucket z 02554; ● 100
Pomponotto Pines; RMC Place; PLYMOUTH; ▲ East Bridgewater; *187 H-15; ★ **BOS**; mail East Bridgewater z 02333; ● 200
Ponakin Mill; RMC Place; WORCESTER; ▲ Lancaster; *187 D-11; elev. 270ft./82m.; ★ **BOS**; mail Lancaster z 01523
Pond Hill; RMC Place; ESSEX; ▲ Amesbury; *187 A-15; ★ **BOS**; mail Amesbury z 01913
Pond Village; RMC Place; BARNSTABLE; *187 J-18; elev. 58ft./18m.; ★ **BARN**
Pondville; RMC Place; NORFOLK; ▲ Norfolk; *187 G-13; elev. 260ft./79m.; ★ **BOS**; mail Norfolk z 02056; ● 200
Pondville; RMC Place; PLYMOUTH; ▲ Plymouth; *187 I-17; elev. 50ft./15m.; ★ **BOS**; mail Buzzards Bay z 02532; ● 200
Pondville; RMC Place; WORCESTER; ▲ Auburn; **187** D-19; elev. 530ft./162m.; ★ **WORC**; mail Auburn z 01501
Ponkapoag; RMC Place; NORFOLK; ▲ Canton; *187 F-14; ★ **BOS**; mail Canton z 02021
Pontoosuc Gardens; RMC Place; BERKSHIRE; *186 D-2; elev. 1,130ft./344m.; ★ **PTSF**; mail Pittsfield z 01201
Pope Beach; RMC Place; BRISTOL; ▲ Fairhaven; *187 K-15; elev. 20ft./6m.; ★ **N.BED**; mail Fairhaven z 02719
Popponesset; CDP-Census Area Only; BARNSTABLE; *187 K-18; ★ **BARN**; Ⓒ 310
Popponesset Beach; RMC Place; BARNSTABLE; ▲ Mashpee; *187 K-18; ★ **BARN**; mail Mashpee z 02649
Popponesset Island; CDP-Census Area Only; BARNSTABLE; *187 K-18; ★ **BARN**; Ⓒ 39
Porter Square; RMC Place; MIDDLESEX; *187 N-20; ★ **BOS**; mail Cambridge z 02140; pop. incl. with Cambridge (Inc. Place)
Potoosuc Lake; RMC Place; BERKSHIRE; ▲ Lanesborough; *186 D-2; ★ **PTSF**; mail Lanesboro z 01237; ● 800
Pottersville; RMC Place; BRISTOL; ▲ Somerset; *187 J-14; ★ **F.R.**; mail Somerset z 02726
Pratt Corner; RMC Place; FRANKLIN; ▲ Shutesbury; *186 E-6; mail Shutesbury z 01072; rural
Precinct; RMC Place; PLYMOUTH; ▲ Lakeville; *187 I-15; elev. 110ft./34m.; ★ **BOS**; mail Middleboro z 02346
Prentice Corner; RMC Place; WORCESTER; ▲ Northbridge; *187 G-11; ★ **WORC**; mail Whitinsville z 01588; ● 30
Prides Crossing; RMC Place; ESSEX; *187 C-16; elev. 51ft./16m.; 🅿; ★ **BOS**; z 01965; pop. incl. with Beverly (Inc. Place)
Princeton; RMC Place; WORCESTER; ▲ Princeton; **186** D-10; elev. 1,175ft./358m.; 🅿; ★ **WORC**; z 01541; ● 1,100
Princeton; MCD-Town; WORCESTER; *186 D-9; elev. 1,175ft./358m.; 🅿; ★ **WORC**; z 01541; Ⓟ 3,189; Ⓒ 3,353; ◆ 3,271
Priscilla Beach; RMC Place; PLYMOUTH; ▲ Plymouth; **187** H-17; elev. 50ft./15m.; ★ **BOS**; mail Plymouth z 02360; ● 450
Proctor; RMC Place; ESSEX; *187 D-15; ★ **BOS**; mail Peabody z 01960; pop. incl. with Peabody (Inc. Place)
Provincetown; CDP; BARNSTABLE; ▲ Provincetown; *187 G-19; 🅿; z 02657; Ⓟ 3,374; Ⓒ 3,192
Provincetown; MCD-Town; BARNSTABLE; *187 G-19; 🅿; z 02657; Ⓟ 3,561; Ⓒ 3,431
Provincetown Wharf; RMC Place; BARNSTABLE; ▲ Provincetown; *187 N-20; mail Provincetown z 02657
Putnamville; RMC Place; ESSEX; ▲ Danvers; *187 C-15; ★ **BOS**; mail Danvers z 01923

Q

Quaise; RMC Place; NANTUCKET; ▲ Nantucket; *187 M-20; elev. 40ft./12m.; mail Nantucket z 02554; ● 40
Queen Lake; RMC Place; WORCESTER; ▲ Phillipston; *186 D-8; mail Athol z 01331; summer pop. 500
Quidnet; RMC Place; NANTUCKET; ▲ Nantucket; **187** M-20; elev. 39ft./12m.; mail Nantucket z 02554; ● 100
Quincy; Inc. Place; NORFOLK; **187** F-14; elev. 20ft./6m.; 🅿 🅷 🅲 1,275 ■; ★ **BOS**; z 02169-71, z 02269; Ⓟ 84,985; Ⓒ 88,025; ◆ 89,734
Quincy Adams; RMC Place; NORFOLK; *187 N-20; ★ **BOS**; mail Quincy z 02169; pop. incl. with Quincy (Inc. Place)
Quincy Center; RMC Place; NORFOLK; *187 F-14; elev. 40ft./12m.; ★ **BOS**; mail Quincy z 02169; pop. incl. with Quincy (Inc. Place)
Quincy Point; RMC Place; NORFOLK; *187 F-15; elev. 20ft./6m.; ★ **BOS**; mail Quincy z 02169; pop. incl. with Quincy (Inc. Place)
Quinsigamond; WORCESTER; see Quinsigamond Village (RMC Place)
Quinsigamond Village (Quinsigamond); RMC Place; WORCESTER; **187** C-19; elev. 500ft./152m.; ★ **WORC**; mail Worcester z 01607; pop. incl. with Worcester (Inc. Place)
Quissett; RMC Place; BARNSTABLE; ▲ Falmouth; **187** K-17; mail Falmouth z 02540; ● 200

R

Rakeville; RMC Place; NORFOLK; ▲ Bellingham; *187 H-12; elev. 225ft./69m.; ★ **BOS**; mail Bellingham z 02019
Randolph; CDP; NORFOLK; ▲ Randolph; **187** F-14; elev. 184ft./56m.; 🅿; ★ **BOS**; z 02368; Ⓟ 30,093; Ⓒ 30,963; ◆ 30,816
Randolph; MCD-Town; NORFOLK; *187 F-14; 🅿; ★ **BOS**; z 02368; Ⓟ 30,093; Ⓒ 30,963; ◆ 30,816
Raynham; RMC Place; BRISTOL; ▲ Raynham; **187** H-14; elev. 81ft./25m.; 🅿; ★ **BOS**; z 02767 & mail Raynham Center z 02768; ● 2,100
Raynham; MCD-Town; BRISTOL; *187 H-14; 🅿; ★ **BOS**; z 02767 & mail Raynham Center z 02768; Ⓟ 9,867; Ⓒ 11,739; ◆ 12,792
Raynham Center; CDP; BRISTOL; ▲ Raynham; **187** H-14; elev. 50ft./15m.; 🅿; ★ **BOS**; z 02768; Ⓟ 3,709; Ⓒ 3,633
Reading; CDP; MIDDLESEX; ▲ Reading; **187** D-14; elev. 129ft./39m.; 🅿; ★ **BOS**; z 01867; Ⓟ 22,539; Ⓒ 23,708; ◆ 23,594
Reading; MCD-Town; MIDDLESEX; *187 D-14; 🅿; ★ **BOS**; z 01867; Ⓟ 22,539; Ⓒ 23,708; ◆ 23,594
Readville; RMC Place; SUFFOLK; *187 F-14; elev. 60ft./18m.; 🅿; ★ **BOS**; z 02136-37; pop. incl. with Boston (Inc. Place)
Rehoboth; RMC Place; BRISTOL; ▲ Rehoboth; **187** I-13; elev. 50ft./15m.; 🅿; ★ **PROV-**; z 02769; ● 400
Rehoboth; MCD-Town; BRISTOL; *187 I-13; 🅿; ★ **PROV-**; z 02769; Ⓟ 8,656; Ⓒ 10,172; ◆ 10,803
Renfrew; RMC Place; BERKSHIRE; ▲ Adams; *186 C-2; elev. 760ft./232m.; ★ **PTSF**; mail Adams z 01220
Reservoir; RMC Place; NORFOLK; ▲ Brookline; *187 E-14; elev. 120ft./37m.; ★ **BOS**; mail Brookline z 02445
Revere; Inc. Place; SUFFOLK; **187** E-14; elev. 20ft./6m.; 🅿; ★ **BOS**; z 02151; Ⓟ 42,786; Ⓒ 47,283; ◆ 57,980
Revere Beach; RMC Place; SUFFOLK; *187 N-20; ★ **BOS**; mail Revere z 02151; pop. incl. with Revere (Inc. Place)
Rexhame; RMC Place; PLYMOUTH; ▲ Marshfield; **187** G-16; elev. 30ft./9m.; ★ **BOS**; mail Marshfield z 02050; ● 600
Rice Square; RMC Place; WORCESTER; **187** B-20; elev. 600ft./183m.; ★ **WORC**; mail Worcester z 01604; pop. incl. with Worcester (Inc. Place)
Richmond; RMC Place; BERKSHIRE; ▲ Richmond; **186** E-1; elev. 1,057ft./322m.; 🅿; ★ **PTSF**; z 01254 & mail Pittsfield z 01201; ● 250
Richmond; MCD-Town; BERKSHIRE; *186 E-1; 🅿; ★ **PTSF**; z 01254 & mail Pittsfield z 01201; Ⓟ 1,677; Ⓒ 1,604; ◆ 1,460
Richmond Furnace; RMC Place; BERKSHIRE; ▲ Richmond; *186 E-1; elev. 1,003ft./306m.; ★ **PTSF**; mail Richmond z 01254
Rings Island; RMC Place; ESSEX; ▲ Salisbury; *187 A-15; elev. 10ft./3m.; ★ **BOS**; mail Newburyport z 01950
Rio Vista; RMC Place; MIDDLESEX; ▲ Billerica; *187 D-13; elev. 190ft./58m.; ★ **BOS**; mail North Billerica z 01862
Rising; BERKSHIRE; see Risingdale (RMC Place)
Risingdale (Rising); RMC Place; BERKSHIRE; ▲ Great Barrington; **186** F-1; elev. 710ft./216m.; mail Great Barrington z 01230; ● 100
Riverdale; RMC Place; ESSEX; *187 C-16; elev. 50ft./15m.; ★ **BOS**; mail Gloucester z 01930; pop. incl. with Gloucester (Inc. Place)
Riverdale; RMC Place; NORFOLK; ▲ Dedham; **186** M-5; elev. 140ft./43m.; ★ **BOS**; mail Dedham z 02026
Riverdale; RMC Place; WORCESTER; ▲ Northbridge; **187** G-11; elev. 300ft./91m.; ★ **WORC**; mail Northbridge z 01534; ● 110
Rivermoor; RMC Place; PLYMOUTH; ▲ Scituate; *187 F-16; elev. 30ft./9m.; ★ **BOS**; mail Scituate z 02066
River Pines; RMC Place; MIDDLESEX; ▲ Billerica; **187** C-13; elev. 130ft./40m.; ★ **BOS**; mail Billerica z 01821; ● 3,600
Riverside; RMC Place; ESSEX; *187 B-14; elev. 21ft./6m.; ★ **BOS**; mail Haverhill z 01830; pop. incl. with Haverhill (Inc. Place)
Riverside; RMC Place; FRANKLIN; ▲ Gill; **186** C-6; elev. 218ft./66m.; mail Newton z 02458, Turners Falls z 01376; ● 350
Riverside; RMC Place; HAMPDEN; *187 N-20; ★ **SPRG**; mail Holyoke z 01040; pop. incl. with Holyoke (Inc. Place)
Riverside; RMC Place; PLYMOUTH; ▲ Wareham; *187 J-17; elev. 30ft./9m.; ★ **BOS**; mail Onset z 02558; ● 320
Riverview; RMC Place; ESSEX; *187 C-16; elev. 50ft./15m.; ★ **BOS**; mail Gloucester z 01930; pop. incl. with Gloucester (Inc. Place)
Riverview; RMC Place; MIDDLESEX; *187 E-13; elev. 55ft./17m.; ★ **BOS**; mail Waltham z 02453; pop. incl. with Waltham (Inc. Place)
Roberts; RMC Place; MIDDLESEX; *187 N-20; ★ **BOS**; mail Waltham z 02453; pop. incl. with Waltham (Inc. Place)
Rochdale; RMC Place; WORCESTER; ▲ Leicester; **186** F-9; elev. 717ft./219m.; 🅿; ★ **WORC**; z 01542; ● 1,150
Rochester; RMC Place; PLYMOUTH; ▲ Rochester; **187** J-16; elev. 29ft./9m.; 🅿; ★ **N.BED**; z 02770; ● 600
Rochester; MCD-Town; PLYMOUTH; *187 J-16; 🅿; ★ **N.BED**; z 02770; Ⓟ 3,921; Ⓒ 4,581; ◆ 4,796
Rock; RMC Place; PLYMOUTH; ▲ Middleborough; **187** I-15; elev. 80ft./24m.; ★ **BOS**; mail Middleboro z 02346; ● 600
Rockdale; RMC Place; BERKSHIRE; ▲ West Stockbridge; *187 N-20; mail Housatonic z 01236, Northbridge z 01534; rural
Rock Harbor; RMC Place; BARNSTABLE; ▲ Orleans; *187 I-20; elev. 40ft./12m.; ★ **BARN**; mail Orleans z 02653; summer pop. 1,000
Rockland; RMC Place; PLYMOUTH; ▲ Rockland; **187** G-15; elev. 140ft./43m.; 🅿; ★ **BOS**; z 02370; ● 16,123
Rockland; MCD-Town; PLYMOUTH; *187 G-15; 🅿; ★ **BOS**; z 02370; Ⓟ 16,123; Ⓒ 17,670; ◆ 17,939
Rockport; CDP; ESSEX; ▲ Rockport; **187** C-17; elev. 77ft./23m.; 🅿; ★ **BOS**; z 01966; Ⓟ 5,448; Ⓒ 5,606
Rockport; MCD-Town; ESSEX; *187 C-17; 🅿; ★ **BOS**; z 01966; Ⓟ 7,482; Ⓒ 7,767; ◆ 7,654
Rocks Village; RMC Place; ESSEX; *187 B-14; elev. 40ft./12m.; ★ **BOS**; mail Haverhill z 01830; pop. incl. with Haverhill (Inc. Place)
Rock Valley; RMC Place; HAMPDEN; *186 F-5; elev. 314ft./96m.; ★ **SPRG**; mail Holyoke z 01040; pop. incl. with Holyoke (Inc. Place)
Rockville; RMC Place; NORFOLK; ▲ Millis; **187** G-13; elev. 140ft./43m.; ★ **BOS**; mail Millis z 02054; ● 300
Rocky Hill; RMC Place; WORCESTER; ▲ Milford; *187 G-12; elev. 270ft./82m.; ★ **BOS**; mail Milford z 01757
Rocky Neck; RMC Place; ESSEX; *187 C-16; ★ **BOS**; mail Gloucester z 01930; pop. incl. with Gloucester (Inc. Place)
Rocky Nook; RMC Place; PLYMOUTH; ▲ Kingston; *187 H-16; elev. 20ft./6m.; ★ **BOS**; mail Kingston z 02364
Rocky Nook Park; RMC Place; PLYMOUTH; ▲ Kingston; *187 H-16; ★ **BOS**; mail Kingston z 02364
Rocky Nook Point; RMC Place; PLYMOUTH; ▲ Kingston; *187 H-16; elev. 30ft./9m.; ★ **BOS**; mail Kingston z 02364
Roosterville; RMC Place; BERKSHIRE; ▲ Sandisfield; **186** G-3; elev. 775ft./236m.; mail Sandisfield z 01255; ● 50
Roslindale; RMC Place; SUFFOLK; *187 F-14; elev. 100ft./30m.; 🅿; ★ **BOS**; z 02131; pop. incl. with Boston (Inc. Place)
Rowe; RMC Place; FRANKLIN; ▲ Rowe; **186** B-4; elev. 1,364ft./416m.; 🅿; z 01367; ● 80
Rowe; MCD-Town; FRANKLIN; *186 B-4; 🅿; z 01367; Ⓟ 378; Ⓒ 351
Rowley; CDP; ESSEX; ▲ Rowley; **187** B-15; elev. 50ft./15m.; 🅿; ★ **BOS**; z 01969; Ⓟ 1,144; Ⓒ 1,434
Rowley; MCD-Town; ESSEX; *187 B-15; 🅿; ★ **BOS**; z 01969; Ⓟ 4,452; Ⓒ 5,500; ◆ 5,613
Roxbury; RMC Place; SUFFOLK; **186** L-7; elev. 100ft./30m.; 🅿; ★ **BOS**; z 02118-20; pop. incl. with Boston (Inc. Place)
Royalston; RMC Place; WORCESTER; ▲ Royalston; **186** C-8; elev. 1,015ft./309m.; 🅿; z 01368 & mail Athol z 01331; ● 370
Royalston; MCD-Town; WORCESTER; *186 C-8; 🅿; z 01368 & mail Athol z 01331; Ⓟ 1,147; Ⓒ 1,254
Russell; RMC Place; HAMPDEN; **186** F-4; elev. 300ft./91m.; 🅿; ★ **SPRG**; z 01071; ● 900
Russell; MCD-Town; HAMPDEN; *186 G-4; 🅿; ★ **SPRG**; z 01071; Ⓟ 1,594; Ⓒ 1,657; ◆ 1,663
Russells Mills (Dartmouth); RMC Place; BRISTOL; ▲ Dartmouth; **187** K-15; ★ **N.BED**; mail Dartmouth z 02714, North Dartmouth z 02747, South Dartmouth z 02748; ● 160
Russellville; RMC Place; HAMPSHIRE; ▲ Southampton; *186 F-4; elev. 262ft./80m.; ★ **SPRG**; mail Westfield z 01085
Rutland; CDP; WORCESTER; ▲ Rutland; **186** E-9; elev. 1,112ft./339m.; 🅿; ★ **WORC**; z 01543; Ⓟ 2,145; Ⓒ 2,205
Rutland; MCD-Town; WORCESTER; *186 E-9; 🅿; ★ **WORC**; z 01543; Ⓟ 4,936; Ⓒ 6,353; ◆ 7,328

S

Saconesset Hills; RMC Place; BARNSTABLE; ▲ Falmouth; *187 K-17; elev. 30ft./9m.; mail Falmouth z 02540; ● 175
Sagamore; CDP; BARNSTABLE; ▲ Bourne; **187** J-17; elev. 35ft./11m.; 🅿; z 02561; Ⓟ 2,589; Ⓒ 3,544
Sagamore Beach; RMC Place; BARNSTABLE; ▲ Bourne; **187** I-17; elev. 51ft./16m.; 🅿; z 02562; summer pop. 2,000; ● 1,100
Sagamore Highlands; RMC Place; BARNSTABLE; ▲ Bourne; **187** I-17; elev. 70ft./21m.; mail Buzzards Bay z 02532, Sagamore Beach z 02562; ● 100
Salem; Inc. Place; ⊡ ESSEX; **187** D-15; elev. 9ft./3m.; 🅿 🅷 🅲 10,230 ■; ★ **BOS**; z 01970-71; Ⓟ 38,091; Ⓒ 40,407; ◆ 40,944
Salem Neck; RMC Place; ESSEX; *187 D-15; elev. 20ft./6m.; ★ **BOS**; mail Salem z 01970
Salem State College; RMC Place; ESSEX; *187 D-15; ★ **BOS**; mail Salem z 01970; pop. incl. with Salem (Inc. Place)
Salisbury (Salisbury Center); CDP; ESSEX; ▲ Salisbury; **187** A-15; elev. 25ft./8m.; 🅿; ★ **BOS**; z 01952; Ⓟ 3,729; Ⓒ 4,484
Salisbury; MCD-Town; ESSEX; *187 A-15; 🅿; ★ **BOS**; z 01952 & mail Newburyport z 01950; Ⓟ 6,882; Ⓒ 7,827; ◆ 8,260
Salisbury Beach; RMC Place; ESSEX; ▲ Salisbury; *187 A-16; elev. 15ft./5m.; 🅿; ★ **BOS**; z 01952
Salisbury Center; ESSEX; see Salisbury (CDP)
Salisbury Heights; RMC Place; WORCESTER; **187** A-18; elev. 900ft./274m.; ★ **WORC**; mail Worcester z 01609; pop. incl. with Worcester (Inc. Place)
Salisbury Plains; RMC Place; ESSEX; ▲ Salisbury; **187** A-15; elev. 90ft./27m.; ★ **BOS**; mail Newburyport z 01950; ● 600
Salisbury Point; RMC Place; ESSEX; ▲ Amesbury; *187 A-15; elev. 50ft./15m.; ★ **BOS**; mail Amesbury z 01913
Salters Point; RMC Place; BRISTOL; ▲ Dartmouth; *187 N-20; ★ **N.BED**; mail South Dartmouth z 02748; summer pop. 150
Sandersdale; RMC Place; WORCESTER; ▲ Southbridge; *186 G-9; elev. 412ft./126m.; ★ **WORC**; mail Southbridge z 01550
Sand Hill; PLYMOUTH; see Sand Hills (RMC Place)
Sand Hills (Sand Hill); RMC Place; PLYMOUTH; ▲ Scituate; **187** F-16; ★ **BOS**; mail Scituate z 02066; ● 1,800
Sandisfield; RMC Place; BERKSHIRE; ▲ Sandisfield; **186** G-2; elev. 1,577ft./481m.; 🅿; z 01255; ● 225
Sandisfield; MCD-Town; BERKSHIRE; *186 G-2; 🅿; z 01255; Ⓟ 667; Ⓒ 824
Sandwich; CDP; BARNSTABLE; ▲ Sandwich; **187** J-18; elev. 20ft./6m.; 🅿; ★ **BARN**; z 02563 & mail Forestdale z 02644; Ⓟ 2,998; Ⓒ 3,058
Sandwich; MCD-Town; BARNSTABLE; *187 J-17; 🅿; ★ **BARN**; z 02563 & mail Forestdale z 02644; Ⓟ 15,489; Ⓒ 20,136; ◆ 19,722
Sandy Beach; RMC Place; NORFOLK; ▲ Cohasset; *187 N-20; ★ **BOS**; mail Cohasset z 02025
Sandy Beach; RMC Place; WORCESTER; ▲ Rutland; **186** E-9; elev. 1,040ft./317m.; ★ **WORC**; mail Rutland z 01543; ● 60
Santuit; RMC Place; BARNSTABLE; *187 K-18; elev. 72ft./22m.; ★ **BARN**; mail Cotuit z 02635; pop. incl. with Barnstable (Inc. Place)
Sassaquin; RMC Place; BRISTOL; *187 N-20; ★ **N.BED**; mail New Bedford z 02745; pop. incl. with New Bedford (Inc. Place)
Saugus; CDP; ESSEX; ▲ Saugus; **187** D-14; elev. 21ft./6m.; 🅿; ★ **BOS**; z 01906; Ⓟ 25,549; Ⓒ 26,078; ◆ 26,527
Saugus; MCD-Town; ESSEX; *187 D-14; 🅿 ■; ★ **BOS**; z 01906; Ⓟ 25,549; Ⓒ 26,078; ◆ 26,527
Saugus Center; RMC Place; ESSEX; ▲ Saugus; *187 N-20; ★ **BOS**; mail Saugus z 01906
Saundersville; RMC Place; WORCESTER; ▲ Grafton; *187 F-11; elev. 300ft./91m.; ★ **WORC**; mail South Grafton z 01560
Savin Hill; RMC Place; SUFFOLK; *187 E-14; elev. 50ft./15m.; ★ **BOS**; mail Boston z 02125; pop. incl. with Boston (Inc. Place)
Savoy; RMC Place; BERKSHIRE; ▲ Savoy; **186** C-3; elev. 1,720ft./524m.; 🅿; z 01256; ● 150
Savoy; MCD-Town; BERKSHIRE; *186 C-3; 🅿; z 01256; Ⓟ 634; Ⓒ 705
Savoy Center; RMC Place; BERKSHIRE; ▲ Savoy; *186 C-3; mail Savoy z 01256; rural
Saxonville; RMC Place; MIDDLESEX; **186** L-2; elev. 190ft./58m.; ★ **BOS**; mail Framingham z 01701, z 01705
Schoosett; RMC Place; PLYMOUTH; ▲ Pembroke; *187 G-16; ★ **BOS**; mail Pembroke z 02359
Scituate; CDP; PLYMOUTH; ▲ Scituate; **187** F-16; elev. 30ft./9m.; 🅿; ★ **BOS**; z 02040, z 02055, z 02060, z 02066; Ⓟ 5,180; Ⓒ 5,069
Scituate; MCD-Town; PLYMOUTH; *187 F-16; 🅿; ★ **BOS**; z 02040, z 02055, z 02060, z 02066; Ⓟ 16,786; Ⓒ 17,863; ◆ 18,252
Scorton Shores; RMC Place; BARNSTABLE; ▲ Sandwich; *187 J-18; elev. 40ft./12m.; ★ **BARN**; mail East Sandwich z 02537; summer pop. 1,200; ● 400
Scott Hill Acres; RMC Place; NORFOLK; ▲ Bellingham; *187 G-12; elev. 270ft./82m.; ★ **BOS**; mail Bellingham z 02019
Seabrook; CDP-Census Area Only; BARNSTABLE; *187 K-17; ★ **BARN**; Ⓒ 477
Searsville; RMC Place; HAMPSHIRE; ▲ Williamsburg; *186 E-5; elev. 680ft./207m.; ★ **SPRG**; mail Williamsburg z 01096; rural
Sea View; RMC Place; PLYMOUTH; ▲ Marshfield; **187** G-16; elev. 30ft./9m.; ★ **BOS**; mail Marshfield z 02050; ● 100
Second Cliff; RMC Place; PLYMOUTH; ▲ Scituate; *187 F-16; elev. 40ft./12m.; ★ **BOS**; mail Scituate z 02066
Seconsett Island; CDP-Census Area Only; BARNSTABLE; *187 K-17; ★ **BARN**; Ⓒ 81
Seekonk; RMC Place; BRISTOL; ▲ Seekonk; **187** I-13; elev. 50ft./15m.; 🅿; ★ **PROV-**; z 02771; ● 13,046
Seekonk; MCD-Town; BRISTOL; *187 I-13; 🅿; ★ **PROV-**; z 02771; Ⓟ 13,046; Ⓒ 13,425; ◆ 13,118
Segreganset; RMC Place; BRISTOL; ▲ Dighton; **187** I-14; elev. 56ft./17m.; ★ **BOS**; mail Dighton z 02715; ● 400
Shaker Village; RMC Place; WORCESTER; ▲ Harvard; *187 D-11; elev. 300ft./91m.; ★ **BOS**; mail Harvard z 01451; rural
Sharon; CDP; NORFOLK; ▲ Sharon; **187** G-14; 🅿; ★ **BOS**; z 02067; Ⓟ 5,893; Ⓒ 5,941
Sharon; MCD-Town; NORFOLK; *187 G-13; 🅿; ★ **BOS**; z 02067; Ⓟ 15,517; Ⓒ 17,408; ◆ 17,693
Sharon Heights; RMC Place; NORFOLK; ▲ Sharon; *187 G-13; elev. 274ft./84m.; ★ **BOS**; mail Sharon z 02067
Shattuckville; RMC Place; FRANKLIN; ▲ Colrain; **186** C-5; elev. 482ft./147m.; 🅿; z 01340; ● 170
Shawkemo; RMC Place; NANTUCKET; ▲ Nantucket; *187 M-20; mail Nantucket z 02554; ● 25
Shawsheen Heights; RMC Place; ESSEX; ▲ Andover; *187 C-14; elev. 170ft./52m.; ★ **BOS**; mail Andover z 01810
Shawsheen Village; RMC Place; ESSEX; ▲ Andover; **187** C-14; elev. 93ft./28m.; ★ **BOS**; mail Andover z 01810; ● 2,600
Sheffield; RMC Place; BERKSHIRE; ▲ Sheffield; **186** G-1; elev. 675ft./206m.; 🅿; z 01257; ● 1,150
Sheffield; MCD-Town; BERKSHIRE; *186 G-1; 🅿; z 01257; Ⓟ 2,910; Ⓒ 3,335
Shelburne (Shelburne Center); RMC Place; FRANKLIN; ▲ Shelburne; **186** C-5; elev. 560ft./171m.; mail Shelburne Falls z 01370; ● 150
Shelburne; MCD-Town; FRANKLIN; *186 C-5; mail Shelburne Falls z 01370; Ⓟ 2,012; Ⓒ 2,058
Shelburne Center; FRANKLIN; see Shelburne (RMC Place)
Shelburne Falls; CDP; FRANKLIN; ▲ Shelburne, Buckland; **186** C-5; elev. 420ft./128m.; 🅿; z 01370; Ⓟ 1,996; Ⓒ 1,951
Sheldonville; RMC Place; NORFOLK; ▲ Wrentham; **187** H-12; elev. 255ft./78m.; 🅿; ★ **BOS**; z 02070; ● 450
Shell Beach; RMC Place; PLYMOUTH; ▲ Mattapoisett; *187 K-16; elev. 10ft./3m.; ★ **N.BED**; mail Mattapoisett z 02739; summer pop. 150; ● 35
Shepardville; RMC Place; NORFOLK; ▲ Plainville; *187 H-13; elev. 220ft./67m.; ★ **BOS**; mail Plainville z 02762
Sherborn; RMC Place; MIDDLESEX; ▲ Sherborn; **187** F-12; elev. 175ft./53m.; 🅿; ★ **BOS**; z 01770; ● 1,400
Sherborn; MCD-Town; MIDDLESEX; *187 F-12; 🅿; ★ **BOS**; z 01770; Ⓟ 3,989; Ⓒ 4,200; ◆ 4,234
Sherwood Forest; RMC Place; BERKSHIRE; ▲ Becket; **186** F-3; mail Becket z 01223, Chester z 01011; ● 400
Sherwood Forest; RMC Place; BRISTOL; ▲ Acushnet; **187** E-20; elev. 130ft./40m.; ★ **N.BED**; mail Acushnet z 02743
Shimmo; RMC Place; NANTUCKET; ▲ Nantucket; *187 M-20; mail Nantucket z 02554; summer pop. 80; ● 25
Shirkshire; RMC Place; FRANKLIN; ▲ Conway; *186 D-5; mail Conway z 01341; rural
Shirley; CDP; MIDDLESEX; ▲ Shirley; **187** D-11; elev. 279ft./85m.; 🅿; ★ **BOS**; z 01464; Ⓟ 1,559; Ⓒ 1,427
Shirley; MCD-Town; MIDDLESEX; *187 C-11; 🅿; ★ **BOS**; z 01464; Ⓟ 6,118; Ⓒ 6,373; Ⓡ 7,616; ◆ 7,910
Shirley Center; RMC Place; MIDDLESEX; ▲ Shirley; **187** C-11; elev. 403ft./123m.; 🅿; ★ **BOS**; z 01464; ● 220
Shore Acres; RMC Place; BRISTOL; ▲ Dartmouth; *187 K-15; elev. 22ft./7m.; ★ **N.BED**; mail South Dartmouth z 02748; ● 50
Shore Acres; RMC Place; PLYMOUTH; ▲ Scituate; **187** F-16; elev. 25ft./8m.; ★ **BOS**; mail Scituate z 02066; ● 1,200
Shrewsbury; RMC Place; WORCESTER; ▲ Shrewsbury; **186** F-10; elev. 668ft./204m.; 🅿; ★ **WORC**; z 01545-46; Ⓟ 24,146; ● 31,600
Shrewsbury; MCD-Town; WORCESTER; *186 F-10; 🅿 ■; ★ **WORC**; z 01545-46; Ⓟ 24,146; Ⓒ 31,640; ◆ 35,178
Shutesbury; RMC Place; FRANKLIN; ▲ Shutesbury; **186** D-6; elev. 1,225ft./373m.; 🅿; z 01072; ● 700
Shutesbury; MCD-Town; FRANKLIN; *186 D-7; 🅿; z 01072; Ⓟ 1,561; Ⓒ 1,810; Ⓡ 1,806
Siasconset; RMC Place; NANTUCKET; ▲ Nantucket; **187** M-20; elev. 37ft./11m.; 🅿; z 02564; summer pop. 2,000; ● 600
Siggsville; RMC Place; BERKSHIRE; ▲ Adams; *186 C-2; ★ **PTSF**; mail Adams z 01220
Silver Beach; RMC Place; BARNSTABLE; ▲ Falmouth; **187** J-17; elev. 20ft./6m.; 🅿; z 02565; ● 1,300
Silver Hill; RMC Place; MIDDLESEX; ▲ Weston; *187 E-13; elev. 161ft./49m.; ★ **BOS**; mail Weston z 02493
Silver Lake; RMC Place; MIDDLESEX; ▲ Wilmington, Tewksbury; **187** C-13; elev. 106ft./32m.; ★ **BOS**; mail Wilmington z 01887; ● 2,900
Silver Lake; RMC Place; PLYMOUTH; ▲ Plympton, Kingston; **187** H-16; elev. 75ft./23m.; ★ **BOS**; mail Kingston z 02364; ● 220
Silver Shell Beach; RMC Place; BRISTOL; ▲ Fairhaven; *187 K-15; elev. 5ft./2m.; ★ **N.BED**; mail Fairhaven z 02719
Silver Spring Beach; RMC Place; BARNSTABLE; ▲ Eastham; *187 N-20; ★ **BARN**; mail North Eastham z 02651
Sippewisset; RMC Place; BARNSTABLE; ▲ Falmouth; **187** K-17; elev. 50ft./15m.; mail Falmouth z 02540; ● 1,500
Sixteen Acres; RMC Place; HAMPDEN; **187** M-13; elev. 220ft./67m.; ★ **SPRG**; mail Springfield z 01101; pop. incl. with Springfield (Inc. Place)
Smith Highlands; RMC Place; HAMPDEN; *186 F-5; elev. 170ft./52m.; ★ **SPRG**; mail Chicopee z 01020; pop. incl. with Chicopee (Inc. Place)
Smith Mills; CDP; BRISTOL; ▲ Dartmouth; **187** K-15; elev. 50ft./15m.; ★ **N.BED**; mail North Dartmouth z 02747; Ⓟ 4,593; Ⓒ 4,432
Smiths Ferry; RMC Place; HAMPDEN; *186 F-5; elev. 125ft./38m.; ★ **SPRG**; mail Holyoke z 01040; pop. incl. with Holyoke (Inc. Place)
Smoke Rise Heights; RMC Place; BRISTOL; ▲ Swansea; *187 J-13; ★ **F.R.**; mail Swansea z 02777; ● 1,750
Snug Harbor; RMC Place; PLYMOUTH; ▲ Duxbury; *187 N-20; ★ **BOS**; mail Duxbury z 02332
Soldiers Field; RMC Place; SUFFOLK; *187 F-14; ★ **BOS**; mail Boston z 02163; pop. incl. with Boston (Inc. Place)
Somerset; CDP; BRISTOL; ▲ Somerset; **187** J-14; elev. 50ft./15m.; 🅿; ★ **F.R.**; z 02725-26; Ⓟ 17,655; Ⓒ 18,234
Somerset; MCD-Town; BRISTOL; *187 J-14; 🅿; ★ **F.R.**; z 02725-26; Ⓟ 17,655; Ⓒ 18,234; ◆ 18,245
Somerset Centre; RMC Place; BRISTOL; ▲ Somerset; *187 N-20; ★ **F.R.**; mail Somerset z 02726
Somerville; Inc. Place; MIDDLESEX; **187** E-14; elev. 12ft./4m.; 🅿 ■; ★ **BOS**; z 02143-45; Ⓟ 76,210; Ⓒ 77,478; ◆ 78,019
South; RMC Place; BRISTOL; *187 J-14; ★ **F.R.**; mail Fall River z 02724; pop. incl. with Fall River (Inc. Place)
South Acton; RMC Place; MIDDLESEX; ▲ Acton; **187** D-12; elev. 202ft./62m.; ★ **BOS**; mail Acton z 01720; ● 3,200
South Amherst; CDP; HAMPSHIRE; ▲ Amherst; **186** E-6; elev. 231ft./70m.; ★ **SPRG**; mail Amherst z 01002; Ⓟ 5,053; Ⓒ 5,039
Southampton; RMC Place; HAMPSHIRE; ▲ Southampton; **186** F-5; elev. 230ft./70m.; 🅿; ★ **SPRG**; z 01073; ● 550
Southampton; MCD-Town; HAMPSHIRE; *186 F-5; 🅿; ★ **SPRG**; z 01073; Ⓟ 4,478; Ⓒ 5,387; ◆ 5,768
South Ashburnham; CDP; WORCESTER; ▲ Ashburnham; **186** C-9; elev. 900ft./274m.; ★ **BOS**; mail Ashburnham z 01430; Ⓟ 1,110; Ⓒ 1,013
South Ashfield; RMC Place; FRANKLIN; ▲ Ashfield; **186** D-4; elev. 988ft./301m.; mail Ashfield z 01330; ● 70
South Athol; RMC Place; WORCESTER; ▲ Athol; *186 D-7; elev. 574ft./175m.; mail Athol z 01331
South Attleboro; RMC Place; BRISTOL; *187 I-12; elev. 100ft./30m.; 🅿 🅷; ★ **PROV-**; z 02703; pop. incl. with Attleboro (Inc. Place)

Entries in **UPPERCASE** are counties.
Entries in **bold** have populations of 2,500 or more.
Names in parentheses are alternate names.

Inc. Place	Incorporated Place
RMC Place	Rand McNally Designated Place
CDP	Census Designated Place
MCD	Minor Civil Division
⊡	County Seat
▲	Minor Civil Division
elev.	Elevation
🅿	Post Office
🅷	Hospital
🅲	College
■	Principal Business Center
★	Ranally Metro Area (RMA) Abbreviation
z	Zip Code(s)
Ⓟ	Previous Census Population
Ⓡ	Revised Census Population
Ⓐ	Annexation Population
●	Rand McNally Population Estimate
Ⓒ	Final Census Population
Ⓢ	Special Census Population
◆	Estimated Population

For additional definitions see Glossary, Volume 1, and Introduction, Volume 2.

South Barre; RMC Place; WORCESTER; ▲ Barre; **186** E-8; elev. 600ft./183m.; 🅿; ★ **WORC**; z 01074; ● 550
South Bellingham; RMC Place; NORFOLK; ▲ Bellingham; ***187** G-12; elev. 200ft./61m.; ★ **BOS**; mail Bellingham z 02019
South Berlin; RMC Place; WORCESTER; ▲ Berlin; **187** E-11; elev. 275ft./84m.; ★ **BOS**; mail Berlin z 01503; ● 300
South Billerica; RMC Place; MIDDLESEX; ▲ Billerica; ***187** D-13; elev. 211ft./64m.; ★ **BOS**; mail Bedford z 01730; rural
South Bolton; RMC Place; WORCESTER; ▲ Bolton; ***187** E-11; elev. 369ft./112m.; ★ **BOS**; mail Bolton z 01740
Southboro; WORCESTER; see Southborough (RMC Place)
Southborough (Southboro); RMC Place; WORCESTER; ▲ Southborough; **187** E-12; elev. 306ft./93m.; 🅿; ★ **BOS**; z 01745, z 01772; ● 1,500
Southborough; MCD-Town; WORCESTER; ***187** F-11; 🅿; ★ **BOS**; z 01745, z 01772; Ⓟ 6,628; © 8,781; ◆ 9,862
South Boston; RMC Place; SUFFOLK; **186** L-7; elev. 30ft./9m.; 🅿; ★ **BOS**; z 02127; pop. incl. with Boston (Inc. Place)
South Braintree; RMC Place; NORFOLK; ▲ Braintree; ***187** F-15; elev. 100ft./30m.; ★ **BOS**; mail Braintree z 02184
Southbridge; CDP; WORCESTER; ▲ Southbridge; **186** G-9; 🅿 🅷; ★ **WORC**; z 01550; Ⓟ 13,631; © 12,878
Southbridge; MCD-Town; WORCESTER; ***186** G-9; 🅿; ★ **WORC**; z 01550; Ⓟ 17,816; © 17,214; ◆ 16,198
South Byfield; RMC Place; ESSEX; ▲ Newbury; **187** B-15; elev. 70ft./21m.; ★ **BOS**; mail Byfield z 01922; ● 50
South Carver; RMC Place; PLYMOUTH; ▲ Carver; ***187** I-16; elev. 97ft./30m.; 🅿; ★ **BOS**; z 02366
South Charlton; RMC Place; WORCESTER; ▲ Charlton; ***186** G-9; elev. 619ft./189m.; ★ **WORC**; mail Charlton z 01507; ● 200
South Chatham; RMC Place; BARNSTABLE; ▲ Chatham; **187** J-20; elev. 59ft./18m.; 🅿; ★ **BARN**; z 02659; summer pop. 2,500; ● 950
South Chelmsford; RMC Place; MIDDLESEX; ▲ Chelmsford; ***187** C-12; elev. 207ft./63m.; ★ **BOS**; mail Chelmsford z 01824
South Dartmouth (Padanaram); RMC Place; BRISTOL; ▲ Dartmouth; **187** G-20; elev. 56ft./17m.; 🅿; ★ **N.BED**; z 02748; ● 9,800
South Deerfield; CDP; FRANKLIN; ▲ Deerfield; **186** D-5; elev. 204ft./62m.; 🅿; z 01373; Ⓟ 1,906; © 1,868
South Dennis; CDP; BARNSTABLE; ▲ Dennis; **187** J-19; elev. 40ft./12m.; 🅿; ★ **BARN**; z 02660; Ⓟ 3,559; © 3,679
South Duxbury; CDP; PLYMOUTH; ▲ Duxbury; **187** H-16; elev. 50ft./15m.; ★ **BOS**; mail Duxbury z 02332; Ⓟ 3,017; © 3,062
South Easton; RMC Place; BRISTOL; ▲ Easton; **187** G-14; elev. 105ft./32m.; 🅿; ★ **BOS**; z 02375; ● 1,500
South Egremont; RMC Place; BERKSHIRE; ▲ Egremont; **186** F-1; elev. 714ft./218m.; 🅿; z 01258; ● 600
South End; RMC Place; HAMPDEN; ***186** G-5; ★ **SPRG**; mail Springfield z 01105; pop. incl. with Springfield (Inc. Place)
South Essex; RMC Place; ESSEX; ▲ Essex; ***187** C-16; elev. 70ft./21m.; ★ **BOS**; mail Essex z 01929
Southfield; RMC Place; BERKSHIRE; ▲ New Marlborough; **186** G-2; elev. 1,223ft./373m.; 🅿; z 01259; ● 200
South Fitchburg; RMC Place; WORCESTER; ***186** C-10; elev. 450ft./137m.; ★ **BOS**; mail Fitchburg z 01420; pop. incl. with Fitchburg (Inc. Place)
South Foxboro; RMC Place; NORFOLK; ▲ Foxborough; ***187** H-13; elev. 194ft./59m.; ★ **BOS**; mail Foxboro z 02035; ● 150
South Framingham; RMC Place; MIDDLESEX; ▲ Framingham; ***187** F-12; ★ **BOS**; mail Framingham z 01704
South Georgetown; RMC Place; ESSEX; ▲ Georgetown; **187** B-15; elev. 102ft./31m.; ★ **BOS**; mail Georgetown z 01833; ● 150
South Grafton; WORCESTER; see Fisherville (RMC Place)
South Groveland; RMC Place; ESSEX; ▲ Groveland; ***187** B-14; ★ **BOS**; mail Groveland z 01834; ● 200
South Hadley; RMC Place; HAMPSHIRE; ▲ South Hadley; **186** F-6; elev. 257ft./78m.; 🅿 🅲 2,235; ★ **SPRG**; z 01075; ● 5,500
South Hadley; MCD-Town; HAMPSHIRE; ***186** F-5; 🅿 🅲 2,235; ★ **SPRG**; z 01075; Ⓟ 16,685; © 17,196; ◆ 17,243
South Hadley Falls; RMC Place; HAMPSHIRE; ▲ South Hadley; **186** F-5; elev. 80ft./24m.; ★ **SPRG**; mail South Hadley z 01075; ● 5,100
South Hamilton; RMC Place; ESSEX; ▲ Hamilton; **187** C-15; elev. 55ft./17m.; 🅿 🅲 2,212; ★ **BOS**; z 01982; ● 2,800
South Hanover; RMC Place; PLYMOUTH; ▲ Hanover; **187** G-15; elev. 80ft./24m.; ★ **BOS**; mail Hanover z 02339; ● 1,000
South Harwich; RMC Place; BARNSTABLE; ▲ Harwich; **187** J-20; elev. 20ft./6m.; 🅿; ★ **BARN**; z 02661; ● 800
South Hingham; RMC Place; PLYMOUTH; ▲ Hingham; **187** F-15; elev. 140ft./43m.; ★ **BOS**; mail Hingham z 02043; ● 4,000
South Lancaster (Thayer); CDP; WORCESTER; ▲ Lancaster; **187** D-11; elev. 280ft./85m.; 🅿 🅲 572; ★ **BOS**; z 01561; Ⓟ 1,772; © 1,742
South Lawrence; RMC Place; ESSEX; ***187** B-14; elev. 59ft./18m.; ★ **BOS**; mail Lawrence z 01842-43; pop. incl. with Lawrence (Inc. Place)
South Lee; RMC Place; BERKSHIRE; ▲ Lee; **186** F-2; elev. 870ft./265m.; 🅿; ★ **PTSF**; z 01260; ● 500
South Lowell; RMC Place; MIDDLESEX; ***187** C-13; elev. 121ft./37m.; ★ **BOS**; mail Tewksbury z 01876; pop. incl. with Lowell (Inc. Place)
South Lynnfield; RMC Place; ESSEX; ▲ Lynnfield; **186** H-8; elev. 129ft./39m.; ★ **BOS**; mail Lynnfield z 01940
South Mashpee; RMC Place; BARNSTABLE; ▲ Mashpee; ***187** K-18; elev. 21ft./6m.; ★ **BARN**; mail Mashpee z 02649
South Middleboro; RMC Place; PLYMOUTH; ▲ Middleborough; **187** I-16; elev. 108ft./33m.; ★ **BOS**; mail Middleboro z 02346; ● 480
South Milford; RMC Place; WORCESTER; ▲ Hopedale; ***187** G-12; elev. 270ft./82m.; ★ **BOS**; mail Hopedale z 01747
South Natick; RMC Place; MIDDLESEX; ▲ Natick; **186** M-3; elev. 124ft./38m.; ★ **BOS**; mail Natick z 01760
South Orleans; RMC Place; BARNSTABLE; ▲ Orleans; **187** J-20; elev. 40ft./12m.; 🅿; ★ **BARN**; z 02662; ● 750
South Peabody; RMC Place; ESSEX; **186** H-9; elev. 72ft./22m.; ★ **BOS**; mail Peabody z 01960; pop. incl. with Peabody (Inc. Place)
South Pond; RMC Place; PLYMOUTH; ▲ Plymouth; ***187** H-17; ★ **BOS**; mail Plymouth z 02360
South Quincy; RMC Place; NORFOLK; **186** N-8; elev. 30ft./9m.; ★ **BOS**; mail Quincy z 02169; pop. incl. with Quincy (Inc. Place)
South Rehoboth; RMC Place; BRISTOL; ▲ Rehoboth; ***187** I-13; ★ **PROV-**; mail Rehoboth z 02769; rural
South Royalston; RMC Place; WORCESTER; ▲ Royalston; **186** C-8; elev. 850ft./259m.; mail Athol z 01331, Royalston z 01368; ● 450
South Salem; RMC Place; ESSEX; ***187** D-15; elev. 16ft./5m.; ★ **BOS**; mail Salem z 01970; pop. incl. with Salem (Inc. Place)
South Sandisfield; RMC Place; BERKSHIRE; ▲ Sandisfield; ***186** G-2; elev. 1,448ft./441m.; mail Sandisfield z 01255
South Sandwich; BARNSTABLE; see Farmersville (RMC Place)
South Springfield; RMC Place; HAMPDEN; ***187** N-20; ★ **SPRG**; mail Springfield z 01101; pop. incl. with Springfield (Inc. Place)
South Stoughton; RMC Place; NORFOLK; ▲ Stoughton; ***187** G-14; elev. 273ft./83m.; ★ **BOS**; mail Stoughton z 02072
South Sudbury; MIDDLESEX; see Sudbury (RMC Place)
South Sutton; RMC Place; WORCESTER; ▲ Sutton; **186** G-10; elev. 448ft./137m.; ★ **WORC**; mail Douglas z 01516; ● 175
South Swansea; RMC Place; BRISTOL; ▲ Swansea; **187** J-13; elev. 50ft./15m.; ★ **F.R.**; mail Swansea z 02777; ● 1,000
South Truro; RMC Place; BARNSTABLE; ▲ Truro; ***187** H-20; elev. 40ft./12m.; mail Truro z 02666
South Uxbridge; WORCESTER; see Ironstone (RMC Place)
Southville; RMC Place; WORCESTER; ▲ Southborough; ***187** F-11; elev. 264ft./80m.; ★ **BOS**; mail Southborough z 01772
South Walpole; RMC Place; NORFOLK; ▲ Walpole; **187** G-13; elev. 223ft./68m.; 🅿; ★ **BOS**; z 02071; ● 1,300
South Waltham; RMC Place; MIDDLESEX; ***187** E-13; elev. 86ft./26m.; 🅿; ★ **BOS**; z 02453; pop. incl. with Waltham (Inc. Place)
South Wareham; RMC Place; PLYMOUTH; ▲ Wareham; ***187** J-16; elev. 32ft./10m.; ★ **BOS**; mail Wareham z 02571, West Wareham z 02576; ● 200
South Wellfleet; RMC Place; BARNSTABLE; ▲ Wellfleet; **187** H-20; elev. 50ft./15m.; 🅿; z 02663; summer pop. 900; ● 600
South Westport; RMC Place; BRISTOL; ▲ Westport; **187** K-14; elev. 65ft./20m.; ★ **F.R.**; mail Westport z 02790; ● 180
South Weymouth; RMC Place; NORFOLK; ▲ Weymouth; ***187** F-15; elev. 143ft./44m.; 🅿 🅷; ★ **BOS**; z 02190
Southwick (Southwick Center); RMC Place; HAMPDEN; ▲ Southwick; **186** G-4; elev. 244ft./74m.; 🅿; ★ **SPRG**; z 01077; ● 1,250
Southwick; MCD-Town; HAMPDEN; ***186** G-4; 🅿; ★ **SPRG**; z 01077; Ⓟ 7,667; © 8,835; ◆ 8,991
Southwick Center; HAMPDEN; see Southwick (RMC Place)
South Williamstown; RMC Place; BERKSHIRE; ▲ Williamstown; ***186** C-2; elev. 869ft./265m.; mail Williamstown z 01267
South Wilmington; RMC Place; MIDDLESEX; ***187** D-14; elev. 105ft./32m.; ★ **BOS**; mail Woburn z 01801; pop. incl. with Woburn (Inc. Place)
South Worthington; RMC Place; HAMPSHIRE; ▲ Worthington; ***186** E-4; elev. 961ft./293m.; mail Huntington z 01050
South Yarmouth; CDP; BARNSTABLE; ▲ Yarmouth; **187** J-19; elev. 20ft./6m.; 🅿; ★ **BARN**; z 02664 & mail West Yarmouth z 02673; Ⓟ 10,358; © 11,603
Spencer; CDP; WORCESTER; ▲ Spencer; **186** F-9; elev. 925ft./282m.; 🅿; ★ **WORC**; z 01562; Ⓟ 6,306; © 6,032
Spencer; MCD-Town; WORCESTER; ***186** F-9; 🅿; ★ **WORC**; z 01562; Ⓟ 11,645; © 11,691; ◆ 11,193
Spindleville; RMC Place; WORCESTER; ▲ Hopedale; ***187** G-12; elev. 230ft./70m.; ★ **BOS**; mail Hopedale z 01747
Springdale; RMC Place; HAMPDEN; **187** K-11; elev. 70ft./21m.; ★ **SPRG**; mail Holyoke z 01040; pop. incl. with Holyoke (Inc. Place)
Springdale; RMC Place; NORFOLK; ▲ Canton; ***187** G-14; ★ **BOS**; mail Canton z 02021
Springfield; Inc. Place; ⊡ HAMPDEN; **186** G-5; elev. 70ft./21m.; 🅿 🅲 10,516 ■; ★ **SPRG**; z 01101-09, z 01111, z 01115, z 01118-19, z 01128-29, z 01138-39, z 01144, z 01151-52, z 01199; Ⓟ 156,983; © 152,082; ◆ 150,970
Spring Hill; RMC Place; MIDDLESEX; ***187** E-14; ★ **BOS**; mail Somerville z 02143; pop. incl. with Somerville (Inc. Place)
Squantum; RMC Place; NORFOLK; **186** L-8; elev. 50ft./15m.; 🅿; ★ **BOS**; z 02171; pop. incl. with Quincy (Inc. Place)
Standish; RMC Place; BRISTOL; ***187** N-20; ★ **BOS**; mail Taunton z 02780; pop. incl. with Taunton (Inc. Place)
Staples Shore; RMC Place; PLYMOUTH; ▲ Lakeville; ***187** I-15; elev. 56ft./17m.; ★ **BOS**; mail Middleboro z 02346
State House; RMC Place; SUFFOLK; ***187** E-14; ★ **BOS**; mail Boston z 02133; pop. incl. with Boston (Inc. Place)
State Line; RMC Place; BERKSHIRE; ▲ West Stockbridge; **186** E-1; elev. 916ft./279m.; mail West Stockbridge z 01266; ● 80
Sterling; RMC Place; WORCESTER; ▲ Sterling; **186** D-10; elev. 502ft./153m.; 🅿; ★ **WORC**; z 01564; ● 1,350
Sterling; MCD-Town; WORCESTER; ***186** D-10; 🅿; ★ **WORC**; z 01564; Ⓟ 6,481; © 7,257; ◆ 7,449
Sterling Junction; RMC Place; WORCESTER; ▲ Sterling; **186** E-10; elev. 441ft./134m.; ★ **WORC**; mail Sterling z 01564; ● 600
Stevens Corner; RMC Place; BERKSHIRE; ▲ Richmond; ***186** E-1; elev. 1,215ft./370m.; ★ **PTSF**; mail Pittsfield z 01201; rural
Still River; RMC Place; WORCESTER; ▲ Harvard; **187** D-11; elev. 415ft./126m.; 🅿; ★ **BOS**; z 01467; ● 300
Stockbridge; RMC Place; BERKSHIRE; ▲ Stockbridge; **186** F-1; elev. 842ft./257m.; 🅿 🅷; ★ **PTSF**; z 01262-63; ● 1,100
Stockbridge; MCD-Town; BERKSHIRE; ***186** E-1; 🅿; ★ **PTSF**; z 01262-63; Ⓟ 2,408; © 2,276; ◆ 2,070
Stoneham; CDP; MIDDLESEX; ▲ Stoneham; **187** D-14; elev. 155ft./47m.; 🅿 🅷; ★ **BOS**; z 02180; Ⓟ 22,203; © 22,219; ◆ 21,613
Stoneham; MCD-Town; MIDDLESEX; ***187** D-14; 🅿; ★ **BOS**; z 02180; Ⓟ 22,203; © 22,219; ◆ 21,613
Stoneville; RMC Place; FRANKLIN; ▲ Erving; ***186** C-7; elev. 477ft./145m.; mail Erving z 01344; rural
Stoneville; RMC Place; WORCESTER; ▲ Auburn; **187** C-18; elev. 601ft./183m.; ★ **WORC**; mail Auburn z 01501
Stony Beach; RMC Place; PLYMOUTH; ▲ Hull; ***187** E-15; elev. 20ft./6m.; ★ **BOS**; mail Greenbush z 02040
Stony Brook; RMC Place; MIDDLESEX; ▲ Weston; **186** K-4; ★ **BOS**; mail Weston z 02493
Stoughton; RMC Place; NORFOLK; ▲ Stoughton; **187** G-14; 🅿; ★ **BOS**; z 02072; Ⓟ 26,777
Stoughton; MCD-Town; NORFOLK; ***187** G-14; 🅿; ★ **BOS**; z 02072; Ⓟ 26,777; © 27,149; ◆ 27,573
Stoughton Junction; RMC Place; NORFOLK; ▲ Stoughton; ***187** G-14; ★ **BOS**; mail Stoughton z 02072
Stow; RMC Place; MIDDLESEX; ▲ Stow; **187** D-12; elev. 231ft./70m.; 🅿; ★ **BOS**; z 01775; ● 1,250
Stow; MCD-Town; MIDDLESEX; ***187** D-12; 🅿; ★ **BOS**; z 01775; Ⓟ 5,328; © 5,902; ◆ 6,220
Straits Pond; RMC Place; PLYMOUTH; ▲ Hull; ***187** F-15; elev. 50ft./15m.; ★ **BOS**; mail Hull z 02045
Sturbridge; CDP; WORCESTER; ▲ Sturbridge; **186** G-8; elev. 619ft./189m.; 🅿; ★ **WORC**; z 01518, z 01566; Ⓟ 2,093; © 2,047
Sturbridge; MCD-Town; WORCESTER; ***186** G-8; 🅿; ★ **WORC**; z 01518, z 01566; Ⓟ 7,775; © 7,837; ◆ 7,880
Sudbury (South Sudbury); RMC Place; MIDDLESEX; ▲ Sudbury; **187** E-12; 🅿; ★ **BOS**; z 01776; ● 1,950
Sudbury; MCD-Town; MIDDLESEX; ***187** E-12; 🅿; ★ **BOS**; z 01776; Ⓟ 14,358; © 16,841; ◆ 18,039
SUFFOLK; **187** F-14; Ⓟ 663,906; © 689,807; ◆ 763,832
Summer Heights; RMC Place; NORFOLK; ▲ Canton; ***187** F-14; ★ **BOS**; mail Canton z 02021
Summit; RMC Place; WORCESTER; **187** A-19; elev. 650ft./198m.; ★ **WORC**; mail Worcester z 01606; pop. incl. with Worcester (Inc. Place)
Summit Grove; RMC Place; BRISTOL; ▲ Dartmouth; ***187** K-15; ★ **N.BED**; mail North Dartmouth z 02747
Sunderland; RMC Place; FRANKLIN; ▲ Sunderland; **186** D-6; elev. 142ft./43m.; 🅿; ★ **SPRG**; z 01375; ● 1,100
Sunderland; MCD-Town; FRANKLIN; ***186** D-6; 🅿; ★ **SPRG**; z 01375; Ⓟ 3,399; © 3,777; ◆ 3,711
Sunderland; RMC Place; WORCESTER; **187** C-20; elev. 500ft./152m.; ★ **WORC**; mail Worcester z 01604; pop. incl. with Worcester (Inc. Place)
Sunken Meadow Beach; RMC Place; BARNSTABLE; ▲ Eastham; ***187** I-20; ★ **BARN**; mail North Eastham z 02651
Sunnyside; RMC Place; WORCESTER; ▲ Dudley; ***186** G-9; elev. 480ft./146m.; ★ **WORC**; mail Dudley z 01571
Surfside; RMC Place; NANTUCKET; ▲ Nantucket; **187** M-20; elev. 20ft./6m.; mail Nantucket z 02554; summer pop. 500; ● 150
Sutton; RMC Place; WORCESTER; ▲ Sutton; **186** G-10; elev. 706ft./215m.; 🅿; ★ **WORC**; z 01590 & mail Millbury z 01527; ● 600
Sutton; MCD-Town; WORCESTER; ***186** G-10; 🅿; ★ **WORC**; z 01590 & mail Millbury z 01527; Ⓟ 6,824; © 8,250; ◆ 9,177
Swampscott; CDP; ESSEX; ▲ Swampscott; **187** D-15; elev. 45ft./14m.; 🅿; ★ **BOS**; z 01907; Ⓟ 13,650; © 14,412
Swampscott; MCD-Town; ESSEX; ***187** D-15; 🅿; ★ **BOS**; z 01907; Ⓟ 13,650; © 14,412; ◆ 14,674
Swansea (Swansea Village); RMC Place; BRISTOL; ▲ Swansea; **187** J-13; elev. 22ft./7m.; 🅿; ★ **F.R.**; z 02777; ● 900
Swansea; MCD-Town; BRISTOL; ***187** J-13; 🅿 ■; ★ **F.R.**; z 02777; Ⓟ 15,411; © 15,901; ◆ 15,686
Swansea Center; RMC Place; BRISTOL; ▲ Swansea; **187** J-13; ★ **F.R.**; mail Swansea z 02777; ● 300
Swansea Village; BRISTOL; see Swansea (RMC Place)
Swanson Corners; RMC Place; HAMPSHIRE; ▲ Southampton; ***186** F-5; ★ **SPRG**; mail Southampton z 01073; rural
Sweets Corner; RMC Place; BERKSHIRE; ▲ Williamstown; ***186** C-2; elev. 752ft./229m.; mail Williamstown z 01267
Swift River; RMC Place; HAMPSHIRE; ▲ Cummington; **186** D-4; elev. 961ft./293m.; mail Cummington z 01026; ● 250
Swifts Beach; RMC Place; PLYMOUTH; ▲ Wareham; ***187** J-16; elev. 10ft./3m.; ★ **BOS**; mail Wareham z 02571
Symmes Corner; RMC Place; MIDDLESEX; ▲ Winchester; ***187** D-14; elev. 130ft./40m.; ★ **BOS**; mail Winchester z 01890

T

Tafts Corner; RMC Place; WORCESTER; ▲ Spencer; **186** F-9; elev. 1,000ft./305m.; ★ **WORC**; mail Spencer z 01562; ● 50
Tahanto Beach; RMC Place; BARNSTABLE; ▲ Bourne; ***187** J-17; elev. 20ft./6m.; mail Pocasset z 02559
Tapleyville; RMC Place; ESSEX; ▲ Danvers; ***187** D-15; elev. 50ft./15m.; ★ **BOS**; mail Danvers z 01923
Tarkiln; RMC Place; PLYMOUTH; ▲ Duxbury; ***187** H-16; ★ **BOS**; mail Duxbury z 02332; ● 120
Tatnuck; RMC Place; WORCESTER; **187** B-18; elev. 630ft./192m.; ★ **WORC**; mail Worcester z 01602; pop. incl. with Worcester (Inc. Place)
Taunton; Inc. Place; ⊡ BRISTOL; **187** I-14; elev. 30ft./9m.; 🅿 🅷 ■; ★ **BOS**; z 02780, z 02783 & mail East Taunton z 02718; Ⓟ 49,832; © 55,976; ◆ 57,321
Teaticket; CDP; BARNSTABLE; ▲ Falmouth; **187** K-17; elev. 24ft./7m.; 🅿; z 02536; Ⓟ 1,856; © 1,907
Templeton; RMC Place; WORCESTER; ▲ Templeton; **186** D-8; elev. 1,141ft./348m.; 🅿; ★ **BOS**; z 01468; ● 1,000
Templeton; MCD-Town; WORCESTER; ***186** C-9; 🅿; ★ **BOS**; z 01468; Ⓟ 6,438; © 6,799; ◆ 6,894
Ten Hills; RMC Place; MIDDLESEX; ***187** E-14; elev. 25ft./8m.; ★ **BOS**; mail Somerville z 02145; pop. incl. with Somerville (Inc. Place)
Tewksbury; RMC Place; MIDDLESEX; ▲ Tewksbury; **187** C-13; elev. 126ft./38m.; 🅿 🅷; ★ **BOS**; z 01876; ● 11,000
Tewksbury; MCD-Town; MIDDLESEX; ***187** C-13; 🅿; ★ **BOS**; z 01876; Ⓟ 27,266; © 28,851; ◆ 29,192
Texas; RMC Place; WORCESTER; ▲ Oxford; **186** G-9; elev. 621ft./189m.; ★ **WORC**; mail North Oxford z 01537; ● 430
Thayer; WORCESTER; see South Lancaster (CDP)
The Green; RMC Place; PLYMOUTH; ▲ Middleborough; ***187** H-15; ★ **BOS**; mail Middleboro z 02346
The Pines; RMC Place; MIDDLESEX; ▲ Billerica; ***187** N-20; ★ **BOS**; mail Pinehurst z 01866
The Plains; RMC Place; ESSEX; ▲ Manchester-by-the-Sea; ***187** C-16; ★ **BOS**; mail Manchester z 01944
Thomastown; RMC Place; PLYMOUTH; ▲ Middleborough; ***187** I-15; elev. 123ft./37m.; ★ **BOS**; mail Middleboro z 02346; ● 50
Thorndike; RMC Place; HAMPDEN; ▲ Palmer; **186** F-7; elev. 347ft./106m.; 🅿; ★ **SPRG**; z 01079; ● 1,150
Three Rivers; CDP; HAMPDEN; ▲ Palmer; **186** F-7; elev. 320ft./98m.; 🅿; ★ **SPRG**; z 01080; Ⓟ 3,006; © 2,939
Thumpertown Beach; RMC Place; BARNSTABLE; ▲ Eastham; ***187** I-20; elev. 30ft./9m.; ★ **BARN**; mail North Eastham z 02651
Tihonet; RMC Place; PLYMOUTH; ▲ Wareham; ***187** I-16; elev. 30ft./9m.; ★ **BOS**; mail Wareham z 02571; ● 100
Tinkertown; RMC Place; PLYMOUTH; ▲ Duxbury; **187** H-16; elev. 67ft./20m.; ★ **BOS**; mail Duxbury z 02332; ● 100
Tinkhamtown; RMC Place; PLYMOUTH; ▲ Mattapoisett; ***187** J-15; elev. 40ft./12m.; ★ **N.BED**; mail Mattapoisett z 02739
Tisbury; DUKES; see Vineyard Haven (CDP)
Tisbury; MCD-Town; DUKES; ***187** L-17; mail Oak Bluffs z 02557, Vineyard Haven z 02568, West Chop z 02573, West Tisbury z 02575; Ⓟ 3,120; © 3,755
Tobeys Island; RMC Place; BARNSTABLE; ▲ Bourne; ***187** J-17; mail Monument Beach z 02553
Tolland; HAMPDEN; see Tolland Center (RMC Place)
Tolland; MCD-Town; HAMPDEN; ***186** G-3; 🅿; z 01034; Ⓟ 289; © 426
Tolland Center (Tolland); RMC Place; HAMPDEN; ▲ Tolland; **186** G-3; mail Granville z 01034; ● 200
Tonset; RMC Place; BARNSTABLE; ▲ Orleans; **187** I-20; elev. 30ft./9m.; ★ **BARN**; mail East Orleans z 02643, Orleans z 02653; ● 500
Topsfield; CDP; ESSEX; ▲ Topsfield; **187** C-15; elev. 63ft./19m.; 🅿; ★ **BOS**; z 01983; Ⓟ 2,711; © 2,826
Topsfield; MCD-Town; ESSEX; ***187** C-15; 🅿; ★ **BOS**; z 01983; Ⓟ 5,754; © 6,141; ◆ 6,118
Touisset; RMC Place; BRISTOL; ▲ Swansea; **187** J-13; elev. 20ft./6m.; ★ **F.R.**; mail Swansea z 02777; ● 1,500
Town Crest Village; RMC Place; BERKSHIRE; ▲ Cheshire; **186** C-2; elev. 1,020ft./311m.; ★ **PTSF**; mail Cheshire z 01225; ● 120
Town Hall; RMC Place; PLYMOUTH; ▲ Hanson; ***187** G-15; elev. 73ft./22m.; ★ **BOS**; mail Hanson z 02341
Townsend; CDP; MIDDLESEX; ▲ Townsend; **186** C-10; elev. 315ft./96m.; 🅿; ★ **BOS**; z 01469, z 01474; Ⓟ 1,164; © 1,043
Townsend; MCD-Town; MIDDLESEX; ***186** C-10; 🅿; ★ **BOS**; z 01469, z 01474; Ⓟ 8,496; © 9,198; ◆ 9,369
Townsend Harbor; RMC Place; MIDDLESEX; ▲ Townsend; **187** C-11; elev. 271ft./83m.; ★ **BOS**; mail Townsend z 01469; ● 900
Townsend Hill; RMC Place; BRISTOL; ***187** J-14; ★ **F.R.**; mail Fall River z 02724
Tozier Corner; RMC Place; ESSEX; ***187** B-14; ★ **BOS**; mail Methuen z 01844; pop. incl. with Methuen (Inc. Place)
Tremont; PLYMOUTH; see West Wareham (CDP)
Truro; RMC Place; BARNSTABLE; ▲ Truro; **187** H-20; elev. 25ft./8m.; 🅿; z 02666; ● 550
Truro; MCD-Town; BARNSTABLE; ***187** H-20; 🅿; z 02666; Ⓟ 1,573; © 2,087
Tufts University; RMC Place; MIDDLESEX; ***187** E-14; elev. 34ft./10m.; 🅿; ★ **BOS**; z 02153; pop. incl. with Medford (Inc. Place)
Tully (Tullyville); RMC Place; FRANKLIN; ▲ Orange; **186** C-7; elev. 588ft./179m.; mail Athol z 01331, Orange z 01364; ● 200
Tullyville; FRANKLIN; see Tully (RMC Place)
Turkey Hill Shores; RMC Place; WORCESTER; ▲ Rutland; **186** E-9; elev. 1,020ft./311m.; ★ **WORC**; mail Rutland z 01543; ● 170
Turners Falls; CDP; FRANKLIN; ▲ Montague; **186** C-6; elev. 326ft./99m.; 🅿; z 01349, z 01376; Ⓟ 4,731; © 4,441
Turnpike; WORCESTER; see Fairlawn (RMC Place)
Tyngsboro; RMC Place; MIDDLESEX; ▲ Tyngsborough; **187** C-12; elev. 150ft./46m.; 🅿; ★ **BOS**; z 01879; ● 250
Tyngsborough; MCD-Town; MIDDLESEX; ***187** C-12; ★ **BOS**; mail Tyngsboro z 01879; Ⓟ 8,642; © 11,081; ◆ 12,075
Tyringham; RMC Place; BERKSHIRE; ▲ Tyringham; **186** F-2; elev. 901ft./275m.; 🅿; z 01264; ● 200
Tyringham; MCD-Town; BERKSHIRE; ***186** F-2; 🅿; z 01264; Ⓟ 369; © 350

U

Union Hill; RMC Place; WORCESTER; ***186** F-10; elev. 600ft./183m.; ★ **WORC**; pop. incl. with Worcester (Inc. Place)
Union Market; RMC Place; MIDDLESEX; ***187** N-20; ★ **BOS**; mail Watertown z 02472; pop. incl. with Watertown (Inc. Place)
Union Point; RMC Place; WORCESTER; ▲ Webster; ***187** N-20; ★ **WORC**; mail Webster z 01570
Unionville; RMC Place; NORFOLK; ***187** G-12; elev. 260ft./79m.; ★ **BOS**; mail Franklin z 02038; pop. incl. with Franklin (Inc. Place)
Unionville; RMC Place; WORCESTER; ▲ Holden; ***186** E-10; elev. 650ft./198m.; ★ **WORC**; mail Holden z 01520; ● 100
University Park; RMC Place; WORCESTER; ***186** F-10; elev. 500ft./152m.; ★ **WORC**; mail Worcester z 01605; pop. incl. with Worcester (Inc. Place)
Uphams Corner; RMC Place; SUFFOLK; ***187** E-14; elev. 45ft./14m.; 🅿; ★ **BOS**; z 02125; pop. incl. with Boston (Inc. Place)
Upper Hill; RMC Place; HAMPDEN; ***186** G-6; ★ **SPRG**; mail Springfield z 01129; pop. incl. with Springfield (Inc. Place)
Upton; RMC Place; WORCESTER; ▲ Upton; **187** F-11; elev. 301ft./92m.; 🅿; ★ **BOS**; z 01568; ● 1,200
Upton; MCD-Town; WORCESTER; ***187** G-11; 🅿; ★ **BOS**; z 01568; Ⓟ 4,677; © 5,642; Ⓡ 5,713; ◆ 5,955
Upton-West Upton; CDP-Census Area Only; WORCESTER; ▲ Upton; ***187** F-11; ★ **BOS**; mail Upton z 01568; Ⓟ 2,347; © 2,326; Ⓡ 2,311
Uxbridge; RMC Place; WORCESTER; ▲ Uxbridge; **187** G-11; elev. 270ft./82m.; 🅿; ★ **WORC**; z 01569; ● 3,500
Uxbridge; MCD-Town; WORCESTER; ***187** G-11; 🅿; ★ **WORC**; z 01569; Ⓟ 10,415; © 11,156; ◆ 11,455

V

Vallersville; RMC Place; PLYMOUTH; ▲ Plymouth; **187** I-17; elev. 31ft./9m.; ★ **BOS**; mail Buzzards Bay z 02532; ● 150
Valley View; RMC Place; NORFOLK; ▲ Bellingham; ***187** G-12; elev. 280ft./85m.; ★ **BOS**; mail Bellingham z 02019
Van Deusenville; RMC Place; BERKSHIRE; ▲ Great Barrington; **186** F-1; elev. 723ft./220m.; mail Great Barrington z 01230, Housatonic z 01236; ● 100
Varnumtown; RMC Place; MIDDLESEX; ▲ Dracut; ***187** B-12; elev. 200ft./61m.; ★ **BOS**; mail Dracut z 01826
Victory Hill; RMC Place; BERKSHIRE; ***186** D-2; elev. 1,230ft./375m.; ★ **PTSF**; mail Pittsfield z 01201; pop. incl. with Pittsfield (Inc. Place)
Village; RMC Place; NORFOLK; ▲ Medway; ***187** G-12; ★ **BOS**; mail Medway z 02053
Village of Nagog Woods; RMC Place; MIDDLESEX; ▲ Acton; ***187** D-12; elev. 250ft./76m.; 🅿; ★ **BOS**; z 01718; ● 275
Vineyard Haven (Tisbury); CDP; DUKES; ▲ Tisbury; **187** L-17; elev. 24ft./7m.; 🅿; z 02568, z 02573 & mail Oak Bluffs z 02557, West Tisbury z 02575; Ⓟ 1,762; © 2,048
Vineyard Highlands; RMC Place; DUKES; ▲ Oak Bluffs; ***187** L-17; elev. 40ft./12m.; mail Oak Bluffs z 02557

W

Waban; RMC Place; MIDDLESEX; **186** L-5; elev. 130ft./40m.; 🅿; ★ **BOS**; z 02468; pop. incl. with Newton (Inc. Place)
Wachusett; RMC Place; WORCESTER; ***186** D-10; elev. 805ft./245m.; ★ **BOS**; mail Fitchburg z 01420
Waites Corner; RMC Place; WORCESTER; ***186** C-10; elev. 700ft./213m.; ★ **BOS**; mail Fitchburg z 01420; pop. incl. with Fitchburg (Inc. Place)
Wakeby; RMC Place; BARNSTABLE; ▲ Sandwich; **187** J-18; elev. 110ft./34m.; ★ **BARN**; mail Sandwich z 02563; ● 100
Wakefield; CDP; MIDDLESEX; ▲ Wakefield; **187** D-14; elev. 100ft./30m.; 🅿; ★ **BOS**; z 01880; Ⓟ 24,825; © 24,804; ◆ 24,973
Wakefield; MCD-Town; MIDDLESEX; ***187** D-14; 🅿; ★ **BOS**; z 01880; Ⓟ 24,825; © 24,804; ◆ 24,973
Wakefield Center; RMC Place; MIDDLESEX; ▲ Wakefield; ***187** N-20; ★ **BOS**; mail Wakefield z 01880
Wakefield Junction; RMC Place; MIDDLESEX; ▲ Wakefield; ***187** D-14; elev. 90ft./27m.; ★ **BOS**; mail Wakefield z 01880
Wales; RMC Place; HAMPDEN; ▲ Wales; **186** G-8; elev. 949ft./289m.; 🅿; z 01081; ● 800
Wales; MCD-Town; HAMPDEN; ***186** G-8; 🅿; z 01081; Ⓟ 1,566; © 1,737
Wallis Street; RMC Place; ESSEX; ***187** D-15; ★ **BOS**; mail Peabody z 01960; pop. incl. with Peabody (Inc. Place)
Walnut Hill; RMC Place; MIDDLESEX; ***187** D-14; elev. 75ft./23m.; ★ **BOS**; mail Woburn z 01801; pop. incl. with Woburn (Inc. Place)
Walpole; CDP; NORFOLK; ▲ Walpole; **187** G-13; elev. 150ft./46m.; 🅿; ★ **BOS**; z 02081 & mail East Walpole z 02032, South Walpole z 02071; Ⓟ 5,495; © 5,867
Walpole; MCD-Town; NORFOLK; ***187** G-13; 🅿; ★ **BOS**; z 02081 & mail East Walpole z 02032, South Walpole z 02071; Ⓟ 20,212; © 22,824; ◆ 23,240
Waltham; Inc. Place; MIDDLESEX; **187** E-13; elev. 50ft./15m.; 🅿 🅷 🅲 10,686 ■; ★ **BOS**; z 02451-54 & mail North Waltham z 02455; Ⓟ 57,878; © 59,226; ◆ 60,706
Waltham Highlands; RMC Place; MIDDLESEX; ***187** E-13; elev. 160ft./49m.; ★ **BOS**; mail Waltham z 02451; pop. incl. with Waltham (Inc. Place)
Wamesit; RMC Place; MIDDLESEX; ▲ Tewksbury; **187** C-13; elev. 137ft./42m.; ★ **BOS**; mail Tewksbury z 01876; ● 2,700
Wampum Corner; RMC Place; NORFOLK; ▲ Wrentham; ***187** G-13; ★ **BOS**; mail Wrentham z 02093
Wapping; RMC Place; FRANKLIN; ▲ Deerfield; **186** D-5; elev. 150ft./46m.; mail Deerfield z 01342; ● 110
Waquoit; BARNSTABLE; see Waquoit Village (RMC Place)
Waquoit Village (Waquoit); RMC Place; BARNSTABLE; ▲ Falmouth; **187** K-17; mail East Falmouth z 02536; ● 500
Ward Hill; RMC Place; ESSEX; ***187** B-14; elev. 64ft./20m.; 🅿; ★ **BOS**; z 01835; pop. incl. with Haverhill (Inc. Place)
Ware; CDP; HAMPSHIRE; ▲ Ware; **186** F-7; elev. 475ft./145m.; 🅿 🅷; ★ **SPRG**; z 01082; Ⓟ 6,533; © 6,174
Ware; MCD-Town; HAMPSHIRE; ***186** F-7; 🅿; ★ **SPRG**; z 01082; Ⓟ 9,808; © 9,707; ◆ 9,902
Ware Center; RMC Place; HAMPSHIRE; ▲ Ware; ***186** F-7; elev. 503ft./153m.; ★ **SPRG**; mail Ware z 01082; rural
Wareham; PLYMOUTH; see Wareham Center (CDP)
Wareham; MCD-Town; PLYMOUTH; ***187** J-16; 🅿; ★ **BOS**; z 02571; Ⓟ 19,232; © 20,335; ◆ 21,399
Wareham Center (Wareham); CDP; PLYMOUTH; ▲ Wareham; **187** J-16; elev. 20ft./6m.; ★ **BOS**; mail Wareham z 02571; Ⓟ 2,607; © 2,874
Warren; CDP; WORCESTER; ▲ Warren; **186** F-8; elev. 605ft./184m.; 🅿; z 01083; Ⓟ 1,516; © 1,452
Warren; MCD-Town; WORCESTER; ***186** F-8; 🅿; z 01083; Ⓟ 4,437; © 4,776
Warrentown; RMC Place; PLYMOUTH; ▲ Middleborough; **187** H-15; elev. 29ft./9m.; ★ **BOS**; mail Middleboro z 02346; ● 370
Warwick; RMC Place; FRANKLIN; ▲ Warwick; **186** C-7; elev. 937ft./286m.; 🅿; z 01364, z 01378; ● 250
Warwick; MCD-Town; FRANKLIN; ***186** C-7; 🅿; z 01364, z 01378; Ⓟ 740; © 750
Washington; RMC Place; BERKSHIRE; ▲ Washington; **186** E-2; elev. 1,412ft./430m.; 🅿; z 01223 & mail Hinsdale z 01235; ● 100
Washington; MCD-Town; BERKSHIRE; ***186** E-2; 🅿; z 01223; Ⓟ 615; © 544
Watertown; Inc. Place; MIDDLESEX; **187** E-13; elev. 36ft./11m.; 🅿; ★ **BOS**; z 02471-72, z 02477; Ⓟ 33,284; © 32,986; ◆ 32,783
Waterville; RMC Place; PLYMOUTH; ▲ Middleborough; **187** H-15; elev. 117ft./36m.; ★ **BOS**; mail Middleboro z 02346; ● 200
Waterville; RMC Place; WORCESTER; ▲ Winchendon; **186** C-8; elev. 910ft./277m.; ★ **BOS**; mail Winchendon z 01475; ● 800
Watuppa; RMC Place; BRISTOL; ***187** N-20; ★ **F.R.**; mail Fall River z 02721; pop. incl. with Fall River (Inc. Place)
Wauwinet; RMC Place; NANTUCKET; ▲ Nantucket; ***187** M-20; elev. 10ft./3m.; mail Nantucket z 02554; summer pop. 500; ● 80
Waverley; RMC Place; MIDDLESEX; ▲ Belmont; ***187** E-13; elev. 70ft./21m.; 🅿; ★ **BOS**; z 02479
Wawela Park; RMC Place; WORCESTER; ▲ Webster; ***186** G-10; elev. 500ft./152m.; ★ **WORC**; mail Webster z 01570
Wayland; RMC Place; MIDDLESEX; ▲ Wayland; **187** E-12; elev. 127ft./39m.; 🅿; ★ **BOS**; z 01778; ● 2,500
Wayland; MCD-Town; MIDDLESEX; ***187** E-12; 🅿; ★ **BOS**; z 01778; Ⓟ 11,874; © 13,100; ◆ 13,857
Wayside Inn; RMC Place; MIDDLESEX; ▲ Sudbury; ***187** E-12; ★ **BOS**; mail Sudbury z 01776; rural
Webster; CDP; WORCESTER; ▲ Webster; **186** G-9; 🅿 🅷; ★ **WORC**; z 01570 & mail Dudley z 01571; Ⓟ 11,849; © 11,600
Webster; MCD-Town; WORCESTER; ***186** G-10; 🅿; ★ **WORC**; z 01570; Ⓟ 16,196; © 16,415; ◆ 15,781
Webster Square; RMC Place; WORCESTER; ***186** F-10; elev. 477ft./145m.; ★ **WORC**; mail Worcester z 01603; pop. incl. with Worcester (Inc. Place)
Wedgemere; RMC Place; MIDDLESEX; ▲ Winchester; ***187** D-14; elev. 25ft./8m.; ★ **BOS**; mail Winchester z 01890
Weir Village; RMC Place; BRISTOL; ***187** I-14; elev. 50ft./15m.; ★ **BOS**; mail Taunton z 02780; pop. incl. with Taunton (Inc. Place)
Wellesley; CDP; NORFOLK; ▲ Wellesley; **187** F-13; elev. 141ft./43m.; 🅿 🅷 🅲 2,237; ★ **BOS**; z 02481-82 & mail Babson Park z 02457; Ⓟ 26,615; © 26,613; ◆ 26,696
Wellesley; MCD-Town; NORFOLK; ***187** E-13; 🅿 🅲 5,596 ■; ★ **BOS**; z 02481-82 & mail Babson Park z 02457; Ⓟ 26,615; © 26,613; ◆ 26,696
Wellesley Farms; RMC Place; NORFOLK; ▲ Wellesley; **186** L-4; elev. 200ft./61m.; ★ **BOS**; mail Wellesley Hills z 02481
Wellesley Fells; RMC Place; NORFOLK; ▲ Wellesley; **186** L-4; elev. 160ft./49m.; ★ **BOS**; mail Wellesley z 02482
Wellesley Hills; RMC Place; NORFOLK; ▲ Wellesley; **186** L-4; elev. 137ft./42m.; 🅿; ★ **BOS**; z 02481
Wellfleet; RMC Place; BARNSTABLE; ▲ Wellfleet; **187** H-20; elev. 50ft./15m.; 🅿; z 02667; ● 1,200
Wellfleet; MCD-Town; BARNSTABLE; ***187** H-20; 🅿; z 02667; Ⓟ 2,493; © 2,749
Wellington; RMC Place; MIDDLESEX; **186** J-7; elev. 8ft./2m.; ★ **BOS**; mail Medford z 02155; pop. incl. with Medford (Inc. Place)
Wellville; RMC Place; WORCESTER; ▲ Ashburnham; **186** C-9; elev. 1,150ft./351m.; ★ **BOS**; mail Ashburnham z 01430; summer pop. 300; ● 110
Wendell; RMC Place; FRANKLIN; ▲ Wendell; **186** D-7; elev. 1,164ft./355m.; 🅿; z 01379; ● 400
Wendell; MCD-Town; FRANKLIN; ***186** D-6; 🅿; z 01379; Ⓟ 899; © 986
Wendell Depot; RMC Place; FRANKLIN; ▲ Wendell; **186** C-7; elev. 500ft./152m.; 🅿; z 01380; ● 90
Wenham; RMC Place; ESSEX; ▲ Wenham; **187** C-15; elev. 60ft./18m.; 🅿 🅲 1,528; ★ **BOS**; z 01984; ● 4,212
Wenham; MCD-Town; ESSEX; ***187** C-15; 🅿 🅲 1,528; ★ **BOS**; z 01984; Ⓟ 4,212; © 4,440; ◆ 4,472
Wenham; RMC Place; PLYMOUTH; ▲ Carver; ***187** H-16; ★ **BOS**; mail North Carver z 02355; ● 200
West Abington; RMC Place; PLYMOUTH; ▲ Abington; ***187** G-15; elev. 147ft./45m.; ★ **BOS**; mail Abington z 02351
West Acton; RMC Place; MIDDLESEX; ▲ Acton; **187** D-12; elev. 222ft./68m.; ★ **BOS**; mail Acton z 01720; ● 5,200
West Andover; RMC Place; ESSEX; ▲ Andover; **187** C-14; elev. 150ft./46m.; ★ **BOS**; mail Andover z 01810; ● 2,000
West Auburn; RMC Place; WORCESTER; ▲ Auburn; ***186** F-10; elev. 626ft./191m.; ★ **WORC**; mail Auburn z 01501
West Barnstable; RMC Place; BARNSTABLE; ***187** J-18; elev. 43ft./13m.; 🅿; ★ **BARN**; z 02668; pop. incl. with Barnstable (Inc. Place)
West Becket; RMC Place; BERKSHIRE; ▲ Becket; **186** F-2; elev. 1,415ft./431m.; mail Lee z 01238; ● 50
West Bedford; RMC Place; MIDDLESEX; ▲ Bedford; ***187** D-13; elev. 136ft./41m.; ★ **BOS**; mail Bedford z 01730
West Berlin; RMC Place; WORCESTER; ▲ Berlin; **187** E-11; elev. 309ft./94m.; ★ **BOS**; mail Berlin z 01503; ● 100
West Billerica; RMC Place; MIDDLESEX; ▲ Billerica; ***187** C-13; ★ **BOS**; mail North Billerica z 01862; ● 1,950
Westborough; CDP; WORCESTER; ▲ Westborough; **187** F-11; 🅿 🅷; ★ **WORC**; z 01580-82; Ⓟ 3,917; © 3,983
Westborough; MCD-Town; WORCESTER; ***187** F-11; 🅿; ★ **WORC**; z 01580-82; Ⓟ 14,133; © 17,997; ◆ 19,458
West Boxford; RMC Place; ESSEX; ▲ Boxford; **187** B-14; elev. 144ft./44m.; 🅿; ★ **BOS**; z 01885; ● 800
West Boylston; RMC Place; WORCESTER; ▲ West Boylston; **186** E-10; elev. 481ft./147m.; 🅿; ★ **WORC**; z 01583; ● 3,300
West Boylston; MCD-Town; WORCESTER; ***186** E-10; 🅿; ★ **WORC**; z 01583; Ⓟ 6,611; © 7,481; ◆ 8,099
West Bridgewater (West Bridgewater Center); RMC Place; PLYMOUTH; ▲ West Bridgewater; **187** H-15; elev. 65ft./20m.; 🅿; ★ **BOS**; z 02379; ● 2,100
West Bridgewater; MCD-Town; PLYMOUTH; ***187** H-14; 🅿; ★ **BOS**; z 02379; Ⓟ 6,389; © 6,634; ◆ 6,514
West Bridgewater Center; PLYMOUTH; see West Bridgewater (RMC Place)
West Brimfield; RMC Place; HAMPDEN; ▲ Brimfield; ***186** F-7; elev. 396ft./121m.; mail Palmer z 01069
West Brookfield; CDP; WORCESTER; ▲ West Brookfield; **186** F-8; elev. 633ft./193m.; 🅿; ★ **WORC**; z 01585; Ⓟ 1,419; © 1,610
West Brookfield; MCD-Town; WORCESTER; ***186** F-8; 🅿; ★ **WORC**; z 01585; Ⓟ 3,532; © 3,804; ◆ 3,772
Westbrook Village (Hancock Village); RMC Place; NORFOLK; ▲ Brookline; ***187** E-14; elev. 165ft./50m.; ★ **BOS**; mail Brookline z 02445
West Cambridge; RMC Place; MIDDLESEX; ***187** N-20; ★ **BOS**; mail Cambridge z 02138; pop. incl. with Cambridge (Inc. Place)
West Chatham; CDP; BARNSTABLE; ▲ Chatham; **187** J-20; elev. 50ft./15m.; 🅿; ★ **BARN**; z 02669; Ⓟ 1,504; © 1,446
West Chelmsford; RMC Place; MIDDLESEX; ▲ Chelmsford; ***187** C-12; elev. 141ft./43m.; ★ **BOS**; mail North Chelmsford z 01863
Westchester; RMC Place; WORCESTER; ***186** F-10; elev. 750ft./229m.; ★ **WORC**; mail Worcester z 01605; pop. incl. with Worcester (Inc. Place)
West Chesterfield; RMC Place; HAMPSHIRE; ▲ Chesterfield; **186** E-4; elev. 770ft./235m.; 🅿; z 01084; ● 200
West Chop; RMC Place; DUKES; ▲ Tisbury; ***187** L-17; elev. 8ft./2m.; 🅿; z 02573
West Concord; CDP; MIDDLESEX; ▲ Concord; **187** D-12; elev. 131ft./40m.; ★ **BOS**; mail Concord z 01742; Ⓟ 5,761; © 5,632
West Cummington; RMC Place; HAMPSHIRE; ▲ Cummington; **186** D-3; elev. 1,200ft./366m.; mail Cummington z 01026; ● 150
Westdale; RMC Place; PLYMOUTH; ▲ East Bridgewater; ***187** H-15; elev. 75ft./23m.; ★ **BOS**; mail East Bridgewater z 02333; ● 800
West Deerfield; RMC Place; FRANKLIN; ▲ Deerfield; ***186** D-5; elev. 301ft./92m.; mail Deerfield z 01342
West Dennis; CDP; BARNSTABLE; ▲ Dennis; **187** J-19; elev. 28ft./9m.; 🅿; ★ **BARN**; z 02670; Ⓟ 2,307; © 2,570
West Dudley; RMC Place; WORCESTER; ▲ Dudley; **186** G-9; elev. 400ft./122m.; ★ **WORC**; mail Dudley z 01571; ● 300
West Duxbury; RMC Place; PLYMOUTH; ▲ Duxbury; ***187** G-16; elev. 123ft./37m.; ★ **BOS**; mail Duxbury z 02332
West Falmouth; CDP; BARNSTABLE; ▲ Falmouth; **187** K-17; elev. 24ft./7m.; 🅿; z 02574; Ⓟ 1,752; © 1,867
West Farms; RMC Place; HAMPSHIRE; ***186** E-5; elev. 314ft./96m.; ★ **SPRG**; mail Florence z 01062; pop. incl. with Northampton (Inc. Place)
Westfield; Inc. Place; HAMPDEN; **186** G-4; elev. 140ft./43m.; 🅿 🅷 🅲 5,345 ■; ★ **SPRG**; z 01085-86; Ⓟ 38,372; © 40,072; ◆ 40,373
West Fitchburg; RMC Place; WORCESTER; ***186** C-10; elev. 670ft./204m.; ★ **BOS**; mail Fitchburg z 01420; pop. incl. with Fitchburg (Inc. Place)
Westford; RMC Place; MIDDLESEX; ▲ Westford; **187** C-12; elev. 406ft./124m.; 🅿; ★ **BOS**; z 01886; ● 1,400
Westford; MCD-Town; MIDDLESEX; ***187** C-12; 🅿; ★ **BOS**; z 01886; Ⓟ 16,392; © 20,754; ◆ 22,406
West Foxboro; RMC Place; NORFOLK; ▲ Foxborough; **187** G-13; elev. 328ft./100m.; ★ **BOS**; mail Foxboro z 02035; ● 1,100
Westgate Park; RMC Place; BRISTOL; ***187** J-15; ★ **N.BED**; mail New Bedford z 02745; pop. incl. with New Bedford (Inc. Place)
West Gloucester; RMC Place; ESSEX; ***187** C-16; elev. 50ft./15m.; ★ **BOS**; mail Gloucester z 01930; pop. incl. with Gloucester (Inc. Place)
West Granville; RMC Place; HAMPDEN; ▲ Granville; **186** G-3; elev. 1,230ft./375m.; mail Granville z 01034; ● 175
West Groton; RMC Place; MIDDLESEX; ▲ Groton; **187** C-11; elev. 240ft./73m.; 🅿; ★ **BOS**; z 01472; ● 900
Westhampton; RMC Place; HAMPSHIRE; ▲ Westhampton; **186** E-4; elev. 730ft./223m.; 🅿; z 01027; ● 300
Westhampton; MCD-Town; HAMPSHIRE; ***186** E-4; 🅿; z 01027; Ⓟ 1,327; © 1,468
West Hanover; RMC Place; PLYMOUTH; ▲ Hanover; **187** G-15; elev. 84ft./26m.; ★ **BOS**; mail Hanover z 02339; ● 1,700
West Harwich; RMC Place; BARNSTABLE; ▲ Harwich; **187** J-20; elev. 20ft./6m.; 🅿; ★ **BARN**; z 02671; ● 1,500
West Hatfield (Hatfield); RMC Place; HAMPSHIRE; ▲ Hatfield; **186** E-5; elev. 160ft./49m.; 🅿; ★ **SPRG**; z 01088 & mail Hatfield z 01038; ● 350
West Hawley; RMC Place; FRANKLIN; ***186** D-3; elev. 1,080ft./329m.; mail Charlemont z 01339
West Hingham; RMC Place; PLYMOUTH; ▲ Hingham; **186** M-9; elev. 40ft./12m.; ★ **BOS**; mail Hingham z 02043
West Hyannisport; RMC Place; BARNSTABLE; ***187** K-19; elev. 15ft./5m.; 🅿; ★ **BARN**; z 02672; pop. incl. with Barnstable (Inc. Place)
Westlands; RMC Place; MIDDLESEX; ▲ Chelmsford; ***187** C-13; elev. 140ft./43m.; ★ **BOS**; mail Chelmsford z 01824
West Leominster; RMC Place; WORCESTER; ***186** D-10; elev. 430ft./131m.; ★ **BOS**; mail Leominster z 01453; pop. incl. with Leominster (Inc. Place)
West Leyden; RMC Place; FRANKLIN; ▲ Leyden; ***186** B-5; elev. 490ft./149m.; mail Bernardston z 01337; rural
West Lynn; RMC Place; ESSEX; **186** I-8; elev. 12ft./4m.; 🅿; ★ **BOS**; z 01905; pop. incl. with Lynn (Inc. Place)
West Manchester; RMC Place; ESSEX; ▲ Manchester-by-the-Sea; ***187** C-16; elev. 20ft./6m.; ★ **BOS**; mail Manchester z 01944
West Mansfield; RMC Place; BRISTOL; ▲ Mansfield; **187** H-13; elev. 142ft./43m.; ★ **BOS**; mail Mansfield z 02048; ● 650
West Medford; RMC Place; MIDDLESEX; **186** J-6; elev. 50ft./15m.; 🅿; ★ **BOS**; z 02156 & mail Medford z 02155; pop. incl. with Medford (Inc. Place)
West Medway; RMC Place; NORFOLK; ▲ Medway; **187** G-12; elev. 200ft./61m.; ★ **BOS**; mail Medway z 02053; ● 2,000
West Millbury; RMC Place; WORCESTER; ▲ Millbury; **186** F-10; elev. 640ft./195m.; 🅿; ★ **WORC**; z 01586; ● 300
Westminster; RMC Place; WORCESTER; ▲ Westminster; **186** D-9; elev. 1,080ft./329m.; 🅿; ★ **BOS**; z 01441, z 01473; ● 1,100
Westminster; MCD-Town; WORCESTER; ***186** D-9; 🅿; ★ **BOS**; z 01441, z 01473; Ⓟ 6,191; © 6,907; ◆ 7,176
West Natick; RMC Place; MIDDLESEX; ▲ Natick; **186** M-3; elev. 160ft./49m.; ★ **BOS**; mail Natick z 01760
West New Boston; RMC Place; BERKSHIRE; ▲ Sandisfield; ***186** G-3; elev. 887ft./270m.; mail Sandisfield z 01255
West Newbury; RMC Place; ESSEX; ▲ West Newbury; **187** B-15; 🅿; ★ **BOS**; z 01985; ● 1,100
West Newbury; MCD-Town; ESSEX; ***187** B-15; 🅿; ★ **BOS**; z 01985; Ⓟ 3,421; © 4,149; ◆ 4,296
West Newton; RMC Place; MIDDLESEX; ***187** E-13; elev. 50ft./15m.; 🅿; ★ **BOS**; z 02465; pop. incl. with Newton (Inc. Place)
Weston; RMC Place; MIDDLESEX; ▲ Weston; **187** E-13; elev. 180ft./55m.; 🅿 🅲 1,314; ★ **BOS**; z 02493; ● 10,200
Weston; MCD-Town; MIDDLESEX; ***187** E-13; 🅿 🅲 1,314; ★ **BOS**; z 02493; Ⓟ 10,200; © 11,469; ◆ 12,250
West Orange; RMC Place; FRANKLIN; ▲ Orange; ***186** C-7; mail Orange z 01364; ● 40
West Otis; RMC Place; BERKSHIRE; ▲ Otis; ***186** F-2; elev. 1,366ft./416m.; 🅿; z 01245
West Peabody; RMC Place; ESSEX; ***187** D-15; elev. 73ft./22m.; ★ **BOS**; mail Peabody z 01960; pop. incl. with Peabody (Inc. Place)
West Pelham; RMC Place; HAMPSHIRE; ▲ Pelham; **186** E-6; elev. 368ft./112m.; mail Amherst z 01002; ● 550
Westport; BRISTOL; see North Westport (CDP-Census Area Only)
Westport; MCD-Town; BRISTOL; ***187** K-14; 🅿; ★ **F.R.**; z 02790; Ⓟ 13,852; © 14,183; ◆ 14,327
Westport Factory; RMC Place; BRISTOL; ▲ Westport; **187** K-14; elev. 50ft./15m.; ★ **N.BED**; mail Westport z 02790; ● 250
Westport Point; RMC Place; BRISTOL; ▲ Westport; **187** K-14; elev. 72ft./22m.; 🅿; ★ **F.R.**; z 02791; ● 600
West Quincy; RMC Place; NORFOLK; ***187** F-14; elev. 45ft./14m.; ★ **BOS**; mail Quincy z 02169; pop. incl. with Quincy (Inc. Place)
West Roxbury; RMC Place; SUFFOLK; **186** M-6; elev. 200ft./61m.; 🅿; ★ **BOS**; z 02132; pop. incl. with Boston (Inc. Place)
West Royalston; RMC Place; WORCESTER; ▲ Royalston; ***186** B-7; elev. 901ft./275m.; mail Athol z 01331; rural
West Side; RMC Place; WORCESTER; ***186** F-10; ★ **WORC**; mail Worcester z 01602; pop. incl. with Worcester (Inc. Place)
West Somerville; RMC Place; MIDDLESEX; ***187** E-14; elev. 30ft./9m.; 🅿; ★ **BOS**; z 02144; pop. incl. with Somerville (Inc. Place)
West Springfield; CDP-Census Area Only; HAMPDEN; ▲ West Springfield; **186** G-5; elev. 65ft./20m.; 🅿; ★ **SPRG**; z 01089-90; Ⓟ 27,537; © 27,899
West Springfield; Inc. Place; HAMPDEN; ***187** N-20; elev. 65ft./20m.; 🅿 ■; z 01089-90; incorporated April 1, 2000; not reported in 2000 Census; ● 27,900; ◆ 28,041
West Sterling; RMC Place; WORCESTER; ▲ Sterling; **186** D-10; elev. 488ft./149m.; ★ **WORC**; mail Sterling z 01564; ● 100
West Stockbridge; RMC Place; BERKSHIRE; ▲ West Stockbridge; **186** E-1; elev. 901ft./275m.; 🅿; z 01266; ● 850
West Stockbridge; MCD-Town; BERKSHIRE; ***186** E-1; 🅿; z 01266; Ⓟ 1,483; © 1,416
West Stockbridge Center; RMC Place; BERKSHIRE; ▲ West Stockbridge; **186** E-1; elev. 1,160ft./354m.; mail West Stockbridge z 01266; ● 120
West Stoughton; RMC Place; NORFOLK; ▲ Stoughton; ***187** G-14; elev. 150ft./46m.; ★ **BOS**; mail Stoughton z 02072
West Sutton; RMC Place; WORCESTER; ▲ Sutton; **186** G-10; elev. 650ft./198m.; ★ **WORC**; mail Millbury z 01527; ● 200
West Tatnuck; RMC Place; WORCESTER; **187** B-18; elev. 900ft./274m.; ★ **WORC**; mail Worcester z 01602; pop. incl. with Worcester (Inc. Place)
West Tisbury; RMC Place; DUKES; ▲ Tisbury; **187** M-16; elev. 37ft./11m.; 🅿; z 02575 & mail Vineyard Haven z 02568; ● 600
West Tisbury; MCD-Town; DUKES; ***187** L-17; 🅿; z 02575 & mail Vineyard Haven z 02568; Ⓟ 1,704; © 2,467
West Townsend; RMC Place; MIDDLESEX; ▲ Townsend; **186** C-10; elev. 331ft./101m.; 🅿; ★ **BOS**; z 01474; ● 700
West Upton; RMC Place; WORCESTER; ▲ Upton; **187** F-11; elev. 300ft./91m.; ★ **BOS**; mail Upton z 01568; ● 1,100
Westview; RMC Place; NORFOLK; ***187** G-12; elev. 250ft./76m.; ★ **BOS**; mail Franklin z 02038; pop. incl. with Franklin (Inc. Place)
Westville; RMC Place; BRISTOL; ***187** I-14; elev. 50ft./15m.; ★ **BOS**; mail Taunton z 02780; pop. incl. with Taunton (Inc. Place)
West Walpole; RMC Place; NORFOLK; ▲ Walpole; **187** G-13; ★ **BOS**; mail Walpole z 02081; ● 150
West Ware; RMC Place; HAMPSHIRE; ▲ Ware; ***186** F-7; ★ **SPRG**; mail Ware z 01082; rural
West Wareham (Tremont); CDP; PLYMOUTH; ▲ Wareham; **187** I-16; elev. 40ft./12m.; 🅿; ★ **BOS**; z 02576; Ⓟ 2,059; © 1,908
West Warren; RMC Place; WORCESTER; ▲ Warren; **186** F-7; elev. 534ft./163m.; 🅿; z 01092; ● 1,300
West Watertown; RMC Place; MIDDLESEX; ***187** N-20; ★ **BOS**; mail Watertown z 02472; pop. incl. with Watertown (Inc. Place)
West Whately; RMC Place; FRANKLIN; ▲ Whately; **186** D-5; elev. 571ft./174m.; 🅿; z 01039; pop. incl. with Easthampton (Inc. Place)
West Wind Shores; RMC Place; PLYMOUTH; ▲ Plymouth; ***187** N-20; ★ **BOS**; mail Buzzards Bay z 02532; ● 200
Westwood; RMC Place; NORFOLK; ▲ Westwood; **187** F-13; 🅿 🅷; ★ **BOS**; z 02090; ● 6,500
Westwood; MCD-Town; NORFOLK; ***187** F-13; 🅿; ★ **BOS**; z 02090; Ⓟ 12,557; © 14,117; ◆ 14,600
West Worthington; RMC Place; HAMPSHIRE; ▲ Worthington; ***186** E-3; elev. 1,504ft./458m.; mail Worthington z 01098; rural
West Wrentham; RMC Place; NORFOLK; **187** H-12; elev. 375ft./114m.; ★ **BOS**; mail Sheldonville z 02070; ● 150
West Yarmouth; CDP; BARNSTABLE; ▲ Yarmouth; **187** J-19; elev. 20ft./6m.; 🅿; ★ **BARN**; z 02673; Ⓟ 5,409; © 6,460
Wethersfield; RMC Place; NORFOLK; ▲ Bellingham; ***187** G-12; elev. 246ft./75m.; ★ **BOS**; mail Bellingham z 02019
Weweantic; CDP-Census Area Only; PLYMOUTH; ▲ Wareham; ***187** J-16; elev. 10ft./3m.; ★ **BOS**; mail Wareham z 02571; Ⓟ 1,812; © 1,903
Weymouth; CDP; NORFOLK; ▲ Weymouth; **187** F-15; elev. 90ft./27m.; 🅿; ★ **BOS**; z 02188-91; Ⓟ 54,063; © 53,988; ◆ 54,144
Weymouth; MCD-Town; NORFOLK; ***187** F-15; 🅿 ■; ★ **BOS**; z 02188-91; Ⓟ 54,063; © 53,988; ◆ 54,144
Weymouth Heights; RMC Place; NORFOLK; ▲ Weymouth; **186** N-9; elev. 35ft./11m.; ★ **BOS**; mail Weymouth z 02188
Weymouth Landing; RMC Place; NORFOLK; ▲ Weymouth; ***187** F-15; elev. 10ft./3m.; ★ **BOS**; mail Weymouth z 02188
Whalom; RMC Place; WORCESTER; ▲ Lunenburg; **186** C-10; elev. 510ft./155m.; ★ **BOS**; mail Fitchburg z 01420; ● 1,400
Whately; RMC Place; FRANKLIN; ▲ Whately; **186** D-5; 🅿; z 01093 & mail South Deerfield z 01373; ● 630
Whately; MCD-Town; FRANKLIN; ***186** D-5; 🅿; z 01093 & mail South Deerfield z 01373; Ⓟ 1,375; © 1,573; Ⓡ 1,563
Wheelockville; RMC Place; WORCESTER; ▲ Uxbridge; **187** G-11; elev. 242ft./74m.; ★ **WORC**; mail Uxbridge z 01569; ● 500
Wheelwright; RMC Place; WORCESTER; ▲ Hardwick; **186** E-8; elev. 590ft./180m.; 🅿; z 01094; ● 500
White City; RMC Place; WORCESTER; ▲ Hopedale; ***187** G-11; elev. 350ft./107m.; ★ **BOS**; mail Hopedale z 01747
White Horse Beach; RMC Place; PLYMOUTH; ▲ Plymouth; **187** H-17; elev. 25ft./8m.; 🅿; ★ **BOS**; z 02381; ● 1,250
White Island Shores; CDP; PLYMOUTH; ▲ Wareham; **187** I-17; elev. 81ft./25m.; ★ **BOS**; mail East Wareham z 02538; Ⓟ 1,827; © 2,133
White Oaks; RMC Place; BERKSHIRE; ▲ Williamstown; ***186** B-2; elev. 656ft./200m.; mail Williamstown z 01267
White Valley; RMC Place; WORCESTER; ▲ Barre; ***186** E-8; ★ **WORC**; mail Barre z 01005; ● 100
Whitins; WORCESTER; see Linwood (RMC Place)
Whitinsville; CDP; WORCESTER; ▲ Northbridge; **187** G-11; elev. 303ft./92m.; 🅿; ★ **WORC**; z 01588; Ⓟ 5,639; © 6,340
Whitman; RMC Place; PLYMOUTH; ▲ Whitman; **187** G-15; elev. 110ft./34m.; 🅿; ★ **BOS**; z 02382; ● 13,240

Entries in **UPPERCASE** are counties.
Entries in **bold** have populations of 2,500 or more.
Names in parentheses are alternate names.

Inc. Place	Incorporated Place
RMC Place	Rand McNally Designated Place
CDP	Census Designated Place
MCD	Minor Civil Division
⊡	County Seat
▲	Minor Civil Division
elev.	Elevation
🅿	Post Office
🅷	Hospital
🅲	College
■	Principal Business Center
★	Ranally Metro Area (RMA) Abbreviation
z	Zip Code(s)
Ⓟ	Previous Census Population
Ⓡ	Revised Census Population
Ⓐ	Annexation Population
●	Rand McNally Population Estimate
©	Final Census Population
Ⓢ	Special Census Population
◆	Estimated Population

For additional definitions see Glossary, Volume 1, and Introduction, Volume 2.

Whitman; MCD-Town; PLYMOUTH; ***187** G-15; 🅿; ★ **BOS**; **z** 02382; Ⓟ 13,240; © 13,882; ◆ 14,027
Whittenton; RMC Place; BRISTOL; ***187** H-14; elev. 57ft./17m.; ★ **BOS**; mail Taunton **z** 02780; pop. incl. with Taunton (Inc. Place)
Wianno; RMC Place; BARNSTABLE; ***187** K-18; elev. 22ft./7m.; ★ **BARN**; mail Osterville **z** 02655; pop. incl. with Barnstable (Inc. Place)
Wigginsville; RMC Place; MIDDLESEX; ***187** N-20; ★ **BOS**; mail Lowell **z** 01850; pop. incl. with Lowell (Inc. Place)
Wilbraham; CDP; HAMPDEN; ▲ Wilbraham; **186** G-6; elev. 290ft./88m.; 🅿; ★ **SPRG**; **z** 01095; Ⓟ 3,352; © 3,544
Wilbraham; MCD-Town; HAMPDEN; ***186** G-6; 🅿; ★ **SPRG**; **z** 01095; Ⓟ 12,635; © 13,473; ◆ 13,764
Wilkinsonville; RMC Place; WORCESTER; ▲ Sutton; **186** F-10; elev. 338ft./103m.; 🅿; ★ **WORC**; **z** 01590 & mail Millbury **z** 01527; ● 900
Williamsburg; RMC Place; HAMPSHIRE; ▲ Williamsburg; **186** E-5; elev. 530ft./162m.; 🅿; ★ **SPRG**; **z** 01096; ● 1,200
Williamsburg; MCD-Town; HAMPSHIRE; ***186** E-5; 🅿; ★ **SPRG**; **z** 01096; Ⓟ 2,515; © 2,427; ◆ 2,446
Williamstown; CDP; BERKSHIRE; ▲ Williamstown; **186** B-2; elev. 638ft./194m.; 🅿 🅲 2,224; **z** 01267; Ⓟ 4,791; © 4,754
Williamstown; MCD-Town; BERKSHIRE; ***186** C-2; 🅿 🅲 2,224; **z** 01267; Ⓟ 8,220; © 8,424
Williamsville; RMC Place; BERKSHIRE; ▲ West Stockbridge; **186** F-1; elev. 791ft./241m.; mail Housatonic **z** 01236; ● 220
Williamsville; RMC Place; WORCESTER; ▲ Hubbardston; **186** D-8; elev. 820ft./250m.; mail Hubbardston **z** 01452; ● 100
Willimansett; RMC Place; HAMPDEN; **187** K-11; elev. 70ft./21m.; 🅿; ★ **SPRG**; **z** 01013; pop. incl. with Chicopee (Inc. Place)
Wilmington; CDP; MIDDLESEX; ▲ Wilmington, Tewksbury; **187** D-14; elev. 96ft./29m.; 🅿; ★ **BOS**; **z** 01887; Ⓟ 17,654; © 21,363; ◆ 22,365
Wilmington; MCD-Town; MIDDLESEX; ***187** C-14; 🅿; ★ **BOS**; **z** 01887; Ⓟ 17,651; © 21,363; ◆ 22,365
Wilson; RMC Place; ESSEX; ***187** N-20; ★ **BOS**; mail Gloucester **z** 01930; pop. incl. with Gloucester (Inc. Place)
Winchendon; CDP; WORCESTER; ▲ Winchendon; **186** C-9; elev. 1,000ft./305m.; 🅿; ★ **BOS**; **z** 01475; Ⓟ 4,316; © 4,246
Winchendon; MCD-Town; WORCESTER; ***186** C-9; 🅿; ★ **BOS**; **z** 01475; Ⓟ 8,805; © 9,611; ◆ 10,214
Winchendon Center; RMC Place; WORCESTER; ▲ Winchendon; ***186** C-9; elev. 1,230ft./375m.; ★ **BOS**; mail Winchendon **z** 01475; ● 100
Winchendon Springs; RMC Place; WORCESTER; ▲ Winchendon; **186** B-9; elev. 1,019ft./311m.; 🅿; ★ **BOS**; **z** 01477; ● 500
Winchester; CDP; MIDDLESEX; ▲ Winchester; **187** D-14; elev. 62ft./19m.; 🅿 🅷; ★ **BOS**; **z** 01890; Ⓟ 20,267; © 20,810; ◆ 21,307
Winchester; MCD-Town; MIDDLESEX; ***187** D-14; 🅿; ★ **BOS**; **z** 01890; Ⓟ 20,267; © 20,810; ◆ 21,307
Winchester Highlands; RMC Place; MIDDLESEX; ▲ Winchester; ***187** D-14; elev. 146ft./45m.; ★ **BOS**; mail Winchester **z** 01890
Windsor; RMC Place; BERKSHIRE; ▲ Windsor; **186** D-3; elev. 2,031ft./619m.; 🅿; **z** 01270; ● 200
Windsor; MCD-Town; BERKSHIRE; ***186** D-3; 🅿; **z** 01270; Ⓟ 770; © 875
Winnecunnet; RMC Place; BRISTOL; ▲ Norton; **187** H-14; elev. 70ft./21m.; ★ **BOS**; mail Norton **z** 02766; ● 450
Winnmere (Wynnmere); RMC Place; MIDDLESEX; ▲ Burlington; ***187** D-13; ★ **BOS**; mail Burlington **z** 01803
Winslows; RMC Place; NORFOLK; ▲ Norwood; ***187** F-13; elev. 170ft./52m.; ★ **BOS**; mail Norwood **z** 02062
Winter Hill; RMC Place; MIDDLESEX; ***187** E-14; elev. 120ft./37m.; 🅿; ★ **BOS**; **z** 02145; pop. incl. with Somerville (Inc. Place)
Winthrop; CDP; SUFFOLK; ▲ Winthrop; **187** E-15; elev. 36ft./11m.; 🅿; ★ **BOS**; **z** 02152; Ⓟ 18,127; © 18,303
Winthrop; MCD-Town; SUFFOLK; ***187** E-15; 🅿; ★ **BOS**; **z** 02152; Ⓟ 18,127; © 18,303; ◆ 20,023
Winthrop Beach; RMC Place; SUFFOLK; ▲ Winthrop; ***187** E-15; ★ **BOS**; mail Winthrop **z** 02152
Winthrop Highlands; RMC Place; SUFFOLK; ▲ Winthrop; ***187** E-15; elev. 70ft./21m.; ★ **BOS**; mail Winthrop **z** 02152
Woburn; Inc. Place; MIDDLESEX; **187** D-14; elev. 100ft./30m.; 🅿 🅷 ■; ★ **BOS**; **z** 01801, **z** 01807, **z** 01813, **z** 01815, **z** 01888; Ⓟ 35,943; © 37,258; ◆ 36,787
Wollaston; RMC Place; NORFOLK; **186** M-8; elev. 27ft./8m.; 🅿; ★ **BOS**; **z** 02170; pop. incl. with Quincy (Inc. Place)
Woodland; RMC Place; WORCESTER; ***187** N-20; ★ **WORC**; pop. incl. with Worcester (Inc. Place)
Woodland Park; RMC Place; WORCESTER; ▲ Auburn; **187** C-19; elev. 550ft./168m.; ★ **WORC**; mail Auburn **z** 01501
Woods Hole; CDP; BARNSTABLE; ▲ Falmouth; **187** K-17; elev. 15ft./5m.; 🅿; **z** 02543; © 925
Woodville; RMC Place; MIDDLESEX; ▲ Hopkinton; **187** F-11; elev. 310ft./94m.; 🅿; ★ **BOS**; **z** 01784; ● 250
Worcester; Inc. Place; ⊡ WORCESTER; **186** F-10; elev. 480ft./146m.; 🅿 🅷 🅲 20,672 ■; ★ **WORC**; **z** 01601-10, **z** 01612-15, **z** 01653-55; Ⓟ 169,759; © 172,648; ◆ 172,480
WORCESTER; **186** D-8; Ⓟ 709,705; © 750,963; Ⓡ 749,973; ◆ 774,010
Woronoco; RMC Place; HAMPDEN; ▲ Russell; **186** G-4; elev. 256ft./78m.; 🅿; ★ **SPRG**; **z** 01097; ● 300
Woronoco Heights; RMC Place; HAMPDEN; ▲ Russell; ***186** G-4; elev. 1,000ft./305m.; ★ **SPRG**; mail Woronoco **z** 01097
Worthington; HAMPSHIRE; see Worthington Corners (RMC Place)
Worthington; MCD-Town; HAMPSHIRE; ***186** E-3; 🅿; **z** 01098; Ⓟ 1,156; © 1,270
Worthington Center; RMC Place; HAMPSHIRE; ▲ Worthington; **186** E-3; elev. 1,433ft./437m.; mail Worthington **z** 01098; ● 125
Worthington Corners (Worthington); RMC Place; HAMPSHIRE; ▲ Worthington; **186** E-3; mail Worthington **z** 01098; ● 550
Wrentham (Wrentham Center); RMC Place; NORFOLK; ▲ Wrentham; **187** G-13; elev. 253ft./77m.; 🅿; ★ **BOS**; **z** 02093 & mail Sheldonville **z** 02070; ● 2,250
Wrentham; MCD-Town; NORFOLK; ***187** G-12; 🅿; ★ **BOS**; **z** 02093 & mail Sheldonville **z** 02070; Ⓟ 9,006; © 10,554; ◆ 10,941
Wrentham Center; NORFOLK; see Wrentham (RMC Place)
Wyben; RMC Place; HAMPDEN; ***186** F-4; elev. 366ft./112m.; ★ **SPRG**; mail Westfield **z** 01085; pop. incl. with Westfield (Inc. Place)
Wynnmere; MIDDLESEX; see Winnmere (RMC Place)
Wyoming; RMC Place; MIDDLESEX; **186** I-7; elev. 55ft./17m.; ★ **BOS**; mail Melrose **z** 02176; pop. incl. with Melrose (Inc. Place)

Y

Yankee Orchards; RMC Place; BERKSHIRE; ***186** D-2; elev. 1,030ft./314m.; ★ **PTSF**; mail Pittsfield **z** 01201; pop. incl. with Pittsfield (Inc. Place)
Yarmouth; RMC Place; BARNSTABLE; ▲ Yarmouth; **187** J-19; elev. 30ft./9m.; ★ **BARN**; mail South Yarmouth **z** 02664, West Yarmouth **z** 02673, Yarmouth Port **z** 02675; ● 1,300
Yarmouth; BARNSTABLE; see Yarmouth Port (CDP)
Yarmouth; MCD-Town; BARNSTABLE; ***187** J-19; ★ **BARN**; mail South Yarmouth **z** 02664, West Yarmouth **z** 02673, Yarmouth Port **z** 02675; Ⓟ 21,174; © 24,807; ◆ 23,901
Yarmouth Port (Yarmouth); CDP; BARNSTABLE; ▲ Yarmouth; **187** J-19; elev. 40ft./12m.; 🅿; ★ **BARN**; **z** 02675 & mail South Yarmouth **z** 02664, West Yarmouth **z** 02673; Ⓟ 4,271; © 5,395

Z

Zoar; RMC Place; FRANKLIN; ▲ Charlemont; ***186** C-4; elev. 640ft./195m.; mail Rowe **z** 01367; rural
Zylonite; RMC Place; BERKSHIRE; ▲ Adams; ***186** C-3; elev. 700ft./213m.; ★ **PTSF**; mail Adams **z** 01220

MICHIGAN

Statistics

Total area (2000) — 96,716 square miles
Land area (2000) — 56,804 square miles
Water area (2000) — 39,912 square miles
Capital — Lansing
Admitted as state — January, 1837

Maps

State maps can be found on pages 142-254 in Vol. 1
County Subdivision maps can be found on pages 255-271 in Vol. 1

Ranally Metro Areas (RMAs) and Abbreviations

Battle Creek, MI — BTLCK
Benton Harbor-St. Joseph, MI — BNTH-
Detroit, MI-CAN. — DET
Elkhart, IN-MI — ELK
Flint, MI — FLN
Grand Rapids, MI — GDR
Holland, MI — HLND
Jackson, MI — JAC
Kalamazoo, MI — KZOO
Lansing, MI — LANS
Monroe, MI — MONR
Muskegon, MI — MUS
Port Huron, MI-CAN. — PTHU
Saginaw-Bay City-Midland, MI — SAG-
Sault Ste. Marie, MI-CAN. — SOO
South Bend, IN-MI — S.B.
Toledo, OH-MI — TOL

Principal Places

Place Name	Place Type	County	Population
Detroit	Inc. Place	WAYNE	◆ 911,811
Grand Rapids	Inc. Place	KENT	◆ 200,507
Warren	Inc. Place	MACOMB	◆ 131,979
Sterling Heights	Inc. Place	MACOMB	◆ 128,059
Ann Arbor	Inc. Place	WASHTENAW	◆ 121,701
Lansing	Inc. Place	INGHAM	◆ 118,970
Flint	Inc. Place	GENESEE	◆ 113,448
Livonia	Inc. Place	WAYNE	◆ 97,721
Clinton	CDP-Census Area Only	MACOMB	◆ 94,605
Clinton	MCD-Charter Township	MACOMB	◆ 94,605
Dearborn	Inc. Place	WAYNE	◆ 93,431
Westland	Inc. Place	WAYNE	◆ 84,949
Farmington Hills	Inc. Place	OAKLAND	◆ 80,776
Troy	Inc. Place	OAKLAND	◆ 79,965
Canton	CDP-Census Area Only	WAYNE	◆ 77,910
Canton	MCD-Charter Township	WAYNE	◆ 77,910
Kalamazoo	Inc. Place	KALAMAZOO	◆ 77,543
Southfield	Inc. Place	OAKLAND	◆ 76,857
Wyoming	Inc. Place	KENT	◆ 73,370
Shelby	CDP-Census Area Only	MACOMB	◆ 72,598
Shelby	MCD-Charter Township	MACOMB	◆ 72,598
Waterford	CDP	OAKLAND	◆ 70,813
Waterford	MCD-Charter Township	OAKLAND	◆ 70,813
Rochester Hills	Inc. Place	OAKLAND	◆ 68,945
West Bloomfield	MCD-Charter Township	OAKLAND	◆ 65,197
West Bloomfield Township	CDP-Census Area Only	OAKLAND	◆ 65,197
Pontiac	Inc. Place	OAKLAND	◆ 61,962
Taylor	Inc. Place	WAYNE	◆ 60,976
Macomb	MCD-Township	MACOMB	◆ 60,504
Saint Clair Shores	Inc. Place	MACOMB	◆ 58,873
Dearborn Heights	Inc. Place	WAYNE	◆ 55,993
Ypsilanti	MCD-Charter Township	WASHTENAW	◆ 55,754
Royal Oak	Inc. Place	OAKLAND	◆ 55,477
Saginaw	Inc. Place	SAGINAW	◆ 55,423
Battle Creek	Inc. Place	CALHOUN	◆ 51,512
Novi	Inc. Place	OAKLAND	◆ 49,909
Kentwood	Inc. Place	KENT	◆ 49,448
East Lansing	Inc. Place	INGHAM	◆ 48,490
Portage	Inc. Place	KALAMAZOO	◆ 47,397
Redford	CDP	WAYNE	◆ 46,700
Redford	MCD-Charter Township	WAYNE	◆ 46,700
Roseville	Inc. Place	MACOMB	◆ 45,117
Georgetown	MCD-Charter Township	OTTAWA	◆ 44,857
Chesterfield	MCD-Charter Township	MACOMB	◆ 43,601
Meridian	MCD-Charter Township	INGHAM	◆ 41,286
Bloomfield	MCD-Township	OAKLAND	◆ 41,126
Bloomfield Township	CDP-Census Area Only	OAKLAND	◆ 41,126
Midland	Inc. Place	MIDLAND	◆ 41,110
Muskegon	Inc. Place	MUSKEGON	◆ 38,741
Saginaw	MCD-Charter Township	SAGINAW	◆ 37,120
Lincoln Park	Inc. Place	WAYNE	◆ 36,473
Commerce	MCD-Charter Township	OAKLAND	◆ 36,125
Pittsfield	MCD-Charter Township	WASHTENAW	◆ 35,880
Jackson	Inc. Place	JACKSON	◆ 35,228
Bay City	Inc. Place	BAY	◆ 34,985
Orion	MCD-Charter Township	OAKLAND	◆ 34,473
Holland	MCD-Charter Township	OTTAWA	◆ 33,737
Holland	Inc. Place	OTTAWA	◆ 33,697
Independence	MCD-Charter Township	OAKLAND	◆ 33,536
Eastpointe	Inc. Place	MACOMB	◆ 33,136
Plainfield	MCD-Charter Township	KENT	◆ 32,696
Flint	MCD-Charter Township	GENESEE	◆ 31,768
Delta	MCD-Charter Township	EATON	◆ 30,737
Grand Blanc	MCD-Charter Township	GENESEE	◆ 30,309
Port Huron	Inc. Place	ST. CLAIR	◆ 30,123
Bedford	MCD-Township	MONROE	◆ 30,085
Burton	Inc. Place	GENESEE	◆ 29,894
White Lake	MCD-Charter Township	OAKLAND	◆ 29,094
Madison Heights	Inc. Place	OAKLAND	◆ 28,866
Oak Park	Inc. Place	OAKLAND	◆ 28,673
Inkster	Inc. Place	WAYNE	◆ 28,215
Mount Pleasant	Inc. Place	ISABELLA	◆ 28,013
Southgate	Inc. Place	WAYNE	◆ 27,903
Garden City	Inc. Place	WAYNE	◆ 27,191
Allen Park	Inc. Place	WAYNE	◆ 26,520
Plymouth	MCD-Charter Township	WAYNE	◆ 25,986
Plymouth Township	CDP-Census Area Only	WAYNE	◆ 25,986
Wyandotte	Inc. Place	WAYNE	◆ 25,304
Delhi	MCD-Charter Township	INGHAM	◆ 24,952
Hamburg	MCD-Township	LIVINGSTON	◆ 24,455
Harrison	CDP-Census Area Only	MACOMB	◆ 24,450
Harrison	MCD-Charter Township	MACOMB	◆ 24,450
Walker	Inc. Place	KENT	◆ 24,427
Brownstown	MCD-Charter Township	WAYNE	◆ 24,035
Blackman	MCD-Charter Township	JACKSON	◆ 23,753
Ypsilanti	Inc. Place	WASHTENAW	◆ 23,392
Norton Shores	Inc. Place	MUSKEGON	◆ 23,178
Okemos	CDP	INGHAM	◆ 23,178
Van Buren	MCD-Charter Township	WAYNE	◆ 23,154
Saginaw Township North	CDP-Census Area Only	SAGINAW	◆ 23,086
Genesee	MCD-Charter Township	GENESEE	◆ 22,936
Kalamazoo	MCD-Charter Township	KALAMAZOO	◆ 22,894
Gaines	MCD-Charter Township	KENT	◆ 22,684
Washington	MCD-Township	MACOMB	◆ 22,332
Forest Hills	CDP-Census Area Only	KENT	◆ 22,323
Romulus	Inc. Place	WAYNE	◆ 22,264
Hamtramck	Inc. Place	WAYNE	◆ 21,984
Summit	MCD-Township	JACKSON	◆ 21,667
Mount Morris	MCD-Charter Township	GENESEE	◆ 21,648
Monroe	Inc. Place	MONROE	◆ 21,007
Northville	MCD-Charter Township	WAYNE	◆ 20,920
Ferndale	Inc. Place	OAKLAND	◆ 20,386
Frenchtown	MCD-Charter Township	MONROE	◆ 20,332
Auburn Hills	Inc. Place	OAKLAND	◆ 19,966
Byron	MCD-Township	KENT	◆ 19,688
Oshtemo	MCD-Charter Township	KALAMAZOO	◆ 19,617
Trenton	Inc. Place	WAYNE	© 19,584
Marquette	Inc. Place	MARQUETTE	◆ 19,341
Adrian	Inc. Place	LENAWEE	◆ 19,111
Wayne	Inc. Place	WAYNE	© 19,051
Hazel Park	Inc. Place	OAKLAND	© 18,963
Highland	MCD-Charter Township	OAKLAND	◆ 18,459
Birmingham	Inc. Place	OAKLAND	◆ 18,060
Muskegon	MCD-Charter Township	MUSKEGON	© 17,737
Davison	MCD-Township	GENESEE	© 17,722
Brighton	MCD-Township	LIVINGSTON	© 17,673
Park	MCD-Township	OTTAWA	© 17,579
Jenison	CDP	OTTAWA	© 17,211
Grosse Pointe Woods	Inc. Place	WAYNE	© 17,080
Mount Clemens	Inc. Place	MACOMB	◆ 16,541
Benton	MCD-Charter Township	BERRIEN	© 16,404
Grandville	Inc. Place	KENT	© 16,263
Waverly	CDP-Census Area Only	EATON	© 16,194
Oxford	MCD-Charter Township	OAKLAND	© 16,025
Genoa	MCD-Township	LIVINGSTON	© 15,901
Scio	MCD-Charter Township	WASHTENAW	© 15,759
Green Oak	MCD-Township	LIVINGSTON	© 15,618
Bangor	MCD-Charter Township	BAY	© 15,547
Berkley	Inc. Place	OAKLAND	© 15,531
Fraser	Inc. Place	MACOMB	© 15,297
Milford	MCD-Charter Township	OAKLAND	© 15,271
Cutlerville	CDP	KENT	© 15,114
Cascade	MCD-Charter Township	KENT	© 15,107
Owosso	Inc. Place	SHIAWASSEE	◆ 14,856
Highland Park	Inc. Place	WAYNE	◆ 14,837
Brandon	MCD-Charter Township	OAKLAND	© 14,765
Northview	CDP-Census Area Only	KENT	© 14,730
Sault Ste. Marie	Inc. Place	CHIPPEWA	◆ 14,728
Southfield	MCD-Township	OAKLAND	© 14,430
Grand Rapids	MCD-Charter Township	KENT	© 14,056
Alpine	MCD-Charter Township	KENT	© 13,976
Lincoln	MCD-Charter Township	BERRIEN	© 13,952
Comstock	MCD-Charter Township	KALAMAZOO	© 13,851
Garfield	MCD-Charter Township	GRAND TRAVERSE	© 13,840
Traverse City	Inc. Place	GRAND TRAVERSE	◆ 13,815
Saginaw Township South	CDP-Census Area Only	SAGINAW	© 13,801
Huron	MCD-Charter Township	WAYNE	© 13,737
Monroe	MCD-Charter Township	MONROE	© 13,491
Leoni	MCD-Township	JACKSON	© 13,459
Springfield	MCD-Charter Township	OAKLAND	© 13,338
Niles	MCD-Township	BERRIEN	© 13,325
Grand Haven	MCD-Charter Township	OTTAWA	© 13,278
Riverview	Inc. Place	WAYNE	© 13,272
Wixom	Inc. Place	OAKLAND	© 13,263
Spring Lake	MCD-Township	OTTAWA	© 13,140
Vienna	MCD-Charter Township	GENESEE	© 13,108
Oakland	MCD-Charter Township	OAKLAND	© 13,071
Allendale	MCD-Charter Township	OTTAWA	© 13,042
Harper Woods	Inc. Place	WAYNE	◆ 12,989
Fenton	MCD-Charter Township	GENESEE	© 12,968
Beecher	CDP	GENESEE	© 12,793
Clawson	Inc. Place	OAKLAND	© 12,732
Coldwater	Inc. Place	BRANCH	© 12,697
Fruitport	MCD-Charter Township	MUSKEGON	© 12,533
Woodhaven	Inc. Place	WAYNE	© 12,530
Grosse Pointe Park	Inc. Place	WAYNE	© 12,443
Escanaba	Inc. Place	DELTA	◆ 12,283
Niles	Inc. Place	BERRIEN	© 12,204
Mundy	MCD-Charter Township	GENESEE	© 12,191
DeWitt	MCD-Charter Township	CLINTON	© 12,143
Cannon	MCD-Township	KENT	© 12,075
Emmett	MCD-Charter Township	CALHOUN	© 11,979
Thomas	MCD-Township	SAGINAW	© 11,877
Sumpter	MCD-Township	WAYNE	© 11,856
Bridgeport	MCD-Charter Township	SAGINAW	© 11,709
Muskegon Heights	Inc. Place	MUSKEGON	◆ 11,619
Allendale	CDP	OTTAWA	© 11,555
Ionia	Inc. Place	IONIA	® 11,528
Holt	CDP	INGHAM	© 11,315
Haslett	CDP	INGHAM	® 11,292
Sturgis	Inc. Place	ST. JOSEPH	© 11,285
Ecorse	Inc. Place	WAYNE	© 11,229
Lyon	MCD-Charter Township	OAKLAND	© 11,041
Hartland	MCD-Township	LIVINGSTON	© 10,996
Texas	MCD-Charter Township	KALAMAZOO	© 10,919
Grosse Ile	CDP	WAYNE	© 10,894
Grosse Ile	MCD-Township	WAYNE	© 10,894
Big Rapids	Inc. Place	MECOSTA	© 10,849
Antwerp	MCD-Township	VAN BUREN	© 10,813
East Grand Rapids	Inc. Place	KENT	© 10,764
Superior	MCD-Charter Township	WASHTENAW	© 10,740
Melvindale	Inc. Place	WAYNE	© 10,735
Benton Harbor	Inc. Place	BERRIEN	◆ 10,692
Fort Gratiot	MCD-Charter Township	ST. CLAIR	© 10,691
Comstock Park	CDP	KENT	© 10,674
Fenton	Inc. Place	GENESEE	© 10,582
Rochester	Inc. Place	OAKLAND	© 10,467
Alpena	Inc. Place	ALPENA	◆ 10,451
Beverly Hills	Inc. Place	OAKLAND	© 10,437
Farmington	Inc. Place	OAKLAND	© 10,423
Grand Haven	Inc. Place	OTTAWA	◆ 10,350
Buena Vista	MCD-Charter Township	SAGINAW	© 10,318
Flushing	MCD-Charter Township	GENESEE	© 10,230
Saint Joseph	MCD-Charter Township	BERRIEN	© 10,042
Holly	MCD-Township	OAKLAND	© 10,037
Monitor	MCD-Charter Township	BAY	© 10,037
South Lyon	Inc. Place	OAKLAND	© 10,036
East Bay	MCD-Township	GRAND TRAVERSE	© 9,919
River Rouge	Inc. Place	WAYNE	© 9,917
Hampton	MCD-Charter Township	BAY	© 9,902
Cadillac	Inc. Place	WEXFORD	◆ 9,896
Ada	MCD-Township	KENT	© 9,882
Oronoko	MCD-Charter Township	BERRIEN	© 9,843
Clay	MCD-Township	ST. CLAIR	© 9,822
Alpena	MCD-Township	ALPENA	© 9,788
Grosse Pointe Farms	Inc. Place	WAYNE	© 9,764
Marysville	Inc. Place	ST. CLAIR	© 9,684
Egelston	MCD-Township	MUSKEGON	© 9,537
Bedford	MCD-Charter Township	CALHOUN	© 9,517
Lambertville	CDP	MONROE	© 9,299
Alma	Inc. Place	GRATIOT	© 9,275
Howell	Inc. Place	LIVINGSTON	© 9,232
Albion	Inc. Place	CALHOUN	© 9,144
Westwood	CDP	KALAMAZOO	© 9,122
Lapeer	Inc. Place	LAPEER	© 9,072
Plymouth	Inc. Place	WAYNE	© 9,022
Caledonia	MCD-Charter Township	KENT	© 8,964
Sparta	MCD-Township	KENT	© 8,938
Pennfield	MCD-Charter Township	CALHOUN	© 8,913
Cooper	MCD-Charter Township	KALAMAZOO	© 8,754
Menominee	Inc. Place	MENOMINEE	◆ 8,701
Kimball	MCD-Township	ST. CLAIR	© 8,628
Port Huron	MCD-Charter Township	ST. CLAIR	© 8,615
Tecumseh	Inc. Place	LENAWEE	© 8,574
Center Line	Inc. Place	MACOMB	© 8,531
Union Lake	RMC Place	OAKLAND	● 8,500
Flat Rock	Inc. Place	WAYNE	© 8,488
Tyrone	MCD-Township	LIVINGSTON	© 8,459
Lansing	MCD-Charter Township	INGHAM	© 8,458
Lenox	MCD-Township	MACOMB	© 8,433
Charlotte	Inc. Place	EATON	© 8,389
Oceola	MCD-Township	LIVINGSTON	© 8,362
Ludington	Inc. Place	MASON	© 8,357
Flushing	Inc. Place	GENESEE	© 8,348
Thetford	MCD-Township	GENESEE	© 8,277
Northfield	MCD-Township	WASHTENAW	© 8,252
Grand Blanc	Inc. Place	GENESEE	© 8,242
Hillsdale	Inc. Place	HILLSDALE	© 8,233
Saint Joseph	Inc. Place	BERRIEN	◆ 8,223
Richfield	MCD-Township	GENESEE	© 8,170
Bruce	MCD-Township	MACOMB	© 8,158
Kinross	MCD-Charter Township	CHIPPEWA	® 8,140
Dalton	MCD-Township	MUSKEGON	© 8,047
Saline	Inc. Place	WASHTENAW	© 8,034
Greenville	Inc. Place	MONTCALM	◆ 7,867
Bridgeport	CDP	SAGINAW	© 7,849
Buena Vista	CDP-Census Area Only	SAGINAW	© 7,845
Fair Plain	CDP	BERRIEN	© 7,828
Grand Ledge	Inc. Place	EATON	® 7,804
Temperance	CDP	MONROE	© 7,757
Saint Johns	Inc. Place	CLINTON	® 7,744
Tittabawassee	MCD-Township	SAGINAW	© 7,706
Mayfield	MCD-Township	LAPEER	© 7,659
Long Lake	MCD-Township	GRAND TRAVERSE	© 7,648
Iron Mountain	Inc. Place	DICKINSON	◆ 7,644
Madison	MCD-Charter Township	LENAWEE	® 7,616
Union	MCD-Charter Township	ISABELLA	© 7,615
Zeeland	MCD-Charter Township	OTTAWA	© 7,613
Ash	MCD-Township	MONROE	© 7,610
Algoma	MCD-Township	KENT	© 7,596
Spring Arbor	MCD-Township	JACKSON	© 7,577
Clayton	MCD-Charter Township	GENESEE	® 7,553
Bath	MCD-Charter Township	CLINTON	© 7,541
Putnam	MCD-Township	LIVINGSTON	© 7,500
Marshall	Inc. Place	CALHOUN	© 7,459
New Baltimore	Inc. Place	MACOMB	© 7,405
York	MCD-Township	WASHTENAW	© 7,392
Laketon	MCD-Township	MUSKEGON	© 7,363
Windsor	MCD-Charter Township	EATON	© 7,340
Three Rivers	Inc. Place	ST. JOSEPH	© 7,328
Schoolcraft	MCD-Township	KALAMAZOO	© 7,260
Atlas	MCD-Township	GENESEE	© 7,257
Oscoda	MCD-Charter Township	IOSCO	© 7,248
Columbia	MCD-Township	JACKSON	© 7,234
Mason	Inc. Place	INGHAM	® 7,164
Hudsonville	Inc. Place	OTTAWA	© 7,160
Hastings	Inc. Place	BARRY	© 7,095
Paw Paw	MCD-Township	VAN BUREN	© 7,091
Handy	MCD-Township	LIVINGSTON	© 7,004
Calumet	MCD-Charter Township	HOUGHTON	® 6,968
Ira	MCD-Township	ST. CLAIR	© 6,966
Napoleon	MCD-Township	JACKSON	© 6,962
Berlin	MCD-Charter Township	MONROE	© 6,924
Tallmadge	MCD-Charter Township	OTTAWA	© 6,881
Marion	MCD-Township	LIVINGSTON	© 6,757
Walled Lake	Inc. Place	OAKLAND	© 6,713
Brighton	Inc. Place	LIVINGSTON	© 6,701
Ishpeming	Inc. Place	MARQUETTE	© 6,686
Thornapple	MCD-Township	BARRY	© 6,685
Carrollton	CDP	SAGINAW	© 6,602
Carrollton	MCD-Township	SAGINAW	© 6,602
Indianfields	MCD-Township	TUSCOLA	® 6,595
Shields	CDP	SAGINAW	© 6,590
Manistee	Inc. Place	MANISTEE	© 6,586
Dorr	MCD-Township	ALLEGAN	© 6,579
Whitmore Lake	CDP	LIVINGSTON	© 6,574
Houghton	Inc. Place	HOUGHTON	◆ 6,549
Argentine	MCD-Township	GENESEE	© 6,521
Raisin	MCD-Charter Township	LENAWEE	© 6,507
Gaines	MCD-Township	GENESEE	© 6,491
Richland	MCD-Township	KALAMAZOO	© 6,491
Grayling	MCD-Township	CRAWFORD	® 6,483
Northville	Inc. Place	WAYNE	© 6,459
Blair	MCD-Township	GRAND TRAVERSE	© 6,448
Addison	MCD-Township	OAKLAND	© 6,439
Sylvan	MCD-Township	WASHTENAW	© 6,425
St. Clair	MCD-Township	ST. CLAIR	© 6,423
South Monroe	CDP-Census Area Only	MONROE	© 6,370
Dundee	MCD-Township	MONROE	© 6,341
Montrose	MCD-Charter Township	GENESEE	© 6,336
Howard	MCD-Township	CASS	© 6,309
Milford	Inc. Place	OAKLAND	© 6,272
Eastwood	CDP	KALAMAZOO	© 6,265
Rose	MCD-Township	OAKLAND	© 6,210
Birch Run	MCD-Township	SAGINAW	© 6,191
Holly	Inc. Place	OAKLAND	® 6,179
Oregon	MCD-Township	LAPEER	© 6,166
Huntington Woods	Inc. Place	OAKLAND	© 6,151
Groveland	MCD-Township	OAKLAND	© 6,150
Chocolay	MCD-Charter Township	MARQUETTE	® 6,095
Petoskey	Inc. Place	EMMET	◆ 6,057
Almont	MCD-Township	LAPEER	© 6,041
Dowagiac	Inc. Place	CASS	® 6,009
Breitung	MCD-Charter Township	DICKINSON	© 5,930
Belding	Inc. Place	IONIA	© 5,877
Ontwa	MCD-Township	CASS	© 5,865
Bagley	MCD-Township	OTSEGO	© 5,838
Pavilion	MCD-Township	KALAMAZOO	© 5,829
Courtland	MCD-Township	KENT	© 5,817
Denton	MCD-Township	ROSCOMMON	© 5,817
Zeeland	Inc. Place	OTTAWA	© 5,805
Saint Clair	Inc. Place	ST. CLAIR	© 5,802
Adrian	MCD-Township	LENAWEE	© 5,749
Deerfield	MCD-Township	LAPEER	© 5,736
Blendon	MCD-Township	OTTAWA	© 5,721
Lodi	MCD-Township	WASHTENAW	© 5,710
Howell	MCD-Township	LIVINGSTON	© 5,679
Ironwood	Inc. Place	GOGEBIC	◆ 5,666
Gun Plain	MCD-Charter Township	ALLEGAN	© 5,637
Comstock	RMC Place	KALAMAZOO	● 5,600
Robinson	MCD-Township	OTTAWA	© 5,588
Salem	MCD-Township	WASHTENAW	© 5,562
Laketown	MCD-Township	ALLEGAN	© 5,561
Kingsford	Inc. Place	DICKINSON	© 5,549
Davison	Inc. Place	GENESEE	© 5,536
Clyde	MCD-Township	ST. CLAIR	© 5,523
Bertrand	RMC Place	BERRIEN	● 5,500
Elba	MCD-Township	LAPEER	© 5,462
Benton Heights	CDP	BERRIEN	© 5,458
Saint Louis	Inc. Place	GRATIOT	® 5,453
Royal Oak	MCD-Charter Township	OAKLAND	© 5,446
Grosse Pointe	Inc. Place	WAYNE	◆ 5,373
Eaton Rapids	Inc. Place	EATON	© 5,330
Cambridge	MCD-Township	LENAWEE	© 5,299
Cheboygan	Inc. Place	CHEBOYGAN	© 5,295
Bear Creek	MCD-Township	EMMET	© 5,269
Peninsula	MCD-Township	GRAND TRAVERSE	© 5,265
Dexter	MCD-Township	WASHTENAW	© 5,248
Armada	MCD-Township	MACOMB	© 5,246
Fruitland	MCD-Township	MUSKEGON	© 5,235
Lowell	MCD-Charter Township	KENT	© 5,219
Coloma	MCD-Charter Township	BERRIEN	© 5,217
Webster	MCD-Township	WASHTENAW	© 5,198
Springfield	Inc. Place	CALHOUN	© 5,189
Freeland	CDP	SAGINAW	© 5,147

Entries in **UPPERCASE** are counties.
Entries in **bold** have populations of 2,500 or more.
Names in parentheses are alternate names.
Inc. Place — Incorporated Place
RMC Place — Rand McNally Designated Place
CDP — Census Designated Place
MCD — Minor Civil Division

⊡ County Seat
▲ Minor Civil Division
elev. Elevation
🅿 Post Office

🄷 Hospital
🄲 College
■ Principal Business Center
★ Ranally Metro Area (RMA) Abbreviation
z Zip Code(s)

Ⓟ Previous Census Population
® Revised Census Population
Ⓐ Annexation Population
● Rand McNally Population Estimate
© Final Census Population
Ⓢ Special Census Population
◆ Estimated Population

For additional definitions see Glossary, Volume 1, and Introduction, Volume 2.

Place Name	Place Type	County	Population
Kawkawlin	MCD-Township	BAY	Ⓒ 5,104
Swartz Creek	Inc. Place	GENESEE	Ⓒ 5,102
Lapeer	MCD-Township	LAPEER	Ⓒ 5,078
Berrien	MCD-Township	BERRIEN	Ⓒ 5,075
Jamestown	MCD-Charter Township	OTTAWA	Ⓒ 5,062
Oakfield	MCD-Township	KENT	Ⓒ 5,058
Ross	MCD-Township	KALAMAZOO	Ⓒ 5,047
Wells	MCD-Township	DELTA	Ⓒ 5,044
Gladstone	Inc. Place	DELTA	Ⓒ 5,032
South Haven	Inc. Place	VAN BUREN	Ⓒ 5,021
Green Lake	MCD-Township	GRAND TRAVERSE	Ⓒ 5,009
La Salle	MCD-Township	MONROE	Ⓒ 5,001
Commerce	RMC Place	OAKLAND	● 5,000

County Business Data

County	FIPS Code	County Seat	Land Area (Sq. Mi.)	Census Population			Wholesale Trade		Manufacturing, 2002			
				4/1/2000	4/1/1990	% Change 1990-2000	Sales, 2002 ($1,000)	% Change 1997-2002	Establish-ments	Total Employees	Value Added ($1,000)	Ranally Mfg. Units
Alcona	001	Harrisville	674	11,719	10,145	15.5	668	(d)	...	(d)	(d)	...
Alger	003	Munising	918	9,862	8,972	9.9	(d)	(d)	9	753	75,441	40
Allegan	005	Allegan	827	105,665	90,509	16.7	788,574	113.5	208	16,614	2,101,598	1,112
Alpena	007	Alpena	574	31,314	30,605	2.3	166,033	15.9	52	1,893	224,722	119
Antrim	009	Bellaire	477	23,110	18,185	27.1	16,192	-50.2	55	1,218	103,212	55
Arenac	011	Standish	367	17,269	14,931	15.7	(d)	(d)	32	576	43,358	23
Baraga	013	L'Anse	904	8,746	7,954	10.0	(d)	(d)	...	(d)	(d)	...
Barry	015	Hastings	556	56,755	50,057	13.4	(d)	(d)	75	3,419	363,253	192
Bay	017	Bay City	444	110,157	111,723	-1.4	570,212	-5.0	138	5,119	512,860	271
Benzie	019	Beulah	321	15,998	12,200	31.1	2,579	-43.4	...	(d)	(d)	...
Berrien	021	St. Joseph	571	162,453	161,378	0.7	1,065,928	13.6	370	14,392	1,257,131	665
Branch	023	Coldwater	507	45,787	41,502	10.3	(d)	(d)	94	3,977	347,710	184
Calhoun	025	Marshall	709	137,985	135,982	1.5	1,410,927	1.3	202	13,970	2,202,344	1,165
Cass	027	Cassopolis	492	51,104	49,477	3.3	239,664	-5.1	87	3,474	269,418	143
Charlevoix	029	Charlevoix	417	26,090	21,468	21.5	29,131	-14.0	58	2,535	343,927	182
Cheboygan	031	Cheboygan	716	26,448	21,398	23.6	83,064	70.0	32	677	40,376	21
Chippewa	033	Sault Ste. Marie	1,561	38,543	34,604	11.4	121,443	387.7	25	(d)	(d)	...
Clare	035	Harrison	567	31,252	24,952	25.2	32,257	-31.6	27	815	51,963	27
Clinton	037	St. Johns	571	64,753	57,883	11.9	(d)	(d)	65	(d)	(d)	...
Crawford	039	Grayling	558	14,273	12,260	16.4	15,802	(d)	18	641	61,047	32
Delta	041	Escanaba	1,170	38,520	37,780	2.0	242,109	153.4	63	2,740	409,537	217
Dickinson	043	Iron Mountain	766	27,472	26,831	2.4	(d)	(d)	51	(d)	(d)	...
Eaton	045	Charlotte	576	103,655	92,879	11.6	712,705	5.8	82	(d)	(d)	...
Emmet	047	Petoskey	468	31,437	25,040	25.5	135,781	80.2	66	1,765	168,677	89
Genesee	049	Flint	640	436,141	430,459	1.3	4,465,101	135.1	347	23,871	2,677,385	1,417
Gladwin	051	Gladwin	507	26,023	21,896	18.8	(d)	(d)	42	1,000	80,577	43
Gogebic	053	Bessemer	1,102	17,370	18,052	-3.8	17,714	-50.0	26	602	36,421	19
Grand Traverse	055	Traverse City	465	77,654	64,273	20.8	660,219	-9.5	206	5,581	544,825	288
Gratiot	057	Ithaca	570	42,285	38,982	8.5	(d)	(d)	60	2,626	211,775	112
Hillsdale	059	Hillsdale	599	46,527	43,431	7.1	221,172	2.6	102	6,076	525,585	278
Houghton	061	Houghton	1,012	36,016	35,446	1.6	(d)	(d)	46	(d)	(d)	...
Huron	063	Bad Axe	837	36,079	34,951	3.2	179,192	-7.9	78	3,487	363,617	192
Ingham	065	Mason	559	279,320	281,912	-0.9	5,106,975	54.1	265	(d)	(d)	...
Ionia	067	Ionia	573	61,518	57,024	7.9	92,615	-35.4	76	3,067	344,720	182
Iosco	069	Tawas City	549	27,339	30,209	-9.5	(d)	(d)	37	1,257	116,257	62
Iron	071	Crystal Falls	1,166	13,138	13,175	-0.3	11,229	-39.0	...	(d)	(d)	...
Isabella	073	Mount Pleasant	574	63,351	54,624	16.0	209,196	-36.2	57	2,606	204,160	108
Jackson	075	Jackson	707	158,422	149,756	5.8	749,590	-28.4	317	10,875	1,177,854	623
Kalamazoo	077	Kalamazoo	562	238,603	223,411	6.8	1,945,859	4.1	385	16,675	4,273,710	2,261
Kalkaska	079	Kalkaska	561	16,571	13,497	22.8	75,697	-0.6	17	790	49,276	26
Kent	081	Grand Rapids	856	574,335	500,631	14.7	16,690,424	5.1	1,183	77,101	7,278,648	3,851
Keweenaw	083	Eagle River	541	2,301	1,701	35.3	(d)	(d)	...	(d)	(d)	...
Lake	085	Baldwin	567	11,333	8,583	32.0	(d)	(d)	...	(d)	(d)	...
Lapeer	087	Lapeer	654	87,904	74,768	17.6	143,486	5.5	133	5,276	516,432	273
Leelanau	089	Leland	348	21,119	16,527	27.8	10,741	-46.4	...	(d)	(d)	...
Lenawee	091	Adrian	751	98,890	91,476	8.1	366,545	-14.7	170	8,044	980,385	519
Livingston	093	Howell	568	156,951	115,645	35.7	1,122,666	5.5	272	10,236	1,364,089	722
Luce	095	Newberry	903	7,024	5,763	21.9	(d)	(d)	...	(d)	(d)	...
Mackinac	097	St. Ignace	1,022	11,943	10,674	11.9	(d)	(d)	...	(d)	(d)	...
Macomb	099	Mount Clemens	480	788,149	717,400	9.9	6,243,694	-5.5	1,959	84,332	9,707,782	5,136
Manistee	101	Manistee	544	24,527	21,265	15.3	33,441	(d)	30	993	158,315	84
Marquette	103	Marquette	1,821	64,634	70,887	-8.8	166,480	4.7	47	884	60,897	32
Mason	105	Ludington	495	28,274	25,537	10.7	(d)	(d)	42	2,484	236,102	125
Mecosta	107	Big Rapids	556	40,553	37,308	8.7	(d)	(d)	34	1,770	195,274	103
Menominee	109	Menominee	1,044	25,326	24,920	1.6	(d)	(d)	62	2,462	246,803	131
Midland	111	Midland	521	82,874	75,651	9.5	(d)	(d)	69	5,742	651,105	344
Missaukee	113	Lake City	567	14,478	12,147	19.2	(d)	(d)	...	(d)	(d)	...
Monroe	115	Monroe	551	145,945	133,600	9.2	1,928,545	163.6	151	9,025	1,142,085	604
Montcalm	117	Stanton	708	61,266	53,059	15.5	102,317	-35.5	80	5,199	433,588	229
Montmorency	119	Atlanta	548	10,315	8,936	15.4	(d)	(d)	...	(d)	(d)	...
Muskegon	121	Muskegon	509	170,200	158,983	7.1	922,018	3.4	332	14,344	1,554,642	823
Newaygo	123	White Cloud	842	47,874	38,202	25.3	(d)	(d)	39	1,428	136,857	72
Oakland	125	Pontiac	873	1,194,156	1,083,592	10.2	62,105,475	-10.2	2,160	79,167	12,578,604	6,655
Oceana	127	Hart	540	26,873	22,454	19.7	17,168	17.5	42	1,417	124,170	66
Ogemaw	129	West Branch	564	21,645	18,681	15.9	74,957	7.2	34	1,040	61,517	33
Ontonagon	131	Ontonagon	1,312	7,818	8,854	-11.7	(d)	(d)	...	(d)	(d)	...
Osceola	133	Reed City	566	23,197	20,146	15.1	51,670	1.0	49	3,062	335,341	177
Oscoda	135	Mio	565	9,418	7,842	20.1	6,768	(d)	...	(d)	(d)	...
Otsego	137	Gaylord	515	23,301	17,957	29.8	(d)	(d)	44	1,504	87,754	46
Ottawa	139	Grand Haven	566	238,314	187,768	26.9	2,038,175	-7.9	616	35,521	4,672,629	2,472
Presque Isle	141	Rogers City	660	14,411	13,743	4.9	25,553	-38.7	...	(d)	(d)	...
Roscommon	143	Roscommon	521	25,469	19,776	28.8	(d)	(d)	...	(d)	(d)	...
Saginaw	145	Saginaw	809	210,039	211,946	-0.9	1,301,531	-19.4	241	17,637	2,768,531	1,465
St. Clair	147	Port Huron	724	164,235	145,607	12.8	599,767	0.6	282	10,294	1,059,083	560
St. Joseph	149	Centreville	504	62,422	58,913	6.0	167,456	-33.6	157	8,977	1,294,691	685
Sanilac	151	Sandusky	964	44,547	39,928	11.6	166,640	67.4	83	3,342	260,862	138
Schoolcraft	153	Manistique	1,178	8,903	8,302	7.2	(d)	(d)	...	(d)	(d)	...
Shiawassee	155	Corunna	539	71,687	69,770	2.7	(d)	(d)	82	3,500	275,895	146
Tuscola	157	Caro	812	58,266	55,498	5.0	(d)	(d)	56	2,008	173,806	92
Van Buren	159	Paw Paw	611	76,263	70,060	8.9	221,354	37.9	104	4,209	762,247	403
Washtenaw	161	Ann Arbor	710	322,895	282,937	14.1	3,024,340	-9.4	393	27,975	3,333,991	1,764
Wayne	163	Detroit	614	2,061,162	2,111,687	-2.4	44,320,325	16.7	2,059	118,362	18,890,667	9,994
Wexford	165	Cadillac	565	30,484	26,360	15.6	(d)	(d)	62	(d)	(d)	...
The State			**56,804**	**9,938,444**	**9,295,297**	**6.9**	**165,958,945**	**4.1**	**15,193**	**736,259**	**97,575,395**	**51,624**

(d) Data not available. Corresponding percentages or Ranally Manufacturing Units are estimates.
... Represents 0 or amount too minimal to be reported.

Administrative Divisions

Townships: All Michigan counties are divided into townships, except for areas within cities. Townships are legally incorporated units and may levy taxes, elect certain officials, and carry on limited governmental functions. "Charter" townships have considerably broader functions and powers than other townships. Only townships with an active government recognized by the U.S. Census of Governments are printed in this index.

Cities and Villages: Incorporated cities do not form part of the townships which adjoin or surround them. Each of the incorporated villages, in contrast, legally forms part of one or more townships.

Index of Places and Counties

A

Abscota; RMC Place; CALHOUN; ▲ Burlington; ***189** S-7; elev. 940ft./287m.; mail Burlington **z** 49029; rural
Ackerson Lake; RMC Place; JACKSON; ▲ Napoleon; ***189** S-9; elev. 970ft./296m.; ★ **JAC**; mail Jackson **z** 49201; ● 250
Acme; RMC Place; GRAND TRAVERSE; ▲ Acme; **188** J-6; 🅿; **z** 49610; ● 500
Acme; MCD-Township; GRAND TRAVERSE; ***188** J-6; 🅿; **z** 49610; Ⓟ 3,447; Ⓒ 4,332
Ada; RMC Place; KENT; ▲ Ada; **189** P-6; 🅿; ★ **GDR**; **z** 49301, **z** 49355-57; ● 2,300
Ada; MCD-Township; KENT; ***189** P-6; 🅿; ★ **GDR**; **z** 49301, **z** 49355-57; Ⓟ 7,578; Ⓒ 9,882
Adair; RMC Place; ST. CLAIR; ▲ Casco; **189** P-14; ★ **DET**; mail Casco **z** 48064; ● 130
Adams; MCD-Township; ARENAC; ***189** L-10; mail Sterling **z** 48659; Ⓟ 417; Ⓒ 550
Adams; MCD-Township; HILLSDALE; ***189** T-9; mail North Adams **z** 49262; Ⓟ 2,339; Ⓒ 2,498
Adams; MCD-Township; HOUGHTON; ***188** A-12; mail South Range **z** 49963; Ⓟ 2,388; Ⓒ 2,747
Adams Park; RMC Place; KALAMAZOO; ▲ Brady; ***189** S-6; ★ **KZOO**; mail Vicksburg **z** 49097; ● 400
Adamsville; RMC Place; CASS; ▲ Ontwa; **189** T-5; ★ **S.B.**; mail Edwardsburg **z** 49112; ● 190
Addison; Inc. Place; LENAWEE; ▲ Woodstock, Rollin; **189** S-9; 🅿 🅷; ★ **JAC**; **z** 49220; Ⓟ 632; Ⓒ 627
Addison; MCD-Township; OAKLAND; ***189** P-12; ★ **DET**; mail Leonard **z** 48367; Ⓟ 5,142; Ⓒ 6,439
Adrian; Inc. Place; ⊡ LENAWEE; **189** T-10; 🅿 🅷 🅲 2,965 ■; **z** 49221; Ⓟ 22,097; Ⓒ 21,574; Ⓡ 22,215; ◆ 19,111
Adrian; MCD-Township; LENAWEE; ***189** S-10; 🅿 🅲 2,965; **z** 49221; does not include the City of Adrian; Ⓟ 4,336; Ⓒ 5,749
Advance; RMC Place; CHARLEVOIX; ▲ Eveline; **188** H-7; mail Boyne City **z** 49712
Aetna; MCD-Township; MECOSTA; ***189** N-6; mail Morley **z** 49336; Ⓟ 1,622; Ⓒ 2,044
Aetna; MCD-Township; MISSAUKEE; ***189** K-7; mail Lake **z** 48632; Ⓟ 416; Ⓒ 491
Aetna; RMC Place; NEWAYGO; ▲ Lincoln, Denver; **189** N-5; mail White Cloud **z** 49349
Afton; RMC Place; CHEBOYGAN; ▲ Koehler, Ellis; **188** H-9; 🅿; **z** 49705; ● 150
Agate; RMC Place; ONTONAGON; ▲ Interior; ***188** C-12; elev. 1,184ft./361m.; mail Trout Creek **z** 49967; rural
Agnew; RMC Place; OTTAWA; ▲ Grand Haven; **189** P-5; mail West Olive **z** 49460; ● 180
Ahmeek; Inc. Place; KEWEENAW; ▲ Allouez; **188** A-13; 🅿; **z** 49901; Ⓟ 148; Ⓒ 157
Ainger; RMC Place; EATON; ▲ Walton; ***189** R-8; mail Olivet **z** 49076; ● 40
Airport Forest; RMC Place; CLARE; ▲ Hayes; ***189** L-8; mail Harrison **z** 48625; ● 200
Akron; Inc. Place; TUSCOLA; ▲ Fairgrove, Akron; **189** N-11; elev. 646ft./197m.; 🅿; **z** 48701; Ⓟ 421; Ⓒ 461
Akron; MCD-Township; TUSCOLA; ***189** N-11; 🅿; **z** 48701; includes part of the Village of Akron; Ⓟ 1,609; Ⓒ 1,589
Alabaster; RMC Place; IOSCO; ▲ Alabaster; **189** L-11; mail Tawas City **z** 48763; ● 110
Alabaster; MCD-Township; IOSCO; ***189** L-11; mail Tawas City **z** 48763; Ⓟ 394; Ⓒ 503
Alaiedon; MCD-Township; INGHAM; ***189** Q-9; ★ **LANS**; mail Mason **z** 48854; Ⓟ 3,173; Ⓒ 3,498; Ⓡ 3,048
Alamo; RMC Place; KALAMAZOO; ▲ Alamo; **189** R-6; elev. 783ft./239m.; ★ **KZOO**; mail Kalamazoo **z** 49009; ● 140
Alamo; MCD-Township; KALAMAZOO; ***189** R-6; ★ **KZOO**; mail Kalamazoo **z** 49009; Ⓟ 3,276; Ⓒ 3,820
Alanson; Inc. Place; EMMET; ▲ Littlefield; **188** G-8; elev. 615ft./187m.; 🅿; **z** 49706; Ⓟ 677; Ⓒ 785
Alaska; RMC Place; KENT; ▲ Caledonia; **189** P-6; elev. 685ft./209m.; ★ **GDR**; mail Alto **z** 49302, Caledonia **z** 49316; ● 280
Alba; RMC Place; ANTRIM; ▲ Star, Chestonia; **188** I-7; elev. 1,179ft./359m.; 🅿; **z** 49611; ● 370
Albee; MCD-Township; SAGINAW; ***189** O-10; mail Saint Charles **z** 48655; Ⓟ 2,402; Ⓒ 2,338
Albert; MCD-Township; MONTMORENCY; ***188** I-9; mail Lewiston **z** 49756; Ⓟ 2,097; Ⓒ 2,695
Alberta; RMC Place; BARAGA; ▲ L'Anse; **188** B-13; elev. 1,319ft./402m.; mail Lanse **z** 49946; ● 30
Albion; Inc. Place; CALHOUN; **189** R-8; elev. 959ft./292m.; 🅿 🅷 🅲 1,941; **z** 49224; Ⓟ 10,066; Ⓒ 9,144
Albion; MCD-Township; CALHOUN; ***189** S-8; 🅿 🅲 1,941; **z** 49224; does not include the City of Albion; Ⓟ 1,256; Ⓒ 1,200
Albion; RMC Place; HOUGHTON; ▲ Calumet; ***188** A-13; elev. 1,207ft./368m.; mail Calumet **z** 49913; ● 130
Albright Shores; RMC Place; GLADWIN; ▲ Billings; **189** M-9; elev. 691ft./211m.; mail Beaverton **z** 48612; summer pop. 600; ● 150
Alcona; RMC Place; ALCONA; ▲ Haynes; ***188** J-12; mail Harrisville **z** 48740
Alcona; MCD-Township; ALCONA; ***188** J-11; mail Black River **z** 48721; Ⓟ 906; Ⓒ 1,089
ALCONA; **188** J-11; Ⓟ 10,145; Ⓒ 11,719; ◆ 11,520
Alden; RMC Place; ANTRIM; ▲ Helena; **188** I-7; elev. 604ft./184m.; 🅿; **z** 49612; ● 450
Algansee; RMC Place; BRANCH; ▲ Algansee; ***189** T-8; elev. 1,047ft./319m.; mail Quincy **z** 49082; ● 100
Algansee; MCD-Township; BRANCH; ***189** T-8; mail Quincy **z** 49082; Ⓟ 1,859; Ⓒ 2,061
Alger; RMC Place; ARENAC; ▲ Moffatt; **189** L-10; elev. 784ft./239m.; 🅿; **z** 48610; ● 180
ALGER; **188** E-3; Ⓟ 8,972; Ⓒ 9,862; ◆ 9,687
Algoma; MCD-Township; KENT; ***189** O-6; ★ **GDR**; mail Rockford **z** 49341; Ⓟ 5,496; Ⓒ 7,596
Algonac; Inc. Place; ST. CLAIR; **189** Q-14; 🅿; ★ **DET**; **z** 48001; Ⓟ 4,551; Ⓒ 4,613
Allegan; Inc. Place; ⊡ ALLEGAN; **189** R-5; elev. 658ft./201m.; 🅿 🅷; **z** 49010; Ⓟ 4,547; Ⓒ 4,838; Ⓡ 4,717
Allegan; MCD-Township; ALLEGAN; ***189** Q-5; 🅿; **z** 49010; does not include the City of Allegan; Ⓟ 3,976; Ⓒ 4,050; Ⓡ 4,185
ALLEGAN; **189** Q-5; Ⓟ 90,509; Ⓒ 105,665; ◆ 110,970
Allen; Inc. Place; HILLSDALE; ▲ Allen; **189** S-8; 🅿; **z** 49227; Ⓟ 201; Ⓒ 225
Allen; MCD-Township; HILLSDALE; ***189** T-8; 🅿; **z** 49227; Ⓟ 1,412; Ⓒ 1,631
Allendale; RMC Place; CLARE; ▲ Hayes; ***189** L-8; mail Harrison **z** 48625; ● 320
Allendale; CDP; OTTAWA; ▲ Allendale; **189** P-5; 🅿 🅲 22,565; ★ **GDR**; **z** 49401; Ⓟ 6,950; Ⓒ 11,555
Allendale; MCD-Charter Township; OTTAWA; ***189** P-5; 🅿 🅲 22,565; ★ **GDR**; **z** 49401; Ⓟ 8,022; Ⓒ 13,042
Allen Park; Inc. Place; WAYNE; **189** R-12; elev. 595ft./181m.; 🅿; ★ **DET**; **z** 48101; Ⓟ 31,092; Ⓒ 29,376; ◆ 26,520
Allenton; RMC Place; ST. CLAIR; ▲ Berlin; **189** P-13; 🅿; **z** 48002; ● 360
Allenville; RMC Place; MACKINAC; ▲ Brevort; **188** F-8; elev. 704ft./215m.; mail Moran **z** 49760
Allis; MCD-Township; PRESQUE ISLE; ***188** H-9; mail Onaway **z** 49765; Ⓟ 887; Ⓒ 1,035
Allouez; RMC Place; KEWEENAW; ▲ Allouez; ***188** A-13; 🅿; **z** 49805; ● 200
Allouez; MCD-Township; KEWEENAW; ***188** A-13; 🅿; **z** 49805; Ⓟ 1,422; Ⓒ 1,584
Allyn; RMC Place; BENZIE; ▲ Inland; ***188** J-5; elev. 800ft./244m.; mail Interlochen **z** 49643; rural
Alma; Inc. Place; GRATIOT; **189** O-8; elev. 736ft./224m.; 🅿 🅷 🅲 1,174; **z** 48801-02; Ⓟ 9,034; Ⓒ 9,275
Almeda Beach; RMC Place; ROSCOMMON; ▲ Gerrish; mail Roscommon **z** 48653; summer pop. 100
Almena; RMC Place; VAN BUREN; ▲ Almena; ***189** R-5; ★ **KZOO**; mail Paw Paw **z** 49079; ● 70
Almena; MCD-Township; VAN BUREN; ***189** R-6; ★ **KZOO**; mail Paw Paw **z** 49079; Ⓟ 3,581; Ⓒ 4,226
Almer; MCD-Township; TUSCOLA; ***189** N-12; mail Caro **z** 48723; Ⓟ 2,628; Ⓒ 3,023
Almira; MCD-Township; BENZIE; ***188** J-5; mail Empire **z** 49630; Ⓟ 1,449; Ⓒ 2,811
Almont; Inc. Place; LAPEER; ▲ Almont; **189** P-13; 🅿; ★ **DET**; **z** 48003; Ⓟ 2,354; Ⓒ 2,803
Almont; MCD-Township; LAPEER; ***189** P-13; 🅿; ★ **DET**; **z** 48003; Ⓟ 4,660; Ⓒ 6,041
Aloha; RMC Place; CHEBOYGAN; ▲ Aloha; **188** G-9; mail Cheboygan **z** 49721; ● 100
Aloha; MCD-Township; CHEBOYGAN; ***188** G-9; mail Cheboygan **z** 49721; Ⓟ 707; Ⓒ 1,041
Alpena; Inc. Place; ⊡ ALPENA; **188** I-11; elev. 593ft./181m.; 🅿 🅷 ■; **z** 49707; Ⓟ 11,354; Ⓒ 11,304; ◆ 10,451
Alpena; MCD-Township; ALPENA; ***188** I-11; 🅿; **z** 49707; does not include the City of Alpena; Ⓟ 9,602; Ⓒ 9,788
ALPENA; **188** I-11; Ⓟ 30,605; Ⓒ 31,314; ◆ 29,396
Alpena Junction; RMC Place; ALPENA; ▲ Alpena; ***188** I-11; mail Alpena **z** 49707; pop. incl. with Alpena (Inc. Place)
Alpha; Inc. Place; IRON; ▲ Mastodon; **188** D-13; 🅿; **z** 49902; Ⓟ 219; Ⓒ 198
Alpine; RMC Place; KENT; ▲ Alpine; **189** P-6; elev. 751ft./229m.; ★ **GDR**; mail Comstock Park **z** 49321; ● 250
Alpine; MCD-Charter Township; KENT; ***189** P-6; ★ **GDR**; mail Comstock Park **z** 49321; Ⓟ 9,863; Ⓒ 13,976
Alston; RMC Place; HOUGHTON; ▲ Laird; ***188** B-12; mail Pelkie **z** 49958; ● 70
Alto; RMC Place; KENT; ▲ Lowell, Bowne; **189** P-7; elev. 817ft./249m.; 🅿; ★ **GDR**; **z** 49302; ● 300
Altona; RMC Place; MECOSTA; ▲ Hinton; **189** N-7; mail Morley **z** 49336; ● 30
Alverno; RMC Place; CHEBOYGAN; ▲ Benton; **188** G-9; elev. 683ft./208m.; mail Cheboygan **z** 49721
Amador; RMC Place; SANILAC; ▲ Worth; ***189** O-14; elev. 730ft./223m.; ★ **PTHU**; mail Croswell **z** 48422; rural
Amasa; RMC Place; IRON; ▲ Hematite; **188** C-13; elev. 1,440ft./439m.; 🅿; **z** 49903; ● 400
Amber; MCD-Township; MASON; ***189** M-4; mail Ludington **z** 49431; Ⓟ 1,684; Ⓒ 2,054
Amble; RMC Place; MONTCALM; ▲ Winfield; **189** N-7; mail Howard City **z** 49329; ● 90
Amboy; MCD-Township; HILLSDALE; ***189** T-9; mail Camden **z** 49232; Ⓟ 978; Ⓒ 1,224
Anchorville; RMC Place; ST. CLAIR; ▲ Ira; **189** Q-13; 🅿; ★ **DET**; **z** 48004; Ⓟ 3,202
Andersonville; RMC Place; OAKLAND; ▲ Springfield; ***189** Q-11; ★ **DET**; mail Davisburg **z** 48350; rural
Andrews (Andrews University); RMC Place; BERRIEN; ▲ Oronoko; ***189** T-4; mail Berrien Springs **z** 49104; ● 700
Andrews University; BERRIEN; see Andrews (RMC Place)
Ann Arbor; Inc. Place; ⊡ WASHTENAW; **189** R-11; elev. 840ft./256m.; 🅿 🅷 🅲 41,814 ■; ★ **DET**; **z** 48103-09, **z** 48113; Ⓟ 109,592; Ⓒ 114,024; ◆ 121,701
Ann Arbor; MCD-Charter Township; WASHTENAW; ***189** R-11; 🅿 🅲 41,814; ★ **DET**; **z** 48103-09, **z** 48113; does not include the City of Ann Arbor; Ⓟ 3,793; Ⓒ 4,720
Antioch; MCD-Township; WEXFORD; ***189** K-6; mail Tustin **z** 49688; Ⓟ 671; Ⓒ 810
Antoine; RMC Place; DICKINSON; ***188** D-13; elev. 1,181ft./360m.; mail Iron Mountain **z** 49801; pop. incl. with Iron Mountain (Inc. Place)
Antrim; RMC Place; ANTRIM; ▲ Mancelona; **188** I-7; mail Mancelona **z** 49659; ● 230
Antrim; MCD-Township; SHIAWASSEE; ***189** P-10; mail Byron **z** 48418; Ⓟ 1,679; Ⓒ 2,050
ANTRIM; **188** I-7; Ⓟ 18,185; Ⓒ 23,110; ◆ 24,159
Antwerp; MCD-Township; VAN BUREN; ***189** S-5; ★ **KZOO**; mail Lawton **z** 49065; Ⓟ 9,293; Ⓒ 10,813
Anvil; RMC Place; GOGEBIC; ▲ Bessemer; ***188** B-10; mail Bessemer **z** 49911; ● 200
Aplin Beach; RMC Place; BAY; ▲ Bangor; ***189** N-10; ★ **SAG-**; mail Bay City **z** 48706
Applegate; Inc. Place; SANILAC; ▲ Washington; **189** N-13; 🅿; **z** 48401; Ⓟ 297; Ⓒ 287
Arbela; MCD-Township; TUSCOLA; ***189** O-11; ★ **FLN**; mail Millington **z** 48746; Ⓟ 3,182; Ⓒ 3,219
Arbutus Beach; RMC Place; OTSEGO; ▲ Otsego Lake, Bagley; **188** I-8; mail Gaylord **z** 49735; ● 250
Arcada; MCD-Township; GRATIOT; ***189** O-8; mail Alma **z** 48801; Ⓟ 1,660; Ⓒ 1,708
Arcade; RMC Place; WASHTENAW; ***189** R-11; ★ **DET**; mail Ann Arbor **z** 48106; pop. incl. with Ann Arbor (Inc. Place)
Arcadia; MCD-Township; LAPEER; ***189** O-12; mail Attica **z** 48412; Ⓟ 2,448; Ⓒ 3,197
Arcadia; RMC Place; MANISTEE; ▲ Arcadia; **189** K-4; elev. 587ft./179m.; 🅿; **z** 49613; ● 320
Arcadia; MCD-Township; MANISTEE; ***189** K-4; 🅿; **z** 49613; Ⓟ 553; Ⓒ 621
Arenac; RMC Place; ARENAC; ▲ Arenac; ***189** L-10; elev. 598ft./182m.; mail Standish **z** 48658; rural
Arenac; MCD-Township; ARENAC; ***189** L-10; mail Standish **z** 48658; Ⓟ 921; Ⓒ 992
ARENAC; **189** L-10; Ⓟ 14,931; Ⓒ 17,269; ◆ 16,154
Argentine; CDP; GENESEE; ▲ Argentine; **189** Q-11; ★ **FLN**; mail Linden **z** 48451; Ⓟ 1,907; Ⓒ 2,285
Argentine; MCD-Township; GENESEE; ***189** P-10; ★ **FLN**; mail Linden **z** 48451; Ⓟ 4,651; Ⓒ 6,521
Argyle; RMC Place; SANILAC; ▲ Argyle; **189** N-13; 🅿; **z** 48410; ● 160
Argyle; MCD-Township; SANILAC; ***189** N-13; 🅿; **z** 48410; Ⓟ 820; Ⓒ 770
Arlington; MCD-Township; VAN BUREN; ***189** R-5; mail Bangor **z** 49013; Ⓟ 1,929; Ⓒ 2,075
Armada; Inc. Place; MACOMB; ▲ Armada; **189** P-13; 🅿; ★ **DET**; **z** 48005; Ⓟ 1,548; Ⓒ 1,573
Armada; MCD-Township; MACOMB; ***189** P-13; 🅿; ★ **DET**; **z** 48005; Ⓟ 4,491; Ⓒ 5,246
Armstrong Corners; RMC Place; VAN BUREN; ▲ Waverly, Almena; ***189** R-5; ★ **KZOO**; mail Paw Paw **z** 49079; rural
Arnheim; RMC Place; BARAGA; ▲ Baraga; ***188** B-13; elev. 654ft./199m.; mail Pelkie **z** 49958; ● 110
Arnold (Mashek); RMC Place; MARQUETTE; ▲ Wells; **188** E-1; elev. 1,032ft./315m.; 🅿; **z** 49819; ● 50
Artesia Beach; RMC Place; ROSCOMMON; ▲ Richfield; ***189** K-9; elev. 1,164ft./355m.; mail Saint Helen **z** 48656; ● 290
Arthur; MCD-Township; CLARE; ***189** M-8; mail Clare **z** 48617; Ⓟ 544; Ⓒ 667
Arthur Bay; RMC Place; MENOMINEE; ▲ Ingallston; ***188** H-1; elev. 592ft./180m.; mail Menominee **z** 49858; rural
Arvon; MCD-Township; BARAGA; ***188** B-13; mail Skanee **z** 49962; Ⓟ 422; Ⓒ 482

Entries in **UPPERCASE** are counties.
Entries in **bold** have populations of 2,500 or more.
Names in parentheses are alternate names.

Inc. Place	Incorporated Place
RMC Place	Rand McNally Designated Place
CDP	Census Designated Place
MCD	Minor Civil Division
⊡	County Seat
▲	Minor Civil Division
elev.	Elevation
🅿	Post Office
🅷	Hospital
🅲	College
■	Principal Business Center
★	Ranally Metro Area (RMA) Abbreviation
z	Zip Code(s)
Ⓟ	Previous Census Population
Ⓡ	Revised Census Population
Ⓐ	Annexation Population
●	Rand McNally Population Estimate
Ⓒ	Final Census Population
Ⓢ	Special Census Population
◆	Estimated Population

For additional definitions see Glossary, Volume 1, and Introduction, Volume 2.

Ash; MCD-Township; MONROE; *189 S-12; ★ DET; mail Carleton z 48117; Ⓟ 7,480; Ⓒ 7,610
Ashland; MCD-Township; NEWAYGO; *189 O-5; mail Grant z 49327; Ⓟ 1,997; Ⓒ 2,570
Ashland Center; RMC Place; NEWAYGO; ▲ Ashland; *189 O-5; mail Grant z 49327; ● 30
Ashley; Inc. Place; GRATIOT; ▲ Elba; 189 O-9; elev. 671ft./205m.; 🅿; z 48806; Ⓟ 518; Ⓒ 526
Ashmore; RMC Place; TUSCOLA; ▲ Columbia; *189 N-12; mail Unionville z 48767; rural
Ashton; RMC Place; OSCEOLA; ▲ Lincoln; 189 L-6; mail Leroy z 49655, Reed City z 49677; ● 110
Askel; RMC Place; HOUGHTON; ▲ Portage; *188 B-13; elev. 622ft./190m.; mail Pelkie z 49958; ● 30
Assinins; RMC Place; BARAGA; 188 B-13; elev. 673ft./205m.
Assyria; RMC Place; BARRY; ▲ Assyria; 189 R-7; mail Bellevue z 49021; ● 50
Assyria; MCD-Township; BARRY; *189 R-7; mail Bellevue z 49021; Ⓟ 1,799; Ⓒ 1,912
Athens; Inc. Place; CALHOUN; ▲ Athens; 189 S-7; elev. 896ft./273m.; 🅿; z 49011; Ⓟ 990; Ⓒ 1,111
Athens; MCD-Township; CALHOUN; *189 S-7; 🅿; z 49011; Ⓟ 2,515; Ⓒ 2,571
Atlanta; CDP; ⊡ MONTMORENCY; ▲ Briley; 188 I-10; 🅿; z 49709; Ⓒ 757
Atlantic Mine; RMC Place; HOUGHTON; ▲ Adams; *188 A-12; 🅿; z 49905; ● 530
Atlas; RMC Place; GENESEE; ▲ Atlas; 189 P-11; elev. 846ft./258m.; 🅿; ★ FLN; z 48411; ● 290
Atlas; MCD-Township; GENESEE; *189 P-11; 🅿; ★ FLN; z 48411 & mail Goodrich z 48438; Ⓟ 5,551; Ⓒ 7,257
Attica; RMC Place; LAPEER; ▲ Attica; 189 P-12; 🅿; ★ DET; z 48412; ● 420
Attica; MCD-Township; LAPEER; *189 P-12; 🅿; ★ DET; z 48412; Ⓟ 3,873; Ⓒ 4,678
Atwood; RMC Place; ANTRIM; ▲ Banks; *188 H-7; mail Ellsworth z 49729; ● 70
Auburn; Inc. Place; BAY; 189 N-10; elev. 620ft./189m.; 🅿; ★ SAG-; z 48611; Ⓟ 1,855; Ⓒ 2,011
Auburn Heights; OAKLAND; see Auburn Hills (Inc. Place)
Auburn Hills (Auburn Heights); Inc. Place; OAKLAND; 190 F-5; 🅿 🅷 🅲 3,740; ★ DET; z 48321, z 48326; Ⓟ 17,076; Ⓒ 19,837; ◆ 19,966
Au Gres; Inc. Place; ARENAC; 189 L-11; elev. 589ft./180m.; 🅿; z 48703; Ⓟ 838; Ⓒ 1,028
Au Gres; MCD-Township; ARENAC; *189 L-11; 🅿; z 48703; does not include the City of Au Gres; Ⓟ 1,007; Ⓒ 1,007
Augusta; Inc. Place; KALAMAZOO; ▲ Charleston, Ross; 189 R-7; 🅿; ★ KZOO; z 49012; Ⓟ 927; Ⓒ 899
Augusta; MCD-Charter Township; WASHTENAW; *189 S-11; ★ DET; mail Milan z 48160, Willis z 48191; Ⓟ 4,415; Ⓒ 4,813
Aura; RMC Place; BARAGA; ▲ L'Anse; *188 B-13; mail Lanse z 49946; ● 100
Aurelius; RMC Place; INGHAM; ▲ Aurelius; 189 Q-9; ★ LANS; mail Mason z 48854; ● 270
Aurelius; MCD-Township; INGHAM; *189 Q-9; ★ LANS; mail Mason z 48854; Ⓟ 2,686; Ⓒ 3,318
Aurora; RMC Place; GOGEBIC; ▲ Ironwood; *188 C-10; elev. 1,582ft./482m.; mail Ironwood z 49938; pop. incl. with Ironwood (Inc. Place)
Au Sable; CDP; IOSCO; ▲ Au Sable; 189 K-12; 🅿; z 48750; Ⓟ 1,542; Ⓒ 1,533
Au Sable; MCD-Charter Township; IOSCO; *189 K-12; 🅿; z 48750; Ⓟ 2,312; Ⓒ 2,230
Au Sable; MCD-Township; ROSCOMMON; *189 K-9; mail Roscommon z 48653; Ⓟ 231; Ⓒ 281
Au Sable River Park; RMC Place; ROSCOMMON; ▲ Richfield; *189 K-9; mail Saint Helen z 48656; ● 180
Austin; RMC Place; HILLSDALE; ▲ Woodbridge, Amboy; *189 T-8; mail Camden z 49232; ● 30
Austin; RMC Place; MARQUETTE; ▲ Forsyth; 188 D-1; elev. 1,150ft./351m.; mail Gwinn z 49841; ● 70
Austin; MCD-Township; MECOSTA; *189 N-7; mail Stanwood z 49346; Ⓟ 1,102; Ⓒ 1,415
Austin; MCD-Township; SANILAC; *189 N-13; mail Ubly z 48475; Ⓟ 639; Ⓒ 673
Austin Center; RMC Place; SANILAC; ▲ Austin; *189 N-13; elev. 791ft./241m.; mail Ubly z 48475; rural
Austin Lake; RMC Place; KALAMAZOO; ★ KZOO; mail Portage z 49081; pop. incl. with Portage (Inc. Place)
Au Train; RMC Place; ALGER; ▲ Au Train; 188 D-3; elev. 612ft./187m.; 🅿; z 49806; ● 490
Au Train; MCD-Township; ALGER; *188 D-3; 🅿; z 49806; Ⓟ 1,047; Ⓒ 1,172
Auvinen Corner; RMC Place; GOGEBIC; ▲ Ironwood; *188 B-10; elev. 1,213ft./370m.; mail Ironwood z 49938; rural
Avalon Beach; RMC Place; MONROE; ▲ Monroe; *189 T-12; ★ MONR; mail Monroe z 48161; ● 410
Averill; RMC Place; MIDLAND; ▲ Lincoln; 189 N-9; ★ SAG-; mail Sanford z 48657; ● 400
Avery; MCD-Township; MONTMORENCY; *188 I-10; mail Atlanta z 49709; Ⓟ 579; Ⓒ 717
Avoca; RMC Place; ST. CLAIR; ▲ Kenockee; 189 O-13; 🅿; z 48006; ● 270
Avondale; RMC Place; OSCEOLA; ▲ Hartwick; *189 L-7; elev. 1,230ft./375m.; mail Evart z 49631; rural
Azalia; RMC Place; MONROE; ▲ Milan; 189 S-11; 🅿; ★ DET; z 48110; ● 120

B

Bach; RMC Place; HURON; ▲ Sebewaing, Brookfield; 189 M-12; mail Sebewaing z 48759; ● 30
Backus; MCD-Township; ROSCOMMON; *189 K-9; mail Saint Helen z 48656; Ⓟ 249; Ⓒ 350
Backus Beach; RMC Place; ALCONA; ▲ Hawes; *188 J-11; mail Spruce z 48762; ● 730
Bad Axe; Inc. Place; ⊡ HURON; 189 M-13; elev. 765ft./233m.; 🅿 🅷; z 48413; Ⓟ 3,484; Ⓒ 3,462
Bagley; RMC Place; MENOMINEE; ▲ Nadeau; *188 G-1; elev. 779ft./237m.; mail Daggett z 49821
Bagley; MCD-Township; OTSEGO; *188 I-8; mail Gaylord z 49735; Ⓟ 4,929; Ⓒ 5,838
Baie de Wasai; RMC Place; CHIPPEWA; ▲ Sugar Island; *188 D-9; mail Sault Sainte Marie z 49783; ● 60
Bailey; RMC Place; MUSKEGON; ▲ Casnovia; 189 O-5; elev. 832ft./254m.; 🅿; z 49303; ● 330
Bainbridge; MCD-Township; BERRIEN; *189 S-4; ★ BNTH-; mail Benton Harbor z 49022; Ⓟ 2,865; Ⓒ 3,132
Bainbridge Center; RMC Place; BERRIEN; ▲ Bainbridge; *189 S-4; elev. 789ft./240m.; ★ BNTH-; mail Benton Harbor z 49022; ● 30
Bakertown; RMC Place; BERRIEN; ▲ Bertrand; *189 T-4; elev. 722ft./220m.; mail Buchanan z 49107; rural
Baldwin; MCD-Township; DELTA; *188 F-2; mail Perkins z 49872; Ⓟ 726; Ⓒ 748
Baldwin; MCD-Township; IOSCO; *189 K-11; mail Whittemore z 48770; Ⓟ 1,670; Ⓒ 1,726
Baldwin; Inc. Place; ⊡ LAKE; ▲ Webber, Pleasant Plains; 189 M-5; elev. 838ft./255m.; 🅿; z 49304; Ⓟ 821; Ⓒ 1,107
Baltic; RMC Place; HOUGHTON; ▲ Adams; *188 A-12; mail Atlantic Mine z 49905; ● 200
Baltimore; MCD-Township; BARRY; *189 Q-7; mail Hastings z 49058; Ⓟ 1,701; Ⓒ 1,845
Baltimore; RMC Place; ONTONAGON; ▲ Stannard; *188 B-11; mail Bruce Crossing z 49912; rural
Bamfields; RMC Place; ALCONA; ▲ Mitchell; *188 J-10; elev. 900ft./274m.; mail Glennie z 48737; ● 40
Banat; RMC Place; MENOMINEE; ▲ Holmes; *188 G-1; elev. 796ft./243m.; mail Daggett z 49821; ● 40
Bancroft; Inc. Place; SHIAWASSEE; ▲ Shiawassee; 189 P-10; elev. 854ft./260m.; 🅿; ★ FLN; z 48414; Ⓟ 599; Ⓒ 616
Banfield; RMC Place; BARRY; ▲ Johnstown; 189 R-7; elev. 967ft./295m.; ★ BTLCK; mail Battle Creek z 49017; ● 40
Bangor; MCD-Charter Township; BAY; *189 N-10; ★ SAG-; mail Bay City z 48706; Ⓟ 16,028; Ⓒ 15,547
Bangor; Inc. Place; VAN BUREN; 189 R-5; elev. 658ft./201m.; 🅿; z 49013; Ⓟ 1,922; Ⓒ 1,933
Bangor; MCD-Township; VAN BUREN; *189 R-5; 🅿; z 49013 & mail Berrien Springs z 49103; does not include the City of Bangor; Ⓟ 1,948; Ⓒ 2,121
Bankers; RMC Place; HILLSDALE; ▲ Hillsdale, Cambria; *189 T-8; mail Hillsdale z 49242; ● 80
Banks; MCD-Township; ANTRIM; *188 H-7; mail Ellsworth z 49729; Ⓟ 1,513; Ⓒ 1,813
Banksons Lake; RMC Place; VAN BUREN; ▲ Porter; mail Lawton z 49065; summer pop. 200
Bannister; RMC Place; GRATIOT; ▲ Elba; 189 O-9; 🅿; z 48807; ● 250
Baraga; Inc. Place; BARAGA; ▲ Baraga; 188 B-13; elev. 614ft./187m.; 🅿; z 49908; Ⓟ 1,231; Ⓒ 1,285
Baraga; MCD-Township; BARAGA; *188 B-13; 🅿; z 49908; Ⓟ 2,832; Ⓒ 3,542
BARAGA; 188 B-13; Ⓟ 7,954; Ⓒ 8,746; ◆ 8,516
Barbeau; RMC Place; CHIPPEWA; ▲ Bruce; 188 D-9; elev. 656ft./200m.; 🅿; z 49710; summer pop. 500; ● 100
Barker Creek; RMC Place; KALKASKA; ▲ Clearwater; *188 J-7; elev. 653ft./199m.; mail Williamsburg z 49690; rural
Bark River; RMC Place; DELTA; ▲ Bark River; 188 G-2; elev. 744ft./227m.; 🅿; z 49807; ● 280
Bark River; MCD-Township; DELTA; *188 F-2; 🅿; z 49807; Ⓟ 1,548; Ⓒ 1,650
Bar Lake; RMC Place; MANISTEE; ▲ Manistee; 189 K-4; mail Manistee z 49660; ● 280
Barnard; RMC Place; CHARLEVOIX; ▲ Norwood, Marion; *188 H-7; mail Charlevoix z 49720
Barnes Lake-Millers Lake; CDP-Census Area Only; LAPEER; ▲ Deerfield; *189 O-12; ★ DET; mail Columbiaville z 48421; Ⓟ 1,304; Ⓒ 1,187
Baroda; Inc. Place; BERRIEN; ▲ Baroda; 189 S-4; 🅿; ★ BNTH-; z 49101; Ⓟ 657; Ⓒ 858
Baroda; MCD-Township; BERRIEN; *189 T-4; 🅿; ★ BNTH-; z 49101; Ⓟ 2,731; Ⓒ 2,880
Barron Lake; RMC Place; CASS; ▲ Howard; 189 T-5; ★ S.B.; mail Niles z 49120; ● 1,570
Barry; MCD-Township; BARRY; *189 R-7; ★ KZOO; mail Hickory Corners z 49060; Ⓟ 3,190; Ⓒ 3,489
BARRY; 189 Q-7; Ⓟ 50,057; Ⓒ 56,755; ◆ 59,379
Barryton; Inc. Place; MECOSTA; ▲ Fork; 189 M-7; elev. 976ft./297m.; 🅿; z 49305; Ⓟ 393; Ⓒ 381
Barton; MCD-Township; NEWAYGO; *189 M-6; mail Paris z 49338; Ⓟ 624; Ⓒ 820
Barton City; RMC Place; ALCONA; ▲ Hawes, Millen; 188 J-11; 🅿; z 48705; ● 350
Barton Hills; Inc. Place; WASHTENAW; ▲ Ann Arbor; 190 A-5; ★ DET; mail Ann Arbor z 48105; Ⓟ 320; Ⓒ 335
Barton Lake; RMC Place; KALAMAZOO; ▲ Schoolcraft; 189 S-6; ★ KZOO; mail Vicksburg z 49097; ● 420
Base Line Lake; RMC Place; ALLEGAN, VAN BUREN; ▲ Pine Grove, Trowbridge; *189 R-5; elev. 750ft./229m.; mail Gobles z 49055; ● 150
Bass Lake; RMC Place; MASON; ▲ Summit; *189 M-4; mail Pentwater z 49449; ● 50
Batavia (Batavia Station); RMC Place; BRANCH; ▲ Batavia; 189 T-7; mail Coldwater z 49036; ● 120
Batavia; MCD-Township; BRANCH; *189 T-7; mail Coldwater z 49036; Ⓟ 1,522; Ⓒ 1,546
Batavia Center; RMC Place; BRANCH; ▲ Batavia; *189 T-7; elev. 927ft./283m.; mail Coldwater z 49036; ● 30
Batavia Station; BRANCH; see Batavia (RMC Place)
Bates; RMC Place; GRAND TRAVERSE; ▲ Acme; 188 J-6; elev. 722ft./220m.; mail Williamsburg z 49690; ● 30
Bates; RMC Place; IRON; ▲ Bates; *188 C-12; elev. 1,601ft./488m.; mail Iron River z 49935; ● 150
Bates; MCD-Township; IRON; *188 C-12; mail Iron River z 49935; Ⓟ 966; Ⓒ 1,021
Bath; RMC Place; CLINTON; ▲ Bath; 189 Q-9; 🅿; ★ LANS; z 48808; ● 730
Bath; MCD-Charter Township; CLINTON; *189 Q-9; 🅿; ★ LANS; z 48808; Ⓟ 6,387; Ⓒ 7,541
Battle Creek; Inc. Place; CALHOUN; 189 R-7; 🅿 🅷 ■; ★ BTLCK; z 49014-18, z 49037; Ⓟ 53,540; Ⓒ 53,364; ◆ 51,512
Bauer; RMC Place; OTTAWA; ▲ Georgetown, Blendon; 189 P-5; ★ GDR; mail Hudsonville z 49426; ● 190
Baw Beese Lake; RMC Place; HILLSDALE; ▲ Hillsdale, Cambria; *189 T-9; elev. 1,100ft./335m.; mail Hillsdale z 49242; ● 210
Bay; MCD-Township; CHARLEVOIX; *188 H-7; mail Boyne City z 49712; Ⓟ 825; Ⓒ 1,068
BAY; 189 M-10; Ⓟ 111,723; Ⓒ 110,157; ◆ 105,505
Bay City; Inc. Place; ⊡ BAY; 189 N-10; 🅿 🅷 🅲 9,543 ■; ★ SAG-; z 48706-08, z 48710; Ⓟ 38,936; Ⓒ 36,817; ◆ 34,985
Bay de Noc; MCD-Township; DELTA; *188 F-3; mail Rapid River z 49878; Ⓟ 320; Ⓒ 329
Bay Harbor; RMC Place; EMMET; 188 H-7; 🅿; z 49770; pop. incl. with Petoskey (Inc. Place)
Bay Mills; RMC Place; CHIPPEWA; ▲ Bay Mills; 188 D-8; elev. 605ft./184m.; mail Brimley z 49715; ● 170
Bay Mills; MCD-Township; CHIPPEWA; *188 D-8; mail Brimley z 49715; Ⓟ 787; Ⓒ 1,214
Bay Mills Reservation; Indian Reservation; CHIPPEWA; mail Brimley z 49715; also location of Indian Agency; Ⓟ 322; Ⓒ 605
Bay Park; RMC Place; TUSCOLA; 189 N-11
Bay Port; RMC Place; HURON; ▲ McKinley, Fairhaven; 189 M-12; 🅿; z 48720; ● 600
Bayshore; RMC Place; CHARLEVOIX, EMMET; ▲ Resort, Hayes; 188 H-7; mail Bay Shore z 49711; ● 260
Bay View; RMC Place; EMMET; ▲ Bear Creek; 188 H-8; 🅿; z 49770; summer pop. 1,000
Beach Grove; RMC Place; MENOMINEE; ▲ Ingallston; *188 H-1; elev. 587ft./179m.; mail Menominee z 49858; rural
Beacon; RMC Place; MARQUETTE; ▲ Champion; *188 B-13; mail Champion z 49814
Beacon Hill; RMC Place; HOUGHTON; ▲ Stanton; *188 A-12; mail Atlantic Mine z 49905; ● 30
Beadle Lake; RMC Place; CALHOUN; ▲ Emmett; 189 R-7; ★ BTLCK; mail Battle Creek z 49014; ● 1,550
Beal City; CDP; ISABELLA; ▲ Nottawa; 189 N-8; elev. 865ft./264m.; mail Mount Pleasant z 48858; Ⓟ 345; Ⓒ 345
Bear Creek; MCD-Township; EMMET; *188 H-8; mail Petoskey z 49770; Ⓟ 3,469; Ⓒ 5,269
Bearinger; MCD-Township; PRESQUE ISLE; *188 G-9; mail Millersburg z 49759; Ⓟ 246; Ⓒ 329
Bear Lake; RMC Place; HILLSDALE; ▲ Cambria; *189 T-8; elev. 1,100ft./335m.; mail Hillsdale z 49242; ● 160
Bear Lake; MCD-Township; KALKASKA; *188 J-8; mail Kalkaska z 49646; Ⓟ 639; Ⓒ 746
Bear Lake; Inc. Place; MANISTEE; ▲ Bear Lake; 189 K-5; 🅿; z 49614; Ⓟ 339; Ⓒ 318
Bear Lake; MCD-Township; MANISTEE; *189 K-5; 🅿; z 49614; Ⓟ 1,419; Ⓒ 1,587
Beaugrand; MCD-Township; CHEBOYGAN; *188 G-9; mail Cheboygan z 49721; Ⓟ 1,004; Ⓒ 1,157
Beaver; MCD-Township; BAY; *189 M-10; ★ SAG-; mail Auburn z 48611; Ⓟ 2,810; Ⓒ 2,806
Beaver; MCD-Township; NEWAYGO; *189 N-5; mail Bitely z 49309; Ⓟ 417; Ⓒ 608
Beaver Creek; MCD-Township; CRAWFORD; *188 J-8; mail Roscommon z 48653; Ⓟ 1,175; Ⓒ 1,486
Beaverdam; RMC Place; OTTAWA; ▲ Zeeland; *189 P-5; elev. 682ft./208m.; ★ HLND; mail Zeeland z 49464; ● 90
Beaver Grove; RMC Place; MARQUETTE; ▲ Chocolay; *188 D-2; mail Marquette z 49855; ● 160
Beaver Island; CHARLEVOIX; see Saint James (RMC Place)
Beaverton; Inc. Place; GLADWIN; 189 M-9; 🅿; z 48612; Ⓟ 1,150; Ⓒ 1,106
Beaverton; MCD-Township; GLADWIN; *189 M-9; 🅿; z 48612; does not include the City of Beaverton; Ⓟ 1,671; Ⓒ 1,815
Bedford; RMC Place; CALHOUN; ▲ Bedford; 189 R-7; 🅿; ★ BTLCK; z 49020; ● 260
Bedford; MCD-Charter Township; CALHOUN; *189 R-7; 🅿; ★ BTLCK; z 49020 & mail Battle Creek z 49017; Ⓟ 9,810; Ⓒ 9,517
Bedford; MCD-Township; MONROE; *189 T-11; ★ TOL; mail Lambertville z 48144, Temperance z 48182; Ⓟ 23,748; Ⓒ 28,606; ◆ 30,085
Beebe; RMC Place; GRATIOT; ▲ Emerson; *189 O-9; mail Ithaca z 48847
Beecher; CDP; GENESEE; ▲ Flint; 190 A-9; ★ FLN; mail Mount Morris z 48458; Ⓟ 14,465; Ⓒ 12,793
Beechwood; RMC Place; IRON; ▲ Iron River; 188 C-12; 🅿; z 49935; ● 30
Beechwood; RMC Place; OGEMAW; ▲ Rose; *189 K-10; elev. 1,026ft./313m.; mail Rose City z 48654; ● 30
Beechwood; CDP-Census Area Only; OTTAWA; ▲ Park, Holland; 189 Q-5; ★ HLND; mail Holland z 49423; Ⓟ 2,676; Ⓒ 2,963
Belding; Inc. Place; IONIA; 189 P-7; elev. 780ft./238m.; 🅿; z 48809, z 48887; Ⓟ 5,969; Ⓒ 5,877
Belknap; MCD-Township; PRESQUE ISLE; *188 H-10; mail Hawks z 49743; Ⓟ 920; Ⓒ 854
Belknap Corner; PRESQUE ISLE; see Nagel Corner (RMC Place)
Bell; RMC Place; PRESQUE ISLE; ▲ Presque Isle; *188 H-11; elev. 600ft./183m.; mail Alpena z 49707; rural
Bellaire; Inc. Place; ⊡ ANTRIM; ▲ Forest Home, Kearney; 188 I-7; elev. 616ft./188m.; 🅿; z 49615; Ⓟ 1,104; Ⓒ 1,164
Belleville; Inc. Place; WAYNE; 189 S-11; elev. 670ft./204m.; 🅿; ★ DET; z 48111-12; Ⓟ 3,270; Ⓒ 3,997
Bellevue; Inc. Place; EATON; ▲ Bellevue; 189 R-8; 🅿; z 49021; Ⓟ 1,401; Ⓒ 1,365
Bellevue; MCD-Township; EATON; *189 R-8; 🅿; z 49021; Ⓟ 2,938; Ⓒ 3,144
Bell Oak; RMC Place; INGHAM; ▲ Locke; 189 Q-10; elev. 922ft./281m.; mail Webberville z 48892; ● 30
Belmont; RMC Place; KENT; ▲ Plainfield; 189 P-6; elev. 667ft./203m.; 🅿; ★ GDR; z 49306; ● 730
Belsay; RMC Place; GENESEE; *189 P-11; elev. 777ft./237m.; ★ FLN; mail Flint z 48503; pop. incl. with Burton (Inc. Place)
Belvedere; RMC Place; CHARLEVOIX; ▲ Charlevoix; mail Charlevoix z 49720; summer pop. 350
Belvidere; MCD-Township; MONTCALM; *189 N-7; mail Six Lakes z 48886; Ⓟ 2,134; Ⓒ 2,438
Bendon; RMC Place; BENZIE; ▲ Inland; 188 J-5; mail Interlochen z 49643; ● 50
Bengal; MCD-Township; CLINTON; *189 P-8; mail Saint Johns z 48879; Ⓟ 989; Ⓒ 1,174
Bennington; RMC Place; SHIAWASSEE; ▲ Bennington; 189 P-9; elev. 792ft./241m.; mail Owosso z 48867; ● 50
Bennington; MCD-Township; SHIAWASSEE; *189 P-10; mail Owosso z 48867; Ⓟ 2,726; Ⓒ 3,017
Benona; MCD-Township; OCEANA; *189 N-4; mail Shelby z 49455; Ⓟ 1,133; Ⓒ 1,520
Bentheim; RMC Place; ALLEGAN; ▲ Reynolds; 189 Q-5; elev. 650ft./198m.; mail Hamilton z 49419; ● 100
Bentley; RMC Place; BAY; ▲ Gibson; 189 M-10; 🅿; z 48613; ● 100
Bentley; MCD-Township; GLADWIN; *189 M-9; mail Rhodes z 48652; Ⓟ 751; Ⓒ 859
Bentleys Corners (Bently Corners); RMC Place; CALHOUN; ▲ Clarendon; *189 S-8; elev. 1,019ft./311m.; mail Homer z 49245; ● 150
Bently Corners; CALHOUN; see Bentleys Corners (RMC Place)
Benton; MCD-Charter Township; BERRIEN; *189 S-4; ★ BNTH-; mail Benton Harbor z 49022; Ⓟ 17,163; Ⓒ 16,404
Benton; MCD-Township; CHEBOYGAN; *188 G-9; mail Cheboygan z 49721; Ⓟ 2,388; Ⓒ 3,080
Benton; MCD-Township; EATON; *189 Q-8; ★ LANS; mail Potterville z 48876; Ⓟ 2,528; Ⓒ 2,712
Benton Harbor; Inc. Place; BERRIEN; ▲ Benton; 189 S-4; 🅿 ■; ★ BNTH-; z 49022-23; Ⓟ 12,818; Ⓒ 11,182; ◆ 10,692
Benton Heights (Euclid Center); CDP; BERRIEN; ▲ Benton; 189 S-4; ★ BNTH-; mail Benton Harbor z 49022; Ⓟ 5,465; Ⓒ 5,458
BENZIE; 188 J-5; Ⓟ 12,200; Ⓒ 15,998; ◆ 17,192
Benzonia; Inc. Place; BENZIE; ▲ Benzonia; 188 J-5; 🅿; z 49616; Ⓟ 449; Ⓒ 519; Ⓡ 480
Benzonia; MCD-Township; BENZIE; *188 J-5; 🅿; z 49616; Ⓟ 2,405; Ⓒ 2,839
Bergland; RMC Place; ONTONAGON; ▲ Bergland; 188 B-11; 🅿; z 49910; ● 670
Bergland; MCD-Township; ONTONAGON; *188 B-11; 🅿; z 49910; Ⓟ 618; Ⓒ 550
Berkley; Inc. Place; OAKLAND; 190 H-5; elev. 680ft./207m.; 🅿; ★ DET; z 48072; Ⓟ 16,960; Ⓒ 15,531
Berlamont; RMC Place; VAN BUREN; ▲ Columbia, Bloomingdale; *189 R-5; elev. 702ft./214m.; mail Bloomingdale z 49026; rural
Berlin; MCD-Township; IONIA; *189 P-7; ★ GDR; mail Ionia z 48846; Ⓟ 3,610; Ⓒ 2,787; Ⓡ 1,828
Berlin; MCD-Charter Township; MONROE; *189 S-12; ★ DET; mail Newport z 48166; Ⓟ 6,286; Ⓒ 6,924
Berlin; MCD-Township; ST. CLAIR; *189 P-13; 🅿; z 48002 & mail Capac z 48014; Ⓟ 2,407; Ⓒ 3,162
Berne; RMC Place; HURON; ▲ McKinley; *189 M-12; elev. 623ft./190m.; mail Pigeon z 48755; ● 50
Berrien; MCD-Township; BERRIEN; *189 T-4; mail Berrien Center z 49102; Ⓟ 4,697; Ⓒ 5,075
BERRIEN; 189 S-4; Ⓟ 161,378; Ⓒ 162,453; ◆ 155,093
Berrien Center; RMC Place; BERRIEN; ▲ Berrien; 189 T-4; 🅿; z 49102; ● 250
Berrien Springs; Inc. Place; BERRIEN; ▲ Oronoko; 189 T-4; 🅿 🅲 3,195; z 49103-04; Ⓟ 1,927; Ⓒ 1,862
Berryville; RMC Place; JACKSON; ▲ Tompkins; *189 R-9; elev. 950ft./290m.; mail Rives Junction z 49277; rural
Bertrand; RMC Place; BERRIEN; ▲ Niles; 189 T-4; ★ S.B.; mail Niles z 49120; ● 5,500
Bertrand; MCD-Township; BERRIEN; *189 T-4; mail Niles z 49120; Ⓟ 2,228; Ⓒ 2,380
Berville; RMC Place; ST. CLAIR; ▲ Berlin; 189 P-13; 🅿; z 48002; ● 310
Bessemer; Inc. Place; ⊡ GOGEBIC; 188 B-10; elev. 1,432ft./436m.; 🅿; z 49911; Ⓟ 2,272; Ⓒ 2,148
Bessemer; MCD-Township; GOGEBIC; *188 C-10; 🅿; z 49911 & mail Ramsay z 49959; does not include the City of Bessemer; Ⓟ 1,374; Ⓒ 1,270
Bete Grise; RMC Place; KEWEENAW; ▲ Grant; 188 A-14; elev. 632ft./193m.; mail Mohawk z 49950
Bethany; MCD-Township; GRATIOT; *189 N-9; mail Saint Louis z 48880; Ⓟ 1,814; Ⓒ 3,492; Ⓡ 2,533
Bethany Beach; RMC Place; BERRIEN; ▲ Chikaming; *189 T-3; mail Sawyer z 49125; ● 60
Bethel; RMC Place; BRANCH; ▲ Bethel; *189 T-7; elev. 997ft./304m.; mail Coldwater z 49036; ● 50
Bethel; MCD-Township; BRANCH; *189 T-7; mail Coldwater z 49036; Ⓟ 1,279; Ⓒ 1,421
Betsy; RMC Place; KEWEENAW; ▲ Grant; *188 A-13; elev. 616ft./188m.; mail Lake Linden z 49945; ● 30
Betzer; RMC Place; HILLSDALE; ▲ Wright, Ransom; *189 T-9; elev. 908ft./277m.; mail Pittsford z 49271; rural
Beulah; Inc. Place; ⊡ BENZIE; ▲ Benzonia; 188 J-5; 🅿; z 49617; Ⓟ 421; Ⓒ 363; Ⓡ 402
Beverly Hills; RMC Place; MARQUETTE; *188 D-1; elev. 1,395ft./425m.; mail Negaunee z 49866; pop. incl. with Negaunee (Inc. Place)
Beverly Hills (Westwood); Inc. Place; OAKLAND; ▲ Southfield; 190 H-5; 🅿; ★ DET; z 48025; Ⓟ 10,610; Ⓒ 10,437
Big Bay; CDP; MARQUETTE; ▲ Powell; 188 B-14; 🅿; z 49808; Ⓒ 265
Big Creek; MCD-Township; OSCODA; *188 J-9; mail Mio z 48647; Ⓟ 2,778; Ⓒ 3,380
Biggs Settlement; RMC Place; OSCODA; ▲ Elmer, Comins; *188 J-10; mail Mio z 48647; rural
Big Prairie; MCD-Township; NEWAYGO; *189 N-6; mail White Cloud z 49349; Ⓟ 1,731; Ⓒ 2,465
Big Rapids; Inc. Place; ⊡ MECOSTA; 189 M-6; 🅿 🅷 🅲 12,575; z 49307; Ⓟ 12,603; Ⓒ 10,849
Big Rapids; MCD-Charter Township; MECOSTA; *189 N-6; 🅿 🅲 12,575; z 49307; does not include the City of Big Rapids; Ⓟ 3,100; Ⓒ 3,249
Big Rock; RMC Place; MONTMORENCY; ▲ Briley; 188 I-9; mail Atlanta z 49709
Billings; MCD-Township; GLADWIN; *189 M-9; mail Beaverton z 48612; Ⓟ 2,305; Ⓒ 2,715
Bingham; MCD-Township; CLINTON; *189 P-9; mail Saint Johns z 48879; Ⓟ 2,546; Ⓒ 2,776; Ⓡ 2,517
Bingham; MCD-Township; HURON; *189 M-13; mail Ubly z 48475; Ⓟ 1,617; Ⓒ 1,751
Bingham; MCD-Township; LEELANAU; *188 I-6; mail Traverse City z 49684; Ⓟ 2,051; Ⓒ 2,425
Bingham Farms; Inc. Place; OAKLAND; ▲ Southfield; 190 H-5; elev. 716ft./218m.; 🅿; ★ DET; z 48025; Ⓟ 1,001; Ⓒ 1,030
Birch Beach; RMC Place; SANILAC; ▲ Worth; 189 O-14; ★ PTHU; mail Lexington z 48450; ● 360
Birch Creek; RMC Place; MENOMINEE; ▲ Menominee; 188 H-1; elev. 649ft./198m.; mail Menominee z 49858
Birch Run; Inc. Place; SAGINAW; ▲ Birch Run; 189 O-11; elev. 635ft./194m.; 🅿; ★ FLN; z 48415; Ⓟ 992; Ⓒ 1,653
Birch Run; MCD-Township; SAGINAW; *189 O-11; 🅿; ★ FLN; z 48415; Ⓟ 5,354; Ⓒ 6,191
Birchwood; RMC Place; BERRIEN; ▲ Chikaming; *189 T-3; mail Harbert z 49115; ● 50
Birchwood; RMC Place; CHEBOYGAN; ▲ Mullett; *188 G-9; mail Cheboygan z 49721; ● 60
Birmingham; Inc. Place; OAKLAND; 189 Q-12; elev. 781ft./238m.; 🅿 ■; ★ DET; z 48009, z 48012; Ⓟ 19,997; Ⓒ 19,291; ◆ 18,060
Bismarck; MCD-Township; PRESQUE ISLE; *188 H-10; mail Rogers City z 49779; Ⓟ 319; Ⓒ 408
Bitely; RMC Place; NEWAYGO; ▲ Lilley; 189 M-5; 🅿; z 49309; ● 200
Black Lake Bluffs; RMC Place; PRESQUE ISLE; ▲ Bearinger; *188 G-9; mail Onaway z 49765; ● 70
Blackman; MCD-Charter Township; JACKSON; *189 R-9; ★ JAC; mail Jackson z 49202; Ⓟ 20,492; Ⓒ 22,800; ◆ 23,753
Black River; RMC Place; ALCONA; ▲ Alcona; 188 I-12; elev. 590ft./180m.; 🅿; z 48721; ● 200
Black River Harbor; RMC Place; GOGEBIC; ▲ Ironwood; *188 B-10; mail Ironwood z 49938; ● 50
Blaine; MCD-Township; BENZIE; *189 K-5; mail Frankfort z 49635; Ⓟ 424; Ⓒ 491
Blaine; RMC Place; ST. CLAIR; ▲ Grant; 189 O-14; elev. 727ft./222m.; mail Jeddo z 48032
Blair; MCD-Township; GRAND TRAVERSE; *188 J-6; mail Traverse City z 49684; Ⓟ 5,249; Ⓒ 6,448
Blanchard; RMC Place; ISABELLA; ▲ Rolland; 189 N-7; 🅿; z 49310; ● 450
Blaney Park; RMC Place; SCHOOLCRAFT; ▲ Mueller; 188 E-5; elev. 738ft./225m.; mail Germfask z 49836; ● 30
Blendon; MCD-Township; OTTAWA; *189 P-5; ★ HLND; mail Hudsonville z 49426; Ⓟ 4,740; Ⓒ 5,721
Bliss; RMC Place; EMMET; ▲ Bliss; 188 G-8; mail Levering z 49755; ● 50
Bliss; MCD-Township; EMMET; *188 G-8; mail Levering z 49755; Ⓟ 483; Ⓒ 572
Blissfield; Inc. Place; LENAWEE; ▲ Blissfield; 189 T-11; elev. 694ft./212m.; 🅿; z 49228; Ⓟ 3,172; Ⓒ 3,223
Blissfield; MCD-Township; LENAWEE; *189 T-11; 🅿; z 49228; Ⓟ 3,849; Ⓒ 3,915
Bloomer; MCD-Township; MONTCALM; *189 O-8; mail Carson City z 48811; Ⓟ 2,922; Ⓒ 3,039; Ⓡ 3,652
Bloomfield; MCD-Township; HURON; *189 M-13; mail Port Hope z 48468; Ⓟ 563; Ⓒ 535
Bloomfield; MCD-Township; MISSAUKEE; *189 K-7; mail Lake City z 49651; Ⓟ 390; Ⓒ 475
Bloomfield; RMC Place; OAKLAND; ▲ Bloomfield; 🅿; ★ DET; z 48301-04; pop. incl. with Bloomfield Hills (Inc. Place)
Bloomfield; MCD-Township; OAKLAND; 190 G-4; 🅿; ★ DET; z 48301-04; Ⓟ 42,137; Ⓒ 43,023; ◆ 41,126
Bloomfield Glens; RMC Place; OAKLAND; ▲ West Bloomfield; ★ DET; mail West Bloomfield z 48322
Bloomfield Hills; Inc. Place; OAKLAND; ▲ Bloomfield; 190 G-5; 🅿; ★ DET; z 48301-04; Ⓟ 4,288; Ⓒ 3,940
Bloomfield Hills North; RMC Place; OAKLAND; ▲ Bloomfield; ★ DET; mail Bloomfield Hills z 48302
Bloomfield Township; CDP-Census Area Only; OAKLAND; ▲ Bloomfield; *189 Q-12; 🅿; ★ DET; z 48301-04; Ⓟ 42,137; Ⓒ 43,021; ◆ 41,126
Bloomfield Town Square; RMC Place; OAKLAND; ▲ Bloomfield; *189 Q-12; ★ DET; mail Bloomfield Hills z 48302
Bloomfield Village; RMC Place; OAKLAND; ▲ Bloomfield; *189 Q-12; 🅿; ★ DET; z 48301
Bloomingdale; Inc. Place; VAN BUREN; ▲ Bloomingdale; 189 R-5; 🅿; z 49026; Ⓟ 503; Ⓒ 528
Bloomingdale; MCD-Township; VAN BUREN; *189 R-5; 🅿; z 49026; Ⓟ 2,854; Ⓒ 3,364
Blue Jacket; RMC Place; HOUGHTON; ▲ Calumet; mail Calumet z 49913; pop. incl. with Calumet (Inc. Place)
Blue Lake; MCD-Township; KALKASKA; *188 J-8; mail Kalkaska z 49646; Ⓟ 378; Ⓒ 428
Blue Lake; MCD-Township; MUSKEGON; *189 N-4; mail Whitehall z 49461; Ⓟ 1,235; Ⓒ 1,990
Blue Water Beach; RMC Place; SANILAC; ▲ Worth; *189 O-14; ★ PTHU; mail Lexington z 48450; ● 310
Bluff Beach; RMC Place; ST. JOSEPH; ▲ White Pigeon; ★ ELK; mail White Pigeon z 49099
Bluffton; RMC Place; MUSKEGON; ★ MUS; pop. incl. with Muskegon (Inc. Place)
Blumfield; MCD-Township; SAGINAW; *189 N-11; mail Reese z 48757; Ⓟ 1,999; Ⓒ 2,014
Blumfield Corners; RMC Place; SAGINAW; ▲ Blumfield; *189 N-11; mail Reese z 48757; rural
Boardman; MCD-Township; KALKASKA; *188 J-7; mail South Boardman z 49680; Ⓟ 1,076; Ⓒ 1,373
Bohemia; MCD-Township; ONTONAGON; *188 B-12; mail Toivola z 49965; Ⓟ 90; Ⓒ 77
Boichot Acres; RMC Place; CLINTON; ▲ DeWitt; *189 Q-9; elev. 850ft./259m.; ★ LANS; mail Lansing z 48906; ● 200
Bois Blanc; MCD-Township; MACKINAC; *188 F-9; mail Pointe aux Pins z 49775; Ⓟ 59; Ⓒ 71
Bolles Harbor; RMC Place; MONROE; ▲ Monroe; *189 T-12; ★ MONR; mail Monroe z 48161; ● 720
Bolton; RMC Place; ALPENA; ▲ Maple Ridge; *188 H-11; elev. 731ft./223m.; mail Alpena z 49707; rural
Bombay; RMC Place; MIDLAND; ▲ Mills, Larkin; *189 M-9; elev. 671ft./205m.; ★ SAG-; mail Midland z 48642; ● 30
Boon; RMC Place; WEXFORD; ▲ Boon; 189 K-6; elev. 1,376ft./419m.; 🅿; z 49618; ● 110
Boon; MCD-Township; WEXFORD; *189 K-6; 🅿; z 49618; Ⓟ 562; Ⓒ 670
Bootjack; RMC Place; HOUGHTON; ▲ Torch Lake; *188 A-13; elev. 673ft./205m.; mail Lake Linden z 49945; ● 30
Borculo; RMC Place; OTTAWA; ▲ Olive, Blendon; 189 P-5; ★ HLND; mail Zeeland z 49464; ● 400
Boston; RMC Place; HOUGHTON; ▲ Franklin; *188 A-13; mail Hancock z 49930; ● 130
Boston; MCD-Township; IONIA; *189 P-7; ★ GDR; mail Saranac z 48881; Ⓟ 4,313; Ⓒ 4,961
Bostwick Lake; RMC Place; KENT; ▲ Cannon; 189 P-6; ★ GDR; mail Rockford z 49341; ● 800
Boulder Park; RMC Place; CHARLEVOIX; ▲ Charlevoix; *188 H-7; elev. 600ft./183m.; mail Charlevoix z 49720; summer pop. 2,000; ● 200
Bourret; MCD-Township; GLADWIN; *189 L-9; mail Alger z 48610; Ⓟ 400; Ⓒ 471
Bowens Mills; RMC Place; BARRY; ▲ Yankee Springs; *189 Q-6; elev. 776ft./237m.; ★ GDR; mail Middleville z 49333; ● 150
Bowne; MCD-Township; KENT; *189 Q-7; mail Alto z 49302; Ⓟ 1,907; Ⓒ 2,743
Boyne City; Inc. Place; CHARLEVOIX; 188 H-7; elev. 600ft./183m.; 🅿; z 49712; Ⓟ 3,478; Ⓒ 3,503
Boyne Falls; Inc. Place; CHARLEVOIX; ▲ Boyne Valley; 188 H-8; 🅿; z 49713; Ⓟ 369; Ⓒ 370
Boyne Valley; MCD-Township; CHARLEVOIX; *188 H-8; mail Boyne Falls z 49713; Ⓟ 1,102; Ⓒ 1,215
Bradley; RMC Place; ALLEGAN; ▲ Wayland; 189 Q-6; elev. 824ft./251m.; 🅿; z 49311; ● 170
Brady; MCD-Township; KALAMAZOO; *189 S-6; ★ KZOO; mail Vicksburg z 49097; Ⓟ 3,857; Ⓒ 4,263
Brady; MCD-Township; SAGINAW; *189 O-10; mail Oakley z 48649; Ⓟ 2,396; Ⓒ 2,344
Brampton; RMC Place; DELTA; ▲ Brampton; 188 F-2; 🅿; z 49837; ● 260
Brampton; MCD-Township; DELTA; *188 F-2; 🅿; z 49837; Ⓟ 1,142; Ⓒ 1,090
Branch; RMC Place; MASON, LAKE; ▲ Sweetwater, Branch; 189 M-5; 🅿; z 49402; ● 140
Branch; MCD-Township; MASON; *189 M-5; 🅿; z 49402 & mail Walhalla z 49458; Ⓟ 973; Ⓒ 1,181
BRANCH; 189 T-7; Ⓟ 41,502; Ⓒ 45,787; ◆ 46,078
Brandon; MCD-Charter Township; OAKLAND; *189 P-12; ★ DET; mail Ortonville z 48462; Ⓟ 12,051; Ⓒ 14,765
Brandywine Lake; RMC Place; VAN BUREN; ▲ Pine Grove; *189 R-5; elev. 782ft./238m.; mail Gobles z 49055; ● 150
Brant; RMC Place; SAGINAW; ▲ Brant; 189 O-9; elev. 613ft./187m.; 🅿; z 48614; ● 80
Brant; MCD-Township; SAGINAW; *189 O-9; 🅿; z 48614; Ⓟ 1,942; Ⓒ 2,023
Brassar; RMC Place; CHIPPEWA; ▲ Sugar Island; *188 D-9; mail Sault Sainte Marie z 49783; rural
Bravo; RMC Place; ALLEGAN; ▲ Clyde; 189 R-5; elev. 667ft./203m.; mail Fennville z 49408; ● 40
Breckenridge; Inc. Place; GRATIOT; ▲ Wheeler; 189 N-9; 🅿; z 48615; Ⓟ 1,301; Ⓒ 1,339
Breedsville; Inc. Place; VAN BUREN; ▲ Columbia; 189 R-5; 🅿; z 49027; Ⓟ 213; Ⓒ 235
Breen; MCD-Township; DICKINSON; *188 F-1; mail Foster City z 49834; Ⓟ 464; Ⓒ 479
Breezy Beach; RMC Place; ST. JOSEPH; ▲ White Pigeon; ★ ELK; mail White Pigeon z 49099
Breitung; MCD-Charter Township; DICKINSON; *188 D-13; mail Quinnesec z 49876; Ⓟ 5,483; Ⓒ 5,930
Brent Creek; RMC Place; GENESEE; ▲ Flushing; *189 O-10; ★ FLN; mail Flushing z 48433; ● 30
Brethren; RMC Place; MANISTEE; ▲ Dickson; 189 K-5; elev. 729ft./222m.; 🅿; z 49619; ● 240
Bretton Woods; RMC Place; EATON; ▲ Delta; ★ LANS; mail Lansing z 48917
Brevort; RMC Place; MACKINAC; ▲ Moran; 188 E-7; mail Moran z 49760; ● 130
Brevort; MCD-Township; MACKINAC; *188 E-8; mail Moran z 49760; Ⓟ 484; Ⓒ 649
Bridgehampton; MCD-Township; SANILAC; *189 N-13; mail Carsonville z 48419; Ⓟ 845; Ⓒ 911
Bridgeport; CDP; SAGINAW; ▲ Bridgeport; 189 O-10; 🅿; ★ SAG-; z 48722; Ⓟ 8,569; Ⓒ 7,849
Bridgeport; MCD-Charter Township; SAGINAW; *189 O-10; 🅿; ★ SAG-; z 48722; Ⓟ 12,747; Ⓒ 11,709
Bridgeton; RMC Place; NEWAYGO; ▲ Bridgeton; 189 O-5; mail Grant z 49327; ● 30
Bridgeton; MCD-Township; NEWAYGO; *189 O-5; mail Grant z 49327; Ⓟ 1,574; Ⓒ 2,098
Bridgeville; RMC Place; GRATIOT; ▲ Washington, Fulton; *189 O-9; elev. 650ft./198m.; mail Saint Johns z 48879; ● 50
Bridgewater; RMC Place; WASHTENAW; ▲ Bridgewater; 189 S-10; 🅿; z 48115; ● 140
Bridgewater; MCD-Township; WASHTENAW; *189 S-10; 🅿; z 48115 & mail Clinton z 49236, Manchester z 48158; Ⓟ 1,304; Ⓒ 1,646
Bridgman; Inc. Place; BERRIEN; 189 T-4; 🅿; z 49106; Ⓟ 2,140; Ⓒ 2,428
Brightmoor; RMC Place; WAYNE; *189 R-12; ★ DET; mail Detroit z 48223; pop. incl. with Detroit (Inc. Place)
Brighton; Inc. Place; LIVINGSTON; 189 Q-11; 🅿 🅷; ★ DET; z 48114, z 48116; Ⓟ 5,686; Ⓒ 6,701
Brighton; MCD-Township; LIVINGSTON; *189 Q-11; 🅿; ★ DET; z 48114, z 48116; does not include the City of Brighton; Ⓟ 14,815; Ⓒ 17,673
Briley; MCD-Township; MONTMORENCY; *188 I-9; mail Atlanta z 49709; Ⓟ 1,831; Ⓒ 2,029
Brimley; RMC Place; CHIPPEWA; ▲ Superior; 188 D-8; elev. 655ft./200m.; 🅿; z 49715; ● 560
Brinton; RMC Place; ISABELLA; ▲ Coldwater; 189 M-7; elev. 1,038ft./316m.; mail Lake z 48632; ● 70
Bristol; RMC Place; LAKE; ▲ Dover; *189 L-6; mail Tustin z 49688; ● 30
Britton; Inc. Place; LENAWEE; ▲ Ridgeway; 189 S-11; 🅿; z 49229; Ⓟ 694; Ⓒ 699
Broad Acres; RMC Place; MACOMB; ▲ Clinton; *189 Q-13; ★ DET; mail Clinton Township z 48035
Broadbridge Station; RMC Place; ST. CLAIR; ▲ Cottrellville; *189 Q-14; elev. 582ft./177m.; ★ DET; mail Marine City z 48039; ● 100
Brockway; RMC Place; ST. CLAIR; ▲ Brockway; 189 O-13; 🅿; z 48097; ● 30
Brockway; MCD-Township; ST. CLAIR; *189 O-13; 🅿; z 48097; Ⓟ 1,609; Ⓒ 1,900
Brohman; RMC Place; NEWAYGO; ▲ Merrill; 189 N-5; 🅿; z 49312; ● 200
Bronson; Inc. Place; BRANCH; 189 T-7; 🅿; z 49028; Ⓟ 2,342; Ⓒ 2,421
Bronson; MCD-Township; BRANCH; *189 T-7; 🅿; z 49028; does not include the City of Bronson; Ⓟ 1,228; Ⓒ 1,358
Brookfield; RMC Place; EATON; ▲ Brookfield; 189 R-8; elev. 928ft./283m.; mail Charlotte z 48813; ● 50
Brookfield; MCD-Township; EATON; *189 R-8; mail Charlotte z 48813; Ⓟ 1,331; Ⓒ 1,429
Brookfield; MCD-Township; HURON; *189 M-12; mail Owendale z 48754; Ⓟ 947; Ⓒ 914
Brooklyn; Inc. Place; JACKSON; ▲ Columbia; 189 S-10; elev. 992ft./302m.; 🅿; ★ JAC; z 49230; Ⓟ 1,027; Ⓒ 1,176
Brooks; MCD-Township; NEWAYGO; *189 N-6; mail Newaygo z 49337; Ⓟ 2,728; Ⓒ 3,671
Brookside; RMC Place; NEWAYGO; ▲ Sheridan; *189 N-5; mail Fremont z 49412; rural
Brookville; RMC Place; WASHTENAW; ▲ Plymouth; *189 R-11; elev. 880ft./268m.; ★ DET; mail Salem z 48175; rural
Broomfield; MCD-Township; ISABELLA; *189 N-7; mail Remus z 49340; Ⓟ 1,266; Ⓒ 1,620
Brown; MCD-Township; MANISTEE; *189 K-5; mail Manistee z 49660; Ⓟ 588; Ⓒ 712
Brown City; Inc. Place; SANILAC, LAPEER; 189 O-13; elev. 813ft./248m.; 🅿; z 48416; Ⓟ 1,244; Ⓒ 1,334
Brownlee Park; CDP; CALHOUN; ▲ Pennfield, Emmett; 189 R-7; ★ BTLCK; mail Battle Creek z 49014; Ⓟ 2,536; Ⓒ 2,588
Brownstown (Brownstown Township); MCD-Charter Township; WAYNE; 190 M-4; 🅿; ★ DET; z 48134, z 48164, z 48173-74, z 48183, z 48193 & mail Wyandotte z 48192; Ⓟ 18,811; Ⓒ 22,989; ◆ 24,035
Brownstown Township; WAYNE; see Brownstown (MCD-Charter Township)
Brownsville; RMC Place; CASS; ▲ Calvin; *189 T-5; mail Cassopolis z 49031; ● 110
Brownwood Lake; RMC Place; VAN BUREN; ▲ Paw Paw; *189 S-5; elev. 700ft./213m.; ★ KZOO; mail Paw Paw z 49079; ● 220
Bruce; MCD-Township; CHIPPEWA; *188 D-9; mail Sault Sainte Marie z 49783; Ⓟ 1,610; Ⓒ 1,940
Bruce (Bruce Township); MCD-Township; MACOMB; *189 P-13; 🅿; ★ DET; z 48065; Ⓟ 6,012; Ⓒ 8,158
Bruce Crossing; RMC Place; ONTONAGON; ▲ Stannard; 188 B-12; elev. 1,144ft./349m.; 🅿; z 49912; ● 300
Bruce Township; MACOMB; see Bruce (MCD-Township)
Bruningville; RMC Place; PRESQUE ISLE; ▲ Rogers; *188 H-10; elev. 756ft./230m.; mail Rogers City z 49779; rural
Brunswick; RMC Place; MUSKEGON, NEWAYGO; ▲ Sheridan, Holton; 189 N-5; 🅿; z 49425; ● 50
Brutus; RMC Place; EMMET; ▲ Maple River; 188 G-8; elev. 680ft./207m.; 🅿; z 49716; ● 160
Bryant; RMC Place; ALCONA; ▲ Curtis; *189 K-11; elev. 844ft./257m.; mail Glennie z 48737; rural
Buchanan; Inc. Place; BERRIEN; 189 T-4; 🅿; z 49107; Ⓟ 4,992; Ⓒ 4,681
Buchanan; MCD-Township; BERRIEN; *189 T-4; 🅿; z 49107; does not include the City of Buchanan; Ⓟ 3,402; Ⓒ 3,510
Buckeye; MCD-Township; GLADWIN; *189 M-9; mail Gladwin z 48624; Ⓟ 996; Ⓒ 1,333
Buckley; Inc. Place; WEXFORD; ▲ Hanover; 189 K-6; 🅿; z 49620; Ⓟ 402; Ⓒ 550
Bucks Corners; RMC Place; OCEANA; ▲ Weare; *189 M-4; elev. 666ft./203m.; mail Pentwater z 49449; rural
Buel; MCD-Township; SANILAC; *189 O-13; mail Croswell z 48422; Ⓟ 844; Ⓒ 1,237
Buena Vista; CDP-Census Area Only; SAGINAW; ▲ Buena Vista; *189 N-10; ★ SAG-; mail Saginaw z 48601; Ⓟ 8,196; Ⓒ 7,845
Buena Vista; MCD-Charter Township; SAGINAW; *189 N-10; ★ SAG-; mail Saginaw z 48601; Ⓟ 10,900; Ⓒ 10,318
Bullock Creek; RMC Place; MIDLAND; ▲ Midland; 189 N-9; elev. 625ft./191m.; ★ SAG-; mail Midland z 48642; ● 750
Bumbletown; RMC Place; KEWEENAW; ▲ Allouez; *188 A-13; mail Allouez z 49805; ● 50
Bunker Hill; RMC Place; INGHAM; ▲ Bunker Hill; 189 R-9; elev. 946ft./288m.; mail Leslie z 49251, Stockbridge z 49285; ● 130
Bunker Hill; MCD-Township; INGHAM; *189 R-9; mail Leslie z 49251; Ⓟ 1,888; Ⓒ 1,979
Bunny Run; RMC Place; OAKLAND; ▲ Orion; *189 P-12; ★ DET; mail Lake Orion z 48362; ● 1,900
Burdell; MCD-Township; OSCEOLA; *189 L-6; mail Tustin z 49688; Ⓟ 1,153; Ⓒ 1,241
Burdickville; RMC Place; LEELANAU; ▲ Empire; 188 J-5; mail Maple City z 49664; ● 30
Burgess; RMC Place; CHARLEVOIX; ▲ Hayes; *188 H-7; mail Charlevoix z 49720; rural
Burleigh; MCD-Township; IOSCO; *189 L-10; mail Whittemore z 48770; Ⓟ 695; Ⓒ 775
Burleigh Corners; RMC Place; CALHOUN; ▲ Pennfield; *189 R-7; elev. 900ft./274m.; ★ BTLCK; mail Battle Creek z 49017; rural
Burlington; Inc. Place; CALHOUN; ▲ Burlington; 189 S-7; elev. 923ft./281m.; 🅿; z 49029; Ⓟ 294; Ⓒ 405
Burlington; MCD-Township; CALHOUN; *189 S-7; 🅿; z 49029; Ⓟ 1,773; Ⓒ 1,929
Burlington; MCD-Township; LAPEER; *189 O-12; mail Clifford z 48727; Ⓟ 1,495; Ⓒ 1,402
Burnips; RMC Place; ALLEGAN; ▲ Salem; 189 Q-5; elev. 699ft./213m.; 🅿; ★ GDR; z 49314; ● 190
Burns; MCD-Township; SHIAWASSEE; *189 P-10; ★ FLN; mail Byron z 48418; Ⓟ 3,019; Ⓒ 3,500
Burnside; RMC Place; LAPEER; ▲ Burnside; *189 O-12; elev. 850ft./259m.; mail Brown City z 48416; ● 50
Burnside; MCD-Township; LAPEER; *189 O-12; mail Brown City z 48416; Ⓟ 1,753; Ⓒ 1,920
Burr Oak; Inc. Place; ST. JOSEPH; ▲ Burr Oak; 189 T-7; elev. 883ft./269m.; 🅿; z 49030; Ⓟ 882; Ⓒ 797
Burr Oak; MCD-Township; ST. JOSEPH; *189 T-7; 🅿; z 49030; Ⓟ 2,542; Ⓒ 2,739
Burt; MCD-Township; ALGER; *188 C-5; mail Grand Marais z 49839; Ⓟ 508; Ⓒ 480
Burt; MCD-Township; CHEBOYGAN; *188 G-8; mail Cheboygan z 49721; Ⓟ 533; Ⓒ 654
Burt; CDP-Census Area Only; SAGINAW; ▲ Taymouth; 189 O-10; 🅿; ★ SAG-; z 48417; Ⓟ 1,169; Ⓒ 1,122
Burtchville; MCD-Township; ST. CLAIR; *189 O-14; 🅿; ★ PTHU; z 48059; Ⓟ 3,559; Ⓒ 3,956
Burt Lake; RMC Place; CHEBOYGAN; ▲ Tuscarora; 188 G-8; 🅿; z 49717; summer pop. 250; ● 120
Burton; Inc. Place; GENESEE; 189 P-11; elev. 780ft./238m.; 🅿 ■; ★ FLN; z 48509, z 48519, z 48529; Ⓟ 27,617; Ⓒ 30,308; ◆ 29,894
Burton; RMC Place; SHIAWASSEE; ▲ Middlebury; 189 P-9; mail Owosso z 48867; ● 30
Burton-Northeast; RMC Place; GENESEE; ★ FLN; mail Burton z 48509; pop. incl. with Burton (Inc. Place)
Burton-Southeast; RMC Place; GENESEE; ★ FLN; mail Burton z 48529; pop. incl. with Burton (Inc. Place)
Bushnell; MCD-Township; MONTCALM; *189 O-8; mail Sheridan z 48884; Ⓟ 1,291; Ⓒ 2,111; Ⓡ 1,498
Butler; RMC Place; BRANCH; ▲ Butler; 189 S-8; elev. 1,014ft./309m.; mail Quincy z 49082; ● 30
Butler; MCD-Township; BRANCH; *189 S-8; mail Quincy z 49082; Ⓟ 1,191; Ⓒ 1,362
Butman; MCD-Township; GLADWIN; *189 L-9; mail Gladwin z 48624; Ⓟ 1,188; Ⓒ 1,947
Butterfield; MCD-Township; MISSAUKEE; *189 K-8; mail Lake z 48632; Ⓟ 452; Ⓒ 548
Butternut; RMC Place; MONTCALM; ▲ Bloomer; 189 O-8; mail Carson City z 48811; ● 130
Byron; MCD-Township; KENT; *189 Q-6; ★ GDR; mail Byron Center z 49315; Ⓟ 13,235; Ⓒ 17,553; ◆ 19,688
Byron; Inc. Place; SHIAWASSEE; ▲ Burns; 189 P-10; 🅿; ★ FLN; z 48418; Ⓟ 573; Ⓒ 595
Byron Center; CDP; KENT; ▲ Byron; 189 Q-6; elev. 757ft./231m.; 🅿; ★ GDR; z 49315; Ⓒ 3,777

C

Cadillac; Inc. Place; ⊡ WEXFORD; 189 L-7; elev. 1,328ft./405m.; 🅿 🅷 🅲 1,640 ■; z 49601; Ⓟ 10,104; Ⓒ 10,000; ◆ 9,896
Cadmus; RMC Place; LENAWEE; ▲ Dover; 189 T-10; 🅿; z 49221; ● 100
Cady; RMC Place; MACOMB; ▲ Clinton; *189 Q-13; ★ DET; mail Clinton Township z 48035
Calcite; RMC Place; PRESQUE ISLE; ▲ Rogers; *188 G-10; mail Rogers City z 49779; pop. incl. with Rogers City (Inc. Place)
Calderwood; RMC Place; ONTONAGON; ▲ Interior; 188 C-12; elev. 1,496ft./456m.; mail Trout Creek z 49967
Caldwell; MCD-Township; MISSAUKEE; *189 K-7; mail Lake City z 49651; Ⓟ 1,104; Ⓒ 1,363
Caledonia; MCD-Township; ALCONA; *188 I-11; mail Spruce z 48762; Ⓟ 987; Ⓒ 1,203
Caledonia; Inc. Place; KENT; ▲ Caledonia; 189 Q-6; elev. 800ft./244m.; 🅿; ★ GDR; z 49316; Ⓟ 885; Ⓒ 1,102
Caledonia; MCD-Charter Township; KENT; *189 Q-6; 🅿; ★ GDR; z 49316; Ⓟ 6,254; Ⓒ 8,964
Caledonia; MCD-Township; SHIAWASSEE; *189 P-10; mail Corunna z 48817; Ⓟ 4,514; Ⓒ 4,427
CALHOUN; 189 S-8; Ⓟ 135,982; Ⓒ 137,985; ◆ 133,535
California; RMC Place; BRANCH; ▲ California; 189 T-8; elev. 1,060ft./323m.; mail Montgomery z 49255; ● 50
California; MCD-Township; BRANCH; *189 T-8; mail Montgomery z 49255; Ⓟ 797; Ⓒ 909
Calumet; Inc. Place; HOUGHTON; ▲ Calumet; 188 A-13; elev. 1,208ft./368m.; 🅿; z 49913, z 49918, z 49942; Ⓟ 818; Ⓒ 879; Ⓡ 850
Calumet; MCD-Charter Township; HOUGHTON; *188 A-13; 🅿; z 49913, z 49918, z 49942; Ⓟ 7,015; Ⓒ 6,997; Ⓡ 6,968
Calvin; MCD-Township; CASS; *189 T-5; mail Cassopolis z 49031; Ⓟ 1,813; Ⓒ 2,041
Calvin Center; RMC Place; CASS; ▲ Calvin; 189 T-5; elev. 880ft./268m.; mail Cassopolis z 49031; ● 70
Cambria; RMC Place; HILLSDALE; ▲ Cambria; 189 T-8; mail Hillsdale z 49242; ● 280
Cambria; MCD-Township; HILLSDALE; *189 T-9; mail Hillsdale z 49242; Ⓟ 2,372; Ⓒ 2,546
Cambridge; MCD-Township; LENAWEE; *189 S-10; ★ JAC; mail Onsted z 49265; Ⓟ 4,429; Ⓒ 5,299
Cambridge Junction; RMC Place; LENAWEE; ▲ Cambridge; *189 S-10; ★ JAC; mail Brooklyn z 49230; ● 400
Camden; Inc. Place; HILLSDALE; ▲ Camden; 189 T-8; 🅿; z 49232; Ⓟ 482; Ⓒ 550
Camden; MCD-Township; HILLSDALE; *189 T-8; 🅿; z 49232; Ⓟ 1,984; Ⓒ 2,088
Campbell; MCD-Township; IONIA; *189 P-7; mail Clarksville z 48815; Ⓟ 1,814; Ⓒ 2,243
Campbell City; CLARE; see Temple (RMC Place)
Campbells Corner; RMC Place; OAKLAND; ▲ Oakland, Addison; *189 P-12; ★ DET; mail Leonard z 48367; ● 50
Campbells Corners; RMC Place; OGEMAW; ▲ West Branch; *189 K-10; mail West Branch z 48661; rural
Canada Corners; RMC Place; MUSKEGON; ▲ Casnovia; *189 O-5; elev. 765ft./233m.; mail Casnovia z 49318; rural
Canada Creek Ranch; CDP-Census Area Only; MONTMORENCY; ▲ Montmorency; *188 H-9; mail Atlanta z 49709; summer pop. 1,200; Ⓒ 405
Canada Shores; RMC Place; BRANCH; ▲ Ovid; *189 T-8; mail Coldwater z 49036; summer pop. 300; ● 30
Canadian Lakes; CDP-Census Area Only; MECOSTA; *189 N-7; 🅿; z 49346; Ⓒ 1,922
Canal Station; RMC Place; CHIPPEWA; *188 D-9; ★ SOO; mail Sault Sainte Marie z 49783; pop. incl. with Sault Ste. Marie (Inc. Place)
Canandaigua; RMC Place; LENAWEE; ▲ Seneca; *189 T-10; elev. 824ft./251m.; mail Clayton z 49235, Hudson z 49247, Stockbridge z 49285; ● 60
Canfield Beach; RMC Place; PRESQUE ISLE; ▲ Bearinger; *188 G-9; mail Onaway z 49765; ● 60
Cannon; MCD-Township; KENT; *189 P-6; ★ GDR; mail Rockford z 49341; Ⓟ 7,928; Ⓒ 12,075
Cannonsburg; RMC Place; KENT; ▲ Cannon; 189 P-6; 🅿; ★ GDR; z 49317; ● 240
Canton; CDP-Census Area Only; WAYNE; ▲ Canton; 190 J-2; elev. 695ft./212m.; 🅿; ★ DET; z 48187-88 & mail Wayne z 48184; Ⓟ 57,047; Ⓒ 76,366; ◆ 77,910
Canton; MCD-Charter Township; WAYNE; *189 R-12; 🅿; ★ DET; z 48187-88 & mail Wayne z 48184; Ⓟ 57,040; Ⓒ 76,366; ◆ 77,910
Capac; Inc. Place; ST. CLAIR; ▲ Mussey; 189 P-13; 🅿; ★ DET; z 48014; Ⓟ 1,583; Ⓒ 1,775
Caribou Lake; RMC Place; CHIPPEWA; ▲ Detour; 188 E-10; mail De Tour Village z 49725; ● 30
Carland; RMC Place; SHIAWASSEE; ▲ Fairfield; 189 P-9; elev. 762ft./232m.; 🅿; z 48831; ● 80
Carleton; Inc. Place; MONROE; 189 S-12; elev. 610ft./186m.; 🅿; ★ DET; z 48117; Ⓟ 2,770; Ⓒ 2,562
Carlisle; RMC Place; KENT; ▲ Byron; *189 P-6; elev. 682ft./208m.; ★ GDR; mail Grand Rapids z 49508
Carlshend; RMC Place; MARQUETTE; ▲ Skandia; 188 D-2; elev. 1,151ft./351m.; mail Skandia z 49885; ● 120
Carlton; MCD-Township; BARRY; *189 Q-7; mail Hastings z 49058; Ⓟ 2,067; Ⓒ 2,331
Carlton Center; RMC Place; BARRY; ▲ Carlton; 189 Q-7; mail Freeport z 49325; ● 70
Carmel; MCD-Township; EATON; *189 Q-8; ★ LANS; mail Charlotte z 48813; Ⓟ 2,433; Ⓒ 2,626
Carney; Inc. Place; MENOMINEE; 188 G-1; 🅿; z 49812; Ⓒ 225
Caro; Inc. Place; ⊡ TUSCOLA; ▲ Almer, Indianfields; 189 N-12; 🅿 🅷; z 48723; Ⓟ 4,054; Ⓒ 4,145
Carp Lake; RMC Place; EMMET; ▲ Carp Lake; 188 G-8; 🅿; z 49718; summer pop. 500; ● 350
Carp Lake; MCD-Township; EMMET; *188 G-8; 🅿; z 49718; Ⓟ 597; Ⓒ 807
Carp Lake; MCD-Township; ONTONAGON; *188 B-11; mail Ontonagon z 49953; Ⓟ 1,193; Ⓒ 891
Carrollton; CDP; SAGINAW; ▲ Carrollton; 189 N-10; 🅿; ★ SAG-; z 48724; Ⓟ 6,521; Ⓒ 6,602
Carrollton; MCD-Township; SAGINAW; *189 N-10; 🅿; ★ SAG-; z 48724; Ⓟ 6,521; Ⓒ 6,602
Carr Settlement; RMC Place; LAKE, MASON; ▲ Logan, Lake; *189 M-5; elev. 725ft./221m.; mail Branch z 49402; rural
Carson City; Inc. Place; MONTCALM; ▲ Bloomer; 189 O-8; 🅿 🅷; z 48811; Ⓟ 1,158; Ⓒ 1,190
Carsonville; Inc. Place; SANILAC; ▲ Bridgehampton, Washington; 189 N-13; elev. 823ft./251m.; 🅿; z 48419; Ⓟ 583; Ⓒ 502
Carter Corners; RMC Place; BENZIE; *188 J-5; elev. 829ft./253m.; mail Interlochen z 49643; rural
Cascade; RMC Place; KENT; ▲ Cascade; 189 P-6; ★ GDR; mail Grand Rapids z 49506, z 49546; ● 2,300
Cascade; MCD-Charter Township; KENT; *189 P-6; ★ GDR; mail Grand Rapids z 49506, z 49546; Ⓟ 12,869; Ⓒ 15,107
Casco; MCD-Township; ALLEGAN; *189 R-5; mail South Haven z 49090; Ⓟ 2,856; Ⓒ 3,019
Casco; MCD-Township; ST. CLAIR; *189 Q-14; 🅿; ★ DET; z 48064; Ⓟ 4,552; Ⓒ 4,747
Case; MCD-Township; PRESQUE ISLE; *188 H-10; mail Millersburg z 49759; Ⓟ 770; Ⓒ 942
Caseville; Inc. Place; HURON; ▲ Caseville; 189 M-12; 🅿; z 48725; Ⓟ 857; Ⓒ 888
Caseville; MCD-Township; HURON; *189 M-12; 🅿; z 48725; Ⓟ 2,139; Ⓒ 2,723
Cash; RMC Place; SANILAC; ▲ Watertown; *189 N-13; mail Sandusky z 48471
Casnovia; Inc. Place; MUSKEGON, KENT; ▲ Tyrone, Casnovia; 189 O-6; elev. 881ft./269m.; 🅿; ★ MUS; z 49318; Ⓟ 376; Ⓒ 315
Casnovia; MCD-Township; MUSKEGON; *189 O-5; 🅿; z 49318 & mail Bailey z 49303; includes part of the Village of Casnovia; Ⓟ 2,361; Ⓒ 2,652
Caspian; Inc. Place; IRON; 188 C-12; elev. 1,492ft./455m.; 🅿; z 49915; Ⓟ 1,031; Ⓒ 997
CASS; 189 S-5; Ⓟ 49,477; Ⓒ 51,104; ◆ 50,078
Cass City; Inc. Place; TUSCOLA; ▲ Elkland; 189 N-12; elev. 743ft./226m.; 🅿 🅷; z 48726; Ⓟ 2,276; Ⓒ 2,643
Cassopolis; Inc. Place; ⊡ CASS; ▲ LaGrange; 189 T-5; elev. 902ft./275m.; 🅿; z 49031; Ⓟ 1,822; Ⓒ 1,740; Ⓡ 1,878
Castle Park; RMC Place; ALLEGAN; ▲ Laketown; 189 Q-5; ★ HLND; mail Holland z 49423; ● 50
Castleton; MCD-Township; BARRY; *189 Q-7; mail Nashville z 49073; Ⓟ 3,379; Ⓒ 3,475
Cathro; RMC Place; ALPENA; ▲ Maple Ridge; 188 H-11; mail Alpena z 49707; ● 290
Cato; MCD-Township; MONTCALM; *189 N-7; mail Lakeview z 48850; Ⓟ 2,500; Ⓒ 2,920
Cedar; RMC Place; LEELANAU; ▲ Solon; 188 J-5; elev. 596ft./182m.; 🅿; z 49621; ● 230
Cedar; MCD-Township; OSCEOLA; *189 M-7; mail Evart z 49631; Ⓟ 267; Ⓒ 406
Cedar Bluff; RMC Place; ALLEGAN; ▲ Casco; *189 R-4; elev. 670ft./204m.; mail South Haven z 49090; ● 150
Cedar Creek; RMC Place; BARRY; ▲ Hope; *189 R-7; mail Delton z 49046; ● 50
Cedar Creek; MCD-Township; MUSKEGON; *189 O-5; ★ MUS; mail Twin Lake z 49457; Ⓟ 2,846; Ⓒ 3,109
Cedar Creek; MCD-Township; WEXFORD; *189 K-6; mail Manton z 49663; Ⓟ 1,013; Ⓒ 1,489
Cedar Lake; RMC Place; MONTCALM; ▲ Home; 189 N-8; elev. 888ft./271m.; 🅿; z 48812; ● 290
Cedar Lake; RMC Place; VAN BUREN; ▲ Porter; *189 S-5; elev. 900ft./274m.; mail Marcellus z 49067; ● 200
Cedar River; RMC Place; MENOMINEE; ▲ Cedarville; 188 G-2; 🅿; z 49887; ● 40
Cedar Run; RMC Place; GRAND TRAVERSE; ▲ Long Lake; *188 J-5; elev. 800ft./244m.; mail Traverse City z 49684; summer pop. 100; ● 30
Cedar Springs; Inc. Place; KENT; ▲ Solon, Nelson; 189 O-6; 🅿; ★ GDR; z 49319; Ⓟ 2,600; Ⓒ 3,112
Cedarville; RMC Place; MACKINAC; ▲ Clark; 188 E-9; 🅿; z 49719; summer pop. 4,000; ● 1,070
Cedarville; MCD-Township; MENOMINEE; *188 G-2; mail Stephenson z 49887; Ⓟ 185; Ⓒ 276
Cement City; Inc. Place; LENAWEE, JACKSON; ▲ Columbia, Woodstock; *189 S-9; 🅿; ★ JAC; z 49233; Ⓟ 493; Ⓒ 452
Centennial Heights; RMC Place; HOUGHTON; ▲ Calumet; *188 A-13; mail Calumet z 49913; ● 100
Center; MCD-Township; EMMET; *188 G-8; mail Pellston z 49769; Ⓟ 517; Ⓒ 499
Center Line; Inc. Place; MACOMB; 190 H-7; elev. 625ft./191m.; 🅿; ★ DET; z 48015; Ⓟ 9,026; Ⓒ 8,531
Centerville; MCD-Township; LEELANAU; *188 I-6; mail Cedar z 49621; Ⓟ 836; Ⓒ 1,095
Central; RMC Place; KEWEENAW; ▲ Houghton; 188 A-13; mail Mohawk z 49950
Central Lake; Inc. Place; ANTRIM; ▲ Central Lake; 188 I-7; elev. 635ft./194m.; 🅿; z 49622; Ⓟ 954; Ⓒ 990
Central Lake; MCD-Township; ANTRIM; *188 I-7; 🅿; z 49622; Ⓟ 1,919; Ⓒ 2,254
Centreville; Inc. Place; ⊡ ST. JOSEPH; ▲ Nottawa, Lockport; 189 T-6; elev. 826ft./252m.; 🅿; z 49032; Ⓟ 1,516; Ⓒ 1,579
Ceresco; RMC Place; CALHOUN; ▲ Emmett, Marshall; 189 R-7; 🅿; ★ BTLCK; z 49033; ● 230
Chamberlains; RMC Place; ST. JOSEPH; ▲ Flowerfield; *189 S-6; elev. 884ft./269m.; mail Marcellus z 49067; rural
Champion; RMC Place; MARQUETTE; ▲ Champion; 188 B-13; elev. 1,598ft./487m.; 🅿; z 49814; ● 450
Champion; MCD-Township; MARQUETTE; *188 B-14; 🅿; z 49814; Ⓟ 346; Ⓒ 297
Chandler; MCD-Township; CHARLEVOIX; *188 H-8; mail Boyne City z 49712; Ⓟ 182; Ⓒ 230
Chandler; MCD-Township; HURON; *189 M-12; mail Elkton z 48731; Ⓟ 509; Ⓒ 501
Channing; RMC Place; DICKINSON; ▲ Sagola; 188 C-13; elev. 1,397ft./426m.; 🅿; z 49815; ● 550
Chapin; RMC Place; SAGINAW; ▲ Chapin; 189 O-9; mail Henderson z 48841; ● 60
Chapin; MCD-Township; SAGINAW; *189 O-9; mail Henderson z 48841; Ⓟ 969; Ⓒ 1,045
Charleston; MCD-Township; KALAMAZOO; *189 R-7; mail Augusta z 49012, Galesburg z 49053; Ⓟ 1,776; Ⓒ 1,813
Charleston; RMC Place; SANILAC; ▲ Delaware; *189 M-13; elev. 749ft./228m.; mail Minden City z 48456
Charlevoix; Inc. Place; ⊡ CHARLEVOIX; 188 H-7; 🅿 🅷; z 49711, z 49720; Ⓟ 3,116; Ⓒ 2,994
Charlevoix; MCD-Township; CHARLEVOIX; *188 H-7; 🅿; z 49711, z 49720; does not include the City of Charlevoix; Ⓟ 1,016; Ⓒ 1,697
CHARLEVOIX; 188 H-7; Ⓟ 21,468; Ⓒ 26,090; ◆ 26,077
Charlotte; Inc. Place; ⊡ EATON; 189 Q-8; elev. 917ft./280m.; 🅿 🅷; ★ LANS; z 48813; Ⓟ 8,083; Ⓒ 8,389

Entries in **UPPERCASE** are counties.
Entries in **bold** have populations of 2,500 or more.
Names in parentheses are alternate names.
Inc. Place — Incorporated Place
RMC Place — Rand McNally Designated Place
CDP — Census Designated Place
MCD — Minor Civil Division
⊡ County Seat
▲ Minor Civil Division
elev. Elevation
🅿 Post Office
🅷 Hospital
🅲 College
■ Principal Business Center
★ Ranally Metro Area (RMA) Abbreviation
z Zip Code(s)
Ⓟ Previous Census Population
Ⓡ Revised Census Population
Ⓐ Annexation Population
● Rand McNally Population Estimate
Ⓒ Final Census Population
Ⓢ Special Census Population
◆ Estimated Population

For additional definitions see Glossary, Volume 1, and Introduction, Volume 2.

Charlton; MCD-Township; OTSEGO; ***188** I-9; mail Johannesburg **Z** 49751; Ⓟ 913; Ⓒ 1,330
Chase; RMC Place; LAKE; ▲ Chase; **189** M-6; 🅿; **Z** 49623; ● 250
Chase; MCD-Township; LAKE; ***189** M-6; 🅿; **Z** 49623; Ⓟ 999; Ⓒ 1,194
Chassell; RMC Place; HOUGHTON; ▲ Chassell; **188** A-13; 🅿; **Z** 49916; ● 710
Chassell; MCD-Township; HOUGHTON; ***188** A-13; 🅿; **Z** 49916; Ⓟ 1,686; Ⓒ 1,822
Chatham; Inc. Place; ALGER; ▲ Rock River; **188** D-3; 🅿; **Z** 49816; Ⓟ 268; Ⓒ 231
Chatham Corners; RMC Place; ALGER; ***188** D-3; mail Chatham **Z** 49816; pop. incl. with Chatham (Inc. Place)
Chauncey; RMC Place; KENT; ▲ Plainfield, Cannon; ***189** P-6; ★ **GDR**; mail Belmont **Z** 49306; rural
Cheboygan; Inc. Place; ⊡ CHEBOYGAN; **188** G-9; 🅿 🅷; **Z** 49721; Ⓟ 4,999; Ⓒ 5,295
CHEBOYGAN; **188** H-9; Ⓟ 21,398; Ⓒ 26,448; ◆ 26,160
Chelsea; Inc. Place; WASHTENAW; **189** R-10; 🅿 🅷; ★ **DET**; **Z** 48118; Ⓟ 3,772; Ⓒ 4,398
Cherry Beach; RMC Place; ST. CLAIR; ▲ Cottrellville; ***189** Q-14; ★ **DET**; mail Marine City **Z** 48039; ● 140
Cherry Bend; RMC Place; LEELANAU; ▲ Elmwood; ***188** J-6; mail Traverse City **Z** 49684
Cherry Grove; MCD-Township; WEXFORD; ***189** L-6; mail Cadillac **Z** 49601; Ⓟ 1,763; Ⓒ 2,328
Cherry Hill; RMC Place; WAYNE; ▲ Canton; ***189** R-11; ★ **DET**; mail Canton **Z** 48187; ● 60
Cherry Island; RMC Place; WAYNE; ★ **DET**; mail Rockwood **Z** 48173
Cherry Valley; MCD-Township; LAKE; ***189** M-6; mail Chase **Z** 49623; Ⓟ 248; Ⓒ 368
Chesaning; Inc. Place; SAGINAW; ▲ Chesaning; **189** O-10; 🅿; **Z** 48616; Ⓟ 2,567; Ⓒ 2,548
Chesaning; MCD-Township; SAGINAW; ***189** O-10; 🅿; **Z** 48616; Ⓟ 4,904; Ⓒ 4,861
Cheshire; MCD-Township; ALLEGAN; ***189** R-5; mail Allegan **Z** 49010; Ⓟ 1,967; Ⓒ 2,335
Cheshire Center; RMC Place; ALLEGAN; ▲ Cheshire; ***189** R-5; elev. 708ft./216m.; mail Allegan **Z** 49010; rural
Chester; RMC Place; EATON; ▲ Chester; **189** Q-8; mail Charlotte **Z** 48813; ● 50
Chester; MCD-Township; EATON; ***189** Q-8; mail Charlotte **Z** 48813; Ⓟ 1,602; Ⓒ 1,778
Chester; MCD-Township; OTSEGO; ***188** I-9; mail Gaylord **Z** 49735; Ⓟ 934; Ⓒ 1,265
Chester; MCD-Township; OTTAWA; ***189** O-5; mail Conklin **Z** 49403; Ⓟ 2,133; Ⓒ 2,315
Chesterfield; RMC Place; MACOMB; ▲ Chesterfield; ***189** Q-13; 🅿; ★ **DET**; **Z** 48047, **Z** 48051; ● 480
Chesterfield; MCD-Charter Township; MACOMB; **190** E-10; 🅿; ★ **DET**; **Z** 48047, **Z** 48051; Ⓟ 25,905; Ⓒ 37,405; ◆ 43,601
Chestonia; MCD-Township; ANTRIM; ***188** I-7; mail Alba **Z** 49611; Ⓟ 401; Ⓒ 546
Chicagon Lake; RMC Place; IRON; ▲ Stambaugh; ***188** D-13; elev. 1,447ft./441m.; mail Crystal Falls **Z** 49920; ● 80
Chicora; RMC Place; ALLEGAN; ▲ Cheshire; ***189** R-5; elev. 698ft./213m.; mail Allegan **Z** 49010, Pullman **Z** 49450; rural
Chief; MANISTEE; see Chief Lake (RMC Place)
Chief Lake (Chief); RMC Place; MANISTEE; ▲ Bear Lake; ***189** K-5; mail Kaleva **Z** 49645; summer pop. 150; ● 30
Chikaming; MCD-Township; BERRIEN; ***189** T-3; mail Lakeside **Z** 49116; Ⓟ 3,717; Ⓒ 3,678
China; MCD-Charter Township; ST. CLAIR; ***189** P-14; 🅿; ★ **DET**; **Z** 48054; Ⓟ 2,644; Ⓒ 3,340
Chippewa; MCD-Township; CHIPPEWA; ***188** D-7; mail Strongs **Z** 49790; Ⓟ 279; Ⓒ 238
Chippewa; MCD-Township; ISABELLA; ***189** N-8; mail Mount Pleasant **Z** 48858; Ⓟ 4,130; Ⓒ 4,617
Chippewa; MCD-Township; MECOSTA; ***189** M-7; mail Chippewa Lake **Z** 49320; Ⓟ 1,035; Ⓒ 1,239
CHIPPEWA; **188** E-9; Ⓟ 34,604; Ⓒ 38,543; ◆ 39,674
Chippewa Lake; RMC Place; MECOSTA; ▲ Chippewa; **189** M-7; 🅿; **Z** 49320; ● 160
Chippewa Vista; RMC Place; MECOSTA; ▲ Fork; ***189** M-7; mail Barryton **Z** 49305; ● 110
Chocolay; MCD-Charter Township; MARQUETTE; ***188** D-2; mail Marquette **Z** 49855; Ⓟ 6,025; Ⓒ 7,148; Ⓡ 6,095
Christie Lake; RMC Place; VAN BUREN; ▲ Lawrence; ***189** S-5; elev. 785ft./239m.; ★ **KZOO**; mail Decatur **Z** 49045, Lawrence **Z** 49064; summer pop. 400; ● 150
Christmas; RMC Place; ALGER; ▲ Au Train; **188** D-3; 🅿; **Z** 49862; ● 200
Churchill; RMC Place; MUSKEGON; ★ **MUS**; mail Muskegon **Z** 49441; pop. incl. with Norton Shores (Inc. Place)
Churchill; MCD-Township; OGEMAW; ***189** K-10; mail West Branch **Z** 48661; Ⓟ 1,130; Ⓒ 1,603
Circle Pine Center; RMC Place; BARRY; ▲ Orangeville; ***189** Q-6; ★ **KZOO**; mail Delton **Z** 49046; rural
Cisco Lake; RMC Place; GOGEBIC; ▲ Watersmeet; mail Watersmeet **Z** 49969
Clam Lake; MCD-Township; WEXFORD; ***189** L-7; mail Cadillac **Z** 49601; Ⓟ 1,739; Ⓒ 2,238
Clam River; RMC Place; ANTRIM; ▲ Forest Home; **188** I-7; mail Bellaire **Z** 49615
Clam Union; MCD-Township; MISSAUKEE; ***189** L-7; mail Lake **Z** 48632; Ⓟ 854; Ⓒ 882
Clare; Inc. Place; CLARE, ISABELLA; **189** M-8; elev. 841ft./256m.; 🅿 🅷; **Z** 48617; Ⓟ 3,021; Ⓒ 3,173
CLARE; **189** M-8; Ⓟ 24,952; Ⓒ 31,252; ◆ 29,941
Clarence; MCD-Township; CALHOUN; ***189** R-8; mail Albion **Z** 49224; Ⓟ 2,051; Ⓒ 2,032
Clarendon; RMC Place; CALHOUN; ▲ Clarendon; ***189** S-8; mail Homer **Z** 49245; ● 50
Clarendon; MCD-Township; CALHOUN; ***189** S-8; mail Homer **Z** 49245; Ⓟ 1,100; Ⓒ 1,114
Clarion; RMC Place; CHARLEVOIX; ▲ Melrose; **188** H-8; mail Boyne Falls **Z** 49713; ● 120
Clark; MCD-Township; MACKINAC; ***188** E-9; mail Cedarville **Z** 49719; Ⓟ 2,012; Ⓒ 2,200
Clarklake; RMC Place; JACKSON; ▲ Columbia; ***189** S-9; 🅿; ★ **JAC**; **Z** 49234; ● 460
Clarksburg; RMC Place; MARQUETTE; ▲ Ely; ***188** C-14; elev. 1,534ft./468m.; mail Champion **Z** 49814; ● 30
Clarkston (Village of Clarkston); Inc. Place; OAKLAND; **189** Q-12; 🅿; ★ **DET**; **Z** 48346-48; Ⓟ 1,005; Ⓒ 962
Clarksville; Inc. Place; IONIA; ▲ Campbell; **189** P-7; elev. 826ft./252m.; 🅿; **Z** 48815; Ⓟ 360; Ⓒ 317
Clawson; Inc. Place; OAKLAND; **190** H-6; elev. 667ft./203m.; 🅿; ★ **DET**; **Z** 48017; Ⓟ 13,874; Ⓒ 12,732
Clay; MCD-Township; ST. CLAIR; ***189** Q-14; 🅿; ★ **DET**; **Z** 48001; Ⓟ 8,862; Ⓒ 9,822
Claybanks; MCD-Township; OCEANA; ***189** N-4; mail Rothbury **Z** 49452; Ⓟ 679; Ⓒ 831
Clayton; MCD-Township; ARENAC; ***189** L-10; mail Sterling **Z** 48659; Ⓟ 908; Ⓒ 1,101
Clayton; MCD-Charter Township; GENESEE; ***189** P-10; ★ **FLN**; mail Swartz Creek **Z** 48473; Ⓟ 7,368; Ⓒ 7,546; Ⓡ 7,553
Clayton; Inc. Place; LENAWEE; ▲ Hudson, Dover; **189** T-10; elev. 891ft./272m.; 🅿; **Z** 49235; Ⓟ 384; Ⓒ 326
Clear Lake; RMC Place; OGEMAW; ▲ Foster; **189** K-9; mail West Branch **Z** 48661; ● 230
Clearwater; MCD-Township; KALKASKA; ***188** J-7; mail Rapid City **Z** 49676; Ⓟ 1,959; Ⓒ 2,382
Clement; MCD-Township; GLADWIN; ***189** L-9; mail Alger **Z** 48610; Ⓟ 822; Ⓒ 994
Cleon; MCD-Township; MANISTEE; ***189** K-5; mail Copemish **Z** 49625; Ⓟ 713; Ⓒ 932
Cleveland; MCD-Township; LEELANAU; ***188** I-5; mail Maple City **Z** 49664; Ⓟ 783; Ⓒ 1,040
Clifford; Inc. Place; LAPEER; ▲ Burlington; **189** O-12; 🅿; **Z** 48727; Ⓟ 354; Ⓒ 324
Climax; Inc. Place; KALAMAZOO; ▲ Climax; **189** S-7; 🅿; **Z** 49034; Ⓟ 677; Ⓒ 791
Climax; MCD-Township; KALAMAZOO; ***189** S-7; 🅿; **Z** 49034; Ⓟ 2,221; Ⓒ 2,412
Clinton; Inc. Place; LENAWEE; ▲ Clinton; **189** S-10; 🅿; **Z** 49236; Ⓟ 2,475; Ⓒ 2,293
Clinton; MCD-Township; LENAWEE; ***189** S-10; 🅿; **Z** 49236; Ⓟ 3,557; Ⓒ 3,624
Clinton; CDP-Census Area Only; MACOMB; ▲ Clinton; **190** G-8; 🅲 5,281; ★ **DET**; mail Clinton Township **Z** 48035-36, **Z** 48038; Ⓟ 85,866; Ⓒ 95,648; ◆ 94,605
Clinton (Clinton Township); MCD-Charter Township; MACOMB; ***189** Q-13; 🅲 5,281; ★ **DET**; mail Clinton Township **Z** 48035-36, **Z** 48038; Ⓟ 10,838; Ⓒ 95,648; ◆ 94,605
Clinton; MCD-Township; OSCODA; ***188** J-10; mail Comins **Z** 48619; Ⓟ 447; Ⓒ 511
CLINTON; **189** P-9; Ⓟ 57,883; Ⓒ 64,753; ◆ 69,197
Clinton Township; MACOMB; see Clinton (MCD-Charter Township)
Clinton Village; RMC Place; CLINTON; ▲ DeWitt; **188** A-3; ★ **LANS**; mail Lansing **Z** 48906; ● 830
Clio; Inc. Place; GENESEE; **189** O-11; elev. 725ft./221m.; 🅿; ★ **FLN**; **Z** 48420; Ⓟ 2,629; Ⓒ 2,483
Cloverdale; RMC Place; BARRY; ▲ Hope; **189** Q-7; 🅿; **Z** 49035; ● 250
Cloverville; RMC Place; MUSKEGON; ▲ Sullivan, Fruitport; **189** O-5; ★ **MUS**; mail Muskegon **Z** 49444; ● 1,950
Clyde; MCD-Township; ALLEGAN; ***189** Q-5; mail Fennville **Z** 49408; Ⓟ 2,001; Ⓒ 2,104
Clyde; RMC Place; OAKLAND; ▲ Highland; **190** E-1; ★ **DET**; mail Highland **Z** 48357; ● 210
Clyde; MCD-Township; ST. CLAIR; ***189** P-14; 🅿; ★ **PTHU**; **Z** 48049; Ⓟ 5,052; Ⓒ 5,523
Coats Grove; RMC Place; BARRY; ▲ Carlton, Castleton, Hastings, Woodland; **189** Q-7; mail Hastings **Z** 49058
Coddes Beach; RMC Place; PRESQUE ISLE; ▲ North Allis; ***188** G-9; mail Onaway **Z** 49765; ● 70
Cody; RMC Place; GENESEE; ***189** P-11; ★ **FLN**; mail Flint **Z** 48507; pop. incl. with Flint (Inc. Place)
Coe; RMC Place; ISABELLA; ▲ Coe; **189** N-8; mail Saint Louis **Z** 48880; ● 40
Coe; MCD-Township; ISABELLA; ***189** N-8; mail Saint Louis **Z** 48880; Ⓟ 2,967; Ⓒ 2,993
Cohoctah; RMC Place; LIVINGSTON; ▲ Cohoctah; **189** Q-10; 🅿; **Z** 48816; ● 110
Cohoctah; MCD-Township; LIVINGSTON; ***189** Q-10; 🅿; **Z** 48816; Ⓟ 2,693; Ⓒ 3,394
Cohoctah Center; RMC Place; LIVINGSTON; ▲ Cohoctah; **189** Q-10; mail Fowlerville **Z** 48836; ● 40
Cold Springs; CHEBOYGAN; see Grand View Beach (RMC Place)
Coldsprings; MCD-Township; KALKASKA; ***188** J-7; mail Kalkaska **Z** 49646; Ⓟ 1,073; Ⓒ 1,449
Coldwater; Inc. Place; ⊡ BRANCH; **189** T-8; elev. 969ft./295m.; 🅿 🅷; **Z** 49036; Ⓟ 9,607; Ⓒ 12,697
Coldwater; MCD-Township; BRANCH; ***189** S-8; 🅿; **Z** 49036; does not include the City of Coldwater; Ⓟ 4,795; Ⓒ 3,678; Ⓡ 3,818
Coldwater; MCD-Township; ISABELLA; ***189** M-7; mail Lake **Z** 48632; Ⓟ 732; Ⓒ 737
Coleman; Inc. Place; MIDLAND; **189** M-9; elev. 757ft./231m.; 🅿; **Z** 48618; Ⓟ 1,237; Ⓒ 1,296
Colfax; MCD-Township; BENZIE; ***189** K-5; mail Thompsonville **Z** 49683; Ⓟ 415; Ⓒ 585
Colfax; MCD-Township; HURON; ***189** M-12; mail Bad Axe **Z** 48413; Ⓟ 1,936; Ⓒ 1,954
Colfax; MCD-Township; MECOSTA; ***189** N-7; mail Big Rapids **Z** 49307; Ⓟ 1,915; Ⓒ 1,975
Colfax; MCD-Township; OCEANA; ***189** M-5; mail Walkerville **Z** 49459; Ⓟ 374; Ⓒ 574
Colfax; MCD-Township; WEXFORD; ***189** K-6; mail Manton **Z** 49663; Ⓟ 556; Ⓒ 763
College Park; RMC Place; WAYNE; ***189** R-12; ★ **DET**; mail Detroit **Z** 48221; pop. incl. with Detroit (Inc. Place)
College Town; RMC Place; BAY; ▲ Hampton; ***189** N-10; elev. 595ft./181m.; ★ **SAG-**; mail Bay City **Z** 48706; ● 680
Colling; RMC Place; TUSCOLA; ▲ Columbia; **189** N-12; elev. 654ft./199m.; mail Unionville **Z** 48767
Collins; RMC Place; IONIA; ▲ Portland, Orange; ***189** P-8; elev. 769ft./234m.; mail Lyons **Z** 48851
Coloma; Inc. Place; BERRIEN; **189** S-4; elev. 649ft./198m.; 🅿; ★ **BNTH-**; **Z** 49038-39; Ⓟ 1,679; Ⓒ 1,595
Coloma; MCD-Charter Township; BERRIEN; ***189** S-4; 🅿; ★ **BNTH-**; **Z** 49038-39; does not include the City of Coloma; Ⓟ 5,123; Ⓒ 5,217
Colon; Inc. Place; ST. JOSEPH; ▲ Colon; **189** S-7; elev. 860ft./262m.; 🅿; **Z** 49040; Ⓟ 1,224; Ⓒ 1,227
Colon; MCD-Township; ST. JOSEPH; ***189** T-7; 🅿; **Z** 49040; Ⓟ 3,217; Ⓒ 3,405
Columbia; MCD-Township; JACKSON; ***189** S-9; ★ **JAC**; mail Brooklyn **Z** 49230; Ⓟ 6,308; Ⓒ 7,234
Columbia; MCD-Township; TUSCOLA; ***189** N-12; mail Unionville **Z** 48767; Ⓟ 1,383; Ⓒ 1,419
Columbia; MCD-Township; VAN BUREN; ***189** R-5; mail Grand Junction **Z** 49056; Ⓟ 2,552; Ⓒ 2,714
Columbia Corners; RMC Place; TUSCOLA; ▲ Columbia; ***189** N-11; elev. 654ft./199m.; mail Unionville **Z** 48767; ● 30
Columbiaville; Inc. Place; LAPEER; ▲ Oregon, Marathon; **189** O-12; elev. 780ft./238m.; 🅿; ★ **FLN**; **Z** 48421; Ⓟ 934; Ⓒ 815
Columbus; MCD-Township; LUCE; ***188** D-6; mail Mc Millan **Z** 49853; Ⓟ 218; Ⓒ 215
Columbus; MCD-Township; ST. CLAIR; ***189** P-13; 🅿; ★ **DET**; **Z** 48063; Ⓟ 3,235; Ⓒ 4,615
Colwood; RMC Place; TUSCOLA; ▲ Elmwood, Columbia; ***189** N-12; elev. 667ft./203m.; mail Unionville **Z** 48767
Comins; OSCODA; see Gomins (RMC Place)
Comins; MCD-Township; OSCODA; ***188** J-10; 🅿; **Z** 48619 & mail Fairview **Z** 48621; Ⓟ 1,785; Ⓒ 2,017
Commerce; RMC Place; OAKLAND; ▲ Commerce; **189** Q-11; ★ **DET**; mail Commerce Township **Z** 48382, Walled Lake **Z** 48390; ● 5,000
Commerce (Commerce Township); MCD-Charter Township; OAKLAND; ***189** Q-11; ★ **DET**; mail Commerce Township **Z** 48382, Walled Lake **Z** 48390; Ⓟ 26,955; Ⓒ 34,764; ◆ 36,125
Commerce Township; OAKLAND; see Commerce (MCD-Charter Township)
Comstock; RMC Place; KALAMAZOO; ▲ Comstock; **189** P-3; 🅿; ★ **KZOO**; **Z** 49041; ● 5,600
Comstock; MCD-Charter Township; KALAMAZOO; ***189** R-6; 🅿; ★ **KZOO**; **Z** 49041; Ⓟ 11,834; Ⓒ 13,851
Comstock Northwest; CDP-Census Area Only; KALAMAZOO; ▲ Comstock; ***189** R-6; elev. 872ft./266m.; ★ **KZOO**; mail Comstock **Z** 49041; Ⓟ 3,402; Ⓒ 4,472
Comstock Park; CDP; KENT; ▲ Plainfield, Alpine; **189** P-6; 🅿; ★ **GDR**; **Z** 49321; Ⓟ 6,530; Ⓒ 10,674
Concord; Inc. Place; JACKSON; ▲ Concord; **189** S-8; 🅿; **Z** 49237; Ⓟ 944; Ⓒ 1,101
Concord; MCD-Township; JACKSON; ***189** S-8; 🅿; **Z** 49237; Ⓟ 2,408; Ⓒ 2,692
Condit; RMC Place; CALHOUN; ▲ Albion; ***189** S-8; elev. 965ft./294m.; mail Homer **Z** 49245
Cone; RMC Place; MONROE; ▲ Milan; ***189** S-11; elev. 693ft./211m.; ★ **DET**; mail Milan **Z** 48160; ● 50
Conklin; RMC Place; OTTAWA; ▲ Chester; **189** O-5; 🅿; **Z** 49403; ● 290
Connorville; RMC Place; GOGEBIC; ▲ Wakefield; ***188** B-10; mail Wakefield **Z** 49968; ● 30
Constantine; Inc. Place; ST. JOSEPH; ▲ Constantine; **189** T-6; 🅿; **Z** 49042; Ⓟ 2,032; Ⓒ 2,095
Constantine; MCD-Township; ST. JOSEPH; ***189** T-6; 🅿; **Z** 49042; Ⓟ 4,152; Ⓒ 4,181
Convis; MCD-Township; CALHOUN; ***189** R-8; mail Battle Creek **Z** 49017; Ⓟ 1,739; Ⓒ 1,666
Conway; RMC Place; EMMET; ▲ Little Traverse; **188** G-8; elev. 607ft./185m.; 🅿; **Z** 49722; ● 350
Conway; MCD-Township; LIVINGSTON; ***189** Q-10; mail Fowlerville **Z** 48836; Ⓟ 1,818; Ⓒ 2,732
Cooks; RMC Place; SCHOOLCRAFT; ▲ Inwood; **188** F-4; 🅿; **Z** 49817; ● 160
Cooks Corners; RMC Place; IONIA; ▲ Otisco; ***189** P-7; elev. 826ft./252m.; mail Belding **Z** 48809; ● 100
Cooper; MCD-Charter Township; KALAMAZOO; ***189** R-6; ★ **KZOO**; mail Kalamazoo **Z** 49004; Ⓟ 8,442; Ⓒ 8,754
Cooper Center; RMC Place; KALAMAZOO; ▲ Cooper; **189** R-6; ★ **KZOO**; mail Kalamazoo **Z** 49004; ● 250
Coopersville; Inc. Place; OTTAWA; **189** P-5; 🅿; ★ **GDR**; **Z** 49404; Ⓟ 3,421; Ⓒ 3,910
Copemish; Inc. Place; MANISTEE; ▲ Cleon; **189** K-5; elev. 808ft./246m.; 🅿; **Z** 49625; Ⓟ 222; Ⓒ 232
Copenhagen Beach; RMC Place; SCHOOLCRAFT; ▲ Hiawatha; ***188** F-4; mail Manistique **Z** 49854
Copper City; Inc. Place; HOUGHTON; ▲ Calumet; ***188** A-13; elev. 877ft./267m.; 🅿; **Z** 49917; Ⓟ 198; Ⓒ 205
Copper Harbor; RMC Place; KEWEENAW; ▲ Grant; **188** A-14; 🅿; **Z** 49918; ● 70
Coral; RMC Place; MONTCALM; ▲ Maple Valley; **189** O-7; 🅿; **Z** 49322; ● 230
Corey; RMC Place; CASS, ST. JOSEPH; ▲ Fabius, Newberg; ***189** T-6; mail Three Rivers **Z** 49093; ● 60
Corinne; RMC Place; MACKINAC; ▲ Newton; **188** E-6; elev. 764ft./233m.; mail Gould City **Z** 49838
Cornell; RMC Place; DELTA; ▲ Cornell; **188** F-2; elev. 817ft./249m.; 🅿; **Z** 49818-19; ● 80
Cornell; MCD-Township; DELTA; ***188** F-2; 🅿; **Z** 49818-19; Ⓟ 529; Ⓒ 557
Corunna; Inc. Place; ⊡ SHIAWASSEE; **189** P-10; elev. 750ft./229m.; 🅿; **Z** 48817; Ⓟ 3,091; Ⓒ 3,381
Corwith; MCD-Township; OTSEGO; ***188** H-9; mail Vanderbilt **Z** 49795; Ⓟ 1,416; Ⓒ 1,719
Coryell Islands; RMC Place; MACKINAC; ▲ Clark; ***188** E-9; mail Cedarville **Z** 49719; summer pop. 120
Cottage Grove; RMC Place; ROSCOMMON; ▲ Lyon, Gerrish; mail Roscommon **Z** 48653; summer pop. 100
Cottage Park; RMC Place; CHIPPEWA; ▲ Dafter; **188** D-9; mail Dafter **Z** 49724; ● 50
Cottrellville; MCD-Township; ST. CLAIR; ***189** Q-14; 🅿; ★ **DET**; **Z** 48039; Ⓟ 3,301; Ⓒ 3,814
County Spur; RMC Place; KALAMAZOO; ★ **KZOO**; pop. incl. with Kalamazoo (Inc. Place)
Court; RMC Place; KALAMAZOO; ***189** R-6; ★ **KZOO**; mail Kalamazoo **Z** 49007; pop. incl. with Kalamazoo (Inc. Place)
Courtland; MCD-Township; KENT; ***189** O-6; ★ **GDR**; mail Rockford **Z** 49341; Ⓟ 3,950; Ⓒ 5,817
Covert; RMC Place; VAN BUREN; ▲ Covert; **189** R-4; elev. 690ft./210m.; 🅿; ★ **BNTH-**; **Z** 49043; ● 640
Covert; MCD-Township; VAN BUREN; ***189** R-4; 🅿; ★ **BNTH-**; **Z** 49043; Ⓟ 2,855; Ⓒ 3,141
Covington; RMC Place; BARAGA; ▲ Covington; **188** B-13; elev. 1,601ft./488m.; 🅿; **Z** 49919; ● 300
Covington; MCD-Township; BARAGA; ***188** B-13; 🅿; **Z** 49919; Ⓟ 651; Ⓒ 569
Cranbrook; RMC Place; OAKLAND; ▲ Bloomfield; ★ **DET**; mail Bloomfield Hills **Z** 48303; pop. incl. with Bloomfield Hills (Inc. Place)
CRAWFORD; **188** J-8; Ⓟ 12,260; Ⓒ 14,273; ◆ 14,180
Crescent Lake Estates; RMC Place; OAKLAND; ▲ Waterford; ***189** Q-12; ★ **DET**; mail Waterford **Z** 48327
Crisp; RMC Place; OTTAWA; ▲ Olive; ***189** P-5; elev. 675ft./206m.; ★ **HLND**; mail Holland **Z** 49423; ● 120
Crockery; MCD-Township; OTTAWA; ***189** P-5; mail Nunica **Z** 49448; Ⓟ 3,599; Ⓒ 3,782
Crofton; RMC Place; KALKASKA; ▲ Boardman; ***188** J-7; mail South Boardman **Z** 49680; rural
Crooked Lake; RMC Place; BARRY; ▲ Prairieville; **189** R-7; ★ **KZOO**; mail Delton **Z** 49046; ● 230
Crooked Lake; RMC Place; LIVINGSTON; ▲ Genoa; ***189** Q-11; elev. 970ft./296m.; ★ **DET**; mail Brighton **Z** 48116; ● 480
Cross Village; RMC Place; EMMET; ▲ Cross Village; **188** G-7; elev. 689ft./210m.; 🅿; **Z** 49723; summer pop. 800; ● 150
Cross Village; MCD-Township; EMMET; ***188** G-7; 🅿; **Z** 49723; Ⓟ 201; Ⓒ 294
Croswell; Inc. Place; SANILAC; **189** O-14; elev. 736ft./224m.; 🅿; **Z** 48422; Ⓟ 2,174; Ⓒ 2,467
Croton; RMC Place; NEWAYGO; ▲ Croton; ***189** N-6; elev. 752ft./229m.; mail Newaygo **Z** 49337; ● 130
Croton; MCD-Township; NEWAYGO; ***189** N-6; mail Newaygo **Z** 49337; Ⓟ 1,965; Ⓒ 3,042
Croton Heights; RMC Place; NEWAYGO; ▲ Croton; ***189** N-6; elev. 746ft./227m.; mail Newaygo **Z** 49337; ● 150
Crump; RMC Place; BAY; ▲ Garfield; **189** M-10; mail Linwood **Z** 48634; ● 60
Crystal; RMC Place; MONTCALM; ▲ Crystal; **189** O-8; 🅿; **Z** 48818; ● 680
Crystal; MCD-Township; MONTCALM; ***189** O-8; 🅿; **Z** 48818; Ⓟ 2,541; Ⓒ 2,824
Crystal; MCD-Township; OCEANA; ***189** M-4; mail Hart **Z** 49420; Ⓟ 658; Ⓒ 832
Crystal Beach; RMC Place; BRANCH; ▲ Ovid; ***189** T-8; mail Coldwater **Z** 49036; ● 50
Crystal Falls; Inc. Place; ⊡ IRON; **188** C-13; 🅿; **Z** 49920; Ⓟ 1,922; Ⓒ 1,791
Crystal Falls; MCD-Township; IRON; ***188** C-13; 🅿; **Z** 49920; does not include the City of Crystal Falls; Ⓟ 1,614; Ⓒ 1,722
Crystal Lake; MCD-Township; BENZIE; ***188** J-4; mail Frankfort **Z** 49635; Ⓟ 759; Ⓒ 960
Crystal Valley; RMC Place; OCEANA; ▲ Crystal; **189** M-4; elev. 754ft./230m.; mail Hart **Z** 49420; ● 110
Cumber; RMC Place; SANILAC; ▲ Austin; **189** N-13; elev. 808ft./246m.; mail Ubly **Z** 48475
Cumming; MCD-Township; OGEMAW; ***189** K-10; mail Lupton **Z** 48635; Ⓟ 686; Ⓒ 796
Cunard; RMC Place; MENOMINEE; ▲ Meyer; ***188** F-1; mail Hermansville **Z** 49847; ● 30
Curran; RMC Place; ALCONA; ▲ Mitchell; **188** J-10; 🅿; **Z** 48728; ● 300
Curtis; MCD-Township; ALCONA; ***188** J-11; mail Glennie **Z** 48737; Ⓟ 1,128; Ⓒ 1,378
Curtis; RMC Place; MACKINAC; ▲ Portage; **188** E-6; 🅿; **Z** 49820; summer pop. 1,200; ● 620
Curtisville; RMC Place; ALCONA; ▲ Curtis; **188** J-10; elev. 955ft./291m.; mail South Branch **Z** 48761; ● 50
Custer; MCD-Township; ANTRIM; ***188** I-7; mail Mancelona **Z** 49659; Ⓟ 630; Ⓒ 988
Custer; Inc. Place; MASON; ▲ Custer; **189** M-4; elev. 698ft./213m.; 🅿; **Z** 49405; Ⓟ 312; Ⓒ 318
Custer; MCD-Township; MASON; ***189** M-4; 🅿; **Z** 49405; Ⓟ 1,176; Ⓒ 1,307
Custer; MCD-Township; SANILAC; ***189** N-13; mail Sandusky **Z** 48471; Ⓟ 1,018; Ⓒ 1,036
Cutlerville; CDP; KENT; ▲ Byron, Gaines; **189** P-6; elev. 678ft./207m.; ★ **GDR**; mail Grand Rapids **Z** 49508, **Z** 49548; Ⓟ 11,228; Ⓒ 15,114

D

Dafter; RMC Place; CHIPPEWA; ▲ Dafter; **188** D-9; 🅿; **Z** 49724; ● 160
Dafter; MCD-Township; CHIPPEWA; ***188** D-9; 🅿; **Z** 49724; Ⓟ 1,083; Ⓒ 1,304
Daggett; Inc. Place; MENOMINEE; ▲ Daggett; **188** G-1; 🅿; **Z** 49821; Ⓟ 260; Ⓒ 270
Daggett; MCD-Township; MENOMINEE; ***188** G-1; 🅿; **Z** 49821; Ⓟ 745; Ⓒ 740
Dailey; RMC Place; CASS; ▲ Jefferson; ***189** T-5; elev. 821ft./250m.; mail Cassopolis **Z** 49031; ● 140
Dallas; MCD-Township; CLINTON; ***189** P-8; mail Fowler **Z** 48835; Ⓟ 2,146; Ⓒ 2,323
Dalton; RMC Place; MUSKEGON; ▲ Dalton; **189** O-4; elev. 659ft./201m.; ★ **MUS**; mail Muskegon **Z** 49445; ● 320
Dalton; MCD-Township; MUSKEGON; ***189** O-4; ★ **MUS**; mail Muskegon **Z** 49445; Ⓟ 6,276; Ⓒ 8,047
Damon; RMC Place; OGEMAW; ▲ Foster; ***189** K-9; mail Rose City **Z** 48654
Danby; MCD-Township; IONIA; ***189** Q-8; mail Sunfield **Z** 48890; Ⓟ 2,371; Ⓒ 2,696
Danish Landing; RMC Place; CRAWFORD; ▲ Grayling; ***188** J-8; mail Grayling **Z** 49738; ● 150
Dansville; Inc. Place; INGHAM; ▲ Ingham; **189** Q-9; 🅿; **Z** 48819; Ⓟ 437; Ⓒ 429
Darragh; RMC Place; KALKASKA; ▲ Excelsior, Coldsprings; **188** J-7; elev. 1,246ft./380m.; mail Kalkaska **Z** 49646
Davis; RMC Place; MACOMB; ▲ Ray; **190** E-8; elev. 651ft./198m.; ★ **DET**; mail Romeo **Z** 48065; ● 160
Davisburg; RMC Place; OAKLAND; ▲ Springfield; **190** D-2; 🅿; ★ **DET**; **Z** 48350; ● 450
Davison; Inc. Place; GENESEE; **189** P-11; elev. 799ft./244m.; 🅿; ★ **FLN**; **Z** 48423; Ⓟ 5,693; Ⓒ 5,536
Davison; MCD-Township; GENESEE; ***189** P-11; 🅿; ★ **FLN**; **Z** 48423; does not include the City of Davison; Ⓟ 14,671; Ⓒ 17,722
Day; MCD-Township; MONTCALM; ***189** O-7; mail McBrides **Z** 48852; Ⓟ 1,196; Ⓒ 1,282
Dayton; RMC Place; BERRIEN; ▲ Bertrand; **189** T-4; mail Galien **Z** 49113; ● 150
Dayton; MCD-Township; NEWAYGO; ***189** N-5; mail Fremont **Z** 49412; Ⓟ 1,971; Ⓒ 2,002
Dayton; MCD-Township; TUSCOLA; ***189** N-12; mail Mayville **Z** 48744; Ⓟ 1,706; Ⓒ 1,869
Dayton Center; RMC Place; NEWAYGO; ▲ Dayton; ***189** N-5; mail Fremont **Z** 49412; rural
Dean; RMC Place; MIDLAND; ***189** N-10; ★ **SAG-**; pop. incl. with Midland (Inc. Place)
Dearborn; Inc. Place; WAYNE; **189** R-12; 🅿 🅷 🅲 8,566 ■; ★ **DET**; **Z** 48120-21, **Z** 48123-24, **Z** 48126, **Z** 48128; Ⓟ 89,286; Ⓒ 97,775; ◆ 93,431
Dearborn Heights; Inc. Place; WAYNE; **190** J-4; elev. 625ft./191m.; 🅿 ■; ★ **DET**; **Z** 48125, **Z** 48127; Ⓟ 60,838; Ⓒ 58,264; ◆ 55,993
Decatur; Inc. Place; VAN BUREN; ▲ Decatur; **189** S-5; 🅿; ★ **KZOO**; **Z** 49045; Ⓟ 1,760; Ⓒ 1,838
Decatur; MCD-Township; VAN BUREN; ***189** S-5; 🅿; ★ **KZOO**; **Z** 49045; Ⓟ 3,616; Ⓒ 3,916
Decker; RMC Place; SANILAC; ▲ Lakefield; **189** N-12; 🅿; **Z** 48426; ● 100
Deckerville; Inc. Place; SANILAC; ▲ Marion; **189** N-13; 🅿 🅷; **Z** 48427; Ⓟ 1,015; Ⓒ 944
Deep River; MCD-Township; ARENAC; ***189** L-10; mail Sterling **Z** 48659; Ⓟ 2,074; Ⓒ 2,244
Deerfield; MCD-Township; ISABELLA; ***189** N-8; mail Mount Pleasant **Z** 48858; Ⓟ 2,598; Ⓒ 3,081
Deerfield; MCD-Township; LAPEER; ***189** O-12; ★ **DET**; mail Columbiaville **Z** 48421; Ⓟ 4,903; Ⓒ 5,736
Deerfield; Inc. Place; LENAWEE; ▲ Deerfield; **189** T-11; elev. 673ft./205m.; 🅿; **Z** 49238; Ⓟ 922; Ⓒ 1,005
Deerfield; MCD-Township; LENAWEE; ***189** T-11; 🅿; **Z** 49238; Ⓟ 1,659; Ⓒ 1,770
Deerfield; MCD-Township; LIVINGSTON; ***189** Q-10; ★ **DET**; mail Linden **Z** 48451; Ⓟ 3,000; Ⓒ 4,087
Deerfield; MCD-Township; MECOSTA; ***189** N-7; mail Morley **Z** 49336; Ⓟ 1,231; Ⓒ 1,630
Deerfield Center; RMC Place; ISABELLA; ▲ Deerfield; ***189** N-8; mail Mount Pleasant **Z** 48858
Deerfield Center; RMC Place; LIVINGSTON; ▲ Deerfield; ***189** Q-10; elev. 897ft./273m.; ★ **DET**; mail Linden **Z** 48451
Deer Park; RMC Place; LUCE; ▲ McMillan; **188** C-6; mail Newberry **Z** 49868; ● 20
Deerton; RMC Place; ALGER; ▲ Onota; **188** D-2; 🅿; **Z** 49822; ● 230
Defiance; DELTA; see Trombly (RMC Place)
Deford; RMC Place; TUSCOLA; ▲ Novesta; **189** N-12; 🅿; **Z** 48729; ● 200
Dehoco; RMC Place; WASHTENAW; ▲ Salem; ***189** R-11; ★ **DET**; mail Salem **Z** 48175
Deibert; RMC Place; KALKASKA; ▲ Springfield; ***188** J-7; mail South Boardman **Z** 49680; rural
Delano; RMC Place; ARENAC; ▲ Whitney; **189** L-11; mail Au Gres **Z** 48703
Delaware; MCD-Township; SANILAC; ***189** M-13; mail Minden City **Z** 48456; Ⓟ 961; Ⓒ 930
Delhi; MCD-Charter Township; INGHAM; ***189** Q-9; ★ **LANS**; mail Ann Arbor **Z** 48103, Holt **Z** 48842; Ⓟ 19,190; Ⓒ 22,569; Ⓡ 22,496; ◆ 24,952
Delray; RMC Place; WAYNE; ★ **DET**; mail Detroit **Z** 48217; pop. incl. with Detroit (Inc. Place)
Delta; MCD-Charter Township; EATON; ***189** Q-8; ★ **LANS**; mail Lansing **Z** 48917; Ⓟ 26,129; Ⓒ 29,682; ◆ 30,737
DELTA; **188** F-3; Ⓟ 37,780; Ⓒ 38,520; ◆ 36,471
Delta Mills; RMC Place; EATON; ▲ Delta; **188** A-1; ★ **LANS**; mail Lansing **Z** 48917; ● 330
Delton; RMC Place; BARRY; ▲ Prairieville, Barry; **189** R-7; 🅿; ★ **KZOO**; **Z** 49046; ● 500
Delwin; RMC Place; ISABELLA; ▲ Denver; ***189** M-8; mail Mount Pleasant **Z** 48858
Denmark; MCD-Township; TUSCOLA; ***189** N-11; mail Richville **Z** 48758; Ⓟ 3,369; Ⓒ 3,249
Denton; MCD-Township; ROSCOMMON; ***189** K-8; mail Prudenville **Z** 48651; Ⓟ 4,290; Ⓒ 5,817
Denton; RMC Place; WAYNE; ▲ Van Buren; **190** L-2; ★ **DET**; mail Belleville **Z** 48111; ● 330
Denver; MCD-Township; ISABELLA; ***189** M-8; mail Mount Pleasant **Z** 48858; Ⓟ 1,019; Ⓒ 1,147
Denver; MCD-Township; NEWAYGO; ***189** N-5; mail Hesperia **Z** 49421; Ⓟ 1,532; Ⓒ 1,971
Derby; RMC Place; BERRIEN; ▲ Lincoln; ***189** S-4; ★ **BNTH-**; mail Stevensville **Z** 49127; ● 30
Detour; MCD-Township; CHIPPEWA; ***188** E-10; mail De Tour Village **Z** 49725; Ⓟ 806; Ⓒ 894
De Tour Village; Inc. Place; CHIPPEWA; ▲ Detour; **188** E-10; 🅿; **Z** 49725; Ⓟ 407; Ⓒ 421
Detroit; Inc. Place; ⊡ WAYNE; **189** R-13; 🅿 🅷 🅲 42,047 ■; ★ **DET**; **Z** 48201-40, **Z** 48242-44, **Z** 48255, **Z** 48260, **Z** 48264-69, **Z** 48272, **Z** 48275, **Z** 48277-79, **Z** 48288; Ⓟ 1,027,974; Ⓒ 951,270; ◆ 911,811
Detroit Beach; CDP; MONROE; ▲ Frenchtown; ***189** S-12; ★ **MONR**; mail Monroe **Z** 48162; Ⓟ 2,113; Ⓒ 2,289
Detroit River; RMC Place; WAYNE; ★ **DET**; mail Detroit **Z** 48222; pop. incl. with Detroit (Inc. Place)
Devereaux; RMC Place; JACKSON; ▲ Parma; **189** R-8; mail Albion **Z** 49224; ● 60
Devils Lake; RMC Place; LENAWEE; ▲ Woodstock; ***189** S-9; ★ **JAC**; mail Manitou Beach **Z** 49253
DeWitt; Inc. Place; CLINTON; **189** P-9; 🅿; ★ **LANS**; **Z** 48820; Ⓟ 3,964; Ⓒ 4,702
DeWitt; MCD-Charter Township; CLINTON; ***189** P-9; 🅿; ★ **LANS**; **Z** 48820 & mail Lansing **Z** 48906; does not include the City of DeWitt; Ⓟ 10,448; Ⓒ 12,143
Dexter; Inc. Place; WASHTENAW; ▲ Webster, Scio; **189** R-10; elev. 862ft./263m.; 🅿; ★ **DET**; **Z** 48130; Ⓟ 1,497; Ⓒ 2,338
Dexter; MCD-Township; WASHTENAW; ***189** R-10; 🅿; ★ **DET**; **Z** 48130 & mail Pinckney **Z** 48169; does not include the Village of Dexter; Ⓟ 4,407; Ⓒ 5,248
Diamond Lake; RMC Place; NEWAYGO; ▲ Lincoln; ***189** N-5; mail White Cloud **Z** 49349; summer pop. 1,000; ● 60
Diamond Shores; RMC Place; CASS; ▲ Penn; ***189** T-5; mail Cassopolis **Z** 49031; ● 60
Diamond Springs; RMC Place; ALLEGAN; ▲ Heath, Monterey, Overisel, Salem; ***189** Q-5; elev. 644ft./196m.; mail Hamilton **Z** 49419; rural
Dice Corners; RMC Place; MIDLAND; ▲ Lee, Homer; ***189** N-9; elev. 643ft./196m.; ★ **SAG-**; mail Hemlock **Z** 48626; rural
DICKINSON; **188** C-14; Ⓟ 26,831; Ⓒ 27,472; ◆ 26,704
Dickson; MCD-Township; MANISTEE; ***189** K-5; mail Brethren **Z** 49619; Ⓟ 735; Ⓒ 929
Diffin; RMC Place; ALGER; ▲ Limestone; **188** E-2; mail Trenary **Z** 49891; rural
Dighton; RMC Place; OSCEOLA; ▲ Sherman; **189** L-7; mail Tustin **Z** 49688; ● 80
Dimondale; Inc. Place; EATON; ▲ Windsor; **189** Q-8; 🅿; ★ **LANS**; **Z** 48821; Ⓟ 1,247; Ⓒ 1,342
Diorite; RMC Place; MARQUETTE; ▲ Ely; **188** B-14; mail Champion **Z** 49814; ● 200
Disco; RMC Place; MACOMB; ▲ Shelby; **190** E-7; ★ **DET**; mail Utica **Z** 48315
Dixboro; RMC Place; WASHTENAW; ▲ Superior; **189** R-11; elev. 819ft./250m.; ★ **DET**; mail Ann Arbor **Z** 48105; ● 500
Dodgeville; RMC Place; HOUGHTON; ▲ Portage; ***188** A-13; 🅿; **Z** 49921; ● 400
Dollar Bay; RMC Place; HOUGHTON; ▲ Osceola; **188** A-13; 🅿; **Z** 49922; ● 1,050
Dollar Settlement; RMC Place; CHIPPEWA; ▲ Bay Mills; ***188** D-8; elev. 649ft./198m.; mail Brimley **Z** 49715; ● 70
Dollarville; RMC Place; LUCE; ▲ McMillan; **188** D-6; elev. 717ft./219m.; mail Newberry **Z** 49868; ● 90
Dolph; RMC Place; MISSAUKEE; ▲ Holland; ***189** L-8; mail Falmouth **Z** 49632; rural
Donaldson; RMC Place; CHIPPEWA; ▲ Bruce; ***188** D-9; elev. 691ft./211m.; mail Sault Sainte Marie **Z** 49783; rural
Donken; RMC Place; HOUGHTON; ▲ Elm River; **188** A-12; mail Toivola **Z** 49965; ● 30
Doriva Beach; RMC Place; CHEBOYGAN; ▲ Grant; ***188** G-9; elev. 613ft./187m.; mail Cheboygan **Z** 49721; rural
Dorr; RMC Place; ALLEGAN; ▲ Dorr; **189** Q-6; 🅿; ★ **GDR**; **Z** 49323; ● 1,600
Dorr; MCD-Township; ALLEGAN; ***189** Q-6; 🅿; ★ **GDR**; **Z** 49323; Ⓟ 5,453; Ⓒ 6,579
Doster; RMC Place; ALLEGAN, BARRY; ▲ Prairieville, Gun Plain; **189** R-6; ★ **KZOO**; mail Plainwell **Z** 49080; ● 40
Doughertys Corners; RMC Place; KALAMAZOO; ▲ Oshtemo; ***189** R-6; ★ **KZOO**; mail Kalamazoo **Z** 49009; rural
Douglas; Inc. Place; ALLEGAN; ▲ Saugatuck; **189** Q-5; 🅿; **Z** 49406; Ⓟ 1,040; Ⓒ 1,214
Douglass; MCD-Township; MONTCALM; ***189** O-7; mail Stanton **Z** 48888; Ⓟ 1,944; Ⓒ 2,377
Dover; MCD-Township; LAKE; ***189** L-6; mail Luther **Z** 49656; Ⓟ 318; Ⓒ 332
Dover; MCD-Township; LENAWEE; ***189** T-10; mail Clayton **Z** 49235; Ⓟ 1,811; Ⓒ 1,787
Dover; MCD-Township; OTSEGO; ***188** I-9; mail Grayling **Z** 49738; Ⓟ 485; Ⓒ 614
Dowagiac; Inc. Place; CASS; **189** S-5; elev. 772ft./235m.; 🅿 🅷; **Z** 49047; Ⓟ 6,409; Ⓒ 6,147; Ⓡ 6,009
Dowling; RMC Place; BARRY; ▲ Baltimore; **189** R-7; elev. 956ft./291m.; 🅿; **Z** 49050; ● 150
Downington; RMC Place; SANILAC; ▲ Marion, Bridgehampton; ***189** N-13; mail Deckerville **Z** 48427; ● 50
Downtown; RMC Place; GENESEE; ***189** P-11; ★ **FLN**; mail Flint **Z** 48502; pop. incl. with Flint (Inc. Place)
Downtown; RMC Place; INGHAM; ***189** Q-9; ★ **LANS**; mail Lansing **Z** 48901, **Z** 48924; pop. incl. with Lansing (Inc. Place)
Downtown; RMC Place; MIDLAND; ***189** N-9; ★ **SAG-**; mail Midland **Z** 48640; pop. incl. with Midland (Inc. Place)
Doyle; MCD-Township; SCHOOLCRAFT; ***188** E-5; mail Gulliver **Z** 49840; Ⓟ 616; Ⓒ 630
Drayton Plains; RMC Place; OAKLAND; ▲ Waterford; **189** Q-12; elev. 970ft./296m.; 🅿; ★ **DET**; **Z** 48330
Drenthe; RMC Place; OTTAWA; ▲ Zeeland; ***189** Q-5; elev. 662ft./202m.; ★ **HLND**; mail Zeeland **Z** 49464; ● 170
Drummond; MCD-Township; CHIPPEWA; ***188** E-11; mail Drummond Island **Z** 49726; Ⓟ 835; Ⓒ 992
Drummond Island; RMC Place; CHIPPEWA; ▲ Drummond; **188** E-10; 🅿; **Z** 49726; summer pop. 1,000; ● 300
Dryburg; RMC Place; CHIPPEWA; ▲ Rudyard; ***188** E-8; mail Rudyard **Z** 49780; rural
Dryden; Inc. Place; LAPEER; **189** P-12; elev. 919ft./280m.; 🅿; ★ **DET**; **Z** 48428; Ⓟ 628; Ⓒ 815
Dryden; MCD-Township; LAPEER; ***189** P-12; 🅿; ★ **DET**; **Z** 48428; Ⓟ 3,399; Ⓒ 4,624
Dublin; RMC Place; MANISTEE; ▲ Norman; **189** L-5; elev. 860ft./262m.; mail Wellston **Z** 49689; ● 50
Duck Lake; RMC Place; ALLEGAN; ▲ Cheshire; ***189** R-5; elev. 750ft./229m.; mail Gobles **Z** 49055; ● 100
Duck Lake; RMC Place; CALHOUN; ▲ Clarence; **189** R-8; mail Albion **Z** 49224; ● 500
Duel; RMC Place; BAY; ▲ Beaver; **189** M-10; elev. 640ft./195m.; ★ **SAG-**; mail Midland **Z** 48640
Duffield; RMC Place; GENESEE; ▲ Gaines; **189** P-10; ★ **FLN**; mail Swartz Creek **Z** 48473; ● 40
Dukes; RMC Place; MARQUETTE; ▲ Skandia; **188** D-2; elev. 1,092ft./333m.; mail Skandia **Z** 49885; rural
Duncan; MCD-Township; HOUGHTON; ***188** B-12; mail Dundee **Z** 48131; Ⓟ 304; Ⓒ 280
Dundee; Inc. Place; MONROE; ▲ Dundee; **189** S-11; 🅿; **Z** 48131; Ⓟ 2,664; Ⓒ 3,522
Dundee; MCD-Township; MONROE; ***189** S-11; 🅿; **Z** 48131; Ⓟ 5,376; Ⓒ 6,341
Dunham Lake; RMC Place; LIVINGSTON, OAKLAND; ▲ Highland, Hartland; ***189** Q-11; elev. 1,000ft./305m.; ★ **DET**; mail Hartland **Z** 48353; ● 910
Dunningville; RMC Place; ALLEGAN; ▲ Heath; ***189** Q-5; elev. 670ft./204m.; mail Allegan **Z** 49010; rural
Dunn Location; RMC Place; IRON; ▲ Mastodon; ***188** C-13; elev. 1,511ft./461m.; mail Crystal Falls **Z** 49920; rural
Duplain; RMC Place; CLINTON; ▲ Duplain; ***189** P-9; mail Saint Johns **Z** 48879; ● 40
Duplain; MCD-Township; CLINTON; ***189** P-9; mail Elsie **Z** 48831; Ⓟ 2,235; Ⓒ 2,329
Durand; Inc. Place; SHIAWASSEE; **189** P-10; elev. 796ft./243m.; 🅿; ★ **FLN**; **Z** 48429; Ⓟ 4,283; Ⓒ 3,933
Dutton; RMC Place; KENT; ▲ Gaines; **189** P-6; elev. 760ft./232m.; 🅿; ★ **GDR**; **Z** 49316; ● 630
Dwight; MCD-Township; HURON; ***189** L-13; mail Kinde **Z** 48445; Ⓟ 917; Ⓒ 930

E

Eagle; Inc. Place; CLINTON; ▲ Eagle; **189** Q-8; 🅿; **Z** 48822; Ⓟ 120; Ⓒ 130
Eagle; MCD-Township; CLINTON; ***189** Q-8; 🅿; **Z** 48822; Ⓟ 2,151; Ⓒ 2,332; Ⓡ 2,343
Eagle Harbor; RMC Place; KEWEENAW; ▲ Eagle Harbor; **188** A-13; 🅿; **Z** 49950; ● 70
Eagle Harbor; MCD-Township; KEWEENAW; 🅿; **Z** 49950; Ⓟ 82; Ⓒ 281; Ⓡ 359
Eagle Lake; RMC Place; CASS; ▲ Ontwa; **189** T-5; ★ **S.B.**; mail Edwardsburg **Z** 49112; ● 1,160
Eagle Lake; RMC Place; VAN BUREN; ▲ Paw Paw; ***189** S-5; elev. 770ft./235m.; ★ **KZOO**; mail Paw Paw **Z** 49079; ● 160
Eagle Mills; RMC Place; KENT; ▲ Grand Rapids; ★ **GDR**; pop. incl. with Grand Rapids (Inc. Place)
Eagle Point; RMC Place; CASS; ▲ Calvin; ***189** T-5; mail Cassopolis **Z** 49031; ● 110
Eagle River; RMC Place; ⊡ KEWEENAW; ▲ Houghton; **188** A-13; 🅿; **Z** 49950; ● 50
Eagles Nest; RMC Place; MENOMINEE; ▲ Menominee; ***188** H-1; elev. 638ft./194m.; mail Menominee **Z** 49858; rural
East Bay; MCD-Township; GRAND TRAVERSE; ***188** J-6; mail Traverse City **Z** 49686; Ⓟ 8,307; Ⓒ 9,919
East China; MCD-Charter Township; ST. CLAIR; ***189** P-14; 🅿 🅷; ★ **DET**; **Z** 48054; Ⓟ 3,216; Ⓒ 3,630
East Cooper; RMC Place; KALAMAZOO; ▲ Cooper; ***189** R-6; elev. 786ft./240m.; ★ **KZOO**; mail Kalamazoo **Z** 49004; ● 2,700
East Dayton; RMC Place; TUSCOLA; ▲ Wells, Dayton; ***189** N-12; elev. 814ft./248m.; mail Caro **Z** 48723
East Detroit; MACOMB; see Eastpointe (Inc. Place)
East Gilead; RMC Place; BRANCH; ▲ Gilead; ***189** T-7; elev. 981ft./299m.; mail Bronson **Z** 49028; ● 50
East Grand Rapids; Inc. Place; KENT; **190** B-3; elev. 756ft./230m.; 🅿; ★ **GDR**; **Z** 49506 & mail Grand Rapids **Z** 49546; Ⓟ 10,807; Ⓒ 10,764
East Houghton; RMC Place; HOUGHTON; ▲ Hancock; mail Houghton **Z** 49931; pop. incl. with Houghton (Inc. Place)
East Jordan; Inc. Place; CHARLEVOIX; **188** H-7; elev. 600ft./183m.; 🅿; **Z** 49727; Ⓟ 2,240; Ⓒ 2,507
East Kingsford; RMC Place; DICKINSON; ▲ Breitung; ***188** D-13; mail Iron Mountain **Z** 49801, Kingsford **Z** 49802; ● 1,000
East Lake; Inc. Place; MANISTEE; ▲ Manistee; **189** L-4; 🅿; **Z** 49626; Ⓟ 473; Ⓒ 441
East Lansing; Inc. Place; INGHAM; **189** Q-9; elev. 850ft./259m.; 🅿 🅲 45,520 ■; ★ **LANS**; **Z** 48823-26; Ⓟ 50,677; Ⓒ 46,525; ◆ 48,490
East Leroy; RMC Place; CALHOUN; ▲ Leroy; **189** S-7; elev. 921ft./281m.; 🅿; ★ **BTLCK**; **Z** 49051; ● 190
Eastmanville; RMC Place; OTTAWA; ▲ Polkton; **189** P-5; mail Coopersville **Z** 49404; ● 60
Easton; MCD-Township; IONIA; ***189** P-7; mail Ionia **Z** 48846; Ⓟ 5,384; Ⓒ 2,835
Easton; RMC Place; SHIAWASSEE; ▲ New Haven; **189** O-10; elev. 728ft./222m.; mail Owosso **Z** 48867; ● 30
East Paris; RMC Place; KENT; ***189** P-6; ★ **GDR**; mail Grand Rapids **Z** 49508; pop. incl. with Kentwood (Inc. Place)
Eastpointe (East Detroit); Inc. Place; MACOMB; **189** R-13; 🅿 ■; ★ **DET**; **Z** 48021; Ⓟ 35,283; Ⓒ 34,077; ◆ 33,136
Eastport; RMC Place; ANTRIM; ▲ Central Lake; **188** I-7; 🅿; **Z** 49627; ● 160
East Rockwood; RMC Place; WAYNE; ▲ Brownstown; ***189** S-12; ★ **DET**; mail Rockwood **Z** 48173; ● 670
East Saugatuck; RMC Place; ALLEGAN; ▲ Manlius, Fillmore; **189** Q-5; elev. 717ft./219m.; ★ **HLND**; mail Hamilton **Z** 49419; ● 100
East Sebewa (Sebewa); RMC Place; IONIA; ▲ Danby, Sebewa; ***189** Q-8; mail Sunfield **Z** 48890; rural
East Side; RMC Place; SAGINAW; ▲ Saginaw; ★ **SAG-**; mail Saginaw **Z** 48601; pop. incl. with Saginaw (Inc. Place)
East Tawas (East Tawas-Tawas City); Inc. Place; IOSCO; **189** K-11; elev. 689ft./210m.; 🅿; **Z** 48730; Ⓟ 2,887; Ⓒ 2,951
East Tawas-Tawas City; IOSCO; see East Tawas (Inc. Place)
Eastview; RMC Place; MACOMB; ▲ Washington; ***189** Q-13; ★ **DET**; mail Romeo **Z** 48065; ● 800
Eastwood; CDP; KALAMAZOO; ▲ Kalamazoo; **189** P-3; ★ **KZOO**; mail Kalamazoo **Z** 49001; Ⓟ 6,340; Ⓒ 6,265
Eaton; MCD-Township; EATON; ***189** Q-8; ★ **LANS**; mail Charlotte **Z** 48813; Ⓟ 3,492; Ⓒ 4,278
EATON; **189** R-8; Ⓟ 92,879; Ⓒ 103,655; ◆ 107,414
Eaton Rapids; Inc. Place; EATON; **189** R-8; elev. 871ft./265m.; 🅿 🅷; ★ **LANS**; **Z** 48827; Ⓟ 4,695; Ⓒ 5,330
Eaton Rapids; MCD-Township; EATON; ***189** Q-8; 🅿; ★ **LANS**; **Z** 48827; does not include the City of Eaton Rapids; Ⓟ 3,003; Ⓒ 3,821
Eau Claire; Inc. Place; BERRIEN; ▲ Pipestone, Berrien; **189** S-4; 🅿; **Z** 49111; Ⓟ 494; Ⓒ 656
Eben; ALGER; see Eben Junction (RMC Place)
Eben Junction (Eben); RMC Place; ALGER; ▲ Rock River; **188** D-3; 🅿; **Z** 49825-26; ● 410
Echo; MCD-Township; ANTRIM; ***188** I-7; mail Central Lake **Z** 49622; Ⓟ 766; Ⓒ 928
Eckerman; RMC Place; CHIPPEWA; ▲ Chippewa; **188** D-7; elev. 778ft./237m.; 🅿; **Z** 49728, **Z** 49790; ● 250
Eckerman Corner; RMC Place; CHIPPEWA; ▲ Chippewa; ***188** D-7; elev. 868ft./265m.; mail Eckerman **Z** 49728; rural
Eckford; RMC Place; CALHOUN; ▲ Eckford; **189** S-8; elev. 953ft./290m.; mail Homer **Z** 49245; ● 70
Eckford; MCD-Township; CALHOUN; ***189** S-8; mail Homer **Z** 49245; Ⓟ 1,217; Ⓒ 1,282
Ecorse; Inc. Place; WAYNE; **190** L-6; elev. 585ft./178m.; 🅿; ★ **DET**; **Z** 48229; Ⓟ 12,180; Ⓒ 11,229
Eden; RMC Place; INGHAM; ▲ Vevay; **189** Q-9; elev. 970ft./296m.; ★ **LANS**; mail Leslie **Z** 49251, Mason **Z** 48854; ● 300
Eden; MCD-Township; LAKE; ***189** L-5; mail Irons **Z** 49644; Ⓟ 235; Ⓒ 377
Eden; MCD-Township; MASON; ***189** M-4; mail Scottville **Z** 49454; Ⓟ 491; Ⓒ 555
Edenville; RMC Place; MIDLAND; ▲ Edenville; **189** M-9; 🅿; **Z** 48620; ● 410
Edenville; MCD-Township; MIDLAND; ***189** M-9; 🅿; **Z** 48620; Ⓟ 2,367; Ⓒ 2,528
Edgemont Park; CDP-Census Area Only; INGHAM; ▲ Lansing; ***189** Q-9; ★ **LANS**; mail Lansing **Z** 48917; Ⓟ 2,532; Ⓒ 2,442
Edgerton; RMC Place; KENT; ▲ Algoma; ***189** O-6; ★ **GDR**; mail Rockford **Z** 49341; rural
Edgewood Beach; RMC Place; MENOMINEE; ▲ Menominee; ***188** H-1; elev. 590ft./180m.; mail Menominee **Z** 49858; rural
Edmore; Inc. Place; MONTCALM; ▲ Home; **189** N-7; elev. 965ft./294m.; 🅿; **Z** 48829; Ⓟ 1,126; Ⓒ 1,244
Edwards; MCD-Township; OGEMAW; ***189** L-9; mail West Branch **Z** 48661; Ⓟ 1,210; Ⓒ 1,390
Edwardsburg; Inc. Place; CASS; ▲ Ontwa; **189** T-5; elev. 829ft./253m.; 🅿; ★ **S.B.**; **Z** 49112, **Z** 49130; Ⓟ 1,142; Ⓒ 1,147
Edwards Corners; RMC Place; ST. JOSEPH; ▲ Flowerfield; ***189** S-6; elev. 880ft./268m.; mail Marcellus **Z** 49067; rural
Egelston; MCD-Township; MUSKEGON; ***189** O-5; elev. 640ft./195m.; ★ **MUS**; mail Muskegon **Z** 49442; Ⓟ 7,640; Ⓒ 9,537
Eight Point Lake; RMC Place; CLARE; ▲ Garfield; ***189** M-7; mail Lake **Z** 48632; ● 160
Elba; MCD-Township; GRATIOT; ***189** O-9; mail Bannister **Z** 48807; Ⓟ 1,390; Ⓒ 1,394
Elba; RMC Place; LAPEER; ▲ Elba; **189** P-12; elev. 854ft./260m.; ★ **DET**; mail Lapeer **Z** 48446; ● 200
Elba; MCD-Township; LAPEER; ***189** P-12; ★ **DET**; mail Lapeer **Z** 48446; Ⓟ 4,536; Ⓒ 5,462
Elberta; Inc. Place; BENZIE; ▲ Gilmore; **188** J-4; 🅿; **Z** 49628; Ⓟ 478; Ⓒ 457
Elbridge; MCD-Township; OCEANA; ***189** N-4; mail Walkerville **Z** 49459; Ⓟ 820; Ⓒ 1,233
Eldorado; RMC Place; CRAWFORD; ▲ South Branch; ***188** J-9; elev. 1,272ft./388m.; mail Roscommon **Z** 48653; rural
Elizabeth Lake Estates; RMC Place; OAKLAND; ▲ Waterford; ***189** Q-12; ★ **DET**; mail Waterford **Z** 48327
Elk; MCD-Township; LAKE; ***189** L-5; mail Irons **Z** 49644; Ⓟ 580; Ⓒ 900
Elk; MCD-Township; SANILAC; ***189** O-13; mail Peck **Z** 48466; Ⓟ 1,465; Ⓒ 1,584
Elkland; MCD-Township; TUSCOLA; ***189** N-12; mail Cass City **Z** 48726; Ⓟ 3,430; Ⓒ 3,659
Elk Rapids; Inc. Place; ANTRIM; ▲ Elk Rapids; **188** I-6; elev. 587ft./179m.; 🅿; **Z** 49629; Ⓟ 1,626; Ⓒ 1,700
Elk Rapids; MCD-Township; ANTRIM; ***188** I-6; 🅿; **Z** 49629; Ⓟ 2,374; Ⓒ 2,741
Elkton; Inc. Place; HURON; ▲ Oliver; **189** M-12; elev. 647ft./197m.; 🅿; **Z** 48731; Ⓟ 958; Ⓒ 863
Ellington; RMC Place; TUSCOLA; ▲ Ellington; ***189** N-12; elev. 788ft./240m.; mail Caro **Z** 48723; rural
Ellington; MCD-Township; TUSCOLA; ***189** N-12; mail Caro **Z** 48723; Ⓟ 1,215; Ⓒ 1,304
Ellis; MCD-Township; CHEBOYGAN; ***188** H-9; mail Afton **Z** 49705; Ⓟ 345; Ⓒ 519
Ellsworth; Inc. Place; ANTRIM; ▲ Banks; **188** H-7; elev. 621ft./189m.; 🅿; **Z** 49729; Ⓟ 418; Ⓒ 483
Ellsworth; MCD-Township; LAKE; ***189** L-6; mail Luther **Z** 49656; Ⓟ 622; Ⓒ 821
Elm; RMC Place; WAYNE; ***189** R-12; ★ **DET**; pop. incl. with Livonia (Inc. Place)
Elmdale; RMC Place; IONIA, KENT; ▲ Bowne, Campbell; **189** P-7; elev. 831ft./253m.; mail Clarksville **Z** 48815; ● 30
Elmer; MCD-Township; OSCODA; ***188** J-9; mail Mio **Z** 48647; Ⓟ 854; Ⓒ 1,095
Elmer; RMC Place; SANILAC; **189** N-13
Elmer; MCD-Township; SANILAC; ***189** N-13; mail Sandusky **Z** 48471; Ⓟ 774; Ⓒ 790
Elm Hall; RMC Place; GRATIOT; ▲ Sumner; **189** O-8; 🅿; **Z** 48830; ● 200
Elmira; RMC Place; OTSEGO, ANTRIM; ▲ Warner, Elmira; **188** I-8; 🅿; **Z** 49730; ● 230
Elmira; MCD-Township; OTSEGO; ***188** I-8; 🅿; **Z** 49730; Ⓟ 1,038; Ⓒ 1,598
Elm River; MCD-Township; HOUGHTON; ***188** B-12; mail Toivola **Z** 49965; Ⓟ 159; Ⓒ 169
Elmwood; MCD-Charter Township; LEELANAU; ***188** J-6; mail Traverse City **Z** 49684; Ⓟ 3,427; Ⓒ 4,264
Elmwood; RMC Place; TUSCOLA; ▲ Elmwood; ***189** N-12; elev. 771ft./235m.; mail Cass City **Z** 48726; rural
Elmwood; MCD-Township; TUSCOLA; ***189** N-12; mail Cass City **Z** 48726; Ⓟ 1,260; Ⓒ 1,213
Elo; RMC Place; HOUGHTON; ▲ Portage; **188** B-12; elev. 877ft./267m.; mail Pelkie **Z** 49958; ● 30
Eloise; RMC Place; WAYNE; ***189** R-12; 🅷; ★ **DET**; pop. incl. with Westland (Inc. Place)
Elsie; Inc. Place; CLINTON; ▲ Duplain; **189** P-9; 🅿; **Z** 48831; Ⓟ 957; Ⓒ 1,055
Elwell; RMC Place; GRATIOT; ▲ Seville; **189** O-8; 🅿; **Z** 48832; ● 270
Ely; MCD-Township; MARQUETTE; ***188** C-14; mail Champion **Z** 49814; Ⓟ 1,946; Ⓒ 2,010
Emerson; MCD-Township; GRATIOT; ***189** O-9; mail Breckenridge **Z** 48615; Ⓟ 1,003; Ⓒ 966
EMMET; **188** G-7; Ⓟ 25,040; Ⓒ 31,437; ◆ 33,135
Emmett; MCD-Charter Township; CALHOUN; ***189** R-7; ★ **BTLCK**; mail Battle Creek **Z** 49014; Ⓟ 10,764; Ⓒ 11,979
Emmett; Inc. Place; ST. CLAIR; ▲ Emmett; **189** P-13; elev. 775ft./236m.; 🅿; **Z** 48022; Ⓟ 297; Ⓒ 251
Emmett; MCD-Township; ST. CLAIR; ***189** P-13; 🅿; **Z** 48022; Ⓟ 1,816; Ⓒ 2,506
Empire; Inc. Place; LEELANAU; ▲ Empire; **188** J-5; elev. 619ft./189m.; 🅿; **Z** 49630; Ⓟ 355; Ⓒ 378
Empire; MCD-Township; LEELANAU; ***188** J-5; 🅿; **Z** 49630; Ⓟ 858; Ⓒ 1,085
Engadine; RMC Place; MACKINAC; ▲ Garfield; **188** E-6; 🅿; **Z** 49827; ● 480
Ensign; RMC Place; DELTA; ▲ Ensign; **188** F-3; elev. 711ft./217m.; mail Rapid River **Z** 49878; ● 40
Ensign; MCD-Township; DELTA; ***188** F-3; mail Rapid River **Z** 49878; Ⓟ 669; Ⓒ 780
Ensley; MCD-Township; NEWAYGO; ***189** O-6; mail Howard City **Z** 49329; Ⓟ 1,984; Ⓒ 2,474
Ensley Center; RMC Place; NEWAYGO; ▲ Ensley; **189** O-6; elev. 990ft./302m.; mail Sand Lake **Z** 49343; ● 30
Enterprise; MCD-Township; MISSAUKEE; ***189** K-8; mail Merritt **Z** 49667; Ⓟ 127; Ⓒ 194
Entrican; RMC Place; MONTCALM; ▲ Douglass; **189** O-7; elev. 901ft./275m.; mail Stanton **Z** 48888; ● 80
Epoufette; RMC Place; MACKINAC; ▲ Hendricks; **188** E-7; elev. 584ft./178m.; mail Naubinway **Z** 49762; ● 70
Epsilon; RMC Place; EMMET; ▲ Springvale; **188** H-8; mail Petoskey **Z** 49770; ● 50
Epworth Heights; MASON; see North Epworth (RMC Place)
Erie; RMC Place; MONROE; ▲ Erie; **189** T-11; 🅿; ★ **TOL**; **Z** 48133; ● 690
Erie; MCD-Township; MONROE; ***189** T-12; 🅿; ★ **TOL**; **Z** 48133; Ⓟ 4,492; Ⓒ 4,850
Erwin; MCD-Township; GOGEBIC; ***188** C-10; mail Ironwood **Z** 49938; Ⓟ 477; Ⓒ 357
Escanaba; Inc. Place; ⊡ DELTA; **188** F-2; elev. 598ft./182m.; 🅿 🅷 ■; **Z** 49829; Ⓟ 13,659; Ⓒ 13,140; ◆ 12,283
Escanaba; MCD-Township; DELTA; ***188** F-2; 🅿; **Z** 49829; does not include the City of Escanaba; Ⓟ 3,340; Ⓒ 3,587
Essex; MCD-Township; CLINTON; ***189** P-8; mail Saint Johns **Z** 48879; Ⓟ 1,677; Ⓒ 1,812
Essexville; Inc. Place; BAY; **189** N-10; elev. 590ft./180m.; 🅿; ★ **SAG-**; **Z** 48732; Ⓟ 4,088; Ⓒ 3,766
Estey; RMC Place; GLADWIN; ▲ Bentley; **189** M-9; mail Rhodes **Z** 48652; ● 100
Estral Beach; Inc. Place; MONROE; ▲ Berlin; **189** S-12; ★ **DET**; mail Newport **Z** 48166; Ⓟ 430; Ⓒ 486
Euclid Center; BERRIEN; see Benton Heights (CDP)
Eureka; RMC Place; CLINTON; ▲ Greenbush; **189** O-9; 🅿; **Z** 48833; ● 210
Eureka; MCD-Charter Township; MONTCALM; ***189** O-7; ★ **GDR**; mail Greenville **Z** 48838; Ⓟ 2,594; Ⓒ 3,271
Evangeline; MCD-Township; CHARLEVOIX; ***188** H-7; mail Boyne City **Z** 49712; Ⓟ 646; Ⓒ 773
Evans; RMC Place; KENT; ▲ Courtland; ***189** O-6; ★ **GDR**; mail Cedar Springs **Z** 49319; rural
Evans Lake; RMC Place; LENAWEE; ▲ Franklin; ***189** S-10; elev. 1,000ft./305m.; mail Tipton **Z** 49287; ● 100
Evart; Inc. Place; OSCEOLA; **189** M-7; 🅿; **Z** 49631; Ⓟ 1,744; Ⓒ 1,738
Evart; MCD-Township; OSCEOLA; ***189** M-7; 🅿; **Z** 49631; does not include the City of Evart; Ⓟ 1,229; Ⓒ 1,513
Eveline; MCD-Township; CHARLEVOIX; ***188** H-7; mail East Jordan **Z** 49727; Ⓟ 1,100; Ⓒ 1,560
Everett; MCD-Township; NEWAYGO; ***189** N-6; mail White Cloud **Z** 49349; Ⓟ 1,519; Ⓒ 1,985
Evergreen; MCD-Township; MONTCALM; ***189** O-8; mail Sheridan **Z** 48884; Ⓟ 2,531; Ⓒ 2,922
Evergreen; MCD-Township; SANILAC; ***189** N-12; mail Decker **Z** 48426; Ⓟ 907; Ⓒ 995
Evergreen Acres; RMC Place; MONROE; ▲ Monroe; ***189** T-12; ★ **MONR**; mail Monroe **Z** 48161; ● 970
Evergreen Shores; RMC Place; MACKINAC; ▲ St. Ignace; **188** F-8; mail Saint Ignace **Z** 49781; ● 180
Ewen; RMC Place; ONTONAGON; ▲ McMillan; **188** B-11; 🅿; **Z** 49925; ● 470
Ewing; MCD-Township; MARQUETTE; ***188** E-2; mail Rock **Z** 49880; Ⓟ 156; Ⓒ 159
Excelsior; MCD-Township; KALKASKA; ***188** J-7; mail Kalkaska **Z** 49646; Ⓟ 714; Ⓒ 855
Exeter; MCD-Township; MONROE; ***189** S-12; ★ **DET**; mail Maybee **Z** 48159; Ⓟ 3,253; Ⓒ 3,727

F

Fabius; MCD-Township; ST. JOSEPH; ***189** T-6; mail Three Rivers **Z** 49093; Ⓟ 3,187; Ⓒ 3,285
Factoryville; RMC Place; ST. JOSEPH; ▲ Leonidas; ***189** S-7; mail Athens **Z** 49011, Leonidas **Z** 49066; rural
Fairbanks; MCD-Township; DELTA; ***188** G-3; mail Cooks **Z** 49817; Ⓟ 309; Ⓒ 321
Fairfax; RMC Place; ST. JOSEPH; ▲ Colon; **189** S-7; mail Colon **Z** 49040; ● 40
Fairfield; RMC Place; LENAWEE; ▲ Fairfield; **189** T-10; mail Adrian **Z** 49221; ● 240
Fairfield; MCD-Township; LENAWEE; ***189** T-10; mail Adrian **Z** 49221; Ⓟ 1,883; Ⓒ 1,756
Fairfield; MCD-Township; SHIAWASSEE; ***189** P-9; mail Elsie **Z** 48831; Ⓟ 790; Ⓒ 745
Fairgrove; Inc. Place; TUSCOLA; ▲ Fairgrove; **189** N-11; 🅿; **Z** 48733; Ⓟ 592; Ⓒ 627
Fairgrove; MCD-Township; TUSCOLA; ***189** N-11; 🅿; **Z** 48733; Ⓟ 1,743; Ⓒ 1,749
Fairhaven; MCD-Township; HURON; ***189** M-11; mail Bay Port **Z** 48720; Ⓟ 1,250; Ⓒ 1,259
Fair Haven; RMC Place; ST. CLAIR; ▲ Ira; **189** Q-14; 🅿; ★ **DET**; **Z** 48023; Ⓟ 1,505
Fair Plain; CDP; BERRIEN; ▲ Saint Joseph, Benton; ***189** S-4; elev. 626ft./191m.; ★ **BNTH-**; mail Benton Harbor **Z** 49022; Ⓟ 8,051; Ⓒ 7,828
Fairplain; MCD-Township; MONTCALM; ***189** O-7; mail Greenville **Z** 48838; Ⓟ 1,575; Ⓒ 1,826
Fairport; RMC Place; DELTA; ▲ Fairbanks; **188** G-3; elev. 602ft./183m.; mail Garden **Z** 49835; ● 100
Fairview; RMC Place; OSCODA; ▲ Comins; **188** J-10; elev. 1,170ft./357m.; 🅿; **Z** 48621; ● 570
Faithorn; RMC Place; MENOMINEE; ▲ Faithorn; ***188** D-14; elev. 849ft./259m.; mail Vulcan **Z** 49892; ● 30
Faithorn; MCD-Township; MENOMINEE; ***188** G-1; mail Vulcan **Z** 49892; Ⓟ 213; Ⓒ 214
Fallasberg; RMC Place; KENT; ▲ Vergennes; ***189** P-7; elev. 680ft./207m.; ★ **GDR**; mail Lowell **Z** 49331; ● 30
Falmouth; RMC Place; MISSAUKEE; ▲ Clam Union; **189** L-7; 🅿; **Z** 49632; ● 280
Fargo; RMC Place; ST. CLAIR; ▲ Greenwood; **189** O-13; 🅿; **Z** 48006; ● 90
Farmers Creek; RMC Place; LAPEER; ▲ Metamora, Hadley; ***189** P-12; ★ **DET**; mail Metamora **Z** 48455; ● 120
Farmington; Inc. Place; OAKLAND; **190** H-3; elev. 750ft./229m.; 🅿; ★ **DET**; **Z** 48331-36; Ⓟ 10,132; Ⓒ 10,423
Farmington Hills; Inc. Place; OAKLAND; **189** R-12; elev. 850ft./259m.; 🅿 🅷 ■; ★ **DET**; **Z** 48331-36; Ⓟ 74,652; Ⓒ 82,111; ◆ 80,776
Farrandville; RMC Place; GENESEE; ▲ Vienna; **189** O-11; ★ **FLN**; mail Clio **Z** 48420; ● 820
Farwell; Inc. Place; CLARE; ▲ Surrey; **189** M-8; 🅿; **Z** 48622; Ⓟ 851; Ⓒ 855
Fawn River; RMC Place; ST. JOSEPH; ▲ Fawn River; **189** T-7; mail Sturgis **Z** 49091; ● 30
Fawn River; MCD-Township; ST. JOSEPH; ***189** T-7; mail Sturgis **Z** 49091; Ⓟ 1,571; Ⓒ 1,648
Fayette; RMC Place; DELTA; ▲ Fairbanks; **188** F-3; mail Garden **Z** 49835; rural
Fayette; MCD-Township; HILLSDALE; ***189** S-9; mail Jonesville **Z** 49250; Ⓟ 3,190; Ⓒ 3,350
Federal Building; RMC Place; SAGINAW; ▲ Saginaw; ***189** N-10; ★ **SAG-**; mail Saginaw **Z** 48606; pop. incl. with Saginaw (Inc. Place)
Felch; RMC Place; DICKINSON; ▲ Felch; **188** D-14; elev. 1,172ft./357m.; 🅿; **Z** 49831, **Z** 49877; ● 300
Felch; MCD-Township; DICKINSON; ***188** C-14; 🅿; **Z** 49831, **Z** 49877; Ⓟ 705; Ⓒ 726
Felch Mountain; RMC Place; DICKINSON; ▲ Felch; **188** D-14; mail Iron Mountain **Z** 49801; ● 40
Fenkell; RMC Place; WAYNE; ***189** R-12; ★ **DET**; mail Detroit **Z** 48238; pop. incl. with Detroit (Inc. Place)
Fennville; Inc. Place; ALLEGAN; ▲ Manlius, Clyde; **189** Q-5; 🅿; **Z** 49408; Ⓟ 1,023; Ⓒ 1,459
Fenton; Inc. Place; GENESEE; ***189** P-11; 🅿; ★ **FLN**; **Z** 48430; Ⓟ 8,444; Ⓒ 10,582
Fenton; MCD-Charter Township; GENESEE; ***189** P-11; 🅿; ★ **FLN**; **Z** 48430; does not include the City of Fenton; Ⓟ 10,055; Ⓒ 12,968
Fenwick; RMC Place; MONTCALM; ▲ Fairplain; **189** O-7; 🅿; **Z** 48834; ● 150
Ferndale; Inc. Place; OAKLAND; **189** R-12; elev. 649ft./198m.; 🅿 🅷; ★ **DET**; **Z** 48220; Ⓟ 25,084; Ⓒ 22,105; ◆ 20,386
Ferris; MCD-Township; MONTCALM; ***189** O-8; mail Vestaburg **Z** 48891; Ⓟ 1,189; Ⓒ 1,379
Ferry; RMC Place; OCEANA; ▲ Ferry; **189** N-4; elev. 717ft./219m.; mail Shelby **Z** 49455; ● 200
Ferry; MCD-Township; OCEANA; ***189** N-4; mail Shelby **Z** 49455; Ⓟ 1,033; Ⓒ 1,296
Ferrysburg; Inc. Place; OTTAWA; **189** P-4; 🅿; **Z** 49409; Ⓟ 2,919; Ⓒ 3,040
Fibre; RMC Place; CHIPPEWA; **188** E-8; elev. 700ft./213m.; 🅿; **Z** 49780; ● 30
Fife Lake; Inc. Place; GRAND TRAVERSE; ▲ Fife Lake; **188** J-7; elev. 1,038ft./316m.; 🅿; **Z** 49633; Ⓟ 394; Ⓒ 466
Fife Lake; MCD-Township; GRAND TRAVERSE; ***188** J-6; 🅿; **Z** 49633; Ⓟ 1,344; Ⓒ 1,517
Filer; MCD-Charter Township; MANISTEE; ***189** L-4; mail Manistee **Z** 49660; Ⓟ 1,966; Ⓒ 2,208
Filer City; RMC Place; MANISTEE; ▲ Filer; **189** L-4; 🅿; **Z** 49634; ● 280
Filion; RMC Place; HURON; ▲ Meade, Lincoln; **189** M-12; 🅿; **Z** 48432; ● 200
Fillmore (Filmore); RMC Place; ALLEGAN; ▲ Fillmore; **189** Q-5; ★ **HLND**; mail Holland **Z** 49423; ● 50
Fillmore; MCD-Township; ALLEGAN; ***189** Q-5; ★ **HLND**; mail Holland **Z** 49423; Ⓟ 2,710; Ⓒ 2,756
Filmore; ALLEGAN; see Fillmore (RMC Place)
Findley; RMC Place; ST. JOSEPH; ▲ Burr Oak; **189** T-7; mail Burr Oak **Z** 49030; ● 40
Fisher; RMC Place; KENT; ★ **GDR**; mail Wyoming **Z** 49509; pop. incl. with Wyoming (Inc. Place)
Fisher Building; RMC Place; WAYNE; ***189** R-13; ★ **DET**; mail Detroit **Z** 48211; pop. incl. with Detroit (Inc. Place)
Fisherville; RMC Place; BAY; ▲ Williams; ***189** N-10; elev. 639ft./195m.; ★ **SAG-**; mail Auburn **Z** 48611; ● 90
Fitchburg; RMC Place; INGHAM; ▲ Bunker Hill; **189** R-9; elev. 945ft./288m.; mail Stockbridge **Z** 49285; ● 80

Entries in **UPPERCASE** are counties.
Entries in **bold** have populations of 2,500 or more.
Names in parentheses are alternate names.

Inc. Place	Incorporated Place
RMC Place	Rand McNally Designated Place
CDP	Census Designated Place
MCD	Minor Civil Division
⊡	County Seat
▲	Minor Civil Division
elev.	Elevation
🅿	Post Office
🅷	Hospital
🅲	College
■	Principal Business Center
★	Ranally Metro Area (RMA) Abbreviation
Z	Zip Code(s)
Ⓟ	Previous Census Population
Ⓡ	Revised Census Population
Ⓐ	Annexation Population
●	Rand McNally Population Estimate
Ⓒ	Final Census Population
Ⓢ	Special Census Population
◆	Estimated Population

For additional definitions see Glossary, Volume 1, and Introduction, Volume 2.

Five Lakes; RMC Place; LAPEER; ▲ Mayfield; ***189** O-12; ★ **DET**; mail Lapeer z 48446; rural
Five Points; RMC Place; SHIAWASSEE; ▲ Owosso; ***189** P-10; elev. 782ft./238m.; mail Owosso z 48867; rural
Flanders (Greeley); RMC Place; ALPENA; ▲ Green; ***188** I-11; mail Lachine z 49753; rural
Flat Rock; RMC Place; DELTA; ▲ Escanaba; ***188** F-2; elev. 772ft./235m.; mail Gladstone z 49837; ● 150
Flat Rock; Inc. Place; WAYNE; **189** S-12; elev. 600ft./183m.; 🅿; ★ **DET**; z 48134; ℗ 7,290; © 8,488
Flint; Inc. Place; ⊡ GENESEE; **189** P-11; 🅿 🅷 🅲 14,631 ■; ★ **FLN**; z 48501-07, z 48509, z 48519, z 48529, z 48531-32, z 48550-57; ℗ 140,761; © 124,943; ◆ 113,448
Flint; MCD-Charter Township; GENESEE; ***189** P-11; 🅿 🅲 14,631; ★ **FLN**; z 48501-07, z 48509, z 48519, z 48529, z 48531-32, z 48550-57, z 98662; does not include the City of Flint; ℗ 34,081; © 33,691; ◆ 31,768
Florence; MCD-Township; ST. JOSEPH; ***189** T-6; mail Constantine z 49042; ℗ 1,518; © 1,436
Florida; RMC Place; HOUGHTON; ▲ Calumet; mail Calumet z 49913; pop. incl. with Laurium (Inc. Place)
Flowerfield; RMC Place; ST. JOSEPH; ▲ Flowerfield; **189** S-6; elev. 859ft./262m.; ★ **KZOO**; mail Three Rivers z 49093; ● 130
Flowerfield; MCD-Township; ST. JOSEPH; ***189** S-6; ★ **KZOO**; mail Three Rivers z 49093; ℗ 1,418; © 1,592
Flower Hills; BERRIEN; see Tower Hill (RMC Place)
Floyd; RMC Place; MIDLAND; ▲ Lee; ***189** N-9; elev. 642ft./196m.; ★ **SAG-**; mail Midland z 48640; rural
Flushing; Inc. Place; GENESEE; ▲ Flushing; **189** P-10; 🅿; ★ **FLN**; z 48433; ℗ 8,542; © 8,348
Flushing; MCD-Charter Township; GENESEE; ***189** O-10; 🅿; ★ **FLN**; z 48433; ℗ 9,223; © 10,230
Flynn; MCD-Township; SANILAC; ***189** O-13; mail Marlette z 48453; ℗ 914; © 1,040
Foote Site Village; RMC Place; IOSCO; ▲ Oscoda; ***189** K-11; elev. 643ft./196m.; mail Oscoda z 48750; ● 350
Ford Lake; RMC Place; MASON; ▲ Sheridan; mail Fountain z 49410; summer pop. 400
Ford River; RMC Place; DELTA; ▲ Ford River; **188** G-2; mail Escanaba z 49829; ● 280
Ford River; MCD-Township; DELTA; ***188** G-2; mail Escanaba z 49829; ℗ 2,002; © 2,241
Forest; MCD-Township; CHEBOYGAN; ***188** H-9; mail Tower z 49792; ℗ 929; © 1,080
Forest; MCD-Township; GENESEE; ***189** O-11; ★ **FLN**; mail Otisville z 48463; ℗ 4,409; © 4,738
Forest; MCD-Township; MISSAUKEE; ***189** K-7; mail Lake City z 49651; ℗ 878; © 1,082
Forester; RMC Place; SANILAC; ▲ Forester; **189** N-14; mail Carsonville z 48419; ● 80
Forester; MCD-Township; SANILAC; ***189** N-14; mail Carsonville z 48419; ℗ 919; © 1,108
Forest Grove; RMC Place; OTTAWA; ▲ Jamestown; ***189** Q-5; elev. 783ft./239m.; ★ **GDR**; mail Hudsonville z 49426; ● 140
Forest Grove Station; RMC Place; OTTAWA; ▲ Jamestown; ***189** Q-5; elev. 698ft./213m.; ★ **GDR**; mail Hudsonville z 49426; rural
Forest Hill; RMC Place; GRATIOT; ▲ Pine River; ***189** N-8; elev. 786ft./240m.; mail Alma z 48801; ● 30
Forest Hills; CDP-Census Area Only; KENT; ▲ Cascade, Ada; **190** B-3; elev. 750ft./229m.; ★ **GDR**; mail Grand Rapids z 49506; ℗ 16,690; © 20,942; ◆ 22,323
Forest Home; MCD-Township; ANTRIM; ***188** I-7; mail Bellaire z 49615; ℗ 1,410; © 1,858
Forest Lake; RMC Place; ALGER; ▲ Au Train; **188** D-3; mail Munising z 49862; ● 60
Forestville; Inc. Place; SANILAC; ▲ Delaware; **189** M-14; elev. 635ft./194m.; 🅿; z 48434; ℗ 153; © 127
Fork; MCD-Township; MECOSTA; ***189** M-7; mail Barryton z 49305; ℗ 1,395; © 1,678
Forsyth; MCD-Township; MARQUETTE; ***188** E-1; mail Little Lake z 49833; ℗ 8,775; © 4,824
Fort Dearborn; RMC Place; WAYNE; ***189** R-12; ★ **DET**; mail Dearborn z 48123-24; pop. incl. with Dearborn (Inc. Place)
Fort Gratiot; MCD-Charter Township; ST. CLAIR; ***189** P-14; 🅿; ★ **PTHU**; z 48059; ℗ 8,968; © 10,691
Fortune Lake; RMC Place; IRON; ▲ Crystal Falls; ***188** C-13; elev. 1,377ft./420m.; mail Crystal Falls z 49920; ● 30
Foster; MCD-Township; OGEMAW; ***189** K-9; mail West Branch z 48661; ℗ 719; © 821
Foster City; RMC Place; DICKINSON; ▲ Breen; **188** D-14; elev. 1,029ft./314m.; 🅿; z 49834; ● 350
Fosters; RMC Place; SAGINAW; ▲ Taymouth; ***189** O-10; ★ **SAG-**; mail Birch Run z 48415; ● 70
Fostoria; RMC Place; TUSCOLA; ▲ Watertown; **189** O-12; 🅿; z 48435; ● 370
Fountain; Inc. Place; MASON; ▲ Sherman; **189** L-5; 🅿; z 49410; ℗ 165; © 175
Fountain Park; RMC Place; HILLSDALE; ▲ Jefferson; ***189** T-9; mail Osseo z 49266; ● 150
Fourmile Corner; RMC Place; LUCE; ▲ McMillan; ***188** D-6; elev. 785ft./239m.; mail Newberry z 49868
Fowler; Inc. Place; CLINTON; ▲ Dallas; **189** P-8; elev. 743ft./226m.; 🅿; z 48835; ℗ 912; © 1,136
Fowlerville; Inc. Place; LIVINGSTON; ▲ Handy; **189** Q-10; 🅿; z 48836; ℗ 2,648; © 2,972
Fox; RMC Place; MENOMINEE; ▲ Cedarville; **188** G-2; elev. 592ft./180m.; mail Stephenson z 49887; rural
Fox Creek; RMC Place; WAYNE; ***189** R-13; ★ **DET**; mail Detroit z 48215; pop. incl. with Detroit (Inc. Place)
Francisco; RMC Place; JACKSON; ▲ Grass Lake; ***189** R-10; ★ **JAC**; mail Grass Lake z 49240; ● 80
Frankenlust; MCD-Township; BAY; ***189** N-10; ★ **SAG-**; mail Bay City z 48706; ℗ 2,281; © 2,530
Frankenmuth; Inc. Place; SAGINAW; **189** O-11; 🅿; ★ **SAG-**; z 48734, z 48787; ℗ 4,408; © 4,838
Frankenmuth; MCD-Township; SAGINAW; ***189** O-11; 🅿; ★ **SAG-**; z 48734, z 48787; does not include the City of Frankenmuth; ℗ 2,122; © 2,049
Frankentrost; RMC Place; SAGINAW; ▲ Blumfield; **189** N-11; elev. 616ft./188m.; mail Saginaw z 48601; ● 50
Frankfort; Inc. Place; BENZIE; **188** J-4; elev. 600ft./183m.; 🅿 🅷; z 49635; ℗ 1,546; © 1,513
Franklin; MCD-Township; CLARE; ***189** L-8; mail Harrison z 48625; ℗ 600; © 809
Franklin; MCD-Township; HOUGHTON; ***188** A-13; mail Hancock z 49930; ℗ 1,164; © 1,320
Franklin; MCD-Township; LENAWEE; ***189** S-10; mail Tipton z 49287; ℗ 2,473; © 2,939
Franklin; Inc. Place; OAKLAND; ▲ Southfield; **190** H-4; elev. 833ft./254m.; 🅿; ★ **DET**; z 48025; ℗ 2,626; © 2,937
Franklin Mine; RMC Place; HOUGHTON; ▲ Franklin; ***188** A-13; mail Hancock z 49930; ● 280
Fraser; MCD-Township; BAY; ***189** M-10; ★ **SAG-**; mail Linwood z 48634; ℗ 3,680; © 3,375
Fraser; Inc. Place; MACOMB; **190** G-8; elev. 610ft./186m.; 🅿; ★ **DET**; z 48026; ℗ 13,899; © 15,297
Freda; RMC Place; HOUGHTON; ▲ Stanton; ***188** A-12; elev. 736ft./224m.; mail Atlantic Mine z 49905; ● 70
Frederic; RMC Place; CRAWFORD; ▲ Frederic; **188** J-8; elev. 1,205ft./367m.; 🅿; z 49733; ● 570
Frederic; MCD-Township; CRAWFORD; ***188** J-8; 🅿; z 49733; ℗ 1,287; © 1,401; ® 1,434
Fredonia; MCD-Township; CALHOUN; ***189** S-8; mail Marshall z 49068; ℗ 1,741; © 1,723
Freedom; RMC Place; CHEBOYGAN; ▲ Mackinaw; ***188** F-8; mail Cheboygan z 49721; rural
Freedom; MCD-Township; WASHTENAW; ***189** S-10; mail Chelsea z 48118, Manchester z 48158; ℗ 1,486; © 1,562
Freeland; CDP; SAGINAW; ▲ Tittabawassee; **189** N-10; elev. 635ft./194m.; 🅿; ★ **SAG-**; z 48623; ℗ 1,421; © 5,147
Freeman; MCD-Township; CLARE; ***189** M-7; mail Lake z 48632; ℗ 613; © 1,118
Freeport; Inc. Place; BARRY; ▲ Carlton, Irving; **189** Q-7; 🅿; z 49325; ℗ 458; © 444
Free Soil; Inc. Place; MASON; ▲ Free Soil; **189** L-4; elev. 677ft./206m.; 🅿; z 49411; ℗ 148; © 177
Free Soil; MCD-Township; MASON; ***189** L-4; 🅿; z 49411; ℗ 860; © 809; ® 938
Freidburger; RMC Place; SANILAC; ▲ Austin; ***189** N-13; elev. 789ft./240m.; mail Ubly z 48475; rural
Fremont; MCD-Township; ISABELLA; ***189** N-8; mail Blanchard z 49310; ℗ 1,217; © 1,358
Fremont; Inc. Place; NEWAYGO; **189** N-5; elev. 823ft./251m.; 🅿 🅷; z 49412-13; ℗ 3,875; © 4,224
Fremont; MCD-Township; SAGINAW; ***189** O-9; mail Saint Charles z 48655; ℗ 2,137; © 2,099
Fremont; MCD-Township; SANILAC; ***189** O-13; mail Yale z 48097; ℗ 787; © 913
Fremont; MCD-Township; TUSCOLA; ***189** O-12; mail Mayville z 48744; ℗ 3,153; © 3,559
French Landing; RMC Place; WAYNE; ★ **DET**; mail Romulus z 48174
Frenchtown; RMC Place; MARQUETTE; ***188** D-1; elev. 1,446ft./441m.; mail Ishpeming z 49849; pop. incl. with Ishpeming (Inc. Place)
Frenchtown; MCD-Charter Township; MONROE; ***189** S-12; 🅿; ★ **MONR**; z 48161 & mail Monroe z 48162; ℗ 18,210; © 20,777; ◆ 20,332
French Town; RMC Place; OCEANA; ▲ Pentwater; ***189** M-4; mail Pentwater z 49449; pop. incl. with Pentwater (Inc. Place)
Friendship; MCD-Township; EMMET; ***188** G-7; mail Harbor Springs z 49740; ℗ 591; © 844
Frontier; RMC Place; HILLSDALE; ▲ Woodbridge; **189** T-9; 🅿; z 49239; ● 210
Frost; MCD-Township; CLARE; ***189** L-8; mail Harrison z 48625; ℗ 826; © 1,159
Frost Corners; RMC Place; IONIA; ▲ Portland; ***189** P-8; elev. 812ft./247m.; mail Portland z 48875; rural
Fruitland; MCD-Township; MUSKEGON; ***189** O-4; ★ **MUS**; mail Whitehall z 49461; ℗ 4,391; © 5,235
Fruitport; Inc. Place; MUSKEGON; ▲ Fruitport; **189** O-5; 🅿; ★ **MUS**; z 49415; ℗ 1,090; © 1,124
Fruitport; MCD-Charter Township; MUSKEGON; ***189** O-5; 🅿; ★ **MUS**; z 49415; ℗ 11,485; © 12,533
Fruitport Siding; RMC Place; MUSKEGON; ★ **MUS**; mail Muskegon z 49444; pop. incl. with Norton Shores (Inc. Place)
Fulton; MCD-Township; GRATIOT; ***189** O-8; mail Perrinton z 48871; ℗ 2,114; © 2,413
Fulton; RMC Place; KALAMAZOO; ▲ Wakeshma; **189** S-7; 🅿; z 49052; ● 400
Fulton; RMC Place; KEWEENAW; ▲ Allouez; ***188** A-13; mail Mohawk z 49950; ● 250

G

Gaastra; Inc. Place; IRON; **188** C-12; elev. 1,660ft./506m.; 🅿; z 49927; ℗ 376; © 339
Gagetown; Inc. Place; TUSCOLA; ▲ Elmwood; **189** M-12; 🅿; z 48735; ℗ 337; © 389
Gaines; Inc. Place; GENESEE; ▲ Gaines; **189** P-10; 🅿; ★ **FLN**; z 48436; ℗ 427; © 366
Gaines; MCD-Township; GENESEE; ***189** P-10; 🅿; ★ **FLN**; z 48436; ℗ 5,391; © 6,491
Gaines; MCD-Charter Township; KENT; ***189** Q-6; ★ **GDR**; mail Grand Rapids z 49508; ℗ 14,533; © 20,112; ◆ 22,684
Galesburg; Inc. Place; KALAMAZOO; **189** R-7; 🅿; ★ **KZOO**; z 49053; ℗ 1,863; © 1,988
Galien; Inc. Place; BERRIEN; ▲ Galien; **189** T-4; elev. 679ft./207m.; 🅿; z 49113; ℗ 596; © 593
Galien; MCD-Township; BERRIEN; ***189** T-4; 🅿; z 49113; ℗ 1,591; © 1,611
Ganges; RMC Place; ALLEGAN; ▲ Ganges; **189** Q-5; elev. 661ft./201m.; mail Fennville z 49408; ● 80
Ganges; MCD-Township; ALLEGAN; ***189** Q-5; mail Fennville z 49408; ℗ 2,124; © 2,524
Garden; Inc. Place; DELTA; ▲ Garden; **188** F-4; elev. 618ft./188m.; 🅿; z 49835; ℗ 268; © 240
Garden; MCD-Township; DELTA; ***188** F-4; 🅿; z 49835; ℗ 783; © 817
Garden City; Inc. Place; WAYNE; **189** R-12; elev. 636ft./194m.; 🅿 🅷; ★ **DET**; z 48135-36; ℗ 31,846; © 30,047; ◆ 27,191
Garden Corners; RMC Place; DELTA; ▲ Garden; **188** F-4; elev. 689ft./210m.; mail Cooks z 49817; ● 110
Gardendale; RMC Place; ST. CLAIR; ▲ Fort Gratiot; ***189** P-14; ★ **PTHU**; mail Fort Gratiot z 48059; ● 160
Gardenville; RMC Place; CHIPPEWA; ▲ Soo; ***188** D-9; ★ **SOO**; mail Sault Sainte Marie z 49783
Gardner; RMC Place; MENOMINEE; ▲ Holmes; ***188** G-1; mail Daggett z 49821; rural
Garfield; MCD-Township; BAY; ***189** M-10; mail Linwood z 48634; ℗ 1,736; © 1,775
Garfield; MCD-Township; CLARE; ***189** M-7; mail Traverse City z 49684; ℗ 1,477; © 1,968
Garfield; MCD-Charter Township; GRAND TRAVERSE; ***188** J-6; mail Traverse City z 49684; ℗ 10,516; © 13,840
Garfield; MCD-Township; KALKASKA; ***188** J-7; mail Fife Lake z 49633; ℗ 596; © 794
Garfield; MCD-Township; MACKINAC; ***188** E-6; mail Engadine z 49827; ℗ 1,156; © 1,251
Garfield; MCD-Township; NEWAYGO; ***189** N-5; mail Newaygo z 49337; ℗ 2,067; © 2,464
Garnet; RMC Place; MACKINAC; ▲ Hudson; **188** E-7; mail Naubinway z 49762; ● 90
Garth; RMC Place; DELTA; ▲ Masonville; ***188** F-3; mail Rapid River z 49878; ● 100
Gay; RMC Place; KEWEENAW; ▲ Sherman; **188** A-13; elev. 653ft./199m.; 🅿; z 49945; ● 60
Gaylord; Inc. Place; ⊡ OTSEGO; **188** I-8; elev. 1,349ft./411m.; 🅿 🅷; z 49734-35; ℗ 3,256; © 3,681
Genesee; RMC Place; GENESEE; ▲ Genesee; **189** O-11; 🅿; ★ **FLN**; z 48437; ● 1,500
Genesee; MCD-Charter Township; GENESEE; ***189** O-11; 🅿; ★ **FLN**; z 48437; ℗ 24,093; © 24,125; ◆ 22,936
GENESEE; **189** P-11; ℗ 430,459; © 436,141; ® 436,148; ◆ 419,287
Geneva; MCD-Township; MIDLAND; ***189** M-9; mail Coleman z 48618; ℗ 1,048; © 1,137
Geneva; MCD-Township; VAN BUREN; ***189** R-5; mail Grand Junction z 49056; ℗ 3,162; © 3,975
Genoa; MCD-Township; LIVINGSTON; ***189** Q-11; ★ **DET**; mail Brighton z 48114, z 48116; ℗ 10,820; © 15,901
Georgetown; MCD-Charter Township; OTTAWA; ***189** P-5; ★ **GDR**; mail Hudsonville z 49426, Jenison z 49428; ℗ 32,672; © 41,658; ◆ 44,857
Gera; RMC Place; SAGINAW; ▲ Frankenmuth; **189** N-11; ★ **SAG-**; mail Frankenmuth z 48734; ● 20
Germfask; RMC Place; SCHOOLCRAFT; ▲ Germfask; **188** E-5; 🅿; z 49836; ● 250
Germfask; MCD-Township; SCHOOLCRAFT; ***188** E-5; 🅿; z 49836; ℗ 542; © 491
Gerrish; MCD-Township; ROSCOMMON; ***189** K-8; mail Roscommon z 48653; ℗ 2,421; © 3,072
Gibbs City; RMC Place; IRON; **188** C-12; elev. 1,488ft./454m.; mail Fowler z 48835
Gibraltar; Inc. Place; WAYNE; **189** S-12; elev. 584ft./178m.; 🅿; ★ **DET**; z 48173; ℗ 4,297; © 4,264
Gibson; RMC Place; ALLEGAN; ▲ Laketown; ***189** Q-5; elev. 647ft./197m.; ★ **HLND**; mail Holland z 49423; ● 50
Gibson; MCD-Township; BAY; ***189** M-10; mail Bentley z 48613; ℗ 1,090; © 1,245
Gilchrist; RMC Place; MACKINAC; ▲ Garfield; **188** E-6; mail Naubinway z 49762; ● 20
Gilead (Gilead Lake); RMC Place; BRANCH; ▲ Gilead; ***189** T-7; mail Bronson z 49028; ● 150
Gilead; MCD-Township; BRANCH; ***189** T-7; mail Bronson z 49028; ℗ 688; © 753
Gilead Lake; BRANCH; see Gilead (RMC Place)
Gilford; RMC Place; TUSCOLA; ▲ Gilford; **189** N-11; 🅿; z 48736; ● 230
Gilford; MCD-Township; TUSCOLA; ***189** N-11; 🅿; z 48736; ℗ 824; © 833
Gilmore; MCD-Township; BENZIE; ***188** J-5; mail Elberta z 49628; ℗ 794; © 850
Gilmore; MCD-Township; ISABELLA; ***189** M-8; mail Farwell z 48622; ℗ 1,072; © 1,376
Gingell; OAKLAND; see Gingellville (RMC Place)
Gingellville (Gingell); RMC Place; OAKLAND; ▲ Orion; ***189** Q-12; ★ **DET**; mail Lake Orion z 48359; ● 320
Girard; RMC Place; BRANCH; ▲ Girard; **189** S-8; mail Coldwater z 49036; ● 200
Girard; MCD-Township; BRANCH; ***189** S-8; mail Coldwater z 49036; ℗ 1,800; © 1,916; ® 1,776
Gladstone; Inc. Place; DELTA; **188** F-2; elev. 601ft./183m.; 🅿; z 49837; ℗ 4,565; © 5,032
Gladwin; Inc. Place; ⊡ GLADWIN; **189** L-9; elev. 786ft./240m.; 🅿 🅷; z 48624; ℗ 2,682; © 3,001
Gladwin; MCD-Township; GLADWIN; ***189** L-9; 🅿; z 48624; does not include the City of Gladwin; ℗ 916; © 1,044
GLADWIN; **189** L-9; ℗ 21,896; © 26,023; ◆ 25,217
Glen Arbor; RMC Place; LEELANAU; ▲ Glen Arbor; **188** I-5; elev. 591ft./180m.; 🅿; z 49636; ● 280
Glen Arbor; MCD-Township; LEELANAU; ***188** I-5; 🅿; z 49636; ℗ 644; © 788
Glencoe Hills Apartments; RMC Place; WASHTENAW; ▲ Pittsfield; ★ **DET**; mail Ann Arbor z 48108; pop. incl. with Ann Arbor (Inc. Place)
Glendale; RMC Place; VAN BUREN; ▲ Waverly; **189** R-5; elev. 768ft./234m.; mail Paw Paw z 49079
Glendora; RMC Place; BERRIEN; ▲ Weesaw; **189** T-4; 🅿; z 49107; ● 40
Glen Haven; RMC Place; LEELANAU; ▲ Glen Arbor; **188** I-5; mail Cedar z 49621; ● 60
Glenn; RMC Place; ALLEGAN; ▲ Ganges; **189** R-4; elev. 652ft./199m.; 🅿; z 49416; ● 270
Glenn Haven Shores; RMC Place; ALLEGAN; ▲ Casco; ***189** R-4; elev. 670ft./204m.; mail South Haven z 49090; ● 100
Glennie; RMC Place; ALCONA; ▲ Curtis; **188** J-11; 🅿; z 48737; ● 400
Glenn Shores; RMC Place; ALLEGAN; ▲ Casco; ***189** R-4; elev. 665ft./203m.; mail South Haven z 49090; ● 80
Glenwood; RMC Place; CASS; ▲ Wayne; ***189** S-5; elev. 769ft./234m.; mail Dowagiac z 49047; rural
Gobles; Inc. Place; VAN BUREN; **189** R-5; elev. 815ft./248m.; 🅿; z 49055; ℗ 769; © 815
Goetzville; RMC Place; CHIPPEWA; ▲ Raber; **188** E-10; elev. 752ft./229m.; 🅿; z 49736; ● 100
GOGEBIC; **188** C-11; ℗ 18,052; © 17,370; ◆ 15,929
Golden; MCD-Township; OCEANA; ***189** N-4; mail Mears z 49436; ℗ 1,302; © 1,810
Golfcrest (Hollywood Golfcrest); RMC Place; MONROE; ▲ Frenchtown; ***189** S-12; ★ **MONR**; mail Monroe z 48162; ● 200
Gomins (Comins); RMC Place; OSCODA; ▲ Clinton; **188** J-10; mail Comins z 48619; ● 170
Goodar; MCD-Township; OGEMAW; ***189** K-10; mail South Branch z 48761; ℗ 381; © 493
Goodells; RMC Place; ST. CLAIR; ▲ Wales; **189** P-13; elev. 707ft./215m.; 🅿; z 48027; ● 340
Good Hart; RMC Place; EMMET; ▲ Readmond; **188** G-7; elev. 708ft./216m.; 🅿; z 49737; summer pop. 700; ● 60
Goodison; RMC Place; OAKLAND; ▲ Oakland; **190** E-6; 🅿; ★ **DET**; z 48306; ● 190
Goodland; MCD-Township; LAPEER; ***189** O-13; mail Imlay City z 48444; ℗ 1,476; © 1,734
Goodrich; Inc. Place; GENESEE; ▲ Atlas; **189** P-11; elev. 894ft./272m.; 🅿; ★ **FLN**; z 48438; ℗ 916; © 1,353
Goodwell; MCD-Township; NEWAYGO; ***189** N-6; mail White Cloud z 49349; ℗ 358; © 551
Gordon Beach; RMC Place; BERRIEN; ▲ New Buffalo; ***189** T-3; mail Union Pier z 49129
Gordonville; RMC Place; MIDLAND; ▲ Mount Haley, Lee; ***189** N-9; elev. 646ft./197m.; ★ **SAG-**; mail Midland z 48640
Gore; MCD-Township; HURON; ***189** L-13; mail Port Hope z 48468; ℗ 125; © 139
Gotts Corners; RMC Place; HURON; ▲ Lake; ***189** M-12; mail Caseville z 48725; rural
Gould City; RMC Place; MACKINAC; ▲ Newton; **188** E-6; elev. 743ft./226m.; 🅿; z 49838; ● 200
Gourley; MCD-Township; MENOMINEE; ***188** G-2; mail Carney z 49812; ℗ 362; © 409
Gowen; RMC Place; MONTCALM; ▲ Montcalm; **189** O-7; elev. 860ft./262m.; 🅿; ★ **GDR**; z 49326; ● 350
Graafschap; RMC Place; ALLEGAN; ▲ Laketown, Fillmore; **189** Q-5; ★ **HLND**; mail Holland z 49423; ● 200
Grace; RMC Place; PRESQUE ISLE; ▲ Bearinger; ***188** G-10; elev. 590ft./180m.; mail Millersburg z 49759; summer pop. 150; ● 20
Graham Lake; RMC Place; CALHOUN; ▲ Leroy; ***189** S-7; elev. 928ft./283m.; ★ **BTLCK**; mail Battle Creek z 49014; ● 210
Grand Beach; Inc. Place; BERRIEN; ▲ New Buffalo; **189** T-3; 🅿; z 49117; ℗ 146; © 221
Grand Blanc; Inc. Place; GENESEE; **189** P-11; 🅿; ★ **FLN**; z 48439, z 48480; ℗ 7,760; © 8,242
Grand Blanc; MCD-Charter Township; GENESEE; ***189** P-11; 🅿; ★ **FLN**; z 48439, z 48480; does not include the City of Grand Blanc; ℗ 25,392; © 29,827; ◆ 30,309
Grand Haven; Inc. Place; ⊡ OTTAWA; **189** P-4; 🅿 🅷 ■; z 49417; ℗ 11,951; © 11,168; ◆ 10,350
Grand Haven; MCD-Charter Township; OTTAWA; ***189** P-5; 🅿; z 49417; does not include the City of Grand Haven; ℗ 9,710; © 13,278
Grand Island; MCD-Township; ALGER; ***188** D-3; mail Munising z 49862; ℗ 21; © 45
Grand Junction; RMC Place; VAN BUREN; ▲ Columbia; **189** R-5; 🅿; z 49056; ● 230
Grand Ledge; Inc. Place; EATON; **189** Q-8; 🅿; ★ **LANS**; z 48837; ℗ 7,579; © 7,813; ® 7,804
Grand Marais; RMC Place; ALGER; ▲ Burt; **188** C-5; 🅿; z 49839; ● 330
Grand Rapids; Inc. Place; ⊡ KENT; **189** P-6; 🅿 🅷 🅲 22,071 ■; ★ **GDR**; z 49501-10, z 49512, z 49514-16, z 49518-19, z 49523, z 49525, z 49528, z 49530, z 49534, z 49544, z 49546, z 49548, z 49550, z 49555, z 49560, z 49588, z 49599; ℗ 189,126; © 197,800; ◆ 200,507
Grand Rapids; MCD-Charter Township; KENT; ***189** P-6; 🅿 🅲 22,071; ★ **GDR**; z 49501-10, z 49512, z 49514-16, z 49518-19, z 49523, z 49525, z 49528, z 49530, z 49534, z 49544, z 49546, z 49548, z 49550, z 49555, z 49560, z 49588, z 49599; does not include the City of Grand Rapids; ℗ 10,760; © 14,056
Grand River; RMC Place; WAYNE; ***189** R-13; ★ **DET**; mail Detroit z 48208; pop. incl. with Detroit (Inc. Place)
Grand Shelby; RMC Place; WAYNE; ★ **DET**; mail Detroit z 48216; pop. incl. with Detroit (Inc. Place)
GRAND TRAVERSE; **188** J-6; ℗ 64,273; © 77,654; ◆ 86,343
Grand Traverse Reservation; Indian Reservation; LEELANAU; © 0
Grand View; RMC Place; MONROE; ▲ La Salle; ***189** T-12; elev. 575ft./175m.; ★ **MONR**; mail La Salle z 48145; ● 100
Grand View Acres; RMC Place; WAYNE; ▲ Northville; ***189** R-12; ★ **DET**; mail Northville z 48167; ● 670
Grand View Beach (Cold Springs); RMC Place; CHEBOYGAN; ▲ Tuscarora; ***188** G-8; mail Indian River z 49749; ● 50
Grandville; Inc. Place; KENT; **189** P-6; elev. 604ft./184m.; 🅿; ★ **GDR**; z 49418, z 49468; ℗ 15,624; © 16,263
Grange Hall; IONIA; see North Bell (RMC Place)
Grant; MCD-Township; CHEBOYGAN; ***188** G-9; mail Cheboygan z 49721; ℗ 686; © 947
Grant; MCD-Township; CLARE; ***189** M-8; mail Clare z 48617; ℗ 2,636; © 3,034
Grant; MCD-Township; GRAND TRAVERSE; ***188** J-6; mail Interlochen z 49643; ℗ 745; © 947
Grant; MCD-Township; HURON; ***189** M-12; mail Cass City z 48726; ℗ 778; © 833
Grant; MCD-Township; IOSCO; ***189** K-11; mail Tawas City z 48763; ℗ 1,154; © 1,560
Grant; MCD-Township; KEWEENAW; ***188** A-14; mail Copper Harbor z 49918; ℗ 104; © 172
Grant; MCD-Township; MASON; ***189** L-4; mail Free Soil z 49411; ℗ 749; © 850
Grant; MCD-Township; MECOSTA; ***189** M-7; mail Big Rapids z 49307; ℗ 644; © 680
Grant; Inc. Place; NEWAYGO; **189** O-5; elev. 835ft./255m.; 🅿; ★ **GDR**; z 49327; ℗ 764; © 881
Grant; MCD-Township; NEWAYGO; ***189** O-6; 🅿; ★ **GDR**; z 49327; does not include the City of Grant; ℗ 2,558; © 3,130
Grant; MCD-Township; OCEANA; ***189** N-4; ★ **MUS**; mail Rothbury z 49452; ℗ 2,578; © 2,932
Grant (Grant Township); MCD-Township; ST. CLAIR; ***189** O-14; mail Jeddo z 48032; ℗ 1,210; © 1,667
Grant Center; RMC Place; MECOSTA; ▲ Grant; ***189** M-7; elev. 990ft./302m.; mail Big Rapids z 49307; ● 30
Grant Township; ST. CLAIR; see Grant (MCD-Township)
Grape; RMC Place; MONROE; ▲ Raisinville; ***189** S-11; ★ **MONR**; mail Monroe z 48162; rural
Grass Lake; RMC Place; GLADWIN; ▲ Sherman; ***189** L-9; elev. 1,090ft./332m.; mail Gladwin z 48624; ● 280
Grass Lake; Inc. Place; JACKSON; ▲ Grass Lake; **189** R-10; elev. 996ft./304m.; 🅿; ★ **JAC**; z 49240; ℗ 903; © 1,082
Grass Lake; MCD-Township; JACKSON; ***189** R-10; 🅿; ★ **JAC**; z 49240; ℗ 3,774; © 4,586
Gratiot; RMC Place; WAYNE; ***189** R-13; ★ **DET**; mail Detroit z 48207; pop. incl. with Detroit (Inc. Place)
GRATIOT; **189** O-8; ℗ 38,982; © 42,285; ◆ 42,452
Grattan (Grattan Center); RMC Place; KENT; ▲ Grattan; **189** P-7; ★ **GDR**; mail Belding z 48809; ● 130
Grattan; MCD-Township; KENT; ***189** P-7; ★ **GDR**; mail Belding z 48809; ℗ 2,876; © 3,551
Grattan Center; KENT; see Grattan (RMC Place)
Gravel Lake; RMC Place; VAN BUREN; ▲ Porter; ***189** S-5; elev. 900ft./274m.; mail Lawton z 49065; summer pop. 500; ● 200
Grawn; RMC Place; GRAND TRAVERSE; ▲ Green Lake, Blair; **188** J-6; 🅿; z 49637; ● 300
Grayling; Inc. Place; ⊡ CRAWFORD; **188** J-8; elev. 1,137ft./347m.; 🅿 🅷; z 49738-39; ℗ 1,944; © 1,952
Grayling; MCD-Township; CRAWFORD; ***188** J-8; 🅿; z 49738-39; does not include the City of Grayling; ℗ 5,647; © 6,516; ® 6,483
Greater Galesburg; CDP-Census Area Only; KALAMAZOO; ▲ Charleston; ***189** R-7; elev. 800ft./244m.; ★ **KZOO**; mail Galesburg z 49053; ℗ 1,260; © 1,631
Great Lake Beach; RMC Place; SANILAC; ▲ Worth; ***189** O-14; elev. 600ft./183m.; ★ **PTHU**; mail Lexington z 48450; ● 460
Great Western; RMC Place; IRON; ▲ Crystal Falls; mail Crystal Falls z 49920; pop. incl. with Crystal Falls (Inc. Place)
Greeley; ALPENA; see Flanders (RMC Place)
Green; MCD-Township; ALPENA; ***188** I-10; mail Lachine z 49753; ℗ 1,095; © 1,205
Green; MCD-Charter Township; MECOSTA; ***189** M-6; mail Paris z 49338; ℗ 2,833; © 3,209
Green; RMC Place; ONTONAGON; ▲ Ontonagon, Carp Lake; ***188** B-11; elev. 616ft./188m.; mail Ontonagon z 49953
Greenbush; RMC Place; ALCONA; ▲ Greenbush; **188** J-12; 🅿; z 48738; summer pop. 2,500; ● 250
Greenbush; MCD-Township; ALCONA; ***188** J-12; 🅿; z 48738; ℗ 1,373; © 1,499
Greenbush; MCD-Township; CLINTON; ***189** P-9; mail Eureka z 48833; ℗ 2,028; © 2,115
Greendale; MCD-Township; MIDLAND; ***189** N-9; mail Shepherd z 48883; ℗ 1,495; © 1,788
Greenfield Village; RMC Place; WAYNE; ***189** R-12; ★ **DET**; mail Dearborn z 48124; pop. incl. with Dearborn (Inc. Place)
Green Lake; RMC Place; ALLEGAN; ▲ Leighton; **189** Q-6; ★ **GDR**; mail Caledonia z 49316; ● 400
Green Lake; MCD-Township; GRAND TRAVERSE; ***188** J-6; mail Interlochen z 49643; ℗ 3,677; © 5,009
Greenland; RMC Place; ONTONAGON; ▲ Greenland; **188** B-12; elev. 1,138ft./347m.; 🅿; z 49929; ● 340
Greenland; MCD-Township; ONTONAGON; ***188** B-12; 🅿; z 49929; ℗ 1,001; © 870
Greenleaf; MCD-Township; SANILAC; ***189** N-12; mail Cass City z 48726; ℗ 667; © 804
Greenmead; RMC Place; WAYNE; ★ **DET**; mail Livonia z 48153; pop. incl. with Livonia (Inc. Place)
Green Oak; MCD-Township; LIVINGSTON; ***189** R-11; ★ **DET**; mail Brighton z 48116; ℗ 11,604; © 15,618
Green River; RMC Place; ANTRIM; ▲ Chestonia; ***188** I-7; mail Mancelona z 49659
Green Road; RMC Place; WASHTENAW; ★ **DET**; mail Ann Arbor z 48105, z 48113; pop. incl. with Ann Arbor (Inc. Place)
Greenville; Inc. Place; MONTCALM; **189** O-7; 🅿 🅷 ■; ★ **GDR**; z 48838; ℗ 8,101; © 7,935; ◆ 7,867
Greenwood; MCD-Township; CLARE; ***189** L-8; mail Harrison z 48625; ℗ 718; © 1,059
Greenwood; RMC Place; MARQUETTE; ▲ Ely; ***188** D-1; mail Ishpeming z 49849; ● 170
Greenwood; MCD-Township; OCEANA; ***189** N-5; mail Fremont z 49412; ℗ 915; © 1,154
Greenwood; RMC Place; OGEMAW; ▲ Horton; ***189** L-10; mail Alger z 48610; ● 40
Greenwood; MCD-Township; OSCODA; ***188** J-9; mail Lewiston z 49756; ℗ 880; © 1,195
Greenwood; MCD-Township; ST. CLAIR; ***189** O-13; 🅿; z 48006; ℗ 1,037; © 1,373
Greenwood; MCD-Township; WEXFORD; ***189** K-6; mail Manton z 49663; ℗ 372; © 542
Gregory; RMC Place; LIVINGSTON; ▲ Unadilla; **189** R-10; 🅿; ★ **DET**; z 48137; ● 420
Greilickville; CDP; LEELANAU; ▲ Elmwood; **188** J-6; mail Traverse City z 49684; ℗ 1,165; © 1,415
Gresham; RMC Place; EATON; ▲ Chester; **189** Q-8; elev. 915ft./279m.; mail Charlotte z 48813
Grim; MCD-Township; GLADWIN; ***189** M-9; mail Rhodes z 48652; ℗ 100; © 129
Grind Stone City; RMC Place; HURON; ▲ Port Austin; **189** L-13; mail Port Austin z 48467; ● 70
Groos; RMC Place; DELTA; ▲ Wells; ***188** F-2; mail Gladstone z 49837
Gros Cap; RMC Place; MACKINAC; ▲ Moran; **188** F-8; mail Saint Ignace z 49781; ● 70
Grosse Ile; CDP; WAYNE; ▲ Grosse Ile; **190** M-6; 🅿; ★ **DET**; z 48138; ℗ 9,781; © 10,894
Grosse Ile; MCD-Township; WAYNE; ***189** S-12; 🅿; ★ **DET**; z 48138; ℗ 9,781; © 10,894
Grosse Pointe; Inc. Place; WAYNE; ▲ Grosse Pointe; **190** J-8; 🅿 🅷 ■; ★ **DET**; z 48215, z 48224, z 48230, z 48236; ℗ 5,681; © 5,670; ◆ 5,373
Grosse Pointe; MCD-Township; WAYNE; ***189** R-13; 🅿; ★ **DET**; z 48215, z 48224, z 48230, z 48236; ℗ 2,850; © 2,743
Grosse Pointe Farms; Inc. Place; WAYNE; **190** I-9; elev. 585ft./178m.; 🅿 🅷; ★ **DET**; z 48230, z 48236; ℗ 10,092; © 9,764
Grosse Pointe Park; Inc. Place; WAYNE; **190** J-8; elev. 580ft./177m.; 🅿; ★ **DET**; z 48215, z 48224, z 48230, z 48236; ℗ 12,857; © 12,443
Grosse Pointe Shores; Inc. Place; WAYNE, MACOMB; **190** I-9; elev. 586ft./179m.; 🅿; ★ **DET**; z 48230, z 48236; ℗ 2,955; © 2,823
Grosse Pointe Woods; Inc. Place; WAYNE; **189** R-13; elev. 587ft./179m.; 🅿; ★ **DET**; z 48230, z 48236; ℗ 17,715; © 17,080
Grosvenor; RMC Place; LENAWEE; ▲ Palmyra; ***189** T-10; elev. 699ft./213m.; mail Blissfield z 49228; rural
Grout; MCD-Township; GLADWIN; ***189** M-9; mail Gladwin z 48624; ℗ 1,626; © 1,869
Groveland; MCD-Township; OAKLAND; ***189** P-11; ★ **DET**; mail Ortonville z 48462; ℗ 4,705; © 6,150
Gulliver; RMC Place; SCHOOLCRAFT; ▲ Doyle; **188** F-5; 🅿; z 49840; ● 100
Gull Lake; RMC Place; KALAMAZOO; ▲ Ross; ***189** R-7; ★ **KZOO**; mail Richland z 49083; ● 150
Gun Plain; MCD-Charter Township; ALLEGAN; ***189** R-6; ★ **KZOO**; mail Plainwell z 49080; ℗ 4,754; © 5,637
Gustin; MCD-Township; ALCONA; ***188** J-11; mail Harrisville z 48740; ℗ 823; © 832
Gwinn; CDP; MARQUETTE; ▲ Forsyth; **188** E-1; elev. 1,090ft./332m.; 🅿; z 49841; ℗ 2,370; © 1,965

H

Hadley; RMC Place; LAPEER; ▲ Hadley; **189** P-12; 🅿; ★ **DET**; z 48440; ● 580
Hadley; MCD-Township; LAPEER; ***189** P-12; 🅿; ★ **DET**; z 48440 & mail Metamora z 48455; ℗ 3,830; © 4,655
Hagar; MCD-Township; BERRIEN; ***189** S-4; ★ **BNTH-**; mail Coloma z 49038; ℗ 4,113; © 3,964
Hagar Shores; BERRIEN; see Lake Michigan Beach (CDP)
Hagensville; RMC Place; PRESQUE ISLE; ▲ Belknap; **188** H-10; elev. 783ft./239m.; mail Rogers City z 49779
Hagerman Lake; RMC Place; IRON; ▲ Stambaugh; ***188** D-12; elev. 1,572ft./479m.; mail Iron River z 49935; ● 100
Haight; MCD-Township; ONTONAGON; ***188** C-12; mail Bruce Crossing z 49912; ℗ 218; © 228
Hale; RMC Place; IOSCO; ▲ Plainfield; **189** K-10; 🅿; z 48739; ● 400
Halfway Corners; RMC Place; HURON; ▲ Sigel; ***189** M-13; mail Harbor Beach z 48441; rural
Hamburg; RMC Place; LIVINGSTON; ▲ Hamburg; **189** R-11; 🅿; ★ **DET**; z 48139 & mail Whitmore Lake z 48189; ● 1,050
Hamburg; MCD-Township; LIVINGSTON; ***189** R-11; 🅿; ★ **DET**; z 48139 & mail Pinckney z 48169, Whitmore Lake z 48189; ℗ 13,083; © 20,627; ◆ 24,455
Hamilton; RMC Place; ALLEGAN; ▲ Heath; **189** Q-5; 🅿; z 49419; ● 1,170
Hamilton; MCD-Township; CLARE; ***189** L-8; mail Harrison z 48625; ℗ 1,546; © 1,988
Hamilton; MCD-Township; GRATIOT; ***189** O-9; mail Ithaca z 48847; ℗ 489; © 491
Hamilton; MCD-Township; VAN BUREN; ***189** S-5; mail Decatur z 49045; ℗ 1,515; © 1,797
Hamlin; MCD-Township; EATON; ***189** R-8; mail Eaton Rapids z 48827; ℗ 2,351; © 2,953
Hamlin; MCD-Township; MASON; ***189** L-4; mail Ludington z 49431; ℗ 2,597; © 3,192
Hammond Bay; PRESQUE ISLE; see Huron Beach (RMC Place)
Hampton; MCD-Charter Township; BAY; ***189** N-11; ★ **SAG-**; mail Essexville z 48732; ℗ 9,520; © 9,902
Hamtramck; Inc. Place; WAYNE; **189** R-13; elev. 628ft./191m.; 🅿; ★ **DET**; z 48211-12; ℗ 18,372; © 22,976; ◆ 21,984
Hancock; Inc. Place; HOUGHTON; **188** A-13; elev. 686ft./209m.; 🅿 🅷 🅲 573; z 49930; ℗ 4,547; © 4,323
Hancock; MCD-Township; HOUGHTON; ***188** A-13; 🅿 🅲 573; z 49930; does not include the City of Hancock; ℗ 287; © 408
Handy; MCD-Township; LIVINGSTON; ***189** Q-10; mail Fowlerville z 48836; ℗ 5,488; © 7,004
Hannah; RMC Place; GRAND TRAVERSE; ▲ Mayfield; **188** J-6; elev. 1,064ft./324m.; mail Kingsley z 49649
Hannahville Community; Indian Reservation; MENOMINEE; mail Wilson z 49896; ℗ 211; © 295
Hanover; Inc. Place; JACKSON; ▲ Hanover; **189** S-9; elev. 1,117ft./340m.; 🅿; ★ **JAC**; z 49241; ℗ 481; © 424
Hanover; MCD-Township; JACKSON; ***189** S-9; 🅿; ★ **JAC**; z 49241; ℗ 3,710; © 3,792
Hanover; MCD-Township; WEXFORD; ***189** K-6; mail Buckley z 49620; ℗ 826; © 1,200
Hansen; RMC Place; MENOMINEE; ▲ Menominee; ***188** H-1; elev. 640ft./195m.; mail Menominee z 49858; rural
Harbert; RMC Place; BERRIEN; ▲ Chikaming; **189** T-3; 🅿; z 49115; ● 600
Harbor Beach; Inc. Place; HURON; **189** M-13; elev. 610ft./186m.; 🅿 🅷; z 48441; ℗ 2,089; © 1,837
Harbor Point; RMC Place; EMMET; ▲ West Traverse; ***188** G-7; 🅿; z 49740; summer pop. 200
Harbor Springs; Inc. Place; EMMET; **188** G-7; elev. 600ft./183m.; 🅿; z 49737, z 49740; ℗ 1,540; © 1,567
Harbor View; RMC Place; PRESQUE ISLE; ▲ Presque Isle; mail Presque Isle z 49777
Hardwood; RMC Place; DICKINSON; ▲ Breen; **188** F-1; 🅿; z 49807; ● 200
Haring; MCD-Charter Township; WEXFORD; ***189** K-7; mail Cadillac z 49601; ℗ 2,501; © 2,962
Harlan; RMC Place; MANISTEE, WEXFORD; ▲ Wexford, Cleon; ***189** K-5; elev. 1,070ft./326m.; mail Copemish z 49625; rural
Harlem; RMC Place; OTTAWA; ▲ Olive; ***189** P-5; ★ **HLND**; mail Holland z 49424; rural
Harper; RMC Place; WAYNE; ***189** R-13; ★ **DET**; mail Detroit z 48213; pop. incl. with Detroit (Inc. Place)
Harper Woods; Inc. Place; WAYNE; **190** I-8; elev. 590ft./180m.; 🅿 ■; ★ **DET**; z 48225; ℗ 14,903; © 14,254; ◆ 12,989
Harrietta; Inc. Place; WEXFORD; ▲ Slagle, Boon; **189** K-6; elev. 1,112ft./339m.; 🅿; z 49638; ℗ 157; © 169
Harris; RMC Place; MENOMINEE; ▲ Harris; **188** G-2; elev. 795ft./242m.; 🅿; z 49845; ● 30
Harris; MCD-Township; MENOMINEE; ***188** F-2; 🅿; z 49845; ℗ 1,542; © 1,895
Harrisburg; RMC Place; OTTAWA; ▲ Chester; **189** O-5; mail Ravenna z 49451
Harrison; Inc. Place; ⊡ CLARE; **189** L-8; elev. 1,186ft./361m.; 🅿; z 48625; ℗ 1,835; © 2,108
Harrison; CDP-Census Area Only; MACOMB; ***189** Q-13; 🅷; ★ **DET**; mail Harrison Township z 48045; ℗ 24,685; © 24,461; ◆ 24,450
Harrison; MCD-Charter Township; MACOMB; ***189** Q-13; ★ **DET**; mail Harrison Township z 48045; ℗ 24,685; © 24,461; ◆ 24,450
Harrison Beach; RMC Place; SCHOOLCRAFT; ▲ Hiawatha; ***188** F-4; elev. 620ft./189m.; mail Manistique z 49854; ● 180
Harrisville; Inc. Place; ⊡ ALCONA; **188** J-12; 🅿; z 48740; ℗ 470; © 514
Harrisville; MCD-Township; ALCONA; ***188** J-12; 🅿; z 48740; does not include the City of Harrisville; ℗ 1,315; © 1,411
Harsens Island; ST. CLAIR; see Sans Souci (RMC Place)
Hart; Inc. Place; ⊡ OCEANA; **189** M-4; 🅿; z 49420; ℗ 1,942; © 1,950
Hart; MCD-Township; OCEANA; ***189** N-4; 🅿; z 49420; does not include the City of Hart; ℗ 1,513; © 2,026
Hartford; Inc. Place; VAN BUREN; ▲ Hartford; **189** S-5; 🅿; ★ **BNTH-**; z 49057; ℗ 2,341; © 2,476
Hartford; MCD-Township; VAN BUREN; ***189** S-5; 🅿; ★ **BNTH-**; z 49057; does not include the City of Hartford; ℗ 3,032; © 3,159
Hartland; RMC Place; LIVINGSTON; ▲ Hartland; **189** Q-11; 🅿; ★ **DET**; z 48353; ● 570
Hartland; MCD-Township; LIVINGSTON; ***189** Q-11; 🅿; ★ **DET**; z 48353 & mail Brighton z 48114; ℗ 6,860; © 10,996
Hartwick; MCD-Township; OSCEOLA; ***189** L-7; mail Evart z 49631; ℗ 456; © 629
Harvard; RMC Place; KENT; ▲ Oakfield; ***189** O-7; ★ **GDR**; mail Cedar Springs z 49319; rural
Harvey; CDP; MARQUETTE; ▲ Chocolay; **188** D-2; 🅿; z 49855; ℗ 1,377; © 1,321
Haslett; CDP; INGHAM; ▲ Meridian; **189** Q-9; 🅿; ★ **LANS**; z 48840; ℗ 10,230; © 11,283; ® 11,292
Hastings; Inc. Place; ⊡ BARRY; **189** Q-7; 🅿 🅷; z 49058; ℗ 6,549; © 7,095
Hastings; MCD-Charter Township; BARRY; ***189** Q-7; 🅿; z 49058; does not include the City of Hastings; ℗ 2,830; © 2,930
Hatmaker; RMC Place; BRANCH; ▲ Bethel; ***189** T-7; elev. 944ft./288m.; mail Coldwater z 49036; ● 30
Hatton; MCD-Township; CLARE; ***189** M-8; mail Harrison z 48625; ℗ 673; © 923
Hautala Corner; RMC Place; GOGEBIC; ▲ Ironwood; ***188** B-10; elev. 1,232ft./376m.; mail Ironwood z 49938; rural
Hawes; MCD-Township; ALCONA; ***188** J-11; mail Lincoln z 48742; ℗ 1,035; © 1,167
Hawkhead; RMC Place; ALLEGAN; ▲ Casco; ***189** R-5; elev. 625ft./191m.; mail Glenn z 49416; rural
Hawkins; RMC Place; NEWAYGO; ▲ Barton; **189** M-6; elev. 1,128ft./344m.; mail Reed City z 49677; ● 20
Hawks (Larocque); RMC Place; PRESQUE ISLE; ▲ Belknap; **188** H-10; 🅿; z 49743; ● 70
Hay; MCD-Township; GLADWIN; ***189** M-9; mail Gladwin z 48624; ℗ 1,173; © 1,402
Hayes; MCD-Township; CHARLEVOIX; ***188** H-7; mail Charlevoix z 49720; ℗ 1,317; © 1,893
Hayes; MCD-Township; CLARE; ***189** L-8; mail Harrison z 48625; ℗ 3,811; © 4,916
Hayes; MCD-Township; OTSEGO; ***188** I-8; mail Gaylord z 49735; ℗ 1,437; © 2,385
Haynes; MCD-Township; ALCONA; ***188** J-12; mail Lincoln z 48742; ℗ 549; © 724
Hazel; RMC Place; HOUGHTON; ▲ Laird; ***188** B-12; mail Pelkie z 49958; rural
Hazelhurst; RMC Place; BERRIEN; ▲ Chikaming; ***189** T-3; elev. 650ft./198m.; mail Harbert z 49115; ● 100
Hazel Park; Inc. Place; OAKLAND; **190** I-7; elev. 634ft./193m.; 🅿; ★ **DET**; z 48030; ℗ 20,051; © 18,963
Hazelton; MCD-Township; SHIAWASSEE; ***189** P-10; ★ **FLN**; mail Flushing z 48433; ℗ 2,294; © 2,206
Heath; MCD-Township; ALLEGAN; ***189** Q-5; mail Hamilton z 49419; ℗ 2,297; © 3,100
Hebron; MCD-Township; CHEBOYGAN; ***188** G-8; mail Levering z 49755; ℗ 202; © 303
Helena; MCD-Township; ANTRIM; ***188** I-7; mail Alden z 49612; ℗ 837; © 878
Helena; RMC Place; HURON; ▲ Sherman, Sand Beach; ***189** M-13; elev. 710ft./216m.; mail Harbor Beach z 48441; ● 30
Hell (Hi Land Lake); RMC Place; LIVINGSTON; ▲ Putnam; **189** R-10; ★ **DET**; mail Pinckney z 48169; ● 40
Helmer; RMC Place; LUCE; ▲ Lakefield; ***188** E-6; elev. 692ft./211m.; mail Mc Millan z 49853
Helps; RMC Place; MENOMINEE; ▲ Spalding; ***188** F-1; elev. 1,026ft./313m.; mail Perronville z 49873; ● 50
Hemans; RMC Place; SANILAC; ▲ Lamotte; ***189** N-12; elev. 778ft./237m.; mail Decker z 48426; ● 60
Hematite; MCD-Township; IRON; ***188** C-13; mail Amasa z 49903; ℗ 366; © 352
Hemlock; CDP; SAGINAW; ▲ Richland; **189** N-9; elev. 653ft./199m.; 🅿; ★ **SAG-**; z 48626; ℗ 1,601; © 1,585
Henderson; RMC Place; SHIAWASSEE; ▲ Rush; **189** P-10; 🅿; z 48841; ● 200
Henderson; MCD-Township; WEXFORD; ***189** L-6; mail Cadillac z 49601; ℗ 162; © 176
Hendricks; MCD-Township; MACKINAC; ***188** E-7; mail Naubinway z 49762; ℗ 161; © 183
Henrietta; MCD-Township; JACKSON; ***189** R-9; ★ **JAC**; mail Munith z 49259, Pleasant Lake z 49272; ℗ 3,858; © 4,483
Henrietta Station; RMC Place; JACKSON; ▲ Henrietta; ***189** R-9; elev. 912ft./278m.; ★ **JAC**; mail Munith z 49259; rural
Herman; RMC Place; BARAGA; ▲ L'Anse; ***188** B-13; mail Lanse z 49946; ● 70
Hermansville; RMC Place; MENOMINEE; ▲ Meyer; **188** F-1; 🅿; z 49847; ● 550
Herron; RMC Place; ALPENA; ▲ Wilson; **188** I-11; 🅿; z 49744; ● 100
Hersey; Inc. Place; OSCEOLA; ▲ Hersey; **189** M-6; 🅿; z 49639; ℗ 354; © 374
Hersey; MCD-Township; OSCEOLA; ***189** M-7; 🅿; z 49639; ℗ 1,455; © 1,846
Hesperia; Inc. Place; OCEANA, NEWAYGO; ▲ Denver, Newfield; **189** N-5; 🅿; z 49421; ℗ 846; © 954
Hessel; RMC Place; MACKINAC; ▲ Clark; **188** E-9; 🅿; z 49745; ● 270
Hetherton; RMC Place; MONTMORENCY, OTSEGO; ▲ Charlton, Vienna; ***188** I-9; elev. 1,372ft./418m.; mail Johannesburg z 49751; rural
Hiawatha; MCD-Township; SCHOOLCRAFT; ***188** E-4; mail Manistique z 49854; ℗ 1,279; © 1,328
Hickory Corners; RMC Place; BARRY; ▲ Barry; **189** R-7; elev. 967ft./295m.; 🅿; ★ **KZOO**; z 49060; ● 250
Higgins; MCD-Township; ROSCOMMON; ***189** K-9; mail Roscommon z 48653; ℗ 1,685; © 2,061
Higgins Lake (Lyon Manor); RMC Place; ROSCOMMON; ▲ Lyon; **189** K-8; 🅿; z 48627; ● 460
Highland; RMC Place; OAKLAND; ▲ Highland; **189** Q-11; 🅿; ★ **DET**; z 48356-57; ● 800
Highland; MCD-Charter Township; OAKLAND; ***189** Q-11; 🅿; ★ **DET**; z 48356-57; ℗ 17,941; © 19,169; ◆ 18,459
Highland; MCD-Township; OSCEOLA; ***189** L-7; mail Marion z 49665; ℗ 1,012; © 1,207
Highland Lakes; RMC Place; WAYNE; ▲ Northville; ***189** R-12; elev. 800ft./244m.; ★ **DET**; mail Northville z 48167; ● 2,000
Highland Park; RMC Place; KALAMAZOO; ▲ Richland; ***189** R-7; ★ **KZOO**; mail Richland z 49083; ● 150
Highland Park; Inc. Place; WAYNE; **189** R-12; elev. 636ft./194m.; 🅿 ■; ★ **DET**; z 48203; ℗ 20,121; © 16,746; ◆ 14,837
Highway; RMC Place; HOUGHTON; ▲ Franklin; ***188** A-13; elev. 1,160ft./354m.; mail Calumet z 49913; rural
Hi Hill Villa; RMC Place; OAKLAND; ▲ Orion; ★ **DET**; mail Lake Orion z 48360; ● 700
Hi Land Lake; LIVINGSTON; see Hell (RMC Place)
Hill; MCD-Township; OGEMAW; ***189** K-10; mail Hale z 48739; ℗ 1,546; © 1,584
Hillcrest; RMC Place; GOGEBIC; ▲ Ironwood; ***188** B-10; elev. 1,390ft./424m.; mail Ironwood z 49938; ● 300
Hillcrest Orchard; RMC Place; MONROE; ▲ La Salle; ***189** T-12; ★ **MONR**; mail La Salle z 48145; ● 350
Hilliards; RMC Place; ALLEGAN; ▲ Hopkins; **189** Q-6; mail Hopkins z 49328; ● 30
Hillman; Inc. Place; MONTMORENCY; ▲ Hillman; **188** I-10; elev. 813ft./248m.; 🅿; z 49746; ℗ 643; © 685
Hillman; MCD-Township; MONTMORENCY; ***188** I-10; 🅿; z 49746; ℗ 2,189; © 2,267
Hillsdale; Inc. Place; ⊡ HILLSDALE; **189** T-9; 🅿 🅷 🅲 1,346; z 49242; ℗ 8,170; © 8,233
Hillsdale; MCD-Township; HILLSDALE; ***189** T-8; 🅿 🅲 1,346; z 49242; does not include the City of Hillsdale; ℗ 1,786; © 1,965
HILLSDALE; **189** T-8; ℗ 43,431; © 46,527; ◆ 46,274
Hinchman; RMC Place; BERRIEN; ▲ Oronoko; ***189** S-4; mail Berrien Springs z 49103; ● 40
Hinton; MCD-Township; MECOSTA; ***189** N-7; mail Lakeview z 48850; ℗ 995; © 1,035
Hockaday; RMC Place; GLADWIN; ▲ Butman; ***189** L-9; elev. 821ft./250m.; mail Gladwin z 48624; rural
Hodunk; RMC Place; BRANCH; ▲ Union; **189** S-7; mail Union City z 49094
Hogstrom; MARQUETTE; see Lawson (RMC Place)
Holland; MCD-Township; MISSAUKEE; ***189** L-8; mail Lake z 48632; ℗ 169; © 223
Holland; Inc. Place; OTTAWA, ALLEGAN; **189** Q-5; 🅿 🅷 🅲 3,203 ■; ★ **HLND**; z 49422-24; ℗ 30,745; © 35,048; ◆ 33,697
Holland; MCD-Charter Township; OTTAWA; ***189** Q-5; 🅿 🅲 3,203; ★ **HLND**; z 49422-24; does not include the City of Holland; ℗ 17,523; © 28,911; ◆ 33,737
Holloway; RMC Place; LENAWEE; ▲ Raisin; ***189** S-10; elev. 749ft./228m.; mail Britton z 49229; ● 50
Holly; Inc. Place; OAKLAND; ▲ Rose, Holly; **189** P-11; elev. 937ft./286m.; 🅿; ★ **DET**; z 48442; ℗ 5,595; © 6,135; ® 6,179
Holly; MCD-Township; OAKLAND; ***189** P-11; 🅿; ★ **DET**; z 48442; includes part of the Village of Holly; ℗ 8,852; © 10,037
Hollywood Golfcrest; MONROE; see Golfcrest (RMC Place)
Holmes; MCD-Township; MENOMINEE; ***188** G-1; mail Daggett z 49821; ℗ 292; © 296
Holt; CDP; INGHAM; ▲ Delhi; **189** Q-9; 🅿; ★ **LANS**; z 48842; ℗ 11,744; © 11,315
Holton; RMC Place; MUSKEGON; ▲ Holton; **189** N-5; 🅿; z 49425; ● 580
Holton; MCD-Township; MUSKEGON; ***189** N-5; 🅿; z 49425; ℗ 2,318; © 2,532
Home; MCD-Township; MONTCALM; ***189** N-7; mail Edmore z 48829; ℗ 2,513; © 2,708
Home; MCD-Township; NEWAYGO; ***189** M-6; mail Bitely z 49309; ℗ 202; © 261
Home Acres; RMC Place; KENT; ★ **GDR**; mail Grand Rapids z 49508; pop. incl. with Wyoming (Inc. Place)
Homer; Inc. Place; CALHOUN; ▲ Homer; **189** S-8; elev. 994ft./303m.; 🅿; z 49245; ℗ 1,758; © 1,851
Homer; MCD-Township; CALHOUN; ***189** S-8; 🅿; z 49245; ℗ 2,875; © 3,010
Homer; MCD-Charter Township; MIDLAND; ***189** N-9; ★ **SAG-**; mail Midland z 48640; ℗ 4,235; © 3,924
Homestead; MCD-Township; BENZIE; ***188** J-5; mail Honor z 49640; ℗ 1,477; © 2,078
Homestead; RMC Place; CHIPPEWA; ▲ Sugar Island; ***188** D-9; mail Sault Sainte Marie z 49783; ● 60
Hongore Bay (Hongore Heights); RMC Place; CHEBOYGAN; ▲ Waverly; ***188** G-9; mail Onaway z 49765; ● 250
Hongore Heights; CHEBOYGAN; see Hongore Bay (RMC Place)
Honor; Inc. Place; BENZIE; ▲ Homestead; **188** J-5; 🅿; z 49640; ℗ 292; © 299
Hooper; RMC Place; ALLEGAN; ▲ Martin, Gun Plain; ***189** R-6; ★ **KZOO**; mail Plainwell z 49080; rural
Hope; MCD-Township; BARRY; ***189** Q-7; mail Hastings z 49058; ℗ 2,993; © 3,283
Hope; RMC Place; MIDLAND; ▲ Hope; **189** M-9; elev. 678ft./207m.; 🅿; z 48628; ● 100
Hope; MCD-Township; MIDLAND; ***189** M-9; 🅿; z 48628; ℗ 1,220; © 1,286
Hopkins; Inc. Place; ALLEGAN; ▲ Hopkins; **189** Q-6; elev. 704ft./215m.; 🅿; z 49328; ℗ 546; © 592
Hopkins; MCD-Township; ALLEGAN; ***189** Q-6; 🅿; z 49328; ℗ 2,350; © 2,671
Hopkinsburg; RMC Place; ALLEGAN; ▲ Hopkins; **189** Q-6; mail Hopkins z 49328; ● 50
Hopwood Acres; RMC Place; INGHAM; ▲ Lansing; ***189** Q-9; ★ **LANS**; mail Lansing z 48912; pop. incl. with Lansing (Inc. Place)
Horton; RMC Place; JACKSON; ▲ Hanover; **189** S-9; elev. 1,042ft./318m.; 🅿; ★ **JAC**; z 49246; ● 380
Horton; MCD-Township; OGEMAW; ***189** L-10; mail West Branch z 48661; ℗ 955; © 997
Horton Bay; RMC Place; CHARLEVOIX; **188** H-7; elev. 669ft./204m.; mail Boyne City z 49712
Houghton; Inc. Place; ⊡ HOUGHTON; **188** A-13; elev. 607ft./185m.; 🅿 🅲 6,510 ■; z 49921, z 49931; ℗ 7,498; © 7,010; ® 7,039; ◆ 6,549
Houghton; MCD-Township; KEWEENAW; mail Mohawk z 49950; ℗ 54; © 204; ® 126
HOUGHTON; **188** A-12; ℗ 35,446; © 36,016; ◆ 34,808
Houghton Lake; CDP; ROSCOMMON; ▲ Denton, Roscommon; **189** K-8; elev. 1,162ft./354m.; 🅿; z 48629; ℗ 3,353; © 3,749
Houghton Lake Heights; RMC Place; ROSCOMMON; ▲ Roscommon; ***189** K-8; 🅿; z 48630
Houghton Point; RMC Place; ROSCOMMON; ▲ Lake; **189** K-8; mail Houghton Lake z 48629; ● 120
Howard; MCD-Township; CASS; ***189** T-5; ★ **S.B.**; mail Niles z 49120; ℗ 6,378; © 6,309
Howard City; Inc. Place; MONTCALM; ▲ Reynolds; **189** O-6; 🅿; z 49329; ℗ 1,351; © 1,585
Howardsville; RMC Place; ST. JOSEPH; ▲ Flowerfield; **189** S-6; mail Marcellus z 49067; ● 40
Howell; Inc. Place; ⊡ LIVINGSTON; **189** Q-10; elev. 922ft./281m.; 🅿 🅷; ★ **DET**; z 48843-44, z 48855, z 48863; ℗ 8,184; © 9,232
Howell; MCD-Township; LIVINGSTON; ***189** Q-10; 🅿; ★ **DET**; z 48843-44, z 48855, z 48863; does not include the City of Howell; ℗ 4,298; © 5,679
Hoxeyville; RMC Place; WEXFORD; ▲ South Branch; **189** L-6; elev. 1,132ft./345m.; 🅿; z 49601; ● 60
Hoytville; RMC Place; EATON; ▲ Roxand; **189** Q-8; elev. 869ft./265m.
Hubbard Lake; CDP-Census Area Only; ALCONA; ***188** J-11; © 993
Hubbard Lake; RMC Place; ALPENA; ▲ Ossineke; **188** I-11; elev. 736ft./224m.; 🅿; z 49747; summer pop. 3,000; ● 210
Hubbardston; Inc. Place; IONIA, CLINTON; ▲ Lebanon, North Plains; **189** P-8; 🅿; z 48845; ℗ 404; © 394
Hubbell; CDP; HOUGHTON; ▲ Osceola, Torch Lake; **188** A-13; 🅿; z 49934; ℗ 1,174; © 1,105
Hudson; MCD-Township; CHARLEVOIX; ***188** H-8; mail Elmira z 49730; ℗ 481; © 639
Hudson; Inc. Place; LENAWEE; **189** T-9; elev. 918ft./280m.; 🅿 🅷; z 49247; ℗ 2,580; © 2,499
Hudson; MCD-Township; LENAWEE; ***189** T-9; 🅿; z 49247; does not include the City of Hudson; ℗ 1,481; © 1,576
Hudson; MCD-Township; MACKINAC; ***188** E-7; mail Naubinway z 49762; ℗ 197; © 214
Hudsonville; Inc. Place; OTTAWA; **189** P-5; 🅿; ★ **GDR**; z 49426; ℗ 6,170; © 7,160
Hulbert; RMC Place; CHIPPEWA; ▲ Hulbert; **188** D-7; 🅿; z 49748; ● 350
Hulbert; MCD-Township; CHIPPEWA; ***188** D-7; 🅿; z 49748; ℗ 208; © 211
Humboldt; MCD-Township; MARQUETTE; ***188** C-14; mail Champion z 49814; ℗ 500; © 469
Hume; MCD-Township; HURON; ***189** L-12; mail Port Austin z 48467; ℗ 714; © 801
Hunters Creek; RMC Place; LAPEER; ▲ Lapeer; ***189** P-12; elev. 902ft./275m.; ★ **DET**; mail Lapeer z 48446; rural
Huntington Woods; Inc. Place; OAKLAND; **190** H-6; elev. 660ft./201m.; 🅿; ★ **DET**; z 48070; ℗ 6,419; © 6,151
Huron; MCD-Township; HURON; ***189** L-13; mail Port Austin z 48467; ℗ 376; © 423
Huron; MCD-Charter Township; WAYNE; ***189** S-12; ★ **DET**; mail Flat Rock z 48134, New Boston z 48164; ℗ 10,447; © 13,737
HURON; **189** M-13; ℗ 34,951; © 36,079; ◆ 32,347
Huron Beach (Hammond Bay); RMC Place; PRESQUE ISLE; ▲ Ocqueoc; ***188** G-10; mail Millersburg z 49759; ● 200
Huron City; RMC Place; HURON; ▲ Huron; ***189** L-13; elev. 646ft./197m.; mail Port Austin z 48467; rural
Huron Gardens (Huron Heights); RMC Place; OAKLAND; ▲ Waterford; ***189** Q-12; ★ **DET**; mail Pontiac z 48341
Huron Heights; OAKLAND; see Huron Gardens (RMC Place)
Huronia Heights; RMC Place; SANILAC; ▲ Worth; **189** O-14; ★ **PTHU**; mail Lexington z 48450; ● 460
Huron Mountain; RMC Place; MARQUETTE; ▲ Powell; **188** B-14; mail Big Bay z 49808; ● 30
Huron Potawatomi Reservation; Indian Reservation; CALHOUN; © 11
Hurontown; RMC Place; HOUGHTON; ▲ Portage; ***188** A-13; mail Houghton z 49931; ● 320

I

Ida; RMC Place; MONROE; ▲ Raisinville, Ida; **189** T-11; elev. 639ft./195m.; 🅿; ★ **TOL**; z 48140; ● 1,020
Ida; MCD-Township; MONROE; ***189** T-11; 🅿; ★ **TOL**; z 48140; ℗ 4,554; © 4,949
Idlewild; RMC Place; LAKE; ▲ Yates; **189** M-6; elev. 856ft./261m.; 🅿; z 49642; ● 270
Imlay; MCD-Township; LAPEER; ***189** P-13; ★ **DET**; mail Imlay City z 48444; does not include the City of Imlay City; ℗ 2,143; © 2,713
Imlay City; Inc. Place; LAPEER; **189** P-12; elev. 830ft./253m.; 🅿; ★ **DET**; z 48444; ℗ 2,921; © 3,869
Imperial Heights; RMC Place; BARAGA; ▲ Benzonia; ***188** B-13; mail Michigamme z 49861; ● 100
Ina; RMC Place; OSCEOLA; ▲ Highland; **189** L-7; elev. 1,346ft./410m.; mail Tustin z 49688
Independence; MCD-Charter Township; OAKLAND; ***189** Q-12; 🅿; ★ **DET**; z 48346, z 48348; ℗ 24,722; © 32,581; ◆ 33,536
Indianfield; RMC Place; KALAMAZOO; ★ **KZOO**; mail Portage z 49081; pop. incl. with Portage (Inc. Place)
Indianfields; MCD-Township; TUSCOLA; ***189** N-12; mail Caro z 48723; ℗ 6,699; © 6,392; ® 6,595
Indian Lake; RMC Place; CASS; ▲ Silver Creek; **189** S-5; mail Dowagiac z 49047; ● 640
Indian River; CDP; CHEBOYGAN; ▲ Tuscarora; **188** G-8; elev. 616ft./188m.; 🅿; z 49749; summer pop. 3,000; © 2,008
Indiantown; RMC Place; SAGINAW; ▲ Buena Vista; ***189** N-10; elev. 587ft./179m.; ★ **SAG-**; mail Saginaw z 48601; ● 60
Ingalls; RMC Place; MENOMINEE; ▲ Mellen; **188** H-1; 🅿; z 49848; ● 160
Ingallston; RMC Place; MENOMINEE; ▲ Ingallston; ***188** H-1; elev. 592ft./180m.; mail Menominee z 49858; rural
Ingallston; MCD-Township; MENOMINEE; ***188** H-1; mail Menominee z 49858; ℗ 1,055; © 1,042
Ingersoll; MCD-Township; MIDLAND; ***189** N-9; ★ **SAG-**; mail Freeland z 48623; ℗ 2,788; © 3,018
Ingham; MCD-Township; INGHAM; ***189** Q-9; mail Dansville z 48819; ℗ 1,942; © 2,061
INGHAM; **189** Q-9; ℗ 281,912; © 279,320; ® 279,414; ◆ 283,880
Ingleside; RMC Place; CHEBOYGAN; ▲ Munro; mail Levering z 49755
Inkster; Inc. Place; WAYNE; **190** K-4; elev. 628ft./191m.; 🅿; ★ **DET**; z 48141; ℗ 30,772; © 30,115; ◆ 28,215
Inland; MCD-Township; BENZIE; ***188** J-5; mail Interlochen z 49643; ℗ 1,096; © 1,587
Inland Corners; RMC Place; BENZIE; ▲ Inland; ***188** J-5; elev. 936ft./285m.; mail Interlochen z 49643; rural
Interior; MCD-Township; ONTONAGON; ***188** C-12; mail Trout Creek z 49967; ℗ 480; © 375
Interlochen; RMC Place; GRAND TRAVERSE; ▲ Green Lake; **188** J-6; elev. 841ft./256m.; 🅿; z 49643; ● 300
Inverness; MCD-Township; CHEBOYGAN; ***188** G-9; mail Cheboygan z 49721; ℗ 1,952; © 2,278
Inwood; MCD-Township; SCHOOLCRAFT; ***188** E-4; mail Cooks z 49817; ℗ 638; © 722

Entries in **UPPERCASE** are counties.
Entries in **bold** have populations of 2,500 or more.
Names in parentheses are alternate names.

Inc. Place	Incorporated Place
RMC Place	Rand McNally Designated Place
CDP	Census Designated Place
MCD	Minor Civil Division

⊡	County Seat
▲	Minor Civil Division
elev.	Elevation
🅿	Post Office
🅷	Hospital
🅲	College
■	Principal Business Center
★	Ranally Metro Area (RMA) Abbreviation
z	Zip Code(s)
℗	Previous Census Population
®	Revised Census Population
Ⓐ	Annexation Population
●	Rand McNally Population Estimate
©	Final Census Population
Ⓢ	Special Census Population
◆	Estimated Population

For additional definitions see Glossary, Volume 1, and Introduction, Volume 2.

Ionia; Inc. Place; ⊡ IONIA; **189** P-7; elev. 660ft./201m.; 🅿 🅷; **z** 48846; Ⓟ 5,935; Ⓒ 10,569; Ⓡ 11,528

Ionia; MCD-Township; IONIA; ***189** P-8; 🅿; **z** 48846; does not include the City of Ionia; Ⓟ 3,153; Ⓒ 3,669

IONIA; **189** P-7; Ⓟ 57,024; Ⓒ 61,518; ◆ 64,037

Iosco; MCD-Township; LIVINGSTON; ***189** Q-10; mail Fowlerville **z** 48836; Ⓟ 1,567; Ⓒ 3,039

IOSCO; **189** K-11; Ⓟ 30,209; Ⓒ 27,339; ◆ 25,601

Ira; MCD-Township; ST. CLAIR; ***189** Q-14; 🅿; ★ **DET**; **z** 48023 & mail Anchorville **z** 48004; Ⓟ 5,587; Ⓒ 6,966

IRON; **188** C-12; Ⓟ 13,175; Ⓒ 13,138; ◆ 11,955

Iron Mountain; Inc. Place; ⊡ DICKINSON; **188** D-13; elev. 1,138ft./347m.; 🅿 🅷 ■; **z** 49801-02, **z** 49831; Ⓟ 8,525; Ⓒ 8,154; ◆ 7,644

Iron River; Inc. Place; IRON; **188** C-12; elev. 1,510ft./460m.; 🅿 🅷; **z** 49935; includes Mineral Hills annexed July 1, 2000, and Stambaugh annexed July 1, 2000; Ⓟ 2,095; Ⓒ 1,929; Ⓐ 3,386

Iron River; MCD-Township; IRON; ***188** C-12; 🅿; **z** 49935; does not include the City of Iron River; Ⓟ 1,398; Ⓒ 1,585

Irons; RMC Place; LAKE; ▲ Elk; **189** L-5; 🅿; **z** 49644; summer pop. 1,200; ● 50

Ironton; RMC Place; CHARLEVOIX; ▲ Eveline; **188** H-7; mail Charlevoix **z** 49720; ● 110

Ironwood; Inc. Place; GOGEBIC; **188** B-10; elev. 1,503ft./458m.; 🅿 🅷 ■; **z** 49938; Ⓟ 6,849; Ⓒ 6,293; ◆ 5,666

Ironwood; MCD-Charter Township; GOGEBIC; ***188** B-10; 🅿; **z** 49938; does not include the City of Ironwood; Ⓟ 2,303; Ⓒ 2,330

Irving; RMC Place; BARRY; ▲ Irving; **189** Q-7; elev. 752ft./229m.; mail Hastings **z** 49058; ● 120

Irving; MCD-Township; BARRY; ***189** Q-7; mail Hastings **z** 49058; Ⓟ 1,905; Ⓒ 2,682

Isabella; RMC Place; DELTA; ▲ Nahma, Garden; ***188** F-4; elev. 627ft./191m.; mail Rapid River **z** 49878; ● 50

Isabella; MCD-Township; ISABELLA; ***189** M-8; mail Rosebush **z** 48878; Ⓟ 2,025; Ⓒ 2,145

ISABELLA; **189** N-8; Ⓟ 54,624; Ⓒ 63,351; ◆ 68,523

Isabella Reservation; Indian Reservation; ISABELLA; mail Mount Pleasant **z** 48858; also location of Indian Agency; Ⓟ 23,020; Ⓒ 25,822

Isadore; RMC Place; LEELANAU; ▲ Centerville; ***188** I-6; mail Cedar **z** 49621; rural

Ishpeming; Inc. Place; MARQUETTE; **188** D-1; elev. 1,411ft./430m.; 🅿 🅷; **z** 49849, **z** 49865; Ⓟ 7,200; Ⓒ 6,686

Ishpeming; MCD-Township; MARQUETTE; ***188** C-1; 🅿; **z** 49849, **z** 49865; does not include the City of Ishpeming; Ⓟ 3,515; Ⓒ 3,522

Ithaca; Inc. Place; ⊡ GRATIOT; **189** O-9; elev. 790ft./241m.; 🅿; **z** 48847; Ⓟ 3,009; Ⓒ 3,098

Iva; RMC Place; SAGINAW; ▲ Richland; ***189** N-9; elev. 646ft./197m.; ★ **SAG-**; mail Hemlock **z** 48626

Ivanrest; RMC Place; KENT; ★ **GDR**; mail Grandville **z** 49418; pop. incl. with Grandville (Inc. Place)

J

Jackson; Inc. Place; ⊡ JACKSON; **189** R-9; elev. 960ft./293m.; 🅿 🅷 🅲 1,730 ■; ★ **JAC**; **z** 49201-04; Ⓟ 37,446; Ⓒ 36,316; ◆ 35,228

JACKSON; **189** R-9; Ⓟ 149,756; Ⓒ 158,422; ◆ 161,208

Jacobsville; RMC Place; HOUGHTON; ▲ Torch Lake; ***188** A-13; mail Lake Linden **z** 49945; ● 70

Jam; RMC Place; MIDLAND; ▲ Mount Haley; ***189** N-9; mail Merrill **z** 48637; rural

James; MCD-Township; SAGINAW; ***189** O-10; ★ **SAG-**; mail Saginaw **z** 48609; Ⓟ 2,005; Ⓒ 1,930

Jamestown; RMC Place; OTTAWA; ▲ Jamestown; **189** Q-5; elev. 715ft./218m.; 🅿; ★ **GDR**; **z** 49427; ● 350

Jamestown; MCD-Charter Township; OTTAWA; ***189** Q-5; 🅿; ★ **GDR**; **z** 49427 & mail Hudsonville **z** 49426; Ⓟ 4,059; Ⓒ 5,062

Jasper; RMC Place; LENAWEE; ▲ Fairfield; **189** T-10; 🅿; **z** 49248; ● 330

Jasper; MCD-Township; MIDLAND; ***189** N-9; mail Saint Louis **z** 48880; Ⓟ 1,096; Ⓒ 1,145

Jeddo; RMC Place; ST. CLAIR; ▲ Grant; **189** O-14; 🅿; **z** 48032; ● 110

Jefferson; MCD-Township; CASS; ***189** T-5; mail Edwardsburg **z** 49112; Ⓟ 2,112; Ⓒ 2,401

Jefferson; MCD-Township; HILLSDALE; ***189** T-9; mail Osseo **z** 49266; Ⓟ 3,083; Ⓒ 3,141

Jefferson; RMC Place; JACKSON; ▲ Columbia; **189** S-9; ★ **JAC**; mail Brooklyn **z** 49230; ● 50

Jefferson; RMC Place; WAYNE; ***189** R-13; ★ **DET**; mail Detroit **z** 48214

Jenison; CDP; OTTAWA; ▲ Georgetown; **189** P-6; elev. 608ft./185m.; 🅿; ★ **GDR**; **z** 49428-29; Ⓟ 17,882; Ⓒ 17,211

Jennings; RMC Place; MISSAUKEE; ▲ Lake; **189** K-7; mail Lake City **z** 49651; ● 70

Jericho Corners; RMC Place; VAN BUREN; ▲ Geneva; ***189** R-5; elev. 628ft./191m.; mail South Haven **z** 49090; ● 210

Jerome; RMC Place; HILLSDALE; ▲ Somerset; **189** S-9; 🅿; **z** 49249; ● 150

Jerome; MCD-Township; MIDLAND; ***189** M-9; ★ **SAG-**; mail Sanford **z** 48657; Ⓟ 4,470; Ⓒ 4,888

Jessieville; RMC Place; GOGEBIC; ▲ Ironwood; ***188** C-10; mail Ironwood **z** 49938; pop. incl. with Ironwood (Inc. Place)

Johannesburg; RMC Place; OTSEGO; ▲ Charlton; **188** I-9; elev. 1,351ft./412m.; 🅿; **z** 49751; ● 250

Johnstown; MCD-Township; BARRY; ***189** R-7; ★ **BTLCK**; mail Dowling **z** 49050; Ⓟ 2,932; Ⓒ 3,067

Johnswood; RMC Place; CHIPPEWA; ▲ Drummond; ***188** F-11; mail Drummond Island **z** 49726; rural

Jones; RMC Place; CASS; ▲ Newberg; **189** T-6; 🅿; **z** 49061; ● 290

Jonesfield; MCD-Township; SAGINAW; ***189** N-9; ★ **SAG-**; mail Merrill **z** 48637; Ⓟ 1,740; Ⓒ 1,710

Jonesville; Inc. Place; HILLSDALE; ▲ Fayette; **189** S-8; 🅿; **z** 49250; Ⓟ 2,283; Ⓒ 2,337

Joppa; RMC Place; CALHOUN; ▲ Leroy; **189** S-7; elev. 931ft./284m.; ★ **BTLCK**; mail East Leroy **z** 49051

Jordan; MCD-Township; ANTRIM; ***188** I-7; mail Ellsworth **z** 49729; Ⓟ 583; Ⓒ 875

Joyfield; MCD-Township; BENZIE; ***189** K-5; mail Benzonia **z** 49616; Ⓟ 626; Ⓒ 777

Joyfield; RMC Place; WAYNE; ***189** R-12; ★ **DET**; mail Detroit **z** 48228; pop. incl. with Detroit (Inc. Place)

Juddville; RMC Place; SHIAWASSEE; ▲ Hazelton; **189** P-10; elev. 728ft./222m.; ★ **FLN**; mail Corunna **z** 48817; ● 30

Jugville; RMC Place; NEWAYGO; ▲ Sherman; ***189** N-5; mail White Cloud **z** 49349; ● 70

Juhl; RMC Place; SANILAC; ▲ Elmer; ***189** N-13; elev. 784ft./239m.; mail Marlette **z** 48453

Juniata; RMC Place; TUSCOLA; ▲ Vassar, Fremont; **189** O-11; elev. 747ft./228m.; ★ **FLN**; mail Mayville **z** 48744; ● 100

Juniata; MCD-Township; TUSCOLA; ***189** N-11; mail Vassar **z** 48768; Ⓟ 1,666; Ⓒ 1,673

K

Kaiserville; RMC Place; LIVINGSTON; ▲ Unadilla; ***189** R-10; ★ **DET**; mail Gregory **z** 48137; ● 210

Kalamazoo; Inc. Place; ⊡ KALAMAZOO; **189** R-6; 🅿 🅷 🅲 26,181 ■; ★ **KZOO**; **z** 49001, **z** 49003-09, **z** 49019, **z** 49048 & mail Portage **z** 49002, **z** 49024; Ⓟ 80,277; Ⓒ 77,145; ◆ 77,543

Kalamazoo; MCD-Charter Township; KALAMAZOO; ***189** R-6; 🅿 🅲 26,181; ★ **KZOO**; **z** 49001, **z** 49003-09, **z** 49019, **z** 49048 & mail Portage **z** 49002, **z** 49024; does not include the City of Kalamazoo; Ⓟ 20,976; Ⓒ 21,675; ◆ 22,894

KALAMAZOO; **189** S-6; Ⓟ 223,411; Ⓒ 238,603; ◆ 253,947

Kalamo; RMC Place; EATON; ▲ Kalamo; **189** Q-8; mail Vermontville **z** 49096; ● 80

Kalamo; MCD-Township; EATON; ***189** Q-8; mail Vermontville **z** 49096; Ⓟ 1,665; Ⓒ 1,742

Kaleva; Inc. Place; MANISTEE; ▲ Maple Grove; **189** K-5; 🅿; **z** 49645; Ⓟ 484; Ⓒ 509

Kalkaska; Inc. Place; ⊡ KALKASKA; ▲ Kalkaska; **188** J-7; elev. 1,035ft./315m.; 🅿 🅷; **z** 49646; Ⓟ 1,952; Ⓒ 2,226

Kalkaska; MCD-Township; KALKASKA; ***188** J-7; 🅿; **z** 49646; Ⓟ 4,269; Ⓒ 4,830

KALKASKA; **188** J-7; Ⓟ 13,497; Ⓒ 16,571; ◆ 16,871

Karlin; RMC Place; GRAND TRAVERSE; ▲ Grant; **188** J-6; elev. 887ft./270m.; 🅿; **z** 49643; ● 100

Kasson; MCD-Township; LEELANAU; ***188** J-5; mail Maple City **z** 49664; Ⓟ 1,135; Ⓒ 1,577

Kawkawlin; RMC Place; BAY; ▲ Monitor, Kawkawlin; **189** N-10; 🅿; ★ **SAG-**; **z** 48631; ● 450

Kawkawlin; MCD-Township; BAY; ***189** M-10; 🅿; ★ **SAG-**; **z** 48631; Ⓟ 4,852; Ⓒ 5,104

Kearney; MCD-Township; ANTRIM; ***188** I-7; mail Bellaire **z** 49615; Ⓟ 1,487; Ⓒ 1,764

Kearsarge; RMC Place; HOUGHTON; ▲ Calumet; **188** A-13; 🅿; **z** 49942; ● 150

Keego Harbor; Inc. Place; OAKLAND; **190** F-4; elev. 930ft./283m.; 🅿; ★ **DET**; **z** 48320; Ⓟ 2,932; Ⓒ 2,769

Keeler; RMC Place; VAN BUREN; ▲ Keeler; **189** S-5; elev. 806ft./246m.; mail Hartford **z** 49057; ● 180

Keeler; MCD-Township; VAN BUREN; ***189** S-5; mail Hartford **z** 49057; Ⓟ 2,344; Ⓒ 2,601

Keene; MCD-Township; IONIA; ***189** P-7; mail Saranac **z** 48881; Ⓟ 1,376; Ⓒ 1,660

Kegomic; RMC Place; EMMET; ▲ Bear Creek; ***188** H-8; mail Petoskey **z** 49770; ● 140

Kellogg; RMC Place; ALLEGAN; ▲ Watson; ***189** R-6; mail Allegan **z** 49010; rural

Kelloggsville; RMC Place; KENT; ★ **GDR**; mail Grand Rapids **z** 49508; pop. incl. with Kentwood (Inc. Place)

Kellys Corners; RMC Place; MUSKEGON; ▲ Moorland; ***189** O-5; mail Ravenna **z** 49451; ● 40

Kelsey Lake; RMC Place; CASS; ▲ LaGrange; ***189** S-5; elev. 850ft./259m.; mail Cassopolis **z** 49031; ● 290

Kendall; RMC Place; VAN BUREN; ▲ Pine Grove; **189** R-6; elev. 799ft./244m.; 🅿; **z** 49062; ● 250

Kenockee; MCD-Township; ST. CLAIR; ***189** P-13; 🅿; **z** 48006; Ⓟ 1,854; Ⓒ 2,423

Kensington; RMC Place; WAYNE; ***189** R-13; ★ **DET**; mail Detroit **z** 48224; pop. incl. with Detroit (Inc. Place)

KENT; **189** O-6; Ⓟ 500,631; Ⓒ 574,335; ◆ 612,271

Kent City; Inc. Place; KENT; ▲ Tyrone; **189** O-6; elev. 800ft./244m.; 🅿; ★ **GDR**; **z** 49330; Ⓟ 899; Ⓒ 1,061

Kenton; RMC Place; HOUGHTON; ▲ Duncan; **188** B-12; elev. 1,179ft./359m.; 🅿; **z** 49967; ● 250

Kentwood; Inc. Place; KENT; **189** P-6; elev. 689ft./210m.; 🅿 ■; ★ **GDR**; **z** 49508, **z** 49512, **z** 49518, **z** 49548, **z** 49588 & mail Grand Rapids **z** 49506, **z** 49546; Ⓟ 37,826; Ⓒ 45,255; ◆ 49,448

Kerby; RMC Place; SHIAWASSEE; ▲ Caledonia; ***189** P-10; elev. 765ft./233m.; mail Corunna **z** 48817

Kessington; RMC Place; CASS; ▲ Mason; ***189** T-5; ★ **ELK**; mail Edwardsburg **z** 49112, Union **z** 49130; ● 170

Kewadin; RMC Place; ANTRIM; ▲ Milton, Elk Rapids; **188** I-7; elev. 609ft./186m.; 🅿; **z** 49648; ● 570

KEWEENAW; **188** A-13; Ⓟ 1,701; Ⓒ 2,301; ◆ 2,206

Keweenaw Bay; RMC Place; BARAGA; ▲ Baraga; ***188** B-13; elev. 680ft./207m.; 🅿; **z** 49908; ● 70

Kibbie Corners; RMC Place; VAN BUREN; ▲ Geneva; ***189** R-5; elev. 627ft./191m.; mail South Haven **z** 49090; rural

Killarney Beach; RMC Place; BAY; ▲ Bangor; ***189** M-10; ★ **SAG-**; mail Bay City **z** 48706

Killmaster; RMC Place; ALCONA; ▲ Gustin; ***188** J-11; mail Harrisville **z** 48740; rural

Kilmanagh; RMC Place; HURON; ▲ Brookfield, Fairhaven, Sebewaing, Winsor; **189** M-12; mail Sebewaing **z** 48759; ● 30

Kimball; RMC Place; ST. CLAIR; ▲ Kimball; ***189** P-14; elev. 639ft./195m.; 🅿; ★ **PTHU**; **z** 48074; ● 30

Kimball; MCD-Township; ST. CLAIR; ***189** P-14; 🅿; ★ **PTHU**; **z** 48074; Ⓟ 7,247; Ⓒ 8,628

Kinde; Inc. Place; HURON; ▲ Meade, Dwight, Lincoln; **189** L-13; 🅿; **z** 48445; Ⓟ 473; Ⓒ 534

Kinderhook; RMC Place; BRANCH; ▲ Kinderhook; **189** T-8; elev. 1,003ft./306m.; mail Coldwater **z** 49036; ● 150

Kinderhook; MCD-Township; BRANCH; ***189** T-8; mail Coldwater **z** 49036; Ⓟ 1,292; Ⓒ 1,614

King Arthur's Court; RMC Place; CLINTON; ▲ DeWitt; ***189** Q-9; ★ **LANS**; mail Lansing **z** 48906; ● 780

Kingsford; Inc. Place; DICKINSON; **188** D-13; elev. 1,100ft./335m.; 🅿; **z** 49802 & mail Iron Mountain **z** 49801; Ⓟ 5,480; Ⓒ 5,549

Kingsley; Inc. Place; GRAND TRAVERSE; ▲ Paradise; **188** J-6; elev. 996ft./304m.; 🅿; **z** 49649; Ⓟ 738; Ⓒ 1,469

Kings Mill; RMC Place; LAPEER; ▲ Arcadia; **189** O-12; elev. 878ft./268m.; mail North Branch **z** 48461; ● 50

Kingston; Inc. Place; TUSCOLA; ▲ Koylton, Kingston; **189** N-12; 🅿; **z** 48741; Ⓟ 439; Ⓒ 450

Kingston; MCD-Township; TUSCOLA; ***189** N-12; 🅿; **z** 48741 & mail Deford **z** 48729; includes part of the Village of Kingston; Ⓟ 1,498; Ⓒ 1,615

Kinneville; RMC Place; INGHAM; ▲ Onondaga; **189** R-9; mail Eaton Rapids **z** 48827; ● 30

Kinross; RMC Place; CHIPPEWA; ▲ Kinross; **188** D-8; 🅿; **z** 49752; ● 50

Kinross; MCD-Charter Township; CHIPPEWA; ***188** D-8; 🅿; **z** 49752; Ⓟ 6,566; Ⓒ 5,922; Ⓡ 8,140

Kipling; RMC Place; DELTA; ▲ Brampton; **188** F-2; elev. 586ft./179m.; mail Gladstone **z** 49837; ● 310

K. I. Sawyer AFB; CDP-Census Area Only; MARQUETTE; ▲ West Branch, Forsyth, Sands; ***188** D-2; Ⓒ 1,443

Kiva; RMC Place; ALGER; ▲ Limestone; **188** E-2; mail Trenary **z** 49891

Klacking; MCD-Township; OGEMAW; ***189** K-9; mail Rose City **z** 48654; Ⓟ 430; Ⓒ 617

Klinger Lake; RMC Place; ST. JOSEPH; ▲ White Pigeon; **189** T-6; ★ **ELK**; mail Sturgis **z** 49091, White Pigeon **z** 49099; ● 1,000

Klingville; RMC Place; HOUGHTON; ▲ Chassell; ***188** A-13; mail Chassell **z** 49916; rural

Kneeland; RMC Place; OSCODA; ▲ Comins; ***188** J-10; elev. 1,074ft./327m.; mail Mio **z** 48647

Knollwood Park; RMC Place; JACKSON; ▲ Leoni, Blackman; ***189** R-9; ★ **JAC**; mail Jackson **z** 49203; ● 210

Kochville; MCD-Township; SAGINAW; ***189** N-10; ★ **SAG-**; mail Saginaw **z** 48604; Ⓟ 2,740; Ⓒ 3,241

Koehler; MCD-Township; CHEBOYGAN; ***188** G-9; mail Afton **z** 49705; Ⓟ 722; Ⓒ 1,168

Koss; RMC Place; MENOMINEE; ▲ Lake; **188** H-1; elev. 718ft./219m.; mail Stephenson **z** 49887; ● 30

Koylton; MCD-Township; TUSCOLA; ***189** N-12; mail Kingston **z** 48741; Ⓟ 1,446; Ⓒ 1,579

Krakow; MCD-Township; PRESQUE ISLE; ***188** H-11; mail Posen **z** 49776; Ⓟ 617; Ⓒ 622

L

La Branche; RMC Place; MENOMINEE; ▲ Spalding; ***188** F-1; elev. 950ft./290m.; mail Perronville **z** 49873; ● 20

Lacey; RMC Place; BARRY; ▲ Johnstown, Assyria; **189** R-7; elev. 998ft./304m.; ★ **BTLCK**; mail Bellevue **z** 49021; ● 80

Lachine; RMC Place; ALPENA; ▲ Long Rapids; **188** I-11; 🅿; **z** 49753; ● 200

Lac La Belle; RMC Place; KEWEENAW; ▲ Allouez; **188** A-13; mail Mohawk **z** 49950; ● 30

Lacota; RMC Place; VAN BUREN; ▲ Geneva; **189** R-5; 🅿; **z** 49063; ● 250

Lac Vieux Desert Reservation; Indian Reservation; GOGEBIC; Ⓒ 135

Lafayette; MCD-Township; GRATIOT; ***189** O-9; mail Wheeler **z** 48662; Ⓟ 683; Ⓒ 656

Lagoon Beach; RMC Place; BAY; ▲ Bangor; ***189** N-10; ★ **SAG-**; mail Bay City **z** 48706

La Grange; RMC Place; CASS; ▲ LaGrange; **189** S-5; mail Cassopolis **z** 49031; ● 120

LaGrange; MCD-Township; CASS; ***189** T-5; mail Cassopolis **z** 49031; Ⓟ 3,406; Ⓒ 3,340; Ⓡ 3,478

Laing; RMC Place; SANILAC; ▲ Argyle; ***189** N-13; elev. 770ft./235m.; mail Snover **z** 48472; rural

Laingsburg; Inc. Place; SHIAWASSEE; **189** P-9; elev. 820ft./250m.; 🅿; **z** 48848; Ⓟ 1,148; Ⓒ 1,223

Laird; MCD-Township; HOUGHTON; ***188** B-12; mail Nisula **z** 49952; Ⓟ 582; Ⓒ 634

Lake; MCD-Township; BENZIE; ***188** J-5; mail Honor **z** 49640; Ⓟ 508; Ⓒ 635

Lake (Lake Charter); MCD-Charter Township; BERRIEN; ***189** T-4; mail Bridgman **z** 49106; Ⓟ 2,487; Ⓒ 3,148

Lake; RMC Place; CLARE; ▲ Garfield; **189** M-7; 🅿; **z** 48632; ● 550

Lake; MCD-Township; HURON; ***189** L-12; mail Caseville **z** 48725; Ⓟ 800; Ⓒ 996

Lake; MCD-Township; LAKE; ***189** M-5; mail Baldwin **z** 49304; Ⓟ 700; Ⓒ 849

Lake; MCD-Township; MACOMB; ***189** R-13; ★ **DET**; mail Grosse Pointe **z** 48236; Ⓟ 105; Ⓒ 80

Lake; MCD-Township; MENOMINEE; ***188** E-14; mail Daggett **z** 49821; Ⓟ 603; Ⓒ 576

Lake; MCD-Township; MISSAUKEE; ***189** K-7; mail Lake City **z** 49651; Ⓟ 1,980; Ⓒ 2,468

Lake; MCD-Township; ROSCOMMON; ***189** K-8; mail Houghton Lake **z** 48629; Ⓟ 1,234; Ⓒ 1,351

LAKE; **189** M-5; Ⓟ 8,583; Ⓒ 11,333; ◆ 10,959

Lake Angeline; RMC Place; MARQUETTE; ▲ Ishpeming; ***188** D-1; elev. 1,439ft./439m.; mail Ishpeming **z** 49849; pop. incl. with Ishpeming (Inc. Place)

Lake Angelus; Inc. Place; OAKLAND; **190** E-4; 🅿; ★ **DET**; **z** 48326; Ⓟ 328; Ⓒ 326

Lake Ann; Inc. Place; BENZIE; ▲ Almira; **188** J-5; 🅿; **z** 49650; Ⓟ 217; Ⓒ 276

Lake Charter; BERRIEN; see Lake (MCD-Charter Township)

Lake City; Inc. Place; ⊡ MISSAUKEE; **189** K-7; elev. 1,260ft./384m.; 🅿; **z** 49651; Ⓟ 858; Ⓒ 923

Lake Fenton; CDP-Census Area Only; GENESEE; ▲ Fenton; **189** P-11; ★ **FLN**; mail Fenton **z** 48430; Ⓟ 4,091; Ⓒ 4,876

Lakefield; MCD-Township; LUCE; ***188** D-6; mail Mc Millan **z** 49853; Ⓟ 869; Ⓒ 1,074

Lakefield; MCD-Township; SAGINAW; ***189** O-9; mail Merrill **z** 48637; Ⓟ 962; Ⓒ 1,030

Lake George; RMC Place; CLARE; ▲ Lincoln; **189** M-8; 🅿; **z** 48633; ● 430

Lake Isabella (Village of Lake Isabella); Inc. Place; ISABELLA; ***189** N-8; 🅿; **z** 48893; Ⓒ 1,243

Lakeland; RMC Place; LIVINGSTON; ▲ Hamburg; **189** R-11; elev. 858ft./262m.; 🅿; ★ **DET**; **z** 48143; ● 1,050

Lake Lansing; RMC Place; INGHAM; ▲ Meridian; ★ **LANS**; mail Haslett **z** 48840

Lake Leelanau; RMC Place; LEELANAU; ▲ Suttons Bay, Leland; **188** I-6; 🅿; **z** 49653; ● 370

Lake Linden; Inc. Place; HOUGHTON; ▲ Schoolcraft; **188** A-13; 🅿; **z** 49945; Ⓟ 1,203; Ⓒ 1,081

Lake Margrethe; RMC Place; CRAWFORD; ▲ Grayling; ***188** J-8; elev. 1,150ft./351m.; mail Grayling **z** 49738; ● 420

Lake Michigan Beach (Hagar Shores); CDP; BERRIEN; ▲ Hagar; **189** S-4; ★ **BNTH-**; mail Hagar Shores **z** 49039; Ⓟ 1,694; Ⓒ 1,509

Lake Mine; RMC Place; ONTONAGON; ▲ Greenland; ***188** B-12; elev. 1,004ft./306m.; mail Mass City **z** 49948; rural

Lake Nepessing; RMC Place; LAPEER; ▲ Elba; **189** P-12; ★ **DET**; mail Lapeer **z** 48446; ● 690

Lake Odessa; Inc. Place; IONIA; ▲ Odessa; **189** Q-7; 🅿; **z** 48849; Ⓟ 2,256; Ⓒ 2,272

Lake Orion; Inc. Place; OAKLAND; ▲ Orion; **189** P-12; 🅿; ★ **DET**; **z** 48359-62; Ⓟ 3,057; Ⓒ 2,715

Lake Orion Heights; RMC Place; OAKLAND; ▲ Orion; ***189** Q-12; ★ **DET**; mail Lake Orion **z** 48361-62

Lake Pleasant; RMC Place; LAPEER; ▲ Attica; ***189** P-12; elev. 880ft./268m.; ★ **DET**; mail Attica **z** 48412; ● 530

Lakeport; RMC Place; ST. CLAIR; ▲ Burtchville; **189** O-14; 🅿; ★ **PTHU**; **z** 48059; ● 350

Lake Roland; RMC Place; HOUGHTON; ▲ Elm River; ***188** B-12; elev. 1,199ft./365m.; mail Wakefield **z** 49968; ● 30

Lakeside; RMC Place; BERRIEN; ▲ Chikaming; **189** T-3; 🅿; **z** 49116; ● 1,100

Lakeside; RMC Place; HURON; ▲ Port Austin; mail Port Austin **z** 48467; pop. incl. with Port Austin (Inc. Place)

Lakeside; RMC Place; MUSKEGON; ★ **MUS**; pop. incl. with Muskegon (Inc. Place)

Lakeside Landing; RMC Place; GENESEE; ▲ Fenton; ***189** P-11; ★ **FLN**; mail Fenton **z** 48430

Laketon; MCD-Township; MUSKEGON; ***189** O-4; ★ **MUS**; mail Muskegon **z** 49445; Ⓟ 6,538; Ⓒ 7,363

Laketown; MCD-Township; ALLEGAN; ***189** Q-5; ★ **HLND**; mail Holland **z** 49423; Ⓟ 4,888; Ⓒ 5,561

Lakeview; RMC Place; BERRIEN; ▲ Chikaming; ***189** T-3; mail Union Pier **z** 49129

Lakeview; RMC Place; CALHOUN; ***189** R-7; ★ **BTLCK**; mail Battle Creek **z** 49015; pop. incl. with Battle Creek (Inc. Place)

Lakeview; Inc. Place; MONTCALM; ▲ Cato; **189** N-7; elev. 953ft./290m.; 🅿 🅷; **z** 48850; Ⓟ 1,108; Ⓒ 1,112

Lakeville; RMC Place; OAKLAND; ▲ Addison; **189** P-12; 🅿; ★ **DET**; **z** 48366; ● 340

Lakewood; RMC Place; ALPENA; ▲ Alpena; ***188** H-11; elev. 660ft./201m.; mail Alpena **z** 49707; rural

Lakewood; RMC Place; KALAMAZOO; ▲ Kalamazoo; ***189** R-6; ★ **KZOO**; mail Portage **z** 49002; ● 1,560

Lakewood; RMC Place; MONROE; ★ **TOL**; mail Luna Pier **z** 48157; pop. incl. with Luna Pier (Inc. Place)

Lakewood Club; Inc. Place; MUSKEGON; ▲ Dalton; **189** O-4; ★ **MUS**; mail Twin Lake **z** 49457; Ⓟ 659; Ⓒ 1,006

Lamar; RMC Place; KENT; ★ **GDR**; mail Wyoming **z** 49509; pop. incl. with Wyoming (Inc. Place)

Lamb; RMC Place; ST. CLAIR; ▲ Wales; **189** P-13; mail Goodells **z** 48027; ● 140

Lambertville; CDP; MONROE; ▲ Bedford; **189** T-11; 🅿; ★ **TOL**; **z** 48144; Ⓟ 7,860; Ⓒ 9,299

Lamont; RMC Place; OTTAWA; ▲ Tallmadge; **189** P-5; elev. 661ft./201m.; 🅿; ★ **GDR**; **z** 49430; ● 300

Lamotte; MCD-Township; SANILAC; ***189** N-12; mail Decker **z** 48426; Ⓟ 949; Ⓒ 981

Lanewood; RMC Place; WASHTENAW; ***189** R-10; ★ **DET**; mail Chelsea **z** 48118; pop. incl. with Chelsea (Inc. Place)

Langston; RMC Place; MONTCALM; ▲ Pine; **189** O-7; elev. 885ft./270m.; mail Stanton **z** 48888; ● 150

L'Anse; Inc. Place; ⊡ BARAGA; ▲ L'Anse; **188** B-13; elev. 682ft./208m.; 🅿 🅷; **z** 49946; Ⓟ 2,151; Ⓒ 2,107

L'Anse; MCD-Township; BARAGA; ***188** B-13; mail Lanse **z** 49946; Ⓟ 3,818; Ⓒ 3,926

L'Anse Reservation; Indian Reservation; BARAGA; ▲ L'Anse; also location of Indian Agency; Ⓟ 3,289; Ⓒ 3,538

Lansing; Inc. Place; **STATE CAPITAL**; INGHAM, CLINTON, EATON; **189** Q-9; 🅿 🅷 🅲 3,281 ■; ★ **LANS**; **z** 48901, **z** 48906, **z** 48908-13, **z** 48915-19, **z** 48921-22, **z** 48924, **z** 48929-30, **z** 48933, **z** 48937, **z** 48950-51, **z** 48956, **z** 48980; Ⓟ 127,321; Ⓒ 119,128; Ⓡ 119,286; ◆ 118,970

Lansing; MCD-Charter Township; INGHAM; ***189** Q-9; 🅿 🅲 3,281; ★ **LANS**; **z** 48901, **z** 48906, **z** 48908-13, **z** 48915-19, **z** 48921-22, **z** 48924, **z** 48929-30, **z** 48933, **z** 48937, **z** 48950-51, **z** 48956, **z** 48980; does not include the City of Lansing; Ⓟ 8,919; Ⓒ 8,458

Lapeer; Inc. Place; ⊡ LAPEER; **189** P-12; 🅿 🅷; ★ **DET**; **z** 48446; Ⓟ 7,759; Ⓒ 9,072

Lapeer; MCD-Township; LAPEER; ***189** P-12; 🅿; ★ **DET**; **z** 48446; does not include the City of Lapeer; Ⓟ 4,519; Ⓒ 5,078

LAPEER; **189** O-12; Ⓟ 74,768; Ⓒ 87,904; ◆ 88,348

Laporte; RMC Place; MIDLAND; ▲ Ingersoll; **189** N-10; ★ **SAG-**; mail Freeland **z** 48623; ● 150

Larkin; MCD-Charter Township; MIDLAND; ***189** M-9; ★ **SAG-**; mail Midland **z** 48642; Ⓟ 3,588; Ⓒ 4,514

Larocque; PRESQUE ISLE; see Hawks (RMC Place)

Larson Beach; RMC Place; ALCONA; ▲ Alcona; ***188** J-11; mail Spruce **z** 48762; ● 30

La Salle; RMC Place; MONROE; ▲ La Salle; **189** T-12; 🅿; ★ **MONR**; **z** 48145; ● 250

La Salle; MCD-Township; MONROE; ***189** T-12; 🅿; ★ **MONR**; **z** 48145; Ⓟ 4,985; Ⓒ 5,001

La Salle Gardens; RMC Place; OAKLAND; ▲ Waterford; ***189** Q-12; ★ **DET**; mail Pontiac **z** 48341

Lathrup Village; Inc. Place; OAKLAND; **190** H-5; elev. 703ft./214m.; 🅿; ★ **DET**; **z** 48076; Ⓟ 4,329; Ⓒ 4,236

Laurium; Inc. Place; HOUGHTON; ▲ Calumet; **188** A-13; elev. 1,246ft./380m.; 🅿 🅷; **z** 49913; Ⓟ 2,268; Ⓒ 2,126

Lawrence; Inc. Place; VAN BUREN; ▲ Lawrence; **189** S-5; 🅿; ★ **KZOO**; **z** 49064; Ⓟ 915; Ⓒ 1,059

Lawrence; MCD-Township; VAN BUREN; ***189** S-5; 🅿; ★ **KZOO**; **z** 49064; Ⓟ 3,030; Ⓒ 3,341

Lawson (Hogstrom); RMC Place; MARQUETTE; ▲ Skandia; ***188** D-2; mail Skandia **z** 49885; rural

Lawton; Inc. Place; VAN BUREN; ▲ Antwerp; **189** S-5; 🅿; ★ **KZOO**; **z** 49065; Ⓟ 1,685; Ⓒ 1,859

Layton Corners; RMC Place; SAGINAW; ▲ Maple Grove; **189** O-10; mail Chelsea **z** 48118; ● 30

Leaton; RMC Place; ISABELLA; ▲ Denver; **189** N-8; mail Mount Pleasant **z** 48858; ● 30

Leavitt; MCD-Township; OCEANA; ***189** N-5; mail Walkerville **z** 49459; Ⓟ 804; Ⓒ 845

Lebanon; MCD-Township; CLINTON; ***189** P-8; mail Hubbardston **z** 48845; Ⓟ 644; Ⓒ 705

Ledyard; RMC Place; KENT; ▲ Grand Rapids; ★ **GDR**; mail Grand Rapids **z** 49523; pop. incl. with Grand Rapids (Inc. Place)

Lee; MCD-Township; ALLEGAN; ***189** R-5; mail Pullman **z** 49450; Ⓟ 2,672; Ⓒ 4,114

Lee; MCD-Township; CALHOUN; ***189** R-8; mail Marshall **z** 49068; Ⓟ 1,281; Ⓒ 1,257

Lee; MCD-Township; MIDLAND; ***189** N-9; ★ **SAG-**; mail Midland **z** 48640; Ⓟ 4,017; Ⓒ 4,411

Lee Center; RMC Place; CALHOUN; ▲ Lee; ***189** R-8; elev. 970ft./296m.; mail Olivet **z** 49076; rural

Leelanau; MCD-Township; LEELANAU; ***188** I-6; mail Northport **z** 49670; Ⓟ 1,694; Ⓒ 2,139

LEELANAU; **188** I-5; Ⓟ 16,527; Ⓒ 21,119; ◆ 21,759

Leer; RMC Place; ALPENA; ▲ Long Rapids; ***188** H-11; elev. 828ft./252m.; mail Posen **z** 49776; rural

Legrand; RMC Place; CHEBOYGAN; ▲ Koehler; ***188** H-9; mail Afton **z** 49705; ● 30

Leighton; MCD-Township; ALLEGAN; ***189** Q-6; ★ **GDR**; mail Caledonia **z** 49316; Ⓟ 3,069; Ⓒ 3,652

Leisure; RMC Place; ALLEGAN; ▲ Casco; ***189** R-5; elev. 685ft./209m.; mail South Haven **z** 49090; ● 150

Leland; RMC Place; ⊡ LEELANAU; ▲ Leland; **188** I-6; elev. 602ft./183m.; 🅿; **z** 49654; ● 680

Leland; MCD-Township; LEELANAU; ***188** I-5; 🅿; **z** 49654; Ⓟ 1,642; Ⓒ 2,033

Lemon Park; RMC Place; KALAMAZOO; ▲ Brady; ***189** S-6; elev. 851ft./259m.; ★ **KZOO**; mail Vicksburg **z** 49097; ● 70

LENAWEE; **189** T-10; Ⓟ 91,476; Ⓒ 98,890; Ⓡ 98,947; ◆ 99,151

Lennon; Inc. Place; GENESEE, SHIAWASSEE; ▲ Clayton, Venice; **189** P-10; 🅿; **z** 48449; Ⓟ 534; Ⓒ 517; Ⓡ 519

Lennon Green Estates; RMC Place; SHIAWASSEE; ▲ Venice; ***189** P-10; elev. 777ft./237m.; ★ **FLN**; mail Lennon **z** 48449; ● 400

Lenox; MCD-Township; MACOMB; ***189** Q-13; 🅿; ★ **DET**; **z** 48048, **z** 48050; Ⓟ 5,400; Ⓒ 8,433

Leonard; Inc. Place; OAKLAND; ▲ Addison; **189** P-12; elev. 1,003ft./306m.; 🅿; ★ **DET**; **z** 48367; Ⓟ 357; Ⓒ 332

Leoni; RMC Place; JACKSON; ▲ Leoni; **189** R-9; ★ **JAC**; mail Jackson **z** 49201; ● 90

Leoni; MCD-Township; JACKSON; ***189** R-9; ★ **JAC**; mail Jackson **z** 49201; Ⓟ 13,435; Ⓒ 13,459

Leonidas; RMC Place; ST. JOSEPH; ▲ Leonidas; **189** S-7; elev. 869ft./265m.; 🅿; **z** 49066; ● 220

Leonidas; MCD-Township; ST. JOSEPH; ***189** S-7; 🅿; **z** 49066; Ⓟ 1,171; Ⓒ 1,239

Leota; RMC Place; CLARE; ▲ Hatton; ***189** L-8; mail Harrison **z** 48625; ● 200

Leroy; MCD-Township; CALHOUN; ***189** S-7; ★ **BTLCK**; mail East Leroy **z** 49051; Ⓟ 3,026; Ⓒ 3,240

Leroy; MCD-Township; INGHAM; ***189** Q-10; mail Webberville **z** 48892; Ⓟ 3,561; Ⓒ 3,653

Le Roy; Inc. Place; OSCEOLA; ▲ Le Roy; **189** L-6; 🅿; **z** 49655; Ⓟ 251; Ⓒ 267

Le Roy; MCD-Township; OSCEOLA; ***189** L-6; mail Leroy **z** 49655; Ⓟ 958; Ⓒ 1,159

Leroy; RMC Place; PRESQUE ISLE; ▲ Krakow; ***188** H-11; elev. 663ft./202m.; mail Alpena **z** 49707; rural

Les Cheneaux Club; RMC Place; MACKINAC; ▲ Clark; ***188** E-9; mail Cedarville **z** 49719; summer pop. 160

Leslie; Inc. Place; INGHAM; **189** R-9; elev. 935ft./285m.; 🅿; ★ **LANS**; **z** 49251; Ⓟ 1,872; Ⓒ 2,044

Leslie; MCD-Township; INGHAM; ***189** R-9; 🅿; ★ **LANS**; **z** 49251; does not include the City of Leslie; Ⓟ 2,436; Ⓒ 2,327

Lesterville; RMC Place; ST. CLAIR; ▲ Berlin; ***189** P-13; elev. 789ft./240m.; mail Allenton **z** 48002; rural

Level Park; RMC Place; CALHOUN; ▲ Bedford; **189** R-7; ★ **BTLCK**; mail Battle Creek **z** 49017; ● 3,490

Level Park-Oak Park; CDP-Census Area Only; CALHOUN; ▲ Bedford; ***189** R-7; ★ **BTLCK**; mail Battle Creek **z** 49017; Ⓟ 3,502; Ⓒ 3,605

Levering; RMC Place; EMMET; ▲ McKinley, Carp Lake; **188** G-8; elev. 756ft./230m.; 🅿; **z** 49755; ● 500

Lewiston; CDP; MONTMORENCY; ▲ Albert; **188** I-9; 🅿; **z** 49756; Ⓒ 990

Lewisville; RMC Place; HURON; ▲ Huron, Bloomfield; ***189** L-13; elev. 704ft./215m.; mail Port Hope **z** 48468; ● 30

Lexington; Inc. Place; SANILAC; ▲ Lexington; **189** O-14; elev. 623ft./190m.; 🅿; **z** 48450; Ⓟ 779; Ⓒ 1,104

Lexington; MCD-Township; SANILAC; ***189** O-14; 🅿; **z** 48450; Ⓟ 3,028; Ⓒ 3,688

Lexington Heights; RMC Place; SANILAC; ▲ Worth; **189** O-14; ★ **PTHU**; mail Lexington **z** 48450; ● 520

Liberty; RMC Place; JACKSON; ▲ Liberty; **189** S-9; ★ **JAC**; mail Cement City **z** 49233; ● 110

Liberty; MCD-Township; JACKSON; ***189** S-9; ★ **JAC**; mail Clarklake **z** 49234; Ⓟ 2,452; Ⓒ 2,903

Liberty; RMC Place; WASHTENAW; ***189** R-11; ★ **DET**; mail Ann Arbor **z** 48107; pop. incl. with Ann Arbor (Inc. Place)

Liberty; MCD-Township; WEXFORD; ***189** K-6; mail Manton **z** 49663; Ⓟ 641; Ⓒ 800

Lilley; RMC Place; NEWAYGO; **189** M-5; elev. 865ft./264m.

Lilley; MCD-Township; NEWAYGO; ***189** M-5; mail Bitely **z** 49309; Ⓟ 565; Ⓒ 788

Lima; MCD-Township; WASHTENAW; ***189** R-10; ★ **DET**; mail Chelsea **z** 48118; Ⓟ 2,585; Ⓒ 3,224

Lima Center; RMC Place; WASHTENAW; ▲ Lima; ***189** R-10; ★ **DET**; mail Chelsea **z** 48118, Dexter **z** 48130; rural

Lime Island; RMC Place; CHIPPEWA; ▲ Raber; ***188** E-10; mail Goetzville **z** 49736; ● 30

Limestone; RMC Place; ALGER; ▲ Limestone; **188** E-3; elev. 912ft./278m.; 🅿; **z** 49816; ● 60

Limestone; MCD-Township; ALGER; ***188** E-3; 🅿; **z** 49816; Ⓟ 334; Ⓒ 407

Lincoln; Inc. Place; ALCONA; ▲ Hawes, Gustin; **188** J-11; 🅿; **z** 48742; Ⓟ 337; Ⓒ 364

Lincoln; MCD-Township; ARENAC; ***189** L-10; ★ **SAG-**; mail Standish **z** 48658; Ⓟ 969; Ⓒ 1,522; Ⓡ 1,007

Lincoln; MCD-Charter Township; BERRIEN; ***189** S-4; ★ **BNTH-**; mail Stevensville **z** 49127; Ⓟ 13,604; Ⓒ 13,952

Lincoln; MCD-Township; CLARE; ***189** M-8; mail Lake George **z** 48633; Ⓟ 1,253; Ⓒ 1,758

Lincoln; MCD-Township; HURON; ***189** M-13; mail Filion **z** 48432; Ⓟ 868; Ⓒ 873

Lincoln; MCD-Township; ISABELLA; ***189** N-8; mail Shepherd **z** 48883; Ⓟ 1,794; Ⓒ 1,936

Lincoln; MCD-Township; MIDLAND; ***189** M-9; ★ **SAG-**; mail Midland **z** 48640; Ⓟ 1,807; Ⓒ 2,277

Lincoln; MCD-Township; NEWAYGO; ***189** N-5; mail White Cloud **z** 49349; Ⓟ 969; Ⓒ 1,338

Lincoln; MCD-Township; OSCEOLA; ***189** M-6; mail Reed City **z** 49677; Ⓟ 1,228; Ⓒ 1,629

Lincoln Park; RMC Place; MUSKEGON; ★ **MUS**; mail Muskegon **z** 49441; pop. incl. with Norton Shores (Inc. Place)

Lincoln Park; Inc. Place; WAYNE; **189** R-12; elev. 587ft./179m.; 🅿 🅷 ■; ★ **DET**; **z** 48146; Ⓟ 41,832; Ⓒ 40,008; ◆ 36,473

Linden; Inc. Place; GENESEE; ▲ Fenton; **189** P-11; 🅿; ★ **FLN**; **z** 48451; Ⓟ 2,415; Ⓒ 2,861

Linkville; RMC Place; HURON; ▲ Winsor, Brookfield; ***189** M-12; mail Pigeon **z** 48755; ● 50

Linwood; RMC Place; BAY; ▲ Kawkawlin, Fraser; **189** M-10; elev. 587ft./179m.; 🅿; ★ **SAG-**; **z** 48634; ● 500

Linwood; RMC Place; WAYNE; ***189** R-12; ★ **DET**; mail Detroit **z** 48206; pop. incl. with Detroit (Inc. Place)

Linwood Beach; RMC Place; BAY; ▲ Kawkawlin; ***189** M-10; ★ **SAG-**; mail Linwood **z** 48634; ● 300

Lisbon; RMC Place; KENT, OTTAWA; ▲ Chester, Sparta; ***189** O-6; ★ **GDR**; mail Conklin **z** 49403; rural

Liske; RMC Place; PRESQUE ISLE; ▲ Pulawski; ***188** H-11; elev. 747ft./228m.; mail Hawks **z** 49743; rural

Litchfield; Inc. Place; HILLSDALE; **189** S-8; 🅿; **z** 49252; Ⓟ 1,317; Ⓒ 1,458

Litchfield; MCD-Township; HILLSDALE; ***189** S-8; 🅿; **z** 49252; does not include the City of Litchfield; Ⓟ 957; Ⓒ 969

Littlefield; MCD-Township; EMMET; ***188** G-8; mail Alanson **z** 49706; Ⓟ 2,310; Ⓒ 2,783

Little Lake; RMC Place; MARQUETTE; ▲ Forsyth; **188** D-2; elev. 1,128ft./344m.; 🅿; **z** 49833; ● 800

Little Point Sable; RMC Place; OCEANA; ▲ Benona; ***189** N-4; mail Shelby **z** 49455; summer pop. 200

Little River Reservation; Indian Reservation; MANISTEE; Ⓒ 2

Little Traverse; MCD-Township; EMMET; ***188** G-8; mail Harbor Springs **z** 49740; Ⓟ 1,805; Ⓒ 2,426

Little Traverse Bay Reservation; Indian Reservation; EMMET; Ⓒ 0

Livernois; RMC Place; WAYNE; ***189** R-12; ★ **DET**; mail Detroit **z** 48210; pop. incl. with Detroit (Inc. Place)

Livingston; MCD-Township; OTSEGO; ***188** I-8; mail Gaylord **z** 49735; Ⓟ 1,755; Ⓒ 2,339

LIVINGSTON; **189** Q-10; Ⓟ 115,645; Ⓒ 156,951; ◆ 180,017

Livonia; Inc. Place; WAYNE; **189** R-12; elev. 638ft./194m.; 🅿 🅷 🅲 3,306 ■; ★ **DET**; **z** 48150-54; Ⓟ 100,850; Ⓒ 100,545; ◆ 97,721

Loch Alpine; RMC Place; WASHTENAW; ▲ Scio; ***189** R-11; elev. 880ft./268m.; ★ **DET**; mail Ann Arbor **z** 48103; ● 1,200

Locke; MCD-Township; INGHAM; ***189** Q-10; mail Williamston **z** 48895; Ⓟ 1,521; Ⓒ 1,671

Lockport; MCD-Township; ST. JOSEPH; ***189** T-6; mail Centreville **z** 49032; Ⓟ 3,395; Ⓒ 3,814

Lockwood; RMC Place; BRANCH; ▲ Ovid; ***189** T-8; elev. 1,006ft./307m.; mail Coldwater **z** 49036; ● 30

Lodi; RMC Place; KALKASKA; ▲ Orange; ***188** J-7; elev. 1,133ft./345m.; mail Kalkaska **z** 49646; ● 60

Lodi; MCD-Township; WASHTENAW; ***189** R-11; ★ **DET**; mail Ann Arbor **z** 48103, Saline **z** 48176; Ⓟ 3,902; Ⓒ 5,710

Logan; MCD-Township; MASON; ***189** M-5; mail Branch **z** 49402; Ⓟ 203; Ⓒ 329

Logan; MCD-Township; OGEMAW; ***189** K-10; mail Prescott **z** 48756; Ⓟ 547; Ⓒ 581

London; MCD-Township; MONROE; ***189** S-11; ★ **DET**; mail Maybee **z** 48159, Milan **z** 48160; Ⓟ 2,915; Ⓒ 3,024

Long Beach; RMC Place; MENOMINEE; ▲ Menominee; ***188** H-1; elev. 584ft./178m.; mail Menominee **z** 49858; rural

Long Lake; RMC Place; CLARE; ▲ Frost; ***189** L-8; mail Harrison **z** 48625; summer pop. 1,200

Long Lake; MCD-Township; GRAND TRAVERSE; ***188** J-6; mail Traverse City **z** 49684; Ⓟ 5,977; Ⓒ 7,648

Long Lake; RMC Place; IONIA; ▲ Orleans; ***189** O-7; elev. 820ft./250m.; mail Orleans **z** 48865; ● 340

Long Lake; RMC Place; IOSCO; ▲ Plainfield; **189** K-10; elev. 918ft./280m.; 🅿; **z** 48743; ● 170

Long Lake Shores; RMC Place; OAKLAND; ▲ Bloomfield; ★ **DET**; mail West Bloomfield **z** 48323

Long Point; RMC Place; CHEBOYGAN; ▲ Mullett; ***188** G-9; elev. 622ft./190m.; mail Cheboygan **z** 49721; ● 110

Long Rapids; RMC Place; ALPENA; ▲ Long Rapids; **188** H-11; elev. 739ft./225m.; mail Lachine **z** 49753; ● 50

Long Rapids; MCD-Township; ALPENA; ***188** H-11; mail Lachine **z** 49753; Ⓟ 1,021; Ⓒ 1,019

Longrie; RMC Place; MENOMINEE; ▲ Lake; ***188** H-1; elev. 728ft./222m.; mail Stephenson **z** 49887; rural

Loomis; RMC Place; ISABELLA; ▲ Wise; **189** M-8; mail Clare **z** 48617; ● 100

Loretto; RMC Place; DICKINSON; ▲ Waucedah; **188** D-14; elev. 909ft./277m.; 🅿; **z** 49852; ● 400

Lost Lake Woods; CDP; ALCONA; ▲ Alcona; ***188** J-11; mail Spruce **z** 48762; Ⓒ 339

Loud; MCD-Township; MONTMORENCY; ***188** I-10; mail Comins **z** 48619; Ⓟ 220; Ⓒ 284

Lovells; RMC Place; CRAWFORD; ▲ Lovells; **188** J-9; elev. 1,162ft./354m.; mail Grayling **z** 49738; ● 130

Lovells; MCD-Township; CRAWFORD; ***188** J-9; mail Grayling **z** 49738; Ⓟ 420; Ⓒ 578

Lowell; Inc. Place; KENT; **189** P-7; 🅿; ★ **GDR**; **z** 49331; Ⓟ 3,983; Ⓒ 4,013

Lowell; MCD-Charter Township; KENT; ***189** P-7; 🅿; ★ **GDR**; **z** 49331; does not include the City of Lowell; Ⓟ 4,774; Ⓒ 5,219

Loxley; RMC Place; ROSCOMMON; ▲ Roscommon; ***189** K-8; elev. 1,127ft./344m.; mail Houghton Lake **z** 48629; ● 50

Lucas; RMC Place; MISSAUKEE; ▲ Richland; **189** L-7; mail Mc Bain **z** 49657; ● 150

LUCE; **188** D-6; Ⓟ 5,763; Ⓒ 7,024; ◆ 6,866

Ludington; Inc. Place; ⊡ MASON; **189** M-4; elev. 584ft./178m.; 🅿 🅷; **z** 49431; Ⓟ 8,507; Ⓒ 8,357

Lulu; RMC Place; MONROE; ▲ Ida; ***189** T-11; elev. 655ft./200m.; ★ **TOL**; mail Ida **z** 48140; ● 160

Lum; RMC Place; LAPEER; ▲ Arcadia; **189** O-12; 🅿; **z** 48412; ● 270

Luna Pier; Inc. Place; MONROE; **189** T-12; elev. 575ft./175m.; 🅿; ★ **TOL**; **z** 48157; Ⓟ 1,507; Ⓒ 1,483

Lupton; RMC Place; OGEMAW; ▲ Rose; **189** K-10; 🅿; **z** 48635; ● 250

Luther; Inc. Place; LAKE; ▲ Ellsworth, Newkirk; **189** L-6; 🅿; **z** 49656; Ⓟ 343; Ⓒ 339

Luzerne; RMC Place; OSCODA; ▲ Big Creek; **188** J-9; elev. 1,076ft./328m.; 🅿; **z** 48636; ● 610

Lyndon; MCD-Township; WASHTENAW; ***189** R-10; mail Chelsea **z** 48118; Ⓟ 2,228; Ⓒ 2,728

Lynn; MCD-Township; ST. CLAIR; ***189** O-13; 🅿; **z** 48097; Ⓟ 921; Ⓒ 1,187

Lyon; MCD-Charter Township; OAKLAND; ***189** R-11; ★ **DET**; mail Northville **z** 48167; Ⓟ 9,450; Ⓒ 11,041

Lyon; MCD-Township; ROSCOMMON; ***189** K-8; mail Roscommon **z** 48653; Ⓟ 1,037; Ⓒ 1,462

Lyon Lake; RMC Place; CALHOUN; ▲ Fredonia; ***189** S-8; elev. 949ft./289m.; mail Marshall **z** 49068; ● 190

Lyon Manor; ROSCOMMON; see Higgins Lake (RMC Place)

Lyons; Inc. Place; IONIA; ▲ Ionia, Lyons; **189** P-8; 🅿; **z** 48851; Ⓟ 824; Ⓒ 726

Lyons; MCD-Township; IONIA; ***189** P-8; 🅿; **z** 48851; includes only part of the Village of Lyons; Ⓟ 3,276; Ⓒ 3,446

M

Mabel; RMC Place; GRAND TRAVERSE; ▲ Whitewater; ***188** J-7; mail Williamsburg **z** 49690; rural

Macatawa; RMC Place; OTTAWA; ▲ Park; ***189** Q-5; 🅿; ★ **HLND**; **z** 49434; ● 200

MACKINAC; **188** E-7; Ⓟ 10,674; Ⓒ 11,943; ◆ 10,614

Mackinac Island; Inc. Place; MACKINAC; **188** F-8; elev. 600ft./183m.; 🅿; **z** 49757; Ⓟ 469; Ⓒ 523

Mackinaw; MCD-Township; CHEBOYGAN; ***188** F-8; mail Mackinaw City **z** 49701; Ⓟ 604; Ⓒ 576

Mackinaw City; Inc. Place; CHEBOYGAN, EMMET; ▲ Wawatam, Mackinaw; **188** F-8; elev. 590ft./180m.; 🅿; **z** 49701; Ⓟ 875; Ⓒ 859

Macomb; RMC Place; MACOMB; ▲ Macomb; **190** E-8; elev. 628ft./191m.; 🅿; ★ **DET**; **z** 48042, **z** 48044; ● 160

Macomb; MCD-Township; MACOMB; ***189** Q-13; 🅿; ★ **DET**; **z** 48042, **z** 48044; Ⓟ 22,714; Ⓒ 50,478; ◆ 60,504

MACOMB; **189** Q-13; Ⓟ 717,400; Ⓒ 788,149; ◆ 825,070

Macon; RMC Place; LENAWEE; ▲ Macon; **189** S-10; elev. 835ft./255m.; mail Clinton **z** 49236; ● 100

Macon; MCD-Township; LENAWEE; ***189** S-11; mail Clinton **z** 49236; Ⓟ 1,421; Ⓒ 1,448

Madison; MCD-Charter Township; LENAWEE; ***189** T-10; mail Adrian **z** 49221; Ⓟ 5,351; Ⓒ 8,200; Ⓡ 7,616

Madison Heights; Inc. Place; OAKLAND; **189** Q-12; elev. 635ft./194m.; 🅿 🅷 ■; ★ **DET**; **z** 48071; Ⓟ 32,196; Ⓒ 31,101; ◆ 28,866

Mancelona; Inc. Place; ANTRIM; ▲ Mancelona; **188** I-7; 🅿; **z** 49659; Ⓟ 1,370; Ⓒ 1,408

Mancelona; MCD-Township; ANTRIM; ***188** I-8; 🅿; **z** 49659; Ⓟ 3,173; Ⓒ 4,100

Manchester; Inc. Place; WASHTENAW; ▲ Manchester; **189** S-10; 🅿; **z** 48158; Ⓟ 1,753; Ⓒ 2,160

Manchester; MCD-Township; WASHTENAW; ***189** S-10; 🅿; **z** 48158; Ⓟ 3,492; Ⓒ 4,102

Manistee; Inc. Place; ⊡ MANISTEE; **189** L-4; 🅿 🅷; **z** 49660; Ⓟ 6,734; Ⓒ 6,586

Manistee; MCD-Township; MANISTEE; ***189** K-4; 🅿; **z** 49660; does not include City of Manistee; Ⓟ 2,952; Ⓒ 3,764

MANISTEE; **189** K-5; Ⓟ 21,265; Ⓒ 24,527; ◆ 24,366

Manistique; Inc. Place; ⊡ SCHOOLCRAFT; **188** F-4; 🅿 🅷; **z** 49854; Ⓟ 3,456; Ⓒ 3,583

Manistique; MCD-Township; SCHOOLCRAFT; ***188** E-5; 🅿; **z** 49854; does not include the City of Manistique; Ⓟ 916; Ⓒ 1,053

Manitou Beach; RMC Place; LENAWEE; ▲ Woodstock, Rollin; **189** S-9; elev. 1,074ft./327m.; 🅿; ★ **JAC**; **z** 49253; ● 1,400

Manitou Beach; RMC Place; PRESQUE ISLE; ▲ Rogers; ***188** G-10; mail Rogers City **z** 49779; summer pop. 4,500

Manitou Beach-Devils Lake; CDP-Census Area Only; LENAWEE; ***189** S-9; ★ **JAC**; mail Manitou Beach **z** 49253; Ⓟ 2,061; Ⓒ 2,080

Manlius; MCD-Township; ALLEGAN; ***189** Q-5; mail Fennville **z** 49408; Ⓟ 1,776; Ⓒ 2,634

Manning; RMC Place; CHEBOYGAN; ▲ Grant; ***188** G-9; elev. 640ft./195m.; mail Cheboygan **z** 49721; rural

Mansfield; RMC Place; IRON; ▲ Mansfield; ***188** C-13; elev. 1,380ft./421m.; mail Crystal Falls **z** 49920; ● 50

Mansfield; MCD-Township; IRON; ***188** C-13; mail Crystal Falls **z** 49920; Ⓟ 248; Ⓒ 243

Manton; Inc. Place; WEXFORD; **189** K-6; elev. 1,120ft./341m.; 🅿; **z** 49663; Ⓟ 1,161; Ⓒ 1,221

Maple; RMC Place; WAYNE; ***189** R-12; ★ **DET**; mail Dearborn **z** 48126; pop. incl. with Dearborn (Inc. Place)

Maple City; RMC Place; LEELANAU; ▲ Kasson; **188** I-5; elev. 716ft./218m.; 🅿; **z** 49664; ● 240

Maple Forest; MCD-Township; CRAWFORD; ***188** J-8; mail Grayling **z** 49738; Ⓟ 407; Ⓒ 498

Maple Grove; RMC Place; BARRY; ▲ Maple Grove; ***189** Q-7; elev. 966ft./294m.; mail Nashville **z** 49073; ● 50

Maple Grove; MCD-Township; BARRY; ***189** Q-7; mail Nashville **z** 49073; Ⓟ 1,398; Ⓒ 1,471

Maple Grove; MCD-Township; MANISTEE; ***189** K-5; mail Kaleva **z** 49645; Ⓟ 1,123; Ⓒ 1,285

Maple Grove; MCD-Township; SAGINAW; ***189** O-10; mail New Lothrop **z** 48460; Ⓟ 2,830; Ⓒ 2,640

Maple Grove Corners; RMC Place; VAN BUREN; ▲ South Haven; ***189** R-4; elev. 690ft./210m.; mail South Haven **z** 49090; rural

Maple Hill; RMC Place; MONTCALM; ▲ Pierson; **189** O-6; mail Pierson **z** 49339

Maple Lake; RMC Place; VAN BUREN; ▲ Paw Paw; ★ **KZOO**; mail Paw Paw **z** 49079; pop. incl. with Paw Paw (Inc. Place)

Maple Rapids; Inc. Place; CLINTON; ▲ Essex; **189** O-8; 🅿; **z** 48853; Ⓟ 680; Ⓒ 643

Maple Ridge; MCD-Township; ALPENA; ***188** H-11; mail Alpena **z** 49707; Ⓟ 1,514; Ⓒ 1,715

Maple Ridge; RMC Place; ARENAC; ▲ Mason, Clayton; **189** L-10; elev. 809ft./247m.; mail Twining **z** 48766; ● 30

Maple Ridge; MCD-Township; DELTA; ***188** E-2; mail Rock **z** 49880; Ⓟ 829; Ⓒ 808

Maple River; MCD-Township; EMMET; ***188** G-8; mail Brutus **z** 49716; Ⓟ 743; Ⓒ 1,232

Mapleton; RMC Place; GRAND TRAVERSE; ▲ Peninsula; **188** I-6; mail Traverse City **z** 49686; summer pop. 400; ● 100

Mapleton (Smiths Crossing); RMC Place; MIDLAND; ▲ Midland, Ingersoll; **189** N-10; ★ **SAG-**; mail Midland **z** 48640; pop. incl. with Midland (Inc. Place)

Maple Valley; MCD-Township; MONTCALM; ***189** O-7; mail Trufant **z** 49347; Ⓟ 1,824; Ⓒ 2,083

Maple Valley; RMC Place; ROSCOMMON; ▲ Richfield, Backus; ***189** K-9; elev. 1,227ft./374m.; mail Saint Helen **z** 48656; ● 50

Maple Valley; MCD-Township; SANILAC; ***189** O-13; mail Brown City **z** 48416; Ⓟ 1,022; Ⓒ 1,114

Maplewood; RMC Place; DELTA; ▲ Masonville; ***188** F-3; mail Rapid River **z** 49878; rural

Marathon; MCD-Township; LAPEER; ***189** O-12; ★ **FLN**; mail Columbiaville **z** 48421; Ⓟ 4,286; Ⓒ 4,701

Marcellus; Inc. Place; CASS; ▲ Marcellus; **189** S-6; 🅿; **z** 49067; Ⓟ 1,193; Ⓒ 1,162

Marcellus; MCD-Township; CASS; ***189** S-6; 🅿; **z** 49067; Ⓟ 2,569; Ⓒ 2,712

Marengo; RMC Place; CALHOUN; ▲ Marengo; ***189** R-8; elev. 925ft./282m.; mail Albion **z** 49224; ● 170

Marengo; MCD-Township; CALHOUN; ***189** R-8; mail Albion **z** 49224; Ⓟ 1,801; Ⓒ 2,131

Marenisco; RMC Place; GOGEBIC; ▲ Marenisco; **188** C-11; elev. 1,515ft./462m.; 🅿; **z** 49947; ● 700

Marenisco; MCD-Township; GOGEBIC; ***188** C-11; 🅿; **z** 49947; Ⓟ 959; Ⓒ 1,051

Marilla; RMC Place; MANISTEE; ▲ Marilla; ***189** K-5; elev. 934ft./285m.; mail Copemish **z** 49625; ● 30

Marilla; MCD-Township; MANISTEE; ***189** K-5; mail Copemish **z** 49625; Ⓟ 268; Ⓒ 362

Marine City; Inc. Place; ST. CLAIR; **189** Q-14; elev. 588ft./179m.; 🅿; ★ **DET**; **z** 48039; Ⓟ 4,556; Ⓒ 4,652

Marion; MCD-Township; CHARLEVOIX; ***188** H-7; mail Charlevoix **z** 49720; Ⓟ 1,130; Ⓒ 1,492

Marion; MCD-Township; LIVINGSTON; ***189** Q-10; ★ **DET**; mail Howell **z** 48843; Ⓟ 4,918; Ⓒ 6,757

Marion; Inc. Place; OSCEOLA; ▲ Marion; **189** L-7; 🅿; **z** 49665; Ⓟ 807; Ⓒ 836

Marion; MCD-Township; OSCEOLA; ***189** L-7; 🅿; **z** 49665; Ⓟ 1,445; Ⓒ 1,580

Marion; MCD-Township; SAGINAW; ***189** O-9; mail Brant **z** 48614; Ⓟ 928; Ⓒ 925

Marion; MCD-Township; SANILAC; ***189** N-13; mail Decker **z** 48426; Ⓟ 1,831; Ⓒ 1,803

Marion Springs; RMC Place; SAGINAW; ▲ Marion; ***189** O-9; elev. 648ft./198m.; mail Brant **z** 48614; ● 30

Markey; RMC Place; ROSCOMMON; ▲ Markey; ***189** K-8; elev. 1,167ft./356m.; mail Houghton Lake **z** 48629; rural

Markey; MCD-Township; ROSCOMMON; ***189** K-8; mail Houghton Lake **z** 48629; Ⓟ 1,768; Ⓒ 2,424

Marlette; Inc. Place; SANILAC; **189** O-12; 🅿 🅷; **z** 48453; Ⓟ 1,924; Ⓒ 2,104

Marlette; MCD-Township; SANILAC; ***189** O-12; 🅿; **z** 48453; Ⓟ 1,910; Ⓒ 2,051

Marne; RMC Place; OTTAWA; ▲ Wright; **189** P-5; elev. 672ft./205m.; 🅿; ★ **GDR**; **z** 49435; ● 490

Marquette; MCD-Township; MACKINAC; ***188** E-9; mail Pickford **z** 49774; Ⓟ 550; Ⓒ 659

Marquette; Inc. Place; ⊡ MARQUETTE; **188** D-2; elev. 628ft./191m.; 🅿 🅷 🅲 9,689 ■; **z** 49855; Ⓟ 21,977; Ⓒ 19,661; Ⓡ 20,714; ◆ 19,341

Marquette; MCD-Charter Township; MARQUETTE; ***188** C-1; 🅿 🅲 9,689; **z** 49855; does not include the City of Marquette; Ⓟ 2,757; Ⓒ 3,286

MARQUETTE; **188** D-1; Ⓟ 70,887; Ⓒ 64,634; ◆ 65,438

Marshall; Inc. Place; ⊡ CALHOUN; **189** R-8; elev. 916ft./279m.; 🅿 🅷; ★ **BTLCK**; **z** 49068-69; Ⓟ 6,891; Ⓒ 7,459

Marshall; MCD-Township; CALHOUN; ***189** R-8; 🅿; ★ **BTLCK**; **z** 49068-69; does not include the City of Marshall; Ⓟ 2,655; Ⓒ 2,922

Martin; Inc. Place; ALLEGAN; ▲ Martin; **189** Q-6; elev. 832ft./254m.; 🅿; **z** 49070; Ⓟ 462; Ⓒ 435

Martin; MCD-Township; ALLEGAN; ***189** Q-6; 🅿; **z** 49070; Ⓟ 2,487; Ⓒ 2,514

Martiny; MCD-Township; MECOSTA; ***189** N-7; mail Rodney **z** 49342; Ⓟ 1,348; Ⓒ 1,606

Marysville; Inc. Place; ST. CLAIR; **189** P-14; elev. 610ft./186m.; 🅿; ★ **PTHU**; **z** 48040; Ⓟ 8,515; Ⓒ 9,684

Mashek; MARQUETTE; see Arnold (RMC Place)

Mason; MCD-Township; ARENAC; ***189** L-10; mail Twining **z** 48766; Ⓟ 865; Ⓒ 994

Mason; MCD-Township; CASS; ***189** T-5; ★ **ELK**; mail Edwardsburg **z** 49112; Ⓟ 2,450; Ⓒ 2,514

Mason; RMC Place; HOUGHTON; ▲ Osceola; ***188** A-13; mail Hancock **z** 49930; ● 60

Mason; Inc. Place; ⊡ INGHAM; **189** Q-9; elev. 880ft./268m.; 🅿; ★ **LANS**; **z** 48854; Ⓟ 6,768; Ⓒ 6,714; Ⓡ 7,164

MASON; **189** L-4; Ⓟ 25,537; Ⓒ 28,274; ◆ 28,452

Masonville; RMC Place; DELTA; **188** F-3; mail Rapid River **z** 49878

Masonville; MCD-Township; DELTA; ***188** E-3; mail Rapid River **z** 49878; Ⓟ 1,709; Ⓒ 1,877

Mass City; RMC Place; ONTONAGON; ▲ Greenland; **188** B-12; 🅿; **z** 49948; ● 430

Mastodon; MCD-Township; IRON; ***188** D-13; mail Alpha **z** 49902; Ⓟ 654; Ⓒ 668

Matchwood; MCD-Township; ONTONAGON; ***188** B-11; mail Ewen **z** 49925; Ⓟ 122; Ⓒ 115

Matherton; RMC Place; CLINTON, IONIA; ▲ North Plains, Lebanon; **189** P-8; mail Hubbardston **z** 48845; ● 140

Mathias; MCD-Township; ALGER; ***188** E-3; mail Trenary **z** 49891; Ⓟ 563; Ⓒ 571

Mattawan; Inc. Place; VAN BUREN; ▲ Antwerp; **189** S-6; 🅿; ★ **KZOO**; **z** 49071; Ⓟ 2,456; Ⓒ 2,536

Matteson; RMC Place; BRANCH; ▲ Matteson; ***189** T-7; elev. 895ft./273m.; mail Bronson **z** 49028; ● 150

Matteson; MCD-Township; BRANCH; ***189** T-7; mail Bronson **z** 49028; Ⓟ 1,231; Ⓒ 1,285

Max Myers Addition; RMC Place; BERRIEN; ▲ Berrien; mail Niles **z** 49120; ● 530

Maxton; RMC Place; CHIPPEWA; ▲ Drummond; ***188** E-11; elev. 600ft./183m.; mail Drummond Island **z** 49726; summer pop. 300; ● 100

Maybee; Inc. Place; MONROE; ▲ Exeter; **189** S-11; 🅿; ★ **DET**; **z** 48159; Ⓟ 500; Ⓒ 505

Mayfield; RMC Place; GRAND TRAVERSE; ▲ Paradise; **188** J-6; elev. 842ft./257m.; 🅿; **z** 49666; ● 170

Mayfield; MCD-Township; GRAND TRAVERSE; ***189** K-6; 🅿; **z** 49666 & mail Kingsley **z** 49649; Ⓟ 967; Ⓒ 1,271

Mayfield; MCD-Township; LAPEER; ***189** O-12; ★ **DET**; mail Lapeer **z** 48446; Ⓟ 7,133; Ⓒ 7,659

Mayflower; RMC Place; HOUGHTON; ▲ Calumet; ***188** A-13; elev. 1,000ft./305m.; mail Calumet **z** 49913; rural

Mayville; Inc. Place; TUSCOLA; ▲ Fremont; **189** O-12; 🅿; **z** 48744; Ⓟ 1,010; Ⓒ 1,055

Maywood; RMC Place; DELTA; ▲ Ensign; ***188** F-3; mail Rapid River **z** 49878; ● 50

McBain; Inc. Place; MISSAUKEE; **189** L-7; elev. 1,240ft./378m.; 🅿; **z** 49657; Ⓟ 692; Ⓒ 584

McBride; Inc. Place; MONTCALM; ▲ Day; **189** O-7; elev. 964ft./294m.; mail McBrides **z** 48852; Ⓟ 236; Ⓒ 232

McCords; RMC Place; KENT; ▲ Cascade; ***189** P-6; elev. 776ft./237m.; ★ **GDR**; mail Alto **z** 49302; ● 30

McDonald; RMC Place; VAN BUREN; ▲ Bangor; ***189** R-5; mail Bangor **z** 49013; ● 30

McFarland (McFarlands); RMC Place; MARQUETTE; ▲ Turin; **188** E-2; elev. 1,089ft./332m.; mail Rock **z** 49880; ● 70

McFarlands; MARQUETTE; see McFarland (RMC Place)

McGregor; RMC Place; SANILAC; ▲ Bridgehampton; **189** N-13; elev. 773ft./236m.; mail Deckerville **z** 48427; ● 60

McGrew; RMC Place; GENESEE; ★ **FLN**; pop. incl. with Flint (Inc. Place)

McIntyre Landing; RMC Place; CRAWFORD; ▲ Grayling; ***188** J-8; mail Grayling **z** 49738; ● 140

McKinley; MCD-Township; EMMET; ***188** G-8; mail Pellston **z** 49769; Ⓟ 1,080; Ⓒ 1,269

McKinley; MCD-Township; HURON; ***189** M-12; mail Pigeon **z** 48755; Ⓟ 527; Ⓒ 503

McKinley; RMC Place; OSCODA; ▲ Mentor; **188** J-10; mail Mio **z** 48647; ● 220

McLean; RMC Place; NEWAYGO; ▲ Bridgeton; ***189** O-5; mail Fremont **z** 49412; rural

McLeods Corner; RMC Place; LUCE; ▲ Pentland; **188** D-6; elev. 743ft./226m.; mail Newberry **z** 49868; rural

McMillan; RMC Place; LUCE; ▲ Lakefield; **188** D-6; elev. 750ft./229m.; 🅿; **z** 49853; ● 200

McMillan; MCD-Township; LUCE; ***188** D-6; mail Newberry **z** 49868; Ⓟ 2,961; Ⓒ 3,947; Ⓡ 3,010

McMillan; MCD-Township; ONTONAGON; ***188** B-11; mail Ewen **z** 49925; Ⓟ 650; Ⓒ 601

McMillan Corner; RMC Place; LUCE; ▲ Lakefield; ***188** D-6; mail Mc Millan **z** 49853; rural

Meade; MCD-Township; HURON; ***189** M-12; mail Filion **z** 48432; Ⓟ 777; Ⓒ 799

Meade; RMC Place; MACOMB; ▲ Ray, Macomb; **190** E-9; ★ **DET**; mail New Haven **z** 48048; ● 160

Meade; MCD-Township; MASON; ***189** L-5; mail Free Soil **z** 49411; Ⓟ 142; Ⓒ 287; Ⓡ 158

Meadowbrook; RMC Place; OAKLAND; ★ **DET**; pop. incl. with Rochester Hills (Inc. Place)

Meads Landing; RMC Place; ROSCOMMON; ▲ Lake; ***189** K-8; mail Houghton Lake **z** 48629; ● 60

Mears; RMC Place; OCEANA; ▲ Golden; **189** N-4; 🅿; **z** 49436; ● 360

Meauwataka; RMC Place; WEXFORD; ▲ Colfax; **189** K-6; elev. 1,370ft./418m.; mail Cadillac **z** 49601

Mecosta; Inc. Place; MECOSTA; ▲ Morton; **189** N-7; 🅿; **z** 49332; Ⓟ 393; Ⓒ 440

Mecosta; MCD-Township; MECOSTA; ***189** N-6; 🅿; **z** 49332 & mail Stanwood **z** 49346; does not include the Village of Mecosta; Ⓟ 1,966; Ⓒ 2,435

MECOSTA; **189** N-7; Ⓟ 37,308; Ⓒ 40,553; ◆ 40,962

Medina; RMC Place; LENAWEE; ▲ Medina; **189** T-10; mail Hudson **z** 49247; ● 70

Medina; MCD-Township; LENAWEE; ***189** T-9; mail Hudson **z** 49247; Ⓟ 1,368; Ⓒ 1,227

Melbourne; RMC Place; SAGINAW; ▲ Zilwaukee; ***189** N-10; ★ **SAG-**; mail Saginaw **z** 48604; rural

Melita; RMC Place; ARENAC; ▲ Clayton; **189** L-10; elev. 834ft./254m.; mail Sterling **z** 48659; ● 30

Mellen; MCD-Township; MENOMINEE; ***188** H-1; mail Ingalls **z** 49848; Ⓟ 1,183; Ⓒ 1,260

Melrose; MCD-Township; CHARLEVOIX; ***188** H-8; mail Walloon Lake **z** 49796; Ⓟ 1,106; Ⓒ 1,388

Melstrand; RMC Place; ALGER; ▲ Munising; **188** D-4; elev. 935ft./285m.; mail Shingleton **z** 49884; ● 60

Melvin; Inc. Place; SANILAC; ▲ Speaker; **189** O-13; 🅿; **z** 48454; Ⓟ 148; Ⓒ 160

Melvindale; Inc. Place; WAYNE; **190** K-5; elev. 590ft./180m.; 🅿; ★ **DET**; **z** 48122; Ⓟ 11,216; Ⓒ 10,735

Memphis; Inc. Place; MACOMB, ST. CLAIR; **189** P-13; elev. 755ft./230m.; 🅿; ★ **DET**; **z** 48041; Ⓟ 1,221; Ⓒ 1,129

Mendon; Inc. Place; ST. JOSEPH; ▲ Mendon; **189** S-6; elev. 852ft./260m.; 🅿; ★ **KZOO**; **z** 49072; Ⓟ 920; Ⓒ 917

Mendon; MCD-Township; ST. JOSEPH; ***189** S-6; 🅿; ★ **KZOO**; **z** 49072; Ⓟ 2,695; Ⓒ 2,775

Menominee; Inc. Place; ⊡ MENOMINEE; **188** I-1; 🅿 ■; **z** 49858; Ⓟ 9,398; Ⓒ 9,131; ◆ 8,701

Menominee; MCD-Township; MENOMINEE; ***188** H-1; 🅿; **z** 49858; does not include the City of Menominee; Ⓟ 3,956; Ⓒ 3,939

MENOMINEE; **188** G-1; Ⓟ 24,920; Ⓒ 25,326; ◆ 23,856

Menonaqua Beach; RMC Place; EMMET; ▲ Little Traverse; ***188** G-8; mail Harbor Springs **z** 49740; summer pop. 500

Mentha; RMC Place; VAN BUREN; ▲ Pine Grove; ***189** R-6; elev. 729ft./222m.; mail Gobles **z** 49055; rural

Mentor; MCD-Township; CHEBOYGAN; ***188** H-8; mail Wolverine **z** 49799; Ⓟ 518; Ⓒ 781

Entries in **UPPERCASE** are counties.
Entries in **bold** have populations of 2,500 or more.
Names in parentheses are alternate names.

Inc. Place	Incorporated Place
RMC Place	Rand McNally Designated Place
CDP	Census Designated Place
MCD	Minor Civil Division
⊡	County Seat
▲	Minor Civil Division
elev.	Elevation
🅿	Post Office
🅷	Hospital
🅲	College
■	Principal Business Center
★	Ranally Metro Area (RMA) Abbreviation
z	Zip Code(s)
Ⓟ	Previous Census Population
Ⓡ	Revised Census Population
Ⓐ	Annexation Population
●	Rand McNally Population Estimate
Ⓒ	Final Census Population
Ⓢ	Special Census Population
◆	Estimated Population

For additional definitions see Glossary, Volume 1, and Introduction, Volume 2.

Mentor; MCD-Township; OSCODA; ***188** J-10; mail Mio z 48647; Ⓟ 1,098; Ⓒ 1,220
Meredith; RMC Place; CLARE, GLADWIN; ▲ Sherman, Franklin; ***189** L-8; elev. 1,075ft./328m.; mail Gladwin z 48624; ● 200
Meridian; MCD-Charter Township; INGHAM; ***189** Q-9; ★ **LANS**; mail East Lansing z 48823; Ⓟ 35,644; Ⓒ 39,116; Ⓡ 39,125; ◆ 41,286
Merle Beach; RMC Place; CLINTON; ▲ Olive; ***189** P-9; elev. 775ft./236m.; mail Dewitt z 48820; rural
Merrill; MCD-Township; NEWAYGO; ***189** N-5; mail Bitely z 49309; Ⓟ 451; Ⓒ 590
Merrill; Inc. Place; SAGINAW; ▲ Jonesfield; **189** N-9; elev. 671ft./205m.; 🅿; ★ **SAG-**; z 48637; Ⓟ 755; Ⓒ 782
Merriman; RMC Place; DICKINSON; ▲ Breitung; ***188** D-13; elev. 1,173ft./358m.; mail Iron Mountain z 49801; ● 30
Merritt; MCD-Township; BAY; ***189** N-11; mail Munger z 48747; Ⓟ 1,510; Ⓒ 1,510
Merritt; RMC Place; MISSAUKEE; ▲ Butterfield; **189** K-8; elev. 1,153ft./351m.; 🅿; z 49667; ● 120
Merriweather; RMC Place; ONTONAGON; ▲ Bergland; **188** B-11; 🅿; z 49947; ● 130
Merson; RMC Place; ALLEGAN; ▲ Trowbridge; ***189** R-5; mail Allegan z 49010; rural
Mesick; Inc. Place; WEXFORD; ▲ Springville; **189** K-6; 🅿; z 49668; Ⓟ 406; Ⓒ 447
Metamora; Inc. Place; LAPEER; ▲ Metamora; **189** P-12; 🅿; ★ **DET**; z 48455; Ⓟ 447; Ⓒ 507
Metamora; MCD-Township; LAPEER; ***189** P-12; 🅿; ★ **DET**; z 48455; Ⓟ 3,544; Ⓒ 4,184
Metropolitan; RMC Place; DICKINSON; ▲ Felch; ***188** D-14; mail Iron Mountain z 49801; ● 40
Metz; RMC Place; PRESQUE ISLE; ▲ Metz; **188** H-10; elev. 829ft./253m.; mail Posen z 49776; ● 90
Metz; MCD-Township; PRESQUE ISLE; ***188** H-10; mail Posen z 49776; Ⓟ 403; Ⓒ 331
Meyer; MCD-Township; MENOMINEE; ***188** F-1; mail Hermansville z 49847; Ⓟ 1,090; Ⓒ 1,036
Miami Park; RMC Place; ALLEGAN; ▲ Casco; ***189** R-4; elev. 650ft./198m.; mail South Haven z 49090; ● 100
Michelson; RMC Place; ROSCOMMON; ▲ Roscommon; ***189** K-8; elev. 1,138ft./347m.; mail Houghton Lake z 48629; ● 180
Michiana; Inc. Place; BERRIEN; ▲ New Buffalo; **189** T-3; 🅿; z 49117; Ⓟ 164; Ⓒ 200
Michigamme; CDP; MARQUETTE; ▲ Michigamme; **188** B-13; 🅿; z 49861; Ⓒ 287
Michigamme; MCD-Township; MARQUETTE; ***188** B-13; 🅿; z 49861; Ⓟ 339; Ⓒ 377
Michigan Center; CDP; JACKSON; ▲ Leoni; **189** S-9; elev. 945ft./288m.; 🅿; ★ **JAC**; z 49254; Ⓟ 4,863; Ⓒ 4,641
Michigan State University; RMC Place; INGHAM; ★ **LANS**; mail East Lansing z 48824; pop. incl. with East Lansing (Inc. Place)
Michigan State University Residence Halls; RMC Place; INGHAM; ★ **LANS**; mail East Lansing z 48825; pop. incl. with East Lansing (Inc. Place)
Middlebelt; RMC Place; WAYNE; ***189** R-12; ★ **DET**; mail Romulus z 48174; pop. incl. with Romulus (Inc. Place)
Middle Branch; MCD-Township; OSCEOLA; ***189** L-7; mail Marion z 49665; Ⓟ 701; Ⓒ 858
Middlebury; MCD-Township; SHIAWASSEE; ***189** P-9; mail Ovid z 48866; Ⓟ 1,536; Ⓒ 1,491
Middleton; RMC Place; GRATIOT; ▲ Fulton; **189** O-8; 🅿; z 48856; ● 500
Middletown; CDP-Census Area Only; SHIAWASSEE; ▲ Caledonia; ***189** P-10; elev. 740ft./226m.; mail Corunna z 48817; Ⓟ 1,010; Ⓒ 966
Middle Village; RMC Place; EMMET; ▲ Readmond, Friendship; ***188** G-7; elev. 732ft./223m.; mail Good Hart z 49737; ● 30
Middleville; Inc. Place; BARRY; ▲ Thornapple; **189** Q-6; elev. 726ft./221m.; 🅿; ★ **GDR**; z 49333; Ⓟ 1,966; Ⓒ 2,721
Midland; Inc. Place; ⊡ MIDLAND, BAY; **189** N-9; elev. 629ft./192m.; 🅿 🅷 🅲 6,418 ■; ★ **SAG-**; z 48640-42, z 48667, z 48670, z 48674, z 48686; Ⓟ 38,053; Ⓒ 41,685; ◆ 41,110
Midland; MCD-Charter Township; MIDLAND; ***189** N-9; 🅿 🅲 6,418; ★ **SAG-**; z 48640-42, z 48667, z 48670, z 48674, z 48686; does not include the City of Midland; Ⓟ 2,221; Ⓒ 2,297
MIDLAND; **189** N-9; Ⓟ 75,651; Ⓒ 82,874; ◆ 80,695
Midland Park; RMC Place; KALAMAZOO; ▲ Ross; **189** R-7; ★ **KZOO**; mail Hickory Corners z 49060; ● 450
Mikado; RMC Place; ALCONA; ▲ Mikado; **188** J-11; elev. 647ft./197m.; 🅿; z 48745; ● 150
Mikado; MCD-Township; ALCONA; ***188** J-11; 🅿; z 48745; Ⓟ 852; Ⓒ 1,043
Milan; MCD-Township; MONROE; ***189** S-11; 🅿; ★ **DET**; z 48160; does not include the City of Milan; Ⓟ 1,659; Ⓒ 1,670
Milan; Inc. Place; WASHTENAW, MONROE; **189** S-11; 🅿; ★ **DET**; z 48160; Ⓟ 4,040; Ⓒ 4,775
Milburg; BERRIEN; see Millburg (RMC Place)
Milford; Inc. Place; OAKLAND; ▲ Milford; **189** Q-11; elev. 945ft./288m.; 🅿; ★ **DET**; z 48380-81; Ⓟ 5,511; Ⓒ 6,272
Milford; MCD-Charter Township; OAKLAND; ***189** Q-11; 🅿; ★ **DET**; z 48380-81; Ⓟ 12,121; Ⓒ 15,271
Millbrook; RMC Place; MECOSTA; ▲ Millbrook; **189** N-7; 🅿; z 49310; ● 110
Millbrook; MCD-Township; MECOSTA; ***189** N-7; 🅿; z 49310; Ⓟ 1,012; Ⓒ 1,081
Millburg (Milburg); RMC Place; BERRIEN; ▲ Benton; **189** S-4; ★ **BNTH-**; mail Benton Harbor z 49022; ● 180
Millecoquins; RMC Place; MACKINAC; ▲ Garfield; ***188** E-6; mail Engadine z 49827; ● 50
Millen; MCD-Township; ALCONA; ***188** J-11; mail Barton City z 48705; Ⓟ 417; Ⓒ 463
Millersburg; Inc. Place; PRESQUE ISLE; ▲ Case; **188** H-10; 🅿; z 49759; Ⓟ 250; Ⓒ 263
Millers Corners; RMC Place; KALKASKA; ▲ Garfield; ***188** J-7; mail Fife Lake z 49633; rural
Millett; RMC Place; EATON; ▲ Delta; **189** Q-9; ★ **LANS**; mail Lansing z 48917; ● 770
Milleville Beach; RMC Place; WAYNE; ▲ Brownstown; ***189** S-12; ★ **DET**; mail Rockwood z 48173; ● 390
Millgrove; RMC Place; ALLEGAN; ▲ Valley, Allegan; ***189** Q-5; elev. 693ft./211m.; mail Allegan z 49010
Millington; Inc. Place; TUSCOLA; ▲ Millington; **189** O-11; 🅿; ★ **FLN**; z 48746; Ⓟ 1,114; Ⓒ 1,137
Millington; MCD-Township; TUSCOLA; ***189** O-11; 🅿; ★ **FLN**; z 48746; Ⓟ 4,199; Ⓒ 4,459
Mill Lake; RMC Place; VAN BUREN; ▲ Bloomingdale; ***189** R-5; elev. 800ft./244m.; mail Gobles z 49055; summer pop. 275; ● 180
Mills; RMC Place; HOUGHTON; ▲ Osceola; ***188** A-13; mail Hubbell z 49934
Mills; MCD-Township; MIDLAND; ***189** M-9; mail Rhodes z 48652; Ⓟ 1,635; Ⓒ 1,871
Mills; MCD-Township; OGEMAW; ***189** L-10; mail Prescott z 48756; Ⓟ 3,174; Ⓒ 4,005
Mills; RMC Place; SANILAC; ▲ Marion; mail Deckerville z 48427; rural
Millville; RMC Place; INGHAM; ▲ White Oak; **189** Q-10; mail Stockbridge z 49285
Milnes; RMC Place; HILLSDALE; ▲ Scipio, Moscow; ***189** S-9; elev. 1,140ft./347m.; mail Jonesville z 49250; rural
Milton; MCD-Township; ANTRIM; ***188** I-7; mail Kewadin z 49648; Ⓟ 1,468; Ⓒ 2,072
Milton; MCD-Township; CASS; ***189** T-5; ★ **S.B.**; mail Niles z 49120; Ⓟ 2,284; Ⓒ 2,646
Milwood; RMC Place; KALAMAZOO; **189** Q-2; ★ **KZOO**; pop. incl. with Kalamazoo (Inc. Place)
Minard; JACKSON; see Minards Mill (RMC Place)
Minards Mill (Minard); RMC Place; JACKSON; ▲ Tompkins; ***189** R-9; elev. 940ft./287m.; mail Parma z 49269; rural
Minden; SANILAC; see Minden City (Inc. Place)
Minden; MCD-Township; SANILAC; ***189** M-13; mail Minden City z 48456; Ⓟ 670; Ⓒ 633
Minden City (Minden); Inc. Place; SANILAC; ▲ Mentor, Minden; **189** M-13; 🅿; z 48456, z 48465; Ⓟ 233; Ⓒ 242
Mineral Hills; RMC Place; IRON; ▲ Iron River; **188** C-12; mail Iron River z 49935; former incorporated place; became part of Iron River July 1, 2000; pop. incl. with Iron River (Inc. Place); Ⓟ 200; Ⓒ 214
Minor Beach; RMC Place; SCHOOLCRAFT; ▲ Thompson; ***188** F-4; elev. 619ft./189m.; mail Manistique z 49854
Mio; CDP; ⊡ OSCODA; ▲ Mentor, Big Creek; **188** J-10; elev. 1,022ft./312m.; 🅿; z 48647; Ⓟ 1,886; summer pop. 5,000; Ⓒ 2,016
MISSAUKEE; **189** K-7; Ⓟ 12,147; Ⓒ 14,478; ◆ 14,902
Missaukee Park; RMC Place; MISSAUKEE; ▲ Lake; ***189** K-7; mail Lake City z 49651; summer pop. 200
Mitchell; MCD-Township; ALCONA; ***188** J-10; mail Curran z 48728; Ⓟ 290; Ⓒ 396
Moddersville; RMC Place; MISSAUKEE; ▲ Holland; **189** L-8; elev. 1,182ft./360m.; mail Lake z 48632; rural
Moffatt; MCD-Township; ARENAC; ***189** L-10; mail Alger z 48610; Ⓟ 780; Ⓒ 1,121
Mohawk; RMC Place; KEWEENAW; ▲ Allouez; **188** A-13; 🅿; z 49950 & mail Allouez z 49805; ● 600
Moline; RMC Place; ALLEGAN; ▲ Leighton, Dorr; **189** Q-6; 🅿; ★ **GDR**; z 49335; ● 750
Moltke; MCD-Township; PRESQUE ISLE; ***188** G-10; mail Rogers City z 49779; Ⓟ 309; Ⓒ 352
Monitor; MCD-Charter Township; BAY; ***189** N-10; ★ **SAG-**; mail Bay City z 48706; Ⓟ 9,512; Ⓒ 10,037
Monongahela Location; RMC Place; IRON; ▲ Crystal Falls; ***188** C-13; mail Crystal Falls z 49920; ● 30
Monroe; Inc. Place; ⊡ MONROE; **189** T-12; 🅿 🅷 ■; ★ **MONR**; z 48161-62 & mail Erie z 48133, Maybee z 48159; Ⓟ 22,902; Ⓒ 22,076; ◆ 21,007
Monroe; MCD-Charter Township; MONROE; ***189** T-12; 🅿; ★ **MONR**; z 48161-62; does not include the City of Monroe; Ⓟ 11,909; Ⓒ 13,491
Monroe; MCD-Township; NEWAYGO; ***189** N-6; mail White Cloud z 49349; Ⓟ 247; Ⓒ 324
MONROE; **189** S-11; Ⓟ 133,600; Ⓒ 145,945; ◆ 150,309
Monroe Center; RMC Place; GRAND TRAVERSE; ▲ Green Lake, Blair; ***188** J-6; elev. 1,040ft./317m.; mail Grawn z 49637; ● 50
Montague; Inc. Place; MUSKEGON; **189** N-4; 🅿; ★ **MUS**; z 49437; Ⓟ 2,276; Ⓒ 2,407
Montague; MCD-Township; MUSKEGON; ***189** N-4; 🅿; ★ **MUS**; z 49437; does not include the City of Montague; Ⓟ 1,429; Ⓒ 1,637
Montcalm; MCD-Township; MONTCALM; ***189** O-7; ★ **GDR**; mail Greenville z 48838; Ⓟ 2,879; Ⓒ 3,178
MONTCALM; **189** O-7; Ⓟ 53,059; Ⓒ 61,266; ◆ 62,262
Monterey; MCD-Township; ALLEGAN; ***189** Q-5; mail Allegan z 49010, Hopkins z 49328; Ⓟ 1,534; Ⓒ 2,065
Monterey Center; RMC Place; ALLEGAN; ▲ Monterey; ***189** Q-5; elev. 899ft./274m.; mail Allegan z 49010; rural
Montgomery; Inc. Place; HILLSDALE; ▲ Camden; **189** T-8; 🅿; z 49255; Ⓟ 388; Ⓒ 386
Montmorency; MCD-Township; MONTMORENCY; ***188** H-10; mail Hillman z 49746; Ⓟ 1,075; Ⓒ 1,202
MONTMORENCY; **188** I-9; Ⓟ 8,936; Ⓒ 10,315; ◆ 10,239
Montrose; Inc. Place; GENESEE; **189** O-10; 🅿; ★ **FLN**; z 48457; Ⓟ 1,811; Ⓒ 1,619
Montrose; MCD-Charter Township; GENESEE; ***189** O-10; 🅿; ★ **FLN**; z 48457; does not include the City of Montrose; Ⓟ 6,236; Ⓒ 6,336
Moore; MCD-Township; SANILAC; ***189** N-13; mail Sandusky z 48471; Ⓟ 1,238; Ⓒ 1,262
Moore Park; RMC Place; ST. JOSEPH; ▲ Park; **189** S-6; ★ **KZOO**; mail Three Rivers z 49093; ● 130
Moores Junction; RMC Place; ARENAC; ▲ Adams; ***189** L-10; elev. 750ft./229m.; mail Sterling z 48659; rural
Moorestown; RMC Place; MISSAUKEE; ▲ Norwich; **189** K-7; elev. 1,216ft./371m.; 🅿; z 49651; ● 100
Mooreville; RMC Place; WASHTENAW; ▲ York; **189** S-11; ★ **DET**; mail Milan z 48160; ● 70
Moorland; RMC Place; MUSKEGON; ▲ Moorland; ***189** O-5; elev. 689ft./210m.; mail Ravenna z 49451; ● 40
Moorland; MCD-Township; MUSKEGON; ***189** O-5; mail Ravenna z 49451; Ⓟ 1,543; Ⓒ 1,616
Moran; RMC Place; MACKINAC; ▲ Brevort; **188** F-8; 🅿; z 49760; ● 200
Moran; MCD-Township; MACKINAC; ***188** E-7; 🅿; z 49760 & mail Saint Ignace z 49781; Ⓟ 838; Ⓒ 1,080
Morenci; Inc. Place; LENAWEE; **189** T-10; elev. 780ft./238m.; 🅿 🅷; z 49256; Ⓟ 2,342; Ⓒ 2,398
Morgan; RMC Place; BARRY; ▲ Castleton; ***189** Q-7; elev. 820ft./250m.; mail Nashville z 49073; ● 50
Morgan Corners; RMC Place; CALHOUN; ▲ Pennfield; ***189** S-7; elev. 944ft./288m.; ★ **BTLCK**; mail Battle Creek z 49017; ● 620
Morley; Inc. Place; MECOSTA; ▲ Deerfield, Aetna; **189** N-6; 🅿; z 49336; Ⓟ 528; Ⓒ 495
Morrice; Inc. Place; SHIAWASSEE; ▲ Perry; **189** P-10; 🅿; ★ **LANS**; z 48857; Ⓟ 630; Ⓒ 882
Morseville; RMC Place; SAGINAW; ▲ Taymouth; **189** O-10; ★ **SAG-**; mail Birch Run z 48415; ● 30
Morton; MCD-Township; MECOSTA; ***189** N-7; mail Mecosta z 49332; Ⓟ 2,122; Ⓒ 3,597
Moscow; RMC Place; HILLSDALE; ▲ Moscow; **189** S-9; 🅿; z 49257; ● 190
Moscow; MCD-Township; HILLSDALE; ***189** S-9; 🅿; z 49257; Ⓟ 1,353; Ⓒ 1,445
Mosherville; RMC Place; HILLSDALE; ▲ Scipio; ***189** S-9; 🅿; z 49258; ● 170
Mosherville Station; RMC Place; HILLSDALE; ▲ Scipio; ***189** S-9; mail Jonesville z 49250; ● 40
Mottley; RMC Place; HOUGHTON; ▲ Laird; ***188** B-12; mail Nisula z 49952; rural
Mott Park; RMC Place; GENESEE; ***189** P-11; ★ **FLN**; mail Flint z 48504; pop. incl. with Flint (Inc. Place)
Mottville; RMC Place; ST. JOSEPH; ▲ Mottville; **189** T-6; 🅿; ★ **ELK**; z 49099; ● 200
Mottville; MCD-Township; ST. JOSEPH; ***189** T-6; ★ **ELK**; mail White Pigeon z 49099; Ⓟ 1,501; Ⓒ 1,499
Mound Spring; RMC Place; ST. JOSEPH; ▲ White Pigeon; ★ **ELK**; mail Sturgis z 49091
Mountain Beach; RMC Place; OTTAWA; ▲ Port Sheldon; ***189** P-4; elev. 650ft./198m.; ★ **HLND**; mail West Olive z 49460; ● 70
Mount Clemens; Inc. Place; ⊡ MACOMB; **189** Q-13; elev. 614ft./187m.; 🅿 🅷 ■; ★ **DET**; z 48043, z 48046; Ⓟ 18,405; Ⓒ 17,312; ◆ 16,541
Mount Elliott; RMC Place; WAYNE; ***189** S-13; ★ **DET**; mail Detroit z 48234
Mount Forest; RMC Place; BAY; ▲ Mount Forest; **189** M-10; mail Pinconning z 48650; ● 30
Mount Forest; MCD-Township; BAY; ***189** M-10; mail Pinconning z 48650; Ⓟ 1,457; Ⓒ 1,405
Mount Haley; MCD-Township; MIDLAND; ***189** N-9; mail Merrill z 48637; Ⓟ 1,656; Ⓒ 1,654
Mount Morris; Inc. Place; GENESEE; **189** O-11; elev. 794ft./242m.; 🅿; ★ **FLN**; z 48458; Ⓟ 3,292; Ⓒ 3,194
Mount Morris; MCD-Charter Township; GENESEE; ***189** O-11; 🅿; ★ **FLN**; z 48458; does not include the City of Mount Morris; Ⓟ 25,198; Ⓒ 23,725; ◆ 21,648
Mount Pleasant; RMC Place; ALLEGAN; ▲ Casco; ***189** R-4; elev. 649ft./198m.; mail South Haven z 49090; ● 50
Mount Pleasant; Inc. Place; ⊡ ISABELLA; **189** N-8; elev. 770ft./235m.; 🅿 🅷 🅲 26,710 ■; z 48804, z 48858-59; Ⓟ 23,285; Ⓒ 25,946; ◆ 28,013
Mount Vernon; RMC Place; MACOMB; ▲ Washington; ***189** Q-12; elev. 840ft./256m.; ★ **DET**; mail Rochester z 48306; ● 60
Mueller; MCD-Township; SCHOOLCRAFT; ***188** E-5; mail Gulliver z 49840; Ⓟ 206; Ⓒ 245
Muir; Inc. Place; IONIA; ▲ Lyons; **189** P-8; elev. 655ft./200m.; 🅿; z 48860; Ⓟ 667; Ⓒ 634
Mullet Lake; RMC Place; CHEBOYGAN; ▲ Inverness; **188** G-9; mail Mullett Lake z 49761; ● 250
Mullett; MCD-Township; CHEBOYGAN; ***188** G-9; mail Topinabee z 49791; Ⓟ 1,056; Ⓒ 1,284
Mulliken; Inc. Place; EATON; ▲ Roxand; **189** Q-8; 🅿; z 48861; Ⓟ 590; Ⓒ 557
Mundy; MCD-Charter Township; GENESEE; ***189** P-11; ★ **FLN**; mail Flint z 48507; Ⓟ 11,511; Ⓒ 12,191
Munger; RMC Place; BAY; ▲ Merritt; **189** N-11; elev. 596ft./182m.; 🅿; z 48747; ● 200
Munising; Inc. Place; ⊡ ALGER; **188** D-3; 🅿 🅷; z 49862; Ⓟ 2,783; Ⓒ 2,539
Munising; MCD-Township; ALGER; ***188** D-4; 🅿; z 49862 & mail Wetmore z 49895; does not include the City of Munising; Ⓟ 2,193; Ⓒ 3,125
Munith; RMC Place; JACKSON; ▲ Waterloo; **189** R-10; 🅿; ★ **JAC**; z 49259; ● 350
Munro; MCD-Township; CHEBOYGAN; ***188** G-8; mail Levering z 49755; Ⓟ 512; Ⓒ 679
Munson; RMC Place; LENAWEE; ▲ Medina; **189** T-9; mail Morenci z 49256; ● 50
Muskegon; Inc. Place; ⊡ MUSKEGON; **189** O-4; 🅿 🅷 🅲 5,021 ■; ★ **MUS**; z 49440-45; Ⓟ 40,283; Ⓒ 40,105; ◆ 38,741
Muskegon; MCD-Charter Township; MUSKEGON; ***189** O-5; 🅿 🅲 5,021; ★ **MUS**; z 49440-45; does not include the City of Muskegon; Ⓟ 15,302; Ⓒ 17,737
MUSKEGON; **189** O-5; Ⓟ 158,983; Ⓒ 170,200; ◆ 172,438
Muskegon Heights; Inc. Place; MUSKEGON; ▲ Muskegon; **189** O-4; 🅿 ■; ★ **MUS**; z 49444; Ⓟ 13,176; Ⓒ 12,049; ◆ 11,619
Mussey; MCD-Township; ST. CLAIR; ***189** P-13; 🅿; ★ **DET**; z 48014; Ⓟ 3,113; Ⓒ 3,740
Muttonville; RMC Place; MACOMB, ST. CLAIR; ▲ Casco, Lenox; ***189** P-13; ★ **DET**; mail Richmond z 48062

N

Nadeau; RMC Place; MENOMINEE; ▲ Nadeau; **188** G-1; elev. 810ft./247m.; 🅿; z 49863; ● 260
Nadeau; MCD-Township; MENOMINEE; ***188** G-1; 🅿; z 49863; Ⓟ 1,161; Ⓒ 1,160
Nagel Corner (Belknap Corner); RMC Place; PRESQUE ISLE; ▲ Belknap; ***188** H-10; elev. 824ft./251m.; mail Hawks z 49743; ● 30
Nahma; RMC Place; DELTA; ▲ Nahma; **188** F-3; 🅿; z 49864; ● 210
Nahma; MCD-Township; DELTA; ***188** F-3; 🅿; z 49864; Ⓟ 491; Ⓒ 499
Napoleon; CDP; JACKSON; ▲ Napoleon; **189** S-10; elev. 962ft./293m.; 🅿; ★ **JAC**; z 49261; Ⓟ 1,332; Ⓒ 1,254
Napoleon; MCD-Township; JACKSON; ***189** S-9; 🅿; ★ **JAC**; z 49261; Ⓟ 6,273; Ⓒ 6,962
Nashville; Inc. Place; BARRY; ▲ Maple Grove, Castleton; **189** Q-7; 🅿; z 49073; Ⓟ 1,654; Ⓒ 1,684
Nathan; RMC Place; MENOMINEE; ▲ Holmes; **188** E-14; elev. 830ft./253m.; mail Daggett z 49821; rural
National; RMC Place; IRON; ▲ Crystal Falls; ***188** C-13; mail Crystal Falls z 49920
National City; RMC Place; IOSCO; ▲ Sherman; **189** L-11; elev. 674ft./205m.; 🅿; z 48748; ● 80
National Mine; RMC Place; MARQUETTE; ▲ Tilden; **188** D-1; 🅿; z 49865; ● 490
Naubinway; RMC Place; MACKINAC; ▲ Garfield; **188** E-6; elev. 595ft./181m.; 🅿; z 49762; ● 350
Needmore; RMC Place; EATON; ▲ Roxand, Chester; **189** Q-8; elev. 902ft./275m.; mail Charlotte z 48813
Neeley; RMC Place; ALLEGAN; ▲ Orangeville; ***189** R-6; ★ **KZOO**; mail Plainwell z 49080; rural
Negaunee; Inc. Place; MARQUETTE; **188** D-1; elev. 1,375ft./419m.; 🅿; z 49866; Ⓟ 4,741; Ⓒ 4,576
Negaunee; MCD-Township; MARQUETTE; ***188** D-1; 🅿; z 49866; does not include City of Negaunee; Ⓟ 2,368; Ⓒ 2,707
Nellsville; RMC Place; ROSCOMMON; ▲ Roscommon; ***189** K-8; elev. 1,159ft./353m.; mail Houghton Lake z 48629; ● 180
Nelson; MCD-Township; KENT; ***189** O-6; ★ **GDR**; mail Sand Lake z 49343; Ⓟ 3,406; Ⓒ 4,192
Nelson; RMC Place; SAGINAW; ▲ Fremont; **189** O-9; mail Hemlock z 48626
Nessen City; RMC Place; BENZIE; ▲ Colfax; **189** K-5; elev. 856ft./261m.; mail Thompsonville z 49683; ● 40
Nester; MCD-Township; ROSCOMMON; ***189** L-9; mail Gladwin z 48624; Ⓟ 225; Ⓒ 263
Nestoria; RMC Place; BARAGA; ▲ Covington; **188** B-13; mail Michigamme z 49861
New Allouez; RMC Place; KEWEENAW; ▲ Allouez; ***188** A-13; elev. 995ft./303m.; mail Ahmeek z 49901; ● 70
Newark; MCD-Township; GRATIOT; ***189** O-8; mail Ithaca z 48847; Ⓟ 1,138; Ⓒ 1,149
Newark; RMC Place; OAKLAND; ▲ Holly; ***189** P-11; elev. 932ft./284m.; ★ **DET**; mail Holly z 48442; rural
Newaygo; Inc. Place; NEWAYGO; **189** N-6; elev. 633ft./193m.; 🅿; z 49337; Ⓟ 1,336; Ⓒ 1,670
NEWAYGO; **189** N-5; Ⓟ 38,202; Ⓒ 47,874; ◆ 48,934
New Baltimore; Inc. Place; MACOMB; **189** Q-13; 🅿 🅷; ★ **DET**; z 48047, z 48051; Ⓟ 5,798; Ⓒ 7,405
Newberg; MCD-Township; CASS; ***189** T-6; mail Jones z 49061; Ⓟ 1,627; Ⓒ 1,703
Newberry; Inc. Place; ⊡ LUCE; ▲ McMillan; **188** D-6; elev. 788ft./240m.; 🅿 🅷; z 49868; Ⓟ 1,873; Ⓒ 2,686; Ⓡ 1,749
New Boston; RMC Place; WAYNE; ▲ Huron; **190** M-3; 🅿; ★ **DET**; z 48164; ● 1,300
New Bristol Location; RMC Place; IRON; ▲ Crystal Falls; ***188** C-13; elev. 1,382ft./421m.; mail Crystal Falls z 49920; ● 50
New Buffalo; Inc. Place; BERRIEN; **189** T-3; 🅿; z 49117; Ⓟ 2,317; Ⓒ 2,200
New Buffalo; MCD-Township; BERRIEN; ***189** T-3; 🅿; z 49117; does not include the City of New Buffalo; Ⓟ 2,419; Ⓒ 2,468
New Era; Inc. Place; OCEANA; ▲ Grant, Shelby; **189** N-4; 🅿; ★ **MUS**; z 49446; Ⓟ 520; Ⓒ 461
Newfield; MCD-Township; OCEANA; ***189** N-5; mail Hesperia z 49421; Ⓟ 2,144; Ⓒ 2,483
New Greenleaf; RMC Place; SANILAC; ▲ Greenleaf; **189** M-12; elev. 756ft./230m.; mail Cass City z 48726; ● 30
New Haven; MCD-Township; GRATIOT; ***189** O-8; mail Sumner z 48889; Ⓟ 972; Ⓒ 1,016
New Haven; Inc. Place; MACOMB; ▲ Lenox; **189** Q-13; 🅿; ★ **DET**; z 48048, z 48050; Ⓟ 2,331; Ⓒ 3,071
New Haven; MCD-Township; SHIAWASSEE; ***189** P-10; mail Owosso z 48867; Ⓟ 1,286; Ⓒ 1,293
New Holland; RMC Place; OTTAWA; ▲ Holland; **189** P-5; elev. 671ft./205m.; ★ **HLND**; mail Holland z 49424; ● 130
New Hudson; RMC Place; OAKLAND; ▲ Lyon; **189** Q-11; 🅿; ★ **DET**; z 48165; ● 110
Newkirk; MCD-Township; LAKE; ***189** L-6; mail Luther z 49656; Ⓟ 586; Ⓒ 719
New Lothrop; Inc. Place; SHIAWASSEE; ▲ Hazelton; **189** O-10; 🅿; ★ **FLN**; z 48460; Ⓟ 596; Ⓒ 603
Newport; RMC Place; MONROE; ▲ Berlin; **189** S-12; 🅿; ★ **DET**; z 48166; ● 1,070
New Richmond; RMC Place; ALLEGAN; ▲ Manlius; **189** Q-5; mail Fennville z 49408; ● 180
New Salem; RMC Place; ALLEGAN; ▲ Salem; ***189** Q-6; elev. 684ft./208m.; ★ **GDR**; mail Byron Center z 49315; rural
New Swanzy; RMC Place; MARQUETTE; ▲ Forsyth; **188** E-2; mail Gwinn z 49841; ● 570
Newton; MCD-Township; CALHOUN; ***189** S-7; mail Battle Creek z 49017; Ⓟ 2,025; Ⓒ 2,493
Newton; MCD-Township; MACKINAC; ***188** E-6; mail Gould City z 49838; Ⓟ 358; Ⓒ 356
New Troy; RMC Place; BERRIEN; ▲ Weesaw; **189** T-4; 🅿; z 49119; ● 500
Nicholsville; RMC Place; CASS; ▲ Volinia; ***189** S-5; mail Marcellus z 49067; ● 40
Niles; Inc. Place; BERRIEN, CASS; **189** T-4; elev. 658ft./201m.; 🅿 🅷; ★ **S.B.**; z 49120-21; Ⓟ 12,458; Ⓒ 12,204
Niles; MCD-Township; BERRIEN; ***189** T-4; 🅿; ★ **S.B.**; z 49120-21; does not include the City of Niles; Ⓟ 12,828; Ⓒ 13,325
Nirvana; RMC Place; LAKE; ▲ Yates, Cherry Valley; **189** M-6; elev. 974ft./297m.; mail Chase z 49623; ● 50
Nisula; RMC Place; HOUGHTON; ▲ Laird; **188** B-12; elev. 1,050ft./320m.; 🅿; z 49952; ● 100
Noble; MCD-Township; BRANCH; ***189** T-7; mail Bronson z 49028; Ⓟ 479; Ⓒ 518
Noordeloos; RMC Place; OTTAWA; ▲ Holland; ***189** P-5; elev. 671ft./205m.; ★ **HLND**; mail Holland z 49424; rural
Norman; MCD-Township; MANISTEE; ***189** L-5; mail Wellston z 49689; Ⓟ 1,189; Ⓒ 1,676
North Adams; Inc. Place; HILLSDALE; ▲ Adams; **189** S-9; 🅿; z 49262; Ⓟ 512; Ⓒ 514
North Allis; MCD-Township; PRESQUE ISLE; ***188** G-9; mail Onaway z 49765; Ⓟ 502; Ⓒ 618
North Bay City; RMC Place; BAY; ▲ Bangor; ★ **SAG-**; mail Bay City z 48706
North Bell (Grange Hall); RMC Place; IONIA; ▲ Boston; ***189** P-7; elev. 850ft./259m.; ★ **GDR**; mail Clarksville z 48815; rural
North Blendon; RMC Place; OTTAWA; ▲ Blendon; ***189** P-5; ★ **HLND**; mail Hudsonville z 49426; rural
North Bradley; RMC Place; MIDLAND; ▲ Geneva; **189** M-9; mail Coleman z 48618; ● 70
North Branch; Inc. Place; LAPEER; **189** O-12; elev. 820ft./250m.; 🅿; ★ **DET**; z 48461; Ⓟ 1,023; Ⓒ 1,027
North Branch; MCD-Township; LAPEER; ***189** O-12; 🅿; ★ **DET**; z 48461; Ⓟ 3,006; Ⓒ 3,595
North Dorr; RMC Place; ALLEGAN, KENT; ▲ Byron, Dorr; ***189** Q-6; ★ **GDR**; mail Dorr z 49323; ● 100
Northeast; RMC Place; GENESEE; ★ **FLN**; mail Burton z 48509, Flint z 48506; pop. incl. with Burton (Inc. Place)
Northeast; RMC Place; KENT; ★ **GDR**; mail Grand Rapids z 49505, z 49515, z 49525; pop. incl. with Grand Rapids (Inc. Place)
Northeast; RMC Place; WAYNE; ***189** R-12; ★ **DET**; mail Livonia z 48152; pop. incl. with Livonia (Inc. Place)
North End; RMC Place; WAYNE; ***189** R-13; ★ **DET**; mail Detroit z 48202, z 48211; pop. incl. with Detroit (Inc. Place)
North Epworth (Epworth Heights); RMC Place; MASON; ▲ Pere Marquette; **189** L-4; mail Ludington z 49431; summer pop. 1,500
Northfield; MCD-Township; WASHTENAW; ***189** R-11; ★ **DET**; mail Whitmore Lake z 48189; Ⓟ 6,732; Ⓒ 8,252
North Flint; RMC Place; GENESEE; ★ **FLN**; pop. incl. with Flint (Inc. Place)
Northgate; RMC Place; KENT; ▲ Plainfield; ***189** P-6; ★ **GDR**; mail Grand Rapids z 49525
North Lake; RMC Place; LAPEER, TUSCOLA; ▲ Watertown, Marathon; **189** O-12; ★ **FLN**; mail Otter Lake z 48464; ● 380
North Lake; RMC Place; MARQUETTE; ▲ Ishpeming; **189** R-5; mail Ishpeming z 49849; ● 120
North Lake; RMC Place; VAN BUREN; ▲ Pine Grove, Almena; **188** B-14; elev. 800ft./244m.; ★ **KZOO**; mail Gobles z 49055; ● 270
North Lakeport; RMC Place; ST. CLAIR; ▲ Burtchville; **189** O-14; 🅿; ★ **PTHU**; z 48059; ● 300
Northland; RMC Place; MARQUETTE; ▲ Wells; **188** E-1; elev. 1,091ft./333m.; ● 60
North Manitou; RMC Place; LEELANAU; ▲ Leland; ***188** I-5; mail Leland z 49654; ● 170
North Morenci; RMC Place; LENAWEE; ▲ Seneca; **189** T-10; elev. 799ft./244m.; mail Morenci z 49256; ● 90
North Muskegon; Inc. Place; MUSKEGON; **189** O-4; elev. 621ft./189m.; 🅿; ★ **MUS**; z 49445; Ⓟ 3,919; Ⓒ 4,031
North Paynesville; RMC Place; ONTONAGON; ▲ Stannard; ***188** B-12; elev. 1,159ft./353m.; mail Bruce Crossing z 49912
North Plains; MCD-Township; IONIA; ***189** P-8; mail Hubbardston z 48845; Ⓟ 1,333; Ⓒ 1,366
Northport; Inc. Place; LEELANAU; ▲ Leelanau; **188** I-6; 🅿 🅷; z 49670; Ⓟ 605; Ⓒ 648
Northport Point; RMC Place; LEELANAU; ▲ Leelanau; **188** H-6; mail Northport z 49670; summer pop. 300; rural
North Shade; MCD-Township; GRATIOT; ***189** O-8; mail Middleton z 48856; Ⓟ 758; Ⓒ 706
North Shore; RMC Place; BERRIEN; ▲ Benton; ***189** S-4; elev. 600ft./183m.; ★ **BNTH-**; mail Benton Harbor z 49022; ● 30
North Shores; RMC Place; MONROE; ▲ La Salle; ***189** T-12; ★ **MONR**; mail La Salle z 48145; ● 300
Northside; RMC Place; GENESEE; ***189** P-11; ★ **FLN**; mail Flint z 48505; pop. incl. with Flint (Inc. Place)
North Star; RMC Place; GRATIOT; ▲ North Star; **189** O-9; 🅿; z 48862; ● 300
North Star; MCD-Township; GRATIOT; ***189** O-9; 🅿; z 48862; Ⓟ 1,055; Ⓒ 996
North Street; RMC Place; ST. CLAIR; ▲ Clyde; **189** O-14; elev. 642ft./196m.; 🅿; ★ **PTHU**; z 48049; ● 80
Northview; CDP-Census Area Only; KENT; ▲ Plainfield; ***189** P-6; ★ **GDR**; mail Grand Rapids z 49525; Ⓟ 13,712; Ⓒ 14,730
Northville; RMC Place; KENT; ▲ Plainfield; 1 mi. E of Plainfield Heights; ★ **GDR**; mail Grand Rapids z 49525
Northville; Inc. Place; WAYNE, OAKLAND; **189** R-11; elev. 829ft./253m.; 🅿 🅷; ★ **DET**; z 48167-68; Ⓟ 6,226; Ⓒ 6,459
Northville (Northville Township); MCD-Charter Township; WAYNE; ***189** R-11; 🅿; ★ **DET**; z 48167-68; does not include the City of Northville; Ⓟ 17,313; Ⓒ 21,036; ◆ 20,920
Northville Commons; RMC Place; WAYNE; ▲ Northville; ***189** R-12; ★ **DET**; mail Northville z 48167; ● 2,900
Northville Township; WAYNE; see Northville (MCD-Charter Township)
Northwest; RMC Place; KENT; ★ **GDR**; mail Flint z 48504, z 48531-32, Grand Rapids z 49504; pop. incl. with Grand Rapids (Inc. Place)
Northwestern; RMC Place; WAYNE; ***189** R-12; ★ **DET**; mail Detroit z 48204; pop. incl. with Detroit (Inc. Place)
North Wheeler; RMC Place; GRATIOT, MIDLAND; ▲ Porter, Wheeler; ***189** N-9; mail Wheeler z 48662
Northwood; RMC Place; KALAMAZOO; ▲ Kalamazoo, Cooper; ***189** R-6; ★ **KZOO**; mail Kalamazoo z 49004; ● 1,100
Norton; RMC Place; WAYNE; ***189** R-12; ★ **DET**; pop. incl. with Livonia (Inc. Place)
Norton Shores; Inc. Place; MUSKEGON; **189** O-4; elev. 612ft./187m.; 🅿; ★ **MUS**; z 49441, z 49444; Ⓟ 21,755; Ⓒ 22,527; ◆ 23,178
Norvell; RMC Place; JACKSON; ▲ Norvell; ***189** S-10; 🅿; ★ **JAC**; z 49263; ● 280
Norvell; MCD-Township; JACKSON; ***189** S-10; 🅿; ★ **JAC**; z 49263; Ⓟ 2,657; Ⓒ 2,922
Norwalk; RMC Place; MANISTEE; ▲ Brown; **189** K-5; elev. 724ft./221m.; mail Manistee z 49660
Norway; Inc. Place; DICKINSON; **188** D-14; 🅿; z 49870; Ⓟ 2,910; Ⓒ 2,959
Norway; MCD-Township; DICKINSON; ***188** D-14; 🅿; z 49870 & mail Vulcan z 49892; does not include the City of Norway; Ⓟ 1,325; Ⓒ 1,639
Norwich; MCD-Township; MISSAUKEE; ***189** K-8; mail Lake City z 49651; Ⓟ 505; Ⓒ 646
Norwich; MCD-Township; NEWAYGO; ***189** M-6; mail Big Rapids z 49307; Ⓟ 499; Ⓒ 557
Norwood; RMC Place; CHARLEVOIX; ▲ Norwood; **188** H-6; mail Charlevoix z 49720; ● 100
Norwood; MCD-Township; CHARLEVOIX; ***188** H-7; mail Charlevoix z 49720; Ⓟ 516; Ⓒ 714
Nottawa; MCD-Township; ISABELLA; ***189** N-8; mail Mount Pleasant z 48858; Ⓟ 1,968; Ⓒ 2,278
Nottawa; RMC Place; ST. JOSEPH; ▲ Nottawa; **189** T-6; elev. 841ft./256m.; 🅿; z 49075; ● 270
Nottawa; MCD-Township; ST. JOSEPH; ***189** T-6; 🅿; z 49075; Ⓟ 3,637; Ⓒ 3,999
Novesta; MCD-Township; TUSCOLA; ***189** N-12; mail Deford z 48729; Ⓟ 1,464; Ⓒ 1,606
Novi; Inc. Place; OAKLAND; **189** R-11; elev. 909ft./277m.; 🅿 ■; ★ **DET**; z 48374-77; Ⓟ 32,998; Ⓒ 47,386; ◆ 49,909
Novi; MCD-Township; OAKLAND; ***189** R-11; 🅿; ★ **DET**; z 48374-77; does not include the City of Novi; Ⓟ 150; Ⓒ 193
Nunda; MCD-Township; CHEBOYGAN; ***188** H-9; mail Wolverine z 49799; Ⓟ 725; Ⓒ 925
Nunica; RMC Place; OTTAWA; ▲ Crockery; **189** P-5; 🅿; z 49448; ● 360

O

Oak; RMC Place; WAYNE; ***189** R-12; ★ **DET**; pop. incl. with Detroit (Inc. Place)
Oakfield; MCD-Township; KENT; ***189** O-7; ★ **GDR**; mail Greenville z 48838; Ⓟ 3,842; Ⓒ 5,058
Oak Grove; RMC Place; LIVINGSTON; ▲ Cohoctah; **189** Q-10; 🅿; z 48863; ● 150
Oak Grove; RMC Place; OTSEGO; ▲ Bagley; ***188** I-8; elev. 1,284ft./391m.; mail Gaylord z 49735; ● 170
Oak Grove; RMC Place; ROSCOMMON; ▲ Gerrish; mail Roscommon z 48653; summer pop. 150
Oak Hill; RMC Place; MANISTEE; ▲ Filer; **189** L-4; mail Manistee z 49660; ● 920
Oakhurst; RMC Place; TUSCOLA; ▲ Wisner; **189** N-11; mail Akron z 48701; ● 50
Oakland; RMC Place; ALLEGAN; ▲ Overisel; ***189** Q-5; elev. 699ft./213m.; mail Hamilton z 49419; rural
Oakland (Oakland Township); MCD-Charter Township; OAKLAND; ***189** Q-12; 🅿; ★ **DET**; z 48306, z 48363; Ⓟ 8,227; Ⓒ 13,071
OAKLAND; **189** P-12; Ⓟ 1,083,592; Ⓒ 1,194,156; ◆ 1,186,334
Oakland Township; OAKLAND; see Oakland (MCD-Charter Township)
Oakley; Inc. Place; SAGINAW; ▲ Brady; **189** O-10; 🅿; z 48649; Ⓟ 362; Ⓒ 339
Oak Manor; RMC Place; BERRIEN; ▲ Niles; ***189** T-4; elev. 740ft./226m.; ★ **S.B.**; mail Niles z 49120; ● 1,400
Oak Park; RMC Place; CALHOUN; ▲ Bedford; ★ **BTLCK**; mail Battle Creek z 49017
Oak Park; Inc. Place; OAKLAND; **189** R-12; elev. 666ft./203m.; 🅿; ★ **DET**; z 48237; Ⓟ 30,462; Ⓒ 29,793; ◆ 28,673
Oak Shade Park; RMC Place; LENAWEE; ▲ Cambridge; ***189** S-10; ★ **JAC**; mail Brooklyn z 49230; ● 40
Oakville; RMC Place; MONROE; ▲ London; **189** S-11; ★ **DET**; mail Milan z 48160; ● 50
Oakwood; RMC Place; KALAMAZOO; ***189** R-6; ★ **KZOO**; pop. incl. with Kalamazoo (Inc. Place)
Oakwood; RMC Place; OAKLAND; ▲ Oxford, Brandon; ***189** P-12; elev. 1,099ft./335m.; ★ **DET**; mail Oxford z 48371; ● 130
Oakwood; RMC Place; ST. JOSEPH; ▲ White Pigeon; ***189** T-6; ★ **ELK**; mail White Pigeon z 49099
Oakwood; RMC Place; WAYNE; ★ **DET**; mail Melvindale z 48122; pop. incl. with Melvindale (Inc. Place)
OCEANA; **189** N-4; Ⓟ 22,454; Ⓒ 26,873; ◆ 27,165
Oceola; MCD-Township; LIVINGSTON; ***189** Q-11; ★ **DET**; mail Howell z 48843-44; Ⓟ 4,825; Ⓒ 8,362
Ocqueoc; RMC Place; PRESQUE ISLE; ▲ Ocqueoc; ***188** G-10; 🅿; z 49759; ● 90
Ocqueoc; MCD-Township; PRESQUE ISLE; ***188** G-10; 🅿; z 49759; Ⓟ 521; Ⓒ 634
Oden; RMC Place; EMMET; ▲ Littlefield; **188** G-8; elev. 613ft./187m.; 🅿; z 49764; ● 350
Odessa; MCD-Township; IONIA; ***189** P-7; mail Lake Odessa z 48849; Ⓟ 3,885; Ⓒ 4,036
Odgers Location; RMC Place; IRON; ▲ Crystal Falls; ***188** C-13; mail Crystal Falls z 49920; ● 60
Ogden; MCD-Township; LENAWEE; ***189** T-10; mail Blissfield z 49228; Ⓟ 1,146; Ⓒ 1,063
Ogden Center; RMC Place; LENAWEE; ▲ Ogden; **189** T-10; elev. 710ft./216m.; mail Blissfield z 49228; ● 90
Ogemaw; MCD-Township; OGEMAW; ***189** K-9; mail West Branch z 48661; Ⓟ 893; Ⓒ 1,118
OGEMAW; **189** K-10; Ⓟ 18,681; Ⓒ 21,645; ◆ 20,880
Ogemaw Springs; RMC Place; OGEMAW; ▲ Ogemaw; ***189** K-9; mail West Branch z 48661; ● 40
Oil City; RMC Place; MIDLAND; ▲ Greendale; **189** N-9; elev. 702ft./214m.; mail Shepherd z 48883
Okemos; CDP; INGHAM; ▲ Meridian; **189** Q-9; elev. 839ft./256m.; 🅿; ★ **LANS**; z 48805, z 48864; Ⓟ 20,216; Ⓒ 22,805; ◆ 23,178
Old Mission; RMC Place; GRAND TRAVERSE; ▲ Peninsula; **188** I-6; 🅿; z 49673; ● 300
Old Redford; RMC Place; WAYNE; ***189** R-12; ★ **DET**; mail Detroit z 48219; pop. incl. with Detroit (Inc. Place)
Olive; MCD-Township; CLINTON; ***189** P-9; mail Saint Johns z 48879; Ⓟ 2,122; Ⓒ 2,322
Olive; MCD-Township; OTTAWA; ***189** P-5; ★ **HLND**; mail West Olive z 49460; Ⓟ 2,866; Ⓒ 4,691
Olive Center; RMC Place; OTTAWA; ▲ Olive; ***189** P-5; elev. 631ft./192m.; ★ **HLND**; mail Holland z 49424; ● 120
Olive Hills; RMC Place; OTTAWA; ▲ Port Sheldon; ★ **HLND**; mail West Olive z 49460; summer pop. 60
Oliver; MCD-Township; HURON; ***189** M-12; mail Elkton z 48731; Ⓟ 1,685; Ⓒ 1,626
Oliver; MCD-Township; KALKASKA; ***188** J-7; mail Kalkaska z 49646; Ⓟ 291; Ⓒ 263
Olivet; Inc. Place; EATON; **189** R-8; elev. 930ft./283m.; 🅿 🅲 1,070; z 49076; Ⓟ 1,604; Ⓒ 1,758
Olson; RMC Place; MIDLAND; ▲ Lee; ***189** N-9; elev. 651ft./198m.; ★ **SAG-**; mail Midland z 48640; rural
Omena; RMC Place; LEELANAU; ▲ Leelanau; **188** I-6; elev. 642ft./196m.; 🅿; z 49674; summer pop. 700; ● 60
Omer; Inc. Place; ARENAC; **189** L-10; elev. 611ft./186m.; 🅿; z 48749; Ⓟ 385; Ⓒ 337
Onaway; Inc. Place; PRESQUE ISLE; **188** H-9; elev. 860ft./262m.; 🅿; z 49765; Ⓟ 1,039; Ⓒ 993
Oneida; MCD-Charter Township; EATON; ***189** Q-8; ★ **LANS**; mail Grand Ledge z 48837; Ⓟ 3,228; Ⓒ 3,703
Onekama; Inc. Place; MANISTEE; ▲ Onekama; **189** K-5; 🅿; z 49675; Ⓟ 515; Ⓒ 647
Onekama; MCD-Township; MANISTEE; ***189** K-4; 🅿; z 49675; Ⓟ 1,266; Ⓒ 1,514
Onondaga; RMC Place; INGHAM; ▲ Onondaga; **189** R-9; 🅿; z 49264; ● 250
Onondaga; MCD-Township; INGHAM; ***189** R-9; 🅿; z 49264; Ⓟ 2,444; Ⓒ 2,958
Onota; RMC Place; ALGER; ▲ Onota; ***188** D-3; elev. 900ft./274m.; mail Deerton z 49822; rural
Onota; MCD-Township; ALGER; ***188** D-3; mail Deerton z 49822; Ⓟ 244; Ⓒ 310
Onsted; Inc. Place; LENAWEE; ▲ Cambridge; **189** S-10; elev. 989ft./301m.; 🅿; ★ **JAC**; z 49265; Ⓟ 801; Ⓒ 813
Ontonagon; Inc. Place; ⊡ ONTONAGON; ▲ Ontonagon; **188** B-11; elev. 642ft./196m.; 🅿 🅷; z 49953; Ⓟ 2,040; Ⓒ 1,769
Ontonagon; MCD-Township; ONTONAGON; ***188** B-11; 🅿; z 49953; Ⓟ 3,238; Ⓒ 2,954
ONTONAGON; **188** B-11; Ⓟ 8,854; Ⓒ 7,818; ◆ 6,684
Ontonagon Reservation; Indian Reservation; ONTONAGON; Ⓒ 0
Ontwa; MCD-Township; CASS; ***189** T-5; ★ **S.B.**; mail Edwardsburg z 49112; Ⓟ 5,592; Ⓒ 5,865
Orange; MCD-Township; IONIA; ***189** P-8; mail Ionia z 48846; Ⓟ 1,047; Ⓒ 1,040
Orange; MCD-Township; KALKASKA; ***188** J-7; mail Kalkaska z 49646; Ⓟ 885; Ⓒ 1,176
Orangeville; RMC Place; BARRY; ▲ Orangeville; **189** Q-6; elev. 777ft./237m.; ★ **KZOO**; mail Plainwell z 49080; ● 250
Orangeville; MCD-Township; BARRY; ***189** Q-6; ★ **KZOO**; mail Plainwell z 49080; Ⓟ 2,880; Ⓒ 3,321
Orchard; RMC Place; PRESQUE ISLE; ▲ Posen, Pulawski; ***188** H-11; elev. 829ft./253m.; mail Posen z 49776; rural
Orchard Beach; RMC Place; CHEBOYGAN; ▲ Benton; ***188** G-9; mail Cheboygan z 49721; ● 120
Orchard Lake (Orchard Lake Village); Inc. Place; OAKLAND; **189** Q-12; elev. 950ft./290m.; 🅿; ★ **DET**; z 48323-24; Ⓟ 2,286; Ⓒ 2,215
Orchard Lake Village; OAKLAND; see Orchard Lake (Inc. Place)
Orchard Park; RMC Place; CALHOUN; ***189** R-7; ★ **BTLCK**; mail Battle Creek z 49017; pop. incl. with Battle Creek (Inc. Place)
Orchard Point; RMC Place; PRESQUE ISLE; ▲ Presque Isle; ***188** H-11; elev. 661ft./201m.; mail Alpena z 49707; rural
Oregon; MCD-Township; LAPEER; ***189** O-12; ★ **FLN**; mail Lapeer z 48446; Ⓟ 5,913; Ⓒ 6,166
Orient; MCD-Township; OSCEOLA; ***189** M-7; mail Sears z 49679; Ⓟ 692; Ⓒ 803
Orion; MCD-Charter Township; OAKLAND; ***189** Q-12; 🅿; ★ **DET**; z 48359-60, z 48362 & mail Lake Orion z 48361; Ⓟ 24,076; Ⓒ 33,463; ◆ 34,473
Orleans; RMC Place; IONIA; ▲ Orleans; **189** P-7; 🅿; z 48865; ● 230
Orleans; MCD-Township; IONIA; ***189** P-7; 🅿; z 48865; Ⓟ 2,548; Ⓒ 2,736
Oronoko; MCD-Charter Township; BERRIEN; ***189** T-4; 🅲 3,195; mail Berrien Springs z 49103; Ⓟ 9,819; Ⓒ 9,843
Ortonville; Inc. Place; OAKLAND; ▲ Brandon; **189** P-11; elev. 941ft./287m.; 🅿; ★ **DET**; z 48462; Ⓟ 1,252; Ⓒ 1,535
Osceola; RMC Place; HOUGHTON; ▲ Osceola; ***188** A-13; mail Calumet z 49913; ● 130
Osceola; MCD-Township; HOUGHTON; ***188** A-13; mail Calumet z 49913; Ⓟ 1,878; Ⓒ 1,908
Osceola; MCD-Township; OSCEOLA; ***189** M-7; mail Evart z 49631; Ⓟ 937; Ⓒ 1,118
OSCEOLA; **189** M-7; Ⓟ 20,146; Ⓒ 23,197; ◆ 22,746
Oscoda; CDP; IOSCO; ▲ Au Sable; **189** K-12; 🅿; z 48750; Ⓟ 1,061; Ⓒ 992
Oscoda; MCD-Charter Township; IOSCO; ***189** K-11; 🅿; z 48750; Ⓟ 11,958; Ⓒ 7,248
OSCODA; **188** J-9; Ⓟ 7,842; Ⓒ 9,418; ◆ 8,795
Oshtemo; RMC Place; KALAMAZOO; ▲ Oshtemo; **189** R-6; 🅿; ★ **KZOO**; z 49077; ● 2,000
Oshtemo; MCD-Charter Township; KALAMAZOO; ***189** R-6; 🅿; ★ **KZOO**; z 49077; Ⓟ 13,401; Ⓒ 17,003; ◆ 19,617
Osier; RMC Place; DELTA; ▲ Masonville; ***188** E-3; mail Rapid River z 49878; rural
Oskar; RMC Place; HOUGHTON; ▲ Stanton; ***188** A-12; mail Houghton z 49931; ● 30
Osseo; RMC Place; HILLSDALE; ▲ Jefferson; **189** T-9; 🅿; z 49266; ● 320
Ossineke; CDP; ALPENA; ▲ Sanborn; **188** I-11; 🅿; z 49766; Ⓟ 1,091; Ⓒ 1,059
Ossineke; MCD-Township; ALPENA; ***188** I-11; 🅿; z 49766 & mail Hubbard Lake z 49747; Ⓟ 1,652; Ⓒ 1,761
Otisco; MCD-Township; IONIA; ***189** P-7; mail Belding z 48809; Ⓟ 1,863; Ⓒ 2,243
Otisville; Inc. Place; GENESEE; ▲ Forest; **189** O-11; 🅿; ★ **FLN**; z 48463; Ⓟ 724; Ⓒ 882
Otsego; Inc. Place; ALLEGAN; **189** R-6; 🅿; z 49078; Ⓟ 3,937; Ⓒ 3,933
Otsego; MCD-Township; ALLEGAN; ***189** R-6; 🅿; z 49078; does not include the City of Otsego; Ⓟ 4,780; Ⓒ 4,854
OTSEGO; **188** I-9; Ⓟ 17,957; Ⓒ 23,301; ◆ 23,829
Otsego Lake; RMC Place; OTSEGO; ▲ Otsego Lake; ***188** I-8; mail Gaylord z 49735; ● 170
Otsego Lake; MCD-Township; OTSEGO; ***188** I-8; mail Gaylord z 49735; Ⓟ 1,794; Ⓒ 2,532
OTTAWA; **189** P-5; Ⓟ 187,768; Ⓒ 238,314; ◆ 261,793
Ottawa Beach; RMC Place; OTTAWA; ▲ Park; ★ **HLND**; mail Holland z 49424; summer pop. 200
Ottawa Center; RMC Place; OTTAWA; ▲ Polkton, Crockery; ***189** P-5; elev. 638ft./194m.; mail Coopersville z 49404; rural
Ottawa Lake; RMC Place; MONROE; ▲ Whiteford; **189** T-11; 🅿; ★ **TOL**; z 49267; ● 190
Otter; RMC Place; HOUGHTON; ▲ Laird; ***188** B-12; mail Nisula z 49952; rural
Otterburn; RMC Place; GENESEE; ★ **FLN**; mail Swartz Creek z 48473; pop. incl. with Swartz Creek (Inc. Place)
Otter Lake; Inc. Place; LAPEER, GENESEE; ▲ Forest, Marathon; **189** O-11; 🅿; ★ **FLN**; z 48464; Ⓟ 474; Ⓒ 437
Otto; MCD-Township; OCEANA; ***189** N-4; mail Hesperia z 49421; Ⓟ 404; Ⓒ 662
Overisel; RMC Place; ALLEGAN; ▲ Overisel; **189** Q-5; mail Holland z 49423; ● 160
Overisel; MCD-Township; ALLEGAN; ***189** Q-5; mail Holland z 49423; Ⓟ 2,324; Ⓒ 2,594
Oviatt; RMC Place; BENZIE; ▲ Almira; ***188** J-5; elev. 872ft./266m.; mail Lake Ann z 49650; rural
Ovid; MCD-Township; BRANCH; ***189** T-8; mail Coldwater z 49036; Ⓟ 2,103; Ⓒ 2,432
Ovid; Inc. Place; CLINTON, SHIAWASSEE; ▲ Ovid, Middlebury; **189** P-9; 🅿; z 48866; Ⓟ 1,442; Ⓒ 1,514
Ovid; MCD-Township; CLINTON; ***189** P-9; 🅿; z 48866; Ⓟ 3,105; Ⓒ 3,490
Owendale; Inc. Place; HURON; ▲ Brookfield; **189** M-12; elev. 643ft./196m.; 🅿; z 48754; Ⓟ 285; Ⓒ 296
Owosso; Inc. Place; SHIAWASSEE; **189** P-10; 🅿 🅷 🅲 2,875 ■; z 48841, z 48867; Ⓟ 16,322; Ⓒ 15,713; ◆ 14,856
Owosso; MCD-Charter Township; SHIAWASSEE; ***189** P-10; 🅿 🅲 2,875; z 48841, z 48867; does not include the City of Owosso; Ⓟ 4,121; Ⓒ 4,670
Owosso Junction; RMC Place; SHIAWASSEE; ▲ Owosso; mail Owosso z 48867; pop. incl. with Owosso (Inc. Place)
Oxbow; RMC Place; BERRIEN; ▲ Sodus; ***189** S-4; elev. 645ft./197m.; ★ **BNTH-**; mail Sodus z 49126; ● 50
Oxbow (Oxbow Lake); RMC Place; OAKLAND; ▲ White Lake; ***189** Q-11; ★ **DET**
Oxbow Lake; OAKLAND; see Oxbow (RMC Place)
Oxford; Inc. Place; OAKLAND; ▲ Oxford; **189** P-12; elev. 1,057ft./322m.; 🅿; ★ **DET**; z 48370-71; Ⓟ 2,929; Ⓒ 3,540
Oxford; MCD-Charter Township; OAKLAND; ***189** P-12; 🅿; ★ **DET**; z 48370-71; Ⓟ 11,933; Ⓒ 16,025
Ozark; RMC Place; MACKINAC; ▲ Moran; ***188** E-7; mail Moran z 49760; rural

P

Paavola; RMC Place; HOUGHTON; ▲ Franklin; ***188** A-13; mail Hancock z 49930; ● 120
Painesdale; RMC Place; HOUGHTON; ▲ Adams; **188** A-12; 🅿; z 49955; ● 450
Paint Creek; RMC Place; WASHTENAW; ▲ Augusta; ***189** S-11; elev. 688ft./210m.; ★ **DET**; mail Willis z 48191, Ypsilanti z 48197; ● 30
Palestine; RMC Place; MENOMINEE; ▲ Stephenson; ***188** H-1; elev. 706ft./215m.; mail Stephenson z 49887; rural
Palisades Park; RMC Place; VAN BUREN; ▲ Covert; ***189** R-4; ★ **BNTH-**; mail Covert z 49043; summer pop. 450
Palmer; CDP; MARQUETTE; ▲ Richmond; **188** D-1; elev. 1,298ft./396m.; 🅿; z 49871; Ⓒ 449
Palms; RMC Place; SANILAC; ▲ Minden; **189** N-13; 🅿; z 48465; ● 30
Palmyra; RMC Place; LENAWEE; ▲ Palmyra; **189** T-10; 🅿; z 49268; ● 370
Palmyra; MCD-Township; LENAWEE; ***189** T-10; 🅿; z 49268; Ⓟ 2,602; Ⓒ 2,366
Palo; RMC Place; IONIA; ▲ Ronald; **189** O-8; elev. 790ft./241m.; 🅿; z 48870; ● 250
Paradise (Tahquamenon); RMC Place; CHIPPEWA; ▲ Whitefish; **188** C-7; 🅿; z 49768; ● 340
Paradise; MCD-Township; GRAND TRAVERSE; ***188** J-6; mail Kingsley z 49649; Ⓟ 2,508; Ⓒ 4,191
Parchment; Inc. Place; KALAMAZOO; **189** O-2; elev. 800ft./244m.; 🅿; ★ **KZOO**; z 49004; Ⓟ 1,958; Ⓒ 1,936
Paris; MCD-Township; HURON; ***189** M-13; mail Ruth z 48470; Ⓟ 624; Ⓒ 557
Paris; RMC Place; MECOSTA; ▲ Green; **189** M-6; 🅿; z 49338; ● 230
Parisville; RMC Place; HURON; ▲ Paris; **189** M-13; elev. 797ft./243m.; mail Ruth z 48470; ● 50
Park; MCD-Township; OTTAWA; ***189** Q-5; ★ **HLND**; mail Holland z 49423; Ⓟ 13,541; Ⓒ 17,579
Park; MCD-Township; ST. JOSEPH; ***189** S-6; ★ **KZOO**; mail Three Rivers z 49093; Ⓟ 2,769; Ⓒ 2,699
Parkdale; RMC Place; MANISTEE; ▲ Manistee; **189** K-4; mail Manistee z 49660; ● 550
Parkers Corners; RMC Place; LIVINGSTON; mail Fowlerville z 48836; ● 40
Park Grove; RMC Place; WAYNE; ***189** R-13; ★ **DET**; mail Detroit z 48205; pop. incl. with Detroit (Inc. Place)
Park Lake; RMC Place; CLINTON; ▲ Bath; **188** A-4; ★ **LANS**; mail Bath z 48808; ● 390
Park Lake; RMC Place; OSCEOLA; ▲ Marion, Highland; ***189** L-7; mail Marion z 49665; rural
Park Plaza; RMC Place; WAYNE; ***189** R-12; ★ **DET**; mail Lincoln Park z 48146; pop. incl. with Lincoln Park (Inc. Place)
Park Shore Resort; RMC Place; CASS; ▲ LaGrange; **189** T-5; mail Cassopolis z 49031; ● 290
Parkville; RMC Place; ST. JOSEPH; ▲ Park; ***189** S-6; ★ **KZOO**; mail Three Rivers z 49093; ● 140
Parma; Inc. Place; JACKSON; ▲ Sandstone, Parma; **189** R-9; elev. 992ft./302m.; 🅿; ★ **JAC**; z 49269; Ⓟ 809; Ⓒ 907
Parma; MCD-Township; JACKSON; ***189** R-8; 🅿; z 49269 & mail Albion z 49224; includes only part of the Village of Parma; Ⓟ 2,491; Ⓒ 2,696
Parnell; RMC Place; KENT; ▲ Grattan; ***189** P-7; elev. 837ft./255m.; ★ **GDR**; mail Ada z 49301; ● 170
Parshallville; RMC Place; LIVINGSTON; ▲ Tyrone, Hartland; **189** Q-11; ★ **DET**; mail Fenton z 48430; ● 80
Partello; RMC Place; CALHOUN; ▲ Lee; **189** R-8; mail Olivet z 49076
Patterson Gardens; RMC Place; MONROE; ▲ Monroe; ***189** T-12; ★ **MONR**; mail Monroe z 48161; ● 2,140
Patterson Lake; RMC Place; LIVINGSTON; ▲ Putnam; ***189** R-10; elev. 900ft./274m.; ★ **DET**; mail Pinckney z 48169; ● 220
Paulding; RMC Place; ONTONAGON; ▲ Haight; **188** C-12; elev. 1,354ft./413m.; mail Bruce Crossing z 49912; ● 100
Pavilion; MCD-Township; KALAMAZOO; ***189** S-6; ★ **KZOO**; mail Scotts z 49088; Ⓟ 5,500; Ⓒ 5,829
Paw Paw; Inc. Place; ⊡ VAN BUREN; ▲ Antwerp, Paw Paw; **189** S-5; 🅿 🅷; ★ **KZOO**; z 49079; Ⓟ 3,169; Ⓒ 3,363
Paw Paw; MCD-Township; VAN BUREN; ***189** S-5; 🅿; ★ **KZOO**; z 49079; includes part of the Village of Paw Paw; Ⓟ 6,701; Ⓒ 7,091
Paw Paw Lake; CDP; BERRIEN; ▲ Watervliet, Coloma; **189** S-4; ★ **BNTH-**; mail Coloma z 49038, Watervliet z 49098; Ⓟ 3,782; Ⓒ 3,944
Payment; RMC Place; CHIPPEWA; ▲ Sugar Island; **188** D-9; mail Sault Sainte Marie z 49783; ● 110
Paynesville; RMC Place; ONTONAGON; ▲ Stannard; **188** B-12; elev. 1,256ft./383m.; mail Bruce Crossing z 49912; ● 30
Peacock; RMC Place; LAKE; ▲ Peacock; **189** L-5; elev. 869ft./265m.; mail Irons z 49644; ● 60
Peacock; MCD-Township; LAKE; ***189** L-5; mail Irons z 49644; Ⓟ 344; Ⓒ 445
Peaine; MCD-Township; CHARLEVOIX; ***188** G-6; mail Beaver Island z 49782; Ⓟ 128; Ⓒ 244
Pearl; RMC Place; ALLEGAN; ▲ Clyde; **189** Q-5; mail Fennville z 49408; ● 60
Pearl Beach; RMC Place; BRANCH; ▲ Ovid; ***189** T-8; mail Coldwater z 49036; summer pop. 300; ● 150
Pearl Beach; CDP; ST. CLAIR; ▲ Clay; **189** Q-14; elev. 581ft./177m.; 🅿; ★ **DET**; z 48001; Ⓟ 3,394; Ⓒ 3,224
Pearl Grange; RMC Place; BERRIEN; ▲ Benton; ***189** S-4; ★ **BNTH-**; mail Benton Harbor z 49022; rural
Peck; Inc. Place; SANILAC; ▲ Elk; **189** O-13; 🅿; z 48466; Ⓟ 558; Ⓒ 599
Pelkie; RMC Place; BARAGA; ▲ Baraga; **188** B-12; elev. 672ft./205m.; 🅿; z 49958; ● 160
Pellston; Inc. Place; EMMET; ▲ Maple River, McKinley; **188** G-8; elev. 702ft./214m.; 🅿; z 49769; Ⓟ 583; Ⓒ 771
Peninsula; MCD-Township; GRAND TRAVERSE; ***188** I-6; mail Traverse City z 49686; Ⓟ 4,340; Ⓒ 5,265
Penn; RMC Place; CASS; ▲ Penn; ***189** T-5; elev. 900ft./274m.; mail Cassopolis z 49031; ● 90
Penn; MCD-Township; CASS; ***189** T-5; mail Cassopolis z 49031; Ⓟ 1,877; Ⓒ 1,902
Pennellwood; RMC Place; BERRIEN; ▲ Berrien; ***189** T-4; mail Berrien Springs z 49103; summer pop. 125
Pennfield; RMC Place; CALHOUN; ▲ Pennfield; **189** R-7; ★ **BTLCK**; mail Battle Creek z 49017; ● 100
Pennfield; MCD-Charter Township; CALHOUN; ***189** R-7; ★ **BTLCK**; mail Battle Creek z 49017; Ⓟ 8,386; Ⓒ 8,913
Penobscot; RMC Place; WAYNE; ***189** R-13; ★ **DET**; mail Detroit z 48226-28; pop. incl. with Detroit (Inc. Place)
Pentland; MCD-Township; LUCE; ***188** D-6; mail Newberry z 49868; Ⓟ 1,715; Ⓒ 1,788; Ⓡ 2,725
Pentoga; RMC Place; IRON; ▲ Stambaugh; ***188** D-13; elev. 1,402ft./427m.; mail Crystal Falls z 49920; rural
Pentwater; Inc. Place; OCEANA; ▲ Pentwater; **189** M-4; elev. 689ft./210m.; 🅿; z 49449; Ⓟ 1,050; Ⓒ 958
Pentwater; MCD-Township; OCEANA; ***189** M-4; 🅿; z 49449; Ⓟ 1,422; Ⓒ 1,513
Pequaming; RMC Place; BARAGA; ▲ L'Anse; ***188** B-13; mail Lanse z 49946; ● 30
Pere Marquette; MCD-Charter Township; MASON; ***189** M-4; mail Ludington z 49431; Ⓟ 2,065; Ⓒ 2,228
Perkins; RMC Place; DELTA; ▲ Baldwin; **188** F-2; 🅿; z 49872; ● 400
Perrinton; Inc. Place; GRATIOT; ▲ Fulton; **189** O-8; 🅿; z 48871; Ⓟ 393; Ⓒ 439
Perronville; RMC Place; MENOMINEE; ▲ Harris; **188** F-2; 🅿; z 49873; ● 60
Perry; Inc. Place; SHIAWASSEE; **189** P-10; elev. 889ft./271m.; 🅿; ★ **LANS**; z 48872; Ⓟ 2,163; Ⓒ 2,065
Perry; MCD-Township; SHIAWASSEE; ***189** Q-10; 🅿; ★ **LANS**; z 48872; does not include the City of Perry; Ⓟ 3,698; Ⓒ 4,438
Perry Acres; RMC Place; OAKLAND; ▲ Orion; ★ **DET**; mail Lake Orion z 48360; ● 320
Perry Lake Heights; RMC Place; OAKLAND; ▲ Brandon; ***189** P-12; ★ **DET**; mail Ortonville z 48462; ● 200
Peshawbestown; RMC Place; LEELANAU; ▲ Suttons Bay; **188** I-6; 🅿; z 49682; ● 90
Peters; RMC Place; ST. CLAIR; ▲ Casco; ***189** Q-14; ★ **DET**; mail Marine City z 48039; ● 50
Petersburg; Inc. Place; MONROE; **189** T-11; elev. 680ft./207m.; 🅿; ★ **TOL**; z 49270; Ⓟ 1,201; Ⓒ 1,157
Petoskey; Inc. Place; ⊡ EMMET; **188** H-7; elev. 786ft./240m.; 🅿 🅷 ■; z 49770; Ⓟ 6,056; Ⓒ 6,080; ◆ 6,057
Pettysville (Rush Lake); RMC Place; LIVINGSTON; ▲ Hamburg; ***189** R-10; elev. 875ft./267m.; ★ **DET**; mail Pinckney z 48169; ● 220
Pewabic; RMC Place; HOUGHTON; ▲ Franklin; ***188** A-13; mail Hancock z 49930
Pewamo; Inc. Place; IONIA; ▲ Lyons; **189** P-8; 🅿; z 48873; Ⓟ 520; Ⓒ 560
Phelps; RMC Place; CHARLEVOIX; ▲ Marion; ***188** H-7; mail Charlevoix z 49720; rural
Phillipsville; RMC Place; HOUGHTON; ▲ Calumet; ***188** A-13; mail Allouez z 49805; ● 30
Phoenix; RMC Place; KEWEENAW; ▲ Houghton; **188** A-13; mail Mohawk z 49950; ● 20
Phoenix; RMC Place; OAKLAND; ***189** Q-12; ★ **DET**; mail Pontiac z 48342; pop. incl. with Pontiac (Inc. Place)
Pickford; RMC Place; CHIPPEWA, MACKINAC; ▲ Marquette, Pickford; **188** E-9; elev. 616ft./188m.; 🅿; z 49774; ● 450
Pickford; MCD-Township; CHIPPEWA; ***188** E-9; 🅿; z 49774; Ⓟ 1,360; Ⓒ 1,584
Pier Cove; RMC Place; ALLEGAN; ▲ Ganges; ***189** Q-4; elev. 625ft./191m.; mail South Haven z 49090; ● 50
Pierport; RMC Place; MANISTEE; ▲ Onekama; **189** K-4; elev. 606ft./185m.; 🅿; z 49614; ● 40
Pierson; Inc. Place; MONTCALM; ▲ Pierson; **189** O-6; elev. 900ft./274m.; 🅿; z 49339; Ⓟ 207; Ⓒ 185
Pierson; MCD-Township; MONTCALM; ***189** O-6; 🅿; z 49339; Ⓟ 2,177; Ⓒ 2,866
Pigeon; Inc. Place; HURON; ▲ Winsor; **189** M-12; 🅿 🅷; z 48755; Ⓟ 1,207; Ⓒ 1,207
Pinckney; Inc. Place; LIVINGSTON; ▲ Putnam; **189** R-10; 🅿; ★ **DET**; z 48169; Ⓟ 1,603; Ⓒ 2,141
Pinconning; Inc. Place; BAY; **189** M-10; 🅿; ★ **SAG-**; z 48650; Ⓟ 1,291; Ⓒ 1,386
Pinconning; MCD-Township; BAY; ***189** M-10; 🅿; ★ **SAG-**; z 48650; does not include the City of Pinconning; Ⓟ 2,647; Ⓒ 2,608
Pine; MCD-Township; MONTCALM; ***189** O-7; mail Stanton z 48888; Ⓟ 1,392; Ⓒ 1,654
Pine Bluffs; RMC Place; ROSCOMMON; ▲ Gerrish; ***189** K-8; elev. 1,180ft./360m.; mail Roscommon z 48653; ● 70
Pine Creek; RMC Place; CALHOUN; ▲ Leroy; **189** S-7; ★ **BTLCK**; mail East Leroy z 49051
Pine Grove; RMC Place; VAN BUREN; ▲ Pine Grove; ***189** R-5; elev. 796ft./243m.; mail Gobles z 49055; ● 150
Pine Grove; MCD-Township; VAN BUREN; ***189** R-6; mail Gobles z 49055; Ⓟ 2,594; Ⓒ 2,773
Pine River; RMC Place; ARENAC; ▲ Standish; ***189** L-10; elev. 604ft./184m.; ★ **SAG-**; mail Standish z 48658; ● 30
Pine River; MCD-Township; GRATIOT; ***189** N-8; mail Alma z 48801; Ⓟ 2,064; Ⓒ 2,451
Pine Run; RMC Place; GENESEE; ▲ Vienna; **189** O-11; ★ **FLN**; mail Clio z 48420; ● 660
Pine Stump Junction; RMC Place; LUCE; ▲ McMillan; ***188** C-6; mail Newberry z 49868; ● 15
Piney Woods; RMC Place; CLARE; ▲ Hayes; ***189** L-8; mail Harrison z 48625; ● 500
Pinnebog; RMC Place; HURON; ▲ Meade, Hume; **189** M-12; mail Kinde z 48445; ● 60
Pinora; MCD-Township; LAKE; ***189** M-6; mail Reed City z 49677; Ⓟ 414; Ⓒ 643
Pioneer; MCD-Township; MISSAUKEE; ***189** K-7; mail Lake City z 49651; Ⓟ 388; Ⓒ 460
Pipestone; MCD-Township; BERRIEN; ***189** S-4; mail Eau Claire z 49111; Ⓟ 2,303; Ⓒ 2,474
Pittsburg; RMC Place; SHIAWASSEE; ▲ Bennington; **189** P-10; elev. 859ft./262m.; mail Owosso z 48867
Pittsfield; RMC Place; WASHTENAW; ▲ Pittsfield; ***189** S-11; elev. 832ft./254m.; ★ **DET**; mail Ann Arbor z 48108, Ypsilanti z 48197; rural
Pittsfield; MCD-Charter Township; WASHTENAW; ***189** S-11; ★ **DET**; mail Ann Arbor z 48104, z 48108, Ypsilanti z 48197; Ⓟ 17,668; Ⓒ 30,167; ◆ 35,880
Pittsford; RMC Place; HILLSDALE; ▲ Pittsford, Jefferson; **189** T-9; 🅿; z 49271; ● 530
Pittsford; MCD-Township; HILLSDALE; ***189** T-9; 🅿; z 49271; Ⓟ 1,595; Ⓒ 1,600
Plainfield; MCD-Township; IOSCO; ***189** K-11; mail Hale z 48739; Ⓟ 3,490; Ⓒ 4,292
Plainfield; MCD-Charter Township; KENT; ***189** P-6; ★ **GDR**; mail Comstock Park z 49321; Ⓟ 24,946; Ⓒ 30,195; ◆ 32,696
Plainfield; RMC Place; LIVINGSTON; ▲ Unadilla; **189** R-10; elev. 955ft./291m.; ★ **DET**; mail Gregory z 48137; ● 40
Plainfield Heights; RMC Place; KENT; ▲ Plainfield; ***189** P-6; ★ **GDR**; mail Grand Rapids z 49525
Plainwell; Inc. Place; ALLEGAN; ▲ Gun Plain; **189** R-6; elev. 730ft./223m.; 🅿; ★ **KZOO**; z 49080; Ⓟ 4,057; Ⓒ 3,933
Platte; MCD-Township; BENZIE; ***188** J-5; mail Honor z 49640; Ⓟ 253; Ⓒ 342
Pleasant Lake; RMC Place; HILLSDALE; ▲ Jefferson; mail Osseo z 49266; summer pop. 500
Pleasant Lake; RMC Place; JACKSON; ▲ Henrietta; ***189** R-9; 🅿; ★ **JAC**; z 49272; ● 710

Entries in **UPPERCASE** are counties.
Entries in **bold** have populations of 2,500 or more.
Names in parentheses are alternate names.
Inc. Place — Incorporated Place
RMC Place — Rand McNally Designated Place
CDP — Census Designated Place
MCD — Minor Civil Division

⊡ County Seat
▲ Minor Civil Division
elev. Elevation
🅿 Post Office
🅷 Hospital
🅲 College
■ Principal Business Center
★ Ranally Metro Area (RMA) Abbreviation
z Zip Code(s)

Ⓟ Previous Census Population
Ⓡ Revised Census Population
Ⓐ Annexation Population
● Rand McNally Population Estimate
Ⓒ Final Census Population
Ⓢ Special Census Population
◆ Estimated Population

For additional definitions see Glossary, Volume 1, and Introduction, Volume 2.

Pleasant Lake; RMC Place; WASHTENAW; ▲ Freedom; ***189** S-10; mail Manchester z 48158; ● 160
Pleasanton; MCD-Township; MANISTEE; ***189** K-5; mail Bear Lake z 49614; Ⓟ 573; Ⓒ 817
Pleasant Plains; MCD-Township; LAKE; ***189** M-5; mail Baldwin z 49304; Ⓟ 1,464; Ⓒ 1,535
Pleasant Ridge; Inc. Place; OAKLAND; **190** H-6; elev. 650ft./198m.; 🅿; ★ **DET**; z 48069; Ⓟ 2,775; Ⓒ 2,594
Pleasant Valley; RMC Place; MIDLAND; ▲ Jasper; **189** N-9; mail Saint Louis z 48880
Pleasant View; RMC Place; EMMET; ▲ Pleasantview; ***188** G-8; mail Harbor Springs z 49740; rural
Pleasantview; MCD-Township; EMMET; ***188** G-8; mail Harbor Springs z 49740; Ⓟ 375; Ⓒ 943
Plymouth; RMC Place; GOGEBIC; ▲ Wakefield; ***188** B-10; mail Wakefield z 49968; pop. incl. with Wakefield (Inc. Place)
Plymouth; Inc. Place; WAYNE; **189** R-12; 🅿; ★ **DET**; z 48170; Ⓟ 9,560; Ⓒ 9,022
Plymouth; MCD-Charter Township; WAYNE; ***189** R-11; 🅿; ★ **DET**; z 48170; does not include the City of Plymouth; Ⓟ 23,648; Ⓒ 27,798; ◆ 25,986
Plymouth Township; CDP-Census Area Only; WAYNE; ▲ Plymouth; ***189** R-11; elev. 809ft./247m.; ★ **DET**; mail Plymouth z 48170; Ⓟ 23,646; Ⓒ 27,798; ◆ 25,986
Pogy; RMC Place; MECOSTA; ▲ Grant; ***189** M-7; mail Hersey z 49639; rural
Point Au Gres; RMC Place; ARENAC; ▲ Au Gres; mail Au Gres z 48703; summer pop. 500
Pointe Aux Barques; RMC Place; HURON; ▲ Pointe Aux Barques; ***189** L-13; mail Port Austin z 48467; summer pop. 300
Pointe Aux Barques; MCD-Township; HURON; ***189** L-13; mail Port Austin z 48467; Ⓟ 15; Ⓒ 10
Pointe aux Peaux Farms; RMC Place; MONROE; ▲ Frenchtown; ★ **MONR**; mail Newport z 48166
Pointe aux Pins; RMC Place; MACKINAC; ▲ Bois Blanc; **188** F-9; elev. 608ft./185m.; 🅿; z 49775; ● 50
Point Mills; RMC Place; HOUGHTON; ▲ Torch Lake; ***188** A-13; elev. 713ft./217m.; mail Dollar Bay z 49922; ● 30
Point Nipigon; RMC Place; CHEBOYGAN; ▲ Beaugrand; ***188** F-8; elev. 625ft./191m.; mail Cheboygan z 49721; summer pop. 60
Pokagon; RMC Place; CASS; ▲ Pokagon; **189** T-5; mail Dowagiac z 49047; ● 140
Pokagon; MCD-Township; CASS; ***189** T-5; mail Dowagiac z 49047; Ⓟ 2,188; Ⓒ 2,199
Polaski; RMC Place; PRESQUE ISLE; ▲ Posen; ***188** H-11; elev. 749ft./228m.; mail Posen z 49776; rural
Polkton; MCD-Charter Township; OTTAWA; ***189** P-5; mail Coopersville z 49404; Ⓟ 2,284; Ⓒ 2,335
Pomona; RMC Place; MANISTEE; ▲ Cleon; ***189** K-5; elev. 878ft./268m.; mail Copemish z 49625
Pompei; GRATIOT; see Pompeii (RMC Place)
Pompeii (Pompei); RMC Place; GRATIOT; ▲ Washington; **189** O-9; 🅿; z 48874; ● 200
Ponchartrain Shores; RMC Place; MACKINAC; ▲ Marquette; ***188** E-8; elev. 590ft./180m.; mail Saint Ignace z 49781; ● 50
Ponshewaing; RMC Place; EMMET; ▲ Littlefield; ***188** G-8; mail Alanson z 49706; ● 290
Pontiac; Inc. Place; ⊡ OAKLAND; **189** Q-12; elev. 943ft./287m.; 🅿 🅷 ■; ★ **DET**; z 48340-43 & mail West Bloomfield z 48322-25; Ⓟ 71,166; Ⓒ 66,337; Ⓡ 67,506; ◆ 61,962
Portage; MCD-Charter Township; HOUGHTON; ***188** A-12; mail Dodgeville z 49921; Ⓟ 2,941; Ⓒ 3,156
Portage; Inc. Place; KALAMAZOO; **189** S-6; 🅿 ■; ★ **KZOO**; z 49002, z 49024, z 49081; Ⓟ 41,042; Ⓒ 44,897; ◆ 47,397
Portage; MCD-Township; MACKINAC; ***188** E-6; mail Curtis z 49820; Ⓟ 890; Ⓒ 1,055
Portage Entry; RMC Place; HOUGHTON; ▲ Chassell; ***188** A-13; mail Chassell z 49916; ● 70
Portage Lake; RMC Place; LIVINGSTON, WASHTENAW; ▲ Hamburg, Dexter, Putnam, Webster; ***189** R-10; elev. 884ft./269m.; ★ **DET**; mail Pinckney z 48169; ● 600
Port Austin; Inc. Place; HURON; ▲ Port Austin; **189** L-12; 🅿; z 48467; Ⓟ 815; Ⓒ 737
Port Austin; MCD-Township; HURON; ***189** L-13; 🅿; z 48467; Ⓟ 1,474; Ⓒ 1,591
Porter; MCD-Township; CASS; ***189** T-6; ★ **ELK**; mail Constantine z 49042; Ⓟ 3,857; Ⓒ 3,794
Porter; MCD-Township; MIDLAND; ***189** N-9; mail Breckenridge z 48615; Ⓟ 1,140; Ⓒ 1,270
Porter; MCD-Township; VAN BUREN; ***189** S-6; mail Lawton z 49065; Ⓟ 2,086; Ⓒ 2,406
Port Gypsum; RMC Place; IOSCO; mail Tawas City z 48763; pop. incl. with Tawas City (Inc. Place)
Port Hope; Inc. Place; HURON; ▲ Rubicon; **189** L-13; 🅿; z 48468; Ⓟ 313; Ⓒ 310
Port Huron; Inc. Place; ⊡ ST. CLAIR; **189** P-14; 🅿 🅷 🅲 1,640 ■; ★ **PTHU**; z 48060-61; Ⓟ 33,694; Ⓒ 32,338; ◆ 30,123
Port Huron; MCD-Charter Township; ST. CLAIR; ***189** P-14; 🅿 🅲 1,640; ★ **PTHU**; z 48060-61; does not include the City of Port Huron; Ⓟ 7,621; Ⓒ 8,615
Portland; Inc. Place; IONIA; **189** P-8; 🅿; z 48875; Ⓟ 3,889; Ⓒ 3,789
Portland; MCD-Township; IONIA; ***189** P-8; 🅿; z 48875; does not include the City of Portland; Ⓟ 2,383; Ⓒ 2,460
Port Sanilac; Inc. Place; SANILAC; ▲ Sanilac; **189** N-14; 🅿; z 48469; Ⓟ 656; Ⓒ 658
Port Sheldon; RMC Place; OTTAWA; ▲ Port Sheldon; **189** P-5; ★ **HLND**; mail West Olive z 49460; ● 180
Port Sheldon; MCD-Township; OTTAWA; ***189** P-5; ★ **HLND**; mail West Olive z 49460; Ⓟ 2,929; Ⓒ 4,503
Portsmouth; MCD-Charter Township; BAY; ***189** N-10; ★ **SAG-**; mail Bay City z 48708; Ⓟ 3,918; Ⓒ 3,619
Posen; Inc. Place; PRESQUE ISLE; ▲ Posen; **188** H-11; 🅿; z 49776; Ⓟ 263; Ⓒ 292
Posen; MCD-Township; PRESQUE ISLE; ***188** H-11; 🅿; z 49776; Ⓟ 972; Ⓒ 959
Poseyville; RMC Place; MIDLAND; ▲ Ingersoll; **189** N-9; elev. 639ft./195m.; ★ **SAG-**; mail Midland z 48640; ● 100
Potters Lake; RMC Place; LAPEER, GENESEE; ▲ Davison, Elba; ***189** P-11; elev. 836ft./255m.; ★ **DET**; mail Davison z 48423; ● 200
Potterville; Inc. Place; EATON; ▲ Benton; **189** Q-8; 🅿; ★ **LANS**; z 48876; Ⓟ 1,523; Ⓒ 2,168
Powell; MCD-Township; MARQUETTE; ***188** B-14; mail Big Bay z 49808; Ⓟ 660; Ⓒ 724
Powers; Inc. Place; MENOMINEE; ▲ Spaulding; **188** G-1; elev. 869ft./265m.; 🅿; z 49874; Ⓟ 271; Ⓒ 430
Prairie Ronde; MCD-Township; KALAMAZOO; ***189** S-6; mail Schoolcraft z 49087; Ⓟ 1,365; Ⓒ 2,086
Prairieville; RMC Place; BARRY; ▲ Orangeville, Prairieville; **189** R-6; ★ **KZOO**; mail Delton z 49046; ● 180
Prairieville; MCD-Township; BARRY; ***189** R-6; ★ **KZOO**; mail Plainwell z 49080; Ⓟ 3,409; Ⓒ 3,175
Prattville; RMC Place; HILLSDALE; ▲ Wright; **189** T-9; elev. 933ft./284m.; 🅿; z 49271; ● 200
Prescott; Inc. Place; OGEMAW; ▲ Richland; **189** L-10; 🅿; z 48756; Ⓟ 314; Ⓒ 286
Presque Isle; RMC Place; PRESQUE ISLE; ▲ Presque Isle; **188** H-11; 🅿; z 49777; summer pop. 1,000; ● 120
Presque Isle; MCD-Township; PRESQUE ISLE; ***188** H-11; 🅿; z 49777; Ⓟ 1,312; Ⓒ 1,691
PRESQUE ISLE; **188** H-10; Ⓟ 13,743; Ⓒ 14,411; ◆ 13,615
Princeton; RMC Place; MARQUETTE; ▲ Forsyth; **188** D-1; 🅿; z 49841; ● 180
Prosper; RMC Place; MISSAUKEE; ▲ Clam Union; ***189** L-7; elev. 1,198ft./365m.; mail Falmouth z 49632; rural
Prudenville; CDP; ROSCOMMON; ▲ Denton; **189** K-8; 🅿; z 48651; Ⓟ 1,513; Ⓒ 1,737
Pulaski; RMC Place; JACKSON; ▲ Pulaski; **189** S-9; elev. 1,088ft./332m.; mail Hanover z 49241; ● 130
Pulaski; MCD-Township; JACKSON; ***189** S-9; mail Hanover z 49241; Ⓟ 1,816; Ⓒ 1,931
Pulawski; MCD-Township; PRESQUE ISLE; ***188** H-11; mail Posen z 49776; Ⓟ 427; Ⓒ 372
Pullman; RMC Place; ALLEGAN; ▲ Lee; **189** R-5; elev. 651ft./198m.; 🅿; z 49450; ● 600
Putnam; MCD-Township; LIVINGSTON; ***189** R-10; ★ **DET**; mail Pinckney z 48169; Ⓟ 6,183; Ⓒ 7,500
Putney Corners; RMC Place; BENZIE; ▲ Blaine; ***189** K-5; elev. 791ft./241m.; mail Frankfort z 49635; ● 30

Q

Quanicassee; RMC Place; TUSCOLA; ▲ Wisner; **189** N-11; mail Fairgrove z 48733; ● 130
Quarry; RMC Place; HURON; ▲ Reno; ***189** M-12; elev. 619ft./189m.; mail Bay Port z 48720; ● 30
Quimby; RMC Place; BARRY; ▲ Hastings; ***189** Q-7; elev. 810ft./247m.; mail Hastings z 49058; ● 30
Quincy; Inc. Place; BRANCH; ▲ Quincy; **189** S-8; elev. 1,017ft./310m.; 🅿; z 49082; Ⓟ 1,680; Ⓒ 1,701
Quincy; MCD-Township; BRANCH; ***189** T-8; 🅿; z 49082; Ⓟ 4,003; Ⓒ 4,411
Quincy; MCD-Township; HOUGHTON; ***188** A-13; mail Hancock z 49930; Ⓟ 223; Ⓒ 251
Quinnesec; CDP; DICKINSON; ▲ Breitung; **188** D-13; 🅿; z 49876; Ⓟ 1,254; Ⓒ 1,187

R

Rabbit Bay; RMC Place; HOUGHTON; ▲ Torch Lake; ***188** A-13; mail Lake Linden z 49945; ● 30
Rabbits Back; RMC Place; MACKINAC; ▲ St. Ignace; ***188** F-8; elev. 604ft./184m.; mail Saint Ignace z 49781; ● 30
Raber; RMC Place; CHIPPEWA; ▲ Raber; ***188** E-10; elev. 594ft./181m.; mail Goetzville z 49736; summer pop. 60
Raber; MCD-Township; CHIPPEWA; ***188** E-10; mail Goetzville z 49736; Ⓟ 569; Ⓒ 670
Raco; RMC Place; CHIPPEWA; ▲ Superior; **188** D-8; 🅿; z 49715; ● 50
Rainy Beach; RMC Place; PRESQUE ISLE; ▲ North Allis, Bearinger; ***188** G-9; mail Onaway z 49765; ● 70
Raisin; MCD-Charter Township; LENAWEE; ***189** S-10; mail Adrian z 49221; Ⓟ 5,648; Ⓒ 6,507
Raisinville; MCD-Township; MONROE; ***189** S-11; ★ **MONR**; mail Monroe z 48161-62; Ⓟ 4,634; Ⓒ 4,896
Ralph; RMC Place; DICKINSON; ▲ West Branch; **188** C-14; elev. 1,138ft./347m.; 🅿; z 49877; ● 60
Rambaultown; RMC Place; HOUGHTON; ▲ Calumet; ***188** A-13; mail Calumet z 49913; ● 260
Ramona Park; RMC Place; EMMET; ▲ Little Traverse; ***188** G-8; mail Harbor Springs z 49740; summer pop. 200; ● 50
Ramsay; RMC Place; GOGEBIC; ▲ Bessemer; **188** B-10; 🅿; z 49959; ● 1,080
Randall Lake; RMC Place; BRANCH; ▲ Coldwater; ***189** S-8; mail Coldwater z 49036; ● 150
Randville; RMC Place; DICKINSON; ▲ Sagola; ***188** D-13; elev. 1,261ft./384m.; mail Iron Mountain z 49801; ● 30
Rankin; RMC Place; GENESEE; ▲ Mundy; **189** P-11; ★ **FLN**; mail Swartz Creek z 48473; ● 220
Ransom; RMC Place; HILLSDALE; ▲ Ransom; **189** T-9; mail Osseo z 49266; ● 130
Ransom; MCD-Township; HILLSDALE; ***189** T-9; mail Osseo z 49266; Ⓟ 911; Ⓒ 982
Rapid City; RMC Place; KALKASKA; ▲ Clearwater; **188** J-7; elev. 626ft./191m.; 🅿; z 49676; ● 420
Rapid River; RMC Place; DELTA; ▲ Masonville; **188** F-3; elev. 591ft./180m.; 🅿; z 49878; ● 800
Rapid River; MCD-Township; KALKASKA; ***188** J-7; mail Mancelona z 49659; Ⓟ 746; Ⓒ 1,005
Rapson; RMC Place; HURON; ▲ Bloomfield, Lincoln, Sigel, Verona; ***189** M-13; elev. 731ft./223m.; mail Bad Axe z 48413; ● 60
Rathbone; RMC Place; GRATIOT; ▲ Lafayette; ***189** O-9; mail Breckenridge z 48615
Ravenna; Inc. Place; MUSKEGON; ▲ Ravenna; **189** O-5; 🅿; z 49451; Ⓟ 919; Ⓒ 1,206
Ravenna; MCD-Township; MUSKEGON; ***189** O-5; 🅿; z 49451; Ⓟ 2,354; Ⓒ 2,856
Ravenswood; RMC Place; INGHAM; ▲ Lansing; ***189** Q-9; ★ **LANS**; mail Lansing z 48917; ● 700
Ray; RMC Place; BRANCH; ▲ California; **189** T-8; mail Fremont z 46737; total pop., including Ray, IN, 120; ● 60
Ray (Ray Twp); MCD-Township; MACOMB; ***189** Q-13; 🅿; ★ **DET**; z 48096; Ⓟ 3,230; Ⓒ 3,740
Ray Center; RMC Place; MACOMB; ▲ Ray; **190** D-9; ★ **DET**; mail Ray z 48096
Raymond Corners; RMC Place; LAKE; ▲ Ellsworth; ***189** L-6; elev. 1,220ft./372m.; mail Luther z 49656; rural
Ray Twp; MACOMB; see Ray (MCD-Township)
Reading; Inc. Place; HILLSDALE; **189** T-8; 🅿; z 49274; Ⓟ 1,127; Ⓒ 1,134
Reading; MCD-Township; HILLSDALE; ***189** T-8; 🅿; z 49274; does not include the City of Reading; Ⓟ 1,768; Ⓒ 1,781
Readmond; MCD-Township; EMMET; ***188** G-7; mail Cross Village z 49723; Ⓟ 374; Ⓒ 493
Redding; MCD-Township; CLARE; ***189** L-7; mail Harrison z 48625; Ⓟ 448; Ⓒ 526
Redford; CDP; WAYNE; ▲ Redford; **189** R-12; 🅿; ★ **DET**; z 48239-40; Ⓒ 51,622; ◆ 46,700
Redford; MCD-Charter Township; WAYNE; ***189** R-12; 🅿; ★ **DET**; z 48239-40; Ⓟ 54,387; Ⓒ 51,622; ◆ 46,700
Redman; RMC Place; HURON; ▲ Bloomfield; ***189** L-13; elev. 713ft./217m.; mail Port Hope z 48468
Red Oak; RMC Place; OSCODA; ▲ Greenwood; **188** J-9; elev. 1,168ft./356m.; mail Lewiston z 49756
Red Park; RMC Place; MANISTEE; ▲ Onekama; ***189** K-4; mail Manistee z 49660; summer pop. 250
Redridge; RMC Place; HOUGHTON; ▲ Stanton; ***188** A-12; mail Atlantic Mine z 49905; ● 40
Reed City; Inc. Place; ⊡ OSCEOLA; **189** M-6; elev. 1,039ft./317m.; 🅿 🅷; z 49677; Ⓟ 2,379; Ⓒ 2,430
Reeder; MCD-Township; MISSAUKEE; ***189** K-7; mail Lake City z 49651; Ⓟ 772; Ⓒ 1,112
Reeds Lake; RMC Place; KENT; ***189** P-6; elev. 750ft./229m.; ★ **GDR**; mail Grand Rapids z 49506; pop. incl. with East Grand Rapids (Inc. Place)
Reeman; RMC Place; NEWAYGO; ▲ Sheridan; **189** N-5; elev. 763ft./233m.; mail Fremont z 49412; ● 110
Reese; Inc. Place; TUSCOLA; ▲ Denmark; **189** N-11; elev. 628ft./191m.; 🅿; z 48757; Ⓟ 1,414; Ⓒ 1,375
Remus; RMC Place; MECOSTA; ▲ Wheatland; **189** N-7; 🅿; z 49340; ● 480
Renaissance Center; RMC Place; WAYNE; ***189** R-13; ★ **DET**; mail Detroit z 48243; pop. incl. with Detroit (Inc. Place)
Reno; MCD-Township; IOSCO; ***189** K-10; mail Whittemore z 48770; Ⓟ 572; Ⓒ 656
Republic; CDP; MARQUETTE; ▲ Republic; **188** C-13; elev. 1,520ft./463m.; 🅿; z 49879; Ⓒ 614
Republic; MCD-Township; MARQUETTE; ***188** C-13; 🅿; z 49879; Ⓟ 1,170; Ⓒ 1,106
Rescue; RMC Place; HURON; ▲ Grant; ***189** M-12; elev. 715ft./218m.; mail Gagetown z 48735
Resort; MCD-Township; EMMET; ***188** H-7; mail Petoskey z 49770; Ⓟ 2,068; Ⓒ 2,479
Rexton; RMC Place; MACKINAC; ▲ Hudson, Hendricks; **188** E-7; mail Naubinway z 49762; ● 160
Reynolds; MCD-Township; MONTCALM; ***189** N-6; mail Howard City z 49329; Ⓟ 3,028; Ⓒ 4,279
Rhodes; RMC Place; GLADWIN; ▲ Bentley; **189** M-10; 🅿; z 48652; ● 130
Rice; RMC Place; BENZIE; ▲ Benzonia; ***188** J-5; elev. 660ft./201m.; mail Benzonia z 49616; rural
Rich; MCD-Township; LAPEER; ***189** O-12; mail Mayville z 48744; Ⓟ 1,162; Ⓒ 1,412
Richfield; MCD-Township; GENESEE; ***189** O-11; ★ **FLN**; mail Davison z 48423; Ⓟ 7,271; Ⓒ 8,170
Richfield; MCD-Township; ROSCOMMON; ***189** K-9; mail Saint Helen z 48656; Ⓟ 3,413; Ⓒ 4,139
Richfield Center; RMC Place; GENESEE; ▲ Richfield; ***189** O-11; elev. 786ft./240m.; ★ **FLN**; mail Davison z 48423; ● 130
Richland; Inc. Place; KALAMAZOO; ▲ Richland; **189** R-6; 🅿; ★ **KZOO**; z 49083; Ⓟ 465; Ⓒ 593
Richland; MCD-Township; KALAMAZOO; ***189** R-6; 🅿; ★ **KZOO**; z 49083; Ⓟ 5,099; Ⓒ 6,491
Richland; MCD-Township; MISSAUKEE; ***189** L-7; mail Mc Bain z 49657; Ⓟ 1,236; Ⓒ 1,445
Richland; MCD-Township; MONTCALM; ***189** N-8; mail Vestaburg z 48891; Ⓟ 2,355; Ⓒ 2,868
Richland; MCD-Township; OGEMAW; ***189** L-10; mail Prescott z 48756; Ⓟ 856; Ⓒ 956
Richland; MCD-Township; SAGINAW; ***189** N-9; ★ **SAG-**; mail Hemlock z 48626; Ⓟ 4,177; Ⓒ 4,281
Richmond; Inc. Place; MACOMB; ▲ Richmond, Lenox; **189** P-13; 🅿; ★ **DET**; z 48062; Ⓟ 4,141; Ⓒ 4,897
Richmond; MCD-Township; MACOMB; ***189** P-13; 🅿; ★ **DET**; z 48062; does not include the City of Richmond; Ⓒ 3,416
Richmond; MCD-Township; MARQUETTE; ***188** D-1; mail Palmer z 49871; Ⓟ 1,095; Ⓒ 974
Richmond; MCD-Township; OSCEOLA; ***189** M-6; mail Reed City z 49677; Ⓟ 1,722; Ⓒ 1,695
Richmondville; RMC Place; SANILAC; ▲ Forester; **189** N-14; mail Deckerville z 48427; ● 30
Richville; RMC Place; TUSCOLA; ▲ Denmark; **189** N-11; 🅿; z 48758; ● 370
Ridgeway; RMC Place; LENAWEE; ▲ Ridgeway; **189** S-11; 🅿; z 49229; ● 200
Ridgeway; MCD-Township; LENAWEE; ***189** S-11; 🅿; z 49229; Ⓟ 1,572; Ⓒ 1,580
Riga; RMC Place; LENAWEE; ▲ Riga; **189** T-11; elev. 696ft./212m.; 🅿; z 49276; ● 400
Riga; MCD-Township; LENAWEE; ***189** T-11; 🅿; z 49276; Ⓟ 1,471; Ⓒ 1,439
Riley; RMC Place; CLINTON; ▲ Riley; ***189** P-8; elev. 750ft./229m.; mail Saint Johns z 48879; rural
Riley; MCD-Township; CLINTON; ***189** P-8; mail Saint Johns z 48879; Ⓟ 1,543; Ⓒ 1,767
Riley; MCD-Township; ST. CLAIR; ***189** P-13; 🅿; z 48041; Ⓟ 2,154; Ⓒ 3,046
Riley Center; RMC Place; ST. CLAIR; ▲ Riley; **189** P-13; elev. 780ft./238m.; mail Memphis z 48041; ● 60
Ripley; RMC Place; HOUGHTON; ▲ Franklin; ***188** A-13; mail Hancock z 49930; ● 350
Riverdale; RMC Place; GRATIOT; ▲ Seville; **189** O-8; 🅿; z 48877; ● 400
River Rouge; Inc. Place; WAYNE; **190** K-6; elev. 584ft./178m.; 🅿; ★ **DET**; z 48218; Ⓟ 11,314; Ⓒ 9,917
Riverside; RMC Place; BERRIEN; ▲ Hagar; **189** S-4; elev. 640ft./195m.; 🅿; ★ **BNTH-**; z 49084; ● 290
Riverside; MCD-Township; MISSAUKEE; ***189** L-7; mail Mc Bain z 49657; Ⓟ 853; Ⓒ 1,050
Riverton; MCD-Township; MASON; ***189** M-4; mail Scottville z 49454; Ⓟ 1,115; Ⓒ 1,335
Riverview; Inc. Place; WAYNE; **189** S-12; elev. 600ft./183m.; 🅿; ★ **DET**; z 48192-93; Ⓟ 13,894; Ⓒ 13,272
Rives; MCD-Township; JACKSON; ***189** R-9; ★ **JAC**; mail Rives Junction z 49277; Ⓟ 4,026; Ⓒ 4,725
Rives Junction; RMC Place; JACKSON; ▲ Rives; **189** R-9; 🅿; ★ **JAC**; z 49277; ● 450
Roaring Brook; RMC Place; EMMET; ▲ Little Traverse; ***188** G-8; mail Harbor Springs z 49740; summer pop. 200; ● 30
Roberts Corners; RMC Place; LUCE; ▲ Pentland; ***188** D-6; elev. 869ft./265m.; mail Newberry z 49868; ● 60
Roberts Landing; RMC Place; ST. CLAIR; ▲ Cottrellville; **189** Q-14; ★ **DET**; mail Algonac z 48001; ● 50
Robin Glen-Indiantown; CDP-Census Area Only; SAGINAW; ▲ Buena Vista; ***189** N-10; elev. 585ft./178m.; ★ **SAG-**; mail Saginaw z 48601; Ⓟ 1,395; Ⓒ 1,158
Robinson; RMC Place; OTTAWA; ▲ Robinson; ***189** P-5; elev. 628ft./191m.; mail West Olive z 49460; rural
Robinson; MCD-Township; OTTAWA; ***189** P-5; mail West Olive z 49460; Ⓟ 3,925; Ⓒ 5,588
Rochester; Inc. Place; OAKLAND; **189** Q-12; elev. 749ft./228m.; 🅿 🅷 🅲 17,737; ★ **DET**; z 48306-09; Ⓟ 7,130; Ⓒ 10,467
Rochester Hills; Inc. Place; OAKLAND; **189** Q-12; 🅿 🅲 1,049; ★ **DET**; z 48306-07, z 48309 & mail Rochester z 48308; Ⓟ 61,766; Ⓒ 68,825; ◆ 68,945
Rock; RMC Place; DELTA; ▲ Maple Ridge; **188** E-2; 🅿; z 49880; ● 440
Rockford; Inc. Place; KENT; **189** O-6; elev. 693ft./211m.; 🅿; ★ **GDR**; z 49341, z 49351; Ⓟ 3,750; Ⓒ 4,626
Rockland; RMC Place; ONTONAGON; ▲ Rockland; **188** B-12; elev. 1,180ft./360m.; 🅿; z 49960; ● 270
Rockland; MCD-Township; ONTONAGON; ***188** B-11; 🅿; z 49960; Ⓟ 371; Ⓒ 324
Rock River; MCD-Township; ALGER; ***188** D-3; mail Eben Junction z 49825; Ⓟ 1,279; Ⓒ 1,213
Rockwood; Inc. Place; WAYNE; **189** S-12; elev. 585ft./178m.; 🅿; ★ **DET**; z 48173; Ⓟ 3,141; Ⓒ 3,442
Rodney; RMC Place; MECOSTA; ▲ Colfax; **189** N-7; elev. 1,081ft./329m.; 🅿; z 49342; ● 160
Rogers; MCD-Township; PRESQUE ISLE; ***188** G-10; mail Rogers City z 49779; Ⓟ 857; Ⓒ 949
Rogers City; Inc. Place; ⊡ PRESQUE ISLE; ▲ Rogers; **188** G-10; elev. 605ft./184m.; 🅿 🅷; z 49779; Ⓟ 3,642; Ⓒ 3,322
Rolland; MCD-Township; ISABELLA; ***189** N-7; mail Blanchard z 49310; Ⓟ 1,138; Ⓒ 1,210
Rolland Center; RMC Place; ISABELLA; ▲ Rolland; ***189** N-8; elev. 931ft./284m.; mail Blanchard z 49310; rural
Rollin; RMC Place; LENAWEE; ▲ Rollin; **189** T-9; elev. 983ft./300m.; 🅿; z 49247; ● 110
Rollin; MCD-Township; LENAWEE; ***189** T-9; mail Hudson z 49247; Ⓟ 3,323; Ⓒ 3,176
Rome; MCD-Township; LENAWEE; ***189** S-10; mail Adrian z 49221; Ⓟ 1,632; Ⓒ 1,772
Rome Center; RMC Place; LENAWEE; ▲ Rome; ***189** S-10; elev. 908ft./277m.; mail Adrian z 49221; ● 50
Romeo; Inc. Place; MACOMB; ▲ Washington, Bruce; **189** P-13; 🅿; ★ **DET**; z 48065; Ⓟ 3,520; Ⓒ 3,721
Romulus; Inc. Place; WAYNE; **189** R-12; 🅿; ★ **DET**; z 48174; Ⓟ 22,897; Ⓒ 22,979; ◆ 22,264
Ronald; MCD-Township; IONIA; ***189** P-8; mail Ionia z 48846; Ⓟ 1,715; Ⓒ 1,903
Rondo; RMC Place; CHEBOYGAN; ▲ Mentor; ***188** H-8; elev. 723ft./220m.; mail Wolverine z 49799
Roosevelt Park; Inc. Place; MUSKEGON; **189** O-4; elev. 625ft./191m.; ★ **MUS**; mail Muskegon z 49441; Ⓟ 3,885; Ⓒ 3,890
Roscommon; Inc. Place; ⊡ ROSCOMMON; **189** K-8; elev. 1,130ft./344m.; 🅿; z 48653; Ⓟ 858; Ⓒ 1,133
Roscommon; MCD-Township; ROSCOMMON; ***189** L-8; 🅿; z 48653; does not include the City of Roscommon; Ⓟ 3,223; Ⓒ 4,249
ROSCOMMON; **189** L-8; Ⓟ 19,776; Ⓒ 25,469; ◆ 24,862
Rose; MCD-Township; OAKLAND; ***189** Q-11; ★ **DET**; mail Holly z 48442; Ⓟ 4,926; Ⓒ 6,210
Rose; MCD-Township; OGEMAW; ***189** K-10; mail Rose City z 48654; Ⓟ 1,260; Ⓒ 1,409
Roseburg; RMC Place; SANILAC; ▲ Fremont; **189** O-13; mail Yale z 48097; ● 30
Rosebush; Inc. Place; ISABELLA; ▲ Isabella; **189** M-8; 🅿; z 48878; Ⓟ 333; Ⓒ 379
Rose Center; RMC Place; OAKLAND; ▲ Rose; **190** E-1; ★ **DET**; mail Holly z 48442; ● 170
Rose City; Inc. Place; OGEMAW; **189** K-10; elev. 950ft./290m.; 🅿; z 48654; Ⓟ 686; Ⓒ 721
Rosedale; RMC Place; CHIPPEWA; ▲ Bruce; **188** D-9; elev. 638ft./194m.; mail Sault Sainte Marie z 49783
Rose Island; RMC Place; HURON; ▲ Fairhaven; ***189** M-11; mail Sebewaing z 48759; ● 30
Rose Lake; MCD-Township; OSCEOLA; ***189** L-7; mail Leroy z 49655; Ⓟ 968; Ⓒ 1,231
Roseville; Inc. Place; MACOMB; **189** Q-13; elev. 615ft./187m.; 🅿 ■; ★ **DET**; z 48066; Ⓟ 51,412; Ⓒ 48,129; ◆ 45,117
Ross; MCD-Township; KALAMAZOO; ***189** R-7; ★ **KZOO**; mail Augusta z 49012; Ⓟ 4,730; Ⓒ 5,047
Rothbury; Inc. Place; OCEANA; ▲ Grant; **189** N-4; elev. 690ft./210m.; 🅿; ★ **MUS**; z 49452; Ⓟ 407; Ⓒ 416
Round Lake; RMC Place; EMMET; ▲ Bear Creek; ***188** H-8; mail Harbor Springs z 49740, Petoskey z 49770; summer pop. 100; ● 30
Round Lake; RMC Place; LENAWEE; ▲ Rollin; mail Manitou Beach z 49253
Round Lake; RMC Place; MASON; ▲ Sheridan; ***189** L-5; elev. 719ft./219m.; mail Fountain z 49410; ● 60
Rousseau; RMC Place; ONTONAGON; ▲ Bohemia; ***188** B-12; mail Mass City z 49948; rural
Rowes Corner; RMC Place; WASHTENAW; ▲ Sharon; ***189** S-10; elev. 1,011ft./308m.; mail Manchester z 48158; rural
Roxand; MCD-Township; EATON; ***189** Q-8; mail Grand Ledge z 48837, Mulliken z 48861; Ⓟ 1,903; Ⓒ 1,903
Royal Oak; Inc. Place; OAKLAND; **189** Q-12; elev. 655ft./200m.; 🅿 🅷 ■; ★ **DET**; z 48067-68, z 48073; Ⓟ 65,410; Ⓒ 60,062; ◆ 55,477
Royal Oak; MCD-Charter Township; OAKLAND; ***189** R-12; 🅿; ★ **DET**; z 48067-68, z 48073 & mail Ferndale z 48220; Ⓟ 5,011; Ⓒ 5,446
Royal Oak Beach; RMC Place; CHEBOYGAN; ▲ Mullett; ***188** G-8; mail Cheboygan z 49721; rural
Royalton; MCD-Township; BERRIEN; ***189** S-4; ★ **BNTH-**; mail Saint Joseph z 49085; Ⓟ 3,135; Ⓒ 3,888
Rubicon; MCD-Township; HURON; ***189** M-13; mail Port Hope z 48468; Ⓟ 766; Ⓒ 778
Ruby; RMC Place; ST. CLAIR; ▲ Clyde; ***189** P-14; 🅿; ★ **PTHU**; z 48049 & mail Goodells z 48027; ● 220
Rudyard; RMC Place; CHIPPEWA; ▲ Rudyard; **188** E-8; elev. 687ft./209m.; 🅿; z 49780; ● 1,100
Rudyard; MCD-Township; CHIPPEWA; ***188** E-8; 🅿; z 49780; Ⓟ 1,270; Ⓒ 1,315
Rumely; RMC Place; ALGER; ▲ Rock River; **188** D-2; 🅿; z 49826; ● 90
Rush; MCD-Township; SHIAWASSEE; ***189** P-10; mail Henderson z 48841; Ⓟ 1,405; Ⓒ 1,409
Rush Lake; LIVINGSTON; see Pettysville (RMC Place)
Rusk; RMC Place; OTTAWA; ▲ Allendale; ***189** P-5; elev. 636ft./194m.; ★ **GDR**; mail Zeeland z 49464; ● 30
Russell Island; RMC Place; ST. CLAIR; ▲ Clay; 🅿; ★ **DET**; z 48001; summer pop. 130
Russellville; RMC Place; GENESEE; ▲ Richfield; **189** O-11; elev. 744ft./227m.; ★ **FLN**; mail Davison z 48423; ● 220
Rust; RMC Place; MONTMORENCY; ▲ Rust; ***188** I-10; mail Hillman z 49746; ● 50
Rust; MCD-Township; MONTMORENCY; ***188** I-10; mail Hillman z 49746; Ⓟ 514; Ⓒ 549
Rustford; RMC Place; MECOSTA; ▲ Deerfield; ***189** N-7; mail Morley z 49336; rural
Ruth; RMC Place; HURON; ▲ Sherman; **189** M-13; elev. 754ft./230m.; 🅿; z 48470; ● 230
Rutland; MCD-Charter Township; BARRY; ***189** Q-7; mail Hastings z 49058; Ⓟ 2,797; Ⓒ 3,646

S

Sac Bay; RMC Place; DELTA; ▲ Fairbanks; ***188** G-3; elev. 630ft./192m.; mail Garden z 49835; ● 20
Saddle Lake; RMC Place; VAN BUREN; ▲ Columbia; ***189** R-5; elev. 700ft./213m.; mail Grand Junction z 49056; summer pop. 400; ● 230
Saganing; RMC Place; ARENAC; ▲ Standish; ***189** M-10; elev. 596ft./182m.; ★ **SAG-**; mail Standish z 48658; rural
Sage; MCD-Township; GLADWIN; ***189** L-9; mail Gladwin z 48624; Ⓟ 2,177; Ⓒ 2,617
Saginaw; Inc. Place; ⊡ SAGINAW; **189** N-10; 🅿 🅷 ■; ★ **SAG-**; z 48601-09, z 48638, z 48663; Ⓟ 69,512; Ⓒ 61,799; Ⓡ 61,792; ◆ 55,423
Saginaw; MCD-Charter Township; SAGINAW; ***189** N-10; 🅿; ★ **SAG-**; z 48601-09, z 48638, z 48663; does not include the City of Saginaw; Ⓟ 37,684; Ⓒ 39,657; ◆ 37,120
SAGINAW; **189** O-10; Ⓟ 211,946; Ⓒ 210,039; Ⓡ 210,042; ◆ 193,951
Saginaw Township North; CDP-Census Area Only; SAGINAW; ▲ Saginaw; ***189** N-10; elev. 626ft./191m.; ★ **SAG-**; mail Saginaw z 48603; Ⓟ 23,018; Ⓒ 24,994; ◆ 23,086
Saginaw Township South; CDP-Census Area Only; SAGINAW; ▲ Saginaw; ***189** N-10; elev. 613ft./187m.; ★ **SAG-**; mail Saginaw z 48603; Ⓟ 13,987; Ⓒ 13,801
Sagola; RMC Place; DICKINSON; ▲ Sagola; **188** C-13; elev. 1,436ft./438m.; 🅿; z 49881; ● 180
Sagola; MCD-Township; DICKINSON; ***188** C-13; 🅿; z 49881; Ⓟ 1,166; Ⓒ 1,169
Saint Anthony; RMC Place; MONROE; ▲ Whiteford; ***189** T-11; ★ **TOL**; mail Temperance z 48182; ● 140
Saint Charles; Inc. Place; SAGINAW; ▲ Swan Creek, St. Charles; **189** O-10; elev. 593ft./181m.; 🅿; ★ **SAG-**; z 48655; Ⓟ 2,144; Ⓒ 2,215
St. Charles; MCD-Township; SAGINAW; ***189** O-10; ★ **SAG-**; mail Saint Charles z 48655; includes part of the Village of Saint Charles; Ⓟ 3,505; Ⓒ 3,393
Saint Clair; Inc. Place; ST. CLAIR; **189** P-14; 🅿; ★ **DET**; z 48079; Ⓟ 5,116; Ⓒ 5,802
St. Clair; MCD-Township; ST. CLAIR; ***189** P-14; ★ **DET**; mail Saint Clair z 48079; does not include the City of Saint Clair; Ⓟ 4,614; Ⓒ 6,423
ST. CLAIR; **189** P-13; Ⓟ 145,607; Ⓒ 164,235; ◆ 166,437
Saint Clair Shores; Inc. Place; MACOMB; **189** Q-13; elev. 585ft./178m.; 🅿 ■; ★ **DET**; z 48080-82; Ⓟ 68,107; Ⓒ 63,096; ◆ 58,873
Saint Helen (Saint Helens); CDP; ROSCOMMON; ▲ Richfield; **189** K-9; 🅿; z 48656; Ⓟ 2,390; Ⓒ 2,993
Saint Helens; ROSCOMMON; see Saint Helen (CDP)
Saint Ignace; Inc. Place; ⊡ MACKINAC; **188** F-8; 🅿 🅷; z 49781; Ⓟ 2,568; Ⓒ 2,678
St. Ignace; MCD-Township; MACKINAC; ***188** E-8; mail Saint Ignace z 49781; does not include the City of Saint Ignace; Ⓟ 932; Ⓒ 1,024
Saint Jacques; RMC Place; DELTA; ▲ Nahma; ***188** F-3; elev. 657ft./200m.; mail Rapid River z 49878; ● 30
Saint James (Beaver Island); RMC Place; CHARLEVOIX; ▲ St. James; **188** F-6; mail Beaver Island z 49782; ● 400
St. James; MCD-Township; CHARLEVOIX; ***188** F-6; mail Beaver Island z 49782; Ⓟ 276; Ⓒ 307
Saint Johns; Inc. Place; ⊡ CLINTON; **189** P-9; elev. 794ft./242m.; 🅿 🅷; z 48879; Ⓟ 7,284; Ⓒ 7,485; Ⓡ 7,744
Saint Joseph; Inc. Place; ⊡ BERRIEN; **189** S-4; 🅿 🅷 ■; ★ **BNTH-**; z 49085; Ⓟ 9,214; Ⓒ 8,789; ◆ 8,223
Saint Joseph; MCD-Charter Township; BERRIEN; ***189** S-4; ★ **BNTH-**; mail Benton Harbor z 49022; does not include the City of Saint Joseph; Ⓟ 9,613; Ⓒ 10,042
ST. JOSEPH; **189** T-6; Ⓟ 58,913; Ⓒ 62,422; ◆ 62,089
Saint Louis; Inc. Place; GRATIOT; **189** N-9; elev. 725ft./221m.; 🅿; z 48880; Ⓟ 3,828; Ⓒ 4,494; Ⓡ 5,453
Saint Marys Lake; RMC Place; CALHOUN; ▲ Pennfield, Bedford; ***189** R-7; ★ **BTLCK**; mail Battle Creek z 49017; ● 380
Saint Marys Transfer; RMC Place; CHIPPEWA; pop. incl. with Sault Ste. Marie (Inc. Place)
Saint Nicholas; RMC Place; DELTA; ▲ Baldwin, Maple Ridge; ***188** F-2; elev. 855ft./261m.; mail Rock z 49880; rural
Salem; MCD-Township; ALLEGAN; ***189** Q-5; ★ **GDR**; mail Burnips z 49314; Ⓟ 2,708; Ⓒ 3,486
Salem; RMC Place; WASHTENAW; ▲ Salem; **190** I-1; 🅿; ★ **DET**; z 48175; ● 350
Salem; MCD-Township; WASHTENAW; ***189** R-11; 🅿; ★ **DET**; z 48175 & mail South Lyon z 48178; Ⓟ 3,734; Ⓒ 5,562
Saline; Inc. Place; WASHTENAW; **189** S-11; 🅿 🅷; ★ **DET**; z 48176; Ⓟ 6,660; Ⓒ 8,034
Saline; MCD-Township; WASHTENAW; ***189** S-11; 🅿; z 48176 & mail Clinton z 49236; does not include the City of Saline; Ⓟ 1,276; Ⓒ 1,302
Salisbury; RMC Place; MARQUETTE; ▲ Ishpeming; ***188** D-1; mail Ishpeming z 49849; pop. incl. with Ishpeming (Inc. Place)
Samaria; RMC Place; MONROE; ▲ Bedford; **189** T-11; elev. 646ft./197m.; 🅿; ★ **TOL**; z 48177; ● 480
Sanborn; MCD-Township; ALPENA; ***188** I-11; mail Ossineke z 49766; Ⓟ 2,196; Ⓒ 2,152
Sand Beach; MCD-Township; HURON; ***189** M-13; mail Harbor Beach z 48441; Ⓟ 1,358; Ⓒ 1,470
Sand Creek; RMC Place; LENAWEE; ▲ Madison; **189** T-10; elev. 779ft./237m.; 🅿; z 49279; ● 110
Sand Lake; RMC Place; IOSCO; ▲ Grant; ***189** K-11; mail National City z 48748; ● 350
Sand Lake; Inc. Place; KENT; ▲ Nelson; **189** O-6; elev. 920ft./280m.; 🅿; ★ **GDR**; z 49343; Ⓟ 456; Ⓒ 492
Sand River; RMC Place; ALGER, MARQUETTE; ▲ Chocolay, Onota; **188** D-2; mail Deerton z 49822; ● 80
Sands; RMC Place; MARQUETTE; ▲ Sands; **188** D-2; mail Gwinn z 49841; ● 60
Sands; MCD-Township; MARQUETTE; ***188** D-2; mail Gwinn z 49841; Ⓟ 2,696; Ⓒ 2,127
Sandstone; MCD-Township; JACKSON; ***189** R-9; ★ **JAC**; mail Jackson z 49201; Ⓟ 3,300; Ⓒ 3,801
Sandusky; Inc. Place; ⊡ SANILAC; **189** N-13; elev. 774ft./236m.; 🅿 🅷; z 48471; Ⓟ 2,403; Ⓒ 2,745
Sandy Beach; RMC Place; ST. JOSEPH; ▲ White Pigeon; ★ **ELK**; mail Sturgis z 49091
Sanford; Inc. Place; MIDLAND; ▲ Jerome; **189** N-9; 🅿; ★ **SAG-**; z 48657; Ⓟ 889; Ⓒ 943
Sanilac; MCD-Township; SANILAC; ***189** N-14; mail Port Sanilac z 48469; Ⓟ 2,362; Ⓒ 2,609
SANILAC; **189** N-13; Ⓟ 39,928; Ⓒ 44,547; ◆ 42,605
San Souci Beach; RMC Place; BRANCH; ▲ Ovid; ***189** T-8; elev. 1,000ft./305m.; mail Coldwater z 49036; ● 50
Sans Souci (Harsens Island); RMC Place; ST. CLAIR; ▲ Clay; ***189** Q-14; ★ **DET**; mail Harsens Island z 48028; summer pop. 5,000; ● 350
Santiago; RMC Place; ARENAC; ▲ Turner; ***189** L-11; mail Turner z 48765
Saranac; Inc. Place; IONIA; ▲ Boston; **189** P-7; elev. 644ft./196m.; 🅿; ★ **GDR**; z 48881; Ⓟ 1,461; Ⓒ 1,326
Sauble; MCD-Township; LAKE; ***189** L-5; mail Branch z 49402; Ⓟ 297; Ⓒ 323
Sauble Station; RMC Place; LAKE; ▲ Sauble; ***189** L-5; elev. 725ft./221m.; mail Branch z 49402; rural
Saugatuck; Inc. Place; ALLEGAN; ▲ Saugatuck; **189** Q-5; 🅿; z 49453; Ⓟ 954; Ⓒ 1,065
Saugatuck; MCD-Township; ALLEGAN; ***189** Q-5; 🅿; z 49453; Ⓟ 2,916; Ⓒ 3,590
Sault Ste. Marie; Inc. Place; ⊡ CHIPPEWA; **188** D-9; elev. 613ft./187m.; 🅷 🅲 2,897 ■; ★ **SOO**; mail Kincheloe z 49784-86, z 49788, Sault Sainte Marie z 49783; location of Michigan Indian Agency; Ⓟ 14,689; Ⓒ 16,542; Ⓡ 14,324; ◆ 14,728
Sault Ste. Marie Reservation; Indian Reservation; CHIPPEWA; mail Sault Sainte Marie z 49783; Ⓒ 354
Sawyer; RMC Place; BERRIEN; ▲ Chikaming; **189** T-4; elev. 654ft./199m.; 🅿; z 49125; ● 500
Sawyer Lake; RMC Place; DICKINSON; ▲ Sagola; ***188** C-13; elev. 1,406ft./429m.; mail Channing z 49815; ● 80
Schaffer; RMC Place; DELTA; ▲ Bark River; **188** F-2; elev. 778ft./237m.; 🅿; z 49807; ● 150
Schoolcraft; MCD-Township; HOUGHTON; ***188** A-13; mail Hubbell z 49934; Ⓟ 2,037; Ⓒ 1,863
Schoolcraft; Inc. Place; KALAMAZOO; ▲ Schoolcraft; **189** S-6; 🅿; ★ **KZOO**; z 49087; Ⓟ 1,517; Ⓒ 1,587
Schoolcraft; MCD-Township; KALAMAZOO; ***189** S-6; 🅿; ★ **KZOO**; z 49087; Ⓟ 6,705; Ⓒ 7,260
SCHOOLCRAFT; **188** E-4; Ⓟ 8,302; Ⓒ 8,903; ◆ 8,199
Schuck Island; HURON; see Valley Island (RMC Place)
Schultz; RMC Place; BARRY; ▲ Hope; ***189** Q-7; elev. 907ft./276m.; mail Hastings z 49058; ● 301
Scio; MCD-Charter Township; WASHTENAW; ***189** R-11; ★ **DET**; mail Ann Arbor z 48103, Dexter z 48130; Ⓟ 11,077; Ⓒ 15,759
Sciota; MCD-Township; SHIAWASSEE; ***189** P-9; mail Laingsburg z 48848; Ⓟ 1,578; Ⓒ 1,801
Scipio; MCD-Township; HILLSDALE; ***189** S-9; mail Jonesville z 49250; Ⓟ 1,479; Ⓒ 1,822
Scofield; RMC Place; MONROE; ▲ Exeter; **189** S-12; ★ **DET**
Scottdale; RMC Place; BERRIEN; ▲ Royalton; ***189** S-4; ★ **BNTH-**; mail Saint Joseph z 49085; ● 550
Scotts; RMC Place; KALAMAZOO; ▲ Pavilion, Climax; **189** S-7; 🅿; ★ **KZOO**; z 49088; ● 350
Scottville; Inc. Place; MASON; **189** M-4; elev. 678ft./207m.; 🅿; z 49454; Ⓟ 1,287; Ⓒ 1,266
Sears; RMC Place; OSCEOLA; ▲ Sylvan, Orient; **189** M-7; 🅿; z 49679; ● 90
Sebewa; IONIA; see East Sebewa (RMC Place)
Sebewa; MCD-Township; IONIA; ***189** P-8; mail Portland z 48875; Ⓟ 1,160; Ⓒ 1,202
Sebewaing; Inc. Place; HURON; ▲ Sebewaing; **189** M-11; elev. 585ft./178m.; 🅿; z 48759; Ⓟ 1,923; Ⓒ 1,974
Sebewaing; MCD-Township; HURON; ***189** M-12; 🅿; z 48759; Ⓟ 2,937; Ⓒ 2,944
Secord; MCD-Township; GLADWIN; ***189** L-9; mail Gladwin z 48624; Ⓟ 914; Ⓒ 1,140
Segwun; RMC Place; KENT; ▲ Lowell; ***189** P-7; elev. 637ft./194m.; ★ **GDR**; mail Lowell z 49331; ● 80
Seidler; RMC Place; BAY; ▲ Beaver; ***189** M-10; elev. 610ft./186m.; ★ **SAG-**; mail Auburn z 48611; rural
Selkirk; RMC Place; OGEMAW; ▲ Churchill; **189** K-10; mail West Branch z 48661; ● 40
Selma; MCD-Township; WEXFORD; ***189** K-6; mail Cadillac z 49601; Ⓟ 1,607; Ⓒ 1,915
Seneca; RMC Place; KEWEENAW; ▲ Allouez; ***188** A-13; elev. 1,000ft./305m.; mail Mohawk z 49950; rural
Seneca; RMC Place; LENAWEE; ▲ Seneca; ***189** T-10; elev. 798ft./243m.; 🅿; z 49256, z 49279; ● 150
Seneca; MCD-Township; LENAWEE; ***189** T-10; 🅿; z 49279 & mail Morenci z 49256; Ⓟ 1,289; Ⓒ 1,303
Seney; RMC Place; SCHOOLCRAFT; ▲ Seney; **188** D-5; 🅿; z 49883; ● 200
Seney; MCD-Township; SCHOOLCRAFT; ***188** D-5; 🅿; z 49883; Ⓟ 185; Ⓒ 180
Senter; RMC Place; HOUGHTON; ▲ Osceola; ***188** A-13; mail Dollar Bay z 49922; ● 30
Seven Harbors; RMC Place; OAKLAND; ▲ Highland; ***189** Q-11; ★ **DET**; mail Highland z 48356; ● 4,700
Seven Oaks; RMC Place; WAYNE; ***189** R-12; ★ **DET**; mail Detroit z 48235; pop. incl. with Detroit (Inc. Place)
Seville; MCD-Township; GRATIOT; ***189** N-8; mail Elwell z 48832; Ⓟ 2,217; Ⓒ 2,375
Seymour Square; RMC Place; KENT; ▲ Grand Rapids; ***189** P-6; ★ **GDR**; mail Grand Rapids z 49510; pop. incl. with Grand Rapids (Inc. Place)
Shabbona; RMC Place; SANILAC; ▲ Evergreen; **189** N-12; mail Decker z 48426; ● 90
Shady Shores; RMC Place; OGEMAW; ▲ Hill; ***189** K-10; mail Lupton z 48635; ● 350
Shadyside; RMC Place; HILLSDALE; ▲ Jefferson; ***189** T-9; mail Osseo z 49266; ● 30
Shaftsburg; RMC Place; SHIAWASSEE; ▲ Woodhull; **189** Q-9; elev. 887ft./270m.; 🅿; ★ **LANS**; z 48882; ● 270
Shaldas Corner; RMC Place; LEELANAU; ▲ Cleveland; ***188** I-5; elev. 630ft./192m.; mail Maple City z 49664; rural
Shallows; RMC Place; CHIPPEWA; ***188** D-9; elev. 608ft./185m.; ★ **SOO**; pop. incl. with Sault Ste. Marie (Inc. Place)
Shanghai Corners; RMC Place; BERRIEN; ▲ Pipestone; ***189** S-4; mail Eau Claire z 49111; rural
Sharon; RMC Place; KALKASKA; ▲ Garfield; ***188** J-7; mail Fife Lake z 49633; rural
Sharon; MCD-Township; WASHTENAW; ***189** S-10; mail Manchester z 48158; Ⓟ 1,366; Ⓒ 1,678
Sharon Hollow; RMC Place; WASHTENAW; ▲ Sharon; ***189** S-10; elev. 922ft./281m.; mail Manchester z 48158
Sharps Corners; RMC Place; ROSCOMMON; ▲ Markey, Gerrish; ***189** K-8; elev. 1,184ft./361m.; mail Roscommon z 48653; rural
Shawnee Shores; RMC Place; BRANCH; ▲ Ovid; mail Coldwater z 49036; ● 100
Sheaffer Location; RMC Place; IRON; ▲ Crystal Falls; ***188** C-13; mail Crystal Falls z 49920; rural
Shelby ; CDP-Census Area Only; MACOMB; ▲ Shelby; **190** F-7; elev. 686ft./209m.; ★ **DET**; mail Utica z 48315-18; Ⓟ 48,655; Ⓒ 65,159; ◆ 72,598
Shelby (Shelby Township); MCD-Charter Township; MACOMB; ***189** Q-13; ★ **DET**; mail Utica z 48315-18; Ⓟ 48,655; Ⓒ 65,159; ◆ 72,598
Shelby; Inc. Place; OCEANA; ▲ Shelby; **189** N-4; 🅿 🅷; z 49455; Ⓟ 1,871; Ⓒ 1,914
Shelby; MCD-Township; OCEANA; ***189** N-4; 🅿; z 49455; Ⓟ 3,692; Ⓒ 3,951
Shelby Township; MACOMB; see Shelby (MCD-Charter Township)
Shelbyville; RMC Place; ALLEGAN; ▲ Wayland, Martin; **189** Q-6; elev. 831ft./253m.; 🅿; z 49344; ● 160
Sheldon; RMC Place; WAYNE; ▲ Canton; **190** K-2; elev. 682ft./208m.; ★ **DET**; mail Belleville z 48111; ● 590
Shepardsville; RMC Place; CLINTON; ▲ Ovid; **189** P-9; mail Ovid z 48866; ● 70
Shepherd; Inc. Place; ISABELLA; ▲ Coe; **189** N-8; 🅿; z 48883; Ⓟ 1,413; Ⓒ 1,536
Sheridan; MCD-Township; CALHOUN; ***189** R-8; mail Albion z 49224; Ⓟ 2,139; Ⓒ 2,116
Sheridan; MCD-Township; CLARE; ***189** M-8; mail Clare z 48617; Ⓟ 1,051; Ⓒ 1,588
Sheridan; MCD-Township; HURON; ***189** M-12; mail Bad Axe z 48413; Ⓟ 694; Ⓒ 736
Sheridan; MCD-Township; MASON; ***189** L-5; mail Fountain z 49410; Ⓟ 837; Ⓒ 969
Sheridan; MCD-Township; MECOSTA; ***189** N-7; mail Barryton z 49305; Ⓟ 1,020; Ⓒ 1,357
Sheridan; Inc. Place; MONTCALM; ▲ Sidney, Bushnell, Evergreen, Fairplain; **189** O-7; 🅿 🅷; z 48884; Ⓟ 730; Ⓒ 705
Sheridan; MCD-Charter Township; NEWAYGO; ***189** N-5; mail Fremont z 49412; Ⓟ 2,252; Ⓒ 2,423
Sherman; MCD-Township; GLADWIN; ***189** L-9; mail Gladwin z 48624; Ⓟ 796; Ⓒ 1,029
Sherman; MCD-Township; HURON; ***189** M-13; mail Minden City z 48456; Ⓟ 1,155; Ⓒ 1,165
Sherman; MCD-Township; IOSCO; ***189** L-11; mail National City z 48748; Ⓟ 502; Ⓒ 493
Sherman; MCD-Township; ISABELLA; ***189** M-7; mail Lake z 48632; Ⓟ 1,725; Ⓒ 2,616
Sherman; MCD-Township; KEWEENAW; ***188** A-13; mail Lake Linden z 49945; Ⓟ 39; Ⓒ 60
Sherman; MCD-Township; MASON; ***189** L-4; mail Fountain z 49410; Ⓟ 952; Ⓒ 1,090
Sherman; MCD-Township; NEWAYGO; ***189** N-5; mail Fremont z 49412; Ⓟ 1,866; Ⓒ 2,159
Sherman; MCD-Township; OSCEOLA; ***189** L-7; mail Tustin z 49688; Ⓟ 948; Ⓒ 1,081
Sherman; MCD-Township; ST. JOSEPH; ***189** T-6; mail Sturgis z 49091; Ⓟ 2,978; Ⓒ 3,248
Sherman; RMC Place; WEXFORD; ▲ Antioch, Hanover, Springville, Wexford; **189** K-6; elev. 912ft./278m.; mail Mesick z 49668; ● 30
Sherman City; RMC Place; ISABELLA; ▲ Coldwater, Sherman; **189** M-7; elev. 963ft./294m.; mail Lake z 48632; ● 30
Sherwood; Inc. Place; BRANCH; ▲ Sherwood; **189** S-7; elev. 883ft./269m.; 🅿; z 49089; Ⓟ 320; Ⓒ 324
Sherwood; MCD-Township; BRANCH; ***189** S-7; 🅿; z 49089; Ⓟ 2,310; Ⓒ 2,284
Sherwood Corners; RMC Place; OSCODA; ▲ Elmer, Comins; ***188** J-10; elev. 1,049ft./320m.; mail Mio z 48647; rural
Shiawassee; MCD-Township; SHIAWASSEE; ***189** P-10; ★ **FLN**; mail Durand z 48429; Ⓟ 2,731; Ⓒ 2,907
SHIAWASSEE; **189** P-10; Ⓟ 69,770; Ⓒ 71,687; ◆ 69,279
Shiawasseetown (Shi-Town); RMC Place; SHIAWASSEE; ▲ Shiawassee; **189** P-10; elev. 818ft./249m.; ★ **FLN**; mail Durand z 48429; ● 80
Shields; CDP; SAGINAW; ▲ Thomas; **189** N-10; ★ **SAG-**; mail Saginaw z 48609; Ⓟ 6,634; Ⓒ 6,590
Shiloh; RMC Place; IONIA; ▲ Orleans; ***189** P-7; elev. 836ft./255m.; mail Orleans z 48865
Shingleton; RMC Place; ALGER; ▲ Munising; **188** D-4; elev. 821ft./250m.; 🅿; z 49884; ● 320
Shi-Town; SHIAWASSEE; see Shiawasseetown (RMC Place)
Shoreham; Inc. Place; BERRIEN; ▲ Saint Joseph; **189** S-4; ★ **BNTH-**; mail Saint Joseph z 49085; Ⓟ 737; Ⓒ 860
Shore Line Junction; RMC Place; HOUGHTON; ▲ Hancock; mail Hancock z 49930; pop. incl. with Hancock (Inc. Place)
Shorewood Hills; RMC Place; BERRIEN; ▲ Chikaming; ***189** T-3; mail Sawyer z 49125; summer pop. 500; ● 150
Shorewood-Tower Hills-Harbert; CDP-Census Area Only; BERRIEN; ▲ Lake, Chikaming; ***189** T-3; mail Harbert z 49115, Sawyer z 49125; Ⓟ 1,636; Ⓒ 1,619
Sibley; RMC Place; WAYNE; ★ **DET**; mail Trenton z 48183; pop. incl. with Trenton (Inc. Place)
Sidnaw; RMC Place; HOUGHTON; ▲ Duncan; **188** B-12; elev. 1,366ft./416m.; 🅿; z 49961; ● 300
Sidney; RMC Place; MONTCALM; ▲ Sidney; **189** O-7; elev. 898ft./274m.; 🅿; z 48885; ● 120
Sidney; MCD-Township; MONTCALM; ***189** O-7; 🅿; z 48885; Ⓟ 2,375; Ⓒ 2,563
Sid Town; RMC Place; IOSCO; ▲ Oscoda; ***189** K-11; elev. 700ft./213m.; mail Oscoda z 48750; ● 100
Sigel; MCD-Township; HURON; ***189** M-13; mail Harbor Beach z 48441; Ⓟ 599; Ⓒ 576
Sigma; RMC Place; KALKASKA; ▲ Oliver; ***188** J-7; mail Kalkaska z 49646; ● 100
Silver City; RMC Place; ONTONAGON; ▲ Carp Lake; **188** B-11; mail Ontonagon z 49953; ● 60
Silver Creek; MCD-Township; CASS; ***189** S-5; mail Dowagiac z 49047; Ⓟ 3,101; Ⓒ 3,491
Silverwood; RMC Place; TUSCOLA, LAPEER; ▲ Rich, Dayton; **189** O-12; elev. 808ft./246m.; 🅿; z 48760; ● 170
Simar; RMC Place; ONTONAGON; ▲ Bohemia; ***188** B-12; mail Mass City z 49948; rural
Sims; MCD-Township; ARENAC; ***189** L-11; mail Au Gres z 48703; Ⓟ 836; Ⓒ 1,091
Sister Lakes; RMC Place; VAN BUREN; ▲ Keeler; ***189** S-5; mail Dowagiac z 49047; summer pop. 5,000; ● 1,780
Sitka; RMC Place; NEWAYGO; ▲ Sheridan, Bridgeton; ***189** O-5; elev. 743ft./226m.; mail Fremont z 49412
Six Lakes; RMC Place; MONTCALM; ▲ Belvidere; **189** N-7; 🅿; z 48886; ● 420
Skandia; RMC Place; MARQUETTE; ▲ Skandia; **188** D-2; 🅿; z 49885; ● 300
Skandia; MCD-Township; MARQUETTE; ***188** D-2; 🅿; z 49885; Ⓟ 933; Ⓒ 907
Skanee; RMC Place; BARAGA; ▲ Arvon; **188** B-13; elev. 747ft./228m.; 🅿; z 49962; ● 100
Skeels; RMC Place; GLADWIN; ▲ Sherman; **189** L-9; elev. 1,004ft./306m.; mail Gladwin z 48624
Skidway Lake; CDP; OGEMAW; ▲ Mills; **189** L-10; 🅿; z 48756; Ⓟ 2,569; Ⓒ 3,147
Slagle; MCD-Township; WEXFORD; ***189** K-6; mail Harrietta z 49638; Ⓟ 470; Ⓒ 569
Slapneck; RMC Place; ALGER; ▲ Rock River; ***188** D-3; mail Chatham z 49816; ● 40
Sleepy Hollow; RMC Place; ONTONAGON; ▲ Haight; ***188** C-11; elev. 1,256ft./383m.; mail Bruce Crossing z 49912; rural
Slocum; RMC Place; MUSKEGON; ▲ Casnovia; ***189** O-5; mail Ravenna z 49451; ● 50
Smith Corners; RMC Place; OCEANA; ▲ Weare; ***189** M-4; mail Hart z 49420; rural
Smiths Creek; RMC Place; ST. CLAIR; ▲ Kimball; ***189** P-14; 🅿; ★ **PTHU**; z 48074; ● 150
Smiths Crossing; MIDLAND; see Mapleton (RMC Place)
Smyrna; RMC Place; IONIA; ▲ Otisco; ***189** P-7; 🅿; z 48887; ● 150
Snover; RMC Place; SANILAC; ▲ Moore; **189** N-13; 🅿; z 48472; ● 300
Snyderville; RMC Place; ST. CLAIR; ▲ Columbus; ***189** P-14; ★ **DET**; mail Columbus z 48063; rural
Sodus; RMC Place; BERRIEN; ▲ Sodus; **189** S-4; elev. 672ft./205m.; 🅿; ★ **BNTH-**; z 49126; ● 180
Sodus; MCD-Township; BERRIEN; ***189** S-4; 🅿; ★ **BNTH-**; z 49126; Ⓟ 2,065; Ⓒ 2,139
Sokol Camp; RMC Place; BERRIEN; ▲ New Buffalo; ***189** T-3; mail New Buffalo z 49117; summer pop. 100
Solon; MCD-Township; KENT; ***189** O-6; ★ **GDR**; mail Cedar Springs z 49319; Ⓟ 3,648; Ⓒ 4,662
Solon; RMC Place; LEELANAU; ▲ Solon; ***188** J-6; mail Cedar z 49621; ● 30
Solon; MCD-Township; LEELANAU; ***188** J-6; mail Cedar z 49621; Ⓟ 1,268; Ⓒ 1,542
Solvay; RMC Place; KENT; ▲ Grand Rapids; ★ **GDR**; pop. incl. with Grand Rapids (Inc. Place)
Somerset; RMC Place; HILLSDALE; ▲ Somerset; **189** S-9; 🅿; z 49281; ● 140
Somerset; MCD-Township; HILLSDALE; ***189** S-9; 🅿; z 49281; Ⓟ 3,416; Ⓒ 4,277
Somerset Center; RMC Place; HILLSDALE; ▲ Somerset; **189** S-9; 🅿; z 49282; ● 440
Sonoma; RMC Place; CALHOUN; ▲ Leroy; ***189** S-7; ★ **BTLCK**; mail Battle Creek z 49017; ● 230
Soo; MCD-Township; CHIPPEWA; ***188** D-9; ★ **SOO**; mail Sault Sainte Marie z 49783; Ⓟ 2,165; Ⓒ 2,652
Soo Junction; RMC Place; LUCE; mail Newberry z 49868; rural
South Arm; MCD-Township; CHARLEVOIX; ***188** H-7; mail East Jordan z 49727; Ⓟ 1,418; Ⓒ 1,844
South Bay City; RMC Place; BAY; ★ **SAG-**; pop. incl. with Bay City (Inc. Place)
South Blendon; RMC Place; OTTAWA; ▲ Blendon; ***189** P-5; elev. 665ft./203m.; ★ **HLND**; mail Hudsonville z 49426; rural
South Boardman; RMC Place; KALKASKA; ▲ Boardman; **188** J-7; elev. 1,010ft./308m.; 🅿; z 49680; ● 250
South Branch; MCD-Township; CRAWFORD; ***188** J-9; mail Roscommon z 48653; Ⓟ 1,380; Ⓒ 1,842
South Branch; RMC Place; OGEMAW; ▲ Goodar; **189** K-10; 🅿; z 48761; ● 150
South Branch; MCD-Township; WEXFORD; ***189** L-6; mail Cadillac z 49601; Ⓟ 306; Ⓒ 330
South Butler; RMC Place; BRANCH; ▲ Butler; ***189** S-8; elev. 1,005ft./306m.; mail Quincy z 49082
Southeast; RMC Place; GENESEE; ★ **FLN**; mail Burton z 48519, z 48529; pop. incl. with Burton (Inc. Place)
Southfield; Inc. Place; OAKLAND; **189** R-12; elev. 684ft./208m.; 🅿 🅷 🅲 4,049 ■; ★ **DET**; z 48033-34, z 48037, z 48075-76, z 48086; Ⓟ 75,728; Ⓒ 78,296; ◆ 76,857
Southfield; MCD-Township; OAKLAND; ***189** Q-12; 🅿 🅲 4,049; ★ **DET**; z 48033-34, z 48037, z 48075-76, z 48086 & mail Birmingham z 48009, Franklin z 48025; does not include the City of Southfield; Ⓟ 14,255; Ⓒ 14,430
Southgate; Inc. Place; WAYNE; **189** S-12; elev. 591ft./180m.; 🅿 ■; ★ **DET**; z 48195; Ⓟ 30,771; Ⓒ 30,136; ◆ 27,903
South Gull Lake; CDP-Census Area Only; KALAMAZOO; ▲ Ross; ***189** R-7; elev. 900ft./274m.; ★ **KZOO**; mail Richland z 49083; Ⓟ 1,453; Ⓒ 1,526
South Haven; Inc. Place; VAN BUREN, ALLEGAN; **189** R-4; 🅿 🅷; z 49090; Ⓟ 5,563; Ⓒ 5,021
South Haven; MCD-Charter Township; VAN BUREN; ***189** R-4; 🅿; z 49090; does not include the City of South Haven; Ⓟ 4,185; Ⓒ 4,046
South Ionia; RMC Place; IONIA; ▲ Ionia; **189** P-7; mail Ionia z 48846; ● 100
South Lyon; Inc. Place; OAKLAND; **189** R-11; elev. 919ft./280m.; 🅿; ★ **DET**; z 48178; Ⓟ 5,857; Ⓒ 10,036
South Monroe; CDP-Census Area Only; MONROE; ▲ Monroe; ***189** T-12; ★ **MONR**; mail Monroe z 48161; Ⓟ 5,266; Ⓒ 6,370
South Monterey; RMC Place; ALLEGAN; ▲ Monterey; ***189** Q-5; mail Allegan z 49010; rural
South Range; Inc. Place; HOUGHTON; ▲ Adams; **188** A-12; elev. 1,140ft./347m.; 🅿; z 49963; Ⓟ 745; Ⓒ 727
South Riley; RMC Place; CLINTON; ▲ Watertown, Riley; ***189** P-8; mail Dewitt z 48820
South Rockwood; Inc. Place; MONROE; ▲ Berlin; **189** S-12; 🅿; ★ **DET**; z 48179; Ⓟ 1,221; Ⓒ 1,284
Spalding; RMC Place; MENOMINEE; ▲ Spaulding; **188** G-1; elev. 853ft./260m.; 🅿; z 49886; ● 590
Spalding; MCD-Township; MENOMINEE; ***188** F-1; 🅿; z 49886; Ⓟ 1,536; Ⓒ 1,761
Sparlingville; RMC Place; ST. CLAIR; ▲ Kimball; **189** P-14; ★ **PTHU**; mail Smiths Creek z 48074; Ⓟ 1,974
Sparr; RMC Place; OTSEGO; ▲ Dover; **188** I-9; mail Gaylord z 49735; ● 30
Sparta; Inc. Place; KENT; ▲ Sparta; **189** O-6; elev. 753ft./230m.; 🅿; ★ **GDR**; z 49345; Ⓟ 3,968; Ⓒ 4,159
Sparta; MCD-Township; KENT; ***189** O-6; 🅿; ★ **GDR**; z 49345; Ⓟ 8,447; Ⓒ 8,938
Spaulding; MCD-Township; SAGINAW; ***189** O-10; ★ **SAG-**; mail Saint Charles z 48655; Ⓟ 2,662; Ⓒ 2,399; Ⓡ 2,409
Speaker; MCD-Township; SANILAC; ***189** O-13; mail Melvin z 48454; Ⓟ 1,171; Ⓒ 1,408
Spencer; RMC Place; KALKASKA; ▲ Orange; ***188** J-7; elev. 1,123ft./342m.; mail Kalkaska z 49646; ● 70
Spencer; MCD-Township; KENT; ***189** O-7; ★ **GDR**; mail Gowen z 49326; Ⓟ 3,184; Ⓒ 3,681
Spinks Corners; RMC Place; BERRIEN; ▲ Bainbridge; ***189** S-4; elev. 739ft./225m.; ★ **BNTH-**; mail Benton Harbor z 49022
Spratt; RMC Place; ALPENA; ▲ Green; **188** I-11; mail Lachine z 49753
Spring Arbor; CDP; JACKSON; ▲ Spring Arbor; **189** S-9; 🅿 🅲 3,714; ★ **JAC**; z 49283; Ⓟ 2,010; Ⓒ 2,188
Spring Arbor; MCD-Township; JACKSON; ***189** S-9; 🅿 🅲 3,714; ★ **JAC**; z 49283; Ⓟ 6,939; Ⓒ 7,577
Spring Beach; RMC Place; CASS; ▲ Penn; ***189** T-5; mail Cassopolis z 49031; ● 40
Springdale; MCD-Township; MANISTEE; ***189** K-5; mail Thompsonville z 49683; Ⓟ 498; Ⓒ 730
Springfield; Inc. Place; CALHOUN; **189** R-7; elev. 850ft./259m.; 🅿; ★ **BTLCK**; z 49015, z 49037; Ⓟ 5,582; Ⓒ 5,189
Springfield; MCD-Township; KALKASKA; ***188** J-7; mail South Boardman z 49680; Ⓟ 871; Ⓒ 1,270
Springfield; RMC Place; OAKLAND; ▲ Springfield; ***189** Q-11; ★ **DET**; mail Clarkston z 48346; ● 120
Springfield; MCD-Charter Township; OAKLAND; ***189** Q-11; ★ **DET**; mail Clarkston z 48346, Davisburg z 48350; Ⓟ 9,927; Ⓒ 13,338
Springfield Place; RMC Place; CALHOUN; ***189** R-7; ★ **BTLCK**; mail Battle Creek z 49015; pop. incl. with Battle Creek (Inc. Place)
Spring Grove; RMC Place; ALLEGAN; ▲ Casco; ***189** R-5; elev. 690ft./210m.; mail Glenn z 49416; ● 50
Spring Lake; Inc. Place; OTTAWA; ▲ Spring Lake; **189** P-5; elev. 594ft./181m.; 🅿; z 49456; Ⓟ 2,537; Ⓒ 2,514
Spring Lake; MCD-Township; OTTAWA; ***189** P-5; 🅿; z 49456; Ⓟ 10,751; Ⓒ 13,140
Springport; Inc. Place; JACKSON; ▲ Springport; **189** R-8; 🅿; z 49284; Ⓟ 707; Ⓒ 704
Springport; MCD-Township; JACKSON; ***189** R-8; 🅿; z 49284; Ⓟ 2,090; Ⓒ 2,182
Springvale; MCD-Township; EMMET; ***188** H-8; mail Petoskey z 49770; Ⓟ 1,300; Ⓒ 1,727
Springville; RMC Place; LENAWEE; ▲ Cambridge; **189** S-10; ★ **JAC**; mail Onsted z 49265; ● 60
Springville; MCD-Township; WEXFORD; ***189** K-6; mail Mesick z 49668; Ⓟ 1,339; Ⓒ 1,673
Springwells; RMC Place; WAYNE; ***189** R-12; ★ **DET**; mail Detroit z 48209; pop. incl. with Detroit (Inc. Place)
Spruce; RMC Place; ALCONA; ▲ Caledonia; **188** I-11; 🅿; z 48762; ● 120
Spurr; MCD-Township; BARAGA; ***188** B-13; mail Michigamme z 49861; Ⓟ 231; Ⓒ 227
Stalwart; RMC Place; CHIPPEWA; ▲ Raber, Pickford; **188** E-9; 🅿; z 49736; ● 60
Stambaugh; RMC Place; IRON; **188** C-12; elev. 1,539ft./469m.; 🅿; z 49964; former incorporated place; became part of Iron River July 1, 2000; pop. incl. with Iron River (Inc. Place); Ⓟ 1,281; Ⓒ 1,243
Stambaugh; MCD-Township; IRON; ***188** C-12; 🅿; z 49964 & mail Iron River z 49935; does not include the City of Stambaugh; Ⓟ 1,224; Ⓒ 1,248
Standale; RMC Place; KENT; ***189** P-6; ★ **GDR**; mail Grand Rapids z 49504, z 49544; pop. incl. with Walker (Inc. Place)
Standish; Inc. Place; ⊡ ARENAC; **189** L-10; elev. 631ft./192m.; 🅿 🅷; ★ **SAG-**; z 48658; Ⓟ 1,377; Ⓒ 1,581; Ⓡ 2,096
Standish; MCD-Township; ARENAC; ***189** L-10; 🅿; ★ **SAG-**; z 48658; does not include the City of Standish; Ⓟ 1,945; Ⓒ 2,026
Stannard; MCD-Township; ONTONAGON; ***188** B-12; mail Bruce Crossing z 49912; Ⓟ 873; Ⓒ 833
Stanton; MCD-Township; HOUGHTON; ***188** A-12; mail Houghton z 49931; Ⓟ 1,184; Ⓒ 1,268
Stanton; Inc. Place; ⊡ MONTCALM; **189** O-7; elev. 919ft./280m.; 🅿; z 48888; Ⓟ 1,504; Ⓒ 1,504
Stanwood; Inc. Place; MECOSTA; ▲ Mecosta; **189** N-6; 🅿; z 49346; Ⓟ 174; Ⓒ 204
Star; MCD-Township; ANTRIM; ***188** I-8; mail Alba z 49611; Ⓟ 575; Ⓒ 745
Star City; RMC Place; MISSAUKEE; ▲ West Branch; ***189** K-8; mail Lake City z 49651; rural
Star Corners; RMC Place; MANISTEE; ▲ Stronach; ***189** L-5; elev. 701ft./214m.; mail Manistee z 49660; rural
Star Corners; RMC Place; MENOMINEE; ▲ Lake, Holmes; ***188** G-1; elev. 787ft./240m.; mail Stephenson z 49887; rural
Stark; RMC Place; WAYNE; ***189** R-12; ★ **DET**; pop. incl. with Livonia (Inc. Place)

Entries in **UPPERCASE** are counties.
Entries in **bold** have populations of 2,500 or more.
Names in parentheses are alternate names.
Inc. Place — Incorporated Place
RMC Place — Rand McNally Designated Place
CDP — Census Designated Place
MCD — Minor Civil Division
⊡ County Seat
▲ Minor Civil Division
elev. Elevation
🅿 Post Office
🅷 Hospital
🅲 College
■ Principal Business Center
★ Ranally Metro Area (RMA) Abbreviation
z Zip Code(s)
Ⓟ Previous Census Population
Ⓡ Revised Census Population
Ⓐ Annexation Population
● Rand McNally Population Estimate
Ⓒ Final Census Population
Ⓢ Special Census Population
◆ Estimated Population

For additional definitions see Glossary, Volume 1, and Introduction, Volume 2.

Starville; RMC Place; ST. CLAIR; ▲ Cottrellville; *189 Q-14; ★ DET; mail Marine City z 48039; ● 100
Steamburg; RMC Place; HILLSDALE; ▲ Cambria; *189 T-9; elev. 1,133ft./345m.; mail Hillsdale z 49242; rural
Stephenson; Inc. Place; MENOMINEE; 188 H-1; 🅿; z 49887; Ⓟ 904; Ⓒ 875
Stephenson; MCD-Township; MENOMINEE; *188 H-1; 🅿; z 49887; does not include the City of Stephenson; Ⓟ 695; Ⓒ 716
Sterling; Inc. Place; ARENAC; ▲ Deep River; 189 L-10; elev. 759ft./231m.; 🅿; z 48659; Ⓟ 520; Ⓒ 533
Sterling; MACOMB; see Sterling Heights (Inc. Place)
Sterling Heights (Sterling); Inc. Place; MACOMB; 189 Q-13; elev. 620ft./189m.; 🅿 ■; ★ DET; z 48310-14; Ⓟ 117,810; Ⓒ 124,471; ◆ 128,059
Steuben; RMC Place; SCHOOLCRAFT; ▲ Inwood; 188 E-4; mail Manistique z 49854; ● 70
Stevensville; Inc. Place; BERRIEN; ▲ Lincoln; 189 S-4; elev. 635ft./194m.; 🅿; ★ BNTH-; z 49127; Ⓟ 1,230; Ⓒ 1,191
Stockbridge; Inc. Place; INGHAM; ▲ Stockbridge; 189 R-10; 🅿; z 49285; Ⓟ 1,202; Ⓒ 1,260
Stockbridge; MCD-Township; INGHAM; *189 R-10; 🅿; z 49285; Ⓟ 2,971; Ⓒ 3,435
Stonington; RMC Place; DELTA; ▲ Bay de Noc; 188 F-3; elev. 620ft./189m.; mail Rapid River z 49878; rural
Stony Creek; RMC Place; WASHTENAW; ▲ Augusta; *189 S-11; ★ DET; mail Milan z 48160, Ypsilanti z 48197; ● 90
Stony Lake; RMC Place; OCEANA; ▲ Benona; 189 N-4; mail Shelby z 49455; ● 50
Stony Point; CDP; MONROE; ▲ Frenchtown; *189 S-12; ★ MONR; mail Newport z 48166; Ⓟ 1,598; Ⓒ 1,775
Strasburg; RMC Place; MONROE; ▲ Raisinville; *189 T-11; ★ MONR; mail Monroe z 48161; rural
Strathmoor; RMC Place; WAYNE; *189 R-12; ★ DET; mail Detroit z 48227; pop. incl. with Detroit (Inc. Place)
Strawberry Point; RMC Place; OTTAWA; ▲ Spring Lake; *189 P-5; elev. 600ft./183m.; mail Spring Lake z 49456; ● 200
Stronach; RMC Place; MANISTEE; ▲ Stronach; 189 L-4; elev. 607ft./185m.; 🅿; z 49660; ● 210
Stronach; MCD-Township; MANISTEE; *189 L-5; 🅿; z 49660; Ⓟ 688; Ⓒ 804
Strongs; RMC Place; CHIPPEWA; ▲ Chippewa; 188 D-7; 🅿; z 49790; ● 380
Strongs Corners; RMC Place; CHIPPEWA; ▲ Chippewa; mail Strongs z 49790
Stuart Lake; RMC Place; CALHOUN; ▲ Eckford; *189 S-8; elev. 928ft./283m.; mail Marshall z 49068; ● 100
Sturgeon Point; RMC Place; ALCONA; ▲ Haynes; *188 J-12; mail Harrisville z 48740; rural
Sturgis; Inc. Place; ST. JOSEPH; 189 T-7; 🅿 🅷; z 49091; Ⓟ 10,130; Ⓒ 11,285
Sturgis; MCD-Township; ST. JOSEPH; *189 T-6; 🅿; z 49091; does not include the City of Sturgis; Ⓟ 1,965; Ⓒ 2,403
Stutsmanville; RMC Place; EMMET; ▲ Friendship; *188 G-7; mail Harbor Springs z 49740; rural
Sugar Island; MCD-Township; CHIPPEWA; *188 D-9; mail Sault Sainte Marie z 49783; Ⓟ 441; Ⓒ 683
Sugar Rapids; RMC Place; GLADWIN; ▲ Butman; *189 L-9; elev. 796ft./243m.; mail Gladwin z 48624; rural
Sullivan; RMC Place; MUSKEGON; ▲ Sullivan; *189 O-5; ★ MUS; mail Ravenna z 49451; ● 100
Sullivan; MCD-Township; MUSKEGON; *189 O-5; ★ MUS; mail Ravenna z 49451; Ⓟ 2,230; Ⓒ 2,477
Summerfield; MCD-Township; CLARE; *189 L-8; mail Harrison z 48625; Ⓟ 316; Ⓒ 453
Summerfield; MCD-Township; MONROE; *189 T-11; ★ TOL; mail Petersburg z 49270; Ⓟ 3,076; Ⓒ 3,233
Summit; MCD-Township; JACKSON; *189 S-9; ★ JAC; mail Jackson z 49203; Ⓟ 21,130; Ⓒ 21,534; ◆ 21,667
Summit; MCD-Township; MASON; *189 M-4; mail Ludington z 49431; Ⓟ 815; Ⓒ 1,021
Summit City; RMC Place; GRAND TRAVERSE; ▲ Paradise; *189 K-6; elev. 1,070ft./326m.; mail Kingsley z 49649; ● 50
Summit Heights; RMC Place; ROSCOMMON; ▲ Denton; *189 K-8; mail Houghton Lake z 48629
Sumner; RMC Place; GRATIOT; ▲ Sumner; 189 O-8; elev. 764ft./233m.; 🅿; z 48889; ● 170
Sumner; MCD-Township; GRATIOT; *189 O-8; 🅿; z 48889; Ⓟ 1,799; Ⓒ 1,911
Sumnerville; RMC Place; CASS; ▲ Pokagon; 189 T-5; mail Niles z 49120; ● 180
Sumpter; MCD-Township; WAYNE; *189 S-12; ★ DET; mail Belleville z 48111; Ⓟ 10,891; Ⓒ 11,856
Sun; RMC Place; NEWAYGO; ▲ Grant; *189 O-6; ★ GDR; mail Grant z 49327; rural
Sunfield; Inc. Place; EATON; ▲ Sunfield; 189 Q-8; elev. 866ft./264m.; 🅿; z 48890; Ⓟ 610; Ⓒ 591
Sunfield; MCD-Township; EATON; *189 Q-8; 🅿; z 48890; Ⓟ 2,086; Ⓒ 2,177
Sunrise Heights; RMC Place; CALHOUN; ▲ Emmett; 189 R-7; ★ BTLCK; mail Battle Creek z 49015; ● 1,350
Sunset Beach; RMC Place; JACKSON; ▲ Norvell; *189 S-10; ★ JAC; mail Brooklyn z 49230; ● 220
Superior; MCD-Township; CHIPPEWA; *188 D-8; mail Brimley z 49715; Ⓟ 990; Ⓒ 1,329
Superior; MCD-Charter Township; WASHTENAW; *189 R-11; ★ DET; mail Ann Arbor z 48105, Ypsilanti z 48197-98; Ⓟ 8,720; Ⓒ 10,740
Surrey; MCD-Township; CLARE; *189 M-8; mail Farwell z 48622; Ⓟ 3,221; Ⓒ 3,555
Sutton Bay; LEELANAU; see Suttons Bay (Inc. Place)
Suttons Bay (Sutton Bay); Inc. Place; LEELANAU; ▲ Suttons Bay; 188 I-6; 🅿; z 49682; Ⓟ 561; Ⓒ 589
Suttons Bay; MCD-Township; LEELANAU; *188 I-6; 🅿; z 49682; Ⓟ 2,150; Ⓒ 2,982
Swains Lake; RMC Place; JACKSON; ▲ Pulaski; *189 S-9; mail Concord z 49237; ● 160
Swan Creek; RMC Place; SAGINAW; ▲ Swan Creek, James; *189 O-10; elev. 594ft./181m.; ★ SAG-; mail Saginaw z 48609; rural
Swan Creek; MCD-Township; SAGINAW; *189 O-10; ★ SAG-; mail Saginaw z 48609; Ⓟ 2,346; Ⓒ 2,536
Swanson; RMC Place; MENOMINEE; ▲ Holmes; *188 G-1; mail Daggett z 49821; rural
Swartz Creek; Inc. Place; GENESEE; 189 P-11; elev. 790ft./241m.; 🅿; ★ FLN; z 48473; Ⓟ 4,851; Ⓒ 5,102
Swedetown; RMC Place; HOUGHTON; ▲ Calumet; *188 A-13; mail Calumet z 49913; ● 130
Sweetwater; MCD-Township; LAKE; *189 M-5; mail Baldwin z 49304; Ⓟ 223; Ⓒ 238
Sylvan; MCD-Township; OSCEOLA; *189 M-7; mail Evart z 49631; Ⓟ 852; Ⓒ 1,033
Sylvan; MCD-Township; WASHTENAW; *189 R-10; mail Chelsea z 48118; Ⓟ 5,827; Ⓒ 6,425
Sylvan Beach; MUSKEGON; see Wabaningo (RMC Place)
Sylvan Center; RMC Place; WASHTENAW; ▲ Sylvan; *189 R-10; mail Chelsea z 48118; ● 70
Sylvan Lake; Inc. Place; OAKLAND; ▲ Oakland; 189 Q-12; 🅿; ★ DET; z 48320; Ⓟ 1,884; Ⓒ 1,735
Sylvester; RMC Place; MECOSTA; ▲ Hinton; *189 N-7; elev. 981ft./299m.; mail Mecosta z 49332; ● 30

T

Tabor; RMC Place; BERRIEN; ▲ Sodus; *189 S-4; elev. 645ft./197m.; ★ BNTH-; mail Sodus z 49126; ● 40
Tahquamenon; CHIPPEWA; see Paradise (RMC Place)
Talbot; RMC Place; MENOMINEE; ▲ Nadeau; *188 G-1; elev. 726ft./221m.; mail Daggett z 49821; rural
Tallmadge; RMC Place; OTTAWA; ▲ Tallmadge; 189 P-5; ★ GDR; mail Grand Rapids z 49544; ● 80
Tallmadge; MCD-Charter Township; OTTAWA; *189 P-5; ★ GDR; mail Grand Rapids z 49544; Ⓟ 6,293; Ⓒ 6,881
Tallman; RMC Place; MASON; ▲ Branch; 189 L-5; mail Fountain z 49410; ● 70
Tamarack; RMC Place; HOUGHTON; ▲ Osceola; *188 A-13; mail Calumet z 49913; ● 200
Tapiola; RMC Place; HOUGHTON; ▲ Portage; 188 B-12; elev. 836ft./255m.; mail Chassell z 49916; rural
Tawas; MCD-Township; IOSCO; *189 K-11; mail Tawas City z 48763; Ⓟ 1,465; Ⓒ 1,684
Tawas City; Inc. Place; ⊡ IOSCO; 189 K-11; elev. 587ft./179m.; 🅿 🅷; z 48763-64; Ⓟ 2,009; Ⓒ 2,005
Taylor; Inc. Place; WAYNE; 190 L-4; elev. 615ft./187m.; 🅿 🅷 ■; ★ DET; z 48180; Ⓟ 70,811; Ⓒ 65,868; ◆ 60,976
Taymouth; MCD-Township; SAGINAW; *189 O-10; ★ SAG-; mail Burt z 48417; Ⓟ 4,524; Ⓒ 4,624
Teapot Dome; RMC Place; VAN BUREN; ▲ Paw Paw; *189 S-5; elev. 790ft./241m.; ★ KZOO; mail Paw Paw z 49079; ● 30
Tecumseh; Inc. Place; LENAWEE; 189 S-10; 🅿 🅷; z 49286; Ⓟ 7,462; Ⓒ 8,574
Tecumseh; MCD-Township; LENAWEE; *189 S-10; 🅿; z 49286; does not include the City of Tecumseh; Ⓟ 1,539; Ⓒ 1,881
Tekonsha; Inc. Place; CALHOUN; ▲ Tekonsha; 189 S-8; 🅿; z 49092; Ⓟ 722; Ⓒ 712
Tekonsha; MCD-Township; CALHOUN; *189 S-8; 🅿; z 49092; Ⓟ 1,749; Ⓒ 1,734
Teleford; RMC Place; WAYNE; *189 R-12; ★ DET; mail Dearborn z 48128; pop. incl. with Dearborn Heights (Inc. Place)
Temperance; CDP; MONROE; ▲ Bedford; 189 T-11; 🅿; ★ TOL; z 48182; Ⓟ 6,542; Ⓒ 7,757
Temple (Campbell City); RMC Place; CLARE; ▲ Redding; 189 L-7; elev. 1,060ft./323m.; mail Harrison z 48625; ● 300
Texas; MCD-Charter Township; KALAMAZOO; *189 S-6; ★ KZOO; mail Kalamazoo z 49009; Ⓟ 7,711; Ⓒ 10,919
Texas Corners; RMC Place; KALAMAZOO; ▲ Texas; *189 S-6; elev. 907ft./276m.; ★ KZOO; mail Kalamazoo z 49009; ● 270
The Fingerboard Corner; RMC Place; CHEBOYGAN; ▲ Walker, Koehler; *188 H-9; mail Afton z 49705; rural
The Heights; RMC Place; JACKSON; ▲ Norvell; *189 S-10; ★ JAC; mail Brooklyn z 49230; ● 180
Theodore; RMC Place; DICKINSON; *188 D-14; mail Iron Mountain z 49801
Thetford; MCD-Township; GENESEE; *189 O-11; ★ FLN; mail Clio z 48420; Ⓟ 8,333; Ⓒ 8,277
Thomas; RMC Place; OAKLAND; ▲ Oxford; *189 P-12; elev. 1,085ft./331m.; ★ DET; mail Oxford z 48371; ● 200
Thomas; MCD-Township; SAGINAW; *189 N-10; ★ SAG-; mail Saginaw z 48609; Ⓟ 10,971; Ⓒ 11,877
Thomaston; RMC Place; GOGEBIC; ▲ Wakefield; 188 B-10; elev. 1,349ft./411m.; mail Wakefield z 49968; ● 80
Thompson; RMC Place; SCHOOLCRAFT; ▲ Thompson; 188 F-4; elev. 597ft./182m.; 🅿; z 49854; ● 200
Thompson; MCD-Township; SCHOOLCRAFT; *188 F-4; 🅿; z 49854; Ⓟ 464; Ⓒ 671
Thompsons Heights; RMC Place; LAKE; ▲ Cherry Valley; *189 M-6; elev. 895ft./273m.; mail Idlewild z 49642; rural
Thompsonville; Inc. Place; BENZIE; ▲ Weldon, Colfax; 189 K-5; elev. 793ft./242m.; 🅿; z 49683; Ⓟ 416; Ⓒ 457
Thornapple; MCD-Township; BARRY; *189 Q-6; ★ GDR; mail Middleville z 49333; Ⓟ 5,226; Ⓒ 6,685
Thornville; RMC Place; LAPEER; ▲ Metamora, Dryden; 189 P-12; ★ DET; mail Metamora z 48455; ● 60
Three Lakes; RMC Place; BARAGA; ▲ Spurr; 188 B-13; elev. 1,620ft./494m.; mail Michigamme z 49861; ● 150
Three Mile Lake; RMC Place; VAN BUREN; ▲ Paw Paw; *189 S-5; elev. 757ft./231m.; ★ KZOO; mail Paw Paw z 49079; ● 220
Three Oaks; Inc. Place; BERRIEN; 189 T-3; elev. 679ft./207m.; 🅿; z 49128; Ⓟ 1,786; Ⓒ 1,829
Three Oaks; MCD-Township; BERRIEN; *189 T-3; 🅿; z 49128; Ⓟ 2,952; Ⓒ 2,949
Three Rivers; Inc. Place; ST. JOSEPH; 189 T-6; elev. 810ft./247m.; 🅿 🅷; z 49093; Ⓟ 7,413; Ⓒ 7,328
Thunder Mountain; RMC Place; VAN BUREN; ▲ Covert; *189 R-4; elev. 615ft./187m.; ★ BNTH-; mail Coloma z 49038; ● 160
Tilden; MCD-Township; MARQUETTE; *188 D-1; mail Ishpeming z 49849; Ⓟ 1,010; Ⓒ 1,003
Tipton; RMC Place; LENAWEE; ▲ Franklin; 189 S-10; elev. 904ft./276m.; 🅿; z 49287; ● 200
Tittabawassee; MCD-Township; SAGINAW; *189 N-10; ★ SAG-; mail Freeland z 48623; Ⓟ 4,627; Ⓒ 7,706
Tobacco; MCD-Township; GLADWIN; *189 M-9; mail Beaverton z 48612; Ⓟ 2,229; Ⓒ 2,552
Tobico Beach; RMC Place; BAY; ▲ Bangor; *189 M-10; ★ SAG-; mail Bay City z 48706
Tobin Location; RMC Place; IRON; ▲ Crystal Falls; *188 C-13; mail Crystal Falls z 49920; ● 200
Tobins Harbor; RMC Place; KEWEENAW; ▲ Houghton; located on Isle Royale; mail Grand Portage z 55605
Toivola; RMC Place; HOUGHTON; ▲ Adams; *188 A-12; elev. 1,275ft./389m.; 🅿; z 49965; ● 130
Tompkins (Tompkins Center); RMC Place; JACKSON; ▲ Tompkins; *189 R-9; mail Rives Junction z 49277; ● 60
Tompkins; MCD-Township; JACKSON; *189 R-9; mail Rives Junction z 49277; Ⓟ 2,321; Ⓒ 2,758
Tompkins Center; JACKSON; see Tompkins (RMC Place)
Topaz; RMC Place; ONTONAGON; ▲ Matchwood; *188 B-11; elev. 1,255ft./383m.; mail Ewen z 49925
Topinabee; RMC Place; CHEBOYGAN; ▲ Mullett; 188 G-8; elev. 611ft./186m.; 🅿; z 49791; ● 400
Toquin; RMC Place; VAN BUREN; ▲ Covert, Bangor; *189 R-4; elev. 673ft./205m.; mail Hartford z 49057; rural
Torch Lake; RMC Place; ANTRIM; ▲ Torch Lake; 188 I-7; elev. 620ft./189m.; mail Eastport z 49627; ● 80
Torch Lake; MCD-Township; ANTRIM; *188 I-7; mail Kewadin z 49648; Ⓟ 762; Ⓒ 1,159
Torch Lake; MCD-Township; HOUGHTON; *188 A-13; mail Hubbell z 49934; Ⓟ 1,553; Ⓒ 1,860
Torch River; RMC Place; ANTRIM, KALKASKA; ▲ Clearwater, Milton; 188 I-7; mail Rapid City z 49676; ● 410
Towar Gardens; RMC Place; INGHAM; *189 Q-9; ★ LANS; mail East Lansing z 48823; ● 2,400
Tower; RMC Place; CHEBOYGAN; ▲ Forest; 188 H-9; 🅿; z 49792; ● 300
Tower Hill (Flower Hills); RMC Place; BERRIEN; ▲ Chikaming; *189 T-3; elev. 612ft./187m.; mail Sawyer z 49125; ● 160
Town Corners; RMC Place; OCEANA; ▲ Claybanks, Benona; *189 N-4; elev. 756ft./230m.; ★ MUS; mail New Era z 49446; rural
Traunik; RMC Place; ALGER; ▲ Limestone; 188 E-3; elev. 925ft./282m.; 🅿; z 49891; ● 100
Traverse Bay; RMC Place; HOUGHTON; ▲ Schoolcraft; 188 A-13; mail Lake Linden z 49945; ● 40
Traverse City; Inc. Place; ⊡ GRAND TRAVERSE, LEELANAU; 188 J-6; elev. 599ft./183m.; 🅿 🅷 ■; z 49684-86, z 49696; Ⓟ 15,155; Ⓒ 14,532; ◆ 13,815
Tremaine Corners; RMC Place; IONIA; ▲ Berlin, Orange; *189 P-7; ★ GDR; mail Ionia z 48846; rural
Trenary; RMC Place; ALGER; ▲ Mathias; 188 E-3; 🅿; z 49891; ● 300
Trent; RMC Place; MUSKEGON; *189 O-5; mail Bailey z 49303; rural
Trenton; Inc. Place; WAYNE; 189 S-12; elev. 590ft./180m.; 🅿 🅷; ★ DET; z 48183; Ⓟ 20,586; Ⓒ 19,584
Trimountain; RMC Place; HOUGHTON; ▲ Adams; *188 A-12; mail Atlantic Mine z 49905; ● 220
Trolley; RMC Place; WAYNE; *189 R-13; ★ DET; mail Detroit z 48231-35; pop. incl. with Detroit (Inc. Place)
Trombly (Defiance); RMC Place; DELTA; ▲ Maple Ridge; 188 E-2; elev. 907ft./276m.; mail Rock z 49880; ● 40
Trout Creek; RMC Place; ONTONAGON; ▲ Interior; 188 B-12; elev. 1,115ft./340m.; 🅿; z 49967; ● 230
Trout Lake; RMC Place; CHIPPEWA; ▲ Trout Lake; 188 E-7; 🅿; z 49793; ● 370
Trout Lake; MCD-Township; CHIPPEWA; *188 E-8; 🅿; z 49793; Ⓟ 429; Ⓒ 465
Trowbridge; MCD-Township; ALLEGAN; *189 R-5; mail Allegan z 49010; Ⓟ 2,328; Ⓒ 2,519; Ⓡ 2,510
Trowbridge Park; CDP; MARQUETTE; ▲ Marquette; 188 D-1; mail Marquette z 49855; Ⓟ 1,831; Ⓒ 2,012
Troy; MCD-Township; NEWAYGO; *189 M-5; mail Bitely z 49309; Ⓟ 173; Ⓒ 243
Troy; Inc. Place; OAKLAND; 189 Q-12; elev. 670ft./204m.; 🅿 🅷 🅲 3,242 ■; ★ DET; z 48007, z 48083-85, z 48098-99; Ⓟ 72,884; Ⓒ 80,959; ◆ 79,965
Trufant; RMC Place; MONTCALM; ▲ Maple Valley; 189 O-7; 🅿; z 49347; ● 500
Turin; MCD-Township; MARQUETTE; *188 E-2; mail Rock z 49880; Ⓟ 156; Ⓒ 131
Turk Lake; RMC Place; MONTCALM; ▲ Montcalm; 189 O-7; ★ GDR; mail Greenville z 48838; ● 350
Turner; Inc. Place; ARENAC; ▲ Turner; 189 L-11; 🅿; z 48765; Ⓟ 158; Ⓒ 139
Turner; MCD-Township; ARENAC; *189 L-11; 🅿; z 48765; Ⓟ 628; Ⓒ 642
Turner Shores; RMC Place; BERRIEN; ▲ Chikaming; *189 T-3; mail Lakeside z 49116; ● 300
Tuscarora; MCD-Township; CHEBOYGAN; *188 G-8; mail Indian River z 49749; Ⓟ 2,297; Ⓒ 3,091
Tuscola; RMC Place; TUSCOLA; ▲ Tuscola; 189 O-11; 🅿; z 48769; ● 100
Tuscola; MCD-Township; TUSCOLA; *189 O-11; 🅿; z 48769; Ⓟ 2,144; Ⓒ 2,152
TUSCOLA; 189 N-11; Ⓟ 55,498; Ⓒ 58,266; ◆ 55,940
Tustin; Inc. Place; OSCEOLA; ▲ Burdell; 189 L-6; 🅿; z 49688; Ⓟ 236; Ⓒ 237
Twelve Corners; RMC Place; BERRIEN; ▲ Benton; *189 S-4; elev. 652ft./199m.; ★ BNTH-; mail Benton Harbor z 49022; rural
Twining; Inc. Place; ARENAC; ▲ Turner, Mason; 189 L-10; 🅿; z 48766; Ⓟ 169; Ⓒ 192
Twin Lake; CDP; MUSKEGON; ▲ Cedar Creek, Dalton; 189 O-5; elev. 688ft./210m.; 🅿; ★ MUS; z 49457; Ⓟ 1,328; Ⓒ 1,613
Twin Lakes; RMC Place; CASS; ▲ Wayne; *189 S-5; mail Dowagiac z 49047; ● 180
Twin Lakes; RMC Place; HOUGHTON; ▲ Elm River; 188 B-12; elev. 1,201ft./366m.; mail Toivola z 49965; ● 150
Two Rivers; RMC Place; ISABELLA; ▲ Deerfield; *189 N-8; mail Mount Pleasant z 48858; rural
Tyre; RMC Place; SANILAC; ▲ Austin; 189 M-13; elev. 781ft./238m.; mail Ubly z 48475; ● 40
Tyrone; MCD-Township; KENT; *189 O-6; ★ GDR; mail Kent City z 49330; Ⓟ 3,757; Ⓒ 4,304
Tyrone; MCD-Township; LIVINGSTON; *189 Q-11; ★ DET; mail Fenton z 48430; Ⓟ 6,854; Ⓒ 8,459
Tyrone Lake; RMC Place; LIVINGSTON; ▲ Tyrone, Hartland; *189 Q-11; elev. 1,000ft./305m.; ★ DET; mail Fenton z 48430; ● 110

U

Ubly; Inc. Place; HURON; ▲ Bingham; 189 M-13; elev. 789ft./240m.; 🅿; z 48475; Ⓟ 821; Ⓒ 873
Unadilla; RMC Place; LIVINGSTON; ▲ Unadilla; 189 R-10; ★ DET; mail Gregory z 48137; ● 100
Unadilla; MCD-Township; LIVINGSTON; *189 R-10; ★ DET; mail Gregory z 48137; Ⓟ 2,949; Ⓒ 3,190
Union; MCD-Township; BRANCH; *189 S-7; mail Union City z 49094; Ⓟ 2,976; Ⓒ 3,121
Union; RMC Place; CASS; ▲ Porter; 189 T-5; 🅿; ★ ELK; z 49130; ● 200
Union; MCD-Township; GRAND TRAVERSE; *188 J-6; mail Fife Lake z 49633; Ⓟ 255; Ⓒ 417
Union; MCD-Charter Township; ISABELLA; *189 N-8; mail Mount Pleasant z 48858; Ⓟ 5,139; Ⓒ 7,615
Union City; Inc. Place; BRANCH, CALHOUN; ▲ Union; 189 S-7; 🅿; z 49094; Ⓟ 1,767; Ⓒ 1,804
Union Lake; RMC Place; OAKLAND; ▲ Commerce, Waterford, West Bloomfield, White Lake; 190 F-3; 🅿; ★ DET; z 48387; ● 8,500
Union Pier; RMC Place; BERRIEN; ▲ New Buffalo, Chikaming; 189 T-3; 🅿; z 49129; ● 1,100
Unionville; Inc. Place; TUSCOLA; ▲ Columbia; 189 N-11; 🅿; z 48767; Ⓟ 590; Ⓒ 605
Upjohn; RMC Place; KALAMAZOO; ★ KZOO; mail Portage z 49081; pop. incl. with Portage (Inc. Place)
Urbandale; RMC Place; CALHOUN; *189 R-7; ★ BTLCK; mail Battle Creek z 49017; pop. incl. with Battle Creek (Inc. Place)
Utica; Inc. Place; MACOMB; 190 F-7; elev. 650ft./198m.; 🅿; ★ DET; z 48315-18; Ⓟ 5,081; Ⓒ 4,577
Utopia Beach; RMC Place; MENOMINEE; ▲ Menominee; *188 H-1; elev. 586ft./179m.; mail Menominee z 49858; rural

V

Valley; MCD-Township; ALLEGAN; *189 Q-5; mail Allegan z 49010; Ⓟ 1,145; Ⓒ 1,831; Ⓡ 1,828
Valley Center; RMC Place; SANILAC; ▲ Maple Valley; 189 O-13; elev. 802ft./244m.; mail Brown City z 48416
Valley Farms; RMC Place; CLINTON; ▲ DeWitt; 188 A-3; ★ LANS; mail Lansing z 48906; ● 950
Valley Island (Schuck Island); RMC Place; HURON; ▲ Fairhaven; *189 M-11; elev. 585ft./178m.; mail Sebewaing z 48759; ● 80
Van; RMC Place; EMMET; ▲ McKinley; *188 G-8; mail Levering z 49755; ● 50
Van Buren; MCD-Charter Township; WAYNE; *189 R-12; ★ DET; mail Belleville z 48111; Ⓟ 21,010; Ⓒ 23,559; ◆ 23,154
VAN BUREN; 189 R-5; Ⓟ 70,060; Ⓒ 76,263; ◆ 75,623
Vandalia; Inc. Place; CASS; ▲ Penn; 189 T-5; elev. 877ft./267m.; 🅿; z 49095; Ⓟ 357; Ⓒ 429
Vanderbilt; Inc. Place; OTSEGO; ▲ Corwith; 188 H-8; 🅿; z 49795; Ⓟ 605; Ⓒ 587
Vandercook Lake; CDP; JACKSON; ▲ Summit; 189 S-9; ★ JAC; mail Jackson z 49203; Ⓟ 4,642; Ⓒ 4,809
Van Meer; RMC Place; ALGER; ▲ Munising; *188 D-4; elev. 887ft./270m.; mail Shingleton z 49884; ● 60
Vantown; RMC Place; INGHAM; ▲ White Oak, Leroy; *189 Q-10; elev. 932ft./284m.; mail Webberville z 48892; ● 30
Vassar; Inc. Place; TUSCOLA; 189 N-11; 🅿; ★ FLN; z 48768 & mail Tuscola z 48769; Ⓟ 2,559; Ⓒ 2,823
Vassar; MCD-Township; TUSCOLA; *189 O-11; 🅿; ★ FLN; z 48768 & mail Tuscola z 48769; does not include the City of Vassar; Ⓟ 3,866; Ⓒ 4,356
Venice; MCD-Township; SHIAWASSEE; *189 P-10; ★ FLN; mail Corunna z 48817; Ⓟ 2,812; Ⓒ 2,588
Vergennes; MCD-Township; KENT; *189 P-7; ★ GDR; mail Lowell z 49331; Ⓟ 2,492; Ⓒ 3,611
Vermontville; Inc. Place; EATON; ▲ Vermontville; 189 Q-8; elev. 928ft./283m.; 🅿; z 49096; Ⓟ 776; Ⓒ 789
Vermontville; MCD-Township; EATON; *189 Q-8; 🅿; z 49096; Ⓟ 1,896; Ⓒ 2,100
Vernon; MCD-Township; ISABELLA; *189 M-8; mail Clare z 48617; Ⓟ 1,308; Ⓒ 1,342
Vernon; Inc. Place; SHIAWASSEE; ▲ Vernon; 189 P-10; 🅿; ★ FLN; z 48476 & mail Durand z 48429; Ⓟ 913; Ⓒ 847
Vernon; MCD-Township; SHIAWASSEE; *189 P-10; 🅿; ★ FLN; z 48476 & mail Durand z 48429; Ⓟ 4,989; Ⓒ 4,980
Vernon Center; ISABELLA; see Vernon City (RMC Place)
Vernon City (Vernon Center); RMC Place; ISABELLA; ▲ Vernon; 189 M-8; mail Clare z 48617; pop. incl. with Clare (Inc. Place)
Verona; RMC Place; CALHOUN; *189 R-7; ★ BTLCK; mail Battle Creek z 49017; pop. incl. with Battle Creek (Inc. Place)
Verona; RMC Place; GOGEBIC; ▲ Wakefield; *188 B-10; elev. 1,530ft./466m.; mail Wakefield z 49968; pop. incl. with Wakefield (Inc. Place)
Verona; RMC Place; HURON; ▲ Verona; 189 M-13; elev. 803ft./245m.; mail Bad Axe z 48413; ● 80
Verona; MCD-Township; HURON; *189 M-13; mail Bad Axe z 48413; Ⓟ 1,196; Ⓒ 1,349
Verona Park; RMC Place; CALHOUN; ▲ Pennfield; *189 R-7; ★ BTLCK; mail Battle Creek z 49017; pop. incl. with Battle Creek (Inc. Place)
Vestaburg; RMC Place; MONTCALM; ▲ Richland; 189 N-8; 🅿; z 48891; ● 420
Vevay; MCD-Township; INGHAM; *189 Q-9; ★ LANS; mail Mason z 48854; Ⓟ 3,668; Ⓒ 3,614
Vickery Landing; RMC Place; BARRY; ▲ Johnstown; *189 R-7; ★ BTLCK; mail Dowling z 49050; ● 50
Vickeryville; RMC Place; MONTCALM; ▲ Bushnell; 189 O-8; elev. 822ft./251m.; mail Sheridan z 48884; ● 100
Vicksburg; Inc. Place; KALAMAZOO; ▲ Schoolcraft, Brady; 189 S-6; elev. 860ft./262m.; 🅿 🅷; ★ KZOO; z 49097; Ⓟ 2,216; Ⓒ 2,320
Victor; MCD-Township; CLINTON; *189 P-9; ★ LANS; mail Laingsburg z 48848; Ⓟ 2,784; Ⓒ 3,275
Victoria; RMC Place; ONTONAGON; ▲ Rockland; *188 B-12; elev. 1,149ft./350m.; mail Rockland z 49960
Victory; MCD-Township; MASON; *189 L-4; mail Scottville z 49454; Ⓟ 1,084; Ⓒ 1,444
Vienna; MCD-Charter Township; GENESEE; *189 O-11; ★ FLN; mail Clio z 48420; Ⓟ 13,210; Ⓒ 13,108
Vienna; RMC Place; MONTMORENCY; ▲ Vienna; *188 I-9; mail Johannesburg z 49751; ● 30
Vienna; MCD-Charter Township; MONTMORENCY; *188 I-9; mail Johannesburg z 49751; Ⓟ 431; Ⓒ 572
Village of Clarkston; OAKLAND; see Clarkston (Inc. Place)
Village of Lake Isabella; ISABELLA; see Lake Isabella (Inc. Place)
Virginia Park; RMC Place; OTTAWA; ▲ Park; *189 Q-5; ★ HLND; mail Holland z 49423; ● 1,800
Vogel Center; RMC Place; MISSAUKEE; ▲ Clam Union; 189 L-7; mail Mc Bain z 49657; ● 110
Volinia; RMC Place; CASS; ▲ Volinia; 189 S-5; elev. 865ft./264m.; mail Decatur z 49045; ● 40
Volinia; MCD-Township; CASS; *189 S-5; mail Decatur z 49045; Ⓟ 1,032; Ⓒ 1,174
Volney; RMC Place; NEWAYGO; ▲ Beaver; *189 M-5; elev. 878ft./268m.; mail Bitely z 49309; ● 30
Vriesland; RMC Place; OTTAWA; ▲ Zeeland; 189 Q-5; ★ HLND; mail Zeeland z 49464; ● 150
Vulcan; RMC Place; DICKINSON; ▲ Norway; 188 D-14; 🅿; z 49852, z 49892; ● 100

W

Wabaningo (Sylvan Beach); RMC Place; MUSKEGON; ▲ Fruitland; *189 O-4; elev. 585ft./178m.; ★ MUS; mail Sylvan Beach z 49463, Whitehall z 49461; summer pop. 100
Wacousta; RMC Place; CLINTON; ▲ Watertown; 189 P-8; elev. 797ft./243m.; ★ LANS; mail Grand Ledge z 48837; ● 310
Wadhams; RMC Place; ST. CLAIR; ▲ Kimball; 189 P-14; ★ PTHU; mail Smiths Creek z 48074; ● 150
Wagarville; RMC Place; GLADWIN; ▲ Gladwin; *189 L-9; elev. 843ft./257m.; mail Gladwin z 48624; ● 30
Wainola; RMC Place; ONTONAGON; ▲ Greenland; *188 B-12; elev. 1,122ft./342m.; mail Mass City z 49948; rural
Wakefield; Inc. Place; GOGEBIC; 188 B-10; elev. 1,550ft./472m.; 🅿; z 49968; Ⓟ 2,318; Ⓒ 2,085
Wakefield; MCD-Township; GOGEBIC; *188 B-10; 🅿; z 49968; does not include the City of Wakefield; Ⓟ 452; Ⓒ 364
Wakelee; RMC Place; CASS; ▲ Marcellus, Newberg, Penn, Volinia; 189 S-5; mail Marcellus z 49067; ● 80
Wakeshma; MCD-Township; KALAMAZOO; *189 S-7; mail Fulton z 49052; Ⓟ 1,378; Ⓒ 1,414
Waldenburg; RMC Place; MACOMB; ▲ Macomb; 190 F-8; elev. 605ft./184m.; ★ DET; mail Macomb z 48044; ● 110
Waldron; Inc. Place; HILLSDALE; ▲ Wright; 189 T-9; elev. 900ft./274m.; 🅿; z 49288; Ⓟ 581; Ⓒ 590
Wales; RMC Place; ST. CLAIR; ▲ Wales; *189 P-13; elev. 700ft./213m.; 🅿; z 48027; rural
Wales; MCD-Township; ST. CLAIR; *189 P-13; 🅿; z 48027; Ⓟ 2,294; Ⓒ 2,986
Walhalla; RMC Place; MASON; ▲ Branch; 189 M-5; 🅿; z 49458; ● 380
Walker; MCD-Township; CHEBOYGAN; *188 H-9; mail Afton z 49705; Ⓟ 256; Ⓒ 292
Walker; Inc. Place; KENT; 190 B-1; elev. 742ft./226m.; 🅿 ■; ★ GDR; z 49534, z 49544 & mail Grand Rapids z 49504, z 49514; Ⓟ 17,279; Ⓒ 21,842; ◆ 24,427
Walkers Point; RMC Place; MACKINAC; ▲ Bois Blanc; mail Cheboygan z 49721
Walkerville; Inc. Place; OCEANA; ▲ Leavitt; 189 M-5; elev. 870ft./265m.; 🅿; z 49459; Ⓟ 262; Ⓒ 254
Wallace; RMC Place; MENOMINEE; ▲ Mellen; 188 H-1; 🅿; z 49893; ● 150
Walled Lake; Inc. Place; OAKLAND; 189 Q-11; elev. 939ft./286m.; 🅿; ★ DET; z 48390-91; Ⓟ 6,278; Ⓒ 6,713
Wallin; RMC Place; BENZIE; ▲ Colfax; *188 J-5; elev. 824ft./251m.; mail Thompsonville z 49683
Wall Lake; RMC Place; BARRY; ▲ Hope; mail Delton z 49046; summer pop. 500
Walloon Lake; RMC Place; CHARLEVOIX; ▲ Melrose; 188 H-8; 🅿; z 49796; ● 240
Walnut Lake; RMC Place; OAKLAND; ▲ West Bloomfield; *189 Q-12; ★ DET; mail Bloomfield Hills z 48301; ● 950
Walnut Point; RMC Place; CALHOUN; ▲ Convis; *189 R-8; elev. 943ft./287m.; mail Marshall z 49068; rural
Walters; RMC Place; OAKLAND; ▲ Independence; *189 Q-12; elev. 1,055ft./322m.; ★ DET; mail Clarkston z 48346; ● 550
Walton; MCD-Township; EATON; *189 R-8; mail Olivet z 49076; Ⓟ 1,729; Ⓒ 2,011
Waltz; RMC Place; WAYNE; ▲ Huron; 190 N-3; ★ DET; mail New Boston z 48164; ● 500
Wardcliff; RMC Place; INGHAM; ▲ Meridian; *189 Q-9; ★ LANS; mail East Lansing z 48823; ● 2,100
Warner; MCD-Township; ANTRIM; *188 I-8; mail Elmira z 49730; Ⓟ 287; Ⓒ 389
Warren; Inc. Place; MACOMB; 189 Q-13; elev. 615ft./187m.; 🅿 🅷 ■; ★ DET; z 48088-93, z 48397; Ⓟ 144,864; Ⓒ 138,247; ◆ 131,979
Warren; MCD-Township; MIDLAND; *189 M-9; mail Coleman z 48618; Ⓟ 1,812; Ⓒ 2,107
Wasepi; RMC Place; ST. JOSEPH; ▲ Nottawa; *189 T-6; mail Centreville z 49032
Washington; MCD-Township; GRATIOT; *189 O-9; mail Ashley z 48806; Ⓟ 1,029; Ⓒ 909
Washington; RMC Place; MACOMB; ▲ Washington; 189 Q-13; elev. 700ft./213m.; 🅿; ★ DET; z 48094-95; ● 1,850
Washington; MCD-Township; MACOMB; *189 Q-13; 🅿; ★ DET; z 48094-95 & mail Romeo z 48065; Ⓟ 13,087; Ⓒ 19,080; ◆ 22,332
Washington; MCD-Township; SANILAC; *189 N-13; mail Applegate z 48401; Ⓟ 1,557; Ⓒ 1,636
Washington Harbor; RMC Place; KEWEENAW; ▲ Eagle Harbor; mail Grand Portage z 55605
Washington Heights; RMC Place; CALHOUN; ★ BTLCK; mail Battle Creek z 49017; pop. incl. with Battle Creek (Inc. Place)
WASHTENAW; 189 R-10; Ⓟ 282,937; Ⓒ 322,895; Ⓡ 322,770; ◆ 361,395
Waterford; CDP; OAKLAND; ▲ Waterford; 189 Q-12; 🅿; ★ DET; z 48327-29 & mail Drayton Plains z 48330; Ⓟ 66,692; Ⓒ 73,150; Ⓡ 71,981; ◆ 70,813
Waterford (Waterford Township); MCD-Charter Township; OAKLAND; *189 Q-12; 🅿; ★ DET; z 48327-29 & mail Drayton Plains z 48330; Ⓟ 66,692; Ⓒ 73,150; Ⓡ 71,981; ◆ 70,813
Waterford Township; OAKLAND; see Waterford (MCD-Charter Township)
Waterloo; RMC Place; JACKSON; ▲ Waterloo; 189 R-10; mail Grass Lake z 49240; ● 190
Waterloo; MCD-Township; JACKSON; *189 R-10; mail Grass Lake z 49240; Ⓟ 2,830; Ⓒ 3,069
Watermill Lake; RMC Place; LAKE; ▲ Yates; *189 M-6; elev. 830ft./253m.; mail Idlewild z 49642; ● 110
Waters; RMC Place; OTSEGO; ▲ Otsego Lake; 188 I-8; elev. 1,265ft./386m.; 🅿; z 49797; ● 150
Watersmeet; RMC Place; GOGEBIC; ▲ Watersmeet; 188 C-12; elev. 1,598ft./487m.; 🅿; z 49969; ● 800
Watersmeet; MCD-Township; GOGEBIC; *188 C-12; 🅿; z 49969; Ⓟ 1,048; Ⓒ 1,472
Watertown; MCD-Charter Township; CLINTON; *189 Q-8; ★ LANS; mail Dewitt z 48820; Ⓟ 3,731; Ⓒ 4,162; Ⓡ 4,160
Watertown; RMC Place; SANILAC; ▲ Watertown; 189 O-13; mail Sandusky z 48471; ● 100
Watertown; MCD-Township; SANILAC; *189 N-13; mail Sandusky z 48471; Ⓟ 1,235; Ⓒ 1,376
Watertown; MCD-Township; TUSCOLA; *189 O-12; mail Fostoria z 48435; Ⓟ 2,132; Ⓒ 2,231
Watervale; RMC Place; BENZIE; ▲ Blaine; *189 K-4; mail Arcadia z 49613; summer pop. 100
Watervliet; Inc. Place; BERRIEN; 189 S-4; 🅿 🅷; ★ BNTH-; z 49098; Ⓟ 1,867; Ⓒ 1,843
Watervliet; MCD-Township; BERRIEN; *189 S-4; 🅿; ★ BNTH-; z 49098; does not include the City of Watervliet; Ⓟ 2,926; Ⓒ 3,392
Watrousville; RMC Place; TUSCOLA; ▲ Juniata; 189 N-11; mail Vassar z 48768; ● 200
Watson; RMC Place; ALLEGAN; ▲ Watson; 189 Q-6; elev. 812ft./247m.; mail Otsego z 49078; ● 30
Watson; MCD-Township; ALLEGAN; *189 Q-6; mail Otsego z 49078; Ⓟ 1,897; Ⓒ 2,086; Ⓡ 2,084
Wattles Park; RMC Place; CALHOUN; ▲ Emmett; *189 R-7; elev. 901ft./275m.; ★ BTLCK; mail Battle Creek z 49014; ● 720
Watton; RMC Place; BARAGA; ▲ Covington; 188 B-12; 🅿; z 49970; ● 150
Waucedah; RMC Place; DICKINSON; ▲ Waucedah; 188 D-14; elev. 900ft./274m.; mail Vulcan z 49892; ● 50
Waucedah; MCD-Township; DICKINSON; *188 D-14; mail Vulcan z 49892; Ⓟ 693; Ⓒ 800
Waverly; MCD-Township; CHEBOYGAN; *188 G-9; mail Onaway z 49765; Ⓟ 371; Ⓒ 472
Waverly; CDP-Census Area Only; EATON; ▲ Delta; *189 Q-9; ★ LANS; mail Lansing z 48917; Ⓟ 15,614; Ⓒ 16,194
Waverly; MCD-Township; VAN BUREN; *189 R-5; mail Paw Paw z 49079; Ⓟ 2,188; Ⓒ 2,467
Wawatam; MCD-Township; EMMET; *188 F-8; mail Mackinaw City z 49701; Ⓟ 563; Ⓒ 705
Wawatam Beach; RMC Place; CHEBOYGAN; mail Mackinaw City z 49701; pop. incl. with Mackinaw City (Inc. Place)
Wayland; Inc. Place; ALLEGAN; 189 Q-6; 🅿; z 49348; Ⓟ 2,751; Ⓒ 3,939
Wayland; MCD-Township; ALLEGAN; *189 Q-6; 🅿; z 49348; does not include the City of Wayland; Ⓟ 2,569; Ⓒ 3,013
Wayne; MCD-Township; CASS; *189 S-5; mail Dowagiac z 49047; Ⓟ 2,780; Ⓒ 2,861
Wayne; Inc. Place; WAYNE; 190 K-3; elev. 658ft./201m.; 🅿 🅷; ★ DET; z 48184; Ⓟ 19,899; Ⓒ 19,051
WAYNE; 189 R-12; Ⓟ 2,111,687; Ⓒ 2,061,162; ◆ 2,005,415
Wayne Junction; RMC Place; WAYNE; ★ DET; pop. incl. with Wayne (Inc. Place)
Weadock; RMC Place; CHEBOYGAN; ▲ Nunda; *188 G-8; mail Levering z 49755; rural
Weale; RMC Place; HURON; ▲ Fairhaven; *189 M-12; mail Bay Port z 48720
Weare; MCD-Township; OCEANA; *189 M-4; mail Hart z 49420; Ⓟ 1,041; Ⓒ 1,261
Webber; MCD-Township; LAKE; *189 M-5; mail Baldwin z 49304; Ⓟ 968; Ⓒ 1,875
Webberville; Inc. Place; INGHAM; ▲ Leroy; 189 Q-10; 🅿; z 48892; Ⓟ 1,698; Ⓒ 1,503
Webster; MCD-Township; WASHTENAW; *189 R-11; ★ DET; mail Dexter z 48130; Ⓟ 3,235; Ⓒ 5,198
Weesaw; MCD-Township; BERRIEN; *189 T-4; mail Three Oaks z 49128; Ⓟ 2,114; Ⓒ 2,065
Weidman; CDP; ISABELLA; ▲ Sherman, Nottawa; 189 M-8; elev. 892ft./272m.; 🅿; z 48893; Ⓟ 696; Ⓒ 879
Welcome Corners; RMC Place; BARRY; ▲ Carlton; *189 Q-7; elev. 844ft./257m.; mail Hastings z 49058; rural
Weldon; MCD-Township; BENZIE; *188 J-5; mail Thompsonville z 49683; Ⓟ 448; Ⓒ 530
Wellington; MCD-Township; ALPENA; *188 H-10; mail Lachine z 49753; Ⓟ 269; Ⓒ 296
Wells; RMC Place; DELTA; ▲ Wells; 188 F-2; elev. 632ft./193m.; 🅿; z 49894; ● 1,000
Wells; MCD-Township; DELTA; *188 F-2; 🅿; z 49894; Ⓟ 5,159; Ⓒ 5,044
Wells; MCD-Township; MARQUETTE; *188 E-1; mail Cornell z 49818; Ⓟ 281; Ⓒ 292
Wells; MCD-Township; TUSCOLA; *189 N-12; mail Caro z 48723; Ⓟ 1,528; Ⓒ 1,946; Ⓡ 1,743
Wellston; RMC Place; MANISTEE; ▲ Norman; 189 L-5; elev. 773ft./236m.; 🅿; z 49689; ● 320
Wellsville; RMC Place; LENAWEE; ▲ Palmyra; *189 T-11; mail Blissfield z 49228; rural
Wenona Beach; RMC Place; BAY; ▲ Bangor; ★ SAG-; mail Bay City z 48706
Wequetonsing; RMC Place; EMMET; ▲ Little Traverse; 188 G-7; 🅿; z 49740; summer pop. 500
West Bloomfield; RMC Place; OAKLAND; ▲ West Bloomfield; 🅿; ★ DET; z 48322-25
West Bloomfield; MCD-Charter Township; OAKLAND; 190 G-3; 🅿; ★ DET; z 48322-25; Ⓟ 54,843; Ⓒ 64,860; ◆ 65,197
West Bloomfield Township; CDP-Census Area Only; OAKLAND; ▲ West Bloomfield; *189 Q-12; ★ DET; mail West Bloomfield z 48323-24; Ⓟ 54,843; Ⓒ 64,862; ◆ 65,197
West Branch; MCD-Township; DICKINSON; *188 E-1; mail Ralph z 49877; Ⓟ 80; Ⓒ 67
West Branch; MCD-Township; MARQUETTE; *188 D-2; mail Skandia z 49885; Ⓟ 2,241; Ⓒ 1,648
West Branch; MCD-Township; MISSAUKEE; *189 K-7; mail Merritt z 49667; Ⓟ 473; Ⓒ 532
West Branch; Inc. Place; ⊡ OGEMAW; 189 K-9; elev. 959ft./292m.; 🅿 🅷; z 48661; Ⓟ 1,914; Ⓒ 1,926
West Branch; MCD-Township; OGEMAW; *189 K-10; 🅿; z 48661; does not include the City of West Branch; Ⓟ 2,294; Ⓒ 2,628
Westchester Village; RMC Place; OAKLAND; ▲ Bloomfield; *189 Q-12; ★ DET; mail Bloomfield Hills z 48301
West Ishpeming; CDP; MARQUETTE; ▲ Ishpeming; *188 D-1; mail Ishpeming z 49849; Ⓒ 2,792
Westland; Inc. Place; WAYNE; 189 R-12; elev. 636ft./194m.; 🅿 🅷 ■; ★ DET; z 48185-86 & mail Wayne z 48184; Ⓟ 84,724; Ⓒ 86,602; ◆ 84,949
West Leroy; RMC Place; CALHOUN; ▲ Leroy; *189 S-7; elev. 979ft./298m.; ★ BTLCK; mail East Leroy z 49051; rural
West Monroe; CDP-Census Area Only; MONROE; ▲ Monroe; *189 T-12; ★ MONR; mail Monroe z 48161-62; Ⓟ 3,919; Ⓒ 3,893
West Olive; RMC Place; OTTAWA; ▲ Port Sheldon; 189 P-5; 🅿; ★ HLND; z 49460; ● 200
Weston; RMC Place; LENAWEE; ▲ Fairfield; 189 T-10; elev. 760ft./232m.; 🅿; z 49289; ● 300
Westphalia; Inc. Place; CLINTON; ▲ Westphalia; 189 P-8; elev. 761ft./232m.; 🅿; z 48894; Ⓟ 780; Ⓒ 876
Westphalia; MCD-Township; CLINTON; *189 P-8; 🅿; z 48894; Ⓟ 2,099; Ⓒ 2,257
West Sebewa; RMC Place; IONIA; ▲ Sebewa; *189 P-7; elev. 863ft./263m.; mail Portland z 48875; rural
West Side; RMC Place; SAGINAW; ▲ Saginaw; ★ SAG-; mail Saginaw z 48603; pop. incl. with Saginaw (Inc. Place)
West Traverse; MCD-Township; EMMET; *188 G-7; mail Harbor Springs z 49740; Ⓟ 968; Ⓒ 1,448
Westville; RMC Place; MONTCALM; ▲ Douglass, Day; 189 O-7; elev. 957ft./292m.; mail Stanton z 48888; ● 50
West Willow; RMC Place; WASHTENAW; ▲ Ypsilanti; *189 R-11; ★ DET; mail Ypsilanti z 48198; ● 4,400
West Windsor; RMC Place; EATON; ▲ Windsor; 189 Q-8; ★ LANS; mail Charlotte z 48813
Westwood; CDP; KALAMAZOO; ▲ Kalamazoo; *189 R-6; ★ KZOO; mail Kalamazoo z 49006, z 49009, z 49019; Ⓟ 8,957; Ⓒ 9,122
Westwood; OAKLAND; see Beverly Hills (Inc. Place)
Westwood Heights; RMC Place; GENESEE; ▲ Mount Morris; *189 P-11; ★ FLN; mail Flint z 48504; ● 860
West Yard; RMC Place; MARQUETTE; ▲ Marquette; pop. incl. with Marquette (Inc. Place)
Wetmore; RMC Place; ALGER; ▲ Munising; 188 D-3; elev. 872ft./266m.; 🅿; z 49895 & mail Kalamazoo z 49006-07, z 49009; ● 480
Wetzel; RMC Place; ANTRIM; ▲ Mancelona; *188 I-7; mail Mancelona z 49659; rural
Wexford; MCD-Township; WEXFORD; *189 K-6; mail Mesick z 49668; Ⓟ 567; Ⓒ 798
WEXFORD; 189 K-6; Ⓟ 26,360; Ⓒ 30,484; ◆ 31,769
Wheatfield; MCD-Township; INGHAM; *189 Q-9; mail Williamston z 48895; Ⓟ 1,571; Ⓒ 1,641
Wheatland; MCD-Township; HILLSDALE; *189 T-9; mail Addison z 49220; Ⓟ 1,225; Ⓒ 1,258
Wheatland; MCD-Township; MECOSTA; *189 N-7; mail Remus z 49340; Ⓟ 1,365; Ⓒ 1,474
Wheatland; MCD-Township; SANILAC; *189 N-13; mail Deckerville z 48427; Ⓟ 513; Ⓒ 530
Wheeler; RMC Place; GRATIOT; ▲ Wheeler; 189 N-9; 🅿; z 48662; ● 320
Wheeler; MCD-Township; GRATIOT; *189 N-9; 🅿; z 48662; Ⓟ 2,926; Ⓒ 2,785
White; RMC Place; HOUGHTON; ▲ Laird; *188 B-12; mail Nisula z 49952; rural
White Cloud; Inc. Place; ⊡ NEWAYGO; 189 N-6; elev. 871ft./265m.; 🅿; z 49349; Ⓟ 1,147; Ⓒ 1,420
Whitefish; MCD-Township; CHIPPEWA; *188 C-7; mail Eckerman z 49728; Ⓟ 517; Ⓒ 588
Whitefish Point; RMC Place; CHIPPEWA; ▲ Whitefish; 188 C-7; mail Paradise z 49768; ● 50
Whiteford; MCD-Township; MONROE; *189 T-11; ★ TOL; mail Ottawa Lake z 49267; Ⓟ 4,433; Ⓒ 4,420
Whiteford Center; RMC Place; MONROE; ▲ Whiteford; *189 T-11; elev. 682ft./208m.; ★ TOL; mail Ottawa Lake z 49267; ● 90
Whitehall; Inc. Place; MUSKEGON; 189 N-4; elev. 593ft./181m.; 🅿; ★ MUS; z 49461, z 49463; Ⓟ 3,027; Ⓒ 2,884
Whitehall; MCD-Township; MUSKEGON; *189 N-4; 🅿; ★ MUS; z 49461, z 49463; does not include the City of Whitehall; Ⓟ 1,464; Ⓒ 1,648
White Lake; RMC Place; OAKLAND; ▲ White Lake; 190 E-2; 🅿; ★ DET; z 48383, z 48386; ● 3,200
White Lake; MCD-Charter Township; OAKLAND; *189 Q-11; 🅿; ★ DET; z 48383, z 48386; Ⓟ 22,608; Ⓒ 28,219; ◆ 29,094
White Oak; MCD-Township; INGHAM; *189 Q-10; mail Dansville z 48819, Stockbridge z 49285; Ⓟ 1,074; Ⓒ 1,177
White Pigeon; Inc. Place; ST. JOSEPH; ▲ White Pigeon; 189 T-6; elev. 815ft./248m.; 🅿; ★ ELK; z 49099; Ⓟ 1,458; Ⓒ 1,627
White Pigeon; MCD-Township; ST. JOSEPH; *189 T-6; 🅿; ★ ELK; z 49099; Ⓟ 3,654; Ⓒ 3,847
White Pine; RMC Place; ONTONAGON; ▲ Carp Lake; 188 B-11; 🅿; z 49971; ● 910
White River; MCD-Township; MUSKEGON; *189 N-4; ★ MUS; mail Montague z 49437; Ⓟ 1,250; Ⓒ 1,338
White Rock; RMC Place; HURON; ▲ Sherman; *189 M-14; elev. 600ft./183m.; mail Harbor Beach z 48441; ● 50
Whites Beach; RMC Place; ARENAC; ▲ Standish; *189 M-10; ★ SAG-; mail Standish z 48658; ● 150
White Star; RMC Place; GLADWIN; ▲ Hay; *189 L-9; elev. 727ft./222m.; mail Gladwin z 48624; ● 50
Whitewater; MCD-Township; GRAND TRAVERSE; *188 J-7; mail Williamsburg z 49690; Ⓟ 1,825; Ⓒ 2,467
Whitmore Lake; CDP; LIVINGSTON, WASHTENAW; ▲ Green Oak, Northfield; 189 R-11; 🅿; ★ DET; z 48189; Ⓟ 3,251; Ⓒ 6,574
Whitney; MCD-Township; ARENAC; *189 L-11; mail Turner z 48765; Ⓟ 981; Ⓒ 1,033
Whitneyville; RMC Place; KENT; ▲ Cascade; *189 P-6; elev. 739ft./225m.; ★ GDR; mail Alto z 49302; ● 50
Whittaker; RMC Place; WASHTENAW; ▲ Augusta; 189 S-11; elev. 677ft./206m.; 🅿; ★ DET; z 48190; ● 240
Whittemore; Inc. Place; IOSCO; 189 L-10; elev. 780ft./238m.; 🅿; z 48770; Ⓟ 463; Ⓒ 476
Wickware; RMC Place; SANILAC; ▲ Greenleaf; *189 N-12; elev. 776ft./237m.; mail Cass City z 48726; rural
Wilber; MCD-Township; IOSCO; *189 K-11; mail East Tawas z 48730; Ⓟ 638; Ⓒ 740
Wilcox; MCD-Township; NEWAYGO; *189 N-6; mail White Cloud z 49349; Ⓟ 831; Ⓒ 1,145
Wildwood; RMC Place; CHEBOYGAN; ▲ Mentor; *188 H-8; elev. 721ft./220m.; mail Alanson z 49706
Wildwood; RMC Place; MANISTEE; ▲ Bear Lake; 189 K-5; mail Bear Lake z 49614; ● 80
Willard; RMC Place; BAY; ▲ Beaver; 189 N-10; elev. 618ft./188m.; ★ SAG-; mail Auburn z 48611
Williams; MCD-Charter Township; BAY; *189 N-10; ★ SAG-; mail Auburn z 48611; Ⓟ 4,278; Ⓒ 4,492
Williamsburg; RMC Place; GRAND TRAVERSE; ▲ Whitewater; 188 J-6; 🅿; z 49690; ● 400
Williamsport; RMC Place; MANISTEE; ▲ Manistee; *189 K-4; mail Manistee z 49660; ● 30
Williamston; Inc. Place; INGHAM; 189 Q-9; 🅿; ★ LANS; z 48895; Ⓟ 2,922; Ⓒ 3,441
Williamstown; MCD-Township; INGHAM; *189 Q-9; ★ LANS; mail Williamston z 48895; does not include the City of Williamston; Ⓟ 4,285; Ⓒ 4,834
Williamsville; RMC Place; CASS; ▲ Porter; *189 T-5; ★ ELK; mail Vandalia z 49095; ● 60
Williamsville; RMC Place; LIVINGSTON; ▲ Unadilla; *189 R-10; elev. 924ft./282m.; ★ DET; mail Gregory z 48137; rural
Willis; RMC Place; WASHTENAW; ▲ Augusta; 190 M-1; elev. 688ft./210m.; 🅿; ★ DET; z 48191; ● 300
Willow; RMC Place; WAYNE; ▲ Huron; 190 N-3; ★ DET; mail New Boston z 48164; ● 430
Wilmot; MCD-Township; CHEBOYGAN; *188 H-8; mail Wolverine z 49799; Ⓟ 592; Ⓒ 826
Wilmot; RMC Place; TUSCOLA; ▲ Kingston; 189 N-12; mail Deford z 48729; ● 140
Wilson; MCD-Township; ALPENA; *188 I-11; mail Alpena z 49707; Ⓟ 1,902; Ⓒ 2,074
Wilson; MCD-Township; CHARLEVOIX; *188 H-7; mail Ellsworth z 49729; Ⓟ 1,391; Ⓒ 2,022
Wilson; RMC Place; MENOMINEE; ▲ Harris; 188 G-1; 🅿; z 49896; ● 150
Windemere; RMC Place; INGHAM; ▲ Lansing; *189 Q-9; ★ LANS; mail Lansing z 48917; ● 1,800
Windsor; MCD-Charter Township; EATON; *189 Q-8; ★ LANS; mail Dimondale z 48821; Ⓟ 6,460; Ⓒ 7,340
Winegars; RMC Place; GLADWIN; ▲ Hay, Buckeye; 189 M-9; elev. 731ft./223m.; mail Gladwin z 48624
Winfield; MCD-Township; MONTCALM; *189 N-7; mail Lakeview z 48850; Ⓟ 1,336; Ⓒ 2,049
Winn; RMC Place; ISABELLA; ▲ Fremont; 189 N-8; 🅿; z 48896; ● 450
Winona; RMC Place; HOUGHTON; ▲ Elm River; 188 B-12; mail Toivola z 49965; ● 40
Winsor; MCD-Township; HURON; *189 M-12; mail Pigeon z 48755; Ⓟ 2,032; Ⓒ 2,044
Winterfield; MCD-Township; CLARE; *189 L-7; mail Marion z 49665; Ⓟ 371; Ⓒ 483
Winters; RMC Place; ALGER; ▲ Mathias; *188 E-3; mail Trenary z 49891; rural
Winthrop Junction; RMC Place; MARQUETTE; ▲ Ishpeming; *188 D-1; mail Ishpeming z 49849; pop. incl. with Ishpeming (Inc. Place)
Wise; MCD-Township; ISABELLA; *189 M-8; mail Coleman z 48618; Ⓟ 1,233; Ⓒ 1,301
Wisner; RMC Place; TUSCOLA; ▲ Wisner, Akron; 189 N-11; mail Akron z 48701; ● 110
Wisner; MCD-Township; TUSCOLA; *189 N-11; mail Fairgrove z 48733; Ⓟ 795; Ⓒ 749
Witch Lake; RMC Place; MARQUETTE; ▲ Republic; 188 C-13; elev. 1,493ft./455m.; mail Republic z 49879; ● 80
Wixom; Inc. Place; OAKLAND; 189 Q-11; elev. 930ft./283m.; 🅿; ★ DET; z 48393; Ⓟ 8,550; Ⓒ 13,263
Wolf Lake; RMC Place; JACKSON; ▲ Grass Lake, Napoleon; *189 S-10; elev. 964ft./294m.; ★ JAC; mail Jackson z 49201; ● 410
Wolf Lake; CDP; MUSKEGON; ▲ Egelston; 189 O-5; elev. 640ft./195m.; ★ MUS; mail Muskegon z 49442; Ⓟ 4,110; Ⓒ 4,455
Wolverine; Inc. Place; CHEBOYGAN; ▲ Wilmot, Nunda; 188 H-8; 🅿; z 49799; Ⓟ 283; Ⓒ 359
Wolverine Lake; Inc. Place; OAKLAND; ▲ Commerce; 190 G-2; 🅿; ★ DET; z 48390; Ⓟ 4,727; Ⓒ 4,415
Woodard Lake; RMC Place; IONIA; ▲ Ronald; *189 P-7; elev. 840ft./256m.; mail Fenwick z 48834; rural
Woodbridge; MCD-Township; HILLSDALE; *189 T-9; mail Hillsdale z 49242; Ⓟ 1,160; Ⓒ 1,337
Woodbury; RMC Place; BARRY, EATON; ▲ Sunfield, Woodland; 189 Q-7; mail Lake Odessa z 48849; ● 80
Wooden Shoe Village; RMC Place; GLADWIN; ▲ Hay; 189 L-9; mail Gladwin z 48624; ● 330
Woodhaven; Inc. Place; WAYNE; 190 M-5; elev. 595ft./181m.; 🅿; ★ DET; z 48183; Ⓟ 11,631; Ⓒ 12,530
Woodhull; MCD-Township; SHIAWASSEE; *189 P-9; ★ LANS; mail Perry z 48872; Ⓟ 3,585; Ⓒ 3,850
Woodland; Inc. Place; BARRY; ▲ Woodland; 189 Q-7; elev. 875ft./267m.; 🅿; z 48897; Ⓟ 466; Ⓒ 495
Woodland; MCD-Township; BARRY; *189 Q-7; 🅿; z 48897; Ⓟ 2,025; Ⓒ 2,129
Woodland Beach; CDP; MONROE; ▲ Frenchtown; *189 S-12; ★ MONR; mail Monroe z 48162; Ⓟ 2,309; Ⓒ 2,179
Woodland Lake; RMC Place; LIVINGSTON; ▲ Brighton; *189 Q-11; ★ DET; mail Brighton z 48114; ● 530
Woodland Park; RMC Place; NEWAYGO; ▲ Merrill; 189 M-5; mail Bitely z 49309; ● 200
Woods; RMC Place; ISABELLA; ▲ Gilmore; *189 M-8; elev. 934ft./285m.; mail Farwell z 48622; rural
Wood Spur; RMC Place; ONTONAGON; ▲ Ontonagon; *188 B-11; elev. 849ft./259m.; mail Ontonagon z 49953; rural
Woodstock; MCD-Township; LENAWEE; *189 S-9; ★ JAC; mail Addison z 49220; Ⓟ 3,155; Ⓒ 3,468
Woodville; RMC Place; NEWAYGO; ▲ Norwich, Monroe; 189 N-6; elev. 998ft./304m.; mail White Cloud z 49349; ● 50
Wooster; RMC Place; NEWAYGO; ▲ Sherman; *189 N-5; mail Fremont z 49412; rural
Worden; RMC Place; WASHTENAW; ▲ Salem; *189 R-11; elev. 972ft./296m.; ★ DET; mail South Lyon z 48178; rural
Worth; RMC Place; ARENAC; ▲ Standish; *189 M-10; elev. 616ft./188m.; ★ SAG-; mail Pinconning z 48650
Worth; MCD-Township; SANILAC; *189 O-14; ★ PTHU; mail Croswell z 48422, Jeddo z 48032; Ⓟ 3,146; Ⓒ 4,021
Wright; MCD-Township; HILLSDALE; *189 T-9; mail Pittsford z 49271; Ⓟ 1,809; Ⓒ 1,788
Wright; RMC Place; OTTAWA; ▲ Wright; *189 P-6; elev. 870ft./265m.; ★ GDR; mail Conklin z 49403; ● 40
Wright; MCD-Township; OTTAWA; *189 P-5; ★ GDR; mail Conklin z 49403; Ⓟ 3,285; Ⓒ 3,286
Wyandotte; Inc. Place; WAYNE; 189 S-12; 🅿 🅷 ■; ★ DET; z 48192-93; Ⓟ 30,938; Ⓒ 28,006; ◆ 25,304
Wyman; RMC Place; MONTCALM; ▲ Home; 189 N-7; mail Blanchard z 49310; ● 50
Wyoming; Inc. Place; KENT; 189 P-6; elev. 646ft./197m.; 🅿 ■; ★ GDR; z 49418, z 49503, z 49508-09, z 49519, z 49548; Ⓟ 63,891; Ⓒ 69,368; ◆ 73,370
Wyoming Park; RMC Place; KENT; *189 P-6; ★ GDR; mail Wyoming z 49509; pop. incl. with Wyoming (Inc. Place)

Y

Yale; RMC Place; GOGEBIC; ▲ Bessemer; *188 B-10; mail Bessemer z 49911; pop. incl. with Bessemer (Inc. Place)
Yale; Inc. Place; ST. CLAIR; 189 O-13; elev. 802ft./244m.; 🅿 🅷; z 48097; Ⓟ 1,977; Ⓒ 2,063
Yankee Springs; MCD-Township; BARRY; *189 Q-6; ★ GDR; mail Middleville z 49333; Ⓟ 2,977; Ⓒ 4,219
Yates; MCD-Township; LAKE; *189 M-6; mail Idlewild z 49642; Ⓟ 585; Ⓒ 714
Yellow Jacket; RMC Place; HOUGHTON; ▲ Calumet; mail Calumet z 49913; pop. incl. with Calumet (Inc. Place)
York; MCD-Township; WASHTENAW; *189 S-11; ★ DET; mail Milan z 48160; Ⓟ 6,225; Ⓒ 7,392
Yorkville; RMC Place; KALAMAZOO; ▲ Ross; *189 R-7; ★ KZOO; mail Richland z 49083; ● 200
Ypsilanti; Inc. Place; WASHTENAW; 189 R-11; 🅿 🅷 🅲 22,974 ■; ★ DET; z 48197-98; Ⓟ 24,846; Ⓒ 22,362; Ⓡ 22,237; ◆ 23,392
Ypsilanti; MCD-Charter Township; WASHTENAW; *189 S-11; 🅿 🅲 22,974; ★ DET; z 48197-98; does not include the City of Ypsilanti; Ⓟ 45,307; Ⓒ 49,182; ◆ 55,754
Yuba; RMC Place; GRAND TRAVERSE; ▲ Acme; *188 J-6; mail Williamsburg z 49690; ● 30
Yuma; RMC Place; WEXFORD; ▲ Springville; 189 K-6; mail Mesick z 49668; ● 80

Z

Zeba; RMC Place; BARAGA; ▲ L'Anse; *188 B-13; mail Lanse z 49946; ● 130
Zeeland; Inc. Place; OTTAWA; 189 Q-5; elev. 646ft./197m.; 🅿 🅷; ★ HLND; z 49464; Ⓟ 5,417; Ⓒ 5,805
Zeeland; MCD-Charter Township; OTTAWA; *189 Q-5; 🅿; ★ HLND; z 49464; does not include the City of Zeeland; Ⓟ 4,472; Ⓒ 7,613
Zilwaukee; Inc. Place; SAGINAW; 189 N-10; elev. 580ft./177m.; ★ SAG-; mail Saginaw z 48604; Ⓟ 1,850; Ⓒ 1,799
Zilwaukee; MCD-Township; SAGINAW; *189 N-10; ★ SAG-; mail Saginaw z 48604; Ⓟ 82; Ⓒ 61
Zutphen; RMC Place; OTTAWA; ▲ Jamestown; *189 P-5; elev. 754ft./230m.; ★ GDR; mail Hudsonville z 49426; rural

MINNESOTA

Statistics

Total area (2000) — 86,939 square miles
Land area (2000) — 79,610 square miles
Water area (2000) — 7,329 square miles
Capital — Saint Paul
Admitted as state — May, 1858

Maps

State maps can be found on pages 142-254 in Vol. 1

Ranally Metro Areas (RMAs) and Abbreviations

Duluth, MN-WI — DUL
Fargo-Moorhead, ND-MN — FAR-
Grand Forks, ND-MN — GDFK
La Crosse, WI-MN — LACRO
Mankato, MN — MNKT
Minneapolis-St. Paul, MN-WI — MPLS-
Rochester, MN — ROCH
St. Cloud, MN — ST.CLD

Principal Places

Place Name	Place Type	County	Population
Minneapolis	Inc. Place	HENNEPIN	◆ 406,088
Saint Paul	Inc. Place	RAMSEY	◆ 301,792
Rochester	Inc. Place	OLMSTED	◆ 103,354
Duluth	Inc. Place	ST. LOUIS	◆ 86,841
Bloomington	Inc. Place	HENNEPIN	◆ 83,413
Brooklyn Park	Inc. Place	HENNEPIN	◆ 73,656
Plymouth	Inc. Place	HENNEPIN	◆ 71,657
Eagan	Inc. Place	DAKOTA	◆ 66,632
Saint Cloud	Inc. Place	STEARNS	◆ 66,055
Woodbury	Inc. Place	WASHINGTON	◆ 61,277
Burnsville	Inc. Place	DAKOTA	◆ 61,276
Eden Prairie	Inc. Place	HENNEPIN	◆ 61,178
Coon Rapids	Inc. Place	ANOKA	◆ 59,931
Lakeville	Inc. Place	DAKOTA	◆ 54,336
Maple Grove	Inc. Place	HENNEPIN	◆ 53,861
Blaine	Inc. Place	ANOKA	◆ 51,139
Minnetonka	Inc. Place	HENNEPIN	◆ 50,876
Apple Valley	Inc. Place	DAKOTA	◆ 50,366
Edina	Inc. Place	HENNEPIN	◆ 48,384
Saint Louis Park	Inc. Place	HENNEPIN	◆ 45,377
Shakopee	Inc. Place	SCOTT	◆ 36,548
Mankato	Inc. Place	BLUE EARTH	◆ 36,141
Maplewood	Inc. Place	RAMSEY	◆ 35,198
Moorhead	Inc. Place	CLAY	◆ 35,080
Inver Grove Heights	Inc. Place	DAKOTA	◆ 34,370
Richfield	Inc. Place	HENNEPIN	◆ 34,125
Cottage Grove	Inc. Place	WASHINGTON	◆ 32,594
Roseville	Inc. Place	RAMSEY	◆ 32,328
Andover	Inc. Place	ANOKA	◆ 32,182
Savage	Inc. Place	SCOTT	◆ 30,728
Brooklyn Center	Inc. Place	HENNEPIN	◆ 29,682
Winona	Inc. Place	WINONA	◆ 27,518
Oakdale	Inc. Place	WASHINGTON	◆ 26,954
Shoreview	Inc. Place	RAMSEY	◆ 25,772
Fridley	Inc. Place	ANOKA	◆ 25,630
Owatonna	Inc. Place	STEELE	◆ 25,027
Chanhassen	Inc. Place	CARVER	◆ 24,930
Champlin	Inc. Place	HENNEPIN	◆ 23,835
White Bear Lake	Inc. Place	RAMSEY	◆ 23,698
Chaska	Inc. Place	CARVER	◆ 23,330
Faribault	Inc. Place	RICE	◆ 22,868
Austin	Inc. Place	MOWER	◆ 22,855
Crystal	Inc. Place	HENNEPIN	◆ 21,944
Ramsey	Inc. Place	ANOKA	◆ 21,807
Elk River	Inc. Place	SHERBURNE	◆ 21,543
New Brighton	Inc. Place	RAMSEY	◆ 21,021
Hastings	Inc. Place	DAKOTA	◆ 20,955
Lino Lakes	Inc. Place	ANOKA	◆ 20,809
Prior Lake	Inc. Place	SCOTT	◆ 20,665
New Hope	Inc. Place	HENNEPIN	◆ 20,460
South Saint Paul	Inc. Place	DAKOTA	◆ 19,807
Golden Valley	Inc. Place	HENNEPIN	◆ 19,761
West Saint Paul	Inc. Place	DAKOTA	◆ 18,735
Columbia Heights	Inc. Place	ANOKA	© 18,520
Rosemount	Inc. Place	DAKOTA	◆ 18,106
Anoka	Inc. Place	ANOKA	© 18,076
Albert Lea	Inc. Place	FREEBORN	◆ 17,383
Hopkins	Inc. Place	HENNEPIN	® 17,367
Willmar	Inc. Place	KANDIYOHI	◆ 17,249
Northfield	Inc. Place	RICE	© 17,147
Hibbing	Inc. Place	ST. LOUIS	◆ 16,129
Red Wing	Inc. Place	GOODHUE	© 16,116
Stillwater	Inc. Place	WASHINGTON	® 15,323
Robbinsdale	Inc. Place	HENNEPIN	© 14,123
Brainerd	Inc. Place	CROW WING	◆ 13,650
Fergus Falls	Inc. Place	OTTER TAIL	◆ 13,156
Hutchinson	Inc. Place	MCLEOD	© 13,080
Vadnais Heights	Inc. Place	RAMSEY	© 13,069
New Ulm	Inc. Place	BROWN	◆ 12,946
Bemidji	Inc. Place	BELTRAMI	◆ 12,915
Mounds View	Inc. Place	RAMSEY	© 12,738
Ham Lake	Inc. Place	ANOKA	© 12,710
Marshall	Inc. Place	LYON	◆ 12,690
Farmington	Inc. Place	DAKOTA	© 12,365
North Saint Paul	Inc. Place	RAMSEY	© 11,929
North Mankato	Inc. Place	NICOLLET	© 11,798
Worthington	Inc. Place	NOBLES	◆ 11,552
Mendota Heights	Inc. Place	DAKOTA	© 11,434
Cloquet	Inc. Place	CARLTON	© 11,201
East Bethel	Inc. Place	ANOKA	© 10,941
Sauk Rapids	Inc. Place	BENTON	© 10,213
Fairmont	Inc. Place	MARTIN	◆ 10,192
Buffalo	Inc. Place	WRIGHT	© 10,097
Little Canada	Inc. Place	RAMSEY	© 9,771
Saint Peter	Inc. Place	NICOLLET	® 9,761
Arden Hills	Inc. Place	RAMSEY	© 9,652
Sartell	Inc. Place	STEARNS	© 9,641
Waseca	Inc. Place	WASECA	® 9,611
Mound	Inc. Place	HENNEPIN	© 9,435
Saint Michael	Inc. Place	WRIGHT	© 9,099
Virginia	Inc. Place	ST. LOUIS	◆ 8,918
Alexandria	Inc. Place	DOUGLAS	© 8,820
Thief River Falls	Inc. Place	PENNINGTON	© 8,410
Crookston	Inc. Place	POLK	© 8,192
Hermantown	Inc. Place	ST. LOUIS	® 8,047
North Branch	Inc. Place	CHISAGO	© 8,023
Saint Anthony	Inc. Place	HENNEPIN	© 8,012
Monticello	Inc. Place	WRIGHT	© 7,868
Grand Rapids	Inc. Place	ITASCA	© 7,764
Little Falls	Inc. Place	MORRISON	© 7,719
Mahtomedi	Inc. Place	WASHINGTON	© 7,563
Orono	Inc. Place	HENNEPIN	© 7,538
East Grand Forks	Inc. Place	POLK	© 7,501
Shorewood	Inc. Place	HENNEPIN	© 7,400
Detroit Lakes	Inc. Place	BECKER	© 7,348
Oak Grove	Inc. Place	ANOKA	© 6,903
Lake Elmo	Inc. Place	WASHINGTON	© 6,863
Waconia	Inc. Place	CARVER	© 6,814
Forest Lake	Inc. Place	WASHINGTON	© 6,798
Spring Lake Park	Inc. Place	ANOKA	© 6,772
International Falls	Inc. Place	KOOCHICHING	© 6,703
Waite Park	Inc. Place	STEARNS	© 6,568
Litchfield	Inc. Place	MEEKER	© 6,562
Otsego	Inc. Place	WRIGHT	© 6,389
Hugo	Inc. Place	WASHINGTON	© 6,363
Big Lake	Inc. Place	SHERBURNE	© 6,063
Corcoran	Inc. Place	HENNEPIN	© 5,630
Falcon Heights	Inc. Place	RAMSEY	© 5,572
Baxter	Inc. Place	CROW WING	© 5,555
Cambridge	Inc. Place	ISANTI	© 5,520
Montevideo	Inc. Place	CHIPPEWA	® 5,462
Redwood Falls	Inc. Place	REDWOOD	© 5,459
Glencoe	Inc. Place	MCLEOD	© 5,453
Stewartville	Inc. Place	OLMSTED	© 5,411
Morris	Inc. Place	STEVENS	® 5,173
Saint Paul Park	Inc. Place	WASHINGTON	© 5,070
Lake City	Inc. Place	WABASHA	® 5,054

County Business Data

County	FIPS Code	County Seat	Land Area (Sq. Mi.)	Census Population			Wholesale Trade		Manufacturing, 2002			
				4/1/2000	4/1/1990	% Change 1990-2000	Sales, 2002 ($1,000)	% Change 1997-2002	Establish-ments	Total Employees	Value Added ($1,000)	Ranally Mfg. Units
Aitkin	001	Aitkin	1,819	15,301	12,425	23.1	81,316	(d)	...	(d)	(d)	...
Anoka	003	Anoka	424	298,084	243,641	22.3	6,833,271	274.6	655	22,944	2,506,784	1,326
Becker	005	Detroit Lakes	1,310	30,000	27,881	7.6	87,392	11.2	41	1,652	142,990	76
Beltrami	007	Bemidji	2,505	39,650	34,384	15.3	118,788	17.3	47	1,470	98,631	52
Benton	009	Foley	408	34,226	30,185	13.4	(d)	(d)	70	3,889	333,636	177
Big Stone	011	Ortonville	497	5,820	6,285	-7.4	63,487	(d)	...	(d)	(d)	...
Blue Earth	013	Mankato	752	55,941	54,044	3.5	898,159	61.0	86	3,993	657,410	348
Brown	015	New Ulm	611	26,911	26,984	-0.3	161,342	-61.4	41	3,689	589,630	312
Carlton	017	Carlton	860	31,671	29,259	8.2	557,239	188.5	37	(d)	(d)	...
Carver	019	Chaska	357	70,205	47,915	46.5	973,630	70.8	157	11,183	1,297,151	686
Cass	021	Walker	2,018	27,150	21,791	24.6	83,472	(d)	...	(d)	(d)	...
Chippewa	023	Montevideo	583	13,088	13,228	-1.1	156,773	-18.1	24	726	56,213	30
Chisago	025	Center City	418	41,101	30,521	34.7	107,801	(d)	98	1,889	126,746	67
Clay	027	Moorhead	1,045	51,229	50,422	1.6	(d)	(d)	40	745	91,746	49
Clearwater	029	Bagley	995	8,423	8,309	1.4	24,300	37.2	17	519	43,977	23
Cook	031	Grand Marais	1,451	5,168	3,868	33.6	(d)	(d)	...	(d)	(d)	...
Cottonwood	033	Windom	640	12,167	12,694	-4.2	51,159	-69.8	22	1,056	110,992	59
Crow Wing	035	Brainerd	997	55,099	44,249	24.5	216,717	21.3	111	2,429	212,507	112
Dakota	037	Hastings	570	355,904	275,227	29.3	7,658,337	37.3	486	18,999	2,290,263	1,212
Dodge	039	Mantorville	440	17,731	15,731	12.7	(d)	(d)	27	1,022	41,806	22
Douglas	041	Alexandria	634	32,821	28,674	14.5	299,462	71.6	89	2,636	316,927	168
Faribault	043	Blue Earth	714	16,181	16,937	-4.5	(d)	(d)	33	1,422	153,127	81
Fillmore	045	Preston	861	21,122	20,777	1.7	262,282	8.9	37	777	49,532	26
Freeborn	047	Albert Lea	708	32,584	33,060	-1.4	272,496	-47.8	62	2,968	250,333	132
Goodhue	049	Red Wing	758	44,127	40,690	8.4	408,699	-39.9	90	4,485	412,114	218
Grant	051	Elbow Lake	546	6,289	6,246	0.7	147,617	-29.4	...	(d)	(d)	...
Hennepin	053	Minneapolis	557	1,116,200	1,032,431	8.1	55,640,960	-7.2	2,107	91,211	9,475,432	5,013
Houston	055	Caledonia	558	19,718	18,497	6.6	(d)	(d)	27	(d)	(d)	...
Hubbard	057	Park Rapids	922	18,376	14,939	23.0	22,116	-23.7	34	1,026	97,050	51
Isanti	059	Cambridge	439	31,287	25,921	20.7	27,399	(d)	72	1,429	116,957	62
Itasca	061	Grand Rapids	2,665	43,992	40,863	7.7	112,923	-75.8	54	1,767	228,093	121
Jackson	063	Jackson	702	11,268	11,677	-3.5	113,494	-13.6	12	(d)	(d)	...
Kanabec	065	Mora	525	14,996	12,802	17.1	(d)	(d)	17	659	38,041	20
Kandiyohi	067	Willmar	796	41,203	38,761	6.3	(d)	(d)	64	2,909	232,399	123
Kittson	069	Hallock	1,097	5,285	5,767	-8.4	82,667	-7.4	...	(d)	(d)	...
Koochiching	071	International Falls	3,102	14,355	16,299	-11.9	(d)	(d)	20	(d)	(d)	...
Lac qui Parle	073	Madison	765	8,067	8,924	-9.6	104,215	-16.4	...	(d)	(d)	...
Lake	075	Two Harbors	2,099	11,058	10,415	6.2	(d)	(d)	...	(d)	(d)	...
Lake of the Woods	077	Baudette	1,297	4,522	4,076	10.9	(d)	(d)	...	(d)	(d)	...
Le Sueur	079	Le Center	448	25,426	23,239	9.4	245,723	59.6	48	2,742	557,357	295
Lincoln	081	Ivanhoe	537	6,429	6,890	-6.7	26,728	-33.6	...	(d)	(d)	...
Lyon	083	Marshall	714	25,425	24,789	2.6	779,096	-14.9	33	1,611	219,795	116
Mahnomen	087	Mahnomen	556	5,190	5,044	2.9	(d)	(d)	...	(d)	(d)	...
Marshall	089	Warren	1,772	10,155	10,993	-7.6	92,016	(d)	...	(d)	(d)	...
Martin	091	Fairmont	709	21,802	22,914	-4.9	391,153	-6.7	45	1,792	146,564	78
McLeod	085	Glencoe	492	34,898	32,030	9.0	(d)	(d)	73	(d)	(d)	...
Meeker	093	Litchfield	609	22,644	20,846	8.6	134,549	33.5	53	1,384	145,121	77
Mille Lacs	095	Milaca	574	22,330	18,670	19.6	(d)	(d)	56	2,107	118,371	63
Morrison	097	Little Falls	1,124	31,712	29,604	7.1	159,608	-1.2	54	2,216	163,680	87
Mower	099	Austin	711	38,603	37,385	3.3	160,849	-63.7	36	4,347	733,771	388
Murray	101	Slayton	704	9,165	9,660	-5.1	87,214	11.0	...	(d)	(d)	...
Nicollet	103	St. Peter	452	29,771	28,076	6.0	178,677	-13.8	40	4,634	299,474	158
Nobles	105	Worthington	715	20,832	20,098	3.7	138,917	(d)	27	2,330	185,374	98
Norman	107	Ada	876	7,442	7,975	-6.7	48,235	-16.3	...	(d)	(d)	...
Olmsted	109	Rochester	653	124,277	106,470	16.7	708,033	17.0	98	12,044	1,340,537	709
Otter Tail	111	Fergus Falls	1,980	57,159	50,714	12.7	251,730	7.9	86	3,572	312,419	165
Pennington	113	Thief River Falls	617	13,584	13,306	2.1	(d)	(d)	24	1,766	172,100	91
Pine	115	Pine City	1,411	26,530	21,264	24.8	21,275	-16.3	...	(d)	(d)	...
Pipestone	117	Pipestone	466	9,895	10,491	-5.7	150,288	-41.3	13	596	79,542	42
Polk	119	Crookston	1,970	31,369	32,498	-3.5	234,886	13.9	37	1,523	235,776	125
Pope	121	Glenwood	670	11,236	10,745	4.6	241,840	25.8	30	722	28,211	15
Ramsey	123	St. Paul	156	511,035	485,765	5.2	13,596,342	45.7	700	31,563	4,900,623	2,593
Red Lake	125	Red Lake Falls	432	4,299	4,525	-5.0	1,308	-96.3	...	(d)	(d)	...
Redwood	127	Redwood Falls	880	16,815	17,254	-2.5	344,624	-13.8	25	1,044	60,253	32
Renville	129	Olivia	983	17,154	17,673	-2.9	282,753	-22.5	33	991	172,907	91
Rice	131	Faribault	498	56,665	49,183	15.2	(d)	(d)	85	4,647	566,649	300
Rock	133	Luverne	483	9,721	9,806	-0.9	75,534	-30.4	...	(d)	(d)	...
Roseau	135	Roseau	1,663	16,338	15,026	8.7	22,897	-67.1	21	(d)	(d)	...
St. Louis	137	Duluth	6,225	200,528	198,213	1.2	1,182,289	(d)	231	5,644	484,921	257
Scott	139	Shakopee	357	89,498	57,846	54.7	2,043,105	6.5	160	5,067	504,749	267
Sherburne	141	Elk River	436	64,417	41,945	53.6	211,494	169.5	125	2,192	221,299	117
Sibley	143	Gaylord	589	15,356	14,366	6.9	35,553	-75.8	25	883	133,198	70
Stearns	145	St. Cloud	1,345	133,166	118,791	12.1	(d)	(d)	255	12,634	1,181,105	625
Steele	147	Owatonna	430	33,680	30,729	9.6	205,155	-9.1	75	5,965	561,382	297
Stevens	149	Morris	562	10,053	10,634	-5.5	97,638	-35.6	...	(d)	(d)	...

Entries in **UPPERCASE** are counties.
Entries in **bold** have populations of 2,500 or more.
Names in parentheses are alternate names.
Inc. Place — Incorporated Place
RMC Place — Rand McNally Designated Place
CDP — Census Designated Place
MCD — Minor Civil Division

⊡ County Seat
▲ Minor Civil Division
elev. Elevation
🅿 Post Office

H Hospital
C College
■ Principal Business Center
★ Ranally Metro Area (RMA) Abbreviation
z Zip Code(s)

Ⓟ Previous Census Population
® Revised Census Population
Ⓐ Annexation Population
● Rand McNally Population Estimate
© Final Census Population
Ⓢ Special Census Population
◆ Estimated Population

For additional definitions see Glossary, Volume 1, and Introduction, Volume 2.

County	FIPS Code	County Seat	Land Area (Sq. Mi.)	Census Population			Wholesale Trade		Manufacturing, 2002			
				4/1/2000	4/1/1990	% Change 1990-2000	Sales, 2002 ($1,000)	% Change 1997-2002	Establish-ments	Total Employees	Value Added ($1,000)	Ranally Mfg. Units
Swift	151	Benson	744	11,956	10,724	11.5	195,995	8.5	...	(d)	(d)	...
Todd	153	Long Prairie	942	24,426	23,363	4.5	(d)	(d)	44	1,643	140,734	74
Traverse	155	Wheaton	574	4,134	4,463	-7.4	64,395	-33.2	...	(d)	(d)	...
Wabasha	157	Wabasha	525	21,610	19,744	9.5	(d)	(d)	34	1,865	199,028	105
Wadena	159	Wadena	535	13,713	13,154	4.2	(d)	(d)	20	715	49,482	26
Waseca	161	Waseca	423	19,526	18,079	8.0	51,455	-17.8	28	2,297	307,642	163
Washington	163	Stillwater	392	201,130	145,896	37.9	3,624,224	78.6	229	11,165	1,424,628	754
Watonwan	165	St. James	435	11,876	11,682	1.7	200,161	-5.5	18	1,047	64,510	34
Wilkin	167	Breckenridge	751	7,138	7,516	-5.0	(d)	(d)	...	(d)	(d)	...
Winona	169	Winona	626	49,985	47,828	4.5	197,584	-52.8	114	5,583	484,631	256
Wright	171	Buffalo	661	89,986	68,710	31.0	675,196	205.2	199	5,250	420,858	223
Yellow Medicine	173	Granite Falls	758	11,080	11,684	-5.2	134,390	46.6	...	(d)	(d)	...
The State			**79,610**	**4,919,479**	**4,375,099**	**12.4**	**108,388,816**	**9.0**	**8,139**	**351,884**	**39,610,449**	**20,957**

(d) Data not available. Corresponding percentages or Ranally Manufacturing Units are estimates.
... Represents 0 or amount too minimal to be reported.

Index of Places and Counties

A

Ada; Inc. Place; ⊡ NORMAN; **192** H-2; elev. 907ft./276m.; 🅿 🅷; z 56510; Ⓟ 1,708; Ⓒ 1,657
Adams; Inc. Place; MOWER; **193** T-11; elev. 1,300ft./396m.; 🅿; z 55909; Ⓟ 756; Ⓒ 800
Adolph; RMC Place; ST. LOUIS; ***192** J-11; elev. 1,277ft./389m.; 🅿; ★ **DUL**; z 55701; pop. incl. with Hermantown (Inc. Place)
Adrian; Inc. Place; NOBLES; **193** T-3; elev. 1,541ft./470m.; 🅿 🅷; z 56110; Ⓟ 1,141; Ⓒ 1,234
Afton; Inc. Place; WASHINGTON; **193** P-10; elev. 700ft./213m.; 🅿; ★ **MPLS-**; z 55001; Ⓟ 2,645; Ⓒ 2,839
Ah-gwah-ching; RMC Place; CASS; **192** I-6; elev. 1,400ft./427m.; 🅿; z 56430; ● 50
Aitkin; Inc. Place; ⊡ AITKIN; **193** K-8; elev. 1,217ft./371m.; 🅿 🅷; z 56431; Ⓟ 1,698; Ⓒ 1,984
AITKIN; **192** J-9; Ⓟ 12,425; Ⓒ 15,301; ◆ 15,710
Akeley; Inc. Place; HUBBARD; **192** I-6; elev. 1,420ft./433m.; 🅿; z 56433; Ⓟ 393; Ⓒ 412
Albany; Inc. Place; STEARNS; **193** M-6; elev. 1,200ft./366m.; 🅿 🅷; z 56307; Ⓟ 1,548; Ⓒ 1,796
Alberta; Inc. Place; STEVENS; **193** N-3; elev. 1,109ft./338m.; 🅿; z 56207; Ⓟ 136; Ⓒ 142
Albert Lea; Inc. Place; ⊡ FREEBORN; **193** T-9; elev. 1,299ft./396m.; 🅿 🅷 ■; z 56007; Ⓟ 18,310; Ⓒ 18,356; ◆ 17,383
Albertville; Inc. Place; WRIGHT; **193** O-8; elev. 960ft./293m.; 🅿; ★ **MPLS-**; z 55301; Ⓟ 1,251; Ⓒ 3,621
Albion Center; RMC Place; WRIGHT; ***193** O-8; mail Annandale z 55302; ● 35
Alborn; RMC Place; ST. LOUIS; **192** I-11; elev. 1,304ft./397m.; 🅿; z 55702; ● 200
Alden; Inc. Place; FREEBORN; **193** T-9; elev. 1,260ft./384m.; 🅿; z 56009; Ⓟ 623; Ⓒ 652
Aldrich; Inc. Place; WADENA; **193** K-6; elev. 1,330ft./405m.; 🅿; z 56434; Ⓟ 70; Ⓒ 53
Alexandria; Inc. Place; ⊡ DOUGLAS; **193** M-5; elev. 1,404ft./428m.; 🅿 🅷; z 56308; Ⓟ 7,838; Ⓒ 8,820
Alida; RMC Place; CLEARWATER; **192** H-5; elev. 1,522ft./464m.; mail Shevlin z 56676; ● 20
Allen Junction; RMC Place; ST. LOUIS; mail Hoyt Lakes z 55750; pop. incl. with Hoyt Lakes (Inc. Place)
Alma City; RMC Place; WASECA; **193** S-8; mail Janesville z 56048; ● 40
Almelund; RMC Place; CHISAGO; **193** N-10; elev. 990ft./302m.; 🅿; z 55002; ● 150
Almora; RMC Place; OTTER TAIL; **193** L-5; mail Henning z 56551; ● 50
Alpha; Inc. Place; JACKSON; **193** T-6; elev. 1,387ft./423m.; 🅿; z 56111; Ⓟ 105; Ⓒ 126
Altura; Inc. Place; WINONA; **193** R-12; elev. 1,180ft./360m.; 🅿; z 55910; Ⓟ 349; Ⓒ 417
Alvarado; Inc. Place; MARSHALL; **192** E-1; elev. 812ft./247m.; 🅿; z 56710; Ⓟ 356; Ⓒ 371
Alvwood; RMC Place; ITASCA; ***192** G-7; elev. 1,380ft./421m.; mail Blackduck z 56630
Amboy; Inc. Place; BLUE EARTH; **193** S-7; elev. 1,044ft./318m.; 🅿; z 56010; Ⓟ 517; Ⓒ 575
Amherst; RMC Place; FILLMORE; ***193** T-12; elev. 1,049ft./320m.; mail Canton z 55922; rural
Amiret; RMC Place; LYON; **193** R-4; elev. 1,280ft./390m.; 🅿; z 56175; ● 60
Amor; RMC Place; OTTER TAIL; ***193** K-4; mail Battle Lake z 56515
Andover; Inc. Place; ANOKA; **193** O-9; elev. 891ft./272m.; 🅿; ★ **MPLS-**; z 55303-04; Ⓟ 15,216; Ⓒ 26,588; ◆ 32,182
Andree; RMC Place; ISANTI; **193** M-9; elev. 959ft./292m.; mail Braham z 55006; ● 30
Andyville; RMC Place; MOWER; ***193** S-10; mail Austin z 55912; rural
Angle Inlet; RMC Place; LAKE OF THE WOODS; **192** B-5; elev. 1,065ft./325m.; 🅿; z 56711; ● 75
Angora (Shermans Corner); RMC Place; ST. LOUIS; **192** G-11; elev. 1,349ft./411m.; 🅿; z 55703; ● 100
Angus; RMC Place; POLK; **192** F-2; elev. 871ft./265m.; 🅿; z 56762; ● 50
Annandale; Inc. Place; WRIGHT; **193** O-7; elev. 1,050ft./320m.; 🅿; z 55302; Ⓟ 2,054; Ⓒ 2,684
Anoka; Inc. Place; ⊡ ANOKA; **193** O-9; elev. 870ft./265m.; 🅿 🅷; ★ **MPLS-**; z 55303-04; Ⓟ 17,192; Ⓒ 18,076
ANOKA; **193** O-9; Ⓟ 243,641; Ⓒ 298,084; ◆ 323,361
Antlers Park; RMC Place; DAKOTA; ***193** Q-9; ★ **MPLS-**; mail Lakeville z 55044; pop. incl. with Lakeville (Inc. Place)
Appleton; Inc. Place; SWIFT; **193** O-3; elev. 1,010ft./308m.; 🅿 🅷; z 56208; Ⓟ 1,552; Ⓒ 2,871
Apple Valley; Inc. Place; DAKOTA; **193** P-9; elev. 955ft./291m.; 🅿; ★ **MPLS-**; z 55124; Ⓟ 34,598; Ⓒ 45,527; ◆ 50,366
Arco; Inc. Place; LINCOLN; **193** Q-3; elev. 1,700ft./518m.; 🅿; z 56113; Ⓟ 104; Ⓒ 100
Arcturus; RMC Place; ITASCA; mail Taconite z 55786; pop. incl. with Taconite (Inc. Place)
Arden Hills; Inc. Place; RAMSEY; **191** D-6; elev. 950ft./290m.; 🅿; ★ **MPLS-**; z 55112, z 55126; Ⓟ 9,199; Ⓒ 9,652
Arendahl; RMC Place; FILLMORE; ***193** S-12; elev. 1,190ft./363m.; mail Peterson z 55962; rural
Argonne; RMC Place; DAKOTA; ***193** P-9; ★ **MPLS-**; mail Lakeville z 55044; pop. incl. with Lakeville (Inc. Place)
Argyle; Inc. Place; MARSHALL; **192** E-2; elev. 847ft./258m.; 🅿; z 56713; Ⓟ 636; Ⓒ 656
Arlington; Inc. Place; SIBLEY; **193** Q-8; elev. 1,000ft./305m.; 🅿 🅷; z 55307; Ⓟ 1,886; Ⓒ 2,048
Armstrong; RMC Place; FREEBORN; ***193** T-9; mail Alden z 56009; ● 30
Arnesen; RMC Place; LAKE OF THE WOODS; ***192** C-5; mail Roosevelt z 56673
Arnold; CDP; ST. LOUIS; **192** J-12; elev. 1,438ft./438m.; ★ **DUL**; mail Duluth z 55803; Ⓟ 2,891; Ⓒ 3,032
Arthyde; RMC Place; AITKIN; ***193** K-10; elev. 1,285ft./392m.; mail Mc Grath z 56350; rural
Artichoke Lake; RMC Place; BIG STONE; ***193** N-3; mail Correll z 56227; rural
Ashby; Inc. Place; GRANT; **193** L-4; elev. 1,295ft./395m.; 🅿; z 56309; Ⓟ 469; Ⓒ 472
Ash Creek; RMC Place; ROCK; ***193** T-3; mail Steen z 56173; ● 25
Ash Lake; RMC Place; ST. LOUIS; **192** E-10; mail Orr z 55771; ● 30
Askov; Inc. Place; PINE; **193** L-10; elev. 1,160ft./354m.; 🅿; z 55704; Ⓟ 343; Ⓒ 368
Assumption; RMC Place; CARVER; ***193** P-8; mail Green Isle z 55338; rural
Atkinson; RMC Place; CARLTON; ***192** J-11; elev. 1,147ft./350m.; mail Carlton z 55718; rural
Atwater; Inc. Place; KANDIYOHI; **193** O-6; elev. 1,215ft./370m.; 🅿; z 56209; Ⓟ 1,053; Ⓒ 1,079
Atwood; RMC Place; HENNEPIN; ***193** P-9; ★ **MPLS-**; mail Minneapolis z 55424; pop. incl. with Edina (Inc. Place)
Audubon; Inc. Place; BECKER; **192** J-3; elev. 1,316ft./401m.; 🅿; z 56511; Ⓟ 411; Ⓒ 445
Augusta; RMC Place; CARVER; ***193** P-8; elev. 982ft./299m.; ★ **MPLS-**; mail Chaska z 55318; ● 100
Aure; RMC Place; BELTRAMI; ***192** G-5; mail Shevlin z 56676; rural
Aurora; Inc. Place; ST. LOUIS; **192** G-11; elev. 1,480ft./451m.; 🅿 🅷; z 55705; Ⓟ 1,965; Ⓒ 1,850
Austin; Inc. Place; ⊡ MOWER; **193** T-10; elev. 1,198ft./365m.; 🅿 🅷 ■; z 55912; Ⓟ 21,907; Ⓒ 23,314; ◆ 22,855
Austin Acres; RMC Place; MOWER; ***193** T-10; mail Austin z 55912; pop. incl. with Austin (Inc. Place)
Auto Club; RMC Place; HENNEPIN; ***193** P-9; ★ **MPLS-**; mail Minneapolis z 55420; pop. incl. with Bloomington (Inc. Place)
Automba; RMC Place; CARLTON; ***193** K-10; elev. 1,270ft./387m.; mail Kettle River z 55757
Averill; RMC Place; CLAY; **192** I-2; elev. 916ft./279m.; mail Glyndon z 56547; ● 40
Avoca; Inc. Place; MURRAY; **193** S-4; elev. 1,530ft./466m.; 🅿; z 56114; Ⓟ 150; Ⓒ 146
Avon; Inc. Place; STEARNS; **193** N-7; elev. 1,129ft./344m.; 🅿; z 56310; Ⓟ 970; Ⓒ 1,242

B

Babbitt; Inc. Place; ST. LOUIS; **192** G-12; elev. 1,486ft./453m.; 🅿; z 55706; Ⓟ 1,562; Ⓒ 1,670
Backus; Inc. Place; CASS; **192** J-7; elev. 1,341ft./409m.; 🅿; z 56435; Ⓟ 240; Ⓒ 311
Badger; Inc. Place; ROSEAU; **192** C-3; elev. 1,082ft./330m.; 🅿; z 56714; Ⓟ 381; Ⓒ 470
Bagley; Inc. Place; ⊡ CLEARWATER; **192** G-5; elev. 1,441ft./439m.; 🅿 🅷; z 56621; Ⓟ 1,388; Ⓒ 1,235
Baker; RMC Place; CLAY; **192** J-2; elev. 936ft./285m.; 🅿; z 56580; ● 90
Balaton; Inc. Place; LYON; **193** R-3; elev. 1,523ft./464m.; 🅿; z 56115; Ⓟ 737; Ⓒ 637
Bald Eagle; RMC Place; RAMSEY; **191** C-9; ★ **MPLS-**; mail Saint Paul z 55110; ● 1,800
Balkan; RMC Place; ST. LOUIS; mail Chisholm z 55719; rural
Ball Bluff; RMC Place; AITKIN; ***192** I-9; elev. 1,247ft./380m.; mail Jacobson z 55752; rural
Ball Club; RMC Place; ITASCA; **192** H-8; elev. 1,300ft./396m.; mail Deer River z 56636; ● 75
Balmoral; RMC Place; OTTER TAIL; mail Battle Lake z 56515
Bancroft; RMC Place; FREEBORN; ***193** T-9; elev. 1,236ft./377m.; mail Albert Lea z 56007; ● 30
Barden; RMC Place; SCOTT; ***193** P-9; ★ **MPLS-**; mail Shakopee z 55379; pop. incl. with Shakopee (Inc. Place)
Barnesville; Inc. Place; CLAY; **192** J-2; elev. 1,024ft./312m.; 🅿; z 56514; Ⓟ 2,066; Ⓒ 2,173
Barnum; Inc. Place; CARLTON; **193** K-11; elev. 1,103ft./336m.; 🅿; z 55707; Ⓟ 482; Ⓒ 525
Barrett; Inc. Place; GRANT; **193** M-4; elev. 1,166ft./355m.; 🅿; z 56311; Ⓟ 350; Ⓒ 355
Barrows; RMC Place; CROW WING; **193** K-7; elev. 1,206ft./368m.; mail Brainerd z 56401; ● 75
Barry; Inc. Place; BIG STONE; **193** N-2; elev. 1,101ft./336m.; 🅿; z 56210; Ⓟ 40; Ⓒ 25
Bassett; RMC Place; ST. LOUIS; **192** H-12; mail Brimson z 55602; ● 50
Basswood; RMC Place; OTTER TAIL; ***193** K-4; mail Richville z 56576; rural
Basswood Grove; RMC Place; WASHINGTON; ***193** P-10; mail Hastings z 55033; rural
Battle Lake; Inc. Place; OTTER TAIL; **193** K-4; elev. 1,372ft./418m.; 🅿; z 56515; Ⓟ 698; Ⓒ 686; Ⓡ 747
Baudette; Inc. Place; ⊡ LAKE OF THE WOODS; **192** D-6; elev. 1,086ft./331m.; 🅿 🅷; z 56623; Ⓟ 1,146; Ⓒ 1,104
Baxter; Inc. Place; CROW WING; **193** K-7; elev. 1,208ft./368m.; 🅿; z 56425 & mail Brainerd z 56401; Ⓟ 3,695; Ⓒ 5,555
Bay Lake; RMC Place; CROW WING; **193** K-8; elev. 1,288ft./393m.; mail Deerwood z 56444; ● 80
Bayport; Inc. Place; WASHINGTON; **193** O-10; elev. 686ft./209m.; 🅿; ★ **MPLS-**; z 55003; Ⓟ 3,200; Ⓒ 3,162
Bayview; RMC Place; MILLE LACS; **193** L-9; mail Onamia z 56359; ● 40
Bayview; RMC Place; ST. LOUIS; ***192** J-12; elev. 1,196ft./365m.; ★ **DUL**; pop. incl. with Duluth (Inc. Place)
Bear Creek; RMC Place; OLMSTED; ★ **ROCH**; mail Rochester z 55904; pop. incl. with Rochester (Inc. Place)
Beardsley; Inc. Place; BIG STONE; **193** N-2; elev. 1,098ft./335m.; 🅿; z 56211; Ⓟ 297; Ⓒ 262
Bear River; RMC Place; ITASCA, ST. LOUIS; ***192** G-10; mail Cook z 55723
Bear Valley; RMC Place; WABASHA; ***193** R-11; mail Lake City z 55041; rural
Beauford; RMC Place; BLUE EARTH; **193** S-8; elev. 1,011ft./308m.; mail Mapleton z 56065; ● 60
Beaulieu; RMC Place; MAHNOMEN; **192** H-4; mail Mahnomen z 56557; ● 30
Beaver; RMC Place; WINONA; ***193** R-12; mail Altura z 55910; rural
Beaver Bay; Inc. Place; LAKE; **192** H-13; elev. 705ft./215m.; 🅿; z 55601; Ⓟ 147; Ⓒ 175
Beaver Creek; Inc. Place; ROCK; **193** T-2; elev. 1,492ft./455m.; 🅿; z 56116; Ⓟ 249; Ⓒ 250
Beaver Falls; RMC Place; RENVILLE; ***193** Q-5; elev. 950ft./290m.; mail Morton z 56270
Bechyn; RMC Place; RENVILLE; **193** Q-5; mail Redwood Falls z 56283; ● 30
Becida; RMC Place; HUBBARD; ***192** H-5; elev. 1,425ft./434m.; 🅿; z 56678; rural
Becker; Inc. Place; SHERBURNE; **193** N-8; elev. 970ft./296m.; 🅿; z 55308; Ⓟ 902; Ⓒ 2,673
BECKER; **192** I-4; Ⓟ 27,881; Ⓒ 30,000; ◆ 31,919
Beckville; RMC Place; MEEKER; ***193** O-6; elev. 1,194ft./364m.; mail Litchfield z 55355
Bejou; Inc. Place; MAHNOMEN; **192** H-3; elev. 1,222ft./372m.; 🅿; z 56516; Ⓟ 110; Ⓒ 94
Belgrade; Inc. Place; STEARNS; **193** N-5; elev. 1,266ft./386m.; 🅿; z 56312; Ⓟ 700; Ⓒ 750
Bellaire; RMC Place; RAMSEY; **191** D-9; ★ **MPLS-**; mail Saint Paul z 55110; ● 1,900
Bellechester; Inc. Place; GOODHUE, WABASHA; **193** Q-11; elev. 1,116ft./340m.; mail Cedar z 55011, Goodhue z 55027; Ⓟ 110; Ⓒ 172
Belle Creek; RMC Place; GOODHUE; ***193** Q-10; elev. 960ft./293m.; mail Goodhue z 55027; rural
Belle Plaine; Inc. Place; SCOTT; **193** Q-8; elev. 860ft./262m.; 🅿; z 56011; Ⓟ 3,149; Ⓒ 3,789
Belle Prairie; RMC Place; MORRISON; **193** L-7; mail Little Falls z 56345; ● 500
Belle River; RMC Place; DOUGLAS; ***193** L-5; elev. 1,362ft./415m.; mail Carlos z 56319
Bellingham; Inc. Place; LAC QUI PARLE; **193** O-3; elev. 1,050ft./320m.; 🅿; z 56212; Ⓟ 247; Ⓒ 205
Beltrami; Inc. Place; POLK; **192** G-2; elev. 903ft./275m.; 🅿; z 56517; Ⓟ 137; Ⓒ 101
BELTRAMI; **192** E-6; Ⓟ 34,384; Ⓒ 39,650; ◆ 43,980
Belvidere Mills; RMC Place; GOODHUE; ***193** Q-11; mail Goodhue z 55027; rural
Belview; Inc. Place; REDWOOD; **193** Q-5; elev. 1,060ft./323m.; 🅿; z 56214; Ⓟ 383; Ⓒ 412
Bemidji; Inc. Place; ⊡ BELTRAMI; **192** H-6; elev. 1,350ft./411m.; 🅿 🅷 🅲 4,974 ■; z 56601, z 56619; Ⓟ 11,245; Ⓒ 11,917; ◆ 12,915
Bena; Inc. Place; CASS; **192** H-7; located on Leech Lake Ind. Res.; elev. 1,308ft./399m.; 🅿; z 56626; Ⓟ 147; Ⓒ 110
Benedict; RMC Place; HUBBARD; **192** I-6; elev. 1,316ft./401m.; 🅿; z 56436; ● 90
Bennettville; RMC Place; AITKIN; ***193** K-8; elev. 1,266ft./386m.; mail Aitkin z 56431; rural
Benson; Inc. Place; ⊡ SWIFT; **193** N-4; elev. 1,050ft./320m.; 🅿 🅷; z 56215; Ⓟ 3,235; Ⓒ 3,376
BENTON; **193** M-8; Ⓟ 30,185; Ⓒ 34,226; Ⓡ 34,227; ◆ 40,324
Benton Meadows; RMC Place; CARVER; ***193** P-8; mail Cologne z 55322; pop. incl. with Cologne (Inc. Place)
Bergen; RMC Place; JACKSON; **193** S-5; mail Windom z 56101; ● 35
Bergville; RMC Place; ITASCA; ***192** G-7; mail Northome z 56661; rural
Berkey; RMC Place; OTTER TAIL; ***193** K-4; mail Underwood z 56586; rural
Bernadotte; RMC Place; NICOLLET; **193** Q-7; mail Lafayette z 56054; ● 25
Berne; RMC Place; DODGE; ***193** R-10; mail West Concord z 55985; ● 25
Berner; RMC Place; CLEARWATER; ***192** G-5; mail Gonvick z 56644; rural
Berning Mill; RMC Place; WRIGHT; ***193** O-9; elev. 878ft./268m.; ★ **MPLS-**; mail Saint Michael z 55376; rural
Beroun; RMC Place; PINE; **193** M-10; elev. 972ft./296m.; 🅿; z 55063; ● 100
Bertha; Inc. Place; TODD; **193** K-5; elev. 1,406ft./429m.; 🅿; z 56437; Ⓟ 507; Ⓒ 470
Bethany; RMC Place; WINONA; ***193** R-12; mail Altura z 55910; ● 50
Bethel; Inc. Place; ANOKA; **193** N-9; elev. 929ft./283m.; 🅿; ★ **MPLS-**; z 55005; Ⓟ 394; Ⓒ 443
Big Bend City; RMC Place; CHIPPEWA; **193** O-4; mail Milan z 56262; ● 60
Bigelow; Inc. Place; NOBLES; **193** T-4; elev. 1,629ft./497m.; 🅿; z 56117; Ⓟ 232; Ⓒ 231
Big Falls; Inc. Place; KOOCHICHING; **192** E-8; elev. 1,217ft./371m.; 🅿; z 56627; Ⓟ 341; Ⓒ 264
Bigfork; Inc. Place; ITASCA; **192** G-8; elev. 1,318ft./402m.; 🅿 🅷; z 56628 & mail Effie z 56639; Ⓟ 384; Ⓒ 469
Big Island; RMC Place; HENNEPIN; ★ **MPLS-**; mail Excelsior z 55331; pop. incl. with Orono (Inc. Place)
Big Lake; Inc. Place; SHERBURNE; **193** N-8; elev. 942ft./287m.; 🅿; ★ **MPLS-**; z 55309; Ⓟ 3,113; Ⓒ 6,063
Big Spring; RMC Place; FILLMORE; ***193** T-12; elev. 1,250ft./381m.; mail Harmony z 55939; rural
BIG STONE; **193** N-2; Ⓟ 6,285; Ⓒ 5,820; ◆ 5,335
Big Stone City; RMC Place; BIG STONE; mail Ortonville z 56278; pop. incl. with Ortonville (Inc. Place)
Big Woods; RMC Place; MARSHALL; ***192** E-1; elev. 801ft./244m.; mail Oslo z 56744; rural
Bingham Lake; Inc. Place; COTTONWOOD; **193** S-5; elev. 1,422ft./433m.; 🅿; z 56118; Ⓟ 155; Ⓒ 167
Birch Beach; RMC Place; LAKE OF THE WOODS; ***192** C-6; elev. 1,066ft./325m.; mail Williams z 56686; summer pop. 150
Birchdale; RMC Place; KOOCHICHING; **192** D-8; elev. 1,160ft./354m.; 🅿; z 56629; ● 30
Birchwood (Birchwood Village); Inc. Place; WASHINGTON; **191** D-9; elev. 960ft./293m.; ★ **MPLS-**; mail Saint Paul z 55110; Ⓟ 1,042; Ⓒ 968
Birchwood Village; WASHINGTON; see Birchwood (Inc. Place)
Bird Island; Inc. Place; RENVILLE; **193** P-6; elev. 1,090ft./332m.; 🅿; z 55310; Ⓟ 1,326; Ⓒ 1,195
Biscay; Inc. Place; MCLEOD; **193** P-7; elev. 1,030ft./314m.; mail Glencoe z 55336; Ⓟ 113; Ⓒ 114
Biwabik; Inc. Place; ST. LOUIS; **192** G-11; elev. 1,448ft./441m.; 🅿; z 55708; Ⓟ 1,097; Ⓒ 954
Bixby; RMC Place; STEELE; **193** S-10; elev. 1,300ft./396m.; mail Blooming Prairie z 55917; ● 100
Blackberry; RMC Place; ITASCA; **192** I-9; mail Grand Rapids z 55744; ● 50
Blackduck; Inc. Place; BELTRAMI; **192** G-7; elev. 1,383ft./422m.; 🅿; z 56630, z 56663; Ⓟ 718; Ⓒ 696
Black Hammer; RMC Place; HOUSTON; **193** T-13; elev. 1,179ft./359m.; mail Spring Grove z 55974; ● 50
Blaine; Inc. Place; ANOKA, RAMSEY; **193** O-9; elev. 900ft./274m.; 🅿 ■; ★ **MPLS-**; z 55014, z 55434, z 55449; Ⓟ 38,975; Ⓒ 44,942; Ⓡ 45,014; ◆ 51,139
Blakeley; RMC Place; SCOTT; **193** Q-8; mail Belle Plaine z 56011; ● 100
Blomford; RMC Place; ISANTI; ***193** N-10; elev. 946ft./288m.; mail Isanti z 55040; rural
Blomkest; Inc. Place; KANDIYOHI; **193** P-5; elev. 1,130ft./344m.; 🅿; z 56216; Ⓟ 183; Ⓒ 186
Bloom Dale; RMC Place; HENNEPIN; ***193** P-9; elev. 830ft./253m.; ★ **MPLS-**; mail Minneapolis z 55431; pop. incl. with Bloomington (Inc. Place)
Blooming Prairie; Inc. Place; STEELE, DODGE; **193** S-10; elev. 1,290ft./393m.; 🅿; z 55917; Ⓟ 2,043; Ⓒ 1,933
Bloomington; Inc. Place; HENNEPIN; **193** P-9; elev. 830ft./253m.; 🅿 🅲 889 ■; ★ **MPLS-**; z 55420, z 55425, z 55431, z 55435, z 55437-38 & mail Minneapolis z 55439; Ⓟ 86,335; Ⓒ 85,172; ◆ 83,413
Bloomington Ferry; RMC Place; HENNEPIN; ***193** P-9; ★ **MPLS-**; mail Minneapolis z 55438; pop. incl. with Bloomington (Inc. Place)
Blue Earth; Inc. Place; ⊡ FARIBAULT; **193** T-7; elev. 1,093ft./333m.; 🅿 🅷; z 56013; Ⓟ 3,745; Ⓒ 3,621
BLUE EARTH; **193** S-7; Ⓟ 54,044; Ⓒ 55,941; ◆ 61,040
Blue Grass; RMC Place; WADENA; ***193** K-5; mail Sebeka z 56477; ● 20
Bluffton; Inc. Place; OTTER TAIL; **193** K-5; elev. 1,350ft./411m.; 🅿; z 56518; Ⓟ 187; Ⓒ 210
Bock; Inc. Place; MILLE LACS; **193** M-9; elev. 1,105ft./337m.; 🅿; z 56313; Ⓟ 115; Ⓒ 106
Bodum; RMC Place; ISANTI; ***193** N-9; elev. 982ft./299m.; mail Isanti z 55040; rural
Boisberg; RMC Place; TRAVERSE; ***193** L-2; elev. 988ft./301m.; mail Wheaton z 56296; rural
Bois Fort; RMC Place; KOOCHICHING; **192** F-9; located on Nett Lake Ind. Res.; mail Nett Lake z 55772; ● 350
Bois Forte Reservation; Indian Reservation; KOOCHICHING, ITASCA, ST. LOUIS; Ⓒ 657
Bombay; RMC Place; GOODHUE; ***193** R-10; elev. 1,178ft./359m.; mail Kenyon z 55946
Bonanza Grove; RMC Place; BIG STONE; ***193** N-2; mail Beardsley z 56211
Bongards; RMC Place; CARVER; ***193** P-8; elev. 984ft./300m.; mail Norwood Young America z 55368
Bonnie Glen; RMC Place; CHISAGO; ***193** N-10; ★ **MPLS-**; mail Chisago City z 55013; ● 150
Border; RMC Place; KOOCHICHING; ***192** D-7; elev. 1,097ft./334m.; mail Baudette z 56623; rural
Borup; Inc. Place; NORMAN; **192** I-2; elev. 912ft./278m.; 🅿; z 56519; Ⓟ 119; Ⓒ 91
Bovey; Inc. Place; ITASCA; **192** H-9; elev. 1,353ft./412m.; 🅿; z 55709; Ⓟ 662; Ⓒ 662
Bovey-Coleraine; RMC Place; ITASCA; ***192** H-9; mail Bovey z 55709; pop. incl. with Bovey (Inc. Place)
Bowlus; Inc. Place; MORRISON; **193** M-7; elev. 1,108ft./338m.; 🅿; z 56314; Ⓟ 260; Ⓒ 260
Bowstring; RMC Place; ITASCA; **192** G-8; elev. 1,314ft./401m.; 🅿; z 56631; ● 25
Boyd; Inc. Place; LAC QUI PARLE; **193** P-3; elev. 1,050ft./320m.; 🅿; z 56218; Ⓟ 251; Ⓒ 210
Boy River; Inc. Place; CASS; **192** I-7; elev. 1,329ft./405m.; 🅿; z 56672; Ⓟ 43; Ⓒ 38
Bradford; RMC Place; ISANTI; **193** N-9; mail Isanti z 55040; ● 40
Braham; Inc. Place; ISANTI, KANABEC; **193** M-10; elev. 950ft./290m.; 🅿; z 55006; Ⓟ 1,139; Ⓒ 1,276
Brainerd; Inc. Place; ⊡ CROW WING; **193** K-7; elev. 1,212ft./369m.; 🅿 🅷 ■; z 56401, z 56425; Ⓟ 12,353; Ⓒ 13,178; Ⓡ 13,382; ◆ 13,650
Branch; RMC Place; CHISAGO; ***193** N-10; elev. 900ft./274m.; mail North Branch z 55056; pop. incl. with North Branch (Inc. Place)
Brandon; Inc. Place; DOUGLAS; **193** L-4; elev. 1,388ft./423m.; 🅿; z 56315; Ⓟ 441; Ⓒ 450
Bratsberg; RMC Place; FILLMORE; ***193** S-13; mail Rushford z 55971
Breckenridge; Inc. Place; ⊡ WILKIN; **193** K-2; elev. 964ft./294m.; 🅿 🅷; z 56520; Ⓟ 3,708; Ⓒ 3,559
Breezy Point; Inc. Place; CROW WING; **192** J-7; elev. 1,220ft./372m.; 🅿; z 56472; Ⓟ 432; Ⓒ 979
Bremen; RMC Place; WABASHA; ***193** R-12; elev. 1,108ft./338m.; mail Millville z 55957; rural
Brennyville; RMC Place; BENTON; **193** M-8; elev. 1,234ft./376m.; mail Foley z 56329; ● 35
Brevik; RMC Place; CASS; **192** I-7; mail Longville z 56655; summer pop. 150; ● 30
Brewster; Inc. Place; NOBLES; **193** T-4; elev. 1,489ft./454m.; 🅿; z 56119; Ⓟ 532; Ⓒ 502
Bricelyn; Inc. Place; FARIBAULT; **193** T-8; elev. 1,181ft./360m.; 🅿; z 56014; Ⓟ 426; Ⓒ 379
Bridgeman; RMC Place; CASS; ***193** K-6; elev. 1,303ft./397m.; mail Pillager z 56473; ● 25
Bridgewater; RMC Place; RICE; ***193** Q-9; mail Faribault z 55021; rural
Brimson; RMC Place; ST. LOUIS; **192** H-12; elev. 1,516ft./462m.; 🅿; z 55602; ● 40
Bristol; RMC Place; FILLMORE; ***193** T-12; elev. 1,334ft./407m.; mail Harmony z 55939
Britt; RMC Place; ST. LOUIS; **192** G-11; elev. 1,479ft./451m.; 🅿; z 55710; ● 80
Brooklyn; RMC Place; ST. LOUIS; ***192** H-10; mail Hibbing z 55746; pop. incl. with Hibbing (Inc. Place)
Brooklyn Center; Inc. Place; HENNEPIN; **191** D-4; elev. 880ft./268m.; 🅿 🅲 700 ■; ★ **MPLS-**; z 55428-30, z 55443-44; Ⓟ 28,887; Ⓒ 29,172; ◆ 29,682
Brooklyn Park; Inc. Place; HENNEPIN; **191** B-3; elev. 872ft./266m.; 🅿; ★ **MPLS-**; z 55428-29, z 55443-45; Ⓟ 56,381; Ⓒ 67,388; ◆ 73,656
Brook Park; Inc. Place; PINE; **193** L-10; elev. 1,020ft./311m.; 🅿; z 55007; Ⓟ 125; Ⓒ 156
Brooks; Inc. Place; RED LAKE; **192** G-3; elev. 1,125ft./343m.; 🅿; z 56715; Ⓟ 158; Ⓒ 141
Brookston; Inc. Place; ST. LOUIS; **192** J-11; located on Fond du Lac Ind. Res.; elev. 1,228ft./374m.; 🅿; z 55711; Ⓟ 107; Ⓒ 98
Brooten; Inc. Place; STEARNS, POPE; **193** N-5; elev. 1,307ft./398m.; 🅿; z 56316; Ⓟ 589; Ⓒ 649
Browerville; Inc. Place; TODD; **193** L-6; elev. 1,283ft./391m.; 🅿; z 56438; Ⓟ 782; Ⓒ 735
BROWN; **193** R-6; Ⓟ 26,984; Ⓒ 26,911; ◆ 25,691
Brownsdale; Inc. Place; MOWER; **193** S-10; elev. 1,275ft./389m.; 🅿; z 55918; Ⓟ 695; Ⓒ 718
Browns Valley; Inc. Place; TRAVERSE; **193** M-1; elev. 984ft./300m.; 🅿; z 56219; Ⓟ 804; Ⓒ 690
Brownsville; Inc. Place; HOUSTON; **193** S-14; elev. 651ft./198m.; 🅿; z 55919; Ⓟ 415; Ⓒ 517
Brownton; Inc. Place; MCLEOD; **193** P-7; elev. 1,021ft./311m.; 🅿; z 55312; Ⓟ 781; Ⓒ 807
Bruno; Inc. Place; PINE; **193** K-11; elev. 1,151ft./351m.; 🅿; z 55712; Ⓟ 89; Ⓒ 102
Brunswick; RMC Place; KANABEC; **193** M-9; elev. 962ft./293m.; mail Mora z 55051; ● 80
Brush Creek; RMC Place; FARIBAULT; ***193** T-8; elev. 1,134ft./346m.; mail Bricelyn z 56014
Brushvale; RMC Place; WILKIN; ***193** K-2; elev. 957ft./292m.; mail Breckenridge z 56520; rural
Buckman; Inc. Place; MORRISON; **193** M-7; elev. 1,200ft./366m.; 🅿; z 56317; Ⓟ 201; Ⓒ 208
Buffalo; Inc. Place; ⊡ WRIGHT; **193** O-8; elev. 967ft./295m.; 🅿 🅷; ★ **MPLS-**; z 55313; Ⓟ 6,856; Ⓒ 10,097
Buffalo Lake; Inc. Place; RENVILLE; **193** P-6; elev. 1,074ft./327m.; 🅿; z 55314; Ⓟ 734; Ⓒ 768
Buhl; Inc. Place; ST. LOUIS; **192** H-10; elev. 1,533ft./467m.; 🅿; z 55713; Ⓟ 915; Ⓒ 983
Bunde; RMC Place; CHIPPEWA; ***193** P-5; elev. 1,079ft./329m.; mail Clara City z 56222; ● 25
Burchard; RMC Place; LYON; ***193** R-3; elev. 1,665ft./507m.; mail Balaton z 56115
Burnett; RMC Place; ST. LOUIS; ***192** I-11; elev. 1,306ft./398m.; 🅿; z 55431 & mail Saginaw z 55779; rural
Burnsville; Inc. Place; DAKOTA; **191** J-4; elev. 975ft./297m.; 🅿 🅷 ■; ★ **MPLS-**; z 55306, z 55337; Ⓟ 51,288; Ⓒ 60,220; ◆ 61,276
Burr; RMC Place; YELLOW MEDICINE; **193** P-2; elev. 1,326ft./404m.; mail Canby z 56220; ● 20
Burschville; RMC Place; HENNEPIN; ***193** O-9; ★ **MPLS-**; mail Loretto z 55357; pop. incl. with Corcoran (Inc. Place)
Burtrum; Inc. Place; TODD; **193** M-6; elev. 1,285ft./392m.; 🅿; z 56318; Ⓟ 172; Ⓒ 146
Bushville; RMC Place; BENTON; ***193** M-8; mail Foley z 56329; rural
Butler; RMC Place; OTTER TAIL; ***192** J-5; elev. 1,462ft./446m.; mail New York Mills z 56567
Butler Quarter; RMC Place; HENNEPIN; ★ **MPLS-**; mail Minneapolis z 55403; pop. incl. with Minneapolis (Inc. Place)
Butterfield; Inc. Place; WATONWAN; **193** S-6; elev. 1,189ft./362m.; 🅿; z 56120; Ⓟ 509; Ⓒ 564
Butternut; RMC Place; BLUE EARTH; **193** R-7; elev. 988ft./301m.; mail Lake Crystal z 56055; ● 30
Buyck; RMC Place; ST. LOUIS; **192** F-11; elev. 1,235ft./376m.; 🅿; z 55771; ● 25
Bygland; RMC Place; POLK; ***192** F-1; mail East Grand Forks z 56721; rural
Byron; Inc. Place; OLMSTED; **193** R-11; elev. 1,262ft./385m.; 🅿; ★ **ROCH**; z 55920; Ⓟ 2,441; Ⓒ 3,500

C

Cable; RMC Place; SHERBURNE; ***193** N-8; ★ **ST.CLD**; mail Saint Cloud z 56304; rural
Caledonia; Inc. Place; ⊡ HOUSTON; **193** T-13; elev. 1,174ft./358m.; 🅿; z 55921; Ⓟ 2,846; Ⓒ 2,965
Callaway; Inc. Place; BECKER; **192** I-4; located on White Earth Ind. Res.; elev. 1,370ft./418m.; 🅿; z 56521; Ⓟ 212; Ⓒ 200
Calumet; Inc. Place; ITASCA; **192** H-9; elev. 1,392ft./424m.; 🅿; z 55716; Ⓟ 382; Ⓒ 383
Cambria; RMC Place; BLUE EARTH; **193** R-7; mail New Ulm z 56073; ● 80
Cambridge; Inc. Place; ⊡ ISANTI; **193** N-9; elev. 962ft./293m.; 🅿 🅷; z 55008; Ⓟ 5,094; Ⓒ 5,520
Camden Place; RMC Place; HENNEPIN; ***193** O-9; ★ **MPLS-**; mail Minneapolis z 55412; pop. incl. with Minneapolis (Inc. Place)
Campbell; Inc. Place; WILKIN; **193** L-2; elev. 985ft./300m.; 🅿; z 56522 & mail Tintah z 56583; Ⓟ 233; Ⓒ 241
Camp Lacupolis; RMC Place; WABASHA; ***193** Q-12; elev. 683ft./208m.; mail Lake City z 55041; summer pop. 100; ● 30
Canby; Inc. Place; YELLOW MEDICINE; **193** P-3; elev. 1,234ft./376m.; 🅿 🅷; z 56220; Ⓟ 1,826; Ⓒ 1,903
Cannon City; RMC Place; RICE; **193** R-9; mail Faribault z 55021; ● 60
Cannon Falls; Inc. Place; GOODHUE; **193** Q-10; elev. 838ft./255m.; 🅿 🅷; z 55009; Ⓟ 3,232; Ⓒ 3,795
Canton; Inc. Place; FILLMORE; **193** T-12; elev. 1,345ft./410m.; 🅿; z 55922; Ⓟ 362; Ⓒ 343
Canyon; RMC Place; ST. LOUIS; **192** I-11; elev. 1,355ft./413m.; 🅿; z 55717; ● 70
Cardigan Junction; RMC Place; RAMSEY; ***193** O-10; ★ **MPLS-**; mail Saint Paul z 55112; pop. incl. with Shoreview (Inc. Place)
Caribou; RMC Place; KITTSON; ***192** C-3; elev. 1,015ft./309m.; mail Lancaster z 56735; rural
Carimona; RMC Place; FILLMORE; ***193** T-12; mail Preston z 55965; rural
Carlisle; RMC Place; OTTER TAIL; **193** K-3; elev. 1,225ft./373m.; 🅿; z 56537; ● 30
Carlos; Inc. Place; DOUGLAS; **193** L-5; elev. 1,370ft./418m.; 🅿; z 56319; Ⓟ 361; Ⓒ 329
Carlton; Inc. Place; ⊡ CARLTON; **192** J-11; elev. 1,091ft./333m.; 🅿; ★ **DUL**; z 55718; Ⓟ 923; Ⓒ 810
CARLTON; **192** J-10; Ⓟ 29,259; Ⓒ 31,671; ◆ 33,436
Carmody; RMC Place; ISANTI; ***193** M-9; mail Cottage Grove z 55016; rural
Carp; RMC Place; LAKE OF THE WOODS; ***192** D-6; mail Baudette z 56623; rural
Carver; Inc. Place; CARVER; **193** P-8; elev. 740ft./226m.; 🅿; ★ **MPLS-**; z 55315; Ⓟ 744; Ⓒ 1,266
CARVER; **193** P-8; Ⓟ 47,915; Ⓒ 70,205; ◆ 89,806
Cashtown; RMC Place; BIG STONE; ***193** N-2; mail Ortonville z 56278; pop. incl. with Ortonville (Inc. Place)
Casino; RMC Place; CASS; ***193** K-7; elev. 1,365ft./416m.; mail Pillager z 56473; ● 30
CASS; **192** J-7; Ⓟ 21,791; Ⓒ 27,150; ◆ 28,249
Cass Lake; Inc. Place; CASS; **192** H-6; located on Leech Lake Ind. Res.; elev. 1,323ft./403m.; 🅿 🅷; z 56633; location of Minnesota Indian Agency; Ⓟ 923; Ⓒ 860
Castle Danger; RMC Place; LAKE; **192** I-13; elev. 634ft./193m.; mail Two Harbors z 55616; ● 35
Castle Rock; RMC Place; DAKOTA; **193** Q-10; elev. 933ft./284m.; 🅿; z 55010; ● 150
Cazenovia; RMC Place; PIPESTONE; ***193** R-2; mail Pipestone z 56164; rural
Cedar; RMC Place; ANOKA; **193** N-9; elev. 607ft./185m.; 🅿; ★ **MPLS-**; z 55011; pop. incl. with Oak Grove (Inc. Place)
Cedar Beach; RMC Place; OLMSTED; ***193** R-11; ★ **ROCH**; mail Oronoco z 55960; ● 35
Cedar Grove; RMC Place; DAKOTA; ***193** P-9; ★ **MPLS-**; mail Saint Paul z 55111; pop. incl. with Eagan (Inc. Place)
Cedar Mills; Inc. Place; MEEKER; **193** P-7; elev. 1,091ft./333m.; mail Hutchinson z 55350; Ⓟ 80; Ⓒ 53
Celina; RMC Place; ST. LOUIS; ***192** F-10; elev. 1,315ft./401m.; mail Cook z 55723; rural
Center City; Inc. Place; ⊡ CHISAGO; **193** N-10; elev. 900ft./274m.; 🅿; ★ **MPLS-**; z 55012 & mail Almelund z 55002; Ⓟ 451; Ⓒ 582
Centerville; Inc. Place; ANOKA; **191** B-8; elev. 909ft./277m.; 🅿; ★ **MPLS-**; z 55038; Ⓟ 1,633; Ⓒ 3,202
Centerville; RMC Place; WINONA; ***193** S-13; mail Winona z 55987; ● 40
Central; RMC Place; WADENA; ***193** K-6; elev. 1,320ft./402m.; mail Verndale z 56481; rural
Central Lakes; RMC Place; ST. LOUIS; ***192** H-11; mail Eveleth z 55734; rural
Ceylon; Inc. Place; MARTIN; **193** T-6; elev. 1,260ft./384m.; 🅿; z 56121; Ⓟ 461; Ⓒ 413
Chamberlain; RMC Place; HUBBARD; ***192** I-6; mail Akeley z 56433; rural
Champlin; Inc. Place; HENNEPIN; **191** A-2; elev. 850ft./259m.; 🅿; ★ **MPLS-**; z 55316; Ⓟ 16,849; Ⓒ 22,193; ◆ 23,835
Chandler; Inc. Place; MURRAY; **193** S-3; elev. 1,651ft./503m.; 🅿; z 56122; Ⓟ 316; Ⓒ 276
Chanhassen; Inc. Place; CARVER, HENNEPIN; **193** P-9; elev. 976ft./297m.; 🅿; ★ **MPLS-**; z 55317; Ⓟ 11,732; Ⓒ 20,321; ◆ 24,930
Charlesville; RMC Place; GRANT, TRAVERSE; ***193** L-3; mail Tintah z 56583; rural
Chaska; Inc. Place; ⊡ CARVER; **193** P-9; elev. 728ft./222m.; 🅿; ★ **MPLS-**; z 55318; Ⓟ 11,339; Ⓒ 17,449; ◆ 23,330
Chatfield; Inc. Place; FILLMORE, OLMSTED; **193** S-12; elev. 1,000ft./305m.; 🅿; z 55923; Ⓟ 2,226; Ⓒ 2,394
Cherry; RMC Place; ST. LOUIS; ***192** H-10; elev. 1,353ft./412m.; mail Iron z 55751, Mountain Iron z 55768; ● 100
Cherry Grove; RMC Place; FILLMORE; **193** T-12; elev. 1,327ft./404m.; mail Spring Valley z 55975; ● 70
Chester; RMC Place; OLMSTED; **193** S-11; elev. 1,120ft./341m.; ★ **ROCH**; mail Rochester z 55904; ● 200
Chicago Bay; RMC Place; COOK; mail Hovland z 55606
Chickamaw Beach; Inc. Place; CASS; **192** J-7; elev. 1,300ft./396m.; mail Pine River z 56474; Ⓟ 132; Ⓒ 148
CHIPPEWA; **193** O-4; Ⓟ 13,228; Ⓒ 13,088; ◆ 12,176
Chippewa City; RMC Place; COOK; ***192** B-12; mail Grand Marais z 55604; rural
CHISAGO; **193** N-10; Ⓟ 30,521; Ⓒ 41,101; ◆ 50,817
Chisago City; Inc. Place; CHISAGO; **193** N-10; elev. 922ft./281m.; 🅿 🅷; ★ **MPLS-**; z 55013; Ⓟ 2,009; Ⓒ 2,622
Chisholm; Inc. Place; ST. LOUIS; **192** H-10; elev. 1,578ft./481m.; 🅿; z 55719; Ⓟ 5,290; Ⓒ 4,960
Choice; RMC Place; FILLMORE; ***193** T-13; elev. 818ft./249m.; mail Mabel z 55954; rural
Chokio; Inc. Place; STEVENS; **193** N-3; elev. 1,127ft./344m.; 🅿; z 56221; Ⓟ 521; Ⓒ 443
Circle Pines; Inc. Place; ANOKA; **191** B-7; elev. 900ft./274m.; 🅿; ★ **MPLS-**; z 55014; Ⓟ 4,704; Ⓒ 4,663
City; RMC Place; OLMSTED; ***193** R-11; ★ **ROCH**; mail Rochester z 55904; pop. incl. with Rochester (Inc. Place)
Civic Center; RMC Place; ST. LOUIS; ***192** J-12; ★ **DUL**; mail Duluth z 55802; pop. incl. with Duluth (Inc. Place)
Clara City; Inc. Place; CHIPPEWA; **193** P-5; elev. 1,062ft./324m.; 🅿; z 56222; Ⓟ 1,307; Ⓒ 1,393
Claremont; Inc. Place; DODGE; **193** R-10; elev. 1,285ft./392m.; 🅿; z 55924; Ⓟ 530; Ⓒ 620
Clarissa; Inc. Place; TODD; **193** L-6; elev. 1,320ft./402m.; 🅿; z 56440; Ⓟ 637; Ⓒ 609
Clarkfield; Inc. Place; YELLOW MEDICINE; **193** P-4; elev. 1,080ft./329m.; 🅿; z 56223; Ⓟ 924; Ⓒ 944
Clarks Grove; Inc. Place; FREEBORN; **193** S-9; elev. 1,300ft./396m.; 🅿; z 56016; Ⓟ 675; Ⓒ 734
CLAY; **192** I-3; Ⓟ 50,422; Ⓒ 51,229; ◆ 55,638
Clearbrook; Inc. Place; CLEARWATER; **192** G-5; elev. 1,350ft./411m.; 🅿; z 56634; Ⓟ 560; Ⓒ 551
Clear Lake; Inc. Place; SHERBURNE; **193** N-8; elev. 991ft./302m.; 🅿; z 55319; Ⓟ 315; Ⓒ 266
Clearwater; Inc. Place; WRIGHT; **193** N-8; elev. 1,000ft./305m.; 🅿; z 55320; Ⓟ 597; Ⓒ 858
CLEARWATER; **192** G-5; Ⓟ 8,309; Ⓒ 8,423; ◆ 8,283
Clements; Inc. Place; REDWOOD; **193** Q-5; elev. 1,050ft./320m.; 🅿; z 56224; Ⓟ 191; Ⓒ 191
Clementson; RMC Place; LAKE OF THE WOODS; **192** D-7; elev. 1,086ft./331m.; mail Baudette z 56623; ● 20
Cleveland; Inc. Place; LE SUEUR; **193** R-8; elev. 1,051ft./320m.; 🅿; z 56017; Ⓟ 699; Ⓒ 673
Cliff; RMC Place; DAKOTA; ★ **MPLS-**; mail Saint Paul z 55118; pop. incl. with Lilydale (Inc. Place)
Clifton; RMC Place; ST. LOUIS; ***192** I-12; mail Duluth z 55804; rural
Climax; Inc. Place; POLK; **192** G-2; elev. 860ft./262m.; 🅿; z 56523; Ⓟ 264; Ⓒ 243
Clinton; Inc. Place; BIG STONE; **193** N-2; elev. 1,150ft./351m.; 🅿; z 56225; Ⓟ 574; Ⓒ 453
Clinton Falls; RMC Place; STEELE; **193** R-9; elev. 1,133ft./345m.; mail Owatonna z 55060; ● 40
Clitherall; Inc. Place; OTTER TAIL; **193** K-4; elev. 1,348ft./411m.; 🅿; z 56524; Ⓟ 109; Ⓒ 118
Clontarf; Inc. Place; SWIFT; **193** N-4; elev. 1,050ft./320m.; 🅿; z 56226; Ⓟ 172; Ⓒ 173
Cloquet; Inc. Place; CARLTON; **192** J-11; elev. 1,204ft./367m.; 🅿 🅷; ★ **DUL**; z 55720; Ⓟ 10,885; Ⓒ 11,201
Clotho; RMC Place; TODD; **193** L-5; mail Long Prairie z 56347; ● 25
Cloverdale; RMC Place; PINE; **193** L-10; elev. 972ft./296m.; mail Hinckley z 55037; ● 40
Cloverton; RMC Place; PINE; **193** L-11; elev. 1,099ft./335m.; mail Sandstone z 55072; ● 35
Clyde; RMC Place; WINONA; ***193** S-12; mail Utica z 55979; rural
Coates; Inc. Place; DAKOTA; **193** P-10; elev. 917ft./280m.; ★ **MPLS-**; mail Rosemount z 55068; Ⓟ 186; Ⓒ 163
Cobden; Inc. Place; BROWN; **193** R-6; elev. 1,040ft./317m.; 🅿; z 56085; Ⓟ 62; Ⓒ 61
Cohasset; Inc. Place; ITASCA; **192** H-8; elev. 1,280ft./390m.; 🅿; z 55721; Ⓟ 1,970; Ⓒ 2,481
Coin; RMC Place; KANABEC; ***193** M-9; elev. 970ft./296m.; mail Ogilvie z 56358; rural
Cokato; Inc. Place; WRIGHT; **193** O-7; elev. 1,052ft./321m.; 🅿; z 55321; Ⓟ 2,180; Ⓒ 2,727
Colby; RMC Place; ST. LOUIS; ***192** G-12; mail Hoyt Lakes z 55750; pop. incl. with Hoyt Lakes (Inc. Place)
Cold Spring; Inc. Place; STEARNS; **193** N-7; elev. 1,091ft./333m.; 🅿; z 56320; Ⓟ 2,459; Ⓒ 2,975
Coleraine; Inc. Place; ITASCA; **192** H-9; elev. 1,324ft./404m.; 🅿; z 55722; Ⓟ 1,041; Ⓒ 1,110
Collegeville (Saint John's University); RMC Place; STEARNS; **193** N-7; elev. 1,094ft./333m.; 🅿 🅲 1,837; ★ **ST.CLD**; z 56321; ● 200
Collis; RMC Place; TRAVERSE; **193** M-2; mail Dumont z 56236; ● 20
Cologne; Inc. Place; CARVER; **193** P-8; elev. 948ft./289m.; 🅿; z 55322; Ⓟ 563; Ⓒ 1,012
Columbia Heights; Inc. Place; ANOKA; **191** D-5; elev. 950ft./290m.; 🅿; ★ **MPLS-**; z 55421; Ⓟ 18,910; Ⓒ 18,520
Columbus; Inc. Place; ANOKA; ***193** N-10; incorporated September 21, 2006; not included in 2000 Census; ● 4,000
Comfrey; Inc. Place; BROWN, COTTONWOOD; **193** R-6; elev. 1,301ft./397m.; 🅿; z 56019; Ⓟ 433; Ⓒ 367
Commerce; RMC Place; HENNEPIN; ***193** P-9; ★ **MPLS-**; mail Minneapolis z 55415; pop. incl. with Minneapolis (Inc. Place)
Como; RMC Place; RAMSEY; ***193** P-10; ★ **MPLS-**; mail Saint Paul z 55108; pop. incl. with Saint Paul (Inc. Place)
Comstock; Inc. Place; CLAY; **192** J-2; elev. 920ft./280m.; 🅿; z 56525; Ⓟ 123; Ⓒ 123
Conception; RMC Place; WABASHA; ***193** R-12; elev. 1,170ft./357m.; mail Kellogg z 55945; rural
Concord; RMC Place; DODGE; **193** R-10; mail West Concord z 55985; ● 60
Conger; Inc. Place; FREEBORN; **193** T-9; elev. 1,289ft./393m.; 🅿; z 56020; Ⓟ 143; Ⓒ 133
Constance; RMC Place; ANOKA; ***193** O-9; elev. 902ft./275m.; ★ **MPLS-**; mail Anoka z 55303; pop. incl. with Andover (Inc. Place)
Cook; Inc. Place; ST. LOUIS; **192** F-10; elev. 1,306ft./398m.; 🅿 🅷; z 55723; Ⓟ 680; Ⓒ 622
COOK; **192** A-11; Ⓟ 3,868; Ⓒ 5,168; ◆ 5,412
Cooley; RMC Place; ITASCA; ***192** H-9; elev. 1,444ft./440m.; mail Nashwauk z 55769; rural
Coon Creek; RMC Place; ANOKA; ***193** O-9; ★ **MPLS-**; mail Minneapolis z 55433; pop. incl. with Coon Rapids (Inc. Place)
Coon Lake Beach; RMC Place; ANOKA; ***193** N-10; ★ **MPLS-**; mail Wyoming z 55092; pop. incl. with East Bethel (Inc. Place)
Coon Rapids; Inc. Place; ANOKA; **193** O-9; elev. 860ft./262m.; 🅿 🅷 ■; ★ **MPLS-**; z 55433, z 55448; Ⓟ 52,978; Ⓒ 61,607; ◆ 59,931
Coopers Corner; RMC Place; ANOKA; ***193** N-9; ★ **MPLS-**; mail Bethel z 55005; pop. incl. with East Bethel (Inc. Place)
Copas; RMC Place; WASHINGTON; ***193** O-10; ★ **MPLS-**; mail Scandia z 55073; ● 50
Corcoran; Inc. Place; HENNEPIN; **193** O-9; elev. 980ft./299m.; 🅿; ★ **MPLS-**; z 55340 & mail Loretto z 55357, Osseo z 55311, Rogers z 55374; Ⓟ 5,199; Ⓒ 5,630
Cordova; RMC Place; LE SUEUR; ***193** R-8; mail Le Center z 56057; ● 50
Cormorant; RMC Place; BECKER; ***192** J-3; mail Detroit Lakes z 56501, Pelican Rapids z 56572
Corning; RMC Place; MOWER; ***193** S-10; mail Austin z 55912
Correll; Inc. Place; BIG STONE; **193** O-3; elev. 980ft./299m.; 🅿; z 56227; Ⓟ 60; Ⓒ 47
Corvuso; RMC Place; MEEKER; **193** P-6; mail Cosmos z 56228; ● 25
Cosmos; Inc. Place; MEEKER; **193** P-6; elev. 1,112ft./339m.; 🅿; z 56228; Ⓟ 610; Ⓒ 582
Cottage Grove; Inc. Place; WASHINGTON; **193** P-10; elev. 800ft./244m.; 🅿; ★ **MPLS-**; z 55016; Ⓟ 22,935; Ⓒ 30,582; ◆ 32,594
Cotton; RMC Place; ST. LOUIS; **192** I-11; elev. 1,329ft./405m.; 🅿; z 55724; ● 200
Cottonwood; Inc. Place; LYON; **193** Q-4; 🅿; z 56229; Ⓟ 982; Ⓒ 1,148
COTTONWOOD; **193** S-5; Ⓟ 12,694; Ⓒ 12,167; ◆ 11,083
Courtland; Inc. Place; NICOLLET; **193** R-7; 🅿; z 56021; Ⓟ 412; Ⓒ 538
Cove; RMC Place; MILLE LACS; **193** L-9; mail Onamia z 56359; ● 75
Craigville; RMC Place; KOOCHICHING; ***192** F-9; mail Effie z 56639
Crane Lake; RMC Place; ST. LOUIS; **192** E-11; elev. 1,160ft./354m.; 🅿; z 55725; summer pop. 2,000; ● 300
Credit River; RMC Place; SCOTT; ***193** P-9; elev. 990ft./302m.; ★ **MPLS-**; mail Prior Lake z 55372; ● 50
Croftville; RMC Place; COOK; **192** B-12; mail Grand Marais z 55604; ● 40
Cromwell; Inc. Place; CARLTON; **192** J-10; elev. 1,311ft./400m.; 🅿; z 55726; Ⓟ 221; Ⓒ 143; Ⓡ 190
Crookston; Inc. Place; ⊡ POLK; **192** G-2; elev. 890ft./271m.; 🅿 🅷 🅲 2,414; z 56716; Ⓟ 8,119; Ⓒ 8,192
Crosby; Inc. Place; CROW WING; **193** K-8; elev. 1,261ft./384m.; 🅿 🅷; z 56441; Ⓟ 2,073; Ⓒ 2,299
Crosby Beach; RMC Place; CROW WING; ***193** K-8; elev. 1,266ft./386m.; mail Deerwood z 56444; ● 350
Cross Lake; Inc. Place; CROW WING; **192** J-7; elev. 1,240ft./378m.; 🅿; z 56442; Ⓟ 1,132; Ⓒ 1,893
Crown; RMC Place; ISANTI; **193** N-9; elev. 953ft./290m.; mail Saint Francis z 55070; ● 50
Crow River; RMC Place; MEEKER; **193** O-6; elev. 1,156ft./352m.; mail Grove City z 56243; ● 20
Crow Wing; RMC Place; CROW WING; **193** K-7; elev. 1,194ft./364m.; mail Brainerd z 56401; ● 25
CROW WING; **192** J-8; Ⓟ 44,249; Ⓒ 55,099; ◆ 62,889
Crystal; Inc. Place; HENNEPIN; **191** E-3; elev. 900ft./274m.; 🅿; ★ **MPLS-**; z 55422, z 55427-29; Ⓟ 23,788; Ⓒ 22,698; ◆ 21,944
Crystal Bay; RMC Place; HENNEPIN; ***193** P-9; 🅿; ★ **MPLS-**; z 55323; pop. incl. with Orono (Inc. Place)
Culver; RMC Place; ST. LOUIS; **192** I-11; elev. 1,289ft./393m.; 🅿; z 55779; ● 30
Cummingsville; RMC Place; OLMSTED; ***193** S-12; mail Chatfield z 55923; rural
Currie; Inc. Place; MURRAY; **193** R-4; elev. 1,500ft./457m.; 🅿; z 56123; Ⓟ 303; Ⓒ 225
Cushing; RMC Place; MORRISON; **193** L-6; elev. 1,240ft./378m.; 🅿; z 56443; ● 70
Cusson; RMC Place; ST. LOUIS; **192** F-10; elev. 1,333ft./406m.; mail Orr z 55771; ● 40
Cutler; RMC Place; AITKIN; **193** K-8; elev. 1,270ft./387m.; mail Aitkin z 56431; ● 100
Cuyuna; Inc. Place; CROW WING; ***193** K-8; elev. 1,250ft./381m.; mail Deerwood z 56444; Ⓟ 172; Ⓒ 231
Cyrus; Inc. Place; POPE; **193** M-4; elev. 1,138ft./347m.; 🅿; z 56323; Ⓟ 328; Ⓒ 303

D

Dakota; Inc. Place; WINONA; **193** S-14; elev. 691ft./211m.; 🅿; ★ **LACRO**; z 55925; Ⓟ 360; Ⓒ 329
DAKOTA; **193** P-9; Ⓟ 275,227; Ⓒ 355,904; ◆ 393,588
Dalbo; RMC Place; ISANTI; **193** M-9; elev. 960ft./293m.; 🅿; z 55017; ● 100
Dale; RMC Place; CLAY; ***192** I-3; mail Hawley z 56549; ● 20
Dalton; Inc. Place; OTTER TAIL; **193** L-4; elev. 1,350ft./411m.; 🅿; z 56324; Ⓟ 234; Ⓒ 258
Danube; Inc. Place; RENVILLE; **193** P-5; elev. 1,082ft./330m.; 🅿; z 56230; Ⓟ 562; Ⓒ 529
Danvers; Inc. Place; SWIFT; **193** O-4; elev. 1,027ft./313m.; 🅿; z 56231; Ⓟ 98; Ⓒ 108
Darfur; Inc. Place; WATONWAN; **193** R-6; elev. 1,148ft./350m.; 🅿; z 56022; Ⓟ 128; Ⓒ 137
Darling; RMC Place; MORRISON; mail Little Falls z 56345; rural
Darwin; Inc. Place; MEEKER; **193** O-7; elev. 1,132ft./345m.; 🅿; z 55324; Ⓟ 252; Ⓒ 276
Dassel; Inc. Place; MEEKER; **193** O-7; elev. 1,091ft./333m.; 🅿; z 55325; Ⓟ 1,082; Ⓒ 1,233
Dawson; Inc. Place; LAC QUI PARLE; **193** P-3; elev. 1,058ft./322m.; 🅿 🅷; z 56232; Ⓟ 1,626; Ⓒ 1,539
Day; RMC Place; ISANTI; ***193** M-9; mail Braham z 55006
Dayton; Inc. Place; HENNEPIN, WRIGHT; **193** O-9; 🅿; ★ **MPLS-**; z 55327 & mail Osseo z 55369; Ⓟ 4,443; Ⓒ 4,699; Ⓡ 4,713
Daytons Bluff; RMC Place; RAMSEY; ***193** P-10; ★ **MPLS-**; mail Saint Paul z 55106; pop. incl. with Saint Paul (Inc. Place)
Debs; RMC Place; BELTRAMI; **192** G-5; elev. 1,343ft./409m.; mail Shevlin z 56676; ● 25
Deephaven; Inc. Place; HENNEPIN; **191** G-1; elev. 950ft./290m.; ★ **MPLS-**; mail Excelsior z 55331, Wayzata z 55391; Ⓟ 3,653; Ⓒ 3,853
Deer Creek; Inc. Place; OTTER TAIL; **193** K-5; elev. 1,393ft./425m.; 🅿; z 56527; Ⓟ 303; Ⓒ 328

Entries in **UPPERCASE** are counties.
Entries in **bold** have populations of 2,500 or more.
Names in parentheses are alternate names.

Inc. Place	Incorporated Place
RMC Place	Rand McNally Designated Place
CDP	Census Designated Place
MCD	Minor Civil Division
⊡	County Seat
▲	Minor Civil Division
elev.	Elevation
🅿	Post Office
🅷	Hospital
🅲	College
■	Principal Business Center
★	Ranally Metro Area (RMA) Abbreviation
z	Zip Code(s)
Ⓟ	Previous Census Population
Ⓡ	Revised Census Population
Ⓐ	Annexation Population
●	Rand McNally Population Estimate
Ⓒ	Final Census Population
Ⓢ	Special Census Population
◆	Estimated Population

For additional definitions see Glossary, Volume 1, and Introduction, Volume 2.

Deerfield; RMC Place; STEELE; *193 R-9; mail Medford z 55049; rural
Deer River; Inc. Place; ITASCA; 192 H-8; elev. 1,291ft./393m.; 🅿 🅷; z 56636 & mail Bowstring z 56631; Ⓟ 838; Ⓒ 903
Deerwood; Inc. Place; CROW WING; 193 K-8; elev. 1,277ft./389m.; 🅿; z 56444; Ⓟ 524; Ⓒ 590
De Graff; Inc. Place; SWIFT; 193 O-4; elev. 1,055ft./322m.; 🅿; z 56271; Ⓟ 149; Ⓒ 133
Delano; Inc. Place; WRIGHT; 193 O-8; elev. 944ft./288m.; 🅿; z 55328; Ⓟ 2,709; Ⓒ 3,837; Ⓡ 3,897
Delavan; Inc. Place; FARIBAULT; 193 S-8; elev. 1,063ft./324m.; 🅿; z 56023; Ⓟ 245; Ⓒ 223
Delft; RMC Place; COTTONWOOD; 193 S-5; elev. 1,450ft./442m.; mail Windom z 56101; ● 100
Delhi; Inc. Place; REDWOOD; 193 Q-5; elev. 1,030ft./314m.; 🅿; z 56283; Ⓟ 69; Ⓒ 69
Dell; RMC Place; FARIBAULT; *193 T-8; mail Blue Earth z 56013; rural
Dellwood; Inc. Place; WASHINGTON; 191 C-9; elev. 950ft./290m.; 🅿; ★ **MPLS-**; z 55110; Ⓟ 887; Ⓒ 1,033
Denham; Inc. Place; PINE; 193 K-10; elev. 1,203ft./367m.; mail Sturgeon Lake z 55783; Ⓟ 36; Ⓒ 40
Dennison; Inc. Place; GOODHUE, RICE; 193 Q-10; elev. 980ft./299m.; 🅿; z 55018; Ⓟ 152; Ⓒ 168
Dent; Inc. Place; OTTER TAIL; 193 K-4; elev. 1,364ft./416m.; 🅿; z 56528; Ⓟ 177; Ⓒ 192
Detroit Lakes; Inc. Place; ⊡ BECKER; 192 J-4; elev. 1,365ft./416m.; 🅿 🅷; z 56501-02; Ⓟ 6,635; Ⓒ 7,348
Dexter; Inc. Place; MOWER; 193 S-11; elev. 1,418ft./432m.; 🅿; z 55926; Ⓟ 303; Ⓒ 333
Diamond Lake; RMC Place; HENNEPIN; *193 P-9; ★ **MPLS-**; mail Minneapolis z 55419; pop. incl. with Minneapolis (Inc. Place)
Dilworth; Inc. Place; CLAY; 192 I-2; elev. 909ft./277m.; 🅿; ★ **FAR-**; z 56529; Ⓟ 2,562; Ⓒ 3,001
Dinkytown; RMC Place; HENNEPIN; *193 P-9; ★ **MPLS-**; mail Minneapolis z 55414; pop. incl. with Minneapolis (Inc. Place)
DODGE; 193 S-10; Ⓟ 15,731; Ⓒ 17,731; ◆ 19,465
Dodge Center; Inc. Place; DODGE; 193 R-10; elev. 1,293ft./394m.; 🅿; ★ **ROCH**; z 55927; Ⓟ 1,954; Ⓒ 2,226
Donaldson; Inc. Place; KITTSON; 192 D-2; elev. 828ft./252m.; 🅿; z 56720; Ⓟ 57; Ⓒ 41
Donnelly; Inc. Place; STEVENS; 193 M-3; elev. 1,133ft./345m.; 🅿; z 56235; Ⓟ 221; Ⓒ 254
Dora Lake; RMC Place; ITASCA; 192 G-8; elev. 1,324ft./404m.; mail Northome z 56661; ● 40
Doran; Inc. Place; WILKIN; 193 L-2; elev. 970ft./296m.; 🅿; z 56522; Ⓟ 78; Ⓒ 59
Dorothy; RMC Place; RED LAKE; 192 F-3; mail Red Lake Falls z 56750; ● 25
Dorset; RMC Place; HUBBARD; 192 I-6; elev. 1,476ft./450m.; mail Park Rapids z 56470; ● 80
Douglas; RMC Place; OLMSTED; 193 R-11; elev. 1,032ft./315m.; ★ **ROCH**; mail Bayport z 55003, Oronoco z 55960; ● 150
DOUGLAS; 193 L-4; Ⓟ 28,674; Ⓒ 32,821; ◆ 36,862
Douglas Lodge; RMC Place; HUBBARD; *192 I-5; elev. 1,550ft./472m.; mail Noyes z 56740
Dover; Inc. Place; OLMSTED; 193 S-12; 🅿; z 55929; Ⓟ 416; Ⓒ 438
Dovray; Inc. Place; MURRAY; 193 R-4; elev. 1,520ft./463m.; 🅿; z 56125; Ⓟ 60; Ⓒ 67
Downer; RMC Place; CLAY; 192 J-2; 🅿; z 56514; ● 90
Dresbach; RMC Place; WINONA; 193 S-14; elev. 689ft./210m.; ★ **LACRO**; mail La Crescent z 55947; ● 150
Duelm; RMC Place; BENTON; 193 N-8; mail Foley z 56329; ● 70
Duluth; Inc. Place; ⊡ ST. LOUIS; 192 J-12; elev. 620ft./189m.; 🅿 🅷 🅲 14,494 ■; ★ **DUL**; z 55701, z 55801-08, z 55810-12, z 55814-16; Ⓟ 85,493; Ⓒ 86,918; Ⓡ 86,319; ◆ 86,841
Duluth Heights; RMC Place; ST. LOUIS; *192 J-12; ★ **DUL**; mail Duluth z 55811; pop. incl. with Duluth (Inc. Place)
Dumfries; RMC Place; WABASHA; *193 Q-12; mail Wabasha z 55981
Dumont; Inc. Place; TRAVERSE; 193 M-2; elev. 1,040ft./317m.; 🅿; z 56236; Ⓟ 126; Ⓒ 122
Dundas; Inc. Place; RICE; 193 Q-9; elev. 958ft./292m.; 🅿; z 55019; Ⓟ 473; Ⓒ 547
Dundee; Inc. Place; NOBLES; 193 S-4; elev. 1,451ft./442m.; 🅿; z 56131; Ⓟ 107; Ⓒ 102
Dunnell; Inc. Place; MARTIN; 193 T-6; elev. 1,320ft./402m.; 🅿; z 56127; Ⓟ 187; Ⓒ 197
Dunvilla; RMC Place; OTTER TAIL; 192 J-3; elev. 1,350ft./411m.; mail Pelican Rapids z 56572; ● 100
Duquette; RMC Place; PINE; 193 K-11; elev. 1,147ft./350m.; 🅿; z 55756; ● 70
Duxbury; RMC Place; PINE; 193 L-11; mail Sandstone z 55072; ● 20

E

Eagan; Inc. Place; DAKOTA; 191 J-7; elev. 900ft./274m.; 🅿 🅲 1,741; ★ **MPLS-**; z 55120-23; Ⓟ 47,409; Ⓒ 63,557; ◆ 66,632
Eagle Bend; Inc. Place; TODD; 193 L-5; elev. 1,369ft./417m.; 🅿; z 56446; Ⓟ 524; Ⓒ 595
Eagle Lake; Inc. Place; BLUE EARTH; 193 R-8; elev. 1,014ft./309m.; 🅿; ★ **MNKT**; z 56024; Ⓟ 1,703; Ⓒ 1,787
East Beaver Bay; RMC Place; LAKE; 192 H-14; mail Beaver Bay z 55601; ● 20
East Bethel; Inc. Place; ANOKA; 193 N-9; elev. 934ft./285m.; 🅿; ★ **MPLS-**; z 55005, z 55011, z 55092; Ⓟ 8,050; Ⓒ 10,941
East Chain; RMC Place; MARTIN; 193 T-7; mail Fairmont z 56031, Granada z 56039; ● 200
East Cottage Grove; RMC Place; WASHINGTON; *193 P-10; ★ **MPLS-**; mail Cottage Grove z 55016; pop. incl. with Cottage Grove (Inc. Place)
Eastern Heights; RMC Place; RAMSEY; *193 P-10; ★ **MPLS-**; mail Saint Paul z 55119, z 55128; pop. incl. with Saint Paul (Inc. Place)
East Grand Forks; Inc. Place; POLK; 192 F-1; elev. 830ft./253m.; 🅿; ★ **GDFK**; z 56721; Ⓟ 8,658; Ⓒ 7,501
East Gull Lake; Inc. Place; CASS; 193 K-7; elev. 1,252ft./382m.; 🅿; z 56401; Ⓟ 687; Ⓒ 978
East Hastings; RMC Place; DAKOTA; ★ **MPLS-**; mail Hastings z 55033; pop. incl. with Hastings (Inc. Place)
East Lake; RMC Place; AITKIN; 193 K-9; mail McGregor z 55760; ● 30
East Lake Francis Shores; RMC Place; ISANTI; *193 N-9; mail Isanti z 55040; ● 170
East Minneapolis; RMC Place; HENNEPIN; ★ **MPLS-**; pop. incl. with Minneapolis (Inc. Place)
East Moorhead; CLAY; see Moorhead (Inc. Place)
Easton; Inc. Place; FARIBAULT; 193 S-8; elev. 1,060ft./323m.; 🅿; z 56025; Ⓟ 229; Ⓒ 214
East Saint Paul; RMC Place; RAMSEY; ★ **MPLS-**; pop. incl. with Saint Paul (Inc. Place)
Eastside; RMC Place; HENNEPIN; *193 O-9; ★ **MPLS-**; mail Minneapolis z 55418; pop. incl. with Minneapolis (Inc. Place)
East Union; RMC Place; CARVER; 193 P-8; mail Carver z 55315; ● 60
Ebro; RMC Place; CLEARWATER; 192 H-4; located on White Earth Ind. Res.; mail Bagley z 56621; ● 70
Echo; Inc. Place; YELLOW MEDICINE; 193 Q-5; elev. 1,080ft./329m.; 🅿; z 56237; Ⓟ 304; Ⓒ 278
Echols; RMC Place; WATONWAN; *193 S-6; mail Saint James z 56081; rural
Eden; RMC Place; DODGE; *193 R-10; ★ **ROCH**; mail Dodge Center z 55927; rural
Eden Prairie; Inc. Place; HENNEPIN; 191 I-1; elev. 880ft./268m.; 🅿; ★ **MPLS-**; z 55343-44, z 55346-47; Ⓟ 39,311; Ⓒ 54,901; ◆ 61,178
Eden Valley; Inc. Place; MEEKER, STEARNS; 193 N-6; elev. 1,110ft./338m.; 🅿; z 55329; Ⓟ 732; Ⓒ 866
Edgerton; Inc. Place; PIPESTONE; 193 S-3; elev. 1,573ft./479m.; 🅿; z 56128; Ⓟ 1,106; Ⓒ 1,033
Edgewood; RMC Place; ISANTI; 193 N-9; elev. 959ft./292m.; mail Cambridge z 55008; ● 120
Edina; Inc. Place; HENNEPIN; 191 H-3; elev. 850ft./259m.; 🅿 ■; ★ **MPLS-**; z 55410, z 55416, z 55423-24, z 55435-36, z 55439 & mail Hopkins z 55343; Ⓟ 46,070; Ⓒ 47,425; ◆ 48,384
Effie; Inc. Place; ITASCA; 192 G-8; elev. 1,381ft./421m.; 🅿; z 56639; Ⓟ 130; Ⓒ 91
Eidswold; RMC Place; SCOTT; *193 Q-9; mail Elko z 55020
Eitzen; Inc. Place; HOUSTON; 193 T-13; elev. 1,140ft./347m.; 🅿; z 55931; Ⓟ 221; Ⓒ 229
Elba; Inc. Place; WINONA; 193 R-12; elev. 744ft./227m.; mail Altura z 55910; Ⓟ 220; Ⓒ 214
Elbow Lake; CDP-Census Area Only; BECKER, CLEARWATER; *192 I-4; Ⓒ 104
Elbow Lake; Inc. Place; ⊡ GRANT; 193 L-3; elev. 1,222ft./372m.; 🅿 🅷; z 56531; Ⓟ 1,186; Ⓒ 1,275
Eldes Corner; RMC Place; ST. LOUIS; *192 J-11; elev. 1,222ft./372m.; ★ **DUL**; mail Duluth z 55810; ● 150
Eldred; RMC Place; POLK; 192 G-2; elev. 866ft./264m.; 🅿; z 56523; ● 50
Elgin; Inc. Place; WABASHA; 193 R-12; elev. 1,060ft./323m.; 🅿; z 55932; Ⓟ 733; Ⓒ 826
Elizabeth; Inc. Place; OTTER TAIL; 193 K-3; elev. 1,256ft./383m.; 🅿; z 56533; Ⓟ 152; Ⓒ 172
Elko; RMC Place; SCOTT; 193 Q-9; elev. 1,132ft./345m.; 🅿; z 55020; former incorporated place; became part of Elko New Market January 1, 2007; pop. incl. with Elko New Market (Inc. Place); Ⓟ 223; Ⓒ 472
Elko New Market; Inc. Place; SCOTT; *193 Q-9; incorporated January 1, 2007; not reported in 2000 Census; ● 1,800
Elk River; Inc. Place; ⊡ SHERBURNE; 193 O-9; elev. 900ft./274m.; 🅿; ★ **MPLS-**; z 55330; Ⓟ 11,143; Ⓒ 16,447; ◆ 21,543
Elkton; Inc. Place; MOWER; 193 T-11; elev. 1,400ft./427m.; 🅿; z 55933; Ⓟ 142; Ⓒ 149
Ellendale; Inc. Place; STEELE; 193 S-9; elev. 1,280ft./390m.; 🅿; z 56026; Ⓟ 549; Ⓒ 590
Ellsworth; Inc. Place; NOBLES; 193 T-3; elev. 1,450ft./442m.; 🅿; z 56129; Ⓟ 580; Ⓒ 540
Elmdale; Inc. Place; MORRISON; 193 M-7; elev. 1,169ft./356m.; mail Bowlus z 56314; Ⓟ 130; Ⓒ 107
Elmer; RMC Place; ST. LOUIS; *192 I-10; mail Meadowlands z 55765; ● 25
Elmore; Inc. Place; FARIBAULT; 193 T-7; elev. 1,114ft./340m.; 🅿; z 56027; Ⓟ 709; Ⓒ 735
Elmwood; RMC Place; HENNEPIN; *193 P-9; elev. 900ft./274m.; ★ **MPLS-**; mail Minneapolis z 55416; pop. incl. with Saint Louis Park (Inc. Place)
Elrosa; Inc. Place; STEARNS; 193 N-6; elev. 1,313ft./400m.; 🅿; z 56325; Ⓟ 205; Ⓒ 166
Elway; RMC Place; RAMSEY; *193 P-10; ★ **MPLS-**; mail Saint Paul z 55105, z 55116; pop. incl. with Saint Paul (Inc. Place)
Ely; Inc. Place; ST. LOUIS; 192 F-12; elev. 1,473ft./449m.; 🅿 🅷; z 55731 & mail Winton z 55796; Ⓟ 3,968; Ⓒ 3,724
Ely Lake; RMC Place; ST. LOUIS; *192 H-11; mail Eveleth z 55734; ● 1,100
Elysian; Inc. Place; LE SUEUR, WASECA; 193 R-8; elev. 1,050ft./320m.; 🅿; z 56028; Ⓟ 445; Ⓒ 486
Embarrass; RMC Place; ST. LOUIS; 192 G-12; elev. 1,421ft./433m.; 🅿; z 55732; ● 100
Emco; RMC Place; ST. LOUIS; mail Hoyt Lakes z 55750; pop. incl. with Hoyt Lakes (Inc. Place)
Emily; Inc. Place; CROW WING; 192 J-8; elev. 1,298ft./396m.; 🅿; z 56447; Ⓟ 613; Ⓒ 847
Emmaville; RMC Place; HUBBARD; *192 I-6; mail Park Rapids z 56470; ● 25
Emmons; Inc. Place; FREEBORN; 193 T-9; elev. 1,280ft./390m.; 🅿; z 56029; Ⓟ 439; Ⓒ 432
Empire (Empire City); RMC Place; DAKOTA; 193 Q-10; mail Farmington z 55024; ● 100
Empire City; DAKOTA; see Empire (RMC Place)
Endion; RMC Place; ST. LOUIS; ★ **DUL**; pop. incl. with Duluth (Inc. Place)
Enfield; RMC Place; WRIGHT; *193 N-8; mail Monticello z 55362; ● 25
Englund; RMC Place; MARSHALL; *192 D-2; elev. 965ft./294m.; mail Strandquist z 56758
Erdahl; RMC Place; GRANT; 193 L-4; elev. 1,265ft./386m.; mail Elbow Lake z 56531; ● 50
Erhard; Inc. Place; OTTER TAIL; 193 K-3; elev. 1,293ft./394m.; 🅿; z 56534; Ⓟ 181; Ⓒ 150
Ericsburg; RMC Place; KOOCHICHING; 192 D-9; elev. 1,115ft./340m.; mail International Falls z 56649; ● 90
Erie; RMC Place; PENNINGTON; mail Goodridge z 56725; rural
Erskine; Inc. Place; POLK; 192 G-3; elev. 1,190ft./363m.; 🅿; z 56535; Ⓟ 422; Ⓒ 437
Esden; RMC Place; CROW WING; *193 K-8; elev. 1,277ft./389m.; mail Deerwood z 56444; rural
Esko; RMC Place; CARLTON; 192 J-11; elev. 1,170ft./357m.; 🅿; ★ **DUL**; z 55733; ● 550
Essig; RMC Place; BROWN; 193 R-6; elev. 1,001ft./305m.; 🅿; z 56030, z 56073; ● 50
Estes Brook; RMC Place; MILLE LACS; 193 M-8; elev. 1,053ft./321m.; mail Oak Park z 56357; ● 35
Etna; RMC Place; FILLMORE; *193 T-11; mail Spring Valley z 55975
Etter; RMC Place; DAKOTA; *193 P-11; mail Welch z 55089; ● 50
Euclid; RMC Place; POLK; 192 F-2; elev. 890ft./271m.; 🅿; z 56722; ● 150
Eureka; RMC Place; HENNEPIN; *193 P-9; ★ **MPLS-**; mail Excelsior z 55331; pop. incl. with Shorewood (Inc. Place)
Evan; Inc. Place; BROWN; 193 Q-6; elev. 1,020ft./311m.; 🅿; z 56085, z 56266; Ⓟ 83; Ⓒ 91
Evansville; Inc. Place; DOUGLAS; 193 L-4; elev. 1,359ft./414m.; 🅿; z 56326; Ⓟ 566; Ⓒ 566
Eveleth; Inc. Place; ST. LOUIS; 192 H-11; elev. 1,610ft./491m.; 🅿; z 55734; Ⓟ 4,064; Ⓒ 3,865
Everdell; RMC Place; WILKIN; *193 K-2; elev. 991ft./302m.; mail Breckenridge z 56520
Evergreen; RMC Place; BECKER; *192 J-5; elev. 1,548ft./472m.; mail Frazee z 56544
Excelsior; Inc. Place; HENNEPIN; 193 P-9; elev. 950ft./290m.; 🅿; ★ **MPLS-**; z 55331; Ⓟ 2,367; Ⓒ 2,393
Eyota; Inc. Place; OLMSTED; 193 S-12; elev. 1,241ft./378m.; 🅿; z 55934; Ⓟ 1,448; Ⓒ 1,644

F

Fairbanks; RMC Place; ST. LOUIS; *192 H-12; elev. 1,653ft./504m.; mail Brimson z 55602; rural
Fairfax; Inc. Place; RENVILLE; 193 Q-6; elev. 1,040ft./317m.; 🅿; z 55332; Ⓟ 1,276; Ⓒ 1,295
Fairhaven; RMC Place; STEARNS; 193 N-7; mail South Haven z 55382; ● 200
Fairmont; Inc. Place; ⊡ MARTIN; 193 T-7; elev. 1,187ft./362m.; 🅿 🅷 ■; z 56031, z 56075; Ⓟ 11,265; Ⓒ 10,889; ◆ 10,192
Faith; RMC Place; NORMAN; *192 H-3; mail Twin Valley z 56584; ● 20
Falcon Heights; Inc. Place; RAMSEY; 191 F-6; elev. 960ft./293m.; 🅿; ★ **MPLS-**; z 55108, z 55113; Ⓟ 5,380; Ⓒ 5,572
Faribault; Inc. Place; ⊡ RICE; 193 R-9; elev. 999ft./304m.; 🅿 🅷; z 55021; Ⓟ 17,085; Ⓒ 20,818; ◆ 22,868
FARIBAULT; 193 T-8; Ⓟ 16,937; Ⓒ 16,181; ◆ 14,415
Farming; RMC Place; STEARNS; 193 N-6; mail Richmond z 56368; ● 50
Farmington; Inc. Place; DAKOTA; 193 Q-10; elev. 904ft./276m.; 🅿 🅷; ★ **MPLS-**; z 55024; Ⓟ 5,940; Ⓒ 12,365
Farris; RMC Place; HUBBARD; *192 H-6; mail Cass Lake z 56633; rural
Farwell; Inc. Place; POPE; 193 M-4; elev. 1,350ft./411m.; 🅿; z 56327; Ⓟ 74; Ⓒ 57
Federal Dam; Inc. Place; CASS; 192 H-7; elev. 1,310ft./399m.; 🅿; z 56641; Ⓟ 118; Ⓒ 101
Felton; Inc. Place; CLAY; 192 I-2; elev. 910ft./277m.; 🅿; z 56536; Ⓟ 211; Ⓒ 216
Fergus Falls; Inc. Place; ⊡ OTTER TAIL; 193 K-3; elev. 1,196ft./365m.; 🅿 🅷 ■; z 56537-38; Ⓟ 12,362; Ⓒ 13,471; ◆ 13,156
Fernando; RMC Place; MCLEOD; 193 Q-7; elev. 1,057ft./322m.; mail Stewart z 55385; ● 25
Fertile; Inc. Place; POLK; 192 G-3; elev. 1,140ft./347m.; 🅿; z 56540; Ⓟ 853; Ⓒ 893
Fifty Lakes; Inc. Place; CROW WING; 192 J-8; elev. 1,277ft./389m.; 🅿; z 56448; Ⓟ 299; Ⓒ 392
Fillmore; RMC Place; FILLMORE; 193 S-12; mail Wykoff z 55990; ● 100
FILLMORE; 193 T-12; Ⓟ 20,777; Ⓒ 21,122; ◆ 21,006
Finland; RMC Place; LAKE; 192 H-14; elev. 1,330ft./405m.; 🅿; z 55603; ● 300
Finlayson; Inc. Place; PINE; 193 L-10; elev. 1,110ft./338m.; 🅿; z 55735; Ⓟ 242; Ⓒ 314
Fisher; Inc. Place; POLK; 192 G-2; elev. 853ft./260m.; 🅿; z 56723; Ⓟ 413; Ⓒ 435
Flensburg; Inc. Place; MORRISON; 193 L-7; elev. 1,220ft./372m.; 🅿; z 56328; Ⓟ 213; Ⓒ 244
Fletcher; RMC Place; HENNEPIN; *193 O-9; ★ **MPLS-**; mail Osseo z 55369; ● 80
Flintwood Hills; RMC Place; ANOKA; *193 O-9; elev. 865ft./264m.; ★ **MPLS-**; mail Anoka z 55303; pop. incl. with Ramsey (Inc. Place)
Flom; RMC Place; NORMAN; 192 I-3; elev. 1,280ft./390m.; 🅿; z 56541; ● 90
Floodwood; Inc. Place; ST. LOUIS; 192 I-10; elev. 1,253ft./382m.; 🅿; z 55736; Ⓟ 574; Ⓒ 503
Florence; Inc. Place; LYON; 193 R-3; elev. 1,720ft./524m.; 🅿; z 56170; Ⓟ 53; Ⓒ 61
Florenton; RMC Place; ST. LOUIS; 192 G-11; mail Virginia z 55792; ● 100
Florian; RMC Place; MARSHALL; *192 D-2; elev. 957ft./292m.; mail Strandquist z 56758
Foley; Inc. Place; ⊡ BENTON; 193 M-8; elev. 1,140ft./347m.; 🅿; z 56329, z 56357; Ⓟ 1,854; Ⓒ 2,154
Fond du Lac; RMC Place; ST. LOUIS; *192 J-11; elev. 607ft./185m.; ★ **DUL**; pop. incl. with Duluth (Inc. Place)
Fond du Lac Reservation; Indian Reservation; CARLTON, ST. LOUIS; mail Cloquet z 55720; Ⓟ 2,853; Ⓒ 3,728
Forada; Inc. Place; DOUGLAS; 193 M-5; elev. 1,414ft./431m.; mail Alexandria z 56308; Ⓟ 171; Ⓒ 197
Forbes; RMC Place; ST. LOUIS; 192 H-11; elev. 1,347ft./411m.; 🅿; z 55738; ● 110
Fordson; RMC Place; DAKOTA; ★ **MPLS-**; mail Saint Paul z 55121; pop. incl. with Eagan (Inc. Place)
Forest City; RMC Place; MEEKER; 193 O-7; mail Litchfield z 55355; ● 80
Forest Grove; RMC Place; KOOCHICHING; *192 F-7; elev. 1,365ft./416m.; mail Mizpah z 56660; rural
Forest Lake; Inc. Place; WASHINGTON; 193 O-10; elev. 909ft./277m.; 🅿 🅷; ★ **MPLS-**; z 55025; Ⓟ 5,833; Ⓒ 6,798
Forest Mills; RMC Place; GOODHUE; *193 R-11; mail Zumbrota z 55992; ● 30
Foreston; Inc. Place; MILLE LACS; 193 M-8; elev. 1,090ft./332m.; 🅿; z 56330; Ⓟ 354; Ⓒ 389
Fork; RMC Place; MARSHALL; *192 E-1; elev. 800ft./244m.; mail Oslo z 56744; rural
Fort Ripley; Inc. Place; CROW WING; 193 L-7; elev. 1,160ft./354m.; 🅿; z 56449; Ⓟ 92; Ⓒ 74
Fosston; Inc. Place; POLK; 192 G-4; elev. 1,298ft./396m.; 🅿 🅷; z 56542; Ⓟ 1,529; Ⓒ 1,575
Fossum; RMC Place; NORMAN; *192 H-3; mail Twin Valley z 56584
Fountain; Inc. Place; FILLMORE; 193 S-12; elev. 1,305ft./398m.; 🅿; z 55935; Ⓟ 327; Ⓒ 343
Four Corners; RMC Place; ST. LOUIS; *192 J-11; ★ **DUL**; mail Duluth z 55811
Four Town; RMC Place; BELTRAMI; *192 E-5; mail Grygla z 56727; rural
Fox; RMC Place; ROSEAU; 192 C-4; mail Roseau z 56751
Foxhome; Inc. Place; WILKIN; 193 K-3; elev. 1,029ft./314m.; 🅿; z 56543; Ⓟ 160; Ⓒ 143
Fox Lake; RMC Place; MARTIN; 193 T-6; mail Welcome z 56181; ● 100
Franconia; RMC Place; CHISAGO; *193 N-11; mail Shafer z 55074; ● 50
Franklin; Inc. Place; RENVILLE; 193 Q-6; elev. 1,004ft./306m.; 🅿; z 55333; Ⓟ 441; Ⓒ 498
Franklin; RMC Place; ST. LOUIS; *192 G-11; elev. 1,498ft./457m.; mail Virginia z 55792; pop. incl. with Virginia (Inc. Place)
Franklin Avenue; RMC Place; HENNEPIN; ★ **MPLS-**; mail Minneapolis z 55404; pop. incl. with Minneapolis (Inc. Place)
Frazee; Inc. Place; BECKER; 192 J-4; elev. 1,399ft./426m.; 🅿; z 56544; Ⓟ 1,176; Ⓒ 1,377
Freeborn; Inc. Place; FREEBORN; 193 S-9; elev. 1,230ft./375m.; 🅿; z 56032; Ⓟ 301; Ⓒ 305
FREEBORN; 193 S-9; Ⓟ 33,060; Ⓒ 32,584; ◆ 30,729
Freeburg; RMC Place; HOUSTON; 193 T-14; mail Caledonia z 55921; ● 60
Freedhem; RMC Place; MORRISON; 193 L-7; mail Little Falls z 56345; ● 50
Freeport; Inc. Place; STEARNS; 193 M-6; elev. 1,240ft./378m.; 🅿; z 56331; Ⓟ 556; Ⓒ 454
Fremont; RMC Place; WINONA; *193 S-12; mail Utica z 55979
French Lake; RMC Place; WRIGHT; 193 O-7; mail Annandale z 55302; ● 30
French River; RMC Place; ST. LOUIS; 192 I-12; mail Duluth z 55804; ● 400
Fridley; Inc. Place; ANOKA; 191 D-5; elev. 880ft./268m.; 🅿 🅷 ■; ★ **MPLS-**; z 55421, z 55432; Ⓟ 28,335; Ⓒ 27,449; ◆ 25,630
Friesland; RMC Place; PINE; *193 L-10; elev. 1,141ft./348m.; mail Hinckley z 55037
Frontenac (Frontenac Station); RMC Place; GOODHUE; 193 Q-11; elev. 717ft./219m.; 🅿; z 55026; ● 300
Frontenac Station; GOODHUE; see Frontenac (RMC Place)
Frost; Inc. Place; FARIBAULT; 193 T-8; elev. 1,130ft./344m.; 🅿; z 56033; Ⓟ 236; Ⓒ 251
Fulda; Inc. Place; MURRAY; 193 S-4; elev. 1,532ft./467m.; 🅿; z 56131; Ⓟ 1,212; Ⓒ 1,283
Funkley; Inc. Place; BELTRAMI; 192 G-7; elev. 1,391ft./424m.; mail Blackduck z 56630; Ⓟ 15; Ⓒ 15

G

Garden City; RMC Place; BLUE EARTH; 193 R-7; elev. 1,011ft./308m.; 🅿; z 56034; ● 200
Garfield; Inc. Place; DOUGLAS; 193 L-4; elev. 1,417ft./432m.; 🅿; z 56332; Ⓟ 203; Ⓒ 281
Garrison; Inc. Place; CROW WING; 193 K-8; elev. 1,260ft./384m.; 🅿; z 56450; Ⓟ 138; Ⓒ 213
Garvin; Inc. Place; LYON; 193 R-4; elev. 1,527ft./465m.; 🅿; z 56132; Ⓟ 149; Ⓒ 159
Gary; Inc. Place; NORMAN; 192 H-3; elev. 1,100ft./335m.; 🅿; z 56545; Ⓟ 200; Ⓒ 215
Gary; RMC Place; ST. LOUIS; *192 J-12; ★ **DUL**; pop. incl. with Duluth (Inc. Place)
Gatzke; RMC Place; MARSHALL; 192 E-4; elev. 1,180ft./360m.; 🅿; z 56724; ● 50
Gaylord; Inc. Place; ⊡ SIBLEY; 193 Q-7; elev. 996ft./304m.; 🅿; z 55334; Ⓟ 1,935; Ⓒ 2,279
Gem Lake; Inc. Place; RAMSEY; 191 D-8; elev. 954ft./291m.; ★ **MPLS-**; mail Saint Paul z 55110; Ⓟ 439; Ⓒ 419
Gemmell; RMC Place; KOOCHICHING; *192 F-7; mail Mizpah z 56660
Geneva; Inc. Place; FREEBORN; 193 S-9; elev. 1,220ft./372m.; 🅿; z 56035 & mail Ellendale z 56026; Ⓟ 444; Ⓒ 449
Genoa; RMC Place; OLMSTED; 193 R-11; mail Byron z 55920; ● 60
Genoa; RMC Place; ST. LOUIS; *192 H-11; mail Eveleth z 55734; pop. incl. with Eveleth (Inc. Place)
Genola; Inc. Place; MORRISON; 193 L-7; elev. 1,161ft./354m.; mail Pierz z 56364; Ⓟ 85; Ⓒ 71
Gentilly; RMC Place; POLK; 192 G-2; elev. 940ft./287m.; mail Crookston z 56716; ● 100
Georgetown; Inc. Place; CLAY; 192 I-2; elev. 880ft./268m.; 🅿; z 56546; Ⓟ 107; Ⓒ 125
Georgeville; RMC Place; STEARNS; 193 N-6; elev. 1,247ft./380m.; mail Belgrade z 56312; ● 30
Gheen; RMC Place; ST. LOUIS; 192 F-10; elev. 1,360ft./415m.; 🅿; z 55771; ● 60
Gheen Corner; RMC Place; ST. LOUIS; *192 F-10; elev. 1,339ft./408m.; mail Orr z 55771; rural
Ghent; Inc. Place; LYON; 193 Q-4; elev. 1,164ft./355m.; 🅿; z 56239; Ⓟ 316; Ⓒ 315
Gibbon; Inc. Place; SIBLEY; 193 Q-6; elev. 1,050ft./320m.; 🅿; z 55335; Ⓟ 712; Ⓒ 808
Giese; RMC Place; AITKIN; *193 L-10; elev. 1,275ft./389m.; mail Finlayson z 55735
Gilbert; Inc. Place; ST. LOUIS; 192 H-11; elev. 1,550ft./472m.; 🅿; z 55741; Ⓟ 1,934; Ⓒ 1,847
Gilfillan; RMC Place; REDWOOD; *193 Q-5; mail Redwood Falls z 56283; rural
Gilman; Inc. Place; BENTON; 193 M-8; elev. 1,190ft./363m.; 🅿; z 56333; Ⓟ 192; Ⓒ 215
Gladstone; RMC Place; RAMSEY; *193 O-10; ★ **MPLS-**; mail Saint Paul z 55109; pop. incl. with Maplewood (Inc. Place)
Glen; RMC Place; AITKIN; 193 K-9; elev. 1,302ft./397m.; mail Aitkin z 56431; ● 100
Glencoe; Inc. Place; ⊡ MCLEOD; 193 P-7; elev. 1,013ft./309m.; 🅿 🅷; z 55336; Ⓟ 4,648; Ⓒ 5,453
Glendale; RMC Place; ST. LOUIS; *192 F-10; mail Orr z 55771
Glendorado; RMC Place; BENTON; 193 N-8; mail Princeton z 55371; ● 20
Glen Lake; RMC Place; HENNEPIN; *193 P-9; ★ **MPLS-**; mail Minnetonka z 55345; pop. incl. with Minnetonka (Inc. Place)
Glenville; Inc. Place; FREEBORN; 193 T-9; elev. 1,230ft./375m.; 🅿; z 56036; Ⓟ 778; Ⓒ 720
Glenwood; Inc. Place; ⊡ POPE; 193 M-5; elev. 1,350ft./411m.; 🅿 🅷; z 56334; Ⓟ 2,573; Ⓒ 2,594
Glenwood Junction; RMC Place; HENNEPIN; *193 O-9; ★ **MPLS-**; mail Minneapolis z 55427; pop. incl. with Golden Valley (Inc. Place)
Glory; RMC Place; AITKIN; *193 K-9; elev. 1,266ft./386m.; mail Aitkin z 56431; rural
Gloster; RMC Place; RAMSEY; *193 O-10; ★ **MPLS-**; mail Saint Paul z 55109; pop. incl. with Maplewood (Inc. Place)
Gluek; RMC Place; CHIPPEWA; *193 O-4; elev. 1,040ft./317m.; mail Maynard z 56260
Glyndon; Inc. Place; CLAY; 192 I-2; elev. 922ft./281m.; 🅿; z 56547; Ⓟ 862; Ⓒ 1,049
Godahl; RMC Place; BROWN, WATONWAN; 193 R-6; mail Saint James z 56081; ● 20
Golden Hill; RMC Place; OLMSTED; *193 S-11; ★ **ROCH**; mail Rochester z 55902; pop. incl. with Rochester (Inc. Place)
Golden Valley; Inc. Place; HENNEPIN; 191 E-3; elev. 900ft./274m.; 🅿 🅷 ■; ★ **MPLS-**; z 55416, z 55422, z 55426-27; Ⓟ 20,971; Ⓒ 20,281; ◆ 19,761
Gonvick; Inc. Place; CLEARWATER; 192 G-4; elev. 1,270ft./387m.; 🅿; z 56644; Ⓟ 302; Ⓒ 294
Goodhue; Inc. Place; GOODHUE; 193 Q-11; elev. 1,140ft./347m.; 🅿; z 55027; Ⓟ 533; Ⓒ 778
GOODHUE; 193 Q-10; Ⓟ 40,690; Ⓒ 44,127; ◆ 46,178
Goodland; RMC Place; ITASCA; 192 I-10; elev. 1,416ft./432m.; 🅿; z 55742; ● 150
Goodridge; Inc. Place; PENNINGTON; 192 F-4; elev. 1,170ft./357m.; 🅿; z 56725; Ⓟ 115; Ⓒ 98
Good Thunder; Inc. Place; BLUE EARTH; 193 S-8; elev. 1,000ft./305m.; 🅿; z 56037; Ⓟ 561; Ⓒ 592
Goodview; Inc. Place; WINONA; 193 R-13; elev. 660ft./201m.; 🅿; z 55987; Ⓟ 2,878; Ⓒ 3,373
Gordon; FREEBORN; see Gordonsville (RMC Place)
Gordonsville (Gordon); RMC Place; FREEBORN; 193 T-9; mail Glenville z 56036; ● 100
Gotha; RMC Place; CARVER; *193 P-8; elev. 969ft./295m.; mail Cologne z 55322; ● 20
Graceton; RMC Place; LAKE OF THE WOODS; 192 D-6; elev. 1,136ft./346m.; mail Williams z 56686; ● 30
Graceville; Inc. Place; BIG STONE; 193 N-2; elev. 1,116ft./340m.; 🅿 🅷; z 56240; Ⓟ 671; Ⓒ 605
Granada; Inc. Place; MARTIN; 193 T-7; elev. 1,124ft./343m.; 🅿; z 56039; Ⓟ 374; Ⓒ 317
Grand Falls; RMC Place; KOOCHICHING; *192 E-8; mail Big Falls z 56627
Grand Lake; ST. LOUIS; see Saginaw (RMC Place)
Grand Marais; Inc. Place; ⊡ COOK; 192 B-12; elev. 688ft./210m.; 🅿 🅷; z 55604; Ⓟ 1,171; Ⓒ 1,353
Grand Meadow; Inc. Place; MOWER; 193 S-11; elev. 1,341ft./409m.; 🅿; z 55936; Ⓟ 967; Ⓒ 945
Grand Portage; RMC Place; COOK; 192 A-13; elev. 610ft./186m.; 🅿; z 55605; ● 200
Grand Portage Reservation; Indian Reservation; COOK; mail Grand Portage z 55605; also location of Indian Agency; Ⓟ 281; Ⓒ 557
Grand Rapids; Inc. Place; ⊡ ITASCA; 192 H-9; elev. 1,290ft./393m.; 🅿 🅷; z 55730, z 55744-45; Ⓟ 7,976; Ⓒ 7,764
Grand View Heights; RMC Place; OTTER TAIL; *192 J-4; mail Perham z 56573
Grandy; RMC Place; ISANTI; 193 M-9; elev. 937ft./286m.; 🅿; z 55029; ● 150
Granger; RMC Place; FILLMORE; 193 T-12; elev. 1,150ft./351m.; 🅿; z 55939; ● 100
Granite Falls; Inc. Place; ⊡ YELLOW MEDICINE, CHIPPEWA; 193 P-4; elev. 920ft./280m.; 🅿 🅷; z 56241; Ⓟ 3,083; Ⓒ 3,070
Grant; Inc. Place; WASHINGTON; 191 D-10; ★ **MPLS-**; mail Saint Paul z 55110, z 55115, Stillwater z 55082; Ⓟ 3,778; Ⓒ 4,026
GRANT; 193 M-3; Ⓟ 6,246; Ⓒ 6,289; ◆ 5,972
Grass Lake; RMC Place; KANABEC; *193 M-10; mail Braham z 55006; rural
Grasston; Inc. Place; KANABEC; 193 M-10; elev. 960ft./293m.; 🅿; z 55030, z 55036; Ⓟ 119; Ⓒ 105
Grattan; RMC Place; ITASCA; 192 F-8; mail Northome z 56661; ● 40
Greaney; RMC Place; ST. LOUIS; 192 F-10; elev. 1,306ft./398m.; mail Orr z 55771; ● 25
Greenbush; Inc. Place; ROSEAU; 192 D-3; elev. 1,075ft./328m.; 🅿; z 56726; Ⓟ 800; Ⓒ 784
Greenfield; Inc. Place; HENNEPIN; 193 O-8; elev. 995ft./303m.; ★ **MPLS-**; mail Loretto z 55357, Rockford z 55373; Ⓟ 1,450; Ⓒ 2,544
Green Isle; Inc. Place; SIBLEY; 193 P-8; elev. 1,000ft./305m.; 🅿; z 55338; Ⓟ 239; Ⓒ 334
Greenland; RMC Place; LE SUEUR; *193 R-8; elev. 1,050ft./320m.; mail Elysian z 56028
Greenleaf; RMC Place; MEEKER; 193 O-7; mail Litchfield z 55355; ● 40
Greenleafton; RMC Place; FILLMORE; 193 T-12; elev. 1,357ft./414m.; mail Preston z 55965; ● 80
Green Valley; RMC Place; LYON; 193 Q-4; mail Marshall z 56258; ● 100
Greenwald; Inc. Place; STEARNS; 193 N-6; elev. 1,263ft./385m.; 🅿; z 56335; Ⓟ 209; Ⓒ 201
Greenwood; Inc. Place; HENNEPIN; *193 P-9; elev. 950ft./290m.; 🅿; ★ **MPLS-**; z 55331 & mail Clearbrook z 56634; Ⓟ 614; Ⓒ 729
Grey Eagle; Inc. Place; TODD; 193 M-6; elev. 1,222ft./372m.; 🅿; z 56336; Ⓟ 353; Ⓒ 335
Grogan; RMC Place; WATONWAN; 193 S-7; elev. 1,043ft./318m.; mail Saint James z 56081; ● 30
Groningen; RMC Place; PINE; *193 L-10; mail Sandstone z 55072; ● 35
Grove City; Inc. Place; MEEKER; 193 O-6; elev. 1,200ft./366m.; 🅿; z 56243; Ⓟ 547; Ⓒ 608
Grove Lake; RMC Place; POPE; 193 N-5; mail Glenwood z 56334; ● 30
Groveland; RMC Place; HENNEPIN; *193 P-9; ★ **MPLS-**; mail Wayzata z 55391; pop. incl. with Minnetonka (Inc. Place)
Grygla; Inc. Place; MARSHALL; 192 E-4; elev. 1,179ft./359m.; 🅿; z 56727; Ⓟ 220; Ⓒ 228
Guckeen; RMC Place; FARIBAULT; 193 T-7; mail Blue Earth z 56013; ● 100
Gully; Inc. Place; POLK; 192 G-4; elev. 1,300ft./396m.; 🅿; z 56646; Ⓟ 128; Ⓒ 106
Gutches Grove (Reynolds); RMC Place; TODD; *193 L-6; mail Long Prairie z 56347
Guthrie; RMC Place; HUBBARD; 192 H-6; elev. 1,420ft./433m.; mail Laporte z 56461; ● 60

H

Hackensack; Inc. Place; CASS; 192 I-7; elev. 1,396ft./426m.; 🅿; z 56452; Ⓟ 245; Ⓒ 285
Hackett; RMC Place; LAKE OF THE WOODS; *192 C-6; elev. 1,073ft./327m.; mail Baudette z 56623; rural
Hader; RMC Place; GOODHUE; 193 Q-10; mail Zumbrota z 55992; ● 30
Hadley; Inc. Place; MURRAY; 193 S-3; elev. 1,700ft./518m.; 🅿; z 56151; Ⓟ 94; Ⓒ 81
Hagan; RMC Place; CHIPPEWA; 193 O-4; mail Milan z 56262; ● 35
Hallock; Inc. Place; ⊡ KITTSON; 192 C-2; elev. 817ft./249m.; 🅿 🅷; z 56728 & mail Noyes z 56740, Saint Vincent z 56755; Ⓟ 1,304; Ⓒ 1,196
Halma; Inc. Place; KITTSON; 192 D-2; elev. 1,001ft./305m.; 🅿; z 56729; Ⓟ 73; Ⓒ 78
Halstad; Inc. Place; NORMAN; 192 H-2; elev. 872ft./266m.; 🅿; z 56548; Ⓟ 611; Ⓒ 622
Hamburg; Inc. Place; CARVER; 193 P-8; elev. 1,000ft./305m.; 🅿; z 55339; Ⓟ 492; Ⓒ 538
Hamel; RMC Place; HENNEPIN; *193 O-9; 🅿; ★ **MPLS-**; z 55340; pop. incl. with Medina (Inc. Place)
Hamel; HENNEPIN; see Medina (Inc. Place)
Hamilton; RMC Place; FILLMORE; *193 S-11; elev. 1,252ft./382m.; mail Spring Valley z 55975
Ham Lake; Inc. Place; ANOKA; 193 O-9; elev. 900ft./274m.; 🅿; ★ **MPLS-**; z 55304; Ⓟ 8,924; Ⓒ 12,710
Hammond; Inc. Place; WABASHA; 193 R-11; elev. 798ft./243m.; 🅿; z 55991; Ⓟ 205; Ⓒ 198
Hampton; Inc. Place; DAKOTA; 193 Q-10; elev. 980ft./299m.; 🅿; z 55031; Ⓟ 363; Ⓒ 434
Hancock; Inc. Place; STEVENS; 193 N-4; elev. 1,151ft./351m.; 🅿; z 56244; Ⓟ 723; Ⓒ 717
Hanley Falls; Inc. Place; YELLOW MEDICINE; 193 P-4; elev. 1,046ft./319m.; 🅿; z 56245; Ⓟ 246; Ⓒ 323
Hanover; Inc. Place; WRIGHT, HENNEPIN; 193 O-8; elev. 900ft./274m.; 🅿; ★ **MPLS-**; z 55341; Ⓟ 787; Ⓒ 1,355
Hanska; Inc. Place; BROWN; 193 R-7; elev. 1,007ft./307m.; 🅿; z 56041; Ⓟ 443; Ⓒ 443
Happyland; RMC Place; KOOCHICHING; mail Littlefork z 56653; rural
Harding; Inc. Place; MORRISON; 193 L-8; elev. 1,260ft./384m.; mail Pierz z 56364; Ⓟ 76; Ⓒ 105
Hardwick; Inc. Place; ROCK; 193 S-3; elev. 607ft./185m.; 🅿; z 56134; Ⓟ 234; Ⓒ 222
Harmony; Inc. Place; FILLMORE; 193 T-12; elev. 1,350ft./411m.; 🅿 🅷; z 55939; Ⓟ 1,081; Ⓒ 1,080
Harnell Park; RMC Place; ST. LOUIS; *192 I-11; mail Saginaw z 55779; ● 50
Harris; Inc. Place; CHISAGO; 193 N-10; elev. 902ft./275m.; 🅿; z 55032; Ⓟ 843; Ⓒ 1,121
Hart; RMC Place; WINONA; *193 S-13; mail Rushford z 55971; rural
Hartland; Inc. Place; FREEBORN; 193 S-9; elev. 1,252ft./382m.; 🅿; z 56042; Ⓟ 270; Ⓒ 288
Hassan; RMC Place; HENNEPIN; *193 O-9; elev. 944ft./288m.; ★ **MPLS-**; mail Dayton z 55327, Osseo z 55311, z 55369, Rogers z 55374; ● 100
Hassman; RMC Place; AITKIN; *192 J-9; elev. 1,206ft./368m.; mail Aitkin z 56431
Hastings; Inc. Place; ⊡ DAKOTA, WASHINGTON; 193 P-10; elev. 730ft./223m.; 🅿 🅷; ★ **MPLS-**; z 55033; Ⓟ 15,445; Ⓒ 18,204; ◆ 20,955
Hasty; RMC Place; WRIGHT; 193 N-8; mail Clearwater z 55320; ● 40
Hatfield; Inc. Place; PIPESTONE; 193 S-3; elev. 1,680ft./512m.; 🅿; z 56164; Ⓟ 66; Ⓒ 47
Havana; RMC Place; STEELE; *193 R-10; elev. 1,223ft./373m.; mail Owatonna z 55060; ● 50
Hawick; RMC Place; KANDIYOHI; 193 N-6; elev. 1,238ft./377m.; 🅿; z 56273; ● 120
Hawley; Inc. Place; CLAY; 192 J-3; elev. 1,150ft./351m.; 🅿; z 56549; Ⓟ 1,655; Ⓒ 1,882
Hay Creek; RMC Place; GOODHUE; 193 Q-11; elev. 832ft./254m.; mail Red Wing z 55066; ● 60
Haydenville; RMC Place; LAC QUI PARLE; *193 O-3; mail Madison z 56256; rural
Hayfield; Inc. Place; DODGE; 193 S-10; elev. 1,320ft./402m.; 🅿; z 55940; Ⓟ 1,283; Ⓒ 1,325
Haypoint; RMC Place; AITKIN; *192 I-9; elev. 1,275ft./389m.; mail Hill City z 55748; rural
Hayward; Inc. Place; FREEBORN; 193 T-9; elev. 1,245ft./379m.; 🅿; z 56043; Ⓟ 246; Ⓒ 249
Hazel Park; RMC Place; RAMSEY; ★ **MPLS-**; pop. incl. with Saint Paul (Inc. Place)
Hazel Run; Inc. Place; YELLOW MEDICINE; 193 P-4; elev. 1,062ft./324m.; 🅿; z 56241; Ⓟ 81; Ⓒ 64
Hazelwood; RMC Place; RICE; *193 Q-9; mail Northfield z 55057; ● 25
Heatwole; RMC Place; MCLEOD; *193 P-7; elev. 1,060ft./323m.; mail Hutchinson z 55350; rural
Hector; Inc. Place; RENVILLE; 193 P-6; elev. 1,078ft./329m.; 🅿; z 55342; Ⓟ 1,145; Ⓒ 1,166
Heiberg; RMC Place; NORMAN; *192 H-3; mail Twin Valley z 56584; rural
Heidelberg; Inc. Place; LE SUEUR; 193 Q-9; elev. 1,050ft./320m.; 🅿; z 56071; Ⓟ 73; Ⓒ 72
Heinola; RMC Place; OTTER TAIL; *193 K-5; elev. 1,415ft./431m.; mail New York Mills z 56567; rural
Henderson; Inc. Place; SIBLEY; 193 Q-8; elev. 737ft./225m.; 🅿; z 56044; Ⓟ 746; Ⓒ 910
Hendricks; Inc. Place; LINCOLN; 193 Q-2; elev. 1,790ft./546m.; 🅿; z 56136; Ⓟ 684; Ⓒ 725
Hendrum; Inc. Place; NORMAN; 192 H-2; elev. 870ft./265m.; 🅿; z 56550; Ⓟ 309; Ⓒ 315
HENNEPIN; 193 O-8; Ⓟ 1,032,431; Ⓒ 1,116,200; Ⓡ 1,116,039; ◆ 1,161,214
Henning; Inc. Place; OTTER TAIL; 193 K-5; elev. 1,432ft./436m.; 🅿; z 56551; Ⓟ 738; Ⓒ 719; Ⓡ 772
Henriette; Inc. Place; PINE; 193 M-10; elev. 996ft./304m.; 🅿; z 55036; Ⓟ 78; Ⓒ 101
Henrytown; RMC Place; FILLMORE; *193 T-12; elev. 1,108ft./338m.; mail Harmony z 55939; rural
Herman; Inc. Place; GRANT; 193 M-3; elev. 1,073ft./327m.; 🅿; z 56248; Ⓟ 485; Ⓒ 452
Hermantown; Inc. Place; ST. LOUIS; 192 J-11; elev. 1,362ft./415m.; 🅿; ★ **DUL**; z 55810-11; Ⓟ 6,761; Ⓒ 7,448; Ⓡ 8,047
Heron Lake; Inc. Place; JACKSON; 193 S-5; elev. 1,420ft./433m.; 🅿; z 56137; Ⓟ 730; Ⓒ 768
Hewitt; Inc. Place; TODD; 193 K-5; elev. 1,372ft./418m.; 🅿; z 56453; Ⓟ 269; Ⓒ 267
Hiawatha Spur; RMC Place; DAKOTA; ★ **MPLS-**; mail Saint Paul z 55111; pop. incl. with Eagan (Inc. Place)
Hibbing; Inc. Place; ST. LOUIS; 192 H-10; elev. 1,489ft./454m.; 🅿 🅷 ■; z 55746-47; Ⓟ 18,046; Ⓒ 17,071; ◆ 16,129
Hidden Creek; RMC Place; ANOKA; *193 O-9; elev. 880ft./268m.; ★ **MPLS-**; mail Anoka z 55303; pop. incl. with Andover (Inc. Place)
High Forest; RMC Place; OLMSTED; 193 S-11; ★ **ROCH**; mail Stewartville z 55976; ● 100
Highland; RMC Place; FILLMORE; *193 T-13; mail Lanesboro z 55949
Highland; RMC Place; HENNEPIN; *193 O-9; ★ **MPLS-**; mail Minneapolis z 55411; pop. incl. with Minneapolis (Inc. Place)
Highland; RMC Place; LAKE; *192 H-13; elev. 1,634ft./498m.; mail Two Harbors z 55616; rural
Highland; RMC Place; WRIGHT; *193 O-8; elev. 1,001ft./305m.; mail Howard Lake z 55349
High Landing; RMC Place; PENNINGTON; *192 F-4; elev. 1,159ft./353m.; mail Goodridge z 56725; rural
Highland Park; RMC Place; RAMSEY; *193 P-10; ★ **MPLS-**; mail Saint Paul z 55116; pop. incl. with Saint Paul (Inc. Place)
Hill City; Inc. Place; AITKIN; 192 I-9; elev. 1,357ft./414m.; 🅿; z 55748; Ⓟ 469; Ⓒ 479
Hillman; Inc. Place; MORRISON; 193 L-8; elev. 1,315ft./401m.; 🅿; z 56338; Ⓟ 45; Ⓒ 29
Hills; Inc. Place; ROCK; 193 T-2; elev. 1,480ft./451m.; 🅿; z 56138; Ⓟ 607; Ⓒ 565
Hilltop; Inc. Place; ANOKA; 191 D-5; elev. 950ft./290m.; 🅿; ★ **MPLS-**; z 55421; Ⓟ 749; Ⓒ 766
Hillview (Paddock); RMC Place; OTTER TAIL; 192 J-5; mail Sebeka z 56477; ● 20
Hinckley; Inc. Place; PINE; 193 L-10; elev. 1,031ft./314m.; 🅿; z 55037; Ⓟ 946; Ⓒ 1,291
Hines; RMC Place; BELTRAMI; 192 G-6; elev. 1,404ft./428m.; 🅿; z 56647; ● 60
Hinsdale; RMC Place; ST. LOUIS; *192 G-12; pop. incl. with Hoyt Lakes (Inc. Place)
Hitterdal; Inc. Place; CLAY; 192 I-3; elev. 1,250ft./381m.; 🅿; z 56552; Ⓟ 242; Ⓒ 201
Hoffman; Inc. Place; GRANT; 193 M-4; elev. 1,254ft./382m.; 🅿; z 56339; Ⓟ 576; Ⓒ 672
Hoffmans Corners; RMC Place; RAMSEY; *193 O-10; ★ **MPLS-**; mail Saint Paul z 55110; pop. incl. with Gem Lake (Inc. Place)
Hokah; Inc. Place; HOUSTON; 193 S-14; elev. 700ft./213m.; 🅿; z 55941; Ⓟ 687; Ⓒ 614
Holdingford; Inc. Place; STEARNS; 193 M-7; elev. 1,150ft./351m.; 🅿; z 56340; Ⓟ 561; Ⓒ 736
Holland; Inc. Place; PIPESTONE; 193 R-3; elev. 1,778ft./542m.; 🅿; z 56139; Ⓟ 216; Ⓒ 215
Hollandale; Inc. Place; FREEBORN; 193 S-9; elev. 1,205ft./367m.; 🅿; z 56045; Ⓟ 289; Ⓒ 292
Holloway; Inc. Place; SWIFT; 193 O-3; elev. 1,034ft./315m.; 🅿; z 56249; Ⓟ 123; Ⓒ 112
Hollywood; RMC Place; CARVER; *193 P-8; elev. 976ft./297m.; mail Watertown z 55388; rural
Holmes City; RMC Place; DOUGLAS; 193 M-4; elev. 1,400ft./427m.; 🅿; z 56341; ● 90
Holt; Inc. Place; MARSHALL; 192 E-3; elev. 1,155ft./352m.; 🅿; z 56738; Ⓟ 88; Ⓒ 89
Holyoke; RMC Place; CARLTON; 193 K-11; elev. 1,037ft./316m.; 🅿; z 55749 & mail Wrenshall z 55797; ● 60
Homer; RMC Place; WINONA; 193 R-13; elev. 658ft./201m.; 🅿; z 55942; ● 150
Hoot Lake; RMC Place; OTTER TAIL; mail Fergus Falls z 56537; pop. incl. with Fergus Falls (Inc. Place)
Hope; RMC Place; STEELE; 193 S-9; elev. 1,200ft./366m.; 🅿; z 56046; ● 120
Hopkins; Inc. Place; HENNEPIN; 191 G-2; elev. 926ft./282m.; 🅿; ★ **MPLS-**; z 55305, z 55343, z 55345; Ⓟ 16,534; Ⓒ 17,145; Ⓡ 17,367
Hopper; RMC Place; ST. LOUIS; *192 H-11; mail Virginia z 55792; pop. incl. with Mountain Iron (Inc. Place)
Houston; Inc. Place; HOUSTON; 193 S-13; elev. 684ft./208m.; 🅿; z 55943; Ⓟ 1,013; Ⓒ 1,020
HOUSTON; 193 S-13; Ⓟ 18,497; Ⓒ 19,718; ◆ 19,283
Hovland; RMC Place; COOK; 192 B-13; elev. 734ft./224m.; 🅿; z 55606; ● 250
Howard Lake; Inc. Place; WRIGHT; 193 O-8; elev. 1,018ft./310m.; 🅿; z 55349, z 55575; Ⓟ 1,343; Ⓒ 1,853
Hoyt Lakes; Inc. Place; ST. LOUIS; 192 G-12; elev. 1,469ft./448m.; 🅿; z 55750; Ⓟ 2,348; Ⓒ 2,082
Hubbard; RMC Place; HUBBARD; 192 J-6; mail Park Rapids z 56470; ● 150
HUBBARD; 192 I-5; Ⓟ 14,939; Ⓒ 18,376; ◆ 18,964
Hugo; Inc. Place; WASHINGTON; 191 B-9; elev. 935ft./285m.; 🅿; ★ **MPLS-**; z 55038; Ⓟ 4,417; Ⓒ 6,363
Humboldt; Inc. Place; KITTSON; 192 C-1; elev. 794ft./242m.; 🅿; z 56731; Ⓟ 74; Ⓒ 61
Humboldt Yard; RMC Place; HENNEPIN; ★ **MPLS-**; pop. incl. with Minneapolis (Inc. Place)
Hunters Park; RMC Place; ST. LOUIS; *192 J-12; ★ **DUL**; pop. incl. with Duluth (Inc. Place)
Huntersville; RMC Place; WADENA; 192 J-6; mail Menahga z 56464; ● 20
Huntley; RMC Place; FARIBAULT; 193 S-7; elev. 1,091ft./333m.; 🅿; z 56047; ● 150
Huot; RMC Place; RED LAKE; *192 F-3; mail Red Lake Falls z 56750; rural
Husby Spur; RMC Place; RAMSEY; ★ **MPLS-**; mail Saint Paul z 55112; pop. incl. with Arden Hills (Inc. Place)
Hutchinson; Inc. Place; MCLEOD; 193 P-7; elev. 1,056ft./322m.; 🅿 🅷; z 55350; Ⓟ 11,523; Ⓒ 13,080
Hutton; RMC Place; FILLMORE; *193 T-12; mail Harmony z 55939; rural
Hydes Lake; RMC Place; CARVER; *193 P-8; elev. 990ft./302m.; mail Cologne z 55322; rural

I

Ideal Corners; RMC Place; CROW WING; *192 J-7; elev. 1,249ft./381m.; mail Pequot Lakes z 56472; rural
Idington; RMC Place; ST. LOUIS; *192 G-11; mail Angora z 55703; ● 25
Ihlen; Inc. Place; PIPESTONE; 193 S-2; elev. 1,650ft./503m.; 🅿; z 56140; Ⓟ 101; Ⓒ 107
Illgen City; RMC Place; LAKE; *192 H-14; elev. 738ft./225m.; mail Silver Bay z 55614; rural
Imogene; RMC Place; MARTIN; 193 T-7; mail Granada z 56039; ● 70
Independence; Inc. Place; HENNEPIN; 193 O-8; elev. 1,000ft./305m.; 🅿; ★ **MPLS-**; z 55357, z 55359 & mail Delano z 55328, Rockford z 55373; Ⓟ 2,822; Ⓒ 3,236
Independence; RMC Place; ST. LOUIS; *192 I-11; elev. 1,308ft./399m.; mail Saginaw z 55779; rural
Indus; RMC Place; KOOCHICHING; *192 D-8; mail Birchdale z 56629; rural
Inger; RMC Place; ITASCA; 192 G-8; elev. 1,328ft./405m.; mail Deer River z 56636; ● 80
Inguadona; RMC Place; CASS; *192 I-7; mail Longville z 56655; ● 30
International Falls; Inc. Place; ⊡ KOOCHICHING; 192 D-9; elev. 1,128ft./344m.; 🅿 🅷; z 56649; Ⓟ 8,325; Ⓒ 6,703
Inver Grove; DAKOTA; see Inver Grove Heights (Inc. Place)
Inver Grove Heights (Inver Grove); Inc. Place; DAKOTA; 191 J-9; elev. 850ft./259m.; 🅿; ★ **MPLS-**; z 55076-77; Ⓟ 22,477; Ⓒ 29,751; ◆ 34,370
Iona; Inc. Place; MURRAY; 193 S-4; elev. 1,640ft./500m.; 🅿; z 56141; Ⓟ 158; Ⓒ 173
Iron; ST. LOUIS; see Iron Junction (Inc. Place)
Ironhub; RMC Place; CROW WING; *193 K-8; elev. 1,247ft./380m.; mail Aitkin z 56431; ● 25
Iron Junction (Iron); Inc. Place; ST. LOUIS; *192 H-11; elev. 1,378ft./420m.; mail Iron z 55751; Ⓟ 133; Ⓒ 93
Ironton; Inc. Place; CROW WING; 193 K-8; elev. 1,233ft./376m.; 🅿; z 56455; Ⓟ 553; Ⓒ 498
Isabella; RMC Place; LAKE; 192 G-13; elev. 1,927ft./587m.; 🅿; z 55607; ● 100
Isanti; Inc. Place; ISANTI; 193 N-9; elev. 940ft./287m.; 🅿; z 55040; Ⓟ 1,228; Ⓒ 2,324
ISANTI; 193 N-9; Ⓟ 25,921; Ⓒ 31,287; ◆ 40,087
Island Lake; RMC Place; BELTRAMI; *192 G-6; elev. 1,342ft./409m.; mail Puposky z 56667; rural
Island Park; RMC Place; HENNEPIN; *193 P-9; ★ **MPLS-**; mail Mound z 55364; pop. incl. with Mound (Inc. Place)
Island View; RMC Place; KOOCHICHING; 192 D-9; elev. 1,138ft./347m.; mail International Falls z 56649; ● 150
Isle; Inc. Place; MILLE LACS; 193 L-9; elev. 1,270ft./387m.; 🅿; z 56342; Ⓟ 566; Ⓒ 707
ITASCA; 192 G-9; Ⓟ 40,863; Ⓒ 43,992; ◆ 44,984
Ivanhoe; Inc. Place; ⊡ LINCOLN; 193 Q-3; elev. 1,677ft./511m.; 🅿 🅷; z 56142; Ⓟ 751; Ⓒ 679
Iverson; RMC Place; CARLTON; *192 J-11; elev. 1,230ft./375m.; ★ **DUL**; mail Carlton z 55718; rural

J

Jackson; Inc. Place; ⊡ JACKSON; 193 T-5; elev. 1,312ft./400m.; 🅿 🅷; z 56143; Ⓟ 3,559; Ⓒ 3,501
JACKSON; 193 T-5; Ⓟ 11,677; Ⓒ 11,268; ◆ 10,752
Jacobson; RMC Place; AITKIN; 192 I-9; elev. 1,251ft./381m.; 🅿; z 55752; ● 150
Jacobs Prairie; RMC Place; STEARNS; *193 N-7; elev. 1,151ft./351m.; mail Cold Spring z 56320
Jakeville; RMC Place; BENTON; *193 M-8; elev. 1,202ft./366m.; mail Foley z 56329; rural
Jameson; RMC Place; KOOCHICHING; *192 D-9; mail International Falls z 56649; rural
Janesville; Inc. Place; WASECA; 193 R-8; elev. 1,069ft./326m.; 🅿; z 56048; Ⓟ 1,969; Ⓒ 2,109
Jarretts; RMC Place; WABASHA; *193 R-11; mail Millville z 55957; ● 50
Jasper; Inc. Place; PIPESTONE, ROCK; 193 S-2; elev. 1,600ft./488m.; 🅿; z 56144; Ⓟ 599; Ⓒ 597
Jaynes; RMC Place; ITASCA; *192 G-8; mail Bigfork z 56628; rural
Jeffers; Inc. Place; COTTONWOOD; 193 R-5; elev. 1,480ft./451m.; 🅿; z 56145; Ⓟ 443; Ⓒ 396
Jenkins; Inc. Place; CROW WING; 192 J-7; elev. 1,263ft./385m.; 🅿; z 56456 & mail Pequot Lakes z 56472; Ⓟ 262; Ⓒ 287
Jennie; RMC Place; MEEKER; *193 O-7; elev. 1,109ft./338m.; mail Dassel z 55325; rural
Jesse Lake; ITASCA; see Jessie Lake (RMC Place)
Jessenland; RMC Place; SIBLEY; *193 Q-8; mail Henderson z 56044; rural
Jessie Lake (Jesse Lake); RMC Place; ITASCA; *192 G-8; mail Talmoon z 56637; rural
Johnsburg; RMC Place; MOWER; 193 T-10; mail Adams z 55909; ● 25
Johnson; Inc. Place; BIG STONE; 193 N-3; elev. 1,128ft./344m.; 🅿; z 56236; Ⓟ 46; Ⓒ 32
Johnsville; RMC Place; ANOKA; *193 O-9; elev. 902ft./275m.; ★ **MPLS-**; mail Minneapolis z 55434; pop. incl. with Blaine (Inc. Place)
Jonathan; RMC Place; CARVER; ★ **MPLS-**; mail Chaska z 55318; pop. incl. with Chaska (Inc. Place)
Jordan; Inc. Place; SCOTT; 193 P-9; elev. 760ft./232m.; 🅿; z 55352; Ⓟ 2,909; Ⓒ 3,833
Judson; RMC Place; BLUE EARTH; 193 R-7; elev. 803ft./245m.; mail Lake Crystal z 56055; ● 150

K

Kabekona; RMC Place; HUBBARD; 192 H-6; elev. 1,364ft./416m.; mail Laporte z 56461; ● 60
Kabetogama (Lake Kabetogama); RMC Place; ST. LOUIS; 192 E-10; 🅿; z 56669; ● 100
KANABEC; 193 M-9; Ⓟ 12,802; Ⓒ 14,996; ◆ 16,091
Kanaranzi; RMC Place; ROCK; 193 T-3; elev. 1,500ft./457m.; 🅿; z 56146; ● 60
Kandiyohi; Inc. Place; KANDIYOHI; 193 O-6; elev. 1,223ft./373m.; 🅿; z 56251; Ⓟ 506; Ⓒ 555
KANDIYOHI; 193 O-5; Ⓟ 38,761; Ⓒ 41,203; ◆ 40,254
Karlstad; Inc. Place; KITTSON; 192 D-2; elev. 1,048ft./319m.; 🅿; z 56732; Ⓟ 881; Ⓒ 794
Kasota; Inc. Place; LE SUEUR; 193 R-8; elev. 800ft./244m.; 🅿; z 56050; Ⓟ 655; Ⓒ 680
Kasson; Inc. Place; DODGE; 193 R-10; elev. 1,242ft./379m.; 🅿; ★ **ROCH**; z 55944; Ⓟ 3,514; Ⓒ 4,398
Katrine; RMC Place; CROW WING; *193 K-8; elev. 1,290ft./393m.; mail Deerwood z 56444; ● 20
Keewatin; Inc. Place; ITASCA; 192 H-10; elev. 1,469ft./448m.; 🅿; z 55753; Ⓟ 1,118; Ⓒ 1,164
Kelliher; Inc. Place; BELTRAMI; 192 F-7; elev. 1,361ft./415m.; 🅿; z 56650; Ⓟ 348; Ⓒ 294
Kellogg; Inc. Place; WABASHA; 193 R-12; elev. 722ft./220m.; 🅿; z 55945; Ⓟ 423; Ⓒ 439
Kelly Lake; RMC Place; ST. LOUIS; *192 H-10; elev. 1,509ft./460m.; 🅿; z 55746; pop. incl. with Hibbing (Inc. Place)
Kelsey; RMC Place; ST. LOUIS; 192 I-11; elev. 1,300ft./396m.; 🅿; z 55724; ● 30
Kennedy; Inc. Place; KITTSON; 192 D-2; elev. 826ft./252m.; 🅿; z 56733; Ⓟ 337; Ⓒ 255
Kenneth; Inc. Place; ROCK; 193 S-3; elev. 1,580ft./482m.; 🅿; z 56147; Ⓟ 81; Ⓒ 61
Kensington; Inc. Place; DOUGLAS; 193 M-4; elev. 1,300ft./396m.; 🅿; z 56343; Ⓟ 295; Ⓒ 286
Kent; Inc. Place; WILKIN; 193 K-2; elev. 950ft./290m.; 🅿; z 56553; Ⓟ 131; Ⓒ 120
Kenwood; RMC Place; HENNEPIN; ★ **MPLS-**; mail Minneapolis z 55403; pop. incl. with Minneapolis (Inc. Place)
Kenwood; RMC Place; ST. LOUIS; ★ **DUL**; mail Duluth z 55811; pop. incl. with Duluth (Inc. Place)
Kenyon; Inc. Place; GOODHUE; 193 R-10; elev. 1,150ft./351m.; 🅿; z 55946; Ⓟ 1,552; Ⓒ 1,661
Kerkhoven; Inc. Place; SWIFT; 193 O-5; elev. 1,109ft./338m.; 🅿; z 56252; Ⓟ 732; Ⓒ 759
Kerr; RMC Place; ST. LOUIS; *192 H-10; elev. 1,520ft./463m.; mail Hibbing z 55746; pop. incl. with Hibbing (Inc. Place)
Kerrick; Inc. Place; PINE; 193 K-11; elev. 1,170ft./357m.; 🅿; z 55756; Ⓟ 56; Ⓒ 71
Kettle River; Inc. Place; CARLTON; 193 K-10; elev. 1,182ft./360m.; 🅿; z 55757; Ⓟ 190; Ⓒ 168
Kiester; Inc. Place; FARIBAULT; 193 T-8; elev. 1,250ft./381m.; 🅿; z 56051; Ⓟ 606; Ⓒ 540
Kilkenny; Inc. Place; LE SUEUR; 193 R-9; elev. 1,060ft./323m.; 🅿; z 56052; Ⓟ 167; Ⓒ 148
Kimball; Inc. Place; STEARNS; 193 N-7; elev. 1,132ft./345m.; 🅿; z 55353; Ⓟ 690; Ⓒ 635
Kimberly; RMC Place; AITKIN; *193 K-9; mail Aitkin z 56431
Kinbrae; Inc. Place; NOBLES; 193 S-4; elev. 1,464ft./446m.; mail Fulda z 56131; Ⓟ 18; Ⓒ 21
Kingsdale; RMC Place; PINE; *193 L-11; mail Sandstone z 55072
Kings Park; RMC Place; OLMSTED; *193 R-11; ★ **ROCH**; mail Oronoco z 55960; rural
Kingston; Inc. Place; MEEKER; 193 O-7; elev. 1,027ft./313m.; 🅿; z 55325; Ⓟ 131; Ⓒ 120
Kinmount; RMC Place; ST. LOUIS; *192 E-10; mail Orr z 55771; rural
Kinney; Inc. Place; ST. LOUIS; 192 H-10; elev. 1,550ft./472m.; 🅿; z 55758; Ⓟ 257; Ⓒ 199
KITTSON; 192 C-2; Ⓟ 5,767; Ⓒ 5,285; ◆ 4,292
Kitzville; RMC Place; ST. LOUIS; *192 H-10; mail Hibbing z 55746; pop. incl. with Hibbing (Inc. Place)
Kjellberg Park; RMC Place; WRIGHT; *193 O-8; elev. 970ft./296m.; ★ **MPLS-**; mail Monticello z 55362; ● 300
Klossner; RMC Place; NICOLLET; 193 Q-7; elev. 1,000ft./305m.; 🅿; z 56073; ● 50
Knapp; RMC Place; WRIGHT; *193 O-7; elev. 1,032ft./315m.; mail Cokato z 55321; ● 25
Knife River; RMC Place; LAKE; 192 I-12; elev. 625ft./191m.; 🅿; z 55609; ● 300
Komensky; RMC Place; MCLEOD; *193 P-7; elev. 1,063ft./324m.; mail Hutchinson z 55350
KOOCHICHING; 192 E-8; Ⓟ 16,299; Ⓒ 14,355; ◆ 13,160
Kragnes; RMC Place; CLAY; 192 I-2; elev. 890ft./271m.; mail Moorhead z 56560; ● 60
Kroschel; RMC Place; KANABEC; *193 L-10; elev. 1,110ft./338m.; mail Hinckley z 55037; rural

L

Lac qui Parle; RMC Place; LAC QUI PARLE; 193 O-3; mail Montevideo z 56265; ● 50
LAC QUI PARLE; 193 O-3; Ⓟ 8,924; Ⓒ 8,067; ◆ 7,193
La Crescent; Inc. Place; HOUSTON; 193 S-14; elev. 675ft./206m.; 🅿; ★ **LACRO**; z 55947; Ⓟ 4,311; Ⓒ 4,923
Lafayette; Inc. Place; NICOLLET; 193 Q-7; elev. 1,014ft./309m.; 🅿; z 56054; Ⓟ 462; Ⓒ 529
Lagoona Beach; RMC Place; BIG STONE; *193 N-2; mail Ortonville z 56278; rural
LAKE; 192 G-13; Ⓟ 10,415; Ⓒ 11,058; ◆ 10,448
Lake Benton; Inc. Place; LINCOLN; 193 R-3; elev. 1,760ft./536m.; 🅿; z 56149; Ⓟ 693; Ⓒ 703
Lake Bronson; Inc. Place; KITTSON; 192 D-2; elev. 959ft./292m.; 🅿; z 56734; Ⓟ 272; Ⓒ 246
Lake Center; RMC Place; BECKER; 192 J-3; elev. 1,393ft./425m.; mail Audubon z 56511; ● 25
Lake City; Inc. Place; WABASHA, GOODHUE; 193 Q-12; elev. 701ft./214m.; 🅿 🅷; z 55041; Ⓟ 4,391; Ⓒ 4,950; Ⓡ 5,054
Lake Crystal; Inc. Place; BLUE EARTH; 193 R-7; elev. 1,000ft./305m.; 🅿; z 56055; Ⓟ 2,084; Ⓒ 2,420
Lake Elmo; Inc. Place; WASHINGTON; 193 O-10; elev. 936ft./285m.; 🅿; ★ **MPLS-**; z 55042; Ⓟ 5,903; Ⓒ 6,863
Lake Eunice; RMC Place; BECKER; *192 J-3; elev. 1,350ft./411m.; mail Lake Park z 56554; rural
Lakefield; Inc. Place; JACKSON; 193 T-5; elev. 1,476ft./450m.; 🅿; z 56150; Ⓟ 1,679; Ⓒ 1,721
Lake Fremont (Zimmerman); Inc. Place; SHERBURNE; 193 N-9; elev. 992ft./302m.; ★ **MPLS-**; mail Zimmerman z 55398; Ⓟ 1,350; Ⓒ 2,851
Lake George; RMC Place; HUBBARD; 192 I-6; elev. 1,429ft./436m.; 🅿; z 56458; ● 200
Lake Henry; Inc. Place; STEARNS; 193 N-6; elev. 1,300ft./396m.; mail Paynesville z 56362; Ⓟ 90; Ⓒ 90
Lake Hubert; RMC Place; CROW WING; 193 K-7; elev. 1,204ft./367m.; 🅿; z 56459, z 56468; ● 300
Lake Itasca; RMC Place; CLEARWATER; 192 H-5; elev. 1,500ft./457m.; 🅿; z 56470; ● 50
Lake Kabetogama; ST. LOUIS; see Kabetogama (RMC Place)
Lakeland; Inc. Place; WASHINGTON; 193 P-10; elev. 720ft./219m.; 🅿; ★ **MPLS-**; z 55043; Ⓟ 2,000; Ⓒ 1,917
Lakeland Shores; Inc. Place; WASHINGTON; *193 P-10; elev. 740ft./226m.; ★ **MPLS-**; mail Lakeland z 55043; Ⓟ 291; Ⓒ 355
Lake Lillian; Inc. Place; KANDIYOHI; 193 P-6; elev. 1,110ft./338m.; 🅿; z 56253; Ⓟ 229; Ⓒ 257
Lake Netta; RMC Place; ANOKA; *193 O-9; ★ **MPLS-**; mail Anoka z 55303; pop. incl. with Ham Lake (Inc. Place)
Lake Nichols; RMC Place; ST. LOUIS; mail Canyon z 55717; rural
LAKE OF THE WOODS; 192 D-5; Ⓟ 4,076; Ⓒ 4,522; ◆ 3,774

Entries in **UPPERCASE** are counties.
Entries in **bold** have populations of 2,500 or more.
Names in parentheses are alternate names.
Inc. Place — Incorporated Place
RMC Place — Rand McNally Designated Place
CDP — Census Designated Place
MCD — Minor Civil Division

⊡ County Seat
▲ Minor Civil Division
elev. Elevation
🅿 Post Office
🅷 Hospital
🅲 College
■ Principal Business Center
★ Ranally Metro Area (RMA) Abbreviation
z Zip Code(s)
Ⓟ Previous Census Population
Ⓡ Revised Census Population
Ⓐ Annexation Population
● Rand McNally Population Estimate
Ⓒ Final Census Population
Ⓢ Special Census Population
◆ Estimated Population

For additional definitions see Glossary, Volume 1, and Introduction, Volume 2.

Lake Park; Inc. Place; BECKER; 192 I-3; elev. 1,320ft./402m.; 🅿; z 56554; Ⓟ 638; © 782
Lake Saint Croix Beach; Inc. Place; WASHINGTON; *193 P-10; elev. 692ft./211m.; ★ **MPLS-**; mail Lakeland z 55043; Ⓟ 1,078; © 1,140
Lake Sarah; RMC Place; HENNEPIN; *193 O-8; elev. 996ft./304m.; ★ **MPLS-**; mail Loretto z 55357; pop. incl. with Greenfield (Inc. Place)
Lake Shore; Inc. Place; CASS; 193 K-7; elev. 1,242ft./379m.; 🅿; z 56468; Ⓟ 693; © 966
Lake Shore Park; RMC Place; RAMSEY; *193 O-10; ★ **MPLS-**; mail Saint Paul z 55110; pop. incl. with White Bear Lake (Inc. Place)
Lakeside; RMC Place; RENVILLE; *193 P-6; elev. 1,070ft./326m.; mail Buffalo Lake z 55314; ● 30
Lakeside; RMC Place; ST. LOUIS; *192 J-12; ★ **DUL**; mail Duluth z 55804; pop. incl. with Duluth (Inc. Place)
Lake Street; RMC Place; HENNEPIN; *193 P-9; ★ **MPLS-**; mail Minneapolis z 55408; pop. incl. with Minneapolis (Inc. Place)
Lakeville; Inc. Place; DAKOTA; 193 Q-9; elev. 974ft./297m.; 🅿; ★ **MPLS-**; z 55044 & mail Rosemount z 55068; Ⓟ 24,854; © 43,128; ◆ 54,336
Lake Wilson; Inc. Place; MURRAY; 193 S-3; elev. 1,650ft./503m.; 🅿; z 56151; Ⓟ 319; © 270
Lakewood; RMC Place; ST. LOUIS; *192 J-12; elev. 662ft./202m.; ★ **DUL**; pop. incl. with Duluth (Inc. Place)
Lamberton; Inc. Place; REDWOOD; 193 R-5; elev. 1,151ft./351m.; 🅿; z 56152; Ⓟ 972; © 859
Lamoille; RMC Place; WINONA; 193 S-13; mail Winona z 55987; ● 50
Lamson; RMC Place; MEEKER; *193 O-7; mail Dassel z 55325; rural
Lancaster; Inc. Place; KITTSON; 192 C-2; elev. 910ft./277m.; 🅿; z 56735; Ⓟ 342; © 363
Landfall; Inc. Place; WASHINGTON; 191 G-9; elev. 980ft./299m.; ★ **MPLS-**; mail Saint Paul z 55128; Ⓟ 685; © 700
Lanesboro; Inc. Place; FILLMORE; 193 S-12; elev. 846ft./258m.; 🅿; z 55949; Ⓟ 858; © 788
Langdon; RMC Place; WASHINGTON; *193 P-10; ★ **MPLS-**; mail Cottage Grove z 55016; pop. incl. with Cottage Grove (Inc. Place)
Lansing; RMC Place; MOWER; 193 S-10; elev. 1,230ft./375m.; 🅿; z 55950; ● 250
Laporte; Inc. Place; HUBBARD; 192 I-6; elev. 1,400ft./427m.; 🅿; z 56461; Ⓟ 101; © 145
La Prairie; Inc. Place; ITASCA; 192 H-9; elev. 1,279ft./390m.; mail Grand Rapids z 55744; Ⓟ 438; © 605
Larsmont; RMC Place; LAKE; 192 I-13; elev. 668ft./204m.; mail Two Harbors z 55616; ● 50
La Salle; Inc. Place; WATONWAN; 193 R-6; elev. 1,040ft./317m.; 🅿; z 56056; Ⓟ 98; © 90
Lastrup; Inc. Place; MORRISON; 193 L-8; elev. 1,240ft./378m.; 🅿; z 56344; Ⓟ 112; © 99
Lauderdale; Inc. Place; RAMSEY; 191 F-6; elev. 960ft./293m.; 🅿; ★ **MPLS-**; z 55108, z 55113; Ⓟ 2,700; © 2,364
Lavinia; RMC Place; ST. LOUIS; *192 H-10; mail Hibbing z 55746; pop. incl. with Hibbing (Inc. Place)
Lawler; RMC Place; AITKIN; 193 K-10; elev. 1,312ft./400m.; mail McGregor z 55760; ● 60
Lawndale; RMC Place; WILKIN; *192 J-3; mail Rothsay z 56579; rural
Lax Lake; RMC Place; LAKE; *192 H-13; mail Silver Bay z 55614
Leader; RMC Place; CASS; 193 K-6; elev. 1,366ft./416m.; mail Motley z 56466; ● 50
Leaf Lake; RMC Place; OTTER TAIL; mail Henning z 56551; summer pop. 200; rural
Leaf Valley; RMC Place; DOUGLAS; *193 L-4; mail Garfield z 56332
Leavenworth; RMC Place; BROWN; 193 R-6; mail Sleepy Eye z 56085; ● 40
Le Center; Inc. Place; ⊡ LE SUEUR; 193 Q-8; elev. 1,052ft./321m.; 🅿; z 56057; Ⓟ 2,006; © 2,240
Leech Lake Reservation; Indian Reservation; CASS, BELTRAMI, HUBBARD, ITASCA; mail Cass Lake z 56633; also location of Minnesota Indian Agency; Ⓟ 8,441; © 10,205
Leetonia; RMC Place; ST. LOUIS; *192 H-10; mail Hibbing z 55746; pop. incl. with Hibbing (Inc. Place)
Le Hillier; RMC Place; BLUE EARTH; *193 R-8; ★ **MNKT**; mail Mankato z 56001; ● 450
Lena; RMC Place; GOODHUE; *193 R-11; mail Pine Island z 55963; rural
Lengby; Inc. Place; POLK; 192 H-4; elev. 1,360ft./415m.; 🅿; z 56651; Ⓟ 112; © 79
Lenora; RMC Place; FILLMORE; 193 T-12; elev. 1,104ft./336m.; mail Canton z 55922; ● 35
Leonard; Inc. Place; CLEARWATER; 192 G-5; elev. 1,500ft./457m.; 🅿; z 56652; Ⓟ 26; © 29
Leonidas; Inc. Place; ST. LOUIS; 192 H-11; elev. 1,450ft./442m.; mail Eveleth z 55734; Ⓟ 70; © 60
Leota; CDP; NOBLES; 193 S-3; elev. 1,720ft./524m.; 🅿; z 56153; © 230
Lerdal; RMC Place; FREEBORN; *193 S-9; elev. 1,269ft./387m.; mail Albert Lea z 56007
Le Roy; Inc. Place; MOWER; 193 T-11; elev. 1,280ft./390m.; 🅿; z 55951; Ⓟ 904; © 925
Lester Park; RMC Place; ST. LOUIS; *192 J-12; ★ **DUL**; pop. incl. with Duluth (Inc. Place)
Lester Prairie; Inc. Place; MCLEOD; 193 P-8; elev. 1,004ft./306m.; 🅿; z 55354; Ⓟ 1,180; © 1,377
Le Sueur; Inc. Place; LE SUEUR, SIBLEY; 193 Q-8; elev. 800ft./244m.; 🅿 🅷; z 56058; Ⓟ 3,714; © 3,922
LE SUEUR; 193 Q-8; Ⓟ 23,239; © 25,426; ◆ 28,744
Lewis Lake; RMC Place; KANABEC; *193 M-9; elev. 1,010ft./308m.; mail Braham z 55006, Ogilvie z 56358; rural
Lewiston; Inc. Place; WINONA; 193 S-12; elev. 1,221ft./372m.; 🅿; z 55952; Ⓟ 1,298; © 1,484
Lewisville; Inc. Place; WATONWAN; 193 S-7; elev. 1,060ft./323m.; 🅿; z 56060; Ⓟ 255; © 274
Lexington; Inc. Place; ANOKA; 191 B-6; elev. 910ft./277m.; ★ **MPLS-**; mail Circle Pines z 55014, Saint Paul z 55112; Ⓟ 2,279; © 2,214; Ⓡ 2,142
Lexington; RMC Place; LE SUEUR; *193 Q-8; mail Le Center z 56057; ● 35
Libby; RMC Place; AITKIN; *192 J-9; elev. 1,260ft./384m.; mail McGregor z 55760, Palisade z 56469; ● 50
Lilydale; Inc. Place; DAKOTA; 191 H-7; elev. 700ft./213m.; ★ **MPLS-**; mail Saint Paul z 55118; Ⓟ 506; © 552
Lime Creek; RMC Place; MURRAY; *193 S-4; mail Fulda z 56131; ● 30
Lincoln; RMC Place; MORRISON; 193 L-6; mail Cushing z 56443; ● 70
LINCOLN; 193 Q-2; Ⓟ 6,890; © 6,429; ◆ 5,756
Linden Grove; RMC Place; ST. LOUIS; *192 F-10; elev. 1,307ft./398m.; mail Cook z 55723; rural
Lindford; RMC Place; KOOCHICHING; *192 E-8; mail Littlefork z 56653; rural
Lindstrom; Inc. Place; CHISAGO; 193 N-10; elev. 900ft./274m.; 🅿; ★ **MPLS-**; z 55045; Ⓟ 2,461; © 3,015
Lino Lakes; Inc. Place; ANOKA; 193 O-10; elev. 910ft./277m.; 🅿; ★ **MPLS-**; z 55014, z 55038 & mail Saint Paul z 55110, z 55126; Ⓟ 8,807; © 16,791; ◆ 20,809
Linwood; RMC Place; ANOKA; *193 N-10; ★ **MPLS-**; mail Bethel z 55005, Wyoming z 55092; ● 50
Lismore; Inc. Place; NOBLES; 193 S-3; elev. 1,690ft./515m.; 🅿; z 56155; Ⓟ 248; © 238
Litchfield; Inc. Place; ⊡ MEEKER; 193 O-7; elev. 1,132ft./345m.; 🅿 🅷; z 55355; Ⓟ 6,041; © 6,562
Litomysl; RMC Place; STEELE; *193 S-10; mail Owatonna z 55060; rural
Little Canada; Inc. Place; RAMSEY; 191 E-8; elev. 950ft./290m.; 🅿; ★ **MPLS-**; z 55109, z 55117; Ⓟ 8,971; © 9,771
Little Chicago; RMC Place; RICE; *193 Q-9; elev. 1,080ft./329m.; mail Northfield z 55057; ● 30
Little Falls; Inc. Place; ⊡ MORRISON; 193 L-7; elev. 1,120ft./341m.; 🅿 🅷; z 56345; Ⓟ 7,232; © 7,719
Littlefork; Inc. Place; KOOCHICHING; 192 E-9; elev. 1,121ft./342m.; 🅿; z 56653; Ⓟ 838; © 680
Little Marais; RMC Place; LAKE; 192 H-14; elev. 641ft./195m.; 🅿; z 55614; ● 50
Little Pine; RMC Place; CROW WING; *192 J-8; elev. 1,276ft./389m.; mail Aitkin z 56431, Emily z 56447; rural
Little Rock; CDP-Census Area Only; BELTRAMI; *192 F-5; elev. 1,203ft./367m.; mail Redlake z 56671; Ⓟ 714; © 1,055
Little Rock; RMC Place; MORRISON; 193 M-7; elev. 1,202ft./366m.; mail Royalton z 56373; ● 30
Little Sauk; RMC Place; TODD; 193 M-6; elev. 1,260ft./384m.; 🅿; z 56347; ● 70
Little Swan; RMC Place; ST. LOUIS; *192 H-10; elev. 1,291ft./393m.; mail Hibbing z 55746; pop. incl. with Hibbing (Inc. Place)
Local; RMC Place; BECKER; *192 J-4; elev. 1,464ft./446m.; mail Detroit Lakes z 56501; ● 30
Lockhart; RMC Place; NORMAN; 192 H-2; 🅿; z 56510; ● 30
Loman; RMC Place; KOOCHICHING; 192 D-8; elev. 1,084ft./330m.; 🅿; z 56654; ● 100
London; RMC Place; FREEBORN; 193 T-10; elev. 1,200ft./366m.; 🅿; z 56036; ● 50
Long Beach; Inc. Place; POPE; ▲ New Russia; 193 M-5; elev. 1,150ft./351m.; mail Glenwood z 56334; Ⓟ 204; © 271
Long Lake; Inc. Place; HENNEPIN; 193 P-9; elev. 981ft./299m.; 🅿; ★ **MPLS-**; z 55356; Ⓟ 1,984; © 1,842
Long Point; RMC Place; LAKE OF THE WOODS; *192 C-6; mail Williams z 56686; summer pop. 150
Long Prairie; Inc. Place; ⊡ TODD; 193 L-6; elev. 1,300ft./396m.; 🅿 🅷; z 56347; Ⓟ 2,786; © 3,040
Long Siding; RMC Place; MILLE LACS; 193 N-9; mail Princeton z 55371; ● 100
Longville; Inc. Place; CASS; 192 I-7; elev. 1,330ft./405m.; 🅿; z 56655; Ⓟ 224; © 180
Lonsdale; Inc. Place; RICE; 193 Q-9; elev. 1,096ft./334m.; 🅿; z 55046; Ⓟ 1,252; © 1,491
Loop; RMC Place; HENNEPIN; *193 P-9; ★ **MPLS-**; mail Minneapolis z 55402; pop. incl. with Minneapolis (Inc. Place)
Loretto; Inc. Place; HENNEPIN; *193 O-9; elev. 1,025ft./312m.; 🅿; ★ **MPLS-**; z 55357, z 55595-99; Ⓟ 404; © 570
Loring; RMC Place; HENNEPIN; *193 P-9; ★ **MPLS-**; mail Minneapolis z 55403, z 55405; pop. incl. with Minneapolis (Inc. Place)
Lost Lake; RMC Place; HENNEPIN; ★ **MPLS-**; mail Minneapolis z 55441-42; pop. incl. with Plymouth (Inc. Place)
Louisburg; Inc. Place; LAC QUI PARLE; 193 O-3; elev. 1,040ft./317m.; 🅿; z 56256; Ⓟ 42; © 26
Louriston; RMC Place; CHIPPEWA; *193 O-4; elev. 1,047ft./319m.; mail Maynard z 56260; rural
Lower Sioux Reservation; Indian Reservation; REDWOOD; mail Morton z 56270; Ⓟ 79; © 335
Lowry; Inc. Place; POPE; 193 M-4; elev. 1,360ft./415m.; 🅿; z 56349 & mail Farwell z 56327; Ⓟ 233; © 271
Lowry Avenue; RMC Place; HENNEPIN; ★ **MPLS-**; mail Minneapolis z 55411-12; pop. incl. with Minneapolis (Inc. Place)
Lucan; Inc. Place; REDWOOD; 193 Q-5; elev. 1,080ft./329m.; 🅿; z 56255; Ⓟ 235; © 226
Lude; RMC Place; LAKE OF THE WOODS; *192 C-6; mail Williams z 56686
Lutsen; RMC Place; COOK; 192 B-11; elev. 671ft./205m.; 🅿; z 55612; ● 260
Luverne; Inc. Place; ⊡ ROCK; 193 T-3; elev. 1,457ft./444m.; 🅿 🅷; z 56156; Ⓟ 4,382; © 4,617
Luxemburg; RMC Place; STEARNS; 193 N-7; elev. 1,106ft./337m.; ★ **ST.CLD**; mail Saint Cloud z 56301; ● 150
Lydia; RMC Place; SCOTT; 193 Q-9; elev. 950ft./290m.; ★ **MPLS-**; mail Jordan z 55352; ● 80
Lyle; Inc. Place; MOWER; 193 T-10; elev. 1,200ft./366m.; 🅿; z 55953; Ⓟ 504; © 566
Lynd; Inc. Place; LYON; 193 Q-3; elev. 1,320ft./402m.; 🅿; z 56157; Ⓟ 287; © 346
Lyndale; RMC Place; HENNEPIN; *193 P-8; ★ **MPLS-**; mail Maple Plain z 55359; pop. incl. with Independence (Inc. Place)
Lyndale Junction; RMC Place; HENNEPIN; ★ **MPLS-**; pop. incl. with Minneapolis (Inc. Place)
Lynwood; RMC Place; ST. LOUIS; mail Hibbing z 55746; pop. incl. with Hibbing (Inc. Place)
LYON; 193 R-4; Ⓟ 24,789; © 25,425; ◆ 24,597

M

Mabel; Inc. Place; FILLMORE; 193 T-13; elev. 1,134ft./346m.; 🅿; z 55954; Ⓟ 745; © 766
Madelia; Inc. Place; WATONWAN; 193 R-7; elev. 1,029ft./314m.; 🅿 🅷; z 56062; Ⓟ 2,237; © 2,340
Madison; Inc. Place; ⊡ LAC QUI PARLE; 193 O-3; elev. 1,090ft./332m.; 🅿 🅷; z 56256; Ⓟ 1,951; © 1,768
Madison Lake; Inc. Place; BLUE EARTH; 193 R-8; elev. 1,050ft./320m.; 🅿; z 56063; Ⓟ 643; © 837
Mae; RMC Place; CASS; *192 J-8; mail Outing z 56662; rural
Magnolia; Inc. Place; ROCK; 193 T-3; elev. 1,520ft./463m.; 🅿; z 56158; Ⓟ 155; © 221
Mahkonce; RMC Place; MAHNOMEN; *192 H-4; mail Mahnomen z 56557; rural
Mahnomen; Inc. Place; ⊡ MAHNOMEN; 192 H-3; elev. 1,214ft./370m.; 🅿 🅷; z 56557; Ⓟ 1,154; © 1,202
MAHNOMEN; 192 H-4; Ⓟ 5,044; © 5,190; ◆ 5,166
Mahoning; RMC Place; ST. LOUIS; *192 H-10; pop. incl. with Hibbing (Inc. Place)
Mahtomedi; Inc. Place; WASHINGTON; 191 D-10; elev. 1,000ft./305m.; 🅿; ★ **MPLS-**; z 55115; Ⓟ 5,569; © 7,563
Mahtowa; RMC Place; CARLTON; 192 J-11; elev. 1,152ft./351m.; 🅿; z 55707; ● 150
Maine; RMC Place; OTTER TAIL; *193 K-4; mail Underwood z 56586; ● 30
Maine Prairie; RMC Place; STEARNS; *193 N-7; elev. 1,155ft./352m.; mail Kimball z 55353; ● 60
Makinen; RMC Place; ST. LOUIS; 192 H-11; elev. 1,405ft./428m.; 🅿; z 55763; ● 50
Mallory; RMC Place; POLK; *192 F-1; mail East Grand Forks z 56721; ● 25
Malmo; RMC Place; AITKIN; 193 K-9; mail Aitkin z 56431; ● 50
Malung; RMC Place; ROSEAU; *192 C-4; mail Roseau z 56751; rural
Manannah; RMC Place; MEEKER; 193 O-6; elev. 1,151ft./351m.; mail Eden Valley z 55329, Grove City z 56243; ● 50
Manchester; Inc. Place; FREEBORN; 193 S-9; elev. 1,283ft./391m.; 🅿; z 56007; Ⓟ 69; © 81
M & D Junction; RMC Place; RAMSEY; ★ **MPLS-**; mail Saint Paul z 55110; pop. incl. with White Bear Lake (Inc. Place)
Manhattan Beach; Inc. Place; CROW WING; 192 J-7; elev. 1,270ft./387m.; 🅿; z 56442; Ⓟ 61; © 50
Manitou; RMC Place; KOOCHICHING; *192 D-8; elev. 1,120ft./341m.; mail Birchdale z 56629; rural
Mankato; Inc. Place; ⊡ BLUE EARTH, LE SUEUR, NICOLLET; 193 R-8; elev. 794ft./242m.; 🅿 🅷 🅲 14,721 ■; ★ **MNKT**; z 56001-03, z 56006; Ⓟ 31,405; © 32,427; ◆ 36,141
Mansfield; RMC Place; FREEBORN; 193 T-9; elev. 1,247ft./380m.; mail Alden z 56009; ● 25
Mantorville; Inc. Place; ⊡ DODGE; 193 R-10; elev. 1,121ft./342m.; 🅿; ★ **ROCH**; z 55955; Ⓟ 874; © 1,054
Maple; RMC Place; CARVER; *193 P-8; elev. 1,000ft./305m.; ★ **MPLS-**; mail Waconia z 55387; rural
Maple Bay; RMC Place; POLK; 192 G-3; mail Mentor z 56736; ● 60
Maple Grove; Inc. Place; HENNEPIN; 193 O-9; elev. 935ft./285m.; 🅿; ★ **MPLS-**; z 55311, z 55369, z 55569; Ⓟ 38,736; © 50,365; ◆ 53,861
Maple Hill; RMC Place; COOK; *192 B-12; mail Grand Marais z 55604; ● 50
Maple Island; RMC Place; FREEBORN; 193 S-10; mail Hollandale z 56045; ● 150
Maple Lake; Inc. Place; WRIGHT; 193 O-8; elev. 1,040ft./317m.; 🅿; z 55358; Ⓟ 1,394; © 1,633
Maple Plain; Inc. Place; HENNEPIN; 193 O-8; elev. 1,001ft./305m.; 🅿; ★ **MPLS-**; z 55348, z 55359, z 55393, z 55570-71, z 55574, z 55576, z 55578-79, z 55592-93 & mail Rockford z 55572, z 55577; Ⓟ 2,005; © 2,088
Mapleton; Inc. Place; BLUE EARTH; 193 S-8; elev. 1,030ft./314m.; 🅿; z 56065; Ⓟ 1,526; © 1,678
Mapleview; Inc. Place; MOWER; 193 S-10; elev. 1,218ft./371m.; mail Austin z 55912; Ⓟ 206; © 189
Maplewood; Inc. Place; RAMSEY; 191 E-8; elev. 1,000ft./305m.; 🅿 🅷 ■; ★ **MPLS-**; z 55109, z 55117, z 55119, z 55144 & mail Saint Paul z 55106; Ⓟ 30,954; © 34,947; Ⓡ 35,258; ◆ 35,198
Marble; Inc. Place; ITASCA; 192 H-9; elev. 1,390ft./424m.; 🅿; z 55764; Ⓟ 618; © 695
Marcell; RMC Place; ITASCA; 192 G-8; elev. 1,386ft./422m.; 🅿; z 56657; ● 100
Margie; RMC Place; KOOCHICHING; 192 F-8; elev. 1,264ft./385m.; 🅿; z 56658; ● 40
Marietta; Inc. Place; LAC QUI PARLE; 193 O-2; elev. 1,108ft./338m.; 🅿; z 56257; Ⓟ 211; © 174
Marine; WASHINGTON; see Marine on Saint Croix (Inc. Place)
Marine on Saint Croix (Marine); Inc. Place; WASHINGTON; 193 O-10; elev. 750ft./229m.; 🅿; ★ **MPLS-**; z 55047; Ⓟ 602; © 602
Marion; RMC Place; OLMSTED; 193 S-11; ★ **ROCH**; mail Rochester z 55904; ● 100
Markham; RMC Place; ST. LOUIS; 192 H-11; elev. 1,465ft./447m.; mail Makinen z 55763; ● 50
Markville; RMC Place; PINE; 193 L-11; elev. 1,005ft./306m.; 🅿; z 55072; ● 80
Marshall; Inc. Place; ⊡ LYON; 193 Q-4; elev. 1,170ft./357m.; 🅿 🅷 🅲 6,097 ■; z 56258; Ⓟ 12,023; © 12,735; Ⓡ 12,717; ◆ 12,690
MARSHALL; 192 E-3; Ⓟ 10,993; © 10,155; ◆ 9,315
MARTIN; 193 S-6; Ⓟ 22,914; © 21,802; ◆ 20,257
Martin Lake; RMC Place; ANOKA; *193 N-10; ★ **MPLS-**; mail Stacy z 55079; ● 150
Marty (Pearl Lake); RMC Place; STEARNS; *193 N-7; mail Kimball z 55353; ● 50
Marysburg; RMC Place; BLUE EARTH, LE SUEUR; *193 R-8; mail Madison Lake z 56063; rural
Marystown; RMC Place; SCOTT; *193 P-9; ★ **MPLS-**; mail Shakopee z 55379; ● 100
Matawan; RMC Place; WASECA; 193 S-8; mail New Richland z 56072; ● 50
Mattson; RMC Place; KITTSON; *192 D-1; elev. 794ft./242m.; mail Hallock z 56728; rural
Mavie; RMC Place; PENNINGTON; *192 E-4; mail Goodridge z 56725; rural
Max; RMC Place; ITASCA; 192 G-8; elev. 1,373ft./418m.; 🅿; z 56659; ● 25
Mayer; Inc. Place; CARVER; 193 P-8; elev. 979ft./298m.; 🅿; z 55360; Ⓟ 471; © 554
Mayhew; RMC Place; BENTON; *193 M-7; mail Sauk Rapids z 56379; ● 30
Mayhew Lake; RMC Place; BENTON; *193 M-8; mail Sauk Rapids z 56379; ● 30
Maynard; Inc. Place; CHIPPEWA; 193 P-4; elev. 1,029ft./314m.; 🅿; z 56260; Ⓟ 419; © 388
Mayowood; RMC Place; OLMSTED; *193 S-11; ★ **ROCH**; mail Rochester z 55902; ● 30
Mayville; RMC Place; MOWER; *193 S-10; mail Austin z 55912; rural
Mazeppa; Inc. Place; WABASHA; 193 R-11; elev. 931ft./284m.; 🅿; z 55956; Ⓟ 722; © 778
McCauleyville; RMC Place; WILKIN; *193 K-2; mail Kent z 56553; ● 20
McGrath; Inc. Place; AITKIN; 193 L-9; elev. 1,240ft./378m.; 🅿; z 56350; Ⓟ 62; © 65
McGregor; Inc. Place; AITKIN; 192 J-9; elev. 1,233ft./376m.; 🅿; z 55760; Ⓟ 376; © 404
McIntosh; Inc. Place; POLK; 192 G-4; elev. 1,223ft./373m.; 🅿; z 56556; Ⓟ 665; © 638
McKee; RMC Place; DAKOTA; ★ **MPLS-**; mail Saint Paul z 55121; pop. incl. with Eagan (Inc. Place)
McKinley; Inc. Place; ST. LOUIS; *192 G-11; elev. 1,438ft./438m.; 🅿; z 55741; Ⓟ 116; © 80
MCLEOD; 193 P-7; Ⓟ 32,030; © 34,898; ◆ 37,506
Meadowlands; Inc. Place; ST. LOUIS; 192 I-10; elev. 1,275ft./389m.; 🅿; z 55765; Ⓟ 92; © 111
Medford; Inc. Place; STEELE; 193 R-9; elev. 1,100ft./335m.; 🅿; z 55049; Ⓟ 733; © 984
Medicine Lake; Inc. Place; HENNEPIN; 191 F-2; elev. 895ft./273m.; 🅿; ★ **MPLS-**; z 55441; Ⓟ 385; © 368
Medina (Hamel); Inc. Place; HENNEPIN; 193 O-9; elev. 1,000ft./305m.; 🅿; ★ **MPLS-**; z 55340 & mail Loretto z 55357, Maple Plain z 55359; Ⓟ 3,096; © 4,005
MEEKER; 193 O-6; Ⓟ 20,846; © 22,644; ◆ 23,040
Meire Grove; Inc. Place; STEARNS; 193 M-6; elev. 1,294ft./394m.; mail Melrose z 56352; Ⓟ 124; © 149
Melby; RMC Place; DOUGLAS; 193 L-4; elev. 1,276ft./389m.; mail Evansville z 56326; ● 40
Melrose; Inc. Place; STEARNS; 193 M-6; elev. 1,213ft./370m.; 🅿 🅷; z 56352; Ⓟ 2,561; © 3,091
Melrude; RMC Place; ST. LOUIS; 192 H-11; elev. 1,348ft./411m.; 🅿; z 55766 & mail Cotton z 55724; ● 35
Menahga; Inc. Place; WADENA; 192 J-5; elev. 1,403ft./428m.; 🅿; z 56464; Ⓟ 1,076; © 1,220
Mendota; Inc. Place; DAKOTA; 191 H-6; elev. 800ft./244m.; 🅿; ★ **MPLS-**; z 55150; Ⓟ 164; © 197
Mendota Heights; Inc. Place; DAKOTA; 191 H-7; elev. 850ft./259m.; 🅿 🅲 1,810; ★ **MPLS-**; z 55118, z 55120; Ⓟ 9,431; © 11,434
Mentor; Inc. Place; POLK; 192 G-3; elev. 1,170ft./357m.; 🅿; z 56736; Ⓟ 94; © 150
Meriden; RMC Place; STEELE; 193 R-9; elev. 1,140ft./347m.; 🅿; z 56093; ● 150
Merriam Park; RMC Place; RAMSEY; ★ **MPLS-**; pop. incl. with Saint Paul (Inc. Place)
Merrifield; RMC Place; CROW WING; 193 K-7; elev. 1,219ft./372m.; 🅿; z 56465; ● 400
Merton; RMC Place; STEELE; *193 R-10; elev. 1,260ft./384m.; mail Owatonna z 55060; rural
Mesaba; RMC Place; ST. LOUIS; *192 G-12; elev. 1,519ft./463m.; mail Hoyt Lakes z 55750; pop. incl. with Hoyt Lakes (Inc. Place)
Middle River; Inc. Place; MARSHALL; 192 E-3; elev. 1,141ft./348m.; 🅿; z 56737; Ⓟ 285; © 319
Midway; RMC Place; BECKER; 192 J-5; elev. 1,522ft./464m.; mail Menahga z 56464; ● 25
Midway; RMC Place; RAMSEY; *193 P-10; ★ **MPLS-**; mail Saint Paul z 55104; pop. incl. with Saint Paul (Inc. Place)
Midway; RMC Place; ST. LOUIS; *192 H-11; mail Virginia z 55792; pop. incl. with Virginia (Inc. Place)
Miesville; Inc. Place; DAKOTA; 193 Q-10; elev. 940ft./287m.; mail Cannon Falls z 55009; Ⓟ 135; © 135
Milaca; Inc. Place; ⊡ MILLE LACS; 193 M-8; elev. 1,079ft./329m.; 🅿; z 56353; Ⓟ 2,182; © 2,580
Milan; Inc. Place; CHIPPEWA; 193 O-3; elev. 1,005ft./306m.; 🅿; z 56262; Ⓟ 353; © 326
MILLE LACS; 193 L-8; Ⓟ 18,670; © 22,330; ◆ 26,750
Mille Lacs Reservation; Indian Reservation; MILLE LACS, AITKIN, CROW WING, PINE; mail Onamia z 56359; © 4,548
Miller Hill; RMC Place; ST. LOUIS; *192 J-12; ★ **DUL**; mail Duluth z 55811; pop. incl. with Duluth (Inc. Place)
Millersburg; RMC Place; RICE; *193 Q-9; mail Faribault z 55021; rural
Millerville; Inc. Place; DOUGLAS; 193 L-4; elev. 1,392ft./424m.; mail Brandon z 56315; Ⓟ 104; © 115
Millville; Inc. Place; WABASHA; 193 R-11; elev. 783ft./239m.; 🅿; z 55957; Ⓟ 163; © 186
Milroy; Inc. Place; REDWOOD; 193 Q-4; elev. 1,110ft./338m.; 🅿; z 56263; Ⓟ 297; © 271
Miltona; Inc. Place; DOUGLAS; 193 L-5; elev. 1,399ft./426m.; 🅿; z 56354; Ⓟ 181; © 279
Mineral Center; RMC Place; COOK; *192 A-13; elev. 1,300ft./396m.; mail Grand Portage z 55605; rural
Minneapolis; Inc. Place; ⊡ HENNEPIN; 193 O-9; elev. 840ft./256m.; 🅿 🅷 🅲 102,762 ■; ★ **MPLS-**; z 55401-50, z 55454-55, z 55458-60, z 55467, z 55470, z 55472-74, z 55478-80, z 55483-88; Ⓟ 368,383; © 382,618; Ⓡ 382,747; ◆ 406,088
Minnehaha; RMC Place; HENNEPIN; *193 P-9; ★ **MPLS-**; mail Minneapolis z 55406; pop. incl. with Minneapolis (Inc. Place)
Minneiska; Inc. Place; WABASHA, WINONA; 193 R-12; elev. 670ft./204m.; 🅿; z 55910; Ⓟ 127; © 116
Minneota; Inc. Place; LYON; 193 Q-3; elev. 1,168ft./356m.; 🅿; z 56264; Ⓟ 1,417; © 1,449
Minnesota City; Inc. Place; WINONA; 193 R-13; elev. 700ft./213m.; 🅿; z 55959; Ⓟ 258; © 235
Minnesota Lake; Inc. Place; FARIBAULT, BLUE EARTH; 193 S-8; elev. 1,050ft./320m.; 🅿; z 56068; Ⓟ 681; © 681
Minnesota Transfer; RMC Place; RAMSEY; *193 P-9; ★ **MPLS-**; mail Saint Paul z 55114; pop. incl. with Saint Paul (Inc. Place)
Minnetonka; Inc. Place; HENNEPIN; 191 G-1; elev. 950ft./290m.; 🅿 ■; ★ **MPLS-**; z 55305, z 55343, z 55345; Ⓟ 48,370; © 51,301; Ⓡ 51,102; ◆ 50,876
Minnetonka Beach; Inc. Place; HENNEPIN; *193 P-9; elev. 950ft./290m.; 🅿; ★ **MPLS-**; z 55361; Ⓟ 573; © 614
Minnetonka Mills; RMC Place; HENNEPIN; *193 P-9; elev. 950ft./290m.; 🅿; ★ **MPLS-**; z 55343 & mail Hopkins z 55305; pop. incl. with Minnetonka (Inc. Place)
Minnetrista; Inc. Place; HENNEPIN; *193 P-8; elev. 1,000ft./305m.; 🅿; ★ **MPLS-**; z 55331, z 55359, z 55364, z 55375, z 55388 & mail Waconia z 55387; Ⓟ 3,439; © 4,358
Minnewawa; RMC Place; AITKIN; *192 J-9; elev. 1,247ft./380m.; mail McGregor z 55760; summer pop. 300; ● 150
Missabe Junction; RMC Place; ST. LOUIS; *192 J-12; ★ **DUL**; pop. incl. with Duluth (Inc. Place)
Mitchell; RMC Place; ST. LOUIS; *192 H-10; pop. incl. with Hibbing (Inc. Place)
Mizpah; Inc. Place; KOOCHICHING; 192 F-7; elev. 1,385ft./422m.; 🅿; z 56660; Ⓟ 100; © 78
Moland; RMC Place; RICE; *193 R-10; mail Kenyon z 55946
Money Creek; RMC Place; HOUSTON; 193 S-13; mail Houston z 55943; ● 80
Montevideo; Inc. Place; ⊡ CHIPPEWA; 193 P-4; elev. 1,016ft./310m.; 🅿 🅷; z 56265; Ⓟ 5,499; © 5,346; Ⓡ 5,462
Montgomery; Inc. Place; LE SUEUR; 193 Q-9; elev. 1,065ft./325m.; 🅿; z 56069; Ⓟ 2,399; © 2,794
Monticello; Inc. Place; WRIGHT; 193 N-8; elev. 940ft./287m.; 🅿 🅷; ★ **MPLS-**; z 55362, z 55365, z 55561, z 55563, z 55565, z 55580-82, z 55584-91; Ⓟ 4,941; © 7,868
Montrose; Inc. Place; WRIGHT; 193 O-8; elev. 985ft./300m.; 🅿; z 55363; Ⓟ 1,008; © 1,143
Moorhead (East Moorhead); Inc. Place; ⊡ CLAY; 192 I-2; elev. 903ft./275m.; 🅿 🅲 10,166; ★ **FAR-**; z 56560-63; Ⓟ 32,295; © 32,177; ◆ 35,080
Moose Lake; Inc. Place; CARLTON; 193 K-10; elev. 1,062ft./324m.; 🅿 🅷; z 55767; Ⓟ 1,206; © 2,239
Mora; Inc. Place; ⊡ KANABEC; 193 M-9; elev. 1,010ft./308m.; 🅿 🅷; z 55051; Ⓟ 2,905; © 3,193
Morgan; Inc. Place; REDWOOD; 193 Q-6; elev. 1,040ft./317m.; 🅿; z 56266; Ⓟ 965; © 903
Morgan Park; RMC Place; ST. LOUIS; *192 J-12; ★ **DUL**; mail Duluth z 55808; pop. incl. with Duluth (Inc. Place)
Morningside; RMC Place; HENNEPIN; ★ **MPLS-**; mail Minneapolis z 55424; pop. incl. with Edina (Inc. Place)
Morrill; RMC Place; MORRISON; 193 M-8; mail Foley z 56329; ● 70
Morris; Inc. Place; ⊡ STEVENS; 193 N-3; elev. 1,133ft./345m.; 🅿 🅷 🅲 1,747; z 56267; Ⓟ 5,613; © 5,068; Ⓡ 5,173
MORRISON; 193 M-8; Ⓟ 29,604; © 31,712; ◆ 32,895
Morristown; Inc. Place; RICE; 193 R-9; elev. 1,000ft./305m.; 🅿; z 55052; Ⓟ 784; © 981
Morton; Inc. Place; RENVILLE; 193 Q-5; elev. 870ft./265m.; 🅿; z 56270; Ⓟ 448; © 442
Moscow; RMC Place; FREEBORN; *193 T-10; mail Austin z 55912; rural
Motley; Inc. Place; MORRISON, CASS; 193 K-6; elev. 1,229ft./375m.; 🅿; z 56466; Ⓟ 441; © 585
Mound; Inc. Place; HENNEPIN; 193 P-8; elev. 942ft./287m.; 🅿; ★ **MPLS-**; z 55364; Ⓟ 9,634; © 9,435
Mound Prairie; RMC Place; HOUSTON; *193 S-13; mail Houston z 55943; rural
Mounds View; Inc. Place; RAMSEY; 191 C-6; elev. 900ft./274m.; 🅿; ★ **MPLS-**; z 55112; Ⓟ 12,541; © 12,738
Mountain Iron; Inc. Place; ST. LOUIS; 192 G-11; elev. 1,474ft./449m.; 🅿; z 55768 & mail Virginia z 55792; Ⓟ 3,362; © 2,999
Mountain Lake; Inc. Place; COTTONWOOD; 193 S-6; elev. 1,305ft./398m.; 🅿; z 56159; Ⓟ 1,906; © 2,082
Mount Royal; RMC Place; ST. LOUIS; *192 J-12; ★ **DUL**; mail Duluth z 55803; pop. incl. with Duluth (Inc. Place)
MOWER; 193 T-11; Ⓟ 37,385; © 38,603; ◆ 37,599
Munger; RMC Place; ST. LOUIS; *192 J-11; elev. 1,367ft./417m.; mail Cloquet z 55720
Murdock; Inc. Place; SWIFT; 193 O-5; elev. 1,090ft./332m.; 🅿; z 56271; Ⓟ 282; © 303
Murphy City; RMC Place; LAKE; 192 G-13; mail Finland z 55603; ● 30
MURRAY; 193 R-4; Ⓟ 9,660; © 9,165; ◆ 8,180
Muskoda; RMC Place; CLAY; *192 J-2; elev. 1,050ft./320m.; mail Glyndon z 56547; rural
Myrtle; Inc. Place; FREEBORN; 193 T-10; elev. 1,250ft./381m.; 🅿; z 56036; Ⓟ 72; © 63

N

Nashua; Inc. Place; WILKIN; 193 L-3; elev. 1,005ft./306m.; 🅿; z 56565; Ⓟ 63; © 69
Nashwauk; Inc. Place; ITASCA; 192 H-9; elev. 1,520ft./463m.; 🅿; z 55769; Ⓟ 1,026; © 935
Nassau; Inc. Place; LAC QUI PARLE; 193 O-2; elev. 1,115ft./340m.; 🅿; z 56257; Ⓟ 83; © 83
Navarre; RMC Place; HENNEPIN; *193 P-9; elev. 940ft./287m.; 🅿; ★ **MPLS-**; z 55392; pop. incl. with Orono (Inc. Place)
Naytahwaush; CDP; MAHNOMEN; 192 H-4; elev. 1,490ft./454m.; 🅿; z 56566; Ⓟ 378; © 583
Nebish; RMC Place; BELTRAMI; 192 G-6; mail Nevis z 56467, Puposky z 56667; ● 30
Nelson; Inc. Place; DOUGLAS; 193 M-5; elev. 1,367ft./417m.; 🅿; z 56355; Ⓟ 177; © 172
Nemadji; RMC Place; CARLTON; *193 K-11; mail Kerrick z 55756; rural
Nerstrand; Inc. Place; RICE; 193 Q-10; elev. 1,192ft./363m.; 🅿; z 55053; Ⓟ 210; © 233
Nett Lake; RMC Place; ST. LOUIS, KOOCHICHING; 192 F-10; located on Nett Lake Ind. Res.; elev. 1,326ft./404m.; 🅿; z 55772; ● 250
Nevis; Inc. Place; HUBBARD; 192 I-6; elev. 1,470ft./448m.; 🅿; z 56467; Ⓟ 375; © 364
New Auburn; Inc. Place; SIBLEY; 193 P-7; elev. 1,002ft./305m.; 🅿; z 55366; Ⓟ 363; © 488
New Brighton; Inc. Place; RAMSEY; 191 D-6; elev. 900ft./274m.; 🅿; ★ **MPLS-**; z 55112; Ⓟ 22,207; © 22,206; ◆ 21,021
Newburg; RMC Place; FILLMORE; 193 T-13; mail Mabel z 55954; ● 40
New Duluth; RMC Place; ST. LOUIS; *192 J-12; ★ **DUL**; pop. incl. with Duluth (Inc. Place)
Newfolden; Inc. Place; MARSHALL; 192 E-3; elev. 1,090ft./332m.; 🅿; z 56738; Ⓟ 345; © 362
New Germany; Inc. Place; CARVER; 193 P-8; elev. 980ft./299m.; 🅿; z 55367; Ⓟ 353; © 346
New Hartford; RMC Place; WINONA; *193 S-13; mail Dakota z 55925
New Hope; Inc. Place; HENNEPIN; 191 D-3; elev. 900ft./274m.; 🅿; ★ **MPLS-**; z 55427-28; Ⓟ 21,853; © 20,873; ◆ 20,460
Newhouse; RMC Place; HOUSTON; *193 T-13; mail Mabel z 55954; rural
New London; Inc. Place; KANDIYOHI; 193 O-6; elev. 1,222ft./372m.; 🅿; z 56273; Ⓟ 971; © 1,066
New Market; RMC Place; SCOTT; 193 Q-9; elev. 1,140ft./347m.; 🅿; z 55054; former incorporated place; became part of Elko New Market January 1, 2007; pop. incl. with Elko New Market (Inc. Place); Ⓟ 227; © 332
New Munich; Inc. Place; STEARNS; 193 M-6; elev. 1,192ft./363m.; 🅿; z 56356; Ⓟ 314; © 352
Newport; Inc. Place; WASHINGTON; 191 I-9; elev. 743ft./226m.; 🅿; ★ **MPLS-**; z 55055; Ⓟ 3,720; © 3,715
New Prague; Inc. Place; LE SUEUR, SCOTT; 193 Q-9; elev. 980ft./299m.; 🅿 🅷; z 56071; Ⓟ 3,569; © 4,559
New Richland; Inc. Place; WASECA; 193 S-9; elev. 1,184ft./361m.; 🅿; z 56072; Ⓟ 1,237; © 1,197
New Rome; RMC Place; SIBLEY; *193 Q-7; elev. 1,000ft./305m.; mail Arlington z 55307; ● 25
Newry; RMC Place; FREEBORN; *193 S-10; elev. 1,270ft./387m.; mail Blooming Prairie z 55917, Hollandale z 56045; rural
New Trier; Inc. Place; DAKOTA; 193 Q-10; elev. 980ft./299m.; 🅿; z 55031; Ⓟ 96; © 116
New Ulm; Inc. Place; ⊡ BROWN; 193 R-7; elev. 896ft./273m.; 🅿 🅷 🅲 731 ■; z 56073; Ⓟ 13,132; © 13,594; ◆ 12,946
New York Mills; Inc. Place; OTTER TAIL; 193 K-5; elev. 1,410ft./430m.; 🅿; z 56567; Ⓟ 940; © 1,158
Nickerson; RMC Place; PINE; 193 K-11; elev. 1,156ft./352m.; mail Wrenshall z 55797; ● 40
Nicollet; Inc. Place; NICOLLET; 193 R-7; elev. 990ft./302m.; 🅿; z 56074; Ⓟ 795; © 889
NICOLLET; 193 Q-7; Ⓟ 28,076; © 29,771; ◆ 32,421
Nicols; RMC Place; DAKOTA; *193 P-9; ★ **MPLS-**; mail Saint Paul z 55121; pop. incl. with Eagan (Inc. Place)
Nicolville; RMC Place; MOWER; *193 T-10; elev. 1,241ft./378m.; 🅿; z 55912; ● 50
Nielsville; Inc. Place; POLK; 192 G-2; elev. 865ft./264m.; 🅿; z 56568; Ⓟ 100; © 91
Nimrod; Inc. Place; WADENA; 192 J-6; elev. 1,330ft./405m.; 🅿; z 56478; Ⓟ 65; © 75
Nininger; RMC Place; DAKOTA; *193 P-10; ★ **MPLS-**; mail Hastings z 55033; ● 50
Nisswa; Inc. Place; CROW WING; 193 K-7; elev. 1,231ft./375m.; 🅿; z 56468 & mail Lake Hubert z 56459; Ⓟ 1,391; © 1,953
NOBLES; 193 T-3; Ⓟ 20,098; © 20,832; ◆ 20,102
Nodine; RMC Place; WINONA; 193 S-13; mail Dakota z 55925; ● 50
Nokomis; RMC Place; HENNEPIN; *193 P-9; ★ **MPLS-**; mail Minneapolis z 55417; pop. incl. with Minneapolis (Inc. Place)
Nopeming; RMC Place; ST. LOUIS; *192 J-11; elev. 1,150ft./351m.; ★ **DUL**; mail Duluth z 55810; ● 200
Norcross; Inc. Place; GRANT; 193 M-3; elev. 1,040ft./317m.; 🅿; z 56274; Ⓟ 86; © 59
NORMAN; 192 H-2; Ⓟ 7,975; © 7,442; ◆ 6,492
Normandale; RMC Place; HENNEPIN; *193 P-9; elev. 850ft./259m.; ★ **MPLS-**; mail Minneapolis z 55435, z 55439; pop. incl. with Edina (Inc. Place)
Norseland; RMC Place; NICOLLET; 193 Q-7; mail Saint Peter z 56082; ● 30
North Benton; RMC Place; BENTON; *193 M-8; elev. 1,236ft./377m.; mail Foley z 56329; rural
North Branch; Inc. Place; CHISAGO; 193 N-10; elev. 896ft./273m.; 🅿; z 55056; Ⓟ 4,267; © 8,023
Northcote; RMC Place; KITTSON; *192 C-1; elev. 802ft./244m.; mail Hallock z 56728
Northdale; RMC Place; ANOKA; *193 O-9; ★ **MPLS-**; mail Minneapolis z 55433; pop. incl. with Coon Rapids (Inc. Place)
North Douglas; RMC Place; HENNEPIN; *193 O-9; ★ **MPLS-**; mail Minneapolis z 55422; pop. incl. with Crystal (Inc. Place)
Northfield; Inc. Place; RICE, DAKOTA; 193 Q-10; elev. 919ft./280m.; 🅿 🅷 🅲 4,942; z 55057; Ⓟ 14,684; © 17,147
North Mankato; Inc. Place; NICOLLET, BLUE EARTH; 193 R-8; elev. 800ft./244m.; 🅿; ★ **MNKT**; z 56003 & mail Mankato z 56002; Ⓟ 10,164; © 11,798
North Oaks; Inc. Place; RAMSEY; 191 D-7; elev. 900ft./274m.; 🅿; ★ **MPLS-**; z 55127 & mail Saint Paul z 55126; Ⓟ 3,386; © 3,883
Northome; Inc. Place; KOOCHICHING; 192 F-7; elev. 1,429ft./436m.; 🅿; z 56661; Ⓟ 283; © 230
North Prairie; RMC Place; MORRISON; 193 M-7; mail Bowlus z 56314; ● 50
North Redwood; RMC Place; REDWOOD; *193 Q-5; elev. 847ft./258m.; 🅿; z 56283; pop. incl. with Redwood Falls (Inc. Place); Ⓟ 203
Northrop; Inc. Place; MARTIN; 193 S-7; elev. 1,141ft./348m.; 🅿; z 56075; Ⓟ 276; © 262
North Saint Paul; Inc. Place; RAMSEY; 191 E-9; elev. 1,000ft./305m.; 🅿; ★ **MPLS-**; z 55109; Ⓟ 12,376; © 11,929
Northside; RMC Place; FREEBORN; mail Albert Lea z 56007; pop. incl. with Albert Lea (Inc. Place)
Northtown; RMC Place; HENNEPIN; ★ **MPLS-**; pop. incl. with Minneapolis (Inc. Place)
Norway Lake; RMC Place; KANDIYOHI; *193 O-5; mail Sunburg z 56289; ● 120
Norwood; RMC Place; CARVER; *193 P-8; 🅿; z 55368, z 55383, z 55554, z 55583; pop. incl. with Norwood Young America (Inc. Place)
Norwood; CARVER; see Norwood Young America (Inc. Place)
Norwood Young America (Norwood); Inc. Place; CARVER; 193 P-8; elev. 983ft./300m.; 🅿; z 55368, z 55397, z 55473 & mail Norwood z 55383, z 55554, z 55583, Young America z 55394; Ⓟ 2,705; © 3,108
Novak's Corner; RMC Place; BENTON; *193 M-8; mail Foley z 56329; rural
Nowthen; RMC Place; ANOKA; *193 N-9; elev. 941ft./287m.; 🅿; ★ **MPLS-**; z 55303, z 55330; ● 50
Noyes; RMC Place; KITTSON; 192 C-1; elev. 789ft./240m.; 🅿; z 56740; ● 25

O

Oak Center; RMC Place; WABASHA; 193 Q-11; elev. 1,154ft./352m.; mail Lake City z 55041; ● 40
Oakdale; Inc. Place; WASHINGTON; 191 F-10; elev. 1,050ft./320m.; 🅿 🅲 1,200; ★ **MPLS-**; z 55128 & mail Lake Elmo z 55042; Ⓟ 18,374; © 26,653; ◆ 26,954
Oak Grove; Inc. Place; ANOKA; 193 N-9; 🅿; ★ **MPLS-**; z 55011, z 55303; Ⓟ 5,488; © 6,903
Oak Island; RMC Place; LAKE OF THE WOODS; 192 B-6; elev. 1,065ft./325m.; 🅿; z 56741; rural
Oak Knoll; RMC Place; HENNEPIN; *193 P-9; ★ **MPLS-**; mail Hopkins z 55305; pop. incl. with Minnetonka (Inc. Place)
Oakland; RMC Place; FREEBORN; 193 T-10; elev. 1,264ft./385m.; 🅿; z 56007; ● 130
Oak Park; RMC Place; ANOKA; *193 O-9; elev. 914ft./279m.; ★ **MPLS-**; mail Minneapolis z 55434; pop. incl. with Blaine (Inc. Place)
Oak Park; RMC Place; BENTON; 193 M-8; elev. 1,130ft./344m.; 🅿; z 56329, z 56357; ● 130
Oak Park Heights; Inc. Place; WASHINGTON; 193 O-10; elev. 750ft./229m.; 🅿; ★ **MPLS-**; z 55082; Ⓟ 3,486; © 3,957; Ⓡ 3,777
Oakport; CDP-Census Area Only; CLAY; *192 I-2; elev. 897ft./273m.; ★ **FAR-**; mail Moorhead z 56560; Ⓟ 1,026; © 1,334
Oak Ridge; RMC Place; WINONA; *193 R-12; elev. 1,226ft./374m.; mail Altura z 55910; rural
Odessa; Inc. Place; BIG STONE; 193 O-3; elev. 962ft./293m.; 🅿; z 56276; Ⓟ 155; © 113
Odin; Inc. Place; WATONWAN; 193 S-6; elev. 1,208ft./368m.; 🅿; z 56160; Ⓟ 102; © 125
Ogema; Inc. Place; BECKER; 192 I-4; located on White Earth Ind. Res.; elev. 1,270ft./387m.; 🅿; z 56569; Ⓟ 164; © 143
Ogilvie; Inc. Place; KANABEC; 193 M-9; elev. 1,047ft./319m.; 🅿; z 56358; Ⓟ 510; © 474
Okabena; Inc. Place; JACKSON; 193 S-5; elev. 1,424ft./434m.; 🅿; z 56161; Ⓟ 223; © 185
Oklee; Inc. Place; RED LAKE; 192 F-4; elev. 1,150ft./351m.; 🅿; z 56742; Ⓟ 441; © 396
Old Frontenac; RMC Place; GOODHUE; 193 Q-11; mail Frontenac z 55026; ● 250
Olga; RMC Place; POLK; *192 G-4; mail Gully z 56646; rural
Olivia; Inc. Place; ⊡ RENVILLE; 193 P-5; elev. 1,083ft./330m.; 🅿 🅷; z 56277; Ⓟ 2,623; © 2,570
OLMSTED; 193 R-11; Ⓟ 106,470; © 124,277; ◆ 143,607
Onamia; Inc. Place; MILLE LACS; 193 L-8; elev. 1,264ft./385m.; 🅿 🅷; z 56359; Ⓟ 676; © 847
Onega; RMC Place; ST. LOUIS; *192 H-10; pop. incl. with Hibbing (Inc. Place)
Oneota; RMC Place; ST. LOUIS; *192 J-12; ★ **DUL**; pop. incl. with Duluth (Inc. Place)
Onigum; RMC Place; CASS; 192 I-7; mail Walker z 56484; ● 60
Opole; RMC Place; STEARNS; 193 M-7; mail Holdingford z 56340; ● 90
Opstead; RMC Place; MILLE LACS; *193 L-9; mail Isle z 56342; rural
Orchard Lake; RMC Place; DAKOTA; ★ **MPLS-**; mail Lakeville z 55044; pop. incl. with Lakeville (Inc. Place)
Org; RMC Place; NOBLES; *193 T-4; elev. 1,650ft./503m.; mail Worthington z 56187
Orleans; RMC Place; KITTSON; 192 C-2; elev. 840ft./256m.; 🅿; z 56735; ● 10
Ormsby; Inc. Place; WATONWAN, MARTIN; 193 S-6; elev. 1,205ft./367m.; 🅿; z 56162; Ⓟ 159; © 154
Orono; Inc. Place; HENNEPIN; 193 P-8; elev. 975ft./297m.; 🅿; ★ **MPLS-**; z 55356 & mail Crystal Bay z 55323, Excelsior z 55331, Maple Plain z 55359, Mound z 55364, Wayzata z 55391; Ⓟ 7,285; © 7,538
Oronoco; Inc. Place; OLMSTED; 193 R-11; elev. 985ft./300m.; 🅿; ★ **ROCH**; z 55960; Ⓟ 727; © 883
Orr; Inc. Place; ST. LOUIS; 192 F-10; elev. 1,304ft./397m.; 🅿; z 55771-72; Ⓟ 265; © 249
Orrock; RMC Place; SHERBURNE; 193 N-8; elev. 987ft./301m.; mail Big Lake z 55309; ● 50
Orth; RMC Place; ITASCA; *192 F-7; mail Northome z 56661; rural
Ortonville; Inc. Place; ⊡ BIG STONE, LAC QUI PARLE; 193 N-2; elev. 1,094ft./333m.; 🅿 🅷; z 56278; Ⓟ 2,205; © 2,158
Osage; RMC Place; BECKER; 192 I-5; elev. 1,500ft./457m.; 🅿; z 56570; ● 300
Osakis; Inc. Place; DOUGLAS, TODD; 193 M-5; elev. 1,350ft./411m.; 🅿; z 56360; Ⓟ 1,256; © 1,567
Oshawa; RMC Place; NICOLLET; *193 R-7; mail Saint Peter z 56082; rural
Oslo; RMC Place; DODGE; *193 S-11; elev. 1,295ft./395m.; mail Hayfield z 55940
Oslo; Inc. Place; MARSHALL; 192 E-1; 🅿; z 56744; Ⓟ 362; © 347
Oslund; RMC Place; ITASCA; *192 G-8; mail Spring Lake z 56680
Osseo; Inc. Place; HENNEPIN; 191 C-2; elev. 880ft./268m.; 🅿; ★ **MPLS-**; z 55311, z 55369, z 55569; Ⓟ 2,704; © 2,434
Oster; RMC Place; WRIGHT; *193 P-8; mail Watertown z 55388; rural
Ostrander; Inc. Place; FILLMORE; 193 T-11; 🅿; z 55961; Ⓟ 276; © 212
Otisco; RMC Place; WASECA; 193 S-9; elev. 1,149ft./350m.; 🅿; z 56093; ● 100
Otisville; RMC Place; WASHINGTON; *193 O-10; elev. 791ft./241m.; ★ **MPLS-**; mail Scandia z 55073; ● 70
Otsego; Inc. Place; WRIGHT; *193 O-9; 🅿; ★ **MPLS-**; z 55301, z 55330, z 55362, z 55374 & mail Dayton z 55327, Wrenshall z 55797; Ⓟ 5,219; © 6,389
Ottawa; RMC Place; LE SUEUR; 193 Q-8; mail Le Sueur z 56058; ● 100
Otter Creek; RMC Place; CARLTON; *192 J-11; elev. 1,150ft./351m.; mail Carlton z 55718; rural
Ottertail; Inc. Place; OTTER TAIL; 193 K-4; elev. 1,355ft./413m.; 🅿; z 56571; Ⓟ 313; © 451
OTTER TAIL; 193 K-3; Ⓟ 50,714; © 57,159; ◆ 56,157
Outing; RMC Place; CASS; 192 J-8; elev. 1,320ft./402m.; 🅿; z 56662; ● 250
Owatonna; Inc. Place; ⊡ STEELE; 193 R-9; elev. 1,154ft./352m.; 🅿 🅷 ■; z 55060; Ⓟ 19,386; © 22,434; ◆ 25,027
Oxboro; RMC Place; HENNEPIN; *193 P-9; ★ **MPLS-**; mail Minneapolis z 55437; pop. incl. with Bloomington (Inc. Place)
Oxlip; RMC Place; ISANTI; *193 N-9; elev. 956ft./291m.; mail Isanti z 55040
Oylen; RMC Place; WADENA; 193 K-6; mail Verndale z 56481; ● 25

P

Paddock; OTTER TAIL; see Hillview (RMC Place)
Padua; RMC Place; STEARNS; 193 N-5; elev. 1,349ft./411m.; mail Sauk Centre z 56378; ● 25
Palisade; Inc. Place; AITKIN; 192 J-9; elev. 1,225ft./373m.; 🅿; z 56469; Ⓟ 144; © 118
Palmdale; RMC Place; CHISAGO; *193 N-11; mail Taylors Falls z 55084; rural
Palmers; RMC Place; ST. LOUIS; *192 I-12; elev. 684ft./208m.; mail Duluth z 55804
Palo; RMC Place; ST. LOUIS; *192 H-11; elev. 1,401ft./427m.; mail Aurora z 55705
Parent; RMC Place; BENTON; *193 M-8; elev. 1,121ft./342m.; mail Foley z 56329; rural
Parkers Prairie; Inc. Place; OTTER TAIL; 193 L-5; elev. 1,464ft./446m.; 🅿; z 56361; Ⓟ 956; © 991
Park Rapids; Inc. Place; ⊡ HUBBARD; 192 I-5; 🅿 🅷; z 56470; Ⓟ 2,863; © 3,276
Park View; RMC Place; POLK; *192 G-2; mail Crookston z 56716; pop. incl. with Crookston (Inc. Place)
Parkville; RMC Place; ST. LOUIS; *192 G-11; elev. 1,481ft./451m.; 🅿; z 55768; pop. incl. with Mountain Iron (Inc. Place)
Parkway Junction; RMC Place; RAMSEY; ★ **MPLS-**; pop. incl. with Saint Paul (Inc. Place)
Payne; RMC Place; ST. LOUIS; *192 I-11; elev. 1,315ft./401m.; mail Meadowlands z 55765; rural
Paynesville; Inc. Place; STEARNS; 193 N-6; elev. 1,170ft./357m.; 🅿 🅷; z 56362; Ⓟ 2,275; © 2,267
Pearl Lake; STEARNS; see Marty (RMC Place)
Pease; Inc. Place; MILLE LACS; 193 M-8; elev. 1,030ft./314m.; 🅿; z 56363; Ⓟ 178; © 163
Pelican Rapids; Inc. Place; OTTER TAIL; 192 J-3; elev. 1,309ft./399m.; 🅿; z 56572; Ⓟ 1,886; © 2,374
Pelland; RMC Place; KOOCHICHING; *192 D-9; elev. 1,111ft./339m.; mail International Falls z 56649; rural
Pemberton; Inc. Place; BLUE EARTH; 193 S-8; elev. 1,043ft./318m.; 🅿; z 56078; Ⓟ 228; © 246
Pencer; RMC Place; ROSEAU; *192 D-4; elev. 1,096ft./334m.; 🅿; z 56751; rural
Pengilly; RMC Place; ITASCA; 192 H-9; elev. 1,350ft./411m.; 🅿; z 55775; ● 850
Pennington; RMC Place; BELTRAMI; 192 H-7; located on Leech Lake Ind. Res.; elev. 1,317ft./401m.; 🅿; z 56663; ● 90
PENNINGTON; 192 F-3; Ⓟ 13,306; © 13,584; ◆ 13,724
Pennock; Inc. Place; KANDIYOHI; 193 O-5; elev. 1,131ft./345m.; 🅿; z 56279; Ⓟ 476; © 504
Pequaywan Lake; RMC Place; ST. LOUIS; *192 I-12; mail Duluth z 55801; summer pop. 120
Pequot Lakes; Inc. Place; CROW WING; 192 J-7; elev. 1,280ft./390m.; 🅿; z 56472; Ⓟ 843; © 947
Perham; Inc. Place; OTTER TAIL; 192 J-4; elev. 1,371ft./418m.; 🅿 🅷; z 56573; Ⓟ 2,075; © 2,559
Perkins; RMC Place; HOUSTON; *193 S-13; elev. 760ft./232m.; mail Houston z 55943; rural
Perley; Inc. Place; NORMAN; 192 H-2; elev. 877ft./267m.; 🅿; z 56574; Ⓟ 132; © 121
Petersburg; RMC Place; JACKSON; 193 T-6; mail Jackson z 56143; ● 35
Peterson; Inc. Place; FILLMORE; 193 S-13; elev. 761ft./232m.; 🅿; z 55962; Ⓟ 259; © 269
Petran; RMC Place; FREEBORN; *193 T-10; mail Hayward z 56043; rural
Phelps; RMC Place; OTTER TAIL; *193 K-4; mail Underwood z 56586; ● 35
Philbrook; RMC Place; TODD; *193 K-6; mail Motley z 56466; ● 75
Pickwick; RMC Place; WINONA; *193 S-13; mail Winona z 55987; ● 150
Piedmont Heights; RMC Place; ST. LOUIS; ★ **DUL**; pop. incl. with Duluth (Inc. Place)
Pierz; Inc. Place; MORRISON; 193 L-7; elev. 1,170ft./357m.; 🅿; z 56364; Ⓟ 1,014; © 1,277
Pigeon River; RMC Place; COOK; *192 A-13; mail Grand Portage z 55605; rural
Pike Lake; RMC Place; ST. LOUIS; *192 J-12; ★ **DUL**; mail Duluth z 55811; pop. incl. with Hermantown (Inc. Place)
Pillager; Inc. Place; CASS; 193 K-7; elev. 1,209ft./369m.; 🅿; z 56473; Ⓟ 306; © 420
Pillsbury; RMC Place; TODD; 193 M-6; elev. 1,183ft./361m.; mail Swanville z 56382; ● 45
Pilot Grove; RMC Place; FARIBAULT; 193 T-7; elev. 1,128ft./344m.; mail Elmore z 56027; ● 25
Pilot Mound; RMC Place; FILLMORE; *193 S-12; elev. 1,000ft./305m.; mail Chatfield z 55923
PINE; 193 K-11; Ⓟ 21,264; © 26,530; ◆ 28,380
Pine Bend; RMC Place; DAKOTA; *193 P-10; elev. 929ft./283m.; ★ **MPLS-**; mail Rosemount z 55068; pop. incl. with Rosemount (Inc. Place)
Pine Brook; RMC Place; ISANTI; *193 N-9; elev. 969ft./295m.; mail Cambridge z 55008; rural
Pine Center; RMC Place; CROW WING; 193 L-8; mail Brainerd z 56401; ● 80
Pine City; Inc. Place; ⊡ PINE; 193 M-10; elev. 950ft./290m.; 🅿; z 55063; Ⓟ 2,613; © 3,043
Pinecreek; RMC Place; ROSEAU; *192 C-4; elev. 1,047ft./319m.; mail Roseau z 56751
Pine Island; Inc. Place; GOODHUE, OLMSTED; 193 R-11; elev. 1,004ft./306m.; 🅿; z 55963; Ⓟ 2,125; © 2,337
Pine Point; CDP; BECKER; *192 I-5; © 337
Pine River; Inc. Place; CASS; 192 J-7; elev. 1,290ft./393m.; 🅿; z 56474 & mail Jenkins z 56456; Ⓟ 871; © 928
Pine Springs; Inc. Place; WASHINGTON; 191 E-10; elev. 950ft./290m.; 🅿; ★ **MPLS-**; z 55115, z 55128; Ⓟ 436; © 421
Pineville; RMC Place; ST. LOUIS; *192 G-11; elev. 1,380ft./421m.; mail Aurora z 55705
Pinewood; RMC Place; BELTRAMI; 192 G-5; elev. 1,450ft./442m.; 🅿; z 56676; ● 60
Pioneer; RMC Place; RAMSEY; *193 P-10; ★ **MPLS-**; mail Saint Paul z 55101; pop. incl. with Saint Paul (Inc. Place)
Pipestone; Inc. Place; ⊡ PIPESTONE; 193 S-2; elev. 1,738ft./530m.; 🅿 🅷; z 56164; Ⓟ 4,554; © 4,280; Ⓡ 4,384
PIPESTONE; 193 R-2; Ⓟ 10,491; © 9,895; ◆ 9,299
Pitt; RMC Place; LAKE OF THE WOODS; 192 D-6; elev. 1,112ft./339m.; 🅿; z 56623; ● 25
Plainview; Inc. Place; WABASHA; 193 R-12; elev. 1,155ft./352m.; 🅿; z 55964; Ⓟ 2,768; © 3,190
Plato; Inc. Place; MCLEOD; 193 P-8; elev. 995ft./303m.; 🅿; z 55370; Ⓟ 355; © 336
Pleasant Grove; RMC Place; OLMSTED; 193 S-11; mail Stewartville z 55976; ● 70
Pleasant Lake; RMC Place; STEARNS; *193 N-7; elev. 1,100ft./335m.; ★ **ST.CLD**; mail Saint Cloud z 56301; former incorporated place; became part of Rockville June 1, 2002; pop. incl. with Rockville (Inc. Place); Ⓟ 79; © 504
Plummer; Inc. Place; RED LAKE; 192 F-3; elev. 1,125ft./343m.; 🅿; z 56748; Ⓟ 277; © 270
Plymouth; Inc. Place; HENNEPIN; 191 E-1; elev. 1,000ft./305m.; 🅿; ★ **MPLS-**; z 55441-42, z 55446-47; Ⓟ 50,889; © 65,894; ◆ 71,657
Point Douglas; RMC Place; WASHINGTON; 193 P-10; ★ **MPLS-**; mail Hastings z 55033; ● 65
POLK; 192 F-2; Ⓟ 32,498; © 31,369; ◆ 30,840
Ponemah; CDP; BELTRAMI; 192 F-6; located on Red Lake Ind. Res.; elev. 1,192ft./363m.; 🅿; z 56666; Ⓟ 704; © 874
Ponsford; RMC Place; BECKER; 192 I-5; elev. 1,536ft./468m.; 🅿; z 56575; ● 200
POPE; 193 N-4; Ⓟ 10,745; © 11,236; ◆ 10,866
Popple Creek; RMC Place; BENTON; *193 M-8; mail Sauk Rapids z 56379
Port Cargill; RMC Place; SCOTT; *193 P-9; ★ **MPLS-**; mail Savage z 55378; pop. incl. with Savage (Inc. Place)
Porter; Inc. Place; YELLOW MEDICINE; 193 Q-3; elev. 1,200ft./366m.; 🅿; z 56280; Ⓟ 210; © 190
Post Town; RMC Place; OLMSTED; *193 R-11; ★ **ROCH**; mail Byron z 55920; rural
Potsdam; RMC Place; OLMSTED; 193 R-11; elev. 1,139ft./347m.; mail Elgin z 55932; ● 30
Powderhorn; RMC Place; HENNEPIN; *193 P-9; ★ **MPLS-**; mail Minneapolis z 55407; pop. incl. with Minneapolis (Inc. Place)
Prairie Island Indian Community; Indian Reservation; GOODHUE; mail Welch z 55089; Ⓟ 111; © 177
Prairieville; RMC Place; RICE; *193 R-10; mail Faribault z 55021
Pratt; RMC Place; STEELE; *193 S-10; mail Owatonna z 55060; ● 40
Predmore; RMC Place; OLMSTED; *193 S-11; ★ **ROCH**; mail Eyota z 55934
Preston; Inc. Place; ⊡ FILLMORE; 193 T-12; elev. 960ft./293m.; 🅿; z 55965; Ⓟ 1,530; © 1,426
Priam; RMC Place; KANDIYOHI; 193 O-5; elev. 1,110ft./338m.; mail Raymond z 56282; ● 30
Princeton; Inc. Place; MILLE LACS, SHERBURNE; 193 N-9; elev. 983ft./300m.; 🅿 🅷; z 55371; Ⓟ 3,719; © 3,933
Prinsburg; Inc. Place; KANDIYOHI; 193 P-5; elev. 1,104ft./336m.; 🅿; z 56281; Ⓟ 502; © 458
Prior Lake; Inc. Place; SCOTT; 193 P-9; elev. 960ft./293m.; 🅿; ★ **MPLS-**; z 55372, z 55379 & mail Savage z 55378; Ⓟ 11,482; © 15,917; ◆ 20,665
Proctor; Inc. Place; ST. LOUIS; 192 J-12; elev. 1,248ft./380m.; 🅿; ★ **DUL**; z 55810 & mail Duluth z 55811; Ⓟ 2,974; © 2,852
Prosit; RMC Place; ST. LOUIS; *192 I-11; mail Alborn z 55702; rural
Prosper; RMC Place; FILLMORE; 193 T-13; elev. 1,357ft./414m.; mail Mabel z 55954; ● 50
Pulaski Lake Shores; RMC Place; WRIGHT; *193 O-8; elev. 1,031ft./314m.; ★ **MPLS-**; mail Buffalo z 55313; pop. incl. with Buffalo (Inc. Place)
Puposky; RMC Place; BELTRAMI; 192 G-6; elev. 1,400ft./427m.; 🅿; z 56667; ● 35

Q

Quamba; Inc. Place; KANABEC; 193 M-9; elev. 1,020ft./311m.; mail Brook Park z 55007, Mora z 55051; Ⓟ 124; © 98

R

Racine; Inc. Place; MOWER; 193 S-11; elev. 1,295ft./395m.; 🅿; z 55967; Ⓟ 288; © 355
Radium; RMC Place; MARSHALL; 192 E-2; elev. 925ft./282m.; 🅿; z 56762; ● 30
Rainy Junction; RMC Place; ST. LOUIS; *192 H-11; mail Virginia z 55792; pop. incl. with Virginia (Inc. Place)
Ramey; RMC Place; MORRISON; 193 M-8; elev. 1,288ft./393m.; mail Foley z 56329; ● 50
Ramsey; Inc. Place; ANOKA; 193 O-9; elev. 890ft./271m.; 🅿; ★ **MPLS-**; z 55303; Ⓟ 12,408; © 18,510; ◆ 21,807
Ramsey; RMC Place; MOWER; *193 S-10; mail Austin z 55912; rural
RAMSEY; 193 O-10; Ⓟ 485,765; © 511,035; Ⓡ 511,202; ◆ 511,676
Randall; Inc. Place; MORRISON; 193 L-7; elev. 1,200ft./366m.; 🅿; z 56475; Ⓟ 571; © 535
Randolph; Inc. Place; DAKOTA; 193 Q-10; elev. 833ft./254m.; 🅿; z 55065; Ⓟ 331; © 318
Ranier; Inc. Place; KOOCHICHING; 192 D-9; elev. 1,120ft./341m.; 🅿; z 56668; Ⓟ 199; © 188
Rapidan; RMC Place; BLUE EARTH; 193 R-8; elev. 986ft./301m.; mail Mankato z 56001; ● 150
Rassat (Rasset); RMC Place; WRIGHT; *193 O-8; mail Buffalo z 55313; ● 20
Rasset; WRIGHT; see Rassat (RMC Place)
Rauch; RMC Place; KOOCHICHING; *192 F-10; mail Orr z 55771; rural
Ray; RMC Place; KOOCHICHING; 192 E-9; elev. 1,155ft./352m.; 🅿; z 56669; ● 80
Raymond; Inc. Place; KANDIYOHI; 193 O-5; elev. 1,086ft./331m.; 🅿; z 56282; Ⓟ 668; © 803
Reading; RMC Place; NOBLES; 193 T-4; elev. 1,710ft./521m.; 🅿; z 56165; ● 150
Reads Landing; RMC Place; WABASHA; 193 Q-12; elev. 688ft./210m.; 🅿; z 55968; ● 250
Redby; CDP; BELTRAMI; 192 F-6; elev. 1,200ft./366m.; 🅿; z 56670; Ⓟ 787; © 957
Red Lake; CDP; BELTRAMI; 192 F-6; located on Red Lake Ind. Res.; elev. 1,200ft./366m.; 🅿 🅷; z 56671; location of Indian Agency; Ⓟ 1,068; © 1,430
RED LAKE; 192 F-3; Ⓟ 4,525; © 4,299; ◆ 4,078
Red Lake Falls; Inc. Place; ⊡ RED LAKE; 192 F-3; elev. 1,037ft./316m.; 🅿; z 56750; Ⓟ 1,481; © 1,590
Red Lake Reservation; Indian Reservation; BELTRAMI, CLEARWATER, KOOCHICHING, LAKE OF THE WOODS, MARSHALL, PENNINGTON, POLK, RED LAKE, ROSEAU; mail Redlake z 56671; Ⓟ 2,979; © 5,162
Red Rock; RMC Place; COOK; *192 A-13; mail Grand Portage z 55605; rural
Redtop; RMC Place; AITKIN; *193 L-9; elev. 1,283ft./391m.; mail Isle z 56342
Red Wing; Inc. Place; ⊡ GOODHUE; 193 Q-11; elev. 750ft./229m.; 🅿 🅷; z 55066; Ⓟ 15,134; © 16,116
REDWOOD; 193 Q-5; Ⓟ 17,254; © 16,815; ◆ 15,184
Redwood Falls; Inc. Place; ⊡ REDWOOD; 193 Q-5; elev. 1,044ft./318m.; 🅿 🅷; z 56283; Ⓟ 4,859; © 5,459

Entries in **UPPERCASE** are counties.
Entries in **bold** have populations of 2,500 or more.
Names in parentheses are alternate names.
Inc. Place — Incorporated Place
RMC Place — Rand McNally Designated Place
CDP — Census Designated Place
MCD — Minor Civil Division

⊡ County Seat
▲ Minor Civil Division
elev. Elevation
🅿 Post Office

🅷 Hospital
🅲 College
■ Principal Business Center
★ Ranally Metro Area (RMA) Abbreviation
z Zip Code(s)

Ⓟ Previous Census Population
Ⓡ Revised Census Population
Ⓐ Annexation Population
● Rand McNally Population Estimate
© Final Census Population
Ⓢ Special Census Population
◆ Estimated Population

For additional definitions see Glossary, Volume 1, and Introduction, Volume 2.

Reformatory; RMC Place; SHERBURNE; ★ **ST.CLD**; mail Saint Cloud z 56301; pop. incl. with Saint Cloud (Inc. Place)
Regal; Inc. Place; KANDIYOHI; **193** N-6; elev. 1,219ft./372m.; mail Belgrade z 56312; Ⓟ 51; © 40
Remer; Inc. Place; CASS; **192** I-8; elev. 1,340ft./408m.; 🅿; z 56672; Ⓟ 342; © 372
Reno; RMC Place; HOUSTON; **193** T-14; mail Brownsville z 55919; ● 40
Renova; RMC Place; MOWER; ***193** S-11; mail Dexter z 55926; rural
Renville; Inc. Place; RENVILLE; **193** P-5; elev. 1,069ft./326m.; 🅿; z 56284; Ⓟ 1,315; © 1,323
RENVILLE; **193** Q-6; Ⓟ 17,673; © 17,154; ◆ 15,713
Revere; Inc. Place; REDWOOD; **193** R-5; elev. 1,151ft./351m.; 🅿; z 56166; Ⓟ 117; © 100
Reynolds; TODD; see Gutches Grove (RMC Place)
Rice; Inc. Place; BENTON; **193** M-7; elev. 1,063ft./324m.; 🅿; ★ **ST.CLD**; z 56367; Ⓟ 610; © 711
RICE; **193** Q-9; Ⓟ 49,183; © 56,665; ◆ 62,807
Riceford; RMC Place; HOUSTON; **193** T-13; elev. 1,019ft./311m.; mail Mabel z 55954; ● 20
Rice Lake; CDP-Census Area Only; CLEARWATER; ***192** H-4; © 226
Rice Street; RMC Place; RAMSEY; ***193** O-10; ★ **MPLS-**; mail Saint Paul z 55101, z 55103, z 55117; pop. incl. with Saint Paul (Inc. Place)
Richfield; Inc. Place; HENNEPIN; **191** H-4; elev. 842ft./257m.; 🅿 🅲 1,069 ■; ★ **MPLS-**; z 55423; Ⓟ 35,710; © 34,439; Ⓡ 34,310; ◆ 34,125
Richmond; Inc. Place; STEARNS; **193** N-7; elev. 1,119ft./341m.; 🅿; z 56368 & mail Roscoe z 56371; Ⓟ 965; © 1,213
Rich Valley; RMC Place; DAKOTA; ***193** P-10; elev. 859ft./262m.; ★ **MPLS-**; mail South Saint Paul z 55075; pop. incl. with Rosemount (Inc. Place)
Richville; Inc. Place; OTTER TAIL; **193** K-4; elev. 1,354ft./413m.; 🅿; z 56576; Ⓟ 121; © 124
Richwood; RMC Place; BECKER; **192** I-4; elev. 1,476ft./450m.; 🅿; z 56577; ● 100
Ridgeway; RMC Place; WINONA; **193** S-13; mail Houston z 55943; ● 40
Rindal; RMC Place; NORMAN, POLK; **192** H-3; elev. 1,158ft./353m.; mail Fertile z 56540; ● 25
Riverside; RMC Place; HENNEPIN; ***193** P-9; ★ **MPLS-**; mail Minneapolis z 55454; pop. incl. with Minneapolis (Inc. Place)
Riverside; RMC Place; ST. LOUIS; ***192** J-12; ★ **DUL**; pop. incl. with Duluth (Inc. Place)
Riverside Heights; RMC Place; FARIBAULT; ***193** T-7; mail Blue Earth z 56013; ● 50
Riverton; Inc. Place; CROW WING; **193** K-8; elev. 1,228ft./374m.; 🅿; z 56455; Ⓟ 122; © 115
Riverview; RMC Place; RAMSEY; ***193** P-10; ★ **MPLS-**; mail Saint Paul z 55107; pop. incl. with Saint Paul (Inc. Place)
Robbin; RMC Place; KITTSON; **192** D-1; mail Drayton z 58225; ● 30
Robbinsdale; Inc. Place; HENNEPIN; **191** E-3; elev. 881ft./269m.; 🅿 🅷; ★ **MPLS-**; z 55422; Ⓟ 14,396; © 14,123
Robinson; RMC Place; ST. LOUIS; ***192** F-12; elev. 1,480ft./451m.; mail Ely z 55731; rural
Rochert; RMC Place; BECKER; **192** J-4; elev. 1,450ft./442m.; 🅿; z 56578; ● 100
Rochester; Inc. Place; ⊡ OLMSTED; **193** S-11; elev. 1,006ft./307m.; 🅿 🅷 🅲 800 ■; ★ **ROCH**; z 55901-06; Ⓟ 70,745; © 85,806; ◆ 103,354
ROCK; **193** S-2; Ⓟ 9,806; © 9,721; ◆ 9,571
Rock Creek; Inc. Place; PINE; **193** M-10; elev. 938ft./286m.; 🅿; z 55067; Ⓟ 1,040; © 1,119
Rock Dell; RMC Place; OLMSTED; **193** S-11; mail Byron z 55920; ● 40
Rockford; Inc. Place; WRIGHT, HENNEPIN; **193** O-8; elev. 916ft./279m.; 🅿; ★ **MPLS-**; z 55373, z 55572, z 55577; Ⓟ 2,665; © 3,484
Rockville; Inc. Place; STEARNS; **193** N-7; elev. 1,084ft./330m.; 🅿; z 56369; includes Pleasant Lake annexed June 1, 2002; Ⓟ 579; © 749; Ⓐ 1,253
Rogers; Inc. Place; HENNEPIN; **193** O-9; 🅿; ★ **MPLS-**; z 55374; Ⓟ 698; © 3,588
Rollag; RMC Place; CLAY; **192** J-3; elev. 1,366ft./416m.; 🅿; z 56549; ● 30
Rollingstone; Inc. Place; WINONA; **193** R-13; elev. 759ft./231m.; 🅿; z 55969; Ⓟ 697; © 697
Rollins; RMC Place; ST. LOUIS; ***192** H-12; elev. 1,504ft./458m.; mail Brimson z 55602; rural
Ronneby; Inc. Place; BENTON; **193** M-8; elev. 1,120ft./341m.; mail Foley z 56329; Ⓟ 58; © 16
Roosevelt; Inc. Place; ROSEAU, LAKE OF THE WOODS; ***192** C-5; elev. 1,163ft./354m.; 🅿; z 56673, z 56682; Ⓟ 180; © 166
Roscoe (Roscoe Center); RMC Place; GOODHUE; ***193** R-10; mail Wanamingo z 55983
Roscoe; Inc. Place; STEARNS; **193** N-6; elev. 1,161ft./354m.; 🅿; z 56371; Ⓟ 141; © 116
Roscoe Center; GOODHUE; see Roscoe (RMC Place)
Roseau; Inc. Place; ⊡ ROSEAU; **192** C-4; elev. 1,048ft./319m.; 🅿 🅷; z 56751; Ⓟ 2,396; © 2,756
ROSEAU; **192** D-4; Ⓟ 15,026; © 16,338; ◆ 15,642
Rose City; RMC Place; DOUGLAS; **193** L-5; elev. 1,431ft./436m.; mail Eagle Bend z 56446; ● 40
Rose Creek; Inc. Place; MOWER; **193** T-10; elev. 1,250ft./381m.; 🅿; z 55970; Ⓟ 363; © 354
Roseland; RMC Place; KANDIYOHI; **193** P-5; mail Blomkest z 56216; ● 250
Rosemount; Inc. Place; DAKOTA; **193** P-10; elev. 970ft./296m.; 🅿; ★ **MPLS-**; z 55068; Ⓟ 8,622; © 14,619; ◆ 18,106
Rosen; RMC Place; LAC QUI PARLE; **193** O-2; mail Bellingham z 56212; ● 40
Rosendale; RMC Place; MEEKER; ***193** O-6; elev. 1,178ft./359m.; mail Grove City z 56243
Roseport; RMC Place; DAKOTA; ***193** P-10; ★ **MPLS-**; mail South Saint Paul z 55075; pop. incl. with Inver Grove Heights (Inc. Place)
Roseville; Inc. Place; RAMSEY; **191** E-7; elev. 950ft./290m.; 🅿 ■; ★ **MPLS-**; z 55113, z 55126 & mail Saint Paul z 55108, z 55112; Ⓟ 33,485; © 33,690; ◆ 32,328
Rosewood; RMC Place; MARSHALL; **192** E-3; mail Thief River Falls z 56701; ● 25
Ross; RMC Place; ROSEAU; **192** C-4; elev. 1,035ft./315m.; 🅿; z 56751; ● 20
Rossburg; RMC Place; AITKIN; ***193** K-9; elev. 1,239ft./378m.; mail Aitkin z 56431; rural
Rothsay; Inc. Place; WILKIN, OTTER TAIL; **193** K-3; elev. 1,209ft./369m.; 🅿; z 56579; Ⓟ 443; © 497
Round Lake; Inc. Place; NOBLES; **193** T-4; elev. 1,550ft./472m.; 🅿; z 56167; Ⓟ 463; © 424
Round Prairie; RMC Place; TODD; ***193** M-6; mail Long Prairie z 56347; ● 30
Rowena; RMC Place; REDWOOD; ***193** Q-5; mail Wabasso z 56293; rural
Rowland; RMC Place; HENNEPIN; ***193** P-9; ★ **MPLS-**; mail Eden Prairie z 55344; pop. incl. with Eden Prairie (Inc. Place)
Royalton; Inc. Place; MORRISON, BENTON; **193** M-7; elev. 1,080ft./329m.; 🅿; z 56373; Ⓟ 802; © 816
Roy Lake; RMC Place; CLEARWATER, MAHNOMEN; **192** H-4; elev. 1,506ft./459m.; mail Mahnomen z 56557; ● 100
Ruby Junction; RMC Place; ST. LOUIS; ***192** H-10; mail Hibbing z 55746; pop. incl. with Hibbing (Inc. Place)
Rush City; Inc. Place; CHISAGO; **193** M-10; elev. 917ft./280m.; 🅿 🅷; z 55069 & mail Rock Creek z 55067; Ⓟ 1,497; © 2,102
Rushford; Inc. Place; FILLMORE; **193** S-13; elev. 726ft./221m.; 🅿; z 55971; Ⓟ 1,485; © 1,696
Rushford Village; Inc. Place; FILLMORE; ***193** S-13; elev. 800ft./244m.; 🅿; z 55962, z 55971; Ⓟ 705; © 714
Rushmore; Inc. Place; NOBLES; **193** T-4; elev. 1,666ft./508m.; 🅿; z 56168; Ⓟ 381; © 376
Rush Point; RMC Place; CHISAGO; **193** M-10; elev. 952ft./290m.; mail Stanchfield z 55080; ● 60
Rush River; RMC Place; SIBLEY; ***193** Q-8; elev. 948ft./289m.; mail Le Sueur z 56058
Ruskin; RMC Place; RICE; ***193** R-10; mail Faribault z 55021; rural
Russell; Inc. Place; LYON; **193** R-3; elev. 1,527ft./465m.; 🅿; z 56169; Ⓟ 394; © 371
Rustad; RMC Place; CLAY; **192** J-2; mail Moorhead z 56560; ● 40
Ruthton; Inc. Place; PIPESTONE; **193** R-3; elev. 1,732ft./528m.; 🅿; z 56170; Ⓟ 328; © 284
Rutledge; Inc. Place; PINE; **193** L-10; elev. 1,032ft./315m.; 🅿; z 55795; Ⓟ 152; © 196

S

Sabin; Inc. Place; CLAY; **192** J-2; elev. 925ft./282m.; 🅿; z 56580; Ⓟ 495; © 421
Sacred Heart; Inc. Place; RENVILLE; **193** P-5; elev. 1,070ft./326m.; 🅿; z 56285; Ⓟ 603; © 549
Saga Hill; RMC Place; HENNEPIN; ***193** P-8; elev. 1,000ft./305m.; ★ **MPLS-**; mail Crystal Bay z 55323; pop. incl. with Orono (Inc. Place)
Saginaw (Grand Lake); RMC Place; ST. LOUIS; **192** J-11; elev. 1,337ft./408m.; 🅿; z 55779; ● 100
Saint Anna; RMC Place; STEARNS; ***193** M-7; mail Avon z 56310; ● 50
Saint Anthony; Inc. Place; HENNEPIN, RAMSEY; **191** E-5; elev. 920ft./280m.; 🅿; ★ **MPLS-**; z 55418 & mail Minneapolis z 55421; Ⓟ 7,727; © 8,012
Saint Anthony; Inc. Place; STEARNS; **193** M-6; elev. 1,266ft./386m.; mail Albany z 56307; Ⓟ 81; © 90
Saint Augusta (Ventura); Inc. Place; STEARNS; **193** N-7; 🅿; ★ **ST.CLD**; z 55320, z 55353, z 55382, z 56301; incorporated May 2, 2000 as Ventura; not reported in 2000 Census; name changed to St. Augusta; ● 2,700
Saint Benedict; RMC Place; SCOTT; ***193** Q-9; elev. 933ft./284m.; mail Jordan z 55352, New Prague z 56071; ● 30
Saint Bonifacius; Inc. Place; HENNEPIN; **193** P-8; elev. 970ft./296m.; 🅿 🅲 1,344; ★ **MPLS-**; z 55375; Ⓟ 1,180; © 1,873
Saint Charles; Inc. Place; WINONA; **193** S-12; elev. 1,142ft./348m.; 🅿; z 55972; Ⓟ 2,642; © 3,295
Saint Clair; Inc. Place; BLUE EARTH; **193** R-8; elev. 1,000ft./305m.; 🅿; z 56080; Ⓟ 633; © 827
Saint Clair; RMC Place; RAMSEY; ★ **MPLS-**; mail Saint Paul z 55116; pop. incl. with Saint Paul (Inc. Place)
Saint Cloud; Inc. Place; ⊡ STEARNS, BENTON, SHERBURNE; **193** N-7; elev. 1,041ft./317m.; 🅿 🅷 🅲 15,400 ■; ★ **ST.CLD**; z 56301-04, z 56372, z 56393, z 56395-99 & mail Waite Park z 56387-88; Ⓟ 48,812; © 59,107; Ⓡ 59,111; ◆ 66,055
Saint Croix Junction; RMC Place; WASHINGTON; ★ **MPLS-**; mail Hastings z 55033; pop. incl. with Hastings (Inc. Place)
Saint Francis; Inc. Place; ANOKA; **193** N-9; elev. 918ft./280m.; 🅿; ★ **MPLS-**; z 55070; Ⓟ 2,538; © 4,910
Saint Francis; RMC Place; STEARNS; ***193** M-6; mail Freeport z 56331
Saint George; RMC Place; NICOLLET; **193** Q-6; mail New Ulm z 56073; ● 60
Saint Henry; RMC Place; LE SUEUR; ***193** Q-8; elev. 1,010ft./308m.; mail Le Center z 56057; ● 30
Saint Hilaire; Inc. Place; PENNINGTON; **192** F-3; elev. 1,089ft./332m.; 🅿; z 56754; Ⓟ 298; © 272
Saint James; Inc. Place; ⊡ WATONWAN; **193** S-6; elev. 1,082ft./330m.; 🅿 🅷; z 56081; Ⓟ 4,364; © 4,695
Saint John's University; STEARNS; see Collegeville (RMC Place)
Saint Joseph; Inc. Place; STEARNS; **193** N-7; elev. 1,100ft./335m.; 🅿 🅲 2,027; ★ **ST.CLD**; z 56374 & mail Saint Stephen z 56375; Ⓟ 3,294; © 4,681
Saint Killian; RMC Place; NOBLES; ***193** S-3; mail Wilmont z 56185; ● 40
Saint Leo; Inc. Place; YELLOW MEDICINE; **193** P-3; elev. 1,119ft./341m.; 🅿; z 56264; Ⓟ 111; © 106
ST. LOUIS; **192** H-10; Ⓟ 198,213; © 200,528; ◆ 197,434
Saint Louis Park; Inc. Place; HENNEPIN; **191** G-3; elev. 906ft./276m.; 🅿 🅷 ■; ★ **MPLS-**; z 55416, z 55424, z 55426, z 55436; Ⓟ 43,787; © 44,126; Ⓡ 44,102; ◆ 45,377
Saint Martin; Inc. Place; STEARNS; **193** N-6; elev. 1,250ft./381m.; 🅿; z 56376; Ⓟ 274; © 278
Saint Marys Point; Inc. Place; WASHINGTON; ***193** P-10; elev. 693ft./211m.; ★ **MPLS-**; mail Lakeland z 55043; Ⓟ 339; © 344
Saint Mathias; RMC Place; CROW WING; ***193** L-7; elev. 1,200ft./366m.; mail Fort Ripley z 56449; rural
Saint Michael; Inc. Place; WRIGHT; **193** O-8; elev. 960ft./293m.; 🅿; ★ **MPLS-**; z 55376; Ⓟ 2,506; © 9,099
Saint Nicholas; RMC Place; STEARNS; **193** N-7; mail Watkins z 55389; ● 50
Saint Patrick; RMC Place; SCOTT; **193** Q-9; elev. 1,005ft./306m.; mail New Prague z 56071; ● 50
Saint Paul; Inc. Place; **STATE CAPITAL**; ⊡ RAMSEY; **193** P-10; elev. 874ft./266m.; 🅿 🅷 🅲 43,850 ■; ★ **MPLS-**; z 55101-30, z 55133, z 55144-46, z 55150, z 55155, z 55164-66, z 55168-72, z 55175, z 55187-88; Ⓟ 272,235; © 287,151; Ⓡ 286,840; ◆ 301,792
Saint Paul Park; Inc. Place; WASHINGTON; **193** P-10; elev. 750ft./229m.; 🅿; ★ **MPLS-**; z 55071; Ⓟ 4,965; © 5,070
Saint Peter; Inc. Place; ⊡ NICOLLET; **193** R-8; elev. 770ft./235m.; 🅿 🅷 🅲 2,618; z 56082; Ⓟ 9,421; © 9,747; Ⓡ 9,761
Saint Rosa; Inc. Place; STEARNS; **193** M-6; elev. 1,260ft./384m.; mail Freeport z 56331; Ⓟ 75; © 44
Saint Stephen; Inc. Place; STEARNS; **193** M-7; elev. 1,200ft./366m.; 🅿; z 56375; Ⓟ 607; © 860
Saint Thomas; RMC Place; LE SUEUR; **193** Q-8; mail Le Sueur z 56058; ● 40
Saint Vincent; Inc. Place; KITTSON; **192** C-1; elev. 780ft./238m.; 🅿; z 56755; Ⓟ 116; © 117
Saint Wendel; RMC Place; STEARNS; **193** M-7; elev. 1,210ft./369m.; mail Avon z 56310; ● 50
Salem Corners; RMC Place; OLMSTED; **193** S-11; mail Byron z 55920; ● 30
Salol; RMC Place; ROSEAU; **192** C-4; elev. 1,077ft./328m.; 🅿; z 56756; ● 80
Sanborn; Inc. Place; REDWOOD; **193** R-5; elev. 1,100ft./335m.; 🅿; z 56083; Ⓟ 459; © 434
Sandstone; Inc. Place; PINE; **193** L-10; elev. 1,060ft./323m.; 🅿 🅷; z 55072; Ⓟ 2,057; © 1,549; Ⓡ 2,396
Sandy Lake Reservation; Indian Reservation; AITKIN; © 70
Santiago; RMC Place; SHERBURNE; **193** N-8; elev. 1,020ft./311m.; 🅿; z 55377; ● 75
Saratoga; RMC Place; WINONA; ***193** S-12; mail Saint Charles z 55972; ● 30
Sargeant; Inc. Place; MOWER; **193** S-10; elev. 1,390ft./424m.; 🅿; z 55973; Ⓟ 78; © 76
Sartell; Inc. Place; STEARNS, BENTON; **193** M-7; elev. 1,022ft./312m.; 🅿; ★ **ST.CLD**; z 56377; Ⓟ 5,393; © 9,641
Sauk Centre; Inc. Place; STEARNS; **193** M-6; elev. 1,246ft./380m.; 🅿 🅷; z 56378, z 56389; Ⓟ 3,581; © 3,930
Sauk Rapids; Inc. Place; BENTON; **193** N-7; elev. 1,080ft./329m.; 🅿; ★ **ST.CLD**; z 56379; Ⓟ 7,825; © 10,213
Saum; RMC Place; BELTRAMI; **192** F-6; elev. 1,200ft./366m.; 🅿; z 56650; ● 40
Savage; Inc. Place; SCOTT; **193** P-9; elev. 730ft./223m.; 🅿; ★ **MPLS-**; z 55378 & mail Prior Lake z 55372; Ⓟ 9,906; © 21,115; ◆ 30,728
Sawbill Landing; RMC Place; LAKE; ***192** G-13
Sawyer; RMC Place; CARLTON; **192** J-11; located on Fond du Lac Ind. Res.; elev. 1,330ft./405m.; 🅿; z 55780; ● 200
Scandia; Inc. Place; WASHINGTON; **193** O-10; elev. 1,034ft./315m.; 🅿; ★ **MPLS-**; z 55073; incorporated January 1, 2007; not reoported in 2000 Census; ● 3,900
Scandia Valley; RMC Place; MORRISON; ***193** L-6; elev. 1,291ft./393m.; mail Cushing z 56443; rural
Scanlon; Inc. Place; CARLTON; **192** J-11; elev. 1,200ft./366m.; ★ **DUL**; mail Cloquet z 55720; Ⓟ 878; © 838
Schley; RMC Place; CASS; ***192** H-7; elev. 1,309ft./399m.; mail Cass Lake z 56633; rural
Schroeder; RMC Place; COOK; **192** C-11; elev. 701ft./214m.; 🅿; z 55613; ● 350
SCOTT; **193** Q-9; Ⓟ 57,846; © 89,498; ◆ 131,074
Scotts Corner; RMC Place; CARLTON; ***192** J-11; elev. 1,106ft./337m.; mail Carlton z 55718, Wrenshall z 55797; rural
Seaforth; Inc. Place; REDWOOD; **193** Q-5; elev. 1,060ft./323m.; 🅿; z 56287; Ⓟ 87; © 77
Searles; RMC Place; BROWN; **193** R-7; elev. 1,000ft./305m.; 🅿; z 56073, z 56084; ● 150
Sebeka; Inc. Place; WADENA; **192** J-5; elev. 1,385ft./422m.; 🅿; z 56477; Ⓟ 662; © 710
Section Thirty; RMC Place; LAKE; ***192** F-12; mail Ely z 55731; ● 50
Sedan; Inc. Place; POPE; **193** N-5; elev. 1,350ft./411m.; 🅿; z 56334; Ⓟ 63; © 65
Sedil; RMC Place; DAKOTA; ***193** P-10; ★ **MPLS-**; mail Rosemount z 55068; ● 50
Shafer; Inc. Place; CHISAGO; **193** N-10; elev. 942ft./287m.; 🅿; z 55074; Ⓟ 368; © 343
Shakopee; Inc. Place; ⊡ SCOTT; **193** P-9; elev. 791ft./241m.; 🅿 🅷; ★ **MPLS-**; z 55372, z 55379; Ⓟ 11,739; © 20,568; ◆ 36,548
Shakopee Mdewakanton Sioux Community; Indian Reservation; SCOTT; © 266
Shaw; RMC Place; ST. LOUIS; ***192** I-11; mail Canyon z 55717; rural
Sheffield Mill; RMC Place; RICE; mail Faribault z 55021; pop. incl. with Faribault (Inc. Place)
Sheldon; RMC Place; HOUSTON; **193** T-13; mail Caledonia z 55921; ● 50
Shelly; Inc. Place; NORMAN; **192** H-2; elev. 865ft./264m.; 🅿; z 56581; Ⓟ 225; © 266
Sherack; RMC Place; POLK; ***192** F-2; mail Euclid z 56722; rural
Sherburn; Inc. Place; MARTIN; **193** T-6; elev. 1,290ft./393m.; 🅿; z 56171; Ⓟ 1,105; © 1,082
SHERBURNE; **193** N-8; Ⓟ 41,945; © 64,417; Ⓡ 64,415; ◆ 88,586
Shermans Corner; ST. LOUIS; see Angora (RMC Place)
Sheshebee; RMC Place; AITKIN; ***192** J-9; mail McGregor z 55760; summer pop. 250; ● 100
Shevlin; Inc. Place; CLEARWATER; **192** G-5; elev. 1,460ft./445m.; 🅿; z 56676; Ⓟ 157; © 160
Shieldsville; RMC Place; RICE; ***193** Q-9; mail Faribault z 55021
Shooks; RMC Place; BELTRAMI; **192** F-7; elev. 1,358ft./414m.; mail Northome z 56661; ● 30
Shoreham; RMC Place; BECKER; ***192** J-4; mail Detroit Lakes z 56501; summer pop. 150
Shoreham; RMC Place; HENNEPIN; ★ **MPLS-**; pop. incl. with Minneapolis (Inc. Place)
Shoreview; Inc. Place; RAMSEY; **191** D-7; elev. 950ft./290m.; 🅿; ★ **MPLS-**; z 55126; Ⓟ 24,587; © 25,924; ◆ 25,772
Shorewood; Inc. Place; HENNEPIN; **193** P-9; elev. 982ft./299m.; ★ **MPLS-**; mail Excelsior z 55331, Mound z 55364; Ⓟ 5,917; © 7,400
Shotley; RMC Place; BELTRAMI; ***192** F-6; elev. 1,210ft./369m.; mail Kelliher z 56650; rural
Shovel Lake; RMC Place; AITKIN; ***192** I-8; elev. 1,340ft./408m.; mail Swatara z 55785; rural
SIBLEY; **193** Q-7; Ⓟ 14,366; © 15,356; ◆ 14,957
Side Lake; RMC Place; ST. LOUIS; **192** G-10; elev. 1,379ft./420m.; 🅿; z 55781; ● 180
Silica; RMC Place; ST. LOUIS; **192** H-10; mail Hibbing z 55746; ● 50
Silo; RMC Place; WINONA; mail Lewiston z 55952; rural
Silver Bay; Inc. Place; LAKE; **192** H-14; elev. 900ft./274m.; 🅿; z 55614; Ⓟ 1,894; © 2,068
Silver Corners; RMC Place; BENTON; ***193** M-8; mail Rice z 56367; rural
Silver Creek; RMC Place; LAKE; ***192** I-13; mail Two Harbors z 55616; rural
Silver Creek; RMC Place; WRIGHT; **193** N-8; elev. 980ft./299m.; 🅿; z 55380; ● 170
Silverdale; RMC Place; KOOCHICHING; ***192** F-10; elev. 1,311ft./400m.; mail Orr z 55771; rural
Silver Lake; Inc. Place; MCLEOD; **193** P-7; elev. 1,050ft./320m.; 🅿; z 55381; Ⓟ 764; © 761
Simpson; RMC Place; OLMSTED; **193** S-11; mail Rochester z 55904; ● 90
Sioux Valley; RMC Place; JACKSON; **193** T-5; elev. 1,474ft./449m.; mail Lake Park z 51347; ● 30
Skibo; RMC Place; ST. LOUIS; ***192** H-12; mail Hoyt Lakes z 55750; rural
Skyburg; RMC Place; GOODHUE; ***193** R-10; mail Kenyon z 55946
Skyline; Inc. Place; BLUE EARTH; ***193** R-8; elev. 850ft./259m.; ★ **MNKT**; mail Mankato z 56001; Ⓟ 272; © 330
Slayton; Inc. Place; ⊡ MURRAY; **193** S-4; elev. 1,608ft./490m.; 🅿 🅷; z 56172; Ⓟ 2,147; © 2,072
Sleepy Eye; Inc. Place; BROWN; **193** R-6; elev. 1,030ft./314m.; 🅿 🅷; z 56085; Ⓟ 3,694; © 3,515; Ⓡ 3,644
Sletten; RMC Place; POLK; mail McIntosh z 56556; rural
Smiths Mill; RMC Place; BLUE EARTH, WASECA; **193** R-8; mail Janesville z 56048; ● 50
Smithville; RMC Place; ST. LOUIS; ***192** J-12; elev. 710ft./216m.; ★ **DUL**; pop. incl. with Duluth (Inc. Place)
Snellman; RMC Place; BECKER; **192** I-5; mail Osage z 56570; ● 20
Sobieski; Inc. Place; MORRISON; **193** M-7; elev. 1,133ft./345m.; mail Little Falls z 56345; Ⓟ 199; © 196
Soderville; RMC Place; ANOKA; ***193** O-9; elev. 900ft./274m.; ★ **MPLS-**; mail Andover z 55304; pop. incl. with Ham Lake (Inc. Place)
Sogn; RMC Place; GOODHUE; **193** Q-10; mail Dennison z 55018; ● 30
Solway; Inc. Place; BELTRAMI; **192** G-5; elev. 1,450ft./442m.; 🅿; z 56678 & mail Wilton z 56687; Ⓟ 74; © 69
Soudan; RMC Place; ST. LOUIS; **192** G-11; elev. 1,480ft./451m.; 🅿; z 55782; ● 900
South Bend; RMC Place; BLUE EARTH; ***193** R-8; elev. 950ft./290m.; ★ **MNKT**; mail Mankato z 56001; ● 110
South Branch; RMC Place; WATONWAN; ***193** S-6; elev. 1,115ft./340m.; mail Saint James z 56081; rural
Southdale; RMC Place; HENNEPIN; ★ **MPLS-**; mail Minneapolis z 55435; pop. incl. with Edina (Inc. Place)
South Haven; Inc. Place; WRIGHT; **193** O-7; elev. 1,100ft./335m.; 🅿; z 55382; Ⓟ 193; © 204
South International Falls; RMC Place; KOOCHICHING; ***192** D-9; elev. 1,150ft./351m.; 🅿; z 56679; pop. incl. with International Falls (Inc. Place)
South Minneapolis; RMC Place; HENNEPIN; ★ **MPLS-**; mail Minneapolis z 55408; pop. incl. with Minneapolis (Inc. Place)
South Saint Paul; Inc. Place; DAKOTA; **191** H-8; elev. 800ft./244m.; 🅿; ★ **MPLS-**; z 55075-77; Ⓟ 20,197; © 20,167; ◆ 19,807
Spafford; RMC Place; JACKSON; ***193** T-5; mail Worthington z 56187
Sparta; RMC Place; ST. LOUIS; ***192** H-11; pop. incl. with Gilbert (Inc. Place)
Spectacle Lake; RMC Place; ISANTI; ***193** N-9; mail Cambridge z 55008; ● 100
Spicer; Inc. Place; KANDIYOHI; **193** O-6; elev. 1,171ft./357m.; 🅿; z 56288; Ⓟ 1,020; © 1,126
Spring Creek; RMC Place; YELLOW MEDICINE; ***193** P-4; mail Clarkfield z 56223; rural
Springfield; Inc. Place; BROWN; **193** R-5; elev. 1,026ft./313m.; 🅿 🅷; z 56087; Ⓟ 2,173; © 2,215
Spring Grove; Inc. Place; HOUSTON; **193** T-13; elev. 1,320ft./402m.; 🅿 🅷; z 55974; Ⓟ 1,153; © 1,304
Spring Hill; Inc. Place; STEARNS; **193** N-6; elev. 1,250ft./381m.; mail Melrose z 56352; Ⓟ 77; © 55
Spring Lake; RMC Place; ISANTI; ***193** N-10; elev. 933ft./284m.; mail North Branch z 55056; rural
Spring Lake; RMC Place; ITASCA; **192** G-8; elev. 1,350ft./411m.; 🅿; z 56680; ● 50
Spring Lake Park; Inc. Place; ANOKA, RAMSEY; **191** C-5; elev. 910ft./277m.; 🅿; ★ **MPLS-**; z 55432; Ⓟ 6,532; © 6,772
Spring Park; Inc. Place; HENNEPIN; ***193** P-9; elev. 950ft./290m.; 🅿; ★ **MPLS-**; z 55384; Ⓟ 1,571; © 1,717
Springsteel Island; RMC Place; ROSEAU; ***192** C-5; elev. 1,067ft./325m.; mail Warroad z 56763; summer pop. 75
Springvale; RMC Place; ISANTI; ***193** M-9; elev. 935ft./285m.; mail Stanchfield z 55080; ● 45
Spring Valley; Inc. Place; FILLMORE; **193** T-11; elev. 1,729ft./527m.; 🅿 🅷; z 55975; Ⓟ 2,461; © 2,518
Spruce Center; RMC Place; DOUGLAS; ***193** L-5; mail Miltona z 56354; ● 25
Squaw Lake; Inc. Place; ITASCA; **192** G-7; located on Leech Lake Ind. Res.; elev. 1,347ft./411m.; 🅿; z 56681; Ⓟ 139; © 99
Stacy; Inc. Place; CHISAGO; **193** N-10; elev. 893ft./272m.; 🅿; ★ **MPLS-**; z 55078-79; Ⓟ 1,081; © 1,278
Stanchfield; RMC Place; ISANTI; **193** M-9; elev. 940ft./287m.; 🅿; z 55080; ● 200
Stanley; RMC Place; ISANTI; ***193** N-10; elev. 984ft./300m.; mail Cambridge z 55008; rural
Stanton; RMC Place; GOODHUE; **193** Q-10; elev. 917ft./280m.; 🅿; z 55018; ● 50
Staples; Inc. Place; TODD, WADENA; **193** K-6; elev. 1,227ft./374m.; 🅿 🅷; z 56479; Ⓟ 2,754; © 3,104
Starbuck; Inc. Place; POPE; **193** N-4; elev. 1,162ft./354m.; 🅿 🅷; z 56381; Ⓟ 1,143; © 1,314
Stark; RMC Place; CHISAGO; **193** N-10; mail Harris z 55032; ● 75
STEARNS; **193** N-6; Ⓟ 118,791; © 133,166; Ⓡ 133,167; ◆ 149,872
STEELE; **193** S-9; Ⓟ 30,729; © 33,680; ◆ 36,648
Steele Center; RMC Place; STEELE; ***193** S-9; mail Owatonna z 55060; rural
Steelton; RMC Place; ST. LOUIS; ***192** J-12; elev. 664ft./202m.; ★ **DUL**; mail Duluth z 55808; pop. incl. with Duluth (Inc. Place)
Steen; Inc. Place; ROCK; **193** T-3; elev. 1,490ft./454m.; 🅿; z 56173; Ⓟ 176; © 182
Stephen; Inc. Place; MARSHALL; **192** D-2; elev. 828ft./252m.; 🅿; z 56757; Ⓟ 707; © 708
Sterling Center; RMC Place; BLUE EARTH; ***193** S-8; elev. 1,009ft./308m.; mail Amboy z 56010
STEVENS; **193** N-3; Ⓟ 10,634; © 10,053; ◆ 9,492
Stewart; RMC Place; LAKE; ***192** I-13; mail Two Harbors z 55616; rural
Stewart; Inc. Place; MCLEOD; **193** P-7; elev. 1,062ft./324m.; 🅿; z 55385; Ⓟ 566; © 564
Stewartville; Inc. Place; OLMSTED; **193** S-11; elev. 1,240ft./378m.; 🅿; ★ **ROCH**; z 55976; Ⓟ 4,520; © 5,411
Stillwater; Inc. Place; ⊡ WASHINGTON; **193** O-10; elev. 700ft./213m.; 🅿 🅷; ★ **MPLS-**; z 55082-83; Ⓟ 13,882; © 15,143; Ⓡ 15,323
Stockholm; RMC Place; WRIGHT; **193** O-7; mail Cokato z 55321; ● 25
Stockton; Inc. Place; WINONA; **193** R-13; elev. 757ft./231m.; 🅿; z 55988; Ⓟ 529; © 682
Storden; Inc. Place; COTTONWOOD; **193** R-5; elev. 1,400ft./427m.; 🅿; z 56174; Ⓟ 283; © 274
Strandquist; Inc. Place; MARSHALL; **192** D-3; elev. 1,062ft./324m.; 🅿; z 56758; Ⓟ 98; © 88
Strathcona; Inc. Place; ROSEAU; **192** D-3; elev. 1,124ft./343m.; 🅿; z 56759; Ⓟ 40; © 29
Strout; RMC Place; MEEKER; ***193** O-6; elev. 1,179ft./359m.; mail Litchfield z 55355; rural
Stubbs Bay; RMC Place; HENNEPIN; ***193** P-9; elev. 935ft./285m.; ★ **MPLS-**; mail Long Lake z 55356; pop. incl. with Orono (Inc. Place)
Sturgeon; RMC Place; ST. LOUIS; ***192** G-10; elev. 1,296ft./395m.; mail Angora z 55703; ● 30
Sturgeon Lake; Inc. Place; PINE; **193** K-10; elev. 1,074ft./327m.; 🅿; z 55783; Ⓟ 230; © 347
Sugar Loaf; RMC Place; WINONA; ***193** R-13; mail Winona z 55987; pop. incl. with Winona (Inc. Place)
Summit; RMC Place; STEELE; ***193** S-10; mail Blackduck z 56630, Blooming Prairie z 55917; rural
Sumter; RMC Place; MCLEOD; ***193** P-7; mail Glencoe z 55336; rural
Sunburg; Inc. Place; KANDIYOHI; **193** N-5; elev. 1,259ft./384m.; 🅿; z 56289; Ⓟ 117; © 110
Sundahl; NORMAN; see Sundal (RMC Place)
Sundal (Sundahl); RMC Place; NORMAN; ***192** H-3; mail Gary z 56545; rural
Sunfish Lake; Inc. Place; DAKOTA; **191** H-7; elev. 950ft./290m.; 🅿; ★ **MPLS-**; z 55118 & mail Inver Grove Heights z 55077; Ⓟ 413; © 504
Sunrise; RMC Place; CHISAGO; ***193** N-10; mail North Branch z 55056; ● 120
Suomi; RMC Place; ITASCA; ***192** H-8; mail Deer River z 56636; rural
Svea; RMC Place; KANDIYOHI; **193** O-5; elev. 1,140ft./347m.; 🅿; z 56216; ● 100
Sveadahl; RMC Place; WATONWAN; ***193** R-6; mail Saint James z 56081
Swanburg; RMC Place; CROW WING; ***192** J-7; elev. 1,310ft./399m.; mail Pine River z 56474; rural
Swan River; RMC Place; ITASCA; **192** I-9; elev. 1,293ft./394m.; 🅿; z 55784; ● 50
Swanville; Inc. Place; MORRISON; **193** M-6; elev. 1,183ft./361m.; 🅿; z 56382; Ⓟ 324; © 351
Swatara; RMC Place; AITKIN; **192** I-8; elev. 1,296ft./395m.; 🅿; z 55785; ● 50
Swift; RMC Place; ROSEAU; **192** C-5; elev. 1,080ft./329m.; 🅿; z 56682 & mail Warroad z 56763; ● 30
SWIFT; **193** O-4; Ⓟ 10,724; © 11,956; ◆ 10,961
Swift Falls; RMC Place; SWIFT; **193** N-5; mail Benson z 56215; ● 70
Sylvan; RMC Place; CASS; ***193** K-7; elev. 1,206ft./368m.; mail Pillager z 56473; ● 50
Syre; RMC Place; NORMAN; ***192** I-3; elev. 1,116ft./340m.; mail Twin Valley z 56584

T

Tabor; RMC Place; POLK; **192** F-2; mail Warren z 56762; ● 40
Taconite; Inc. Place; ITASCA; **192** H-9; elev. 1,403ft./428m.; 🅿; z 55786; Ⓟ 310; © 315
Taconite Harbor; RMC Place; COOK; ***192** C-11; mail Schroeder z 55613; rural
Talmoon; RMC Place; ITASCA; **192** G-8; elev. 1,359ft./414m.; 🅿; z 56637; ● 60
Tamarack; Inc. Place; AITKIN; **192** J-10; elev. 1,269ft./387m.; 🅿; z 55787; Ⓟ 53; © 59
Taopi; Inc. Place; MOWER; **193** T-11; elev. 1,350ft./411m.; 🅿; z 55977; Ⓟ 83; © 93
Taunton; Inc. Place; LYON; **193** Q-3; elev. 1,175ft./358m.; 🅿; z 56291; Ⓟ 175; © 207
Taylors Falls; Inc. Place; CHISAGO; **193** N-11; elev. 744ft./227m.; 🅿; z 55084; Ⓟ 694; © 951
Tenney; Inc. Place; WILKIN; **193** L-2; elev. 990ft./302m.; 🅿; z 56583; Ⓟ 4; © 6
Tenstrike; Inc. Place; BELTRAMI; **192** G-6; elev. 1,403ft./428m.; 🅿; z 56683; Ⓟ 184; © 195
Terrace; RMC Place; POPE; **193** N-5; mail Glenwood z 56334; ● 40
Terrebonne; RMC Place; RED LAKE; **192** F-3; mail Red Lake Falls z 56750; ● 25
The Arches; RMC Place; WINONA; ***193** S-13; mail Lewiston z 55952; ● 45
Theilman; RMC Place; WABASHA; **193** R-12; elev. 740ft./226m.; 🅿; z 55945; ● 70
The Lakes; CDP-Census Area Only; MURRAY; ***193** R-4; © 619
Thief River Falls; Inc. Place; ⊡ PENNINGTON; **192** F-3; elev. 1,133ft./345m.; 🅿 🅷; z 56701; Ⓟ 8,010; © 8,410
Third Crow Wing Lake; RMC Place; HUBBARD; mail Nevis z 56467; rural
Thompsonburg; RMC Place; LINCOLN; ***193** Q-2; mail Ivanhoe z 56142; rural
Thompson Grove; RMC Place; WASHINGTON; ★ **MPLS-**; mail Cottage Grove z 55016; pop. incl. with Cottage Grove (Inc. Place)
Thompson Heights; RMC Place; ANOKA; ***193** O-9; elev. 870ft./265m.; ★ **MPLS-**; mail Minneapolis z 55433; pop. incl. with Coon Rapids (Inc. Place)
Thompson Park; RMC Place; ANOKA; ***193** O-9; elev. 870ft./265m.; ★ **MPLS-**; mail Minneapolis z 55433; pop. incl. with Coon Rapids (Inc. Place)
Thompson Riverview Terrace; RMC Place; ANOKA; **191** B-4; ★ **MPLS-**; mail Minneapolis z 55433; pop. incl. with Coon Rapids (Inc. Place)
Thomson; Inc. Place; CARLTON; ***192** J-11; elev. 1,050ft./320m.; ★ **DUL**; mail Carlton z 55718; Ⓟ 132; © 153
Thor; RMC Place; AITKIN; ***193** K-9; elev. 1,270ft./387m.; mail Aitkin z 56431; rural
Thorhult; RMC Place; BELTRAMI; ***192** E-5; elev. 1,236ft./377m.; mail Grygla z 56727; rural
Tintah; Inc. Place; TRAVERSE; **193** L-3; elev. 996ft./304m.; 🅿; z 56583; Ⓟ 74; © 79
Toad Lake; RMC Place; BECKER; ***192** J-4; elev. 1,523ft./464m.; mail Frazee z 56544; rural
TODD; **193** L-6; Ⓟ 23,363; © 24,426; ◆ 23,985
Tofte; RMC Place; COOK; **192** C-11; elev. 629ft./192m.; 🅿; z 55615; ● 250
Togo; RMC Place; ITASCA; ***192** G-9; elev. 1,357ft./414m.; 🅿; z 55723; rural
Toimi; RMC Place; LAKE; ***192** H-12; elev. 1,738ft./530m.; mail Brimson z 55602; rural
Toivola; RMC Place; ST. LOUIS; **192** I-10; elev. 1,289ft./393m.; 🅿; z 55765; ● 30
Tonka Bay; Inc. Place; HENNEPIN; ***193** P-9; elev. 938ft./286m.; ★ **MPLS-**; mail Excelsior z 55331; Ⓟ 1,472; © 1,547
Tower; Inc. Place; ST. LOUIS; **192** G-11; elev. 1,400ft./427m.; 🅿; z 55790; Ⓟ 502; © 479
Tracy; Inc. Place; LYON; **193** R-4; elev. 1,398ft./426m.; 🅿 🅷; z 56175; Ⓟ 2,059; © 2,268
Traffic; RMC Place; HENNEPIN; ***193** P-9; ★ **MPLS-**; mail Minneapolis z 55403; pop. incl. with Minneapolis (Inc. Place)
Trail; Inc. Place; POLK; **192** G-4; elev. 1,250ft./381m.; 🅿; z 56684; Ⓟ 67; © 62
Trails End; RMC Place; COOK; ***192** A-11; mail Grand Marais z 55604; summer pop. 100; rural
Traverse; RMC Place; NICOLLET; ***193** Q-8; mail Saint Peter z 56082; ● 30
TRAVERSE; **193** M-2; Ⓟ 4,463; © 4,134; ◆ 3,561
Trimont; Inc. Place; MARTIN; **193** S-6; elev. 1,236ft./377m.; 🅿; z 56176; Ⓟ 745; © 754
Trommald; Inc. Place; CROW WING; **193** K-8; elev. 1,225ft./373m.; mail Crosby z 56441; Ⓟ 80; © 125
Trosky; Inc. Place; PIPESTONE; **193** S-3; elev. 1,698ft./518m.; 🅿; z 56144, z 56177; Ⓟ 120; © 116
Trout Brook Junction; RMC Place; RAMSEY; ★ **MPLS-**; pop. incl. with Saint Paul (Inc. Place)
Troy; RMC Place; WINONA; ***193** S-12; mail Saint Charles z 55972
Truman; Inc. Place; MARTIN; **193** S-7; elev. 1,110ft./338m.; 🅿; z 56088; Ⓟ 1,292; © 1,259
Turtle River; Inc. Place; BELTRAMI; **192** G-6; elev. 1,350ft./411m.; 🅿; z 56601; Ⓟ 62; © 75
Twig; RMC Place; ST. LOUIS; **192** I-11; elev. 1,370ft./418m.; 🅿; z 55791; ● 200
Twin Cities; RMC Place; HENNEPIN; ***193** P-9; elev. 820ft./250m.; ★ **MPLS-**; mail Saint Paul z 55111
Twin Lakes; Inc. Place; FREEBORN; **193** T-9; elev. 1,271ft./387m.; 🅿; z 56089; Ⓟ 154; © 168
Twin Valley; Inc. Place; NORMAN; **192** H-3; elev. 1,090ft./332m.; 🅿; z 56584; Ⓟ 821; © 865
Two Harbors; Inc. Place; ⊡ LAKE; **192** I-13; elev. 699ft./213m.; 🅿 🅷; z 55616; Ⓟ 3,651; © 3,613
Two Inlets; RMC Place; BECKER; ***192** I-5; elev. 1,486ft./453m.; mail Park Rapids z 56470; ● 30
Tyler; Inc. Place; LINCOLN; **193** R-3; elev. 1,733ft./528m.; 🅿 🅷; z 56178; Ⓟ 1,257; © 1,218

U

Ulen; Inc. Place; CLAY; **192** I-3; elev. 1,150ft./351m.; 🅿; z 56585; Ⓟ 547; © 532
Underwood; Inc. Place; OTTER TAIL; **193** K-4; elev. 1,343ft./409m.; 🅿; z 56586; Ⓟ 284; © 319
Union Hill; RMC Place; LE SUEUR, SCOTT; ***193** Q-8; elev. 1,006ft./307m.; mail New Prague z 56071
Upper Grey Cloud Island; RMC Place; WASHINGTON; ***193** P-10; ★ **MPLS-**; mail Cottage Grove z 55016, Saint Paul Park z 55071; rural
Upper Sioux Reservation; Indian Reservation; YELLOW MEDICINE; mail Granite Falls z 56241; Ⓟ 54; © 57
Upsala; Inc. Place; MORRISON; **193** M-6; elev. 1,220ft./372m.; 🅿; z 56384; Ⓟ 371; © 424
Uptown; RMC Place; RAMSEY; ***193** P-10; ★ **MPLS-**; mail Saint Paul z 55102; pop. incl. with Saint Paul (Inc. Place)
Urbank; Inc. Place; OTTER TAIL; **193** L-4; elev. 1,477ft./450m.; mail Parkers Prairie z 56361; Ⓟ 73; © 59
Utica; Inc. Place; WINONA; **193** S-12; elev. 1,173ft./358m.; 🅿; z 55979; Ⓟ 220; © 230

V

Vadnais Heights; Inc. Place; RAMSEY; **191** D-8; elev. 900ft./274m.; 🅿; ★ **MPLS-**; z 55110, z 55127; Ⓟ 11,041; © 13,069
Valley Ridge; RMC Place; DAKOTA; elev. 1,000ft./305m.; ★ **MPLS-**; mail Burnsville z 55337; pop. incl. with Burnsville (Inc. Place)
Vasa; RMC Place; GOODHUE; **193** Q-11; mail Welch z 55089; ● 70
Ventura; STEARNS; see Saint Augusta (Inc. Place)
Verdi; RMC Place; LINCOLN; **193** R-2; elev. 1,764ft./538m.; 🅿; z 56164; ● 70
Vergas; Inc. Place; OTTER TAIL; **192** J-4; elev. 1,400ft./427m.; 🅿; z 56587; Ⓟ 287; © 311
Vermillion; Inc. Place; DAKOTA; **193** P-10; 🅿; z 55085; Ⓟ 510; © 437
Vermillion Dam; RMC Place; ST. LOUIS; ***192** F-11; mail Orr z 55771; summer pop. 150; ● 70
Verndale; Inc. Place; WADENA; **193** K-6; elev. 1,349ft./411m.; 🅿; z 56481; Ⓟ 560; © 575
Vernon Center; Inc. Place; BLUE EARTH; **193** S-7; elev. 1,030ft./314m.; 🅿; z 56090; Ⓟ 339; © 359
Veseli; RMC Place; RICE; ***193** Q-9; elev. 1,080ft./329m.; 🅿; z 55046 & mail Webster z 55088; ● 200
Vesta; Inc. Place; REDWOOD; **193** Q-5; elev. 1,060ft./323m.; 🅿; z 56292 & mail Seaforth z 56287; Ⓟ 302; © 339
Victoria; Inc. Place; CARVER; **193** P-8; elev. 1,000ft./305m.; 🅿; ★ **MPLS-**; z 55386; Ⓟ 2,354; © 4,025
Viking; Inc. Place; MARSHALL; **192** E-3; elev. 1,070ft./326m.; 🅿; z 56760; Ⓟ 103; © 92
Villard; Inc. Place; POPE; **193** M-5; elev. 1,365ft./416m.; 🅿; z 56385; Ⓟ 247; © 244
Vineland; CDP; MILLE LACS; ***193** L-8; elev. 1,261ft./384m.; mail Onamia z 56359; Ⓟ 438; © 607
Vining; Inc. Place; OTTER TAIL; **193** K-4; elev. 1,387ft./423m.; 🅿; z 56588; Ⓟ 84; © 68
Viola; RMC Place; OLMSTED; **193** R-12; elev. 1,160ft./354m.; 🅿; z 55934; ● 90
Virginia; Inc. Place; ST. LOUIS; **192** G-11; elev. 1,437ft./438m.; 🅿 🅷 ■; z 55777, z 55792; Ⓟ 9,410; © 9,157; ◆ 8,918
Vista; RMC Place; WASECA; ***193** S-9; elev. 1,178ft./359m.; mail Waseca z 56093; rural

W

Wabasha; Inc. Place; ⊡ WABASHA; **193** Q-12; elev. 704ft./215m.; 🅿 🅷; z 55981; Ⓟ 2,384; © 2,599
WABASHA; **193** Q-12; Ⓟ 19,744; © 21,610; ◆ 21,315
Wabasso; Inc. Place; REDWOOD; **193** Q-5; elev. 1,078ft./329m.; 🅿; z 56293; Ⓟ 684; © 643; Ⓡ 682
Wabedo; RMC Place; CASS; ***192** I-7; elev. 1,350ft./411m.; mail Longville z 56655; ● 30
Waconia; Inc. Place; CARVER; **193** P-8; elev. 991ft./302m.; 🅿 🅷; z 55387; Ⓟ 3,498; © 6,814
Wacouta; RMC Place; GOODHUE; **193** Q-11; mail Red Wing z 55066; ● 80
Wadena; Inc. Place; ⊡ WADENA, OTTER TAIL; **193** K-5; elev. 1,350ft./411m.; 🅿 🅷; z 56482; Ⓟ 4,131; © 4,294
WADENA; **193** K-6; Ⓟ 13,154; © 13,713; ◆ 13,431
Wahkon; Inc. Place; MILLE LACS; **193** L-9; elev. 1,260ft./384m.; 🅿; z 56386; Ⓟ 197; © 314
Waite Park; Inc. Place; STEARNS; **193** N-7; elev. 1,070ft./326m.; 🅿; ★ **ST.CLD**; z 56387-88; Ⓟ 5,020; © 6,568
Walbo; RMC Place; ISANTI; ***193** N-9; mail Cambridge z 55008; rural
Waldo; RMC Place; LAKE; ***192** I-13; mail Two Harbors z 55616; rural
Waldorf; Inc. Place; WASECA; **193** S-8; elev. 1,080ft./329m.; 🅿; z 56091; Ⓟ 243; © 242
Wales; RMC Place; LAKE; ***192** H-13; mail Two Harbors z 55616; rural
Walker; Inc. Place; ⊡ CASS; **192** I-6; elev. 1,336ft./407m.; 🅿; z 56484 & mail Benedict z 56436; Ⓟ 950; © 1,069
Walnut Grove; Inc. Place; REDWOOD; **193** R-4; elev. 1,212ft./369m.; 🅿; z 56180; Ⓟ 625; © 599
Walters; Inc. Place; FARIBAULT; **193** T-8; elev. 1,250ft./381m.; 🅿; z 56097; Ⓟ 86; © 88
Waltham; Inc. Place; MOWER; **193** S-10; elev. 1,320ft./402m.; 🅿; z 55982; Ⓟ 170; © 196
Wanamingo; Inc. Place; GOODHUE; **193** R-10; elev. 1,050ft./320m.; 🅿; z 55983; Ⓟ 847; © 1,007
Wanda; Inc. Place; REDWOOD; **193** R-5; elev. 1,100ft./335m.; 🅿; z 56294; Ⓟ 103; © 103
Wannaska; RMC Place; ROSEAU; **192** D-4; elev. 1,105ft./337m.; 🅿; z 56761; ● 90
Warba; Inc. Place; ITASCA; **192** I-9; elev. 1,280ft./390m.; 🅿; z 55793; Ⓟ 137; © 183
Ward Springs; RMC Place; TODD; **193** M-6; mail Grey Eagle z 56336; ● 60
Warman; RMC Place; KANABEC; **193** L-9; mail Mora z 55051; ● 30
Warren; Inc. Place; ⊡ MARSHALL; **192** E-2; elev. 854ft./260m.; 🅿 🅷; z 56762; Ⓟ 1,813; © 1,678
Warroad; Inc. Place; ROSEAU; **192** C-5; elev. 1,070ft./326m.; 🅿; z 56763 & mail Oak Island z 56741; Ⓟ 1,679; © 1,722
Warsaw; RMC Place; RICE; **193** R-9; elev. 1,000ft./305m.; 🅿; z 55087; ● 250
Waseca; Inc. Place; ⊡ WASECA; **193** R-9; elev. 1,151ft./351m.; 🅿 🅷; z 56093; Ⓟ 8,385; © 8,493; Ⓡ 9,611
WASECA; **193** S-8; Ⓟ 18,079; © 19,526; ◆ 19,695
Washington; RMC Place; FILLMORE; ***193** S-11; elev. 1,148ft./350m.; mail Spring Valley z 55975; ● 25
WASHINGTON; **193** O-10; Ⓟ 145,896; © 201,130; ◆ 228,306
Wasioja; RMC Place; DODGE; **193** R-10; ★ **ROCH**; mail Dodge Center z 55927; ● 70
Waskish; RMC Place; BELTRAMI; **192** E-7; elev. 1,200ft./366m.; 🅿; z 56685; ● 75
Wastedo; RMC Place; GOODHUE; ***193** Q-10; mail Cannon Falls z 55009; rural
Waterford; RMC Place; DAKOTA; **193** Q-10; mail Northfield z 55057; ● 75
Watertown; Inc. Place; CARVER; **193** P-8; elev. 960ft./293m.; 🅿; z 55388; Ⓟ 2,408; © 3,029
Waterville; Inc. Place; LE SUEUR; **193** R-9; elev. 1,010ft./308m.; 🅿; z 56096; Ⓟ 1,771; © 1,833
Watkins; Inc. Place; MEEKER; **193** N-7; elev. 1,150ft./351m.; 🅿; z 55389; Ⓟ 849; © 880
WATONWAN; **193** S-6; Ⓟ 11,682; © 11,876; ◆ 10,685
Watson; Inc. Place; CHIPPEWA; **193** O-4; elev. 1,031ft./314m.; 🅿; z 56295; Ⓟ 211; © 209
Waubun; Inc. Place; MAHNOMEN; **192** I-4; elev. 1,240ft./378m.; 🅿; z 56589; Ⓟ 330; © 403
Waverly; Inc. Place; WRIGHT; **193** O-8; elev. 998ft./304m.; 🅿; z 55390; Ⓟ 600; © 732
Wawina; RMC Place; ITASCA; **192** I-10; elev. 1,267ft./386m.; 🅿; z 55736; ● 25
Wayzata; Inc. Place; HENNEPIN; **191** F-1; elev. 940ft./287m.; 🅿; ★ **MPLS-**; z 55391; Ⓟ 3,806; © 4,113
Wayzata Boulevard; RMC Place; HENNEPIN; ★ **MPLS-**; mail Minneapolis z 55416; pop. incl. with Saint Louis Park (Inc. Place)
Wealthwood; RMC Place; AITKIN; **193** K-9; elev. 1,274ft./388m.; mail Aitkin z 56431; ● 30
Weaver; RMC Place; WABASHA; **193** R-12; elev. 686ft./209m.; mail Altura z 55910; ● 50
Weber; RMC Place; ISANTI; ***193** N-10; mail North Branch z 55056; rural
Webster; RMC Place; RICE; **193** Q-9; elev. 1,060ft./323m.; 🅿; z 55088; ● 150
Wegdahl; RMC Place; CHIPPEWA; **193** P-4; mail Montevideo z 56265; ● 100
Welch; RMC Place; GOODHUE; **193** Q-11; elev. 714ft./218m.; 🅿; z 55089; ● 80
Welcome; Inc. Place; MARTIN; **193** T-6; elev. 1,235ft./376m.; 🅿; z 56181; Ⓟ 790; © 721
Wells; Inc. Place; FARIBAULT; **193** S-8; elev. 1,160ft./354m.; 🅿; z 56097; Ⓟ 2,465; © 2,494
Weme; RMC Place; CLEARWATER; ***192** G-4; elev. 1,353ft./412m.; mail Clearbrook z 56634; rural
Wendell; Inc. Place; GRANT; **193** L-3; elev. 1,151ft./351m.; 🅿; z 56590; Ⓟ 159; © 177
Wertheimer Siding; RMC Place; WASHINGTON; ★ **MPLS-**; pop. incl. with Saint Paul Park (Inc. Place)
West Albany; RMC Place; WABASHA; ***193** R-12; elev. 800ft./244m.; mail Millville z 55957; ● 40
West Albion; RMC Place; WRIGHT; ***193** O-7; mail Annandale z 55302
West Bloomington; RMC Place; HENNEPIN; ★ **MPLS-**; mail Minneapolis z 55437-38; pop. incl. with Bloomington (Inc. Place)
Westbrook; Inc. Place; COTTONWOOD; **193** R-4; elev. 1,422ft./433m.; 🅿 🅷; z 56183; Ⓟ 853; © 755
Westbury; RMC Place; BECKER; ***192** I-4; mail Detroit Lakes z 56501
West Concord; Inc. Place; DODGE; **193** R-10; elev. 1,240ft./378m.; 🅿; z 55985; Ⓟ 871; © 836
West Duluth; RMC Place; ST. LOUIS; ***192** J-12; ★ **DUL**; mail Duluth z 55807; pop. incl. with Duluth (Inc. Place)
West Duluth Junction; RMC Place; ST. LOUIS; ★ **DUL**; pop. incl. with Duluth (Inc. Place)
West Edina; RMC Place; HENNEPIN; ★ **MPLS-**; mail Minneapolis z 55436; pop. incl. with Edina (Inc. Place)
West End; RMC Place; RAMSEY; ***193** P-10; ★ **MPLS-**; mail Saint Paul z 55102; pop. incl. with Saint Paul (Inc. Place)
West Lake Francis Shores; RMC Place; ISANTI; ***193** N-9; elev. 927ft./283m.; mail Isanti z 55040; rural
West Lynn; RMC Place; MCLEOD; ***193** P-7; elev. 1,069ft./326m.; mail Hutchinson z 55350; rural
West Newton; RMC Place; WABASHA; ***193** R-12; mail Kellogg z 55945
West Point; RMC Place; ISANTI; ***193** N-9; mail Cambridge z 55008; rural
Westport; Inc. Place; POPE; **193** M-5; elev. 1,335ft./407m.; mail Villard z 56385; Ⓟ 47; © 72
West Rock; RMC Place; PINE; ***193** M-10; mail Pine City z 55063; pop. incl. with Rock Creek (Inc. Place)
West Saint Paul; Inc. Place; DAKOTA; **191** H-7; elev. 800ft./244m.; 🅿 ■; ★ **MPLS-**; z 55107, z 55118; Ⓟ 19,248; © 19,405; ◆ 18,735
West Union; Inc. Place; TODD; **193** M-5; elev. 1,338ft./408m.; 🅿; z 56389 & mail Sauk Centre z 56378; Ⓟ 54; © 87
West Virginia; RMC Place; ST. LOUIS; ***192** G-11; mail Virginia z 55792; pop. incl. with Mountain Iron (Inc. Place)
Whalan; Inc. Place; FILLMORE; **193** S-12; elev. 793ft./242m.; 🅿; z 55949; Ⓟ 94; © 64
Wheatland; RMC Place; RICE; ***193** Q-9; elev. 1,050ft./320m.; mail Montgomery z 56069; rural
Wheaton; Inc. Place; ⊡ TRAVERSE; **193** M-2; elev. 1,019ft./311m.; 🅿 🅷; z 56296; Ⓟ 1,615; © 1,619
Wheeler's Point; RMC Place; LAKE OF THE WOODS; **192** C-6; mail Baudette z 56623; summer pop. 500; ● 220
Whipholt; RMC Place; CASS; **192** I-7; elev. 1,310ft./399m.; 🅿; z 56484; ● 130
White Bear Beach; RMC Place; RAMSEY; **191** C-9; ★ **MPLS-**; mail Saint Paul z 55110; ● 500
White Bear Lake; Inc. Place; RAMSEY, WASHINGTON; **193** O-10; elev. 950ft./290m.; 🅿; ★ **MPLS-**; z 55110, z 55115 & mail Saint Paul z 55127; Ⓟ 24,704; © 24,325; ◆ 23,698
White Earth; CDP; BECKER; **192** I-4; located on White Earth Ind. Res.; elev. 1,515ft./462m.; 🅿; z 56591; Ⓟ 319; © 424
White Earth Reservation; Indian Reservation; MAHNOMEN, BECKER, CLEARWATER; mail White Earth z 56591; Ⓟ 9,506; © 9,188
Whiteface; RMC Place; ST. LOUIS; ***192** I-11; mail Melrude z 55766; rural
White Rock; RMC Place; GOODHUE; **193** Q-10; mail Cannon Falls z 55009; ● 50
Whyte; RMC Place; LAKE; ***192** H-13; mail Two Harbors z 55616; rural
Wig Wam Bay; RMC Place; MILLE LACS; ***193** L-8; mail Onamia z 56359; rural
Wilbert; RMC Place; MARTIN; **193** T-6; mail Ceylon z 56121; ● 40
Wilder; Inc. Place; JACKSON; **193** S-5; elev. 1,470ft./448m.; 🅿; z 56101; Ⓟ 83; © 69
Wildwood; RMC Place; KOOCHICHING; ***192** F-8; mail Northome z 56661; rural
WILKIN; **193** K-2; Ⓟ 7,516; © 7,138; ◆ 6,260
Wilkinson; RMC Place; CASS; ***192** H-6; mail Cass Lake z 56633; rural
Willernie; Inc. Place; WASHINGTON; **191** D-10; elev. 950ft./290m.; 🅿; ★ **MPLS-**; z 55090; Ⓟ 584; © 549
Williams; Inc. Place; LAKE OF THE WOODS; **192** D-6; elev. 1,150ft./351m.; 🅿; z 56686; Ⓟ 212; © 210
Willmar; Inc. Place; ⊡ KANDIYOHI; **193** O-5; elev. 1,130ft./344m.; 🅿 🅷 ■; z 56201; Ⓟ 17,531; © 18,351; Ⓡ 18,488; ◆ 17,249
Willow Creek; RMC Place; BLUE EARTH; ***193** S-7; mail Amboy z 56010, Vernon Center z 56090; rural
Willow River; Inc. Place; PINE; **193** K-10; elev. 1,038ft./316m.; 🅿; z 55795; Ⓟ 284; © 309
Wilmington; RMC Place; HOUSTON; ***193** T-13; mail Caledonia z 55921; rural
Wilmont; Inc. Place; NOBLES; **193** S-4; elev. 1,730ft./527m.; 🅿; z 56185; Ⓟ 351; © 332
Wilno; RMC Place; LINCOLN; **193** Q-3; mail Ivanhoe z 56142; ● 35
Wilpen; RMC Place; ST. LOUIS; ***192** H-10; elev. 1,427ft./435m.; mail Hibbing z 55746; pop. incl. with Hibbing (Inc. Place)
Wilson; RMC Place; WINONA; ***193** S-13; mail Pine River z 56474, Winona z 55987; ● 40
Wilton; Inc. Place; BELTRAMI; **192** H-6; elev. 1,400ft./427m.; 🅿; z 56601, z 56687; Ⓟ 171; © 186
Wilton; RMC Place; WASECA; ***193** S-9; elev. 1,109ft./338m.; mail Waseca z 56093
Windom; Inc. Place; ⊡ COTTONWOOD; **193** S-5; elev. 1,364ft./416m.; 🅿 🅷; z 56101 & mail Bingham Lake z 56118; Ⓟ 4,283; © 4,490
Winger; Inc. Place; POLK; **192** G-3; elev. 1,230ft./375m.; 🅿; z 56592; Ⓟ 167; © 205
Winnebago; Inc. Place; FARIBAULT; **193** S-7; elev. 1,110ft./338m.; 🅿; z 56098 & mail Huntley z 56047; Ⓟ 1,565; © 1,487
Winnipeg Junction; RMC Place; CLAY; ***192** I-3; mail Hawley z 56549; ● 40
Winona; Inc. Place; ⊡ WINONA; **193** R-13; elev. 666ft./203m.; 🅿 🅷 🅲 13,752 ■; z 55987 & mail Stockton z 55988; Ⓟ 25,399; © 27,069; ◆ 27,518
WINONA; **193** S-12; Ⓟ 47,828; © 49,985; ◆ 50,345
Winsted; Inc. Place; MCLEOD; **193** P-8; elev. 1,010ft./308m.; 🅿; z 55395; Ⓟ 1,581; © 2,094
Winthrop; Inc. Place; SIBLEY; **193** Q-7; elev. 1,018ft./310m.; 🅿; z 55396; Ⓟ 1,279; © 1,367
Winton; Inc. Place; ST. LOUIS; **192** F-12; elev. 1,335ft./407m.; 🅿; z 55796; Ⓟ 169; © 185
Wirock; RMC Place; MURRAY; **193** S-4; mail Iona z 56141; ● 25
Wirt; RMC Place; ITASCA; **192** G-8; elev. 1,330ft./405m.; 🅿; z 56688; ● 30
Withrow; RMC Place; WASHINGTON; ***193** O-10; ★ **MPLS-**; mail Stillwater z 55082; ● 50
Witoka; RMC Place; WINONA; **193** S-13; mail Winona z 55987; ● 90
Wolf; RMC Place; ST. LOUIS; ***192** H-11; mail Iron z 55751, Mountain Iron z 55768; ● 50
Wolf Lake; Inc. Place; BECKER; **192** J-5; elev. 1,570ft./479m.; 🅿; z 56593; Ⓟ 35; © 31
Wolford; RMC Place; CROW WING; ***193** K-8; elev. 1,215ft./370m.; mail Crosby z 56441; ● 70
Wolverton; Inc. Place; WILKIN; **192** J-2; elev. 926ft./282m.; 🅿; z 56594; Ⓟ 158; © 122
Woodbury; Inc. Place; WASHINGTON; **191** G-10; elev. 1,065ft./325m.; 🅿; ★ **MPLS-**; z 55125, z 55129 & mail Saint Paul z 55128; Ⓟ 20,075; © 46,463; ◆ 61,277
Wood Lake; Inc. Place; YELLOW MEDICINE; **193** P-4; elev. 1,050ft./320m.; 🅿; z 56297; Ⓟ 406; © 436
Woodland; Inc. Place; HENNEPIN; **191** G-1; elev. 950ft./290m.; ★ **MPLS-**; mail Wayzata z 55391; Ⓟ 496; © 480
Woodland; RMC Place; KANABEC; ***193** L-9; elev. 1,241ft./378m.; mail Isle z 56342
Woodland; RMC Place; ST. LOUIS; ***192** J-12; ★ **DUL**; mail Duluth z 55803; pop. incl. with Duluth (Inc. Place)
Woodland Park; RMC Place; OTTER TAIL; mail Henning z 56551
Woodland Terrace; RMC Place; ANOKA; ***193** O-9; elev. 878ft./268m.; ★ **MPLS-**; mail Anoka z 55303; pop. incl. with Andover (Inc. Place)
Woodstock; Inc. Place; PIPESTONE; **193** R-3; elev. 1,824ft./556m.; 🅿; z 56186; Ⓟ 159; © 132
Worthington; Inc. Place; ⊡ NOBLES; **193** T-4; elev. 1,593ft./486m.; 🅿 🅷 ■; z 56187; Ⓟ 9,977; © 11,283; ◆ 11,552
Wrenshall; Inc. Place; CARLTON; **192** J-11; elev. 1,041ft./317m.; 🅿; z 55749, z 55797; Ⓟ 296; © 308
Wright; Inc. Place; CARLTON; **192** J-10; elev. 1,303ft./397m.; 🅿; z 55798; Ⓟ 144; © 93
WRIGHT; **193** O-7; Ⓟ 68,710; © 89,986; Ⓡ 89,993; ◆ 121,975
Wrightstown; RMC Place; OTTER TAIL; **193** K-5; elev. 1,425ft./434m.; mail Hewitt z 56453; ● 30
Wyattville; RMC Place; WINONA; ***193** S-13; elev. 1,246ft./380m.; mail Lewiston z 55952; rural
Wykoff; Inc. Place; FILLMORE; **193** S-12; elev. 1,322ft./403m.; 🅿; z 55990; Ⓟ 493; © 460
Wylie; RMC Place; RED LAKE; ***192** F-3; mail Red Lake Falls z 56750; rural
Wyman; RMC Place; ST. LOUIS; ***192** G-12; mail Hoyt Lakes z 55750; pop. incl. with Hoyt Lakes (Inc. Place)
Wyoming; Inc. Place; CHISAGO; **193** N-10; elev. 900ft./274m.; 🅿; ★ **MPLS-**; z 55092; Ⓟ 2,142; © 3,048

Y

YELLOW MEDICINE; **193** P-3; Ⓟ 11,684; © 11,080; ◆ 9,855
York; RMC Place; FILLMORE; ***193** T-12; mail Harmony z 55939; rural
Yorktown; RMC Place; HENNEPIN; ***193** P-9; elev. 850ft./259m.; ★ **MPLS-**; mail Minneapolis z 55435; pop. incl. with Edina (Inc. Place)
Young America; RMC Place; CARVER; ***193** P-8; elev. 1,000ft./305m.; 🅿; z 55394, z 55397, z 55399, z 55550-53, z 55555-60, z 55562, z 55564, z 55566-68, z 55573, z 55594 & mail Minneapolis z 55473, Norwood Young America z 55368; pop. incl. with Norwood Young America (Inc. Place)
Yucatan; RMC Place; HOUSTON; ***193** T-13; mail Houston z 55943; rural

Z

Zemple; Inc. Place; ITASCA; **192** H-8; elev. 1,284ft./391m.; mail Deer River z 56636; Ⓟ 63; © 75
Zerkel; RMC Place; CLEARWATER; ***192** H-5; elev. 1,565ft./477m.; mail Bagley z 56621
Zim; RMC Place; ST. LOUIS; **192** H-11; elev. 1,339ft./408m.; 🅿; z 55738; ● 100
Zimmerman; SHERBURNE; see Lake Fremont (Inc. Place)
Zumbra Heights; RMC Place; CARVER; mail Victoria z 55386; pop. incl. with Victoria (Inc. Place)
Zumbro Falls; Inc. Place; WABASHA; **193** R-11; 🅿; z 55991; Ⓟ 237; © 177
Zumbrota; Inc. Place; GOODHUE; **193** R-11; elev. 1,005ft./306m.; 🅿 🅷; z 55992; Ⓟ 2,312; © 2,789

Entries in **UPPERCASE** are counties.
Entries in **bold** have populations of 2,500 or more.
Names in parentheses are alternate names.
Inc. Place — Incorporated Place
RMC Place — Rand McNally Designated Place
CDP — Census Designated Place
MCD — Minor Civil Division

⊡ County Seat
▲ Minor Civil Division
elev. Elevation
🅿 Post Office
🅷 Hospital
🅲 College
■ Principal Business Center
★ Ranally Metro Area (RMA) Abbreviation
z Zip Code(s)

Ⓟ Previous Census Population
Ⓡ Revised Census Population
Ⓐ Annexation Population
● Rand McNally Population Estimate
© Final Census Population
Ⓢ Special Census Population
◆ Estimated Population

For additional definitions see Glossary, Volume 1, and Introduction, Volume 2.

MISSISSIPPI

Statistics

Total area (2000) — 48,430 square miles
Land area (2000) — 46,907 square miles
Water area (2000) — 1,523 square miles
Capital — Jackson
Admitted as state — December, 1817

Maps

State maps can be found on pages 142-254 in Vol. 1

Ranally Metro Areas (RMAs) and Abbreviations

Biloxi-Gulfport, MS — BIL-
Columbus, MS — COL
Greenville, MS — GRNV
Hattiesburg, MS — HATT
Jackson, MS — JAC
Laurel, MS — LAUR
Memphis, TN-AR-MS — MEM
Meridian, MS — MRID
Natchez, MS-LA — NCHZ
Pascagoula, MS — PSCG
Vicksburg, MS-LA — VICK

Principal Places

Place Name	Place Type	County	Population
Jackson	Inc. Place	HINDS	◆ 177,006
Gulfport	Inc. Place	HARRISON	◆ 71,207
Hattiesburg	Inc. Place	FORREST	◆ 50,299
Biloxi	Inc. Place	HARRISON	◆ 48,420
Southaven	Inc. Place	DESOTO	◆ 44,677
Olive Branch	Inc. Place	DESOTO	◆ 40,071
Meridian	Inc. Place	LAUDERDALE	◆ 38,833
Tupelo	Inc. Place	LEE	◆ 37,139
Greenville	Inc. Place	WASHINGTON	◆ 36,391
Vicksburg	Inc. Place	WARREN	◆ 24,612
Horn Lake	Inc. Place	DESOTO	◆ 24,318
Columbus	Inc. Place	LOWNDES	◆ 24,280
Pascagoula	Inc. Place	JACKSON	◆ 24,168
Starkville	Inc. Place	OKTIBBEHA	◆ 24,160
Clinton	Inc. Place	HINDS	◆ 23,547
Ridgeland	Inc. Place	MADISON	◆ 22,700
Pearl	Inc. Place	RANKIN	◆ 22,235
Brandon	Inc. Place	RANKIN	◆ 20,721
Laurel	Inc. Place	JONES	◆ 19,794
Clarksdale	Inc. Place	COAHOMA	◆ 18,609
Long Beach	Inc. Place	HARRISON	© 17,320
Ocean Springs	Inc. Place	JACKSON	© 17,225
Moss Point	Inc. Place	JACKSON	© 15,851
Greenwood	Inc. Place	LEFLORE	◆ 15,795
Natchez	Inc. Place	ADAMS	◆ 15,694
Grenada	Inc. Place	GRENADA	© 14,879
Madison	Inc. Place	MADISON	© 14,692
Yazoo City	Inc. Place	YAZOO	® 14,141
Corinth	Inc. Place	ALCORN	◆ 14,115
Cleveland	Inc. Place	BOLIVAR	© 13,841
McComb	Inc. Place	PIKE	◆ 12,945
Canton	Inc. Place	MADISON	© 12,911
West Point	Inc. Place	CLAY	© 12,145
Indianola	Inc. Place	SUNFLOWER	© 12,066
Oxford	Inc. Place	LAFAYETTE	© 11,756
Gautier	Inc. Place	JACKSON	© 11,681
Picayune	Inc. Place	PEARL RIVER	© 10,535
Brookhaven	Inc. Place	LINCOLN	◆ 9,935
Booneville	Inc. Place	PRENTISS	© 8,625
Bay Saint Louis	Inc. Place	HANCOCK	© 8,209
Holly Springs	Inc. Place	MARSHALL	© 7,957
D'Iberville	Inc. Place	HARRISON	© 7,608
New Albany	Inc. Place	UNION	© 7,607
Petal	Inc. Place	FORREST	© 7,579
Byram	CDP	HINDS	© 7,386
Kosciusko	Inc. Place	ATTALA	© 7,372
Philadelphia	Inc. Place	NESHOBA	© 7,303
Batesville	Inc. Place	PANOLA	© 7,113
Louisville	Inc. Place	WINSTON	© 7,006
Amory	Inc. Place	MONROE	© 6,956
Hernando	Inc. Place	DESOTO	© 6,812
Senatobia	Inc. Place	TATE	© 6,682
Saint Martin	CDP	JACKSON	© 6,676
Waveland	Inc. Place	HANCOCK	© 6,674
Columbia	Inc. Place	MARION	© 6,603
Pass Christian	Inc. Place	HARRISON	© 6,579
Aberdeen	Inc. Place	MONROE	© 6,415
West Hattiesburg	CDP-Census Area Only	LAMAR	© 6,305
Richland	Inc. Place	RANKIN	© 6,027
Forest	Inc. Place	SCOTT	© 5,987
Diamondhead	CDP	HANCOCK	© 5,912
Gulf Hills	CDP	JACKSON	© 5,900
Crystal Springs	Inc. Place	COPIAH	© 5,873
Leland	Inc. Place	WASHINGTON	© 5,502
Winona	Inc. Place	MONTGOMERY	© 5,482
Ripley	Inc. Place	TIPPAH	© 5,478
Pontotoc	Inc. Place	PONTOTOC	© 5,253
Waynesboro	Inc. Place	WAYNE	© 5,197

County Business Data

County	FIPS Code	County Seat	Land Area (Sq. Mi.)	Census Population			Wholesale Trade		Manufacturing, 2002			
				4/1/2000	4/1/1990	% Change 1990-2000	Sales, 2002 ($1,000)	% Change 1997-2002	Establish-ments	Total Employees	Value Added ($1,000)	Ranally Mfg. Units
Adams	001	Natchez	460	34,340	35,356	-2.9	(d)	(d)	26	(d)	(d)	...
Alcorn	003	Corinth	400	34,558	31,722	8.9	287,506	8.8	52	3,981	281,516	149
Amite	005	Liberty	730	13,599	13,328	2.0	17,264	(d)	11	742	52,762	28
Attala	007	Kosciusko	735	19,661	18,481	6.4	50,805	10.0	21	972	47,121	25
Benton	009	Ashland	407	8,026	8,046	-0.2	(d)	(d)	...	(d)	(d)	...
Bolivar	011	Cleveland, Rosedale	876	40,633	41,875	-3.0	321,811	-9.5	24	2,116	152,207	81
Calhoun	013	Pittsboro	587	15,069	14,908	1.1	15,982	-41.4	28	1,454	127,070	67
Carroll	015	Carrollton, Vaiden	628	10,769	9,237	16.6	(d)	(d)	...	(d)	(d)	...
Chickasaw	017	Houston, Okolona	502	19,440	18,085	7.5	74,324	11.6	74	3,984	160,137	85
Choctaw	019	Ackerman	419	9,758	9,071	7.6	(d)	(d)	...	(d)	(d)	...
Claiborne	021	Port Gibson	487	11,831	11,370	4.1	(d)	(d)	...	(d)	(d)	...
Clarke	023	Quitman	691	17,955	17,313	3.7	(d)	(d)	20	861	51,285	27
Clay	025	West Point	409	21,979	21,120	4.1	200,497	-64.3	26	4,027	215,980	114
Coahoma	027	Clarksdale	554	30,622	31,665	-3.3	197,658	-2.7	21	(d)	(d)	...
Copiah	029	Hazlehurst	777	28,757	27,592	4.2	(d)	(d)	32	2,285	182,117	96
Covington	031	Collins	414	19,407	16,527	17.4	177,001	-58.5	12	1,578	77,344	41
DeSoto	033	Hernando	478	107,199	67,910	57.9	1,342,475	(d)	124	5,511	638,080	338
Forrest	035	Hattiesburg	467	72,604	68,314	6.3	(d)	(d)	81	4,105	453,733	240
Franklin	037	Meadville	565	8,448	8,377	0.8	(d)	(d)	...	(d)	(d)	...
George	039	Lucedale	478	19,144	16,673	14.8	(d)	(d)	...	(d)	(d)	...
Greene	041	Leakesville	713	13,299	10,220	30.1	(d)	(d)	...	(d)	(d)	...
Grenada	043	Grenada	422	23,263	21,555	7.9	127,138	3.2	26	3,022	147,201	78
Hancock	045	Bay Saint Louis	477	42,967	31,760	35.3	(d)	(d)	29	(d)	(d)	...
Harrison	047	Biloxi, Gulfport	581	189,601	165,365	14.7	695,325	6.8	135	(d)	(d)	...
Hinds	049	Jackson, Raymond	869	250,800	254,441	-1.4	2,734,653	5.2	183	8,284	634,634	336
Holmes	051	Lexington	756	21,609	21,604	0.0	15,273	-32.0	9	635	23,972	13
Humphreys	053	Belzoni	418	11,206	12,134	-7.6	35,718	(d)	4	(d)	(d)	...
Issaquena	055	Mayersville	413	2,274	1,909	19.1	(d)	(d)	...	(d)	(d)	...
Itawamba	057	Fulton	532	22,770	20,017	13.8	(d)	(d)	35	1,071	149,450	79
Jackson	059	Pascagoula	727	131,420	115,243	14.0	(d)	(d)	86	(d)	(d)	...
Jasper	061	Bay Springs, Paulding	676	18,149	17,114	6.0	(d)	(d)	13	(d)	(d)	...
Jefferson	063	Fayette	519	9,740	8,653	12.6	5,048	(d)	...	(d)	(d)	...
Jefferson Davis	065	Prentiss	408	13,962	14,051	-0.6	1,603	-20.1	...	(d)	(d)	...
Jones	067	Ellisville, Laurel	694	64,958	62,031	4.7	(d)	(d)	76	(d)	(d)	...
Kemper	069	De Kalb	766	10,453	10,356	0.9	(d)	(d)	...	(d)	(d)	...
Lafayette	071	Oxford	631	38,744	31,826	21.7	59,091	26.4	23	1,781	151,596	80
Lamar	073	Purvis	497	39,070	30,424	28.4	(d)	(d)	20	567	43,526	23
Lauderdale	075	Meridian	704	78,161	75,555	3.4	1,200,121	23.3	74	3,693	295,891	157
Lawrence	077	Monticello	431	13,258	12,458	6.4	(d)	(d)	9	(d)	(d)	...
Leake	079	Carthage	583	20,940	18,436	13.6	21,646	22.4	13	3,826	262,621	139
Lee	081	Tupelo	450	75,755	65,581	15.5	975,556	17.4	159	14,131	1,169,302	619
Leflore	083	Greenwood	592	37,947	37,341	1.6	(d)	(d)	39	(d)	(d)	...
Lincoln	085	Brookhaven	586	33,166	30,278	9.5	(d)	(d)	27	1,209	130,685	69
Lowndes	087	Columbus	502	61,586	59,308	3.8	(d)	(d)	72	5,510	501,549	265
Madison	089	Canton	717	74,674	53,794	38.8	1,925,487	63.2	72	3,800	240,959	127
Marion	091	Columbia	542	25,595	25,544	0.2	78,120	(d)	26	1,245	60,249	32
Marshall	093	Holly Springs	706	34,993	30,361	15.3	(d)	(d)	32	1,103	73,047	39
Monroe	095	Aberdeen	764	38,014	36,582	3.9	120,761	15.5	59	3,574	580,270	307
Montgomery	097	Winona	407	12,189	12,388	-1.6	(d)	(d)	21	579	49,227	26
Neshoba	099	Philadelphia	570	28,684	24,800	15.7	94,663	11.0	24	1,209	122,846	65
Newton	101	Decatur	578	21,838	20,291	7.6	17,205	(d)	23	1,858	100,116	53
Noxubee	103	Macon	695	12,548	12,604	-0.4	18,435	-12.8	22	997	66,862	35
Oktibbeha	105	Starkville	458	42,902	38,375	11.8	62,094	145.0	28	1,502	116,053	61
Panola	107	Batesville, Sardis	684	34,274	29,996	14.3	305,251	23.1	40	2,566	278,914	148
Pearl River	109	Poplarville	811	48,621	38,714	25.6	(d)	(d)	47	786	92,136	49
Perry	111	New Augusta	647	12,138	10,865	11.7	(d)	(d)	8	925	134,680	71
Pike	113	Magnolia	409	38,940	36,882	5.6	154,159	-6.0	34	3,080	148,761	79
Pontotoc	115	Pontotoc	497	26,726	22,237	20.2	(d)	(d)	83	6,616	493,640	261
Prentiss	117	Booneville	415	25,556	23,278	9.8	84,150	-1.3	52	3,843	418,230	221
Quitman	119	Marks	405	10,117	10,490	-3.6	(d)	(d)	...	(d)	(d)	...
Rankin	121	Brandon	775	115,327	87,161	32.3	1,303,711	-19.0	121	4,940	821,462	435
Scott	123	Forest	609	28,423	24,137	17.8	55,241	-46.7	32	6,016	721,372	382
Sharkey	125	Rolling Fork	428	6,580	7,066	-6.9	52,296	185.0	...	(d)	(d)	...
Simpson	127	Mendenhall	589	27,639	23,953	15.4	(d)	(d)	...	(d)	(d)	...
Smith	129	Raleigh	636	16,182	14,798	9.4	30,788	(d)	15	1,310	93,644	50
Stone	131	Wiggins	445	13,622	10,750	26.7	(d)	(d)	11	(d)	(d)	...
Sunflower	133	Indianola	694	34,369	32,867	4.6	(d)	(d)	23	1,157	212,686	113
Tallahatchie	135	Charleston, Sumner	644	14,903	15,210	-2.0	23,257	-4.0	...	(d)	(d)	...
Tate	137	Senatobia	404	25,370	21,432	18.4	(d)	(d)	14	1,154	92,838	49
Tippah	139	Ripley	458	20,826	19,523	6.7	64,783	8.2	33	3,027	197,558	105
Tishomingo	141	Iuka	424	19,163	17,683	8.4	61,159	-26.0	34	2,562	148,096	78
Tunica	143	Tunica	455	9,227	8,164	13.0	(d)	(d)	8	548	18,179	10
Union	145	New Albany	415	25,362	22,085	14.8	79,856	-76.1	36	3,217	153,597	81
Walthall	147	Tylertown	404	15,156	14,352	5.6	38,530	-27.7	21	726	31,065	16
Warren	149	Vicksburg	587	49,644	47,880	3.7	286,437	89.0	50	4,716	473,124	250
Washington	151	Greenville	724	62,977	67,935	-7.3	380,181	-3.5	55	2,672	343,992	182
Wayne	153	Waynesboro	810	21,216	19,517	8.7	137,715	-21.0	20	991	111,466	59
Webster	155	Walthall	422	10,294	10,222	0.7	1,691	(d)	15	516	49,268	26
Wilkinson	157	Woodville	677	10,312	9,678	6.6	28,415	4.1	...	(d)	(d)	...
Winston	159	Louisville	607	20,160	19,433	3.7	148,913	52.0	20	1,315	81,880	43
Yalobusha	161	Coffeeville, Water Valley	467	13,051	12,033	8.5	15,574	-68.1	12	1,573	129,726	69
Yazoo	163	Yazoo City	919	28,149	25,506	10.4	85,159	-9.0	25	1,612	104,249	55
The State			**46,907**	**2,844,658**	**2,573,216**	**10.5**	**19,215,751**	**4.2**	**2,796**	**182,822**	**16,126,629**	**8,532**

(d) Data not available. Corresponding percentages or Ranally Manufacturing Units are estimates.
... Represents 0 or amount too minimal to be reported.

Entries in **UPPERCASE** are counties.
Entries in **bold** have populations of 2,500 or more.
Names in parentheses are alternate names.
Inc. Place — Incorporated Place
RMC Place — Rand McNally Designated Place
CDP — Census Designated Place
MCD — Minor Civil Division

⊡ County Seat
▲ Minor Civil Division
elev. Elevation
🅿 Post Office

H Hospital
C College
■ Principal Business Center
★ Ranally Metro Area (RMA) Abbreviation
z Zip Code(s)

Ⓟ Previous Census Population
® Revised Census Population
Ⓐ Annexation Population
● Rand McNally Population Estimate
© Final Census Population
Ⓢ Special Census Population
◆ Estimated Population

For additional definitions see Glossary, Volume 1, and Introduction, Volume 2.

Index of Places and Counties

A

Abbeville; Inc. Place; LAFAYETTE; **194** C-7; elev. 361ft./110m.; 🄿; z 38601; Ⓟ 399; Ⓒ 423
Abbott; RMC Place; CLAY; ***194** E-9; elev. 251ft./77m.; mail West Point z 39773; rural
Aberdeen; Inc. Place; ⊡ MONROE; **194** D-9; 🄿 🄷; z 39730; Ⓟ 6,837; Ⓒ 6,415
Ackerman; Inc. Place; ⊡ CHOCTAW; **194** F-8; elev. 520ft./158m.; 🄿 🄷; z 39735; Ⓟ 1,573; Ⓒ 1,696
Acona; RMC Place; HOLMES; **194** F-6; mail Lexington z 39095; ● 50
Adams; RMC Place; HINDS; ***194** H-5; elev. 270ft./82m.; mail Utica z 39175; rural
ADAMS; **194** J-3; Ⓟ 35,356; Ⓒ 34,340; ◆ 30,336
Adaton; RMC Place; OKTIBBEHA; ***194** E-8; mail Starkville z 39759; rural
Addie; RMC Place; ISSAQUENA; ***194** F-4; mail Glen Allan z 38744; rural
Agricola; RMC Place; GEORGE; **194** L-9; elev. 218ft./66m.; 🄿; z 39452; ● 200
A H Mccoy Federal Bldg; RMC Place; HINDS; ★ **JAC**; mail Jackson z 39269; pop. incl. with Jackson (Inc. Place)
Airey; RMC Place; HARRISON; ***194** L-8; mail Saucier z 39574; rural
Albeison; JONES; see Moselle (RMC Place)
Albin; RMC Place; TALLAHATCHIE; ***194** D-5; mail Webb z 38966; rural
Alcorn; RMC Place; CLAIBORNE; **194** I-4; mail Lorman z 39096; ● 200
ALCORN; **194** B-9; Ⓟ 31,722; Ⓒ 34,558; ◆ 35,618
Algoma; Inc. Place; PONTOTOC; **194** C-8; 🄿; z 38820; Ⓟ 420; Ⓒ 508
Allen; RMC Place; COPIAH; ***194** I-5; elev. 473ft./144m.; mail Hazlehurst z 39083; rural
Alligator; Inc. Place; BOLIVAR; **194** D-5; 🄿; z 38720; Ⓟ 187; Ⓒ 220
Alpine; RMC Place; UNION; ***194** C-9; elev. 431ft./131m.; mail Blue Springs z 38828, Guntown z 38849; rural
Altitude; RMC Place; PRENTISS; ***194** B-9; mail Booneville z 38829; ● 60
Alva; RMC Place; MONTGOMERY; ***194** E-7; mail Duck Hill z 38925; rural
AMITE; **194** K-4; Ⓟ 13,328; Ⓒ 13,599; ◆ 12,922
Amory; Inc. Place; MONROE; **194** D-9; 🄿 🄷; z 38821; Ⓟ 7,093; Ⓒ 6,956
Amory Junction; MONROE; see Colsub (RMC Place)
Anchor; RMC Place; CHICKASAW; ***194** D-8; elev. 336ft./102m.; mail Woodland z 39776; rural
Anchorage; RMC Place; HUMPHREYS; ***194** F-5; mail Yazoo City z 39194; rural
Anding; RMC Place; YAZOO; **194** G-5; mail Bentonia z 39040; ● 60
Anguilla; Inc. Place; SHARKEY; **194** F-4; 🄿; z 38721; Ⓟ 883; Ⓒ 907
Anse; RMC Place; RANKIN; ***194** I-6; ★ **JAC**; mail Florence z 39073; ● 160
Ansley; RMC Place; HANCOCK; **194** M-7; mail Lakeshore z 39558; ● 270
Antioch; JASPER; see Turnerville (RMC Place)
Antioch; RMC Place; JONES; ***194** J-8; ★ **LAUR**; mail Laurel z 39440, z 39443; rural
Apple Ridge; RMC Place; HINDS; ★ **JAC**; mail Jackson z 39204; pop. incl. with Jackson (Inc. Place)
Arcola; Inc. Place; WASHINGTON; **194** F-4; 🄿; z 38722; Ⓟ 564; Ⓒ 563
Ariel; RMC Place; AMITE; ***194** K-4; elev. 365ft./111m.; mail Gloster z 39638; rural
Arkabutla; RMC Place; TATE; **194** B-6; 🄿; z 38602; ● 380
Arlington; RMC Place; LINCOLN; ***194** J-5; mail Bogue Chitto z 39629; rural
Arlington; RMC Place; NESHOBA; ***194** G-8; mail Philadelphia z 39350; rural
Arm; RMC Place; LAWRENCE; **194** J-6; elev. 259ft./79m.; mail Silver Creek z 39663; ● 80
Arnold Line; RMC Place; LAMAR; **194** E-1; ★ **HATT**; mail Hattiesburg z 39401-02; ● 60
Artesia; Inc. Place; LOWNDES; **194** E-9; elev. 244ft./74m.; 🄿; z 39736; Ⓟ 484; Ⓒ 498
Ashland; Inc. Place; ⊡ BENTON; **194** B-8; elev. 645ft./197m.; 🄿; z 38603; Ⓟ 490; Ⓒ 577
Askew; RMC Place; PANOLA; **194** B-6; 🄿; z 38621; ● 150
Athens; RMC Place; MONROE; ***194** D-9; elev. 301ft./92m.; mail Aberdeen z 39730; rural
Atlanta; RMC Place; CHICKASAW; ***194** D-8; elev. 404ft./123m.; mail Woodland z 39776; rural
ATTALA; **194** F-7; Ⓟ 18,481; Ⓒ 19,661; ◆ 19,579
Atway; RMC Place; MARSHALL; ***194** B-7; mail Holly Springs z 38635; rural
Auburn; RMC Place; LEE; ***194** C-9; mail Tupelo z 38804; ● 30
Auburn; RMC Place; LINCOLN; **194** J-5; mail Summit z 39666
Austin; RMC Place; TUNICA; **194** B-5; mail Tunica z 38676; ● 70
Avalon; RMC Place; CARROLL; **194** E-6; 🄿; z 38930; ● 100
Avent; GREENE; see Benjoe (RMC Place)
Avera; RMC Place; GREENE; **194** K-9; elev. 320ft./98m.; mail Leakesville z 39451; ● 60
Avon (Pettit); RMC Place; WASHINGTON; **194** F-4; 🄿; z 38723; ● 150

B

Bailey; RMC Place; LAUDERDALE; **194** H-9; 🄿; ★ **MRID**; z 39320; ● 150
Baird; RMC Place; SUNFLOWER; ***194** E-5; 🄿; z 38751
Baker; RMC Place; UNION; ***194** C-8; mail New Albany z 38652
Bald Hill; RMC Place; UNION; ***194** C-8; mail New Albany z 38652; rural
Baldwyn; Inc. Place; PRENTISS, LEE; **194** B-9; 🄿; z 38824; Ⓟ 3,204; Ⓒ 3,321
Ballard; RMC Place; MADISON; ***194** G-6; elev. 226ft./69m.; mail Canton z 39046; pop. incl. with Canton (Inc. Place)
Ballardsville; RMC Place; ITAWAMBA; ***194** C-9; mail Tupelo z 38801; ● 30
Ballentine; RMC Place; PANOLA; ***194** C-6; mail Crenshaw z 38621; rural
Ballground; RMC Place; WARREN; ***194** G-5; mail Redwood z 39156
Baltzer; RMC Place; SUNFLOWER; ***194** D-5; elev. 146ft./45m.; mail Anguilla z 38721, Clarksdale z 38614, Cleveland z 38732; rural
Banks; RMC Place; TUNICA; **194** B-6; elev. 199ft./61m.; mail Robinsonville z 38664
Banner; RMC Place; CALHOUN; **194** D-7; elev. 353ft./108m.; 🄿; z 38913; ● 100
Barlow; RMC Place; COPIAH; ***194** I-5; elev. 311ft./95m.; mail Hazlehurst z 39083
Barnes; RMC Place; LEAKE; ***194** G-7; mail Carthage z 39051; rural
Barnesville; RMC Place; DESOTO; ***194** A-6; ★ **MEM**; mail Memphis z 38109; ● 50
Barnett; RMC Place; CLARKE; ***194** I-9; mail Pachuta z 39347; rural
Barr; RMC Place; TATE; ***194** B-7; mail Senatobia z 38668; rural
Barrontown; RMC Place; FORREST; ***194** J-8; ★ **HATT**; mail Hattiesburg z 39401, Petal z 39465; ● 50
Bartahatchie; RMC Place; MONROE; mail Caledonia z 39740; rural
Barth; RMC Place; PEARL RIVER; ***194** L-8; mail Poplarville z 39470; rural
Barto; RMC Place; PIKE; ***194** K-5; elev. 289ft./88m.; mail McComb z 39648; rural
Barton; RMC Place; GEORGE; ***194** L-9; elev. 127ft./39m.; mail Lucedale z 39452; rural
Barton; RMC Place; MARSHALL; **194** A-7; elev. 388ft./118m.; mail Collierville z 38017; ● 60
Basic; RMC Place; CLARKE; ***194** H-9; mail Enterprise z 39330; rural
Basin; RMC Place; GEORGE; ***194** L-9; elev. 141ft./43m.; mail Lucedale z 39452; ● 30
Bassfield; Inc. Place; JEFFERSON DAVIS; **194** J-7; 🄿; z 39421; Ⓟ 249; Ⓒ 315
Batesville; Inc. Place; ⊡ PANOLA; **194** C-6; 🄿 🄷; z 38606; Ⓟ 6,403; Ⓒ 7,113
Batson; RMC Place; FORREST; ***194** K-8; elev. 150ft./46m.; ★ **HATT**; mail Hattiesburg z 39401; rural
Battlefield; RMC Place; HINDS; ***194** H-6; ★ **JAC**; mail Jackson z 39204; pop. incl. with Jackson (Inc. Place)
Battle Field; RMC Place; NEWTON; ***194** G-8; mail Collinsville z 39325; rural
Battles; RMC Place; WAYNE; **194** J-9; elev. 143ft./44m.; mail State Line z 39362
Baugh; RMC Place; COAHOMA; ***194** C-5; mail Sherard z 38669; rural
Baxter; RMC Place; JASPER; ***194** H-8; mail Louin z 39338; rural
Baxterville; RMC Place; LAMAR; **194** K-7; mail Lumberton z 39455; ● 320
Bayland; RMC Place; YAZOO; ***194** G-5; mail Yazoo City z 39194; rural
Bay Saint Louis; Inc. Place; ⊡ HANCOCK; **194** M-8; 🄿 🄷; ★ **BIL-**; z 39520-22, z 39525, z 39529; Ⓟ 8,063; Ⓒ 8,209
Bayside Park; RMC Place; HANCOCK; ***194** M-7; ★ **BIL-**; mail Bay Saint Louis z 39520; ● 680
Bay Springs; Inc. Place; ⊡ JASPER; **194** I-8; 🄿 🄷; z 39422; Ⓟ 1,729; Ⓒ 2,097
Beacon Hill; RMC Place; UNION; ***194** C-8; mail New Albany z 38652; ● 100
Beans Ferry; RMC Place; ITAWAMBA; ***194** C-10; mail Fulton z 38843
Bear Town; RMC Place; PIKE; **194** K-5; mail McComb z 39648; pop. incl. with McComb (Inc. Place)
Beasley; RMC Place; CLAY; ***194** E-8; mail Pheba z 39755; rural
Beatline; RMC Place; NESHOBA; ***194** G-8; elev. 480ft./146m.; mail Philadelphia z 39350; rural
Beatty; RMC Place; CARROLL; ***194** F-7; mail Vaiden z 39176; rural
Beaumont; Inc. Place; PERRY; **194** K-9; elev. 95ft./29m.; 🄿; z 39423; Ⓟ 1,054; Ⓒ 977
Beauregard; Inc. Place; COPIAH; **194** I-5; elev. 476ft./145m.; mail Wesson z 39191; Ⓟ 206; Ⓒ 265
Beauvoir; RMC Place; HARRISON; ***194** M-8; ★ **BIL-**; pop. incl. with Biloxi (Inc. Place)
Becker; RMC Place; MONROE; **194** D-9; elev. 235ft./72m.; 🄿; z 38825; ● 260
Beech Springs; RMC Place; LEE; ***194** C-9; mail Saltillo z 38866; ● 230
Beechwood; RMC Place; AMITE; ***194** K-4; elev. 269ft./82m.; mail Liberty z 39645; rural
Bee Lake; RMC Place; HOLMES; ***194** F-5; mail Tchula z 39169; rural
Belden; RMC Place; LEE; **194** C-9; 🄿; z 38826; pop. incl. with Tupelo (Inc. Place)
Belen; RMC Place; QUITMAN; **194** C-5; 🄿; z 38609; ● 250
Bellefontaine; RMC Place; WEBSTER; **194** E-8; 🄿; z 39737; ● 250
Belle Isle; RMC Place; HANCOCK; ★ **N.O.**; mail Pearlington z 39572; ● 270
Belleville; RMC Place; PERRY; ***194** K-8; elev. 121ft./37m.; mail New Augusta z 39462; rural
Bellewood; RMC Place; HUMPHREYS; ***194** F-5; elev. 112ft./34m.; mail Isola z 38754; rural
Bells School; RMC Place; OKTIBBEHA; mail Starkville z 39759; rural
Belmont; Inc. Place; TISHOMINGO; **194** C-10; 🄿; z 38827; Ⓟ 1,554; Ⓒ 1,961
Belzoni; Inc. Place; ⊡ HUMPHREYS; **194** F-5; 🄿 🄷; z 39038; Ⓟ 2,536; Ⓒ 2,663
Benjoe (Avent); RMC Place; GREENE; ***194** K-9; mail Mc Lain z 39456; rural
Benndale; RMC Place; GEORGE; ***194** L-9; elev. 92ft./28m.; 🄿; z 39456 & mail Lucedale z 39452; rural
Benoit; Inc. Place; BOLIVAR; **194** E-4; 🄿; z 38725; Ⓟ 641; Ⓒ 611
Benson; RMC Place; JONES; ***194** J-8; elev. 262ft./80m.; mail Ellisville z 39437; rural
Bentley; RMC Place; CALHOUN; ***194** D-8; mail Mantee z 39751; rural
Bent Oak; RMC Place; LOWNDES; ***194** E-9; mail Columbus z 39701; rural
Benton; RMC Place; YAZOO; **194** G-6; 🄿; z 39039; ● 400
BENTON; **194** B-8; Ⓟ 8,046; Ⓒ 8,026; ◆ 8,048
Bentonia; Inc. Place; YAZOO; **194** G-5; elev. 188ft./57m.; 🄿; z 39040; Ⓟ 390; Ⓒ 500
Benwood; RMC Place; YALOBUSHA; ***194** D-7; mail Coffeeville z 38922; ● 60
Berclair; RMC Place; LEFLORE; ***194** E-5; mail Itta Bena z 38941
Bertice (McDonald); RMC Place; LEAKE; ***194** G-7; mail Lena z 39094; rural
Berwick; RMC Place; AMITE; ***194** K-4; elev. 350ft./107m.; mail Liberty z 39645; rural
Bethany; RMC Place; LEE; ***194** B-9; mail Baldwyn z 38824, Guntown z 38849; ● 30
Betheden; RMC Place; WINSTON; ***194** F-8; mail Louisville z 39339; rural
Bethel; RMC Place; NEWTON; ***194** H-8; mail Newton z 39345; rural
Bethlehem; RMC Place; MARSHALL; **194** B-8; mail Potts Camp z 38659; ● 120
Bethlehem; PONTOTOC; see Possum Trot (RMC Place)
Bethsaida; RMC Place; NESHOBA; ***194** G-8; mail Philadelphia z 39350; rural
Bett; RMC Place; TATE; ***194** B-7; mail Coldwater z 38618
Beulah; Inc. Place; BOLIVAR; **194** D-4; 🄿; z 38726; Ⓟ 460; Ⓒ 473
Beulah; RMC Place; NEWTON; ***194** H-8; elev. 500ft./152m.; mail Little Rock z 39337; ● 110
Beulah Hubbard; RMC Place; NEWTON; ***194** H-8; mail Little Rock z 39337; rural
Beverly (Davenport); RMC Place; COAHOMA; ***194** C-5; mail Clarksdale z 38614; ● 50
Bewelcome; RMC Place; AMITE; ***194** K-4; elev. 398ft./121m.; mail Gloster z 39638; rural
Bexley; RMC Place; GEORGE; ***194** K-9; mail Lucedale z 39452; rural
Bigbee; RMC Place; MONROE; ***194** D-9; mail Amory z 38821
Bigbee Valley; RMC Place; NOXUBEE; **194** F-10; 🄿; z 39739; ● 80
Big Creek; Inc. Place; CALHOUN; **194** D-7; 🄿; z 38914; Ⓟ 123; Ⓒ 127
Biggersville; RMC Place; ALCORN; **194** B-9; mail Corinth z 38834; ● 300
Big Level; RMC Place; STONE; ***194** L-8; mail Perkinston z 39573, Wiggins z 39577; rural
Big Point; CDP; JACKSON; **194** L-9; mail Pascagoula z 39567, z 39581; Ⓒ 115
Billups; RMC Place; LOWNDES; ***194** E-9; mail Columbus z 39701; rural
Biloxi; Inc. Place; ⊡ HARRISON; **194** M-9; 🄿 🄷 ■; ★ **BIL-**; z 39530-35, z 39540; Ⓟ 46,319; Ⓒ 50,644; ◆ 48,420
Binford; RMC Place; MONROE; ***194** D-9; elev. 262ft./80m.; mail Aberdeen z 39730; rural
Binnsville; RMC Place; KEMPER; ***194** F-10; elev. 232ft./71m.; mail Scooba z 39358; rural
Birmingham Ridge; RMC Place; LEE; ***194** C-9; elev. 370ft./113m.; mail Blue Springs z 38828; rural
Bissell; RMC Place; LEE; **194** C-9; mail Tupelo z 38801; pop. incl. with Tupelo (Inc. Place)
Black Bayou Junction; RMC Place; LEFLORE; ***194** D-6; mail Glendora z 38928; rural
Black Hawk; RMC Place; CARROLL; **194** E-6; mail Coila z 38923; ● 100
Blackjack; RMC Place; OKTIBBEHA; ***194** E-9; mail Starkville z 39759; rural
Blackland; RMC Place; PRENTISS; ***194** B-9; elev. 426ft./130m.; mail Booneville z 38829; ● 100
Blackwater; RMC Place; KEMPER; **194** G-9; elev. 315ft./96m.; mail Daleville z 39326; ● 80
Blackwater; RMC Place; MARSHALL; ***194** G-7; mail Waterford z 38685; rural
Blaine; RMC Place; SUNFLOWER; **194** E-5; elev. 125ft./38m.; mail Sunflower z 38778; ● 50
Blair; RMC Place; LEE; **194** C-9; elev. 362ft./110m.; mail Guntown z 38849; ● 60
Blakely; RMC Place; WARREN; **194** H-4; ★ **VICK**; mail Vicksburg z 39183; rural
Blanton; RMC Place; SHARKEY; ***194** G-4; mail Rolling Fork z 39159; rural
Bloody Springs; RMC Place; TISHOMINGO; ***194** B-10; elev. 542ft./165m.; mail Belmont z 38827; rural
Bloomfield; RMC Place; KEMPER; ***194** G-9; elev. 406ft./124m.; mail De Kalb z 39328; rural
Bloomfield; RMC Place; NESHOBA; ***194** G-8; elev. 520ft./158m.; mail Philadelphia z 39350; rural
Blue Hills; RMC Place; CLAIBORNE; mail Pattison z 39144; ● 100
Blue Lake; RMC Place; TALLAHATCHIE; ***194** D-5; mail Drew z 38737; rural
Blue Mountain; Inc. Place; TIPPAH; **194** B-8; 🄿 🄲 366; z 38610; Ⓟ 667; Ⓒ 670
Blue Springs; Inc. Place; UNION; **194** C-9; 🄿; z 38828; Ⓟ 140; Ⓒ 144
Bluff Springs; RMC Place; KEMPER; ***194** G-9; mail De Kalb z 39328; rural
Bluff Springs; RMC Place; PANOLA; ***194** C-7; elev. 380ft./116m.; mail Sardis z 38666; rural
Bobo; RMC Place; COAHOMA; **194** C-5; mail Clarksdale z 38614; ● 100
Bobo; RMC Place; QUITMAN; ***194** C-6; mail Marks z 38646; rural
Boggan Bend; RMC Place; LEE; ***194** C-9; elev. 349ft./106m.; mail Guntown z 38849; rural
Bogue Chitto; CDP; KEMPER, NESHOBA; ***194** G-8; elev. 450ft./137m.; mail Philadelphia z 39350, Preston z 39354; Ⓟ 689; Ⓒ 533
Bogue Chitto; RMC Place; LINCOLN; **194** J-5; 🄿; z 39629; ● 700
Boice; RMC Place; WAYNE; ***194** I-9; mail Waynesboro z 39367; rural
Bolatusha; RMC Place; LEAKE; ***194** F-7; mail Sallis z 39160; rural
Bolivar; RMC Place; BOLIVAR; ***194** E-4; elev. 144ft./44m.; mail Benoit z 38725; ● 100
BOLIVAR; **194** D-4; Ⓟ 41,875; Ⓒ 40,633; ◆ 36,730
Bolton; Inc. Place; HINDS; **194** H-5; elev. 217ft./66m.; 🄿; ★ **JAC**; z 39041; Ⓟ 637; Ⓒ 629
Bond; RMC Place; NESHOBA; ***194** G-8; elev. 481ft./147m.; mail Philadelphia z 39350; rural
Bond; RMC Place; STONE; **194** L-8; elev. 302ft./92m.; mail Wiggins z 39577; ● 500
Bonhomme; RMC Place; FORREST; ***194** K-8; ★ **HATT**; mail Hattiesburg z 39401; pop. incl. with Hattiesburg (Inc. Place)
Bonita; RMC Place; LAUDERDALE; ***194** H-9; ★ **MRID**; mail Meridian z 39301; pop. incl. with Meridian (Inc. Place)
Boon; RMC Place; WINSTON; ***194** F-8; elev. 500ft./152m.; mail Louisville z 39339; rural
Booneville; Inc. Place; ⊡ PRENTISS; **194** B-9; 🄿 🄷; z 38829; Ⓟ 7,955; Ⓒ 8,625
Bothwell; RMC Place; GREENE; ***194** J-9; elev. 295ft./90m.; mail Richton z 39476; rural
Bounds Crossroads; RMC Place; ITAWAMBA; ***194** C-10; elev. 435ft./133m.; mail Red Bay z 35582; rural
Bourbon; RMC Place; WASHINGTON; ***194** E-5; mail Leland z 38756
Bovina; RMC Place; WARREN; **194** H-5; elev. 244ft./74m.; ★ **VICK**; mail Vicksburg z 39180; ● 140
Bowdre; RMC Place; TUNICA; ***194** B-5; mail Robinsonville z 38664; rural
Bowling Green; RMC Place; HOLMES; ***194** F-6; elev. 324ft./99m.; mail Durant z 39063
Bowman; RMC Place; TATE; ***194** B-6; mail Coldwater z 38618; rural
Boyer; RMC Place; SUNFLOWER; ***194** E-5; elev. 126ft./38m.; mail Indianola z 38751; rural
Boyette; RMC Place; ATTALA; ***194** F-7; elev. 276ft./84m.; mail Sallis z 39160; rural
Boyle; Inc. Place; BOLIVAR; **194** E-5; elev. 139ft./42m.; 🄿; z 38730; Ⓟ 651; Ⓒ 720
Bradley; RMC Place; OKTIBBEHA; ***194** E-8; elev. 328ft./100m.; mail Starkville z 39759
Branch; RMC Place; SCOTT; ***194** H-7; mail Morton z 39117; rural
Brandon; Inc. Place; ⊡ RANKIN; **194** H-6; elev. 486ft./148m.; 🄿 🄷; ★ **JAC**; z 39042-43, z 39047; Ⓟ 11,077; Ⓒ 16,436; ◆ 20,721
Branyan; RMC Place; UNION; ***194** C-9; mail Blue Springs z 38828; rural
Brasfield; RMC Place; JEFFERSON; ***194** I-4; mail Lorman z 39096; rural
Bratton; RMC Place; HINDS; ★ **JAC**; pop. incl. with Jackson (Inc. Place)
Braxton; Inc. Place; SIMPSON; **194** I-6; 🄿; z 39044; Ⓟ 141; Ⓒ 181
Brazil (Stover); RMC Place; TALLAHATCHIE; ***194** D-6; mail Tutwiler z 38963
Brewer; RMC Place; CLARKE; ***194** I-9; elev. 345ft./105m.; mail Quitman z 39355; rural
Brewer; RMC Place; LEE; ***194** C-9; mail Shannon z 38868; rural
Brewer; RMC Place; PERRY; ***194** J-9; elev. 234ft./71m.; mail Richton z 39476; rural
Bright; RMC Place; DESOTO; ***194** B-6; mail Hernando z 38632; rural
Bristers Store; RMC Place; LAWRENCE; ***194** J-6; mail Jayess z 39641; ● 30
Brockton; RMC Place; LAUDERDALE; ***194** H-9; ★ **MRID**; mail Meridian z 39301
Brody; RMC Place; BENTON; ***194** A-8; elev. 604ft./184m.; mail Ashland z 38603; rural
Brookhaven; Inc. Place; ⊡ LINCOLN; **194** J-5; elev. 487ft./148m.; 🄿 🄷 ■; z 39601-03; Ⓟ 10,243; Ⓒ 9,861; ◆ 9,935
Brookhaven West; RMC Place; LINCOLN; mail Brookhaven z 39603; pop. incl. with Brookhaven (Inc. Place)
Brookhollow Place; RMC Place; HINDS; ***194** H-5; ★ **JAC**; mail Jackson z 39212; rural
Brooklyn; RMC Place; FORREST; **194** K-8; 🄿; z 39425; ● 900
Brooks; RMC Place; SUNFLOWER; ***194** D-5; mail Drew z 38737; rural
Brooksville; Inc. Place; NOXUBEE; **194** F-9; elev. 277ft./84m.; 🄿; z 39739; Ⓟ 1,098; Ⓒ 1,182
Brownfield; RMC Place; TIPPAH; **194** A-9; elev. 460ft./140m.; mail Walnut z 38683; ● 250
Browning; RMC Place; LEFLORE; ***194** E-6; mail Greenwood z 38930; rural
Brownsville; RMC Place; HINDS; **194** H-5; mail Bolton z 39041; ● 40
Brown Town; RMC Place; GREENE; **194** K-10; elev. 269ft./82m.; mail Leakesville z 39451, Lucedale z 39452; total pop. 100 includes 50 in Alabama; ● 50
Brozville; RMC Place; HOLMES; ***194** F-6; mail Lexington z 39095; rural
Bruce; Inc. Place; CALHOUN; **194** D-8; 🄿 🄷; z 38915, z 38949; Ⓟ 2,127; Ⓒ 2,097
Brunswick; RMC Place; WARREN; ***194** G-4; mail Vicksburg z 39183; rural
Bryant; RMC Place; YALOBUSHA; ***194** D-7; mail Coffeeville z 38922; ● 60
Bucatunna; WAYNE; see Buckatunna (RMC Place)
Buchannan; RMC Place; PONTOTOC; ***194** C-8; mail Pontotoc z 38863; rural
Buckatunna (Bucatunna); RMC Place; WAYNE; **194** J-9; elev. 148ft./45m.; 🄿; z 39322; ● 600
Buckhorn; RMC Place; PONTOTOC; ***194** D-8; mail Randolph z 38864; ● 70
Bude; Inc. Place; FRANKLIN; **194** J-4; elev. 232ft./71m.; 🄿; z 39630; Ⓟ 969; Ⓒ 1,037
Buena Vista; RMC Place; CHICKASAW; **194** D-9; mail Houston z 38851; ● 70
Buena Vista; RMC Place; TIPPAH; **194** B-8; mail Ripley z 38663
Buena Vista Lakes; RMC Place; DESOTO; ***194** B-6; elev. 300ft./91m.; mail Hernando z 38632; ● 380
Bunker Hill; RMC Place; MARION; **194** J-7; mail Columbia z 39429; ● 150
Bunkley; RMC Place; FRANKLIN; ***194** J-4; elev. 194ft./59m.; mail Meadville z 39653; rural
Burgess; RMC Place; LAFAYETTE; ***194** C-7; mail Oxford z 38655; ● 50
Burns; RMC Place; SMITH; ***194** H-7; mail Raleigh z 39153; rural
Burnside; RMC Place; NESHOBA; ***194** G-8; mail Philadelphia z 39350; rural
Burnsville; Inc. Place; TISHOMINGO; **194** B-10; elev. 465ft./142m.; 🄿; z 38833; Ⓟ 949; Ⓒ 1,034
Burrell; RMC Place; QUITMAN; mail Falcon z 38628; ● 50
Burtons; RMC Place; PRENTISS; ***194** B-10; mail Booneville z 38829; ● 30
Bush; RMC Place; SIMPSON; ***194** I-6; mail Pinola z 39149; rural
Busy Corner; RMC Place; AMITE; ***194** K-4; mail Gloster z 39638, Liberty z 39645
Butler; RMC Place; HOLMES; ***194** F-6; mail Tchula z 39169; rural
Byhalia; Inc. Place; MARSHALL; **194** B-7; elev. 369ft./112m.; 🄿; z 38611; Ⓟ 955; Ⓒ 706
Byram; CDP; HINDS; **194** H-6; elev. 265ft./81m.; 🄿; ★ **JAC**; z 39272; Ⓒ 7,386

C

Cadamy; RMC Place; ITAWAMBA; ***194** C-10; elev. 360ft./110m.; mail Tremont z 38876; rural
Cadaretta; RMC Place; WEBSTER; ***194** E-7; mail Gore Springs z 38929; rural
Caesar; RMC Place; PEARL RIVER; **194** L-7; elev. 172ft./52m.; mail Carriere z 39426, Picayune z 39466; ● 250
Caile; RMC Place; SUNFLOWER; ***194** F-5; elev. 112ft./34m.; mail Isola z 38754; rural
Cairo; RMC Place; PRENTISS; ***194** B-10; mail Tishomingo z 38873; ● 60
Caledonia; Inc. Place; LOWNDES; **194** E-10; elev. 339ft./103m.; 🄿; z 39740; Ⓟ 821; Ⓒ 1,015
Calhoun; RMC Place; JONES; ***194** J-8; elev. 284ft./87m.; ★ **LAUR**; mail Laurel z 39440, z 39443
Calhoun; RMC Place; NEWTON; ***194** H-8; mail Newton z 39345
CALHOUN; **194** D-7; Ⓟ 14,908; Ⓒ 15,069; ◆ 14,327
Calhoun City; Inc. Place; CALHOUN; **194** D-8; 🄿 🄷; z 38916, z 38955; Ⓟ 1,838; Ⓒ 1,872
Calyx; RMC Place; NOXUBEE; ***194** F-9; mail Shuqualak z 39361; rural
Cambridge; RMC Place; LAFAYETTE; ***194** C-7; mail Abbeville z 38601; rural
Camden; RMC Place; MADISON; **194** G-7; 🄿; z 39045; ● 700
Cameron; RMC Place; MADISON; ***194** G-6; elev. 365ft./111m.; mail Pickens z 39146; rural
Cameta; RMC Place; SHARKEY; ***194** F-4; mail Rolling Fork z 39159; rural
Campbell; RMC Place; TIPPAH; mail Ripley z 38663; pop. incl. with Ripley (Inc. Place)
Canaan; RMC Place; BENTON; **194** A-8; elev. 613ft./187m.; 🄿; z 38603; ● 40
Candlestick; RMC Place; HINDS; ★ **JAC**; mail Jackson z 39212; pop. incl. with Jackson (Inc. Place)
Candlestick Park; RMC Place; HINDS; ★ **JAC**; mail Jackson z 39212, z 39282; pop. incl. with Jackson (Inc. Place)
Cannonsburg; RMC Place; JEFFERSON; ***194** J-4; mail Natchez z 39120; ● 130
Canton; Inc. Place; ⊡ MADISON; **194** G-6; 🄿 🄷; z 39046; Ⓟ 10,062; Ⓒ 12,911
Cardsville; RMC Place; ITAWAMBA; ***194** C-10; mail Nettleton z 38858; rural
Carlisle; RMC Place; CLAIBORNE; **194** I-4; mail Hermanville z 39086; ● 90
Carlos; RMC Place; LINCOLN; ***194** J-5; mail Wesson z 39191; rural
Carmack; RMC Place; ATTALA; ***194** F-7; mail Vaiden z 39176; ● 30
Carmichael; RMC Place; CLARKE; ***194** I-9; elev. 335ft./102m.; mail Shubuta z 39360; ● 50
Carmichael; RMC Place; PERRY; mail Beaumont z 39423; rural
Carnes; RMC Place; FORREST; **194** K-8; elev. 313ft./95m.; mail Lumberton z 39455; ● 150
Carolina; RMC Place; ITAWAMBA; ***194** C-9; elev. 348ft./106m.; mail Nettleton z 38858; rural
Carpenter; RMC Place; COPIAH; **194** I-5; elev. 162ft./49m.; mail Hermanville z 39086; ● 110
Carriere; RMC Place; PEARL RIVER; **194** L-7; elev. 166ft./51m.; 🄿; z 39426; ● 880
CARROLL; **194** E-6; Ⓟ 9,237; Ⓒ 10,769; ◆ 10,401
Carrollton; Inc. Place; ⊡ CARROLL; **194** E-6; 🄿; z 38917; Ⓟ 221; Ⓒ 408
Carrollton; CARROLL; see North Carrollton (Inc. Place)
Carson; RMC Place; JEFFERSON DAVIS; **194** J-7; 🄿; z 39427; ● 500
Carter; RMC Place; YAZOO; **194** F-5; mail Yazoo City z 39194; ● 80
Carterville; RMC Place; FORREST; ***194** K-8; ★ **HATT**; mail Hattiesburg z 39401, Petal z 39465; pop. incl. with Petal (Inc. Place)
Carthage; Inc. Place; ⊡ LEAKE; **194** G-7; elev. 400ft./122m.; 🄿 🄷; z 39051; Ⓟ 3,819; Ⓒ 4,637
Cary; Inc. Place; SHARKEY; **194** G-4; 🄿; z 39054; Ⓟ 392; Ⓒ 427
Cascilla; RMC Place; TALLAHATCHIE; **194** D-6; 🄿; z 38920; ● 100
Caseyville; RMC Place; LINCOLN; ***194** J-5; mail Union Church z 39668, Wesson z 39191; rural
Catchings; SHARKEY; see Delta City (RMC Place)
Cato; RMC Place; RANKIN; ***194** I-6; mail Brandon z 39042, Braxton z 39044; rural
Cayce; RMC Place; MARSHALL; ***194** A-7; elev. 420ft./128m.; mail Collierville z 38017
Cayuga; RMC Place; HINDS; ***194** H-5; elev. 276ft./84m.; mail Utica z 39175; ● 40
Cedar Bluff; RMC Place; CLAY; **194** E-9; 🄿; z 39741; ● 450
Cedar Hill; RMC Place; MADISON; ***194** H-6; elev. 407ft./124m.; mail Flora z 39071
Cedar Hill; RMC Place; MONTGOMERY; ***194** E-7; mail Duck Hill z 38925; rural
Cedars; RMC Place; WARREN; ***194** H-4; ★ **VICK**; mail Vicksburg z 39180; pop. incl. with Vicksburg (Inc. Place)
Cedarview; RMC Place; DESOTO; ***194** A-7; ★ **MEM**; mail Olive Branch z 38654; ● 150
Center; RMC Place; ATTALA; ***194** F-7; mail Kosciusko z 39090; rural
Center; RMC Place; UNION; ***194** C-8; elev. 570ft./174m.; mail Blue Springs z 38828, New Albany z 38652; rural
Center Hill; RMC Place; LAUDERDALE; ***194** G-9; elev. 365ft./111m.; ★ **MRID**; mail Meridian z 39305; ● 50
Center Point; COPIAH; see Glancy (RMC Place)
Center Ridge; RMC Place; NEWTON; ***194** H-8; mail Chunky z 39323; ● 30
Center Ridge; RMC Place; SMITH; **194** I-7; elev. 449ft./137m.; mail Taylorsville z 39168
Center Ridge; RMC Place; WINSTON; ***194** F-8; mail Louisville z 39339; rural
Centerville; RMC Place; ITAWAMBA; **194** C-9; mail Mantachie z 38855; pop. incl. with Mantachie (Inc. Place)
Central Academy; RMC Place; PANOLA; ***194** C-7; mail Batesville z 38606; ● 90
Centralgrove; RMC Place; MONROE; ***194** D-9; mail Aberdeen z 39730, Nettleton z 38858; rural
Centreville; Inc. Place; WILKINSON, AMITE; **194** K-4; elev. 380ft./116m.; 🄿 🄷; z 39631; Ⓟ 1,771; Ⓒ 1,680
Chalybeate; RMC Place; TIPPAH; **194** A-9; mail Walnut z 38683; ● 320
Champion Hill; RMC Place; HINDS; ***194** H-5; elev. 196ft./60m.; mail Edwards z 39066; ● 30
Chapel Hill; RMC Place; HINDS; ***194** I-5; mail Utica z 39175; ● 50
Charleston; Inc. Place; ⊡ TALLAHATCHIE; **194** D-6; 🄿 🄷; z 38921, z 38958; Ⓟ 2,328; Ⓒ 2,198
Chatawa; RMC Place; PIKE; **194** K-5; 🄿; z 39632; ● 160
Chatham; RMC Place; WASHINGTON; **194** F-4; 🄿; z 38731; ● 40
Cheraw; RMC Place; MARION; ***194** K-6; mail Foxworth z 39483
Cherrycreek; RMC Place; PONTOTOC; ***194** C-8; mail Blue Springs z 38828; rural
Chester; RMC Place; CHOCTAW; **194** E-8; mail Ackerman z 39735; ● 220
Chesterville; RMC Place; LEE, PONTOTOC; ***194** C-9; mail Belden z 38826, Tupelo z 38801; ● 30
CHICKASAW; **194** D-8; Ⓟ 18,085; Ⓒ 19,440; ◆ 18,740
Chicora; RMC Place; WAYNE; **194** J-9; mail Buckatunna z 39322
Chiwapa; RMC Place; PONTOTOC; ***194** C-8; elev. 453ft./138m.; mail Pontotoc z 38863; rural
Choctaw; RMC Place; BOLIVAR; **194** E-4; elev. 129ft./39m.; mail Shaw z 38773; ● 250
Choctaw; RMC Place; JONES; ***194** J-8; 🄿; ★ **LAUR**; z 39350 & mail Laurel z 39440-42; pop. incl. with Laurel (Inc. Place)
CHOCTAW; **194** E-8; Ⓟ 9,071; Ⓒ 9,758; ◆ 8,660
Chulahoma; RMC Place; MARSHALL; ***194** B-7; mail Holly Springs z 38635
Chunky; Inc. Place; NEWTON; **194** H-8; elev. 316ft./96m.; 🄿; z 39323; Ⓟ 292; Ⓒ 344
Church Hill; RMC Place; JEFFERSON; **194** I-4; elev. 208ft./63m.; 🄿; z 39120; ● 40
Clack; RMC Place; TUNICA; ***194** B-6; mail Robinsonville z 38664; rural
CLAIBORNE; **194** I-4; Ⓟ 11,370; Ⓒ 11,831; ◆ 10,136
Clara; RMC Place; WAYNE; **194** J-9; 🄿; z 39324; ● 400
Claremont; RMC Place; COAHOMA; ***194** C-5; mail Clarksdale z 38614; rural
CLARKE; **194** I-9; Ⓟ 17,313; Ⓒ 17,955; ◆ 16,934
Clarksburg; RMC Place; RANKIN, SCOTT; ***194** H-7; mail Morton z 39117; rural
Clarksdale; Inc. Place; ⊡ COAHOMA; **194** C-5; 🄿 🄷 ■; z 38614, z 38669; Ⓟ 19,717; Ⓒ 20,645; ◆ 18,609
Clarkson; RMC Place; WEBSTER; ***194** E-8; elev. 510ft./155m.; mail Mathiston z 39752; rural
Clay; RMC Place; ITAWAMBA; ***194** C-10; mail Fulton z 38843; rural
CLAY; **194** E-9; Ⓟ 21,120; Ⓒ 21,979; ◆ 20,544
Clayrysville; RMC Place; TIPPAH; ***194** B-8; mail Ripley z 38663; rural
Clayton; RMC Place; TUNICA; ***194** B-5; mail Dundee z 38626; rural
Clayton Village; RMC Place; OKTIBBEHA; ***194** E-9; mail Starkville z 39759; ● 340
Claytown; RMC Place; WINSTON; ***194** F-8; elev. 449ft./137m.; mail Louisville z 39339; rural
Clear Creek Ranch; GRENADA; see Glenwild (RMC Place)
Cleary (Hoover Lake and Park); RMC Place; RANKIN; **194** H-6; ★ **JAC**; mail Florence z 39073; ● 1,150
Clem; RMC Place; JEFFERSON DAVIS; **194** J-7; mail Prentiss z 39474; ● 50
Cleo; RMC Place; JONES; ***194** J-8; elev. 234ft./71m.; ★ **LAUR**; mail Laurel z 39440, z 39443; rural
Clermont Harbor; RMC Place; HANCOCK; **194** M-7; 🄿; ★ **BIL-**; z 39558; summer pop. 550; ● 470
Cleveland; Inc. Place; ⊡ BOLIVAR; **194** D-5; elev. 142ft./43m.; 🄿 🄷 🄲 4,217; z 38732-33; Ⓟ 15,384; Ⓒ 13,841
Cleveland; RMC Place; KEMPER; ***194** G-9; elev. 531ft./162m.; mail De Kalb z 39328; rural
Clifton; RMC Place; SCOTT; ***194** H-7; mail Forest z 39074; rural
Cliftonville; RMC Place; NOXUBEE; **194** F-10; mail Brooksville z 39739; ● 90
Clinton; Inc. Place; HINDS; **194** H-5; elev. 381ft./116m.; 🄿 🄲 4,038; ★ **JAC**; z 39056, z 39058, z 39060; Ⓟ 21,847; Ⓒ 23,347; ◆ 23,547
Cloverdale; RMC Place; ADAMS; **194** J-3; elev. 145ft./44m.; ★ **NCHZ**; mail Natchez z 39120; ● 340
Clover Hill; RMC Place; COAHOMA; ***194** C-5; mail Lyon z 38645; rural
Coahoma; Inc. Place; COAHOMA; **194** C-5; elev. 179ft./55m.; 🄿; z 38617; Ⓟ 254; Ⓒ 325
COAHOMA; **194** C-5; Ⓟ 31,665; Ⓒ 30,622; ◆ 26,669
Coalville; HARRISON; see Wool Market (RMC Place)
Coats; RMC Place; SIMPSON; ***194** I-7; mail Mount Olive z 39119; rural
Cobbs; RMC Place; LINCOLN; ***194** J-5; elev. 398ft./121m.; mail Brookhaven z 39601; rural
Cobbville; RMC Place; MADISON; ***194** G-6; mail Canton z 39046; rural
Cockrum; RMC Place; DESOTO; ***194** B-7; mail Hernando z 38632; ● 200
Coffeeville; Inc. Place; ⊡ YALOBUSHA; **194** D-7; 🄿; z 38922; Ⓟ 825; Ⓒ 930
Cohay; RMC Place; SMITH; ***194** I-7; mail Raleigh z 39153; rural
Coila; RMC Place; CARROLL; **194** E-6; 🄿; z 38923; ● 50
Colby; RMC Place; YAZOO; ***194** G-5; mail Yazoo City z 39194; ● 40
Coldwater; RMC Place; NESHOBA; ***194** G-8; mail Philadelphia z 39350; rural
Coldwater; Inc. Place; TATE; **194** B-6; 🄿; z 38618; Ⓟ 1,502; Ⓒ 1,674
Coles; RMC Place; AMITE; **194** K-4; elev. 237ft./72m.; mail Crosby z 39633, Gloster z 39638; ● 60
College Hill; RMC Place; LAFAYETTE; ***194** C-7; mail Oxford z 38655; ● 200
College Hill Station; RMC Place; LAFAYETTE; ***194** C-7; mail Oxford z 38655; ● 80
Collins; Inc. Place; ⊡ COVINGTON; **194** J-7; 🄿 🄷; z 39428; Ⓟ 2,541; Ⓒ 2,683
Collinsville; CDP; LAUDERDALE; **194** H-9; elev. 450ft./137m.; 🄿; ★ **MRID**; z 39325; Ⓟ 1,364; Ⓒ 1,823
Colonial; RMC Place; HINDS; ***194** H-6; ★ **JAC**; mail Jackson z 39211; pop. incl. with Jackson (Inc. Place)
Colony Town; RMC Place; LEFLORE; ***194** E-5; mail Itta Bena z 38941; rural
Colsub (Amory Junction); RMC Place; MONROE; mail Amory z 38821; pop. incl. with Amory (Inc. Place)
Columbia; Inc. Place; ⊡ MARION; **194** K-7; 🄿 🄷; z 39429; Ⓟ 6,815; Ⓒ 6,603
Columbus; Inc. Place; ⊡ LOWNDES; **194** E-9; 🄿 🄷 🄲 2,428 ■; ★ **COL**; z 39701-05, z 39710; Ⓟ 23,799; Ⓒ 25,944; ◆ 24,280
Columbus AFB; CDP-Census Area Only; LOWNDES; ***194** E-9; 🄿; ★ **COL**; z 39701, z 39710 & mail Columbus z 39705; Ⓟ 2,890; Ⓒ 2,060
Commerce; RMC Place; TUNICA; **194** B-5; mail Robinsonville z 38664; rural
Como; Inc. Place; PANOLA; **194** C-6; 🄿; z 38619; Ⓟ 1,387; Ⓒ 1,310
Concord; RMC Place; UNION; ***194** B-8; mail New Albany z 38652; rural
Conehatta; CDP; NEWTON; **194** H-8; 🄿; z 39057; Ⓟ 925; Ⓒ 997
Conway; RMC Place; LEAKE; ***194** G-7; elev. 465ft./142m.; mail Carthage z 39051; rural
Cooksville; RMC Place; NOXUBEE; ***194** F-10; mail Macon z 39341; rural
Cooperville; RMC Place; SCOTT; ***194** H-7; mail Morton z 39117; rural
Coosa; RMC Place; LEAKE; ***194** G-7; elev. 461ft./141m.; mail Carthage z 39051; rural
COPIAH; **194** I-5; Ⓟ 27,592; Ⓒ 28,757; ◆ 29,137
Corinth; Inc. Place; ⊡ ALCORN; **194** A-9; elev. 455ft./139m.; 🄿 🄷 ■; z 38834-35; Ⓟ 11,820; Ⓒ 14,054; ◆ 14,115
Cornersville; RMC Place; MARSHALL; ***194** B-8; mail Hickory Flat z 38633, Potts Camp z 38659
Corrona; RMC Place; LEE; ***194** C-9; mail Guntown z 38849; rural
Cotton Plant; RMC Place; TIPPAH; **194** B-8; mail Blue Mountain z 38610; ● 40
Cottonville; RMC Place; TATE; ***194** B-6; mail Coldwater z 38618
Country Life School; RANKIN; see Piney Woods (RMC Place)
Counts; RMC Place; COAHOMA; ***194** D-5; elev. 158ft./48m.; mail Clarksdale z 38614; rural
Courthouse; RMC Place; HARRISON; ★ **BIL-**; mail Gulfport z 39501; pop. incl. with Gulfport (Inc. Place)
Courtland; Inc. Place; PANOLA; **194** C-6; 🄿; z 38620; Ⓟ 329; Ⓒ 460
COVINGTON; **194** J-7; Ⓟ 16,527; Ⓒ 19,407; ◆ 20,322
Cowart; RMC Place; TALLAHATCHIE; ***194** D-6; mail Charleston z 38921
Coxburg; RMC Place; HOLMES; **194** F-6; elev. 334ft./102m.; mail Lexington z 39095; ● 30
Coxs Ferry; RMC Place; HINDS; ***194** G-5; elev. 154ft./47m.; mail Bolton z 39041; rural
Coy; RMC Place; KEMPER, NESHOBA; ***194** G-8; mail Preston z 39354; rural
Craigside; RMC Place; LEFLORE; ***194** E-6; mail Greenwood z 38930
Craig Springs; RMC Place; OKTIBBEHA; ***194** E-8; mail Sturgis z 39769; rural
Crandall; RMC Place; CLARKE; ***194** I-9; elev. 254ft./77m.; mail Quitman z 39355; rural
Crane Creek; RMC Place; HANCOCK; ***194** L-8; mail Perkinston z 39573; rural
Cranfield; RMC Place; ADAMS; **194** J-4; elev. 394ft./120m.; mail Roxie z 39661; ● 140
Crawford; Inc. Place; LOWNDES; **194** F-9; elev. 321ft./98m.; 🄿; z 39743; Ⓟ 668; Ⓒ 655
Crenshaw; Inc. Place; QUITMAN, PANOLA; **194** C-6; 🄿; z 38621; Ⓟ 978; Ⓒ 916
Crockett; RMC Place; TATE; ***194** B-6; mail Senatobia z 38668
Crosby; Inc. Place; AMITE, WILKINSON; **194** K-4; elev. 168ft./51m.; 🄿; z 39633; Ⓟ 465; Ⓒ 360
Crossgates; RMC Place; RANKIN; ★ **JAC**; mail Brandon z 39042; pop. incl. with Brandon (Inc. Place)
Crossroad; RMC Place; LEAKE; ***194** G-7; elev. 518ft./158m.; mail Carthage z 39051; rural
Crossroads; RMC Place; GEORGE; ***194** L-9; elev. 160ft./49m.; mail Lucedale z 39452; rural
Crossroads; RMC Place; NESHOBA; ***194** G-8; elev. 590ft./180m.; mail Philadelphia z 39350, Union z 39365; rural
Crossroads; RMC Place; PEARL RIVER; ***194** L-7; elev. 193ft./59m.; mail Greenville z 38701, Poplarville z 39470
Cross Roads; RMC Place; RANKIN; ***194** H-7; mail Pelahatchie z 39145; rural
Cross Roads; RMC Place; TISHOMINGO; ***194** A-10; mail Iuka z 38852; rural
Crossroads; RMC Place; WASHINGTON; ***194** E-4; ★ **GRNV**; mail Greenville z 38701, z 38703, Poplarville z 39470; pop. incl. with Greenville (Inc. Place)
Crotts; RMC Place; JONES; ***194** J-8; mail Ellisville z 39437; rural
Crowder; Inc. Place; QUITMAN, PANOLA; **194** C-6; 🄿; z 38622; Ⓟ 758; Ⓒ 766
Crown Zellerback; ISSAQUENA; see New Fitler (RMC Place)
Cruger; Inc. Place; HOLMES; **194** E-6; 🄿; z 38924; Ⓟ 548; Ⓒ 449
Crupp; RMC Place; YAZOO; ***194** G-5; mail Yazoo City z 39194; ● 80
Crystal Springs; Inc. Place; COPIAH; **194** I-5; elev. 464ft./141m.; 🄿; z 39059; Ⓟ 5,643; Ⓒ 5,873
Cuba; RMC Place; ALCORN; ***194** A-9; elev. 410ft./125m.; mail Corinth z 38834; rural
Cub Lake; RMC Place; DESOTO; ***194** B-6; elev. 220ft./67m.; mail Hernando z 38632; ● 30
Cuevas (Pineville); RMC Place; HARRISON; **194** M-8; ★ **BIL-**; mail Pass Christian z 39571; ● 170
Cumberland; RMC Place; WEBSTER; ***194** E-8; elev. 465ft./142m.; mail Maben z 39750; ● 110
Curtis Station; RMC Place; PANOLA; **194** C-6; mail Batesville z 38606; ● 140
Cybur; RMC Place; PEARL RIVER; ***194** L-7; elev. 74ft./23m.; mail Carriere z 39426, Picayune z 39466; ● 50
Cynthia; RMC Place; HINDS; ***194** H-6; ★ **JAC**; mail Jackson z 39206; rural

D

Dahomey; RMC Place; BOLIVAR; ***194** E-4; mail Benoit z 38725; rural
Daisy-Vestry; JACKSON; see Vestry (RMC Place)
Daleville; RMC Place; LAUDERDALE; **194** G-9; elev. 386ft./118m.; 🄿; z 39326; ● 150
Damascus; RMC Place; KEMPER; ***194** G-9; elev. 534ft./163m.; mail De Kalb z 39328; rural
Damascus; RMC Place; SCOTT; ***194** G-7; mail Walnut Grove z 39189; rural
Dancy; RMC Place; WEBSTER; ***194** E-8; mail Mantee z 39751; rural
Daniel; RMC Place; SMITH; ***194** H-7; mail Puckett z 39151; rural
Darbun; RMC Place; WALTHALL; ***194** K-6; mail Kokomo z 39643
Darden; RMC Place; UNION; ***194** C-8; mail Myrtle z 38650; rural
Darling; RMC Place; QUITMAN; **194** C-6; 🄿; z 38623; ● 230
Darlove; RMC Place; WASHINGTON; ***194** F-5; elev. 105ft./32m.; mail Hollandale z 38748
Darracott; RMC Place; MONROE; ***194** D-9; mail Aberdeen z 39730; rural
Darrington; RMC Place; WILKINSON; ***194** K-4; mail Crosby z 39633; rural
Davenport; COAHOMA; see Beverly (RMC Place)
Davis; RMC Place; MADISON; ***194** G-6; mail Canton z 39046; rural
Days; RMC Place; DESOTO; ***194** A-6; ★ **MEM**; mail Lake Cormorant z 38641; rural
Days; MONROE; see East Aberdeen (RMC Place)
Deans Corner; RMC Place; DESOTO; ***194** B-6; ★ **MEM**; mail Lake Cormorant z 38641; rural
Deasonville; RMC Place; YAZOO; ***194** G-6; elev. 286ft./87m.; mail Vaughan z 39179; rural
Decatur; Inc. Place; ⊡ NEWTON; **194** H-8; 🄿; z 39327; Ⓟ 1,248; Ⓒ 1,426
Dedeaux (Vidalia); RMC Place; HANCOCK, HARRISON; ***194** M-8; mail Pass Christian z 39571; rural
Deemer; RMC Place; NESHOBA; **194** G-8; mail Philadelphia z 39350; ● 90
Deemer Station; RMC Place; NESHOBA; ***194** G-8; elev. 410ft./125m.; mail Bailey z 39320; rural
Deerbrook; RMC Place; NOXUBEE; ***194** F-9; elev. 260ft./79m.; mail Brooksville z 39739; ● 30
Deeson; RMC Place; BOLIVAR; **194** D-4; mail Duncan z 38740; ● 30
De Kalb; Inc. Place; ⊡ KEMPER; **194** G-9; elev. 464ft./141m.; 🄿 🄷; z 39328; Ⓟ 1,073; Ⓒ 972
Delay; RMC Place; LAFAYETTE; ***194** C-7; elev. 376ft./115m.; mail Oxford z 38655; rural
De Lisle; RMC Place; HARRISON; **194** M-8; elev. 23ft./7m.; ★ **BIL-**; mail Pass Christian z 39571; ● 680
Delta; RMC Place; PANOLA; ***194** C-6; mail Crenshaw z 38621; rural
Delta City (Catchings); RMC Place; SHARKEY; **194** F-5; 🄿; z 39061; ● 250
Delta Drive; RMC Place; HINDS; ★ **JAC**; mail Jackson z 39213, z 39283; pop. incl. with Jackson (Inc. Place)
Delta State University; RMC Place; BOLIVAR; ***194** D-5; mail Cleveland z 38732-33; pop. incl. with Cleveland (Inc. Place)
Denham; RMC Place; WAYNE; ***194** J-9; elev. 178ft./54m.; mail Waynesboro z 39367
Denmark; RMC Place; LAFAYETTE; **194** C-8; elev. 395ft./120m.; mail Oxford z 38655; ● 70
Dennis; RMC Place; TISHOMINGO; **194** B-10; 🄿; z 38838; ● 280
Dennis Settlement; RMC Place; SCOTT; ***194** H-8; elev. 430ft./131m.; mail Lake z 39092; rural
Dentontown; RMC Place; CALHOUN; ***194** D-7; mail Calhoun City z 38916, Slate Spring z 38955
Dentville; RMC Place; COPIAH; **194** I-5; elev. 263ft./80m.; mail Hermanville z 39086; ● 100
Deovolente; RMC Place; HUMPHREYS; ***194** F-5; mail Belzoni z 39038; rural
Derby; RMC Place; PEARL RIVER; ***194** L-7; mail Poplarville z 39470; ● 50
Derma; Inc. Place; CALHOUN; **194** D-8; 🄿; z 38839; Ⓟ 959; Ⓒ 1,023
De Soto; RMC Place; CLARKE; **194** I-9; elev. 210ft./64m.; mail Shubuta z 39360; ● 200
DESOTO; **194** B-6; Ⓟ 67,910; Ⓒ 107,199; ◆ 156,779
Deweese; RMC Place; NESHOBA; ***194** G-8; elev. 598ft./182m.; mail Philadelphia z 39350; rural
Dexter; RMC Place; WALTHALL; ***194** K-6; mail Tylertown z 39667; rural
Diamondhead; CDP; HANCOCK; **194** M-8; 🄿; ★ **BIL-**; z 39525; Ⓟ 2,661; Ⓒ 5,912
D'Iberville (North Biloxi); Inc. Place; HARRISON, JACKSON; **194** M-9; 🄿; ★ **BIL-**; z 39540 & mail Biloxi z 39532; Ⓟ 6,566; Ⓒ 7,608
Dinsmore; RMC Place; NOXUBEE; ***194** F-10; elev. 200ft./61m.; mail Macon z 39341; rural
Divide; RMC Place; LAWRENCE; ***194** J-6; mail Monticello z 39654; ● 30
Dixie; RMC Place; FORREST; ***194** K-8; mail Hattiesburg z 39401; rural
Dixie Pine; RMC Place; FORREST; ***194** K-8; ★ **HATT**; mail Hattiesburg z 39401; pop. incl. with Hattiesburg (Inc. Place)
Dixon; RMC Place; NESHOBA; ***194** G-8; elev. 584ft./178m.; mail Philadelphia z 39350; rural
D'Lo; Inc. Place; SIMPSON; **194** I-6; elev. 293ft./89m.; 🄿; z 39062; Ⓟ 421; Ⓒ 394
Doddsville; Inc. Place; SUNFLOWER; **194** E-5; elev. 128ft./39m.; 🄿; z 38736; Ⓟ 149; Ⓒ 108
Doloroso; RMC Place; WILKINSON; **194** K-3; elev. 298ft./91m.; mail Woodville z 39669; ● 45
Donegal; RMC Place; WILKINSON; ***194** K-3; mail Woodville z 39669; rural
Doolittle; RMC Place; NEWTON; ***194** H-8; mail Newton z 39345; pop. incl. with Newton (Inc. Place)
Dorion; DESOTO; see Lake View (RMC Place)
Dorsey; RMC Place; ITAWAMBA; **194** C-9; mail Fulton z 38843; ● 100
Doskie; RMC Place; TISHOMINGO; ***194** A-10; elev. 458ft./140m.; mail Burnsville z 38833, Iuka z 38852; rural
Dossville; RMC Place; LEAKE; ***194** F-7; mail Carthage z 39051; rural
Dover; RMC Place; NESHOBA; ***194** G-8; mail Union z 39365; rural
Dover; RMC Place; YAZOO; ***194** G-5; elev. 259ft./79m.; mail Bentonia z 39040; ● 30
Dowdville; RMC Place; NESHOBA; ***194** G-8; mail Philadelphia z 39350; rural
Downtown; RMC Place; HARRISON; ★ **BIL-**; mail Gulfport z 39501; pop. incl. with Gulfport (Inc. Place)
Downtown; RMC Place; HINDS; ★ **JAC**; mail Jackson z 39201, z 39207, z 39215, z 39225; pop. incl. with Jackson (Inc. Place)
Downtown; RMC Place; LEE; ***194** C-9; mail Tupelo z 38801; pop. incl. with Tupelo (Inc. Place)
Drew; Inc. Place; SUNFLOWER; **194** D-5; elev. 139ft./42m.; 🄿; z 38737 & mail Parchman z 38738; Ⓟ 2,349; Ⓒ 2,434
Dubard; RMC Place; GRENADA; ***194** D-6; mail Grenada z 38901; rural
Dubbs; RMC Place; TUNICA; ***194** B-5; mail Dundee z 38626
Dublin; RMC Place; COAHOMA; **194** D-5; elev. 158ft./48m.; 🄿; z 38739; ● 160
Duck Hill; Inc. Place; MONTGOMERY; **194** E-7; 🄿; z 38925; Ⓟ 586; Ⓒ 746
Duffee; RMC Place; NEWTON; **194** H-8; mail Little Rock z 39337; ● 110
Dumas; Inc. Place; TIPPAH; **194** B-9; elev. 623ft./190m.; 🄿; z 38625; Ⓟ 407; Ⓒ 452
Duncan; Inc. Place; BOLIVAR; **194** D-5; 🄿; z 38740; Ⓟ 416; Ⓒ 578
Dundee; RMC Place; TUNICA; **194** B-5; 🄿; z 38626; ● 200
Dunleith; RMC Place; WASHINGTON; ***194** E-4; mail Leland z 38756
Durant; Inc. Place; HOLMES; **194** F-7; elev. 269ft./82m.; 🄿 🄷; z 39063; Ⓟ 2,838; Ⓒ 2,932
Dwiggins; RMC Place; SUNFLOWER; ***194** D-5; elev. 143ft./44m.; mail Drew z 38737; rural
Dwyer; RMC Place; SUNFLOWER; ***194** E-5; elev. 122ft./37m.; mail Sunflower z 38778; rural

E

Eagle Lake; RMC Place; WARREN; ***194** H-4; mail Vicksburg z 39183; ● 200
Early Grove; RMC Place; MARSHALL; ***194** A-7; elev. 496ft./151m.; mail Lamar z 38642; ● 50
East Aberdeen (Days); RMC Place; MONROE; ***194** D-9; mail Aberdeen z 39730; rural
Eastabuchie; RMC Place; JONES; **194** J-8; 🄿; z 39436; ● 210
East Fork; RMC Place; AMITE; ***194** K-5; elev. 345ft./105m.; mail Smithdale z 39664; rural
East Heights; RMC Place; LEE; ***194** C-9; mail Tupelo z 38801; pop. incl. with Tupelo (Inc. Place)
East Hillsboro; RMC Place; SCOTT; ***194** H-7; elev. 439ft./134m.; mail Forest z 39074; rural
Eastlawn; RMC Place; JACKSON; mail Pascagoula z 39567, z 39569; pop. incl. with Pascagoula (Inc. Place)
East Lincoln; RMC Place; LINCOLN; ***194** J-6; mail Brookhaven z 39601; ● 30
East Moss Point; RMC Place; JACKSON; mail Moss Point z 39563; pop. incl. with Moss Point (Inc. Place)
Eastport; RMC Place; TISHOMINGO; **194** B-10; mail Iuka z 38852; ● 300
East Side; RMC Place; PERRY; ***194** J-9; mail Richton z 39476
East Tupelo; RMC Place; LEE; mail Tupelo z 38801; pop. incl. with Tupelo (Inc. Place)
Eatonville; RMC Place; FORREST; ***194** J-8; elev. 283ft./86m.; ★ **HATT**; mail Hattiesburg z 39401; ● 30
Ebenezer; RMC Place; HOLMES; **194** F-6; elev. 321ft./98m.; mail Lexington z 39095; ● 60
Ecru; Inc. Place; PONTOTOC; **194** C-8; 🄿; z 38841; Ⓟ 696; Ⓒ 947
Eddiceton; RMC Place; FRANKLIN; **194** J-4; mail Mc Call Creek z 39647; ● 150
Eden; Inc. Place; YAZOO; **194** F-5; mail Yazoo City z 39194; Ⓟ 88; Ⓒ 126
Edgewater Park; RMC Place; HARRISON; ***194** M-8; ★ **BIL-**; pop. incl. with Biloxi (Inc. Place)
Edinburg; RMC Place; LEAKE; **194** G-8; elev. 387ft./118m.; 🄿; z 39051; ● 110
Edwards; Inc. Place; HINDS; **194** H-5; 🄿; z 39066; Ⓟ 1,279; Ⓒ 1,347
Eggville; RMC Place; LEE; ***194** C-9; mail Saltillo z 38866, Tupelo z 38804; rural
Egremont; RMC Place; SHARKEY; ***194** G-4; mail Rolling Fork z 39159
Egypt; RMC Place; CHICKASAW; **194** D-9; elev. 302ft./92m.; 🄿; z 38860; ● 80
Egypt; RMC Place; HOLMES; ***194** E-6; mail Cruger z 38924; ● 40
Electric Mills; RMC Place; KEMPER; **194** G-9; mail Scooba z 39358; ● 50
Elizabeth; RMC Place; WASHINGTON; **194** E-4; elev. 127ft./39m.; 🄿; z 38756; ● 140
Ellard; RMC Place; CALHOUN; ***194** D-7; elev. 275ft./84m.; mail Bruce z 38915; rural
Elliott; RMC Place; GRENADA; **194** E-7; 🄿; z 38926; ● 1,100
Ellistown; RMC Place; UNION; **194** C-9; elev. 365ft./111m.; mail Dennis z 38838; ● 120
Ellisville; Inc. Place; ⊡ JONES; **194** J-8; elev. 258ft./79m.; 🄿; ★ **LAUR**; z 39437; Ⓟ 3,634; Ⓒ 3,465
Ellisville Junction; RMC Place; JONES; **194** J-8; ★ **LAUR**; mail Ellisville z 39437; ● 30
Elsie; RMC Place; CALHOUN; mail Vardaman z 38878; rural
Elton; RMC Place; HINDS; ***194** H-6; elev. 261ft./80m.; ★ **JAC**; mail Jackson z 39212; pop. incl. with Jackson (Inc. Place)
Elwood; RMC Place; CLARKE; ***194** I-9; mail Quitman z 39355; ● 30
Emory; RMC Place; HOLMES; ***194** F-6; elev. 464ft./141m.; mail Lexington z 39095; rural
Endville; RMC Place; PONTOTOC; ***194** C-9; elev. 445ft./136m.; mail Blue Springs z 38828; rural
Energy; RMC Place; CLARKE; ***194** H-9; mail Meridian z 39301; rural
Enid; RMC Place; TALLAHATCHIE; **194** D-6; 🄿; z 38927; ● 140
Enon; RMC Place; WALTHALL; **194** K-6; mail Jayess z 39641; ● 40
Enondale; RMC Place; KEMPER; **194** G-9; elev. 209ft./64m.; mail Porterville z 39352; ● 50
Enterprise; RMC Place; AMITE; ***194** K-4; elev. 389ft./119m.; mail Liberty z 39645; rural
Enterprise; Inc. Place; CLARKE; **194** H-9; 🄿; z 39330; Ⓟ 477; Ⓒ 474
Enterprise; RMC Place; LINCOLN; ***194** J-5; elev. 442ft./135m.; mail Bogue Chitto z 39629, Brookhaven z 39601; ● 50
Enterprise; RMC Place; UNION; **194** C-8; elev. 329ft./100m.; mail Myrtle z 38650; ● 200
Enzor; RMC Place; LAUDERDALE; ***194** H-9; ★ **MRID**; mail Meridian z 39301; ● 150
Errata; RMC Place; JONES; ***194** I-8; elev. 308ft./94m.; ★ **LAUR**; mail Laurel z 39440, z 39443; rural
Erwin; RMC Place; WASHINGTON; ***194** F-4; mail Chatham z 38731, Glen Allan z 38744
Escatawpa; CDP; JACKSON; **194** M-9; 🄿; ★ **PSCG**; z 39552; Ⓟ 3,902; Ⓒ 3,566
Eset (Pine Bluff); RMC Place; WAYNE; mail State Line z 39362; ● 100
Eskridge; RMC Place; MONTGOMERY; ***194** E-7; mail Duck Hill z 38925, Winona z 38967; ● 30
Esperanza; PONTOTOC; see Hurricane (RMC Place)
Essex; RMC Place; QUITMAN; ***194** C-6; mail Darling z 38623; rural
Estes; RMC Place; WINSTON; ***194** F-8; mail Louisville z 39339; rural
Estesmill; RMC Place; LEAKE; ***194** G-7; elev. 476ft./145m.; mail Carthage z 39051, Walnut Grove z 39189; rural
Estill; RMC Place; WASHINGTON; ***194** F-4; elev. 120ft./37m.; mail Hollandale z 38748
Ethel; Inc. Place; ATTALA; **194** F-7; elev. 439ft./134m.; 🄿; z 39067; Ⓟ 454; Ⓒ 452
Etta; RMC Place; UNION; **194** C-8; 🄿; z 38627
Eucutta; RMC Place; WAYNE; **194** I-9; mail Shubuta z 39360
Eudora; RMC Place; DESOTO; **194** B-6; elev. 301ft./92m.; mail Hernando z 38632; ● 200
Eunice; RMC Place; AMITE; ***194** K-4; elev. 207ft./63m.; mail Gloster z 39638; rural
Eupora; Inc. Place; WEBSTER; **194** E-8; 🄿 🄷; z 39744; Ⓟ 2,145; Ⓒ 2,326
Eureka Springs; RMC Place; PANOLA; ***194** C-6; mail Courtland z 38620; rural
Evansville; RMC Place; TATE; ***194** B-6; mail Coldwater z 38618, Tunica z 38676; rural
Evansville; RMC Place; TUNICA; **194** B-5; mail Coldwater z 38618, Tunica z 38676; ● 75
Everett; RMC Place; SIMPSON; ***194** I-7; elev. 348ft./106m.; mail Mendenhall z 39114; rural
Evergreen; RMC Place; ITAWAMBA; **194** C-9; mail Fulton z 38843; ● 80
Expose; RMC Place; MARION; ***194** K-6; mail Columbia z 39429; ● 40

F

Fairfield; RMC Place; UNION; **194** C-9; mail Blue Springs z 38828; ● 90
Fairground; RMC Place; NESHOBA; mail Philadelphia z 39350; rural
Fairhaven; RMC Place; DESOTO; ***194** A-7; ★ **MEM**; mail Olive Branch z 38654; pop. incl. with Olive Branch (Inc. Place)
Fairhill; RMC Place; NOXUBEE; ***194** F-9; mail Shuqualak z 39361; rural
Fair Oaks Springs; RMC Place; LINCOLN; ***194** J-5; mail Brookhaven z 39601; rural
Fair River; RMC Place; LINCOLN; ***194** J-6; mail Brookhaven z 39601, Sontag z 39665; rural
Fairview; RMC Place; ITAWAMBA; **194** C-10; elev. 517ft./158m.; mail Golden z 38847, Indianola z 38751; ● 200
Fairview; RMC Place; SUNFLOWER; ***194** E-5; mail Golden z 38847, Indianola z 38751; rural
Falcon; Inc. Place; QUITMAN; **194** C-6; 🄿; z 38628, z 38670; Ⓟ 167; Ⓒ 317
Falkner; Inc. Place; TIPPAH; **194** B-8; 🄿; z 38629; Ⓟ 232; Ⓒ 212
Fame; RMC Place; WEBSTER; ***194** E-8; mail Eupora z 39744; rural
Fannin; RMC Place; RANKIN; ***194** H-6; elev. 386ft./118m.; mail Brandon z 39047
Farmhaven (Millville); RMC Place; MADISON; ***194** G-7; elev. 378ft./115m.; mail Canton z 39046; rural
Farmington; Inc. Place; ALCORN; **194** A-9; elev. 530ft./162m.; mail Corinth z 38834; Ⓒ 1,810
Farrell; RMC Place; COAHOMA; **194** C-5; 🄿; z 38630; ● 250
Fayette; Inc. Place; ⊡ JEFFERSON; **194** J-4; elev. 290ft./88m.; 🄿 🄷; z 39069 & mail Harriston z 39081; Ⓟ 1,853; Ⓒ 2,242
Fenton; RMC Place; HANCOCK; ***194** M-8; ★ **BIL-**; mail Kiln z 39556; rural
Fentress; RMC Place; CHOCTAW; **194** F-8; mail Ackerman z 39735; ● 90
Fenwick; RMC Place; ADAMS; ***194** J-3; mail Natchez z 39120
Fernwood; RMC Place; PIKE; **194** K-5; 🄿; z 39635; ● 400
Fikestown; RMC Place; SCOTT; ***194** H-7; elev. 470ft./143m.; mail Lake z 39092; rural
Fitler; RMC Place; ISSAQUENA; **194** G-4; elev. 101ft./31m.; 🄿; z 39159; ● 30
Fitzhugh; RMC Place; SUNFLOWER; ***194** D-5; mail Drew z 38737; rural
Flora; Inc. Place; MADISON; **194** G-6; elev. 256ft./78m.; 🄿; z 39071; Ⓟ 1,482; Ⓒ 1,546
Florence; Inc. Place; RANKIN; **194** H-6; elev. 316ft./96m.; 🄿; ★ **JAC**; z 39073; Ⓟ 1,831; Ⓒ 2,396
Flowerdale; RMC Place; LEE; ***194** C-9; mail Tupelo z 38801; pop. incl. with Tupelo (Inc. Place)
Floweree; RMC Place; WARREN; ***194** G-4; elev. 97ft./30m.; mail Redwood z 39156; rural
Flowood; Inc. Place; RANKIN; **194** C-3; elev. 271ft./83m.; 🄿; ★ **JAC**; z 39232 & mail Pearl z 39208, z 39288; Ⓟ 2,860; Ⓒ 4,750
Floyd; RMC Place; BENTON; ***194** B-8; mail Ashland z 38603; rural
Fondren; RMC Place; HINDS; ***194** H-6; ★ **JAC**; mail Jackson z 39216, z 39296; pop. incl. with Jackson (Inc. Place)
Fords Creek; RMC Place; PEARL RIVER; ***194** K-7; mail Poplarville z 39470; rural
Fordyke; RMC Place; YAZOO; ***194** G-6; mail Benton z 39039; rural
Forest; Inc. Place; ⊡ SCOTT; **194** H-7; elev. 485ft./148m.; 🄿 🄷; z 39074; Ⓟ 5,060; Ⓒ 5,987

Entries in **UPPERCASE** are counties.
Entries in **bold** have populations of 2,500 or more.
Names in parentheses are alternate names.
Inc. Place — Incorporated Place
RMC Place — Rand McNally Designated Place
CDP — Census Designated Place
MCD — Minor Civil Division

⊡ County Seat
▲ Minor Civil Division
elev. Elevation
🄿 Post Office
🄷 Hospital
🄲 College
■ Principal Business Center
★ Ranally Metro Area (RMA) Abbreviation
z Zip Code(s)
Ⓟ Previous Census Population
Ⓡ Revised Census Population
Ⓐ Annexation Population
● Rand McNally Population Estimate
Ⓒ Final Census Population
Ⓢ Special Census Population
◆ Estimated Population

For additional definitions see Glossary, Volume 1, and Introduction, Volume 2.

Forestdale; RMC Place; NESHOBA; *194 G-8; mail Union Z 39365; rural
Forest Grove; RMC Place; LEAKE; *194 G-7; mail Carthage Z 39051; rural
Forest Hill; RMC Place; HINDS; *194 H-6; ★ JAC; mail Jackson Z 39212; pop. incl. with Jackson (Inc. Place)
Forkville; RMC Place; SCOTT; 194 H-7; mail Morton Z 39117; ● 150
FORREST; 194 K-8; Ⓟ 68,314; Ⓒ 72,604; ◆ 81,016
Fort Adams; RMC Place; WILKINSON; 194 K-3; elev. 56ft./17m.; mail Woodville Z 39669; ● 80
Fort Stephens; RMC Place; KEMPER; mail Bailey Z 39320; rural
Fountainebleau; RMC Place; JACKSON; *194 M-9; ★ PSCG; mail Ocean Springs Z 39564; ● 100
Four Corners; RMC Place; ATTALA, LEAKE, NESHOBA, WINSTON; mail Kosciusko Z 39090; rural
Four Mile; RMC Place; HUMPHREYS; *194 F-5; mail Belzoni Z 39038; rural
Foxworth; RMC Place; MARION; 194 K-6; 🅿; Z 39483; ● 600
Franklin; RMC Place; FRANKLIN; *194 J-4; mail Roxie Z 39661; rural
FRANKLIN; 194 J-4; Ⓟ 8,377; Ⓒ 8,448; ◆ 8,332
Frankstown; RMC Place; PRENTISS; *194 B-9; mail Baldwyn Z 38824; ● 100
Freeny; RMC Place; LEAKE; *194 G-7; mail Carthage Z 39051; ● 110
Freerun; RMC Place; YAZOO; *194 F-6; mail Yazoo City Z 39194; rural
Freetrade; RMC Place; LEAKE; *194 G-7; mail Carthage Z 39051; rural
Freeze Corner; RMC Place; DESOTO; *194 B-6; mail Hernando Z 38632; rural
French Camp; Inc. Place; CHOCTAW; 194 F-7; 🅿; Z 39745; Ⓟ 320; Ⓒ 393
French Store; RMC Place; RANKIN; *194 H-6; ★ JAC; mail Florence Z 39073; rural
Friars Point; Inc. Place; COAHOMA; 194 C-5; 🅿; Z 38631; Ⓟ 1,334; Ⓒ 1,480
Friendship; RMC Place; LINCOLN; mail Brookhaven Z 39601, Ecru Z 38841
Friendship; RMC Place; PONTOTOC; 194 C-8; elev. 402ft./123m.; mail Brookhaven Z 39601, Ecru Z 38841, Pontotoc Z 38863; ● 200
Frog Island; RMC Place; LEE; *194 C-9; mail Saltillo Z 38866; rural
Frostbridge; RMC Place; WAYNE; *194 I-9; mail Waynesboro Z 39367; rural
Fruitland Park; RMC Place; FORREST; *194 L-8; elev. 304ft./93m.; mail Wiggins Z 39577
Fugate; RMC Place; YAZOO; *194 G-6; elev. 232ft./71m.; mail Benton Z 39039; rural
Fulton; Inc. Place; ⊡ ITAWAMBA; 194 C-10; elev. 341ft./104m.; 🅿; Z 38843; Ⓟ 3,387; Ⓒ 3,882
Furrs; RMC Place; PONTOTOC; 194 C-9; mail Pontotoc Z 38863; ● 150
Futheyville; RMC Place; GRENADA; 194 D-7; mail Grenada Z 38901; pop. incl. with Grenada (Inc. Place)

G

Gallman; RMC Place; COPIAH; 194 I-5; elev. 463ft./141m.; 🅿; Z 39077; ● 400
Garden City; RMC Place; FRANKLIN; *194 J-4; mail Roxie Z 39661
Garlandville; RMC Place; JASPER; *194 H-8; elev. 455ft./139m.; mail Newton Z 39345
Gaston; RMC Place; PRENTISS; *194 B-9; mail Booneville Z 38829; pop. incl. with Booneville (Inc. Place)
Gatesville; RMC Place; COPIAH; 194 I-6; mail Crystal Springs Z 39059; ● 80
Gatewood; RMC Place; YALOBUSHA; *194 D-7; mail Coffeeville Z 38922; ● 60
Gatman; MONROE; see Gattman (Inc. Place)
Gattman (Gatman); Inc. Place; MONROE; 194 D-10; elev. 291ft./89m.; 🅿; Z 38844; Ⓟ 120; Ⓒ 114
Gault; RMC Place; LAFAYETTE; *194 C-7; mail Oxford Z 38655; ● 80
Gautier; Inc. Place; JACKSON; 194 M-9; 🅿; ★ PSCG; Z 39553; Ⓟ 10,088; Ⓒ 11,681
Geeslin Corner; RMC Place; GRENADA; *194 D-6; mail Grenada Z 38901; pop. incl. with Grenada (Inc. Place)
Geeville; RMC Place; PRENTISS; *194 B-9; elev. 466ft./142m.; mail Baldwyn Z 38824
Geneill; RMC Place; WASHINGTON; *194 E-5; mail Leland Z 38756; rural
GEORGE; 194 L-9; Ⓟ 16,673; Ⓒ 19,144; ◆ 22,484
Georgetown; Inc. Place; COPIAH; 194 I-6; elev. 236ft./72m.; 🅿; Z 39078; Ⓟ 332; Ⓒ 344
Geren; LEFLORE; see Ruby (RMC Place)
Gholson; RMC Place; NOXUBEE; *194 F-9; elev. 557ft./170m.; mail Shuqualak Z 39361
Gibson; RMC Place; MONROE; 194 D-9; elev. 263ft./80m.; mail Aberdeen Z 39730; ● 100
Gift; RMC Place; ALCORN; *194 A-9; elev. 405ft./123m.; mail Corinth Z 38834; ● 110
Giles; RMC Place; KEMPER; *194 G-10; elev. 203ft./62m.; mail Scooba Z 39358; rural
Gill (Pleasant Hill); RMC Place; LEAKE; *194 G-7; mail Carthage Z 39051; rural
Gillsburg; RMC Place; AMITE; *194 K-5; mail Osyka Z 39657
Gitano; RMC Place; JONES; *194 I-8; mail Taylorsville Z 39168
Glade; RMC Place; JONES; *194 J-8; ★ LAUR; mail Laurel Z 39440; ● 140
Glancy (Center Point); RMC Place; COPIAH; *194 I-5; elev. 330ft./101m.; mail Hazlehurst Z 39083; rural
Glen; ALCORN; see Glens (Inc. Place)
Glen Allan; RMC Place; WASHINGTON; 194 F-4; 🅿; Z 38744; ● 500
Glendale; RMC Place; FORREST; 194 J-8; elev. 169ft./52m.; ★ HATT; mail Hattiesburg Z 39401; ● 1,300
Glendora; Inc. Place; TALLAHATCHIE; 194 D-6; 🅿; Z 38928; Ⓟ 165; Ⓒ 285
Glenfield; RMC Place; UNION; *194 B-8; mail New Albany Z 38652; pop. incl. with New Albany (Inc. Place)
Glens (Glen); Inc. Place; ALCORN; 194 B-10; mail Glen Z 38846; Ⓟ 221; Ⓒ 286
Glenville; RMC Place; PANOLA; *194 B-7; mail Como Z 38619; rural
Glenwild (Clear Creek Ranch); RMC Place; GRENADA; *194 D-7; mail Grenada Z 38901; rural
Gloster; Inc. Place; AMITE; 194 K-4; elev. 434ft./132m.; 🅿; Z 39638; Ⓟ 1,323; Ⓒ 1,073
Glover; RMC Place; DESOTO; 194 A-6; mail Walls Z 38680; ● 50
Gluckstadt; RMC Place; MADISON; 194 H-6; elev. 273ft./83m.; mail Madison Z 39110; ● 210
Golden; Inc. Place; TISHOMINGO; 194 C-10; 🅿; Z 38847; Ⓟ 202; Ⓒ 201
Golden Grove; RMC Place; NESHOBA; *194 G-8; elev. 580ft./177m.; mail Union Z 39365; rural
Goldfield; RMC Place; SUNFLOWER; *194 D-5; mail Drew Z 38737; rural
Gooden Lake; RMC Place; HUMPHREYS; *194 F-5; mail Belzoni Z 39038; rural
Good Hope; RMC Place; LEAKE; 194 G-7; elev. 370ft./113m.; mail Lena Z 39094; ● 110
Good Hope; RMC Place; NESHOBA; *194 G-8; mail Philadelphia Z 39350; rural
Good Hope; RMC Place; PERRY; *194 J-8; elev. 267ft./81m.; mail Richton Z 39476; rural
Goodman; Inc. Place; HOLMES; 194 F-6; 🅿; Z 39079 & mail Thomastown Z 39171; Ⓟ 1,256; Ⓒ 1,252
Goodwater; RMC Place; CLARKE; *194 I-9; mail Vossburg Z 39366; rural
Goodyear; RMC Place; PEARL RIVER; mail Picayune Z 39466; pop. incl. with Picayune (Inc. Place)
Gore Springs; RMC Place; GRENADA; 194 D-7; 🅿; Z 38929; ● 110
Goshen Springs (New Goshen Springs); RMC Place; RANKIN; *194 H-6; mail Brandon Z 39047; rural
Goss; RMC Place; MARION; 194 J-6; mail Columbia Z 39429; ● 100
Grace; RMC Place; ISSAQUENA; 194 F-4; 🅿; Z 38745; ● 270
Grady; RMC Place; WEBSTER; *194 E-8; mail Eupora Z 39744; rural
Graham; RMC Place; UNION; *194 B-9; elev. 523ft./159m.; mail Baldwyn Z 38824; rural
Grand Gulf; RMC Place; CLAIBORNE; 194 I-4; elev. 248ft./76m.; mail Port Gibson Z 39150; ● 60
Grange; RMC Place; LAWRENCE; *194 J-6; elev. 321ft./98m.; mail Newhebron Z 39140; rural
Grange Hall; RMC Place; WARREN; *194 H-4; elev. 315ft./96m.; ★ VICK; mail Vicksburg Z 39180; rural
Grapeland; RMC Place; BOLIVAR; *194 E-4; mail Benoit Z 38725; rural
Gravel Hill; RMC Place; CARROLL; *194 E-6; mail Greenwood Z 38930; rural
Graves; RMC Place; LEE; *194 C-9; mail Blue Springs Z 38828; rural
Gravestown; RMC Place; TIPPAH; 194 B-8; mail Ripley Z 38663; ● 200
Greenbrier Park; RMC Place; PEARL RIVER; *194 M-7; mail Picayune Z 39466; ● 250
GREENE; 194 K-9; Ⓟ 10,220; Ⓒ 13,299; ◆ 14,921
Greenfield; RMC Place; RANKIN; *194 H-6; ★ JAC; mail Brandon Z 39042; rural
Greenfield Addition; RMC Place; WASHINGTON; ★ GRNV; mail Greenville Z 38701; pop. incl. with Greenville (Inc. Place)
Green Grove; RMC Place; COAHOMA; *194 C-5; elev. 160ft./49m.; mail Rena Lara Z 38767; rural
Greenland; RMC Place; NEWTON; *194 G-8; mail Union Z 39365; rural
Greenville; Inc. Place; ⊡ WASHINGTON; 194 E-4; 🅿 🅷 ■; ★ GRNV; Z 38701-04, Z 38731; Ⓟ 45,226; Ⓒ 41,633; ◆ 36,391
Greenville North; RMC Place; WASHINGTON; ★ GRNV; mail Greenville Z 38701; pop. incl. with Greenville (Inc. Place)
Greenwood; RMC Place; ITAWAMBA; *194 C-9; mail Fulton Z 38843; rural
Greenwood; Inc. Place; ⊡ LEFLORE; 194 E-6; 🅿 🅷 ■; Z 38930, Z 38935; Ⓟ 18,906; Ⓒ 18,425; ◆ 15,795
Greenwood Springs; RMC Place; MONROE; 194 D-10; elev. 298ft./91m.; 🅿; Z 38848; ● 260
Grenada; Inc. Place; ⊡ GRENADA; 194 D-7; 🅿 🅷; Z 38901-02; Ⓟ 10,864; Ⓒ 14,879
GRENADA; 194 E-6; Ⓟ 21,555; Ⓒ 23,263; ◆ 22,916
Griffith; RMC Place; CLAY; *194 E-9; mail Cedarbluff Z 39741; ● 30
Gulde; RMC Place; RANKIN; *194 H-6; elev. 372ft./113m.; mail Brandon Z 39042; rural
Gulf Hills; CDP; JACKSON; *194 M-9; ★ BIL-; mail Ocean Springs Z 39564; Ⓟ 5,004; Ⓒ 5,900
Gulf Hills Country Club; RMC Place; JACKSON; *194 M-9; ★ BIL-; mail Ocean Springs Z 39564; ● 920
Gulf Park Estates; CDP; JACKSON; *194 M-9; ★ BIL-; mail Ocean Springs Z 39564; Ⓟ 2,314; Ⓒ 4,272
Gulfport; Inc. Place; ⊡ HARRISON; 194 M-8; 🅿 🅷 ■; ★ BIL-; Z 39501-03, Z 39505-07; Ⓟ 40,775; Ⓒ 71,127; ◆ 71,207
Gum Grove; RMC Place; HOLMES; *194 F-5; elev. 114ft./35m.; mail Tchula Z 39169; rural
Gums; RMC Place; YALOBUSHA; *194 D-7; mail Coffeeville Z 38922; rural
Gum Springs; RMC Place; SCOTT; *194 H-7; mail Forest Z 39074; rural
Gunnison; Inc. Place; BOLIVAR; 194 D-4; elev. 155ft./47m.; 🅿; Z 38746; Ⓟ 611; Ⓒ 633
Guntown; Inc. Place; LEE; 194 C-9; elev. 384ft./117m.; 🅿; Z 38849; Ⓟ 692; Ⓒ 1,183
Gwin; RMC Place; HOLMES; *194 F-6; mail Tchula Z 39169; pop. incl. with Tchula (Inc. Place)
Gwinville; RMC Place; JEFFERSON DAVIS; *194 I-6; mail Newhebron Z 39140; ● 50

H

Hale; RMC Place; CLARKE; *194 I-9; elev. 294ft./90m.; mail Shubuta Z 39360; ● 130
Halltown; RMC Place; UNION; *194 B-9; elev. 453ft./138m.; mail Guntown Z 38849; rural
Hamburg; RMC Place; FRANKLIN; 194 J-4; elev. 403ft./123m.; mail Roxie Z 39661; ● 120
Hamilton (New Hamilton); RMC Place; MONROE; 194 D-9; elev. 247ft./75m.; 🅿; Z 39746; ● 630
Hampton; RMC Place; WASHINGTON; *194 F-4; mail Glen Allan Z 38744; rural
HANCOCK; 194 M-7; Ⓟ 31,760; Ⓒ 42,967; ◆ 41,000
Handle; RMC Place; WINSTON; *194 F-9; elev. 465ft./142m.; mail Louisville Z 39339; rural
Handsboro; RMC Place; HARRISON; *194 M-8; ★ BIL-; mail Gulfport Z 39501; pop. incl. with Gulfport (Inc. Place)
Handy Corner; RMC Place; DESOTO; *194 A-7; elev. 376ft./115m.; ★ MEM; mail Olive Branch Z 38654; ● 130
Hard Cash; RMC Place; HUMPHREYS; *194 F-5; mail Belzoni Z 39038; rural
Hardy; RMC Place; GRENADA; 194 D-7; mail Grenada Z 38901; ● 80
Harleston; RMC Place; JACKSON; *194 L-9; elev. 127ft./39m.; mail Lucedale Z 39452; ● 30
Harmontown; RMC Place; LAFAYETTE; 194 B-7; elev. 392ft./119m.; mail Como Z 38619; ● 200
Harmony; RMC Place; CLARKE; *194 I-9; mail Quitman Z 39355; rural
Harperville; RMC Place; SCOTT; 194 H-7; 🅿; Z 39080; ● 170
HARRISON; 194 L-8; Ⓟ 165,365; Ⓒ 189,601; ◆ 182,330
Harriston; RMC Place; JEFFERSON; 194 I-4; elev. 216ft./66m.; 🅿; Z 39081; ● 340
Harrisville; RMC Place; SIMPSON; 194 I-6; 🅿; Z 39082; ● 380
Harvey; RMC Place; FORREST; *194 J-8; elev. 150ft./46m.; ★ HATT; mail Petal Z 39465; pop. incl. with Petal (Inc. Place)
Hathorn; RMC Place; MARION; *194 J-6; mail Columbia Z 39429; rural
Hatley; Inc. Place; MONROE; 194 D-10; mail Amory Z 38821; Ⓟ 529; Ⓒ 476
Hattiesburg; Inc. Place; ⊡ FORREST, LAMAR; 194 K-8; elev. 161ft./49m.; 🅿 🅷 🅲 17,336 ■; ★ HATT; Z 39401-04, Z 39406-07; Ⓟ 41,882; Ⓒ 44,779; ◆ 50,299
Hayes Crossing; RMC Place; PANOLA; *194 C-7; elev. 320ft./98m.; mail Sardis Z 38666; rural
Hays; RMC Place; SCOTT; *194 G-8; elev. 432ft./132m.; mail Conehatta Z 39057; rural
Hazel; RMC Place; NEWTON; *194 H-8; elev. 450ft./137m.; mail Lake Z 39092; rural
Hazlehurst; Inc. Place; ⊡ COPIAH; 194 I-5; elev. 479ft./146m.; 🅿 🅷; Z 39083; Ⓟ 4,221; Ⓒ 4,400
Heads; RMC Place; WASHINGTON; *194 E-4; elev. 122ft./37m.; mail Leland Z 38756; rural
Heathman; RMC Place; SUNFLOWER; *194 E-5; mail Indianola Z 38751; rural
Hebron; RMC Place; JEFFERSON DAVIS; 194 I-6; elev. 368ft./112m.; mail Newhebron Z 39140; ● 80
Hebron; RMC Place; JONES; *194 J-8; elev. 276ft./84m.; mail Taylorsville Z 39168; ● 50
Heidelberg; Inc. Place; JASPER; 194 I-8; elev. 324ft./99m.; 🅿; Z 39439; Ⓟ 981; Ⓒ 840
Helena; CDP; JACKSON; *194 M-9; ★ PSCG; mail Pascagoula Z 39567, Z 39581; Ⓒ 778
Helm; RMC Place; WASHINGTON; *194 E-4; elev. 120ft./37m.; mail Leland Z 38756; rural
Henderson Point; HARRISON; see Henderson's Point (RMC Place)
Henderson's Point (Henderson Point); RMC Place; HARRISON; *194 M-8; ★ BIL-; mail Pass Christian Z 39571
Hendrix; RMC Place; MONTGOMERY; *194 E-7; mail Kilmichael Z 39747; rural
Henleyfield; RMC Place; PEARL RIVER; *194 L-7; elev. 223ft./68m.; mail Carriere Z 39426; rural
Herbert Springs; RMC Place; NESHOBA; *194 G-8; mail Collinsville Z 39325; rural
Hermanville; RMC Place; CLAIBORNE; 194 I-4; 🅿; Z 39086; ● 400
Hernando; Inc. Place; ⊡ DESOTO; 194 B-6; 🅿; ★ MEM; Z 38632; Ⓟ 3,125; Ⓒ 6,812
Hero; RMC Place; JASPER; *194 H-8; mail Newton Z 39345; rural
Hesterville; RMC Place; ATTALA; *194 F-7; elev. 434ft./132m.; mail West Z 39192; rural
Heucks; LINCOLN; see Heucks Retreat (RMC Place)
Heucks Retreat (Heucks); RMC Place; LINCOLN; *194 J-5; mail Brookhaven Z 39601, Wesson Z 39191; rural
Hickory; Inc. Place; NEWTON; 194 H-8; elev. 326ft./99m.; 🅿; Z 39332; Ⓟ 493; Ⓒ 499
Hickory Flat; Inc. Place; BENTON; 194 B-8; 🅿; Z 38633; Ⓟ 535; Ⓒ 565
Hickory Hills; CDP-Census Area Only; JACKSON; *194 M-9; ★ PSCG; Ⓒ 3,046
Hideaway Hills; RMC Place; PANOLA; *194 C-6; elev. 366ft./112m.; mail Sardis Z 38666; ● 50
Hidi; RMC Place; HUMPHREYS; *194 F-5; elev. 110ft./34m.; mail Silver City Z 39166; rural
Higgins; RMC Place; LAMAR; *194 J-7; mail Sumrall Z 39482; rural
High Hill; RMC Place; LEAKE; *194 G-8; mail Philadelphia Z 39350; rural
Highlandale; RMC Place; LEFLORE; *194 E-5; mail Minter City Z 38944, Schlater Z 38952; rural
Highpoint; RMC Place; WINSTON; 194 F-8; mail Louisville Z 39339
Hightown; RMC Place; ALCORN; 194 B-9; mail Corinth Z 38834; ● 150
Hillhouse; RMC Place; COAHOMA; *194 C-4; mail Alligator Z 38720; rural
Hillman; RMC Place; GREENE; 194 K-9; mail Leakesville Z 39451; ● 40
Hillsboro; RMC Place; SCOTT; 194 H-7; elev. 448ft./137m.; 🅿; Z 39087; ● 230
Hillsdale; RMC Place; PEARL RIVER; *194 L-7; elev. 243ft./74m.; mail Poplarville Z 39470; rural
Hinchcliff; RMC Place; QUITMAN; *194 C-6; elev. 168ft./51m.; mail Marks Z 38646
HINDS; 194 H-5; Ⓟ 254,441; Ⓒ 250,800; ◆ 246,479
Hinkle; RMC Place; ALCORN; 194 B-9; mail Rienzi Z 38865; ● 160
Hintonville; RMC Place; PERRY; 194 K-9; mail Beaumont Z 39423, New Augusta Z 39462; ● 340
Hinze; RMC Place; WINSTON; *194 F-8; elev. 470ft./143m.; mail Mc Cool Z 39108; rural
Hiram; RMC Place; TALLAHATCHIE; *194 D-6; mail Tutwiler Z 38963; rural
Hiwannee; RMC Place; WAYNE; 194 I-9; elev. 215ft./66m.; mail Waynesboro Z 39367
Hobo Station; RMC Place; PRENTISS; *194 B-9; elev. 412ft./126m.; mail Booneville Z 38829; ● 30
Hohenlinden; RMC Place; WEBSTER; *194 D-8; mail Mantee Z 39751
Holcomb; RMC Place; GRENADA; 194 D-6; 🅿; Z 38940; ● 900
Holcut; RMC Place; TISHOMINGO; *194 B-10; mail Iuka Z 38852; rural
Hollandale; Inc. Place; WASHINGTON; 194 F-4; 🅿; Z 38748; Ⓟ 3,576; Ⓒ 3,437
Hollis; RMC Place; CALHOUN; *194 D-8; mail Vardaman Z 38878; rural
Holly Bluff; RMC Place; YAZOO; 194 G-5; 🅿; Z 39088; ● 300
Holly Grove; RMC Place; CARROLL; *194 E-6; mail Sidon Z 38954
Holly Ridge; RMC Place; SUNFLOWER; 194 E-5; elev. 120ft./37m.; 🅿; Z 38749; ● 100
Holly Springs; Inc. Place; ⊡ MARSHALL; 194 B-7; elev. 609ft./186m.; 🅿 🅷 🅲 920; Z 38634-35, Z 38649; Ⓟ 7,261; Ⓒ 7,957
Hollywood; RMC Place; TUNICA; 194 B-5; mail Tunica Z 38676; ● 80
HOLMES; 194 F-6; Ⓟ 21,604; Ⓒ 21,609; ◆ 20,001
Holmesville; RMC Place; PIKE; *194 K-5; mail McComb Z 39648
Holts Spur; RMC Place; TISHOMINGO; *194 B-10; mail Burnsville Z 38833; rural
Homewood; RMC Place; SCOTT; 194 H-7; mail Forest Z 39074; ● 75
Homochitto; RMC Place; AMITE; *194 K-4; mail Gloster Z 39638, Meadville Z 39653
Honey Island; RMC Place; HUMPHREYS; *194 F-5; mail Belzoni Z 39038, Tchula Z 39169; rural
Hoover Lake and Park; RANKIN; see Cleary (RMC Place)
Hope; RMC Place; NESHOBA; *194 G-8; elev. 497ft./151m.; mail Philadelphia Z 39350
Hopedale; RMC Place; ISSAQUENA; *194 F-4; mail Mayersville Z 39113; rural
Hopewell (Laird); RMC Place; BENTON; *194 A-8; elev. 646ft./197m.; mail Saulsbury Z 38067; rural
Hopewell; RMC Place; COPIAH; *194 I-6; mail Crystal Springs Z 39059; ● 30
Hopoca; RMC Place; LEAKE; *194 G-7; mail Carthage Z 39051; rural
Horn Lake; Inc. Place; DESOTO; 194 A-6; 🅿; ★ MEM; Z 38637 & mail Southaven Z 38671; Ⓟ 9,069; Ⓒ 14,099; ◆ 24,318
Horseshoe; RMC Place; HOLMES; *194 F-6; mail Tchula Z 39169; rural
Horseshoe; RMC Place; SCOTT; *194 G-7; mail Walnut Grove Z 39189; rural
Hortontown; RMC Place; PONTOTOC; *194 C-8; mail Pontotoc Z 38863; rural
Hot Coffee; RMC Place; COVINGTON; *194 I-7; elev. 279ft./85m.; mail Collins Z 39428
Houlka (New Houlka); Inc. Place; CHICKASAW; 194 D-8; 🅿; Z 38850; Ⓟ 558; Ⓒ 710
House; RMC Place; NESHOBA; 194 G-8; mail Union Z 39365; ● 100
Houston; Inc. Place; ⊡ CHICKASAW; 194 D-8; 🅿 🅷; Z 38851; Ⓟ 3,903; Ⓒ 4,079
Howard; RMC Place; HOLMES; 194 F-6; elev. 143ft./44m.; mail Lexington Z 39095; ● 30
Howell; RMC Place; GEORGE; *194 L-10; elev. 150ft./46m.; mail Lucedale Z 39452; ● 60
Howison; RMC Place; HARRISON; *194 L-8; elev. 178ft./54m.; mail Saucier Z 39574; rural
Hoy; RMC Place; JONES; *194 I-8; elev. 279ft./85m.; ★ LAUR; mail Laurel Z 39440, Z 39443; rural
Hub; RMC Place; MARION; *194 K-7; mail Columbia Z 39429
Hubbard; RMC Place; HINDS; *194 H-5; elev. 217ft./66m.; mail Edwards Z 39066
Hudsonville; RMC Place; MARSHALL; *194 B-7; elev. 473ft./144m.; mail Holly Springs Z 38635; rural
Humber; RMC Place; COAHOMA; *194 C-5; mail Clarksdale Z 38614; rural
HUMPHREYS; 194 F-5; Ⓟ 12,134; Ⓒ 11,206; ◆ 9,712
Huntsville; RMC Place; MONTGOMERY; *194 E-7; mail French Camp Z 39745; rural
Hurley; CDP; JACKSON; 194 L-9; elev. 100ft./30m.; 🅿; Z 39555; Ⓒ 985
Hurricane (Esperanza); RMC Place; PONTOTOC; 194 C-8; mail Pontotoc Z 38863, Thaxton Z 38871; ● 200
Hurricane Creek; RMC Place; CLARKE; *194 H-9; mail Meridian Z 39301; rural
Hushpuckena; RMC Place; BOLIVAR; 194 D-5; mail Shelby Z 38774; ● 60

I

Improve; RMC Place; MARION; *194 J-7; mail Columbia Z 39429
Increase; RMC Place; LAUDERDALE; *194 H-9; elev. 405ft./123m.; mail Meridian Z 39301
Inda; RMC Place; STONE; *194 L-8; mail Perkinston Z 39573, Wiggins Z 39577; rural
Independence; RMC Place; SCOTT; *194 H-7; mail Morton Z 39117; rural
Independence; RMC Place; TATE; 194 B-7; 🅿; Z 38638; ● 350
Indian Hills; RMC Place; LEE; *194 C-9; mail Saltillo Z 38866; ● 290
Indianola; Inc. Place; ⊡ SUNFLOWER; 194 E-5; 🅿 🅷; Z 38749, Z 38751; Ⓟ 11,809; Ⓒ 12,066
Indian Springs; RMC Place; PERRY; *194 K-8; elev. 226ft./69m.; mail Glen Z 38846, Hattiesburg Z 39401; rural
Industrial; RMC Place; PEARL RIVER; *194 L-7; mail Picayune Z 39466; ● 200
Ingomar; RMC Place; UNION; 194 C-8; elev. 369ft./112m.; mail New Albany Z 38652; ● 250
Ingrams Mill; RMC Place; DESOTO; 194 B-7; mail Byhalia Z 38611; ● 50
Inverness; Inc. Place; SUNFLOWER; 194 E-5; elev. 119ft./36m.; 🅿; Z 38753; Ⓟ 1,174; Ⓒ 1,153
Isola; Inc. Place; HUMPHREYS; 194 F-5; elev. 116ft./35m.; 🅿; Z 38754; Ⓟ 732; Ⓒ 768
ISSAQUENA; 194 G-4; Ⓟ 1,909; Ⓒ 2,274; ◆ 1,467
ITAWAMBA; 194 C-9; Ⓟ 20,017; Ⓒ 22,770; ◆ 22,848
Itta Bena; Inc. Place; LEFLORE; 194 E-6; 🅿 🅲 3,162; Z 38941; Ⓟ 2,377; Ⓒ 2,208
Iuka; Inc. Place; ⊡ TISHOMINGO; 194 B-10; elev. 569ft./173m.; 🅿 🅷; Z 38852; Ⓟ 3,122; Ⓒ 3,059

J

Jacinto; RMC Place; ALCORN; 194 B-9; mail Rienzi Z 38865; ● 220
Jack; RMC Place; COPIAH; *194 I-5; elev. 238ft./73m.; mail Utica Z 39175; rural
Jackson; Inc. Place; STATE CAPITAL; ⊡ HINDS, MADISON, RANKIN; 194 H-6; elev. 294ft./90m.; 🅿 🅷 🅲 15,461 ■; ★ JAC; Z 39201-13, Z 39215-18, Z 39225, Z 39232, Z 39236, Z 39250, Z 39269, Z 39271-72, Z 39282-84, Z 39286, Z 39288-89, Z 39296, Z 39298 & mail Whitfield Z 39193; Ⓟ 196,637; Ⓒ 184,256; ◆ 177,006
JACKSON; 194 L-9; Ⓟ 115,243; Ⓒ 131,420; ◆ 127,553
Jackson State University; RMC Place; HINDS; ★ JAC; mail Jackson Z 39217; pop. incl. with Jackson (Inc. Place)
Jago; RMC Place; DESOTO; *194 A-6; ★ MEM; mail Horn Lake Z 38637, Southaven Z 38671; pop. incl. with Southaven (Inc. Place)
Jaketown; RMC Place; HUMPHREYS; *194 F-5; mail Belzoni Z 39038; rural
James; RMC Place; WASHINGTON; *194 F-4; mail Hollandale Z 38748
Jamestown; RMC Place; MARION; *194 K-6; mail Foxworth Z 39483; rural
Janice; RMC Place; PERRY; *194 K-8; mail Brooklyn Z 39425; rural
JASPER; 194 I-8; Ⓟ 17,114; Ⓒ 18,149; ◆ 18,025
Jayess; RMC Place; LAWRENCE; 194 J-6; 🅿; Z 39641; ● 110
Jeannette; RMC Place; ADAMS; *194 J-3; mail Natchez Z 39120; rural
Jeff Davis; RMC Place; WARREN; *194 H-4; ★ VICK; mail Vicksburg Z 39180; rural
Jefferson; RMC Place; CARROLL; *194 E-6; mail Carrollton Z 38917; rural
JEFFERSON; 194 I-4; Ⓟ 8,653; Ⓒ 9,740; ◆ 8,861
JEFFERSON DAVIS; 194 J-6; Ⓟ 14,051; Ⓒ 13,962; ◆ 12,333
Jeffries; RMC Place; COAHOMA; *194 C-5; mail Dundee Z 38626; rural
Jenkins; RMC Place; JONES; *194 J-8; elev. 216ft./66m.; ★ LAUR; mail Ellisville Z 39437; rural
Jericho; RMC Place; UNION; *194 B-9; mail Baldwyn Z 38824; rural
Johns; RMC Place; RANKIN; *194 H-7; mail Brandon Z 39042
Johnson; RMC Place; JONES; 194 J-8; elev. 349ft./106m.; mail Ellisville Z 39437; ● 30
Johnston; PIKE; see Johnstons Station (RMC Place)
Johnstons Station (Johnston); RMC Place; PIKE; *194 J-5; mail Summit Z 39666
Jonathan; RMC Place; GREENE; *194 K-9; elev. 119ft./36m.; mail Leakesville Z 39451; ● 50
JONES; 194 J-8; Ⓟ 62,031; Ⓒ 64,958; ◆ 72,746
Jonestown; Inc. Place; COAHOMA; 194 C-5; 🅿; Z 38639; Ⓟ 1,467; Ⓒ 1,701
Jonestown; RMC Place; YAZOO; 194 G-5; mail Yazoo City Z 39194; pop. incl. with Yazoo City (Inc. Place)
Jug Fork; RMC Place; LEE, UNION; *194 C-9; mail Blue Springs Z 38828; rural
Jumpertown; Inc. Place; PRENTISS; 194 B-9; elev. 589ft./180m.; mail Booneville Z 38829; Ⓟ 438; Ⓒ 404
Junction City; RMC Place; CLARKE; *194 I-9; elev. 277ft./84m.; mail Quitman Z 39355; rural

K

Kalem; RMC Place; SCOTT; *194 H-7; mail Morton Z 39117
Keirn; RMC Place; HOLMES; *194 F-6; mail Cruger Z 38924; rural
Kellis Store; RMC Place; KEMPER; *194 G-9; mail Preston Z 39354; rural
Kelona; RMC Place; JASPER; *194 I-8; mail Vossburg Z 39366; rural
KEMPER; 194 G-9; Ⓟ 10,356; Ⓒ 10,453; ◆ 9,883
Kendrick; RMC Place; ALCORN; 194 A-10; elev. 461ft./141m.; mail Corinth Z 38834; ● 270
Keownville; RMC Place; UNION; *194 B-8; mail New Albany Z 38652
Kewanee; RMC Place; LAUDERDALE; 194 H-10; mail Toomsuba Z 39364; ● 60
Key Field; RMC Place; LAUDERDALE; ★ MRID; mail Meridian Z 39301; pop. incl. with Meridian (Inc. Place)
Kilmichael; Inc. Place; MONTGOMERY; 194 E-7; elev. 357ft./109m.; 🅿 🅷; Z 39747; Ⓟ 826; Ⓒ 830
Kiln; CDP; HANCOCK; 194 M-7; elev. 20ft./6m.; 🅿; Z 39556; Ⓟ 1,262; Ⓒ 2,040
King and Anderson; RMC Place; COAHOMA; *194 C-5; mail Clarksdale Z 38614; rural
Kings; RMC Place; WARREN; *194 H-4; ★ VICK; mail Vicksburg Z 39183; pop. incl. with Vicksburg (Inc. Place)
Kingston; RMC Place; ADAMS; 194 J-3; mail Natchez Z 39120; ● 390
Kinlock; RMC Place; SUNFLOWER; *194 F-5; mail Indianola Z 38751; rural
Kipling; RMC Place; KEMPER; *194 G-9; mail De Kalb Z 39328; rural
Kirby; RMC Place; FRANKLIN; *194 J-4; mail Roxie Z 39661
Kirkville; RMC Place; ITAWAMBA; *194 C-9; mail Baldwyn Z 38824, Fulton Z 38843; rural
Kittrell; RMC Place; PERRY; *194 K-9; mail Beaumont Z 39423; rural
Klem; RMC Place; SMITH; *194 H-7; mail Forest Z 39074; rural
Klondike; RMC Place; KEMPER; *194 G-9; elev. 491ft./150m.; mail Bailey Z 39320
Knobtown; RMC Place; GREENE; *194 J-9; elev. 142ft./43m.; mail State Line Z 39362; rural
Knoxo; RMC Place; WALTHALL; *194 K-6; mail Tylertown Z 39667; rural
Knoxville; RMC Place; FRANKLIN; 194 J-4; mail Roxie Z 39661; ● 100
Kokomo; RMC Place; MARION; 194 K-6; 🅿; Z 39643; ● 210
Kola; RMC Place; COVINGTON; *194 J-7; elev. 267ft./81m.; mail Collins Z 39428; rural
Kolola Springs; RMC Place; LOWNDES; *194 E-10; elev. 225ft./69m.; ★ COL; mail Caledonia Z 39740; ● 160
Kosciusko; Inc. Place; ⊡ ATTALA; 194 F-7; elev. 488ft./149m.; 🅿 🅷; Z 39090; Ⓟ 6,986; Ⓒ 7,372
Kossuth; Inc. Place; ALCORN; 194 B-9; 🅿; Z 38834; Ⓟ 245; Ⓒ 170
Kreole; RMC Place; JACKSON; *194 M-9; elev. 8ft./2m.; 🅿; ★ PSCG; Z 39563 & mail Pascagoula Z 39567; pop. incl. with Moss Point (Inc. Place)

L

Lackey (Lackie); RMC Place; MONROE; *194 D-9; elev. 217ft./66m.; mail Aberdeen Z 39730; rural
Lackie; MONROE; see Lackey (RMC Place)
LAFAYETTE; 194 C-7; Ⓟ 31,826; Ⓒ 38,744; ◆ 43,555
Lafayette Springs; RMC Place; LAFAYETTE; *194 C-8; elev. 451ft./137m.; mail Oxford Z 38655; ● 30
Laird; BENTON; see Hopewell (RMC Place)
Lake; Inc. Place; SCOTT, NEWTON; 194 H-8; elev. 440ft./134m.; 🅿; Z 39092; Ⓟ 369; Ⓒ 408
Lake Carrier; PANOLA; see Locke Station (RMC Place)
Lake Center; RMC Place; MARSHALL; *194 B-8; mail Potts Camp Z 38659; ● 370
Lake City; RMC Place; PRENTISS; mail Booneville Z 38829; pop. incl. with Booneville (Inc. Place)
Lake City; RMC Place; YAZOO; *194 F-5; mail Yazoo City Z 39194; rural
Lake Como; RMC Place; JASPER; *194 I-8; elev. 350ft./107m.; mail Bay Springs Z 39422; rural
Lake Cormorant; RMC Place; DESOTO; 194 A-6; 🅿; Z 38641 & mail Horn Lake Z 38637; ● 270
Lakeland; RMC Place; RANKIN; *194 H-6; ★ JAC; mail Richland Z 39218; pop. incl. with Richland (Inc. Place)
Lake of Hills; RMC Place; DESOTO; *194 B-6; mail Hernando Z 38632; seasonal pop. 350; ● 200
Lakeshore; RMC Place; HANCOCK; 194 M-7; 🅿; ★ BIL-; Z 39558; ● 1,200
Lake View (Dorion); RMC Place; DESOTO; 194 A-6; elev. 222ft./68m.; mail Walls Z 38680; ● 200
Lamar; RMC Place; BENTON; 194 B-8; 🅿; Z 38642; ● 150
LAMAR; 194 K-7; Ⓟ 30,424; Ⓒ 39,070; ◆ 50,478
Lamar Park; RMC Place; LAMAR; 194 F-1; ★ HATT; mail Hattiesburg Z 39401-02; pop. incl. with Hattiesburg (Inc. Place)
Lambert; Inc. Place; QUITMAN; 194 C-6; 🅿; Z 38643; Ⓟ 1,131; Ⓒ 1,967
Lamkin; RMC Place; HUMPHREYS; *194 F-5; mail Silver City Z 39166; rural
Lamont; RMC Place; BOLIVAR; 194 E-4; 🅿; Z 38703 & mail Greenville Z 38701; ● 70
Lampton; RMC Place; MARION; 194 K-7; mail Columbia Z 39429; ● 130
Landon; RMC Place; HARRISON; *194 M-8; ★ BIL-; mail Gulfport Z 39503; pop. incl. with Gulfport (Inc. Place)
Langford; RMC Place; RANKIN; *194 H-6; ★ JAC; mail Brandon Z 39042; ● 300
Langsdale; RMC Place; CLARKE; *194 I-9; elev. 307ft./94m.; mail Shubuta Z 39360; ● 30
Larue; RMC Place; JACKSON; *194 L-9; mail Ocean Springs Z 39564, Vancleave Z 39565; rural
Latimer; CDP; JACKSON; 194 L-9; mail Ocean Springs Z 39564, Vancleave Z 39565; Ⓟ 3,222; Ⓒ 4,288
Latonia; RMC Place; GEORGE; *194 L-10; mail Lucedale Z 39452; rural
Lauderdale; RMC Place; LAUDERDALE; 194 G-9; elev. 215ft./66m.; 🅿; Z 39335; ● 650
LAUDERDALE; 194 H-9; Ⓟ 75,555; Ⓒ 78,161; ◆ 76,923
Laurel; Inc. Place; ⊡ JONES; 194 J-8; elev. 264ft./80m.; 🅿 🅷 ■; ★ LAUR; Z 39440-43; Ⓟ 18,827; Ⓒ 18,393; ◆ 19,794
Laurel Hill; RMC Place; NESHOBA; *194 G-8; elev. 429ft./131m.; mail Philadelphia Z 39350; rural
Lawrence; RMC Place; NEWTON; 194 H-8; elev. 455ft./139m.; 🅿; Z 39336; ● 200
LAWRENCE; 194 J-6; Ⓟ 12,458; Ⓒ 13,258; ◆ 13,318
Laws Hill; RMC Place; MARSHALL; 194 B-7; elev. 590ft./180m.; mail Waterford Z 38685; ● 170
Leaf; RMC Place; GREENE; 194 K-9; elev. 96ft./29m.; 🅿; Z 39456; ● 120
LEAKE; 194 G-7; Ⓟ 18,436; Ⓒ 20,940; ◆ 23,023
Leakesville; Inc. Place; ⊡ GREENE; 194 K-9; 🅿; Z 39451; Ⓟ 1,129; Ⓒ 1,026
Learned; Inc. Place; HINDS; 194 H-5; elev. 204ft./62m.; 🅿; Z 39154; Ⓟ 111; Ⓒ 50
Lebanon; RMC Place; HINDS; *194 H-5; elev. 307ft./94m.; mail Potts Camp Z 38659, Raymond Z 39154; rural
LEE; 194 C-9; Ⓟ 65,581; Ⓒ 75,755; ◆ 80,625
Lee Donald; RMC Place; JASPER; mail Vossburg Z 39366; rural
Leedy; RMC Place; TISHOMINGO; 194 B-10; mail Burnsville Z 38833; ● 100
Leesburg; RMC Place; RANKIN; *194 H-7; mail Morton Z 39117
Leesdale; RMC Place; ADAMS; *194 J-4; mail Roxie Z 39661; rural
Leeville; RMC Place; FORREST; *194 J-8; elev. 220ft./67m.; ★ HATT; mail Hattiesburg Z 39401; rural
Lefleur; RMC Place; HINDS; mail Jackson Z 39211, Z 39236; pop. incl. with Jackson (Inc. Place)
Leflore; RMC Place; GRENADA; 194 E-6; mail Holcomb Z 38940; ● 50
LEFLORE; 194 E-5; Ⓟ 37,341; Ⓒ 37,947; ◆ 34,746
Leland; Inc. Place; WASHINGTON; 194 E-4; elev. 126ft./38m.; 🅿; Z 38756; Ⓟ 6,366; Ⓒ 5,502
Lemon; RMC Place; SMITH; *194 H-7; mail Forest Z 39074; rural
Lena; Inc. Place; LEAKE; 194 G-7; 🅿; Z 39094; Ⓟ 175; Ⓒ 167
Lessley; RMC Place; WILKINSON; *194 K-3; mail Woodville Z 39669; rural
Le Tourneau; RMC Place; WARREN; 194 H-4; ★ VICK; mail Vicksburg Z 39180; ● 200
Leverett; RMC Place; TALLAHATCHIE; *194 D-6; mail Cascilla Z 38920; rural
Lewisburg; RMC Place; DESOTO; 194 B-7; ★ MEM; mail Olive Branch Z 38654; ● 120
Lexie; RMC Place; WALTHALL; *194 K-6; elev. 251ft./77m.; mail Tylertown Z 39667
Lexington; Inc. Place; ⊡ HOLMES; 194 F-6; 🅿 🅷; Z 39095; Ⓟ 2,227; Ⓒ 2,025
Liberty; Inc. Place; ⊡ AMITE; 194 K-4; elev. 361ft./110m.; 🅿; Z 39645; Ⓟ 624; Ⓒ 633
Liberty; RMC Place; KEMPER; *194 G-9; mail De Kalb Z 39328; rural
Lightsey; RMC Place; WAYNE; *194 I-8; mail Laurel Z 39440; rural
Lillian; RMC Place; SCOTT; *194 H-7; mail Forest Z 39074; rural
LINCOLN; 194 J-5; Ⓟ 30,278; Ⓒ 33,166; ◆ 34,733
Linn; RMC Place; SUNFLOWER; *194 E-5; mail Doddsville Z 38736; rural
Linwood; RMC Place; NESHOBA; *194 G-8; elev. 542ft./165m.; mail Union Z 39365; ● 100
Linwood; RMC Place; YAZOO; *194 G-6; elev. 287ft./87m.; mail Vaughan Z 39179; ● 100
Little Creek; RMC Place; PERRY; *194 K-9; mail Beaumont Z 39423
Little Italy; RMC Place; SCOTT; *194 H-8; elev. 423ft./129m.; mail Lake Z 39092; rural
Little Rock; RMC Place; NEWTON; 194 G-8; 🅿; Z 39337; ● 230
Little Texas; RMC Place; TUNICA; *194 B-6; mail Tunica Z 38676; rural
Little Yazoo; RMC Place; YAZOO; 194 G-5; elev. 332ft./101m.; mail Bentonia Z 39040; ● 110
Litton; RMC Place; BOLIVAR; 194 E-4; mail Shaw Z 38773; rural
Lizana; RMC Place; HARRISON; *194 L-8; mail Gulfport Z 39503; ● 60
Lobdell; RMC Place; BOLIVAR; *194 D-4; mail Beulah Z 38726; rural
Lobutcha; RMC Place; WINSTON; *194 F-8; mail Mc Cool Z 39108; rural
Loch Leven; RMC Place; WILKINSON; *194 K-3; elev. 56ft./17m.; mail Woodville Z 39669; rural
Locke Station (Lake Carrier); RMC Place; PANOLA; *194 C-6; mail Batesville Z 38606; rural
Lockhart; RMC Place; LAUDERDALE; *194 H-9; mail Lauderdale Z 39335; rural
Lodi; RMC Place; HUMPHREYS; *194 F-5; elev. 110ft./34m.; mail Silver City Z 39166; rural
Lodi; RMC Place; MONTGOMERY; *194 E-7; mail Stewart Z 39767; ● 50
Lombardy; RMC Place; SUNFLOWER; *194 D-5; elev. 145ft./44m.; mail Shelby Z 38774; rural
Long (Longs Switch); RMC Place; WASHINGTON; *194 E-5; elev. 118ft./36m.; mail Leland Z 38756; rural
Long Beach; Inc. Place; HARRISON; 194 M-8; 🅿; ★ BIL-; Z 39560; Ⓟ 15,804; Ⓒ 17,320
Longino; RMC Place; NESHOBA; *194 G-8; mail Philadelphia Z 39350; rural
Long Lake; RMC Place; COAHOMA; *194 C-5; mail Coahoma Z 38617; rural
Long Lake; RMC Place; WARREN; *194 H-4; ★ VICK; mail Vicksburg Z 39183; ● 100
Longshot; RMC Place; BOLIVAR; *194 E-4; elev. 130ft./40m.; mail Benoit Z 38725, Shaw Z 38773; rural
Longs Switch; WASHINGTON; see Long (RMC Place)
Longtown; RMC Place; PANOLA; 194 C-6; mail Sarah Z 38665; ● 250
Longview; RMC Place; OKTIBBEHA; 194 E-8; elev. 293ft./89m.; mail Starkville Z 39759; ● 390
Longview; RMC Place; PONTOTOC; *194 C-8; elev. 400ft./122m.; mail Pontotoc Z 38863; rural
Looxahoma; RMC Place; TATE; 194 B-7; elev. 379ft./116m.; mail Senatobia Z 38668; ● 110
Lorena; RMC Place; SMITH; *194 H-7; mail Forest Z 39074
Lorenzen; RMC Place; SHARKEY; *194 F-4; mail Rolling Fork Z 39159; rural
Lorman; RMC Place; JEFFERSON; 194 I-4; 🅿 🅲 3,587; Z 39096; ● 560
Louin; Inc. Place; JASPER; 194 I-8; 🅿; Z 39338; Ⓟ 289; Ⓒ 339
Louise; Inc. Place; HUMPHREYS; 194 F-5; 🅿; Z 39097; Ⓟ 343; Ⓒ 315
Louisville; Inc. Place; ⊡ WINSTON; 194 F-8; 🅿 🅷; Z 39339; Ⓟ 7,169; Ⓒ 7,006
Love; RMC Place; DESOTO; *194 B-6; mail Hernando Z 38632; rural
LOWNDES; 194 E-9; Ⓟ 59,308; Ⓒ 61,586; ◆ 58,655
Loyd; RMC Place; CALHOUN; *194 D-8; mail Vardaman Z 38878; rural
Loyd Star; RMC Place; LINCOLN; *194 J-5; mail Brookhaven Z 39601; ● 30
Lucas; RMC Place; JEFFERSON DAVIS; 194 J-6; elev. 302ft./92m.; mail Prentiss Z 39474; ● 30
Lucedale; Inc. Place; ⊡ GEORGE; 194 L-9; elev. 282ft./86m.; 🅿 🅷; Z 39452; Ⓟ 2,592; Ⓒ 2,458
Lucern; RMC Place; NEWTON; *194 H-8; mail Union Z 39365; rural
Lucien; RMC Place; FRANKLIN; 194 J-5; mail Brookhaven Z 39601; ● 50
Luckney; RMC Place; RANKIN; *194 H-6; elev. 302ft./92m.; ★ JAC; mail Pearl Z 39208; pop. incl. with Flowood (Inc. Place)
Ludlow; RMC Place; SCOTT; 194 G-7; 🅿; Z 39098; ● 240
Lula; Inc. Place; COAHOMA; 194 C-5; 🅿; Z 38644; Ⓟ 224; Ⓒ 370
Lumberton; Inc. Place; LAMAR, PEARL RIVER; 194 K-7; elev. 297ft./91m.; 🅿; Z 39455; Ⓟ 2,121; Ⓒ 2,228
Lurand; RMC Place; COAHOMA; *194 C-5; mail Clarksdale Z 38614; ● 130
Lux; RMC Place; COVINGTON; *194 J-7; elev. 191ft./58m.; mail Hattiesburg Z 39401; rural
Lyman; RMC Place; HARRISON; *194 M-8; elev. 95ft./29m.; ★ BIL-; mail Gulfport Z 39503; pop. incl. with Gulfport (Inc. Place)
Lyman; CDP-Census Area Only; HARRISON; *194 M-8; mail Gulfport Z 39503; Ⓒ 1,081
Lynchburg; CDP; DESOTO; 194 A-6; elev. 300ft./91m.; ★ MEM; mail Memphis Z 38109; Ⓟ 2,071; Ⓒ 2,959
Lynn Creek; RMC Place; NOXUBEE; *194 F-9; elev. 240ft./73m.; mail Brooksville Z 39739; rural
Lynville; RMC Place; KEMPER; *194 G-9; mail Preston Z 39354
Lyon; Inc. Place; COAHOMA; 194 C-5; 🅿; Z 38645; Ⓟ 446; Ⓒ 418

M

Maben; Inc. Place; OKTIBBEHA, WEBSTER; 194 E-8; 🅿; Z 39750; Ⓟ 752; Ⓒ 803
Macedonia; RMC Place; FORREST; *194 J-8; elev. 235ft./72m.; mail Hattiesburg Z 39401
Macedonia; RMC Place; LEE; *194 C-9; elev. 383ft./117m.; mail Tupelo Z 38804; rural
Macedonia; RMC Place; UNION; *194 C-8; elev. 370ft./113m.; mail Myrtle Z 38650; rural
Macel; RMC Place; TALLAHATCHIE; *194 D-6; mail Philipp Z 38950; rural
Macon; Inc. Place; ⊡ NOXUBEE; 194 F-9; 🅿 🅷; Z 39341; Ⓟ 2,256; Ⓒ 2,461
Madden; RMC Place; LEAKE; 194 G-8; elev. 453ft./138m.; 🅿; Z 39109; ● 319
Madison; Inc. Place; MADISON; 194 H-6; elev. 335ft./102m.; 🅿; ★ JAC; Z 39110, Z 39130; Ⓟ 7,471; Ⓒ 14,692
MADISON; 194 G-6; Ⓟ 53,794; Ⓒ 74,674; ◆ 92,158
Madisonville; RMC Place; MADISON; *194 G-6; mail Canton Z 39046; rural
Magee; Inc. Place; SIMPSON; 194 I-7; elev. 430ft./131m.; 🅿 🅷; Z 39111; Ⓟ 3,607; Ⓒ 4,200
Magnolia; Inc. Place; ⊡ PIKE; 194 K-5; elev. 319ft./97m.; 🅿 🅷; Z 39652; Ⓟ 2,245; Ⓒ 2,071
Mahned; RMC Place; PERRY; 194 K-8; elev. 117ft./36m.; mail New Augusta Z 39462; ● 150
Main; RMC Place; LAUDERDALE; mail Meridian Z 39302; pop. incl. with Meridian (Inc. Place)
Malone; RMC Place; MARSHALL; *194 B-7; mail Waterford Z 38685; rural
Malvina; RMC Place; BOLIVAR; 194 D-4; mail Rosedale Z 38769; ● 30
Mannassa; RMC Place; CLARKE; *194 I-9; elev. 326ft./99m.; mail Quitman Z 39355; rural
Mantachie; Inc. Place; ITAWAMBA; 194 C-9; elev. 356ft./109m.; 🅿; Z 38855; Ⓟ 651; Ⓒ 1,107
Mantee; Inc. Place; WEBSTER; 194 D-8; 🅿; Z 39751; Ⓟ 134; Ⓒ 169
Marcella; RMC Place; HOLMES; *194 F-6; mail Tchula Z 39169; rural
Marianna; RMC Place; MARSHALL; *194 B-7; mail Holly Springs Z 38635; rural
Marie; RMC Place; SUNFLOWER; mail Indianola Z 38751; rural
Marietta; Inc. Place; PRENTISS; 194 C-9; elev. 382ft./116m.; 🅿; Z 38856; Ⓟ 287; Ⓒ 248
Marion; Inc. Place; LAUDERDALE; 194 H-9; 🅿; ★ MRID; Z 39342; Ⓟ 1,359; Ⓒ 1,305
MARION; 194 K-6; Ⓟ 25,544; Ⓒ 25,595; ◆ 25,894
Maris Town; RMC Place; MADISON; *194 G-6; mail Canton Z 39046
Markette; RMC Place; LAFAYETTE; *194 C-7; elev. 325ft./99m.; mail Oxford Z 38655; rural
Markham; RMC Place; SUNFLOWER; *194 E-5; mail Moorhead Z 38761; rural
Marks; Inc. Place; ⊡ QUITMAN; 194 C-6; elev. 166ft./51m.; 🅿 🅷; Z 38646 & mail Belen Z 38609; Ⓟ 1,758; Ⓒ 1,551; Ⓡ 2,047
MARSHALL; 194 B-7; Ⓟ 30,361; Ⓒ 34,993; ◆ 37,575
Mars Hill; RMC Place; AMITE; *194 K-5; mail Summit Z 39666; rural
Martin; RMC Place; LAUDERDALE; 194 G-9; mail Collinsville Z 39325; ● 110
Martin Bluff; RMC Place; JACKSON; *194 M-9; ★ PSCG; mail Gautier Z 39553; Ⓟ 1,928; ● 1,900
Martinsville; RMC Place; COPIAH; *194 I-5; elev. 436ft./133m.; mail Hazlehurst Z 39083; rural
Martintown; RMC Place; UNION; *194 C-8; elev. 360ft./110m.; mail New Albany Z 38652; ● 80
Martinville; RMC Place; SIMPSON; *194 I-7; mail Mendenhall Z 39114; rural
Marydell; RMC Place; LEAKE; *194 G-7; mail Carthage Z 39051; rural
Mashulaville; RMC Place; NOXUBEE; 194 F-9; elev. 260ft./79m.; mail Macon Z 39341; ● 60
Matherville; RMC Place; WAYNE; 194 I-9; 🅿; Z 39360; ● 50
Mathiston; Inc. Place; WEBSTER, CHOCTAW; 194 E-8; 🅿; Z 39752; Ⓟ 818; Ⓒ 720
Mattson; RMC Place; COAHOMA; 194 D-5; elev. 165ft./50m.; 🅿; Z 38614; ● 150
Mauvella; GEORGE; see Movella (RMC Place)
Maxie; RMC Place; FORREST; *194 K-8; elev. 223ft./68m.; mail Brooklyn Z 39425; ● 40
Maybank; RMC Place; FORREST; 194 J-8; ★ HATT; mail Hattiesburg Z 39401; ● 30
Mayersville; Inc. Place; ⊡ ISSAQUENA; 194 G-4; 🅿; Z 39113; Ⓟ 329; Ⓒ 795
Mayhew; RMC Place; LOWNDES; 194 E-9; elev. 209ft./64m.; 🅿; Z 39753; ● 110
Mayton; RMC Place; RANKIN; *194 I-7; elev. 384ft./117m.; mail Brandon Z 39042; rural
Maywood; RMC Place; DESOTO; *194 A-6; ★ MEM; mail Olive Branch Z 38654; pop. incl. with Olive Branch (Inc. Place)
McAdams; RMC Place; ATTALA; 194 F-7; 🅿; Z 39107; ● 250
McBride; RMC Place; JEFFERSON; *194 I-5; elev. 342ft./104m.; mail Pattison Z 39144; ● 80
McCall Creek; RMC Place; FRANKLIN; 194 J-5; 🅿; Z 39647; ● 140
McCallum; RMC Place; FORREST; *194 K-8; elev. 141ft./43m.; mail Hattiesburg Z 39401; rural
McCarley; RMC Place; CARROLL; 194 E-7; 🅿; Z 38943; ● 150
McComb; Inc. Place; PIKE; 194 K-5; 🅿 🅷 ■; Z 39648-49; Ⓟ 11,591; Ⓒ 13,337; ◆ 12,945
McCondy; RMC Place; CHICKASAW; 194 D-9; ● 120
McCool; Inc. Place; ATTALA; 194 F-8; elev. 470ft./143m.; 🅿; Z 39108; Ⓟ 169; Ⓒ 182
McCrary; RMC Place; LOWNDES; *194 E-10; ★ COL; mail Columbus Z 39701; rural
McCutcheon; RMC Place; WASHINGTON; *194 F-4; mail Arcola Z 38722; rural
McDonald; LEAKE; see Bertice (RMC Place)
McDonald; RMC Place; NESHOBA; 194 G-8; mail Union Z 39365; ● 50
McElveen; RMC Place; AMITE; *194 K-5; mail Summit Z 39666; rural
McHenry; RMC Place; STONE; 194 L-8; elev. 267ft./81m.; 🅿; Z 39561; ● 160
McLain; Inc. Place; GREENE; 194 K-9; 🅿; Z 39456; Ⓟ 536; Ⓒ 603
McLaurin; RMC Place; FORREST; 194 K-8; elev. 354ft./108m.; mail Hattiesburg Z 39401; ● 530
McLaurin Heights; RMC Place; RANKIN; *194 H-6; ★ JAC; mail Pearl Z 39208; pop. incl. with Pearl (Inc. Place)
McLeod; RMC Place; NOXUBEE; *194 F-9; elev. 227ft./69m.; mail Macon Z 39341; rural
McMillan; RMC Place; WINSTON; *194 F-8; mail Louisville Z 39339; rural
McNair; RMC Place; JEFFERSON; 194 J-4; elev. 421ft./128m.; mail Fayette Z 39069; ● 100
McNeal; RMC Place; JASPER; *194 I-8; elev. 446ft./136m.; mail Louin Z 39338; rural
McNeill; RMC Place; PEARL RIVER; 194 L-7; 🅿; Z 39457; ● 1,050
McSwain; RMC Place; PERRY; *194 K-8; mail Richton Z 39476; rural
McVille; RMC Place; ATTALA, LEAKE; *194 F-7; mail Kosciusko Z 39090; rural
Meadville; Inc. Place; ⊡ FRANKLIN; 194 J-4; 🅿 🅷; Z 39653; Ⓟ 453; Ⓒ 519
Mechanicsburg; RMC Place; YAZOO; *194 G-5; mail Bentonia Z 39040; ● 50
Meehan (Meehan Junction); RMC Place; LAUDERDALE; *194 H-9; mail Meridian Z 39307; ● 150
Meehan Junction; LAUDERDALE; see Meehan (RMC Place)
Meeks; RMC Place; HOLMES; *194 F-6; elev. 121ft./37m.; mail Cruger Z 38924; rural
Melba; RMC Place; LAMAR; mail Sumrall Z 39482; ● 50
Meltonville; RMC Place; MADISON; *194 H-6; elev. 260ft./79m.; mail Canton Z 39046; rural
Memphis; DESOTO; see Walls (Inc. Place)
Mendenhall; Inc. Place; ⊡ SIMPSON; 194 I-6; elev. 323ft./98m.; 🅿 🅷; Z 39114; Ⓟ 2,463; Ⓒ 2,555
Meridian; Inc. Place; ⊡ LAUDERDALE; 194 H-9; 🅿 🅷 ■; ★ MRID; Z 39301-05, Z 39307, Z 39309; Ⓟ 41,036; Ⓒ 39,968; ◆ 38,833
Meridian Station; CDP-Census Area Only; LAUDERDALE; *194 G-9; mail Meridian Z 39309; Ⓟ 2,503; Ⓒ 1,849
Merigold; Inc. Place; BOLIVAR; 194 D-5; elev. 141ft./43m.; 🅿; Z 38759; Ⓟ 572; Ⓒ 664
Merit; RMC Place; SIMPSON; *194 I-6; mail Mendenhall Z 39114; rural
Merrill; RMC Place; GEORGE; 194 K-9; elev. 58ft./18m.; mail Lucedale Z 39452; ● 100
Mesa; RMC Place; WALTHALL; *194 K-6; elev. 392ft./119m.; mail Tylertown Z 39667
Metcalfe; Inc. Place; WASHINGTON; 194 E-4; elev. 131ft./40m.; 🅿; ★ GRNV; Z 38760; Ⓟ 1,092; Ⓒ 1,109
Meyers; RMC Place; FORREST; *194 K-8; ★ HATT; mail Hattiesburg Z 39401; pop. incl. with Hattiesburg (Inc. Place)
Michigan City; RMC Place; BENTON; 194 A-8; 🅿; Z 38647; ● 250
Midnight; RMC Place; HUMPHREYS; 194 F-5; elev. 109ft./33m.; 🅿; Z 39115; ● 230
Midway (Peetsville); RMC Place; COPIAH; *194 J-5; mail Wesson Z 39191; ● 80
Midway; RMC Place; HINDS; *194 H-5; ★ JAC; mail Terry Z 39170
Midway; RMC Place; LEAKE; *194 G-7; elev. 477ft./145m.; mail Carthage Z 39051; rural
Midway; RMC Place; SCOTT; *194 G-7; mail Forest Z 39074; rural
Midway; RMC Place; TISHOMINGO; *194 B-10; mail Iuka Z 38852; ● 80
Midway; RMC Place; YAZOO; *194 G-6; mail Benton Z 39039; ● 80
Mileston; RMC Place; HOLMES; *194 F-6; mail Tchula Z 39169
Millard; RMC Place; PEARL RIVER; *194 L-7; elev. 186ft./57m.; mail Poplarville Z 39470; rural
Mill Creek; RMC Place; JONES; *194 J-8; elev. 329ft./100m.; ★ LAUR; mail Laurel Z 39440
Mill Creek; RMC Place; PEARL RIVER; *194 L-7; elev. 162ft./49m.; mail Carriere Z 39426
Mill Creek; RMC Place; RANKIN; *194 H-6; ★ JAC; mail Brandon Z 39047; ● 250
Millcreek; RMC Place; WINSTON; *194 F-8; elev. 429ft./131m.; mail Louisville Z 39339; rural
Mill Creek Cabin Area; RMC Place; TISHOMINGO; *194 B-10; mail Iuka Z 38852; ● 90
Miller; RMC Place; DESOTO; 194 B-7; ★ MEM; mail Olive Branch Z 38654; ● 80
Millington; RMC Place; KEMPER; *194 G-10; elev. 216ft./66m.; mail Scooba Z 39358; rural
Millsaps College; RMC Place; HINDS; ★ JAC; mail Jackson Z 39210; pop. incl. with Jackson (Inc. Place)
Mill Town; RMC Place; MADISON; *194 G-6; mail Canton Z 39046
Millville; MADISON; see Farmhaven (RMC Place)
Mimms; PANOLA; see Mims (RMC Place)
Mims (Mimms); RMC Place; PANOLA; *194 C-6; mail Batesville Z 38606; rural
Mineral Wells; RMC Place; DESOTO; *194 A-6; 🅿; ★ MEM; Z 38654; pop. incl. with Olive Branch (Inc. Place)
Mingo; RMC Place; TISHOMINGO; *194 B-10; mail Tishomingo Z 38873; rural
Minter City; RMC Place; LEFLORE; 194 D-6; 🅿; Z 38944; ● 200
Missionary; RMC Place; JASPER; *194 I-8; elev. 575ft./175m.; mail Rose Hill Z 39356; rural
Mississippi Choctaw Reservation; Indian Reservation; NESHOBA, ATTALA, JONES, KEMPER, LEAKE, NEWTON, SCOTT; mail Philadelphia Z 39350; also location of Indian Agency; Ⓟ 2,866; Ⓒ 4,311
Mississippi City; RMC Place; HARRISON; *194 M-8; elev. 19ft./6m.; ★ BIL-; mail Gulfport Z 39501; pop. incl. with Gulfport (Inc. Place)
Mississippi College; RMC Place; HINDS; *194 H-5; ★ JAC; mail Clinton Z 39058; pop. incl. with Clinton (Inc. Place)
Mitchell; RMC Place; TIPPAH; *194 B-9; mail Ripley Z 38663; rural
Mize; Inc. Place; SMITH; 194 I-7; elev. 299ft./91m.; 🅿; Z 39116; Ⓟ 312; Ⓒ 285
Money; RMC Place; LEFLORE; 194 E-6; 🅿; Z 38945; ● 120
Monroe; RMC Place; FRANKLIN; *194 J-4; mail Meadville Z 39653; ● 70
MONROE; 194 D-9; Ⓟ 36,582; Ⓒ 38,014; ◆ 36,465
Monterey; RMC Place; RANKIN; *194 H-6; ★ JAC; mail Florence Z 39073
Monte Vista; RMC Place; WEBSTER; *194 E-8; elev. 460ft./140m.; mail Eupora Z 39744, Walthall Z 39771; rural
Montgomery; RMC Place; LINCOLN; *194 J-5; mail Wesson Z 39191; rural
MONTGOMERY; 194 E-7; Ⓟ 12,388; Ⓒ 12,189; ◆ 11,105
Monticello; Inc. Place; ⊡ LAWRENCE; 194 J-6; 🅿 🅷; Z 39654; Ⓟ 1,755; Ⓒ 1,726
Montpelier; RMC Place; CLAY; 194 D-8; 🅿; Z 39754; ● 160
Montrose; Inc. Place; JASPER; 194 H-8; mail Louin Z 39338; Ⓟ 106; Ⓒ 127
Moon; RMC Place; COAHOMA; *194 C-5; mail Coahoma Z 38617; rural
Moores Mill; RMC Place; TISHOMINGO; *194 C-10; elev. 338ft./103m.; mail Dennis Z 38838; rural
Mooreville; RMC Place; LEE; 194 C-9; 🅿; Z 38857; ● 380
Moorhead; Inc. Place; SUNFLOWER; 194 E-5; elev. 117ft./36m.; 🅿; Z 38761; Ⓟ 2,417; Ⓒ 2,573
Morgan City; Inc. Place; LEFLORE; 194 E-5; 🅿; Z 38946; Ⓟ 139; Ⓒ 305
Morgans; HINDS; see Morgans Store (RMC Place)
Morgans Store (Morgans); RMC Place; HINDS; *194 I-5; mail Terry Z 39170
Morgantown; RMC Place; ADAMS; 194 J-3; ★ NCHZ; mail Natchez Z 39120; ● 2,900
Morgantown; RMC Place; MARION; 194 K-6; elev. 164ft./50m.; 🅿; Z 39483 & mail Sturgis Z 39769; ● 300
Morgantown; RMC Place; OKTIBBEHA; *194 F-8; elev. 311ft./95m.; 🅿; Z 39483 & mail Sturgis Z 39769; ● 30
Morning Star; RMC Place; HINDS; *194 H-5; elev. 175ft./53m.; mail Edwards Z 39066; rural
Morriston; RMC Place; FORREST; *194 J-8; ★ HATT; mail Hattiesburg Z 39401
Morton; Inc. Place; SCOTT; 194 H-7; elev. 465ft./142m.; 🅿; Z 39117; Ⓟ 3,212; Ⓒ 3,482
Moscow; RMC Place; KEMPER; 194 G-9; mail De Kalb Z 39328; ● 110
Moselle (Albeison); RMC Place; JONES; 194 J-8; 🅿; Z 39459; ● 700
Moss; RMC Place; JASPER; 194 I-8; 🅿; Z 39460; ● 250
Moss Point; Inc. Place; JACKSON; 194 M-9; elev. 22ft./7m.; 🅿; ★ PSCG; Z 39562-63 & mail Pascagoula Z 39581; Ⓟ 17,837; Ⓒ 15,851
Mossy Lake; RMC Place; LEFLORE; *194 E-5; mail Swiftown Z 38959; ● 50
Mound Bayou; Inc. Place; BOLIVAR; 194 D-5; elev. 143ft./44m.; 🅿; Z 38762; Ⓟ 2,222; Ⓒ 2,102
Mound City; RMC Place; BOLIVAR; *194 D-4; elev. 142ft./43m.; mail Beulah Z 38726, Blue Springs Z 38828; rural
Mound City; RMC Place; UNION; *194 C-8; mail Beulah Z 38726, Blue Springs Z 38828
Mount Carmel; RMC Place; JEFFERSON DAVIS; *194 J-7; mail Prentiss Z 39474; ● 30
Mount Nebo; RMC Place; KEMPER; *194 G-9; mail De Kalb Z 39328; rural
Mount Olive; Inc. Place; COVINGTON; 194 I-7; 🅿; Z 39119; Ⓟ 914; Ⓒ 893
Mount Olive; RMC Place; FRANKLIN; *194 J-4; elev. 267ft./81m.; mail Meadville Z 39653; rural
Mount Olive; RMC Place; JONES; *194 I-8; ★ LAUR; mail Laurel Z 39440; rural
Mount Pleasant; RMC Place; ITAWAMBA; mail Tremont Z 38876; rural
Mount Pleasant; RMC Place; MARSHALL; 194 A-7; elev. 470ft./143m.; 🅿; Z 38635, Z 38649; ● 400
Mount Vernon; RMC Place; LEE; *194 C-9; mail Tupelo Z 38801, Z 38804; rural
Mount Zion; RMC Place; SIMPSON; *194 I-7; mail Magee Z 39111, Mount Olive Z 39119; rural
Movella (Mauvella); RMC Place; GEORGE; *194 L-9; elev. 62ft./19m.; mail Lucedale Z 39452; ● 50
Muldon; RMC Place; MONROE; *194 D-9; elev. 302ft./92m.; mail Aberdeen Z 39730; rural
Murphy; RMC Place; WASHINGTON; *194 F-5; mail Hollandale Z 38748
Murry; RMC Place; TIPPAH; *194 B-8; mail Ripley Z 38663; rural
Muskegon; RMC Place; SCOTT; *194 H-8; elev. 440ft./134m.; mail Lake Z 39092
Myrick; RMC Place; JONES; 194 J-8; elev. 264ft./80m.; ★ LAUR; mail Laurel Z 39440; ● 110
Myrleville; RMC Place; YAZOO; *194 G-6; elev. 267ft./81m.; mail Benton Z 39039; ● 30
Myrtle; Inc. Place; UNION; 194 B-8; elev. 398ft./121m.; 🅿; Z 38650; Ⓟ 358; Ⓒ 407

N

Nancy; RMC Place; CLARKE; *194 I-9; mail Vossburg Z 39366; rural
Nason; RMC Place; GRENADA; *194 D-6; mail Holcomb Z 38940; rural
Natchez; Inc. Place; ⊡ ADAMS; 194 J-3; 🅿 🅷 ■; ★ NCHZ; Z 39120-22; Ⓟ 19,460; Ⓒ 18,464; ◆ 15,694
National Cemetery; RMC Place; WARREN; ★ VICK; mail Vicksburg Z 39180; pop. incl. with Vicksburg (Inc. Place)
Necaise; RMC Place; HANCOCK; *194 L-7; mail Perkinston Z 39573
Neely; RMC Place; GREENE; 194 K-9; elev. 228ft./69m.; 🅿; Z 39461; ● 200
Nellieburg; CDP; LAUDERDALE; 194 G-1; ★ MRID; mail Meridian Z 39307; Ⓟ 1,208; Ⓒ 1,354
Nesbit; RMC Place; DESOTO; 194 B-6; 🅿; ★ MEM; Z 38651 & mail Horn Lake Z 38637; pop. incl. with Hernando (Inc. Place)
Neshoba; RMC Place; NESHOBA; 194 G-8; mail Union Z 39365; ● 150
NESHOBA; 194 G-8; Ⓟ 24,800; Ⓒ 28,684; ◆ 30,217
Nettleton; Inc. Place; MONROE, LEE; 194 D-9; elev. 266ft./81m.; 🅿; Z 38858; Ⓟ 2,462; Ⓒ 1,932; Ⓡ 2,013
Nevada; RMC Place; HINDS; *194 G-5; elev. 156ft./48m.; mail Bolton Z 39041; rural
New Albany; Inc. Place; ⊡ UNION; 194 C-8; elev. 364ft./111m.; 🅿 🅷; Z 38652; Ⓟ 6,775; Ⓒ 7,607
New Augusta; Inc. Place; ⊡ PERRY; 194 K-8; elev. 108ft./33m.; 🅿; Z 39462; Ⓟ 668; Ⓒ 715
New Byram; RMC Place; HINDS; 194 H-6; elev. 326ft./99m.; ★ JAC; mail Jackson Z 39212; ● 500
New Canaan; RMC Place; BENTON; *194 A-8; elev. 570ft./174m.; mail Ashland Z 38603; rural

---

Entries in **UPPERCASE** are counties.
Entries in **bold** have populations of 2,500 or more.
Names in parentheses are alternate names.

Inc. Place	Incorporated Place
RMC Place	Rand McNally Designated Place
CDP	Census Designated Place
MCD	Minor Civil Division
⊡	County Seat
▲	Minor Civil Division
elev.	Elevation
🅿	Post Office
🅷	Hospital
🅲	College
■	Principal Business Center
★	Ranally Metro Area (RMA) Abbreviation
Z	Zip Code(s)
Ⓟ	Previous Census Population
Ⓡ	Revised Census Population
Ⓐ	Annexation Population
●	Rand McNally Population Estimate
Ⓒ	Final Census Population
Ⓢ	Special Census Population
◆	Estimated Population

For additional definitions see Glossary, Volume 1, and Introduction, Volume 2.

New Fitler (Crown Zellerback); RMC Place; ISSAQUENA; *194 G-4; mail Rolling Fork z 39159; rural
New Garden; RMC Place; TATE; *194 B-7; mail Coldwater z 38618; rural
New Goshen Springs; RANKIN; see Goshen Springs (RMC Place)
New Hamilton; MONROE; see Hamilton (RMC Place)
New Harmony; RMC Place; UNION; 194 C-8; mail Blue Springs z 38828; ● 100
New Hebron; Inc. Place; LAWRENCE; 194 I-6; 🅿; z 39140; Ⓟ 373; © 447
New Hope; CDP; LOWNDES; 194 E-10; ★ **COL**; mail Columbus z 39701-02; Ⓟ 1,663; © 1,964
New Houlka; CHICKASAW; see Houlka (Inc. Place)
Newman; RMC Place; HINDS; *194 H-5; elev. 184ft./56m.; mail Edwards z 39066; rural
Newmans; RMC Place; WARREN; *194 H-5; ★ **VICK**; mail Vicksburg z 39180
Newmans Grove; RMC Place; WARREN; *194 H-5; ★ **VICK**; mail Raymond z 39154; rural
Newport; RMC Place; ATTALA; *194 F-7; elev. 320ft./98m.; mail Sallis z 39160; rural
Newport; RMC Place; DESOTO; *194 B-6; mail Lake Cormorant z 38641; ● 30
New Salem; RMC Place; ITAWAMBA; *194 C-10; elev. 410ft./125m.; mail Fulton z 38843; rural
New Sight; RMC Place; LINCOLN; *194 J-5; mail Brookhaven z 39601; rural
New Site; RMC Place; PRENTISS; 194 B-10; 🅿; z 38859; ● 250
Newton; Inc. Place; NEWTON; 194 H-8; elev. 415ft./126m.; 🅿; z 39345; Ⓟ 3,701; © 3,699
NEWTON; 194 H-8; Ⓟ 20,291; © 21,838; ◆ 22,528
New Town; RMC Place; TATE; *194 B-6; mail Senatobia z 38668
New Wren; RMC Place; MONROE; 194 D-9; elev. 306ft./93m.; mail Aberdeen z 39730; ● 210
Nichols; RMC Place; LEFLORE; *194 E-5; mail Swiftown z 38959; ● 25
Nicholson; RMC Place; PEARL RIVER; 194 M-7; 🅿; z 39463; ● 1,000
Nida; RMC Place; HOLMES; mail Tchula z 39169
Nitta Yuma; RMC Place; SHARKEY; 194 F-4; 🅿; z 38721; ● 80
Nixon; RMC Place; PONTOTOC; *194 C-8; mail Pontotoc z 38863; rural
Nod; RMC Place; YAZOO; *194 G-6; elev. 217ft./66m.; mail Benton z 39039; ● 50
Nola; RMC Place; LAWRENCE; 194 J-6; mail Sontag z 39665; ● 130
Norfield; RMC Place; LINCOLN; *194 J-5; mail Bogue Chitto z 39629; rural
Norfolk; RMC Place; DESOTO; *194 A-6; mail Lake Cormorant z 38641; ● 30
Norris; RMC Place; SCOTT; 194 H-7; elev. 519ft./158m.; mail Forest z 39074; rural
North; RMC Place; HINDS; *194 H-6; ★ **JAC**; mail Jackson z 39206; pop. incl. with Jackson (Inc. Place)
North; RMC Place; LAUDERDALE; *194 H-9; ★ **MRID**; mail Jackson z 39286, Meridian z 39305; pop. incl. with Meridian (Inc. Place)
North Bay; RMC Place; HARRISON; ★ **BIL-**; mail Biloxi z 39532; pop. incl. with D'Iberville (Inc. Place)
North Bend; RMC Place; NESHOBA; *194 G-8; mail Philadelphia z 39350; rural
North Biloxi; HARRISON, JACKSON; see D'Iberville (Inc. Place)
North Carrollton (Carrollton); Inc. Place; CARROLL; 194 E-6; 🅿; z 38947 & mail Carrollton z 38917; Ⓟ 578; © 499
North Crossroads; RMC Place; TISHOMINGO; 194 A-10; mail Iuka z 38852; ● 50
North Greenville; RMC Place; WASHINGTON; *194 E-4; ★ **GRNV**; mail Greenville z 38701
North Gulfport; RMC Place; HARRISON; 194 M-1; elev. 25ft./8m.; ★ **BIL-**; mail Gulfport z 39503; pop. incl. with Gulfport (Inc. Place)
North Haven; RMC Place; UNION; *194 B-8; mail New Albany z 38652; ● 270
North Long Beach; RMC Place; HARRISON; *194 M-8; ★ **BIL-**; mail Long Beach z 39560; pop. incl. with Long Beach (Inc. Place)
North Tunica; CDP-Census Area Only; TUNICA; 194 B-5; mail Tunica z 38676; Ⓟ 1,314; © 1,450
Norton; RMC Place; TIPPAH; *194 B-8; mail Ripley z 38663; rural
Noxapater; Inc. Place; WINSTON; 194 F-8; elev. 491ft./150m.; 🅿; z 39346; Ⓟ 441; © 419
NOXUBEE; 194 F-9; Ⓟ 12,604; © 12,548; ◆ 11,706

O

Oak Bowery; RMC Place; JONES; *194 J-8; elev. 386ft./118m.; mail Ellisville z 39437; rural
Oak Grove; RMC Place; HOLMES; *194 F-6; mail Tchula z 39169; rural
Oak Grove; RMC Place; JONES; *194 J-8; mail Ellisville z 39437, Hattiesburg z 39401, Moselle z 39459; ● 250
Oak Grove; RMC Place; LAMAR; 194 K-7; elev. 405ft./123m.; ★ **HATT**; mail Hattiesburg z 39401; ● 640
Oak Grove; RMC Place; PERRY; *194 K-8; mail Beaumont z 39423; rural
Oakland; RMC Place; ITAWAMBA; *194 C-10; elev. 410ft./125m.; mail Fulton z 38843; rural
Oakland; RMC Place; PIKE; *194 K-5; mail Summit z 39666; rural
Oakland; Inc. Place; YALOBUSHA; 194 D-6; 🅿; z 38948; Ⓟ 553; © 586
Oakley (Oakley Training School); RMC Place; HINDS; 194 H-5; elev. 192ft./59m.; ★ **JAC**; mail Raymond z 39154; ● 250
Oakley Training School; HINDS; see Oakley (RMC Place)
Oak Ridge; RMC Place; WARREN; *194 H-5; mail Vicksburg z 39183; rural
Oak Vale; RMC Place; LAWRENCE, JEFFERSON DAVIS; 194 J-6; 🅿; z 39656; ● 160
Obadiah; RMC Place; LAUDERDALE; 194 H-9; mail Bailey z 39320; ● 170
Ocean Springs; Inc. Place; JACKSON; 194 M-9; 🅿 🅷; ★ **BIL-**; z 39564-66; Ⓟ 14,658; © 17,225
Ocobla; RMC Place; NESHOBA; *194 G-8; mail Philadelphia z 39350; rural
Ofahoma; RMC Place; LEAKE; 194 G-7; mail Carthage z 39051; ● 220
Oil City; RMC Place; YAZOO; 194 G-5; elev. 341ft./104m.; mail Bentonia z 39040; ● 75
Okahola; RMC Place; LAMAR; *194 K-8; elev. 231ft./70m.; ★ **HATT**; mail Purvis z 39475; rural
Oklahoma; RMC Place; CARROLL; *194 E-6; elev. 135ft./41m.; mail Carrollton z 38917; rural
Okolona; Inc. Place; ⊡ CHICKASAW; 194 D-9; 🅿 🅷; z 38860; Ⓟ 3,267; © 3,056
OKTIBBEHA; 194 E-8; Ⓟ 38,375; © 42,902; ◆ 44,940
Oktoc; RMC Place; OKTIBBEHA; *194 E-9; elev. 292ft./89m.; mail Starkville z 39759; rural
Old Cairo; RMC Place; PRENTISS; mail Booneville z 38829; ● 30
Old Dominion; RMC Place; LEFLORE; *194 E-5; mail Morgan City z 38946; rural
Oldenburg; RMC Place; FRANKLIN; *194 J-4; elev. 334ft./102m.; mail Roxie z 39661; rural
Oldham; RMC Place; TISHOMINGO; *194 B-10; mail Iuka z 38852; ● 60
Old Hamilton; RMC Place; MONROE; 194 D-10; mail Hamilton z 39746; ● 60
Old Houlka; RMC Place; CHICKASAW; 194 D-8; mail Houlka z 38850; ● 30
Old Red Star; RMC Place; LINCOLN; *194 J-5; mail Brookhaven z 39601; rural
Old Union; RMC Place; LEE; *194 C-9; elev. 310ft./94m.; mail Shannon z 38868; rural
Olive Branch; Inc. Place; DESOTO; 194 A-7; 🅿 🅷; ★ **MEM**; z 38654; Ⓟ 3,567; © 21,054; ◆ 40,071
Oloh; RMC Place; LAMAR; 194 K-7; mail Sumrall z 39482; ● 100
Oma; RMC Place; LAWRENCE; 194 I-6; mail Monticello z 39654; ● 30
Omega; RMC Place; HOLMES; *194 F-5; mail Tchula z 39169; rural
Onward; RMC Place; SHARKEY; *194 G-4; mail Rolling Fork z 39159; rural
Ora; RMC Place; COVINGTON; 194 J-7; elev. 278ft./85m.; mail Collins z 39428; pop. incl. with Collins (Inc. Place)
Orange; RMC Place; CLARKE, JASPER; *194 I-9; mail Pachuta z 39347
Orange Grove; RMC Place; HARRISON; *194 M-8; ★ **BIL-**; mail Gulfport z 39503, Pascagoula z 39567; pop. incl. with Gulfport (Inc. Place)
Orange Grove; RMC Place; JACKSON; 194 M-10; ★ **PSCG**; mail Gulfport z 39503, Pascagoula z 39567, z 39581; ● 570
O'Reilly; RMC Place; BOLIVAR; *194 E-5; mail Boyle z 38730; ● 30
Orwood; RMC Place; LAFAYETTE; *194 C-7; mail Oxford z 38655; ● 30
Osborn; RMC Place; OKTIBBEHA; 194 E-9; elev. 266ft./81m.; mail Starkville z 39759; ● 80
Osborne Creek; RMC Place; PRENTISS; *194 B-9; mail Booneville z 38829; ● 60
Osyka; Inc. Place; PIKE; 194 K-5; 🅿; z 39657; Ⓟ 483; © 481
Ovett; RMC Place; JONES; 194 J-8; 🅿; z 39464; ● 630
Owens Wells; RMC Place; HOLMES; *194 F-6; mail Lexington z 39095; rural
Oxberry; RMC Place; GRENADA; *194 D-6; mail Holcomb z 38940; rural
Oxford; RMC Place; AMITE; *194 K-4; elev. 422ft./129m.; mail Gloster z 39638; rural
Oxford; Inc. Place; ⊡ LAFAYETTE; 194 C-7; elev. 416ft./127m.; 🅿 🅷 🅲 13,990; z 38655; Ⓟ 9,984; © 11,756
Ozona; RMC Place; PEARL RIVER; *194 L-7; elev. 129ft./39m.; mail Carriere z 39426

P

Pace; Inc. Place; BOLIVAR; 194 D-4; elev. 140ft./43m.; 🅿; z 38764; Ⓟ 354; © 364
Pachuta; Inc. Place; CLARKE; 194 I-9; 🅿; z 39347; Ⓟ 268; © 245
Paden; Inc. Place; TISHOMINGO; 194 B-10; elev. 452ft./138m.; mail Tishomingo z 38873; Ⓟ 123; © 106
Palmer; FORREST; see Palmers Crossing (RMC Place)
Palmers Crossing (Palmer); RMC Place; FORREST; 194 K-8; ★ **HATT**; mail Hattiesburg z 39401; pop. incl. with Hattiesburg (Inc. Place)
Palmetto; RMC Place; LEE; *194 C-9; elev. 323ft./98m.; mail Tupelo z 38801; ● 50
PANOLA; 194 C-6; Ⓟ 29,996; © 34,274; ◆ 35,547
Panther Burn; RMC Place; SHARKEY; 194 F-4; elev. 114ft./35m.; 🅿; z 38765; ● 90
Parham; RMC Place; MONROE; 194 D-10; mail Amory z 38821, Greenwood Springs z 38848, Smithville z 38870; ● 290
Paris; RMC Place; LAFAYETTE; 194 C-7; elev. 375ft./114m.; 🅿; z 38949; ● 160
Parks; RMC Place; UNION; *194 C-9; mail New Albany z 38652; rural
Parksplace; RMC Place; PANOLA; *194 B-6; mail Como z 38619; ● 80
Pascagoula; Inc. Place; ⊡ JACKSON; 194 M-9; elev. 16ft./5m.; 🅿 🅷 ■; ★ **PSCG**; z 39563, z 39567-69, z 39581, z 39595 & mail Moss Point z 39562; Ⓟ 25,899; © 26,200; ◆ 24,168
Pascagoula River Estates; RMC Place; GEORGE; *194 L-9; elev. 30ft./9m.; mail Lucedale z 39452; rural
Pass Christian; Inc. Place; HARRISON; 194 M-8; elev. 10ft./3m.; 🅿; ★ **BIL-**; z 39571; Ⓟ 5,557; © 6,579
Patosi; RMC Place; YAZOO; *194 F-5; mail Yazoo City z 39194; ● 100
Pattison; RMC Place; CLAIBORNE; 194 I-4; elev. 185ft./56m.; 🅿; z 39144; ● 330
Paul; RMC Place; TALLAHATCHIE; *194 D-6; mail Cascilla z 38920; rural
Paulding; RMC Place; ⊡ JASPER; 194 I-8; 🅿; z 39348; ● 150
Paulette; RMC Place; NOXUBEE; 194 F-10; mail Macon z 39341; ● 30
Paynes; RMC Place; TALLAHATCHIE; 194 D-6; mail Cascilla z 38920
Pearl; Inc. Place; RANKIN; 194 H-6; elev. 272ft./83m.; 🅿; ★ **JAC**; z 39208, z 39288; Ⓟ 19,588; © 21,961; ◆ 22,235
Pearl; RMC Place; SIMPSON; *194 I-6; elev. 251ft./77m.; mail Florence z 39073; rural
Pearl City; RMC Place; RANKIN; ★ **JAC**; mail Pearl z 39208; pop. incl. with Pearl (Inc. Place)
Pearlington; CDP; HANCOCK; 194 M-7; elev. 8ft./2m.; 🅿; ★ **N.O.**; z 39572; Ⓟ 1,603; © 1,684
Pearl River; CDP; NESHOBA; *194 G-8; elev. 524ft./160m.; mail Philadelphia z 39350; Ⓟ 2,136; © 3,156
PEARL RIVER; 194 K-7; Ⓟ 38,714; © 48,621; ◆ 57,826
Pearson; RMC Place; RANKIN; 194 D-3; elev. 301ft./92m.; ★ **JAC**; mail Pearl z 39208; pop. incl. with Pearl (Inc. Place)
Pecan; RMC Place; JACKSON; 194 M-10; elev. 7ft./2m.; ★ **PSCG**; mail Pascagoula z 39567, z 39581; ● 80
Pecan Grove; RMC Place; JONES; *194 J-8; elev. 280ft./85m.; ★ **LAUR**; mail Ellisville z 39437; rural
Peetsville; COPIAH; see Midway (RMC Place)
Pelahatchie; Inc. Place; RANKIN; 194 H-7; elev. 359ft./109m.; 🅿; z 39145; Ⓟ 1,553; © 1,461
Penantly; RMC Place; JASPER; *194 H-8; mail Rose Hill z 39356; rural
Pendorff; RMC Place; JONES; *194 J-8; ★ **LAUR**; mail Laurel z 39440; rural
Penns; RMC Place; LOWNDES; *194 E-9; elev. 299ft./91m.; mail Crawford z 39743; rural
Penton; RMC Place; DESOTO; *194 B-6; mail Robinsonville z 38664; ● 50
Peoples; RMC Place; TIPPAH; 194 B-9; mail Ripley z 38663
Peoria (Robinson); RMC Place; AMITE; *194 K-5; mail Liberty z 39645; rural
Percy; RMC Place; WASHINGTON; 194 F-4; 🅿; z 38748
Perdue; RMC Place; NEWTON; *194 H-8; elev. 398ft./121m.; mail Little Rock z 39337; rural
Perkinston; RMC Place; STONE; 194 L-8; elev. 133ft./41m.; 🅿; z 39573; ● 100
PERRY; 194 K-8; Ⓟ 10,865; © 12,138; ◆ 12,510
Perrytown; RMC Place; WILKINSON; *194 J-4; elev. 154ft./47m.; mail Crosby z 39633; rural
Perth; RMC Place; JEFFERSON; *194 J-4; mail Fayette z 39069; rural
Perthshire; RMC Place; BOLIVAR; 194 D-4; mail Gunnison z 38746; ● 50
Petal; Inc. Place; FORREST; 194 J-8; 🅿; ★ **HATT**; z 39465; Ⓟ 7,883; © 7,579
Peteet; RMC Place; LEFLORE; *194 E-5; mail Morgan City z 38946; ● 20
Pettit; WASHINGTON; see Avon (RMC Place)
Peyton; RMC Place; CLAIBORNE; *194 I-4; mail Pattison z 39144; rural
Pheba; RMC Place; CLAY; 194 E-8; 🅿; z 39755; ● 700
Philadelphia; Inc. Place; ⊡ NESHOBA; 194 G-8; elev. 424ft./129m.; 🅿 🅷; z 39350; location of Choctaw Indian Agency; Ⓟ 6,758; © 7,303
Philipp; RMC Place; TALLAHATCHIE; 194 D-6; 🅿; z 38950; ● 350
Phillipstown; RMC Place; LEFLORE; *194 E-6; mail Sidon z 38954; rural
Phoenix; RMC Place; YAZOO; *194 G-5; mail Bentonia z 39040; ● 100
Piave; RMC Place; GREENE; *194 J-9; mail Leakesville z 39451, Richton z 39476; ● 30
Picayune; Inc. Place; PEARL RIVER; 194 M-7; elev. 61ft./19m.; 🅿 🅷; z 39466; Ⓟ 10,633; © 10,535
Pickens; Inc. Place; HOLMES; 194 G-6; elev. 232ft./71m.; 🅿; z 39146, z 39179; Ⓟ 1,285; © 1,325
Pickwick; RMC Place; MARION; *194 K-7; mail Foxworth z 39483; rural
Pierce Crossroads; RMC Place; YAZOO; *194 G-6; mail Yazoo City z 39194; rural
Piggtown; RMC Place; LEAKE; *194 G-7; mail Lena z 39094; rural
PIKE; 194 K-5; Ⓟ 36,882; © 38,940; ◆ 39,220
Piketown; RMC Place; SCOTT; *194 H-8; elev. 448ft./137m.; mail Forest z 39074; rural
Pinckneyville; RMC Place; WILKINSON; *194 K-3; mail Woodville z 39669; rural
Pinebluff; RMC Place; CLAY; *194 E-8; mail Mantee z 39751; rural
Pine Bluff; WAYNE; see Eset (RMC Place)
Pinebur; RMC Place; MARION; 194 K-7; mail Columbia z 39429; ● 70
Pinedale; RMC Place; UNION; 194 C-8; mail Etta z 38627
Pine Flat; RMC Place; LAFAYETTE; *194 C-7; mail Water Valley z 38965; rural
Pine Flat; RMC Place; TISHOMINGO; *194 A-10; mail Iuka z 38852; rural
Pine Grove; RMC Place; BENTON; *194 B-8; mail Hickory Flat z 38633; rural
Pine Grove; RMC Place; LAMAR; *194 K-7; elev. 373ft./114m.; mail Purvis z 39475; rural
Pine Grove; RMC Place; LEE, MONROE; *194 D-9; mail Booneville z 38829, Pontotoc z 38863, Shannon z 38868; ● 30
Pine Grove; RMC Place; TIPPAH; 194 B-9; elev. 674ft./205m.; mail Booneville z 38829; rural
Pine Ridge; RMC Place; ADAMS; *194 J-3; ★ **NCHZ**; mail Natchez z 39120
Pine Ridge; RMC Place; LAMAR; *194 K-7; mail Purvis z 39475; rural
Pine Springs; RMC Place; LAUDERDALE; *194 H-9; ★ **MRID**; mail Meridian z 39305; ● 50
Pine Valley; RMC Place; YALOBUSHA; *194 D-7; mail Water Valley z 38965; rural
Pineview; RMC Place; JONES; *194 I-8; ★ **LAUR**; mail Laurel z 39440; rural
Pineville; HARRISON; see Cuevas (RMC Place)
Pineville; RMC Place; SMITH; *194 H-7; mail Forest z 39074; rural
Piney Woods (Country Life School); RMC Place; RANKIN; 194 I-6; 🅿; z 39148; ● 100
Pinola; RMC Place; SIMPSON; 194 I-6; 🅿; z 39149; ● 130
Pisgah; RMC Place; GREENE; *194 K-9; elev. 303ft./92m.; mail Lucedale z 39452; rural
Pisgah; RMC Place; PRENTISS; *194 B-9; elev. 515ft./157m.; mail Rienzi z 38865; ● 180
Pisgah; RMC Place; RANKIN; *194 H-6; mail Brandon z 39047; rural
Pistol Ridge; RMC Place; FORREST; *194 K-8; mail Lumberton z 39455; ● 30
Pittman; RMC Place; MARION; mail Foxworth z 39483; rural
Pittsboro; Inc. Place; ⊡ CALHOUN; 194 D-8; 🅿; z 38951; Ⓟ 277; © 212
Plain; RANKIN; see Richland (Inc. Place)
Plainview; RMC Place; RANKIN; ★ **JAC**; mail Richland z 39218; pop. incl. with Richland (Inc. Place)
Plantersville; Inc. Place; LEE; 194 C-9; elev. 300ft./91m.; 🅿; z 38862; Ⓟ 1,046; © 1,144
Plattsburg; RMC Place; WINSTON; *194 F-8; elev. 555ft./169m.; mail Philadelphia z 39350
Pleasant Grove; RMC Place; PANOLA; 194 C-6; mail Sardis z 38666; ● 110
Pleasant Hill; RMC Place; COPIAH; *194 I-5; elev. 491ft./150m.; mail Union Church z 39668; rural
Pleasant Hill; RMC Place; DESOTO; 194 B-6; ★ **MEM**; mail Nesbit z 38651; ● 100
Pleasant Hill; LEAKE; see Gill (RMC Place)
Pleasant Hill; RMC Place; UNION; *194 B-8; mail New Albany z 38652; rural
Pleasant Ridge; RMC Place; JONES; *194 J-8; mail Laurel z 39440; rural
Pleasant Ridge; RMC Place; UNION; *194 B-9; mail Baldwyn z 38824, Dumas z 38625, New Albany z 38652; rural
Plum Point; RMC Place; DESOTO; *194 A-6; ★ **MEM**; mail Southaven z 38671; pop. incl. with Southaven (Inc. Place)
Pluto; RMC Place; HOLMES; *194 F-5; mail Tchula z 39169; rural
Poagville; RMC Place; TATE; *194 B-6; elev. 369ft./112m.; mail Coldwater z 38618; rural
Pocahontas; RMC Place; HINDS; 194 H-6; 🅿; z 39072; ● 100
Pokal; RMC Place; SIMPSON; *194 I-6; mail Newhebron z 39140; rural
Polfrey; RMC Place; JACKSON; *194 M-9; ★ **BIL-**; mail Ocean Springs z 39564; ● 120
Polkville; Inc. Place; SMITH; 194 H-7; elev. 510ft./155m.; mail Morton z 39117; Ⓟ 129; © 132
Pollock; RMC Place; SUNFLOWER; *194 E-5; mail Indianola z 38751; rural
Pond; RMC Place; WILKINSON; *194 K-3; mail Woodville z 39669; rural
Ponta; RMC Place; LAUDERDALE; *194 G-9; mail Meridian z 39305; rural
Pontotoc; Inc. Place; ⊡ PONTOTOC; 194 C-8; elev. 501ft./153m.; 🅿 🅷; z 38863; Ⓟ 4,570; © 5,253
PONTOTOC; 194 C-8; Ⓟ 22,237; © 26,726; ◆ 28,870
Poolville; RMC Place; UNION; *194 C-8; mail Myrtle z 38650; rural
Pope; Inc. Place; PANOLA; 194 C-6; 🅿; z 38658; Ⓟ 171; © 241
Poplar Corners; RMC Place; DESOTO; *194 A-6; elev. 309ft./94m.; mail Walls z 38680; ● 30
Poplar Creek; RMC Place; MONTGOMERY; 194 E-7; elev. 412ft./126m.; mail Kilmichael z 39747; ● 70
Poplar Springs; RMC Place; HOLMES; *194 F-6; mail Durant z 39063; rural
Poplar Springs; RMC Place; MONTGOMERY; *194 E-7; elev. 324ft./99m.; mail Kilmichael z 39747; rural
Poplar Springs; RMC Place; NEWTON; *194 H-8; mail Newton z 39345; rural
Poplarville; Inc. Place; ⊡ PEARL RIVER; 194 L-7; elev. 317ft./97m.; 🅿 🅷; z 39470; Ⓟ 2,561; © 2,601
Porterville; RMC Place; KEMPER; 194 G-9; elev. 200ft./61m.; 🅿; z 39352; ● 100
Port Gibson; Inc. Place; ⊡ CLAIBORNE; 194 I-4; 🅿 🅷; z 39150; Ⓟ 1,810; © 1,840
Posey Mound; RMC Place; QUITMAN; *194 C-6; mail Darling z 38623, Marks z 38646; rural
Possum Trot (Bethlehem); RMC Place; PONTOTOC; *194 C-8; mail Pontotoc z 38863; rural
Post; RMC Place; LAUDERDALE; 194 G-9; mail Collinsville z 39325; ● 30
Potts Camp; Inc. Place; MARSHALL; 194 B-8; 🅿; z 38659; Ⓟ 483; © 494
Powell; RMC Place; COAHOMA; *194 C-5; elev. 184ft./56m.; mail Dundee z 38626; rural
Powers; RMC Place; JONES; *194 J-8; ★ **LAUR**; mail Laurel z 39440; rural
Prairie; RMC Place; MONROE; 194 D-9; 🅿; z 39756; ● 210
Prairie Point; RMC Place; NOXUBEE; *194 F-10; elev. 195ft./59m.; 🅿; z 39341; ● 50
Prentiss; Inc. Place; ⊡ JEFFERSON DAVIS; 194 J-6; elev. 336ft./102m.; 🅿 🅷; z 39474; Ⓟ 1,487; © 1,158
PRENTISS; 194 B-9; Ⓟ 23,278; © 25,556; ◆ 25,264
Presidential Hills; RMC Place; HINDS; ★ **JAC**; mail Jackson z 39213; pop. incl. with Jackson (Inc. Place)
Preston; RMC Place; KEMPER; 194 G-9; elev. 535ft./163m.; 🅿; z 39354; ● 100
Pricedale; RMC Place; PIKE; 194 K-6; elev. 336ft./102m.; mail Summit z 39666; ● 100
Prichard; RMC Place; TUNICA; 194 B-6; mail Tunica z 38676; ● 30
Prince Chapel; RMC Place; KEMPER; *194 G-9; mail Preston z 39354; rural
Priscilla; RMC Place; WASHINGTON; *194 E-4; mail Greenville z 38701; rural
Prismatic; RMC Place; KEMPER; *194 G-9; elev. 484ft./148m.; mail Bailey z 39320, Daleville z 39326; rural
Progress; RMC Place; JEFFERSON DAVIS; *194 J-6; mail Prentiss z 39474; ● 30
Progress; RMC Place; PERRY; *194 K-9; mail Beaumont z 39423; rural
Progress; RMC Place; PIKE; 194 K-5; mail Magnolia z 39652, McComb z 39648, Osyka z 39657, Tylertown z 39667; ● 210
Prospect; RMC Place; NEWTON; *194 G-8; elev. 510ft./155m.; mail Conehatta z 39057; rural
Puckett; Inc. Place; RANKIN; 194 I-7; 🅿; z 39151; Ⓟ 294; © 354
Pulaski; RMC Place; SCOTT; 194 H-7; 🅿; z 39152; ● 140
Pumpkin Center; RMC Place; UNION; *194 B-8; mail New Albany z 38652; ● 70
Purvis; Inc. Place; ⊡ LAMAR; 194 K-7; elev. 381ft./116m.; 🅿; z 39475; Ⓟ 2,140; © 2,164
Pyland; RMC Place; CHICKASAW; 194 D-8; elev. 291ft./89m.; mail Houston z 38851; ● 130

Q

Quentin; RMC Place; FRANKLIN; *194 J-5; mail Mc Call Creek z 39647; ● 50
Quincy; RMC Place; MONROE; 194 D-10; mail Aberdeen z 39730, Amory z 38821, Greenwood Springs z 38848; ● 160
Quitman; Inc. Place; ⊡ CLARKE; 194 I-9; elev. 434ft./132m.; 🅿 🅷; z 39355; Ⓟ 2,736; © 2,463
QUITMAN; 194 D-5; Ⓟ 10,490; © 10,117; Ⓡ 10,115; ◆ 8,362
Quito; RMC Place; LEFLORE; 194 E-6; mail Itta Bena z 38941; ● 60
Quofaloma; RMC Place; HOLMES; *194 F-5; elev. 112ft./34m.; mail Tchula z 39169; rural

R

Rainey; RMC Place; JONES; *194 J-8; mail Moselle z 39459; ● 210,
Raleigh; Inc. Place; ⊡ SMITH; 194 I-7; elev. 544ft./166m.; 🅿; z 39153; Ⓟ 1,291; © 1,255
Ramsey Springs; RMC Place; STONE; *194 L-9; elev. 95ft./29m.; mail Perkinston z 39573
Randolph; RMC Place; PONTOTOC; 194 C-8; 🅿; z 38864; ● 400
Rankin; RMC Place; RANKIN; *194 H-6; mail Brandon z 39042; rural
RANKIN; 194 H-6; Ⓟ 87,161; © 115,327; ◆ 141,725
Ratliff; RMC Place; ITAWAMBA; *194 C-9; elev. 354ft./108m.; mail Baldwyn z 38824, Guntown z 38849, Mantachie z 38855; ● 120
Rawls Springs; RMC Place; FORREST; 194 J-7; ★ **HATT**; mail Hattiesburg z 39401-02; ● 800
Raworth; RMC Place; SCOTT; *194 H-7; elev. 503ft./153m.; mail Morton z 39117; rural
Raymond; Inc. Place; ⊡ HINDS; 194 H-5; elev. 321ft./98m.; 🅿; ★ **JAC**; z 39154; Ⓟ 2,275; © 1,664; Ⓡ 2,044
Raytown; RMC Place; MADISON; *194 G-7; mail Canton z 39046; ● 140
Red Banks; RMC Place; MARSHALL; 194 B-7; elev. 449ft./137m.; 🅿; z 38661; ● 580
Redbone; RMC Place; WARREN; *194 H-4; elev. 160ft./49m.; ★ **VICK**; mail Vicksburg z 39180
Reddoch; RMC Place; COVINGTON; *194 J-7; mail Taylorsville z 39168; rural
Red Lick; RMC Place; JEFFERSON; 194 I-4; elev. 288ft./88m.; mail Lorman z 39096; ● 150
Redwater; CDP; LEAKE; *194 G-7; elev. 386ft./118m.; mail Carthage z 39051; Ⓟ 289; © 409
Redwood; RMC Place; WARREN; 194 H-4; 🅿; z 39156; ● 200
Reedtown; RMC Place; HINDS; *194 I-5; elev. 219ft./67m.; mail Utica z 39175; ● 30
Reform; RMC Place; CHOCTAW; 194 E-8; 🅿; z 39735; ● 110
Refuge; RMC Place; WASHINGTON; *194 F-4; elev. 124ft./38m.; ★ **GRNV**; mail Greenville z 38701
Reid; RMC Place; CALHOUN; *194 D-8; elev. 471ft./144m.; mail Pittsboro z 38951, Vardaman z 38878; rural
Remus; RMC Place; LEAKE; *194 G-8; elev. 483ft./147m.; mail Carthage z 39051; rural
Rena Lara; RMC Place; COAHOMA; 194 C-5; 🅿; z 38767; ● 270
Renfroe; RMC Place; LEAKE; *194 G-7; mail Carthage z 39051
Renova; Inc. Place; BOLIVAR; 194 D-5; mail Cleveland z 38732; Ⓟ 636; © 623
Revive; RMC Place; MADISON; *194 G-7; mail Camden z 39045; rural
Rexburg; RMC Place; WASHINGTON; *194 E-4; mail Leland z 38756; rural
Rexford; RMC Place; SIMPSON; *194 I-6; mail Florence z 39073; rural
Rhodes; RMC Place; PERRY; *194 J-8; elev. 272ft./83m.; mail Richton z 39476; rural
Riceville; RMC Place; HARRISON; *194 L-8; mail Perkinston z 39573; rural
Rich; RMC Place; COAHOMA; 194 C-5; 🅿; z 38617; ● 100
Richardson; RMC Place; PEARL RIVER; *194 L-7; elev. 70ft./21m.; mail Carriere z 39426, Picayune z 39466; ● 100
Richland; RMC Place; HOLMES; 194 F-6; elev. 325ft./99m.; mail Goodman z 39079; ● 30
Richland; RMC Place; HUMPHREYS; *194 F-5; mail Silver City z 39166; rural
Richland (Plain); Inc. Place; RANKIN; 194 H-6; 🅿; ★ **JAC**; z 39218; Ⓟ 4,014; © 6,027
Richmond; RMC Place; LEE; *194 C-9; mail Fulton z 38843, Plantersville z 38862, Tupelo z 38804
Richton; Inc. Place; PERRY; 194 J-8; elev. 160ft./49m.; 🅿 🅷; z 39476; Ⓟ 1,034; © 1,038
Ridgeland; Inc. Place; MADISON; 194 H-6; elev. 353ft./108m.; 🅿; ★ **JAC**; z 39157-58; Ⓟ 11,714; © 20,173; ◆ 22,700
Rienzi; Inc. Place; ALCORN; 194 B-9; elev. 437ft./133m.; 🅿; z 38865; Ⓟ 339; © 330
Ripley; Inc. Place; ⊡ TIPPAH; 194 B-8; 🅿 🅷; z 38663; Ⓟ 5,371; © 5,478
Rising Sun; RMC Place; LEFLORE; *194 E-6; mail Greenwood z 38930
Riverton; RMC Place; COAHOMA; mail Clarksdale z 38614; pop. incl. with Clarksdale (Inc. Place)
Riverview Estates; RMC Place; GEORGE; *194 L-9; elev. 100ft./30m.; mail Lucedale z 39452; rural
Robbs; RMC Place; PONTOTOC; *194 D-8; elev. 411ft./125m.; mail Randolph z 38864; ● 100
Roberts; RMC Place; NEWTON; *194 H-8; elev. 431ft./131m.; mail Lawrence z 39336; ● 50
Robinson; AMITE; see Peoria (RMC Place)
Robinson Gin; RMC Place; DESOTO; *194 B-6; elev. 256ft./78m.; mail Hernando z 38632; ● 30
Robinsonville; RMC Place; TUNICA; 194 B-6; 🅿; z 38664; ● 260
Robinwood; RMC Place; LAWRENCE; *194 J-6; mail Monticello z 39654; rural
Rock Creek; RMC Place; NEWTON; *194 G-8; mail Union z 39365; rural
Rock Hill; RMC Place; ALCORN; mail Corinth z 38834; ● 150
Rock Hill; RMC Place; FORREST; *194 K-8; elev. 333ft./101m.; mail Purvis z 39475; rural
Rock Hill; OKTIBBEHA; see Rocky Hill (RMC Place)
Rock Hill; RMC Place; PANOLA; *194 C-6; mail Sardis z 38666; ● 30
Rock Hill; RMC Place; RANKIN; *194 H-6; ★ **JAC**; mail Brandon z 39042; rural
Rockport; RMC Place; COPIAH; *194 I-6; elev. 222ft./68m.; mail Hazlehurst z 39083; rural
Rocky Hill (Rock Hill); RMC Place; OKTIBBEHA; *194 E-9; mail Starkville z 39759; rural
Rocky Springs; RMC Place; CLAIBORNE; *194 I-4; elev. 315ft./96m.; mail Hermanville z 39086; ● 30
Rodney; RMC Place; JEFFERSON; 194 I-4; mail Lorman z 39096; ● 90
Roebuck; RMC Place; LEFLORE; *194 E-6; mail Sidon z 38954; rural
Rogerslacy; RMC Place; JASPER; mail Sandersville z 39477; rural
Rolling Fork; Inc. Place; ⊡ SHARKEY; 194 F-4; 🅿; z 39159; Ⓟ 2,444; © 2,486
Rome; RMC Place; SUNFLOWER; 194 D-5; 🅿; z 38768; ● 180
Roseacres; RMC Place; COAHOMA; *194 C-5; mail Coahoma z 38617
Rosebloom; RMC Place; TALLAHATCHIE; *194 D-6; mail Cascilla z 38920; rural
Rosebud; RMC Place; LEAKE; *194 G-7; elev. 440ft./134m.; mail Walnut Grove z 39189; rural
Rosedale; Inc. Place; ⊡ BOLIVAR; 194 D-4; elev. 145ft./44m.; 🅿; z 38769; Ⓟ 2,595; © 2,414
Rose Hill; RMC Place; JASPER; 194 I-8; 🅿; z 39356; ● 250
Rosella; RMC Place; LAWRENCE; *194 J-6; mail Monticello z 39654; rural
Rosemary; RMC Place; HINDS; *194 I-6; elev. 255ft./78m.; ★ **JAC**; mail Terry z 39170
Rosetta; RMC Place; WILKINSON; 194 K-4; elev. 171ft./52m.; mail Crosby z 39633; ● 40
Rough Edge; RMC Place; PONTOTOC; *194 C-8; elev. 538ft./164m.; mail Pontotoc z 38863; pop. incl. with Pontotoc (Inc. Place)
Roundaway; RMC Place; COAHOMA; *194 D-5; elev. 154ft./47m.; mail Clarksdale z 38614; ● 120
Roundlake; RMC Place; BOLIVAR; 194 D-4; mail Duncan z 38740; ● 100
Rounsaville; RMC Place; GREENE; *194 K-10; elev. 240ft./73m.; mail Leakesville z 39451; rural
Roxie; Inc. Place; FRANKLIN; 194 J-4; elev. 232ft./71m.; 🅿; z 39661; Ⓟ 568; © 569
Ruby (Geren); RMC Place; LEFLORE; *194 E-6; mail Philipp z 38950; rural
Rudyard; RMC Place; COAHOMA; *194 C-5; mail Coahoma z 38617; rural
Ruleville; Inc. Place; SUNFLOWER; 194 D-5; elev. 135ft./41m.; 🅿 🅷; z 38771; Ⓟ 3,245; © 3,234
Runnelstown; RMC Place; PERRY; *194 J-8; mail Hattiesburg z 39401
Rural Hill; RMC Place; WINSTON; *194 F-8; elev. 540ft./165m.; mail Mc Cool z 39108; rural
Russell; RMC Place; LAUDERDALE; 194 G-3; elev. 420ft./128m.; ★ **MRID**; mail Meridian z 39301; ● 110
Russum; RMC Place; CLAIBORNE; 194 I-4; mail Lorman z 39096; ● 90
Ruth; RMC Place; LINCOLN; 194 J-5; 🅿; z 39662; ● 230
Ryan; ITAWAMBA; see Sandy Springs (RMC Place)

S

Sabino; RMC Place; QUITMAN; *194 C-5; mail Marks z 38646; ● 50
Sabougla; RMC Place; CALHOUN; *194 D-7; mail Calhoun City z 38916, Slate Spring z 38955; rural
Saint Ann; RMC Place; LEAKE; *194 G-7; mail Carthage z 39051; rural
Saint Martin; CDP; JACKSON; *194 M-9; elev. 20ft./6m.; ★ **BIL-**; mail Biloxi z 39533; Ⓟ 6,349; © 6,676
Salem; RMC Place; LEAKE; *194 G-8; mail Walnut Grove z 39189; rural
Salem; RMC Place; WALTHALL; *194 K-6; mail Tylertown z 39667; rural
Sallis; Inc. Place; ATTALA; 194 F-7; 🅿; z 39160 & mail Mc Adams z 39107; Ⓟ 139; © 114
Saltillo; Inc. Place; LEE; 194 C-9; 🅿; z 38866; Ⓟ 1,782; © 3,393
Sanatorium; RMC Place; SIMPSON; *194 I-7; elev. 539ft./164m.; 🅿; z 39111; ● 500
Sandersville; Inc. Place; JONES; 194 I-8; elev. 286ft./87m.; 🅿; ★ **LAUR**; z 39477; Ⓟ 853; © 789
Sand Hill; RMC Place; COPIAH; *194 I-5; elev. 352ft./107m.; mail Wesson z 39191; rural
Sand Hill; RMC Place; GREENE; 194 J-9; elev. 316ft./96m.; mail Richton z 39476; ● 150
Sand Hill; RMC Place; JONES; *194 J-8; elev. 308ft./94m.; mail Ellisville z 39437, Richton z 39476; rural
Sand Hill; RMC Place; RANKIN; 194 H-6; 🅿; z 39161; ● 250
Sandtown; RMC Place; NESHOBA; *194 G-8; elev. 594ft./181m.; mail Philadelphia z 39350; rural
Sandy Hook; RMC Place; MARION; 194 K-7; 🅿; z 39478; ● 210
Sandy Springs (Ryan); RMC Place; ITAWAMBA; *194 C-10; mail Fulton z 38843; rural
Sanford; RMC Place; COVINGTON; *194 J-7; mail Seminary z 39479; ● 150
Sapa; RMC Place; WEBSTER; *194 E-8; elev. 411ft./125m.; mail Eupora z 39744; rural
Sarah; RMC Place; TATE; 194 B-6; 🅿; z 38665; ● 230
Saratoga; RMC Place; SIMPSON; *194 I-7; elev. 342ft./104m.; mail Magee z 39111; rural
Sardis; RMC Place; COPIAH; *194 I-5; elev. 379ft./116m.; mail Hazlehurst z 39083; rural
Sardis; Inc. Place; ⊡ PANOLA; 194 C-6; 🅿; z 38666; Ⓟ 2,128; © 2,038
Sarepta; RMC Place; CALHOUN; 194 C-8; 🅿; z 38864; ● 50
Sartinsville; WALTHALL; see Sartinville (RMC Place)
Sartinville (Sartinsville); RMC Place; WALTHALL; 194 K-6; mail Jayess z 39641
Satartia; Inc. Place; YAZOO; 194 G-5; 🅿; z 39162; Ⓟ 59; © 68
Saucier; CDP; HARRISON; 194 L-8; elev. 155ft./47m.; 🅿; z 39574; © 1,303
Saukum; RMC Place; WILKINSON; *194 K-4; mail Crosby z 39633; rural
Savage; RMC Place; TATE; 194 B-6; 🅿; z 38665; ● 160
Savannah; RMC Place; PEARL RIVER; *194 L-7; elev. 317ft./97m.; mail Poplarville z 39470; rural
Savannah Grove; RMC Place; LAUDERDALE; ★ **MRID**; mail Meridian z 39301; pop. incl. with Meridian (Inc. Place)
Savoy; RMC Place; LAUDERDALE; *194 H-9; mail Meridian z 39307; ● 50
Schamberville; RMC Place; LAUDERDALE; *194 H-9; mail Collinsville z 39325; rural
Schlater; Inc. Place; LEFLORE; 194 E-5; 🅿; z 38952; Ⓟ 404; © 388
Schley; RMC Place; SIMPSON; *194 I-6; mail Newhebron z 39140; rural
Scobey; RMC Place; YALOBUSHA; 194 D-7; 🅿; z 38953; ● 90
Scooba; Inc. Place; KEMPER; 194 G-9; 🅿; z 39358; Ⓟ 541; © 632
Scotland; RMC Place; YAZOO; *194 G-6; mail Bentonia z 39040; ● 30
Scott; RMC Place; BOLIVAR; 194 E-4; 🅿; z 38772; ● 300
SCOTT; 194 H-7; Ⓟ 24,137; © 28,423; ◆ 28,875
Sebastopol; Inc. Place; SCOTT, LEAKE; 194 G-8; 🅿; z 39359; Ⓟ 281; © 233
Sellers; RMC Place; HANCOCK; *194 L-8; mail Perkinston z 39573; rural
Sels Prairie; RMC Place; CLARKE; *194 I-9; elev. 381ft./116m.; mail Shubuta z 39360; rural
Seminary; Inc. Place; COVINGTON; 194 J-7; elev. 268ft./82m.; 🅿; z 39479; Ⓟ 231; © 335
Senatobia; Inc. Place; ⊡ TATE; 194 B-6; 🅿 🅷; z 38668 & mail Sarah z 38665; Ⓟ 4,772; © 6,682
Senatobia Lakes; RMC Place; TATE; *194 B-6; elev. 290ft./88m.; mail Senatobia z 38668; ● 200
Seneca; RMC Place; LAMAR; *194 K-7; elev. 328ft./100m.; mail Lumberton z 39455; ● 50
Sessums; RMC Place; OKTIBBEHA; 194 E-9; mail Starkville z 39759; ● 170
Seven Springs; RMC Place; HINDS; *194 H-5; ★ **JAC**; mail Raymond z 39154; rural
Shackleford; RMC Place; HOLMES; *194 F-6; mail Tchula z 39169; rural
Shady Grove; RMC Place; COPIAH; *194 I-5; elev. 453ft./138m.; mail Hazlehurst z 39083; ● 30
Shady Grove; RMC Place; JONES; 194 I-8; ★ **LAUR**; mail Laurel z 39440; ● 420
Shannon; Inc. Place; LEE; 194 C-9; 🅿; z 38868; Ⓟ 1,419; © 1,657
Sharkey; RMC Place; TALLAHATCHIE; 194 D-6; mail Charleston z 38921
SHARKEY; 194 G-4; Ⓟ 7,066; © 6,580; ◆ 5,096
Sharon; RMC Place; JONES; 194 I-8; ★ **LAUR**; mail Laurel z 39440; ● 180
Sharon; RMC Place; MADISON; 194 G-6; 🅿; z 39163 & mail Canton z 39046; ● 420
Sharpsburg; RMC Place; MADISON; *194 G-6; mail Pickens z 39146; rural
Shaw; Inc. Place; BOLIVAR, SUNFLOWER; 194 E-5; elev. 134ft./41m.; 🅿; z 38773; Ⓟ 2,349; © 2,312
Shelby; Inc. Place; BOLIVAR; 194 D-5; elev. 157ft./48m.; 🅿; z 38774; Ⓟ 2,806; © 2,926
Shellmound; RMC Place; LEFLORE; *194 E-6; mail Greenwood z 38930
Shelton; RMC Place; JONES; *194 J-8; elev. 345ft./105m.; mail Moselle z 39459; rural
Sheppard Town; RMC Place; LEFLORE; *194 E-5; mail Morgan City z 38946; rural
Sherard; RMC Place; COAHOMA; 194 C-5; 🅿; z 38669; ● 150
Sherman; Inc. Place; PONTOTOC, UNION; 194 C-9; elev. 363ft./111m.; 🅿; z 38869; Ⓟ 528; © 548
Sherwood; RMC Place; CHOCTAW; 194 E-8; mail Mathiston z 39752; ● 30
Sherwood Forest; RMC Place; RANKIN; *194 H-6; ★ **JAC**; mail Brandon z 39042; ● 250
Shiloh; RMC Place; ITAWAMBA; *194 C-9; mail Mantachie z 38855; ● 30
Shiloh; RMC Place; RANKIN; *194 H-7; mail Pelahatchie z 39145; rural
Shipman; RMC Place; GEORGE; *194 L-10; mail Lucedale z 39452; rural
Shivers; RMC Place; SIMPSON; *194 I-6; elev. 466ft./142m.; mail Pinola z 39149
Shoccoe; RMC Place; MADISON; *194 G-6; mail Canton z 39046; rural
Shoreline Park; CDP-Census Area Only; HANCOCK; *194 M-7; elev. 5ft./2m.; ★ **BIL-**; mail Waveland z 39576; Ⓟ 2,775; © 4,058
Shubuta; Inc. Place; CLARKE; 194 I-9; elev. 197ft./60m.; 🅿; z 39360; Ⓟ 577; © 651
Shucktown; RMC Place; LAUDERDALE; *194 G-9; elev. 407ft./124m.; mail Meridian z 39305; ● 50
Shuford; RMC Place; PANOLA; *194 C-7; mail Courtland z 38620; rural
Shuqualak (Shuqulak); Inc. Place; NOXUBEE; 194 F-9; elev. 217ft./66m.; 🅿; z 39361; Ⓟ 570; © 562
Shuqulak; NOXUBEE; see Shuqualak (Inc. Place)
Sibley; RMC Place; ADAMS; 194 J-3; 🅿; z 39165; ● 290
Sibleyton; RMC Place; MONTGOMERY; *194 E-7; elev. 350ft./107m.; mail Kilmichael z 39747; rural
Sidon; Inc. Place; LEFLORE; 194 E-6; 🅿; z 38954; Ⓟ 596; © 672
Signal; RMC Place; WARREN; *194 H-4; ★ **VICK**; mail Vicksburg z 39180; pop. incl. with Vicksburg (Inc. Place)
Silver City; Inc. Place; HUMPHREYS; 194 F-5; 🅿; z 39166 & mail Midnight z 39115; Ⓟ 348; © 337
Silver Creek; Inc. Place; LAWRENCE; 194 J-6; 🅿; z 39663; Ⓟ 190; © 209
Silver Run; RMC Place; PEARL RIVER; *194 L-8; elev. 180ft./55m.; mail Perkinston z 39573; ● 30
SIMPSON; 194 I-6; Ⓟ 23,953; © 27,639; ◆ 27,389
Singleton; RMC Place; LEAKE; *194 G-7; mail Carthage z 39051
Singleton Settlement; RMC Place; SCOTT; *194 H-7; elev. 440ft./134m.; mail Forest z 39074; rural
Skene; RMC Place; BOLIVAR; 194 E-5; elev. 134ft./41m.; 🅿; z 38730; ● 200
Skuna; RMC Place; CALHOUN; *194 D-7; mail Bruce z 38915; rural
Skyline; RMC Place; LEE; *194 C-9; mail Tupelo z 38804; ● 50
Slate Spring (Slate Springs); Inc. Place; CALHOUN; 194 D-8; 🅿; z 38955; Ⓟ 118; © 121
Slate Springs; CALHOUN; see Slate Spring (Inc. Place)
Slayden; RMC Place; MARSHALL; 194 A-7; mail Lamar z 38642; ● 120
Sledge; Inc. Place; QUITMAN; 194 C-6; 🅿; z 38670; Ⓟ 577; © 529
Sloan; RMC Place; MADISON; *194 G-6; mail Canton z 39046; rural
Smith; RMC Place; COVINGTON; *194 I-7; mail Collins z 39428; rural
Smith; RMC Place; LAUDERDALE; *194 H-9; elev. 293ft./89m.; mail Toomsuba z 39364; rural
SMITH; 194 I-7; Ⓟ 14,798; © 16,182; ◆ 15,731
Smithdale; RMC Place; AMITE; 194 J-5; 🅿; z 39664; ● 100
Smiths; RMC Place; HINDS; *194 H-5; mail Edwards z 39066; rural
Smithville; Inc. Place; MONROE; 194 D-10; 🅿; z 38870; Ⓟ 871; © 882
Smyrna; RMC Place; ATTALA; *194 F-7; elev. 517ft./158m.; mail Kosciusko z 39090; rural
Smyrna; RMC Place; COPIAH; *194 I-5; elev. 293ft./89m.; mail Hazlehurst z 39083; rural
Snell; RMC Place; CLARKE; *194 H-9; mail Meridian z 39301; ● 30
Snow Lake Shores; Inc. Place; BENTON; *194 B-8; mail Ashland z 38603; © 300
Somerville; RMC Place; LEFLORE; *194 D-6; mail Minter City z 38944; rural
Sonora; RMC Place; CHICKASAW; *194 D-8; mail Houston z 38851; rural
Sontag; RMC Place; LAWRENCE; 194 J-6; elev. 257ft./78m.; 🅿; z 39665; ● 220
Soso; Inc. Place; JONES; 194 I-8; elev. 312ft./95m.; 🅿; ★ **LAUR**; z 39480; Ⓟ 366; © 379
South Amory; RMC Place; MONROE; mail Amory z 38821; pop. incl. with Amory (Inc. Place)
Southaven; Inc. Place; DESOTO; 194 A-6; 🅿 🅷; ★ **MEM**; z 38671-72; Ⓟ 17,949; © 28,977; ◆ 44,677
South McComb; RMC Place; PIKE; mail McComb z 39648; pop. incl. with McComb (Inc. Place)
Spanish Fort; RMC Place; SHARKEY; *194 G-5; mail Holly Bluff z 39088; rural
Sparta; RMC Place; CHICKASAW; *194 D-8; elev. 331ft./101m.; mail Woodland z 39776; rural
Splinter; RMC Place; LAFAYETTE; *194 C-7; elev. 380ft./116m.; mail Taylor z 38673; ● 30
Splunge; RMC Place; MONROE; 194 D-10; elev. 332ft./101m.; mail Greenwood Springs z 38848; ● 210
Spring Cottage; RMC Place; MARION; *194 K-7; mail Columbia z 39429; ● 80
Spring Creek; RMC Place; NESHOBA; *194 G-8; mail Philadelphia z 39350; rural
Springdale; RMC Place; LAFAYETTE; *194 C-7; mail Water Valley z 38965; rural
Springdale Lakes; RMC Place; UNION; *194 B-8; mail Myrtle z 38650; rural
Spring Hill; RMC Place; BENTON; *194 A-8; elev. 488ft./149m.; mail Michigan City z 38647, Toccopola z 38874; rural
Springhill; RMC Place; JONES; *194 I-8; ★ **LAUR**; mail Laurel z 39440; rural
Spring Hill; RMC Place; LAFAYETTE; *194 C-8; mail Michigan City z 38647, Oxford z 38655, Thaxton z 38871, Toccopola z 38874; ● 50
Spring Hill; RMC Place; NESHOBA; *194 G-8; elev. 520ft./158m.; mail Philadelphia z 39350; rural
Springville; RMC Place; PONTOTOC; 194 C-8; mail Pontotoc z 38863; ● 80
Stallo; RMC Place; NESHOBA; *194 F-8; mail Philadelphia z 39350
Stamper; NEWTON; see Stratton (RMC Place)
Stampley; RMC Place; JEFFERSON; *194 J-4; elev. 219ft./67m.; mail Fayette z 39069; ● 150
Standing Pine; CDP; LEAKE; *194 G-7; mail Carthage z 39051; Ⓟ 346; © 509
Stanton; RMC Place; ADAMS; *194 J-4; elev. 309ft./94m.; ★ **NCHZ**; mail Natchez z 39120; rural
Star; RMC Place; RANKIN; 194 I-6; elev. 420ft./128m.; 🅿; ★ **JAC**; z 39167; ● 550
Starkville; Inc. Place; ⊡ OKTIBBEHA; 194 E-9; elev. 374ft./114m.; 🅿 🅷 ■; z 39759-60; Ⓟ 18,458; © 21,869; ◆ 24,160
State Line; Inc. Place; GREENE, WAYNE; 194 J-9; 🅿; z 39362; Ⓟ 395; © 555
Steele; RMC Place; SCOTT; *194 H-7; mail Forest z 39074
Steens; RMC Place; LOWNDES; 194 E-10; 🅿; ★ **COL**; z 39766; ● 210
Steiner; RMC Place; SUNFLOWER; *194 E-5; mail Shaw z 38773; rural
Stewart; RMC Place; MONTGOMERY; 194 E-7; 🅿; z 39767; ● 280
Stokes; RMC Place; MADISON; *194 G-6; elev. 230ft./70m.; mail Canton z 39046; rural
STONE; 194 L-8; Ⓟ 10,750; © 13,622; ◆ 15,681
Stoneville; RMC Place; WASHINGTON; 194 E-4; 🅿; z 38776; ● 250
Stonewall; Inc. Place; CLARKE; 194 H-9; elev. 235ft./72m.; 🅿; z 39363; Ⓟ 1,148; © 1,149
Stonewall; RMC Place; DESOTO; *194 B-7; mail Byhalia z 38611; rural
Stonewall; RMC Place; HOLMES; *194 F-5; elev. 110ft./34m.; mail Tchula z 39169; rural
Stovall; RMC Place; COAHOMA; 194 C-5; 🅿; z 38614; ● 30
Stover; TALLAHATCHIE; see Brazil (RMC Place)
Straight Bayou; RMC Place; SHARKEY; *194 F-5; mail Anguilla z 38721; rural
Stratton (Stamper); RMC Place; NEWTON; 194 H-8; elev. 449ft./137m.; mail Union z 39365; ● 1,250
Strayhorn; RMC Place; TATE; *194 B-6; mail Sarah z 38665; ● 250
Strengthford; RMC Place; WAYNE; *194 J-9; elev. 223ft./68m.; mail Laurel z 39440; rural
Strickland; RMC Place; ALCORN; *194 B-9; mail Corinth z 38834
Stringer; RMC Place; JASPER; 194 I-8; 🅿; z 39481; ● 430
Stringtown; RMC Place; BOLIVAR; *194 E-4; mail Benoit z 38725
Strong (Strongs); RMC Place; MONROE; *194 E-9; mail Aberdeen z 39730; rural
Stronghope; RMC Place; COPIAH; *194 I-6; elev. 318ft./97m.; mail Wesson z 39191; rural
Strongs; MONROE; see Strong (RMC Place)
Sturgis; Inc. Place; OKTIBBEHA; 194 E-8; elev. 336ft./102m.; 🅿; z 39769; Ⓟ 198; © 206
Sucarnochee; RMC Place; KEMPER; *194 G-9; mail Porterville z 39352; rural
Success; RMC Place; HARRISON; *194 L-8; elev. 181ft./55m.; mail Saucier z 39574
Sumbax; RMC Place; MARION; *194 K-6; elev. 231ft./70m.; mail Foxworth z 39483; rural
Summerland; RMC Place; SMITH; 194 I-8; mail Taylorsville z 39168
Summit; Inc. Place; PIKE; 194 K-5; elev. 431ft./131m.; 🅿; z 39666; Ⓟ 1,566; © 1,428
Sumner; Inc. Place; ⊡ TALLAHATCHIE; 194 D-5; 🅿; z 38957; Ⓟ 368; © 407
Sumrall; Inc. Place; LAMAR; 194 J-7; elev. 290ft./88m.; 🅿; z 39482; Ⓟ 903; © 1,005
Sunflower; RMC Place; PRENTISS; mail Booneville z 38829; pop. incl. with Booneville (Inc. Place)
Sunflower; Inc. Place; SUNFLOWER; 194 E-5; 🅿; z 38778; Ⓟ 729; © 696
SUNFLOWER; 194 E-5; Ⓟ 32,867; © 34,369; ◆ 30,553
Sunnycrest; RMC Place; GRENADA; *194 D-7; mail Grenada z 38901; pop. incl. with Grenada (Inc. Place)
Sunnyside; RMC Place; LEFLORE; *194 E-6; mail Minter City z 38944, Schlater z 38952
Sunrise; RMC Place; FORREST; *194 K-8; ★ **HATT**; mail Hattiesburg z 39401; ● 50
Sunrise; RMC Place; LEAKE; *194 G-7; mail Carthage z 39051
Suqualena; RMC Place; LAUDERDALE; *194 H-9; elev. 399ft./122m.; ★ **MRID**; mail Meridian z 39305; ● 50
Swan Lake; RMC Place; TALLAHATCHIE; 194 D-6; 🅿; z 38958; ● 80
Sweatman; RMC Place; MONTGOMERY; *194 E-7; mail Duck Hill z 38925; rural
Swiftown; RMC Place; LEFLORE; 194 F-5; 🅿; z 38959; ● 110
Swiftwater; RMC Place; WASHINGTON; *194 E-4; ★ **GRNV**; mail Greenville z 38701; rural
Sylvarena; Inc. Place; SMITH; 194 I-8; elev. 367ft./112m.; mail Raleigh z 39153; Ⓟ 110; © 120
Symonds; RMC Place; BOLIVAR; 194 D-4; elev. 144ft./44m.; mail Rosedale z 38769; ● 100

T

TALLAHATCHIE; 194 D-6; Ⓟ 15,210; © 14,903; ◆ 12,648
Tallula; RMC Place; ISSAQUENA; 194 G-4; mail Rolling Fork z 39159; ● 60
Talowah; RMC Place; LAMAR; 194 K-7; mail Lumberton z 39455; ● 150
TATE; 194 B-6; Ⓟ 21,432; © 25,370; ◆ 26,998
Tatum; RMC Place; AMITE; *194 K-4; mail Gloster z 39638; rural
Taylor; Inc. Place; LAFAYETTE; 194 C-7; elev. 325ft./99m.; 🅿; z 38673; Ⓟ 288; © 289
Taylorsville; Inc. Place; SMITH; 194 I-7; 🅿; z 39168; Ⓟ 1,412; © 1,341
Tchula; Inc. Place; HOLMES; 194 F-6; 🅿; z 39169; Ⓟ 2,186; © 2,332
Teasdale; RMC Place; TALLAHATCHIE; *194 C-6; mail Enid z 38927; rural
Ted; RMC Place; SMITH; *194 I-8; mail Louin z 39338; rural
Ten Mile; RMC Place; STONE; 194 L-8; mail Perkinston z 39573; rural
Teoc; RMC Place; CARROLL; *194 E-6; elev. 160ft./49m.; mail Carrollton z 38917; rural
Terry; Inc. Place; HINDS; 194 I-6; elev. 295ft./90m.; 🅿; ★ **JAC**; z 39170; Ⓟ 613; © 664
Thaxton; Inc. Place; PONTOTOC; 194 C-8; elev. 436ft./133m.; 🅿; z 38871; Ⓟ 431; © 513
Theo; RMC Place; ALCORN; *194 A-9; elev. 520ft./158m.; mail Walnut z 38683; rural
Thomastown; RMC Place; LEAKE; 194 G-7; elev. 405ft./123m.; 🅿; z 39171; ● 200
Thomasville; RMC Place; RANKIN; *194 H-6; ★ **JAC**; mail Florence z 39073; rural
Thompson; RMC Place; AMITE; 194 K-5; mail Smithdale z 39664; ● 30
Thompsonville; RMC Place; HINDS; *194 I-5; elev. 286ft./87m.; mail Crystal Springs z 39059; rural
Thorn; RMC Place; CHICKASAW; 194 D-8; mail Houston z 38851; ● 50
Thornton; RMC Place; HOLMES; 194 F-6; 🅿; z 39169; ● 200
Thrashers; RMC Place; PRENTISS; 194 B-9; mail Booneville z 38829; ● 250
Threadville; RMC Place; CLARKE; *194 I-9; mail Quitman z 39355; ● 30
Three Rivers; RMC Place; JACKSON; 194 L-9; mail Pascagoula z 39567, z 39581; ● 200
Thyatira; RMC Place; TATE; *194 B-7; mail Senatobia z 38668
Tibbee; RMC Place; CLAY; *194 E-9; mail West Point z 39773; rural
Tibbs; RMC Place; TUNICA; *194 C-6; mail Sledge z 38670; ● 40
Tie Plant; RMC Place; GRENADA; 194 D-7; 🅿; z 38960; pop. incl. with Grenada (Inc. Place)
Tilden; RMC Place; ITAWAMBA; *194 C-10; elev. 456ft./139m.; mail Fulton z 38843; rural
Tillatoba; Inc. Place; YALOBUSHA; 194 D-6; 🅿; z 38961; Ⓟ 41; © 121
Tillman; RMC Place; CLAIBORNE; *194 I-4; mail Port Gibson z 39150
Tilton; RMC Place; LAWRENCE; *194 J-6; elev. 186ft./57m.; mail Monticello z 39654; rural
Tinsley; RMC Place; YAZOO; 194 G-5; 🅿; z 39173; ● 260
Tiplersville; RMC Place; TIPPAH; 194 B-9; 🅿; z 38674; ● 120
Tippah; RMC Place; BENTON; *194 B-8; mail Ashland z 38603; rural
TIPPAH; 194 B-8; Ⓟ 19,523; © 20,826; ◆ 21,089
Tippo; RMC Place; TALLAHATCHIE; 194 D-6; 🅿; z 38962; ● 120
Tishomingo; Inc. Place; TISHOMINGO; 194 B-10; 🅿; z 38873; Ⓟ 332; © 316
TISHOMINGO; 194 B-10; Ⓟ 17,683; © 19,163; ◆ 18,983
Toccopola; Inc. Place; PONTOTOC; 194 C-8; elev. 412ft./126m.; 🅿; z 38874; Ⓟ 154; © 189
Tocowa; RMC Place; PANOLA; *194 C-6; mail Courtland z 38620; rural
Tomnolen; RMC Place; WEBSTER; 194 E-8; 🅿; z 39744; ● 120
Toomsuba; RMC Place; LAUDERDALE; 194 H-9; elev. 315ft./96m.; 🅿; z 39364; ● 370
Topeka; RMC Place; LAWRENCE; 194 J-6; mail Jayess z 39641; ● 60
Topisaw; RMC Place; PIKE; *194 K-6; mail Ruth z 39662, Summit z 39666; rural
Topton; RMC Place; LAUDERDALE; *194 H-9; elev. 429ft./131m.; mail Meridian z 39305; rural
Touchstone; RMC Place; SIMPSON; *194 I-6; mail Braxton z 39044; rural
Tougaloo; RMC Place; HINDS, MADISON; *194 H-6; 🅿; ★ **JAC**; z 39174; pop. incl. with Jackson (Inc. Place)
Town of Walls; DESOTO; see Walls (Inc. Place)
Townsend; RMC Place; KEMPER; *194 G-9; elev. 244ft./74m.; mail Porterville z 39352; ● 60
Tralake; RMC Place; WASHINGTON; 194 F-5; elev. 110ft./34m.; mail Leland z 38756; ● 50
Trapp; RMC Place; NESHOBA; *194 G-8; mail Philadelphia z 39350; rural
Traxler; RMC Place; SMITH; *194 I-7; mail Magee z 39111; rural
Trebloc; RMC Place; CHICKASAW; 194 D-9; 🅿; z 38875; ● 100
Tremont; Inc. Place; ITAWAMBA; 194 C-10; 🅿; z 38876; Ⓟ 342; © 390
Tribbett; RMC Place; WASHINGTON; 194 E-5; mail Leland z 38756; ● 35
Trinity; RMC Place; DESOTO; *194 B-6; elev. 315ft./96m.; mail Hernando z 38632; ● 50
Trinity; RMC Place; LOWNDES; *194 E-9; mail Crawford z 39743; rural
Troy; RMC Place; PONTOTOC; 194 D-9; elev. 505ft./154m.; mail Pontotoc z 38863; ● 180
Truitt; RMC Place; MADISON; *194 G-6; elev. 341ft./104m.; mail Pickens z 39146; rural
Tucker; CDP; NESHOBA; *194 G-8; mail Philadelphia z 39350; Ⓟ 459; © 534
Tuckers Crossing; RMC Place; JONES; *194 J-8; ★ **LAUR**; mail Laurel z 39440; rural
Tula; RMC Place; LAFAYETTE; 194 C-8; elev. 489ft./149m.; 🅿; z 38675; ● 120
Tunica; Inc. Place; ⊡ TUNICA; 194 B-5; 🅿; z 38676; Ⓟ 1,175; © 1,132
TUNICA; 194 B-5; Ⓟ 8,164; © 9,227; ◆ 10,464
Tunica North; RMC Place; TUNICA; *194 B-5; ● 1,200
Tupelo; Inc. Place; ⊡ LEE; 194 C-9; elev. 290ft./88m.; 🅿 🅷 ■; z 38801-04; Ⓟ 30,685; © 34,211; ◆ 37,139
Turnbull; RMC Place; WILKINSON; *194 K-3; mail Woodville z 39669; rural
Turnerville (Antioch); RMC Place; JASPER; *194 I-8; mail Louin z 39338; rural
Turon; RMC Place; ITAWAMBA; *194 C-10; mail Smithville z 38870; rural
Tuscola; RMC Place; LEAKE; 194 G-7; elev. 349ft./106m.; mail Lena z 39094; ● 60
Tutwiler; Inc. Place; TALLAHATCHIE; 194 D-5; 🅿; z 38963; Ⓟ 1,391; © 1,364
Twin; RMC Place; MARION; 194 K-7; mail Sandy Hook z 39478; ● 80
Twin Lakes; RMC Place; DESOTO; *194 A-6; elev. 280ft./85m.; ★ **MEM**; mail Walls z 38680; ● 4,700
Tylertown; Inc. Place; ⊡ WALTHALL; 194 K-6; elev. 293ft./89m.; 🅿 🅷; z 39667; Ⓟ 1,938; © 1,910
Tyro; RMC Place; TATE; 194 B-7; elev. 444ft./135m.; mail Senatobia z 38668; ● 100

U

Union; RMC Place; JONES; *194 J-8; elev. 291ft./89m.; mail Ellisville z 39437; rural
Union; RMC Place; LEE; *194 C-9; mail Plantersville z 38862; rural
Union; Inc. Place; NEWTON, NESHOBA; 194 G-8; elev. 471ft./144m.; 🅿 🅷; z 39365; Ⓟ 1,875; © 2,021
Union; RMC Place; SIMPSON; *194 I-6; mail Pinola z 39149; ● 30
UNION; 194 B-8; Ⓟ 22,085; © 25,362; ◆ 26,658
Union Church; RMC Place; JEFFERSON; 194 J-4; 🅿; z 39668; ● 200
Union Hall; RMC Place; LINCOLN; *194 J-5; mail Brookhaven z 39601; rural
Unity; RMC Place; LEE; *194 C-9; mail Guntown z 38849; rural
Usrytown; RMC Place; SCOTT; *194 H-8; mail Forest z 39074
Utica; Inc. Place; HINDS; 194 I-5; 🅿; z 39175; Ⓟ 1,033; © 966

V

Vaiden; Inc. Place; ⊡ CARROLL; 194 E-7; 🅿; z 39176; Ⓟ 789; © 840
Valewood; RMC Place; ISSAQUENA; *194 F-4; mail Glen Allan z 38744; rural
Valley; RMC Place; YAZOO; *194 G-5; mail Yazoo City z 39194; ● 30
Valley Hill; RMC Place; CARROLL; *194 E-6; mail Carrollton z 38917, Greenwood z 38930; rural
Valley Park; RMC Place; ISSAQUENA; 194 G-4; 🅿; z 39177; ● 230
Value; RMC Place; RANKIN; *194 H-6; ★ **JAC**; mail Brandon z 39042; pop. incl. with Brandon (Inc. Place)
Van Buren; RMC Place; ITAWAMBA; *194 C-10; elev. 266ft./81m.; mail Nettleton z 38858; ● 50
Vance; RMC Place; QUITMAN; 194 D-5; elev. 151ft./46m.; 🅿; z 38964; ● 250
Vancleave; CDP; JACKSON; 194 L-9; 🅿; ★ **PSCG**; z 39565; Ⓟ 3,214; © 4,910
Van Vleet; RMC Place; CHICKASAW; 194 D-9; elev. 374ft./114m.; 🅿; z 38877; ● 200
Van Winkle; RMC Place; HINDS; *194 H-6; ★ **JAC**; pop. incl. with Jackson (Inc. Place)
Vardaman; Inc. Place; CALHOUN; 194 D-8; 🅿; z 38878; Ⓟ 920; © 1,065
Vaughan; RMC Place; YAZOO; 194 G-6; 🅿; z 39179; ● 260
Vaughn; RMC Place; LINCOLN; *194 J-5; mail Brookhaven z 39601; rural
Velma; RMC Place; YALOBUSHA; *194 D-7; mail Water Valley z 38965; rural
Vernal; RMC Place; GREENE; *194 K-9; mail Lucedale z 39452; rural
Vernon; RMC Place; MADISON; *194 G-5; mail Louisville z 39339
Vernon; RMC Place; WINSTON; *194 F-8; mail Louisville z 39339
Verona; Inc. Place; LEE; 194 C-9; 🅿; z 38879; Ⓟ 2,893; © 3,334
Vestry (Daisy-Vestry); RMC Place; JACKSON; *194 L-9; mail Perkinston z 39573; ● 70
Vickland; RMC Place; SHARKEY; *194 F-4; mail Rolling Fork z 39159; rural
Vicksburg; Inc. Place; ⊡ WARREN; 194 H-4; 🅿 🅷 ■; ★ **VICK**; z 39180-83; Ⓟ 20,908; © 26,407; ◆ 24,612
Victoria; RMC Place; MARSHALL; 194 B-7; 🅿; z 38679; ● 570
Vidalia; HANCOCK, HARRISON; see Dedeaux (RMC Place)
Vimville; RMC Place; LAUDERDALE; *194 H-9; ★ **MRID**; mail Meridian z 39301; ● 80
Virlilia; RMC Place; MADISON; *194 G-6; mail Canton z 39046; rural
Vossburg; RMC Place; JASPER; 194 I-8; 🅿; z 39366; ● 250

Entries in **UPPERCASE** are counties.
Entries in **bold** have populations of 2,500 or more.
Names in parentheses are alternate names.

Inc. Place	Incorporated Place
RMC Place	Rand McNally Designated Place
CDP	Census Designated Place
MCD	Minor Civil Division

⊡ County Seat
▲ Minor Civil Division
elev. Elevation
🅿 Post Office
🅷 Hospital
🅲 College
■ Principal Business Center
★ Ranally Metro Area (RMA) Abbreviation
z Zip Code(s)
Ⓟ Previous Census Population
Ⓡ Revised Census Population
Ⓐ Annexation Population
● Rand McNally Population Estimate
© Final Census Population
Ⓢ Special Census Population
◆ Estimated Population

For additional definitions see Glossary, Volume 1, and Introduction, Volume 2.

W

Waco; SUNFLOWER; see Waco Plantation (RMC Place)
Waco Plantation (Waco); RMC Place; SUNFLOWER; ***194** E-5; mail Inverness **z** 38753; rural
Waddell; RMC Place; CLAY; ***194** E-9; mail Cedarbluff **z** 39741; ● 40
Wade; CDP; JACKSON; **194** L-9; elev. 46ft./14m.; mail Drew **z** 38737, Pascagoula **z** 39567, **z** 39581; Ⓒ 491
Wade; RMC Place; SUNFLOWER; ***194** D-5; mail Drew **z** 38737, Pascagoula **z** 39567; rural
Wahalak; RMC Place; KEMPER; ***194** G-9; elev. 186ft./57m.; mail Scooba **z** 39358; rural
Wakefield; RMC Place; TATE; ***194** B-7; elev. 391ft./119m.; mail Coldwater **z** 38618; rural
Wakeland; RMC Place; LEFLORE; ***194** E-6; mail Greenwood **z** 38930, Money **z** 38945; rural
Waldrup; RMC Place; JASPER; ***194** I-8; mail Bay Springs **z** 39422; rural
Wallerville; RMC Place; UNION; ***194** C-8; elev. 543ft./166m.; mail New Albany **z** 38652; rural
Wallhill; RMC Place; MARSHALL; ***194** B-7; mail Coldwater **z** 38618; rural
Walls (Memphis, Town of Walls); Inc. Place; DESOTO; ***194** A-6; 🅿; **z** 38680, **z** 38686; Ⓟ 70; Ⓒ 87
Walnut; RMC Place; QUITMAN; ***194** C-5; elev. 162ft./49m.; mail Vance **z** 38964; rural
Walnut; Inc. Place; TIPPAH; **194** A-8; 🅿; **z** 38683; Ⓟ 523; Ⓒ 754
Walnut Grove; RMC Place; COAHOMA; ***194** C-5; elev. 155ft./47m.; mail Rena Lara **z** 38767; rural
Walnut Grove; Inc. Place; LEAKE; **194** G-7; elev. 365ft./111m.; 🅿; **z** 39189; Ⓟ 389; Ⓒ 488
Walters; RMC Place; JONES; ***194** J-8; elev. 212ft./65m.; ★ **LAUR**; mail Ellisville **z** 39437; ● 160
Waltersville; RMC Place; WARREN; **194** H-4; ★ **VICK**; mail Vicksburg **z** 39183; pop. incl. with Vicksburg (Inc. Place)
Walthall; Inc. Place; ⊡ WEBSTER; **194** E-8; 🅿; **z** 39771; Ⓟ 167; Ⓒ 170
WALTHALL; **194** K-6; Ⓟ 14,352; Ⓒ 15,156; ◆ 15,027
Wanilla; RMC Place; LAWRENCE; **194** J-6; elev. 212ft./65m.; mail Monticello **z** 39654; ● 80
Wardwell; RMC Place; CALHOUN; mail Vardaman **z** 38878; rural
WARREN; **194** H-5; Ⓟ 47,880; Ⓒ 49,644; ◆ 47,598
Warrenton; RMC Place; WARREN; ***194** H-4; elev. 103ft./31m.; ★ **VICK**; mail Vicksburg **z** 39180; pop. incl. with Vicksburg (Inc. Place)
Warsaw; RMC Place; MARSHALL; **194** B-7; mail Byhalia **z** 38611; ● 60
Washington; RMC Place; ADAMS; **194** J-3; 🅿; **z** 39190; ● 750
WASHINGTON; **194** E-4; Ⓟ 67,935; Ⓒ 62,977; ◆ 53,349
Waterford; RMC Place; MARSHALL; **194** B-7; 🅿; **z** 38685; ● 350
Water Oak; RMC Place; WAYNE; ***194** J-9; mail Waynesboro **z** 39367; rural
Water Valley; Inc. Place; ⊡ YALOBUSHA; **194** C-7; 🅿 🅷; **z** 38965; Ⓟ 3,610; Ⓒ 3,677
Watson; RMC Place; MARSHALL; **194** B-7; elev. 386ft./118m.; mail Byhalia **z** 38611; ● 120
Wautubbee; RMC Place; CLARKE; ***194** I-9; elev. 356ft./109m.; mail Enterprise **z** 39330; rural
Waveland; Inc. Place; HANCOCK; **194** M-8; 🅿; ★ **BIL-**; **z** 39576; Ⓟ 5,369; Ⓒ 6,674
Waxhaw; RMC Place; BOLIVAR; ***194** D-4; mail Gunnison **z** 38746; rural
Way; RMC Place; MADISON; ***194** G-6; mail Canton **z** 39046
WAYNE; **194** I-9; Ⓟ 19,517; Ⓒ 21,216; ◆ 21,059
Waynesboro; Inc. Place; ⊡ WAYNE; **194** J-9; elev. 190ft./58m.; 🅿 🅷; **z** 39367; Ⓟ 5,143; Ⓒ 5,197
Wayside; RMC Place; WASHINGTON; **194** F-4; elev. 120ft./37m.; 🅿; **z** 38780; ● 300
Weathersby; RMC Place; SIMPSON; **194** I-7; mail Mendenhall **z** 39114; pop. incl. with Mendenhall (Inc. Place)
Webb; Inc. Place; TALLAHATCHIE; **194** D-6; 🅿; **z** 38966; Ⓟ 605; Ⓒ 587
WEBSTER; **194** E-7; Ⓟ 10,222; Ⓒ 10,294; ◆ 9,588
Weir; Inc. Place; CHOCTAW; **194** F-8; elev. 467ft./142m.; 🅿; **z** 39772; Ⓟ 525; Ⓒ 553
Wells; RMC Place; LOWNDES; mail Caledonia **z** 39740
Wells Town; RMC Place; LAWRENCE; mail Lumberton **z** 39455; ● 100
Wenasoga; RMC Place; ALCORN; **194** A-9; elev. 494ft./151m.; mail Corinth **z** 38834; ● 220
Wesson; Inc. Place; COPIAH; **194** J-5; elev. 461ft./141m.; 🅿; **z** 39191; Ⓟ 1,510; Ⓒ 1,693
West; Inc. Place; HOLMES; **194** F-7; 🅿; **z** 39192; Ⓟ 184; Ⓒ 220
West; RMC Place; LAUDERDALE; ★ **MRID**; mail Meridian **z** 39305; pop. incl. with Meridian (Inc. Place)
West Biloxi; RMC Place; HARRISON; ★ **BIL-**; mail Biloxi **z** 39531; pop. incl. with Biloxi (Inc. Place)
West Days; RMC Place; DESOTO; ***194** A-6; elev. 244ft./74m.; ★ **MEM**; mail Lake Cormorant **z** 38641; rural
West Gulfport; RMC Place; HARRISON; ***194** M-8; ★ **BIL-**; mail Gulfport **z** 39501; pop. incl. with Gulfport (Inc. Place)
West Hattiesburg; CDP-Census Area Only; LAMAR; ***194** K-8; elev. 219ft./67m.; ★ **HATT**; mail Hattiesburg **z** 39401; Ⓟ 5,450; Ⓒ 6,305
West Hill; RMC Place; HOLMES; ***194** F-6; elev. 370ft./113m.; mail Durant **z** 39063; rural
West Jackson; RMC Place; HINDS; ***194** H-6; ★ **JAC**; mail Jackson **z** 39207; pop. incl. with Jackson (Inc. Place)
Westland; RMC Place; HINDS; ***194** H-6; ★ **JAC**; mail Jackson **z** 39209, **z** 39289; pop. incl. with Jackson (Inc. Place)
West Lincoln; RMC Place; LINCOLN; ***194** J-5; mail Brookhaven **z** 39601; ● 50
West Marks; RMC Place; QUITMAN; ***194** C-6; mail Marks **z** 38646; ● 300
West Point; Inc. Place; ⊡ CLAY; **194** E-9; 🅿 🅷; **z** 39773; Ⓟ 8,489; Ⓒ 12,145
West Poplarville; RMC Place; PEARL RIVER; ***194** L-7; mail Poplarville **z** 39470; ● 130
Westside; RMC Place; CLAIBORNE; ***194** I-4; mail Port Gibson **z** 39150; ● 90
West Union; RMC Place; UNION; mail Myrtle **z** 38650
Westville; RMC Place; SIMPSON; ***194** I-6; mail Mendenhall **z** 39114; rural
Wheeler (Wheelers); RMC Place; PRENTISS; **194** B-9; 🅿; **z** 38880; ● 600
Wheelers; PRENTISS; see Wheeler (RMC Place)
Whistler; RMC Place; WAYNE; **194** J-9; mail Waynesboro **z** 39367; ● 150
White Apple; RMC Place; FRANKLIN; ***194** J-4; mail Roxie **z** 39661
White Bluff; RMC Place; MARION; ***194** J-6; mail Foxworth **z** 39483; rural
White Cap; RMC Place; AMITE; ***194** K-4; elev. 418ft./127m.; mail Gloster **z** 39638; rural
Whitehead; RMC Place; TALLAHATCHIE; ***194** D-6; mail Glendora **z** 38928; rural
White Oak; RMC Place; SMITH; ***194** I-7; elev. 425ft./130m.; mail Magee **z** 39111; ● 100
Whites; RMC Place; CLAY; **194** E-9; mail West Point **z** 39773; ● 120
Whites; RMC Place; RANKIN; ***194** I-6; elev. 362ft./110m.; ★ **JAC**; mail Florence **z** 39073; rural
Whitesand; RMC Place; JEFFERSON DAVIS; ***194** J-6; mail Newhebron **z** 39140; rural
White Sand; RMC Place; PEARL RIVER; ***194** L-7; mail Caledonia **z** 39740, Poplarville **z** 39470
Whites Crossing; RMC Place; STONE; ***194** L-8; elev. 258ft./79m.; mail Wiggins **z** 39577; rural
Whitfield; RMC Place; JONES; **194** J-8; elev. 302ft./92m.; mail Ovett **z** 39464; ● 120
Whitney; RMC Place; SUNFLOWER; ***194** D-5; mail Drew **z** 38737
Whitten Town; RMC Place; TIPPAH; ***194** B-8; mail Ripley **z** 38663; rural
Whynot; RMC Place; LAUDERDALE; **194** H-9; mail Meridian **z** 39301; ● 50
Wickware; RMC Place; NEWTON; mail Newton **z** 39345; rural
Wiggins; RMC Place; LEAKE; ***194** G-7; mail Carthage **z** 39051; rural
Wiggins; Inc. Place; ⊡ STONE; ***194** L-8; elev. 276ft./84m.; 🅿; **z** 39577; Ⓟ 3,185; Ⓒ 3,849
Wilco Estates; RMC Place; DESOTO; ***194** B-6; elev. 320ft./98m.; mail Hernando **z** 38632; ● 80
Wildwood; RMC Place; LEFLORE; ***194** E-6; elev. 135ft./41m.; mail Greenwood **z** 38930; rural
Wilkinson; RMC Place; WILKINSON; **194** K-3; mail Woodville **z** 39669; rural
WILKINSON; **194** K-3; Ⓟ 9,678; Ⓒ 10,312; ◆ 9,998
Willet; RMC Place; WASHINGTON; ***194** F-5; mail Hollandale **z** 38748; rural
Williamsburg; RMC Place; COVINGTON; **194** J-7; elev. 337ft./103m.; mail Collins **z** 39428; ● 135
Williamsville; RMC Place; ATTALA; **194** F-7; mail Kosciusko **z** 39090; ● 320
Williamsville; RMC Place; NESHOBA; **194** G-8; mail Philadelphia **z** 39350; pop. incl. with Philadelphia (Inc. Place)
Willowood; RMC Place; HINDS; ***194** H-6; ★ **JAC**; mail Jackson **z** 39212; pop. incl. with Jackson (Inc. Place)
Willows; RMC Place; CLAIBORNE; ***194** I-4; elev. 301ft./92m.; mail Port Gibson **z** 39150; rural
Winborn; RMC Place; BENTON; **194** B-8; mail Hickory Flat **z** 38633, Potts Camp **z** 38659; ● 60
Winchester; RMC Place; WAYNE; **194** J-9; elev. 166ft./51m.; mail Waynesboro **z** 39367; ● 100
Windsor Park; RMC Place; JACKSON; ***194** M-9; ★ **BIL-**; mail Ocean Springs **z** 39564; ● 580
Wingate; RMC Place; PERRY; ***194** K-8; elev. 115ft./35m.; mail New Augusta **z** 39462; pop. incl. with New Augusta (Inc. Place)
Winona; Inc. Place; ⊡ MONTGOMERY; **194** E-7; elev. 392ft./119m.; 🅿 🅷; **z** 38967; Ⓟ 5,724; Ⓒ 5,482
WINSTON; **194** F-8; Ⓟ 19,433; Ⓒ 20,160; ◆ 19,654
Winstonville; Inc. Place; BOLIVAR; **194** D-5; elev. 147ft./45m.; 🅿; **z** 38781; Ⓟ 277; Ⓒ 319
Winterville; RMC Place; WASHINGTON; ***194** E-4; 🅿; **z** 38782; ● 100
Wolf Springs; RMC Place; LAUDERDALE; ***194** H-9; ★ **MRID**; mail Meridian **z** 39301; rural
Woodburn; SUNFLOWER; see Woodburn Plantation (RMC Place)
Woodburn Plantation (Woodburn); RMC Place; SUNFLOWER; ***194** E-5; mail Indianola **z** 38751, Inverness **z** 38753; rural
Woodland; Inc. Place; CHICKASAW; **194** D-8; 🅿; **z** 39776; Ⓟ 182; Ⓒ 159
Woodland; RMC Place; PONTOTOC; ***194** C-8; mail Pontotoc **z** 38863; rural
Woodland Lake; RMC Place; DESOTO; ***194** B-6; mail Hernando **z** 38632; ● 200
Woodville; Inc. Place; ⊡ WILKINSON; **194** K-3; elev. 410ft./125m.; 🅿; **z** 39669; Ⓟ 1,393; Ⓒ 1,192
Woodwards; RMC Place; WAYNE; ***194** J-9; mail Waynesboro **z** 39367; rural
Wool Market (Coalville); RMC Place; HARRISON; **194** L-3; ★ **BIL-**; mail Biloxi **z** 39532; pop. incl. with Biloxi (Inc. Place); Ⓟ 1,166
Wortham; RMC Place; HARRISON; ***194** L-8; mail Saucier **z** 39574; rural
Wren; RMC Place; MONROE; ***194** D-9; elev. 284ft./87m.; mail Aberdeen **z** 39730; rural
Wright; RMC Place; BOLIVAR; ***194** D-4; mail Gunnison **z** 38746, Rosedale **z** 38769
Wyatte; RMC Place; TATE; ***194** B-7; mail Senatobia **z** 38668

Y

YALOBUSHA; **194** D-7; Ⓟ 12,033; Ⓒ 13,051; ◆ 13,804
YAZOO; **194** G-6; Ⓟ 25,506; Ⓒ 28,149; ◆ 28,276
Yazoo City; Inc. Place; ⊡ YAZOO; **194** G-5; 🅿 🅷; **z** 39194; Ⓟ 12,427; Ⓒ 14,550; Ⓡ 14,141
Yocona; RMC Place; LAFAYETTE; ***194** C-7; mail Oxford **z** 38655; ● 150
Yokena; RMC Place; WARREN; ***194** H-4; elev. 103ft./31m.; ★ **VICK**; mail Vicksburg **z** 39180; rural
Youngs; RMC Place; GRENADA; ***194** D-7; mail Coffeeville **z** 38922; rural

Z

Zama; RMC Place; ATTALA; **194** F-8; mail Kosciusko **z** 39090; ● 100
Zemuly; RMC Place; ATTALA; ***194** F-7; mail Sallis **z** 39160; rural
Zero; RMC Place; LAUDERDALE; ***194** H-9; ★ **MRID**; mail Meridian **z** 39301; ● 50
Zetus; RMC Place; LINCOLN; ***194** J-5; mail Brookhaven **z** 39601; ● 30
Zieglerville; RMC Place; YAZOO; ***194** F-6; mail Benton **z** 39039, Lexington **z** 39095; rural
Zion; RMC Place; PONTOTOC; ***194** C-9; elev. 319ft./97m.; mail Pontotoc **z** 38863
Zumbro; RMC Place; BOLIVAR; ***194** D-5; mail Cleveland **z** 38732; ● 30

Entries in **UPPERCASE** are counties.
Entries in **bold** have populations of 2,500 or more.
Names in parentheses are alternate names.
Inc. Place — Incorporated Place
RMC Place — Rand McNally Designated Place
CDP — Census Designated Place
MCD — Minor Civil Division

⊡ County Seat
▲ Minor Civil Division
elev. Elevation
🅿 Post Office

🅷 Hospital
🅲 College
■ Principal Business Center
★ Ranally Metro Area (RMA) Abbreviation
z Zip Code(s)

Ⓟ Previous Census Population
Ⓡ Revised Census Population
Ⓐ Annexation Population
● Rand McNally Population Estimate
Ⓒ Final Census Population
Ⓢ Special Census Population
◆ Estimated Population

For additional definitions see Glossary, Volume 1, and Introduction, Volume 2.

MISSOURI

NE IA IL KS Jefferson City KY OK AR TN

Statistics

Total area (2000) — 69,704 square miles
Land area (2000) — 68,886 square miles
Water area (2000) — 818 square miles
Capital — Jefferson City
Admitted as state — August, 1821

Maps

State maps can be found on pages 142-254 in Vol. 1

Ranally Metro Areas (RMAs) and Abbreviations

Cape Girardeau, MO — CPGIR
Columbia, MO — COL
Jefferson City, MO — JFCY
Joplin, MO-KS — JOP
Kansas City, MO-KS — K.C.
St. Joseph, MO-KS — ST.JO
St. Louis, MO-IL — ST.L
Springfield, MO — SPRG

Principal Places

Place Name	Place Type	County	Population
Kansas City	Inc. Place	JACKSON	◆ 464,872
Saint Louis	Independent City		◆ 356,533
Springfield	Inc. Place	GREENE	◆ 169,858
Independence	Inc. Place	JACKSON	◆ 113,766
Columbia	Inc. Place	BOONE	◆ 108,823
Saint Joseph	Inc. Place	BUCHANAN	◆ 78,447
O'Fallon	Inc. Place	ST. CHARLES	◆ 77,058
Lees Summit	Inc. Place	JACKSON	◆ 75,194
Saint Charles	Inc. Place	ST. CHARLES	◆ 64,847
Saint Peters	Inc. Place	ST. CHARLES	◆ 54,969
Joplin	Inc. Place	JASPER	◆ 51,825
Blue Springs	Inc. Place	JACKSON	◆ 49,892
Florissant	Inc. Place	ST. LOUIS	◆ 46,886
Chesterfield	Inc. Place	ST. LOUIS	◆ 46,238
Jefferson City	Inc. Place	COLE	◆ 41,473
Cape Girardeau	Inc. Place	CAPE GIRARDEAU	◆ 37,329
University City	Inc. Place	ST. LOUIS	◆ 35,284
Oakville	CDP	ST. LOUIS	◆ 34,070
Wildwood	Inc. Place	ST. LOUIS	◆ 33,064
Liberty	Inc. Place	CLAY	◆ 30,842
Ballwin	Inc. Place	ST. LOUIS	◆ 30,258
Raytown	Inc. Place	JACKSON	◆ 29,961
Gladstone	Inc. Place	CLAY	◆ 28,139
Mehlville	CDP	ST. LOUIS	◆ 27,805
Kirkwood	Inc. Place	ST. LOUIS	◆ 26,114
Hazelwood	Inc. Place	ST. LOUIS	◆ 25,384
Maryland Heights	Inc. Place	ST. LOUIS	◆ 24,743
Grandview	Inc. Place	JACKSON	◆ 24,712
Belton	Inc. Place	CASS	◆ 23,832
Webster Groves	Inc. Place	ST. LOUIS	◆ 22,571
Ferguson	Inc. Place	ST. LOUIS	◆ 21,266
Spanish Lake	CDP	ST. LOUIS	◆ 20,584
Sedalia	Inc. Place	PETTIS	◆ 20,124
Affton	CDP	ST. LOUIS	◆ 19,863
Arnold	Inc. Place	JEFFERSON	◆ 19,704
Manchester	Inc. Place	ST. LOUIS	© 19,161
Rolla	Inc. Place	PHELPS	◆ 18,010
Lemay	CDP	ST. LOUIS	© 17,215
Hannibal	Inc. Place	MARION	◆ 16,899
Overland	Inc. Place	ST. LOUIS	© 16,838
Sikeston	Inc. Place	SCOTT	◆ 16,836
Concord	CDP	ST. LOUIS	© 16,689
Kirksville	Inc. Place	ADAIR	◆ 16,569
Creve Coeur	Inc. Place	ST. LOUIS	◆ 16,381
Warrensburg	Inc. Place	JOHNSON	© 16,340
Clayton	Inc. Place	ST. LOUIS	◆ 16,030
Poplar Bluff	Inc. Place	BUTLER	◆ 15,367
Jennings	Inc. Place	ST. LOUIS	◆ 14,790
Bridgeton	Inc. Place	ST. LOUIS	◆ 14,656
Moberly	Inc. Place	RANDOLPH	◆ 14,244
Farmington	Inc. Place	ST. FRANCOIS	© 13,924
Fort Leonard Wood	CDP-Census Area Only	PULASKI	© 13,666
Washington	Inc. Place	FRANKLIN	© 13,243
Carthage	Inc. Place	JASPER	© 12,668
Saint Ann	Inc. Place	ST. LOUIS	◆ 12,663
Marshall	Inc. Place	SALINE	© 12,433
Lebanon	Inc. Place	LACLEDE	© 12,155
Fulton	Inc. Place	CALLAWAY	© 12,128
Nixa	Inc. Place	CHRISTIAN	© 12,124
Jackson	Inc. Place	CAPE GIRARDEAU	© 11,947
Wentzville	Inc. Place	ST. CHARLES	◆ 11,692
Crestwood	Inc. Place	ST. LOUIS	◆ 11,271
Kennett	Inc. Place	DUNKLIN	© 11,260
Raymore	Inc. Place	CASS	© 11,146
Bellefontaine Neighbors	Inc. Place	ST. LOUIS	® 11,088
Town and Country	Inc. Place	ST. LOUIS	© 10,894
Excelsior Springs	Inc. Place	CLAY	© 10,847
West Plains	Inc. Place	HOWELL	◆ 10,766
Maryville	Inc. Place	NODAWAY	© 10,581
Neosho	Inc. Place	NEWTON	© 10,505
Mexico	Inc. Place	AUDRAIN	◆ 10,173
Lake Saint Louis	Inc. Place	ST. CHARLES	© 10,169
Berkeley	Inc. Place	ST. LOUIS	© 10,063
Webb City	Inc. Place	JASPER	© 9,812
Cameron	Inc. Place	CLINTON	® 9,788
Ozark	Inc. Place	CHRISTIAN	© 9,665
Festus	Inc. Place	JEFFERSON	© 9,660
Richmond Heights	Inc. Place	ST. LOUIS	© 9,602
Clinton	Inc. Place	HENRY	© 9,311
Maplewood	Inc. Place	ST. LOUIS	© 9,228
Bolivar	Inc. Place	POLK	© 9,143
Ellisville	Inc. Place	ST. LOUIS	© 9,104
Murphy	CDP	JEFFERSON	© 9,048
Chillicothe	Inc. Place	LIVINGSTON	© 8,968
Harrisonville	Inc. Place	CASS	© 8,946
Nevada	Inc. Place	VERNON	© 8,607
Des Peres	Inc. Place	ST. LOUIS	◆ 8,601
Republic	Inc. Place	GREENE	© 8,438
Ladue	Inc. Place	ST. LOUIS	® 8,413
Sunset Hills	Inc. Place	ST. LOUIS	© 8,267
Boonville	Inc. Place	COOPER	© 8,202
Park Hills	Inc. Place	ST. FRANCOIS	© 7,861
Union	Inc. Place	FRANKLIN	© 7,757
Brentwood	Inc. Place	ST. LOUIS	© 7,693
Eureka	Inc. Place	ST. LOUIS	© 7,676
Perryville	Inc. Place	PERRY	© 7,667
Olivette	Inc. Place	ST. LOUIS	© 7,438
Dexter	Inc. Place	STODDARD	® 7,430
Monett	Inc. Place	BARRY	© 7,396
Sappington	CDP	ST. LOUIS	© 7,287
Aurora	Inc. Place	LAWRENCE	© 7,014
Saint Johns	Inc. Place	ST. LOUIS	© 6,871
Black Jack	Inc. Place	ST. LOUIS	© 6,792
Caruthersville	Inc. Place	PEMISCOT	© 6,760
Troy	Inc. Place	LINCOLN	© 6,737
Shrewsbury	Inc. Place	ST. LOUIS	© 6,644
Valley Park	Inc. Place	ST. LOUIS	© 6,518
De Soto	Inc. Place	JEFFERSON	© 6,375
Sullivan	Inc. Place	FRANKLIN	© 6,351
Trenton	Inc. Place	GRUNDY	© 6,216
Richmond	Inc. Place	RAY	© 6,116
Barnhart	CDP	JEFFERSON	© 6,108
Branson	Inc. Place	TANEY	© 6,050
North Kansas City	Inc. Place	CLAY	◆ 5,897
Glendale	Inc. Place	ST. LOUIS	© 5,767
Marshfield	Inc. Place	WEBSTER	© 5,720
Pleasant Hill	Inc. Place	CASS	© 5,582
Macon	Inc. Place	MACON	© 5,538
Oak Grove	Inc. Place	JACKSON	© 5,535
Smithville	Inc. Place	CLAY	© 5,514
Pacific	Inc. Place	FRANKLIN	© 5,482
Kearney	Inc. Place	CLAY	© 5,472
Carl Junction	Inc. Place	JASPER	© 5,294
Warrenton	Inc. Place	WARREN	© 5,281
Weldon Spring	Inc. Place	ST. CHARLES	© 5,270
Dellwood	Inc. Place	ST. LOUIS	© 5,255
Normandy	Inc. Place	ST. LOUIS	® 5,247
Glasgow Village	CDP	ST. LOUIS	© 5,234
Bowling Green	Inc. Place	PIKE	® 5,166
Grain Valley	Inc. Place	JACKSON	© 5,160

County and Independent City Business Data

County	FIPS Code	County Seat	Land Area (Sq. Mi.)	Census Population			Wholesale Trade		Manufacturing, 2002			
				4/1/2000	4/1/1990	% Change 1990-2000	Sales, 2002 ($1,000)	% Change 1997-2002	Establish-ments	Total Employees	Value Added ($1,000)	Ranally Mfg. Units
Adair	001	Kirksville	567	24,977	24,577	1.6	(d)	(d)	13	(d)	(d)	...
Andrew	003	Savannah	435	16,492	14,632	12.7	36,555	(d)	...	(d)	(d)	...
Atchison	005	Rock Port	545	6,430	7,457	-13.8	(d)	(d)	...	(d)	(d)	...
Audrain	007	Mexico	693	25,853	23,599	9.6	111,106	-11.2	32	1,531	190,196	101
Barry	009	Cassville	779	34,010	27,547	23.5	196,025	99.8	55	6,000	423,255	224
Barton	011	Lamar	594	12,541	11,312	10.9	59,165	(d)	18	2,042	170,486	90
Bates	013	Butler	848	16,653	15,025	10.8	81,618	13.3	...	(d)	(d)	...
Benton	015	Warsaw	706	17,180	13,859	24.0	(d)	(d)	...	(d)	(d)	...
Bollinger	017	Marble Hill	621	12,029	10,619	13.3	(d)	(d)	...	(d)	(d)	...
Boone	019	Columbia	685	135,454	112,379	20.5	(d)	(d)	95	5,234	732,218	387
Buchanan	021	Saint Joseph	410	85,998	83,083	3.5	1,622,139	(d)	85	(d)	(d)	...
Butler	023	Poplar Bluff	698	40,867	38,765	5.4	156,382	-8.0	56	3,298	226,340	120
Caldwell	025	Kingston	429	8,969	8,380	7.0	(d)	(d)	...	(d)	(d)	...
Callaway	027	Fulton	839	40,766	32,809	24.3	48,128	-63.0	35	790	57,738	31
Camden	029	Camdenton	655	37,051	27,495	34.8	86,505	-2.2	59	1,178	75,912	40
Cape Girardeau	031	Jackson	579	68,693	61,633	11.5	1,173,811	81.4	105	(d)	(d)	...
Carroll	033	Carrollton	695	10,285	10,748	-4.3	91,552	16.1	...	(d)	(d)	...
Carter	035	Van Buren	508	5,941	5,515	7.7	8,967	92.7	...	(d)	(d)	...
Cass	037	Harrisonville	699	82,092	63,808	28.7	198,914	(d)	87	1,507	143,823	76
Cedar	039	Stockton	476	13,733	12,093	13.6	(d)	(d)	...	(d)	(d)	...
Chariton	041	Keytesville	756	8,438	9,202	-8.3	(d)	(d)	...	(d)	(d)	...
Christian	043	Ozark	563	54,285	32,644	66.3	155,156	15.5	113	2,073	134,512	71
Clark	045	Kahoka	507	7,416	7,547	-1.7	40,565	-41.3	...	(d)	(d)	...
Clay	047	Liberty	396	184,006	153,411	19.9	6,606,705	14.4	230	14,442	3,364,943	1,780
Clinton	049	Plattsburg	419	18,979	16,595	14.4	(d)	(d)	...	(d)	(d)	...
Cole	051	Jefferson City	391	71,397	63,579	12.3	441,277	-50.8	61	3,572	830,935	440
Cooper	053	Boonville	565	16,670	14,835	12.4	73,708	16.5	...	(d)	(d)	...
Crawford	055	Steelville	743	22,804	19,173	18.9	29,580	-36.1	43	1,521	117,453	62
Dade	057	Greenfield	490	7,923	7,449	6.4	(d)	(d)	...	(d)	(d)	...
Dallas	059	Buffalo	542	15,661	12,646	23.8	24,630	3.3	...	(d)	(d)	...
Daviess	061	Gallatin	567	8,016	7,865	1.9	41,083	-1.3	...	(d)	(d)	...
DeKalb	063	Maysville	424	11,597	9,967	16.4	(d)	(d)	...	(d)	(d)	...
Dent	065	Salem	754	14,927	13,702	8.9	(d)	(d)	27	692	58,971	31
Douglas	067	Ava	815	13,084	11,876	10.2	(d)	(d)	12	529	44,850	24
Dunklin	069	Kennett	546	33,155	33,112	0.1	99,503	-25.9	29	942	114,995	61
Franklin	071	Union	923	93,807	80,603	16.4	359,537	94.0	217	9,697	1,078,963	571
Gasconade	073	Hermann	521	15,342	14,006	9.5	27,700	(d)	39	1,436	105,941	56
Gentry	075	Albany	492	6,861	6,848	0.2	21,068	(d)	...	(d)	(d)	...
Greene	077	Springfield	675	240,391	207,949	15.6	5,419,866	6.2	345	15,546	1,604,662	849
Grundy	079	Trenton	436	10,432	10,536	-1.0	41,774	-29.3	13	814	48,848	26
Harrison	081	Bethany	725	8,850	8,469	4.5	47,240	-36.7	...	(d)	(d)	...
Henry	083	Clinton	702	21,997	20,044	9.7	99,147	-54.6	39	1,614	137,660	73
Hickory	085	Hermitage	399	8,940	7,335	21.9	(d)	(d)	...	(d)	(d)	...
Holt	087	Oregon	462	5,351	6,034	-11.3	33,200	-27.4	...	(d)	(d)	...
Howard	089	Fayette	466	10,212	9,631	6.0	(d)	(d)	...	(d)	(d)	...
Howell	091	West Plains	928	37,238	31,447	18.4	226,471	-17.2	90	3,556	279,818	148
Iron	093	Ironton	551	10,697	10,726	-0.3	13,283	(d)	...	(d)	(d)	...
Jackson	095	Independence	605	654,880	633,232	3.4	18,289,127	61.8	824	32,174	5,831,043	3,085
Jasper	097	Carthage	640	104,686	90,465	15.7	1,453,158	62.0	199	10,798	1,085,831	574
Jefferson	099	Hillsboro	657	198,099	171,380	15.6	613,631	74.0	185	4,450	515,128	273
Johnson	101	Warrensburg	830	48,258	42,514	13.5	(d)	(d)	29	1,576	107,704	57
Knox	103	Edina	506	4,361	4,482	-2.7	(d)	(d)	...	(d)	(d)	...
Laclede	105	Lebanon	766	32,513	27,158	19.7	192,899	52.7	62	5,062	398,252	211
Lafayette	107	Lexington	629	32,960	31,107	6.0	(d)	(d)	38	1,059	105,855	56
Lawrence	109	Mount Vernon	613	35,204	30,236	16.4	239,671	16.6	51	1,402	148,010	78
Lewis	111	Monticello	505	10,494	10,233	2.6	(d)	(d)	...	(d)	(d)	...
Lincoln	113	Troy	630	38,944	28,892	34.8	106,953	-25.8	43	1,397	219,843	116
Linn	115	Linneus	620	13,754	13,885	-0.9	95,499	180.5	21	1,620	122,602	65
Livingston	117	Chillicothe	535	14,558	14,592	-0.2	131,974	-32.8	24	868	71,856	38
Macon	121	Macon	804	15,762	15,345	2.7	54,292	-34.5	10	537	20,296	11
Madison	123	Fredericktown	497	11,800	11,127	6.0	14,794	-22.0	...	(d)	(d)	...
Maries	125	Vienna	528	8,903	7,976	11.6	74,387	-14.5	...	(d)	(d)	...
Marion	127	Palmyra	438	28,289	27,682	2.2	(d)	(d)	46	(d)	(d)	...
McDonald	119	Pineville	540	21,681	16,938	28.0	74,595	(d)	31	2,778	215,928	114
Mercer	129	Princeton	454	3,757	3,723	0.9	(d)	(d)	...	(d)	(d)	...
Miller	131	Tuscumbia	592	23,564	20,700	13.8	109,113	73.7	24	785	68,517	36
Mississippi	133	Charleston	413	13,427	14,442	-7.0	217,757	-30.5	...	(d)	(d)	...
Moniteau	135	California	417	14,827	12,298	20.6	(d)	(d)	24	788	46,271	24
Monroe	137	Paris	646	9,311	9,104	2.3	37,293	119.8	8	895	60,820	32
Montgomery	139	Montgomery City	537	12,136	11,355	6.9	75,625	-19.3	29	564	45,030	24
Morgan	141	Versailles	597	19,309	15,574	24.0	33,470	7.7	29	559	35,343	19
New Madrid	143	New Madrid	678	19,760	20,928	-5.6	635,863	104.8	17	2,431	168,929	89
Newton	145	Neosho	626	52,636	44,445	18.4	227,133	16.4	72	3,932	338,415	179
Nodaway	147	Maryville	877	21,912	21,709	0.9	103,421	-56.9	22	2,082	391,251	207

Entries in **UPPERCASE** are counties.
Entries in **bold** have populations of 2,500 or more.
Names in parentheses are alternate names.
Inc. Place — Incorporated Place
RMC Place — Rand McNally Designated Place
CDP — Census Designated Place
MCD — Minor Civil Division

⊡ County Seat
▲ Minor Civil Division
elev. Elevation
🅿 Post Office

🄷 Hospital
🄲 College
■ Principal Business Center
★ Ranally Metro Area (RMA) Abbreviation
z Zip Code(s)

Ⓟ Previous Census Population
® Revised Census Population
Ⓐ Annexation Population
● Rand McNally Population Estimate
© Final Census Population
Ⓢ Special Census Population
◆ Estimated Population

For additional definitions see Glossary, Volume 1, and Introduction, Volume 2.

County	FIPS Code	County Seat	Land Area (Sq. Mi.)	Census Population 4/1/2000	Census Population 4/1/1990	Census Population % Change 1990-2000	Wholesale Trade Sales, 2002 ($1,000)	Wholesale Trade % Change 1997-2002	Manufacturing, 2002 Establish-ments	Manufacturing, 2002 Total Employees	Manufacturing, 2002 Value Added ($1,000)	Manufacturing, 2002 Ranally Mfg. Units
Oregon	149	Alton	791	10,344	9,470	9.2	24,441	-15.8	...	(d)	(d)	...
Osage	151	Linn	606	13,062	12,018	8.7	(d)	(d)	28	766	120,048	64
Ozark	153	Gainesville	742	9,542	8,598	11.0	(d)	(d)	...	(d)	(d)	...
Pemiscot	155	Caruthersville	493	20,047	21,921	-8.5	189,651	-11.3	14	838	49,385	26
Perry	157	Perryville	475	18,132	16,648	8.9	56,960	45.6	36	3,001	276,789	146
Pettis	159	Sedalia	685	39,403	35,437	11.2	216,174	2.2	64	4,943	479,456	254
Phelps	161	Rolla	673	39,825	35,248	13.0	104,241	5.3	53	1,564	114,929	61
Pike	163	Bowling Green	673	18,351	15,969	14.9	137,212	(d)	28	626	103,082	55
Platte	165	Platte City	420	73,781	57,867	27.5	4,821,464	44.6	51	1,845	203,600	108
Polk	167	Bolivar	637	26,992	21,826	23.7	80,338	-33.2	34	762	74,560	39
Pulaski	169	Waynesville	547	41,165	41,307	-0.3	(d)	(d)	...	(d)	(d)	...
Putnam	171	Unionville	518	5,223	5,079	2.8	(d)	(d)	...	(d)	(d)	...
Ralls	173	New London	471	9,626	8,476	13.6	(d)	(d)	...	(d)	(d)	...
Randolph	175	Huntsville	482	24,663	24,370	1.2	93,684	21.8	28	1,372	95,348	50
Ray	177	Richmond	569	23,354	21,971	6.3	(d)	(d)	18	554	52,771	28
Reynolds	179	Centerville	811	6,689	6,661	0.4	2,931	-64.7	...	(d)	(d)	...
Ripley	181	Doniphan	629	13,509	12,303	9.8	(d)	(d)	39	547	20,908	11
St. Charles	183	Saint Charles	560	283,883	212,907	33.3	4,681,369	155.6	273	14,717	2,494,300	1,320
St. Clair	185	Osceola	677	9,652	8,457	14.1	(d)	(d)	...	(d)	(d)	...
St. Francois	187	Farmington	449	55,641	48,904	13.8	(d)	(d)	57	2,466	168,060	89
Ste. Genevieve	186	Sainte Genevieve	502	17,842	16,037	11.3	49,357	36.9	35	1,581	130,874	69
St. Louis	189	Clayton	508	1,016,315	993,529	2.3	30,548,854	-23.2	1,141	66,208	7,123,344	3,769
Saline	195	Marshall	756	23,756	23,523	1.0	158,518	-29.9	24	1,485	216,040	114
Schuyler	197	Lancaster	308	4,170	4,236	-1.6	(d)	(d)	...	(d)	(d)	...
Scotland	199	Memphis	438	4,983	4,822	3.3	12,564	-50.3	...	(d)	(d)	...
Scott	201	Benton	421	40,422	39,376	2.7	325,108	-48.4	76	2,595	288,150	152
Shannon	203	Eminence	1,004	8,324	7,613	9.3	8,406	-62.4	...	(d)	(d)	...
Shelby	205	Shelbyville	501	6,799	6,942	-2.1	23,854	-26.2	...	(d)	(d)	...
Stoddard	207	Bloomfield	827	29,705	28,895	2.8	(d)	(d)	43	2,621	453,102	240
Stone	209	Galena	463	28,658	19,078	50.2	12,619	-54.9	...	(d)	(d)	...
Sullivan	211	Milan	651	7,219	6,326	14.1	(d)	(d)	4	(d)	(d)	...
Taney	213	Forsyth	632	39,703	25,561	55.3	58,718	-19.5	56	568	39,005	21
Texas	215	Houston	1,179	23,003	21,476	7.1	23,549	-64.7	46	889	54,787	29
Vernon	217	Nevada	834	20,454	19,041	7.4	44,374	-21.1	21	1,351	268,399	142
Warren	219	Warrenton	431	24,525	19,534	25.6	(d)	(d)	36	1,893	133,211	70
Washington	221	Potosi	760	23,344	20,380	14.5	(d)	(d)	23	628	34,422	18
Wayne	223	Greenville	761	13,259	11,543	14.9	4,733	32.4	...	(d)	(d)	...
Webster	225	Marshfield	593	31,045	23,753	30.7	60,912	135.7	57	969	95,760	51
Worth	227	Grant City	267	2,382	2,440	-2.4	(d)	(d)	...	(d)	(d)	...
Wright	229	Hartville	682	17,955	16,758	7.1	67,838	-28.5	22	630	32,799	17
Independent City												
St. Louis	510		62	348,189	396,685	-12.2	10,618,881	0.3	685	25,531	4,870,268	2,577
The State			**68,886**	**5,595,211**	**5,117,073**	**9.3**	**95,603,561**	**4.6**	**7,210**	**319,974**	**41,528,244**	**21,971**

(d) Data not available. Corresponding percentages or Ranally Manufacturing Units are estimates.
... Represents 0 or amount too minimal to be reported.

Index of Places and Counties

A

Aaron; RMC Place; BATES; *196 G-10; elev. 906ft./276m.; mail Adrian z 64720; rural
Abadyl; RMC Place; CHRISTIAN; *197 K-12; mail Bruner z 65620; rural
Abesville; RMC Place; STONE; 197 L-11; elev. 1,138ft./347m.; mail Galena z 65656; ● 100
Abo; RMC Place; LACLEDE; *197 I-13; mail Lebanon z 65536; rural
Acorn Corner; RMC Place; PEMISCOT; *197 N-19; elev. 260ft./79m.; mail Steele z 63877; ● 30
Acorn Ridge; RMC Place; STODDARD; 197 K-19; elev. 388ft./118m.; mail Puxico z 63960; ● 30
Adair; RMC Place; ADAIR; *197 B-13; mail Brashear z 63533
ADAIR; 197 C-13; Ⓟ 24,577; Ⓒ 24,977; ◆ 24,504
Adrian; Inc. Place; BATES; 196 G-9; elev. 871ft./265m.; 🅿; z 64720; Ⓟ 1,582; Ⓒ 1,780
Advance; Inc. Place; STODDARD; 197 K-19; elev. 361ft./110m.; 🅿; z 63730; Ⓟ 1,139; Ⓒ 1,244
Affton; CDP; ST. LOUIS; 195 G-5; elev. 609ft./186m.; 🅿; ★ ST.L; z 63123; Ⓟ 21,106; Ⓒ 20,535; ◆ 19,863
Agency; Inc. Place; BUCHANAN; 196 D-8; elev. 840ft./256m.; 🅿; ★ ST.JO; z 64401; Ⓟ 642; Ⓒ 599
Aid; RMC Place; STODDARD; *197 K-19; mail Bloomfield z 63825; ● 50
Airline Acres; RMC Place; MISSISSIPPI; *197 L-20; elev. 1,308ft./399m.; mail Charleston z 63834; rural
Airport Drive; Inc. Place; JASPER; 195 L-2; elev. 964ft./294m.; ★ JOP; mail Joplin z 64801; Ⓟ 818; Ⓒ 622
Akers; RMC Place; SHANNON; *197 J-15; mail Salem z 65560; rural
Alanthus Grove; RMC Place; GENTRY; *196 B-9; elev. 279ft./85m.; mail Stanberry z 64489; ● 30
Alba; Inc. Place; JASPER; 196 J-9; elev. 989ft./301m.; 🅿; ★ JOP; z 64830; Ⓟ 465; Ⓒ 588
Albany; Inc. Place; ⊡ GENTRY; 196 B-9; elev. 915ft./279m.; 🅿 🅷; z 64402; Ⓟ 1,958; Ⓒ 1,937
Albany; RMC Place; RAY; *196 E-10; mail Orrick z 64077; ● 30
Aldrich; Inc. Place; POLK; 197 J-11; elev. 900ft./274m.; 🅿; z 65601; Ⓟ 76; Ⓒ 75
Alexandria; Inc. Place; CLARK; 197 B-15; elev. 490ft./149m.; 🅿; z 63430; Ⓟ 341; Ⓒ 166
Alfalfa Center; RMC Place; MISSISSIPPI; *197 K-20; elev. 316ft./96m.; mail Charleston z 63834; rural
Algonquin; RMC Place; ST. LOUIS; ★ ST.L; mail Saint Louis z 63119; pop. incl. with Webster Groves (Inc. Place)
Allbright; RMC Place; MADISON; *197 J-18; elev. 479ft./146m.; mail Marquand z 63655; rural
Allendale; Inc. Place; WORTH; 196 B-9; elev. 1,063ft./324m.; 🅿; z 64420; Ⓟ 58; Ⓒ 54
Allenton; RMC Place; ST. LOUIS; 195 G-1; elev. 492ft./150m.; 🅿; ★ ST.L; z 63001; pop. incl. with Eureka (Inc. Place)
Allenville; Inc. Place; CAPE GIRARDEAU; *197 J-19; elev. 352ft./107m.; mail Chaffee z 63740; Ⓟ 69; Ⓒ 104
Alley Spring; RMC Place; SHANNON; *197 K-16; elev. 679ft./207m.; mail Eminence z 65466; rural
All Saints Village; RMC Place; ST. CHARLES; 195 C-1; elev. 532ft./162m.; ★ ST.L; mail Saint Peters z 63376; ● 550
Alma; Inc. Place; LAFAYETTE; 197 E-11; elev. 800ft./244m.; 🅿; z 64001; Ⓟ 446; Ⓒ 399
Almartha; RMC Place; OZARK; 197 L-13; mail Wasola z 65773
Almon; RMC Place; HICKORY; *197 I-12; elev. 828ft./252m.; mail Preston z 65732; rural
Alpha; RMC Place; GRUNDY; *197 C-11; mail Laredo z 64652; rural
Altamont; Inc. Place; DAVIESS; 196 C-10; elev. 1,004ft./306m.; 🅿; z 64620; Ⓟ 188; Ⓒ 218
Altenburg; Inc. Place; PERRY; 197 I-20; elev. 560ft./171m.; 🅿; z 63732; Ⓟ 307; Ⓒ 309
Altheim; RMC Place; ST. LOUIS; *197 G-17; ★ ST.L; mail Saint Louis z 63141; pop. incl. with Town and Country (Inc. Place)
Alton; Inc. Place; ⊡ OREGON; 197 L-16; elev. 779ft./237m.; 🅿; z 65606; Ⓟ 692; Ⓒ 668
Altona; RMC Place; BATES; *196 G-9; elev. 900ft./274m.; mail Adrian z 64720
Amazonia; Inc. Place; ANDREW; 196 C-8; elev. 842ft./257m.; 🅿; z 64421; Ⓟ 257; Ⓒ 277
Americus; RMC Place; MONTGOMERY; 197 F-15; mail Rhineland z 65069; ● 60
Amity; Inc. Place; DEKALB; 196 C-9; elev. 1,000ft./305m.; 🅿; z 64422; Ⓟ 99; Ⓒ 70
Amoret; Inc. Place; BATES; 196 H-9; elev. 852ft./260m.; 🅿; z 64722; Ⓟ 212; Ⓒ 211
Amsterdam; Inc. Place; BATES; 196 G-9; elev. 880ft./268m.; 🅿; z 64723; Ⓟ 237; Ⓒ 281
Amy; RMC Place; HOWELL; *197 L-14; elev. 1,192ft./363m.; mail Caulfield z 65626; rural
Anabel; RMC Place; MACON; 197 D-14; elev. 838ft./255m.; 🅿; z 63431; ● 30
Anaconda; RMC Place; FRANKLIN; *197 H-16; elev. 841ft./256m.; mail Saint Clair z 63077; ● 180
Anderson; Inc. Place; MCDONALD; 196 L-9; elev. 890ft./271m.; 🅿; z 64831; Ⓟ 1,432; Ⓒ 1,856
ANDREW; 196 C-8; Ⓟ 14,632; Ⓒ 16,492; ◆ 16,855
Annada; Inc. Place; PIKE; 197 E-17; elev. 449ft./137m.; 🅿; z 63330; Ⓟ 70; Ⓒ 48
Annapolis; Inc. Place; IRON; 197 J-17; elev. 691ft./211m.; 🅿; z 63620; Ⓟ 363; Ⓒ 310
Anniston; Inc. Place; MISSISSIPPI; 197 L-20; elev. 310ft./94m.; 🅿; z 63820; Ⓟ 288; Ⓒ 285
Anson; RMC Place; CLARK; *197 A-15; mail Farmington z 52626; rural
Anthonies Mill; RMC Place; WASHINGTON; 197 H-16; mail Bourbon z 65441; rural
Antioch; RMC Place; CLARK; *197 B-15; elev. 698ft./213m.; mail Kahoka z 63445; rural
Antioch; RMC Place; CLAY; *196 E-9; ★ K.C.; mail Kansas City z 64119, z 64157-58, z 64167; pop. incl. with Kansas City (Inc. Place)
Antonia; RMC Place; JEFFERSON; *197 G-18; elev. 520ft./158m.; 🅿; ★ ST.L; z 63052; ● 650
Anutt; RMC Place; DENT; 197 I-15; elev. 1,217ft./371m.; ● 60
Apache Flats; RMC Place; COLE; *197 G-14; ★ JFCY; mail Jefferson City z 65101; ● 230
Apple Creek (Schnurbusch); RMC Place; PERRY; *197 I-19; mail Perryville z 63775; ● 30
Appleton; CAPE GIRARDEAU; see Old Appleton (Inc. Place)
Appleton City; Inc. Place; ST. CLAIR; 196 H-10; elev. 836ft./255m.; 🅿 🅷; z 64724; Ⓟ 1,280; Ⓒ 1,314
Aquilla; RMC Place; STODDARD; *197 K-19; mail Bloomfield z 63825
Arab; RMC Place; BOLLINGER; 197 K-19; elev. 362ft./110m.; 🅿; z 63787; ● 130
Arbela; Inc. Place; SCOTLAND; 197 B-14; elev. 671ft./205m.; 🅿; z 63432, z 63442; Ⓟ 40; Ⓒ 40
Arbor; RMC Place; CAPE GIRARDEAU; *197 K-19; elev. 340ft./104m.; mail Chaffee z 63740
Arbor Terrace; RMC Place; ST. LOUIS; *197 F-18; ★ ST.L; mail Saint Louis z 63121; pop. incl. with Northwoods (Inc. Place)
Arbyrd; Inc. Place; DUNKLIN; 197 N-18; elev. 245ft./75m.; 🅿; z 63821; Ⓟ 597; Ⓒ 528
Arcadia (Arcadia Ironton); Inc. Place; IRON; 197 J-17; elev. 910ft./277m.; 🅿; z 63621; Ⓟ 609; Ⓒ 567
Arcadia Ironton; IRON; see Arcadia (Inc. Place)
Archie; Inc. Place; CASS; 196 G-9; elev. 832ft./254m.; 🅿; z 64725; Ⓟ 799; Ⓒ 890
Arcola; Inc. Place; DADE; 196 J-10; elev. 1,013ft./309m.; 🅿; z 65603; Ⓟ 72; Ⓒ 45
Ardeola; RMC Place; STODDARD; *197 K-19; mail Advance z 63730; ● 40
Arditta; RMC Place; HOWELL; *197 L-14; elev. 1,092ft./333m.; mail Caulfield z 65626; rural
Ardmore; RMC Place; MACON; *197 D-13; mail Excello z 65247; rural
Argo; RMC Place; CRAWFORD; *197 H-16; elev. 952ft./290m.; mail Bourbon z 65441; rural
Argyle; Inc. Place; OSAGE, MARIES; 197 H-14; elev. 719ft./219m.; 🅿; z 65001; Ⓟ 178; Ⓒ 164
Arkmo; RMC Place; DUNKLIN; *197 N-18; elev. 340ft./104m.; mail Arbyrd z 63821; rural
Arkoe; Inc. Place; NODAWAY; 196 B-8; elev. 980ft./299m.; mail Maryville z 64468; Ⓟ 64; Ⓒ 58
Arley; RMC Place; CLAY; *196 D-9; ★ K.C.; mail Kearney z 64060
Arlington; RMC Place; PHELPS; *197 I-14; mail Newburg z 65550; rural
Armstrong; Inc. Place; HOWARD; 197 E-13; elev. 830ft./253m.; 🅿; z 65230; Ⓟ 310; Ⓒ 287
Arnica; RMC Place; CEDAR; *197 I-11; elev. 958ft./292m.; mail Humansville z 65674; rural
Arnold; Inc. Place; JEFFERSON; 197 G-18; elev. 550ft./168m.; 🅿; ★ ST.L; z 63010; Ⓟ 18,828; Ⓒ 19,965; ◆ 19,704
Aroma; RMC Place; NEWTON; *196 L-9; elev. 1,227ft./374m.; mail Granby z 64844; ● 100
Arroll; RMC Place; TEXAS; *197 K-15; elev. 1,203ft./367m.; mail Summersville z 65571; ● 30
Arrowhead Beach; RMC Place; MILLER; *197 H-13; mail Lake Ozark z 65049; pop. incl. with Lake Ozark (Inc. Place)
Arrow Point; Inc. Place; BARRY; *197 L-11; mail Golden z 65658; Ⓒ 133
Arrow Rock; Inc. Place; SALINE; 197 E-12; elev. 700ft./213m.; 🅿; z 65320; Ⓟ 70; Ⓒ 79
Arthur; RMC Place; VERNON; *196 H-9; elev. 767ft./234m.; mail Rich Hill z 64779; rural
Asbury; Inc. Place; JASPER; 196 J-9; elev. 900ft./274m.; 🅿; ★ JOP; z 64832; Ⓟ 220; Ⓒ 218
Ashburn; RMC Place; PIKE; 197 D-16; elev. 474ft./144m.; 🅿; z 63433; disincorporated since 2000 Census; Ⓟ 51; Ⓒ 51
Asherville; RMC Place; STODDARD; 197 K-18; elev. 441ft./134m.; mail Puxico z 63960; ● 40
Ash Grove; Inc. Place; GREENE; 197 J-11; elev. 1,042ft./318m.; 🅿; z 65604; Ⓟ 1,128; Ⓒ 1,430
Ash Hill; RMC Place; BUTLER; 197 L-18; mail Fisk z 63940; ● 30
Ashland; Inc. Place; BOONE; 197 F-14; elev. 905ft./276m.; 🅿; z 65010; Ⓟ 1,252; Ⓒ 1,869; Ⓡ 2,201
Ashley; RMC Place; PIKE; 197 E-16; elev. 725ft./221m.; mail Bowling Green z 63334; ● 150
Ashley Creek; RMC Place; TEXAS; *197 J-15; elev. 982ft./299m.; mail Raymondville z 65555; ● 30
Ashton; RMC Place; CLARK; 197 B-15; elev. 722ft./220m.; mail Luray z 63453; ● 40
Aspenhoff; RMC Place; WARREN; *197 F-16; mail Marthasville z 63357; ● 110
ATCHISON; 196 B-7; Ⓟ 7,457; Ⓒ 6,430; Ⓡ 6,431; ◆ 6,113
Athens; RMC Place; CLARK; *197 A-15; mail Revere z 63465; rural
Atherton; RMC Place; JACKSON; 196 G-7; ★ K.C.; mail Independence z 64050; ● 200
Athol; RMC Place; JACKSON; *196 E-9; mail Kansas City z 64125; pop. incl. with Kansas City (Inc. Place)
Atlanta; Inc. Place; MACON; 197 C-13; elev. 902ft./275m.; 🅿; z 63530; Ⓟ 411; Ⓒ 450
Atlas; RMC Place; JASPER; *196 K-9; ★ JOP; mail Carthage z 64836; ● 130
Auburn; RMC Place; LINCOLN; *197 E-16; mail Elsberry z 63343, Silex z 63377; rural
Aud; RMC Place; OSAGE; *197 G-15; elev. 652ft./199m.; mail Chamois z 65024; rural
AUDRAIN; 197 E-14; Ⓟ 23,599; Ⓒ 25,853; ◆ 25,408
Augusta; Inc. Place; ST. CHARLES; 197 G-17; elev. 520ft./158m.; 🅿; z 63332; Ⓟ 263; Ⓒ 218
Aullville; Inc. Place; LAFAYETTE; 197 F-11; elev. 730ft./223m.; mail Higginsville z 64037; Ⓟ 72; Ⓒ 86
Aurora; Inc. Place; LAWRENCE; 196 K-10; elev. 1,368ft./417m.; 🅿 🅷; z 65605; Ⓟ 6,459; Ⓒ 7,014
Aurora Springs; RMC Place; MILLER; *197 H-13; mail Eldon z 65026; ● 100
Austin; RMC Place; CASS; *196 G-9; 🅿; z 64725; ● 150
Auxvasse; Inc. Place; CALLAWAY; 197 F-15; elev. 870ft./265m.; 🅿; z 65231; Ⓟ 821; Ⓒ 901
Ava; Inc. Place; ⊡ DOUGLAS; 197 K-13; elev. 1,283ft./391m.; 🅿; z 65608; Ⓟ 2,938; Ⓒ 3,021
Avalon; RMC Place; LIVINGSTON; 197 D-11; elev. 860ft./262m.; 🅿; z 64601; ● 70
Avenue City; RMC Place; ANDREW; 196 C-8; elev. 890ft./271m.; ★ ST.JO; mail Saint Joseph z 64505; ● 90
Avert; RMC Place; STODDARD; *197 K-19; mail Bloomfield z 63825; rural
Avery; RMC Place; HICKORY, BENTON; *197 H-11; elev. 842ft./257m.; mail Warsaw z 65355, Wheatland z 65779; rural
Avilla; Inc. Place; JASPER; 196 K-10; elev. 1,117ft./340m.; 🅿; z 64833; Ⓟ 99; Ⓒ 137
Avon; RMC Place; STE. GENEVIEVE; *197 I-18; mail Farmington z 63640; rural
Avondale; Inc. Place; CLAY; 196 H-4; elev. 781ft./238m.; 🅿; ★ K.C.; z 64117; Ⓟ 550; Ⓒ 529
Axtell; RMC Place; MACON; *197 C-13; mail Macon z 63552; rural
Azen; RMC Place; SCOTLAND; *197 A-14; mail Arbela z 63432; rural

B

Babbtown; RMC Place; OSAGE; *197 G-14; elev. 913ft./278m.; mail Meta z 65058, Westphalia z 65085
Bachelor; RMC Place; CALLAWAY; *197 F-15; elev. 822ft./251m.; mail Auxvasse z 65231; rural
Bacon; RMC Place; MONITEAU; *197 F-13; mail Jamestown z 65046; rural
Baden; RMC Place; ST. LOUIS (Independent City); *197 F-18; ★ ST.L; mail Saint Louis z 63147; pop. incl. with Saint Louis (Independent City)
Baderville; RMC Place; NEW MADRID; *197 L-19; elev. 286ft./87m.; mail Lilbourn z 63862; rural
Bado; RMC Place; TEXAS; *197 J-14; mail Cabool z 65689
Bagnell; Inc. Place; MILLER; *197 H-13; elev. 586ft./179m.; mail Eldon z 65026; Ⓟ 89; Ⓒ 86
Bahner; RMC Place; PETTIS; *197 G-12; elev. 893ft./272m.; mail Smithton z 65350; rural
Baker; RMC Place; STODDARD; *197 L-19; elev. 292ft./89m.; mail Essex z 63846; disincorporated since 2000 Census; Ⓟ 8; Ⓒ 5
Bakersfield; Inc. Place; OZARK; 197 L-14; elev. 718ft./219m.; 🅿; z 65609; Ⓟ 292; Ⓒ 285
Bakersville; PEMISCOT; see Bakerville (RMC Place)
Bakerville (Bakersville); RMC Place; PEMISCOT; *197 M-19; mail Bragg City z 63827
Baldwin Lake; CASS; see Baldwin Park (Inc. Place)
Baldwin Park (Baldwin Lake); Inc. Place; CASS; *196 F-9; elev. 890ft./271m.; ★ K.C.; mail Pleasant Hill z 64080; Ⓟ 85; Ⓒ 115
Ballard; RMC Place; BATES; 196 G-10; elev. 926ft./282m.; mail Butler z 64730; ● 80
Ballwin; Inc. Place; ST. LOUIS; 197 G-17; elev. 659ft./201m.; 🅿; ★ ST.L; z 63011, z 63021-22, z 63024; Ⓟ 21,406; Ⓒ 31,283; ◆ 30,258
Bancroft; RMC Place; DAVIESS; *196 C-10; elev. 981ft./299m.; mail Gilman City z 64642; rural
Banner; RMC Place; IRON; *197 I-17; elev. 1,035ft./315m.; mail Belleview z 63623; ● 40
Bannister; RMC Place; CAMDEN; *197 H-12; elev. 769ft./234m.; mail Macks Creek z 65786; rural
Bardley; RMC Place; RIPLEY, OREGON; *197 L-16; mail Doniphan z 63935; rural
Baring; Inc. Place; KNOX; 197 B-14; elev. 820ft./250m.; 🅿; z 63531; Ⓟ 182; Ⓒ 159
Barnard; Inc. Place; NODAWAY; 196 B-8; elev. 940ft./287m.; 🅿; z 64423; Ⓟ 234; Ⓒ 257
Barnesville; RMC Place; MACON; *197 C-13; elev. 896ft./273m.; mail Atlanta z 63530; rural
Barnett; Inc. Place; MORGAN; 197 G-13; elev. 970ft./296m.; 🅿; z 65011; Ⓟ 215; Ⓒ 207
Barnhart; CDP; JEFFERSON; 197 G-18; elev. 550ft./168m.; 🅿; ★ ST.L; z 63012; Ⓟ 4,911; Ⓒ 6,108
Barretts; RMC Place; ST. LOUIS; *197 G-18; ★ ST.L; mail Saint Louis z 63122; ● 150
Barry; RMC Place; CLAY, PLATTE; *196 E-9; elev. 990ft./302m.; ★ K.C.; mail Kansas City z 64155; pop. incl. with Kansas City (Inc. Place)
BARRY; 196 L-10; Ⓟ 27,547; Ⓒ 34,010; ◆ 36,383
Bartlett; RMC Place; SHANNON; *197 K-16; mail Birch Tree z 65438; rural
BARTON; 196 J-9; Ⓟ 11,312; Ⓒ 12,541; ◆ 12,310
Barwick; RMC Place; CALDWELL; *196 D-10; elev. 939ft./286m.; mail Kidder z 64649; rural
Baryties; RMC Place; WASHINGTON; *197 H-17; elev. 700ft./213m.; mail Blackwell z 63626; rural
Bassville; RMC Place; GREENE; *197 J-12; elev. 1,262ft./385m.; ★ SPRG; mail Strafford z 65757; rural
BATES; 196 H-9; Ⓟ 15,025; Ⓒ 16,653; ◆ 16,925
Bates City; Inc. Place; LAFAYETTE; *196 F-10; elev. 880ft./268m.; 🅿; z 64011; Ⓟ 197; Ⓒ 245
Batesville; RMC Place; BUTLER; *197 L-18; elev. 322ft./98m.; mail Broseley z 63932; ● 30
Battlefield; Inc. Place; GREENE; 197 K-11; elev. 1,258ft./383m.; 🅿; ★ SPRG; z 65619; Ⓟ 1,526; Ⓒ 2,385
Baxter; RMC Place; STONE; *197 L-11; mail Lampe z 65681; rural
Bay; RMC Place; GASCONADE; *197 G-15; elev. 572ft./174m.; mail Hermann z 65041; ● 100
Bayshore; RMC Place; JEFFERSON; *197 G-18; ★ ST.L; mail Arnold z 63010; pop. incl. with Arnold (Inc. Place)
Beach; RMC Place; WEBSTER; *197 J-12; elev. 1,250ft./381m.; mail Conway z 65632; rural
Beaman; RMC Place; PETTIS; 197 F-12; elev. 833ft./254m.; mail Smithton z 65350
Bean Lake; PLATTE; see Bean Lake Station (RMC Place)
Bean Lake Station (Bean Lake); RMC Place; PLATTE; 196 D-8; mail Rushville z 64484; ● 100
Bearcreek; RMC Place; CEDAR; *197 I-11; elev. 1,059ft./323m.; mail Fair Play z 65649
Beaufort; RMC Place; FRANKLIN; 197 G-16; elev. 882ft./269m.; 🅿; z 63013; ● 260
Beckville; RMC Place; WAYNE; *197 K-17; mail Piedmont z 63957; pop. incl. with Piedmont (Inc. Place)
Bedford; RMC Place; LIVINGSTON; 197 D-11; mail Hale z 64643; ● 40
Bedison; RMC Place; NODAWAY; *196 B-8; elev. 1,094ft./333m.; mail Conception Junction z 64434; rural
Belews Creek; RMC Place; JEFFERSON; *197 H-17; ★ ST.L; mail Hillsboro z 63050; rural
Belfast; RMC Place; NEWTON; *196 K-9; mail Neosho z 64850; ● 220
Belgique; RMC Place; PERRY; *197 I-19; elev. 372ft./113m.; mail Perryville z 63775
Belgrade; RMC Place; WASHINGTON; 197 I-17; elev. 888ft./271m.; 🅿; z 63622; ● 250
Bellair; RMC Place; COOPER; *197 F-12; elev. 781ft./238m.; mail Bunceton z 65237; rural
Bellamy; RMC Place; VERNON; *196 I-9; elev. 950ft./290m.; mail Sheldon z 64784; rural
Bella Villa; Inc. Place; ST. LOUIS; 195 G-6; elev. 450ft./137m.; ★ ST.L; mail Saint Louis z 63125; Ⓟ 708; Ⓒ 687
Bell City; Inc. Place; STODDARD; 197 K-19; elev. 326ft./99m.; 🅿; z 63735; Ⓟ 469; Ⓒ 461
Belle; Inc. Place; MARIES, OSAGE; 197 H-15; elev. 1,039ft./317m.; 🅿; z 65013; Ⓟ 1,218; Ⓒ 1,344
Belle Center; RMC Place; JASPER; *196 K-9; elev. 956ft./291m.; ★ JOP; mail Joplin z 64801
Bellefontaine; RMC Place; ST. LOUIS; *197 G-17; ★ ST.L; mail Chesterfield z 63017; pop. incl. with Chesterfield (Inc. Place)
Bellefontaine; RMC Place; WASHINGTON; *197 H-17; elev. 791ft./241m.; mail Cadet z 63630; rural
Bellefontaine Neighbors; Inc. Place; ST. LOUIS; 195 C-6; elev. 500ft./152m.; ★ ST.L; mail Saint Louis z 63137; Ⓟ 10,922; Ⓒ 11,271; Ⓡ 11,088
Bellerive; Inc. Place; ST. LOUIS; *197 F-18; elev. 650ft./198m.; ★ ST.L; mail Saint Louis z 63121; Ⓟ 238; Ⓒ 254
Bellerive Estates; RMC Place; ST. LOUIS; *197 G-18; ★ ST.L; mail Saint Louis z 63141; pop. incl. with Town and Country (Inc. Place)
Belleview; RMC Place; IRON; 197 I-17; elev. 1,040ft./317m.; 🅿; z 63623; ● 200
Belleville; RMC Place; JASPER; *196 K-9; ★ JOP; mail Joplin z 64801; ● 100
Bellflower; Inc. Place; MONTGOMERY; 197 F-16; elev. 760ft./232m.; 🅿; z 63333; Ⓟ 413; Ⓒ 427
Bel-Nor; Inc. Place; ST. LOUIS; 195 D-5; elev. 600ft./183m.; ★ ST.L; mail Saint Louis z 63133; Ⓟ 2,935; Ⓒ 1,598
Bel-Ridge; Inc. Place; ST. LOUIS; 195 D-5; elev. 600ft./183m.; ★ ST.L; mail Saint Louis z 63133; Ⓟ 3,199; Ⓒ 3,082
Belton; Inc. Place; CASS; 196 F-9; elev. 1,102ft./336m.; 🅿 🅷; ★ K.C.; z 64012; Ⓟ 18,150; Ⓒ 21,730; ◆ 23,832
Belvidere; RMC Place; JACKSON; *196 F-9; ★ K.C.; mail Grandview z 64030; pop. incl. with Grandview (Inc. Place)
Bem; RMC Place; GASCONADE; *197 H-15; elev. 836ft./255m.; mail Owensville z 65066
Ben Avis; RMC Place; ST. LOUIS; ★ ST.L; mail Saint Louis z 63135; pop. incl. with Ferguson (Inc. Place)
Benbow; RMC Place; MARION; *197 C-15; elev. 700ft./213m.; mail Ewing z 63440; rural
Benbush (Seven Pines); RMC Place; ST. LOUIS; *197 F-18; ★ ST.L; mail Saint Louis z 63141; ● 2,000
Bendavis; RMC Place; TEXAS; *197 J-14; elev. 1,500ft./457m.; 🅿; z 65444; ● 40
Benjamin; RMC Place; LEWIS; *197 B-15; elev. 588ft./179m.; mail Canton z 63435; rural
Bennett Springs; RMC Place; DALLAS, LACLEDE; *197 I-12; mail Lebanon z 65536; ● 100
Benton; Inc. Place; ⊡ SCOTT; 197 K-20; elev. 440ft./134m.; 🅿; z 63736; Ⓟ 575; Ⓒ 732
BENTON; 197 G-11; Ⓟ 13,859; Ⓒ 17,180; ◆ 18,696
Benton City; Inc. Place; AUDRAIN; 197 E-15; elev. 822ft./251m.; 🅿; z 65232; Ⓟ 139; Ⓒ 122
Benton Park; RMC Place; ST. LOUIS (Independent City); *197 G-18; ★ ST.L; mail Saint Louis z 63104; pop. incl. with Saint Louis (Independent City)
Bentonville; RMC Place; BENTON; *197 H-11; elev. 932ft./284m.; mail Warsaw z 65355; rural
Berdell Hills; ST. LOUIS; see Normandy (Inc. Place)
Berger; Inc. Place; FRANKLIN; *197 G-16; elev. 512ft./156m.; 🅿; z 63014; Ⓟ 247; Ⓒ 206
Berkeley; Inc. Place; ST. LOUIS; 195 C-5; elev. 600ft./183m.; 🅿; ★ ST.L; z 63134, z 63140; Ⓟ 12,450; Ⓒ 10,063
Berlin; RMC Place; GENTRY; *196 C-9; elev. 1,006ft./307m.; mail King City z 64463; rural
Bernheimer; RMC Place; WARREN; *197 G-16; elev. 504ft./154m.; mail Marthasville z 63357; rural
Bernie; Inc. Place; STODDARD; 197 L-19; elev. 305ft./93m.; 🅿; z 63822; Ⓟ 1,847; Ⓒ 1,777
Berryman; RMC Place; CRAWFORD; 197 I-16; elev. 750ft./229m.; 🅿; z 65565; rural
Bertrand; Inc. Place; MISSISSIPPI; 197 K-20; elev. 320ft./98m.; 🅿; z 63823; Ⓟ 692; Ⓒ 740
Berwick; RMC Place; NEWTON; *196 K-10; mail Pierce City z 65723; rural
Bessville; RMC Place; BOLLINGER; *197 J-18; elev. 595ft./181m.; mail Marble Hill z 63764; rural
Bethany; Inc. Place; ⊡ HARRISON; 196 B-10; elev. 904ft./276m.; 🅿 🅷; z 64424; Ⓟ 3,005; Ⓒ 3,087
Bethel; Inc. Place; SHELBY; 197 C-14; elev. 739ft./225m.; 🅿; z 63434; Ⓟ 117; Ⓒ 121
Bethpage; RMC Place; MCDONALD; *196 L-9; mail Stella z 64867; rural
Beulah; RMC Place; MADISON; *197 J-18; elev. 548ft./167m.; mail Des Arc z 63636; rural
Beulah; RMC Place; PHELPS; *197 I-14; elev. 1,141ft./348m.; 🅿; z 65436; rural
Beverly; RMC Place; PLATTE; 196 E-8; mail Platte City z 64079; rural
Beverly Hills; Inc. Place; ST. LOUIS; 195 D-6; elev. 640ft./195m.; ★ ST.L; mail Saint Louis z 63121; Ⓟ 660; Ⓒ 603
Bevier; Inc. Place; MACON; 197 D-13; elev. 791ft./241m.; 🅿; z 63532; Ⓟ 643; Ⓒ 723
Bible Grove; RMC Place; SCOTLAND; 197 B-14; mail Baring z 63531; ● 40
Biehle; RMC Place; PERRY; 197 I-19; mail Perryville z 63775; former incorporated place; disincorporated November 6, 2003; Ⓒ 11
Bigelow; Inc. Place; HOLT; 196 B-7; elev. 858ft./262m.; 🅿; z 64437; Ⓟ 32; Ⓒ 38
Big Lake; Inc. Place; HOLT; 196 C-7; mail Craig z 64437; Ⓟ 170; Ⓒ 127
Big Piney; RMC Place; PULASKI; *197 I-14; mail Newburg z 65550
Big Spring; RMC Place; MONTGOMERY; 197 F-15; elev. 553ft./169m.; mail New Florence z 63363; ● 120
Billings; Inc. Place; CHRISTIAN; 197 K-11; elev. 1,359ft./414m.; 🅿; z 65610; Ⓟ 989; Ⓒ 1,091
Billingsville; RMC Place; COOPER; *197 F-13; mail Boonville z 65233; rural
Billman Spur; RMC Place; ST. LOUIS; ★ ST.L; mail Saint Louis z 63123; pop. incl. with Grantwood Village (Inc. Place)
Billmore; RMC Place; OREGON; *197 L-16; mail Couch z 65690; rural
Birch Tree; Inc. Place; SHANNON; 197 K-15; elev. 991ft./302m.; 🅿; z 65438; Ⓟ 599; Ⓒ 634
Birds Corner (Birds Corners); RMC Place; STODDARD; *197 K-19; elev. 305ft./93m.; mail Essex z 63846; rural
Birds Corners; STODDARD; see Birds Corner (RMC Place)
Birds Point; RMC Place; MISSISSIPPI; *197 K-20; mail Charleston z 63834; rural
Bird Springs; RMC Place; OZARK; *197 L-14; mail Dora z 65637; rural
Birmingham; Inc. Place; CLAY; 196 H-5; elev. 735ft./224m.; 🅿; ★ K.C.; z 64161; Ⓟ 222; Ⓒ 214
Bismarck; Inc. Place; ST. FRANCOIS; 197 I-17; elev. 1,023ft./312m.; 🅿; z 63624; Ⓟ 1,579; Ⓒ 1,470
Bixby; RMC Place; IRON; 197 I-16; elev. 1,401ft./427m.; 🅿; z 65439; ● 100
Black; RMC Place; REYNOLDS; 197 J-17; elev. 803ft./245m.; 🅿; z 63625; ● 210
Blackburn; Inc. Place; SALINE; 197 E-11; elev. 805ft./245m.; 🅿; z 65321; Ⓟ 308; Ⓒ 284
Blackjack; RMC Place; ST. CLAIR; *196 I-10; elev. 800ft./244m.; mail Stockton z 65785; rural
Black Jack; Inc. Place; ST. LOUIS; 195 C-6; elev. 596ft./182m.; ★ ST.L; mail Florissant z 63033-34; Ⓟ 6,128; Ⓒ 6,792
Black Walnut; RMC Place; ST. CHARLES; 195 B-5; mail Saint Charles z 63301; rural
Blackwater; Inc. Place; COOPER; *197 F-12; elev. 610ft./186m.; 🅿; z 65322; Ⓟ 221; Ⓒ 199
Blackwell; RMC Place; ST. FRANCOIS; 197 H-17; elev. 588ft./179m.; 🅿; z 63626; ● 80
Blairstown; Inc. Place; HENRY; 196 G-10; elev. 760ft./232m.; 🅿; z 64726; Ⓟ 185; Ⓒ 141
Bland; Inc. Place; GASCONADE, OSAGE; 197 H-15; elev. 1,023ft./312m.; 🅿; z 65014, z 65062; Ⓟ 651; Ⓒ 565
Blendville; RMC Place; JASPER; ★ JOP; mail Joplin z 64801; pop. incl. with Joplin (Inc. Place)
Bliss (Kingston); RMC Place; WASHINGTON; *197 H-17; elev. 643ft./196m.; mail Blackwell z 63626; rural
Blodgett; Inc. Place; SCOTT; 197 K-20; elev. 325ft./99m.; 🅿; z 63824; Ⓟ 202; Ⓒ 265
Blomeyer; RMC Place; CAPE GIRARDEAU; *197 J-19; elev. 336ft./102m.; mail Chaffee z 63740; rural
Bloomfield; Inc. Place; ⊡ STODDARD; 197 K-19; elev. 497ft./151m.; 🅿; z 63825; Ⓟ 1,800; Ⓒ 1,952
Blooming Rose; RMC Place; PHELPS; *197 I-14; mail Beulah z 65436; rural
Bloomington; RMC Place; MACON; *197 C-13; mail Bevier z 63532; rural
Bloomsdale; Inc. Place; STE. GENEVIEVE; 197 H-18; elev. 506ft./154m.; 🅿; z 63627; Ⓟ 353; Ⓒ 419
Blosser; RMC Place; SALINE; *197 E-11; elev. 670ft./204m.; mail Malta Bend z 65339; rural
Blue Branch; RMC Place; BENTON; *197 H-11; mail Warsaw z 65355; ● 265
Blue Eye; Inc. Place; STONE; 197 M-11; elev. 1,300ft./396m.; 🅿; z 65611; Ⓟ 112; Ⓒ 129
Blue Lick; RMC Place; SALINE; *197 F-12; elev. 783ft./239m.; mail Marshall z 65340; rural
Blue Mills; RMC Place; JACKSON; *196 E-9; mail Independence z 64058; rural
Blue Mound; RMC Place; LIVINGSTON; *197 D-11; elev. 985ft./300m.; mail Dawn z 64638; rural
Blue Ridge; RMC Place; HARRISON; 196 B-10; elev. 1,000ft./305m.; mail Bethany z 64424; ● 30
Blue Springs; Inc. Place; JACKSON; 196 F-9; elev. 950ft./290m.; 🅿 🅷 ■; ★ K.C.; z 64013-15, z 64029, z 64064; Ⓟ 40,153; Ⓒ 48,080; ◆ 49,892
Blue Summit; RMC Place; JACKSON; 196 I-5; ★ K.C.; mail Kansas City z 64126; ● 1,200
Blue Vue; RMC Place; JACKSON; ★ K.C.; mail Kansas City z 64133; pop. incl. with Kansas City (Inc. Place)
Bluffton; RMC Place; MONTGOMERY; *197 F-15; elev. 526ft./160m.; mail Rhineland z 65069; rural
Blythedale; Inc. Place; HARRISON; 196 B-10; elev. 1,087ft./331m.; 🅿; z 64426; Ⓟ 130; Ⓒ 233
Boaz; RMC Place; CHRISTIAN; *197 K-11; mail Clever z 65631; ● 100
Boekerton; RMC Place; NEW MADRID; *197 M-19; mail Portageville z 63873; rural
Bogard; Inc. Place; CARROLL; 197 D-11; elev. 860ft./262m.; 🅿; z 64622; Ⓟ 228; Ⓒ 234
Bois D'Arc; RMC Place; GREENE; 197 J-11; elev. 1,203ft./367m.; 🅿; z 65612; ● 500
Bolckow; Inc. Place; ANDREW; 196 C-8; elev. 930ft./283m.; 🅿; z 64427; Ⓟ 253; Ⓒ 234
Boles; RMC Place; FRANKLIN; *197 G-17; ★ ST.L; mail Labadie z 63055; ● 100
Bolivar; Inc. Place; ⊡ POLK; 197 I-11; elev. 1,056ft./322m.; 🅿 🅷 🅲 3,503; z 65613, z 65727; Ⓟ 6,845; Ⓒ 9,143
BOLLINGER; 197 J-18; Ⓟ 10,619; Ⓒ 12,029; ◆ 12,072
Bona; RMC Place; DADE; 197 J-11; elev. 1,053ft./321m.; mail Aldrich z 65601; ● 30
Bonanza; RMC Place; CALDWELL; *196 D-10; mail Kingston z 64650; rural
Bonne Terre; Inc. Place; ST. FRANCOIS; 197 I-17; elev. 830ft./253m.; 🅿 🅷; z 63628; Ⓟ 3,871; Ⓒ 4,039
Bonnots Mill; RMC Place; OSAGE; *197 G-14; elev. 544ft./166m.; 🅿; z 65016; ● 130
BOONE; 197 E-13; Ⓟ 112,379; Ⓒ 135,454; ◆ 164,561
Boonesboro; RMC Place; HOWARD; 197 E-12; mail Franklin z 65250; ● 60
Boonville; Inc. Place; ⊡ COOPER; 197 F-13; elev. 660ft./201m.; 🅿 🅷; z 65233; Ⓟ 7,095; Ⓒ 8,202
Boschertown; RMC Place; ST. CHARLES; *197 F-18; elev. 450ft./137m.; ★ ST.L; mail Saint Charles z 63301; ● 100
Bosky Dell; RMC Place; MCDONALD; *196 L-9; mail Anderson z 64831; pop. incl. with Lanagan (Inc. Place)
Boss; RMC Place; DENT; 197 I-16; elev. 1,069ft./326m.; 🅿; z 65440; ● 100
Boston; RMC Place; BARTON; *196 J-9; mail Lamar z 64759; rural
Bosworth; Inc. Place; CARROLL; 197 D-11; elev. 750ft./229m.; 🅿; z 64623; Ⓟ 334; Ⓒ 382
Boulder City; RMC Place; NEWTON; *196 L-9; mail Granby z 64844
Bourbon; Inc. Place; CRAWFORD; 197 H-16; elev. 932ft./284m.; 🅿; z 65441; Ⓟ 1,188; Ⓒ 1,348
Bowen; RMC Place; HENRY, JOHNSON; *197 G-11; mail Windsor z 65360
Bowers Mill; RMC Place; LAWRENCE; *196 K-10; elev. 1,030ft./314m.; mail La Russell z 64848; rural
Bowling Green; Inc. Place; ⊡ PIKE; 197 E-16; elev. 899ft./274m.; 🅿; z 63334; Ⓟ 2,976; Ⓒ 3,260; Ⓡ 5,166
Bowmansville; RMC Place; JOHNSON; *197 F-11; mail Warrensburg z 64093; ● 250
Boydsville; RMC Place; CALLAWAY; *197 F-14; elev. 847ft./258m.; mail Fulton z 65251; rural
Boyer; RMC Place; WRIGHT; *197 J-13; elev. 1,500ft./457m.; mail Hartville z 65667; rural
Boynton; RMC Place; SULLIVAN; 197 B-12; mail Milan z 63556
Boys Town; RMC Place; PHELPS; *197 H-15; elev. 900ft./274m.; mail Saint James z 65559; ● 200
Bracken; RMC Place; WEBSTER; *197 J-13; elev. 1,350ft./411m.; mail Marshfield z 65706; rural
Bradleyville; Inc. Place; TANEY; 197 L-12; elev. 843ft./257m.; 🅿; z 65614; incorporated August 20, 2002; not reported in 2000 Census; ● 100
Braggadocio; RMC Place; PEMISCOT; 197 M-19; elev. 266ft./81m.; 🅿; z 63826; ● 200
Bragg City; Inc. Place; PEMISCOT; 197 M-19; elev. 255ft./78m.; 🅿; z 63827; Ⓟ 117; Ⓒ 189
Braley; RMC Place; CLINTON; *196 D-9; mail Plattsburg z 64477
Branch; RMC Place; CAMDEN; 197 I-12; elev. 1,105ft./337m.; mail Macks Creek z 65786; ● 200
Brandon; RMC Place; BENTON; *197 G-11; elev. 912ft./278m.; mail Windsor z 65360; rural
Brandsville; Inc. Place; HOWELL; 197 L-15; elev. 949ft./289m.; 🅿; z 65688; Ⓟ 167; Ⓒ 174
Branson; Inc. Place; TANEY; 197 L-12; elev. 722ft./220m.; 🅿 🅷; z 65615-16; Ⓟ 3,706; Ⓒ 6,050
Branson West (Lakeview); Inc. Place; STONE; *197 L-11; elev. 1,362ft./415m.; 🅿; z 65737; Ⓟ 37; Ⓒ 408
Brashear; Inc. Place; ADAIR; 197 B-13; elev. 850ft./259m.; 🅿; z 63533; Ⓟ 318; Ⓒ 280
Brasher; PEMISCOT; see Cottonwood Point (RMC Place)
Braymer; Inc. Place; CALDWELL; 196 D-10; elev. 780ft./238m.; 🅿; z 64624; Ⓟ 886; Ⓒ 910
Brays; RMC Place; MILLER; *197 H-14; mail Iberia z 65486; rural
Brazeau; RMC Place; PERRY; 197 I-19; elev. 550ft./168m.; 🅿; z 63737; ● 90
Brazil; RMC Place; WASHINGTON; *197 I-16; elev. 871ft./265m.; mail Potosi z 63664; rural
Brazito; RMC Place; COLE; 197 G-14; mail Jefferson City z 65101, z 65109; ● 80
Breckenridge; Inc. Place; CALDWELL; 196 D-10; elev. 927ft./283m.; 🅿; z 64625; Ⓟ 418; Ⓒ 454
Breckenridge Hills; Inc. Place; ST. LOUIS; 195 D-5; elev. 600ft./183m.; 🅿; ★ ST.L; z 63114; Ⓟ 5,404; Ⓒ 4,817
Breen Acres; RMC Place; PLATTE; *196 E-9; ★ K.C.; mail Kansas City z 64152; pop. incl. with Kansas City (Inc. Place)
Brentwood; Inc. Place; ST. LOUIS; 195 F-5; elev. 493ft./150m.; 🅿; ★ ST.L; z 63144; Ⓟ 8,150; Ⓒ 7,693
Brewer; RMC Place; PERRY; 197 I-19; mail Perryville z 63775; ● 115
Briar; RMC Place; RIPLEY; 197 L-17; elev. 666ft./203m.; 🅿; z 63931
Bricefield; BARRY; see Pulaskifield (RMC Place)
Brickeys; RMC Place; STE. GENEVIEVE; *197 H-18; mail Bloomsdale z 63627; rural
Bridgeton; Inc. Place; ST. LOUIS; 195 C-4; elev. 550ft./168m.; 🅿 🅷 ■; ★ ST.L; z 63044 & mail Earth City z 63045; Ⓟ 17,779; Ⓒ 15,550; ◆ 14,656
Bridgeton Terrace; RMC Place; ST. LOUIS; *197 F-18; elev. 550ft./168m.; ★ ST.L; mail Bridgeton z 63044; pop. incl. with Bridgeton (Inc. Place)
Brighton; RMC Place; POLK; 197 J-11; elev. 1,179ft./359m.; 🅿; z 65617; ● 220
Brimson; Inc. Place; GRUNDY; 197 B-11; elev. 776ft./237m.; 🅿; z 64642; Ⓟ 72; Ⓒ 63
Brinktown; RMC Place; MARIES; 197 H-14; elev. 1,040ft./317m.; 🅿; z 65443; ● 100
Briscoe; RMC Place; LINCOLN; *197 E-16; mail Troy z 63379
Bristow; RMC Place; VERNON; *196 I-9; elev. 861ft./262m.; mail Nevada z 64772; rural
Brixey; RMC Place; OZARK; 197 L-13; elev. 991ft./302m.; 🅿; z 65618; rural
Broadway; RMC Place; ST. LOUIS (Independent City); *197 G-18; ★ ST.L; mail Saint Louis z 63147; pop. incl. with Saint Louis (Independent City)
Brock; RMC Place; SCOTLAND; *197 A-14; elev. 800ft./244m.; mail Memphis z 63555; rural
Bronaugh; Inc. Place; VERNON; 196 I-9; elev. 900ft./274m.; 🅿; z 64728; Ⓟ 211; Ⓒ 245
Brookdale; RMC Place; ST. LOUIS; *197 F-18; ★ ST.L; mail Saint Louis z 63141; ● 1,750
Brookfield; Inc. Place; LINN; 197 C-12; elev. 767ft./234m.; 🅿 🅷; z 64628; Ⓟ 4,888; Ⓒ 4,769
Brookline (Brookline Station); Inc. Place; GREENE; *197 K-11; elev. 1,286ft./392m.; 🅿; ★ SPRG; z 65619; Ⓟ 283; Ⓒ 326
Brookline Station; GREENE; see Brookline (Inc. Place)
Brooklyn; RMC Place; HARRISON; *196 B-10; elev. 946ft./288m.; mail Ridgeway z 64481
Brooklyn Heights; Inc. Place; JASPER; *196 K-9; elev. 1,000ft./305m.; ★ JOP; mail Carthage z 64836; Ⓟ 116; Ⓒ 125
Brookside; RMC Place; CAPE GIRARDEAU; *197 J-19; mail Jackson z 63755; rural
Broseley; RMC Place; BUTLER; 197 L-18; elev. 320ft./98m.; 🅿; z 63932; ● 200
Brownbranch; RMC Place; TANEY; 197 L-12; elev. 878ft./268m.; mail Ava z 65608; rural
Brownfield; RMC Place; LACLEDE; *197 I-14; mail Richland z 65556; rural

---

Entries in **UPPERCASE** are counties.
Entries in **bold** have populations of 2,500 or more.
Names in parentheses are alternate names.

Inc. Place	Incorporated Place
RMC Place	Rand McNally Designated Place
CDP	Census Designated Place
MCD	Minor Civil Division
⊡	County Seat
▲	Minor Civil Division
elev.	Elevation
🅿	Post Office
🅷	Hospital
🅲	College
■	Principal Business Center
★	Ranally Metro Area (RMA) Abbreviation
z	Zip Code(s)
Ⓟ	Previous Census Population
Ⓡ	Revised Census Population
Ⓐ	Annexation Population
●	Rand McNally Population Estimate
Ⓒ	Final Census Population
Ⓢ	Special Census Population
◆	Estimated Population

For additional definitions see Glossary, Volume 1, and Introduction, Volume 2.

Browning; Inc. Place; LINN, SULLIVAN; 197 C-12; elev. 760ft./232m.; 🅿; z 64630; Ⓟ 331; Ⓒ 317
Brownington; Inc. Place; HENRY; 197 H-11; elev. 721ft./220m.; mail Deepwater z 64740; Ⓟ 84; Ⓒ 119
Browns; RMC Place; BOONE; 197 F-14; ★ COL; mail Columbia z 65202; ● 100
Browns Spring; RMC Place; STONE; *197 K-11; mail Billings z 65610; ● 80
Brownwood; RMC Place; STODDARD; *197 K-19; elev. 353ft./108m.; 🅿; z 63738; ● 200
Brumley; Inc. Place; MILLER; 197 H-13; elev. 751ft./229m.; 🅿; z 65017; Ⓟ 81; Ⓒ 102
Bruner; RMC Place; CHRISTIAN; 197 K-12; elev. 1,468ft./447m.; 🅿; z 65620; ● 100
Brunot; RMC Place; WAYNE; *197 J-17; elev. 515ft./157m.; mail Des Arc z 63636; rural
Brunswick; Inc. Place; CHARITON; 197 D-12; elev. 769ft./234m.; 🅿; z 65236; Ⓟ 1,074; Ⓒ 925
Brush Creek; RMC Place; LACLEDE; *197 I-13; mail Lebanon z 65536; ● 100
Brushyknob; RMC Place; DOUGLAS; *197 K-13; mail Ava z 65608; rural
BUCHANAN; 196 D-8; Ⓟ 83,083; Ⓒ 85,998; ◆ 89,191
Buck Donic; RMC Place; DUNKLIN; *197 N-18; mail Cardwell z 63829; rural
Buckhart; RMC Place; DOUGLAS; *197 K-14; elev. 875ft./267m.; mail Ava z 65608; rural
Buckhorn; RMC Place; MADISON; *197 J-18; elev. 566ft./173m.; mail Marquand z 63655, Waynesville z 65583; rural
Buckhorn; RMC Place; PULASKI; *197 I-14; mail Marquand z 63655, Waynesville z 65583; ● 300
Bucklin; Inc. Place; LINN; 197 C-12; elev. 910ft./277m.; 🅿; z 64631; Ⓟ 616; Ⓒ 524
Buckner; Inc. Place; JACKSON; 196 E-10; elev. 750ft./229m.; 🅿; ★ K.C.; z 64016; Ⓟ 2,873; Ⓒ 2,725
Bucoda; RMC Place; DUNKLIN; *197 N-18; mail Senath z 63876; rural
Bucyrus; RMC Place; TEXAS; 197 J-14; elev. 1,226ft./374m.; 🅿; z 65444; ● 50
Buell; RMC Place; MONTGOMERY; 197 F-15; elev. 740ft./226m.; 🅿; z 63361; ● 70
Buffalo; Inc. Place; ⊡ DALLAS; 197 I-12; elev. 1,200ft./366m.; 🅿; z 65622; Ⓟ 2,414; Ⓒ 2,781
Buffington; RMC Place; STODDARD; *197 L-19; elev. 300ft./91m.; mail Essex z 63846; rural
Bull Creek; Inc. Place; TANEY; *197 L-12; mail Branson z 65616; Ⓟ 156; Ⓒ 225
Bullion; RMC Place; ADAIR; *197 B-13; elev. 951ft./290m.; mail Brashear z 63533, Kirksville z 63501; rural
Bunceton; Inc. Place; COOPER; 197 F-13; elev. 800ft./244m.; 🅿; z 65237; Ⓟ 341; Ⓒ 348
Bunker; Inc. Place; REYNOLDS, DENT; 197 J-16; elev. 1,400ft./427m.; 🅿; z 63629; Ⓟ 390; Ⓒ 427
Bunker Hill; RMC Place; HOWARD; *197 E-13; mail Higbee z 65257; rural
Bunker Hill; RMC Place; SCHUYLER; *197 A-13; elev. 820ft./250m.; mail Downing z 63536; rural
Burbank; RMC Place; WAYNE; *197 K-18; mail Greenville z 63944; rural
Burdett; RMC Place; BATES; *196 G-9; elev. 855ft./261m.; mail Adrian z 64720; rural
Burfordville; RMC Place; CAPE GIRARDEAU; 197 J-19; elev. 389ft./119m.; 🅿; z 63739; ● 80
Burgess; Inc. Place; BARTON; *196 J-9; elev. 893ft./272m.; mail Mindenmines z 64769; Ⓟ 97; Ⓒ 70
Burke City; RMC Place; ST. LOUIS; *197 F-18; ★ ST.L; mail Saint Louis z 63135; pop. incl. with Hazelwood (Inc. Place)
Burksville; RMC Place; SHELBY; *197 C-14; elev. 733ft./223m.; mail Shelbyville z 63469; rural
Burlington Junction; Inc. Place; NODAWAY; 196 B-8; elev. 944ft./288m.; 🅿; z 64428; Ⓟ 634; Ⓒ 632
Burnham; RMC Place; HOWELL; *197 K-14; elev. 1,340ft./408m.; mail Willow Springs z 65793; ● 120
Burns; RMC Place; POLK; *197 I-11; mail Bolivar z 65613; rural
Burr; RMC Place; RIPLEY; *197 M-17; mail Warm Springs z 72478
Burton; RMC Place; HOWARD; *197 E-13; elev. 676ft./206m.; mail Fayette z 65248; rural
Burtville; RMC Place; JOHNSON; *197 G-11; mail Knob Noster z 65336; rural
Butcher; RMC Place; HICKORY; *197 I-11; elev. 307ft./94m.; mail Weaubleau z 65774; rural
Butler; Inc. Place; ⊡ BATES; 196 H-9; elev. 860ft./262m.; 🅿 🄷; z 64730; Ⓟ 4,099; Ⓒ 4,209
BUTLER; 197 L-18; Ⓟ 38,765; Ⓒ 40,867; ◆ 40,749
Butler Hill Estates; RMC Place; ST. LOUIS; *197 G-18; elev. 550ft./168m.; ★ ST.L; mail Saint Louis z 63128; ● 1,500
Butterfield; Inc. Place; BARRY; 196 L-10; elev. 1,520ft./463m.; 🅿; z 65625 & mail Butterfld z 65623; Ⓟ 248; Ⓒ 397
Butts; RMC Place; CRAWFORD; *197 H-16; mail Bourbon z 65441; rural
Byers; RMC Place; JEFFERSON; *197 G-18; mail Arnold z 63010; ● 750
Bynumville; RMC Place; CHARITON; 197 D-13; mail Salisbury z 65281; ● 50
Byrnes Mill; Inc. Place; JEFFERSON; 195 I-2; 🅿; ★ ST.L; z 63025, z 63049, z 63051; Ⓟ 1,578; Ⓒ 2,376
Byron; RMC Place; OSAGE; *197 G-15; mail Belle z 65013; rural

C

Cabanne; RMC Place; ST. LOUIS (Independent City); ★ ST.L; mail Saint Louis z 63112; pop. incl. with Saint Louis (Independent City)
Cabool; Inc. Place; TEXAS; 197 K-14; elev. 1,253ft./382m.; 🅿; z 65689; Ⓟ 2,006; Ⓒ 2,168
Caddo; RMC Place; WEBSTER; *197 J-12; elev. 1,317ft./401m.; mail Marshfield z 65706; rural
Cadet; RMC Place; WASHINGTON; 197 H-17; elev. 803ft./245m.; 🅿; z 63630; ● 150
Cainesville; HARRISON; see Cainsville (Inc. Place)
Cainsville (Cainesville); Inc. Place; HARRISON; 196 B-10; elev. 850ft./259m.; 🅿; z 64632; Ⓟ 387; Ⓒ 370
Cairo; Inc. Place; RANDOLPH; 197 D-13; elev. 864ft./263m.; 🅿; z 65239; Ⓟ 282; Ⓒ 293
CALDWELL; 196 D-10; Ⓟ 8,380; Ⓒ 8,969; ◆ 9,351
Caledonia; Inc. Place; WASHINGTON; 197 I-17; elev. 924ft./282m.; 🅿; z 63631; Ⓟ 142; Ⓒ 158
Calhoun; Inc. Place; HENRY; 197 G-11; elev. 800ft./244m.; 🅿; z 65323; Ⓟ 450; Ⓒ 491
California; Inc. Place; ⊡ MONITEAU; 197 G-13; elev. 874ft./266m.; 🅿; z 65018, z 65042; Ⓟ 3,465; Ⓒ 4,005
Callao; Inc. Place; MACON; 197 D-13; elev. 819ft./250m.; 🅿; z 63534; Ⓟ 332; Ⓒ 291
CALLAWAY; 197 F-14; Ⓟ 32,809; Ⓒ 40,766; ◆ 43,525
Calm; RMC Place; OREGON; *197 L-16; elev. 502ft./153m.; mail Gatewood z 63942; rural
Calumet; RMC Place; PIKE; *197 E-16; mail Clarksville z 63336; rural
Calverton Park; Inc. Place; ST. LOUIS; 195 C-5; elev. 600ft./183m.; ★ ST.L; mail Saint Louis z 63135-36; Ⓟ 1,404; Ⓒ 1,322
Calwood; RMC Place; CALLAWAY; 197 F-15; elev. 815ft./248m.; mail Fulton z 65251; ● 100
Cambridge; RMC Place; SALINE; *197 E-12; mail Gilliam z 65330; rural
Camden; Inc. Place; RAY; 196 E-10; elev. 713ft./217m.; 🅿; z 64017; Ⓟ 238; Ⓒ 209
CAMDEN; 197 I-13; Ⓟ 27,495; Ⓒ 37,051; ◆ 41,146
Camden Point; Inc. Place; PLATTE; 196 D-8; elev. 950ft./290m.; 🅿; z 64018; Ⓟ 373; Ⓒ 484
Camdenton; Inc. Place; ⊡ CAMDEN; 197 H-13; elev. 1,043ft./318m.; 🅿; z 65020; Ⓟ 2,561; Ⓒ 2,779
Cameron; Inc. Place; CLINTON, DEKALB; 196 D-9; elev. 1,036ft./316m.; 🅿 🄷; z 64429; Ⓟ 4,831; Ⓒ 8,312; Ⓡ 9,788
Campbell; Inc. Place; DUNKLIN; 197 L-19; elev. 310ft./94m.; 🅿; z 63933; Ⓟ 2,165; Ⓒ 1,883
Campbellton; RMC Place; FRANKLIN; *197 G-16; mail New Haven z 63068, Washington z 63090; ● 100
Canaan; RMC Place; GASCONADE; 197 H-15; elev. 1,047ft./319m.; mail Bland z 65014; ● 110
Canalou; Inc. Place; NEW MADRID; 197 L-19; elev. 289ft./88m.; 🅿; z 63828; Ⓟ 319; Ⓒ 348
Cane Hill; RMC Place; CEDAR; *196 J-10; mail Dadeville z 65635; ● 80
Caney Creek; RMC Place; SCOTT; *197 K-19; elev. 334ft./102m.; mail Oran z 63771; rural
Cannon Mines; RMC Place; WASHINGTON; *197 H-17; elev. 794ft./242m.; mail Cadet z 63630; ● 85
Canton; Inc. Place; LEWIS; 197 B-15; elev. 485ft./148m.; 🅿 🄲 869; z 63435; Ⓟ 2,623; Ⓒ 2,557
Cantwell; RMC Place; ST. FRANCOIS; *197 I-18; elev. 787ft./240m.; mail Park Hills z 63601; pop. incl. with Desloge (Inc. Place)
Cape Fair; RMC Place; STONE; 197 L-11; elev. 968ft./295m.; 🅿; z 65624; ● 600
Cape Girardeau; Inc. Place; CAPE GIRARDEAU, SCOTT; 197 J-20; elev. 400ft./122m.; 🅿 🄷 🄲 10,477 ■; ★ CPGIR; z 63701-03; Ⓟ 34,438; Ⓒ 35,349; ◆ 37,329
CAPE GIRARDEAU; 197 J-19; Ⓟ 61,633; Ⓒ 68,693; ◆ 74,142
Caplinger Mills; RMC Place; CEDAR; 196 I-10; elev. 800ft./244m.; 🅿; z 65607
Cappeln; RMC Place; ST. CHARLES; *197 F-17; elev. 824ft./251m.; mail Foristell z 63348, New Melle z 63365
Capps; RMC Place; MILLER; *197 H-14; elev. 563ft./172m.; mail Tuscumbia z 65082
Cardwell; Inc. Place; DUNKLIN; 197 N-18; elev. 245ft./75m.; 🅿; z 63829; Ⓟ 792; Ⓒ 789
Carl Junction; Inc. Place; JASPER; 196 K-9; elev. 904ft./276m.; 🅿; ★ JOP; z 64834; Ⓟ 4,123; Ⓒ 5,294
Carlow; RMC Place; DAVIESS; *196 C-10; mail Jamesport z 64648; rural
Carmack; RMC Place; GENTRY; *196 B-9; elev. 910ft./277m.; mail Albany z 64402; rural
Carola; RMC Place; BUTLER; *197 L-18; elev. 318ft./97m.; mail Qulin z 63961; rural
Carondelet; RMC Place; ST. LOUIS (Independent City); *197 G-18; ★ ST.L; mail Saint Louis z 63111; pop. incl. with Saint Louis (Independent City)
Carr; RMC Place; ST. LOUIS; ★ ST.L; mail Florissant z 63031; pop. incl. with Florissant (Inc. Place)
Carrington; RMC Place; CALLAWAY; *197 F-14; mail Fulton z 65251; ● 90
Carr Lane; RMC Place; STONE; *197 M-11; elev. 1,132ft./345m.; mail Berryville z 72616; ● 80
CARROLL; 197 D-11; Ⓟ 10,748; Ⓒ 10,285; ◆ 9,658
Carrollton; Inc. Place; ⊡ CARROLL; 197 E-11; elev. 754ft./230m.; 🅿 🄷; z 64633; Ⓟ 4,406; Ⓒ 4,122
Carsonville; RMC Place; ST. LOUIS; 195 D-5; ★ ST.L; mail Saint Louis z 63121; ● 2,000
CARTER; 197 K-17; Ⓟ 5,515; Ⓒ 5,941; ◆ 5,946
Carterville; Inc. Place; JASPER; 195 L-3; elev. 1,000ft./305m.; 🅿; ★ JOP; z 64835; Ⓟ 2,013; Ⓒ 1,850
Carthage; Inc. Place; ⊡ JASPER; 196 K-9; elev. 1,002ft./305m.; 🅿 🄷; ★ JOP; z 64836; Ⓟ 10,747; Ⓒ 12,668
Caruth; RMC Place; DUNKLIN; 197 M-19; mail Kennett z 63857; ● 100
Caruthersville; Inc. Place; ⊡ PEMISCOT; 197 M-20; elev. 282ft./86m.; 🅿; z 63830; Ⓟ 7,389; Ⓒ 6,760
Carytown; Inc. Place; JASPER; 196 J-9; elev. 938ft./286m.; ★ JOP; mail Carthage z 64836; Ⓟ 149; Ⓒ 217
Cascade; RMC Place; WAYNE; 197 J-18; elev. 528ft./161m.; 🅿; z 63632
Case; RMC Place; WARREN; *197 F-16; mail Hermann z 65041; rural
Cash; RMC Place; MACON; *197 C-13; mail Callao z 63534; rural
CASS; 196 F-9; Ⓟ 63,808; Ⓒ 82,092; ◆ 99,462
Cassidy; RMC Place; CHRISTIAN; *197 K-12; ★ SPRG; mail Nixa z 65714; pop. incl. with Fremont Hills (Inc. Place)
Cassville; Inc. Place; ⊡ BARRY; 196 L-10; elev. 1,324ft./404m.; 🅿 🄷; z 65623, z 65625; Ⓟ 2,371; Ⓒ 2,890
Castle Point; CDP-Census Area Only; ST. LOUIS; *197 F-18; ★ ST.L; mail Saint Louis z 63136; Ⓟ 4,975; Ⓒ 4,559
Castle Rock; RMC Place; JASPER; ★ JOP; mail Joplin z 64801; pop. incl. with Joplin (Inc. Place)
Castlewood; RMC Place; ST. LOUIS; *197 G-17; ★ ST.L; mail Ballwin z 63021; ● 400
Catawba; RMC Place; CALDWELL; *196 D-10; elev. 865ft./264m.; mail Braymer z 64624
Catawissa; RMC Place; FRANKLIN; *197 G-17; elev. 530ft./162m.; 🅿; ★ ST.L; z 63015; ● 240
Catherine Place (Slabtown); RMC Place; MADISON; *197 J-18; mail Fredericktown z 63645; pop. incl. with Fredericktown (Inc. Place)
Cato; RMC Place; BARRY; *197 L-11; elev. 1,219ft./372m.; mail Aurora z 65605; rural
Catron; Inc. Place; NEW MADRID; 197 L-19; elev. 280ft./85m.; 🅿; z 63833; Ⓟ 81; Ⓒ 68
Caulfield; RMC Place; HOWELL; 197 L-14; elev. 1,029ft./314m.; 🅿; z 65626; ● 110
Cave; Inc. Place; LINCOLN; *197 F-16; elev. 543ft./166m.; mail Troy z 63379; Ⓟ 10; Ⓒ 7
Cave Hill; RMC Place; GASCONADE; *197 G-15; elev. 600ft./183m.; mail Hermann z 65041; ● 90
Caverna; RMC Place; MCDONALD; *196 M-9; mail Hiwasse z 72739
Cave Spring; RMC Place; GREENE; *197 J-11; mail Walnut Grove z 65770, Willard z 65781; ● 135
Cawood; RMC Place; ANDREW; *196 C-8; mail Bolckow z 64427; rural
CEDAR; 196 I-10; Ⓟ 12,093; Ⓒ 13,733; ◆ 13,358
Cedar City; RMC Place; CALLAWAY; *197 G-14; elev. 550ft./168m.; 🅿; ★ JFCY; z 65101; pop. incl. with Jefferson City (Inc. Place)
Cedarcreek; RMC Place; TANEY; 197 L-12; elev. 970ft./296m.; 🅿; z 65627; ● 100
Cedar Gap; RMC Place; WRIGHT; *197 K-13; elev. 1,694ft./516m.; mail Seymour z 65746; ● 40
Cedar Hill; CDP; JEFFERSON; 197 G-17; elev. 500ft./152m.; 🅿; ★ ST.L; z 63016; Ⓟ 1,966; Ⓒ 1,703
Cedar Hill Lakes; Inc. Place; JEFFERSON; *197 G-17; elev. 550ft./168m.; ★ ST.L; mail Cedar Hill z 63016; Ⓟ 227; Ⓒ 229
Cedar Ridge; RMC Place; DALLAS; *197 I-12; elev. 1,140ft./347m.; mail Long Lane z 65590; rural
Cedar Springs; RMC Place; CEDAR; 196 I-10; elev. 902ft./275m.; mail El Dorado Springs z 64744; ● 85
Cedar Valley; RMC Place; BUTLER; *197 L-18; elev. 400ft./122m.; mail Poplar Bluff z 63901; ● 50
Cedarville; RMC Place; DADE; *196 J-10; mail Jerico Springs z 64756; rural
Celt; RMC Place; DALLAS; *197 I-12; mail Tunas z 65764; rural
Centaur; RMC Place; ST. LOUIS; *197 G-17; mail Chesterfield z 63005; pop. incl. with Wildwood (Inc. Place)
Center; Inc. Place; RALLS; 197 D-15; elev. 719ft./219m.; 🅿; z 63436; Ⓟ 552; Ⓒ 644
Center Square; RMC Place; JACKSON; *196 E-9; ★ K.C.; mail Kansas City z 64196; pop. incl. with Kansas City (Inc. Place)
Centertown; Inc. Place; COLE; 197 G-13; elev. 848ft./258m.; 🅿; z 65023; Ⓟ 356; Ⓒ 257
Centerview; Inc. Place; JOHNSON; 196 F-10; elev. 870ft./265m.; 🅿; z 64019; Ⓟ 214; Ⓒ 249
Centerville; Inc. Place; ⊡ REYNOLDS; 197 J-17; elev. 742ft./226m.; 🅿; z 63633; Ⓟ 89; Ⓒ 171
Central; RMC Place; JACKSON; *196 E-9; ★ K.C.
Central; RMC Place; MADISON; *197 J-18; elev. 1,070ft./326m.; mail Fredericktown z 63645; rural
Central City; RMC Place; JASPER; *196 K-9; elev. 987ft./301m.; ★ JOP; mail Joplin z 64801; ● 100
Centralia; Inc. Place; BOONE, AUDRAIN; 197 E-14; elev. 891ft./272m.; 🅿; z 65240; Ⓟ 3,414; Ⓒ 3,774
Centropolis; RMC Place; JACKSON; *196 E-9; ★ K.C.; mail Kansas City z 64120, z 64125-26; pop. incl. with Kansas City (Inc. Place)
Chadwick; RMC Place; CHRISTIAN; 197 K-12; elev. 1,378ft./420m.; 🅿; z 65629; ● 190
Chaffee; Inc. Place; SCOTT; 197 K-19; elev. 340ft./104m.; 🅿; ★ CPGIR; z 63740; Ⓟ 3,059; Ⓒ 3,044
Chain of Rocks; Inc. Place; LINCOLN; *197 F-17; elev. 438ft./134m.; mail Old Monroe z 63369; Ⓒ 91
Chain-O-Lakes; Inc. Place; BARRY; *196 L-10; mail Cassville z 65625; Ⓟ 111; Ⓒ 127
Chambersburg; RMC Place; CLARK; *197 A-15; mail Kahoka z 63445; rural
Chamois; Inc. Place; OSAGE; 197 G-15; elev. 530ft./162m.; 🅿; z 65024; Ⓟ 449; Ⓒ 456
Champ; Inc. Place; ST. LOUIS; 195 D-4; elev. 607ft./185m.; ★ ST.L; mail Hazelwood z 63042; Ⓟ 11; Ⓒ 12
Champion; RMC Place; DOUGLAS; *197 K-13; elev. 892ft./272m.; mail Norwood z 65717; rural
Champion City; RMC Place; FRANKLIN; *197 H-16; elev. 752ft./229m.; mail Leslie z 63056; rural
Chandler; RMC Place; CLAY; *196 E-9; ★ K.C.; mail Kearney z 64060; rural
Chapel Hill; RMC Place; LAFAYETTE; *196 F-10; mail Bates City z 64011; rural
Chariton; RMC Place; PUTNAM; *197 A-13; mail Unionville z 63565; rural
CHARITON; 197 D-12; Ⓟ 9,202; Ⓒ 8,438; ◆ 7,573
Charity; RMC Place; DALLAS; 197 J-12; elev. 1,188ft./362m.; mail Elkland z 65644; ● 120
Charlack; Inc. Place; ST. LOUIS; 195 D-5; elev. 650ft./198m.; ★ ST.L; mail Saint Louis z 63114; Ⓟ 1,388; Ⓒ 1,431
Charles Nagel; RMC Place; ST. LOUIS (Independent City); *197 F-18; ★ ST.L; mail Saint Louis z 63115; pop. incl. with Saint Louis (Independent City)
Charleston; Inc. Place; ⊡ MISSISSIPPI; 197 K-20; elev. 327ft./100m.; 🅿; z 63834; Ⓟ 5,085; Ⓒ 4,732
Charter Oak; RMC Place; STODDARD; *197 L-19; elev. 291ft./89m.; mail Catron z 63833; ● 30
Cheltenham; RMC Place; ST. LOUIS (Independent City); pop. incl. with Saint Louis (Independent City)
Cherokee Pass; RMC Place; MADISON; *197 J-18; elev. 978ft./298m.; mail Fredericktown z 63645; ● 300
Cherry Box; RMC Place; SHELBY; *197 C-14; elev. 832ft./254m.; mail Clarence z 63437, Leonard z 63451
Cherry Valley Estates; RMC Place; GREENE; *197 K-12; ★ SPRG; mail Springfield z 65804; ● 200
Cherryville; RMC Place; CRAWFORD; 197 I-16; elev. 1,020ft./311m.; 🅿; z 65446; ● 135
Chesapeake; RMC Place; LAWRENCE; 197 K-11; mail Mount Vernon z 65712; ● 100
Chesterfield; Inc. Place; ST. LOUIS; 197 G-17; elev. 462ft./141m.; 🅿 🄷 🄲 1,098; ★ ST.L; z 63005-06, z 63017; Ⓟ 38,630; Ⓒ 46,802; ◆ 46,238
Chestnutridge; RMC Place; CHRISTIAN; *197 L-12; elev. 1,320ft./402m.; 🅿; z 65630; ● 150
Chicopee; RMC Place; CARTER; 197 K-16; mail Van Buren z 63965; ● 60
Chilhowee; Inc. Place; JOHNSON; 196 G-10; elev. 885ft./270m.; 🅿; z 64733; Ⓟ 335; Ⓒ 329
Chillicothe; Inc. Place; ⊡ LIVINGSTON; 197 C-11; elev. 798ft./243m.; 🅿 🄷; z 64601; Ⓟ 8,804; Ⓒ 8,968
Chilton; RMC Place; CARTER; *197 K-17; elev. 433ft./132m.; mail Van Buren z 63965; ● 30
Chitwood; RMC Place; JASPER; *196 K-9; ★ JOP; mail Joplin z 64801; pop. incl. with Joplin (Inc. Place)
Chouteau; RMC Place; ST. LOUIS (Independent City); *197 G-18; ★ ST.L; mail Saint Louis z 63110; pop. incl. with Saint Louis (Independent City)
CHRISTIAN; 197 K-12; Ⓟ 32,644; Ⓒ 54,285; ◆ 77,875
Christian Center; RMC Place; CHRISTIAN; *197 K-12; elev. 1,390ft./424m.; mail Ozark z 65721; rural
Chula; Inc. Place; LIVINGSTON; 197 C-11; elev. 800ft./244m.; 🅿; z 64635; Ⓟ 183; Ⓒ 198
Circle City; RMC Place; STODDARD; *197 K-19; mail Essex z 63846; ● 155
Civic Center; RMC Place; JACKSON; *196 E-9; ★ K.C.; mail Kansas City z 64106; pop. incl. with Kansas City (Inc. Place)
Civil Bend; RMC Place; DAVIESS; *196 C-10; elev. 867ft./264m.; mail Pattonsburg z 64670; rural
Clapper; RMC Place; MONROE; *197 D-15; elev. 754ft./230m.; mail Monroe City z 63456; rural
Clara; RMC Place; TEXAS; *197 J-14; elev. 1,271ft./387m.; mail Houston z 65483; rural
Clarence; Inc. Place; SHELBY; 197 D-14; elev. 820ft./250m.; 🅿; z 63437; Ⓟ 1,026; Ⓒ 915
Clark; Inc. Place; RANDOLPH; 197 E-13; elev. 867ft./264m.; 🅿; z 65243; Ⓟ 257; Ⓒ 275
CLARK; 197 B-15; Ⓟ 7,547; Ⓒ 7,416; ◆ 7,240
Clark City; RMC Place; CLARK; *197 B-15; elev. 691ft./211m.; mail Kahoka z 63445; rural
Clarksburg; Inc. Place; MONITEAU; 197 G-13; elev. 897ft./273m.; 🅿; z 65025; Ⓟ 358; Ⓒ 375
Clarksdale; Inc. Place; DEKALB; 196 C-9; elev. 900ft./274m.; 🅿; z 64430; Ⓟ 287; Ⓒ 351
Clarkson Valley; Inc. Place; ST. LOUIS; 195 F-2; elev. 640ft./195m.; ★ ST.L; mail Chesterfield z 63005, z 63017; Ⓟ 2,508; Ⓒ 2,675
Clarksville; Inc. Place; PIKE; 197 E-17; elev. 461ft./141m.; 🅿; z 63336; Ⓟ 480; Ⓒ 490
Clarkton; Inc. Place; DUNKLIN; 197 M-19; elev. 280ft./85m.; 🅿; z 63837; Ⓟ 1,113; Ⓒ 1,330
Claryville; RMC Place; PERRY; *197 I-19; mail Perryville z 63775; rural
CLAY; 196 E-9; Ⓟ 153,411; Ⓒ 184,006; ◆ 221,100
Claycomo; Inc. Place; CLAY; 196 G-4; elev. 800ft./244m.; ★ K.C.; mail Kansas City z 64119; Ⓟ 1,668; Ⓒ 1,267
Claysville; RMC Place; BOONE; *197 G-14; elev. 558ft./170m.; mail Hartsburg z 65039; rural
Clayton; Inc. Place; ⊡ ST. LOUIS; 197 G-18; elev. 550ft./168m.; 🅿 ■; ★ ST.L; z 63105, z 63124; Ⓟ 13,874; Ⓒ 12,825; Ⓡ 15,935; ◆ 16,030
Clear Creek; RMC Place; COOPER; *197 F-12; elev. 800ft./244m.; mail Pilot Grove z 65276; rural
Clearmont; Inc. Place; NODAWAY; 196 A-8; elev. 963ft./294m.; 🅿; z 64431; Ⓟ 175; Ⓒ 191
Clear Spring; RMC Place; CARTER; *197 K-16; elev. 556ft./169m.; mail Van Buren z 63965; rural
Clear Springs; RMC Place; TEXAS; *197 K-15; mail Willow Springs z 65793; rural
Clearwater; RMC Place; STE. GENEVIEVE; *197 I-18; elev. 528ft./161m.; mail Sainte Genevieve z 63670; rural
Cleavesville; RMC Place; GASCONADE; *197 H-15; elev. 901ft./275m.; mail Bland z 65014; rural
Clementine; RMC Place; PHELPS; *197 I-14; elev. 1,000ft./305m.; mail Newburg z 65550; rural
Cleveland; Inc. Place; CASS; 196 F-9; elev. 980ft./299m.; 🅿; z 64734; Ⓟ 506; Ⓒ 592
Clever; Inc. Place; CHRISTIAN; 197 K-11; elev. 1,398ft./426m.; 🅿; z 65631; Ⓟ 580; Ⓒ 1,010
Cliff Village; Inc. Place; NEWTON; *196 K-9; elev. 900ft./274m.; ★ JOP; mail Joplin z 64804; Ⓟ 19; Ⓒ 33
Clifton City; RMC Place; COOPER; 197 F-12; elev. 763ft./233m.; mail Otterville z 65348
Clifton Hill; Inc. Place; RANDOLPH; 197 D-13; elev. 722ft./220m.; 🅿; z 65244; Ⓟ 108; Ⓒ 124
Climax Springs; Inc. Place; CAMDEN; 197 H-12; elev. 966ft./294m.; 🅿; z 65324; Ⓟ 91; Ⓒ 80
Clines Island; RMC Place; STODDARD; *197 K-19; elev. 312ft./95m.; mail Essex z 63846; rural
Clinton; Inc. Place; ⊡ HENRY; 196 G-10; elev. 803ft./245m.; 🅿 🄷; z 64735; Ⓟ 8,703; Ⓒ 9,311
CLINTON; 196 D-9; Ⓟ 16,595; Ⓒ 18,979; ◆ 21,871
Cliquot; RMC Place; POLK; *197 I-11; mail Dunnegan z 65640; ● 100
Clover Bottom; RMC Place; FRANKLIN; *197 G-16; mail Washington z 63090
Cloverdale; RMC Place; DALLAS; *197 I-12; elev. 1,174ft./358m.; mail Buffalo z 65622; rural
Clubb; RMC Place; WAYNE; 197 K-18; elev. 546ft./166m.; 🅿; z 63934; rural
Clyde; Inc. Place; NODAWAY; 196 B-9; elev. 986ft./301m.; 🅿; z 64432; Ⓟ 71; Ⓒ 74
Coal; RMC Place; HENRY; 197 G-11; mail Clinton z 64735
Coal Hill; RMC Place; CEDAR; *196 I-10; elev. 950ft./290m.; mail El Dorado Springs z 64744; rural
Coatsville; RMC Place; SCHUYLER; 197 A-13; elev. 950ft./290m.; 🅿; z 63535
Cobalt; MADISON; see Cobalt Village (Inc. Place)
Cobalt City; MADISON; see Cobalt Village (Inc. Place)
Cobalt Village (Cobalt, Cobalt City); Inc. Place; MADISON; 197 J-18; elev. 800ft./244m.; mail Fredericktown z 63645; Ⓟ 254; Ⓒ 189
Cobbler; RMC Place; JACKSON; *196 E-9; mail Independence z 64058; rural
Cody; RMC Place; GREENE; *197 K-12; elev. 1,428ft./435m.; ★ SPRG; mail Rogersville z 65742; rural
Coffey (Salem); Inc. Place; DAVIESS; 196 C-10; elev. 933ft./284m.; 🅿; z 64636; Ⓟ 131; Ⓒ 140
Coffeyton; RMC Place; CRAWFORD; *197 H-16; elev. 1,021ft./311m.; mail Bourbon z 65441; ● 150
Coffman; RMC Place; STE. GENEVIEVE; 197 I-18; mail Sainte Genevieve z 63670; ● 80
Coldspring; RMC Place; DOUGLAS; *197 K-13; mail Norwood z 65717; rural
Cold Springs; RMC Place; BENTON; *197 H-11; mail Warsaw z 65355; ● 135
Coldwater; RMC Place; WAYNE; 197 J-18; elev. 502ft./153m.; mail Silva z 63964
COLE; 197 G-13; Ⓟ 63,579; Ⓒ 71,397; ◆ 74,214
Cole Camp; Inc. Place; BENTON; 197 G-12; elev. 1,018ft./310m.; 🅿; z 65325; Ⓟ 1,054; Ⓒ 1,028
Coleman; RMC Place; CASS; *196 F-9; elev. 1,017ft./310m.; mail Peculiar z 64078; rural
College Mound; RMC Place; MACON; 197 D-13; elev. 844ft./257m.; mail Excello z 65247; ● 50
Collins; Inc. Place; ST. CLAIR; 197 I-11; elev. 851ft./259m.; 🅿; z 64738; Ⓟ 144; Ⓒ 176
Coloma; RMC Place; CARROLL; 197 D-11; mail Bogard z 64622; ● 30
Colony; RMC Place; KNOX; 197 B-14; mail Baring z 63531, Rutledge z 63563; ● 30
Columbia; Inc. Place; ⊡ BOONE; 197 F-14; elev. 758ft./231m.; 🅿 🄷 🄲 30,254 ■; ★ COL; z 65201-03, z 65205, z 65211-12, z 65215-18, z 65299; Ⓟ 69,101; Ⓒ 84,531; ◆ 108,823
Columbus; RMC Place; JOHNSON; *196 F-10; mail Centerview z 64019; ● 100
Comet; RMC Place; DADE; *197 J-11; elev. 950ft./290m.; mail Everton z 65646, Walnut Grove z 65770; rural
Commerce; Inc. Place; SCOTT; 197 K-20; elev. 330ft./101m.; 🅿; z 63742; Ⓟ 173; Ⓒ 110
Commerce Tower; RMC Place; JACKSON; *196 E-9; ★ K.C.; mail Kansas City z 64199; pop. incl. with Kansas City (Inc. Place)
Commercial; RMC Place; GREENE; *197 K-11; ★ SPRG; mail Springfield z 65803; pop. incl. with Springfield (Inc. Place)
Competition; RMC Place; LACLEDE; 197 J-13; mail Falcon z 65470
Conception; RMC Place; NODAWAY; *196 B-9; elev. 1,106ft./337m.; 🅿; z 64433; ● 150
Conception Junction; Inc. Place; NODAWAY; 196 B-9; elev. 1,001ft./305m.; 🅿; z 64434; Ⓟ 236; Ⓒ 202
Conclay; RMC Place; ST. LOUIS; *197 G-18; elev. 540ft./165m.; ★ ST.L; mail Saint Louis z 63124; pop. incl. with Ladue (Inc. Place)
Concord; RMC Place; CALLAWAY; *197 F-14; elev. 910ft./277m.; mail Auxvasse z 65231; rural
Concord; CDP; ST. LOUIS; 195 G-5; ★ ST.L; mail Saint Louis z 63128; Ⓟ 19,859; Ⓒ 16,689
Concord Hill; RMC Place; WARREN; *197 G-16; mail Marthasville z 63357; ● 85
Concordia; Inc. Place; LAFAYETTE; 197 F-11; elev. 787ft./240m.; 🅿; z 64020; Ⓟ 2,160; Ⓒ 2,360
Coney Island; Inc. Place; STONE; *197 L-11; mail Kimberling City z 65686; Ⓒ 94
Connelsville; RMC Place; ADAIR; 197 B-13; elev. 778ft./237m.; mail Novinger z 63559; ● 120
Conran; RMC Place; NEW MADRID; *197 L-20; elev. 286ft./87m.; 🅿; z 63873; ● 100
Converse; RMC Place; CLINTON; *196 D-9; mail Lathrop z 64465; rural
Conway; Inc. Place; LACLEDE; 197 J-12; elev. 1,404ft./428m.; 🅿; z 65632; Ⓟ 629; Ⓒ 743
Cook Station; RMC Place; CRAWFORD; 197 I-15; elev. 892ft./272m.; mail Cook Sta z 65449
Cool Valley; Inc. Place; ST. LOUIS; 195 D-6; elev. 550ft./168m.; ★ ST.L; mail Saint Louis z 63135; Ⓟ 1,407; Ⓒ 1,081
COOPER; 197 F-12; Ⓟ 14,835; Ⓒ 16,670; ◆ 17,777
Cooper Chapel; HOWARD; see Petersburg (RMC Place)
Cooper Hill; RMC Place; OSAGE; *197 G-15; elev. 561ft./171m.; mail Bland z 65014; ● 60
Cooter; Inc. Place; PEMISCOT; 197 N-19; elev. 260ft./79m.; 🅿; z 63839; Ⓟ 451; Ⓒ 440
Cora; RMC Place; SULLIVAN; *197 C-12; mail Milan z 63556
Corder; Inc. Place; LAFAYETTE; 197 E-11; elev. 860ft./262m.; 🅿; z 64021; Ⓟ 485; Ⓒ 427
Cornelia; RMC Place; JOHNSON; *196 G-10; elev. 886ft./270m.; mail Warrensburg z 64093
Corning; Inc. Place; HOLT; 196 B-7; elev. 875ft./267m.; 🅿; z 64437; Ⓟ 88; Ⓒ 21
Cornwall; RMC Place; MADISON; *197 J-18; mail Fredericktown z 63645; ● 50
Corridon; RMC Place; REYNOLDS; 197 J-16; mail Centerville z 63633; ● 50
Corry; RMC Place; DADE; *196 J-10; mail Dadeville z 65635; rural
Corsicana; RMC Place; BARRY; *196 L-10; elev. 1,290ft./393m.; mail Purdy z 65734; rural
Corso; RMC Place; LINCOLN; *197 E-16; elev. 692ft./211m.; mail Silex z 63377; rural
Corticelli; RMC Place; MONITEAU; *197 G-13; elev. 922ft./281m.; mail Russellville z 65074; rural
Cosby; Inc. Place; ANDREW; 196 C-9; elev. 953ft./290m.; 🅿; z 64436; Ⓟ 121; Ⓒ 143
Cossville; RMC Place; JASPER; *196 J-9; mail Oronogo z 64855; rural
Cottage Farm; RMC Place; JEFFERSON; *197 H-17; mail Hillsboro z 63050; rural
Cottleville; Inc. Place; ST. CHARLES; 195 D-1; elev. 517ft./158m.; 🅿; ★ ST.L; z 63304, z 63338, z 63366, z 63376; Ⓟ 2,936; Ⓒ 1,928
Cotton Plant; RMC Place; DUNKLIN; *197 N-19; mail Hornersville z 63855; rural
Cottonwood Point (Brasher); RMC Place; PEMISCOT; *197 N-19; elev. 264ft./80m.; mail Caruthersville z 63830; ● 30
Couch; RMC Place; OREGON; 197 L-16; elev. 641ft./195m.; 🅿; z 65690; ● 80
Country Club; ANDREW; see Country Club Village (Inc. Place)
Country Club; RMC Place; JACKSON; *196 F-9; ★ K.C.; mail Kansas City z 64113; pop. incl. with Kansas City (Inc. Place)
Country Club Hills; Inc. Place; ST. LOUIS; 195 D-6; elev. 600ft./183m.; ★ ST.L; mail Saint Louis z 63136; Ⓟ 1,316; Ⓒ 1,381
Country Club Village (Country Club); Inc. Place; ANDREW; 196 C-8; elev. 1,060ft./323m.; ★ ST.JO; mail Saint Joseph z 64505; Ⓟ 1,755; Ⓒ 1,846
Country Life Acres; Inc. Place; ST. LOUIS; 195 E-4; elev. 670ft./204m.; ★ ST.L; mail Saint Louis z 63131; Ⓟ 101; Ⓒ 81
Countryside; RMC Place; PLATTE; ★ K.C.; mail Kansas City z 64152; pop. incl. with Kansas City (Inc. Place)
Courtney; RMC Place; JACKSON; *196 E-9; ★ K.C.; mail Independence z 64050; pop. incl. with Sugar Creek (Inc. Place)
Courtois; RMC Place; WASHINGTON; 197 I-16; elev. 900ft./274m.; 🅿; z 65565; rural
Cowgill; Inc. Place; CALDWELL; 196 D-10; elev. 960ft./293m.; 🅿; z 64637; Ⓟ 257; Ⓒ 247
Coy; RMC Place; MCDONALD; *196 L-9; elev. 943ft./287m.; mail Anderson z 64831; ● 120
Crabbs (Peawee); RMC Place; WEBSTER; *197 K-13; elev. 1,633ft./498m.; mail Seymour z 65746; rural
Craig; Inc. Place; HOLT; 196 B-7; elev. 868ft./265m.; 🅿; z 64437; Ⓟ 346; Ⓒ 309
Crane; Inc. Place; STONE; 197 K-11; elev. 1,122ft./342m.; 🅿; z 65633; Ⓟ 1,218; Ⓒ 1,390
Crawford; RMC Place; SCOTLAND; *197 B-14; elev. 720ft./219m.; mail Memphis z 63555; rural
CRAWFORD; 197 I-16; Ⓟ 19,173; Ⓒ 22,804; ◆ 24,360
Creighton; Inc. Place; CASS; 196 G-10; elev. 800ft./244m.; 🅿; z 64739; Ⓟ 289; Ⓒ 322
Crescent; RMC Place; ST. LOUIS; 195 G-2; elev. 500ft./152m.; 🅿; ★ ST.L; z 63025; ● 200
Crescent Hill; RMC Place; BATES; *196 G-9; elev. 900ft./274m.; mail Adrian z 64720; ● 115
Crescent Lake; RMC Place; CLAY; *196 E-9; ★ K.C.; mail Excelsior Springs z 64024; pop. incl. with Excelsior Springs (Inc. Place)
Crestwood; Inc. Place; ST. LOUIS; 195 F-5; elev. 621ft./189m.; ■; ★ ST.L; mail Saint Louis z 63126; Ⓟ 11,234; Ⓒ 11,863; ◆ 11,271
Cretcher; RMC Place; SALINE; *197 F-11; elev. 794ft./242m.; mail Sweet Springs z 65351; rural
Creve Coeur; Inc. Place; ST. LOUIS; 197 F-18; elev. 644ft./196m.; 🅿 ■; ★ ST.L; z 63141; Ⓟ 12,304; Ⓒ 16,500; Ⓡ 16,759; ◆ 16,381
Crider; RMC Place; HOWELL; *197 L-14; elev. 1,096ft./334m.; mail Pottersville z 65790; rural
Crites Corner; RMC Place; CARTER; *197 K-17; elev. 886ft./270m.; mail Ellsinore z 63937; ● 30
Crocker; Inc. Place; PULASKI; 197 I-14; elev. 1,124ft./343m.; 🅿; z 65452; Ⓟ 1,077; Ⓒ 1,033
Crockerville; RMC Place; BENTON; *197 G-12; elev. 1,024ft./312m.; mail Cole Camp z 65325; rural
Cross Keys; RMC Place; ST. LOUIS; *197 F-18; ★ ST.L; mail Florissant z 63033; pop. incl. with Florissant (Inc. Place)
Cross Roads; RMC Place; DOUGLAS; *197 L-12; elev. 1,239ft./378m.; mail Ava z 65608; rural
Cross Roads; RMC Place; OZARK; *197 L-14; mail Dora z 65637; rural
Cross Timbers; Inc. Place; HICKORY; 197 H-12; elev. 1,030ft./314m.; 🅿; z 65634; Ⓟ 168; Ⓒ 185
Crosstown; RMC Place; PERRY; *197 I-19; elev. 570ft./174m.; mail Perryville z 63775; ● 100
Cross Way; RMC Place; WEBSTER; *197 J-12; elev. 1,348ft./411m.; mail Marshfield z 65706; rural
Crowder; RMC Place; SCOTT; *197 K-19; mail Sikeston z 63801; ● 100
Crown; RMC Place; WEBSTER; *197 J-12; elev. 1,308ft./399m.; mail Marshfield z 65706; ● 100
Cruise Mill; RMC Place; WASHINGTON; *197 H-17; mail Blackwell z 63626; rural
Crump; RMC Place; CAPE GIRARDEAU; *197 J-19; elev. 388ft./118m.; mail Whitewater z 63785; ● 100
Crystal City; Inc. Place; JEFFERSON; 197 H-18; elev. 432ft./132m.; 🅿 🄷; ★ ST.L; z 63019; Ⓟ 4,088; Ⓒ 4,247
Crystal Lake Park; Inc. Place; ST. LOUIS; 195 E-4; elev. 600ft./183m.; ★ ST.L; mail Saint Louis z 63131; Ⓟ 506; Ⓒ 457
Crystal Lakes; Inc. Place; RAY; *196 E-10; 🅿; ★ K.C.; z 64024; Ⓟ 255; Ⓒ 383
Cuba; Inc. Place; CRAWFORD; 197 H-16; elev. 1,015ft./309m.; 🅿; z 65453; Ⓟ 2,537; Ⓒ 3,230
Cunningham; RMC Place; CHARITON; *197 D-12; mail Sumner z 64681; ● 30
Cunningham; RMC Place; PEMISCOT; *197 M-19; elev. 267ft./81m.; mail Hayti z 63851; rural
Curdton; RMC Place; STODDARD; *197 K-19; mail Puxico z 63960; rural
Cureall; RMC Place; HOWELL; *197 L-14; elev. 943ft./287m.; mail Pottersville z 65790; rural
Current View; RMC Place; RIPLEY; 197 M-17; elev. 328ft./100m.; mail Doniphan z 63935; ● 85
Curryville; Inc. Place; PIKE; 197 E-16; elev. 816ft./249m.; 🅿; z 63339; Ⓟ 261; Ⓒ 251
Custer; RMC Place; DENT; *197 J-15; elev. 1,250ft./381m.; mail Salem z 65560; rural
Cyclone; RMC Place; MCDONALD; *196 L-9; mail Pineville z 64856; rural
Cyrene; RMC Place; PIKE; 197 E-16; elev. 859ft./262m.; mail Bowling Green z 63334; ● 90

D

DADE; 196 J-10; Ⓟ 7,449; Ⓒ 7,923; ◆ 7,311
Dadeville; Inc. Place; DADE; 197 J-11; elev. 1,080ft./329m.; 🅿; z 65635; Ⓟ 220; Ⓒ 224
Daisy; RMC Place; CAPE GIRARDEAU; 197 J-19; elev. 600ft./183m.; 🅿; z 63743
DALLAS; 197 I-12; Ⓟ 12,646; Ⓒ 15,661; ◆ 17,481
Dalton; Inc. Place; CHARITON; 197 E-12; elev. 725ft./221m.; 🅿; z 65246; Ⓟ 38; Ⓒ 27
Damascus; RMC Place; ST. CLAIR; *197 H-11; elev. 856ft./261m.; mail Osceola z 64776; rural
Dameron; RMC Place; LINCOLN; *197 E-17; mail Elsberry z 63343; rural
Damsel; RMC Place; CAMDEN; *197 H-13; elev. 840ft./256m.; mail Osage Beach z 65065; pop. incl. with Osage Beach (Inc. Place)
Danby; RMC Place; JEFFERSON; 197 H-18; mail Bloomsdale z 63627; ● 60
Danforth; RMC Place; ADAIR; *197 B-13; elev. 800ft./244m.; mail Novinger z 63559; rural
Danville; RMC Place; MONTGOMERY; 197 F-15; elev. 817ft./249m.; 🅿; z 63361; ● 60
Dardenne; RMC Place; ST. CHARLES; *197 F-17; elev. 617ft./188m.; ★ ST.L; mail O Fallon z 63366; pop. incl. with Dardenne Prairie (Inc. Place)
Dardenne Prairie; Inc. Place; ST. CHARLES; *197 F-17; 🅿; ★ ST.L; z 63366, z 63368; Ⓟ 1,769; Ⓒ 4,384
Darien; RMC Place; DENT; *197 J-15; elev. 1,360ft./415m.; mail Salem z 65560; rural
Darksville; RMC Place; RANDOLPH; *197 D-13; mail Huntsville z 65259
Darlington; Inc. Place; GENTRY; 196 B-9; elev. 836ft./255m.; 🅿; z 64438; Ⓟ 76; Ⓒ 113
Daugherty (Eight Mile); RMC Place; CASS; 196 G-9; elev. 882ft./269m.; mail Harrisonville z 64701; ● 130
DAVIESS; 196 C-10; Ⓟ 7,865; Ⓒ 8,016; ◆ 7,736
Davis; RMC Place; LINCOLN; 197 E-16; mail Troy z 63379; ● 100
Davis; RMC Place; ST. FRANCOIS; *197 I-17; elev. 1,010ft./308m.; mail Park Hills z 63601; rural
Davisville; RMC Place; CRAWFORD; 197 I-16; elev. 1,020ft./311m.; 🅿; z 65456; rural
Dawn; RMC Place; LIVINGSTON; 197 D-11; elev. 765ft./233m.; 🅿; z 64638; ● 130
Dawson; NODAWAY; see Dawsonville (RMC Place)
Dawson; RMC Place; WRIGHT; 197 J-14; mail Mountain Grove z 65711; ● 40
Dawsonville (Dawson); RMC Place; NODAWAY; *196 B-8; elev. 929ft./283m.; mail Burlington Junction z 64428; rural
Dawt; RMC Place; OZARK; *197 L-14; mail Tecumseh z 65760; ● 80
Dayton; RMC Place; CASS; 196 G-9; mail Garden City z 64747; ● 120
Daytown; RMC Place; ST. FRANCOIS; *197 I-17; elev. 746ft./227m.; mail Leadwood z 63653; pop. incl. with Leadwood (Inc. Place)
Dean; RMC Place; ANDREW; mail Saint Joseph z 64505; ● 200
Dean Lake; CHARITON; see Snyder (RMC Place)
Dearborn; Inc. Place; PLATTE, BUCHANAN; 196 D-8; elev. 950ft./290m.; 🅿; z 64439; Ⓟ 480; Ⓒ 529
Decaturville; RMC Place; CAMDEN; *197 I-13; elev. 1,052ft./321m.; mail Lebanon z 65536
Deckard-Y; RMC Place; OREGON; *197 L-16; elev. 640ft./195m.; mail Couch z 65690, Myrtle z 65778; ● 100
Dederick; RMC Place; VERNON; 196 I-10; mail El Dorado Springs z 64744; ● 30
Deepwater; Inc. Place; HENRY; 196 H-10; elev. 750ft./229m.; 🅿; z 64740; Ⓟ 441; Ⓒ 507
Deer; RMC Place; OSAGE; *197 G-15; elev. 596ft./182m.; mail Chamois z 65024; rural
Deerfield; Inc. Place; VERNON; 196 I-9; elev. 785ft./239m.; 🅿; z 64741; Ⓟ 85; Ⓒ 75
Deering; RMC Place; PEMISCOT; 197 M-19; elev. 259ft./79m.; 🅿; z 63840; ● 100
Deer Land; RMC Place; DUNKLIN; *197 M-19; mail Kennett z 63857; rural
Deer Park; RMC Place; BOONE; 197 F-14; mail Columbia z 65201; rural
Deer Ridge; RMC Place; LEWIS; *197 B-14; elev. 733ft./223m.; mail La Belle z 63447; rural
Defiance; RMC Place; ST. CHARLES; 197 G-17; elev. 480ft./146m.; 🅿; z 63341; ● 300
Deicke; RMC Place; ST. LOUIS; ★ ST.L; mail Eureka z 63025
De Kalb; Inc. Place; BUCHANAN; 196 D-8; elev. 1,130ft./344m.; 🅿; z 64440; Ⓟ 222; Ⓒ 257
DEKALB; 196 C-9; Ⓟ 9,967; Ⓒ 11,597; Ⓡ 13,073; ◆ 12,032
De Lassus; RMC Place; ST. FRANCOIS; *197 I-18; mail Farmington z 63640; ● 230
Delaware; RMC Place; SHANNON; *197 K-16; elev. 735ft./224m.; mail Birch Tree z 65438; rural
Delbridge; RMC Place; WASHINGTON; *197 I-16; elev. 1,229ft./375m.; mail Potosi z 63664; rural
Dell Junction; RMC Place; BENTON; *197 H-11; elev. 880ft./268m.; mail Warsaw z 65355; ● 100
Dellwood; Inc. Place; ST. LOUIS; 195 C-6; elev. 537ft./164m.; ★ ST.L; mail Saint Louis z 63135-36; Ⓟ 5,245; Ⓒ 5,255
Delmar; RMC Place; HENRY; *196 G-10; elev. 819ft./250m.; mail Clinton z 64735; rural
Delmo; RMC Place; NEW MADRID; *197 L-19; mail Sikeston z 63801; ● 200
Delta; Inc. Place; CAPE GIRARDEAU; 197 K-19; elev. 339ft./103m.; 🅿; z 63744; Ⓟ 450; Ⓒ 517
Dennis Acres; Inc. Place; NEWTON; 195 N-2; elev. 1,060ft./323m.; ★ JOP; mail Joplin z 64804; Ⓟ 157; Ⓒ 68
DENT; 197 I-15; Ⓟ 13,702; Ⓒ 14,927; ◆ 14,807
Denton; RMC Place; JOHNSON; *196 G-10; mail Holden z 64040; rural
Denton; RMC Place; PEMISCOT; 197 N-19; elev. 260ft./79m.; mail Steele z 63877; ● 120
Denver; Inc. Place; WORTH; 196 B-9; elev. 898ft./274m.; 🅿; z 64441; Ⓟ 53; Ⓒ 40
Derby; RMC Place; ST. FRANCOIS; *197 I-17; mail Park Hills z 63601; rural
Dermott; RMC Place; WEBSTER; *197 J-12; elev. 1,279ft./390m.; mail Marshfield z 65706; rural
Derrahs; RMC Place; LEWIS; *197 B-15; elev. 607ft./185m.; mail Williamstown z 63473; rural
Des Arc; Inc. Place; IRON; 197 J-17; elev. 588ft./179m.; 🅿; z 63636; Ⓟ 173; Ⓒ 187
Desloge; Inc. Place; ST. FRANCOIS; 197 I-17; elev. 800ft./244m.; 🅿; z 63601, z 63628; Ⓟ 4,150; Ⓒ 4,802
De Soto; Inc. Place; JEFFERSON; 197 H-17; elev. 503ft./153m.; 🅿; ★ ST.L; z 63020; Ⓟ 5,993; Ⓒ 6,375
Des Peres; Inc. Place; ST. LOUIS; 195 F-4; elev. 600ft./183m.; 🅿 ■; ★ ST.L; z 63131 & mail Saint Louis z 63122; Ⓟ 8,388; Ⓒ 8,592; ◆ 8,601
Dessa; RMC Place; NEWTON; *196 L-9; elev. 1,135ft./346m.; mail Neosho z 64850; rural
Detmold; RMC Place; FRANKLIN; *197 G-16; mail New Haven z 63068; ● 100
Devils Elbow; RMC Place; PULASKI; 197 I-14; elev. 803ft./245m.; 🅿; z 65457; ● 200
De Witt; Inc. Place; CARROLL; 197 E-12; elev. 720ft./219m.; 🅿; z 64639; Ⓟ 125; Ⓒ 120
Dexter; Inc. Place; STODDARD; 197 L-19; elev. 387ft./118m.; 🅿 🄷; z 63841; Ⓟ 7,559; Ⓒ 7,356; Ⓡ 7,430
Diamond; Inc. Place; NEWTON; 196 K-9; elev. 1,180ft./360m.; 🅿; z 64840; Ⓟ 775; Ⓒ 807
Dickens; RMC Place; TANEY; *197 L-12; elev. 1,032ft./315m.; mail Taneyville z 65759; rural
Diehlstadt; Inc. Place; SCOTT; 197 K-20; elev. 325ft./99m.; mail Charleston z 63834; Ⓟ 145; Ⓒ 163
Diggins; Inc. Place; WEBSTER; *197 K-12; elev. 1,651ft./503m.; 🅿; z 65636; Ⓟ 258; Ⓒ 298
Dillard; RMC Place; CRAWFORD; *197 I-16; elev. 897ft./273m.; mail Davisville z 65456; rural
Dillon; RMC Place; PHELPS; *197 H-15; mail Rolla z 65401; rural
Dissen; RMC Place; FRANKLIN; *197 G-16; mail New Haven z 63068; ● 100
Dittmer; RMC Place; JEFFERSON; 197 G-17; elev. 720ft./219m.; 🅿; ★ ST.L; z 63023; ● 600
Dixie; RMC Place; CALLAWAY; *197 F-14; elev. 819ft./250m.; mail New Bloomfield z 65063; rural
Dixon; Inc. Place; PULASKI; 197 H-14; elev. 1,167ft./356m.; 🅿; z 65459; Ⓟ 1,585; Ⓒ 1,570
Dockery; RMC Place; RAY; *196 E-10; mail Richmond z 64085; ● 40
Dodson; RMC Place; JACKSON; *196 F-9; ★ K.C.; pop. incl. with Kansas City (Inc. Place)
Doe Run; RMC Place; ST. FRANCOIS; 197 I-18; elev. 940ft./287m.; 🅿; z 63637; ● 300
Dogwood; RMC Place; DOUGLAS; *197 K-12; elev. 1,686ft./514m.; mail Seymour z 65746; rural
Dogwood; RMC Place; MISSISSIPPI; *197 L-20; mail East Prairie z 63845; ● 30
Dolly Siding; RMC Place; ST. FRANCOIS; mail Bonne Terre z 63628; pop. incl. with Bonne Terre (Inc. Place)
Dongola; RMC Place; BOLLINGER; 197 K-19; mail Advance z 63730; ● 80
Doniphan; Inc. Place; ⊡ RIPLEY; 197 L-17; elev. 467ft./142m.; 🅿 🄷; z 63935; Ⓟ 1,713; Ⓒ 1,932
Doolittle; Inc. Place; PHELPS; 197 I-14; elev. 1,008ft./307m.; mail Rolla z 65401; Ⓟ 599; Ⓒ 644
Dora; RMC Place; OZARK; 197 L-14; elev. 1,040ft./317m.; 🅿; z 65637; ● 80
Dorena; RMC Place; MISSISSIPPI; *197 L-20; mail East Prairie z 63845; rural
Doss; RMC Place; DENT; *197 J-15; mail Salem z 65560; ● 30
Dotham; RMC Place; ATCHISON; *196 B-7; elev. 963ft./294m.; mail Fairfax z 64446; rural
DOUGLAS; 197 K-13; Ⓟ 11,876; Ⓒ 13,084; ◆ 13,282
Dove; RMC Place; LACLEDE; *197 I-13; mail Lebanon z 65536; ● 100
Dover; Inc. Place; LAFAYETTE; 197 E-11; elev. 817ft./249m.; 🅿; z 64022; Ⓟ 115; Ⓒ 108
Dover; RMC Place; LEWIS; *197 C-15; mail La Grange z 63448; rural
Downing; Inc. Place; SCHUYLER; 197 B-13; elev. 873ft./266m.; 🅿; z 63536; Ⓟ 359; Ⓒ 396
Drake; RMC Place; GASCONADE; 197 G-15; elev. 868ft./265m.; mail Owensville z 65066
Dresden; RMC Place; PETTIS; 197 F-11; mail La Monte z 65337, Sedalia z 65301; ● 300
Drexel; Inc. Place; CASS, BATES; 196 G-9; elev. 992ft./302m.; 🅿; z 64742; Ⓟ 936; Ⓒ 1,090
Dripping Spring; RMC Place; BOONE; *197 E-13; elev. 664ft./202m.; mail Columbia z 65202; rural
Drury; RMC Place; DOUGLAS; 197 K-14; elev. 1,200ft./366m.; 🅿; z 65638; rural
Dudenville; RMC Place; DADE, JASPER; *196 J-10; mail Golden City z 64748; ● 50
Dudley; Inc. Place; STODDARD; 197 L-18; elev. 343ft./105m.; 🅿; z 63936; Ⓟ 271; Ⓒ 289
Duenweg; Inc. Place; JASPER; *196 K-9; elev. 1,074ft./327m.; 🅿; ★ JOP; z 64841; Ⓟ 940; Ⓒ 1,034
Dugginsville; RMC Place; OZARK; *197 M-13; elev. 720ft./219m.; 🅿; z 65761; ● 90
Duke; RMC Place; PHELPS; 197 I-14; elev. 1,115ft./340m.; 🅿; z 65461; rural
Duncan; RMC Place; WRIGHT, WEBSTER; *197 J-13; elev. 1,446ft./441m.; mail Marshfield z 65706; rural
Duncans Bridge; RMC Place; MONROE; 197 D-14; mail Clarence z 63437; ● 30
Dundee; RMC Place; FRANKLIN; *197 G-16; mail Washington z 63090; rural
DUNKLIN; 197 N-19; Ⓟ 33,112; Ⓒ 33,155; ◆ 31,138
Dunksburg; RMC Place; JOHNSON, PETTIS; *197 F-11; elev. 748ft./228m.; mail Sweet Springs z 65351
Dunlap; RMC Place; GRUNDY; 197 C-11; mail Trenton z 64683; ● 50
Dunn; RMC Place; NEW MADRID; *197 M-19; elev. 267ft./81m.; mail Gideon z 63848; rural
Dunn (Impo); RMC Place; TEXAS; *197 K-14; mail Mountain Grove z 65711; ● 30
Dunnegan; RMC Place; POLK; 197 I-11; elev. 930ft./283m.; 🅿; z 65640; ● 200
Duquesne; Inc. Place; JASPER; 195 M-3; elev. 1,072ft./327m.; ★ JOP; mail Joplin z 64801; Ⓟ 1,229; Ⓒ 1,640
Durham; RMC Place; LEWIS; 197 C-15; elev. 649ft./198m.; 🅿; z 63438; ● 190
Dutchtown; Inc. Place; CAPE GIRARDEAU; 197 J-19; elev. 356ft./109m.; 🅿; z 63745; Ⓒ 99
Dutzow; RMC Place; WARREN; 197 G-16; elev. 491ft./150m.; 🅿; z 63342; ● 250
Dye; RMC Place; PLATTE; *196 D-8; elev. 977ft./298m.; mail Weston z 64098; rural
Dykes; RMC Place; TEXAS; *197 J-14; elev. 1,463ft./446m.; mail Bucyrus z 65444; rural

E

Eagle Rock; RMC Place; BARRY; 196 L-10; elev. 931ft./284m.; 🅿; z 65641; ● 300
Eagleville; Inc. Place; HARRISON; 196 B-10; elev. 1,097ft./334m.; 🅿; z 64442; Ⓟ 275; Ⓒ 321
Easley; RMC Place; BOONE; 197 F-13; mail Columbia z 65203
East Atchison; BUCHANAN; see Winthrop (RMC Place)
East Bonne Terre; RMC Place; ST. FRANCOIS; *197 I-17; mail Bonne Terre z 63628; ● 500
East End; RMC Place; IRON; *197 I-16; mail Belleview z 63623; rural
East Independence; RMC Place; JACKSON; *196 E-9; ★ K.C.; mail Independence z 64056; pop. incl. with Independence (Inc. Place)
East Kansas City; CLAY; see Randolph (Inc. Place)
East Kirkwood; RMC Place; ST. LOUIS; ★ ST.L; mail Saint Louis z 63122; pop. incl. with Kirkwood (Inc. Place)
East Leavenworth; RMC Place; PLATTE; *196 E-8; mail Platte City z 64079; rural
East Lynne; Inc. Place; CASS; 196 G-9; elev. 850ft./259m.; 🅿; z 64743; Ⓟ 289; Ⓒ 300
East Mexico; RMC Place; AUDRAIN; mail Mexico z 65265; pop. incl. with Mexico (Inc. Place)
Easton; Inc. Place; BUCHANAN; 196 D-9; elev. 920ft./280m.; 🅿; z 64443; Ⓟ 232; Ⓒ 258
East Prairie; Inc. Place; MISSISSIPPI; 197 L-20; elev. 307ft./94m.; 🅿; z 63845; Ⓟ 3,416; Ⓒ 3,227
East Purdy; RMC Place; BARRY; *196 L-10; elev. 1,449ft./442m.; mail Purdy z 65734; rural
Eastside; RMC Place; BUCHANAN; ★ ST.JO; mail Saint Joseph z 64508; pop. incl. with Saint Joseph (Inc. Place)
Eastville; RMC Place; CALLAWAY; *197 F-14; elev. 877ft./267m.; mail Kingdom City z 65262; rural
Eastwood; RMC Place; CARTER; 197 K-16; elev. 918ft./280m.; mail Van Buren z 63965; ● 40
Ebenezer; RMC Place; GREENE; *197 J-11; mail Springfield z 65803; ● 120
Ebo; RMC Place; WASHINGTON; *197 H-17; elev. 901ft./275m.; mail Potosi z 63664; rural
Eccles; RMC Place; CHARITON; *197 D-12; elev. 550ft./168m.; mail Keytesville z 65261; rural
Economy; RMC Place; MACON; *197 C-13; elev. 884ft./269m.; mail Atlanta z 63530
Ectonville; RMC Place; CLAY; *196 E-9; elev. 1,020ft./311m.; ★ K.C.; mail Smithville z 64089; rural
Edgar Springs; Inc. Place; PHELPS; 197 I-15; elev. 1,210ft./369m.; 🅿; z 65462; Ⓟ 215; Ⓒ 190
Edgehill; RMC Place; REYNOLDS; *197 J-17; elev. 832ft./254m.; mail Black z 63625; rural
Edgerton; Inc. Place; PLATTE; 196 D-9; elev. 850ft./259m.; 🅿; z 64444; Ⓟ 565; Ⓒ 533
Edgerton Junction; RMC Place; PLATTE; *196 D-9; mail Dearborn z 64439; rural
Edgewater Beach; RMC Place; TANEY; *197 L-12; elev. 724ft./221m.; mail Forsyth z 65653; summer pop. 200; ● 100
Edgewood; RMC Place; PIKE; *197 E-16; mail Bowling Green z 63334
Edina; Inc. Place; ⊡ KNOX; 197 B-14; elev. 816ft./249m.; 🅿; z 63537; Ⓟ 1,283; Ⓒ 1,233
Edinburg; RMC Place; GRUNDY; 197 C-11; elev. 958ft./292m.; mail Trenton z 64683; ● 40
Edmonson; RMC Place; BENTON; *197 H-12; elev. 766ft./233m.; mail Lincoln z 65338; rural
Edmundson; Inc. Place; ST. LOUIS; 195 D-5; elev. 600ft./183m.; ★ ST.L; mail Saint Louis z 63134; Ⓟ 1,111; Ⓒ 840
Edwards; RMC Place; BENTON; 197 H-12; elev. 800ft./244m.; 🅿; z 65326; ● 40
Egypt Grove; RMC Place; HOWELL; *197 L-14; elev. 1,151ft./351m.; mail Caulfield z 65626; rural
Egypt Mills; RMC Place; CAPE GIRARDEAU; 197 J-20; elev. 376ft./115m.; mail Cape Girardeau z 63701; ● 120
Eight Mile; CASS; see Daugherty (RMC Place)
Eldon; Inc. Place; MILLER; 197 G-13; elev. 933ft./284m.; 🅿; z 65026, z 65072; Ⓟ 4,419; Ⓒ 4,895
El Dorado Springs; Inc. Place; CEDAR; 196 I-10; elev. 901ft./275m.; 🅿 🄷; z 64744; Ⓟ 3,830; Ⓒ 3,775
Eldridge; RMC Place; LACLEDE; 197 I-13; elev. 1,194ft./364m.; 🅿; z 65463
Elgin; RMC Place; SHELBY; *197 C-14; elev. 765ft./233m.; mail Bethel z 63434; rural
Elijah; RMC Place; OZARK; *197 L-14; mail Caulfield z 65626; rural
Elk Creek; RMC Place; TEXAS; 197 K-14; elev. 1,149ft./350m.; 🅿; z 65464; ● 85
Elkhead; RMC Place; CHRISTIAN; *197 K-12; elev. 1,536ft./468m.; mail Sparta z 65753; rural
Elkhorn; RMC Place; RAY; *196 E-10; elev. 1,024ft./312m.; ★ K.C.; mail Orrick z 64077; ● 100
Elkhurst; RMC Place; BOONE; *197 F-14; mail Columbia z 65201; rural
Elkland; RMC Place; WEBSTER; 197 J-12; elev. 1,336ft./407m.; 🅿; z 65644; ● 200
Elk Prairie; RMC Place; PHELPS; ● 20
Elk Springs; RMC Place; MCDONALD; *196 L-9; mail Noel z 64854; rural
Elkton; RMC Place; HICKORY; 197 I-11; mail Flemington z 65650
Ellington; Inc. Place; REYNOLDS; 197 J-17; elev. 667ft./203m.; 🅿 🄷; z 63638; Ⓟ 994; Ⓒ 1,045
Ellis; RMC Place; VERNON; *196 I-9; elev. 829ft./253m.; mail Nevada z 64772; rural
Ellis Prairie; RMC Place; TEXAS; *197 J-14; elev. 1,212ft./369m.; mail Bucyrus z 65444
Ellisville; Inc. Place; ST. LOUIS; 195 F-2; elev. 720ft./219m.; 🅿; ★ ST.L; z 63011, z 63021, z 63038; Ⓟ 7,545; Ⓒ 9,104
Ellsinore (Elsinore); Inc. Place; CARTER; 197 K-17; elev. 711ft./217m.; 🅿; z 63937; Ⓟ 405; Ⓒ 363
Elm; RMC Place; JOHNSON; *196 F-10; elev. 896ft./273m.; mail Kingsville z 64061; ● 90
Elmdale Village; RMC Place; ST. LOUIS; ★ ST.L; mail Saint Louis z 63114; pop. incl. with Saint Johns (Inc. Place)
Elmer; Inc. Place; MACON; 197 C-13; elev. 800ft./244m.; 🅿; z 63538; Ⓟ 91; Ⓒ 98
Elmira; Inc. Place; RAY; 196 D-10; elev. 900ft./274m.; 🅿; z 64062; Ⓟ 70; Ⓒ 82
Elmo; Inc. Place; NODAWAY; 196 A-8; elev. 1,000ft./305m.; 🅿; z 64445; Ⓟ 179; Ⓒ 166
Elmont; RMC Place; FRANKLIN; *197 H-16; elev. 974ft./297m.; mail Sullivan z 63080; rural
Elmwood; RMC Place; SALINE; *197 E-11; mail Blackburn z 65321; ● 40
Elsberry; Inc. Place; LINCOLN; 197 E-17; elev. 449ft./137m.; 🅿; z 63343; Ⓟ 1,898; Ⓒ 2,047
Elsey; RMC Place; STONE; 197 L-11; mail Crane z 65633; ● 200
Elsinore; CARTER; see Ellsinore (Inc. Place)
Elston; RMC Place; COLE; *197 G-14; ★ JFCY; mail Jefferson City z 65101, z 65109; ● 120
Elvins; RMC Place; ST. FRANCOIS; *197 I-17; elev. 765ft./233m.; 🅿; z 63601; pop. incl. with Park Hills (Inc. Place)
Elwood; RMC Place; GREENE; *197 K-11; ★ SPRG; mail Springfield z 65802; ● 150
Ely; RMC Place; MARION; *197 D-15; mail Palmyra z 63461; ● 30
Emden; RMC Place; SHELBY; 197 C-15; elev. 740ft./226m.; 🅿; z 63439; ● 40
Emerald Beach; Inc. Place; BARRY; *197 L-11; mail Golden z 65658; Ⓟ 172; Ⓒ 250
Emerson; RMC Place; MARION; 197 C-15; elev. 673ft./205m.; mail Maywood z 63454; ● 70
Eminence; Inc. Place; ⊡ SHANNON; 197 K-16; elev. 677ft./206m.; 🅿; z 65466; Ⓟ 582; Ⓒ 548
Emma; Inc. Place; SALINE, LAFAYETTE; 197 F-11; elev. 759ft./231m.; 🅿; z 65327; Ⓟ 194; Ⓒ 243
Empire Prairie; RMC Place; ANDREW; *196 C-9; elev. 1,093ft./333m.; mail King City z 64463; rural
Englewood; RMC Place; BOONE; *197 F-14; elev. 873ft./266m.; mail Ashland z 65010; ● 110
Englewood; RMC Place; JACKSON; *196 E-9; ★ K.C.; mail Independence z 64052; pop. incl. with Independence (Inc. Place)
Enon; RMC Place; MONITEAU; 197 G-13; mail Russellville z 65074; ● 80
Enon; RMC Place; ST. CHARLES; *197 F-17; elev. 460ft./140m.; ★ ST.L; mail Wentzville z 63385
Enyart; RMC Place; GENTRY; *196 B-9; elev. 910ft./277m.; mail Gentry z 64453; rural
Eolia; Inc. Place; PIKE; 197 E-16; elev. 833ft./254m.; 🅿; z 63344; Ⓟ 389; Ⓒ 435
Epworth; RMC Place; SHELBY; *197 C-14; elev. 780ft./238m.; mail Shelbyville z 63469
Erie; RMC Place; MCDONALD; *196 L-9; elev. 1,000ft./305m.; mail Goodman z 64843; rural
Ernestville; RMC Place; LAFAYETTE; *197 F-11; elev. 740ft./226m.; mail Concordia z 64020; rural
Essex; Inc. Place; STODDARD; 197 L-19; elev. 300ft./91m.; 🅿; z 63846; Ⓟ 531; Ⓒ 524
Estes; RMC Place; PIKE; *197 E-16; mail Middletown z 63359
Esther; RMC Place; ST. FRANCOIS; *197 I-18; elev. 800ft./244m.; mail Park Hills z 63601; pop. incl. with Park Hills (Inc. Place)
Estill; RMC Place; HOWARD; *197 F-13; elev. 660ft./201m.; mail New Franklin z 65274; rural
Ethel; Inc. Place; MACON; 197 C-13; elev. 850ft./259m.; 🅿; z 63539; Ⓟ 71; Ⓒ 100
Ethlyn; RMC Place; LINCOLN; *197 F-17; elev. 499ft./152m.; mail Old Monroe z 63369; ● 100
Etlah; RMC Place; FRANKLIN; *197 G-16; mail Berger z 63014; rural
Etna; RMC Place; SCOTLAND; *197 B-14; elev. 756ft./230m.; mail Arbela z 63432; rural
Etterville; RMC Place; MILLER; 197 G-13; elev. 880ft./268m.; 🅿; z 65026; ● 150
Eudora; RMC Place; POLK; 197 J-11; elev. 1,104ft./336m.; 🅿; z 65645; ● 200
Eugene; RMC Place; COLE; 197 G-13; elev. 800ft./244m.; 🅿; z 65032; Ⓟ 141; ● 150
Eunice; RMC Place; TEXAS; 197 J-15; elev. 1,353ft./412m.; 🅿; z 65468; ● 40
Eureka; Inc. Place; ST. LOUIS; 197 G-17; elev. 450ft./137m.; 🅿; ★ ST.L; z 63025; Ⓟ 4,683; Ⓒ 7,676
Evans; RMC Place; DOUGLAS; *197 K-13; mail Ava z 65608; rural
Evansville; RMC Place; BUCHANAN; *196 D-8; elev. 884ft./269m.; ★ ST.JO; mail Saint Joseph z 64507; rural
Evansville; RMC Place; MONROE; *197 D-14; mail Moberly z 65270; rural
Eve; RMC Place; VERNON; *196 I-9; elev. 808ft./246m.; mail Deerfield z 64741; rural
Evening Shade; RMC Place; TEXAS; *197 J-14; elev. 1,345ft./410m.; mail Plato z 65552, Roby z 65557; ● 350
Everett; RMC Place; CASS; *196 G-9; mail Archie z 64725; rural
Evergreen (Twin Bridges); Inc. Place; LACLEDE; *197 J-13; mail Lebanon z 65536; Ⓒ 42
Eversonville; RMC Place; LINN, LIVINGSTON; *197 C-11; elev. 802ft./244m.; mail Wheeling z 64688; rural

Entries in **UPPERCASE** are counties.
Entries in **bold** have populations of 2,500 or more.
Names in parentheses are alternate names.

Inc. Place	Incorporated Place
RMC Place	Rand McNally Designated Place
CDP	Census Designated Place
MCD	Minor Civil Division
⊡	County Seat
▲	Minor Civil Division
elev.	Elevation
🅿	Post Office
🄷	Hospital
🄲	College
■	Principal Business Center
★	Ranally Metro Area (RMA) Abbreviation
z	Zip Code(s)
Ⓟ	Previous Census Population
Ⓡ	Revised Census Population
Ⓐ	Annexation Population
●	Rand McNally Population Estimate
Ⓒ	Final Census Population
Ⓢ	Special Census Population
◆	Estimated Population

For additional definitions see Glossary, Volume 1, and Introduction, Volume 2.

Everton; Inc. Place; DADE; 197 J-11; elev. 1,038ft./316m.; 🅿; Z 65646; Ⓟ 325; Ⓒ 322
Ewing; Inc. Place; LEWIS; 197 C-15; elev. 680ft./207m.; 🅿; Z 63440; Ⓟ 463; Ⓒ 464
Excello; RMC Place; MACON; 197 D-13; elev. 868ft./265m.; 🅿; Z 65247
Excelsior; RMC Place; MORGAN; *197 G-13; mail Versailles Z 65084
Excelsior Estates; Inc. Place; RAY, CLAY; *196 E-10; ★ K.C.; mail Excelsior Springs Z 64024, Lawson Z 64062; Ⓟ 274; Ⓒ 263
Excelsior Springs; Inc. Place; CLAY, RAY; 196 E-9; elev. 900ft./274m.; 🅿 🅷; ★ K.C.; Z 64024; Ⓟ 10,354; Ⓒ 10,847
Executive Park; RMC Place; JACKSON; ★ K.C.; mail Kansas City Z 64120; pop. incl. with Kansas City (Inc. Place)
Exeter; Inc. Place; BARRY; 196 L-10; elev. 1,559ft./475m.; 🅿; Z 65647; Ⓟ 597; Ⓒ 707

F

Fagus; RMC Place; BUTLER; 197 L-18; elev. 305ft./93m.; 🅿; Z 63938; ● 100
Fairdealing; RMC Place; RIPLEY; 197 L-17; elev. 460ft./140m.; 🅿; Z 63939; ● 350
Fairfax; Inc. Place; ATCHISON; 196 B-7; elev. 900ft./274m.; 🅿 🅷; Z 64446; Ⓟ 699; Ⓒ 645
Fairgrounds; RMC Place; ST. LOUIS (Independent City); *197 G-18; ★ ST.L; mail Saint Louis Z 63107; pop. incl. with Saint Louis (Independent City)
Fair Grove; Inc. Place; GREENE; 197 J-12; elev. 1,250ft./381m.; 🅿; Z 65648; Ⓟ 919; Ⓒ 1,107
Fair Haven; RMC Place; VERNON; *196 H-10; elev. 814ft./248m.; mail Harwood Z 64750; ● 30
Fairleigh; RMC Place; BUCHANAN; *196 C-8; ★ ST.JO; mail Saint Joseph Z 64506; pop. incl. with Saint Joseph (Inc. Place)
Fairmont; RMC Place; CLARK; 197 B-14; elev. 770ft./235m.; mail Wyaconda Z 63474; ● 30
Fairmount; RMC Place; JACKSON; *196 E-9; ★ K.C.; mail Independence Z 64053; pop. incl. with Independence (Inc. Place)
Fair Play; Inc. Place; POLK; 197 I-11; elev. 994ft./303m.; 🅿; Z 65649; Ⓟ 442; Ⓒ 418
Fairport; RMC Place; DEKALB; 196 C-9; elev. 1,000ft./305m.; 🅿; Z 64469; ● 90
Fairview; Inc. Place; NEWTON; 196 L-10; elev. 1,284ft./391m.; 🅿; Z 64842; Ⓟ 298; Ⓒ 395
Fairview; RMC Place; TANEY; *197 L-12; elev. 1,315ft./401m.; mail Bradleyville Z 65614, Rueter Z 65744; rural
Fairview; RMC Place; TEXAS; 197 J-14; mail Cabool Z 65689; ● 30
Fairview Acres; RMC Place; ST. FRANCOIS; *197 I-17; elev. 880ft./268m.; mail Park Hills Z 63601; pop. incl. with Park Hills (Inc. Place)
Fairville; RMC Place; SALINE; *197 E-12; elev. 784ft./239m.; mail Slater Z 65349; rural
Falcon; RMC Place; LACLEDE; 197 I-13; elev. 1,158ft./353m.; 🅿; Z 65470; rural
Fanchon; RMC Place; HOWELL; *197 L-15; elev. 922ft./281m.; mail Peace Valley Z 65788; rural
Fanning; RMC Place; CRAWFORD; *197 H-15; elev. 1,047ft./319m.; mail Cuba Z 65453; ● 90
Farber; Inc. Place; AUDRAIN; 197 E-15; elev. 767ft./234m.; 🅿; Z 63345; Ⓟ 418; Ⓒ 411
Farewell; RMC Place; OREGON; *197 M-16; elev. 779ft./237m.; mail Skidmore Z 64487; rural
Farley; Inc. Place; PLATTE; 196 E-8; elev. 761ft./232m.; 🅿; Z 64028; Ⓟ 217; Ⓒ 226
Farmer; RMC Place; PIKE; *197 E-16; mail Curryville Z 63339
Farmersville; RMC Place; LIVINGSTON; 197 C-11; mail Trenton Z 64683; ● 30
Farmington; Inc. Place; ⊡ ST. FRANCOIS; 197 I-18; elev. 918ft./280m.; 🅿 🅷; Z 63640; Ⓟ 11,598; Ⓒ 13,924
Farrar; RMC Place; PERRY; 197 I-19; elev. 510ft./155m.; 🅿; Z 63746; ● 60
Farrenberg; NEW MADRID; see Farrenburg (RMC Place)
Farrenburg (Farrenberg); RMC Place; NEW MADRID; *197 L-20; mail New Madrid Z 63869; ● 40
Faucett; RMC Place; BUCHANAN; 196 D-8; elev. 968ft./295m.; 🅿; Z 64448; ● 350
Fayette; Inc. Place; ⊡ HOWARD; 197 E-13; elev. 700ft./213m.; 🅿 🅲 3,161; Z 65248; Ⓟ 2,888; Ⓒ 2,793
Fayetteville; RMC Place; JOHNSON; 196 F-10; elev. 854ft./260m.; mail Warrensburg Z 64093; ● 100
Federal; RMC Place; ST. FRANCOIS; *197 I-18; elev. 900ft./274m.; mail Park Hills Z 63601; pop. incl. with Park Hills (Inc. Place)
Fee Fee; RMC Place; ST. LOUIS; *197 F-18; ★ ST.L; mail Saint Louis Z 63141
Fegley; RMC Place; ADAIR; *197 B-13; elev. 946ft./288m.; mail Kirksville Z 63501; rural
Femme Osage; RMC Place; ST. CHARLES; *197 G-17; mail Augusta Z 63332
Fenton; Inc. Place; ST. LOUIS; 195 G-4; elev. 415ft./126m.; 🅿 🅲 2,535; ★ ST.L; Z 63026, Z 63099; Ⓟ 3,346; Ⓒ 4,360
Fenwick; RMC Place; JOHNSON; *196 G-10; mail Holden Z 64040; rural
Ferguson; Inc. Place; ST. LOUIS; 195 D-5; elev. 554ft./169m.; 🅿; ★ ST.L; Z 63135 & mail Saint Louis Z 63136, Z 63145; Ⓟ 22,286; Ⓒ 22,406; ◆ 21,266
Fernridge; RMC Place; ST. LOUIS; *197 F-18; ★ ST.L; mail Saint Louis Z 63141; pop. incl. with Creve Coeur (Inc. Place)
Fernview Estates; RMC Place; ST. LOUIS; *197 I-18; elev. 543ft./166m.; mail Saint Louis Z 63141
Ferrelview; Inc. Place; PLATTE; 196 E-2; elev. 950ft./290m.; 🅿; ★ K.C.; Z 64163; Ⓟ 338; Ⓒ 593
Fertile; RMC Place; WASHINGTON; 197 H-17; elev. 762ft./232m.; mail Cadet Z 63630; ● 90
Festus; Inc. Place; JEFFERSON; 197 H-18; elev. 468ft./143m.; 🅿; ★ ST.L; Z 63028; Ⓟ 8,105; Ⓒ 9,660
Fidelity; Inc. Place; JASPER; 196 K-9; elev. 1,121ft./342m.; ★ JOP; mail Carthage Z 64836; Ⓟ 235; Ⓒ 252
Field; RMC Place; ST. LOUIS (Independent City); *197 G-18; ★ ST.L; mail Saint Louis Z 63108; pop. incl. with Saint Louis (Independent City)
Filley; RMC Place; CEDAR; 196 I-10; elev. 873ft./266m.; mail El Dorado Springs Z 64744; ● 80
Fillmore; Inc. Place; ANDREW; 196 C-8; elev. 920ft./280m.; 🅿; Z 64449; Ⓟ 256; Ⓒ 211
Finey; RMC Place; HENRY; *197 H-11; elev. 912ft./278m.; mail Deepwater Z 64740; ● 80
Fisk; Inc. Place; BUTLER; 197 L-18; elev. 325ft./99m.; 🅿; Z 63940; Ⓟ 422; Ⓒ 363
Flag Spring; RMC Place; PHELPS; 197 H-15; mail Saint James Z 65559; ● 120
Flag Springs; RMC Place; ANDREW; *196 C-9; elev. 998ft./304m.; mail Union Star Z 64494; rural
Flat; RMC Place; PHELPS; 197 I-14; mail Newburg Z 65550; ● 80
Flat River; RMC Place; ST. FRANCOIS; *197 I-18; elev. 733ft./223m.; 🅿; Z 63601, Z 63653; pop. incl. with Park Hills (Inc. Place)
Flatwood; RMC Place; SHANNON; *197 K-16; elev. 1,092ft./333m.; mail Eminence Z 65466; rural
Fleming; Inc. Place; RAY; *196 E-10; elev. 710ft./216m.; mail Orrick Z 64077; Ⓟ 130; Ⓒ 122
Flemington; Inc. Place; POLK; 197 I-11; elev. 1,126ft./343m.; 🅿; Z 65650; Ⓟ 141; Ⓒ 124
Fletcher; RMC Place; JEFFERSON; 197 H-17; elev. 572ft./174m.; 🅿; Z 63030; ● 320
Flint Hill; Inc. Place; ST. CHARLES; 197 F-17; elev. 576ft./176m.; 🅿; ★ ST.L; Z 63346; Ⓟ 229; Ⓒ 379
Flordell Hills; Inc. Place; ST. LOUIS; 195 D-6; elev. 493ft./150m.; ★ ST.L; mail Saint Louis Z 63136; Ⓟ 950; Ⓒ 931
Florence; RMC Place; BUCHANAN; ★ ST.JO; mail Saint Joseph Z 64504; pop. incl. with Saint Joseph (Inc. Place)
Florence; RMC Place; MORGAN; 197 G-12; elev. 942ft./287m.; 🅿; Z 65329; ● 140
Florida; Inc. Place; MONROE; *197 D-15; 🅿; Z 65283; Ⓒ 9
Florissant; Inc. Place; ST. LOUIS; 195 C-5; elev. 550ft./168m.; 🅿 ■; ★ ST.L; Z 63031-34; Ⓟ 51,206; Ⓒ 50,497; ◆ 46,886
Floyd; RMC Place; RAY; *196 E-10; mail Orrick Z 64077; rural
Flucom; RMC Place; JEFFERSON; *197 H-18; mail De Soto Z 63020; ● 100
Foil; RMC Place; OZARK; *197 L-13; elev. 920ft./280m.; mail Squires Z 65755; rural
Foley; Inc. Place; LINCOLN; 197 E-17; elev. 442ft./135m.; 🅿; Z 63347; Ⓟ 209; Ⓒ 178
Folk; RMC Place; OSAGE; *197 G-14; elev. 800ft./244m.; mail Westphalia Z 65085; ● 30
Foose; RMC Place; DALLAS; 197 J-12; mail Buffalo Z 65622; ● 110
Forbes; RMC Place; HOLT; 196 C-8; elev. 858ft./262m.; mail Oregon Z 64473; ● 70
Ford City; RMC Place; GENTRY; *196 C-9; elev. 1,043ft./318m.; mail King City Z 64463; ● 40
Fordland; Inc. Place; WEBSTER; 197 K-12; elev. 1,608ft./490m.; 🅿; Z 65652; Ⓟ 523; Ⓒ 684
Forest City; Inc. Place; HOLT; 196 C-7; elev. 856ft./261m.; 🅿; Z 64451; Ⓟ 380; Ⓒ 338
Forest Green; RMC Place; CHARITON; 197 E-12; elev. 649ft./198m.; mail Salisbury Z 65281; ● 40
Forest Hills; RMC Place; BENTON; elev. 210ft./64m.; mail Warsaw Z 65355
Forest Mills; RMC Place; JASPER; *196 K-9; elev. 1,000ft./305m.; mail Reeds Z 64859; rural
Foristell; Inc. Place; ST. CHARLES, WARREN; 197 F-17; elev. 707ft./215m.; 🅿; ★ ST.L; Z 63348; Ⓟ 144; Ⓒ 331
Forker; RMC Place; LINN; *197 D-12; mail Laclede Z 64651
Forkners Hill; RMC Place; WEBSTER; *197 J-12; elev. 1,250ft./381m.; mail Conway Z 65632; rural
Fornfelt; SCOTT, CAPE GIRARDEAU; see Scott City (Inc. Place)
Forsyth; Inc. Place; ⊡ TANEY; 197 L-12; elev. 947ft./289m.; 🅿; Z 65653; Ⓟ 1,175; Ⓒ 1,686
Fort Bellefontaine; RMC Place; ST. LOUIS; *197 F-18; mail Florissant Z 63034; ● 135
Fortescue; Inc. Place; HOLT; 196 C-7; elev. 860ft./262m.; 🅿; Z 64437; Ⓟ 46; Ⓒ 51
Fort Henry; RMC Place; RANDOLPH; *197 D-13; elev. 772ft./235m.; mail Huntsville Z 65259; rural
Fort Leonard Wood; CDP-Census Area Only; PULASKI; *197 I-14; 🅿; Z 65473; Ⓟ 15,863; Ⓒ 13,666
Fortuna; RMC Place; MONITEAU; 197 G-13; elev. 961ft./293m.; 🅿; Z 65034; ● 165
Fort Zumwalt; RMC Place; ST. CHARLES; ★ ST.L; mail O Fallon Z 63366; pop. incl. with O'Fallon (Inc. Place)
Foster; Inc. Place; BATES; 196 H-9; elev. 850ft./259m.; 🅿; Z 64745; Ⓟ 161; Ⓒ 130
Fountain Grove; RMC Place; LINN; *197 D-11; mail Meadville Z 64659
Fountain N' Lakes; Inc. Place; LINCOLN; *197 F-17; mail Moscow Mills Z 63362; Ⓒ 129
Four Seasons (Village of Four Seasons); Inc. Place; CAMDEN; *197 H-13; elev. 253ft./77m.; 🅿; Z 65049; Ⓟ 805; Ⓒ 1,493
Fox Creek; RMC Place; ST. LOUIS; *197 G-17; elev. 768ft./234m.; ★ ST.L; mail Pacific Z 63069; pop. incl. with Wildwood (Inc. Place)
Frailie; RMC Place; NEW MADRID; *197 M-19; mail Gideon Z 63848; rural
Frankclay; RMC Place; ST. FRANCOIS; 197 I-17; elev. 900ft./274m.; 🅿; Z 63601; ● 300
Frankenstein; RMC Place; OSAGE; *197 G-15; elev. 794ft./242m.; mail Bonnots Mill Z 65016; ● 50
Frankford; Inc. Place; PIKE; 197 D-16; elev. 630ft./192m.; 🅿; Z 63441; Ⓟ 396; Ⓒ 351
Franklin; Inc. Place; HOWARD; *197 F-13; elev. 600ft./183m.; 🅿; Z 65250; Ⓟ 181; Ⓒ 112
FRANKLIN; 197 G-16; Ⓟ 80,603; Ⓒ 93,807; ◆ 99,626
Franks; RMC Place; PULASKI; *197 I-14; mail Dixon Z 65459; rural
Frazier; RMC Place; BUCHANAN; *196 D-9; elev. 938ft./286m.; mail Agency Z 64401; ● 30
Fredericksburg; RMC Place; GASCONADE, OSAGE; *197 G-15; mail Morrison Z 65061; rural
Fredericktown; Inc. Place; ⊡ MADISON; 197 J-18; elev. 743ft./226m.; 🅿 🅷; Z 63645; Ⓟ 3,950; Ⓒ 3,928
Fredville; RMC Place; NEWTON; *196 K-9; elev. 1,135ft./346m.; mail Neosho Z 64850; rural
Freeburg; Inc. Place; OSAGE; 197 H-14; elev. 899ft./274m.; 🅿; Z 65035; Ⓟ 446; Ⓒ 423
Freedom; RMC Place; CAMDEN; *197 H-13; elev. 270ft./82m.; mail Montreal Z 65591; rural
Freedom; RMC Place; OSAGE; *197 G-15; elev. 745ft./227m.; mail Chamois Z 65024
Freeman; Inc. Place; CASS; 196 G-9; elev. 349ft./106m.; 🅿; Z 64746; Ⓟ 480; Ⓒ 521
Freistatt; Inc. Place; LAWRENCE; 196 K-10; elev. 1,330ft./405m.; 🅿; Z 65654; Ⓟ 166; Ⓒ 184
Fremont; RMC Place; CARTER; 197 K-16; elev. 621ft./189m.; 🅿; Z 63941; ● 120
Fremont Hills; Inc. Place; CHRISTIAN; *197 K-12; elev. 1,298ft./396m.; ★ SPRG; mail Nixa Z 65714; Ⓟ 201; Ⓒ 597
French Village; RMC Place; ST. FRANCOIS; 197 H-18; elev. 899ft./274m.; 🅿; Z 63036; ● 300
Friedheim; RMC Place; CAPE GIRARDEAU; 197 J-19; elev. 540ft./165m.; 🅿; Z 63747; ● 135
Friendly Valley; RMC Place; PERRY; *197 I-19; elev. 620ft./189m.; mail Perryville Z 63775; rural
Frisbee; RMC Place; DUNKLIN; 197 M-19; mail Holcomb Z 63852; ● 50
Frisco; RMC Place; STODDARD; *197 L-19; elev. 294ft./90m.; mail Essex Z 63846; rural
Fristoe; RMC Place; BENTON; 197 H-11; elev. 944ft./288m.; mail Warsaw Z 65355; ● 120
Frohna; Inc. Place; PERRY; 197 I-19; elev. 550ft./168m.; 🅿; Z 63748; Ⓟ 162; Ⓒ 192
Frontenac; Inc. Place; ST. LOUIS; 195 E-4; elev. 550ft./168m.; 🅿 ■; ★ ST.L; Z 63131; Ⓟ 3,374; Ⓒ 3,483; ◆ 3,519
Fruitland; RMC Place; CAPE GIRARDEAU; 197 J-19; mail Jackson Z 63755; ● 200
Fruitland; RMC Place; GREENE; *197 J-12; elev. 1,214ft./370m.; mail Fair Grove Z 65648; ● 130
Frumet; RMC Place; JEFFERSON; *197 H-17; mail De Soto Z 63020; rural
Fulton; Inc. Place; ⊡ CALLAWAY; 197 F-14; elev. 770ft./235m.; 🅿 🅷 🅲 3,244; Z 65251; Ⓟ 10,033; Ⓒ 12,128
Furner; RMC Place; BOONE; *197 F-13; mail Columbia Z 65203; ● 200

G

Gaines; RMC Place; HENRY; *197 H-11; elev. 756ft./230m.; mail Clinton Z 64735; rural
Gainesville; Inc. Place; ⊡ OZARK; 197 L-13; elev. 759ft./231m.; 🅿; Z 65655; Ⓟ 659; Ⓒ 632
Galena; Inc. Place; ⊡ STONE; 197 L-11; elev. 985ft./300m.; 🅿; Z 65624, Z 65656; Ⓟ 401; Ⓒ 451
Galesburg; RMC Place; JASPER; *196 J-9; ★ JOP; mail Oronogo Z 64855; ● 100
Gallatin; Inc. Place; ⊡ DAVIESS; 196 C-10; elev. 931ft./284m.; 🅿; Z 64640; Ⓟ 1,864; Ⓒ 1,789
Galloway; RMC Place; GREENE; *197 K-12; elev. 1,175ft./358m.; ★ SPRG; mail Springfield Z 65804; pop. incl. with Springfield (Inc. Place)
Galmey; RMC Place; HICKORY; *197 I-11; elev. 973ft./297m.; mail Wheatland Z 65779; ● 270
Galt; Inc. Place; GRUNDY; 197 C-11; elev. 854ft./260m.; 🅿; Z 64641; Ⓟ 296; Ⓒ 275
Gamburg; RMC Place; RIPLEY; *197 L-17; mail Oxly Z 63955; rural
Game; PEMISCOT; see Stubtown (RMC Place)
Gamma; RMC Place; MONTGOMERY; *197 E-16; elev. 705ft./215m.; mail Bellflower Z 63333; rural
Garden City; Inc. Place; CASS; 196 G-9; elev. 916ft./279m.; 🅿; Z 64747; Ⓟ 1,225; Ⓒ 1,500
Gardenview; RMC Place; ST. LOUIS; ★ ST.L; mail Florissant Z 63033
Garfield; RMC Place; OREGON; *197 L-16; mail Couch Z 65690; rural
Garland; RMC Place; HENRY; *196 G-10; elev. 798ft./243m.; mail Clinton Z 64735; rural
Garrison; RMC Place; CHRISTIAN; 197 L-12; elev. 891ft./272m.; 🅿; Z 65657
Garwood; RMC Place; REYNOLDS; *197 K-17; elev. 899ft./274m.; mail Piedmont Z 63957, Van Buren Z 63965; rural
Gasconade; Inc. Place; GASCONADE; 197 G-15; elev. 527ft./161m.; 🅿; Z 65036, Z 65061; Ⓟ 253; Ⓒ 267
GASCONADE; 197 G-15; Ⓟ 14,006; Ⓒ 15,342; ◆ 15,224
Gascondy; RMC Place; OSAGE; *197 H-15; elev. 672ft./205m.; mail Belle Z 65013; rural
Gashland; RMC Place; CLAY; *196 E-9; elev. 1,016ft./310m.; ★ K.C.; mail Kansas City Z 64155; pop. incl. with Kansas City (Inc. Place)
Gateway Drive; RMC Place; NEWTON; *196 K-9; ★ JOP; mail Joplin Z 64801; pop. incl. with Joplin (Inc. Place)
Gatewood; RMC Place; RIPLEY; 197 L-16; elev. 543ft./166m.; 🅿; Z 63942; rural
Gaynor; RMC Place; NODAWAY; *196 A-9; elev. 1,216ft./371m.; mail Parnell Z 64475; rural
Gazette; RMC Place; PIKE; *197 E-16; mail Middletown Z 63359
Gentry; Inc. Place; GENTRY; 196 B-9; elev. 888ft./271m.; 🅿; Z 64453; Ⓟ 95; Ⓒ 101
GENTRY; 196 B-9; Ⓟ 6,848; Ⓒ 6,861; ◆ 6,041
Gentryville; RMC Place; DOUGLAS; *197 L-13; elev. 1,112ft./339m.; mail Ava Z 65608; rural
Gentryville; RMC Place; GENTRY; 196 B-9; elev. 829ft./253m.; mail Albany Z 64402; ● 30
Georgetown; RMC Place; PETTIS; 197 F-12; elev. 828ft./252m.; mail Sedalia Z 65301; ● 130
Georgia City; RMC Place; JASPER; *196 J-9; elev. 873ft./266m.; ★ JOP; mail Asbury Z 64832; rural
Gerald; Inc. Place; FRANKLIN; 197 G-16; elev. 895ft./273m.; 🅿; Z 63037; Ⓟ 888; Ⓒ 1,171
Germantown (Noah); RMC Place; HENRY; *196 H-10; mail Montrose Z 64770; rural
Gerster; Inc. Place; ST. CLAIR; 197 I-11; elev. 857ft./261m.; mail Osceola Z 64776; Ⓟ 40; Ⓒ 35
Gibbs; Inc. Place; ADAIR; 197 C-13; elev. 900ft./274m.; 🅿; Z 63540; Ⓟ 89; Ⓒ 100
Gibson; RMC Place; DUNKLIN; *197 M-19; elev. 280ft./85m.; 🅿; Z 63847; ● 150
Gideon; Inc. Place; NEW MADRID; 197 M-19; elev. 269ft./82m.; 🅿; Z 63848; Ⓟ 1,104; Ⓒ 1,113
Gifford (South Gifford); Inc. Place; MACON; 197 C-13; elev. 760ft./232m.; mail La Plata Z 63549; Ⓟ 64; Ⓒ 72
Gilbert; RMC Place; DUNKLIN; *197 N-19; mail Hornersville Z 63855; rural
Gilliam; Inc. Place; SALINE; 197 E-12; elev. 813ft./248m.; 🅿; Z 65330; Ⓟ 212; Ⓒ 229
Gilman City; Inc. Place; HARRISON, DAVIESS; 196 B-10; elev. 979ft./298m.; 🅿; Z 64642; Ⓟ 393; Ⓒ 380
Gilmore; RMC Place; ST. CHARLES; *197 F-17; ★ ST.L; mail Wentzville Z 63385; ● 100
Ginger Blue; Inc. Place; MCDONALD; *196 L-9; mail Noel Z 64854; incorporated January 21, 1965; not reported in 2000 Census; ● 230
Gipsy; RMC Place; BOLLINGER; 197 K-18; elev. 400ft./122m.; 🅿; Z 63750; rural
Girdner; RMC Place; DOUGLAS; *197 L-13; mail Ava Z 65608; rural
Gladden; RMC Place; DENT; *197 J-15; elev. 1,290ft./393m.; mail Salem Z 65560; rural
Gladstone (Linden); Inc. Place; CLAY; 196 E-9; elev. 950ft./290m.; 🅿; ★ K.C.; Z 64118-19 & mail Kansas City Z 64116, Z 64155-56, Z 64165-66, Z 64188; Ⓟ 26,243; Ⓒ 26,365; ◆ 28,139
Glasgow; Inc. Place; HOWARD, CHARITON; 197 E-12; elev. 650ft./198m.; 🅿; Z 65254; Ⓟ 1,295; Ⓒ 1,263
Glasgow Village; CDP; ST. LOUIS; *197 F-18; ★ ST.L; mail Saint Louis Z 63137; Ⓟ 5,199; Ⓒ 5,234
Glenaire; Inc. Place; CLAY; 196 G-5; elev. 800ft./244m.; ★ K.C.; mail Liberty Z 64068; Ⓟ 597; Ⓒ 553
Glenallen; Inc. Place; BOLLINGER; 197 J-19; elev. 456ft./139m.; 🅿; Z 63751; Ⓟ 96; Ⓒ 145
Glencoe; RMC Place; ST. LOUIS; *197 G-17; elev. 453ft./138m.; 🅿; ★ ST.L; Z 63038; pop. incl. with Wildwood (Inc. Place)
Glendale; RMC Place; PUTNAM; *197 B-13; elev. 825ft./251m.; mail Livonia Z 63551; rural
Glendale; Inc. Place; ST. LOUIS; 195 F-5; elev. 585ft./178m.; ★ ST.L; mail Saint Louis Z 63122; Ⓟ 5,945; Ⓒ 5,767
Glen Echo Park; Inc. Place; ST. LOUIS; *197 F-18; elev. 650ft./198m.; ★ ST.L; mail Saint Louis Z 63121; Ⓟ 304; Ⓒ 166
Glennon; RMC Place; BOLLINGER; *197 K-19; elev. 544ft./166m.; mail Marble Hill Z 63764; ● 100
Glennonville; RMC Place; DUNKLIN; 197 L-18; mail Campbell Z 63933; ● 140
Glen Park; RMC Place; JEFFERSON; *197 G-18; elev. 400ft./122m.; ★ ST.L; mail Pevely Z 63070; pop. incl. with Glen Park (Inc. Place)
Glensted; RMC Place; MORGAN; 197 G-12; elev. 972ft./296m.; mail Versailles Z 65084; ● 100
Glenstone; RMC Place; GREENE; *197 K-12; ★ SPRG; mail Springfield Z 65804; pop. incl. with Springfield (Inc. Place)
Glenwood; Inc. Place; SCHUYLER; 197 A-13; elev. 950ft./290m.; 🅿; Z 63541; Ⓟ 195; Ⓒ 203
Glenwood Junction; RMC Place; SCHUYLER; *197 A-13; mail Glenwood Z 63541
Glidewell; RMC Place; GREENE; 197 J-11; elev. 1,170ft./357m.; mail Springfield Z 65803; ● 70
Glover; RMC Place; IRON; 197 J-17; elev. 848ft./258m.; 🅿; Z 63620; rural
Gobler; RMC Place; PEMISCOT; *197 M-19; elev. 250ft./76m.; 🅿; Z 63849
Golden; RMC Place; BARRY; 197 L-11; elev. 1,165ft./355m.; 🅿; Z 65658; ● 130
Golden City; Inc. Place; BARTON; 196 J-10; elev. 1,050ft./320m.; 🅿; Z 64748; Ⓟ 794; Ⓒ 884
Golden Oak; RMC Place; CLAY; ★ K.C.; mail Kansas City Z 64117; pop. incl. with Kansas City (Inc. Place)
Goldman; RMC Place; JEFFERSON; 197 H-17; elev. 481ft./147m.; ★ ST.L; mail Hillsboro Z 63050; ● 150
Goldsberry; RMC Place; MACON; *197 C-13; elev. 987ft./301m.; mail Ethel Z 63539
Gooch Mill; RMC Place; COOPER; *197 F-13; mail Boonville Z 65233, Prairie Home Z 65068; rural
Goodhope; RMC Place; DOUGLAS; *197 K-12; elev. 1,274ft./388m.; mail Ava Z 65608; ● 90
Goodland; RMC Place; IRON; *197 I-16; mail Belleview Z 63623; rural
Goodman; Inc. Place; MCDONALD; 196 L-9; elev. 1,254ft./382m.; 🅿; Z 64843; Ⓟ 1,094; Ⓒ 1,183
Goodnight; Inc. Place; POLK; elev. 1,050ft./320m.; incorporated February 24, 2003; not reported in 2000 Census
Good Samaritan Ranch; RMC Place; POLK; *197 J-11; elev. 1,013ft./309m.; mail Brighton Z 65617; ● 220
Goodson; RMC Place; POLK; 197 I-12; elev. 1,050ft./320m.; 🅿; Z 65663; ● 85
Gordonville; Inc. Place; CAPE GIRARDEAU; 197 J-19; elev. 400ft./122m.; 🅿; Z 63752 & mail Cape Girardeau Z 63701; Ⓟ 345; Ⓒ 425
Gorin (South Gorin); Inc. Place; SCOTLAND; 197 B-14; elev. 700ft./213m.; 🅿; Z 63543; Ⓟ 130; Ⓒ 143
Goshen; RMC Place; MERCER; *197 B-11; mail Princeton Z 64673; rural
Gospel Ridge; RMC Place; PULASKI; *197 I-14; mail Saint Robert Z 65584; pop. incl. with Saint Robert (Inc. Place)
Goss; Inc. Place; MONROE; *197 D-14; mail Paris Z 65275; incorporated March 26, 2001; not reported in 2000 Census
Gower; Inc. Place; CLINTON, BUCHANAN; 196 D-9; elev. 941ft./287m.; 🅿; Z 64454; Ⓟ 1,249; Ⓒ 1,399
Graff; RMC Place; WRIGHT; 197 J-14; elev. 1,348ft./411m.; 🅿; Z 65660; ● 50
Graham; Inc. Place; NODAWAY; 196 B-8; elev. 880ft./268m.; 🅿; Z 64455; Ⓟ 204; Ⓒ 191
Grain Valley; Inc. Place; JACKSON; 196 F-9; elev. 800ft./244m.; 🅿; ★ K.C.; Z 64029; Ⓟ 1,898; Ⓒ 5,160
Granby; Inc. Place; NEWTON; 196 K-9; elev. 1,150ft./351m.; 🅿; Z 64844; Ⓟ 1,945; Ⓒ 2,121
Grand Center; RMC Place; RANDOLPH; *197 D-13; elev. 781ft./238m.; mail Callao Z 63534; rural
Grand Falls Plaza; Inc. Place; NEWTON; *196 K-9; elev. 892ft./272m.; ★ JOP; mail Joplin Z 64804; Ⓟ 122; Ⓒ 104
Grandin; Inc. Place; CARTER; 197 L-17; elev. 585ft./178m.; 🅿; Z 63943; Ⓟ 233; Ⓒ 236
Grand Pass; Inc. Place; SALINE; 197 E-11; elev. 666ft./203m.; 🅿; Z 65339; Ⓟ 53; Ⓒ 53
Grandview; Inc. Place; JACKSON; 196 F-9; elev. 1,036ft./316m.; 🅿; ★ K.C.; Z 64030; Ⓟ 24,967; Ⓒ 24,881; ◆ 24,712
Granger; Inc. Place; SCOTLAND; 197 B-14; elev. 760ft./232m.; 🅿; Z 63442; Ⓟ 63; Ⓒ 44
Graniteville; RMC Place; IRON; 197 I-17; mail Ironton Z 63650; ● 30
Grant City; Inc. Place; ⊡ WORTH; 196 B-9; elev. 1,136ft./346m.; 🅿; Z 64456; Ⓟ 998; Ⓒ 926
Grantwood Village; Inc. Place; ST. LOUIS; 195 G-5; elev. 605ft./184m.; ★ ST.L; mail Saint Louis Z 63123; Ⓟ 904; Ⓒ 883
Granville; RMC Place; MONROE; *197 D-14; mail Holliday Z 65258, Paris Z 65275
Grassy; RMC Place; BOLLINGER; 197 J-18; elev. 706ft./215m.; 🅿; Z 63751; rural
Grave Hill (Gravelhill); RMC Place; CAPE GIRARDEAU; *197 J-19; elev. 426ft./130m.; mail Burfordville Z 63739, Whitewater Z 63785
Gravelhill; CAPE GIRARDEAU; see Grave Hill (RMC Place)
Gravelton; RMC Place; WAYNE; *197 J-18; mail Marquand Z 63655; rural
Gravois; RMC Place; ST. LOUIS (Independent City); *197 G-18; ★ ST.L; mail Saint Louis Z 63116; pop. incl. with Saint Louis (Independent City)
Gravois Mills; Inc. Place; MORGAN; 197 H-12; elev. 667ft./203m.; 🅿; Z 65037-38; Ⓟ 101; Ⓒ 208
Grayridge; RMC Place; STODDARD; *197 L-19; elev. 295ft./90m.; 🅿; Z 63850; ● 140
Grayson; RMC Place; CLINTON; 196 D-9; elev. 980ft./299m.; mail Trimble Z 64492; ● 125
Grays Point; RMC Place; LAWRENCE; *196 J-10; elev. 1,183ft./361m.; mail Miller Z 65707; rural
Gray Summit; CDP; FRANKLIN; 197 G-17; elev. 552ft./168m.; 🅿; ★ ST.L; Z 63039; Ⓟ 2,505; Ⓒ 2,640
Graysville; RMC Place; PUTNAM; 197 B-13; elev. 999ft./304m.; mail Livonia Z 63551, Unionville Z 63565; ● 40
Green Bay Terrace; RMC Place; CAMDEN; *197 H-13; mail Sunrise Beach Z 65079; ● 100
Greenbrier; RMC Place; BOLLINGER; *197 K-19; elev. 366ft./112m.; mail Advance Z 63730
Green Castle; Inc. Place; SULLIVAN; 197 B-12; elev. 1,048ft./319m.; 🅿; Z 63544; Ⓟ 254; Ⓒ 308
Green City; Inc. Place; SULLIVAN; 197 B-12; elev. 1,059ft./323m.; 🅿; Z 63545; Ⓟ 671; Ⓒ 688
Green Cox; RMC Place; CAPE GIRARDEAU; *197 K-19; mail Advance Z 63730; rural
Greendale; Inc. Place; ST. LOUIS; 195 D-5; elev. 600ft./183m.; ★ ST.L; mail Saint Louis Z 63133; Ⓟ 426; Ⓒ 722
GREENE; 197 J-11; Ⓟ 207,949; Ⓒ 240,391; ◆ 281,275
Greenfield; Inc. Place; ⊡ DADE; 196 J-10; elev. 1,087ft./331m.; 🅿; Z 65661; Ⓟ 1,416; Ⓒ 1,358
Green Forest; RMC Place; BUTLER; *197 L-18; elev. 467ft./142m.; mail Poplar Bluff Z 63901; ● 70
Green Grove; RMC Place; ADAIR; *197 B-13; elev. 900ft./274m.; mail Novinger Z 63559; rural
Greenlawn; RMC Place; RALLS; *197 D-15; mail Perry Z 63462; rural
Green Mound Ridge; RMC Place; CHRISTIAN; *197 K-12; elev. 1,305ft./398m.; mail Highlandville Z 65669; ● 100
Green Mountain; RMC Place; WRIGHT; *197 J-14; elev. 1,430ft./436m.; mail Mountain Grove Z 65711; rural
Green Oaks; RMC Place; STODDARD; *197 L-18; mail Dudley Z 63936; rural
Green Park; Inc. Place; ST. LOUIS; 195 G-5; ★ ST.L; mail Saint Louis Z 63128; Ⓒ 2,666
Green Ridge; Inc. Place; PETTIS; 197 G-11; elev. 909ft./277m.; 🅿; Z 65332; Ⓟ 452; Ⓒ 445
Greensburg; RMC Place; KNOX; 197 B-14; elev. 792ft./241m.; mail Baring Z 63531; ● 30
Greenstreet; RMC Place; FRANKLIN; *197 G-16; mail Beaufort Z 63013; ● 100
Greentop; Inc. Place; SCHUYLER, ADAIR; 197 B-13; elev. 991ft./302m.; 🅿; Z 63546; Ⓟ 425; Ⓒ 427
Green Trail; RMC Place; ST. LOUIS; *197 G-17; ★ ST.L; mail Chesterfield Z 63017; pop. incl. with Chesterfield (Inc. Place)
Greenville; RMC Place; CLAY; *196 E-9; ★ K.C.; mail Kearney Z 64060; ● 100
Greenville; Inc. Place; ⊡ WAYNE; 197 K-18; elev. 406ft./124m.; 🅿; Z 63944; Ⓟ 437; Ⓒ 451
Greenwood; Inc. Place; JACKSON; 196 F-9; elev. 953ft./290m.; 🅿; ★ K.C.; Z 64034; Ⓟ 1,505; Ⓒ 3,952
Greer; RMC Place; OREGON; *197 L-16; elev. 853ft./260m.; mail Alton Z 65606
Gregory; CLARK; see Gregory Landing (RMC Place)
Gregory Landing (Gregory); RMC Place; CLARK; *197 B-15; mail Canton Z 63435
Gretna; RMC Place; TANEY; *197 L-11; mail Branson Z 65616; rural
Grimmet; RMC Place; HOWELL; *197 L-14; mail West Plains Z 65775; rural
Grisham; RMC Place; BOLLINGER; *197 J-18; mail Marble Hill Z 63764; rural
Grogan; RMC Place; TEXAS; *197 K-15; elev. 1,200ft./366m.; mail Elk Creek Z 65464; ● 30
Grover; RMC Place; ST. LOUIS; *197 G-17; elev. 794ft./242m.; 🅿; ★ ST.L; Z 63040; pop. incl. with Wildwood (Inc. Place)
Grovespring; RMC Place; WRIGHT; 197 J-13; elev. 1,300ft./396m.; 🅿; Z 65662
Grubville; RMC Place; JEFFERSON; 197 H-17; elev. 901ft./275m.; 🅿; Z 63041; ● 200
GRUNDY; 197 B-11; Ⓟ 10,536; Ⓒ 10,432; ◆ 10,143
Guilford; Inc. Place; NODAWAY; 196 B-8; elev. 980ft./299m.; 🅿; Z 64457; Ⓟ 93; Ⓒ 87
Gulfton; RMC Place; JASPER; *196 K-9; mail Carl Junction Z 64834; ● 200
Gumbo; RMC Place; ST. FRANCOIS; *197 I-17; mail Chesterfield Z 63005, Park Hills Z 63601; ● 200
Gunn City; Inc. Place; CASS; 196 G-10; elev. 860ft./262m.; mail Garden City Z 64747; Ⓟ 65; Ⓒ 85
Guthrie; RMC Place; CALLAWAY; 197 F-14; mail New Bloomfield Z 65063; ● 150

H

Hagers Grove; RMC Place; SHELBY; *197 C-14; mail Clarence Z 63437; rural
Hahn; RMC Place; BOLLINGER; *197 K-19; mail Marble Hill Z 63764; rural
Hailey; RMC Place; BARRY; *196 L-10; mail Aurora Z 65605; rural
Hale; Inc. Place; CARROLL; 197 D-11; elev. 770ft./235m.; 🅿; Z 64643; Ⓟ 480; Ⓒ 473
Half Rock; RMC Place; MERCER; *197 B-11; mail Spickard Z 64679; rural
Halfway; Inc. Place; POLK; 197 I-12; elev. 1,077ft./328m.; 🅿; Z 65663; Ⓟ 171; Ⓒ 176
Halls; RMC Place; BUCHANAN; 196 D-8; elev. 802ft./244m.; mail Saint Joseph Z 64504; ● 50
Hallsville; Inc. Place; BOONE; 197 E-14; elev. 916ft./279m.; 🅿; Z 65255; Ⓟ 917; Ⓒ 978
Halltown; Inc. Place; LAWRENCE; 197 K-11; 🅿; Z 65664; Ⓟ 161; Ⓒ 189
Hamilton; Inc. Place; CALDWELL; 196 D-10; elev. 994ft./303m.; 🅿; Z 64644; Ⓟ 1,737; Ⓒ 1,813
Hammond; RMC Place; OZARK; *197 L-13; elev. 744ft./227m.; mail Thornfield Z 65762; ● 90
Hams Prairie; RMC Place; CALLAWAY; 197 F-14; elev. 851ft./259m.; mail Fulton Z 65251; ● 100
Hancock; RMC Place; PULASKI; 197 H-14; elev. 1,109ft./338m.; mail Crocker Z 65452; ● 50
Handy; RMC Place; RIPLEY; 197 L-16; mail Fremont Z 63941; rural
Hanley Hills; Inc. Place; ST. LOUIS; 195 E-5; elev. 594ft./181m.; ★ ST.L; mail Saint Louis Z 63133; Ⓟ 2,325; Ⓒ 2,124
Hannibal; Inc. Place; MARION, RALLS; 197 D-16; elev. 491ft./150m.; 🅿 🅷 🅲 1,111 ■; Z 63401; Ⓟ 18,004; Ⓒ 17,757; ◆ 16,899
Hannon; RMC Place; BARTON; *196 I-9; elev. 869ft./265m.; mail Liberal Z 64762; rural
Happy Hollow; RMC Place; WASHINGTON; *197 H-17; elev. 876ft./267m.; mail Cadet Z 63630; ● 150
Hardeman; RMC Place; SALINE; *197 E-12; elev. 765ft./233m.; mail Marshall Z 65340; rural
Hardenville; RMC Place; OZARK; *197 L-13; elev. 963ft./294m.; 🅿; Z 65666
Hardin; Inc. Place; RAY; 196 E-10; elev. 690ft./210m.; 🅿; Z 64035; Ⓟ 598; Ⓒ 614
Harg; RMC Place; BOONE; *197 F-14; ★ COL; mail Columbia Z 65201; rural
Harlem; RMC Place; CLAY; *196 E-9; mail Kansas City Z 64116; pop. incl. with Kansas City (Inc. Place)
Harold; RMC Place; GREENE; *197 J-11; elev. 1,179ft./359m.; mail Walnut Grove Z 65770; rural
Harper; RMC Place; ST. CLAIR; *197 H-11; elev. 941ft./287m.; mail Osceola Z 64776; rural
Harris; Inc. Place; SULLIVAN; 197 B-11; elev. 900ft./274m.; 🅿; Z 64645; Ⓟ 102; Ⓒ 105
Harrisburg; Inc. Place; BOONE; 197 E-13; elev. 841ft./256m.; 🅿; Z 65256; Ⓟ 169; Ⓒ 184
HARRISON; 196 B-10; Ⓟ 8,469; Ⓒ 8,850; ◆ 8,983
Harrisonville; Inc. Place; ⊡ CASS; 196 G-9; elev. 904ft./276m.; 🅿 🅷; Z 64701; Ⓟ 7,683; Ⓒ 8,946
Hart; RMC Place; MCDONALD; *196 L-8; mail Seneca Z 64865; ● 100
Hartford; RMC Place; PUTNAM; 197 B-12; mail Unionville Z 63565; ● 30
Hartsburg; Inc. Place; BOONE; 197 F-14; elev. 564ft./172m.; 🅿; Z 65039; Ⓟ 131; Ⓒ 108
Hartshorn; RMC Place; TEXAS; *197 J-15; elev. 1,300ft./396m.; 🅿; Z 65479
Hartville; Inc. Place; ⊡ WRIGHT; 197 J-13; elev. 1,170ft./357m.; 🅿; Z 65667; Ⓟ 495; Ⓒ 607
Hartwell; RMC Place; HENRY; *196 G-10; mail Urich Z 64788; disincorporated March 2, 1995; Ⓒ 16
Hartzell; RMC Place; NEW MADRID; *197 M-19; mail Gideon Z 63848; ● 60
Harvester; RMC Place; ST. CHARLES; *197 F-17; elev. 612ft./187m.; ★ ST.L; mail Saint Charles Z 63303-04; pop. incl. with Saint Peters (Inc. Place)
Harviell; RMC Place; BUTLER; *197 L-18; elev. 318ft./97m.; 🅿; Z 63945; ● 200
Harwood; Inc. Place; VERNON; 196 I-10; elev. 840ft./256m.; 🅿; Z 64750; Ⓟ 89; Ⓒ 90
Haseltine; RMC Place; GREENE; *197 K-11; ★ SPRG; mail Springfield Z 65802; rural
Hassard; RMC Place; RALLS; *197 D-15; mail Monroe City Z 63456; rural
Hastain; RMC Place; BENTON; *197 H-12; elev. 696ft./212m.; mail Edwards Z 65326; rural
Hatfield; RMC Place; HARRISON; 196 A-10; elev. 1,152ft./351m.; 🅿; Z 64458; ● 50
Hatton; RMC Place; CALLAWAY; 197 F-14; mail Auxvasse Z 65231; ● 110
Havenhurst; RMC Place; MCDONALD; *196 L-9; mail Pineville Z 64856; pop. incl. with Pineville (Inc. Place)
Hawkeye; RMC Place; PULASKI; *197 H-13; elev. 1,108ft./338m.; mail Crocker Z 65452; rural
Hawk Point; Inc. Place; LINCOLN; 197 F-16; elev. 720ft./219m.; 🅿; Z 63349; Ⓟ 472; Ⓒ 459
Hayden; RMC Place; MARIES; *197 H-14; mail Dixon Z 65459; rural
Hayes Park; RMC Place; JACKSON; ★ K.C.; mail Sibley Z 64088; pop. incl. with Sibley (Inc. Place)
Hayti; Inc. Place; PEMISCOT; 197 M-19; elev. 273ft./83m.; 🅿 🅷; Z 63851; Ⓟ 3,280; Ⓒ 3,207
Hayti Heights; Inc. Place; PEMISCOT; *197 M-19; elev. 270ft./82m.; 🅿; Z 63851; Ⓟ 893; Ⓒ 771
Hayward; RMC Place; PEMISCOT; *197 M-20; mail Portageville Z 63873; disincorporated January 24, 2000; Ⓟ 103; Ⓒ 123
Haywood City; Inc. Place; SCOTT; 197 K-20; elev. 330ft./101m.; mail Benton Z 63736, Oran Z 63771; Ⓟ 263; Ⓒ 239
Hazelgreen (Hazlegreen); RMC Place; LACLEDE; *197 I-13; mail Richland Z 65556; rural
Hazel Run; RMC Place; ST. FRANCOIS; *197 I-18; elev. 788ft./240m.; mail Bonne Terre Z 63628; rural
Hazelwood; Inc. Place; ST. LOUIS; 195 C-5; elev. 550ft./168m.; 🅿; ★ ST.L; Z 63042-44 & mail Earth City Z 63045, Saint Louis Z 63135; Ⓟ 15,324; Ⓒ 26,206; ◆ 25,384
Hazlegreen; LACLEDE; see Hazelgreen (RMC Place)
Heatonville; RMC Place; LAWRENCE; *196 K-10; mail Miller Z 65707; rural
Hebron; RMC Place; DOUGLAS; *197 L-14; elev. 953ft./290m.; mail West Plains Z 65775; rural
Hecla; RMC Place; LINN; *197 C-11; elev. 814ft./248m.; mail Linneus Z 64653; rural
Hedge City; RMC Place; KNOX; *197 C-14; elev. 800ft./244m.; mail Novelty Z 63460; rural
Helena; RMC Place; ANDREW; 196 C-9; elev. 1,060ft./323m.; 🅿; Z 64459; ● 200
Helm; RMC Place; PULASKI; *197 H-14; mail Dixon Z 65459; rural
Heman Park; RMC Place; ST. LOUIS; ★ ST.L; mail Saint Louis Z 63130; pop. incl. with University City (Inc. Place)
Hematite; RMC Place; JEFFERSON; 197 H-18; elev. 440ft./134m.; 🅿; ★ ST.L; Z 63047; ● 250
Hemple; RMC Place; CLINTON; *196 D-9; elev. 1,034ft./315m.; 🅿; Z 64490; ● 150
Henderson; RMC Place; WEBSTER; *197 K-12; mail Rogersville Z 65742; rural
Hendrickson; RMC Place; BUTLER; 197 K-18; mail Williamsville Z 63967; ● 60
Henley; RMC Place; COLE; 197 G-14; elev. 600ft./183m.; 🅿; Z 65040; ● 100
Henrietta; Inc. Place; RAY; 196 E-10; elev. 702ft./214m.; 🅿; Z 64036; Ⓟ 412; Ⓒ 457
HENRY; 197 G-11; Ⓟ 20,044; Ⓒ 21,997; ◆ 22,188
Henry Winfield Wheeler; RMC Place; ST. LOUIS (Independent City); *197 G-18; ★ ST.L; mail Saint Louis Z 63101; pop. incl. with Saint Louis (Independent City)
Herculaneum; Inc. Place; JEFFERSON; 197 H-18; elev. 422ft./129m.; 🅿; ★ ST.L; Z 63048; Ⓟ 2,263; Ⓒ 2,805
Hercules; RMC Place; TANEY; *197 L-12; mail Bradleyville Z 65614; rural
Hermann; Inc. Place; ⊡ GASCONADE; 197 F-15; elev. 519ft./158m.; 🅿 🅷; Z 65041; Ⓟ 2,754; Ⓒ 2,674
Hermitage; Inc. Place; ⊡ HICKORY; 197 I-11; elev. 822ft./251m.; 🅿; Z 65668; Ⓟ 512; Ⓒ 406; Ⓡ 496
Hermondale; RMC Place; PEMISCOT; *197 N-19; elev. 251ft./77m.; mail Steele Z 63877; rural
Hickman Mills; RMC Place; JACKSON; *196 F-9; ★ K.C.; mail Kansas City Z 64134, Z 64137, Z 64192; pop. incl. with Kansas City (Inc. Place)
Hickory; GRUNDY; see Hickory Creek (RMC Place)
HICKORY; 197 H-12; Ⓟ 7,335; Ⓒ 8,940; ◆ 9,067
Hickory Barren; RMC Place; GREENE; *197 J-12; elev. 1,300ft./396m.; ★ SPRG; mail Springfield Z 65803; rural
Hickory Creek (Hickory); RMC Place; GRUNDY; *197 C-11; mail Trenton Z 64683; rural
Hickory Hill; RMC Place; COLE; *197 G-13; elev. 861ft./262m.; mail Henley Z 65040
Higbee; Inc. Place; RANDOLPH; 197 E-13; elev. 880ft./268m.; 🅿; Z 65257; Ⓟ 639; Ⓒ 623
Higdon; RMC Place; MADISON; *197 I-18; mail Fredericktown Z 63645; ● 30
Higginsville; Inc. Place; LAFAYETTE; 197 E-11; elev. 836ft./255m.; 🅿; Z 64037; Ⓟ 4,693; Ⓒ 4,682
High Gate; RMC Place; MARIES; 197 H-15; elev. 1,085ft./331m.; mail Saint James Z 65559
High Hill; Inc. Place; MONTGOMERY; 197 F-16; elev. 894ft./272m.; 🅿; Z 63350; Ⓟ 204; Ⓒ 231
Highland; RMC Place; PERRY; *197 I-19; elev. 676ft./206m.; mail Perryville Z 63775; rural
Highlandville; Inc. Place; CHRISTIAN; 197 K-11; elev. 1,380ft./421m.; 🅿; Z 65669; Ⓒ 872
Highley Heights; RMC Place; ST. FRANCOIS; *197 I-18; elev. 761ft./232m.; mail Park Hills Z 63601; pop. incl. with Desloge (Inc. Place)
High Point; RMC Place; MONITEAU; 197 G-13; elev. 903ft./275m.; 🅿; Z 65042; ● 100
High Ridge; CDP; JEFFERSON; 197 G-17; elev. 927ft./283m.; 🅿; ★ ST.L; Z 63049; Ⓟ 4,423; Ⓒ 4,236
Hilda; RMC Place; TANEY; *197 L-12; elev. 995ft./303m.; mail Kissee Mills Z 65680; rural
Hilderbrand; RMC Place; CAPE GIRARDEAU; *197 I-19; elev. 569ft./173m.; mail Perryville Z 63775; rural
Hill City; RMC Place; BARRY; *197 L-11; elev. 1,400ft./427m.; mail Cassville Z 65625; rural
Hillhouse Addition; RMC Place; CAMDEN; elev. 1,115ft./340m.; mail Richland Z 65556
Hilliard; RMC Place; BUTLER; *197 L-18; elev. 355ft./108m.; mail Poplar Bluff Z 63901; rural
Hillsboro; Inc. Place; ⊡ JEFFERSON; 197 H-17; elev. 802ft./244m.; 🅿; ★ ST.L; Z 63050; Ⓟ 1,625; Ⓒ 1,675
Hillsdale; Inc. Place; ST. LOUIS; 195 D-6; elev. 600ft./183m.; ★ ST.L; mail Saint Louis Z 63133; Ⓟ 1,948; Ⓒ 1,477
Hill Top; RMC Place; RIPLEY; 197 L-17; mail Doniphan Z 63935; ● 110
Hinch; RMC Place; CRAWFORD; *197 H-16; mail Bourbon Z 65441; rural
Hinton; RMC Place; BOONE; 197 E-14; mail Columbia Z 65202; ● 150
Hiram; RMC Place; WAYNE; *197 K-18; elev. 500ft./152m.; 🅿; Z 63944
Hitt; RMC Place; SCOTLAND; *197 A-14; mail Memphis Z 63555; rural
Hoberg; Inc. Place; LAWRENCE; *196 K-10; elev. 1,180ft./360m.; mail Mount Vernon Z 65712; Ⓟ 62; Ⓒ 60
Hobson; RMC Place; DENT; *197 I-15; mail Salem Z 65560; rural
Hocomo; RMC Place; HOWELL; *197 L-14; elev. 1,101ft./336m.; mail Caulfield Z 65626; rural
Hodge; RMC Place; LAFAYETTE; *197 E-11; mail Waverly Z 64096; rural
Hoene Spring; RMC Place; JEFFERSON; 195 H-2; ★ ST.L; mail Eureka Z 63025; ● 450
Hoffman Junction; RMC Place; ST. FRANCOIS; *197 I-17; elev. 890ft./271m.; mail Bonne Terre Z 63628; rural
Holcomb; Inc. Place; DUNKLIN; 197 M-19; elev. 275ft./84m.; 🅿; Z 63852; Ⓟ 531; Ⓒ 696
Holden; Inc. Place; JOHNSON; 196 F-10; elev. 883ft./269m.; 🅿; Z 64040; Ⓟ 2,389; Ⓒ 2,510
Holland; Inc. Place; PEMISCOT; 197 N-19; elev. 250ft./76m.; 🅿; Z 63853; Ⓟ 237; Ⓒ 246
Holliday; Inc. Place; MONROE; 197 D-14; elev. 788ft./240m.; 🅿; Z 65258; Ⓟ 139; Ⓒ 129
Holliday Landing; RMC Place; WAYNE; *197 K-18; mail Greenville Z 63944; rural
Hollister; Inc. Place; TANEY; 197 L-12; elev. 733ft./223m.; 🅿; Z 65672-73; Ⓟ 2,628; Ⓒ 3,867
Hollow; RMC Place; ST. LOUIS; *197 G-17; ★ ST.L; mail Pacific Z 63069; pop. incl. with Wildwood (Inc. Place)
Hollywood; RMC Place; DUNKLIN; *197 N-18; elev. 245ft./75m.; mail Arbyrd Z 63821; ● 50
Holman; RMC Place; WEBSTER; *197 J-12; elev. 1,500ft./457m.; mail Strafford Z 65757; rural
Holmes Park; RMC Place; JACKSON; ★ K.C.; mail Kansas City Z 64131; pop. incl. with Kansas City (Inc. Place)
Holstein; RMC Place; WARREN; 197 G-16; mail Marthasville Z 63357; ● 90
Holt; Inc. Place; CLAY, CLINTON; 196 D-9; elev. 900ft./274m.; 🅿; ★ K.C.; Z 64048; Ⓟ 311; Ⓒ 405
HOLT; 196 B-7; Ⓟ 6,034; Ⓒ 5,351; ◆ 4,989
Holts Summit; Inc. Place; CALLAWAY; 197 G-14; elev. 864ft./263m.; 🅿; ★ JFCY; Z 65043; Ⓟ 2,292; Ⓒ 2,935
Homestead; Inc. Place; RAY; *196 E-10; ★ K.C.; mail Excelsior Springs Z 64024; Ⓟ 177; Ⓒ 181
Homestown; Inc. Place; PEMISCOT; *197 M-19; elev. 265ft./81m.; 🅿; Z 63879; Ⓟ 230; Ⓒ 181
Honey Creek; RMC Place; COLE; *197 G-14; elev. 800ft./244m.; mail Jefferson City Z 65101; ● 110
Hooker; RMC Place; PULASKI; *197 I-14; mail Newburg Z 65550; rural
Hoover; RMC Place; PLATTE; 196 D-2; ★ K.C.; mail Platte City Z 64079; ● 150
Hope; RMC Place; OSAGE; *197 G-15; elev. 587ft./179m.; mail Morrison Z 65061; rural
Hopewell (Hopewell Academy); RMC Place; WARREN; *197 F-16; elev. 569ft./173m.; mail Marthasville Z 63357; ● 120
Hopewell; RMC Place; WASHINGTON; *197 I-17; elev. 858ft./262m.; mail Mineral Point Z 63660; ● 300
Hopewell Academy; WARREN; see Hopewell (RMC Place)
Hopkins; Inc. Place; NODAWAY; 196 A-8; elev. 1,046ft./319m.; 🅿; Z 64461; Ⓟ 575; Ⓒ 579
Horine; CDP; JEFFERSON; 197 H-18; elev. 420ft./128m.; ★ ST.L; mail Pevely Z 63070; Ⓟ 1,043; Ⓒ 923
Hornersville; Inc. Place; DUNKLIN; 197 N-19; elev. 245ft./75m.; 🅿; Z 63855; Ⓟ 629; Ⓒ 686
Hornet; RMC Place; NEWTON; *196 K-9; ★ JOP; mail Seneca Z 64865; ● 90
Horton; RMC Place; VERNON; 196 H-9; elev. 766ft./233m.; 🅿; Z 64778; ● 50
House Creek; RMC Place; CARTER; *197 K-16; mail Van Buren Z 63965; ● 40
House Springs; RMC Place; JEFFERSON; 197 G-17; elev. 474ft./144m.; 🅿; ★ ST.L; Z 63051; ● 300
Houston; Inc. Place; ⊡ TEXAS; 197 J-14; elev. 1,180ft./360m.; 🅿 🅷; Z 65483; Ⓟ 2,118; Ⓒ 1,992
Houstonia; Inc. Place; PETTIS; 197 F-11; elev. 760ft./232m.; 🅿; Z 65333; Ⓟ 283; Ⓒ 275
Houston Lake; Inc. Place; PLATTE; 196 G-3; elev. 850ft./259m.; 🅿; ★ K.C.; Z 64151 & mail Kansas City Z 64152; Ⓟ 303; Ⓒ 284
HOWARD; 197 E-13; Ⓟ 9,631; Ⓒ 10,212; ◆ 9,757
Howards Ridge; RMC Place; OZARK; *197 L-14; elev. 884ft./269m.; mail Gainesville Z 65655; rural
Howardville; Inc. Place; NEW MADRID; *197 L-20; elev. 290ft./88m.; mail New Madrid Z 63869; Ⓟ 440; Ⓒ 342
Howell; RMC Place; ST. CHARLES; *197 F-17; elev. 506ft./154m.; ★ ST.L; mail Saint Charles Z 63303; pop. incl. with Saint Peters (Inc. Place)
HOWELL; 197 L-14; Ⓟ 31,447; Ⓒ 37,238; ◆ 39,032
Howes Mill; RMC Place; DENT; *197 I-16; elev. 1,080ft./329m.; mail Salem Z 65560; rural
Hudson; RMC Place; BATES; *196 H-10; elev. 850ft./259m.; mail Appleton City Z 64724; rural
Huggins; RMC Place; TEXAS; *197 J-14; elev. 1,492ft./455m.; 🅿; Z 65484; ● 50
Hughesville; Inc. Place; PETTIS; 197 F-11; elev. 808ft./246m.; 🅿; Z 65334; Ⓟ 174; Ⓒ 174
Hugo; RMC Place; CAMDEN; *197 H-13; elev. 944ft./288m.; mail Linn Creek Z 65052; rural
Humansville; Inc. Place; POLK; 197 I-11; elev. 950ft./290m.; 🅿; Z 65674; Ⓟ 1,084; Ⓒ 946
Hume; Inc. Place; BATES; 196 H-9; elev. 894ft./272m.; 🅿; Z 64752; Ⓟ 287; Ⓒ 337
Humphreys; Inc. Place; SULLIVAN; 197 C-11; elev. 928ft./283m.; 🅿; Z 64646; Ⓟ 98; Ⓒ 164
Hunnewell; Inc. Place; SHELBY; 197 D-15; elev. 750ft./229m.; 🅿; Z 63443; Ⓟ 219; Ⓒ 227
Hunter; RMC Place; CARTER; 197 K-17; elev. 724ft./221m.; mail Grandin Z 63943; ● 150
Hunters Mill; RMC Place; WASHINGTON; *197 I-17; elev. 836ft./255m.; mail Potosi Z 63664; ● 100
Hunterville; RMC Place; STODDARD; *197 L-19; mail Essex Z 63846; rural
Huntingdale; RMC Place; HENRY; *196 G-10; mail Clinton Z 64735
Huntington; RMC Place; RALLS; *197 D-15; elev. 729ft./222m.; mail Monroe City Z 63456; rural
Huntleigh; Inc. Place; ST. LOUIS; 195 F-4; elev. 610ft./186m.; ★ ST.L; mail Saint Louis Z 63131; Ⓟ 392; Ⓒ 323
Huntsdale; Inc. Place; BOONE; 197 F-13; mail Columbia Z 65203; incorporated February 1, 2003; not reported in 2000 Census; ● 140
Huntsville; Inc. Place; ⊡ RANDOLPH; 197 D-13; elev. 800ft./244m.; 🅿; Z 65259; Ⓟ 1,567; Ⓒ 1,553
Hurdland; Inc. Place; KNOX; 197 B-14; elev. 889ft./271m.; 🅿; Z 63547; Ⓟ 212; Ⓒ 239
Hurley; Inc. Place; STONE; 197 K-11; elev. 1,080ft./329m.; 🅿; Z 65675; Ⓟ 87; Ⓒ 157
Hurlingen; RMC Place; BUCHANAN; *196 C-9; elev. 938ft./286m.; mail Easton Z 64443; rural
Huron; RMC Place; POLK; *197 I-11; elev. 1,133ft./345m.; mail Bolivar Z 65613; ● 100
Hurricane; RMC Place; BOLLINGER; *197 J-19; elev. 674ft./205m.; mail Marble Hill Z 63764; rural
Hurricane Deck; RMC Place; CAMDEN; *197 H-13; elev. 775ft./236m.; mail Sunrise Beach Z 65079; ● 300
Hurryville; RMC Place; ST. FRANCOIS; *197 I-18; elev. 851ft./259m.; mail Farmington Z 63640; ● 100
Hutton Valley; RMC Place; HOWELL; *197 K-15; elev. 1,153ft./351m.; mail Willow Springs Z 65793; ● 80
Hy-Tex; RMC Place; JACKSON; ★ K.C.; pop. incl. with Kansas City (Inc. Place)

I

Iantha; RMC Place; BARTON; *196 J-9; elev. 985ft./300m.; 🅿; Z 64759; ● 150
Iatan; Inc. Place; PLATTE; 196 D-8; mail Weston Z 64098; Ⓟ 47; Ⓒ 54
Iberia; Inc. Place; MILLER; 197 H-14; elev. 932ft./284m.; 🅿; Z 65486; Ⓟ 650; Ⓒ 605; Ⓡ 651
Iconium; RMC Place; ST. CLAIR; *197 H-11; mail Osceola Z 64776
Idalia; RMC Place; STODDARD; *197 K-19; mail Bloomfield Z 63825; ● 50
Idlewild; RMC Place; STODDARD; *197 K-18; elev. 345ft./105m.; mail Puxico Z 63960
Ilasco; RMC Place; RALLS; 197 D-16; mail Hannibal Z 63401, Saverton Z 63467; ● 80
Illmo; RMC Place; SCOTT; *197 J-20; elev. 390ft./119m.; ★ CPGIR; mail Scott City Z 63780; pop. incl. with Scott City (Inc. Place)
Imperial; CDP; JEFFERSON; *197 G-18; elev. 446ft./136m.; 🅿; ★ ST.L; Z 63052-53; Ⓟ 4,156; Ⓒ 4,373
Impo; TEXAS; see Dunn (RMC Place)
Independence; Inc. Place; ⊡ JACKSON, CLAY; 196 E-9; elev. 900ft./274m.; 🅿 🅷 ■; ★ K.C.; Z 64050-58; Ⓟ 112,301; Ⓒ 113,288; ◆ 113,766
Indian Creek; RMC Place; MONROE; *197 D-15; elev. 697ft./212m.; mail Monroe City Z 63456; ● 30
Indian Ford Lakes; RMC Place; MARIES; *197 H-14; elev. 620ft./189m.; mail Vienna Z 65582; rural
Indian Grove; RMC Place; CHARITON; 197 D-12; elev. 796ft./243m.; mail Brunswick Z 65236; ● 40
Indian Hills; RMC Place; JACKSON; *196 F-9; ★ K.C.; mail Kansas City Z 64114
Indian Lake; RMC Place; CRAWFORD; *197 H-15; elev. 900ft./274m.; mail Cuba Z 65453; ● 800
Indian Point; Inc. Place; STONE; *197 L-11; mail Branson Z 65616; Ⓟ 435; Ⓒ 588
Indian Springs; RMC Place; VERNON; *196 H-10; elev. 803ft./245m.; mail Schell City Z 64783; rural
Ink; RMC Place; SHANNON; *197 J-15; mail Eminence Z 65466; rural
Innsbrook; Inc. Place; WARREN; *197 F-16; 🅿; Z 63390; Ⓒ 469
Ionia; Inc. Place; BENTON, PETTIS; *197 G-11; elev. 946ft./288m.; 🅿; Z 65335; Ⓟ 126; Ⓒ 108
Irena; Inc. Place; WORTH; *196 A-9; Ⓒ 33
IRON; 197 I-16; Ⓟ 10,726; Ⓒ 10,697; ◆ 9,680
Irondale (Savoy); Inc. Place; WASHINGTON; 197 I-17; elev. 820ft./250m.; 🅿; Z 63648; Ⓟ 474; Ⓒ 437
Iron Gates; RMC Place; JASPER; *196 K-9; elev. 1,040ft./317m.; ★ JOP; mail Joplin Z 64801; pop. incl. with Joplin (Inc. Place)
Iron Mountain; RMC Place; ST. FRANCOIS; 197 I-17; elev. 1,100ft./335m.; mail Ironton Z 63650
Iron Mountain Lake; Inc. Place; ST. FRANCOIS; *197 I-17; mail Bismarck Z 63624; Ⓟ 632; Ⓒ 693
Ironton; Inc. Place; ⊡ IRON; 197 I-17; elev. 900ft./274m.; 🅿; Z 63650; Ⓟ 1,539; Ⓒ 1,471
Irwin; RMC Place; BARTON; 196 I-9; elev. 974ft./297m.; 🅿; Z 64759; ● 80
Isabella; RMC Place; OZARK; 197 L-13; elev. 958ft./292m.; 🅿; Z 65676; summer pop. 500; rural
Isadora; RMC Place; WORTH; *196 A-9; mail Grant City Z 64456; rural
Ishmael; RMC Place; WASHINGTON; *197 I-16; elev. 900ft./274m.; mail Potosi Z 63664; rural
Island City; RMC Place; GENTRY; *196 B-9; elev. 300ft./91m.; mail Stanberry Z 64489; rural
Ives; RMC Place; STODDARD; *197 L-18; mail Dudley Z 63936; rural

J

Jack; RMC Place; DENT; *197 J-15; elev. 1,340ft./408m.; mail Salem Z 65560; rural
Jacket; RMC Place; MCDONALD; *196 L-10; elev. 1,120ft./341m.; mail Seligman Z 65745; rural
Jacks Fork; RMC Place; SHANNON; *197 K-16; mail Eminence Z 65466; rural
Jackson; Inc. Place; ⊡ CAPE GIRARDEAU; 197 J-19; elev. 497ft./151m.; 🅿; ★ CPGIR; Z 63755; Ⓟ 9,256; Ⓒ 11,947
JACKSON; 196 F-9; Ⓟ 633,232; Ⓒ 654,880; ◆ 669,955
Jacksonville; Inc. Place; RANDOLPH; 197 D-13; elev. 867ft./264m.; 🅿; Z 65260; Ⓟ 115; Ⓒ 163
Jadwin; RMC Place; DENT; *197 J-15; elev. 1,300ft./396m.; 🅿; Z 65501; ● 60
Jake Prairie; RMC Place; CRAWFORD; *197 H-15; elev. 929ft./283m.; mail Cuba Z 65453; rural
James Crews; RMC Place; JACKSON; *196 E-9; ★ K.C.; mail Kansas City Z 64127; pop. incl. with Kansas City (Inc. Place)
Jameson; Inc. Place; DAVIESS; 196 C-10; elev. 797ft./243m.; 🅿; Z 64647; Ⓟ 149; Ⓒ 120
Jamesport; Inc. Place; DAVIESS; 196 C-10; elev. 990ft./302m.; 🅿; Z 64648; Ⓟ 570; Ⓒ 505
Jamestown; Inc. Place; MONITEAU; 197 F-13; elev. 880ft./268m.; 🅿; Z 65046; Ⓟ 298; Ⓒ 382
Jamesville; RMC Place; STONE; *197 K-11; mail Clever Z 65631; rural
J&G Junction; RMC Place; JASPER; ★ JOP; mail Joplin Z 64801; pop. incl. with Joplin (Inc. Place)
Jane; RMC Place; MCDONALD; 196 L-9; elev. 998ft./304m.; 🅿; Z 64856; ● 120
Japan; RMC Place; FRANKLIN; 197 H-16; elev. 935ft./285m.; mail Sullivan Z 63080; ● 90
Jarvis; RMC Place; JEFFERSON; *197 H-18; ★ ST.L; mail Hillsboro Z 63050; rural
Jasper; Inc. Place; JASPER; 196 J-9; elev. 946ft./288m.; 🅿; Z 64755; Ⓟ 994; Ⓒ 1,011
JASPER; 196 J-9; Ⓟ 90,465; Ⓒ 104,686; ◆ 120,253
Jaudon; RMC Place; CASS; *196 F-9; elev. 1,026ft./313m.; ★ K.C.; mail Belton Z 64012; ● 30
Jaywye; RMC Place; NEW MADRID; 197 L-19; elev. 278ft./85m.; mail Portageville Z 63873; ● 30
Jedburg; ST. LOUIS; see Sherman (RMC Place)
JEFFERSON; 197 H-17; Ⓟ 171,380; Ⓒ 198,099; ◆ 214,480
Jefferson City; Inc. Place; **STATE CAPITAL**; ⊡ COLE, CALLAWAY; 197 G-14; elev. 702ft./214m.; 🅿 🅷 🅲 3,224 ■; ★ JFCY; Z 65101-11; Ⓟ 35,481; Ⓒ 39,636; Ⓡ 38,053; ◆ 41,473
Jefferson Memorial; RMC Place; ST. LOUIS (Independent City); *197 G-18; ★ ST.L; mail Saint Louis Z 63102; pop. incl. with Saint Louis (Independent City)
Jenkins; RMC Place; BARRY; 197 L-11; elev. 1,100ft./335m.; 🅿; Z 65605; ● 90
Jennings; Inc. Place; ST. LOUIS; 195 D-6; elev. 515ft./157m.; 🅿 ■; ★ ST.L; Z 63136; Ⓟ 15,905; Ⓒ 15,469; ◆ 14,790
Jerico; RMC Place; WRIGHT; *197 K-13; elev. 1,428ft./435m.; mail Seymour Z 65746; rural
Jerico Springs; Inc. Place; CEDAR; 196 I-10; 🅿; Z 64756; Ⓟ 247; Ⓒ 259
Jerktail; RMC Place; WRIGHT; *197 J-13; elev. 1,306ft./398m.; mail Hartville Z 65667; rural
Jerome; RMC Place; PHELPS; 197 I-14; elev. 700ft./213m.; 🅿; Z 65529; ● 250
Jewett; RMC Place; MADISON; *197 J-18; mail Annapolis Z 63620; ● 30
JOHNSON; 196 G-10; Ⓟ 42,514; Ⓒ 48,258; ◆ 52,286
Johnson City; RMC Place; ST. CLAIR; *196 H-10; elev. 798ft./243m.; mail Appleton City Z 64724; rural
Johnstown; RMC Place; BATES; *196 H-10; mail Montrose Z 64770; rural
Johnstown; RMC Place; JASPER; ★ JOP; mail Carterville Z 64835; pop. incl. with Carterville (Inc. Place)
Jonesburg; Inc. Place; MONTGOMERY; 197 F-16; elev. 897ft./273m.; 🅿; Z 63351; Ⓟ 630; Ⓒ 695
Joplin; Inc. Place; JASPER, NEWTON; 196 K-9; elev. 972ft./296m.; 🅿 🅷 🅲 6,418 ■; ★ JOP; Z 64801-04; Ⓟ 40,961; Ⓒ 45,504; ◆ 51,825
Jordan; RMC Place; HICKORY; *197 H-12; elev. 852ft./260m.; mail Cross Timbers Z 65634; rural
Jordan W Chambers; RMC Place; ST. LOUIS (Independent City); *197 G-18; ★ ST.L; mail Saint Louis Z 63106; pop. incl. with Saint Louis (Independent City)
Josephville; Inc. Place; ST. CHARLES; *197 F-17; ★ ST.L; mail Wentzville Z 63385; Ⓟ 445; Ⓒ 270
Judge; RMC Place; OSAGE; *197 G-15; mail Linn Z 65051; ● 30
Junction City; Inc. Place; MADISON; 197 J-18; elev. 784ft./239m.; mail Fredericktown Z 63645; Ⓟ 326; Ⓒ 319
Junland; RMC Place; BUTLER; *197 L-18; elev. 322ft./98m.; mail Poplar Bluff Z 63901; rural

K

Kahoka; Inc. Place; ⊡ CLARK; 197 B-15; elev. 703ft./214m.; 🅿; Z 63445; Ⓟ 2,195; Ⓒ 2,241
Kaiser; RMC Place; MILLER; *197 H-13; elev. 913ft./278m.; 🅿; Z 65047; rural
Kampville; RMC Place; ST. CHARLES; 197 F-17; ★ ST.L; mail Saint Charles Z 63301; ● 100
Kampville Beach; RMC Place; ST. CHARLES; ★ ST.L; mail Saint Charles Z 63301
Kampville Court; RMC Place; ST. CHARLES; ★ ST.L; mail Saint Charles Z 63301
Kansas City; Inc. Place; JACKSON, CASS, CLAY, PLATTE; 196 E-9; elev. 800ft./244m.; 🅿 🅷 🅲 23,948 ■; ★ K.C.; Z 64101-02, Z 64105-06, Z 64108-14, Z 64116-21, Z 64123-34, Z 64136-39, Z 64141, Z 64144-58, Z 64161, Z 64163-68, Z 64170-72, Z 64179-80, Z 64183-84, Z 64187-88, Z 64190-93, Z 64195-99, Z 64999; Ⓟ 435,146; Ⓒ 441,545; ◆ 464,872
Kaseyville; RMC Place; MACON; *197 D-13; elev. 759ft./231m.; mail Callao Z 63534; rural
Kearney; Inc. Place; CLAY; 196 E-9; elev. 849ft./259m.; 🅿; ★ K.C.; Z 64060; Ⓟ 1,790; Ⓒ 5,472
Keener Cave; RMC Place; WAYNE; *197 K-18; mail Williamsville Z 63967; rural

Entries in **UPPERCASE** are counties.
Entries in **bold** have populations of 2,500 or more.
Names in parentheses are alternate names.
Inc. Place — Incorporated Place
RMC Place — Rand McNally Designated Place
CDP — Census Designated Place
MCD — Minor Civil Division

⊡ County Seat
▲ Minor Civil Division
elev. Elevation
🅿 Post Office

🅷 Hospital
🅲 College
■ Principal Business Center
★ Ranally Metro Area (RMA) Abbreviation
Z Zip Code(s)

Ⓟ Previous Census Population
Ⓡ Revised Census Population
Ⓐ Annexation Population
● Rand McNally Population Estimate
Ⓒ Final Census Population
Ⓢ Special Census Population
◆ Estimated Population

For additional definitions see Glossary, Volume 1, and Introduction, Volume 2.

Keethtown; RMC Place; MILLER; *197 H-13; mail Iberia z 65486; rural

Kellerville; RMC Place; SHELBY; *197 C-14; elev. 774ft./236m.; mail Shelbyville z 63469; rural

Kelso; Inc. Place; SCOTT; 197 K-20; elev. 400ft./122m.; 🅿; ★ **CPGIR**; z 63758; Ⓟ 526; Ⓒ 527

Keltner; RMC Place; CHRISTIAN; *197 K-12; elev. 1,103ft./336m.; mail Oldfield z 65720; rural

Kendricktown; RMC Place; JASPER; 196 K-9; ★ **JOP**; mail Carthage z 64836; ● 200

Kenmoor; RMC Place; BUCHANAN; mail Saint Joseph z 64504; ● 110

Kennett; Inc. Place; ⊡ DUNKLIN; 197 M-19; elev. 265ft./81m.; 🅿 🅷; z 63857; Ⓟ 10,941; Ⓒ 11,260

Kenoma; RMC Place; BARTON; 196 J-9; elev. 970ft./296m.; mail Lamar z 64759; ● 110

Keota; RMC Place; MACON; *197 D-13; mail Bevier z 63532; rural

Kerr; RMC Place; CALDWELL; *196 D-10; elev. 902ft./275m.; mail Cameron z 64429; rural

Kerrville; RMC Place; PLATTE; *196 E-8; mail Platte City z 64079; ● 190

Kersey Coates; RMC Place; JACKSON; ★ **K.C.**; mail Kansas City z 64105; pop. incl. with Kansas City (Inc. Place)

Ketterman; RMC Place; VERNON; *196 H-9; elev. 760ft./232m.; mail Walker z 64790; rural

Kewanee; RMC Place; NEW MADRID; 197 L-20; elev. 302ft./92m.; 🅿; z 63860; ● 220

Keyes Summit; RMC Place; ST. LOUIS; *197 G-18; ★ **ST.L**; mail Saint Louis z 63122; ● 250

Keysville; RMC Place; CRAWFORD; *197 I-16; elev. 892ft./272m.; mail Steelville z 65565; rural

Keytesville; Inc. Place; ⊡ CHARITON; 197 D-12; elev. 709ft./216m.; 🅿; z 65261; Ⓟ 564; Ⓒ 533

Kidder; Inc. Place; CALDWELL; 196 C-10; elev. 1,009ft./308m.; 🅿; z 64649; Ⓟ 241; Ⓒ 271

Kiel; RMC Place; FRANKLIN; *197 G-16; elev. 755ft./230m.; mail New Haven z 63068; rural

Killarney Shores; RMC Place; IRON; *197 I-17; mail Ironton z 63650; ● 70

Kilwinning; RMC Place; SCOTLAND; *197 A-14; elev. 863ft./263m.; mail Downing z 63536; rural

Kimberling City; Inc. Place; STONE; 197 L-11; elev. 1,016ft./310m.; 🅿; z 65686; Ⓟ 1,590; Ⓒ 2,253

Kimberling Hills; RMC Place; STONE; mail Kimberling City z 65686; pop. incl. with Kimberling City (Inc. Place)

Kimble; RMC Place; TEXAS; *197 J-15; mail Licking z 65542; rural

Kime; RMC Place; WAYNE; *197 K-18; mail Greenville z 63944; rural

Kimmswick; Inc. Place; JEFFERSON; *197 G-18; elev. 411ft./125m.; 🅿; ★ **ST.L**; z 63053; Ⓟ 135; Ⓒ 94

Kinder; RMC Place; STODDARD; *197 K-19; elev. 343ft./105m.; mail Puxico z 63960; ● 30

Kinderpost; RMC Place; TEXAS; *197 J-14; elev. 1,200ft./366m.; mail Licking z 65542; rural

Kinfolks Ridge; RMC Place; PEMISCOT; *197 M-20; elev. 263ft./80m.; mail Caruthersville z 63830; rural

King City; Inc. Place; GENTRY; 196 C-9; elev. 1,100ft./335m.; 🅿; z 64463; Ⓟ 986; Ⓒ 1,012

Kingdom City (McCredie); Inc. Place; CALLAWAY; 197 F-14; elev. 862ft./263m.; 🅿; z 65262; Ⓟ 112; Ⓒ 121

Kings Lake; RMC Place; LINCOLN; *197 E-17; mail Foley z 63347; ● 100

Kings Point; RMC Place; DADE; *196 J-10; mail Lockwood z 65682; rural

Kingston; Inc. Place; ⊡ CALDWELL; 196 D-10; elev. 900ft./274m.; 🅿; z 64650; Ⓟ 279; Ⓒ 287

Kingston; WASHINGTON; see Bliss (RMC Place)

Kingsville; Inc. Place; JOHNSON; 196 F-10; elev. 914ft./279m.; 🅿; z 64061; Ⓟ 279; Ⓒ 257

Kinloch; Inc. Place; ST. LOUIS; *197 F-18; 🅿; ★ **ST.L**; z 63140; Ⓒ 449

Kinsey; RMC Place; STE. GENEVIEVE; *197 H-18; mail Bloomsdale z 63627; ● 100

Kirbyville; Inc. Place; TANEY; 197 L-12; elev. 1,000ft./305m.; 🅿; z 65679; incorporated June 4, 2001; not reported in 2000 Census; ● 100

Kirksville; Inc. Place; ⊡ ADAIR; 197 B-13; elev. 981ft./299m.; 🅿 🅷 🅲 8,079 ■; z 63501; Ⓟ 17,152; Ⓒ 16,988; ◆ 16,569

Kirkwood; Inc. Place; ST. LOUIS; 195 F-4; elev. 636ft./194m.; 🅿 ■; ★ **ST.L**; z 63122; Ⓟ 27,291; Ⓒ 27,324; ◆ 26,114

Kirschner; RMC Place; BUCHANAN; *196 D-8; ★ **ST.JO**; mail Saint Joseph z 64504; pop. incl. with Saint Joseph (Inc. Place)

Kissee Mills; RMC Place; TANEY; *197 L-12; elev. 986ft./301m.; 🅿; z 65680; ● 350

Kliever; RMC Place; MONITEAU; 197 F-13; elev. 783ft./239m.; mail California z 65018; ● 100

Klondike; RMC Place; JASPER; *196 K-9; elev. 881ft./269m.; ★ **JOP**; mail Carl Junction z 64834; rural

Knights; RMC Place; JASPER; *196 K-9; mail Carthage z 64836; ● 150

Knobby; RMC Place; BENTON; *197 H-12; elev. 300ft./91m.; mail Edwards z 65326; rural

Knob Lick; RMC Place; ST. FRANCOIS; 197 I-18; elev. 930ft./283m.; 🅿; z 63651; ● 110

Knob Noster; Inc. Place; JOHNSON; 197 F-11; elev. 793ft./242m.; 🅿; z 65336 & mail Whiteman Air Force Base z 65305; Ⓟ 2,261; Ⓒ 2,462

Knobtown; RMC Place; JACKSON; *196 F-9; ★ **K.C.**; mail Kansas City z 64138; pop. incl. with Kansas City (Inc. Place)

Knolls; RMC Place; CAMDEN; elev. 217ft./66m.; mail Osage Beach z 65065

Knorpp; RMC Place; JEFFERSON; *197 H-18; elev. 600ft./183m.; mail De Soto z 63020; rural

KNOX; 197 C-14; Ⓟ 4,482; Ⓒ 4,361; ◆ 3,993

Knox City; Inc. Place; KNOX; 197 B-14; elev. 764ft./233m.; 🅿; z 63446; Ⓟ 262; Ⓒ 223

Knoxville; RMC Place; RAY; 196 D-10; mail Rayville z 64084; ● 85

Kodiak; RMC Place; ANDREW; *196 C-8; mail Savannah z 64485; rural

Koeltztown; RMC Place; OSAGE; 197 G-14; elev. 931ft./284m.; 🅿; z 65048; ● 130

Koenig; RMC Place; OSAGE; *197 G-15; elev. 700ft./213m.; mail Belle z 65013; rural

Koester Spring; RMC Place; ST. FRANCOIS; *197 H-18; elev. 700ft./213m.; mail French Village z 63036; rural

Koshkonong; Inc. Place; OREGON; 197 L-15; elev. 970ft./296m.; 🅿; z 65692; Ⓟ 198; Ⓒ 205

Krakow; RMC Place; FRANKLIN; *197 G-16; elev. 764ft./233m.; mail Washington z 63090; ● 100

Kurreville; RMC Place; CAPE GIRARDEAU; *197 J-19; elev. 548ft./167m.; mail Millersville z 63766; rural

Kyle; RMC Place; BUCHANAN; *196 D-8; mail Saint Joseph z 64504; ● 300

L

Labadie; RMC Place; FRANKLIN; 197 G-17; elev. 526ft./160m.; 🅿; ★ **ST.L**; z 63055; ● 600

La Belle; Inc. Place; LEWIS; 197 C-14; elev. 738ft./225m.; 🅿; z 63447; Ⓟ 655; Ⓒ 669

Laclede; Inc. Place; LINN; 197 C-12; elev. 785ft./239m.; 🅿; z 64651; Ⓟ 410; Ⓒ 415

LACLEDE; 197 I-13; Ⓟ 27,158; Ⓒ 32,513; ◆ 36,127

Lacyville; RMC Place; BATES; *196 G-9; elev. 893ft./272m.; mail Adrian z 64720; rural

Laddonia; Inc. Place; AUDRAIN; 197 E-15; elev. 780ft./238m.; 🅿; z 63352; Ⓟ 581; Ⓒ 620

La Due; RMC Place; HENRY; *196 H-10; mail Clinton z 64735; disincorporated since 2000 Census; Ⓟ 20; Ⓒ 39

Ladue; Inc. Place; ST. LOUIS; 195 E-5; elev. 540ft./165m.; ★ **ST.L**; mail Saint Louis z 63124; Ⓟ 8,847; Ⓒ 8,645; Ⓡ 8,413

LAFAYETTE; 196 F-10; Ⓟ 31,107; Ⓒ 32,960; ◆ 32,363

Laflin; RMC Place; BOLLINGER; *197 J-19; elev. 396ft./121m.; mail Leopold z 63760

La Forge; RMC Place; NEW MADRID; *197 L-20; mail New Madrid z 63869; rural

Lagonda; RMC Place; CHARITON; *197 D-13; mail New Cambria z 63558; rural

La Grange; Inc. Place; LEWIS; 197 C-15; elev. 500ft./152m.; 🅿; z 63448; Ⓟ 1,102; Ⓒ 1,000

Laguna Beach; RMC Place; CAMDEN; *197 H-13; mail Osage Beach z 65065; pop. incl. with Osage Beach (Inc. Place)

Lake Adelle; RMC Place; JEFFERSON; *197 G-17; elev. 704ft./215m.; mail Cedar Hill z 63016; ● 330

Lake Annette; Inc. Place; CASS; *196 G-9; 🅿; z 64746; Ⓟ 157; Ⓒ 163

Lake Arrowhead; RMC Place; FRANKLIN; *197 G-17; elev. 626ft./191m.; ★ **ST.L**; mail Lonedell z 63060; ● 200

Lake City; RMC Place; JACKSON; *196 E-9; elev. 752ft./229m.; ★ **K.C.**; mail Buckner z 64016; pop. incl. with Independence (Inc. Place)

Lake Contrary; RMC Place; BUCHANAN; *196 D-8; ★ **ST.JO**; mail Saint Joseph z 64504; ● 500

Lake Creek; RMC Place; BENTON; *197 G-12; elev. 978ft./298m.; mail Cole Camp z 65325; rural

Lake Junction; RMC Place; ST. LOUIS; *197 G-18; ★ **ST.L**; mail Saint Louis z 63119; pop. incl. with Webster Groves (Inc. Place)

Lake Lafayette; Inc. Place; LAFAYETTE; *196 F-10; elev. 900ft./274m.; mail Odessa z 64076; Ⓟ 267; Ⓒ 346

Lakeland; RMC Place; MILLER; *197 H-13; mail Eldon z 65026; pop. incl. with Lake Ozark (Inc. Place); Ⓟ 351

Lake Lotawana (Lotawana Lake); Inc. Place; JACKSON; 196 F-9; elev. 900ft./274m.; 🅿; ★ **K.C.**; z 64086 & mail Lees Summit z 64063; Ⓟ 2,141; Ⓒ 1,872

Lake Mykee Town; Inc. Place; CALLAWAY; *197 G-14; mail Holts Summit z 65043; Ⓟ 257; Ⓒ 326

Lakenan; RMC Place; SHELBY; 197 D-14; mail Shelbina z 63468; ● 70

Lake of the Ozarks; MILLER, CAMDEN; see Lake Ozark (Inc. Place)

Lake Ozark (Lake of the Ozarks); Inc. Place; MILLER, CAMDEN; 197 H-13; elev. 703ft./214m.; 🅿; z 65049; Ⓟ 681; Ⓒ 1,489

Lake Saint Louis; Inc. Place; ST. CHARLES; 197 F-17; elev. 620ft./189m.; 🅿 🅷; ★ **ST.L**; z 63367; Ⓟ 7,400; Ⓒ 10,169

Lake Sherwood (Lake Sherwood Estates); RMC Place; WARREN; *197 G-16; elev. 800ft./244m.; 🅿; z 63357; rural

Lake Sherwood Estates; WARREN; see Lake Sherwood (RMC Place)

Lakeshire; Inc. Place; ST. LOUIS; 195 G-5; elev. 500ft./152m.; ★ **ST.L**; mail Saint Louis z 63125; Ⓟ 1,467; Ⓒ 1,375

Lakeside; RMC Place; JASPER; *196 K-9; ★ **JOP**; mail Joplin z 64801; ● 300

Lakeside; Inc. Place; MILLER; *197 H-13; elev. 600ft./183m.; mail Eldon z 65026; Ⓟ 38; Ⓒ 37

Lake Spring; RMC Place; DENT; 197 I-15; elev. 995ft./303m.; 🅿; z 65532; rural

Lake Tapawingo; Inc. Place; JACKSON; 196 J-7; elev. 850ft./259m.; 🅿; ★ **K.C.**; z 64015; Ⓟ 761; Ⓒ 843

Lake Tekakwitha; RMC Place; JEFFERSON; *197 G-17; elev. 607ft./185m.; ★ **ST.L**; mail Pacific z 63069; ● 300

Lakeview; RMC Place; CASS; *196 F-9; elev. 1,069ft./326m.; ★ **K.C.**; mail Raymore z 64083; pop. incl. with Raymore (Inc. Place)

Lakeview; RMC Place; MILLER; *197 H-13; elev. 800ft./244m.; mail Eldon z 65026; pop. incl. with Lake Ozark (Inc. Place); Ⓟ 110

Lakeview; RMC Place; RAY; *196 E-10; elev. 680ft./207m.; mail Hardin z 64035, Norborne z 64668; rural

Lakeview; STONE; see Branson West (Inc. Place)

Lakeview Heights; RMC Place; BENTON; 197 H-12; mail Lincoln z 65338; ● 100

Lake Viking; RMC Place; DAVIESS; *196 C-10; elev. 888ft./271m.; mail Gallatin z 64640; ● 230

Lake Waukomis; Inc. Place; PLATTE; 196 G-3; elev. 950ft./290m.; 🅿; ★ **K.C.**; z 64151 & mail Kansas City z 64152; Ⓟ 1,027; Ⓒ 917

Lake Winnebago; Inc. Place; CASS; 196 M-6; elev. 900ft./274m.; 🅿; ★ **K.C.**; z 64034; Ⓟ 748; Ⓒ 902

Lake Wittona; RMC Place; GRUNDY; *197 C-11; elev. 915ft./279m.; mail Trenton z 64683; rural

Lamar; Inc. Place; ⊡ BARTON; 196 J-9; elev. 985ft./300m.; 🅿; z 64759, z 64766; Ⓟ 4,168; Ⓒ 4,425

Lamar Heights; Inc. Place; BARTON; *196 J-9; elev. 971ft./296m.; mail Lamar z 64759; Ⓟ 176; Ⓒ 216

Lambert; RMC Place; SCOTT; *197 K-20; elev. 350ft./107m.; mail Benton z 63736; disincorporated since 2000 Census; Ⓟ 36; Ⓒ 49

Lamine; RMC Place; COOPER; 197 F-12; elev. 611ft./186m.; mail Boonville z 65233

La Monte; Inc. Place; PETTIS; 197 F-11; elev. 860ft./262m.; 🅿; z 65337; Ⓟ 995; Ⓒ 1,064

Lampe; RMC Place; STONE; 197 L-11; elev. 1,313ft./400m.; 🅿; z 65681; ● 400

Lanagan; Inc. Place; MCDONALD; 196 L-9; elev. 850ft./259m.; 🅿; z 64847; Ⓟ 501; Ⓒ 411

Lancaster; Inc. Place; ⊡ SCHUYLER; 197 A-13; elev. 950ft./290m.; 🅿; z 63548; Ⓟ 785; Ⓒ 737

Lanes Prairie; RMC Place; MARIES; *197 H-15; mail Belle z 65013; rural

Langdon; RMC Place; ATCHISON; *196 B-7; elev. 891ft./272m.; mail Fairfax z 64446

Lanton; RMC Place; HOWELL; 197 L-15; elev. 900ft./274m.; mail West Plains z 65775; ● 40

La Plata; Inc. Place; MACON; 197 C-13; elev. 941ft./287m.; 🅿; z 63549; Ⓟ 1,401; Ⓒ 1,486

Laquey; RMC Place; PULASKI; 197 I-14; elev. 1,050ft./320m.; 🅿; z 65534; ● 300

Laredo; Inc. Place; GRUNDY; 197 C-11; elev. 808ft./246m.; 🅿; z 64652; Ⓟ 205; Ⓒ 250

Larimore; RMC Place; ST. LOUIS; *197 F-18; ★ **ST.L**; mail Saint Louis z 63138

La Russell; Inc. Place; JASPER; *196 K-10; elev. 1,100ft./335m.; 🅿; z 64848; Ⓟ 114; Ⓒ 138

Latham; RMC Place; MONITEAU; 197 G-13; elev. 884ft./269m.; 🅿; z 65050; ● 140

Lathrop; Inc. Place; CLINTON; 196 D-9; elev. 1,060ft./323m.; 🅿; z 64465; Ⓟ 1,794; Ⓒ 2,092

Latour; Inc. Place; JOHNSON; 196 G-10; elev. 800ft./244m.; 🅿; z 64747; Ⓟ 87; Ⓒ 65

Latty; RMC Place; WASHINGTON; *197 H-17; elev. 815ft./248m.; mail Potosi z 63664; ● 200

Laurel Heights; RMC Place; JACKSON; ★ **K.C.**; mail Kansas City z 64133; pop. incl. with Raytown (Inc. Place)

Laurie; Inc. Place; MORGAN; *197 H-12; elev. 968ft./295m.; 🅿; z 65037-38; Ⓟ 507; Ⓒ 663

LaValle; RMC Place; STODDARD; *197 L-19; mail Catron z 63833; rural

Lavin Spur; RMC Place; COLE; pop. incl. with Jefferson City (Inc. Place)

LAWRENCE; 196 K-10; Ⓟ 30,236; Ⓒ 35,204; ◆ 38,469

Lawrenceburg; RMC Place; LAWRENCE; *197 J-11; elev. 1,220ft./372m.; mail Everton z 65646; ● 80

Lawrenceton; RMC Place; STE. GENEVIEVE; 197 H-18; elev. 561ft./171m.; mail Bloomsdale z 63627; ● 80

Lawson; Inc. Place; RAY, CLAY; 196 D-10; elev. 1,077ft./328m.; 🅿; ★ **K.C.**; z 64062; Ⓟ 1,876; Ⓒ 2,336

Leadington; Inc. Place; ST. FRANCOIS; 197 I-18; elev. 880ft./268m.; 🅿; z 63601; Ⓟ 201; Ⓒ 206

Leadmine; RMC Place; DALLAS; *197 I-12; mail Tunas z 65764

Leadwood; Inc. Place; ST. FRANCOIS; 197 I-17; elev. 723ft./220m.; 🅿; z 63601, z 63653; Ⓟ 1,247; Ⓒ 1,160

Leann; RMC Place; BARRY; *197 L-11; mail Aurora z 65605; rural

Leasburg; Inc. Place; CRAWFORD; 197 H-16; elev. 1,020ft./311m.; 🅿; z 65535; Ⓟ 289; Ⓒ 323

Leawood; Inc. Place; NEWTON; 195 N-2; elev. 940ft./287m.; ★ **JOP**; mail Joplin z 64801; Ⓟ 736; Ⓒ 904

Lebanon; Inc. Place; ⊡ LACLEDE; 197 I-13; elev. 1,266ft./386m.; 🅿 🅷; z 65536; Ⓟ 9,983; Ⓒ 12,155

Lebeck; RMC Place; CEDAR; *196 I-10; elev. 950ft./290m.; mail El Dorado Springs z 64744; rural

Lebo; RMC Place; HOWELL; *197 L-14; mail West Plains z 65775; rural

Lecoma; RMC Place; DENT; 197 I-15; elev. 1,176ft./358m.; 🅿; z 65401; ● 60

Leeds; RMC Place; JACKSON; *196 E-9; ★ **K.C.**; mail Kansas City z 64129; pop. incl. with Kansas City (Inc. Place)

Leemon; RMC Place; CAPE GIRARDEAU; *197 J-20; mail Jackson z 63755; rural

Leeper; RMC Place; WAYNE; 197 K-17; mail Piedmont z 63957; ● 160

Lees Summit; Inc. Place; JACKSON, CASS; 196 L-6; elev. 1,043ft./318m.; 🅿 🅷; ★ **K.C.**; z 64002, z 64063-65, z 64081-83, z 64086; Ⓟ 46,418; Ⓒ 70,700; ◆ 75,194

Leesville; RMC Place; HENRY; 197 G-11; mail Clinton z 64735; ● 100

Leeton; Inc. Place; JOHNSON; 197 G-11; elev. 955ft./291m.; 🅿; z 64761; Ⓟ 632; Ⓒ 619

Lemay (Luxemburg); CDP; ST. LOUIS; 195 G-6; elev. 540ft./165m.; 🅿; ★ **ST.L**; z 63125; Ⓟ 18,005; Ⓒ 17,215

Lemons; RMC Place; PUTNAM; 197 B-12; mail Unionville z 63565; ● 100

Lenox; RMC Place; DENT; 197 I-15; elev. 1,230ft./375m.; 🅿; z 65541

Lentner; RMC Place; SHELBY; 197 D-14; elev. 791ft./241m.; 🅿; z 63450

Leonard; Inc. Place; SHELBY; 197 C-14; elev. 764ft./233m.; 🅿; z 63451; Ⓟ 90; Ⓒ 66

Leon Mercer Jordan; RMC Place; PLATTE; ★ **K.C.**; mail Kansas City z 64128; pop. incl. with Kansas City (Inc. Place)

Leopold; RMC Place; BOLLINGER; *197 J-19; elev. 639ft./195m.; 🅿; z 63760; ● 300

Leora; RMC Place; STODDARD; 197 K-19; mail Bloomfield z 63825; ● 30

Leota; RMC Place; HOWELL; *197 L-14; mail Caulfield z 65626; rural

Leslie; Inc. Place; FRANKLIN; *197 G-16; elev. 819ft./250m.; 🅿; z 63056; Ⓟ 134; Ⓒ 87

Lesterville; RMC Place; REYNOLDS; 197 J-17; elev. 712ft./217m.; 🅿; z 63654; ● 180

LeVance Spur; RMC Place; JACKSON; ★ **K.C.**; pop. incl. with Kansas City (Inc. Place)

Levasy; Inc. Place; JACKSON; *196 E-10; elev. 709ft./216m.; 🅿; ★ **K.C.**; z 64066; Ⓟ 279; Ⓒ 108

Levick Mill (Levicks Mill); RMC Place; RANDOLPH; *197 D-14; elev. 750ft./229m.; mail Jacksonville z 65260; rural

Levicks Mill; RANDOLPH; see Levick Mill (RMC Place)

Lewis; RMC Place; HENRY; 197 G-11; elev. 796ft./243m.; mail Clinton z 64735; ● 80

LEWIS; 197 B-15; Ⓟ 10,233; Ⓒ 10,494; ◆ 9,896

Lewis and Clark Village; Inc. Place; BUCHANAN; 196 D-8; elev. 785ft./239m.; mail Rushville z 64484; Ⓟ 142; Ⓒ 155

Lewistown; Inc. Place; LEWIS; 197 C-15; elev. 725ft./221m.; 🅿; z 63452; Ⓟ 453; Ⓒ 595

Lexington; Inc. Place; ⊡ LAFAYETTE; 196 E-10; elev. 849ft./259m.; 🅿 🅷; z 64067; Ⓟ 4,860; Ⓒ 4,453

Liberal; Inc. Place; BARTON; 196 J-9; elev. 894ft./272m.; 🅿; z 64762; Ⓟ 684; Ⓒ 779

Liberty; RMC Place; CALLAWAY; *197 G-14; elev. 650ft./198m.; mail New Bloomfield z 65063; rural

Liberty; Inc. Place; ⊡ CLAY; 196 E-9; elev. 879ft./268m.; 🅿 🅷 🅲 1,404; ★ **K.C.**; z 64068-69; Ⓟ 20,459; Ⓒ 26,232; ◆ 30,842

Libertyville; RMC Place; ST. FRANCOIS; *197 I-18; elev. 912ft./278m.; mail Farmington z 63640; ● 120

Lick (Prairie Lick); RMC Place; COOPER; *197 F-12; mail Boonville z 65233; rural

Licking; Inc. Place; TEXAS; 197 J-15; elev. 1,259ft./384m.; 🅿; z 65542; Ⓟ 1,328; Ⓒ 1,471

Liege; RMC Place; MONTGOMERY; mail Bellflower z 63333; pop. incl. with Bellflower (Inc. Place)

Liguori; RMC Place; JEFFERSON; *197 G-18; elev. 560ft./171m.; 🅿; ★ **ST.L**; z 63057; ● 100

Lilbourn; Inc. Place; NEW MADRID; 197 L-20; elev. 285ft./87m.; 🅿; z 63862; Ⓟ 1,378; Ⓒ 1,303

Lilly; RMC Place; CLINTON; *196 D-9; mail Plattsburg z 64477; rural

Lincoln; Inc. Place; BENTON; 197 G-11; elev. 950ft./290m.; 🅿; z 65338; Ⓟ 874; Ⓒ 1,026

LINCOLN; 197 F-16; Ⓟ 28,892; Ⓒ 38,944; ◆ 54,899

Lindbergh; RMC Place; CALLAWAY; *197 F-14; mail Columbia z 65202; ● 160

Linden; RMC Place; CHRISTIAN; 197 K-12; mail Rogersville z 65742; ● 125

Linden; CLAY; see Gladstone (Inc. Place)

Lindenwood; RMC Place; ST. LOUIS (Independent City); pop. incl. with Saint Louis (Independent City)

Lindley; RMC Place; GRUNDY; *197 C-11; elev. 901ft./275m.; mail Laredo z 64652; rural

Lingo; RMC Place; MACON; *197 D-12; elev. 816ft./249m.; mail Bucklin z 64631; ● 30

Linkville; RMC Place; PLATTE; *196 E-9; ★ **K.C.**; mail Kansas City z 64152; pop. incl. with Kansas City (Inc. Place)

Linn; Inc. Place; ⊡ OSAGE; 197 G-15; elev. 706ft./215m.; 🅿; z 65051; Ⓟ 1,148; Ⓒ 1,354; Ⓡ 1,402

LINN; 197 C-12; Ⓟ 13,885; Ⓒ 13,754; ◆ 12,436

Linn Creek; Inc. Place; CAMDEN; 197 H-13; elev. 698ft./213m.; 🅿; z 65052; Ⓟ 232; Ⓒ 280

Linneus; Inc. Place; ⊡ LINN; 197 C-12; elev. 837ft./255m.; 🅿; z 64653; Ⓟ 364; Ⓒ 369

Lisbon; RMC Place; HOWARD; *197 E-12; mail Glasgow z 65254; rural

Lisle; RMC Place; CASS; *196 G-9; elev. 972ft./296m.; mail Drexel z 64742; rural

Lithium; RMC Place; PERRY; *197 I-19; elev. 400ft./122m.; mail Perryville z 63775; disincorporated since 2000 Census; Ⓟ 7; ● 75

Little Blue; RMC Place; JACKSON; *196 F-9; elev. 789ft./240m.; ★ **K.C.**; mail Kansas City z 64133; pop. incl. with Kansas City (Inc. Place)

Little Village; RMC Place; CLAY; ★ **K.C.**; mail Kansas City z 64118; pop. incl. with Kansas City (Inc. Place)

LIVINGSTON; 197 C-11; Ⓟ 14,592; Ⓒ 14,558; ◆ 14,276

Livonia; Inc. Place; PUTNAM; 197 B-13; elev. 820ft./250m.; 🅿; z 63551; Ⓟ 126; Ⓒ 114

Loch Lloyd; Inc. Place; CASS; mail Belton z 64012; incorporated September 4, 2003; not reported in 2000 Census

Lock Springs; Inc. Place; DAVIESS; 196 C-10; elev. 717ft./219m.; 🅿; z 64654; Ⓟ 57; Ⓒ 69

Lockwood; Inc. Place; DADE; 196 J-10; elev. 1,078ft./329m.; 🅿; z 65682; Ⓟ 1,041; Ⓒ 989

Locust Hill; RMC Place; KNOX; *197 C-14; elev. 863ft./263m.; mail Hurdland z 63547, Novelty z 63460; rural

Lodi; RMC Place; WAYNE; 197 J-18; elev. 432ft./132m.; 🅿; z 63950

Logan; RMC Place; LAWRENCE; *197 K-11; mail Marionville z 65705; ● 110

Lohman; Inc. Place; COLE; *197 G-13; elev. 649ft./198m.; 🅿; z 65053; Ⓟ 154; Ⓒ 168

Loma Linda; RMC Place; BUTLER; *197 L-18; elev. 457ft./139m.; mail Poplar Bluff z 63901; pop. incl. with Poplar Bluff (Inc. Place)

Loma Linda; Inc. Place; NEWTON; *196 K-9; 🅿; ★ **JOP**; z 64804; Ⓒ 507

Lonedell; RMC Place; FRANKLIN; 197 H-17; elev. 580ft./177m.; 🅿; z 63060; ● 400

Lone Elm; RMC Place; COOPER; 197 F-13; elev. 827ft./252m.; mail Bunceton z 65237; ● 80

Lone Elm; RMC Place; JASPER; 195 L-1; ★ **JOP**; mail Joplin z 64801; ● 140

Lone Hill; RMC Place; BUTLER; *197 L-18; mail Poplar Bluff z 63901; rural

Lone Jack; Inc. Place; JACKSON; 196 F-10; elev. 1,110ft./338m.; 🅿; ★ **K.C.**; z 64070; Ⓟ 392; Ⓒ 528

Lone Tree; RMC Place; CASS; *196 G-9; mail Harrisonville z 64701; rural

Long Beach; RMC Place; TANEY; *197 L-12; mail Branson z 65616; ● 300

Long Lane; RMC Place; DALLAS; 197 I-12; elev. 1,139ft./347m.; 🅿; z 65590; ● 125

Longrun; RMC Place; OZARK; *197 L-13; elev. 863ft./263m.; mail Theodosia z 65761; rural

Longtown; Inc. Place; PERRY; 197 I-19; elev. 620ft./189m.; mail Perryville z 63775; Ⓟ 107; Ⓒ 76

Longview; RMC Place; JACKSON; *196 F-9; ★ **K.C.**; mail Kansas City z 64138-39; pop. incl. with Kansas City (Inc. Place)

Longview; RMC Place; MCDONALD; *196 L-9; elev. 1,300ft./396m.; mail Rocky Comfort z 64861; rural

Longwood; RMC Place; PETTIS; *197 F-12; mail Hughesville z 65334, Marshall z 65340, Sedalia z 65301

Loose Creek; RMC Place; OSAGE; 197 G-14; elev. 819ft./250m.; 🅿; z 65054

Loring; RMC Place; WRIGHT; *197 J-13; elev. 1,460ft./445m.; mail Hartville z 65667; rural

Lotawana Lake; JACKSON; see Lake Lotawana (Inc. Place)

Loughboro; RMC Place; ST. FRANCOIS; *197 I-18; elev. 940ft./287m.; mail Park Hills z 63601; ● 100

Louisburg; Inc. Place; DALLAS; 197 I-12; elev. 1,175ft./358m.; 🅿; z 65685; Ⓟ 115; Ⓒ 147

Louisiana; Inc. Place; PIKE; 197 D-16; elev. 1,477ft./450m.; 🅿 🅷; z 63353; Ⓟ 3,967; Ⓒ 3,863

Louisville; RMC Place; LINCOLN; *197 E-16; mail Bowling Green z 63334

Lowground; RMC Place; PUTNAM; *197 B-13; mail Novinger z 63559; rural

Lowndes; RMC Place; WAYNE; 197 K-18; elev. 425ft./130m.; 🅿; z 63951

Lowry City; Inc. Place; ST. CLAIR; 197 H-11; elev. 885ft./270m.; 🅿; z 64763; Ⓟ 723; Ⓒ 728

Low Wassie; RMC Place; SHANNON; *197 K-16; elev. 808ft./246m.; mail Winona z 65588

Lucas; RMC Place; HENRY; *196 G-10; mail Urich z 64788

Lucas and Hunt Village; RMC Place; ST. LOUIS; *197 F-18; elev. 550ft./168m.; ★ **ST.L**; mail Saint Louis z 63121; ● 850

Lucerne; Inc. Place; PUTNAM; 197 B-12; elev. 950ft./290m.; 🅿; z 64655; Ⓟ 51; Ⓒ 92

Ludlow; Inc. Place; LIVINGSTON; 197 D-11; elev. 737ft./225m.; 🅿; z 64656; Ⓟ 147; Ⓒ 204

Luebbering; RMC Place; FRANKLIN; *197 H-17; elev. 759ft./231m.; 🅿; z 63061 & mail Lonedell z 63060; ● 165

Lulu; RMC Place; OREGON; *197 L-16; mail Alton z 65606; rural

Luna; RMC Place; OZARK; *197 L-14; elev. 819ft./250m.; mail Gainesville z 65655; rural

Lupus; Inc. Place; MONITEAU; *197 F-13; elev. 574ft./175m.; mail Jamestown z 65046; Ⓟ 39; Ⓒ 29

Luray; Inc. Place; CLARK; 197 B-14; elev. 737ft./225m.; 🅿; z 63453; Ⓟ 70; Ⓒ 102

Lutesville; RMC Place; BOLLINGER; *197 J-19; elev. 417ft./127m.; 🅿; z 63764; pop. incl. with Marble Hill (Inc. Place)

Luxemburg; ST. LOUIS; see Lemay (CDP)

Luystown; RMC Place; OSAGE; *197 G-15; mail Bonnots Mill z 65016; rural

Lynchburg; RMC Place; LACLEDE; 197 J-14; elev. 1,351ft./412m.; 🅿; z 65543

Lyon; RMC Place; FRANKLIN; *197 G-16; mail New Haven z 63068; ● 130

M

Macedonia; RMC Place; PHELPS; *197 H-15; elev. 986ft./301m.; mail Rolla z 65401; rural

Machens; RMC Place; ST. CHARLES; *197 F-18; mail Portage Des Sioux z 63373; rural

Mackenzie; Inc. Place; ST. LOUIS; *197 G-18; elev. 450ft./137m.; ★ **ST.L**; mail Saint Louis z 63123; Ⓟ 148; Ⓒ 137

Macks Camp; RMC Place; BENTON; *197 H-11; elev. 249ft./76m.; mail Warsaw z 65355; ● 100

Macks Creek; Inc. Place; CAMDEN; 197 I-12; elev. 875ft./267m.; 🅿; z 65786; Ⓟ 272; Ⓒ 267

Macomb; RMC Place; WRIGHT; *197 K-13; elev. 1,517ft./462m.; 🅿; z 65702; ● 60

Macon; Inc. Place; ⊡ MACON; 197 D-13; elev. 859ft./262m.; 🅿 🅷; z 63552; Ⓟ 5,571; Ⓒ 5,538

MACON; 197 C-13; Ⓟ 15,345; Ⓒ 15,762; ◆ 15,546

Madison; Inc. Place; MONROE; 197 D-14; elev. 796ft./243m.; 🅿; z 65263; Ⓟ 518; Ⓒ 586

MADISON; 197 J-18; Ⓟ 11,127; Ⓒ 11,800; ◆ 12,414

Madisonville; RMC Place; RALLS; *197 D-15; mail Center z 63436; rural

Madry; RMC Place; BARRY; *196 L-10; mail Aurora z 65605; rural

Magnolia; RMC Place; JOHNSON; *196 G-10; mail Holden z 64040

Main City; RMC Place; CASS; *196 G-9; elev. 992ft./302m.; mail Drexel z 64742; rural

Maitland; Inc. Place; HOLT; 196 B-8; elev. 900ft./274m.; 🅿; z 64466; Ⓟ 338; Ⓒ 342

Majorville; RMC Place; BENTON; *197 H-12; elev. 900ft./274m.; mail Warsaw z 65355; rural

Malden; Inc. Place; DUNKLIN; 197 L-19; elev. 290ft./88m.; 🅿; z 63863; Ⓟ 5,123; Ⓒ 4,782

Malta Bend; Inc. Place; SALINE; 197 E-11; elev. 684ft./208m.; 🅿; z 65339; Ⓟ 289; Ⓒ 249

Mammoth; RMC Place; OZARK; *197 L-13; mail Gainesville z 65655

Manchester; Inc. Place; ST. LOUIS; 195 F-3; elev. 531ft./162m.; 🅿; ★ **ST.L**; z 63011, z 63021, z 63088; Ⓟ 6,542; Ⓒ 19,161

Mandeville; RMC Place; CARROLL; *197 D-11; elev. 974ft./297m.; mail Bogard z 64622; rural

Manes; RMC Place; WRIGHT; 197 J-13; elev. 1,324ft./404m.; mail Mountain Grove z 65711; ● 50

Mano; RMC Place; BARRY; *197 L-11; elev. 1,069ft./326m.; mail Cassville z 65625; summer pop. 300; ● 115

Mansfield; Inc. Place; WRIGHT; 197 K-13; elev. 1,488ft./454m.; 🅿; z 65704; Ⓟ 1,429; Ⓒ 1,349

Many Springs; RMC Place; OREGON; *197 L-16; mail Alton z 65606

Mapaville; RMC Place; JEFFERSON; *197 H-18; elev. 677ft./206m.; 🅿; ★ **ST.L**; z 63065; ● 400

Maple Grove; RMC Place; JASPER; *196 J-10; elev. 1,096ft./334m.; mail Golden City z 64748; rural

Maple Park; RMC Place; CLAY; *196 E-9; mail Kansas City z 64119; pop. incl. with Kansas City (Inc. Place)

Maples; RMC Place; TEXAS; *197 J-15; elev. 1,363ft./415m.; mail Licking z 65542, Salem z 65560; rural

Maplewood; RMC Place; PETTIS; *197 G-12; elev. 852ft./260m.; mail Sedalia z 65301; ● 500

Maplewood; Inc. Place; ST. LOUIS; 195 F-5; elev. 508ft./155m.; 🅿; ★ **ST.L**; z 63143; Ⓟ 9,962; Ⓒ 9,228

Marble Hill; Inc. Place; ⊡ BOLLINGER; 197 J-19; elev. 422ft./129m.; 🅿; z 63764; Ⓟ 1,447; Ⓒ 1,502

Marceline; Inc. Place; LINN, CHARITON; 197 D-12; elev. 850ft./259m.; 🅿; z 64658; Ⓟ 2,645; Ⓒ 2,558

March; RMC Place; DALLAS; *197 J-12; mail Elkland z 65644; ● 125

Marco; RMC Place; STODDARD; *197 L-19; elev. 292ft./89m.; mail Parma z 63870; rural

Margona Village; RMC Place; ST. LOUIS; ★ **ST.L**; mail Saint Louis z 63114; pop. incl. with Saint Johns (Inc. Place)

MARIES; 197 H-14; Ⓟ 7,976; Ⓒ 8,903; ◆ 9,247

Marion; RMC Place; COLE; 197 F-13; mail Centertown z 65023; rural

MARION; 197 C-15; Ⓟ 27,682; Ⓒ 28,289; ◆ 27,927

Marionville; Inc. Place; LAWRENCE; 197 K-11; elev. 1,359ft./414m.; 🅿; z 65705; Ⓟ 1,920; Ⓒ 2,113

Marlborough; Inc. Place; ST. LOUIS; 195 F-5; elev. 500ft./152m.; ★ **ST.L**; mail Saint Louis z 63123; Ⓟ 1,949; Ⓒ 2,235

Marling; RMC Place; MONTGOMERY; *197 E-16; elev. 727ft./222m.; mail Middletown z 63359; rural

Marquand; Inc. Place; MADISON; 197 J-18; elev. 571ft./174m.; 🅿; z 63655; Ⓟ 278; Ⓒ 251

Marshall; Inc. Place; ⊡ SALINE; 197 E-12; elev. 770ft./235m.; 🅿 🅷 🅲 1,384; z 65340; Ⓟ 12,711; Ⓒ 12,433

Marshfield; Inc. Place; ⊡ WEBSTER; 197 J-12; elev. 1,494ft./455m.; 🅿; z 65706; Ⓟ 4,374; Ⓒ 5,720

Marston; Inc. Place; NEW MADRID; 197 L-20; elev. 289ft./88m.; 🅿; z 63866; Ⓟ 691; Ⓒ 610

Marthasville; Inc. Place; WARREN; 197 G-16; elev. 496ft./151m.; 🅿; z 63357; Ⓟ 674; Ⓒ 837

Martin City; RMC Place; JACKSON; *196 F-9; 🅿; ★ **K.C.**; z 64147 & mail Kansas City z 64114, z 64145-46, z 64149; pop. incl. with Kansas City (Inc. Place)

Martinsburg; Inc. Place; AUDRAIN; 197 E-15; elev. 807ft./246m.; 🅿; z 65264; Ⓟ 337; Ⓒ 326

Martinstown; RMC Place; PUTNAM; *197 B-13; mail Novinger z 63559, Unionville z 63565; ● 30

Martinsville; RMC Place; HARRISON; 196 B-10; elev. 1,076ft./328m.; 🅿; z 64467; ● 30

Marvel Cave (Marvel Cave Park); RMC Place; STONE; *197 L-11; mail Branson z 65616

Marvel Cave Park; STONE; see Marvel Cave (RMC Place)

Marvin; RMC Place; MORGAN; *197 G-13; elev. 1,020ft./311m.; mail Barnett z 65011, Versailles z 65084; rural

Marvin Terrace; RMC Place; ST. LOUIS; ★ **ST.L**; mail Saint Louis z 63114; pop. incl. with Saint Johns (Inc. Place)

Maryden; RMC Place; WASHINGTON; *197 I-17; elev. 879ft./268m.; mail Bismarck z 63624; ● 150

Maryknoll; RMC Place; LINCOLN; 197 F-17; mail Old Monroe z 63369; ● 220

Maryland Heights; Inc. Place; ST. LOUIS; 195 D-4; elev. 500ft./152m.; 🅿; ★ **ST.L**; z 63043; Ⓟ 25,407; Ⓒ 25,756; ◆ 24,743

Marys Home; RMC Place; MILLER; 197 H-14; elev. 783ft./239m.; mail Eugene z 65032

Maryville; Inc. Place; ⊡ NODAWAY; 196 B-8; elev. 1,136ft./346m.; 🅿 🅷 🅲 6,232; z 64468; Ⓟ 10,663; Ⓒ 10,581

Maryville Gardens; RMC Place; ST. LOUIS (Independent City); *197 G-18; ★ **ST.L**; mail Saint Louis z 63111, z 63118; pop. incl. with Saint Louis (Independent City)

Masters; RMC Place; CEDAR; *197 I-11; mail Fair Play z 65649; rural

Matson; RMC Place; ST. CHARLES; 197 G-17; mail Defiance z 63341; ● 80

Mattese; RMC Place; ST. LOUIS; 195 H-5; ★ **ST.L**; mail Saint Louis z 63129; ● 2,500

Matthews; Inc. Place; NEW MADRID; 197 L-20; elev. 310ft./94m.; 🅿; z 63867; Ⓟ 614; Ⓒ 605

Maud; RMC Place; SHELBY; *197 D-14; mail Clarence z 63437

Maupin; RMC Place; FRANKLIN; *197 H-17; elev. 601ft./183m.; mail Luebbering z 63061; rural

Maxey; RMC Place; BUCHANAN; *196 D-8; mail Saint Joseph z 64507; ● 100

Maxville; RMC Place; JASPER; *196 K-9; mail Arnold z 63010, Carthage z 64836; ● 200

Mayesburg; RMC Place; BATES; *196 G-10; mail Urich z 64788; rural

Mayfield; RMC Place; BOLLINGER; *197 J-19; mail Patton z 63662; ● 100

Maysville; Inc. Place; ⊡ DEKALB; 196 C-9; elev. 974ft./297m.; 🅿; z 64469; Ⓟ 1,176; Ⓒ 1,212

Mayview; Inc. Place; LAFAYETTE; 196 E-10; elev. 905ft./276m.; 🅿; z 64071; Ⓟ 279; Ⓒ 294

Maywood; RMC Place; LEWIS; *197 C-15; elev. 516ft./157m.; 🅿; z 63454; ● 200

McAllister Springs Access Point; RMC Place; SALINE; *197 F-11; elev. 743ft./226m.; mail Houstonia z 65333; rural

McBaine; Inc. Place; BOONE; *197 F-13; elev. 571ft./174m.; mail Columbia z 65203; Ⓟ 29; Ⓒ 17

McBride; RMC Place; PERRY; *197 I-19; elev. 370ft./113m.; 🅿; z 63776

McCarty; RMC Place; PEMISCOT; *197 N-19; elev. 263ft./80m.; mail Caruthersville z 63830; rural

McClurg; RMC Place; TANEY; *197 L-13; elev. 1,120ft./341m.; 🅿; z 65701; rural

McCord Bend; Inc. Place; STONE; *197 L-11; elev. 1,000ft./305m.; mail Galena z 65656; Ⓟ 206; Ⓒ 292

McCracken; RMC Place; CHRISTIAN; *197 K-12; elev. 1,377ft./420m.; mail Sparta z 65753; ● 130

McCredie; CALLAWAY; see Kingdom City (Inc. Place)

McCurry; RMC Place; GENTRY; *196 B-9; elev. 274ft./84m.; mail Darlington z 64438; rural

MCDONALD; 196 L-9; Ⓟ 16,938; Ⓒ 21,681; ◆ 22,727

McDowell; RMC Place; BARRY; 196 L-10; elev. 1,161ft./354m.; mail Verona z 65769; ● 80

McElhany; RMC Place; NEWTON; *196 L-9; mail Neosho z 64850; ● 150

McFall; Inc. Place; GENTRY; 196 C-10; elev. 960ft./293m.; 🅿; z 64657; Ⓟ 142; Ⓒ 135

McGee; RMC Place; WAYNE; 197 K-18; elev. 395ft./120m.; 🅿; z 63763; ● 80

McGirk; RMC Place; MONITEAU; *197 G-13; elev. 833ft./254m.; 🅿; z 65055; ● 120

McGuire; RMC Place; DUNKLIN; *197 L-19; elev. 286ft./87m.; mail Clarkton z 63837; ● 30

McKinley; RMC Place; LAWRENCE; *197 K-11; elev. 1,370ft./418m.; mail Marionville z 65705; rural

McKittrick; Inc. Place; MONTGOMERY; *197 F-15; elev. 513ft./156m.; 🅿; z 65041; Ⓟ 66; Ⓒ 72

McMullin; RMC Place; SCOTT; *197 K-20; mail Sikeston z 63801; ● 30

McNatt; RMC Place; MCDONALD; *196 L-9; mail Stella z 64867; rural

Meacham Park; RMC Place; ST. LOUIS; *197 G-18; ★ **ST.L**; mail Saint Louis z 63122; pop. incl. with Kirkwood (Inc. Place)

Meadowbrook Downs; RMC Place; ST. LOUIS; ★ **ST.L**; mail Saint Louis z 63114; pop. incl. with Overland (Inc. Place)

Meadville; Inc. Place; LINN; 197 C-11; elev. 756ft./230m.; 🅿; z 64659; Ⓟ 360; Ⓒ 457

Medford; RMC Place; JOHNSON; *196 G-10; mail Holden z 64040

Medill; RMC Place; CLARK; 197 B-15; mail Kahoka z 63445; ● 150

Medoc; RMC Place; JASPER; *196 J-9; mail Oronogo z 64855; rural

Mehlville; CDP; ST. LOUIS; 195 G-5; elev. 638ft./194m.; ★ **ST.L**; mail Saint Louis z 63129; Ⓟ 27,557; Ⓒ 28,822; ◆ 27,805

Meinert; RMC Place; DADE; *196 J-10; elev. 1,158ft./353m.; mail Lockwood z 65682

Melbourne; RMC Place; HARRISON; *196 B-10; mail Gilman City z 64642; ● 30

Melrose; RMC Place; ST. LOUIS; *197 G-17; elev. 776ft./237m.; ★ **ST.L**; mail Pacific z 63069; pop. incl. with Wildwood (Inc. Place)

Memphis; Inc. Place; ⊡ SCOTLAND; 197 B-14; elev. 801ft./244m.; 🅿 🅷; z 63555; Ⓟ 2,094; Ⓒ 2,061

Mendon; Inc. Place; CHARITON; 197 D-12; elev. 698ft./213m.; 🅿; z 64660; Ⓟ 207; Ⓒ 208

Mendota; RMC Place; PUTNAM; *197 A-12; elev. 900ft./274m.; mail Unionville z 63565; rural

Menfro; RMC Place; PERRY; 197 I-19; elev. 371ft./113m.; mail Perryville z 63775; ● 30

Mentor; RMC Place; GREENE; *197 K-12; elev. 1,342ft./409m.; ★ **SPRG**; mail Rogersville z 65742; rural

Mercer; Inc. Place; MERCER; 197 A-11; elev. 1,074ft./327m.; 🅿; z 64661; Ⓟ 297; Ⓒ 342

MERCER; 197 B-11; Ⓟ 3,723; Ⓒ 3,757; ◆ 3,483

Mercyville; RMC Place; MACON; *197 C-13; mail Elmer z 63538; rural

Merriam Woods; Inc. Place; TANEY; *197 L-12; elev. 960ft./293m.; mail Forsyth z 65653, Rockaway Beach z 65740; Ⓟ 601; Ⓒ 1,142

Merritt; RMC Place; DOUGLAS; *197 K-12; mail Oldfield z 65720; rural

Merwin; Inc. Place; BATES; 196 G-9; elev. 883ft./269m.; mail Amsterdam z 64723; Ⓟ 75; Ⓒ 83

Mesler; STODDARD; see Messler (RMC Place)

Messler (Mesler); RMC Place; STODDARD; *197 K-19; elev. 323ft./98m.; ● 30

Meta; Inc. Place; OSAGE; 197 H-14; elev. 610ft./186m.; 🅿; z 65058; Ⓟ 249; Ⓒ 249

Metz; Inc. Place; VERNON; 196 H-9; elev. 785ft./239m.; 🅿; z 64765; Ⓟ 91; Ⓒ 67

Mexico; Inc. Place; ⊡ AUDRAIN; 197 E-14; elev. 802ft./244m.; 🅿 🅷 ■; z 65265; Ⓟ 11,290; Ⓒ 11,320; ◆ 10,173

Miami; Inc. Place; SALINE; 197 E-12; elev. 707ft./215m.; 🅿; z 65344; Ⓟ 142; Ⓒ 160

Miami Station; RMC Place; CARROLL; *197 E-12; mail Carrollton z 64633; rural

Michelles Corner; RMC Place; TEXAS; *197 J-14; elev. 1,433ft./437m.; mail Bucyrus z 65444; ● 30

Micola; RMC Place; PEMISCOT; *197 M-19; mail Steele z 63877; rural

Middlebrook; RMC Place; IRON; *197 I-17; elev. 1,140ft./347m.; 🅿; z 63656; ● 200

Middle Grove; RMC Place; MONROE; 197 E-14; elev. 784ft./239m.; mail Madison z 65263; ● 30

Middletown; Inc. Place; MONTGOMERY; 197 E-16; elev. 713ft./217m.; 🅿; z 63359; Ⓟ 217; Ⓒ 199

Midland; ADAIR; see Tipperary (RMC Place)

Midridge; RMC Place; SHANNON; *197 J-16; elev. 1,231ft./375m.; mail Bunker z 63629; rural

Midvale; RMC Place; TEXAS; *197 K-15; elev. 1,376ft./419m.; mail Summersville z 65571; ● 40

Midway; RMC Place; ANDREW; *196 C-8; elev. 996ft./304m.; mail Bolckow z 64427; rural

Midway; RMC Place; BOONE; 197 F-13; elev. 652ft./199m.; mail Columbia z 65202; ● 200

Midway; RMC Place; LEWIS; *197 B-15; elev. 723ft./220m.; mail Lewistown z 63452; rural

Midway; RMC Place; NEWTON; *196 K-9; elev. 1,050ft./320m.; ★ **JOP**; pop. incl. with Joplin (Inc. Place)

Mike; RMC Place; CHARITON; *197 D-12; mail Marceline z 64658; ● 30

Milan; Inc. Place; ⊡ SULLIVAN; 197 B-12; elev. 969ft./295m.; 🅿 🅷; z 63556; Ⓟ 1,767; Ⓒ 1,958

Mildred; RMC Place; TANEY; *197 L-12; elev. 985ft./300m.; mail Kirbyville z 65679; ● 250

Milford; Inc. Place; BARTON; 196 J-10; elev. 924ft./282m.; 🅿; z 64766; Ⓟ 22; Ⓒ 52

Millard; Inc. Place; ADAIR; 197 C-13; mail Kirksville z 63501; Ⓟ 71; Ⓒ 75

Millcreek; RMC Place; MADISON; *197 J-18; 🅿; z 63645; ● 190

Miller; Inc. Place; LAWRENCE; 196 K-10; elev. 1,300ft./396m.; 🅿; z 65707; Ⓟ 753; Ⓒ 754

MILLER; 197 H-13; Ⓟ 20,700; Ⓒ 23,564; ◆ 24,960

Millersburg; RMC Place; CALLAWAY; 197 F-14; elev. 813ft./248m.; mail Fulton z 65251; ● 235

Millersville; RMC Place; CAPE GIRARDEAU; 197 J-19; elev. 460ft./140m.; 🅿; z 63766; ● 250

Mill Grove; RMC Place; MERCER; 197 B-11; elev. 820ft./250m.; mail Princeton z 64673

Millheim; RMC Place; PERRY; *197 I-19; elev. 600ft./183m.; mail Perryville z 63775; rural

Mill Spring; Inc. Place; WAYNE; 197 K-17; elev. 431ft./131m.; 🅿; z 63952; Ⓟ 252; Ⓒ 219

Millville; RMC Place; RAY; 196 D-10; mail Richmond z 64085

Millwood; RMC Place; LINCOLN; 197 E-16; elev. 644ft./196m.; mail Silex z 63377

Milo; Inc. Place; VERNON; 196 I-9; elev. 878ft./268m.; 🅿; z 64767; Ⓟ 76; Ⓒ 84

Milton; RMC Place; ATCHISON; *196 B-7; elev. 898ft./274m.; mail Fairfax z 64446; rural

Milton; RMC Place; RANDOLPH; *197 D-14; mail Moberly z 65270

Mincy; RMC Place; TANEY; *197 L-12; elev. 918ft./280m.; mail Kirbyville z 65679; rural

Mindenmines; Inc. Place; BARTON; 196 J-9; elev. 962ft./293m.; 🅿; z 64769; Ⓟ 346; Ⓒ 409

Mine La Motte; RMC Place; MADISON; *197 I-18; elev. 879ft./268m.; 🅿; z 63645; ● 140

Mineola; RMC Place; MONTGOMERY; *197 F-15; elev. 567ft./173m.; 🅿; z 63361; ● 40

Miner; Inc. Place; SCOTT; 197 K-20; elev. 310ft./94m.; 🅿; z 63801; Ⓟ 1,218; Ⓒ 1,056

Mineral City; RMC Place; ST. FRANCOIS; *197 I-17; elev. 1,188ft./362m.; mail Doe Run z 63637; rural

Mineral Point; Inc. Place; WASHINGTON; *197 I-17; elev. 867ft./264m.; 🅿; z 63660; Ⓟ 384; Ⓒ 363

Mineral Spring; RMC Place; BARRY; *196 L-10; mail Cassville z 65625; ● 155

Mineville; RMC Place; CLAY; *196 E-9; ★ **K.C.**; mail Kansas City z 64161; pop. incl. with Kansas City (Inc. Place)

Mingo; RMC Place; STODDARD; *197 K-18; mail Puxico z 63960; rural

Minimum; RMC Place; IRON; *197 J-17; elev. 613ft./187m.; mail Annapolis z 63620; ● 30

Minnie; RMC Place; BOONE; *197 E-13; mail Harrisburg z 65256; rural

Minnith; RMC Place; STE. GENEVIEVE; *197 I-19; elev. 437ft./133m.; mail Saint Mary z 63673; ● 85

Mint Hill; RMC Place; OSAGE; *197 G-15; elev. 931ft./284m.; mail Chamois z 65024; rural

Mirabile; RMC Place; CALDWELL; 196 D-10; mail Polo z 64671; ● 50

Miramiguoa Park; Inc. Place; FRANKLIN; *197 H-16; mail Sullivan z 63080; Ⓒ 127

Missionary Acres; RMC Place; WAYNE; *197 K-18; mail Greenville z 63944; ● 80

MISSISSIPPI; 197 K-20; Ⓟ 14,442; Ⓒ 13,427; ◆ 13,260

Missouri City; Inc. Place; CLAY; 196 E-9; elev. 897ft./273m.; 🅿; ★ **K.C.**; z 64072; Ⓟ 348; Ⓒ 295

Mitchell; RMC Place; ST. FRANCOIS; *197 I-17; elev. 903ft./275m.; mail Park Hills z 63601; ● 110

Moberly; Inc. Place; RANDOLPH; 197 D-13; elev. 877ft./267m.; 🅿 🅷 🅲 530 ■; z 65270; Ⓟ 12,839; Ⓒ 11,945; Ⓡ 13,741; ◆ 14,244

Modena; RMC Place; MERCER; 197 B-11; mail Princeton z 64673; ● 60

Mokane; Inc. Place; CALLAWAY; 197 G-15; elev. 534ft./163m.; 🅿; z 65059; Ⓟ 186; Ⓒ 188

Moline Acres; Inc. Place; ST. LOUIS; 195 C-6; elev. 450ft./137m.; ★ **ST.L**; mail Saint Louis z 63136; Ⓟ 2,710; Ⓒ 2,662

Molino; RMC Place; AUDRAIN; 197 E-14; mail Mexico z 65265; ● 80

Monark Springs; RMC Place; NEWTON; *196 L-9; mail Neosho z 64850; ● 100

Monegaw Springs; RMC Place; ST. CLAIR; 196 H-10; elev. 758ft./231m.; mail Osceola z 64776

Monett; Inc. Place; BARRY, LAWRENCE; 196 K-10; elev. 1,317ft./401m.; 🅿 🅷; z 65708; Ⓟ 6,529; Ⓒ 7,396

MONITEAU; 197 G-13; Ⓟ 12,298; Ⓒ 14,827; ◆ 15,199

Monkey Run; RMC Place; RALLS; *197 D-16; mail Hannibal z 63401, Saverton z 63467

MONROE; 197 D-14; Ⓟ 9,104; Ⓒ 9,311; ◆ 9,134

Monroe City; Inc. Place; MONROE, MARION, RALLS; 197 D-15; elev. 749ft./228m.; 🅿; z 63456; Ⓟ 2,701; Ⓒ 2,588

Montague; RMC Place; CHRISTIAN; *197 K-11; mail Highlandville z 65669; ● 120

Montague Hill; RMC Place; SALINE; *197 E-12; elev. 756ft./230m.; mail Marshall z 65340

Montevallo; RMC Place; VERNON; 196 I-10; elev. 959ft./292m.; mail Milo z 64767; ● 50

Montgomery; MONTGOMERY; see Montgomery City (Inc. Place)

MONTGOMERY; 197 F-15; Ⓟ 11,355; Ⓒ 12,136; ◆ 11,806

Montgomery City (Montgomery); Inc. Place; ⊡ MONTGOMERY; 197 F-15; elev. 816ft./249m.; 🅿; z 63361; Ⓟ 2,281; Ⓒ 2,442

Monticello; Inc. Place; ⊡ LEWIS; 197 C-15; 🅿; z 63457; Ⓟ 106; Ⓒ 126

Montier; RMC Place; SHANNON; *197 K-15; elev. 1,039ft./317m.; 🅿; z 65546; ● 200

Montreal; RMC Place; CAMDEN; 197 H-13; elev. 1,029ft./314m.; 🅿; z 65591; ● 150

Montrose; Inc. Place; HENRY; 196 H-10; elev. 836ft./255m.; 🅿; z 64770; Ⓟ 440; Ⓒ 417

Montserrat; RMC Place; JOHNSON; 197 F-11; elev. 802ft./244m.; mail Knob Noster z 65336; ● 80

Moody; RMC Place; HOWELL; 197 L-14; elev. 983ft./300m.; 🅿; z 65777; ● 80

Mooresville; Inc. Place; LIVINGSTON; 197 D-11; elev. 920ft./280m.; 🅿; z 64664; Ⓟ 100; Ⓒ 89

Mora; RMC Place; BENTON; 197 G-12; elev. 1,040ft./317m.; 🅿; z 65345; ● 80

Morehouse; Inc. Place; NEW MADRID; 197 L-19; elev. 302ft./92m.; 🅿; z 63868; Ⓟ 1,068; Ⓒ 1,015

Morgan; RMC Place; LACLEDE; 197 J-13; elev. 1,249ft./381m.; mail Conway z 65632; ● 100

MORGAN; 197 G-12; Ⓟ 15,574; Ⓒ 19,309; ◆ 21,122

Morgan Heights; RMC Place; JASPER; *196 K-9; elev. 1,047ft./319m.; ★ **JOP**; mail Carthage z 64836; ● 250

Morley; Inc. Place; SCOTT; 197 K-20; elev. 343ft./105m.; 🅿; z 63767; Ⓟ 683; Ⓒ 792

Morrison; Inc. Place; GASCONADE; 197 G-15; elev. 527ft./161m.; 🅿; z 65036, z 65061; Ⓟ 160; Ⓒ 123

Morrisville; Inc. Place; POLK; 197 J-11; elev. 1,160ft./354m.; 🅿; z 65645, z 65710; Ⓟ 293; Ⓒ 344

Morse Mill; RMC Place; JEFFERSON; *197 H-17; elev. 495ft./151m.; 🅿; z 63066; ● 400

Morton; RMC Place; RAY; *196 E-10; elev. 803ft./245m.; mail Richmond z 64085; rural

Mosby (Moseby); Inc. Place; CLAY; 196 E-9; elev. 756ft./230m.; 🅿; ★ **K.C.**; z 64024, z 64073; Ⓟ 194; Ⓒ 242

Moscow Mills; Inc. Place; LINCOLN; 197 F-17; elev. 500ft./152m.; 🅿; z 63362; Ⓟ 924; Ⓒ 1,742

Moseby; CLAY; see Mosby (Inc. Place)

Moselle; RMC Place; FRANKLIN; 197 G-17; elev. 493ft./150m.; mail Union z 63084; ● 160

Mosher; RMC Place; STE. GENEVIEVE; *197 H-18; mail Sainte Genevieve z 63670; rural

Motley; RMC Place; JASPER; *196 K-9; mail Sarcoxie z 64862; ● 100

Mound City; Inc. Place; HOLT; 196 B-7; elev. 900ft./274m.; 🅿; z 64470; Ⓟ 1,273; Ⓒ 1,193

Moundville; Inc. Place; VERNON; 196 I-9; elev. 840ft./256m.; 🅿; z 64771; Ⓟ 140; Ⓒ 103

Mountain; RMC Place; MCDONALD; *196 L-10; elev. 1,080ft./329m.; mail Washburn z 65772; rural

Mountain Grove; Inc. Place; WRIGHT, TEXAS; 197 K-14; elev. 1,423ft./434m.; 🅿; z 65711; Ⓟ 4,182; Ⓒ 4,574

Mountain View; Inc. Place; HOWELL; 197 K-15; elev. 1,144ft./349m.; 🅿 🅷; z 65548; Ⓟ 2,036; Ⓒ 2,430

Mount Airy; RMC Place; RANDOLPH; 197 E-13; elev. 745ft./227m.; mail Huntsville z 65259; ● 30

Mount Freedom; RMC Place; JEFFERSON; *197 H-17; elev. 740ft./226m.; mail Hillsboro z 63050; rural

Mount Hope; RMC Place; FRANKLIN; *197 H-17; elev. 703ft./214m.; mail Saint Clair z 63077; rural

Mount Hulda; RMC Place; BENTON; *197 G-12; mail Cole Camp z 65325; rural

Mount Leonard; Inc. Place; SALINE; 197 E-11; elev. 810ft./247m.; mail Malta Bend z 65339; Ⓟ 96; Ⓒ 123

Mount Moriah; Inc. Place; HARRISON; 196 B-10; elev. 830ft./253m.; 🅿; z 64481; Ⓟ 104; Ⓒ 143

Mount Pleasant; RMC Place; MILLER; *197 G-13; elev. 949ft./289m.; mail Eldon z 65026; ● 150

Mount Shira; RMC Place; MCDONALD; *196 L-9; elev. 834ft./254m.; mail Noel z 64854

Mount Sterling; RMC Place; GASCONADE; 197 G-15; elev. 591ft./180m.; 🅿; z 65062

Mount Vernon; Inc. Place; ⊡ LAWRENCE; 196 K-10; elev. 1,176ft./358m.; 🅿 🅷; z 65712; Ⓟ 3,726; Ⓒ 4,017

Mount Zion; RMC Place; DOUGLAS; *197 K-13; elev. 1,272ft./388m.; mail Ava z 65608; ● 120

Mount Zion; RMC Place; HENRY; *197 H-11; elev. 880ft./268m.; mail Deepwater z 64740

Muffittville; BUTLER; see Oglesville (RMC Place)

Mulberry; RMC Place; BARTON; 🅿; z 66756; pop. incl. with Burgess (Inc. Place)

Mulberry; RMC Place; BATES; *196 H-9; elev. 782ft./238m.; mail Amoret z 64722; rural

Munsell; RMC Place; SHANNON; *197 K-16; mail Eminence z 65466; rural

Murphy; CDP; JEFFERSON; 195 H-3; ★ **ST.L**; mail Fenton z 63026, High Ridge z 63049; Ⓟ 9,342; Ⓒ 9,048

Murry; RMC Place; BOONE; 197 F-14; ★ **COL**; mail Columbia z 65202, Hallsville z 65255; ● 80

Musicks Ferry; RMC Place; ST. LOUIS; 195 B-5; ★ **ST.L**; mail Florissant z 63034; ● 100

Musselfork; RMC Place; CHARITON; *197 D-12; mail Keytesville z 65261; rural

Myrtle; RMC Place; OREGON; 197 M-16; elev. 566ft./173m.; 🅿; z 65778; ● 120

Mystic; RMC Place; SULLIVAN; *197 B-12; mail Green City z 63545; rural

N

Napier; RMC Place; HOLT; *196 C-7; elev. 850ft./259m.; mail Forest City z 64451; rural

Napoleon; Inc. Place; LAFAYETTE; *196 E-10; elev. 768ft./234m.; 🅿; z 64074; Ⓟ 233; Ⓒ 208

Napton; RMC Place; SALINE; 197 E-12; elev. 643ft./196m.; 🅿; z 65340; ● 50

Nashua; RMC Place; CLAY; *196 E-9; ★ **K.C.**; mail Kansas City z 64155; pop. incl. with Kansas City (Inc. Place)

Nashville; RMC Place; BARTON; 196 J-9; mail Oronogo z 64855; ● 100

Naylor; Inc. Place; RIPLEY; 197 L-17; elev. 304ft./93m.; 🅿; z 63953; Ⓟ 642; Ⓒ 610

Nebo; RMC Place; LACLEDE; 197 J-14; elev. 1,100ft./335m.; mail Falcon z 65470

Neck; JASPER; see Neck City (Inc. Place)

Neck City (Neck); Inc. Place; JASPER; *196 J-9; elev. 934ft./285m.; 🅿; ★ **JOP**; z 64849; Ⓟ 132; Ⓒ 119

Neelys; CAPE GIRARDEAU; see Neelys Landing (RMC Place)

Neelys Landing (Neelys); RMC Place; CAPE GIRARDEAU; 197 J-20; mail Jackson z 63755

Neelyville; Inc. Place; BUTLER; 197 L-18; elev. 303ft./92m.; 🅿; z 63954; Ⓟ 381; Ⓒ 487

Neeper; RMC Place; CLARK; *197 B-15; elev. 719ft./219m.; mail Kahoka z 63445; rural

Neier; RMC Place; FRANKLIN; *197 G-16; elev. 816ft./249m.; mail Union z 63084; rural

Nelson; Inc. Place; SALINE; 197 F-12; elev. 650ft./198m.; 🅿; z 65347; Ⓟ 181; Ⓒ 212

Nelsonville; RMC Place; MARION; *197 C-15; elev. 719ft./219m.; mail Ewing z 63440; rural

Nemo; RMC Place; HICKORY; *197 I-12; elev. 989ft./301m.; mail Pittsburg z 65724; ● 200

Neola; RMC Place; DADE; *196 J-10; mail Greenfield z 65661; rural

Neosho; Inc. Place; ⊡ NEWTON; 196 K-9; elev. 998ft./304m.; 🅿 🅷; z 64850, z 64853; Ⓟ 9,254; Ⓒ 10,505

Netherlands; RMC Place; PEMISCOT; *197 M-19; mail Hayti z 63851; rural

Nettleton; RMC Place; CALDWELL; *196 D-10; elev. 962ft./293m.; mail Hamilton z 64644; ● 50

Nevada; Inc. Place; ⊡ VERNON; 196 I-9; elev. 880ft./268m.; 🅿 🅷; z 64772; Ⓟ 8,597; Ⓒ 8,607

Newark; Inc. Place; KNOX; 197 C-14; elev. 700ft./213m.; 🅿; z 63458; Ⓟ 82; Ⓒ 100

New Bloomfield; Inc. Place; CALLAWAY; 197 F-14; elev. 841ft./256m.; 🅿; z 65063; Ⓟ 480; Ⓒ 599

New Boston; RMC Place; LINN; 197 C-12; elev. 964ft./294m.; 🅿; z 63557; ● 60

Newburg; Inc. Place; PHELPS; 197 I-14; elev. 711ft./217m.; 🅿; z 65550; Ⓟ 589; Ⓒ 484

New Cambria; Inc. Place; MACON; 197 D-13; elev. 855ft./261m.; 🅿; z 63558; Ⓟ 223; Ⓒ 222

New Florence; Inc. Place; MONTGOMERY; 197 F-15; elev. 874ft./266m.; 🅿; z 63363; Ⓟ 801; Ⓒ 764

New Frankfort; RMC Place; SALINE; *197 E-12; elev. 683ft./208m.; mail Slater z 65349; rural

New Franklin; Inc. Place; HOWARD; 197 F-13; elev. 655ft./200m.; 🅿; z 65274; Ⓟ 1,107; Ⓒ 1,145

New Hamburg; RMC Place; SCOTT; 197 K-20; elev. 459ft./140m.; mail Benton z 63736; ● 250

New Hampton; Inc. Place; HARRISON; 196 B-10; elev. 958ft./292m.; 🅿; z 64471; Ⓟ 320; Ⓒ 349

New Harmony; RMC Place; PIKE; *197 E-16; mail Curryville z 63339; rural

New Hartford; RMC Place; PIKE; 197 E-16; elev. 600ft./183m.; 🅿; z 63359

New Haven; Inc. Place; FRANKLIN; 197 G-16; elev. 600ft./183m.; 🅿; z 63068; Ⓟ 1,757; Ⓒ 1,867

New Hope; RMC Place; DENT; *197 J-15; elev. 1,300ft./396m.; mail Salem z 65560; rural

New Hope; RMC Place; LINCOLN; 197 E-17; elev. 715ft./218m.; mail Elsberry z 63343; ● 90

New Lebanon; RMC Place; COOPER; *197 F-12; mail Bunceton z 65237; rural

New Liberty; RMC Place; OREGON; *197 L-16; mail Winona z 65588; rural

New London; Inc. Place; ⊡ RALLS; 197 D-16; elev. 675ft./206m.; 🅿; z 63459; Ⓟ 988; Ⓒ 1,001

New Madrid; Inc. Place; ⊡ NEW MADRID; 197 L-20; elev. 305ft./93m.; 🅿; z 63869; Ⓟ 3,350; Ⓒ 3,334

NEW MADRID; 197 L-19; Ⓟ 20,928; Ⓒ 19,760; ◆ 17,474

New Market; RMC Place; PLATTE; 196 D-8; mail Dearborn z 64439; ● 80

New Melle; Inc. Place; ST. CHARLES; 197 F-17; elev. 789ft./240m.; 🅿; z 63365; Ⓟ 486; Ⓒ 124; Ⓡ 287

New Offenburg; RMC Place; STE. GENEVIEVE; *197 I-18; elev. 760ft./232m.; 🅿; z 63670; ● 200

New Piper; RMC Place; HENRY; *196 G-10; elev. 827ft./252m.; mail Urich z 64788; rural

New Point; RMC Place; HOLT; 196 C-8; elev. 874ft./266m.; 🅿; z 64473; ● 50

Newport; RMC Place; BARTON; *196 J-10; elev. 1,006ft./307m.; mail Lamar z 64759

New Santa Fe; RMC Place; JACKSON; *196 F-9; ★ **K.C.**; mail Kansas City z 64145; pop. incl. with Kansas City (Inc. Place)

New Survey; RMC Place; PEMISCOT; *197 N-19; elev. 255ft./78m.; mail Steele z 63877; rural

NEWTON; 196 K-9; Ⓟ 44,445; Ⓒ 52,636; ◆ 56,928

Newtonia; Inc. Place; NEWTON; *196 K-9; elev. 1,203ft./367m.; 🅿; z 64853; Ⓟ 204; Ⓒ 231

Newtown; Inc. Place; SULLIVAN; 197 B-11; elev. 950ft./290m.; 🅿; z 64667; Ⓟ 115; Ⓒ 209

New Truxton; RMC Place; WARREN; *197 F-16; elev. 710ft./216m.; mail Truxton z 63381

New Wells; RMC Place; CAPE GIRARDEAU; 197 J-19; elev. 400ft./122m.; 🅿; z 63732; ● 90

New Woollam (Woollam); RMC Place; GASCONADE; *197 G-15; elev. 679ft./207m.; mail Owensville z 65066; rural

New York; RMC Place; CALDWELL; *196 D-10; elev. 802ft./244m.; mail Hamilton z 64644; rural

Niangua; Inc. Place; WEBSTER; 197 J-12; elev. 1,435ft./437m.; 🅿; z 65713; Ⓟ 459; Ⓒ 445

Niangua Junction; RMC Place; WEBSTER; *197 J-12; elev. 1,433ft./437m.; mail Niangua z 65713; rural

Nichols; RMC Place; GREENE; *197 K-11; ★ **SPRG**; mail Springfield z 65802; pop. incl. with Springfield (Inc. Place)

Nind; RMC Place; ADAIR; *197 C-13; mail Kirksville z 63501; rural

Nishnabotna; RMC Place; ATCHISON; 196 B-7; mail Fairfax z 64446; rural

Nixa; Inc. Place; CHRISTIAN; 197 K-11; elev. 1,300ft./396m.; 🅿; ★ **SPRG**; z 65714; Ⓟ 4,707; Ⓒ 12,124

Noah; HENRY; see Germantown (RMC Place)

Noble; RMC Place; OZARK; *197 L-13; elev. 1,060ft./323m.; 🅿; z 65715; rural

Nodaway; RMC Place; ANDREW; 196 C-8; mail Amazonia z 64421; ● 125

NODAWAY; 196 B-8; Ⓟ 21,709; Ⓒ 21,912; ◆ 22,082

Noel; Inc. Place; MCDONALD; 196 L-9; elev. 827ft./252m.; 🅿; z 64854; Ⓟ 1,169; Ⓒ 1,480

Nona; RMC Place; ST. CHARLES; *197 G-17; elev. 489ft./149m.; mail Augusta z 63332; rural

Norborne; Inc. Place; CARROLL; 197 E-11; elev. 692ft./211m.; 🅿; z 64668, z 64680; Ⓟ 856; Ⓒ 805

Entries in **UPPERCASE** are counties.
Entries in **bold** have populations of 2,500 or more.
Names in parentheses are alternate names.

Inc. Place	Incorporated Place
RMC Place	Rand McNally Designated Place
CDP	Census Designated Place
MCD	Minor Civil Division
⊡	County Seat
▲	Minor Civil Division
elev.	Elevation
🅿	Post Office
🅷	Hospital
🅲	College
■	Principal Business Center
★	Ranally Metro Area (RMA) Abbreviation
z	Zip Code(s)
Ⓟ	Previous Census Population
Ⓡ	Revised Census Population
Ⓐ	Annexation Population
●	Rand McNally Population Estimate
Ⓒ	Final Census Population
Ⓢ	Special Census Population
◆	Estimated Population

For additional definitions see Glossary, Volume 1, and Introduction, Volume 2.

Normandy (Berdell Hills); Inc. Place; ST. LOUIS; **195** D-6; elev. 600ft./183m.; 🅿; ★ **ST.L**; z 63121; Ⓟ 4,480; © 5,153; Ⓡ 5,247
Norris; RMC Place; HENRY; ***196** G-10; mail Blairstown z 64726; rural
Northeast; RMC Place; JACKSON; ***196** E-9; ★ **K.C.**; mail Kansas City z 64123; pop. incl. with Kansas City (Inc. Place)
Northern Heights; RMC Place; PLATTE; ***196** E-9; ★ **K.C.**; mail Kansas City z 64152; pop. incl. with Kansas City (Inc. Place)
North Kansas City; Inc. Place; CLAY; **196** H-3; elev. 744ft./227m.; 🅿 🅷 🅲 611 ■; ★ **K.C.**; z 64116 & mail Kansas City z 64117-18, z 64161; Ⓟ 4,130; © 4,714; ◆ 5,897
North Lilbourn; Inc. Place; NEW MADRID; ***197** L-20; elev. 280ft./85m.; mail Lilbourn z 63862; Ⓟ 157; © 95
Northmoor; Inc. Place; PLATTE; **196** G-3; elev. 850ft./259m.; 🅿; ★ **K.C.**; z 64150-51 & mail Kansas City z 64152; Ⓟ 441; © 399
North Noel; RMC Place; MCDONALD; mail Noel z 64854; pop. incl. with Noel (Inc. Place)
North Patton; RMC Place; BOLLINGER; ***197** J-19; mail Patton z 63662; ● 140
North Salem; RMC Place; LINN; ***197** C-12; mail Winigan z 63566
North Shores; RMC Place; BENTON; elev. 240ft./73m.; mail Warsaw z 65355
Northview; RMC Place; WEBSTER; **197** J-12; elev. 1,441ft./439m.; mail Marshfield z 65706; ● 150
North Wardell; Inc. Place; PEMISCOT; ***197** M-19; elev. 270ft./82m.; mail Wardell z 63879; Ⓟ 135; © 170
Northwoods; Inc. Place; ST. LOUIS; **195** D-6; elev. 550ft./168m.; ★ **ST.L**; mail Saint Louis z 63121; Ⓟ 5,106; © 4,643
Northwye; RMC Place; PHELPS; **197** H-15; elev. 1,114ft./340m.; mail Rolla z 65401; ● 200
Norwood; Inc. Place; WRIGHT; **197** K-13; elev. 1,496ft./456m.; 🅿; z 65717; Ⓟ 449; © 552
Norwood Court; Inc. Place; ST. LOUIS; ***197** F-18; elev. 622ft./190m.; ★ **ST.L**; mail Saint Louis z 63121; Ⓟ 888; © 1,061
Nottinghill; RMC Place; OZARK; ***197** L-13; elev. 1,042ft./318m.; 🅿; z 65762; rural
Novelty; Inc. Place; KNOX; **197** C-14; elev. 830ft./253m.; 🅿; z 63460; Ⓟ 143; © 119
Novinger; Inc. Place; ADAIR; **197** B-13; elev. 770ft./235m.; 🅿; z 63559; Ⓟ 542; © 534
Nyhart; RMC Place; BATES; ***196** H-9; elev. 772ft./235m.; mail Butler z 64730; rural
Nyssa; RMC Place; BUTLER; ***197** L-18; elev. 325ft./99m.; mail Broseley z 63932; rural

O

Oak; RMC Place; DEKALB; ***196** C-9; elev. 963ft./294m.; mail Amity z 64422; rural
Oak Grove; FRANKLIN; see Oak Grove Village (Inc. Place)
Oak Grove; Inc. Place; JACKSON, LAFAYETTE; **196** F-10; elev. 870ft./265m.; 🅿; ★ **K.C.**; z 64075; Ⓟ 4,563; © 5,535
Oak Grove; RMC Place; MADISON; ***197** J-18; elev. 727ft./222m.; mail Fredericktown z 63645; rural
Oak Grove Heights; RMC Place; GREENE; ***197** K-12; elev. 1,407ft./429m.; ★ **SPRG**; mail Springfield z 65801; ● 160
Oak Grove Village (Oak Grove); Inc. Place; FRANKLIN; **197** H-16; elev. 922ft./281m.; mail Sullivan z 63080; Ⓟ 402; © 382
Oak Hill; RMC Place; CRAWFORD; ***197** H-16; mail Cuba z 65453; ● 80
Oakland; RMC Place; LACLEDE; ***197** I-13; elev. 1,265ft./386m.; mail Lebanon z 65536; rural
Oakland; Inc. Place; ST. LOUIS; **195** F-5; elev. 616ft./188m.; ★ **ST.L**; mail Saint Louis z 63122; Ⓟ 1,593; © 1,540
Oakland Park; RMC Place; JASPER; ***196** K-9; elev. 1,000ft./305m.; ★ **JOP**; mail Webb City z 64870; pop. incl. with Webb City (Inc. Place)
Oak Ridge; Inc. Place; CAPE GIRARDEAU; **197** J-19; elev. 600ft./183m.; 🅿; z 63769; Ⓟ 202; © 202
Oaks; Inc. Place; CLAY; **196** G-3; elev. 950ft./290m.; ★ **K.C.**; mail Kansas City z 64118; Ⓟ 130; © 136
Oakside; RMC Place; SHANNON; ***197** K-15; mail Mountain View z 65548; rural
Oakton; RMC Place; BARTON; ***196** J-9; elev. 975ft./297m.; mail Lamar z 64759
Oakvale; RMC Place; JEFFERSON; ***197** H-18; elev. 587ft./179m.; ★ **ST.L**; mail De Soto z 63020; rural
Oakview; Inc. Place; CLAY; **196** G-3; elev. 1,000ft./305m.; ★ **K.C.**; mail Kansas City z 64118; Ⓟ 351; © 386
Oakville; CDP; ST. LOUIS; **195** H-6; elev. 605ft./184m.; ★ **ST.L**; mail Saint Louis z 63129; Ⓟ 31,750; © 35,309; ◆ 34,070
Oakwood; Inc. Place; CLAY; **196** G-3; elev. 1,000ft./305m.; ★ **K.C.**; mail Kansas City z 64116; Ⓟ 212; © 197
Oakwood; RMC Place; MARION; mail Hannibal z 63401; pop. incl. with Hannibal (Inc. Place)
Oakwood Manor; RMC Place; CLAY; ***196** E-9; elev. 980ft./299m.; ★ **K.C.**; pop. incl. with Gladstone (Inc. Place)
Oakwood Park; Inc. Place; CLAY; **196** G-3; elev. 990ft./302m.; ★ **K.C.**; mail Kansas City z 64116; Ⓟ 213; © 183
Oates; RMC Place; REYNOLDS; **197** J-16; elev. 994ft./303m.; mail Black z 63625
Ocie; RMC Place; OZARK; **197** L-13; elev. 743ft./226m.; mail Theodosia z 65761; rural
Octa; RMC Place; DUNKLIN; ***197** M-19; mail Senath z 63876; ● 30
Odessa; Inc. Place; LAFAYETTE; **196** F-10; elev. 930ft./283m.; 🅿; z 64076; Ⓟ 3,695; © 4,818
Odin; RMC Place; WRIGHT; ***197** J-13; mail Hartville z 65667
Oermann; RMC Place; JEFFERSON; ***197** H-17; elev. 790ft./241m.; mail Dittmer z 63023; ● 80
O'Fallon; Inc. Place; ST. CHARLES; **197** F-17; elev. 543ft./166m.; 🅿; ★ **ST.L**; z 63366-68; Ⓟ 18,698; © 46,169; ◆ 77,058
Ogborn; RMC Place; ST. FRANCOIS; ***197** I-18; elev. 954ft./291m.; mail Farmington z 63640; rural
Oglesville (Muffittville); RMC Place; BUTLER; ***197** L-18; mail Qulin z 63961; ● 70
Ohio; RMC Place; ST. CLAIR; ***196** H-10; elev. 838ft./255m.; mail Lowry City z 64763; rural
Okete; RMC Place; LINCOLN; ***197** E-17; mail Troy z 63379; rural
Olathia; RMC Place; DOUGLAS; ***197** K-13; elev. 248ft./76m.; mail Mansfield z 65704; rural
Old Appleton (Appleton); Inc. Place; CAPE GIRARDEAU; ***197** I-19; elev. 400ft./122m.; 🅿; z 63770; Ⓟ 82; © 82
Old Bland; RMC Place; GASCONADE; ***197** H-15; elev. 772ft./235m.; mail Bland z 65014; rural
Old Chilhowee; RMC Place; JOHNSON; ***196** G-10; mail Chilhowee z 64733; ● 100
Olden; RMC Place; HOWELL; **197** L-14; elev. 1,243ft./379m.; mail Pomona z 65789; ● 80
Oldfield; RMC Place; CHRISTIAN; ***197** K-12; elev. 1,380ft./421m.; 🅿; z 65720; ● 125
Old Fredonia; RMC Place; BENTON; ***197** H-12; elev. 701ft./214m.; mail Warsaw z 65355; rural
Oldham; RMC Place; BOONE; ***197** F-14; elev. 885ft./270m.; mail Ashland z 65010; ● 80
Old Linn Creek; RMC Place; CAMDEN; ***197** H-13; elev. 700ft./213m.; mail Linn Creek z 65052; rural
Old Merritt; RMC Place; DOUGLAS; ***197** K-12; elev. 1,242ft./379m.; mail Oldfield z 65720; ● 100
Old Mines; RMC Place; WASHINGTON; **197** H-17; elev. 797ft./243m.; mail Cadet z 63630; ● 200
Old Monroe; Inc. Place; LINCOLN; **197** F-17; elev. 425ft./130m.; 🅿; z 63369; Ⓟ 242; © 250
Old Orchard; RMC Place; ST. LOUIS; ★ **ST.L**; mail Saint Louis z 63119; pop. incl. with Webster Groves (Inc. Place)
Old Woollam; RMC Place; GASCONADE; ***197** G-15; elev. 762ft./232m.; mail Owensville z 65066; rural
Olean; Inc. Place; MILLER; ***197** G-13; elev. 769ft./234m.; 🅿; z 65064; Ⓟ 106; © 157
Olive; RMC Place; DALLAS; ***197** J-12; elev. 1,312ft./400m.; mail Fair Grove z 65648; ● 100
Olive; RMC Place; ST. LOUIS (Independent City); ***197** G-18; ★ **ST.L**; mail Saint Louis z 63101; pop. incl. with Saint Louis (Independent City)
Olivette; Inc. Place; ST. LOUIS; **195** E-5; elev. 660ft./201m.; 🅿; ★ **ST.L**; z 63132; Ⓟ 7,573; © 7,438
Olney; RMC Place; LINCOLN; **197** E-16; elev. 714ft./218m.; 🅿; z 63370
Olympia; RMC Place; CEDAR; ***196** I-10; elev. 950ft./290m.; mail El Dorado Springs z 64744; rural
Olympian Village; Inc. Place; JEFFERSON; **197** H-18; elev. 700ft./213m.; mail De Soto z 63020; Ⓟ 752; © 669
Omaha; RMC Place; PUTNAM; ***197** A-13; elev. 996ft./304m.; mail Unionville z 63565; rural
Ongo; RMC Place; DOUGLAS; ***197** K-12; elev. 1,280ft./390m.; mail Sparta z 65753; rural
Oran; Inc. Place; SCOTT; **197** K-19; elev. 347ft./106m.; 🅿; z 63771; Ⓟ 1,164; © 1,264
Orange; RMC Place; LAWRENCE; ***196** K-10; mail Aurora z 65605; rural
Orchard Farm; RMC Place; ST. CHARLES; **195** B-4; mail Saint Charles z 63301; ● 300
Orchard Lakes; RMC Place; ST. LOUIS; ***197** F-18; ★ **ST.L**; mail Saint Louis z 63141; ● 1,750
Orearville; RMC Place; SALINE; ***197** E-12; elev. 780ft./238m.; mail Slater z 65349; rural
Oregon; Inc. Place; ⊡ HOLT; **196** C-8; elev. 1,094ft./333m.; 🅿; z 64473; Ⓟ 935; © 935
OREGON; **197** L-16; Ⓟ 9,470; © 10,344; ◆ 10,188
Oriole; RMC Place; CAPE GIRARDEAU; ***197** J-20; mail Cape Girardeau z 63701; ● 140
Orla; RMC Place; LACLEDE; ***197** J-13; elev. 1,052ft./321m.; mail Lebanon z 65536; rural
Oronogo; Inc. Place; JASPER; ***196** K-9; elev. 950ft./290m.; 🅿; ★ **JOP**; z 64855; Ⓟ 595; © 976
Orrick; Inc. Place; RAY; **196** E-10; elev. 720ft./219m.; 🅿; z 64077; Ⓟ 935; © 889
Orrsburg; RMC Place; NODAWAY; ***196** B-8; elev. 1,159ft./353m.; mail Parnell z 64475; rural
OSAGE; **197** G-14; Ⓟ 12,018; © 13,062; ◆ 13,114
Osage Beach; Inc. Place; CAMDEN, MILLER; **197** H-13; elev. 895ft./273m.; 🅿 🅷; z 65065; Ⓟ 2,599; © 3,662
Osage Bend; RMC Place; COLE; ***197** G-14; elev. 730ft./223m.; mail Jefferson City z 65101; ● 90
Osage Bluff; RMC Place; COLE; ***197** G-14; mail Jefferson City z 65101; ● 110
Osage City; RMC Place; COLE; ***197** G-14; ★ **JFCY**; mail Jefferson City z 65101; ● 150
Osage Hill; RMC Place; ST. LOUIS; ★ **ST.L**; mail Saint Louis z 63122; pop. incl. with Kirkwood (Inc. Place)
Osborn; Inc. Place; DEKALB, CLINTON; **196** D-9; elev. 1,035ft./315m.; 🅿; z 64474; Ⓟ 400; © 455
Oscar; RMC Place; TEXAS; ***197** J-15; mail Licking z 65542; rural
Osceola; Inc. Place; ⊡ ST. CLAIR; **197** H-11; elev. 763ft./233m.; 🅿 🅷; z 64776; Ⓟ 755; © 835
Osgood; Inc. Place; SULLIVAN; **197** B-11; elev. 820ft./250m.; mail Galt z 64641; Ⓟ 53; © 51
Osiris; RMC Place; CEDAR; ***196** I-10; mail Jerico Springs z 64756; rural
Oskaloosa; RMC Place; BARTON; **196** I-9; elev. 866ft./264m.; mail Liberal z 64762
Otterville; Inc. Place; COOPER; **197** F-12; elev. 722ft./220m.; 🅿; z 65348; Ⓟ 507; © 476
Otto; RMC Place; JEFFERSON; **197** G-18; elev. 879ft./268m.; 🅿; ★ **ST.L**; z 63052; ● 500
Overland; Inc. Place; ST. LOUIS; **195** D-4; elev. 641ft./195m.; 🅿; ★ **ST.L**; z 63114; Ⓟ 17,987; © 16,838
Overton; RMC Place; COOPER; ***197** F-13; mail Boonville z 65233; rural
Owens; RMC Place; WRIGHT; ***197** K-13; elev. 1,320ft./402m.; mail Norwood z 65717; ● 30
Owensville; Inc. Place; GASCONADE; **197** G-15; elev. 935ft./285m.; 🅿; z 65066; Ⓟ 2,325; © 2,500
Owls Bend; RMC Place; SHANNON; ***197** K-16; mail Eminence z 65466; rural
Owsley; RMC Place; JOHNSON; ***197** G-11; elev. 889ft./271m.; mail Green Ridge z 65332; rural
Oxford; RMC Place; WORTH; ***196** B-9; mail Parnell z 64475
Oxly; RMC Place; RIPLEY; **197** L-17; elev. 320ft./98m.; 🅿; z 63955; ● 220
Oyer; RMC Place; ST. CLAIR; ***196** H-10; elev. 853ft./260m.; mail El Dorado Springs z 64744; rural
Ozark; Inc. Place; ⊡ CHRISTIAN; **197** K-12; elev. 1,178ft./359m.; 🅿; ★ **SPRG**; z 65721; Ⓟ 4,381; © 9,665
OZARK; **197** L-13; Ⓟ 8,598; © 9,542; ◆ 8,946
Ozark Beach; RMC Place; TANEY; ***197** L-12; mail Forsyth z 65653; ● 200
Ozark Springs; RMC Place; PULASKI; ***197** I-14; mail Waynesville z 65583; summer pop. 100; ● 30
Ozark View; RMC Place; ST. LOUIS; ***197** G-18; ★ **ST.L**; mail Saint Louis z 63122; ● 1,000

P

Pacific; Inc. Place; FRANKLIN, ST. LOUIS; **197** G-17; elev. 466ft./142m.; 🅿; ★ **ST.L**; z 63055, z 63069; Ⓟ 4,350; © 5,482
Pack; RMC Place; MCDONALD; ***196** L-9; elev. 1,126ft./343m.; mail Noel z 64854; rural
Pagedale; Inc. Place; ST. LOUIS; **195** E-5; elev. 577ft./176m.; ★ **ST.L**; mail Saint Louis z 63133; Ⓟ 3,771; © 3,616; Ⓡ 3,522
Painton; RMC Place; STODDARD; **197** K-19; elev. 320ft./98m.; 🅿; z 63771; ● 50
Palace; RMC Place; PULASKI; ***197** I-14; mail Newburg z 65550, Plato z 65552; ● 30
Palisades; RMC Place; ST. LOUIS; ★ **ST.L**; mail Ballwin z 63011
Palmer; RMC Place; WASHINGTON; ***197** I-16; elev. 901ft./275m.; mail Potosi z 63664; rural
Palmetto; RMC Place; GREENE; ***197** K-12; mail Rogersville z 65742; rural
Palmyra; Inc. Place; ⊡ MARION; **197** C-15; elev. 641ft./195m.; 🅿; z 63461; Ⓟ 3,371; © 3,467
Palo Pinto; RMC Place; BENTON; ***197** G-11; elev. 779ft./237m.; mail Lincoln z 65338; rural
Papin; RMC Place; JEFFERSON; ***197** H-18; mail De Soto z 63020; ● 120
Papinsville; BATES; see Papinville (RMC Place)
Papinville (Papinsville); RMC Place; BATES; ***196** H-9; mail Rockville z 64780; ● 80
Paradise; RMC Place; CLAY; ***196** D-9; ★ **K.C.**; mail Smithville z 64089; ● 100
Paris; Inc. Place; ⊡ MONROE; **197** D-14; elev. 696ft./212m.; 🅿; z 65275; Ⓟ 1,486; © 1,529
Paris Springs; RMC Place; LAWRENCE; ***197** K-11; mail Everton z 65646; rural
Parkcrest Village; RMC Place; GREENE; ★ **SPRG**; mail Springfield z 65807; pop. incl. with Springfield (Inc. Place)
Parkdale; Inc. Place; JEFFERSON; **195** H-3; elev. 700ft./213m.; ★ **ST.L**; mail High Ridge z 63049; Ⓟ 212; © 205
Parkdale; RMC Place; PLATTE; ***196** E-9; ★ **K.C.**; mail Kansas City z 64152; pop. incl. with Kansas City (Inc. Place)
Parker Lake; RMC Place; PERRY; ***197** I-18; mail Perryville z 63775; summer pop. 600; ● 110
Park Forest; RMC Place; PLATTE; ★ **K.C.**; mail Kansas City z 64152; pop. incl. with Kansas City (Inc. Place)
Park Hills; Inc. Place; ST. FRANCOIS; **197** I-17; 🅿; z 63601, z 63653; Ⓟ 7,744; © 7,861
Parkville; Inc. Place; PLATTE; **196** E-8; elev. 758ft./231m.; 🅿 🅲 13,275; ★ **K.C.**; z 64152 & mail Kansas City z 64151, z 64163-64, z 64190; Ⓟ 2,402; © 4,059
Parkway; Inc. Place; FRANKLIN; ***197** G-17; elev. 748ft./228m.; mail Saint Clair z 63077; Ⓟ 277; © 280
Parkway; RMC Place; JACKSON; ***196** F-9; ★ **K.C.**; mail Kansas City z 64129-30; pop. incl. with Kansas City (Inc. Place)
Parma; Inc. Place; NEW MADRID; **197** L-19; elev. 281ft./86m.; 🅿; z 63870; Ⓟ 995; © 852
Parnell; Inc. Place; NODAWAY; **196** B-9; elev. 1,060ft./323m.; 🅿; z 64475; Ⓟ 157; © 197
Parshley; RMC Place; JASPER; ***196** K-9; elev. 1,044ft./318m.; mail Carthage z 64836, Sarcoxie z 64862; rural
Pasadena Hills; Inc. Place; ST. LOUIS; **195** D-6; elev. 650ft./198m.; ★ **ST.L**; mail Saint Louis z 63121; Ⓟ 1,165; © 1,147
Pasadena Park; Inc. Place; ST. LOUIS; ***197** F-18; elev. 630ft./192m.; ★ **ST.L**; mail Saint Louis z 63121; Ⓟ 532; © 489
Pascola; Inc. Place; PEMISCOT; **197** M-19; elev. 268ft./82m.; 🅿; z 63851; Ⓟ 120; © 138
Passaic; Inc. Place; BATES; **196** G-9; elev. 865ft./264m.; 🅿; z 64730; Ⓟ 40; © 40
Patterson; RMC Place; WAYNE; **197** K-18; elev. 440ft./134m.; 🅿; z 63956; ● 250
Patton; RMC Place; BOLLINGER; **197** J-19; elev. 605ft./184m.; 🅿; z 63662; ● 120
Patton Junction; RMC Place; BOLLINGER; **197** J-19; elev. 684ft./208m.; mail Patton z 63662; ● 90
Pattonsburg; Inc. Place; DAVIESS; **196** C-10; elev. 776ft./237m.; 🅿; z 64670; Ⓟ 414; © 261
Paulding; RMC Place; DUNKLIN; ***197** N-18; mail Arbyrd z 63821; rural
Paulina Hills; RMC Place; JEFFERSON; **195** H-4; ★ **ST.L**; mail Arnold z 63010; ● 230
Paydown; RMC Place; MARIES; ***197** H-15; elev. 620ft./189m.; mail Belle z 65013, Vienna z 65582; rural
Paynesville; Inc. Place; PIKE; **197** E-17; elev. 564ft./172m.; 🅿; z 63336; Ⓟ 54; © 91
Peace Valley; RMC Place; HOWELL; **197** L-15; elev. 1,093ft./333m.; 🅿; z 65788
Peach Orchard; RMC Place; PEMISCOT; ***197** M-19; elev. 264ft./80m.; mail Gideon z 63848, Holcomb z 63852
Peaksville; RMC Place; CLARK; **197** A-15; elev. 699ft./213m.; mail Revere z 63465; ● 30
Pea Ridge; RMC Place; WASHINGTON; ***197** H-16; mail Sullivan z 63080; ● 30
Pearl; RMC Place; GREENE; ***197** J-11; elev. 1,147ft./350m.; mail Walnut Grove z 65770; rural
Peawee; WEBSTER; see Crabbs (RMC Place)
Pebble Acres; RMC Place; ST. LOUIS; ***197** G-18; ★ **ST.L**; mail Saint Louis z 63141; pop. incl. with Town and Country (Inc. Place)
Peculiar; Inc. Place; CASS; **196** F-9; elev. 1,004ft./306m.; 🅿; ★ **K.C.**; z 64078; Ⓟ 1,777; © 2,604
Peerless Park; RMC Place; ST. LOUIS; **195** G-3; elev. 410ft./125m.; ★ **ST.L**; mail Fenton z 63026, Valley Park z 63088; Ⓟ 33; ● 80
Peers; RMC Place; WARREN; ***197** G-16; mail Marthasville z 63357
PEMISCOT; **197** M-19; Ⓟ 21,921; © 20,047; ◆ 18,442
Pendleton; Inc. Place; WARREN; ***197** F-16; mail Warrenton z 63383; incorporated August 10, 1999; not reported in 2000 Census; Ⓡ 52
Penermon; Inc. Place; STODDARD; ***197** L-19; elev. 295ft./90m.; mail Essex z 63846; Ⓟ 94; © 75
Pennsboro; RMC Place; DADE; **196** J-10; mail South Greenfield z 65752; ● 30
Pennville; RMC Place; SULLIVAN; ***197** B-12; mail Green City z 63545; rural
Peoria; RMC Place; WASHINGTON; ***197** I-17; mail Belgrade z 63622; rural
Pepsin; RMC Place; NEWTON; ***196** K-9; elev. 1,124ft./343m.; mail Granby z 64844; rural
Perkins; RMC Place; SCOTT; ***197** K-19; elev. 329ft./100m.; 🅿; z 63774; ● 200
Perrin; RMC Place; CLINTON; ***196** D-9; elev. 1,035ft./315m.; mail Plattsburg z 64477; ● 80
Perry; Inc. Place; RALLS; **197** D-15; elev. 683ft./208m.; 🅿; z 63462; Ⓟ 711; © 666
PERRY; **197** I-19; Ⓟ 16,648; © 18,132; ◆ 19,245
Perryville; Inc. Place; ⊡ PERRY; **197** I-19; elev. 580ft./177m.; 🅿 🅷; z 63747, z 63775-76 & mail Uniontown z 63783; Ⓟ 6,933; © 7,667
Pershing; RMC Place; GASCONADE; **197** G-15; mail Morrison z 65061
Peru; RMC Place; BATES; ***196** H-9; elev. 812ft./247m.; mail Butler z 64730; rural
Peruque; RMC Place; ST. CHARLES; **197** F-17; elev. 433ft./132m.; mail Saint Charles z 63301; ● 80
Petersburg (Cooper Chapel); RMC Place; HOWARD; ***197** E-12; mail Franklin z 65250; rural
Petersville; RMC Place; FRANKLIN; ***197** G-17; ★ **ST.L**; mail Labadie z 63055; rural
PETTIS; **197** F-11; Ⓟ 35,437; © 39,403; ◆ 41,139
Pevely; Inc. Place; JEFFERSON; **197** H-18; elev. 440ft./134m.; 🅿; ★ **ST.L**; z 63070; Ⓟ 2,831; © 3,768
Phelps; ATCHISON; see Phelps City (RMC Place)
Phelps; RMC Place; LAWRENCE; **196** K-10; elev. 1,195ft./364m.; mail La Russell z 64848; ● 80
PHELPS; **197** I-15; Ⓟ 35,248; © 39,825; ◆ 42,360
Phelps City (Phelps); RMC Place; ATCHISON; **196** B-7; elev. 887ft./270m.; mail Rock Port z 64482; Ⓟ 32
Phenix; RMC Place; GREENE; ***197** J-11; elev. 1,050ft./320m.; mail Ash Grove z 65604, Walnut Grove z 65770; rural
Philadelphia; RMC Place; MARION; **197** C-15; elev. 710ft./216m.; 🅿; z 63463; ● 265
Phillipsburg; Inc. Place; LACLEDE; **197** J-13; elev. 1,400ft./427m.; 🅿; z 65722; Ⓟ 170; © 201
Pickering; Inc. Place; NODAWAY; **196** B-8; elev. 1,022ft./312m.; 🅿; z 64476; Ⓟ 171; © 154
Piedmont; Inc. Place; WAYNE; **197** K-17; elev. 502ft./153m.; 🅿; z 63957; Ⓟ 2,166; © 1,992
Pierce City; Inc. Place; LAWRENCE; **196** K-10; elev. 1,199ft./365m.; 🅿; z 65723; Ⓟ 1,382; © 1,385
Pierpont; Inc. Place; BOONE; ***197** F-14; elev. 772ft./235m.; mail Columbia z 65201; incorporated November 3, 2004; not reported in 2000 Census
Pierre Laclede; RMC Place; ST. LOUIS (Independent City); ***197** G-18; ★ **ST.L**; mail Saint Louis z 63108; pop. incl. with Saint Louis (Independent City)
PIKE; **197** D-16; Ⓟ 15,969; © 18,351; ◆ 18,023
Pilot Grove; Inc. Place; COOPER; **197** F-12; elev. 850ft./259m.; 🅿; z 65276; Ⓟ 714; © 723
Pilot Knob; Inc. Place; IRON; **197** I-17; elev. 1,000ft./305m.; 🅿 🅷; z 63663; Ⓟ 783; © 697
Pinckney; RMC Place; WARREN; ***197** G-16; mail Marthasville z 63357; rural
Pine Crest; RMC Place; TEXAS; **197** K-15; elev. 1,212ft./369m.; mail Summersville z 65571; ● 40
Pine Lawn; Inc. Place; ST. LOUIS; **195** D-6; elev. 550ft./168m.; ★ **ST.L**; mail Saint Louis z 63120; Ⓟ 5,092; © 4,204
Pine Ridge; RMC Place; CHRISTIAN; ***197** L-12; mail Forsyth z 65653; rural
Pineville; Inc. Place; ⊡ MCDONALD; **196** L-9; elev. 899ft./274m.; 🅿; z 64856; Ⓟ 580; © 768
Piney Park; RMC Place; FRANKLIN; ***197** H-17; elev. 743ft./226m.; mail Saint Clair z 63077
Pinhook; Inc. Place; MISSISSIPPI; ***197** L-20; elev. 301ft./92m.; mail East Prairie z 63845; © 48
Pioneer; RMC Place; BARRY; ***196** L-10; mail Purdy z 65734
Piper; RMC Place; HENRY; ***196** G-10; elev. 801ft./244m.; mail Montrose z 64770; rural
Pisgah; RMC Place; COOPER; ***197** F-13; elev. 858ft./262m.; mail Bunceton z 65237; rural
Pittsburg; RMC Place; HICKORY; **197** I-11; elev. 1,035ft./315m.; 🅿; z 65724; ● 200
Pittsville; RMC Place; JOHNSON; **196** F-10; elev. 859ft./262m.; mail Holden z 64040; ● 80
Plad; RMC Place; DALLAS; **197** I-12; mail Tunas z 65764; rural
Plano; RMC Place; GREENE; ***197** K-11; mail Bois D Arc z 65612; ● 160
Plato; Inc. Place; TEXAS; **197** J-14; elev. 1,063ft./324m.; 🅿; z 65552; incorporated January 1, 2000; not reported in 2000 Census; Ⓡ 64
PLATTE; **196** D-8; Ⓟ 57,867; © 73,781; ◆ 88,185
Platte City; Inc. Place; ⊡ PLATTE; **196** E-8; elev. 850ft./259m.; 🅿; ★ **K.C.**; z 64079; Ⓟ 2,947; © 3,866
Platte Woods; Inc. Place; PLATTE; **196** G-2; elev. 1,000ft./305m.; 🅿; ★ **K.C.**; z 64151; Ⓟ 427; © 474
Plattin; RMC Place; JEFFERSON; ***197** H-18; mail Festus z 63028; rural
Plattsburg; Inc. Place; ⊡ CLINTON; **196** D-9; elev. 953ft./290m.; 🅿; z 64477; Ⓟ 2,248; © 2,354
Pleasant Gap; RMC Place; BATES; ***196** H-10; mail Butler z 64730; rural
Pleasant Green; RMC Place; COOPER; ***197** F-12; elev. 800ft./244m.; mail Pilot Grove z 65276; rural
Pleasant Grove; RMC Place; COOPER; ***197** F-13; elev. 811ft./247m.; mail Prairie Home z 65068; rural
Pleasant Hill; Inc. Place; CASS; **196** F-9; elev. 909ft./277m.; 🅿; ★ **K.C.**; z 64080; Ⓟ 3,827; © 5,582
Pleasant Hope; Inc. Place; POLK; **197** J-11; elev. 1,101ft./336m.; 🅿; z 65725; Ⓟ 360; © 548
Pleasant Ridge; RMC Place; BARRY; ***196** K-10; elev. 1,440ft./439m.; mail Verona z 65769; ● 120
Pleasant Ridge; RMC Place; BATES; ***196** H-10; elev. 978ft./298m.; mail Rockville z 64780; rural
Pleasant Valley; Inc. Place; CLAY; **196** G-5; elev. 800ft./244m.; 🅿; ★ **K.C.**; z 64068; Ⓟ 2,731; © 3,321
Pleasant Valley; RMC Place; JASPER; ***196** K-9; ★ **JOP**; mail Carthage z 64836; ● 170
Plevna; RMC Place; KNOX; ***197** C-14; elev. 790ft./241m.; 🅿; z 63464; ● 50
Plew; RMC Place; LAWRENCE; ***196** K-10; elev. 1,182ft./360m.; mail La Russell z 64848; rural
Plymouth; RMC Place; CARROLL; ***197** D-11; elev. 804ft./245m.; mail Braymer z 64624; rural
Pocahontas; Inc. Place; CAPE GIRARDEAU; **197** J-19; elev. 620ft./189m.; 🅿; z 63779; Ⓟ 90; © 127
Point Lookout; RMC Place; TANEY; **195** J-9; elev. 929ft./283m.; 🅿 🅲 1,350; z 65726; ● 1,200
Point Pleasant; RMC Place; NEW MADRID; **197** M-20; elev. 290ft./88m.; mail Portageville z 63873
Polk; RMC Place; POLK; ***197** I-11; elev. 1,040ft./317m.; 🅿; z 65727; ● 90
POLK; **197** I-11; Ⓟ 21,826; © 26,992; ◆ 31,076
Pollock; Inc. Place; SULLIVAN; **197** B-12; elev. 936ft./285m.; 🅿; z 63560; Ⓟ 66; © 131
Polo; Inc. Place; CALDWELL; **196** D-10; elev. 1,000ft./305m.; 🅿; z 64671; Ⓟ 539; © 582
Pomona; RMC Place; HOWELL; **197** L-14; elev. 1,241ft./378m.; 🅿; z 65789; ● 300
Pom-o-sa Heights; RMC Place; BENTON; ***197** H-11; mail Warsaw z 65355; ● 90
Ponce de Leon; RMC Place; STONE; ***197** L-11; elev. 1,100ft./335m.; 🅿; z 65728; ● 120
Pond; RMC Place; ST. LOUIS; **197** G-17; elev. 799ft./244m.; ★ **ST.L**; mail Glencoe z 63038, Grover z 63040; pop. incl. with Wildwood (Inc. Place)
Ponder; RMC Place; RIPLEY; ***197** L-17; elev. 440ft./134m.; mail Doniphan z 63935; rural
Pondfork; RMC Place; OZARK; ***197** L-13; mail Thornfield z 65762; rural
Pontiac; RMC Place; OZARK; **197** M-13; elev. 825ft./251m.; 🅿; z 65729; summer pop. 600; ● 150
Pony Express; RMC Place; BUCHANAN; ***196** D-8; ★ **ST.JO**; mail Saint Joseph z 64503; pop. incl. with Saint Joseph (Inc. Place)
Poplar; RMC Place; BENTON; ***197** H-11; elev. 267ft./81m.; mail Warsaw z 65355; rural
Poplar Bluff; Inc. Place; ⊡ BUTLER; **197** L-18; elev. 344ft./105m.; 🅿 🅷 ■; z 63901-02; Ⓟ 16,996; © 16,651; ◆ 15,367
Portage Des Sioux; Inc. Place; ST. CHARLES; **195** A-5; elev. 433ft./132m.; 🅿; z 63373; Ⓟ 503; © 351
Portageville; Inc. Place; NEW MADRID, PEMISCOT; **197** M-19; elev. 281ft./86m.; 🅿; z 63873; Ⓟ 3,401; © 3,295
Port Hudson; RMC Place; FRANKLIN; ***197** G-16; mail New Haven z 63068; rural
Portland; RMC Place; CALLAWAY; **197** F-15; elev. 541ft./165m.; 🅿; z 65067; ● 130
Possum Walk; RMC Place; NODAWAY; ***196** A-8; elev. 1,103ft./336m.; mail Burlington Junction z 64428; rural
Post Oak; RMC Place; JOHNSON; **196** G-10; elev. 996ft./304m.; mail Leeton z 64761
Potosi; Inc. Place; ⊡ WASHINGTON; **197** I-17; elev. 900ft./274m.; 🅿 🅷; z 63664; Ⓟ 2,683; © 2,662
Pottersville; RMC Place; HOWELL; **197** L-14; elev. 962ft./293m.; 🅿; z 65790
Powe; RMC Place; STODDARD; **197** L-19; mail Bernie z 63822; ● 110
Powell; RMC Place; MCDONALD; **196** L-9; elev. 998ft./304m.; 🅿; z 65730; ● 85
Powellville; RMC Place; PHELPS; ***197** I-14; elev. 1,000ft./305m.; mail Newburg z 65550; rural
Powersite; RMC Place; TANEY; ***197** L-12; elev. 926ft./282m.; 🅿; z 65731; ● 280
Powersville; Inc. Place; PUTNAM; **197** A-11; elev. 1,000ft./305m.; 🅿; z 64672; Ⓟ 38; © 86
Poynor; RMC Place; RIPLEY; **197** L-17; elev. 428ft./130m.; 🅿; z 63935; ● 100
Prairie City; RMC Place; BATES; **196** H-10; elev. 772ft./235m.; mail Rockville z 64780
Prairie Hill; RMC Place; CHARITON; **197** D-13; elev. 729ft./222m.; mail Salisbury z 65281; ● 90
Prairie Home; Inc. Place; COOPER; **197** F-13; elev. 897ft./273m.; 🅿; z 65068; Ⓟ 215; © 220
Prairie Lick; COOPER; see Lick (RMC Place)
Prathersville; RMC Place; BOONE; ***197** F-14; ★ **COL**; mail Columbia z 65202; ● 120
Prathersville; Inc. Place; CLAY; ***196** E-9; elev. 760ft./232m.; ★ **K.C.**; mail Excelsior Springs z 64024; Ⓟ 130; © 111
Pratt; RMC Place; RIPLEY; ***197** L-17; mail Doniphan z 63935; rural
Prescott; RMC Place; TEXAS; ***197** J-14; elev. 1,160ft./354m.; mail Houston z 65483, Licking z 65542; rural
Preston; Inc. Place; HICKORY; **197** I-12; elev. 1,046ft./319m.; 🅿; z 65732; Ⓟ 136; © 113
Preston; RMC Place; JASPER; ***196** J-9; elev. 920ft./280m.; ★ **JOP**; mail Carthage z 64836; rural
Prices Branch; RMC Place; MONTGOMERY; ***197** F-16; elev. 750ft./229m.; mail New Florence z 63363; rural
Princeton; Inc. Place; ⊡ MERCER; **197** B-11; elev. 932ft./284m.; 🅿; z 64673; Ⓟ 1,021; © 1,047
Proctor; RMC Place; MORGAN; ***197** H-12; elev. 210ft./64m.; mail Gravois Mills z 65037; ● 80
Prospect; RMC Place; JACKSON; ★ **K.C.**
Prospect Hill; RMC Place; ST. LOUIS; ***197** F-18; ★ **ST.L**; mail Saint Louis z 63137; pop. incl. with Riverview (Inc. Place)
Prosperity; RMC Place; JASPER; **195** L-3; elev. 1,028ft./313m.; ★ **JOP**; mail Joplin z 64801; ● 120
Protem; RMC Place; TANEY; **197** L-12; elev. 706ft./215m.; 🅿; z 65733; rural
Providence; RMC Place; DUNKLIN; ***197** L-19; elev. 285ft./87m.; mail Malden z 63863; rural
Pulaski; RMC Place; RIPLEY; ***197** L-17; elev. 433ft./132m.; mail Doniphan z 63935; rural
PULASKI; **197** I-14; Ⓟ 41,307; © 41,165; ◆ 45,214
Pulaskifield (Bricefield); RMC Place; BARRY; ***196** K-10; elev. 1,265ft./386m.; mail Monett z 65708; rural
Pumpkin Center; RMC Place; NODAWAY; ***196** B-8; elev. 1,036ft./316m.; mail Barnard z 64423
Purcell; Inc. Place; JASPER; ***196** J-9; elev. 960ft./293m.; 🅿; ★ **JOP**; z 64857; Ⓟ 359; © 357
Purdin; Inc. Place; LINN; **197** C-12; elev. 833ft./254m.; 🅿; z 64674; Ⓟ 217; © 223
Purdy; Inc. Place; BARRY; **196** L-10; elev. 1,484ft./452m.; 🅿; z 65734; Ⓟ 977; © 1,103
Pure Air; RMC Place; ADAIR; ***197** B-13; mail Novinger z 63559; rural
Purina Farm; RMC Place; FRANKLIN; ★ **ST.L**; mail Gray Summit z 63039
Purman; RMC Place; RIPLEY; ***197** L-17; elev. 371ft./113m.; mail Doniphan z 63935; rural
Purvis; RMC Place; CAMDEN; ***197** H-12; mail Sunrise Beach z 65079; summer pop. 300; ● 140
PUTNAM; **197** A-12; Ⓟ 5,079; © 5,223; ◆ 4,619
Puxico; Inc. Place; STODDARD; **197** K-18; elev. 370ft./113m.; 🅿; z 63960; Ⓟ 819; © 1,145
Pyletown; RMC Place; STODDARD; ***197** L-19; mail Dexter z 63841; rural
Pyrmont; RMC Place; MORGAN; ***197** G-12; mail Stover z 65078; rural

Q

Quaker; RMC Place; WASHINGTON; ***197** I-16; elev. 1,000ft./305m.; mail Potosi z 63664; rural
Quarles; RMC Place; HENRY; ***196** G-10; elev. 876ft./267m.; mail Clinton z 64735; rural
Queen City; Inc. Place; SCHUYLER; **197** B-13; elev. 1,003ft./306m.; 🅿; z 63561; Ⓟ 704; © 638
Quincy; RMC Place; HICKORY; **197** H-11; elev. 960ft./293m.; 🅿; z 65735
Quitman; Inc. Place; NODAWAY; **196** B-8; elev. 913ft./278m.; 🅿; z 64487; Ⓟ 47; © 46
Qulin; Inc. Place; BUTLER; **197** L-18; elev. 315ft./96m.; 🅿; z 63961 & mail Fagus z 63938; Ⓟ 384; © 467

R

Racine; RMC Place; NEWTON; **196** K-9; elev. 960ft./293m.; 🅿; z 64858; ● 200
Racket; RMC Place; BENTON; ***197** H-11; elev. 837ft./255m.; mail Warsaw z 65355
Racola; RMC Place; WASHINGTON; ***197** H-17; elev. 740ft./226m.; mail Cadet z 63630; ● 300
Rader; RMC Place; WEBSTER; **197** J-13; elev. 1,142ft./348m.; mail Niangua z 65713; rural
Ralls; RMC Place; RALLS; ***197** D-16; elev. 536ft./163m.; mail Hannibal z 63401; pop. incl. with Hannibal (Inc. Place)
RALLS; **197** D-15; Ⓟ 8,476; © 9,626; ◆ 9,924
Randles; RMC Place; CAPE GIRARDEAU; **197** K-19; mail Chaffee z 63740; ● 130
Randolph (East Kansas City); Inc. Place; CLAY; **196** H-5; elev. 800ft./244m.; 🅿; ★ **K.C.**; z 64117, z 64161; Ⓟ 60; © 47
RANDOLPH; **197** D-13; Ⓟ 24,370; © 24,663; ◆ 25,811
Randolph Springs; RMC Place; RANDOLPH; ***197** D-13; elev. 699ft./213m.; mail Huntsville z 65259; rural
Ravanna; RMC Place; MERCER; **197** B-11; mail Princeton z 64673; ● 100
Ravena; RMC Place; CLAY; ★ **K.C.**; mail Liberty z 64068; pop. incl. with Pleasant Valley (Inc. Place)
Ravena Gardens; RMC Place; CLAY; ★ **K.C.**; mail Liberty z 64068; pop. incl. with Pleasant Valley (Inc. Place)
Ravenwood; Inc. Place; NODAWAY; **196** B-9; elev. 1,040ft./317m.; 🅿; z 64479; Ⓟ 409; © 448
RAY; **196** E-10; Ⓟ 21,971; © 23,354; ◆ 23,006
Raymondville; Inc. Place; TEXAS; **197** J-15; elev. 1,320ft./402m.; 🅿; z 65555; Ⓟ 425; © 442
Raymore; Inc. Place; CASS; **196** F-9; elev. 1,104ft./336m.; 🅿; ★ **K.C.**; z 64083; Ⓟ 5,592; © 11,146
Raytown; Inc. Place; JACKSON; **196** F-9; elev. 950ft./290m.; 🅿; ★ **K.C.**; z 64129, z 64133, z 64138 & mail Kansas City z 64136; Ⓟ 30,601; © 30,388; ◆ 29,961
Rayville; Inc. Place; RAY; ***196** E-10; elev. 968ft./295m.; 🅿; z 64084; Ⓟ 170; © 204
Rea; Inc. Place; ANDREW; **196** C-8; elev. 1,059ft./323m.; 🅿; z 64480; Ⓟ 62; © 56
Readsville; RMC Place; CALLAWAY; **197** F-15; elev. 830ft./253m.; mail Portland z 65067; rural
Rector; RMC Place; SHANNON; ***197** J-15; mail Salem z 65560; rural
Redbird; RMC Place; GASCONADE; ***197** H-15; mail Bland z 65014; rural
Red Bridge; RMC Place; JACKSON; ***196** F-9; ★ **K.C.**; mail Kansas City z 64131; pop. incl. with Kansas City (Inc. Place)
Redford; RMC Place; REYNOLDS; **197** J-17; elev. 695ft./212m.; 🅿; z 63665; ● 100
Redings Mill; Inc. Place; NEWTON; ***196** K-9; elev. 900ft./274m.; ★ **JOP**; mail Joplin z 64801; Ⓟ 204; © 159
Redman; RMC Place; MACON; ***197** C-14; elev. 828ft./252m.; mail Anabel z 63431; rural
Redmondville; RMC Place; IRON; ***197** I-17; elev. 1,000ft./305m.; mail Belleview z 63623; rural
Red Oak; RMC Place; LAWRENCE; ***196** K-10; mail La Russell z 64848
Red Top; RMC Place; WEBSTER; ***197** J-12; elev. 1,461ft./445m.; mail Strafford z 65757; ● 120
Reeds; Inc. Place; JASPER; **196** K-9; elev. 1,125ft./343m.; 🅿; z 64859; Ⓟ 88; © 103
Reeds Spring; Inc. Place; STONE; **197** L-11; elev. 1,199ft./365m.; 🅿; z 65737; Ⓟ 411; © 465
Reform; RMC Place; CALLAWAY; ***197** F-15; mail Steedman z 65077; rural
Regal; RMC Place; RAY; ***196** D-10; elev. 850ft./259m.; mail Braymer z 64624; rural
Reger; RMC Place; SULLIVAN; **197** B-12; mail Milan z 63556; ● 80
Renick; Inc. Place; RANDOLPH; **197** E-13; elev. 874ft./266m.; 🅿; z 65278; Ⓟ 195; © 221
Rensselaer; Inc. Place; RALLS; ***197** D-15; elev. 724ft./221m.; mail Hannibal z 63401; Ⓟ 94; © 145
Republic; Inc. Place; GREENE; **197** K-11; elev. 1,311ft./400m.; 🅿; ★ **SPRG**; z 65738; Ⓟ 6,292; © 8,438
Rescue; RMC Place; LAWRENCE; ***196** K-10; mail La Russell z 64848; ● 90
Revere; Inc. Place; CLARK; **197** B-15; elev. 680ft./207m.; 🅿; z 63465; Ⓟ 133; © 121
Reynolds; RMC Place; REYNOLDS; **197** J-16; elev. 1,255ft./383m.; 🅿; z 63666; ● 100
REYNOLDS; **197** J-16; Ⓟ 6,661; © 6,689; ◆ 6,323
Reynolds Ford; RMC Place; CAPE GIRARDEAU; ***197** J-19; mail Millersville z 63766; rural
Rhineland; Inc. Place; MONTGOMERY; **197** F-15; elev. 517ft./158m.; 🅿; z 65069; Ⓟ 157; © 176
Rhyse; RMC Place; DENT; ***197** J-15; mail Salem z 65560; rural
Richards; Inc. Place; VERNON; **196** I-9; elev. 840ft./256m.; 🅿; z 64778; Ⓟ 106; © 95
Rich Fountain; RMC Place; OSAGE; **197** G-15; elev. 612ft./187m.; mail Freeburg z 65035; ● 220
Rich Hill; Inc. Place; BATES; **196** H-9; elev. 787ft./240m.; 🅿; z 64779; Ⓟ 1,317; © 1,461
Richie; RMC Place; BUCHANAN; ***196** D-8; mail Saint Joseph z 64507; ● 120
Richland; Inc. Place; PULASKI, CAMDEN, LACLEDE; **197** I-13; elev. 1,119ft./341m.; 🅿; z 65556; Ⓟ 2,029; © 1,805
Richmond; Inc. Place; ⊡ RAY; **196** E-10; elev. 826ft./252m.; 🅿 🅷; z 64085; Ⓟ 5,738; © 6,116
Richmond Heights; Inc. Place; ST. LOUIS; **195** E-5; elev. 469ft./143m.; 🅿; ★ **ST.L**; z 63117; Ⓟ 10,448; © 9,602
Richville; RMC Place; DOUGLAS; ***197** L-14; elev. 1,184ft./361m.; mail Dora z 65637; rural
Richville; RMC Place; HOLT; ***196** C-8; elev. 1,034ft./315m.; mail Oregon z 64473; rural
Richwoods; RMC Place; WASHINGTON; **197** H-17; elev. 770ft./235m.; 🅿; z 63071; ● 300
Ridgedale; RMC Place; TANEY; **197** L-11; elev. 1,388ft./423m.; 🅿; z 65739; ● 450
Ridgely; Inc. Place; PLATTE; **196** D-9; elev. 955ft./291m.; mail Edgerton z 64444; Ⓟ 57; © 64
Ridgeway; Inc. Place; HARRISON; **196** B-10; elev. 1,057ft./322m.; 🅿; z 64481; Ⓟ 379; © 530
Ridgley; RMC Place; BARRY; **196** L-10; elev. 1,481ft./451m.; mail Exeter z 65647; ● 120
Riggs; RMC Place; BOONE; ***197** E-14; mail Sturgeon z 65284; rural
Rimby; RMC Place; POLK; ***197** I-12; mail Half Way z 65663; rural
Ripley; RMC Place; JACKSON; ***196** E-9; ★ **K.C.**; mail Independence z 64056; pop. incl. with Independence (Inc. Place)
RIPLEY; **197** L-17; Ⓟ 12,303; © 13,509; ◆ 13,348
Risco; Inc. Place; NEW MADRID; **197** L-19; elev. 275ft./84m.; 🅿; z 63874; Ⓟ 434; © 392
Ritchey; Inc. Place; NEWTON; **196** K-9; elev. 1,086ft./331m.; mail Granby z 64844; Ⓟ 62; © 76
Ritter; RMC Place; GREENE; ***197** J-11; mail Columbia z 65203; ● 140
River Aux Vases; RMC Place; STE. GENEVIEVE; **197** I-18; mail Sainte Genevieve z 63670; ● 110
River Bend; Inc. Place; JACKSON; **196** G-6; ★ **K.C.**; mail Independence z 64058; © 10
River Bend Estates; RMC Place; ST. LOUIS; ***197** F-17; ★ **ST.L**; mail Chesterfield z 63017; pop. incl. with Chesterfield (Inc. Place)
Riverdale; RMC Place; CHRISTIAN; ***197** K-11; elev. 1,100ft./335m.; ★ **SPRG**; mail Ozark z 65721; rural
Rivermines; RMC Place; ST. FRANCOIS; ***197** I-17; elev. 800ft./244m.; 🅿; z 63601; pop. incl. with Park Hills (Inc. Place)
Riverside; RMC Place; DUNKLIN; ***197** N-18; mail Cardwell z 63829; ● 30
Riverside; Inc. Place; PLATTE; **196** G-3; elev. 800ft./244m.; 🅿; ★ **K.C.**; z 64150-51, z 64168; Ⓟ 3,010; © 2,979
Riverside Inn; RMC Place; MCDONALD; ***196** L-9; elev. 880ft./268m.; mail Noel z 64854; rural
Riverton; RMC Place; OREGON; **197** L-16; elev. 441ft./134m.; mail Alton z 65606; rural
Riverview; Inc. Place; ST. LOUIS; **195** C-7; elev. 500ft./152m.; ★ **ST.L**; mail Saint Louis z 63137; Ⓟ 3,242; © 3,146
Riverview Estates; Inc. Place; CASS; incorporated September 25, 2007; not reported in 2000 Census; ● 70
Rives; Inc. Place; DUNKLIN; ***197** N-19; elev. 245ft./75m.; 🅿; z 63875; Ⓟ 89; © 88
Roach; RMC Place; CAMDEN; **197** H-12; elev. 991ft./302m.; 🅿; z 65787; summer pop. 800; ● 200
Roads; RMC Place; CARROLL; ***197** D-11; elev. 765ft./233m.; mail Norborne z 64668
Roanoke; RMC Place; HOWARD, RANDOLPH; **197** E-13; elev. 840ft./256m.; mail Armstrong z 65230; ● 30
Roanridge; RMC Place; PLATTE; ★ **K.C.**; mail Kansas City z 64152; pop. incl. with Kansas City (Inc. Place)
Robbins; RMC Place; JOHNSON; ***196** F-10; elev. 880ft./268m.; mail Warrensburg z 64093; ● 90
Robertson; RMC Place; ST. LOUIS; **195** C-5; ★ **ST.L**; mail Hazelwood z 63042; pop. incl. with Hazelwood (Inc. Place)
Robertsville; RMC Place; FRANKLIN; **197** G-17; elev. 501ft./153m.; 🅿; ★ **ST.L**; z 63072; ● 250
Robinwood East; RMC Place; ST. LOUIS; ***197** F-18; ★ **ST.L**; mail Saint Louis z 63141; ● 850
Robinwood West; RMC Place; ST. LOUIS; ***197** F-18; ★ **ST.L**; mail Saint Louis z 63141; ● 1,000
Roby; RMC Place; TEXAS; **197** J-14; elev. 1,384ft./422m.; 🅿; z 65557; ● 150
Rocheport; Inc. Place; BOONE; **197** F-13; elev. 597ft./182m.; 🅿; z 65279; Ⓟ 255; © 208
Rochester; RMC Place; ANDREW; **196** C-9; mail Helena z 64459; ● 200
Rockaway Beach; Inc. Place; TANEY; ***197** L-12; elev. 800ft./244m.; 🅿; z 65740; Ⓟ 275; © 577
Rockbridge; RMC Place; OZARK; ***197** L-13; elev. 764ft./233m.; 🅿; z 65741
Rock Creek; RMC Place; JEFFERSON; ***197** G-18; elev. 800ft./244m.; ★ **ST.L**; mail Arnold z 63010; ● 100
Rock Creek Junction; RMC Place; JACKSON; ***196** E-9; elev. 748ft./228m.; ★ **K.C.**; pop. incl. with Kansas City (Inc. Place)
Rock Hill; Inc. Place; ST. LOUIS; **195** F-5; elev. 550ft./168m.; ★ **ST.L**; mail Saint Louis z 63119, z 63124; Ⓟ 5,217; © 4,765
Rockingham; RMC Place; RAY; ***196** E-10; mail Hardin z 64035; rural
Rock Port; Inc. Place; ⊡ ATCHISON; **196** B-7; elev. 930ft./283m.; 🅿; z 64482; Ⓟ 1,438; © 1,395; Ⓡ 1,403
Rock Springs; RMC Place; ST. FRANCOIS; ***197** I-18; mail Park Hills z 63601; ● 130
Rockview; RMC Place; SCOTT; ***197** K-19; ★ **CPGIR**; mail Chaffee z 63740; ● 160
Rockville; Inc. Place; BATES; **196** H-10; elev. 784ft./239m.; 🅿; z 64780; Ⓟ 193; © 162
Rocky Comfort; RMC Place; MCDONALD; **196** L-10; elev. 1,331ft./406m.; 🅿; z 64861; ● 190
Rocky Mount; RMC Place; MORGAN; **197** H-13; elev. 865ft./264m.; 🅿; z 65026, z 65072; summer pop. 1,300; ● 130
Rocky Ridge; STE. GENEVIEVE; see Rocky Ridge Ranch (RMC Place)
Rocky Ridge Ranch (Rocky Ridge); RMC Place; STE. GENEVIEVE; ***197** I-18; elev. 800ft./244m.; mail Sainte Genevieve z 63670; ● 500
Rogersville; Inc. Place; WEBSTER, GREENE; **197** K-12; elev. 1,460ft./445m.; 🅿; z 65742; Ⓟ 995; © 1,508
Rolla; Inc. Place; ⊡ PHELPS; **197** I-15; elev. 1,119ft./341m.; 🅿 🅷 🅲 5,602 ■; z 65401-02, z 65409; Ⓟ 14,090; © 16,367; ◆ 18,010
Rombauer; RMC Place; BUTLER; ***197** L-18; elev. 335ft./102m.; 🅿; z 63901, z 63962; ● 200
Rome; RMC Place; DOUGLAS; ***197** L-13; mail Ava z 65608; rural
Rondo; RMC Place; POLK; ***197** I-11; elev. 1,071ft./326m.; mail Flemington z 65650; rural
Roosterville; RMC Place; CLAY; ***196** E-9; elev. 940ft./287m.; ★ **K.C.**; mail Liberty z 64068
Rosati; RMC Place; PHELPS; ***197** H-15; elev. 1,077ft./328m.; mail Saint James z 65559; ● 100
Roscoe; Inc. Place; ST. CLAIR; **196** I-10; elev. 763ft./233m.; 🅿; z 64781; Ⓟ 100; © 112
Rosebud; Inc. Place; GASCONADE; **197** G-16; elev. 883ft./269m.; 🅿; z 63091; Ⓟ 380; © 364
Rosedale; RMC Place; ST. LOUIS (Independent City); mail Saint Louis z 63112; pop. incl. with Saint Louis (Independent City)
Roseland; RMC Place; HENRY; ***197** G-11; mail Calhoun z 65323; rural
Roselle; RMC Place; MADISON; **197** I-18; elev. 837ft./255m.; mail Fredericktown z 63645, Ironton z 63650; ● 60
Rosendale; Inc. Place; ANDREW; **196** C-8; elev. 910ft./277m.; 🅿; z 64483; Ⓟ 186; © 180
Rothville; Inc. Place; CHARITON; **197** D-12; elev. 696ft./212m.; 🅿; z 64676; Ⓟ 100; © 93
Roubidoux; RMC Place; TEXAS; ***197** J-14; elev. 1,139ft./347m.; mail Bucyrus z 65444; rural
Round Grove; RMC Place; LAWRENCE; ***196** J-10; elev. 1,265ft./386m.; mail Miller z 65707; rural
Round Spring; RMC Place; SHANNON; ***197** J-16; elev. 700ft./213m.; mail Eminence z 65466; rural
Rover; RMC Place; OREGON; ***197** L-15; elev. 966ft./294m.; mail West Plains z 65775
Rowena; RMC Place; AUDRAIN; ***197** E-14; mail Centralia z 65240
Royal; RMC Place; PHELPS; ***197** H-15; elev. 960ft./293m.; mail Saint James z 65559; rural
Royal Heights; RMC Place; JASPER; ★ **JOP**; mail Joplin z 64801; pop. incl. with Joplin (Inc. Place)
Royal Oak; RMC Place; OREGON; ***197** L-15; elev. 908ft./277m.; mail Alton z 65606; rural
Ruble; RMC Place; REYNOLDS; ***197** K-17; mail Ellington z 63638; rural
Rucker; RMC Place; BOONE; ***197** E-13; mail Clark z 65243; rural
Rueter; RMC Place; TANEY; **197** L-12; elev. 1,313ft./400m.; 🅿; z 65744; rural
Running Deer; RMC Place; CAMDEN; elev. 217ft./66m.; mail Osage Beach z 65065
Rush Hill; Inc. Place; AUDRAIN; **197** E-15; elev. 788ft./240m.; 🅿; z 65280; Ⓟ 121; © 130
Rush Tower; RMC Place; JEFFERSON; ***197** H-18; elev. 397ft./121m.; mail Festus z 63028; rural
Rushville; Inc. Place; BUCHANAN; **196** D-8; elev. 810ft./247m.; 🅿; z 64484; Ⓟ 306; © 280
Ruskin Heights; RMC Place; JACKSON; ***196** F-9; ★ **K.C.**; mail Kansas City z 64134; pop. incl. with Kansas City (Inc. Place)
Russ; RMC Place; LACLEDE; ***197** J-13; mail Lebanon z 65536; rural
Russellville; Inc. Place; COLE; **197** G-13; elev. 888ft./271m.; 🅿; z 65074; Ⓟ 869; © 758
Russellville; RMC Place; RAY; ***196** E-10; mail Norborne z 64668; rural
Rutledge; Inc. Place; SCOTLAND; **197** B-14; elev. 750ft./229m.; 🅿; z 63563; Ⓟ 74; © 103

S

Sabula; RMC Place; IRON; **197** J-17; elev. 690ft./210m.; mail Annapolis z 63620; ● 50
Saco; RMC Place; MADISON; ***197** J-18; elev. 500ft./152m.; mail Fredericktown z 63645; rural
Sacville; RMC Place; GREENE; ***197** J-11; mail Willard z 65781; ● 200
Saddlebrooke; Inc. Place; CHRISTIAN, TANEY; 🅿; z 65630; incorporated March 1, 2003; not reported in 2000 Census; ● 15
Safe; RMC Place; MARIES; ***197** H-15; elev. 924ft./282m.; mail Saint James z 65559; rural
Sage Hill; RMC Place; LAWRENCE; ***197** K-11; elev. 1,472ft./449m.; mail Aurora z 65605; rural
Saginaw; Inc. Place; NEWTON; **196** K-9; elev. 950ft./290m.; 🅿; ★ **JOP**; z 64864; Ⓟ 384; © 276
Saint Albans; RMC Place; FRANKLIN; ***197** G-17; elev. 483ft./147m.; 🅿; ★ **ST.L**; z 63073; ● 150
Saint Ann; Inc. Place; ST. LOUIS; **195** D-5; elev. 600ft./183m.; 🅿 🅲 6,400 ■; ★ **ST.L**; z 63074; Ⓟ 14,489; © 13,607; ◆ 12,663
Saint Anthony; RMC Place; MILLER; **197** H-14; elev. 951ft./290m.; mail Iberia z 65486; ● 130
Saint Aubert; RMC Place; OSAGE; ***197** G-15; elev. 544ft./166m.; mail Chamois z 65024; rural
Saint Catharine (Saint Catherine); RMC Place; LINN; **197** C-12; elev. 802ft./244m.; 🅿; z 64628; ● 90
Saint Catherine; LINN; see Saint Catharine (RMC Place)
Saint Charles; Inc. Place; ⊡ ST. CHARLES; **197** F-18; elev. 536ft./163m.; 🅿 🅷 🅲 14,000 ■; ★ **ST.L**; z 63301-04; Ⓟ 54,555; © 60,321; ◆ 64,847
ST. CHARLES; **197** F-17; Ⓟ 212,907; © 283,883; Ⓡ 283,893; ◆ 353,076
Saint Clair; Inc. Place; FRANKLIN; **197** G-16; elev. 769ft./234m.; 🅿; z 63077; Ⓟ 3,917; © 4,390
ST. CLAIR; **196** H-10; Ⓟ 8,457; © 9,652; ◆ 9,408
Saint Clement; RMC Place; PIKE; **197** E-16; elev. 815ft./248m.; mail Bowling Green z 63334; ● 110
Saint Cloud; Inc. Place; CRAWFORD; ***197** H-16; elev. 966ft./294m.; mail Bourbon z 65441; Ⓟ 59; © 56
Sainte Genevieve; Inc. Place; ⊡ STE. GENEVIEVE; **197** H-19; elev. 401ft./122m.; 🅿 🅷; z 63670; Ⓟ 4,411; © 4,476
Saint Elizabeth; Inc. Place; MILLER; **197** H-14; elev. 812ft./247m.; 🅿; z 65075; Ⓟ 257; © 297
Saint Francisville; RMC Place; CLARK; **197** B-15; elev. 522ft./159m.; mail Alexandria z 63430; ● 150
Saint Francois; RMC Place; ST. FRANCOIS; mail Park Hills z 63601; pop. incl. with Park Hills (Inc. Place)
ST. FRANCOIS; **197** I-17; Ⓟ 48,904; © 55,641; ◆ 63,868
STE. GENEVIEVE; **197** I-18; Ⓟ 16,037; © 17,842; ◆ 17,635
Saint George; Inc. Place; ST. LOUIS; **195** G-5; elev. 500ft./152m.; ★ **ST.L**; mail Saint Louis z 63125; Ⓟ 1,270; © 1,288
Saint George; RMC Place; WRIGHT; ***197** J-13; mail Hartville z 65667; rural
Saint James; Inc. Place; PHELPS; **197** H-15; elev. 1,088ft./332m.; 🅿; z 65559; Ⓟ 3,256; © 3,704
Saint John; ST. LOUIS; see Saint Johns (Inc. Place)
Saint Johns (Saint John); Inc. Place; ST. LOUIS; **195** D-5; elev. 600ft./183m.; ★ **ST.L**; mail Saint Louis z 63114; Ⓟ 7,466; © 6,871
Saint Johns Station; RMC Place; ST. LOUIS; ★ **ST.L**; mail Saint Louis z 63114; pop. incl. with Saint Johns (Inc. Place)
Saint Joseph; Inc. Place; ⊡ BUCHANAN; **196** D-8; elev. 833ft./254m.; 🅿 🅷 🅲 5,295 ■; ★ **ST.JO**; z 64501-08; Ⓟ 71,852; © 73,990; ◆ 78,447
Saint Joseph Stock Yards; RMC Place; BUCHANAN; ★ **ST.JO**; mail Saint Joseph z 64501; pop. incl. with Saint Joseph (Inc. Place)
Saint Jude Acres; RMC Place; STE. GENEVIEVE; pop. incl. with Sainte Genevieve (Inc. Place)
Saint Louis; Independent City; **197** G-18; elev. 470ft./143m.; 🅿 🅷 🅲 60,226 ■; ★ **ST.L**; z 63101-41, z 63143-47, z 63150-51, z 63155-58, z 63160, z 63163-64, z 63166-67, z 63169, z 63171, z 63177-80, z 63182, z 63188, z 63190, z 63195, z 63197-99; Ⓟ 396,685; © 348,189; ◆ 356,533
ST. LOUIS; **197** G-17; Ⓟ 993,529; © 1,016,315; Ⓡ 1,016,300; ◆ 980,632
Saint Luke; RMC Place; WEBSTER; ***197** J-12; elev. 1,300ft./396m.; mail Conway z 65632; rural
Saint Martins; Inc. Place; COLE; **197** G-14; elev. 760ft./232m.; ★ **JFCY**; mail Jefferson City z 65101, z 65109; Ⓟ 717; © 1,023
Saint Mary (Saint Marys); Inc. Place; STE. GENEVIEVE; **197** I-19; elev. 440ft./134m.; 🅿; z 63673; Ⓟ 461; © 377
Saint Marys; STE. GENEVIEVE; see Saint Mary (Inc. Place)
Saint Patrick; RMC Place; CLARK; **197** B-15; elev. 681ft./208m.; 🅿; z 63466; ● 30
Saint Paul; Inc. Place; ST. CHARLES; **197** F-17; elev. 520ft./158m.; 🅿; ★ **ST.L**; z 63366; Ⓟ 1,192; © 1,634
Saint Peters; Inc. Place; ST. CHARLES; **197** F-17; elev. 443ft./135m.; 🅿 🅷; ★ **ST.L**; z 63303-04, z 63366, z 63376; Ⓟ 45,779; © 51,381; ◆ 54,969
Saint Robert; Inc. Place; PULASKI; **197** I-14; elev. 1,085ft./331m.; 🅿; z 65584 & mail Waynesville z 65583; Ⓟ 1,730; © 2,760
Saint Thomas; Inc. Place; COLE; **197** G-14; elev. 750ft./229m.; 🅿; z 65076; Ⓟ 263; © 287
Salcedo; RMC Place; SCOTT; **197** K-19; elev. 304ft./93m.; mail Sikeston z 63801; ● 90
Salem; DAVIESS; see Coffey (Inc. Place)
Salem; Inc. Place; ⊡ DENT; **197** I-15; elev. 1,182ft./360m.; 🅿 🅷; z 65560; Ⓟ 4,486; © 4,854
Saline; RMC Place; MERCER; ***197** A-11; mail Cainsville z 64632; rural
SALINE; **197** E-12; Ⓟ 23,523; © 23,756; ◆ 22,363
Saline City; RMC Place; SALINE; ***197** E-12; mail Slater z 65349; rural
Salisbury; Inc. Place; CHARITON; **197** D-13; elev. 700ft./213m.; 🅿; z 65281; Ⓟ 1,881; © 1,726
Salt Springs; RMC Place; SALINE; ***197** E-11; elev. 721ft./220m.; mail Malta Bend z 65339; rural
Samford; RMC Place; PEMISCOT; ***197** N-19; elev. 256ft./78m.; mail Steele z 63877; rural
Sampsel; RMC Place; LIVINGSTON; ***197** C-11; elev. 708ft./216m.; mail Chillicothe z 64601
Sampson; RMC Place; WEBSTER; ***197** J-12; elev. 1,401ft./427m.; mail Niangua z 65713; rural
San Antonio; RMC Place; BUCHANAN; ***196** C-9; elev. 974ft./297m.; mail Easton z 64443; ● 30
Sand Hill; RMC Place; SCOTLAND; ***197** B-14; mail Rutledge z 63563; rural
Sandstone; RMC Place; VERNON; ***196** I-9; elev. 854ft./260m.; mail Milo z 64767; ● 30
Sandy Hook; RMC Place; MONITEAU; **197** F-13; mail Jamestown z 65046
Santa Fe; RMC Place; MONROE; **197** E-15; elev. 718ft./219m.; 🅿; z 65282; ● 100
Santa Rosa; RMC Place; DEKALB; **196** C-10; mail Pattonsburg z 64670
Sapp; RMC Place; BOONE; ***197** F-14; mail Columbia z 65203; ● 80
Sappington; CDP; ST. LOUIS; **195** G-5; elev. 597ft./182m.; 🅿; ★ **ST.L**; z 63126-28; Ⓟ 10,917; © 7,287
Saratoga; RMC Place; MCDONALD; ***196** L-9; elev. 1,021ft./311m.; mail Noel z 64854; ● 80
Sarcoxie; Inc. Place; JASPER; **196** K-10; elev. 1,150ft./351m.; 🅿; z 64862; Ⓟ 1,330; © 1,354
Sarvis Point; RMC Place; WEBSTER; ***197** K-12; elev. 1,394ft./425m.; mail Seymour z 65746; rural
Savannah; Inc. Place; ⊡ ANDREW; **196** C-8; elev. 1,115ft./340m.; 🅿; ★ **ST.JO**; z 64485; Ⓟ 4,352; © 4,762
Saverton; RMC Place; RALLS; **197** D-16; elev. 489ft./149m.; 🅿; z 63467; ● 80
Savoy; WASHINGTON; see Irondale (Inc. Place)
Saxton; RMC Place; BUCHANAN; ***196** D-8; elev. 889ft./271m.; ★ **ST.JO**; mail Saint Joseph z 64507; pop. incl. with Saint Joseph (Inc. Place)
Schell City; Inc. Place; VERNON; **196** H-10; elev. 747ft./228m.; 🅿; z 64783; Ⓟ 292; © 286
Schlatitz; RMC Place; BOLLINGER; ***197** K-19; elev. 436ft./133m.; mail Advance z 63730; rural
Schluersburg; RMC Place; ST. CHARLES; ***197** G-17; elev. 512ft./156m.; mail Augusta z 63332; rural
Schnurbusch; PERRY; see Apple Creek (RMC Place)
Schofield; RMC Place; POLK; ***197** J-12; mail Half Way z 65663; rural
Scholten; RMC Place; BARRY; ***197** L-11; mail Aurora z 65605; ● 90
Schubert; RMC Place; COLE; ***197** G-14; ★ **JFCY**; mail Jefferson City z 65101; rural
Schuermann Heights; RMC Place; ST. LOUIS; ***197** F-18; elev. 600ft./183m.; ★ **ST.L**; mail Saint Louis z 63114
Schult; RMC Place; PEMISCOT; ***197** M-19; elev. 268ft./82m.; mail Hayti z 63851; rural
SCHUYLER; **197** B-13; Ⓟ 4,236; © 4,170; ◆ 4,113
Scobeville; RMC Place; DUNKLIN; ***197** M-19; mail Kennett z 63857; rural
Scopus; RMC Place; BOLLINGER; **197** J-19; elev. 684ft./208m.; 🅿; z 63764; ● 160
Scotland; RMC Place; JASPER; ***196** K-9; elev. 1,033ft./315m.; ★ **JOP**; mail Carthage z 64836; ● 100
SCOTLAND; **197** B-14; Ⓟ 4,822; © 4,983; ◆ 4,827
Scotsdale; Inc. Place; JEFFERSON; **195** I-2; ★ **ST.L**; mail House Springs z 63051; Ⓟ 193; © 211
SCOTT; **197** K-20; Ⓟ 39,376; © 40,422; ◆ 40,750
Scott City (Fornfelt); Inc. Place; SCOTT, CAPE GIRARDEAU; **197** J-20; elev. 400ft./122m.; 🅿; ★ **CPGIR**; z 63780; Ⓟ 4,292; © 4,591
Scotts Corner; RMC Place; AUDRAIN; ***197** E-15; mail Laddonia z 63352; rural
Scrivner; RMC Place; COLE; ***197** G-13; mail Russellville z 65074; rural
Seaton; RMC Place; PHELPS; ***197** I-15; mail Salem z 65560; rural
Seckman; RMC Place; JEFFERSON; ***197** G-18; mail Imperial z 63052; ● 200
Sedalia; Inc. Place; ⊡ PETTIS; **197** F-12; elev. 919ft./280m.; 🅿 🅷 ■; z 65301-02; Ⓟ 19,800; © 20,339; ◆ 20,124

Entries in **UPPERCASE** are counties.
Entries in **bold** have populations of 2,500 or more.
Names in parentheses are alternate names.
Inc. Place — Incorporated Place
RMC Place — Rand McNally Designated Place
CDP — Census Designated Place
MCD — Minor Civil Division

⊡ County Seat
▲ Minor Civil Division
elev. Elevation
🅿 Post Office

🅷 Hospital
🅲 College
■ Principal Business Center
★ Ranally Metro Area (RMA) Abbreviation
z Zip Code(s)

Ⓟ Previous Census Population
Ⓡ Revised Census Population
Ⓐ Annexation Population
● Rand McNally Population Estimate

© Final Census Population
Ⓢ Special Census Population
◆ Estimated Population

For additional definitions see Glossary, Volume 1, and Introduction, Volume 2.

Sedgewickville; Inc. Place; BOLLINGER; **197** J-19; elev. 642ft./196m.; 🄿; z 63781; Ⓟ 138; Ⓒ 197

Seligman; Inc. Place; BARRY; **196** L-10; elev. 1,540ft./469m.; 🄿; z 65745; Ⓟ 593; Ⓒ 877

Selma; RMC Place; JEFFERSON; ***197** H-18; mail Festus z 63028; ● 200

Selmore; RMC Place; CHRISTIAN; ***197** K-12; elev. 1,322ft./403m.; ★ **SPRG**; mail Ozark z 65721

Selsa; RMC Place; JACKSON; ***196** E-9; ★ **K.C.**; mail Independence z 64057; pop. incl. with Independence (Inc. Place)

Senate Grove; RMC Place; FRANKLIN; ***197** G-16; elev. 622ft./190m.; mail Berger z 63014; rural

Senath; Inc. Place; DUNKLIN; **197** M-18; elev. 265ft./81m.; 🄿; z 63876; Ⓟ 1,622; Ⓒ 1,650

Seneca; Inc. Place; NEWTON; **196** L-9; elev. 853ft./260m.; 🄿; z 64865; Ⓟ 1,885; Ⓒ 2,135

Sequoita; RMC Place; GREENE; ★ **SPRG**; mail Springfield z 65804; pop. incl. with Springfield (Inc. Place)

Sereno; RMC Place; PERRY; ***197** I-19; elev. 621ft./189m.; mail Perryville z 63775; ● 30

Seven Pines; ST. LOUIS; see Benbush (RMC Place)

Seymour; Inc. Place; WEBSTER; **197** K-13; elev. 1,653ft./504m.; 🄿; z 65746; Ⓟ 1,636; Ⓒ 1,834

Shackelford; SALINE; see Shackleford (RMC Place)

Shackleford (Shackelford); RMC Place; SALINE; ***197** E-11; mail Marshall z 65340; ● 30

Shade; RMC Place; PEMISCOT; ***197** M-19; mail Hayti z 63851; rural

Shady Dell; RMC Place; BUTLER; ***197** L-18; mail Poplar Bluff z 63901; rural

Shady Grove; RMC Place; CHRISTIAN; ***197** K-12; elev. 1,361ft./415m.; mail Sparta z 65753; ● 100

Shady Grove; RMC Place; PULASKI; ***197** I-14; mail Waynesville z 65583; rural

Shamrock; RMC Place; CALLAWAY; ***197** F-15; elev. 768ft./234m.; mail Auxvasse z 65231, Montgomery City z 63361; rural

SHANNON; **197** K-15; Ⓟ 7,613; Ⓒ 8,324; ◆ 8,585

Shannondale; RMC Place; CHARITON; ***197** E-12; mail Salisbury z 65281; rural

Shannondale; RMC Place; SHANNON; ***197** J-16; elev. 1,153ft./351m.; mail Salem z 65560; rural

Sharon; RMC Place; SALINE; ***197** E-12; elev. 750ft./229m.; mail Slater z 65349; rural

Shaw; RMC Place; BOONE; **197** F-14; ★ **COL**; mail Columbia z 65202; ● 80

Shawnee Mound; RMC Place; HENRY; ***196** G-10; elev. 927ft./283m.; mail Chilhowee z 64733

Shawneetown; RMC Place; CAPE GIRARDEAU; ***197** J-19; mail Jackson z 63755; ● 140

Shearwood; RMC Place; LIVINGSTON; ***197** C-11; elev. 910ft./277m.; mail Jamesport z 64648; rural

Sheffield; RMC Place; JACKSON; ★ **K.C.**; mail Kansas City z 64125; pop. incl. with Kansas City (Inc. Place)

Shelbina; Inc. Place; SHELBY; **197** D-14; elev. 779ft./237m.; 🄿; z 63468; Ⓟ 2,172; Ⓒ 1,943

Shelby; RMC Place; LINN; ***197** C-12; mail Purdin z 64674; rural

SHELBY; **197** C-14; Ⓟ 6,942; Ⓒ 6,799; ◆ 6,386

Shelbyville; Inc. Place; ⊡ SHELBY; **197** C-14; elev. 768ft./234m.; 🄿; z 63469; Ⓟ 582; Ⓒ 682

Sheldon; Inc. Place; VERNON; **196** I-9; elev. 915ft./279m.; 🄿; z 64784; Ⓟ 464; Ⓒ 529

Shell Knob; CDP; BARRY; **197** L-11; elev. 1,149ft./350m.; 🄿; z 65747; Ⓒ 1,393

Sheridan; Inc. Place; WORTH; **196** A-9; elev. 1,040ft./317m.; 🄿; z 64486; Ⓟ 174; Ⓒ 185

Sherman (Jedburg); RMC Place; ST. LOUIS; **195** G-2; ★ **ST.L**; mail Ballwin z 63011, z 63021; ● 250

Sherrill; RMC Place; TEXAS; ***197** J-15; mail Licking z 65542; rural

Shibboleth; RMC Place; WASHINGTON; ***197** H-17; elev. 799ft./244m.; mail Cadet z 63630; rural

Shibleys Point; RMC Place; ADAIR; ***197** B-13; mail Novinger z 63559; rural

Shirley; RMC Place; WASHINGTON; **197** I-17; elev. 885ft./270m.; mail Potosi z 63664; ● 120

Shoal Creek Drive; Inc. Place; NEWTON; **195** N-2; elev. 950ft./290m.; ★ **JOP**; mail Joplin z 64801; Ⓟ 296; Ⓒ 346

Shoal Creek Estates; Inc. Place; NEWTON; ***196** K-9; ★ **JOP**; mail Joplin z 64801; Ⓟ 21; Ⓒ 51

Shook; RMC Place; WAYNE; ***197** K-18; elev. 395ft./120m.; 🄿; z 63963; ● 80

Short Bend; RMC Place; DENT; ***197** I-16; elev. 990ft./302m.; mail Salem z 65560; rural

Shoveltown; RMC Place; ST. LOUIS; ***197** F-18; elev. 520ft./158m.; ★ **ST.L**; mail Florissant z 63033

Shrewsbury; Inc. Place; ST. LOUIS; **195** F-5; elev. 500ft./152m.; ★ **ST.L**; mail Saint Louis z 63119; Ⓟ 6,416; Ⓒ 6,644

Sibley; Inc. Place; JACKSON; ***196** E-10; elev. 786ft./240m.; 🄿; ★ **K.C.**; z 64088; Ⓟ 367; Ⓒ 347

Sigsbee; RMC Place; SHELBY; ***197** C-15; elev. 741ft./226m.; mail Bethel z 63434; rural

Sikeston; Inc. Place; SCOTT, NEW MADRID; **197** K-20; elev. 325ft./99m.; 🄿 🄷 ■; z 63801; Ⓟ 17,641; Ⓒ 16,992; ◆ 16,836

Silex; Inc. Place; LINCOLN; **197** E-16; elev. 508ft./155m.; 🄿; z 63377; Ⓟ 197; Ⓒ 206

Silica; RMC Place; JEFFERSON; ***197** H-18; elev. 425ft./130m.; ★ **ST.L**; mail Festus z 63028; rural

Siloam Springs; RMC Place; HOWELL; ***197** L-14; mail West Plains z 65775; rural

Silva; RMC Place; WAYNE; ***197** K-18; elev. 403ft./123m.; 🄿; z 63934, z 63964; ● 300

Silver Creek; Inc. Place; NEWTON; **195** N-2; elev. 1,050ft./320m.; ★ **JOP**; mail Joplin z 64801; Ⓟ 513; Ⓒ 608

Silver Dollar City; RMC Place; STONE; ***197** L-11; elev. 1,332ft./406m.; mail Branson z 65616; ● 80

Silver Lake; RMC Place; PERRY; **197** I-19; mail Perryville z 63775; ● 30

Silver Mine; RMC Place; MADISON; ***197** J-18; mail Fredericktown z 63645; ● 30

Simco; MCDONALD; see Simcoe (RMC Place)

Simcoe (Simco); RMC Place; MCDONALD; ***196** L-9; elev. 1,272ft./388m.; mail Rocky Comfort z 64861; rural

Simmons; RMC Place; TEXAS; **197** K-14; elev. 1,120ft./341m.; mail Cabool z 65689, Houston z 65483; ● 30

Sinsabaugh; RMC Place; RIPLEY; ***197** M-17; elev. 291ft./89m.; mail Naylor z 63953; rural

Sitze Store; RMC Place; BOLLINGER; ***197** J-18; elev. 561ft./171m.; rural

Skidmore; Inc. Place; NODAWAY; **196** B-8; elev. 925ft./282m.; 🄿; z 64487; Ⓟ 404; Ⓒ 342

Slabtown; MADISON; see Catherine Place (RMC Place)

Slabtown; RMC Place; TEXAS; ***197** J-14; elev. 900ft./274m.; mail Licking z 65542; rural

Slagle; RMC Place; POLK; ***197** J-11; mail Bolivar z 65613; ● 80

Slater; Inc. Place; SALINE; **197** E-12; elev. 853ft./260m.; 🄿; z 65349; Ⓟ 2,186; Ⓒ 2,083

Sleeper; RMC Place; LACLEDE; **197** I-13; mail Lebanon z 65536; ● 100

Sligo; RMC Place; DENT; ***197** I-16; elev. 1,069ft./326m.; mail Salem z 65560; ● 30

Smallett; RMC Place; DOUGLAS; ***197** L-13; elev. 1,056ft./322m.; mail Ava z 65608; rural

Smelter Hill; RMC Place; JASPER; ★ **JOP**; mail Joplin z 64801; pop. incl. with Joplin (Inc. Place)

Smithfield; RMC Place; JASPER; ***196** K-9; elev. 862ft./263m.; ★ **JOP**; mail Carl Junction z 64834; ● 200

Smithton; Inc. Place; PETTIS; **197** G-12; elev. 888ft./271m.; 🄿; z 65350; Ⓟ 532; Ⓒ 510

Smithville; Inc. Place; CLAY; **196** E-9; elev. 810ft./247m.; 🄿 🄷; ★ **K.C.**; z 64089; Ⓟ 2,525; Ⓒ 5,514

Smittle; RMC Place; WRIGHT; ***197** J-13; elev. 1,240ft./378m.; mail Grovespring z 65662; rural

Smoky Hollow; RMC Place; DENT; ***197** I-15; elev. 1,260ft./384m.; mail Salem z 65560; rural

Sni Mills; RMC Place; JACKSON; ***196** F-10; ★ **K.C.**; mail Oak Grove z 64075

Snow Hollow Lake; RMC Place; IRON; ***197** I-17; mail Middle Brook z 63656; ● 50

Snyder (Dean Lake); RMC Place; CHARITON; ***197** D-12; mail Triplett z 65286; ● 30

Solo; RMC Place; TEXAS; ***197** K-14; elev. 1,224ft./373m.; 🄿; z 65564; ● 100

Souder; RMC Place; OZARK; ***197** L-13; elev. 865ft./264m.; 🄿; z 65773; rural

Soulard; RMC Place; ST. LOUIS (Independent City); ***197** G-18; ★ **ST.L**; mail Saint Louis z 63157; pop. incl. with Saint Louis (Independent City)

South Carrollton; RMC Place; CARROLL; ***197** E-11; elev. 664ft./202m.; mail Carrollton z 64633; pop. incl. with Carrollton (Inc. Place)

South Cedar City; RMC Place; CALLAWAY; pop. incl. with Jefferson City (Inc. Place)

Southeast; RMC Place; JACKSON; ***196** F-9; ★ **K.C.**; mail Kansas City z 64132; pop. incl. with Kansas City (Inc. Place)

Southeast Junction; RMC Place; ST. LOUIS (Independent City); pop. incl. with Saint Louis (Independent City)

South Fork; RMC Place; HOWELL; **197** L-14; elev. 1,091ft./333m.; 🄿; z 65776; ● 130

South Gifford; MACON; see Gifford (Inc. Place)

South Gorin; SCOTLAND; see Gorin (Inc. Place)

South Greenfield (Watkins); Inc. Place; DADE; ***196** J-10; elev. 943ft./287m.; 🄿; z 65752 & mail Greenfield z 65661; Ⓟ 112; Ⓒ 136

South Lee; RMC Place; JACKSON; ***196** F-9; ★ **K.C.**; mail Lees Summit z 64081; pop. incl. with Lees Summit (Inc. Place)

South Liberty; RMC Place; CLAY; ***196** E-9; ★ **K.C.**; mail Liberty z 64068; pop. incl. with Liberty (Inc. Place)

South Lineville; Inc. Place; MERCER; **197** A-11; elev. 1,093ft./333m.; mail Lineville z 50147; Ⓟ 40; Ⓒ 37

South Point; RMC Place; FRANKLIN; mail Washington z 63090; pop. incl. with Washington (Inc. Place)

South Saint Joseph; RMC Place; BUCHANAN; ***196** D-8; ★ **ST.JO**; mail Saint Joseph z 64504; pop. incl. with Saint Joseph (Inc. Place)

South Shore; RMC Place; ST. CHARLES; **197** F-18; mail Saint Charles z 63301; ● 200

South Side; RMC Place; GREENE; ***197** K-11; ★ **SPRG**; mail Springfield z 65806; pop. incl. with Springfield (Inc. Place)

South Troost; RMC Place; JACKSON; ***196** F-9; ★ **K.C.**; mail Kansas City z 64110, z 64112, z 64131; pop. incl. with Kansas City (Inc. Place)

South Troy; RMC Place; LINCOLN; ***197** F-16; mail Troy z 63379; rural

South Van Buren; RMC Place; CARTER; ***197** K-16; mail Van Buren z 63965; ● 300

Southwest; RMC Place; GREENE; ★ **SPRG**; mail Springfield z 65817; pop. incl. with Springfield (Inc. Place)

Southwest; RMC Place; ST. LOUIS (Independent City); ***197** G-18; ★ **ST.L**; mail Saint Louis z 63139; pop. incl. with Saint Louis (Independent City)

South West City; Inc. Place; MCDONALD; **196** L-8; elev. 949ft./289m.; 🄿; z 64863; Ⓟ 600; Ⓒ 855

Spalding; RMC Place; RALLS; ***197** D-15; mail Hannibal z 63401; rural

Spanish Lake; CDP; ST. LOUIS; **195** C-7; elev. 538ft./164m.; ★ **ST.L**; mail Saint Louis z 63138; Ⓟ 20,322; Ⓒ 21,337; ◆ 20,584

Sparta; Inc. Place; CHRISTIAN; **197** K-12; elev. 1,407ft./429m.; 🄿; z 65753; Ⓟ 751; Ⓒ 1,144

Speed; RMC Place; COOPER; ***197** F-13; mail Boonville z 65233; ● 100

Spencerburg; RMC Place; PIKE; ***197** D-16; mail Curryville z 63339

Sperry; RMC Place; ADAIR; ***197** B-13; elev. 956ft./291m.; mail Kirksville z 63501

Spickard (Spickards); Inc. Place; GRUNDY; **197** B-11; elev. 800ft./244m.; 🄿; z 64679; Ⓟ 326; Ⓒ 315

Spickards; GRUNDY; see Spickard (Inc. Place)

Splitlog; RMC Place; MCDONALD; ***196** L-9; elev. 1,220ft./372m.; mail Goodman z 64843; ● 100

Spokane; CDP; CHRISTIAN; **197** L-11; elev. 1,360ft./415m.; 🄿; z 65754; Ⓒ 133

Sprague; RMC Place; BATES; ***196** H-9; mail Rich Hill z 64779

Spring Bluff; RMC Place; FRANKLIN; ***197** H-16; elev. 910ft./277m.; mail Sullivan z 63080; rural

Spring City; RMC Place; NEWTON; ***196** K-9; elev. 1,112ft./339m.; ★ **JOP**; mail Joplin z 64801; ● 130

Spring Creek; RMC Place; PHELPS; ***197** I-14; mail Duke z 65461; rural

Springfield; Inc. Place; ⊡ GREENE, CHRISTIAN; **197** K-11; elev. 1,316ft./401m.; 🄿 🄷 🄲 29,949 ■; ★ **SPRG**; z 65801-10, z 65814, z 65817, z 65890, z 65897-99 & mail Ozark z 65721, Rogersville z 65742; Ⓟ 140,494; Ⓒ 151,580; ◆ 169,858

Spring Fork; RMC Place; PETTIS; ***197** G-12; elev. 900ft./274m.; mail Sedalia z 65301; rural

Spring Garden; RMC Place; MILLER; ***197** G-13; mail Eugene z 65032; ● 100

Springhill; RMC Place; LIVINGSTON; ***197** C-11; mail Chillicothe z 64601

Springtown; RMC Place; WASHINGTON; ***197** I-17; elev. 1,053ft./321m.; mail Mineral Point z 63660; ● 530

Spring Valley; RMC Place; CAMDEN; ***197** H-12; elev. 700ft./213m.; mail Osage Beach z 65065; ● 100

Spring Valley; RMC Place; MCDONALD; elev. 825ft./251m.; mail Noel z 64854; pop. incl. with Noel (Inc. Place)

Sprott; RMC Place; STE. GENEVIEVE; ***197** I-18; elev. 1,052ft./321m.; mail Sainte Genevieve z 63670

Spruce; RMC Place; BATES; **196** H-10; elev. 835ft./255m.; mail Butler z 64730; ● 80

Spurgeon; RMC Place; NEWTON; ***196** K-9; ★ **JOP**; mail Neosho z 64850; ● 100

Squires; RMC Place; DOUGLAS; **197** L-13; elev. 380ft./116m.; 🄿; z 65755; ● 110

Stahl; RMC Place; ADAIR; ***197** B-13; mail Novinger z 63559; rural

Stanberry; Inc. Place; GENTRY; **196** B-9; elev. 886ft./270m.; 🄿; z 64489; Ⓟ 1,310; Ⓒ 1,243

Stanhope; RMC Place; SALINE; ***197** E-12; mail Malta Bend z 65339; rural

Stanton; RMC Place; FRANKLIN; **197** H-16; elev. 872ft./266m.; 🄿; z 63079; ● 200

Star City; RMC Place; BARRY; ***196** L-10; elev. 1,190ft./363m.; mail Purdy z 65734; rural

Stark; RMC Place; PIKE; **197** E-16; elev. 644ft./196m.; mail Louisiana z 63353

Stark City; Inc. Place; NEWTON; **196** L-9; elev. 1,225ft./373m.; 🄿; z 64866; Ⓟ 127; Ⓒ 156

Starkenburg; RMC Place; MONTGOMERY; ***197** F-15; elev. 719ft./219m.; mail Rhineland z 65069

State Line; RMC Place; PEMISCOT; ***197** N-19; elev. 253ft./77m.; mail Steele z 63877; rural

Steedman; RMC Place; CALLAWAY; **197** F-15; elev. 527ft./161m.; 🄿; z 65077; ● 135

Steele; Inc. Place; PEMISCOT; **197** N-19; elev. 260ft./79m.; 🄿; z 63877; Ⓟ 2,395; Ⓒ 2,263

Steeles; RMC Place; RIPLEY; ***197** L-17; elev. 562ft./171m.; mail Doniphan z 63935; rural

Steelville; Inc. Place; ⊡ CRAWFORD; **197** H-16; elev. 750ft./229m.; 🄿; z 65565-66; Ⓟ 1,465; Ⓒ 1,429

Steffenville; RMC Place; LEWIS; **197** C-14; elev. 700ft./213m.; 🄿; z 63447; ● 30

Steinmetz; RMC Place; HOWARD; ***197** E-13; mail Glasgow z 65254; rural

Stella; Inc. Place; NEWTON; ***196** L-9; elev. 1,150ft./351m.; 🄿; z 64867; Ⓟ 132; Ⓒ 178

Stephens; RMC Place; BOONE; ***197** F-14; elev. 855ft./261m.; ★ **COL**; mail Columbia z 65202; ● 240

Stephens; RMC Place; CALLAWAY; **197** F-14; elev. 875ft./267m.; mail Columbia z 65201; ● 140

Stet; RMC Place; CARROLL, RAY; **196** D-10; elev. 790ft./241m.; 🄿; z 64680; ● 30

Stewartsville; Inc. Place; DEKALB; **196** D-9; elev. 958ft./292m.; 🄿; z 64490; Ⓟ 732; Ⓒ 759

Stillings; RMC Place; PLATTE; ***196** E-8; mail Platte City z 64079; rural

Stinson; RMC Place; LAWRENCE; ***196** J-10; elev. 1,134ft./346m.; mail Miller z 65707; rural

Stockdale; RMC Place; CLAY; ***196** E-9; mail Liberty z 64068; ● 200

Stockton; Inc. Place; ⊡ CEDAR; **196** I-10; elev. 965ft./294m.; 🄿; z 65785; Ⓟ 1,579; Ⓒ 1,960

Stockton Hills; RMC Place; CEDAR; elev. 1,000ft./305m.; mail Stockton z 65785

Stockyards; RMC Place; BUCHANAN; ***196** D-8; ★ **ST.JO**; mail Saint Joseph z 64504; pop. incl. with Saint Joseph (Inc. Place)

Stockyards; RMC Place; JACKSON; ***196** E-9; ★ **K.C.**; mail Kansas City z 64101-02; pop. incl. with Kansas City (Inc. Place)

STODDARD; **197** L-19; Ⓟ 28,895; Ⓒ 29,705; ◆ 29,423

STONE; **197** L-11; Ⓟ 19,078; Ⓒ 28,658; ◆ 32,052

Stone Hill; RMC Place; DENT; ***197** I-16; elev. 1,150ft./351m.; mail Salem z 65560; rural

Stoneridge; RMC Place; STONE; ***197** L-11; mail Powersite z 65731, Reeds Spring z 65737; ● 100

Stony Dell; RMC Place; PHELPS; ***197** I-14; elev. 750ft./229m.; mail Jerome z 65529; rural

Stony Hill; RMC Place; GASCONADE; **197** G-16; mail New Haven z 63068; ● 90

Stotesbury; Inc. Place; VERNON; **196** H-9; elev. 770ft./235m.; 🄿; z 64752; Ⓟ 42; Ⓒ 43

Stotts City; Inc. Place; LAWRENCE; ***196** K-10; elev. 1,150ft./351m.; 🄿; z 65756; Ⓟ 235; Ⓒ 250

Stoutland; Inc. Place; CAMDEN, LACLEDE; **197** I-13; elev. 1,171ft./357m.; 🄿; z 65567; Ⓟ 207; Ⓒ 177

Stoutsville; Inc. Place; MONROE; **197** D-15; elev. 613ft./187m.; 🄿; z 65283; Ⓟ 26; Ⓒ 44

Stover; Inc. Place; MORGAN; **197** G-12; elev. 1,052ft./321m.; 🄿; z 65078; Ⓟ 964; Ⓒ 968

Strafford; Inc. Place; GREENE; **197** J-12; elev. 1,482ft./452m.; 🄿; ★ **SPRG**; z 65757; Ⓟ 1,166; Ⓒ 1,845

Strain; RMC Place; FRANKLIN; ***197** H-16; mail Sullivan z 63080

Strasburg; Inc. Place; CASS; **196** F-10; elev. 840ft./256m.; 🄿; z 64090; Ⓟ 124; Ⓒ 136

Stringtown; RMC Place; BUTLER; ***197** L-17; elev. 477ft./145m.; mail Poplar Bluff z 63901; ● 50

Stringtown; RMC Place; COLE; ***197** G-13; mail Lohman z 65053; ● 120

Stringtown; RMC Place; JASPER; ***196** K-9; elev. 886ft./270m.; ★ **JOP**; mail Carl Junction z 64834; ● 110

Strother; RMC Place; MONROE; ***197** D-14; elev. 739ft./225m.; mail Paris z 65275; ● 30

Stubbs; RMC Place; PLATTE; ***196** D-8; mail Camden Point z 64018; rural

Stubtown (Game); RMC Place; PEMISCOT; ***197** M-19; mail Caruthersville z 63830; rural

Stults; STONE; see Stutts (RMC Place)

Stultz; RMC Place; TEXAS; ***197** K-14; elev. 1,200ft./366m.; mail Elk Creek z 65464; ● 30

Sturdivant; RMC Place; BOLLINGER; **197** K-19; elev. 349ft./106m.; 🄿; z 63782; ● 100

Sturgeon; Inc. Place; BOONE; **197** E-14; elev. 851ft./259m.; 🄿; z 65284; Ⓟ 838; Ⓒ 944

Sturges; RMC Place; LIVINGSTON; ***197** C-11; mail Chillicothe z 64601

Stutts (Stults); RMC Place; STONE; ***197** L-11; mail Reeds Spring z 65737; ● 180

Sublette; RMC Place; ADAIR; **197** B-13; elev. 984ft./300m.; mail Greentop z 63546; ● 30

Success; RMC Place; TEXAS; **197** J-14; elev. 1,404ft./428m.; 🄿; z 65570

Sue City; RMC Place; MACON; ***197** C-13; mail La Plata z 63549; rural

Sugar Creek; Inc. Place; JACKSON, CLAY; **196** I-5; elev. 850ft./259m.; 🄿; ★ **K.C.**; z 64050, z 64053-54, z 64056, z 64058; Ⓟ 3,982; Ⓒ 3,839

Sugar Lake; RMC Place; BUCHANAN; ***196** D-8; mail Rushville z 64484; ● 200

Sugartree; RMC Place; CARROLL; ***197** E-11; mail Norborne z 64668; rural

Sullivan; Inc. Place; FRANKLIN, CRAWFORD; **197** H-16; elev. 987ft./301m.; 🄿 🄷; z 63080; Ⓟ 5,661; Ⓒ 6,351

SULLIVAN; **197** B-12; Ⓟ 6,326; Ⓒ 7,219; ◆ 6,425

Sulphur Springs; RMC Place; JEFFERSON; ***197** G-18; elev. 420ft./128m.; 🄿; ★ **ST.L**; z 63052; ● 200

Sumach; RMC Place; DUNKLIN; ***197** M-19; elev. 270ft./82m.; mail Holcomb z 63852; rural

Summerfield; RMC Place; MARIES; ***197** H-15; elev. 854ft./260m.; mail Belle z 65013

Summersville; Inc. Place; TEXAS, SHANNON; **197** K-15; elev. 1,238ft./377m.; 🄿; z 65571; Ⓟ 571; Ⓒ 544

Sumner; Inc. Place; CHARITON; **197** D-12; elev. 682ft./208m.; 🄿; z 64681; Ⓟ 140; Ⓒ 142

Sundown (Theodosia Hills); RMC Place; OZARK; ***197** L-13; mail Theodosia z 65761; disincorporated November, 2001; Ⓟ 35; Ⓒ 38

Sunland Hills; RMC Place; ST. LOUIS; ***197** F-18; ★ **ST.L**; mail Florissant z 63033; ● 700

Sunlight; RMC Place; WASHINGTON; ***197** I-17; mail Belgrade z 63622; rural

Sunny Slope; RMC Place; JACKSON; ***196** E-9; ★ **K.C.**; mail Kansas City z 64110; pop. incl. with Kansas City (Inc. Place)

Sunnyvale; RMC Place; NEWTON, JASPER; ***196** K-9; elev. 1,050ft./320m.; ★ **JOP**; mail Joplin z 64801; pop. incl. with Joplin (Inc. Place)

Sunrise; RMC Place; DUNKLIN; ***197** N-19; mail Hornersville z 63855; rural

Sunrise Beach; Inc. Place; CAMDEN, MORGAN; **197** H-13; elev. 700ft./213m.; 🄿; z 65079; Ⓟ 181; Ⓒ 368

Sunset Hills; Inc. Place; ST. LOUIS; **195** G-4; elev. 600ft./183m.; ★ **ST.L**; mail Saint Louis z 63127; Ⓟ 4,915; Ⓒ 8,267

Susanna; RMC Place; WEBSTER; ***197** J-13; mail Niangua z 65713; rural

Sutherland; RMC Place; JOHNSON; ***197** G-11; elev. 977ft./298m.; mail Windsor z 65360; rural

Swan; RMC Place; TANEY; ***197** L-12; elev. 816ft./249m.; mail Taneyville z 65759; rural

Swart; RMC Place; VERNON; ***196** I-9; elev. 826ft./252m.; mail Moundville z 64771; rural

Swedeborg; RMC Place; PULASKI; **197** I-14; elev. 1,121ft./342m.; 🄿; z 65556; ● 200

Sweden; RMC Place; DOUGLAS; ***197** L-13; mail Ava z 65608; ● 125

Sweet Springs; Inc. Place; SALINE; **197** F-11; elev. 683ft./208m.; 🄿; z 65351; Ⓟ 1,595; Ⓒ 1,628

Sweetwater; RMC Place; NEWTON; ***196** L-9; elev. 1,269ft./387m.; mail Neosho z 64850; rural

Sweetwater; RMC Place; REYNOLDS; ***197** J-16; elev. 986ft./301m.; mail Ellington z 63638; rural

Swift; RMC Place; PEMISCOT; ***197** M-19; mail Hayti z 63851; rural

Swinton; RMC Place; STODDARD; ***197** K-19; mail Advance z 63730; ● 30

Swiss; RMC Place; GASCONADE; ***197** G-15; mail Hermann z 65041

Switzler; RMC Place; BOONE; ***197** F-14; mail Columbia z 65202; pop. incl. with Columbia (Inc. Place)

Sycamore; RMC Place; OZARK; **197** L-14; elev. 820ft./250m.; 🄿; z 65760; ● 80

Sycamore Hills; Inc. Place; ST. LOUIS; **195** D-5; elev. 655ft./200m.; ★ **ST.L**; mail Saint Louis z 63114; Ⓟ 667; Ⓒ 722

Syenite; RMC Place; ST. FRANCOIS; ***197** I-18; mail Knob Lick z 63651; ● 100

Sylvania; RMC Place; DADE; ***196** J-10; elev. 1,072ft./327m.; mail Lockwood z 65682; rural

Syracuse; Inc. Place; MORGAN; **197** G-12; elev. 911ft./278m.; 🄿; z 65354; Ⓟ 185; Ⓒ 172

T

Taberville; RMC Place; ST. CLAIR; ***196** H-10; elev. 742ft./226m.; mail Rockville z 64780; ● 80

Table Rock; RMC Place; TANEY; ***197** L-11; elev. 900ft./274m.; mail Branson z 65616; former incorporated place; merged into Branson May 24, 2004; pop. incl. with Branson (Inc. Place); Ⓟ 100; Ⓒ 229

Taitsville; RMC Place; RAY; ***196** D-10; mail Polo z 64671; rural

Tallapoosa (Tallipoosa); Inc. Place; NEW MADRID; ***197** L-19; elev. 270ft./82m.; 🄿; z 63878; Ⓟ 174; Ⓒ 204

Tallipoosa; NEW MADRID; see Tallapoosa (Inc. Place)

TANEY; **197** L-12; Ⓟ 25,561; Ⓒ 39,703; ◆ 48,535

Taneyville; Inc. Place; TANEY; **197** L-12; elev. 1,075ft./328m.; 🄿; z 65759; Ⓟ 279; Ⓒ 359

Tanner; RMC Place; SCOTT; ***197** K-19; mail Sikeston z 63801; ● 60

Tanyard; RMC Place; NEWTON; ***196** K-9; elev. 943ft./287m.; ★ **JOP**; mail Joplin z 64801; pop. incl. with Joplin (Inc. Place)

Taos; RMC Place; BUCHANAN; ***196** D-8; mail Faucett z 64448, Jefferson City z 65101; ● 60

Taos; Inc. Place; COLE; **197** G-14; elev. 728ft./222m.; ★ **JFCY**; mail Faucett z 64448, Jefferson City z 65101; Ⓟ 802; Ⓒ 870

Tara; RMC Place; ST. LOUIS; ★ **ST.L**; mail Saint Louis z 63123

Tarkio; Inc. Place; ATCHISON; **196** B-7; elev. 940ft./287m.; 🄿; z 64491; Ⓟ 2,243; Ⓒ 1,935

Tarrants; RMC Place; PIKE; ***197** E-16; elev. 740ft./226m.; mail Bowling Green z 63334; disincorporated since 2000 Census; Ⓟ 43; Ⓒ 30

Tarsney Lakes; RMC Place; JACKSON; ***196** F-10; elev. 850ft./259m.; ★ **K.C.**; mail Oak Grove z 64075; ● 380

Taskee Station; RMC Place; WAYNE; ***197** K-18; elev. 400ft./122m.; mail Williamsville z 63967; rural

Tauria; RMC Place; STONE; ***197** L-11; mail Reeds Spring z 65737; rural

Taylor; RMC Place; MARION; **197** C-15; elev. 489ft./149m.; 🄿; z 63471; ● 150

Tea; RMC Place; GASCONADE; ***197** H-16; mail Rosebud z 63091; rural

Teal Bend; RMC Place; BENTON; ***197** H-11; elev. 265ft./81m.; mail Warsaw z 65355; ● 150

Tebbetts; RMC Place; CALLAWAY; **197** G-14; elev. 550ft./168m.; 🄿; z 65080; ● 170

Tecumseh; RMC Place; OZARK; **197** L-14; elev. 585ft./178m.; 🄿; z 65760; ● 100

Tempo; RMC Place; ST. LOUIS; **195** E-4; ★ **ST.L**; mail Saint Louis z 63141; ● 1,600

Ten Brook; RMC Place; JEFFERSON; ***197** G-18; ★ **ST.L**; mail Arnold z 63010; pop. incl. with Arnold (Inc. Place)

Ten Mile; RMC Place; MACON; ***197** C-13; elev. 853ft./260m.; mail Macon z 63552; rural

Teresita; RMC Place; SHANNON; **197** K-15; elev. 1,155ft./352m.; 🄿; z 65438; ● 100

Terre Du Lac; RMC Place; ST. FRANCOIS; ***197** I-17; elev. 1,000ft./305m.; mail Bonne Terre z 63628; ● 700

Terrell; RMC Place; CHRISTIAN; ***197** K-11; mail Billings z 65610; ● 140

Terry; RMC Place; PEMISCOT; ***197** M-19; elev. 265ft./81m.; mail Hayti z 63851; rural

TEXAS; **197** J-14; Ⓟ 21,476; Ⓒ 23,003; ◆ 24,474

Thayer; Inc. Place; OREGON; **197** L-15; elev. 532ft./162m.; 🄿; z 65791; Ⓟ 1,996; Ⓒ 2,201

The Landing; RMC Place; RALLS; ***197** D-15; mail Monroe City z 63456; Ⓟ 8; ● 100

Theodosia; Inc. Place; OZARK; **197** L-13; elev. 900ft./274m.; 🄿; z 65761; Ⓟ 235; Ⓒ 240

Theodosia Hills; OZARK; see Sundown (RMC Place)

Thomas Hill; RMC Place; RANDOLPH; ***197** D-13; elev. 752ft./229m.; mail Clifton Hill z 65244

Thomasville; RMC Place; OREGON; **197** L-15; elev. 643ft./196m.; mail Birch Tree z 65438; ● 80

Thompson; RMC Place; AUDRAIN; **197** E-14; elev. 840ft./256m.; 🄿; z 65285; ● 200

Thoms; RMC Place; JASPER; ***196** K-9; elev. 945ft./288m.; ★ **JOP**; mail Carl Junction z 64834, Joplin z 64801; ● 100

Thornfield; RMC Place; OZARK; ***197** L-13; elev. 800ft./244m.; 🄿; z 65762; ● 80

Thorpe; RMC Place; WEBSTER, DALLAS; ***197** J-12; elev. 1,214ft./370m.; mail Elkland z 65644; rural

Thox Rock; RMC Place; PHELPS; ***197** H-14; elev. 680ft./207m.; mail Newburg z 65550; rural

Thrush; RMC Place; HENRY; ***197** G-11; elev. 809ft./247m.; mail Clinton z 64735; rural

Tiff; RMC Place; WASHINGTON; ***197** H-17; elev. 640ft./195m.; 🄿; z 63674

Tiffany Springs; RMC Place; PLATTE; ***196** E-8; elev. 1,025ft./312m.; ★ **K.C.**; mail Kansas City z 64152; pop. incl. with Kansas City (Inc. Place)

Tiff City; RMC Place; MCDONALD; **196** L-9; elev. 841ft./256m.; 🄿; z 64868; ● 120

Tiffin; RMC Place; ST. CLAIR; **196** I-10; elev. 842ft./257m.; mail El Dorado Springs z 64744; ● 80

Tightwad; Inc. Place; HENRY; **197** H-11; elev. 872ft./266m.; mail Clinton z 64735; Ⓟ 50; Ⓒ 63

Tillman; RMC Place; STODDARD; ***197** K-19; mail Advance z 63730; rural

Tilsit; RMC Place; CAPE GIRARDEAU; ***197** J-19; mail Jackson z 63755; ● 110

Timber; RMC Place; SHANNON; ***197** J-16; mail Salem z 65560; rural

Times Beach; RMC Place; ST. LOUIS; ***197** G-17; elev. 430ft./131m.; ★ **ST.L**; mail Eureka z 63025; rural

Tina; Inc. Place; CARROLL; **197** D-11; elev. 740ft./226m.; 🄿; z 64682; Ⓟ 199; Ⓒ 193

Tindall; Inc. Place; GRUNDY; **197** B-11; elev. 787ft./240m.; mail Trenton z 64683; Ⓟ 46; Ⓒ 65

Tinkerville; RMC Place; DUNKLIN, DUNKLIN; ***197** M-19; elev. 255ft./78m.; mail Kennett z 63857; rural

Tinney Grove; RMC Place; RAY; ***196** D-10; elev. 913ft./278m.; mail Braymer z 64624; rural

Tin Town; RMC Place; POLK; ***197** J-12; mail Buffalo z 65622; ● 90

Tipperary (Midland); RMC Place; ADAIR; ***197** B-13; mail Novinger z 63559; rural

Tipton; Inc. Place; MONITEAU; **197** G-13; elev. 926ft./282m.; 🄿; z 65081; Ⓟ 2,026; Ⓒ 3,261

Tipton Ford; RMC Place; NEWTON; ***196** K-9; elev. 941ft./287m.; ★ **JOP**; mail Joplin z 64801; rural

Toga; RMC Place; STODDARD; ***197** K-19; mail Advance z 63730; ● 20

Toledo; RMC Place; OZARK; ***197** L-13; elev. 891ft./272m.; mail Squires z 65755; rural

Tolona; RMC Place; LEWIS; ***197** C-15; elev. 693ft./211m.; mail Lewistown z 63452

Torch; RMC Place; RIPLEY; ***197** L-17; elev. 293ft./89m.; mail Naylor z 63953; rural

Toronto; RMC Place; CAMDEN; ***197** H-13; elev. 227ft./69m.; mail Montreal z 65591; rural

Tower Grove; RMC Place; ST. LOUIS (Independent City); ***197** G-18; ★ **ST.L**; mail Saint Louis z 63163; pop. incl. with Saint Louis (Independent City)

Town and Country; Inc. Place; ST. LOUIS; **195** E-3; elev. 650ft./198m.; 🄿 🄷; ★ **ST.L**; z 63017 & mail Ballwin z 63011, Saint Louis z 63131; Ⓟ 9,503; Ⓒ 10,894

Tracy; Inc. Place; PLATTE; **196** E-8; elev. 780ft./238m.; mail Platte City z 64079; Ⓟ 287; Ⓒ 213

Trask; RMC Place; HOWELL; ***197** K-15; elev. 1,198ft./365m.; mail Mountain View z 65548

Treloar; RMC Place; WARREN; **197** G-16; elev. 505ft./154m.; 🄿; z 63378; ● 130

Trenton; Inc. Place; ⊡ GRUNDY; **197** C-11; elev. 841ft./256m.; 🄿 🄷; z 64683; Ⓟ 6,129; Ⓒ 6,216

Trimble; Inc. Place; CLINTON; **196** D-9; elev. 931ft./284m.; 🄿; z 64492; Ⓟ 405; Ⓒ 451

Triplett; Inc. Place; CHARITON; **197** D-12; elev. 660ft./201m.; 🄿; z 65286; Ⓟ 58; Ⓒ 64

Troutt; RMC Place; WASHINGTON; ***197** H-17; elev. 901ft./275m.; mail Potosi z 63664; rural

Troy; Inc. Place; ⊡ LINCOLN; **197** F-16; elev. 572ft./174m.; 🄿 🄷; z 63379; Ⓟ 3,811; Ⓒ 6,737

Truesdail; WARREN; see Truesdale (Inc. Place)

Truesdale (Truesdail); Inc. Place; WARREN; ***197** F-16; elev. 863ft./263m.; mail Warrenton z 63383; Ⓟ 285; Ⓒ 397

Truxton; Inc. Place; LINCOLN; **197** F-16; elev. 733ft./223m.; 🄿; z 63381; Ⓟ 90; Ⓒ 96

Tuckahoe; RMC Place; JASPER; **195** L-1; elev. 998ft./304m.; ★ **JOP**; mail Joplin z 64801; ● 90

Tucker; RMC Place; RIPLEY; ***197** L-16; mail Gatewood z 63942; rural

Tuckers Corner; RMC Place; JASPER; ***196** J-9; mail Oronogo z 64855; rural

Tunas; RMC Place; DALLAS; **197** I-12; elev. 920ft./280m.; 🄿; z 65764

Turley; RMC Place; TEXAS; ***197** J-14; elev. 1,125ft./343m.; mail Plato z 65552; rural

Turner; GREENE; see Turners (RMC Place)

Turners (Turner); RMC Place; GREENE; ***197** K-12; elev. 1,190ft./363m.; 🄿; z 65765; ● 275

Turnerville; RMC Place; HOWELL; ***197** K-15; mail Mountain View z 65548; rural

Turney; Inc. Place; CLINTON; **196** D-9; elev. 1,035ft./315m.; 🄿; z 64493; Ⓟ 155; Ⓒ 155

Turtle; RMC Place; DENT; ***197** J-16; elev. 1,392ft./424m.; mail Salem z 65560; ● 50

Tuscumbia; Inc. Place; ⊡ MILLER; **197** H-13; elev. 742ft./226m.; 🄿; z 65082; Ⓟ 148; Ⓒ 218

Tuxedo Park; RMC Place; ST. LOUIS; ★ **ST.L**; mail Saint Louis z 63119; pop. incl. with Webster Groves (Inc. Place)

Twelvemile; RMC Place; MADISON; ***197** J-18; elev. 633ft./193m.; mail Fredericktown z 63645; ● 30

Twin Bridges; LACLEDE; see Evergreen (Inc. Place)

Twin Oaks; Inc. Place; ST. LOUIS; **195** F-3; elev. 613ft./187m.; 🄿; ★ **ST.L**; z 63088 & mail Ballwin z 63021; Ⓟ 506; Ⓒ 362

Twin Springs; RMC Place; FRANKLIN; ***197** H-16; mail Stanton z 63079; rural

Tyler; RMC Place; PEMISCOT; ***197** N-19; elev. 259ft./79m.; mail Steele z 63877; ● 30

Tyrone; RMC Place; TEXAS; ***197** K-15; mail Elk Creek z 65464, Houston z 65483; ● 40

U

Udall; RMC Place; OZARK; **197** L-14; elev. 840ft./256m.; 🄿; z 65766; summer pop. 200; ● 120

Ulman; RMC Place; MILLER; ***197** H-13; elev. 940ft./287m.; 🄿; z 65083; ● 150

Umber; RMC Place; CEDAR; ***196** I-10; mail Stockton z 65785; rural

Umber View Heights; Inc. Place; CEDAR; ***196** I-10; mail Stockton z 65785; Ⓟ 34; Ⓒ 52

Union; Inc. Place; ⊡ FRANKLIN; **197** G-16; elev. 545ft./166m.; 🄿; z 63084; Ⓟ 5,909; Ⓒ 7,757

Union; RMC Place; RAY; ***196** D-10; elev. 970ft./296m.; ★ **K.C.**; mail Lawson z 64062; rural

Union City; RMC Place; STONE; ***197** K-11; elev. 1,338ft./408m.; mail Billings z 65610

Union Star; Inc. Place; DEKALB; **196** C-9; elev. 960ft./293m.; 🄿; z 64494; Ⓟ 432; Ⓒ 433

Uniontown; RMC Place; PERRY; **197** I-19; elev. 576ft./176m.; 🄿; z 63783; ● 60

Unionville; Inc. Place; ⊡ PUTNAM; **197** B-12; elev. 1,067ft./325m.; 🄿; z 63565; Ⓟ 1,989; Ⓒ 2,041

Unity Village; Inc. Place; JACKSON; **196** K-6; elev. 850ft./259m.; 🄿; ★ **K.C.**; z 64065 & mail Lees Summit z 64063-64; Ⓟ 138; Ⓒ 140

University City; Inc. Place; ST. LOUIS; **195** E-5; elev. 550ft./168m.; 🄿; ★ **ST.L**; z 63130 & mail Saint Louis z 63105, z 63124, z 63132; Ⓟ 40,087; Ⓒ 37,428; Ⓡ 37,644; ◆ 35,284

Uplands Park; Inc. Place; ST. LOUIS; ***197** F-18; elev. 600ft./183m.; ★ **ST.L**; mail Saint Louis z 63121; Ⓟ 499; Ⓒ 460

Upton; RMC Place; TEXAS; ***197** J-14; mail Plato z 65552; rural

Urbana; Inc. Place; DALLAS; **197** I-12; elev. 1,050ft./320m.; 🄿; z 65767; Ⓟ 350; Ⓒ 407

Urbandale; RMC Place; RANDOLPH; ***197** E-13; elev. 872ft./266m.; mail Moberly z 65270; pop. incl. with Moberly (Inc. Place)

Urich; Inc. Place; HENRY; **196** G-10; elev. 780ft./238m.; 🄿; z 64788; Ⓟ 498; Ⓒ 499

Useful; RMC Place; OSAGE; ***197** G-15; elev. 796ft./243m.; mail Linn z 65051; rural

Utica; Inc. Place; LIVINGSTON; **197** D-11; elev. 748ft./228m.; 🄿; z 64686; Ⓟ 299; Ⓒ 274

V

Vale; RMC Place; JACKSON; ***196** F-9; ★ **K.C.**; mail Kansas City z 64138; pop. incl. with Kansas City (Inc. Place)

Valles Mines; RMC Place; JEFFERSON; **197** H-18; elev. 746ft./227m.; 🄿; z 63087 & mail De Soto z 63020; ● 500

Valley City; RMC Place; JOHNSON; ***197** F-11; elev. 707ft./215m.; mail Knob Noster z 65336

Valley Park; Inc. Place; ST. LOUIS; **195** G-3; elev. 421ft./128m.; 🄿; ★ **ST.L**; z 63088; Ⓟ 4,165; Ⓒ 6,518

Valley Ridge; RMC Place; DUNKLIN; ***197** L-19; elev. 335ft./102m.; mail Campbell z 63933; ● 50

Valley View; RMC Place; BENTON; ***197** H-11; mail Warsaw z 65355; ● 100

Valley View; RMC Place; STE. GENEVIEVE; **197** H-18; elev. 528ft./161m.; mail Bloomsdale z 63627; ● 300

Valley Water Mills; RMC Place; GREENE; ***197** J-12; ★ **SPRG**; mail Springfield z 65803; rural

Van; RMC Place; POLK; ***197** J-11; elev. 1,050ft./320m.; mail Bolivar z 65613

Van Buren; Inc. Place; ⊡ CARTER; **197** K-16; elev. 475ft./145m.; 🄿; z 63965; Ⓟ 893; Ⓒ 845

Vance; RMC Place; WEBSTER; ***197** J-13; elev. 1,272ft./388m.; mail Niangua z 65713; rural

Van Cleve; RMC Place; MARIES; ***197** H-14; mail Meta z 65058; rural

Vandalia; Inc. Place; AUDRAIN, RALLS; **197** E-15; elev. 766ft./233m.; 🄿; z 63382; Ⓟ 2,683; Ⓒ 2,529; Ⓡ 3,863

Vandiver; Inc. Place; AUDRAIN; **197** E-15; elev. 760ft./232m.; mail Mexico z 65265; Ⓟ 75; Ⓒ 83

Vanduser; Inc. Place; SCOTT; ***197** K-19; elev. 313ft./95m.; 🄿; z 63784; Ⓟ 187; Ⓒ 217

Vanzant; RMC Place; DOUGLAS; **197** K-14; elev. 1,177ft./359m.; 🄿; z 65768; ● 80

Vastus; RMC Place; BUTLER; ***197** L-18; elev. 300ft./91m.; mail Neelyville z 63954; ● 30

Velda City; ST. LOUIS; see Velda Village (Inc. Place)

Velda Village (Velda City); Inc. Place; ST. LOUIS; **195** D-6; elev. 630ft./192m.; ★ **ST.L**; mail Saint Louis z 63121, z 63133; Ⓟ 1,597; Ⓒ 1,616

Velda Village Hills; Inc. Place; ST. LOUIS; **195** D-6; elev. 570ft./174m.; ★ **ST.L**; mail Saint Louis z 63121; Ⓟ 1,315; Ⓒ 1,090

Vera; RMC Place; PIKE; ***197** E-16; elev. 620ft./189m.; mail Bowling Green z 63334

Verdella; RMC Place; BARTON; ***196** I-9; mail Liberal z 64762

VERNON; **196** I-9; Ⓟ 19,041; Ⓒ 20,454; ◆ 19,717

Verona; Inc. Place; LAWRENCE; **196** K-10; elev. 1,267ft./386m.; 🄿; z 65769; Ⓟ 546; Ⓒ 714

Verona Hills; RMC Place; JACKSON; ★ **K.C.**; mail Kansas City z 64145; pop. incl. with Kansas City (Inc. Place)

Versailles; Inc. Place; ⊡ MORGAN; **197** G-12; elev. 1,036ft./316m.; 🄿; z 65084; Ⓟ 2,365; Ⓒ 2,565

Vibbard; RMC Place; RAY; **196** E-10; ★ **K.C.**; mail Lawson z 64062; ● 210

Viburnum; Inc. Place; IRON; **197** I-16; elev. 1,274ft./388m.; 🄿; z 65566; Ⓟ 743; Ⓒ 825

Vichy; RMC Place; MARIES; **197** H-15; elev. 1,118ft./341m.; 🄿; z 65580; ● 220

Victoria; RMC Place; JEFFERSON; ***197** H-17; elev. 469ft./143m.; ★ **ST.L**; mail De Soto z 63020; ● 350

Vida; RMC Place; PHELPS; ***197** I-15; elev. 1,046ft./319m.; mail Newburg z 65550, Rolla z 65401; ● 100

Vienna; Inc. Place; ⊡ MARIES; **197** H-14; elev. 873ft./266m.; 🄿; z 65582; Ⓟ 611; Ⓒ 628

Vigus; RMC Place; ST. LOUIS; ***197** F-18; ★ **ST.L**; mail Hazelwood z 63042; pop. incl. with Maryland Heights (Inc. Place)

Village of Charlack; RMC Place; ST. LOUIS; ***197** F-18; ★ **ST.L**; mail Saint Louis z 63114; ● 1,200

Village of Four Seasons; CAMDEN; see Four Seasons (Inc. Place)

Villa Heights; RMC Place; JASPER; ★ **JOP**; mail Joplin z 64801; pop. incl. with Joplin (Inc. Place)

Villa Ridge; CDP; FRANKLIN; ***197** G-17; elev. 637ft./194m.; 🄿; ★ **ST.L**; z 63089; Ⓟ 1,865; Ⓒ 2,417

Vineland; RMC Place; JEFFERSON; **197** H-17; elev. 695ft./212m.; mail De Soto z 63020; ● 120

Vinita Park; Inc. Place; ST. LOUIS; **195** D-5; elev. 561ft./171m.; ★ **ST.L**; mail Saint Louis z 63114; Ⓟ 2,001; Ⓒ 1,924

Vinita Terrace; Inc. Place; ST. LOUIS; **195** D-5; elev. 600ft./183m.; ★ **ST.L**; mail Saint Louis z 63114; Ⓟ 338; Ⓒ 292

Vinson; RMC Place; STODDARD; ***197** L-19; elev. 289ft./88m.; mail Dexter z 63841; rural

Viola; RMC Place; STONE, BARRY; ***197** M-11; mail Shell Knob z 65747

Virgil City; RMC Place; CEDAR, VERNON; ***196** I-10; mail El Dorado Springs z 64744

Virginia; RMC Place; BATES; **196** H-9; elev. 875ft./267m.; mail Butler z 64730

Vista; Inc. Place; ST. CLAIR; **197** H-11; elev. 860ft./262m.; 🄿; z 64776; Ⓟ 50; Ⓒ 55

Vulcan; RMC Place; IRON; ***197** J-17; elev. 558ft./170m.; 🄿; z 63675; rural

W

Waco; Inc. Place; JASPER; ***196** J-9; elev. 900ft./274m.; 🄿; ★ **JOP**; z 64869; Ⓟ 86; Ⓒ 86

Wagoner; RMC Place; CEDAR; ***196** I-10; mail Stockton z 65785; rural

Wainwright; RMC Place; CALLAWAY; **197** G-14; ★ **JFCY**; mail Holts Summit z 65043; ● 85

Wakenda; RMC Place; CARROLL; **197** E-11; elev. 652ft./199m.; Ⓟ 89

Waldo; RMC Place; JACKSON; ***196** F-9; ★ **K.C.**; mail Kansas City z 64114; pop. incl. with Kansas City (Inc. Place)

Waldron; RMC Place; PLATTE; **196** E-8; elev. 760ft./232m.; 🄿; ★ **K.C.**; z 64092; ● 200

Walker; Inc. Place; VERNON; **196** I-9; elev. 852ft./260m.; 🄿; z 64790; Ⓟ 283; Ⓒ 275

Wallace; RMC Place; BUCHANAN; **196** D-8; mail Dearborn z 64439; ● 115

Wall Street; RMC Place; DALLAS; ***197** I-12; mail Long Lane z 65590; rural

Walnut Grove; Inc. Place; GREENE; **197** J-11; elev. 1,200ft./366m.; 🄿; z 65770; Ⓟ 549; Ⓒ 630

Walnut Shade; RMC Place; TANEY; **197** L-12; elev. 755ft./230m.; 🄿; z 65771; ● 300

Wanamaker; RMC Place; SALINE; ***197** F-12; elev. 799ft./244m.; mail Marshall z 65340; rural

Wanda; RMC Place; NEWTON; ***196** L-9; elev. 1,176ft./358m.; mail Stark City z 64866; ● 80

Wappapello; RMC Place; WAYNE; **197** K-18; elev. 350ft./107m.; 🄿; z 63966; summer pop. 3,000; ● 150

Wardell; Inc. Place; PEMISCOT; **197** M-19; elev. 270ft./82m.; 🄿; z 63879; Ⓟ 325; Ⓒ 278

Wardsville; Inc. Place; COLE; **197** G-14; elev. 803ft./245m.; ★ **JFCY**; mail Jefferson City z 65101; Ⓟ 513; Ⓒ 976

Ware; RMC Place; JEFFERSON; ***197** H-17; elev. 552ft./168m.; mail Hillsboro z 63050; rural

Warren; RMC Place; MARION; ***197** D-15; elev. 727ft./222m.; mail Monroe City z 63456

WARREN; **197** F-16; Ⓟ 19,534; Ⓒ 24,525; ◆ 32,180

Warrensburg; Inc. Place; ⊡ JOHNSON; **196** F-10; elev. 880ft./268m.; 🄿 🄷 🄲 10,711; z 64093; Ⓟ 15,244; Ⓒ 16,340

Warrenton; Inc. Place; ⊡ WARREN; **197** F-16; elev. 828ft./252m.; 🄿; z 63383; Ⓟ 3,596; Ⓒ 5,281

Warsaw; Inc. Place; ⊡ BENTON; **197** H-11; elev. 709ft./216m.; 🄿; z 65355; Ⓟ 1,696; Ⓒ 2,070

Warson Woods; Inc. Place; ST. LOUIS; **195** F-4; elev. 600ft./183m.; ★ **ST.L**; mail Saint Louis z 63122; Ⓟ 2,049; Ⓒ 1,983

Washburn; Inc. Place; BARRY; **196** L-10; elev. 1,480ft./451m.; 🄿; z 65772; Ⓟ 362; Ⓒ 448

Washington; Inc. Place; FRANKLIN; **197** G-16; elev. 568ft./173m.; 🄿; z 63090; Ⓟ 10,704; Ⓒ 13,243

WASHINGTON; **197** H-16; Ⓟ 20,380; Ⓒ 23,344; ◆ 24,582

Washington Center; RMC Place; HARRISON; ***196** B-10; elev. 1,053ft./321m.; mail Martinsville z 64467; rural

Wasola; RMC Place; OZARK; **197** L-13; elev. 1,294ft./394m.; 🄿; z 65773; ● 110

Waterloo; RMC Place; LAFAYETTE; ***196** E-10; mail Wellington z 64097; rural

Watkins; DADE; see South Greenfield (Inc. Place)

Watson; Inc. Place; ATCHISON; **196** A-7; elev. 894ft./272m.; 🄿; z 64496; Ⓟ 137; Ⓒ 121

Waverly; Inc. Place; LAFAYETTE; **197** E-11; elev. 808ft./246m.; 🄿; z 64096; Ⓟ 837; Ⓒ 806

Wayland; Inc. Place; CLARK; **197** B-15; elev. 535ft./163m.; 🄿; z 63472; Ⓟ 391; Ⓒ 425

Wayne; RMC Place; BARRY; ***196** L-10; mail Washburn z 65772; ● 140

WAYNE; **197** K-18; Ⓟ 11,543; Ⓒ 13,259; ◆ 12,348

Waynesville; Inc. Place; ⊡ PULASKI; **197** I-14; elev. 805ft./245m.; 🄿; z 65583; Ⓟ 3,207; Ⓒ 3,507

Weatherby; Inc. Place; DEKALB; **196** C-9; elev. 885ft./270m.; 🄿; z 64497; Ⓟ 91; Ⓒ 123

Weatherby Lake; Inc. Place; PLATTE; **196** G-2; elev. 950ft./290m.; 🄿; ★ **K.C.**; z 64152-53; Ⓟ 1,613; Ⓒ 1,873

Weaubleau; Inc. Place; HICKORY; **197** I-11; elev. 980ft./299m.; 🄿; z 65774; Ⓟ 436; Ⓒ 518

Webb City; Inc. Place; JASPER; **196** K-9; elev. 1,000ft./305m.; 🄿; ★ **JOP**; z 64870; Ⓟ 7,449; Ⓒ 9,812

Weber Hill; RMC Place; JEFFERSON; **195** H-3; elev. 778ft./237m.; ★ **ST.L**; mail House Springs z 63051; ● 800

WEBSTER; **197** J-12; Ⓟ 23,753; Ⓒ 31,045; ◆ 37,544

Webster Groves; Inc. Place; ST. LOUIS; **195** F-5; elev. 581ft./177m.; 🄿 🄲 20,620; ★ **ST.L**; z 63119; Ⓟ 22,987; Ⓒ 23,230; ◆ 22,571

Webster Park; RMC Place; ST. LOUIS; ★ **ST.L**; mail Saint Louis z 63119; pop. incl. with Webster Groves (Inc. Place)

Wedgewood; RMC Place; ST. LOUIS; ***197** F-18; ★ **ST.L**; mail Florissant z 63031; ● 1,000

Wedgewood Green; RMC Place; ST. LOUIS; ***197** F-18; ★ **ST.L**; mail Florissant z 63031; ● 1,100

Weingarten; RMC Place; STE. GENEVIEVE; **197** I-18; elev. 833ft./254m.; mail Sainte Genevieve z 63670; ● 100

Wela; NEWTON; see Wela Park (RMC Place)

Wela Park (Wela); RMC Place; NEWTON; ***196** K-9; mail Seneca z 64865; rural

Weldon Spring; Inc. Place; ST. CHARLES; **197** F-17; 🄿; ★ **ST.L**; z 63304; Ⓟ 1,470; Ⓒ 5,270

Weldon Spring Heights; Inc. Place; ST. CHARLES; **195** D-1; elev. 620ft./189m.; ★ **ST.L**; mail Saint Charles z 63304; Ⓟ 82; Ⓒ 79

Wellington; Inc. Place; LAFAYETTE; **196** E-10; elev. 717ft./219m.; 🄿; z 64097; Ⓟ 779; Ⓒ 784

Wellston; Inc. Place; ST. LOUIS; **195** E-6; elev. 517ft./158m.; ★ **ST.L**; mail Saint Louis z 63112, z 63133; Ⓟ 3,612; Ⓒ 2,460

Wellsville; Inc. Place; MONTGOMERY; **197** E-15; elev. 822ft./251m.; 🄿; z 63384; Ⓟ 1,430; Ⓒ 1,423

Wentworth; Inc. Place; NEWTON; **196** K-10; elev. 1,220ft./372m.; 🄿; z 64873; Ⓟ 138; Ⓒ 141

Wentzville; Inc. Place; ST. CHARLES; **197** F-17; elev. 603ft./184m.; 🄿 🄷 🄲 495; ★ **ST.L**; z 63385; Ⓟ 5,088; Ⓒ 6,896; ◆ 11,692

Wesco; RMC Place; CRAWFORD; **197** I-16; elev. 864ft./263m.; 🄿; z 65586

West Alton; Inc. Place; ST. CHARLES; **197** F-18; elev. 434ft./132m.; 🄿; z 63386; Ⓟ 1,067; Ⓒ 573

West Aurora; RMC Place; MILLER; ***197** H-13; mail Eldon z 65026; rural

Westboro; Inc. Place; ATCHISON; **196** A-7; elev. 992ft./302m.; 🄿; z 64498; Ⓟ 182; Ⓒ 163

West Ely; RMC Place; MARION; ***197** D-15; elev. 715ft./218m.; mail Hannibal z 63401; ● 40

West Eminence; RMC Place; SHANNON; ***197** K-16; mail Eminence z 65466; ● 110

West Hermondale; RMC Place; PEMISCOT; ***197** N-19; elev. 251ft./77m.; mail Steele z 63877; ● 30

West Line; Inc. Place; CASS; **196** G-9; elev. 900ft./274m.; 🄿; z 64734; Ⓟ 98; Ⓒ 95

Weston; Inc. Place; PLATTE; **196** D-8; elev. 800ft./244m.; 🄿; z 64098; Ⓟ 1,528; Ⓒ 1,631

Westphalia; Inc. Place; OSAGE; **197** G-14; elev. 622ft./190m.; 🄿; z 65085; Ⓟ 287; Ⓒ 320

West Plains; Inc. Place; ⊡ HOWELL; **197** L-15; elev. 991ft./302m.; 🄿 🄷 ■; z 65775-76; Ⓟ 8,913; Ⓒ 10,866; ◆ 10,766

Westport; RMC Place; JACKSON; ***196** E-9; ★ **K.C.**; mail Kansas City z 64111, z 64171; pop. incl. with Kansas City (Inc. Place)

West Quincy; RMC Place; MARION; **197** C-15; mail Taylor z 63471; ● 30

West Sullivan; Inc. Place; CRAWFORD; ***197** H-16; Ⓒ 78

Westview; RMC Place; NEWTON; **196** L-9; mail Neosho z 64850; ● 110

Westville; RMC Place; CHARITON; ***197** D-12; elev. 819ft./250m.; mail Marceline z 64658; rural

Westwood; Inc. Place; ST. LOUIS; **195** E-4; elev. 600ft./183m.; ★ **ST.L**; mail Saint Louis z 63131; Ⓟ 309; Ⓒ 284

Wet Glaize; RMC Place; CAMDEN; ***197** I-13; mail Stoutland z 65567; rural

Wheatland; Inc. Place; HICKORY; **197** I-11; elev. 1,030ft./314m.; 🄿; z 65779; Ⓟ 363; Ⓒ 388

Wheaton; Inc. Place; BARRY; **196** L-10; elev. 1,387ft./423m.; 🄿; z 64874; Ⓟ 637; Ⓒ 721

Wheelerville; RMC Place; BARRY; ***197** L-11; mail Aurora z 65605; ● 200

Wheeling; Inc. Place; LIVINGSTON; **197** C-11; elev. 749ft./228m.; 🄿; z 64688; Ⓟ 284; Ⓒ 268

Whispering Hills; RMC Place; ST. LOUIS; ***197** F-18; ★ **ST.L**; mail Saint Louis z 63141; ● 1,000

Whitakerville; RMC Place; BENTON; **197** H-11; elev. 812ft./247m.; mail Warsaw z 65355; ● 100

White Branch; RMC Place; BENTON; ***197** H-11; mail Warsaw z 65355; ● 260

White Church; RMC Place; HOWELL; **197** L-15; elev. 1,075ft./328m.; mail Pomona z 65789

White Cloud; RMC Place; HICKORY; ***197** H-11; elev. 990ft./302m.; mail Wheatland z 65779; rural

White Hall Fields; RMC Place; CLAY; ★ **K.C.**; mail Liberty z 64068; pop. incl. with Liberty (Inc. Place)

Whiteman AFB; CDP-Census Area Only; JOHNSON; ***197** F-11; 🄿; z 65305; Ⓟ 4,174; Ⓒ 3,814

White Oak; RMC Place; DUNKLIN; **197** M-19; elev. 265ft./81m.; 🄿; z 63880; ● 50

Whiteside; Inc. Place; LINCOLN; **197** E-16; elev. 800ft./244m.; 🄿; z 63387; Ⓟ 79; Ⓒ 67

Whitesville; RMC Place; ANDREW; **196** C-8; mail Rea z 64480; ● 80

Whitewater; Inc. Place; CAPE GIRARDEAU; **197** J-19; elev. 370ft./113m.; 🄿; z 63785; Ⓟ 103; Ⓒ 113

Whiting; RMC Place; MISSISSIPPI; **197** L-20; mail East Prairie z 63845; ● 150

Whitman; RMC Place; CHARITON; ***197** D-12; elev. 657ft./200m.; mail Triplett z 65286; ● 10

Wien; RMC Place; CHARITON; ***197** D-13; elev. 825ft./251m.; mail New Cambria z 63558; ● 60

Wilbur Park; Inc. Place; ST. LOUIS; **195** F-6; ★ **ST.L**; mail Saint Louis z 63123; Ⓟ 522; Ⓒ 475

Wilcox; RMC Place; NODAWAY; **196** B-8; elev. 500ft./152m.; mail Maryville z 64468; ● 70

Wilderness; RMC Place; OREGON; **197** L-16; elev. 843ft./257m.; mail Fremont z 63941

Wildwood; RMC Place; HARRISON; ***196** B-10; elev. 895ft./273m.; mail Bethany z 64424; rural

Wildwood; Inc. Place; ST. LOUIS; **195** F-1; 🄿; ★ **ST.L**; z 63005, z 63011, z 63021, z 63025, z 63038, z 63040, z 63069; Ⓒ 32,884; ◆ 33,064

Wildwood Estates; RMC Place; GREENE; ***197** K-11; ★ **SPRG**; mail Springfield z 65804; pop. incl. with Springfield (Inc. Place)

Wildwood Lake; RMC Place; JACKSON; ★ **K.C.**; mail Kansas City z 64133; pop. incl. with Raytown (Inc. Place)

Wilhelmina; RMC Place; DUNKLIN; ***197** L-18; mail Campbell z 63933; ● 40

Willard; Inc. Place; GREENE; **197** J-11; elev. 1,231ft./375m.; 🄿; ★ **SPRG**; z 65781; Ⓟ 2,177; Ⓒ 3,193

William M Chick; RMC Place; JACKSON; ***196** E-9; ★ **K.C.**; mail Kansas City z 64124; pop. incl. with Kansas City (Inc. Place)

Williamsburg; RMC Place; CALLAWAY; **197** F-15; elev. 826ft./252m.; 🄿; z 63388; ● 100

Williamstown; RMC Place; LEWIS; **197** B-15; elev. 721ft./220m.; 🄿; z 63473

Williamsville; Inc. Place; WAYNE; **197** K-17; elev. 392ft./119m.; 🄿; z 63967; Ⓟ 391; Ⓒ 379

Willmathsville; RMC Place; ADAIR; ***197** B-13; elev. 939ft./286m.; mail Greentop z 63546

Willow Brook; RMC Place; BUCHANAN; ***196** D-8; ★ **ST.JO**; mail Faucett z 64448

Willow Springs; Inc. Place; HOWELL; **197** K-14; elev. 1,257ft./383m.; 🄿; z 65793; Ⓟ 2,038; Ⓒ 2,147

Wilson City; Inc. Place; MISSISSIPPI; **197** K-20; elev. 315ft./96m.; mail Wyatt z 63882; Ⓟ 210; Ⓒ 165

Wilton; RMC Place; BOONE; **197** F-13; mail Hartsburg z 65039; ● 80

Winchester; RMC Place; CLARK; **197** B-15; elev. 673ft./205m.; mail Canton z 63435; ● 110

Winchester; Inc. Place; ST. LOUIS; **195** F-3; elev. 600ft./183m.; ★ **ST.L**; mail Ballwin z 63011, z 63021; Ⓟ 1,678; Ⓒ 1,651

Windsor; Inc. Place; HENRY, PETTIS; **197** G-11; elev. 900ft./274m.; 🄿; z 65360; Ⓟ 3,044; Ⓒ 3,087

Windsor Place; Inc. Place; COOPER; incorporated February 28, 2006; not reported in 2000 Census; ● 200

Windsor Springs; RMC Place; ST. LOUIS; ***197** G-18; ★ **ST.L**; mail Saint Louis z 63122; pop. incl. with Kirkwood (Inc. Place)

Windyville; RMC Place; DALLAS; **197** I-12; elev. 1,078ft./329m.; 🄿; z 65783

Winfield; Inc. Place; LINCOLN; **197** F-17; elev. 446ft./136m.; 🄿; z 63389; Ⓟ 672; Ⓒ 723

Winigan; RMC Place; SULLIVAN; **197** C-12; elev. 993ft./303m.; 🄿; z 63566

Winner; RMC Place; CLAY; ***196** E-9; mail Kansas City z 64166; rural

Winnipeg; RMC Place; LACLEDE; ***197** J-14; elev. 1,119ft./341m.; mail Laquey z 65534; rural

Winnwood; RMC Place; CLAY; ★ **K.C.**; mail Kansas City z 64117; pop. incl. with Kansas City (Inc. Place)

Winnwood Gardens; RMC Place; CLAY; ***196** E-9; elev. 877ft./267m.; ★ **K.C.**; mail Kansas City z 64117; pop. incl. with Kansas City (Inc. Place)

Winnwood Lake; RMC Place; CLAY; ★ **K.C.**; mail Kansas City z 64117; pop. incl. with Kansas City (Inc. Place)

Winona; Inc. Place; SHANNON; **197** K-16; elev. 920ft./280m.; 🄿; z 65588; Ⓟ 1,081; Ⓒ 1,290

Winston; Inc. Place; DAVIESS; **196** C-10; elev. 1,040ft./317m.; 🄿; z 64689; Ⓟ 251; Ⓒ 247

Winthrop (East Atchison); RMC Place; BUCHANAN; **196** D-8; mail Rushville z 64484; ● 60

Wisdom; RMC Place; BENTON; ***197** H-11; elev. 763ft./233m.; mail Warsaw z 65355; rural

Wishart; RMC Place; POLK; **197** J-11; elev. 979ft./298m.; mail Morrisville z 65710

Withers Mill; RMC Place; MARION; **197** D-15; mail Hannibal z 63401, Palmyra z 63461; ● 30

Wittenberg; RMC Place; PERRY; **197** I-20; elev. 380ft./116m.; 🄿; z 63748; ● 60

Wolf Island; RMC Place; MISSISSIPPI; **197** L-20; elev. 305ft./93m.; 🄿; z 63881; ● 30

Womack; RMC Place; STE. GENEVIEVE; **197** I-18; mail Fredericktown z 63645; rural

Woodbine Heights; RMC Place; ST. LOUIS; ★ **ST.L**; mail Saint Louis z 63122; pop. incl. with Kirkwood (Inc. Place)

Woodcliffe; RMC Place; GREENE; ★ **SPRG**; mail Springfield z 65804

Wood Heights (Woods Heights); Inc. Place; RAY; **196** E-10; elev. 900ft./274m.; 🄿; ★ **K.C.**; z 64024; Ⓟ 708; Ⓒ 742

Woodhill; RMC Place; CLAY; ***196** E-9; mail Kansas City z 64117; pop. incl. with Kansas City (Inc. Place)

Woodland; RMC Place; MARION; ***197** D-15; elev. 681ft./208m.; mail Palmyra z 63461; ● 30

Woodlandville; RMC Place; BOONE; ***197** E-13; mail Harrisburg z 65256, Rocheport z 65279; rural

Woodlawn; RMC Place; MONROE; elev. 786ft./240m.; mail Madison z 65263

Woodridge; RMC Place; ST. LOUIS; ★ **ST.L**; mail Florissant z 63033

Woodruff; RMC Place; PLATTE; ***196** D-8; mail Weston z 64098; rural

Woods Heights; RAY; see Wood Heights (Inc. Place)

Woodson Terrace; Inc. Place; ST. LOUIS; **195** D-5; elev. 600ft./183m.; ★ **ST.L**; mail Saint Louis z 63134; Ⓟ 4,362; Ⓒ 4,189

Woodville; RMC Place; MACON; ***197** D-14; elev. 812ft./247m.; mail Excello z 65247

Wooldridge; Inc. Place; COOPER; **197** F-13; elev. 579ft./176m.; 🄿; z 65287; Ⓟ 54; Ⓒ 47

Woollam; GASCONADE; see New Woollam (RMC Place)

Worland; RMC Place; BATES; ***196** H-9; elev. 818ft./249m.; mail Hume z 64752; ● 80

Wornall; RMC Place; JACKSON; ***196** F-9; ★ **K.C.**; mail Kansas City z 64113-14; pop. incl. with Kansas City (Inc. Place)

Worth; Inc. Place; WORTH; **196** B-9; elev. 923ft./281m.; 🄿; z 64499; Ⓟ 103; Ⓒ 94

WORTH; **196** B-9; Ⓟ 2,440; Ⓒ 2,382; ◆ 2,095

Wortham; RMC Place; ST. FRANCOIS; ***197** I-17; mail Park Hills z 63601; ● 350

Worthington; Inc. Place; PUTNAM; **197** B-13; elev. 800ft./244m.; 🄿; z 63567; Ⓟ 86; Ⓒ 89

WRIGHT; **197** J-13; Ⓟ 16,758; Ⓒ 17,955; ◆ 18,406

Wright City; Inc. Place; WARREN; **197** F-16; elev. 727ft./222m.; 🄿; z 63390; Ⓟ 1,250; Ⓒ 1,532

Wyaconda; Inc. Place; CLARK; **197** B-14; elev. 756ft./230m.; 🄿; z 63474; Ⓟ 347; Ⓒ 310

Wyatt; Inc. Place; MISSISSIPPI; **197** K-20; elev. 315ft./96m.; 🄿; z 63882; Ⓟ 376; Ⓒ 364

Wyatt Park; RMC Place; BUCHANAN; ***196** C-8; ★ **ST.JO**; mail Saint Joseph z 64507; pop. incl. with Saint Joseph (Inc. Place)

Wyeth; RMC Place; ANDREW; ***196** C-8; mail Rosendale z 64483; rural

Y

Yancy Mills; RMC Place; PHELPS; ***197** I-15; mail Rolla z 65401; rural

Yarrow; RMC Place; ADAIR; ***197** C-13; mail Kirksville z 63501; rural

Yates; RMC Place; RANDOLPH; ***197** E-13; mail Higbee z 65257; ● 50

Yonkerville; RMC Place; BARRY; ***196** K-10; elev. 1,300ft./396m.; mail Pierce City z 65723; rural

Youngstown; RMC Place; ADAIR; ***197** B-13; mail Novinger z 63559

Yount; RMC Place; PERRY; ***197** I-19; elev. 632ft./193m.; mail Perryville z 63775; rural

Yukon; RMC Place; TEXAS; **197** J-15; elev. 1,316ft./401m.; 🄿; z 65589; ● 60

Z

Zalma; Inc. Place; BOLLINGER; **197** K-19; elev. 380ft./116m.; 🄿; z 63787; Ⓟ 83; Ⓒ 93

Zanoni; RMC Place; OZARK; **197** L-14; elev. 700ft./213m.; 🄿; z 65784; rural

Zell; RMC Place; STE. GENEVIEVE; ***197** H-18; elev. 614ft./187m.; mail Sainte Genevieve z 63670; ● 130

Zion; RMC Place; MADISON; ***197** J-18; mail Fredericktown z 63645; ● 30

Zora; RMC Place; BENTON; ***197** H-12; mail Stover z 65078; rural

---

Entries in **UPPERCASE** are counties.
Entries in **bold** have populations of 2,500 or more.
Names in parentheses are alternate names.

Inc. Place	Incorporated Place
RMC Place	Rand McNally Designated Place
CDP	Census Designated Place
MCD	Minor Civil Division

⊡ County Seat
▲ Minor Civil Division
elev. Elevation
🄿 Post Office

🄷 Hospital
🄲 College
■ Principal Business Center
★ Ranally Metro Area (RMA) Abbreviation
z Zip Code(s)

Ⓟ Previous Census Population
Ⓡ Revised Census Population
Ⓐ Annexation Population
● Rand McNally Population Estimate
Ⓒ Final Census Population
Ⓢ Special Census Population
◆ Estimated Population

For additional definitions see Glossary, Volume 1, and Introduction, Volume 2.

MONTANA

CANADA
ND
Helena
ID
SD
WY

Statistics

Total area (2000) — 147,042 square miles
Land area (2000) — 145,552 square miles
Water area (2000) — 1,490 square miles
Capital — Helena
Admitted as state — November, 1889

Ranally Metro Areas (RMAs) and Abbreviations

Billings, MT — BIL
Butte, MT — BUT
Great Falls, MT — GTFA
Missoula, MT — MSLA

Maps

State maps can be found on pages 142-254 in Vol. 1

Principal Places

Place Name	Place Type	County	Population
Billings	Inc. Place	YELLOWSTONE	◆ 99,694
Missoula	Inc. Place	MISSOULA	◆ 64,504
Great Falls	Inc. Place	CASCADE	◆ 59,233
Bozeman	Inc. Place	GALLATIN	◆ 45,443
Butte	Inc. Place	SILVER BOW	◆ 31,600
Helena	Inc. Place	LEWIS AND CLARK	◆ 28,042
Kalispell	Inc. Place	FLATHEAD	◆ 18,503
Anaconda	Inc. Place	DEER LODGE	© 9,417

Place Name	Place Type	County	Population
Havre	Inc. Place	HILL	◆ 9,022
Miles City	Inc. Place	CUSTER	© 8,487
Helena Valley Southeast	CDP-Census Area Only	LEWIS AND CLARK	© 7,141
Helena Valley West Central	CDP-Census Area Only	LEWIS AND CLARK	© 6,983
Livingston	Inc. Place	PARK	© 6,851
Laurel	Inc. Place	YELLOWSTONE	© 6,255
Evergreen	CDP	FLATHEAD	© 6,215
Billings Heights	RMC Place	YELLOWSTONE	● 6,000

Place Name	Place Type	County	Population
Lewistown	Inc. Place	FERGUS	© 5,813
Belgrade	Inc. Place	GALLATIN	© 5,728
Orchard Homes	CDP	MISSOULA	© 5,199
Whitefish	Inc. Place	FLATHEAD	© 5,032

County Business Data

County	FIPS Code	County Seat	Land Area (Sq. Mi.)	Census Population			Wholesale Trade		Manufacturing, 2002			
				4/1/2000	4/1/1990	% Change 1990-2000	Sales, 2002 ($1,000)	% Change 1997-2002	Establish-ments	Total Employees	Value Added ($1,000)	Ranally Mfg. Units
Beaverhead	001	Dillon	5,542	9,202	8,424	9.2	25,735	57.6	...	(d)	(d)	...
Big Horn	003	Hardin	4,995	12,671	11,337	11.8	12,032	(d)	...	(d)	(d)	...
Blaine	005	Chinook	4,226	7,009	6,728	4.2	24,703	-57.6	...	(d)	(d)	...
Broadwater	007	Townsend	1,191	4,385	3,318	32.2	13,957	-62.3	...	(d)	(d)	...
Carbon	009	Red Lodge	2,048	9,552	8,080	18.2	(d)	(d)	...	(d)	(d)	...
Carter	011	Ekalaka	3,340	1,360	1,503	-9.5	(d)	(d)	...	(d)	(d)	...
Cascade	013	Great Falls	2,698	80,357	77,691	3.4	906,765	-18.7	76	808	84,296	45
Chouteau	015	Fort Benton	3,973	5,970	5,452	9.5	29,767	-72.6	...	(d)	(d)	...
Custer	017	Miles City	3,783	11,696	11,697	-0.0	81,951	-13.1	...	(d)	(d)	...
Daniels	019	Scobey	1,426	2,017	2,266	-11.0	6,477	-72.6	...	(d)	(d)	...
Dawson	021	Glendive	2,373	9,059	9,505	-4.7	61,621	55.2	...	(d)	(d)	...
Deer Lodge	023	Anaconda	737	9,417	10,278	-8.4	(d)	(d)	...	(d)	(d)	...
Fallon	025	Baker	1,620	2,837	3,103	-8.6	17,745	17.2	...	(d)	(d)	...
Fergus	027	Lewistown	4,339	11,893	12,083	-1.6	257,294	37.0	...	(d)	(d)	...
Flathead	029	Kalispell	5,098	74,471	59,218	25.8	488,523	40.7	153	3,287	267,563	142
Gallatin	031	Bozeman	2,606	67,831	50,463	34.4	454,938	-4.5	165	2,353	183,790	97
Garfield	033	Jordan	4,668	1,279	1,589	-19.5	(d)	(d)	...	(d)	(d)	...
Glacier	035	Cut Bank	2,995	13,247	12,121	9.3	34,361	-52.4	...	(d)	(d)	...
Golden Valley	037	Ryegate	1,175	1,042	912	14.3	(d)	(d)	...	(d)	(d)	...
Granite	039	Philipsburg	1,727	2,830	2,548	11.1	(d)	(d)	...	(d)	(d)	...
Hill	041	Havre	2,896	16,673	17,654	-5.6	104,611	-28.0	...	(d)	(d)	...
Jefferson	043	Boulder	1,657	10,049	7,939	26.6	7,915	15.0	...	(d)	(d)	...
Judith Basin	045	Stanford	1,870	2,329	2,282	2.1	11,223	(d)	...	(d)	(d)	...
Lake	047	Polson	1,494	26,507	21,041	26.0	7,155	-79.0	42	778	68,398	36
Lewis and Clark	049	Helena	3,461	55,716	47,495	17.3	264,196	21.7	...	(d)	(d)	...
Liberty	051	Chester	1,430	2,158	2,295	-6.0	(d)	(d)	...	(d)	(d)	...
Lincoln	053	Libby	3,613	18,837	17,481	7.8	7,030	44.0	27	601	34,796	18
Madison	057	Virginia City	3,587	6,851	5,989	14.4	(d)	(d)	...	(d)	(d)	...
McCone	055	Circle	2,643	1,977	2,276	-13.1	(d)	(d)	...	(d)	(d)	...
Meagher	059	White Sulphur Springs	2,392	1,932	1,819	6.2	(d)	(d)	...	(d)	(d)	...
Mineral	061	Superior	1,220	3,884	3,315	17.2	(d)	(d)	...	(d)	(d)	...
Missoula	063	Missoula	2,598	95,802	78,687	21.8	715,323	-7.8	116	2,536	245,709	130
Musselshell	065	Roundup	1,867	4,497	4,106	9.5	10,174	30.0	...	(d)	(d)	...
Park	067	Livingston	2,802	15,694	14,562	7.8	23,798	-29.8	...	(d)	(d)	...
Petroleum	069	Winnett	1,654	493	519	-5.0	(d)	(d)	...	(d)	(d)	...
Phillips	071	Malta	5,140	4,601	5,163	-10.9	43,716	178.4	...	(d)	(d)	...
Pondera	073	Conrad	1,625	6,424	6,433	-0.1	36,015	-34.8	...	(d)	(d)	...
Powder River	075	Broadus	3,297	1,858	2,090	-11.1	(d)	(d)	...	(d)	(d)	...
Powell	077	Deer Lodge	2,326	7,180	6,620	8.5	(d)	(d)	...	(d)	(d)	...
Prairie	079	Terry	1,737	1,199	1,383	-13.3	(d)	(d)	...	(d)	(d)	...
Ravalli	081	Hamilton	2,394	36,070	25,010	44.2	134,121	-19.4	91	968	64,174	34
Richland	083	Sidney	2,084	9,667	10,716	-9.8	252,710	33.9	...	(d)	(d)	...
Roosevelt	085	Wolf Point	2,356	10,620	10,999	-3.4	55,299	-3.8	...	(d)	(d)	...
Rosebud	087	Forsyth	5,012	9,383	10,505	-10.7	(d)	(d)	...	(d)	(d)	...
Sanders	089	Thompson Falls	2,762	10,227	8,669	18.0	26,118	-59.8	...	(d)	(d)	...
Sheridan	091	Plentywood	1,677	4,105	4,732	-13.3	22,735	-48.4	...	(d)	(d)	...
Silver Bow	093	Butte	718	34,606	33,941	2.0	136,324	-29.0	...	(d)	(d)	...
Stillwater	095	Columbus	1,795	8,195	6,536	25.4	12,491	105.6	...	(d)	(d)	...
Sweet Grass	097	Big Timber	1,855	3,609	3,154	14.4	3,515	(d)	...	(d)	(d)	...
Teton	099	Choteau	2,273	6,445	6,271	2.8	9,470	-69.6	...	(d)	(d)	...
Toole	101	Shelby	1,911	5,267	5,046	4.4	69,269	-3.1	...	(d)	(d)	...
Treasure	103	Hysham	979	861	874	-1.5	(d)	(d)	...	(d)	(d)	...
Valley	105	Glasgow	4,921	7,675	8,239	-6.8	69,884	-1.8	...	(d)	(d)	...
Wheatland	107	Harlowton	1,423	2,259	2,246	0.6	5,459	43.2	...	(d)	(d)	...
Wibaux	109	Wibaux	889	1,068	1,191	-10.3	(d)	(d)	...	(d)	(d)	...
Yellowstone	111	Billings	2,635	129,352	113,471	14.0	(d)	(d)	179	3,289	420,070	222
The State			**145,552**	**902,195**	**799,065**	**12.9**	**7,223,420**	**-4.9**	**1,234**	**18,582**	**1,673,980**	**886**

(d) Data not available. Corresponding percentages or Ranally Manufacturing Units are estimates.
... Represents 0 or amount too minimal to be reported.

Index of Places and Counties

A

Absarokee; CDP; STILLWATER; **199** I-11; elev. 4,029ft./1,228m.; 🅿; z 59001; Ⓟ 1,067; © 1,234
Acton; RMC Place; YELLOWSTONE; **199** I-12; elev. 3,800ft./1,158m.; 🅿; z 59002; ● 60
Agawam; RMC Place; TETON; ***198** D-7; mail Choteau z 59422
Agency; CDP-Census Area Only; HILL; ***199** C-11; © 324
Agency; RMC Place; SANDERS; **198** E-3; located on Flathead Ind. Res.; elev. 2,540ft./774m.; mail Dixon z 59831; ● 100
Alberton; Inc. Place; MINERAL; **198** F-3; elev. 3,140ft./957m.; 🅿; z 59820; Ⓟ 354; © 374
Albion; RMC Place; CARTER; ***199** J-20; mail Alzada z 59311; rural
Alder; CDP; MADISON; **198** J-7; elev. 5,108ft./1,557m.; 🅿; z 59710; © 116
Alhambra; RMC Place; JEFFERSON; ***198** G-7; elev. 4,265ft./1,300m.; mail Clancy z 59634
Alpine; RMC Place; CARBON; ***199** J-11; elev. 6,219ft./1,896m.; mail Roscoe z 59071; summer pop. 200; ● 2
Alzada; RMC Place; CARTER; **199** J-20; elev. 3,622ft./1,104m.; 🅿; z 59311; ● 30
Amazon; RMC Place; JEFFERSON; ***198** H-7; elev. 5,464ft./1,665m.; mail Boulder z 59632; rural
Amsterdam; RMC Place; GALLATIN; **198** I-8; mail Manhattan z 59741; ● 100
Amsterdam-Churchill; CDP-Census Area Only; GALLATIN; ***198** I-8; © 727
Anaconda (Anaconda-Deer Lodge County); Inc. Place; ⊡ DEER LODGE; **198** H-6; elev. 5,265ft./1,605m.; 🅿 🅷; z 59711; Ⓟ 10,278; © 9,417
Anaconda-Deer Lodge County; DEER LODGE; see Anaconda (Inc. Place)
Anceney; RMC Place; GALLATIN; ***198** I-8; mail Manhattan z 59741; rural
Andes; RMC Place; RICHLAND; ***199** D-19; mail Culbertson z 59218; rural
Angela; RMC Place; ROSEBUD; **199** F-16; elev. 2,919ft./890m.; 🅿; z 59312; ● 10
Antelope; CDP; SHERIDAN; **199** B-19; elev. 2,042ft./622m.; 🅿; z 59211; © 43
Apgar; RMC Place; FLATHEAD; ***198** B-4; mail West Glacier z 59936; summer pop. 100; ● 2
Argenta; RMC Place; BEAVERHEAD; ***198** J-6; mail Dillon z 59725
Arlee; CDP; LAKE; **198** E-4; located on Flathead Ind. Res.; elev. 3,080ft./939m.; 🅿; z 59821; Ⓟ 484; © 602
Armington; RMC Place; CASCADE; **198** E-9; elev. 3,562ft./1,086m.; mail Belt z 59412; ● 75
Ashland; CDP; ROSEBUD; **199** I-16; elev. 2,940ft./896m.; 🅿; z 59003-04; Ⓟ 484; © 464
Ashuelot; RMC Place; CASCADE; ***198** E-7; mail Fort Shaw z 59443; ● 40
Augusta; CDP; LEWIS AND CLARK; **198** E-6; elev. 4,067ft./1,240m.; 🅿; z 59410; © 284
Avon; CDP; POWELL; **198** G-6; elev. 4,706ft./1,434m.; 🅿; z 59713; © 124
Azure; CDP-Census Area Only; HILL; ***199** C-11; © 253

B

Babb; RMC Place; GLACIER; **198** B-5; located on Blackfeet Ind. Res.; elev. 4,520ft./1,378m.; 🅿; z 59411; ● 45
Bainville; Inc. Place; ROOSEVELT; **199** C-19; elev. 1,962ft./598m.; 🅿; z 59212; Ⓟ 165; © 153
Baker; Inc. Place; ⊡ FALLON; **199** G-20; elev. 2,929ft./893m.; 🅿 🅷; z 59313 & mail Willard z 59354; Ⓟ 1,818; © 1,695
Ballantine; CDP; YELLOWSTONE; **199** H-13; elev. 3,004ft./916m.; 🅿; z 59006; © 346
Bannack; RMC Place; BEAVERHEAD; **198** J-5; mail Dillon z 59725; ● 25
Basin; CDP; JEFFERSON; **198** H-7; elev. 6,355ft./1,937m.; 🅿; z 59631; © 255
Bearcreek; Inc. Place; CARBON; **199** J-12; elev. 4,578ft./1,395m.; 🅿; z 59007; Ⓟ 37; © 83
Bearmouth; RMC Place; GRANITE; ***198** G-5; mail Drummond z 59832; rural
Bear Spring; RMC Place; FERGUS; mail Denton z 59430; rural
Beaver Creek; CDP-Census Area Only; HILL; ***199** B-11; © 291
BEAVERHEAD; **198** K-6; Ⓟ 8,424; © 9,202; ◆ 8,686
Beaverton; RMC Place; VALLEY; ***199** C-15; mail Saco z 59261; rural
Beehive; RMC Place; STILLWATER; ***199** J-11; mail Nye z 59061; rural
Belfry; CDP; CARBON; **199** J-12; elev. 3,862ft./1,177m.; 🅿; z 59008; © 219
Belgrade; Inc. Place; GALLATIN; **198** I-8; elev. 4,454ft./1,358m.; 🅿; z 59714; Ⓟ 3,411; © 5,728
Belknap; RMC Place; SANDERS; ***198** D-2; elev. 2,392ft./729m.; mail Trout Creek z 59874
Bell Crossing; RMC Place; RAVALLI; ***198** G-4; mail Stevensville z 59870; rural
Belle Creek; RMC Place; POWDER RIVER; **199** J-18; elev. 3,560ft./1,085m.; mail Broadus z 59317; ● 20
Belmont; RMC Place; GOLDEN VALLEY; ***199** H-12; mail Lavina z 59046; rural
Belt; Inc. Place; CASCADE; **198** E-9; elev. 3,571ft./1,088m.; 🅿; z 59412; Ⓟ 571; © 633
Belton; FLATHEAD; see West Glacier (RMC Place)
Benchland; RMC Place; JUDITH BASIN; **198** F-10; mail Moccasin z 59462; ● 10
Benteen; RMC Place; BIG HORN; ***199** J-15; mail Garryowen z 59031; ● 30
Biddle; RMC Place; POWDER RIVER; **199** J-18; elev. 3,318ft./1,011m.; 🅿; z 59314; ● 15
Big Arm; CDP; LAKE; **198** D-4; located on Flathead Ind. Res.; elev. 2,944ft./897m.; 🅿; z 59910; © 131
Bigfork; CDP; FLATHEAD; **198** C-4; elev. 2,968ft./905m.; 🅿; z 59911; © 1,421
Bighorn; RMC Place; TREASURE; **199** H-14; elev. 2,695ft./821m.; 🅿; z 59010; ● 15
BIG HORN; **199** J-13; Ⓟ 11,337; © 12,671; ◆ 12,721
Big Sandy; Inc. Place; CHOUTEAU; **198** C-10; elev. 2,712ft./827m.; 🅿 🅷; z 59520; Ⓟ 740; © 703
Big Sky; CDP-Census Area Only; GALLATIN; **198** J-8; elev. 5,934ft./1,809m.; 🅿; z 59716; © 1,221
Big Timber; Inc. Place; ⊡ SWEET GRASS; **198** I-10; elev. 4,081ft./1,244m.; 🅿 🅷; z 59011; Ⓟ 1,557; © 1,650
Billings; Inc. Place; ⊡ YELLOWSTONE; **199** I-13; elev. 3,124ft./952m.; 🅿 🅷 🅲 5,697 ■; ★ **BIL**; z 59101-08, z 59111-12, z 59114-17; Ⓟ 81,151; © 89,847; ◆ 99,694
Billings Heights; RMC Place; YELLOWSTONE; **199** M-19; elev. 3,181ft./970m.; ★ **BIL**; mail Billings z 59105; ● 6,000
Birch Creek Colony; RMC Place; PONDERA; ***198** C-6; mail Valier z 59486; ● 50
Birney; CDP; ROSEBUD; **199** J-16; elev. 3,159ft./963m.; 🅿; z 59012; © 108
Black Eagle; CDP; CASCADE; **198** E-8; elev. 3,400ft./1,036m.; 🅿; ★ **GTFA**; z 59414; © 914
Blackfeet Reservation; Indian Reservation; GLACIER, PONDERA; mail Browning z 59417; also location of Indian Agency; Ⓟ 6,660; © 10,100
Blackfoot; RMC Place; GLACIER; **198** B-6; located on Blackfeet Ind. Res.; elev. 4,160ft./1,268m.; mail Browning z 59417; ● 80
BLAINE; **199** C-12; Ⓟ 6,728; © 7,009; ◆ 6,345
Bloomfield; RMC Place; DAWSON; ***199** E-18; elev. 2,615ft./797m.; 🅿; z 59315; ● 15
Blossburg; RMC Place; POWELL; ***198** G-7; mail Elliston z 59728; rural
Boneau; CDP-Census Area Only; CHOUTEAU; ***199** C-11; © 190
Bonner; RMC Place; MISSOULA; **198** F-4; elev. 3,296ft./1,005m.; 🅿; z 59823; ● 200
Bonner-West Riverside; CDP-Census Area Only; MISSOULA; ***198** F-4; mail Bonner z 59823, Missoula z 59802; Ⓟ 1,669; © 1,693
Boulder; Inc. Place; ⊡ JEFFERSON; **198** H-7; elev. 4,904ft./1,495m.; 🅿; z 59632; Ⓟ 1,316; © 1,300
Box Elder; CDP; HILL; **198** C-10; elev. 2,680ft./817m.; 🅿; z 59521; location of Rocky Boys Indian Agency; © 794
Boyd; RMC Place; CARBON; **199** J-12; elev. 4,033ft./1,229m.; 🅿; z 59013; ● 200
Boyes; RMC Place; CARTER; **199** J-18; elev. 3,400ft./1,036m.; 🅿; z 59316; ● 25
Bozeman; Inc. Place; ⊡ GALLATIN; **198** I-9; elev. 4,810ft./1,466m.; 🅿 🅷 🅲 16,274 ■; z 59715, z 59717-19, z 59771-72; Ⓟ 22,660; © 27,509; ◆ 45,443
Bozeman Hot Springs; RMC Place; GALLATIN; **198** I-8; mail Bozeman z 59715; ● 75
Brady; RMC Place; PONDERA; **198** D-7; elev. 3,530ft./1,076m.; 🅿; z 59416; ● 150
Brandon; RMC Place; MADISON; ***198** J-7; elev. 5,609ft./1,710m.; mail Sheridan z 59749
Bridger; Inc. Place; CARBON; **199** J-12; elev. 3,680ft./1,122m.; 🅿; z 59014; Ⓟ 692; © 745
Bridger; RMC Place; GALLATIN; mail Bozeman z 59772; pop. incl. with Bozeman (Inc. Place)
Broadus; Inc. Place; ⊡ POWDER RIVER; **199** I-18; elev. 3,029ft./923m.; 🅿; z 59317; Ⓟ 572; © 451
Broadview; Inc. Place; YELLOWSTONE; **199** H-12; elev. 3,800ft./1,158m.; 🅿; z 59015; Ⓟ 133; © 150
BROADWATER; **198** G-8; Ⓟ 3,318; © 4,385; ◆ 4,673
Brock Creek; RMC Place; POWELL; ***198** G-6; mail Garrison z 59731
Brockton; Inc. Place; ROOSEVELT; **199** C-18; located on Fort Peck Ind. Res.; elev. 1,959ft./597m.; 🅿; z 59213; Ⓟ 365; © 245
Brockway; RMC Place; MCCONE; **199** E-17; elev. 2,593ft./790m.; 🅿; z 59214; ● 35
Brooks; RMC Place; FERGUS; ***199** F-11; mail Lewistown z 59457
Brown; RMC Place; DEER LODGE; mail Anaconda z 59711; pop. incl. with Anaconda (Inc. Place)
Brown Addition; RMC Place; CASCADE; ***198** E-8; mail Sand Coulee z 59472; ● 30
Browning; Inc. Place; GLACIER; **198** B-6; located on Blackfeet Ind. Res.; elev. 4,362ft./1,330m.; 🅿 🅷; z 59417; location of Indian Agency; Ⓟ 1,170; © 1,065
Brusett; RMC Place; GARFIELD; **199** E-15; elev. 3,000ft./914m.; 🅿; z 59318; ● 5
Buffalo; RMC Place; FERGUS; **199** F-11; elev. 4,311ft./1,314m.; 🅿; z 59418; ● 6
Busby; CDP; BIG HORN; **199** I-15; elev. 3,434ft./1,047m.; 🅿; z 59016; Ⓟ 409; © 695
Butte (Butte-Silver Bow); Inc. Place; ⊡ SILVER BOW; **198** H-6; elev. 5,549ft./1,691m.; 🅿 🅷 🅲 2,357 ■; ★ **BUT**; z 59701-03, z 59707, z 59750; Ⓟ 33,336; © 33,892; ◆ 31,600
Butte-Silver Bow; SILVER BOW; see Butte (Inc. Place)
Buxton; RMC Place; SILVER BOW; ***198** H-6; ★ **BUT**; mail Butte z 59750; pop. incl. with Butte (Inc. Place)
Bynum; RMC Place; TETON; **198** D-7; elev. 3,972ft./1,211m.; 🅿; z 59419; ● 120

C

Camas; RMC Place; SANDERS; ***198** D-3; located on Flathead Ind. Res.; elev. 2,834ft./864m.; mail Hot Springs z 59845
Camas Prairie; RMC Place; SANDERS; ***198** E-3; located on Flathead Ind. Res.; elev. 2,827ft./862m.; mail Plains z 59859; rural
Cameron; RMC Place; MADISON; **198** J-8; elev. 5,400ft./1,646m.; 🅿; z 59720; ● 10
Camp Three; CDP-Census Area Only; MUSSELSHELL; ***199** G-13; © 138
Canyon Creek; RMC Place; LEWIS AND CLARK; **198** F-7; elev. 4,325ft./1,318m.; 🅿; z 59633; ● 250
Canyon Ferry; RMC Place; LEWIS AND CLARK; ***198** G-8; mail Helena z 59601
Capitol; RMC Place; CARTER; **199** I-20; elev. 3,200ft./975m.; 🅿; z 59319 & mail Camp Crook z 57724; ● 5
Capitol; RMC Place; LEWIS AND CLARK; ***198** G-7; mail Helena z 59620; pop. incl. with Helena (Inc. Place)
CARBON; **199** J-12; Ⓟ 8,080; © 9,552; ◆ 9,580
Cardwell; CDP; JEFFERSON; **198** I-7; elev. 4,271ft./1,302m.; 🅿; z 59721; © 40
Carlyle; RMC Place; WIBAUX; **199** F-20; elev. 2,900ft./884m.; mail Wibaux z 59353; rural
Carter; CDP; CHOUTEAU; **198** D-9; elev. 3,109ft./948m.; 🅿; z 59420; © 62
CARTER; **199** I-19; Ⓟ 1,503; © 1,360; ◆ 1,232
Cartersville; RMC Place; ROSEBUD; ***199** H-16; mail Rosebud z 59347
Cascade; Inc. Place; CASCADE; **198** E-8; elev. 3,378ft./1,030m.; 🅿; z 59421; Ⓟ 729; © 819
CASCADE; **198** F-8; Ⓟ 77,691; © 80,357; ◆ 85,309
Castle Rock; RMC Place; ROSEBUD; ***199** I-16; mail Forsyth z 59327; rural
Cat Creek; RMC Place; PETROLEUM; **199** F-13; 🅿; z 59087
Centennial; RMC Place; YELLOWSTONE; mail Billings z 59102, z 59108; pop. incl. with Billings (Inc. Place)
Centerville; RMC Place; CASCADE; **198** E-8; elev. 3,474ft./1,059m.; mail Sand Coulee z 59472; ● 25
Centerville; RMC Place; SILVER BOW; ***198** H-6; ★ **BUT**; mail Butte z 59701; pop. incl. with Butte (Inc. Place)
Central Park; RMC Place; GALLATIN; ***198** I-8; mail Belgrade z 59714
Chapman; RMC Place; PHILLIPS; ***199** B-13; mail Loring z 59537; rural
Charlo; CDP; LAKE; **198** E-4; located on Flathead Ind. Res.; elev. 2,935ft./895m.; 🅿; z 59824; Ⓟ 358; © 439
Charlos Heights; RMC Place; RAVALLI; ***198** H-4; elev. 3,742ft./1,141m.; mail Hamilton z 59840
Checkerboard; RMC Place; MEAGHER; **198** G-9; elev. 5,246ft./1,599m.; mail Martinsdale z 59053; ● 20
Chester; Inc. Place; ⊡ LIBERTY; **198** B-9; elev. 3,132ft./955m.; 🅿 🅷; z 59522; Ⓟ 942; © 871
Chico Hot Springs; RMC Place; PARK; **198** J-9; mail Pray z 59065
Chinook; Inc. Place; ⊡ BLAINE; **199** B-11; elev. 2,438ft./743m.; 🅿; z 59523 & mail Lloyd z 59535; Ⓟ 1,512; © 1,386
Choteau; Inc. Place; ⊡ TETON; **198** D-7; elev. 3,820ft./1,164m.; 🅿 🅷; z 59422; Ⓟ 1,741; © 1,781
CHOUTEAU; **198** C-8; Ⓟ 5,452; © 5,970; ◆ 5,156
Christina; RMC Place; FERGUS; **199** E-11; elev. 3,600ft./1,097m.; mail Hilger z 59451; ● 20
Churchill; RMC Place; GALLATIN; **198** I-8; mail Manhattan z 59741; ● 300
Circle; Inc. Place; ⊡ MCCONE; **199** E-17; elev. 2,450ft./747m.; 🅿 🅷; z 59215; Ⓟ 805; © 644
Clancey; JEFFERSON; see Clancy (CDP)
Clancy (Clancey); CDP; JEFFERSON; ***198** G-7; elev. 4,226ft./1,288m.; 🅿; z 59634; © 1,406
Clinton; CDP; MISSOULA; **198** F-4; elev. 3,478ft./1,060m.; 🅿; z 59825; © 549
Clyde Park; Inc. Place; PARK; **198** I-9; elev. 4,868ft./1,484m.; 🅿; z 59018; Ⓟ 282; © 310
Coalridge; RMC Place; SHERIDAN; ***199** B-19; elev. 2,195ft./669m.; mail Dagmar z 59219; rural
Coalwood; RMC Place; POWDER RIVER; ***199** I-18; elev. 3,345ft./1,020m.; mail Volborg z 59351
Cobden; MINERAL; see Lozeau (RMC Place)
Coffee Creek; RMC Place; FERGUS; **198** E-10; elev. 3,608ft./1,100m.; 🅿; z 59424; ● 65
Cohagen; RMC Place; GARFIELD; **199** F-16; elev. 2,720ft./829m.; 🅿; z 59322; ● 15
Cold Springs; RMC Place; MISSOULA; ***198** F-4; ★ **MSLA**; mail Missoula z 59803; pop. incl. with Missoula (Inc. Place)
Collins; RMC Place; TETON; **198** D-7; mail Dutton z 59433; rural
Colstrip; Inc. Place; ROSEBUD; **199** H-16; elev. 3,232ft./985m.; 🅿; z 59323; Ⓟ 3,035; © 2,346
Columbia Falls; Inc. Place; FLATHEAD; **198** C-4; elev. 3,080ft./939m.; 🅿; z 59912; Ⓟ 2,942; © 3,645
Columbia Heights; RMC Place; FLATHEAD; **198** C-4; mail Columbia Falls z 59912; ● 110
Columbus; Inc. Place; ⊡ STILLWATER; **199** I-12; elev. 3,600ft./1,097m.; 🅿 🅷; z 59019; Ⓟ 1,573; © 1,748
Comanche; RMC Place; YELLOWSTONE; ***199** H-12; mail Broadview z 59015; rural
Condon (Swan Valley); RMC Place; MISSOULA; **198** E-4; elev. 3,713ft./1,132m.; 🅿; z 59826; ● 40
Conner; RMC Place; RAVALLI; **198** H-4; elev. 4,030ft./1,228m.; 🅿; z 59827; ● 35
Conrad; Inc. Place; ⊡ PONDERA; **198** C-7; elev. 3,510ft./1,070m.; 🅿 🅷; z 59425; Ⓟ 2,891; © 2,753
Cooke City; RMC Place; PARK; **198** K-10; elev. 7,651ft./2,332m.; 🅿; z 59020, z 59081; summer pop. 125; ● 70
Cooke City-Silver Gate; CDP-Census Area Only; PARK; ***198** K-10; © 140
Coram; CDP; FLATHEAD; **198** C-4; elev. 3,200ft./975m.; 🅿; z 59913; © 337
Corbin; RMC Place; JEFFERSON; **198** G-7; elev. 4,769ft./1,454m.; mail Jefferson City z 59638
Corvallis; CDP; RAVALLI; **198** G-4; elev. 3,476ft./1,059m.; 🅿; z 59828; © 443
Corwin Springs; RMC Place; PARK; **198** J-9; elev. 5,125ft./1,562m.; mail Gardiner z 59030; ● 40
Crackerville; RMC Place; DEER LODGE; ***198** H-6; mail Anaconda z 59711; pop. incl. with Anaconda (Inc. Place)
Craig; RMC Place; LEWIS AND CLARK; **198** F-7; elev. 3,455ft./1,053m.; 🅿; z 59648; ● 90
Crane; RMC Place; RICHLAND; **199** D-19; elev. 1,950ft./594m.; 🅿; z 59217; ● 75

Entries in **UPPERCASE** are counties.
Entries in **bold** have populations of 2,500 or more.
Names in parentheses are alternate names.
Inc. Place — Incorporated Place
RMC Place — Rand McNally Designated Place
CDP — Census Designated Place
MCD — Minor Civil Division

⊡ County Seat
▲ Minor Civil Division
elev. Elevation
🅿 Post Office

🅷 Hospital
🅲 College
■ Principal Business Center
★ Ranally Metro Area (RMA) Abbreviation
z Zip Code(s)

Ⓟ Previous Census Population
Ⓡ Revised Census Population
Ⓐ Annexation Population
● Rand McNally Population Estimate
© Final Census Population
Ⓢ Special Census Population
◆ Estimated Population

For additional definitions see Glossary, Volume 1, and Introduction, Volume 2.

Creston; RMC Place; FLATHEAD; 198 C-4; elev. 2,954ft./900m.; 🅿; z 59901; ● 70
Crow Agency; CDP; BIG HORN; 199 I-14; located on Crow Ind. Res.; elev. 3,039ft./926m.; 🅿 🅷; z 59022; location of Indian Agency; Ⓟ 1,446; © 1,552
Crow Reservation; Indian Reservation; BIG HORN, YELLOWSTONE; mail Crow Agency z 59022; also location of Indian Agency; Ⓟ 5,973; © 6,894
Culbertson; Inc. Place; ROOSEVELT; 199 C-19; elev. 1,933ft./589m.; 🅿 🅷; z 59218; Ⓟ 796; © 716
Cushman; RMC Place; GOLDEN VALLEY; *199 H-12; mail Lavina z 59046
Custer; CDP; YELLOWSTONE; 199 H-14; elev. 2,735ft./834m.; 🅿; z 59024; © 145
CUSTER; 199 H-17; Ⓟ 11,697; © 11,696; ◆ 11,191
Cut Bank; Inc. Place; ⊡ GLACIER; 198 B-7; elev. 3,760ft./1,146m.; 🅿 🅷; z 59427; Ⓟ 3,329; © 3,105

D

Dagmar; RMC Place; SHERIDAN; 199 B-19; elev. 2,044ft./623m.; 🅿; z 59219; ● 50
DANIELS; 199 A-17; Ⓟ 2,266; © 2,017; ◆ 1,515
Danvers; RMC Place; FERGUS; 199 E-11; elev. 3,554ft./1,083m.; mail Lewistown z 59457; rural
Darby; Inc. Place; RAVALLI; 198 H-4; elev. 3,888ft./1,185m.; 🅿; z 59829; Ⓟ 625; © 710
Dawson; RMC Place; SILVER BOW; ★ **BUT**; mail Ramsay z 59748; pop. incl. with Butte (Inc. Place)
DAWSON; 199 E-18; Ⓟ 9,505; © 9,059; ◆ 8,511
Dayton; CDP; LAKE; 198 D-4; elev. 2,917ft./889m.; 🅿; z 59914; © 95
Dean; RMC Place; STILLWATER; *199 J-11; mail Fishtail z 59028; rural
Dearborn; RMC Place; LEWIS AND CLARK; *198 F-7; mail Wolf Creek z 59648; rural
De Borgia; CDP; MINERAL; 198 E-2; elev. 3,004ft./916m.; 🅿; z 59830; © 69
Decker; RMC Place; BIG HORN; 199 K-15; elev. 3,570ft./1,088m.; 🅿; z 59025; ● 20
Deerfield Colony; RMC Place; FERGUS; *199 E-11; mail Lewistown z 59457; ● 50
Deer Lodge; Inc. Place; ⊡ POWELL; 198 G-6; elev. 4,521ft./1,378m.; 🅿 🅷; z 59722; Ⓟ 3,378; © 3,421
DEER LODGE; 198 H-5; Ⓟ 10,278; © 9,417; ◆ 8,775
Del Bonita; RMC Place; GLACIER; *198 A-6; located on Blackfeet Ind. Res.; mail Cut Bank z 59427; rural
Dell; RMC Place; BEAVERHEAD; 198 K-6; elev. 6,006ft./1,831m.; 🅿; z 59724; ● 25
Delphia; RMC Place; MUSSELSHELL; 199 G-13; elev. 3,050ft./930m.; mail Roundup z 59073; ● 20
Denton; Inc. Place; FERGUS; 198 E-10; elev. 3,603ft./1,098m.; 🅿; z 59430; Ⓟ 350; © 301
Devon; RMC Place; TOOLE; 198 C-8; elev. 3,109ft./948m.; mail Shelby z 59474; ● 4
Dewey; RMC Place; BEAVERHEAD; 198 I-6; mail Divide z 59727; ● 50
Dillon; Inc. Place; ⊡ BEAVERHEAD; 198 J-6; elev. 5,096ft./1,553m.; 🅿 🅷 🅲 1,176; z 59725; Ⓟ 3,991; © 3,752; Ⓡ 4,147
Divide; RMC Place; SILVER BOW; *198 I-6; elev. 5,395ft./1,644m.; 🅿; ★ **BUT**; z 59727; pop. incl. with Butte (Inc. Place)
Dixon; CDP; SANDERS; 198 E-3; located on Flathead Ind. Res.; elev. 2,524ft./769m.; 🅿; z 59831; © 216
Dodson; Inc. Place; PHILLIPS; 199 C-13; elev. 2,290ft./698m.; 🅿; z 59524; Ⓟ 137; © 122
Donald; RMC Place; SILVER BOW; *198 I-6; ★ **BUT**; mail Whitehall z 59759; pop. incl. with Butte (Inc. Place)
Dover; RMC Place; JUDITH BASIN; *198 E-10; mail Stanford z 59479; rural
Dovetail; RMC Place; PETROLEUM; *199 E-13; mail Winnett z 59087; rural
Downtown; RMC Place; YELLOWSTONE; *199 I-13; ★ **BIL**; mail Billings z 59101, z 59103; pop. incl. with Billings (Inc. Place)
Drummond; Inc. Place; GRANITE; 198 G-5; elev. 3,948ft./1,203m.; 🅿; z 59832; Ⓟ 264; © 318
Dunkirk; RMC Place; TOOLE; *198 C-8; mail Shelby z 59474; ● 14
Dupuyer; RMC Place; PONDERA; 198 C-6; elev. 4,122ft./1,256m.; 🅿; z 59432; ● 100
Durant; RMC Place; SILVER BOW; *198 H-6; ★ **BUT**; mail Ramsay z 59748; pop. incl. with Butte (Inc. Place)
Dutton; Inc. Place; TETON; 198 D-8; elev. 3,716ft./1,133m.; 🅿; z 59433; Ⓟ 392; © 389

E

Eagleton; RMC Place; CHOUTEAU; *199 D-11; mail Big Sandy z 59520; rural
East Butte; RMC Place; SILVER BOW; *198 H-6; ★ **BUT**; mail Butte z 59701; pop. incl. with Butte (Inc. Place)
East Glacier Park; GLACIER; see East Glacier Park Village (CDP)
East Glacier Park Village (East Glacier Park, Glacier Park); CDP; GLACIER; 198 C-5; located on Blackfeet Ind. Res.; elev. 4,795ft./1,462m.; mail East Glacier Park z 59434; Ⓟ 326; © 396
East Helena; Inc. Place; LEWIS AND CLARK; 198 G-7; elev. 3,874ft./1,181m.; 🅿; z 59635; Ⓟ 1,538; © 1,642
East Missoula; CDP; MISSOULA; *198 F-4; ★ **MSLA**; mail Missoula z 59801-02; © 2,070
Eaton Addition; RMC Place; CASCADE; *198 E-8; ★ **GTFA**; mail Great Falls z 59405
Eden; RMC Place; CASCADE; *198 E-8; mail Great Falls z 59405; rural
Edgar; RMC Place; CARBON; *199 J-12; elev. 3,462ft./1,055m.; 🅿; z 59026; ● 60
Ekalaka; Inc. Place; ⊡ CARTER; 199 H-19; elev. 3,031ft./924m.; 🅿; z 59324; Ⓟ 439; © 410
Elkhorn Hot Springs; RMC Place; BEAVERHEAD; 198 J-5; mail Polaris z 59746; ● 60
Elliston; CDP; POWELL; 198 G-6; elev. 5,040ft./1,536m.; 🅿; z 59728; © 225
Elmdale; RMC Place; RICHLAND; *199 D-19; mail Brockton z 59213; rural
Elmo; CDP; LAKE; 198 D-3; located on Flathead Ind. Res.; elev. 2,912ft./888m.; 🅿; z 59915; © 143
Emigrant; RMC Place; PARK; 198 J-9; elev. 4,855ft./1,480m.; 🅿; z 59027; ● 60
Enid; RMC Place; RICHLAND; 199 D-19; elev. 2,500ft./762m.; mail Lambert z 59243; rural
Ennis; Inc. Place; MADISON; 198 J-7; elev. 4,939ft./1,505m.; 🅿 🅷; z 59729; Ⓟ 773; © 840
Essex; RMC Place; FLATHEAD; 198 C-5; elev. 3,860ft./1,177m.; 🅿; z 59916; ● 30
Ethridge; RMC Place; TOOLE; 198 B-7; elev. 3,544ft./1,080m.; 🅿; z 59435; ● 15
Eureka; Inc. Place; LINCOLN; 198 A-2; elev. 2,566ft./782m.; 🅿; z 59917; Ⓟ 1,043; © 1,017
Evaro; CDP; MISSOULA; 198 F-4; elev. 3,956ft./1,206m.; mail Missoula z 59801-02; © 329
Evergreen; CDP; FLATHEAD; 198 C-4; elev. 2,920ft./890m.; 🅿; z 59901; Ⓟ 4,109; © 6,215
Everson; RMC Place; FERGUS; *199 E-11; mail Denton z 59430; rural

F

Fairfield; Inc. Place; TETON; 198 E-7; elev. 3,977ft./1,212m.; 🅿; z 59436; Ⓟ 660; © 659
Fairview; Inc. Place; RICHLAND; 199 D-20; elev. 1,902ft./580m.; 🅿; z 59221; Ⓟ 869; © 709
Fallon; CDP; PRAIRIE; 199 F-18; elev. 2,207ft./673m.; 🅿; z 59326, z 59341; © 138
FALLON; 199 H-19; Ⓟ 3,103; © 2,837; ◆ 2,750
Farmington; RMC Place; TETON; 198 D-7; mail Choteau z 59422
Feely; RMC Place; SILVER BOW; *198 I-6; ★ **BUT**; pop. incl. with Butte (Inc. Place)
Ferdig; RMC Place; TOOLE; 198 B-8; elev. 3,516ft./1,072m.; 🅿; z 59466
Fergus; RMC Place; FERGUS; 199 E-12; elev. 3,700ft./1,128m.; mail Hilger z 59451; rural
FERGUS; 199 E-12; Ⓟ 12,083; © 11,893; ◆ 10,958
Finley Point; CDP-Census Area Only; LAKE; *198 D-4; elev. 2,943ft./897m.; mail Polson z 59860; Ⓟ 395; © 493
Fishtail; RMC Place; STILLWATER; 199 J-11; elev. 4,455ft./1,358m.; 🅿; z 59028; ● 85
FLATHEAD; 198 D-5; Ⓟ 59,218; © 74,471; ◆ 88,241
Flathead Reservation; Indian Reservation; LAKE, FLATHEAD, MISSOULA, SANDERS; mail Ronan z 59864; also location of Indian Agency; Ⓟ 19,628; © 26,172
Flatwillow; RMC Place; PETROLEUM; *199 F-13; mail Winnett z 59087; rural
Flaxville; Inc. Place; DANIELS; 199 B-18; elev. 2,800ft./853m.; 🅿; z 59222; Ⓟ 88; © 87
Floral Park; RMC Place; SILVER BOW; *198 H-6; ★ **BUT**; mail Butte z 59701; pop. incl. with Butte (Inc. Place)
Florence; CDP; RAVALLI; 198 G-4; elev. 3,259ft./993m.; 🅿; z 59833; © 901
Floweree; RMC Place; CHOUTEAU; 198 D-9; elev. 3,215ft./980m.; 🅿; z 59440; ● 25
Forestgrove; RMC Place; FERGUS; 199 F-12; elev. 4,111ft./1,253m.; 🅿; z 59441; ● 60
Forest Park; RMC Place; DAWSON; 199 F-19; mail Glendive z 59330; ● 1,000
Forsyth; Inc. Place; ⊡ ROSEBUD; 199 H-16; elev. 2,526ft./770m.; 🅿 🅷; z 59327; Ⓟ 2,178; © 1,944
Fort Belknap; BLAINE; see Fort Belknap Agency (CDP)
Fort Belknap Agency (Fort Belknap); CDP; BLAINE; 199 C-12; located on Fort Belknap Ind. Res.; mail Harlem z 59526; Ⓟ 422; © 1,262
Fort Belknap Reservation; Indian Reservation; PHILIPS, BLAINE; mail Harlem z 59526; Indian Agency located in Harlem, MT; Ⓟ 2,060; © 2,959
Fort Benton; Inc. Place; ⊡ CHOUTEAU; 198 D-9; elev. 2,632ft./802m.; 🅿 🅷; z 59442; Ⓟ 1,660; © 1,594
Fortine; CDP; LINCOLN; 198 B-3; elev. 2,960ft./902m.; 🅿; z 59918; © 169
Fort Keogh; RMC Place; CUSTER; *199 G-17; mail Miles City z 59301; rural
Fort Kipp; RMC Place; ROOSEVELT; *199 C-19; located on Fort Peck Ind. Res.; elev. 1,941ft./592m.; mail Brockton z 59213; ● 40
Fort Peck; Inc. Place; VALLEY; 199 C-16; elev. 2,100ft./640m.; 🅿; z 59223; Ⓟ 325; © 240
Fort Peck Reservation; Indian Reservation; ROOSEVELT, DANIELS, SHERIDAN, VALLEY; mail Poplar z 59255; also location of Indian Agency; Ⓟ 9,921; © 10,321
Fort Shaw; CDP; CASCADE; 198 E-7; elev. 3,518ft./1,072m.; 🅿; z 59443; © 274
Fort Smith (Yellowtail); CDP; BIG HORN; 199 J-14; elev. 3,280ft./1,000m.; 🅿; z 59035; summer pop. 450; © 122
Four Buttes; RMC Place; DANIELS; 199 B-17; elev. 2,488ft./758m.; 🅿; z 59263; ● 20
Four Corners; CDP; GALLATIN; *198 I-8; © 1,828
Four Corners; RMC Place; TOOLE; *198 B-8; elev. 3,922ft./1,195m.; mail Oilmont z 59466; rural
Fox Lake; CDP-Census Area Only; RICHLAND; *199 D-19; © 157
Frazer; CDP; VALLEY; 199 C-17; located on Fort Peck Ind. Res.; elev. 2,060ft./628m.; 🅿; z 59225; Ⓟ 403; © 452
Frenchtown; CDP; MISSOULA; 198 F-3; elev. 3,044ft./928m.; 🅿; z 59834; © 883
Froid; Inc. Place; ROOSEVELT; 199 C-19; elev. 2,026ft./618m.; 🅿; z 59226; Ⓟ 195; © 195
Fromberg; Inc. Place; CARBON; 199 J-12; elev. 3,527ft./1,075m.; 🅿; z 59029; Ⓟ 370; © 486

G

Galata; RMC Place; TOOLE; 198 C-8; elev. 3,100ft./945m.; 🅿; z 59444; ● 25
Galen; RMC Place; DEER LODGE; *198 H-6; elev. 4,733ft./1,443m.; pop. incl. with Anaconda (Inc. Place)
GALLATIN; 198 J-8; Ⓟ 50,463; © 67,831; ◆ 103,096
Gallatin Gateway; RMC Place; GALLATIN; 198 I-8; elev. 4,941ft./1,506m.; 🅿; z 59730; ● 400
Gardiner; CDP; PARK; 198 K-9; elev. 5,314ft./1,620m.; 🅿; z 59030; © 851
GARFIELD; 199 F-15; Ⓟ 1,589; © 1,279; ◆ 1,191
Garland; RMC Place; CUSTER; *199 H-17; mail Miles City z 59301; rural
Garneill; RMC Place; FERGUS; 199 G-11; elev. 4,420ft./1,347m.; 🅿; z 59453; ● 12
Garrison; CDP; POWELL; 198 G-6; elev. 4,360ft./1,329m.; 🅿; z 59731; © 112
Garryowen; RMC Place; BIG HORN; 199 I-15; elev. 3,124ft./952m.; 🅿; z 59031; ● 60
Georgetown; RMC Place; DEER LODGE; *198 H-5; mail Anaconda z 59711; pop. incl. with Anaconda (Inc. Place)
Geraldine; Inc. Place; CHOUTEAU; 198 E-10; elev. 3,135ft./956m.; 🅿; z 59446; Ⓟ 299; © 284
Geyser; RMC Place; JUDITH BASIN; 198 E-9; elev. 4,173ft./1,272m.; 🅿; z 59447; ● 85
Gibson Flats; RMC Place; CASCADE; 199 N-17; mail Great Falls z 59405; ● 100
Gildford; CDP; HILL; 198 B-10; elev. 2,835ft./864m.; 🅿; z 59525; © 185
Gilman; RMC Place; LEWIS AND CLARK; *198 E-6; mail Augusta z 59410; rural
Gilt Edge; RMC Place; FERGUS; *199 F-12; elev. 4,492ft./1,369m.; mail Lewistown z 59457; rural
GLACIER; 198 A-6; Ⓟ 12,121; © 13,247; ◆ 12,987
Glacier Colony; RMC Place; GLACIER; *198 B-7; mail Cut Bank z 59427; rural
Glacier Park; GLACIER; see East Glacier Park Village (CDP)
Glasgow; Inc. Place; ⊡ VALLEY; 199 C-16; elev. 2,090ft./637m.; 🅿 🅷; z 59230-31; Ⓟ 3,572; © 3,253
Glen; RMC Place; BEAVERHEAD; 198 J-6; elev. 4,980ft./1,518m.; 🅿; z 59732; ● 30
Glendive; Inc. Place; ⊡ DAWSON; 199 F-19; elev. 2,078ft./633m.; 🅿 🅷; z 59330; Ⓟ 4,802; © 4,729; Ⓡ 4,878
Glentana; RMC Place; VALLEY; 199 B-16; elev. 3,082ft./939m.; 🅿; z 59240; ● 11
Goldcreek; RMC Place; POWELL; 198 G-6; elev. 4,196ft./1,279m.; 🅿; z 59733; ● 10
GOLDEN VALLEY; 199 G-11; Ⓟ 912; © 1,042; ◆ 1,162
Goldstone; RMC Place; HILL; *198 B-9; elev. 3,024ft./922m.; mail Rudyard z 59540; rural
Gordon (Mount Ellis); RMC Place; GALLATIN; *198 I-9; mail Bozeman z 59715
GRANITE; 198 G-5; Ⓟ 2,548; © 2,830; ◆ 2,723
Grant; RMC Place; BEAVERHEAD; 198 K-5; elev. 5,814ft./1,772m.; mail Dillon z 59725; ● 25
Grantsdale; RMC Place; RAVALLI; 198 H-4; elev. 3,678ft./1,121m.; 🅿; z 59835; ● 175
Grass Range; Inc. Place; FERGUS; 199 F-12; elev. 3,488ft./1,063m.; 🅿; z 59032 & mail Forest Grove z 59441; Ⓟ 159; © 149
Great Falls; Inc. Place; ⊡ CASCADE; 198 E-8; elev. 3,334ft./1,016m.; 🅿 🅷 🅲 778 ■; ★ **GTFA**; z 59401-06; Ⓟ 55,097; © 56,690; ◆ 59,233
Greenfield; RMC Place; TETON; *198 D-7; elev. 3,940ft./1,201m.; mail Fairfield z 59436
Greenough; RMC Place; MISSOULA; 198 F-5; elev. 4,155ft./1,266m.; 🅿; z 59823
Gregson; RMC Place; SILVER BOW; *198 H-6; ★ **BUT**; mail Ramsay z 59748; pop. incl. with Butte (Inc. Place)
Greycliff; CDP; SWEET GRASS; 199 I-11; elev. 3,927ft./1,197m.; 🅿; z 59033; © 56

H

Hackney; RMC Place; SILVER BOW; *198 H-6; elev. 5,140ft./1,567m.; ★ **BUT**; mail Ramsay z 59748; pop. incl. with Butte (Inc. Place)
Halfmoon; RMC Place; FLATHEAD; 198 M-1; mail Columbia Falls z 59912; ● 100
Hall; RMC Place; GRANITE; 198 G-5; elev. 4,198ft./1,280m.; 🅿; z 59837; ● 100
Hamilton; Inc. Place; ⊡ RAVALLI; 198 H-4; elev. 3,572ft./1,089m.; 🅿 🅷; z 59840; Ⓟ 2,737; © 3,705
Hammond; RMC Place; CARTER; 199 J-19; elev. 3,712ft./1,131m.; 🅿; z 59332; ● 15
Hammond Valley; RMC Place; ROSEBUD; *199 H-15; mail Forsyth z 59327; rural
Happy's Inn; RMC Place; LINCOLN; 198 C-2; mail Libby z 59923; ● 50
Happy Valley; RMC Place; FLATHEAD; mail Whitefish z 59937; rural
Hardin; Inc. Place; ⊡ BIG HORN; 199 I-14; elev. 2,902ft./885m.; 🅿 🅷; z 59034; Ⓟ 2,940; © 3,384
Hardy; RMC Place; CASCADE; *198 F-7; mail Cascade z 59421
Harlem; Inc. Place; BLAINE; 199 B-12; elev. 2,371ft./723m.; 🅿 🅷; z 59526; location of Fort Belknap Indian Agency; Ⓟ 882; © 848
Harlowton; Inc. Place; ⊡ WHEATLAND; 199 G-11; elev. 4,167ft./1,270m.; 🅿 🅷; z 59036; Ⓟ 1,049; © 1,062
Harrison; CDP; MADISON; 198 I-7; elev. 4,915ft./1,498m.; 🅿; z 59735; © 162
Hathaway; RMC Place; ROSEBUD; 199 H-16; elev. 2,437ft./743m.; 🅿; z 59333; ● 30
Haugan; RMC Place; MINERAL; 198 E-2; elev. 3,130ft./954m.; 🅿; z 59842; ● 90
Havre; Inc. Place; ⊡ HILL; 199 B-11; elev. 2,494ft./760m.; 🅿 🅷 🅲 1,388 ■; z 59501; Ⓟ 10,201; © 9,621; ◆ 9,022
Havre North; CDP-Census Area Only; HILL; 199 B-11; mail Havre z 59501; Ⓟ 1,110; © 973
Hays; CDP; BLAINE; 199 D-12; located on Fort Belknap Ind. Res.; elev. 3,540ft./1,079m.; 🅿; z 59527; Ⓟ 333; © 702
Heart Butte; CDP; PONDERA; 198 C-6; elev. 4,462ft./1,360m.; 🅿; z 59448; Ⓟ 499; © 698
Heath; RMC Place; FERGUS; *199 F-11; mail Lewistown z 59457; rural
Hedgesville; RMC Place; WHEATLAND; *199 G-11; mail Shawmut z 59078; rural
Helena; Inc. Place; **STATE CAPITAL**; ⊡ LEWIS AND CLARK; 198 G-7; elev. 4,090ft./1,247m.; 🅿 🅷 🅲 1,392 ■; z 59601-02, z 59604, z 59620, z 59623-26; Ⓟ 24,569; © 25,780; ◆ 28,042
Helena Valley Northeast; CDP-Census Area Only; LEWIS AND CLARK; *198 G-7; elev. 3,668ft./1,118m.; mail Helena z 59602; Ⓟ 1,585; © 2,122
Helena Valley Northwest; CDP-Census Area Only; LEWIS AND CLARK; *198 G-7; elev. 3,992ft./1,217m.; mail Helena z 59602; Ⓟ 1,251; © 2,082
Helena Valley Southeast; CDP-Census Area Only; LEWIS AND CLARK; *198 G-7; elev. 3,778ft./1,152m.; mail Helena z 59601; Ⓟ 4,601; © 7,141
Helena Valley West Central; CDP-Census Area Only; LEWIS AND CLARK; *198 G-7; elev. 3,826ft./1,166m.; mail Helena z 59601; Ⓟ 6,327; © 6,983
Helena West Side; CDP-Census Area Only; LEWIS AND CLARK; *198 G-7; elev. 4,600ft./1,402m.; mail Helena z 59601; Ⓟ 1,847; © 1,711
Hellgate; RMC Place; MISSOULA; *198 F-4; ★ **MSLA**; mail Missoula z 59802, z 59808; pop. incl. with Missoula (Inc. Place)
Helmville; RMC Place; POWELL; 198 F-6; elev. 4,306ft./1,312m.; 🅿; z 59843; ● 80
Henderson Heights; RMC Place; CASCADE; *198 E-8; ★ **GTFA**; mail Great Falls z 59404; pop. incl. with Great Falls (Inc. Place)
Heron; CDP; SANDERS; 198 C-1; elev. 2,253ft./687m.; 🅿; z 59844; © 149
Herron; CDP-Census Area Only; HILL; *199 B-11; © 100
Herron Park; RMC Place; HILL; *199 B-11; mail Havre z 59501
Hesper; RMC Place; YELLOWSTONE; *199 I-12; ★ **BIL**; mail Billings z 59102, z 59106
Highwood; CDP; CHOUTEAU; 198 E-9; elev. 3,386ft./1,032m.; 🅿; z 59450; © 189
Hilger; RMC Place; FERGUS; 199 E-11; elev. 4,080ft./1,244m.; 🅿; z 59451; ● 40
HILL; 198 C-10; Ⓟ 17,654; © 16,673; ◆ 16,513
Hillview Heights; RMC Place; MISSOULA; *198 F-4; ★ **MSLA**; mail Missoula z 59803; pop. incl. with Missoula (Inc. Place)
Hingham; Inc. Place; HILL; 198 B-10; elev. 3,032ft./924m.; 🅿; z 59528; Ⓟ 181; © 157
Hinsdale; RMC Place; VALLEY; 199 C-15; elev. 2,180ft./664m.; 🅿; z 59241; ● 250
Hobson; Inc. Place; JUDITH BASIN; 199 F-11; elev. 4,078ft./1,243m.; 🅿; z 59452; Ⓟ 226; © 244
Hodges; RMC Place; DAWSON; *199 F-19; mail Wibaux z 59353; rural
Hogeland; RMC Place; BLAINE; 199 B-12; elev. 3,150ft./960m.; 🅿; z 59529; ● 60
Holter Dam; RMC Place; LEWIS AND CLARK; *198 F-7; mail Wolf Creek z 59648
Homestead; RMC Place; SHERIDAN; 199 B-19; elev. 1,984ft./605m.; 🅿; z 59242; ● 50
Hot Springs; Inc. Place; SANDERS; 198 D-3; elev. 2,829ft./862m.; 🅿; z 59845, z 59848; Ⓟ 411; © 531
Howard; RMC Place; ROSEBUD; *199 H-15; mail Forsyth z 59327
Hughesville; RMC Place; JUDITH BASIN; *198 F-9; mail Monarch z 59463; rural
Hungry Horse; CDP; FLATHEAD; 198 C-4; elev. 3,100ft./945m.; 🅿; z 59919; © 934
Huntley; CDP; YELLOWSTONE; 199 I-13; elev. 3,014ft./919m.; 🅿; z 59037; © 411
Huson; RMC Place; MISSOULA; 198 F-3; elev. 3,015ft./919m.; 🅿; z 59846; ● 75
Hysham; Inc. Place; ⊡ TREASURE; 199 H-15; elev. 2,661ft./811m.; 🅿; z 59038, z 59076; Ⓟ 361; © 330

I

Iliad; RMC Place; CHOUTEAU; *199 D-11; mail Big Sandy z 59520; rural
Ingomar; RMC Place; ROSEBUD; 199 G-15; elev. 3,041ft./927m.; 🅿; z 59039; ● 20
Inverness; CDP; HILL; 198 B-9; elev. 3,306ft./1,008m.; 🅿; z 59530; © 103
Ismay; Inc. Place; CUSTER; 199 G-19; elev. 2,540ft./774m.; 🅿; z 59336; Ⓟ 19; © 26

J

Jackson; RMC Place; BEAVERHEAD; 198 J-5; elev. 6,400ft./1,951m.; 🅿; z 59736; ● 50
Janney; RMC Place; SILVER BOW; *198 I-6; elev. 5,882ft./1,793m.; ★ **BUT**; mail Butte z 59701; pop. incl. with Butte (Inc. Place)
Jardine; RMC Place; PARK; 198 K-9; mail Gardiner z 59030; ● 25
Jeffers; RMC Place; MADISON; 198 J-8; mail Ennis z 59729; ● 80
JEFFERSON; 198 H-7; Ⓟ 7,939; © 10,049; ◆ 11,373
Jefferson City; CDP; JEFFERSON; 198 G-7; elev. 4,558ft./1,389m.; 🅿; z 59638; © 295
Jefferson Island; RMC Place; MADISON; *198 I-7; mail Cardwell z 59721
Jette; CDP-Census Area Only; LAKE; *198 D-4; © 267
Joliet; Inc. Place; CARBON; 199 J-12; elev. 3,740ft./1,140m.; 🅿; z 59041; Ⓟ 522; © 575
Joplin; CDP; LIBERTY; 198 B-9; elev. 3,320ft./1,012m.; 🅿; z 59531; © 210
Jordan; Inc. Place; ⊡ GARFIELD; 199 E-15; elev. 2,598ft./792m.; 🅿; z 59337; Ⓟ 494; © 364
JUDITH BASIN; 198 F-9; Ⓟ 2,282; © 2,329; ◆ 1,849
Judith Gap; Inc. Place; WHEATLAND; 199 G-11; elev. 4,582ft./1,397m.; 🅿; z 59453; Ⓟ 133; © 164

K

Kalispell; Inc. Place; ⊡ FLATHEAD; 198 C-4; elev. 2,955ft./901m.; 🅿 🅷 ■; z 59901, z 59903-04; Ⓟ 11,917; © 14,223; ◆ 18,503
Kerr; CDP-Census Area Only; LAKE; *198 D-4; © 17
Kevin; Inc. Place; TOOLE; 198 B-7; elev. 3,329ft./1,015m.; 🅿; z 59454; Ⓟ 185; © 178
Kicking Horse; CDP-Census Area Only; LAKE; *198 E-4; elev. 3,060ft./933m.; mail Ronan z 59864; Ⓟ 281; © 80
Kila; RMC Place; FLATHEAD; 198 C-3; elev. 3,255ft./992m.; 🅿; z 59920; ● 100
Kingsbury Colony; RMC Place; PONDERA; *198 C-6; mail Valier z 59486; ● 40
Kings Point; CDP-Census Area Only; LAKE; *198 D-4; © 169
Kinsey; RMC Place; CUSTER; 199 G-17; elev. 2,318ft./707m.; 🅿; z 59338; ● 25
Kiowa; RMC Place; GLACIER; *198 B-5; mail Browning z 59417
Kirby; RMC Place; BIG HORN; *199 J-15; elev. 3,874ft./1,181m.; mail Busby z 59016; rural
Klein; CDP; MUSSELSHELL; *199 G-13; mail Roundup z 59072; © 188
Knife River; CDP-Census Area Only; RICHLAND; *199 E-19; © 297
Kolin; RMC Place; JUDITH BASIN; *199 F-11; elev. 3,944ft./1,202m.; mail Hilger z 59451; rural
Kremlin; CDP; HILL; 198 B-10; elev. 2,850ft./869m.; 🅿; z 59532; © 126

L

LAKE; 198 D-3; Ⓟ 21,041; © 26,507; ◆ 28,063
Lake McDonald; RMC Place; FLATHEAD; 198 B-4; elev. 3,225ft./983m.; 🅿; z 59921; summer pop. 150; ● 5
Lakeside; CDP; FLATHEAD; 198 C-4; elev. 2,900ft./884m.; 🅿; z 59922; © 1,679
Lakeview; RMC Place; BEAVERHEAD; 198 L-7; mail Lima z 59739; ● 11
Lambert; RMC Place; RICHLAND; 199 D-19; elev. 2,346ft./715m.; 🅿; z 59243; ● 160
Lame Deer; CDP; ROSEBUD; 199 I-16; located on Northern Cheyenne Ind. Res.; elev. 3,380ft./1,030m.; 🅿; z 59043; location of Indian Agency; Ⓟ 1,918; © 2,018
Landusky; RMC Place; PHILLIPS; 199 D-12; elev. 3,992ft./1,217m.; mail Dodson z 59524
Larslan; RMC Place; VALLEY; 199 B-16; located on Fort Peck Ind. Res.; elev. 3,000ft./914m.; 🅿; z 59244; ● 25
La Salle; RMC Place; FLATHEAD; *198 C-4; mail Columbia Falls z 59912
Last Chance; RMC Place; LEWIS AND CLARK; *198 G-7; mail Helena z 59601; pop. incl. with Helena (Inc. Place)
Laurel; Inc. Place; YELLOWSTONE; 199 I-12; elev. 3,297ft./1,005m.; 🅿; ★ **BIL**; z 59044; Ⓟ 5,686; © 6,255
Laurin; RMC Place; MADISON; 198 J-7; elev. 5,054ft./1,540m.; mail Sheridan z 59749; ● 60
Lavina; Inc. Place; GOLDEN VALLEY; 199 H-12; elev. 3,443ft./1,049m.; 🅿; z 59046; Ⓟ 151; © 209
Lebo; RMC Place; MEAGHER; *198 H-10; mail Martinsdale z 59053; rural
Ledger; RMC Place; PONDERA; 198 C-7; elev. 3,278ft./999m.; 🅿; z 59456; ● 25
Leisure Highlands; RMC Place; MISSOULA; *198 F-4; ★ **MSLA**; mail Missoula z 59803
Lennep; RMC Place; MEAGHER; *198 G-9; mail Martinsdale z 59053; rural
LEWIS AND CLARK; 198 E-6; Ⓟ 47,495; © 55,716; ◆ 61,050
Lewistown; Inc. Place; ⊡ FERGUS; 199 F-11; elev. 3,963ft./1,208m.; 🅿 🅷; z 59457 & mail Forest Grove z 59441; Ⓟ 6,051; © 5,813
Lewistown Heights; CDP-Census Area Only; FERGUS; *199 F-11; © 365
Libby; Inc. Place; ⊡ LINCOLN; 198 B-2; elev. 2,086ft./636m.; 🅿 🅷; z 59923; Ⓟ 2,532; © 2,626
LIBERTY; 198 B-9; Ⓟ 2,295; © 2,158; ◆ 1,690
Lima; Inc. Place; BEAVERHEAD; 198 K-6; elev. 6,256ft./1,907m.; 🅿; z 59739; Ⓟ 265; © 242
Limestone; RMC Place; STILLWATER; *198 J-10; mail Nye z 59061; rural
Lincoln; CDP; LEWIS AND CLARK; 198 F-6; elev. 4,536ft./1,383m.; 🅿; z 59639; © 1,100
LINCOLN; 198 B-2; Ⓟ 17,481; © 18,837; ◆ 18,926
Linda Vista; RMC Place; MISSOULA; *198 F-4; ★ **MSLA**; mail Missoula z 59803; pop. incl. with Missoula (Inc. Place)
Lindsay; RMC Place; DAWSON; 199 E-18; elev. 2,203ft./671m.; 🅿; z 59339; ● 50
Livingston; Inc. Place; ⊡ PARK; 198 I-9; elev. 4,503ft./1,373m.; 🅿 🅷; z 59047; Ⓟ 6,701; © 6,851
Lloyd; RMC Place; BLAINE; 199 C-11; elev. 3,880ft./1,183m.; 🅿; z 59535; ● 8
Lockwood; CDP-Census Area Only; YELLOWSTONE; 199 I-13; ★ **BIL**; mail Billings z 59101; Ⓟ 3,967; © 4,306
Lodge Grass; Inc. Place; BIG HORN; 199 J-15; elev. 3,363ft./1,025m.; 🅿; z 59050; Ⓟ 517; © 510
Lodge Pole; CDP; BLAINE; 199 D-13; located on Fort Belknap Ind. Res.; mail Dodson z 59524; © 214
Logan; RMC Place; GALLATIN; 198 I-8; elev. 4,101ft./1,250m.; mail Manhattan z 59741; ● 125
Lohman; RMC Place; BLAINE; *199 B-11; elev. 2,441ft./744m.; mail Chinook z 59523
Lolo; CDP; MISSOULA; 198 F-4; elev. 3,189ft./972m.; 🅿; ★ **MSLA**; z 59847; Ⓟ 2,746; © 3,388
Lolo Hot Springs; RMC Place; MISSOULA; 198 F-3; mail Lolo z 59847; ● 10
Loma; CDP; CHOUTEAU; 198 D-9; elev. 2,574ft./785m.; 🅿; z 59460; © 92
Lonepine; CDP; SANDERS; 198 D-3; elev. 2,857ft./871m.; 🅿; z 59848; © 137
Loring; RMC Place; PHILLIPS; 199 B-14; elev. 2,800ft./853m.; 🅿; z 59537; ● 11
Lost Creek; RMC Place; DEER LODGE; *198 H-6; elev. 5,438ft./1,658m.; mail Anaconda z 59711; pop. incl. with Anaconda (Inc. Place)
Lothair; RMC Place; LIBERTY; 198 C-8; elev. 3,310ft./1,009m.; 🅿; z 59461, z 59474; ● 15
Lozeau (Cobden); RMC Place; MINERAL; *198 F-3; mail Superior z 59872; rural
Lustre; RMC Place; VALLEY; 199 C-17; located on Fort Peck Ind. Res.; elev. 2,800ft./853m.; 🅿; z 59225; ● 25
Luther; RMC Place; CARBON; 199 J-11; elev. 5,200ft./1,585m.; 🅿; z 59068

M

MADISON; 198 J-7; Ⓟ 5,989; © 6,851; ◆ 7,705
Madoc; RMC Place; DANIELS; 199 B-18; mail Flaxville z 59222; ● 15
Maiden; RMC Place; FERGUS; *199 F-12; elev. 4,814ft./1,467m.; mail Lewistown z 59457
Maiden Rock; RMC Place; SILVER BOW; *198 I-6; ★ **BUT**; mail Melrose z 59743; pop. incl. with Butte (Inc. Place)
Malmstrom AFB; CDP-Census Area Only; CASCADE; *198 E-8; 🅿; ★ **GTFA**; z 59402; Ⓟ 5,938; © 4,544
Malta; Inc. Place; ⊡ PHILLIPS; 199 C-14; elev. 2,255ft./687m.; 🅿 🅷; z 59538; Ⓟ 2,340; © 2,120
Manchester; RMC Place; CASCADE; *198 E-8; elev. 3,353ft./1,022m.; ★ **GTFA**; mail Great Falls z 59404; rural
Manhattan; Inc. Place; GALLATIN; 198 I-8; elev. 4,243ft./1,293m.; 🅿; z 59741; Ⓟ 1,034; © 1,396
Manicke; RMC Place; LINCOLN; *198 C-2; mail Libby z 59923; rural
Many Glacier Hotel; RMC Place; GLACIER; *198 B-5; mail East Glacier Park z 59434; summer pop. 400
Marion; RMC Place; FLATHEAD; 198 C-3; elev. 3,940ft./1,201m.; 🅿; z 59925; ● 80
Marsh; RMC Place; DAWSON; *199 F-18; mail Fallon z 59326
Martin City; CDP; FLATHEAD; 198 C-4; elev. 3,200ft./975m.; 🅿; z 59926; © 331
Martinsdale; RMC Place; MEAGHER; 198 G-10; elev. 4,822ft./1,470m.; 🅿; z 59053; ● 65
Marysville; RMC Place; LEWIS AND CLARK; 198 G-7; elev. 5,366ft./1,636m.; 🅿; z 59640; ● 85
Maudlow; RMC Place; GALLATIN; 198 H-8; elev. 4,385ft./1,337m.; mail Belgrade z 59714; ● 5
Maxville; RMC Place; GRANITE; 198 G-5; elev. 4,828ft./1,472m.; mail Philipsburg z 59858; ● 90
McAllister; RMC Place; MADISON; 198 J-7; elev. 4,905ft./1,495m.; 🅿; z 59740; ● 100
McCabe; RMC Place; ROOSEVELT; 199 C-19; elev. 2,200ft./671m.; 🅿; z 59218; ● 20
McClellans Creek; RMC Place; LEWIS AND CLARK; mail East Helena z 59635; rural
MCCONE; 199 D-17; Ⓟ 2,276; © 1,977; ◆ 1,674
McLeod; RMC Place; SWEET GRASS; 198 I-10; elev. 4,809ft./1,466m.; 🅿; z 59052; ● 7
McQueen; RMC Place; SILVER BOW; *198 H-6; ★ **BUT**; mail Butte z 59701; pop. incl. with Butte (Inc. Place)
MEAGHER; 198 F-8; Ⓟ 1,819; © 1,932; ◆ 1,825
Medicine Lake; Inc. Place; SHERIDAN; 199 B-19; elev. 1,951ft./595m.; 🅿; z 59247; Ⓟ 357; © 269
Melrose; RMC Place; SILVER BOW; *198 I-6; elev. 5,181ft./1,579m.; 🅿; ★ **BUT**; z 59743; pop. incl. with Butte (Inc. Place)
Melstone; Inc. Place; MUSSELSHELL; 199 G-14; elev. 2,910ft./887m.; 🅿; z 59054; Ⓟ 166; © 136
Melville; RMC Place; SWEET GRASS; 198 H-10; elev. 5,000ft./1,524m.; 🅿; z 59055; ● 20
Mildred; RMC Place; PRAIRIE; 199 G-18; elev. 2,400ft./732m.; 🅿; z 59341; ● 30
Miles City; Inc. Place; ⊡ CUSTER; 199 G-17; elev. 2,358ft./719m.; 🅿 🅷; z 59301; Ⓟ 8,461; © 8,487
Milford Colony; RMC Place; LEWIS AND CLARK; 198 E-7; mail Wolf Creek z 59648; ● 130
Mill Creek; RMC Place; DEER LODGE; *198 H-6; mail Anaconda z 59711; pop. incl. with Anaconda (Inc. Place)
Miller Colony; RMC Place; TETON; 198 D-7; mail Choteau z 59422; ● 70
Mill Iron; RMC Place; CARTER; 199 H-20; elev. 3,400ft./1,036m.; 🅿; z 59324; rural
Milltown; RMC Place; MISSOULA; 198 F-4; elev. 3,282ft./1,000m.; 🅿; z 59851; ● 175
Miner; RMC Place; PARK; *198 J-9; mail Emigrant z 59027; rural
MINERAL; 198 F-3; Ⓟ 3,315; © 3,884; ◆ 3,650
Missoula; Inc. Place; ⊡ MISSOULA; 198 F-4; elev. 3,200ft./975m.; 🅿 🅷 🅲 15,251 ■; ★ **MSLA**; z 59801-04, z 59806-08, z 59812; Ⓟ 42,918; © 57,053; ◆ 64,504
MISSOULA; 198 F-4; Ⓟ 78,687; © 95,802; ◆ 112,108
Missoula Southwest; RMC Place; MISSOULA; *198 F-4; ★ **MSLA**; mail Missoula z 59804; pop. incl. with Missoula (Inc. Place)
Mizpah; RMC Place; CUSTER; *199 H-18; mail Miles City z 59301; rural
Moccasin; RMC Place; JUDITH BASIN; 198 F-10; elev. 4,174ft./1,272m.; 🅿; z 59462; ● 35
Moffit Canyon; RMC Place; GALLATIN; *198 I-9; mail Bozeman z 59715; rural
Moiese; RMC Place; LAKE; 198 E-4; located on Flathead Ind. Res.; elev. 2,600ft./792m.; 🅿; z 59824; ● 5
Molt; RMC Place; STILLWATER; 199 I-12; elev. 3,960ft./1,207m.; 🅿; z 59002, z 59057; ● 23
Mona; RMC Place; RICHLAND; *199 C-19; mail Brockton z 59213; rural
Monarch; RMC Place; CASCADE; 198 F-9; elev. 4,560ft./1,390m.; 🅿; z 59463; ● 80
Monida; RMC Place; BEAVERHEAD; *198 L-6; mail Lima z 59739; ● 7
Montague; RMC Place; CHOUTEAU; *198 D-10; mail Fort Benton z 59442; ● 15
Montana City; CDP; JEFFERSON; *198 G-7; elev. 4,040ft./1,231m.; 🅿; z 59634; © 2,094
Moore; Inc. Place; FERGUS; 199 F-11; elev. 4,171ft./1,271m.; 🅿; z 59464; Ⓟ 211; © 186
Morgan; RMC Place; PHILLIPS; *199 A-14; mail Loring z 59537; ● 3
Mosby; RMC Place; GARFIELD; 199 F-14; elev. 2,510ft./765m.; 🅿; z 59058; ● 15
Moulton; RMC Place; FERGUS; *199 E-11; mail Hilger z 59451; rural
Mountain View; RMC Place; GALLATIN; *198 I-8; mail Bozeman z 59718; ● 250
Mount Ellis; GALLATIN; see Gordon (RMC Place)
Muddy; CDP; BIG HORN; *199 I-16; elev. 3,474ft./1,059m.; mail Busby z 59016; Ⓟ 387; © 627
Mullan; RMC Place; MISSOULA; ★ **MSLA**; mail Missoula z 59808; pop. incl. with Missoula (Inc. Place)
Musselshell; CDP; MUSSELSHELL; 199 G-13; elev. 2,994ft./913m.; 🅿; z 59059; © 60
MUSSELSHELL; 199 G-13; Ⓟ 4,106; © 4,497; ◆ 4,422
Myers; RMC Place; TREASURE; *199 H-15; elev. 2,681ft./817m.; mail Hysham z 59038; rural
Mystic Heights; RMC Place; GALLATIN; *198 K-9; mail Bozeman z 59715; ● 175

N

Nashua; Inc. Place; VALLEY; 199 C-16; elev. 2,063ft./629m.; 🅿; z 59248; Ⓟ 375; © 325
Navajo; RMC Place; DANIELS; *199 B-18; mail Flaxville z 59222; rural
Neihart; Inc. Place; CASCADE; 198 F-9; elev. 5,635ft./1,718m.; 🅿; z 59465; Ⓟ 53; © 91
Nevada City; RMC Place; MADISON; *198 J-7; mail Virginia City z 59755; ● 10
New Chicago; RMC Place; GRANITE; *198 G-5; elev. 4,017ft./1,224m.; mail Drummond z 59832
Newcomb; RMC Place; SILVER BOW; *198 H-6; ★ **BUT**; mail Butte z 59701; pop. incl. with Butte (Inc. Place)
New Miami Colony; RMC Place; PONDERA; *198 C-7; mail Conrad z 59425; ● 90
New Rockport Colony; RMC Place; TETON; *198 D-7; mail Choteau z 59422; ● 80
Niarada; CDP; SANDERS, FLATHEAD; 198 D-3; elev. 2,860ft./872m.; 🅿; z 59845; © 50
Nibbe; RMC Place; YELLOWSTONE; *199 H-14; mail Worden z 59088; rural
Nickwall; RMC Place; MCCONE; *199 C-18; mail Wolf Point z 59201; rural
Ninemile; RMC Place; MISSOULA; *198 F-3; elev. 3,020ft./920m.; mail Huson z 59846; rural
Nissler; RMC Place; SILVER BOW; *198 H-6; ★ **BUT**; mail Butte z 59701; pop. incl. with Butte (Inc. Place)
Nohle; RICHLAND; see Nohly (RMC Place)
Nohly (Nohle); RMC Place; RICHLAND; *199 C-20; mail Fairview z 59221; rural
Norris; RMC Place; MADISON; 198 I-8; elev. 4,850ft./1,478m.; 🅿; z 59745; ● 60
North Browning; CDP-Census Area Only; GLACIER; *198 B-6; elev. 4,370ft./1,332m.; mail Browning z 59417; Ⓟ 1,630; © 2,200
Northern Cheyenne Reservation; Indian Reservation; ROSEBUD, BIG HORN; mail Lame Deer z 59043; also location of Indian Agency; Ⓟ 3,664; © 4,470
Northridge Heights; RMC Place; FLATHEAD; *198 C-3; mail Kalispell z 59901; pop. incl. with Kalispell (Inc. Place)
North Riverview Terrace; RMC Place; CASCADE; *198 E-8; ★ **GTFA**; mail Great Falls z 59404; pop. incl. with Great Falls (Inc. Place)
Noxon; CDP; SANDERS; 198 C-1; elev. 2,189ft./667m.; 🅿; z 59853; © 230
Nye; RMC Place; STILLWATER; 199 J-11; elev. 4,845ft./1,477m.; 🅿; z 59061; ● 30

O

Oilmont; RMC Place; TOOLE; 198 B-7; elev. 3,507ft./1,069m.; 🅿; z 59466; ● 35
Old Agency; CDP-Census Area Only; SANDERS; *198 E-3; © 95
Olive; RMC Place; POWDER RIVER; 199 I-18; elev. 3,300ft./1,006m.; 🅿; z 59343; ● 5
Ollie; RMC Place; FALLON; *199 G-20; mail Baker z 59313; rural
Olney; RMC Place; FLATHEAD; 198 B-3; elev. 3,200ft./975m.; 🅿; z 59927; ● 165
Opheim; Inc. Place; VALLEY; 199 B-16; elev. 3,265ft./995m.; 🅿; z 59250; Ⓟ 145; © 111
Opportunity; RMC Place; DEER LODGE; *198 H-6; elev. 4,948ft./1,508m.; mail Anaconda z 59711; pop. incl. with Anaconda (Inc. Place)
Orchard Homes; CDP; MISSOULA; 199 M-12; ★ **MSLA**; mail Missoula z 59801, z 59804; Ⓟ 10,317; © 5,199
Ossette; RMC Place; DANIELS; *199 B-17; mail Richland z 59260; rural
Oswego; RMC Place; VALLEY; 199 C-17; located on Fort Peck Ind. Res.; mail Wolf Point z 59201; ● 30
Otter; RMC Place; POWDER RIVER; 199 J-17; elev. 3,500ft./1,067m.; 🅿; z 59062; ● 5
Outlook; Inc. Place; SHERIDAN; 199 A-18; elev. 2,400ft./732m.; 🅿; z 59252; Ⓟ 109; © 82
Ovando; CDP; POWELL; 198 F-5; elev. 4,100ft./1,250m.; 🅿; z 59854; © 71

P

Pablo; CDP; LAKE; 198 D-4; located on Flathead Ind. Res.; elev. 3,085ft./940m.; 🅿 🅲 1,096; z 59855; location of Indian Agency; Ⓟ 1,298; © 1,814
Painted Hills; RMC Place; GALLATIN; *198 I-9; mail Bozeman z 59715; ● 200
Paradise; CDP; SANDERS; 198 E-3; elev. 2,489ft./759m.; 🅿; z 59856; © 184
PARK; 198 I-9; Ⓟ 14,562; © 15,694; ◆ 16,243
Park City; CDP; STILLWATER; 199 I-12; elev. 3,400ft./1,036m.; 🅿; z 59063; © 870
Parker School; CDP-Census Area Only; HILL, CHOUTEAU; *199 C-11; © 352
Park Grove; RMC Place; VALLEY; *199 C-16; mail Nashua z 59248; ● 50
Peerless; RMC Place; DANIELS; 199 B-17; elev. 2,835ft./864m.; 🅿; z 59253; ● 70
Pendroy; RMC Place; TETON; 198 C-7; elev. 4,275ft./1,303m.; 🅿; z 59467; ● 35
Perma; RMC Place; SANDERS; 198 E-3; located on Flathead Ind. Res.; elev. 2,503ft./763m.; mail Plains z 59859; rural
PETROLEUM; 199 E-13; Ⓟ 519; © 493; ◆ 374
Petrolia; RMC Place; PETROLEUM; mail Winnett z 59087; rural
Philipsburg; Inc. Place; ⊡ GRANITE; 198 G-5; elev. 5,270ft./1,606m.; 🅿 🅷; z 59858; Ⓟ 925; © 914
PHILLIPS; 199 B-13; Ⓟ 5,163; © 4,601; ◆ 3,835
Piegan; RMC Place; GLACIER; *198 C-6; mail Babb z 59411; rural
Piltzville; RMC Place; MISSOULA; 198 F-4; elev. 3,293ft./1,004m.; ★ **MSLA**; mail Bonner z 59823, Missoula z 59802; ● 700
Pine Creek; RMC Place; PARK; *198 I-9; elev. 4,856ft./1,480m.; mail Livingston z 59047
Pinegrove; RMC Place; MISSOULA; *198 F-4; ★ **MSLA**; mail Missoula z 59802; ● 150
Pinesdale; Inc. Place; RAVALLI; 198 G-3; elev. 4,000ft./1,219m.; 🅿; z 59840-41; Ⓟ 670; © 742
Pinnacle; RMC Place; FLATHEAD; *198 C-5; mail Essex z 59916; ● 15
Pioneer; RMC Place; YELLOWSTONE; *199 I-13; ★ **BIL**; mail Billings z 59102, z 59104, z 59106; pop. incl. with Billings (Inc. Place)
Pioneer Junction; RMC Place; LINCOLN; *198 C-2; mail Libby z 59923; ● 40
Plains; Inc. Place; SANDERS; 198 E-3; elev. 2,468ft./752m.; 🅿 🅷; z 59859; Ⓟ 992; © 1,126
Pleasant Prairie; RMC Place; DANIELS; *199 B-18; mail Flaxville z 59222; rural
Plentywood; Inc. Place; ⊡ SHERIDAN; 199 B-19; elev. 2,024ft./617m.; 🅿 🅷; z 59254; Ⓟ 2,136; © 2,061
Plevna; Inc. Place; FALLON; 199 G-19; elev. 2,757ft./840m.; 🅿; z 59344; Ⓟ 140; © 138
Plum Creek; RMC Place; FERGUS; *199 E-11; mail Lewistown z 59457; rural
Polaris; RMC Place; BEAVERHEAD; 198 J-5; elev. 6,355ft./1,937m.; 🅿; z 59746; ● 10
Polebridge; RMC Place; FLATHEAD; 198 B-4; 🅿; z 59928; ● 30
Polson; Inc. Place; ⊡ LAKE; 198 D-4; located on Flathead Ind. Res.; elev. 2,931ft./893m.; 🅿 🅷; z 59860; Ⓟ 3,283; © 4,041
Pompeys Pillar; RMC Place; YELLOWSTONE; 199 H-14; elev. 2,880ft./878m.; 🅿; z 59064; ● 70
PONDERA; 198 C-7; Ⓟ 6,433; © 6,424; ◆ 5,788
Pony; RMC Place; MADISON; 198 I-7; elev. 5,440ft./1,658m.; 🅿; z 59747; ● 150
Poplar; Inc. Place; ROOSEVELT; 199 C-18; located on Fort Peck Ind. Res.; elev. 1,993ft./607m.; 🅿; z 59255; location of Indian Agency; Ⓟ 881; © 911
Portage; RMC Place; CASCADE; *198 D-9; elev. 3,388ft./1,033m.; mail Floweree z 59440
Porters Corner; RMC Place; GRANITE; *198 H-5; elev. 3,882ft./1,183m.; mail Philipsburg z 59858; rural
Post Creek; RMC Place; LAKE; *198 E-4; located on Flathead Ind. Res.; elev. 2,774ft./846m.; mail Saint Ignatius z 59865; rural
Potomac; RMC Place; MISSOULA; 198 F-5; elev. 3,619ft./1,103m.; 🅿; z 59823; ● 30
POWDER RIVER; 199 J-17; Ⓟ 2,090; © 1,858; ◆ 1,598
Powderville; RMC Place; POWDER RIVER; 199 I-18; elev. 2,828ft./862m.; 🅿; z 59345; ● 10
POWELL; 198 G-6; Ⓟ 6,620; © 7,180; ◆ 7,369
Power; CDP; TETON; 198 D-8; elev. 3,682ft./1,122m.; 🅿; z 59468; © 171
PRAIRIE; 199 F-17; Ⓟ 1,383; © 1,199; ◆ 997
Pray; RMC Place; PARK; 198 J-9; elev. 5,000ft./1,524m.; 🅿; z 59065; ● 15
Proctor; RMC Place; LAKE; 198 D-4; elev. 3,160ft./963m.; 🅿; z 59914, z 59929; ● 75
Pryor; CDP; BIG HORN; 199 J-13; elev. 4,065ft./1,239m.; 🅿; z 59066; Ⓟ 654; © 628

Q

Quietus; RMC Place; BIG HORN; *199 J-16; mail Otter z 59062; rural
Quinn; RMC Place; SILVER BOW; *198 I-6; ★ **BUT**; pop. incl. with Butte (Inc. Place)

R

Racetrack; RMC Place; POWELL; *198 H-6; elev. 4,697ft./1,432m.; mail Deer Lodge z 59722; rural
Radersburg; CDP; BROADWATER; 198 H-8; elev. 4,320ft./1,317m.; 🅿; z 59641; © 70
Ramsay; RMC Place; SILVER BOW; *198 H-6; elev. 5,309ft./1,618m.; 🅿; ★ **BUT**; z 59748; pop. incl. with Butte (Inc. Place)
Rapelje; RMC Place; STILLWATER; 199 H-12; elev. 4,077ft./1,243m.; 🅿; z 59067; ● 225
Rattlesnake; RMC Place; MISSOULA; *198 F-4; ★ **MSLA**; mail Missoula z 59808; pop. incl. with Missoula (Inc. Place)
Ravalli; CDP; LAKE; 198 E-4; located on Flathead Ind. Res.; elev. 2,696ft./822m.; 🅿; z 59863; © 119
RAVALLI; 198 H-4; Ⓟ 25,010; © 36,070; ◆ 40,661
Raymond; RMC Place; SHERIDAN; 199 A-19; elev. 2,400ft./732m.; 🅿; z 59256; ● 12
Raynesford; RMC Place; JUDITH BASIN; 198 E-9; elev. 4,063ft./1,238m.; 🅿; z 59469; ● 50
Red Bluff; RMC Place; MADISON; *198 I-8; elev. 4,768ft./1,453m.; mail Norris z 59745; ● 10
Red Lodge; Inc. Place; ⊡ CARBON; 199 J-12; elev. 5,553ft./1,693m.; 🅿 🅷; z 59068; Ⓟ 1,958; © 2,177
Redstone; RMC Place; SHERIDAN; 199 B-18; elev. 2,200ft./671m.; 🅿; z 59257; ● 50
Reed Point; CDP; STILLWATER; 199 I-11; elev. 3,744ft./1,141m.; 🅿; z 59069; © 185
Regina; RMC Place; PHILLIPS; 199 D-14; elev. 2,580ft./786m.; mail Malta z 59538; ● 10
Reserve; CDP; SHERIDAN; 199 B-19; located on Fort Peck Ind. Res.; elev. 1,960ft./597m.; 🅿; z 59258; © 37
Rexford; Inc. Place; LINCOLN; 198 A-2; elev. 2,338ft./713m.; 🅿; z 59930; Ⓟ 132; © 151
Richey; Inc. Place; DAWSON; 199 D-18; elev. 2,500ft./762m.; 🅿; z 59259; Ⓟ 259; © 189
Richland; RMC Place; VALLEY; 199 B-16; elev. 2,790ft./850m.; 🅿; z 59260; ● 60
RICHLAND; 199 D-19; Ⓟ 10,716; © 9,667; ◆ 9,191
Ridge; RMC Place; CARTER; *199 J-19; mail Alzada z 59311; rural
Ridgelawn; RMC Place; RICHLAND; mail Sidney z 59270; ● 25
Ridgeway; RMC Place; CARTER; *199 I-19; mail Hammond z 59332; rural
Rimini; RMC Place; LEWIS AND CLARK; *198 G-7; mail Helena z 59601
Ringling; RMC Place; MEAGHER; 198 H-9; elev. 5,311ft./1,619m.; 🅿; z 59642; ● 60
Rising Sun; RMC Place; GLACIER; *198 B-5; mail East Glacier Park z 59434; summer pop. 250
Riverbend; CDP-Census Area Only; MINERAL; *198 E-3; © 442
Riverside; RMC Place; RAVALLI; *198 H-4; elev. 3,519ft./1,073m.; mail Hamilton z 59840; rural
Rivulet; RMC Place; MINERAL; 198 F-3; elev. 2,915ft./888m.; mail Alberton z 59820; rural
Roberts; RMC Place; CARBON; 199 J-12; elev. 4,580ft./1,396m.; 🅿; z 59070; ● 320
Rocker; RMC Place; SILVER BOW; *198 H-6; ★ **BUT**; mail Butte z 59701; pop. incl. with Butte (Inc. Place)
Rockport Colony; RMC Place; TETON; 198 C-6; mail Pendroy z 59467; ● 50
Rock Springs; RMC Place; ROSEBUD; 199 F-16; elev. 2,958ft./902m.; mail Angela z 59312; ● 20
Rockvale; RMC Place; CARBON; *199 I-12; elev. 3,474ft./1,059m.; mail Joliet z 59041
Rocky Boy; RMC Place; HILL; 199 C-11; located on Rocky Boy's Ind. Res.; mail Box Elder z 59521; ● 170
Rocky Boy's Reservation; Indian Reservation; CHOUTEAU, HILL; mail Box Elder z 59521; also location of Indian Agency; Ⓟ 1,650; © 1,605
Rocky Point; CDP-Census Area Only; LAKE; *198 D-4; © 107
Rollins; CDP; LAKE; 198 D-4; elev. 3,040ft./927m.; 🅿; z 59931; © 183
Ronan; Inc. Place; LAKE; 198 E-4; located on Flathead Ind. Res.; elev. 3,050ft./930m.; 🅿 🅷; z 59864; Ⓟ 1,547; © 1,812
ROOSEVELT; 199 C-18; Ⓟ 10,999; © 10,620; ◆ 9,784
Roosville; RMC Place; LINCOLN; *198 A-2; elev. 2,699ft./823m.; mail Eureka z 59917; ● 3
Roscoe; RMC Place; CARBON; 199 J-11; elev. 4,997ft./1,523m.; 🅿; z 59071; ● 35
Rosebud; RMC Place; ROSEBUD; 199 H-16; elev. 2,485ft./757m.; 🅿; z 59347; ● 120
ROSEBUD; 199 G-16; Ⓟ 10,505; © 9,383; ◆ 9,129
Ross Fork; RMC Place; FERGUS; *199 F-11; elev. 3,794ft./1,156m.; mail Lewistown z 59457; rural
Roundup; Inc. Place; ⊡ MUSSELSHELL; 199 G-13; elev. 3,226ft./983m.; 🅿 🅷; z 59072-73; Ⓟ 1,808; © 1,931
Roy; RMC Place; FERGUS; 199 E-12; elev. 3,500ft./1,067m.; 🅿; z 59471; ● 175
Ruby; RMC Place; MADISON; *198 J-7; elev. 5,171ft./1,576m.; mail Alder z 59710; ● 40
Rudyard; CDP; HILL; 198 B-9; elev. 3,109ft./948m.; 🅿; z 59540; © 275
Ryegate; Inc. Place; ⊡ GOLDEN VALLEY; 199 H-12; elev. 3,641ft./1,110m.; 🅿; z 59074; Ⓟ 260; © 268

S

Saco; Inc. Place; PHILLIPS; 199 C-14; elev. 2,175ft./663m.; 🅿; z 59261; Ⓟ 261; © 224
Saddle Butte; CDP-Census Area Only; HILL; *199 B-11; © 138
Sage Creek Colony; RMC Place; LIBERTY; *198 A-9; mail Chester z 59522; rural
Saint Ignatius; Inc. Place; LAKE; 198 E-4; located on Flathead Ind. Res.; elev. 2,940ft./896m.; 🅿; z 59865; Ⓟ 778; © 788
Saint Labre Mission; RMC Place; ROSEBUD; 199 I-16; mail Ashland z 59004; ● 400
Saint Marie; CDP; VALLEY; 199 C-16; 🅿; z 59230-31; © 183
Saint Mary; RMC Place; GLACIER; 198 B-5; elev. 4,520ft./1,378m.; 🅿; z 59417; ● 20
Saint Peter; RMC Place; CASCADE; *198 E-7; mail Cascade z 59421; rural
Saint Phillip; RMC Place; WIBAUX; *199 F-20; mail Wibaux z 59353; rural
Saint Pierre; CDP-Census Area Only; HILL; *199 C-11; © 289
Saint Regis; CDP; MINERAL; 198 E-2; elev. 2,649ft./807m.; 🅿; z 59866; © 315
Saint Xavier; CDP; BIG HORN; 199 J-14; located on Crow Ind. Res.; elev. 3,074ft./937m.; 🅿; z 59075; © 67
Salmon Prairie; RMC Place; LAKE; *198 D-4; elev. 3,453ft./1,052m.; mail Bigfork z 59911; rural
Saltese; RMC Place; MINERAL; 198 E-2; elev. 3,371ft./1,027m.; 🅿; z 59867; ● 40
Sand Coulee; RMC Place; CASCADE; 198 E-8; elev. 3,465ft./1,056m.; 🅿; z 59472; ● 250
Sand Creek; RMC Place; MCCONE; *199 D-17; mail Wolf Point z 59201; rural
Sanders; RMC Place; TREASURE; 199 H-15; elev. 2,602ft./793m.; 🅿; z 59038, z 59076; ● 20
SANDERS; 198 D-2; Ⓟ 8,669; © 10,227; ◆ 11,096
Sand Springs; RMC Place; GARFIELD; 199 F-14; elev. 3,199ft./975m.; 🅿; z 59077; ● 20
Sangrey; CDP-Census Area Only; HILL; *199 C-11; © 263
Santa Rita; RMC Place; GLACIER; 198 B-7; elev. 3,790ft./1,155m.; 🅿; z 59427; ● 75
Sapphire Village; RMC Place; JUDITH BASIN; *198 F-10; mail Hobson z 59452; ● 50
Savage; RMC Place; RICHLAND; 199 E-19; elev. 1,980ft./604m.; 🅿; z 59262; ● 300
Savoy; RMC Place; BLAINE; *199 C-13; elev. 2,330ft./710m.; mail Harlem z 59526; rural
Scobey; Inc. Place; ⊡ DANIELS; 199 B-17; elev. 2,507ft./764m.; 🅿 🅷; z 59263; Ⓟ 1,154; © 1,082
Sedan; RMC Place; GALLATIN; *198 H-9; mail Wilsall z 59086
Seeley Lake; CDP; MISSOULA; 198 E-5; elev. 4,028ft./1,228m.; 🅿; z 59868; © 1,436
Shawmut; RMC Place; WHEATLAND; 199 H-11; elev. 3,857ft./1,176m.; 🅿; z 59078; ● 130
Shelby; Inc. Place; ⊡ TOOLE; 198 B-7; elev. 3,286ft./1,002m.; 🅿 🅷; z 59474 & mail Lothair z 59461; Ⓟ 2,763; © 3,216
Shepherd; CDP; YELLOWSTONE; 199 H-13; elev. 3,106ft./947m.; 🅿; z 59079; © 193
Sheridan; Inc. Place; MADISON; 198 J-7; elev. 5,100ft./1,554m.; 🅿 🅷; z 59749; Ⓟ 652; © 659
SHERIDAN; 199 A-19; Ⓟ 4,732; © 4,105; ◆ 3,255
Shonkin; RMC Place; CHOUTEAU; 198 E-9; elev. 3,400ft./1,036m.; 🅿; z 59450; rural
Sidney; Inc. Place; ⊡ RICHLAND; 199 D-20; elev. 1,931ft./589m.; 🅿 🅷; z 59270; Ⓟ 5,217; © 4,774
Silesia; RMC Place; CARBON; 199 I-12; elev. 3,390ft./1,033m.; 🅿; z 59041; ● 50
Silver Bow; RMC Place; SILVER BOW; *198 H-6; elev. 5,380ft./1,640m.; ★ **BUT**; mail Butte z 59750; pop. incl. with Butte (Inc. Place)
SILVER BOW; 198 I-6; Ⓟ 33,941; © 34,606; ◆ 32,105
Silver Bow Park; RMC Place; SILVER BOW; *198 H-6; ★ **BUT**; mail Butte z 59701; pop. incl. with Butte (Inc. Place)
Silver Gate; RMC Place; PARK; 198 K-10; elev. 7,389ft./2,252m.; 🅿; z 59081; summer pop. 150; ● 27
Silver Star; RMC Place; MADISON; 198 I-7; elev. 4,520ft./1,378m.; 🅿; z 59751; ● 100
Simms; CDP; CASCADE; 198 E-7; elev. 3,566ft./1,087m.; 🅿; z 59477; © 373
Simpson; RMC Place; HILL; *198 A-10; mail Havre z 59501; rural
Sipple; RMC Place; JUDITH BASIN; *199 F-11; mail Moore z 59464; rural
Sleeping Buffalo; RMC Place; PHILLIPS; *199 B-14; elev. 2,224ft./678m.; mail Saco z 59261; rural
Somers; CDP; FLATHEAD; 198 C-4; elev. 2,910ft./887m.; 🅿; z 59932; © 556
Sonnette; RMC Place; POWDER RIVER; 199 J-17; elev. 3,800ft./1,158m.; 🅿; z 59317; ● 5
Sourdough Creek; RMC Place; GALLATIN; *198 I-9; mail Bozeman z 59715; ● 200
South Browning; CDP-Census Area Only; GLACIER; *198 B-6; elev. 4,400ft./1,341m.; mail Browning z 59417; Ⓟ 1,748; © 1,677
Southern Cross; RMC Place; DEER LODGE; *198 H-5; mail Anaconda z 59711; pop. incl. with Anaconda (Inc. Place)
Spring Creek Colony; RMC Place; FERGUS; *199 F-11; mail Lewistown z 59457; ● 30
Springdale; RMC Place; PARK; 198 I-10; elev. 4,222ft./1,287m.; 🅿; z 59082; ● 30
Springdale Colony; RMC Place; MEAGHER; *198 G-9; mail White Sulphur Springs z 59645; ● 90
Square Butte; RMC Place; CHOUTEAU; *198 E-10; 🅿; z 59446 & mail Fort Benton z 59442; ● 25
Stanford; Inc. Place; ⊡ JUDITH BASIN; 198 F-10; elev. 4,284ft./1,306m.; 🅿; z 59479; Ⓟ 529; © 454
Stark; RMC Place; MISSOULA; *198 F-3; elev. 3,305ft./1,007m.; mail Huson z 59846; rural
Starr School; CDP; GLACIER; *198 B-5; located on Blackfeet Ind. Res.; mail Browning z 59417; Ⓟ 260; © 248
Staton; RMC Place; DEER LODGE; *198 H-6; elev. 5,442ft./1,659m.; pop. incl. with Anaconda (Inc. Place)
Stemple; RMC Place; LEWIS AND CLARK; *198 F-6; mail Lincoln z 59639; rural
Stevensville; Inc. Place; RAVALLI; 198 G-4; elev. 3,370ft./1,027m.; 🅿; z 59870; Ⓟ 1,221; © 1,553
STILLWATER; 199 H-12; Ⓟ 6,536; © 8,195; ◆ 8,805
Stockett; RMC Place; CASCADE; 198 E-8; elev. 3,671ft./1,119m.; 🅿; z 59480; ● 200
Straw; RMC Place; FERGUS; *199 F-11; mail Buffalo z 59418
Stryker; RMC Place; LINCOLN; 198 B-3; elev. 3,290ft./1,003m.; 🅿; z 59933; ● 50
Stump Town; RMC Place; DEER LODGE; *198 H-5; mail Anaconda z 59711; pop. incl. with Anaconda (Inc. Place)
Suffolk; RMC Place; FERGUS; 199 E-11; mail Hilger z 59451; ● 15
Sula; RMC Place; RAVALLI; 198 I-4; elev. 4,422ft./1,348m.; 🅿; z 59871; ● 100
Sumatra; RMC Place; ROSEBUD; 199 G-14; elev. 3,202ft./976m.; 🅿; z 59083; ● 2
Summit; RMC Place; GLACIER; *198 C-5; mail East Glacier Park z 59434; rural
Sunburst; Inc. Place; TOOLE; 198 B-7; elev. 3,348ft./1,020m.; 🅿; z 59482; Ⓟ 437; © 415
Sunnyside; RMC Place; DEER LODGE; *198 H-5; mail Anaconda z 59711; pop. incl. with Anaconda (Inc. Place)
Sun Prairie; CDP-Census Area Only; CASCADE; *198 E-8; elev. 3,350ft./1,021m.; ★ **GTFA**; mail Vaughn z 59487; Ⓟ 1,424; © 1,772
Sun Prairie; RMC Place; PHILLIPS; *199 D-14; mail Malta z 59538
Sun River; CDP; CASCADE; 198 E-8; elev. 3,418ft./1,042m.; 🅿; z 59483; © 131
Sun River Park; RMC Place; CASCADE; *198 E-8; ★ **GTFA**; mail Great Falls z 59404
Sunset; RMC Place; MISSOULA; *198 F-5; mail Bonner z 59823; rural

Entries in **UPPERCASE** are counties.
Entries in **bold** have populations of 2,500 or more.
Names in parentheses are alternate names.
Inc. Place — Incorporated Place
RMC Place — Rand McNally Designated Place
CDP — Census Designated Place
MCD — Minor Civil Division

⊡ County Seat
▲ Minor Civil Division
elev. Elevation
🅿 Post Office

🅷 Hospital
🅲 College
■ Principal Business Center
★ Ranally Metro Area (RMA) Abbreviation
z Zip Code(s)

Ⓟ Previous Census Population
Ⓡ Revised Census Population
Ⓐ Annexation Population
● Rand McNally Population Estimate
© Final Census Population
Ⓢ Special Census Population
◆ Estimated Population

For additional definitions see Glossary, Volume 1, and Introduction, Volume 2.

Superior; Inc. Place; ⊡ MINERAL; **198** E-3; elev. 2,744ft./836m.; 🅿 🅷; **z** 59872; Ⓟ 881; Ⓒ 893

Swan Lake; RMC Place; LAKE; **198** D-4; elev. 3,086ft./941m.; 🅿; **z** 59911; ● 125

Swan Valley; MISSOULA; see Condon (RMC Place)

Sweet Grass; RMC Place; TOOLE; **198** A-7; elev. 3,467ft./1,057m.; 🅿; **z** 59484; ● 125

SWEET GRASS; **199** H-11; Ⓟ 3,154; Ⓒ 3,609; ◆ 3,938

Swiftcurrent; RMC Place; GLACIER; ***198** B-5; mail East Glacier Park **z** 59434; summer pop. 200

T

Tampico; RMC Place; VALLEY; **199** C-15; mail Glasgow **z** 59230; ● 15

Tarkio; RMC Place; MINERAL; ***198** F-3; mail Superior **z** 59872; rural

Teigen; RMC Place; PETROLEUM; **199** F-13; elev. 3,300ft./1,006m.; 🅿; **z** 59084; ● 10

Terry; Inc. Place; ⊡ PRAIRIE; **199** F-18; elev. 2,253ft./687m.; 🅿 🅷; **z** 59349; Ⓟ 659; Ⓒ 611

TETON; **198** D-6; Ⓟ 6,271; Ⓒ 6,445; ◆ 5,887

Thompson Falls; Inc. Place; ⊡ SANDERS; **198** D-2; elev. 2,419ft./737m.; 🅿; **z** 59873; Ⓟ 1,319; Ⓒ 1,321

Three Forks; Inc. Place; GALLATIN; **198** I-8; elev. 4,080ft./1,244m.; 🅿; **z** 59752; Ⓟ 1,203; Ⓒ 1,728

TOOLE; **198** B-8; Ⓟ 5,046; Ⓒ 5,267; ◆ 5,253

Toston; CDP; BROADWATER; **198** H-8; elev. 3,910ft./1,192m.; 🅿; **z** 59643 & mail Radersburg **z** 59641; Ⓒ 105

Townsend; Inc. Place; ⊡ BROADWATER; **198** H-8; elev. 3,848ft./1,173m.; 🅿 🅷; **z** 59644; Ⓟ 1,635; Ⓒ 1,867

Tracy; RMC Place; CASCADE; **198** E-8; elev. 3,426ft./1,044m.; 🅿; **z** 59472; ● 225

TREASURE; **199** H-15; Ⓟ 874; Ⓒ 861; ◆ 583

Trego; RMC Place; LINCOLN; **198** B-3; elev. 3,117ft./950m.; 🅿; **z** 59934; ● 30

Trident; RMC Place; GALLATIN; **198** H-8; elev. 4,036ft./1,230m.; mail Three Forks **z** 59752; ● 15

Trout Creek; CDP; SANDERS; **198** D-1; elev. 2,368ft./722m.; 🅿; **z** 59874; Ⓒ 261

Troy; Inc. Place; LINCOLN; **198** B-1; elev. 1,888ft./575m.; 🅿; **z** 59935; Ⓟ 953; Ⓒ 957

Truly; RMC Place; CASCADE; ***198** E-8; mail Ulm **z** 59485; rural

Turah; RMC Place; MISSOULA; ***198** F-4; elev. 3,320ft./1,012m.; mail Clinton **z** 59825

Turner; RMC Place; BLAINE; **199** B-13; elev. 3,040ft./927m.; 🅿; **z** 59542; ● 100

Turner Colony; RMC Place; BLAINE; ***199** B-13; mail Turner **z** 59542; ● 40

Turtle Lake; CDP-Census Area Only; LAKE; ***198** D-4; Ⓒ 194

Twin Bridges; Inc. Place; MADISON; **198** I-6; elev. 4,627ft./1,410m.; 🅿; **z** 59754; Ⓟ 374; Ⓒ 400

Twin Creeks; RMC Place; MISSOULA; ***198** F-4; mail Bonner **z** 59823; rural

Twodot; RMC Place; WHEATLAND; **198** G-10; elev. 4,432ft./1,351m.; 🅿; **z** 59085; ● 35

U

Ulm; CDP; CASCADE; **198** E-8; elev. 3,346ft./1,020m.; 🅿; **z** 59485; Ⓒ 750

Unionville; RMC Place; LEWIS AND CLARK; ***198** G-7; mail Helena **z** 59601

Utica; RMC Place; JUDITH BASIN; **198** F-10; elev. 4,468ft./1,362m.; mail Hobson **z** 59452; ● 20

V

Valier; Inc. Place; PONDERA; **198** C-7; elev. 3,805ft./1,160m.; 🅿; **z** 59486; Ⓟ 519; Ⓒ 498

Valley; RMC Place; LEWIS AND CLARK; mail Helena **z** 59602; pop. incl. with Helena (Inc. Place)

VALLEY; **199** B-15; Ⓟ 8,239; Ⓒ 7,675; ◆ 6,741

Valley Grove; RMC Place; GALLATIN; ***198** I-8; mail Bozeman **z** 59718; ● 250

Vananda; RMC Place; ROSEBUD; ***199** G-15; mail Forsyth **z** 59327

Vandalia; RMC Place; VALLEY; **199** C-15; elev. 2,125ft./648m.; 🅿; **z** 59273; ● 20

Varney; RMC Place; MADISON; ***198** J-7; elev. 5,200ft./1,585m.; mail Ennis **z** 59729

Vaughn; CDP; CASCADE; **198** E-8; elev. 3,370ft./1,027m.; 🅿; **z** 59487; Ⓒ 701

Victor; CDP; RAVALLI; **198** G-4; elev. 3,400ft./1,036m.; 🅿; **z** 59875; Ⓒ 859

Vida; RMC Place; MCCONE; **199** D-17; elev. 2,400ft./732m.; 🅿; **z** 59274; ● 50

Virgelle; RMC Place; CHOUTEAU; ***198** D-10; mail Big Sandy **z** 59520; rural

Virginia City; Inc. Place; ⊡ MADISON; **198** J-7; elev. 5,822ft./1,775m.; 🅿; **z** 59755; Ⓟ 142; Ⓒ 130

Volborg; RMC Place; CUSTER; **199** H-17; elev. 2,307ft./703m.; 🅿; **z** 59351; ● 5

Volt; RMC Place; ROOSEVELT; ***199** C-17; located on Fort Peck Ind. Res.; mail Wolf Point **z** 59201; rural

W

Wagner; RMC Place; PHILLIPS; **199** C-13; elev. 2,300ft./701m.; mail Malta **z** 59538

Walkerville; Inc. Place; SILVER BOW; **198** H-6; elev. 6,468ft./1,971m.; 🅿; ★ **BUT**; **z** 59701; Walkerville continues to function as a separate municipality within the consolidated government of Butte-Silver Bow; Ⓟ 605; Ⓒ 714

Wan-i-gan; RMC Place; PARK; ***198** J-9; mail Pray **z** 59065; rural

Ware; RMC Place; FERGUS; ***199** F-11; elev. 3,600ft./1,097m.; mail Lewistown **z** 59457; rural

Warm Springs; RMC Place; DEER LODGE; ***198** H-6; elev. 4,814ft./1,467m.; 🅿 🅷; **z** 59756; pop. incl. with Anaconda (Inc. Place)

Warrick; RMC Place; CHOUTEAU; ***199** C-11; mail Big Sandy **z** 59520; rural

Washoe; RMC Place; CARBON; ***199** J-12; 🅿; **z** 59007 & mail Red Lodge **z** 59068

Waterloo; RMC Place; MADISON; **198** I-7; mail Whitehall **z** 59759; ● 50

Wayne; RMC Place; CASCADE; ***198** E-9; mail Belt **z** 59412, Great Falls **z** 59405; rural

Webster; RMC Place; FALLON; ***199** H-20; mail Baker **z** 59313; rural

Westby; Inc. Place; SHERIDAN; **199** A-20; elev. 2,000ft./610m.; 🅿; **z** 59275; Ⓟ 253; Ⓒ 172

West Glacier (Belton); RMC Place; FLATHEAD; **198** B-4; elev. 3,215ft./980m.; 🅿; **z** 59921, **z** 59936; summer pop. 1,500; ● 425

West Glendive; CDP-Census Area Only; DAWSON; ***199** F-19; Ⓒ 1,833

West Havre; CDP-Census Area Only; HILL; ***199** B-11; Ⓒ 284

West Riverside; RMC Place; MISSOULA; **198** F-4; mail Missoula **z** 59802; ● 800

West Valley; RMC Place; DEER LODGE; ***198** H-5; elev. 5,504ft./1,678m.; mail Anaconda **z** 59711; pop. incl. with Anaconda (Inc. Place)

West Yellowstone; Inc. Place; GALLATIN; **198** K-8; elev. 6,667ft./2,032m.; 🅿; **z** 59758; Ⓟ 913; Ⓒ 1,177

Whately; RMC Place; VALLEY; ***199** C-16; mail Nashua **z** 59248; rural

WHEATLAND; **199** H-11; Ⓟ 2,246; Ⓒ 2,259; ◆ 2,052

Whitefish; Inc. Place; FLATHEAD; **198** C-4; elev. 3,036ft./925m.; 🅿 🅷; **z** 59937; Ⓟ 4,368; Ⓒ 5,032

Whitehall; Inc. Place; JEFFERSON; **198** I-7; elev. 4,360ft./1,329m.; 🅿; **z** 59759; Ⓟ 1,067; Ⓒ 1,044

White Haven; RMC Place; LINCOLN; **198** C-2; mail Libby **z** 59923; ● 140

White Pine; RMC Place; SANDERS; **198** D-2; elev. 2,582ft./787m.; mail Trout Creek **z** 59874

White Sulphur Springs; Inc. Place; ⊡ MEAGHER; **198** G-9; elev. 5,100ft./1,554m.; 🅿 🅷; **z** 59645; Ⓟ 963; Ⓒ 984

Whitetail; RMC Place; DANIELS; **199** A-18; elev. 2,500ft./762m.; 🅿; **z** 59276; ● 110

Whitewater; RMC Place; PHILLIPS; **199** B-14; elev. 2,400ft./732m.; 🅿; **z** 59544; ● 90

Whitlash; RMC Place; LIBERTY; **198** B-8; elev. 3,943ft./1,202m.; 🅿; **z** 59545; ● 35

Wibaux; Inc. Place; ⊡ WIBAUX; **199** F-20; elev. 2,634ft./803m.; 🅿; **z** 59353; Ⓟ 628; Ⓒ 567

WIBAUX; **199** F-19; Ⓟ 1,191; Ⓒ 1,068; ◆ 894

Wickes; RMC Place; JEFFERSON; **198** H-7; elev. 5,165ft./1,574m.; mail Jefferson City **z** 59638; ● 30

Willard; RMC Place; FALLON; **199** H-19; elev. 3,400ft./1,036m.; 🅿; **z** 59354; ● 5

Williamsburg; RMC Place; SILVER BOW; ***198** H-6; ★ **BUT**; mail Butte **z** 59701; pop. incl. with Butte (Inc. Place)

Willow Creek; CDP; GALLATIN; **198** I-8; elev. 4,200ft./1,280m.; 🅿; **z** 59760; Ⓒ 209

Wilsall; CDP; PARK; **198** H-9; elev. 5,060ft./1,542m.; 🅿; **z** 59086; Ⓒ 237

Windham; RMC Place; JUDITH BASIN; **198** F-10; elev. 4,268ft./1,301m.; mail Stanford **z** 59479; ● 35

Winifred; Inc. Place; FERGUS; **199** E-11; elev. 3,300ft./1,006m.; 🅿; **z** 59489; Ⓟ 150; Ⓒ 156

Winnett; Inc. Place; ⊡ PETROLEUM; **199** F-13; elev. 2,960ft./902m.; 🅿; **z** 59084, **z** 59087; Ⓟ 188; Ⓒ 185

Winston; CDP; BROADWATER; **198** G-8; elev. 4,350ft./1,326m.; 🅿; **z** 59647; Ⓒ 73

Wisdom; CDP; BEAVERHEAD; **198** I-5; elev. 6,058ft./1,846m.; 🅿; **z** 59761; Ⓒ 114

Wise River; RMC Place; BEAVERHEAD; **198** I-5; elev. 5,681ft./1,732m.; 🅿; **z** 59762; ● 60

Wolf Creek; RMC Place; LEWIS AND CLARK; **198** F-7; elev. 3,571ft./1,088m.; 🅿; **z** 59648; ● 150

Wolf Point; Inc. Place; ⊡ ROOSEVELT; **199** C-17; located on Fort Peck Ind. Res.; elev. 1,997ft./609m.; 🅿 🅷; **z** 59201; Ⓟ 2,880; Ⓒ 2,663

Woodland Heights; RMC Place; MISSOULA; ***198** F-4; ★ **MSLA**; mail Missoula **z** 59804

Woods Bay; CDP; LAKE; **198** D-4; mail Bigfork **z** 59911; Ⓒ 748

Woodside; RMC Place; RAVALLI; ***198** G-4; elev. 3,488ft./1,063m.; mail Victor **z** 59875

Woodworth; RMC Place; POWELL, MISSOULA; **198** F-5; elev. 4,238ft./1,292m.; mail Bonner **z** 59823; rural

Worden; CDP; YELLOWSTONE; **199** H-13; elev. 2,959ft./902m.; 🅿; **z** 59088; Ⓒ 506

Wornath; RMC Place; MISSOULA; ***198** F-4; ★ **MSLA**; mail Missoula **z** 59804; ● 100

Wye; CDP-Census Area Only; MISSOULA; ***198** F-4; ★ **MSLA**; Ⓒ 381

Wyola; CDP; BIG HORN; **199** J-15; located on Crow Ind. Res.; elev. 3,711ft./1,131m.; 🅿; **z** 59089; Ⓒ 186

Y

Yaak; RMC Place; LINCOLN; ***198** A-1; mail Troy **z** 59935

YELLOWSTONE; **199** H-13; Ⓟ 113,471; Ⓒ 129,352; ◆ 141,091

Yellowtail; BIG HORN; see Fort Smith (CDP)

York; RMC Place; LEWIS AND CLARK; ***198** G-7; mail Helena **z** 59601

Z

Zortman; RMC Place; PHILLIPS; **199** D-13; elev. 4,000ft./1,219m.; 🅿; **z** 59546; ● 100

Zurich; RMC Place; BLAINE; **199** B-12; elev. 2,381ft./726m.; 🅿; **z** 59547; ● 50

NEBRASKA

SD
WY
IA
Lincoln
CO
KS
MO

Statistics

Total area (2000) — 77,354 square miles
Land area (2000) — 76,872 square miles
Water area (2000) — 482 square miles
Capital — Lincoln
Admitted as state — March, 1867

Maps

State maps can be found on pages 142-254 in Vol. 1

Ranally Metro Areas (RMAs) and Abbreviations

Grand Island, NE — GDIS
Lincoln, NE — LINC
Omaha, NE-IA — OMA
Sioux City, IA-NE-SD — SXCY

Principal Places

Place Name	Place Type	County	Population
Omaha	Inc. Place	DOUGLAS	◆ 419,706
Lincoln	Inc. Place	LANCASTER	◆ 269,866
Bellevue	Inc. Place	SARPY	◆ 50,878
Grand Island	Inc. Place	HALL	◆ 45,823
Kearney	Inc. Place	BUFFALO	◆ 29,338
Hastings	Inc. Place	ADAMS	◆ 26,773
Fremont	Inc. Place	DODGE	◆ 24,833
North Platte	Inc. Place	LINCOLN	◆ 23,600
Papillion	Inc. Place	SARPY	◆ 22,086
Norfolk	Inc. Place	MADISON	◆ 21,079
Columbus	Inc. Place	PLATTE	◆ 21,053
Scottsbluff	Inc. Place	SCOTTS BLUFF	◆ 14,463
Beatrice	Inc. Place	GAGE	◆ 12,533
South Sioux City	Inc. Place	DAKOTA	© 11,925
La Vista	Inc. Place	SARPY	© 11,699
Chalco	CDP	SARPY	© 10,736
Lexington	Inc. Place	DAWSON	© 10,011
Alliance	Inc. Place	BOX BUTTE	© 8,959
Offutt AFB	CDP-Census Area Only	SARPY	© 8,901
York	Inc. Place	YORK	© 8,081
Gering	Inc. Place	SCOTTS BLUFF	© 7,751
Blair	Inc. Place	WASHINGTON	© 7,512
McCook	Inc. Place	RED WILLOW	◆ 7,316
Nebraska City	Inc. Place	OTOE	© 7,228
Plattsmouth	Inc. Place	CASS	© 6,887
Seward	Inc. Place	SEWARD	© 6,319
Ralston	Inc. Place	DOUGLAS	© 6,314
Sidney	Inc. Place	CHEYENNE	© 6,282
Elkhorn	Inc. Place	DOUGLAS	© 6,062
Crete	Inc. Place	SALINE	© 6,028
Holdrege	Inc. Place	PHELPS	© 5,636
Chadron	Inc. Place	DAWES	© 5,634
Wayne	Inc. Place	WAYNE	© 5,583
Schuyler	Inc. Place	COLFAX	© 5,371

County Business Data

County	FIPS Code	County Seat	Land Area (Sq. Mi.)	Census Population			Wholesale Trade		Manufacturing, 2002			
				4/1/2000	4/1/1990	% Change 1990-2000	Sales, 2002 ($1,000)	% Change 1997-2002	Establish-ments	Total Employees	Value Added ($1,000)	Ranally Mfg. Units
Adams	001	Hastings	563	31,151	29,625	5.2	(d)	(d)	61	(d)	(d)	...
Antelope	003	Neligh	857	7,452	7,965	-6.4	102,728	16.2	...	(d)	(d)	...
Arthur	005	Arthur	715	444	462	-3.9	(d)	(d)	...	(d)	(d)	...
Banner	007	Harrisburg	746	819	852	-3.9	(d)	(d)	...	(d)	(d)	...
Blaine	009	Brewster	711	583	675	-13.6	(d)	(d)	...	(d)	(d)	...
Boone	011	Albion	687	6,259	6,667	-6.1	113,362	-31.2	...	(d)	(d)	...
Box Butte	013	Alliance	1,075	12,158	13,130	-7.4	79,076	-5.9	...	(d)	(d)	...
Boyd	015	Butte	540	2,438	2,835	-14.0	(d)	(d)	...	(d)	(d)	...
Brown	017	Ainsworth	1,221	3,525	3,657	-3.6	(d)	(d)	...	(d)	(d)	...
Buffalo	019	Kearney	968	42,259	37,447	12.9	(d)	(d)	56	(d)	(d)	...
Burt	021	Tekamah	493	7,791	7,868	-1.0	34,065	-34.7	...	(d)	(d)	...
Butler	023	David City	584	8,767	8,601	1.9	15,920	(d)	...	(d)	(d)	...
Cass	025	Plattsmouth	559	24,334	21,318	14.1	(d)	(d)	...	(d)	(d)	...
Cedar	027	Hartington	740	9,615	10,131	-5.1	56,941	-28.6	...	(d)	(d)	...
Chase	029	Imperial	894	4,068	4,381	-7.1	107,447	-9.3	...	(d)	(d)	...
Cherry	031	Valentine	5,961	6,148	6,307	-2.5	82,265	121.4	...	(d)	(d)	...
Cheyenne	033	Sidney	1,196	9,830	9,494	3.5	31,422	(d)	...	(d)	(d)	...
Clay	035	Clay Center	573	7,039	7,123	-1.2	(d)	(d)	...	(d)	(d)	...
Colfax	037	Schuyler	413	10,441	9,139	14.2	35,069	-56.9	6	(d)	(d)	...
Cuming	039	West Point	572	10,203	10,117	0.9	(d)	(d)	19	(d)	(d)	...
Custer	041	Broken Bow	2,576	11,793	12,270	-3.9	58,001	-22.0	...	(d)	(d)	...
Dakota	043	Dakota City	264	20,253	16,742	21.0	(d)	(d)	37	(d)	(d)	...
Dawes	045	Chadron	1,396	9,060	9,021	0.4	51,889	(d)	...	(d)	(d)	...
Dawson	047	Lexington	1,013	24,365	19,940	22.2	(d)	(d)	28	(d)	(d)	...
Deuel	049	Chappell	440	2,098	2,237	-6.2	(d)	(d)	...	(d)	(d)	...
Dixon	051	Ponca	476	6,339	6,143	3.2	(d)	(d)	2	(d)	(d)	...
Dodge	053	Fremont	534	36,160	34,500	4.8	565,086	-3.8	70	3,652	382,457	202
Douglas	055	Omaha	331	463,585	416,444	11.3	11,277,986	-2.3	520	24,127	3,151,364	1,667
Dundy	057	Benkelman	920	2,292	2,582	-11.2	7,677	(d)	...	(d)	(d)	...
Fillmore	059	Geneva	576	6,634	7,103	-6.6	75,105	-9.5	...	(d)	(d)	...
Franklin	061	Franklin	576	3,574	3,938	-9.2	(d)	(d)	...	(d)	(d)	...
Frontier	063	Stockville	975	3,099	3,101	-0.1	(d)	(d)	...	(d)	(d)	...
Furnas	065	Beaver City	718	5,324	5,553	-4.1	(d)	(d)	...	(d)	(d)	...
Gage	067	Beatrice	855	22,993	22,794	0.9	134,880	-9.0	41	1,991	177,462	94
Garden	069	Oshkosh	1,704	2,292	2,460	-6.8	(d)	(d)	...	(d)	(d)	...
Garfield	071	Burwell	570	1,902	2,141	-11.2	8,004	(d)	...	(d)	(d)	...
Gosper	073	Elwood	458	2,143	1,928	11.2	(d)	(d)	...	(d)	(d)	...
Grant	075	Hyannis	776	747	769	-2.9	(d)	(d)	...	(d)	(d)	...
Greeley	077	Greeley	570	2,714	3,006	-9.7	(d)	(d)	...	(d)	(d)	...
Hall	079	Grand Island	546	53,534	48,925	9.4	677,625	-1.8	86	(d)	(d)	...
Hamilton	081	Aurora	544	9,403	8,862	6.1	(d)	(d)	20	640	154,701	82
Harlan	083	Alma	553	3,786	3,810	-0.6	(d)	(d)	...	(d)	(d)	...
Hayes	085	Hayes Center	713	1,068	1,222	-12.6	(d)	(d)	...	(d)	(d)	...
Hitchcock	087	Trenton	710	3,111	3,750	-17.0	(d)	(d)	...	(d)	(d)	...
Holt	089	O'Neill	2,413	11,551	12,599	-8.3	75,202	-54.8	...	(d)	(d)	...
Hooker	091	Mullen	721	783	793	-1.3	(d)	(d)	...	(d)	(d)	...
Howard	093	St. Paul	569	6,567	6,055	8.5	(d)	(d)	...	(d)	(d)	...
Jefferson	095	Fairbury	573	8,333	8,759	-4.9	(d)	(d)	...	(d)	(d)	...
Johnson	097	Tecumseh	376	4,488	4,673	-4.0	15,785	-45.7	...	(d)	(d)	...
Kearney	099	Minden	516	6,882	6,629	3.8	(d)	(d)	...	(d)	(d)	...
Keith	101	Ogallala	1,061	8,875	8,584	3.4	148,915	-21.9	...	(d)	(d)	...
Keya Paha	103	Springview	773	983	1,029	-4.5	(d)	(d)	...	(d)	(d)	...
Kimball	105	Kimball	952	4,089	4,108	-0.5	11,754	(d)	...	(d)	(d)	...
Knox	107	Center	1,108	9,374	9,534	-1.7	75,723	(d)	...	(d)	(d)	...
Lancaster	109	Lincoln	839	250,291	213,641	17.2	2,250,158	(d)	271	15,174	2,048,203	1,084
Lincoln	111	North Platte	2,564	34,632	32,508	6.5	(d)	(d)	...	(d)	(d)	...
Logan	113	Stapleton	571	774	878	-11.8	(d)	(d)	...	(d)	(d)	...
Loup	115	Taylor	570	712	683	4.2	(d)	(d)	...	(d)	(d)	...
Madison	119	Madison	573	35,226	32,655	7.9	(d)	(d)	62	5,711	453,867	240
McPherson	117	Tryon	859	533	546	-2.4	(d)	(d)	...	(d)	(d)	...
Merrick	121	Central City	485	8,204	8,042	2.0	(d)	(d)	...	(d)	(d)	...
Morrill	123	Bridgeport	1,424	5,440	5,423	0.3	45,026	46.7	...	(d)	(d)	...
Nance	125	Fullerton	441	4,038	4,275	-5.5	30,291	(d)	...	(d)	(d)	...
Nemaha	127	Auburn	409	7,576	7,980	-5.1	29,774	(d)	...	(d)	(d)	...
Nuckolls	129	Nelson	575	5,057	5,786	-12.6	44,243	-1.5	...	(d)	(d)	...
Otoe	131	Nebraska City	616	15,396	14,252	8.0	106,213	-19.1	13	1,471	119,164	63
Pawnee	133	Pawnee City	432	3,087	3,317	-6.9	5,575	(d)	...	(d)	(d)	...
Perkins	135	Grant	883	3,200	3,367	-5.0	70,436	-48.5	...	(d)	(d)	...
Phelps	137	Holdrege	540	9,747	9,715	0.3	156,713	(d)	7	(d)	(d)	...
Pierce	139	Pierce	574	7,857	7,827	0.4	(d)	(d)	...	(d)	(d)	...
Platte	141	Columbus	678	31,662	29,820	6.2	274,683	-15.4	74	5,542	756,911	400
Polk	143	Osceola	439	5,639	5,675	-0.6	140,491	19.9	...	(d)	(d)	...
Red Willow	145	McCook	717	11,448	11,705	-2.2	101,447	(d)	...	(d)	(d)	...
Richardson	147	Falls City	553	9,531	9,937	-4.1	70,786	-4.4	...	(d)	(d)	...
Rock	149	Bassett	1,008	1,756	2,019	-13.0	66,298	(d)	...	(d)	(d)	...
Saline	151	Wilber	575	13,843	12,715	8.9	73,611	1.3	20	2,717	182,816	97
Sarpy	153	Papillion	241	122,595	102,583	19.5	3,657,043	(d)	70	3,013	287,877	152
Saunders	155	Wahoo	754	19,830	18,285	8.4	94,333	30.8	...	(d)	(d)	...
Scotts Bluff	157	Gering	739	36,951	36,025	2.6	293,777	30.1	43	1,092	57,196	30
Seward	159	Seward	575	16,496	15,450	6.8	56,481	-40.0	14	677	65,753	35
Sheridan	161	Rushville	2,441	6,198	6,750	-8.2	87,061	-25.7	...	(d)	(d)	...
Sherman	163	Loup City	566	3,318	3,718	-10.8	(d)	(d)	...	(d)	(d)	...
Sioux	165	Harrison	2,067	1,475	1,549	-4.8	(d)	(d)	...	(d)	(d)	...
Stanton	167	Stanton	430	6,455	6,244	3.4	(d)	(d)	...	(d)	(d)	...
Thayer	169	Hebron	575	6,055	6,635	-8.7	81,932	-14.7	...	(d)	(d)	...
Thomas	171	Thedford	713	729	851	-14.3	(d)	(d)	...	(d)	(d)	...
Thurston	173	Pender	394	7,171	6,936	3.4	70,309	123.7	...	(d)	(d)	...
Valley	175	Ord	568	4,647	5,169	-10.1	40,678	-59.9	...	(d)	(d)	...
Washington	177	Blair	390	18,780	16,607	13.1	(d)	(d)	24	1,074	(d)	
Wayne	179	Wayne	443	9,851	9,364	5.2	23,734	(d)	14	758	50,825	27
Webster	181	Red Cloud	575	4,061	4,279	-5.1	33,650	-30.5	...	(d)	(d)	...
Wheeler	183	Bartlett	575	886	948	-6.5	(d)	(d)	...	(d)	(d)	...
York	185	York	576	14,598	14,428	1.2	217,138	4.7	25	1,059	87,072	46
The State			**76,872**	**1,711,263**	**1,578,385**	**8.4**	**26,155,770**	**-31.2**	**1,976**	**103,029**	**11,469,004**	**6,068**

(d) Data not available. Corresponding percentages or Ranally Manufacturing Units are estimates.
... Represents 0 or amount too minimal to be reported.

Index of Places and Counties

Entries in **UPPERCASE** are counties.
Entries in **bold** have populations of 2,500 or more.
Names in parentheses are alternate names.

Inc. Place	Incorporated Place
RMC Place	Rand McNally Designated Place
CDP	Census Designated Place
MCD	Minor Civil Division
⊡	County Seat
▲	Minor Civil Division
elev.	Elevation
🅿	Post Office
🅷	Hospital
🅲	College
■	Principal Business Center
★	Ranally Metro Area (RMA) Abbreviation
z	Zip Code(s)
Ⓟ	Previous Census Population
Ⓡ	Revised Census Population
Ⓐ	Annexation Population
●	Rand McNally Population Estimate
©	Final Census Population
Ⓢ	Special Census Population
◆	Estimated Population

For additional definitions see Glossary, Volume 1, and Introduction, Volume 2.

Aloys; RMC Place; CUMING; *201 H-17; mail West Point Z 68788; rural
Altona; RMC Place; WAYNE; *201 G-16; mail Wayne Z 68787; rural
Alvo; Inc. Place; CASS; **201** K-18; elev. 1,340ft./408m.; [P]; Z 68304; Ⓟ 164; Ⓒ 142
Amelia; RMC Place; HOLT; **201** G-12; elev. 2,200ft./671m.; [P]; Z 68711; ● 30
Ames; RMC Place; DODGE; **201** I-17; [P]; Z 68621; ● 35
Ames Avenue; RMC Place; DOUGLAS; ***201** I-19; ★ **OMA**; mail Omaha Z 68110-11; pop. incl. with Omaha (Inc. Place)
Amherst; Inc. Place; BUFFALO; **201** K-11; elev. 2,240ft./683m.; [P]; Z 68812; Ⓟ 231; Ⓒ 277
Amick Acres; RMC Place; HALL; ***201** K-13; elev. 1,907ft./581m.; mail Doniphan Z 68832; ● 200
Angora; RMC Place; MORRILL; **200** H-3; elev. 4,263ft./1,299m.; [P]; Z 69331; ● 20
Angus; RMC Place; NUCKOLLS; **201** M-14; mail Nelson Z 68961; ● 40
Anoka; Inc. Place; BOYD; **201** E-12; elev. 1,650ft./503m.; mail Butte Z 68722; Ⓟ 10; Ⓒ 10
Anselmo; Inc. Place; CUSTER; **200** I-10; elev. 2,608ft./795m.; [P]; Z 68813; Ⓟ 189; Ⓒ 159
Ansley; Inc. Place; CUSTER; **201** J-11; elev. 2,307ft./703m.; [P]; Z 68814; Ⓟ 555; Ⓒ 520
ANTELOPE; **201** G-14; Ⓟ 7,965; Ⓒ 7,452; ◆ 6,522
Antioch; RMC Place; SHERIDAN; ***200** G-4; elev. 3,882ft./1,183m.; mail Ellsworth Z 69340
Arapahoe; Inc. Place; FURNAS; **200** M-10; elev. 2,175ft./663m.; [P]; Z 68922; Ⓟ 1,001; Ⓒ 1,028
Arborville; RMC Place; YORK; ***201** J-15; elev. 1,703ft./519m.; mail Polk Z 68654; rural
Arcadia; Inc. Place; VALLEY; **201** I-12; elev. 2,157ft./657m.; [P]; Z 68815; Ⓟ 385; Ⓒ 359
Archer; RMC Place; MERRICK; **201** J-14; elev. 1,743ft./531m.; [P]; Z 68816; ● 80
Arizona; RMC Place; BURT; ***201** H-18; elev. 1,034ft./315m.; mail Tekamah Z 68061; rural
Arlington; Inc. Place; WASHINGTON; **201** I-18; elev. 1,200ft./366m.; [P]; Z 68002; Ⓟ 1,178; Ⓒ 1,197
Arnold; Inc. Place; CUSTER; **200** I-9; elev. 2,700ft./823m.; [P]; Z 69120; Ⓟ 679; Ⓒ 630
Arnold Heights; RMC Place; LANCASTER; ★ **LINC**; pop. incl. with Lincoln (Inc. Place)
Arthur; Inc. Place; ⊡ ARTHUR; **200** I-6; elev. 3,647ft./1,112m.; [P]; Z 69121; Ⓟ 128; Ⓒ 145
ARTHUR; **200** I-5; Ⓟ 462; Ⓒ 444; ◆ 330
Ashby; RMC Place; GRANT; **200** G-5; elev. 3,848ft./1,173m.; [P]; Z 69333; ● 100
Ashland; Inc. Place; SAUNDERS; **201** J-18; elev. 1,096ft./334m.; [P]; Z 68003; Ⓟ 2,136; Ⓒ 2,262
Ashton; Inc. Place; SHERMAN; **201** J-12; elev. 2,038ft./621m.; [P]; Z 68817; Ⓟ 251; Ⓒ 237
Assumption; RMC Place; ADAMS; **201** L-13; mail Juniata Z 68955; ● 30
Aten; RMC Place; CEDAR; ***201** E-15; mail Crofton Z 68730; ● 60
Atkinson; Inc. Place; HOLT; **201** F-12; elev. 2,105ft./642m.; [P] [H]; Z 68713; Ⓟ 1,380; Ⓒ 1,244
Atlanta; Inc. Place; PHELPS; **201** L-11; elev. 2,339ft./713m.; [P]; Z 68923; Ⓟ 114; Ⓒ 130
Auburn; Inc. Place; ⊡ NEMAHA; **201** L-19; elev. 994ft./303m.; [P] [H]; Z 68305; Ⓟ 3,443; Ⓒ 3,350
Aurora; Inc. Place; ⊡ HAMILTON; **201** K-14; [P] [H]; Z 68818; Ⓟ 3,810; Ⓒ 4,225
Autumn Hills; RMC Place; DOUGLAS; ★ **OMA**; mail Omaha Z 68134; pop. incl. with Omaha (Inc. Place)
Avoca; Inc. Place; CASS; **201** K-18; elev. 1,172ft./357m.; [P]; Z 68307; Ⓟ 254; Ⓒ 270
Axtell; Inc. Place; KEARNEY; **201** L-12; elev. 2,220ft./677m.; [P]; Z 68924; Ⓟ 707; Ⓒ 696
Ayr; Inc. Place; ADAMS; **201** L-13; elev. 1,850ft./564m.; [P]; Z 68925; Ⓟ 101; Ⓒ 98

B

Bancroft; Inc. Place; CUMING; **201** G-17; elev. 1,325ft./404m.; [P]; Z 68004; Ⓟ 494; Ⓒ 520
BANNER; **200** I-1; Ⓟ 852; Ⓒ 819; ◆ 705
Barada; Inc. Place; RICHARDSON; **201** M-20; elev. 1,110ft./338m.; mail Falls City Z 68355; Ⓟ 24; Ⓒ 28
Barneston; Inc. Place; GAGE; **201** M-18; elev. 1,210ft./369m.; [P]; Z 68309; Ⓟ 122; Ⓒ 122
Bartlett; Inc. Place; ⊡ WHEELER; **201** H-13; elev. 2,162ft./659m.; [P]; Z 68622; Ⓟ 131; Ⓒ 128
Bartley; Inc. Place; RED WILLOW; **200** M-9; elev. 2,340ft./713m.; [P]; Z 69020; Ⓟ 339; Ⓒ 355
Bassett; Inc. Place; ⊡ ROCK; **201** F-11; elev. 2,343ft./714m.; [P] [H]; Z 68714; Ⓟ 739; Ⓒ 743
Battle Creek; Inc. Place; MADISON; **201** H-15; elev. 1,590ft./485m.; [P]; Z 68715; Ⓟ 997; Ⓒ 1,158
Bayard; Inc. Place; MORRILL; **200** H-2; elev. 3,790ft./1,155m.; [P]; Z 69334 & mail McGrew Z 69353; Ⓟ 1,196; Ⓒ 1,247
Bazile Mills; Inc. Place; KNOX; **201** F-14; elev. 1,750ft./533m.; mail Creighton Z 68729; Ⓟ 34; Ⓒ 26
Beacon View; RMC Place; SARPY; ***201** J-18; elev. 1,062ft./324m.; mail Gretna Z 68028; ● 20
Beatrice; Inc. Place; ⊡ GAGE; **201** M-17; elev. 1,284ft./391m.; [P] [H] ■; Z 68310; Ⓟ 12,354; Ⓒ 12,496; Ⓡ 12,510; ◆ 12,533
Beaver City; Inc. Place; ⊡ FURNAS; **200** M-10; elev. 2,170ft./661m.; [P]; Z 68926; Ⓟ 707; Ⓒ 641
Beaver Crossing; Inc. Place; SEWARD; **201** K-16; elev. 1,460ft./445m.; [P]; Z 68313; Ⓟ 448; Ⓒ 457
Bee; Inc. Place; SEWARD; **201** J-16; elev. 1,560ft./475m.; [P]; Z 68314; Ⓟ 209; Ⓒ 223
Beemer; Inc. Place; CUMING; **201** H-17; elev. 1,370ft./418m.; [P]; Z 68716; Ⓟ 672; Ⓒ 773
Belden; Inc. Place; CEDAR; **201** F-16; elev. 1,580ft./482m.; [P]; Z 68717; Ⓟ 149; Ⓒ 131
Belgrade; Inc. Place; NANCE; **201** I-14; [P]; Z 68623; Ⓟ 157; Ⓒ 134
Bellevue; Inc. Place; SARPY; **201** J-19; elev. 1,061ft./323m.; [P] [C] 6,808 ■; ★ **OMA**; Z 68005, Z 68123, Z 68133, Z 68147, Z 68157; Ⓟ 30,928; Ⓒ 44,382; ◆ 50,878
Bellwood; Inc. Place; BUTLER; **201** I-16; elev. 1,450ft./442m.; [P]; Z 68624; Ⓟ 395; Ⓒ 446
Belmont; RMC Place; LANCASTER; ★ **LINC**; pop. incl. with Lincoln (Inc. Place)
Belvidere; Inc. Place; THAYER; **201** M-15; elev. 1,498ft./457m.; [P]; Z 68315; Ⓟ 117; Ⓒ 98
Benedict; Inc. Place; YORK; **201** K-15; elev. 1,685ft./514m.; [P]; Z 68316; Ⓟ 230; Ⓒ 278
Benkelman; Inc. Place; ⊡ DUNDY; **200** M-6; elev. 2,980ft./908m.; [P] [H]; Z 69021; Ⓟ 1,193; Ⓒ 1,006
Bennet (Bennett); Inc. Place; LANCASTER; **201** K-18; elev. 1,300ft./396m.; [P]; Z 68317; Ⓟ 544; Ⓒ 570
Bennett; LANCASTER; see Bennet (Inc. Place)
Bennington; Inc. Place; DOUGLAS; **201** I-18; elev. 1,100ft./335m.; [P]; ★ **OMA**; Z 68007; Ⓟ 866; Ⓒ 937
Benson; RMC Place; DOUGLAS; ***201** J-19; ★ **OMA**; mail Omaha Z 68104; pop. incl. with Omaha (Inc. Place)
Benson Acres; RMC Place; DOUGLAS; ★ **OMA**; pop. incl. with Omaha (Inc. Place)
Benson Gardens; RMC Place; DOUGLAS; ★ **OMA**; pop. incl. with Omaha (Inc. Place)
Berea; RMC Place; BOX BUTTE; **200** G-3; mail Alliance Z 69301; ● 40
Bertha; RMC Place; BURT; ***201** H-18; elev. 1,379ft./420m.; mail Craig Z 68019; rural
Bertrand; Inc. Place; PHELPS; **201** L-11; elev. 2,517ft./767m.; [P]; Z 68927; Ⓟ 708; Ⓒ 786
Berwyn; Inc. Place; CUSTER; **201** J-11; [P]; Z 68814; Ⓟ 122; Ⓒ 134
Bethany; RMC Place; LANCASTER; ***201** K-17; ★ **LINC**; mail Lincoln Z 68505; pop. incl. with Lincoln (Inc. Place)
Bethany Heights; RMC Place; LANCASTER; ★ **LINC**; pop. incl. with Lincoln (Inc. Place)
Big Springs; Inc. Place; DEUEL; **200** J-5; elev. 3,367ft./1,026m.; [P]; Z 69122; Ⓟ 495; Ⓒ 418
Bingham; RMC Place; SHERIDAN; **200** G-5; [P]; Z 69335; ● 40
Bixby; RMC Place; FILLMORE; ***201** L-15; mail Sutton Z 68979; rural
Bladen; Inc. Place; WEBSTER; **201** M-13; elev. 1,980ft./604m.; [P]; Z 68928; Ⓟ 280; Ⓒ 291
BLAINE; **200** H-9; Ⓟ 675; Ⓒ 583; ◆ 387
Blair; Inc. Place; ⊡ WASHINGTON; **201** I-18; elev. 1,075ft./328m.; [P] [H] [C] 589; Z 68008-09; Ⓟ 6,860; Ⓒ 7,512
Bloomfield; Inc. Place; KNOX; **201** F-15; elev. 1,703ft./519m.; [P]; Z 68718; Ⓟ 1,181; Ⓒ 1,126
Bloomington; Inc. Place; FRANKLIN; **201** M-12; elev. 1,848ft./563m.; [P]; Z 68929; Ⓟ 129; Ⓒ 124
Blue Hill; Inc. Place; WEBSTER; **201** M-13; elev. 1,972ft./601m.; [P]; Z 68930; Ⓟ 810; Ⓒ 867
Blue River Lodge; RMC Place; SALINE; mail Crete Z 68333
Blue Springs; Inc. Place; GAGE; **201** M-17; elev. 1,208ft./368m.; [P]; Z 68318; Ⓟ 431; Ⓒ 383
Boelus (Howard City); Inc. Place; HOWARD; **201** J-13; elev. 1,916ft./584m.; [P]; Z 68820; Ⓟ 203; Ⓒ 221
Boone; RMC Place; BOONE; **201** I-14; elev. 1,695ft./517m.; [P]; Z 68620; ● 20
BOONE; **201** H-14; Ⓟ 6,667; Ⓒ 6,259; ◆ 5,364
Bostwick; RMC Place; NUCKOLLS; ***201** M-14; mail Superior Z 68978
Bow Valley; RMC Place; CEDAR; **201** E-16; mail Hartington Z 68739; ● 50
BOX BUTTE; **200** G-2; Ⓟ 13,130; Ⓒ 12,158; ◆ 10,893
BOYD; **201** E-12; Ⓟ 2,835; Ⓒ 2,438; ◆ 2,036
Boys Town; Inc. Place; DOUGLAS; **201** J-18; elev. 1,200ft./366m.; [P]; ★ **OMA**; Z 68010; Ⓟ 794; Ⓒ 818
Bradshaw; Inc. Place; YORK; **201** K-15; elev. 1,720ft./524m.; [P]; Z 68319; Ⓟ 330; Ⓒ 336
Brady; Inc. Place; LINCOLN; **200** J-9; elev. 2,654ft./809m.; [P]; Z 69123; Ⓟ 331; Ⓒ 366
Brainard; Inc. Place; BUTLER; **201** J-16; elev. 1,675ft./511m.; [P]; Z 68626; Ⓟ 326; Ⓒ 351
Brandon; RMC Place; PERKINS; **200** K-5; elev. 3,512ft./1,070m.; mail Grant Z 69140; ● 10
Breslau; RMC Place; PIERCE; ***201** F-15; mail Osmond Z 68765
Brewster; Inc. Place; ⊡ BLAINE; **200** H-10; elev. 2,494ft./760m.; [P]; Z 68821; Ⓟ 22; Ⓒ 29
Bridgeport; Inc. Place; ⊡ MORRILL; **200** H-3; elev. 3,666ft./1,117m.; [P] [H]; Z 69336; Ⓟ 1,581; Ⓒ 1,594
Briggs; RMC Place; DOUGLAS; ***201** I-19; ★ **OMA**; mail Omaha Z 68122; ● 160
Bristow; Inc. Place; BOYD; **201** E-13; elev. 1,480ft./451m.; [P]; Z 68719; Ⓟ 107; Ⓒ 88
Broadwater; Inc. Place; MORRILL; **200** I-3; elev. 3,586ft./1,093m.; [P]; Z 69125; Ⓟ 160; Ⓒ 140
Brock; Inc. Place; NEMAHA; **201** L-19; [P]; Z 68320; Ⓟ 143; Ⓒ 162
Broken Bow; Inc. Place; ⊡ CUSTER; **200** I-10; elev. 2,475ft./754m.; [P] [H]; Z 68822; Ⓟ 3,778; Ⓒ 3,491
BROWN; **200** F-10; Ⓟ 3,657; Ⓒ 3,525; ◆ 3,006
Brownlee; RMC Place; CHERRY; **200** G-8; elev. 2,864ft./873m.; [P]; Z 69166; ● 40
Brownson; RMC Place; CHEYENNE; **200** J-3; mail Sidney Z 69162; ● 20
Brownville; Inc. Place; NEMAHA; **201** L-20; elev. 1,000ft./305m.; [P]; Z 68321; Ⓟ 148; Ⓒ 146
Brule; Inc. Place; KEITH; **200** J-5; elev. 3,290ft./1,003m.; [P]; Z 69127; Ⓟ 411; Ⓒ 372
Bruning; Inc. Place; THAYER; **201** M-15; elev. 1,583ft./482m.; [P]; Z 68322; Ⓟ 332; Ⓒ 300
Bruno; Inc. Place; BUTLER; **201** J-17; elev. 1,500ft./457m.; [P]; Z 68014; Ⓟ 141; Ⓒ 112
Brunswick; Inc. Place; ANTELOPE; **201** G-14; elev. 1,854ft./565m.; [P]; Z 68720; Ⓟ 182; Ⓒ 179
BUFFALO; **201** K-12; Ⓟ 37,447; Ⓒ 42,259; ◆ 45,399
Burchard; Inc. Place; PAWNEE; **201** M-18; elev. 1,400ft./427m.; [P]; Z 68323 & mail Lewiston Z 68380; Ⓟ 105; Ⓒ 103
Burr; Inc. Place; OTOE; **201** L-18; elev. 1,150ft./351m.; [P]; Z 68324; Ⓟ 75; Ⓒ 66
Burress; RMC Place; FILLMORE; ***201** L-15; mail Fairmont Z 68354; rural
BURT; **201** H-18; Ⓟ 7,868; Ⓒ 7,791; ◆ 6,810
Burton; Inc. Place; KEYA PAHA; **201** E-11; elev. 2,139ft./652m.; mail Springview Z 68778; Ⓟ 9; Ⓒ 11
Burwell; Inc. Place; ⊡ GARFIELD; **201** H-12; elev. 2,173ft./662m.; [P]; Z 68823; Ⓟ 1,278; Ⓒ 1,130
Bushnell; Inc. Place; KIMBALL; **200** J-1; elev. 4,871ft./1,485m.; [P]; Z 69128; Ⓟ 119; Ⓒ 162
BUTLER; **201** J-16; Ⓟ 8,601; Ⓒ 8,767; ◆ 8,230
Butte; Inc. Place; ⊡ BOYD; **201** E-12; elev. 1,811ft./552m.; [P]; Z 68722; Ⓟ 452; Ⓒ 366
Byron; Inc. Place; THAYER; **201** M-15; elev. 1,670ft./509m.; [P]; Z 68325; Ⓟ 140; Ⓒ 144

C

Cadams; RMC Place; NUCKOLLS; ***201** M-14; mail Superior Z 68978
Cairo; Inc. Place; HALL; **201** K-13; elev. 1,952ft./595m.; [P]; Z 68824; Ⓟ 733; Ⓒ 790
Callaway; Inc. Place; CUSTER; **200** J-10; elev. 2,556ft./779m.; [P] [H]; Z 68825; Ⓟ 539; Ⓒ 637
Cambridge; Inc. Place; FURNAS; **200** M-9; elev. 2,263ft./690m.; [P] [H]; Z 69022; Ⓟ 1,107; Ⓒ 1,041
Campbell; Inc. Place; FRANKLIN; **201** M-13; elev. 2,050ft./625m.; [P]; Z 68932; Ⓟ 432; Ⓒ 387
Carleton; Inc. Place; THAYER; **201** M-15; elev. 1,560ft./475m.; [P]; Z 68326; Ⓟ 144; Ⓒ 136
Carroll; Inc. Place; WAYNE; **201** G-16; elev. 1,600ft./488m.; [P]; Z 68723; Ⓟ 237; Ⓒ 238
CASS; **201** K-18; Ⓟ 21,318; Ⓒ 24,334; ◆ 25,314
CEDAR; **201** F-16; Ⓟ 10,131; Ⓒ 9,615; ◆ 8,106
Cedar Bluffs; Inc. Place; SAUNDERS; **201** I-17; elev. 1,296ft./395m.; [P]; Z 68015; Ⓟ 591; Ⓒ 615
Cedar Creek; Inc. Place; CASS; **201** J-19; elev. 1,030ft./314m.; [P]; Z 68016; Ⓟ 334; Ⓒ 396
Cedar Rapids; Inc. Place; BOONE; **201** I-14; elev. 1,776ft./541m.; [P]; Z 68627 & mail Primrose Z 68655; Ⓟ 396; Ⓒ 407
Center; Inc. Place; ⊡ KNOX; **201** F-14; elev. 1,700ft./518m.; [P]; Z 68724; Ⓟ 112; Ⓒ 90
Central City; Inc. Place; ⊡ MERRICK; **201** J-14; elev. 1,703ft./519m.; [P] [H]; Z 68826; Ⓟ 2,868; Ⓒ 2,998
Ceresco; Inc. Place; SAUNDERS; **201** J-17; elev. 1,220ft./372m.; [P]; Z 68017; Ⓟ 825; Ⓒ 920
Chadron; Inc. Place; ⊡ DAWES; **200** E-3; elev. 3,380ft./1,030m.; [P] [H] [C] 2,767; Z 69337; Ⓟ 5,588; Ⓒ 5,634
Chalco; CDP; SARPY; ***201** J-18; ★ **OMA**; mail Papillion Z 68046; Ⓟ 7,337; Ⓒ 10,736
Chambers; Inc. Place; HOLT; **201** G-12; elev. 2,100ft./640m.; [P]; Z 68725; Ⓟ 341; Ⓒ 333
Champion; RMC Place; CHASE; **200** L-6; elev. 3,300ft./1,006m.; [P]; Z 69023; ● 140
Chapman; Inc. Place; MERRICK; **201** J-14; elev. 1,764ft./538m.; [P]; Z 68827; Ⓟ 292; Ⓒ 341
Chappell; Inc. Place; ⊡ DEUEL; **200** J-4; elev. 3,697ft./1,127m.; [P]; Z 69129; Ⓟ 979; Ⓒ 983
CHASE; **200** L-5; Ⓟ 4,381; Ⓒ 4,068; ◆ 3,509
Cheney; LANCASTER; see Cheneys (RMC Place)
Cheneys (Cheney); RMC Place; LANCASTER; ***201** K-17; ★ **LINC**; mail Lincoln Z 68526; ● 100
CHERRY; **200** F-7; Ⓟ 6,307; Ⓒ 6,148; ◆ 5,458
Chester; Inc. Place; THAYER; **201** M-15; elev. 1,627ft./496m.; [P]; Z 68327 & mail Hubbell Z 68375, Reynolds Z 68429; Ⓟ 351; Ⓒ 294
CHEYENNE; **200** J-2; Ⓟ 9,494; Ⓒ 9,830; ◆ 10,197
Cisco; CDP-Census Area Only; GARDEN; ***200** I-4; Ⓒ 68
Clarks; Inc. Place; MERRICK; **201** J-15; elev. 1,623ft./495m.; [P]; Z 68628; Ⓟ 379; Ⓒ 361
Clarkson; Inc. Place; COLFAX; **201** H-16; elev. 1,500ft./457m.; [P]; Z 68629; Ⓟ 699; Ⓒ 685
Clatonia; Inc. Place; GAGE; **201** L-17; elev. 1,400ft./427m.; [P]; Z 68328; Ⓟ 296; Ⓒ 275
CLAY; **201** L-14; Ⓟ 7,123; Ⓒ 7,039; ◆ 6,147
Clay Center; Inc. Place; ⊡ CLAY; **201** L-14; elev. 1,775ft./541m.; [P]; Z 68933; Ⓟ 825; Ⓒ 861
Clearwater; Inc. Place; ANTELOPE; **201** G-14; elev. 1,793ft./547m.; [P]; Z 68726; Ⓟ 401; Ⓒ 384
Clinton; Inc. Place; SHERIDAN; **200** E-4; mail Gordon Z 69343; Ⓟ 33; Ⓒ 30
Cody; Inc. Place; CHERRY; **200** E-7; elev. 3,099ft./945m.; [P]; Z 69211; Ⓟ 177; Ⓒ 149
Coleridge; Inc. Place; CEDAR; **201** F-16; elev. 1,560ft./475m.; [P]; Z 68727; Ⓟ 596; Ⓒ 541
COLFAX; **201** I-16; Ⓟ 9,139; Ⓒ 10,441; ◆ 9,744
College View; RMC Place; LANCASTER; ***201** K-17; ★ **LINC**; mail Lincoln Z 68506; pop. incl. with Lincoln (Inc. Place)
Colon; Inc. Place; SAUNDERS; **201** J-17; elev. 1,245ft./379m.; [P]; Z 68018; Ⓟ 128; Ⓒ 138
Colton; RMC Place; CHEYENNE; ***200** J-3; mail Sidney Z 69162
Columbus; Inc. Place; ⊡ PLATTE; **201** I-16; elev. 1,449ft./442m.; [P] [H] ■; Z 68601-02; Ⓟ 19,480; Ⓒ 20,971; ◆ 21,053
Comstock; Inc. Place; CUSTER; **201** I-11; elev. 2,250ft./686m.; [P]; Z 68828; Ⓟ 135; Ⓒ 110
Concord; Inc. Place; DIXON; **201** F-16; [P]; Z 68728; Ⓟ 156; Ⓒ 160
Constance; RMC Place; CEDAR; ***201** E-15; mail Crofton Z 68730; rural
Cook; Inc. Place; JOHNSON; **201** L-18; elev. 1,061ft./323m.; [P]; Z 68329; Ⓟ 333; Ⓒ 322
Cordova; Inc. Place; SEWARD; **201** K-16; elev. 1,560ft./475m.; [P]; Z 68330; Ⓟ 147; Ⓒ 127
Cornlea; Inc. Place; PLATTE; **201** I-15; elev. 1,722ft./525m.; [P]; Z 68642; Ⓟ 39; Ⓒ 41
Cortland; Inc. Place; GAGE; **201** L-17; elev. 1,446ft./441m.; [P]; Z 68331; Ⓟ 393; Ⓒ 488
Cotesfield; Inc. Place; HOWARD; **201** I-13; elev. 1,892ft./577m.; [P]; Z 68835; Ⓟ 60; Ⓒ 66
Cowles; Inc. Place; WEBSTER; **201** M-13; elev. 1,792ft./546m.; [P]; Z 68930; Ⓟ 42; Ⓒ 48
Cozad; Inc. Place; DAWSON; **200** K-10; elev. 2,490ft./759m.; [P] [H]; Z 69130; Ⓟ 3,823; Ⓒ 4,163
Crab Orchard; Inc. Place; JOHNSON; **201** L-18; elev. 1,282ft./391m.; [P]; Z 68332; Ⓟ 47; Ⓒ 49
Craig; Inc. Place; BURT; **201** H-18; elev. 1,349ft./411m.; [P]; Z 68019; Ⓟ 228; Ⓒ 241
Crawford; Inc. Place; DAWES; **200** E-2; elev. 3,673ft./1,120m.; [P] [H]; Z 69339; Ⓟ 1,115; Ⓒ 1,107
Creighton; Inc. Place; KNOX; **201** F-14; elev. 1,600ft./488m.; [P] [H]; Z 68729; Ⓟ 1,223; Ⓒ 1,270
Creston; Inc. Place; PLATTE; **201** H-16; elev. 1,620ft./494m.; [P]; Z 68631; Ⓟ 220; Ⓒ 215
Crete; Inc. Place; SALINE; **201** L-17; elev. 1,360ft./415m.; [P] [H] [C] 2,482; Z 68333; Ⓟ 4,841; Ⓒ 6,028
Crofton; Inc. Place; KNOX; **201** E-15; elev. 1,440ft./439m.; [P]; Z 68730; Ⓟ 820; Ⓒ 754
Crookston; Inc. Place; CHERRY; **200** E-8; [P]; Z 69212; Ⓟ 99; Ⓒ 98
Crowell; RMC Place; DODGE; ***201** H-17; mail Scribner Z 68057
Crown Point; RMC Place; DOUGLAS; ★ **OMA**; mail Omaha Z 68122; pop. incl. with Omaha (Inc. Place)
Culbertson; Inc. Place; HITCHCOCK; **200** M-8; elev. 2,600ft./792m.; [P]; Z 69024; Ⓟ 795; Ⓒ 594
CUMING; **201** H-17; Ⓟ 10,117; Ⓒ 10,203; ◆ 8,996
Curtis; Inc. Place; FRONTIER; **200** L-8; elev. 2,580ft./786m.; [P]; Z 69025; Ⓟ 791; Ⓒ 832
Cushing; Inc. Place; HOWARD; **201** J-13; elev. 1,780ft./543m.; mail Saint Paul Z 68873; Ⓟ 25; Ⓒ 31
CUSTER; **200** J-10; Ⓟ 12,270; Ⓒ 11,793; ◆ 10,479

D

DAKOTA; **201** F-17; Ⓟ 16,742; Ⓒ 20,253; ◆ 20,396
Dakota City; Inc. Place; ⊡ DAKOTA; **201** F-18; elev. 1,102ft./336m.; [P]; Z 68731; Ⓟ 1,470; Ⓒ 1,821
Dalton; Inc. Place; CHEYENNE; **200** I-3; elev. 4,270ft./1,301m.; [P]; Z 69131; Ⓟ 282; Ⓒ 332
Danbury; Inc. Place; RED WILLOW; **200** M-9; elev. 2,476ft./755m.; [P]; Z 69026 & mail Lebanon Z 69036; Ⓟ 109; Ⓒ 127
Dannebrog; Inc. Place; HOWARD; **201** J-13; elev. 1,850ft./564m.; [P]; Z 68831; Ⓟ 324; Ⓒ 352
Darr; RMC Place; DAWSON; ***200** K-10; mail Cozad Z 69130
Davenport; Inc. Place; THAYER; **201** M-15; elev. 1,654ft./504m.; [P]; Z 68335; Ⓟ 383; Ⓒ 339
Davey; Inc. Place; LANCASTER; **201** J-17; elev. 1,300ft./396m.; [P]; Z 68336; Ⓟ 160; Ⓒ 153
David City; Inc. Place; ⊡ BUTLER; **201** J-16; [P] [H]; Z 68632; Ⓟ 2,522; Ⓒ 2,597
DAWES; **200** E-3; Ⓟ 9,021; Ⓒ 9,060; ◆ 8,964
Dawson; Inc. Place; RICHARDSON; **201** M-19; elev. 1,000ft./305m.; [P]; Z 68337; Ⓟ 157; Ⓒ 209
DAWSON; **200** K-10; Ⓟ 19,940; Ⓒ 24,365; ◆ 24,315
Daykin; Inc. Place; JEFFERSON; **201** M-16; elev. 1,530ft./466m.; [P]; Z 68338; Ⓟ 188; Ⓒ 177
Debolt; RMC Place; DOUGLAS; ***201** I-19; ★ **OMA**; mail Omaha Z 68152; pop. incl. with Omaha (Inc. Place)
Decatur; Inc. Place; BURT; **201** G-18; elev. 1,100ft./335m.; [P]; Z 68020; Ⓟ 641; Ⓒ 618
Denman; RMC Place; BUFFALO; ***201** K-13; mail Kenesaw Z 68956; rural
Denton; Inc. Place; LANCASTER; **201** K-17; elev. 1,234ft./376m.; [P]; Z 68339; Ⓟ 161; Ⓒ 189
Deshler; Inc. Place; THAYER; **201** M-15; elev. 1,550ft./472m.; [P]; Z 68340; Ⓟ 892; Ⓒ 879
De Soto; RMC Place; WASHINGTON; **201** I-19; mail Fort Calhoun Z 68023; ● 30
DEUEL; **200** J-5; Ⓟ 2,237; Ⓒ 2,098; ◆ 1,847
Deweese; Inc. Place; CLAY; **201** L-14; elev. 1,687ft./514m.; [P]; Z 68934; Ⓟ 74; Ⓒ 80
De Witt; Inc. Place; SALINE; **201** L-17; elev. 1,290ft./393m.; [P]; Z 68341; Ⓟ 598; Ⓒ 572
Dickens; RMC Place; LINCOLN; **200** K-7; elev. 3,127ft./953m.; [P]; Z 69132, Z 69170; Ⓟ 16
Diller; Inc. Place; JEFFERSON; **201** M-17; elev. 1,350ft./411m.; [P]; Z 68342 & mail Steele City Z 68440; Ⓟ 298; Ⓒ 287
Dix; Inc. Place; KIMBALL; **200** J-2; elev. 4,554ft./1,388m.; [P]; Z 69133; Ⓟ 229; Ⓒ 267
Dixon; Inc. Place; DIXON; **201** F-16; elev. 1,460ft./445m.; [P]; Z 68732; Ⓟ 87; Ⓒ 108
DIXON; **201** F-17; Ⓟ 6,143; Ⓒ 6,339; ◆ 6,288
Dodge; Inc. Place; DODGE; **201** H-17; elev. 1,400ft./427m.; [P]; Z 68633; Ⓟ 693; Ⓒ 700
DODGE; **201** I-17; Ⓟ 34,500; Ⓒ 36,160; ◆ 35,684
Doniphan; Inc. Place; HALL; **201** K-13; elev. 1,940ft./591m.; [P]; Z 68832; Ⓟ 736; Ⓒ 763
Dorchester; Inc. Place; SALINE; **201** L-16; elev. 1,484ft./452m.; [P]; Z 68343; Ⓟ 614; Ⓒ 615
Douglas; Inc. Place; OTOE; **201** L-18; elev. 1,250ft./381m.; [P]; Z 68344; Ⓟ 199; Ⓒ 231
DOUGLAS; **201** J-18; Ⓟ 416,444; Ⓒ 463,585; ◆ 503,249
Downtown; RMC Place; DOUGLAS; ***201** J-19; ★ **OMA**; mail Omaha Z 68101; pop. incl. with Omaha (Inc. Place)
Du Bois; Inc. Place; PAWNEE; **201** M-19; elev. 1,068ft./326m.; [P]; Z 68345; Ⓟ 119; Ⓒ 166
Duff; RMC Place; ROCK; ***201** G-11; elev. 2,503ft./763m.; mail Bassett Z 68714; rural
Dunbar; Inc. Place; OTOE; **201** K-19; [P]; Z 68346, Z 68382; Ⓟ 171; Ⓒ 237
Duncan; Inc. Place; PLATTE; **201** I-15; elev. 1,492ft./455m.; [P]; Z 68634; Ⓟ 387; Ⓒ 359
DUNDY; **200** M-6; Ⓟ 2,582; Ⓒ 2,292; ◆ 1,952
Dunning; Inc. Place; BLAINE; **200** H-9; elev. 2,624ft./800m.; [P]; Z 68833; Ⓟ 131; Ⓒ 109
Dustin; RMC Place; HOLT; ***201** E-12; elev. 1,927ft./587m.; mail Atkinson Z 68713; rural
Dwight; Inc. Place; BUTLER; **201** J-16; elev. 1,623ft./495m.; [P]; Z 68635; Ⓟ 227; Ⓒ 259

E

Eagle; Inc. Place; CASS; **201** K-18; elev. 1,350ft./411m.; [P]; Z 68347; Ⓟ 1,047; Ⓒ 1,105
East Omaha; RMC Place; DOUGLAS; ***201** J-19; ★ **OMA**; pop. incl. with Omaha (Inc. Place)
Eddyville; Inc. Place; DAWSON; **200** K-10; elev. 2,450ft./747m.; [P]; Z 68834; Ⓟ 102; Ⓒ 96
Edgar; Inc. Place; CLAY; **201** L-14; elev. 1,728ft./527m.; [P]; Z 68935; Ⓟ 600; Ⓒ 539
Edholm; RMC Place; BUTLER; ***201** I-16; elev. 1,367ft./417m.; mail Linwood Z 68036; rural
Edison; Inc. Place; FURNAS; **200** M-10; elev. 2,116ft./645m.; [P]; Z 68936; Ⓟ 148; Ⓒ 154
Elba; Inc. Place; HOWARD; **201** J-13; elev. 1,850ft./564m.; [P]; Z 68835; Ⓟ 196; Ⓒ 243
Eldorado; RMC Place; CLAY; ***201** K-14; elev. 1,770ft./539m.; mail Aurora Z 68818; rural
Elgin; Inc. Place; ANTELOPE; **201** H-14; elev. 1,921ft./586m.; [P]; Z 68636; Ⓟ 731; Ⓒ 735
Eli; RMC Place; CHERRY; **200** E-6; elev. 3,192ft./973m.; mail Valentine Z 69201; rural
Elk City; RMC Place; DOUGLAS; **201** I-18; mail Valley Z 68064; ● 50
Elk Creek; Inc. Place; JOHNSON; **201** M-19; elev. 1,080ft./329m.; [P]; Z 68348; Ⓟ 116; Ⓒ 112
Elkhorn; Inc. Place; DOUGLAS; **201** J-18; elev. 1,200ft./366m.; [P]; ★ **OMA**; Z 68022; Ⓟ 1,398; Ⓒ 6,062
Ellis; RMC Place; GAGE; **201** M-17; mail Beatrice Z 68310; ● 70
Ellsworth; RMC Place; SHERIDAN; **200** G-5; elev. 3,912ft./1,192m.; [P]; Z 69340; ● 30
Elm Creek; Inc. Place; BUFFALO; **201** K-11; elev. 2,262ft./689m.; [P]; Z 68836; Ⓟ 852; Ⓒ 894
Elmwood; Inc. Place; CASS; **201** K-18; elev. 1,250ft./381m.; [P]; Z 68349; Ⓟ 584; Ⓒ 668
Elmwood Park; RMC Place; DOUGLAS; ***201** J-19; ★ **OMA**; mail Omaha Z 68105-06; pop. incl. with Omaha (Inc. Place)
Elsie; Inc. Place; PERKINS; **200** K-6; elev. 3,385ft./1,032m.; [P]; Z 69134; Ⓟ 153; Ⓒ 139
Elsmere; RMC Place; CHERRY; **200** G-9; elev. 2,685ft./818m.; [P]; Z 69135; ● 30
Elwood; Inc. Place; ⊡ GOSPER; **200** L-10; [P]; Z 68937; Ⓟ 679; Ⓒ 761
Elyria; Inc. Place; VALLEY; **201** I-12; [P]; Z 68837; Ⓟ 61; Ⓒ 54
Emerald; RMC Place; LANCASTER; **201** K-17; mail Lincoln Z 68528; ● 170
Emerick; RMC Place; MADISON; ***201** H-15; elev. 1,849ft./564m.; mail Meadow Grove Z 68752; rural
Emerson; Inc. Place; DIXON, DAKOTA, THURSTON; **201** G-17; elev. 1,431ft./436m.; [P]; Z 68733; Ⓟ 791; Ⓒ 817
Emmet; Inc. Place; HOLT; **201** F-12; [P]; Z 68734; Ⓟ 70; Ⓒ 77
Enders; RMC Place; CHASE; **200** L-6; elev. 3,076ft./938m.; [P]; Z 69027; ● 60
Endicott; Inc. Place; JEFFERSON; **201** M-16; elev. 1,350ft./411m.; [P]; Z 68350; Ⓟ 163; Ⓒ 139
Enola; RMC Place; MADISON; **201** H-15; mail Norfolk Z 68701; ● 40
Ericson; Inc. Place; WHEELER; **201** H-13; elev. 2,027ft./618m.; [P]; Z 68637; Ⓟ 111; Ⓒ 104
Ericson Lake; RMC Place; WHEELER; ***201** H-13; elev. 2,018ft./615m.; mail Ericson Z 68637; summer pop. 250; ● 20
Eustis; Inc. Place; FRONTIER; **200** L-10; elev. 2,640ft./805m.; [P]; Z 69028; Ⓟ 452; Ⓒ 464
Ewing; Inc. Place; HOLT; **201** G-13; elev. 1,850ft./564m.; [P]; Z 68735; Ⓟ 449; Ⓒ 433
Exeter; Inc. Place; FILLMORE; **201** L-16; elev. 2,552ft./778m.; [P]; Z 68351; Ⓟ 661; Ⓒ 712

F

Fairbury; Inc. Place; ⊡ JEFFERSON; **201** M-16; elev. 1,317ft./401m.; [P] [H]; Z 68352; Ⓟ 4,335; Ⓒ 4,262
Fairfield; Inc. Place; CLAY; **201** L-14; elev. 1,780ft./543m.; [P]; Z 68938; Ⓟ 458; Ⓒ 467
Fairmont; Inc. Place; FILLMORE; **201** L-15; elev. 1,641ft./500m.; [P]; Z 68354; Ⓟ 708; Ⓒ 691
Fairview Heights; RMC Place; SARPY; ***201** J-19; elev. 1,200ft./366m.; mail Omaha Z 68138; ● 70
Falls City; Inc. Place; ⊡ RICHARDSON; **201** M-20; elev. 1,100ft./335m.; [P] [H]; Z 68355; Ⓟ 4,769; Ⓒ 4,671
Farnam; Inc. Place; DAWSON; **200** K-9; elev. 2,740ft./835m.; [P]; Z 69029; Ⓟ 188; Ⓒ 223
Farwell; Inc. Place; HOWARD; **201** J-13; elev. 2,000ft./610m.; [P]; Z 68838; Ⓟ 152; Ⓒ 148
Filley; Inc. Place; GAGE; **201** M-18; elev. 1,400ft./427m.; [P]; Z 68357; Ⓟ 157; Ⓒ 174
FILLMORE; **201** L-15; Ⓟ 7,103; Ⓒ 6,634; ◆ 5,815
Firth; Inc. Place; LANCASTER; **201** L-17; elev. 1,350ft./411m.; [P]; Z 68358; Ⓟ 471; Ⓒ 564
Florence; RMC Place; DOUGLAS; ***201** I-19; ★ **OMA**; mail Omaha Z 68112, Z 68152; pop. incl. with Omaha (Inc. Place)
Fontanelle; RMC Place; WASHINGTON; **201** I-18; [P]; Z 68044; ● 80
Fordyce; Inc. Place; CEDAR; **201** E-15; elev. 1,380ft./421m.; [P]; Z 68736; Ⓟ 190; Ⓒ 182
Fort Calhoun; Inc. Place; WASHINGTON; **201** I-19; elev. 1,110ft./338m.; [P]; Z 68023; Ⓟ 648; Ⓒ 856
Fort Omaha; RMC Place; DOUGLAS; ★ **OMA**; pop. incl. with Omaha (Inc. Place)
Fort Robinson; RMC Place; DAWES; **200** E-2; mail Crawford Z 69339; ● 60
Foster; Inc. Place; PIERCE; **201** G-15; elev. 1,643ft./501m.; [P]; Z 68765; Ⓟ 57; Ⓒ 63
Foxley; RMC Place; DOUGLAS; ★ **OMA**; pop. incl. with Omaha (Inc. Place)
Franklin; Inc. Place; ⊡ FRANKLIN; **201** M-12; elev. 1,820ft./555m.; [P] [H]; Z 68939; Ⓟ 1,112; Ⓒ 1,026
FRANKLIN; **201** M-12; Ⓟ 3,938; Ⓒ 3,574; ◆ 2,861
Fremont; Inc. Place; ⊡ DODGE; **201** I-18; elev. 1,198ft./365m.; [P] [H] [C] 1,052 ■; Z 68025-26; Ⓟ 23,680; Ⓒ 25,174; ◆ 24,833
Friend; Inc. Place; SALINE; **201** L-16; elev. 1,557ft./475m.; [P] [H]; Z 68359; Ⓟ 1,111; Ⓒ 1,174
FRONTIER; **200** L-8; Ⓟ 3,101; Ⓒ 3,099; ◆ 2,531
Fullerton; Inc. Place; ⊡ NANCE; **201** I-14; elev. 1,657ft./505m.; [P]; Z 68638; Ⓟ 1,452; Ⓒ 1,378
Funk; Inc. Place; PHELPS; **201** L-11; elev. 2,250ft./686m.; [P]; Z 68940; Ⓟ 198; Ⓒ 204
FURNAS; **200** M-9; Ⓟ 5,553; Ⓒ 5,324; ◆ 4,463

G

GAGE; **201** L-17; Ⓟ 22,794; Ⓒ 22,993; ◆ 23,017
Gandy; Inc. Place; LOGAN; **200** I-9; mail Stapleton Z 69163; Ⓟ 51; Ⓒ 30
GARDEN; **200** I-5; Ⓟ 2,460; Ⓒ 2,292; ◆ 1,645
GARFIELD; **201** H-12; Ⓟ 2,141; Ⓒ 1,902; ◆ 1,622
Garland; Inc. Place; SEWARD; **201** K-17; elev. 1,560ft./475m.; [P]; Z 68360; Ⓟ 247; Ⓒ 247
Garrison; Inc. Place; BUTLER; **201** J-16; elev. 1,590ft./485m.; [P]; Z 68632; Ⓟ 71; Ⓒ 67
Gates; RMC Place; CUSTER; ***200** I-10; elev. 2,448ft./746m.; mail Broken Bow Z 68822; rural
Gateway; RMC Place; LANCASTER; ★ **LINC**; mail Lincoln Z 68505; pop. incl. with Lincoln (Inc. Place)
Geneva; Inc. Place; ⊡ FILLMORE; **201** L-15; [P] [H]; Z 68361; Ⓟ 2,310; Ⓒ 2,226
Genoa; Inc. Place; NANCE; **201** I-15; elev. 1,600ft./488m.; [P] [H]; Z 68640; Ⓟ 1,082; Ⓒ 981
Gering; Inc. Place; ⊡ SCOTTS BLUFF; **200** H-1; elev. 3,914ft./1,193m.; [P]; Z 69341; Ⓟ 7,946; Ⓒ 7,751
Gibbon; Inc. Place; BUFFALO; **201** K-12; elev. 2,060ft./628m.; [P]; Z 68840; Ⓟ 1,525; Ⓒ 1,759
Gilead; Inc. Place; THAYER; **201** M-16; elev. 1,550ft./472m.; [P]; Z 68362; Ⓟ 37; Ⓒ 40
Giltner; Inc. Place; HAMILTON; **201** K-14; elev. 1,835ft./559m.; [P]; Z 68841; Ⓟ 367; Ⓒ 389
Gladstone; RMC Place; JEFFERSON; **201** M-16; elev. 1,540ft./469m.; [P]; Z 68352; ● 30
Glen; RMC Place; SIOUX; ***200** F-2; elev. 4,196ft./1,279m.; mail Crawford Z 69339, Harrison Z 69346; rural
Glenover; RMC Place; GAGE; ***201** M-17; mail Beatrice Z 68310; pop. incl. with Beatrice (Inc. Place)
Glenvil (Glenville); Inc. Place; CLAY; **201** L-14; elev. 1,850ft./564m.; [P]; Z 68941; Ⓟ 304; Ⓒ 332
Glenville; CLAY; see Glenvil (Inc. Place)
Glenwood Park; RMC Place; BUFFALO; **201** K-12; mail Kearney Z 68847; ● 250
Goehner; Inc. Place; SEWARD; **201** K-16; elev. 1,545ft./471m.; [P]; Z 68364; Ⓟ 192; Ⓒ 186
Good Samaritan Village; RMC Place; ADAMS; ***201** L-13; mail Hastings Z 68901; pop. incl. with Hastings (Inc. Place)
Gordon; Inc. Place; SHERIDAN; **200** E-5; elev. 3,550ft./1,082m.; [P] [H]; Z 69343; Ⓟ 1,803; Ⓒ 1,756
GOSPER; **200** L-10; Ⓟ 1,928; Ⓒ 2,143; ◆ 1,996
Gothenburg; Inc. Place; DAWSON; **200** K-9; elev. 2,567ft./782m.; [P] [H]; Z 69138; Ⓟ 3,232; Ⓒ 3,619
Grafton; Inc. Place; FILLMORE; **201** L-15; elev. 1,687ft./514m.; [P]; Z 68365; Ⓟ 167; Ⓒ 152
Grainton; RMC Place; PERKINS; **200** K-7; elev. 3,300ft./1,006m.; mail Wallace Z 69169; Ⓟ 16; ● 25
Grand Island; Inc. Place; ⊡ HALL; **201** K-13; elev. 1,870ft./570m.; [P] [H] ■; ★ **GDIS**; Z 68801-03; Ⓟ 39,386; Ⓒ 42,940; ◆ 45,823
Grant; Inc. Place; ⊡ PERKINS; **200** K-6; elev. 3,418ft./1,042m.; [P] [H]; Z 69140; Ⓟ 1,239; Ⓒ 1,225
GRANT; **200** H-5; Ⓟ 769; Ⓒ 747; ◆ 558
Greeley (Greeley Center); Inc. Place; ⊡ GREELEY; **201** I-13; elev. 2,010ft./613m.; [P]; Z 68842; Ⓟ 562; Ⓒ 531
GREELEY; **201** I-13; Ⓟ 3,006; Ⓒ 2,714; ◆ 2,141
Greeley Center; GREELEY; see Greeley (Inc. Place)
Green Meadows; RMC Place; DOUGLAS; ***201** J-18; ★ **OMA**; mail Omaha Z 68164; ● 100
Greenwood; Inc. Place; CASS; **201** K-18; elev. 1,128ft./344m.; [P]; Z 68366; Ⓟ 531; Ⓒ 544
Gresham; Inc. Place; YORK; **201** J-16; elev. 1,623ft./495m.; [P]; Z 68367; Ⓟ 253; Ⓒ 270
Gretna; Inc. Place; SARPY; **201** J-18; elev. 1,248ft./380m.; [P]; Z 68028; Ⓟ 2,249; Ⓒ 2,355
Gross; Inc. Place; BOYD; **201** E-13; elev. 1,770ft./539m.; mail Bristow Z 68719; Ⓟ 7; Ⓒ 5
Grover; RMC Place; SEWARD; ***201** K-16; mail Milford Z 68405; ● 40
Guide Rock; Inc. Place; WEBSTER; **201** M-14; elev. 1,650ft./503m.; [P]; Z 68942; Ⓟ 290; Ⓒ 245
Gurley; Inc. Place; CHEYENNE; **200** I-3; elev. 4,300ft./1,311m.; [P]; Z 69141; Ⓟ 198; Ⓒ 228

H

Hadar; Inc. Place; PIERCE; **201** G-15; elev. 1,550ft./472m.; [P]; Z 68701, Z 68738; Ⓟ 291; Ⓒ 312
Haig; RMC Place; SCOTTS BLUFF; ***200** H-1; mail Mitchell Z 69357; ● 30
Haigler; Inc. Place; DUNDY; **200** M-5; elev. 3,264ft./995m.; [P]; Z 69030; Ⓟ 225; Ⓒ 211
HALL; **201** K-13; Ⓟ 48,925; Ⓒ 53,534; ◆ 55,945
Hallam; Inc. Place; LANCASTER; **201** L-17; elev. 1,490ft./454m.; [P]; Z 68368; Ⓟ 309; Ⓒ 276
Halsey; Inc. Place; THOMAS, BLAINE; **200** H-9; elev. 2,697ft./822m.; [P]; Z 69142; Ⓟ 110; Ⓒ 59
HAMILTON; **201** K-14; Ⓟ 8,862; Ⓒ 9,403; ◆ 9,255
Hamlet; Inc. Place; HAYES; **200** L-7; elev. 2,829ft./862m.; Ⓟ 60; Ⓒ 54
Hampton; Inc. Place; HAMILTON; **201** K-14; elev. 1,760ft./536m.; [P]; Z 68843; Ⓟ 432; Ⓒ 439
Hansen; RMC Place; ADAMS; **201** K-13; mail Hastings Z 68901; ● 50
Harbine; Inc. Place; JEFFERSON; **201** M-17; elev. 1,440ft./439m.; mail Jansen Z 68377; Ⓟ 66; Ⓒ 56
Hardy; Inc. Place; NUCKOLLS; **201** M-14; elev. 1,539ft./469m.; [P]; Z 68943; Ⓟ 206; Ⓒ 179
HARLAN; **201** M-11; Ⓟ 3,810; Ⓒ 3,786; ◆ 3,337
Harrisburg; CDP; ⊡ BANNER; **200** I-1; elev. 4,000ft./1,219m.; [P]; Z 69345; Ⓒ 75
Harrison; Inc. Place; ⊡ SIOUX; **200** E-1; elev. 4,857ft./1,480m.; [P]; Z 69346; Ⓟ 291; Ⓒ 279
Hartington; Inc. Place; ⊡ CEDAR; **201** F-16; elev. 1,400ft./427m.; [P]; Z 68739; Ⓟ 1,583; Ⓒ 1,640
Harvard; Inc. Place; CLAY; **201** L-14; elev. 1,803ft./550m.; [P]; Z 68944; Ⓟ 976; Ⓒ 998
Hastings; Inc. Place; ⊡ ADAMS; **201** L-13; elev. 1,931ft./589m.; [P] [H] [C] 1,137 ■; Z 68901-02; Ⓟ 22,837; Ⓒ 24,064; ◆ 26,773
Havelock; RMC Place; LANCASTER; ***201** K-17; ★ **LINC**; mail Lincoln Z 68529; pop. incl. with Lincoln (Inc. Place)
Havens; RMC Place; MERRICK; ***201** J-15; elev. 1,586ft./483m.; mail Clarks Z 68628; rural
HAYES; **200** L-7; Ⓟ 1,222; Ⓒ 1,068; ◆ 944
Hayes Center; Inc. Place; ⊡ HAYES; **200** L-7; elev. 2,800ft./853m.; [P]; Z 69032; Ⓟ 259; Ⓒ 240
Hay Springs; Inc. Place; SHERIDAN; **200** E-4; elev. 3,830ft./1,167m.; [P]; Z 69347 & mail Whitney Z 69367; Ⓟ 693; Ⓒ 652
Hazard; Inc. Place; SHERMAN; **201** J-12; elev. 2,110ft./643m.; [P]; Z 68844; Ⓟ 78; Ⓒ 66
Heartwell; Inc. Place; KEARNEY; **201** L-12; elev. 2,090ft./637m.; [P]; Z 68945; Ⓟ 69; Ⓒ 80
Hebron; Inc. Place; ⊡ THAYER; **201** M-15; elev. 1,460ft./445m.; [P] [H]; Z 68370; Ⓟ 1,765; Ⓒ 1,565
Hemingford; Inc. Place; BOX BUTTE; **200** G-3; elev. 4,280ft./1,305m.; [P]; Z 69348; Ⓟ 953; Ⓒ 993
Henderson; Inc. Place; YORK; **201** K-15; elev. 1,715ft./523m.; [P] [H]; Z 68371; Ⓟ 999; Ⓒ 986
Hendley; Inc. Place; FURNAS; **200** M-10; elev. 2,231ft./680m.; [P]; Z 68946; Ⓟ 42; Ⓒ 38
Henry; Inc. Place; SCOTTS BLUFF; **200** G-1; elev. 4,040ft./1,231m.; [P]; Z 69358; Ⓟ 145; Ⓒ 162
Herman; Inc. Place; WASHINGTON; **201** H-18; elev. 1,042ft./318m.; [P]; Z 68029; Ⓟ 186; Ⓒ 310
Hershey; Inc. Place; LINCOLN; **200** J-7; elev. 2,895ft./882m.; [P]; Z 69143; Ⓟ 579; Ⓒ 572
Hickman; Inc. Place; LANCASTER; **201** L-17; elev. 1,250ft./381m.; [P]; Z 68372; Ⓟ 1,081; Ⓒ 1,084; Ⓡ 1,111
Hideaway Acres; RMC Place; KNOX; ***201** E-15; elev. 1,380ft./421m.; mail Crofton Z 68730; ● 40
Hildreth; Inc. Place; FRANKLIN; **201** M-12; elev. 2,170ft./661m.; [P]; Z 68947; Ⓟ 364; Ⓒ 370
Hillerage; RMC Place; SCOTTS BLUFF; ***200** H-2; mail Scottsbluff Z 69361; ● 150
HITCHCOCK; **200** M-7; Ⓟ 3,750; Ⓒ 3,111; ◆ 2,719
Holbrook; Inc. Place; FURNAS; **200** M-10; elev. 2,207ft./673m.; [P]; Z 68948; Ⓟ 233; Ⓒ 225
Holdrege; Inc. Place; ⊡ PHELPS; **201** L-11; elev. 2,335ft./712m.; [P] [H]; Z 68949, Z 68969; Ⓟ 5,671; Ⓒ 5,636
Holland; RMC Place; LANCASTER; ***201** L-17; [P]; Z 68372; ● 150
Hollinger; RMC Place; FURNAS; ***200** M-10; mail Oxford Z 68967
Holmesville; RMC Place; GAGE; **201** M-17; elev. 1,250ft./381m.; [P]; Z 68310; ● 100
Holstein; Inc. Place; ADAMS; **201** L-13; elev. 2,010ft./613m.; [P]; Z 68950; Ⓟ 207; Ⓒ 229
HOLT; **201** G-12; Ⓟ 12,599; Ⓒ 11,551; ◆ 10,028
Homer; Inc. Place; DAKOTA; **201** F-18; elev. 1,113ft./339m.; [P]; Z 68030; Ⓟ 553; Ⓒ 590
HOOKER; **200** H-7; Ⓟ 793; Ⓒ 783; ◆ 694
Hooper; Inc. Place; DODGE; **201** I-17; elev. 1,229ft./375m.; [P]; Z 68031; Ⓟ 850; Ⓒ 827
Hordville; Inc. Place; HAMILTON; **201** J-14; elev. 1,780ft./543m.; [P]; Z 68846; Ⓟ 164; Ⓒ 150
Hoskins; Inc. Place; WAYNE; **201** G-16; elev. 1,665ft./507m.; [P]; Z 68740; Ⓟ 307; Ⓒ 283
HOWARD; **201** J-13; Ⓟ 6,055; Ⓒ 6,567; ◆ 6,621
Howard City; HOWARD; see Boelus (Inc. Place)
Howe; RMC Place; NEMAHA; **201** L-19; mail Auburn Z 68305; ● 30
Howells; Inc. Place; COLFAX; **201** H-16; elev. 1,500ft./457m.; [P]; Z 68641; Ⓟ 615; Ⓒ 632
Hubbard; Inc. Place; DAKOTA; **201** F-17; elev. 1,172ft./357m.; [P]; Z 68741; Ⓟ 199; Ⓒ 234
Hubbell; Inc. Place; THAYER; **201** M-15; elev. 1,460ft./445m.; [P]; Z 68375; Ⓟ 55; Ⓒ 73
Humboldt; Inc. Place; RICHARDSON; **201** M-19; elev. 1,010ft./308m.; [P] [H]; Z 68376; Ⓟ 1,003; Ⓒ 941
Humphrey; Inc. Place; PLATTE; **201** H-15; elev. 1,644ft./501m.; [P]; Z 68642; Ⓟ 741; Ⓒ 786
Huntley; Inc. Place; HARLAN; **201** M-11; elev. 2,124ft./647m.; [P]; Z 68971; Ⓟ 58; Ⓒ 67
Hyannis; Inc. Place; ⊡ GRANT; **200** H-6; elev. 3,747ft./1,142m.; [P]; Z 69350; Ⓟ 210; Ⓒ 287

I

Imperial; Inc. Place; ⊡ CHASE; **200** L-6; elev. 3,284ft./1,001m.; [P] [H]; Z 69033; Ⓟ 2,007; Ⓒ 1,982
Inavale; RMC Place; WEBSTER; **201** M-13; elev. 1,726ft./526m.; [P]; Z 68952; ● 130
Indianola; Inc. Place; RED WILLOW; **200** M-9; elev. 2,379ft./725m.; [P]; Z 69034; Ⓟ 672; Ⓒ 642
Indian Village; RMC Place; LANCASTER; ★ **LINC**; mail Lincoln Z 68502, Z 68542; pop. incl. with Lincoln (Inc. Place)
Inglewood; Inc. Place; DODGE; **201** I-18; elev. 1,192ft./363m.; mail Fremont Z 68025; Ⓟ 286; Ⓒ 382
Inland; RMC Place; CLAY; **201** L-14; [P]; Z 68954; ● 100
Inman; Inc. Place; HOLT; **201** F-13; elev. 1,925ft./587m.; [P]; Z 68742; Ⓟ 159; Ⓒ 148
Iowa Reservation; Indian Reservation; RICHARDSON; Reservation extends into KS; Ⓒ 22
Irvington; RMC Place; DOUGLAS; **201** A-17; ★ **OMA**; mail Omaha Z 68134; ● 150
Ithaca; Inc. Place; SAUNDERS; **201** J-17; elev. 1,150ft./351m.; [P]; Z 68033 & mail Memphis Z 68042; Ⓟ 133; Ⓒ 168

J

Jacinto; RMC Place; KIMBALL; ***200** J-2; mail Dix Z 69133; rural
Jackson; Inc. Place; DAKOTA; **201** F-17; elev. 1,120ft./341m.; [P]; Z 68743; Ⓟ 230; Ⓒ 205
Jamison; RMC Place; KEYA PAHA; ***201** E-11; mail Newport Z 68759
Jansen; Inc. Place; JEFFERSON; **201** M-16; elev. 1,463ft./446m.; [P]; Z 68377; Ⓟ 140; Ⓒ 143
JEFFERSON; **201** M-16; Ⓟ 8,759; Ⓒ 8,333; ◆ 7,064
Johnson; Inc. Place; NEMAHA; **201** L-19; elev. 1,243ft./379m.; [P]; Z 68378-79; Ⓟ 323; Ⓒ 280
JOHNSON; **201** L-18; Ⓟ 4,673; Ⓒ 4,488; ◆ 4,209
Johnson Lake; RMC Place; GOSPER; [P]; Z 68937; summer pop. 800
Johnstown; Inc. Place; BROWN; **200** F-9; elev. 2,594ft./791m.; [P]; Z 69214; Ⓟ 48; Ⓒ 53
Julian; Inc. Place; NEMAHA; **201** L-19; elev. 1,050ft./320m.; [P]; Z 68378-79; Ⓟ 71; Ⓒ 63
Juniata; Inc. Place; ADAMS; **201** L-13; [P]; Z 68955; Ⓟ 811; Ⓒ 693

K

Kearney; Inc. Place; ⊡ BUFFALO; **201** K-12; elev. 2,153ft./656m.; [P] [H] [C] 6,468 ■; Z 68845, Z 68847-49; Ⓟ 24,396; Ⓒ 27,431; ◆ 29,338
KEARNEY; **201** L-12; Ⓟ 6,629; Ⓒ 6,882; ◆ 6,596
Keene; RMC Place; KEARNEY; ***201** L-12; mail Axtell Z 68924
KEITH; **200** J-6; Ⓟ 8,584; Ⓒ 8,875; ◆ 7,922
Kenesaw; Inc. Place; ADAMS; **201** L-13; elev. 2,050ft./625m.; [P]; Z 68956; Ⓟ 818; Ⓒ 873
Kennard; Inc. Place; WASHINGTON; **201** I-18; elev. 1,144ft./349m.; [P]; Z 68034; Ⓟ 371; Ⓒ 371
KEYA PAHA; **200** E-10; Ⓟ 1,029; Ⓒ 983; ◆ 797
Keystone; RMC Place; KEITH; **200** J-6; elev. 3,100ft./945m.; [P]; Z 69144; ● 90
Kilgore; Inc. Place; CHERRY; **200** E-8; elev. 2,919ft./890m.; [P]; Z 69216; Ⓟ 79; Ⓒ 99
Kimball; Inc. Place; ⊡ KIMBALL; **200** J-1; elev. 4,709ft./1,435m.; [P] [H]; Z 69145; Ⓟ 2,574; Ⓒ 2,559
KIMBALL; **200** J-1; Ⓟ 4,108; Ⓒ 4,089; ◆ 3,325
King Lake; RMC Place; DOUGLAS; ***201** I-18; ★ **OMA**; mail Valley Z 68064; ● 350
Knievels Corner; RMC Place; HOLT; ***201** G-13; mail Ewing Z 68735; rural
KNOX; **201** F-15; Ⓟ 9,534; Ⓒ 9,374; ◆ 8,547
Kohles Acres; RMC Place; KNOX; ***201** E-15; elev. 1,250ft./381m.; mail Crofton Z 68730; ● 60
Kramer; RMC Place; LANCASTER; **201** L-17; mail Crete Z 68333; ● 60
Kronborg; RMC Place; HAMILTON; ***201** K-14; mail Marquette Z 68854
Kuesters Lake; RMC Place; HALL; ***201** K-14; ★ **GDIS**; mail Grand Island Z 68801; ● 150

L

Lake Forest Estates; RMC Place; DOUGLAS; **201** B-17; ★ **OMA**; mail Omaha Z 68134; pop. incl. with Omaha (Inc. Place)
Lakeside; RMC Place; SHERIDAN; **200** G-4; elev. 3,884ft./1,184m.; [P]; Z 69351; ● 30
Lamar; Inc. Place; CHASE; **200** L-5; elev. 3,300ft./1,006m.; [P]; Z 69023; Ⓟ 31; Ⓒ 19
LANCASTER; **201** K-17; Ⓟ 213,641; Ⓒ 250,291; ◆ 290,075
Lanham; RMC Place; GAGE; **201** M-17; mail Odell Z 68415; ● 30
La Platte; RMC Place; SARPY; **201** J-19; ★ **OMA**; mail Bellevue Z 68123; ● 200
Laurel; Inc. Place; CEDAR; **201** F-16; elev. 1,480ft./451m.; [P]; Z 68745; Ⓟ 981; Ⓒ 986
La Vista; Inc. Place; SARPY; **201** D-17; elev. 1,050ft./320m.; [P]; ★ **OMA**; Z 68128, Z 68138; Ⓟ 9,840; Ⓒ 11,699
Lawrence; Inc. Place; NUCKOLLS; **201** M-14; elev. 1,881ft./573m.; [P]; Z 68957; Ⓟ 323; Ⓒ 312
Lebanon; Inc. Place; RED WILLOW; **200** M-9; elev. 2,396ft./730m.; [P]; Z 69036; Ⓟ 75; Ⓒ 70
Lee Valley; RMC Place; DOUGLAS; ★ **OMA**; mail Omaha Z 68134; pop. incl. with Omaha (Inc. Place)
Leigh; Inc. Place; COLFAX; **201** H-16; elev. 1,600ft./488m.; [P]; Z 68643; Ⓟ 447; Ⓒ 442
Lemoyne; RMC Place; KEITH; **200** J-6; elev. 3,300ft./1,006m.; [P]; Z 69146; ● 170
Leshara; Inc. Place; SAUNDERS; **201** I-18; elev. 1,165ft./355m.; [P]; Z 68064; Ⓟ 118; Ⓒ 111
Lewellen; Inc. Place; GARDEN; **200** I-5; elev. 3,300ft./1,006m.; [P]; Z 69147; Ⓟ 307; Ⓒ 282
Lewiston; Inc. Place; PAWNEE; **201** M-18; elev. 1,450ft./442m.; [P]; Z 68380; Ⓟ 64; Ⓒ 86
Lexington; Inc. Place; ⊡ DAWSON; **200** K-10; elev. 2,390ft./728m.; [P] [H]; Z 68850; Ⓟ 6,601; Ⓒ 10,011
Liberty; Inc. Place; GAGE; **201** M-18; elev. 1,300ft./396m.; [P]; Z 68381; Ⓟ 74; Ⓒ 86
Lillian; RMC Place; CUSTER; ***200** I-10; elev. 2,557ft./779m.; mail Broken Bow Z 68822; rural
Lincoln; Inc. Place; **STATE CAPITAL**; ⊡ LANCASTER; **201** K-17; elev. 1,176ft./358m.; [P] [H] [C] 25,901 ■; ★ **LINC**; Z 68501-10, Z 68512, Z 68514, Z 68516-17, Z 68520-24, Z 68526-29, Z 68531-32, Z 68542, Z 68583, Z 68588; Ⓟ 191,972; Ⓒ 225,581; ◆ 269,866
LINCOLN; **200** K-7; Ⓟ 32,508; Ⓒ 34,632; ◆ 35,072
Lindsay; Inc. Place; PLATTE; **201** H-15; elev. 1,660ft./506m.; [P]; Z 68644; Ⓟ 321; Ⓒ 276
Lindy; RMC Place; KNOX; **201** E-15; mail Bloomfield Z 68718; ● 20
Linoma Beach; RMC Place; SARPY; ***201** J-18; elev. 1,064ft./324m.; mail Gretna Z 68028; rural
Linwood; Inc. Place; BUTLER; **201** I-17; elev. 1,341ft./409m.; [P]; Z 68036; Ⓟ 91; Ⓒ 118
Lisco; RMC Place; GARDEN; **200** I-4; [P]; Z 69148; ● 110
Litchfield; Inc. Place; SHERMAN; **201** J-12; elev. 2,170ft./661m.; [P]; Z 68852; Ⓟ 314; Ⓒ 280
Lodgepole; Inc. Place; CHEYENNE; **200** J-4; elev. 3,830ft./1,167m.; [P]; Z 69149; Ⓟ 368; Ⓒ 348
LOGAN; **200** I-9; Ⓟ 878; Ⓒ 774; ◆ 736
Loma; RMC Place; BUTLER; **201** J-17; mail Brainard Z 68626; ● 30
Londer; RMC Place; KEARNEY; ***201** L-12; elev. 2,158ft./658m.; mail Kearney Z 68847; ● 80
Long Pine; Inc. Place; BROWN; **200** F-10; elev. 2,402ft./732m.; [P]; Z 69217; Ⓟ 396; Ⓒ 341
Loomis; Inc. Place; PHELPS; **201** L-11; elev. 2,420ft./738m.; [P]; Z 68958; Ⓟ 376; Ⓒ 397
Lorenzo; RMC Place; CHEYENNE; **200** J-3; elev. 4,390ft./1,338m.; mail Sidney Z 69162; ● 20
Loretto; RMC Place; BOONE; **201** H-14; mail Albion Z 68620; ● 30
Lorton (Lorton Village); Inc. Place; OTOE; **201** L-19; elev. 1,030ft./314m.; [P]; Z 68346, Z 68382; Ⓟ 61; Ⓒ 39
Lorton Village; OTOE; see Lorton (Inc. Place)
Louisville; Inc. Place; CASS; **201** J-18; elev. 1,044ft./318m.; [P]; Z 68037; Ⓟ 998; Ⓒ 1,046
LOUP; **201** H-11; Ⓟ 683; Ⓒ 712; ◆ 631
Loup City; Inc. Place; ⊡ SHERMAN; **201** J-12; elev. 2,072ft./632m.; [P]; Z 68853; Ⓟ 1,104; Ⓒ 996
Lowell; RMC Place; KEARNEY; **201** L-12; elev. 2,063ft./629m.; mail Gibbon Z 68840; ● 30
Lushton; Inc. Place; YORK; **201** K-15; elev. 1,675ft./511m.; mail Henderson Z 68371; Ⓟ 28; Ⓒ 33
Lyman; Inc. Place; SCOTTS BLUFF; **200** H-1; elev. 1,640ft./500m.; [P]; Z 69352; Ⓟ 452; Ⓒ 421
Lynch; Inc. Place; BOYD; **201** E-13; elev. 1,400ft./427m.; [P] [H]; Z 68746; Ⓟ 296; Ⓒ 269
Lyons; Inc. Place; BURT; **201** H-18; elev. 1,280ft./390m.; [P]; Z 68038; Ⓟ 1,144; Ⓒ 963

M

Macon; RMC Place; FRANKLIN; **201** M-12; mail Franklin Z 68939; ● 30
Macy; CDP; THURSTON; **201** G-18; elev. 1,110ft./338m.; [P]; Z 68039; Ⓟ 836; Ⓒ 956
Madison; Inc. Place; ⊡ MADISON; **201** H-15; elev. 1,581ft./482m.; [P]; Z 68748; Ⓟ 2,135; Ⓒ 2,367
MADISON; **201** H-15; Ⓟ 32,655; Ⓒ 35,226; ◆ 31,602
Madrid; Inc. Place; PERKINS; **200** K-6; elev. 3,300ft./1,006m.; [P]; Z 69150; Ⓟ 288; Ⓒ 265
Magnet; Inc. Place; CEDAR; **201** F-15; elev. 1,820ft./555m.; [P]; Z 68749; Ⓟ 69; Ⓒ 79
Malcolm; Inc. Place; LANCASTER; **201** K-17; elev. 1,300ft./396m.; [P]; Z 68402; Ⓟ 181; Ⓒ 413
Malmo; Inc. Place; SAUNDERS; **201** J-17; elev. 1,250ft./381m.; [P]; Z 68040; Ⓟ 114; Ⓒ 109
Manley; Inc. Place; CASS; **201** K-18; elev. 1,280ft./390m.; [P]; Z 68403; Ⓟ 170; Ⓒ 191
Maple Hills; RMC Place; DOUGLAS; ★ **OMA**; mail Omaha Z 68134; pop. incl. with Omaha (Inc. Place)
Mariaville; RMC Place; ROCK; ***201** E-11; elev. 1,914ft./583m.; mail Newport Z 68759; rural
Marion; RMC Place; RED WILLOW; **200** N-9; mail Danbury Z 69026; ● 40
Marquette; Inc. Place; HAMILTON; **201** K-14; elev. 1,829ft./557m.; [P]; Z 68854; Ⓟ 211; Ⓒ 282
Marsland; RMC Place; DAWES; **200** F-2; elev. 4,157ft./1,267m.; [P]; Z 69354; ● 10
Martell; RMC Place; LANCASTER; **201** L-17; elev. 1,350ft./411m.; [P]; Z 68404; ● 100
Martinsburg; Inc. Place; DIXON; **201** F-17; elev. 1,252ft./382m.; mail Allen Z 68710, Ponca Z 68770; Ⓟ 90; Ⓒ 103
Mascot; RMC Place; HARLAN; ***201** M-11; mail Oxford Z 68967
Maskell; Inc. Place; DIXON; **201** E-16; elev. 1,290ft./393m.; [P]; Z 68751; Ⓟ 54; Ⓒ 67
Mason; CUSTER; see Mason City (Inc. Place)
Mason City (Mason); Inc. Place; CUSTER; **201** J-11; elev. 2,250ft./686m.; [P]; Z 68855; Ⓟ 160; Ⓒ 178
Max; RMC Place; DUNDY; **200** M-6; elev. 2,895ft./882m.; [P]; Z 69037; ● 90
Maxwell; Inc. Place; LINCOLN; **200** J-8; elev. 2,711ft./826m.; [P]; Z 69151; Ⓟ 285; Ⓒ 315
Maywood; Inc. Place; FRONTIER; **200** L-8; elev. 2,693ft./821m.; [P]; Z 69038; Ⓟ 313; Ⓒ 331
McCook; Inc. Place; ⊡ RED WILLOW; **200** M-8; elev. 2,576ft./785m.; [P] [H] ■; Z 69001; Ⓟ 8,112; Ⓒ 7,994; Ⓡ 7,996; ◆ 7,316
McCool Junction; Inc. Place; YORK; **201** K-15; elev. 1,557ft./475m.; [P]; Z 68401; Ⓟ 372; Ⓒ 385
McGrew; Inc. Place; SCOTTS BLUFF; **200** H-2; elev. 3,780ft./1,152m.; [P]; Z 69353; Ⓟ 99; Ⓒ 103
McLean; Inc. Place; PIERCE; **201** F-15; elev. 1,820ft./555m.; [P]; Z 68747; Ⓟ 49; Ⓒ 38
MCPHERSON; **200** I-7; Ⓟ 546; Ⓒ 533; ◆ 540
Mead; Inc. Place; SAUNDERS; **201** J-18; elev. 1,200ft./366m.; [P]; Z 68041; Ⓟ 513; Ⓒ 564
Meadow; SARPY; see Meadow Oaks (RMC Place)
Meadow Grove; Inc. Place; MADISON; **201** G-15; elev. 1,638ft./499m.; [P]; Z 68752; Ⓟ 332; Ⓒ 311
Meadow Oaks (Meadow); RMC Place; SARPY; ***201** J-18; elev. 1,026ft./313m.; mail Springfield Z 68059; ● 120
Melbeta; Inc. Place; SCOTTS BLUFF; **200** H-2; elev. 3,825ft./1,166m.; [P]; Z 69355; Ⓟ 116; Ⓒ 138
Memphis; Inc. Place; SAUNDERS; **201** J-18; elev. 1,100ft./335m.; [P]; Z 68042; Ⓟ 117; Ⓒ 106
Menominee; RMC Place; CEDAR; **201** E-15; mail Fordyce Z 68736; ● 30
Merna; Inc. Place; CUSTER; **200** I-10; elev. 2,669ft./814m.; [P]; Z 68856; Ⓟ 377; Ⓒ 391
MERRICK; **201** J-14; Ⓟ 8,042; Ⓒ 8,204; ◆ 7,412
Merriman; Inc. Place; CHERRY; **200** E-6; elev. 3,260ft./994m.; [P]; Z 69218; Ⓟ 151; Ⓒ 118
Milburn; RMC Place; CUSTER; **200** H-10; elev. 2,472ft./753m.; [P]; Z 68813; rural
Milford; Inc. Place; SEWARD; **201** K-16; [P]; Z 68405; Ⓟ 1,886; Ⓒ 2,070
Millard; RMC Place; DOUGLAS, SARPY; ***201** J-18; [P]; ★ **OMA**; Z 68144-45 & mail Omaha Z 68137; pop. incl. with Omaha (Inc. Place)
Millard Highlands; RMC Place; DOUGLAS; ★ **OMA**; mail Omaha Z 68137, Z 68144-45; pop. incl. with Omaha (Inc. Place)
Miller; Inc. Place; BUFFALO; **201** K-11; elev. 2,311ft./704m.; [P]; Z 68858; Ⓟ 130; Ⓒ 156
Milligan; Inc. Place; FILLMORE; **201** L-16; elev. 1,600ft./488m.; [P]; Z 68406; Ⓟ 328; Ⓒ 315
Millis Beach; RMC Place; DAKOTA; ***201** F-18; elev. 1,097ft./334m.; ★ **SXCY**; mail Dakota City Z 68731; ● 30
Mills; RMC Place; KEYA PAHA; ***201** E-11; elev. 1,920ft./585m.; [P]; Z 68753
Milton Store; RMC Place; BUFFALO; ***201** J-11; elev. 2,233ft./681m.; mail Miller Z 68858; rural
Minatare; Inc. Place; SCOTTS BLUFF; **200** H-2; elev. 3,822ft./1,165m.; [P]; Z 69356; Ⓟ 807; Ⓒ 810
Minden; Inc. Place; ⊡ KEARNEY; **201** L-12; elev. 2,172ft./662m.; [P] [H]; Z 68959; Ⓟ 2,749; Ⓒ 2,964
Minersville; RMC Place; OTOE; ***201** L-19; elev. 931ft./284m.; mail Nebraska City Z 68410; rural
Mitchell; Inc. Place; SCOTTS BLUFF; **200** H-1; [P]; Z 69357; Ⓟ 1,743; Ⓒ 1,831
Monowi; Inc. Place; BOYD; **201** E-13; elev. 1,325ft./404m.; mail Lynch Z 68746; Ⓟ 6; Ⓒ 2
Monroe; Inc. Place; PLATTE; **201** I-15; elev. 1,522ft./464m.; [P]; Z 68647; Ⓟ 309; Ⓒ 307
Monterey; RMC Place; CUMING; ***201** H-17; mail West Point Z 68788; rural
Moorefield; Inc. Place; FRONTIER; **200** L-9; elev. 2,824ft./861m.; [P]; Z 69039; Ⓟ 52; Ⓒ 52
Morrill; Inc. Place; SCOTTS BLUFF; **200** G-1; elev. 3,988ft./1,216m.; [P]; Z 69358; Ⓟ 974; Ⓒ 957
MORRILL; **200** H-3; Ⓟ 5,423; Ⓒ 5,440; ◆ 5,011
Morse Bluff; Inc. Place; SAUNDERS; **201** I-17; elev. 1,295ft./395m.; [P]; Z 68648; Ⓟ 128; Ⓒ 134

Entries in **UPPERCASE** are counties.
Entries in **bold** have populations of 2,500 or more.
Names in parentheses are alternate names.

Inc. Place	Incorporated Place
RMC Place	Rand McNally Designated Place
CDP	Census Designated Place
MCD	Minor Civil Division
⊡	County Seat
▲	Minor Civil Division
elev.	Elevation
[P]	Post Office
[H]	Hospital
[C]	College
■	Principal Business Center
★	Ranally Metro Area (RMA) Abbreviation
Z	Zip Code(s)
Ⓟ	Previous Census Population
Ⓡ	Revised Census Population
Ⓐ	Annexation Population
●	Rand McNally Population Estimate
Ⓒ	Final Census Population
Ⓢ	Special Census Population
◆	Estimated Population

For additional definitions see Glossary, Volume 1, and Introduction, Volume 2.

Mount Michael; RMC Place; DOUGLAS; ***201** I-18; elev. 1,200ft./366m.; ★ **OMA**; mail Elkhorn Z 68022; ● 200

Mullen; Inc. Place; ⊡ HOOKER; **200** G-7; elev. 3,217ft./981m.; 🅿; Z 69152; ℗ 554; © 491

Murdock; Inc. Place; CASS; **201** K-18; elev. 1,280ft./390m.; 🅿; Z 68407; ℗ 267; © 269

Murphy; RMC Place; HAMILTON; ***201** K-14; mail Phillips Z 68865; rural

Murray; Inc. Place; CASS; **201** K-19; elev. 1,145ft./349m.; 🅿; Z 68409; ℗ 418; © 481

Mynard; RMC Place; CASS; **201** J-19; mail Plattsmouth Z 68048; ● 60

N

NANCE; **201** I-14; ℗ 4,275; © 4,038; ◆ 3,398

Naper; Inc. Place; BOYD; **201** E-12; elev. 1,980ft./604m.; 🅿; Z 68755; ℗ 130; © 105

Naponee; Inc. Place; FRANKLIN; **201** M-12; elev. 1,877ft./572m.; 🅿; Z 68960; ℗ 97; © 132

Nashville; RMC Place; WASHINGTON; ***201** I-19; elev. 1,085ft./331m.; mail Omaha Z 68112; ● 100

Nebraska City; Inc. Place; ⊡ OTOE; **201** K-19; elev. 1,029ft./314m.; 🅿 🅷; Z 68410; ℗ 6,547; © 7,228

Nehawka; Inc. Place; CASS; **201** K-19; elev. 992ft./302m.; 🅿; Z 68413; ℗ 260; © 232

Neligh; Inc. Place; ⊡ ANTELOPE; **201** G-14; elev. 1,750ft./533m.; 🅿 🅷; Z 68756; ℗ 1,742; © 1,651

Nelson; Inc. Place; ⊡ NUCKOLLS; **201** M-14; elev. 1,686ft./514m.; 🅿; Z 68961 & mail Oak Z 68964; ℗ 627; © 587

Nemaha; Inc. Place; NEMAHA; **201** L-20; elev. 914ft./279m.; 🅿; Z 68414; ℗ 188; © 178

NEMAHA; **201** L-19; ℗ 7,980; © 7,576; ◆ 6,788

Nenzel; Inc. Place; CHERRY; **200** E-7; elev. 3,114ft./949m.; 🅿; Z 69219; ℗ 8; © 13

Newark; RMC Place; KEARNEY; ***201** L-12; elev. 2,104ft./641m.; mail Gibbon Z 68840, Kearney Z 68847; ● 30

Newcastle (Ponce); Inc. Place; DIXON; **201** F-17; elev. 1,310ft./399m.; 🅿; Z 68757; ℗ 271; © 299

Newman Grove; Inc. Place; MADISON, PLATTE; **201** H-15; elev. 1,740ft./530m.; 🅿; Z 68758; ℗ 787; © 797

Newport; Inc. Place; ROCK; **201** F-11; elev. 2,233ft./681m.; 🅿; Z 68759; ℗ 136; © 98

Nickerson; Inc. Place; DODGE; **201** I-18; elev. 1,199ft./365m.; 🅿; Z 68044; ℗ 291; © 431

Nimburg; RMC Place; BUTLER; ***201** I-17; elev. 1,429ft./436m.; mail Linwood Z 68036; rural

Nim City; RMC Place; RICHARDSON; ***201** M-19; elev. 1,000ft./305m.; mail Dawson Z 68337; rural

Niobrara; Inc. Place; KNOX; **201** E-14; elev. 1,226ft./374m.; 🅿; Z 68760; ℗ 376; © 379

Nora; Inc. Place; NUCKOLLS; **201** M-14; elev. 1,752ft./534m.; 🅿; Z 68961; ℗ 24; © 20

Norfolk; Inc. Place; MADISON; **201** G-15; elev. 1,527ft./465m.; 🅿 ■; Z 68701-02; ℗ 21,476; © 23,516; ◆ 21,079

Norman; Inc. Place; KEARNEY; **201** L-12; elev. 2,075ft./632m.; 🅿; Z 68959; ℗ 48; © 49

North Auburn; RMC Place; NEMAHA; mail Auburn Z 68305; pop. incl. with Auburn (Inc. Place)

North Bend; Inc. Place; DODGE; **201** I-17; elev. 1,273ft./388m.; 🅿; Z 68649; ℗ 1,249; © 1,213

North Loup; Inc. Place; VALLEY; **201** I-12; elev. 1,960ft./597m.; 🅿; Z 68859; ℗ 361; © 339

North Oaks; RMC Place; DOUGLAS; ***201** I-19; ★ **OMA**; mail Omaha Z 68122; ● 900

North Omaha; RMC Place; DOUGLAS; ★ **OMA**; mail Omaha Z 68112; pop. incl. with Omaha (Inc. Place)

North Platte; Inc. Place; ⊡ LINCOLN; **200** J-8; elev. 2,800ft./853m.; 🅿 🅷 ■; Z 69101, Z 69103; ℗ 22,605; © 23,878; ◆ 23,600

Northport; RMC Place; MORRILL; **200** H-3; mail Bridgeport Z 69336; ● 80

North Shore; RMC Place; DAKOTA; ***201** F-18; ★ **SXCY**; mail South Sioux City Z 68776; ● 80

Northwest; RMC Place; DOUGLAS; ***201** I-19; ★ **OMA**; mail Omaha Z 68122, Z 68134, Z 68142, Z 68164; pop. incl. with Omaha (Inc. Place)

NUCKOLLS; **201** M-14; ℗ 5,786; © 5,057; ◆ 4,337

O

Oak; Inc. Place; NUCKOLLS; **201** M-14; elev. 1,592ft./485m.; 🅿; Z 68964; ℗ 68; © 60

Oakdale; Inc. Place; ANTELOPE; **201** G-14; elev. 1,707ft./520m.; 🅿; Z 68761; ℗ 362; © 345

Oakland; Inc. Place; BURT; **201** H-18; elev. 1,287ft./392m.; 🅿 🅷; Z 68045; ℗ 1,279; © 1,367

Obert; Inc. Place; CEDAR; **201** E-16; elev. 1,336ft./407m.; 🅿; Z 68757; ℗ 39; © 49

Oconto; Inc. Place; CUSTER; **200** J-10; elev. 2,566ft./782m.; 🅿; Z 68860; ℗ 147; © 141

Octavia; Inc. Place; BUTLER; **201** I-16; elev. 1,410ft./430m.; 🅿; Z 68632; ℗ 132; © 145

Odell; Inc. Place; GAGE; **201** M-17; 🅿; Z 68415; ℗ 291; © 345

Odessa; RMC Place; BUFFALO; **201** K-11; elev. 2,220ft./677m.; 🅿; Z 68861; ● 140

Offutt AFB (Offutt AFB West); CDP-Census Area Only; SARPY; ***201** J-19; 🅿; ★ **OMA**; Z 68113; ℗ 10,883; © 8,901

Offutt AFB West; SARPY; see Offutt AFB (CDP-Census Area Only)

Ogallala; Inc. Place; ⊡ KEITH; **200** J-6; elev. 3,223ft./982m.; 🅿 🅷; Z 69153; ℗ 5,095; © 4,930

Ohiowa; Inc. Place; FILLMORE; **201** L-16; elev. 1,590ft./485m.; 🅿; Z 68416; ℗ 146; © 142

Old Mill; RMC Place; DOUGLAS; ★ **OMA**; mail Omaha Z 68134; pop. incl. with Omaha (Inc. Place)

Olean; RMC Place; COLFAX; ***201** H-17; mail Dodge Z 68633; rural

Omaha; Inc. Place; ⊡ DOUGLAS; **201** J-19; elev. 1,040ft./317m.; 🅿 🅷 🅲 26,996 ■; ★ **OMA**; Z 68101-14, Z 68116-20, Z 68122, Z 68124, Z 68127, Z 68130-32, Z 68134-39, Z 68142, Z 68144-45, Z 68147, Z 68152, Z 68154-55, Z 68157, Z 68164, Z 68172, Z 68175-76, Z 68178-80, Z 68182-83, Z 68197-98 & mail Papillion Z 68046, Z 68133; ℗ 335,719; © 390,007; ◆ 419,706

Omaha Reservation; Indian Reservation; THURSTON, BURT, CUMING; Reservation extends into IA; mail Macy Z 68039; also location of Indian Agency; ℗ 5,459; © 5,194

O'Neill; Inc. Place; ⊡ HOLT; **201** F-13; elev. 2,000ft./610m.; 🅿 🅷; Z 68763; ℗ 3,852; © 3,733

Ong; Inc. Place; CLAY; **201** L-15; elev. 1,680ft./512m.; 🅿; Z 68452; ℗ 69; © 67

Orchard; Inc. Place; ANTELOPE; **201** G-14; elev. 1,946ft./593m.; 🅿; Z 68764; ℗ 439; © 391

Ord; Inc. Place; ⊡ VALLEY; **201** I-12; elev. 2,049ft./625m.; 🅿 🅷; Z 68862; ℗ 2,481; © 2,269

Orleans; Inc. Place; HARLAN; **201** M-11; elev. 1,996ft./608m.; 🅿; Z 68966; ℗ 490; © 425

Orum; RMC Place; WASHINGTON; **201** I-18; mail Blair Z 68008; ● 30

Osceola; Inc. Place; ⊡ POLK; **201** J-15; elev. 1,627ft./496m.; 🅿 🅷; Z 68651; ℗ 879; © 921

Oshkosh; Inc. Place; ⊡ GARDEN; **200** I-4; elev. 3,600ft./1,097m.; 🅿 🅷; Z 69154, Z 69190; ℗ 986; © 887

Osmond; Inc. Place; PIERCE; **201** F-15; 🅿 🅷; Z 68765; ℗ 774; © 796

Otoe; Inc. Place; OTOE; **201** K-19; elev. 1,118ft./341m.; 🅿; Z 68417; ℗ 196; © 217

OTOE; **201** K-18; ℗ 14,252; © 15,396; ◆ 15,678

Overton; Inc. Place; DAWSON; **201** K-11; elev. 2,316ft./706m.; 🅿; Z 68863 & mail Eddyville Z 68834; ℗ 547; © 646

Oxford; Inc. Place; FURNAS, HARLAN; **200** M-10; elev. 2,075ft./632m.; 🅿; Z 68967; ℗ 949; © 876

P

Page; Inc. Place; HOLT; **201** F-13; elev. 1,956ft./596m.; 🅿; Z 68766; ℗ 191; © 157

Palisade; Inc. Place; HITCHCOCK; **200** M-7; elev. 2,765ft./843m.; 🅿; Z 69040; ℗ 381; © 386

Palmer; Inc. Place; MERRICK; **201** J-14; 🅿; Z 68864; ℗ 753; © 472

Palmyra; Inc. Place; OTOE; **201** K-18; elev. 1,133ft./345m.; 🅿; Z 68418; ℗ 545; © 546

Panama; Inc. Place; LANCASTER; **201** L-18; elev. 1,400ft./427m.; 🅿; Z 68419; ℗ 207; © 253

Papillion; Inc. Place; ⊡ SARPY; **201** J-19; elev. 1,029ft./314m.; 🅿 🅷; ★ **OMA**; Z 68046, Z 68133 & mail Omaha Z 68157; ℗ 10,378; © 16,363; ◆ 22,086

Parks; RMC Place; DUNDY; **200** M-6; elev. 3,096ft./944m.; 🅿; Z 69041; ● 50

Parkview; RMC Place; HALL; ***201** K-13; ★ **GDIS**; mail Grand Island Z 68801; pop. incl. with Grand Island (Inc. Place)

Paul; RMC Place; OTOE; ***201** L-19; mail Nebraska City Z 68410

Pauline; RMC Place; ADAMS; **201** L-13; mail Glenvil Z 68941; ● 60

Pawnee; PAWNEE; see Pawnee City (Inc. Place)

PAWNEE; **201** N-18; ℗ 3,317; © 3,087; ◆ 2,617

Pawnee City (Pawnee); Inc. Place; ⊡ PAWNEE; **201** M-19; elev. 1,190ft./363m.; 🅿 🅷; Z 68420; ℗ 1,008; © 1,033

Paxton; Inc. Place; KEITH; **200** J-7; 🅿; Z 69155; ℗ 536; © 614

Pecks Grove; RMC Place; LANCASTER; ★ **LINC**; pop. incl. with Lincoln (Inc. Place)

Pender; Inc. Place; ⊡ THURSTON; **201** G-17; elev. 1,331ft./406m.; 🅿 🅷; Z 68047; ℗ 1,208; © 1,148

PERKINS; **200** K-6; ℗ 3,367; © 3,200; ◆ 2,874

Peru; Inc. Place; NEMAHA; **201** L-19; elev. 1,000ft./305m.; 🅿 🅲 2,127; Z 68421; ℗ 1,110; © 569; ® 922

Petersburg; Inc. Place; BOONE; **201** H-14; elev. 1,898ft./579m.; 🅿; Z 68652; ℗ 388; © 374

PHELPS; **201** L-11; ℗ 9,715; © 9,747; ◆ 8,734

Phillips; Inc. Place; HAMILTON; **201** K-14; elev. 1,880ft./573m.; 🅿; Z 68865; ℗ 316; © 336

Pickrell; Inc. Place; GAGE; **201** L-17; elev. 1,321ft./403m.; 🅿; Z 68422; ℗ 201; © 182

Pierce; Inc. Place; ⊡ PIERCE; **201** G-15; elev. 1,579ft./481m.; 🅿; Z 68767; ℗ 1,615; © 1,774

PIERCE; **201** G-15; ℗ 7,827; © 7,857; ◆ 6,986

Pilger; Inc. Place; STANTON; **201** G-16; elev. 1,407ft./429m.; 🅿; Z 68768; ℗ 361; © 378

Pine Ridge; CDP-Census Area Only; SHERIDAN; ***200** D-4; © 14

Plainview; Inc. Place; PIERCE; **201** F-15; elev. 1,690ft./515m.; 🅿 🅷; Z 68769; ℗ 1,333; © 1,353

PLATTE; **201** I-15; ℗ 29,820; © 31,662; ◆ 32,358

Platte Center; Inc. Place; PLATTE; **201** I-15; elev. 1,550ft./472m.; 🅿; Z 68653; ℗ 387; © 359

Plattsmouth; Inc. Place; ⊡ CASS; **201** J-19; elev. 1,000ft./305m.; 🅿; Z 68048; ℗ 6,412; © 6,887

Pleasant Dale; Inc. Place; SEWARD; **201** K-17; elev. 1,300ft./396m.; 🅿; Z 68423; ℗ 253; © 245

Pleasant Hill; RMC Place; SALINE; ***201** L-16; mail Dorchester Z 68343; ● 30

Pleasanton; Inc. Place; BUFFALO; **201** K-12; elev. 2,080ft./634m.; 🅿; Z 68866; ℗ 372; © 360

Pleasant Valley; RMC Place; CEDAR; ***201** F-15; elev. 1,570ft./479m.; mail Hartington Z 68739; rural

Plymouth; Inc. Place; JEFFERSON; **201** M-17; elev. 1,431ft./436m.; 🅿; Z 68424; ℗ 455; © 477

Polk; Inc. Place; POLK; **201** J-15; elev. 1,740ft./530m.; 🅿; Z 68654; ℗ 345; © 322

POLK; **201** J-15; ℗ 5,675; © 5,639; ◆ 5,143

Ponca; Inc. Place; ⊡ DIXON; **201** F-17; elev. 1,143ft./348m.; 🅿; Z 68770; ℗ 877; © 1,062

Ponce; DIXON; see Newcastle (Inc. Place)

Poole; RMC Place; BUFFALO; **201** K-12; mail Ravenna Z 68869

Potter; Inc. Place; CHEYENNE; **200** J-2; elev. 4,389ft./1,338m.; 🅿; Z 69156; ℗ 388; © 390

Powell; RMC Place; JEFFERSON; **201** M-16; mail Fairbury Z 68352; ● 20

Prague; Inc. Place; SAUNDERS; **201** J-17; elev. 1,350ft./411m.; 🅿; Z 68050; ℗ 282; © 346

Prairie Home; RMC Place; LANCASTER; **201** K-18; mail Lincoln Z 68527; ● 70

Precept; RMC Place; FURNAS; ***200** M-10; mail Stamford Z 68977; rural

Preston; Inc. Place; RICHARDSON; **201** M-20; elev. 880ft./268m.; mail Falls City Z 68355; ℗ 40; © 50

Primrose; Inc. Place; BOONE; **201** I-14; elev. 1,830ft./558m.; 🅿; Z 68655; ℗ 69; © 69

Princeton; RMC Place; LANCASTER; **201** L-17; mail Martell Z 68404; ● 50

Prosser; Inc. Place; ADAMS; **201** L-13; elev. 2,050ft./625m.; 🅿; Z 68883; ℗ 77; © 94

Purdum; RMC Place; BLAINE; **200** G-9; elev. 2,698ft./822m.; 🅿; Z 69157; ● 20

R

Raeville; RMC Place; BOONE; **201** H-14; elev. 1,950ft./594m.; mail Petersburg Z 68652; ● 20

Ragan; Inc. Place; HARLAN; **201** M-11; elev. 2,330ft./710m.; 🅿; Z 68949, Z 68969; ℗ 59; © 46

Ralston; Inc. Place; DOUGLAS; **201** C-17; elev. 1,100ft./335m.; 🅿; ★ **OMA**; Z 68127-28 & mail Omaha Z 68117; ℗ 6,236; © 6,314

Randolph; Inc. Place; CEDAR; **201** F-16; elev. 1,660ft./506m.; 🅿; Z 68771; ℗ 983; © 955

Ravenna; Inc. Place; BUFFALO; **201** J-12; elev. 2,018ft./615m.; 🅿; Z 68869; ℗ 1,317; © 1,341

Raymond; Inc. Place; LANCASTER; **201** K-17; elev. 1,220ft./372m.; 🅿; Z 68428; ℗ 167; © 186

Red Cloud; Inc. Place; ⊡ WEBSTER; **201** M-13; 🅿 🅷; Z 68970; ℗ 1,204; © 1,131

Redington; RMC Place; MORRILL; ***200** I-2; mail Bridgeport Z 69336; ● 30

RED WILLOW; **200** M-8; ℗ 11,705; © 11,448; ® 11,450; ◆ 10,351

Regency; RMC Place; DOUGLAS; ★ **OMA**; mail Omaha Z 68114; pop. incl. with Omaha (Inc. Place)

Republican; HARLAN; see Republican City (Inc. Place)

Republican City (Republican); Inc. Place; HARLAN; **201** M-11; elev. 1,942ft./592m.; 🅿; Z 68971; ℗ 199; © 209

Reynolds; Inc. Place; JEFFERSON; **201** M-16; 🅿; Z 68429; ℗ 104; © 88

RICHARDSON; **201** M-19; ℗ 9,937; © 9,531; ◆ 7,923

Richfield; RMC Place; SARPY; ***201** J-19; elev. 1,200ft./366m.; 🅿; Z 68059; ● 30

Richland; Inc. Place; COLFAX; **201** I-16; elev. 1,399ft./426m.; 🅿; Z 68601; ℗ 96; © 89

Ringgold; RMC Place; MCPHERSON; ***200** I-8; mail Tryon Z 69167

Rising City; Inc. Place; BUTLER; **201** J-16; elev. 1,590ft./485m.; 🅿; Z 68658; ℗ 341; © 386

Riverdale; Inc. Place; BUFFALO; **201** K-12; elev. 2,181ft./665m.; 🅿; Z 68870; ℗ 208; © 213

Riverside Lakes; RMC Place; DOUGLAS; ***201** J-18; elev. 1,115ft./340m.; ★ **OMA**; mail Waterloo Z 68069; ● 480

Riverside Park; RMC Place; SEWARD; ***201** K-16; elev. 1,410ft./430m.; mail Central City Z 68826, Milford Z 68405; ● 30

Riverton; Inc. Place; FRANKLIN; **201** M-13; elev. 1,768ft./539m.; 🅿; Z 68972; ℗ 162; © 145

Roanoke; RMC Place; DOUGLAS; ★ **OMA**; mail Omaha Z 68134; pop. incl. with Omaha (Inc. Place)

Roca; Inc. Place; LANCASTER; **201** K-17; elev. 1,250ft./381m.; 🅿; Z 68430; ℗ 84; © 220

ROCK; **201** G-11; ℗ 2,019; © 1,756; ◆ 1,489

Rockford; RMC Place; GAGE; ***201** M-18; mail Beatrice Z 68310

Rockville; Inc. Place; SHERMAN; **201** J-12; elev. 1,970ft./600m.; 🅿; Z 68871; ℗ 87; © 111

Rogers; Inc. Place; COLFAX; **201** I-17; 🅿; Z 68659; ℗ 89; © 95

Rokeby; RMC Place; LANCASTER; ***201** K-17; ★ **LINC**; mail Lincoln Z 68523; rural

Rosalie; Inc. Place; THURSTON; **201** G-17; elev. 1,350ft./411m.; 🅿; Z 68055; ℗ 178; © 194

Roscoe; RMC Place; KEITH; **200** J-6; mail Ogallala Z 69153; ● 50

Rose; RMC Place; ROCK; **201** G-11; elev. 2,500ft./762m.; 🅿; Z 68714; ● 10

Roseland; Inc. Place; ADAMS; **201** L-13; elev. 1,972ft./601m.; 🅿; Z 68973; ℗ 247; © 242

Rosemont; RMC Place; WEBSTER; **201** M-13; elev. 1,949ft./594m.; 🅿; Z 68930; ● 20

Rosenburg; RMC Place; PLATTE; ***201** I-15; mail Lindsay Z 68644; rural

Round Valley; RMC Place; CUSTER; ***201** I-11; elev. 2,669ft./814m.; mail Broken Bow Z 68822; rural

Royal; Inc. Place; ANTELOPE; **201** G-14; elev. 1,869ft./570m.; 🅿; Z 68773; ℗ 81; © 75

Rulo; Inc. Place; RICHARDSON; **201** M-20; elev. 923ft./281m.; 🅿; Z 68431; ℗ 191; © 226

Rushville; Inc. Place; ⊡ SHERIDAN; **200** E-4; elev. 3,746ft./1,142m.; 🅿; Z 69360 & mail Whiteclay Z 69365; ℗ 1,127; © 999

Ruskin; Inc. Place; NUCKOLLS; **201** M-15; elev. 1,680ft./512m.; 🅿; Z 68974; ℗ 187; © 195

S

Sac and Fox Reservation; Indian Reservation; RICHARDSON; Reservation extends into KS; mail Falls City Z 68355, Rulo Z 68431; ℗ 920; © 131

Sacramento; RMC Place; PHELPS; ***201** L-11; elev. 2,265ft./690m.; mail Holdrege Z 68949; rural

Saddle Creek (West Dodge); RMC Place; DOUGLAS; ***201** J-19; ★ **OMA**; mail Omaha Z 68131-32; pop. incl. with Omaha (Inc. Place)

Saint Bernard; RMC Place; PLATTE; **201** H-15; mail Lindsay Z 68644; ● 30

Saint Columbans; RMC Place; SARPY; ***201** J-19; elev. 965ft./294m.; ★ **OMA**; mail St Columbans Z 68056; ● 30

Saint Edward; Inc. Place; BOONE; **201** I-14; elev. 1,660ft./506m.; 🅿; Z 68660; ℗ 822; © 796

Saint Helena; Inc. Place; CEDAR; **201** E-16; elev. 1,242ft./379m.; 🅿; Z 68774; ℗ 87; © 86

Saint James; RMC Place; CEDAR; ***201** E-16; mail Wynot Z 68792; ● 30

Saint Libory; RMC Place; HOWARD; **201** J-13; elev. 1,863ft./568m.; 🅿; Z 68872; ● 270

Saint Mary; RMC Place; JOHNSON; **201** L-18; elev. 1,150ft./351m.; 🅿; Z 68443; ● 50

Saint Paul; Inc. Place; ⊡ HOWARD; **201** J-13; elev. 1,811ft./552m.; 🅿 🅷; Z 68873; ℗ 2,009; © 2,218

Saint Stephens; RMC Place; NUCKOLLS; ***201** M-14; mail Lawrence Z 68957; rural

Salem; Inc. Place; RICHARDSON; **201** M-20; elev. 1,000ft./305m.; 🅿; Z 68433; ℗ 160; © 138

SALINE; **201** L-16; ℗ 12,715; © 13,843; ◆ 13,781

Santee; Inc. Place; KNOX; **201** E-14; elev. 1,250ft./381m.; mail Niobrara Z 68760; ℗ 365; © 302

Santee Reservation; Indian Reservation; KNOX; mail Niobrara Z 68760; also location of Indian Agency; ℗ 914; © 878

Sarben; RMC Place; KEITH; **200** J-7; mail Paxton Z 69155; ● 30

Sargent; Inc. Place; CUSTER; **201** I-11; elev. 2,314ft./705m.; 🅿 🅷; Z 68874; ℗ 710; © 649

Saronville; Inc. Place; CLAY; **201** L-14; elev. 1,746ft./532m.; 🅿; Z 68975; ℗ 38; © 61

SARPY; **201** J-18; ℗ 102,583; © 122,595; ◆ 153,561

SAUNDERS; **201** J-17; ℗ 18,285; © 19,830; ◆ 20,041

Schaupps; RMC Place; SHERMAN; ***201** J-12; elev. 2,085ft./636m.; mail Ashton Z 68817; rural

Schuyler; Inc. Place; ⊡ COLFAX; **201** I-16; elev. 1,354ft./413m.; 🅿 🅷; Z 68661; ℗ 4,052; © 5,371

Scotia; Inc. Place; GREELEY; **201** I-13; elev. 1,924ft./586m.; 🅿; Z 68875; ℗ 318; © 308

Scottsbluff; Inc. Place; SCOTTS BLUFF; **200** H-1; elev. 3,885ft./1,184m.; 🅿 🅷 ■; Z 69361, Z 69363 & mail McGrew Z 69353; ℗ 13,711; © 14,732; ◆ 14,463

SCOTTS BLUFF; **200** H-1; ℗ 36,025; © 36,951; ◆ 36,234

Scribner; Inc. Place; DODGE; **201** H-17; elev. 1,255ft./383m.; 🅿; Z 68057; ℗ 950; © 971

Seneca; Inc. Place; THOMAS; **200** G-8; elev. 2,974ft./906m.; 🅿; Z 69161; ℗ 78; © 51

Seward; Inc. Place; ⊡ SEWARD; **201** K-16; elev. 1,452ft./443m.; 🅿 🅷 🅲 1,251; Z 68434; ℗ 5,634; © 6,319

SEWARD; **201** K-16; ℗ 15,450; © 16,496; ◆ 16,087

Seymour; RMC Place; DOUGLAS; ★ **OMA**; pop. incl. with Omaha (Inc. Place)

Seymour Park; RMC Place; DOUGLAS; ***201** J-19; ★ **OMA**; mail Omaha Z 68127; pop. incl. with Ralston (Inc. Place)

Shelby; Inc. Place; POLK; **201** J-15; elev. 1,640ft./500m.; 🅿; Z 68662; ℗ 690; © 690

Shelton; Inc. Place; BUFFALO; **201** K-13; elev. 2,018ft./615m.; 🅿; Z 68876; ℗ 954; © 1,140

SHERIDAN; **200** F-4; ℗ 6,750; © 6,198; ◆ 5,288

SHERMAN; **201** J-12; ℗ 3,718; © 3,318; ◆ 2,904

Shickley; Inc. Place; FILLMORE; **201** L-15; elev. 1,650ft./503m.; 🅿; Z 68436; ℗ 360; © 376

Sholes; Inc. Place; WAYNE; **201** G-16; elev. 1,720ft./524m.; mail Randolph Z 68771; ℗ 22; © 24

Shubert; Inc. Place; RICHARDSON; **201** M-20; elev. 1,123ft./342m.; 🅿; Z 68437; ℗ 237; © 252

Sidney; Inc. Place; ⊡ CHEYENNE; **200** J-3; elev. 4,085ft./1,245m.; 🅿 🅷; Z 69160, Z 69162; ℗ 5,959; © 6,282

Silver Creek; Inc. Place; MERRICK; **201** J-15; elev. 1,547ft./472m.; 🅿; Z 68663; ℗ 625; © 441

SIOUX; **200** F-1; ℗ 1,549; © 1,475; ◆ 1,294

Skyline; RMC Place; DOUGLAS; ***201** J-18; elev. 1,250ft./381m.; ★ **OMA**; mail Elkhorn Z 68022; pop. incl. with Elkhorn (Inc. Place); ℗ 2,563

Smithfield; Inc. Place; GOSPER; **200** L-10; elev. 2,545ft./776m.; 🅿; Z 68976; ℗ 53; © 68

Smyrna; RMC Place; NUCKOLLS; ***201** M-14; elev. 1,790ft./546m.; mail Superior Z 68978; rural

Snyder; Inc. Place; DODGE; **201** H-17; elev. 1,340ft./408m.; 🅿; Z 68664; ℗ 280; © 318

South Bend; Inc. Place; CASS; **201** J-18; elev. 1,050ft./320m.; 🅿; Z 68058; ℗ 93; © 86

South Minden; RMC Place; KEARNEY; mail Minden Z 68959; pop. incl. with Minden (Inc. Place)

South Omaha; RMC Place; DOUGLAS; ***201** J-19; ★ **OMA**; mail Omaha Z 68107; pop. incl. with Omaha (Inc. Place)

South Sioux City; Inc. Place; DAKOTA; **201** F-18; elev. 1,096ft./334m.; 🅿; ★ **SXCY**; Z 68776; ℗ 9,677; © 11,925

South Yankton; RMC Place; CEDAR; ***201** E-15; mail Saint Helena Z 68774, Yankton Z 57078; ● 50

Spalding; Inc. Place; GREELEY; **201** H-13; elev. 1,900ft./579m.; 🅿; Z 68665; ℗ 592; © 537

Sparks; RMC Place; CHERRY; ***200** E-9; elev. 2,596ft./791m.; 🅿; Z 69220; ● 10

Sparta; RMC Place; KNOX; ***201** F-14; mail Verdigre Z 68783; rural

Spencer; Inc. Place; BOYD; **201** E-13; elev. 1,684ft./513m.; 🅿; Z 68777; ℗ 536; © 541

Spencer Park; RMC Place; ADAMS; mail Hastings Z 68901; pop. incl. with Hastings (Inc. Place)

Sprague; Inc. Place; LANCASTER; **201** L-17; elev. 1,258ft./383m.; 🅿; Z 68438; ℗ 157; © 146

Springfield; Inc. Place; SARPY; **201** J-18; elev. 1,100ft./335m.; 🅿; Z 68059; ℗ 1,426; © 1,450

Springview; Inc. Place; ⊡ KEYA PAHA; **200** E-10; elev. 2,448ft./746m.; 🅿; Z 68778; ℗ 304; © 244

Stamford; Inc. Place; HARLAN; **201** M-11; elev. 2,050ft./625m.; 🅿; Z 68977; ℗ 188; © 202

Stanton; Inc. Place; ⊡ STANTON; **201** H-16; elev. 1,473ft./449m.; 🅿; Z 68779; ℗ 1,549; © 1,627

STANTON; **201** H-16; ℗ 6,244; © 6,455; ◆ 6,184

Staplehurst; Inc. Place; SEWARD; **201** K-16; elev. 1,500ft./457m.; 🅿; Z 68439; ℗ 281; © 270

Stapleton; Inc. Place; ⊡ LOGAN; **200** I-9; elev. 3,000ft./914m.; 🅿; Z 69163; ℗ 299; © 301

State House; RMC Place; LANCASTER; ★ **LINC**; mail Lincoln Z 68509; pop. incl. with Lincoln (Inc. Place)

Steele City; Inc. Place; JEFFERSON; **201** M-17; elev. 1,300ft./396m.; 🅿; Z 68440; ℗ 101; © 84

Steinauer; Inc. Place; PAWNEE; **201** M-18; elev. 1,210ft./369m.; 🅿; Z 68441; ℗ 92; © 74

Stella; Inc. Place; RICHARDSON; **201** M-19; elev. 1,000ft./305m.; 🅿; Z 68442; ℗ 248; © 220

Sterling; Inc. Place; JOHNSON; **201** L-18; elev. 1,179ft./359m.; 🅿; Z 68443 & mail Burr Z 68324; ℗ 451; © 507

Still Meadow; RMC Place; DOUGLAS; ★ **OMA**; mail Omaha Z 68122; pop. incl. with Omaha (Inc. Place)

Stockham; Inc. Place; HAMILTON; **201** K-14; elev. 1,700ft./518m.; mail Aurora Z 68818; ℗ 64; © 60

Stockville; Inc. Place; ⊡ FRONTIER; **200** L-9; 🅿; Z 69042; ℗ 32; © 36

Stock Yards; RMC Place; DOUGLAS; ***201** J-19; ★ **OMA**; mail Omaha Z 68107; pop. incl. with Omaha (Inc. Place)

Strang; Inc. Place; FILLMORE; **201** L-15; elev. 1,620ft./494m.; 🅿; Z 68444; ℗ 42; © 32

Stratton; Inc. Place; HITCHCOCK; **200** M-7; elev. 2,798ft./853m.; 🅿; Z 69043; ℗ 427; © 396

Stromsburg; Inc. Place; POLK; **201** J-15; elev. 1,678ft./511m.; 🅿; Z 68666; ℗ 1,241; © 1,232

Stuart; Inc. Place; HOLT; **201** F-12; elev. 2,150ft./655m.; 🅿; Z 68780; ℗ 650; © 625

Summit; RMC Place; DOUGLAS; ★ **OMA**; pop. incl. with Omaha (Inc. Place)

Sumner; Inc. Place; DAWSON; **201** K-11; elev. 2,370ft./722m.; 🅿; Z 68878; ℗ 210; © 237

Sunnyslope; RMC Place; DOUGLAS; ★ **OMA**; mail Omaha Z 68134; pop. incl. with Omaha (Inc. Place)

Sunol; RMC Place; CHEYENNE; **200** J-3; mail Lodgepole Z 69149; ● 100

Superior; Inc. Place; NUCKOLLS; **201** M-14; elev. 1,573ft./479m.; 🅿 🅷; Z 68978; ℗ 2,397; © 2,055

Surprise; Inc. Place; BUTLER; **201** J-16; elev. 1,550ft./472m.; 🅿; Z 68667; ℗ 55; © 44

Sutherland; Inc. Place; LINCOLN; **200** J-7; elev. 2,569ft./783m.; 🅿; Z 69165; ℗ 1,032; © 1,129

Sutton; Inc. Place; CLAY; **201** L-15; elev. 1,680ft./512m.; 🅿; Z 68979; ℗ 1,353; © 1,447

Swanton; Inc. Place; SALINE; **201** L-16; elev. 1,341ft./409m.; 🅿; Z 68445; ℗ 145; © 106

Swedeburg; RMC Place; SAUNDERS; **201** J-17; mail Wahoo Z 68066; ● 40

Sybrant; RMC Place; ROCK; ***201** G-11; elev. 2,442ft./744m.; mail Bassett Z 68714; rural

Syracuse; Inc. Place; OTOE; **201** K-18; elev. 1,050ft./320m.; 🅿 🅷; Z 68446; ℗ 1,646; © 1,762

T

Table Rock; Inc. Place; PAWNEE; **201** M-19; elev. 1,038ft./316m.; 🅿; Z 68447; ℗ 308; © 264

Talmage; Inc. Place; OTOE; **201** L-19; elev. 980ft./299m.; 🅿; Z 68448; ℗ 246; © 268

Tamora; RMC Place; SEWARD; **201** K-16; elev. 1,550ft./472m.; mail Seward Z 68434; ℗ 51

Tarnov; Inc. Place; PLATTE; **201** I-15; elev. 1,650ft./503m.; 🅿; Z 68642; ℗ 61; © 63

Taylor; Inc. Place; ⊡ LOUP; **201** H-11; elev. 2,269ft./692m.; 🅿; Z 68879; ℗ 186; © 207

Tecumseh; Inc. Place; ⊡ JOHNSON; **201** L-18; elev. 1,142ft./348m.; 🅿 🅷; Z 68450; ℗ 1,702; © 1,716

Tekamah; Inc. Place; ⊡ BURT; **201** H-18; elev. 1,058ft./322m.; 🅿; Z 68061; ℗ 1,852; © 1,892

Telbasta; RMC Place; WASHINGTON; ***201** I-18; mail Arlington Z 68002

Terrytown; Inc. Place; SCOTTS BLUFF; **200** H-1; elev. 3,870ft./1,180m.; mail Gering Z 69341; ℗ 656; © 646

Thayer; Inc. Place; YORK; **201** K-15; elev. 1,600ft./488m.; mail Waco Z 68460; ℗ 64; © 71

THAYER; **201** M-15; ℗ 6,635; © 6,055; ◆ 5,108

Thedford; Inc. Place; ⊡ THOMAS; **200** H-8; elev. 2,848ft./868m.; 🅿; Z 69166; ℗ 243; © 211

THOMAS; **200** H-8; ℗ 851; © 729; ◆ 588

Thompson; RMC Place; JEFFERSON; ***201** M-16; mail Fairbury Z 68352

Thurston; Inc. Place; THURSTON; **201** G-17; elev. 1,400ft./427m.; 🅿; Z 68062; ℗ 98; © 125

THURSTON; **201** G-17; ℗ 6,936; © 7,171; ◆ 7,080

Tilden; Inc. Place; MADISON, ANTELOPE; **201** G-15; elev. 1,681ft./512m.; 🅿 🅷; Z 68781; ℗ 895; © 1,078

Tobias; Inc. Place; SALINE; **201** L-16; elev. 1,600ft./488m.; 🅿; Z 68453; ℗ 127; © 158

Tomahawk Hills; RMC Place; DOUGLAS; ★ **OMA**; pop. incl. with Omaha (Inc. Place)

Touhy; RMC Place; SAUNDERS; **201** J-17; mail Valparaiso Z 68065; ● 30

Trenton; Inc. Place; ⊡ HITCHCOCK; **200** M-7; elev. 2,674ft./815m.; 🅿; Z 69044; ℗ 656; © 507

Trumbull; Inc. Place; CLAY, ADAMS; **201** L-14; elev. 1,875ft./572m.; 🅿; Z 68980; ℗ 225; © 212

Tryon; RMC Place; ⊡ MCPHERSON; **200** I-8; elev. 3,266ft./995m.; 🅿; Z 69167; ● 150

U

Uehling; Inc. Place; DODGE; **201** H-18; elev. 1,250ft./381m.; 🅿; Z 68063; ℗ 273; © 275

Ulysses; Inc. Place; BUTLER; **201** J-16; elev. 1,520ft./463m.; 🅿; Z 68667, Z 68669; ℗ 256; © 276

Unadilla; Inc. Place; OTOE; **201** K-18; elev. 1,100ft./335m.; 🅿; Z 68454; ℗ 294; © 342

Underwood Hills; RMC Place; DOUGLAS; ★ **OMA**; pop. incl. with Omaha (Inc. Place)

Union; Inc. Place; CASS; **201** K-19; elev. 1,000ft./305m.; 🅿; Z 68455; ℗ 299; © 260

University Place; RMC Place; LANCASTER; ***201** K-17; ★ **LINC**; mail Lincoln Z 68504; pop. incl. with Lincoln (Inc. Place)

Upland; Inc. Place; FRANKLIN; **201** M-12; elev. 2,160ft./658m.; 🅿; Z 68981; ℗ 169; © 179

Utica; Inc. Place; SEWARD; **201** K-16; elev. 1,590ft./485m.; 🅿; Z 68456; ℗ 718; © 844

V

Valentine; Inc. Place; ⊡ CHERRY; **200** E-8; elev. 2,579ft./786m.; 🅿 🅷; Z 69201; ℗ 2,826; © 2,820

Valley; Inc. Place; DOUGLAS; **201** I-18; elev. 1,137ft./347m.; 🅿; ★ **OMA**; Z 68064; ℗ 1,775; © 1,788

VALLEY; **201** I-12; ℗ 5,169; © 4,647; ◆ 4,164

Valparaiso; Inc. Place; SAUNDERS; **201** J-17; 🅿; Z 68065; ℗ 481; © 563

Venango; Inc. Place; PERKINS; **200** K-5; elev. 3,597ft./1,096m.; 🅿; Z 69168; ℗ 192; © 175

Venice; RMC Place; DOUGLAS; **201** J-18; ★ **OMA**; mail Waterloo Z 68069; ● 180

Verdel; Inc. Place; KNOX; **201** E-14; elev. 1,258ft./383m.; 🅿; Z 68760; ℗ 59; © 58

Verdigre; Inc. Place; KNOX; **201** F-14; elev. 1,352ft./412m.; 🅿; Z 68783; ℗ 607; © 519

Verdon; Inc. Place; RICHARDSON; **201** M-20; elev. 950ft./290m.; 🅿; Z 68457 & mail Salem Z 68433; ℗ 242; © 223

Vesta; RMC Place; JOHNSON; ***201** L-18; elev. 1,231ft./375m.; mail Tecumseh Z 68450; ● 20

Villa Springs; RMC Place; SARPY; ***201** J-19; elev. 989ft./301m.; mail Springfield Z 68059; ● 50

Virginia; Inc. Place; GAGE; **201** M-18; elev. 1,540ft./469m.; 🅿; Z 68458; ℗ 94; © 67

Vorhees; RMC Place; BOONE; ***201** I-14; elev. 1,732ft./528m.; mail Albion Z 68620; rural

W

Wabash; RMC Place; CASS; ***201** K-18; mail Murdock Z 68407; ● 50

Waco; Inc. Place; YORK; **201** K-15; elev. 1,625ft./495m.; 🅿; Z 68460; ℗ 211; © 256

Wagners Lake; RMC Place; PLATTE; ***201** I-16; mail Columbus Z 68601; pop. incl. with Columbus (Inc. Place)

Wahoo; Inc. Place; ⊡ SAUNDERS; **201** J-17; elev. 1,200ft./366m.; 🅿 🅷; Z 68066; ℗ 3,681; © 3,942

Wakefield; Inc. Place; DIXON, WAYNE; **201** G-17; elev. 1,383ft./422m.; 🅿; Z 68784; ℗ 1,082; © 1,411

Walkers Valley View; RMC Place; KNOX; ***201** E-15; elev. 1,220ft./372m.; mail Crofton Z 68730; ● 40

Wallace; Inc. Place; LINCOLN; **200** K-7; elev. 3,108ft./947m.; 🅿; Z 69169; ℗ 308; © 329

Walthill; Inc. Place; THURSTON; **201** G-18; elev. 1,302ft./397m.; 🅿; Z 68067; ℗ 747; © 909

Walton; RMC Place; LANCASTER; **201** K-18; elev. 1,200ft./366m.; 🅿; ★ **LINC**; Z 68461; ● 80

Walworth; RMC Place; CUSTER; ***201** I-11; elev. 2,729ft./832m.; mail Sargent Z 68874; rural

Wann; RMC Place; SAUNDERS; **201** J-18; mail Ashland Z 68003; ● 20

Washington; Inc. Place; WASHINGTON; **201** I-18; elev. 1,150ft./351m.; 🅿; Z 68068; ℗ 125; © 126

WASHINGTON; **201** I-18; ℗ 16,607; © 18,780; ◆ 19,982

Waterbury; Inc. Place; DIXON; **201** F-17; elev. 1,283ft./391m.; 🅿; Z 68785; ℗ 95; © 89

Waterloo; Inc. Place; DOUGLAS; **201** J-18; elev. 1,128ft./344m.; 🅿; ★ **OMA**; Z 68069; ℗ 479; © 459

Wauneta; Inc. Place; CHASE; **200** L-7; elev. 2,938ft./896m.; 🅿; Z 69045; ℗ 675; © 625

Wausa; Inc. Place; KNOX; **201** F-15; elev. 1,771ft./540m.; 🅿; Z 68786; ℗ 598; © 636

Waverly; Inc. Place; LANCASTER; **201** K-18; elev. 1,120ft./341m.; 🅿; Z 68462; ℗ 1,869; © 2,448

Wayne; Inc. Place; ⊡ WAYNE; **201** G-16; elev. 1,500ft./457m.; 🅿 🅷 🅲 3,415; Z 68787; ℗ 5,142; © 5,583

WAYNE; **201** G-16; ℗ 9,364; © 9,851; ◆ 8,804

Wayside; RMC Place; DAWES; ***200** D-2; mail Chadron Z 69337; rural

WEBSTER; **201** M-13; ℗ 4,279; © 4,061; ◆ 3,530

Weeping Water; Inc. Place; CASS; **201** K-18; 🅿; Z 68463; ℗ 1,008; © 1,103

Wee Town; RMC Place; PIERCE; ***201** G-15; elev. 1,657ft./505m.; mail Pierce Z 68767; rural

Weissert; RMC Place; CUSTER; **201** I-11; elev. 2,428ft./740m.; 🅿; Z 68814; ● 30

Wellfleet; Inc. Place; LINCOLN; **200** K-8; elev. 2,810ft./856m.; 🅿; Z 69170; ℗ 63; © 76

West Benson; RMC Place; DOUGLAS; ★ **OMA**; pop. incl. with Omaha (Inc. Place)

West Dodge; DOUGLAS; see Saddle Creek (RMC Place)

Western; Inc. Place; SALINE; **201** L-16; elev. 1,450ft./442m.; 🅿; Z 68464; ℗ 264; © 287

Westerville; RMC Place; CUSTER; **201** I-11; elev. 2,333ft./711m.; 🅿; Z 68881; ● 30

West Lincoln; RMC Place; LANCASTER; ***201** K-17; ★ **LINC**; pop. incl. with Lincoln (Inc. Place)

West Omaha; RMC Place; DOUGLAS; ***201** J-19; ★ **OMA**; mail Omaha Z 68114, Z 68124; pop. incl. with Omaha (Inc. Place)

Weston; Inc. Place; SAUNDERS; **201** J-17; elev. 1,255ft./383m.; 🅿; Z 68070; ℗ 299; © 310

West Point; Inc. Place; ⊡ CUMING; **201** H-17; elev. 1,335ft./407m.; 🅿 🅷; Z 68788; ℗ 3,250; © 3,660

WHEELER; **201** H-13; ℗ 948; © 886; ◆ 813

Whiteclay; RMC Place; SHERIDAN; **200** E-4; elev. 3,300ft./1,006m.; 🅿; Z 69365; ● 30

Whitman; RMC Place; GRANT; **200** G-6; elev. 3,588ft./1,094m.; 🅿; Z 69366; ● 140

Whitney; Inc. Place; DAWES; **200** E-3; elev. 3,411ft./1,040m.; 🅿; Z 69367; ℗ 38; © 87

Wilber; Inc. Place; ⊡ SALINE; **201** L-17; elev. 1,329ft./405m.; 🅿; Z 68465; ℗ 1,527; © 1,761

Wilcox; Inc. Place; KEARNEY; **201** L-12; elev. 2,220ft./677m.; 🅿; Z 68982; ℗ 349; © 360

Willis; RMC Place; DAKOTA; ***201** F-17; mail Jackson Z 68743

Willow Island; RMC Place; DAWSON; **200** K-9; elev. 2,523ft./769m.; 🅿; Z 69171; ● 20

Wilsonville; Inc. Place; FURNAS; **200** M-9; elev. 2,304ft./702m.; 🅿; Z 69046; ℗ 136; © 118

Winnebago; Inc. Place; THURSTON; **201** G-18; located on Winnebago Ind. Res.; elev. 1,200ft./366m.; 🅿 🅷; Z 68071; location of Indian Agency; ℗ 705; © 768

Winnebago Reservation; Indian Reservation; THURSTON, DIXON; Reservation extends into IA; mail Winnebago Z 68071; also location of Indian Agency; ℗ 2,554; © 2,588

Winnetoon; Inc. Place; KNOX; **201** F-14; elev. 1,645ft./501m.; 🅿; Z 68789; ℗ 59; © 70

Winside; Inc. Place; WAYNE; **201** G-16; elev. 1,618ft./493m.; 🅿; Z 68790; ℗ 434; © 468

Winslow; Inc. Place; DODGE; **201** I-18; elev. 1,215ft./370m.; 🅿; Z 68072; ℗ 140; © 104

Wisner; Inc. Place; CUMING; **201** H-17; elev. 1,379ft./420m.; 🅿; Z 68791; ℗ 1,253; © 1,270

Wolbach; Inc. Place; GREELEY; **201** I-13; elev. 1,900ft./579m.; 🅿; Z 68882; ℗ 280; © 287

Wood Lake; Inc. Place; CHERRY; **200** F-9; elev. 2,700ft./823m.; 🅿; Z 69221; ℗ 59; © 72

Woodland Park; RMC Place; STANTON; ***201** G-16; elev. 1,669ft./509m.; mail Norfolk Z 68701; ● 550

Wood River; Inc. Place; HALL; **201** K-13; elev. 1,965ft./599m.; 🅿; Z 68883; ℗ 1,156; © 1,204

Worms; RMC Place; MERRICK; **201** J-14; mail Saint Libory Z 68872; ● 30

Wymore; Inc. Place; GAGE; **201** M-17; elev. 1,241ft./378m.; 🅿; Z 68466; ℗ 1,611; © 1,656

Wynot; Inc. Place; CEDAR; **201** E-16; elev. 1,200ft./366m.; 🅿; Z 68792; ℗ 213; © 191

Y

York; Inc. Place; ⊡ YORK; **201** K-15; elev. 1,609ft./490m.; 🅿 🅷 🅲 440; Z 68467; ℗ 7,884; © 8,081

YORK; **201** K-15; ℗ 14,428; © 14,598; ◆ 14,300

Yossem's Paradise Valley; RMC Place; DOUGLAS; ★ **OMA**; mail Omaha Z 68134; pop. incl. with Omaha (Inc. Place)

Yutan; Inc. Place; SAUNDERS; **201** J-18; elev. 1,174ft./358m.; 🅿; Z 68073; ℗ 626; © 1,216

Entries in **UPPERCASE** are counties.
Entries in **bold** have populations of 2,500 or more.
Names in parentheses are alternate names.

Inc. Place	Incorporated Place
RMC Place	Rand McNally Designated Place
CDP	Census Designated Place
MCD	Minor Civil Division
⊡	County Seat
▲	Minor Civil Division
elev.	Elevation
🅿	Post Office
🅷	Hospital
🅲	College
■	Principal Business Center
★	Ranally Metro Area (RMA) Abbreviation
Z	Zip Code(s)
℗	Previous Census Population
®	Revised Census Population
Ⓐ	Annexation Population
●	Rand McNally Population Estimate
©	Final Census Population
Ⓢ	Special Census Population
◆	Estimated Population

For additional definitions see Glossary, Volume 1, and Introduction, Volume 2.

NEVADA

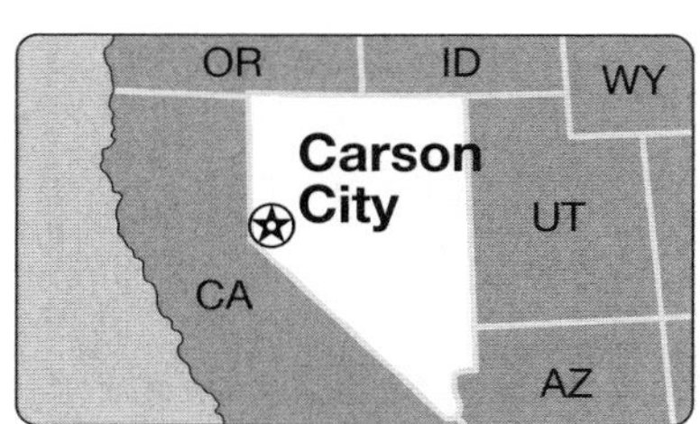

Statistics

Total area (2000) — 110,561 square miles
Land area (2000) — 109,826 square miles
Water area (2000) — 735 square miles
Capital — Carson City
Admitted as state — October, 1864

Maps

State maps can be found on pages 142-254 in Vol. 1

Ranally Metro Areas (RMAs) and Abbreviations

Las Vegas, NV — LASV
Reno, NV — RENO

Principal Places

Place Name	Place Type	County	Population
Las Vegas	Inc. Place	CLARK	◆ 594,689
Paradise	CDP	CLARK	◆ 263,642
Henderson	Inc. Place	CLARK	◆ 252,552
Reno	Inc. Place	WASHOE	◆ 230,192
Sunrise Manor	CDP-Census Area Only	CLARK	◆ 221,195
North Las Vegas	Inc. Place	CLARK	◆ 207,942
Spring Valley	CDP-Census Area Only	CLARK	◆ 166,327
Sparks	Inc. Place	WASHOE	◆ 86,208
Carson City	Independent City		◆ 53,870
Winchester	CDP	CLARK	◆ 38,196
Pahrump	CDP	NYE	◆ 32,581
Sun Valley	CDP	WASHOE	© 19,461
Whitney	CDP-Census Area Only	CLARK	© 18,273
Elko	Inc. Place	ELKO	© 16,708
Boulder City	Inc. Place	CLARK	© 14,966
Enterprise	CDP-Census Area Only	CLARK	© 14,676
East Las Vegas	RMC Place	CLARK	Ⓟ 11,087
Gardnerville Ranchos	CDP-Census Area Only	DOUGLAS	© 11,054
Spring Creek	CDP	ELKO	© 10,548
Incline Village-Crystal Bay	CDP-Census Area Only	WASHOE	© 9,952
Mesquite	Inc. Place	CLARK	© 9,389
Spanish Springs	CDP-Census Area Only	WASHOE	© 9,018
Fernley	Inc. Place	LYON	● 8,900
Nellis AFB	CDP-Census Area Only	CLARK	© 8,896
Fernley	CDP-Census Area Only	LYON	K 8,543
Fallon	Inc. Place	CHURCHILL	© 7,536
Winnemucca	Inc. Place	HUMBOLDT	© 7,174
Laughlin	CDP	CLARK	© 7,076
Lemmon Valley-Golden Valley	CDP-Census Area Only	WASHOE	© 6,855
Dayton	CDP	LYON	© 5,907
Moapa Valley	CDP-Census Area Only	CLARK	© 5,784
Incline Village	RMC Place	WASHOE	● 5,500

County and Independent City Business Data

County	FIPS Code	County Seat	Land Area (Sq. Mi.)	Census Population 4/1/2000	Census Population 4/1/1990	Census Population % Change 1990-2000	Wholesale Trade Sales, 2002 ($1,000)	Wholesale Trade % Change 1997-2002	Manufacturing, 2002 Establish-ments	Manufacturing, 2002 Total Employees	Manufacturing, 2002 Value Added ($1,000)	Manufacturing, 2002 Ranally Mfg. Units
Churchill	001	Fallon	4,929	23,982	17,938	33.7	25,467	-13.2	...	(d)	(d)	...
Clark	003	Las Vegas	7,910	1,375,765	741,459	85.5	(d)	(d)	926	19,776	2,214,524	1,172
Douglas	005	Minden	710	41,259	27,637	49.3	(d)	(d)	63	2,438	221,833	117
Elko	007	Elko	17,179	45,291	33,530	35.1	(d)	(d)	...	(d)	(d)	...
Esmeralda	009	Goldfield	3,589	971	1,344	-27.8	(d)	(d)	...	(d)	(d)	...
Eureka	011	Eureka	4,176	1,651	1,547	6.7	(d)	(d)	...	(d)	(d)	...
Humboldt	013	Winnemucca	9,648	16,106	12,844	25.4	33,537	-47.8	...	(d)	(d)	...
Lander	015	Battle Mountain	5,494	5,794	6,266	-7.5	(d)	(d)	...	(d)	(d)	...
Lincoln	017	Pioche	10,634	4,165	3,775	10.3	(d)	(d)	...	(d)	(d)	...
Lyon	019	Yerington	1,994	34,501	20,001	72.5	94,715	105.8	66	1,725	195,717	104
Mineral	021	Hawthorne	3,756	5,071	6,475	-21.7	(d)	(d)	...	(d)	(d)	...
Nye	023	Tonopah	18,147	32,485	17,781	82.7	(d)	(d)	...	(d)	(d)	...
Pershing	027	Lovelock	6,037	6,693	4,336	54.4	(d)	(d)	...	(d)	(d)	...
Storey	029	Virginia City	263	3,399	2,526	34.6	(d)	(d)	...	(d)	(d)	...
Washoe	031	Reno	6,342	339,486	254,667	33.3	(d)	(d)	449	(d)	(d)	...
White Pine	033	Ely	8,876	9,181	9,264	-0.9	10,941	-37.8	...	(d)	(d)	...
Independent City												
Carson City	510		143	52,457	40,443	29.7	203,264	-8.6	163	3,654	360,680	191
The State			**109,826**	**1,998,257**	**1,201,833**	**66.3**	**16,513,814**	**28.9**	**1,764**	**42,503**	**4,654,748**	**2,463**

(d) Data not available. Corresponding percentages or Ranally Manufacturing Units are estimates.
... Represents 0 or amount too minimal to be reported.

Index of Places and Counties

A

Alamo; RMC Place; LINCOLN; **202** J-8; elev. 3,449ft./1,051m.; 🅿; z 89001; ● 400
Amargosa Valley (Lathrop Wells); RMC Place; NYE; **202** K-6; elev. 2,660ft./811m.; 🅿; z 89020; ● 380
Arthur; RMC Place; ELKO; ***202** C-8; mail Ruby Valley z 89833, Wells z 89835; rural
Ashmeadow; RMC Place; NYE; ***202** L-7; mail Amargosa Valley z 89020; rural
Ash Springs; RMC Place; LINCOLN; **202** J-8; mail Hiko z 89017; ● 50
Aspen; RMC Place; ELKO; mail Elko z 89801; pop. incl. with Elko (Inc. Place)
Atlanta; RMC Place; LINCOLN; ***202** H-9; elev. 6,675ft./2,035m.; mail Pioche z 89043; rural
Austin; RMC Place; LANDER; **202** F-5; elev. 6,527ft./1,989m.; 🅿; z 89310; ● 350

B

Baker; RMC Place; WHITE PINE; **202** G-10; elev. 5,400ft./1,646m.; 🅿; z 89311; ● 100
Basalt; RMC Place; MINERAL; ***202** I-4; elev. 6,348ft./1,935m.; mail Benton z 93512; rural
Battle Mountain; CDP; ⊡ LANDER; **202** D-6; elev. 4,512ft./1,375m.; 🅿 🅷; z 89820; Ⓟ 3,542; © 2,871
Battle Mountain Reservation; Indian Reservation; LANDER; © 124
Beatty; CDP; NYE; **202** K-6; elev. 3,284ft./1,001m.; 🅿; z 89003; Ⓟ 1,623; © 1,154
Belmont; RMC Place; NYE; **202** H-6; elev. 7,663ft./2,336m.; mail Manhattan z 89022, Tonopah z 89049; ● 25
Beowawe; RMC Place; EUREKA; **202** D-6; elev. 4,696ft./1,431m.; 🅿; z 89821; ● 280
Black Springs; RMC Place; WASHOE; **202** F-2; ★ **RENO**; mail Reno z 89506; ● 230
Blue Diamond; CDP; CLARK; **202** L-8; elev. 3,400ft./1,036m.; 🅿; z 89004; © 282
Bluffs; RMC Place; ELKO; ***202** C-7; elev. 5,200ft./1,585m.; mail Elko z 89801; pop. incl. with Elko (Inc. Place)
Bonanza; RMC Place; CLARK; ***202** L-8; ★ **LASV**; mail Las Vegas z 89106, z 89127; pop. incl. with Las Vegas (Inc. Place)
Border Town; RMC Place; WASHOE; ***202** E-1; ★ **RENO**; mail Reno z 89506; ● 100
Boulder City; Inc. Place; CLARK; **202** L-9; elev. 2,500ft./762m.; 🅿 🅷; ★ **LASV**; z 89005-06; Ⓟ 12,567; © 14,966
Buckeye; RMC Place; DOUGLAS; ***202** G-2; elev. 4,800ft./1,463m.; mail Gardnerville z 89410; rural
Bullion; RMC Place; ELKO; ***202** D-7; mail Elko z 89801; ● 70
Bunkerville; CDP; CLARK; **202** K-10; elev. 1,552ft./473m.; 🅿; z 89007; © 1,014

C

Cactus Springs; RMC Place; CLARK; ***202** K-7; mail Las Vegas z 89124; rural
Calico Ridge; RMC Place; CLARK; mail Henderson z 89015; pop. incl. with Henderson (Inc. Place)
Caliente; Inc. Place; LINCOLN; **202** I-9; elev. 4,395ft./1,340m.; 🅿; z 89008; Ⓟ 1,111; © 1,123
Cal-Nev-Ari; CDP; CLARK; **202** M-9; 🅿; z 89039; © 278
Campbell Ranch; Indian Reservation; LYON; © 446
Carlin; Inc. Place; ELKO; **202** D-7; elev. 4,920ft./1,500m.; 🅿; z 89822 & mail Crescent Valley z 89821; Ⓟ 2,220; © 2,161
Carp; RMC Place; LINCOLN; ***202** J-9; mail Caliente z 89008; rural
Carson City; Independent City; **STATE CAPITAL**; **202** F-2; elev. 4,687ft./1,429m.; 🅿 🅷 ■; z 89701-06, z 89711-14, z 89721; location of Western Nevada Indian Agency; Ⓟ 40,443; © 52,457; ◆ 53,870
Carson Colony; Indian Reservation; CARSON CITY (Independent City); mail Carson City z 89701; © 286
Carson Meadows; RMC Place; CARSON CITY (Independent City); ***202** F-2; elev. 4,651ft./1,418m.; mail Carson City z 89701; pop. incl. with Carson City (Independent City)
Carvers; RMC Place; NYE; ***202** G-5; mail Round Mountain z 89045
Caselton; RMC Place; LINCOLN; **202** I-9; mail Pioche z 89043; ● 40
Centerville; RMC Place; DOUGLAS; ***202** G-2; elev. 4,720ft./1,439m.; mail Gardnerville z 89410, z 89460; rural
Chaparral Ridge; RMC Place; ELKO; ***202** C-7; elev. 5,066ft./1,544m.; mail Elko z 89801; pop. incl. with Elko (Inc. Place)
Charleston; RMC Place; ELKO; ***202** B-8; mail Mountain City z 89831; rural
Charleston Park; RMC Place; CLARK; ***202** L-8; mail Las Vegas z 89108; ● 100
Cherry Creek; RMC Place; WHITE PINE; **202** E-9; mail Ely z 89301; ● 30
CHURCHILL; **202** F-4; Ⓟ 17,938; © 23,982; ◆ 25,052
CLARK; **202** K-8; Ⓟ 741,459; © 1,375,765; ◆ 1,949,304
Clear Creek; RMC Place; CARSON CITY (Independent City); ***202** G-2; mail Carson City z 89701, z 89705; pop. incl. with Carson City (Independent City)
Clover Hills; RMC Place; ELKO; ***202** C-7; elev. 5,066ft./1,544m.; mail Elko z 89801; pop. incl. with Elko (Inc. Place)
Coaldale; RMC Place; ESMERALDA; **202** I-4; elev. 4,636ft./1,413m.; mail Tonopah z 89049; ● 20
Cobre; RMC Place; ELKO; ***202** C-9; mail Wells z 89835; rural
Cold Springs; RMC Place; CHURCHILL; **202** F-4; mail Fallon z 89406; ● 20
Cold Springs; CDP-Census Area Only; WASHOE; ***202** E-1; 🅿; z 89506; © 3,834
Contact; RMC Place; ELKO; ***202** B-9; mail Jackpot z 89825; rural
Cosgrave; RMC Place; PERSHING; ***202** C-4; mail Winnemucca z 89445; ● 50
Cottonwood Cove; RMC Place; CLARK; **202** M-9; elev. 800ft./244m.; mail Searchlight z 89046; ● 180
Country Lane Estates; RMC Place; DOUGLAS; ***202** G-2; elev. 4,780ft./1,457m.; mail Gardnerville z 89460; rural
Crescent Valley; RMC Place; EUREKA; **202** D-6; elev. 4,800ft./1,463m.; 🅿; z 89821; ● 100
Crestview; RMC Place; ELKO; mail Elko z 89801; pop. incl. with Elko (Inc. Place)
Crystal; RMC Place; NYE; ***202** K-7; mail Pahrump z 89041, z 89048; rural
Crystal Bay; RMC Place; WASHOE; **202** F-1; elev. 6,400ft./1,951m.; 🅿; z 89402; seasonal pop. 5,000; ● 1,500
Crystal Springs; RMC Place; LINCOLN; ***202** I-8; mail Hiko z 89017; rural
Currant; RMC Place; NYE; ***202** G-8; elev. 6,183ft./1,885m.; mail Ely z 89301
Currie; RMC Place; ELKO; ***202** D-9; mail Ely z 89301

D

Dayton; CDP; LYON; **202** F-2; elev. 4,379ft./1,335m.; 🅿; z 89403; Ⓟ 2,217; © 5,907
Dayton Valley; RMC Place; LYON; ***202** F-2; elev. 4,361ft./1,329m.; mail Dayton z 89403; ● 900
Deep Creek; RMC Place; ELKO; ***202** B-7; mail Elko z 89801; rural
Deeth; RMC Place; ELKO; **202** C-8; elev. 5,340ft./1,628m.; 🅿; z 89823; ● 100
Denio; RMC Place; HUMBOLDT; **202** A-3; elev. 4,200ft./1,280m.; 🅿; z 89404; ● 35
Denio Junction; RMC Place; HUMBOLDT; ***202** A-3; mail Denio z 89404; rural
Divide; RMC Place; STOREY; ***202** F-2; mail Virginia City z 89440; ● 120
Dixie Valley; RMC Place; CHURCHILL; **202** E-4; mail Fallon z 89406; ● 20
DOUGLAS; **202** G-2; Ⓟ 27,637; © 41,259; ◆ 44,867
Downtown; RMC Place; CLARK; ***202** L-8; ★ **LASV**; mail Las Vegas z 89101, z 89125; pop. incl. with Las Vegas (Inc. Place)
Downtown; RMC Place; WASHOE; ★ **RENO**; mail Reno z 89501, z 89504-05; pop. incl. with Reno (Inc. Place)
Dresslerville; RMC Place; DOUGLAS; ***202** G-2; mail Gardnerville z 89410, z 89460; ● 250
Dresslerville Colony; Indian Reservation; DOUGLAS; © 315
Duck Valley Reservation; Indian Reservation; ELKO; Reservation extends into ID; mail Owyhee z 89832; Ⓟ 846; © 1,017
Duckwater; RMC Place; NYE; **202** G-7; located on Duckwater Ind. Res.; elev. 5,460ft./1,664m.; 🅿; z 89314; ● 25
Duckwater Reservation; Indian Reservation; NYE; mail Duckwater z 89314; Ⓟ 106; © 149
Dunphy; RMC Place; EUREKA; **202** D-6; mail Battle Mountain z 89820, Crescent Valley z 89821; ● 25
Dyer (Fish Lake Valley); RMC Place; ESMERALDA; **202** I-4; elev. 4,886ft./1,489m.; 🅿; z 89010; ● 110

E

East Elko; RMC Place; ELKO; mail Elko z 89802; pop. incl. with Elko (Inc. Place)
East Ely; RMC Place; WHITE PINE; ***202** F-9; elev. 6,386ft./1,946m.; mail Ely z 89315; pop. incl. with Ely (Inc. Place)
Eastgate; RMC Place; CHURCHILL; ***202** F-4; mail Fallon z 89406; rural
Eastland Hills; RMC Place; ELKO; ***202** C-7; elev. 5,220ft./1,591m.; mail Elko z 89801; pop. incl. with Elko (Inc. Place)
East Las Vegas; RMC Place; CLARK; **202** L-4; elev. 1,660ft./506m.; ★ **LASV**; mail Las Vegas z 89112, z 89121-22, z 89160; Ⓟ 11,087
Echo Bay; RMC Place; CLARK; ***202** L-9; mail Overton z 89040; ● 30
Edgewood; RMC Place; DOUGLAS; ***202** G-1; elev. 6,308ft./1,923m.; mail Stateline z 89449
Elburz; RMC Place; ELKO; ***202** C-8; mail Elko z 89801, Halleck z 89824; ● 40
Elgin; RMC Place; LINCOLN; ***202** J-9; mail Caliente z 89008; rural
Elko; Inc. Place; ⊡ ELKO; **202** C-7; elev. 5,067ft./1,544m.; 🅿 🅷 🅲 3,282; z 89801-03 & mail Spring Creek z 89815; location of Eastern Nevada Indian Agency; Ⓟ 14,736; © 16,708
ELKO; **202** C-7; Ⓟ 33,530; © 45,291; ◆ 49,121
Elko Colony; Indian Reservation; ELKO; © 729
Elko Summit Estates; RMC Place; ELKO; ***202** C-7; mail Spring Creek z 89815
Elk Point; RMC Place; DOUGLAS; **149** C-2; elev. 6,240ft./1,902m.; mail Zephyr Cove z 89448; ● 250
Ely; Inc. Place; ⊡ WHITE PINE; **202** F-9; elev. 6,427ft./1,959m.; 🅿 🅷; z 89301, z 89315; Ⓟ 4,756; © 4,041
Ely Reservation; Indian Reservation; WHITE PINE; © 133
Empire; RMC Place; WASHOE; **202** D-2; elev. 4,040ft./1,231m.; 🅿; z 89405; ● 370
Enterprise; CDP-Census Area Only; CLARK; ***202** L-8; elev. 2,374ft./724m.; 🅿; ★ **LASV**; z 89124 & mail Las Vegas z 89118; Ⓟ 6,412; © 14,676
ESMERALDA; **202** I-5; Ⓟ 1,344; © 971; ◆ 573
Etna; RMC Place; LINCOLN; ***202** I-9; elev. 4,216ft./1,285m.; mail Caliente z 89008; rural
Eureka; RMC Place; ⊡ EUREKA; **202** F-7; elev. 6,481ft./1,975m.; 🅿; z 89316; ● 600
EUREKA; **202** E-6; Ⓟ 1,547; © 1,651; ◆ 1,755

F

Fallon; Inc. Place; ⊡ CHURCHILL; **202** F-3; elev. 3,963ft./1,208m.; 🅿 🅷; z 89406-07, z 89496; Ⓟ 6,438; © 7,536
Fallon Paiute-Shoshone Colony; Indian Reservation; CHURCHILL; © 123
Fallon Paiute-Shoshone Reservation; Indian Reservation; CHURCHILL; mail Fallon z 89406; Ⓟ 279; © 620
Fallon Station; CDP-Census Area Only; CHURCHILL; ***202** F-3; mail Fallon z 89406; Ⓟ 1,092; © 1,265
Federal; RMC Place; CLARK; ***202** L-8; ★ **LASV**; mail Las Vegas z 89101; pop. incl. with Las Vegas (Inc. Place)
Fernley; Inc. Place; LYON; **202** F-2; elev. 4,153ft./1,266m.; 🅿; z 89408; incorporated July 1, 2001; not reported in 2000 Census; ● 8,900
Fernley; CDP-Census Area Only; LYON; **202** F-2; elev. 4,151ft./1,265m.; 🅿; z 89408; Ⓟ 5,164; © 8,543
Fish Lake Valley; ESMERALDA; see Dyer (RMC Place)
Fish Spring; RMC Place; DOUGLAS; ***202** G-2; elev. 5,115ft./1,559m.; mail Gardnerville z 89410; rural
Flanigan; RMC Place; WASHOE; ***202** E-2; elev. 4,002ft./1,220m.; mail Reno z 89506; rural
Fort McDermitt Reservation; Indian Reservation; HUMBOLDT; Reservation extends into OR; mail Mc Dermitt z 89421; also location of Indian Agency; Ⓟ 472; © 309
Fort Mojave Reservation; Indian Reservation; CLARK; Reservation extends into AZ and CA; mail Needles z 92363; © 19

G

Gabbs; RMC Place; NYE; **202** G-4; elev. 4,680ft./1,426m.; 🅿; z 89409; disincorporated May 8, 2001; Ⓟ 667; © 318
Galena; RMC Place; WASHOE; ★ **RENO**; mail Reno z 89511; pop. incl. with Reno (Inc. Place)
Galena Forest Estates; RMC Place; WASHOE; ***202** F-2; elev. 5,455ft./1,663m.; ★ **RENO**; mail Reno z 89511; ● 300
Gardnerville; CDP; DOUGLAS; **202** G-2; elev. 4,746ft./1,447m.; 🅿; z 89410, z 89460; Ⓟ 2,177; © 3,357
Gardnerville Ranchos; CDP-Census Area Only; DOUGLAS; ***202** G-2; mail Gardnerville z 89460; Ⓟ 7,455; © 11,054
Garside; RMC Place; CLARK; ***202** L-8; ★ **LASV**; mail Las Vegas z 89102, z 89107, z 89126, z 89146; pop. incl. with Las Vegas (Inc. Place)
Genoa; RMC Place; DOUGLAS; **149** C-3; elev. 4,788ft./1,459m.; 🅿; z 89411; ● 220
Gerlach; RMC Place; WASHOE; **202** D-2; elev. 3,951ft./1,204m.; 🅿; z 89412; ● 300
Gerlach-Empire; CDP-Census Area Only; WASHOE; ***202** D-2; © 499
Glenbrook; RMC Place; DOUGLAS; **202** G-1; elev. 6,260ft./1,908m.; 🅿; z 89413; ● 500
Glendale; RMC Place; CLARK; **202** K-9; elev. 1,521ft./464m.; mail Moapa z 89025; ● 50
Glendale; RMC Place; WASHOE; ***202** F-2; ★ **RENO**; mail Sparks z 89431; pop. incl. with Sparks (Inc. Place)
Golconda; RMC Place; HUMBOLDT; **202** C-5; elev. 4,400ft./1,341m.; 🅿; z 89414; ● 230
Golden Valley; RMC Place; WASHOE; ***202** F-2; elev. 5,100ft./1,554m.; ★ **RENO**; mail Reno z 89506; ● 1,200
Goldfield; RMC Place; ⊡ ESMERALDA; **202** I-5; elev. 5,689ft./1,734m.; 🅿; z 89013; ● 500
Gold Hill; RMC Place; STOREY; ***202** F-2; mail Virginia City z 89440; ● 100
Gold Point; RMC Place; ESMERALDA; **202** J-5; elev. 5,388ft./1,642m.; mail Goldfield z 89013; ● 20
Goodsprings; CDP; CLARK; **202** M-8; elev. 3,718ft./1,133m.; 🅿; z 89019; © 232
Goshute Reservation; Indian Reservation; WHITE PINE; Reservation extends into UT; mail Ibapah z 84034; Ⓟ 25; © 15
Greenbrae; RMC Place; WASHOE; ★ **RENO**; mail Sparks z 89431; pop. incl. with Sparks (Inc. Place)
Green Valley; RMC Place; CLARK; ★ **LASV**; mail Henderson z 89014; pop. incl. with Henderson (Inc. Place)

H

Hadley; RMC Place; NYE; ***202** G-5; mail Round Mountain z 89045
Halleck; RMC Place; ELKO; **202** C-8; elev. 5,230ft./1,594m.; 🅿; z 89824; ● 40
Hamilton; RMC Place; WHITE PINE; ***202** F-8; mail Ely z 89301; rural
Hawthorne; CDP; ⊡ MINERAL; **202** H-3; elev. 4,320ft./1,317m.; 🅿 🅷; z 89415; Ⓟ 4,162; © 3,311
Hazen; RMC Place; CHURCHILL; **202** F-3; elev. 4,004ft./1,220m.; mail Fernley z 89408; ● 50
Henderson; Inc. Place; CLARK; **202** L-9; elev. 1,960ft./597m.; 🅿 🅷 🅲 1,032; ★ **LASV**; z 89002, z 89009, z 89011-12, z 89014-16, z 89044, z 89052-53, z 89074, z 89077; Ⓟ 64,942; © 175,381; ◆ 252,552
Hidden Valley; RMC Place; WASHOE; ***202** F-2; ★ **RENO**; mail Reno z 89502, z 89511; ● 1,000
Highland; RMC Place; ELKO; ***202** D-7; mail Elko z 89801; ● 40
Highland Park; RMC Place; WASHOE; ★ **RENO**; pop. incl. with Reno (Inc. Place)
Hiko; RMC Place; LINCOLN; **202** I-8; elev. 3,869ft./1,179m.; 🅿; z 89017; ● 80
Holbrook Junction; RMC Place; DOUGLAS; ***202** G-2; mail Gardnerville z 89410; rural
Horizon Hills; RMC Place; WASHOE; ***202** F-2; elev. 5,300ft./1,615m.; ★ **RENO**; mail Reno z 89506; ● 150
Huffakers; RMC Place; WASHOE; ***202** F-2; elev. 4,482ft./1,366m.; ★ **RENO**; mail Reno z 89501; pop. incl. with Reno (Inc. Place)
Humboldt; RMC Place; PERSHING; ***202** D-4; mail Imlay z 89418, Lovelock z 89419; rural
HUMBOLDT; **202** C-4; Ⓟ 12,844; © 16,106; ◆ 17,933
Huntridge; RMC Place; CLARK; ***202** L-8; ★ **LASV**; mail Las Vegas z 89104, z 89116, z 89185; pop. incl. with Las Vegas (Inc. Place)

I

Imlay; RMC Place; PERSHING; **202** D-4; elev. 4,195ft./1,279m.; 🅿; z 89418; ● 250
Incline Village; RMC Place; WASHOE; **149** A-2; elev. 6,360ft./1,939m.; 🅿 🅲 677; z 89450-52; seasonal pop. 8,000; ● 5,500
Incline Village-Crystal Bay; CDP-Census Area Only; WASHOE; ***202** F-1; mail Incline Village z 89450; Ⓟ 7,119; © 9,952
Indian Hills; CDP-Census Area Only; DOUGLAS; ***202** G-2; elev. 4,743ft./1,446m.; mail Carson City z 89705; Ⓟ 2,544; © 4,407
Indian Springs; CDP; CLARK; **202** K-8; elev. 3,100ft./945m.; 🅿; z 89018, z 89070; Ⓟ 1,164; © 1,302
Ione; RMC Place; NYE; **202** G-5; mail Austin z 89310; ● 20

J

Jack Creek; RMC Place; ELKO; ***202** B-7; mail Tuscarora z 89834; rural
Jackpot; RMC Place; ELKO; **202** A-9; elev. 5,240ft./1,597m.; 🅿; z 89825; ● 600
Jacks Valley; RMC Place; DOUGLAS; **149** C-3; elev. 5,145ft./1,568m.; mail Carson City z 89701, z 89705; ● 250
Jarbidge; RMC Place; ELKO; **202** B-8; elev. 6,200ft./1,890m.; 🅿; z 89826; ● 80
Jean; RMC Place; CLARK; **202** M-8; elev. 2,840ft./866m.; 🅿; z 89019, z 89026; ● 200
Jiggs; RMC Place; ELKO; **202** D-7; elev. 5,480ft./1,670m.; 🅿; z 89801, z 89815; ● 30
Johnnie; RMC Place; NYE; ***202** K-7; mail Pahrump z 89041, z 89048; rural
Johnson Lane; CDP-Census Area Only; DOUGLAS; ***202** G-2; elev. 4,800ft./1,463m.; mail Minden z 89423; Ⓟ 2,551; © 4,837

K

Kingsbury; CDP; DOUGLAS; ***202** G-1; mail Stateline z 89449, Zephyr Cove z 89448; Ⓟ 2,238; © 2,624
Kingsbury Meadows; RMC Place; DOUGLAS; ***202** G-1; mail Stateline z 89449; ● 50
Kingsbury Village; RMC Place; DOUGLAS; ***202** G-1; mail Stateline z 89449; ● 900
Kingston; RMC Place; LANDER; **202** F-6; elev. 6,144ft./1,873m.; mail Austin z 89310; ● 60

L

Lakeridge; RMC Place; DOUGLAS; **149** C-2; mail Stateline z 89449, Zephyr Cove z 89448; ● 200
Lakeview; RMC Place; CARSON CITY (Independent City); ***202** F-2; mail Carson City z 89701, z 89703
Lake Village; RMC Place; DOUGLAS; ***202** G-1; elev. 6,485ft./1,977m.; mail Stateline z 89449, Zephyr Cove z 89448; ● 250
Lamoille; RMC Place; ELKO; **202** D-8; elev. 5,887ft./1,794m.; 🅿; z 89828; ● 120
LANDER; **202** E-6; Ⓟ 6,266; © 5,794; ◆ 5,243
Lane City; RMC Place; WHITE PINE; **202** F-8; mail Ely z 89301
Las Vegas; Inc. Place; ⊡ CLARK; **202** L-8; elev. 2,020ft./616m.; 🅿 🅷 🅲 63,452 ■; ★ **LASV**; z 89044, z 89054, z 89101-57, z 89159-66, z 89169-70, z 89173, z 89177-80, z 89183, z 89185, z 89191, z 89193, z 89195, z 89199; Ⓟ 258,295; © 478,434; Ⓡ 479,137; ◆ 594,689
Las Vegas Colony; Indian Reservation; CLARK; © 108
Lathrop Wells; NYE; see Amargosa Valley (RMC Place)
Laughlin; CDP; CLARK; **147** T-8; elev. 520ft./158m.; 🅿; z 89028-29; Ⓟ 4,791; © 7,076
Lawton; RMC Place; WASHOE; ***202** F-1; elev. 4,774ft./1,455m.; ★ **RENO**; mail Reno z 89503; pop. incl. with Reno (Inc. Place)
Lee; RMC Place; ELKO; **202** D-8; elev. 5,760ft./1,756m.; 🅿; z 89801; ● 100
Leeteville; RMC Place; CHURCHILL; ***202** F-3; mail Fallon z 89406; rural
Lemmon Valley; RMC Place; WASHOE; ***202** F-2; elev. 4,940ft./1,506m.; ★ **RENO**; mail Reno z 89506; ● 4,500
Lemmon Valley-Golden Valley; CDP-Census Area Only; WASHOE; ***202** E-2; ★ **RENO**; © 6,855
Lida; RMC Place; ESMERALDA; ***202** J-5; elev. 6,161ft./1,878m.; mail Goldfield z 89013
LINCOLN; **202** I-9; Ⓟ 3,775; © 4,165; ◆ 5,083
Lincoln Park; RMC Place; DOUGLAS; ***202** G-1; mail Glenbrook z 89413; ● 50
Lockwood; RMC Place; STOREY; ***202** F-2; 🅿; z 89434 & mail Sparks z 89431; ● 120
Logandale; RMC Place; CLARK; **202** K-9; elev. 1,379ft./420m.; 🅿; z 89021; ● 1,000
Lone Mountain; RMC Place; CLARK; ***202** L-8; ★ **LASV**; mail Las Vegas z 89129; pop. incl. with Las Vegas (Inc. Place)
Lovelock; Inc. Place; ⊡ PERSHING; **202** E-3; elev. 3,977ft./1,212m.; 🅿 🅷; z 89419; Ⓟ 2,069; © 2,003
Lovelock Colony; Indian Reservation; PERSHING; © 103
Lower Gold Hill; RMC Place; STOREY; ***202** F-2; mail Virginia City z 89440; ● 60
Lund; RMC Place; WHITE PINE; **202** G-8; elev. 5,600ft./1,707m.; 🅿; z 89317; ● 200
Luning; RMC Place; MINERAL; **202** H-4; elev. 4,605ft./1,404m.; 🅿; z 89420; ● 60
LYON; **202** F-2; Ⓟ 20,001; © 34,501; ◆ 56,389

M

Majors Place; RMC Place; WHITE PINE; ***202** G-9; elev. 6,494ft./1,979m.; mail Ely z 89301; rural
Manhattan; RMC Place; NYE; **202** H-5; elev. 7,000ft./2,134m.; 🅿; z 89022; ● 70
Mark Twain; RMC Place; STOREY; ***202** F-2; mail Dayton z 89403; rural
Mason; RMC Place; LYON; **202** G-2; elev. 4,423ft./1,348m.; mail Yerington z 89447; ● 400
Mayberry-Highland Park; RMC Place; WASHOE; ***202** F-2; elev. 4,600ft./1,402m.; ★ **RENO**; mail Reno z 89501
McDermitt; CDP; HUMBOLDT; **202** A-5; elev. 4,424ft./1,348m.; 🅿; z 89421; Ⓟ 373; © 269
McGill; CDP; WHITE PINE; **202** F-9; elev. 6,200ft./1,890m.; 🅿; z 89318; Ⓟ 1,258; © 1,054
Meadow Mesa; RMC Place; CLARK; ★ **LASV**; mail North Las Vegas z 89031-33; pop. incl. with North Las Vegas (Inc. Place)
Mercury; RMC Place; NYE; **202** K-7; elev. 3,780ft./1,152m.; 🅿; z 89023; ● 50
Mesquite; Inc. Place; CLARK; **202** K-10; elev. 1,608ft./490m.; 🅿; z 89024, z 89027, z 89034; Ⓟ 1,871; © 9,389
Midas; RMC Place; ELKO; ***202** C-6; elev. 5,745ft./1,751m.; 🅿; z 89414; ● 70
Middlegate; RMC Place; CHURCHILL; ***202** F-4; mail Fallon z 89406; rural
Mill City; RMC Place; PERSHING; ***202** D-4; elev. 4,225ft./1,288m.; 🅿; z 89418
Mina; RMC Place; MINERAL; **202** H-4; elev. 4,546ft./1,386m.; 🅿; z 89422; ● 350
Minden; CDP; ⊡ DOUGLAS; **202** G-2; elev. 4,721ft./1,439m.; 🅿; z 89423; Ⓟ 1,441; © 2,836
MINERAL; **202** H-3; Ⓟ 6,475; © 5,071; ◆ 4,756
Moapa; RMC Place; CLARK; **202** K-9; elev. 1,709ft./521m.; 🅿; z 89025, z 89037, z 89067; ● 300
Moapa River Reservation; Indian Reservation; CLARK; mail Moapa z 89025; Ⓟ 185; © 206
Moapa Town; CDP-Census Area Only; CLARK; ***202** K-9; © 928
Moapa Valley; CDP-Census Area Only; CLARK; ***202** K-9; elev. 1,334ft./407m.; 🅿; z 89021, z 89040; Ⓟ 3,640; © 5,784
Mogul; RMC Place; WASHOE; ***202** F-1; elev. 4,701ft./1,433m.; ★ **RENO**; mail Reno z 89523; rural
Montello; RMC Place; ELKO; **202** C-9; elev. 4,875ft./1,486m.; 🅿; z 89830; ● 200
Mottsville; RMC Place; DOUGLAS; ***202** G-2; elev. 4,760ft./1,451m.; mail Gardnerville z 89460; rural
Moundhouse; RMC Place; LYON; ***202** F-2; 🅿; z 89706; ● 350
Mountain City; RMC Place; ELKO; **202** B-7; elev. 5,641ft./1,719m.; 🅿; z 89831; ● 100
Mountain Springs; RMC Place; CLARK; ***202** L-8; 🅿; z 89124 & mail Las Vegas z 89101; ● 100
Mountain View Estates; RMC Place; ELKO; ***202** C-7; elev. 5,200ft./1,585m.; mail Elko z 89801; pop. incl. with Elko (Inc. Place)
Mount Charleston; CDP; CLARK; ***202** L-8; 🅿; z 89124; © 285
Mount Montgomery; RMC Place; MINERAL; ***202** I-4; mail Benton z 93512
Mustang; RMC Place; WASHOE; ***202** F-2; elev. 4,500ft./1,372m.; mail Sparks z 89431, z 89434; ● 50

N

Nellis AFB; CDP-Census Area Only; CLARK; ***202** L-8; 🅿; ★ **LASV**; z 89191; Ⓟ 8,377; © 8,896
Nelson; RMC Place; CLARK; **202** M-9; elev. 2,954ft./900m.; mail Searchlight z 89046; ● 70
New Empire; RMC Place; CARSON CITY (Independent City); ***202** F-2; mail Carson City z 89701; pop. incl. with Carson City (Independent City)

Entries in **UPPERCASE** are counties.
Entries in **bold** have populations of 2,500 or more.
Names in parentheses are alternate names.

Inc. Place	Incorporated Place
RMC Place	Rand McNally Designated Place
CDP	Census Designated Place
MCD	Minor Civil Division
⊡	County Seat
▲	Minor Civil Division
elev.	Elevation
🅿	Post Office
🅷	Hospital
🅲	College
■	Principal Business Center
★	Ranally Metro Area (RMA) Abbreviation
z	Zip Code(s)
Ⓟ	Previous Census Population
Ⓡ	Revised Census Population
Ⓐ	Annexation Population
●	Rand McNally Population Estimate
©	Final Census Population
Ⓢ	Special Census Population
◆	Estimated Population

For additional definitions see Glossary, Volume 1, and Introduction, Volume 2.

New Washoe City; RMC Place; WASHOE; **149** A-3; elev. 5,096ft./1,553m.; mail Carson City **z** 89701, Washoe Valley **z** 89704; Ⓟ 2,875
Nixon; CDP; WASHOE; **202** E-2; located on Pyramid Lake Ind. Res.; elev. 3,938ft./1,200m.; 🅿; **z** 89424; © 418
North 7 Estates; RMC Place; ELKO; ***202** C-7; elev. 5,200ft./1,585m.; mail Elko **z** 89801; pop. incl. with Elko (Inc. Place)
North Battle Mountain; RMC Place; LANDER; ***202** D-6; mail Battle Mountain **z** 89820; ● 40
North Fork; RMC Place; ELKO; ***202** B-7; mail Elko **z** 89801, Mountain City **z** 89831; rural
North Las Vegas; Inc. Place; CLARK; **202** L-8; elev. 1,850ft./564m.; 🅿 🄷; ★ **LASV**; **z** 89030-33, **z** 89036, **z** 89081, **z** 89084-87; Ⓟ 47,707; © 115,488; ◆ 207,942
Northridge; RMC Place; ELKO; ***202** C-7; elev. 5,277ft./1,608m.; mail Elko **z** 89801; pop. incl. with Elko (Inc. Place)
North Valley; RMC Place; WASHOE; ★ **RENO**; mail Reno **z** 89506; pop. incl. with Reno (Inc. Place)
NYE; **202** H-6; Ⓟ 17,781; © 32,485; ◆ 47,433

O

Oasis; RMC Place; ELKO; ***202** C-9; 🅿; **z** 89835; rural
Olinghouse; RMC Place; WASHOE; ***202** F-2; mail Wadsworth **z** 89442; rural
Oreana; RMC Place; PERSHING; **202** D-4; elev. 4,158ft./1,267m.; mail Lovelock **z** 89419; ● 100
Orovada; RMC Place; HUMBOLDT; **202** B-5; elev. 4,337ft./1,322m.; 🅿; **z** 89425; ● 250
Overton; RMC Place; CLARK; **202** K-9; elev. 1,270ft./387m.; 🅿; **z** 89040; ● 1,200
Owyhee; CDP; ELKO; **202** A-7; elev. 5,397ft./1,645m.; 🅿 🄷; **z** 89832; Ⓟ 908; © 1,017

P

Pahrump; CDP; NYE; **202** L-7; elev. 2,640ft./805m.; 🅿; **z** 89041, **z** 89048, **z** 89060-61; Ⓟ 7,424; © 24,631; ◆ 32,581
Palomino Valley; RMC Place; WASHOE; ***202** E-2; elev. 1,320ft./402m.; mail Reno **z** 89510; ● 200
Panaca; RMC Place; LINCOLN; **202** I-9; elev. 4,738ft./1,444m.; 🅿; **z** 89042; ● 600
Panther Valley; RMC Place; WASHOE; ***202** F-2; elev. 5,200ft./1,585m.; ★ **RENO**; mail Reno **z** 89501, **z** 89506; pop. incl. with Reno (Inc. Place)
Paradise; CDP; CLARK; ***202** L-8; ★ **LASV**; mail Las Vegas **z** 89109; Ⓟ 124,682; © 186,070; ◆ 263,642
Paradise Hill; RMC Place; HUMBOLDT; ***202** C-5; elev. 4,498ft./1,371m.; mail Winnemucca **z** 89445; rural
Paradise Valley; RMC Place; CLARK; ***202** L-8; ★ **LASV**; mail Las Vegas **z** 89109, **z** 89119, **z** 89132
Paradise Valley; RMC Place; HUMBOLDT; **202** B-5; elev. 4,520ft./1,378m.; 🅿; **z** 89426; ● 150
Park Terrace; RMC Place; CARSON CITY (Independent City); ***202** F-2; elev. 4,662ft./1,421m.; mail Carson City **z** 89701; pop. incl. with Carson City (Independent City)
Patrick; RMC Place; WASHOE; ***202** F-2; mail Sparks **z** 89431, **z** 89434; rural
Peavine; RMC Place; WASHOE; ★ **RENO**; mail Reno **z** 89523, **z** 89533; pop. incl. with Reno (Inc. Place)
PERSHING; **202** D-3; Ⓟ 4,336; © 6,693; ◆ 6,269
Pine Grove; RMC Place; LYON; ***202** G-3; mail Yerington **z** 89447; ● 20
Pinenut; RMC Place; DOUGLAS; ***202** G-2; elev. 4,940ft./1,506m.; mail Gardnerville **z** 89410; ● 100
Pinion Hills; RMC Place; CARSON CITY (Independent City); ***202** F-2; mail Carson City **z** 89701; pop. incl. with Carson City (Independent City)
Pioche; RMC Place; ⊡ LINCOLN; **202** I-9; elev. 6,064ft./1,848m.; 🅿; **z** 89043; ● 800
Pittman; RMC Place; CLARK; ***202** L-9; ★ **LASV**; mail Henderson **z** 89015; pop. incl. with Henderson (Inc. Place)
Pleasant Valley; RMC Place; ELKO; ***202** D-8; mail Spring Creek **z** 89815; ● 100
Pleasant Valley; RMC Place; WASHOE; ***202** F-2; ★ **RENO**; mail Reno **z** 89511, **z** 89521; ● 200
Preston; RMC Place; WHITE PINE; ***202** G-8; mail Ely **z** 89301
Primm (State Line); RMC Place; CLARK; ***202** M-8; 🅿; **z** 89019; ● 50
Pyramid Lake Reservation; Indian Reservation; WASHOE, LYON, STOREY; mail Nixon **z** 89424; Ⓟ 853; © 1,734

Q

Quail Ridge; RMC Place; LYON; ***202** F-2; elev. 4,351ft./1,326m.; mail Dayton **z** 89403
Quinn River Crossing; RMC Place; HUMBOLDT; ***202** B-4; mail Denio **z** 89404, Winnemucca **z** 89445; rural

R

Rachel; RMC Place; LINCOLN; **202** I-7; mail Alamo **z** 89001; ● 70
Raleigh Heights; RMC Place; WASHOE; ***202** F-2; elev. 5,260ft./1,603m.; ★ **RENO**; mail Reno **z** 89506; pop. incl. with Reno (Inc. Place)
Rancho Estates; RMC Place; DOUGLAS; ***202** G-2; elev. 4,800ft./1,463m.; mail Gardnerville **z** 89460; ● 280
Rancho Haven; RMC Place; WASHOE; ***202** E-1; elev. 1,472ft./449m.; ★ **RENO**; mail Reno **z** 89506; ● 250
Rancho Vista; RMC Place; LYON; ***202** F-2; elev. 4,800ft./1,463m.; mail Dayton **z** 89403
Red Rock Estates; RMC Place; WASHOE; ***202** E-2; elev. 5,200ft./1,585m.; ★ **RENO**; mail Reno **z** 89506; ● 250
Red Rock Vista; RMC Place; CLARK; ★ **LASV**; mail Las Vegas **z** 89108, **z** 89129-31, **z** 89133; pop. incl. with Las Vegas (Inc. Place)
Reno; Inc. Place; ⊡ WASHOE; **202** F-2; elev. 4,498ft./1,371m.; 🅿 🄷 🄲 16,663 ■; ★ **RENO**; **z** 89501-13, **z** 89515, **z** 89519-21, **z** 89523, **z** 89533, **z** 89555, **z** 89557, **z** 89570, **z** 89595, **z** 89599; Ⓟ 133,850; © 180,480; ◆ 230,192
Reno Park; RMC Place; WASHOE; ***202** E-1; mail Reno **z** 89506; ● 550
Reno-Sparks Colony; Indian Reservation; WASHOE; © 881
Riverside; RMC Place; CLARK; ***202** K-10; mail Bunkerville **z** 89007; rural
River Village; RMC Place; LYON; ***202** F-2; elev. 4,361ft./1,329m.; mail Dayton **z** 89403
Rixie's; RMC Place; EUREKA; ***202** D-6; mail Battle Mountain **z** 89820; rural
Round Hill Village; RMC Place; DOUGLAS; **149** C-2; elev. 6,600ft./2,012m.; mail Zephyr Cove **z** 89448; ● 400
Round Mountain; RMC Place; NYE; **202** G-6; elev. 6,400ft./1,951m.; 🅿; **z** 89045; ● 220
Rowland; RMC Place; ELKO; ***202** A-7; elev. 4,922ft./1,500m.; mail Bruneau **z** 83604; rural
Ruby Valley; RMC Place; ELKO; **202** D-8; elev. 6,050ft./1,844m.; 🅿; **z** 89833; ● 100
Ruby Vista; RMC Place; ELKO; mail Elko **z** 89801; pop. incl. with Elko (Inc. Place)
Ruth; RMC Place; WHITE PINE; **202** F-8; elev. 6,880ft./2,097m.; 🅿; **z** 89319; ● 500

S

Sagecrest Complex; RMC Place; ELKO; ***202** C-7; elev. 5,100ft./1,554m.; mail Elko **z** 89801; pop. incl. with Elko (Inc. Place)
Sage Hills 2; RMC Place; ELKO; ***202** C-7; elev. 5,059ft./1,542m.; mail Elko **z** 89801; pop. incl. with Elko (Inc. Place)
Saint Clair; RMC Place; CHURCHILL; ***202** F-3; mail Fallon **z** 89406; rural
Salt Wells; RMC Place; CHURCHILL; ***202** F-3; elev. 3,957ft./1,206m.; mail Fallon **z** 89406; rural
Sandy Valley; CDP; CLARK; **202** M-8; 🅿; **z** 89019; © 1,804
San Jacinto; RMC Place; ELKO; ***202** B-9; mail Jackpot **z** 89825; rural
Satalite Hills; RMC Place; WASHOE; ***202** F-2; elev. 4,500ft./1,372m.; ★ **RENO**; mail Sparks **z** 89436; pop. incl. with Sparks (Inc. Place)
Schurz; CDP; MINERAL; **202** G-3; located on Walker River Ind. Res.; elev. 4,126ft./1,258m.; 🅿; **z** 89427; Ⓟ 617; © 721
Scotty's Junction; RMC Place; NYE; **202** J-6; mail Goldfield **z** 89013; ● 10
Searchlight; CDP; CLARK; **202** M-9; elev. 3,520ft./1,073m.; 🅿; **z** 89039, **z** 89046; © 576
Shafter; RMC Place; ELKO; ***202** C-9; elev. 5,591ft./1,704m.; mail Wells **z** 89835; rural
Sheridan; RMC Place; DOUGLAS; ***202** G-2; elev. 4,806ft./1,465m.; mail Gardnerville **z** 89410, **z** 89460; ● 200
Shoshone; RMC Place; WHITE PINE; ***202** G-9; mail Ely **z** 89301; rural
Sierra; RMC Place; WASHOE; ★ **RENO**; mail Reno **z** 89506; pop. incl. with Reno (Inc. Place)
Silverado; RMC Place; CLARK; ★ **LASV**; mail Las Vegas **z** 89120, **z** 89123; pop. incl. with Las Vegas (Inc. Place)
Silver City; RMC Place; LYON; **202** F-2; elev. 5,040ft./1,536m.; 🅿; **z** 89428; ● 150
Silver Peak; RMC Place; ESMERALDA; **202** I-5; elev. 4,320ft./1,317m.; 🅿; **z** 89047; ● 200
Silver Springs; CDP; LYON; **202** F-2; elev. 4,198ft./1,280m.; 🅿; **z** 89429; Ⓟ 2,253; © 4,708
Skyland; RMC Place; DOUGLAS; **149** C-2; mail Glenbrook **z** 89413, Zephyr Cove **z** 89448; ● 350
Sloan; RMC Place; CLARK; ***202** L-8; elev. 2,830ft./863m.; 🅿; **z** 89054, **z** 89124 & mail Las Vegas **z** 89103; ● 80
Smith; RMC Place; LYON; **202** G-2; elev. 4,780ft./1,457m.; 🅿; **z** 89430; ● 160
Smith Valley; CDP-Census Area Only; LYON; ***202** G-2; elev. 4,789ft./1,460m.; mail Smith **z** 89430; Ⓟ 1,033; © 1,425
South Fork Reservation; Indian Reservation; ELKO; © 83
Southgate; RMC Place; ELKO; ***202** C-7; elev. 5,136ft./1,565m.; mail Elko **z** 89801; pop. incl. with Elko (Inc. Place)
South Hills; RMC Place; WASHOE; **203** J-2; elev. 4,600ft./1,402m.; ★ **RENO**; mail Reno **z** 89501; ● 1,100
Spanish Springs; CDP-Census Area Only; WASHOE; ***202** F-2; 🅿; **z** 89436, **z** 89441; © 9,018
Spanish Springs Valley; RMC Place; WASHOE; ***202** F-2; elev. 4,460ft./1,359m.; mail Sparks **z** 89436; ● 650
Sparks; Inc. Place; WASHOE; **202** F-2; elev. 4,417ft./1,346m.; 🅿 🄷 ■; ★ **RENO**; **z** 89431-32, **z** 89434-36, **z** 89441 & mail Sun Valley **z** 89433; Ⓟ 53,367; © 66,346; ◆ 86,208
Spring Creek; CDP; ELKO; **202** D-8; 🅿; **z** 89815; Ⓟ 5,866; © 10,548
Spring Valley; CDP-Census Area Only; CLARK; **202** L-2; elev. 2,414ft./736m.; ★ **LASV**; mail Las Vegas **z** 89103, **z** 89113, **z** 89117, **z** 89135, **z** 89147, **z** 89180; Ⓟ 51,726; © 117,390; ◆ 166,327
Stagecoach; RMC Place; LYON; **202** F-2; 🅿; **z** 89429; ● 150
Stanton Park; RMC Place; CARSON CITY (Independent City); mail Carson City **z** 89701; pop. incl. with Carson City (Independent City)
State Line; CLARK; see Primm (RMC Place)
Stateline; CDP; DOUGLAS; **202** G-1; elev. 6,360ft./1,939m.; 🅿; **z** 89449; Ⓟ 1,379; © 1,215
Steamboat; RMC Place; WASHOE; **202** F-2; elev. 4,600ft./1,402m.; ★ **RENO**; mail Reno **z** 89511, **z** 89521; ● 300
Steptoe; RMC Place; WHITE PINE; ***202** F-9; mail Mc Gill **z** 89318; rural
Stewart; RMC Place; CARSON CITY (Independent City); ***202** G-2; elev. 4,713ft./1,437m.; mail Carson City **z** 89701; pop. incl. with Carson City (Independent City)
Stewart Community; Indian Reservation; DOUGLAS, CARSON CITY; © 196
Stewarts Point; RMC Place; CLARK; ***202** L-9; mail Overton **z** 89040
Stillwater; RMC Place; CHURCHILL; **202** F-3; mail Fallon **z** 89406; ● 200
STOREY; **202** F-2; Ⓟ 2,526; © 3,399; ◆ 4,372
Strawberry; RMC Place; WHITE PINE; ***202** E-7; mail Ely **z** 89301; rural
Strip Station; RMC Place; CLARK; ★ **LASV**; mail Las Vegas **z** 89114
Summerlin; RMC Place; CLARK; ★ **LASV**; mail Las Vegas **z** 89128, **z** 89134, **z** 89137-38; pop. incl. with Las Vegas (Inc. Place)
Summerlin South; CDP-Census Area Only; CLARK; ***202** L-8; © 3,735
Summit Lake Reservation; Indian Reservation; HUMBOLDT; mail Denio **z** 89404; © 15
Summit Village; RMC Place; DOUGLAS; **149** C-3; mail Stateline **z** 89449; ● 1,000
Suncrest; RMC Place; ELKO; ***202** C-7; elev. 5,100ft./1,554m.; mail Elko **z** 89801; pop. incl. with Elko (Inc. Place)
Sundance Estates; RMC Place; ELKO; ***202** C-7; elev. 5,228ft./1,593m.; mail Elko **z** 89801; pop. incl. with Elko (Inc. Place)
Sunnyside; RMC Place; NYE; ***202** H-8; mail Lund **z** 89317; ● 30
Sunridge Heights; RMC Place; DOUGLAS; ***202** G-2; mail Carson City **z** 89705; ● 300
Sunrise; RMC Place; CLARK; ★ **LASV**; mail Las Vegas **z** 89110, **z** 89115; pop. incl. with Las Vegas (Inc. Place)
Sunrise Manor; CDP-Census Area Only; CLARK; **202** K-4; ★ **LASV**; mail Las Vegas **z** 89110; Ⓟ 95,362; © 156,120; ◆ 221,195
Sun Valley; CDP; WASHOE; **203** G-2; 🅿; ★ **RENO**; **z** 89433 & mail Sparks **z** 89431; Ⓟ 11,391; © 19,461
Sutcliffe; CDP; WASHOE; **202** E-2; located on Pyramid Lake Ind. Res.; elev. 3,900ft./1,189m.; mail Reno **z** 89510; © 281

T

Tahoe Village; RMC Place; DOUGLAS; ***202** G-1; elev. 6,400ft./1,951m.; mail Stateline **z** 89449
Tempiute; RMC Place; LINCOLN; ***202** I-8; mail Alamo **z** 89001; rural
The Lakes; RMC Place; CLARK; 🅿; ★ **LASV**; **z** 88901, **z** 88905, **z** 89163 & mail Las Vegas **z** 89117, **z** 89164; pop. incl. with Las Vegas (Inc. Place)
Thomas Creek Estates; RMC Place; WASHOE; ***202** F-2; elev. 4,900ft./1,494m.; ★ **RENO**; mail Reno **z** 89511; ● 200
Timberline Estates; RMC Place; CARSON CITY (Independent City); mail Carson City **z** 89703; pop. incl. with Carson City (Independent City)
Tollhouse; RMC Place; HUMBOLDT; ***202** C-5; mail Winnemucca **z** 89445; rural
Tonopah; CDP; ⊡ NYE; **202** H-5; elev. 6,030ft./1,838m.; 🅿 🄷; **z** 89049; Ⓟ 3,616; © 2,627
Topaz Lake; RMC Place; DOUGLAS; ***202** G-2; mail Gardnerville **z** 89410; ● 200
Topaz Ranch Estates; RMC Place; DOUGLAS; ***202** G-2; mail Wellington **z** 89444; ● 700
Tracy; WASHOE; see Tracy-Clark (RMC Place)
Tracy-Clark (Tracy); RMC Place; WASHOE; ***202** F-2; elev. 1,300ft./396m.; mail Sparks **z** 89434; rural
Tuscarora; RMC Place; ELKO; **202** C-7; elev. 6,118ft./1,865m.; 🅿; **z** 89834; ● 100
Twin Bridges; RMC Place; ELKO; ***202** D-7; mail Spring Creek **z** 89815; rural
Twin Flat; RMC Place; LYON; ***202** F-2; mail Silver City **z** 89428; ● 100
Tyrolean Village; RMC Place; WASHOE; ***202** F-1; elev. 7,000ft./2,134m.; mail Incline Village **z** 89450; ● 280

U

Unionville; RMC Place; PERSHING; **202** D-4; 🅿; **z** 89418; ● 35
Ursine; RMC Place; LINCOLN; **202** I-10; mail Pioche **z** 89043; ● 50

V

Valle Verde; RMC Place; CLARK; ★ **LASV**; mail Henderson **z** 89052-53; pop. incl. with Henderson (Inc. Place)
Valmy; RMC Place; HUMBOLDT; **202** C-5; elev. 4,510ft./1,375m.; 🅿; **z** 89438; ● 140
Verdi; RMC Place; WASHOE; **202** F-1; elev. 4,905ft./1,495m.; 🅿; ★ **RENO**; **z** 89439; ● 1,500
Verdi-Mogul; CDP-Census Area Only; WASHOE; ***202** F-1; ★ **RENO**; © 2,949
Virginia City; RMC Place; ⊡ STOREY; **202** F-2; elev. 6,220ft./1,896m.; 🅿; **z** 89440; ● 930
Virginia City Highlands; RMC Place; STOREY; ***202** F-2; mail Reno **z** 89511, **z** 89521; rural
Vista; RMC Place; WASHOE; ***202** F-2; elev. 4,396ft./1,340m.; ★ **RENO**; mail Sparks **z** 89434; pop. incl. with Sparks (Inc. Place)
Vya; RMC Place; WASHOE; ***202** B-2; elev. 5,561ft./1,695m.; mail Cedarville **z** 96104; rural

W

Wabuska; RMC Place; LYON; **202** F-2; elev. 4,299ft./1,310m.; mail Yerington **z** 89447; ● 100
Wadsworth; CDP; WASHOE; **202** F-2; located on Pyramid Lake Ind. Res.; elev. 4,076ft./1,242m.; 🅿; **z** 89442; Ⓟ 640; © 881
Walker Lake; RMC Place; MINERAL; **202** G-3; 🅿; **z** 89415; ● 400
Walker River Reservation; Indian Reservation; MINERAL, CHURCHILL, LYON; mail Schurz **z** 89427; Ⓟ 571; © 853
Warm Springs; RMC Place; NYE; **202** H-7; elev. 541ft./165m.; mail Tonopah **z** 89049; rural
Washington; RMC Place; WASHOE; ★ **RENO**; mail Reno **z** 89503, **z** 89513; pop. incl. with Reno (Inc. Place)
WASHOE; **202** D-2; Ⓟ 254,667; © 339,486; ◆ 423,970
Washoe City; RMC Place; WASHOE; **202** F-2; ★ **RENO**; mail Washoe Valley **z** 89704; ● 500
Washoe Valley; RMC Place; WASHOE; 🅿; **z** 89704 & mail Carson City **z** 89701
Weed Heights; RMC Place; LYON; **202** G-2; elev. 4,640ft./1,414m.; mail Yerington **z** 89447; ● 240
Wellington; RMC Place; LYON; **202** G-2; elev. 4,808ft./1,465m.; 🅿; **z** 89444; ● 300
Wells; Inc. Place; ELKO; **202** C-8; elev. 5,626ft./1,715m.; 🅿; **z** 89835; Ⓟ 1,256; © 1,346
Wells Colony; Indian Reservation; ELKO; © 54
West Reno; RMC Place; WASHOE; ***202** F-2; elev. 4,561ft./1,390m.; ★ **RENO**; mail Reno **z** 89509; pop. incl. with Reno (Inc. Place)
West Wendover; Inc. Place; ELKO; **202** D-10; elev. 4,305ft./1,312m.; 🅿; **z** 89883; Ⓟ 2,154; © 4,721
Westwood Village; RMC Place; DOUGLAS; ***202** G-2; elev. 4,697ft./1,432m.; mail Minden **z** 89423; rural
WHITE PINE; **202** F-8; Ⓟ 9,264; © 9,181; ◆ 9,098
Whitney; RMC Place; CLARK; ***202** L-8; ★ **LASV**; mail Las Vegas **z** 89122; pop. incl. with Henderson (Inc. Place)
Whitney; CDP-Census Area Only; CLARK; ***202** L-9; ★ **LASV**; mail Las Vegas **z** 89122; © 18,273
Wilkins; RMC Place; ELKO; ***202** B-9; mail Wells **z** 89835; rural
Willow Beach; RMC Place; CLARK; mail Boulder City **z** 89005; summer pop. 300; ● 25
Winchester; CDP; CLARK; ***202** L-8; elev. 2,000ft./610m.; ★ **LASV**; mail Las Vegas **z** 89101, **z** 89109; Ⓟ 23,365; © 26,958; ◆ 38,196
Winnemucca; Inc. Place; ⊡ HUMBOLDT; **202** C-5; elev. 4,299ft./1,310m.; 🅿 🄷; **z** 89445-46; Ⓟ 6,134; © 7,174
Winnemucca Colony; Indian Reservation; HUMBOLDT; mail Winnemucca **z** 89445; © 62

Y

Yerington; Inc. Place; ⊡ LYON; **202** G-3; elev. 4,384ft./1,336m.; 🅿 🄷; **z** 89447; Ⓟ 2,367; © 2,883
Yerington Colony; Indian Reservation; LYON; mail Yerington **z** 89447; Ⓟ 421; © 139
Yomba Reservation; Indian Reservation; NYE; mail Austin **z** 89310; Ⓟ 60; © 96

Z

Zephyr Cove; RMC Place; DOUGLAS; **202** G-1; 🅿; **z** 89448 & mail Stateline **z** 89449; seasonal pop. 6,000; ● 1,000
Zephyr Cove-Round Hill Village; CDP-Census Area Only; DOUGLAS; ***202** G-1; mail Zephyr Cove **z** 89448; Ⓟ 1,434; © 1,649

NEW HAMPSHIRE

Statistics

Total area (2000) — 9,350 square miles
Land area (2000) — 8,968 square miles
Water area (2000) — 382 square miles
Capital — Concord
One of Thirteen Original States

Maps

State maps can be found on pages 142-254 in Vol. 1
County Subdivision maps can be found on pages 255-271 in Vol. 1

Ranally Metro Areas (RMAs) and Abbreviations

Boston, MA-NH — BOS
Concord, NH — CONC
Manchester, NH — MNCH
Portsmouth-Dover-Rochester, NH-ME — PTSM-

Principal Places

Place Name	Place Type	County	Population
Manchester	Inc. Place	HILLSBOROUGH	◆ 108,446
Nashua	Inc. Place	HILLSBOROUGH	◆ 87,518
Concord	Inc. Place	MERRIMACK	◆ 40,999
Derry	MCD-Town	ROCKINGHAM	◆ 36,434
Rochester	Inc. Place	STRAFFORD	◆ 31,109
Salem	MCD-Town	ROCKINGHAM	◆ 29,145
Dover	Inc. Place	STRAFFORD	◆ 28,830
Merrimack	MCD-Town	HILLSBOROUGH	◆ 25,943
Londonderry	MCD-Town	ROCKINGHAM	◆ 25,512
Hudson	MCD-Town	HILLSBOROUGH	◆ 24,286
Derry	CDP	ROCKINGHAM	◆ 23,332
Keene	Inc. Place	CHESHIRE	◆ 22,800
Bedford	MCD-Town	HILLSBOROUGH	◆ 21,234
Portsmouth	Inc. Place	ROCKINGHAM	◆ 19,696
Goffstown	MCD-Town	HILLSBOROUGH	◆ 17,524
Hampton	MCD-Town	ROCKINGHAM	◆ 16,875
Laconia	Inc. Place	BELKNAP	◆ 14,981
Exeter	MCD-Town	ROCKINGHAM	◆ 14,863
Milford	MCD-Town	HILLSBOROUGH	◆ 14,573
Hooksett	MCD-Town	MERRIMACK	◆ 14,197
Durham	MCD-Town	STRAFFORD	◆ 13,903
Lebanon	Inc. Place	GRAFTON	◆ 12,810
Windham	MCD-Town	ROCKINGHAM	◆ 12,423
Claremont	Inc. Place	SULLIVAN	◆ 12,233
Somersworth	Inc. Place	STRAFFORD	◆ 12,074

Place Name	Place Type	County	Population
Salem	RMC Place	ROCKINGHAM	● 12,000
Amherst	MCD-Town	HILLSBOROUGH	◆ 11,644
Pelham	MCD-Town	HILLSBOROUGH	◆ 11,546
Londonderry	CDP	ROCKINGHAM	© 11,417
Hanover	MCD-Town	GRAFTON	© 10,850
Berlin	Inc. Place	COOS	© 10,331
Exeter	CDP	ROCKINGHAM	© 9,759
Raymond	MCD-Town	ROCKINGHAM	◆ 9,711
Seabrook	MCD-Town	ROCKINGHAM	◆ 9,345
Hampstead	MCD-Town	ROCKINGHAM	◆ 9,334
Hampton	CDP	ROCKINGHAM	© 9,126
Newmarket	MCD-Town	ROCKINGHAM	◆ 9,101
Durham	CDP	STRAFFORD	© 9,024
Barrington	MCD-Town	STRAFFORD	◆ 8,775
Weare	MCD-Town	HILLSBOROUGH	◆ 8,737
Conway	MCD-Town	CARROLL	© 8,604
Franklin	Inc. Place	MERRIMACK	© 8,405
Litchfield	MCD-Town	HILLSBOROUGH	◆ 8,355
Milford	CDP	HILLSBOROUGH	© 8,293
Hanover	CDP	GRAFTON	© 8,162
Hudson	CDP	HILLSBOROUGH	© 7,814
Plaistow	MCD-Town	ROCKINGHAM	◆ 7,607
Hollis	MCD-Town	HILLSBOROUGH	◆ 7,440
Stratham	MCD-Town	ROCKINGHAM	◆ 7,385
Bow	MCD-Town	MERRIMACK	© 7,138

Place Name	Place Type	County	Population
Pembroke	MCD-Town	MERRIMACK	© 6,897
Gilford	MCD-Town	BELKNAP	© 6,803
Swanzey	MCD-Town	CHESHIRE	© 6,800
Belmont	MCD-Town	BELKNAP	© 6,716
Farmington	MCD-Town	STRAFFORD	◆ 6,289
Newport	MCD-Town	SULLIVAN	© 6,269
Atkinson	MCD-Town	ROCKINGHAM	◆ 6,212
Wolfeboro	MCD-Town	CARROLL	© 6,083
Meredith	MCD-Town	BELKNAP	© 5,943
Plymouth	MCD-Town	GRAFTON	© 5,892
Kingston	MCD-Town	ROCKINGHAM	◆ 5,887
Peterborough	MCD-Town	HILLSBOROUGH	© 5,883
Littleton	MCD-Town	GRAFTON	© 5,845
Sandown	MCD-Town	ROCKINGHAM	◆ 5,789
Rye	MCD-Town	ROCKINGHAM	◆ 5,787
Pinardville	CDP	HILLSBOROUGH	© 5,779
Epping	MCD-Town	ROCKINGHAM	◆ 5,592
Jaffrey	MCD-Town	CHESHIRE	© 5,476
Rindge	MCD-Town	CHESHIRE	© 5,451
Hopkinton	MCD-Town	MERRIMACK	© 5,399
Suncook	CDP	MERRIMACK	© 5,362
South Hooksett	CDP	MERRIMACK	© 5,282
Newmarket	CDP	ROCKINGHAM	© 5,124
Auburn	MCD-Town	ROCKINGHAM	◆ 5,079

County Business Data

County	FIPS Code	County Seat	Land Area (Sq. Mi.)	Census Population 4/1/2000	Census Population 4/1/1990	Census Population % Change 1990-2000	Wholesale Trade Sales, 1997 ($1,000)	Wholesale Trade % Change 1992-97	Manufacturing, 1997 Establish-ments	Manufacturing, 1997 Total Employees	Manufacturing, 1997 Value Added ($1,000)	Manufacturing, 1997 Ranally Mfg. Units
Belknap	001	Laconia	401	56,325	49,216	14.4	158,138	-13.0	121	3,343	267,679	142
Carroll	003	Ossipee	934	43,666	35,410	23.3	(d)	(d)	85	1,053	65,028	34
Cheshire	005	Keene	707	73,825	70,121	5.3	379,271	-6.0	170	6,415	555,335	294
Coos	007	Lancaster	1,800	33,111	34,828	-4.9	(d)	(d)	39	1,392	105,826	56
Grafton	009	Woodsville	1,713	81,743	74,929	9.1	391,104	17.3	138	5,430	457,035	242
Hillsborough	011	Manchester, Nashua	876	380,841	336,073	13.3	5,018,069	4.7	678	31,667	3,418,772	1,809
Merrimack	013	Concord	934	136,225	120,005	13.5	2,197,833	174.9	220	7,869	644,114	341
Rockingham	015	Exeter	695	277,359	245,845	12.8	4,898,183	13.2	493	16,061	2,128,331	1,126
Strafford	017	Dover	369	112,233	104,233	7.7	403,106	43.4	155	6,338	497,778	263
Sullivan	019	Newport	537	40,458	38,592	4.8	115,907	31.1	114	3,977	388,028	205
The State			**8,968**	**1,235,786**	**1,109,252**	**11.4**	**13,741,876**	**20.8**	**2,213**	**83,545**	**8,527,926**	**4,512**

(d) Data not available. Corresponding percentages or Ranally Manufacturing Units are estimates.
... Represents 0 or amount too minimal to be reported.

Administrative Divisions

Towns: Although all New Hampshire counties have towns, they may not cover the entire area of each county. Although legally incorporated, towns are not treated as incorporated places by the U.S. Census because the population often is scattered among several localities and rural areas rather than being concentrated in a single place. Only towns with an active government recognized by the U.S. Census of Governments are printed in this index.

Unincorporated County Subdivisions: Grants, Locations, Purchases, Unorganized Locations and Unorganized Townships do not possess governmental and taxing powers, and they are not listed in this index.

Cities: Incorporated cities do not form part of the towns which adjoin or surround them.

Index of Places and Counties

A

B

C

D

Entries in **UPPERCASE** are counties.
Entries in **bold** have populations of 2,500 or more.
Names in parentheses are alternate names.

Inc. Place	Incorporated Place
RMC Place	Rand McNally Designated Place
CDP	Census Designated Place
MCD	Minor Civil Division
⊡	County Seat
▲	Minor Civil Division
elev.	Elevation
▣	Post Office
🅷	Hospital
🅲	College
■	Principal Business Center
★	Ranally Metro Area (RMA) Abbreviation
z	Zip Code(s)
Ⓟ	Previous Census Population
Ⓡ	Revised Census Population
Ⓐ	Annexation Population
●	Rand McNally Population Estimate
©	Final Census Population
Ⓢ	Special Census Population
◆	Estimated Population

For additional definitions see Glossary, Volume 1, and Introduction, Volume 2.

Deerfield; RMC Place; ROCKINGHAM; ▲ Deerfield; 203 L-8; elev. 552ft./168m.; [P]; z 03037; ● 200

Deerfield; MCD-Town; ROCKINGHAM; *203 L-8; [P]; z 03037; Ⓟ 3,124; Ⓒ 3,678

Deerfield Center; RMC Place; ROCKINGHAM; *203 L-8; elev. 475ft./145m.; mail Deerfield z 03037; ● 350

Deerfield Parade (James City); RMC Place; ROCKINGHAM; ▲ Deerfield; 203 L-8; mail Deerfield z 03037; ● 200

Deering; RMC Place; HILLSBOROUGH; ▲ Deering; 203 L-6; elev. 1,078ft./329m.; [P]; z 03244; ● 100

Deering; MCD-Town; HILLSBOROUGH; *203 L-6; [P]; z 03244; Ⓟ 1,707; Ⓒ 1,875

Derry; CDP; ROCKINGHAM; 203 M-8; [P] [H]; ★ **BOS**; z 03038; Ⓟ 20,446; Ⓒ 22,661; ◆ 23,332

Derry; MCD-Town; ROCKINGHAM; *203 M-8; [P]; ★ **BOS**; z 03038; Ⓟ 29,603; Ⓒ 34,021; ◆ 36,434

Derry Village; RMC Place; ROCKINGHAM; ▲ Derry; *203 M-8; ★ **BOS**; mail Derry z 03038; ● 900

Dixville Notch; RMC Place; COOS; ▲ Dixville; 203 C-8; mail Colebrook z 03576; ● 20

Dorchester; RMC Place; GRAFTON; ▲ Dorchester; 203 I-6; elev. 1,368ft./417m.; [P]; z 03266; ● 60

Dorchester; MCD-Town; GRAFTON; *203 I-6; [P]; z 03266; Ⓟ 392; Ⓒ 353

Dorrs Corner; RMC Place; CARROLL; ▲ Ossipee; *203 I-8; mail Center Ossipee z 03814; ● 45

Dover; Inc. Place; ⊡ STRAFFORD; 203 K-10; elev. 57ft./17m.; [P] [H] ■; ★ **PTSM-**; z 03820-22; Ⓟ 25,042; Ⓒ 26,884; ◆ 28,830

Dover Point; RMC Place; STRAFFORD; *203 L-10; ★ **PTSM-**; mail Dover z 03820; pop. incl. with Dover (Inc. Place)

Dows Corner; RMC Place; ROCKINGHAM; ▲ Exeter; *203 L-10; ★ **PTSM-**; mail Exeter z 03833; ● 30

Drewsville; RMC Place; CHESHIRE; ▲ Walpole; 203 L-4; elev. 475ft./145m.; [P]; z 03604; ● 150

Dublin; RMC Place; CHESHIRE; ▲ Dublin; 203 M-5; elev. 1,439ft./439m.; [P] [H]; z 03444; ● 650

Dublin; MCD-Town; CHESHIRE; *203 M-5; [P]; z 03444; Ⓟ 1,474; Ⓒ 1,476

Ducks Head; RMC Place; CARROLL; ▲ Jackson; *203 G-8; mail Jackson z 03846

Dummer; RMC Place; COOS; ▲ Dummer; *203 E-8; [P]; z 03588; ● 100

Dummer; MCD-Town; COOS; *203 D-8; [P]; z 03588; Ⓟ 327; Ⓒ 309

Dunbarton; MERRIMACK; see Dunbarton Center (RMC Place)

Dunbarton; MCD-Town; MERRIMACK; *203 L-7; [P]; z 03046 & mail Concord z 03301, Goffstown z 03045; Ⓟ 1,759; Ⓒ 2,226

Dunbarton Center (Dunbarton); RMC Place; MERRIMACK; ▲ Dunbarton; 203 L-7; mail Dunbarton z 03046; ● 230

Durham; CDP; STRAFFORD; ▲ Durham; 203 L-9; [P] [C] 13,957; ★ **PTSM-**; z 03824; Ⓟ 9,236; Ⓒ 9,024

Durham; MCD-Town; STRAFFORD; *203 L-9; [P] [C] 13,957; ★ **PTSM-**; z 03824; Ⓟ 11,818; Ⓒ 12,664; ◆ 13,903

E

East Alstead; RMC Place; CHESHIRE; ▲ Alstead; 203 L-5; elev. 1,281ft./390m.; mail Alstead z 03602; ● 200

East Alton; RMC Place; BELKNAP; ▲ Alton; *203 J-8; mail Alton z 03809

East Andover; RMC Place; MERRIMACK; ▲ Andover; 203 J-7; elev. 652ft./199m.; [P]; z 03231; ● 350

East Barrington; RMC Place; STRAFFORD; *203 K-9; ★ **PTSM-**; mail Barrington z 03825; ● 200

East Candia; RMC Place; ROCKINGHAM; ▲ Candia; 203 L-8; [P]; ★ **MNCH**; z 03040; ● 125

East Concord; RMC Place; MERRIMACK; *203 K-7; elev. 314ft./96m.; ★ **CONC**; mail Concord z 03301; pop. incl. with Concord (Inc. Place)

East Conway; RMC Place; CARROLL; ▲ Conway; 203 G-9; elev. 410ft./125m.; mail Center Conway z 03813; ● 135

East Deering; RMC Place; HILLSBOROUGH; ▲ Deering; *203 L-6; elev. 807ft./246m.; mail Hillsborough z 03244; rural

East Derry; RMC Place; ROCKINGHAM; ▲ Derry; 203 M-8; [P]; ★ **BOS**; z 03041; ● 850

East Freedom; RMC Place; CARROLL; ▲ Freedom; *203 I-9; mail Freedom z 03836; rural

East Grafton; RMC Place; GRAFTON; ▲ Grafton; *203 J-6; mail Grafton z 03240

East Grantham; RMC Place; SULLIVAN; ▲ Grantham; *203 J-5; mail Grantham z 03753; ● 60

East Hampstead; RMC Place; ROCKINGHAM; ▲ Hampstead; 203 M-9; [P]; ★ **BOS**; z 03826; ● 1,400

East Haverhill; RMC Place; GRAFTON; ▲ Haverhill; 203 G-6; mail Pike z 03780; ● 110

East Hebron; RMC Place; GRAFTON; ▲ Hebron; 203 I-6; [P]; z 03241; ● 150

East Holderness; RMC Place; GRAFTON; ▲ Holderness; *203 I-7; mail Ashland z 03217; ● 120

East Kingston; RMC Place; ROCKINGHAM; ▲ East Kingston; *203 M-9; elev. 124ft./38m.; [P]; ★ **PTSM-**; z 03827; ● 300

East Kingston; MCD-Town; ROCKINGHAM; *203 M-9; [P]; ★ **PTSM-**; z 03827; Ⓟ 1,352; Ⓒ 1,784; ◆ 1,859

East Lempster; RMC Place; SULLIVAN; ▲ Lempster; 203 K-5; elev. 1,230ft./375m.; [P]; z 03605; ● 300

East Merrimack; CDP-Census Area Only; HILLSBOROUGH; ▲ Merrimack; *203 M-7; ★ **BOS**; mail Merrimack z 03054; Ⓟ 3,656; Ⓒ 3,784

East Milford; RMC Place; HILLSBOROUGH; ▲ Milford; *203 M-7; ★ **BOS**; mail Milford z 03055

Easton; RMC Place; GRAFTON; ▲ Easton; *203 G-6; elev. 1,167ft./356m.; mail Franconia z 03580, Woodsville z 03785; rural

Easton; MCD-Town; GRAFTON; *203 G-6; mail Franconia z 03580, Woodsville z 03785; Ⓟ 223; Ⓒ 256

East Plainfield; RMC Place; SULLIVAN; ▲ Plainfield; *203 J-5; elev. 1,016ft./310m.; mail Plainfield z 03781; rural

East Rindge; RMC Place; CHESHIRE; ▲ Rindge; 203 N-6; mail Rindge z 03461; ● 250

East Rochester; RMC Place; STRAFFORD; *203 K-9; ★ **PTSM-**; mail Rochester z 03868; pop. incl. with Rochester (Inc. Place)

East Sandwich; RMC Place; CARROLL; ▲ Sandwich; *203 H-8; mail Center Sandwich z 03227; rural

East Sullivan; RMC Place; CHESHIRE; ▲ Sullivan; 203 L-5; elev. 1,023ft./312m.; mail Sullivan z 03445; ● 175

East Sutton; RMC Place; MERRIMACK; ▲ Sutton; *203 K-6; elev. 586ft./179m.; mail Warner z 03278

East Swanzey; RMC Place; CHESHIRE; ▲ Swanzey; 203 M-5; [P]; z 03446; ● 350

East Tilton; RMC Place; BELKNAP; ▲ Tilton; *203 J-7; elev. 543ft./166m.; mail Tilton z 03276; ● 100

East Unity; RMC Place; SULLIVAN; ▲ Unity; 203 K-5; elev. 1,201ft./366m.; mail Newport z 03773; ● 130

Eastview; RMC Place; CHESHIRE; ▲ Harrisville; *203 M-5; elev. 1,014ft./309m.; mail Harrisville z 03450; rural

East Wakefield (Burleyville); RMC Place; CARROLL; ▲ Wakefield; 203 I-9; elev. 685ft./209m.; [P]; z 03830; ● 90

East Washington; RMC Place; SULLIVAN; ▲ Washington; 203 K-6; elev. 939ft./286m.; mail Washington z 03280; ● 60

East Westmoreland; RMC Place; CHESHIRE; ▲ Westmoreland; *203 L-4; mail Westmoreland z 03467; ● 180

East Wilder; RMC Place; GRAFTON; *203 I-5; mail West Lebanon z 03784; pop. incl. with Lebanon (Inc. Place)

East Wolfeboro; RMC Place; CARROLL; ▲ Wolfeboro; *203 I-9; mail Wolfeboro z 03894; rural

Eaton; MCD-Town; CARROLL; *203 H-9; mail Eaton Center z 03832; Ⓟ 362; Ⓒ 375

Eaton Center; RMC Place; CARROLL; ▲ Eaton; 203 H-9; elev. 529ft./161m.; [P]; z 03832; ● 100

Effingham; RMC Place; CARROLL; ▲ Effingham; 203 I-9; [P]; z 03882 & mail Center Ossipee z 03814; ● 75

Effingham; MCD-Town; CARROLL; *203 I-9; [P]; z 03882 & mail Center Ossipee z 03814; Ⓟ 941; Ⓒ 1,273

Effingham Falls; RMC Place; CARROLL; ▲ Effingham; 203 I-9; mail Center Ossipee z 03814; ● 100

Elkins; RMC Place; MERRIMACK; ▲ New London; 203 J-6; [P]; z 03233; ● 120

Ellsworth; MCD-Town; GRAFTON; *203 H-6; [P]; z 03223 & mail Plymouth z 03264, Rumney z 03266; Ⓟ 74; Ⓒ 87

Elmwood; RMC Place; HILLSBOROUGH; ▲ Hancock; *203 L-6; elev. 783ft./239m.; mail Hancock z 03449; rural

Elmwood; RMC Place; MERRIMACK; ▲ Danbury; 203 J-6; mail Danbury z 03230; ● 80

Elmwood Corners; RMC Place; ROCKINGHAM; ▲ Hampton; *203 M-10; ★ **PTSM-**; mail Hampton z 03842

Elwyn Park; RMC Place; ROCKINGHAM; *203 L-10; ★ **PTSM-**; mail Portsmouth z 03801; pop. incl. with Portsmouth (Inc. Place)

Enfield; CDP; GRAFTON; ▲ Enfield; 203 I-5; elev. 776ft./237m.; [P]; z 03748; Ⓟ 1,560; Ⓒ 1,698

Enfield; MCD-Town; GRAFTON; *203 I-5; [P]; z 03748; Ⓟ 3,979; Ⓒ 4,618

Enfield Center; RMC Place; GRAFTON; ▲ Enfield; 203 J-5; elev. 853ft./260m.; [P]; z 03749; ● 250

Epping; CDP; ROCKINGHAM; ▲ Epping; 203 L-9; [P]; ★ **PTSM-**; z 03042; Ⓟ 1,384; Ⓒ 1,673

Epping; MCD-Town; ROCKINGHAM; *203 L-9; [P]; ★ **PTSM-**; z 03042; Ⓟ 5,162; Ⓒ 5,476; ◆ 5,592

Epsom; RMC Place; MERRIMACK; ▲ Epsom; 203 K-8; [P]; ★ **CONC**; z 03234; ● 250

Epsom; MCD-Town; MERRIMACK; *203 K-8; [P]; ★ **CONC**; z 03234; Ⓟ 3,591; Ⓒ 4,021

Errol; RMC Place; COOS; ▲ Errol; 203 D-9; elev. 1,228ft./374m.; [P]; z 03579; ● 170

Errol; MCD-Town; COOS; *203 D-9; [P]; z 03579; Ⓟ 292; Ⓒ 298

Etna; RMC Place; GRAFTON; ▲ Hanover; 203 I-5; elev. 782ft./238m.; [P]; z 03750; ● 350

Exeter; CDP; ⊡ ROCKINGHAM; ▲ Exeter; 203 L-9; [P] [H]; ★ **PTSM-**; z 03833; Ⓟ 9,556; Ⓒ 9,759

Exeter; MCD-Town; ROCKINGHAM; *203 L-9; [P]; ★ **PTSM-**; z 03833; Ⓟ 12,481; Ⓒ 14,058; ◆ 14,863

Exeter Hampton Mobile Village; RMC Place; ROCKINGHAM; ▲ Exeter; ★ **PTSM-**; mail Exeter z 03833; ● 150

Exeter Villa; RMC Place; ROCKINGHAM; ▲ Exeter; *203 M-9; ★ **PTSM-**; mail Exeter z 03833; ● 50

Exeter West; RMC Place; ROCKINGHAM; ▲ Exeter; ★ **PTSM-**; mail Exeter z 03833

F

Fabyan; RMC Place; COOS; ▲ Carroll; *203 F-8; mail Twin Mountain z 03595

Fairhill Manor; RMC Place; ROCKINGHAM; ▲ Rye; *203 L-10; ★ **PTSM-**; mail Rye z 03870; ● 250

Farmington; CDP; STRAFFORD; ▲ Farmington; 203 J-9; [P]; ★ **PTSM-**; z 03835; Ⓟ 3,567; Ⓒ 3,468

Farmington; MCD-Town; STRAFFORD; *203 K-9; [P]; ★ **PTSM-**; z 03835; Ⓟ 5,739; Ⓒ 5,774; ◆ 6,289

Fitzwilliam; RMC Place; CHESHIRE; ▲ Fitzwilliam; 203 M-5; elev. 1,205ft./367m.; [P]; z 03447; ● 650

Fitzwilliam; MCD-Town; CHESHIRE; *203 M-5; [P]; z 03447; Ⓟ 2,011; Ⓒ 2,141

Fitzwilliam Depot; RMC Place; CHESHIRE; ▲ Fitzwilliam; 203 M-5; mail Fitzwilliam z 03447; ● 500

Fogg Corner; RMC Place; ROCKINGHAM; ▲ North Hampton; *203 M-10; ★ **PTSM-**; mail North Hampton z 03862; ● 150

Forest Lake; RMC Place; CHESHIRE; ▲ Winchester; *203 M-4; mail Winchester z 03470; summer pop. 200; ● 100

Fosters Corners; RMC Place; ROCKINGHAM; ▲ Salem; *203 M-8; ★ **BOS**; mail Salem z 03079; ● 100

Foundry; RMC Place; STRAFFORD; *203 K-10; ★ **PTSM-**; mail Somersworth z 03878; pop. incl. with Somersworth (Inc. Place)

Foyes Corner; RMC Place; ROCKINGHAM; ▲ Rye; *203 L-10; ★ **PTSM-**; mail Rye z 03870; ● 90

Francestown; RMC Place; HILLSBOROUGH; ▲ Francestown; 203 L-6; [P]; z 03043; ● 250

Francestown; MCD-Town; HILLSBOROUGH; *203 L-6; [P]; z 03043; Ⓟ 1,217; Ⓒ 1,480

Franconia; RMC Place; GRAFTON; ▲ Franconia; 203 F-7; [P]; z 03580; ● 600

Franconia; MCD-Town; GRAFTON; *203 G-7; [P]; z 03580; Ⓟ 811; Ⓒ 924

Franklin; Inc. Place; MERRIMACK; 203 J-7; elev. 335ft./102m.; [P] [H]; z 03235; Ⓟ 8,304; Ⓒ 8,405

Freedom; RMC Place; CARROLL; ▲ Freedom; 203 H-9; elev. 452ft./138m.; [P]; z 03836; ● 400

Freedom; MCD-Town; CARROLL; *203 H-9; [P]; z 03836; Ⓟ 935; Ⓒ 1,303

Fremont; RMC Place; ROCKINGHAM; ▲ Fremont; 203 L-9; elev. 158ft./48m.; [P]; ★ **BOS**; z 03044; ● 900

Fremont; MCD-Town; ROCKINGHAM; *203 L-9; [P]; ★ **BOS**; z 03044; Ⓟ 2,576; Ⓒ 3,510; ◆ 3,951

G

Gardners Grove; RMC Place; BELKNAP; ▲ Belmont; *203 J-7; mail Belmont z 03220; rural

Gates Corner; RMC Place; STRAFFORD; *203 K-10; ★ **PTSM-**; mail Dover z 03820; pop. incl. with Dover (Inc. Place)

Gaza; RMC Place; BELKNAP; ▲ Sanbornton; *203 J-7; mail Sanbornton z 03269; ● 30

Georges Mills; RMC Place; SULLIVAN; ▲ Sunapee; 203 J-5; [P]; z 03751; ● 400

Gerrish (North Boscawen); RMC Place; MERRIMACK; ▲ Boscawen; *203 K-7; elev. 79ft./24m.; ★ **CONC**; mail Concord z 03303

Gilford; RMC Place; BELKNAP; ▲ Gilford; 203 J-8; elev. 741ft./226m.; [P]; z 03249 & mail Laconia z 03246-47; ● 600

Gilford; MCD-Town; BELKNAP; *203 J-8; [P]; z 03249 & mail Laconia z 03246-47; Ⓟ 5,867; Ⓒ 6,803

Gilmans Corner; RMC Place; GRAFTON; ▲ Orford; *203 H-6; elev. 920ft./280m.; mail Orford z 03777

Gilmanton; RMC Place; BELKNAP; ▲ Gilmanton; 203 J-8; elev. 998ft./304m.; [P]; z 03237 & mail Gilmanton Iron Works z 03837; ● 700

Gilmanton; MCD-Town; BELKNAP; *203 J-8; [P]; z 03237 & mail Gilmanton Iron Works z 03837; Ⓟ 2,609; Ⓒ 3,060

Gilmanton Ironworks; RMC Place; BELKNAP; ▲ Gilmanton; 203 J-8; elev. 629ft./192m.; [P]; z 03837; ● 600

Gilsum; RMC Place; CHESHIRE; ▲ Gilsum; 203 L-5; [P]; z 03448; ● 400

Gilsum; MCD-Town; CHESHIRE; *203 L-5; [P]; z 03448; Ⓟ 745; Ⓒ 777

Glen; RMC Place; CARROLL; ▲ Bartlett; 203 G-8; [P]; z 03838; ● 250

Glencliff; RMC Place; GRAFTON; ▲ Warren; 203 H-6; [P]; z 03238; ● 90

Glendale; RMC Place; BELKNAP; ▲ Gilford; 203 J-8; elev. 520ft./158m.; mail Laconia z 03246; ● 400

Glenmere Village; RMC Place; STRAFFORD; ▲ Lee; *203 L-9; elev. 93ft./28m.; ★ **PTSM-**; mail Durham z 03824; ● 40

Goffs Falls; RMC Place; HILLSBOROUGH; *203 M-8; ★ **MNCH**; mail Manchester z 03103; pop. incl. with Manchester (Inc. Place)

Goffstown; RMC Place; HILLSBOROUGH; ▲ Goffstown; 203 L-7; elev. 306ft./93m.; [P]; ★ **MNCH**; z 03045 & mail Dunbarton z 03046; ● 3,200

Goffstown; MCD-Town; HILLSBOROUGH; *203 L-7; [P]; ★ **MNCH**; z 03045 & mail Dunbarton z 03046; Ⓟ 14,621; Ⓒ 16,929; ◆ 17,524

Gonic; RMC Place; STRAFFORD; *203 K-9; ★ **PTSM-**; mail Rochester z 03839; pop. incl. with Rochester (Inc. Place)

Goodrich Falls; RMC Place; CARROLL; ▲ Bartlett; *203 G-8; mail Jackson z 03846; ● 60

Goose Hollow; RMC Place; GRAFTON; ▲ Campton; *203 H-7; elev. 780ft./238m.; mail Campton z 03223; rural

Gorham; CDP; COOS; ▲ Gorham; 203 F-8; elev. 801ft./244m.; [P]; z 03581 & mail Randolph z 03593; Ⓟ 1,910; Ⓒ 1,773

Gorham; MCD-Town; COOS; *203 F-8; [P]; z 03581 & mail Randolph z 03593; Ⓟ 3,173; Ⓒ 2,895

Goshen; RMC Place; SULLIVAN; ▲ Goshen; 203 K-5; [P]; z 03752; ● 350

Goshen; MCD-Town; SULLIVAN; *203 K-5; [P]; z 03752; Ⓟ 742; Ⓒ 741

Goshen Four Corners; RMC Place; SULLIVAN; ▲ Goshen; mail Goshen z 03752; rural

Gossville; RMC Place; MERRIMACK; ▲ Epsom; 203 K-8; ★ **CONC**; mail Epsom z 03234; ● 350

Governors Lake; RMC Place; ROCKINGHAM; ▲ Raymond; *203 L-8; ★ **BOS**; mail Raymond z 03077; summer pop. 250

Grafton; RMC Place; GRAFTON; ▲ Grafton; 203 J-6; [P]; z 03240; ● 225

Grafton; MCD-Town; GRAFTON; *203 J-6; [P]; z 03240; Ⓟ 923; Ⓒ 1,138

GRAFTON; 203 H-6; Ⓟ 74,929; Ⓒ 81,743; ◆ 86,200

Grafton Center; RMC Place; GRAFTON; ▲ Grafton; 203 J-6; mail Grafton z 03240; ● 50

Grange; RMC Place; COOS; ▲ Lancaster; *203 E-7; elev. 979ft./298m.; mail Lancaster z 03584

Granite; RMC Place; CARROLL; ▲ Ossipee; *203 I-9; mail Ossipee z 03864

Grantham; RMC Place; SULLIVAN; ▲ Grantham; 203 J-5; elev. 962ft./293m.; [P]; z 03753; ● 300

Grantham; MCD-Town; SULLIVAN; *203 J-5; [P]; z 03753; Ⓟ 1,247; Ⓒ 2,167

Grasmere; RMC Place; HILLSBOROUGH; ▲ Goffstown; *203 L-7; ★ **MNCH**; mail Goffstown z 03045; ● 500

Great Boars Head; RMC Place; ROCKINGHAM; ▲ Hampton; *203 M-10; ★ **PTSM-**; mail Hampton z 03842; ● 70

Greenfield; RMC Place; HILLSBOROUGH; ▲ Greenfield; 203 M-6; elev. 843ft./257m.; [P] [H]; z 03047; ● 900

Greenfield; MCD-Town; HILLSBOROUGH; *203 M-6; [P]; z 03047; Ⓟ 1,519; Ⓒ 1,657

Greenland; RMC Place; ROCKINGHAM; ▲ Greenland; 203 L-10; [P]; ★ **PTSM-**; z 03840; ● 1,400

Greenland; MCD-Town; ROCKINGHAM; *203 L-10; [P]; ★ **PTSM-**; z 03840; Ⓟ 2,768; Ⓒ 3,208; ◆ 3,553

Greenland Station; RMC Place; ROCKINGHAM; ▲ Greenland; *203 L-10; ★ **PTSM-**; mail Greenland z 03840

Greenville; CDP; HILLSBOROUGH; ▲ Greenville; 203 M-6; [P]; ★ **BOS**; z 03048; Ⓟ 1,135; Ⓒ 1,131

Greenville; MCD-Town; HILLSBOROUGH; *203 N-6; [P]; ★ **BOS**; z 03048; Ⓟ 2,231; Ⓒ 2,224; ◆ 2,135

Groton; RMC Place; GRAFTON; ▲ Groton; 203 I-6; mail Hebron z 03241, Rumney z 03266; ● 140

Groton; MCD-Town; GRAFTON; *203 I-6; mail Hebron z 03241, Rumney z 03266; Ⓟ 318; Ⓒ 456

Groveton; CDP; COOS; ▲ Northumberland; 203 E-7; elev. 884ft./269m.; [P]; z 03582; Ⓟ 1,255; Ⓒ 1,197

Guild; RMC Place; SULLIVAN; ▲ Newport; 203 K-5; [P]; z 03754; ● 325

H

Hampstead; RMC Place; ROCKINGHAM; ▲ Hampstead; 203 M-9; elev. 329ft./100m.; [P] [H]; ★ **BOS**; z 03841; ● 900

Hampstead; MCD-Town; ROCKINGHAM; *203 M-9; [P]; ★ **BOS**; z 03841; Ⓟ 6,732; Ⓒ 8,297; ◆ 9,334

Hampton; CDP; ROCKINGHAM; ▲ Hampton; 203 M-10; [P]; ★ **PTSM-**; z 03842-43; Ⓟ 7,989; Ⓒ 9,126

Hampton; MCD-Town; ROCKINGHAM; *203 M-10; [P]; ★ **PTSM-**; z 03842-43; Ⓟ 12,278; Ⓒ 14,937; ◆ 16,875

Hampton Beach; RMC Place; ROCKINGHAM; ▲ Hampton; 203 M-10; ★ **PTSM-**; mail Hampton z 03842-43; summer pop. 1,800; ● 600

Hampton Falls; RMC Place; ROCKINGHAM; ▲ Hampton Falls; 203 M-10; [P]; ★ **PTSM-**; z 03844; ● 550

Hampton Falls; MCD-Town; ROCKINGHAM; *203 M-10; [P]; ★ **PTSM-**; z 03844; Ⓟ 1,503; Ⓒ 1,880; ◆ 2,160

Hancock; RMC Place; HILLSBOROUGH; ▲ Hancock; 203 L-6; [P]; z 03449; ● 500

Hancock; MCD-Town; HILLSBOROUGH; *203 L-6; [P]; z 03449; Ⓟ 1,604; Ⓒ 1,739

Hanover; CDP; GRAFTON; ▲ Hanover; 203 I-5; elev. 531ft./162m.; [P] [H] [C] 5,753; z 03755; Ⓟ 6,538; Ⓒ 8,162

Hanover; MCD-Town; GRAFTON; *203 I-5; [P] [C] 5,753; z 03755; Ⓟ 9,212; Ⓒ 10,850

Hanover Center; RMC Place; GRAFTON; ▲ Hanover; 203 I-5; elev. 1,162ft./354m.; mail Hanover z 03755; ● 60

Happy Corner; RMC Place; COOS; ▲ Pittsburg; *203 B-8; elev. 1,541ft./470m.; mail Pittsburg z 03592

Happy Valley; RMC Place; HILLSBOROUGH; ▲ Peterborough; *203 M-6; elev. 724ft./221m.; mail Peterborough z 03458; ● 70

Harrisville; RMC Place; CHESHIRE; ▲ Harrisville; 203 M-5; [P]; z 03450; ● 500

Harrisville; MCD-Town; CHESHIRE; *203 M-5; [P]; z 03450; Ⓟ 981; Ⓒ 1,075

Hart's Location; MCD-Town; CARROLL; *203 G-8; [P]; z 03812 & mail North Conway z 03860; Ⓟ 36; Ⓒ 37

Hastings; RMC Place; MERRIMACK; ▲ New London; *203 J-6; elev. 1,166ft./355m.; mail New London z 03257; ● 40

Haverhill; RMC Place; GRAFTON; ▲ Haverhill; 203 G-5; [P]; z 03765; ● 400

Haverhill; MCD-Town; GRAFTON; *203 G-6; [P]; z 03765 & mail North Haverhill z 03774; Ⓟ 4,164; Ⓒ 4,416

Hayes; STRAFFORD; see North Rochester (RMC Place)

Haynes Corner; RMC Place; ROCKINGHAM; ▲ Exeter; *203 L-9; ★ **PTSM-**; mail Exeter z 03833

Hebron; RMC Place; GRAFTON; ▲ Hebron; 203 I-6; [P]; z 03241; ● 150

Hebron; MCD-Town; GRAFTON; *203 I-6; [P]; z 03241; Ⓟ 386; Ⓒ 459

Hell Hollow; RMC Place; SULLIVAN; ▲ Plainfield; *203 J-4; elev. 680ft./207m.; mail Cornish Flat z 03746; rural

Henniker; CDP; MERRIMACK; ▲ Henniker; 203 K-6; [P] [C] 1,281; z 03242; Ⓟ 1,693; Ⓒ 1,627

Henniker; MCD-Town; MERRIMACK; *203 K-6; [P] [C] 1,281; z 03242; Ⓟ 4,151; Ⓒ 4,433

High Bridge; RMC Place; HILLSBOROUGH; ▲ New Ipswich; 203 N-6; elev. 869ft./265m.; ★ **BOS**; mail New Ipswich z 03071; ● 100

Hill; RMC Place; MERRIMACK; ▲ Hill; 203 J-7; [P]; z 03243; ● 275

Hill; MCD-Town; MERRIMACK; *203 J-6; [P]; z 03243; Ⓟ 814; Ⓒ 992

Hill Center; RMC Place; MERRIMACK; ▲ Hill; *203 J-7; mail Hill z 03243

Hillsboro; RMC Place; HILLSBOROUGH; ▲ Hillsborough; *203 L-6; ● 1,500

Hillsborough; CDP-Census Area Only; HILLSBOROUGH; ▲ Hillsborough; 203 L-6; elev. 580ft./177m.; [P]; z 03244; Ⓟ 1,826; Ⓒ 1,842

Hillsborough; MCD-Town; HILLSBOROUGH; *203 L-6; [P]; z 03244; Ⓟ 4,498; Ⓒ 4,928

HILLSBOROUGH; 203 M-6; Ⓟ 336,073; Ⓒ 380,841; ◆ 400,358

Hillsborough Center; RMC Place; HILLSBOROUGH; ▲ Hillsborough; 203 L-6; mail Hillsborough z 03244; ● 150

Hillsborough Lower Village; RMC Place; HILLSBOROUGH; ▲ Hillsborough; 203 L-6; mail Hillsborough z 03244; ● 250

Hillsborough Upper Village; RMC Place; HILLSBOROUGH; ▲ Hillsborough; 203 L-6; mail Hillsborough z 03244; ● 345

Hills Corner; RMC Place; STRAFFORD; ▲ Strafford; *203 K-9; mail Center Strafford z 03815; rural

Hinsdale; CDP; CHESHIRE; ▲ Hinsdale; 203 M-4; [P]; z 03451; Ⓟ 1,718; Ⓒ 1,713

Hinsdale; MCD-Town; CHESHIRE; *203 M-4; [P]; z 03451; Ⓟ 3,936; Ⓒ 4,082

Holderness; RMC Place; GRAFTON; ▲ Holderness; 203 I-7; [P]; z 03245; ● 400

Holderness; MCD-Town; GRAFTON; *203 I-7; [P]; z 03245; Ⓟ 1,694; Ⓒ 1,930

Hollis; RMC Place; HILLSBOROUGH; ▲ Hollis; 203 N-7; [P]; ★ **BOS**; z 03049; ● 600

Hollis; MCD-Town; HILLSBOROUGH; *203 N-7; [P]; ★ **BOS**; z 03049; Ⓟ 5,705; Ⓒ 7,015; ◆ 7,440

Hooksett; CDP; MERRIMACK; ▲ Hooksett; 203 L-8; elev. 199ft./61m.; [P]; ★ **MNCH**; z 03106; Ⓒ 3,609

Hooksett; MCD-Town; MERRIMACK; *203 L-8; [P]; ★ **MNCH**; z 03106; Ⓟ 8,767; Ⓒ 11,721; ◆ 14,197

Hopkinton; RMC Place; MERRIMACK; ▲ Hopkinton; 203 K-7; elev. 505ft./154m.; [P]; ★ **CONC**; z 03229; ● 400

Hopkinton; MCD-Town; MERRIMACK; *203 K-7; [P]; ★ **CONC**; z 03229; Ⓟ 4,806; Ⓒ 5,399

Horses Corner; RMC Place; MERRIMACK; ▲ Chichester; *203 K-8; ★ **CONC**; mail Chichester z 03258; rural

Howards Grove; RMC Place; ROCKINGHAM; ▲ Derry; *203 M-8; ★ **BOS**; mail Derry z 03038; ● 20

Hudson; CDP; HILLSBOROUGH; ▲ Hudson; 203 M-8; [P]; ★ **BOS**; z 03051 & mail Litchfield z 03052; Ⓟ 7,626; Ⓒ 7,814

Hudson; MCD-Town; HILLSBOROUGH; *203 M-8; [P]; ★ **BOS**; z 03051 & mail Litchfield z 03052; Ⓟ 19,530; Ⓒ 22,928; ◆ 24,286

Hudson Center; RMC Place; HILLSBOROUGH; ▲ Hudson; *203 M-8; elev. 199ft./61m.; ★ **BOS**; mail Hudson z 03051

I

Interlaken Park; RMC Place; BELKNAP; *203 I-8; mail Laconia z 03246; pop. incl. with Laconia (Inc. Place)

Intervale; RMC Place; CARROLL; ▲ Conway, Bartlett; 203 G-9; elev. 547ft./167m.; [P]; z 03845; ● 300

J

Jackson; RMC Place; CARROLL; ▲ Jackson; 203 G-8; [P]; z 03846; ● 350

Jackson; MCD-Town; CARROLL; *203 G-8; [P]; z 03846; Ⓟ 678; Ⓒ 835

Jackson Falls; RMC Place; CARROLL; ▲ Jackson; *203 G-8; mail Jackson z 03846

Jady Hill; RMC Place; ROCKINGHAM; ▲ Exeter; *203 L-9; ★ **PTSM-**; mail Exeter z 03833

Jaffrey; CDP; CHESHIRE; ▲ Jaffrey; 203 M-6; elev. 1,013ft./309m.; [P]; z 03452; Ⓟ 2,558; Ⓒ 2,802

Jaffrey; MCD-Town; CHESHIRE; *203 M-5; [P]; z 03452; Ⓟ 5,361; Ⓒ 5,476

Jaffrey Center; RMC Place; CHESHIRE; ▲ Jaffrey; 203 M-5; elev. 1,126ft./343m.; mail Jaffrey z 03452; ● 400

James City; ROCKINGHAM; see Deerfield Parade (RMC Place)

Jefferson; RMC Place; COOS; ▲ Jefferson; 203 F-7; [P]; z 03583; ● 225

Jefferson; MCD-Town; COOS; *203 F-7; [P]; z 03583; Ⓟ 965; Ⓒ 1,006

Jefferson Highlands; RMC Place; COOS; ▲ Jefferson; *203 F-8; mail Jefferson z 03583; rural

Jones Corner; RMC Place; CHESHIRE; ▲ Rindge; *203 N-6; elev. 1,247ft./380m.; mail Rindge z 03461; rural

K

Kearsarge; RMC Place; CARROLL; ▲ Bartlett, Conway; 203 G-9; [P]; z 03847; ● 100

Keene; Inc. Place; ⊡ CHESHIRE; 203 M-5; elev. 486ft./148m.; [P] [H] [C] 6,150 ■; z 03431, z 03435; Ⓟ 22,430; Ⓒ 22,563; ◆ 22,800

Keewayden; RMC Place; CARROLL; ▲ Wolfeboro; *203 I-8; mail Wolfeboro z 03894; rural

Kelleys Corner; RMC Place; MERRIMACK; ▲ Chichester; *203 K-8; elev. 580ft./177m.; ★ **CONC**; mail Chichester z 03258

Kellyville; RMC Place; SULLIVAN; ▲ Newport; 203 K-5; mail Newport z 03773; ● 200

Kelwyn Park; RMC Place; STRAFFORD; ▲ Rollinsford; *203 K-10; ★ **PTSM-**; mail Rollinsford z 03869; ● 120

Kensington; RMC Place; ROCKINGHAM; ▲ Kensington; 203 M-9; [P]; ★ **PTSM-**; z 03833 & mail East Kingston z 03827; ● 240

Kensington; MCD-Town; ROCKINGHAM; *203 M-9; [P]; ★ **PTSM-**; z 03833 & mail East Kingston z 03827; Ⓟ 1,631; Ⓒ 1,893; ◆ 2,231

Kidderville; RMC Place; COOS; ▲ Colebrook; *203 C-8; elev. 1,322ft./403m.; mail Colebrook z 03576

Kingston; RMC Place; ROCKINGHAM; ▲ Kingston; 203 M-9; elev. 139ft./42m.; [P]; ★ **BOS**; z 03848; ● 1,400

Kingston; MCD-Town; ROCKINGHAM; *203 M-9; [P]; ★ **BOS**; z 03848; Ⓟ 5,591; Ⓒ 5,862; ◆ 5,887

L

Laconia; Inc. Place; ⊡ BELKNAP; 203 J-7; elev. 570ft./174m.; [P] [H] ■; z 03246-47 & mail Gilford z 03249; Ⓟ 15,743; Ⓒ 16,411; ◆ 14,981

Lakeport; RMC Place; BELKNAP; *203 J-8; elev. 521ft./159m.; mail Laconia z 03246-47; pop. incl. with Laconia (Inc. Place)

Lancaster; CDP; ⊡ COOS; ▲ Lancaster; 203 E-7; elev. 867ft./264m.; [P] [H]; z 03584; Ⓟ 1,859; Ⓒ 1,695

Lancaster; MCD-Town; COOS; *203 E-7; [P]; z 03584; Ⓟ 3,522; Ⓒ 3,280

Landaff; GRAFTON; see Landaff Center (RMC Place)

Landaff; MCD-Town; GRAFTON; *203 G-6; [P]; z 03585 & mail Woodsville z 03785; Ⓟ 350; Ⓒ 378

Landaff Center (Landaff); RMC Place; GRAFTON; ▲ Landaff; 203 G-6; elev. 1,138ft./347m.; mail Lisbon z 03585, Woodsville z 03785; ● 30

Langdon; RMC Place; SULLIVAN; ▲ Langdon; 203 L-4; [P]; z 03602; ● 200

Langdon; MCD-Town; SULLIVAN; *203 L-4; [P]; z 03602; Ⓟ 580; Ⓒ 586

Langs Corner; RMC Place; ROCKINGHAM; ▲ Rye; *203 L-10; elev. 52ft./16m.; ★ **PTSM-**; mail Rye z 03870

Laskey Corner; RMC Place; STRAFFORD; ▲ Milton; *203 J-9; elev. 426ft./130m.; ★ **PTSM-**; mail Union z 03887; rural

Laurel Lake; RMC Place; CHESHIRE; ▲ Fitzwilliam; *203 N-5; mail Fitzwilliam z 03447; summer pop. 250

Lawrence Corner; RMC Place; HILLSBOROUGH; ▲ Merrimack; *203 M-7; ★ **BOS**; mail Merrimack z 03054; ● 40

Leavitts Hill; RMC Place; ROCKINGHAM; ▲ Deerfield; *203 L-8; mail Deerfield z 03037; rural

Lebanon; Inc. Place; GRAFTON; 203 I-5; elev. 595ft./181m.; [P] [H] ■; z 03756, z 03766; Ⓟ 12,183; Ⓒ 12,568; ◆ 12,810

Lee; RMC Place; STRAFFORD; ▲ Lee; 203 L-9; [P]; ★ **PTSM-**; z 03824, z 03861; ● 150

Lee; MCD-Town; STRAFFORD; *203 L-9; [P]; ★ **PTSM-**; z 03824, z 03861; Ⓟ 3,729; Ⓒ 4,145; ◆ 4,493

Lempster; RMC Place; SULLIVAN; ▲ Lempster; 203 K-5; elev. 1,416ft./432m.; [P]; z 03605; ● 170

Lempster; MCD-Town; SULLIVAN; *203 K-5; [P]; z 03605; Ⓟ 947; Ⓒ 971

Lincoln; RMC Place; GRAFTON; ▲ Lincoln; 203 G-7; elev. 811ft./247m.; [P]; z 03251; ● 900

Lincoln; MCD-Town; GRAFTON; *203 G-7; [P]; z 03251; Ⓟ 1,229; Ⓒ 1,271

Lincoln Park; RMC Place; HILLSBOROUGH; *203 N-7; ★ **BOS**; mail Nashua z 03063; pop. incl. with Nashua (Inc. Place)

Lisbon; CDP; GRAFTON; ▲ Lisbon; 203 G-6; elev. 599ft./183m.; [P]; z 03585; Ⓟ 1,246; Ⓒ 1,070

Lisbon; MCD-Town; GRAFTON; *203 F-6; [P]; z 03585; Ⓟ 1,664; Ⓒ 1,587

Litchfield; RMC Place; HILLSBOROUGH; ▲ Litchfield; *203 M-7; elev. 127ft./39m.; [P]; ★ **BOS**; z 03052; ● 200

Litchfield; MCD-Town; HILLSBOROUGH; *203 M-8; [P]; ★ **BOS**; z 03052; Ⓟ 5,516; Ⓒ 7,360; ◆ 8,355

Little Boars Head; RMC Place; ROCKINGHAM; ▲ North Hampton; 203 L-10; ★ **PTSM-**; mail North Hampton z 03862; ● 120

Little Island Pond; RMC Place; HILLSBOROUGH; ▲ Pelham; *203 N-8; ★ **BOS**; mail Pelham z 03076; ● 600

Littleton; CDP; GRAFTON; ▲ Littleton; 203 F-6; elev. 822ft./251m.; [P] [H]; z 03561; Ⓟ 4,633; Ⓒ 4,431

Littleton; MCD-Town; GRAFTON; *203 F-6; [P]; z 03561; Ⓟ 5,827; Ⓒ 5,845

Lochmere; RMC Place; BELKNAP; ▲ Tilton; 203 J-7; [P]; z 03252; ● 200

Lockehaven; RMC Place; GRAFTON; ▲ Enfield; mail Enfield z 03748; rural

Londonderry; CDP; ROCKINGHAM; ▲ Londonderry; 203 M-8; elev. 371ft./113m.; [P]; ★ **MNCH**; z 03053; Ⓟ 10,114; Ⓒ 11,417

Londonderry; MCD-Town; ROCKINGHAM; *203 M-8; [P]; ★ **MNCH**; z 03053; Ⓟ 19,781; Ⓒ 23,236; ◆ 25,512

Long Sands; RMC Place; CARROLL; ▲ Ossipee; *203 I-9; mail Center Ossipee z 03814; ● 60

Lost Nation; RMC Place; COOS; ▲ Lancaster; *203 E-7; mail Lancaster z 03584; rural

Loudon; RMC Place; MERRIMACK; ▲ Loudon; 203 K-7; elev. 369ft./112m.; [P]; ★ **CONC**; z 03307 & mail Concord z 03301; ● 150

Loudon; MCD-Town; MERRIMACK; *203 K-8; [P]; ★ **CONC**; z 03307 & mail Concord z 03301; Ⓟ 4,114; Ⓒ 4,481

Loudon Center; RMC Place; MERRIMACK; ▲ Loudon; *203 K-8; ★ **CONC**; mail Concord z 03301

Lower Bartlett; RMC Place; CARROLL; ▲ Bartlett; *203 G-9; mail Intervale z 03845; ● 30

Lower Gilmanton; RMC Place; BELKNAP; ▲ Gilmanton; *203 K-8; elev. 1,087ft./331m.; mail Pittsfield z 03263

Lower Village; RMC Place; CHESHIRE; ▲ Gilsum; *203 L-5; mail Gilsum z 03448; ● 75

Lower Village; RMC Place; MERRIMACK; ▲ Warner; *203 K-6; elev. 412ft./126m.; mail Warner z 03278

Lucas Pond; RMC Place; ROCKINGHAM; ▲ Northwood; *203 K-9; mail Northwood z 03261; summer pop. 125

Lyman; GRAFTON; see Parker Hill (RMC Place)

Lyman; MCD-Town; GRAFTON; *203 F-6; [P]; z 03585; Ⓟ 388; Ⓒ 487

Lyme; RMC Place; GRAFTON; ▲ Lyme; 203 H-5; elev. 563ft./172m.; [P]; z 03768; ● 450

Lyme; MCD-Town; GRAFTON; *203 H-5; [P]; z 03768; Ⓟ 1,496; Ⓒ 1,679

Lyme Center; RMC Place; GRAFTON; ▲ Lyme; 203 H-5; elev. 839ft./256m.; [P]; z 03769; ● 125

Lyndeborough; RMC Place; HILLSBOROUGH; ▲ Lyndeborough; 203 M-6; elev. 892ft./272m.; [P]; z 03082; ● 100

Lyndeborough; MCD-Town; HILLSBOROUGH; *203 M-6; [P]; z 03082; Ⓟ 1,294; Ⓒ 1,585

M

Madbury; RMC Place; STRAFFORD; ▲ Madbury; 203 K-9; elev. 104ft./32m.; [P]; ★ **PTSM-**; z 03823 & mail Dover z 03820; ● 150

Madbury; MCD-Town; STRAFFORD; *203 K-9; [P]; ★ **PTSM-**; z 03823 & mail Dover z 03820; Ⓟ 1,404; Ⓒ 1,509; ◆ 1,617

Madison; RMC Place; CARROLL; ▲ Madison; 203 H-9; elev. 673ft./205m.; [P]; z 03849 & mail Silver Lake z 03875; ● 250

Madison; MCD-Town; CARROLL; *203 H-9; [P]; z 03849 & mail Silver Lake z 03875; Ⓟ 1,704; Ⓒ 1,984

Manchester; Inc. Place; ⊡ HILLSBOROUGH; 203 L-8; elev. 225ft./69m.; [P] [H] [C] 13,602 ■; ★ **MNCH**; z 03101-09, z 03111 & mail Bedford z 03110; Ⓟ 99,567; Ⓒ 107,006; ◆ 108,446

Maplehaven; RMC Place; ROCKINGHAM; *203 L-10; ★ **PTSM-**; mail Portsmouth z 03801; pop. incl. with Portsmouth (Inc. Place)

Maplewood; RMC Place; GRAFTON; ▲ Bethlehem; *203 F-7; mail Bethlehem z 03574; ● 30

Marlborough; CDP; CHESHIRE; ▲ Marlborough; 203 M-5; [P]; z 03455; Ⓟ 1,211; Ⓒ 1,089

Marlborough; MCD-Town; CHESHIRE; *203 M-5; [P]; z 03455; Ⓟ 1,927; Ⓒ 2,009

Marlow; RMC Place; CHESHIRE; ▲ Marlow; 203 L-5; [P]; z 03456; ● 450

Marlow; MCD-Town; CHESHIRE; *203 L-5; [P]; z 03456; Ⓟ 650; Ⓒ 747

Marshall Corner; RMC Place; ROCKINGHAM; ▲ Brentwood; 203 L-9; ★ **PTSM-**; mail Exeter z 03833; ● 80

Marshall Farms; RMC Place; ROCKINGHAM; ▲ Exeter; ★ **PTSM-**; mail Exeter z 03833; ● 60

Martin; RMC Place; MERRIMACK; ▲ Hooksett; *203 L-8; ★ **MNCH**; mail Hooksett z 03106

Mascoma; RMC Place; GRAFTON; *203 I-5; elev. 761ft./232m.; mail Enfield z 03748; pop. incl. with Lebanon (Inc. Place)

Mason; RMC Place; HILLSBOROUGH; ▲ Mason; 203 N-6; [P]; ★ **BOS**; z 03048; ● 200

Mason; MCD-Town; HILLSBOROUGH; *203 N-7; [P]; ★ **BOS**; z 03048; Ⓟ 1,212; Ⓒ 1,147; ◆ 1,236

Masons; RMC Place; COOS; ▲ Stratford; *203 D-7; mail North Stratford z 03590; rural

Massabesic; RMC Place; HILLSBOROUGH; *203 L-8; ★ **MNCH**; mail Manchester z 03104; pop. incl. with Manchester (Inc. Place)

Mast Yard; RMC Place; MERRIMACK; *203 K-7; ★ **CONC**; mail Concord z 03303; pop. incl. with Concord (Inc. Place)

Meaderboro Corner; RMC Place; STRAFFORD; *203 K-9; ★ **PTSM-**; mail Rochester z 03867; pop. incl. with Rochester (Inc. Place)

Meadowbrook; RMC Place; ROCKINGHAM; *203 L-10; ★ **PTSM-**; mail Portsmouth z 03801; pop. incl. with Portsmouth (Inc. Place)

Melrose Corner; RMC Place; STRAFFORD; *203 K-9; ★ **PTSM-**; mail Rochester z 03868; pop. incl. with Rochester (Inc. Place)

Melvin Mills; RMC Place; MERRIMACK; ▲ Warner; *203 K-6; elev. 639ft./195m.; mail Warner z 03278

Melvin Village; RMC Place; CARROLL; ▲ Tuftonboro; 203 I-8; elev. 20ft./6m.; [P]; z 03850; summer pop. 1,500; ● 500

Meredith; CDP; BELKNAP; ▲ Meredith; 203 I-7; elev. 549ft./167m.; [P]; z 03253; Ⓟ 1,654; Ⓒ 1,739

Meredith; MCD-Town; BELKNAP; *203 I-7; [P]; z 03253; Ⓟ 4,837; Ⓒ 5,943

Meredith Center; RMC Place; BELKNAP; ▲ Meredith; 203 I-7; elev. 525ft./160m.; mail Meredith z 03253; ● 225

Meriden; RMC Place; SULLIVAN; ▲ Plainfield; 203 J-5; elev. 931ft./284m.; [P]; z 03770; ● 500

Merrill Corners; RMC Place; STRAFFORD; ▲ Farmington; *203 K-9; ★ **PTSM-**; mail New Durham z 03855; rural

Merrimack; RMC Place; HILLSBOROUGH; ▲ Merrimack; 203 M-7; [P]; ★ **BOS**; z 03054; ● 2,400

Merrimack; MCD-Town; HILLSBOROUGH; *203 M-7; [P]; ★ **BOS**; z 03054; Ⓟ 22,156; Ⓒ 25,119; ◆ 25,943

MERRIMACK; 203 K-6; Ⓟ 120,005; Ⓒ 136,225; ◆ 148,988

Merrymeeting Lake; RMC Place; STRAFFORD; ▲ New Durham; *203 J-9; mail New Durham z 03855; ● 200

Middleton; STRAFFORD; see Middleton Corners (RMC Place)

Middleton; MCD-Town; STRAFFORD; *203 J-9; [P]; z 03887; Ⓟ 1,183; Ⓒ 1,440

Middleton Corners (Middleton); RMC Place; STRAFFORD; ▲ Middleton; 203 J-9; mail Union z 03887; summer pop. 800; ● 150

Milan; RMC Place; COOS; ▲ Milan; 203 E-8; elev. 1,134ft./346m.; [P]; z 03588; ● 225

Milan; MCD-Town; COOS; *203 E-8; [P]; z 03588; Ⓟ 1,295; Ⓒ 1,331

Milford; CDP; HILLSBOROUGH; ▲ Milford; 203 M-7; elev. 263ft./80m.; [P]; ★ **BOS**; z 03055; Ⓟ 8,014; Ⓒ 8,293

Milford; MCD-Town; HILLSBOROUGH; *203 M-7; [P]; ★ **BOS**; z 03055; Ⓟ 11,795; Ⓒ 13,535; ◆ 14,573

Mill Hollow; RMC Place; CHESHIRE; ▲ Alstead; *203 L-5; elev. 1,191ft./363m.; mail Alstead z 03602; ● 100

Mill Village; RMC Place; CHESHIRE; ▲ Stoddard; *203 L-5; mail Stoddard z 03464; rural

Mill Village; RMC Place; SULLIVAN; ▲ Plainfield; *203 J-4; elev. 560ft./171m.; mail Plainfield z 03781; rural

Millville (Millville Lake); RMC Place; ROCKINGHAM; ▲ Salem; *203 M-8; ★ **BOS**; mail Salem z 03079; ● 900

Millville Lake; ROCKINGHAM; see Millville (RMC Place)

Milton; RMC Place; STRAFFORD; ▲ Milton; 203 J-9; [P]; ★ **PTSM-**; z 03851 & mail Milton Mills z 03852; ● 1,100

Milton; MCD-Town; STRAFFORD; *203 J-9; [P]; ★ **PTSM-**; z 03851 & mail Milton Mills z 03852; Ⓟ 3,691; Ⓒ 3,910; ◆ 4,198

Milton Mills; RMC Place; STRAFFORD; ▲ Milton; 203 J-9; [P]; ★ **PTSM-**; z 03852; ● 400

Mirror Lake; RMC Place; CARROLL; ▲ Tuftonboro; 203 I-8; elev. 527ft./161m.; [P]; z 03853; ● 300

Monroe; RMC Place; GRAFTON; ▲ Monroe; 203 F-5; [P]; z 03771; ● 275

Monroe; MCD-Town; GRAFTON; *203 F-6; [P]; z 03771; Ⓟ 746; Ⓒ 759

Mont Vernon; RMC Place; HILLSBOROUGH; ▲ Mont Vernon; 203 M-7; [P]; ★ **BOS**; z 03057; ● 600

Mont Vernon; MCD-Town; HILLSBOROUGH; *203 M-7; [P]; ★ **BOS**; z 03057; Ⓟ 1,812; Ⓒ 2,034; ◆ 2,122

Moultonboro; CARROLL; see Moultonborough (RMC Place)

Moultonborough (Moultonboro); RMC Place; CARROLL; ▲ Moultonborough; 203 I-8; [P]; z 03254; ● 350

Moultonborough; MCD-Town; CARROLL; *203 I-8; [P]; z 03254; Ⓟ 2,956; Ⓒ 4,484

Moultonborough Falls; RMC Place; CARROLL; ▲ Moultonborough; *203 I-8; elev. 537ft./164m.; mail Moultonborough z 03254

Moultonville; RMC Place; CARROLL; ▲ Ossipee; *203 I-9; mail Center Ossipee z 03814; ● 150

Mountain Lake; RMC Place; GRAFTON; ▲ Haverhill; *203 G-6; mail North Haverhill z 03774; ● 300

Mount Sunapee; RMC Place; MERRIMACK; ▲ Newbury; 203 K-5; elev. 1,126ft./343m.; [P]; z 03255; ● 250

Mount Washington; RMC Place; COOS; ▲ Sargents Purchase; *203 F-8; [P]; z 03589

Munsonville; RMC Place; CHESHIRE; ▲ Nelson; 203 L-5; [P]; z 03457; ● 230

Murray Hill; RMC Place; MERRIMACK; ▲ Hill; *203 J-6; mail Hill z 03243; rural

N

Nashua; Inc. Place; ⊡ HILLSBOROUGH; 203 M-7; elev. 169ft./52m.; [P] [H] [C] 2,007 ■; ★ **BOS**; z 03060-64; Ⓟ 79,662; Ⓒ 86,605; ◆ 87,518

Nelson; RMC Place; CHESHIRE; ▲ Nelson; 203 L-5; [P]; z 03457 & mail Sullivan z 03445; ● 125

Nelson; MCD-Town; CHESHIRE; *203 L-5; [P]; z 03457 & mail Sullivan z 03445; Ⓟ 535; Ⓒ 634

New Boston; RMC Place; HILLSBOROUGH; ▲ New Boston; 203 L-7; elev. 469ft./143m.; [P]; z 03070; ● 850

New Boston; MCD-Town; HILLSBOROUGH; *203 L-7; [P]; z 03070; Ⓟ 3,214; Ⓒ 4,138

Newbury; RMC Place; MERRIMACK; ▲ Newbury; 203 K-6; elev. 1,106ft./337m.; [P]; z 03255 & mail South Newbury z 03272; ● 200

Newbury; MCD-Town; MERRIMACK; *203 K-6; [P]; z 03255 & mail South Newbury z 03272; Ⓟ 1,347; Ⓒ 1,702

New Castle; RMC Place; ROCKINGHAM; ▲ New Castle; 203 L-10; [P]; ★ **PTSM-**; z 03854; ● 840

New Castle; MCD-Town; ROCKINGHAM; *203 L-10; [P]; ★ **PTSM-**; z 03854; Ⓟ 840; Ⓒ 1,010; ◆ 1,093

New Durham; RMC Place; STRAFFORD; ▲ New Durham; 203 J-9; elev. 541ft./165m.; [P]; z 03855; ● 350

New Durham; MCD-Town; STRAFFORD; *203 J-9; [P]; z 03855; Ⓟ 1,974; Ⓒ 2,220

Newfields; RMC Place; ROCKINGHAM; ▲ Newfields; 203 L-9; elev. 46ft./14m.; [P]; ★ **PTSM-**; z 03856; ● 700

Newfields; MCD-Town; ROCKINGHAM; *203 L-9; [P]; ★ **PTSM-**; z 03856; Ⓟ 888; Ⓒ 1,551; ◆ 1,853

New Hampton; RMC Place; BELKNAP; ▲ New Hampton; 203 I-7; elev. 531ft./162m.; [P]; z 03256; ● 275

New Hampton; MCD-Town; BELKNAP; *203 I-7; [P]; z 03256; Ⓟ 1,606; Ⓒ 1,950

Newington; MCD-Town; ROCKINGHAM; *203 L-10; [P]; ★ **PTSM-**; z 03801, z 03805; Ⓟ 990; Ⓒ 775; ◆ 765

New Ipswich (New Ipswich Center); RMC Place; HILLSBOROUGH; ▲ New Ipswich; 203 N-6; [P]; ★ **BOS**; z 03071; ● 800

New Ipswich; MCD-Town; HILLSBOROUGH; *203 N-6; [P]; ★ **BOS**; z 03071; Ⓟ 4,014; Ⓒ 4,289; ◆ 4,563

New Ipswich Center; HILLSBOROUGH; see New Ipswich (RMC Place)

New London; RMC Place; MERRIMACK; ▲ New London; 203 J-6; [P] [H] [C] 898; z 03257; ● 1,400

New London; MCD-Town; MERRIMACK; *203 J-6; [P] [C] 898; z 03257; Ⓟ 3,180; Ⓒ 4,116

Newmarket; CDP; ROCKINGHAM; ▲ Newmarket; 203 L-9; elev. 40ft./12m.; [P]; ★ **PTSM-**; z 03857; Ⓟ 4,917; Ⓒ 5,124

Newmarket; MCD-Town; ROCKINGHAM; *203 L-9; [P]; ★ **PTSM-**; z 03857; Ⓟ 7,157; Ⓒ 8,027; ◆ 9,101

Newport; CDP; ⊡ SULLIVAN; ▲ Newport; 203 K-5; elev. 797ft./243m.; [P]; z 03773; Ⓟ 3,772; Ⓒ 4,008

Newport; MCD-Town; SULLIVAN; *203 K-5; [P]; z 03773; Ⓟ 6,110; Ⓒ 6,269

New Rye; RMC Place; MERRIMACK; ▲ Epsom; *203 K-8; elev. 559ft./170m.; ★ **CONC**; mail Epsom z 03234

Newton; RMC Place; ROCKINGHAM; ▲ Newton; 203 M-9; [P]; ★ **BOS**; z 03858; ● 650

Newton; MCD-Town; ROCKINGHAM; *203 M-9; [P]; ★ **BOS**; z 03858; Ⓟ 3,473; Ⓒ 4,289; ◆ 4,922

Newton Junction; RMC Place; ROCKINGHAM; ▲ Newton; *203 M-9; [P]; ★ **BOS**; z 03859; ● 500

Noone; RMC Place; HILLSBOROUGH; ▲ Peterborough; 203 M-6; mail Peterborough z 03458; ● 80

North Barnstead; RMC Place; BELKNAP; ▲ Barnstead; *203 K-8; elev. 775ft./236m.; mail Center Barnstead z 03225

North Beach; RMC Place; ROCKINGHAM; ▲ Hampton; *203 M-10; ★ **PTSM-**; mail Hampton z 03842; summer pop. 500; ● 200

North Boscawen; MERRIMACK; see Gerrish (RMC Place)

North Branch; RMC Place; HILLSBOROUGH; ▲ Antrim; 203 L-6; elev. 914ft./279m.; mail Antrim z 03440; ● 150

North Brookline; RMC Place; HILLSBOROUGH; ▲ Brookline; *203 M-7; elev. 288ft./88m.; ★ **BOS**; mail Milford z 03055; rural

North Charlestown; RMC Place; SULLIVAN; ▲ Charlestown; 203 K-4; mail Charlestown z 03603; ● 150

North Chatham; RMC Place; CARROLL; ▲ Chatham; 203 F-9; mail Center Conway z 03813; ● 80

North Chester; RMC Place; ROCKINGHAM; ▲ Chester; *203 L-8; ★ **BOS**; mail Chester z 03036; rural

North Chichester; RMC Place; MERRIMACK; ▲ Chichester; 203 K-8; ★ **CONC**; mail Chichester z 03258, Epsom z 03234; ● 250

North Conway; CDP; CARROLL; ▲ Conway; 203 G-9; elev. 531ft./162m.; [P] [H]; z 03860 & mail Intervale z 03845, Kearsarge z 03847; Ⓟ 2,032; Ⓒ 2,069

North Danville; RMC Place; ROCKINGHAM; ▲ Danville; *203 M-9; elev. 279ft./85m.; ★ **BOS**; mail Danville z 03819; rural

Northfield; RMC Place; MERRIMACK; ▲ Northfield; 203 J-7; [P]; z 03276; ● 1,500

Northfield; MCD-Town; MERRIMACK; *203 J-7; [P]; z 03276; Ⓟ 4,263; Ⓒ 4,548

North Grantham; RMC Place; SULLIVAN; ▲ Grantham; *203 J-5; elev. 1,218ft./371m.; mail Grantham z 03753

North Groton; RMC Place; GRAFTON; ▲ Groton; *203 I-6; elev. 1,237ft./377m.; mail Rumney z 03266

North Hampton; RMC Place; ROCKINGHAM; ▲ North Hampton; 203 L-10; [P]; ★ **PTSM-**; z 03862; ● 500

North Hampton; MCD-Town; ROCKINGHAM; *203 L-10; [P]; ★ **PTSM-**; z 03862; Ⓟ 3,637; Ⓒ 4,259; ◆ 4,574

North Hampton Center; RMC Place; ROCKINGHAM; ▲ North Hampton; *203 L-10; ★ **PTSM-**; mail North Hampton z 03862; ● 800

North Haverhill; RMC Place; GRAFTON; ▲ Haverhill; 203 G-6; elev. 499ft./152m.; [P]; z 03774; ● 450

North Hinsdale; RMC Place; CHESHIRE; ▲ Hinsdale; mail Hinsdale z 03451; rural

North Littleton; RMC Place; GRAFTON; ▲ Littleton; *203 F-6; mail Littleton z 03561; rural

North Londonderry; RMC Place; ROCKINGHAM; ▲ Londonderry; *203 M-8; ★ **MNCH**; mail Londonderry z 03053; ● 300

North Newport; RMC Place; SULLIVAN; ▲ Newport; 203 J-5; mail Newport z 03773; ● 200

North Pelham; RMC Place; HILLSBOROUGH; ▲ Pelham; 203 M-8; elev. 192ft./59m.; ★ **BOS**; mail Pelham z 03076; ● 400

North Pembroke; RMC Place; MERRIMACK; ▲ Pembroke; *203 K-8; elev. 694ft./212m.; ★ **CONC**; mail Suncook z 03275

North Richmond; RMC Place; CHESHIRE; ▲ Richmond; *203 M-5; mail Winchester z 03470

North Rochester (Hayes); RMC Place; STRAFFORD; *203 K-9; ★ **PTSM-**; mail Rochester z 03867; pop. incl. with Rochester (Inc. Place)

North Salem; RMC Place; ROCKINGHAM; ▲ Salem; 203 M-8; elev. 186ft./57m.; [P]; ★ **BOS**; z 03073; ● 300

North Sanbornton; RMC Place; BELKNAP; ▲ Sanbornton; 203 J-7; elev. 632ft./193m.; mail Sanbornton z 03269; ● 300

North Sandwich; RMC Place; CARROLL; ▲ Sandwich; 203 H-8; elev. 694ft./212m.; [P]; z 03259; ● 100

North Stratford; RMC Place; COOS; ▲ Stratford; 203 D-7; [P]; z 03590; ● 400

North Sutton; RMC Place; MERRIMACK; ▲ Sutton; 203 K-6; elev. 917ft./280m.; [P]; z 03260; ● 275

North Swanzey; RMC Place; CHESHIRE; ▲ Swanzey; *203 M-5; [P]; z 03431; pop. incl. with Keene (Inc. Place)

Northumberland; RMC Place; COOS; ▲ Northumberland; 203 E-7; [P]; z 03582 & mail Jefferson z 03583; ● 100

Northumberland; MCD-Town; COOS; *203 E-7; [P]; z 03582 & mail Jefferson z 03583, Lancaster z 03584; Ⓟ 2,492; Ⓒ 2,438

North Village; RMC Place; HILLSBOROUGH; ▲ Peterborough; 203 M-6; elev. 706ft./215m.; mail Peterborough z 03458; ● 160

North Wakefield; RMC Place; CARROLL; ▲ Wakefield; *203 I-9; mail Ossipee z 03864; rural

North Walpole; RMC Place; CHESHIRE; ▲ Walpole; 203 L-4; elev. 300ft./91m.; [P]; z 03609; ● 800

North Weare; RMC Place; HILLSBOROUGH; ▲ Weare; *203 L-7; ★ **MNCH**; mail Weare z 03281; ● 150

North Wilmot; RMC Place; MERRIMACK; ▲ Wilmot; *203 J-6; mail Danbury z 03230; rural

North Wolfeboro; RMC Place; CARROLL; ▲ Wolfeboro; *203 I-9; mail Wolfeboro z 03894

Northwood; RMC Place; ROCKINGHAM; ▲ Northwood; 203 K-9; elev. 559ft./170m.; [P]; z 03261; ● 650

Northwood; MCD-Town; ROCKINGHAM; *203 K-8; [P]; z 03261; Ⓟ 3,124; Ⓒ 3,640

Northwood Center; RMC Place; ROCKINGHAM; ▲ Northwood; 203 K-8; elev. 631ft./192m.; mail Northwood z 03261; ● 275

Northwood Narrows; RMC Place; ROCKINGHAM; *203 K-8; mail Northwood z 03261; ● 450

Northwood Ridge; RMC Place; ROCKINGHAM; ▲ Northwood; 203 K-8; mail Northwood z 03261; ● 250

North Woodstock; RMC Place; GRAFTON; ▲ Woodstock; 203 G-7; elev. 738ft./225m.; [P]; z 03262; ● 600

Nottingham; RMC Place; ROCKINGHAM; ▲ Nottingham; 203 L-9; elev. 260ft./79m.; [P]; z 03290; ● 275

Nottingham; MCD-Town; ROCKINGHAM; *203 L-9; [P]; z 03290; Ⓟ 2,939; Ⓒ 3,701

Noyes Terrace; RMC Place; ROCKINGHAM; ▲ Salem; *203 N-8; ★ **BOS**; mail Salem z 03079; ● 300

Nuttings Beach; RMC Place; GRAFTON; ▲ Bristol, Alexandria; *203 I-6; mail Bristol z 03222; summer pop. 130

O

Onway Lake; RMC Place; ROCKINGHAM; ▲ Raymond; *203 L-8; ★ **BOS**; mail Raymond z 03077; summer pop. 200

Orange; RMC Place; GRAFTON; ▲ Orange; 203 I-6; elev. 1,214ft./370m.; [P]; z 03741; ● 120

Orange; MCD-Town; GRAFTON; *203 I-6; [P]; z 03741; Ⓟ 237; Ⓒ 299

Orford; RMC Place; GRAFTON; ▲ Orford; 203 H-5; elev. 419ft./128m.; [P]; z 03777; ● 400

Orford; MCD-Town; GRAFTON; *203 H-5; [P]; z 03777; Ⓟ 1,008; Ⓒ 1,091

Orfordville; RMC Place; GRAFTON; ▲ Orford; 203 H-5; mail Orford z 03777; ● 120

Ossipee; RMC Place; ⊡ CARROLL; ▲ Ossipee; 203 I-9; elev. 581ft./177m.; [P]; z 03864; ● 250

Ossipee; MCD-Town; CARROLL; *203 I-9; [P]; z 03864 & mail Center Ossipee z 03814; Ⓟ 3,309; Ⓒ 4,211

Ossipee Lake Shores; RMC Place; CARROLL; ▲ Ossipee; *203 H-9; mail Center Ossipee z 03814; ● 100

Ossipee Valley; RMC Place; CARROLL; ▲ Ossipee; *203 I-8; mail Center Ossipee z 03814; rural

P

Pages Corner; RMC Place; MERRIMACK; ▲ Dunbarton; 203 L-7; elev. 455ft./139m.; mail Concord z 03301; ● 90

Pannaway Manor; RMC Place; ROCKINGHAM; *203 L-10; ★ **PTSM-**; mail Portsmouth z 03801; pop. incl. with Portsmouth (Inc. Place)

Entries in **UPPERCASE** are counties.
Entries in **bold** have populations of 2,500 or more.
Names in parentheses are alternate names.

Inc. Place	Incorporated Place
RMC Place	Rand McNally Designated Place
CDP	Census Designated Place
MCD	Minor Civil Division

⊡	County Seat
▲	Minor Civil Division
elev.	Elevation
[P]	Post Office
[H]	Hospital
[C]	College
■	Principal Business Center
★	Ranally Metro Area (RMA) Abbreviation
z	Zip Code(s)
Ⓟ	Previous Census Population
Ⓡ	Revised Census Population
Ⓐ	Annexation Population
●	Rand McNally Population Estimate
Ⓒ	Final Census Population
Ⓢ	Special Census Population
◆	Estimated Population

For additional definitions see Glossary, Volume 1, and Introduction, Volume 2.

Parker; RMC Place; HILLSBOROUGH; ▲ Goffstown; ***203** L-7; ★ **MNCH**; mail Goffstown **z** 03045; ● 125
Parker Hill (Lyman); RMC Place; GRAFTON; ▲ Lyman; ***203** F-6; elev. 1,214ft./370m.; mail Lisbon **z** 03585
Park Hill; RMC Place; CHESHIRE; ▲ Westmoreland; ***203** L-4; mail Westmoreland **z** 03467; ● 60
Partridge Lake; RMC Place; GRAFTON; ▲ Littleton; ***203** F-6; mail Littleton **z** 03561; summer pop. 125; ● 30
Passaconaway; RMC Place; CARROLL; ▲ Albany; **203** H-8; mail Conway **z** 03818; ● 40
Pearls Corner; RMC Place; MERRIMACK; ▲ Loudon; ***203** K-7; elev. 449ft./137m.; ★ **CONC**; mail Concord **z** 03301
Pelham; RMC Place; HILLSBOROUGH; ▲ Pelham; ***203** N-8; elev. 152ft./46m.; 🅿; ★ **BOS**; **z** 03076; ● 1,200
Pelham; MCD-Town; HILLSBOROUGH; ***203** N-8; 🅿; ★ **BOS**; **z** 03076; Ⓟ 9,408; Ⓒ 10,914; ◆ 11,546
Pembroke; RMC Place; MERRIMACK; ▲ Pembroke; ***203** L-8; 🅿; ★ **CONC**; **z** 03275; ● 400
Pembroke; MCD-Town; MERRIMACK; ***203** K-8; 🅿; ★ **CONC**; **z** 03275; Ⓟ 6,561; Ⓒ 6,897
Pembroke Hill; RMC Place; MERRIMACK; ▲ Pembroke; ***203** L-8; ★ **CONC**; mail Suncook **z** 03275; rural
Penacook; RMC Place; MERRIMACK; ***203** K-7; elev. 336ft./102m.; 🅿; ★ **CONC**; **z** 03303; pop. incl. with Concord (Inc. Place)
Pendleton Beach; RMC Place; BELKNAP; ***203** I-8; mail Laconia **z** 03246; pop. incl. with Laconia (Inc. Place)
Pequawket; RMC Place; CARROLL; ▲ Tamworth; ***203** H-8; mail Chocorua **z** 03817
Percy; RMC Place; COOS; ▲ Stark; **203** E-8; mail Groveton **z** 03582; ● 60
Perkins Hill; RMC Place; ROCKINGHAM; ▲ Exeter; ***203** M-9; ★ **PTSM-**; mail Exeter **z** 03833; rural
Peterborough; CDP; HILLSBOROUGH; ▲ Peterborough; **203** M-6; 🅿 🅷; **z** 03458; Ⓟ 2,685; Ⓒ 2,944
Peterborough; MCD-Town; HILLSBOROUGH; ***203** M-6; 🅿; **z** 03458; Ⓟ 5,239; Ⓒ 5,883
Pickering; RMC Place; STRAFFORD; ***203** K-9; elev. 152ft./46m.; ★ **PTSM-**; mail Rochester **z** 03867; pop. incl. with Rochester (Inc. Place)
Pierce Bridge; RMC Place; GRAFTON; ▲ Bethlehem; ***203** F-7; elev. 1,191ft./363m.; mail Bethlehem **z** 03574; ● 40
Piermont; RMC Place; GRAFTON; ▲ Piermont; **203** H-5; elev. 568ft./173m.; 🅿; **z** 03779; ● 200
Piermont; MCD-Town; GRAFTON; ***203** H-6; 🅿; **z** 03779; Ⓟ 624; Ⓒ 709
Pike; RMC Place; GRAFTON; ▲ Hanover; **203** G-6; 🅿; **z** 03780; ● 225
Pinardville; CDP; HILLSBOROUGH; ▲ Goffstown; **203** B-4; ★ **MNCH**; mail Manchester **z** 03102; Ⓟ 4,654; Ⓒ 5,779
Pine Grove Park; RMC Place; ROCKINGHAM; ▲ Salem; ***203** M-8; ★ **BOS**; mail Salem **z** 03079
Pine River; RMC Place; CARROLL; ▲ Effingham; ***203** I-9; mail Center Ossipee **z** 03814; ● 15
Pine Valley; RMC Place; HILLSBOROUGH; ▲ Milford; ***203** M-7; ★ **BOS**; mail Wilton **z** 03086
Pittsburg; RMC Place; COOS; ▲ Pittsburg; **203** B-8; elev. 1,331ft./406m.; 🅿; **z** 03592; ● 400
Pittsburg; MCD-Town; COOS; ***203** B-8; 🅿; **z** 03592; Ⓟ 901; Ⓒ 867
Pittsfield; CDP; MERRIMACK; ▲ Pittsfield; **203** K-8; elev. 501ft./153m.; 🅿; ★ **CONC**; **z** 03263; Ⓟ 1,717; Ⓒ 1,669
Pittsfield; MCD-Town; MERRIMACK; ***203** K-8; 🅿; ★ **CONC**; **z** 03263; Ⓟ 3,701; Ⓒ 3,931
Plaice Cove; RMC Place; ROCKINGHAM; ▲ Hampton; ***203** M-10; ★ **PTSM-**; mail Hampton **z** 03842; summer pop. 150; ● 50
Plainfield; RMC Place; SULLIVAN; ▲ Plainfield; **203** J-4; elev. 528ft./161m.; 🅿; **z** 03781; ● 400
Plainfield; MCD-Town; SULLIVAN; ***203** J-5; 🅿; **z** 03781; Ⓟ 2,056; Ⓒ 2,241
Plaistow; RMC Place; ROCKINGHAM; ▲ Plaistow; **203** M-9; elev. 104ft./32m.; 🅿; ★ **BOS**; **z** 03865; ● 2,200
Plaistow; MCD-Town; ROCKINGHAM; ***203** M-9; 🅿; ★ **BOS**; **z** 03865; Ⓟ 7,316; Ⓒ 7,747; ◆ 7,607
Plymouth; CDP; GRAFTON; ▲ Plymouth; **203** I-7; elev. 514ft./157m.; 🅿 🅷 🅲 5,376; **z** 03264; Ⓟ 3,967; Ⓒ 3,528
Plymouth; MCD-Town; GRAFTON; ***203** I-7; 🅿 🅲 5,376; **z** 03264; Ⓟ 5,811; Ⓒ 5,892
Ponemah; RMC Place; HILLSBOROUGH; ▲ Amherst; ***203** M-7; ★ **BOS**; mail Milford **z** 03055
Poocham; RMC Place; CHESHIRE; ▲ Westmoreland; mail Westmoreland **z** 03467; rural
Portsmouth; Inc. Place; ROCKINGHAM; **203** L-10; elev. 21ft./6m.; 🅿 🅷 ■; ★ **PTSM-**; **z** 03801-05; Ⓟ 25,925; Ⓒ 20,784; ◆ 19,696
Portsmouth Plains; RMC Place; ROCKINGHAM; ***203** L-10; ★ **PTSM-**; mail Portsmouth **z** 03801; pop. incl. with Portsmouth (Inc. Place)
Potter Place; RMC Place; MERRIMACK; ▲ Andover; **203** J-6; ● 60
Puckershire; RMC Place; SULLIVAN; ***203** K-5; elev. 592ft./180m.; mail Claremont **z** 03743; pop. incl. with Claremont (Inc. Place)

Q

Quaker City; RMC Place; SULLIVAN; ▲ Unity; ***203** K-4; mail Charlestown **z** 03603; rural
Quincy; RMC Place; GRAFTON; ▲ Rumney; ***203** I-6; elev. 515ft./157m.; mail Rumney **z** 03266

R

Rand; RMC Place; CHESHIRE; ▲ Rindge; ***203** N-5; elev. 1,130ft./344m.; mail Rindge **z** 03461; rural
Randolph; RMC Place; COOS; ▲ Randolph; **203** F-8; 🅿; **z** 03593 & mail Berlin **z** 03570; ● 200
Randolph; MCD-Town; COOS; ***203** F-8; 🅿; **z** 03593 & mail Berlin **z** 03570, Jefferson **z** 03583; Ⓟ 371; Ⓒ 339
Raymond; CDP; ROCKINGHAM; ▲ Raymond; **203** L-8; elev. 205ft./62m.; 🅿; ★ **BOS**; **z** 03077; Ⓟ 2,516; Ⓒ 2,839
Raymond; MCD-Town; ROCKINGHAM; ***203** L-8; 🅿; ★ **BOS**; **z** 03077; Ⓟ 8,713; Ⓒ 9,674; ◆ 9,711
Redstone; RMC Place; CARROLL; ▲ Conway; **203** G-9; mail Center Conway **z** 03813; ● 150
Reed Road Parcel; RMC Place; ROCKINGHAM; ▲ Sandown; ***203** M-8; ★ **BOS**; mail Sandown **z** 03873; ● 200
Reeds Ferry; RMC Place; HILLSBOROUGH; ▲ Merrimack; ***203** M-7; ★ **BOS**; mail Merrimack **z** 03054; ● 700
Richardson; RMC Place; HILLSBOROUGH; ▲ Milford; ***203** M-7; ★ **BOS**; mail Milford **z** 03055; ● 50
Richmond; RMC Place; CHESHIRE; ▲ Richmond; **203** N-5; elev. 1,062ft./324m.; 🅿; **z** 03470; ● 125
Richmond; MCD-Town; CHESHIRE; ***203** M-5; 🅿; **z** 03470; Ⓟ 877; Ⓒ 1,077
Rindge; RMC Place; CHESHIRE; ▲ Rindge; **203** N-6; 🅿 🅲 2,698; **z** 03461; ● 400
Rindge; MCD-Town; CHESHIRE; ***203** N-6; 🅿 🅲 2,698; **z** 03461; Ⓟ 4,941; Ⓒ 5,451
Rings Corner; RMC Place; MERRIMACK; ▲ Pittsfield; ***203** K-8; ★ **CONC**; mail Pittsfield **z** 03263; ● 25
Rivercrest; RMC Place; GRAFTON; ▲ Hanover; ***203** I-5; elev. 510ft./155m.; mail Hanover **z** 03755; ● 100
Riverdale; RMC Place; HILLSBOROUGH; ▲ Weare, New Boston; **203** L-7; elev. 309ft./94m.; ★ **MNCH**; mail Weare **z** 03281; ● 50
Riverhill; RMC Place; MERRIMACK; ***203** K-7; elev. 358ft./109m.; ★ **CONC**; mail Concord **z** 03301; pop. incl. with Concord (Inc. Place)
Riverside; RMC Place; ROCKINGHAM; ▲ Seabrook; ***203** M-10; ★ **BOS**; mail Seabrook **z** 03874; rural
Riverton; RMC Place; COOS; ▲ Jefferson; mail Jefferson **z** 03583; rural
Robinson Corner; RMC Place; GRAFTON; ▲ Grafton; ***203** J-6; elev. 1,076ft./328m.; mail Grafton **z** 03240; rural
Roby; RMC Place; MERRIMACK; ▲ Warner; ***203** K-6; elev. 511ft./156m.; mail Warner **z** 03278; rural
Rochester; Inc. Place; STRAFFORD; **203** K-9; elev. 200ft./61m.; 🅿 🅷 ■; ★ **PTSM-**; **z** 03839, **z** 03866-68; Ⓟ 26,630; Ⓒ 28,461; ◆ 31,109
ROCKINGHAM; **203** L-8; Ⓟ 245,845; Ⓒ 277,359; ◆ 295,671
Rockwold; RMC Place; GRAFTON; ▲ Holderness; ***203** I-7; elev. 570ft./174m.; mail Holderness **z** 03245; summer pop. 150; ● 20
Rollinsford (Salmon Falls); RMC Place; STRAFFORD; ▲ Rollinsford; **203** K-10; 🅿; ★ **PTSM-**; **z** 03805, **z** 03869; ● 1,500
Rollinsford; MCD-Town; STRAFFORD; ***203** K-10; 🅿; ★ **PTSM-**; **z** 03805, **z** 03869; Ⓟ 2,645; Ⓒ 2,648; ◆ 2,845
Roundys Corner; RMC Place; CHESHIRE; ▲ Gilsum; ***203** L-5; mail Gilsum **z** 03448; rural
Rowes Corner; RMC Place; ROCKINGHAM; ▲ Newton; ***203** M-9; ★ **BOS**; mail Newton **z** 03858; ● 40
Roxbury; MCD-Town; CHESHIRE; ***203** M-5; 🅿; **z** 03431; Ⓟ 248; Ⓒ 237
Rumney; RMC Place; GRAFTON; ▲ Rumney; **203** H-6; 🅿; **z** 03266; ● 425
Rumney; MCD-Town; GRAFTON; ***203** H-6; 🅿; **z** 03266; Ⓟ 1,446; Ⓒ 1,480
Rumney Depot; RMC Place; GRAFTON; ▲ Rumney; **203** I-6; elev. 511ft./156m.; mail Rumney **z** 03266; ● 325
Ryder Corner; RMC Place; SULLIVAN; ▲ Newport; ***203** J-5; mail Newport **z** 03773; rural
Rye; RMC Place; ROCKINGHAM; ▲ Rye; **203** L-10; 🅿; ★ **PTSM-**; **z** 03870; ● 850
Rye; MCD-Town; ROCKINGHAM; ***203** L-10; 🅿; ★ **PTSM-**; **z** 03870; Ⓟ 4,612; Ⓒ 5,182; ◆ 5,787
Rye Beach; RMC Place; ROCKINGHAM; ▲ Rye; **203** L-10; 🅿; ★ **PTSM-**; **z** 03871; ● 450
Rye North Beach; RMC Place; ROCKINGHAM; ▲ Rye; ***203** L-10; ★ **PTSM-**; mail Rye **z** 03870; ● 120

S

Sachem Village; RMC Place; GRAFTON; ***203** I-5; mail West Lebanon **z** 03784; pop. incl. with Lebanon (Inc. Place)
Salem; RMC Place; ROCKINGHAM; ▲ Salem; **203** M-8; elev. 131ft./40m.; 🅿 🅷; ★ **BOS**; **z** 03079; ● 12,000
Salem; MCD-Town; ROCKINGHAM; ***203** M-8; 🅿 ■; ★ **BOS**; **z** 03079; Ⓟ 25,746; Ⓒ 28,112; ◆ 29,145
Salem Depot; RMC Place; ROCKINGHAM; ▲ Salem; ***203** M-8; ★ **BOS**; mail Salem **z** 03079
Salisbury; RMC Place; MERRIMACK; ▲ Salisbury; **203** K-7; 🅿; **z** 03268; ● 330
Salisbury; MCD-Town; MERRIMACK; ***203** J-6; 🅿; **z** 03268; Ⓟ 1,061; Ⓒ 1,137
Salisbury Heights; RMC Place; MERRIMACK; ▲ Salisbury; **203** J-7; mail Salisbury **z** 03268; ● 100
Salmon Falls; STRAFFORD; see Rollinsford (RMC Place)
Sanbornton; RMC Place; BELKNAP; ▲ Sanbornton; **203** J-7; elev. 822ft./251m.; 🅿; **z** 03269; ● 320
Sanbornton; MCD-Town; BELKNAP; ***203** J-7; 🅿; **z** 03269; Ⓟ 2,136; Ⓒ 2,581
Sanbornville; RMC Place; CARROLL; ▲ Wakefield; **203** J-9; elev. 581ft./177m.; 🅿; **z** 03872; ● 1,200
Sandown; RMC Place; ROCKINGHAM; ▲ Sandown; **203** M-8; 🅿; ★ **BOS**; **z** 03873; ● 600
Sandown; MCD-Town; ROCKINGHAM; ***203** M-9; 🅿; ★ **BOS**; **z** 03873; Ⓟ 4,060; Ⓒ 5,143; ◆ 5,789
Sandwich; RMC Place; CARROLL; ▲ Sandwich; **203** I-8; 🅿; **z** 03227; ● 60
Sandwich; MCD-Town; CARROLL; ***203** H-8; 🅿; **z** 03227; Ⓟ 1,066; Ⓒ 1,286
Sawyer Lake; RMC Place; BELKNAP; ▲ Gilmanton; ***203** J-8; mail Gilmanton **z** 03237; summer pop. 125; ● 50
Sawyers; RMC Place; STRAFFORD; ***203** K-10; ★ **PTSM-**; mail Dover **z** 03820; pop. incl. with Dover (Inc. Place)
Scotland; RMC Place; CHESHIRE; ▲ Winchester; **203** N-4; mail Winchester **z** 03470; ● 70
Seabrook; RMC Place; ROCKINGHAM; ▲ Seabrook; **203** M-10; elev. 56ft./17m.; 🅿; ★ **BOS**; **z** 03874; ● 900
Seabrook; MCD-Town; ROCKINGHAM; ***203** M-10; 🅿; ★ **BOS**; **z** 03874; Ⓟ 6,503; Ⓒ 7,934; ◆ 9,345
Seabrook Beach; RMC Place; ROCKINGHAM; ▲ Seabrook; ***203** M-10; ★ **BOS**; mail Seabrook **z** 03874; ● 100
Seacrest Village; RMC Place; ROCKINGHAM; ***203** L-10; ★ **PTSM-**; mail Portsmouth **z** 03801; pop. incl. with Portsmouth (Inc. Place)
Severance; RMC Place; ROCKINGHAM; ▲ Auburn; ***203** L-8; ★ **MNCH**; mail Auburn **z** 03032; ● 475
Sharon; RMC Place; HILLSBOROUGH; ▲ Sharon; **203** M-6; elev. 1,185ft./361m.; 🅿; **z** 03458; ● 75
Sharon; MCD-Town; HILLSBOROUGH; ***203** M-6; 🅿; **z** 03458; Ⓟ 299; Ⓒ 360
Shelburne; RMC Place; COOS; ▲ Shelburne; **203** F-9; 🅿; **z** 03581
Shelburne; MCD-Town; COOS; ***203** F-9; 🅿; **z** 03581; Ⓟ 437; Ⓒ 379
Shellcamp Pond; RMC Place; BELKNAP; ▲ Gilmanton; ***203** J-8; mail Gilmanton **z** 03237; summer pop. 125; ● 60
Sherwood Forest; RMC Place; ROCKINGHAM; ▲ Exeter; ***203** L-9; ★ **PTSM-**; mail Exeter **z** 03833
Short Falls; RMC Place; MERRIMACK; ▲ Epsom; **203** K-8; ★ **CONC**; mail Chichester **z** 03258, Epsom **z** 03234; ● 90
Silver Lake; RMC Place; CARROLL; ▲ Madison; **203** H-8; elev. 474ft./144m.; 🅿; **z** 03875; ● 300
Smith Colony; RMC Place; ROCKINGHAM; ▲ Hampton; ***203** M-10; ★ **PTSM-**; mail Hampton **z** 03842; ● 250
Smithtown; RMC Place; ROCKINGHAM; ▲ Seabrook; ***203** M-10; ★ **BOS**; mail Seabrook **z** 03874; ● 350
Smithville; RMC Place; HILLSBOROUGH; ▲ New Ipswich; ***203** N-6; elev. 1,056ft./322m.; ★ **BOS**; mail New Ipswich **z** 03071; ● 125
Snowville; RMC Place; CARROLL; ▲ Eaton; **203** H-9; mail Eaton Center **z** 03832; ● 50
Snumshire; RMC Place; SULLIVAN; ▲ Charlestown; ***203** K-4; mail Charlestown **z** 03603; rural
Somersworth; Inc. Place; STRAFFORD; **203** K-10; elev. 204ft./62m.; 🅿; ★ **PTSM-**; **z** 03878; Ⓟ 11,249; Ⓒ 11,477; ◆ 12,074
Soo Nipi; RMC Place; MERRIMACK; ▲ New London; mail New London **z** 03257; summer pop. 100
South Acworth; RMC Place; SULLIVAN; ▲ Acworth; **203** K-5; 🅿; **z** 03607; ● 200
South Barnstead; RMC Place; BELKNAP; ▲ Barnstead; **203** K-8; elev. 725ft./221m.; mail Center Barnstead **z** 03225; ● 70
South Brookline; RMC Place; HILLSBOROUGH; ▲ Brookline; ***203** N-7; elev. 240ft./73m.; ★ **BOS**; mail Brookline **z** 03033; ● 125
South Charlestown; RMC Place; SULLIVAN; ▲ Charlestown; ***203** K-4; mail Charlestown **z** 03603
South Chatham; RMC Place; CARROLL; ▲ Chatham; **203** G-9; elev. 418ft./127m.; mail Center Conway **z** 03813, Fryeburg **z** 04037; ● 90
South Conway; RMC Place; CARROLL; ▲ Conway; ***203** H-9; elev. 635ft./194m.; mail Center Conway **z** 03813
South Cornish; RMC Place; SULLIVAN; ▲ Cornish; ***203** J-5; elev. 961ft./293m.; mail Cornish **z** 03745; rural
South Danbury; RMC Place; MERRIMACK; ▲ Danbury; ***203** J-6; mail Danbury **z** 03230; rural
South Danville; RMC Place; ROCKINGHAM; ▲ Danville; **203** M-9; elev. 217ft./66m.; ★ **BOS**; mail Danville **z** 03819; ● 250
South Deerfield; RMC Place; ROCKINGHAM; ▲ Deerfield; ***203** L-8; mail Deerfield **z** 03037
South Effingham; RMC Place; CARROLL; ▲ Effingham; **203** I-9; mail Effingham **z** 03882; ● 120
South Hampton; RMC Place; ROCKINGHAM; ▲ South Hampton; ***203** M-9; elev. 202ft./62m.; 🅿; ★ **BOS**; **z** 03827; ● 125
South Hampton; MCD-Town; ROCKINGHAM; ***203** M-9; 🅿; ★ **BOS**; **z** 03827; Ⓟ 740; Ⓒ 844; ◆ 843
South Hooksett; CDP; MERRIMACK; ▲ Hooksett; **203** L-8; ★ **MNCH**; mail Hooksett **z** 03106; Ⓟ 3,638; Ⓒ 5,282
South Keene; RMC Place; CHESHIRE; ***203** M-5; mail Keene **z** 03431; pop. incl. with Keene (Inc. Place)
South Kingston; RMC Place; ROCKINGHAM; ▲ Kingston; ***203** M-9; ★ **BOS**; mail Kingston **z** 03848
South Lee; RMC Place; STRAFFORD; ▲ Lee; ***203** L-9; elev. 169ft./52m.; ★ **PTSM-**; mail Durham **z** 03824; rural
South Lyndeboro; RMC Place; HILLSBOROUGH; ▲ Lyndeborough; **203** M-6; mail Lyndeborough **z** 03082; ● 250
South Merrimack; RMC Place; HILLSBOROUGH; ▲ Merrimack; **203** M-7; elev. 218ft./66m.; ★ **BOS**; mail Merrimack **z** 03054; ● 200
South Milford; RMC Place; HILLSBOROUGH; ▲ Milford; ***203** M-7; ★ **BOS**; mail Milford **z** 03055
South Newbury; RMC Place; MERRIMACK; ▲ Newbury; **203** K-6; 🅿; **z** 03272; ● 150
South Pittsfield; RMC Place; MERRIMACK; ▲ Pittsfield; ***203** K-8; ★ **CONC**; mail Pittsfield **z** 03263
South Seabrook; RMC Place; ROCKINGHAM; ▲ Seabrook; ***203** M-10; ★ **BOS**; mail Seabrook **z** 03874; ● 250
South Stoddard; RMC Place; CHESHIRE; ▲ Stoddard; ***203** L-5; elev. 1,291ft./393m.; mail Stoddard **z** 03464
South Sutton; RMC Place; MERRIMACK; ▲ Sutton; **203** K-6; 🅿; **z** 03273; ● 170
South Tamworth; RMC Place; CARROLL; ▲ Tamworth; **203** H-8; elev. 588ft./179m.; 🅿; **z** 03883; ● 200
South Weare; RMC Place; HILLSBOROUGH; ▲ Weare; **203** L-7; elev. 630ft./192m.; ★ **MNCH**; mail Weare **z** 03281; ● 250
South Wolfeboro; RMC Place; CARROLL; ▲ Wolfeboro; **203** J-9; mail Wolfeboro **z** 03894; ● 400
Spofford; RMC Place; CHESHIRE; ▲ Chesterfield; **203** M-4; 🅿; **z** 03462; ● 500
Spofford Lake; RMC Place; CHESHIRE; ▲ Chesterfield; ***203** M-4; mail Spofford **z** 03462; summer pop. 600; ● 150
Springfield; RMC Place; SULLIVAN; ▲ Springfield; **203** J-6; elev. 1,427ft./435m.; 🅿; **z** 03284; ● 75
Springfield; MCD-Town; SULLIVAN; ***203** J-5; 🅿; **z** 03284; Ⓟ 788; Ⓒ 945
Spring Haven; RMC Place; BELKNAP; ▲ Alton; ***203** J-8; mail Alton **z** 03809; ● 175
Squag City; RMC Place; SULLIVAN; ▲ Cornish; ***203** J-4; mail Cornish **z** 03745; rural
Squantum; RMC Place; CHESHIRE; ▲ Jaffrey; **203** M-6; elev. 1,044ft./318m.; mail Jaffrey **z** 03452; ● 120
Stark; RMC Place; COOS; ▲ Stark; **203** E-8; 🅿; **z** 03582; ● 125
Stark; MCD-Town; COOS; ***203** E-8; 🅿; **z** 03582; Ⓟ 518; Ⓒ 516
State Line; RMC Place; CHESHIRE; mail Fitzwilliam **z** 03447; ● 20
Stewartstown; RMC Place; COOS; ▲ Stewartstown; **203** C-7; 🅿; **z** 03576; ● 175
Stewartstown; MCD-Town; COOS; ***203** C-8; 🅿; **z** 03576; Ⓟ 1,048; Ⓒ 1,012
Stewartstown Hollow; RMC Place; COOS; ▲ Stewartstown; **203** C-8; elev. 1,277ft./389m.; mail Colebrook **z** 03576; ● 35
Stinson Lake; RMC Place; GRAFTON; ▲ Rumney; **203** H-6; 🅿; **z** 03274; summer pop. 200; ● 60
Stockbridge Corners; RMC Place; BELKNAP; ▲ Alton; ***203** J-8; mail Alton **z** 03809; rural
Stoddard; RMC Place; CHESHIRE; ▲ Stoddard; **203** L-5; 🅿; **z** 03464 & mail Nelson **z** 03457; ● 300
Stoddard; MCD-Town; CHESHIRE; ***203** L-5; 🅿; **z** 03464 & mail Nelson **z** 03457; Ⓟ 622; Ⓒ 928
Strafford (Bow Lake Village); RMC Place; STRAFFORD; ▲ Strafford; **203** K-8; 🅿; **z** 03884; ● 300
Strafford; MCD-Town; STRAFFORD; ***203** K-9; 🅿; **z** 03884; Ⓟ 2,965; Ⓒ 3,626
STRAFFORD; **203** K-9; Ⓟ 104,233; Ⓒ 112,233; ◆ 125,097
Strafford Corner; RMC Place; STRAFFORD; ▲ Strafford; ***203** K-9; mail Center Strafford **z** 03815; rural
Stratford; RMC Place; COOS; ▲ Stratford; **203** D-7; 🅿; **z** 03590; ● 150
Stratford; MCD-Town; COOS; ***203** D-7; 🅿; **z** 03590; Ⓟ 927; Ⓒ 942
Stratham; RMC Place; ROCKINGHAM; ▲ Stratham; **203** L-9; 🅿; ★ **PTSM-**; **z** 03885; ● 800
Stratham; MCD-Town; ROCKINGHAM; ***203** L-10; 🅿; ★ **PTSM-**; **z** 03885; Ⓟ 4,955; Ⓒ 6,355; ◆ 7,385
Sugar Hill; RMC Place; GRAFTON; ▲ Lisbon; **203** F-6; 🅿; **z** 03586 & mail Lisbon **z** 03585; ● 200
Sugar Hill; MCD-Town; GRAFTON; ***203** F-6; 🅿; **z** 03586 & mail Lisbon **z** 03585; Ⓟ 464; Ⓒ 563
Suissevale; RMC Place; CARROLL; ▲ Moultonborough; ***203** I-8; mail Moultonborough **z** 03254; ● 300
Sullivan; RMC Place; CHESHIRE; ▲ Sullivan; ***203** L-5; elev. 1,409ft./429m.; 🅿; **z** 03445; ● 300
Sullivan; MCD-Town; CHESHIRE; ***203** L-5; 🅿; **z** 03445; Ⓟ 706; Ⓒ 746
SULLIVAN; **203** K-4; Ⓟ 38,592; Ⓒ 40,458; ◆ 42,528
Sunapee; RMC Place; SULLIVAN; ▲ Sunapee; **203** J-5; elev. 1,008ft./307m.; 🅿; **z** 03782; ● 1,000
Sunapee; MCD-Town; SULLIVAN; ***203** J-5; 🅿; **z** 03782; Ⓟ 2,559; Ⓒ 3,055
Suncook; CDP; MERRIMACK; ▲ Allenstown, Pembroke; **203** L-8; 🅿; ★ **CONC**; **z** 03275; Ⓟ 5,214; Ⓒ 5,362
Sunrise Lake; RMC Place; STRAFFORD; ▲ Middleton; ***203** J-9; mail Union **z** 03887; summer pop. 500; ● 250
Surry; RMC Place; CHESHIRE; ▲ Surry; **203** L-4; 🅿; **z** 03431; ● 150
Surry; MCD-Town; CHESHIRE; ***203** L-4; 🅿; **z** 03431; Ⓟ 667; Ⓒ 673
Sutton; RMC Place; MERRIMACK; ▲ Sutton; **203** K-6; mail Bradford **z** 03221; ● 200
Sutton; MCD-Town; MERRIMACK; ***203** K-6; mail Bradford **z** 03221; Ⓟ 1,457; Ⓒ 1,544
Swanzey (Swanzey Center); RMC Place; CHESHIRE; ▲ Swanzey; ***203** M-5; 🅿; **z** 03446 & mail Keene **z** 03431; ● 900
Swanzey; MCD-Town; CHESHIRE; ***203** M-5; 🅿; **z** 03446 & mail Keene **z** 03431; Ⓟ 6,236; Ⓒ 6,800
Swanzey Center; CHESHIRE; see Swanzey (RMC Place)
Swetts Mills; RMC Place; MERRIMACK; ▲ Webster; ***203** K-7; mail Concord **z** 03303; rural
Swiftwater; RMC Place; GRAFTON; ▲ Bath; **203** G-6; elev. 689ft./210m.; mail Woodsville **z** 03785; ● 125

T

Tamworth; RMC Place; CARROLL; ▲ Tamworth; **203** H-8; 🅿; **z** 03886; ● 600
Tamworth; MCD-Town; CARROLL; ***203** H-8; 🅿; **z** 03886; Ⓟ 2,165; Ⓒ 2,510
Tavern Village; RMC Place; HILLSBOROUGH; ▲ Weare; ***203** L-7; ★ **MNCH**; mail Weare **z** 03281; ● 50
Temple; RMC Place; HILLSBOROUGH; ▲ Temple; **203** M-6; elev. 1,005ft./306m.; 🅿; **z** 03084; ● 400
Temple; MCD-Town; HILLSBOROUGH; ***203** M-6; 🅿; **z** 03084; Ⓟ 1,194; Ⓒ 1,297
The Five Corners; RMC Place; ROCKINGHAM; ▲ Hampton; ***203** M-10; ★ **PTSM-**; mail Hampton **z** 03842
The Glen; RMC Place; COOS; ▲ Pittsburg; ***203** B-8; mail Pittsburg **z** 03592; summer pop. 75
The Plains; RMC Place; BELKNAP; ▲ Tilton; ***203** J-7; mail Tilton **z** 03276; ● 40
Thomas; RMC Place; CHESHIRE; ***203** N-5; elev. 1,130ft./344m.; mail Rindge **z** 03461
Thornton; RMC Place; GRAFTON; ▲ Thornton; **203** H-7; 🅿; **z** 03223, **z** 03285; ● 100
Thornton; MCD-Town; GRAFTON; ***203** H-7; 🅿; **z** 03223, **z** 03285; Ⓟ 1,505; Ⓒ 1,843
Thorntons Ferry; RMC Place; HILLSBOROUGH; ▲ Merrimack; ***203** M-7; ★ **BOS**; mail Merrimack **z** 03054; ● 200
Tilton; RMC Place; BELKNAP; ▲ Tilton; **203** J-7; elev. 458ft./140m.; 🅿; **z** 03276, **z** 03298-99; ● 1,300
Tilton; MCD-Town; BELKNAP; ***203** J-7; 🅿; **z** 03276, **z** 03298-99; Ⓟ 3,240; Ⓒ 3,477
Tilton-Northfield; CDP-Census Area Only; MERRIMACK, BELKNAP; ***203** J-7; mail Tilton **z** 03276; Ⓟ 3,081; Ⓒ 3,231
Tinkerville; RMC Place; COOS; ▲ Columbia; ***203** D-7; mail North Stratford **z** 03590; rural
Tinkerville; RMC Place; GRAFTON; ▲ Lyman; ***203** F-6; elev. 923ft./281m.; mail Lisbon **z** 03585
Trapshire; RMC Place; SULLIVAN; ▲ Charlestown; ***203** K-4; elev. 326ft./99m.; mail Charlestown **z** 03603; rural
Troy; RMC Place; CHESHIRE; ▲ Troy; **203** M-5; elev. 1,009ft./308m.; 🅿; **z** 03465; ● 1,200
Troy; MCD-Town; CHESHIRE; ***203** M-5; 🅿; **z** 03465; Ⓟ 2,097; Ⓒ 1,962
Tuftonboro; RMC Place; CARROLL; ▲ Tuftonboro; **203** I-8; elev. 998ft./304m.; mail Center Tuftonboro **z** 03816, Melvin Village **z** 03850, Mirror Lake **z** 03853, Ossipee **z** 03864, Wolfeboro **z** 03894; ● 70
Tuftonboro; MCD-Town; CARROLL; ***203** I-8; mail Center Tuftonboro **z** 03816, Melvin Village **z** 03850, Mirror Lake **z** 03853, Ossipee **z** 03864, Wolfeboro **z** 03894; Ⓟ 1,842; Ⓒ 2,148
Twin Mountain; RMC Place; COOS; ▲ Carroll; **203** F-7; elev. 1,442ft./440m.; 🅿; **z** 03595; ● 300

U

Union; RMC Place; CARROLL; ▲ Wakefield; **203** J-9; 🅿; **z** 03887; ● 550
Union Wharf; RMC Place; CARROLL; ▲ Tuftonboro; ***203** I-8; mail Center Tuftonboro **z** 03816; ● 30
Unity; RMC Place; SULLIVAN; ▲ Unity; **203** K-5; mail Charlestown **z** 03603, Claremont **z** 03743, Newport **z** 03773; ● 150
Unity; MCD-Town; SULLIVAN; ***203** K-5; mail Charlestown **z** 03603, Claremont **z** 03743, Newport **z** 03773; Ⓟ 1,341; Ⓒ 1,530
Upper Kidderville; RMC Place; COOS; ▲ Colebrook; ***203** C-8; elev. 1,443ft./440m.; mail Colebrook **z** 03576
Upper Village; RMC Place; COOS; ***203** F-8; mail Gorham **z** 03581

W

Wadley Falls; RMC Place; STRAFFORD; ▲ Lee; ***203** L-9; elev. 95ft./29m.; ★ **PTSM-**; mail Durham **z** 03824
Wakefield; RMC Place; CARROLL; ▲ Wakefield; **203** J-9; elev. 681ft./208m.; mail East Wakefield **z** 03830, Sanbornville **z** 03872, Union **z** 03887; ● 140
Wakefield; MCD-Town; CARROLL; ***203** I-9; mail East Wakefield **z** 03830, Sanbornville **z** 03872, Union **z** 03887; Ⓟ 3,057; Ⓒ 4,252
Wallis Sands; RMC Place; ROCKINGHAM; ▲ Rye; ***203** L-10; ★ **PTSM-**; mail Rye **z** 03870; ● 200
Walpole; RMC Place; CHESHIRE; ▲ Walpole; **203** L-4; 🅿; **z** 03608; ● 800
Walpole; MCD-Town; CHESHIRE; ***203** L-4; 🅿; **z** 03608; Ⓟ 3,210; Ⓒ 3,594
Warner; RMC Place; MERRIMACK; ▲ Warner; **203** K-6; elev. 445ft./136m.; 🅿; **z** 03278; ● 750
Warner; MCD-Town; MERRIMACK; ***203** K-6; 🅿; **z** 03278; Ⓟ 2,250; Ⓒ 2,760
Warren; RMC Place; GRAFTON; ▲ Warren; **203** H-6; 🅿; **z** 03279; ● 550
Warren; MCD-Town; GRAFTON; ***203** H-6; 🅿; **z** 03279; Ⓟ 820; Ⓒ 873
Washington; RMC Place; SULLIVAN; ▲ Washington; **203** K-5; 🅿; **z** 03280; ● 150
Washington; MCD-Town; SULLIVAN; ***203** K-5; 🅿; **z** 03280; Ⓟ 628; Ⓒ 895
Waterloo; RMC Place; MERRIMACK; ▲ Warner; **203** K-6; elev. 446ft./136m.; mail Warner **z** 03278; ● 65
Water Village; RMC Place; CARROLL; ▲ Ossipee; **203** I-8; elev. 790ft./241m.; mail Ossipee **z** 03864; ● 50
Waterville Valley; RMC Place; GRAFTON; ▲ Waterville Valley; **203** H-7; elev. 1,519ft./463m.; 🅿; **z** 03215; ● 120
Waterville Valley; MCD-Town; GRAFTON; ***203** H-7; 🅿; **z** 03215; Ⓟ 151; Ⓒ 257
Wawbeek; RMC Place; CARROLL; ▲ Tuftonboro; **203** I-8; mail Center Tuftonboro **z** 03816; ● 25
Weare; RMC Place; HILLSBOROUGH; ▲ Weare; **203** L-7; 🅿; ★ **MNCH**; **z** 03281; ● 300
Weare; MCD-Town; HILLSBOROUGH; ***203** L-7; 🅿; ★ **MNCH**; **z** 03281; Ⓟ 6,193; Ⓒ 7,776; ◆ 8,737
Weare Corner; RMC Place; ROCKINGHAM; ▲ Seabrook; ***203** M-9; ★ **BOS**; mail Seabrook **z** 03874; ● 120
Webster; RMC Place; MERRIMACK; ▲ Webster; **203** K-7; 🅿; **z** 03303; ● 120
Webster; MCD-Town; MERRIMACK; ***203** K-7; 🅿; **z** 03303; Ⓟ 1,405; Ⓒ 1,579
Webster Lake; RMC Place; MERRIMACK; ***203** J-7; elev. 450ft./137m.; mail Franklin **z** 03235; pop. incl. with Franklin (Inc. Place)
Webster Place; RMC Place; MERRIMACK; ***203** J-7; mail Franklin **z** 03235; pop. incl. with Franklin (Inc. Place)
Websters Mill; RMC Place; MERRIMACK; ▲ Chichester; ***203** K-8; ★ **CONC**; mail Pittsfield **z** 03263; ● 30
Weirs Beach; RMC Place; BELKNAP; ***203** I-8; mail Laconia **z** 03246-47; pop. incl. with Laconia (Inc. Place)
Welshs Corner; RMC Place; STRAFFORD; ▲ Strafford; ***203** K-9; mail Center Strafford **z** 03815; rural
Wendell; RMC Place; SULLIVAN; ▲ Sunapee; **203** K-5; mail Sunapee **z** 03782; ● 125
Wentworth; RMC Place; GRAFTON; ▲ Wentworth; **203** H-6; 🅿; **z** 03282; ● 280
Wentworth; MCD-Town; GRAFTON; ***203** H-6; 🅿; **z** 03282; Ⓟ 630; Ⓒ 798
Wentworth Acres; RMC Place; ROCKINGHAM; ***203** L-10; ★ **PTSM-**; mail Portsmouth **z** 03801; pop. incl. with Portsmouth (Inc. Place)
Wentworths Location; RMC Place; COOS; ▲ Wentworth Location; ***203** C-9; 🅿; **z** 03579; rural
Wentworth Terrace; RMC Place; STRAFFORD; ***203** L-10; ★ **PTSM-**; mail Dover **z** 03820; pop. incl. with Dover (Inc. Place)
West Alton; RMC Place; BELKNAP; ▲ Alton; ***203** J-8; mail Alton **z** 03809, Alton Bay **z** 03810
West Andover; RMC Place; MERRIMACK; ▲ Andover; ***203** J-6
West Barrington; RMC Place; STRAFFORD; ▲ Barrington; ***203** K-9; elev. 400ft./122m.; ★ **PTSM-**; mail Barrington **z** 03825; ● 100
Westboro; GRAFTON; see West Lebanon (RMC Place)
West Campton; RMC Place; GRAFTON; ▲ Campton; **203** H-7; elev. 576ft./176m.; mail Campton **z** 03223; ● 140
West Canaan; RMC Place; GRAFTON; ▲ Canaan; **203** I-5; mail Canaan **z** 03741; ● 125
West Center Harbor; RMC Place; BELKNAP; ▲ Center Harbor; **203** I-7; mail Ashland **z** 03217; ● 75
West Chesterfield; RMC Place; CHESHIRE; ▲ Chesterfield; **203** M-4; elev. 374ft./114m.; 🅿; **z** 03466; ● 550
West Claremont; RMC Place; SULLIVAN; ***203** J-4; elev. 502ft./153m.; mail Claremont **z** 03743; pop. incl. with Claremont (Inc. Place)
West Concord; RMC Place; MERRIMACK; ***203** K-7; elev. 349ft./106m.; ★ **CONC**; pop. incl. with Concord (Inc. Place)
West Deering; RMC Place; HILLSBOROUGH; ▲ Deering; ***203** L-6; elev. 599ft./183m.; mail Antrim **z** 03440; ● 125
West Dummer; RMC Place; COOS; ▲ Dummer; mail Milan **z** 03588; rural
West Epping; RMC Place; ROCKINGHAM; ▲ Epping; **203** L-9; ★ **PTSM-**; mail Epping **z** 03042; ● 350
West Franklin; RMC Place; MERRIMACK; ***203** J-7; mail Franklin **z** 03235; pop. incl. with Franklin (Inc. Place)
West Gonic; RMC Place; STRAFFORD; ***203** K-9; ★ **PTSM-**; mail Rochester **z** 03839; pop. incl. with Rochester (Inc. Place)
West Hampstead; RMC Place; ROCKINGHAM; ▲ Hampstead; **203** M-8; elev. 282ft./86m.; ★ **BOS**; mail Hampstead **z** 03841; ● 200
West Henniker; RMC Place; MERRIMACK; ▲ Henniker; **203** L-6; mail Henniker **z** 03242; ● 300
West Hopkinton; RMC Place; MERRIMACK; ▲ Hopkinton; **203** K-7; elev. 384ft./117m.; ★ **CONC**; mail Contoocook **z** 03229; ● 30
West Kingston; RMC Place; ROCKINGHAM; ▲ Kingston; ***203** M-9; ★ **BOS**; mail Kingston **z** 03848; ● 75
West Lebanon (Westboro); RMC Place; GRAFTON; ***203** I-5; 🅿; **z** 03784; pop. incl. with Lebanon (Inc. Place)
West Milan; RMC Place; COOS; ▲ Milan; **203** E-8; elev. 1,006ft./307m.; mail Milan **z** 03588; ● 100
Westmoreland; RMC Place; CHESHIRE; ▲ Westmoreland; **203** M-4; elev. 422ft./129m.; 🅿; **z** 03467; ● 300
Westmoreland; MCD-Town; CHESHIRE; ***203** L-4; 🅿; **z** 03467; Ⓟ 1,596; Ⓒ 1,747
West Nottingham; RMC Place; ROCKINGHAM; ▲ Nottingham; **203** K-9; elev. 358ft./109m.; 🅿; **z** 03291; ● 175
West Ossipee; RMC Place; CARROLL; ▲ Ossipee; **203** H-8; 🅿; **z** 03890; ● 150
West Peterborough; RMC Place; HILLSBOROUGH; ▲ Peterborough; **203** M-6; 🅿; **z** 03468; ● 500
West Plymouth; RMC Place; GRAFTON; ▲ Plymouth; ***203** I-6; elev. 514ft./157m.; mail Plymouth **z** 03264
Westport; RMC Place; CHESHIRE; ▲ Swanzey; **203** M-4; mail West Swanzey **z** 03469; ● 500
West Rindge; RMC Place; CHESHIRE; ▲ Rindge; **203** M-6; elev. 1,076ft./328m.; mail Rindge **z** 03461; ● 330
West Rumney; RMC Place; GRAFTON; ▲ Rumney; **203** H-6; elev. 539ft./164m.; mail Rumney **z** 03266; ● 150
West Rye; RMC Place; ROCKINGHAM; ▲ Rye; **203** L-10; ★ **PTSM-**; mail Rye **z** 03870; ● 300
West Salisbury; RMC Place; MERRIMACK; ▲ Salisbury; ***203** J-6; mail Salisbury **z** 03268
West Springfield; RMC Place; SULLIVAN; ▲ Springfield; **203** J-5; elev. 1,303ft./397m.; mail Springfield **z** 03284; ● 90
West Stewartstown; RMC Place; COOS; ▲ Stewartstown; **203** C-7; 🅿; **z** 03597; ● 250
West Swanzey; CDP; CHESHIRE; ▲ Swanzey; **203** M-4; 🅿; **z** 03469; Ⓟ 1,055; Ⓒ 1,118
West Thornton; RMC Place; GRAFTON; ▲ Thornton; **203** H-7; mail Campton **z** 03223; ● 160
West Unity; RMC Place; SULLIVAN; ▲ Unity; ***203** K-5; elev. 853ft./260m.; mail Claremont **z** 03743; rural
Westville; RMC Place; ROCKINGHAM; ▲ Plaistow; **203** M-9; elev. 161ft./49m.; ★ **BOS**; mail Plaistow **z** 03865; ● 400
West Wilton; RMC Place; HILLSBOROUGH; ▲ Wilton; **203** M-6; elev. 668ft./204m.; ★ **BOS**; mail Wilton **z** 03086; ● 200
West Windham; RMC Place; ROCKINGHAM; ▲ Windham; ***203** M-8; elev. 224ft./68m.; ★ **BOS**; mail Windham **z** 03087; ● 75
Whiteface; RMC Place; CARROLL; ▲ Sandwich; ***203** H-8; mail North Sandwich **z** 03259
Whitefield; CDP; COOS; ▲ Whitefield; **203** F-7; elev. 956ft./291m.; 🅿; **z** 03598; Ⓟ 1,041; Ⓒ 1,089
Whitefield; MCD-Town; COOS; ***203** F-7; 🅿; **z** 03598; Ⓟ 1,909; Ⓒ 2,038
Whittier; RMC Place; CARROLL; ▲ Tamworth; **203** H-8; mail Tamworth **z** 03886; ● 50
Willey House; RMC Place; CARROLL; ▲ Hart's Location; ***203** G-8; elev. 1,070ft./326m.; mail Bartlett **z** 03812; rural
Wilmot; RMC Place; MERRIMACK; ▲ Wilmot; **203** J-6; 🅿; **z** 03287; ● 120
Wilmot; MCD-Town; MERRIMACK; ***203** J-6; 🅿; **z** 03287; Ⓟ 935; Ⓒ 1,144
Wilmot Flat; RMC Place; MERRIMACK; ▲ Wilmot; **203** J-6; elev. 683ft./208m.; mail Wilmot **z** 03287; ● 350
Wilton; CDP; HILLSBOROUGH; ▲ Wilton, Milford; **203** M-7; elev. 357ft./109m.; 🅿; ★ **BOS**; **z** 03086; Ⓟ 1,165; Ⓒ 1,236
Wilton; MCD-Town; HILLSBOROUGH; ***203** M-6; 🅿; ★ **BOS**; **z** 03086; Ⓟ 3,122; Ⓒ 3,743; ◆ 4,100
Wilton Center; RMC Place; HILLSBOROUGH; ▲ Wilton; ***203** M-6; elev. 712ft./217m.; ★ **BOS**; mail Wilton **z** 03086; ● 100
Winchester; CDP; CHESHIRE; ▲ Winchester; **203** M-4; elev. 457ft./139m.; 🅿; **z** 03470; Ⓟ 1,735; Ⓒ 1,832
Winchester; MCD-Town; CHESHIRE; ***203** M-4; 🅿; **z** 03470; Ⓟ 4,038; Ⓒ 4,144
Windham; RMC Place; ROCKINGHAM; ▲ Windham; ***203** M-8; 🅿; ★ **BOS**; **z** 03087; ● 300
Windham; MCD-Town; ROCKINGHAM; ***203** M-8; 🅿; ★ **BOS**; **z** 03087; Ⓟ 9,000; Ⓒ 10,709; ◆ 12,423
Windham Depot; RMC Place; ROCKINGHAM; ***203** M-8; elev. 327ft./100m.; ★ **BOS**; mail Windham **z** 03087; ● 175
Windsor; MCD-Town; HILLSBOROUGH; ***203** L-6; 🅿; **z** 03244; Ⓟ 107; Ⓒ 201
Winniconic; RMC Place; ROCKINGHAM; ▲ Stratham; ***203** L-10; ★ **PTSM-**; mail Stratham **z** 03885; rural
Winnicut Mills; RMC Place; ROCKINGHAM; ▲ Stratham; ***203** L-10; ★ **PTSM-**; mail Stratham **z** 03885; rural
Winnisquam; RMC Place; BELKNAP; ▲ Belmont, Sanbornton, Tilton; **203** J-7; elev. 499ft./152m.; 🅿; **z** 03289; ● 650
Winona; RMC Place; BELKNAP; ▲ New Hampton; ***203** I-7; elev. 562ft./171m.; mail Ashland **z** 03217; rural
Wolfeboro; CDP; CARROLL; ▲ Wolfeboro; **203** J-8; 🅿 🅷; **z** 03894; Ⓟ 2,783; Ⓒ 2,979
Wolfeboro; MCD-Town; CARROLL; ***203** I-9; 🅿; **z** 03894; Ⓟ 4,807; Ⓒ 6,083
Wolfeboro Center; RMC Place; CARROLL; ▲ Wolfeboro; ***203** I-9; mail Wolfeboro **z** 03894
Wolfeboro Falls; RMC Place; CARROLL; ▲ Wolfeboro; **203** I-8; 🅿; **z** 03896; ● 600
Wonalancet; RMC Place; CARROLL; ▲ Tamworth; **203** H-8; elev. 109ft./33m.; 🅿; **z** 03897; ● 60
Woodland Park; RMC Place; HILLSBOROUGH; ▲ Merrimack; ***203** M-7; ★ **BOS**; mail Merrimack **z** 03054; ● 500
Woodman; RMC Place; CARROLL; ▲ Wakefield; **203** I-9; mail East Wakefield **z** 03830; ● 80
Woodmere; RMC Place; CHESHIRE; ▲ Rindge; ***203** M-6; elev. 1,052ft./321m.; mail Rindge **z** 03461; ● 120
Woodstock; RMC Place; GRAFTON; ▲ Woodstock; **203** H-7; elev. 701ft./214m.; 🅿; **z** 03293; ● 275
Woodstock; MCD-Town; GRAFTON; ***203** H-7; 🅿; **z** 03293; Ⓟ 1,167; Ⓒ 1,139
Woodsville; CDP; ⊡ GRAFTON; ▲ Haverhill; **203** G-6; elev. 157ft./48m.; 🅿 🅷; **z** 03785; Ⓟ 1,122; Ⓒ 1,081

NEW JERSEY

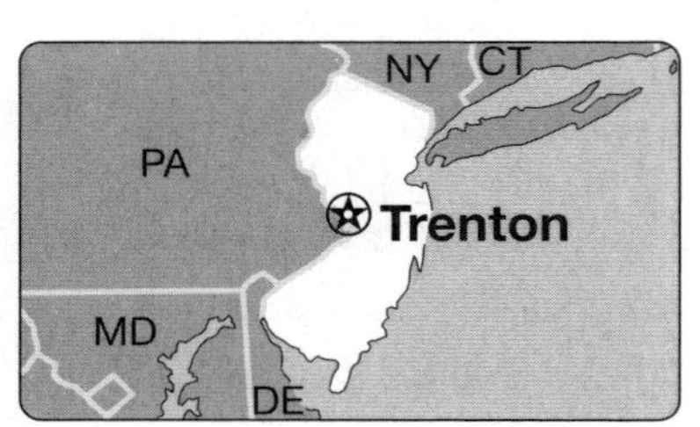

Statistics

Total area (2000) — 8,721 square miles
Land area (2000) — 7,417 square miles
Water area (2000) — 1,304 square miles
Capital — Trenton
One of Thirteen Original States

Maps

State maps can be found on pages 142-254 in Vol. 1
County Subdivision maps can be found on pages 255-271 in Vol. 1

Ranally Metro Areas (RMAs) and Abbreviations

Allentown-Bethlehem, PA-NJ — ALL-
Atlantic City, NJ — ATCY
New York, NY-NJ-CT — N.Y.
Philadelphia-Trenton-Wilmington, PA-NJ-DE-MD — PHIL-
Vineland, NJ — VINL

Principal Places

Place Name	Place Type	County	Population
Newark	Inc. Place	ESSEX	◆ 269,798
Jersey City	Inc. Place	HUDSON	◆ 226,057
Paterson	Inc. Place	PASSAIC	◆ 146,443
Elizabeth	Inc. Place	UNION	◆ 122,214
Edison	CDP	MIDDLESEX	◆ 102,546
Edison	MCD-Township	MIDDLESEX	◆ 102,546
Woodbridge	MCD-Township	MIDDLESEX	◆ 100,133
Toms River	CDP	OCEAN	◆ 96,616
Toms River	MCD-Township	OCEAN	◆ 96,616
Hamilton	MCD-Township	MERCER	◆ 86,593
Trenton	Inc. Place	MERCER	◆ 81,001
Lakewood	MCD-Township	OCEAN	◆ 80,592
Clifton	Inc. Place	PASSAIC	◆ 79,098
Camden	Inc. Place	CAMDEN	◆ 78,384
Brick	MCD-Township	OCEAN	◆ 77,430
Cherry Hill	MCD-Township	CAMDEN	◆ 69,819
Middletown	MCD-Township	MONMOUTH	◆ 68,726
Passaic	Inc. Place	PASSAIC	◆ 68,224
Union City	Inc. Place	HUDSON	◆ 67,126
Old Bridge	MCD-Township	MIDDLESEX	◆ 65,475
East Orange	Inc. Place	ESSEX	◆ 64,860
Gloucester	MCD-Township	CAMDEN	◆ 64,539
Vineland	Inc. Place	CUMBERLAND	◆ 58,641
North Bergen	MCD-Township	HUDSON	◆ 58,147
Irvington	CDP	ESSEX	◆ 57,286
Irvington	MCD-Township	ESSEX	◆ 57,286
Bayonne	Inc. Place	HUDSON	◆ 55,300
Howell	MCD-Township	MONMOUTH	◆ 54,812
Franklin	MCD-Township	SOMERSET	◆ 54,666
Wayne	CDP	PASSAIC	◆ 54,547
Wayne	MCD-Township	PASSAIC	◆ 54,547
Union	CDP	UNION	◆ 54,504
Union	MCD-Township	UNION	◆ 54,504
Piscataway	MCD-Township	MIDDLESEX	◆ 53,969
Washington	MCD-Township	GLOUCESTER	◆ 51,603
New Brunswick	Inc. Place	MIDDLESEX	◆ 51,409
Perth Amboy	Inc. Place	MIDDLESEX	◆ 50,854
Piscataway	RMC Place	MIDDLESEX	● 50,500
Parsippany-Troy Hills	MCD-Township	MORRIS	◆ 50,303
Jackson	MCD-Township	OCEAN	◆ 49,785
East Brunswick	CDP-Census Area Only	MIDDLESEX	◆ 49,774
East Brunswick	MCD-Township	MIDDLESEX	◆ 49,774
West New York	Inc. Place	HUDSON	◆ 49,027
North Bergen	RMC Place	HUDSON	℗ 48,414
Evesham	MCD-Township	BURLINGTON	◆ 46,316
Plainfield	Inc. Place	UNION	◆ 46,220
Bridgewater	MCD-Township	SOMERSET	◆ 46,060
Bloomfield	CDP	ESSEX	◆ 44,969
Bloomfield	MCD-Township	ESSEX	◆ 44,969
West Orange	CDP	ESSEX	◆ 43,398
West Orange	MCD-Township	ESSEX	◆ 43,398
Sayreville	Inc. Place	MIDDLESEX	◆ 43,009
Mount Laurel	MCD-Township	BURLINGTON	◆ 42,932
Hackensack	Inc. Place	BERGEN	◆ 42,502
Atlantic City	Inc. Place	ATLANTIC	◆ 42,262
South Brunswick	MCD-Township	MIDDLESEX	◆ 41,753
Hoboken	Inc. Place	HUDSON	◆ 40,731
Lakewood	CDP	OCEAN	◆ 40,363
Manchester	MCD-Township	OCEAN	◆ 40,153
Kearny	Inc. Place	HUDSON	◆ 40,109
Marlboro	MCD-Township	MONMOUTH	◆ 40,091
Linden	Inc. Place	UNION	◆ 39,645
Hillsborough	MCD-Township	SOMERSET	◆ 39,313
Egg Harbor	MCD-Township	ATLANTIC	◆ 38,991
North Brunswick	MCD-Township	MIDDLESEX	◆ 38,964
North Brunswick Township	CDP-Census Area Only	MIDDLESEX	◆ 38,964
Berkeley	MCD-Township	OCEAN	◆ 38,750
Montclair	CDP	ESSEX	◆ 37,972
Montclair	MCD-Township	ESSEX	◆ 37,972
Teaneck	CDP	BERGEN	◆ 37,824
Teaneck	MCD-Township	BERGEN	◆ 37,824
Galloway	MCD-Township	ATLANTIC	◆ 36,894
Manalapan	MCD-Township	MONMOUTH	◆ 36,772
Willingboro	RMC Place	BURLINGTON	℗ 36,291
Fort Lee	Inc. Place	BERGEN	◆ 36,008
Winslow	MCD-Township	CAMDEN	◆ 35,563
Pennsauken	CDP	CAMDEN	◆ 35,018
Pennsauken	MCD-Township	CAMDEN	◆ 35,018
Ewing	CDP	MERCER	◆ 35,007
Ewing	MCD-Township	MERCER	◆ 35,007
Belleville	CDP	ESSEX	◆ 34,514
Belleville	MCD-Township	ESSEX	◆ 34,514
Freehold	MCD-Township	MONMOUTH	◆ 33,926
Long Branch	Inc. Place	MONMOUTH	◆ 33,799
Monroe	MCD-Township	MIDDLESEX	◆ 32,878
Deptford	MCD-Township	GLOUCESTER	◆ 32,683
Monroe	MCD-Township	GLOUCESTER	◆ 32,504
City of Orange	MCD-Township	ESSEX	◆ 31,723
Orange	CDP	ESSEX	◆ 31,312
Fair Lawn	Inc. Place	BERGEN	◆ 30,916
Willingboro	MCD-Township	BURLINGTON	◆ 30,751
Stafford	MCD-Township	OCEAN	◆ 30,188
Garfield	Inc. Place	BERGEN	◆ 29,525
Lawrence	MCD-Township	MERCER	◆ 29,401
Voorhees	MCD-Township	CAMDEN	◆ 28,769
Westfield	Inc. Place	UNION	◆ 28,751
Millville	Inc. Place	CUMBERLAND	◆ 28,726
Ocean	MCD-Township	MONMOUTH	◆ 28,541
Neptune	MCD-Township	MONMOUTH	◆ 28,458
Englewood	Inc. Place	BERGEN	◆ 27,314
Wall	MCD-Township	MONMOUTH	◆ 27,245
Mercerville-Hamilton Square	CDP-Census Area Only	MERCER	◆ 27,198
Bernards	MCD-Township	SOMERSET	◆ 27,015
West Milford	CDP	PASSAIC	◆ 26,959
West Milford	MCD-Township	PASSAIC	◆ 26,959
Rahway	Inc. Place	UNION	◆ 26,944
Pemberton	MCD-Township	BURLINGTON	◆ 26,657
Livingston	CDP	ESSEX	◆ 26,348
Livingston	MCD-Township	ESSEX	◆ 26,348
Lacey	MCD-Township	OCEAN	◆ 26,136
Bergenfield	Inc. Place	BERGEN	◆ 26,011
Vernon	MCD-Township	SUSSEX	◆ 25,922
East Windsor	MCD-Township	MERCER	◆ 25,811
Nutley	CDP	ESSEX	◆ 25,753
Nutley	MCD-Township	ESSEX	◆ 25,753
Mount Olive	MCD-Township	MORRIS	◆ 25,335
Randolph	MCD-Township	MORRIS	◆ 25,208
Paramus	Inc. Place	BERGEN	◆ 25,055
Bridgeton	Inc. Place	CUMBERLAND	◆ 24,989
Somerset	CDP-Census Area Only	SOMERSET	◆ 24,962
Mahwah	MCD-Township	BERGEN	◆ 24,471
Ridgewood	Inc. Place	BERGEN	◆ 24,167
Old Bridge	CDP	MIDDLESEX	◆ 24,102
Hamilton	MCD-Township	ATLANTIC	◆ 24,072
Rockaway	MCD-Township	MORRIS	◆ 24,024
Middletown	RMC Place	MONMOUTH	● 24,000
Lodi	Inc. Place	BERGEN	◆ 23,874
West Windsor	MCD-Township	MERCER	◆ 23,653
South Plainfield	Inc. Place	MIDDLESEX	◆ 23,247
Cliffside Park	Inc. Place	BERGEN	◆ 23,187
Roxbury	MCD-Township	MORRIS	◆ 23,140
Burlington	MCD-Township	BURLINGTON	◆ 23,032
Raritan	MCD-Township	HUNTERDON	◆ 22,589
Medford	MCD-Township	BURLINGTON	◆ 22,492
Maplewood	CDP	ESSEX	◆ 22,474
Maplewood	MCD-Township	ESSEX	◆ 22,474
Carteret	Inc. Place	MIDDLESEX	◆ 22,198
Scotch Plains	CDP	UNION	◆ 22,190
Scotch Plains	MCD-Township	UNION	◆ 22,190
Plainsboro	MCD-Township	MIDDLESEX	◆ 21,969
Hazlet	MCD-Township	MONMOUTH	◆ 21,758
Cranford	CDP	UNION	◆ 21,632
Cranford	MCD-Township	UNION	◆ 21,632
Moorestown	MCD-Township	BURLINGTON	◆ 21,261
Hillside	CDP	UNION	◆ 21,170
Hillside	MCD-Township	UNION	◆ 21,170
Summit	Inc. Place	UNION	◆ 21,014
Roselle	Inc. Place	UNION	◆ 20,986
West Deptford	MCD-Township	GLOUCESTER	◆ 20,907
Morris	MCD-Township	MORRIS	◆ 20,906
Montville	MCD-Township	MORRIS	◆ 20,769
North Plainfield	Inc. Place	SOMERSET	◆ 20,740
Jefferson	MCD-Township	MORRIS	◆ 20,681
Lower	MCD-Township	CAPE MAY	◆ 20,552
Montgomery	MCD-Township	SOMERSET	◆ 20,325
Pleasantville	Inc. Place	ATLANTIC	◆ 20,324
New Market	RMC Place	MIDDLESEX	● 20,000
Millburn	CDP	ESSEX	© 19,765
Little Egg Harbor	MCD-Township	OCEAN	◆ 19,505
Lyndhurst	CDP	BERGEN	© 19,383
Lyndhurst	MCD-Township	BERGEN	© 19,383
Point Pleasant	Inc. Place	OCEAN	◆ 19,317
Morristown	Inc. Place	MORRIS	◆ 19,133
Maple Shade	MCD-Township	BURLINGTON	© 19,079
Glassboro	Inc. Place	GLOUCESTER	© 19,068
Moorestown	RMC Place	BURLINGTON	● 19,000
Neptune	RMC Place	MONMOUTH	● 19,000
Elmwood Park	Inc. Place	BERGEN	© 18,925
Millburn	MCD-Township	ESSEX	◆ 18,833
Maple Shade	RMC Place	BURLINGTON	● 18,700
Barnegat	MCD-Township	OCEAN	◆ 18,632
Woodbridge	CDP	MIDDLESEX	© 18,309
Hawthorne	Inc. Place	PASSAIC	© 18,218
Rutherford	Inc. Place	BERGEN	© 18,110
Sparta	MCD-Township	SUSSEX	® 18,013
Colonia	CDP	MIDDLESEX	© 17,811
Dover	Inc. Place	MORRIS	◆ 17,775
Washington	MCD-Township	MORRIS	◆ 17,592
Avenel	CDP	MIDDLESEX	© 17,552
Dumont	Inc. Place	BERGEN	© 17,503
Aberdeen	MCD-Township	MONMOUTH	© 17,454
Lindenwold	Inc. Place	CAMDEN	© 17,414
Asbury Park	Inc. Place	MONMOUTH	◆ 17,355
Palisades Park	Inc. Place	BERGEN	© 17,073
South Orange	CDP-Census Area Only	ESSEX	© 16,964
South Orange Village	MCD-Township	ESSEX	© 16,964
Iselin	CDP	MIDDLESEX	© 16,698
Princeton	MCD-Township	MERCER	® 16,662
Wyckoff	CDP	BERGEN	© 16,508
Wyckoff	MCD-Township	BERGEN	© 16,508
Middle	MCD-Township	CAPE MAY	© 16,405
New Milford	Inc. Place	BERGEN	© 16,400
Secaucus	Inc. Place	HUDSON	◆ 16,227
Hopewell	MCD-Township	MERCER	© 16,105
Hopatcong	Inc. Place	SUSSEX	© 15,888
Denville	MCD-Township	MORRIS	© 15,824
Readington	MCD-Township	HUNTERDON	© 15,803
Holmdel	MCD-Township	MONMOUTH	© 15,781
Delran	MCD-Township	BURLINGTON	© 15,536
Franklin	MCD-Township	GLOUCESTER	© 15,466
Madison	Inc. Place	MORRIS	® 15,460
Ocean City	Inc. Place	CAPE MAY	© 15,378
South River	Inc. Place	MIDDLESEX	© 15,322
North Arlington	Inc. Place	BERGEN	© 15,181
Phillipsburg	Inc. Place	WARREN	© 15,166
Tinton Falls	Inc. Place	MONMOUTH	© 15,053
Fords	CDP	MIDDLESEX	© 15,032
Mercerville	RMC Place	MERCER	● 15,000
Eatontown	Inc. Place	MONMOUTH	◆ 14,757
Haddon	MCD-Township	CAMDEN	© 14,651
Clark	CDP	UNION	© 14,597
Clark	MCD-Township	UNION	© 14,597
Cinnaminson	MCD-Township	BURLINGTON	© 14,595
Cinnaminson	RMC Place	BURLINGTON	℗ 14,583
Branchburg	MCD-Township	SOMERSET	© 14,566
Springfield	CDP	UNION	© 14,429
Springfield	MCD-Township	UNION	© 14,429
Harrison	Inc. Place	HUDSON	© 14,424
Springdale	CDP	CAMDEN	© 14,409
Ramsey	Inc. Place	BERGEN	© 14,351
Collingswood	Inc. Place	CAMDEN	© 14,326
Warren	MCD-Township	SOMERSET	© 14,259
Mantua	MCD-Township	GLOUCESTER	© 14,217
Highland Park	Inc. Place	MIDDLESEX	© 13,999
Princeton	Inc. Place	MERCER	◆ 13,907
Pequannock	MCD-Township	MORRIS	© 13,888
Holiday City-Berkeley	CDP-Census Area Only	OCEAN	© 13,884
Moorestown-Lenola	CDP-Census Area Only	BURLINGTON	© 13,860
Denville	RMC Place	MORRIS	● 13,812
Tenafly	Inc. Place	BERGEN	© 13,806
Middlesex	Inc. Place	MIDDLESEX	© 13,717
Verona	CDP	ESSEX	© 13,533
Verona	MCD-Township	ESSEX	© 13,533
Weehawken	MCD-Township	HUDSON	© 13,501
Princeton Meadows	CDP-Census Area Only	MIDDLESEX	© 13,436
Berkeley Heights	CDP	UNION	© 13,407
Berkeley Heights	MCD-Township	UNION	© 13,407
Roselle Park	Inc. Place	UNION	© 13,281
Fairview	Inc. Place	BERGEN	© 13,255
Cherry Hill Mall	CDP-Census Area Only	CAMDEN	© 13,238
Pennsville	MCD-Township	SALEM	© 13,194
Delran	RMC Place	BURLINGTON	● 13,178
Ocean Acres	CDP-Census Area Only	OCEAN	© 13,155
Saddle Brook	CDP	BERGEN	© 13,155
Saddle Brook	MCD-Township	BERGEN	© 13,155
Clinton	MCD-Township	HUNTERDON	© 12,957
Ventnor City	Inc. Place	ATLANTIC	© 12,910
Hanover	MCD-Township	MORRIS	© 12,898
Somerville	Inc. Place	SOMERSET	◆ 12,887
Ridgefield Park	Inc. Place	BERGEN	© 12,873
Metuchen	Inc. Place	MIDDLESEX	© 12,840
Red Bank	Inc. Place	MONMOUTH	◆ 12,621
Hammonton	Inc. Place	ATLANTIC	© 12,604
Brigantine	Inc. Place	ATLANTIC	© 12,594
Succasunna-Kenvil	CDP-Census Area Only	MORRIS	© 12,569
West Freehold	CDP	MONMOUTH	© 12,498
Oakland	Inc. Place	BERGEN	© 12,466
Ringwood	Inc. Place	PASSAIC	© 12,396
Weehawken	RMC Place	HUDSON	℗ 12,385
Cedar Grove	CDP	ESSEX	© 12,300
Cedar Grove	MCD-Township	ESSEX	© 12,300
Upper	MCD-Township	CAPE MAY	© 12,115
Hazlet	RMC Place	MONMOUTH	● 12,000
Mahwah	RMC Place	BERGEN	● 12,000
New Providence	Inc. Place	UNION	© 11,907
Williamstown	CDP	GLOUCESTER	© 11,812
Little Falls	CDP	PASSAIC	® 11,793
Little Falls	MCD-Township	PASSAIC	® 11,793
Hasbrouck Heights	Inc. Place	BERGEN	© 11,662
Haddonfield	Inc. Place	CAMDEN	© 11,659
Pennsville	CDP	SALEM	© 11,657
Somers Point	Inc. Place	ATLANTIC	© 11,614
Wallington	Inc. Place	BERGEN	© 11,583
Glen Rock	Inc. Place	BERGEN	© 11,546
Hanover Township	RMC Place	MORRIS	℗ 11,538
Greentree	CDP-Census Area Only	CAMDEN	© 11,536
Gloucester City	Inc. Place	CAMDEN	© 11,484
East Hanover	MCD-Township	MORRIS	© 11,393
Bellmawr	Inc. Place	CAMDEN	© 11,262
Browns Mills	CDP	BURLINGTON	© 11,257
Morganville	CDP	MONMOUTH	© 11,255
West Caldwell	CDP	ESSEX	© 11,233
West Caldwell	MCD-Township	ESSEX	© 11,233
Colts Neck	MCD-Township	MONMOUTH	® 11,179
Leisure Village West-Pine Lake Park	CDP-Census Area Only	OCEAN	© 11,085
Hamilton Square	RMC Place	MERCER	● 11,000
Westwood	Inc. Place	BERGEN	© 10,999
West Paterson	Inc. Place	PASSAIC	© 10,987
Freehold	Inc. Place	MONMOUTH	© 10,976
River Edge	Inc. Place	BERGEN	© 10,946
Lincoln Park	Inc. Place	MORRIS	© 10,930
Pine Hill	Inc. Place	CAMDEN	© 10,880
Ridgefield	Inc. Place	BERGEN	© 10,830
Guttenberg	Inc. Place	HUDSON	© 10,807
Little Ferry	Inc. Place	BERGEN	© 10,800
Florence	MCD-Township	BURLINGTON	© 10,746
Keansburg	Inc. Place	MONMOUTH	© 10,732
Barclay-Kingston	CDP-Census Area Only	CAMDEN	© 10,728
Mount Holly	MCD-Township	BURLINGTON	© 10,728
Pompton Lakes	Inc. Place	PASSAIC	© 10,640
Mount Holly	RMC Place	BURLINGTON	℗ 10,639
Waterford	MCD-Township	CAMDEN	© 10,494
Lumberton	MCD-Township	BURLINGTON	© 10,461
Echelon	CDP-Census Area Only	CAMDEN	© 10,440
Franklin Lakes	Inc. Place	BERGEN	© 10,422
Southampton	MCD-Township	BURLINGTON	© 10,388
Wantage	MCD-Township	SUSSEX	© 10,387
Beachwood	Inc. Place	OCEAN	© 10,375
Manville	Inc. Place	SOMERSET	© 10,343
Florham Park	Inc. Place	MORRIS	® 10,296
Robbinsville	MCD-Township	MERCER	© 10,275
Wanaque	Inc. Place	PASSAIC	© 10,266
Marlton	CDP	BURLINGTON	© 10,260
Woodbury	Inc. Place	GLOUCESTER	◆ 10,248
Bound Brook	Inc. Place	SOMERSET	© 10,155
Hillsdale	Inc. Place	BERGEN	© 10,087
Chatham	MCD-Township	MORRIS	© 10,086
Kirkwood Voorhees	RMC Place	CAMDEN	● 10,000
Sayerwood South	RMC Place	MIDDLESEX	● 10,000
East Hanover	RMC Place	MORRIS	℗ 9,926
Totowa	Inc. Place	PASSAIC	© 9,892
Lake Mohawk	CDP-Census Area Only	SUSSEX	© 9,755
New Hanover	MCD-Township	BURLINGTON	© 9,744
Burlington	Inc. Place	BURLINGTON	◆ 9,646
Waldwick	Inc. Place	BERGEN	© 9,622
Maywood	Inc. Place	BERGEN	© 9,523
River Vale	CDP	BERGEN	© 9,449
River Vale	MCD-Township	BERGEN	© 9,449
White Horse	CDP	MERCER	© 9,373
Kinnelon	Inc. Place	MORRIS	© 9,365
Pitman	Inc. Place	GLOUCESTER	© 9,331
Yardville-Groveville	CDP-Census Area Only	MERCER	© 9,208
Audubon	Inc. Place	CAMDEN	© 9,182
Villas	CDP	CAPE MAY	© 9,064
White Meadow Lake	CDP-Census Area Only	MORRIS	© 9,052
Kendall Park	CDP	MIDDLESEX	© 9,006
Hackettstown	Inc. Place	WARREN	® 8,984
Millstone	MCD-Township	MONMOUTH	© 8,970
Washington	MCD-Township	BERGEN	© 8,938
Washington Township	CDP-Census Area Only	BERGEN	© 8,938
Leonia	Inc. Place	BERGEN	© 8,914
Matawan	Inc. Place	MONMOUTH	© 8,910
Pittsgrove	MCD-Township	SALEM	© 8,893
Harrison	MCD-Township	GLOUCESTER	© 8,788
Long Hill	MCD-Township	MORRIS	© 8,777
East Rutherford	Inc. Place	BERGEN	© 8,716
Park Ridge	Inc. Place	BERGEN	© 8,708
Mystic Island	CDP	OCEAN	© 8,694
Gilford Park	RMC Place	OCEAN	℗ 8,668
Runnemede	Inc. Place	CAMDEN	© 8,533
Boonton	Inc. Place	MORRIS	© 8,496
Chatham	Inc. Place	MORRIS	© 8,460
Crestwood Village	CDP	OCEAN	© 8,392
Closter	Inc. Place	BERGEN	© 8,383
Bordentown	MCD-Township	BURLINGTON	© 8,380
Ashland	CDP	CAMDEN	© 8,375
Byram	MCD-Township	SUSSEX	® 8,321
Bedminster	MCD-Township	SOMERSET	© 8,302
West Long Branch	Inc. Place	MONMOUTH	© 8,258
Haledon	Inc. Place	PASSAIC	© 8,252
Bogota	Inc. Place	BERGEN	© 8,249
Newton	Inc. Place	SUSSEX	© 8,244
Florence-Roebling	CDP-Census Area Only	BURLINGTON	© 8,200
Margate City	Inc. Place	ATLANTIC	© 8,193
Erlton-Ellisburg	CDP-Census Area Only	CAMDEN	© 8,168
Budd Lake	CDP	MORRIS	© 8,100
Mansfield	MCD-Township	WARREN	® 8,072
Oradell	Inc. Place	BERGEN	© 8,047
Holiday City at Berkeley	RMC Place	OCEAN	● 8,000
Riverside	RMC Place	BURLINGTON	℗ 7,974
North Haledon	Inc. Place	PASSAIC	© 7,920
South Amboy	Inc. Place	MIDDLESEX	© 7,913
Riverside	MCD-Township	BURLINGTON	© 7,911
Spotswood	Inc. Place	MIDDLESEX	© 7,880
Edgewater Park	MCD-Township	BURLINGTON	© 7,864
Cresskill	Inc. Place	BERGEN	© 7,746
Upper Saddle River	Inc. Place	BERGEN	© 7,741
Northfield	Inc. Place	ATLANTIC	© 7,725
Carneys Point	MCD-Township	SALEM	© 7,684
Edgewater	Inc. Place	BERGEN	© 7,677
Kenilworth	Inc. Place	UNION	© 7,675
Wood-Ridge	Inc. Place	BERGEN	© 7,644

Entries in UPPERCASE are counties.
Entries in **bold** have populations of 2,500 or more.
Names in (parentheses) are alternate names.
Inc. Place — Incorporated Place
RMC Place — Rand McNally Designated Place
CDP — Census Designated Place
MCD — Minor Civil Division

⊡ County Seat
▲ Minor Civil Division
elev. Elevation
⊠ Post Office

⊞ Hospital
⊟ College
■ Principal Business Center
★ Ranally Metro Area (RMA) Abbreviation
z Zip Code(s)

℗ Previous Census Population
® Revised Census Population
Ⓐ Annexation Population
● Rand McNally Population Estimate
© Final Census Population
Ⓢ Special Census Population
◆ Estimated Population

For additional definitions see Glossary, Volume 1, and Introduction, Volume 2.

Place Name	Place Type	County	Population
Absecon	Inc. Place	ATLANTIC	© 7,638
Bloomingdale	Inc. Place	PASSAIC	© 7,610
Caldwell	Inc. Place	ESSEX	© 7,584
Keyport	Inc. Place	MONMOUTH	© 7,568
Upper Deerfield	MCD-Township	CUMBERLAND	© 7,556
Haddon Heights	Inc. Place	CAMDEN	© 7,547
Fort Dix	CDP	BURLINGTON	© 7,464
Buena Vista	MCD-Township	ATLANTIC	© 7,436
Twin Rivers	CDP	MERCER	© 7,422
Butler	Inc. Place	MORRIS	© 7,420
North Caldwell	Inc. Place	ESSEX	© 7,375
Maurice River	MCD-Township	CUMBERLAND	Ⓡ 7,374
North Hanover	MCD-Township	BURLINGTON	© 7,347
Bernardsville	Inc. Place	SOMERSET	© 7,345
Chester	MCD-Township	MORRIS	© 7,282
Plumsted	MCD-Township	OCEAN	© 7,275
Glen Ridge	Inc. Place	ESSEX	© 7,271
Stratford	Inc. Place	CAMDEN	© 7,271
Westampton	MCD-Township	BURLINGTON	© 7,217
Emerson	Inc. Place	BERGEN	© 7,197
Fanwood	Inc. Place	UNION	© 7,174
Linwood	Inc. Place	ATLANTIC	© 7,172
Tabernacle	MCD-Township	BURLINGTON	Ⓡ 7,167
Clayton	Inc. Place	GLOUCESTER	© 7,139
Rumson	Inc. Place	MONMOUTH	© 7,137
Palmyra	Inc. Place	BURLINGTON	© 7,091
Barrington	Inc. Place	CAMDEN	© 7,084
Fairfield	CDP-Census Area Only	ESSEX	© 7,063
Fairfield	MCD-Township	ESSEX	© 7,063
Montvale	Inc. Place	BERGEN	© 7,034
Bridgewater	RMC Place	SOMERSET	● 7,000
Milltown	Inc. Place	MIDDLESEX	© 7,000
Midland Park	Inc. Place	BERGEN	© 6,947
Madison Park	CDP	MIDDLESEX	© 6,929
Carneys Point	CDP	SALEM	© 6,914
Dunellen	Inc. Place	MIDDLESEX	© 6,823
Strathmore	CDP	MONMOUTH	© 6,740

Place Name	Place Type	County	Population
Washington	Inc. Place	WARREN	© 6,712
Yorketown	CDP-Census Area Only	MONMOUTH	© 6,712
Allendale	Inc. Place	BERGEN	© 6,699
Union Beach	Inc. Place	MONMOUTH	© 6,649
Mountainside	Inc. Place	UNION	© 6,602
Dennis	MCD-Township	CAPE MAY	© 6,492
McGuire AFB	CDP-Census Area Only	BURLINGTON	© 6,478
Rockaway	Inc. Place	MORRIS	© 6,473
Shamong	MCD-Township	BURLINGTON	© 6,462
Ocean	MCD-Township	OCEAN	© 6,450
Raritan	Inc. Place	SOMERSET	© 6,338
Manasquan	Inc. Place	MONMOUTH	© 6,310
Wharton	Inc. Place	MORRIS	© 6,298
Fairfield	MCD-Township	CUMBERLAND	© 6,283
Lincroft	CDP	MONMOUTH	© 6,255
Washington	MCD-Township	WARREN	© 6,248
Dayton	CDP	MIDDLESEX	© 6,235
Laurence Harbor	CDP	MIDDLESEX	© 6,227
Eastampton	MCD-Township	BURLINGTON	© 6,202
Hardyston	MCD-Township	SUSSEX	© 6,171
Little Silver	Inc. Place	MONMOUTH	© 6,170
Paulsboro	Inc. Place	GLOUCESTER	© 6,160
Union	MCD-Township	HUNTERDON	© 6,160
Berlin	Inc. Place	CAMDEN	© 6,149
Belmar	Inc. Place	MONMOUTH	© 6,045
Andover	MCD-Township	SUSSEX	© 6,033
Logan	MCD-Township	GLOUCESTER	© 6,032
Jamesburg	Inc. Place	MIDDLESEX	© 6,025
Ramblewood	CDP	BURLINGTON	© 6,003
Slackwoods	RMC Place	MERCER	● 6,000
Chesterfield	MCD-Township	BURLINGTON	© 5,955
Fair Haven	Inc. Place	MONMOUTH	© 5,937
Ramtown	CDP	MONMOUTH	© 5,932
Carlstadt	Inc. Place	BERGEN	© 5,917
Mullica	MCD-Township	ATLANTIC	© 5,912
Salem	Inc. Place	SALEM	© 5,857

Place Name	Place Type	County	Population
Lebanon	MCD-Township	HUNTERDON	© 5,816
Oceanport	Inc. Place	MONMOUTH	© 5,807
Watchung	Inc. Place	SOMERSET	◆ 5,806
Prospect Park	Inc. Place	PASSAIC	© 5,779
Lopatcong	MCD-Township	WARREN	© 5,765
Norwood	Inc. Place	BERGEN	© 5,751
Blairstown	MCD-Township	WARREN	© 5,747
Woodcliff Lake	Inc. Place	BERGEN	© 5,745
Green Brook	MCD-Township	SOMERSET	© 5,654
Independence	MCD-Township	WARREN	© 5,603
Tewksbury	MCD-Township	HUNTERDON	© 5,541
Rochelle Park	CDP	BERGEN	© 5,528
Rochelle Park	MCD-Township	BERGEN	© 5,528
Florence	RMC Place	BURLINGTON	● 5,500
Westmont	RMC Place	CAMDEN	● 5,500
Old Tappan	Inc. Place	BERGEN	© 5,482
Wildwood	Inc. Place	CAPE MAY	© 5,436
East Greenwich	MCD-Township	GLOUCESTER	© 5,430
Frankford	MCD-Township	SUSSEX	© 5,420
Mendham	MCD-Township	MORRIS	© 5,400
Englewood Cliffs	Inc. Place	BERGEN	© 5,322
Point Pleasant Beach	Inc. Place	OCEAN	© 5,314
Roseland	Inc. Place	ESSEX	© 5,298
Berlin	MCD-Township	CAMDEN	© 5,290
Commercial	MCD-Township	CUMBERLAND	© 5,259
Morris Plains	Inc. Place	MORRIS	© 5,236
Spring Lake Heights	Inc. Place	MONMOUTH	© 5,227
Neptune City	Inc. Place	MONMOUTH	© 5,218
Hightstown	Inc. Place	MERCER	© 5,216
Somerdale	Inc. Place	CAMDEN	© 5,192
Franklin	Inc. Place	SUSSEX	© 5,160
Holland	MCD-Township	HUNTERDON	© 5,124
Highlands	Inc. Place	MONMOUTH	© 5,097
Mendham	Inc. Place	MORRIS	© 5,097
Mansfield	MCD-Township	BURLINGTON	© 5,090
Highland Lake	CDP	SUSSEX	© 5,051

County Business Data

County	FIPS Code	County Seat	Land Area (Sq. Mi.)	Census Population			Wholesale Trade		Manufacturing, 2002			
				4/1/2000	4/1/1990	% Change 1990-2000	Sales, 2002 ($1,000)	% Change 1997-2002	Establish-ments	Total Employees	Value Added ($1,000)	Ranally Mfg. Units
Atlantic	001	Mays Landing	561	252,552	224,327	12.6	(d)	(d)	155	4,551	381,713	202
Bergen	003	Hackensack	234	884,118	825,380	7.1	69,612,667	11.5	1,581	55,288	7,352,552	3,890
Burlington	005	Mount Holly	805	423,394	395,066	7.2	17,363,293	7.1	468	21,101	2,623,652	1,388
Camden	007	Camden	222	508,932	502,824	1.2	6,495,060	5.8	590	17,008	2,382,791	1,261
Cape May	009	Cape May Court House	255	102,326	95,089	7.6	(d)	(d)	86	737	66,403	35
Cumberland	011	Bridgeton	489	146,438	138,053	6.1	(d)	(d)	200	10,154	1,282,657	679
Essex	013	Newark	126	793,633	778,206	2.0	18,657,856	6.0	1,090	32,794	5,185,679	2,744
Gloucester	015	Woodbury	325	254,673	230,082	10.7	8,059,944	33.8	283	11,791	2,664,772	1,410
Hudson	017	Jersey City	47	608,975	553,099	10.1	13,366,713	18.6	687	16,110	1,601,479	847
Hunterdon	019	Flemington	430	121,989	107,776	13.2	929,769	-22.6	177	4,348	460,947	244
Mercer	021	Trenton	226	350,761	325,824	7.7	(d)	(d)	315	8,600	1,457,405	771
Middlesex	023	New Brunswick	310	750,162	671,780	11.7	29,517,691	21.7	908	46,656	5,306,723	2,808
Monmouth	025	Freehold	472	615,301	553,124	11.2	5,664,506	-10.1	525	9,928	1,091,568	578
Morris	027	Morristown	469	470,212	421,353	11.6	26,778,948	27.9	685	23,347	3,567,401	1,887
Ocean	029	Toms River	636	510,916	433,203	17.9	(d)	(d)	346	6,885	724,543	383
Passaic	031	Paterson	185	489,049	453,060	7.9	8,218,129	-9.5	981	29,478	3,491,981	1,847
Salem	033	Salem	338	64,285	65,294	-1.5	(d)	(d)	44	3,902	654,486	346
Somerset	035	Somerville	305	297,490	240,279	23.8	21,926,742	19.9	363	23,999	2,882,195	1,525
Sussex	037	Newton	521	144,166	130,943	10.1	(d)	(d)	139	2,140	233,860	124
Union	039	Elizabeth	103	522,541	493,819	5.8	15,830,565	0.8	884	35,230	7,039,805	3,725
Warren	041	Belvidere	358	102,437	91,607	11.8	3,976,750	(d)	149	5,764	1,149,676	608
The State			**7,417**	**8,414,350**	**7,730,188**	**8.9**	**256,925,492**	**13.0**	**10,656**	**369,811**	**51,602,288**	**27,301**

(d) Data not available. Corresponding percentages or Ranally Manufacturing Units are estimates.
… Represents 0 or amount too minimal to be reported.

Administrative Divisions

Townships: All New Jersey counties are divided into townships, except for areas within municipal governments. Although legally incorporated, townships are not treated as incorporated places by the U.S. Census because the population often is scattered among several localities and rural areas rather than being concentrated in a single place. Only towns with an active government recognized by the U.S. Census of Governments are printed in this index.

Boroughs, Cities, Towns and Villages: These places do not form part of the townships which adjoin or surround them.

Index of Places and Counties

A

Aberdeen; MCD-Township; MONMOUTH; ***204** H-12; 🅿; ★ **N.Y.**; **z** 07747; Ⓟ 17,038; © 17,454
Abertown; RMC Place; SUSSEX; ▲ Sandyston; ***204** B-8; mail Montague **z** 07827; rural
Absecon; Inc. Place; ATLANTIC; **205** P-10; elev. 25ft./8m.; 🅿; ★ **ATCY**; **z** 08201, **z** 08205; Ⓟ 7,298; © 7,638
Absecon Highlands; RMC Place; ATLANTIC; ▲ Galloway; ***205** P-10; elev. 34ft./10m.; ★ **ATCY**; mail Absecon **z** 08201, **z** 08205; ● 180
Ackors Corner; RMC Place; MERCER; ▲ Hopewell; ***204** I-8; elev. 260ft./79m.; ★ **PHIL-**; mail Pennington **z** 08534
A Country Place; RMC Place; OCEAN; ▲ Lakewood; ***205** K-12; elev. 60ft./18m.; ★ **N.Y.**; mail Lakewood **z** 08701
Adams; RMC Place; MIDDLESEX; ▲ South Brunswick; ***204** H-10; elev. 119ft./36m.; ★ **N.Y.**; mail North Brunswick **z** 08902
Adamston; RMC Place; OCEAN; ▲ Brick; **205** K-13; ★ **N.Y.**; mail Brick **z** 08723
Adelphia; RMC Place; MONMOUTH; ▲ Howell; **204** J-12; 🅿; ★ **N.Y.**; **z** 07710; ● 150
Afton; RMC Place; MORRIS; ***204** F-11; ★ **N.Y.**; mail Florham Park **z** 07932; pop. incl. with Florham Park (Inc. Place)
Albion; RMC Place; CAMDEN; ▲ Winslow; **205** M-7; elev. 143ft./44m.; ★ **PHIL-**; mail Berlin **z** 08009; pop. incl. with Pine Hill (Inc. Place)
Albion Place; RMC Place; PASSAIC; ***204** E-12; ★ **N.Y.**; mail Clifton **z** 07013; pop. incl. with Clifton (Inc. Place)
Aldene; RMC Place; UNION; **210** J-4; ★ **N.Y.**; mail Roselle Park **z** 07204; pop. incl. with Roselle Park (Inc. Place)
Alderbrook Homes; RMC Place; MONMOUTH; ***204** I-13; ★ **N.Y.**; mail Little Silver **z** 07739; pop. incl. with Little Silver (Inc. Place)
Aldine; RMC Place; SALEM; ▲ Alloway; **205** O-5; mail Elmer **z** 08318; ● 50
Alexandria; MCD-Township; HUNTERDON; ***204** G-7; mail Milford **z** 08848, Pittstown **z** 08867; Ⓟ 3,594; © 4,698
Alexauken; RMC Place; HUNTERDON; mail Lambertville **z** 08530; ● 170
Allamuchy; RMC Place; WARREN; ▲ Allamuchy; **204** D-8; 🅿; ★ **N.Y.**; **z** 07820; ● 200
Allamuchy; MCD-Township; WARREN; ***204** E-8; 🅿; ★ **N.Y.**; **z** 07820 & mail Hackettstown **z** 07840; Ⓟ 3,484; © 3,877
Allamuchy-Panther Valley; CDP-Census Area Only; WARREN; ▲ Allamuchy; ***204** E-8; elev. 800ft./244m.; ★ **N.Y.**; mail Allamuchy **z** 07820; Ⓟ 2,764; © 3,125
Allendale; Inc. Place; BERGEN; **204** D-12; elev. 375ft./114m.; 🅿; ★ **N.Y.**; **z** 07401; Ⓟ 5,900; © 6,699
Allenhurst; Inc. Place; MONMOUTH; **204** J-13; elev. 24ft./7m.; 🅿; ★ **N.Y.**; **z** 07709, **z** 07711; Ⓟ 759; © 718
Allentown; Inc. Place; MONMOUTH; **204** J-10; elev. 82ft./25m.; 🅿; ★ **PHIL-**; **z** 08501; Ⓟ 1,828; © 1,882
Allenwood; CDP; MONMOUTH; ▲ Wall; ***205** K-12; 🅿; ★ **N.Y.**; **z** 08720; © 935
Allerton; RMC Place; HUNTERDON; ▲ Clinton; **204** G-8; ★ **N.Y.**; mail Lebanon **z** 08833; ● 100
Allison Acres; RMC Place; PASSAIC; ▲ West Milford; ***204** C-10; ★ **N.Y.**; mail Newfoundland **z** 07435; ● 100
Alloway; CDP; SALEM; ▲ Alloway; **205** O-5; 🅿; **z** 08001; Ⓟ 1,371; © 1,128
Alloway; MCD-Township; SALEM; ***205** O-5; 🅿; **z** 08001; Ⓟ 2,795; © 2,774
Allwood; RMC Place; PASSAIC; ***204** E-12; elev. 145ft./44m.; ★ **N.Y.**; mail Clifton **z** 07012; pop. incl. with Clifton (Inc. Place)
Almonesson; RMC Place; GLOUCESTER; ▲ Deptford; **205** M-6; ★ **PHIL-**; mail Woodbury **z** 08096; ● 800
Alpha; Inc. Place; WARREN; **204** G-6; elev. 273ft./83m.; 🅿; ★ **ALL-**; **z** 08865; Ⓟ 2,530; © 2,482
Alphano; RMC Place; WARREN; ▲ Independence, Allamuchy; ***204** E-8; ★ **N.Y.**; mail Great Meadows **z** 07838
Alpine; Inc. Place; BERGEN; **204** D-14; elev. 410ft./125m.; 🅿; ★ **N.Y.**; **z** 07620; Ⓟ 1,716; © 2,183
Amon Heights; RMC Place; CAMDEN; ▲ Pennsauken; ★ **PHIL-**; mail Pennsauken **z** 08110
Ampere; RMC Place; ESSEX; ***204** F-12; ★ **N.Y.**; mail East Orange **z** 07017; pop. incl. with East Orange (Inc. Place)
Amwell; RMC Place; HUNTERDON; mail Ringoes **z** 08551, Skillman **z** 08558; ● 100
Ancora; RMC Place; CAMDEN; ▲ Winslow; ***205** N-8; ★ **PHIL-**; mail Hammonton **z** 08037; rural
Anderson; RMC Place; WARREN; ▲ Mansfield; **204** F-8; ★ **N.Y.**; mail Port Murray **z** 07865; ● 350
Andover; Inc. Place; SUSSEX; **204** D-9; elev. 646ft./197m.; 🅿; ★ **N.Y.**; **z** 07821; Ⓟ 700; © 658
Andover; MCD-Township; SUSSEX; ***204** D-9; 🅿; ★ **N.Y.**; **z** 07821 & mail Newton **z** 07860; does not include the Borough of Andover; Ⓟ 5,438; © 6,033
Anglesea; RMC Place; CAPE MAY; ***205** S-8; mail Wildwood **z** 08260; pop. incl. with North Wildwood (Inc. Place)
Annandale; CDP; HUNTERDON; ▲ Clinton; **204** G-8; 🅿; ★ **N.Y.**; **z** 08801; Ⓟ 1,074; © 1,276
Anthony; RMC Place; HUNTERDON; ▲ Lebanon; ***204** F-8; ★ **N.Y.**; mail Glen Gardner **z** 08826
Applegarth; RMC Place; MIDDLESEX; ▲ Monroe; ***204** J-10; ★ **N.Y.**; mail Cranbury **z** 08512; rural
Apple Hill; RMC Place; CAMDEN; ▲ Cherry Hill; ★ **PHIL-**; mail Cherry Hill **z** 08002
Apshawa; RMC Place; PASSAIC; ▲ West Milford; ***204** D-11; ★ **N.Y.**; mail Butler **z** 07405; ● 50
Arcola; RMC Place; BERGEN; ***204** D-12; ★ **N.Y.**; mail Paramus **z** 07652; pop. incl. with Paramus (Inc. Place)
Ardena; RMC Place; MONMOUTH; ▲ Howell; ***204** J-12; ★ **N.Y.**; mail Freehold **z** 07728; rural
Ardmore Estates; RMC Place; MONMOUTH; mail Freehold **z** 07728; ● 260
Arlington; RMC Place; HUDSON; ***204** F-12; ★ **N.Y.**; mail Kearny **z** 07032; pop. incl. with Kearny (Inc. Place)
Arneys Mount; RMC Place; BURLINGTON; ▲ Springfield; ***205** L-9; elev. 132ft./40m.; ★ **PHIL-**; mail Pemberton **z** 08068
Arneytown; RMC Place; BURLINGTON, MONMOUTH; ▲ Upper Freehold, North Hanover; ***205** K-10; ★ **PHIL-**; mail Allentown **z** 08501
Arrowhead Lake; RMC Place; MORRIS; ▲ Denville; ***204** E-10; ★ **N.Y.**; mail Denville **z** 07834
Arrowhead Village; RMC Place; OCEAN; ▲ Brick; ***205** K-12; ★ **N.Y.**; mail Brick **z** 08723
Asbury; RMC Place; WARREN, HUNTERDON; ▲ Bethlehem, Franklin; **204** F-7; 🅿; ★ **N.Y.**; **z** 08802; ● 450
Asbury Park; Inc. Place; MONMOUTH; **204** J-13; elev. 21ft./6m.; 🅿 ■; ★ **N.Y.**; **z** 07712; Ⓟ 16,799; © 16,930; ◆ 17,355
Ashland; CDP; CAMDEN; ***205** M-7; ★ **PHIL-**; mail Cherry Hill **z** 08034, Voorhees **z** 08043; © 8,375
Atco; RMC Place; CAMDEN; ▲ Waterford; **205** N-8; 🅿; ★ **PHIL-**; **z** 08004; ● 3,500
Athenia; RMC Place; PASSAIC; ***204** E-12; ★ **N.Y.**; mail Clifton **z** 07013; pop. incl. with Clifton (Inc. Place)
ATLANTIC; **205** P-8; Ⓟ 224,327; © 252,552; ◆ 268,530
Atlantic City; Inc. Place; ATLANTIC; **204** I-2; elev. 8ft./2m.; 🅿 🅷 ■; ★ **ATCY**; **z** 08401, **z** 08404-05 & mail Longport **z** 08403, Margate City **z** 08402, Ventnor City **z** 08406; Ⓟ 37,986; © 40,517; ◆ 42,262
Atlantic Highlands; Inc. Place; MONMOUTH; **204** H-13; elev. 17ft./5m.; 🅿; ★ **N.Y.**; **z** 07716; Ⓟ 4,629; © 4,705
Atlantis; RMC Place; OCEAN; ▲ Little Egg Harbor; ***205** O-11; elev. 10ft./3m.; ★ **ATCY**; mail Tuckerton **z** 08087; pop. incl. with Tuckerton (Inc. Place)
Atsion; RMC Place; BURLINGTON; ▲ Shamong; **205** N-9; ★ **PHIL-**; mail Vincentown **z** 08088; rural
Auburn; RMC Place; SALEM; ▲ Oldmans; **205** N-5; elev. 77ft./23m.; ★ **PHIL-**; mail Swedesboro **z** 08085; ● 150
Audubon; Inc. Place; CAMDEN; **205** M-7; elev. 58ft./18m.; 🅿; ★ **PHIL-**; **z** 08106; Ⓟ 9,205; © 9,182
Audubon Park; Inc. Place; CAMDEN; **228** F-6; elev. 20ft./6m.; ★ **PHIL-**; mail Audubon **z** 08106; Ⓟ 1,150; © 1,102
Augusta; RMC Place; SUSSEX; ▲ Frankford; **204** C-9; elev. 498ft./152m.; 🅿; ★ **N.Y.**; **z** 07822; ● 100
Aura; RMC Place; GLOUCESTER; ▲ Elk; ***205** N-6; elev. 147ft./45m.; ★ **PHIL-**; mail Glassboro **z** 08028, Monroeville **z** 08343
Avalon; Inc. Place; CAPE MAY; **205** R-4; elev. 6ft./2m.; 🅿; **z** 08202; Ⓟ 1,809; © 2,143
Avenel; CDP; MIDDLESEX; ▲ Woodbridge; **204** G-11; elev. 84ft./26m.; 🅿; ★ **N.Y.**; **z** 07001; Ⓟ 15,504; © 17,552
Avis Mills; RMC Place; GLOUCESTER; mail Mullica Hill **z** 08062; ● 45
Avon-by-the-Sea; Inc. Place; MONMOUTH; **204** J-13; elev. 22ft./7m.; 🅿; ★ **N.Y.**; **z** 07717; Ⓟ 2,165; © 2,244
Avondale; RMC Place; ESSEX; ***204** E-12; ★ **N.Y.**; mail Nutley **z** 07110
Awosting; RMC Place; PASSAIC; ▲ West Milford; **204** C-11; ★ **N.Y.**; mail Hewitt **z** 07421; ● 500

B

Babbitt; RMC Place; HUDSON; ***204** E-13; ★ **N.Y.**; mail North Bergen **z** 07047
Bacons Neck; RMC Place; CUMBERLAND; ▲ Greenwich; ***205** P-5; mail Bridgeton **z** 08302; rural
Bakersville; RMC Place; MERCER; ▲ Lawrence; **205** S-12; elev. 57ft./17m.; ★ **PHIL-**; mail Lawrence Township **z** 08648; ● 200
Baldwins Corner; RMC Place; MERCER; ▲ Hopewell; ***204** I-8; elev. 190ft./58m.; ★ **PHIL-**; mail Pennington **z** 08534; ● 40
Baleville; RMC Place; SUSSEX; ▲ Hampton; **204** C-8; ★ **N.Y.**; mail Newton **z** 07860; ● 90
Baltusrol; RMC Place; UNION; ▲ Springfield; ***204** F-11; ★ **N.Y.**; mail Springfield **z** 07081
Bamber Lake; RMC Place; OCEAN; ▲ Lacey; **205** M-11; ★ **N.Y.**; mail Forked River **z** 08731; ● 250
Baptistown; RMC Place; HUNTERDON; ▲ Kingwood; **204** H-7; elev. 503ft./153m.; 🅿; **z** 08803; ● 200
Barber (Maurer); RMC Place; MIDDLESEX; ★ **N.Y.**; pop. incl. with Perth Amboy (Inc. Place)
Barbertown; RMC Place; HUNTERDON; ▲ Kingwood; ***204** H-7; mail Frenchtown **z** 08825
Barclay Farm; RMC Place; CAMDEN; ▲ Cherry Hill; ***205** L-7; ★ **PHIL-**; mail Cherry Hill **z** 08034
Barclay-Kingston; CDP-Census Area Only; CAMDEN; ***205** L-7; ★ **PHIL-**; © 10,728
Bargaintown; RMC Place; ATLANTIC; ▲ Egg Harbor; **205** Q-10; ★ **ATCY**; mail Egg Harbor Township **z** 08234, Pleasantville **z** 08232; ● 1,600
Barley Sheaf; RMC Place; HUNTERDON; ▲ Readington; ***204** G-8; ★ **N.Y.**; mail Flemington **z** 08822
Barnegat; CDP; OCEAN; ▲ Barnegat; **205** N-12; elev. 43ft./13m.; 🅿; ★ **N.Y.**; **z** 08005; Ⓟ 1,160; © 1,690
Barnegat; MCD-Township; OCEAN; ***205** N-11; 🅿; ★ **N.Y.**; **z** 08005; Ⓟ 12,235; © 15,270; ◆ 18,632
Barnegat Bay; RMC Place; OCEAN; mail Barnegat **z** 08005; ● 200
Barnegat Beach; RMC Place; OCEAN; ▲ Ocean; **205** M-12; ★ **N.Y.**; mail Waretown **z** 08758; ● 300
Barnegat Estates; RMC Place; OCEAN; mail Barnegat **z** 08005; ● 500
Barnegat Light; Inc. Place; OCEAN; **205** N-12; elev. 10ft./3m.; 🅿; ★ **N.Y.**; **z** 08006; Ⓟ 675; summer pop. 3,000; © 764
Barnegat Pines; RMC Place; OCEAN; ▲ Lacey; **205** M-12; ★ **N.Y.**; mail Forked River **z** 08731; ● 400
Barnsboro; RMC Place; GLOUCESTER; ▲ Mantua; **205** N-6; elev. 150ft./46m.; ★ **PHIL-**; mail Sewell **z** 08080; ● 700
Barrington; Inc. Place; CAMDEN; **205** M-7; elev. 81ft./25m.; 🅿; ★ **PHIL-**; **z** 08007; Ⓟ 6,774; © 7,084
Barry Lakes; RMC Place; SUSSEX; ▲ Vernon; ***204** B-10; ★ **N.Y.**; mail Highland Lakes **z** 07422; ● 1,500
Bartles Corner; RMC Place; HUNTERDON; ▲ Raritan; ***204** G-8; ★ **N.Y.**; mail Flemington **z** 08822; rural
Bartley; RMC Place; MORRIS; ▲ Mount Olive; **204** E-9; ★ **N.Y.**; mail Flanders **z** 07836
Basking Ridge; RMC Place; SOMERSET; ▲ Bernards; **204** F-10; 🅿; ★ **N.Y.**; **z** 07920, **z** 07939; ● 4,000
Bass River; MCD-Township; BURLINGTON; ***205** N-10; mail New Gretna **z** 08224; Ⓟ 1,580; © 1,510
Bates Mill; RMC Place; CAMDEN; ▲ Winslow; ***205** N-8; elev. 103ft./31m.; ★ **PHIL-**; mail Hammonton **z** 08037; ● 150
Batesville; RMC Place; CAMDEN; ***205** M-7; ★ **PHIL-**; mail Cherry Hill **z** 08034
Batsto; RMC Place; BURLINGTON; ▲ Washington; **205** O-9; 🅿; **z** 08037; ● 10
Bay Harbor Estates; RMC Place; OCEAN; ▲ Brick; ***205** L-12; ★ **N.Y.**; mail Brick **z** 08723
Bay Head; Inc. Place; OCEAN; **205** K-13; elev. 5ft./2m.; 🅿; ★ **N.Y.**; **z** 08742; Ⓟ 1,226; © 1,238
Bayonne; Inc. Place; HUDSON; **204** F-12; elev. 27ft./8m.; 🅿 🅷 ■; ★ **N.Y.**; **z** 07002; Ⓟ 61,444; © 61,842; ◆ 55,300
Bay Point; RMC Place; CUMBERLAND; ▲ Lawrence; ***205** Q-5; mail Cedarville **z** 08311; ● 20
Bay Shore; RMC Place; OCEAN; ▲ Toms River; **205** L-12; ★ **N.Y.**; mail Toms River **z** 08753
Bay Side; RMC Place; CUMBERLAND; ▲ Greenwich; ***205** Q-5; elev. 5ft./2m.; mail Bridgeton **z** 08302
Bay Side; RMC Place; OCEAN; ▲ Stafford; ***205** N-12; ★ **N.Y.**; mail Manahawkin **z** 08050; ● 50
Bayview Heights; RMC Place; OCEAN; ▲ Toms River; ***205** L-12; elev. 20ft./6m.; ★ **N.Y.**; mail Toms River **z** 08753; ● 500
Bayville; RMC Place; OCEAN; ▲ Berkeley; **205** L-12; 🅿; ★ **N.Y.**; **z** 08721; ● 900
Bayway; RMC Place; UNION; ***204** G-12; ★ **N.Y.**; mail Elizabeth **z** 07202; pop. incl. with Elizabeth (Inc. Place)
Baywood; RMC Place; OCEAN; ▲ Brick; ***205** L-13; ★ **N.Y.**; mail Brick **z** 08723
Beach Glen; RMC Place; MORRIS; ▲ Rockaway; ***204** D-10; ★ **N.Y.**; mail Rockaway **z** 07866; ● 40
Beach Haven; Inc. Place; OCEAN; **205** O-12; elev. 10ft./3m.; 🅿; ★ **N.Y.**; **z** 08008; Ⓟ 1,475; © 1,278
Beach Haven Crest; RMC Place; OCEAN; ▲ Long Beach; **205** O-12; ★ **N.Y.**; mail Beach Haven **z** 08008; summer pop. 1,000; ● 100
Beach Haven Gardens; RMC Place; OCEAN; ▲ Long Beach; ***205** O-12; ★ **N.Y.**; mail Beach Haven **z** 08008; summer pop. 1,000; ● 200
Beach Haven Heights; RMC Place; OCEAN; ▲ Long Beach; **205** O-11; ★ **N.Y.**; mail Beach Haven **z** 08008; summer pop. 1,000; ● 300
Beach Haven Park; OCEAN; see Long Beach (RMC Place)
Beach Haven Park; RMC Place; OCEAN; mail Beach Haven **z** 08008; ● 160
Beach Haven Terrace; RMC Place; OCEAN; ▲ Long Beach; **205** O-12; ★ **N.Y.**; mail Beach Haven **z** 08008; summer pop. 2,000; ● 400
Beach Haven West; CDP; OCEAN; ▲ Stafford; ***205** N-12; ★ **N.Y.**; mail Manahawkin **z** 08050; Ⓟ 4,237; © 4,444
Beach View; RMC Place; OCEAN; ▲ Stafford; ***205** N-12; elev. 47ft./14m.; ★ **N.Y.**; mail Barnegat **z** 08005; rural
Beachwood; Inc. Place; OCEAN; **205** L-12; elev. 25ft./8m.; 🅿; ★ **N.Y.**; **z** 08722; Ⓟ 9,324; © 10,375
Beattystown; RMC Place; WARREN; ▲ Mansfield; **204** E-8; ★ **N.Y.**; ● 1,000
Beatyestown; CDP-Census Area Only; WARREN; ▲ Mansfield; **204** E-8; elev. 690ft./210m.; ★ **N.Y.**; mail Hackettstown **z** 07840; Ⓟ 3,966; © 3,223; Ⓡ 4,642
Beaufort; RMC Place; ESSEX; ***204** E-11; ★ **N.Y.**; mail Roseland **z** 07068; pop. incl. with Roseland (Inc. Place)
Beaver Dam; RMC Place; SALEM; ▲ Pennsville; ***205** N-4; ★ **PHIL-**; mail Pennsville **z** 08070; ● 200
Beaver Lake; RMC Place; SUSSEX; ▲ Hardyston; **204** C-10; elev. 992ft./302m.; ★ **N.Y.**; mail Franklin **z** 07416; ● 250
Beaver Run; RMC Place; SUSSEX; ▲ Hardyston; ***204** C-9; ★ **N.Y.**; mail Hamburg **z** 07419; rural
Beckerville; RMC Place; OCEAN; ▲ Manchester; ★ **N.Y.**; mail Lakehurst **z** 08733; rural
Beckett; CDP-Census Area Only; GLOUCESTER; ▲ Logan; ***205** N-5; elev. 20ft./6m.; ★ **PHIL-**; mail Swedesboro **z** 08085; Ⓟ 3,815; © 4,726
Bedminster; RMC Place; SOMERSET; ▲ Bedminster; **204** F-9; 🅿; ★ **N.Y.**; **z** 07921; ● 3,000
Bedminster; MCD-Township; SOMERSET; ***204** F-9; 🅿; ★ **N.Y.**; **z** 07921; Ⓟ 7,086; © 8,302
Beemerville; RMC Place; SUSSEX; ▲ Wantage; ***204** B-9; ★ **N.Y.**; mail Sussex **z** 07461; ● 150
Beesleys Point; RMC Place; CAPE MAY; ▲ Upper; **205** Q-9; ★ **ATCY**; mail Marmora **z** 08223; ● 850
Belcher Creek; PASSAIC; see Crescent Park (RMC Place)
Belcoville; RMC Place; ATLANTIC; ▲ Weymouth; **205** P-9; ★ **ATCY**; mail Mays Landing **z** 08330; ● 200
Belford; CDP; MONMOUTH; ▲ Middletown; **204** H-13; 🅿; ★ **N.Y.**; **z** 07718; © 1,340
Belle Mead; RMC Place; SOMERSET; ▲ Montgomery, Hillsborough; **204** H-9; 🅿 🅷; ★ **N.Y.**; **z** 08502; ● 600
Belleplain; RMC Place; CAPE MAY; ▲ Dennis; **205** R-8; mail Woodbine **z** 08270; ● 600
Belleville; CDP; ESSEX; ▲ Belleville; **204** E-12; elev. 69ft./21m.; 🅿 🅷; ★ **N.Y.**; **z** 07109; Ⓟ 34,213; © 35,928; ◆ 34,514
Belleville; MCD-Township; ESSEX; ***204** E-12; 🅿 ■; ★ **N.Y.**; **z** 07109; Ⓟ 34,213; © 35,928; ◆ 34,514
Bellmawr; Inc. Place; CAMDEN; **205** M-6; elev. 44ft./13m.; 🅿; ★ **PHIL-**; **z** 08031, **z** 08099; Ⓟ 12,603; © 11,262
Bells Crossing; RMC Place; HUNTERDON; ***204** F-7; ★ **N.Y.**; mail Glen Gardner **z** 08826; pop. incl. with Glen Gardner (Inc. Place)
Bells Lake; RMC Place; GLOUCESTER; ▲ Washington; ***205** N-7; ★ **PHIL-**; mail Blackwood **z** 08012; ● 1,800
Bellview; RMC Place; BURLINGTON; ▲ Cinnaminson; ★ **PHIL-**; mail Riverton **z** 08077
Belmar; Inc. Place; MONMOUTH; **204** J-13; elev. 19ft./6m.; 🅿; ★ **N.Y.**; **z** 07715, **z** 07719; Ⓟ 5,877; © 6,045
Belvidere; Inc. Place; ⊡ WARREN; **204** E-7; elev. 257ft./78m.; 🅿; ★ **N.Y.**; **z** 07823; Ⓟ 2,669; © 2,771
Belwood Park; RMC Place; ESSEX; ***204** E-12; ★ **N.Y.**; mail Belleville **z** 07109
Bennetts Mill; RMC Place; CUMBERLAND
Bennetts Mills; RMC Place; OCEAN; ▲ Jackson; ***205** K-11; ★ **N.Y.**; mail Jackson **z** 08527; ● 250
Bergen; RMC Place; HUDSON; ***204** F-13; ★ **N.Y.**; mail Jersey City **z** 07304; pop. incl. with Jersey City (Inc. Place)
BERGEN; **204** C-12; Ⓟ 825,380; © 884,118; ◆ 879,389
Bergenfield; Inc. Place; BERGEN; **204** D-13; elev. 93ft./28m.; 🅿; ★ **N.Y.**; **z** 07621; Ⓟ 24,458; © 26,247; ◆ 26,011
Bergenline; RMC Place; HUDSON; ***204** F-13; ★ **N.Y.**; mail Union City **z** 07087; pop. incl. with Union City (Inc. Place)
Bergen Point; RMC Place; HUDSON; ***204** G-12; ★ **N.Y.**; mail Bayonne **z** 07002; pop. incl. with Bayonne (Inc. Place)
Berkeley; MCD-Township; OCEAN; ***205** M-12; ★ **N.Y.**; mail Bayville **z** 08721, Toms River **z** 08757; Ⓟ 37,319; © 39,991; ◆ 38,750
Berkeley Heights; CDP; UNION; ▲ Berkeley Heights; **204** F-10; 🅿 🅷; ★ **N.Y.**; **z** 07922; Ⓟ 11,980; © 13,407
Berkeley Heights; MCD-Township; UNION; ***204** F-10; 🅿; ★ **N.Y.**; **z** 07922; Ⓟ 11,980; © 13,407
Berkshire Valley; RMC Place; MORRIS; ▲ Roxbury; ***204** D-9; ★ **N.Y.**; mail Wharton **z** 07885; ● 400
Berlin; Inc. Place; CAMDEN; **205** M-7; elev. 155ft./47m.; 🅿 🅷; ★ **PHIL-**; **z** 08009; Ⓟ 5,672; © 6,149
Berlin; MCD-Township; CAMDEN; ***205** M-7; 🅿; ★ **PHIL-**; **z** 08009 & mail West Berlin **z** 08091; does not include the Borough of Berlin; Ⓟ 5,466; © 5,290
Berlin Estates; RMC Place; CAMDEN; ▲ Berlin; ***205** M-7; ★ **PHIL-**; mail Berlin **z** 08009; ● 500
Berlin Heights; RMC Place; CAMDEN; ★ **PHIL-**; mail Berlin **z** 08009; pop. incl. with Berlin (Inc. Place)
Bernards; MCD-Township; SOMERSET; ***204** F-10; ★ **N.Y.**; mail Basking Ridge **z** 07920; Ⓟ 17,199; © 24,575; ◆ 27,015
Bernardsville; Inc. Place; SOMERSET; **204** F-10; elev. 400ft./122m.; 🅿; ★ **N.Y.**; **z** 07924; Ⓟ 6,597; © 7,345
Berryland; RMC Place; GLOUCESTER; ▲ Monroe; ***205** O-8; ★ **PHIL-**; mail Williamstown **z** 08094; rural
Bertrand Island; RMC Place; MORRIS; ***204** D-9; ★ **N.Y.**; mail Mount Arlington **z** 07856; pop. incl. with Mount Arlington (Inc. Place)
Bethlehem; MCD-Township; HUNTERDON; ***204** F-7; ★ **N.Y.**; mail Asbury **z** 08802; Ⓟ 3,104; © 3,820
Beverly; Inc. Place; BURLINGTON; **205** K-7; elev. 28ft./9m.; 🅿; ★ **PHIL-**; **z** 08010; Ⓟ 2,973; © 2,661
Billingsport; RMC Place; GLOUCESTER; ***205** M-6; ★ **PHIL-**; mail Paulsboro **z** 08066; pop. incl. with Paulsboro (Inc. Place)
Birches; RMC Place; GLOUCESTER; ▲ Washington; ***205** N-7; ★ **PHIL-**; mail Blackwood **z** 08012; ● 2,100
Birches West; RMC Place; GLOUCESTER; ▲ Washington; ***205** N-7; ★ **PHIL-**; mail Pitman **z** 08071; ● 1,600
Birch Hills; RMC Place; MORRIS; ▲ Hanover; ***204** E-10; ★ **N.Y.**; mail Whippany **z** 07981; ● 750
Birchwood Lakes; RMC Place; BURLINGTON; ▲ Medford; ***205** M-8; ★ **PHIL-**; mail Medford **z** 08055; ● 500
Birchwood Park; RMC Place; OCEAN; ▲ Brick; ***205** K-12; ★ **N.Y.**; mail Brick **z** 08723
Birmingham; RMC Place; BURLINGTON; ▲ Pemberton; ***205** L-9; 🅿; ★ **PHIL-**; **z** 08011; ● 75
Bissell; RMC Place; HUNTERDON; mail Lebanon **z** 08833; ● 400
Bivalve; RMC Place; CUMBERLAND; ▲ Commercial; **205** R-7; ★ **VINL**; mail Port Norris **z** 08349; ● 50
Black Horse; RMC Place; MIDDLESEX; mail North Brunswick **z** 08902; ● 940
Blackwells Mills; RMC Place; SOMERSET; ▲ Franklin; ***204** H-10; elev. 50ft./15m.; ★ **N.Y.**; mail Somerset **z** 08873; rural
Blackwood; CDP; CAMDEN; ▲ Gloucester; **205** M-7; 🅿 🅷; ★ **PHIL-**; **z** 08012; Ⓟ 5,120; © 4,692
Blackwood Terrace; RMC Place; GLOUCESTER; ▲ Deptford; ***205** M-6; 🅿; ★ **PHIL-**; **z** 08096; ● 1,200
Blairstown; RMC Place; WARREN; ▲ Blairstown; **204** D-7; 🅿; ★ **N.Y.**; **z** 07825; ● 1,100
Blairstown; MCD-Township; WARREN; ***204** D-7; 🅿; ★ **N.Y.**; **z** 07825; Ⓟ 5,331; © 5,747
Blansingburg; RMC Place; MONMOUTH; ▲ Wall; ***205** K-13; ★ **N.Y.**; mail Sea Girt **z** 08750; ● 250
Blawenburg; RMC Place; SOMERSET; ▲ Montgomery; **204** I-9; elev. 156ft./48m.; 🅿; **z** 08504; ● 200
Blenheim; RMC Place; CAMDEN; ▲ Gloucester; ***205** M-7; ★ **PHIL-**; mail Blackwood **z** 08012; ● 1,100
Bloomfield; CDP; ESSEX; ▲ Bloomfield; **204** E-12; elev. 131ft./40m.; 🅿 🅲 2,084; ★ **N.Y.**; **z** 07003; Ⓟ 45,061; © 47,683; ◆ 44,969
Bloomfield; MCD-Township; ESSEX; ***204** E-12; 🅿 🅲 2,084 ■; ★ **N.Y.**; **z** 07003; Ⓟ 45,061; © 47,683; ◆ 44,969
Bloomingdale (Bloomingdale Riverdale); RMC Place; MORRIS; ★ **N.Y.**; mail Riverdale **z** 07457; pop. incl. with Riverdale (Inc. Place)
Bloomingdale; Inc. Place; PASSAIC; **204** D-11; elev. 257ft./78m.; 🅿; ★ **N.Y.**; **z** 07403; Ⓟ 7,530; © 7,610

Entries in **UPPERCASE** are counties.
Entries in **bold** have populations of 2,500 or more.
Names in parentheses are alternate names.

Inc. Place	Incorporated Place
RMC Place	Rand McNally Designated Place
CDP	Census Designated Place
MCD	Minor Civil Division
⊡	County Seat
▲	Minor Civil Division
elev.	Elevation
🅿	Post Office
🅷	Hospital
🅲	College
■	Principal Business Center
★	Ranally Metro Area (RMA) Abbreviation
z	Zip Code(s)
Ⓟ	Previous Census Population
Ⓡ	Revised Census Population
Ⓐ	Annexation Population
●	Rand McNally Population Estimate
©	Final Census Population
Ⓢ	Special Census Population
◆	Estimated Population

For additional definitions see Glossary, Volume 1, and Introduction, Volume 2.

Bloomingdale Riverdale; MORRIS; see Bloomingdale (RMC Place)
Bloomsbury; Inc. Place; HUNTERDON; **204** G-6; elev. 279ft./85m.; 🄿; ★ **ALL-**; z 08804; Ⓟ 890; © 886
Blue Anchor; RMC Place; CAMDEN; ▲ Winslow; **205** N-8; ★ **PHIL-**; mail Hammonton z 08037
Blue Bell; RMC Place; GLOUCESTER; ▲ Franklin; ***205** O-7; ★ **VINL**; mail Newfield z 08344
Bogota; Inc. Place; BERGEN; **204** A-5; elev. 100ft./30m.; 🄿; ★ **N.Y.**; z 07603; Ⓟ 7,824; © 8,249
Bon Air; RMC Place; CAMDEN; ▲ Pennsauken; ***205** L-7; ★ **PHIL-**; mail Pennsauken z 08110
Bonhamtown; RMC Place; MIDDLESEX; ▲ Edison; ***204** H-11; ★ **N.Y.**; mail Edison z 08817
Boonton; Inc. Place; MORRIS; **204** E-11; elev. 431ft./131m.; 🄿; ★ **N.Y.**; z 07005; Ⓟ 8,343; © 8,496
Boonton; MCD-Township; MORRIS; ***204** D-10; 🄿; ★ **N.Y.**; z 07005; does not include the Town of Boonton; Ⓟ 3,566; © 4,287
Bordentown; Inc. Place; BURLINGTON; **205** S-14; elev. 72ft./22m.; 🄿; ★ **PHIL-**; z 08505; Ⓟ 4,341; © 3,969
Bordentown; MCD-Township; BURLINGTON; ***205** K-9; 🄿; ★ **PHIL-**; z 08505; does not include the City of Bordentown; Ⓟ 7,683; © 8,380
Bossert Estates; RMC Place; BURLINGTON; ▲ Bordentown; ***205** K-9; ★ **PHIL-**; mail Bordentown z 08505; ● 1,900
Bound Brook; Inc. Place; SOMERSET; **204** G-10; elev. 48ft./15m.; 🄿; ★ **N.Y.**; z 08805; Ⓟ 9,487; © 10,155
Braddock; RMC Place; CAMDEN; ▲ Winslow; ***205** N-8; ★ **PHIL-**; mail Hammonton z 08037; ● 150
Bradevelt; RMC Place; MONMOUTH; **204** I-12; ★ **N.Y.**; mail Marlboro z 07746; ● 150
Bradley Beach; Inc. Place; MONMOUTH; **204** J-13; elev. 26ft./8m.; 🄿; ★ **N.Y.**; z 07720; Ⓟ 4,475; © 4,793
Bradley Gardens; RMC Place; SOMERSET; ▲ Bridgewater; ***204** G-9; ★ **N.Y.**; mail Bridgewater z 08807; ● 2,900
Bradley Park; RMC Place; MONMOUTH; ▲ Neptune; ***204** J-13; ★ **N.Y.**; mail Neptune z 07753
Brady Park; RMC Place; MORRIS; mail Lake Hopatcong z 07849; ● 165
Braeburn Heights; RMC Place; MERCER; ▲ Ewing; ***204** J-8; ★ **PHIL-**; mail Trenton z 08638
Brainards; RMC Place; WARREN; ▲ Harmony; **204** F-6; ★ **ALL-**; mail Phillipsburg z 08865; ● 150
Brainy Boro; RMC Place; MIDDLESEX; ***204** G-11; ★ **N.Y.**; mail Metuchen z 08840; pop. incl. with Metuchen (Inc. Place)
Branchburg; MCD-Township; SOMERSET; ***204** G-9; 🄿; ★ **N.Y.**; z 08853, z 08876; Ⓟ 10,888; © 14,566
Branchville; Inc. Place; SUSSEX; **204** C-9; elev. 529ft./161m.; 🄿; ★ **N.Y.**; z 07826-27, z 07890; Ⓟ 851; © 845
Brant Beach; RMC Place; OCEAN; ▲ Long Beach; **205** O-12; ★ **N.Y.**; mail Beach Haven z 08008; summer pop. 2,500; ● 300
Brass Castle; CDP; WARREN; ▲ Washington; **204** F-7; ★ **N.Y.**; mail Washington z 07882; Ⓟ 1,419; © 1,507
Brenton Woods; OCEAN; see Breton Woods (RMC Place)
Breton Woods (Brenton Woods); RMC Place; OCEAN; ▲ Brick; **205** K-12; ★ **N.Y.**; mail Brick z 08723
Brick; OCEAN; see Laurelton (RMC Place)
Brick; MCD-Township; OCEAN; ***205** K-12; 🄿 ■; ★ **N.Y.**; z 08723-24; Ⓟ 66,473; © 76,119; ◆ 77,430
Brick Church; RMC Place; ESSEX; ***204** F-12; ★ **N.Y.**; mail East Orange z 07018; pop. incl. with East Orange (Inc. Place)
Bricksboro; RMC Place; CUMBERLAND; ▲ Maurice River; **205** Q-7; elev. 5ft./2m.; mail Millville z 08332; ● 40
Bridgeboro; RMC Place; BURLINGTON; ▲ Delran; **205** K-7; ★ **PHIL-**; mail Riverside z 08075
Bridgepoint; RMC Place; SOMERSET; ▲ Montgomery; ***204** H-9; ★ **N.Y.**; mail Belle Mead z 08502; rural
Bridgeport; RMC Place; GLOUCESTER; ▲ Logan; **205** M-5; 🄿; ★ **PHIL-**; z 08014; ● 700
Bridgeton; Inc. Place; ⊡ CUMBERLAND; **205** M-1; elev. 40ft./12m.; 🄿 🄷; ★ **VINL**; z 08302; Ⓟ 18,942; © 22,771; ◆ 24,989
Bridgeton Junction; RMC Place; CUMBERLAND; ***205** P-6; ★ **VINL**; mail Bridgeton z 08302; pop. incl. with Bridgeton (Inc. Place)
Bridgeville; RMC Place; WARREN; ▲ White; **204** E-7; ★ **N.Y.**; mail Belvidere z 07823; ● 250
Bridgewater; RMC Place; SOMERSET; ▲ Bridgewater; **204** G-9; 🄿; ★ **N.Y.**; z 08807; ● 7,000
Bridgewater (Bridgewater Township); MCD-Township; SOMERSET; ***204** G-9; 🄿 ■; ★ **N.Y.**; z 08807; Ⓟ 32,509; © 42,940; ◆ 46,060
Bridgewater Township; SOMERSET; see Bridgewater (MCD-Township)
Brielle; Inc. Place; MONMOUTH; **205** K-13; elev. 12ft./4m.; 🄿; ★ **N.Y.**; z 08730; Ⓟ 4,406; © 4,893
Brigantine; Inc. Place; ATLANTIC; **204** H-4; elev. 8ft./2m.; 🄿; ★ **ATCY**; z 08203; Ⓟ 11,354; © 12,594
Brighton Beach; RMC Place; OCEAN; ▲ Long Beach; ***205** O-12; ★ **N.Y.**; mail Beach Haven z 08008; summer pop. 1,000; ● 150
Brills; RMC Place; ESSEX; ***204** F-12; ★ **N.Y.**; pop. incl. with Newark (Inc. Place)
Broad Lane; RMC Place; GLOUCESTER; ***205** N-7; elev. 110ft./34m.; ★ **PHIL-**; mail Williamstown z 08094
Broadway; RMC Place; WARREN; ▲ Franklin; **204** F-7; 🄿; ★ **N.Y.**; z 08808; ● 300
Brookdale; RMC Place; ESSEX; ▲ Bloomfield; ***204** E-12; ★ **N.Y.**; mail Bloomfield z 07003
Brookfield; RMC Place; CAMDEN; ▲ Cherry Hill; ***205** M-7; ★ **PHIL-**; mail Cherry Hill z 08034
Brooklawn; Inc. Place; CAMDEN; **228** G-5; elev. 24ft./7m.; 🄿; ★ **PHIL-**; z 08030; Ⓟ 1,805; © 2,354
Brookside; RMC Place; MORRIS; ▲ Mendham; **204** E-10; 🄿; ★ **N.Y.**; z 07926; ● 1,800
Brook Tree; RMC Place; MERCER; ▲ East Windsor; ***204** J-10; elev. 100ft./30m.; ★ **N.Y.**; mail Hightstown z 08520
Brook Valley; RMC Place; MORRIS; ***204** D-11; ★ **N.Y.**; mail Butler z 07405; pop. incl. with Kinnelon (Inc. Place)
Brookview; RMC Place; MIDDLESEX; ***204** H-10; elev. 99ft./30m.; ★ **N.Y.**; mail East Brunswick z 08816
Brookville; RMC Place; HUNTERDON; ▲ Delaware; ***204** I-7; elev. 100ft./30m.; mail Stockton z 08559; ● 25
Brookville; RMC Place; OCEAN; ▲ Ocean, Barnegat; **205** M-11; elev. 137ft./42m.; ★ **N.Y.**; mail Barnegat z 08005
Brookwood; RMC Place; OCEAN; ▲ Jackson; **205** K-11; ★ **N.Y.**; mail Jackson z 08527; ● 4,000
Brotmanville; RMC Place; SALEM; ▲ Pittsgrove; **205** K-3; ★ **VINL**; mail Bridgeton z 08302; ● 150
Browns; RMC Place; PASSAIC; mail Hewitt z 07421; ● 350
Browns Mills; CDP; BURLINGTON; ▲ Pemberton; **205** L-10; 🄿 🄷; ★ **PHIL-**; z 08015; Ⓟ 11,429; © 11,257
Browntown; RMC Place; MIDDLESEX; ▲ Old Bridge; **204** I-11; elev. 62ft./19m.; ★ **N.Y.**; mail Old Bridge z 08857; ● 2,400
Brownville; CDP-Census Area Only; MIDDLESEX; ***204** I-11; ★ **N.Y.**; © 2,660
Brunswick Acres; RMC Place; MIDDLESEX; ▲ South Brunswick; ***204** H-10; ★ **N.Y.**; mail Monmouth Junction z 08852; ● 2,600
Brunswick Gardens; RMC Place; MIDDLESEX; ▲ Old Bridge; ***204** I-11; ★ **N.Y.**; mail Old Bridge z 08857
Brush Hollow; RMC Place; BURLINGTON; ▲ Evesham; ***205** M-8; ★ **PHIL-**; mail Medford z 08055; ● 2,000
Buckingham; RMC Place; OCEAN; ▲ Manchester; ***205** L-10; ★ **N.Y.**; mail Manchester Township z 08759; rural
Buckshutem; RMC Place; CUMBERLAND; ▲ Commercial; **205** Q-7; ★ **VINL**; mail Millville z 08332; ● 100
Budd Lake; CDP; MORRIS; ▲ Mount Olive; **204** E-9; 🄿; ★ **N.Y.**; z 07828; Ⓟ 7,272; © 8,100
Buddtown; RMC Place; BURLINGTON; ▲ Southampton; **205** L-9; ★ **PHIL-**; mail Vincentown z 08088; ● 70
Buena; Inc. Place; ATLANTIC; **205** P-7; elev. 108ft./33m.; 🄿; ★ **VINL**; z 08310; Ⓟ 4,441; © 3,873
Buena Vista; MCD-Township; ATLANTIC; ***205** O-8; ★ **VINL**; mail Buena z 08310; Ⓟ 7,655; © 7,436
Bulltown; RMC Place; BURLINGTON; ▲ Washington; ***205** O-9; mail Egg Harbor City z 08215; rural
Bunker Hill; RMC Place; GLOUCESTER; ▲ Washington; ***205** N-6; ★ **PHIL-**; mail Sewell z 08080; rural
Bunnvale; RMC Place; HUNTERDON; ▲ Lebanon; **204** F-8; ★ **N.Y.**; mail Califon z 07830; ● 400
Burleigh; RMC Place; CAPE MAY; ▲ Middle; **205** S-2; mail Cape May Court House z 08210; ● 700
Burlington (Burlington City); Inc. Place; BURLINGTON; **205** K-8; elev. 12ft./4m.; 🄿 ■; ★ **PHIL-**; z 08016; Ⓟ 9,835; © 9,736; ◆ 9,646
Burlington (Burlington Township); MCD-Township; BURLINGTON; ***205** K-8; 🄿; ★ **PHIL-**; z 08016; does not include the City of Burlington; Ⓟ 12,454; © 20,294; ◆ 23,032
BURLINGTON; **205** M-9; Ⓟ 395,066; © 423,394; Ⓡ 423,391; ◆ 439,225
Burlington City; BURLINGTON; see Burlington (Inc. Place)
Burlington Heights; RMC Place; MONMOUTH; mail Freehold z 07728; ● 600
Burlington Township; BURLINGTON; see Burlington (MCD-Township)
Burnt Mills; RMC Place; SOMERSET; ▲ Bedminster; ***204** G-9; elev. 100ft./30m.; ★ **N.Y.**; mail Bedminster z 07921, Pluckemin z 07978; rural
Bustleton; RMC Place; BURLINGTON; ▲ Florence; ***205** K-8; ★ **PHIL-**; mail Burlington z 08016
Butler; Inc. Place; MORRIS; **204** D-11; elev. 315ft./96m.; 🄿; ★ **N.Y.**; z 07405; Ⓟ 7,392; © 7,420
Butler Park; RMC Place; WARREN; ▲ Washington; ***204** F-7; ★ **N.Y.**; mail Washington z 07882; ● 180
Butlers Park; RMC Place; HUNTERDON; ▲ Lebanon; ***204** F-7; ★ **N.Y.**; mail Washington z 07882; rural
Butterworth Farms; RMC Place; MORRIS; ▲ Morris; ***204** E-10; ★ **N.Y.**; mail Dover z 07801; ● 2,100
Buttzville; RMC Place; WARREN; ▲ White; **204** E-7; 🄿; ★ **N.Y.**; z 07829; ● 300
Byram; RMC Place; HUNTERDON; ▲ Kingwood; **204** H-7; mail Stockton z 08559; rural
Byram; MCD-Township; SUSSEX; ***204** D-9; ★ **N.Y.**; mail Andover z 07821; Ⓟ 8,048; © 8,254; Ⓡ 8,321
Byram Cove; RMC Place; SUSSEX; ***204** D-9; ★ **N.Y.**; mail Hopatcong z 07843; pop. incl. with Hopatcong (Inc. Place)

C

Caldwell; Inc. Place; ESSEX; **204** E-11; elev. 411ft./125m.; 🄿 🄲 2,291; ★ **N.Y.**; z 07006-07; Ⓟ 7,549; © 7,584
Califon; Inc. Place; HUNTERDON; **204** F-8; elev. 471ft./144m.; 🄿; ★ **N.Y.**; z 07830; Ⓟ 1,073; © 1,055
Cambridge; RMC Place; BURLINGTON; ▲ Delran; ***205** K-7; ★ **PHIL-**; mail Riverside z 08075
Cambridge Park; RMC Place; BURLINGTON; ▲ Evesham; ***205** M-8; elev. 80ft./24m.; ★ **PHIL-**; mail Marlton z 08053; ● 2,200
Camden; Inc. Place; ⊡ CAMDEN; **205** L-6; elev. 23ft./7m.; 🄿 🄷 🄲 5,165 ■; ★ **PHIL-**; z 08101-05 & mail Audubon z 08106, Collingswood z 08108, Merchantville z 08109, Oaklyn z 08107, Pennsauken z 08110; Ⓟ 87,492; © 79,904; ◆ 78,384
CAMDEN; **205** N-8; Ⓟ 502,824; © 508,932; ◆ 507,316
Camp Columbus; RMC Place; OCEAN; mail Forked River z 08731; ● 75
Campgaw; RMC Place; BERGEN; ***204** D-12; ★ **N.Y.**; pop. incl. with Franklin Lakes (Inc. Place)
Candlewood; RMC Place; MONMOUTH; ▲ Howell; **205** K-12; ★ **N.Y.**; mail Howell z 07731; ● 4,000
Canterbury at Piscataway; RMC Place; MIDDLESEX; ▲ Piscataway; ★ **N.Y.**; mail Piscataway z 08854
Canton; RMC Place; SALEM; ▲ Lower Alloways Creek; **205** P-4; mail Salem z 08079; ● 350
Cape May; Inc. Place; CAPE MAY; **205** T-1; elev. 14ft./4m.; 🄿; z 08204; Ⓟ 4,668; © 4,034
CAPE MAY; **205** R-8; Ⓟ 95,089; © 102,326; ◆ 93,841
Cape May Court House; CDP; ⊡ CAPE MAY; ▲ Middle; **205** R-2; elev. 19ft./6m.; 🄿 🄷; z 08210; Ⓟ 4,426; © 4,704
Cape May Point; Inc. Place; CAPE MAY; **205** T-1; elev. 9ft./3m.; 🄿; z 08212; Ⓟ 248; © 241
Capitol Hill; RMC Place; BURLINGTON; ▲ Edgewater Park; ***205** K-8; ★ **PHIL-**; mail Beverly z 08010; ● 2,500
Cardiff; RMC Place; ATLANTIC; ▲ Egg Harbor; **205** P-10; ★ **ATCY**; mail Egg Harbor Township z 08234, Pleasantville z 08232; ● 400
Carlls Corner; RMC Place; CUMBERLAND; ▲ Upper Deerfield; **205** L-1; elev. 108ft./33m.; ★ **VINL**; mail Bridgeton z 08302; ● 900
Carlstadt; Inc. Place; BERGEN; **204** B-4; elev. 94ft./29m.; 🄿; ★ **N.Y.**; z 07072; Ⓟ 5,510; © 5,917
Carlton Hill; RMC Place; BERGEN; **210** E-8; ★ **N.Y.**; mail East Rutherford z 07073; pop. incl. with East Rutherford (Inc. Place)
Carmel; RMC Place; CUMBERLAND; ▲ Deerfield; **205** L-2; ★ **VINL**; mail Millville z 08332; ● 150
Carmerville; RMC Place; MONMOUTH; ▲ Wall; ***204** J-12; ★ **N.Y.**; mail Belmar z 07719; ● 200
Carneys Point; CDP; SALEM; ▲ Carneys Point; **205** N-4; 🄿; ★ **PHIL-**; z 08069; Ⓟ 7,686; © 6,914
Carneys Point; MCD-Township; SALEM; ***205** N-4; 🄿; ★ **PHIL-**; z 08069; Ⓟ 8,443; © 7,684
Carpenterville; RMC Place; WARREN; ▲ Pohatcong; **204** G-6; ★ **ALL-**; mail Phillipsburg z 08865; ● 90
Carriage Pointe; RMC Place; MIDDLESEX; ▲ Piscataway; ***204** H-10; ★ **N.Y.**; mail Piscataway z 08854
Carteret; Inc. Place; MIDDLESEX; **204** G-12; elev. 12ft./4m.; 🄿; ★ **N.Y.**; z 07008; Ⓟ 19,025; © 20,709; Ⓡ 20,705; ◆ 22,198
Cassville (Jackson); RMC Place; OCEAN; ***205** K-11; ★ **N.Y.**; mail Jackson z 08527; ● 800
Castle Point; RMC Place; HUDSON; ***204** F-13; ★ **N.Y.**; mail Hoboken z 07030; pop. incl. with Hoboken (Inc. Place)
Caven Point; RMC Place; HUDSON; ***204** F-13; ★ **N.Y.**; pop. incl. with Jersey City (Inc. Place)
Cecil; RMC Place; GLOUCESTER; ▲ Monroe; **205** O-7; ★ **PHIL-**; mail Williamstown z 08094
Cedar Beach; RMC Place; OCEAN; ▲ Berkeley; ***205** M-12; ★ **N.Y.**; mail Bayville z 08721, Port Monmouth z 07758; ● 250
Cedar Bonnet Island; RMC Place; OCEAN; ▲ Stafford; ***205** N-12; ★ **N.Y.**; mail Manahawkin z 08050; ● 30
Cedar Bridge; RMC Place; OCEAN; mail Brick z 08723; ● 570
Cedar Bridge Manor; RMC Place; OCEAN; ▲ Brick; ***205** K-12; ★ **N.Y.**; mail Brick z 08723
Cedar Brook; RMC Place; CAMDEN; ▲ Winslow; **205** N-8; 🄿; ★ **PHIL-**; z 08018; ● 800
Cedar Crest Manor; RMC Place; SALEM; ▲ Carneys Point; **205** N-4; elev. 18ft./5m.; ★ **PHIL-**; mail Penns Grove z 08069; ● 150
Cedar Glen Homes East; RMC Place; OCEAN; ▲ Manchester; ***205** L-12; elev. 80ft./24m.; ★ **N.Y.**; mail Toms River z 08757; ● 600
Cedar Glen Lakes; CDP-Census Area Only; OCEAN; ▲ Manchester; ***205** L-11; ★ **N.Y.**; mail Manchester Township z 08759; Ⓟ 1,611; © 1,617
Cedar Glen West; CDP; OCEAN; ▲ Manchester; ***205** K-11; elev. 100ft./30m.; ★ **N.Y.**; mail Lakehurst z 08733; Ⓟ 1,396; © 1,376
Cedar Grove; RMC Place; CAPE MAY; ▲ Dennis; ***205** R-8; elev. 24ft./7m.; mail Cape May Court House z 08210
Cedar Grove; CDP; ESSEX; ▲ Cedar Grove; **204** E-12; 🄿 🄷; ★ **N.Y.**; z 07009; Ⓟ 12,053; © 12,300
Cedar Grove; MCD-Township; ESSEX; ***204** E-12; 🄿; ★ **N.Y.**; z 07009; Ⓟ 12,053; © 12,300
Cedar Grove; RMC Place; GLOUCESTER; ▲ South Harrison; ***205** N-6; ★ **PHIL-**; mail Mullica Hill z 08062; rural
Cedar Grove; RMC Place; OCEAN; ▲ Toms River; ***205** L-12; ★ **N.Y.**; mail Toms River z 08753; ● 200
Cedar Heights; RMC Place; HUNTERDON; ▲ Clinton; ***204** G-8; ★ **N.Y.**; mail Annandale z 08801; ● 200
Cedar Knolls; RMC Place; MORRIS; ▲ Hanover; **204** E-10; 🄿; ★ **N.Y.**; z 07927
Cedar Lake; RMC Place; MORRIS; ▲ Denville; ***204** E-10; ★ **N.Y.**; mail Denville z 07834
Cedar Run; RMC Place; OCEAN; ▲ Stafford; **205** N-11; ★ **N.Y.**; mail West Creek z 08092; ● 400
Cedarville; CDP; CUMBERLAND; ▲ Lawrence; **205** Q-6; 🄿; z 08311; © 793
Cedarville; RMC Place; SALEM; ▲ Pilesgrove; ***205** O-5; elev. 61ft./19m.; mail Woodstown z 08098; rural
Cedarwood Park; RMC Place; OCEAN; ▲ Brick; ***205** K-12; ★ **N.Y.**; mail Brick z 08723
Centennial Lake; RMC Place; BURLINGTON; ▲ Medford; ***205** M-8; ★ **PHIL-**; mail Marlton z 08053; ● 500
Center Grove; CUMBERLAND; see Centre Grove (RMC Place)
Center Square; RMC Place; GLOUCESTER; ▲ Logan; **205** N-5; elev. 22ft./7m.; ★ **PHIL-**; mail Swedesboro z 08085; ● 150
Centerton; RMC Place; BURLINGTON; ▲ Mount Laurel; ***205** L-8; ★ **PHIL-**; mail Mount Laurel z 08054; ● 30
Centerton; RMC Place; SALEM; ▲ Pittsgrove; **205** O-6; ★ **VINL**; mail Elmer z 08318; ● 150
Centerville; RMC Place; HUNTERDON, SOMERSET; ▲ Readington, Branchburg; **204** G-8; elev. 180ft./55m.; ★ **N.Y.**; mail Neshanic Station z 08853; ● 150
Centerville; RMC Place; MERCER; ▲ Hopewell; ***204** I-8; elev. 200ft./61m.; ★ **PHIL-**; mail Pennington z 08534; rural
Central; RMC Place; ESSEX; ***204** F-12; ★ **N.Y.**; mail East Orange z 07018; pop. incl. with East Orange (Inc. Place)
Central Park; RMC Place; SALEM; ▲ Pennsville; ***205** N-4; ★ **PHIL-**; mail Pennsville z 08070
Centre City; RMC Place; GLOUCESTER; ▲ Mantua; **205** M-6; ★ **PHIL-**; mail Mantua z 08051; ● 1,800
Centre Grove (Center Grove); RMC Place; CUMBERLAND; ▲ Lawrence; **205** Q-6; mail Millville z 08332
Ceramics; RMC Place; MIDDLESEX; ▲ Edison; ★ **N.Y.**
Chadwick; RMC Place; OCEAN; mail Lavallette z 08735; ● 250
Chadwick Beach; RMC Place; OCEAN; ▲ Toms River; ***205** L-13; ★ **N.Y.**; mail Lavallette z 08735; ● 1,200
Chairville; RMC Place; BURLINGTON; ▲ Medford; ***205** M-8; ★ **PHIL-**; mail Medford z 08055
Chambersburg; RMC Place; MERCER; ***204** J-9; ★ **PHIL-**; mail Trenton z 08611; pop. incl. with Trenton (Inc. Place)
Chambers Corners; RMC Place; BURLINGTON; ▲ Springfield; **205** L-9; ★ **PHIL-**; mail Mount Holly z 08060
Changewater; RMC Place; WARREN, HUNTERDON; ▲ Lebanon, Washington; **204** F-7; 🄿; ★ **N.Y.**; z 07831; ● 250
Chapel Heights; RMC Place; GLOUCESTER; ▲ Washington; ***205** N-6; ★ **PHIL-**; mail Sewell z 08080; rural
Charleston; RMC Place; BURLINGTON; ▲ Willingboro; ***205** K-7; ★ **PHIL-**; mail Willingboro z 08046
Charlotteburg; RMC Place; PASSAIC; ▲ West Milford; ***204** D-10; ★ **N.Y.**; mail Newfoundland z 07435; rural
Chatham; Inc. Place; MORRIS; **204** F-11; elev. 244ft./74m.; 🄿; ★ **N.Y.**; z 07928; Ⓟ 8,007; © 8,460
Chatham; MCD-Township; MORRIS; ***204** F-10; 🄿; ★ **N.Y.**; z 07928; does not include the Borough of Chatham; Ⓟ 9,361; © 10,086
Chatsworth; RMC Place; BURLINGTON; ▲ Woodland; **205** M-10; 🄿; z 08019; ● 500
Cheesequake; RMC Place; MIDDLESEX; ▲ Old Bridge; **204** H-11; ★ **N.Y.**; mail Old Bridge z 08857; ● 300
Chelsea Heights; RMC Place; ATLANTIC; ***205** Q-10; ★ **ATCY**; mail Atlantic City z 08401; pop. incl. with Atlantic City (Inc. Place)
Cherry Hill; RMC Place; CAMDEN; ▲ Cherry Hill; **205** L-7; 🄿 🄷; ★ **PHIL-**; z 08002-03, z 08034; Ⓟ 69,319; ● 2,100
Cherry Hill; MCD-Township; CAMDEN; ***205** L-7; 🄿 ■; ★ **PHIL-**; z 08002-03, z 08034; Ⓟ 69,319; © 69,965; ◆ 69,819
Cherry Hill Estates; RMC Place; CAMDEN; ▲ Cherry Hill; ***205** L-7; ★ **PHIL-**; mail Cherry Hill z 08002
Cherry Hill Mall; CDP-Census Area Only; CAMDEN; ***205** L-7; ★ **PHIL-**; mail Cherry Hill z 08002; © 13,238
Cherry Quay; RMC Place; OCEAN; ▲ Brick; ***205** L-12; ★ **N.Y.**; mail Brick z 08723
Cherryville; RMC Place; HUNTERDON; ▲ Franklin; **204** G-8; ★ **N.Y.**; mail Flemington z 08822; ● 50
Cherrywood; RMC Place; CAMDEN; ▲ Gloucester; ***205** M-7; ★ **PHIL-**; mail Blackwood z 08012; ● 1,600
Chesilhurst; Inc. Place; CAMDEN; **205** N-8; elev. 158ft./48m.; 🄿; ★ **PHIL-**; z 08089; Ⓟ 1,526; © 1,520
Chester; Inc. Place; MORRIS; **204** F-9; elev. 846ft./258m.; 🄿; ★ **N.Y.**; z 07930; Ⓟ 1,214; © 1,635
Chester; MCD-Township; MORRIS; ***204** F-9; 🄿; ★ **N.Y.**; z 07930; does not include the Borough of Chester; Ⓟ 5,958; © 7,282
Chesterfield; RMC Place; BURLINGTON; ▲ Chesterfield; **205** K-9; 🄿; ★ **PHIL-**; z 08515 & mail Bordentown z 08505, Trenton z 08650; ● 200
Chesterfield; MCD-Township; BURLINGTON; ***205** K-9; 🄿; ★ **PHIL-**; z 08515 & mail Bordentown z 08505, Trenton z 08650; Ⓟ 5,152; © 5,955
Chestnut; RMC Place; UNION; ▲ Union; ***204** F-11; ★ **N.Y.**; mail Union z 07083
Chewalla Park; RMC Place; MERCER; ▲ Hamilton; ***204** J-9; ★ **PHIL-**; mail Trenton z 08619
Chews Landing; RMC Place; CAMDEN; ▲ Gloucester; ***205** M-7; ★ **PHIL-**; mail Blackwood z 08012
Chrome; RMC Place; MIDDLESEX; **210** L-5; ★ **N.Y.**; mail Carteret z 07008; pop. incl. with Carteret (Inc. Place)
Churchtown; RMC Place; SALEM; ▲ Pennsville; ***205** N-4; ★ **PHIL-**; mail Pennsville z 08070; ● 200
Cinnaminson; RMC Place; BURLINGTON; ▲ Cinnaminson; **205** L-7; 🄿; ★ **PHIL-**; z 08077; Ⓟ 14,583
Cinnaminson; MCD-Township; BURLINGTON; ***205** L-7; 🄿; ★ **PHIL-**; z 08077; Ⓟ 14,583; © 14,595
City of Orange (Orange); MCD-Township; ESSEX; ***204** F-12; ■; ★ **N.Y.**; mail Orange z 07050-51; Ⓟ 29,925; © 32,868; ◆ 31,723
Clara Barton; RMC Place; MIDDLESEX; mail Edison z 08837; ● 565
Clark; CDP; UNION; ▲ Clark; **204** G-11; 🄿; ★ **N.Y.**; z 07066; Ⓟ 14,629; © 14,597
Clark; MCD-Township; UNION; ***204** G-11; 🄿; ★ **N.Y.**; z 07066; Ⓟ 14,629; © 14,597
Clarksboro; RMC Place; GLOUCESTER; ▲ East Greenwich; **205** M-6; elev. 56ft./17m.; 🄿; ★ **PHIL-**; z 08020; ● 1,700
Clarksburg; RMC Place; MONMOUTH; ▲ Millstone; **204** J-10; 🄿; ★ **PHIL-**; z 08510; ● 400
Clarks Landing; RMC Place; OCEAN; ***205** K-13; ★ **N.Y.**; mail Point Pleasant Beach z 08742; pop. incl. with Point Pleasant (Inc. Place)
Clarkstown; RMC Place; ATLANTIC; ▲ Hamilton; **205** P-9; ★ **ATCY**; mail Mays Landing z 08330; ● 200
Clayton; Inc. Place; GLOUCESTER; **205** N-6; elev. 130ft./40m.; 🄿; ★ **PHIL-**; z 08312; Ⓟ 6,155; © 7,139
Claytons Corner; RMC Place; MONMOUTH; ▲ Marlboro; ***204** I-11; elev. 120ft./37m.; ★ **N.Y.**; mail Marlboro z 07746, Morganville z 07751; ● 3,000
Clayville; RMC Place; CUMBERLAND; ★ **VINL**; mail Vineland z 08360; pop. incl. with Vineland (Inc. Place)
Clearbrook Park; CDP-Census Area Only; MIDDLESEX; ▲ Monroe; ***204** I-10; elev. 120ft./37m.; ★ **N.Y.**; mail Cranbury z 08512; Ⓟ 2,853; © 3,053
Clear View Lake; RMC Place; SUSSEX; ▲ Hampton; ***204** C-8; ★ **N.Y.**; mail Newton z 07860; ● 200
Clearwater; RMC Place; SUSSEX; ▲ Andover; ***204** D-9; ★ **N.Y.**; mail Sparta z 07871; ● 150
Clementon; Inc. Place; CAMDEN; **205** M-7; elev. 57ft./17m.; 🄿; ★ **PHIL-**; z 08021; Ⓟ 5,601; © 4,986
Clermont; RMC Place; BURLINGTON; ▲ Hainesport; ***205** L-8; ★ **PHIL-**; mail Mount Holly z 08060; ● 300
Clermont; RMC Place; CAPE MAY; ▲ Dennis; **205** R-8; mail Cape May Court House z 08210; ● 100
Cliff Park; RMC Place; BERGEN; ***204** E-13; ★ **N.Y.**; mail Cliffside Park z 07010; pop. incl. with Cliffside Park (Inc. Place)
Cliffside Park; Inc. Place; BERGEN; **204** E-13; elev. 300ft./91m.; 🄿; ★ **N.Y.**; z 07010; Ⓟ 20,393; © 23,007; ◆ 23,187
Cliffwood; RMC Place; MONMOUTH; ▲ Aberdeen; **204** H-12; 🄿; ★ **N.Y.**; z 07721; ● 1,500
Cliffwood Beach; CDP; MONMOUTH; ▲ Aberdeen; **204** H-12; ★ **N.Y.**; mail Keyport z 07735; Ⓟ 3,543; © 3,538
Cliffwood Lake; RMC Place; SUSSEX; ▲ Hardyston; ***204** C-10; ★ **N.Y.**; mail Stockholm z 07460; ● 550
Clifton; Inc. Place; PASSAIC; **204** E-12; elev. 70ft./21m.; 🄿 ■; ★ **N.Y.**; z 07011-15; Ⓟ 71,742; © 78,672; Ⓡ 79,062; ◆ 79,098
Clinton; RMC Place; ESSEX; ▲ Fairfield; ***204** E-11; ★ **N.Y.**; mail Fairfield z 07004
Clinton; Inc. Place; HUNTERDON; **204** G-8; elev. 195ft./59m.; 🄿; ★ **N.Y.**; z 08809; Ⓟ 2,054; © 2,632
Clinton; MCD-Township; HUNTERDON; ***204** G-8; 🄿; ★ **N.Y.**; z 08809 & mail Annandale z 08801; does not include the Town of Clinton; Ⓟ 10,816; © 12,957
Clinton Hill; RMC Place; ESSEX; ***204** F-12; ★ **N.Y.**; mail Newark z 07108; pop. incl. with Newark (Inc. Place)
Closter; Inc. Place; BERGEN; **204** D-13; elev. 51ft./16m.; 🄿; ★ **N.Y.**; z 07624; Ⓟ 8,094; © 8,383
Cloverhill; RMC Place; HUNTERDON, SOMERSET; ▲ Hillsborough, Raritan; ***204** H-8; ★ **N.Y.**; mail Flemington z 08822, Hillsborough z 08844; ● 150
Clover Hill; RMC Place; MONMOUTH; ▲ Holmdel; ***204** I-12; ★ **N.Y.**; mail Holmdel z 07733; ● 600
Cloverhill; RMC Place; SOMERSET; mail Flemington z 08822; ● 600
Clover Leaf Lakes; RMC Place; ATLANTIC; ▲ Hamilton; **205** P-9; ★ **ATCY**; mail Mays Landing z 08330; ● 900
Cobbs Corner; RMC Place; MORRIS; ▲ Parsippany-Troy Hills; ***204** E-11; ★ **N.Y.**; mail Parsippany z 07054
Cohansey; RMC Place; CUMBERLAND, SALEM; ▲ Alloway, Hopewell, Stow Creek; **205** P-5; ★ **VINL**; mail Bridgeton z 08302; ● 50
Cokesbury; RMC Place; HUNTERDON; ▲ Tewksbury, Clinton; **204** F-8; ★ **N.Y.**; mail Lebanon z 08833; ● 150
Cold Indian Springs; RMC Place; MONMOUTH; ▲ Ocean; ***204** J-13; ★ **N.Y.**; mail Asbury Park z 07712; ● 900
Cold Spring; RMC Place; CAPE MAY; ▲ Lower; **205** T-1; mail Cape May z 08204; ● 600
Colemans Hollow; RMC Place; MORRIS; ▲ Randolph; ***204** E-9; ★ **N.Y.**; mail Mount Freedom z 07970; rural
Colesville; RMC Place; SUSSEX; ▲ Wantage; **204** B-9; ★ **N.Y.**; mail Sussex z 07461; ● 120
Collings Lakes; CDP; ATLANTIC; ▲ Buena Vista; ***205** O-8; ★ **VINL**; mail Williamstown z 08094; Ⓟ 2,046; © 1,726
Collingswood; Inc. Place; CAMDEN; **205** L-7; elev. 20ft./6m.; 🄿; ★ **PHIL-**; z 08107-08; Ⓟ 15,289; © 14,326
Collingwood Park; RMC Place; MONMOUTH; ▲ Wall; **204** J-12; ★ **N.Y.**; mail Farmingdale z 07727; ● 200
Collinsville; RMC Place; MORRIS; ▲ Morris; ***204** E-10; ★ **N.Y.**; mail Morristown z 07960; pop. incl. with Morristown (Inc. Place)
Cologne; RMC Place; ATLANTIC; ▲ Galloway; **205** P-9; 🄿; ★ **ATCY**; z 08213; ● 1,100
Colonia; CDP; MIDDLESEX; ▲ Woodbridge; **204** G-11; 🄿; ★ **N.Y.**; z 07067; Ⓟ 18,238; © 17,811
Colonial Arms; RMC Place; OCEAN; ▲ Jackson; ***205** K-11; elev. 100ft./30m.; ★ **N.Y.**; mail Jackson z 08527; ● 75
Colonial Manor; RMC Place; GLOUCESTER; ▲ West Deptford; **228** G-4; ★ **PHIL-**; mail Woodbury z 08096; ● 2,000
Colonial Park; RMC Place; MERCER; ▲ West Windsor; ***204** I-9; ★ **N.Y.**; mail Princeton Junction z 08550; ● 900
Colonial Terrace; RMC Place; MONMOUTH; ▲ Ocean; ***204** J-13; ★ **N.Y.**; mail Asbury Park z 07712
Colts Neck; RMC Place; MONMOUTH; ▲ Colts Neck; **204** I-12; 🄿; ★ **N.Y.**; z 07722; ● 800
Colts Neck; MCD-Township; MONMOUTH; ***204** I-12; 🄿; ★ **N.Y.**; z 07722; Ⓟ 8,559; © 12,331; Ⓡ 11,179
Columbia; RMC Place; WARREN; ▲ Knowlton; **204** D-6; 🄿; ★ **N.Y.**; z 07832; ● 300
Columbia Lakes; RMC Place; CAMDEN; ▲ Cherry Hill; ***205** L-7; ★ **PHIL-**; mail Cherry Hill z 08002
Columbus; RMC Place; BURLINGTON; ▲ Mansfield; **205** K-9; 🄿; ★ **PHIL-**; z 08022; ● 700
Colwick; RMC Place; CAMDEN; ▲ Cherry Hill; ***205** L-7; ★ **PHIL-**; mail Cherry Hill z 08002
Commercial; MCD-Township; CUMBERLAND; ***205** Q-7; ★ **VINL**; mail Port Norris z 08349; Ⓟ 5,026; © 5,259
Communipaw; RMC Place; HUDSON; ***204** F-13; ★ **N.Y.**; mail Jersey City z 07304; pop. incl. with Jersey City (Inc. Place)
Concordia; CDP-Census Area Only; MIDDLESEX; ▲ Monroe; ***204** I-10; elev. 140ft./43m.; ★ **N.Y.**; mail Cranbury z 08512; Ⓟ 2,683; © 3,658
Conovertown; RMC Place; ATLANTIC; ▲ Galloway; **205** P-10; ★ **ATCY**; mail Absecon z 08205; ● 250
Constable Hook; RMC Place; HUDSON; ***204** G-12; ★ **N.Y.**; mail Bayonne z 07002; pop. incl. with Bayonne (Inc. Place)
Constable Junction; RMC Place; HUDSON; ★ **N.Y.**; mail Bayonne z 07002; pop. incl. with Bayonne (Inc. Place)
Convent Station; RMC Place; MORRIS; ▲ Morris; **204** F-10; elev. 382ft./116m.; 🄿; ★ **N.Y.**; z 07961; ● 1,800
Cookstown; RMC Place; BURLINGTON; ▲ North Hanover, New Hanover; **205** K-10; 🄿; ★ **PHIL-**; z 08511; ● 300
Coontown; RMC Place; SOMERSET; ▲ Warren; ***204** G-10; ★ **N.Y.**; mail Plainfield z 07060; rural
Cooper Park Village; RMC Place; CAMDEN; ▲ Cherry Hill; ★ **PHIL-**; mail Cherry Hill z 08002
Copper Hill; RMC Place; HUNTERDON; ▲ Raritan; ***204** H-8; elev. 159ft./48m.; ★ **N.Y.**; mail Ringoes z 08551; ● 180
Corbin City; Inc. Place; ATLANTIC; **205** Q-8; elev. 13ft./4m.; 🄿; z 08270; Ⓟ 412; © 468
Cornish; RMC Place; WARREN; ▲ White; **204** E-7; ★ **N.Y.**; mail Belvidere z 07823
Cottageville; RMC Place; MIDDLESEX; mail East Brunswick z 08816; ● 250
Cottrell Corners; RMC Place; MIDDLESEX; ▲ Old Bridge; ***204** I-11; ★ **N.Y.**; mail Old Bridge z 08857; rural
Country Farms; RMC Place; MONMOUTH; ▲ Holmdel; ***204** I-12; ★ **N.Y.**; mail Holmdel z 07733; ● 175
Country Lake Estates; CDP; BURLINGTON; ▲ Pemberton; **205** L-10; ★ **PHIL-**; mail Browns Mills z 08015; Ⓟ 4,492; © 4,012
Country Woods; RMC Place; MONMOUTH; ▲ Holmdel; ***204** I-12; ★ **N.Y.**; mail Holmdel z 07733; ● 800
Coytesville; RMC Place; BERGEN; ***204** E-13; ★ **N.Y.**; mail Fort Lee z 07024; pop. incl. with Fort Lee (Inc. Place)
Cozy Lake; RMC Place; MORRIS; ▲ Jefferson; ***204** D-10; ★ **N.Y.**; mail Oak Ridge z 07438; ● 900
Cragmere Park; RMC Place; BERGEN; ▲ Mahwah; ***204** C-12; ★ **N.Y.**; mail Mahwah z 07430
Cramer Hill; RMC Place; CAMDEN; ***205** L-6; ★ **PHIL-**; mail Camden z 08105; pop. incl. with Camden (Inc. Place)
Cranberry Lake; RMC Place; SUSSEX; ▲ Byram; **204** D-9; ★ **N.Y.**; mail Andover z 07821; ● 1,000
Cranbury; CDP; MIDDLESEX; ▲ Monroe, Cranbury; **204** I-10; elev. 103ft./31m.; 🄿; ★ **N.Y.**; z 08512; © 2,008
Cranbury; MCD-Township; MIDDLESEX; ***204** I-10; 🄿; ★ **N.Y.**; z 08512; Ⓟ 2,500; © 3,227
Cranbury Manor; RMC Place; MERCER; ▲ East Windsor; ***204** I-10; ★ **N.Y.**; mail Cranbury z 08512; ● 800
Cranbury Station; RMC Place; MIDDLESEX; ▲ Cranbury; ***204** I-10; ★ **N.Y.**; mail Cranbury z 08512; ● 20
Crandon Lakes; CDP-Census Area Only; SUSSEX; ▲ Stillwater, Hampton; **204** C-8; ★ **N.Y.**; mail Newton z 07860; Ⓟ 1,177; © 1,180
Cranford; CDP; UNION; ▲ Cranford; **204** G-11; 🄿; ★ **N.Y.**; z 07016; Ⓟ 22,624; © 22,578; ◆ 21,632
Cranford; MCD-Township; UNION; ***204** G-11; 🄿; ★ **N.Y.**; z 07016; Ⓟ 22,624; © 22,578; ◆ 21,632
Cranford Junction; RMC Place; UNION; ▲ Cranford; ***204** F-11; ★ **N.Y.**; mail Cranford z 07016
Cream Ridge; RMC Place; MONMOUTH; ▲ Upper Freehold; **205** K-10; 🄿; ★ **PHIL-**; z 08514; ● 150
Crescent Heights; RMC Place; BURLINGTON; ▲ Southampton; ***205** L-9; ★ **PHIL-**; mail Vincentown z 08088; ● 200
Crescent Park (Belcher Creek); RMC Place; PASSAIC; ▲ West Milford; ***204** C-11; ★ **N.Y.**; mail West Milford z 07480; ● 400
Cresskill; Inc. Place; BERGEN; **204** D-13; elev. 43ft./13m.; 🄿; ★ **N.Y.**; z 07626; Ⓟ 7,558; © 7,746
Crestmere; RMC Place; PASSAIC; ▲ West Milford; ***204** C-10; ★ **N.Y.**; mail Newfoundland z 07435; ● 250
Crestmoor; RMC Place; MORRIS; ▲ Washington; ***204** F-8; ★ **N.Y.**; mail Long Valley z 07853; rural
Creston; RMC Place; MERCER; ▲ Hamilton; ***204** J-9; ★ **PHIL-**; mail Trenton z 08619
Crestwood Village; CDP; OCEAN; ▲ Manchester; **205** L-11; ★ **N.Y.**; mail Manchester Township z 08759; Ⓟ 8,030; © 8,392
Cropwell; RMC Place; BURLINGTON; ▲ Evesham; ***205** M-7; ★ **PHIL-**; mail Marlton z 08053; rural
Cross Keys; RMC Place; GLOUCESTER; ▲ Monroe, Washington; **205** N-7; ★ **PHIL-**; mail Sewell z 08080; ● 600
Crossroads; RMC Place; BURLINGTON; ▲ Medford; ***205** L-8; elev. 69ft./21m.; ★ **PHIL-**; mail Medford z 08055
Crosswicks; RMC Place; BURLINGTON; ▲ Chesterfield; **205** K-9; 🄿; ★ **PHIL-**; z 08515; ● 800
Croton; RMC Place; HUNTERDON; ▲ Raritan, Delaware; **204** H-7; ★ **N.Y.**; mail Flemington z 08822; ● 60
Croxton; RMC Place; HUDSON; ★ **N.Y.**; pop. incl. with Jersey City (Inc. Place)
Crystal Lake; RMC Place; BERGEN; ***204** D-12; ★ **N.Y.**; mail Oakland z 07436; pop. incl. with Oakland (Inc. Place)
Crystal Lake; RMC Place; OCEAN; ▲ Berkeley; ***205** M-12; ★ **N.Y.**; mail Bayville z 08721
Culvers Lake; RMC Place; SUSSEX; ▲ Frankford; **204** C-8; ★ **N.Y.**; mail Branchville z 07826; ● 1,100
Cumberland; RMC Place; CUMBERLAND; ▲ Maurice River; **205** Q-7; elev. 38ft./12m.; mail Millville z 08332; ● 100
CUMBERLAND; **205** Q-6; Ⓟ 138,053; © 146,438; ◆ 156,865
Cuthbert Manor; RMC Place; CAMDEN; ▲ Haddon; ★ **PHIL-**; mail Collingswood z 08108

D

Da Costa; RMC Place; ATLANTIC; ***205** O-8; ★ **ATCY**; mail Hammonton z 08037; pop. incl. with Hammonton (Inc. Place)
Danceys Corner; RMC Place; SALEM; ▲ Carneys Point; ***205** N-4; ★ **PHIL-**; mail Penns Grove z 08069; ● 40
Daretown; RMC Place; SALEM; ▲ Upper Pittsgrove; **205** O-5; mail Elmer z 08318; ● 125
Darlington; RMC Place; BERGEN; ▲ Mahwah; ***204** C-12; ★ **N.Y.**; mail Mahwah z 07430, Ramsey z 07446; ● 100
Darts Mills; RMC Place; HUNTERDON; ▲ Readington; ***204** G-8; ★ **N.Y.**; mail Flemington z 08822
Davis; RMC Place; MONMOUTH; ▲ Upper Freehold; ***205** K-10; ★ **PHIL-**; mail Cream Ridge z 08514; rural
Davis Bridge; RMC Place; MORRIS; ▲ Long Hill; ***204** F-10; ★ **N.Y.**; mail Millington z 07946
Dayton; CDP; MIDDLESEX; ▲ South Brunswick; **204** I-10; 🄿; ★ **N.Y.**; z 08810; Ⓟ 4,321; © 6,235
Deacons; RMC Place; BURLINGTON; ***205** K-8; elev. 85ft./26m.; ★ **PHIL-**; mail Mount Holly z 08060; rural
Deal; Inc. Place; MONMOUTH; **204** J-13; elev. 33ft./10m.; 🄿; ★ **N.Y.**; z 07723; Ⓟ 1,179; © 1,070
Deal Park; RMC Place; MONMOUTH; ▲ Ocean; ***204** J-13; ★ **N.Y.**; mail Deal z 07723; ● 600
Deans; RMC Place; MIDDLESEX; ▲ South Brunswick; **204** I-10; ★ **N.Y.**; mail Monmouth Junction z 08852; ● 600
De Cou Village; RMC Place; MERCER; ▲ Hamilton; ★ **PHIL-**; mail Trenton z 08610
Deepwater (Deepwater Point); RMC Place; SALEM; ▲ Pennsville; **205** N-4; 🄿; ★ **PHIL-**; z 08023; ● 500
Deepwater Point; SALEM; see Deepwater (RMC Place)
Deerfield (Deerfield Street); RMC Place; CUMBERLAND; ▲ Upper Deerfield; ***205** O-6; ★ **VINL**; mail Deerfield Street z 08313; ● 350
Deerfield; MCD-Township; CUMBERLAND; ***205** P-6; ★ **VINL**; mail Rosenhayn z 08352; Ⓟ 2,933; © 2,927
Deerfield Park; RMC Place; OCEAN; ▲ Little Egg Harbor; ***205** O-11; ★ **ATCY**; mail Tuckerton z 08087; ● 100
Deerfield Street; CUMBERLAND; see Deerfield (RMC Place)
Deer Park; RMC Place; CAMDEN; ▲ Cherry Hill; ***205** L-7; ★ **PHIL-**; mail Cherry Hill z 08003
Deer Trail Lake; RMC Place; SUSSEX; ▲ Hardyston; ***204** C-10; ★ **N.Y.**; mail Stockholm z 07460; ● 250
DeKays; RMC Place; SUSSEX; ▲ Vernon; ***204** B-10; ★ **N.Y.**; mail Vernon z 07462; ● 25
Delair; RMC Place; CAMDEN; ▲ Pennsauken; ***205** L-7; elev. 33ft./10m.; 🄿; ★ **PHIL-**; z 08110
Delanco; RMC Place; BURLINGTON; ▲ Delanco; **205** K-7; 🄿; ★ **PHIL-**; z 08075; Ⓟ 3,316
Delanco; MCD-Township; BURLINGTON; ***205** K-7; 🄿; ★ **PHIL-**; z 08075; Ⓟ 3,316; © 3,237
Delawanna; RMC Place; PASSAIC; ***204** E-12; ★ **N.Y.**; mail Clifton z 07014; pop. incl. with Clifton (Inc. Place)
Delaware; MCD-Township; HUNTERDON; ***204** H-7; mail Stockton z 08559; Ⓟ 4,512; © 4,478
Delaware; RMC Place; WARREN; ▲ Knowlton; **204** E-7; 🄿; ★ **N.Y.**; z 07833; ● 250
Delaware Gardens; RMC Place; CAMDEN; ▲ Pennsauken; ***205** L-7; ★ **PHIL-**; mail Pennsauken z 08110
Delaware Park; RMC Place; WARREN; ▲ Lopatcong; ***204** F-6; ★ **ALL-**; mail Phillipsburg z 08865; ● 650
Del Haven; RMC Place; CAPE MAY; ▲ Middle; **205** S-1; 🄿; z 08251; ● 1,200
Delmont; RMC Place; CUMBERLAND; ▲ Maurice River; **205** R-7; elev. 11ft./3m.; 🄿; z 08314; ● 650
Delran; RMC Place; BURLINGTON; ▲ Delran; **205** L-7; 🄿; ★ **PHIL-**; z 08075; ● 13,178
Delran; MCD-Township; BURLINGTON; ***205** L-7; 🄿; ★ **PHIL-**; z 08075; Ⓟ 13,178; © 15,536
Delwood; RMC Place; CAMDEN; ▲ Cherry Hill; ★ **PHIL-**; mail Cherry Hill z 08002
Demarest; Inc. Place; BERGEN; **211** B-11; elev. 38ft./12m.; 🄿; ★ **N.Y.**; z 07627; Ⓟ 4,800; © 4,845
Dennis; MCD-Township; CAPE MAY; ***205** R-8; mail Dennisville z 08214; Ⓟ 5,574; © 6,492
Dennisville; RMC Place; CAPE MAY; ▲ Dennis; **205** R-8; elev. 13ft./4m.; 🄿; z 08214; ● 600
Denville; RMC Place; MORRIS; ▲ Denville; **204** E-10; 🄿 🄷; ★ **N.Y.**; z 07834; ● 13,812
Denville; MCD-Township; MORRIS; ***204** E-10; 🄿; ★ **N.Y.**; z 07834; Ⓟ 13,812; © 15,824
Deptford; RMC Place; GLOUCESTER; ▲ Deptford; **205** M-6; 🄿; ★ **PHIL-**; z 08096; ● 900
Deptford; MCD-Township; GLOUCESTER; ***205** M-6; 🄿; ★ **PHIL-**; z 08096; Ⓟ 24,137; © 26,763; ◆ 32,683
Devonshire; RMC Place; ATLANTIC; ▲ Mullica; **205** O-9; elev. 73ft./22m.; ★ **ATCY**; mail Egg Harbor City z 08215; ● 250
Diamond Beach; CDP-Census Area Only; CAPE MAY; ***205** T-8; © 218
Diamond Hill; RMC Place; WARREN; ▲ Mansfield; ***204** E-8; ★ **N.Y.**; mail Hackettstown z 07840; ● 500
Dias Creek; RMC Place; CAPE MAY; ▲ Middle; **205** S-2; mail Cape May Court House z 08210
Dicktown; RMC Place; CAMDEN; ▲ Berlin; ***205** N-7; elev. 146ft./45m.; ★ **PHIL-**; mail Sicklerville z 08081
Dividing Creek; RMC Place; CUMBERLAND; ▲ Downe; **205** Q-6; 🄿; z 08315; ● 500
Doddtown; RMC Place; ESSEX; ***204** F-12; ★ **N.Y.**; mail East Orange z 07017; pop. incl. with East Orange (Inc. Place)
Dogs Corner; RMC Place; MONMOUTH; ***204** I-13; mail Asbury Park z 07712; ● 1,100
Dorchester; RMC Place; CUMBERLAND; ▲ Maurice River; **205** R-7; 🄿; z 08316; ● 600
Dorothy; RMC Place; ATLANTIC; ▲ Weymouth; **205** P-8; 🄿; ★ **ATCY**; z 08317; ● 900
Dover; Inc. Place; MORRIS; **204** E-10; elev. 585ft./178m.; 🄿 ■; ★ **N.Y.**; z 07801-03, z 07806, z 07869; Ⓟ 15,115; © 18,188; ◆ 17,775
Dover; OCEAN; see Toms River (MCD-Township)
Dover Beaches North; CDP-Census Area Only; OCEAN; ***205** L-13; ★ **N.Y.**; © 1,785
Dover Beaches South; CDP-Census Area Only; OCEAN; ***205** L-13; ★ **N.Y.**; © 1,594
Dover Walk; RMC Place; OCEAN; ▲ Toms River; ***205** L-12; ★ **N.Y.**; mail Toms River z 08753; ● 150
Downe; MCD-Township; CUMBERLAND; ***205** R-6; mail Dividing Creek z 08315; Ⓟ 1,702; © 1,631
Downer; RMC Place; GLOUCESTER; ▲ Monroe; ***205** N-7; elev. 15ft./5m.; ★ **PHIL-**; mail Williamstown z 08094; rural
Downs Farms; RMC Place; CAMDEN; ▲ Cherry Hill; ***205** M-7; ★ **PHIL-**; mail Cherry Hill z 08002
Downtown; RMC Place; MERCER; ***204** J-8; ★ **PHIL-**; mail Trenton z 08608; pop. incl. with Trenton (Inc. Place)
Drakestown; RMC Place; MORRIS; ▲ Washington; ***204** E-8; ★ **N.Y.**; mail Hackettstown z 07840; ● 150
Dumont; Inc. Place; BERGEN; **204** D-13; elev. 104ft./32m.; 🄿; ★ **N.Y.**; z 07628; Ⓟ 17,187; © 17,503
Dunbarton; RMC Place; CAMDEN; ▲ Waterford; ***205** N-8; ★ **PHIL-**; mail Atco z 08004
Dundee; RMC Place; PASSAIC; ***204** E-12; ★ **N.Y.**; mail Passaic z 07055; pop. incl. with Passaic (Inc. Place)
Dunellen; Inc. Place; MIDDLESEX; **204** G-10; elev. 58ft./18m.; 🄿; ★ **N.Y.**; z 08812; Ⓟ 6,528; © 6,823
Dunhams Corner; RMC Place; MIDDLESEX; ▲ East Brunswick; ***204** H-11; ★ **N.Y.**; mail East Brunswick z 08816
Dunham Siding; RMC Place; HUDSON; ▲ North Bergen; ★ **N.Y.**; mail North Bergen z 07047
Durham; RMC Place; MIDDLESEX; ▲ Edison; ★ **N.Y.**
Dutch Neck; RMC Place; MERCER; ▲ West Windsor; **204** I-9; ★ **N.Y.**; mail Princeton Junction z 08550; ● 175
Dutchtown; RMC Place; SOMERSET; ▲ Montgomery; ***204** H-9; elev. 120ft./37m.; ★ **N.Y.**; mail Asbury z 08802; rural

E

Eagleswood; MCD-Township; OCEAN; ***205** N-11; ★ **N.Y.**; mail West Creek z 08092; Ⓟ 1,476; © 1,441
Eastampton (Eastampton Township); MCD-Township; BURLINGTON; ***205** L-9; 🄿; ★ **PHIL-**; z 08060; Ⓟ 4,962; © 6,202
Eastampton Township; BURLINGTON; see Eastampton (MCD-Township)
East Amwell; MCD-Township; HUNTERDON; ***204** H-8; ★ **PHIL-**; mail Ringoes z 08551; Ⓟ 4,332; © 4,455
East Berlin; RMC Place; CAMDEN; ▲ Berlin; ***205** M-8; ★ **PHIL-**; mail Berlin z 08009; ● 300
East Brunswick; CDP-Census Area Only; MIDDLESEX; ▲ East Brunswick; **204** H-11; 🄿; ★ **N.Y.**; z 08816; Ⓟ 43,548; © 46,756; ◆ 49,774
East Brunswick; MCD-Township; MIDDLESEX; ***204** H-10; 🄿 ■; ★ **N.Y.**; z 08816; Ⓟ 43,548; © 46,756; ◆ 49,774
East Burlington; RMC Place; BURLINGTON; ***205** K-8; ★ **PHIL-**; mail Burlington z 08016; pop. incl. with Burlington (Inc. Place)
East Camden; RMC Place; CAMDEN; ***205** L-6; ★ **PHIL-**; mail Camden z 08105; pop. incl. with Camden (Inc. Place)
East Freehold; CDP; MONMOUTH; ▲ Marlboro, Freehold; ***204** J-12; ★ **N.Y.**; mail Freehold z 07728; Ⓟ 3,842; © 4,936
East Greenwich; MCD-Township; GLOUCESTER; ***205** M-5; ★ **PHIL-**; mail Clarksboro z 08020; Ⓟ 5,258; © 5,430
East Hanover; RMC Place; MORRIS; ▲ East Hanover; **204** E-11; 🄿; ★ **N.Y.**; z 07936; Ⓟ 9,926
East Hanover; MCD-Township; MORRIS; ***204** E-11; 🄿; ★ **N.Y.**; z 07936; Ⓟ 9,926; © 11,393
East Keansburg; RMC Place; MONMOUTH; ▲ Middletown; ***204** H-12; ★ **N.Y.**; mail Keansburg z 07734; ● 3,000
East Long Branch; RMC Place; MONMOUTH; ***204** I-13; ★ **N.Y.**; mail Long Branch z 07740; pop. incl. with Long Branch (Inc. Place)
East Millstone; RMC Place; SOMERSET; ▲ Franklin; **204** H-10; 🄿; ★ **N.Y.**; z 08875 & mail Somerset z 08873; ● 500
East Newark; Inc. Place; HUDSON; **204** D-3; 🄿; ★ **N.Y.**; z 07029; Ⓟ 2,157; © 2,377
East Orange; Inc. Place; ESSEX; **204** F-12; elev. 166ft./51m.; 🄿 🄷 ■; ★ **N.Y.**; z 07017-19; Ⓟ 73,552; © 69,824; ◆ 64,860
East Pennsauken; RMC Place; CAMDEN; ▲ Pennsauken; ***205** L-7; ★ **PHIL-**; mail Pennsauken z 08110
East Riverton; RMC Place; BURLINGTON; ▲ Cinnaminson; ***205** L-7; ★ **PHIL-**; mail Riverton z 08077
East Rutherford; Inc. Place; BERGEN; **204** B-4; elev. 48ft./15m.; 🄿; ★ **N.Y.**; z 07073; Ⓟ 7,902; © 8,716
East Side; RMC Place; CUMBERLAND; ***205** P-6; ★ **VINL**; mail Bridgeton z 08302; pop. incl. with Bridgeton (Inc. Place)
East Spotswood; RMC Place; MIDDLESEX; ▲ Old Bridge; ***204** H-11; ★ **N.Y.**; mail Old Bridge z 08857
East Trenton Heights; RMC Place; MERCER; ▲ Hamilton; ***204** J-9; ★ **PHIL-**; mail Trenton z 08619; ● 1,000
East Vineland; RMC Place; ATLANTIC; ▲ Buena Vista; **205** P-8; ★ **VINL**; mail Vineland z 08360; ● 300
East Windsor; RMC Place; MERCER; ▲ East Windsor; **204** J-10; 🄿; ★ **N.Y.**; z 08512, z 08520; ● 4,000
East Windsor; MCD-Township; MERCER; ***204** J-10; 🄿; ★ **N.Y.**; z 08512, z 08520; Ⓟ 22,353; © 24,919; ◆ 25,811
Eatontown; Inc. Place; MONMOUTH; **204** I-13; elev. 46ft./14m.; 🄿 ■; ★ **N.Y.**; z 07724, z 07799; Ⓟ 13,800; © 14,008; ◆ 14,757
Echelon; CDP-Census Area Only; CAMDEN; ***205** M-7; ★ **PHIL-**; mail Voorhees z 08043; © 10,440
Edgar; RMC Place; MIDDLESEX; ▲ Woodbridge; ***204** G-11; elev. 60ft./18m.; ★ **N.Y.**; mail Woodbridge z 07095
Edgebrook; RMC Place; MIDDLESEX; ***204** H-11; ★ **N.Y.**; mail New Brunswick z 08901; pop. incl. with New Brunswick (Inc. Place)
Edgewater; Inc. Place; BERGEN; **204** B-6; elev. 55ft./17m.; 🄿; ★ **N.Y.**; z 07020; Ⓟ 5,001; © 7,677
Edgewater Park; RMC Place; BURLINGTON; ▲ Edgewater Park; **205** K-8; 🄿; ★ **PHIL-**; z 08010; ● 2,000
Edgewater Park; MCD-Township; BURLINGTON; ***205** K-8; 🄿; ★ **PHIL-**; z 08010; Ⓟ 8,388; © 7,864
Edinburg; RMC Place; MERCER; ▲ West Windsor; **204** J-9; ★ **N.Y.**; mail Trenton z 08691
Edison; CDP; MIDDLESEX; ▲ Edison; **204** H-11; 🄿 🄷; ★ **N.Y.**; z 08817-18, z 08820, z 08837, z 08899; Ⓟ 88,680; © 97,687; Ⓡ 97,597; ◆ 102,546
Edison; MCD-Township; MIDDLESEX; ***204** G-11; 🄿 ■; ★ **N.Y.**; z 08817-18, z 08820, z 08837, z 08899; Ⓟ 88,680; © 97,687; Ⓡ 97,597; ◆ 102,546
Egg Harbor (Egg Harbor Township); MCD-Township; ATLANTIC; ***205** Q-9; ★ **ATCY**; mail Egg Harbor City z 08215, Egg Harbor Township z 08234, Pleasantville z 08232; not adjacent to Egg Harbor City; Ⓟ 24,544; © 30,726; ◆ 38,991
Egg Harbor City; Inc. Place; ATLANTIC; **205** O-9; elev. 58ft./18m.; 🄿; ★ **ATCY**; z 08215; Ⓟ 4,583; © 4,545
Egg Harbor Township; ATLANTIC; see Egg Harbor (MCD-Township)
Eilers Corner; RMC Place; MERCER; ▲ East Windsor; ***204** J-10; ★ **N.Y.**; mail Hightstown z 08520; ● 100
Elberon; RMC Place; MONMOUTH; ***204** J-13; ★ **N.Y.**; mail Long Branch z 07740; pop. incl. with Long Branch (Inc. Place)
Elberon Park; RMC Place; MONMOUTH; ▲ Ocean; ***204** J-13; ★ **N.Y.**; mail Long Branch z 07740, Oakhurst z 07755; ● 400
Eldora; RMC Place; CAPE MAY; ▲ Dennis; **205** R-8; elev. 16ft./5m.; mail Woodbine z 08270; ● 120
Eldridge Hill (Eldridges Hill); RMC Place; SALEM; ▲ Pilesgrove; ***205** N-5; mail Woodstown z 08098
Eldridge Park; RMC Place; MERCER; ▲ Lawrence; **205** S-12; ★ **PHIL-**; mail Trenton z 08638; ● 3,000
Eldridges Hill; SALEM; see Eldridge Hill (RMC Place)
Elizabeth; Inc. Place; ⊡ UNION; **204** F-12; elev. 36ft./11m.; 🄿 🄷 ■; ★ **N.Y.**; z 07201-02, z 07206-08; Ⓟ 110,002; © 120,568; ◆ 122,214
Elizabethport; RMC Place; UNION; ***204** G-12; 🄿; ★ **N.Y.**; z 07206; pop. incl. with Elizabeth (Inc. Place)
Elk; MCD-Township; GLOUCESTER; ***205** N-6; ★ **PHIL-**; mail Glassboro z 08028; Ⓟ 3,806; © 3,514
Elks Terrace; RMC Place; SALEM; ▲ Quinton; ***205** O-4; mail Salem z 08079; ● 100
Ellisburg; RMC Place; CAMDEN; ▲ Cherry Hill; ***205** L-7; elev. 61ft./19m.; ★ **PHIL-**; mail Cherry Hill z 08002
Ellisdale; RMC Place; BURLINGTON, MONMOUTH; ▲ Upper Freehold, North Hanover; ***205** K-10; ★ **PHIL-**; mail Allentown z 08501; ● 75
Elm; RMC Place; CAMDEN; ▲ Winslow; **205** N-8; ★ **PHIL-**; mail Hammonton z 08037; ● 200
Elmer; Inc. Place; SALEM; **205** O-6; elev. 118ft./36m.; 🄿; z 08318; Ⓟ 1,571; © 1,384
Elmora; RMC Place; UNION; ***204** F-12; ★ **N.Y.**; mail Elizabeth z 07202; pop. incl. with Elizabeth (Inc. Place)
Elmwood Park; Inc. Place; BERGEN; **204** A-3; elev. 50ft./15m.; 🄿; ★ **N.Y.**; z 07407; Ⓟ 17,623; © 18,925
Elsinboro; MCD-Township; SALEM; ***205** O-4; ★ **PHIL-**; mail Salem z 08079; Ⓟ 1,170; © 1,092
Elwood; RMC Place; ATLANTIC; ▲ Mullica; **205** O-9; 🄿; ★ **ATCY**; z 08217; ● 800
Elwood-Magnolia; CDP-Census Area Only; ATLANTIC; ▲ Mullica; ***205** O-9; ★ **ATCY**; mail Elwood z 08217; Ⓟ 1,487; © 1,392
Emerson; Inc. Place; BERGEN; **204** D-13; elev. 46ft./14m.; 🄿; ★ **N.Y.**; z 07630; Ⓟ 6,930; © 7,197
Emmelsville; RMC Place; ATLANTIC; mail Mays Landing z 08330; ● 45
Englewood; Inc. Place; BERGEN; **204** E-13; elev. 44ft./13m.; 🄿 🄷 ■; ★ **N.Y.**; z 07631-32; Ⓟ 24,850; © 26,203; ◆ 27,314
Englewood Annex; RMC Place; BERGEN; ★ **N.Y.**; mail Englewood z 07631; pop. incl. with Englewood (Inc. Place)
Englewood Cliffs; Inc. Place; BERGEN; **204** E-13; elev. 371ft./113m.; 🄿; ★ **N.Y.**; z 07632; Ⓟ 5,634; © 5,322
English Creek; RMC Place; ATLANTIC; ▲ Egg Harbor; **205** Q-9; ★ **ATCY**; mail Egg Harbor Township z 08234, Mays Landing z 08330; rural
Englishtown; Inc. Place; MONMOUTH; **204** I-11; elev. 70ft./21m.; 🄿; ★ **N.Y.**; z 07726; Ⓟ 1,268; © 1,764
Erial; RMC Place; CAMDEN; ▲ Gloucester; **205** M-7; elev. 180ft./55m.; 🄿; ★ **PHIL-**; z 08081; ● 2,500
Erlton; RMC Place; CAMDEN; ▲ Cherry Hill; ***205** L-7; ★ **PHIL-**; mail Cherry Hill z 08002
Erlton-Ellisburg; CDP-Census Area Only; CAMDEN; ***205** L-7; ★ **PHIL-**; © 8,168
Erma; CDP; CAPE MAY; ▲ Lower; **205** T-1; mail Cape May z 08204; Ⓟ 2,045; © 2,088
Erma Park; RMC Place; CAPE MAY; ▲ Lower; ***205** T-8; mail Cape May z 08204; ● 600
Ernston; RMC Place; MIDDLESEX; ***204** H-11; ★ **N.Y.**; mail Parlin z 08859; pop. incl. with Sayreville (Inc. Place)
Erskine; RMC Place; PASSAIC; ***204** C-11; ★ **N.Y.**; mail Ringwood z 07456; pop. incl. with Ringwood (Inc. Place)
Erskine Lakes; RMC Place; PASSAIC; ***204** C-12; ★ **N.Y.**; mail Ringwood z 07456; pop. incl. with Ringwood (Inc. Place)
Espanong; MORRIS; see Lake Hopatcong (RMC Place)
ESSEX; **204** E-12; Ⓟ 778,206; © 793,633; Ⓡ 792,305; ◆ 756,146
Essex Fells; Inc. Place; ESSEX; ***204** E-11; elev. 387ft./118m.; 🄿; ★ **N.Y.**; z 07021; Ⓟ 2,139; © 2,162
Estell Manor; Inc. Place; ATLANTIC; **205** Q-8; elev. 78ft./24m.; 🄿; z 08319; Ⓟ 1,404; © 1,585; Ⓡ 1,588
Estelville; RMC Place; ATLANTIC; ***205** Q-9; mail Estell Manor z 08319; pop. incl. with Estell Manor (Inc. Place)
Etra; RMC Place; MERCER; ▲ East Windsor; **204** J-10; ★ **N.Y.**; mail Hightstown z 08520; ● 30
Everett; RMC Place; MONMOUTH; ▲ Holmdel; ***204** I-12; ★ **N.Y.**; mail Lincroft z 07738; ● 100

Entries in **UPPERCASE** are counties.
Entries in **bold** have populations of 2,500 or more.
Names in parentheses are alternate names.

Inc. Place	Incorporated Place
RMC Place	Rand McNally Designated Place
CDP	Census Designated Place
MCD	Minor Civil Division

⊡ County Seat
▲ Minor Civil Division
elev. Elevation
🄿 Post Office
🄷 Hospital
🄲 College
■ Principal Business Center
★ Ranally Metro Area (RMA) Abbreviation
z Zip Code(s)
Ⓟ Previous Census Population
Ⓡ Revised Census Population
Ⓐ Annexation Population
● Rand McNally Population Estimate
© Final Census Population
Ⓢ Special Census Population
◆ Estimated Population

For additional definitions see Glossary, Volume 1, and Introduction, Volume 2.

Everittstown; RMC Place; HUNTERDON; ▲ Alexandria; 204 G-7; mail Pittstown z 08867; ● 90
Evesboro; RMC Place; BURLINGTON; ▲ Evesham; 205 L-8; ★ PHIL-; mail Marlton z 08053; ● 100
Evesham; MCD-Township; BURLINGTON; *205 M-8; 🅿; ★ PHIL-; z 08053; Ⓟ 35,309; Ⓒ 42,275; ◆ 46,316
Ewan; RMC Place; GLOUCESTER; ▲ Harrison; 205 N-6; elev. 111ft./34m.; 🅿; ★ PHIL-; z 08025; ● 250
Ewansville; RMC Place; BURLINGTON; ▲ Pemberton, Southampton; 205 L-9; ★ PHIL-; mail Mount Holly z 08060; ● 300
Ewing; CDP; MERCER; ▲ Ewing; 205 R-13; 🅿 🅲 6,934; ★ PHIL-; z 08560, z 08618, z 08628, z 08638; Ⓟ 34,185; Ⓒ 35,707; ◆ 35,007
Ewing; MCD-Township; MERCER; *204 J-8; 🅿 🅲 6,934; ★ PHIL-; z 08560, z 08618, z 08628, z 08638; Ⓟ 34,185; Ⓒ 35,707; ◆ 35,007
Ewing Park; RMC Place; MERCER; ▲ Ewing; *204 J-8; ★ PHIL-; mail Trenton z 08638
Ewingville; RMC Place; MERCER; ▲ Ewing; 205 R-12; elev. 140ft./43m.; ★ PHIL-; mail Trenton z 08628, z 08638
Extonville; RMC Place; MERCER; ▲ Hamilton; *205 K-9; ★ PHIL-; mail Trenton z 08620

F

Fairfield; MCD-Township; CUMBERLAND; *205 Q-5; ★ VINL; mail Fairton z 08320; Ⓟ 5,699; Ⓒ 6,283
Fairfield; CDP-Census Area Only; ESSEX; ▲ Fairfield; 204 E-11; elev. 411ft./125m.; 🅿; ★ N.Y.; z 07004; Ⓟ 7,615; Ⓒ 7,063
Fairfield; MCD-Township; ESSEX; *204 E-11; 🅿; ★ N.Y.; z 07004; Ⓟ 7,615; Ⓒ 7,063
Fairfield; RMC Place; MONMOUTH; ▲ Howell; *204 J-12; ★ N.Y.; mail Freehold z 07728; rural
Fair Haven; Inc. Place; MONMOUTH; 204 I-13; elev. 30ft./9m.; 🅿; ★ N.Y.; z 07704; Ⓟ 5,270; Ⓒ 5,937
Fair Lawn; Inc. Place; BERGEN; 204 D-12; elev. 100ft./30m.; 🅿; ★ N.Y.; z 07410; Ⓟ 30,548; Ⓒ 31,637; ◆ 30,916
Fairmount; RMC Place; HUNTERDON; ▲ Tewksbury; 204 F-8; ★ N.Y.; mail Califon z 07830; rural
Fairmount; RMC Place; MORRIS; ▲ Washington; *204 F-8; ★ N.Y.; mail Long Valley z 07853; ● 60
Fairton; CDP; CUMBERLAND; ▲ Fairfield; 205 Q-6; 🅿; ★ VINL; z 08320; Ⓟ 1,359; Ⓒ 2,253; Ⓡ 1,168
Fairview; Inc. Place; BERGEN; 204 C-6; elev. 308ft./94m.; 🅿; ★ N.Y.; z 07022; Ⓟ 10,733; Ⓒ 13,255
Fairview; RMC Place; BURLINGTON; ▲ Delran; 205 M-8; ★ PHIL-; mail Medford z 08055; ● 125
Fairview; RMC Place; BURLINGTON; ▲ Medford; *205 L-7; ★ PHIL-; mail Riverside z 08075
Fairview; RMC Place; CAMDEN; *205 L-6; ★ PHIL-; mail Camden z 08104; pop. incl. with Camden (Inc. Place)
Fairview; RMC Place; GLOUCESTER; ▲ Washington, Deptford; 205 M-6; ★ PHIL-; mail Sewell z 08080
Fairview; CDP; MONMOUTH; ▲ Middletown; *204 I-13; ★ N.Y.; mail Red Bank z 07701; Ⓟ 3,853; Ⓒ 3,942
Fairview Knolls; RMC Place; MIDDLESEX; *204 H-11; mail East Brunswick z 08816; ● 1,250
Fairway Mews; RMC Place; MONMOUTH; *204 J-13; ★ N.Y.; mail Spring Lake z 07762; pop. incl. with Spring Lake Heights (Inc. Place)
Fanwood; Inc. Place; UNION; 204 G-11; elev. 157ft./48m.; 🅿; ★ N.Y.; z 07023; Ⓟ 7,115; Ⓒ 7,174
Fardale; RMC Place; BERGEN; ▲ Mahwah; *204 C-12; ★ N.Y.; mail Mahwah z 07430; ● 50
Far Hills; Inc. Place; SOMERSET; 204 F-9; elev. 220ft./67m.; 🅿; ★ N.Y.; z 07931; Ⓟ 657; Ⓒ 859
Farmcrest Acres; RMC Place; PASSAIC; ▲ West Milford; *204 C-10; ★ N.Y.; mail Oak Ridge z 07438; ● 200
Farmersville; RMC Place; HUNTERDON; ▲ Tewksbury; *204 F-8; ★ N.Y.; mail Califon z 07830; rural
Farmingdale; Inc. Place; MONMOUTH; 204 J-12; elev. 79ft./24m.; 🅿; ★ N.Y.; z 07727; Ⓟ 1,462; Ⓒ 1,587
Farmington; RMC Place; ATLANTIC; ▲ Egg Harbor; 204 H-1; ★ ATCY; mail Egg Harbor Township z 08234, Pleasantville z 08232; ● 450
Farrington Lake Heights; RMC Place; MIDDLESEX; ▲ East Brunswick; *204 H-10; ★ N.Y.; mail Milltown z 08850
Fawn Lakes; RMC Place; OCEAN; ▲ Stafford; *205 N-11; elev. 100ft./30m.; ★ N.Y.; mail Manahawkin z 08050; ● 600
Fayson Lakes; RMC Place; MORRIS; *204 D-11; ★ N.Y.; mail Butler z 07405; pop. incl. with Kinnelon (Inc. Place)
Fellowship; RMC Place; BURLINGTON; ▲ Mount Laurel; *205 L-7; ★ PHIL-; mail Moorestown z 08057; ● 2,500
Fenwick; RMC Place; SALEM; ▲ Pilesgrove, Alloway; 205 O-5; mail Woodstown z 08098
Fernwood; RMC Place; MERCER; ▲ Ewing; *204 J-8; ★ PHIL-; mail Trenton z 08618, z 08628
Ferrell; RMC Place; GLOUCESTER; ▲ Elk; 205 N-6; elev. 138ft./42m.; ★ PHIL-; mail Monroeville z 08343; ● 80
Fieldsboro; Inc. Place; BURLINGTON; 205 S-14; elev. 10ft./3m.; 🅿; ★ PHIL-; z 08505; Ⓟ 579; Ⓒ 522
Fieldville; RMC Place; MIDDLESEX; *204 G-10; mail Somerset z 08873; ● 2,000
Finderne; RMC Place; SOMERSET; ▲ Bridgewater; 204 G-10; ★ N.Y.; mail Bridgewater z 08807, Somerville z 08876; ● 3,000
Finesville; RMC Place; WARREN; ▲ Pohatcong; 204 G-6; ★ ALL-; mail Phillipsburg z 08865; ● 200
Fishing Creek; RMC Place; CAPE MAY; ▲ Lower; *205 S-7; mail Cape May z 08204
Five Corners; RMC Place; HUDSON; ★ N.Y.; mail Jersey City z 07308; pop. incl. with Jersey City (Inc. Place)
Five Points; RMC Place; SALEM; ▲ Oldmans; *205 N-4; ★ PHIL-; mail Pedricktown z 08067
Five Points; RMC Place; SUSSEX; ▲ Stillwater; 204 C-8; ★ N.Y.; mail Newton z 07860
Flagtown; RMC Place; SOMERSET; ▲ Hillsborough; 204 H-9; 🅿; ★ N.Y.; z 08821; ● 600
Flanders; RMC Place; MORRIS; ▲ Mount Olive; 204 E-9; elev. 679ft./207m.; 🅿; ★ N.Y.; z 07836; ● 1,200
Flanders Valley; RMC Place; MORRIS; *204 E-9; ★ N.Y.; mail Flanders z 07836; ● 800
Flatbrookville; RMC Place; SUSSEX; ▲ Walpack; 204 C-7; mail Columbia z 07832; ● 5
Flemington; Inc. Place; ⊡ HUNTERDON; 204 H-8; elev. 160ft./49m.; 🅿 🅷 ■; ★ N.Y.; z 08822; Ⓟ 4,047; Ⓒ 4,200; ◆ 4,199
Flemington Junction; RMC Place; HUNTERDON; ▲ Raritan; *204 H-8; ★ N.Y.; mail Flemington z 08822
Floral Hill; RMC Place; MORRIS; *204 F-11; mail Chatham z 07928; ● 2,000
Florence; RMC Place; BURLINGTON; ▲ Florence; 205 K-8; 🅿; ★ PHIL-; z 08518; ● 5,500
Florence; MCD-Township; BURLINGTON; *205 K-8; 🅿; ★ PHIL-; z 08518; Ⓟ 10,266; Ⓒ 10,746
Florence; RMC Place; CAMDEN; ▲ Winslow; 205 N-7; ★ PHIL-; mail Berlin z 08009; rural
Florence-Roebling; CDP-Census Area Only; BURLINGTON; ▲ Florence; *205 K-8; ★ PHIL-; mail Florence z 08518, Roebling z 08554; Ⓟ 8,564; Ⓒ 8,200
Florham Park; Inc. Place; MORRIS; 204 F-11; elev. 200ft./61m.; 🅿; ★ N.Y.; z 07932; Ⓟ 8,521; Ⓒ 8,857; Ⓡ 10,296
Folsom; Inc. Place; ATLANTIC; 205 O-8; elev. 74ft./23m.; ★ ATCY; mail Hammonton z 08037; Ⓟ 2,181; Ⓒ 1,972
Fords; CDP; MIDDLESEX; ▲ Woodbridge; 204 H-11; elev. 116ft./35m.; 🅿; ★ N.Y.; z 08863; Ⓟ 14,392; Ⓒ 15,032
Forest Grove; RMC Place; GLOUCESTER; ▲ Franklin; 205 K-3; ★ VINL; mail Vineland z 08360; rural
Forest Hill; RMC Place; CAMDEN; ▲ Cherry Hill; ★ PHIL-; mail Cherry Hill z 08003
Forest Hill; RMC Place; ESSEX; ★ N.Y.; mail Newark z 07104; pop. incl. with Newark (Inc. Place)
Forest Lake; RMC Place; SUSSEX; ▲ Byram, Andover; *204 D-9; ★ N.Y.; mail Andover z 07821; ● 200
Forked River; CDP; OCEAN; ▲ Lacey; 205 M-12; elev. 17ft./5m.; 🅿; ★ N.Y.; z 08731; Ⓟ 4,243; Ⓒ 4,914
Forked River Beach; RMC Place; OCEAN; ▲ Lacey; *205 M-12; ★ N.Y.; mail Forked River z 08731; ● 900
Forrest Lake Estates; RMC Place; GLOUCESTER; ▲ Franklin; ★ VINL; mail Malaga z 08328
Fort Dix; CDP; BURLINGTON; ▲ Springfield, New Hanover, Pemberton; *205 K-9; 🅿; ★ PHIL-; z 08640; Ⓟ 10,205; Ⓒ 7,464
Fort Elfsborg; RMC Place; SALEM; ▲ Elsinboro; *205 O-4; ★ PHIL-; mail Salem z 08079; ● 300
Fortescue; RMC Place; CUMBERLAND; ▲ Downe; 205 R-6; elev. 6ft./2m.; 🅿; z 08321; summer pop. 1,000; ● 500
Fort Lee; Inc. Place; BERGEN; 204 E-13; elev. 313ft./95m.; 🅿; ★ N.Y.; z 07024; Ⓟ 31,997; Ⓒ 35,461; ◆ 36,008
Fort Mott; RMC Place; SALEM; ▲ Pennsville; *205 O-4; ★ PHIL-; mail Salem z 08079; ● 60
Fort Plains; RMC Place; MONMOUTH; ▲ Howell; *204 J-12; ★ N.Y.; mail Freehold z 07728
Forty-Fifth Street; RMC Place; HUDSON; *204 F-13; ★ N.Y.; mail Union City z 07087; pop. incl. with Union City (Inc. Place)
Foster Village; RMC Place; BERGEN; *204 E-13; ★ N.Y.; mail Bergenfield z 07621; pop. incl. with Bergenfield (Inc. Place)
Foul Rift; RMC Place; WARREN; ▲ White; 204 E-6; ★ N.Y.; mail Belvidere z 07823; ● 40
Four Bridges; RMC Place; MORRIS; ▲ Washington; *204 E-9; elev. 600ft./183m.; ★ N.Y.; mail Long Valley z 07853; rural
Fox Chase; RMC Place; BURLINGTON; ▲ Tabernacle; *205 M-9; ★ PHIL-; mail Vincentown z 08088; ● 300
Fox Hill; RMC Place; MORRIS; *204 E-10; ★ N.Y.; mail Mountain Lakes z 07046; pop. incl. with Mountain Lakes (Inc. Place)
Fox Hollow Woods; RMC Place; CAMDEN; ▲ Cherry Hill; *205 M-7; ★ PHIL-; mail Cherry Hill z 08003
Francis Mills; RMC Place; OCEAN; ▲ Jackson; *205 K-11; ★ N.Y.; mail Jackson z 08527; rural
Frankford; MCD-Township; SUSSEX; *204 C-9; ★ N.Y.; mail Branchville z 07826; Ⓟ 5,114; Ⓒ 5,420
Franklin; MCD-Township; GLOUCESTER; *205 O-7; ★ PHIL-; mail Franklinville z 08322; Ⓟ 14,482; Ⓒ 15,466
Franklin; MCD-Township; HUNTERDON; *204 G-8; ★ N.Y.; mail Pittstown z 08867; Ⓟ 2,851; Ⓒ 2,990
Franklin; RMC Place; SOMERSET; ▲ Franklin; *204 H-10; ★ N.Y.; mail Somerset z 08873
Franklin; MCD-Township; SOMERSET; *204 H-10; ★ N.Y.; mail Somerset z 08873; Ⓟ 42,780; Ⓒ 50,903; ◆ 54,666
Franklin; Inc. Place; SUSSEX; 204 C-10; elev. 621ft./189m.; 🅿; ★ N.Y.; z 07416; Ⓟ 4,977; Ⓒ 5,160
Franklin; MCD-Township; WARREN; *204 F-7; ★ N.Y.; mail Broadway z 08808; Ⓟ 2,404; Ⓒ 2,768
Franklin Lakes; Inc. Place; BERGEN; 204 D-12; elev. 399ft./122m.; 🅿; ★ N.Y.; z 07417; Ⓟ 9,873; Ⓒ 10,422
Franklin Park; RMC Place; MIDDLESEX, SOMERSET; ▲ Franklin; 204 H-10; 🅿; ★ N.Y.; z 08823; ● 1,200
Franklinville; RMC Place; GLOUCESTER; ▲ Franklin; 205 O-7; 🅿; ★ PHIL-; z 08322; ● 1,500
Frazier Park; RMC Place; OCEAN; ▲ Long Beach; *205 N-12; ★ N.Y.; mail Beach Haven z 08008
Fredon (Fredon Township); MCD-Township; SUSSEX; *204 D-8; 🅿; ★ N.Y.; z 07860; Ⓟ 2,763; Ⓒ 2,860
Fredon Township; SUSSEX; see Fredon (MCD-Township)
Free Acres; RMC Place; UNION; ▲ Berkeley Heights; *204 G-10; ★ N.Y.; mail Berkeley Heights z 07922
Freehold; Inc. Place; ⊡ MONMOUTH; 204 J-11; elev. 178ft./54m.; 🅿 🅷; ★ N.Y.; z 07728; Ⓟ 10,742; Ⓒ 10,976
Freehold; MCD-Township; MONMOUTH; *204 J-11; 🅿; ★ N.Y.; z 07728; does not include the Borough of Freehold; Ⓟ 24,710; Ⓒ 31,537; ◆ 33,926
Freewood Acres; RMC Place; MONMOUTH; ▲ Howell; 204 J-12; ★ N.Y.; mail Howell z 07731; ● 1,900
Frelinghuysen; MCD-Township; WARREN; *204 D-8; ★ N.Y.; mail Andover z 07821, Blairstown z 07825; Ⓟ 1,779; Ⓒ 2,083
Frenchtown; Inc. Place; HUNTERDON; 204 H-7; elev. 141ft./43m.; 🅿; z 08825; Ⓟ 1,528; Ⓒ 1,488
Freneau; RMC Place; MONMOUTH; *204 I-12; ★ N.Y.; mail Matawan z 07747; pop. incl. with Matawan (Inc. Place)
Fresh Ponds; RMC Place; MIDDLESEX; ▲ South Brunswick; *204 I-10; ★ N.Y.; mail East Brunswick z 08816; rural
Friendship; RMC Place; SALEM; ▲ Upper Pittsgrove; *205 O-6; mail Elmer z 08318; rural
Friendship Station; RMC Place; SALEM; ▲ Carneys Point; *205 N-4; elev. 133ft./41m.; ★ PHIL-; mail Penns Grove z 08069; ● 130
Fries Mill (Fries Mills); RMC Place; GLOUCESTER; ▲ Franklin; 205 N-7; ★ PHIL-; mail Franklinville z 08322; ● 200
Fries Mills; GLOUCESTER; see Fries Mill (RMC Place)

G

Galilee; RMC Place; MONMOUTH; *204 I-13; ★ N.Y.; mail Monmouth Beach z 07750; pop. incl. with Monmouth Beach (Inc. Place)
Galloway; MCD-Township; ATLANTIC; *205 P-10; 🅿 🅲 6,727; ★ ATCY; z 08205 & mail Absecon z 08201, Egg Harbor City z 08215; Ⓟ 23,330; Ⓒ 31,209; ◆ 36,894
Gandys Beach; RMC Place; CUMBERLAND; ▲ Downe; 205 Q-6; mail Newport z 08345; summer pop. 160; ● 60
Garden City; RMC Place; GLOUCESTER; ▲ Deptford; *205 N-7; ★ PHIL-; mail Blackwood z 08012
Gardendale; RMC Place; GLOUCESTER; ▲ Washington; *205 N-7; ★ PHIL-; mail Salem z 08079; ● 350
Gardens of Pleasant Plains; RMC Place; OCEAN; ▲ Toms River; *205 L-12; elev. 50ft./15m.; ★ N.Y.; mail Toms River z 08755; ● 1,100
Gardenville; RMC Place; GLOUCESTER; ▲ Deptford; *205 M-6; ★ PHIL-; mail Woodbury z 08096; ● 1,800
Gardenville Center; RMC Place; GLOUCESTER; ▲ Deptford; *205 M-6; ★ PHIL-; mail Woodbury z 08096; ● 1,500
Garfield; Inc. Place; BERGEN; 204 E-12; elev. 80ft./24m.; 🅿; ★ N.Y.; z 07026; Ⓟ 26,727; Ⓒ 29,786; ◆ 29,525
Garwood; Inc. Place; UNION; 210 J-3; elev. 86ft./26m.; 🅿; ★ N.Y.; z 07027; Ⓟ 4,227; Ⓒ 4,153
Genasco; RMC Place; MIDDLESEX; ▲ Woodbridge; ★ N.Y.
General Lafayette; RMC Place; HUDSON; *204 F-13; ★ N.Y.; mail Jersey City z 07309; pop. incl. with Jersey City (Inc. Place)
Georgetown; RMC Place; BURLINGTON; ▲ Mansfield; 205 K-9; ★ PHIL-; mail Columbus z 08022; ● 60
Georgia; RMC Place; MONMOUTH; ▲ Freehold; *204 J-11; ★ N.Y.; mail Freehold z 07728
Germania; RMC Place; ATLANTIC; ▲ Galloway; 205 P-9; ★ ATCY; mail Egg Harbor City z 08215
Germania Gardens; RMC Place; ATLANTIC; ▲ Galloway; *205 P-9; ★ ATCY; mail Cologne z 08213
Gibbsboro; Inc. Place; CAMDEN; 205 M-7; elev. 89ft./27m.; 🅿; ★ PHIL-; z 08026; Ⓟ 2,383; Ⓒ 2,435
Gibbstown; CDP; GLOUCESTER; ▲ Greenwich; 205 M-5; elev. 15ft./5m.; 🅿; ★ PHIL-; z 08027; Ⓟ 3,902; Ⓒ 3,758
Giffordtown; RMC Place; OCEAN; ▲ Little Egg Harbor; *205 O-11; elev. 81ft./25m.; ★ ATCY; mail Tuckerton z 08087; ● 150
Gilford Park; RMC Place; OCEAN; ▲ Toms River; 205 L-12; ★ N.Y.; mail Toms River z 08753; Ⓟ 8,668
Gillespie; RMC Place; MIDDLESEX; *204 H-11; ★ N.Y.; mail Sayreville z 08872; pop. incl. with Sayreville (Inc. Place)
Gillette; RMC Place; MORRIS; ▲ Long Hill; 204 F-10; 🅿; ★ N.Y.; z 07933; ● 900
Gillilandtown; RMC Place; MIDDLESEX; *204 I-11; mail East Brunswick z 08816; ● 2,800
Gilman Lake; RMC Place; GLOUCESTER; ▲ Elk; *205 N-6; ★ PHIL-; mail Monroeville z 08343; ● 200
Gladstone; RMC Place; SOMERSET; *204 F-9; elev. 300ft./91m.; 🅿; ★ N.Y.; z 07934; pop. incl. with Peapack and Gladstone (Inc. Place)
Glassboro; Inc. Place; GLOUCESTER; 205 N-6; elev. 144ft./44m.; 🅿 🅲 9,578; ★ PHIL-; z 08028; Ⓟ 15,614; Ⓒ 19,068
Glasser; RMC Place; SUSSEX; *204 D-9; 🅿; ★ N.Y.; z 07837; pop. incl. with Hopatcong (Inc. Place)
Glen Cove; RMC Place; OCEAN; ▲ Berkeley; *205 M-12; ★ N.Y.; mail Bayville z 08721; ● 200
Glendale; RMC Place; CAMDEN; ▲ Voorhees; *205 M-7; elev. 105ft./32m.; ★ PHIL-; mail Voorhees z 08043
Glendola; RMC Place; MONMOUTH; ▲ Wall; 204 J-13; ★ N.Y.; mail Belmar z 07719; ● 2,400
Glendora; CDP; CAMDEN; ▲ Gloucester; *205 M-7; 🅿; ★ PHIL-; z 08029; Ⓟ 5,201; Ⓒ 4,907
Glen Gardner; Inc. Place; HUNTERDON; 204 F-7; elev. 415ft./126m.; 🅿 🅷; ★ N.Y.; z 08826; Ⓟ 1,665; Ⓒ 1,902
Glen Oaks; RMC Place; CAMDEN; ▲ Gloucester; *205 M-7; ★ PHIL-; mail Clementon z 08021; ● 3,300
Glen Ridge; Inc. Place; ESSEX; 204 C-2; elev. 187ft./57m.; 🅿; ★ N.Y.; z 07028; Ⓟ 7,076; Ⓒ 7,271
Glen Rock; Inc. Place; BERGEN; 204 D-12; elev. 114ft./35m.; 🅿; ★ N.Y.; z 07452; Ⓟ 10,883; Ⓒ 11,546
Glenside; RMC Place; SALEM; ▲ Pennsville; *205 N-4; ★ PHIL-; mail Pennsville z 08070; ● 350
Glenwood; RMC Place; SUSSEX; ▲ Vernon; 204 B-10; 🅿; ★ N.Y.; z 07418; ● 200
Gloucester; CAMDEN; see Gloucester City (Inc. Place)
Gloucester; MCD-Township; CAMDEN; *205 M-7; ★ PHIL-; mail Bellmawr z 08031, Blackwood z 08012, Gloucester City z 08030; not adjacent to Gloucester City; Ⓟ 53,797; Ⓒ 64,350; ◆ 64,539
GLOUCESTER; 205 O-7; Ⓟ 230,082; Ⓒ 254,673; ◆ 293,153
Gloucester City (Gloucester); Inc. Place; CAMDEN; 205 M-6; elev. 19ft./6m.; 🅿; ★ PHIL-; z 08030 & mail Bellmawr z 08031; Ⓟ 12,649; Ⓒ 11,484
Gloucester Heights; RMC Place; CAMDEN; *205 M-6; ★ PHIL-; pop. incl. with Gloucester City (Inc. Place)
Golden Triangle; CDP-Census Area Only; CAMDEN; *205 L-7; ★ PHIL-; Ⓒ 3,511
Golf Manor; RMC Place; SALEM; ▲ Carneys Point; *205 N-4; ★ PHIL-; mail Penns Grove z 08069; ● 200
Golf View; RMC Place; SALEM; ▲ Carneys Point; *205 N-4; ★ PHIL-; mail Penns Grove z 08069; ● 500
Gordon Lakes; RMC Place; PASSAIC; ▲ West Milford; *204 C-11; elev. 100ft./30m.; ★ N.Y.; mail Butler z 07405, West Milford z 07480; ● 200
Gordons Corner; RMC Place; MONMOUTH; mail Freehold z 07728; ● 660
Goshen; RMC Place; CAPE MAY; ▲ Middle; 205 R-2; elev. 12ft./4m.; 🅿; z 08218; ● 600
Gouldtown; RMC Place; CUMBERLAND; ▲ Fairfield; 205 M-2; ★ VINL; mail Bridgeton z 08302; ● 700
Grandin; RMC Place; HUNTERDON; ▲ Union, Franklin; *204 G-7; ★ N.Y.; mail Annandale z 08801; rural
Granton Junction; RMC Place; HUDSON; ▲ North Bergen; ★ N.Y.; mail North Bergen z 07047
Grasselli; RMC Place; UNION; *204 G-12; ★ N.Y.; mail Linden z 07036; pop. incl. with Linden (Inc. Place)
Grassy Sound; RMC Place; CAPE MAY; 205 S-3; mail Stone Harbor z 08247; ● 80
Gravel Hill; RMC Place; MIDDLESEX; ▲ Monroe; *204 I-11; ★ N.Y.; mail Englishtown z 07726
Greater Cross Roads (Larger Cross Roads); RMC Place; SOMERSET; ▲ Bedminster; *204 F-9; ★ N.Y.; mail Bedminster z 07921; rural
Great Meadows; RMC Place; WARREN; ▲ Independence; 204 E-8; elev. 548ft./167m.; 🅿; ★ N.Y.; z 07838; ● 250
Great Meadows-Vienna; CDP-Census Area Only; WARREN; ▲ Independence; *204 E-8; elev. 528ft./161m.; ★ N.Y.; mail Great Meadows z 07838, Vienna z 07880; Ⓟ 1,108; Ⓒ 1,264
Great Notch; RMC Place; PASSAIC; ▲ Little Falls; 204 A-2; ★ N.Y.; mail Little Falls z 07424
Green; MCD-Township; SUSSEX; *204 D-8; ★ N.Y.; mail Andover z 07821; Ⓟ 2,709; Ⓒ 3,220
Green Bank; RMC Place; BURLINGTON; ▲ Washington; 205 O-10; mail Egg Harbor City z 08215; ● 150
Greenbriar; RMC Place; OCEAN; ▲ Brick; *205 K-12; ★ N.Y.; mail Brick z 08723
Greenbrook; RMC Place; PASSAIC; ▲ West Milford; *204 C-11; ★ N.Y.; mail West Milford z 07480; ● 100
Green Brook; RMC Place; SOMERSET; ▲ Green Brook; 204 G-10; 🅿; ★ N.Y.; z 08812; ● 2,400
Green Brook; MCD-Township; SOMERSET; *204 G-10; 🅿; ★ N.Y.; z 08812; Ⓟ 4,460; Ⓒ 5,654
Green Creek; RMC Place; CAPE MAY; ▲ Middle; 205 S-2; 🅿; z 08219; ● 900
Greendell; RMC Place; SUSSEX; ▲ Green; 204 D-8; 🅿; ★ N.Y.; z 07839; ● 200
Greenfield; RMC Place; CAPE MAY; ▲ Upper; *205 R-9; ★ ATCY; mail Ocean View z 08230; ● 200
Greenfield Heights; RMC Place; GLOUCESTER; ▲ West Deptford; *205 M-6; ★ PHIL-; mail Woodbury z 08096; ● 700
Greenfields Village; RMC Place; GLOUCESTER; ▲ West Deptford; *205 M-6; ★ PHIL-; mail Woodbury z 08096; ● 1,500
Green Grove; RMC Place; MONMOUTH; ▲ Ocean; *204 J-13; ★ N.Y.; mail Asbury Park z 07712; ● 400
Greenhaven; RMC Place; CAMDEN; ▲ Cherry Hill; *205 L-7; ★ PHIL-; mail Cherry Hill z 08002
Green Hills; RMC Place; SOMERSET; ▲ Hillsborough; *204 G-9; elev. 60ft./18m.; ★ N.Y.; mail Somerville z 08876; ● 500
Green Island; RMC Place; OCEAN; ▲ Toms River; *205 L-12; ★ N.Y.; mail Toms River z 08753; ● 1,400
Green Knoll; RMC Place; SOMERSET; ▲ Bridgewater; *204 G-9; ★ N.Y.; mail Somerville z 08876
Greenland; RMC Place; CAMDEN; *205 M-7; ★ PHIL-; mail Magnolia z 08049; pop. incl. with Magnolia (Inc. Place)
Green Pond; RMC Place; MORRIS; ▲ Rockaway; 204 D-10; ★ N.Y.; mail Newfoundland z 07435; ● 900
Green Pond Junction; RMC Place; MORRIS; *204 D-11; elev. 681ft./208m.; ★ N.Y.; mail Butler z 07405; pop. incl. with Kinnelon (Inc. Place)
Greensand; RMC Place; MIDDLESEX; ▲ Edison; ★ N.Y.; mail Edison z 08817
Greentree; CDP-Census Area Only; CAMDEN; *205 M-7; ★ PHIL-; Ⓒ 11,536
Green Village; RMC Place; MORRIS; ▲ Harding, Chatham; 204 F-10; elev. 254ft./77m.; 🅿; ★ N.Y.; z 07935; ● 400
Greenville; RMC Place; HUDSON; *204 F-12; ★ N.Y.; mail Jersey City z 07305; pop. incl. with Jersey City (Inc. Place)
Greenville; RMC Place; OCEAN; ▲ Lakewood; *205 K-12; ★ N.Y.; mail Lakewood z 08701; rural
Greenville; RMC Place; SALEM; ▲ Pittsgrove; *205 O-6; ★ VINL; mail Elmer z 08318; rural
Greenwich; RMC Place; CUMBERLAND; ▲ Greenwich; 205 P-5; 🅿; z 08323; ● 700
Greenwich; MCD-Township; CUMBERLAND; *205 Q-5; 🅿; z 08323; Ⓟ 911; Ⓒ 847
Greenwich; MCD-Township; GLOUCESTER; *205 M-5; ★ PHIL-; mail Gibbstown z 08027; Ⓟ 5,102; Ⓒ 4,879
Greenwich; MCD-Township; WARREN; *204 F-6; ★ ALL-; mail Stewartsville z 08886; Ⓟ 1,899; Ⓒ 4,365
Greenwich Pier; RMC Place; CUMBERLAND; ▲ Greenwich; *205 Q-5; mail Greenwich z 08323
Greenwood Park; RMC Place; GLOUCESTER; ▲ Washington; *205 N-7; ★ PHIL-; mail Pitman z 08071; ● 2,000
Grenloch; RMC Place; CAMDEN; ▲ Gloucester; 205 M-7; 🅿; ★ PHIL-; z 08032; ● 450
Grenloch Terrace; RMC Place; GLOUCESTER; ▲ Washington; *205 M-7; ★ PHIL-; mail Grenloch z 08032; ● 350
Griggstown; RMC Place; SOMERSET; ▲ Franklin; 204 H-9; ★ N.Y.; mail Princeton z 08540; ● 900
Grove; RMC Place; ESSEX; *204 F-12; ★ N.Y.; mail Bloomfield z 07003
Grovers Mill; RMC Place; MERCER; ▲ West Windsor; *204 I-9; ★ N.Y.; mail Princeton Junction z 08550; ● 120
Groveville; RMC Place; MERCER; ▲ Hamilton; 205 T-14; ★ PHIL-; mail Trenton z 08620; ● 2,500
Gum Tree Corner; RMC Place; CUMBERLAND; ▲ Stow Creek; *205 P-5; elev. 38ft./12m.; mail Bridgeton z 08302; rural
Guttenberg; Inc. Place; HUDSON; 204 C-5; elev. 240ft./73m.; 🅿; ★ N.Y.; z 07093; Ⓟ 8,268; Ⓒ 10,807

H

Hackensack; Inc. Place; ⊡ BERGEN; 204 E-13; elev. 22ft./7m.; 🅿 🅷 ■; ★ N.Y.; z 07601-02; Ⓟ 37,049; Ⓒ 42,677; ◆ 42,502
Hackettstown; Inc. Place; WARREN; 204 E-8; elev. 571ft./174m.; 🅿 🅷 🅲 2,662; ★ N.Y.; z 07840; Ⓟ 8,120; Ⓒ 10,403; Ⓡ 8,984
Hacklebarney; RMC Place; MORRIS; ▲ Chester; *204 F-9; ★ N.Y.; mail Chester z 07930; rural
Haddon; MCD-Township; CAMDEN; *205 L-7; ★ PHIL-; mail Audubon z 08106, Camden z 08104, Collingswood z 08108, Oaklyn z 08107; Ⓟ 14,837; Ⓒ 14,651
Haddonfield; Inc. Place; CAMDEN; 205 M-7; elev. 95ft./29m.; 🅿; ★ PHIL-; z 08033; Ⓟ 11,628; Ⓒ 11,659
Haddon Heights; Inc. Place; CAMDEN; *205 M-7; elev. 81ft./25m.; 🅿; ★ PHIL-; z 08035; Ⓟ 7,860; Ⓒ 7,547
Haddon Hills; RMC Place; CAMDEN; ▲ Haddon; *205 M-7; ★ PHIL-; mail Haddonfield z 08033; ● 500
Haddon Leigh; RMC Place; CAMDEN; *205 M-7; ★ PHIL-; mail Haddonfield z 08033; pop. incl. with Haddonfield (Inc. Place)
Haddontowne; RMC Place; CAMDEN; ▲ Cherry Hill; *205 M-7; ★ PHIL-; mail Cherry Hill z 08034
Hainesburg; RMC Place; WARREN; ▲ Knowlton; 204 D-7; ★ N.Y.; mail Columbia z 07832; ● 70
Haines Corner; RMC Place; MERCER; ▲ Hamilton; *204 J-9; ★ PHIL-; mail Trenton z 08690
Hainesport; RMC Place; BURLINGTON; ▲ Hainesport; 205 L-8; elev. 41ft./12m.; 🅿; ★ PHIL-; z 08036; ● 1,200
Hainesport; MCD-Township; BURLINGTON; *205 L-8; 🅿; ★ PHIL-; z 08036 & mail Mount Holly z 08060; Ⓟ 3,249; Ⓒ 4,126
Hainesville; RMC Place; SUSSEX; ▲ Sandyston; 204 B-8; mail Branchville z 07826; ● 100
Haledon; Inc. Place; PASSAIC; 204 D-12; elev. 150ft./46m.; 🅿; ★ N.Y.; z 07508, z 07538; Ⓟ 6,951; Ⓒ 8,252
Haleyville; RMC Place; CUMBERLAND; ▲ Commercial; 205 Q-7; ★ VINL; mail Port Norris z 08349; ● 120
Halsey; RMC Place; SUSSEX; ▲ Hampton; 204 C-9; ★ N.Y.; mail Newton z 07860; ● 60
Hamburg; Inc. Place; SUSSEX; 204 C-10; elev. 453ft./138m.; 🅿; ★ N.Y.; z 07419; Ⓟ 2,566; Ⓒ 3,105
Hamden; RMC Place; HUNTERDON; ▲ Clinton; 204 G-8; ★ N.Y.; mail Annandale z 08801
Hamilton; MCD-Township; ATLANTIC; *205 P-9; ★ ATCY; mail Mays Landing z 08330; Ⓟ 16,012; Ⓒ 20,499; ◆ 24,072
Hamilton; MCD-Township; MERCER; *204 J-9; 🅿; ★ PHIL-; z 08609-11, z 08619-20, z 08629, z 08650, z 08690-91; Ⓟ 86,553; Ⓒ 87,109; ◆ 86,593
Hamilton; RMC Place; MONMOUTH; ▲ Neptune; ★ N.Y.; mail Neptune z 07753
Hamilton; RMC Place; SOMERSET; mail Belle Mead z 08502; ● 400
Hamilton Square; RMC Place; MERCER; ▲ Hamilton; 205 T-13; 🅿 🅷; ★ PHIL-; z 08690; ● 11,000
Hammonton; Inc. Place; ATLANTIC; 205 O-8; elev. 100ft./30m.; 🅿 🅷; ★ ATCY; z 08037; Ⓟ 12,208; Ⓒ 12,604
Hampton; Inc. Place; HUNTERDON; 204 F-7; elev. 496ft./151m.; 🅿; ★ N.Y.; z 08827; Ⓟ 1,515; Ⓒ 1,546
Hampton; MCD-Township; SUSSEX; *204 C-8; ★ N.Y.; mail Newton z 07860; Ⓟ 4,438; Ⓒ 4,943
Hancocks Bridge; RMC Place; SALEM; ▲ Lower Alloways Creek; 205 P-4; 🅿; z 08038; ● 350
Hanover; MCD-Township; MORRIS; *204 E-10; ★ N.Y.; mail Whippany z 07981; Ⓟ 11,538; Ⓒ 12,898
Hanover Neck; RMC Place; MORRIS; ▲ East Hanover; *204 E-11; ★ N.Y.; mail East Hanover z 07936
Hanover Township; RMC Place; MORRIS; ▲ Hanover; *204 E-10; ★ N.Y.; mail Whippany z 07981; Ⓟ 11,538
Harbourton; RMC Place; MERCER; ▲ Hopewell; 205 Q-11; ★ PHIL-; mail Lambertville z 08530
Harding; MCD-Township; MORRIS; *204 F-10; ★ N.Y.; mail East Hanover z 07936; Ⓟ 3,640; Ⓒ 3,180
Harding Lakes; RMC Place; ATLANTIC; ▲ Hamilton; 205 P-9; ★ ATCY; mail Mays Landing z 08330; ● 1,000
Hardingville; RMC Place; GLOUCESTER; ▲ Elk; *205 N-6; ★ PHIL-; mail Monroeville z 08343
Hardistonville; RMC Place; SUSSEX; 204 C-10; ★ N.Y.; mail Hamburg z 07419; pop. incl. with Hamburg (Inc. Place)
Hardwick; MCD-Township; WARREN; *204 D-7; 🅿; ★ N.Y.; z 07825; Ⓟ 1,255; Ⓒ 1,464
Hardyston; MCD-Township; SUSSEX; *204 C-10; 🅿; ★ N.Y.; z 07460; Ⓟ 5,275; Ⓒ 6,171
Harlingen; RMC Place; SOMERSET; ▲ Montgomery; 204 H-9; mail Belle Mead z 08502; ● 300
Harmersville; RMC Place; SALEM; ▲ Lower Alloways Creek; 205 P-4; mail Salem z 08079
Harmony; RMC Place; MONMOUTH; ▲ Middletown; *204 H-12; ★ N.Y.; mail Middletown z 07748
Harmony; RMC Place; OCEAN; ▲ Jackson; *205 K-11; ★ N.Y.; mail Jackson z 08527; ● 120
Harmony; RMC Place; WARREN; ▲ Harmony; 204 F-6; ★ ALL-; mail Phillipsburg z 08865; ● 200
Harmony; MCD-Township; WARREN; *204 F-6; ★ ALL-; mail Phillipsburg z 08865; Ⓟ 2,653; Ⓒ 2,729
Harrington Park; Inc. Place; BERGEN; 210 A-10; elev. 50ft./15m.; 🅿; ★ N.Y.; z 07640; Ⓟ 4,623; Ⓒ 4,740
Harrison; MCD-Township; GLOUCESTER; *205 N-6; ★ PHIL-; mail Mullica Hill z 08062; Ⓟ 4,715; Ⓒ 8,788
Harrison; Inc. Place; HUDSON; 204 F-12; elev. 30ft./9m.; 🅿; ★ N.Y.; z 07029; Ⓟ 13,425; Ⓒ 14,424
Harrisonville; RMC Place; GLOUCESTER; ▲ South Harrison; 205 N-5; elev. 83ft./25m.; 🅿; ★ PHIL-; z 08039; ● 500
Harrisonville; RMC Place; SALEM; ▲ Pennsville; 205 O-4; ★ PHIL-; mail Salem z 08079; rural
Hartford; RMC Place; BURLINGTON; ▲ Mount Laurel; 205 L-8; elev. 45ft./14m.; ★ PHIL-; mail Moorestown z 08057; ● 300
Harvey Cedars; Inc. Place; OCEAN; 205 N-12; elev. 5ft./2m.; 🅿; ★ N.Y.; z 08008; Ⓟ 362; summer pop. 3,000; Ⓒ 359
Hasbrouck Heights; Inc. Place; BERGEN; 204 E-13; elev. 130ft./40m.; 🅿; ★ N.Y.; z 07604; Ⓟ 11,488; Ⓒ 11,662
Haskell; RMC Place; PASSAIC; *204 D-11; elev. 218ft./66m.; 🅿; ★ N.Y.; z 07420; pop. incl. with Wanaque (Inc. Place)
Haven Beach; RMC Place; OCEAN; ▲ Long Beach; *205 O-12; ★ N.Y.; mail Beach Haven z 08008; summer pop. 1,000; ● 200
Haven Homes; RMC Place; MIDDLESEX; *204 H-11; mail Edison z 08817; ● 1,850
Haworth; Inc. Place; BERGEN; 210 B-10; elev. 69ft./21m.; 🅿; ★ N.Y.; z 07641; Ⓟ 3,384; Ⓒ 3,390
Hawthorne; Inc. Place; PASSAIC; 204 D-12; elev. 50ft./15m.; 🅿; ★ N.Y.; z 07506-07; Ⓟ 17,084; Ⓒ 18,218
Hazelton; RMC Place; MIDDLESEX; ▲ Woodbridge; *204 G-11; ★ N.Y.; mail Avenel z 07001
Hazen; RMC Place; WARREN; ▲ White; 204 E-7; ★ N.Y.; mail Belvidere z 07823; ● 30
Hazlet; RMC Place; MONMOUTH; ▲ Hazlet; 204 H-12; 🅿; ★ N.Y.; z 07730; ● 12,000
Hazlet; MCD-Township; MONMOUTH; *204 H-12; 🅿; ★ N.Y.; z 07730; Ⓟ 21,976; Ⓒ 21,378; ◆ 21,758
Head Of River; RMC Place; ATLANTIC; *205 Q-8; mail Woodbine z 08270; pop. incl. with Estell Manor (Inc. Place)
Headquarters; RMC Place; HUNTERDON; ▲ Delaware; *204 H-7; elev. 263ft./80m.; mail Sergeantsville z 08557; rural
Heathcote; CDP-Census Area Only; MIDDLESEX; ▲ South Brunswick; *204 I-10; elev. 264ft./80m.; ★ N.Y.; mail Kingston z 08528, Princeton z 08540; Ⓟ 3,112; Ⓒ 4,755
Hedding; RMC Place; BURLINGTON; ▲ Mansfield; 205 K-9; ★ PHIL-; mail Bordentown z 08505; ● 150
Heislerville; RMC Place; CUMBERLAND; ▲ Maurice River; 205 R-7; 🅿; z 08324; ● 500
Helmetta; Inc. Place; MIDDLESEX; 204 I-10; elev. 40ft./12m.; 🅿; ★ N.Y.; z 08828; Ⓟ 1,211; Ⓒ 1,825
Hendrickson Corners; RMC Place; MONMOUTH; *204 H-13; mail Holmdel z 07733, Middletown z 07748; ● 1,200
Hensfoot; RMC Place; HUNTERDON; ▲ Union; *204 G-7; ★ N.Y.; mail Hampton z 08827; rural
Herberts; RMC Place; MIDDLESEX; mail East Brunswick z 08816; ● 500
Herbertsville; RMC Place; OCEAN; ▲ Brick; *205 K-12; ★ N.Y.; mail Brick z 08723
Heritage Village; RMC Place; BURLINGTON; ▲ Evesham; *205 M-8; ★ PHIL-; mail Marlton z 08053; ● 2,500
Herman (Hermon); RMC Place; BURLINGTON; ▲ Washington; *205 O-9; mail Egg Harbor City z 08215; rural
Hermon; BURLINGTON; see Herman (RMC Place)
Herwood; RMC Place; CAMDEN; ▲ Cherry Hill; *205 L-7; ★ PHIL-; mail Cherry Hill z 08002
Hesstown; RMC Place; CUMBERLAND; ▲ Maurice River; *205 Q-7; mail Millville z 08332; ● 50
Hewitt; RMC Place; PASSAIC; ▲ West Milford; 204 C-11; 🅿; ★ N.Y.; z 07421; ● 200
Heyden; RMC Place; MIDDLESEX; ▲ Woodbridge; ★ N.Y.
Hibernia; RMC Place; MORRIS; ▲ Rockaway; 204 D-10; 🅿; ★ N.Y.; z 07842; ● 200
Hickory Acres; RMC Place; MERCER; ▲ East Windsor; *204 J-10; elev. 100ft./30m.; ★ N.Y.; mail Hightstown z 08520
Hickory Tree; RMC Place; MORRIS; ▲ Chatham; *204 F-10; ★ N.Y.; mail Chatham z 07928; ● 400
Hickstown; RMC Place; CAMDEN; ▲ Gloucester; *205 M-7; ★ PHIL-; mail Blackwood z 08012
High Bridge; Inc. Place; HUNTERDON; 204 F-8; elev. 332ft./101m.; 🅿; ★ N.Y.; z 08829; Ⓟ 3,886; Ⓒ 3,776
High Crest Lake; RMC Place; PASSAIC; ▲ West Milford; *204 D-11; ★ N.Y.; mail West Milford z 07480; ● 300
Highland Lake (Highland Lakes); CDP; SUSSEX; ▲ Vernon; 204 B-10; ★ N.Y.; mail Highland Lakes z 07422; Ⓟ 4,550; summer pop. 12,000; Ⓒ 5,051
Highland Lakes; SUSSEX; see Highland Lake (CDP)
Highland Park; RMC Place; CAMDEN; *205 M-6; ★ PHIL-; mail Gloucester City z 08030; pop. incl. with Gloucester City (Inc. Place)
Highland Park; Inc. Place; MIDDLESEX; 204 H-11; elev. 99ft./30m.; 🅿; ★ N.Y.; z 08904; Ⓟ 13,279; Ⓒ 13,999
Highlands; Inc. Place; MONMOUTH; 204 I-13; elev. 104ft./32m.; 🅿; ★ N.Y.; z 07732; Ⓟ 4,849; Ⓒ 5,097
Highlands Beach; RMC Place; CAPE MAY; ▲ Lower; *205 T-7; mail Villas z 08251
High Point; RMC Place; OCEAN; *205 N-12; ★ N.Y.; mail Beach Haven z 08008, Sussex z 07461; pop. incl. with Harvey Cedars (Inc. Place)
Highs Beach; RMC Place; CAPE MAY; ▲ Middle; *205 S-8; mail Cape May Court House z 08210; ● 20
Hightstown; Inc. Place; MERCER; 204 J-10; elev. 84ft./26m.; 🅿; ★ N.Y.; z 08520; Ⓟ 5,126; Ⓒ 5,216
Hightstown Heights; RMC Place; MERCER; ▲ East Windsor; *204 J-10; elev. 103ft./31m.; ★ N.Y.; mail Hightstown z 08520; ● 100
Highview; RMC Place; PASSAIC; ▲ West Milford; *204 C-11; ★ N.Y.; mail West Milford z 07480; ● 200
Highview Park; RMC Place; MONMOUTH; ▲ Wall; *205 K-13; ★ N.Y.; mail Manasquan z 08736; ● 800
Hillcrest; RMC Place; MERCER; *204 J-8; ★ PHIL-; mail Trenton z 08618; pop. incl. with Trenton (Inc. Place)
Hillcrest; RMC Place; PASSAIC; *204 D-12; ★ N.Y.; mail Paterson z 07502; pop. incl. with Paterson (Inc. Place)
Hillsborough; RMC Place; SOMERSET; ▲ Hillsborough; *204 H-9; 🅿; ★ N.Y.; z 08844; rural
Hillsborough; MCD-Township; SOMERSET; *204 H-9; 🅿; ★ N.Y.; z 08844; Ⓟ 28,808; Ⓒ 36,634; ◆ 39,313
Hillsdale; Inc. Place; BERGEN; 204 D-13; elev. 83ft./25m.; 🅿; ★ N.Y.; z 07642 & mail Township Of Washington z 07676; Ⓟ 9,750; Ⓒ 10,087
Hillsdale Manor; RMC Place; BERGEN; *204 D-13; ★ N.Y.; mail Hillsdale z 07642; pop. incl. with Hillsdale (Inc. Place)
Hillside; CDP; UNION; ▲ Hillside; 204 F-12; 🅿; ★ N.Y.; z 07205; Ⓟ 21,044; Ⓒ 21,747; ◆ 21,170
Hillside; MCD-Township; UNION; *204 F-12; 🅿; ★ N.Y.; z 07205; Ⓟ 21,044; Ⓒ 21,747; ◆ 21,170
Hilltop; RMC Place; CAMDEN; ▲ Gloucester; *205 M-7; ★ PHIL-; mail Blackwood z 08012; ● 2,200
Hilltop Terrace; RMC Place; MIDDLESEX; ▲ East Brunswick; ★ N.Y.; mail East Brunswick z 08816
Hilltown; RMC Place; MORRIS; ▲ Rockaway; *204 D-10; ★ N.Y.; mail Wharton z 07885
Hi-Lo Acres; RMC Place; PASSAIC; ▲ West Milford; *204 C-10; ★ N.Y.; mail Newfoundland z 07435; ● 150
Hi-Nella; Inc. Place; CAMDEN; *205 M-7; elev. 83ft./25m.; 🅿; ★ PHIL-; z 08083; Ⓟ 1,045; Ⓒ 1,029
Hoboken; Inc. Place; HUDSON; 204 F-13; elev. 5ft./2m.; 🅿 🅷 🅲 5,082 ■; ★ N.Y.; z 07030; Ⓟ 33,397; Ⓒ 38,577; ◆ 40,731
Hoffmans; RMC Place; HUNTERDON; ▲ Lebanon; *204 F-8; ★ N.Y.; mail Califon z 07830; ● 80
Ho-Ho-Kus; Inc. Place; BERGEN; *204 D-12; elev. 111ft./34m.; 🅿; ★ N.Y.; z 07423; Ⓟ 3,935; Ⓒ 4,060
Holgate; RMC Place; OCEAN; ▲ Long Beach; 205 O-12; ★ N.Y.; mail Beach Haven z 08008
Holiday Beach; RMC Place; OCEAN; ▲ Barnegat; *205 M-12; ★ N.Y.; mail Forked River z 08731; ● 700
Holiday City; RMC Place; OCEAN; ▲ Toms River; 205 L-12; ★ N.Y.; mail Toms River z 08753; ● 800
Holiday City at Berkeley; RMC Place; OCEAN; ▲ Berkeley; *205 L-12; elev. 50ft./15m.; ★ N.Y.; mail Toms River z 08757; ● 8,000
Holiday City-Berkeley; CDP-Census Area Only; OCEAN; ▲ Berkeley; *205 L-11; ★ N.Y.; mail Toms River z 08757; Ⓟ 14,293; Ⓒ 13,884
Holiday City South; CDP-Census Area Only; OCEAN; ▲ Berkeley; *205 L-12; elev. 34ft./10m.; ★ N.Y.; mail Toms River z 08757; Ⓟ 5,452; Ⓒ 4,047
Holiday City West; RMC Place; OCEAN; ▲ Berkeley; *205 L-11; elev. 50ft./15m.; ★ N.Y.; mail Toms River z 08757; ● 3,000
Holiday Heights; CDP-Census Area Only; OCEAN; ▲ Berkeley; *205 L-12; elev. 50ft./15m.; ★ N.Y.; mail Toms River z 08757; Ⓟ 703; Ⓒ 2,389
Holiday on the Bay; RMC Place; OCEAN; ▲ Toms River; *205 L-12; ★ N.Y.; mail Toms River z 08753; ● 400
Holland; RMC Place; HUNTERDON; ▲ Holland; *204 G-6; mail Milford z 08848; ● 40
Holland; MCD-Township; HUNTERDON; *204 G-6; mail Milford z 08848; Ⓟ 4,892; Ⓒ 5,124
Holland (Lake Stockholm); RMC Place; SUSSEX, MORRIS; ▲ Hardyston, Jefferson; *204 C-10; ★ N.Y.; mail Stockholm z 07460; ● 350
Holly Park; RMC Place; OCEAN; ▲ Berkeley; 205 M-12; ★ N.Y.; mail Bayville z 08721; ● 700
Holmansville; RMC Place; OCEAN; ▲ Jackson; *205 K-11; ★ N.Y.; mail Jackson z 08527; rural
Holmdel; RMC Place; MONMOUTH; ▲ Holmdel; 204 I-12; 🅿 🅷; ★ N.Y.; z 07733; ● 900
Holmdel; MCD-Township; MONMOUTH; *204 I-12; 🅿; ★ N.Y.; z 07733; Ⓟ 11,532; Ⓒ 15,781
Holmeson; RMC Place; MONMOUTH; ▲ Millstone; 204 J-11; ★ PHIL-; mail Millstone Township z 08510
Homes Mills; RMC Place; MONMOUTH; ▲ Upper Freehold; *205 K-10; elev. 60ft./18m.; ★ PHIL-; mail Cream Ridge z 08514; rural
Homestead Park; RMC Place; MORRIS; ▲ Long Hill; *204 F-10; ★ N.Y.; mail Gillette z 07933; ● 450
Homestead Run; RMC Place; OCEAN; ▲ Toms River; *205 K-12; elev. 80ft./24m.; ★ N.Y.; mail Toms River z 08755; ● 600
Hoot Owl Estates; RMC Place; BURLINGTON; ▲ Medford; *205 M-8; ★ PHIL-; mail Medford z 08055; ● 800
Hopatcong; Inc. Place; SUSSEX; 204 D-9; elev. 1,100ft./335m.; 🅿; ★ N.Y.; z 07843; Ⓟ 15,586; Ⓒ 15,888
Hopatcong Heights; RMC Place; SUSSEX; *204 D-9; ★ N.Y.; mail Hopatcong z 07843; pop. incl. with Hopatcong (Inc. Place)
Hopatcong Hills; RMC Place; SUSSEX; *204 D-9; ★ N.Y.; mail Hopatcong z 07843; pop. incl. with Hopatcong (Inc. Place)
Hope; RMC Place; WARREN; ▲ Hope; 204 E-7; 🅿; ★ N.Y.; z 07844; ● 500
Hope; MCD-Township; WARREN; *204 E-7; 🅿; ★ N.Y.; z 07844; Ⓟ 1,719; Ⓒ 1,891
Hopelawn; RMC Place; MIDDLESEX; ▲ Woodbridge; 210 M-4; 🅿; ★ N.Y.; z 08861; ● 800
Hopewell; MCD-Township; CUMBERLAND; *205 P-5; mail Bridgeton z 08302; Ⓟ 4,215; Ⓒ 4,434
Hopewell; Inc. Place; MERCER; 204 I-8; elev. 180ft./55m.; 🅿; ★ PHIL-; z 08525; Ⓟ 1,968; Ⓒ 2,035
Hopewell; MCD-Township; MERCER; *204 I-8; 🅿; ★ PHIL-; z 08525 & mail Titusville z 08560; does not include the Borough of Hopewell; Ⓟ 11,590; Ⓒ 16,105
Hornerstown; RMC Place; MONMOUTH; ▲ Upper Freehold; 205 K-10; ★ PHIL-; mail Cream Ridge z 08514; ● 150
Howell; RMC Place; MONMOUTH; ▲ Howell; 205 K-12; 🅿; ★ N.Y.; z 07731; rural
Howell; MCD-Township; MONMOUTH; *204 J-12; 🅿; ★ N.Y.; z 07731 & mail Farmingdale z 07727; Ⓟ 38,987; Ⓒ 48,903; ◆ 54,812
HUDSON; 204 F-13; Ⓟ 553,099; Ⓒ 608,975; ◆ 592,282
Hudson City; RMC Place; HUDSON; *204 F-13; ★ N.Y.; mail Jersey City z 07307
Hudson Heights; RMC Place; HUDSON; ▲ North Bergen; *204 E-13; ★ N.Y.; mail North Bergen z 07047
Hughesville; RMC Place; HUNTERDON; ▲ Holland; *204 G-6; mail Milford z 08848; ● 50
HUNTERDON; 204 G-7; Ⓟ 107,776; Ⓒ 121,989; ◆ 126,427
Hunter's Crossing; RMC Place; HUNTERDON; ▲ Readington; *204 H-8; ★ N.Y.; mail Three Bridges z 08887
Huntsburg; RMC Place; SUSSEX; ▲ Green; *204 D-8; ★ N.Y.; mail Newton z 07860; rural
Huntsville; RMC Place; SUSSEX; ▲ Green; *204 D-8; ★ N.Y.; mail Andover z 07821; ● 60
Hunt Tract; RMC Place; CAMDEN; ▲ Cherry Hill; ★ PHIL-; mail Cherry Hill z 08034
Hurdtown; RMC Place; MORRIS; ▲ Jefferson; 204 D-9; ★ N.Y.; mail Wharton z 07885
Hurffville; RMC Place; GLOUCESTER; ▲ Washington; 205 N-6; ★ PHIL-; mail Sewell z 08080; ● 350
Hutchinson; RMC Place; WARREN; ▲ Harmony; 204 F-6; ★ ALL-; mail Phillipsburg z 08865; ● 100
Hutchinson Mills; RMC Place; MERCER; ▲ Hamilton; *204 J-9; ★ PHIL-; mail Trenton z 08619
Hyson; RMC Place; OCEAN; ▲ Jackson; *205 K-11; ★ N.Y.; mail Jackson z 08527; ● 2,000

I

Idell; RMC Place; HUNTERDON; *204 H-7; mail Frenchtown z 08825; rural
Imlaystown; RMC Place; MONMOUTH; ▲ Upper Freehold; 204 J-10; 🅿; ★ PHIL-; z 08526; ● 250
Independence; MCD-Township; WARREN; *204 E-8; ★ N.Y.; mail Hackettstown z 07840; Ⓟ 3,940; Ⓒ 5,603
Independence Corner; RMC Place; SUSSEX; ▲ Vernon; *204 B-10; ★ N.Y.; mail Sussex z 07461; ● 250
Indian Lake; RMC Place; MORRIS; ▲ Denville; *204 E-10; ★ N.Y.; mail Denville z 07834
Indian Mills; RMC Place; BURLINGTON; ▲ Shamong; 205 M-9; ★ PHIL-; mail Vincentown z 08088; ● 150
Interlaken; Inc. Place; MONMOUTH; 204 J-13; elev. 21ft./6m.; 🅿; ★ N.Y.; z 07712; Ⓟ 910; Ⓒ 900
Iona; RMC Place; GLOUCESTER; ▲ Franklin; 205 O-7; ★ PHIL-; mail Franklinville z 08322
Ironbound; RMC Place; ESSEX; *204 F-12; ★ N.Y.; mail Newark z 07105; pop. incl. with Newark (Inc. Place)
Ironia; RMC Place; MORRIS; ▲ Chester, Randolph; 204 E-9; 🅿; ★ N.Y.; z 07845; ● 800
Iron Rock; RMC Place; CAMDEN; ▲ Pennsauken; *205 L-7; ★ PHIL-; mail Merchantville z 08109
Irvington; CDP; ESSEX; ▲ Irvington; 204 F-12; elev. 185ft./56m.; 🅿 🅷; ★ N.Y.; z 07111; Ⓟ 59,774; Ⓒ 60,695; ◆ 57,286
Irvington; MCD-Township; ESSEX; *204 F-12; 🅿 ■; ★ N.Y.; z 07111; Ⓟ 61,018; Ⓒ 60,695; ◆ 57,286
Iselin; CDP; MIDDLESEX; ▲ Woodbridge; 204 G-11; 🅿; ★ N.Y.; z 08830; Ⓟ 16,141; Ⓒ 16,698
Island Heights; Inc. Place; OCEAN; 205 L-12; elev. 17ft./5m.; 🅿; ★ N.Y.; z 08732; Ⓟ 1,470; Ⓒ 1,751
Ivystone Farms; RMC Place; CAMDEN; ▲ Waterford; *205 N-8; ★ PHIL-; mail Atco z 08004; ● 1,100
Ivywood; RMC Place; BURLINGTON; ▲ Cinnaminson; *205 L-7; ★ PHIL-; mail Riverton z 08077

J

Jackson; RMC Place; CAMDEN; ▲ Waterford; *205 N-8; elev. 125ft./38m.; ★ PHIL-; mail Atco z 08004
Jackson; RMC Place; HUDSON; *204 F-12; ★ N.Y.; mail Jersey City z 07305; pop. incl. with Jersey City (Inc. Place)
Jackson; OCEAN; see Cassville (RMC Place)
Jackson; MCD-Township; OCEAN; *205 K-11; 🅿; ★ N.Y.; z 08527; Ⓟ 33,233; Ⓒ 42,816; ◆ 49,785
Jacksonburg; RMC Place; WARREN; ▲ Blairstown; 204 D-7; ★ N.Y.; mail Blairstown z 07825; ● 200
Jackson Estates; RMC Place; OCEAN; ▲ Jackson; *205 K-11; elev. 100ft./30m.; ★ N.Y.; mail Jackson z 08527; ● 250
Jacksons Mills; RMC Place; OCEAN; ▲ Jackson; 205 K-11; ★ N.Y.; mail Jackson z 08527
Jacksonville; RMC Place; BURLINGTON; ▲ Springfield; 205 K-8; ★ PHIL-; mail Bordentown z 08505; ● 125
Jacksonville; RMC Place; MORRIS; *204 D-11; ★ N.Y.; mail Lincoln Park z 07035; pop. incl. with Lincoln Park (Inc. Place)
Jacobstown; RMC Place; BURLINGTON; ▲ North Hanover; 205 K-10; ★ PHIL-; mail Wrightstown z 08562; ● 150
Jamesburg; Inc. Place; MIDDLESEX; 204 I-10; elev. 65ft./20m.; 🅿; ★ N.Y.; z 08831; Ⓟ 5,294; Ⓒ 6,025
Jamesburg Gardens; RMC Place; MIDDLESEX; mail Monroe Township z 08831; ● 250
Janvier; RMC Place; GLOUCESTER; ▲ Franklin; *205 O-7; elev. 129ft./39m.; ★ PHIL-; mail Franklinville z 08322
Jefferson; RMC Place; GLOUCESTER; ▲ Harrison; 205 N-6; ★ PHIL-; mail Mullica Hill z 08062; ● 125
Jefferson; MCD-Township; MORRIS; *204 D-9; ★ N.Y.; mail Lake Hopatcong z 07849, Oak Ridge z 07438; Ⓟ 17,825; Ⓒ 19,717; ◆ 20,681
Jenkins; RMC Place; BURLINGTON; ▲ Washington; 205 N-10; elev. 42ft./13m.; mail Chatsworth z 08019; ● 60
Jersey City; Inc. Place; ⊡ HUDSON; 204 F-13; elev. 11ft./3m.; 🅿 🅷 🅲 11,639 ■; ★ N.Y.; z 07097, z 07302-11, z 07395, z 07399; Ⓟ 228,537; Ⓒ 240,055; ◆ 226,057
Jerseyville; RMC Place; MONMOUTH; ▲ Howell; 204 J-12; ★ N.Y.; mail Freehold z 07728; ● 50
Jobstown; RMC Place; BURLINGTON; ▲ Springfield; 205 K-9; 🅿; ★ PHIL-; z 08041; ● 100
Johnsonburg; RMC Place; WARREN; ▲ Frelinghuysen; 204 D-8; 🅿; ★ N.Y.; z 07846; ● 250
Jones Island; RMC Place; CUMBERLAND; ▲ Lawrence; *205 Q-6; mail Cedarville z 08311; rural
Jordantown; RMC Place; CAMDEN; ▲ Pennsauken; *205 L-7; ★ PHIL-; mail Merchantville z 08109
Journal Square; RMC Place; HUDSON; *204 F-13; ★ N.Y.; mail Jersey City z 07306; pop. incl. with Jersey City (Inc. Place)
Juliustown; RMC Place; BURLINGTON; ▲ Springfield; 205 L-9; 🅿; ★ PHIL-; z 08042; ● 330
Jutland; RMC Place; HUNTERDON; ▲ Union; *204 G-7; mail Hampton z 08827; ● 80

K

Karrsville; RMC Place; WARREN; ▲ Mansfield; *204 E-7; ★ N.Y.; mail Port Murray z 07865
Kay Gardens; RMC Place; SALEM; ▲ Oldmans; *205 N-4; ★ PHIL-; mail Pedricktown z 08067; ● 150
Keansburg (Keyport); Inc. Place; MONMOUTH; 204 H-12; elev. 13ft./4m.; 🅿; ★ N.Y.; z 07734; Ⓟ 11,069; Ⓒ 10,732
Kearny; Inc. Place; HUDSON; 204 F-12; elev. 104ft./32m.; 🅿 🅷 ■; ★ N.Y.; z 07032, z 07099; Ⓟ 34,874; Ⓒ 40,513; ◆ 40,109
Keasbey (Keasbeys); RMC Place; MIDDLESEX; ▲ Woodbridge; *204 H-11; 🅿; ★ N.Y.; z 08832
Keasbeys; MIDDLESEX; see Keasbey (RMC Place)
Kemah Lake; RMC Place; SUSSEX; ▲ Hampton; *204 C-8; ★ N.Y.; mail Newton z 07860; ● 300
Kendall Park; CDP; MIDDLESEX; ▲ South Brunswick; 204 H-10; 🅿; ★ N.Y.; z 08824; Ⓟ 7,127; Ⓒ 9,006
Kenilworth; Inc. Place; UNION; 210 I-4; elev. 91ft./28m.; 🅿; ★ N.Y.; z 07033; Ⓟ 7,574; Ⓒ 7,675
Kenvil; RMC Place; MORRIS; ▲ Roxbury; 204 E-9; elev. 719ft./219m.; 🅿; ★ N.Y.; z 07847; ● 2,500
Keswick Grove; RMC Place; OCEAN; ▲ Manchester; *205 L-11; ★ N.Y.; mail Manchester Township z 08759; seasonal pop. 300
Keyport; Inc. Place; MONMOUTH; 204 H-12; elev. 25ft./8m.; 🅿; ★ N.Y.; z 07735; Ⓟ 7,586; Ⓒ 7,568
Keyport; MONMOUTH; see Keansburg (Inc. Place)
Kingsland; RMC Place; BERGEN; ▲ Lyndhurst; 204 C-3; ★ N.Y.; mail Lyndhurst z 07071
Kingston; CDP-Census Area Only; MIDDLESEX; *204 I-9; ★ N.Y.; Ⓒ 1,292
Kingston; RMC Place; SOMERSET; ▲ Franklin; 204 I-9; 🅿; ★ N.Y.; z 08528; ● 700
Kingston Estates; RMC Place; CAMDEN; ▲ Cherry Hill; *205 L-7; ★ PHIL-; mail Cherry Hill z 08034
Kings Woods; RMC Place; BERGEN; *204 D-13; ★ N.Y.; mail Alpine z 07620; pop. incl. with Alpine (Inc. Place)
Kingwood; MCD-Township; HUNTERDON; *204 H-7; mail Frenchtown z 08825; Ⓟ 3,325; Ⓒ 3,782
Kinkora; RMC Place; BURLINGTON; ▲ Mansfield; *205 K-9; ★ PHIL-; mail Bordentown z 08505; ● 80
Kinnelon; Inc. Place; MORRIS; 204 D-11; elev. 760ft./232m.; 🅿; ★ N.Y.; z 07405; Ⓟ 8,470; Ⓒ 9,365
Kirbys Mill; RMC Place; BURLINGTON; ▲ Medford; *205 L-8; ★ PHIL-; mail Medford z 08055; ● 100
Kirkwood; RMC Place; CAMDEN; 205 M-7; 🅿; ★ PHIL-; z 08043; pop. incl. with Lindenwold (Inc. Place)
Kirkwood Voorhees (Voorhees); RMC Place; CAMDEN; ▲ Voorhees; *205 M-7; 🅷; ★ PHIL-; mail Voorhees z 08043; ● 10,000
Kitchell Lake; RMC Place; PASSAIC; ▲ West Milford; *204 C-11; ★ N.Y.; mail West Milford z 07480; ● 300
Kittatinny Lake; RMC Place; SUSSEX; ▲ Sandyston; *204 B-8; mail Branchville z 07826; ● 400
Klinesville; RMC Place; HUNTERDON; ▲ Raritan; *204 G-8; ★ N.Y.; mail Flemington z 08822
Knollwood; RMC Place; CAMDEN; ▲ Cherry Hill; ★ PHIL-; mail Cherry Hill z 08002
Knowlton; RMC Place; WARREN; ▲ Knowlton; *204 D-7; ★ N.Y.; mail Columbia z 07832; rural
Knowlton; MCD-Township; WARREN; *204 D-7; ★ N.Y.; mail Columbia z 07832; Ⓟ 2,543; Ⓒ 2,977
Kresson; RMC Place; BURLINGTON, CAMDEN; ▲ Voorhees, Evesham; *205 M-7; ★ PHIL-; mail Marlton z 08053; ● 200

Entries in **UPPERCASE** are counties.
Entries in **bold** have populations of 2,500 or more.
Names in parentheses are alternate names.

Inc. Place	Incorporated Place
RMC Place	Rand McNally Designated Place
CDP	Census Designated Place
MCD	Minor Civil Division
⊡	County Seat
▲	Minor Civil Division
elev.	Elevation
🅿	Post Office
🅷	Hospital
🅲	College
■	Principal Business Center
★	Ranally Metro Area (RMA) Abbreviation
z	Zip Code(s)
Ⓟ	Previous Census Population
Ⓡ	Revised Census Population
Ⓐ	Annexation Population
●	Rand McNally Population Estimate
Ⓒ	Final Census Population
Ⓢ	Special Census Population
◆	Estimated Population

For additional definitions see Glossary, Volume 1, and Introduction, Volume 2.

L

Lacey; MCD-Township; OCEAN; ***205** M-11; ★ **N.Y.**; mail Forked River **z** 08731, Lanoka Harbor **z** 08734; Ⓟ 22,141; © 25,346; ◆ 26,136

Lafayette; RMC Place; SUSSEX; ▲ Lafayette; **204** C-9; [P]; ★ **N.Y.**; **z** 07848; ● 350

Lafayette; MCD-Township; SUSSEX; ***204** C-9; [P]; ★ **N.Y.**; **z** 07848; Ⓟ 1,902; © 2,300

La Gorce Square; RMC Place; BURLINGTON; ▲ Burlington; ***205** K-8; ★ **PHIL-**; mail Burlington **z** 08016; ● 1,500

Lahiere; RMC Place; MIDDLESEX; ***204** G-10; mail Edison **z** 08817; ● 1,250

Lake Club; RMC Place; MONMOUTH; mail Howell **z** 07731; ● 265

Lake Como (South Belmar); Inc. Place; MONMOUTH; **204** J-13; elev. 14ft./4m.; [P]; ★ **N.Y.**; **z** 07719; Ⓟ 1,482; © 1,806

Lake Forest; RMC Place; MORRIS; ▲ Jefferson; ***204** D-9; ★ **N.Y.**; mail Lake Hopatcong **z** 07849; ● 1,000

Lake Grinnell; RMC Place; SUSSEX; ▲ Sparta; ***204** C-9; ★ **N.Y.**; mail Sparta **z** 07871; ● 150

Lake Hiawatha; RMC Place; MORRIS; ▲ Parsippany-Troy Hills; **204** E-11; [P]; ★ **N.Y.**; **z** 07034

Lake Hopatcong (Espanong); RMC Place; MORRIS; ▲ Jefferson; **204** D-9; [P]; ★ **N.Y.**; **z** 07849; ● 3,000

Lakehurst; Inc. Place; OCEAN; **205** L-11; elev. 72ft./22m.; [P]; ★ **N.Y.**; **z** 08733, **z** 08759; Ⓟ 3,078; © 2,522

Lake Iliff; RMC Place; SUSSEX; ▲ Andover; ***204** D-9; ★ **N.Y.**; mail Newton **z** 07860; ● 500

Lake Lackawanna; RMC Place; SUSSEX; ▲ Byram; ***204** D-9; ★ **N.Y.**; mail Stanhope **z** 07874; ● 900

Lakeland; RMC Place; CAMDEN; ▲ Gloucester; ***205** M-7; [H]; ★ **PHIL-**; mail Blackwood **z** 08012; ● 400

Lake Lenape; RMC Place; SUSSEX; ▲ Andover; **204** D-9; ★ **N.Y.**; mail Newton **z** 07860; ● 700

Lake Mohawk; CDP-Census Area Only; SUSSEX; ▲ Sparta; **204** D-9; ★ **N.Y.**; mail Sparta **z** 07871; Ⓟ 8,930; © 9,755

Lake Neepaulin; RMC Place; SUSSEX; ▲ Wantage; ***204** B-9; ★ **N.Y.**; mail Sussex **z** 07461; ● 900

Lake Nelson; RMC Place; MIDDLESEX; ▲ Piscataway; ***204** H-10; ★ **N.Y.**; mail Piscataway **z** 08854

Lake Owassa; RMC Place; SUSSEX; ▲ Frankford; ***204** C-8; ★ **N.Y.**; mail Newton **z** 07860; ● 250

Lake Pine; RMC Place; BURLINGTON; ▲ Medford; **205** M-8; ★ **PHIL-**; mail Marlton **z** 08053; ● 500

Lakeridge; RMC Place; MIDDLESEX; ▲ Old Bridge; ***204** H-12; ★ **N.Y.**; mail Matawan **z** 07747; ● 1,300

Lake Riviera; RMC Place; OCEAN; ▲ Brick; **205** K-12; ★ **N.Y.**; mail Brick **z** 08723

Lake Rogerine; RMC Place; MORRIS; ***204** E-9; ★ **N.Y.**; mail Mount Arlington **z** 07856; pop. incl. with Mount Arlington (Inc. Place)

Lake Shawnee; RMC Place; MORRIS; ▲ Jefferson; ***204** D-9; ★ **N.Y.**; mail Wharton **z** 07885; ● 1,250

Lakeside; RMC Place; PASSAIC; ▲ West Milford; **204** B-11; ★ **N.Y.**; mail Hewitt **z** 07421; ● 400

Lakeside Park; RMC Place; MERCER; ▲ Hamilton; ***204** J-9; ★ **PHIL-**; mail Trenton **z** 08610

Lake Stockholm; SUSSEX, MORRIS; see Holland (RMC Place)

Lake Swannanoa (Swannanoa); RMC Place; MORRIS; ▲ Jefferson; **204** D-10; ★ **N.Y.**; mail Oak Ridge **z** 07438; ● 1,600

Lake Tamarack; RMC Place; SUSSEX; ▲ Hardyston; **204** C-10; ★ **N.Y.**; mail Stockholm **z** 07460; ● 800

Lake Telemark; CDP; MORRIS; ▲ Rockaway; **204** D-10; ★ **N.Y.**; mail Rockaway **z** 07866; Ⓟ 1,121; © 1,202

Lake Tranquility; RMC Place; SUSSEX; ▲ Green; ***204** D-8; ★ **N.Y.**; mail Andover **z** 07821; ● 300

Lakeview; RMC Place; BURLINGTON; ▲ Eastampton; ***205** L-8; ★ **PHIL-**; mail Mount Holly **z** 08060; ● 1,500

Lake View; RMC Place; PASSAIC; ***204** E-12; ★ **N.Y.**; pop. incl. with Paterson (Inc. Place)

Lake Villa Estates; RMC Place; CAMDEN; ▲ Voorhees; ★ **PHIL-**; mail Voorhees **z** 08043; ● 600

Lake Wallkill; RMC Place; SUSSEX; ▲ Vernon; ***204** B-10; ★ **N.Y.**; mail Sussex **z** 07461; ● 800

Lakewood; CDP; OCEAN; ▲ Lakewood; **205** K-12; [P] [H] [C] 7,938; ★ **N.Y.**; **z** 08701; Ⓟ 26,095; © 36,065; ◆ 40,363

Lakewood; MCD-Township; OCEAN; ***205** K-12; [P] [C] 7,938 ■; ★ **N.Y.**; **z** 08701; Ⓟ 45,048; © 60,352; ◆ 80,592

Lambertville; Inc. Place; HUNTERDON; **204** I-7; elev. 71ft./22m.; [P]; ★ **PHIL-**; **z** 08530; Ⓟ 3,927; © 3,868

Lambs Terrace; RMC Place; CAMDEN; ▲ Gloucester; ***205** N-7; ★ **PHIL-**; mail Sicklerville **z** 08081; ● 250

Lamington; RMC Place; SOMERSET; ▲ Bedminster; **204** F-9; ★ **N.Y.**; mail Bedminster **z** 07921; ● 150

Landing; RMC Place; MORRIS; ▲ Roxbury; ***204** E-9; [P]; ★ **N.Y.**; **z** 07850; ● 3,000

Landisville; RMC Place; ATLANTIC; ***205** O-7; elev. 113ft./34m.; [P]; ★ **VINL**; **z** 08326; pop. incl. with Buena (Inc. Place)

Land of Pines; RMC Place; MONMOUTH; ▲ Howell; ***204** J-12; ★ **N.Y.**; mail Leonardo **z** 07737; ● 700

Landsdown; RMC Place; HUNTERDON; ▲ Franklin; ***204** G-8; ★ **N.Y.**; mail Annandale **z** 08801; rural

Lanes Mills; RMC Place; OCEAN; ▲ Lakewood; ***205** K-12; ★ **N.Y.**; mail Lakewood **z** 08701; rural

Lanoka Harbor; RMC Place; OCEAN; ▲ Lacey; **205** M-12; [P]; ★ **N.Y.**; **z** 08734; ● 2,500

Larger Cross Roads; SOMERSET; see Greater Cross Roads (RMC Place)

Larison's Corner; RMC Place; HUNTERDON; ▲ Raritan, East Amwell; **204** H-8; ★ **PHIL-**; mail Ringoes **z** 08551; ● 15

Larrabees; RMC Place; MONMOUTH; mail Howell **z** 07731; ● 200

Laureldale; RMC Place; ATLANTIC; ▲ Hamilton; **205** P-9; ★ **ATCY**; mail Mays Landing **z** 08330; ● 300

Laurel Harbor; RMC Place; OCEAN; ▲ Lacey; ***205** M-12; ★ **N.Y.**; mail Lanoka Harbor **z** 08734

Laurel Lake; CDP; CUMBERLAND; ▲ Commercial; ***205** Q-7; ★ **VINL**; mail Millville **z** 08332; © 2,929

Laurel Springs; Inc. Place; CAMDEN; ***205** M-7; elev. 82ft./25m.; [P]; ★ **PHIL-**; **z** 08021; Ⓟ 2,341; © 1,970

Laurelton (Brick); RMC Place; OCEAN; ▲ Brick; **205** K-12; ★ **N.Y.**; mail Brick **z** 08723-24

Laurelton Gardens; RMC Place; OCEAN; ▲ Brick; ***205** K-12; ★ **N.Y.**; mail Brick **z** 08723

Laurence Harbor; CDP; MIDDLESEX; ▲ Old Bridge; **204** H-12; [P]; ★ **N.Y.**; **z** 08879; Ⓟ 6,361; © 6,227

Lavallette; Inc. Place; OCEAN; **205** L-13; elev. 5ft./2m.; [P]; ★ **N.Y.**; **z** 08735; Ⓟ 2,299; summer pop. 5,000; © 2,665

Lawnside; Inc. Place; CAMDEN; ***205** M-7; elev. 112ft./34m.; [P]; ★ **PHIL-**; **z** 08045; Ⓟ 2,841; © 2,692

Lawrence; MCD-Township; CUMBERLAND; ***205** Q-6; mail Cedarville **z** 08311; Ⓟ 2,433; © 2,721

Lawrence; MCD-Township; MERCER; ***204** I-9; [P] [C] 5,801; ★ **PHIL-**; **z** 08648; Ⓟ 25,787; © 29,159; ◆ 29,401

Lawrence Brook Manor; RMC Place; MIDDLESEX; ▲ East Brunswick; ***204** H-11; ★ **N.Y.**; mail East Brunswick **z** 08816

Lawrenceville; CDP; MERCER; ▲ Lawrence; **205** S-12; [P] [H] [C] 5,801; ★ **PHIL-**; **z** 08648; Ⓟ 6,446; © 4,081

Layton; RMC Place; SUSSEX; ▲ Sandyston; **204** B-8; [P]; **z** 07851; ● 250

Lebanon; Inc. Place; HUNTERDON; **204** G-8; elev. 296ft./90m.; [P]; ★ **N.Y.**; **z** 08833; Ⓟ 1,036; © 1,065

Lebanon; MCD-Township; HUNTERDON; ***204** F-8; [P]; ★ **N.Y.**; **z** 08833 & mail Califon **z** 07830, Glen Gardner **z** 08826; not adjacent to the Borough of Lebanon; Ⓟ 5,679; © 5,816

Lebanon Lake Estates; RMC Place; BURLINGTON; ▲ Woodland; ***205** L-10; mail Browns Mills **z** 08015

Ledgewood; RMC Place; MORRIS; ▲ Roxbury; **204** E-9; [P]; ★ **N.Y.**; **z** 07852; ● 1,200

Leeds Point; RMC Place; ATLANTIC; ▲ Galloway; **205** P-10; [P]; ★ **ATCY**; **z** 08220; ● 400

Leektown; RMC Place; BURLINGTON; ▲ Bass River; **205** O-10; mail Egg Harbor City **z** 08215

Leesburg; RMC Place; CUMBERLAND; ▲ Maurice River; **205** R-7; [P]; **z** 08327; ● 750

Legler; RMC Place; OCEAN; mail Jackson **z** 08527; ● 260

Leisure Knoll; CDP-Census Area Only; OCEAN; ▲ Manchester; ***205** L-11; elev. 70ft./21m.; ★ **N.Y.**; mail Lakehurst **z** 08733; Ⓟ 2,707; © 2,467

Leisuretowne; CDP; BURLINGTON; ▲ Southampton; ***205** M-9; ★ **PHIL-**; mail Vincentown **z** 08088; Ⓟ 2,552; © 2,535

Leisure Village; CDP; OCEAN; ▲ Lakewood; ***205** K-12; ★ **N.Y.**; mail Lakewood **z** 08701; Ⓟ 4,295; © 4,443

Leisure Village East; CDP; OCEAN; ▲ Lakewood; ***205** K-12; elev. 50ft./15m.; ★ **N.Y.**; mail Toms River **z** 08753; Ⓟ 1,989; © 4,597

Leisure Village West; RMC Place; OCEAN; ▲ Manchester; ***205** L-11; elev. 70ft./21m.; ★ **N.Y.**; mail Lakehurst **z** 08733; ● 4,000

Leisure Village West-Pine Lake Park; CDP-Census Area Only; OCEAN; ▲ Manchester; ***205** L-12; elev. 85ft./26m.; ★ **N.Y.**; mail Toms River **z** 08753; Ⓟ 10,139; © 11,085

Lenola; RMC Place; BURLINGTON; ▲ Moorestown; ***205** L-7; ★ **PHIL-**; mail Moorestown **z** 08057; ● 2,500

Leonardo; CDP; MONMOUTH; ▲ Middletown; **204** H-13; [P]; ★ **N.Y.**; **z** 07737; Ⓟ 3,788; © 2,823; Ⓡ 3,975

Leonardville; RMC Place; MONMOUTH; ▲ Middletown; ***204** I-13; ★ **N.Y.**; mail Leonardo **z** 07737; ● 400

Leonia; Inc. Place; BERGEN; **204** B-6; elev. 31ft./9m.; [P]; ★ **N.Y.**; **z** 07605; Ⓟ 8,365; © 8,914

Lewisville; RMC Place; MERCER; ▲ Lawrence; ***204** I-9; ★ **PHIL-**; mail Lawrence Township **z** 08648; ● 100

Liberty; MCD-Township; WARREN; ***204** E-7; ★ **N.Y.**; mail Oxford **z** 07863; Ⓟ 2,493; © 2,765

Liberty Corner; RMC Place; SOMERSET; ▲ Bernards; **204** F-10; [P]; ★ **N.Y.**; **z** 07938; ● 800

Libertyville; RMC Place; SUSSEX; ▲ Wantage; ***204** B-9; ★ **N.Y.**; mail Sussex **z** 07461; rural

Lincoln; RMC Place; GLOUCESTER; ▲ South Harrison; ***205** N-6; elev. 135ft./41m.; ★ **PHIL-**; mail Mullica Hill **z** 08062

Lincoln Park; Inc. Place; MORRIS; **204** D-11; elev. 200ft./61m.; [P]; ★ **N.Y.**; **z** 07035; Ⓟ 10,978; © 10,930

Lincroft; CDP; MONMOUTH; ▲ Middletown; **204** I-12; [P]; ★ **N.Y.**; **z** 07738; Ⓟ 6,193; © 6,255

Linden; Inc. Place; UNION; **204** G-12; elev. 37ft./11m.; [P] ■; ★ **N.Y.**; **z** 07036; Ⓟ 36,701; © 39,394; ◆ 39,645

Linden Junction; RMC Place; UNION; ★ **N.Y.**; mail Linden **z** 07036; pop. incl. with Linden (Inc. Place)

Lindenwold; Inc. Place; CAMDEN; **205** M-7; elev. 50ft./15m.; [P]; ★ **PHIL-**; **z** 08021; Ⓟ 18,734; © 17,414

Lindy's Lake; RMC Place; PASSAIC; ▲ West Milford; ***204** C-11; elev. 1,000ft./305m.; ★ **N.Y.**; mail West Milford **z** 07480; ● 450

Linvale; RMC Place; HUNTERDON; ▲ West Amwell, East Amwell; **204** I-8; ★ **PHIL-**; mail Ringoes **z** 08551; ● 30

Linwood; Inc. Place; ATLANTIC; **205** Q-10; elev. 28ft./9m.; [P]; ★ **ATCY**; **z** 08221; Ⓟ 6,866; © 7,172

Little Egg Harbor (Little Egg Harbor Twp); MCD-Township; OCEAN; ***205** O-11; [P]; ★ **ATCY**; **z** 08087; Ⓟ 13,333; © 15,945; ◆ 19,505

Little Egg Harbor Twp; OCEAN; see Little Egg Harbor (MCD-Township)

Little Falls; CDP; PASSAIC; ▲ Little Falls; **204** E-12; [P]; ★ **N.Y.**; **z** 07424; Ⓟ 11,294; © 10,855; Ⓡ 11,793

Little Falls; MCD-Township; PASSAIC; ***204** E-12; [P]; ★ **N.Y.**; **z** 07424; Ⓟ 11,294; © 10,855; Ⓡ 11,793

Little Ferry; Inc. Place; BERGEN; **204** B-5; elev. 10ft./3m.; [P]; ★ **N.Y.**; **z** 07643; Ⓟ 9,989; © 10,800

Little Ferry Junction; RMC Place; BERGEN; ★ **N.Y.**; pop. incl. with Ridgefield Park (Inc. Place)

Little Rocky Hill; RMC Place; MIDDLESEX; ▲ South Brunswick; ***204** I-10; elev. 240ft./73m.; ★ **N.Y.**; mail Princeton **z** 08540; ● 350

Little Silver; Inc. Place; MONMOUTH; **204** I-13; elev. 38ft./12m.; [P]; ★ **N.Y.**; **z** 07739; Ⓟ 5,721; © 6,170

Little Silver Point; RMC Place; MONMOUTH; ***204** I-13; ★ **N.Y.**; mail Little Silver **z** 07739; pop. incl. with Little Silver (Inc. Place)

Littleton; RMC Place; MORRIS; ***204** E-10; ★ **N.Y.**; mail Morris Plains **z** 07950

Little York; RMC Place; HUNTERDON; ▲ Holland, Alexandria; **204** G-7; [P]; **z** 08834; ● 150

Livingston; CDP; ESSEX; ▲ Livingston; **204** E-11; elev. 307ft./94m.; [P] [H]; ★ **N.Y.**; **z** 07039; Ⓟ 26,609; © 27,391; ◆ 26,348

Livingston; MCD-Township; ESSEX; ***204** F-11; [P] ■; ★ **N.Y.**; **z** 07039; Ⓟ 26,609; © 27,391; ◆ 26,348

Loch Arbour; Inc. Place; MONMOUTH; **204** J-13; elev. 24ft./7m.; [P]; ★ **N.Y.**; **z** 07711; Ⓟ 380; © 280

Locktown; RMC Place; HUNTERDON; ▲ Delaware; ***204** H-7; mail Flemington **z** 08822, Frenchtown **z** 08825

Lockwood; RMC Place; SUSSEX; ***204** E-9; mail Stanhope **z** 07874; ● 1,400

Locust; RMC Place; MONMOUTH; ▲ Middletown; ***204** I-13; [P]; ★ **N.Y.**; **z** 07760; ● 600

Locust Corner; RMC Place; MERCER; mail Cranbury **z** 08512; ● 20

Locust Grove; RMC Place; CAMDEN; ▲ Cherry Hill; ***205** M-7; ★ **PHIL-**; mail Cherry Hill **z** 08003

Lodi; Inc. Place; BERGEN; **204** E-13; elev. 43ft./13m.; [P] [C] 1,992; ★ **N.Y.**; **z** 07644; Ⓟ 22,355; © 23,971; ◆ 23,874

Lodi Junction; RMC Place; BERGEN; ★ **N.Y.**; pop. incl. with Hackensack (Inc. Place)

Logan; MCD-Township; GLOUCESTER; ***205** M-5; ★ **PHIL-**; mail Bridgeport **z** 08014, Swedesboro **z** 08085; Ⓟ 5,147; © 6,032

Lommasons Glen; RMC Place; WARREN; ▲ White; ***204** E-7; ★ **N.Y.**; mail Belvidere **z** 07823; ● 40

London Terrace; RMC Place; MIDDLESEX; ▲ Old Bridge; ***204** H-11; elev. 50ft./15m.; ★ **N.Y.**; mail Parlin **z** 08859; ● 2,800

Long Beach (Beach Haven Park); RMC Place; OCEAN; ▲ Long Beach; **205** O-12; [P]; ★ **N.Y.**; **z** 08008; pop. incl. with Harvey Cedars (Inc. Place) summer pop. 2,000

Long Beach (Long Beach Township); MCD-Township; OCEAN; ***205** O-12; [P]; ★ **N.Y.**; **z** 08008; Ⓟ 3,407; © 3,329

Long Beach Park; RMC Place; OCEAN; ***205** N-12; ★ **N.Y.**; mail Beach Haven **z** 08008

Long Beach Township; OCEAN; see Long Beach (MCD-Township)

Long Branch; Inc. Place; MONMOUTH; **204** I-13; elev. 19ft./6m.; [P] [H] ■; ★ **N.Y.**; **z** 07740; Ⓟ 28,658; © 31,340; ◆ 33,799

Long Bridge; RMC Place; WARREN; ▲ Allamuchy; ***204** D-8; ★ **N.Y.**; mail Great Meadows **z** 07838; rural

Long Hill; RMC Place; MORRIS; ▲ Chatham; **210** I-1; elev. 300ft./91m.; ★ **N.Y.**; mail Chatham **z** 07928; ● 300

Long Hill (Passaic); MCD-Township; MORRIS; ***204** F-10; ★ **N.Y.**; mail Millington **z** 07946; Ⓟ 7,826; © 8,777

Longport; Inc. Place; ATLANTIC; **204** J-1; elev. 6ft./2m.; [P]; ★ **ATCY**; **z** 08403; Ⓟ 1,224; © 1,054

Long Valley; CDP; MORRIS; ▲ Washington; **204** F-8; [P]; ★ **N.Y.**; **z** 07853; Ⓟ 1,744; © 1,818

Longwood Lake; RMC Place; MORRIS; ▲ Jefferson; ***204** D-10; ★ **N.Y.**; mail Oak Ridge **z** 07438; ● 250

Lookover Lake; RMC Place; PASSAIC; ▲ West Milford; ***204** C-11; ★ **N.Y.**; mail Hewitt **z** 07421; ● 80

Lopatcong; MCD-Township; WARREN; ***204** F-6; ★ **ALL-**; mail Phillipsburg **z** 08865; Ⓟ 5,052; © 5,765

Louden; RMC Place; CAMDEN; ▲ Waterford; ***205** N-8; elev. 140ft./43m.; ★ **PHIL-**; mail Atco **z** 08004

Loveladies; RMC Place; OCEAN; ▲ Long Beach; **205** N-12; ★ **N.Y.**; mail Beach Haven **z** 08008; summer pop. 1,500; ● 200

Lower; MCD-Township; CAPE MAY; ***205** T-8; mail Cape May **z** 08204; Ⓟ 20,820; © 22,945; ◆ 20,552

Lower Alloways Creek; MCD-Township; SALEM; ***205** P-4; mail Hancocks Bridge **z** 08038; Ⓟ 1,858; © 1,851

Lower Bank; RMC Place; BURLINGTON; ▲ Washington; **205** O-10; mail Egg Harbor City **z** 08215; ● 200

Lower Harmony; RMC Place; WARREN; ▲ Harmony; ***204** F-6; ★ **ALL-**; mail Phillipsburg **z** 08865; ● 150

Lower Montville; RMC Place; MORRIS; ▲ Montville; ***204** E-11; ★ **N.Y.**; mail Montville **z** 07045; ● 600

Lower Squankum; RMC Place; MONMOUTH; ▲ Howell; **205** K-12; ★ **N.Y.**; mail Farmingdale **z** 07727

Lower Valley; RMC Place; HUNTERDON; ***204** F-8; elev. 593ft./181m.; ★ **N.Y.**; mail Califon **z** 07830; pop. incl. with Califon (Inc. Place)

Lows Hollow; RMC Place; WARREN; ▲ Lopatcong; ***204** F-6; ★ **ALL-**; mail Stewartsville **z** 08886; rural

Lucaston; RMC Place; CAMDEN; ***205** M-7; ★ **PHIL-**; mail Berlin **z** 08009; pop. incl. with Lindenwold (Inc. Place)

Lumberton; RMC Place; BURLINGTON; ▲ Lumberton; **205** L-8; [P]; ★ **PHIL-**; **z** 08048; ● 900

Lumberton; MCD-Township; BURLINGTON; ***205** L-8; [P]; ★ **PHIL-**; **z** 08048 & mail Mount Holly **z** 08060; Ⓟ 6,705; © 10,461

Lumistown; RMC Place; CUMBERLAND; ▲ Lawrence; ***205** Q-6; mail Cedarville **z** 08311; rural

Lyndhurst; CDP; BERGEN; ▲ Lyndhurst; **204** E-12; [P]; ★ **N.Y.**; **z** 07071; Ⓟ 18,262; © 19,383

Lyndhurst; MCD-Township; BERGEN; ***204** E-12; [P]; ★ **N.Y.**; **z** 07071; Ⓟ 18,262; © 19,383

Lynn Woodoaks; RMC Place; MIDDLESEX; ▲ Woodbridge; ***204** G-11; ★ **N.Y.**; mail Colonia **z** 07067

Lyons; RMC Place; SOMERSET; ▲ Bernards; ***204** F-10; [P]; ★ **N.Y.**; **z** 07939

Lyonsville; RMC Place; MORRIS; ▲ Rockaway; ***204** D-10; ★ **N.Y.**; mail Boonton **z** 07005

M

Macedonia; RMC Place; MONMOUTH; ***204** I-12; ★ **N.Y.**; mail Eatontown **z** 07724; pop. incl. with Tinton Falls (Inc. Place)

Macopin; RMC Place; PASSAIC; ▲ West Milford; **204** C-11; ★ **N.Y.**; mail Butler **z** 07405; ● 100

Madison; Inc. Place; MORRIS; **204** F-11; elev. 261ft./80m.; [P] [C] 2,647; ★ **N.Y.**; **z** 07940; Ⓟ 15,850; © 16,530; Ⓡ 15,460

Madison Park; CDP; MIDDLESEX; ▲ Old Bridge; ***204** H-11; ★ **N.Y.**; mail Parlin **z** 08859; Ⓟ 7,490; © 6,929

Madisonville; RMC Place; SOMERSET; ▲ Bernards; ***204** F-10; ★ **N.Y.**; mail Basking Ridge **z** 07920

Magnolia; RMC Place; ATLANTIC; ▲ Mullica; ***205** O-9; ★ **ATCY**; mail Elwood **z** 08217; ● 600

Magnolia; RMC Place; BURLINGTON; ▲ Pemberton; ***205** L-9; ★ **PHIL-**; mail Pemberton **z** 08068; rural

Magnolia; Inc. Place; CAMDEN; **205** M-7; elev. 79ft./24m.; [P]; ★ **PHIL-**; **z** 08049; Ⓟ 4,861; © 4,409

Mahoneyville; RMC Place; SALEM; ▲ Pennsville; ***205** O-4; ★ **PHIL-**; mail Pennsville **z** 08070; ● 200

Mahwah; RMC Place; BERGEN; ▲ Mahwah; **204** C-12; [P] [C] 4,886; ★ **N.Y.**; **z** 07430, **z** 07495; ● 12,000

Mahwah; MCD-Township; BERGEN; ***204** C-12; [P] [C] 4,886; ★ **N.Y.**; **z** 07430, **z** 07495; Ⓟ 17,905; © 24,062; ◆ 24,471

Main Avenue; RMC Place; PASSAIC; ***204** E-12; ★ **N.Y.**; mail Clifton **z** 07011; pop. incl. with Clifton (Inc. Place)

Malaga; RMC Place; GLOUCESTER; ▲ Franklin; **205** O-7; [P]; ★ **VINL**; **z** 08328; ● 2,100

Malapardis; RMC Place; MORRIS; ▲ Hanover; ***204** E-10; elev. 275ft./84m.; ★ **N.Y.**; mail Whippany **z** 07981

Manahawkin; CDP; OCEAN; ▲ Stafford; **205** N-12; [P] [H]; ★ **N.Y.**; **z** 08050; Ⓟ 1,594; © 2,004

Manalapan; RMC Place; MONMOUTH; ▲ Manalapan; **204** J-11; [P]; ★ **N.Y.**; **z** 07726; ● 90

Manalapan; MCD-Township; MONMOUTH; ***204** I-11; [P]; ★ **N.Y.**; **z** 07726; Ⓟ 26,716; © 33,423; ◆ 36,772

Manasquan; Inc. Place; MONMOUTH; **205** K-13; elev. 28ft./9m.; [P]; ★ **N.Y.**; **z** 08736; Ⓟ 5,369; © 6,310

Manasquan Park; RMC Place; MONMOUTH; ▲ Wall; ***205** K-13; ★ **N.Y.**; mail Manasquan **z** 08736; pop. incl. with Brielle (Inc. Place)

Manasquan Shores; RMC Place; MONMOUTH; ▲ Wall; ***205** K-13; ★ **N.Y.**; mail Manasquan **z** 08736; ● 600

Manchester; MCD-Township; OCEAN; ***205** L-10; [P]; ★ **N.Y.**; **z** 08759 & mail Lakehurst **z** 08733; Ⓟ 35,976; © 38,928; ◆ 40,153

Mandalay; RMC Place; OCEAN; ▲ Brick; ***205** L-13; ★ **N.Y.**; mail Brick **z** 08723

Mannington; MCD-Township; SALEM; ***205** N-4; [P]; **z** 08079; Ⓟ 1,693; © 1,559

Mansfield; RMC Place; BURLINGTON; ▲ Mansfield; **205** K-9; ★ **PHIL-**; mail Columbus **z** 08022; ● 40

Mansfield; MCD-Township; BURLINGTON; ***205** K-9; ★ **PHIL-**; mail Columbus **z** 08022; Ⓟ 3,874; © 5,090

Mansfield; MCD-Township; WARREN; ***204** E-8; ★ **N.Y.**; mail Hackettstown **z** 07840, Port Murray **z** 07865; Ⓟ 7,154; © 6,653; Ⓡ 8,072

Mansfield Square; RMC Place; BURLINGTON; ▲ Bordentown, Mansfield; **205** K-9; ★ **PHIL-**; mail Columbus **z** 08022

Mantoloking; Inc. Place; OCEAN; **205** K-13; elev. 7ft./2m.; [P]; ★ **N.Y.**; **z** 08738; Ⓟ 334; © 423

Mantoloking Estates; RMC Place; OCEAN; ▲ Brick; ***205** L-13; ★ **N.Y.**; mail Mantoloking **z** 08738

Mantoloking Shores; RMC Place; OCEAN; ▲ Brick; ***205** L-13; ★ **N.Y.**; mail Mantoloking **z** 08738

Mantua; RMC Place; GLOUCESTER; ▲ Mantua; **205** M-6; elev. 38ft./12m.; [P]; ★ **PHIL-**; **z** 08051; ● 2,400

Mantua; MCD-Township; GLOUCESTER; ***205** N-6; [P]; ★ **PHIL-**; **z** 08051; Ⓟ 10,074; © 14,217

Mantua Grove; RMC Place; GLOUCESTER; ▲ West Deptford; ***205** M-6; ★ **PHIL-**; mail Mount Royal **z** 08061; rural

Mantua Terrace; RMC Place; GLOUCESTER; ▲ West Deptford; ***205** M-6; ★ **PHIL-**; mail Mantua **z** 08051; ● 500

Manunkachunk; RMC Place; WARREN; ▲ White; **204** E-7; ★ **N.Y.**; mail Columbia **z** 07832; ● 150

Manville; Inc. Place; SOMERSET; **204** G-10; elev. 44ft./13m.; [P]; ★ **N.Y.**; **z** 08835; Ⓟ 10,567; © 10,343

Maplecrest; RMC Place; ESSEX; ▲ Maplewood; ***204** F-11; ★ **N.Y.**; mail Maplewood **z** 07040

Maple Glen; RMC Place; OCEAN; ▲ Jackson; ***205** K-11; elev. 100ft./30m.; ★ **N.Y.**; mail Jackson **z** 08527; ● 200

Maple Grange; RMC Place; SUSSEX; ▲ Vernon; ***204** B-10; ★ **N.Y.**; mail Vernon **z** 07462; ● 40

Maple Meade; RMC Place; MIDDLESEX; ▲ North Brunswick; ***204** H-10; ★ **N.Y.**; mail North Brunswick **z** 08902

Maple Shade; RMC Place; BURLINGTON; ▲ Maple Shade; **205** L-7; [P]; ★ **PHIL-**; **z** 08052; Ⓟ 19,211; ● 18,700

Maple Shade; MCD-Township; BURLINGTON; ***205** L-7; [P]; ★ **PHIL-**; **z** 08052; Ⓟ 19,211; © 19,079

Maple Tree; RMC Place; OCEAN; ▲ Toms River; ***205** L-12; ★ **N.Y.**; mail Toms River **z** 08753; ● 3,300

Maple View; RMC Place; MIDDLESEX; ▲ Old Bridge; ***204** I-11; elev. 35ft./11m.; ★ **N.Y.**; mail Old Bridge **z** 08857; ● 600

Maplewood; CDP; ESSEX; ▲ Maplewood; **210** H-4; [P]; ★ **N.Y.**; **z** 07040; Ⓟ 21,756; © 23,868; ◆ 22,474

Maplewood; MCD-Township; ESSEX; ***204** F-11; [P]; ★ **N.Y.**; **z** 07040; Ⓟ 21,756; © 23,868; ◆ 22,474

Marcella; RMC Place; MORRIS; ▲ Rockaway; **204** D-10; elev. 1,073ft./327m.; ★ **N.Y.**; mail Rockaway **z** 07866

Margate City; Inc. Place; ATLANTIC; **204** J-1; elev. 8ft./2m.; [P]; ★ **ATCY**; **z** 08402; Ⓟ 8,431; © 8,193

Marion; RMC Place; HUDSON; ***204** F-13; ★ **N.Y.**; pop. incl. with Jersey City (Inc. Place)

Marksboro; RMC Place; WARREN; ▲ Frelinghuysen; **204** D-8; ★ **N.Y.**; mail Blairstown **z** 07825; ● 150

Marlboro; RMC Place; BURLINGTON; ▲ Evesham; ***205** L-7; elev. 90ft./27m.; ★ **PHIL-**; mail Marlton **z** 08053; ● 250

Marlboro; RMC Place; CUMBERLAND; ▲ Stow Creek; ***205** P-5; mail Bridgeton **z** 08302; ● 60

Marlboro; RMC Place; MONMOUTH; ▲ Marlboro; **204** I-12; elev. 173ft./53m.; [P] [H]; ★ **N.Y.**; **z** 07746; ● 1,100

Marlboro; MCD-Township; MONMOUTH; ***204** I-11; [P]; ★ **N.Y.**; **z** 07746; Ⓟ 27,974; © 36,398; ◆ 40,091

Marlboro Heights; RMC Place; MONMOUTH; ▲ Manalapan; ***204** I-11; ★ **N.Y.**; mail Englishtown **z** 07726; ● 2,600

Marlton; CDP; BURLINGTON; ▲ Evesham; **205** M-8; [P] [H]; ★ **PHIL-**; **z** 08053; Ⓟ 10,228; © 10,260

Marlton Heights; RMC Place; SALEM; ▲ Pilesgrove; ***205** N-5; elev. 54ft./16m.; mail Woodstown **z** 08098

Marlton Lakes; RMC Place; BURLINGTON; ▲ Evesham; ***205** M-8; ★ **PHIL-**; mail Atco **z** 08004, Marlton **z** 08053; ● 1,900

Marlyn Manor; RMC Place; CAPE MAY; ▲ Middle; ***205** S-8; mail Rio Grande **z** 08242

Marmora; RMC Place; CAPE MAY; ▲ Upper; **205** R-9; [P]; ★ **ATCY**; **z** 08223; ● 1,700

Marshalls Corner; RMC Place; MERCER; ▲ Hopewell; **205** R-11; elev. 226ft./69m.; ★ **PHIL-**; mail Hopewell **z** 08525

Marshalltown; RMC Place; SALEM; ▲ Mannington; **205** O-4; elev. 6ft./2m.; mail Salem **z** 08079; rural

Marshallville; RMC Place; CAPE MAY; ▲ Upper; ***205** Q-8; ★ **ATCY**; mail Woodbine **z** 08270; ● 150

Martins Beach; RMC Place; BURLINGTON; ▲ Willingboro; ***205** L-8; ★ **PHIL-**; mail Willingboro **z** 08046

Martinsville; RMC Place; SOMERSET; ▲ Bridgewater; **204** G-10; elev. 306ft./93m.; [P]; ★ **N.Y.**; **z** 08836; ● 1,500

Maryland; RMC Place; OCEAN; ▲ Jackson; ***205** K-11; ★ **N.Y.**; mail Jackson **z** 08527; rural

Masonicus; RMC Place; BERGEN; ▲ Mahwah; ***204** C-12; ★ **N.Y.**; mail Mahwah **z** 07430; rural

Masonville; RMC Place; BURLINGTON; ▲ Mount Laurel; **205** L-8; ★ **PHIL-**; mail Mount Laurel **z** 08054; ● 400

Matawan; Inc. Place; MONMOUTH; **204** I-12; elev. 55ft./17m.; [P]; ★ **N.Y.**; **z** 07747; Ⓟ 9,270; © 8,910

Matchaponix; RMC Place; MIDDLESEX; ▲ Monroe; ***204** I-11; ★ **N.Y.**; mail Monroe Township **z** 08831; rural

Maurer; MIDDLESEX; see Barber (RMC Place)

Maurice River; MCD-Township; CUMBERLAND; ***205** Q-7; mail Leesburg **z** 08327; Ⓟ 6,648; © 6,928; Ⓡ 7,374

Mauricetown; RMC Place; CUMBERLAND; ▲ Commercial; **205** Q-7; [P]; ★ **VINL**; **z** 08329; ● 550

Maxim; RMC Place; MONMOUTH; ▲ Howell; ***205** K-12; ★ **N.Y.**; mail Lakewood **z** 08701; rural

Mayetta; RMC Place; OCEAN; ▲ Stafford; **205** N-11; ★ **N.Y.**; mail West Creek **z** 08092; ● 250

Mays Landing; CDP; ⊡ ATLANTIC; ▲ Hamilton; **205** P-9; elev. 20ft./6m.; [P]; ★ **ATCY**; **z** 08330; Ⓟ 2,090; © 2,321

Mayville; RMC Place; CAPE MAY; ▲ Middle; ***205** S-8; mail Cape May Court House **z** 08210

Maywood; Inc. Place; BERGEN; **204** A-4; elev. 94ft./29m.; [P]; ★ **N.Y.**; **z** 07607; Ⓟ 9,473; © 9,523

McAfee; RMC Place; SUSSEX; ▲ Vernon; **204** B-10; [P]; ★ **N.Y.**; **z** 07428; ● 1,400

McCoys Corner; RMC Place; SUSSEX; ▲ Wantage; ***204** B-9; ★ **N.Y.**; mail Sussex **z** 07461; ● 75

McGuire AFB; CDP-Census Area Only; BURLINGTON; ▲ North Hanover, New Hanover; ***205** K-10; [P]; ★ **PHIL-**; **z** 08641; Ⓟ 7,580; © 6,478

McKee City; RMC Place; ATLANTIC; ▲ Egg Harbor; **205** P-9; [P]; ★ **ATCY**; **z** 08232 & mail Egg Harbor Township **z** 08234; ● 1,200

Meadford Farms; RMC Place; BURLINGTON; ▲ Tabernacle; **205** M-9; ★ **PHIL-**; mail Vincentown **z** 08088; ● 100

Meadowbrook; RMC Place; CAMDEN; ▲ Pennsauken; ***205** L-7; ★ **PHIL-**; mail Merchantville **z** 08109

Meadowbrook Village; RMC Place; OCEAN; ▲ Jackson; **205** K-11; ★ **N.Y.**; mail Jackson **z** 08527; ● 150

Meadows; RMC Place; HUDSON; ★ **N.Y.**; mail Secaucus **z** 07094, **z** 07096; pop. incl. with Secaucus (Inc. Place)

Meadowview; RMC Place; HUDSON; ▲ North Bergen; ***204** E-13; ★ **N.Y.**; mail North Bergen **z** 07047

Meadow Village; RMC Place; ESSEX; ▲ Cedar Grove; ***204** E-12; ★ **N.Y.**; mail Cedar Grove **z** 07009

Mechanicsville; RMC Place; MIDDLESEX; ***204** H-12; ★ **N.Y.**; mail South Amboy **z** 08879; pop. incl. with South Amboy (Inc. Place)

Mechanicsville; RMC Place; MONMOUTH; ▲ Hazlet; ★ **N.Y.**; mail Hazlet **z** 07730

Medford; RMC Place; BURLINGTON; ▲ Medford; **205** L-8; [P]; ★ **PHIL-**; **z** 08055; ● 2,400

Medford; MCD-Township; BURLINGTON; ***205** M-8; [P]; ★ **PHIL-**; **z** 08055; Ⓟ 20,526; © 22,253; ◆ 22,492

Medford Lakes; Inc. Place; BURLINGTON; **205** M-8; elev. 57ft./17m.; [P]; ★ **PHIL-**; **z** 08055; Ⓟ 4,462; © 4,173

Melrose; RMC Place; BURLINGTON; ***205** M-8; elev. 63ft./19m.; ★ **PHIL-**; mail Medford **z** 08055

Melrose; RMC Place; MIDDLESEX; ***204** H-11; ★ **N.Y.**; mail South Amboy **z** 08879; pop. incl. with Sayreville (Inc. Place)

Mendham; Inc. Place; MORRIS; **204** F-9; elev. 648ft./198m.; [P]; ★ **N.Y.**; **z** 07945; Ⓟ 4,890; © 5,097

Mendham; MCD-Township; MORRIS; ***204** E-10; [P]; ★ **N.Y.**; **z** 07945 & mail Brookside **z** 07926; does not include the Borough of Mendham; Ⓟ 4,537; © 5,400

Menlo Park; RMC Place; MIDDLESEX; ▲ Edison; ***204** G-11; ★ **N.Y.**; mail Edison **z** 08837

Menlo Park Terrace; RMC Place; MIDDLESEX; ▲ Woodbridge; **210** M-3; ★ **N.Y.**; mail Metuchen **z** 08840

MERCER; **204** I-8; Ⓟ 325,824; © 350,761; ◆ 361,073

Mercerville; RMC Place; MERCER; ▲ Hamilton; **205** S-13; elev. 90ft./27m.; [P]; ★ **PHIL-**; **z** 08619; ● 15,000

Mercerville-Hamilton Square; CDP-Census Area Only; MERCER; ▲ Hamilton; ***204** J-9; ★ **PHIL-**; mail Trenton **z** 08619, **z** 08690; Ⓟ 26,873; © 26,419; ◆ 27,198

Merchantville; Inc. Place; CAMDEN; **205** L-7; elev. 82ft./25m.; [P]; ★ **PHIL-**; **z** 08109; Ⓟ 4,095; © 3,801

Meriden; RMC Place; MORRIS; ▲ Rockaway; **204** D-10; ★ **N.Y.**; mail Boonton **z** 07005; ● 80

Metedeconk; RMC Place; OCEAN; ▲ Brick; **205** K-13; ★ **N.Y.**; mail Brick **z** 08723

Metropark; RMC Place; MIDDLESEX; ▲ Woodbridge; ★ **N.Y.**

Mettler; RMC Place; SOMERSET; ▲ Franklin; ***204** H-10; elev. 118ft./36m.; ★ **N.Y.**; mail Somerset **z** 08873; ● 80

Metuchen; Inc. Place; MIDDLESEX; **204** G-11; elev. 117ft./36m.; [P]; ★ **N.Y.**; **z** 08840; Ⓟ 12,804; © 12,840

Meyersville; RMC Place; MORRIS; ▲ Long Hill; ***204** F-10; ★ **N.Y.**; mail Gillette **z** 07933; ● 750

Miami Beach; RMC Place; CAPE MAY; ▲ Lower; ***205** S-7; mail Villas **z** 08251

Mickleton; RMC Place; GLOUCESTER; ▲ East Greenwich; **205** M-6; elev. 68ft./21m.; [P]; ★ **PHIL-**; **z** 08056; ● 1,200

Middle; MCD-Township; CAPE MAY; ***205** S-8; mail Cape May Court House **z** 08210; Ⓟ 14,771; © 16,405

Middlebush; RMC Place; SOMERSET; ▲ Franklin; **204** H-10; ★ **N.Y.**; mail Somerset **z** 08873; ● 600

Middlesex; Inc. Place; MIDDLESEX; **204** G-10; elev. 61ft./19m.; [P]; ★ **N.Y.**; **z** 08846; Ⓟ 13,055; © 13,717

MIDDLESEX; **204** I-11; Ⓟ 671,780; © 750,162; ◆ 791,697

Middlesex Downs; RMC Place; MIDDLESEX; mail Monroe Township **z** 08831; ● 250

Middletown; RMC Place; MONMOUTH; ▲ Middletown; **204** I-12; [P]; ★ **N.Y.**; **z** 07748; ● 24,000

Middletown; MCD-Township; MONMOUTH; ***204** I-13; [P]; ★ **N.Y.**; **z** 07748; Ⓟ 68,183; © 66,327; Ⓡ 67,479; ◆ 68,726

Middletown; RMC Place; MORRIS; ▲ Rockaway; ***204** D-10; ★ **N.Y.**; mail Rockaway **z** 07866

Middle Valley; RMC Place; MORRIS; ▲ Washington; **204** F-8; ★ **N.Y.**; mail Long Valley **z** 07853; ● 150

Middleville; RMC Place; SUSSEX; ▲ Stillwater; **204** C-8; [P]; ★ **N.Y.**; **z** 07855; ● 100

Midland Park; Inc. Place; BERGEN; **204** D-12; elev. 347ft./106m.; [P]; ★ **N.Y.**; **z** 07432; Ⓟ 7,047; © 6,947

Midstreams Park; RMC Place; OCEAN; ▲ Brick; ★ **N.Y.**; mail Brick **z** 08723

Midtown; RMC Place; ESSEX; ***204** F-12; ★ **N.Y.**; mail Newark **z** 07102; pop. incl. with Newark (Inc. Place)

Milford; Inc. Place; HUNTERDON; **204** G-6; elev. 139ft./42m.; [P]; **z** 08848; Ⓟ 1,273; © 1,195

Millbridge; RMC Place; CAMDEN; ▲ Gloucester; ***205** M-7; ★ **PHIL-**; mail Clementon **z** 08021; ● 2,000

Mill Brook; RMC Place; MORRIS; ***204** E-10; ● 1,700

Millbrook; RMC Place; WARREN; **204** C-7; elev. 659ft./201m.; mail Columbia **z** 07832; ● 5

Millburn; CDP; ESSEX; ▲ Millburn; **204** F-11; [P]; ★ **N.Y.**; **z** 07041; Ⓟ 18,630; © 19,765

Millburn; MCD-Township; ESSEX; ***204** F-11; [P] ■; ★ **N.Y.**; **z** 07041 & mail Short Hills **z** 07078; Ⓟ 18,630; © 19,765; ◆ 18,833

Millhurst; RMC Place; MONMOUTH; ▲ Manalapan; **204** J-11; elev. 146ft./45m.; ★ **N.Y.**; mail Freehold **z** 07728; ● 100

Millington; RMC Place; MORRIS; ▲ Long Hill; **204** F-10; [P]; ★ **N.Y.**; **z** 07946; ● 2,500

Millside Heights; RMC Place; BURLINGTON; ▲ Delran; ***205** L-7; ★ **PHIL-**; mail Riverside **z** 08075

Millstone; MCD-Township; MONMOUTH; ***204** J-11; ★ **PHIL-**; mail Englishtown **z** 07726, Millstone Township **z** 08510, **z** 08535; Ⓟ 5,069; © 8,970

Millstone; Inc. Place; SOMERSET; **204** H-10; elev. 97ft./30m.; ★ **N.Y.**; mail Hillsborough **z** 08844, Somerville **z** 08876; Ⓟ 450; © 410

Milltown; Inc. Place; MIDDLESEX; **204** H-10; elev. 65ft./20m.; [P]; ★ **N.Y.**; **z** 08850; Ⓟ 6,968; © 7,000

Milltown; RMC Place; MORRIS; ▲ Chester; ***204** F-9; ★ **N.Y.**; mail Chester **z** 07930; rural

Millville; Inc. Place; CUMBERLAND; **205** M-3; elev. 37ft./11m.; [P] ■; ★ **VINL**; **z** 08332; Ⓟ 25,992; © 26,847; ◆ 28,726

Milmay; RMC Place; ATLANTIC; ▲ Buena Vista; **205** P-8; [P]; ★ **VINL**; **z** 08340; ● 350

Milton; RMC Place; MORRIS; ▲ Jefferson; **204** D-10; ★ **N.Y.**; mail Oak Ridge **z** 07438; ● 400

Mimosa Lake; RMC Place; BURLINGTON; ▲ Medford; ***205** M-8; ★ **PHIL-**; mail Marlton **z** 08053; ● 150

Mine Brook; RMC Place; SOMERSET; ***204** F-9; ★ **N.Y.**; mail Far Hills **z** 07931; rural

Mine Hill; RMC Place; MORRIS; ▲ Mine Hill; **204** E-9; [P]; ★ **N.Y.**; **z** 07803; ● 2,800

Mine Hill; MCD-Township; MORRIS; ***204** E-9; [P]; ★ **N.Y.**; **z** 07803; Ⓟ 3,333; © 3,679

Minotola; RMC Place; ATLANTIC; ***205** P-7; elev. 122ft./37m.; [P]; ★ **VINL**; **z** 08341; pop. incl. with Buena (Inc. Place)

Mizpah; RMC Place; ATLANTIC; ▲ Hamilton; **205** P-8; [P]; ★ **ATCY**; **z** 08342; ● 1,000

Moe; RMC Place; PASSAIC; mail Hewitt **z** 07421; ● 400

Money Island; RMC Place; CUMBERLAND; ▲ Downe; ***205** Q-6; mail Newport **z** 08345; ● 25

Monitor; RMC Place; HUDSON; ***204** E-13; ★ **N.Y.**; mail West New York **z** 07093; pop. incl. with West New York (Inc. Place)

MONMOUTH; **204** I-12; Ⓟ 553,124; © 615,301; ◆ 655,588

Monmouth Beach; Inc. Place; MONMOUTH; **204** I-13; elev. 12ft./4m.; [P]; ★ **N.Y.**; **z** 07750; Ⓟ 3,303; © 3,595

Monmouth Heights at Manalapan; RMC Place; MONMOUTH; ***204** I-12; elev. 160ft./49m.; ★ **N.Y.**; mail Marlboro **z** 07746; ● 2,400

Monmouth Heights at Marlboro; RMC Place; MONMOUTH; mail Marlboro **z** 07746; ● 350

Monmouth Hills; RMC Place; MONMOUTH; ▲ Middletown; ***204** I-13; ★ **N.Y.**; mail Highlands **z** 07732; ● 200

Monmouth Junction; CDP; MIDDLESEX; ▲ South Brunswick; **204** I-10; elev. 91ft./28m.; [P]; ★ **N.Y.**; **z** 08852; Ⓟ 1,570; © 2,721

Monroe; MCD-Township; GLOUCESTER; ***205** O-7; ★ **PHIL-**; mail Williamstown **z** 08094; Ⓟ 26,703; © 28,967; ◆ 32,504

Monroe (Monroe Township); MCD-Township; MIDDLESEX; ***204** I-11; [P]; ★ **N.Y.**; **z** 08831 & mail Hightstown **z** 08520; Ⓟ 22,255; © 27,999; ◆ 32,878

Monroe; RMC Place; MORRIS; ▲ Hanover; ***204** E-10; ★ **N.Y.**; mail Whippany **z** 07981

Monroe; RMC Place; SUSSEX; ▲ Sparta, Hardyston; **204** C-9; ★ **N.Y.**; mail Sparta **z** 07871; ● 75

Monroe Township; MIDDLESEX; see Monroe (MCD-Township)

Monroeville; RMC Place; SALEM; ▲ Upper Pittsgrove; **205** O-6; [P]; **z** 08343; ● 200

Montague; RMC Place; SUSSEX; ▲ Montague; **204** A-8; [P]; **z** 07827; ● 40

Montague; MCD-Township; SUSSEX; ***204** B-9; [P]; **z** 07827 & mail Port Jervis **z** 12771; Ⓟ 2,832; © 3,412

Montana; RMC Place; WARREN; ▲ Harmony; ***204** F-7; ★ **ALL-**; mail Phillipsburg **z** 08865; rural

Montclair; CDP; ESSEX; ▲ Montclair; **204** E-12; elev. 337ft./103m.; [P] [H] [C] 16,076; ★ **N.Y.**; **z** 07042-43; Ⓟ 37,729; © 38,977; Ⓡ 38,658; ◆ 37,972

Montclair; MCD-Township; ESSEX; ***204** E-12; [P] [C] 16,076 ■; ★ **N.Y.**; **z** 07042-43; Ⓟ 37,729; © 38,977; Ⓡ 38,658; ◆ 37,972

Montclair Heights; RMC Place; ESSEX; ***204** E-12; ★ **N.Y.**; mail Montclair **z** 07042

Montgomery; MCD-Township; SOMERSET; ***204** H-9; mail Belle Mead **z** 08502, Princeton **z** 08540, Rocky Hill **z** 08553, Skillman **z** 08558; Ⓟ 9,612; © 17,481; ◆ 20,325

Montrose; RMC Place; MONMOUTH; ▲ Colts Neck; ***204** I-12; elev. 160ft./49m.; ★ **N.Y.**; mail Colts Neck **z** 07722; rural

Montvale; Inc. Place; BERGEN; **204** D-13; elev. 187ft./57m.; [P]; ★ **N.Y.**; **z** 07645; Ⓟ 6,946; © 7,034

Montville; RMC Place; MORRIS; ▲ Montville; **204** D-11; [P]; ★ **N.Y.**; **z** 07045; ● 2,600

Montville; MCD-Township; MORRIS; ***204** D-11; [P]; ★ **N.Y.**; **z** 07045; Ⓟ 15,600; © 20,839; ◆ 20,769

Moonachie; Inc. Place; BERGEN; **204** B-5; elev. 7ft./2m.; [P]; ★ **N.Y.**; **z** 07074; Ⓟ 2,817; © 2,754

Moores Corner; RMC Place; SALEM; mail Salem **z** 08079; ● 50

Moorestown; RMC Place; BURLINGTON; ▲ Moorestown; **205** L-7; elev. 76ft./23m.; [P]; ★ **PHIL-**; **z** 08057; ● 19,000

Moorestown; MCD-Township; BURLINGTON; ***205** L-7; [P] ■; ★ **PHIL-**; **z** 08057; © 19,017; ◆ 21,261

Moorestown-Lenola; CDP-Census Area Only; BURLINGTON; ▲ Moorestown; ***205** L-7; ★ **PHIL-**; mail Moorestown **z** 08057; Ⓟ 13,242; © 13,860

Moosepack Pond; RMC Place; MORRIS; ▲ Jefferson; ***204** D-10; ★ **N.Y.**; mail Ogdensburg **z** 07439; ● 250

Morehousetown; RMC Place; ESSEX; ▲ Livingston; ***204** E-11; elev. 193ft./59m.; ★ **N.Y.**; mail Livingston **z** 07039

Morgan; RMC Place; MIDDLESEX; ***204** H-11; ★ **N.Y.**; mail South Amboy **z** 08879; pop. incl. with Sayreville (Inc. Place)

Morgan Beach; RMC Place; MIDDLESEX; ***204** H-12; ★ **N.Y.**; mail South Amboy **z** 08879

Morganville; CDP; MONMOUTH; ▲ Marlboro; **204** I-12; [P]; ★ **N.Y.**; **z** 07751; © 11,255

Morris; RMC Place; CAMDEN; ▲ Pennsauken; ***205** L-7; ★ **PHIL-**; mail Pennsauken **z** 08110

Morris; MCD-Township; MORRIS; ***204** F-10; ★ **N.Y.**; mail Morristown **z** 07961; Ⓟ 19,952; © 21,796; Ⓡ 21,427; ◆ 20,906

MORRIS; **204** E-10; Ⓟ 421,353; © 470,212; ◆ 479,204

Morris Beach; RMC Place; ATLANTIC; ▲ Egg Harbor; ***205** Q-9; ★ **ATCY**; mail Egg Harbor Township **z** 08234; ● 30

Morris Park; RMC Place; WARREN; ▲ Lopatcong; ***204** F-6; ★ **ALL-**; mail Phillipsburg **z** 08865; ● 600

Morris Plains; Inc. Place; MORRIS; **204** E-10; elev. 399ft./122m.; [P]; ★ **N.Y.**; **z** 07950; Ⓟ 5,219; © 5,236

Morris Street; RMC Place; MORRIS; ***204** E-10; ★ **N.Y.**; mail Morristown **z** 07960; pop. incl. with Morristown (Inc. Place)

Morristown; RMC Place; MIDDLESEX; ▲ Old Bridge; ***204** H-12; ★ **N.Y.**; mail Matawan **z** 07747; ● 500

Morristown; Inc. Place; ⊡ MORRIS; **204** E-10; elev. 327ft./100m.; [P] [H] [C] 1,982 ■; ★ **N.Y.**; **z** 07960-63; Ⓟ 16,189; © 18,544; ◆ 19,133

Morrisville; RMC Place; CAMDEN; ▲ Pennsauken; ***205** L-7; ★ **PHIL-**; mail Pennsauken **z** 08110

Morsemere; RMC Place; BERGEN; ***204** E-13; ★ **N.Y.**; mail Ridgefield **z** 07657; pop. incl. with Ridgefield (Inc. Place)

Mountain Lake; RMC Place; WARREN; ▲ Liberty; ***204** E-7; ★ **N.Y.**; mail Belvidere **z** 07823; ● 200

Mountain Lakes; Inc. Place; MORRIS; **204** E-11; elev. 513ft./156m.; [P]; ★ **N.Y.**; **z** 07046; Ⓟ 3,847; © 4,256

Mountainside; Inc. Place; UNION; **204** F-11; elev. 142ft./43m.; [P] [H]; ★ **N.Y.**; **z** 07092; Ⓟ 6,657; © 6,602

Mountain Spring Lakes; RMC Place; PASSAIC; ▲ West Milford; ***204** D-11; ★ **N.Y.**; mail Butler **z** 07405; ● 150

Mountain View; RMC Place; PASSAIC; ▲ Wayne; **204** D-11; elev. 204ft./62m.; ★ **N.Y.**; mail Wayne **z** 07470

Mountainville; RMC Place; HUNTERDON; ▲ Tewksbury; **204** F-8; ★ **N.Y.**; mail Lebanon **z** 08833; ● 75

Mount Airy; RMC Place; HUNTERDON; ▲ West Amwell; **204** I-8; ★ **PHIL-**; mail Lambertville **z** 08530; ● 60

Mount Arlington; Inc. Place; MORRIS; **204** D-9; elev. 1,096ft./334m.; [P]; ★ **N.Y.**; **z** 07856; Ⓟ 3,630; © 4,663

Mount Bethel; RMC Place; SOMERSET; ▲ Warren; ***204** G-10; ★ **N.Y.**; mail Warren **z** 07059

Mount Bethel; RMC Place; WARREN; ▲ Mansfield; ***204** E-8; ★ **N.Y.**; mail Port Murray **z** 07865; rural

Mount Ephraim; Inc. Place; CAMDEN; **228** G-6; elev. 59ft./18m.; [P]; ★ **PHIL-**; **z** 08059; Ⓟ 4,517; © 4,495

Mount Fern; RMC Place; MORRIS; ▲ Randolph; ***204** E-10; ★ **N.Y.**; mail Dover **z** 07801; ● 1,200

Mount Freedom; RMC Place; MORRIS; ▲ Randolph; **204** E-10; [P]; ★ **N.Y.**; **z** 07970; ● 1,900

Mount Hermon; RMC Place; WARREN; ▲ Hope; **204** D-7; ★ **N.Y.**; mail Blairstown **z** 07825

Mount Holly; RMC Place; ⊡ BURLINGTON; ▲ Mount Holly; **205** L-8; elev. 52ft./16m.; [P] [H]; ★ **PHIL-**; **z** 08060; Ⓟ 10,639

Mount Holly; MCD-Township; BURLINGTON; ***205** L-8; [P]; ★ **PHIL-**; **z** 08060; Ⓟ 10,639; © 10,728

Mount Hope; RMC Place; MORRIS; ▲ Rockaway; **204** D-10; ★ **N.Y.**; mail Wharton **z** 07885; ● 375

Mount Horeb; RMC Place; SOMERSET; ▲ Warren; ***204** G-10; ★ **N.Y.**; mail Warren **z** 07059; rural

Mount Joy; RMC Place; HUNTERDON; ▲ Holland; ***204** G-6; mail Milford **z** 08848; ● 100

Mount Kemble Lake; RMC Place; MORRIS; ▲ Harding; ***204** F-10; ★ **N.Y.**; mail Morristown **z** 07960; ● 400

Mount Laurel; RMC Place; BURLINGTON; ▲ Mount Laurel; **205** L-8; [P]; ★ **PHIL-**; **z** 08054; ● 300

Mount Laurel; MCD-Township; BURLINGTON; ***205** L-8; [P]; ★ **PHIL-**; **z** 08054; Ⓟ 30,270; © 40,221; ◆ 42,932

Mount Lebanon; RMC Place; HUNTERDON; mail Glen Gardner **z** 08826; ● 280

Mount Olive; RMC Place; MORRIS; ▲ Mount Olive; ***204** E-9; ★ **N.Y.**; mail Budd Lake **z** 07828

Mount Olive; MCD-Township; MORRIS; ***204** E-8; ★ **N.Y.**; mail Budd Lake **z** 07828; Ⓟ 21,282; © 24,193; ◆ 25,335

Mount Pleasant; RMC Place; CAPE MAY; **205** R-8; elev. 38ft./12m.; mail Woodbine **z** 08270; pop. incl. with Woodbine (Inc. Place)

Mount Pleasant; RMC Place; HUNTERDON; ▲ Holland, Alexandria; **204** G-7; mail Milford **z** 08848; ● 120

Mount Pleasant; RMC Place; WARREN; ▲ Knowlton; ***204** D-7; ★ **N.Y.**; mail Columbia **z** 07832; rural

Mount Rose; RMC Place; MERCER; ▲ Hopewell; ***204** I-9; ★ **PHIL-**; mail Hopewell **z** 08525

Mount Royal; RMC Place; GLOUCESTER; ▲ East Greenwich; **205** M-6; elev. 39ft./12m.; [P]; ★ **PHIL-**; **z** 08061; ● 900

Mount Salem; RMC Place; SUSSEX; ▲ Wantage; ***204** A-9; ★ **N.Y.**; mail Sussex **z** 07461; rural

Mounts Mills; RMC Place; MIDDLESEX; ***204** I-11; elev. 60ft./18m.; ★ **N.Y.**; mail Monroe Township **z** 08831; ● 150

Mount Tabor; MORRIS; see Tabor (RMC Place)

Mount Vernon; RMC Place; WARREN; ▲ Blairstown; ***204** D-7; ★ **N.Y.**; mail Columbia **z** 07832; rural

Muhlenberg; RMC Place; UNION; ***204** G-10; ★ **N.Y.**; mail Plainfield **z** 07060; pop. incl. with Plainfield (Inc. Place)

Mullica; MCD-Township; ATLANTIC; ***205** O-9; ★ **ATCY**; mail Egg Harbor City **z** 08215, Hammonton **z** 08037; Ⓟ 5,896; © 5,912

Mullica Hill; CDP; GLOUCESTER; ▲ Harrison; **205** N-6; [P]; ★ **PHIL-**; **z** 08062; Ⓟ 1,117; © 1,658

Murray Grove; RMC Place; OCEAN; ▲ Lacey; ***205** M-12; ★ **N.Y.**; mail Forked River **z** 08731; ● 150

Murray Hill; RMC Place; UNION; ***204** F-11; ★ **N.Y.**; mail New Providence **z** 07974; pop. incl. with New Providence (Inc. Place)

Myrtle Grove; RMC Place; SUSSEX; ▲ Hampton; **204** C-8; ★ **N.Y.**; mail Newton **z** 07860; rural

Mystic Island (Mystic Islands); CDP; OCEAN; ▲ Little Egg Harbor; **205** O-11; ★ **ATCY**; mail Tuckerton **z** 08087; Ⓟ 7,400; © 8,694

Mystic Islands; OCEAN; see Mystic Island (CDP)

Mystic Shores; RMC Place; OCEAN; ▲ Little Egg Harbor; ***205** O-11; elev. 30ft./9m.; ★ **ATCY**; mail Tuckerton **z** 08087

N

National Park; Inc. Place; GLOUCESTER; **205** M-6; elev. 20ft./6m.; [P]; ★ **PHIL-**; **z** 08063; Ⓟ 3,413; © 3,205

Naughright; RMC Place; MORRIS; ▲ Washington; **204** E-9; elev. 560ft./171m.; ★ **N.Y.**; mail Long Valley **z** 07853; ● 100

Navesink; CDP; MONMOUTH; ▲ Middletown; **204** I-13; [P]; ★ **N.Y.**; **z** 07752; © 1,962

Navesink Beach; RMC Place; MONMOUTH; ***204** I-13; ★ **N.Y.**; mail Rumson **z** 07760; pop. incl. with Sea Bright (Inc. Place)

Neptune; RMC Place; MONMOUTH; ▲ Neptune; **204** J-13; [P] [H]; ★ **N.Y.**; **z** 07753-54; ● 19,000

Neptune (Neptune Township); MCD-Township; MONMOUTH; ***204** J-13; [P]; ★ **N.Y.**; **z** 07753-54; Ⓟ 28,148; © 27,690; ◆ 28,458

Neptune City; Inc. Place; MONMOUTH; **204** J-13; elev. 15ft./5m.; [P]; ★ **N.Y.**; **z** 07753; Ⓟ 4,997; © 5,218

Neptune Township; MONMOUTH; see Neptune (MCD-Township)

Nesco; RMC Place; ATLANTIC; ▲ Mullica; **205** O-9; ★ **ATCY**; mail Hammonton **z** 08037

Neshanic; RMC Place; SOMERSET; ▲ Hillsborough; **204** H-9; ★ **N.Y.**; mail Neshanic Station **z** 08853; ● 150

Neshanic Station; RMC Place; SOMERSET; ▲ Branchburg; **204** H-9; [P]; ★ **N.Y.**; **z** 08853; ● 500

Netcong; Inc. Place; MORRIS; **204** E-9; elev. 882ft./269m.; [P]; ★ **N.Y.**; **z** 07857; Ⓟ 3,311; © 2,580; Ⓡ 3,236

Netcong Heights; RMC Place; MORRIS; ▲ Roxbury; ***204** E-9; ★ **N.Y.**; mail Netcong **z** 07857; ● 200

Netherwood; RMC Place; UNION; ***204** G-11; ★ **N.Y.**; mail Plainfield **z** 07062; pop. incl. with Plainfield (Inc. Place)

New Albany; RMC Place; BURLINGTON; ▲ Cinnaminson; ***205** L-7; ★ **PHIL-**; mail Riverton **z** 08077

New Amsterdam Village; RMC Place; MIDDLESEX; ▲ Old Bridge; ***204** H-11; ★ **N.Y.**; mail South Amboy **z** 08879; ● 1,900

Newark; Inc. Place; ⊡ ESSEX; **204** F-12; elev. 146ft./45m.; [P] [H] [C] 23,802 ■; ★ **N.Y.**; **z** 07101-08, **z** 07112, **z** 07114, **z** 07175, **z** 07184, **z** 07188-89, **z** 07191-93, **z** 07195, **z** 07198-99; Ⓟ 275,221; © 273,546; Ⓡ 272,537; ◆ 269,798

Newark Heights; RMC Place; ESSEX; ▲ Maplewood; ***204** F-11; ★ **N.Y.**; mail Maplewood **z** 07040

Newbakers Corners; RMC Place; WARREN; ▲ Hardwick; ***204** D-8; ★ **N.Y.**; mail Blairstown **z** 07825; rural

New Bedford; RMC Place; MONMOUTH; ▲ Wall; ***204** J-13; ★ **N.Y.**; mail Belmar **z** 07719

Newbolds Corner; RMC Place; BURLINGTON; ***205** L-8; ★ **PHIL-**; mail Mount Holly **z** 08060

New Bridge; RMC Place; BERGEN; ***204** D-13; ★ **N.Y.**; mail New Milford **z** 07646; pop. incl. with New Milford (Inc. Place)

New Brooklyn; RMC Place; CAMDEN, GLOUCESTER; ▲ Monroe, Winslow; **205** N-7; ★ **PHIL-**; mail Sicklerville **z** 08081; ● 4,000

New Brunswick; Inc. Place; ⊡ MIDDLESEX; **204** H-10; elev. 42ft./13m.; [P] [H] [C] 34,392 ■; ★ **N.Y.**; **z** 08901-06, **z** 08922, **z** 08933, **z** 08988-89; Ⓟ 41,711; © 48,573; Ⓡ 48,591; ◆ 51,409

New Canton; RMC Place; MERCER, MONMOUTH; ▲ Robbinsville, Upper Freehold; ★ **PHIL-**; mail Allentown **z** 08501; rural

New Durham; RMC Place; HUDSON; ***204** F-13; ★ **N.Y.**; mail North Bergen **z** 07047

New Durham; RMC Place; MIDDLESEX; ***204** G-11; ★ **N.Y.**; mail Edison **z** 08837

New Egypt; CDP; OCEAN; ▲ Plumsted; **205** K-10; [P]; ★ **PHIL-**; **z** 08533; Ⓟ 2,327; © 2,519

Newfield; Inc. Place; GLOUCESTER; **205** K-3; elev. 110ft./34m.; [P]; ★ **VINL**; **z** 08344; Ⓟ 1,592; © 1,616

Newfoundland; RMC Place; PASSAIC, MORRIS; ▲ West Milford, Jefferson; **204** C-10; [P]; ★ **N.Y.**; **z** 07435; ● 400

New Freedom; RMC Place; CAMDEN; ▲ Berlin; ***205** N-7; elev. 170ft./52m.; ★ **PHIL-**; mail Berlin **z** 08009; rural

New Gretna; RMC Place; BURLINGTON; ▲ Bass River; **205** O-10; [P]; **z** 08224; ● 600

New Hampton; RMC Place; HUNTERDON; ▲ Lebanon; **204** F-7; ★ **N.Y.**; mail Hampton **z** 08827; ● 200

New Hanover; MCD-Township; BURLINGTON; ***205** L-10; ★ **PHIL-**; mail Cookstown **z** 08511; Ⓟ 9,546; © 9,744

New Jersey & New York Junction; RMC Place; BERGEN; ★ **N.Y.**; pop. incl. with East Rutherford (Inc. Place)

New Lisbon; RMC Place; BURLINGTON; ▲ Pemberton; **205** L-9; [P]; ★ **PHIL-**; **z** 08064; ● 350

New Market; RMC Place; MIDDLESEX; ***204** G-10; ★ **N.Y.**; mail Piscataway **z** 08854; ● 20,000

New Market; MIDDLESEX; see Piscataway (RMC Place)

New Milford; Inc. Place; BERGEN; **210** B-10; elev. 33ft./10m.; [P]; ★ **N.Y.**; **z** 07646; Ⓟ 15,990; © 16,400

New Monmouth; RMC Place; MONMOUTH; ▲ Middletown; ***204** H-12; [P]; ★ **N.Y.**; **z** 07748

Newport; RMC Place; CUMBERLAND; ▲ Downe; **205** Q-6; elev. 9ft./3m.; [P]; **z** 08345; ● 700

Newport; RMC Place; HUNTERDON; ▲ Lebanon; ***204** F-8; ★ **N.Y.**; mail Glen Gardner **z** 08826; rural

New Providence; Inc. Place; UNION; **204** F-11; elev. 220ft./67m.; [P]; ★ **N.Y.**; **z** 07974; Ⓟ 11,439; © 11,907

New Russia; MORRIS; see Russia (RMC Place)

New Sharon; RMC Place; GLOUCESTER; ▲ Deptford; ***205** M-6; ★ **PHIL-**; mail Sewell **z** 08080

New Sharon; RMC Place; MERCER, MONMOUTH; ▲ Upper Freehold, Robbinsville; **204** J-10; ★ **PHIL-**; mail Trenton **z** 08691

Newton; Inc. Place; ⊡ SUSSEX; **204** C-9; elev. 608ft./185m.; [P] [H] ■; ★ **N.Y.**; **z** 07860; Ⓟ 7,521; © 8,244; ◆ 8,244

Newton Heights; RMC Place; MIDDLESEX; ***204** H-11; mail East Brunswick **z** 08816; ● 1,550

Newtonville; RMC Place; ATLANTIC; ▲ Buena Vista; **205** O-8; [P]; ★ **VINL**; **z** 08346; ● 200

Newtown; RMC Place; MIDDLESEX; ▲ Piscataway; ***204** G-10; ★ **N.Y.**; mail Piscataway **z** 08854

New Vernon; RMC Place; MORRIS; ▲ Harding; **204** F-10; [P]; ★ **N.Y.**; **z** 07976; ● 600

New Village; RMC Place; WARREN; ▲ Franklin; **204** F-7; ★ **N.Y.**; mail Stewartsville **z** 08886; ● 400

Nixon; RMC Place; MIDDLESEX; ▲ Edison; ***204** H-11; ★ **N.Y.**; mail Edison **z** 08817

Norma; RMC Place; SALEM; ▲ Pittsgrove; **205** L-2; [P]; ★ **VINL**; **z** 08347; ● 400

Normandie; RMC Place; MONMOUTH; ***204** I-13; ★ **N.Y.**; mail Rumson **z** 07760; pop. incl. with Sea Bright (Inc. Place)

Normandy Beach; RMC Place; OCEAN; ▲ Brick; **205** L-13; [P]; ★ **N.Y.**; **z** 08739

North; RMC Place; ESSEX; ***204** F-12; ★ **N.Y.**; mail Newark **z** 07104; pop. incl. with Newark (Inc. Place)

North Arlington; Inc. Place; BERGEN; **204** C-3; elev. 122ft./37m.; [P]; ★ **N.Y.**; **z** 07031; Ⓟ 13,790; © 15,181

North Beach; RMC Place; OCEAN; ▲ Long Beach; ***205** N-12; ★ **N.Y.**; mail Beach Haven **z** 08008; summer pop. 1,000; ● 200

North Beach Haven; CDP; OCEAN; ▲ Long Beach; **205** O-12; ★ **N.Y.**; mail Beach Haven **z** 08008; Ⓟ 2,413; © 2,427

North Bergen; RMC Place; HUDSON; ▲ North Bergen; **204** E-13; elev. 43ft./13m.; [P] [H]; ★ **N.Y.**; **z** 07047; Ⓟ 48,414

Entries in **UPPERCASE** are counties.
Entries in **bold** have populations of 2,500 or more.
Names in parentheses are alternate names.

Inc. Place	Incorporated Place
RMC Place	Rand McNally Designated Place
CDP	Census Designated Place
MCD	Minor Civil Division
⊡	County Seat
▲	Minor Civil Division
elev.	Elevation
[P]	Post Office
[H]	Hospital
[C]	College
■	Principal Business Center
★	Ranally Metro Area (RMA) Abbreviation
z	Zip Code(s)
Ⓟ	Previous Census Population
Ⓡ	Revised Census Population
Ⓐ	Annexation Population
●	Rand McNally Population Estimate
©	Final Census Population
Ⓢ	Special Census Population
◆	Estimated Population

For additional definitions see Glossary, Volume 1, and Introduction, Volume 2.

North Bergen; MCD-Township; HUDSON; *204 E-13; 🄿 ■; ★ N.Y.; z 07047; Ⓟ 48,414; Ⓒ 58,092; ◆ 58,147
North Branch; RMC Place; SOMERSET; ▲ Branchburg; 204 G-9; elev. 76ft./23m.; 🄿; ★ N.Y.; z 08876; ● 1,300
North Branch Depot; RMC Place; SOMERSET; *204 G-9; ★ N.Y.; mail Somerville z 08876; ● 1,200
North Brunswick; MIDDLESEX; see North Brunswick Township (CDP-Census Area Only)
North Brunswick; MCD-Township; MIDDLESEX; *204 H-10; 🄿 🄲 1,417; ★ N.Y.; z 08902; Ⓟ 31,287; Ⓒ 36,287; ◆ 38,964
North Brunswick Township (North Brunswick); CDP-Census Area Only; MIDDLESEX; ▲ North Brunswick; 204 H-10; 🄲 1,417; ★ N.Y.; mail North Brunswick z 08902; Ⓟ 31,287; Ⓒ 36,287; ◆ 38,964
North Caldwell; Inc. Place; ESSEX; 204 E-12; elev. 245ft./75m.; 🄿; ★ N.Y.; z 07006; Ⓟ 6,706; Ⓒ 7,375
North Cape May; CDP; CAPE MAY; ▲ Lower; 205 T-1; 🄿; z 08204; Ⓟ 3,574; Ⓒ 3,618
North Center; RMC Place; ESSEX; *204 E-12; ★ N.Y.; mail Bloomfield z 07003
North Centerville; RMC Place; MONMOUTH; *204 I-12; mail Hazlet z 07730; ● 1,100
North Church; RMC Place; SUSSEX; ▲ Hardyston; 204 C-9; ★ N.Y.; mail Franklin z 07416; ● 100
North Church Estates; RMC Place; SUSSEX; ▲ Hardyston; *204 C-9; ★ N.Y.; mail Franklin z 07416; ● 200
North Crosswicks; RMC Place; MERCER; ▲ Hamilton; *204 J-9; ★ PHIL-; mail Trenton z 08620; ● 100
North Dennis; RMC Place; CAPE MAY; ▲ Dennis; *205 R-8; elev. 14ft./4m.; mail Dennisville z 08214
North Edison; RMC Place; MIDDLESEX; ▲ Edison; *204 G-11; ★ N.Y.; mail Edison z 08817
North Elizabeth; RMC Place; UNION; *204 F-12; ★ N.Y.; mail Elizabeth z 07208; pop. incl. with Elizabeth (Inc. Place)
Northfield; Inc. Place; ATLANTIC; 205 Q-10; elev. 33ft./10m.; 🄿; ★ ATCY; z 08225; Ⓟ 7,305; Ⓒ 7,725
Northfield; RMC Place; ESSEX; ▲ Livingston; *204 F-11; elev. 263ft./80m.; ★ N.Y.; mail Livingston z 07039
North Hackensack; RMC Place; BERGEN; *204 D-13; ★ N.Y.; mail River Edge z 07661; pop. incl. with River Edge (Inc. Place)
North Haledon; Inc. Place; PASSAIC; 204 D-12; elev. 259ft./79m.; 🄿; ★ N.Y.; z 07508 & mail Haledon z 07538; Ⓟ 7,987; Ⓒ 7,920
North Hanover; MCD-Township; BURLINGTON; *205 K-9; ★ PHIL-; mail Wrightstown z 08562; Ⓟ 9,994; Ⓒ 7,347
North Hawthorne; RMC Place; PASSAIC; *204 D-12; ★ N.Y.; mail Hawthorne z 07507; pop. incl. with Hawthorne (Inc. Place)
North Long Branch; RMC Place; MONMOUTH; *204 I-13; ★ N.Y.; mail Long Branch z 07740; pop. incl. with Long Branch (Inc. Place)
North Middletown; CDP-Census Area Only; MONMOUTH; ▲ Middletown; 204 H-12; elev. 12ft./4m.; 🄿; ★ N.Y.; z 07748 & mail Keansburg z 07734; Ⓟ 3,160; Ⓒ 3,165
Northmont; RMC Place; CAMDEN; *205 M-6; ★ PHIL-; mail Mount Ephraim z 08059; pop. incl. with Mount Ephraim (Inc. Place)
North Newark; RMC Place; ESSEX; *204 F-12; ★ N.Y.; mail Newark z 07104; pop. incl. with Newark (Inc. Place)
North Plainfield; Inc. Place; SOMERSET; 204 G-10; elev. 17ft./5m.; 🄿; ★ N.Y.; z 07060, z 07062-63 & mail Watchung z 07069; Ⓟ 18,820; Ⓒ 21,103; ◆ 20,740
North Port Norris; RMC Place; CUMBERLAND; ▲ Commercial; *205 R-7; ★ VINL; mail Port Norris z 08349; ● 100
North Princeton; RMC Place; MERCER; *204 I-9; mail Princeton z 08540; ● 1,500
North Stelton; RMC Place; MIDDLESEX; *204 G-10; mail Piscataway z 08854; ● 3,000
Northvale; Inc. Place; BERGEN; 204 D-13; elev. 82ft./25m.; 🄿; ★ N.Y.; z 07647; Ⓟ 4,563; Ⓒ 4,460
North Vineland; RMC Place; CUMBERLAND; *205 O-7; ★ VINL; mail Vineland z 08360; pop. incl. with Vineland (Inc. Place)
North Wildwood; Inc. Place; CAPE MAY; 205 T-3; elev. 6ft./2m.; 🄿; z 08260; Ⓟ 5,017; Ⓒ 4,935
North Woodbury; RMC Place; GLOUCESTER; *205 M-6; ★ PHIL-; mail Woodbury z 08096; ● 1,200
Norton; RMC Place; HUNTERDON; ▲ Union, Bethlehem; 204 G-7; ★ N.Y.; mail Hampton z 08827; ● 60
Nortonville; RMC Place; GLOUCESTER; ▲ Logan; 205 M-5; ★ PHIL-; mail Swedesboro z 08085; ● 100
Norwood; Inc. Place; BERGEN; 211 A-11; elev. 90ft./27m.; 🄿; ★ N.Y.; z 07648; Ⓟ 4,858; Ⓒ 5,751
Nottingham; RMC Place; MERCER; ▲ Hamilton; *204 J-9; ★ PHIL-; mail Trenton z 08619
Nugentown; RMC Place; OCEAN; ▲ Little Egg Harbor; *205 O-11; elev. 21ft./6m.; ★ ATCY; mail Tuckerton z 08087; ● 150
Nummytown; RMC Place; CAPE MAY; ▲ Middle; *205 S-8
Nutley; CDP; ESSEX; ▲ Nutley; 204 E-12; elev. 91ft./28m.; 🄿; ★ N.Y.; z 07110; Ⓟ 27,099; Ⓒ 27,362; ◆ 25,753
Nutley; MCD-Township; ESSEX; *204 E-12; 🄿; ★ N.Y.; z 07110; Ⓟ 27,099; Ⓒ 27,362; ◆ 25,753

O

Oak Glen; RMC Place; MONMOUTH; ▲ Howell; *204 J-12; ★ N.Y.; mail Howell z 07731; rural
Oak Hill; RMC Place; MONMOUTH; ▲ Middletown; *204 I-13; ★ N.Y.; mail Middletown z 07748
Oakhurst; CDP; MONMOUTH; ▲ Ocean; 204 J-13; 🄿; ★ N.Y.; z 07755; Ⓟ 4,130; Ⓒ 4,152
Oakhurst Manor; RMC Place; MONMOUTH; mail Oakhurst z 07755; ● 750
Oak Island; RMC Place; ESSEX; *204 F-12; ★ N.Y.; pop. incl. with Newark (Inc. Place)
Oak Island Junction; RMC Place; ESSEX; *204 F-12; ★ N.Y.; pop. incl. with Newark (Inc. Place)
Oakland; Inc. Place; BERGEN; 204 D-12; elev. 282ft./86m.; 🄿; ★ N.Y.; z 07436; Ⓟ 11,997; Ⓒ 12,466
Oaklyn; Inc. Place; CAMDEN; 228 F-6; elev. 28ft./9m.; 🄿; ★ PHIL-; z 08107; Ⓟ 4,430; Ⓒ 4,188
Oak Ridge; RMC Place; PASSAIC; ▲ West Milford; *204 C-10; 🄿; ★ N.Y.; z 07438; ● 900
Oak Ridge Estates; RMC Place; OCEAN; ▲ Toms River; 204 C-10; ★ N.Y.; mail Toms River z 08755; ● 1,600
Oak Ridge Lake; MORRIS; see Woodstock (RMC Place)
Oak Shades; RMC Place; MONMOUTH; ▲ Aberdeen; *204 H-12; elev. 40ft./12m.; ★ N.Y.; mail Matawan z 07747; ● 400
Oak Tree; RMC Place; MIDDLESEX; ▲ Edison; *204 G-11; ★ N.Y.; mail Edison z 08817
Oak Tree; RMC Place; OCEAN; ▲ Jackson; *205 K-11; elev. 150ft./46m.; ★ N.Y.; mail Jackson z 08527; ● 300
Oak Valley; CDP; GLOUCESTER; ▲ Deptford; *205 M-6; ★ PHIL-; mail Wenonah z 08090; Ⓟ 4,055; Ⓒ 3,747
Oakwood Beach; RMC Place; SALEM; ▲ Elsinboro; 205 O-4; ★ PHIL-; mail Salem z 08079; ● 200
Oakwood Lakes; RMC Place; BURLINGTON; *205 M-8; ★ PHIL-; mail Medford z 08055; ● 600
Oakwood Park; RMC Place; UNION; *204 F-11; ★ N.Y.; mail New Providence z 07974; pop. incl. with New Providence (Inc. Place)
Ocean; MCD-Township; MONMOUTH; *204 J-13; 🄿 ■; ★ N.Y.; z 07712 & mail Oakhurst z 07755; Ⓟ 25,058; Ⓒ 26,959; ◆ 28,541
Ocean; MCD-Township; OCEAN; *205 M-11; ★ N.Y.; mail Waretown z 08758; Ⓟ 5,416; Ⓒ 6,450
OCEAN; 205 L-11; Ⓟ 433,203; Ⓒ 510,916; ◆ 571,817
Ocean Acres; CDP-Census Area Only; OCEAN; ▲ Stafford, Barnegat; *205 N-11; ★ N.Y.; mail Manahawkin z 08050; Ⓟ 5,587; Ⓒ 13,155
Ocean Beach; RMC Place; OCEAN; ▲ Toms River; 205 L-13; ★ N.Y.; mail Lavallette z 08735; summer pop. 5,000; ● 1,800
Ocean City; Inc. Place; CAPE MAY; 205 Q-10; elev. 4ft./1m.; 🄿; ★ ATCY; z 08226; Ⓟ 15,512; Ⓒ 15,378
Ocean Gate; Inc. Place; OCEAN; 205 L-12; elev. 7ft./2m.; 🄿; ★ N.Y.; z 08740; Ⓟ 2,078; Ⓒ 2,076
Ocean Grove; CDP; MONMOUTH; ▲ Neptune; 204 J-13; 🄿; ★ N.Y.; z 07756; Ⓟ 4,818; Ⓒ 4,256
Ocean Heights; RMC Place; ATLANTIC; *205 Q-10; ★ ATCY; mail Somers Point z 08244; pop. incl. with Somers Point (Inc. Place)
Oceanport; Inc. Place; MONMOUTH; 204 I-13; elev. 12ft./4m.; 🄿; ★ N.Y.; z 07757; Ⓟ 6,146; Ⓒ 5,807
Ocean View; RMC Place; CAPE MAY; ▲ Dennis; 205 R-9; 🄿; z 08230; ● 200
Oceanville; RMC Place; ATLANTIC; ▲ Galloway; 205 P-10; elev. 41ft./12m.; 🄿; ★ ATCY; z 08231; ● 300
Ogdensburg; Inc. Place; SUSSEX; 204 C-9; elev. 677ft./206m.; 🄿; ★ N.Y.; z 07439; Ⓟ 2,722; Ⓒ 2,638
Old Bridge; CDP; MIDDLESEX; ▲ Old Bridge; 204 H-11; 🄿; ★ N.Y.; z 08857; Ⓟ 22,151; Ⓒ 22,833; ◆ 24,102
Old Bridge; MCD-Township; MIDDLESEX; *204 I-11; 🄿; ★ N.Y.; z 08857; Ⓟ 56,475; Ⓒ 60,456; ◆ 65,475
Old Forge Village; RMC Place; MORRIS; ▲ Morris; *204 E-10; ★ N.Y.; mail Morristown z 07960; ● 1,200
Old Manor; RMC Place; MONMOUTH; ▲ Holmdel; *204 H-12; ★ N.Y.; mail Holmdel z 07733; ● 1,000
Oldmans; MCD-Township; SALEM; *205 N-5; ★ PHIL-; mail Pedricktown z 08067; Ⓟ 1,683; Ⓒ 1,798
Old Milford Estates; RMC Place; PASSAIC; ▲ West Milford; *204 C-11; ★ N.Y.; mail West Milford z 07480; ● 150
Old Tappan; Inc. Place; BERGEN; 204 D-13; elev. 50ft./15m.; 🄿; ★ N.Y.; z 07675; Ⓟ 4,254; Ⓒ 5,482
Oldwick; RMC Place; HUNTERDON; ▲ Tewksbury; 204 F-9; 🄿; ★ N.Y.; z 08858; ● 200
Olivet; CDP; SALEM; ▲ Pittsgrove; 205 O-6; ★ VINL; mail Elmer z 08318; Ⓟ 1,315; Ⓒ 1,420
Oradell; Inc. Place; BERGEN; 204 D-13; elev. 110ft./34m.; 🄿; ★ N.Y.; z 07649; Ⓟ 8,024; Ⓒ 8,047
Orange; CDP; ESSEX; ▲ City of Orange; 204 F-12; elev. 204ft./62m.; 🄿 🄷; ★ N.Y.; z 07050-51; Ⓟ 29,925; Ⓒ 32,868; ◆ 31,312
Orange; ESSEX; see City of Orange (MCD-Township)
Orchard Estates; RMC Place; MONMOUTH; mail Freehold z 07728; ● 130
Orchard Heights; RMC Place; MIDDLESEX; *204 H-11; mail East Brunswick z 08816; ● 1,700
Orchard View; RMC Place; BURLINGTON; ▲ Burlington; *205 K-8; ★ PHIL-; mail Burlington z 08016; ● 400
Ortley Beach; RMC Place; OCEAN; ▲ Toms River; 205 L-13; ★ N.Y.; mail Seaside Heights z 08751; summer pop. 3,000; ● 1,500
Osage; RMC Place; CAMDEN; ▲ Voorhees; *205 M-7; ★ PHIL-; mail Voorhees z 08043
Osbornes Mills; RMC Place; MONMOUTH; mail Belmar z 07719; ● 800
Osbornsville; RMC Place; OCEAN; ▲ Brick; 205 K-12; ★ N.Y.; mail Brick z 08723
Osbornville; RMC Place; OCEAN; mail Brick z 08723; ● 850
Othello; RMC Place; CUMBERLAND; ▲ Greenwich; 205 P-5; mail Bridgeton z 08302
Outcalt; RMC Place; MIDDLESEX; ▲ Monroe; *204 I-11; ★ N.Y.; mail Monroe Township z 08831; ● 700
Outwater; RMC Place; BERGEN; *204 E-12; ★ N.Y.; mail Garfield z 07026; pop. incl. with Garfield (Inc. Place)
Overbrook; RMC Place; CAMDEN; *205 M-7; ★ PHIL-; mail Clementon z 08021; pop. incl. with Lindenwold (Inc. Place)
Overbrook; RMC Place; ESSEX; ▲ Cedar Grove; *204 E-12; ★ N.Y.; mail Cedar Grove z 07009
Oxford (Oxford Furnace); CDP; WARREN; ▲ Oxford; 204 E-7; 🄿; ★ N.Y.; z 07863; Ⓟ 1,767; Ⓒ 2,283
Oxford; MCD-Township; WARREN; *204 E-7; 🄿; ★ N.Y.; z 07863; Ⓟ 1,790; Ⓒ 2,307
Oxford Furnace; WARREN; see Oxford (CDP)
Oyster Creek; RMC Place; ATLANTIC; ▲ Galloway; 205 P-11; ★ ATCY; mail Absecon z 08205

P

Packanack Lake; RMC Place; PASSAIC; ▲ Wayne; *204 D-11; ★ N.Y.; mail Wayne z 07470
Palatine; RMC Place; SALEM; ▲ Pittsgrove; *205 O-6; ★ VINL; mail Elmer z 08318
Palermo; RMC Place; CAPE MAY; ▲ Upper; 205 R-9; ★ ATCY; mail Marmora z 08223; ● 1,200
Palisade; RMC Place; BERGEN; ★ N.Y.; mail Fort Lee z 07024; pop. incl. with Fort Lee (Inc. Place)
Palisades Park; Inc. Place; BERGEN; 204 E-13; elev. 150ft./46m.; 🄿; ★ N.Y.; z 07650; Ⓟ 14,536; Ⓒ 17,073
Palmer Square; RMC Place; MERCER; *204 I-9; mail Princeton z 08540; pop. incl. with Princeton (Inc. Place)
Palmyra; Inc. Place; BURLINGTON; 205 L-7; elev. 20ft./6m.; 🄿; ★ PHIL-; z 08065; Ⓟ 7,056; Ⓒ 7,091
Palmyra; RMC Place; HUNTERDON; mail Pittstown z 08867; rural
Pamrapo; RMC Place; HUDSON; *204 G-12; ★ N.Y.; mail Bayonne z 07002; pop. incl. with Bayonne (Inc. Place)
Pancoast; RMC Place; ATLANTIC; ▲ Buena Vista; *205 O-8; ★ VINL; mail Buena z 08310; rural
Panther Lake; RMC Place; SUSSEX; ▲ Byram; *204 D-9; ★ N.Y.; mail Andover z 07821; ● 200
Paradise Lakes; RMC Place; SALEM; ▲ Quinton, Alloway; 205 O-5; mail Alloway z 08001, Salem z 08079; ● 150
Paramus; Inc. Place; BERGEN; 204 D-13; elev. 58ft./18m.; 🄿 🄷 ■; ★ N.Y.; z 07652-53; Ⓟ 25,067; Ⓒ 25,737; ◆ 25,055
Park; RMC Place; PASSAIC; *204 E-12; ★ N.Y.; mail Paterson z 07513, z 07543; pop. incl. with Paterson (Inc. Place)
Park Avenue; RMC Place; HUDSON; ▲ Weehawken; *204 F-13; ★ N.Y.; mail Weehawken z 07086
Parker; RMC Place; MORRIS; ▲ Washington; *204 F-8; ★ N.Y.; mail Long Valley z 07853
Parkertown; RMC Place; OCEAN; ▲ Little Egg Harbor; 205 O-11; ★ ATCY; mail Tuckerton z 08087; ● 800
Park Ridge; Inc. Place; BERGEN; *204 D-13; elev. 226ft./69m.; 🄿; ★ N.Y.; z 07656; Ⓟ 8,102; Ⓒ 8,708
Park Ridge Farms; RMC Place; BURLINGTON; ▲ Bordentown; *204 J-9; ★ PHIL-; mail Bordentown z 08505; ● 1,270
Parkside; RMC Place; CAMDEN; *205 L-6; ★ PHIL-; pop. incl. with Camden (Inc. Place)
Park Village; RMC Place; UNION; ▲ Cranford; *204 G-11; elev. 75ft./23m.; ★ N.Y.; mail Cranford z 07016
Parkway Pines; RMC Place; MONMOUTH, OCEAN; ▲ Brick, Howell; 205 K-12; ★ N.Y.; mail Lakewood z 08701; ● 1,100
Parkway Village; RMC Place; MERCER; ▲ Ewing; *204 J-8; ★ PHIL-; mail Trenton z 08628
Parlin; RMC Place; MIDDLESEX; *204 H-11; elev. 90ft./27m.; 🄿; ★ N.Y.; z 08859; pop. incl. with Sayreville (Inc. Place)
Parry; RMC Place; BURLINGTON; ▲ Cinnaminson; *205 L-7; ★ PHIL-; mail Riverton z 08077
Parsippany; RMC Place; MORRIS; ▲ Parsippany-Troy Hills; 204 E-10; 🄿; ★ N.Y.; z 07054, z 07834
Parsippany-Troy Hills; MCD-Township; MORRIS; *204 E-10; ■; ★ N.Y.; mail Boonton z 07005; Ⓟ 48,478; Ⓒ 50,649; ◆ 50,303
Parsonville; RMC Place; BURLINGTON; ▲ Bordentown; *204 J-9; ★ PHIL-; mail Bordentown z 08505; ● 600
Pasadena; OCEAN; see Wheatland (RMC Place)
Passaic; MORRIS; see Long Hill (MCD-Township)
Passaic; Inc. Place; PASSAIC; 204 E-12; elev. 115ft./35m.; 🄿 🄷 ■; ★ N.Y.; z 07055; Ⓟ 58,041; Ⓒ 67,861; ◆ 68,224
PASSAIC; 204 C-11; Ⓟ 453,060; Ⓒ 489,049; Ⓡ 490,377; ◆ 482,223
Passaic Junction; RMC Place; BERGEN; ▲ Saddle Brook; *204 E-12; ★ N.Y.
Passaic Park; RMC Place; PASSAIC; *204 E-12; ★ N.Y.; mail Passaic z 07055; pop. incl. with Passaic (Inc. Place)
Paterson; Inc. Place; ⊡ PASSAIC; 204 D-12; elev. 100ft./30m.; 🄿 🄷 ■; ★ N.Y.; z 07501-14, z 07522, z 07524, z 07533, z 07538, z 07543-44; Ⓟ 140,891; Ⓒ 149,222; ◆ 146,443
Patricks Corners; RMC Place; MIDDLESEX; ▲ East Brunswick; *204 H-10; ★ N.Y.; mail East Brunswick z 08816
Pattenburg; RMC Place; HUNTERDON; ▲ Union; 204 G-7; mail Asbury z 08802; ● 150
Paulas Corners; RMC Place; MIDDLESEX; ▲ East Brunswick; *204 H-10; ★ N.Y.; mail East Brunswick z 08816
Paulina; RMC Place; WARREN; ▲ Blairstown; 204 D-7; ★ N.Y.; mail Blairstown z 07825; ● 100
Paulins Kill; RMC Place; SUSSEX; ▲ Stillwater; *204 C-8; ★ N.Y.; mail Newton z 07860; ● 1,300
Paulsboro; Inc. Place; GLOUCESTER; 205 M-6; elev. 9ft./3m.; 🄿; ★ PHIL-; z 08066; Ⓟ 6,577; Ⓒ 6,160
Pavonia; RMC Place; CAMDEN; *205 L-6; ★ PHIL-; mail Camden z 08105; pop. incl. with Camden (Inc. Place)
Peahala Park; RMC Place; OCEAN; ▲ Long Beach; *205 O-12; ★ N.Y.; mail Beach Haven z 08008; summer pop. 2,000; ● 250
Peapack; RMC Place; SOMERSET; *204 F-9; elev. 300ft./91m.; 🄿 🄷; ★ N.Y.; z 07977; pop. incl. with Peapack and Gladstone (Inc. Place)
Peapack; SOMERSET; see Peapack and Gladstone (Inc. Place)
Peapack and Gladstone (Peapack); Inc. Place; SOMERSET; 204 F-9; ★ N.Y.; mail Gladstone z 07934, Peapack z 07977; Ⓟ 2,111; Ⓒ 2,433
Pebble Beach; RMC Place; OCEAN; ▲ Ocean, Barnegat; *205 N-12; ★ N.Y.; mail Barnegat z 08005; ● 2,000
Pecks Corner; RMC Place; SALEM; ▲ Quinton; *205 P-5; mail Salem z 08079; rural
Pedricktown; RMC Place; SALEM; ▲ Oldmans; 205 N-5; 🄿; ★ PHIL-; z 08067; ● 1,100
Pelican Island; RMC Place; OCEAN; ▲ Toms River, Berkeley; *205 L-13; ★ N.Y.; mail Seaside Heights z 08751; ● 250
Pellettown; RMC Place; SUSSEX; ▲ Frankford; 204 C-9; ★ N.Y.; mail Augusta z 07822; ● 50
Pemberton; Inc. Place; BURLINGTON; 205 L-9; elev. 46ft./14m.; 🄿; ★ PHIL-; z 08068; Ⓟ 1,367; Ⓒ 1,210
Pemberton; MCD-Township; BURLINGTON; *205 L-9; 🄿; ★ PHIL-; z 08068 & mail Browns Mills z 08015; does not include the Borough of Pemberton; Ⓟ 31,342; Ⓒ 28,691; Ⓡ 28,569; ◆ 26,657
Pemberton Heights; CDP; BURLINGTON; ▲ Pemberton; *205 L-9; ★ PHIL-; mail Pemberton z 08068; Ⓟ 2,941; Ⓒ 2,512
Penbryn; RMC Place; CAMDEN; ▲ Winslow; *205 N-7; ★ PHIL-; mail Berlin z 08009; rural
Penekum; RMC Place; CAMDEN; ▲ Gloucester; *205 M-7; ★ PHIL-; mail Blackwood z 08012; ● 800
Penn Beach; RMC Place; SALEM; ▲ Pennsville; *205 O-4; ★ PHIL-; mail Pennsville z 08070; ● 1,800
Pennington; Inc. Place; MERCER; 205 R-12; elev. 211ft./64m.; 🄿; ★ PHIL-; z 08534; Ⓟ 2,537; Ⓒ 2,696
Pennsauken; CDP; CAMDEN; ▲ Pennsauken; 205 L-7; 🄿; ★ PHIL-; z 08109-10; Ⓟ 34,738; Ⓒ 35,737; ◆ 35,018
Pennsauken; MCD-Township; CAMDEN; *205 L-7; 🄿 ■; ★ PHIL-; z 08109-10; Ⓟ 34,738; Ⓒ 35,737; ◆ 35,018
Penns Grove; Inc. Place; SALEM; 205 N-4; elev. 12ft./4m.; 🄿; ★ PHIL-; z 08069; Ⓟ 5,228; Ⓒ 4,886
Penns Neck; RMC Place; MERCER; ▲ West Windsor; *204 I-9; ★ N.Y.; mail Princeton z 08540; ● 800
Pennsville; CDP; SALEM; ▲ Pennsville; 205 N-4; 🄿; ★ PHIL-; z 08070; Ⓟ 12,218; Ⓒ 11,657
Pennsville; MCD-Township; SALEM; *205 N-4; 🄿; ★ PHIL-; z 08070; Ⓟ 13,794; Ⓒ 13,194
Penny Pot; RMC Place; ATLANTIC; 205 O-8; ★ ATCY; mail Hammonton z 08037; pop. incl. with Folsom (Inc. Place)
Penton; RMC Place; SALEM; ▲ Mannington, Alloway; 205 O-5; mail Salem z 08079; ● 70
Penwell; RMC Place; HUNTERDON; ▲ Lebanon; 204 F-8; ★ N.Y.; mail Port Murray z 07865; ● 50
Pequannock; RMC Place; MORRIS; ▲ Pequannock; 204 D-11; 🄿; ★ N.Y.; z 07440
Pequannock; MCD-Township; MORRIS; *204 D-11; 🄿; ★ N.Y.; z 07440 & mail Pompton Plains z 07444; Ⓟ 12,844; Ⓒ 13,888
Pequest; RMC Place; WARREN; ▲ White; *204 E-7; ★ N.Y.; mail Oxford z 07863; rural
Perkintown; RMC Place; SALEM; ▲ Oldmans; *205 N-4; ★ PHIL-; mail Pedricktown z 08067; rural
Perrineville; RMC Place; MONMOUTH; ▲ Millstone; 204 J-10; 🄿; ★ PHIL-; z 08535; ● 400
Perth Amboy; Inc. Place; MIDDLESEX; 204 H-11; elev. 65ft./20m.; 🄿 🄷 ■; ★ N.Y.; z 08861-63; Ⓟ 41,967; Ⓒ 47,303; ◆ 50,854
Petersburg; RMC Place; CAPE MAY; ▲ Upper; 205 R-9; ★ ATCY; mail Woodbine z 08270; ● 900
Petersburg; RMC Place; MORRIS; mail Oak Ridge z 07438; ● 260
Petersburg; RMC Place; WARREN; ▲ Independence; *204 E-8; ★ N.Y.; mail Hackettstown z 07840; rural
Phalanx; RMC Place; MONMOUTH; *204 I-12; ★ N.Y.; mail Colts Neck z 07722; ● 200
Pheasant Run; RMC Place; BURLINGTON; ▲ Cinnaminson; *205 L-7; ★ PHIL-; mail Riverton z 08077
Philips Mills; RMC Place; MONMOUTH; ▲ Holmdel; *204 H-12; elev. 25ft./8m.; ★ N.Y.; mail Keansburg z 07734; ● 150
Phillipsburg; Inc. Place; WARREN; 204 F-6; elev. 314ft./96m.; 🄿 🄷; ★ ALL-; z 08865; Ⓟ 15,757; Ⓒ 15,166
Phoenix; RMC Place; MIDDLESEX; ▲ Edison; *204 H-11; ★ N.Y.; mail Sayreville z 08871
Pierces Point; RMC Place; CAPE MAY; ▲ Middle; 205 R-2; mail Cape May Court House z 08210; ● 40
Pilesgrove (Pilesgrove Township); MCD-Township; SALEM; *205 N-5; 🄿; z 08098; Ⓟ 3,250; Ⓒ 3,923
Pilesgrove Township; SALEM; see Pilesgrove (MCD-Township)
Pine Beach; Inc. Place; OCEAN; 205 L-12; elev. 17ft./5m.; 🄿; ★ N.Y.; z 08741; Ⓟ 1,954; Ⓒ 1,950
Pine Brook; RMC Place; MONMOUTH; *204 J-13; ★ N.Y.; mail Eatontown z 07724; pop. incl. with Tinton Falls (Inc. Place)
Pine Brook; RMC Place; MORRIS; ▲ Montville; *204 E-11; elev. 183ft./56m.; 🄿; ★ N.Y.; z 07058; ● 700
Pine Brook; RMC Place; SOMERSET; ▲ Montgomery; *204 H-9; elev. 100ft./30m.; ★ N.Y.; mail Hillsborough z 08844; ● 250
Pine Cliff Lake; RMC Place; PASSAIC; ▲ West Milford; *204 C-11; ★ N.Y.; mail West Milford z 07480; ● 300
Pine Grove; RMC Place; BURLINGTON; ▲ Medford; *205 M-8; ★ PHIL-; mail Marlton z 08053, Medford z 08055; ● 250
Pine Hill; Inc. Place; CAMDEN; 205 M-7; elev. 170ft./52m.; 🄿; ★ PHIL-; z 08021; Ⓟ 9,854; Ⓒ 10,880
Pinehurst; RMC Place; ATLANTIC; ▲ Galloway; *205 P-10; ★ ATCY; mail Absecon z 08201, z 08205; ● 1,600
Pine Lake Park; RMC Place; OCEAN; ▲ Manchester; 205 L-12; ★ N.Y.; mail Toms River z 08753; ● 3,000
Pine Ridge at Crestwood; CDP-Census Area Only; OCEAN; ▲ Manchester; *205 L-11; elev. 87ft./27m.; ★ N.Y.; mail Manchester Township z 08759; Ⓟ 2,372; Ⓒ 2,025
Pines Lake; RMC Place; PASSAIC; ▲ Wayne; *204 D-11; ★ N.Y.; mail Wayne z 07470
Pine Terrace; RMC Place; OCEAN; ▲ Toms River; *205 L-12; ★ N.Y.; mail Toms River z 08753; ● 600
Pine Valley; Inc. Place; CAMDEN; *205 M-7; elev. 164ft./50m.; 🄿; ★ PHIL-; z 08021; Ⓟ 19; Ⓒ 20
Pinewald; RMC Place; OCEAN; ▲ Berkeley; 205 M-12; ★ N.Y.; mail Bayville z 08721; ● 1,700
Pinkneyville; RMC Place; SUSSEX; *204 C-9; ★ N.Y.; mail Sparta z 07871; rural
Piscataway (New Market); RMC Place; MIDDLESEX; ▲ Piscataway; 204 G-10; 🄿 🄷 🄲 1,070; ★ N.Y.; z 08854-55; ● 50,500
Piscataway; MCD-Township; MIDDLESEX; *204 G-10; 🄿 🄲 1,070; ★ N.Y.; z 08854-55; Ⓒ 50,482; Ⓡ 50,558; ◆ 53,969
Pitman; Inc. Place; GLOUCESTER; 205 N-6; elev. 132ft./40m.; 🄿; ★ PHIL-; z 08071; Ⓟ 9,365; Ⓒ 9,331
Pittsgrove; MCD-Township; SALEM; *205 O-6; 🄿; ★ VINL; z 08318 & mail Norma z 08347; Ⓟ 8,121; Ⓒ 8,893
Pittstown; RMC Place; HUNTERDON; ▲ Franklin, Alexandria; 204 G-7; 🄿; ★ N.Y.; z 08867; ● 600
Plainfield; Inc. Place; UNION; 204 G-11; elev. 118ft./36m.; 🄿 🄷 ■; ★ N.Y.; z 07060-63, z 07069; Ⓟ 46,567; Ⓒ 47,829; ◆ 46,220
Plainsboro; RMC Place; MIDDLESEX; ▲ Plainsboro; 204 I-9; elev. 80ft./24m.; 🄿; ★ N.Y.; z 08536; ● 2,000
Plainsboro; MCD-Township; MIDDLESEX; *204 I-10; 🄿; ★ N.Y.; z 08536; Ⓟ 14,213; Ⓒ 20,215; ◆ 21,969
Plainsboro Center; CDP-Census Area Only; MIDDLESEX; *204 I-9; ★ N.Y.; Ⓒ 2,209
Plainville; RMC Place; GLOUCESTER; ▲ Franklin; *205 O-7; ★ PHIL-; mail Franklinville z 08322; rural
Plainville; RMC Place; SOMERSET; ▲ Montgomery; *204 H-9; ★ N.Y.; mail Belle Mead z 08502; ● 80
Plaza Park; RMC Place; BURLINGTON; ▲ Burlington; *205 K-8; ★ PHIL-; mail Burlington z 08016; ● 180
Pleasant Gardens; RMC Place; OCEAN; ▲ Jackson; *205 K-11; elev. 100ft./30m.; ★ N.Y.; mail Jackson z 08527; ● 200
Pleasant Grove; RMC Place; MORRIS; ▲ Washington; 204 F-8; ★ N.Y.; mail Long Valley z 07853
Pleasant Grove; RMC Place; OCEAN; ▲ Jackson; *205 K-11; ★ N.Y.; mail Jackson z 08527; rural
Pleasant Hill; RMC Place; MORRIS; ▲ Chester; *204 E-9; ★ N.Y.; mail Succasunna z 07876
Pleasant Mills; RMC Place; ATLANTIC; ▲ Mullica; 205 O-9; ★ ATCY; mail Hammonton z 08037
Pleasant Plains; RMC Place; OCEAN; ▲ Toms River; 205 L-12; ★ N.Y.; mail Toms River z 08755; Ⓟ 2,577
Pleasant Run; RMC Place; HUNTERDON; ▲ Readington; 204 G-8; ★ N.Y.; mail Flemington z 08822, Neshanic Station z 08853
Pleasant Valley; RMC Place; MORRIS; ▲ Mendham; *204 F-9; ★ N.Y.; mail Mendham z 07945; rural
Pleasant Valley; RMC Place; WARREN; ▲ Washington; 204 F-7; ★ N.Y.; mail Washington z 07882; ● 200
Pleasant View; RMC Place; SOMERSET; ▲ Hillsborough; *204 H-9; elev. 104ft./32m.; ★ N.Y.; mail Hillsborough z 08844; ● 200
Pleasantville; Inc. Place; ATLANTIC; 204 H-1; elev. 22ft./7m.; 🄿 ■; ★ ATCY; z 08232 & mail Egg Harbor Township z 08234; Ⓟ 16,027; Ⓒ 19,012; ◆ 20,324
Pluckemin; RMC Place; SOMERSET; ▲ Bedminster; 204 G-9; 🄿; ★ N.Y.; z 07978; ● 300
Plumbsock; RMC Place; SUSSEX; ▲ Wantage; 204 B-9; ★ N.Y.; mail Sussex z 07461
Plumsted; MCD-Township; OCEAN; *205 K-10; ★ N.Y.; mail New Egypt z 08533; Ⓟ 6,005; Ⓒ 7,275
Pohatcong; MCD-Township; WARREN; *204 G-6; ★ ALL-; mail Bloomsbury z 08804; Ⓟ 3,591; Ⓒ 3,416
Pointers; RMC Place; SALEM; ▲ Mannington; 205 O-4; mail Salem z 08079; ● 200
Point Pleasant; Inc. Place; OCEAN; 205 K-13; elev. 18ft./5m.; ★ N.Y.; mail Point Pleasant Beach z 08742; Ⓟ 18,177; Ⓒ 19,306; ◆ 19,317
Point Pleasant; RMC Place; SUSSEX; *204 D-9; ★ N.Y.; mail Hopatcong z 07843; pop. incl. with Hopatcong (Inc. Place)
Point Pleasant Beach; Inc. Place; OCEAN; 205 K-13; elev. 14ft./4m.; 🄿; ★ N.Y.; z 08742; Ⓟ 5,112; Ⓒ 5,314
Pole Tavern; RMC Place; SALEM; *205 O-6; mail Elmer z 08318
Polkville; RMC Place; WARREN; ▲ Knowlton; 204 D-7; ★ N.Y.; mail Columbia z 07832
Pomona; CDP; ATLANTIC; ▲ Galloway; 205 P-10; 🄿 🄷 🄲 6,727; ★ ATCY; z 08240; Ⓟ 2,624; Ⓒ 4,019
Pompton Junction; RMC Place; PASSAIC; *204 D-11; ★ N.Y.; mail Pompton Lakes z 07442, Riverdale z 07457; pop. incl. with Pompton Lakes (Inc. Place)
Pompton Lakes; Inc. Place; PASSAIC; 204 D-11; elev. 211ft./64m.; 🄿; ★ N.Y.; z 07442; Ⓟ 10,539; Ⓒ 10,640
Pompton Plains; RMC Place; MORRIS; ▲ Pequannock; 204 D-11; 🄿 🄷; ★ N.Y.; z 07444
Pompton Riverdale; MORRIS; see Riverdale (Inc. Place)
Porchtown; RMC Place; GLOUCESTER; ▲ Franklin; *205 O-6; ★ PHIL-; mail Newfield z 08344
Port-au-Peck; RMC Place; MONMOUTH; *204 I-13; ★ N.Y.; mail Oceanport z 07757; pop. incl. with Oceanport (Inc. Place)
Port Bridgeton; RMC Place; CUMBERLAND; ★ VINL; pop. incl. with Bridgeton (Inc. Place)
Port Colden; RMC Place; WARREN; ▲ Washington; 204 F-7; ★ N.Y.; mail Washington z 07882; ● 180
Port Elizabeth; RMC Place; CUMBERLAND; ▲ Maurice River; 205 Q-7; elev. 15ft./5m.; 🄿; z 08348; ● 650
Portertown; RMC Place; SALEM; ▲ Mannington; *205 O-5; mail Woodstown z 08098
Port Johnson; RMC Place; HUDSON; *204 G-12; ★ N.Y.; mail Bayonne z 07002; pop. incl. with Bayonne (Inc. Place)
Port Monmouth; CDP; MONMOUTH; ▲ Middletown; 204 H-12; 🄿; ★ N.Y.; z 07758; Ⓟ 3,558; Ⓒ 3,742
Port Morris; RMC Place; MORRIS; ▲ Roxbury; *204 E-9; ★ N.Y.; mail Landing z 07850; ● 700
Port Murray; RMC Place; WARREN; ▲ Mansfield; 204 E-8; elev. 594ft./181m.; 🄿; ★ N.Y.; z 07865; ● 450
Port Newark; RMC Place; ESSEX; *204 F-12; ★ N.Y.; mail Newark z 07114; pop. incl. with Newark (Inc. Place)
Port Norris; CDP; CUMBERLAND; ▲ Commercial; 205 R-7; 🄿; ★ VINL; z 08349; Ⓟ 1,701; Ⓒ 1,507
Port Reading; CDP; MIDDLESEX; ▲ Woodbridge; 204 G-12; 🄿; ★ N.Y.; z 07064; Ⓟ 3,977; Ⓒ 3,829
Port Republic; Inc. Place; ATLANTIC; 205 O-10; elev. 17ft./5m.; 🄿; ★ ATCY; z 08241; Ⓟ 992; Ⓒ 1,037
Port Warren; RMC Place; WARREN; ▲ Greenwich; *204 F-6; ★ ALL-; mail Stewartsville z 08886; rural
Possumtown; RMC Place; MIDDLESEX; ▲ Piscataway; *204 G-10; ★ N.Y.; mail Piscataway z 08854
Potters; RMC Place; MIDDLESEX; ▲ Edison; *204 G-11; ★ N.Y.; mail Edison z 08817
Potterstown; RMC Place; HUNTERDON; ▲ Readington, Clinton; 204 G-8; ★ N.Y.; mail Lebanon z 08833; ● 100
Pottersville; RMC Place; SOMERSET, HUNTERDON; ▲ Tewksbury, Bedminster; 204 F-9; 🄿; ★ N.Y.; z 07979; ● 600
Powerville; RMC Place; MORRIS; ▲ Boonton; *204 D-10; ★ N.Y.; mail Boonton z 07005; rural
Prallsville; RMC Place; HUNTERDON; *204 I-7; elev. 100ft./30m.; mail Stockton z 08559
Preakness; RMC Place; PASSAIC; ▲ Wayne; *204 D-12; ★ N.Y.; mail Wayne z 07470
Presidential Lakes; BURLINGTON; see Presidential Lakes Estates (CDP-Census Area Only)
Presidential Lakes Estates (Presidential Lakes); CDP-Census Area Only; BURLINGTON; ▲ Pemberton; *205 L-10; mail Browns Mills z 08015; Ⓟ 2,450; Ⓒ 2,332
Prices Switch; RMC Place; SUSSEX; ▲ Vernon; *204 B-10; ★ N.Y.; mail Vernon z 07462; ● 40
Princeton; Inc. Place; MERCER; 205 T-11; elev. 215ft./66m.; 🄿 🄷 🄲 7,990 ■; z 08540-44; Ⓟ 12,016; Ⓒ 14,203; Ⓡ 13,568; ◆ 13,907
Princeton; MCD-Township; MERCER; *204 I-9; 🄿 🄲 7,990; z 08540-44; does not include the City of Princeton; Ⓟ 13,198; Ⓒ 16,027; Ⓡ 16,662
Princeton Ivy East; RMC Place; MERCER; ▲ West Windsor; *204 I-9; ★ N.Y.; mail Hightstown z 08520; ● 300
Princeton Junction; CDP; MERCER; ▲ West Windsor; 205 T-11; 🄿; ★ N.Y.; z 08550 & mail Princeton z 08540; Ⓟ 2,362; Ⓒ 2,382
Princeton Meadows; CDP-Census Area Only; MIDDLESEX; *204 I-10; ★ N.Y.; Ⓒ 13,436
Princeton North; CDP-Census Area Only; MERCER; ▲ Princeton; *204 I-9; mail Princeton z 08540; Ⓟ 4,386; Ⓒ 4,528
Prospect Heights; RMC Place; MERCER; ▲ Ewing; *204 J-8; ★ PHIL-; mail Trenton z 08638
Prospect Park; Inc. Place; PASSAIC; 210 B-6; elev. 232ft./71m.; 🄿; ★ N.Y.; z 07508 & mail Haledon z 07538; Ⓟ 5,053; Ⓒ 5,779
Prospect Plains; RMC Place; MIDDLESEX; ▲ Monroe; *204 I-10; ★ N.Y.; mail Cranbury z 08512; ● 40
Prospect Point; RMC Place; MORRIS; ▲ Jefferson; *204 D-9; ★ N.Y.; mail Lake Hopatcong z 07849; ● 1,400
Prospertown; RMC Place; MONMOUTH, OCEAN; ▲ Plumsted, Upper Freehold; *205 K-10; ★ PHIL-; mail Cream Ridge z 08514; ● 40
Pullentown; RMC Place; MONMOUTH; ▲ Upper Freehold; *204 J-10; ★ PHIL-; mail Allentown z 08501
Pumptown; RMC Place; MIDDLESEX; *204 G-11; mail Edison z 08820; ● 2,000

Q

Quaker Gardens; RMC Place; MERCER; ▲ Hamilton; *204 J-9; ★ PHIL-; mail Trenton z 08619; ● 1,500
Quakertown; RMC Place; HUNTERDON; ▲ Franklin; 204 G-7; 🄿; ★ N.Y.; z 08868; ● 200
Quarryville; RMC Place; SUSSEX; ▲ Wantage; 204 B-10; elev. 558ft./170m.; ★ N.Y.; mail Sussex z 07461; rural
Quinton; RMC Place; SALEM; ▲ Quinton; 205 O-4; elev. 17ft./5m.; 🄿; z 08072; ● 500
Quinton; MCD-Township; SALEM; *205 O-5; 🄿; ★ PHIL-; z 08072; Ⓟ 2,511; Ⓒ 2,786

R

Racoon Island; RMC Place; MORRIS; ▲ Jefferson; *204 D-9; ★ N.Y.; mail Lake Hopatcong z 07849; ● 300
Radburn; RMC Place; BERGEN; *204 D-12; ★ N.Y.; mail Fair Lawn z 07410; pop. incl. with Fair Lawn (Inc. Place)
Rahway; Inc. Place; UNION; 204 G-11; elev. 25ft./8m.; 🄿 🄷; ★ N.Y.; z 07065; Ⓟ 25,325; Ⓒ 26,500; ◆ 26,944
Rainbow Lakes; RMC Place; MORRIS; ▲ Parsippany-Troy Hills; *204 E-10; ★ N.Y.; mail Denville z 07834
Raines Corner; RMC Place; SALEM; ▲ Carneys Point; *205 N-4; elev. 24ft./7m.; ★ PHIL-; mail Penns Grove z 08069; ● 40
Ralston; RMC Place; MORRIS; ▲ Mendham; 204 F-9; ★ N.Y.; mail Mendham z 07945; ● 150
Ramblewood; CDP; BURLINGTON; ▲ Mount Laurel; 205 L-7; ★ PHIL-; mail Mount Laurel z 08054; Ⓟ 6,181; Ⓒ 6,003
Ramsey; Inc. Place; BERGEN; 204 C-12; elev. 373ft./114m.; 🄿; ★ N.Y.; z 07446; Ⓟ 13,228; Ⓒ 14,351
Ramseysburg; RMC Place; WARREN; ▲ Knowlton; *204 E-7; elev. 289ft./88m.; ★ N.Y.; mail Columbia z 07832; rural
Ramtown; CDP; MONMOUTH; ▲ Howell; *205 K-12; ★ N.Y.; mail Howell z 07731; Ⓒ 5,932
Rancocas; RMC Place; BURLINGTON; ▲ Westampton; 205 L-8; 🄿; ★ PHIL-; z 08073; ● 500
Rancocas Heights; RMC Place; BURLINGTON; ▲ Hainesport; 228 D-10; ★ PHIL-; mail Mount Holly z 08060; ● 750
Rancocas Woods; RMC Place; BURLINGTON; ▲ Mount Laurel; 228 D-10; ★ PHIL-; mail Mount Laurel z 08054; ● 1,400
Randolph; MCD-Township; MORRIS; *204 E-10; 🄿; ★ N.Y.; z 07869; Ⓟ 19,974; Ⓒ 24,847; ◆ 25,208
Randolphville; RMC Place; MIDDLESEX; *204 H-10; mail Piscataway z 08854; ● 1,100
Rankokus Reservation; Indian Reservation; BURLINGTON; State Reservation; Ⓒ 0
Raritan; MCD-Township; HUNTERDON; *204 H-8; ★ N.Y.; mail Flemington z 08822; Ⓟ 15,616; Ⓒ 19,809; ◆ 22,589
Raritan; Inc. Place; SOMERSET; 204 G-9; elev. 76ft./23m.; 🄿; ★ N.Y.; z 08869; Ⓟ 5,798; Ⓒ 6,338
Raritan Gardens; RMC Place; MIDDLESEX; *204 H-11; ★ N.Y.; mail North Brunswick z 08902; pop. incl. with New Brunswick (Inc. Place)
Raritan Manor; RMC Place; MIDDLESEX; *204 H-11; mail Edison z 08837; ● 1,000
Raven Rock; RMC Place; HUNTERDON; ▲ Delaware; 204 H-7; mail Stockton z 08559
Readington; RMC Place; HUNTERDON; ▲ Readington; 204 G-9; 🄿; ★ N.Y.; z 08870; ● 500
Readington; MCD-Township; HUNTERDON; *204 G-8; 🄿; ★ N.Y.; z 08870 & mail Whitehouse Station z 08889; Ⓟ 13,400; Ⓒ 15,803
Reaville; RMC Place; HUNTERDON; ▲ Raritan, East Amwell; 204 H-8; ★ N.Y.; mail Flemington z 08822, Ringoes z 08551; ● 250
Red Bank; RMC Place; GLOUCESTER; ▲ West Deptford; 228 G-4; ★ PHIL-; mail National Park z 08063; ● 1,100
Red Bank; Inc. Place; MONMOUTH; 204 I-13; elev. 53ft./16m.; 🄿 ■; ★ N.Y.; z 07701-04, z 07709; Ⓟ 10,636; Ⓒ 11,844; ◆ 12,621
Red Lion; RMC Place; BURLINGTON; ▲ Southampton; 205 M-9; ★ PHIL-; mail Vincentown z 08088
Red Lion; RMC Place; MIDDLESEX; ▲ North Brunswick; *204 H-10; ★ N.Y.; mail North Brunswick z 08902
Redshaw Corner; RMC Place; MIDDLESEX; ▲ Old Bridge; *204 I-11; ★ N.Y.; mail Old Bridge z 08857; rural
Reeds Beach; RMC Place; CAPE MAY; ▲ Middle; 205 R-2; mail Cape May Court House z 08210; ● 70
Reevytown; RMC Place; MONMOUTH; *204 J-12; ★ N.Y.; mail Neptune z 07753; pop. incl. with Tinton Falls (Inc. Place)
Repaupo; RMC Place; GLOUCESTER; ▲ Logan; 205 M-5; ★ PHIL-; mail Paulsboro z 08066; ● 100
Repaupo Station; RMC Place; GLOUCESTER; ▲ Logan; *205 M-5; ★ PHIL-; mail Swedesboro z 08085; rural
Retreat; RMC Place; BURLINGTON; ▲ Southampton; *205 L-9; ★ PHIL-; mail Vincentown z 08088
Rhode Hall; RMC Place; MIDDLESEX; ▲ South Brunswick; *204 I-10; ★ N.Y.; mail Helmetta z 08828; rural
Richard Mine; RMC Place; MORRIS; ▲ Rockaway; *204 D-10; ★ N.Y.; mail Wharton z 07885; ● 300
Richfield; RMC Place; PASSAIC; *204 E-12; ★ N.Y.; mail Clifton z 07013; pop. incl. with Clifton (Inc. Place)
Richland; RMC Place; ATLANTIC; ▲ Buena Vista; 205 P-8; 🄿; ★ VINL; z 08350; ● 600
Richwood; RMC Place; GLOUCESTER; ▲ Harrison; 205 N-6; elev. 152ft./46m.; 🄿; ★ PHIL-; z 08074; ● 500
Ridgefield; Inc. Place; BERGEN; 204 E-13; elev. 150ft./46m.; 🄿; ★ N.Y.; z 07657; Ⓟ 9,996; Ⓒ 10,830
Ridgefield Park; Inc. Place; BERGEN; 204 B-5; elev. 96ft./29m.; 🄿; ★ N.Y.; z 07660; Ⓟ 12,454; Ⓒ 12,873
Ridgeway; RMC Place; OCEAN; ▲ Manchester; 205 K-11; ★ N.Y.; mail Lakehurst z 08733
Ridgewood; Inc. Place; BERGEN; 204 D-12; elev. 144ft./44m.; 🄿 🄷 ■; ★ N.Y.; z 07450-51 & mail Glen Rock z 07452; Ⓟ 24,152; Ⓒ 24,936; ◆ 24,167
Riegel Ridge; RMC Place; HUNTERDON; ▲ Holland; 204 G-6; elev. 600ft./183m.; mail Milford z 08848; ● 250
Riegelsville; RMC Place; WARREN; ▲ Pohatcong; 204 G-6; ★ ALL-; mail Milford z 08848; ● 150
Ringoes; RMC Place; HUNTERDON; ▲ West Amwell, East Amwell; 204 H-8; elev. 226ft./69m.; 🄿; ★ PHIL-; z 08551; ● 600
Ringwood; Inc. Place; PASSAIC; 204 C-11; elev. 508ft./155m.; 🄿; ★ N.Y.; z 07456; Ⓟ 12,623; Ⓒ 12,396
Rio Grande; CDP; CAPE MAY; ▲ Middle; 205 S-2; elev. 22ft./7m.; 🄿; z 08242; Ⓟ 2,505; Ⓒ 2,444
Ritz; RMC Place; BERGEN; *204 E-12; ★ N.Y.; mail Garfield z 07026; pop. incl. with Garfield (Inc. Place)
River Bank; RMC Place; OCEAN; ▲ Berkeley; *205 L-12; ★ N.Y.; mail Pine Beach z 08741; ● 350
Riverdale (Pompton Riverdale); Inc. Place; MORRIS; 204 D-11; elev. 232ft./71m.; 🄿; ★ N.Y.; z 07457; Ⓟ 2,370; Ⓒ 2,498
River Edge; Inc. Place; BERGEN; 204 D-13; elev. 35ft./11m.; 🄿; ★ N.Y.; z 07661; Ⓟ 10,603; Ⓒ 10,946
River Plaza; RMC Place; MONMOUTH; ▲ Middletown; 204 I-13; ★ N.Y.; mail Red Bank z 07701; ● 1,900
River Road; RMC Place; BERGEN; *204 D-12; ★ N.Y.; mail Fair Lawn z 07410; pop. incl. with Fair Lawn (Inc. Place)
Riverside; RMC Place; BURLINGTON; ▲ Riverside; 205 K-7; 🄿; ★ PHIL-; z 08075; Ⓟ 7,974
Riverside; MCD-Township; BURLINGTON; *205 K-7; 🄿; ★ PHIL-; z 08075; Ⓟ 7,974; Ⓒ 7,911
Riverside Park; RMC Place; BURLINGTON; ▲ Delran; *205 K-7; ★ PHIL-; mail Riverside z 08075
River Street; RMC Place; PASSAIC; *204 D-12; ★ N.Y.; mail Paterson z 07524, z 07544; pop. incl. with Paterson (Inc. Place)
Riverton; Inc. Place; BURLINGTON; 205 L-7; elev. 60ft./18m.; 🄿; ★ PHIL-; z 08076-77; Ⓟ 2,775; Ⓒ 2,759
River Vale; CDP; BERGEN; ▲ River Vale; 204 D-13; 🄿; ★ N.Y.; z 07675; Ⓟ 9,410; Ⓒ 9,449
River Vale; MCD-Township; BERGEN; *204 D-13; 🄿; ★ N.Y.; z 07675; Ⓟ 9,410; Ⓒ 9,449
Riverview Manor; RMC Place; MIDDLESEX; mail Piscataway z 08854; ● 660
Riverwood; RMC Place; OCEAN; ▲ Toms River; *205 K-12; elev. 100ft./30m.; ★ N.Y.; mail Toms River z 08755; ● 400
Riviera Beach; RMC Place; OCEAN; ▲ Brick; *205 K-12; ★ N.Y.; mail Brick z 08723
Roadstown; RMC Place; CUMBERLAND; ▲ Stow Creek, Hopewell; 205 P-5; mail Bridgeton z 08302; ● 200
Robbinsville; RMC Place; MERCER; ▲ Robbinsville; 204 J-9; 🄿; ★ PHIL-; z 08691; ● 600
Robbinsville (Washington); MCD-Township; MERCER; *204 J-9; ★ PHIL-; mail Trenton z 08691; Ⓟ 5,815; Ⓒ 10,275
Robertsville; RMC Place; MONMOUTH; ▲ Marlboro; 204 I-11; ★ N.Y.; mail Morganville z 07751; ● 2,500
Robins Estates; RMC Place; OCEAN; ▲ Jackson; *205 K-11; ★ N.Y.; mail Jackson z 08527; ● 950
Rochelle Park; CDP; BERGEN; ▲ Rochelle Park; 204 A-4; 🄿; ★ N.Y.; z 07662 & mail Saddle Brook z 07663; Ⓟ 5,587; Ⓒ 5,528
Rochelle Park; MCD-Township; BERGEN; *204 E-13; 🄿; ★ N.Y.; z 07662; Ⓟ 5,587; Ⓒ 5,528
Rockaway; Inc. Place; MORRIS; 204 E-10; elev. 534ft./163m.; 🄿; ★ N.Y.; z 07866; Ⓟ 6,243; Ⓒ 6,473
Rockaway; MCD-Township; MORRIS; *204 D-10; 🄿; ★ N.Y.; z 07866; does not include the Borough of Rockaway; Ⓟ 19,572; Ⓒ 22,930; ◆ 24,024
Rockaway Neck; RMC Place; MORRIS; ▲ Parsippany-Troy Hills; *204 E-11; ★ N.Y.; mail Parsippany z 07054
Rockaway Valley; RMC Place; MORRIS; ▲ Boonton; *204 D-10; ★ N.Y.; mail Boonton z 07005
Rockleigh; Inc. Place; BERGEN; *204 D-13; elev. 50ft./15m.; 🄿; ★ N.Y.; z 07647; Ⓟ 270; Ⓒ 391
Rockport; RMC Place; WARREN; ▲ Mansfield; *204 E-8; ★ N.Y.; mail Hackettstown z 07840; ● 60
Rock Ridge Lake; RMC Place; MORRIS; ▲ Denville; *204 E-10; ★ N.Y.; mail Denville z 07834
Rocktown; RMC Place; HUNTERDON; ▲ West Amwell, East Amwell; *204 I-8; ★ PHIL-; mail Ringoes z 08551; ● 30
Rocky Hill; Inc. Place; SOMERSET; 204 I-9; elev. 120ft./37m.; 🄿; z 08553; Ⓟ 693; Ⓒ 662
Roebling; RMC Place; BURLINGTON; ▲ Florence; 205 K-8; 🄿; ★ PHIL-; z 08554; ● 3,000
Roosevelt; Inc. Place; MONMOUTH; 204 J-10; elev. 152ft./46m.; 🄿; ★ PHIL-; z 08555; Ⓟ 884; Ⓒ 933
Roosevelt City; RMC Place; OCEAN; ▲ Manchester; 205 L-11; ★ N.Y.; mail Manchester Township z 08759; ● 35
Roosevelt Park; RMC Place; CUMBERLAND; *205 Q-7; ★ VINL; mail Millville z 08332; pop. incl. with Millville (Inc. Place)
Rosedale; RMC Place; ATLANTIC; *205 O-8; ★ ATCY; mail Hammonton z 08037; pop. incl. with Hammonton (Inc. Place)
Rosedale; RMC Place; MERCER; ▲ Lawrence; *204 I-9; ★ PHIL-; mail Princeton z 08540; rural
Rose Hill Heights; RMC Place; WARREN; ▲ Lopatcong; *204 F-6; ★ ALL-; mail Phillipsburg z 08865; ● 800
Roseland; Inc. Place; ESSEX; *204 E-11; elev. 356ft./109m.; 🄿; ★ N.Y.; z 07068; Ⓟ 4,847; Ⓒ 5,298
Roselle; Inc. Place; UNION; 204 G-11; elev. 51ft./16m.; 🄿; ★ N.Y.; z 07203; Ⓟ 20,314; Ⓒ 21,274; ◆ 20,986
Roselle Park; Inc. Place; UNION; 210 J-4; elev. 85ft./26m.; 🄿; ★ N.Y.; z 07204; Ⓟ 12,805; Ⓒ 13,281
Rosemont; RMC Place; HUNTERDON; ▲ Delaware; 204 H-7; 🄿; z 08556; ● 185
Rosemont; RMC Place; MERCER; ▲ Hamilton; *204 J-9; ★ PHIL-; mail Trenton z 08619
Rosenhayn; CDP; CUMBERLAND; ▲ Deerfield; 205 L-2; elev. 109ft./33m.; 🄿; ★ VINL; z 08352; Ⓟ 1,053; Ⓒ 1,099
Roseville; RMC Place; ESSEX; *204 F-12; ★ N.Y.; mail Newark z 07107; pop. incl. with Newark (Inc. Place)
Roseville; RMC Place; SUSSEX; mail Stanhope z 07874; ● 355
Ross Corner; RMC Place; SUSSEX; ▲ Frankford; 204 C-9; elev. 515ft./157m.; ★ N.Y.; mail Augusta z 07822; ● 50
Rossmoor; CDP-Census Area Only; MIDDLESEX; ▲ Monroe; *204 I-10; ★ N.Y.; mail Monroe Township z 08831; Ⓟ 3,231; Ⓒ 3,129
Round Top; RMC Place; SOMERSET; ▲ Warren; *204 G-10; ★ N.Y.; mail Warren z 07059; rural
Roxburg; RMC Place; WARREN; ▲ Harmony; 204 E-7; ★ ALL-; mail Phillipsburg z 08865; ● 120
Roxbury; RMC Place; MORRIS; ▲ Roxbury; *204 E-9; ★ N.Y.
Roxbury; MCD-Township; MORRIS; *204 E-9; ★ N.Y.; mail Flanders z 07836, Succasunna z 07876; Ⓟ 20,429; Ⓒ 23,883; Ⓡ 23,227; ◆ 23,140
Royce Valley; RMC Place; SOMERSET; mail Somerville z 08876; ● 250
Rudeville; RMC Place; SUSSEX; ▲ Hardyston; 204 C-10; ★ N.Y.; mail Hamburg z 07419
Rumson; Inc. Place; MONMOUTH; 204 I-13; elev. 15ft./5m.; 🄿; ★ N.Y.; z 07760; Ⓟ 6,701; Ⓒ 7,137
Runnemede; Inc. Place; CAMDEN; 205 M-7; elev. 132ft./40m.; 🄿; ★ PHIL-; z 08078; Ⓟ 9,042; Ⓒ 8,533
Runyon; RMC Place; MIDDLESEX; ▲ Old Bridge; *204 H-11; ★ N.Y.; mail Old Bridge z 08857; pop. incl. with Sayreville (Inc. Place)
Russia (New Russia); RMC Place; MORRIS; ▲ Jefferson; *204 D-10; ★ N.Y.; mail Oak Ridge z 07438; ● 100
Rutgers; RMC Place; MIDDLESEX; *204 H-11; elev. 50ft./15m.; ★ N.Y.; mail New Brunswick z 08901; pop. incl. with New Brunswick (Inc. Place)
Rutherford; Inc. Place; BERGEN; 204 E-12; elev. 98ft./30m.; 🄿; ★ N.Y.; z 07070; Ⓟ 17,790; Ⓒ 18,110

S

Saddle Brook; CDP; BERGEN; ▲ Saddle Brook; 204 A-4; 🄿; ★ N.Y.; z 07663; Ⓟ 13,296; Ⓒ 13,155
Saddle Brook; MCD-Township; BERGEN; *204 E-12; 🄿; ★ N.Y.; z 07663; Ⓟ 13,296; Ⓒ 13,155
Saddle River; Inc. Place; BERGEN; *204 D-12; elev. 175ft./53m.; 🄿; ★ N.Y.; z 07458; Ⓟ 2,950; Ⓒ 3,201
Saint Cloud; RMC Place; ESSEX; ▲ West Orange; *204 F-11; ★ N.Y.; mail West Orange z 07052
Saint Vladimirs; RMC Place; OCEAN; mail Jackson z 08527; ● 500
Salem; Inc. Place; ⊡ SALEM; 205 O-4; elev. 19ft./6m.; 🄿 🄷; ★ PHIL-; z 08079; Ⓟ 6,883; Ⓒ 5,857
SALEM; 205 O-5; Ⓟ 65,294; Ⓒ 64,285; ◆ 64,865
Salem Hill; RMC Place; MONMOUTH; ▲ Howell; *204 J-12; ★ N.Y.; mail Lakewood z 08701
Salina; RMC Place; GLOUCESTER; ▲ Mantua; *205 N-6; elev. 60ft./18m.; ★ PHIL-; mail Sewell z 08080
Sand Brook; RMC Place; HUNTERDON; ▲ Delaware; 204 H-8; mail Stockton z 08559
Sand Hills; RMC Place; MIDDLESEX; ▲ South Brunswick; *204 I-10; elev. 260ft./79m.; ★ N.Y.; mail Monmouth Junction z 08852; rural
Sands Point; RMC Place; MONMOUTH; *204 I-13; ★ N.Y.; mail Oceanport z 07757; pop. incl. with Oceanport (Inc. Place)
Sandyston; MCD-Township; SUSSEX; *204 B-8; 🄿; z 07826-27, z 07851; Ⓟ 1,732; Ⓒ 1,825
Sarepta; RMC Place; WARREN; ▲ White; *204 E-7; ★ N.Y.; mail Belvidere z 07823; ● 35
Saxton Falls; RMC Place; WARREN; ▲ Allamuchy; 204 E-8; ★ N.Y.; mail Stanhope z 07874; ● 100
Sayerwood South; RMC Place; MIDDLESEX; ▲ Old Bridge; 204 I-11; ★ N.Y.; mail Old Bridge z 08857; ● 10,000
Sayres Neck; RMC Place; CUMBERLAND; ▲ Lawrence; *205 Q-6; mail Cedarville z 08311; rural
Sayreville; Inc. Place; MIDDLESEX; 204 H-11; elev. 41ft./12m.; 🄿; ★ N.Y.; z 08871-72; Ⓟ 34,986; Ⓒ 40,377; ◆ 43,009
Sayre Woods; RMC Place; MIDDLESEX; *204 H-11; ★ N.Y.; mail Parlin z 08859; pop. incl. with Sayreville (Inc. Place)
Schooleys Mountain; RMC Place; MORRIS; ▲ Washington; 204 E-8; 🄿; ★ N.Y.; z 07870; ● 200
Scobeyville; RMC Place; MONMOUTH; ▲ Colts Neck; 204 I-12; ★ N.Y.; mail Colts Neck z 07722; ● 15
Scotch Bonnet; RMC Place; CAPE MAY; mail Cape May Court House z 08210; ● 35
Scotch Plains; CDP; UNION; ▲ Scotch Plains; 204 F-11; 🄿; ★ N.Y.; z 07076; Ⓟ 21,160; Ⓒ 22,732; ◆ 22,190
Scotch Plains; MCD-Township; UNION; *204 G-11; 🄿; ★ N.Y.; z 07076; Ⓟ 21,160; Ⓒ 22,732; ◆ 22,190
Scotts Corner; RMC Place; MIDDLESEX; ▲ Plainsboro; *204 I-10; ★ N.Y.; mail Plainsboro z 08536; ● 900
Scudders Falls; RMC Place; MERCER; ▲ Ewing; *204 J-8; ★ PHIL-; mail Trenton z 08628
Scullville; RMC Place; ATLANTIC; ▲ Egg Harbor; 205 Q-9; ★ ATCY; mail Egg Harbor Township z 08234, Mays Landing z 08330; ● 40
Seaboard; RMC Place; HUDSON; ★ N.Y.; mail Kearny z 07032; pop. incl. with Kearny (Inc. Place)
Sea Breeze; RMC Place; CUMBERLAND; ▲ Fairfield; 205 Q-5; ★ VINL; mail Bridgeton z 08302; ● 50
Sea Bright; Inc. Place; MONMOUTH; 204 I-13; elev. 4ft./1m.; 🄿; ★ N.Y.; z 07760; Ⓟ 1,693; Ⓒ 1,818
Seabrook; RMC Place; CUMBERLAND; ▲ Upper Deerfield; 205 P-5; ★ VINL; ● 1,340
Seabrook Farms; CDP-Census Area Only; CUMBERLAND; ▲ Upper Deerfield; 205 L-1; ★ VINL; mail Bridgeton z 08302; Ⓟ 1,457; Ⓒ 1,719
Sea Girt; Inc. Place; MONMOUTH; 205 K-13; elev. 19ft./6m.; 🄿; ★ N.Y.; z 08750; Ⓟ 2,099; Ⓒ 2,148
Sea Girt Estates; RMC Place; MONMOUTH; ▲ Wall; *205 K-13; ★ N.Y.; mail Sea Girt z 08750; ● 250
Sea Isle City; Inc. Place; CAPE MAY; 205 R-9; elev. 6ft./2m.; 🄿; z 08243; Ⓟ 2,692; Ⓒ 2,835
Seaside Heights; Inc. Place; OCEAN; 205 L-13; elev. 7ft./2m.; 🄿; ★ N.Y.; z 08751; Ⓟ 2,366; Ⓒ 3,155
Seaside Park; Inc. Place; OCEAN; 205 L-13; elev. 6ft./2m.; 🄿; ★ N.Y.; z 08752; Ⓟ 1,871; Ⓒ 2,263
Seaview Park; RMC Place; ATLANTIC; ▲ Galloway; *205 P-10; ★ ATCY; mail Absecon z 08205; ● 200
Seaville; RMC Place; CAPE MAY; ▲ Upper; 205 R-9; ★ ATCY; mail Ocean View z 08230; ● 300
Secaucus; Inc. Place; HUDSON; 204 E-13; elev. 12ft./4m.; 🄿 🄷 ■; ★ N.Y.; z 07094, z 07096; Ⓟ 14,061; Ⓒ 15,931; ◆ 16,227
Seeley; RMC Place; CUMBERLAND; ▲ Upper Deerfield; *205 P-5; ★ VINL; mail Bridgeton z 08302; ● 50
Sergeantsville; RMC Place; HUNTERDON; ▲ Delaware; 204 H-7; 🄿; z 08557; ● 400
Seven Stars; RMC Place; OCEAN; ▲ Lakewood; *205 K-12; ★ N.Y.; mail Lakewood z 08701; ● 120
Sewaren; CDP; MIDDLESEX; ▲ Woodbridge; 210 M-4; 🄿; ★ N.Y.; z 07077; Ⓟ 2,569; Ⓒ 2,780
Sewell; RMC Place; GLOUCESTER; ▲ Mantua; 205 N-6; 🄿; ★ PHIL-; z 08080; ● 2,000
Shady Lake; RMC Place; PASSAIC; ▲ West Milford; *204 C-11; ★ N.Y.; mail West Milford z 07480; ● 250
Shafto Corners; RMC Place; MONMOUTH; *204 J-12; ★ N.Y.; mail Farmingdale z 07727; pop. incl. with Tinton Falls (Inc. Place)
Shamong; MCD-Township; BURLINGTON; *205 N-9; 🄿; ★ PHIL-; z 08088; Ⓟ 5,765; Ⓒ 6,462
Shark River Hills; CDP; MONMOUTH; ▲ Neptune; *204 J-13; elev. 65ft./20m.; ★ N.Y.; mail Neptune z 07753; Ⓟ 4,228; Ⓒ 3,878
Sharptown; RMC Place; SALEM; ▲ Pilesgrove; 205 N-5; mail Woodstown z 08098; ● 120
Shaw Crest; RMC Place; CAPE MAY; ▲ Lower; *205 T-8; mail Wildwood z 08260; ● 200

Entries in **UPPERCASE** are counties.
Entries in **bold** have populations of 2,500 or more.
Names in parentheses are alternate names.

Inc. Place	Incorporated Place
RMC Place	Rand McNally Designated Place
CDP	Census Designated Place
MCD	Minor Civil Division
⊡	County Seat
▲	Minor Civil Division
elev.	Elevation
🄿	Post Office
🄷	Hospital
🄲	College
■	Principal Business Center
★	Ranally Metro Area (RMA) Abbreviation
z	Zip Code(s)
Ⓟ	Previous Census Population
Ⓡ	Revised Census Population
Ⓐ	Annexation Population
●	Rand McNally Population Estimate
Ⓒ	Final Census Population
Ⓢ	Special Census Population
◆	Estimated Population

For additional definitions see Glossary, Volume 1, and Introduction, Volume 2.

Shaytown; RMC Place; SUSSEX; ▲ Sandyston; ***204** B-8; mail Montague z 07827; rural
Sheffield; RMC Place; PASSAIC; ▲ Wayne; ***204** D-11; ★ **N.Y.**; mail Wayne z 07470
Sherwood on the Green; RMC Place; GLOUCESTER; ▲ West Deptford; ***205** M-6; ★ **PHIL-**; mail Woodbury z 08096; ● 1,100
Shiloh; Inc. Place; CUMBERLAND; **205** P-5; elev. 118ft./36m.; 🅿; z 08353; Ⓟ 408; © 534
Shimer Manor; RMC Place; WARREN; ▲ Pohatcong; ***204** F-6; ★ **ALL-**; mail Phillipsburg z 08865; ● 1,900
Ship Bottom; Inc. Place; OCEAN; **205** N-12; elev. 10ft./3m.; 🅿; ★ **N.Y.**; z 08008; Ⓟ 1,352; summer pop. 7,000; © 1,384
Shippenport; RMC Place; MORRIS; ▲ Roxbury; ***204** E-9; ★ **N.Y.**; mail Landing z 07850
Shirley; RMC Place; SALEM; ▲ Upper Pittsgrove; **205** K-1; elev. 144ft./44m.; mail Elmer z 08318
Shongum; RMC Place; MORRIS; ▲ Randolph; ***204** E-10; ★ **N.Y.**; mail Mount Freedom z 07970; ● 2,400
Shore Acres; RMC Place; OCEAN; ▲ Brick; **205** L-12; ★ **N.Y.**; mail Brick z 08723
Shore Hills; RMC Place; MORRIS; mail Landing z 07850; ● 500
Shore Road Estates; RMC Place; MIDDLESEX; mail Monroe Township z 08831; ● 685
Shore View; RMC Place; MIDDLESEX; ▲ Woodbridge; ***204** H-11; ★ **N.Y.**; mail Colonia z 07067
Short Hills; RMC Place; ESSEX; ▲ Millburn; ***204** F-11; 🅿; ★ **N.Y.**; z 07078
Shrewsbury; RMC Place; MONMOUTH; ▲ Upper Freehold; ***204** J-10; 🅿; ★ **PHIL-**; z 07702 & mail Allentown z 08501; rural
Shrewsbury; Inc. Place; MONMOUTH; **204** I-13; elev. 25ft./8m.; 🅿; ★ **N.Y.**; z 07702; Ⓟ 3,096; © 3,590
Shrewsbury; MCD-Township; MONMOUTH; ***204** I-13; 🅿; ★ **N.Y.**; z 07702 & mail Eatontown z 07724; Ⓟ 1,098; © 1,098
Sicklerville; RMC Place; CAMDEN; ▲ Winslow; **205** N-7; elev. 142ft./43m.; 🅿; ★ **PHIL-**; z 08081; ● 1,800
Sidney; RMC Place; HUNTERDON; ▲ Franklin; **204** G-8; ★ **N.Y.**; mail Pittstown z 08867; ● 250
Siloam; RMC Place; MONMOUTH; ▲ Freehold; ***204** J-11; ★ **N.Y.**; mail Freehold z 07728; rural
Silver Bay; RMC Place; OCEAN; ▲ Toms River; ***205** L-12; ★ **N.Y.**; mail Toms River z 08753; ● 1,600
Silver Beach; RMC Place; OCEAN; ▲ Toms River; ***205** L-13; ★ **N.Y.**; mail Lavallette z 08735; ● 700
Silver Lake; RMC Place; ESSEX; ▲ Belleville; ***204** F-12; ★ **N.Y.**
Silver Lake; RMC Place; WARREN; ▲ Hope; ***204** D-7; ★ **N.Y.**; mail Blairstown z 07825; ● 300
Silver Ridge (Silver Ridge Park); CDP-Census Area Only; OCEAN; ▲ Berkeley; ***205** L-12; elev. 25ft./8m.; ★ **N.Y.**; mail Toms River z 08753; Ⓟ 1,138; © 1,211
Silver Ridge Park; OCEAN; see Silver Ridge (CDP-Census Area Only)
Silver Ridge Park West; RMC Place; OCEAN; ▲ Berkeley; ***205** L-12; elev. 25ft./8m.; ★ **N.Y.**; mail Toms River z 08757; ● 1,800
Silver Springs; RMC Place; MORRIS; ▲ Roxbury; ***204** D-9; ★ **N.Y.**; mail Landing z 07850
Silverton; RMC Place; OCEAN; ▲ Toms River; **205** L-12; elev. 15ft./5m.; ★ **N.Y.**; mail Toms River z 08753; ● 4,800
Simons Lake; RMC Place; SUSSEX; ▲ Wantage; ***204** B-9; ★ **N.Y.**; mail Sussex z 07461; ● 150
Sim Place; RMC Place; BURLINGTON; ▲ Bass River; ***205** N-11; elev. 90ft./27m.; mail Barnegat z 08005; rural
Singac; RMC Place; PASSAIC; ▲ Little Falls; **204** A-1; ★ **N.Y.**; mail Little Falls z 07424
Sinnickson Landing; RMC Place; SALEM; ▲ Elsinboro; ***205** O-4; ★ **PHIL-**; mail Salem z 08079; ● 200
Sixmile Run; RMC Place; MIDDLESEX, SOMERSET; mail Somerset z 08873; ● 370
Six Points; RMC Place; SALEM; ▲ Pittsgrove; ***205** O-6; ★ **VINL**; mail Bridgeton z 08302
Skillman; RMC Place; SOMERSET; ▲ Montgomery; **204** H-9; 🅿; z 08558; ● 300
Skyline Lakes; RMC Place; PASSAIC; ***204** C-11; ★ **N.Y.**; mail Ringwood z 07456, Wanaque z 07465; pop. incl. with Ringwood (Inc. Place)
Slackwoods; RMC Place; MERCER; ▲ Lawrence; **205** S-13; elev. 84ft./26m.; ★ **PHIL-**; mail Trenton z 08638; ● 6,000
Smalleytown; RMC Place; SOMERSET; ***204** G-10; elev. 275ft./84m.; ★ **N.Y.**; mail Warren z 07059; rural
Smithburg; RMC Place; MONMOUTH; ▲ Millstone, Freehold; **204** J-11; ★ **N.Y.**; mail Freehold z 07728
Smiths Mills; RMC Place; PASSAIC; ▲ West Milford; ***204** D-11; ★ **N.Y.**; mail Butler z 07405; ● 70
Smithville; RMC Place; ATLANTIC; ▲ Galloway; **205** P-10; 🅿; ★ **ATCY**; z 08205 & mail Absecon z 08201; ● 3,000
Smithville; RMC Place; BURLINGTON; ▲ Eastampton; ***205** L-9; ★ **PHIL-**; mail Mount Holly z 08060; ● 150
Smoke Rise; RMC Place; MORRIS; ***204** D-11; ★ **N.Y.**; mail Butler z 07405; pop. incl. with Kinnelon (Inc. Place)
Snow Hill; RMC Place; CAMDEN; ***205** M-7; ★ **PHIL-**; mail Lawnside z 08045; pop. incl. with Lawnside (Inc. Place)
Society Hill; CDP-Census Area Only; MIDDLESEX; ▲ Piscataway; ***204** H-10; elev. 100ft./30m.; ★ **N.Y.**; mail Edison z 08817; Ⓟ 3,577; © 3,804
Somerdale; Inc. Place; CAMDEN; **205** M-7; elev. 83ft./25m.; 🅿; ★ **PHIL-**; z 08083; Ⓟ 5,440; © 5,192
Somerset; RMC Place; MERCER; ▲ Ewing; ***204** J-8; elev. 120ft./37m.; ★ **PHIL-**; mail Trenton z 08628
Somerset; CDP-Census Area Only; SOMERSET; ▲ Franklin; **204** H-10; 🅿; ★ **N.Y.**; z 08873, z 08875 & mail Zarephath z 08890; Ⓟ 22,070; © 23,040; ◆ 24,962
SOMERSET; **204** H-9; Ⓟ 240,279; © 297,490; ◆ 322,313
Somers Point; Inc. Place; ATLANTIC; **205** Q-9; elev. 31ft./9m.; 🅿 🅷; ★ **ATCY**; z 08244; Ⓟ 11,216; © 11,614
Somerville; Inc. Place; ⊡ SOMERSET; **204** G-9; elev. 54ft./16m.; 🅿 🅷 ■; ★ **N.Y.**; z 08876; Ⓟ 11,632; © 12,423; ◆ 12,887
South; RMC Place; ESSEX; ***204** F-12; ★ **N.Y.**; mail Newark z 07112, z 07114; pop. incl. with Newark (Inc. Place)
South Amboy; Inc. Place; MIDDLESEX; **204** H-11; elev. 54ft./16m.; 🅿 🅷; ★ **N.Y.**; z 08879; Ⓟ 7,863; © 7,913
Southampton; MCD-Township; BURLINGTON; ***205** L-9; 🅿; ★ **PHIL-**; z 08088; Ⓟ 10,202; © 10,388
Southard; RMC Place; MONMOUTH; ▲ Howell; ***205** K-12; ★ **N.Y.**; mail Howell z 07731; rural
South Belmar; MONMOUTH; see Lake Como (Inc. Place)
South Bound Brook; Inc. Place; SOMERSET; **204** G-10; elev. 45ft./14m.; 🅿; ★ **N.Y.**; z 08880; Ⓟ 4,185; © 4,492
South Branch; RMC Place; SOMERSET; ▲ Hillsborough; **204** I-10; ★ **N.Y.**; mail Somerville z 08876; ● 150
South Brunswick; MCD-Township; MIDDLESEX; ***204** I-10; ★ **N.Y.**; mail Dayton z 08810, Monmouth Junction z 08852; Ⓟ 25,792; © 37,734; ◆ 41,753
South Brunswick Terrace; RMC Place; MIDDLESEX; ***204** I-9; mail Monmouth Junction z 08852; ● 1,050
South Camden; RMC Place; CAMDEN; ***205** L-6; ★ **PHIL-**; mail Camden z 08104; pop. incl. with Camden (Inc. Place)
South Dennis; RMC Place; CAPE MAY; ▲ Dennis; **205** R-8; 🅿; z 08245; ● 350
South Egg Harbor; RMC Place; ATLANTIC; ▲ Galloway; **205** O-9; ★ **ATCY**; mail Egg Harbor City z 08215; ● 600
South Hackensack; RMC Place; BERGEN; ▲ South Hackensack; **204** A-5; 🅿; ★ **N.Y.**; z 07606; ● 2,106
South Hackensack; MCD-Township; BERGEN; ***204** E-13; 🅿; ★ **N.Y.**; z 07606; Ⓟ 2,106; © 2,249
South Harrison; MCD-Township; GLOUCESTER; ***205** N-5; ★ **PHIL-**; mail Harrisonville z 08039, Mullica Hill z 08062; Ⓟ 1,919; © 2,417
South Lakewood; RMC Place; OCEAN; ▲ Lakewood; ***205** K-12; ★ **N.Y.**; mail Lakewood z 08701; rural
South Mantoloking Beach; RMC Place; OCEAN; ▲ Brick; ***205** L-13; ★ **N.Y.**; mail Mantoloking z 08738
South Ogdensburg; RMC Place; SUSSEX; ***204** C-9; ★ **N.Y.**; pop. incl. with Ogdensburg (Inc. Place)
South Old Bridge; RMC Place; MIDDLESEX; ***204** I-11; ★ **N.Y.**; mail Old Bridge z 08857
South Orange; CDP-Census Area Only; ESSEX; ▲ South Orange Village; **204** F-12; elev. 141ft./43m.; 🅿 🅲 9,522; ★ **N.Y.**; z 07079; Ⓟ 16,390; © 16,964
South Orange Village; MCD-Township; ESSEX; ***204** F-12; 🅲 9,522; ★ **N.Y.**; mail South Orange z 07079; Ⓟ 16,390; © 16,964
South Paterson; RMC Place; PASSAIC; ***204** E-12; ★ **N.Y.**; mail Paterson z 07503, z 07533; pop. incl. with Paterson (Inc. Place)
South Pemberton; RMC Place; BURLINGTON; ***205** L-9; ★ **PHIL-**; mail Pemberton z 08068; pop. incl. with Pemberton (Inc. Place)
South Penns Grove; RMC Place; SALEM; ▲ Carneys Point; ***205** N-4; elev. 10ft./3m.; ★ **PHIL-**; mail Penns Grove z 08069; ● 300
South Plainfield; Inc. Place; MIDDLESEX; **204** G-11; elev. 67ft./20m.; 🅿 ■; ★ **N.Y.**; z 07080; Ⓟ 20,489; © 21,810; ◆ 23,247
South River; Inc. Place; MIDDLESEX; **204** H-11; elev. 50ft./15m.; 🅿; ★ **N.Y.**; z 08882; Ⓟ 13,692; © 15,322
South Seaside Park; RMC Place; OCEAN; ▲ Berkeley; **205** L-13; ★ **N.Y.**; mail Seaside Park z 08752; summer pop. 2,000; ● 400
South Seaville; RMC Place; CAPE MAY; ▲ Dennis; **205** R-8; elev. 22ft./7m.; 🅿; z 08246; ● 500
South Toms River; Inc. Place; OCEAN; **205** L-12; elev. 31ft./9m.; ★ **N.Y.**; mail Toms River z 08757; Ⓟ 3,869; © 3,634
South Vineland; RMC Place; CUMBERLAND; ***205** P-7; elev. 89ft./27m.; ★ **VINL**; mail Vineland z 08360; pop. incl. with Vineland (Inc. Place)
South Westville; RMC Place; GLOUCESTER; ***205** M-6; ★ **PHIL-**; mail Westville z 08093; pop. incl. with Westville (Inc. Place)
Southwind; RMC Place; OCEAN; ▲ Jackson; ***205** K-11; elev. 96ft./29m.; ★ **N.Y.**; mail Jackson z 08527; ● 300
Southwood; RMC Place; MIDDLESEX; ▲ Old Bridge; ***204** I-11; ★ **N.Y.**; mail Old Bridge z 08857; ● 2,800
Sparta; RMC Place; SUSSEX; ▲ Sparta; **204** C-9; ★ **N.Y.**; ● 1,900
Sparta; MCD-Township; SUSSEX; ***204** D-9; 🅿; ★ **N.Y.**; z 07871; Ⓟ 15,157; © 18,080; Ⓡ 18,013
Sparta Junction; RMC Place; SUSSEX; ▲ Sparta; ***204** C-9; elev. 576ft./176m.; ★ **N.Y.**; mail Sparta z 07871; rural
Sparta Lake; RMC Place; SUSSEX; ▲ Sparta; ***204** C-10; ★ **N.Y.**; mail Sparta z 07871; ● 100
Sperry Springs; RMC Place; SUSSEX; ***204** D-9; ★ **N.Y.**; mail Hopatcong z 07843; pop. incl. with Hopatcong (Inc. Place)
Spotswood; Inc. Place; MIDDLESEX; **204** I-11; elev. 30ft./9m.; 🅿; ★ **N.Y.**; z 08884; Ⓟ 7,983; © 7,880
Spotswood Manor; RMC Place; MIDDLESEX; ***204** I-11; mail Monroe Township z 08831; ● 3,000
Spray Beach; RMC Place; OCEAN; ▲ Long Beach; **205** O-12; ★ **N.Y.**; mail Beach Haven z 08008; summer pop. 1,000; ● 200
Springdale; CDP; CAMDEN; ***205** M-7; ★ **PHIL-**; © 14,409
Springdale; RMC Place; SOMERSET; ▲ Warren; ***204** G-10; ★ **N.Y.**; mail Warren z 07059; rural
Springdale; RMC Place; SUSSEX; ▲ Andover; **204** D-8; ★ **N.Y.**; mail Newton z 07860; ● 400
Springfield; MCD-Township; BURLINGTON; ***205** K-8; ★ **PHIL-**; mail Jobstown z 08041; Ⓟ 3,028; © 3,227
Springfield; CDP; UNION; ▲ Springfield; **204** F-11; elev. 97ft./30m.; 🅿; ★ **N.Y.**; z 07081; Ⓟ 13,420; © 14,429
Springfield; MCD-Township; UNION; ***204** F-11; 🅿; ★ **N.Y.**; z 07081; Ⓟ 13,420; © 14,429
Spring Lake (Spring Lake Beach); Inc. Place; MONMOUTH; **204** J-13; elev. 25ft./8m.; 🅿; ★ **N.Y.**; z 07762; Ⓟ 3,499; © 3,567
Spring Lake Beach; MONMOUTH; see Spring Lake (Inc. Place)
Spring Lake Heights; Inc. Place; MONMOUTH; **204** J-13; elev. 54ft./16m.; ★ **N.Y.**; mail Spring Lake z 07762; Ⓟ 5,341; © 5,227
Spring Mill; RMC Place; MONMOUTH; mail Allentown z 08501; ● 165
Spring Mills; RMC Place; HUNTERDON; ▲ Holland; **204** G-6; elev. 300ft./91m.; mail Milford z 08848; ● 125
Springside; RMC Place; BURLINGTON; ▲ Burlington; **205** K-8; elev. 66ft./20m.; ★ **PHIL-**; mail Burlington z 08016; ● 1,600
Springtown; RMC Place; CUMBERLAND; ▲ Greenwich; ***205** P-5; mail Bridgeton z 08302
Springtown; RMC Place; MORRIS; ▲ Washington; ***204** E-8; ★ **N.Y.**; mail Long Valley z 07853
Springtown; RMC Place; WARREN; ▲ Pohatcong; **204** G-6; ★ **ALL-**; mail Phillipsburg z 08865; ● 100
Springville; RMC Place; BURLINGTON; ▲ Mount Laurel; **205** L-8; ★ **PHIL-**; mail Moorestown z 08057; ● 200
Squire Village; RMC Place; OCEAN; ▲ Toms River; ***205** L-12; ★ **N.Y.**; mail Toms River z 08753; ● 500
Stafford (Stafford Township); MCD-Township; OCEAN; ***205** N-11; ★ **N.Y.**; mail Manahawkin z 08050; Ⓟ 13,325; © 22,532; ◆ 30,188
Stafford Township; OCEAN; see Stafford (MCD-Township)
Staffordville; RMC Place; OCEAN; ▲ Eagleswood; **205** N-11; elev. 28ft./9m.; ★ **N.Y.**; mail West Creek z 08092; ● 150
Stanhope; Inc. Place; SUSSEX; **204** D-9; elev. 882ft./269m.; 🅿; ★ **N.Y.**; z 07874; Ⓟ 3,393; © 3,584
Stanton; RMC Place; HUNTERDON; ▲ Readington; **204** G-8; 🅿; ★ **N.Y.**; z 08885; ● 100
Stanton Station; RMC Place; HUNTERDON; ▲ Readington; **204** G-8; ★ **N.Y.**; mail Flemington z 08822
Stanwick; RMC Place; BURLINGTON; ▲ Moorestown; ***205** L-7; ★ **PHIL-**; mail Moorestown z 08057; ● 900
Stanwick Glen; RMC Place; BURLINGTON; ▲ Moorestown; ***205** L-7; ★ **PHIL-**; mail Moorestown z 08057; ● 300
Star Cross; RMC Place; GLOUCESTER; ▲ Franklin; **205** O-7; elev. 134ft./41m.; ★ **PHIL-**; mail Franklinville z 08322; ● 150
Staten Island Junction; RMC Place; UNION; ▲ Cranford; ***204** G-11; ★ **N.Y.**; mail Cranford z 07016
Steelmantown; RMC Place; CAPE MAY; ▲ Upper; ***205** R-8; ★ **ATCY**; mail Woodbine z 08270; rural
Steelmanville; RMC Place; ATLANTIC; ▲ Egg Harbor; **205** Q-9; ★ **ATCY**; mail Egg Harbor Township z 08234, Linwood z 08221; pop. incl. with Linwood (Inc. Place)
Stelton; RMC Place; MIDDLESEX; ***204** H-11; ★ **N.Y.**; mail Edison z 08837
Stephensburg; RMC Place; MORRIS; ▲ Washington; **204** E-8; ★ **N.Y.**; mail Port Murray z 07865; ● 100
Sterling Woods; RMC Place; MONMOUTH; mail Manasquan z 08736; ● 600
Stevens; RMC Place; BURLINGTON; ▲ Burlington; **205** K-8; ★ **PHIL-**; mail Burlington z 08016; ● 300
Stewartsville; RMC Place; WARREN; ▲ Greenwich; **204** F-6; 🅿; ★ **ALL-**; z 08886; ● 800
Still Valley; RMC Place; WARREN; ▲ Pohatcong, Greenwich; ***204** F-6; ★ **ALL-**; mail Phillipsburg z 08865; ● 100
Stillwater; RMC Place; SUSSEX; ▲ Stillwater; **204** C-8; 🅿; ★ **N.Y.**; z 07875; ● 200
Stillwater; MCD-Township; SUSSEX; ***204** C-8; 🅿; ★ **N.Y.**; z 07875; Ⓟ 4,253; © 4,267
Stirling; RMC Place; MORRIS; ▲ Long Hill; **204** F-10; 🅿; ★ **N.Y.**; z 07980; ● 1,800
Stockholm; RMC Place; SUSSEX; ▲ Hardyston; **204** C-10; 🅿; ★ **N.Y.**; z 07460; ● 200
Stockton; Inc. Place; HUNTERDON; **204** H-7; elev. 85ft./26m.; 🅿; z 08559; Ⓟ 629; © 560
Stone Church; RMC Place; MONMOUTH; mail Atlantic Highlands z 07716; ● 300
Stone Harbor; Inc. Place; CAPE MAY; **205** S-3; elev. 5ft./2m.; 🅿; z 08247; Ⓟ 1,025; © 1,128
Stone House; RMC Place; SOMERSET; ▲ Bernards; ***204** F-10; elev. 220ft./67m.; ★ **N.Y.**; mail Millington z 07946; ● 500
Stonehurst East; RMC Place; MONMOUTH; ***204** J-11; mail Freehold z 07728; ● 3,000
Stonehurst West; RMC Place; MONMOUTH; ***204** J-12; mail Freehold z 07728; ● 2,500
Stone Tavern; RMC Place; MONMOUTH; ▲ Millstone; ***204** J-10; ★ **PHIL-**; mail Cream Ridge z 08514; rural
Stonetown; RMC Place; PASSAIC; ***204** C-11; ★ **N.Y.**; mail Wanaque z 07465; pop. incl. with Ringwood (Inc. Place)
Stony Hill; RMC Place; UNION; ▲ Berkeley Heights; ***204** F-10; elev. 407ft./124m.; ★ **N.Y.**; mail Berkeley Heights z 07922
Stoutsburg; RMC Place; MERCER; ▲ Montgomery, Hopewell; ***204** I-9; ★ **PHIL-**; mail Hopewell z 08525
Stow Creek; MCD-Township; CUMBERLAND; ***205** P-5; mail Bridgeton z 08302; Ⓟ 1,437; © 1,429
Stow Creek Landing; RMC Place; CUMBERLAND; ▲ Stow Creek; ***205** P-5; mail Bridgeton z 08302; rural
Stratford; Inc. Place; CAMDEN; **205** M-7; elev. 69ft./21m.; 🅿 🅲 397; ★ **PHIL-**; z 08084; Ⓟ 7,614; © 7,271
Strathmere; CDP; CAPE MAY; ▲ Upper; **205** R-9; 🅿; ★ **ATCY**; z 08248; summer pop. 2,000; © 175
Strathmore; CDP; MONMOUTH; ▲ Aberdeen; ***204** I-12; ★ **N.Y.**; mail Matawan z 07747; Ⓟ 7,060; © 6,740
Suburban; RMC Place; MONMOUTH; ▲ Middletown; ***204** I-13; ★ **N.Y.**; mail Red Bank z 07701
Succasunna; RMC Place; MORRIS; ▲ Roxbury; **204** E-9; 🅿; ★ **N.Y.**; z 07876; ● 4,000
Succasunna-Kenvil; CDP-Census Area Only; MORRIS; ▲ Roxbury; ***204** E-9; ★ **N.Y.**; mail Kenvil z 07847, Succasunna z 07876; Ⓟ 11,781; © 12,569
Summerfield; RMC Place; WARREN; ▲ White; ***204** F-7; ★ **N.Y.**; mail Belvidere z 07823; rural
Summit; Inc. Place; UNION; **204** F-11; elev. 388ft./118m.; 🅿 🅷 ■; ★ **N.Y.**; z 07901-02; Ⓟ 19,757; © 21,131; ◆ 21,014
Summit Avenue; RMC Place; HUDSON; ★ **N.Y.**; mail Union City z 07087; pop. incl. with Union City (Inc. Place)
Sunbury; RMC Place; BURLINGTON; ▲ Pemberton; ***205** L-9; ★ **PHIL-**; mail Pemberton z 08068; ● 850
Sunnyside; RMC Place; HUNTERDON; ▲ Clinton; ***204** G-8; ★ **N.Y.**; mail Annandale z 08801; rural
Sunrise Beach; RMC Place; OCEAN; ▲ Lacey; ***205** M-12; ★ **N.Y.**; mail Forked River z 08731; ● 1,200
Sunset Beach; RMC Place; GLOUCESTER; ▲ Deptford; ***205** M-6; ★ **PHIL-**; mail Blackwood z 08012; ● 1,100
Sunset Hill Garden; RMC Place; SOMERSET; ***204** H-10; ★ **N.Y.**; mail Princeton z 08540; ● 200
Surf City; Inc. Place; OCEAN; **205** N-12; elev. 6ft./2m.; 🅿; ★ **N.Y.**; z 08008; Ⓟ 1,375; summer pop. 5,000; © 1,442
Sussex; Inc. Place; SUSSEX; **204** B-9; elev. 464ft./141m.; 🅿; ★ **N.Y.**; z 07461; Ⓟ 2,201; © 2,145
SUSSEX; **204** C-9; Ⓟ 130,943; © 144,166; ◆ 147,748
Sutton Park; RMC Place; MORRIS; ▲ Mount Olive; ★ **N.Y.**; mail Flanders z 07836
Swainton; RMC Place; CAPE MAY; ▲ Middle; **205** R-3; elev. 22ft./7m.; mail Cape May Court House z 08210
Swannanoa; MORRIS; see Lake Swannanoa (RMC Place)
Swartswood; RMC Place; SUSSEX; ▲ Stillwater; **204** C-8; 🅿; ★ **N.Y.**; z 07877; ● 250
Swartswood Lake; RMC Place; SUSSEX; ▲ Stillwater; ***204** C-8; ★ **N.Y.**; mail Newton z 07860; ● 300
Swedesboro; Inc. Place; GLOUCESTER; **205** N-5; elev. 68ft./21m.; 🅿; ★ **PHIL-**; z 08085; Ⓟ 2,024; © 2,055
Sweetwater; RMC Place; ATLANTIC; ▲ Mullica; **205** O-9; ★ **ATCY**; mail Hammonton z 08037; ● 150
Sykesville; RMC Place; BURLINGTON; ▲ Chesterfield; **205** K-9; ★ **PHIL-**; mail Wrightstown z 08562; ● 60
Sylvan Glen; RMC Place; BURLINGTON; ▲ Bordentown; ***204** J-9; ★ **PHIL-**; mail Bordentown z 08505; ● 250
Sylvan Lake; RMC Place; BURLINGTON; ▲ Burlington; ***205** K-8; ★ **PHIL-**; mail Burlington z 08016; ● 300

T

Tabernacle; RMC Place; BURLINGTON; ▲ Tabernacle; **205** M-9; elev. 98ft./30m.; 🅿; ★ **PHIL-**; z 08088; ● 150
Tabernacle; MCD-Township; BURLINGTON; ***205** M-9; 🅿; ★ **PHIL-**; z 08088; Ⓟ 7,360; © 7,170; Ⓡ 7,167
Tabor (Mount Tabor); RMC Place; MORRIS; ▲ Parsippany-Troy Hills; ***204** E-10; ★ **N.Y.**; mail Mount Tabor z 07878
Tanglewood Farms; RMC Place; MONMOUTH; ▲ Holmdel; ***204** I-12; ★ **N.Y.**; mail Holmdel z 07733; ● 600
Tanners Corners; RMC Place; MIDDLESEX; ▲ East Brunswick; ***204** H-11; ★ **N.Y.**; mail East Brunswick z 08816
Tansboro; RMC Place; CAMDEN; ▲ Winslow; **205** N-8; ★ **PHIL-**; mail Atco z 08004, Berlin z 08009; ● 300
Taunton Lake (Taunton Lakes); RMC Place; BURLINGTON; ▲ Medford; **205** M-8; ★ **PHIL-**; mail Marlton z 08053; ● 250
Taunton Lakes; BURLINGTON; see Taunton Lake (RMC Place)
Taurus; RMC Place; HUDSON; ★ **N.Y.**; mail West New York z 07093; pop. incl. with West New York (Inc. Place)
Tavistock; Inc. Place; CAMDEN; ***205** M-7; elev. 40ft./12m.; ★ **PHIL-**; mail Haddonfield z 08033; Ⓟ 35; © 24
Taylors Mills; RMC Place; MONMOUTH; mail Englishtown z 07726; ● 210
Taylortown; RMC Place; MORRIS; ▲ Montville, Boonton; **204** D-11; ★ **N.Y.**; mail Boonton z 07005; ● 150
Teaneck; CDP; BERGEN; ▲ Teaneck; **204** E-13; 🅿 🅷 🅲 12,112; ★ **N.Y.**; z 07666; Ⓟ 37,825; © 39,260; ◆ 37,824
Teaneck; MCD-Township; BERGEN; ***204** E-13; 🅿 🅲 12,112 ■; ★ **N.Y.**; z 07666; Ⓟ 6,233; © 39,260; ◆ 37,824
Tenafly; Inc. Place; BERGEN; **204** D-13; elev. 52ft./16m.; 🅿; ★ **N.Y.**; z 07670; Ⓟ 13,326; © 13,806
Ten Mile Run; RMC Place; MIDDLESEX; ***204** H-10; mail Kendall Park z 08824; ● 1,100
Tennent; RMC Place; MONMOUTH; ▲ Manalapan; **204** I-11; 🅿; ★ **N.Y.**; z 07763; ● 100
Teterboro; Inc. Place; BERGEN; **204** E-13; elev. 37ft./11m.; 🅿; ★ **N.Y.**; z 07608, z 07699; Ⓟ 22; © 18
Tewksbury; MCD-Township; HUNTERDON; ***204** F-8; ★ **N.Y.**; mail Califon z 07830, Lebanon z 08833; Ⓟ 4,803; © 5,541
The Orchards; RMC Place; MERCER; ▲ Hamilton; ***204** J-9; ★ **PHIL-**; mail Trenton z 08619
Thompsons Beach; RMC Place; CUMBERLAND; ▲ Maurice River; **205** R-7; mail Heislerville z 08324; rural
Thorofare (Thoroughfare); RMC Place; GLOUCESTER; ▲ West Deptford; **205** M-6; elev. 19ft./6m.; 🅿; ★ **PHIL-**; z 08086; ● 1,700
Thoroughfare; GLOUCESTER; see Thorofare (RMC Place)
Three Bridges; RMC Place; HUNTERDON; ▲ Readington; **204** H-8; 🅿; ★ **N.Y.**; z 08887; ● 500
Tierneys Corner; RMC Place; MORRIS; ▲ Jefferson; ***204** D-9; ★ **N.Y.**; mail Lake Hopatcong z 07849; ● 40
Timber Lakes; RMC Place; GLOUCESTER; ▲ Monroe; ***205** O-7; elev. 110ft./34m.; ★ **PHIL-**; mail Williamstown z 08094; ● 650
Timbuctoo; RMC Place; BURLINGTON; ▲ Westampton; ***205** L-8; ★ **PHIL-**; mail Mount Holly z 08060; ● 70
Tinton Falls; Inc. Place; MONMOUTH; **204** J-13; elev. 88ft./27m.; 🅿; ★ **N.Y.**; z 07701, z 07712, z 07724, z 07727, z 07753; Ⓟ 12,361; © 15,053
Titusville; RMC Place; MERCER; ▲ Hopewell; **205** Q-12; 🅿; ★ **PHIL-**; z 08560; ● 900
Toms River; CDP; ⊡ OCEAN; ▲ Toms River; **205** L-12; 🅿 🅷; ★ **N.Y.**; z 08753-57; Ⓟ 7,524; © 86,327; ◆ 96,616
Toms River (Dover); MCD-Township; OCEAN; ***205** L-12; ■; ★ **N.Y.**; mail Toms River z 08753; Ⓟ 76,371; © 89,706; ◆ 96,616
Totowa; Inc. Place; PASSAIC; **204** E-12; elev. 260ft./79m.; 🅿; ★ **N.Y.**; z 07502, z 07511-12; Ⓟ 10,177; © 9,892
Towaco; RMC Place; MORRIS; ▲ Montville; **204** D-11; 🅿; ★ **N.Y.**; z 07082; ● 1,200
Town Bank; RMC Place; CAPE MAY; ▲ Lower; **205** T-1; mail Cape May z 08204; ● 1,500
Town Brook; RMC Place; MONMOUTH; mail Middletown z 07748; ● 300
Town Center; RMC Place; ESSEX; ▲ West Orange; ***204** F-12; ★ **N.Y.**; mail West Orange z 07052
Town Estates; RMC Place; BURLINGTON; ▲ Burlington; ***205** K-8; ★ **PHIL-**; mail Burlington z 08016; ● 1,200
Townley; RMC Place; UNION; ▲ Union; **204** F-1; ★ **N.Y.**; mail Union z 07083
Townsbury; RMC Place; WARREN; ▲ Liberty; **204** E-7; ★ **N.Y.**; mail Oxford z 07863; ● 50
Townsends Inlet; RMC Place; CAPE MAY; **205** S-9; 🅿; z 08243; pop. incl. with Sea Isle City (Inc. Place)
Tranquility; RMC Place; SUSSEX; ▲ Green; **204** D-8; 🅿; ★ **N.Y.**; z 07879; ● 100
Tremley; RMC Place; UNION; ***204** G-12; ★ **N.Y.**; mail Linden z 07036; pop. incl. with Linden (Inc. Place)
Tremley Point; RMC Place; UNION; ***204** G-12; ★ **N.Y.**; mail Linden z 07036
Trenton; Inc. Place; **STATE CAPITAL**; ⊡ MERCER; **205** J-8; elev. 50ft./15m.; 🅿 🅷 🅲 13,173 ■; ★ **PHIL-**; z 08601-11, z 08618-20, z 08625, z 08628-29, z 08638, z 08640-41, z 08645-48, z 08650, z 08666, z 08690-91, z 08695; Ⓟ 88,675; © 85,403; ◆ 81,001
Trenton Gardens; RMC Place; MERCER; ▲ Hamilton; ***204** J-9; ★ **PHIL-**; mail Trenton z 08610; ● 3,000
Troy Hills; RMC Place; MORRIS; ▲ Parsippany-Troy Hills; **204** E-11; ★ **N.Y.**; mail Parsippany z 07054
Tuckahoe; RMC Place; CAPE MAY; ▲ Upper; **205** Q-8; elev. 20ft./6m.; 🅿; ★ **ATCY**; z 08250; ● 800
Tuckerton; Inc. Place; OCEAN; **205** O-11; elev. 23ft./7m.; 🅿; ★ **ATCY**; z 08087; Ⓟ 3,048; © 3,517
Turkey Point Corner; RMC Place; CUMBERLAND; ▲ Downe; ***205** Q-6; mail Port Norris z 08349; ● 50
Turnersville; CDP; GLOUCESTER; ▲ Washington; **205** N-7; 🅿; ★ **PHIL-**; z 08012; Ⓟ 3,843; © 3,867
Tuttles Corner; RMC Place; SUSSEX; ▲ Sandyston; **204** B-8; elev. 583ft./178m.; mail Branchville z 07826; rural
Twin Rivers; CDP; MERCER; ▲ East Windsor; **204** J-10; ★ **N.Y.**; mail Hightstown z 08520; Ⓟ 7,715; © 7,422
Tyler Park; RMC Place; HUDSON; ▲ North Bergen; ★ **N.Y.**; mail North Bergen z 07047

U

Ukrainian Village; RMC Place; SOMERSET; ▲ Franklin; ***204** H-10; ★ **N.Y.**; mail Somerset z 08873; ● 300
Union; MCD-Township; HUNTERDON; ***204** G-7; ★ **N.Y.**; mail Asbury z 08802, Pittstown z 08867; Ⓟ 5,078; © 6,160
Union; CDP; UNION; ▲ Union; **204** F-11; 🅿 🅷 🅲 13,050; ★ **N.Y.**; z 07083; Ⓟ 50,024; © 54,405; ◆ 54,504
Union; MCD-Township; UNION; ***204** F-11; 🅿 🅲 13,050 ■; ★ **N.Y.**; z 07083; Ⓟ 50,024; © 54,405; ◆ 54,504
UNION; **204** F-11; Ⓟ 493,819; © 522,541; ◆ 512,066
Union Beach; Inc. Place; MONMOUTH; **204** H-12; elev. 9ft./3m.; 🅿; ★ **N.Y.**; z 07735; Ⓟ 6,156; © 6,649
Unionburg; RMC Place; UNION; ***204** F-11; ★ **N.Y.**; mail Union z 07083
Union Center; RMC Place; UNION; ▲ Union; ***204** F-11; ★ **N.Y.**; mail Union z 07083
Union City; Inc. Place; HUDSON; **204** F-13; elev. 175ft./53m.; 🅿 ■; ★ **N.Y.**; z 07087 & mail Weehawken z 07086; Ⓟ 58,012; © 67,088; ◆ 67,126
Union Hill; RMC Place; MORRIS; ▲ Denville; ***204** E-10; ★ **N.Y.**; mail Dover z 07801
Union Mills; RMC Place; BURLINGTON; ***205** L-8; elev. 25ft./8m.; ★ **PHIL-**; mail Mount Holly z 08060
Union Square; RMC Place; UNION; ***204** G-12; ★ **N.Y.**; mail Elizabeth z 07201; pop. incl. with Elizabeth (Inc. Place)
Uniontown; RMC Place; WARREN; ▲ Lopatcong; **204** F-6; ★ **ALL-**; mail Phillipsburg z 08865; ● 120
Union Valley; RMC Place; MIDDLESEX; ▲ Monroe; ***204** I-10; ★ **N.Y.**; mail Cranbury z 08512
Union Village; RMC Place; UNION; ***204** F-10; ★ **N.Y.**; mail Berkeley Heights z 07922
Unionville; RMC Place; BURLINGTON; ▲ Eastampton; ***205** L-8; elev. 57ft./17m.; ★ **PHIL-**; mail Mount Holly z 08060; ● 50
Unionville; RMC Place; HUNTERDON; mail Ringoes z 08551; ● 200
Upper; MCD-Township; CAPE MAY; ***205** R-9; ★ **ATCY**; mail Tuckahoe z 08250; Ⓟ 10,681; © 12,115
Upper Deerfield; MCD-Township; CUMBERLAND; ***205** P-6; ★ **VINL**; mail Deerfield Street z 08313; Ⓟ 6,927; © 7,556
Upper Freehold; MCD-Township; MONMOUTH; ***204** J-10; ★ **PHIL-**; mail Allentown z 08501, Cream Ridge z 08514, Princeton z 08544; Ⓟ 3,277; © 4,282
Upper Greenwood Lake; RMC Place; PASSAIC; ▲ West Milford; ***204** B-11; ★ **N.Y.**; mail Hewitt z 07421; ● 2,800
Upper Macopin; RMC Place; PASSAIC; mail Hewitt z 07421; ● 940
Upper Mohawk; RMC Place; SUSSEX; ▲ Sparta; ***204** D-9; ★ **N.Y.**; mail Sparta z 07871
Upper Montclair; RMC Place; ESSEX; ▲ Montclair; ***204** E-12; 🅿; ★ **N.Y.**; z 07043
Upper Montvale; RMC Place; BERGEN; ***204** C-13; ★ **N.Y.**; mail Montvale z 07645; pop. incl. with Montvale (Inc. Place)
Upper Pittsgrove; MCD-Township; SALEM; ***205** O-6; mail Elmer z 08318; Ⓟ 3,140; © 3,468
Upper Saddle River; Inc. Place; BERGEN; **204** C-12; elev. 220ft./67m.; 🅿; ★ **N.Y.**; z 07458; Ⓟ 7,198; © 7,741
Uptown; RMC Place; HUDSON; ***204** F-13; ★ **N.Y.**; mail Hoboken z 07030; pop. incl. with Hoboken (Inc. Place)

V

Vail (Vails); RMC Place; WARREN; ▲ Blairstown; **204** D-7; ★ **N.Y.**; mail Columbia z 07832; ● 30
Vails; WARREN; see Vail (RMC Place)
Vailsburg; RMC Place; ESSEX; ***204** F-12; ★ **N.Y.**; mail Newark z 07106; pop. incl. with Newark (Inc. Place)
Valentine; RMC Place; MIDDLESEX; ▲ Edison; ***204** H-11; ★ **N.Y.**; mail Edison z 08817
Valley; RMC Place; PASSAIC; ▲ Wayne; ***204** D-12; ★ **N.Y.**; mail Wayne z 07470
Vanhiseville; RMC Place; OCEAN; ▲ Jackson; **205** K-11; ★ **N.Y.**; mail Jackson z 08527; ● 80
Vasa Home; RMC Place; MORRIS; ▲ Mount Olive; ***204** E-8; ★ **N.Y.**; mail Hackettstown z 07840; ● 300
Vauxhall; RMC Place; UNION; ▲ Union; ***204** F-11; elev. 133ft./41m.; 🅿; ★ **N.Y.**; z 07088
Ventnor City; Inc. Place; ATLANTIC; **204** J-2; elev. 11ft./3m.; 🅿; ★ **ATCY**; z 08406; Ⓟ 11,005; © 12,910
Ventnor Heights; RMC Place; ATLANTIC; ***205** Q-10; ★ **ATCY**; mail Ventnor City z 08406; pop. incl. with Ventnor City (Inc. Place)
Verga; RMC Place; GLOUCESTER; ▲ West Deptford; ***205** M-6; ★ **PHIL-**; mail Westville z 08093; ● 800
Vernon; RMC Place; SUSSEX; ▲ Vernon; **204** B-10; elev. 564ft./172m.; 🅿; ★ **N.Y.**; z 07462; ● 250
Vernon; MCD-Township; SUSSEX; ***204** B-10; 🅿; ★ **N.Y.**; z 07462; Ⓟ 21,211; © 24,686; ◆ 25,922
Vernon Valley; CDP-Census Area Only; SUSSEX; ▲ Vernon; ***204** B-10; ★ **N.Y.**; mail Glenwood z 07418; Ⓟ 1,696; © 1,737
Vernoy; RMC Place; HUNTERDON; ▲ Tewksbury; ***204** F-8; ★ **N.Y.**; mail Califon z 07830; ● 50
Verona; CDP; ESSEX; ▲ Verona; **204** E-12; elev. 348ft./106m.; 🅿; ★ **N.Y.**; z 07044; Ⓟ 13,597; © 13,533
Verona; MCD-Township; ESSEX; ***204** E-12; 🅿; ★ **N.Y.**; z 07044; Ⓟ 13,597; © 13,533
Victoria; RMC Place; GLOUCESTER; ▲ Franklin; **205** O-8; ★ **PHIL-**; mail Newfield z 08344; rural
Victory Gardens; Inc. Place; MORRIS; **204** E-10; elev. 600ft./183m.; ★ **N.Y.**; mail Dover z 07801; Ⓟ 1,314; © 1,546
Victory Lakes; CDP-Census Area Only; GLOUCESTER; ▲ Monroe; ***205** O-7; elev. 120ft./37m.; ★ **PHIL-**; mail Williamstown z 08094; Ⓟ 2,160; © 2,118
Vienna; RMC Place; WARREN; ▲ Independence; **204** E-8; 🅿; ★ **N.Y.**; z 07880; ● 400
Vienna Gardens; RMC Place; ATLANTIC; ▲ Galloway; ***205** P-9; ★ **ATCY**; mail Cologne z 08213
Villas; CDP; CAPE MAY; ▲ Lower; **205** S-1; 🅿; z 08251; Ⓟ 8,136; © 9,064
Vincentown; RMC Place; BURLINGTON; ▲ Southampton; **205** L-9; elev. 40ft./12m.; 🅿; ★ **PHIL-**; z 08088; ● 900
Vineland; Inc. Place; CUMBERLAND; **205** L-3; elev. 106ft./32m.; 🅿 🅷 ■; ★ **VINL**; z 08360-62; Ⓟ 54,780; © 56,271; Ⓡ 55,825; ◆ 58,641
Vista Center; CDP-Census Area Only; OCEAN; ***204** J-11; ★ **N.Y.**; © 541
Voorhees; CAMDEN; see Kirkwood Voorhees (RMC Place)
Voorhees; MCD-Township; CAMDEN; ***205** M-7; 🅿; ★ **PHIL-**; z 08043; Ⓟ 24,559; © 28,126; ◆ 28,769
Voorhees; RMC Place; SOMERSET; mail Somerset z 08873; ● 430
Voorhees Corner; RMC Place; HUNTERDON; ▲ Raritan; ***204** H-8; ★ **N.Y.**; mail Flemington z 08822; rural
Vulcanite; RMC Place; WARREN; ***204** F-6; ★ **ALL-**; mail Phillipsburg z 08865; pop. incl. with Alpha (Inc. Place)

W

Wading River; RMC Place; BURLINGTON; ▲ Washington; **205** O-10; mail Egg Harbor City z 08215; ● 30
Waldwick; Inc. Place; BERGEN; **204** D-12; elev. 181ft./55m.; 🅿; ★ **N.Y.**; z 07463; Ⓟ 9,757; © 9,622
Wall; RMC Place; MONMOUTH; ▲ Wall; ***204** J-13; 🅿; ★ **N.Y.**; z 07719
Wall; MCD-Township; MONMOUTH; ***204** J-13; 🅿; ★ **N.Y.**; z 07719 & mail Brick z 08724, Farmingdale z 07727, Howell z 07731, Neptune z 07753; Ⓟ 20,244; © 25,261; ◆ 27,245
Wallington; Inc. Place; BERGEN; **204** B-4; elev. 14ft./4m.; 🅿; ★ **N.Y.**; z 07057; Ⓟ 10,828; © 11,583
Wallpack Center; RMC Place; SUSSEX; ▲ Walpack; **204** C-8; elev. 461ft./141m.; 🅿; z 07881; ● 20
Wallworth Park; RMC Place; CAMDEN; ▲ Cherry Hill; ***205** L-7; ★ **PHIL-**; mail Cherry Hill z 08002
Walnford; RMC Place; MONMOUTH; ▲ Upper Freehold; ***205** K-10; elev. 70ft./21m.; ★ **PHIL-**; mail Allentown z 08501; rural
Walnut Valley; RMC Place; WARREN; ▲ Blairstown; **204** D-7; ★ **N.Y.**; mail Columbia z 07832; ● 80
Walpack; MCD-Township; SUSSEX; ***204** C-8; mail Wallpack Center z 07881; Ⓟ 67; © 41
Wanamassa; CDP; MONMOUTH; ▲ Ocean; **204** J-13; ★ **N.Y.**; mail Asbury Park z 07712; Ⓟ 4,530; © 4,551
Wanaque (Wanaque-Midvale); Inc. Place; PASSAIC; **204** C-11; elev. 240ft./73m.; 🅿; ★ **N.Y.**; z 07465; Ⓟ 9,711; © 10,266
Wanaque-Midvale; RMC Place; PASSAIC; ***204** C-11; ★ **N.Y.**; mail Wanaque z 07465; pop. incl. with Wanaque (Inc. Place)
Wanaque-Midvale; PASSAIC; see Wanaque (Inc. Place)
Wantage; MCD-Township; SUSSEX; ***204** B-9; ★ **N.Y.**; mail Sussex z 07461; Ⓟ 9,487; © 10,387
Waretown; CDP; OCEAN; ▲ Ocean; **205** M-12; elev. 15ft./5m.; 🅿; ★ **N.Y.**; z 08758; Ⓟ 1,283; © 1,582
Warners; RMC Place; UNION; ★ **N.Y.**; mail Linden z 07036; pop. incl. with Linden (Inc. Place)
Warren; SOMERSET; see Warrenville (RMC Place)
Warren; MCD-Township; SOMERSET; ***204** G-10; 🅿; ★ **N.Y.**; z 07059 & mail Plainfield z 07060; Ⓟ 10,830; © 14,259
WARREN; **204** F-7; Ⓟ 91,607; © 102,437; ◆ 107,390
Warren Glen; RMC Place; WARREN; ▲ Pohatcong; **204** G-6; ★ **ALL-**; mail Bloomsbury z 08804; ● 300
Warren Grove; RMC Place; OCEAN; ▲ Stafford; **205** N-11; ★ **N.Y.**; mail Barnegat z 08005
Warren Point; RMC Place; BERGEN; ***204** D-12; ★ **N.Y.**; mail Fair Lawn z 07410; pop. incl. with Fair Lawn (Inc. Place)
Warrenville (Warren); RMC Place; SOMERSET; ▲ Warren; **204** G-10; ★ **N.Y.**; mail Warren z 07059; ● 1,000
Washington; MCD-Township; BERGEN; ***204** D-13; ★ **N.Y.**; mail Township Of Washington z 07676; Ⓟ 9,245; © 8,938
Washington; MCD-Township; BURLINGTON; ***205** N-10; mail Egg Harbor City z 08215; Ⓟ 805; © 621
Washington; MCD-Township; GLOUCESTER; ***205** N-7; ★ **PHIL-**; mail Sewell z 08080; Ⓟ 41,960; © 47,114; ◆ 51,603
Washington; MERCER; see Robbinsville (MCD-Township)
Washington; MCD-Township; MORRIS; ***204** E-8; ★ **N.Y.**; mail Long Valley z 07853; Ⓟ 15,592; © 17,592
Washington; Inc. Place; WARREN; **204** F-7; elev. 463ft./141m.; 🅿; ★ **N.Y.**; z 07882; Ⓟ 6,474; © 6,712
Washington; MCD-Township; WARREN; ***204** F-7; 🅿; ★ **N.Y.**; z 07882; does not include the Borough of Washington; Ⓟ 5,367; © 6,248
Washington Corners; RMC Place; MORRIS; ▲ Mendham; ***204** F-10; ★ **N.Y.**; mail Mendham z 07945; rural
Washington Crossing; RMC Place; MERCER; ▲ Hopewell; **205** Q-12; ★ **PHIL-**; mail Titusville z 08560; ● 500
Washington Heights; RMC Place; MIDDLESEX; ***204** H-11; mail East Brunswick z 08816; ● 2,500
Washington Park; RMC Place; ESSEX; ***204** F-12; ★ **N.Y.**; mail Newark z 07102; pop. incl. with Newark (Inc. Place)
Washington Park; RMC Place; MIDDLESEX; mail Edison z 08817; ● 970
Washington Street; RMC Place; HUDSON; ***204** F-13; ★ **N.Y.**; mail Hoboken z 07030; pop. incl. with Hoboken (Inc. Place)
Washington Township; CDP-Census Area Only; BERGEN; ▲ Washington; ***204** D-13; ★ **N.Y.**; mail Township Of Washington z 07676; Ⓟ 9,245; © 8,938
Washington Valley; RMC Place; MORRIS; ▲ Morris, Mendham; ***204** E-10; ★ **N.Y.**; mail Morristown z 07960; ● 500
Watchung; Inc. Place; SOMERSET; **204** G-10; elev. 181ft./55m.; 🅿 ■; ★ **N.Y.**; z 07069 & mail Plainfield z 07060; Ⓟ 5,110; © 5,613; ◆ 5,806
Waterford; MCD-Township; CAMDEN; ***205** N-8; ★ **PHIL-**; mail Atco z 08004, Waterford Works z 08089; Ⓟ 10,940; © 10,494
Waterford Works; RMC Place; CAMDEN; ▲ Winslow, Waterford; **205** N-8; 🅿; ★ **PHIL-**; z 08089; ● 1,000
Waterloo; RMC Place; SUSSEX; ▲ Byram; ***204** E-9; ★ **N.Y.**; mail Stanhope z 07874; ● 60
Watsessing; RMC Place; ESSEX; ▲ Bloomfield; ***204** F-12; ★ **N.Y.**; mail Bloomfield z 07003
Wayne; CDP; PASSAIC; ▲ Wayne; **204** D-11; 🅿 🅷 🅲 10,600; ★ **N.Y.**; z 07470, z 07474; Ⓟ 47,025; © 54,069; ◆ 54,547
Wayne; MCD-Township; PASSAIC; 🅿 🅲 10,600 ■; ★ **N.Y.**; z 07470, z 07474, z 98662; Ⓟ 47,025; © 54,069; ◆ 54,547
Wayside; RMC Place; MONMOUTH; ▲ Ocean; ***204** J-13; ★ **N.Y.**; mail Asbury Park z 07712; pop. incl. with Tinton Falls (Inc. Place)
Wedgewood; RMC Place; GLOUCESTER; ▲ Washington; ***205** N-7; ★ **PHIL-**; mail Pitman z 08071; ● 2,000
Weehawken; RMC Place; HUDSON; ▲ Weehawken; **204** D-5; 🅿; ★ **N.Y.**; z 07086 & mail Union City z 07087, Villas z 08251; Ⓟ 12,385
Weehawken; MCD-Township; HUDSON; ***204** F-13; 🅿; ★ **N.Y.**; z 07086 & mail Union City z 07087; Ⓟ 12,385; © 13,501
Weekstown; RMC Place; ATLANTIC; ▲ Mullica; **205** O-9; ★ **ATCY**; mail Egg Harbor City z 08215, Hammonton z 08037; ● 140
Weequahic; RMC Place; ESSEX; ★ **N.Y.**; mail Newark z 07112; pop. incl. with Newark (Inc. Place)
Weirtown; RMC Place; WARREN; mail Allamuchy z 07820; ● 210
Wellington Park; RMC Place; BURLINGTON; ▲ Cinnaminson; ***205** L-7; ★ **PHIL-**; mail Riverton z 08077
Wellwood; RMC Place; CAMDEN; ***205** L-7; ★ **PHIL-**; mail Merchantville z 08109; pop. incl. with Merchantville (Inc. Place)
Wenonah; Inc. Place; GLOUCESTER; **205** M-6; elev. 27ft./8m.; 🅿; ★ **PHIL-**; z 08090; Ⓟ 2,331; © 2,317
Wescoatville; RMC Place; ATLANTIC; ***205** O-9; ★ **ATCY**; mail Hammonton z 08037; rural
West; RMC Place; ESSEX; ***204** F-12; ★ **N.Y.**; mail Newark z 07103; pop. incl. with Newark (Inc. Place)
West Allenhurst; RMC Place; MONMOUTH; ▲ Ocean; ***204** J-13; 🅿; ★ **N.Y.**; z 07711; ● 500
Westampton; MCD-Township; BURLINGTON; ***205** L-8; 🅿 🅷; ★ **PHIL-**; z 08060; Ⓟ 6,004; © 7,217
West Amwell; MCD-Township; HUNTERDON; ***204** I-8; ★ **PHIL-**; mail Lambertville z 08530; Ⓟ 2,251; © 2,383
West Atco; RMC Place; CAMDEN; ▲ Waterford; ***205** N-8; ★ **PHIL-**; mail Atco z 08004; ● 900
West Atlantic City; RMC Place; ATLANTIC; ▲ Egg Harbor; **204** H-1; ★ **ATCY**; mail Egg Harbor Township z 08234, Pleasantville z 08232; ● 900
West Belmar; CDP; MONMOUTH; ▲ Wall; ***204** J-13; ★ **N.Y.**; mail Belmar z 07719; Ⓟ 2,498; © 2,606
West Bergen; RMC Place; HUDSON; ***204** F-13; ★ **N.Y.**; pop. incl. with Jersey City (Inc. Place)
West Berlin; RMC Place; CAMDEN; ▲ Berlin; **205** M-7; 🅿; ★ **PHIL-**; z 08091; ● 3,000
Westboro; RMC Place; MONMOUTH; ***204** I-13; ★ **N.Y.**; mail Red Bank z 07701; pop. incl. with Red Bank (Inc. Place)
West Caldwell; CDP; ESSEX; ▲ West Caldwell; ***204** E-11; elev. 240ft./73m.; 🅿; ★ **N.Y.**; z 07006-07; Ⓟ 10,422; © 11,233
West Caldwell; MCD-Township; ESSEX; ***204** E-11; 🅿; ★ **N.Y.**; z 07006-07; Ⓟ 10,422; © 11,233
West Cape May; Inc. Place; CAPE MAY; **205** T-1; elev. 6ft./2m.; 🅿; z 08204; Ⓟ 1,026; © 1,095
West Carteret; RMC Place; MIDDLESEX; ***204** G-12; ★ **N.Y.**; mail Carteret z 07008; pop. incl. with Carteret (Inc. Place)
West Collingswood; RMC Place; CAMDEN; ▲ Haddon; ***205** L-6; 🅿; ★ **PHIL-**; z 08107; ● 900
West Collingswood Heights; RMC Place; CAMDEN; ▲ Haddon; ***205** M-6; 🅿; ★ **PHIL-**; z 08059; ● 1,000
West Creek; RMC Place; OCEAN; ▲ Eagleswood; **205** O-11; 🅿; ★ **N.Y.**; z 08092; ● 800
West Deal; RMC Place; MONMOUTH; ▲ Ocean; ***204** J-13; elev. 40ft./12m.; ★ **N.Y.**; mail Asbury Park z 07712; ● 200
West Deptford; MCD-Township; GLOUCESTER; ***205** M-6; 🅿; ★ **PHIL-**; z 08051, z 08063, z 08066, z 08086, z 08093, z 08096; Ⓟ 19,380; © 19,368; ◆ 20,907
West End; RMC Place; GLOUCESTER; ***205** M-6; ★ **PHIL-**; mail Woodbury z 08096; pop. incl. with Woodbury (Inc. Place)
West End; RMC Place; MONMOUTH; ***204** I-13; ★ **N.Y.**; mail Long Branch z 07740; pop. incl. with Long Branch (Inc. Place)
West Englewood; RMC Place; BERGEN; ▲ Teaneck; ***204** E-13; ★ **N.Y.**; mail Teaneck z 07666
West Farms; RMC Place; MONMOUTH; ▲ Howell; ***204** J-12; ★ **N.Y.**; mail Farmingdale z 07727; rural
Westfield; Inc. Place; UNION; **204** G-11; elev. 126ft./38m.; 🅿; ★ **N.Y.**; z 07090-91; Ⓟ 28,870; © 29,644; ◆ 28,751
West Freehold; CDP; MONMOUTH; ▲ Freehold; ***204** J-11; ★ **N.Y.**; mail Freehold z 07728; Ⓟ 11,166; © 12,498
West Grove; RMC Place; MONMOUTH; ▲ Neptune; ***204** J-13; ★ **N.Y.**; mail Neptune z 07753
West Haddonfield; RMC Place; CAMDEN; ***205** M-7; ★ **PHIL-**; mail Haddonfield z 08033; pop. incl. with Haddonfield (Inc. Place)
West Hudson; RMC Place; HUDSON; ***204** F-12; ★ **N.Y.**; mail Kearny z 07032; pop. incl. with Kearny (Inc. Place)
West Keansburg; RMC Place; MONMOUTH; ▲ Hazlet; **204** H-12; ★ **N.Y.**; mail Keansburg z 07734; ● 1,500
West Long Branch; Inc. Place; MONMOUTH; **204** I-13; elev. 27ft./8m.; 🅿 🅲 6,399; ★ **N.Y.**; z 07764; Ⓟ 7,690; © 8,258
West Mahwah; RMC Place; BERGEN; ▲ Mahwah; ***204** C-12; ★ **N.Y.**; mail Mahwah z 07430
West Mantoloking; RMC Place; OCEAN; ▲ Brick; ***205** K-13; ★ **N.Y.**; mail Brick z 08723
West Milford; CDP; PASSAIC; ▲ West Milford; **204** C-11; 🅿; ★ **N.Y.**; z 07480; Ⓟ 25,430; © 26,410; ◆ 26,959
West Milford; MCD-Township; PASSAIC; ***204** C-11; 🅿; ★ **N.Y.**; z 07480; Ⓟ 25,430; © 26,410; ◆ 26,959
Westmont; RMC Place; CAMDEN; ▲ Haddon; ***205** L-7; 🅿; ★ **PHIL-**; z 08108; ● 5,500
West Moorestown; RMC Place; BURLINGTON; ***205** L-7; ★ **PHIL-**; mail Moorestown z 08057; ● 4,500
West New York; Inc. Place; HUDSON; **204** E-13; elev. 185ft./56m.; 🅿 ■; ★ **N.Y.**; z 07093; Ⓟ 38,125; © 45,768; ◆ 49,027
Weston; RMC Place; SOMERSET; ***204** H-9; ★ **N.Y.**; mail Manville z 08835; pop. incl. with Manville (Inc. Place)
Westons Mills; RMC Place; MIDDLESEX; ***204** H-11; ★ **N.Y.**; mail East Brunswick z 08816; pop. incl. with New Brunswick (Inc. Place)
West Orange; CDP; ESSEX; ▲ West Orange; **204** F-12; elev. 368ft./112m.; 🅿 🅷; ★ **N.Y.**; z 07052; Ⓟ 39,103; © 44,943; ◆ 43,398
West Orange; MCD-Township; ESSEX; ***204** E-12; 🅿 ■; ★ **N.Y.**; z 07052; Ⓟ 39,103; © 44,943; ◆ 43,398
West Paterson; Inc. Place; PASSAIC; **204** A-2; elev. 400ft./122m.; 🅿 🅲 2,729; ★ **N.Y.**; z 07424; Ⓟ 10,982; © 10,987
West Point Island; RMC Place; OCEAN; ▲ Toms River; ***205** L-13; ★ **N.Y.**; mail Lavallette z 08735; pop. incl. with Lavallette (Inc. Place)
West Portal; RMC Place; HUNTERDON; ▲ Bethlehem; **204** F-7; mail Asbury z 08802; ● 100
West Side; RMC Place; HUDSON; ***204** F-13; ★ **N.Y.**; mail Jersey City z 07304; pop. incl. with Jersey City (Inc. Place)
West Side; RMC Place; HUDSON; ***204** F-13; ★ **N.Y.**; mail Jersey City z 07304; pop. incl. with Hoboken (Inc. Place)
West Trenton; RMC Place; MERCER; ▲ Ewing; ***204** J-8; 🅿; ★ **PHIL-**; z 08628
West Tuckerton; RMC Place; OCEAN; ▲ Little Egg Harbor; **205** O-11; ★ **ATCY**; mail Tuckerton z 08087; ● 700
West View; RMC Place; BERGEN; ***204** E-13; ★ **N.Y.**; mail Ridgefield Park z 07660; pop. incl. with Ridgefield Park (Inc. Place)
West Village; RMC Place; CUMBERLAND; ▲ Upper Deerfield; ***205** P-6; ★ **VINL**; mail Bridgeton z 08302
Westville; Inc. Place; GLOUCESTER; **205** M-6; elev. 16ft./5m.; 🅿; ★ **PHIL-**; z 08093; Ⓟ 4,573; © 4,500
Westville Grove; RMC Place; GLOUCESTER; ▲ Deptford; **228** G-5; ★ **PHIL-**; mail Westville z 08093; ● 1,500
West Wildwood; Inc. Place; CAPE MAY; **205** T-2; elev. 5ft./2m.; 🅿; z 08260; Ⓟ 453; © 448
West Windsor; MCD-Township; MERCER; ***204** I-9; 🅿; ★ **N.Y.**; z 08550; Ⓟ 16,021; © 21,907; ◆ 23,653
Westwood; Inc. Place; BERGEN; **204** D-13; elev. 75ft./23m.; 🅿 🅷; ★ **N.Y.**; z 07675, z 07677 & mail Township Of Washington z 07676; Ⓟ 10,446; © 10,999
Weymouth; RMC Place; ATLANTIC; ▲ Hamilton; **205** P-8; ★ **ATCY**; mail Mays Landing z 08330; ● 200
Weymouth; MCD-Township; ATLANTIC; ***205** P-8; ★ **ATCY**; mail Dorothy z 08317, Mays Landing z 08330; Ⓟ 1,957; © 2,257; Ⓡ 2,254
Whale Beach; RMC Place; CAPE MAY; ▲ Upper; ***205** R-9; ★ **ATCY**; mail Strathmere z 08248
Wharton; Inc. Place; MORRIS; **204** E-10; elev. 700ft./213m.; 🅿; ★ **N.Y.**; z 07885; Ⓟ 5,405; © 6,298
Wheatland (Pasadena); RMC Place; OCEAN; ***205** M-10; ★ **N.Y.**; mail Manchester Township z 08759; rural
Whippany; RMC Place; MORRIS; ▲ Hanover; **204** E-11; 🅿; ★ **N.Y.**; z 07981, z 07999
White; MCD-Township; WARREN; ***204** E-7; ★ **N.Y.**; mail Belvidere z 07823; Ⓟ 3,603; © 4,245
Whitehall; RMC Place; SUSSEX; ▲ Byram; ***204** D-9; ★ **N.Y.**; mail Andover z 07821; ● 75
White Horse; CDP; MERCER; ▲ Hamilton; **205** S-14; ★ **PHIL-**; mail Trenton z 08610; Ⓟ 9,397; © 9,373
Whitehouse; RMC Place; HUNTERDON; ▲ Readington; **204** G-8; 🅿; ★ **N.Y.**; z 08888; ● 800
White House Station; CDP; HUNTERDON; ▲ Readington; **204** G-8; 🅿; ★ **N.Y.**; z 08889 & mail Whitehouse z 08888; Ⓟ 1,287; © 1,951
White Meadow Lake; CDP-Census Area Only; MORRIS; ▲ Rockaway; ***204** D-10; ★ **N.Y.**; mail Rockaway z 07866; Ⓟ 8,002; © 9,052
White Rock Lake; RMC Place; MORRIS; ▲ Jefferson; ***204** D-10; ★ **N.Y.**; mail Ogdensburg z 07439; ● 1,200
Whitesbog; RMC Place; BURLINGTON; ▲ Pemberton; **205** L-10; ★ **PHIL-**; mail Browns Mills z 08015
Whitesboro; RMC Place; CAPE MAY; ▲ Middle; **205** S-2; 🅿; z 08252; ● 1,100
Whitesboro-Burleigh; CDP-Census Area Only; CAPE MAY; ▲ Middle; ***205** S-8; mail Cape May Court House z 08210, Whitesboro z 08252; Ⓟ 2,080; © 1,836
Whitesville; RMC Place; MONMOUTH; ▲ Neptune; ***204** J-13; ★ **N.Y.**; mail Neptune z 07753
Whitesville; RMC Place; OCEAN; ▲ Jackson; **205** K-11; ★ **N.Y.**; mail Jackson z 08527; ● 120
Whiting (Whitings); RMC Place; OCEAN; ▲ Manchester; **205** L-11; 🅿; ★ **N.Y.**; z 08759; ● 950
Whitings; OCEAN; see Whiting (RMC Place)
Whitman Park; RMC Place; CAMDEN; ***205** L-6; ★ **PHIL-**; mail Camden z 08104; pop. incl. with Camden (Inc. Place)
Whitman Square; RMC Place; GLOUCESTER; ▲ Washington; **205** N-7; ★ **PHIL-**; mail Blackwood z 08012; ● 3,500
Whittier Oaks; RMC Place; MONMOUTH; ***204** I-11; mail Englishtown z 07726; ● 1,000
Whittingham; CDP-Census Area Only; MIDDLESEX; ***204** I-10; ★ **N.Y.**; © 2,483
Wickatunk; RMC Place; MONMOUTH; ▲ Marlboro; **204** I-12; 🅿; ★ **N.Y.**; z 07765; ● 300
Wilburtha; RMC Place; MERCER; ▲ Ewing; ***204** J-8; ★ **PHIL-**; mail Trenton z 08628
Wildwood; Inc. Place; CAPE MAY; **205** T-3; elev. 8ft./2m.; 🅿; z 08260; Ⓟ 4,484; © 5,436
Wildwood Crest; Inc. Place; CAPE MAY; **205** T-2; elev. 9ft./3m.; 🅿; z 08260; Ⓟ 3,631; © 3,980
Wildwood Gardens; RMC Place; CAPE MAY; ***205** S-8; elev. 22ft./7m.
Williamstown; CDP; GLOUCESTER; ▲ Monroe; **205** N-7; 🅿; ★ **PHIL-**; z 08094; Ⓟ 10,891; © 11,812
Williamstown Junction; RMC Place; CAMDEN; ▲ Winslow; ***205** N-7; ★ **PHIL-**; mail Berlin z 08009; rural
Willingboro; RMC Place; BURLINGTON; ▲ Willingboro; **205** K-8; 🅿 🅷; ★ **PHIL-**; z 08046; Ⓟ 36,291
Willingboro; MCD-Township; BURLINGTON; ***205** L-8; 🅿 ■; ★ **PHIL-**; z 08046; Ⓟ 36,291; © 33,008; ◆ 30,751
Willowdale; RMC Place; CAMDEN; ▲ Cherry Hill; ***205** M-8; ★ **PHIL-**; mail Cherry Hill z 08003
Willow Grove; RMC Place; SALEM; ▲ Pittsgrove; **205** K-3; ★ **VINL**; mail Newfield z 08344
Windsor; RMC Place; MERCER; ▲ Robbinsville; **204** J-9; 🅿; ★ **PHIL-**; z 08561; ● 250
Winfield; RMC Place; UNION; ▲ Winfield; ***204** G-11; ★ **N.Y.**; mail Linden z 07036; ● 1,500
Winfield; MCD-Township; UNION; ***204** G-11; ★ **N.Y.**; mail Linden z 07036; Ⓟ 1,576; © 1,514
Winslow; RMC Place; CAMDEN; ▲ Winslow; **205** N-8; 🅿; ★ **PHIL-**; z 08095; ● 800
Winslow; MCD-Township; CAMDEN; ***205** N-8; 🅿; ★ **PHIL-**; z 08095; Ⓟ 30,087; © 34,611; ◆ 35,563
Winslow Junction; RMC Place; CAMDEN; ▲ Winslow; ***205** N-8; ★ **PHIL-**; mail Winslow z 08095
Winston Park; RMC Place; MONMOUTH; mail Howell z 07731; ● 350
Wonder Lake; RMC Place; PASSAIC; ▲ West Milford; ***204** D-11; ★ **N.Y.**; mail West Milford z 07480; ● 150
Woodbine; Inc. Place; CAPE MAY; **205** R-8; elev. 40ft./12m.; 🅿; z 08270; Ⓟ 2,678; © 2,716
Woodbridge; CDP; MIDDLESEX; ▲ Woodbridge; **204** G-11; 🅿 🅷; ★ **N.Y.**; z 07095; Ⓟ 17,434; © 18,309
Woodbridge (Woodbridge Township); MCD-Township; MIDDLESEX; ***204** G-11; 🅿 ■; ★ **N.Y.**; z 07095; Ⓟ 93,086; © 97,203; ◆ 100,133
Woodbridge Oaks; RMC Place; MIDDLESEX; ▲ Woodbridge; ***204** G-11; ★ **N.Y.**; mail Iselin z 08830
Woodbridge Township; MIDDLESEX; see Woodbridge (MCD-Township)
Woodbury; Inc. Place; ⊡ GLOUCESTER; **205** M-6; elev. 57ft./17m.; 🅿 🅷 ■; ★ **PHIL-**; z 08096-97; Ⓟ 10,904; © 10,307; ◆ 10,248
Woodbury Gardens; RMC Place; GLOUCESTER; ▲ Deptford; ***205** M-6; ★ **PHIL-**; mail Woodbury z 08096; ● 700
Woodbury Heights; Inc. Place; GLOUCESTER; **205** M-6; elev. 74ft./23m.; 🅿; ★ **PHIL-**; z 08097; Ⓟ 3,392; © 2,988
Woodcliff; RMC Place; HUDSON; ***204** E-13; ★ **N.Y.**; mail North Bergen z 07047
Woodcliff Lake; Inc. Place; BERGEN; ***204** D-13; elev. 249ft./76m.; 🅿; ★ **N.Y.**; z 07677; Ⓟ 5,303; © 5,745
Woodcrest; RMC Place; CAMDEN; ▲ Cherry Hill; ***205** M-7; ★ **PHIL-**; mail Cherry Hill z 08003
Woodglen; RMC Place; HUNTERDON; ▲ Lebanon; **204** F-8; ★ **N.Y.**; mail Califon z 07830; ● 150
Woodland; MCD-Township; BURLINGTON; ***205** M-10; mail Chatsworth z 08019; Ⓟ 2,063; © 1,170; Ⓡ 1,292
Woodland Ridge; RMC Place; MORRIS; ▲ Randolph; ***204** E-10; ★ **N.Y.**; mail Dover z 07801; ● 1,200

Entries in **UPPERCASE** are counties.
Entries in **bold** have populations of 2,500 or more.
Names in parentheses are alternate names.
Inc. Place — Incorporated Place
RMC Place — Rand McNally Designated Place
CDP — Census Designated Place
MCD — Minor Civil Division

⊡ County Seat
▲ Minor Civil Division
elev. Elevation
🅿 Post Office
🅷 Hospital
🅲 College
■ Principal Business Center
★ Ranally Metro Area (RMA) Abbreviation
z Zip Code(s)
Ⓟ Previous Census Population
Ⓡ Revised Census Population
Ⓐ Annexation Population
● Rand McNally Population Estimate
© Final Census Population
Ⓢ Special Census Population
◆ Estimated Population

For additional definitions see Glossary, Volume 1, and Introduction, Volume 2.

Wood-Lynne; Inc. Place; CAMDEN; **228** F-5; elev. 15ft./5m.; ★ **PHIL-**; mail Oaklyn **z** 08107; Ⓟ 2,547; © 2,796
Woodmere; RMC Place; OCEAN; ▲ Jackson; ***205** K-11; elev. 100ft./30m.; ★ **N.Y.**; mail Jackson **z** 08527; ● 150
Woodport; RMC Place; MORRIS; ▲ Jefferson; **204** D-9; ★ **N.Y.**; mail Wharton **z** 07885; ● 200
Wood-Ridge; Inc. Place; BERGEN; **204** B-4; elev. 188ft./57m.; 🅿; ★ **N.Y.**; **z** 07075; Ⓟ 7,506; © 7,644
Woodruff; RMC Place; CUMBERLAND; ▲ Upper Deerfield; **205** L-2; ★ **VINL**; mail Bridgeton **z** 08302; ● 70
Woods Tavern; RMC Place; SOMERSET; ▲ Hillsborough; **204** H-9; elev. 100ft./30m.; ★ **N.Y.**; mail Somerville **z** 08876; ● 200
Woodstock (Oak Ridge Lake); RMC Place; MORRIS; ▲ Jefferson; ***204** D-10; ★ **N.Y.**; mail Oak Ridge **z** 07438; ● 750
Woodstown; Inc. Place; SALEM; **205** N-5; elev. 47ft./14m.; 🅿; **z** 08098; Ⓟ 3,154; © 3,136
Woodstream; RMC Place; BURLINGTON; ▲ Evesham; ***205** M-7; ★ **PHIL-**; mail Marlton **z** 08053; ● 3,300
Woodsville; RMC Place; MERCER; ▲ Hopewell; ***204** I-8; ★ **PHIL-**; mail Hopewell **z** 08525
Woolwich (Woolwich Township); MCD-Township; GLOUCESTER; ***205** N-5; ★ **PHIL-**; mail Swedesboro **z** 08085; Ⓟ 1,459; © 3,032
Woolwich Township; GLOUCESTER; see Woolwich (MCD-Township)
Wortendyke; RMC Place; BERGEN; ***204** D-12; ★ **N.Y.**; mail Midland Park **z** 07432; pop. incl. with Midland Park (Inc. Place)
Wrights Mill; RMC Place; GLOUCESTER; ▲ Elk; ***205** N-6; ★ **PHIL-**; mail Monroeville **z** 08343
Wrightstown; Inc. Place; BURLINGTON; **205** K-9; elev. 133ft./41m.; 🅿; ★ **PHIL-**; **z** 08562; Ⓟ 3,843; © 748
Wrightsville; RMC Place; BURLINGTON; ▲ Cinnaminson; ***205** L-7; ★ **PHIL-**; mail Riverton **z** 08077
Wrightsville; RMC Place; MONMOUTH; ▲ Upper Freehold; ***204** J-10; ★ **PHIL-**; mail Allentown **z** 08501; rural
Wyckoff; CDP; BERGEN; ▲ Wyckoff; **204** D-12; elev. 355ft./108m.; 🅿 🅷; ★ **N.Y.**; **z** 07481; Ⓟ 15,372; © 16,508
Wyckoff; MCD-Township; BERGEN; ***204** D-12; 🅿; ★ **N.Y.**; **z** 07481; Ⓟ 15,372; © 16,508
Wyckoff Mills; RMC Place; MONMOUTH; ▲ Howell; ***204** J-12; ★ **N.Y.**; mail Freehold **z** 07728
Wyckoffs Mills; RMC Place; MIDDLESEX; ***204** J-10; elev. 100ft./30m.; ★ **N.Y.**; mail Cranbury **z** 08512; rural
Wykertown; RMC Place; SUSSEX; ▲ Frankford; ***204** B-9; ★ **N.Y.**; mail Branchville **z** 07826; rural

Y

Yardville; RMC Place; MERCER; ▲ Hamilton; **205** T-14; 🅿; ★ **PHIL-**; **z** 08620; ● 3,500
Yardville-Groveville; CDP-Census Area Only; MERCER; ▲ Hamilton; ***204** J-9; ★ **PHIL-**; mail Trenton **z** 08620; Ⓟ 9,248; © 9,208
Yardville Heights; RMC Place; MERCER; ▲ Hamilton; ***204** J-9; ★ **PHIL-**; mail Trenton **z** 08620; ● 2,500
Yellow Frame; RMC Place; SUSSEX, WARREN; ▲ Frelinghuysen, Fredon, Green; **204** D-8; elev. 874ft./266m.; ★ **N.Y.**; mail Newton **z** 07860
Yorketown; CDP-Census Area Only; MONMOUTH; ▲ Manalapan; ***204** I-11; ★ **N.Y.**; mail Englishtown **z** 07726; Ⓟ 6,313; © 6,712
Yorktown; RMC Place; SALEM; ▲ Pilesgrove; **205** O-5; mail Woodstown **z** 08098; ● 50

Z

Zarephath; RMC Place; SOMERSET; ▲ Franklin; ***204** G-10; elev. 41ft./12m.; 🅿; ★ **N.Y.**; **z** 08890; ● 50
Zion; RMC Place; SOMERSET; ▲ Montgomery, Hillsborough; **204** H-9; ★ **N.Y.**; mail Skillman **z** 08558; rural

NEW MEXICO

UT CO KS OK AZ Santa Fe TX

Statistics

Total area (2000) — 121,590 square miles
Land area (2000) — 121,356 square miles
Water area (2000) — 234 square miles
Capital — Santa Fe
Admitted as state — January, 1912

Maps

State maps can be found on pages 142-254 in Vol. 1

Ranally Metro Areas (RMAs) and Abbreviations

Albuquerque, NM — ALBU
Clovis, NM — CLOV
El Paso, TX-NM-MEX. — ELP
Farmington, NM — FARM
Las Cruces, NM — LSCR
Roswell, NM — RSWL
Santa Fe, NM — S.FE

Principal Places

Place Name	Place Type	County	Population
Albuquerque	Inc. Place	BERNALILLO	◆ 538,583
Las Cruces	Inc. Place	DONA ANA	◆ 90,821
Rio Rancho	Inc. Place	SANDOVAL	◆ 84,140
Santa Fe	Inc. Place	SANTA FE	◆ 66,137
South Valley	CDP-Census Area Only	BERNALILLO	◆ 46,022
Roswell	Inc. Place	CHAVES	◆ 45,663
Alamogordo	Inc. Place	OTERO	◆ 40,895
Farmington	Inc. Place	SAN JUAN	◆ 38,185
Hobbs	Inc. Place	LEA	◆ 32,737
Clovis	Inc. Place	CURRY	◆ 31,566
Carlsbad	Inc. Place	EDDY	◆ 25,764
Gallup	Inc. Place	MCKINLEY	◆ 16,331
Armijo	RMC Place	BERNALILLO	● 15,000
Las Vegas	Inc. Place	SAN MIGUEL	© 14,565
Deming	Inc. Place	LUNA	© 14,116
Sunland Park	Inc. Place	DONA ANA	© 13,309
North Valley	CDP-Census Area Only	BERNALILLO	© 11,923
Los Alamos	CDP	LOS ALAMOS	© 11,909
Portales	Inc. Place	ROOSEVELT	© 11,131
Artesia	Inc. Place	EDDY	© 10,692
Silver City	Inc. Place	GRANT	© 10,545
Los Lunas	Inc. Place	VALENCIA	© 10,034
Espanola	Inc. Place	RIO ARRIBA	© 9,688
Lovington	Inc. Place	LEA	© 9,471
Socorro	Inc. Place	SOCORRO	© 8,877
Grants	Inc. Place	CIBOLA	© 8,806
Shiprock	CDP	SAN JUAN	© 8,156
Anthony	CDP	DONA ANA	© 7,904
Ruidoso	Inc. Place	LINCOLN	© 7,698
Corrales	Inc. Place	SANDOVAL	© 7,334
Truth or Consequences	Inc. Place	SIERRA	© 7,289
Raton	Inc. Place	COLFAX	© 7,282
Belen	Inc. Place	VALENCIA	© 6,901
Sandia	RMC Place	BERNALILLO	Ⓟ 6,742
Bernalillo	Inc. Place	SANDOVAL	© 6,611
Bloomfield	Inc. Place	SAN JUAN	© 6,417
Aztec	Inc. Place	SAN JUAN	© 6,378
Zuni Pueblo	CDP	MCKINLEY	© 6,367
Kirtland	CDP	SAN JUAN	© 6,190
Chaparral	CDP	DONA ANA	© 6,117
White Rock	CDP	LOS ALAMOS	© 6,045
Alameda	RMC Place	BERNALILLO	● 6,000
Tucumcari	Inc. Place	QUAY	© 5,989
Eldorado at Santa Fe	CDP-Census Area Only	SANTA FE	© 5,799
Paradise Hills	RMC Place	BERNALILLO	Ⓟ 5,513
El Cerro-Monterey Park	CDP-Census Area Only	VALENCIA	© 5,483
Los Ranchos de Albuquerque	Inc. Place	BERNALILLO	© 5,092
Los Chaves	CDP	VALENCIA	© 5,033

County Business Data

County	FIPS Code	County Seat	Land Area (Sq. Mi.)	Census Population			Wholesale Trade		Manufacturing, 2002			
				4/1/2000	4/1/1990	% Change 1990-2000	Sales, 2002 ($1,000)	% Change 1997-2002	Establish-ments	Total Employees	Value Added ($1,000)	Ranally Mfg. Units
Bernalillo	001	Albuquerque	1,166	556,678	480,577	15.8	5,988,723	30.4	668	(d)	(d)	...
Catron	003	Reserve	6,928	3,543	2,563	38.2	(d)	(d)	...	(d)	(d)	...
Chaves	005	Roswell	6,071	61,382	57,849	6.1	170,925	-26.1	51	1,644	194,636	103
Cibola	006	Grants	4,539	25,595	23,794	7.6	23,361	7.3	...	(d)	(d)	...
Colfax	007	Raton	3,757	14,189	12,925	9.8	20,574	(d)	...	(d)	(d)	...
Curry	009	Clovis	1,406	45,044	42,207	6.7	119,627	-0.8	...	(d)	(d)	...
De Baca	011	Fort Sumner	2,325	2,240	2,252	-0.5	(d)	(d)	...	(d)	(d)	...
Dona Ana	013	Las Cruces	3,807	174,682	135,510	28.9	306,226	8.0	137	2,473	330,183	175
Eddy	015	Carlsbad	4,182	51,658	48,605	6.3	95,391	-65.3	34	985	554,927	294
Grant	017	Silver City	3,966	31,002	27,676	12.0	(d)	(d)	...	(d)	(d)	...
Guadalupe	019	Santa Rosa	3,030	4,680	4,156	12.6	(d)	(d)	...	(d)	(d)	...
Harding	021	Mosquero	2,125	810	987	-17.9	(d)	(d)	...	(d)	(d)	...
Hidalgo	023	Lordsburg	3,446	5,932	5,958	-0.4	(d)	(d)	...	(d)	(d)	...
Lea	025	Lovington	4,393	55,511	55,765	-0.5	316,640	2.6	37	673	80,533	43
Lincoln	027	Carrizozo	4,831	19,411	12,219	58.9	17,654	129.8	...	(d)	(d)	...
Los Alamos	028	Los Alamos	109	18,343	18,115	1.3	98,213	137.2	...	(d)	(d)	...
Luna	029	Deming	2,965	25,016	18,110	38.1	37,330	-24.3	...	(d)	(d)	...
McKinley	031	Gallup	5,449	74,798	60,686	23.3	134,040	-30.1	36	656	70,981	38
Mora	033	Mora	1,931	5,180	4,264	21.5	(d)	(d)	...	(d)	(d)	...
Otero	035	Alamogordo	6,627	62,298	51,928	20.0	33,716	13.7	...	(d)	(d)	...
Quay	037	Tucumcari	2,875	10,155	10,823	-6.2	1,185	-73.4	...	(d)	(d)	...
Rio Arriba	039	Tierra Amarilla	5,858	41,190	34,365	19.9	23,925	-40.5	...	(d)	(d)	...
Roosevelt	041	Portales	2,448	18,018	16,702	7.9	53,713	59.2	...	(d)	(d)	...
Sandoval	043	Bernalillo	3,709	89,908	63,319	42.0	182,673	-26.4	72	(d)	(d)	...
San Juan	045	Aztec	5,514	113,801	91,605	24.2	686,934	79.9	76	1,153	92,681	49
San Miguel	047	Las Vegas	4,717	30,126	25,743	17.0	(d)	(d)	...	(d)	(d)	...
Santa Fe	049	Santa Fe	1,909	129,292	98,928	30.7	463,678	36.3	166	1,199	71,056	38
Sierra	051	Truth or Consequences	4,180	13,270	9,912	33.9	(d)	(d)	...	(d)	(d)	...
Socorro	053	Socorro	6,646	18,078	14,764	22.4	(d)	(d)	...	(d)	(d)	...
Taos	055	Taos	2,203	29,979	23,118	29.7	15,419	30.3	...	(d)	(d)	...
Torrance	057	Estancia	3,345	16,911	10,285	64.4	99,682	856.4	...	(d)	(d)	...
Union	059	Clayton	3,830	4,174	4,124	1.2	(d)	(d)	...	(d)	(d)	...
Valencia	061	Los Lunas	1,068	66,152	45,235	46.2	37,656	-1.2	29	(d)	(d)	...
The State			**121,356**	**1,819,046**	**1,515,069**	**20.1**	**8,993,729**	**21.6**	**1,587**	**33,085**	**5,990,566**	**3,169**

(d) Data not available. Corresponding percentages or Ranally Manufacturing Units are estimates.
... Represents 0 or amount too minimal to be reported.

Index of Places and Counties

Entries in **UPPERCASE** are counties.
Entries in **bold** have populations of 2,500 or more.
Names in parentheses are alternate names.

Inc. Place	Incorporated Place
RMC Place	Rand McNally Designated Place
CDP	Census Designated Place
MCD	Minor Civil Division
⊡	County Seat
▲	Minor Civil Division
elev.	Elevation
🄿	Post Office
🄷	Hospital
🄲	College
■	Principal Business Center
★	Ranally Metro Area (RMA) Abbreviation
z	Zip Code(s)
Ⓟ	Previous Census Population
Ⓡ	Revised Census Population
Ⓐ	Annexation Population
●	Rand McNally Population Estimate
©	Final Census Population
Ⓢ	Special Census Population
◆	Estimated Population

For additional definitions see Glossary, Volume 1, and Introduction, Volume 2.

Cowles; RMC Place; SAN MIGUEL; ***206** D-6; elev. 8,165ft./2,489m.; mail Tererro **z** 87573; summer pop. 150
Coyote; RMC Place; RIO ARRIBA; **206** C-5; elev. 6,724ft./2,049m.; [P]; **z** 87012; ● 120
Coyote Canyon (Brimhall); RMC Place; MCKINLEY; **206** D-2; located on Navajo Nation Ind. Res.; elev. 6,124ft./1,867m.; mail Brimhall **z** 87310; ● 200
Cree Meadows Heights; RMC Place; LINCOLN; mail Ruidoso **z** 88345; pop. incl. with Ruidoso (Inc. Place)
Crossroads; RMC Place; LEA; **206** H-10; elev. 4,118ft./1,255m.; [P]; **z** 88114; ● 50
Crownpoint; CDP; MCKINLEY; **206** D-2; elev. 6,971ft./2,125m.; [P] [H]; **z** 87313; location of Eastern Navajo Indian Agency; Ⓟ 2,108; © 2,630
Cruzville; RMC Place; CATRON; ***206** G-1; mail Reserve **z** 87830
Crystal; CDP; SAN JUAN; ***206** C-1; located on Navajo Nation Ind. Res.; mail Navajo **z** 87328; © 347
Cuartelez; CDP-Census Area Only; SANTA FE; ***206** C-5; © 452
Cuba; Inc. Place; SANDOVAL; **206** C-4; elev. 6,908ft./2,106m.; [P]; **z** 87013; Ⓟ 760; © 590
Cubero; RMC Place; CIBOLA; **206** E-3; elev. 6,200ft./1,890m.; [P]; **z** 87014; ● 500
Cuchillo; RMC Place; SIERRA; **206** H-3; elev. 4,780ft./1,457m.; [P]; **z** 87901; ● 70
Cuervo; RMC Place; GUADALUPE; **206** E-8; elev. 4,819ft./1,469m.; [P]; **z** 88417; ● 90
Cundiyo; CDP; SANTA FE; ***206** C-6; elev. 6,640ft./2,024m.; [P]; **z** 87522; © 95
CURRY; **206** F-10; Ⓟ 42,207; © 45,044; ◆ 43,843
Cuyamungue; CDP; SANTA FE; ***206** C-5; mail Santa Fe **z** 87501, **z** 87506; Ⓟ 329; © 421

D

Dahlia; RMC Place; GUADALUPE; ***206** E-7; mail Anton Chico **z** 87711; rural
Dalies; RMC Place; VALENCIA; ***206** E-4; elev. 5,305ft./1,617m.; mail Los Lunas **z** 87031; rural
Dalton Pass; RMC Place; MCKINLEY; ***206** D-2; mail Crownpoint **z** 87313; ● 100
Datil; RMC Place; CATRON; **206** G-3; elev. 7,341ft./2,238m.; [P]; **z** 87821; ● 300
DE BACA; **206** F-8; Ⓟ 2,252; © 2,240; ◆ 1,882
Del Norte; RMC Place; LINCOLN; mail Ruidoso **z** 88345; pop. incl. with Ruidoso (Inc. Place)
Deming; Inc. Place; ⊡ LUNA; **206** J-3; elev. 4,336ft./1,322m.; [P] [H]; **z** 88030-31; Ⓟ 10,970; © 14,116
Derry; RMC Place; SIERRA; **206** I-4; elev. 4,117ft./1,255m.; [P]; **z** 87933; ● 120
Des Moines; Inc. Place; UNION; **206** B-9; elev. 6,640ft./2,024m.; [P]; **z** 88418; Ⓟ 168; © 177
De Vargas Station; RMC Place; SANTA FE; ***206** D-6; ★ **S.FE**; mail Santa Fe **z** 87594; pop. incl. with Santa Fe (Inc. Place)
Dexter; Inc. Place; CHAVES; **206** H-8; elev. 3,462ft./1,055m.; [P]; **z** 88230; Ⓟ 898; © 1,235
Dilia; RMC Place; GUADALUPE; **206** E-7; mail La Loma **z** 87724; ● 80
Dixon; RMC Place; RIO ARRIBA; **206** C-6; elev. 6,020ft./1,835m.; [P]; **z** 87527; ● 850
Dog Canyon Estates; RMC Place; OTERO; ***206** I-6; elev. 4,070ft./1,241m.; mail Alamogordo **z** 88310
Domingo; RMC Place; SANDOVAL; ***206** D-5; located on Santo Domingo Pueblo Ind. Res.; elev. 5,272ft./1,607m.; mail Algodones **z** 87001, Santo Domingo Pueblo **z** 87052; ● 60
Dona Ana; CDP; DONA ANA; **206** J-4; elev. 3,925ft./1,196m.; [P]; ★ **LSCR**; **z** 88032; Ⓟ 1,202; © 1,379
DONA ANA; **206** I-4; Ⓟ 135,510; © 174,682; ◆ 208,124
Dora; Inc. Place; ROOSEVELT; **206** G-10; elev. 4,288ft./1,307m.; [P]; **z** 88115; Ⓟ 167; © 130
Double Crossing; RMC Place; LINCOLN; ***206** H-6; mail Lincoln **z** 88338; rural
Downtown; RMC Place; BERNALILLO; ***206** E-5; ★ **ALBU**; mail Albuquerque **z** 87103; pop. incl. with Albuquerque (Inc. Place)
Drolet; SAN JUAN; see Newcomb (CDP)
Dulce; CDP; RIO ARRIBA; **206** B-4; located on Jicarilla Apache Ind. Res.; elev. 6,769ft./2,063m.; [P]; **z** 87528; location of Indian Agency; Ⓟ 2,438; © 2,623
Dunken; RMC Place; CHAVES; ***206** I-7; elev. 5,463ft./1,665m.; mail Pinon **z** 88344; rural
Dunlap; RMC Place; DE BACA; ***206** G-8; mail Fort Sumner **z** 88119; rural
Duran; RMC Place; TORRANCE; **206** F-6; elev. 6,000ft./1,829m.; [P]; **z** 88301; ● 100
Dusty; RMC Place; SOCORRO; **206** H-3; elev. 6,440ft./1,963m.; mail Winston **z** 87943; ● 25
Dwyer; GRANT; see Faywood (RMC Place)

E

Eagle Nest (Therma); Inc. Place; COLFAX; **206** B-7; elev. 8,203ft./2,500m.; [P]; **z** 87710, **z** 87718; Ⓟ 189; © 306
East Grand Plains; RMC Place; CHAVES; ***206** H-8; ★ **RSWL**; mail Roswell **z** 88201; rural
East Pecos; RMC Place; SAN MIGUEL; ***206** D-6; mail Pecos **z** 87552; ● 200
EDDY; **206** J-8; Ⓟ 48,605; © 51,658; ◆ 51,442
Edgewood; Inc. Place; SANTA FE; **206** E-5; elev. 6,645ft./2,025m.; [P]; **z** 87015; © 1,893
El Alto; RMC Place; MORA; ***206** C-7; mail Mora **z** 87732; ● 100
El Ancon; RMC Place; SAN MIGUEL; ***206** D-6; mail Ribera **z** 87560; ● 30
El Barranco; SAN MIGUEL; see Lower Pueblo (RMC Place)
El Cerrito; RMC Place; SAN MIGUEL; ***206** E-7; mail Villanueva **z** 87583; ● 45
El Cerro; RMC Place; VALENCIA; ***206** F-4; ★ **ALBU**; mail Los Lunas **z** 87031; ● 600
El Cerro-Monterey Park; CDP-Census Area Only; VALENCIA; ***206** E-5; © 5,483
Eldorado; RMC Place; BERNALILLO; ★ **ALBU**; mail Albuquerque **z** 87111, **z** 87154, **z** 87191; pop. incl. with Albuquerque (Inc. Place)
Eldorado at Santa Fe; CDP-Census Area Only; SANTA FE; ***206** D-6; ★ **S.FE**; mail Santa Fe **z** 87505; Ⓟ 2,260; © 5,799
El Duende; RMC Place; RIO ARRIBA; ***206** C-5; mail Hernandez **z** 87537; ● 50
Elephant Butte; Inc. Place; SIERRA; **206** H-4; elev. 4,534ft./1,382m.; [P]; **z** 87935; © 1,390
Elephant Butte Estates; RMC Place; SIERRA; ***206** H-4; elev. 4,470ft./1,362m.; mail Elephant Butte **z** 87935; ● 250
El Gauche; RMC Place; RIO ARRIBA; ***206** C-5; mail Ohkay Owingeh **z** 87566; pop. incl. with Espanola (Inc. Place)
El Guique; RIO ARRIBA; see Guique (RMC Place)
El Huerfano Trading Post; RMC Place; SAN JUAN; ***206** B-3; mail Bloomfield **z** 87413; rural
Elida; Inc. Place; ROOSEVELT; **206** G-9; elev. 4,350ft./1,326m.; [P]; **z** 88116 & mail Kenna **z** 88122; Ⓟ 201; © 183
Elizabethtown; RMC Place; COLFAX; ***206** B-7; mail Eagle Nest **z** 87718; rural
Elk; RMC Place; CHAVES; **206** I-7; mail Mayhill **z** 88339
Elkins; RMC Place; CHAVES; ***206** G-8; mail Roswell **z** 88201; rural
Elk Silver; RMC Place; OTERO; ***206** I-6; mail Bent **z** 88314; rural
El Llanito; RMC Place; SANDOVAL; ***206** D-5; ★ **ALBU**; mail Bernalillo **z** 87004; ● 200
El Llano; RMC Place; RIO ARRIBA; ***206** C-5; mail Espanola **z** 87532; ● 300
El Llano; RMC Place; SAN MIGUEL; ***206** D-7; mail Las Vegas **z** 87701; ● 90
El Morro; RMC Place; CIBOLA; **206** E-2; located on Ramah Navajo Ind. Res.; mail Pueblo of Acoma **z** 87034; ● 100
El Oro; RMC Place; MORA; ***206** C-6; mail Mora **z** 87732; rural
El Porvenir; RMC Place; SAN MIGUEL; **206** D-6; elev. 7,287ft./2,221m.; mail Montezuma **z** 87731; ● 100
El Prado; RMC Place; TAOS; ***206** B-6; elev. 7,000ft./2,134m.; [P]; **z** 87529; ● 900
El Pueblo; RMC Place; SAN MIGUEL; **206** D-6; mail Ribera **z** 87560; ● 50
El Pueblo; SAN MIGUEL; see Upper Pueblo (RMC Place)
El Rancho; CDP; SANTA FE; ***206** C-5; mail Espanola **z** 87532, Santa Fe **z** 87506; © 817
El Rancho Loma Linda; RMC Place; TAOS; mail Vadito **z** 87579; rural
El Rincon de los Trujillos; RMC Place; RIO ARRIBA; ***206** C-6; mail Chimayo **z** 87522
El Rito; RMC Place; RIO ARRIBA; **206** C-5; elev. 6,870ft./2,094m.; [P]; **z** 87530; ● 200
El Turquillo (Turquillo); RMC Place; MORA; ***206** C-7; mail Guadalupita **z** 87722; rural
El Vado; RMC Place; RIO ARRIBA; ***206** B-4; mail Tierra Amarilla **z** 87575; summer pop. 200
El Valle; RMC Place; TAOS; ***206** C-6; mail Chamisal **z** 87521; ● 45
El Valle de Arroyo Seco; CDP-Census Area Only; SANTA FE; ***206** C-5; © 1,149
Embudo; RMC Place; RIO ARRIBA; ***206** C-6; elev. 5,815ft./1,772m.; [P]; **z** 87531; ● 25
Emplazado; RMC Place; SAN MIGUEL; ***206** D-7; elev. 6,820ft./2,079m.; mail Sapello **z** 87745; ● 100
Enchanted Hills; RMC Place; LINCOLN; mail Ruidoso **z** 88345; pop. incl. with Ruidoso (Inc. Place)
Encinal; CDP; CIBOLA; ***206** E-3; located on Laguna Pueblo Ind. Res.; mail Cubero **z** 87014; © 200
Encino; Inc. Place; TORRANCE; **206** F-6; elev. 6,200ft./1,890m.; [P]; **z** 88321; Ⓟ 131; © 94
Engele; SIERRA; see Engle (RMC Place)
Engle (Engele); RMC Place; SIERRA; ***206** H-4; mail Elephant Butte **z** 87935; rural
Ensenada; RMC Place; RIO ARRIBA; **206** B-5; elev. 7,536ft./2,297m.; mail Tierra Amarilla **z** 87575; ● 130
Escabosa; RMC Place; BERNALILLO; **206** E-5; elev. 7,313ft./2,229m.; mail Tijeras **z** 87059; ● 150
Escondida; RMC Place; SOCORRO; ***206** G-4; mail Socorro **z** 87801; ● 60
Espanola; Inc. Place; RIO ARRIBA, SANTA FE; **206** C-5; elev. 5,589ft./1,704m.; [P] [H] [C] 2,002; **z** 87532-33; location of Northern Pueblos Indian Agency; Ⓟ 8,389; © 9,688
Estaca; RMC Place; RIO ARRIBA; ***206** C-5; mail Ohkay Owingeh **z** 87566; ● 60
Estancia; Inc. Place; ⊡ TORRANCE; **206** E-5; elev. 6,107ft./1,861m.; [P]; **z** 87016 & mail Cedarvale **z** 87009; Ⓟ 792; © 1,584
Eunice; Inc. Place; LEA; **206** J-10; elev. 3,450ft./1,052m.; [P]; **z** 88231; Ⓟ 2,676; © 2,562

F

Fairacres; RMC Place; DONA ANA; **206** M-1; elev. 3,896ft./1,188m.; [P]; ★ **LSCR**; **z** 88033; ● 750
Fairview; RMC Place; RIO ARRIBA; ***206** C-5; [P]; **z** 87533; pop. incl. with Espanola (Inc. Place)
Farley; RMC Place; COLFAX; ***206** C-8; elev. 6,056ft./1,846m.; mail Gladstone **z** 88422
Farmington; Inc. Place; SAN JUAN; **206** B-2; elev. 5,311ft./1,619m.; [P] [H] ■; ★ **FARM**; **z** 87401-02, **z** 87499; Ⓟ 33,997; © 37,844; ◆ 38,185
Faywood (Dwyer); RMC Place; GRANT; **206** I-2; elev. 5,200ft./1,585m.; [P]; **z** 88034; rural
Faywood Hot Springs; RMC Place; GRANT; ***206** I-2; mail Faywood **z** 88034; rural
Fence Lake; RMC Place; CIBOLA; **206** F-2; elev. 7,032ft./2,143m.; [P]; **z** 87315; ● 60
Field; RMC Place; CURRY; ***206** F-9; mail Melrose **z** 88124; rural
Fierro; RMC Place; GRANT; **206** I-2; mail Hanover **z** 88041; ● 50
Five Points; RMC Place; BERNALILLO; **206** M-8; ★ **ALBU**; mail Albuquerque **z** 87105, **z** 87121, **z** 87195; ● 4,200
Flora Vista; CDP; SAN JUAN; **206** B-2; elev. 5,507ft./1,679m.; [P]; ★ **FARM**; **z** 87415; Ⓟ 1,021; © 1,383
Florida; RMC Place; SOCORRO; **206** G-4; mail Socorro **z** 87801; pop. incl. with Socorro (Inc. Place)
Floyd; Inc. Place; ROOSEVELT; **206** F-9; elev. 4,150ft./1,265m.; [P]; **z** 88118; Ⓟ 117; © 78
Flume Canyon; RMC Place; LINCOLN; mail Ruidoso **z** 88345; pop. incl. with Ruidoso (Inc. Place)
Flying H; RMC Place; CHAVES; **206** I-7; elev. 5,044ft./1,537m.; [P]; **z** 88339; ● 50
Folsom; Inc. Place; UNION; **206** B-9; elev. 6,406ft./1,953m.; [P]; **z** 88419; Ⓟ 71; © 75
Foothills; RMC Place; BERNALILLO; ★ **ALBU**; mail Albuquerque **z** 87123; pop. incl. with Albuquerque (Inc. Place)
Forest Heights; RMC Place; LINCOLN; mail Ruidoso **z** 88345; pop. incl. with Ruidoso (Inc. Place)
Forest Park; RMC Place; BERNALILLO; ***206** E-5; ★ **ALBU**; mail Cedar Crest **z** 87008; ● 110
Forrest; RMC Place; QUAY; **206** E-9; mail Mcalister **z** 88427; ● 60
Fort Stanton; RMC Place; LINCOLN; **206** H-6; elev. 6,240ft./1,902m.; [P]; **z** 88323; ● 100
Fort Sumner; Inc. Place; ⊡ DE BACA; **206** F-8; elev. 4,049ft./1,234m.; [P] [H]; **z** 88119; Ⓟ 1,269; © 1,249
Fort Wingate; RMC Place; MCKINLEY; ***206** D-2; elev. 6,980ft./2,128m.; [P]; **z** 87316; ● 950
French Corners; RMC Place; COLFAX; ***206** B-8; elev. 5,975ft./1,821m.; mail Springer **z** 87747; rural
Fruitland; RMC Place; SAN JUAN; **206** B-2; elev. 5,120ft./1,561m.; [P]; ★ **FARM**; **z** 87416; ● 800

G

Gabaldon (Ojitos Frios); RMC Place; SAN MIGUEL; ***206** D-7; mail Las Vegas **z** 87701; rural
Galisteo; CDP; SANTA FE; **206** D-6; [P]; **z** 87540; © 265
Gallegos; RMC Place; HARDING; ***206** D-9; elev. 4,137ft./1,261m.; mail Logan **z** 88426; rural
Gallina; RMC Place; RIO ARRIBA; **206** C-4; elev. 7,580ft./2,310m.; [P]; **z** 87017; ● 430
Gallinas; RMC Place; SAN MIGUEL; ***206** D-6; mail Montezuma **z** 87731; ● 40
Gallup; Inc. Place; ⊡ MCKINLEY; **206** D-1; elev. 6,508ft./1,984m.; [P] [H] ■; **z** 87301-02, **z** 87305, **z** 87310, **z** 87317, **z** 87319, **z** 87326, **z** 87375 & mail Mexican Springs **z** 87320; Ⓟ 19,154; © 20,209; ◆ 16,331
Gamerco; RMC Place; MCKINLEY; **206** D-1; elev. 6,740ft./2,054m.; [P]; **z** 87317; ● 400
Garanbuio; RMC Place; SAN MIGUEL; ***206** D-6; mail Ribera **z** 87560; rural
Garfield; RMC Place; DONA ANA; **206** I-4; elev. 4,100ft./1,250m.; [P]; **z** 87936; ● 200
Garita; SAN MIGUEL; see Variadero (RMC Place)
Garrison; RMC Place; ROOSEVELT; ***206** G-10; elev. 4,131ft./1,259m.; mail Rogers **z** 88132; rural
Gary; RMC Place; HIDALGO; ***206** J-1; mail Lordsburg **z** 88045; rural
Gascon; RMC Place; MORA; ***206** C-6; mail Rociada **z** 87742
Gavilan; RMC Place; RIO ARRIBA; ***206** B-4; mail Lindrith **z** 87029; rural
Gila; RMC Place; GRANT; **206** I-2; elev. 4,564ft./1,391m.; [P]; **z** 88038; ● 350
Gila Hot Springs; RMC Place; GRANT; **206** H-2; mail Silver City **z** 88061; ● 35
Gladstone; RMC Place; UNION; **206** C-8; elev. 5,876ft./1,791m.; [P]; **z** 88422; ● 50
Glencoe; RMC Place; LINCOLN; ***206** H-6; elev. 5,725ft./1,745m.; [P]; **z** 88324; ● 50
Glen Grove; RMC Place; LINCOLN; mail Ruidoso **z** 88345; pop. incl. with Ruidoso (Inc. Place)
Glenrio; RMC Place; QUAY; **206** E-10; elev. 3,853ft./1,174m.; [P]; **z** 88434; ● 25
Glenwood; RMC Place; CATRON; **206** H-1; elev. 4,712ft./1,436m.; [P]; **z** 88039; ● 250
Glorieta; CDP; SANTA FE; **206** D-6; elev. 7,443ft./2,269m.; [P]; **z** 87535; © 859
Gobernador; RMC Place; RIO ARRIBA; ***206** B-4; mail Blanco **z** 87412; rural
Golden; RMC Place; SANTA FE; **206** E-5; [P]; **z** 87047; ● 70
Golondrinas; RMC Place; MORA; ***206** C-7; elev. 6,833ft./2,083m.; mail Buena Vista **z** 87712; rural
Gonzales Ranch; RMC Place; SAN MIGUEL; **206** E-6; elev. 6,483ft./1,976m.; [P]; **z** 87560; ● 40
Grady; Inc. Place; CURRY; **206** E-10; elev. 4,600ft./1,402m.; [P]; **z** 88120; Ⓟ 110; © 98
Gran Quivira; RMC Place; TORRANCE; ***206** F-5; elev. 6,348ft./1,935m.; mail Mountainair **z** 87036
GRANT; **206** I-1; Ⓟ 27,676; © 31,002; ◆ 30,260
Grants; Inc. Place; ⊡ CIBOLA; **206** E-3; elev. 6,454ft./1,967m.; [P] [H]; **z** 87020; Ⓟ 8,626; © 8,806
Greenfield; RMC Place; CHAVES; **206** H-8; mail Dexter **z** 88230; ● 150
Green Meadows; RMC Place; LINCOLN; mail Ruidoso **z** 88345; pop. incl. with Ruidoso (Inc. Place)
Green's Gap; RMC Place; CATRON; ***206** G-2; mail Datil **z** 87821; rural
Grenville; Inc. Place; UNION; **206** B-9; elev. 5,975ft./1,821m.; [P]; **z** 88424; Ⓟ 24; © 25
Grier; RMC Place; CURRY; ***206** F-9; mail Clovis **z** 88101; rural
Guachupangue; RMC Place; RIO ARRIBA; ***206** C-5; located on Santa Clara Pueblo Ind. Res.; mail Espanola **z** 87532; ● 220
GUADALUPE; **206** F-7; Ⓟ 4,156; © 4,680; ◆ 4,488
Guadalupita; RMC Place; MORA; **206** C-7; elev. 7,540ft./2,298m.; [P]; **z** 87722; ● 250
Guique (El Guique); RMC Place; RIO ARRIBA; ***206** C-5; mail Ohkay Owingeh **z** 87566; ● 300

H

Hachita; RMC Place; GRANT; **206** K-2; elev. 4,514ft./1,376m.; [P]; **z** 88040; ● 100
Hacienda Acres; RMC Place; DONA ANA; **206** J-4; ★ **ELP**; mail Las Cruces **z** 88011; ● 600
Hagerman; Inc. Place; CHAVES; **206** H-8; elev. 3,425ft./1,044m.; [P]; **z** 88232; Ⓟ 961; © 1,168
Hagerman Acres; RMC Place; EDDY; ***206** J-8; mail Carlsbad **z** 88220; pop. incl. with Carlsbad (Inc. Place)
Hahn; RMC Place; BERNALILLO; ***206** E-5; ★ **ALBU**
Hamilton Terrace; RMC Place; LINCOLN; mail Ruidoso **z** 88345; pop. incl. with Ruidoso (Inc. Place)
Hanover; RMC Place; GRANT; **206** I-2; elev. 6,350ft./1,935m.; [P]; **z** 88041; ● 450
Hanover Junction; GRANT; see Vanadium (RMC Place)
Happy Valley; RMC Place; EDDY; ***206** J-8; mail Carlsbad **z** 88220; ● 750
HARDING; **206** C-9; Ⓟ 987; © 810; ◆ 675
Hatch; Inc. Place; DONA ANA; **206** I-4; elev. 4,057ft./1,237m.; [P]; **z** 87937; Ⓟ 1,136; © 1,673
Hayden; RMC Place; UNION; ***206** C-10; mail Amistad **z** 88410
Hernandez; RMC Place; RIO ARRIBA; ***206** C-5; elev. 5,695ft./1,736m.; [P]; **z** 87537; ● 200
HIDALGO; **206** K-1; Ⓟ 5,958; © 5,932; ◆ 5,031
Highland; RMC Place; BERNALILLO; ★ **ALBU**; mail Albuquerque **z** 87106, **z** 87108, **z** 87198; pop. incl. with Albuquerque (Inc. Place)
High Lonesome; RMC Place; CHAVES; ***206** H-8; mail Roswell **z** 88201; rural
High Rolls (High Rolls Mountain Park); RMC Place; OTERO; **206** I-6; elev. 6,575ft./2,004m.; mail High Rolls Mountain Park **z** 88325; ● 450
High Rolls Mountain Park; OTERO; see High Rolls (RMC Place)
Hill; RMC Place; DONA ANA; ***206** J-4; mail Las Cruces **z** 88005
Hillburn City; RMC Place; LEA; ***206** H-10; mail Lovington **z** 88260; rural
Hillsboro; RMC Place; SIERRA; **206** I-3; elev. 5,254ft./1,601m.; [P]; **z** 88042; ● 200
Hobbies; RMC Place; BERNALILLO; ***206** E-5; ★ **ALBU**; mail Tijeras **z** 87059; rural
Hobbs; Inc. Place; LEA; **206** I-10; elev. 3,625ft./1,105m.; [P] [H] [C] 526 ■; **z** 88240-42, **z** 88244; Ⓟ 29,115; © 28,657; ◆ 32,737
Hoffman Town; RMC Place; BERNALILLO; ***206** E-5; ★ **ALBU**; mail Albuquerque **z** 87112; pop. incl. with Albuquerque (Inc. Place)
Holloman AFB; CDP-Census Area Only; OTERO; ***206** I-5; [P]; **z** 88330; Ⓟ 5,891; © 2,076
Hollywood; RMC Place; LINCOLN; ***206** H-6; mail Ruidoso **z** 88345; pop. incl. with Ruidoso (Inc. Place)
Holman; RMC Place; MORA; **206** C-6; elev. 7,640ft./2,329m.; [P]; **z** 87723; ● 250
Hondo; RMC Place; LINCOLN; **206** H-7; elev. 5,234ft./1,595m.; [P]; **z** 88336; ● 250
Hooverville; RMC Place; SAN MIGUEL; ***206** D-8; mail Conchas Dam **z** 88416; ● 70
Hope; Inc. Place; EDDY; **206** I-7; elev. 4,086ft./1,245m.; [P]; **z** 88250; Ⓟ 101; © 107
Hospah; RMC Place; MCKINLEY; **206** D-3; mail Crownpoint **z** 87313; ● 160
Hot Springs; RMC Place; SAN MIGUEL; ***206** D-7; elev. 6,760ft./2,060m.; mail Montezuma **z** 87731; ● 100
Hot Springs; SIERRA; see Truth or Consequences (Inc. Place)
Hot Springs Landing; RMC Place; SIERRA; ***206** H-4; mail Elephant Butte **z** 87935; ● 350
House; Inc. Place; QUAY; **206** F-9; elev. 4,750ft./1,448m.; [P]; **z** 88121; Ⓟ 85; © 72
Huerfano; CDP-Census Area Only; SAN JUAN; ***206** B-3; © 104
Humble City (Kimbrough); RMC Place; LEA; **206** I-10; elev. 3,708ft./1,130m.; mail Hobbs **z** 88240; ● 50
Hurley; Inc. Place; GRANT; **206** I-2; elev. 5,700ft./1,737m.; [P]; **z** 88043; Ⓟ 1,534; © 1,464
Hyde Park Estates; RMC Place; SANTA FE; ***206** D-6; ★ **S.FE**; mail Santa Fe **z** 87501; ● 100

I

Idlewild; RMC Place; COLFAX; ***206** B-7; mail Eagle Nest **z** 87718; summer pop. 350; ● 10
Ilfeld; RMC Place; SAN MIGUEL; **206** D-6; elev. 6,535ft./1,992m.; [P]; **z** 87538; ● 100
Ima; RMC Place; QUAY; ***206** E-8; mail Cuervo **z** 88417; rural
Indian Hills; RMC Place; LINCOLN; mail Ruidoso **z** 88345; pop. incl. with Ruidoso (Inc. Place)
Isleta (Isleta Pueblo); RMC Place; BERNALILLO; **206** E-5; elev. 4,893ft./1,491m.; [P]; ★ **ALBU**; **z** 87022; Ⓟ 1,703
Isleta Pueblo; BERNALILLO; see Isleta (RMC Place)
Isleta Pueblo; Indian Reservation; BERNALILLO, TORRANCE, VALENCIA; ★ **ALBU**; mail Isleta **z** 87022; Ⓟ 2,412; © 3,166
Isleta Village Proper; CDP-Census Area Only; BERNALILLO; ***206** E-4; ★ **ALBU**; © 496
Iyanbito; RMC Place; MCKINLEY; ***206** D-2; mail Fort Wingate **z** 87316; rural

J

Jacona; RMC Place; SANTA FE; ***206** C-5; mail Santa Fe **z** 87501, **z** 87506; ● 130
Jaconita; CDP; SANTA FE; ***206** C-5; elev. 5,711ft./1,741m.; [P]; **z** 87506; Ⓟ 375; © 343
Jal; Inc. Place; LEA; **206** J-10; elev. 3,029ft./923m.; [P]; **z** 88252; Ⓟ 2,156; © 1,996
Jamestown; RMC Place; MCKINLEY; ● 240
Jarales; CDP; VALENCIA; ***206** F-4; elev. 4,789ft./1,460m.; [P]; **z** 87023; © 1,434
Jemez Pueblo; CDP; SANDOVAL; **206** D-4; located on Jemez Pueblo Ind. Res.; elev. 5,602ft./1,707m.; [P]; **z** 87024; Ⓟ 1,301; © 1,953
Jemez Pueblo; Indian Reservation; SANDOVAL; [P]; **z** 87024; Ⓟ 1,515; © 1,958
Jemez Springs; Inc. Place; SANDOVAL; **206** D-4; elev. 6,200ft./1,890m.; [P]; **z** 87025; Ⓟ 413; © 375
Jicarilla; RMC Place; LINCOLN; ***206** G-6; [P]; **z** 88301; rural
Jicarilla Apache Reservation; Indian Reservation; SANDOVAL, RIO ARRIBA; mail Dulce **z** 87528; also location of Indian Agency; Ⓟ 1,996; © 2,755
Jordan; RMC Place; QUAY; ***206** E-9; mail Mcalister **z** 88427; rural
Jornada North; RMC Place; DONA ANA; ***206** J-4; ★ **LSCR**; mail Las Cruces **z** 88012; rural
Jornada South; RMC Place; DONA ANA; ***206** J-4; ★ **LSCR**; mail Las Cruces **z** 88011; pop. incl. with Las Cruces (Inc. Place)
Juan Tomas; RMC Place; BERNALILLO; ***206** E-5; mail Tijeras **z** 87059; rural
June Acres; RMC Place; DONA ANA; ***206** J-4; ★ **LSCR**; mail Las Cruces **z** 88011; pop. incl. with Las Cruces (Inc. Place)
Junta; RIO ARRIBA; see La Junta (RMC Place)

K

Kenna; RMC Place; ROOSEVELT; **206** G-9; elev. 4,200ft./1,280m.; [P]; **z** 88122; ● 25
Kimbeto; RMC Place; SAN JUAN; ***206** C-3; mail Nageezi **z** 87037; rural
Kimbrough; LEA; see Humble City (RMC Place)
Kingston; RMC Place; SIERRA; **206** I-3; mail Hillsboro **z** 88042; ● 60
Kingswood; RMC Place; LINCOLN; mail Ruidoso **z** 88345; pop. incl. with Ruidoso (Inc. Place)
Kirtland; CDP; SAN JUAN; **206** B-2; elev. 5,180ft./1,579m.; [P]; ★ **FARM**; **z** 87417; Ⓟ 3,552; © 6,190
Knowles; RMC Place; LEA; ***206** I-10; mail Hobbs **z** 88240; rural

L

La Bolsa; RMC Place; RIO ARRIBA; ***206** C-6; mail Embudo **z** 87531; rural
La Canova; RIO ARRIBA; see Canova (RMC Place)
La Cienega; CDP; SANTA FE; **206** D-5; ★ **S.FE**; mail Santa Fe **z** 87507; Ⓟ 1,066; © 3,007
La Constancia; RMC Place; VALENCIA; ***206** F-4; elev. 4,829ft./1,472m.; ★ **ALBU**; mail Belen **z** 87002; rural
La Cueva; RMC Place; MORA; ***206** C-7; mail Buena Vista **z** 87712; rural
La Cueva; RMC Place; SANTA FE; ***206** D-6; mail Glorieta **z** 87535; rural
La Fraqua; RMC Place; SAN MIGUEL; ***206** D-6; mail Ribera **z** 87560; ● 50
Laguna; CIBOLA; see New Laguna (RMC Place)
Laguna (Laguna Pueblo); CDP; CIBOLA; **206** E-3; located on Laguna Pueblo Ind. Res.; elev. 5,860ft./1,786m.; [P]; **z** 87026; location of Indian Agency; Ⓟ 434; © 423
Laguna Pueblo; CIBOLA; see Laguna (CDP)
Laguna Pueblo; Indian Reservation; CIBOLA, BERNALILLO, SANDOVAL, VALENCIA; mail Laguna **z** 87026; also location of Indian Agency; © 3,815
Lagunita; RMC Place; SAN MIGUEL; ***206** D-7; mail Ribera **z** 87560; rural
La Huerta; RMC Place; EDDY; ***206** J-8; elev. 3,113ft./949m.; mail Carlsbad **z** 88220
La Jara; CDP; SANDOVAL; **206** C-4; elev. 7,124ft./2,171m.; [P]; **z** 87027; © 209
La Joya; RMC Place; SOCORRO; **206** F-4; elev. 4,740ft./1,445m.; [P]; **z** 87028; ● 120
La Junta (Junta); RMC Place; RIO ARRIBA; ***206** C-6; elev. 5,871ft./1,789m.; mail Embudo **z** 87531; rural
Lake Arthur; Inc. Place; CHAVES; **206** I-8; elev. 3,378ft./1,030m.; [P]; **z** 88253; Ⓟ 336; © 432
Lake Sumner; CDP; DE BACA; ***206** F-8; [P]; **z** 88119; © 86
Lake Valley; RMC Place; SAN JUAN; **206** C-2; mail Crownpoint **z** 87313; ● 300
Lake View Pines; RMC Place; COLFAX; ***206** B-7; mail Eagle Nest **z** 87718; summer pop. 120
Lakewood; RMC Place; EDDY; **206** I-8; elev. 3,291ft./1,003m.; [P]; **z** 88254; ● 100
La Ladera; RMC Place; VALENCIA; ***206** F-4; ★ **ALBU**; mail Los Lunas **z** 87031; rural
La Loma; GUADALUPE; see Llano Viejo (RMC Place)
La Luz; CDP; OTERO; **206** I-6; elev. 4,744ft./1,446m.; [P]; **z** 88337; Ⓟ 1,625; © 1,615
Lama; RMC Place; TAOS; ***206** B-6; mail Questa **z** 87556; ● 35
LaMadera; RMC Place; RIO ARRIBA; **206** C-5; elev. 6,500ft./1,981m.; [P]; **z** 87539; ● 200
La Madera; RMC Place; SANDOVAL; ***206** E-5; elev. 6,922ft./2,110m.; mail Sandia Park **z** 87047; ● 100
La Manga; RMC Place; SAN MIGUEL; ***206** D-7; mail Las Vegas **z** 87701; rural
La Mesa; RMC Place; DONA ANA; **206** J-4; elev. 3,825ft./1,166m.; [P]; **z** 88044; ● 1,000
La Mesilla; DONA ANA; see Mesilla (Inc. Place)
La Mesilla; RIO ARRIBA; see Mesilla (RMC Place)
Lamy; CDP; SANTA FE; **206** D-6; elev. 6,482ft./1,976m.; [P]; **z** 87540; © 137
La Plata; RMC Place; SAN JUAN; **206** B-2; elev. 5,781ft./1,762m.; [P]; **z** 87418; ● 100
La Puebla; CDP; SANTA FE; ***206** C-6; mail Espanola **z** 87532; © 1,296
La Puente; RMC Place; RIO ARRIBA; **206** B-5; mail Tierra Amarilla **z** 87575; ● 80
Las Collinas; RMC Place; DONA ANA; ***206** J-4; ★ **LSCR**; mail Las Cruces **z** 88012; pop. incl. with Las Cruces (Inc. Place)
Las Cruces; Inc. Place; ⊡ DONA ANA; **206** J-4; elev. 3,896ft./1,188m.; [P] [H] [C] 16,415 ■; ★ **LSCR**; **z** 88001-07, **z** 88011-13; Ⓟ 62,126; © 74,267; Ⓡ 73,539; ◆ 90,821
Las Dispensas; RMC Place; SAN MIGUEL; ***206** D-6; mail Sapello **z** 87745; rural
La Senda; RMC Place; LOS ALAMOS; ***206** D-5; mail Los Alamos **z** 87544
Las Mochas; RMC Place; TAOS; ***206** C-6; mail Vadito **z** 87579; summer pop. 100; ● 30
Las Nutrias (Nutrias); RMC Place; RIO ARRIBA; ***206** B-5; mail Tierra Amarilla **z** 87575; rural
Las Nutrias; RMC Place; SOCORRO; **206** F-4; mail Veguita **z** 87062; ● 35
Las Palomas; RMC Place; SIERRA; ***206** I-4; mail Williamsburg **z** 87942
Las Placitas; RMC Place; RIO ARRIBA; ***206** C-5; elev. 6,672ft./2,034m.; mail El Rito **z** 87530
Las Tablas; RMC Place; RIO ARRIBA; **206** B-5; elev. 7,530ft./2,295m.; [P]; **z** 87581; ● 25
Las Trampas; TAOS; see Trampas (RMC Place)
Las Tusas; RMC Place; SAN MIGUEL; ***206** D-7; mail Sapello **z** 87745; rural
Las Vegas; Inc. Place; ⊡ SAN MIGUEL; **206** D-7; elev. 6,436ft./1,962m.; [P] [H] [C] 3,726; **z** 87701, **z** 87745; Ⓟ 14,753; © 14,565
La Union; RMC Place; DONA ANA; **206** K-5; ★ **ELP**; mail Anthony **z** 88021; ● 700
La Villita; RMC Place; RIO ARRIBA; ***206** C-5; elev. 5,701ft./1,738m.; mail Alcalde **z** 87511; ● 80
LEA; **206** H-9; Ⓟ 55,765; © 55,511; ◆ 60,281
Ledoux; RMC Place; MORA; **206** C-6; elev. 7,419ft./2,261m.; [P]; **z** 87732; ● 175
Lemitar; RMC Place; SOCORRO; **206** G-4; elev. 4,673ft./1,424m.; [P]; **z** 87823; ● 450
Lesbia; RMC Place; QUAY; ***206** E-9; elev. 3,991ft./1,216m.; mail Tucumcari **z** 88401; rural
Levy; RMC Place; MORA; ***206** C-7; mail Wagon Mound **z** 87752; rural
Leyba; RMC Place; SAN MIGUEL; ***206** E-6; elev. 6,380ft./1,945m.; mail Ribera **z** 87560; rural
Lincoln; RMC Place; LINCOLN; **206** H-6; elev. 5,720ft./1,743m.; [P]; **z** 88338; ● 130
LINCOLN; **206** G-6; Ⓟ 12,219; © 19,411; ◆ 20,435
Lindrith; RMC Place; RIO ARRIBA; **206** C-4; elev. 7,249ft./2,209m.; [P]; **z** 87029; ● 50
Lingo; RMC Place; ROOSEVELT; **206** G-10; elev. 3,982ft./1,214m.; [P]; **z** 88123; ● 20
Little Walnut Village; RMC Place; GRANT; ***206** I-2; mail Silver City **z** 88061; ● 100
Little Water; RMC Place; SAN JUAN; ***206** B-2; located on Navajo Nation Ind. Res.; mail Shiprock **z** 87420; rural
Llano; RMC Place; TAOS; ***206** C-6; elev. 8,140ft./2,481m.; [P]; **z** 87543; ● 160
Llano del Medio; RMC Place; GUADALUPE; ***206** E-7; mail La Loma **z** 87724
Llano Largo; RMC Place; TAOS; ***206** C-6; rural
Llano Quemado; RMC Place; TAOS; ***206** C-6; mail Ranchos De Taos **z** 87557; ● 400
Llano Viejo (La Loma); RMC Place; GUADALUPE; ***206** E-7; elev. 5,220ft./1,591m.; mail La Loma **z** 87724; ● 120
Llaves; RMC Place; RIO ARRIBA; ***206** C-4; elev. 7,013ft./2,138m.; mail La Jara **z** 87027; rural
Loco Hills; RMC Place; EDDY; **206** I-9; elev. 3,646ft./1,111m.; [P]; **z** 88255; ● 250
Logan; Inc. Place; QUAY; **206** D-9; elev. 3,819ft./1,164m.; [P]; **z** 88426; Ⓟ 870; © 1,094
Lordsburg; Inc. Place; ⊡ HIDALGO; **206** J-1; elev. 4,258ft./1,298m.; [P]; **z** 88009, **z** 88045, **z** 88055; Ⓟ 2,951; © 3,379
Los Alamos; CDP; ⊡ LOS ALAMOS; **206** C-5; elev. 7,300ft./2,225m.; [P] [H]; **z** 87544-45; Ⓟ 11,455; © 11,909
Los Alamos; RMC Place; SAN MIGUEL; ***206** D-7; mail Sapello **z** 87745; rural
LOS ALAMOS; **206** C-5; Ⓟ 18,115; © 18,343; ◆ 18,079
Los Brazos; RIO ARRIBA; see Brazos (RMC Place)
Los Candelarias; RMC Place; BERNALILLO; ***206** E-5; ★ **ALBU**; mail Albuquerque **z** 87107; pop. incl. with Albuquerque (Inc. Place)
Los Cerrillos; CDP-Census Area Only; SANTA FE; **206** D-5; elev. 5,888ft./1,795m.; mail Cerrillos **z** 87010; © 229
Los Chaves (Los Chavez); CDP; VALENCIA; **206** F-4; elev. 4,822ft./1,470m.; mail Belen **z** 87002; Ⓟ 3,872; © 5,033
Los Chavez; VALENCIA; see Los Chaves (CDP)
Los Cordovas; RMC Place; TAOS; ***206** C-6; elev. 6,742ft./2,055m.; mail Taos **z** 87571; ● 150
Los Duranes; RMC Place; BERNALILLO; ***206** E-5; ★ **ALBU**; mail Albuquerque **z** 87104; pop. incl. with Albuquerque (Inc. Place)
Los Febres; RMC Place; MORA; ***206** C-7; mail Ocate **z** 87734; rural
Los Griegos; RMC Place; BERNALILLO; ***206** E-5; ★ **ALBU**; mail Albuquerque **z** 87107; pop. incl. with Albuquerque (Inc. Place)
Los Hueros; RMC Place; MORA; ***206** C-7; mail Ocate **z** 87734; rural
Los Lentes; RMC Place; VALENCIA; ***206** E-4; elev. 4,855ft./1,480m.; ★ **ALBU**; mail Los Lunas **z** 87031; pop. incl. with Los Lunas (Inc. Place)
Los Luceros; RMC Place; RIO ARRIBA; ***206** C-5; mail Alcalde **z** 87511; rural
Los Lunas; Inc. Place; ⊡ VALENCIA; **206** E-4; elev. 4,852ft./1,479m.; [P] [H]; ★ **ALBU**; **z** 87031; Ⓟ 6,013; © 10,034
Los Montoyas; RMC Place; SAN MIGUEL; ***206** D-7; mail Las Vegas **z** 87701
Los Ojos (Park View); RMC Place; RIO ARRIBA; ***206** B-5; elev. 7,348ft./2,240m.; [P]; **z** 87551; ● 250
Los Pachecos; RMC Place; RIO ARRIBA; ***206** C-6; mail Chimayo **z** 87522, Pecos **z** 87552
Los Padillas; RMC Place; BERNALILLO; **206** E-4; ★ **ALBU**; mail Albuquerque **z** 87105; ● 2,500
Los Pinos; RMC Place; RIO ARRIBA; **206** A-5; elev. 8,043ft./2,452m.; mail Antonito **z** 81120; ● 25
Los Ranchitos; GUADALUPE; see Upper Anton Chico (RMC Place)
Los Ranchos; RMC Place; BERNALILLO; ***206** E-5; ★ **ALBU**; mail Albuquerque **z** 87101; pop. incl. with Los Ranchos de Albuquerque (Inc. Place)
Los Ranchos de Albuquerque; Inc. Place; BERNALILLO; **206** L-8; elev. 4,988ft./1,520m.; [P]; ★ **ALBU**; **z** 87107, **z** 87114; Ⓟ 3,955; © 5,092
Lost Lodge; RMC Place; OTERO; ***206** I-6; elev. 8,700ft./2,652m.; mail Cloudcroft **z** 88317; ● 35
Los Trujillos; RMC Place; VALENCIA; ***206** F-4; ★ **ALBU**; mail Belen **z** 87002; ● 250
Los Trujillos-Gabaldon; CDP-Census Area Only; VALENCIA; ***206** F-4; elev. 4,803ft./1,464m.; ★ **ALBU**; mail Belen **z** 87002; Ⓟ 1,841; © 2,166
Los Vigiles; RMC Place; SAN MIGUEL; ***206** D-7; mail Las Vegas **z** 87701; ● 50
Lourdes; RMC Place; SAN MIGUEL; mail Las Vegas **z** 87701; rural
Lovato; RMC Place; SAN MIGUEL; ***206** E-6; mail Ribera **z** 87560; ● 30
Loving; Inc. Place; EDDY; **206** J-8; elev. 3,050ft./930m.; [P]; **z** 88256; Ⓟ 1,243; © 1,326
Lovington; Inc. Place; ⊡ LEA; **206** I-10; elev. 3,909ft./1,191m.; [P] [H]; **z** 88260; Ⓟ 9,322; © 9,471
Lower Colonias (Pine); RMC Place; SAN MIGUEL; ***206** D-6; mail Pecos **z** 87552; rural
Lower La Posada; RMC Place; SAN MIGUEL; ***206** D-6; mail Pecos **z** 87552; rural
Lower Nutria; RMC Place; MCKINLEY; ***206** E-2; located on Zuni Ind. Res.; mail Zuni **z** 87327
Lower Pueblo (El Barranco); RMC Place; SAN MIGUEL; ***206** D-6; mail Ribera **z** 87560; rural
Lower Ranchito; RMC Place; TAOS; ***206** B-6; mail Vallecitos **z** 87581; rural
Lower Rociada; RMC Place; SAN MIGUEL; mail Rociada **z** 87742; rural
Lucero; RMC Place; MORA; ***206** C-7; elev. 7,126ft./2,172m.; mail Rainsville **z** 87736; rural
Lucy; RMC Place; TORRANCE; ***206** F-6; elev. 6,181ft./1,884m.; mail Willard **z** 87063; rural
Luis Lopez; RMC Place; SOCORRO; **206** G-4; mail Socorro **z** 87801; ● 200
Lumberton; RMC Place; RIO ARRIBA; **206** B-4; elev. 6,845ft./2,086m.; [P]; **z** 87528; ● 100
Luna; RMC Place; CATRON; **206** G-1; elev. 7,040ft./2,146m.; [P]; **z** 87824; ● 200
LUNA; **206** J-2; Ⓟ 18,110; © 25,016; ◆ 27,463
Lybrook; RMC Place; RIO ARRIBA; ***206** C-3; mail Cuba **z** 87013; rural
Lyden; RMC Place; RIO ARRIBA; ***206** C-5; elev. 5,724ft./1,745m.; mail Velarde **z** 87582; ● 120

M

Macimiliano Luna (Camp Luna); RMC Place; SAN MIGUEL; ***206** D-7; mail Las Vegas **z** 87701; ● 300
Madrid; CDP; SANTA FE; **206** D-5; [P]; **z** 87010; © 149
Maes; RMC Place; SAN MIGUEL; ***206** D-8; elev. 6,068ft./1,850m.; mail Las Vegas **z** 87701; rural
Magdalena; Inc. Place; SOCORRO; **206** G-4; elev. 6,573ft./2,003m.; [P]; **z** 87825; Ⓟ 861; © 913
Malaga; RMC Place; EDDY; **206** J-8; elev. 3,003ft./915m.; [P]; **z** 88263; ● 150
Maljamar; RMC Place; LEA; **206** I-9; elev. 4,041ft./1,232m.; [P]; **z** 88264; ● 200
Mangas; RMC Place; CATRON; ***206** G-2; elev. 7,340ft./2,237m.; mail Datil **z** 87821; rural
Mangas Springs; RMC Place; GRANT; ***206** I-2; mail Silver City **z** 88061; rural
Manuelitas; RMC Place; SAN MIGUEL; ***206** D-7; mail Sapello **z** 87745; rural
Manuelito; RMC Place; MCKINLEY; ***206** D-1; [P]; **z** 87301 & mail Mentmore **z** 87319
Manzano; RMC Place; BERNALILLO; ★ **ALBU**; mail Albuquerque **z** 87112, **z** 87153, **z** 87192; pop. incl. with Albuquerque (Inc. Place)
Manzano; CDP; TORRANCE; **206** F-5; elev. 6,857ft./2,090m.; mail Mountainair **z** 87036; © 54
Mariano Lake; RMC Place; MCKINLEY; ***206** D-2; mail Gallup **z** 87301
Maxwell; Inc. Place; COLFAX; **206** B-8; elev. 5,931ft./1,808m.; [P]; **z** 87728; Ⓟ 247; © 274
Mayhill; RMC Place; OTERO; **206** I-6; elev. 6,561ft./2,000m.; [P]; **z** 88339; ● 280
McAlister; RMC Place; QUAY; **206** F-9; elev. 4,724ft./1,440m.; [P]; **z** 88427; ● 60
McCartys; RMC Place; CIBOLA; **206** E-3; located on Acoma Pueblo Ind. Res.; mail San Fidel **z** 87049; ● 300
McDonald; RMC Place; LEA; **206** H-10; elev. 3,962ft./1,208m.; [P]; **z** 88262; ● 50
McGaffey; RMC Place; MCKINLEY; ***206** D-2; mail Fort Wingate **z** 87316
McIntosh; RMC Place; TORRANCE; **206** E-5; elev. 6,140ft./1,871m.; [P]; **z** 87032; ● 100
MCKINLEY; **206** D-3; Ⓟ 60,686; © 74,798; ◆ 66,298
McNew; RMC Place; EDDY; ***206** J-8; mail Carlsbad **z** 88220; ● 100
Meadow Lake; CDP; VALENCIA; ***206** E-5; elev. 5,450ft./1,661m.; mail Los Lunas **z** 87031; Ⓟ 1,590; © 4,491
Meadow Vista; DONA ANA; see Sunland Park (Inc. Place)
Medanales; RMC Place; RIO ARRIBA; **206** C-5; elev. 5,840ft./1,780m.; [P]; **z** 87548; ● 200
Melrose; Inc. Place; CURRY; **206** F-9; elev. 4,400ft./1,341m.; [P]; **z** 88124; Ⓟ 662; © 736
Mentmore; RMC Place; MCKINLEY; **206** D-1; elev. 6,420ft./1,957m.; [P]; **z** 87319; ● 200
Mesa Poleo; RMC Place; RIO ARRIBA; mail Coyote **z** 87012; rural
Mescalero; CDP; OTERO; **206** H-6; located on Mescalero Ind. Res.; elev. 6,605ft./2,013m.; [P] [H]; **z** 88340; location of Indian Agency; Ⓟ 1,159; © 1,233
Mescalero Reservation; Indian Reservation; OTERO, LINCOLN; mail Mescalero **z** 88340; also location of Indian Agency; Ⓟ 2,101; © 3,156
Mesilla (La Mesilla); Inc. Place; DONA ANA; **206** J-4; elev. 3,888ft./1,185m.; [P]; ★ **LSCR**; **z** 88046; Ⓟ 1,975; © 2,180
Mesilla (La Mesilla); RMC Place; RIO ARRIBA; ***206** C-5; mail Espanola **z** 87532
Mesilla Park; RMC Place; DONA ANA; ***206** J-4; elev. 3,877ft./1,182m.; [P]; ★ **LSCR**; **z** 88047; pop. incl. with Las Cruces (Inc. Place)
Mesita; CDP; CIBOLA; ***206** E-4; located on Laguna Pueblo Ind. Res.; mail Laguna **z** 87026; Ⓟ 627; © 776
Mesquite; CDP; DONA ANA; **206** J-4; elev. 3,836ft./1,169m.; [P]; **z** 88048 & mail Vado **z** 88072; © 948
Mexican Springs; MCKINLEY; see Nakaibito (CDP-Census Area Only)
Miami; RMC Place; COLFAX; **206** C-7; elev. 6,196ft./1,889m.; [P]; **z** 87729; ● 100
Mid Valley Air Park; RMC Place; VALENCIA; ***206** E-4; ★ **ALBU**; mail Los Lunas **z** 87031; ● 150
Midway; RMC Place; CHAVES; ***206** H-8; ★ **RSWL**; mail Dexter **z** 88230; ● 250
Miera; RMC Place; BERNALILLO; ***206** E-5; mail Tijeras **z** 87059; rural
Milagro; RMC Place; GUADALUPE; ***206** E-7; mail Encino **z** 88321; rural
Milan; Inc. Place; CIBOLA; **206** E-3; elev. 6,520ft./1,987m.; [P]; **z** 87021; Ⓟ 1,911; © 1,891
Mills; RMC Place; HARDING; **206** C-8; elev. 6,120ft./1,865m.; [P]; **z** 87730; ● 50
Milnesand; RMC Place; ROOSEVELT; **206** G-10; elev. 4,188ft./1,277m.; [P]; **z** 88125; ● 30
Mimbres; RMC Place; GRANT; **206** I-2; elev. 5,970ft./1,820m.; [P]; **z** 88049; ● 100
Mimbres Hot Springs; RMC Place; GRANT; mail Hanover **z** 88041; rural
Mineral Hill; RMC Place; SAN MIGUEL; ***206** D-6; mail Las Vegas **z** 87701
Mission Park; RMC Place; VALENCIA; ***206** E-5; mail Los Lunas **z** 87031; ● 200
Mogollon; RMC Place; CATRON; **206** H-1; [P]; **z** 88039; ● 60
Monero; RMC Place; RIO ARRIBA; ***206** B-4; elev. 7,325ft./2,233m.; mail Dulce **z** 87528
Monte Aplanado; RMC Place; MORA; ***206** C-6; elev. 7,763ft./2,366m.; mail Mora **z** 87732; rural
Monte Verde; RMC Place; COLFAX; mail Angel Fire **z** 87710; pop. incl. with Angel Fire (Inc. Place)
Montezuma; RMC Place; SAN MIGUEL; **206** D-7; elev. 6,744ft./2,056m.; [P]; **z** 87731; ● 200
Monticello; RMC Place; SIERRA; **206** H-3; elev. 5,240ft./1,597m.; [P]; **z** 87939; ● 60
Montoya; RMC Place; QUAY; **206** E-8; elev. 4,320ft./1,317m.; mail Tucumcari **z** 88401; ● 25
Monument; RMC Place; LEA; **206** I-10; elev. 3,573ft./1,089m.; [P]; **z** 88265; ● 100
Moqino; RMC Place; CIBOLA; ***206** E-3; elev. 6,120ft./1,865m.; mail Paguate **z** 87040; ● 40
Mora; RMC Place; ⊡ MORA; **206** C-6; elev. 7,179ft./2,188m.; [P]; **z** 87732; ● 1,200
MORA; **206** C-7; Ⓟ 4,264; © 5,180; ◆ 5,045
Moriarty; Inc. Place; TORRANCE; **206** E-5; elev. 6,217ft./1,895m.; [P]; **z** 87035; Ⓟ 1,399; © 1,765
Mosquero; Inc. Place; ⊡ HARDING, SAN MIGUEL; **206** D-9; elev. 5,688ft./1,734m.; [P]; **z** 87733; Ⓟ 164; © 120
Mountainair; Inc. Place; TORRANCE; **206** F-5; elev. 6,499ft./1,981m.; [P]; **z** 87036; Ⓟ 926; © 1,116
Mountain Park; RMC Place; OTERO; **206** I-6; elev. 6,940ft./2,115m.; mail High Rolls Mountain Park **z** 88325; ● 200
Mountain View; RMC Place; BERNALILLO; ***206** E-5; elev. 4,948ft./1,508m.; ★ **ALBU**; mail Albuquerque **z** 87105; ● 2,350
Mountain View; RMC Place; CHAVES; ***206** H-8; ★ **RSWL**; mail Roswell **z** 88201; pop. incl. with Roswell (Inc. Place)
Mount Dora; RMC Place; UNION; **206** B-9; elev. 5,700ft./1,737m.; [P]; **z** 88424; ● 100
Mule Creek; RMC Place; GRANT; **206** H-1; elev. 5,217ft./1,590m.; [P]; **z** 88051; ● 25

N

Nadine; RMC Place; LEA; ***206** I-10; mail Hobbs **z** 88240; ● 120
Nageezi; CDP; SAN JUAN; **206** C-3; elev. 6,920ft./2,109m.; [P]; **z** 87037; © 296
Nakaibito (Mexican Springs); CDP-Census Area Only; MCKINLEY; **206** D-1; located on Navajo Nation Ind. Res.; elev. 6,440ft./1,963m.; mail Mexican Springs **z** 87320; Ⓟ 242; © 455
Nambe; RMC Place; SANTA FE; **206** C-6; located on Nambe Pueblo Ind. Res.; [P]; **z** 87506 & mail Santa Fe **z** 87501; Ⓟ 1,246
Nambe Pueblo; RMC Place; SANTA FE; ***206** C-6; located on Nambe Pueblo Ind. Res.; mail Santa Fe **z** 87506
Nambe Pueblo; Indian Reservation; SANTA FE; mail Santa Fe **z** 87506; Ⓟ 386; © 1,764
Napi HQ; CDP-Census Area Only; SAN JUAN; ***206** B-2; © 706
Nara Visa; RMC Place; QUAY; **206** D-10; elev. 4,187ft./1,276m.; [P]; **z** 88430; ● 200
Naschitti; CDP; SAN JUAN; **206** C-2; located on Navajo Nation Ind. Res.; mail Tohatchi **z** 87325; Ⓟ 323; © 360
Navajo; CDP; MCKINLEY; **206** C-1; located on Navajo Nation Ind. Res.; elev. 7,083ft./2,159m.; [P]; **z** 87328; Ⓟ 1,985; © 2,097
Navajo Dam (Archuleta); RMC Place; SAN JUAN; ***206** B-3; elev. 5,704ft./1,739m.; [P]; **z** 87419; ● 100
Navajo Estates; RMC Place; MCKINLEY; ***206** D-1; elev. 6,630ft./2,021m.; mail Yatahey **z** 87375; ● 300
Navajo Nation Reservation; Indian Reservation; SAN JUAN, BERNALILLO, CIBOLA, MCKINLEY, SANDOVAL, SOCORRO; Reservation extends into AZ and UT; mail Window Rock **z** 86515; Ⓟ 29,604; © 44,636
Navajo Wingate Village; RMC Place; MCKINLEY; mail Church Rock **z** 87311
Nenahnezad; CDP-Census Area Only; SAN JUAN; ***206** B-2; ★ **FARM**; © 726
Newcomb (Drolet); CDP; SAN JUAN; **206** C-2; located on Navajo Nation Ind. Res.; elev. 5,560ft./1,695m.; [P]; **z** 87455; Ⓟ 388; © 387
Newkirk; RMC Place; GUADALUPE; **206** E-8; elev. 4,557ft./1,389m.; [P]; **z** 88431; ● 60
New Laguna (Laguna); RMC Place; CIBOLA; ***206** E-3; located on Laguna Pueblo Ind. Res.; elev. 5,872ft./1,790m.; [P]; **z** 87038 & mail Laguna **z** 87026; ● 160
New York; RMC Place; CIBOLA; ***206** E-3; located on Laguna Pueblo Ind. Res.; mail Cubero **z** 87014; rural
Nogal; RMC Place; LINCOLN; **206** H-6; elev. 6,476ft./1,974m.; [P]; **z** 88341; ● 150
North Acomita Village; CDP-Census Area Only; CIBOLA; ***206** E-3; elev. 6,100ft./1,859m.; mail Pueblo of Acoma **z** 87034; Ⓟ 314; © 288
North Carmen; RMC Place; MORA; ***206** C-6; mail Mora **z** 87732; rural
North Hurley; RMC Place; GRANT; ***206** I-2; mail Hurley **z** 88043; ● 170
North San Ysidro; RMC Place; SAN MIGUEL; ***206** D-6; mail Ilfeld **z** 87538; ● 120
North Valley; CDP-Census Area Only; BERNALILLO; ***206** E-5; ★ **ALBU**; mail Albuquerque **z** 87107, **z** 87109; Ⓟ 12,507; © 11,923
Nutrias; RIO ARRIBA; see Las Nutrias (RMC Place)

O

Ocate; RMC Place; MORA; **206** C-7; elev. 7,200ft./2,195m.; [P]; **z** 87734; ● 50
Oil Center; RMC Place; LEA; ***206** J-10; elev. 3,580ft./1,091m.; [P]; **z** 88240
Ojito; RMC Place; RIO ARRIBA; ***206** B-4; mail Lindrith **z** 87029
Ojito; RMC Place; TAOS; ***206** C-6; elev. 8,048ft./2,453m.; mail Chamisal **z** 87521; ● 30
Ojitos Frios; RMC Place; SAN MIGUEL; ***206** D-7; mail Las Vegas **z** 87701; rural
Ojitos Frios; SAN MIGUEL; see Gabaldon (RMC Place)
Ojo Amarillo; CDP-Census Area Only; SAN JUAN; ***206** B-2; elev. 5,449ft./1,661m.; ★ **FARM**; mail Kirtland **z** 87417; Ⓟ 955; © 829
Ojo Caliente; RMC Place; CIBOLA; ***206** E-1; located on Zuni Ind. Res.; mail Zuni **z** 87327; summer pop. 600
Ojo Caliente; RMC Place; TAOS; **206** C-5; elev. 6,261ft./1,908m.; [P]; **z** 87549; ● 350
Ojo Feliz; RMC Place; MORA; **206** C-7; elev. 7,540ft./2,298m.; [P]; **z** 87735; ● 75
Ojo Sarco; RMC Place; RIO ARRIBA; **206** C-6; elev. 7,400ft./2,256m.; [P]; **z** 87521; ● 120
Old Albuquerque (Old Town); RMC Place; BERNALILLO; ***206** E-5; ★ **ALBU**; mail Albuquerque **z** 87104, **z** 87194; pop. incl. with Albuquerque (Inc. Place)
Old Horse Springs; RMC Place; CATRON; ***206** G-2; mail Datil **z** 87821
Old Picacho; RMC Place; DONA ANA; **206** M-1; ★ **LSCR**; mail Fairacres **z** 88033; ● 200
Old Town; BERNALILLO; see Old Albuquerque (RMC Place)
Omega; RMC Place; CATRON; **206** F-2; elev. 7,109ft./2,167m.; mail Quemado **z** 87829; ● 30
Organ; RMC Place; DONA ANA; **206** J-5; elev. 5,100ft./1,554m.; [P]; ★ **LSCR**; **z** 88052; ● 500
Orogrande; RMC Place; OTERO; **206** J-5; elev. 4,183ft./1,275m.; [P]; **z** 88342; ● 80
Oscura (Oscuro); RMC Place; LINCOLN; ***206** H-5; mail Carrizozo **z** 88301; rural
Oscuro; LINCOLN; see Oscura (RMC Place)
OTERO; **206** I-6; Ⓟ 51,928; © 62,298; ◆ 63,122
Otis; RMC Place; EDDY; **206** J-8; elev. 3,098ft./944m.; mail Carlsbad **z** 88220; ● 150

P

Paguate; CDP; CIBOLA; **206** E-3; located on Laguna Pueblo Ind. Res.; elev. 6,160ft./1,878m.; [P]; **z** 87040; Ⓟ 492; © 474
Pajarito; RMC Place; BERNALILLO; **206** E-4; elev. 4,912ft./1,497m.; ★ **ALBU**; mail Albuquerque **z** 87105; ● 1,500
Pajarito; RMC Place; SANTA FE; ***206** C-5; located on San Ildefonso Pueblo Ind. Res.; mail Espanola **z** 87532; rural
Pajarito Acres; RMC Place; LOS ALAMOS; ***206** D-5; mail Los Alamos **z** 87544
Paradise Hills; RMC Place; BERNALILLO; **206** K-7; elev. 5,350ft./1,631m.; ★ **ALBU**; mail Albuquerque **z** 87114; Ⓟ 5,513
Paraje (Casa Blanca); CDP; CIBOLA; **206** E-3; located on Laguna Pueblo Ind. Res.; elev. 5,920ft./1,804m.; mail Casa Blanca **z** 87007; Ⓟ 622; © 669
Park Springs; RMC Place; SAN MIGUEL; ***206** E-7; mail Las Vegas **z** 87701; rural
Park View; RIO ARRIBA; see Los Ojos (RMC Place)
Pastura; RMC Place; GUADALUPE; **206** E-7; elev. 6,000ft./1,829m.; [P]; **z** 88435; ● 25
Paxton Springs; RMC Place; CIBOLA; ***206** E-2; elev. 7,690ft./2,344m.; mail Grants **z** 87020; rural
Pecos; Inc. Place; SAN MIGUEL; **206** D-6; elev. 6,923ft./2,110m.; [P]; **z** 87552; Ⓟ 1,012; © 1,441
Pena Blanca; CDP; SANDOVAL; **206** D-5; located on Cochiti Pueblo Ind. Res.; elev. 5,238ft./1,597m.; [P]; **z** 87041; Ⓟ 300; © 661
Penasco; CDP; TAOS; **206** C-6; elev. 7,678ft./2,340m.; [P]; **z** 87553; Ⓟ 648; © 572
Penasco Blanco; RMC Place; SAN MIGUEL; ***206** C-6; mail Rociada **z** 87742; rural
Pendaries; RMC Place; SAN MIGUEL; mail Rociada **z** 87742; summer pop. 150
Pep; RMC Place; ROOSEVELT; **206** G-10; elev. 4,237ft./1,291m.; [P]; **z** 88126; ● 25
Peralta; Inc. Place; VALENCIA; **206** E-5; elev. 4,859ft./1,481m.; ★ **ALBU**; incorporated July 1, 2007; not reported in 2000 Census; ● 3,600
Peralta; CDP-Census Area Only; VALENCIA; **206** E-5; elev. 4,859ft./1,481m.; [P]; ★ **ALBU**; **z** 87042, **z** 87068; Ⓟ 3,182; © 3,750
Perea; RMC Place; MCKINLEY; ***206** D-2; mail Fort Wingate **z** 87316; rural
Pescado; RMC Place; MCKINLEY; ***206** E-2; located on Zuni Ind. Res.; mail Zuni **z** 87327; rural
Petaca; RMC Place; RIO ARRIBA; **206** B-5; elev. 7,280ft./2,219m.; [P]; **z** 87554; ● 90
Philadelphia; RMC Place; CIBOLA; ***206** E-3; located on Laguna Pueblo Ind. Res.; mail Cubero **z** 87014; rural
Picacho; RMC Place; LINCOLN; **206** H-7; elev. 4,946ft./1,508m.; [P]; **z** 88343; ● 100
Picuris; TAOS; see Picuris Pueblo (CDP)
Picuris Pueblo (Picuris, San Lorenzo Pueblo); CDP; TAOS; ***206** C-6; located on Picuris Pueblo Ind. Res.; mail Penasco **z** 87553; © 86
Picuris Pueblo; Indian Reservation; TAOS; mail Penasco **z** 87553; Ⓟ 337; © 1,801
Pie Town; RMC Place; CATRON; **206** F-2; elev. 7,778ft./2,371m.; [P]; **z** 87827; ● 70
Pilar; RMC Place; TAOS; **206** C-6; elev. 6,082ft./1,854m.; mail Taos **z** 87571; ● 80
Pine; SAN MIGUEL; see Lower Colonias (RMC Place)
Pinedale; RMC Place; MCKINLEY; ***206** D-2; mail Gallup **z** 87301
Pinehill; CDP-Census Area Only; CIBOLA; **206** E-2; located on Ramah Navajo Ind. Res.; [P]; **z** 87357; © 116
Pine View; RMC Place; TAOS; mail Vadito **z** 87579; rural
Pineywoods Estates; RMC Place; OTERO; mail High Rolls Mountain Park **z** 88325; ● 90
Pino; RMC Place; BERNALILLO; mail Albuquerque **z** 87114, **z** 87120; pop. incl. with Albuquerque (Inc. Place)
Pinon; RMC Place; OTERO; **206** I-6; elev. 6,063ft./1,848m.; [P]; **z** 88344; ● 100
Pinos Altos; RMC Place; GRANT; **206** I-2; elev. 7,040ft./2,146m.; [P]; **z** 88053; ● 200
Pinos Wells; RMC Place; TORRANCE; ***206** F-6; mail Willard **z** 87063; rural
Pintada (Pintado); RMC Place; GUADALUPE; ***206** E-7; mail Santa Rosa **z** 88435; rural
Pintado; GUADALUPE; see Pintada (RMC Place)
Placita; SIERRA; see Placitas (RMC Place)
Placita; TAOS; see Rio Pueblo (RMC Place)
Placitas; RMC Place; DONA ANA; ***206** I-4; elev. 4,080ft./1,244m.; mail Hatch **z** 87937
Placitas; RMC Place; RIO ARRIBA; ***206** B-5; mail Canjilon **z** 87515; rural
Placitas; CDP; SANDOVAL; **206** D-5; elev. 5,900ft./1,798m.; [P]; **z** 87043; Ⓟ 1,611; © 3,452
Placitas (Placita); RMC Place; SIERRA; ***206** H-3; mail Monticello **z** 87939; ● 45
Playas; RMC Place; HIDALGO; **206** J-2; elev. 4,311ft./1,314m.; [P]; **z** 88009; ● 700
Pleasant Hill; RMC Place; CURRY; ***206** F-10; elev. 4,235ft./1,291m.; mail Texico **z** 88135; rural
Pleasanton; RMC Place; CATRON; **206** H-1; mail Glenwood **z** 88039; ● 100
Pojoaque (Pojoaque Valley); CDP; SANTA FE; **206** C-5; elev. 5,600ft./1,707m.; [P]; **z** 87501 & mail Santa Fe **z** 87506; Ⓟ 1,037; © 1,261
Pojoaque Pueblo; SANTA FE; Indian Reservation; mail Santa Fe **z** 87506; Ⓟ 1,191; © 2,712
Pojoaque Valley; SANTA FE; see Pojoaque (CDP)
Polvadera; RMC Place; SOCORRO; **206** F-4; elev. 4,660ft./1,420m.; [P]; **z** 87828; ● 250
Ponderosa; CDP; SANDOVAL; **206** D-5; elev. 6,000ft./1,829m.; [P]; **z** 87044; © 310
Ponderosa Heights; RMC Place; LINCOLN; ***206** H-6; mail Ruidoso **z** 88345; pop. incl. with Ruidoso (Inc. Place)
Ponderosa Pines; RMC Place; BERNALILLO; ***206** E-5; mail Tijeras **z** 87059; rural
Portales; Inc. Place; ⊡ ROOSEVELT; **206** F-10; elev. 4,009ft./1,222m.; [P] [H] [C] 4,135; **z** 88123, **z** 88130; Ⓟ 10,690; © 11,131
Pot Creek; RMC Place; TAOS; ***206** C-6; mail Taos **z** 87571; rural
Potrero (Sanctuario); RMC Place; SANTA FE; ***206** C-6; mail Chimayo **z** 87522; ● 250
Prairieview; RMC Place; LEA; ***206** H-10; mail Lovington **z** 88260; rural
Prewitt (Baca); RMC Place; MCKINLEY; **206** D-3; elev. 6,820ft./2,079m.; [P]; **z** 87045; ● 460
Progresso; RMC Place; TORRANCE; ***206** F-6; mail Willard **z** 87063; rural
Pueblito; RMC Place; RIO ARRIBA; ***206** C-5; mail Ohkay Owingeh **z** 87566; rural
Pueblitos; RMC Place; VALENCIA; ***206** F-4; elev. 4,792ft./1,461m.; mail Belen **z** 87002; ● 120
Pueblo of Acoma; CIBOLA; see Acoma Village (RMC Place)
Pueblo of Sandia Village; CDP-Census Area Only; SANDOVAL; ***206** E-5; ★ **ALBU**; © 344
Pueblo Pintado; CDP; MCKINLEY; **206** C-3; mail Cuba **z** 87013; © 247
Puerto De Luna; RMC Place; GUADALUPE; **206** E-8; elev. 4,500ft./1,372m.; mail Santa Rosa **z** 88435; ● 100
Punta; TORRANCE; see Punta de Agua (RMC Place)
Punta de Agua (Punta); RMC Place; TORRANCE; **206** F-5; mail Mountainair **z** 87036; ● 30

Q

Quarris Acres; RMC Place; OTERO; ***206** I-6; elev. 8,140ft./2,481m.; mail Cloudcroft **z** 88317; ● 30
Quarteles; RMC Place; SANTA FE; ***206** C-5; mail Espanola **z** 87532; rural
Quay; RMC Place; QUAY; ***206** E-9; elev. 4,292ft./1,308m.; [P]; **z** 88433; rural
QUAY; **206** E-9; Ⓟ 10,823; © 10,155; ◆ 8,820
Queen; RMC Place; EDDY; ***206** J-7; mail Carlsbad **z** 88220; rural
Quemado; RMC Place; CATRON; **206** F-2; elev. 6,890ft./2,100m.; [P]; **z** 87829; ● 350
Querinda Park; RMC Place; TAOS; mail Red River **z** 87558; rural
Questa; Inc. Place; TAOS; **206** B-6; elev. 7,392ft./2,253m.; [P]; **z** 87556; Ⓟ 1,707; © 1,864

Entries in **UPPERCASE** are counties.
Entries in **bold** have populations of 2,500 or more.
Names in parentheses are alternate names.
Inc. Place — Incorporated Place
RMC Place — Rand McNally Designated Place
CDP — Census Designated Place
MCD — Minor Civil Division

⊡ County Seat
▲ Minor Civil Division
elev. Elevation
[P] Post Office
[H] Hospital
[C] College
■ Principal Business Center
★ Ranally Metro Area (RMA) Abbreviation
z Zip Code(s)
Ⓟ Previous Census Population
Ⓡ Revised Census Population
Ⓐ Annexation Population
● Rand McNally Population Estimate
© Final Census Population
Ⓢ Special Census Population
◆ Estimated Population

For additional definitions see Glossary, Volume 1, and Introduction, Volume 2.

R

Radium Springs; CDP; DONA ANA; **206** J-4; elev. 4,000ft./1,219m.; 🅿; z 88054; © 1,518
Ragland; RMC Place; QUAY; ***206** E-9; mail Quay z 88433; rural
Rainsville; RMC Place; MORA; **206** C-7; elev. 7,060ft./2,152m.; 🅿; z 87736; ● 150
Ramah; CDP; MCKINLEY; **206** E-2; located on Ramah Navajo Ind. Res.; elev. 6,900ft./2,103m.; 🅿; z 87321, z 87357; location of Indian Agency; © 407
Ramon; RMC Place; LINCOLN; ***206** F-7; mail Yeso z 88136; rural
Ranches of Taos; TAOS; see Ranchos de Taos (CDP)
Ranchito; RMC Place; TAOS; ***206** B-6; elev. 6,840ft./2,085m.; mail Taos z 87571; ● 200
Ranchitos; RMC Place; RIO ARRIBA; ***206** C-5; mail Bernalillo z 87004, Espanola z 87532, Ohkay Owingeh z 87566; pop. incl. with Espanola (Inc. Place)
Rancho Grande Estates; RMC Place; CATRON; ***206** G-1; elev. 6,360ft./1,939m.; mail Reserve z 87830; ● 120
Ranchos de Taos (Ranches of Taos); CDP; TAOS; **206** C-6; elev. 6,920ft./2,109m.; 🅿; z 87557; Ⓟ 1,779; © 2,390
Ranchos Lake Conchas; RMC Place; SAN MIGUEL; mail Newkirk z 88431; rural
Rancho West; RMC Place; SANDOVAL; ★ **ALBU**; mail Rio Rancho z 87124; pop. incl. with Rio Rancho (Inc. Place)
Ranchvale; RMC Place; CURRY; ***206** F-10; elev. 4,485ft./1,367m.; mail Clovis z 88101; rural
Raton; Inc. Place; ⊡ COLFAX; **206** B-8; elev. 6,680ft./2,036m.; 🅿 🅷; z 87740; Ⓟ 7,372; © 7,282
Red Hill; RMC Place; CATRON; **206** F-1; elev. 7,261ft./2,213m.; mail Quemado z 87829; ● 75
Red River; Inc. Place; TAOS; **206** B-6; elev. 8,650ft./2,637m.; 🅿; z 87558; Ⓟ 387; winter pop. 2,500; © 484
Redrock; RMC Place; GRANT; **206** I-1; elev. 4,000ft./1,219m.; 🅿; z 88055; ● 50
Red Rock; RMC Place; MCKINLEY; ***206** D-1; mail Shiprock z 87420; rural
Regina; CDP; SANDOVAL; **206** C-4; elev. 7,500ft./2,286m.; 🅿; z 87046; © 99
Rehoboth; RMC Place; MCKINLEY; **206** D-2; elev. 6,600ft./2,012m.; 🅿; z 87322; ● 200
Rencona; RMC Place; SAN MIGUEL; ***206** D-6; elev. 7,155ft./2,181m.; mail Rowe z 87562; rural
Reserve; Inc. Place; ⊡ CATRON; **206** G-1; elev. 5,749ft./1,752m.; 🅿; z 87830; Ⓟ 319; © 387
Ribera; RMC Place; SAN MIGUEL; **206** D-6; elev. 6,040ft./1,841m.; 🅿; z 87560; ● 150
Rincon; CDP; DONA ANA; **206** I-4; elev. 4,061ft./1,238m.; 🅿; z 87940; © 220
Rinconada; RMC Place; RIO ARRIBA; ***206** C-6; mail Embudo z 87531; rural
Rincon Montoso; RMC Place; SAN MIGUEL; mail Sapello z 87745; rural
RIO ARRIBA; **206** B-4; Ⓟ 34,365; © 41,190; ◆ 40,678
Rio Chiquito; CDP; SANTA FE; ***206** C-6; mail Chimayo z 87522; © 103
Rio Communities; CDP-Census Area Only; VALENCIA; ***206** F-4; elev. 4,904ft./1,495m.; ★ **ALBU**; mail Belen z 87002; Ⓟ 3,233; © 4,213
Rio Communities North; CDP-Census Area Only; VALENCIA; ***206** F-5; © 1,588
Rio en Medio; CDP-Census Area Only; SANTA FE; ***206** D-6; © 131
Rio Grande Estates; RMC Place; VALENCIA; ***206** F-4; ★ **ALBU**; mail Belen z 87002; ● 1,500
Rio Lucio; CDP; TAOS; ***206** C-6; located on Picuris Pueblo Ind. Res.; elev. 7,267ft./2,215m.; mail Penasco z 87553; © 379
Rio Pueblo (Placita); RMC Place; TAOS; ***206** C-6; mail Vadito z 87579; ● 50
Rio Puerco; RMC Place; RIO ARRIBA; ***206** C-5; mail Youngsville z 87064; rural
Rio Rancho (Rio Rancho Estates); Inc. Place; SANDOVAL, BERNALILLO; **206** E-5; elev. 5,300ft./1,615m.; 🅿; ★ **ALBU**; z 87124, z 87144, z 87174; Ⓟ 32,505; © 51,765; ◆ 84,140
Rio Rancho Estates; SANDOVAL, BERNALILLO; see Rio Rancho (Inc. Place)
Rito de las Sillas; RMC Place; RIO ARRIBA; ***206** C-5; mail Youngsville z 87064; rural
Riverside; RMC Place; EDDY; **206** I-8; mail Artesia z 88210; ● 80
Riverside; RMC Place; GRANT; ***206** I-2; mail Cliff z 88028; rural
Riverside; RMC Place; LINCOLN; ***206** H-7; elev. 4,817ft./1,468m.; mail Roswell z 88201; rural
Road Forks; RMC Place; HIDALGO; ***206** J-1; 🅿; z 88045; ● 50
Robin Hood Park; RMC Place; OTERO; ***206** I-6; elev. 7,640ft./2,329m.; mail Mayhill z 88339; ● 100
Rociada; RMC Place; SAN MIGUEL; **206** C-6; elev. 7,543ft./2,299m.; 🅿; z 87742; ● 80
Rock Canyon; RMC Place; SIERRA; ***206** H-4; elev. 4,512ft./1,375m.; mail Elephant Butte z 87935; ● 100
Rock Springs; CDP-Census Area Only; MCKINLEY; ***206** D-1; mail Yatahey z 87375; © 558
Rodarte; RMC Place; TAOS; ***206** C-6; elev. 7,911ft./2,411m.; mail Vadito z 87579; ● 150
Rodeo; RMC Place; HIDALGO; **206** K-1; elev. 4,128ft./1,258m.; 🅿; z 88056; ● 200
Rodey; RMC Place; DONA ANA; ***206** I-4; mail Hatch z 87937; ● 200
Rogers; RMC Place; ROOSEVELT; **206** G-10; elev. 4,223ft./1,287m.; 🅿; z 88132; ● 50
Romeroville; RMC Place; SAN MIGUEL; ***206** D-7; mail Las Vegas z 87701
ROOSEVELT; **206** G-9; Ⓟ 16,702; © 18,018; ◆ 19,650
Rosebud; RMC Place; HARDING; ***206** C-9; elev. 4,821ft./1,469m.; mail Amistad z 88410; rural
Roswell; Inc. Place; ⊡ CHAVES; **206** H-8; elev. 3,573ft./1,089m.; 🅿 🅷 ■; ★ **RSWL**; z 88201-03; Ⓟ 44,654; © 45,293; ◆ 45,663
Rowe; RMC Place; SAN MIGUEL; **206** D-6; elev. 6,824ft./2,080m.; 🅿; z 87562; ● 250
Roy; Inc. Place; HARDING; **206** C-8; elev. 5,888ft./1,795m.; 🅿; z 87743; Ⓟ 362; © 304
Ruidoso; Inc. Place; LINCOLN; **206** H-6; elev. 6,800ft./2,073m.; 🅿 🅷; z 88345, z 88355; Ⓟ 4,600; © 7,698
Ruidoso Downs; Inc. Place; LINCOLN; **206** H-6; elev. 6,400ft./1,951m.; 🅿; z 88346; Ⓟ 920; © 1,824
Rutheron; RMC Place; RIO ARRIBA; **206** B-5; elev. 7,261ft./2,213m.; 🅿; z 87551; ● 100

S

Sabinal; RMC Place; SOCORRO; ***206** F-4; mail Bosque z 87006; rural
Sabinoso; RMC Place; SAN MIGUEL; ***206** D-8; mail Solano z 87746
Sacramento; RMC Place; OTERO; **206** I-6; elev. 7,400ft./2,256m.; 🅿; z 88347; ● 100
Saint Vrain; RMC Place; CURRY; **206** F-9; elev. 4,400ft./1,341m.; 🅿; z 88133; ● 30
Salem; CDP; DONA ANA; **206** I-4; elev. 4,092ft./1,247m.; 🅿; z 87941; © 795
San Acacia; RMC Place; SOCORRO; ***206** F-4; elev. 4,680ft./1,426m.; 🅿; z 87831; ● 110
San Antonio; RMC Place; BERNALILLO; ***206** E-5; ★ **ALBU**; mail Cedar Crest z 87008; rural
San Antonio; RMC Place; SAN MIGUEL; ***206** D-7; mail Las Vegas z 87701; ● 120
San Antonio; RMC Place; SOCORRO; **206** G-4; elev. 4,550ft./1,387m.; 🅿; z 87832; ● 450
San Antonio de Padua del Rancho; RMC Place; SANTA FE; ***206** C-5; mail Santa Fe z 87508; ● 500
San Antonito; RMC Place; BERNALILLO; ***206** E-5; elev. 6,864ft./2,092m.; 🅿; z 87047; ● 180
Sanchez; RMC Place; SAN MIGUEL; ***206** D-8; elev. 4,642ft./1,415m.; mail Solano z 87746; rural
San Cristobal; RMC Place; TAOS; **206** B-6; elev. 7,450ft./2,271m.; 🅿; z 87564; ● 100
Sanctuario; SANTA FE; see Potrero (RMC Place)
Sandia; RMC Place; BERNALILLO; ***206** E-5; ★ **ALBU**; mail Sandia Park z 87047; location of Indian Agency; Ⓟ 6,742
Sandia Knolls; RMC Place; BERNALILLO; ***206** E-5; mail Sandia Park z 87047; ● 800
Sandia Park; RMC Place; BERNALILLO; **206** E-5; elev. 7,060ft./2,152m.; 🅿; z 87047; ● 700
Sandia Pueblo; RMC Place; SANDOVAL; ***206** E-5; located on Sandia Pueblo Ind. Res.; 🅿; ★ **ALBU**; z 87004; ● 450
Sandia Pueblo; Indian Reservation; SANDOVAL, BERNALILLO; 🅿; ★ **ALBU**; z 87004; Ⓟ 683; © 4,414
SANDOVAL; **206** D-4; Ⓟ 63,319; © 89,908; ◆ 125,512
San Felipe; SANDOVAL; see San Felipe Pueblo (CDP)
San Felipe Pueblo (San Felipe); CDP; SANDOVAL; **206** D-5; located on San Felipe Pueblo Ind. Res.; mail Algodones z 87001; Ⓟ 1,557; © 2,080
San Felipe Pueblo; Indian Reservation; SANDOVAL; mail Bernalillo z 87004; Ⓟ 2,266; © 3,185
San Felipe/Santa Ana joint use area; SANDOVAL; Indian Reservation; © 0
San Felipe/Santo Domingo joint use area; Indian Reservation; SANDOVAL; © 0
San Fidel; RMC Place; CIBOLA; **206** E-3; elev. 6,160ft./1,878m.; 🅿 🅷; z 87049; ● 150
San Francisco; RMC Place; SOCORRO; ***206** F-4; mail Bosque z 87006; rural
San Francisco Plaza; RMC Place; CATRON; mail Reserve z 87830; ● 50
San Geronimo; RMC Place; SAN MIGUEL; ***206** D-6; mail Las Vegas z 87701; rural
San Ignacio; RMC Place; GUADALUPE; ***206** E-7; mail Santa Rosa z 88435; rural
San Ignacio; RMC Place; SAN MIGUEL; ***206** D-6; mail Sapello z 87745
San Ildefonso Pueblo; CDP; SANTA FE; ***206** C-5; located on San Ildefonso Pueblo Ind. Res.; mail Santa Fe z 87501, z 87506; Ⓟ 447; © 458
San Ildefonso Pueblo; Indian Reservation; SANTA FE, SANDOVAL; mail Santa Fe z 87502; Ⓟ 1,491; © 1,524
San Jon; Inc. Place; QUAY; **206** E-9; elev. 4,022ft./1,226m.; 🅿; z 88411, z 88434; Ⓟ 277; © 306
San Jose; RMC Place; BERNALILLO; ***206** J-5; ★ **ELP**; mail Albuquerque z 87102; pop. incl. with Albuquerque (Inc. Place)
San Jose; RMC Place; EDDY; ***206** J-8; mail Carlsbad z 88220; pop. incl. with Carlsbad (Inc. Place)
San Jose; RMC Place; RIO ARRIBA; ***206** C-5; mail Hernandez z 87537; ● 230
San Jose; RMC Place; SAN MIGUEL; ***206** D-6; elev. 6,193ft./1,888m.; 🅿; z 87565; ● 150
San Juan (Sherman); RMC Place; GRANT; ***206** I-3; mail Hanover z 88041
San Juan; CDP; RIO ARRIBA; ***206** C-5; elev. 5,660ft./1,725m.; mail Ohkay Owingeh z 87566; Ⓟ 465; © 592
San Juan; RMC Place; SAN MIGUEL; ***206** E-6; mail San Jose z 87565; rural
SAN JUAN; **206** B-2; Ⓟ 91,605; © 113,801; ◆ 114,333
San Juan Pueblo; RMC Place; RIO ARRIBA; **206** C-5; elev. 5,660ft./1,725m.; 🅿; z 87566; ● 800
San Juan Pueblo; Indian Reservation; RIO ARRIBA; 🅿; z 87566; Ⓟ 4,365; © 6,748
San Lorenzo; RMC Place; GRANT; **206** I-3; elev. 5,860ft./1,786m.; 🅿; z 88041; ● 100
San Lorenzo Pueblo; TAOS; see Picuris Pueblo (CDP)
San Luis; RMC Place; SANDOVAL; ***206** D-4; mail Cuba z 87013; ● 30
San Mateo; RMC Place; CIBOLA; **206** D-3; elev. 7,298ft./2,224m.; 🅿; z 87020; ● 220
San Miguel; RMC Place; DONA ANA; ***206** J-4; elev. 3,841ft./1,171m.; 🅿; z 88058; ● 500
San Miguel; RMC Place; RIO ARRIBA; ***206** A-5; mail Antonito z 81120
San Miguel; RMC Place; SAN MIGUEL; ***206** D-6; mail Ribera z 87560; rural
SAN MIGUEL; **206** D-7; Ⓟ 25,743; © 30,126; ◆ 28,304
Sanostee; CDP; SAN JUAN; **206** B-1; located on Navajo Nation Ind. Res.; elev. 6,000ft./1,829m.; 🅿; z 87461; Ⓟ 626; © 429
San Pablo; RMC Place; SAN MIGUEL; ***206** D-6; elev. 6,846ft./2,087m.; mail Las Vegas z 87701; rural
San Patricio; RMC Place; LINCOLN; **206** H-6; elev. 5,400ft./1,646m.; 🅿; z 88348; ● 200
San Pedro; RMC Place; RIO ARRIBA; ***206** C-5; located on Santa Clara Pueblo Ind. Res.; mail Espanola z 87532; pop. incl. with Espanola (Inc. Place)
San Rafael; RMC Place; CIBOLA; **206** E-3; elev. 6,462ft./1,970m.; 🅿; z 87051; ● 600
San Rafael; RMC Place; SAN MIGUEL; ***206** D-8; mail Trementina z 88439; rural
San Sebastian; RMC Place; SANTA FE; ***206** D-6; ★ **S.FE**; mail Santa Fe z 87505; ● 130
Santa Ana Pueblo; CDP; SANDOVAL; ***206** D-5; located on Santa Ana Pueblo Ind. Res.; 🅿; z 87004; Ⓟ 476; © 479
Santa Ana Pueblo; Indian Reservation; SANDOVAL; 🅿; z 87004; Ⓟ 409; © 487
Santa Clara (Central); Inc. Place; GRANT; **206** I-2; elev. 5,975ft./1,821m.; 🅿; z 88026; Ⓟ 1,835; © 1,944
Santa Clara Pueblo; CDP; RIO ARRIBA; ***206** C-5; located on Santa Clara Pueblo Ind. Res.; mail Espanola z 87532; Ⓟ 1,156; © 980
Santa Clara Pueblo; Indian Reservation; RIO ARRIBA, SANDOVAL, SANTA FE; mail Espanola z 87532; Ⓟ 6,740; © 10,658
Santa Cruz; CDP; SANTA FE; **206** C-5; elev. 5,644ft./1,720m.; 🅿; z 87567; Ⓟ 2,504; © 423
Santa Fe; Inc. Place; **STATE CAPITAL**; ⊡ SANTA FE; **206** D-6; elev. 6,989ft./2,130m.; 🅿 🅷 🅲 2,368 ■; ★ **S.FE**; z 87501-09, z 87540, z 87592, z 87594; Ⓟ 55,859; © 62,203; ◆ 66,137
SANTA FE; **206** E-5; Ⓟ 98,928; © 129,292; ◆ 143,681
Santa Rosa; Inc. Place; ⊡ GUADALUPE; **206** E-7; elev. 4,599ft./1,402m.; 🅿; z 88435; Ⓟ 2,263; © 2,744
Santa Teresa; CDP; DONA ANA; **206** K-5; 🅿 🅷; ★ **ELP**; z 88008 & mail Sunland Park z 88063; © 2,607
Santo Domingo Pueblo; CDP; SANDOVAL; **206** D-5; located on Santo Domingo Pueblo Ind. Res.; elev. 5,180ft./1,579m.; 🅿; z 87052; Ⓟ 2,866; © 2,550
Santo Domingo Pueblo; Indian Reservation; SANDOVAL, SANTA FE; 🅿; z 87052; Ⓟ 2,162; © 3,166
Santo Nino; RMC Place; RIO ARRIBA, SANTA FE; ***206** C-5; elev. 5,605ft./1,708m.; mail Espanola z 87532, Santa Cruz z 87567; pop. incl. with Espanola (Inc. Place)
Santo Tomas; RMC Place; DONA ANA; ***206** J-4; mail La Mesa z 88044; ● 400
San Ysidro; Inc. Place; SANDOVAL; **206** D-4; elev. 5,470ft./1,667m.; 🅿; z 87053; Ⓟ 233; © 238
Sapello; RMC Place; SAN MIGUEL; **206** D-7; elev. 6,963ft./2,122m.; 🅿; z 87745; ● 120
Seama; CDP; CIBOLA; ***206** E-3; located on Laguna Pueblo Ind. Res.; mail Cubero z 87014; Ⓟ 403; © 333
Seboyeta (Cebolleta); RMC Place; CIBOLA; **206** E-3; elev. 6,400ft./1,951m.; 🅿; z 87014; ● 200
Sedan; RMC Place; UNION; **206** C-10; elev. 4,587ft./1,398m.; 🅿; z 88436; ● 50
Sedillo; RMC Place; BERNALILLO; ***206** E-5; mail Tijeras z 87059; rural
Sena; RMC Place; SAN MIGUEL; ***206** D-6; elev. 5,960ft./1,817m.; 🅿; z 87560; ● 120
Seneca; RMC Place; UNION; **206** B-10; elev. 4,990ft./1,521m.; 🅿; z 88415; ● 30
Separ; RMC Place; GRANT; ***206** J-2; mail Lordsburg z 88045; rural
Serafina; RMC Place; SAN MIGUEL; **206** D-7; elev. 6,276ft./1,913m.; 🅿; z 87569; ● 60
Servilleta Plaza; RMC Place; RIO ARRIBA; ***206** B-6; mail La Madera z 87539; ● 40
Seton Village; RMC Place; SANTA FE; ***206** D-6; ★ **S.FE**; mail Santa Fe z 87501, z 87505, z 87508; ● 100
Seven Lakes; RMC Place; MCKINLEY; ***206** D-3; mail Crownpoint z 87313; rural
Seven Rivers; RMC Place; EDDY; ***206** I-8; mail Lakewood z 88254; rural
Seven Springs; RMC Place; SANDOVAL; ***206** C-4; mail Jemez Springs z 87025; rural
Shady Brook; RMC Place; TAOS; ***206** C-6; mail Taos z 87571; rural
Sheep Springs; CDP; SAN JUAN; ***206** C-2; 🅿; z 87364; © 237
Sherman; GRANT; see San Juan (RMC Place)
Shiprock; CDP; SAN JUAN; **206** B-2; located on Navajo Nation Ind. Res.; elev. 4,900ft./1,494m.; 🅿 🅷; z 87420 & mail Sanostee z 87461; location of Shiprock Indian Agency; Ⓟ 7,687; © 8,156
SIERRA; **206** I-4; Ⓟ 9,912; © 13,270; ◆ 11,983
Sierra Vista; RMC Place; LINCOLN; ***206** H-6; mail Alto z 88312; rural
Sierra Vista Estates; RMC Place; BERNALILLO; ***206** E-5; mail Cedar Crest z 87008; ● 220
Sile; RMC Place; SANDOVAL; **206** D-5; mail Pena Blanca z 87041
Silver Acres; RMC Place; GRANT; ***206** I-2; elev. 5,720ft./1,743m.; mail Silver City z 88061; ● 200
Silver City; Inc. Place; ⊡ GRANT; **206** I-2; elev. 5,938ft./1,810m.; 🅿 🅷 🅲 2,844; z 88022, z 88036, z 88053, z 88061-62; Ⓟ 10,683; © 10,545
Sipapu; RMC Place; TAOS; ***206** C-6; mail Vadito z 87579
Sixmile Hill (Sixmile Station); RMC Place; CHAVES; ***206** H-8; ★ **RSWL**; mail Roswell z 88201; rural
Sixmile Station; CHAVES; see Sixmile Hill (RMC Place)
Sixteen Springs; RMC Place; OTERO; ***206** I-6; elev. 8,000ft./2,438m.; mail Cloudcroft z 88317; ● 50
Sky City; CIBOLA; see Acoma (RMC Place)
Skyline-Ganipa; CDP-Census Area Only; CIBOLA; ***206** E-3; elev. 6,039ft./1,841m.; mail Pueblo of Acoma z 87034; Ⓟ 946; © 1,035
Smith Lake (Smiths Lake); RMC Place; MCKINLEY; **206** D-2; 🅿; z 87365; ● 200
Smiths Lake; MCKINLEY; see Smith Lake (RMC Place)
Socorro; Inc. Place; ⊡ SOCORRO; **206** G-4; elev. 4,600ft./1,402m.; 🅿 🅷 🅲 1,889; z 87801; Ⓟ 8,159; © 8,877
SOCORRO; **206** G-5; Ⓟ 14,764; © 18,078; ◆ 18,017
Sofia; RMC Place; UNION; ***206** B-9; elev. 6,218ft./1,895m.; mail Grenville z 88424; rural
Soham; RMC Place; SAN MIGUEL; ***206** D-6; mail San Jose z 87565; rural
Solana; HARDING; see Solano (RMC Place)
Solano (Solana); RMC Place; HARDING; **206** C-8; elev. 5,628ft./1,715m.; 🅿; z 87746; ● 25
Sombrillo; CDP; SANTA FE; ***206** C-5; mail Espanola z 87532; © 493
South Carmen; RMC Place; MORA; ***206** C-6; elev. 7,335ft./2,236m.; mail Mora z 87732; rural
South San Ysidro; RMC Place; SAN MIGUEL; ***206** D-6; mail Ilfeld z 87538, San Jose z 87565; ● 35
South Springs Acres; RMC Place; CHAVES; **206** H-8; ★ **RSWL**; mail Roswell z 88201; ● 60
South Valley; CDP-Census Area Only; BERNALILLO; ***206** E-5; ★ **ALBU**; mail Albuquerque z 87102; Ⓟ 35,701; © 39,060; ◆ 46,022
Spencerville; RMC Place; SAN JUAN; ***206** B-3; ★ **FARM**; mail Aztec z 87410; ● 200
Springer; Inc. Place; COLFAX; **206** C-8; elev. 5,832ft./1,778m.; 🅿; z 87729, z 87747; Ⓟ 1,262; © 1,285
Springstead; RMC Place; MCKINLEY; ***206** D-2; mail Church Rock z 87311, Gallup z 87301; ● 100
Squirrel Springs; RMC Place; MCKINLEY; ***206** C-1; elev. 7,833ft./2,387m.; mail Tohatchi z 87325; rural
Standing Rock; RMC Place; MCKINLEY; ***206** D-2; located on Navajo Nation Ind. Res.; mail Crownpoint z 87313
Stanley; RMC Place; SANTA FE; **206** E-6; elev. 6,334ft./1,931m.; 🅿; z 87056; ● 130
Star Lake; RMC Place; MCKINLEY; mail Cuba z 87013; rural
State College; DONA ANA; see University Park (CDP)
Stead; RMC Place; UNION; ***206** C-10; elev. 4,614ft./1,406m.; 🅿; z 88415; rural
Sumner Lake State Park; RMC Place; DE BACA; ***206** F-8; elev. 4,297ft./1,310m.; mail Fort Sumner z 88119; ● 60
Sunland Park (Meadow Vista); Inc. Place; DONA ANA; **206** K-5; elev. 3,800ft./1,158m.; 🅿; ★ **ELP**; z 88063 & mail Santa Teresa z 88008; Ⓟ 8,179; © 13,309
Sunset; RMC Place; LINCOLN; ***206** H-7; mail Picacho z 88343; rural
Sunshine; RMC Place; LUNA; ***206** J-3; elev. 4,245ft./1,294m.; mail Deming z 88030; rural
Sunspot; RMC Place; OTERO; **206** I-6; elev. 9,200ft./2,804m.; 🅿; z 88349; ● 70
Sun Valley; RMC Place; LINCOLN; ***206** H-6; elev. 7,440ft./2,268m.; mail Alto z 88312; ● 230

T

Taiban; RMC Place; DE BACA; **206** F-9; elev. 4,126ft./1,258m.; 🅿; z 88134; ● 35
Tajique; CDP; TORRANCE; **206** E-5; elev. 6,700ft./2,042m.; 🅿; z 87016; © 148
Talpa; RMC Place; TAOS; **206** C-6; elev. 7,041ft./2,146m.; mail Ranchos De Taos z 87557; ● 450
Taos; Inc. Place; ⊡ TAOS; **206** C-6; elev. 6,952ft./2,119m.; 🅿 🅷; z 87571; Ⓟ 4,065; © 4,700
TAOS; **206** B-6; Ⓟ 23,118; © 29,979; ◆ 31,821
Taos Pueblo; CDP; TAOS; **206** B-6; located on Taos Pueblo Ind. Res.; mail Taos z 87571; Ⓟ 1,187; © 1,264
Taos Pueblo; Indian Reservation; TAOS; mail Taos z 87571; © 4,484
Taos Ski Valley; Inc. Place; TAOS; ***206** B-6; elev. 9,390ft./2,862m.; 🅿; z 87525; © 56
Tatum; Inc. Place; LEA; **206** H-10; elev. 3,995ft./1,218m.; 🅿; z 88213, z 88267; Ⓟ 768; © 683
Tecolote; RMC Place; SAN MIGUEL; ***206** D-7; mail Las Vegas z 87701; ● 150
Tecolotito; RMC Place; SAN MIGUEL; **206** E-7; elev. 5,382ft./1,640m.; mail Anton Chico z 87711; ● 150
Tererro; RMC Place; SAN MIGUEL; **206** D-6; elev. 7,656ft./2,334m.; 🅿; z 87573; ● 80
Tesuque; CDP; SANTA FE; ***206** D-6; elev. 6,759ft./2,060m.; 🅿; ★ **S.FE**; z 87574; Ⓟ 1,490; © 909
Tesuque Pueblo; RMC Place; SANTA FE; ***206** D-6; located on Tesuque Pueblo Ind. Res.; ★ **S.FE**; mail Santa Fe z 87501, z 87506; ● 150
Tesuque Pueblo; Indian Reservation; SANTA FE; mail Santa Fe z 87506; Ⓟ 252; © 806
Texico; Inc. Place; CURRY; **206** F-10; elev. 4,140ft./1,262m.; 🅿; z 88135; Ⓟ 966; © 1,065
Therma; COLFAX; see Eagle Nest (Inc. Place)
Thomas; RMC Place; UNION; ***206** C-10; elev. 5,015ft./1,529m.; mail Clayton z 88415; rural
Thoreau; CDP; MCKINLEY; **206** D-2; elev. 7,134ft./2,174m.; 🅿; z 87323; © 1,863
Three Rivers; RMC Place; OTERO; ***206** H-5; elev. 4,568ft./1,392m.; mail Tularosa z 88352; rural
Tierra Amarilla; RMC Place; ⊡ RIO ARRIBA; **206** B-5; elev. 7,524ft./2,293m.; 🅿; z 87575; ● 700
Tierra Monte; RMC Place; SAN MIGUEL; ***206** C-6; mail Rociada z 87742; rural
Tijeras; Inc. Place; BERNALILLO; **206** E-5; elev. 6,360ft./1,939m.; 🅿; ★ **ALBU**; z 87059; Ⓟ 340; © 474
Timberon; CDP; OTERO; ***206** I-6; elev. 6,880ft./2,097m.; 🅿; z 88350; © 309
Tinian; RMC Place; MCKINLEY; ***206** C-4; mail Cuba z 87013; rural
Tinnie; RMC Place; LINCOLN; **206** H-7; elev. 5,149ft./1,569m.; 🅿; z 88351; ● 140
Tinsley Crossing; RMC Place; ROOSEVELT; ***206** G-9; mail Portales z 88130; rural
Tiptonville; RMC Place; MORA; ***206** D-7; mail Watrous z 87753; rural
Toadlena; RMC Place; SAN JUAN; **206** C-1; located on Navajo Nation Ind. Res.; elev. 6,767ft./2,063m.; mail Newcomb z 87455; ● 200
Tocito; RMC Place; SAN JUAN; ***206** B-1; located on Navajo Nation Ind. Res.; mail Sanostee z 87461, Shiprock z 87420; rural
Tohatchi; CDP; MCKINLEY; **206** C-1; located on Navajo Nation Ind. Res.; elev. 6,440ft./1,963m.; 🅿; z 87325; Ⓟ 661; © 1,037
Tohlakai; RMC Place; MCKINLEY; ***206** D-1; located on Navajo Nation Ind. Res.; mail Gallup z 87301, Tohatchi z 87325; rural
Tolar; RMC Place; ROOSEVELT; ***206** F-9; mail Taiban z 88134
Tome; RMC Place; VALENCIA; **206** F-4; elev. 4,825ft./1,471m.; 🅿; ★ **ALBU**; z 87060; ● 600
Tome-Adelino; CDP-Census Area Only; VALENCIA; ***206** F-4; elev. 4,822ft./1,470m.; ★ **ALBU**; mail Tome z 87060; Ⓟ 1,695; © 2,211
Top of the World; MCKINLEY; see Continental Divide (RMC Place)
T-O Ranch; RMC Place; COLFAX; ***206** B-8; mail Raton z 87740
TORRANCE; **206** F-6; Ⓟ 10,285; © 16,911; ◆ 16,211
Torreon; CDP-Census Area Only; SANDOVAL; ***206** D-4; mail Cuba z 87013; © 297
Torreon; CDP; TORRANCE; **206** F-5; elev. 6,700ft./2,042m.; 🅿; z 87061; © 244
Tortugas; RMC Place; DONA ANA; **206** N-2; ★ **LSCR**; mail Mesilla Park z 88047; ● 500
Totavi; RMC Place; SANTA FE; ***206** C-5; mail Los Alamos z 87544; rural
Trampas (Las Trampas); RMC Place; TAOS; ***206** C-6; elev. 7,436ft./2,266m.; 🅿; z 87576; ● 180
Trementina; RMC Place; SAN MIGUEL; **206** D-8; elev. 5,000ft./1,524m.; 🅿; z 88439; ● 80
Tres Piedras; RMC Place; TAOS; **206** B-6; elev. 8,081ft./2,463m.; 🅿; z 87577; ● 200
Tres Ritos; RMC Place; TAOS; ***206** C-6; mail Vadito z 87579; summer pop. 300; ● 50
Truchas; RMC Place; RIO ARRIBA; **206** C-6; elev. 8,037ft./2,450m.; 🅿; z 87578; ● 500
Trujillo; RMC Place; SAN MIGUEL; ***206** D-7; mail Las Vegas z 87701; rural
Truth or Consequences (Hot Springs); Inc. Place; ⊡ SIERRA; **206** H-4; elev. 4,242ft./1,293m.; 🅿 🅷; z 87901; Ⓟ 6,221; © 7,289
Tse Bonito; CDP; MCKINLEY; ***206** D-1; mail Gallup z 87301; © 261
Tucumcari; Inc. Place; ⊡ QUAY; **206** E-9; elev. 4,086ft./1,245m.; 🅿 🅷; z 88401, z 88416 & mail Newkirk z 88431, Quay z 88433; Ⓟ 6,831; © 5,989
Tularosa; Inc. Place; OTERO; **206** I-5; elev. 4,500ft./1,372m.; 🅿; z 88352; Ⓟ 2,615; © 2,864
Turley; RMC Place; SAN JUAN; ***206** B-3; mail Blanco z 87412
Turn; VALENCIA; see Casa Colorada (CDP)
Turquillo; MORA; see El Turquillo (RMC Place)
Twin Forks Estates; OTERO; see Wimsatt (RMC Place)
Twin Lakes; CDP; MCKINLEY; ***206** D-1; located on Navajo Nation Ind. Res.; mail Gallup z 87301; © 1,069
Two Gray Hills; RMC Place; SAN JUAN; ***206** C-1; mail Tohatchi z 87325; rural
Two Wells; RMC Place; MCKINLEY; ***206** D-1; mail Vanderwagen z 87326; rural
Tyrone; RMC Place; GRANT; **206** I-2; elev. 5,825ft./1,775m.; 🅿; z 88065; ● 950

U

UNION; **206** B-9; Ⓟ 4,124; © 4,174; ◆ 3,759
University Park (State College); CDP; DONA ANA; **206** J-4; elev. 3,884ft./1,184m.; ★ **LSCR**; mail Las Cruces z 88003; Ⓟ 4,520; © 2,732; Ⓡ 3,460
Upper Anton Chico (Los Ranchitos); RMC Place; GUADALUPE; ***206** E-7; mail Anton Chico z 87711; ● 75
Upper Dilia; RMC Place; GUADALUPE; ***206** E-7; mail La Loma z 87724
Upper Fruitland; CDP-Census Area Only; SAN JUAN; ***206** B-2; © 1,664
Upper Nutria; RMC Place; MCKINLEY; ***206** D-2; mail Zuni z 87327; ● 100
Upper Pueblo (El Pueblo); RMC Place; SAN MIGUEL; ***206** D-6; mail Ribera z 87560; rural
Upper Rociada; RMC Place; SAN MIGUEL; ***206** C-6; mail Rociada z 87742; ● 50
Uptown; RMC Place; BERNALILLO; ★ **ALBU**; mail Albuquerque z 87110, z 87176, z 87190; pop. incl. with Albuquerque (Inc. Place)
Ute Mountain Reservation; Indian Reservation; SAN JUAN; Reservation extends into CO and UT; mail Towaoc z 81334; © 0
Ute Park; RMC Place; COLFAX; **206** B-7; elev. 7,413ft./2,259m.; 🅿; z 87749; summer pop. 200; ● 70

V

Vadito; CDP; TAOS; ***206** C-6; elev. 7,528ft./2,295m.; 🅿; z 87579; Ⓟ 283; © 242
Vado; CDP; DONA ANA; **206** J-4; elev. 3,819ft./1,164m.; 🅿; z 88072 & mail Mesquite z 88048; © 3,003
Valdez; RMC Place; TAOS; **206** B-6; elev. 7,400ft./2,256m.; 🅿; z 87580; ● 180
Valencia; CDP; VALENCIA; ***206** E-4; ★ **ALBU**; mail Los Lunas z 87031; Ⓟ 3,917; © 4,500
VALENCIA; **206** F-4; Ⓟ 45,235; © 66,152; ◆ 67,058
Vallecitos; RMC Place; MORA; ***206** C-6; mail Cleveland z 87715; rural
Vallecitos; RMC Place; RIO ARRIBA; **206** B-5; elev. 7,791ft./2,375m.; 🅿; z 87581; ● 140
Vallecitos de los Indios; RMC Place; SANDOVAL; ***206** D-5; mail Jemez Springs z 87025; rural
Valle Escondido; RMC Place; TAOS; ***206** C-6; mail Taos z 87571; ● 80
Valmora; RMC Place; MORA; **206** D-7; elev. 6,340ft./1,932m.; 🅿; z 87750; ● 35
Val Verde; RMC Place; COLFAX; mail Eagle Nest z 87718; ● 100
Vanadium (Hanover Junction); RMC Place; GRANT; **206** I-2; elev. 5,929ft./1,807m.; 🅿; z 88023; ● 100
Vanderwagen (Whitewater); RMC Place; MCKINLEY; **206** E-1; elev. 7,140ft./2,176m.; 🅿; z 87326; ● 300
Variadero (Garita); RMC Place; SAN MIGUEL; ***206** D-8; elev. 4,440ft./1,353m.; mail Garita z 88421; ● 50
Vaughn; Inc. Place; GUADALUPE; **206** F-7; elev. 5,965ft./1,818m.; 🅿; z 88353; Ⓟ 633; © 539
Veguita; RMC Place; SOCORRO; **206** F-4; elev. 4,769ft./1,454m.; 🅿; z 87062; ● 230
Velarde; RMC Place; RIO ARRIBA; **206** C-6; elev. 5,757ft./1,755m.; 🅿; z 87582; ● 450
Vermejo Park; RMC Place; COLFAX; ***206** B-7; mail Raton z 87740; rural
Via Linda; RMC Place; SANTA FE; ★ **S.FE**; mail Santa Fe z 87592; pop. incl. with Santa Fe (Inc. Place)
Villa Madonna; RMC Place; LINCOLN; ***206** H-6; elev. 8,500ft./2,591m.; mail Alto z 88312; rural
Villanueva; RMC Place; SAN MIGUEL; **206** E-6; elev. 6,000ft./1,829m.; 🅿; z 87583; ● 280
Virden; Inc. Place; HIDALGO; **206** I-1; 🅿; z 88045 & mail Duncan z 85534; Ⓟ 108; © 143
Volcano Cliffs; RMC Place; BERNALILLO; ***206** E-4; ★ **ALBU**; mail Albuquerque z 87105; pop. incl. with Albuquerque (Inc. Place)

W

Wagon Mound; Inc. Place; MORA; **206** C-7; elev. 6,195ft./1,888m.; 🅿; z 87735, z 87752; Ⓟ 319; © 369
Walker; RMC Place; CHAVES; ***206** H-8; elev. 3,650ft./1,113m.; ★ **RSWL**; mail Roswell z 88201; pop. incl. with Roswell (Inc. Place)
Waterfall; RMC Place; OTERO; ***206** I-6; elev. 8,200ft./2,499m.; mail Cloudcroft z 88317; ● 90
Waterflow; RMC Place; SAN JUAN; **206** B-2; elev. 5,060ft./1,542m.; 🅿; ★ **FARM**; z 87421; ● 320
Watrous; RMC Place; MORA; **206** D-7; elev. 6,416ft./1,956m.; 🅿; z 87750, z 87753; ● 130
Weed; RMC Place; OTERO; **206** I-6; elev. 7,018ft./2,139m.; 🅿; z 88354; ● 40
West Carlsbad; RMC Place; EDDY; ***206** J-8; pop. incl. with Carlsbad (Inc. Place)
Westgate Heights; RMC Place; BERNALILLO; ***206** E-4; ★ **ALBU**; mail Albuquerque z 87105; pop. incl. with Albuquerque (Inc. Place)
West Las Vegas; RMC Place; SAN MIGUEL; ***206** D-7; elev. 6,500ft./1,981m.; mail Las Vegas z 87701; pop. incl. with Las Vegas (Inc. Place)
Wheatland (Cameron); RMC Place; QUAY; ***206** E-9; mail Grady z 88120; rural
Whiskey Creek; GRANT; see Arenas Valley (RMC Place)
Whitehorse; RMC Place; MCKINLEY; ***206** D-3; mail Cuba z 87013
White Lakes; RMC Place; SANTA FE; ***206** E-6; elev. 6,819ft./2,078m.; mail Stanley z 87056; rural
White Oaks; RMC Place; LINCOLN; ***206** G-6; 🅿; z 88301; rural
White Rock; CDP; LOS ALAMOS; ***206** D-5; 🅿; z 87544; Ⓟ 6,192; © 6,045
White Rock; RMC Place; SAN JUAN; ***206** C-2; mail Crownpoint z 87313; rural
White Sands; CDP; DONA ANA; ***206** J-5; elev. 4,295ft./1,309m.; 🅿; z 88002 & mail Los Alamos z 87544; Ⓟ 2,616; © 1,323
Whites City; RMC Place; EDDY; **206** J-8; elev. 3,648ft./1,112m.; 🅿; z 88268; ● 50
White Signal; RMC Place; GRANT; ***206** I-2; mail Silver City z 88061; rural
Whitetail; RMC Place; OTERO; ***206** H-6; mail Mescalero z 88340; rural
Whitewater; MCKINLEY; see Vanderwagen (RMC Place)
Willard; Inc. Place; TORRANCE; **206** F-5; elev. 6,107ft./1,861m.; 🅿; z 87063; Ⓟ 183; © 240
Williams Acres; RMC Place; MCKINLEY; ***206** D-1; mail Gallup z 87301; ● 150
Williamsburg; Inc. Place; SIERRA; **206** H-4; elev. 4,240ft./1,292m.; 🅿; z 87942; Ⓟ 456; © 527
Willow Creek; RMC Place; CATRON; mail Glenwood z 88039; summer pop. 150
Wimsatt (Twin Forks Estates); RMC Place; OTERO; ***206** I-6; elev. 7,880ft./2,402m.; mail Cloudcroft z 88317; ● 150
Window Rock Junction; MCKINLEY; see Yah-Ta-Hey (CDP)
Winston; RMC Place; SIERRA; **206** H-3; elev. 6,157ft./1,877m.; 🅿; z 87943; ● 100

Y

Yah-Ta-Hey (Window Rock Junction, Yatahey); CDP; MCKINLEY; **206** D-1; mail Yatahey z 87375; © 580
Yatahey; MCKINLEY; see Yah-Ta-Hey (CDP)
Yeso; RMC Place; DE BACA; **206** F-8; elev. 4,773ft./1,455m.; 🅿; z 88136; ● 10
Youngsville; RMC Place; RIO ARRIBA; **206** C-5; elev. 6,800ft./2,073m.; 🅿; z 87064; ● 70

Z

Zamora; RMC Place; BERNALILLO; ***206** E-5; mail Tijeras z 87059; ● 90
Zia Pueblo; CDP; SANDOVAL; ***206** D-4; located on Zia Pueblo Ind. Res.; 🅿; z 87053; Ⓟ 637; © 646
Zia Pueblo; Indian Reservation; SANDOVAL; 🅿; z 87053; Ⓟ 524; © 646
Zuni; MCKINLEY; see Zuni Pueblo (CDP)
Zuni Pueblo (Zuni); CDP; MCKINLEY; **206** E-1; located on Zuni Ind. Res.; elev. 6,275ft./1,913m.; 🅷; mail Zuni z 87327; location of Indian Agency; Ⓟ 5,857; © 6,367
Zuni Reservation; Indian Reservation; MCKINLEY, CATRON, CIBOLA; Reservation extends into AZ; mail Zuni z 87327; also location of Indian Agency; Ⓟ 6,291; © 7,758

NEW YORK

Statistics

Total area (2000) — 54,556 square miles
Land area (2000) — 47,214 square miles
Water area (2000) — 7,342 square miles
Capital — Albany
One of Thirteen Original States

Maps

State maps can be found on pages 142-254 in Vol. 1
County Subdivision maps can be found on pages 255-271 in Vol. 1

Ranally Metro Areas (RMAs) and Abbreviations

Albany-Schenectady-Troy, NY — A-S-T
Binghamton, NY-PA — BING
Buffalo, NY-CAN. — BUF
Elmira, NY — ELM
Glens Falls, NY — GLFLS
Ithaca, NY — ITH
Jamestown, NY — JMST
Kingston, NY — KNGST
Lockport, NY — LOCK
Middletown, NY — MIDD
New York, NY-NJ-CT — N.Y.
Newburgh, NY — NWBG
Plattsburgh, NY — PLATT
Poughkeepsie, NY — POK
Rochester, NY — ROCH
Syracuse, NY — SYR
Utica-Rome, NY — UT-R
Watertown, NY — WATN

Principal Places

Place Name	Place Type	County	Population
New York	Inc. Place	NEW YORK	◆ 8,384,203
Hempstead	MCD-Town	NASSAU	◆ 732,355
Brookhaven	MCD-Town	SUFFOLK	◆ 461,604
Islip	MCD-Town	SUFFOLK	◆ 320,016
Oyster Bay	MCD-Town	NASSAU	◆ 277,530
Buffalo	Inc. Place	ERIE	◆ 263,423
North Hempstead	MCD-Town	NASSAU	◆ 217,366
Rochester	Inc. Place	MONROE	◆ 211,093
Babylon	MCD-Town	SUFFOLK	◆ 205,848
Yonkers	Inc. Place	WESTCHESTER	◆ 203,408
Huntington	MCD-Town	SUFFOLK	◆ 186,959
Syracuse	Inc. Place	ONONDAGA	◆ 140,401
Ramapo	MCD-Town	ROCKLAND	◆ 115,839
Amherst	MCD-Town	ERIE	◆ 115,346
Smithtown	MCD-Town	SUFFOLK	◆ 111,563
Albany	Inc. Place	ALBANY	◆ 97,679
Greece	MCD-Town	MONROE	◆ 93,665
Greenburgh	MCD-Town	WESTCHESTER	◆ 89,854
Cheektowaga	MCD-Town	ERIE	◆ 86,015
Clarkstown	MCD-Town	ROCKLAND	◆ 84,809
Colonie	MCD-Town	ALBANY	◆ 81,260
Cheektowaga	CDP	ERIE	◆ 75,461
New Rochelle	Inc. Place	WESTCHESTER	◆ 74,315
Tonawanda	MCD-Town	ERIE	◆ 70,803
Mount Vernon	Inc. Place	WESTCHESTER	◆ 69,769
Schenectady	Inc. Place	SCHENECTADY	◆ 62,396
Utica	Inc. Place	ONEIDA	◆ 59,145
Southampton	MCD-Town	SUFFOLK	◆ 58,594
Clay	MCD-Town	ONONDAGA	◆ 58,381
Town Of Tonawanda	CDP-Census Area Only	ERIE	◆ 58,230
Hamburg	MCD-Town	ERIE	◆ 55,849
Hempstead	Inc. Place	NASSAU	◆ 55,658
White Plains	Inc. Place	WESTCHESTER	◆ 55,394
Union	MCD-Town	BROOME	◆ 55,159
Brentwood	CDP	SUFFOLK	◆ 53,904
Niagara Falls	Inc. Place	NIAGARA	◆ 51,647
Irondequoit	CDP	MONROE	◆ 51,066
Irondequoit	MCD-Town	MONROE	◆ 51,066
Levittown	CDP	NASSAU	◆ 50,397
Orangetown	MCD-Town	ROCKLAND	◆ 49,274
Troy	Inc. Place	RENSSELAER	◆ 48,524
Amherst	RMC Place	ERIE	● 45,800
Binghamton	Inc. Place	BROOME	◆ 45,771
Rye	MCD-Town	WESTCHESTER	◆ 45,499
Mount Pleasant	MCD-Town	WESTCHESTER	◆ 45,143
Perinton	MCD-Town	MONROE	◆ 44,939
West Babylon	CDP	SUFFOLK	◆ 43,436
West Seneca	CDP	ERIE	◆ 42,760
West Seneca	MCD-Town	ERIE	◆ 42,760
Poughkeepsie	MCD-Town	DUTCHESS	◆ 42,330
Freeport	Inc. Place	NASSAU	◆ 42,329
Monroe	MCD-Town	ORANGE	◆ 42,080
Henrietta	MCD-Town	MONROE	◆ 40,445
Cortlandt	MCD-Town	WESTCHESTER	◆ 40,139
Webster	MCD-Town	MONROE	◆ 39,974
Hicksville	CDP	NASSAU	◆ 39,183
Lancaster	MCD-Town	ERIE	◆ 38,512
Ossining	MCD-Town	WESTCHESTER	◆ 38,054
Yorktown	MCD-Town	WESTCHESTER	◆ 37,939
Commack	CDP	SUFFOLK	◆ 36,358
Penfield	MCD-Town	MONROE	◆ 35,845
Brighton	CDP	MONROE	◆ 35,721
Brighton	MCD-Town	MONROE	◆ 35,721
Haverstraw	MCD-Town	ROCKLAND	◆ 35,596
East Meadow	CDP	NASSAU	◆ 35,582
New City	CDP	ROCKLAND	◆ 35,521
Valley Stream	Inc. Place	NASSAU	◆ 34,927
Clifton Park	MCD-Town	SARATOGA	◆ 34,925
Coram	CDP	SUFFOLK	◆ 34,918
Long Beach	Inc. Place	NASSAU	◆ 34,250
Carmel	MCD-Town	PUTNAM	◆ 34,152
Guilderland	MCD-Town	ALBANY	® 34,045
Warwick	MCD-Town	ORANGE	◆ 33,772
Rome	Inc. Place	ONEIDA	◆ 33,759
Bethlehem	MCD-Town	ALBANY	◆ 33,060
Salina	MCD-Town	ONONDAGA	◆ 32,648
Eastchester	MCD-Town	WESTCHESTER	◆ 32,402
North Tonawanda	Inc. Place	NIAGARA	◆ 32,152
Central Islip	CDP	SUFFOLK	◆ 31,941
Manlius	MCD-Town	ONONDAGA	◆ 31,742
Oceanside	CDP	NASSAU	◆ 31,086
Elmont	CDP	NASSAU	◆ 31,017
Ithaca	Inc. Place	TOMPKINS	◆ 30,909
Newburgh	MCD-Town	ORANGE	◆ 30,639
Newburgh	Inc. Place	ORANGE	◆ 30,198
Riverhead	MCD-Town	SUFFOLK	◆ 30,110
Huntington Station	CDP	SUFFOLK	◆ 29,902
Poughkeepsie	Inc. Place	DUTCHESS	◆ 29,870
Glenville	MCD-Town	SCHENECTADY	◆ 29,778
Rotterdam	MCD-Town	SCHENECTADY	◆ 29,748
Mamaroneck	MCD-Town	WESTCHESTER	◆ 29,737
Gates Center	RMC Place	MONROE	● 29,300
Elmira	Inc. Place	CHEMUNG	◆ 29,084
West Islip	CDP	SUFFOLK	◆ 28,897
Gates	MCD-Town	MONROE	◆ 28,855
Cicero	MCD-Town	ONONDAGA	◆ 28,587
Port Chester	Inc. Place	WESTCHESTER	◆ 28,580
Saratoga Springs	Inc. Place	SARATOGA	◆ 28,496
Deer Park	CDP	SUFFOLK	◆ 28,306
Orchard Park	MCD-Town	ERIE	◆ 28,255
Franklin Square	CDP	NASSAU	◆ 27,866
Jamestown	Inc. Place	CHAUTAUQUA	◆ 27,662
Pittsford	MCD-Town	MONROE	◆ 27,623
Lindenhurst	Inc. Place	SUFFOLK	◆ 27,590
Holbrook	CDP	SUFFOLK	◆ 27,506
Queensbury	MCD-Town	WARREN	◆ 27,366
Chili	MCD-Town	MONROE	◆ 27,301
Centereach	CDP	SUFFOLK	◆ 27,274
Smithtown	CDP	SUFFOLK	◆ 26,893
East Fishkill	MCD-Town	DUTCHESS	◆ 26,832
Watertown	Inc. Place	JEFFERSON	◆ 26,808
Middletown	Inc. Place	ORANGE	◆ 26,780
Clarence	MCD-Town	ERIE	◆ 26,493
Auburn	Inc. Place	CAYUGA	◆ 26,465
Vestal	MCD-Town	BROOME	◆ 26,358
Spring Valley	Inc. Place	ROCKLAND	◆ 26,142
Glen Cove	Inc. Place	NASSAU	◆ 26,141
Dix Hills	CDP-Census Area Only	SUFFOLK	◆ 26,019
Wallkill	MCD-Town	ORANGE	◆ 25,798
Wappinger	MCD-Town	DUTCHESS	◆ 25,467
Shirley	CDP	SUFFOLK	◆ 25,386
Harrison	Inc. Place	WESTCHESTER	◆ 25,352
Harrison	MCD-Town	WESTCHESTER	◆ 25,352
Ossining	Inc. Place	WESTCHESTER	◆ 24,964
Plainview	CDP	NASSAU	◆ 24,347
Peekskill	Inc. Place	WESTCHESTER	◆ 23,953
Bay Shore	CDP	SUFFOLK	◆ 23,841
New Windsor	MCD-Town	ORANGE	◆ 23,750
Montgomery	MCD-Town	ORANGE	◆ 23,636
De Witt	MCD-Town	ONONDAGA	◆ 23,624
Camillus	MCD-Town	ONONDAGA	◆ 23,231
Rockville Centre	Inc. Place	NASSAU	◆ 22,784
Kingston	Inc. Place	ULSTER	◆ 22,629
Fishkill	MCD-Town	DUTCHESS	◆ 22,573
Baldwin	CDP	NASSAU	◆ 22,277
Medford	CDP	SUFFOLK	◆ 21,976
Copiague	CDP	SUFFOLK	◆ 21,918
Le Ray	MCD-Town	JEFFERSON	◆ 21,896
Halfmoon	MCD-Town	SARATOGA	◆ 21,867
Selden	CDP	SUFFOLK	◆ 21,860
Uniondale	CDP	NASSAU	◆ 21,855
Merrick	CDP	NASSAU	◆ 21,618
Massapequa	CDP	NASSAU	◆ 21,520
Niskayuna	MCD-Town	SCHENECTADY	◆ 21,433
Onondaga	MCD-Town	ONONDAGA	◆ 21,347
Rotterdam	CDP	SCHENECTADY	◆ 21,219
New Hartford	MCD-Town	ONEIDA	◆ 21,176
East Hampton	MCD-Town	SUFFOLK	◆ 21,045
East Northport	CDP	SUFFOLK	◆ 20,842
East Patchogue	CDP	SUFFOLK	◆ 20,826
Lockport	Inc. Place	NIAGARA	◆ 20,807
Islip	CDP	SUFFOLK	◆ 20,568
Garden City	Inc. Place	NASSAU	◆ 20,425
Southold	MCD-Town	SUFFOLK	◆ 20,120
Hauppauge	CDP	SUFFOLK	◆ 20,097
Ronkonkoma	CDP	SUFFOLK	◆ 20,024
Lynbrook	Inc. Place	NASSAU	© 19,911
Lysander	MCD-Town	ONONDAGA	◆ 19,854
Lockport	MCD-Town	NIAGARA	◆ 19,770
Lake Ronkonkoma	CDP	SUFFOLK	© 19,701
Owego	MCD-Town	TIOGA	◆ 19,692
East Massapequa	CDP-Census Area Only	NASSAU	© 19,565
Horseheads	MCD-Town	CHEMUNG	© 19,561
Hyde Park	MCD-Town	DUTCHESS	◆ 19,407
Plattsburgh	Inc. Place	CLINTON	◆ 19,396
Ithaca	MCD-Town	TOMPKINS	◆ 19,322
North Massapequa	CDP	NASSAU	© 19,152
North Bellmore	CDP	NASSAU	◆ 19,069
Lackawanna	Inc. Place	ERIE	© 19,064
Wantagh	CDP	NASSAU	© 18,971
Saugerties	MCD-Town	ULSTER	® 18,821
Mamaroneck	Inc. Place	WESTCHESTER	© 18,752
West Hempstead	CDP	NASSAU	© 18,713
Whitestown	MCD-Town	ONEIDA	© 18,635
Grand Island	MCD-Town	ERIE	© 18,621
Eastchester	CDP	WESTCHESTER	© 18,564
Cortland	Inc. Place	CORTLAND	◆ 18,549
Syosset	CDP	NASSAU	© 18,544
Ogden	MCD-Town	MONROE	© 18,492
Huntington	CDP	SUFFOLK	© 18,403
Somers	MCD-Town	WESTCHESTER	© 18,346
Mineola	Inc. Place	NASSAU	◆ 18,143
Bedford	MCD-Town	WESTCHESTER	© 18,133
North Babylon	CDP	SUFFOLK	© 17,877
Scarsdale	Inc. Place	WESTCHESTER	© 17,823
Kiryas Joel	Inc. Place	ORANGE	◆ 17,804
Geddes	MCD-Town	ONONDAGA	© 17,740
Evans	MCD-Town	ERIE	© 17,594
Amsterdam	Inc. Place	MONTGOMERY	◆ 17,503
Massapequa Park	Inc. Place	NASSAU	© 17,499
New Castle	MCD-Town	WESTCHESTER	© 17,491
Blooming Grove	MCD-Town	ORANGE	© 17,351
Southeast	MCD-Town	PUTNAM	© 17,316
Oswego	Inc. Place	OSWEGO	◆ 17,227
Milton	MCD-Town	SARATOGA	© 17,103
Holtsville	CDP	SUFFOLK	© 17,006
Sayville	CDP	SUFFOLK	© 16,735
Nanuet	CDP	ROCKLAND	© 16,707
Depew	Inc. Place	ERIE	© 16,629
North Amityville	CDP	SUFFOLK	© 16,572
Bethpage	CDP	NASSAU	© 16,543
Farmingville	CDP	SUFFOLK	© 16,458
Woodmere	CDP	NASSAU	© 16,447
Bellmore	CDP	NASSAU	© 16,441
Kenmore	Inc. Place	ERIE	© 16,426
Lewiston	MCD-Town	NIAGARA	© 16,257
Tonawanda	Inc. Place	ERIE	© 16,136
Batavia	Inc. Place	GENESEE	◆ 16,035
Kings Park	CDP	SUFFOLK	® 15,976
Floral Park	Inc. Place	NASSAU	© 15,967
Potsdam	MCD-Town	ST. LAWRENCE	® 15,945
Setauket-East Setauket	CDP-Census Area Only	SUFFOLK	© 15,931
Roosevelt	CDP	NASSAU	© 15,854
Seaford	CDP	NASSAU	© 15,791
North Valley Stream	CDP	NASSAU	© 15,789
East Greenbush	MCD-Town	RENSSELAER	© 15,560
Pearl River	CDP	ROCKLAND	© 15,553
Cohoes	Inc. Place	ALBANY	© 15,521
Mastic	CDP	SUFFOLK	© 15,436
Gloversville	Inc. Place	FULTON	◆ 15,286
Port Washington	CDP	NASSAU	© 15,215
Gates-North Gates	CDP-Census Area Only	MONROE	© 15,138
Johnson City	Inc. Place	BROOME	◆ 15,121
South Farmingdale	CDP	NASSAU	© 15,061
North Bay Shore	CDP	SUFFOLK	© 14,992
Sullivan	MCD-Town	MADISON	© 14,991
Malone	MCD-Town	FRANKLIN	© 14,981
Rye	Inc. Place	WESTCHESTER	© 14,955
La Grange	MCD-Town	DUTCHESS	© 14,928
Jefferson Valley-Yorktown	CDP-Census Area Only	WESTCHESTER	© 14,891
Arcadia	MCD-Town	WAYNE	© 14,889
Parma	MCD-Town	MONROE	© 14,822
Beacon	Inc. Place	DUTCHESS	® 14,810
Pomfret	MCD-Town	CHAUTAUQUA	© 14,703
Greece	CDP	MONROE	© 14,614
North New Hyde Park	CDP	NASSAU	© 14,542
Melville	CDP	SUFFOLK	© 14,533
Monsey	CDP	ROCKLAND	© 14,504
Westbury	Inc. Place	NASSAU	© 14,263
Stony Point	MCD-Town	ROCKLAND	© 14,244
Thompson	MCD-Town	SULLIVAN	© 14,189
Glens Falls	Inc. Place	WARREN	◆ 14,164
Wheatfield	MCD-Town	NIAGARA	© 14,086
East Islip	CDP	SUFFOLK	© 14,078
Kent	MCD-Town	PUTNAM	© 14,009
Aurora	MCD-Town	ERIE	© 13,996
Wawarsing	MCD-Town	ULSTER	® 13,936
Stony Brook	CDP	SUFFOLK	© 13,727
Sweden	MCD-Town	MONROE	© 13,716
Beekman	MCD-Town	DUTCHESS	® 13,655
Olean	Inc. Place	CATTARAUGUS	◆ 13,653
German Flatts	MCD-Town	HERKIMER	© 13,629
Moreau	MCD-Town	SARATOGA	® 13,549
Dryden	MCD-Town	TOMPKINS	© 13,532
Geneva	Inc. Place	ONTARIO	◆ 13,383
Ridge	CDP	SUFFOLK	© 13,380
New Cassel	CDP	NASSAU	© 13,298
Greenlawn	CDP	SUFFOLK	© 13,286
Oneonta	Inc. Place	OTSEGO	◆ 13,272
Saint James	CDP	SUFFOLK	© 13,268
Massena	MCD-Town	ST. LAWRENCE	© 13,121
Jericho	CDP	NASSAU	© 13,045
Malta	MCD-Town	SARATOGA	© 13,005
Goshen	MCD-Town	ORANGE	© 12,913
New Paltz	MCD-Town	ULSTER	© 12,830
Endicott	Inc. Place	BROOME	◆ 12,688
Van Buren	MCD-Town	ONONDAGA	© 12,667
Babylon	Inc. Place	SUFFOLK	© 12,615
Ulster	MCD-Town	ULSTER	© 12,544
Wilton	MCD-Town	SARATOGA	® 12,541
Schodack	MCD-Town	RENSSELAER	© 12,536
Highlands	MCD-Town	ORANGE	© 12,484
Arlington	CDP	DUTCHESS	© 12,481
Ogdensburg	Inc. Place	ST. LAWRENCE	© 12,364
Salisbury	CDP-Census Area Only	NASSAU	© 12,341
Lewisboro	MCD-Town	WESTCHESTER	© 12,324
Cornwall	MCD-Town	ORANGE	© 12,307
South Salem	RMC Place	WESTCHESTER	● 12,300
Hampton Bays	CDP	SUFFOLK	® 12,240
Fallsburg	MCD-Town	SULLIVAN	© 12,234
North Wantagh	CDP	NASSAU	© 12,156
Chester	MCD-Town	ORANGE	© 12,140
Fort Drum	CDP-Census Area Only	JEFFERSON	© 12,123
Bath	MCD-Town	STEUBEN	© 12,097
Shawangunk	MCD-Town	ULSTER	© 12,022
Nesconset	CDP	SUFFOLK	© 11,992
Patchogue	Inc. Place	SUFFOLK	◆ 11,931
Dunkirk	Inc. Place	CHAUTAUQUA	◆ 11,901
Pelham	MCD-Town	WESTCHESTER	© 11,866
Fulton	Inc. Place	OSWEGO	© 11,855
Catskill	MCD-Town	GREENE	© 11,849
North Merrick	CDP	NASSAU	© 11,844
North Lindenhurst	CDP	SUFFOLK	© 11,767
Stony Point	CDP	ROCKLAND	© 11,744
Endwell	CDP	BROOME	© 11,706
Brunswick	MCD-Town	RENSSELAER	© 11,664
Mastic Beach	CDP	SUFFOLK	© 11,543
Chenango	MCD-Town	BROOME	© 11,454
Canandaigua	Inc. Place	ONTARIO	® 11,418
Patterson	MCD-Town	PUTNAM	© 11,306
Elma	MCD-Town	ERIE	© 11,304
Massena	Inc. Place	ST. LAWRENCE	© 11,209
Plattsburgh	MCD-Town	CLINTON	© 11,190
Lancaster	Inc. Place	ERIE	© 11,188
Southport	MCD-Town	CHEMUNG	© 11,185
Kingsbury	MCD-Town	WASHINGTON	© 11,171
Manorville	CDP	SUFFOLK	© 11,131
Tarrytown	Inc. Place	WESTCHESTER	© 11,090
Suffern	Inc. Place	ROCKLAND	© 11,006
Mamakating	MCD-Town	SULLIVAN	© 11,002
Oneida	Inc. Place	MADISON	© 10,987
Elwood	CDP	SUFFOLK	℗ 10,916
North Castle	MCD-Town	WESTCHESTER	© 10,849
Loudonville	RMC Place	ALBANY	℗ 10,822
North Greenbush	MCD-Town	RENSSELAER	© 10,805
Fairmount	CDP	ONONDAGA	© 10,795
Roessleville	RMC Place	ALBANY	℗ 10,753
Fredonia	Inc. Place	CHAUTAUQUA	© 10,706
Larchmont North	RMC Place	WESTCHESTER	● 10,700
Putnam Valley	MCD-Town	PUTNAM	© 10,686
Northeast Henrietta	RMC Place	MONROE	● 10,650
Dobbs Ferry	Inc. Place	WESTCHESTER	© 10,622
Terryville	CDP	SUFFOLK	© 10,589
Farmington	MCD-Town	ONTARIO	© 10,585
Miller Place	CDP	SUFFOLK	© 10,580
Mount Kisco	Inc. Place	WESTCHESTER	◆ 10,550
Wyandanch	CDP	SUFFOLK	© 10,546
Lansing	MCD-Town	TOMPKINS	© 10,521
Riverhead	CDP	SUFFOLK	© 10,513
Alden	MCD-Town	ERIE	© 10,470
East Rockaway	Inc. Place	NASSAU	© 10,414
Red Hook	MCD-Town	DUTCHESS	© 10,408
Canton	MCD-Town	ST. LAWRENCE	© 10,334
West Haverstraw	Inc. Place	ROCKLAND	© 10,295
Lake Grove	Inc. Place	SUFFOLK	© 10,250
Watervliet	Inc. Place	ALBANY	© 10,207
Rocky Point	CDP	SUFFOLK	© 10,185
Kirkland	MCD-Town	ONEIDA	© 10,138
Corning	Inc. Place	STEUBEN	◆ 10,133
Haverstraw	Inc. Place	ROCKLAND	© 10,117
Hamburg	Inc. Place	ERIE	© 10,116
Herkimer	MCD-Town	HERKIMER	© 9,962
Lloyd	MCD-Town	ULSTER	© 9,941
Plattekill	MCD-Town	ULSTER	© 9,892
Bohemia	CDP	SUFFOLK	© 9,871
Hartsdale	CDP	WESTCHESTER	© 9,830
Victor	MCD-Town	ONTARIO	® 9,823
Sound Beach	CDP	SUFFOLK	© 9,807
Ontario	MCD-Town	WAYNE	© 9,778
Middle Island	CDP	SUFFOLK	© 9,702
Locust Grove	RMC Place	NASSAU	● 9,700
Newark	Inc. Place	WAYNE	© 9,682
Newfane	MCD-Town	NIAGARA	© 9,657
Geneseo	MCD-Town	LIVINGSTON	© 9,654
Fort Salonga	CDP	SUFFOLK	© 9,634
Liberty	MCD-Town	SULLIVAN	© 9,632
Great Neck	Inc. Place	NASSAU	© 9,538
New Hyde Park	Inc. Place	NASSAU	© 9,523
Westbury South	RMC Place	NASSAU	● 9,500
Marcy	MCD-Town	ONEIDA	® 9,481

Entries in **UPPERCASE** are counties.
Entries in **bold** have populations of 2,500 or more.
Names in parentheses are alternate names.
Inc. Place — Incorporated Place
RMC Place — Rand McNally Designated Place
CDP — Census Designated Place
MCD — Minor Civil Division

⊡ County Seat
▲ Minor Civil Division
elev. Elevation
P Post Office

H Hospital
C College
■ Principal Business Center
★ Ranally Metro Area (RMA) Abbreviation
z Zip Code(s)

℗ Previous Census Population
® Revised Census Population
Ⓐ Annexation Population
● Rand McNally Population Estimate
© Final Census Population
Ⓢ Special Census Population
◆ Estimated Population

For additional definitions see Glossary, Volume 1, and Introduction, Volume 2.

Place Name	Place Type	County	Population
Chappaqua	CDP	WESTCHESTER	© 9,468
South Huntington	CDP	SUFFOLK	© 9,465
Woodbury	MCD-Town	ORANGE	© 9,460
Amityville	Inc. Place	SUFFOLK	© 9,441
Philipstown	MCD-Town	PUTNAM	© 9,422
Potsdam	Inc. Place	ST. LAWRENCE	® 9,413
Albion	MCD-Town	ORLEANS	® 9,409
Hamlin	MCD-Town	MONROE	© 9,355
Seneca Falls	MCD-Town	SENECA	© 9,347
Esopus	MCD-Town	ULSTER	© 9,331
Inwood	CDP	NASSAU	© 9,325
Ellicott	MCD-Town	CHAUTAUQUA	© 9,280
Valley Cottage	CDP	ROCKLAND	© 9,269
Manchester	MCD-Town	ONTARIO	© 9,258
Sleepy Hollow	Inc. Place	WESTCHESTER	© 9,212
Plainedge	CDP	NASSAU	© 9,195
New Windsor	CDP	ORANGE	© 9,077
Barton	MCD-Town	TIOGA	© 9,066
Pleasant Valley	MCD-Town	DUTCHESS	© 9,066
Woodbury	CDP	NASSAU	© 9,010
North Bellport	CDP	SUFFOLK	© 9,007
Niagara	MCD-Town	NIAGARA	© 8,978
Scotchtown	CDP	ORANGE	© 8,954
Sodus	MCD-Town	WAYNE	© 8,949
Malverne	Inc. Place	NASSAU	© 8,934
Woodbury	Inc. Place	ORANGE	● 8,900
Coxsackie	MCD-Town	GREENE	© 8,884
Port Jervis	Inc. Place	ORANGE	© 8,860
Hastings	MCD-Town	OSWEGO	© 8,803
Mount Sinai	CDP	SUFFOLK	© 8,734
Ballston	MCD-Town	SARATOGA	© 8,729
West Webster	RMC Place	MONROE	● 8,700
Macedon	MCD-Town	WAYNE	© 8,688
Lenox	MCD-Town	MADISON	© 8,665
Lake Carmel	CDP	PUTNAM	© 8,663
Bayport	CDP	SUFFOLK	© 8,662
North Elba	MCD-Town	ESSEX	© 8,661
Greenville	CDP	WESTCHESTER	© 8,648
New Scotland	MCD-Town	ALBANY	© 8,626
Ilion	Inc. Place	HERKIMER	© 8,610
Johnstown	Inc. Place	FULTON	® 8,610
Rye Brook	Inc. Place	WESTCHESTER	© 8,602
Schroeppel	MCD-Town	OSWEGO	© 8,566
Dover	MCD-Town	DUTCHESS	© 8,565
South Lockport	CDP	NIAGARA	© 8,552
San Remo	RMC Place	SUFFOLK	● 8,550
Concord	MCD-Town	ERIE	© 8,526
Waterford	MCD-Town	SARATOGA	© 8,515
Mahopac	CDP	PUTNAM	© 8,478
Hornell	Inc. Place	STEUBEN	◆ 8,421
Newstead	MCD-Town	ERIE	© 8,404
Walworth	MCD-Town	WAYNE	© 8,402
Farmingdale	Inc. Place	NASSAU	© 8,399
Mendon	MCD-Town	MONROE	© 8,370
Manhasset	CDP	NASSAU	© 8,362
Collins	MCD-Town	ERIE	© 8,307
Congers	CDP	ROCKLAND	© 8,303
Kinderhook	MCD-Town	COLUMBIA	© 8,296
Delmar	CDP	ALBANY	© 8,292
Marlborough	MCD-Town	ULSTER	© 8,263
De Witt	RMC Place	ONONDAGA	Ⓟ 8,244
Allegany	MCD-Town	CATTARAUGUS	© 8,230
Coeymans	MCD-Town	ALBANY	© 8,151
Baldwin Harbor	CDP	NASSAU	© 8,147
Brockport	Inc. Place	MONROE	© 8,103
Eden	MCD-Town	ERIE	© 8,076
Oakdale	CDP	SUFFOLK	© 8,075
Glens Falls North	CDP-Census Area Only	WARREN	© 8,061
Nassau Shores	RMC Place	NASSAU	● 8,000
South Setauket	RMC Place	SUFFOLK	● 8,000
Sand Lake	MCD-Town	RENSSELAER	© 7,987
Yorktown Heights	CDP	WESTCHESTER	© 7,972
Scotia	Inc. Place	SCHENECTADY	© 7,957
Cortlandville	MCD-Town	CORTLAND	© 7,919
Colonie	Inc. Place	ALBANY	© 7,916
Boston	MCD-Town	ERIE	© 7,897
Crawford	MCD-Town	ORANGE	© 7,875
Waterloo	MCD-Town	SENECA	© 7,866
Deerpark	MCD-Town	ORANGE	© 7,858
Port Jefferson	Inc. Place	SUFFOLK	© 7,837
Chestnut Ridge	Inc. Place	ROCKLAND	© 7,829
North Patchogue	CDP	SUFFOLK	© 7,825
Attica	MCD-Town	WYOMING	® 7,806
Airmont	Inc. Place	ROCKLAND	© 7,799
Le Roy	MCD-Town	GENESEE	© 7,790
Monroe	Inc. Place	ORANGE	© 7,780
Rhinebeck	MCD-Town	DUTCHESS	© 7,762
Rensselaer	Inc. Place	RENSSELAER	© 7,761
Busti	MCD-Town	CHAUTAUQUA	© 7,760
Hastings-on-Hudson	Inc. Place	WESTCHESTER	® 7,715
Royalton	MCD-Town	NIAGARA	© 7,710
Briarcliff Manor	Inc. Place	WESTCHESTER	© 7,696
Wellsville	MCD-Town	ALLEGANY	© 7,678
Palmyra	MCD-Town	WAYNE	© 7,672
Canandaigua	MCD-Town	ONTARIO	© 7,649
Hanover	MCD-Town	CHAUTAUQUA	© 7,638
Croton-on-Hudson	Inc. Place	WESTCHESTER	© 7,606
Northport	Inc. Place	SUFFOLK	© 7,606
Geneseo	Inc. Place	LIVINGSTON	© 7,579
Baywood	CDP-Census Area Only	SUFFOLK	© 7,571
Garden City Park	CDP	NASSAU	© 7,554
Port Jefferson Station	CDP	SUFFOLK	© 7,527
Hudson	Inc. Place	COLUMBIA	© 7,524
Stillwater	MCD-Town	SARATOGA	© 7,522
Pawling	MCD-Town	DUTCHESS	© 7,521

Place Name	Place Type	County	Population
Herkimer	Inc. Place	HERKIMER	© 7,498
Frankfort	MCD-Town	HERKIMER	© 7,478
Schaghticoke	MCD-Town	RENSSELAER	© 7,456
Gouverneur	MCD-Town	ST. LAWRENCE	© 7,418
Southport	CDP	CHEMUNG	© 7,396
Greenfield	MCD-Town	SARATOGA	© 7,362
Norwich	Inc. Place	CHENANGO	© 7,355
Skaneateles	MCD-Town	ONONDAGA	© 7,323
Oswego	MCD-Town	OSWEGO	© 7,287
Livonia	MCD-Town	LIVINGSTON	© 7,286
Williston Park	Inc. Place	NASSAU	© 7,261
Erwin	MCD-Town	STEUBEN	© 7,227
Big Flats	MCD-Town	CHEMUNG	© 7,224
Elmira	MCD-Town	CHEMUNG	© 7,199
Scriba	MCD-Town	OSWEGO	® 7,189
Westmere	CDP	ALBANY	© 7,188
Pleasantville	Inc. Place	WESTCHESTER	© 7,172
West Point	CDP	ORANGE	© 7,138
Bayville	Inc. Place	NASSAU	© 7,135
Hillcrest	CDP	ROCKLAND	© 7,106
Johnstown	MCD-Town	FULTON	® 7,067
Hewlett	CDP	NASSAU	© 7,060
Baldwinsville	Inc. Place	ONONDAGA	© 7,053
Milo	MCD-Town	YATES	© 7,026
Rochester	MCD-Town	ULSTER	© 7,018
Phelps	MCD-Town	ONTARIO	© 7,017
Granby	MCD-Town	OSWEGO	© 7,009
Hudson Falls	Inc. Place	WASHINGTON	© 6,927
Porter	MCD-Town	NIAGARA	© 6,920
Fenton	MCD-Town	BROOME	© 6,909
Ridgeway	MCD-Town	ORLEANS	© 6,886
Lee	MCD-Town	ONEIDA	© 6,875
North Syracuse	Inc. Place	ONONDAGA	© 6,862
Seneca Falls	Inc. Place	SENECA	© 6,861
Solvay	Inc. Place	ONONDAGA	© 6,845
East Hills	Inc. Place	NASSAU	© 6,842
Oyster Bay	CDP	NASSAU	© 6,826
East Half Hollow Hills	RMC Place	SUFFOLK	● 6,800
Williamson	MCD-Town	WAYNE	© 6,777
Hoosick	MCD-Town	RENSSELAER	© 6,759
Tappan	CDP	ROCKLAND	© 6,757
Nyack	Inc. Place	ROCKLAND	© 6,737
West Glens Falls	CDP	WARREN	© 6,721
Jefferson Valley	RMC Place	WESTCHESTER	● 6,700
East Aurora	Inc. Place	ERIE	© 6,673
Wading River	CDP	SUFFOLK	© 6,668
Center Moriches	CDP	SUFFOLK	© 6,655
East Rochester	Inc. Place	MONROE	© 6,650
Mount Hope	MCD-Town	ORANGE	© 6,639
Irvington	Inc. Place	WESTCHESTER	© 6,631
Horseheads	Inc. Place	CHEMUNG	® 6,566
Hurley	MCD-Town	ULSTER	© 6,564
Bronxville	Inc. Place	WESTCHESTER	© 6,543
Mount Ivy	CDP	ROCKLAND	© 6,536
Lawrence	Inc. Place	NASSAU	© 6,522
Monticello	Inc. Place	SULLIVAN	© 6,512
Larchmont	Inc. Place	WESTCHESTER	© 6,485
Cazenovia	MCD-Town	MADISON	© 6,481
Granville	MCD-Town	WASHINGTON	© 6,456
Avon	MCD-Town	LIVINGSTON	© 6,443
Great Neck Plaza	Inc. Place	NASSAU	© 6,433
Mayfield	MCD-Town	FULTON	© 6,432
Corning	MCD-Town	STEUBEN	© 6,426
Verona	MCD-Town	ONEIDA	© 6,425
Windsor	MCD-Town	BROOME	© 6,421
Fort Ann	MCD-Town	WASHINGTON	© 6,417
Medina	Inc. Place	ORLEANS	© 6,415
Warwick	Inc. Place	ORANGE	© 6,412
Cobleskill	MCD-Town	SCHOHARIE	© 6,407
Claverack	MCD-Town	COLUMBIA	© 6,401
Pelham	Inc. Place	WESTCHESTER	© 6,400
Peru	MCD-Town	CLINTON	© 6,370
Mattydale	CDP	ONONDAGA	© 6,367
Homer	MCD-Town	CORTLAND	© 6,363
Cairo	MCD-Town	GREENE	© 6,355
Rosendale	MCD-Town	ULSTER	© 6,352
Marcellus	MCD-Town	ONONDAGA	© 6,319
Penfield	RMC Place	MONROE	● 6,300
Roslyn Heights	CDP	NASSAU	© 6,295
Wawayanda	MCD-Town	ORANGE	© 6,273
Corinth	MCD-Town	SARATOGA	® 6,259
Woodstock	MCD-Town	ULSTER	© 6,241
Wilna	MCD-Town	JEFFERSON	© 6,235
Tuckahoe	Inc. Place	WESTCHESTER	© 6,211
Westmoreland	MCD-Town	ONEIDA	© 6,207
Bayberry	RMC Place	ONONDAGA	● 6,200
East Vestal	RMC Place	BROOME	● 6,200
South Stony Brook	RMC Place	SUFFOLK	● 6,200
Cedarhurst	Inc. Place	NASSAU	© 6,164
Walden	Inc. Place	ORANGE	© 6,164
Pompey	MCD-Town	ONONDAGA	© 6,159
Manorhaven	Inc. Place	NASSAU	© 6,138
Tupper Lake	MCD-Town	FRANKLIN	© 6,137
Sidney	MCD-Town	DELAWARE	© 6,109
Salamanca	Inc. Place	CATTARAUGUS	© 6,097
Volney	MCD-Town	OSWEGO	© 6,094
Elbridge	MCD-Town	ONONDAGA	© 6,091
Orange Lake	CDP	ORANGE	© 6,085
Malone	Inc. Place	FRANKLIN	© 6,075
Clarkson	MCD-Town	MONROE	© 6,072
East Glenville	CDP	SCHENECTADY	© 6,064
Mechanicstown	CDP	ORANGE	© 6,061
Pendleton	MCD-Town	NIAGARA	© 6,050
New Paltz	Inc. Place	ULSTER	© 6,034
South Hill	CDP	TOMPKINS	© 6,003

Place Name	Place Type	County	Population
Albion	Inc. Place	ORLEANS	® 5,992
Thornwood	CDP	WESTCHESTER	© 5,980
Lake Mohegan	CDP-Census Area Only	WESTCHESTER	© 5,979
Conklin	MCD-Town	BROOME	© 5,940
Viola	CDP	ROCKLAND	© 5,931
Batavia	MCD-Town	GENESEE	© 5,915
Fort Edward	MCD-Town	WASHINGTON	© 5,892
Hilton	Inc. Place	MONROE	© 5,856
Marbletown	MCD-Town	ULSTER	© 5,854
Washingtonville	Inc. Place	ORANGE	© 5,851
Brownville	MCD-Town	JEFFERSON	© 5,843
Wilson	MCD-Town	NIAGARA	© 5,840
Lyons	MCD-Town	WAYNE	© 5,831
Richland	MCD-Town	OSWEGO	© 5,824
Amsterdam	MCD-Town	MONTGOMERY	© 5,820
Vienna	MCD-Town	ONEIDA	© 5,819
East Shoreham	CDP-Census Area Only	SUFFOLK	© 5,809
Duanesburg	MCD-Town	SCHENECTADY	© 5,808
Groton	MCD-Town	TOMPKINS	© 5,794
Champlain	MCD-Town	CLINTON	© 5,791
Fairport	Inc. Place	MONROE	© 5,740
North Dansville	MCD-Town	LIVINGSTON	© 5,738
Hamilton	MCD-Town	MADISON	© 5,733
Greene	MCD-Town	CHENANGO	© 5,729
Marilla	MCD-Town	ERIE	© 5,709
Calverton	CDP	SUFFOLK	© 5,704
Canton	Inc. Place	ST. LAWRENCE	® 5,698
Goshen	Inc. Place	ORANGE	© 5,676
Kirkwood	MCD-Town	BROOME	© 5,651
Carmel Hamlet	CDP-Census Area Only	PUTNAM	© 5,650
Pittstown	MCD-Town	RENSSELAER	© 5,644
Bath	Inc. Place	STEUBEN	© 5,641
Islip Terrace	CDP	SUFFOLK	© 5,641
South Valley Stream	CDP-Census Area Only	NASSAU	© 5,638
Lakeview	CDP	NASSAU	© 5,607
Walton	MCD-Town	DELAWARE	© 5,607
West Hills	CDP	SUFFOLK	© 5,607
Harrietstown	MCD-Town	FRANKLIN	© 5,575
Williamsville	Inc. Place	ERIE	© 5,573
Ballston Spa	Inc. Place	SARATOGA	© 5,556
Myers Corner	CDP	DUTCHESS	© 5,546
Portland	MCD-Town	CHAUTAUQUA	© 5,502
Yorktown	RMC Place	WESTCHESTER	● 5,500
Pelham Manor	Inc. Place	WESTCHESTER	© 5,466
Southold	CDP	SUFFOLK	© 5,465
Maine	MCD-Town	BROOME	© 5,459
Centerport	CDP	SUFFOLK	© 5,446
Colesville	MCD-Town	BROOME	© 5,441
Riga	MCD-Town	MONROE	© 5,437
Warsaw	MCD-Town	WYOMING	© 5,423
Fairview	CDP	DUTCHESS	© 5,421
Shelby	MCD-Town	ORLEANS	© 5,420
East Farmingdale	CDP-Census Area Only	SUFFOLK	© 5,400
Old Bethpage	CDP	NASSAU	© 5,400
Cambria	MCD-Town	NIAGARA	© 5,393
Valhalla	CDP	WESTCHESTER	© 5,379
Dickinson	MCD-Town	BROOME	© 5,335
Vernon	MCD-Town	ONEIDA	© 5,335
Beekmantown	MCD-Town	CLINTON	© 5,326
Candor	MCD-Town	TIOGA	© 5,317
Ghent	MCD-Town	COLUMBIA	© 5,276
Carle Place	CDP	NASSAU	© 5,247
Gardiner	MCD-Town	ULSTER	© 5,238
Westfield	MCD-Town	CHAUTAUQUA	© 5,232
Penn Yan	Inc. Place	YATES	© 5,219
Webster	Inc. Place	MONROE	© 5,216
Albertson	CDP	NASSAU	© 5,200
Blauvelt	CDP	ROCKLAND	® 5,200
West Bellport	RMC Place	SUFFOLK	● 5,200
Little Falls	Inc. Place	HERKIMER	© 5,188
Mexico	MCD-Town	OSWEGO	© 5,181
North Salem	MCD-Town	WESTCHESTER	© 5,173
Wellsville	Inc. Place	ALLEGANY	© 5,171
Ticonderoga	MCD-Town	ESSEX	© 5,167
Westvale	CDP	ONONDAGA	© 5,166
Dannemora	MCD-Town	CLINTON	© 5,149
Wheatland	MCD-Town	MONROE	© 5,149
Constantia	MCD-Town	OSWEGO	© 5,141
Alfred	MCD-Town	ALLEGANY	© 5,140
West Elmira	CDP	CHEMUNG	© 5,136
Schuyler Falls	MCD-Town	CLINTON	© 5,128
Saratoga	MCD-Town	SARATOGA	® 5,114
Waterloo	Inc. Place	SENECA	© 5,111
Newfield	MCD-Town	TOMPKINS	© 5,108
Hawthorne	CDP	WESTCHESTER	© 5,083
Kings Point	Inc. Place	NASSAU	© 5,076
Broadalbin	MCD-Town	FULTON	© 5,066
Sea Cliff	Inc. Place	NASSAU	© 5,066
Highland	CDP	ULSTER	© 5,060
Saranac Lake	Inc. Place	FRANKLIN	© 5,041
Searingtown	CDP	NASSAU	© 5,034
Yaphank	CDP	SUFFOLK	© 5,025
Mechanicville	Inc. Place	SARATOGA	© 5,019
Camden	MCD-Town	ONEIDA	® 5,018
Wheatley Heights	CDP-Census Area Only	SUFFOLK	© 5,013
West Sayville	CDP	SUFFOLK	© 5,003
Pitcher Hill	RMC Place	ONONDAGA	● 5,000
Vestal	RMC Place	BROOME	● 5,000

County Business Data

County	FIPS Code	County Seat	Land Area (Sq. Mi.)	Census Population			Wholesale Trade		Manufacturing, 2002			
				4/1/2000	4/1/1990	% Change 1990-2000	Sales, 2002 ($1,000)	% Change 1997-2002	Establish-ments	Total Employees	Value Added ($1,000)	Ranally Mfg. Units
Albany	001	Albany	523	294,565	292,594	0.7	4,964,014	14.5	260	9,410	1,521,615	805
Allegany	003	Belmont	1,030	49,927	50,470	-1.1	32,957	-39.9	54	2,679	309,633	164
Bronx	005	Bronx	42	1,332,650	1,203,789	10.7	(d)	(d)	465	10,504	790,349	418
Broome	007	Binghamton	707	200,536	212,160	-5.5	2,065,588	(d)	225	16,714	1,547,469	819
Cattaraugus	009	Little Valley	1,310	83,955	84,234	-0.3	518,673	26.8	98	5,023	504,348	267
Cayuga	011	Auburn	693	81,963	82,313	-0.4	187,511	-6.8	100	3,510	318,755	169
Chautauqua	013	Mayville	1,062	139,750	141,895	-1.5	616,134	-17.7	226	12,349	1,504,507	796
Chemung	015	Elmira	408	91,070	95,195	-4.3	359,573	-19.6	94	6,648	601,441	318
Chenango	017	Norwich	894	51,401	51,768	-0.7	90,782	41.1	79	2,683	667,444	353
Clinton	019	Plattsburgh	1,039	79,894	85,969	-7.1	656,556	61.3	103	4,624	405,144	214
Columbia	021	Hudson	636	63,094	62,982	0.2	219,402	-12.5	80	1,898	165,216	87
Cortland	023	Cortland	500	48,599	48,963	-0.7	112,062	-42.7	73	3,819	309,161	164
Delaware	025	Delhi	1,446	48,055	47,225	1.8	187,517	24.3	55	4,350	611,073	323
Dutchess	027	Poughkeepsie	802	280,150	259,462	8.0	985,585	(d)	209	19,317	3,197,716	1,692
Erie	029	Buffalo	1,044	950,265	968,532	-1.9	(d)	(d)	1,146	57,645	6,925,165	3,664
Essex	031	Elizabethtown	1,797	38,851	37,152	4.6	21,769	-56.2	33	1,105	185,874	98
Franklin	033	Malone	1,631	51,134	46,540	9.9	129,992	2.6	28	658	44,181	23
Fulton	035	Johnstown	496	55,073	54,191	1.6	366,490	9.0	102	2,675	272,901	144
Genesee	037	Batavia	494	60,370	60,060	0.5	(d)	(d)	98	3,464	300,051	159
Greene	039	Catskill	648	48,195	44,739	7.7	275,983	24.0	39	817	90,063	48
Hamilton	041	Lake Pleasant	1,720	5,379	5,279	1.9	(d)	(d)	...	(d)	(d)	...
Herkimer	043	Herkimer	1,411	64,427	65,797	-2.1	(d)	(d)	68	3,471	455,219	241
Jefferson	045	Watertown	1,272	111,738	110,943	0.7	328,683	17.1	89	2,916	263,750	140
Kings	047	Brooklyn	71	2,465,326	2,300,664	7.2	11,579,249	1.8	2,327	32,402	3,881,178	2,053
Lewis	049	Lowville	1,275	26,944	26,796	0.6	83,693	21.7	28	1,327	182,003	96
Livingston	051	Geneseo	632	64,328	62,372	3.1	258,890	21.8	60	2,441	245,503	130
Madison	053	Wampsville	656	69,441	69,120	0.5	(d)	(d)	71	2,763	312,640	165
Monroe	055	Rochester	659	735,343	713,968	3.0	9,778,063	5.0	973	58,454	9,107,331	4,818
Montgomery	057	Fonda	405	49,708	51,981	-4.4	102,069	-31.3	70	3,637	364,140	193
Nassau	059	Mineola	287	1,334,544	1,287,348	3.7	(d)	(d)	1,446	36,111	5,914,795	3,129
New York	061	New York	23	1,537,195	1,487,536	3.3	140,669,286	-7.3	3,523	58,920	5,122,003	2,710
Niagara	063	Lockport	523	219,846	220,756	-0.4	(d)	(d)	291	13,327	1,628,410	862
Oneida	065	Utica	1,213	235,469	250,836	-6.1	(d)	(d)	271	13,876	1,078,748	571
Onondaga	067	Syracuse	780	458,336	468,973	-2.3	15,081,639	35.1	513	27,536	3,197,380	1,692
Ontario	069	Canandaigua	644	100,224	95,101	5.4	635,960	34.9	162	7,446	796,323	421
Orange	071	Goshen	816	341,367	307,647	11.0	6,766,015	(d)	341	8,585	880,801	466
Orleans	073	Albion	391	44,171	41,846	5.6	55,170	52.0	45	1,646	182,897	97

Entries in **UPPERCASE** are counties.
Entries in **bold** have populations of 2,500 or more.
Names in parentheses are alternate names.
Inc. Place — Incorporated Place
RMC Place — Rand McNally Designated Place
CDP — Census Designated Place
MCD — Minor Civil Division

⊡ County Seat
▲ Minor Civil Division
elev. Elevation
Ⓟ Post Office

H Hospital
C College
■ Principal Business Center
★ Ranally Metro Area (RMA) Abbreviation
z Zip Code(s)

Ⓟ Previous Census Population
® Revised Census Population
Ⓐ Annexation Population
● Rand McNally Population Estimate
© Final Census Population
Ⓢ Special Census Population
◆ Estimated Population

For additional definitions see Glossary, Volume 1, and Introduction, Volume 2.

County	FIPS Code	County Seat	Land Area (Sq. Mi.)	Census Population			Wholesale Trade		Manufacturing, 2002			
				4/1/2000	4/1/1990	% Change 1990-2000	Sales, 2002 ($1,000)	% Change 1997-2002	Establish-ments	Total Employees	Value Added ($1,000)	Ranally Mfg. Units
Oswego	075	Oswego	953	122,377	121,771	0.5	(d)	(d)	96	4,350	559,004	296
Otsego	077	Cooperstown	1,003	61,676	60,517	1.9	304,286	206.2	72	1,271	135,786	72
Putnam	079	Carmel	231	95,745	83,941	14.1	(d)	(d)	87	1,900	230,409	122
Queens	081	Jamaica	109	2,229,379	1,951,598	14.2	13,868,922	7.2	1,755	40,019	3,376,319	1,786
Rensselaer	083	Troy	654	152,538	154,429	-1.2	842,492	7.9	113	3,330	328,996	174
Richmond	085	St. George	58	443,728	378,977	17.1	(d)	(d)	158	1,366	188,312	100
Rockland	087	New City	174	286,753	265,475	8.0	(d)	(d)	292	10,166	5,450,809	2,884
St. Lawrence	089	Canton	2,686	111,931	111,974	-0.0	288,179	-8.9	79	4,081	814,427	431
Saratoga	091	Ballston Spa	812	200,635	181,276	10.7	2,655,159	72.5	128	5,684	736,522	390
Schenectady	093	Schenectady	206	146,555	149,285	-1.8	405,319	-34.5	115	5,607	1,918,864	1,015
Schoharie	095	Schoharie	622	31,582	31,859	-0.9	37,049	51.6	...	(d)	(d)	...
Schuyler	097	Watkins Glen	329	19,224	18,662	3.0	(d)	(d)	...	(d)	(d)	...
Seneca	099	Waterloo	325	33,342	33,683	-1.0	(d)	(d)	36	1,311	189,137	100
Steuben	101	Bath	1,393	98,726	99,088	-0.4	435,750	384.6	84	6,517	722,527	382
Suffolk	103	Riverhead	912	1,419,369	1,321,864	7.4	31,089,261	41.6	2,527	63,055	10,072,735	5,329
Sullivan	105	Monticello	970	73,966	69,277	6.8	220,761	-6.4	51	698	50,961	27
Tioga	107	Owego	519	51,784	52,337	-1.1	352,489	(d)	41	2,070	175,171	93
Tompkins	109	Ithaca	476	96,501	94,097	2.6	182,157	-24.0	91	3,309	452,053	239
Ulster	111	Kingston	1,126	177,749	165,304	7.5	(d)	(d)	211	5,574	450,597	238
Warren	113	Lake George	869	63,303	59,209	6.9	250,706	(d)	92	4,450	467,837	248
Washington	115	Hudson Falls	835	61,042	59,330	2.9	86,197	(d)	105	3,406	394,717	209
Wayne	117	Lyons	604	93,765	89,123	5.2	257,686	-21.2	150	7,436	897,275	475
Westchester	119	White Plains	433	923,459	874,866	5.6	37,819,511	58.1	793	17,700	2,056,105	1,088
Wyoming	121	Warsaw	593	43,424	42,507	2.2	104,972	-2.3	57	1,859	167,572	89
Yates	123	Penn Yan	338	24,621	22,810	7.9	77,531	(d)	31	721	71,403	38
The State			**47,214**	**18,976,457**	**17,990,455**	**5.5**	**343,663,041**	**7.5**	**21,066**	**641,434**	**83,874,558**	**44,375**

(d) Data not available. Corresponding percentages or Ranally Manufacturing Units are estimates.
... Represents 0 or amount too minimal to be reported.

Administrative Divisions

Towns: All New York counties are divided into towns, except for areas within cities or Indian reservations. Although legally incorporated, towns are not treated as incorporated places by the U.S. Census because the population often is scattered among several localities and rural areas rather than being concentrated in a single place. Only towns with an active government recognized by the U.S. Census of Governments are printed in this index.

Cities and Villages: Incorporated cities do not form part of the townships which adjoin or surround them. Each of the incorporated villages, in contrast, legally forms part of one or more townships.

Index of Places and Counties

A

Abbotts; RMC Place; CATTARAUGUS; ▲ Ischua; ***208** NL-5; elev. 1,639ft./500m.; mail Cuba **z** 14727
Academy; RMC Place; ALBANY; ★ **A-S-T**; mail Albany **z** 12208; pop. incl. with Albany (Inc. Place)
Academy; RMC Place; ONTARIO; ▲ Canandaigua; ***208** NJ-8; mail Canandaigua **z** 14424; rural
Accord; CDP; ULSTER; ▲ Rochester; **209** NN-18; elev. 249ft./76m.; [P]; **z** 12404; © 622
Acidalia; RMC Place; SULLIVAN; ▲ Fremont; ***207** SA-2; mail Long Eddy **z** 12760; rural
Acra; RMC Place; GREENE; ▲ Cairo; **209** NL-18; [P]; **z** 12405; ● 575
Adams; Inc. Place; JEFFERSON; ▲ Brownville; **209** NF-12; [P]; ★ **WATN**; **z** 13605; Ⓟ 1,753; © 1,624
Adams; MCD-Town; JEFFERSON; ***209** NF-12; [P]; ★ **WATN**; **z** 13605; Ⓟ 4,977; © 4,782
Adams Basin; RMC Place; MONROE; ▲ Ogden; ***208** NH-7; [P]; ★ **ROCH**; **z** 14410; ● 300
Adams Center; CDP; JEFFERSON; ▲ Adams; **209** NF-12; [P]; ★ **WATN**; **z** 13606; Ⓟ 1,675; © 1,500
Adams Corners; RMC Place; PUTNAM; ▲ Putnam Valley; ***207** SC-7; ★ **N.Y.**; mail Putnam Valley **z** 10579; rural
Adams Cove; RMC Place; JEFFERSON; ▲ Brownville; ***209** NE-12; ★ **WATN**; mail Dexter **z** 13634; rural
Adamsville; RMC Place; WASHINGTON; ▲ Kingsbury, Hartford; ***209** NH-20; elev. 364ft./111m.; ★ **GLFLS**; mail Fort Ann **z** 12827; rural
Addison; Inc. Place; STEUBEN; ▲ Tuscarora; **208** NM-8; [P]; **z** 14801; Ⓟ 1,842; © 1,797
Addison; MCD-Town; STEUBEN; ***208** NM-8; [P]; **z** 14801; Ⓟ 2,645; © 2,640
Addison Hill; RMC Place; STEUBEN; ▲ Tuscarora; ***208** NM-8; mail Elkland **z** 16920; rural
Adelphi; RMC Place; KINGS; ***207** SF-7; elev. 82ft./25m.; ★ **N.Y.**; mail Brooklyn **z** 11238; pop. incl. with New York (Inc. Place)
Aden; RMC Place; SULLIVAN; ▲ Neversink; ***207** SA-4; mail Parksville **z** 12768; rural
Adirondack; RMC Place; WARREN; ▲ Horicon; **209** NF-19; elev. 842ft./257m.; [P]; **z** 12808; ● 200
Adrian; RMC Place; STEUBEN; ▲ Canisteo; **208** NL-8; mail Canisteo **z** 14823; ● 95
Afton; Inc. Place; CHENANGO; ▲ Afton; **209** NL-14; [P]; **z** 13730; Ⓟ 838; © 836
Afton; MCD-Town; CHENANGO; ***209** NL-14; [P]; **z** 13730; Ⓟ 2,972; © 2,977
Afton Lake; RMC Place; CHENANGO; ▲ Afton; ***209** NL-14; mail Afton **z** 13730; ● 125
Airmont; Inc. Place; ROCKLAND; ▲ Ramapo; ***207** SD-6; elev. 500ft./152m.; [P]; ★ **N.Y.**; **z** 10901, **z** 10952; Ⓟ 7,674; © 7,799
Airmont Heights; RMC Place; ROCKLAND; ▲ Ramapo; ★ **N.Y.**; mail Suffern **z** 10901; pop. incl. with Airmont (Inc. Place)
Akins Corners; RMC Place; PUTNAM; ▲ Patterson; ***207** SB-8; elev. 460ft./140m.; ★ **N.Y.**; mail Patterson **z** 12563; rural
Akron; Inc. Place; ERIE; ▲ Newstead; **208** NI-5; [P]; **z** 14001; Ⓟ 2,906; © 3,085
Alabama; RMC Place; GENESEE; ▲ Alabama; **208** NI-5; [P]; **z** 14013; ● 300
Alabama; MCD-Town; GENESEE; ***208** NI-5; [P]; **z** 14013; Ⓟ 1,998; © 1,881
Albany; Inc. Place; **STATE CAPITAL**; ⊡ ALBANY; **209** NK-19; elev. 150ft./46m.; [P] [H] [C] 54,510 ■; ★ **A-S-T**; **z** 12201-12, **z** 12214, **z** 12220, **z** 12222-50, **z** 12252, **z** 12255-57, **z** 12260-61, **z** 12288; Ⓟ 101,082; © 95,658; Ⓡ 94,301; ◆ 97,679
ALBANY; **209** NK-18; Ⓟ 292,594; © 294,565; ◆ 302,552
Albany Medical Center; RMC Place; ALBANY; ★ **A-S-T**; mail Albany **z** 12208; pop. incl. with Albany (Inc. Place)
Albertson; CDP; NASSAU; ▲ North Hempstead; **207** SF-8; [P]; ★ **N.Y.**; **z** 11507; Ⓟ 5,166; © 5,200
Albia; RMC Place; RENSSELAER; **207** SI-6; ★ **A-S-T**; mail Troy **z** 12180
Albion; Inc. Place; ⊡ ORLEANS; ▲ Gaines, Albion; **208** NH-6; [P]; **z** 14411; Ⓟ 5,863; © 7,438; Ⓡ 5,992
Albion; MCD-Town; ORLEANS; ***208** NH-5; [P]; **z** 14411; includes part of the Village of Albion; Ⓟ 8,178; © 8,042; Ⓡ 9,409
Albion; MCD-Town; OSWEGO; ***209** NG-12; mail Altmar **z** 13302; Ⓟ 2,043; © 2,083
Alburg; RMC Place; FRANKLIN; ▲ Moira; ***209** NB-16; mail Brushton **z** 12916; rural
Alcove; RMC Place; ALBANY; ▲ Coeymans; **209** NK-18; [P]; ★ **A-S-T**; **z** 12007; ● 220
Alden; Inc. Place; ERIE; ▲ Alden; **208** NJ-5; elev. 866ft./264m.; [P]; ★ **BUF**; **z** 14004; Ⓟ 2,457; © 2,666
Alden; MCD-Town; ERIE; ***208** NJ-5; [P]; ★ **BUF**; **z** 14004; Ⓟ 10,372; © 10,470
Alden Center; RMC Place; ERIE; ▲ Alden; ***208** NJ-5; elev. 828ft./252m.; ★ **BUF**; mail Alden **z** 14004; ● 380
Alden Manor; RMC Place; NASSAU; ▲ Hempstead; **211** I-16; [P]; ★ **N.Y.**; **z** 11003
Alder Bend; RMC Place; CLINTON; ▲ Altona; ***209** NB-19; mail Altona **z** 12910; ● 200
Alder Creek; RMC Place; ONEIDA; ▲ Boonville; **209** NH-14; elev. 1,199ft./365m.; [P]; **z** 13301; summer pop. 1,000; ● 450
Alexander; Inc. Place; GENESEE; ▲ Alexander; **208** NJ-5; elev. 940ft./287m.; [P]; **z** 14005; Ⓟ 445; © 481
Alexander; MCD-Town; GENESEE; ***208** NJ-5; [P]; **z** 14005; Ⓟ 2,233; © 2,451
Alexander Corners; RMC Place; JEFFERSON; ▲ Henderson; ***209** NF-11; elev. 333ft./101m.; mail Henderson **z** 13650; rural
Alexandria; MCD-Town; JEFFERSON; ***209** ND-12; mail Alexandria Bay **z** 13607; Ⓟ 3,949; © 4,097
Alexandria Bay; Inc. Place; JEFFERSON; ▲ Alexandria; **209** ND-12; elev. 284ft./87m.; [P] [H]; **z** 13607; Ⓟ 1,194; © 1,088
Alfred; Inc. Place; ALLEGANY; ▲ Alfred; **208** NL-7; elev. 1,762ft./537m.; [P] [C] 5,511; **z** 14802; Ⓟ 4,559; © 3,954
Alfred; ALLEGANY; see Alfred Station (RMC Place)
Alfred; MCD-Town; ALLEGANY; ***208** NL-7; [P] [C] 5,511; **z** 14802; Ⓟ 5,791; © 5,140
Alfred Station (Alfred); RMC Place; ALLEGANY; ▲ Alfred; **208** NL-7; [P]; **z** 14803 & mail Alfred **z** 14802; ● 350
Allaben; RMC Place; ULSTER; ▲ Shandaken; **209** NM-17; mail Shandaken **z** 12480; ● 250
Allard Corners; RMC Place; ORANGE; ▲ Montgomery; ***207** SB-5; mail Walden **z** 12586; rural
Allegany; Inc. Place; CATTARAUGUS; **208** NM-5; elev. 1,420ft./433m.; [P]; **z** 14706; Ⓟ 1,980; © 1,883
Allegany; MCD-Town; CATTARAUGUS; ***208** NM-4; [P] [C] 2,375; **z** 14706; Ⓟ 8,327; © 8,230
ALLEGANY; **208** NL-6; Ⓟ 50,470; © 49,927; ◆ 49,352
Allegany Reservation; Indian Reservation; CATTARAUGUS; ▲ Allegany; mail Irving **z** 14081; Ⓟ 7,681; © 6,804
Allen; MCD-Town; ALLEGANY; ***208** NL-6; mail Angelica **z** 14709; Ⓟ 406; © 462
Allen Center; RMC Place; ALLEGANY; ▲ Allen; ***208** NL-6; mail Fillmore **z** 14735; rural
Allens Hill; RMC Place; ONTARIO; ▲ Richmond; ***208** NJ-8; elev. 1,026ft./313m.; mail Bloomfield **z** 14469; ● 80
Allentown; RMC Place; ALLEGANY; ▲ Alma; **208** NM-6; elev. 1,851ft./564m.; [P]; **z** 14707; ● 350
Allentown; RMC Place; SARATOGA; ▲ Day; ***209** NH-18; ★ **GLFLS**; mail Hadley **z** 12835; ● 140
Allenwood; NASSAU; see Great Neck Gardens (CDP-Census Area Only)
Allerton; RMC Place; BRONX; ★ **N.Y.**; mail Bronx **z** 10467; pop. incl. with New York (Inc. Place)
Alligerville; RMC Place; ULSTER; ▲ Rochester; **207** SA-6; elev. 220ft./67m.; mail High Falls **z** 12440; ● 135
Alloway; RMC Place; WAYNE; ▲ Lyons; **208** NI-9; elev. 437ft./133m.; mail Lyons **z** 14489; ● 100
Alma; RMC Place; ALLEGANY; ▲ Alma; **208** NM-6; elev. 1,552ft./473m.; [P]; **z** 14708 & mail Bolivar **z** 14715; ● 225
Alma; MCD-Town; ALLEGANY; ***208** NM-6; [P]; **z** 14708 & mail Bolivar **z** 14715; Ⓟ 846; © 847
Almond; Inc. Place; ALLEGANY, STEUBEN; ▲ Almond, Hornellsville; **208** NL-7; [P]; **z** 14804; Ⓟ 458; © 461
Almond; MCD-Town; ALLEGANY; ***208** NL-7; [P]; **z** 14804; includes part of the Village of Almond; Ⓟ 1,640; © 1,604
Aloquin; RMC Place; ONTARIO; ▲ Hornellsville; ***208** NJ-9; mail Stanley **z** 14561; ● 50
Alpine; RMC Place; SCHUYLER; ▲ Catharine; **208** NL-10; elev. 1,169ft./356m.; [P]; **z** 14805; ● 250
Alplaus; RMC Place; SCHENECTADY; ▲ Glenville; ***209** NJ-18; [P]; ★ **A-S-T**; **z** 12008
Alps; RMC Place; RENSSELAER; ▲ Nassau; **209** NK-20; ★ **A-S-T**; mail Averill Park **z** 12018; ● 100
Alsen; RMC Place; GREENE; ▲ Catskill; ***209** NM-18; ★ **KNGST**; mail Catskill **z** 12414; rural
Altamont; Inc. Place; ALBANY; ▲ Guilderland; **209** NJ-18; elev. 451ft./137m.; [P]; ★ **A-S-T**; **z** 12009; Ⓟ 1,519; © 1,737
Altamont; FRANKLIN; see Tupper Lake (Inc. Place)
Altamont; FRANKLIN; see Tupper Lake (MCD-Town)
Altay; RMC Place; SCHUYLER; ▲ Tyrone; **208** NL-9; elev. 1,239ft./378m.; mail Dundee **z** 14837; ● 100
Altmar; Inc. Place; OSWEGO; ▲ Albion; **209** NG-12; elev. 577ft./176m.; [P]; **z** 13302; Ⓟ 336; © 351
Alton; RMC Place; WAYNE; ▲ Sodus; **208** NH-9; [P]; ★ **ROCH**; **z** 14413; ● 550
Altona; CDP; CLINTON; ▲ Altona; **209** NA-19; [P]; **z** 12910; Ⓟ 1,003; © 1,056
Altona; MCD-Town; CLINTON; ***209** NB-19; [P]; **z** 12910; Ⓟ 2,775; © 3,160
Amagansett; CDP; SUFFOLK; ▲ East Hampton; **207** SE-13; elev. 32ft./10m.; [P]; **z** 11930; summer pop. 6,000; © 1,067
Amawalk; RMC Place; WESTCHESTER; ▲ Yorktown, Somers; **207** SD-7; [P]; ★ **N.Y.**; **z** 10501; ● 1,390
Amber; RMC Place; ONONDAGA; ▲ Otisco; **209** NJ-11; ★ **SYR**; mail Marietta **z** 13110; ● 350
Amblerville; RMC Place; CHENANGO; ▲ New Berlin; ***209** NK-14; mail South New Berlin **z** 13843; rural
Amboy; RMC Place; ONONDAGA; ▲ Camillus; **208** NF-7; ★ **SYR**; mail Camillus **z** 13031; ● 600
Amboy; MCD-Town; OSWEGO; ***209** NH-12; mail Williamstown **z** 13493; Ⓟ 1,010; © 1,312
Amboy Center; RMC Place; OSWEGO; ▲ Amboy; **209** NH-12; mail Williamstown **z** 13493
Amenia; CDP; DUTCHESS; ▲ Amenia; **209** NN-20; elev. 573ft./175m.; [P]; **z** 12501; Ⓟ 1,057; © 1,115
Amenia; MCD-Town; DUTCHESS; ***207** SA-8; [P]; **z** 12501; Ⓟ 5,195; © 4,048
Amenia Union; RMC Place; DUTCHESS; ▲ Amenia; **207** SA-8; elev. 474ft./144m.; mail Amenia **z** 12501; ● 80
Ames; Inc. Place; MONTGOMERY; ▲ Canajoharie; **209** NJ-16; elev. 713ft./217m.; [P]; **z** 13317; Ⓟ 166; © 173
Amherst; RMC Place; ERIE; ▲ Amherst; **208** NI-4; [P] [C] 2,841; ★ **BUF**; **z** 14221, **z** 14226, **z** 14228, **z** 14260-61 & mail Buffalo **z** 14225, **z** 14231, East Amherst **z** 14051, Getzville **z** 14068; ● 45,800
Amherst; MCD-Town; ERIE; ***208** NI-4; [P] [C] 2,841; ★ **BUF**; **z** 14221, **z** 14226, **z** 14228, **z** 14260-61 & mail Buffalo **z** 14225, East Amherst **z** 14051, Getzville **z** 14068; Ⓟ 111,711; © 116,510; ◆ 115,346
Amity; MCD-Town; ALLEGANY; ***208** NL-6; mail Belmont **z** 14813; Ⓟ 2,255; © 2,245
Amity; RMC Place; ORANGE; ▲ Warwick; **207** SD-5; ★ **N.Y.**; mail Warwick **z** 10990; ● 60
Amity Harbor; RMC Place; SUFFOLK; ▲ Babylon; ***207** SF-9; [P]; ★ **N.Y.**; **z** 11701
Amityville; Inc. Place; SUFFOLK; ▲ Babylon; **207** SF-8; elev. 25ft./8m.; [P] [H]; ★ **N.Y.**; **z** 11701, **z** 11708; Ⓟ 9,286; © 9,441
Amsdell Heights; RMC Place; ERIE; ▲ Hamburg; ***208** NJ-3; ★ **BUF**; mail Hamburg **z** 14075; ● 550
Amsterdam; Inc. Place; MONTGOMERY; **209** NI-18; [P] [H] ■; ★ **A-S-T**; **z** 12010; Ⓟ 20,714; © 18,355; ◆ 17,503
Amsterdam; MCD-Town; MONTGOMERY; ***209** NI-18; [P]; ★ **A-S-T**; **z** 12010; does not include the City of Amsterdam; Ⓟ 5,962; © 5,820
Ancram; RMC Place; COLUMBIA; ▲ Ancram; **209** NM-19; [P]; **z** 12502; ● 450
Ancram; MCD-Town; COLUMBIA; ***209** NM-20; [P]; **z** 12502; Ⓟ 1,510; © 1,513
Ancramdale; RMC Place; COLUMBIA; ▲ Ancram; **209** NM-19; [P]; **z** 12503; ● 500
Andes; RMC Place; DELAWARE; ▲ Andes; **209** NM-16; [P]; **z** 13731 & mail Bovina Center **z** 13740; former incorporated place; disincorporated Decmber 31, 2003; Ⓟ 292; © 289
Andes; MCD-Town; DELAWARE; ***209** NM-16; [P]; **z** 13731; Ⓟ 1,291; © 1,356
Andover; Inc. Place; ALLEGANY; ▲ Andover; **208** NM-7; elev. 1,665ft./507m.; [P]; **z** 14806; Ⓟ 1,125; © 1,073
Andover; MCD-Town; ALLEGANY; ***208** NM-7; [P]; **z** 14806; Ⓟ 1,981; © 1,945
Andrea Park Estates; RMC Place; WESTCHESTER; ▲ Yorktown; ★ **N.Y.**; mail Yorktown Heights **z** 10598
Angelica; Inc. Place; ALLEGANY; ▲ Angelica; **208** NL-6; [P]; **z** 14709; Ⓟ 963; © 903
Angelica; MCD-Town; ALLEGANY; ***208** NL-6; [P]; **z** 14709; Ⓟ 1,446; © 1,411
Angola; Inc. Place; ERIE; ▲ Evans; **208** NK-3; elev. 689ft./210m.; [P]; ★ **BUF**; **z** 14006; Ⓟ 2,231; © 2,266
Angola-on-the-Lake; CDP; ERIE; ▲ Evans; **208** NK-3; ★ **BUF**; mail Angola **z** 14006; © 1,771
Annadale; RMC Place; RICHMOND; **210** M-6; ★ **N.Y.**; mail Staten Island **z** 10312; pop. incl. with New York (Inc. Place)
Annandale-on-Hudson; RMC Place; DUTCHESS; ▲ Red Hook; **209** NM-19; [P] [C] 2,012; **z** 12504; ● 100
Annsville; MCD-Town; ONEIDA; ***209** NH-13; mail Taberg **z** 13471; Ⓟ 2,786; © 2,956
Annsville; RMC Place; WESTCHESTER; ▲ Cortlandt; ***207** SC-7; ★ **N.Y.**; mail Peekskill **z** 10566; ● 200
Ansonia; RMC Place; NEW YORK; ★ **N.Y.**; mail New York **z** 10023; pop. incl. with New York (Inc. Place)
Antwerp; Inc. Place; JEFFERSON; ▲ Antwerp; **209** ND-13; elev. 545ft./166m.; [P]; **z** 13608 & mail Oxbow **z** 13671; Ⓟ 739; © 716
Antwerp; MCD-Town; JEFFERSON; ***209** ND-13; [P]; **z** 13608 & mail Oxbow **z** 13671; Ⓟ 1,856; © 1,793
Apalachin; CDP; TIOGA; ▲ Owego; **209** NM-12; [P]; ★ **BING**; **z** 13732; Ⓟ 1,208; © 1,126
Apex; RMC Place; DELAWARE; ▲ Tompkins; ***209** NM-14; mail Hancock **z** 13783; rural
Appleton; RMC Place; NIAGARA; ▲ Newfane; **208** NH-4; elev. 339ft./103m.; [P]; ★ **LOCK**; **z** 14008; ● 200
Apulia; RMC Place; ONONDAGA; ▲ Fabius; ***209** NJ-12; mail Tully **z** 13159; ● 100
Apulia; ONONDAGA; see Apulia Station (RMC Place)
Apulia Station (Apulia); RMC Place; ONONDAGA; ▲ Fabius; **209** NJ-12; elev. 1,245ft./379m.; [P]; **z** 13020; ● 300
Aquebogue; CDP; SUFFOLK; ▲ Riverhead; ***207** SE-11; [P]; **z** 11931; Ⓟ 2,060; © 2,254
Aqueduct; RMC Place; SCHENECTADY; ***209** NJ-18; ★ **A-S-T**; mail Schenectady **z** 12308
Aquetuck; RMC Place; ALBANY; ▲ Coeymans; ***209** NK-19; elev. 318ft./97m.; ★ **A-S-T**; mail Ravena **z** 12143; rural
Arcade; Inc. Place; WYOMING; ▲ Arcade; **208** NK-5; [P]; **z** 14009; Ⓟ 2,081; © 2,026
Arcade; MCD-Town; WYOMING; ***208** NK-5; [P]; **z** 14009; Ⓟ 3,938; © 4,184
Arcade Junction; RMC Place; WYOMING; mail Arcade **z** 14009; pop. incl. with Arcade (Inc. Place)
Arcadia; MCD-Town; WAYNE; ***208** NI-9; mail Newark **z** 14513; Ⓟ 14,855; © 14,889
Arcadia Hills; RMC Place; ORANGE; ▲ Goshen; ***207** SC-5; ★ **N.Y.**; mail Goshen **z** 10924; ● 500
Archdale; RMC Place; WASHINGTON; ▲ Cambridge; ***209** NI-20; elev. 570ft./174m.; mail Greenwich **z** 12834; rural
Archer Ave; RMC Place; QUEENS; ★ **N.Y.**; mail Jamaica **z** 11435; pop. incl. with New York (Inc. Place)
Archville; RMC Place; WESTCHESTER; ▲ Mount Pleasant; ***207** SD-7; ★ **N.Y.**; mail Briarcliff Manor **z** 10510; ● 80
Arden; RMC Place; ORANGE; ▲ Tuxedo; **207** SD-6; elev. 521ft./159m.; [P]; ★ **N.Y.**; **z** 10910; ● 100
Arden Heights; RMC Place; RICHMOND; ***207** SG-6; elev. 53ft./16m.; ★ **N.Y.**; mail Staten Island **z** 10312; pop. incl. with New York (Inc. Place)
Ardonia; RMC Place; ULSTER; ▲ Plattekill; **207** SB-6; ★ **NWBG**; mail Clintondale **z** 12515; ● 120
Ardsley; Inc. Place; WESTCHESTER; ▲ Greenburgh; ***207** SE-7; [P]; ★ **N.Y.**; **z** 10502; Ⓟ 4,272; © 4,269
Ardsley On Hudson; RMC Place; WESTCHESTER; ***207** SE-7; elev. 200ft./61m.; [P]; ★ **N.Y.**; **z** 10503; pop. incl. with Irvington (Inc. Place)
Argusville; RMC Place; SCHOHARIE; ▲ Sharon, Carlisle; ***209** NJ-17; mail Sharon Springs **z** 13459; rural
Argyle; Inc. Place; WASHINGTON; ▲ Hornellsville, Argyle; **209** NH-20; [P]; **z** 12809; Ⓟ 295; © 289
Argyle; MCD-Town; WASHINGTON; ***209** NH-20; [P]; **z** 12809; Ⓟ 3,031; © 3,688
Arietta; MCD-Town; HAMILTON; ***209** NG-16; mail Piseco **z** 12139; Ⓟ 300; © 293
Arkport; Inc. Place; STEUBEN; ▲ Hornellsville; **208** NL-7; elev. 1,194ft./364m.; [P]; **z** 14807; Ⓟ 770; © 832
Arkville; RMC Place; DELAWARE; ▲ Middletown; **209** NM-16; [P]; **z** 12406; ● 500
Arkwright; MCD-Town; CHAUTAUQUA; ***208** NL-2; mail Cassadaga **z** 14718; Ⓟ 1,040; © 1,126
Arlington; CDP; DUTCHESS; ▲ Poughkeepsie; **207** SB-7; [P]; ★ **POK**; **z** 12603; Ⓟ 11,948; © 12,481
Arlington; RMC Place; RICHMOND; ***207** SG-6; elev. 31ft./9m.; ★ **N.Y.**; mail Staten Island **z** 10303; pop. incl. with New York (Inc. Place)
Arlyn Oaks; RMC Place; NASSAU; ▲ Oyster Bay; ***207** SF-8; ★ **N.Y.**; mail Massapequa **z** 11758; ● 4,500
Armonk; CDP; WESTCHESTER; ▲ North Castle; **207** SD-7; elev. 386ft./118m.; [P]; ★ **N.Y.**; **z** 10504; Ⓟ 2,745; © 3,461
Armor; RMC Place; ERIE; ▲ Orchard Park, Hamburg; **208** NJ-4; ★ **BUF**; mail Hamburg **z** 14075; ● 1,550
Arnolds Mill; RMC Place; COLUMBIA; ▲ Ghent; ***209** NL-19; elev. 466ft./142m.; ★ **A-S-T**; mail Chatham **z** 12037; rural
Arrochar; RMC Place; RICHMOND; ***207** SG-6; ★ **N.Y.**; mail Staten Island **z** 10305; pop. incl. with New York (Inc. Place)
Arshamonaque (Jersey Colony); RMC Place; SUFFOLK; ▲ Southold; ***207** SD-12; mail Southold **z** 11971; ● 75
Arthur Manor; RMC Place; WESTCHESTER; ***207** SE-7; ★ **N.Y.**; mail Scarsdale **z** 10583; pop. incl. with Scarsdale (Inc. Place)
Arthursburg; RMC Place; DUTCHESS; ▲ La Grange; **207** SB-7; elev. 338ft./103m.; ★ **POK**; mail Hopewell Junction **z** 12533; ● 215
Arverne; RMC Place; QUEENS; **211** L-14; [P]; ★ **N.Y.**; **z** 11692; pop. incl. with New York (Inc. Place)
Ashantee; RMC Place; LIVINGSTON; ▲ Avon; ***208** NJ-7; elev. 585ft./178m.; ★ **ROCH**; mail Avon **z** 14414; rural
Asharoken; Inc. Place; SUFFOLK; ▲ Huntington; **207** SE-9; ★ **N.Y.**; mail Northport **z** 11768; Ⓟ 807; © 625
Ashford; RMC Place; CATTARAUGUS; **208** NL-4; mail Ellicottville **z** 14731; ● 70
Ashford; MCD-Town; CATTARAUGUS; ***208** NK-4; mail West Valley **z** 14171; Ⓟ 2,162; © 2,223
Ashford Hollow; RMC Place; CATTARAUGUS; ▲ Ashford; ***208** NL-4; elev. 1,518ft./463m.; mail West Valley **z** 14171; ● 90
Ash Grove; RMC Place; WASHINGTON; ▲ White Creek; ***209** NI-20; mail Cambridge **z** 12816; rural
Ashland; MCD-Town; CHEMUNG; ***208** NM-10; ★ **ELM**; mail Wellsburg **z** 14894; Ⓟ 1,966; © 1,951
Ashland; RMC Place; GREENE; ▲ Ashland; **209** NL-17; elev. 1,423ft./434m.; [P]; **z** 12407; ● 200
Ashland; MCD-Town; GREENE; ***209** NL-17; [P]; **z** 12407; Ⓟ 803; © 752
Ashokan; RMC Place; ULSTER; ▲ Olive; **209** NM-18; elev. 679ft./207m.; mail Shokan **z** 12481; ● 300
Ashville; RMC Place; CHAUTAUQUA; ▲ North Harmony; **208** NM-2; [P]; **z** 14710; ● 800
Ashville Bay; RMC Place; CHAUTAUQUA; ▲ North Harmony; ***208** NM-2; mail Ashville **z** 14710; ● 90
Ashwood; RMC Place; ORLEANS; ▲ Yates, Carlton; ***208** NH-5; mail Lyndonville **z** 14098; ● 100
Aspenwood; RMC Place; SARATOGA; ▲ Clifton Park; ***209** NJ-19; ★ **A-S-T**; mail Clifton Park **z** 12065
Aspinwall Corners; RMC Place; JEFFERSON; ▲ Henderson; ***209** NF-12; elev. 360ft./110m.; mail Henderson **z** 13650; rural
Assembly Point; RMC Place; WARREN; ▲ Queensbury; ***209** NG-19; ★ **GLFLS**; mail Lake George **z** 12845; summer pop. 200
Association Island; RMC Place; JEFFERSON; ▲ Henderson; mail Henderson Harbor **z** 13651; summer pop. 300
Astoria; RMC Place; QUEENS; **211** G-11; [P]; ★ **N.Y.**; **z** 11101-06; pop. incl. with New York (Inc. Place)
Athens; Inc. Place; GREENE; ▲ Athens; **209** NL-19; [P]; **z** 12015; Ⓟ 1,708; © 1,695
Athens; MCD-Town; GREENE; ***209** NL-19; [P]; **z** 12015; Ⓟ 3,561; © 3,991
Athol; RMC Place; WARREN; ▲ Thurman; **209** NG-19; [P]; **z** 12810; ● 250
Athol Springs; RMC Place; ERIE; ▲ Hamburg; ***208** NJ-3; [P]; ★ **BUF**; **z** 14010; ● 700
Atlanta; RMC Place; STEUBEN; ▲ Cohocton; **208** NK-8; [P]; **z** 14808; ● 700
Atlantic Beach; Inc. Place; NASSAU; ▲ Hempstead; **207** SG-7; [P]; ★ **N.Y.**; **z** 11509; Ⓟ 1,933; © 1,986
Atlantique; RMC Place; SUFFOLK; ▲ Islip; ***207** SG-9; ★ **N.Y.**; mail Bay Shore **z** 11706; summer pop. 100; ● 10
Attica; Inc. Place; WYOMING, GENESEE; ▲ Alexander, Attica; **208** NJ-5; [P]; **z** 14011; Ⓟ 2,630; © 2,597
Attica; MCD-Town; WYOMING; ***208** NJ-5; [P]; **z** 14011; includes part of the Village of Attica; Ⓟ 7,383; © 6,028; Ⓡ 7,806
Attica Center; RMC Place; WYOMING; ▲ Attica; ***208** NJ-5; elev. 1,541ft./470m.; mail Attica **z** 14011; rural
Attlebury; RMC Place; DUTCHESS; ▲ Stanford; ***209** NN-19; mail Stanfordville **z** 12581; rural
Atwater; RMC Place; CAYUGA; ▲ Genoa; ***208** NK-10; mail King Ferry **z** 13081; ● 30
Atwell; RMC Place; HERKIMER; ▲ Ohio; **209** NG-15; elev. 1,828ft./557m.; mail Forestport **z** 13338; ● 20
Atwood; RMC Place; ULSTER; ▲ Marbletown; ***207** SA-6; ★ **KNGST**; mail Stone Ridge **z** 12484; rural
Auburn; Inc. Place; ⊡ CAYUGA; **208** NJ-10; elev. 708ft./216m.; [P] [H] ■; ★ **SYR**; **z** 13021-22, **z** 13024; Ⓟ 31,258; © 28,574; ◆ 26,465
Auburndale; RMC Place; QUEENS; ★ **N.Y.**; pop. incl. with New York (Inc. Place)
Auburn Southeast; CAYUGA; see Melrose Park (CDP)
Audubon; RMC Place; ERIE; ▲ Amherst; ***208** NI-4; ★ **BUF**; mail Getzville **z** 14068
Audubon; RMC Place; NEW YORK; ★ **N.Y.**; mail New York **z** 10032; pop. incl. with New York (Inc. Place)
Augusta; RMC Place; ONEIDA; ▲ Augusta; **209** NI-14; ★ **UT-R**; mail Oriskany Falls **z** 13425; ● 150
Augusta; MCD-Town; ONEIDA; ***209** NI-14; ★ **UT-R**; mail Oriskany Falls **z** 13425; Ⓟ 2,070; © 1,966
Aurelius; MCD-Town; CAYUGA; ***208** NJ-10; ★ **SYR**; mail Auburn **z** 13021, Cayuga **z** 13034; Ⓟ 2,913; © 2,936
Auriesville; RMC Place; MONTGOMERY; ▲ Glen; ***209** NI-17; [P]; **z** 12016 & mail Fultonville **z** 12072; ● 65
Aurora; Inc. Place; CAYUGA; ▲ Ledyard; **208** NJ-10; [P] [C] 564; **z** 13026; Ⓟ 687; © 720
Aurora; MCD-Town; ERIE; ***208** NJ-4; ★ **BUF**; mail East Aurora **z** 14052; Ⓟ 13,433; © 13,996
Aurora Tract; RMC Place; ONONDAGA; ▲ Clay; ***209** NI-11; ★ **SYR**; mail Liverpool **z** 13088; ● 2,100
Au Sable; MCD-Town; CLINTON; ***209** NC-19; mail Keeseville **z** 12944; Ⓟ 2,870; © 3,015
Ausable Chasm; RMC Place; CLINTON; ▲ Au Sable; ***209** NC-20; [P]; **z** 12911; ● 95
Au Sable Forks; CDP; ESSEX, CLINTON; ▲ Black Brook, Jay; **209** NC-19; [P]; **z** 12912; © 670
Austerlitz; RMC Place; COLUMBIA; ▲ Austerlitz; **209** NL-20; [P]; **z** 12017; ● 400
Austerlitz; MCD-Town; COLUMBIA; ***209** NL-20; [P]; **z** 12017; Ⓟ 1,456; © 1,453
Ava; RMC Place; ONEIDA; ▲ Ava; **209** NH-14; [P]; **z** 13303; ● 300
Ava; MCD-Town; ONEIDA; ***209** NH-14; [P]; **z** 13303; Ⓟ 792; © 725
Averill Park; CDP; RENSSELAER; ▲ Sand Lake; **209** NK-19; [P]; ★ **A-S-T**; **z** 12018; Ⓟ 2,656; © 1,517
Avoca; Inc. Place; STEUBEN; ▲ Avoca; **208** NL-8; elev. 1,192ft./363m.; [P]; **z** 14809; Ⓟ 1,033; © 1,008
Avoca; MCD-Town; STEUBEN; ***208** NL-8; [P]; **z** 14809; Ⓟ 2,269; © 2,314
Avon; Inc. Place; LIVINGSTON; ▲ Avon; **208** NJ-7; elev. 651ft./198m.; [P]; ★ **ROCH**; **z** 14414; Ⓟ 2,995; © 2,977
Avon; MCD-Town; LIVINGSTON; ***208** NJ-7; [P]; ★ **ROCH**; **z** 14414; Ⓟ 6,283; © 6,443
Axeville; RMC Place; CATTARAUGUS; ▲ Conewango; ***208** NL-3; elev. 1,696ft./517m.; mail Conewango Valley **z** 14726; rural
Axton Landing; RMC Place; FRANKLIN; ▲ Harrietstown; ***209** NC-17; mail Tupper Lake **z** 12986

B

Babcock Hill; RMC Place; ONEIDA; ▲ Bridgewater; ***209** NJ-14; mail Cassville **z** 13318; rural
Babcock Lake; RMC Place; RENSSELAER; ▲ Grafton; ***209** NJ-20; mail Petersburg **z** 12138; ● 100
Babylon; Inc. Place; SUFFOLK; ▲ Babylon; **207** SF-9; [P]; ★ **N.Y.**; **z** 11702-04, **z** 11707; Ⓟ 12,249; © 12,615
Babylon; MCD-Town; SUFFOLK; ***207** SG-9; [P]; ★ **N.Y.**; **z** 11702-04, **z** 11707; Ⓟ 202,889; © 211,792; ◆ 205,848
Bacon Hill; RMC Place; SARATOGA; ▲ Northumberland; ***209** NI-19; ★ **GLFLS**; mail Schuylerville **z** 12871; rural
Baggs Corner; RMC Place; JEFFERSON; ▲ Hounsfield; ***209** NE-12; elev. 386ft./118m.; mail Watertown **z** 13601; rural
Bainbridge; Inc. Place; CHENANGO; ▲ Bainbridge; **209** NL-14; elev. 1,006ft./307m.; [P]; **z** 13733; Ⓟ 1,550; © 1,365
Bainbridge; MCD-Town; CHENANGO; ***209** NL-14; [P]; **z** 13733; Ⓟ 3,445; © 3,401
Baiting Hollow; CDP; SUFFOLK; ▲ Riverhead; **207** SE-11; elev. 104ft./32m.; [P]; **z** 11933; © 1,449
Bakers Mills; RMC Place; WARREN; ▲ Johnsburg; **209** NG-18; [P]; **z** 12811; ● 280
Bakerstand; RMC Place; CATTARAUGUS; ▲ Machias; ***208** NL-4; elev. 1,730ft./527m.; mail Machias **z** 14101; rural
Balcom (Balcom Corners); RMC Place; CHAUTAUQUA; ▲ Villenova; ***208** NL-3; elev. 1,322ft./403m.; mail South Dayton **z** 14138; ● 60
Balcom Beach; RMC Place; ALLEGANY; ▲ Rushford; ***208** NL-5; elev. 1,463ft./446m.; mail Rushford **z** 14777; ● 50
Balcom Corners; CHAUTAUQUA; see Balcom (RMC Place)
Bald Mountain; RMC Place; WASHINGTON; ▲ Greenwich; ***209** NI-19; ★ **GLFLS**; mail Greenwich **z** 12834; rural
Baldwin; MCD-Town; CHEMUNG; ***208** NM-10; mail Lowman **z** 14861; Ⓟ 829; © 853
Baldwin; CDP; NASSAU; ▲ Hempstead; **207** SG-8; elev. 27ft./8m.; [P]; ★ **N.Y.**; **z** 11510; Ⓟ 22,719; © 23,455; ◆ 22,277
Baldwin Harbor; CDP; NASSAU; ▲ Hempstead; **211** J-18; ★ **N.Y.**; mail Baldwin **z** 11510; Ⓟ 7,899; © 8,147
Baldwin Heights; RMC Place; CATTARAUGUS; ***208** NM-5; mail Olean **z** 14760; pop. incl. with Olean (Inc. Place)
Baldwin Place; RMC Place; PUTNAM, WESTCHESTER; ▲ Carmel, Somers; ***207** SC-7; [P]; ★ **N.Y.**; **z** 10505; ● 1,500
Baldwinsville; Inc. Place; ONONDAGA; ▲ Van Buren, Lysander; **209** NI-11; [P]; ★ **SYR**; **z** 13027; Ⓟ 6,591; © 7,053
Ballina; RMC Place; MADISON; ▲ Cazenovia; ***209** NJ-13; ★ **SYR**; mail Cazenovia **z** 13035; rural
Ballston; SARATOGA; see Ballston Center (RMC Place)
Ballston; MCD-Town; SARATOGA; ***209** NI-18; ★ **A-S-T**; mail Ballston Lake **z** 12019; Ⓟ 8,078; © 8,729
Ballston Center (Ballston); RMC Place; SARATOGA; ▲ Ballston; ***209** NI-19; elev. 402ft./123m.; ★ **A-S-T**; mail Ballston Lake **z** 12019, Ballston Spa **z** 12020; rural
Ballston Lake; RMC Place; SARATOGA; ▲ Clifton Park, Ballston; **209** NJ-18; [P]; ★ **A-S-T**; **z** 12019; ● 700
Ballston Spa; Inc. Place; ⊡ SARATOGA; ▲ Milton, Ballston; **209** NI-19; elev. 288ft./88m.; [P]; ★ **A-S-T**; **z** 12020; Ⓟ 4,937; © 5,556
Balltown; RMC Place; CHAUTAUQUA; ▲ Hanover; ***208** NK-3; mail Forestville **z** 14062; rural
Balmat; RMC Place; ST. LAWRENCE; ▲ Fowler; **209** ND-14; elev. 681ft./208m.; mail Gouverneur **z** 13642; ● 100
Balmville; CDP; ORANGE; ▲ Newburgh; **207** SB-6; ★ **NWBG**; mail Newburgh **z** 12550; Ⓟ 2,963; © 3,339
Baltimore; RMC Place; CORTLAND; ▲ Preble; ***209** NJ-12; elev. 1,190ft./363m.; mail Preble **z** 13141; ● 30
Bangall; RMC Place; DUTCHESS; ▲ Stanford; **209** NN-19; [P]; **z** 12506; ● 200
Bangall; RMC Place; ONONDAGA; ▲ Van Buren; ***209** NI-11; ★ **SYR**; mail Memphis **z** 13112; rural
Bangor; RMC Place; FRANKLIN; ▲ Bangor; **209** NB-17; [P]; **z** 12966; ● 300
Bangor; MCD-Town; FRANKLIN; ***209** NB-17; [P]; **z** 12966; Ⓟ 2,080; © 2,147
Bangor Station; RMC Place; FRANKLIN; ▲ Bangor; ***209** NB-17; mail North Bangor **z** 12966; rural
Barberville; RMC Place; RENSSELAER; ▲ Poestenkill; ***209** NJ-20; elev. 806ft./246m.; ★ **A-S-T**; mail Averill Park **z** 12018; rural
Barbourville; RMC Place; DELAWARE; ***209** NM-14; mail Deposit **z** 13754; rural
Barcelona; RMC Place; CHAUTAUQUA; ▲ Westfield; ***208** NL-1; mail Westfield **z** 14787; ● 90
Barclay Heights; RMC Place; ULSTER; ★ **KNGST**; mail Saugerties **z** 12477; pop. incl. with Saugerties (Inc. Place)
Bardonia; CDP; ROCKLAND; ▲ Clarkstown; ***207** SD-6; [P]; ★ **N.Y.**; **z** 10954; Ⓟ 4,487; © 4,367
Bardwells Mill; RMC Place; ONEIDA; ▲ Remsen; ***209** NH-15; mail Remsen **z** 13438; rural
Barker; MCD-Town; BROOME; ***209** NL-12; mail Chenango Forks **z** 13746; Ⓟ 2,714; © 2,738
Barker; Inc. Place; NIAGARA; ▲ Somerset; **208** NH-4; elev. 331ft./101m.; [P]; ★ **LOCK**; **z** 14012; Ⓟ 569; © 577
Barkers Grove; RMC Place; WASHINGTON; ▲ Easton; ***209** NI-19; elev. 452ft./138m.; mail Schaghticoke **z** 12154; rural
Barkersville; RMC Place; SARATOGA; ▲ Providence; ***209** NI-18; mail Middle Grove **z** 12850; rural
Barkertown; RMC Place; LIVINGSTON; ▲ Nunda; ***208** NK-6; mail Dalton **z** 14836; rural
Barnard; RMC Place; MONROE; ***208** NH-7; ★ **ROCH**; pop. incl. with Rochester (Inc. Place)
Barnegat; RMC Place; DUTCHESS; ▲ Poughkeepsie; ***207** SB-6; elev. 30ft./9m.; ★ **POK**; mail Poughkeepsie **z** 12603; rural
Barnerville; RMC Place; SCHOHARIE; ▲ Cobleskill; ***209** NJ-17; mail Howes Cave **z** 12092; ● 135
Barnes Corners; RMC Place; LEWIS; ▲ Pinckney; **209** NF-13; elev. 1,400ft./427m.; [P]; **z** 13626; ● 150
Barnes Hole; RMC Place; SUFFOLK; ▲ East Hampton; ***207** SE-13; mail Amagansett **z** 11930
Barneveld (Trenton); Inc. Place; ONEIDA; ▲ Trenton; **209** NH-15; [P]; ★ **UT-R**; **z** 13304; Ⓟ 272; © 332
Barnum Island (North Long Beach); CDP-Census Area Only; NASSAU; ▲ Hempstead; **211** K-17; ★ **N.Y.**; mail Island Park **z** 11558; Ⓟ 2,624; © 2,487
Barre; ORLEANS; see Barre Center (RMC Place)
Barre; MCD-Town; ORLEANS; ***208** NI-5; mail Albion **z** 14411; Ⓟ 2,093; © 2,124
Barre Center (Barre); RMC Place; ORLEANS; ▲ Barre; **208** NH-6; elev. 692ft./211m.; mail Albion **z** 14411; ● 160
Barrington; MCD-Town; YATES; ***208** NK-9; mail Dundee **z** 14837; Ⓟ 1,195; © 1,396
Barrytown; RMC Place; DUTCHESS; ▲ Red Hook; ***209** NM-18; [P]; **z** 12507; ● 170
Barryville; RMC Place; SULLIVAN; ▲ Highland; **207** SC-3; [P]; **z** 12719; ● 600
Bartlett; RMC Place; ONEIDA; ▲ Westmoreland; ***209** NI-14; elev. 543ft./166m.; ★ **UT-R**; mail Rome **z** 13440; rural
Bartlett Corners; RMC Place; MONROE; ▲ Parma; ***208** NH-7; elev. 279ft./85m.; ★ **ROCH**; mail Hilton **z** 14468; rural
Bartlett Hollow; RMC Place; DELAWARE; ▲ Franklin; ***209** NL-15; mail Franklin **z** 13775; rural
Barton; RMC Place; TIOGA; ▲ Barton; **209** NM-11; [P]; **z** 13734; ● 300
Barton; MCD-Town; TIOGA; ***209** NM-11; [P]; **z** 13734; Ⓟ 8,925; © 9,066
Basket; RMC Place; SULLIVAN; ▲ Fremont; ***207** SA-2; mail Long Eddy **z** 12760; rural
Basom; RMC Place; GENESEE; ▲ Alabama; **208** NI-5; elev. 716ft./218m.; [P]; **z** 14013; ● 200
Batavia; Inc. Place; ⊡ GENESEE; **208** NI-6; elev. 895ft./273m.; [P] [H] ■; **z** 14020-21; Ⓟ 16,310; © 16,256; ◆ 16,035
Batavia; MCD-Town; GENESEE; ***208** NI-5; [P]; **z** 14020-21; does not include the City of Batavia; Ⓟ 6,055; © 5,915
Batchellerville; RMC Place; SARATOGA; ▲ Edinburg; **209** NH-18; mail Northville **z** 12134; ● 70
Bates; RMC Place; SCHOHARIE; ▲ Broome; ***209** NK-17; mail Preston Hollow **z** 12469; ● 75
Bath; Inc. Place; ⊡ STEUBEN; ▲ Bath; **208** NL-8; elev. 1,106ft./337m.; [P] [H]; **z** 14810; Ⓟ 5,801; © 5,641
Bath; MCD-Town; STEUBEN; ***208** NL-8; [P]; **z** 14810; Ⓟ 12,724; © 12,097
Bath Beach; RMC Place; KINGS; **210** K-10; ★ **N.Y.**; mail Brooklyn **z** 11214; pop. incl. with New York (Inc. Place)
Bathgate; RMC Place; BRONX; ★ **N.Y.**; mail Bronx **z** 10457; pop. incl. with New York (Inc. Place)
Battenville; RMC Place; WASHINGTON; ▲ Greenwich; ***209** NI-20; ★ **GLFLS**; mail Greenwich **z** 12834; ● 120
Battery Park City; RMC Place; NEW YORK; ***207** SF-6; ★ **N.Y.**; mail New York **z** 10007; pop. incl. with New York (Inc. Place)
Baxter Estates; Inc. Place; NASSAU; ▲ North Hempstead; **211** E-16; ★ **N.Y.**; mail Port Washington **z** 11050; Ⓟ 961; © 1,006
Bay; RMC Place; KINGS; ★ **N.Y.**; mail Brooklyn **z** 11235; pop. incl. with New York (Inc. Place)
Bayberry; RMC Place; ONONDAGA; ▲ Clay; **208** ND-7; [P]; ★ **SYR**; **z** 13090 & mail Liverpool **z** 13088; ● 6,200
Bayberry Dunes; RMC Place; SUFFOLK; ▲ Brookhaven; ***207** SF-10; elev. 6ft./2m.; ★ **N.Y.**; mail Patchogue **z** 11772; summer pop. 125
Bayberry Park; RMC Place; WESTCHESTER; ***207** SE-7; ★ **N.Y.**; mail New Rochelle **z** 10804; pop. incl. with New Rochelle (Inc. Place)
Baychester; RMC Place; BRONX; **211** D-13; ★ **N.Y.**; mail Bronx **z** 10469; pop. incl. with New York (Inc. Place)
Bay Park; CDP; NASSAU; ▲ Hempstead; **211** J-17; ★ **N.Y.**; mail East Rockaway **z** 11518; © 2,300
Bay Point; RMC Place; SUFFOLK; ▲ Southampton; ***207** SE-13; mail Sag Harbor **z** 11963; ● 450
Bayport; CDP; SUFFOLK; ▲ Islip; **207** SI-14; [P]; ★ **N.Y.**; **z** 11705; Ⓟ 7,702; © 8,662
Bay Ridge; RMC Place; KINGS; **210** K-9; ★ **N.Y.**; mail Brooklyn **z** 11220; pop. incl. with New York (Inc. Place)
Bay Shore; CDP; SUFFOLK; ▲ Islip; **207** SF-9; [P] [H]; ★ **N.Y.**; **z** 11706; Ⓟ 21,279; © 23,852; ◆ 23,841
Bay Shores; RMC Place; ONONDAGA; ▲ Otisco; ***209** NJ-11; ★ **SYR**; mail Marietta **z** 13110; ● 25
Bayside; RMC Place; QUEENS; **211** G-15; [P]; ★ **N.Y.**; **z** 11359-61; pop. incl. with New York (Inc. Place)
Bayside Annex; RMC Place; QUEENS; ★ **N.Y.**; mail Bayside **z** 11361; pop. incl. with New York (Inc. Place)
Bayswater; RMC Place; QUEENS; ***207** SG-7; ★ **N.Y.**; mail Far Rockaway **z** 11691; pop. incl. with New York (Inc. Place)
Bay Terrace; RMC Place; QUEENS; ★ **N.Y.**; mail Bayside **z** 11360; pop. incl. with New York (Inc. Place)
Bay View; RMC Place; ERIE; ▲ Hamburg; ***208** NJ-3; ★ **BUF**; mail Hamburg **z** 14075; ● 1,200
Bayview; RMC Place; SUFFOLK; ▲ Southold; ***207** SE-12; mail Southold **z** 11971; ● 900
Bayville; Inc. Place; NASSAU; ▲ Oyster Bay; **207** SE-8; elev. 40ft./12m.; [P]; ★ **N.Y.**; **z** 11709; Ⓟ 7,193; © 7,135
Baywood; CDP-Census Area Only; SUFFOLK; ▲ Islip; ***207** SF-9; elev. 60ft./18m.; ★ **N.Y.**; mail Bay Shore **z** 11706; Ⓟ 7,351; © 7,571
Beach Hampton; RMC Place; SUFFOLK; ▲ East Hampton; ***207** SE-13; mail Amagansett **z** 11930
Beach Ridge; RMC Place; NIAGARA; ▲ Pendleton; **208** NB-4; elev. 579ft./176m.; ★ **BUF**; mail North Tonawanda **z** 14120
Beachville; RMC Place; STEUBEN; ▲ Dansville; ***208** NK-7; mail Arkport **z** 14807
Beacon; Inc. Place; DUTCHESS; **207** SC-6; elev. 144ft./44m.; [P] [H]; ★ **POK**; **z** 12508; Ⓟ 13,243; © 13,808; Ⓡ 14,810
Beacon Hill; RMC Place; DUTCHESS; ▲ Fishkill; ***207** SB-7; ★ **POK**; mail Beacon **z** 12508; ● 800
Beantown; RMC Place; CHEMUNG; ▲ Chemung; ***208** NM-10; mail Lockwood **z** 14859; rural
Beantown (Chemung Center); RMC Place; CHEMUNG; ▲ Chemung; ***208** NM-10; mail Chemung **z** 14825; rural

Entries in **UPPERCASE** are counties.
Entries in **bold** have populations of 2,500 or more.
Names in parentheses are alternate names.

Inc. Place	Incorporated Place
RMC Place	Rand McNally Designated Place
CDP	Census Designated Place
MCD	Minor Civil Division
⊡	County Seat
▲	Minor Civil Division
elev.	Elevation
[P]	Post Office
[H]	Hospital
[C]	College
■	Principal Business Center
★	Ranally Metro Area (RMA) Abbreviation
z	Zip Code(s)
Ⓟ	Previous Census Population
Ⓡ	Revised Census Population
Ⓐ	Annexation Population
●	Rand McNally Population Estimate
©	Final Census Population
Ⓢ	Special Census Population
◆	Estimated Population

For additional definitions see Glossary, Volume 1, and Introduction, Volume 2.

Bear Mountain; RMC Place; ROCKLAND; ▲ Stony Point; *207 SC-6; 🅿; ★ N.Y.; z 10911; ● 75
Bearsville; RMC Place; ULSTER; ▲ Woodstock; 209 NM-18; 🅿; z 12409; ● 550
Beaver Brook; RMC Place; SULLIVAN; ▲ Tusten; *207 SB-3; mail Narrowsburg z 12764; ● 50
Beaver Dam; RMC Place; ORANGE; ▲ Montgomery; *207 SB-5; mail Montgomery z 12549; rural
Beaver Dam; SCHUYLER; see Beaver Dams (RMC Place)
Beaverdam Lake-Salisbury Mills; CDP-Census Area Only; ORANGE; ▲ New Windsor, Blooming Grove, Cornwall; *207 SC-6; ★ NWBG; mail New Windsor z 12553; Ⓟ 1,719; © 2,779
Beaver Dams (Beaver Dam); RMC Place; SCHUYLER; ▲ Dix; 208 NL-9; 🅿; z 14812; ● 600
Beaver Falls; RMC Place; LEWIS; ▲ New Bremen, Croghan; 209 NF-14; 🅿; z 13305; ● 700
Beaverkill; RMC Place; SULLIVAN; ▲ Rockland; *209 NM-16; mail Livingston Manor z 12758; rural
Beaver Meadow; RMC Place; CHENANGO; ▲ Smyrna, Otselic; 209 NK-13; mail Plymouth z 13832; ● 100
Beaver River; RMC Place; HERKIMER; ▲ Webb; *209 NF-15; elev. 1,692ft./516m.; 🅿; z 13367; ● 200
Beaver Valley; RMC Place; CHEMUNG; ▲ Catlin; *208 NL-9; mail Beaver Dams z 14812; rural
Beckers Corners; RMC Place; ALBANY; ▲ Bethlehem; *209 NK-19; ★ A-S-T; mail Selkirk z 12158; ● 350
Becks Grove; RMC Place; ONEIDA; *209 NH-13; ★ UT-R; mail Blossvale z 13308; pop. incl. with Rome (Inc. Place)
Bedell; RMC Place; DELAWARE; ▲ Middletown; *209 NM-17; mail Fleischmanns z 12430; rural
Bedford; RMC Place; KINGS; *207 SF-7; ★ N.Y.; mail Brooklyn z 11210; pop. incl. with New York (Inc. Place)
Bedford; CDP; WESTCHESTER; ▲ Bedford; 207 SD-8; 🅿; ★ N.Y.; z 10506; Ⓟ 1,828; © 1,724
Bedford; MCD-Town; WESTCHESTER; *207 SD-8; 🅿; ★ N.Y.; z 10506; Ⓟ 16,906; © 18,133
Bedford Hills; RMC Place; WESTCHESTER; ▲ Bedford; 207 SD-7; 🅿; ★ N.Y.; z 10507; ● 3,200
Bedford Park; RMC Place; BRONX; *207 SF-7; ★ N.Y.; mail Bronx z 10458; pop. incl. with New York (Inc. Place)
Bedford-Stuyvesant; RMC Place; KINGS; ★ N.Y.; mail Brooklyn z 11233; pop. incl. with New York (Inc. Place)
Beecher Corners; RMC Place; GREENE; ▲ Jewett; *209 NL-17; elev. 1,690ft./515m.; mail Hunter z 12442; rural
Beechertown; RMC Place; ST. LAWRENCE; ▲ Stockholm; *209 NB-16; elev. 549ft./167m.; mail Winthrop z 13697; rural
Beech Hill; RMC Place; WESTCHESTER; *207 SE-7; ★ N.Y.; mail Yonkers z 10710; pop. incl. with Yonkers (Inc. Place)
Beechhurst; RMC Place; QUEENS; 🅿; ★ N.Y.; z 11357; pop. incl. with New York (Inc. Place)
Beechmont; RMC Place; WESTCHESTER; *207 SE-7; ★ N.Y.; mail New Rochelle z 10804; pop. incl. with New Rochelle (Inc. Place)
Beechmont Woods; RMC Place; WESTCHESTER; *207 SE-7; ★ N.Y.; mail New Rochelle z 10804; pop. incl. with New Rochelle (Inc. Place)
Beechwood; RMC Place; MONROE; ★ ROCH; mail Rochester z 14609; pop. incl. with Rochester (Inc. Place)
Beekman; RMC Place; DUTCHESS; ▲ Beekman; *207 SB-7; elev. 380ft./116m.; mail Hopewell Junction z 12533; ● 70
Beekman; MCD-Town; DUTCHESS; *207 SB-7; mail Poughquag z 12570; Ⓟ 10,447; © 11,452; Ⓡ 13,655
Beekman Corners; RMC Place; SCHOHARIE; ▲ Sharon; *209 NJ-16; elev. 1,414ft./431m.; mail Sharon Springs z 13459; rural
Beekmantown; RMC Place; CLINTON; ▲ Beekmantown; 209 NB-19; ★ PLATT; mail Plattsburgh z 12901; ● 300
Beekmantown; MCD-Town; CLINTON; *209 NB-19; ★ PLATT; mail Plattsburgh z 12901; Ⓟ 5,108; © 5,326
Beixedon Estates; RMC Place; SUFFOLK; ▲ Southold; *207 SD-12; mail Southold z 11971
Belcher; RMC Place; WASHINGTON; ▲ Hebron; *209 NH-20; mail Salem z 12865; ● 55
Belcoda; RMC Place; MONROE; ▲ Wheatland; *208 NI-7; ★ ROCH; mail Scottsville z 14546; rural
Belden; RMC Place; BROOME; ▲ Colesville; 209 NM-13; ★ BING; mail Harpursville z 13787; ● 50
Belfast; RMC Place; ALLEGANY; ▲ Belfast; 208 NL-6; 🅿; z 14711; ● 1,100
Belfast; MCD-Town; ALLEGANY; *208 NL-6; 🅿; z 14711; Ⓟ 1,539; © 1,714
Belfort; RMC Place; LEWIS; ▲ Croghan; 209 NE-14; mail Croghan z 13327; ● 50
Belfort Heights; RMC Place; ROCKLAND; ▲ Ramapo; ★ N.Y.; mail Spring Valley z 10977; pop. incl. with Hempstead (Inc. Place)
Belgium; RMC Place; ONONDAGA; ▲ Clay; 209 NI-11; ★ SYR; mail Baldwinsville z 13027; ● 115
Bellaire; RMC Place; QUEENS; *207 SF-7; ★ N.Y.; mail Queens Village z 11429; pop. incl. with New York (Inc. Place)
Belle Harbor; RMC Place; QUEENS; *207 SG-7; 🅿; ★ N.Y.; z 11694; pop. incl. with New York (Inc. Place)
Belle Isle; RMC Place; ONONDAGA; ▲ Camillus; *209 NI-11; ★ SYR; mail Syracuse z 13209; ● 100
Bellerose; Inc. Place; NASSAU; ▲ Hempstead; 211 H-16; ★ N.Y.; mail Floral Park z 11001; Ⓟ 1,101; © 1,173
Bellerose; RMC Place; QUEENS; 🅿; ★ N.Y.; z 11426; pop. incl. with New York (Inc. Place)
Bellerose Terrace; CDP; NASSAU; ▲ Hempstead; 211 H-16; ★ N.Y.; mail Bellerose z 11426, Floral Park z 11001; © 2,157
Belle Terre; Inc. Place; SUFFOLK; ▲ Brookhaven; 207 SE-10; ★ N.Y.; mail Port Jefferson z 11777; Ⓟ 839; © 832
Belleview; RMC Place; CHAUTAUQUA; ▲ Ellery; *208 NM-2; elev. 1,330ft./405m.; ★ JMST; mail Bemus Point z 14712; rural
Belleville; RMC Place; JEFFERSON; ▲ Ellisburg; 209 NF-12; elev. 451ft./137m.; 🅿; z 13611; ● 350
Bellevue; RMC Place; ERIE; ▲ Cheektowaga; *208 NJ-4; ★ BUF; mail Buffalo z 14225
Bellevue; RMC Place; SCHENECTADY; *209 NJ-18; ★ A-S-T; mail Schenectady z 12306; pop. incl. with Schenectady (Inc. Place)
Bellevue Gardens; RMC Place; SARATOGA; ▲ Malta; *209 NI-19; elev. 320ft./98m.; ★ A-S-T; mail Round Lake z 12151; ● 600
Bellmont; MCD-Town; FRANKLIN; *209 NB-18; mail Burke z 12917; Ⓟ 1,246; © 1,423
Bellmont Center; RMC Place; FRANKLIN; ▲ Bellmont; *209 NB-18; elev. 1,298ft./396m.; mail Chateaugay z 12920; rural
Bellmore; CDP; NASSAU; ▲ Hempstead; 211 I-20; elev. 24ft./7m.; 🅿; ★ N.Y.; z 11710; Ⓟ 16,438; © 16,441
Bellona (Gage); RMC Place; YATES; ▲ Benton; *208 NJ-9; 🅿; z 14415; ● 250
Bellow Corners; RMC Place; CATTARAUGUS; ▲ Ashford; *208 NL-4; elev. 1,268ft./386m.; mail West Valley z 14171; rural
Bellport; Inc. Place; SUFFOLK; ▲ Brookhaven; 207 SF-10; elev. 26ft./8m.; 🅿; ★ N.Y.; z 11713; Ⓟ 2,572; © 2,363
Bellvale; RMC Place; ORANGE; ▲ Warwick; 207 SD-5; 🅿; ★ N.Y.; z 10912; ● 200
Bellville; RMC Place; ALLEGANY; ▲ New Hudson; *208 NL-5; mail Caneadea z 14717; rural
Belmont; Inc. Place; ⊡ ALLEGANY; ▲ Amity; 208 NL-6; elev. 1,418ft./432m.; 🅿; z 14813; Ⓟ 1,006; © 952
Belmont; RMC Place; BRONX; *207 SF-7; ★ N.Y.; mail Bronx z 10458; pop. incl. with New York (Inc. Place)
Belvidere; RMC Place; ALLEGANY; ▲ Amity; *208 NL-6; elev. 1,379ft./420m.; mail Belmont z 14813; ● 75
Bemis Heights; RMC Place; SARATOGA; ▲ Stillwater; 209 NI-19; ★ A-S-T; mail Stillwater z 12170; ● 115
Bemus Point; Inc. Place; CHAUTAUQUA; ▲ Ellery; 208 NM-2; 🅿; ★ JMST; z 14712; Ⓟ 383; © 340
Benedict Beach; RMC Place; MONROE; ▲ Hamlin; *208 NH-7; ★ ROCH; mail Hamlin z 14464
Bennett Bridge; RMC Place; OSWEGO; ▲ Orwell; *209 NG-12; mail Altmar z 13302; rural
Bennettsburg; RMC Place; SCHUYLER; ▲ Hector; 208 NL-10; mail Burdett z 14818; ● 110
Bennetts Corner; RMC Place; ORLEANS; ▲ Clarendon; *208 NH-6; ★ ROCH; mail Holley z 14470; rural
Bennettsville; RMC Place; CHENANGO; ▲ Bainbridge; *209 NL-14; mail Bainbridge z 13733; ● 50
Bennington; RMC Place; WYOMING; ▲ Bennington; 208 NJ-5; elev. 1,208ft./368m.; mail Attica z 14011; ● 200
Bennington; MCD-Town; WYOMING; *208 NJ-5; mail Attica z 14011; Ⓟ 3,046; © 3,349
Benson; RMC Place; HAMILTON; ▲ Benson; 209 NH-17; elev. 1,156ft./352m.; mail Northville z 12134; ● 100
Benson; MCD-Town; HAMILTON; *209 NH-17; mail Northville z 12134; Ⓟ 168; © 201
Bensonhurst; RMC Place; KINGS; *207 SG-6; ★ N.Y.; mail Brooklyn z 11223; pop. incl. with New York (Inc. Place)
Benson Mines; RMC Place; ST. LAWRENCE; ▲ Clifton; *209 ND-15; mail Star Lake z 13690; rural
Benton; YATES; see Benton Center (RMC Place)
Benton; MCD-Town; YATES; *208 NJ-9; mail Penn Yan z 14527; Ⓟ 2,380; © 2,640
Benton Center (Benton); RMC Place; YATES; ▲ Benton; 208 NJ-9; mail Penn Yan z 14527; ● 220
Berea; RMC Place; ORANGE; ▲ Montgomery; *207 SB-6; elev. 409ft./125m.; mail Montgomery z 12549; rural
Bergen; Inc. Place; GENESEE; ▲ Bergen; 208 NI-6; elev. 606ft./185m.; 🅿; ★ ROCH; z 14416; Ⓟ 1,103; © 1,240
Bergen; MCD-Town; GENESEE; *208 NI-6; 🅿; ★ ROCH; z 14416; Ⓟ 2,794; © 3,182
Bergen Beach; RMC Place; KINGS; *207 SG-7; ★ N.Y.; mail Brooklyn z 11234; pop. incl. with New York (Inc. Place)
Bergen Beach; RMC Place; SENECA; ▲ Covert; *208 NK-10; ★ ITH; mail Interlaken z 14847; ● 30
Bergen Park; RMC Place; SUFFOLK; ▲ Huntington; ★ N.Y.; mail Huntington Station z 11746
Bergholtz; RMC Place; NIAGARA; ▲ Wheatfield; 208 NB-3; ★ BUF; mail Niagara Falls z 14304; ● 700
Berkshire; RMC Place; FULTON; ▲ Johnstown; *209 NI-17; mail Gloversville z 12078; ● 200
Berkshire (Berkshire Association); RMC Place; ONONDAGA; ▲ Manlius; *209 NI-12; ★ SYR; mail Fayetteville z 13066; ● 1,700
Berkshire; RMC Place; TIOGA; ▲ Berkshire; 209 NL-12; elev. 1,056ft./322m.; 🅿; z 13736; ● 350
Berkshire; MCD-Town; TIOGA; *209 NL-12; 🅿; z 13736; Ⓟ 1,303; © 1,366
Berkshire Association; ONONDAGA; see Berkshire (RMC Place)
Berkshire Terrace; RMC Place; PUTNAM; ▲ Kent; *207 SB-7; ★ N.Y.; mail Carmel z 10512; ● 100
Berlin; RMC Place; RENSSELAER; ▲ Berlin; 209 NJ-20; elev. 852ft./260m.; 🅿; z 12022; ● 1,200
Berlin; MCD-Town; RENSSELAER; *209 NJ-20; 🅿; z 12022; Ⓟ 1,929; © 1,901
Berne; RMC Place; ALBANY; ▲ Berne; 209 NK-18; 🅿; z 12023; ● 600
Berne; MCD-Town; ALBANY; *209 NK-18; 🅿; z 12023; Ⓟ 3,053; © 2,846
Bernhards Bay; RMC Place; OSWEGO; ▲ Constantia; 209 NH-12; 🅿; ★ SYR; z 13028; ● 400
Berryville; RMC Place; MONTGOMERY; ▲ Mohawk; *209 NI-17; elev. 380ft./116m.; ★ A-S-T; mail Fonda z 12068; rural
Berwyn; RMC Place; ONONDAGA; ▲ Pompey; *209 NJ-12; ★ SYR; mail La Fayette z 13084; rural
Best; RMC Place; RENSSELAER; ▲ Sand Lake, East Greenbush; *209 NK-19; ★ A-S-T; mail Averill Park z 12018; rural
Bethany; GENESEE; see Bethany Center (RMC Place)
Bethany; MCD-Town; GENESEE; *208 NJ-6; mail East Bethany z 14054; Ⓟ 1,808; © 1,760
Bethany Center (Bethany); RMC Place; GENESEE; ▲ Bethany; 208 NJ-6; mail East Bethany z 14054; ● 200
Bethel; RMC Place; DUTCHESS; ▲ Pine Plains; *209 NM-19; mail Pine Plains z 12567; rural
Bethel; RMC Place; SULLIVAN; ▲ Bethel; 207 SB-3; 🅿; z 12720; ● 350
Bethel; MCD-Town; SULLIVAN; *207 SB-3; 🅿; z 12720; Ⓟ 3,693; © 4,362
Bethel Corners; RMC Place; CAYUGA; ▲ Ira; *208 NH-10; mail Martville z 13111; rural
Bethel Grove; RMC Place; TOMPKINS; ▲ Dryden; *209 NL-11; ★ ITH; mail Ithaca z 14850; ● 100
Bethford; RMC Place; ERIE; ▲ Hamburg; *208 NJ-4; ★ BUF; mail Buffalo z 14219; ● 2,100
Bethlehem; MCD-Town; ALBANY; *209 NK-19; ★ A-S-T; mail Delmar z 12054; Ⓟ 27,552; © 31,304; ◆ 33,060
Bethlehem Center; RMC Place; ALBANY; ▲ Bethlehem; *209 NK-19; elev. 195ft./59m.; ★ A-S-T; mail Glenmont z 12077
Bethlehem Heights; RMC Place; ALBANY; ▲ Bethlehem; *209 NK-19; ★ A-S-T; mail South Bethlehem z 12161
Bethpage; CDP; NASSAU; ▲ Oyster Bay; 207 SF-8; 🅿 🅷 🅲 2,363; ★ N.Y.; z 11714; Ⓟ 15,761; © 16,543

Beukendaal; RMC Place; SCHENECTADY; ▲ Glenville; *209 NJ-18; ★ A-S-T; mail Schenectady z 12302; ● 150
Beverly Inn Corners; RMC Place; OTSEGO; ▲ Burlington; *209 NJ-16; elev. 1,295ft./395m.; mail Burlington Flats z 13315; rural
Bible School Park; RMC Place; BROOME; *209 NM-12; elev. 890ft./271m.; 🅿; ★ BING; z 13737
Bidwell; RMC Place; ERIE; ★ BUF; mail Buffalo z 14222; pop. incl. with Buffalo (Inc. Place)
Big Brook; RMC Place; ONEIDA; ▲ Western; *209 NH-14; elev. 704ft./215m.; mail Westernville z 13486; rural
Bigelow; RMC Place; ST. LAWRENCE; ▲ De Kalb; *209 NC-14; mail Richville z 13681; ● 75
Big Flats; CDP; CHEMUNG; ▲ Big Flats; 208 NM-9; elev. 910ft./277m.; 🅿; ★ ELM; z 14814; Ⓟ 2,658; © 2,482
Big Flats; MCD-Town; CHEMUNG; *208 NM-9; 🅿; ★ ELM; z 14814; Ⓟ 7,596; © 7,224
Big Flats Airport; CDP-Census Area Only; CHEMUNG; ▲ Big Flats; *208 NM-9; elev. 975ft./297m.; ★ ELM; mail Big Flats z 14814; Ⓟ 2,248; © 2,184
Big Fresh Pond; RMC Place; SUFFOLK; ▲ Southampton; *207 SE-12; mail Southampton z 11968; ● 300
Big Indian; RMC Place; ULSTER; ▲ Shandaken; 209 NM-17; 🅿; z 12410; ● 350
Big Island; RMC Place; ORANGE; ▲ Warwick; *207 SC-5; elev. 416ft./127m.; ★ N.Y.; mail Goshen z 10924; rural
Big Moose; RMC Place; HERKIMER; ▲ Webb; 209 NF-15; elev. 2,035ft./620m.; mail Eagle Bay z 13331; ● 75
Big Tree; RMC Place; ERIE; ▲ Hamburg; 208 NJ-4; elev. 721ft./220m.; ★ BUF; mail Buffalo z 14219; ● 1,000
Big Wolf Lake; RMC Place; FRANKLIN; ▲ Tupper Lake; mail Tupper Lake z 12986; ● 50
Billings; RMC Place; DUTCHESS; ▲ La Grange; 207 SB-7; elev. 404ft./123m.; 🅿; ★ POK; z 12510; ● 480
Billington Bay; RMC Place; MADISON; ▲ Sullivan; *209 NI-12; ★ SYR; mail Bridgeport z 13030; ● 500
Billington Heights; CDP-Census Area Only; ERIE; ▲ Elma, Aurora; *208 NJ-4; ★ BUF; mail East Aurora z 14052; Ⓟ 1,729; © 1,691
Biltmore Shores; RMC Place; NASSAU; ▲ Oyster Bay; *207 SG-8; ★ N.Y.; mail Massapequa z 11758
Bingham Mills; RMC Place; COLUMBIA; ▲ Germantown; *209 NM-19; mail Germantown z 12526; rural
Binghamton; Inc. Place; ⊡ BROOME; 209 NM-12; 🅿 🅷 🅲 14,373 ■; ★ BING; z 13901-05; Ⓟ 53,008; © 47,380; ◆ 45,771
Binghamton; MCD-Town; BROOME; *209 NM-12; 🅿 🅲 14,373; ★ BING; z 13901-05; does not include the City of Binghamton; Ⓟ 5,006; © 4,969
Bingley; RMC Place; MADISON; ▲ Cazenovia; *209 NI-13; ★ SYR; mail Cazenovia z 13035; rural
Binnewater; RMC Place; ULSTER; ▲ Rosendale; *207 SA-6; elev. 204ft./62m.; ★ KNGST; mail Kingston z 12401; ● 320
Birchwood Estates; RMC Place; COLUMBIA; ▲ Kinderhook; *209 NK-19; elev. 311ft./95m.; ★ A-S-T; mail Valatie z 12184; ● 220
Birdsall; RMC Place; ALLEGANY; ▲ Birdsall; 208 NL-6; elev. 1,695ft./517m.; mail Angelica z 14709; ● 50
Birdsall; MCD-Town; ALLEGANY; *208 NL-6; mail Angelica z 14709; Ⓟ 232; © 268
Birmingham Corners; RMC Place; HERKIMER; ▲ Winfield; *209 NJ-16; mail West Winfield z 13491; rural
Bishopville; RMC Place; ALLEGANY; ▲ Almond; *208 NL-7; mail Arkport z 14807; rural
Black Brook; RMC Place; CLINTON; ▲ Black Brook; 209 NC-19; elev. 966ft./294m.; mail Au Sable Forks z 12912; ● 200
Black Brook; MCD-Town; CLINTON; *209 NC-19; mail Au Sable Forks z 12912; Ⓟ 1,556; © 1,660
Black Corners; RMC Place; CHAUTAUQUA; ▲ Arkwright; *208 NL-2; mail Forestville z 14062; rural
Black Creek; RMC Place; ALLEGANY; ▲ New Hudson; 208 NL-5; 🅿; z 14714; ● 250
Blackmans Corners; RMC Place; CLINTON; ▲ Mooers; mail Mooers Forks z 12959; ● 50
Black River; Inc. Place; JEFFERSON; ▲ Rutland, Le Ray; 209 NE-13; 🅿; ★ WATN; z 13612; Ⓟ 1,349; © 1,285
Black Rock; RMC Place; ERIE; ★ BUF; mail Buffalo z 14207; pop. incl. with Buffalo (Inc. Place)
Blackwatch Hills; RMC Place; MONROE; ▲ Perinton; *208 NI-8; ★ ROCH; mail Fairport z 14450; ● 2,850
Blakeley; RMC Place; ERIE; ▲ Aurora; *208 NJ-4; ★ BUF; mail East Aurora z 14052; ● 100
Blasdell; Inc. Place; ERIE; ▲ Hamburg; 208 NJ-4; 🅿; ★ BUF; z 14219; Ⓟ 2,900; © 2,718
Blauvelt; CDP; ROCKLAND; ▲ Orangetown; 207 SE-6; elev. 197ft./60m.; 🅿; ★ N.Y.; z 10913; Ⓟ 4,838; © 5,207; Ⓡ 5,200
Bleecker; RMC Place; FULTON; ▲ Bleecker; 209 NI-17; mail Gloversville z 12078; ● 115
Bleecker; MCD-Town; FULTON; *209 NH-17; mail Gloversville z 12078; Ⓟ 515; © 573
Blenheim; MCD-Town; SCHOHARIE; *209 NK-17; mail North Blenheim z 12131; Ⓟ 332; © 330
Bliss; QUEENS; see Blissville (RMC Place)
Bliss; RMC Place; WYOMING; ▲ Eagle; 208 NK-5; elev. 746ft./227m.; 🅿; z 14024; ● 300
Bliss Corner; RMC Place; FULTON; ▲ Stratford; *209 NI-16; mail Stratford z 13470; rural
Blissville (Bliss); RMC Place; QUEENS; ★ N.Y.; pop. incl. with New York (Inc. Place)
Blockville; RMC Place; CHAUTAUQUA; ▲ Harmony; *208 NM-2; mail Ashville z 14710
Blodgett Mills; RMC Place; CORTLAND; ▲ Cortlandville; 209 NK-12; 🅿; z 13738; ● 160
Bloomerville; RMC Place; STEUBEN; ▲ Avoca; *208 NL-8; mail Avoca z 14809; rural
Bloomfield; ONTARIO; see Holcomb (Inc. Place)
Bloomfield; RMC Place; RICHMOND; *207 SG-6; ★ N.Y.; mail Staten Island z 10314; pop. incl. with New York (Inc. Place)
Bloomingburg; Inc. Place; SULLIVAN; ▲ Mamakating; 207 SB-5; elev. 516ft./157m.; 🅿; ★ MIDD; z 12721; Ⓟ 316; © 353
Bloomingdale; RMC Place; ESSEX; ▲ St. Armand; 209 NC-18; elev. 1,535ft./468m.; 🅿; z 12913; ● 600
Blooming Grove; RMC Place; ORANGE; ▲ Blooming Grove; 207 SC-6; elev. 360ft./110m.; 🅿; ★ N.Y.; z 10914; ● 500
Blooming Grove; MCD-Town; ORANGE; *207 SC-6; 🅿; ★ N.Y.; z 10914; partly in ★ NWBG; Ⓟ 16,673; © 17,351
Bloomington; RMC Place; ULSTER; ▲ Rosendale; 209 NN-18; 🅿; ★ KNGST; z 12411; ● 800
Bloomville; RMC Place; DELAWARE; ▲ Kortright; 209 NL-16; elev. 1,455ft./443m.; 🅿; z 13739; ● 300
Blossvale; RMC Place; ONEIDA; ▲ Annsville; 209 NH-13; 🅿; z 13308 & mail Mc Connellsville z 13401; ● 300
Blue Mountain; RMC Place; ULSTER; ▲ Saugerties; *209 NM-18; ★ KNGST; mail Saugerties z 12477; rural
Blue Mountain Lake; RMC Place; HAMILTON; ▲ Indian Lake; 209 NF-17; elev. 1,829ft./557m.; 🅿; z 12812; summer pop. 400; ● 220
Blue Point; CDP; SUFFOLK; ▲ Brookhaven; 207 SI-14; 🅿; ★ N.Y.; z 11715; Ⓟ 4,230; © 4,407
Blue Ridge; RMC Place; COLUMBIA; ▲ Greenport; *209 NL-19; mail Hudson z 12534; ● 200
Blue Ridge; RMC Place; ESSEX; 209 NE-19; mail North Hudson z 12855, Schroon Lake z 12870
Blue Store; RMC Place; COLUMBIA; ▲ Livingston; *209 NM-19; mail Germantown z 12526
Bluff Point; RMC Place; YATES; ▲ Jerusalem; 208 NK-9; 🅿; z 14478; ● 350
Blythebourne; RMC Place; KINGS; ★ N.Y.; mail Brooklyn z 11219; pop. incl. with New York (Inc. Place)
Boardmanville; RMC Place; CATTARAUGUS; *208 NM-5; elev. 1,428ft./435m.; mail Olean z 14760; pop. incl. with Olean (Inc. Place)
Boght Corners; RMC Place; ALBANY; ▲ Colonie; 207 SG-5; elev. 359ft./109m.; ★ A-S-T; mail Cohoes z 12047; ● 1,150
Bohemia; CDP; SUFFOLK; ▲ Islip; 207 SI-13; elev. 65ft./20m.; 🅿; ★ N.Y.; z 11716; Ⓟ 9,556; © 9,871
Boiceville; RMC Place; ULSTER; ▲ Olive; 209 NM-17; 🅿; z 12412; ● 800
Bolivar; Inc. Place; ALLEGANY; ▲ Bolivar; 208 NM-6; 🅿; z 14715; Ⓟ 1,261; © 1,173
Bolivar; MCD-Town; ALLEGANY; *208 NM-6; 🅿; z 14715; Ⓟ 2,361; © 2,223
Bolton; RMC Place; WARREN; ▲ Bolton; 209 NG-19; mail Diamond Point z 12824; ● 300
Bolton; MCD-Town; WARREN; *209 NG-19; mail Diamond Point z 12824; Ⓟ 1,855; © 2,117
Bolton Landing; RMC Place; WARREN; ▲ Bolton; 209 NG-19; 🅿; z 12814; ● 1,600
Bolts Corners; RMC Place; CAYUGA; ▲ Scipio; *208 NJ-10; elev. 1,060ft./323m.; mail Scipio Center z 13147; rural
Bombay; RMC Place; FRANKLIN; ▲ Bombay; 209 NA-16; elev. 189ft./58m.; 🅿; z 12914 & mail Hogansburg z 13655; ● 300
Bombay; MCD-Town; FRANKLIN; *209 NA-16; 🅿; z 12914 & mail Hogansburg z 13655; Ⓟ 1,158; © 1,192
Bon Air Heights; RMC Place; ROCKLAND; ★ N.Y.; mail Suffern z 10901; pop. incl. with Suffern (Inc. Place)
Bonaparte; LEWIS; see Lake Bonaparte (RMC Place)
Bonney; RMC Place; CHENANGO; ▲ Smyrna; *209 NJ-13; mail Smyrna z 13464; rural
Bonni Castle; RMC Place; WAYNE; ▲ Huron; *208 NH-9; mail Wolcott z 14590; ● 40
Bonnie Crest; RMC Place; WESTCHESTER; *207 SE-7; ★ N.Y.; mail New Rochelle z 10804; pop. incl. with New Rochelle (Inc. Place)
Bonny Lee Estates; RMC Place; COLUMBIA; ▲ Kinderhook; *209 NK-19; elev. 323ft./98m.; ★ A-S-T; mail Valatie z 12184; ● 100
Boomertown; RMC Place; CHAUTAUQUA; *208 NM-2; ★ JMST; mail Ashville z 14710; rural
Boonville; Inc. Place; ONEIDA; ▲ Boonville; 209 NG-14; elev. 1,146ft./349m.; 🅿; z 13309; Ⓟ 2,220; © 2,138
Boonville; MCD-Town; ONEIDA; *209 NG-14; 🅿; z 13309; Ⓟ 4,246; © 4,572
Borden; RMC Place; STEUBEN; ▲ Woodhull; 208 NM-8; elev. 1,354ft./413m.; mail Addison z 14801; ● 40
Border City; RMC Place; SENECA; ▲ Waterloo; 208 NJ-9; mail Geneva z 14456; ● 250
Borodino; RMC Place; ONONDAGA; ▲ Spafford; 209 NJ-11; elev. 110ft./34m.; mail Skaneateles z 13152; ● 100
Borough Hall; RMC Place; QUEENS; ★ N.Y.; mail Jamaica z 11424; pop. incl. with New York (Inc. Place)
Borough Park; RMC Place; KINGS; *207 SG-6; ★ N.Y.; mail Brooklyn z 11219; pop. incl. with New York (Inc. Place)
Boston; RMC Place; ERIE; ▲ Boston; 208 NK-4; 🅿; ★ BUF; z 14025; ● 500
Boston; MCD-Town; ERIE; *208 NK-4; 🅿; ★ BUF; z 14025; Ⓟ 7,445; © 7,897
Boston Corners; RMC Place; COLUMBIA; ▲ Ancram; *209 NM-20; mail Millerton z 12546; rural
Botanical; RMC Place; BRONX; ★ N.Y.; mail Bronx z 10458; pop. incl. with New York (Inc. Place)
Bouckville; RMC Place; MADISON; ▲ Madison; 209 NJ-13; elev. 1,150ft./351m.; 🅿; z 13310; ● 450
Boughton Hill; RMC Place; ONTARIO; ▲ Victor; *208 NI-8; elev. 818ft./249m.; ★ ROCH; mail Victor z 14564; rural
Boulevard; RMC Place; BRONX; ★ N.Y.; mail Bronx z 10459, z 10474; pop. incl. with New York (Inc. Place)
Boultons Beach; RMC Place; JEFFERSON; *209 NE-12; mail Sackets Harbor z 13685
Bouquet; RMC Place; ESSEX; ▲ Essex; *209 ND-20; elev. 248ft./76m.; mail Essex z 12936
Bournes Beach; RMC Place; CHAUTAUQUA; ▲ Westfield; *208 NL-1; mail Westfield z 14787
Bovina; DELAWARE; see Bovina Center (RMC Place)
Bovina; MCD-Town; DELAWARE; *209 NL-16; mail Bovina Center z 13740; Ⓟ 550; © 664
Bovina Center (Bovina); RMC Place; DELAWARE; ▲ Bovina; 209 NL-16; 🅿; z 13740; ● 200
Bowens Corners; RMC Place; OSWEGO; ▲ Granby; *209 NH-11; mail Fulton z 13069; ● 85
Bowerstown; RMC Place; OTSEGO; ▲ Middlefield; *209 NK-15; mail Cooperstown z 13326; ● 35
Bowling Green; RMC Place; NEW YORK; 🅿; ★ N.Y.; z 10004 & mail New York z 10274; pop. incl. with New York (Inc. Place)
Bowmansville; RMC Place; ERIE; ▲ Lancaster; 208 NI-4; 🅿; ★ BUF; z 14026; ● 600
Boylston; MCD-Town; OSWEGO; *209 NG-12; mail Lacona z 13083; Ⓟ 443; © 505
Boylston Center; RMC Place; OSWEGO; ▲ Boylston; *209 NG-12; mail Lacona z 13083; ● 75
Boyntonville; RMC Place; RENSSELAER; ▲ Pittstown; *209 NJ-20; ★ A-S-T; mail Hoosick Falls z 12090
Boysen Bay; RMC Place; ONONDAGA; ▲ Cicero; *209 NH-12; ★ SYR; mail Cicero z 13039; ● 400
Braddock Heights; RMC Place; MONROE; ▲ Greece; 208 NH-7; ★ ROCH; mail Rochester z 14612; ● 700
Bradford; RMC Place; STEUBEN; ▲ Bradford; 208 NL-9; 🅿; z 14815; ● 200
Bradford; MCD-Town; STEUBEN; *208 NL-9; 🅿; z 14815; Ⓟ 699; © 763
Bradley; RMC Place; SULLIVAN; ▲ Neversink; *207 SA-4; mail Liberty z 12754; ● 200
Braeside; RMC Place; RENSSELAER; ▲ Schodack; *209 NK-19; ★ A-S-T; mail Nassau z 12123; ● 950
Brainard; RMC Place; RENSSELAER; ▲ Nassau; 209 NK-20; 🅿; ★ A-S-T; z 12024; pop. incl. with East Nassau (Inc. Place)
Brainards Corners; RMC Place; OTSEGO; ▲ Exeter; *209 NJ-16; mail Burlington Flats z 13315; rural
Brainardsville; RMC Place; FRANKLIN; ▲ Bellmont; 209 NB-18; elev. 1,347ft./411m.; 🅿; z 12915; ● 250

Braman Corners; RMC Place; SCHENECTADY; ▲ Duanesburg; *209 NJ-17; mail Delanson z 12053; rural
Bramans Corners; RMC Place; ALBANY; ▲ New Scotland; *209 NK-18; elev. 1,500ft./457m.; mail Voorheesville z 12186; rural
Bramanville; RMC Place; SCHOHARIE; ▲ Cobleskill; *209 NJ-17; mail Howes Cave z 12092; rural
Brambler Ridge; RMC Place; MONROE; ▲ Perinton; *208 NI-8; ★ ROCH; mail Fairport z 14450; ● 2,250
Branchport; RMC Place; YATES; ▲ Jerusalem; 208 NK-9; elev. 736ft./224m.; 🅿; z 14418; ● 400
Brandon; MCD-Town; FRANKLIN; *209 NB-17; mail North Bangor z 12966; Ⓟ 394; © 542
Brandon Center; RMC Place; FRANKLIN; ▲ Brandon; *209 NB-17; elev. 1,042ft./318m.; mail North Bangor z 12966; rural
Brandreth; RMC Place; HERKIMER; ▲ Webb; *209 NE-15; elev. 1,700ft./518m.; mail Long Lake z 12847
Brant; RMC Place; ERIE; ▲ Brant; 208 NK-3; elev. 756ft./230m.; 🅿; ★ BUF; z 14027; ● 600
Brant; MCD-Town; ERIE; *208 NK-3; 🅿; ★ BUF; z 14027; Ⓟ 2,119; © 1,906
Brantingham; RMC Place; LEWIS; ▲ Greig; 209 NF-14; 🅿; z 13312; ● 500
Brant Lake (Horicon); RMC Place; WARREN; ▲ Horicon; 209 NF-19; elev. 800ft./244m.; 🅿; z 12815; ● 850
Brasher; ST. LAWRENCE; see Brasher Center (RMC Place)
Brasher; MCD-Town; ST. LAWRENCE; *209 NA-16; mail Brasher Falls z 13613; Ⓟ 2,124; © 2,337
Brasher Center (Brasher); RMC Place; ST. LAWRENCE; ▲ Brasher; 209 NB-16; elev. 262ft./80m.; mail Brasher Falls z 13613; ● 85
Brasher Falls; RMC Place; ST. LAWRENCE; ▲ Brasher; 209 NB-16; 🅿; z 13613; ● 750
Brasher Falls-Winthrop; CDP-Census Area Only; ST. LAWRENCE; ▲ Stockholm, Brasher; *209 NB-16; mail Brasher Falls z 13613; Ⓟ 1,271; © 1,140
Brasher Iron Works; RMC Place; ST. LAWRENCE; 209 NA-16; elev. 263ft./80m.; mail Brasher Falls z 13613; ● 175
Brasie Corners; RMC Place; ST. LAWRENCE; ▲ Macomb; 209 NC-13; elev. 384ft./117m.; mail Gouverneur z 13642; ● 30
Breakabeen; RMC Place; SCHOHARIE; ▲ Fulton; 209 NK-17; elev. 754ft./230m.; mail Middleburgh z 12122; ● 80
Breesport; RMC Place; CHEMUNG; ▲ Horseheads; 208 NM-10; 🅿; ★ ELM; z 14816; ● 750
Breezy Point; RMC Place; QUEENS; 211 L-11; 🅿; ★ N.Y.; z 11697; pop. incl. with New York (Inc. Place)
Brentwood; CDP; SUFFOLK; ▲ Islip; 207 SF-9; 🅿 🅷 🅲 903; ★ N.Y.; z 11717; Ⓟ 45,218; © 53,917; ◆ 53,904
Brevoort; RMC Place; KINGS; ★ N.Y.; mail Brooklyn z 11216; pop. incl. with New York (Inc. Place)
Brewerton; CDP; ONONDAGA, OSWEGO; ▲ West Monroe, Cicero, Hastings; 209 NH-12; 🅿; ★ SYR; z 13029; Ⓟ 2,954; © 3,453
Brewster; Inc. Place; PUTNAM; ▲ Southeast; 207 SC-8; elev. 395ft./120m.; 🅿; ★ N.Y.; z 10509; Ⓟ 1,566; © 2,162
Brewster Heights; RMC Place; PUTNAM; ▲ Southeast; *207 SC-8; elev. 621ft./189m.; ★ N.Y.; mail Brewster z 10509; ● 1,000
Brewster Hill (Tonetta Lake Heights); CDP-Census Area Only; PUTNAM; ▲ Southeast; *207 SC-8; ★ N.Y.; mail Brewster z 10509; Ⓟ 2,226; © 2,226
Briarcliff Manor; Inc. Place; WESTCHESTER; ▲ Mount Pleasant, Ossining; 207 SD-7; elev. 266ft./81m.; 🅿; ★ N.Y.; z 10510; Ⓟ 7,070; © 7,696
Bridge (Suspension Bridge); RMC Place; NIAGARA; ★ BUF; mail Niagara Falls z 14305; pop. incl. with Niagara Falls (Inc. Place)
Bridgehampton; CDP; SUFFOLK; ▲ Southampton; 207 SE-13; elev. 41ft./12m.; 🅿; z 11932; Ⓟ 1,997; summer pop. 5,000; © 1,381
Bridgeport; CDP; MADISON, ONONDAGA; ▲ Sullivan, Cicero; 209 NI-12; 🅿; ★ SYR; z 13030; Ⓟ 2,107; © 1,665
Bridgeville; RMC Place; SULLIVAN; ▲ Thompson; *207 SB-4; elev. 1,081ft./329m.; mail Monticello z 12701; rural
Bridgewater; Inc. Place; ONEIDA; ▲ Bridgewater; 209 NJ-14; 🅿; z 13313; Ⓟ 537; © 579
Bridgewater; MCD-Town; ONEIDA; *209 NJ-14; 🅿; z 13313; Ⓟ 1,591; © 1,671
Brier Hill; RMC Place; ST. LAWRENCE; ▲ Morristown; 209 NC-13; 🅿; z 13614; ● 400
Brighton; MCD-Town; FRANKLIN; *209 NC-17; 🅲 910; mail Paul Smiths z 12970; Ⓟ 1,511; © 1,682
Brighton; RMC Place; KINGS; ★ N.Y.; mail Brooklyn z 11235; pop. incl. with New York (Inc. Place)
Brighton; CDP; MONROE; ▲ Brighton; 208 NC-9; ★ ROCH; mail Rochester z 14610, z 14618; Ⓟ 34,455; © 35,584; ◆ 35,721
Brighton; MCD-Town; MONROE; *208 NI-7; ★ ROCH; mail Rochester z 14610; Ⓟ 34,455; © 35,588; ◆ 35,721
Brighton (Brighton Corners); RMC Place; OTSEGO; ▲ Richfield; *209 NJ-16; mail Richfield Springs z 13439; rural
Brighton Beach; RMC Place; KINGS; 210 L-10; ★ N.Y.; mail Brooklyn z 11235; pop. incl. with New York (Inc. Place)
Brighton Corners; OTSEGO; see Brighton (RMC Place)
Brightside; RMC Place; HAMILTON; ▲ Long Lake; mail Raquette Lake z 13436
Brightwaters; Inc. Place; SUFFOLK; ▲ Islip; 207 SF-9; 🅿; ★ N.Y.; z 11718; Ⓟ 3,265; © 3,248
Brinckerhoff; CDP; DUTCHESS; ▲ Fishkill; *207 SB-7; ★ POK; mail Fishkill z 12524; Ⓟ 2,756; © 2,734
Brisben; RMC Place; CHENANGO; ▲ Greene; 209 NL-13; 🅿; z 13830 & mail Greene z 13778; ● 100
Briscoe; RMC Place; SULLIVAN; ▲ Bethel; *207 SA-3; mail Swan Lake z 12783; ● 100
Bristol; RMC Place; ONTARIO; ▲ Bristol; 208 NJ-8; elev. 1,169ft./356m.; mail Bloomfield z 14469; ● 100
Bristol; MCD-Town; ONTARIO; *208 NJ-8; mail Bloomfield z 14469; Ⓟ 2,071; © 2,421
Bristol Center; RMC Place; ONTARIO; ▲ Bristol; *208 NJ-8; mail Canandaigua z 14424; ● 100
Bristol Springs; RMC Place; ONTARIO; ▲ South Bristol; 208 NJ-8; mail Naples z 14512; ● 120
Broadacres; RMC Place; BROOME; ▲ Chenango; 207 SA-11; ★ BING; mail Binghamton z 13905; ● 1,280
Broadalbin; Inc. Place; FULTON; ▲ Mayfield, Broadalbin; 209 NI-18; 🅿; ★ A-S-T; z 12025; Ⓟ 1,397; © 1,411
Broadalbin; MCD-Town; FULTON; *209 NI-18; 🅿; ★ A-S-T; z 12025; includes part of the Village of Broadalbin; Ⓟ 4,397; © 5,066
Broad Channel; RMC Place; QUEENS; 211 K-14; 🅿; ★ N.Y.; z 11693; pop. incl. with New York (Inc. Place)
Broadway; RMC Place; QUEENS; *207 SF-7; ★ N.Y.; mail Astoria z 11106; pop. incl. with New York (Inc. Place)
Brockport; Inc. Place; MONROE; ▲ Clarkson, Sweden; 208 NH-6; 🅿 🅷 🅲 8,315; ★ ROCH; z 14420; Ⓟ 8,749; © 8,103
Brockville; RMC Place; ORLEANS; ▲ Murray; *208 NH-6; ★ ROCH; mail Albion z 14411; ● 85
Brocton; Inc. Place; CHAUTAUQUA; ▲ Portland; 208 NL-2; 🅿; z 14716; Ⓟ 1,387; © 1,547
Brodhead; RMC Place; ULSTER; ▲ Olive; *209 NN-17; mail West Shokan z 12494; rural
Bronx; RMC Place; ⊡ BRONX; *207 SF-7; elev. 60ft./18m.; 🅿; ★ N.Y.; z 10451-75, z 10499; pop. incl. with New York (Inc. Place)
BRONX; 211 E-13; Ⓟ 1,203,789; © 1,332,650; ◆ 1,396,428
Bronxdale; RMC Place; BRONX; *207 SF-7; ★ N.Y.; mail Bronx z 10462; pop. incl. with New York (Inc. Place)
Bronxville; Inc. Place; WESTCHESTER; ▲ Eastchester; 211 B-13; 🅿 🅷 🅲 2,463; ★ N.Y.; z 10708; Ⓟ 6,028; © 6,543
Bronxville Heights; RMC Place; WESTCHESTER; *207 SE-7; ★ N.Y.; mail Bronxville z 10708; pop. incl. with Yonkers (Inc. Place)
Brookdale; RMC Place; ST. LAWRENCE; ▲ Stockholm; *209 NB-15; elev. 322ft./98m.; mail Norwood z 13668; ● 35
Brookfield; RMC Place; MADISON; ▲ Brookfield; 209 NJ-14; 🅿; z 13314; ● 600
Brookfield; MCD-Town; MADISON; *209 NJ-14; 🅿; z 13314; Ⓟ 2,225; © 2,403
Brookhaven; CDP; SUFFOLK; ▲ Brookhaven; *207 SF-10; 🅿; ★ N.Y.; z 11719; Ⓟ 3,118; © 3,570
Brookhaven; MCD-Town; SUFFOLK; *207 SF-10; 🅿 🅲 26,607; ★ N.Y.; z 11719; Ⓟ 407,779; © 448,248; ◆ 461,604
Brooklyn; RMC Place; DELAWARE; ▲ Franklin; *209 NL-15; elev. 1,200ft./366m.; mail Franklin z 13775; rural
Brooklyn; RMC Place; ⊡ KINGS; *207 SF-6; elev. 66ft./20m.; 🅿; ★ N.Y.; z 11201-26, z 11228-43, z 11245, z 11247, z 11249, z 11251-52, z 11256; pop. incl. with New York (Inc. Place)
Brooklyn Heights; RMC Place; KINGS; *207 SF-6; ★ N.Y.; mail Brooklyn z 11201; pop. incl. with New York (Inc. Place)
Brooks Avenue Station; RMC Place; MONROE; *208 NI-7; ★ ROCH; mail Rochester z 14624
Brooksburg; RMC Place; GREENE; ▲ Windham; *209 NL-18; mail Windham z 12496; rural
Brooks Grove; RMC Place; LIVINGSTON; ▲ Mount Morris; *208 NK-6; mail Mount Morris z 14510; rural
Brooktondale; RMC Place; TOMPKINS; ▲ Caroline; 209 NL-11; 🅿; z 14817; ● 500
Brookview; RMC Place; RENSSELAER; ▲ Schodack; *209 NK-19; 🅿; ★ A-S-T; z 12033; ● 100
Brookville; Inc. Place; NASSAU; ▲ Oyster Bay; 211 F-19; 🅲 8,494; ★ N.Y.; mail Glen Head z 11545, Greenvale z 11548; Ⓟ 3,716; © 2,126; Ⓡ 3,365
Broome; MCD-Town; SCHOHARIE; *209 NK-17; mail Middleburgh z 12122; Ⓟ 926; © 947
BROOME; 209 NM-14; Ⓟ 212,160; © 200,536; ◆ 195,199
Broome Center; RMC Place; SCHOHARIE; ▲ Gilboa; *209 NK-17; mail Gilboa z 12076; rural
Broughton Park; RMC Place; TIOGA; ▲ Owego; *209 NM-12; ★ BING; mail Endicott z 13760; ● 550
Browns Bridge; RMC Place; ST. LAWRENCE; ▲ Pierrepont; *209 NC-15; mail Colton z 13625; rural
Browns Hollow; RMC Place; MONTGOMERY; ▲ Root; *209 NJ-17; elev. 982ft./299m.; mail Canajoharie z 13317; rural
Brownsville; RMC Place; KINGS; 211 J-12; elev. 32ft./10m.; ★ N.Y.; mail Brooklyn z 11212; pop. incl. with New York (Inc. Place)
Brownsville; RMC Place; ONTARIO; ▲ Farmington; *208 NI-8; ★ ROCH; mail Victor z 14564; rural
Brownville; Inc. Place; JEFFERSON; ▲ Brownville; 209 NE-12; elev. 354ft./108m.; 🅿; ★ WATN; z 13615; Ⓟ 1,138; © 1,022
Brownville; MCD-Town; JEFFERSON; *209 NE-12; 🅿; ★ WATN; z 13615; Ⓟ 5,604; © 5,843
Bruceville; RMC Place; ULSTER; ▲ Rosendale; *207 SA-6; ★ KNGST; mail High Falls z 12440
Brunswick; RMC Place; RENSSELAER; ▲ Brunswick; 209 NJ-19; ★ A-S-T; mail Troy z 12180; ● 800
Brunswick; MCD-Town; RENSSELAER; *209 NJ-19; ★ A-S-T; mail Troy z 12180; Ⓟ 11,093; © 11,664
Brushton; Inc. Place; FRANKLIN; ▲ Moira; 209 NB-16; 🅿; z 12916; Ⓟ 522; © 479
Brutus; MCD-Town; CAYUGA; *208 NI-10; ★ SYR; mail Weedsport z 13166; Ⓟ 5,013; © 4,777
Bruynswick; RMC Place; ULSTER; ▲ Shawangunk; 207 SB-5; mail Wallkill z 12589; rural
Bryant; RMC Place; NEW YORK; ★ N.Y.; mail New York z 10036; pop. incl. with New York (Inc. Place)
Bryn Mawr Park; RMC Place; WESTCHESTER; *207 SE-7; ★ N.Y.; mail Yonkers z 10701; pop. incl. with Yonkers (Inc. Place)
Buchanan; Inc. Place; WESTCHESTER; ▲ Cortlandt; 207 SD-6; 🅿; ★ N.Y.; z 10511; Ⓟ 1,970; © 2,189
Buckleyville; RMC Place; COLUMBIA; ▲ Ghent; *209 NL-19; ★ A-S-T; mail Chatham z 12037; rural
Bucks Bridge; RMC Place; ST. LAWRENCE; ▲ Potsdam; 209 NB-15; mail Canton z 13617, Madrid z 13660; ● 40
Buck Settlement; RMC Place; STEUBEN; ▲ Bath; *208 NL-8; mail Bath z 14810; rural
Buckton; RMC Place; ST. LAWRENCE; ▲ Stockholm; *209 NB-16; mail Winthrop z 13697; rural
Buel; RMC Place; MONTGOMERY; ▲ Canajoharie; *209 NJ-16; mail Canajoharie z 13317; rural
Buellville; RMC Place; ONONDAGA; ▲ Pompey; *209 NI-12; ★ SYR; mail Manlius z 13104; rural
Buena Vista; RMC Place; STEUBEN; ▲ Howard; *208 NL-8; mail Canisteo z 14823; rural
Buffalo; Inc. Place; ⊡ ERIE; 208 NJ-3; elev. 600ft./183m.; 🅿 🅷 🅲 46,523 ■; ★ BUF; z 14201-28, z 14231, z 14233, z 14240-41, z 14260-61, z 14263-65, z 14267, z 14269-70, z 14272-73, z 14276, z 14280; Ⓟ 328,123; © 292,648; ◆ 263,423
Buffalo Creek; RMC Place; ERIE; ★ BUF; mail Buffalo z 14224; pop. incl. with Buffalo (Inc. Place)
Buffalo Junction; RMC Place; ERIE; ★ BUF; mail Buffalo z 14201; pop. incl. with Buffalo (Inc. Place)
Buffalo Lake; RMC Place; ERIE; ★ BUF; mail Buffalo z 14222; pop. incl. with Buffalo (Inc. Place)
Bull Hill; RMC Place; HERKIMER; ▲ Ohio; *209 NH-15; elev. 1,423ft./434m.; mail Cold Brook z 13324; rural
Bulls Head; RMC Place; MONROE; ★ ROCH; pop. incl. with Rochester (Inc. Place)
Bulls Head; RMC Place; RICHMOND; *207 SG-6; elev. 33ft./10m.; ★ N.Y.; mail Staten Island z 10314; pop. incl. with New York (Inc. Place)

Bullville; RMC Place; ORANGE; ▲ Crawford; 207 SB-5; elev. 518ft./158m.; 🅿; z 10915; ● 900
Bundy Crossing (Bundys); RMC Place; OSWEGO; ▲ Volney; *209 NH-11; mail Oswego z 13126; ● 175
Bundys; OSWEGO; see Bundy Crossing (RMC Place)
Burden; RMC Place; COLUMBIA; ▲ Clermont; *209 NM-19; mail Germantown z 12526; rural
Burden Lake; RMC Place; RENSSELAER; ▲ Sand Lake, Nassau; *209 NK-19; ★ A-S-T; mail Averill Park z 12018; ● 370
Burdett; Inc. Place; SCHUYLER; ▲ Hector; 208 NL-10; 🅿; z 14818; Ⓟ 372; © 357
Burgoyne; RMC Place; SARATOGA; ▲ Saratoga; *209 NI-19; ★ A-S-T; mail Schuylerville z 12871; rural
Burke; Inc. Place; FRANKLIN; ▲ Burke; 209 NA-17; 🅿; z 12917; Ⓟ 209; © 213
Burke; MCD-Town; FRANKLIN; *209 NA-17; 🅿; z 12917; Ⓟ 1,231; © 1,359
Burke Center; RMC Place; FRANKLIN; ▲ Burke; *209 NA-17; elev. 726ft./221m.; mail Burke z 12917; rural
Burlingham; RMC Place; SULLIVAN; ▲ Mamakating; 207 SB-5; 🅿; ★ MIDD; z 12722; ● 500
Burlington; RMC Place; OTSEGO; ▲ Burlington; *209 NJ-16; elev. 1,542ft./470m.; mail Burlington Flats z 13315; ● 85
Burlington; MCD-Town; OTSEGO; *209 NJ-16; mail Burlington Flats z 13315; Ⓟ 1,036; © 1,085
Burlington Flats; RMC Place; OTSEGO; ▲ Burlington; 209 NJ-15; elev. 1,282ft./391m.; 🅿; z 13315 & mail Garrattsville z 13342; ● 100
Burnhams; RMC Place; CHAUTAUQUA; *208 NL-2; mail Cassadaga z 14718; pop. incl. with Cassadaga (Inc. Place)
Burns; RMC Place; ALLEGANY; ▲ Burns; 208 NL-7; elev. 1,198ft./365m.; mail Arkport z 14807; ● 150
Burns; MCD-Town; ALLEGANY; *208 NL-7; mail Arkport z 14807; Ⓟ 1,299; © 1,248
Burnside; RMC Place; ORANGE; ▲ Hamptonburgh; *207 SC-6; elev. 340ft./104m.; ★ N.Y.; mail Rock Tavern z 12575; rural
Burns-Whitney Estates; ALBANY; see Whitney Estates (RMC Place)
Burnt Hills; RMC Place; SARATOGA; ▲ Ballston; 209 NI-18; 🅿; ★ A-S-T; z 12019, z 12027; ● 1,620
Burnwood; RMC Place; DELAWARE; ▲ Hancock; *209 NN-15; mail East Branch z 13756; ● 80
Burrs Mills (Burrville); RMC Place; JEFFERSON; ▲ Watertown; 209 NE-13; ★ WATN; mail Watertown z 13601; ● 100
Burrville; JEFFERSON; see Burrs Mills (RMC Place)
Burt; RMC Place; NIAGARA; ▲ Newfane; 208 NH-4; 🅿; ★ LOCK; z 14028; ● 400
Burtonsville; RMC Place; MONTGOMERY; ▲ Charleston; 209 NJ-17; elev. 518ft./158m.; mail Esperance z 12066; ● 100
Bushes Landing; RMC Place; LEWIS; ▲ Watson; *209 NF-14; elev. 763ft./233m.; mail Lowville z 13367; rural
Bushnell Basin; RMC Place; MONROE; ▲ Perinton; *208 NI-8; elev. 469ft./143m.; ★ ROCH; mail Pittsford z 14534; ● 200
Bushnellsville; RMC Place; ULSTER; ▲ Shandaken; 209 NM-17; mail Shandaken z 12480; ● 200
Bush Terminal; RMC Place; KINGS; ★ N.Y.; mail Brooklyn z 11232; pop. incl. with New York (Inc. Place)
Bushville; RMC Place; GENESEE; ▲ Batavia; *208 NI-5; elev. 879ft./268m.; mail Batavia z 14020; ● 75
Bushville; RMC Place; SULLIVAN; ▲ Bethel; *207 SB-4; elev. 1,187ft./362m.; mail Monticello z 12701; rural
Bushwick; RMC Place; KINGS; 211 I-12; ★ N.Y.; mail Brooklyn z 11221; pop. incl. with New York (Inc. Place)
Buskirk; RMC Place; RENSSELAER; ▲ Hoosick; *209 NI-20; 🅿; z 12028; ● 200
Busti; RMC Place; CHAUTAUQUA; ▲ Busti; 208 NM-2; elev. 1,368ft./417m.; ★ JMST; mail Jamestown z 14701; ● 300
Busti; MCD-Town; CHAUTAUQUA; *208 NM-2; ★ JMST; mail Jamestown z 14701; Ⓟ 8,050; © 7,760
Butler; WAYNE; see Butler Center (RMC Place)
Butler; MCD-Town; WAYNE; *208 NI-10; mail Wolcott z 14590; Ⓟ 2,152; © 2,277
Butler Center (Butler); RMC Place; WAYNE; ▲ Butler; *208 NI-10; mail Wolcott z 14590; ● 45
Butlerville; RMC Place; WESTCHESTER; ▲ Somers; *207 SC-7; ★ N.Y.; mail Croton Falls z 10519, Somers z 10589; ● 350
Butterfield; RMC Place; ONEIDA; ★ UT-R; mail Utica z 13503; pop. incl. with Utica (Inc. Place)
Butternut Grove; RMC Place; DELAWARE; ▲ Colchester; *209 NM-15; mail Roscoe z 12776; rural
Butternuts; MCD-Town; OTSEGO; *209 NK-14; mail Gilbertsville z 13776; Ⓟ 1,626; © 1,792
Byersville; RMC Place; LIVINGSTON; ▲ West Sparta; *208 NK-7; mail Nunda z 14517; rural
Byron; RMC Place; GENESEE; ▲ Byron; 208 NI-6; elev. 616ft./188m.; 🅿; ★ ROCH; z 14422; ● 400
Byron; MCD-Town; GENESEE; *208 NI-6; 🅿; ★ ROCH; z 14422; Ⓟ 2,345; © 2,493

C

Cabinhill; RMC Place; DELAWARE; ▲ Andes; mail Delancey z 13752; rural
Cadiz; RMC Place; CATTARAUGUS; ▲ Franklinville; *208 NL-5; mail Franklinville z 14737
Cadosia; RMC Place; DELAWARE; ▲ Hancock; 209 NM-14; 🅿; z 13783; ● 300
Cadyville; RMC Place; CLINTON; ▲ Plattsburgh; 209 NB-19; elev. 747ft./228m.; 🅿; ★ PLATT; z 12918; ● 900
Cahoonzie; RMC Place; ORANGE; ▲ Deerpark; 207 SC-4; mail Sparrow Bush z 12780; ● 350
Cairo; CDP; GREENE; ▲ Cairo; 209 NL-18; elev. 343ft./105m.; 🅿; z 12413; Ⓟ 1,273; © 1,390
Cairo; MCD-Town; GREENE; *209 NL-18; 🅿; z 12413; Ⓟ 5,418; © 6,355
Calcium; CDP; JEFFERSON; ▲ Le Ray; *209 NE-13; elev. 472ft./144m.; 🅿; ★ WATN; z 13616; Ⓟ 2,465; © 3,346
Calcutta; RMC Place; OTSEGO; ▲ Worcester; *209 NK-16; mail East Worcester z 12064; ● 25
Caledonia; Inc. Place; LIVINGSTON; ▲ Caledonia; 208 NI-7; elev. 666ft./203m.; 🅿; ★ ROCH; z 14423; Ⓟ 2,262; © 2,327
Caledonia; MCD-Town; LIVINGSTON; *208 NI-7; 🅿; ★ ROCH; z 14423; Ⓟ 4,441; © 4,567
Calico Colony; RMC Place; SARATOGA; ▲ Clifton Park; *209 NJ-19; ★ A-S-T; mail Clifton Park z 12065; ● 700
Callicoon; CDP; SULLIVAN; ▲ Delaware; 209 NN-15; elev. 781ft./238m.; 🅿; z 12723; © 216
Callicoon; MCD-Town; SULLIVAN; *207 SA-3; 🅿; z 12723 & mail Youngsville z 12791; Ⓟ 3,024; © 3,052
Callicoon Center; RMC Place; SULLIVAN; ▲ Callicoon; 209 NN-15; elev. 1,258ft./383m.; 🅿; z 12724; ● 430
Calverton; CDP; SUFFOLK; ▲ Riverhead; 207 SE-11; 🅿; ★ N.Y.; z 11933; Ⓟ 4,759; © 5,704
Cambria; MCD-Town; NIAGARA; *208 NH-4; ★ BUF; mail Lockport z 14094; Ⓟ 4,779; © 5,393
Cambria Heights; RMC Place; QUEENS; 211 I-15; 🅿; ★ N.Y.; z 11411; pop. incl. with New York (Inc. Place)
Cambridge; Inc. Place; WASHINGTON; ▲ Cambridge, White Creek; 209 NI-20; elev. 496ft./151m.; 🅿 🅷; z 12816; Ⓟ 1,906; © 1,925
Cambridge; MCD-Town; WASHINGTON; *209 NI-20; 🅿; z 12816; includes part of the Village of Cambridge; Ⓟ 1,938; © 2,152
Camby; RMC Place; DUTCHESS; ▲ Union Vale; *207 SA-7; mail Millbrook z 12545; rural
Camden; Inc. Place; ONEIDA; ▲ Camden; 209 NH-13; 🅿; z 13316; Ⓟ 2,552; © 2,330
Camden; MCD-Town; ONEIDA; *209 NH-13; 🅿; z 13316; Ⓟ 5,134; © 5,028; Ⓡ 5,018
Cameron; RMC Place; STEUBEN; ▲ Cameron; 208 NM-8; elev. 1,051ft./320m.; 🅿; z 14819; ● 200
Cameron; MCD-Town; STEUBEN; *208 NL-8; 🅿; z 14819; Ⓟ 916; © 1,034
Cameron Mills; RMC Place; STEUBEN; ▲ Rathbone; 208 NM-8; 🅿; z 14820 & mail Cameron z 14819; ● 125
Camillus; Inc. Place; ONONDAGA; ▲ Camillus; 209 NI-11; 🅿; ★ SYR; z 13031; Ⓟ 1,150; © 1,249
Camillus; MCD-Town; ONONDAGA; *209 NI-11; 🅿; ★ SYR; z 13031; Ⓟ 23,625; © 23,152; ◆ 23,231
Campbell; RMC Place; STEUBEN; ▲ Campbell; 208 NL-8; 🅿; z 14821; ● 300
Campbell; MCD-Town; STEUBEN; *208 NL-9; 🅿; z 14821; Ⓟ 3,658; © 3,691
Campbell Hall; RMC Place; ORANGE; ▲ Hamptonburgh; 207 SC-5; 🅿; ★ N.Y.; z 10916; ● 650
Camp Hemlock; RMC Place; SULLIVAN; ▲ Mamakating; mail Bloomingburg z 12721; ● 130
Camp Hill; RMC Place; ROCKLAND; *207 SD-6; elev. 538ft./164m.; ★ N.Y.; mail Pomona z 10970
Camps Mills; RMC Place; JEFFERSON; ▲ Hounsfield; *209 NE-12; mail Watertown z 13601; rural
Campville; RMC Place; TIOGA; ▲ Owego; 209 NM-12; ★ BING; mail Endicott z 13760; ● 350
Camroden; RMC Place; ONEIDA; ▲ Floyd; *209 NH-14; elev. 866ft./264m.; ★ UT-R; mail Rome z 13440; rural
Canaan; RMC Place; COLUMBIA; ▲ Canaan; 209 NL-20; elev. 847ft./258m.; 🅿; z 12029; ● 450
Canaan; MCD-Town; COLUMBIA; *209 NL-20; 🅿; z 12029; Ⓟ 1,773; © 1,820
Canaan Center; RMC Place; COLUMBIA; ▲ Canaan; *209 NL-20; mail Canaan z 12029; ● 70
Canada Lake; RMC Place; FULTON; ▲ Caroga; *209 NH-17; mail Caroga Lake z 12032
Canadice; RMC Place; ONTARIO; ▲ Canadice; *208 NJ-7; mail Springwater z 14560; ● 200
Canadice; MCD-Town; ONTARIO; *208 NJ-7; mail Springwater z 14560; Ⓟ 1,857; © 1,846
Canajoharie; Inc. Place; MONTGOMERY; ▲ Canajoharie; 209 NJ-16; elev. 311ft./95m.; 🅿; z 13317; Ⓟ 2,278; © 2,257
Canajoharie; MCD-Town; MONTGOMERY; *209 NJ-16; 🅿; z 13317; Ⓟ 3,909; © 3,797
Canal Street; RMC Place; NEW YORK; 🅿; ★ N.Y.; z 10013, z 10213; pop. incl. with New York (Inc. Place)
Canandaigua; Inc. Place; ⊡ ONTARIO; 208 NJ-8; elev. 767ft./234m.; 🅿 🅷; z 14424-25; Ⓟ 10,725; © 11,264; Ⓡ 11,418
Canandaigua; MCD-Town; ONTARIO; *208 NJ-8; 🅿; z 14424-25; does not include City of Canandaigua; Ⓟ 7,160; © 7,649
Canarsie; RMC Place; KINGS; 211 J-12; ★ N.Y.; mail Brooklyn z 11236; pop. incl. with New York (Inc. Place)
Canaseraga; Inc. Place; ALLEGANY; ▲ Burns; 208 NK-7; 🅿; z 14822; Ⓟ 684; © 594
Canastota; Inc. Place; MADISON; ▲ Lenox; 209 NI-13; 🅿; ★ SYR; z 13032; Ⓟ 4,673; © 4,425
Canawaugus; RMC Place; LIVINGSTON; ▲ Caledonia; *208 NJ-7; ★ ROCH; mail Caledonia z 14423; rural
Candor; Inc. Place; TIOGA; ▲ Candor; 209 NL-11; 🅿; z 13743; Ⓟ 869; © 855
Candor; MCD-Town; TIOGA; *209 NL-11; 🅿; z 13743; Ⓟ 5,310; © 5,317
Caneadea; RMC Place; ALLEGANY; ▲ Caneadea; 208 NL-6; 🅿; z 14717; ● 500
Caneadea; MCD-Town; ALLEGANY; *208 NL-6; 🅿 🅲 1,353; z 14717; Ⓟ 2,551; © 2,694
Canisteo; Inc. Place; STEUBEN; ▲ Canisteo; 208 NL-7; elev. 1,132ft./345m.; 🅿; z 14823; Ⓟ 2,421; © 2,336
Canisteo; MCD-Town; STEUBEN; *208 NL-7; 🅿; z 14823; Ⓟ 3,636; © 3,583
Canisteo Center (Carson); RMC Place; STEUBEN; ▲ Canisteo; *208 NL-7; mail Canisteo z 14823; ● 25
Cannon Corners; RMC Place; CLINTON; ▲ Mooers; *209 NA-19; mail Mooers Forks z 12959; ● 50
Canoe Place; RMC Place; SUFFOLK; ▲ Southampton; *207 SE-12; mail Hampton Bays z 11946
Canoga; RMC Place; SENECA; ▲ Fayette; *208 NJ-10; mail Seneca Falls z 13148; ● 90
Canterbury Hill; RMC Place; ONEIDA; *209 NH-14; elev. 587ft./179m.; ★ UT-R; mail Rome z 13440; pop. incl. with Rome (Inc. Place)
Canterbury Woods; RMC Place; ONONDAGA; ▲ Manlius; *209 NI-12; ★ SYR; mail Minoa z 13116; rural
Canton; Inc. Place; ⊡ ST. LAWRENCE; ▲ Canton; 209 NC-15; elev. 409ft./125m.; 🅿 🅲 4,766; z 13617; Ⓟ 6,379; © 5,882; Ⓡ 5,698
Canton; MCD-Town; ST. LAWRENCE; *209 NC-14; 🅿 🅲 4,766; z 13617; Ⓟ 11,120; © 10,334
Cape Vincent; Inc. Place; JEFFERSON; ▲ Cape Vincent; 209 NE-11; elev. 253ft./77m.; 🅿; z 13618; Ⓟ 683; © 760
Cape Vincent; MCD-Town; JEFFERSON; *209 NE-11; 🅿; z 13618; Ⓟ 2,768; © 3,345
Capitol; RMC Place; ALBANY; ★ A-S-T; mail Albany z 12224; pop. incl. with Albany (Inc. Place)
Capitol Annex; RMC Place; ALBANY; ★ A-S-T; mail Albany z 12225; pop. incl. with Albany (Inc. Place)
Cardiff; RMC Place; ONONDAGA; ▲ LaFayette; 209 NJ-12; ★ SYR; mail La Fayette z 13084; ● 150
Carle Place; CDP; NASSAU; ▲ North Hempstead; 211 G-18; 🅿; ★ N.Y.; z 11514; Ⓟ 5,107; © 5,247
Carle Terrace; RMC Place; ULSTER; ▲ Ulster; ★ KNGST; mail Lake Katrine z 12449

Entries in **UPPERCASE** are counties.
Entries in **bold** have populations of 2,500 or more.
Names in parentheses are alternate names.
Inc. Place — Incorporated Place
RMC Place — Rand McNally Designated Place
CDP — Census Designated Place
MCD — Minor Civil Division

⊡ County Seat
▲ Minor Civil Division
elev. Elevation
🅿 Post Office

🅷 Hospital
🅲 College
■ Principal Business Center
★ Ranally Metro Area (RMA) Abbreviation
z Zip Code(s)

Ⓟ Previous Census Population
Ⓡ Revised Census Population
Ⓐ Annexation Population
● Rand McNally Population Estimate
© Final Census Population
Ⓢ Special Census Population
◆ Estimated Population

For additional definitions see Glossary, Volume 1, and Introduction, Volume 2.

Carleys Mills; RMC Place; OSWEGO; ▲ Palermo; *209 NH-12; ★ SYR; mail Hastings z 13076; rural
Carlisle; RMC Place; SCHOHARIE; ▲ Carlisle; 209 NJ-17; elev. 1,290ft./393m.; 🅿; z 12031; ● 700
Carlisle; MCD-Town; SCHOHARIE; *209 NJ-17; 🅿; z 12031; Ⓟ 1,672; © 1,758
Carlisle Center; RMC Place; SCHOHARIE; ▲ Carlisle; *209 NJ-17; mail Central Bridge z 12035; rural
Carlisle Gardens; RMC Place; NIAGARA; ▲ Lockport; *208 NH-4; ★ LOCK; mail Lockport z 14094; ● 700
Carlton; RMC Place; ORLEANS; ▲ Carlton; *208 NH-6; mail Albion z 14411; ● 170
Carlton; MCD-Town; ORLEANS; *208 NH-5; mail Albion z 14411; Ⓟ 2,808; © 2,960
Carman; RMC Place; SCHENECTADY; ▲ Rotterdam; *209 NJ-18; ★ A-S-T; mail Schenectady z 12303
Carmel; RMC Place; ⊡ PUTNAM; ▲ Carmel; 207 SC-7; ★ N.Y.; ● 3,600
Carmel; MCD-Town; PUTNAM; *207 SC-7; 🅿; ★ N.Y.; z 10512; Ⓟ 28,816; © 33,006; ◆ 34,152
Carmel Hamlet; CDP-Census Area Only; PUTNAM; ▲ Kent, Carmel; 207 SC-7; 🅷; ★ N.Y.; mail Carmel z 10512; Ⓟ 4,800; © 5,650
Carmel Park Estates; RMC Place; PUTNAM; ▲ Kent; *207 SC-7; elev. 891ft./272m.; ★ N.Y.; mail Carmel z 10512; ● 200
Carnegie; RMC Place; ERIE; ▲ Hamburg; *208 NJ-4; ★ BUF; mail Hamburg z 14075; ● 1,450
Caroga; MCD-Town; FULTON; *209 NI-17; mail Caroga Lake z 12032; Ⓟ 1,337; © 1,407
Caroga Lake; RMC Place; FULTON; ▲ Caroga; 209 NI-17; 🅿; z 12032; summer pop. 1,000; ● 800
Caroline; RMC Place; TOMPKINS; ▲ Caroline; 209 NL-11; elev. 1,277ft./389m.; mail Brooktondale z 14817; ● 20
Caroline; RMC Place; TOMPKINS; ▲ Caroline; ● 70
Caroline; MCD-Town; TOMPKINS; *209 NL-11; mail Brooktondale z 14817; Ⓟ 3,044; © 2,910
Caroline Center; RMC Place; TOMPKINS; ▲ Caroline; *209 NL-11; elev. 1,590ft./485m.; mail Brooktondale z 14817
Carroll; MCD-Town; CHAUTAUQUA; *208 NM-3; ★ JMST; mail Frewsburg z 14738; Ⓟ 3,539; © 3,635
Carrollton; RMC Place; CATTARAUGUS; ▲ Allegany; 208 NM-4; mail Kill Buck z 14748; ● 100
Carrollton; MCD-Town; CATTARAUGUS; *208 NM-4; mail Limestone z 14753; Ⓟ 1,555; © 1,410
Carson; STEUBEN; see Canisteo Center (RMC Place)
Carterville; RMC Place; OSWEGO; ▲ Amboy; *209 NH-12; mail Williamstown z 13493; rural
Carthage; Inc. Place; JEFFERSON; ▲ Wilna; 209 NE-13; elev. 743ft./226m.; 🅿 🅷; z 13619; Ⓟ 4,344; © 3,721
Cascade; RMC Place; CAYUGA; ▲ Venice; *209 NJ-11; mail Moravia z 13118; ● 65
Case; RMC Place; ONONDAGA; ▲ Otisco; *209 NJ-12; ★ SYR; mail La Fayette z 13084; rural
Casowasco; RMC Place; CAYUGA; ▲ Scipio; *209 NJ-11; mail Moravia z 13118; summer pop. 300
Cassadaga; Inc. Place; CHAUTAUQUA; ▲ Stockton; 208 NL-2; elev. 1,316ft./401m.; 🅿; z 14718; Ⓟ 768; © 676
Cassville (Richfield Junction); RMC Place; ONEIDA; ▲ Paris; 209 NI-14; elev. 1,210ft./369m.; 🅿; ★ UT-R; z 13318; ● 250
Castile; Inc. Place; WYOMING; ▲ Castile; 208 NK-6; 🅿; z 14427; Ⓟ 1,078; © 1,051
Castile; MCD-Town; WYOMING; *208 NK-6; 🅿; z 14427; Ⓟ 3,042; © 2,873
Castile Center; RMC Place; WYOMING; ▲ Castile; *208 NK-6; elev. 1,517ft./462m.; mail Castile z 14427; rural
Castle Creek; RMC Place; BROOME; ▲ Chenango; 209 NL-12; 🅿; ★ BING; z 13744; ● 400
Castle Hill; RMC Place; BRONX; ★ N.Y.; mail Bronx z 10462; pop. incl. with New York (Inc. Place)
Castle Point; RMC Place; DUTCHESS; ▲ Fishkill; *207 SB-6; 🅿 🅷; ★ POK; z 12511; ● 200
Castleton Corners; RMC Place; RICHMOND; 210 K-7; elev. 183ft./56m.; ★ N.Y.; mail Staten Island z 10314; pop. incl. with New York (Inc. Place)
Castleton-on-Hudson; Inc. Place; RENSSELAER; 209 NK-19; elev. 150ft./46m.; 🅿; ★ A-S-T; z 12033; Ⓟ 1,491; © 1,619
Castorland; Inc. Place; LEWIS; ▲ Denmark; 209 NF-14; elev. 739ft./225m.; 🅿; z 13620; Ⓟ 292; © 306
Catatonk; RMC Place; TIOGA; ▲ Tioga, Candor; *209 NM-11; mail Owego z 13827; ● 90
Catharine (Catherine); RMC Place; SCHUYLER; ▲ Catharine; 208 NL-10; mail Odessa z 14869; ● 100
Catharine; MCD-Town; SCHUYLER; *208 NL-10; mail Odessa z 14869; Ⓟ 1,991; © 1,930
Cathedral; RMC Place; NEW YORK; ★ N.Y.; mail New York z 10025; pop. incl. with New York (Inc. Place)
Catherine; SCHUYLER; see Catharine (RMC Place)
Catherineville; RMC Place; ST. LAWRENCE; *209 NC-16; mail Parishville z 13672; rural
Catlin; MCD-Town; CHEMUNG; *208 NL-9; mail Beaver Dams z 14812; Ⓟ 2,626; © 2,649
Cato; Inc. Place; CAYUGA; ▲ Cato; 208 NI-10; 🅿; ★ SYR; z 13033; Ⓟ 581; © 601
Cato; MCD-Town; CAYUGA; *208 NI-10; 🅿; ★ SYR; z 13033; Ⓟ 2,452; © 2,744
Caton; RMC Place; STEUBEN; ▲ Caton; 208 NM-9; mail Corning z 14830; ● 150
Caton; MCD-Town; STEUBEN; *208 NM-9; mail Corning z 14830; Ⓟ 1,888; © 2,097
Catskill; Inc. Place; ⊡ GREENE; ▲ Catskill; 209 NL-19; elev. 47ft./14m.; 🅿; ★ KNGST; z 12414; Ⓟ 4,690; © 4,392
Catskill; MCD-Town; GREENE; *209 NL-18; 🅿; ★ KNGST; z 12414; Ⓟ 11,965; © 11,849
Cattaraugus; Inc. Place; CATTARAUGUS; ▲ New Albion; 208 NL-3; elev. 1,383ft./422m.; 🅿; z 14719; Ⓟ 1,100; © 1,075
CATTARAUGUS; 208 NL-4; Ⓟ 84,234; © 83,955; ◆ 77,192
Cattaraugus Reservation; Indian Reservation; ERIE, CATTARAUGUS, CHAUTAUQUA; mail Gowanda z 14070, Irving z 14081; Ⓟ 1,994; © 2,412
Cattown; RMC Place; OTSEGO; ▲ Otsego; *209 NJ-16; mail Fly Creek z 13337; rural
Caughdenoy; RMC Place; OSWEGO; ▲ Hastings; 209 NH-12; ★ SYR; mail Central Square z 13036; ● 150
Cayuga; Inc. Place; CAYUGA; ▲ Aurelius; 208 NJ-10; 🅿; ★ SYR; z 13034; Ⓟ 556; © 509
CAYUGA; 209 NJ-11; Ⓟ 82,313; © 81,963; ◆ 77,718
Cayuga Heights; Inc. Place; TOMPKINS; ▲ Ithaca; 209 NK-11; ★ ITH; mail Ithaca z 14850; Ⓟ 3,457; © 3,273; Ⓡ 3,738
Cayuta; RMC Place; SCHUYLER; ▲ Cayuta; 208 NL-10; elev. 1,107ft./337m.; 🅿; z 14824; ● 200
Cayuta; MCD-Town; SCHUYLER; *208 NL-10; 🅿; z 14824; Ⓟ 599; © 545
Cayutaville; RMC Place; SCHUYLER; ▲ Hector, Catharine; *208 NL-10; elev. 1,401ft./427m.; mail Alpine z 14805; rural
Caywood; RMC Place; SENECA; ▲ Lodi; *208 NK-10; mail Lodi z 14860
Cazenovia; Inc. Place; MADISON; ▲ Cazenovia; 209 NJ-13; 🅿 🅲 874; ★ SYR; z 13035; Ⓟ 3,007; © 2,614
Cazenovia; MCD-Town; MADISON; *209 NJ-13; 🅿 🅲 874; ★ SYR; z 13035; Ⓟ 6,514; © 6,481
Cecil Park; RMC Place; WESTCHESTER; *207 SE-7; ★ N.Y.; mail Tuckahoe z 10707; pop. incl. with Yonkers (Inc. Place)
Cedar Cliff; RMC Place; ORANGE; ▲ Newburgh; *207 SB-6; elev. 70ft./21m.; ★ NWBG; mail Marlboro z 12542; rural
Cedarcrest; RMC Place; LIVINGSTON; ▲ Livonia; *208 NJ-7; ★ ROCH; mail Livonia z 14487; ● 80
Cedar Flats; RMC Place; ROCKLAND; ▲ Stony Point; *207 SD-6; elev. 224ft./68m.; ★ N.Y.; mail Stony Point z 10980
Cedar Hill; RMC Place; ALBANY; ▲ Bethlehem; 209 NK-19; ★ A-S-T; mail Selkirk z 12158; ● 300
Cedarhurst; Inc. Place; NASSAU; ▲ Hempstead; 211 K-16; 🅿; ★ N.Y.; z 11516; Ⓟ 5,716; © 6,164
Cedar Knolls; RMC Place; WESTCHESTER; *207 SE-7; ★ N.Y.; mail Bronxville z 10708; pop. incl. with Yonkers (Inc. Place)
Cedarvale; RMC Place; ONONDAGA; ▲ Onondaga; *209 NI-11; ★ SYR; mail Syracuse z 13215; rural
Cedarville; RMC Place; HERKIMER; ▲ Litchfield, Columbia; 209 NJ-15; mail Ilion z 13357; ● 200
Celoron; Inc. Place; CHAUTAUQUA; 208 NM-2; elev. 1,330ft./405m.; 🅿; ★ JMST; z 14720; Ⓟ 1,232; © 1,295
Cementon (Smith Landing); RMC Place; GREENE; ▲ Catskill; 209 NM-18; elev. 122ft./37m.; 🅿; ★ KNGST; z 12414; ● 375
Centenary; RMC Place; ROCKLAND; ▲ Clarkstown; *207 SD-6; ★ N.Y.; mail New City z 10956
Center Avenue; RMC Place; NASSAU; ▲ Hempstead; ★ N.Y.; mail East Rockaway z 11518; pop. incl. with East Rockaway (Inc. Place)
Center Berlin; RMC Place; RENSSELAER; *209 NJ-20; mail Berlin z 12022
Centereach; CDP; SUFFOLK; ▲ Brookhaven; 207 SE-10; 🅿; ★ N.Y.; z 11720; Ⓟ 26,720; © 27,285; ◆ 27,274
Center Falls; RMC Place; WASHINGTON; ▲ Greenwich; *209 NI-20; ★ GLFLS; mail Greenwich z 12834; ● 90
Centerfield; RMC Place; ONTARIO; ▲ Canandaigua; *208 NJ-8; elev. 944ft./288m.; mail Canandaigua z 14424; rural
Center Lisle; RMC Place; BROOME; ▲ Lisle; *209 NL-12; mail Lisle z 13797; ● 85
Center Moriches; CDP; SUFFOLK; ▲ Brookhaven; 207 SF-11; 🅿; ★ N.Y.; z 11934; Ⓟ 5,987; © 6,655
Centerport; RMC Place; CAYUGA; ▲ Mentz, Brutus; *208 NI-10; ★ SYR; mail Weedsport z 13166; rural
Centerport; CDP; SUFFOLK; ▲ Huntington; 207 SE-9; 🅿; ★ N.Y.; z 11721; Ⓟ 5,333; © 5,446
Center Valley; RMC Place; OTSEGO; ▲ Cherry Valley; *209 NJ-16; mail Cherry Valley z 13320; rural
Center Village (Centre Village); RMC Place; BROOME; ▲ Colesville; *209 NM-13; ★ BING; mail Harpursville z 13787; ● 100
Centerville; RMC Place; ALLEGANY; ▲ Centerville; 208 NK-5; 🅿; z 14029; ● 250
Centerville; MCD-Town; ALLEGANY; *208 NK-5; 🅿; z 14029; Ⓟ 678; © 762
Centerville; RMC Place; DELAWARE; ▲ Hancock; *209 NM-15; elev. 1,040ft./317m.; mail East Branch z 13756; ● 60
Center White Creek; RMC Place; WASHINGTON; ▲ White Creek; *209 NI-20; mail Eagle Bridge z 12057; rural
Central Bridge; RMC Place; SCHOHARIE; ▲ Schoharie, Esperance; 209 NJ-17; elev. 621ft./189m.; 🅿; z 12035; ● 800
Centralia; RMC Place; CHAUTAUQUA; ▲ Stockton; *208 NL-2; elev. 1,352ft./412m.; mail Sinclairville z 14782; rural
Central Islip; CDP; SUFFOLK; ▲ Islip; 207 SF-9; 🅿 🅲 488; ★ N.Y.; z 11722, z 11749 & mail Islandia z 11760; Ⓟ 26,028; © 31,950; ◆ 31,941
Central Nyack; RMC Place; ROCKLAND; ▲ Clarkstown; *207 SD-7; ★ N.Y.; mail Nyack z 10960; ● 1,980
Central Park; RMC Place; ERIE; ★ BUF; mail Buffalo z 14214-15; pop. incl. with Buffalo (Inc. Place)
Central Square; Inc. Place; OSWEGO; ▲ Hastings; 209 NH-12; 🅿; ★ SYR; z 13036; Ⓟ 1,671; © 1,646
Central Valley; CDP; ORANGE; ▲ Woodbury; 207 SC-6; 🅿; ★ N.Y.; z 10917; Ⓟ 1,929; © 1,857
Centre Island; Inc. Place; NASSAU; ▲ Oyster Bay; 211 C-20; elev. 35ft./11m.; ★ N.Y.; mail Oyster Bay z 11771; Ⓟ 439; © 444
Centre Village; BROOME; see Center Village (RMC Place)
Centuck; RMC Place; WESTCHESTER; ★ N.Y.; mail Yonkers z 10710; pop. incl. with Yonkers (Inc. Place)
Ceres; RMC Place; ALLEGANY; ▲ Genesee; 208 NM-5; 🅿; z 14721; ● 400
Chadwicks; RMC Place; ONEIDA; ▲ New Hartford; 209 NI-14; 🅿; ★ UT-R; z 13319; ● 2,100
Chaffee; RMC Place; ERIE; ▲ Sardinia; 208 NK-5; 🅿; z 14030; ● 350
Chamberlain Corners; RMC Place; ST. LAWRENCE; ▲ Waddington, Madrid; *209 NB-15; elev. 267ft./81m.; mail Madrid z 13660; rural
Chambers; RMC Place; CHEMUNG; ▲ Catlin; 208 NL-9; elev. 1,201ft./366m.; mail Beaver Dams z 14812; ● 550
Champion; RMC Place; JEFFERSON; ▲ Champion; 209 NE-13; mail Carthage z 13619; ● 100
Champion; MCD-Town; JEFFERSON; *209 NE-13; mail Carthage z 13619; Ⓟ 4,574; © 4,361
Champlain; Inc. Place; CLINTON; ▲ Champlain; 209 NA-20; 🅿; z 12919; Ⓟ 1,273; © 1,173
Champlain; MCD-Town; CLINTON; *209 NA-20; 🅿; z 12919; Ⓟ 5,796; © 5,791
Champlain Park; RMC Place; CLINTON; ▲ Plattsburgh; 209 NB-20; ★ PLATT; mail Plattsburgh z 12901; ● 1,200
Chapel Hill Estates; RMC Place; WESTCHESTER; ▲ Yorktown; ★ N.Y.; mail Yorktown Heights z 10598
Chapin; RMC Place; ONTARIO; ▲ Hopewell; 208 NJ-8; mail Canandaigua z 14424; ● 180
Chappaqua; CDP; WESTCHESTER; ▲ New Castle; 207 SD-7; elev. 496ft./151m.; 🅿; ★ N.Y.; z 10514; © 9,468
Charleston; MCD-Town; MONTGOMERY; *209 NJ-17; mail Esperance z 12066; Ⓟ 1,107; © 1,292
Charleston; RMC Place; RICHMOND; 210 M-5; ★ N.Y.; mail Staten Island z 10309; pop. incl. with New York (Inc. Place)
Charleston Four Corners; RMC Place; MONTGOMERY; ▲ Charleston; 209 NJ-17; elev. 1,092ft./333m.; mail Sprakers z 12166; ● 200
Charlesworth Corners; RMC Place; MONTGOMERY; ▲ Minden; *209 NI-16; mail Fort Plain z 13339; ● 60
Charlotte; CHAUTAUQUA; see Charlotte Center (RMC Place)
Charlotte; MCD-Town; CHAUTAUQUA; *208 NL-2; mail Sinclairville z 14782; Ⓟ 1,528; © 1,713
Charlotte; RMC Place; MONROE; *208 NH-7; ★ ROCH; mail Rochester z 14612; pop. incl. with Rochester (Inc. Place)
Charlotte Center (Charlotte); RMC Place; CHAUTAUQUA; ▲ Charlotte; *208 NL-2; mail Sinclairville z 14782; ● 50
Charlotteville; RMC Place; SCHOHARIE; ▲ Summit; 209 NK-16; 🅿; z 12036; ● 250
Charlton; RMC Place; SARATOGA; ▲ Charlton; 209 NI-18; elev. 498ft./152m.; 🅿; ★ A-S-T; z 12019; ● 320
Charlton; MCD-Town; SARATOGA; *209 NI-18; 🅿; ★ A-S-T; z 12019; Ⓟ 3,984; © 3,954
Charwood Manor; RMC Place; SARATOGA; ▲ Clifton Park; *209 NI-18; elev. 400ft./122m.; ★ A-S-T; mail Clifton Park z 12065; ● 550
Chase Lake; RMC Place; LEWIS; ▲ Watson; 209 NF-14; mail Glenfield z 13343; ● 75
Chase Mills; RMC Place; ST. LAWRENCE; ▲ Waddington, Louisville; 209 NB-15; elev. 272ft./83m.; 🅿; z 13621; ● 250
Chaseville; RMC Place; OTSEGO; ▲ Maryland; *209 NK-16; mail Maryland z 12116; rural
Chasm Falls; RMC Place; FRANKLIN; ▲ Malone; 209 NB-17; mail Malone z 12953
Chateaugay; Inc. Place; FRANKLIN; ▲ Chateaugay; 209 NA-18; elev. 972ft./296m.; 🅿; z 12920; Ⓟ 845; © 798
Chateaugay; MCD-Town; FRANKLIN; *209 NA-18; 🅿; z 12920; Ⓟ 1,659; © 2,036
Chatham; Inc. Place; COLUMBIA; ▲ Ghent, Chatham; 209 NL-19; elev. 473ft./144m.; 🅿; ★ A-S-T; z 12037; Ⓟ 1,920; © 1,758
Chatham; MCD-Town; COLUMBIA; *209 NL-19; 🅿; ★ A-S-T; z 12037; includes part of the village of Chatham; Ⓟ 4,413; © 4,249
Chatham Center; RMC Place; COLUMBIA; ▲ Chatham; 209 NK-19; ★ A-S-T; mail Valatie z 12184; ● 350
Chaumont; Inc. Place; JEFFERSON; ▲ Lyme; 209 NE-12; elev. 293ft./89m.; 🅿; z 13622; Ⓟ 593; © 592
Chautauqua (Chautauqua Institution); RMC Place; CHAUTAUQUA; ▲ Chautauqua; 208 NL-2; 🅿; z 14722; ● 500
Chautauqua; MCD-Town; CHAUTAUQUA; *208 NL-1; 🅿; z 14722; Ⓟ 4,554; © 4,666
CHAUTAUQUA; 208 NL-2; Ⓟ 141,895; © 139,750; ◆ 131,066
Chautauqua Institution; CHAUTAUQUA; see Chautauqua (RMC Place)
Chazy; RMC Place; CLINTON; ▲ Chazy; 209 NA-20; 🅿; z 12921; ● 1,000
Chazy; MCD-Town; CLINTON; *209 NB-19; 🅿; z 12921; Ⓟ 3,890; © 4,181
Chazy Lake; RMC Place; CLINTON; ▲ Dannemora; *209 NB-18; mail Ellenburg Depot z 12935; rural
Chazy Landing; RMC Place; CLINTON; ▲ Chazy; 209 NA-20; mail Chazy z 12921; ● 100
Chedwel; RMC Place; CHAUTAUQUA; ▲ Ellery; *208 NL-2; ★ JMST; mail Bemus Point z 14712; ● 120
Cheektowaga; CDP; ERIE; ▲ Cheektowaga; 208 NE-5; 🅿 🅷; ★ BUF; z 14206, z 14215, z 14225, z 14227 & mail Buffalo z 14211-12, Depew z 14043; Ⓟ 84,387; © 79,988; ◆ 75,461
Cheektowaga; MCD-Town; ERIE; *208 NJ-4; 🅿; ★ BUF; z 14206, z 14215, z 14225, z 14227 & mail Buffalo z 14211-12, Depew z 14043; Ⓟ 99,314; © 94,019; ◆ 86,015
Cheektowaga Northwest; RMC Place; ERIE; ▲ Cheektowaga; ★ BUF; mail Buffalo z 14225
Cheektowaga Southwest; RMC Place; ERIE; ▲ Cheektowaga; ★ BUF; mail Buffalo z 14227
Chelsea; RMC Place; DUTCHESS; ▲ Wappinger; 207 SB-6; 🅿; ★ POK; z 12512; ● 485
Chelsea; RMC Place; RICHMOND; *207 SG-6; ★ N.Y.; mail Staten Island z 10314; pop. incl. with New York (Inc. Place)
Chemung; RMC Place; CHEMUNG; ▲ Chemung; 208 NM-10; elev. 847ft./258m.; 🅿; z 14825; ● 600
Chemung; MCD-Town; CHEMUNG; *208 NM-10; 🅿; z 14825; Ⓟ 2,540; © 2,665
CHEMUNG; 208 NM-10; Ⓟ 95,195; © 91,070; ◆ 86,720
Chemung Center; CHEMUNG; see Beantown (RMC Place)
Chenango; MCD-Town; BROOME; *209 NM-12; ★ BING; mail Chenango Bridge z 13745; Ⓟ 12,310; © 11,454
CHENANGO; 209 NK-13; Ⓟ 51,768; © 51,401; ◆ 51,080
Chenango Bridge; RMC Place; BROOME; ▲ Chenango; 209 NM-12; 🅿; ★ BING; z 13745; ● 2,890
Chenango Forks; RMC Place; BROOME; ▲ Barker, Chenango; 209 NL-13; 🅿; ★ BING; z 13746; ● 500
Chenango Lake; RMC Place; CHENANGO; ▲ New Berlin; *209 NK-14; mail Norwich z 13815; ● 200
Cheneys Point; RMC Place; CHAUTAUQUA; ▲ North Harmony; 208 NM-2; mail Ashville z 14710; ● 250
Cheningo; RMC Place; CORTLAND; ▲ Truxton; *209 NK-12; mail Truxton z 13158
Chepachet; RMC Place; HERKIMER; ▲ Winfield; *209 NJ-16; mail West Winfield z 13491
Cherokee; RMC Place; NEW YORK; ★ N.Y.; mail New York z 10021; pop. incl. with New York (Inc. Place)
Cherry Creek; Inc. Place; CHAUTAUQUA; ▲ Cherry Creek; 208 NL-3; elev. 1,306ft./398m.; 🅿; z 14723; Ⓟ 539; © 551
Cherry Creek; MCD-Town; CHAUTAUQUA; *208 NL-3; 🅿; z 14723; Ⓟ 1,064; © 1,152
Cherry Grove; RMC Place; SUFFOLK; ▲ Brookhaven; *207 SF-10; 🅿; ★ N.Y.; z 11782; ● 550
Cherry Lane; RMC Place; CHAUTAUQUA; ▲ Pomfret; mail Fredonia z 14063; pop. incl. with Fredonia (Inc. Place)
Cherryplain; RMC Place; RENSSELAER; ▲ Berlin; 209 NK-20; 🅿; z 12040; ● 300
Cherrytown; RMC Place; ULSTER; ▲ Rochester; *207 SA-5; mail Kerhonkson z 12446; rural
Cherry Valley; Inc. Place; OTSEGO; ▲ Cherry Valley; 209 NJ-16; elev. 1,326ft./404m.; 🅿; z 13320 & mail Roseboom z 13450; Ⓟ 617; © 592
Cherry Valley; MCD-Town; OTSEGO; *209 NJ-16; 🅿; z 13320 & mail Roseboom z 13450; Ⓟ 1,210; © 1,266
Cherry Valley Junction; RMC Place; SCHOHARIE; ▲ Richmondville; *209 NK-17; mail Cherry Valley z 13320, Cobleskill z 12043; ● 500
Cheshire; RMC Place; ONTARIO; ▲ Canandaigua; 208 NJ-8; mail Canandaigua z 14424; ● 250
Chester; Inc. Place; ORANGE; ▲ Chester; 207 SC-5; 🅿; ★ N.Y.; z 10918; Ⓟ 3,270; © 3,445
Chester; MCD-Town; ORANGE; *207 SC-5; 🅿; ★ N.Y.; z 10918; Ⓟ 9,138; © 12,140
Chester; MCD-Town; WARREN; *209 NF-18; mail Pottersville z 12860; Ⓟ 3,465; © 3,614
Chesterfield; MCD-Town; ESSEX; *209 NC-19; mail Keeseville z 12944; Ⓟ 2,267; © 2,409
Chester Hill Park; RMC Place; WESTCHESTER; *207 SE-7; ★ N.Y.; mail Mount Vernon z 10550; pop. incl. with Mount Vernon (Inc. Place)
Chestertown; RMC Place; WARREN; ▲ Chester; 209 NF-19; elev. 827ft./252m.; 🅿; z 12817; ● 900
Chestnut Hill; RMC Place; ONONDAGA; ▲ Salina; *209 NI-12; ★ SYR; mail Liverpool z 13088; ● 1,230
Chestnut Ridge; RMC Place; DUTCHESS; ▲ Union Vale; *207 SA-8; mail Millbrook z 12545; rural
Chestnut Ridge; RMC Place; NIAGARA; ▲ Lockport; *208 NI-4; ★ LOCK; mail Lockport z 14094
Chestnut Ridge; Inc. Place; ROCKLAND; ▲ Ramapo; *207 SE-6; 🅿; ★ N.Y.; z 10977 & mail Monsey z 10952, Pearl River z 10965; Ⓟ 7,517; © 7,829
Cheviot; RMC Place; COLUMBIA; ▲ Germantown; *209 NM-18; mail Germantown z 12526; ● 80
Chichester; RMC Place; ULSTER; ▲ Shandaken; *209 NM-17; 🅿; z 12416; ● 270
Childs (Fair Haven); RMC Place; ORLEANS; ▲ Gaines; *208 NH-6; elev. 423ft./129m.; mail Albion z 14411; ● 50
Childwold; RMC Place; ST. LAWRENCE; ▲ Piercefield; 209 ND-16; elev. 1,628ft./496m.; 🅿; z 12922; ● 100
Chili; MCD-Town; MONROE; *208 NI-7; ★ ROCH; mail Churchville z 14428; Ⓟ 25,178; © 27,638; ◆ 27,301
Chili Center; RMC Place; MONROE; ▲ Chili; 208 NI-7; ★ ROCH; mail Rochester z 14624; ● 4,350
Chiloway; RMC Place; DELAWARE; ▲ Hancock; *209 NM-15; mail Roscoe z 12776; rural
Chilson; RMC Place; ESSEX; ▲ Ticonderoga; *209 NF-19; elev. 1,004ft./306m.; mail Ticonderoga z 12883
Chinatown; RMC Place; NEW YORK; *207 SF-6; 🅿; ★ N.Y.; z 10013; pop. incl. with New York (Inc. Place)
Chipman; RMC Place; ST. LAWRENCE; *209 NB-14; mail Madrid z 13660; ● 60
Chipmonk; RMC Place; CATTARAUGUS; ▲ Allegany; *208 NM-4; mail Allegany z 14706; rural
Chippewa Bay; RMC Place; ST. LAWRENCE; ▲ Hammond; 209 NC-13; elev. 283ft./86m.; 🅿; z 13623; ● 350
Chittenango; Inc. Place; MADISON; ▲ Sullivan; 209 NI-13; 🅿; ★ SYR; z 13037; Ⓟ 4,734; © 4,855
Chittenango Falls; RMC Place; MADISON; ▲ Cazenovia; *209 NI-13; ★ SYR; mail Cazenovia z 13035; rural
Choconut Center; RMC Place; BROOME; ▲ Union; 207 SB-11; ★ BING; mail Binghamton z 13905; ● 250
Church Street; RMC Place; NEW YORK; ★ N.Y.; mail New York z 10007, z 10249; pop. incl. with New York (Inc. Place)
Churchtown; RMC Place; COLUMBIA; ▲ Claverack, Livingston, Taghkanic; 209 NM-19; elev. 322ft./98m.; mail Craryville z 12521; ● 300
Churchville; Inc. Place; MONROE; ▲ Riga; 208 NI-6; 🅿; ★ ROCH; z 14428; Ⓟ 1,731; © 1,887
Churchville; RMC Place; ONEIDA; ▲ Verona; *209 NH-13; ★ UT-R; mail Verona z 13478; rural
Churubusco; RMC Place; CLINTON; ▲ Clinton; 209 NA-18; elev. 1,194ft./364m.; 🅿; z 12923; ● 200
Cicero; RMC Place; ONONDAGA; ▲ Cicero; 209 NI-12; 🅿; ★ SYR; z 13039; ● 1,100
Cicero; MCD-Town; ONONDAGA; *209 NI-12; 🅿; ★ SYR; z 13039; Ⓟ 25,560; © 27,982; ◆ 28,587
Cicero Center; RMC Place; ONONDAGA; ▲ Cicero; *209 NI-12; elev. 400ft./122m.; ★ SYR; mail Clay z 13041
Cincinnatus; RMC Place; CORTLAND; ▲ Cincinnatus; 209 NK-12; elev. 1,046ft./319m.; 🅿; z 13040; ● 400
Cincinnatus; MCD-Town; CORTLAND; *209 NK-12; 🅿; z 13040; Ⓟ 1,122; © 1,051
Circleville; RMC Place; ORANGE; ▲ Wallkill; 207 SB-5; 🅿; ★ MIDD; z 10919; ● 1,350
City Island; RMC Place; BRONX; *207 SF-7; elev. 19ft./6m.; ★ N.Y.; mail Bronx z 10464; pop. incl. with New York (Inc. Place)
Clairemont Farms; RMC Place; ONONDAGA; ▲ Salina; *209 NI-12; ★ SYR; mail Liverpool z 13088; ● 2,900
Clare; MCD-Town; ST. LAWRENCE; *209 ND-15; mail Russell z 13684; Ⓟ 78; © 112
Claremont Park; RMC Place; BRONX; ★ N.Y.; mail Bronx z 10457; pop. incl. with New York (Inc. Place)
Clarence; RMC Place; ERIE; ▲ Clarence; 208 NI-4; 🅿; ★ BUF; z 14031 & mail Buffalo z 14221; ● 2,100
Clarence; MCD-Town; ERIE; *208 NI-4; 🅿; ★ BUF; z 14031 & mail Buffalo z 14221; Ⓟ 20,041; © 26,123; ◆ 26,493
Clarence Center; CDP; ERIE; ▲ Clarence; 208 NI-4; elev. 635ft./194m.; 🅿; ★ BUF; z 14032; Ⓟ 1,376; © 1,747
Clarendon; RMC Place; ORLEANS; ▲ Clarendon; 208 NH-6; 🅿; ★ ROCH; z 14429; ● 350
Clarendon; MCD-Town; ORLEANS; *208 NI-6; 🅿; ★ ROCH; z 14429; Ⓟ 2,705; © 3,392
Clark Heights; RMC Place; DUTCHESS; ▲ Pleasant Valley; *207 SA-7; ★ POK; mail Pleasant Valley z 12569
Clark Mills; CDP; ONEIDA; ▲ Kirkland; *209 NI-14; 🅿; ★ UT-R; z 13321; Ⓟ 1,303; © 1,424
Clarksburg; RMC Place; ERIE; ▲ Eden; *208 NK-4; ★ BUF; mail Eden z 14057; rural
Clarks Chapel; RMC Place; RENSSELAER; ▲ Schodack; *209 NK-19; ★ A-S-T; mail Nassau z 12123; ● 100
Clarks Corners; RMC Place; CHAUTAUQUA; ▲ Poland; *208 NM-3; ★ JMST; mail Kennedy z 14747; rural
Clarks Mills; RMC Place; WASHINGTON; ▲ Greenwich; 209 NI-19; ★ GLFLS; mail Greenwich z 12834; ● 130
Clarkson; RMC Place; MONROE; ▲ Clarkson; 208 NH-6; elev. 429ft./131m.; 🅿; ★ ROCH; z 14430; ● 600
Clarkson; MCD-Town; MONROE; *208 NH-6; 🅿; ★ ROCH; z 14430; Ⓟ 4,517; © 6,072
Clarkstown; MCD-Town; ROCKLAND; *207 SD-6; ★ N.Y.; mail New City z 10956; Ⓟ 79,346; © 82,082; ◆ 84,809
Clarksville; RMC Place; ALBANY; ▲ New Scotland; 209 NK-18; 🅿; ★ A-S-T; z 12041; ● 800
Clarksville; MCD-Town; ALLEGANY; *208 NM-5; mail West Clarksville z 14786; Ⓟ 1,041; © 1,146
Clarkville; RMC Place; SARATOGA; ▲ Edinburg; *209 NH-18; mail Northville z 12134; rural
Claryville; RMC Place; SULLIVAN; ▲ Neversink; 209 NN-17; 🅿; z 12725; ● 100
Clason Point; RMC Place; BRONX; *207 SF-7; ★ N.Y.; mail Bronx z 10473; pop. incl. with New York (Inc. Place)
Claverack; RMC Place; COLUMBIA; ▲ Claverack; 209 NL-19; 🅿; z 12513; ● 1,000
Claverack; MCD-Town; COLUMBIA; *209 NL-19; 🅿; z 12513; Ⓟ 6,414; © 6,401
Claverack-Red Mills; CDP-Census Area Only; COLUMBIA; ▲ Claverack; *209 NL-19; mail Claverack z 12513; Ⓟ 1,110; © 1,061
Clay; RMC Place; ONONDAGA; ▲ Clay; 209 NH-12; 🅿; ★ SYR; z 13041 & mail Cicero z 13039; ● 700
Clay; MCD-Town; ONONDAGA; *209 NI-12; 🅿; ★ SYR; z 13041; Ⓟ 59,749; © 58,805; ◆ 58,381
Clayburg; RMC Place; CLINTON; ▲ Saranac, Black Brook; 209 NC-18; mail Saranac z 12981; ● 100
Clayton; Inc. Place; JEFFERSON; ▲ Clayton; 209 ND-12; elev. 260ft./79m.; 🅿; z 13624; Ⓟ 2,160; © 1,821
Clayton; MCD-Town; JEFFERSON; *209 ND-12; elev. 260ft./79m.; 🅿; z 13624; Ⓟ 4,629; © 4,817
Clayville; Inc. Place; ONEIDA; ▲ Paris; 209 NI-14; 🅿; ★ UT-R; z 13322; Ⓟ 463; © 445
Clear Creek; RMC Place; CATTARAUGUS, CHAUTAUQUA; ▲ Ellington, Conewango; *208 NL-3; mail Conewango Valley z 14726; ● 40
Clearfield; RMC Place; ERIE; ▲ Amherst; *208 NI-4; ★ BUF; mail Buffalo z 14221
Clemmons; RMC Place; JEFFERSON; ▲ Rutland; *209 NE-13; mail Felts Mills z 13638; rural
Clemons; RMC Place; WASHINGTON; ▲ Dresden; 209 NG-20; 🅿; z 12819; ● 100
Clermont; RMC Place; COLUMBIA; ▲ Clermont; 209 NM-19; elev. 228ft./69m.; mail Germantown z 12526; ● 500
Clermont; MCD-Town; COLUMBIA; *209 NM-19; mail Germantown z 12526; Ⓟ 1,443; © 1,726
Cleveland; Inc. Place; OSWEGO; ▲ Constantia; 209 NH-12; 🅿; ★ SYR; z 13042; Ⓟ 784; © 758
Cleveland Hill; RMC Place; ERIE; ▲ Cheektowaga; *208 NI-4; ★ BUF; mail Buffalo z 14225
Cleverdale; RMC Place; WARREN; ▲ Queensbury; 209 NG-19; 🅿; ★ GLFLS; z 12820; ● 500
Cliff Haven; RMC Place; CLINTON; ▲ Plattsburgh; *209 NB-20; ★ PLATT; mail Plattsburgh z 12901; ● 475
Clifford; RMC Place; OSWEGO; ▲ Palermo; *209 NH-11; elev. 436ft./133m.; ★ SYR; mail Fulton z 13069
Cliffside; RMC Place; OTSEGO; ▲ Milford; *209 NK-15; mail Maryland z 12116; ● 500
Clifton; RMC Place; MONROE; ▲ Chili; 208 NI-7; 🅿; ★ ROCH; z 14428; ● 150
Clifton; RMC Place; RICHMOND; 210 K-8; ★ N.Y.; mail Staten Island z 10304; pop. incl. with New York (Inc. Place)
Clifton; MCD-Town; ST. LAWRENCE; *209 ND-15; mail Newton Falls z 13666; Ⓟ 917; © 791
Clifton Gardens; RMC Place; SARATOGA; ▲ Clifton Park; *209 NJ-19; ★ A-S-T; mail Clifton Park z 12065; ● 1,400
Clifton Heights; RMC Place; ERIE; ▲ Hamburg; *208 NJ-3; ★ BUF; mail Lake View z 14085
Clifton Knolls; RMC Place; SARATOGA; ▲ Clifton Park; *209 NJ-19; ★ A-S-T; mail Clifton Park z 12065; ● 4,300
Clifton Park; RMC Place; SARATOGA; ▲ Halfmoon, Clifton Park; 209 NJ-19; 🅿; ★ A-S-T; z 12065; ● 1,200
Clifton Park; MCD-Town; SARATOGA; *209 NJ-19; 🅿; ★ A-S-T; z 12065; Ⓟ 30,117; © 32,995; Ⓡ 33,110; ◆ 34,925
Clifton Park Center; RMC Place; SARATOGA; ▲ Clifton Park; *209 NJ-19; elev. 321ft./98m.; ★ A-S-T; mail Clifton Park z 12065; ● 25
Clifton Springs; Inc. Place; ONTARIO; ▲ Phelps, Manchester; 208 NI-9; 🅿 🅷; z 14432; Ⓟ 2,175; © 2,223
Climax; RMC Place; GREENE; ▲ Coxsackie; 209 NL-19; elev. 254ft./77m.; 🅿; z 12042; ● 165
Clinton; MCD-Town; CLINTON; *209 NA-18; mail Churubusco z 12923; Ⓟ 663; © 727
Clinton; MCD-Town; DUTCHESS; *207 SA-7; ★ POK; mail Clinton Corners z 12514; Ⓟ 3,760; © 4,010
Clinton; Inc. Place; ONEIDA; ▲ Kirkland; 209 NI-14; 🅿 🅲 1,799; ★ UT-R; z 13323; Ⓟ 2,238; © 1,952
CLINTON; 209 NB-18; Ⓟ 85,969; © 79,894; ◆ 82,280
Clinton Corners; RMC Place; DUTCHESS; ▲ Clinton; 209 NN-19; elev. 304ft./93m.; 🅿; ★ POK; z 12514; ● 450
Clintondale; CDP; ULSTER; ▲ Plattekill, Lloyd; 207 SB-6; 🅿; ★ POK; z 12515; Ⓟ 1,394; © 1,424
Clinton Heights; RMC Place; RENSSELAER; ▲ East Greenbush; *209 NK-19; ★ A-S-T; mail Rensselaer z 12144; ● 850
Clinton Hollow; RMC Place; DUTCHESS; ▲ Clinton; *207 SA-7; elev. 328ft./100m.; ★ POK; mail Salt Point z 12578; ● 250
Clinton Park; RMC Place; RENSSELAER; ▲ East Greenbush; 207 SJ-5; ★ A-S-T; mail Rensselaer z 12144; ● 880
Clinton Square; ONONDAGA; see Downtown (RMC Place)
Clintonville; RMC Place; CLINTON; ▲ Au Sable; 209 NC-19; 🅿; z 12924; ● 200
Clockville; RMC Place; MADISON; ▲ Lincoln; *209 NI-13; 🅿; z 13043; ● 300
Clough Corners; RMC Place; BROOME; ▲ Triangle; *209 NL-12; elev. 1,322ft./403m.; mail Whitney Point z 13862; rural
Clove; RMC Place; DUTCHESS; ▲ Union Vale; 207 SB-7; mail Millbrook z 12545
Clove; RMC Place; SCHOHARIE; ▲ Seward; *209 NK-16; mail Cobleskill z 12043; rural
Clover Bank; RMC Place; ERIE; ▲ Hamburg; *208 NJ-3; ★ BUF; mail Hamburg z 14075
Cloverville (Covesville); RMC Place; DELAWARE; ▲ Middletown; *209 NM-17; elev. 1,460ft./445m.; mail Fleischmanns z 12430; ● 85
Clyde; Inc. Place; WAYNE; ▲ Galen; 208 NI-10; elev. 400ft./122m.; 🅿; z 14433; Ⓟ 2,409; © 2,269
Clymer; RMC Place; CHAUTAUQUA; ▲ Clymer; 208 NM-1; elev. 1,468ft./447m.; 🅿; z 14724; ● 600
Clymer; MCD-Town; CHAUTAUQUA; *208 NM-1; 🅿; z 14724; Ⓟ 1,474; © 1,501
Cobb; RMC Place; SUFFOLK; ▲ Southampton; *207 SE-12; mail Water Mill z 11976
Cobleskill; Inc. Place; SCHOHARIE; ▲ Cobleskill; 209 NK-17; elev. 932ft./284m.; 🅿 🅷 🅲 2,482; z 12043; Ⓟ 5,268; © 4,533
Cobleskill; MCD-Town; SCHOHARIE; *209 NK-17; 🅿 🅲 2,482; z 12043; Ⓟ 7,270; © 6,407
Cochecton; RMC Place; SULLIVAN; ▲ Cochecton; 207 SB-2; 🅿; z 12726; ● 200
Cochecton; MCD-Town; SULLIVAN; *207 SB-3; 🅿; z 12726; Ⓟ 1,318; © 1,328
Cochecton Center; RMC Place; SULLIVAN; ▲ Cochecton; 207 SB-3; elev. 960ft./293m.; 🅿; z 12727; ● 250
Coeymans; CDP; ALBANY; ▲ Coeymans; 209 NK-19; 🅿; ★ A-S-T; z 12045; © 835
Coeymans; MCD-Town; ALBANY; *209 NK-19; 🅿; ★ A-S-T; z 12045; Ⓟ 8,158; © 8,151
Coeymans Hollow; RMC Place; ALBANY; ▲ Coeymans; 209 NK-18; 🅿; ★ A-S-T; z 12046; ● 550
Coffins Mills; RMC Place; ST. LAWRENCE; ▲ Fine; *209 ND-15; elev. 1,364ft./416m.; mail Oswegatchie z 13670; rural
Cohocton; Inc. Place; STEUBEN; ▲ Cohocton; 208 NK-8; 🅿; z 14826; Ⓟ 859; © 854
Cohocton; MCD-Town; STEUBEN; *208 NK-8; 🅿; z 14826; Ⓟ 2,520; © 2,626
Cohoes; Inc. Place; ALBANY; 209 NJ-19; elev. 100ft./30m.; 🅿; ★ A-S-T; z 12047; Ⓟ 16,825; © 15,521
Cokertown; RMC Place; DUTCHESS; ▲ Milan; *209 NM-19; elev. 263ft./80m.; mail Red Hook z 12571; rural
Colchester; RMC Place; DELAWARE; ▲ Walton; *209 NM-15; mail Downsville z 13755, Walton z 13856; ● 25
Colchester; MCD-Town; DELAWARE; *209 NM-15; mail Downsville z 13755, Walton z 13856; Ⓟ 1,928; © 2,042
Cold Brook; Inc. Place; HERKIMER; ▲ Russia; 209 NH-15; 🅿; z 13324; Ⓟ 310; © 336
Coldbrook; RMC Place; SCHENECTADY; ▲ Rotterdam; *209 NJ-18; ★ A-S-T; mail Schenectady z 12303
Colden; RMC Place; ERIE; ▲ Colden; 208 NK-4; 🅿; ★ BUF; z 14033; ● 550
Colden; MCD-Town; ERIE; *208 NK-4; 🅿; ★ BUF; z 14033; Ⓟ 2,899; © 3,323
Coldenham; RMC Place; ORANGE; ▲ Newburgh, Montgomery; 207 SB-6; ★ NWBG; mail Montgomery z 12549; ● 330
Coldspring; MCD-Town; CATTARAUGUS; *208 NM-3; mail Steamburg z 14783; Ⓟ 732; © 751
Cold Spring; ONONDAGA; see Cold Springs (RMC Place)
Cold Spring; Inc. Place; PUTNAM; ▲ Philipstown; 207 SC-6; elev. 108ft./33m.; 🅿; ★ N.Y.; z 10516; Ⓟ 1,998; © 1,983
Cold Spring Harbor; CDP; SUFFOLK; ▲ Huntington; 207 SH-10; 🅿; ★ N.Y.; z 11724; Ⓟ 4,789; © 4,975
Cold Springs (Cold Spring); RMC Place; ONONDAGA; ▲ Lysander; 208 NE-7; ★ SYR; mail Baldwinsville z 13027; ● 650
Cold Springs; RMC Place; STEUBEN; ▲ Urbana; *208 NL-8; mail Bath z 14810; rural
Cold Spring Terrace; RMC Place; SUFFOLK; ▲ Huntington; *207 SF-8; ★ N.Y.; mail Huntington z 11743; ● 2,400
Coldwater; RMC Place; MONROE; ▲ Gates; *208 NI-7; ★ ROCH; mail Rochester z 14624
Colemans; ONEIDA; see Colemans Mills (RMC Place)
Colemans Mills (Colemans); RMC Place; ONEIDA; ▲ Whitestown; *209 NI-14; elev. 477ft./145m.; ★ UT-R; mail Whitesboro z 13492; ● 50
Coleman Station; RMC Place; DUTCHESS; ▲ North East; *207 SA-8; mail Millerton z 12546; rural
Colesville; MCD-Town; BROOME; *209 NM-13; ★ BING; mail Harpursville z 13787; Ⓟ 5,590; © 5,441
Colgate; RMC Place; MADISON; mail Hamilton z 13346; pop. incl. with Hamilton (Inc. Place)
Collabar; RMC Place; ORANGE; ▲ Crawford; *207 SB-5; mail Montgomery z 12549; rural
Collamer; RMC Place; ONONDAGA; ▲ De Witt; *209 NI-12; ★ SYR; mail East Syracuse z 13057; ● 300
College Park; RMC Place; DUTCHESS; ▲ Red Hook; *209 NM-19; mail Red Hook z 12571; ● 430
College Point; RMC Place; QUEENS; 211 F-13; 🅿; ★ N.Y.; z 11356; pop. incl. with New York (Inc. Place)
Colliers; OTSEGO; see Colliersville (RMC Place)
Colliersville (Colliers); RMC Place; OTSEGO; ▲ Milford; 209 NK-15; elev. 1,120ft./341m.; 🅿; z 13747; ● 150
Collingwood; RMC Place; ONONDAGA; ▲ LaFayette; *209 NJ-12; elev. 919ft./280m.; ★ SYR; mail La Fayette z 13084; ● 50
Collingwood Estates; RMC Place; NIAGARA; ▲ Porter; *208 NH-3; ★ BUF; mail Youngstown z 14174; ● 200
Collins; RMC Place; ERIE; ▲ Collins; 208 NK-3; elev. 883ft./269m.; 🅿; z 14034; ● 500
Collins; MCD-Town; ERIE; *208 NK-3; 🅿; z 14034; Ⓟ 6,020; © 8,307
Collins Center; RMC Place; ERIE; ▲ Collins; 208 NK-4; elev. 1,106ft./337m.; 🅿; z 14035; ● 480
Collins Landing; RMC Place; JEFFERSON; ▲ Orleans; *209 ND-12; mail Alexandria Bay z 13607; ● 110
Collinsville; RMC Place; LEWIS; ▲ West Turin; *209 NG-14; elev. 1,206ft./368m.; mail Port Leyden z 13433; ● 30
Colonial Acres; RMC Place; ALBANY; ▲ Bethlehem; ★ A-S-T; mail Glenmont z 12077
Colonial Green; RMC Place; SARATOGA; ▲ Halfmoon; *209 NJ-19; elev. 300ft./91m.; ★ A-S-T; mail Waterford z 12188; ● 1,350
Colonial Heights; RMC Place; DUTCHESS; ▲ Poughkeepsie; *207 SA-7; ★ POK; mail Poughkeepsie z 12603
Colonial Heights; RMC Place; WESTCHESTER; *207 SE-7; ★ N.Y.; mail Bronxville z 10708; pop. incl. with Yonkers (Inc. Place)
Colonial Park; RMC Place; NEW YORK; ★ N.Y.; mail New York z 10039; pop. incl. with New York (Inc. Place)
Colonial Village; RMC Place; NIAGARA; ▲ Lewiston; 208 NA-2; ★ BUF; mail Niagara Falls z 14304
Colonie; Inc. Place; ALBANY; ▲ Colonie; 209 NJ-19; 🅿; ★ A-S-T; z 12205; Ⓟ 8,019; © 7,916
Colonie; MCD-Town; ALBANY; *209 NJ-19; 🅿 🅲 3,220; ★ A-S-T; z 12205 & mail Albany z 12212; Ⓟ 76,494; © 79,258; ◆ 81,260
Colosse; RMC Place; OSWEGO; ▲ Mexico; 209 NH-12; elev. 422ft./129m.; mail Parish z 13131; ● 120
Colton; RMC Place; ST. LAWRENCE; ▲ Colton; 209 NC-15; elev. 864ft./263m.; 🅿; z 13625; ● 700
Colton; MCD-Town; ST. LAWRENCE; *209 ND-16; 🅿; z 13625; Ⓟ 1,274; © 1,453
Columbia; HERKIMER; see Columbia Center (RMC Place)
Columbia; MCD-Town; HERKIMER; *209 NJ-16; mail Ilion z 13357; Ⓟ 1,587; © 1,630
COLUMBIA; 209 NL-20; Ⓟ 62,982; © 63,094; ◆ 61,676
Columbia Center (Columbia); RMC Place; HERKIMER; ▲ Columbia; *209 NJ-16; mail Ilion z 13357; ● 80
Columbia University; RMC Place; NEW YORK; ★ N.Y.; mail New York z 10025; pop. incl. with New York (Inc. Place)
Columbiaville; RMC Place; COLUMBIA; ▲ Stockport; 209 NL-19; 🅿; ★ A-S-T; z 12050; ● 500
Columbus; RMC Place; CHENANGO; ▲ Columbus; 209 NK-14; mail New Berlin z 13411; ● 150
Columbus; MCD-Town; CHENANGO; *209 NJ-14; mail New Berlin z 13411; Ⓟ 869; © 931
Columbus Circle; RMC Place; NEW YORK; ★ N.Y.; mail New York z 10023; pop. incl. with New York (Inc. Place)
Colvin Elmwood; RMC Place; ONONDAGA; ★ SYR; mail Syracuse z 13205, z 13207; pop. incl. with Syracuse (Inc. Place)
Commack; CDP; SUFFOLK; ▲ Smithtown, Huntington; 207 SF-9; 🅿; ★ N.Y.; z 11725; Ⓟ 36,124; © 36,367; ◆ 36,358
Comstock (Great Meadow Correctional Facility); RMC Place; WASHINGTON; ▲ Fort Ann; 209 NG-20; elev. 131ft./40m.; 🅿; z 12821; ● 350
Comstock Tract; RMC Place; ONONDAGA; ▲ Van Buren; *209 NI-11; ★ SYR; mail Baldwinsville z 13027; ● 500
Concord; MCD-Town; ERIE; *208 NK-4; ★ BUF; mail Springville z 14141; Ⓟ 8,387; © 8,526
Concord; RMC Place; RICHMOND; *207 SG-6; ★ N.Y.; mail Staten Island z 10304; pop. incl. with New York (Inc. Place)
Conesus; RMC Place; LIVINGSTON; ▲ Conesus; 208 NJ-7; elev. 1,199ft./365m.; 🅿; z 14435; ● 400
Conesus; MCD-Town; LIVINGSTON; *208 NJ-7; 🅿; z 14435; Ⓟ 2,196; © 2,353
Conesville; RMC Place; SCHOHARIE; ▲ Conesville; 209 NL-17; elev. 1,387ft./423m.; mail Gilboa z 12076; ● 150
Conesville; MCD-Town; SCHOHARIE; *209 NL-17; mail Gilboa z 12076; Ⓟ 684; © 726
Conewango; RMC Place; CATTARAUGUS; ▲ Conewango; 208 NL-3; elev. 1,294ft./394m.; mail Conewango Valley z 14726; ● 150
Conewango; MCD-Town; CATTARAUGUS; *208 NL-3; mail Conewango Valley z 14726; Ⓟ 1,702; © 1,732
Conewango; CHAUTAUQUA, CATTARAUGUS; see Conewango Valley (RMC Place)
Conewango Valley (Conewango); RMC Place; CHAUTAUQUA, CATTARAUGUS; ▲ Ellington, Conewango; 208 NL-3; 🅿; z 14726; ● 300
Coney Island; RMC Place; KINGS; 210 L-10; ★ N.Y.; mail Brooklyn z 11224; pop. incl. with New York (Inc. Place)
Conger Corners; RMC Place; ONEIDA; ▲ Sangerfield; *209 NJ-14; elev. 1,298ft./396m.; mail Waterville z 13480; rural
Congers; CDP; ROCKLAND; ▲ Clarkstown; 207 SD-7; elev. 191ft./58m.; 🅿; ★ N.Y.; z 10920; Ⓟ 8,003; © 8,303
Conifer; RMC Place; ST. LAWRENCE; ▲ Piercefield; 209 ND-16; elev. 1,657ft./505m.; mail Tupper Lake z 12986; ● 75
Conklin; RMC Place; BROOME; ▲ Conklin; 209 NM-13; 🅿; ★ BING; z 13748; ● 1,800
Conklin; MCD-Town; BROOME; *209 NM-13; 🅿; ★ BING; z 13748; Ⓟ 6,265; © 5,940
Conklin Cove (Koenig's Point); RMC Place; CAYUGA; ▲ Owasco; *209 NJ-11; ★ SYR; mail Auburn z 13021; rural
Conklin Forks; RMC Place; BROOME; ▲ Conklin; *209 NM-13; ★ BING; mail Binghamton z 13903; ● 200
Conklingville; RMC Place; SARATOGA; ▲ Day; *209 NH-18; mail Hadley z 12835; rural
Connelly; RMC Place; ULSTER; ▲ Esopus; *207 SA-6; 🅿; ★ KNGST; z 12417; ● 600
Connelly Park; RMC Place; CHAUTAUQUA; ▲ North Harmony; 208 NM-2; mail Ashville z 14710; ● 100
Conquest; RMC Place; CAYUGA; ▲ Conquest; 208 NI-10; elev. 441ft./134m.; mail Port Byron z 13140; ● 75
Conquest; MCD-Town; CAYUGA; *208 NI-10; mail Port Byron z 13140; Ⓟ 1,859; © 1,925
Constable; RMC Place; FRANKLIN; ▲ Constable; 209 NA-17; 🅿; z 12926; ● 350
Constable; MCD-Town; FRANKLIN; *209 NA-17; 🅿; z 12926; Ⓟ 1,203; © 1,428
Constableville; Inc. Place; LEWIS; ▲ West Turin; 209 NG-14; 🅿; z 13325; Ⓟ 307; © 305
Constantia; CDP; OSWEGO; ▲ Constantia; 209 NH-12; 🅿; ★ SYR; z 13044; Ⓟ 1,140; © 1,107
Constantia; MCD-Town; OSWEGO; *209 NH-12; 🅿; ★ SYR; z 13044; Ⓟ 4,868; © 5,141
Constantia Center; RMC Place; OSWEGO; ▲ Constantia; *209 NH-12; elev. 576ft./176m.; ★ SYR; mail Bernhards Bay z 13028
Continental Village; RMC Place; PUTNAM, WESTCHESTER; ▲ Cortlandt, Philipstown; *207 SC-7; elev. 172ft./52m.; ★ N.Y.; mail Cortlandt Manor z 10567; ● 1,650
Cook Corners; RMC Place; ST. LAWRENCE; ▲ Pierrepont; *209 ND-15; elev. 1,481ft./451m.; mail Colton z 13625; rural
Cooksburg; RMC Place; ALBANY; ▲ Rensselaerville; *209 NL-18; mail Preston Hollow z 12469; ● 45
Cooks Falls; RMC Place; DELAWARE; ▲ Colchester; 209 NN-15; mail Roscoe z 12776; ● 200
Cookville; RMC Place; GENESEE; ▲ Pembroke; *208 NI-5; mail Corfu z 14036
Cooley; RMC Place; SULLIVAN; ▲ Liberty; *207 SA-4; mail Parksville z 12768; ● 80
Coolidge Beach; RMC Place; NIAGARA; ▲ Wilson; *208 NH-4; elev. 274ft./84m.; ★ BUF; mail Wilson z 14172; ● 20
Coonrod; RMC Place; ONEIDA; *209 NH-14; ★ UT-R; mail Rome z 13440; pop. incl. with Rome (Inc. Place)
Co-op City; RMC Place; BRONX; ★ N.Y.; mail Bronx z 10475; pop. incl. with New York (Inc. Place)
Cooper; RMC Place; NEW YORK; ★ N.Y.; mail New York z 10003, z 10211, z 10276; pop. incl. with New York (Inc. Place)
Coopers Plains; RMC Place; STEUBEN; ▲ Campbell, Erwin; 208 NM-9; elev. 1,992ft./607m.; 🅿; z 14827; ● 750
Cooperstown; Inc. Place; ⊡ OTSEGO; ▲ Middlefield, Otsego; 209 NJ-15; elev. 1,264ft./385m.; 🅿 🅷; z 13326; Ⓟ 2,180; © 2,032
Cooperstown Junction; RMC Place; OTSEGO; ▲ Milford, Maryland; *209 NK-15; elev. 1,130ft./344m.; mail Maryland z 12116; ● 130
Coopersville; RMC Place; CLINTON; ▲ Champlain; 209 NA-20; mail Champlain z 12919; ● 210
Coopersville; RMC Place; LIVINGSTON; ▲ Nunda; *208 NK-6; elev. 847ft./258m.; mail Nunda z 14517; rural
Copake; RMC Place; COLUMBIA; ▲ Copake; 209 NM-20; elev. 550ft./168m.; 🅿; z 12516, z 12593; ● 1,200
Copake; MCD-Town; COLUMBIA; *209 NM-20; 🅿; z 12516, z 12593; Ⓟ 3,118; © 3,278
Copake Falls; RMC Place; COLUMBIA; ▲ Copake; 209 NM-20; 🅿; z 12517; ● 500
Copake Lake; CDP-Census Area Only; COLUMBIA; ▲ Copake; *209 NM-19; mail Craryville z 12521; summer pop. 1,500; © 762
Copenhagen; Inc. Place; LEWIS; ▲ Denmark; 209 NF-13; elev. 1,174ft./358m.; 🅿; z 13626 & mail Deer River z 13627; Ⓟ 876; © 865
Copiague; CDP; SUFFOLK; ▲ Babylon; *207 SF-9; 🅿; ★ N.Y.; z 11726; Ⓟ 20,769; © 21,922; ◆ 21,918
Coram; CDP; SUFFOLK; ▲ Brookhaven; 207 SE-10; elev. 99ft./30m.; 🅿; ★ N.Y.; z 11727; Ⓟ 30,111; © 34,923; ◆ 34,918
Coram Hill; RMC Place; SUFFOLK; ▲ Brookhaven; *207 SE-10; ★ N.Y.; mail Medford z 11763; ● 1,600
Corbett; RMC Place; DELAWARE; ▲ Colchester; 209 NM-15; elev. 1,113ft./339m.; mail Downsville z 13755; ● 150
Corbettsville; RMC Place; BROOME; ▲ Conklin; 209 NM-13; 🅿; ★ BING; z 13749; ● 460
Cordova; RMC Place; CHAUTAUQUA; ▲ Pomfret; *208 NK-2; mail Fredonia z 14063; pop. incl. with Fredonia (Inc. Place)
Coreys; RMC Place; FRANKLIN; ▲ Harrietstown; 209 ND-17; elev. 1,598ft./487m.; mail Tupper Lake z 12986; ● 130
Corfu; Inc. Place; GENESEE; ▲ Pembroke; 208 NI-5; elev. 861ft./262m.; 🅿; z 14036; Ⓟ 755; © 795
Corinth; Inc. Place; SARATOGA; ▲ Corinth; 209 NH-19; 🅿; ★ GLFLS; z 12822; Ⓟ 2,760; © 2,474
Corinth; MCD-Town; SARATOGA; *209 NH-18; 🅿; ★ GLFLS; z 12822; Ⓟ 5,935; © 5,985; Ⓡ 6,259
Cornell; RMC Place; BRONX; ★ N.Y.; mail Bronx z 10473; pop. incl. with New York (Inc. Place)
Corning; Inc. Place; STEUBEN; 208 NM-9; elev. 937ft./286m.; 🅿 🅷 ■; z 14830-31; Ⓟ 11,938; © 10,842; ◆ 10,133
Corning; MCD-Town; STEUBEN; *208 NM-9; 🅿; z 14830-31; does not include the City of Corning; Ⓟ 6,367; © 6,426
Corning Manor; RMC Place; STEUBEN; ▲ Corning; *208 NM-9; mail Corning z 14830; ● 250
Cornwall; MCD-Town; ORANGE; *207 SC-6; 🅿; ★ NWBG; z 12518; Ⓟ 11,270; © 12,307
Cornwall-on-Hudson; Inc. Place; ORANGE; ▲ Cornwall; 207 SC-6; 🅿; ★ NWBG; z 12520; Ⓟ 3,093; © 3,058
Cornwallville; RMC Place; GREENE; ▲ Durham; 209 NL-18; 🅿; z 12418; ● 130
Corona; RMC Place; QUEENS; 211 G-13; 🅿; ★ N.Y.; z 11368; pop. incl. with New York (Inc. Place)
Corona-A; RMC Place; QUEENS; ★ N.Y.; mail Corona z 11368; pop. incl. with New York (Inc. Place)
Cortland; Inc. Place; ⊡ CORTLAND; 209 NK-12; elev. 1,120ft./341m.; 🅿 🅷 🅲 6,995 ■; z 13045; Ⓟ 19,801; © 18,740; ◆ 18,549
CORTLAND; 209 NK-12; Ⓟ 48,963; © 48,599; ◆ 48,464
Cortlandt; MCD-Town; WESTCHESTER; *207 SD-7; ★ N.Y.; mail Croton On Hudson z 10520; Ⓟ 37,357; © 38,467; ◆ 40,139
Cortlandt Manor; WESTCHESTER; see Van Cortlandtville (RMC Place)
Cortlandville; MCD-Town; CORTLAND; *209 NK-12; mail Cortland z 13045; Ⓟ 8,054; © 7,919
Cortland West; CDP-Census Area Only; CORTLAND; ▲ Cortlandville; *209 NK-11; mail Cortland z 13045; Ⓟ 1,270; © 1,345
Cosmos Heights; RMC Place; CORTLAND; ▲ Homer; *209 NK-11; mail Cortland z 13045; ● 95
Cossayuna; RMC Place; WASHINGTON; ▲ Greenwich; 209 NH-20; elev. 474ft./144m.; 🅿; ★ GLFLS; z 12823; ● 350
Coss Corners; RMC Place; STEUBEN; ▲ Bath; *208 NL-8; elev. 1,784ft./544m.; mail Bath z 14810; rural
Cottage; RMC Place; CATTARAUGUS; ▲ Dayton; 208 NL-3; elev. 1,342ft./409m.; mail South Dayton z 14138; ● 110
Cottage City; RMC Place; ONTARIO; ▲ Gorham; *208 NJ-8; mail Canandaigua z 14424; summer pop. 100
Cottage Park; RMC Place; CHAUTAUQUA; ▲ Busti; *208 NL-2; ★ JMST; mail Lakewood z 14750
Cottam Hill; RMC Place; DUTCHESS; ▲ Poughkeepsie; *207 SB-7; ★ POK; mail Wappingers Falls z 12590; ● 1,000
Cottekill; RMC Place; ULSTER; ▲ Rosendale, Marbletown; 207 SA-6; 🅿; ★ KNGST; z 12419; ● 400
Cottonwood Point; RMC Place; LIVINGSTON; ▲ Groveland; *208 NJ-7; ★ ROCH; mail Conesus z 14435; ● 75
Council Meadows; RMC Place; SARATOGA; ▲ Ballston; *209 NJ-18; ★ A-S-T; mail Burnt Hills z 12027
Country Knolls; CDP-Census Area Only; SARATOGA; ▲ Clifton Park; *209 NJ-19; ★ A-S-T; mail Ballston Lake z 12019; Ⓟ 2,287; © 2,155
Country Knolls; RMC Place; SARATOGA; ▲ Malta; *209 NI-19; elev. 250ft./76m.; ★ A-S-T; mail Round Lake z 12151; ● 1,100
Country Knolls South; RMC Place; SARATOGA; ▲ Clifton Park; *209 NJ-19; elev. 250ft./76m.; ★ A-S-T; mail Clifton Park z 12065; ● 1,900
Country Life Press; RMC Place; NASSAU; ★ N.Y.; mail Garden City z 11530; pop. incl. with Garden City (Inc. Place)
Country Ridge Estates; RMC Place; WESTCHESTER; ▲ Rye; *207 SE-7; ★ N.Y.; mail Port Chester z 10573; pop. incl. with Rye Brook (Inc. Place)
County Line; RMC Place; NIAGARA, ORLEANS; ▲ Yates, Somerset; *208 NH-5; elev. 322ft./98m.; ★ LOCK; mail Lyndonville z 14098; ● 85
Cove Neck; Inc. Place; NASSAU; ▲ Oyster Bay; 211 D-20; elev. 22ft./7m.; ★ N.Y.; mail Oyster Bay z 11771; Ⓟ 332; © 300
Coventry; RMC Place; CHENANGO; ▲ Coventry; 209 NL-13; elev. 1,665ft./507m.; mail Greene z 13778; ● 250
Coventry; MCD-Town; CHENANGO; *209 NL-13; mail Greene z 13778; Ⓟ 1,517; © 1,589
Coventryville; RMC Place; CHENANGO; ▲ Coventry; 209 NL-13; elev. 1,436ft./438m.; mail Bainbridge z 13733; ● 85
Covert; RMC Place; SENECA; ▲ Covert; *208 NK-10; elev. 913ft./278m.; ★ ITH; mail Interlaken z 14847; ● 80
Covert; MCD-Town; SENECA; *208 NK-10; ★ ITH; mail Interlaken z 14847; Ⓟ 2,246; © 2,227
Covesville; DELAWARE; see Cloverville (RMC Place)
Coveytown Corners; RMC Place; FRANKLIN; ▲ Burke; *209 NA-17; elev. 513ft./156m.; mail Burke z 12917; rural
Covington; RMC Place; WYOMING; ▲ Covington; 208 NJ-6; elev. 1,107ft./337m.; mail Pavilion z 14525; ● 180
Covington; MCD-Town; WYOMING; *208 NJ-6; mail Pavilion z 14525; Ⓟ 1,266; © 1,357
Cowlesville; RMC Place; WYOMING; ▲ Bennington; 208 NJ-5; elev. 948ft./289m.; 🅿; z 14037 & mail Attica z 14011; ● 500
Coxsackie; Inc. Place; GREENE; ▲ Coxsackie; 209 NL-19; 🅿; z 12051 & mail West Coxsackie z 12192; Ⓟ 2,789; © 2,895
Coxsackie; MCD-Town; GREENE; *209 NL-19; 🅿; z 12051 & mail West Coxsackie z 12192; Ⓟ 7,633; © 8,884
Crab Meadow (Waterside Park); RMC Place; SUFFOLK; ▲ Huntington; *207 SE-9; ★ N.Y.; mail Northport z 11768; ● 900
Crafts; RMC Place; PUTNAM; ▲ Carmel; *207 SC-7; ★ N.Y.; mail Carmel z 10512; rural
Cragsmoor; CDP; ULSTER; ▲ Wawarsing; 207 SB-5; 🅿; z 12420; © 474
Craigville; RMC Place; ORANGE; ▲ Blooming Grove; *207 SC-5; ★ N.Y.; mail Chester z 10918; rural
Crains Mills; RMC Place; CORTLAND; ▲ Truxton; *209 NJ-12; mail Truxton z 13158; rural
Cranberry Creek; RMC Place; FULTON; ▲ Mayfield; 209 NI-17; ★ A-S-T; mail Mayfield z 12117; ● 225
Cranberry Lake; RMC Place; ST. LAWRENCE; ▲ Clifton; 209 ND-16; elev. 1,497ft./456m.; 🅿; z 12927; ● 500
Crandall Corners; RMC Place; WASHINGTON; ▲ Easton; *209 NI-19; mail Schaghticoke z 12154; rural
Cranes Corners; RMC Place; HERKIMER; ▲ Litchfield; *209 NI-15; mail Frankfort z 13340; rural
Cranesville; RMC Place; MONTGOMERY; ▲ Amsterdam; 209 NI-18; ★ A-S-T; mail Amsterdam z 12010; ● 125
Cranford; RMC Place; BRONX; ★ N.Y.; mail Bronx z 10470; pop. incl. with New York (Inc. Place)
Crary Mills; RMC Place; ST. LAWRENCE; ▲ Canton, Pierrepont, Potsdam; 209 NC-15; elev. 464ft./141m.; mail Canton z 13617; ● 120
Craryville; RMC Place; COLUMBIA; ▲ Copake; 209 NM-19; elev. 635ft./194m.; 🅿; z 12521; ● 600
Craterclub; RMC Place; ESSEX; ▲ Essex; *209 ND-20; mail Essex z 12936; rural
Crawford; MCD-Town; ORANGE; *207 SB-5; mail Pine Bush z 12566; Ⓟ 6,394; © 7,875
Creek Locks; RMC Place; ULSTER; ▲ Rosendale; *207 SA-6; ★ KNGST; mail Bloomington z 12411; ● 200
Crescent; RMC Place; SARATOGA; ▲ Halfmoon; 207 SF-5; ★ A-S-T; mail Waterford z 12188; ● 530
Crescent Beach; RMC Place; MONROE; ▲ Greece; *208 NH-7; elev. 249ft./76m.; ★ ROCH; mail Rochester z 14612; ● 350

Entries in UPPERCASE are counties.
Entries in **bold** have populations of 2,500 or more.
Names in parentheses are alternate names.

Inc. Place	Incorporated Place
RMC Place	Rand McNally Designated Place
CDP	Census Designated Place
MCD	Minor Civil Division

⊡	County Seat
▲	Minor Civil Division
elev.	Elevation
🅿	Post Office
🅷	Hospital
🅲	College
■	Principal Business Center
★	Ranally Metro Area (RMA) Abbreviation
z	Zip Code(s)
Ⓟ	Previous Census Population
Ⓡ	Revised Census Population
Ⓐ	Annexation Population
●	Rand McNally Population Estimate
©	Final Census Population
Ⓢ	Special Census Population
◆	Estimated Population

For additional definitions see Glossary, Volume 1, and Introduction, Volume 2.

Crescent Estates; RMC Place; SARATOGA; ▲ Clifton Park; ***209** NJ-19; elev. 293ft./89m.; ★ **A-S-T**; mail Clifton Park z 12065; ● 2,600
Crescent Estates North; RMC Place; SARATOGA; ▲ Clifton Park; ***209** NJ-19; elev. 280ft./85m.; ★ **A-S-T**; mail Clifton Park z 12065; ● 1,150
Crestview Heights; RMC Place; TIOGA; ▲ Owego; ***209** NM-12; ★ **BING**; mail Endicott z 13760; ● 2,250
Crestwood; RMC Place; WESTCHESTER; ***207** SE-7; ★ **N.Y.**; mail Yonkers z 10710; pop. incl. with Yonkers (Inc. Place)
Crestwood Gardens; RMC Place; WESTCHESTER; ***207** SE-7; ★ **N.Y.**; mail Yonkers z 10710; pop. incl. with Yonkers (Inc. Place)
Crittenden; RMC Place; ERIE; ▲ Alden; **208** NI-5; elev. 854ft./260m.; 🅿; ★ **BUF**; z 14038; ● 250
Crocketts; RMC Place; CAYUGA; ▲ Sterling; ***208** NH-10; mail Sterling z 13156; rural
Croghan; Inc. Place; LEWIS; ▲ New Bremen, Croghan; **209** NF-14; 🅿; z 13327; Ⓟ 664; Ⓒ 665
Croghan; MCD-Town; LEWIS; ***209** NE-14; 🅿; z 13327; includes part of the Village of Croghan; Ⓟ 3,071; Ⓒ 3,161
Crompond; CDP; WESTCHESTER; ▲ Cortlandt; ***207** SD-7; 🅿; ★ **N.Y.**; z 10517; Ⓒ 2,050
Cropseyville; RMC Place; RENSSELAER; ▲ Brunswick; **209** NJ-19; 🅿; ★ **A-S-T**; z 12052; ● 200
Cross River; RMC Place; WESTCHESTER; ▲ Lewisboro; **207** SD-8; elev. 338ft./103m.; 🅿; ★ **N.Y.**; z 10518; ● 980
Cross Roads Estates; RMC Place; WESTCHESTER; ▲ Yorktown; ★ **N.Y.**; mail Yorktown Heights z 10598
Crotona Park; RMC Place; BRONX; ★ **N.Y.**; mail Bronx z 10460; pop. incl. with New York (Inc. Place)
Croton Falls; RMC Place; WESTCHESTER; ▲ Somers, North Salem; **207** SC-8; elev. 244ft./74m.; 🅿; ★ **N.Y.**; z 10519; ● 970
Croton-Harmon; WESTCHESTER; see Croton-on-Hudson (Inc. Place)
Croton Heights; RMC Place; WESTCHESTER; ▲ Yorktown; ***207** SD-7; ★ **N.Y.**; mail Yorktown Heights z 10598
Croton-on-Hudson (Croton-Harmon); Inc. Place; WESTCHESTER; ▲ Cortlandt; **207** SD-7; 🅿; ★ **N.Y.**; z 10520-21; Ⓟ 7,018; Ⓒ 7,606
Crotonville; RMC Place; WESTCHESTER; ▲ Ossining; ***207** SD-7; ★ **N.Y.**; mail Ossining z 10562; ● 950
Crown Heights (Van Keurens); CDP-Census Area Only; DUTCHESS; ▲ Poughkeepsie; ***207** SB-6; ★ **POK**; mail Poughkeepsie z 12603; Ⓟ 3,200; Ⓒ 2,992
Crown Heights; RMC Place; KINGS; ***207** SG-7; elev. 100ft./30m.; ★ **N.Y.**; mail Brooklyn z 11213; pop. incl. with New York (Inc. Place)
Crown Point; RMC Place; ESSEX; ▲ Crown Point; **209** NE-20; elev. 214ft./65m.; 🅿; z 12928; ● 1,000
Crown Point; MCD-Town; ESSEX; ***209** NE-19; 🅿; z 12928; Ⓟ 1,963; Ⓒ 2,119
Crown Point Center (Crown Point Centre); RMC Place; ESSEX; ▲ Crown Point; ***209** NE-20; mail Crown Point z 12928
Crown Point Centre; ESSEX; see Crown Point Center (RMC Place)
Crown Village; RMC Place; NASSAU; ▲ Oyster Bay; ***207** SF-8; ★ **N.Y.**; mail Massapequa Park z 11762; ● 2,000
Crugers; CDP; WESTCHESTER; ▲ Cortlandt; **207** SD-7; 🅿; ★ **N.Y.**; z 10521; Ⓒ 1,752
Crum Creek; RMC Place; FULTON; ▲ Oppenheim; ***209** NI-16; mail Saint Johnsville z 13452; rural
Crystal Brook; RMC Place; SUFFOLK; ▲ Brookhaven; ***207** SE-10; ★ **N.Y.**; mail Mount Sinai z 11766; pop. incl. with Port Jefferson (Inc. Place)
Crystal Dale; RMC Place; LEWIS; ▲ Watson, New Bremen; ***209** NF-14; mail Lowville z 13367; rural
Crystal Lake; RMC Place; ALBANY; ▲ Rensselaerville; ***209** NK-18; mail Middleburgh z 12122, Rensselaerville z 12147; ● 60
Cuba; Inc. Place; ALLEGANY; ▲ Cuba; **208** NL-5; elev. 1,500ft./457m.; 🅿 🅷; z 14727; Ⓟ 1,690; Ⓒ 1,633
Cuba; MCD-Town; ALLEGANY; ***208** NL-5; 🅿; z 14727; Ⓟ 3,401; Ⓒ 3,392
Cuddebackville; RMC Place; ORANGE; ▲ Deerpark; **207** SC-4; 🅿; z 12729; ● 1,100
Cullen; RMC Place; HERKIMER; ▲ Warren; ***209** NJ-16; mail Richfield Springs z 13439; rural
Culvertown; RMC Place; SULLIVAN; ▲ Mamakating; ***207** SB-4; mail Westbrookville z 12785; rural
Cumberland Head; CDP-Census Area Only; CLINTON; ▲ Plattsburgh; ***209** NB-20; elev. 190ft./58m.; ★ **PLATT**; mail Plattsburgh z 12901; Ⓟ 1,698; Ⓒ 1,532
Cummingsville; RMC Place; LIVINGSTON; ▲ North Dansville; **208** NK-7; mail Dansville z 14437; ● 180
Curriers; RMC Place; WYOMING; ▲ Java; **208** NK-5; elev. 1,535ft./468m.; mail Arcade z 14009; ● 110
Curry; RMC Place; SULLIVAN; ▲ Neversink; **207** SA-4; elev. 1,167ft./356m.; mail Neversink z 12765
Currytown; RMC Place; MONTGOMERY; ▲ Root; ***209** NJ-17; mail Sprakers z 12166; rural
Curtis; RMC Place; HERKIMER; ▲ Salisbury; ***209** NI-16; mail Salisbury Center z 13454; rural
Curtis; RMC Place; STEUBEN; ▲ Campbell; ***208** NM-9; mail Campbell z 14821; rural
Cutchogue; CDP; SUFFOLK; ▲ Southold; **207** SE-12; 🅿; z 11935 & mail New Suffolk z 11956; Ⓟ 2,627; Ⓒ 2,849
Cutting; RMC Place; CHAUTAUQUA; ▲ French Creek; **208** NM-1; elev. 1,449ft./442m.; mail Clymer z 14724; ● 90
Cuyler; RMC Place; CORTLAND; ▲ Cuyler; **209** NJ-12; 🅿; z 13158; ● 150
Cuyler; MCD-Town; CORTLAND; ***209** NJ-12; 🅿; z 13158; Ⓟ 850; Ⓒ 1,036
Cuyler Hill; RMC Place; CORTLAND; ▲ Cuyler; ***209** NJ-12; mail Truxton z 13158; rural
Cuylerville; RMC Place; LIVINGSTON; ▲ Leicester; **208** NJ-7; elev. 571ft./174m.; mail Leicester z 14481; ● 420
Cypress Hills; RMC Place; KINGS; ★ **N.Y.**; mail Brooklyn z 11208; pop. incl. with New York (Inc. Place)

D

Dadville; RMC Place; LEWIS; ▲ Lowville; ***209** NF-14; elev. 741ft./226m.; mail Lowville z 13367; ● 90
Dag Hammarskjold; RMC Place; NEW YORK; ★ **N.Y.**; mail New York z 10017; pop. incl. with New York (Inc. Place)
Dahlia; RMC Place; SULLIVAN; ▲ Liberty; ***207** SA-3; mail Livingston Manor z 12758; rural
Dairyland; RMC Place; ULSTER; ▲ Wawarsing; **207** SA-4; mail Greenfield Park z 12435; ● 65
Dale; RMC Place; WYOMING; ▲ Middlebury; **208** NJ-6; elev. 1,201ft./366m.; 🅿; z 14039; ● 100
Dalton; RMC Place; LIVINGSTON; ▲ Portage, Nunda; **208** NK-6; 🅿; z 14836; ● 620
Damascus; RMC Place; BROOME; ▲ Windsor; **209** NM-13; ★ **BING**; mail Windsor z 13865; ● 200
Danby; RMC Place; TOMPKINS; ▲ Danby; **209** NL-11; mail Ithaca z 14850; ● 250
Danby; MCD-Town; TOMPKINS; ***209** NL-11; mail Ithaca z 14850; Ⓟ 2,858; Ⓒ 3,007
Dannemora; Inc. Place; CLINTON; ▲ Saranac, Dannemora; **209** NB-19; elev. 1,439ft./439m.; 🅿; z 12929; Ⓟ 4,005; Ⓒ 4,129
Dannemora; MCD-Town; CLINTON; ***209** NB-18; 🅿; z 12929; includes part of the Village of Dannemora; Ⓟ 5,232; Ⓒ 5,149
Dansville; Inc. Place; LIVINGSTON; ▲ North Dansville; **208** NK-7; 🅿 🅷; z 14437; Ⓟ 5,002; Ⓒ 4,832
Dansville; MCD-Town; STEUBEN; ***208** NK-7; mail Arkport z 14807; Ⓟ 1,811; Ⓒ 1,977
Danube; MCD-Town; HERKIMER; ***209** NI-16; mail Little Falls z 13365; Ⓟ 1,077; Ⓒ 1,098
Danville; RMC Place; BROOME; ▲ Sanford; ***209** NM-14; mail Deposit z 13754; rural
Darien; RMC Place; GENESEE; ▲ Darien; **208** NJ-5; elev. 1,001ft./305m.; mail Darien Center z 14040; ● 300
Darien; MCD-Town; GENESEE; ***208** NJ-5; mail Darien Center z 14040; Ⓟ 2,979; Ⓒ 3,061
Darien Center; RMC Place; GENESEE; ▲ Darien; **208** NJ-5; elev. 1,019ft./311m.; 🅿; z 14040; ● 700
Darrowsville; RMC Place; WARREN; ▲ Chester; ***209** NG-19; mail Chestertown z 12817
Davenport; RMC Place; DELAWARE; ▲ Davenport; **209** NK-16; elev. 1,309ft./399m.; 🅿; z 13750; ● 400
Davenport; MCD-Town; DELAWARE; ***209** NK-15; 🅿; z 13750; Ⓟ 2,438; Ⓒ 2,774
Davenport Center; RMC Place; DELAWARE; ▲ Davenport; **209** NK-15; 🅿; z 13751; ● 220
Davis Park; RMC Place; SUFFOLK; ▲ Brookhaven; **207** SJ-14; elev. 11ft./3m.; 🅿; ★ **N.Y.**; z 11772; summer pop. 300
Daws; RMC Place; GENESEE; ▲ Elba, Batavia; ***208** NI-6; elev. 833ft./254m.; mail Batavia z 14020
Day; MCD-Town; SARATOGA; ***209** NH-18; mail Hadley z 12835; Ⓟ 746; Ⓒ 920
Day Center; RMC Place; SARATOGA; ▲ Day; ***209** NH-18; mail Hadley z 12835
Days Rock; RMC Place; HERKIMER; ▲ German Flatts; ***209** NI-15; mail Mohawk z 13407; rural
Dayton; RMC Place; CATTARAUGUS; ▲ Dayton; **208** NL-3; 🅿; z 14041; ● 350
Dayton; MCD-Town; CATTARAUGUS; ***208** NL-3; 🅿; z 14041; Ⓟ 1,915; Ⓒ 1,945
Daytonville; RMC Place; ONEIDA; ▲ Marshall; ***209** NI-14; mail Waterville z 13480; rural
Dean; RMC Place; CHAUTAUQUA; ▲ Chautauqua; ***208** NL-2; mail Stockton z 14784; rural
Deansboro; RMC Place; ONEIDA; ▲ Marshall; **209** NI-14; 🅿; z 13328; ● 500
Debruce; RMC Place; SULLIVAN; ▲ Rockland; **207** SA-4; mail Livingston Manor z 12758; rural
Decatur; RMC Place; OTSEGO; ▲ Decatur; ***209** NK-16; mail Worcester z 12197; ● 50
Decatur; MCD-Town; OTSEGO; ***209** NK-16; mail Worcester z 12197; Ⓟ 356; Ⓒ 410
Deck; RMC Place; HERKIMER; ▲ Stark; ***209** NI-15; mail Mohawk z 13407; rural
Deckertown; RMC Place; SULLIVAN; ▲ Rockland; ***207** SA-3; mail Livingston Manor z 12758
Deerfield; MCD-Town; ONEIDA; ***209** NH-15; 🅿; ★ **UT-R**; z 13502 & mail Utica z 13503; Ⓟ 3,942; Ⓒ 3,906; Ⓡ 3,909
Deerland; RMC Place; HAMILTON; ▲ Long Lake; ***209** NE-17; elev. 1,662ft./507m.; mail Long Lake z 12847
Deerpark; MCD-Town; ORANGE; ***207** SC-4; mail Cuddebackville z 12729; Ⓟ 7,832; Ⓒ 7,858
Deer Park; CDP; SUFFOLK; ▲ Babylon; **207** SF-9; elev. 74ft./23m.; 🅿; ★ **N.Y.**; z 11729 & mail Huntington Station z 11746; Ⓟ 28,840; Ⓒ 28,316; ◆ 28,306
Deer River; RMC Place; LEWIS; ▲ Denmark; **209** NE-13; 🅿; z 13627; ● 300
Deferiet; Inc. Place; JEFFERSON; ▲ Wilna; **209** NE-13; 🅿; z 13628; Ⓟ 293; Ⓒ 309
Defreestville; RMC Place; RENSSELAER; ▲ North Greenbush; **209** NK-19; ★ **A-S-T**; mail Rensselaer z 12144; ● 960
Degrasse; RMC Place; ST. LAWRENCE; ▲ Russell; **209** ND-15; 🅿; z 13684; ● 140
De Kalb (Old DeKalb); RMC Place; ST. LAWRENCE; ▲ De Kalb; **209** NC-14; mail De Kalb Junction z 13630; ● 100
De Kalb; MCD-Town; ST. LAWRENCE; ***209** NC-14; mail De Kalb Junction z 13630; Ⓟ 2,153; Ⓒ 2,213
De Kalb Junction; RMC Place; ST. LAWRENCE; ▲ De Kalb; **209** NC-14; 🅿; z 13630; ● 375
De Lancey; RMC Place; DELAWARE; ▲ Hamden; **209** NL-15; 🅿; z 13752; ● 110
Delanson; Inc. Place; SCHENECTADY; ▲ Duanesburg; **209** NJ-18; 🅿; z 12053; Ⓟ 361; Ⓒ 385
Delaware; RMC Place; ALBANY; ★ **A-S-T**; mail Albany z 12209; pop. incl. with Albany (Inc. Place)
Delaware; MCD-Town; SULLIVAN; ***207** SA-3; mail Callicoon z 12723; Ⓟ 2,633; Ⓒ 2,719
DELAWARE; **209** NL-15; Ⓟ 47,225; Ⓒ 48,055; ◆ 45,996
Delevan; Inc. Place; CATTARAUGUS; ▲ Yorkshire; **208** NK-5; 🅿; z 14042; Ⓟ 1,214; Ⓒ 1,089
Delhi; Inc. Place; ⊡ DELAWARE; ▲ Delhi; **209** NL-15; elev. 1,370ft./418m.; 🅿 🅲 2,519; z 13753; Ⓟ 3,064; Ⓒ 2,583
Delhi; MCD-Town; DELAWARE; ***209** NL-15; 🅿 🅲 2,519; z 13753; Ⓟ 5,015; Ⓒ 4,629
Delmar; CDP; ALBANY; ▲ Bethlehem; **209** NK-19; 🅿; ★ **A-S-T**; z 12054; Ⓟ 8,360; Ⓒ 8,292
Delphi Falls; RMC Place; ONONDAGA; ▲ Pompey; **209** NJ-12; elev. 952ft./290m.; 🅿; ★ **SYR**; z 13051; ● 500
Delray; RMC Place; ERIE; ▲ West Seneca; ★ **BUF**; mail Buffalo z 14224
Dempster Beach; RMC Place; OSWEGO; ▲ New Haven; ***209** NG-11; mail Oswego z 13126; ● 25
Demster; RMC Place; OSWEGO; ▲ New Haven; ***209** NG-11; mail Oswego z 13126; ● 30
Denmark; RMC Place; LEWIS; ▲ Denmark; **209** NF-13; 🅿; z 13631; ● 150
Denmark; MCD-Town; LEWIS; ***209** NF-13; 🅿; z 13631; Ⓟ 2,718; Ⓒ 2,747
Dennies Hollow; RMC Place; FULTON; ▲ Mayfield; ***209** NI-17; ★ **A-S-T**; mail Mayfield z 12117; rural
Denning; RMC Place; ULSTER; ▲ Denning; ***209** NM-17; mail Claryville z 12725; ● 150
Denning; MCD-Town; ULSTER; ***209** NN-17; mail Claryville z 12725; Ⓟ 524; Ⓒ 516
Dennison Corners; RMC Place; HERKIMER; ▲ German Flatts, Columbia; ***209** NI-15; elev. 1,316ft./401m.; mail Mohawk z 13407; rural
Denton; RMC Place; ORANGE; ▲ Wawayanda; ***207** SC-5; elev. 451ft./137m.; ★ **MIDD**; mail New Hampton z 10958; ● 400
Denver; RMC Place; DELAWARE; ▲ Middletown; ***209** NL-16; 🅿; z 12421; ● 400
Depauville; CDP; JEFFERSON; ▲ Clayton; **209** NE-12; elev. 298ft./91m.; 🅿; z 13632; Ⓒ 512
Depew; Inc. Place; ERIE; ▲ Lancaster, Cheektowaga; **208** NJ-4; 🅿; ★ **BUF**; z 14043; Ⓟ 17,673; Ⓒ 16,629
De Peyster; RMC Place; ST. LAWRENCE; ▲ De Peyster; **209** NC-14; elev. 376ft./115m.; 🅿; z 13633; ● 300
De Peyster; MCD-Town; ST. LAWRENCE; ***209** NC-14; 🅿; z 13633; Ⓟ 913; Ⓒ 936
Deposit; Inc. Place; BROOME, DELAWARE; ▲ Deposit, Sanford; **209** NM-14; elev. 991ft./302m.; 🅿; z 13754; Ⓟ 1,936; Ⓒ 1,699
Deposit; MCD-Town; DELAWARE; ***209** NM-14; 🅿; z 13754; includes part of the Village of Deposit; Ⓟ 1,824; Ⓒ 1,687
Derby; RMC Place; ERIE; ▲ Evans; **208** NJ-3; elev. 707ft./215m.; 🅿; ★ **BUF**; z 14047; ● 1,200
Dering Harbor; Inc. Place; SUFFOLK; ▲ Shelter Island; ***207** SD-12; mail Shelter Island z 11964; Ⓟ 28; Ⓒ 13
DeRuyter; Inc. Place; MADISON; ▲ DeRuyter; **209** NJ-12; elev. 1,296ft./395m.; 🅿; z 13052; Ⓟ 568; Ⓒ 531
DeRuyter; MCD-Town; MADISON; ***209** NJ-13; mail De Ruyter z 13052; Ⓟ 1,458; Ⓒ 1,532
Deuels Corners; RMC Place; ERIE; ▲ Orchard Park; ***208** NJ-4; ★ **BUF**; mail Orchard Park z 14127; ● 300
Devereux; RMC Place; CATTARAUGUS; ▲ Franklinville; ***208** NL-4; mail Ellicottville z 14731; rural
Devon; RMC Place; SUFFOLK; ▲ East Hampton; ***207** SE-13; mail Amagansett z 11930; summer pop. 100
Dewey; RMC Place; MONROE; ★ **ROCH**; mail Rochester z 14613; pop. incl. with Rochester (Inc. Place)
Dewey Bridge; RMC Place; WASHINGTON; ▲ Fort Ann; mail Fort Ann z 12827; rural
De Witt; RMC Place; ONONDAGA; ▲ De Witt; **209** NI-12; 🅿; ★ **SYR**; z 13214; Ⓟ 8,244
De Witt; MCD-Town; ONONDAGA; ***209** NI-12; 🅿; ★ **SYR**; z 13214; Ⓟ 25,148; Ⓒ 24,071; Ⓡ 24,942; ◆ 23,624
Dewittville; RMC Place; CHAUTAUQUA; ▲ Chautauqua; **208** NL-2; elev. 1,328ft./405m.; 🅿; z 14728 & mail Maple Springs z 14756; ● 350
Dexter; Inc. Place; JEFFERSON; ▲ Brownville; **209** NE-12; elev. 325ft./99m.; 🅿; ★ **WATN**; z 13634 & mail Limerick z 13657; Ⓟ 1,030; Ⓒ 1,120
Dexterville; RMC Place; OSWEGO; ▲ Granby; ***209** NH-11; elev. 472ft./144m.; mail Fulton z 13069; ● 55
Diamond Point; RMC Place; WARREN; ▲ Lake George; **209** NG-19; elev. 354ft./108m.; 🅿; ★ **GLFLS**; z 12824; ● 400
Diana; MCD-Town; LEWIS; ***209** NE-14; mail Harrisville z 13648; Ⓟ 1,743; Ⓒ 1,661
Dibbletown; RMC Place; ONEIDA; ▲ Vienna; ***209** NH-13; ★ **UT-R**; mail Blossvale z 13308; rural
Dickersonville; RMC Place; NIAGARA; ▲ Lewiston; ***208** NH-3; elev. 392ft./119m.; ★ **BUF**; mail Ransomville z 14131; ● 200
Dickinson; MCD-Town; BROOME; ***209** NM-12; ★ **BING**; mail Binghamton z 13905; Ⓟ 5,486; Ⓒ 5,335
Dickinson; FRANKLIN; see Dickinson Center (RMC Place)
Dickinson; MCD-Town; FRANKLIN; ***209** NB-16; mail Dickinson Center z 12930; Ⓟ 751; Ⓒ 739
Dickinson Center (Dickinson); RMC Place; FRANKLIN; ▲ Dickinson; **209** NB-16; elev. 938ft./286m.; 🅿; z 12930; ● 300
Dick Urban; RMC Place; ERIE; ▲ Cheektowaga; ***208** NJ-4; ★ **BUF**; mail Depew z 14043; pop. incl. with Depew (Inc. Place)
Dimmick Corners; RMC Place; SARATOGA; ▲ Wilton; ***209** NH-19; elev. 305ft./93m.; ★ **GLFLS**; mail Gansevoort z 12831; rural
Dineharts; RMC Place; STEUBEN; ▲ Wheeler; ***208** NL-8; elev. 1,305ft./398m.; mail Bath z 14810; rural
Divine Corners; RMC Place; SULLIVAN; ▲ Fallsburg; ***207** SA-4; elev. 1,586ft./483m.; mail Loch Sheldrake z 12759; rural
Dix; RMC Place; ONEIDA; ▲ Westmoreland; ***209** NI-14; ★ **UT-R**; mail Rome z 13440; rural
Dix; MCD-Town; SCHUYLER; ***208** NL-9; mail Watkins Glen z 14891; Ⓟ 4,130; Ⓒ 4,197
Dix Hills; CDP-Census Area Only; SUFFOLK; ▲ Huntington; **207** SH-11; 🅿 🅷 🅲 1,254; ★ **N.Y.**; z 11746; Ⓟ 25,849; Ⓒ 26,024; ◆ 26,019
Dobbs Ferry; Inc. Place; WESTCHESTER; ▲ Greenburgh; **207** SE-7; elev. 210ft./64m.; 🅿 🅷 🅲 9,120; ★ **N.Y.**; z 10522; Ⓟ 9,940; Ⓒ 10,622
Dodge; RMC Place; CHAUTAUQUA; ▲ Carroll; ***208** NM-3; ★ **JMST**; mail Frewsburg z 14738; rural
Dogtail Corners; RMC Place; DUTCHESS; ***207** SB-8; mail Wingdale z 12594; rural
Dolgeville; Inc. Place; HERKIMER, FULTON; ▲ Oppenheim, Manheim; **209** NI-16; elev. 802ft./244m.; 🅿; z 13329; Ⓟ 2,452; Ⓒ 2,166
Dongan Hills; RMC Place; RICHMOND; ***207** SG-6; elev. 40ft./12m.; ★ **N.Y.**; mail Staten Island z 10304; pop. incl. with New York (Inc. Place)
Doraville; RMC Place; BROOME; ▲ Colesville; ***209** NM-13; ★ **BING**; mail Nineveh z 13813
Doris Park; RMC Place; OSWEGO; ▲ Constantia; ***209** NH-12; ★ **SYR**; mail Constantia z 13044
Dorloo; RMC Place; SCHOHARIE; ▲ Seward; **209** NJ-16; mail Cobleskill z 12043; ● 450
Dormansville; RMC Place; ALBANY; ▲ Westerlo; **209** NK-18; 🅿; z 12055; ● 100
Dorwood Park; RMC Place; NIAGARA; ▲ Wilson; ***208** NH-4; elev. 356ft./109m.; ★ **BUF**; mail Ransomville z 14131; ● 300
Douglass; ESSEX; see Port Douglas (RMC Place)
Douglaston; RMC Place; QUEENS; **211** G-15; 🅿; ★ **N.Y.**; z 11362-63; pop. incl. with New York (Inc. Place)
Dover; MCD-Town; DUTCHESS; ***207** SB-8; mail Dover Plains z 12522; Ⓟ 7,778; Ⓒ 8,565
Dover Furnace; RMC Place; DUTCHESS; ▲ Dover; **207** SB-8; mail Dover Plains z 12522
Dover Plains; CDP; DUTCHESS; ▲ Washington, Amenia, Dover; **207** SA-8; 🅿; z 12522; Ⓟ 1,847; Ⓒ 1,996
Downsville; RMC Place; DELAWARE; ▲ Colchester; **209** NM-15; 🅿; z 13755; ● 1,100
Downtown; RMC Place; CHEMUNG; ★ **ELM**; mail Elmira z 14901; pop. incl. with Elmira (Inc. Place)
Downtown; RMC Place; MONROE; ★ **ROCH**; mail Rochester z 14603; pop. incl. with Rochester (Inc. Place)
Downtown (Clinton Square); RMC Place; ONONDAGA; ★ **SYR**; mail Syracuse z 13201; pop. incl. with Syracuse (Inc. Place)
Doyle; RMC Place; ERIE; ▲ Cheektowaga; ***208** NJ-4; ★ **BUF**; mail Buffalo z 14206
Dreiser Loop; RMC Place; BRONX; ★ **N.Y.**; mail Bronx z 10475; pop. incl. with New York (Inc. Place)
Dresden (Dresden Station); RMC Place; WASHINGTON; ▲ Dresden; ***209** NF-20; mail Whitehall z 12887
Dresden; MCD-Town; WASHINGTON; ***209** NG-20; mail Whitehall z 12887; Ⓟ 561; Ⓒ 677
Dresden; Inc. Place; YATES; ▲ Torrey; **208** NK-9; 🅿; z 14441; Ⓟ 339; Ⓒ 307
Dresden Station; WASHINGTON; see Dresden (RMC Place)
Dresserville; RMC Place; CAYUGA; ▲ Sempronius; ***209** NJ-11; elev. 1,288ft./393m.; mail Moravia z 13118; rural
Drews Corner; RMC Place; ST. LAWRENCE; ▲ Waddington; ***209** NB-15; mail Waddington z 13694; rural
Dryden; Inc. Place; TOMPKINS; ▲ Dryden; **209** NK-11; 🅿; ★ **ITH**; z 13053; Ⓟ 1,908; Ⓒ 1,832
Dryden; MCD-Town; TOMPKINS; ***209** NK-11; 🅿; ★ **ITH**; z 13053; Ⓟ 13,251; Ⓒ 13,532
Duane; MCD-Town; FRANKLIN; ***209** NC-17; mail Malone z 12953; Ⓟ 152; Ⓒ 159
Duane Center; RMC Place; FRANKLIN; mail Malone z 12953; rural
Duane Lake; CDP-Census Area Only; SCHENECTADY; ***209** NJ-18; Ⓒ 357
Duanesburg; CDP; SCHENECTADY; ▲ Duanesburg; **209** NJ-18; elev. 722ft./220m.; 🅿; z 12056; Ⓒ 339
Duanesburg; MCD-Town; SCHENECTADY; ***209** NJ-18; 🅿; z 12056; Ⓟ 5,474; Ⓒ 5,808
Dublin; RMC Place; SENECA; ▲ Junius; ***208** NI-9; mail Clyde z 14433; ● 45
Dugway; RMC Place; OSWEGO; ▲ Albion; ***209** NG-12; elev. 514ft./157m.; mail Parish z 13131; ● 100
Dunbar; RMC Place; BROOME; ▲ Windsor; ***209** NM-13; elev. 1,403ft./428m.; ★ **BING**; mail Windsor z 13865; rural
Dundee; Inc. Place; YATES; ▲ Starkey; **208** NK-9; elev. 994ft./303m.; 🅿; z 14837; Ⓟ 1,588; Ⓒ 1,690
Dunewood; RMC Place; SUFFOLK; ▲ Islip; ★ **N.Y.**; mail Bay Shore z 11706; summer pop. 120; ● 10
Dunham Hollow; RMC Place; RENSSELAER; ▲ Nassau; ***209** NK-20; ★ **A-S-T**; mail Averill Park z 12018; ● 110
Dunham Manor; RMC Place; ONEIDA; ▲ Whitestown; ★ **UT-R**; mail Whitesboro z 13492
Dunkirk; Inc. Place; CHAUTAUQUA; **208** NK-2; elev. 598ft./182m.; 🅿 🅷 ■; z 14048, z 14166; Ⓟ 13,989; Ⓒ 13,131; ◆ 11,901
Dunkirk; MCD-Town; CHAUTAUQUA; ***208** NK-2; 🅿; z 14048, z 14166; does not include the City of Dunkirk; Ⓟ 1,482; Ⓒ 1,387
Dunnsville; RMC Place; ALBANY; ▲ Guilderland; **207** SH-1; elev. 359ft./109m.; ★ **A-S-T**; mail Altamont z 12009
Dunraven; RMC Place; DELAWARE; ▲ Middletown; ***209** NM-16; mail Margaretville z 12455; rural
Dunsbach Ferry; RMC Place; ALBANY; ▲ Colonie; **207** SG-5; ★ **A-S-T**; mail Cohoes z 12047; ● 650
Dunwoodie; RMC Place; WESTCHESTER; ***207** SE-7; ★ **N.Y.**; mail Yonkers z 10701; pop. incl. with Yonkers (Inc. Place)
Dunwoody Heights; RMC Place; WESTCHESTER; ★ **N.Y.**; mail Yonkers z 10701; pop. incl. with Yonkers (Inc. Place)
Durham; RMC Place; GREENE; ▲ Durham; **209** NL-18; 🅿; z 12422; ● 150
Durham; MCD-Town; GREENE; ***209** NL-18; 🅿; z 12422; Ⓟ 2,324; Ⓒ 2,592
Durhamville; RMC Place; ONEIDA; ▲ Verona; **209** NI-13; 🅿; ★ **UT-R**; z 13054; ● 500
Durkeetown; RMC Place; WASHINGTON; ▲ Fort Edward; ***209** NH-19; ★ **GLFLS**; mail Fort Edward z 12828; rural
Durlandville; RMC Place; ORANGE; ▲ Goshen; **207** SC-5; elev. 421ft./128m.; ★ **N.Y.**; mail Goshen z 10924; ● 160
DUTCHESS; **207** SA-8; Ⓟ 259,462; Ⓒ 280,150; ◆ 287,783
Dutchess Junction; RMC Place; DUTCHESS; ▲ Fishkill; ***207** SC-6; ★ **POK**; mail Beacon z 12508; ● 125
Dutch Flats; RMC Place; WYOMING; ▲ Orangeville; ***208** NJ-5; elev. 1,493ft./455m.; mail Varysburg z 14167; rural
Dutch Hollow; RMC Place; WYOMING; ▲ Sheldon; ***208** NJ-5; elev. 1,265ft./386m.; mail Strykersville z 14145; rural
Dutch Meadows; RMC Place; SARATOGA; ▲ Clifton Park; ***209** NJ-19; elev. 356ft./109m.; ★ **A-S-T**; mail Clifton Park z 12065; ● 780
Dutch Settlement; RMC Place; JEFFERSON; ▲ Le Ray; ***209** NE-13; ★ **WATN**; mail Evans Mills z 13637; rural
Dwaar Kill; RMC Place; ULSTER; ▲ Shawangunk; ***207** SB-5; mail Pine Bush z 12566; rural
Dyke; RMC Place; STEUBEN; ▲ Hornby; ***208** NL-9; elev. 1,529ft./466m.; mail Corning z 14830; rural
Dykemans; RMC Place; PUTNAM; ▲ Southeast; ***207** SC-8; ★ **N.Y.**; mail Brewster z 10509; ● 100
Dyker Heights; RMC Place; KINGS; ***207** SG-6; ★ **N.Y.**; mail Brooklyn z 11228; pop. incl. with New York (Inc. Place)

E

Eagle; RMC Place; WYOMING; ▲ Eagle; **208** NK-5; mail Arcade z 14009; ● 150
Eagle; MCD-Town; WYOMING; ***208** NK-5; mail Arcade z 14009; Ⓟ 1,155; Ⓒ 1,194
Eagle Bay; RMC Place; HERKIMER; ▲ Webb; **209** NF-16; 🅿; z 13331; ● 200
Eagle Bridge; RMC Place; RENSSELAER; ▲ Hoosick; **209** NI-20; elev. 414ft./126m.; 🅿; z 12057; ● 350
Eagle Center; RMC Place; WYOMING; ▲ Eagle; ***208** NK-5; elev. 1,871ft./570m.; mail Bliss z 14024; rural
Eagle Harbor; RMC Place; ORLEANS; ▲ Gaines; **208** NH-5; 🅿; z 14411; ● 250
Eagle Lake; RMC Place; ESSEX; ▲ Ticonderoga; mail Ticonderoga z 12883; summer pop. 100
Eagle Mills; RMC Place; RENSSELAER; ▲ Brunswick; **209** NJ-19; ★ **A-S-T**; mail Troy z 12180; ● 530
Eagle Point; RMC Place; LIVINGSTON; ▲ Geneseo; ***208** NJ-7; ★ **ROCH**; mail Geneseo z 14454; rural
Eagle Valley; RMC Place; ORANGE; ▲ Tuxedo; ***207** SD-5; ★ **N.Y.**; mail Tuxedo Park z 10987; ● 300
Eagle Village; RMC Place; ONONDAGA; ▲ Manlius; ***209** NI-12; ★ **SYR**; mail Manlius z 13104; ● 200
Eagleville (East Salem); RMC Place; WASHINGTON; ▲ Salem; **209** NI-20; mail Shushan z 12873; ● 60
Earlton; RMC Place; GREENE; ▲ Coxsackie; **209** NL-18; 🅿; z 12058; ● 255
Earlville; RMC Place; FRANKLIN; ***209** NA-18; mail Chateaugay z 12920; rural
Earlville; Inc. Place; MADISON, CHENANGO; ▲ Sherburne, Hamilton; **209** NJ-13; 🅿; z 13332; Ⓟ 883; Ⓒ 791
East; RMC Place; WESTCHESTER; ★ **N.Y.**; mail Yonkers z 10704; pop. incl. with Yonkers (Inc. Place)
East Amherst (Transit); RMC Place; ERIE; ▲ Amherst, Clarence; **208** NC-6; 🅿; ★ **BUF**; z 14051; ● 700
East Arcade; RMC Place; WYOMING; ▲ Arcade; ***208** NK-5; elev. 1,597ft./487m.; mail Arcade z 14009; rural
East Atlantic Beach; CDP-Census Area Only; NASSAU; ▲ Hempstead; **211** L-16; 🅿; ★ **N.Y.**; z 11561 & mail Atlantic Beach z 11509; Ⓒ 2,257
East Aurora; Inc. Place; ERIE; ▲ Aurora; **208** NJ-4; elev. 917ft./280m.; 🅿; ★ **BUF**; z 14052; Ⓟ 6,647; Ⓒ 6,673
East Avon; RMC Place; LIVINGSTON; ▲ Avon; **208** NJ-7; ★ **ROCH**; mail Avon z 14414; ● 430
East Bay; RMC Place; WAYNE; ▲ Huron; ***208** NH-9; mail Wolcott z 14590; ● 100
East Beekmantown; RMC Place; CLINTON; ▲ Beekmantown; **209** NB-19; ★ **PLATT**; mail Plattsburgh z 12901; ● 125
East Bend Park; RMC Place; DUTCHESS; ▲ La Grange; ★ **POK**; mail Poughkeepsie z 12603
East Berkshire; RMC Place; TIOGA; ▲ Berkshire; ***209** NL-12; mail Berkshire z 13736; rural
East Berne; RMC Place; ALBANY; ▲ Berne; **209** NK-18; 🅿; z 12059; ● 200
East Bethany; RMC Place; GENESEE; ▲ Bethany; **208** NJ-6; elev. 1,006ft./307m.; 🅿; z 14054; ● 150
East Bloomfield; RMC Place; ONTARIO; ▲ East Bloomfield; ***208** NJ-8; 🅿; ★ **ROCH**; z 14443 & mail Bloomfield z 14469; pop. incl. with Holcomb (Inc. Place)
East Bloomfield; MCD-Town; ONTARIO; ***208** NJ-8; 🅿; ★ **ROCH**; z 14443 & mail Bloomfield z 14469; Ⓟ 3,258; Ⓒ 3,361
East Branch; RMC Place; DELAWARE; ▲ Hancock; **209** NM-15; 🅿; z 13756; ● 400
East Brentwood; RMC Place; SUFFOLK; ▲ Islip; ***207** SF-9; ★ **N.Y.**; mail Brentwood z 11717
East Buffalo; RMC Place; ERIE; ▲ Cheektowaga; mail Buffalo z 14225
East Buskirk (Tiashoke); RMC Place; RENSSELAER; ▲ Hoosick; ***209** NI-20; elev. 445ft./136m.; mail Buskirk z 12028; rural
East Campbell; RMC Place; STEUBEN; ▲ Campbell; ***208** NL-9; elev. 1,033ft./315m.; mail Painted Post z 14870
East Cayuga Heights; RMC Place; TOMPKINS; ▲ Ithaca; ***209** NK-11; ★ **ITH**; mail Ithaca z 14850
East Chatham; RMC Place; COLUMBIA; ▲ Canaan, Chatham; **209** NL-20; 🅿; ★ **A-S-T**; z 12060; ● 500
Eastchester; RMC Place; BRONX; ***207** SE-7; ★ **N.Y.**; mail Bronx z 10466; pop. incl. with New York (Inc. Place)
East Chester; RMC Place; ORANGE; ***207** SC-5; ★ **N.Y.**; mail Chester z 10918; pop. incl. with Chester (Inc. Place)
Eastchester; CDP; WESTCHESTER; ▲ Eastchester; **211** B-14; 🅿; ★ **N.Y.**; z 10707, z 10709; Ⓟ 18,537; Ⓒ 18,564
Eastchester; MCD-Town; WESTCHESTER; ***207** SE-7; 🅿 🅲 2,463; ★ **N.Y.**; z 10707, z 10709; Ⓟ 30,867; Ⓒ 31,318; ◆ 32,402
East Cobleskill; RMC Place; SCHOHARIE; ▲ Cobleskill, Middleburgh, Schoharie; ***209** NK-17; mail Schoharie z 12157; ● 50
East Coldenham; RMC Place; ORANGE; ▲ Newburgh; ***207** SB-6; elev. 500ft./152m.; ★ **NWBG**; mail Newburgh z 12550
East Concord; RMC Place; ERIE; ▲ Concord; ***208** NK-4; elev. 1,456ft./444m.; 🅿; ★ **BUF**; z 14055; ● 160
East Corning; RMC Place; STEUBEN; ▲ Corning; **208** NM-9; mail Corning z 14830; ● 650
East De Kalb; RMC Place; ST. LAWRENCE; ▲ De Kalb; ***209** NC-14; elev. 474ft./144m.; mail De Kalb Junction z 13630; rural
East Durham; RMC Place; GREENE; ▲ Durham; **209** NL-18; 🅿; z 12423; ● 600
East Eden; RMC Place; ERIE; ▲ Eden; **208** NK-4; ★ **BUF**; mail Eden z 14057; ● 300
East Elmhurst; RMC Place; QUEENS; **211** G-12; 🅿; ★ **N.Y.**; z 11369-71; pop. incl. with New York (Inc. Place)
Eastern Parkway; RMC Place; KINGS; ***207** SG-7; ★ **N.Y.**; mail Brooklyn z 11213; pop. incl. with New York (Inc. Place)
East Farmingdale; CDP-Census Area Only; SUFFOLK; ▲ Babylon; ***207** SF-9; ★ **N.Y.**; mail Cincinnatus z 13040, Farmingdale z 11735; Ⓟ 4,510; Ⓒ 5,400
East Fishkill; MCD-Town; DUTCHESS; ***207** SB-7; 🅿; ★ **POK**; z 12533; Ⓟ 22,101; Ⓒ 25,589; ◆ 26,832
East Flatbush; RMC Place; KINGS; ***207** SG-7; ★ **N.Y.**; mail Brooklyn z 11203; pop. incl. with New York (Inc. Place)
East Floyd; RMC Place; ONEIDA; ▲ Floyd; ***209** NH-14; elev. 982ft./299m.; ★ **UT-R**; mail Holland Patent z 13354; rural
East Frankfort; RMC Place; HERKIMER; ▲ Frankfort; ***209** NI-15; ★ **UT-R**; mail Frankfort z 13340; rural
East Freetown; RMC Place; CORTLAND; ▲ Freetown; ***209** NK-12; 🅿; z 13040; ● 30
East Gaines; RMC Place; ORLEANS; ▲ Gaines; ***208** NH-6; elev. 431ft./131m.; mail Albion z 14411; rural
East Galway; RMC Place; SARATOGA; ▲ Galway; ***209** NI-18; ★ **A-S-T**; mail Middle Grove z 12850; ● 300
East Garden City; CDP-Census Area Only; NASSAU; ***207** SF-8; ★ **N.Y.**; Ⓒ 979; Ⓡ 4,406
East Genoa; RMC Place; CAYUGA; ▲ Genoa; ***209** NK-11; mail Locke z 13092; rural
East Glenville; CDP; SCHENECTADY; ▲ Glenville; **209** NJ-18; ★ **A-S-T**; mail Schenectady z 12302; Ⓟ 6,518; Ⓒ 6,064
East Greenbush; CDP; RENSSELAER; ▲ East Greenbush; **209** NK-19; 🅿; ★ **A-S-T**; z 12061; Ⓟ 3,784; Ⓒ 4,085
East Greenbush; MCD-Town; RENSSELAER; ***209** NK-19; 🅿; ★ **A-S-T**; z 12061; Ⓟ 14,076; Ⓒ 15,560
East Greenlawn; RMC Place; SUFFOLK; ▲ Huntington; ***207** SE-9; ★ **N.Y.**; mail East Northport z 11731
East Greenwich; RMC Place; WASHINGTON; ▲ Greenwich; **209** NI-20; 🅿; ★ **GLFLS**; z 12865; ● 220
East Guilford (New Berlin Junction); RMC Place; CHENANGO; ▲ Guilford; ***209** NL-14; mail Bainbridge z 13733; rural
East Half Hollow Hills; RMC Place; SUFFOLK; ▲ Huntington; ***207** SF-9; ★ **N.Y.**; mail Huntington Station z 11746; ● 6,800
East Hamilton; RMC Place; MADISON; ▲ Hamilton; ***209** NJ-14; mail Hubbardsville z 13355; ● 65
East Hampton; Inc. Place; SUFFOLK; ▲ East Hampton; **207** SE-13; elev. 36ft./11m.; 🅿; z 11937; Ⓟ 1,402; Ⓒ 1,334
East Hampton; MCD-Town; SUFFOLK; ***207** SD-14; 🅿; z 11937; Ⓟ 16,132; Ⓒ 19,719; ◆ 21,045
East Hampton North; CDP-Census Area Only; SUFFOLK; ▲ East Hampton; ***207** SE-13; elev. 65ft./20m.; mail East Hampton z 11937; Ⓟ 2,780; Ⓒ 3,587
East Hartford; RMC Place; WASHINGTON; ▲ Hartford; ***209** NH-20; mail Granville z 12832
East Hebron; RMC Place; WASHINGTON; ▲ Hebron; ***209** NH-20; elev. 610ft./186m.; mail Salem z 12865; ● 60
East Herkimer; RMC Place; HERKIMER; ▲ Herkimer; ***209** NI-15; mail Herkimer z 13350; ● 900
East Hill; RMC Place; TOMPKINS; ▲ Ithaca; ***209** NL-11; ★ **ITH**; mail Ithaca z 14850; ● 800
East Hills; Inc. Place; NASSAU; ▲ Oyster Bay, North Hempstead; **207** SF-8; ★ **N.Y.**; mail Greenvale z 11548, Roslyn z 11576, Roslyn Heights z 11577; Ⓟ 6,746; Ⓒ 6,842
East Hillsdale; RMC Place; COLUMBIA; ▲ Hillsdale; ***209** NL-20; elev. 731ft./223m.; mail Hillsdale z 12529; rural
East Homer; RMC Place; CORTLAND; ▲ Homer; **209** NK-12; 🅿; z 13056, z 13158; ● 200
East Hoosick; RMC Place; RENSSELAER; ▲ Hoosick; ***209** NI-20; elev. 897ft./273m.; mail Hoosick Falls z 12090; rural
East Hounsfield; RMC Place; JEFFERSON; ▲ Hounsfield; ***209** NE-12; mail Watertown z 13601
East Huntington; RMC Place; SUFFOLK; ▲ Huntington; ***207** SE-9; ★ **N.Y.**; mail Huntington z 11743; ● 4,500
East Irvington; RMC Place; WESTCHESTER; ▲ Greenburgh; ***207** SE-7; ★ **N.Y.**; mail Irvington z 10533; ● 1,000
East Islip; CDP; SUFFOLK; ▲ Islip; **207** SI-12; 🅿; ★ **N.Y.**; z 11730; Ⓟ 14,325; Ⓒ 14,078
East Ithaca; CDP; TOMPKINS; ▲ Ithaca; ***209** NL-11; elev. 1,000ft./305m.; ★ **ITH**; mail Ithaca z 14850; Ⓟ 2,152; Ⓒ 2,192
East Java; WYOMING; see Java Lake (RMC Place)
East Jefferson; RMC Place; SCHOHARIE; ***209** NK-16; elev. 1,607ft./490m.; mail Jefferson z 12093; rural
East Jewett; RMC Place; GREENE; ▲ Jewett; **209** NL-18; 🅿; z 12424; ● 200
East Kingston; CDP; ULSTER; ▲ Kingston; ***209** NM-18; ★ **KNGST**; mail Kingston z 12401; Ⓒ 285
East Koy; RMC Place; WYOMING; ▲ Pike; ***208** NK-6; elev. 1,459ft./445m.; mail Portageville z 14536; ● 30
East Lansing; RMC Place; TOMPKINS; ▲ Lansing; ***209** NK-11; ★ **ITH**; mail Ithaca z 14852; ● 150
East Leon; RMC Place; CATTARAUGUS; ▲ Leon, Dayton; ***208** NL-3; elev. 1,337ft./408m.; mail Cattaraugus z 14719
East Line; RMC Place; SARATOGA; ▲ Malta, Ballston; ***209** NI-19; ★ **A-S-T**; mail Ballston Spa z 12020; rural
East Marion; CDP; SUFFOLK; ▲ Southold; **207** SD-12; elev. 32ft./10m.; 🅿; z 11939; summer pop. 4,000; Ⓒ 756
East Martinsburg; RMC Place; LEWIS; ▲ Martinsburg; ***209** NF-14; elev. 758ft./231m.; mail Lowville z 13367; ● 120
East Masonville; RMC Place; DELAWARE; ▲ Masonville; ***209** NL-14; mail Sidney Center z 13839; rural
East Massapequa; CDP-Census Area Only; NASSAU; ▲ Oyster Bay; ***207** SF-8; ★ **N.Y.**; mail Massapequa z 11758; Ⓟ 19,550; Ⓒ 19,565
East Mattituck; RMC Place; SUFFOLK; ▲ Southold; ***207** SE-12; mail Mattituck z 11952
East McDonough; RMC Place; CHENANGO; ▲ McDonough; ***209** NK-13; mail Oxford z 13830; ● 70
East Meadow; CDP; NASSAU; ▲ Hempstead; **207** SF-8; 🅿 🅷; ★ **N.Y.**; z 11554; Ⓟ 36,909; Ⓒ 37,461; ◆ 35,582
East Meredith; RMC Place; DELAWARE; ▲ Meredith; **209** NL-15; 🅿; z 13757; ● 200
East Middletown; RMC Place; ORANGE; ★ **MIDD**
Eastmor (Eastmore); RMC Place; RENSSELAER; ▲ North Greenbush; ***209** NJ-19; ★ **A-S-T**; mail Troy z 12180; ● 1,000
Eastmore; RENSSELAER; see Eastmor (RMC Place)
East Moriches; CDP; SUFFOLK; ▲ Brookhaven; ***207** SF-11; elev. 29ft./9m.; 🅿; ★ **N.Y.**; z 11940; Ⓟ 4,021; Ⓒ 4,550
East Nassau; Inc. Place; RENSSELAER; ▲ Nassau; **209** NK-20; elev. 571ft./174m.; 🅿; ★ **A-S-T**; z 12062; Ⓒ 571
East Neck; RMC Place; SUFFOLK; ▲ Huntington; ***207** SE-9; ★ **N.Y.**; mail Huntington z 11743; pop. incl. with Huntington Bay (Inc. Place)
East New York; RMC Place; KINGS; **211** I-12; ★ **N.Y.**; mail Brooklyn z 11207; pop. incl. with New York (Inc. Place)
East Nichols; RMC Place; TIOGA; ▲ Nichols; ***209** NM-11; elev. 1,351ft./412m.; mail Nichols z 13812; rural
East Northport; CDP; SUFFOLK; ▲ Huntington; **207** SE-9; elev. 228ft./69m.; 🅿; ★ **N.Y.**; z 11731; Ⓟ 20,411; Ⓒ 20,845; ◆ 20,842
East Norwich; CDP; NASSAU; ▲ Oyster Bay; **211** E-19; elev. 208ft./63m.; 🅿; ★ **N.Y.**; z 11732; Ⓟ 2,698; Ⓒ 2,675
East Olean; RMC Place; CATTARAUGUS; ***208** NM-5; elev. 1,429ft./436m.; mail Olean z 14760; pop. incl. with Olean (Inc. Place)
Easton; MCD-Town; WASHINGTON; ***209** NI-19; mail Greenwich z 12834, Schaghticoke z 12154; Ⓟ 2,203; Ⓒ 2,259
East Otto; RMC Place; CATTARAUGUS; ▲ East Otto; **208** NL-4; 🅿; z 14729; ● 300
East Otto; MCD-Town; CATTARAUGUS; ***208** NL-4; 🅿; z 14729; Ⓟ 1,003; Ⓒ 1,105
East Palermo; RMC Place; OSWEGO; ▲ Palermo; ***209** NH-11; elev. 459ft./140m.; ★ **SYR**; mail Central Square z 13036; rural
East Palmyra; RMC Place; WAYNE; ▲ Palmyra; **208** NI-9; 🅿; z 14513; ● 135
East Park; RMC Place; DUTCHESS; ▲ Hyde Park; ***207** SA-7; elev. 232ft./71m.; ★ **POK**; mail Hyde Park z 12538
East Part; RMC Place; ST. LAWRENCE; ▲ Stockholm; ***209** NB-16; elev. 376ft./115m.; mail Winthrop z 13697; rural
East Patchogue; CDP; SUFFOLK; ▲ Brookhaven; ***207** SF-10; 🅿; ★ **N.Y.**; z 11772; Ⓟ 20,195; Ⓒ 20,824; ◆ 20,826
East Pembroke; RMC Place; GENESEE; ▲ Pembroke, Batavia; **208** NI-5; 🅿; z 14056; ● 600
East Penfield; RMC Place; MONROE; ▲ Penfield; **208** NI-8; ★ **ROCH**; mail Fairport z 14450; ● 200
East Pharsalia; RMC Place; CHENANGO; ▲ Pharsalia; **209** NK-13; 🅿; z 13758; ● 160
East Pitcairn; RMC Place; ST. LAWRENCE; ▲ Pitcairn; ***209** ND-14; elev. 796ft./243m.; mail Harrisville z 13648; rural
East Pittstown; RMC Place; RENSSELAER; ▲ Pittstown; ***209** NJ-20; elev. 643ft./196m.; ★ **A-S-T**; mail Buskirk z 12028; rural
East Poestenkill; RMC Place; RENSSELAER; ▲ Poestenkill; **209** NJ-20; elev. 1,087ft./331m.; ★ **A-S-T**; mail Averill Park z 12018; ● 150
Eastport; CDP; SUFFOLK; ▲ Southampton, Brookhaven; **207** SF-11; 🅿; ★ **N.Y.**; z 11941; Ⓒ 1,454; Ⓡ 1,486
East Quogue; CDP; SUFFOLK; ▲ Southampton; ***207** SF-12; 🅿; z 11942; Ⓟ 4,372; Ⓒ 4,265; Ⓡ 4,251
East Quoque; RMC Place; SUFFOLK; ▲ Southampton; **207** SE-12; mail East Quogue z 11942; ● 3,150
East Randolph; Inc. Place; CATTARAUGUS; ▲ Conewango, Randolph; **208** NM-3; 🅿; z 14730; Ⓟ 629; Ⓒ 630
East Ridge; RMC Place; SULLIVAN; ▲ Fremont; ***207** SA-2; mail Hankins z 12741; ● 50
East Ripley; RMC Place; CHAUTAUQUA; ▲ Ripley; ***208** NL-1; elev. 731ft./223m.; mail Ripley z 14775; rural
East River; RMC Place; CORTLAND; ▲ Homer; ***209** NK-12; elev. 1,135ft./346m.; mail Cortland z 13045; ● 80
East Rochester; Inc. Place; MONROE; ▲ Pittsford, Perinton; **208** NI-8; 🅿; ★ **ROCH**; z 14445; Ⓟ 6,932; Ⓒ 6,650
East Rockaway; Inc. Place; NASSAU; ▲ Hempstead; **211** J-17; 🅿; ★ **N.Y.**; z 11518; Ⓟ 10,152; Ⓒ 10,414
East Rodman; RMC Place; JEFFERSON; ▲ Rodman; ***209** NF-13; elev. 926ft./282m.; mail Rodman z 13682, Watertown z 13601
East Salamanca; RMC Place; CATTARAUGUS; mail Salamanca z 14779; pop. incl. with Salamanca (Inc. Place)
East Salem; WASHINGTON; see Eagleville (RMC Place)
East Schodack; RMC Place; RENSSELAER; ▲ Schodack; **209** NK-19; 🅿; ★ **A-S-T**; z 12063; ● 500
East Schuyler; RMC Place; HERKIMER; ▲ Schuyler; ***209** NI-15; ★ **UT-R**; mail Frankfort z 13340; rural
East Seneca; RMC Place; ERIE; ▲ West Seneca; ***208** NJ-4; ★ **BUF**; mail Buffalo z 14224
East Setauket (Setauket); RMC Place; SUFFOLK; ▲ Brookhaven; ***207** SE-10; elev. 63ft./19m.; 🅿; ★ **N.Y.**; z 11733; ● 1,350
East Shelby; RMC Place; ORLEANS; ▲ Shelby; ***208** NI-5; elev. 663ft./202m.; mail Medina z 14103; ● 65
East Shoreham; CDP-Census Area Only; SUFFOLK; ▲ Brookhaven; ***207** SE-10; ★ **N.Y.**; mail Shoreham z 11786; Ⓟ 5,461; Ⓒ 5,809
East Side; RMC Place; BROOME; ★ **BING**; mail Binghamton z 13904; pop. incl. with Binghamton (Inc. Place)
East Side; RMC Place; ERIE; ★ **BUF**; mail Buffalo z 14206, z 14211-12; pop. incl. with Buffalo (Inc. Place)
Eastside; RMC Place; SUFFOLK; ▲ East Hampton; ***207** SE-13; elev. 12ft./4m.; mail East Hampton z 11937
East Sidney; RMC Place; DELAWARE; ▲ Sidney; ***209** NL-14; mail Franklin z 13775; rural
East Springfield; RMC Place; OTSEGO; ▲ Springfield; **209** NJ-16; elev. 1,325ft./404m.; 🅿; z 13333; ● 220
East Steamburg; RMC Place; SCHUYLER; ▲ Hector; ***208** NK-10; mail Trumansburg z 14886; rural
East Stone Arabia; RMC Place; MONTGOMERY; ▲ Palatine; ***209** NI-17; mail Palatine Bridge z 13428; rural
East Syracuse; Inc. Place; ONONDAGA; ▲ De Witt; **208** NF-9; 🅿; ★ **SYR**; z 13057; Ⓟ 3,343; Ⓒ 3,178
East Taghkanic; RMC Place; COLUMBIA; ▲ Taghkanic; ***209** NM-19; elev. 570ft./174m.; mail Ancram z 12502; rural
East Tremont; RMC Place; BRONX; ***207** SF-7; ★ **N.Y.**; mail Bronx z 10460; pop. incl. with New York (Inc. Place)
East Varick; RMC Place; SENECA; ▲ Varick; ***208** NJ-10; mail Romulus z 14541
East Vestal; RMC Place; BROOME; ▲ Vestal; ***209** NM-12; ★ **BING**; mail Binghamton z 13902-03; ● 6,200
East Victor; RMC Place; ONTARIO; ▲ Victor; ***208** NI-8; ★ **ROCH**; mail Victor z 14564; ● 100
East View; RMC Place; WESTCHESTER; ▲ Mount Pleasant; ***207** SE-7; ★ **N.Y.**; mail Valhalla z 10595; rural
East Watertown; RMC Place; JEFFERSON; ▲ Watertown; ***209** NE-13; elev. 1,753ft./534m.; ★ **WATN**; mail Watertown z 13601; rural
East Wawarsing; ULSTER; see Port Ben (RMC Place)
East White Plains; RMC Place; WESTCHESTER; ***207** SE-7; elev. 150ft./46m.; ★ **N.Y.**; mail West Harrison z 10604; pop. incl. with Harrison (Inc. Place)
East Williamson; RMC Place; WAYNE; ▲ Williamson; **208** NH-9; elev. 454ft./138m.; 🅿; ★ **ROCH**; z 14449; ● 500
East Williston; Inc. Place; NASSAU; ▲ North Hempstead; **211** G-17; elev. 119ft./36m.; 🅿; ★ **N.Y.**; z 11596; Ⓟ 2,515; Ⓒ 2,503
East Windham; RMC Place; GREENE; ▲ Durham; ***209** NL-18; 🅿; z 12439; ● 65
East Windsor; RMC Place; BROOME; ▲ Windsor; **209** NM-13; ★ **BING**; mail Windsor z 13865; ● 50
East Winfield; RMC Place; HERKIMER; ▲ Winfield; ***209** NJ-16; elev. 1,239ft./378m.; mail West Winfield z 13491; rural
Eastwood; RMC Place; ONONDAGA; ***209** NI-12; ★ **SYR**; mail Syracuse z 13206; pop. incl. with Syracuse (Inc. Place)
East Woods; RMC Place; WESTCHESTER; ▲ Pound Ridge; ***207** SD-8; ★ **N.Y.**; mail Pound Ridge z 10576; ● 250
East Worcester; RMC Place; OTSEGO; ▲ Worcester; **209** NK-16; 🅿; z 12064; ● 300
Eaton; RMC Place; MADISON; ▲ Eaton; **209** NJ-13; elev. 1,200ft./366m.; 🅿; z 13334; ● 500
Eaton; MCD-Town; MADISON; ***209** NJ-13; 🅿 🅲 3,048; z 13334; Ⓟ 5,362; Ⓒ 4,826
Eatons Neck; CDP-Census Area Only; SUFFOLK; ▲ Huntington; ***207** SE-9; ★ **N.Y.**; mail Northport z 11768; Ⓟ 1,499; Ⓒ 1,388
Eatonville; RMC Place; HERKIMER; ▲ Herkimer; ***209** NI-15; mail Little Falls z 13365; rural
Eavesport; RMC Place; ULSTER; ▲ Saugerties; ***209** NM-18; ★ **KNGST**; mail West Camp z 12490
Ebenezer; RMC Place; ERIE; ▲ West Seneca; **208** NG-5; ★ **BUF**; mail Buffalo z 14224
Ebenezer Junction; RMC Place; ERIE; ▲ West Seneca; ★ **BUF**; mail Buffalo z 14224
Echota; RMC Place; NIAGARA; ★ **BUF**; mail Niagara Falls z 14302; pop. incl. with Niagara Falls (Inc. Place)
Eddy; RMC Place; ST. LAWRENCE; ▲ Canton; ***209** NC-14; mail Canton z 13617; rural
Eddyville; RMC Place; CATTARAUGUS; ▲ Mansfield; **208** NL-4; elev. 1,401ft./427m.; mail Little Valley z 14755; ● 55
Eddyville; RMC Place; ULSTER; ▲ Esopus; **207** SA-6; 🅿; ★ **KNGST**; z 12401; ● 500
Eden (Eden Center); CDP; ERIE; ▲ Eden; **208** NK-3; 🅿; ★ **BUF**; z 14057; Ⓟ 3,088; Ⓒ 3,579
Eden; MCD-Town; ERIE; ***208** NK-3; 🅿; ★ **BUF**; z 14057; Ⓟ 7,416; Ⓒ 8,076
Eden Center; ERIE; see Eden (CDP)
Edenville; RMC Place; ORANGE; ▲ Warwick; **207** SD-5; elev. 473ft./144m.; ★ **N.Y.**; mail Warwick z 10990; ● 150
Edenwald; RMC Place; BRONX; ***207** SE-7; ★ **N.Y.**; mail Bronx z 10466; pop. incl. with New York (Inc. Place)
Edgemere; RMC Place; QUEENS; **211** L-15; 🅿; ★ **N.Y.**; z 11690; pop. incl. with New York (Inc. Place)
Edgemont; RMC Place; WESTCHESTER; ▲ Greenburgh; ***207** SE-7; ★ **N.Y.**; mail Scarsdale z 10583
Edgewater Beach; RMC Place; ONEIDA; ▲ Vienna; ***209** NH-13; ★ **UT-R**; mail Blossvale z 13308; ● 100
Edgewater Park; RMC Place; ST. LAWRENCE; ▲ Morristown; ***209** NC-13; mail Ogdensburg z 13669
Edgewood; RMC Place; GREENE; ▲ Hunter; ***209** NM-18; mail Lanesville z 12450; rural
Edgewood; RMC Place; SUFFOLK; ▲ Islip; 🅿; ★ **N.Y.**; z 11717
Edgewood Garden; RMC Place; ONONDAGA; ▲ Camillus; ***209** NI-11; ★ **SYR**; mail Warners z 13164; ● 110
Edinburg; RMC Place; SARATOGA; ▲ Edinburg; **209** NH-18; mail Northville z 12134; ● 300
Edinburg; MCD-Town; SARATOGA; ***209** NH-18; mail Northville z 12134; Ⓟ 1,041; Ⓒ 1,384
Edmeston; RMC Place; OTSEGO; ▲ Edmeston; **209** NJ-14; 🅿; z 13335; ● 600
Edmeston; MCD-Town; OTSEGO; ***209** NJ-14; 🅿; z 13335; Ⓟ 1,717; Ⓒ 1,824
Edson; RMC Place; BROOME; ▲ Windsor; ***209** NM-13; elev. 1,261ft./384m.; ★ **BING**; mail Windsor z 13865; rural
Edwards; Inc. Place; ST. LAWRENCE; ▲ Edwards; **209** ND-14; 🅿; z 13635; Ⓟ 487; Ⓒ 465
Edwards; MCD-Town; ST. LAWRENCE; ***209** ND-14; 🅿; z 13635; Ⓟ 1,083; Ⓒ 1,148
Edwards Hill; RMC Place; WARREN; ▲ Johnsburg; ***209** NG-18; mail Bakers Mills z 12811; rural
Edwards Park; RMC Place; COLUMBIA; ▲ Canaan; ***209** NL-20; mail Canaan z 12029; rural
Edwardsville; RMC Place; ST. LAWRENCE; ▲ Morristown; **209** NC-13; mail Hammond z 13646; ● 110
Eggertsville; RMC Place; ERIE; ▲ Amherst; **208** ND-4; elev. 653ft./199m.; 🅿; ★ **BUF**; z 14226
Egypt; RMC Place; MONROE; ▲ Perinton; ***208** NI-8; ★ **ROCH**; mail Fairport z 14450; ● 90
Einstein; RMC Place; BRONX; ★ **N.Y.**; mail Bronx z 10475; pop. incl. with New York (Inc. Place)
Elayne Meadows; RMC Place; SARATOGA; ▲ Waterford; ***209** NJ-19; ★ **A-S-T**; mail Waterford z 12188; ● 140
Elba; Inc. Place; GENESEE; ▲ Elba; **208** NI-6; elev. 761ft./232m.; 🅿; z 14058; Ⓟ 703; Ⓒ 696
Elba; MCD-Town; GENESEE; ***208** NI-6; 🅿; z 14058; Ⓟ 2,407; Ⓒ 2,439
Elbridge; Inc. Place; ONONDAGA; ▲ Elbridge; **209** NI-11; 🅿; ★ **SYR**; z 13060; Ⓟ 1,219; Ⓒ 1,103
Elbridge; MCD-Town; ONONDAGA; ***209** NI-11; 🅿; ★ **SYR**; z 13060; Ⓟ 6,192; Ⓒ 6,091
Eldred; RMC Place; SULLIVAN; ▲ Highland; **207** SB-3; 🅿; z 12732; ● 750
Elizabethtown; RMC Place; ⊡ ESSEX; ▲ Elizabethtown; **209** ND-19; elev. 591ft./180m.; 🅿 🅷; z 12932; ● 950
Elizabethtown; MCD-Town; ESSEX; ***209** ND-19; 🅿; z 12932; Ⓟ 1,314; Ⓒ 1,315
Elizaville; RMC Place; COLUMBIA; ▲ Gallatin, Clermont; **209** NM-19; elev. 284ft./87m.; 🅿; z 12523; ● 600
Elka Park; RMC Place; GREENE; ▲ Hunter; ***209** NM-18; 🅿; z 12427; ● 100
Elk Brook; RMC Place; DELAWARE; ▲ Hancock; ***209** NM-15; mail Roscoe z 12776; rural
Elk Creek; RMC Place; OTSEGO; ▲ Maryland; ***209** NK-16; elev. 1,333ft./406m.; mail Schenevus z 12155; ● 50
Elkdale; RMC Place; CATTARAUGUS; ▲ Little Valley; ***208** NL-4; elev. 1,481ft./451m.; mail Salamanca z 14779
Ellenburg; RMC Place; CLINTON; ▲ Ellenburg; **209** NA-18; 🅿; z 12933; ● 300
Ellenburg; MCD-Town; CLINTON; ***209** NB-18; 🅿; z 12933; Ⓟ 1,847; Ⓒ 1,812
Ellenburg Center; RMC Place; CLINTON; ▲ Ellenburg; **209** NB-18; elev. 1,203ft./367m.; 🅿; z 12934; ● 400
Ellenburg Depot; RMC Place; CLINTON; ▲ Altona, Ellenburg; **209** NA-18; 🅿; z 12935 & mail Ellenburg z 12933; ● 600
Ellenville; Inc. Place; ULSTER; ▲ Wawarsing, Shawangunk; **207** SA-5; 🅿 🅷; z 12428; Ⓟ 4,243; Ⓒ 4,130
Ellery; MCD-Town; CHAUTAUQUA; ***208** NL-2; ★ **JMST**; mail Maple Springs z 14756; Ⓟ 4,534; Ⓒ 4,576
Ellery Center; RMC Place; CHAUTAUQUA; ▲ Ellery; ***208** NL-2; elev. 1,758ft./536m.; ★ **JMST**; mail Bemus Point z 14712; ● 80
Ellicott; MCD-Town; CHAUTAUQUA; ***208** NM-2; ★ **JMST**; mail Falconer z 14733; Ⓟ 9,455; Ⓒ 9,280
Ellicott; RMC Place; ERIE; ▲ Orchard Park; **208** NJ-4; ★ **BUF**; mail Orchard Park z 14127; ● 550
Ellicottville; Inc. Place; CATTARAUGUS; ▲ Ellicottville; **208** NL-4; elev. 1,549ft./472m.; 🅿; z 14731; Ⓟ 513; Ⓒ 472
Ellicottville; MCD-Town; CATTARAUGUS; ***208** NL-4; 🅿; z 14731; Ⓟ 1,607; Ⓒ 1,738
Ellington; RMC Place; CHAUTAUQUA; ▲ Ellington; **208** NL-3; 🅿; z 14732; ● 500
Ellington; MCD-Town; CHAUTAUQUA; ***208** NL-3; 🅿; z 14732; Ⓟ 1,615; Ⓒ 1,639
Ellisburg; Inc. Place; JEFFERSON; ▲ Ellisburg; **209** NF-12; 🅿; z 13636; Ⓟ 246; Ⓒ 269
Ellisburg; MCD-Town; JEFFERSON; ***209** NF-12; 🅿; z 13636; Ⓟ 3,386; Ⓒ 3,541
Ellis Hollow; RMC Place; TOMPKINS; ▲ Dryden; ★ **ITH**; mail Ithaca z 14850; ● 100
Ellistown; RMC Place; TIOGA; ▲ Barton; ***209** NM-11; mail Waverly z 14892; ● 200
Elma; RMC Place; ERIE; ★ **BUF**
Elma; MCD-Town; ERIE; ***208** NJ-4; 🅿; ★ **BUF**; z 14059; Ⓟ 10,355; Ⓒ 11,304
Elma Center; CDP; ERIE; ▲ Elma; **208** NJ-4; ★ **BUF**; mail Elma z 14059; Ⓟ 2,354; Ⓒ 2,491
Elm Beach; RMC Place; SENECA; ▲ Romulus; ***208** NJ-10; mail Ovid z 14521; ● 100
Elmdale; RMC Place; ST. LAWRENCE; ▲ Gouverneur; ***209** ND-13; mail Gouverneur z 13642; rural
Elm Grove; RMC Place; OTSEGO; ▲ Morris; ***209** NK-14; mail Morris z 13808; ● 100
Elmhurst; RMC Place; CHAUTAUQUA; ▲ Ellicott; ***208** NM-2; ★ **JMST**; mail Jamestown z 14701
Elmhurst; RMC Place; QUEENS; **211** G-13; 🅿; ★ **N.Y.**; z 11373, z 11380 & mail Middle Village z 11379; pop. incl. with New York (Inc. Place)
Elmhurst A; RMC Place; QUEENS; 🅿; ★ **N.Y.**; z 11380; pop. incl. with New York (Inc. Place)
Elmira; Inc. Place; ⊡ CHEMUNG; **208** NM-10; elev. 873ft./266m.; 🅿 🅷 🅲 1,864 ■; ★ **ELM**; z 14901-05, z 14925; Ⓟ 33,724; Ⓒ 30,940; ◆ 29,084
Elmira; MCD-Town; CHEMUNG; ***208** NM-10; 🅿 🅲 1,864; ★ **ELM**; z 14901-05, z 14925; does not include the City of Elmira; Ⓟ 7,440; Ⓒ 7,199
Elmira Heights; Inc. Place; CHEMUNG; ▲ Horseheads, Elmira; **208** NM-10; 🅿; ★ **ELM**; z 14903; Ⓟ 4,359; Ⓒ 4,170
Elmira Heights North; RMC Place; CHEMUNG; ▲ Elmira; ***208** NM-10; ★ **ELM**; mail Elmira z 14903; pop. incl. with Horseheads (Inc. Place)
Elmont; CDP; NASSAU; ▲ Hempstead; **207** SF-7; elev. 43ft./13m.; 🅿; ★ **N.Y.**; z 11003; Ⓟ 28,612; Ⓒ 32,657; ◆ 31,017
Elm Park; RMC Place; RICHMOND; ***207** SG-6; ★ **N.Y.**; mail Staten Island z 10303; pop. incl. with New York (Inc. Place)
Elmsford; Inc. Place; WESTCHESTER; ▲ Greenburgh; **207** SH-7; 🅿; ★ **N.Y.**; z 10523; Ⓟ 3,938; Ⓒ 4,676
Elm Valley; RMC Place; ALLEGANY; ▲ Wellsville, Andover; **208** NM-6; mail Andover z 14806; ● 75
Elmwood; RMC Place; ONONDAGA; ★ **SYR**; mail Syracuse z 13207; pop. incl. with Syracuse (Inc. Place)
Elnora; RMC Place; SARATOGA; ▲ Clifton Park; ***209** NJ-19; ★ **A-S-T**; mail Clifton Park z 12065; ● 350
Elpis; RMC Place; ONEIDA; ▲ Vienna; ***209** NH-13; ★ **UT-R**; mail Camden z 13316; rural
Elsmere; RMC Place; ALBANY; ▲ Bethlehem; **209** NK-19; ★ **A-S-T**; mail Delmar z 12054; ● 4,200
Elsmere; RMC Place; WESTCHESTER; ★ **N.Y.**; pop. incl. with Mount Vernon (Inc. Place)
Eltingville; RMC Place; RICHMOND; **210** M-6; ★ **N.Y.**; mail Staten Island z 10312; pop. incl. with New York (Inc. Place)
Elton; RMC Place; CATTARAUGUS; ▲ Freedom; **208** NK-5; elev. 1,680ft./512m.; mail Delevan z 14042; ● 110
Elwood; CDP; SUFFOLK; ▲ Huntington; ***207** SF-9; 🅿; ★ **N.Y.**; z 11731; Ⓟ 10,916; Ⓒ 10,916
Elwood Farms; RMC Place; SUFFOLK; ▲ Huntington; ★ **N.Y.**; mail East Northport z 11731

Entries in **UPPERCASE** are counties.
Entries in **bold** have populations of 2,500 or more.
Names in parentheses are alternate names.

Inc. Place	Incorporated Place
RMC Place	Rand McNally Designated Place
CDP	Census Designated Place
MCD	Minor Civil Division

⊡ County Seat
▲ Minor Civil Division
elev. Elevation
🅿 Post Office
🅷 Hospital
🅲 College
■ Principal Business Center
★ Ranally Metro Area (RMA) Abbreviation
z Zip Code(s)
Ⓟ Previous Census Population
Ⓡ Revised Census Population
Ⓐ Annexation Population
● Rand McNally Population Estimate
Ⓒ Final Census Population
Ⓢ Special Census Population
◆ Estimated Population

For additional definitions see Glossary, Volume 1, and Introduction, Volume 2.

Embogcht; RMC Place; GREENE; ▲ Catskill; ***209** NM-19; ★ **KNGST**; mail Catskill z 12414; rural
Emerson; RMC Place; CAYUGA; ▲ Conquest; ***208** NI-10; elev. 408ft./124m.; mail Port Byron z 13140; rural
Emerson Hill; RMC Place; RICHMOND; ***207** SG-6; elev. 300ft./91m.; ★ **N.Y.**; mail Staten Island z 10304; pop. incl. with New York (Inc. Place)
Emeryville; RMC Place; ST. LAWRENCE; ▲ Fowler; ***209** ND-14; elev. 614ft./187m.; mail Gouverneur z 13642; rural
Eminence; RMC Place; SCHOHARIE; ▲ Summit, Blenheim; ***209** NK-17; elev. 2,024ft./617m.; mail Summit z 12175; ● 150
Emmons; RMC Place; OTSEGO; ▲ Oneonta; **209** NK-15; mail Oneonta z 13820; ● 150
Empeyville; RMC Place; ONEIDA; ▲ Florence; ***209** NH-13; elev. 1,000ft./305m.; mail Camden z 13316
Empire State; RMC Place; NEW YORK; ★ **N.Y.**; mail New York z 10001; pop. incl. with New York (Inc. Place)
Endicott; Inc. Place; BROOME; ▲ Union; **209** NM-12; 🅿 ■; ★ **BING**; z 13760-61, z 13763; Ⓟ 13,531; Ⓒ 13,038; ◆ 12,688
Endwell (Hooper); CDP; BROOME; ▲ Union; **209** NM-12; 🅿; ★ **BING**; z 13760, z 13762; Ⓟ 12,602; Ⓒ 11,706
Enfield (Enfield Center); RMC Place; TOMPKINS; ▲ Enfield; **208** NL-10; ★ **ITH**; mail Ithaca z 14850; ● 200
Enfield; MCD-Town; TOMPKINS; ***208** NL-10; ★ **ITH**; mail Ithaca z 14850; Ⓟ 3,054; Ⓒ 3,369
Enfield Center; TOMPKINS; see Enfield (RMC Place)
Ensenore; RMC Place; CAYUGA; ▲ Scipio; mail Moravia z 13118; rural
Ephratah; RMC Place; FULTON; ▲ Ephratah; **209** NI-17; elev. 666ft./203m.; mail Fort Plain z 13339; ● 160
Ephratah; MCD-Town; FULTON; ***209** NI-16; mail Fort Plain z 13339; Ⓟ 1,556; Ⓒ 1,693
ERIE; **208** NK-3; Ⓟ 968,532; Ⓒ 950,265; ◆ 896,428
Erieville; RMC Place; MADISON; ▲ Nelson; **209** NJ-13; 🅿; z 13061; ● 400
Erin; RMC Place; CHEMUNG; ▲ Erin; **208** NM-10; 🅿; z 14838; ● 350
Erin; MCD-Town; CHEMUNG; ***208** NM-10; 🅿; z 14838; Ⓟ 2,002; Ⓒ 2,054
Erwin; MCD-Town; STEUBEN; ***208** NM-9; mail Painted Post z 14870; Ⓟ 6,763; Ⓒ 7,227
Erwins; RMC Place; STEUBEN; ▲ Erwin; ***208** NM-9; mail Painted Post z 14870; rural
Escarpment; RMC Place; NIAGARA; ▲ Lewiston; **208** NA-2; ★ **BUF**; mail Lewiston z 14092; ● 1,200
Esopus; RMC Place; ULSTER; ▲ Esopus; **209** NN-18; 🅿; ★ **KNGST**; z 12429; ● 650
Esopus; MCD-Town; ULSTER; ***207** SA-6; 🅿; ★ **KNGST**; z 12429; Ⓟ 8,860; Ⓒ 9,331
Esperance; Inc. Place; SCHOHARIE; ▲ Esperance; **209** NJ-17; 🅿; z 12066; Ⓟ 324; Ⓒ 380
Esperance; MCD-Town; SCHOHARIE; ***209** NJ-17; 🅿; z 12066; Ⓟ 2,101; Ⓒ 2,043
Esplanade; RMC Place; BRONX; ★ **N.Y.**; mail Bronx z 10469; pop. incl. with New York (Inc. Place)
Essex; RMC Place; ESSEX; ▲ Essex; **209** ND-20; 🅿; z 12936; ● 400
Essex; MCD-Town; ESSEX; ***209** ND-20; 🅿; z 12936; Ⓟ 687; Ⓒ 713
ESSEX; **209** NE-19; Ⓟ 37,152; Ⓒ 38,851; ◆ 37,319
Etna; RMC Place; TOMPKINS; ▲ Dryden; **209** NK-11; 🅿; ★ **ITH**; z 13062; ● 550
Euclid; RMC Place; ONONDAGA; ▲ Clay; **209** NH-11; ★ **SYR**; mail Clay z 13041; ● 180
Evans; MCD-Town; ERIE; ***208** NK-3; ★ **BUF**; mail Angola z 14006; Ⓟ 17,478; Ⓒ 17,594
Evans Center; RMC Place; ERIE; ▲ Evans; ***208** NK-3; elev. 605ft./184m.; ★ **BUF**; mail Angola z 14006; ● 200
Evans Mills; Inc. Place; JEFFERSON; ▲ Le Ray; **209** NE-13; elev. 430ft./131m.; 🅿; ★ **WATN**; z 13637; Ⓟ 661; Ⓒ 605
Exeter; MCD-Town; OTSEGO; ***209** NJ-16; mail Burlington Flats z 13315; Ⓟ 967; Ⓒ 954
Exeter Center; RMC Place; OTSEGO; ▲ Exeter; ***209** NJ-16; mail Burlington Flats z 13315; ● 70

F

Fabius; Inc. Place; ONONDAGA; ▲ Fabius; **209** NJ-12; 🅿; z 13063; Ⓟ 310; Ⓒ 355
Fabius; MCD-Town; ONONDAGA; ***209** NJ-12; 🅿; z 13063; Ⓟ 1,760; Ⓒ 1,974
Factory Village; RMC Place; SARATOGA; ▲ Milton; **209** NI-18; ★ **A-S-T**; mail Ballston Spa z 12020; ● 115
Factoryville; RMC Place; ESSEX; ▲ Crown Point; ***209** NE-20; elev. 187ft./57m.; mail Crown Point z 12928
Fairdale; RMC Place; OSWEGO; ▲ Hannibal; ***208** NH-10; ★ **SYR**; mail Hannibal z 13074; rural
Fairfield; RMC Place; HERKIMER; ▲ Fairfield; **209** NI-15; mail Middleville z 13406; ● 150
Fairfield; MCD-Town; HERKIMER; ***209** NI-15; mail Middleville z 13406; Ⓟ 1,442; Ⓒ 1,607
Fairfield Gardens; RMC Place; ALBANY; ▲ Colonie; ★ **A-S-T**; mail Albany z 12205
Fair Harbor; RMC Place; SUFFOLK; ▲ Islip; ***207** SG-9; 🅿; ★ **N.Y.**; z 11706; summer pop. 1,000; ● 10
Fair Haven; Inc. Place; CAYUGA; ▲ Sterling; **208** NH-10; 🅿; z 13064; Ⓟ 895; Ⓒ 884
Fair Haven; ORLEANS; see Childs (RMC Place)
Fairlawn Estates; RMC Place; ALBANY; ▲ Colonie; ***209** NJ-19; ★ **A-S-T**; mail Latham z 12110; ● 2,040
Fairmount; CDP; ONONDAGA; ▲ Geddes, Camillus; **209** NI-11; ★ **SYR**; mail Camillus z 13031, Syracuse z 13219; Ⓟ 12,266; Ⓒ 10,795
Fair Oaks; RMC Place; ORANGE; ▲ Wallkill; ***207** SB-5; ★ **MIDD**; mail Middletown z 10940; ● 200
Fairport; Inc. Place; MONROE; ▲ Perinton; **208** NI-8; 🅿; ★ **ROCH**; z 14450; Ⓟ 5,943; Ⓒ 5,740
Fairview; RMC Place; ALLEGANY, CATTARAUGUS; ▲ Centerville, Centerville, Farmersville, Freedom, Rushford; ***208** NL-5; elev. 1,992ft./607m.; mail Farmersville Station z 14060; rural
Fairview; CDP; DUTCHESS; ▲ Poughkeepsie, Hyde Park; ***207** SA-7; ★ **POK**; mail Poughkeepsie z 12601; Ⓟ 4,811; Ⓒ 5,421
Fairview; CDP; WESTCHESTER; ▲ Greenburgh; **207** SI-7; ★ **N.Y.**; mail White Plains z 10603; Ⓒ 2,887
Fairview; RMC Place; WYOMING; ▲ Castile; ***208** NK-6; mail Castile z 14427; ● 70
Falconer; Inc. Place; CHAUTAUQUA; ▲ Ellicott; **208** NM-2; elev. 1,262ft./385m.; 🅿; ★ **JMST**; z 14733; Ⓟ 2,653; Ⓒ 2,540
Falcon Manor; RMC Place; NIAGARA; ▲ Niagara; ***208** NI-3; ★ **BUF**; mail Niagara Falls z 14304; ● 300
Falconwood; RMC Place; ERIE; ▲ Grand Island; **208** ND-2; ★ **BUF**; mail Grand Island z 14072; ● 1,500
Falls; RMC Place; NIAGARA; ★ **BUF**; mail Niagara Falls z 14303; pop. incl. with Niagara Falls (Inc. Place)
Fallsburg; RMC Place; SULLIVAN; ▲ Fallsburg; **207** SA-4; elev. 1,162ft./354m.; 🅿; z 12733; ● 800
Fallsburg; MCD-Town; SULLIVAN; ***207** SA-4; 🅿; z 12733; Ⓟ 11,445; Ⓒ 12,234
Fancher; RMC Place; ORLEANS; ▲ Murray; **208** NH-6; elev. 569ft./173m.; 🅿; ★ **ROCH**; z 14452; ● 300
Fargo; RMC Place; GENESEE; ▲ Darien; ***208** NJ-5; mail Corfu z 14036; rural
Farleys (Farleys Point); RMC Place; CAYUGA; ▲ Springport; ***208** NJ-10; ★ **SYR**; mail Union Springs z 13160; ● 50
Farleys Point; CAYUGA; see Farleys (RMC Place)
Farmers Mills; RMC Place; PUTNAM; ▲ Kent; **207** SC-7; ★ **N.Y.**; mail Carmel z 10512; ● 375
Farmersville; MCD-Town; CATTARAUGUS; ***208** NL-5; mail Farmersville Station z 14060; Ⓟ 869; Ⓒ 1,028
Farmersville Station; RMC Place; CATTARAUGUS; ▲ Farmersville; **208** NL-5; elev. 1,730ft./527m.; 🅿; z 14060; ● 300
Farmingdale; Inc. Place; NASSAU; ▲ Oyster Bay; **207** SJ-10; 🅿 🅲 6,253; ★ **N.Y.**; z 11735-37, z 11774; Ⓟ 8,022; Ⓒ 8,399
Farmington; RMC Place; ONTARIO; ▲ Farmington; **208** NI-8; 🅿; ★ **ROCH**; z 14425; ● 100
Farmington; MCD-Town; ONTARIO; ***208** NI-8; 🅿; ★ **ROCH**; z 14425; Ⓟ 10,381; Ⓒ 10,585
Farmingville; CDP; SUFFOLK; ▲ Brookhaven; **207** SF-10; elev. 105ft./32m.; 🅿; ★ **N.Y.**; z 11738; Ⓟ 14,842; Ⓒ 16,458
Farnham; Inc. Place; ERIE; ▲ Brant; **208** NK-3; elev. 631ft./192m.; 🅿; ★ **BUF**; z 14061; Ⓟ 427; Ⓒ 322
Farragut; RMC Place; KINGS; ★ **N.Y.**; mail Brooklyn z 11203; pop. incl. with New York (Inc. Place)
Far Rockaway; RMC Place; QUEENS; **211** K-15; elev. 25ft./8m.; 🅿; ★ **N.Y.**; z 11096, z 11690-95, z 11697; pop. incl. with New York (Inc. Place)
Fawn Ridge; RMC Place; ONONDAGA; ▲ Van Buren; ***209** NI-11; ★ **SYR**; mail Baldwinsville z 13027; ● 2,850
Fayette; RMC Place; SENECA; ▲ Fayette; **208** NJ-10; elev. 613ft./187m.; 🅿; z 13065; ● 430
Fayette; MCD-Town; SENECA; ***208** NJ-10; 🅿; z 13065; Ⓟ 3,636; Ⓒ 3,643
Fayetteville; Inc. Place; ONONDAGA; ▲ Manlius; **209** NI-12; 🅿; ★ **SYR**; z 13066; Ⓟ 4,248; Ⓒ 4,190
Fayville; RMC Place; SARATOGA; ▲ Providence; ***209** NI-18; mail Broadalbin z 12025; ● 250
Federal; RMC Place; MONROE; ★ **ROCH**; mail Rochester z 14614; pop. incl. with Rochester (Inc. Place)
Felts Mills; RMC Place; JEFFERSON; ▲ Rutland; **209** NE-13; 🅿; z 13638; ● 500
Fenimore; RMC Place; SARATOGA; ▲ Moreau; ***209** NH-19; ★ **GLFLS**; mail Glens Falls z 12801; ● 250
Fenner; MCD-Town; MADISON; ***209** NI-13; mail Cazenovia z 13035; Ⓟ 1,694; Ⓒ 1,680
Fenton; MCD-Town; BROOME; ***209** NM-13; ★ **BING**; mail Port Crane z 13833; Ⓟ 7,236; Ⓒ 6,909
Fentonville; RMC Place; CHAUTAUQUA; ▲ Aurora; ***208** NM-3; elev. 1,259ft./384m.; ★ **JMST**; mail Frewsburg z 14738; rural
Ferenbaugh; RMC Place; STEUBEN; ▲ Hornby; ***208** NM-9; elev. 1,092ft./333m.; mail Corning z 14830
Fergusons Corners; RMC Place; YATES; ▲ Benton; ***208** NJ-9; mail Geneva z 14456; rural
Fergusonville; RMC Place; DELAWARE; ▲ Davenport; ***209** NK-16; mail Schenevus z 12155; ● 35
Ferndale; RMC Place; SULLIVAN; ▲ Liberty; **209** NN-16; elev. 1,444ft./440m.; 🅿; z 12734; ● 850
Fernwood; RMC Place; OSWEGO; ▲ Richland; **209** NG-12; mail Pulaski z 13142; ● 200
Fernwood; RMC Place; SARATOGA; ***209** NH-19; mail South Glens Falls z 12803; ● 2,400
Fernwood; RMC Place; SULLIVAN; ▲ Fremont; ***207** SA-2; elev. 1,217ft./371m.; mail Long Eddy z 12760; rural
Ferry Village; RMC Place; ERIE; ▲ Grand Island; **208** ND-3; ★ **BUF**; mail Grand Island z 14072; ● 200
Feura Bush; RMC Place; ALBANY; ▲ New Scotland; **209** NK-18; 🅿; ★ **A-S-T**; z 12067; ● 450
Fieldston; RMC Place; BRONX; ★ **N.Y.**; mail Bronx z 10463; pop. incl. with New York (Inc. Place)
Filer Corners; RMC Place; OTSEGO; ▲ Morris; ***209** NK-14; mail Morris z 13808; rural
Fillmore; RMC Place; ALLEGANY; ▲ Hume; **208** NK-6; elev. 1,213ft./370m.; 🅿; z 14735; ● 400
Finchville; RMC Place; ORANGE; ▲ Mount Hope; ***207** SC-4; ★ **MIDD**; mail Middletown z 10940; rural
Findley Lake; RMC Place; CHAUTAUQUA; ▲ Mina; **208** NM-1; 🅿; z 14736; ● 800
Fine; RMC Place; ST. LAWRENCE; ▲ Fine; **209** ND-15; elev. 960ft./293m.; 🅿; z 13639; ● 300
Fine; MCD-Town; ST. LAWRENCE; ***209** NE-15; 🅿; z 13639; Ⓟ 1,813; Ⓒ 1,622
Fineview; RMC Place; JEFFERSON; ▲ Orleans; ***209** ND-12; 🅿; z 13640 & mail Thousand Island Park z 13692; ● 200
Finger Lakes Manor; RMC Place; ONTARIO; mail Canandaigua z 14424; pop. incl. with Canandaigua (Inc. Place)
Fink Basin; RMC Place; HERKIMER; ▲ Danube; ***209** NI-16; mail Little Falls z 13365; rural
Finnegans Corners; RMC Place; ORANGE; ▲ Goshen; ***207** SC-5; elev. 452ft./138m.; ★ **N.Y.**; mail Goshen z 10924; rural
Fire Island; CDP-Census Area Only; SUFFOLK; ***207** SG-10; ★ **N.Y.**; mail Ocean Beach z 11770; Ⓒ 310
Fire Island Pines; RMC Place; SUFFOLK; ▲ Brookhaven; **207** SF-10; 🅿; ★ **N.Y.**; z 11782; ● 900
Firthcliffe; CDP; ORANGE; ▲ New Windsor, Cornwall; ***207** SC-6; 🅷; ★ **NWBG**; mail Cornwall z 12518; Ⓟ 4,427; Ⓒ 4,970
Firthcliffe Heights; RMC Place; ORANGE; ▲ Cornwall; ***207** SC-6; ★ **NWBG**; mail Vails Gate z 12584; ● 350
Fish Creek; RMC Place; LEWIS; ▲ West Turin, Lewis; ***209** NG-13; mail Constableville z 13325; rural
Fish Creek; RMC Place; ULSTER; ▲ Saugerties; ***209** NM-18; ★ **KNGST**; mail Saugerties z 12477; rural
Fish Creek Landing; RMC Place; ONEIDA; ▲ Vienna; ***209** NH-13; ★ **UT-R**; mail Blossvale z 13308; rural
Fishers; RMC Place; ONTARIO; ▲ Victor; **208** NI-8; 🅿; ★ **ROCH**; z 14453; ● 400
Fishers Island; CDP; SUFFOLK; ▲ Southold; **207** SC-14; 🅿; z 06390; Ⓒ 289
Fishers Landing; RMC Place; JEFFERSON; ▲ Orleans; **209** ND-12; 🅿; z 13641; ● 180
Fisherville; RMC Place; CHEMUNG; ▲ Big Flats; ***208** NM-9; elev. 928ft./283m.; ★ **ELM**; mail Elmira z 14903; ● 200
Fish House; RMC Place; FULTON; ▲ Northampton; ***209** NI-18; ★ **A-S-T**; mail Broadalbin z 12025
Fishkill; Inc. Place; DUTCHESS; ▲ Fishkill; **207** SB-7; 🅿; ★ **POK**; z 12524; Ⓟ 1,957; Ⓒ 1,735
Fishkill; MCD-Town; DUTCHESS; ***207** SB-7; 🅿; ★ **POK**; z 12524; Ⓟ 17,655; Ⓒ 20,258; Ⓡ 19,256; ◆ 22,573
Fishkill Plains; RMC Place; DUTCHESS; ▲ East Fishkill; **207** SB-7; elev. 274ft./84m.; ★ **POK**; mail Wappingers Falls z 12590; ● 175
Fishs Eddy; RMC Place; DELAWARE; ▲ Hancock; **209** NM-15; 🅿; z 13774; ● 350
Five Corners; RMC Place; CAYUGA; ***208** NK-10; mail Genoa z 13071; rural
Five Corners; RMC Place; GENESEE; ▲ Oakfield; ***208** NI-6; mail Oakfield z 14125; rural
Five Corners; RMC Place; MADISON; ***209** NJ-14; mail Oneida z 13421; pop. incl. with Oneida (Inc. Place)
Five Corners; RMC Place; ONEIDA; ▲ Sangerfield; ***209** NJ-14; elev. 1,409ft./429m.; mail Waterville z 13480; rural
Fivemile Point; RMC Place; BROOME; ▲ Kirkwood; ***209** NM-13; ★ **BING**; mail Kirkwood z 13795; ● 400
Five Points; RMC Place; ONTARIO; ▲ Phelps; ***208** NI-9; mail Geneva z 14456; rural
Flackville; RMC Place; ST. LAWRENCE; ▲ Lisbon; **209** NB-14; elev. 364ft./111m.; mail Ogdensburg z 13669; ● 110
Flanders; CDP; SUFFOLK; ▲ Southampton; **207** SE-11; elev. 12ft./4m.; 🅿; z 11901; Ⓟ 3,231; Ⓒ 3,646; Ⓡ 3,643
Flatbrook; RMC Place; COLUMBIA; ▲ Canaan; ***209** NL-20; elev. 949ft./289m.; mail Canaan z 12029; rural
Flatbush; RMC Place; KINGS; **211** J-11; ★ **N.Y.**; mail Brooklyn z 11226; pop. incl. with New York (Inc. Place)
Flatbush; RMC Place; ULSTER; ▲ Saugerties; ***209** NM-18; elev. 204ft./62m.; ★ **KNGST**; mail Saugerties z 12477; rural
Flat Creek; RMC Place; MONTGOMERY; ▲ Root; ***209** NJ-17; mail Canajoharie z 13317; rural
Flat Creek; RMC Place; SCHOHARIE; ▲ Gilboa; ***209** NL-17; mail Gilboa z 12076; rural
Flatlands; RMC Place; KINGS; ***207** SG-7; ★ **N.Y.**; mail Brooklyn z 11234; pop. incl. with New York (Inc. Place)
Fleetwood; RMC Place; WESTCHESTER; ***207** SE-7; 🅿; ★ **N.Y.**; z 10552; pop. incl. with Mount Vernon (Inc. Place)
Fleischmanns; Inc. Place; DELAWARE; **209** NM-17; elev. 1,500ft./457m.; 🅿; z 12430; Ⓟ 351; Ⓒ 351
Fleming; RMC Place; CAYUGA; ▲ Fleming; **208** NJ-10; elev. 908ft./277m.; ★ **SYR**; mail Auburn z 13021; ● 220
Fleming; MCD-Town; CAYUGA; ***208** NJ-10; ★ **SYR**; mail Auburn z 13021; Ⓟ 2,644; Ⓒ 2,647
Flemingsville; TIOGA; see Flemingville (RMC Place)
Flemingville (Flemingsville); RMC Place; TIOGA; ▲ Owego; ***209** NM-11; ★ **BING**; mail Owego z 13827; rural
Flint; RMC Place; ONTARIO; ▲ Seneca; ***208** NJ-9; mail Stanley z 14561; ● 100
Floral Park; Inc. Place; NASSAU; ▲ North Hempstead, Hempstead; **211** H-16; 🅿; ★ **N.Y.**; z 11001-05; Ⓟ 15,947; Ⓒ 15,967
Florence; RMC Place; ONEIDA; ▲ Florence; **209** NG-13; mail Camden z 13316; ● 130
Florence; MCD-Town; ONEIDA; ***209** NH-13; mail Camden z 13316; Ⓟ 852; Ⓒ 1,086
Florence Hill; RMC Place; ONEIDA; ▲ Florence; ***209** NH-13; mail Camden z 13316; rural
Florida; MCD-Town; MONTGOMERY; ***209** NJ-17; mail Amsterdam z 12010; Ⓟ 2,637; Ⓒ 2,731
Florida; Inc. Place; ORANGE; ▲ Goshen, Warwick; **207** SC-5; 🅿; ★ **N.Y.**; z 10921; Ⓟ 2,497; Ⓒ 2,571
Floridaville; RMC Place; CAYUGA; ▲ Ira; ***209** NH-11; mail Cato z 13033; rural
Flower Hill; Inc. Place; NASSAU; ▲ North Hempstead; **211** F-16; ★ **N.Y.**; mail Port Washington z 11050; Ⓟ 4,490; Ⓒ 4,508
Flowers; RMC Place; BROOME; ▲ Windsor; ***209** NM-13; ★ **BING**; mail Windsor z 13865; rural
Floyd; RMC Place; ONEIDA; ▲ Floyd; **209** NH-14; elev. 565ft./172m.; ★ **UT-R**; mail Rome z 13440; ● 300
Floyd; MCD-Town; ONEIDA; ***209** NH-14; ★ **UT-R**; mail Rome z 13440; Ⓟ 3,856; Ⓒ 3,869
Flushing; RMC Place; QUEENS; **211** G-13; elev. 50ft./15m.; 🅿; ★ **N.Y.**; z 11351-52, z 11354-75, z 11377-81, z 11385-86, z 11390; pop. incl. with New York (Inc. Place)
Fluvanna; RMC Place; CHAUTAUQUA; ▲ Ellicott; **208** NM-2; ★ **JMST**; mail Jamestown z 14701; ● 900
Fly Creek; RMC Place; OTSEGO; ▲ Otsego; **209** NJ-15; 🅿; z 13337; ● 350
Flying Point; RMC Place; SUFFOLK; ▲ Southampton; ***207** SE-12; mail Water Mill z 11976
Fly Summit; RMC Place; WASHINGTON; ▲ Cambridge; ***209** NI-20; mail Greenwich z 12834
Folsomdale; RMC Place; WYOMING; ***208** NJ-5; elev. 981ft./299m.; mail Cowlesville z 14037; rural
Fonda; Inc. Place; ⊡ MONTGOMERY; ▲ Mohawk; **209** NI-17; elev. 294ft./90m.; 🅿; ★ **A-S-T**; z 12068; Ⓟ 1,007; Ⓒ 810
Foots Corners; RMC Place; LIVINGSTON; ▲ Conesus; ***208** NJ-7; mail Conesus z 14435; rural
Ford Corners; RMC Place; ALBANY; ▲ Westerlo; ***209** NK-18; mail Westerlo z 12193; rural
Fordham; RMC Place; BRONX; ***207** SF-7; ★ **N.Y.**; mail Bronx z 10458; pop. incl. with New York (Inc. Place)
Forest; RMC Place; CLINTON; ▲ Altona; **209** NA-19; elev. 801ft./244m.; mail Ellenburg Depot z 12935; ● 40
Forestburg (Forestburgh); RMC Place; SULLIVAN; ▲ Forestburgh; **207** SB-4; elev. 1,241ft./378m.; mail Forestburgh z 12777; ● 100
Forestburgh; SULLIVAN; see Forestburg (RMC Place)
Forestburgh; MCD-Town; SULLIVAN; ***207** SB-4; 🅿; z 12777 & mail Monticello z 12701; Ⓟ 614; Ⓒ 833
Forest Glen; RMC Place; ERIE; ***208** NJ-4; ★ **BUF**; mail Hamburg z 14075; pop. incl. with Hamburg (Inc. Place)
Forest Hills; RMC Place; QUEENS; 🅿; ★ **N.Y.**; z 11375; pop. incl. with New York (Inc. Place)
Forest Home; CDP; TOMPKINS; ▲ Ithaca; ***209** NL-11; ★ **ITH**; mail Ithaca z 14850; Ⓟ 1,125; Ⓒ 941
Forest Knolls; RMC Place; WESTCHESTER; ***207** SE-7; ★ **N.Y.**; mail New Rochelle z 10804; pop. incl. with New Rochelle (Inc. Place)
Forest Lawn; RMC Place; MONROE; ▲ Webster; ***208** NH-8; ★ **ROCH**; mail Webster z 14580; ● 300
Forest Park; RMC Place; CHAUTAUQUA; ▲ Westfield; ***208** NL-1; elev. 622ft./190m.; mail Westfield z 14787; summer pop. 150; rural
Forest Park; RMC Place; DUTCHESS; ▲ Red Hook; ***207** SA-7; ★ **POK**; mail Rhinebeck z 12572; ● 450
Forestport; RMC Place; ONEIDA; ▲ Forestport; **209** NG-14; 🅿; z 13338; ● 900
Forestport; MCD-Town; ONEIDA; ***209** NG-15; 🅿; z 13338; Ⓟ 1,556; Ⓒ 1,692
Forestport Station; RMC Place; ONEIDA; ▲ Forestport; ***209** NG-15; elev. 1,209ft./369m.; mail Forestport z 13338; ● 100
Forestville; Inc. Place; CHAUTAUQUA; ▲ Hanover; **208** NK-3; elev. 928ft./283m.; 🅿; z 14062; Ⓟ 738; Ⓒ 770
Forge Hollow; RMC Place; ONEIDA; ▲ Marshall; ***209** NI-14; mail Deansboro z 13328; rural
Forks; RMC Place; ERIE; ▲ Cheektowaga; ***208** NJ-4; elev. 659ft./201m.; ★ **BUF**; mail Buffalo z 14225
Forsonville; RMC Place; PUTNAM; ▲ Philipstown; ***207** SC-7; ★ **N.Y.**; mail Garrison z 10524; ● 85
Forsyth; RMC Place; CHAUTAUQUA; ▲ Ripley; ***208** NL-1; mail Ripley z 14775
Fort Ann; Inc. Place; WASHINGTON; ▲ Fort Ann; **209** NG-20; elev. 138ft./42m.; 🅿; z 12827; Ⓟ 419; Ⓒ 471
Fort Ann; MCD-Town; WASHINGTON; ***209** NG-20; 🅿; z 12827; Ⓟ 6,368; Ⓒ 6,417
Fort Covington; RMC Place; FRANKLIN; ▲ Fort Covington; **209** NA-16; elev. 181ft./55m.; 🅿; z 12937; ● 1,200
Fort Covington; MCD-Town; FRANKLIN; ***209** NA-16; 🅿; z 12937; Ⓟ 1,676; Ⓒ 1,645
Fort Covington Center; RMC Place; FRANKLIN; ▲ Fort Covington; ***209** NA-17; elev. 205ft./62m.; mail Fort Covington z 12937; rural
Fort Drum; CDP-Census Area Only; JEFFERSON; ▲ Le Ray; ***209** NE-13; elev. 650ft./198m.; 🅿; ★ **WATN**; z 13602-03; Ⓟ 11,578; Ⓒ 12,123
Fort Edward; Inc. Place; WASHINGTON; ▲ Fort Edward; **209** NH-19; elev. 144ft./44m.; 🅿; ★ **GLFLS**; z 12828; Ⓟ 3,561; Ⓒ 3,141
Fort Edward; MCD-Town; WASHINGTON; ***209** NH-19; 🅿; ★ **GLFLS**; z 12828; Ⓟ 6,330; Ⓒ 5,892
Fort George; RMC Place; NEW YORK; ★ **N.Y.**; mail New York z 10040; pop. incl. with New York (Inc. Place)
Fort Greene; RMC Place; KINGS; ***207** SF-7; ★ **N.Y.**; pop. incl. with New York (Inc. Place)
Fort Hamilton; RMC Place; KINGS; ***207** SG-6; 🅿; ★ **N.Y.**; z 11252 & mail Brooklyn z 11209; pop. incl. with New York (Inc. Place)
Fort Herkimer; RMC Place; HERKIMER; ▲ German Flatts; ***209** NI-15; mail Mohawk z 13407; rural
Fort Hunter; RMC Place; ALBANY; ▲ Guilderland; ***209** NJ-18; ★ **A-S-T**; mail Schenectady z 12303; ● 1,250
Fort Hunter; RMC Place; MONTGOMERY; ▲ Florida; **209** NI-17; 🅿; ★ **A-S-T**; z 12069; ● 325
Fort Jackson; RMC Place; ST. LAWRENCE; ▲ Lawrence, Hopkinton; **209** NB-16; elev. 598ft./182m.; 🅿; z 12965; ● 135
Fort Johnson; Inc. Place; MONTGOMERY; ▲ Amsterdam; **209** NI-17; 🅿; ★ **A-S-T**; z 12070; Ⓟ 615; Ⓒ 491
Fort Miller; RMC Place; WASHINGTON; ▲ Fort Edward; ***209** NH-19; ★ **GLFLS**; mail Fort Edward z 12828; ● 90
Fort Montgomery; CDP; ORANGE; ▲ Highlands; **207** SC-6; 🅿; ★ **N.Y.**; z 10922; Ⓟ 1,450; Ⓒ 1,418
Fort Niagara Beach; RMC Place; NIAGARA; ▲ Porter; ***208** NH-3; elev. 282ft./86m.; ★ **BUF**; mail Youngstown z 14174; ● 100
Fort Orange; RMC Place; ALBANY; ★ **A-S-T**; mail Albany z 12206; pop. incl. with Albany (Inc. Place)
Fort Plain (South Fort Plain); Inc. Place; MONTGOMERY; ▲ Canajoharie, Minden; **209** NJ-16; elev. 317ft./97m.; 🅿; z 13339; Ⓟ 2,416; Ⓒ 2,288
Fort Salonga; CDP; SUFFOLK; ▲ Smithtown, Huntington; **207** SG-11; elev. 31ft./9m.; 🅿; ★ **N.Y.**; z 11768; Ⓟ 9,176; Ⓒ 9,634
Fortsville; RMC Place; SARATOGA; ▲ Moreau; ***209** NH-19; ★ **GLFLS**; mail Gansevoort z 12831; rural
Fort Washington; RMC Place; NEW YORK; ★ **N.Y.**; mail New York z 10032; pop. incl. with New York (Inc. Place)
Foster; RMC Place; TIOGA; ▲ Owego; ***209** NM-12; ★ **BING**; mail Owego z 13827; rural
Fosterdale; RMC Place; SULLIVAN; ▲ Cochecton; **207** SB-3; elev. 1,294ft./394m.; mail Cochecton z 12726; ● 150
Fosterville; RMC Place; CAYUGA; ▲ Aurelius; ***208** NI-10; ★ **SYR**; mail Auburn z 13021; rural
Foster Wheeler Junction; RMC Place; LIVINGSTON; mail Dansville z 14437; pop. incl. with Dansville (Inc. Place)
Fourth Lake; RMC Place; WARREN; ▲ Lake Luzerne; **209** NH-19; elev. 690ft./210m.; mail Lake Luzerne z 12846; ● 300
Fowler; RMC Place; ST. LAWRENCE; ▲ Fowler; **209** ND-14; elev. 588ft./179m.; mail Gouverneur z 13642; ● 300
Fowler; MCD-Town; ST. LAWRENCE; ***209** ND-14; mail Gouverneur z 13642; Ⓟ 1,885; Ⓒ 2,180
Fowlersville; RMC Place; LEWIS; ▲ Lyonsdale; ***209** NG-14; mail Port Leyden z 13433; rural
Fowlerville; RMC Place; LIVINGSTON; ▲ York; **208** NJ-7; elev. 639ft./195m.; ★ **ROCH**; mail Caledonia z 14423; ● 175
Fowlerville; RMC Place; SULLIVAN; ▲ Forestburgh; ***207** SB-3; mail Forestburgh z 12777; rural
Fox Hill; RMC Place; SARATOGA; ▲ Edinburg; ***209** NH-18; mail Northville z 12134; rural
Fox Hills; RMC Place; RICHMOND; **210** K-8; ★ **N.Y.**; mail Staten Island z 10304; pop. incl. with New York (Inc. Place)
Fox Meadows; RMC Place; WESTCHESTER; ★ **N.Y.**; mail Scarsdale z 10583; pop. incl. with Scarsdale (Inc. Place)
Frankfort; Inc. Place; HERKIMER; ▲ Frankfort; **209** NI-15; 🅿; ★ **UT-R**; z 13340; Ⓟ 2,693; Ⓒ 2,537
Frankfort; MCD-Town; HERKIMER; ***209** NI-15; 🅿; ★ **UT-R**; z 13340; Ⓟ 7,494; Ⓒ 7,478
Frankfort Center; RMC Place; HERKIMER; ▲ Frankfort; ***209** NI-15; ★ **UT-R**; mail Frankfort z 13340; rural
Franklin; Inc. Place; DELAWARE; ▲ Franklin; **209** NL-15; 🅿; z 13775, z 13846; Ⓟ 409; Ⓒ 402
Franklin; MCD-Town; DELAWARE; ***209** NL-15; 🅿; z 13775, z 13846; Ⓟ 2,471; Ⓒ 2,621
Franklin; MCD-Town; FRANKLIN; ***209** NC-18; mail Bloomingdale z 12913; Ⓟ 1,016; Ⓒ 1,197
Franklin; RMC Place; ONONDAGA; mail Syracuse z 13218; pop. incl. with Syracuse (Inc. Place)
FRANKLIN; **209** NC-17; Ⓟ 46,540; Ⓒ 51,134; ◆ 50,646
Franklin Park; RMC Place; ONONDAGA; ▲ De Witt; **208** NE-9; ★ **SYR**; mail East Syracuse z 13057; ● 2,600
Franklin Springs; RMC Place; ONEIDA; ▲ Kirkland; **209** NI-14; 🅿; ★ **UT-R**; z 13341; ● 300
Franklin Square; CDP; NASSAU; ▲ Hempstead; **211** H-17; elev. 68ft./21m.; 🅿; ★ **N.Y.**; z 11010; Ⓟ 28,205; Ⓒ 29,342; ◆ 27,866
Franklinton; RMC Place; SCHOHARIE; ▲ Broome; ***209** NK-17; mail Middleburgh z 12122; ● 25
Franklinville; Inc. Place; CATTARAUGUS; ▲ Franklinville; **208** NL-5; 🅿; z 14737; Ⓟ 1,739; Ⓒ 1,855
Franklinville; MCD-Town; CATTARAUGUS; ***208** NL-5; 🅿; z 14737; Ⓟ 2,968; Ⓒ 3,128
Fraser; RMC Place; DELAWARE; ▲ Delhi; **209** NL-15; mail Delhi z 13753; ● 30
Frear Park; RMC Place; RENSSELAER; ***209** NJ-19; ★ **A-S-T**; pop. incl. with Troy (Inc. Place)
Fredonia; Inc. Place; CHAUTAUQUA; ▲ Pomfret; **208** NK-2; elev. 728ft./222m.; 🅿 🅲 5,406; z 14063; Ⓟ 10,436; Ⓒ 10,706
Freedom; RMC Place; CATTARAUGUS; ▲ Freedom; **208** NK-5; 🅿; z 14065; ● 200
Freedom; MCD-Town; CATTARAUGUS; ***208** NK-5; 🅿; z 14065; Ⓟ 2,018; Ⓒ 2,493
Freedom Plains; RMC Place; DUTCHESS; ▲ La Grange; ***207** SB-7; ★ **POK**; mail Pleasant Valley z 12569; ● 160
Freehold; RMC Place; GREENE; ▲ Greenville; **209** NL-18; elev. 428ft./130m.; 🅿; z 12431; ● 500
Freeman; RMC Place; STEUBEN; ▲ Tuscarora; ***208** NM-8; mail Addison z 14801; ● 75
Freeport; Inc. Place; NASSAU; ▲ Hempstead; **207** SG-8; 🅿 ■; ★ **N.Y.**; z 11520; Ⓟ 39,894; Ⓒ 43,783; ◆ 42,329
Freetown; MCD-Town; CORTLAND; ***209** NK-12; mail Marathon z 13803; Ⓟ 688; Ⓒ 789
Freetown; RMC Place; SUFFOLK; ▲ East Hampton; ***207** SE-13; mail East Hampton z 11937
Freetown Corners; RMC Place; CORTLAND; ▲ Freetown; ***209** NK-12; mail Marathon z 13803; rural
Freeville; Inc. Place; TOMPKINS; ▲ Dryden; **209** NK-11; elev. 1,048ft./319m.; 🅿; ★ **ITH**; z 13068; Ⓟ 437; Ⓒ 505
Fremont; RMC Place; STEUBEN; ▲ Fremont; ***208** NL-7; mail Arkport z 14807; ● 100
Fremont; MCD-Town; STEUBEN; ***208** NL-7; mail Arkport z 14807; Ⓟ 912; Ⓒ 964
Fremont; SULLIVAN; see Fremont Center (RMC Place)
Fremont; MCD-Town; SULLIVAN; ***207** SA-2; mail Fremont Center z 12736; Ⓟ 1,332; Ⓒ 1,391
Fremont Center (Fremont); RMC Place; SULLIVAN; ▲ Fremont; **209** NN-15; elev. 1,248ft./380m.; 🅿; z 12736; ● 130
Fremont Heights; RMC Place; ONONDAGA; ▲ Manlius; **208** NF-10; ★ **SYR**; mail East Syracuse z 13057; ● 150
Fremont Hills; RMC Place; ONONDAGA; ▲ Manlius; ***209** NI-12; ★ **SYR**; mail East Syracuse z 13057; ● 1,100
French Creek; MCD-Town; CHAUTAUQUA; ***208** NM-1; mail Clymer z 14724; Ⓟ 916; Ⓒ 935
Frenchville; RMC Place; ONEIDA; ▲ Western; ***209** NH-14; mail Westernville z 13486; ● 80
French Woods; RMC Place; DELAWARE; ▲ Hancock; ***207** SA-2; mail Hancock z 13783; ● 130
Fresh Meadows; RMC Place; QUEENS; **211** H-14; 🅿; ★ **N.Y.**; z 11365-66; pop. incl. with New York (Inc. Place)
Fresh Pond; RMC Place; QUEENS; ***207** SF-7; ★ **N.Y.**; mail Ridgewood z 11385; pop. incl. with New York (Inc. Place)
Fresh Pond Junction; RMC Place; QUEENS; ***207** SF-7; ★ **N.Y.**; pop. incl. with New York (Inc. Place)
Frewsburg; CDP; CHAUTAUQUA; ▲ Carroll; **208** NM-3; 🅿; ★ **JMST**; z 14738; Ⓟ 1,817; Ⓒ 1,965
Freysbush; RMC Place; MONTGOMERY; ▲ Minden; ***209** NJ-16; mail Fort Plain z 13339; ● 60
Friend; RMC Place; YATES; ▲ Jerusalem; ***208** NK-9; elev. 997ft./304m.; mail Penn Yan z 14527; rural
Friendship; CDP; ALLEGANY; ▲ Friendship; **208** NL-6; elev. 1,514ft./461m.; 🅿; z 14739; Ⓟ 1,423; Ⓒ 1,176
Friendship; MCD-Town; ALLEGANY; ***208** NL-6; 🅿; z 14739; Ⓟ 2,185; Ⓒ 1,927
Friends Point; RMC Place; WARREN; ▲ Hague; ***209** NF-20; mail Hague z 12836; rural
Frontenac; RMC Place; JEFFERSON; ▲ Clayton; ***209** ND-12; elev. 260ft./79m.; 🅿; z 13624; summer pop. 250
Fruitland; RMC Place; WAYNE; ▲ Ontario; ***208** NH-8; ★ **ROCH**; mail Ontario z 14519; rural
Fruit Valley; RMC Place; OSWEGO; ▲ Oswego; **208** NG-10; elev. 266ft./81m.; mail Oswego z 13126; ● 50
Fullerville; RMC Place; ST. LAWRENCE; ▲ Fowler; ***209** ND-14; elev. 708ft./216m.; mail Gouverneur z 13642; ● 100
Fulmer Valley; RMC Place; ALLEGANY; ▲ Independence; ***208** NM-7; elev. 1,851ft./564m.; mail Andover z 14806; rural
Fulton; Inc. Place; OSWEGO; **209** NH-11; elev. 364ft./111m.; 🅿 🅷; z 13069; Ⓟ 12,929; Ⓒ 11,855
Fulton; MCD-Town; SCHOHARIE; ***209** NK-17; mail Middleburgh z 12122; Ⓟ 1,514; Ⓒ 1,495
FULTON; **209** NI-17; Ⓟ 54,191; Ⓒ 55,073; ◆ 55,044
Fultonham; RMC Place; SCHOHARIE; ▲ Fulton; **209** NK-17; elev. 706ft./215m.; 🅿; z 12071; ● 400
Fultonville; Inc. Place; MONTGOMERY; ▲ Glen; **209** NI-17; 🅿; z 12016, z 12072; Ⓟ 748; Ⓒ 710
Furnace Brook; RMC Place; ORANGE; ▲ Warwick; ★ **N.Y.**; mail Greenwood Lake z 10925
Furnaceville; RMC Place; WAYNE; ▲ Ontario; ***208** NH-8; elev. 352ft./107m.; ★ **ROCH**; mail Ontario z 14519
Furnace Woods; RMC Place; WESTCHESTER; ▲ Cortlandt; ***207** SD-7; ★ **N.Y.**; mail Cortlandt Manor z 10567; ● 650
Furniss; RMC Place; OSWEGO; ▲ Oswego; ***209** NH-11; mail Oswego z 13126; rural

G

Gabriels; RMC Place; FRANKLIN; ▲ Brighton; **209** NC-17; 🅿; z 12939; ● 250
Gage; YATES; see Bellona (RMC Place)
Gaines; RMC Place; ORLEANS; ▲ Gaines; **208** NH-6; elev. 428ft./130m.; mail Albion z 14411; ● 200
Gaines; MCD-Town; ORLEANS; ***208** NH-6; mail Albion z 14411; Ⓟ 3,025; Ⓒ 3,740
Gainesville; Inc. Place; WYOMING; ▲ Gainesville; **208** NK-6; 🅿; z 14066; Ⓟ 340; Ⓒ 304
Gainesville; MCD-Town; WYOMING; ***208** NK-6; 🅿; z 14066; Ⓟ 2,288; Ⓒ 2,333
Galatia; RMC Place; CORTLAND; ▲ Marathon, Freetown; ***209** NK-12; mail Marathon z 13803; rural
Gale; RMC Place; ST. LAWRENCE; ▲ Piercefield; ***209** ND-16; elev. 1,528ft./466m.; mail Piercefield z 12973; rural
Galen; MCD-Town; WAYNE; ***208** NI-9; mail Clyde z 14433; Ⓟ 4,413; Ⓒ 4,439
Galena; CHENANGO; see North Norwich (RMC Place)
Galeville; CDP; ONONDAGA; ▲ Salina; **208** NE-8; ★ **SYR**; mail Liverpool z 13088; Ⓒ 4,476
Galeville; RMC Place; ULSTER; ▲ Shawangunk; ***207** SB-6; mail Wallkill z 12589; rural
Gallatin; COLUMBIA; see Gallatinville (RMC Place)
Gallatin; MCD-Town; COLUMBIA; ***209** NM-19; mail Pine Plains z 12567; Ⓟ 1,658; Ⓒ 1,499
Gallatinville (Gallatin); RMC Place; COLUMBIA; ▲ Gallatin; ***209** NM-19; mail Pine Plains z 12567; ● 160
Gallupville; RMC Place; SCHOHARIE; ▲ Wright; **209** NK-17; 🅿; z 12073; ● 325
Galway; Inc. Place; SARATOGA; ▲ Galway; **209** NI-18; 🅿; ★ **A-S-T**; z 12074; Ⓟ 151; Ⓒ 214
Galway; MCD-Town; SARATOGA; ***209** NI-18; 🅿; ★ **A-S-T**; z 12074; Ⓟ 3,266; Ⓒ 3,589
Galway Lake; RMC Place; SARATOGA; ▲ Galway; ***209** NI-18; ★ **A-S-T**; mail Broadalbin z 12025, Galway z 12074; rural
Ganahgote; RMC Place; ULSTER; ▲ Gardiner; ***207** SB-6; mail Gardiner z 12525; rural
Gang Mills; CDP; STEUBEN; ▲ Erwin; **208** NM-9; mail Painted Post z 14870; Ⓟ 2,738; Ⓒ 3,304
Gansevoort; RMC Place; SARATOGA; ▲ Northumberland; **209** NH-19; 🅿; ★ **GLFLS**; z 12831; ● 600
Garbutt; RMC Place; MONROE; ▲ Wheatland; ***208** NI-7; ★ **ROCH**; mail Scottsville z 14546; ● 100
Garden City; Inc. Place; NASSAU; ▲ North Hempstead, Hempstead; **211** H-18; 🅿 🅲 8,333 ■; ★ **N.Y.**; z 11530-31, z 11535, z 11599; Ⓟ 21,686; Ⓒ 21,672; ◆ 20,425
Garden City Park; CDP; NASSAU; ▲ North Hempstead; **211** H-17; 🅿; ★ **N.Y.**; z 11040; Ⓟ 7,437; Ⓒ 7,554
Garden City South; CDP; NASSAU; ▲ Hempstead; **211** H-17; 🅿; ★ **N.Y.**; z 11530; Ⓟ 4,073; Ⓒ 3,974
Gardenville; RMC Place; ERIE; ▲ West Seneca; ★ **BUF**; mail Buffalo z 14224
Gardiner; CDP; ULSTER; ▲ Gardiner; **207** SB-6; elev. 308ft./94m.; 🅿; z 12525; Ⓒ 856
Gardiner; MCD-Town; ULSTER; ***207** SB-6; 🅿; z 12525; Ⓟ 4,278; Ⓒ 5,238
Gardiners Bay Estates; RMC Place; SUFFOLK; ▲ Southold; mail East Marion z 11939; ● 100
Gardnersville; RMC Place; SCHOHARIE; ▲ Seward; ***209** NJ-16; elev. 1,219ft./372m.; mail Cobleskill z 12043; ● 75
Gardnertown; CDP; ORANGE; ▲ Newburgh; **207** SB-6; ★ **NWBG**; mail Albany z 12250; Ⓟ 4,209; Ⓒ 4,533
Garfield; RMC Place; RENSSELAER; ▲ Stephentown; ***209** NK-20; mail Stephentown z 12168; rural
Garland; RMC Place; MONROE; ▲ Clarkson; ***208** NH-6; elev. 431ft./131m.; ★ **ROCH**; mail Brockport z 14420; ● 60
Garlinghouse; RMC Place; ONTARIO; ▲ Naples; ***208** NK-8; mail Naples z 14512; rural
Garnerville; RMC Place; ROCKLAND; ***207** SD-6; elev. 200ft./61m.; 🅿; ★ **N.Y.**; z 10923; pop. incl. with West Haverstraw (Inc. Place)
Garnet Lake; RMC Place; WARREN; ▲ Johnsburg; **209** NG-18; mail Johnsburg z 12843; rural
Garoga; RMC Place; FULTON; ▲ Ephratah; ***209** NI-17; mail Johnstown z 12095; ● 90
Garrattsville; RMC Place; OTSEGO; ▲ New Lisbon; **209** NK-15; 🅿; z 13342; ● 150
Garrison; RMC Place; PUTNAM; ▲ Philipstown; **207** SC-6; elev. 21ft./6m.; 🅿; ★ **N.Y.**; z 10524; ● 800
Garrison Four Corners; RMC Place; PUTNAM; ▲ Philipstown; ***207** SC-6; elev. 150ft./46m.; ★ **N.Y.**; mail Garrison z 10524; rural
Garwoods (Whitney Crossings); RMC Place; ALLEGANY; ▲ Burns; ***208** NK-7; elev. 1,273ft./388m.; mail Canaseraga z 14822
Gaskill; RMC Place; TIOGA; ▲ Owego; ***209** NM-12; ★ **BING**; mail Owego z 13827
Gasport; CDP; NIAGARA; ▲ Royalton; **208** NH-4; 🅿; z 14067; Ⓟ 1,336; Ⓒ 1,248
Gates; MCD-Town; MONROE; ***208** NI-7; ★ **ROCH**; mail Rochester z 14624; Ⓒ 29,275; ◆ 28,855
Gates Center; RMC Place; MONROE; ▲ Gates; **208** NI-7; ★ **ROCH**; mail Rochester z 14624; ● 29,300
Gates-North Gates; CDP-Census Area Only; MONROE; ▲ Gates; ***208** NI-7; ★ **ROCH**; mail Rochester z 14626; Ⓟ 14,995; Ⓒ 15,138
Gay Ridge Estates; RMC Place; WESTCHESTER; ▲ Yorktown; ★ **N.Y.**; mail Yorktown Heights z 10598
Gayville; RMC Place; OSWEGO; ▲ Constantia; ***209** NH-12; elev. 471ft./144m.; ★ **SYR**; mail Constantia z 13044
Geddes; MCD-Town; ONONDAGA; ***209** NI-11; ★ **SYR**; mail Syracuse z 13209; Ⓟ 17,677; Ⓒ 17,740
Gedney; RMC Place; WESTCHESTER; ★ **N.Y.**; mail White Plains z 10605; pop. incl. with White Plains (Inc. Place)
Geers Corners; RMC Place; ST. LAWRENCE; ▲ Pitcairn; ***209** ND-14; elev. 776ft./237m.; mail Harrisville z 13648; rural
Genegantslet; RMC Place; CHENANGO; ▲ Greene; ***209** NL-13; mail Greene z 13778; ● 65
Genesee; MCD-Town; ALLEGANY; ***208** NM-5; mail Little Genesee z 14754; Ⓟ 1,672; Ⓒ 1,803
GENESEE; **208** NJ-6; Ⓟ 60,060; Ⓒ 60,370; ◆ 57,586
Genesee Falls; MCD-Town; WYOMING; ***208** NK-6; mail Portageville z 14536; Ⓟ 488; Ⓒ 460
Geneseo; Inc. Place; ⊡ LIVINGSTON; ▲ Geneseo; **208** NJ-7; 🅿 🅲 5,530; ★ **ROCH**; z 14454; Ⓟ 7,187; Ⓒ 7,579
Geneseo; MCD-Town; LIVINGSTON; ***208** NJ-7; 🅿 🅲 5,530; ★ **ROCH**; z 14454; Ⓟ 9,178; Ⓒ 9,654
Geneva; Inc. Place; ONTARIO, SENECA; **208** NJ-9; 🅿 🅷 🅲 1,928 ■; z 14456; Ⓟ 14,143; Ⓒ 13,617; ◆ 13,383
Geneva; MCD-Town; ONTARIO; ***208** NJ-9; 🅿 🅲 1,928; z 14456; does not include the City of Geneva; Ⓟ 2,967; Ⓒ 3,289
Genoa; RMC Place; CAYUGA; ▲ Genoa; **209** NK-11; 🅿; z 13071; ● 500
Genoa; MCD-Town; CAYUGA; ***208** NK-10; 🅿; z 13071; Ⓟ 1,868; Ⓒ 1,914
Georgetown; RMC Place; MADISON; ▲ Georgetown; **209** NJ-13; 🅿; z 13072; ● 500
Georgetown; MCD-Town; MADISON; ***209** NJ-13; 🅿; z 13072; Ⓟ 932; Ⓒ 946
Georgetown; RMC Place; MONROE; ▲ Perinton; ***208** NI-8; ★ **ROCH**; mail Fairport z 14450; ● 1,050
Georgtown Station; RMC Place; MADISON; ▲ Georgetown; ***209** NJ-13; mail Eaton z 13334; rural
German; RMC Place; CHENANGO; ▲ German; **209** NK-13; mail Cincinnatus z 13040; ● 60
German; MCD-Town; CHENANGO; ***209** NK-13; mail Cincinnatus z 13040; Ⓟ 311; Ⓒ 378
German Flatts; MCD-Town; HERKIMER; ***209** NI-15; mail Mohawk z 13407; Ⓟ 14,345; Ⓒ 13,629
Germantown; CDP; COLUMBIA; ▲ Germantown; **209** NM-19; elev. 138ft./42m.; 🅿; z 12526; Ⓒ 862
Germantown; MCD-Town; COLUMBIA; ***209** NM-19; 🅿; z 12526; Ⓟ 2,010; Ⓒ 2,018
Germantown; RMC Place; ORANGE; ***207** SC-4; elev. 445ft./136m.; mail Port Jervis z 12771; pop. incl. with Port Jervis (Inc. Place)
German Village; RMC Place; MONROE; ▲ Irondequoit; ***208** NH-7; ★ **ROCH**; mail Rochester z 14617
Germonds; RMC Place; ROCKLAND; ▲ Clarkstown; ***207** SD-6; elev. 290ft./88m.; ★ **N.Y.**; mail New City z 10956
Gerritsen; RMC Place; KINGS; **211** L-11; ★ **N.Y.**; pop. incl. with New York (Inc. Place)
Gerry; RMC Place; CHAUTAUQUA; ▲ Gerry; **208** NL-2; elev. 1,302ft./397m.; 🅿; z 14740; ● 800
Gerry; MCD-Town; CHAUTAUQUA; ***208** NL-2; 🅿; z 14740; Ⓟ 2,147; Ⓒ 2,054
Getman Corners; RMC Place; HERKIMER; ▲ Columbia; ***209** NI-15; mail Mohawk z 13407; rural
Getzville; RMC Place; ERIE; ▲ Amherst; **208** NI-4; elev. 582ft./177m.; 🅿; ★ **BUF**; z 14068; ● 2,300
Geyser Crest; RMC Place; SARATOGA; ▲ Milton; ***209** NI-19; elev. 334ft./102m.; ★ **A-S-T**; mail Saratoga Springs z 12866; pop. incl. with Saratoga Springs (Inc. Place)
Ghent; CDP; COLUMBIA; ▲ Ghent; **209** NL-19; 🅿; ★ **A-S-T**; z 12075; Ⓒ 586
Ghent; MCD-Town; COLUMBIA; ***209** NL-19; 🅿; ★ **A-S-T**; z 12075; Ⓟ 4,812; Ⓒ 5,276
Gibson; RMC Place; NASSAU; ★ **N.Y.**; mail Valley Stream z 11580; pop. incl. with Valley Stream (Inc. Place)
Gibson; RMC Place; STEUBEN; ▲ Corning; **208** NM-9; mail Corning z 14830; ● 500
Gifford; RMC Place; SCHENECTADY; ▲ Princetown; ***209** NJ-18; ★ **A-S-T**; mail Duanesburg z 12056; rural
Gilbert Mills; RMC Place; OSWEGO; ▲ Schroeppel; ***209** NH-11; elev. 418ft./127m.; ★ **SYR**; mail Phoenix z 13135; rural
Gilbertsville; Inc. Place; OTSEGO; ▲ Butternuts; **209** NK-14; elev. 1,108ft./338m.; 🅿; z 13776; Ⓟ 388; Ⓒ 375
Gilboa; RMC Place; SCHOHARIE; ▲ Gilboa; **209** NL-17; 🅿; z 12076; ● 200
Gilboa; MCD-Town; SCHOHARIE; ***209** NL-17; 🅿; z 12076; Ⓟ 1,207; Ⓒ 1,215
Gilgo Beach; RMC Place; SUFFOLK; ▲ Babylon; ***207** SG-9; 🅿; ★ **N.Y.**; z 11702; ● 100
Gilgo-Oak Beach-Captree; CDP-Census Area Only; SUFFOLK; ***207** SG-9; ★ **N.Y.**; Ⓒ 333
Gilmantown; RMC Place; HAMILTON; ▲ Wells; ***209** NG-17; elev. 1,715ft./523m.; mail Wells z 12190; ● 60
Glasco; CDP; ULSTER; ▲ Saugerties; **209** NM-18; 🅿; ★ **KNGST**; z 12432; Ⓟ 1,538; Ⓒ 1,692
Glass Lake; RMC Place; RENSSELAER; ▲ Sand Lake; ***209** NK-20; ★ **A-S-T**; mail Averill Park z 12018; ● 380
Glen; RMC Place; MONTGOMERY; ▲ Glen; **209** NJ-17; mail Fultonville z 12072; ● 180
Glen; MCD-Town; MONTGOMERY; ***209** NJ-17; mail Fultonville z 12072; Ⓟ 1,950; Ⓒ 2,222
Glen Aubrey; RMC Place; BROOME; ▲ Nanticoke; **209** NL-12; 🅿; ★ **BING**; z 13777; ● 500
Glen Castle; RMC Place; BROOME; ▲ Chenango; **207** SA-11; ★ **BING**; mail Binghamton z 13901; ● 300
Glenclyffe; RMC Place; PUTNAM; ▲ Philipstown; ***207** SC-6; elev. 120ft./37m.; ★ **N.Y.**; mail Garrison z 10524; ● 50
Glencoe Mills; COLUMBIA; see Glenco Mills (RMC Place)
Glenco Mills (Glencoe Mills); RMC Place; COLUMBIA; ▲ Livingston; ***209** NM-19; mail Hudson z 12534; ● 100
Glen Cove; Inc. Place; NASSAU; **207** SF-8; elev. 133ft./41m.; 🅿 🅷 ■; ★ **N.Y.**; z 11542; Ⓟ 24,149; Ⓒ 26,622; ◆ 26,141
Glendale; RMC Place; LEWIS; ▲ Martinsburg; ***209** NF-14; mail Glenfield z 13343; ● 100
Glendale; RMC Place; QUEENS; **211** I-13; 🅿; ★ **N.Y.**; z 11385; pop. incl. with New York (Inc. Place)
Glendale; RMC Place; WESTCHESTER; ▲ New Castle; ***207** SD-7; ★ **N.Y.**; mail Ossining z 10562; ● 75
Glendale Manor; RMC Place; ONEIDA; ★ **UT-R**; mail Rome z 13440; pop. incl. with Rome (Inc. Place)
Glenerie; RMC Place; ULSTER; ▲ Saugerties; ***209** NM-18; ★ **KNGST**; mail Saugerties z 12477; ● 100
Glenfield; RMC Place; LEWIS; ▲ Martinsburg; **209** NF-14; 🅿; z 13312, z 13343; ● 430
Glenford; RMC Place; ULSTER; ▲ Hurley; **209** NM-18; 🅿; ★ **KNGST**; z 12433; ● 550
Glenham; RMC Place; DUTCHESS; ▲ Fishkill; **207** SB-7; 🅿; ★ **POK**; z 12527; ● 2,000
Glen Haven; RMC Place; CAYUGA
Glen Haven; RMC Place; MONROE; ▲ Irondequoit; ***208** NH-8; ★ **ROCH**; mail Rochester z 14617
Glenhaven; RMC Place; ONEIDA; ▲ Whitestown, New Hartford; ★ **UT-R**; mail Whitesboro z 13492; ● 750
Glen Head; CDP; NASSAU; ▲ Oyster Bay; **211** E-18; 🅿; ★ **N.Y.**; z 11545; Ⓟ 4,488; Ⓒ 4,625
Glen Island; RMC Place; WARREN; ▲ Bolton; mail Bolton Landing z 12814
Glen Lake; RMC Place; WARREN; ▲ Queensbury; ***209** NH-19; ★ **GLFLS**; mail Lake George z 12845, Queensbury z 12804; ● 725
Glenmark; RMC Place; WAYNE; ▲ Rose; ***208** NH-9; elev. 312ft./95m.; mail North Rose z 14516; rural
Glenmont; RMC Place; ALBANY; ▲ Bethlehem; **209** NK-19; 🅿; ★ **A-S-T**; z 12077; ● 1,200
Glenmore; RMC Place; ESSEX; ▲ Keene; ***209** ND-19; mail Keene z 12942; rural
Glenmore; RMC Place; ONEIDA; ▲ Annsville; ***209** NH-13; mail Taberg z 13471; ● 30
Glen Oaks; RMC Place; QUEENS; **211** G-16; elev. 104ft./32m.; 🅿; ★ **N.Y.**; z 11004; pop. incl. with New York (Inc. Place)
Glenora; RMC Place; YATES; ▲ Starkey; ***208** NK-9; mail Dundee z 14837; ● 65
Glen Park; Inc. Place; JEFFERSON; ▲ Pamelia, Brownville; ***209** NE-12; elev. 347ft./106m.; 🅿; ★ **WATN**; z 13601; Ⓟ 527; Ⓒ 487
Glenridge; RMC Place; SCHENECTADY; ▲ Glenville; ***209** NJ-18; elev. 300ft./91m.; ★ **A-S-T**; mail Schenectady z 12302; rural
Glens Falls; Inc. Place; WARREN; ▲ Queensbury; **209** NH-19; elev. 348ft./106m.; 🅿 🅷 ■; ★ **GLFLS**; z 12801, z 12803-04; Ⓟ 15,023; Ⓒ 14,354; ◆ 14,164
Glens Falls North; CDP-Census Area Only; WARREN; ▲ Queensbury; ***209** NH-19; ★ **GLFLS**; mail Glens Falls z 12801; Ⓟ 7,978; Ⓒ 8,061
Glen Spey; RMC Place; SULLIVAN; ▲ Lumberland; **207** SC-3; 🅿; z 12737; ● 500
Glen Street; RMC Place; NASSAU; ★ **N.Y.**; mail Sea Cliff z 11579; pop. incl. with Sea Cliff (Inc. Place)
Glenville; MCD-Town; SCHENECTADY; ***209** NJ-18; 🅿 🅷; ★ **A-S-T**; z 12302, z 12325; Ⓟ 28,771; Ⓒ 28,183; ◆ 29,778
Glenville; RMC Place; WESTCHESTER; ▲ Greenburgh; ***207** SE-7; ★ **N.Y.**; mail Tarrytown z 10591; ● 500
Glen Wild; RMC Place; SULLIVAN; ▲ Thompson, Fallsburg; **207** SB-4; elev. 1,313ft./400m.; 🅿; z 12738; ● 370
Glenwood; RMC Place; ERIE; ▲ Colden; **208** NK-4; elev. 1,195ft./364m.; 🅿; ★ **BUF**; z 14069; ● 500
Glenwood; RMC Place; WESTCHESTER; ***207** SE-7; ★ **N.Y.**; mail Yonkers z 10701; pop. incl. with Yonkers (Inc. Place)
Glenwood Landing; CDP; NASSAU; ▲ Oyster Bay, North Hempstead; **211** E-17; 🅿; ★ **N.Y.**; z 11547; Ⓟ 3,407; Ⓒ 3,541
Gloversville; Inc. Place; FULTON; **209** NI-17; elev. 820ft./250m.; 🅿 🅷 ■; z 12078; Ⓟ 16,656; Ⓒ 15,413; ◆ 15,286
Godeffroy; RMC Place; ORANGE; ▲ Deerpark; **207** SC-4; 🅿; z 12729; ● 550
Golden Glow Heights; RMC Place; CHEMUNG; ▲ Big Flats; **208** NM-9; ★ **ELM**; mail Elmira z 14905; ● 450
Golden's Bridge; CDP; WESTCHESTER; ▲ Lewisboro; **207** SC-7; 🅿; ★ **N.Y.**; z 10526; Ⓟ 1,589; Ⓒ 1,578
Goodyears Corners; RMC Place; CAYUGA; ▲ Genoa; ***208** NK-10; mail King Ferry z 13081; rural
Goose Bay Estates; RMC Place; SUFFOLK; ▲ Southold; mail Southold z 11971
Goose Island; RMC Place; WASHINGTON; ▲ Salem; ***209** NH-20; elev. 720ft./219m.; mail Argyle z 12809; ● 30
Gordon Heights; CDP; SUFFOLK; ***207** SE-10; ★ **N.Y.**; mail Coram z 11727, Medford z 11763; Ⓒ 3,094
Gorham; RMC Place; ONTARIO; ▲ Gorham; **208** NJ-9; 🅿; z 14461; ● 950
Gorham; MCD-Town; ONTARIO; ***208** NJ-8; 🅿; z 14461; Ⓟ 3,497; Ⓒ 3,776
Goshen; Inc. Place; ⊡ ORANGE; ▲ Goshen; **207** SC-5; 🅿 🅷; ★ **N.Y.**; z 10924; Ⓟ 5,255; Ⓒ 5,676
Goshen; MCD-Town; ORANGE; ***207** SC-5; 🅿; ★ **N.Y.**; z 10924; Ⓟ 11,500; Ⓒ 12,913
Goshen Hills; RMC Place; ORANGE; ▲ Goshen; ***207** SC-5; ★ **N.Y.**; mail Goshen z 10924; rural
Gothicville; RMC Place; OTSEGO; ▲ Worcester; ***209** NK-16; mail Worcester z 12197; rural
Goulds; RMC Place; DELAWARE; ▲ Hancock; ***207** SA-2; elev. 1,879ft./573m.; mail Long Eddy z 12760; rural
Goulds Mill; RMC Place; LEWIS; ▲ Lyonsdale; ***209** NG-14; mail Lyons Falls z 13368; rural
Gouverneur; Inc. Place; ST. LAWRENCE; ▲ Gouverneur; **209** ND-14; elev. 447ft./136m.; 🅿 🅷; z 13642; Ⓟ 4,604; Ⓒ 4,263
Gouverneur; MCD-Town; ST. LAWRENCE; ***209** ND-14; 🅿; z 13642; Ⓟ 6,985; Ⓒ 7,418
Governors Island; RMC Place; NEW YORK; ***207** SF-6; elev. 20ft./6m.; ★ **N.Y.**; mail New York z 10004; pop. incl. with New York (Inc. Place)
Gowanda; Inc. Place; CATTARAUGUS, ERIE; ▲ Collins, Persia; **208** NK-3; 🅿 🅷; z 14070; Ⓟ 2,901; Ⓒ 2,842
Gracie; RMC Place; CORTLAND; ▲ Cortlandville; ***209** NK-11; elev. 1,188ft./362m.; mail Cortland z 13045; rural
Gracie; RMC Place; NEW YORK; ★ **N.Y.**; mail New York z 10028, z 10130; pop. incl. with New York (Inc. Place)
Grafton; RMC Place; RENSSELAER; ▲ Grafton; **209** NJ-20; elev. 1,472ft./449m.; 🅿; z 12082; ● 600
Grafton; MCD-Town; RENSSELAER; ***209** NJ-20; 🅿; z 12082; Ⓟ 1,917; Ⓒ 1,987
Graham Hill; RMC Place; WESTCHESTER; ▲ Mount Pleasant; ***207** SD-7; ★ **N.Y.**; mail Lake Peekskill z 10537; ● 500
Grahamsville; RMC Place; SULLIVAN; ▲ Neversink; **209** NN-17; elev. 952ft./290m.; 🅿; z 12740; ● 700
Granby; OSWEGO; see Granby Center (RMC Place)
Granby; MCD-Town; OSWEGO; ***209** NH-11; mail Fulton z 13069; Ⓟ 7,013; Ⓒ 7,009
Granby Center (Granby); RMC Place; OSWEGO; ▲ Granby; **209** NH-11; mail Fulton z 13069; ● 100
Grand Gorge; RMC Place; DELAWARE; ▲ Roxbury; **209** NL-17; elev. 1,411ft./430m.; 🅿; z 12434; ● 1,000
Grand Hotel; ULSTER; see Highmount (RMC Place)
Grand Island; RMC Place; ERIE; ▲ Grand Island; **208** NI-3; 🅿; ★ **BUF**; z 14072; ● 800
Grand Island; MCD-Town; ERIE; ***208** NI-3; 🅿; ★ **BUF**; z 14072; Ⓟ 17,561; Ⓒ 18,621
Grand Station; RMC Place; QUEENS; ★ **N.Y.**; mail Astoria z 11103; pop. incl. with New York (Inc. Place)
Grand View; ROCKLAND; see Grand View-on-Hudson (Inc. Place)
Grand View Beach; RMC Place; MONROE; ▲ Greece; ***208** NH-7; ★ **ROCH**; mail Rochester z 14612
Grand View Heights; RMC Place; MONROE; ▲ Greece; ***208** NH-7; ★ **ROCH**; mail Rochester z 14612; ● 1,200
Grand View-on-Hudson (Grand View); Inc. Place; ROCKLAND; ▲ Orangetown; ***207** SE-7; ★ **N.Y.**; mail Nyack z 10960; Ⓟ 271; Ⓒ 284
Grandview Park; RMC Place; JEFFERSON; ▲ Orleans; ***209** ND-12; mail Wellesley Island z 13640; summer pop. 55
Grandyle Village; RMC Place; ERIE; ▲ Grand Island; **208** ND-2; ★ **BUF**; mail Grand Island z 14072; ● 1,500
Granger; MCD-Town; ALLEGANY; ***208** NK-6; mail Fillmore z 14735; Ⓟ 515; Ⓒ 577
Grangerville; RMC Place; SARATOGA; ▲ Saratoga; ***209** NI-19; ★ **A-S-T**; mail Schuylerville z 12871; ● 75
Granite; RMC Place; ULSTER; ▲ Rochester; **207** SA-5; mail Kerhonkson z 12446; ● 165
Granite Springs; RMC Place; WESTCHESTER; ▲ Somers; ***207** SC-7; 🅿; ★ **N.Y.**; z 10527; ● 850
Graniteville; RMC Place; RICHMOND; **210** K-7; elev. 56ft./17m.; ★ **N.Y.**; mail Staten Island z 10314; pop. incl. with New York (Inc. Place)
Grant; RMC Place; HERKIMER; ▲ Russia; ***209** NH-15; elev. 1,237ft./377m.; mail Cold Brook z 13324; ● 85
Grant Avenue; RMC Place; CAYUGA; ★ **SYR**; mail Auburn z 13021; pop. incl. with Auburn (Inc. Place)
Grant City; RMC Place; RICHMOND; ***207** SG-6; ★ **N.Y.**; mail Staten Island z 10304; pop. incl. with New York (Inc. Place)
Grant Hollow; RMC Place; RENSSELAER; ▲ Schaghticoke; ***209** NJ-19; elev. 323ft./98m.; ★ **A-S-T**; mail Melrose z 12121; ● 135
Grant Park; RMC Place; NASSAU; ▲ Hempstead; ★ **N.Y.**; mail Hewlett z 11557
Granville; Inc. Place; WASHINGTON; ▲ Granville; **209** NG-20; elev. 407ft./124m.; 🅿; z 12832; Ⓟ 2,646; Ⓒ 2,644
Granville; MCD-Town; WASHINGTON; ***209** NG-20; 🅿; z 12832; Ⓟ 5,935; Ⓒ 6,456
Grapeville; RMC Place; GREENE; ▲ New Baltimore; ***209** NL-18; ★ **A-S-T**; mail Climax z 12042; ● 135
Graphite; RMC Place; WARREN; ▲ Hague; ***209** NF-19; elev. 1,521ft./464m.; mail Hague z 12836; ● 50
Grasmere; RMC Place; RICHMOND; ***207** SG-6; ★ **N.Y.**; mail Staten Island z 10304; pop. incl. with New York (Inc. Place)
Grassy Point; RMC Place; ROCKLAND; ▲ Stony Point; ***207** SD-6; ★ **N.Y.**; mail Stony Point z 10980; ● 385
Gravesend; RMC Place; KINGS; **211** K-11; ★ **N.Y.**; mail Brooklyn z 11223; pop. incl. with New York (Inc. Place)
Gravesville; RMC Place; HERKIMER; ▲ Russia; **209** NH-15; elev. 786ft./240m.; mail Poland z 13431; ● 120
Gray; RMC Place; HERKIMER; ▲ Ohio, Norway; **209** NH-15; elev. 1,290ft./393m.; mail Cold Brook z 13324; ● 75
Graymoor; RMC Place; PUTNAM; ▲ Philipstown; ***207** SC-7; elev. 480ft./146m.; ★ **N.Y.**; mail Garrison z 10524; ● 150
Gray Oaks; RMC Place; WESTCHESTER; ***207** SE-7; ★ **N.Y.**; mail Yonkers z 10703; pop. incl. with Yonkers (Inc. Place)
Great Bend; CDP; JEFFERSON; ▲ Champion; **209** NE-13; 🅿; z 13643; Ⓒ 801

Entries in **UPPERCASE** are counties.
Entries in **bold** have populations of 2,500 or more.
Names in parentheses are alternate names.
Inc. Place — Incorporated Place
RMC Place — Rand McNally Designated Place
CDP — Census Designated Place
MCD — Minor Civil Division

⊡ County Seat
▲ Minor Civil Division
elev. Elevation
🅿 Post Office

🅷 Hospital
🅲 College
■ Principal Business Center
★ Ranally Metro Area (RMA) Abbreviation
z Zip Code(s)

Ⓟ Previous Census Population
Ⓡ Revised Census Population
Ⓐ Annexation Population
● Rand McNally Population Estimate
Ⓒ Final Census Population
Ⓢ Special Census Population
◆ Estimated Population

For additional definitions see Glossary, Volume 1, and Introduction, Volume 2.

Great Kills; RMC Place; RICHMOND; ***207** SG-6; ★ **N.Y.**; mail Staten Island **Z** 10308; pop. incl. with New York (Inc. Place)

Great Meadow Correctional Facility; WASHINGTON; see Comstock (RMC Place)

Great Neck; Inc. Place; NASSAU; ▲ North Hempstead; **207** SF-7; 🅿; ★ **N.Y.**; **Z** 11020-24, **Z** 11026-27; Ⓟ 8,745; Ⓒ 9,538

Great Neck Estates; Inc. Place; NASSAU; ▲ North Hempstead; **211** F-15; ★ **N.Y.**; mail Great Neck **Z** 11021; Ⓟ 2,790; Ⓒ 2,756

Great Neck Gardens (Allenwood); CDP-Census Area Only; NASSAU; ▲ North Hempstead; ***207** SF-7; ★ **N.Y.**; mail Great Neck **Z** 11021; Ⓒ 1,089

Great Neck Plaza; Inc. Place; NASSAU; **211** F-16; 2 mi. SE of Great Neck; ★ **N.Y.**; mail Great Neck **Z** 11020; Ⓟ 5,897; Ⓒ 6,433

Great River; CDP; SUFFOLK; ▲ Islip; ***207** SF-9; 🅿; ★ **N.Y.**; **Z** 11739; Ⓒ 1,546

Great Valley; RMC Place; CATTARAUGUS; ▲ Great Valley; **208** NL-4; elev. 1,464ft./446m.; 🅿; **Z** 14741; ● 250

Great Valley; MCD-Town; CATTARAUGUS; ***208** NL-4; 🅿; **Z** 14741; Ⓟ 2,090; Ⓒ 2,145

Greece (Ridgemont); CDP; MONROE; ▲ Greece; ***208** NH-7; 🅿; ★ **ROCH**; **Z** 14612, **Z** 14615-16, **Z** 14626; Ⓟ 15,632; Ⓒ 14,614

Greece; MCD-Town; MONROE; ***208** NH-7; 🅿; ★ **ROCH**; **Z** 14612, **Z** 14615-16, **Z** 14626; Ⓟ 90,106; Ⓒ 94,141; ◆ 93,665

Greeley Square; RMC Place; NEW YORK; ★ **N.Y.**; mail New York **Z** 10001; pop. incl. with New York (Inc. Place)

Green Acres; RMC Place; CHAUTAUQUA; ▲ Pomfret; mail Fredonia **Z** 14063; pop. incl. with Fredonia (Inc. Place)

Green Acres Valley; RMC Place; ERIE; ***208** NI-4; ★ **BUF**; mail Buffalo **Z** 14226

Greenburgh; MCD-Town; WESTCHESTER; ***207** SE-7; 🅲 9,120; ★ **N.Y.**; mail Tarrytown **Z** 10591, White Plains **Z** 10607; Ⓟ 83,816; Ⓒ 86,764; Ⓡ 86,831; ◆ 89,854

Green Corners; RMC Place; SCHENECTADY; ▲ Glenville; ***209** NI-18; elev. 769ft./234m.; ★ **A-S-T**; mail Amsterdam **Z** 12010; rural

Green Crest; RMC Place; CHAUTAUQUA; ▲ Portland; ***208** NK-2; mail Fredonia **Z** 14063; ● 150

Greendale; RMC Place; COLUMBIA; ▲ Greenport; ***209** NL-19; mail Hudson **Z** 12534; rural

Greene; Inc. Place; CHENANGO; ▲ Greene; **209** NL-13; elev. 924ft./282m.; 🅿; **Z** 13778; Ⓟ 1,812; Ⓒ 1,701

Greene; MCD-Town; CHENANGO; ***209** NL-13; 🅿; **Z** 13778; Ⓟ 6,053; Ⓒ 5,729

GREENE; **209** NL-17; Ⓟ 44,739; Ⓒ 48,195; ◆ 48,862

Greenfield; MCD-Town; SARATOGA; ***209** NI-18; ★ **A-S-T**; mail Greenfield Center **Z** 12833; Ⓟ 6,338; Ⓒ 7,362

Greenfield Center; RMC Place; SARATOGA; ▲ Greenfield; **209** NI-19; 🅿; ★ **A-S-T**; **Z** 12833; ● 700

Greenfield Park; RMC Place; ULSTER; ▲ Wawarsing; **207** SA-4; 🅿; **Z** 12435; ● 500

Greenhaven; RMC Place; WESTCHESTER; ***207** SE-7; ★ **N.Y.**; mail Rye **Z** 10580; pop. incl. with Rye (Inc. Place)

Greenhurst; RMC Place; CHAUTAUQUA; ▲ Ellery; **208** NM-2; 🅿; ★ **JMST**; **Z** 14742; ● 600

Green Island; Inc. Place; ALBANY; ▲ Green Island; **209** NJ-19; 🅿; ★ **A-S-T**; **Z** 12183; Ⓟ 2,490; Ⓒ 2,278

Green Island; MCD-Town; ALBANY; ***209** NJ-19; 🅿; ★ **A-S-T**; **Z** 12183; Ⓟ 2,490; Ⓒ 2,278

Greenlawn; CDP; SUFFOLK; ▲ Huntington; **207** SH-11; 🅿; ★ **N.Y.**; **Z** 11740; Ⓟ 13,208; Ⓒ 13,286

Greenpoint; RMC Place; KINGS; **211** H-11; ★ **N.Y.**; mail Brooklyn **Z** 11222; pop. incl. with New York (Inc. Place)

Greenport; MCD-Town; COLUMBIA; ***209** NL-19; mail Hudson **Z** 12534; Ⓟ 4,101; Ⓒ 4,180

Greenport; Inc. Place; SUFFOLK; ▲ Southold; **207** SD-12; 🅿 🅷; **Z** 11944; Ⓟ 2,070; Ⓒ 2,048

Greenport West; CDP-Census Area Only; SUFFOLK; ▲ Southold; ***207** SD-12; mail Greenport **Z** 11944; Ⓟ 1,614; Ⓒ 1,679

Greenridge; RMC Place; RICHMOND; ***207** SG-6; elev. 11ft./3m.; ★ **N.Y.**; mail Staten Island **Z** 10312; pop. incl. with New York (Inc. Place)

Green River; RMC Place; COLUMBIA; ▲ Hillsdale; **209** NL-20; mail Hillsdale **Z** 12529; ● 200

Greenvale (North Roslyn); CDP; NASSAU; ▲ Oyster Bay, North Hempstead; **211** F-18; 🅿; ★ **N.Y.**; **Z** 11548; Ⓒ 2,231; Ⓡ 992

Greenville; CDP; GREENE; ▲ Greenville; **209** NL-18; elev. 708ft./216m.; 🅿; **Z** 12083; Ⓒ 493

Greenville; MCD-Town; GREENE; ***209** NL-18; 🅿; **Z** 12083; Ⓟ 3,135; Ⓒ 3,316

Greenville; MCD-Town; ORANGE; ***207** SC-4; ★ **MIDD**; mail Port Jervis **Z** 12771; Ⓟ 3,120; Ⓒ 3,800

Greenville; RMC Place; STEUBEN; ▲ Avoca; ***208** NL-8; mail Cohocton **Z** 14826; rural

Greenville; CDP; WESTCHESTER; ▲ Greenburgh; **207** SI-7; ★ **N.Y.**; mail Scarsdale **Z** 10583; Ⓟ 9,528; Ⓒ 8,648

Greenville Center; RMC Place; GREENE; ▲ Greenville; ***209** NL-18; elev. 722ft./220m.; mail Greenville **Z** 12083; rural

Greenway; RMC Place; ONEIDA; ***209** NI-13; elev. 466ft./142m.; ★ **UT-R**; mail Rome **Z** 13440, Verona **Z** 13478; pop. incl. with Rome (Inc. Place)

Greenwich; Inc. Place; WASHINGTON; ▲ Easton, Greenwich; **209** NI-20; 🅿; ★ **GLFLS**; **Z** 12834; Ⓟ 1,961; Ⓒ 1,902

Greenwich; MCD-Town; WASHINGTON; ***209** NI-20; 🅿; ★ **GLFLS**; **Z** 12834; includes part of the Village of Greenwich; Ⓟ 4,557; Ⓒ 4,896

Greenwich Village; RMC Place; NEW YORK; ***207** SF-6; ★ **N.Y.**; pop. incl. with New York (Inc. Place)

Greenwood; RMC Place; KINGS; ★ **N.Y.**; pop. incl. with New York (Inc. Place)

Greenwood; RMC Place; STEUBEN; ▲ Greenwood; **208** NM-7; 🅿; **Z** 14839; ● 520

Greenwood; MCD-Town; STEUBEN; ***208** NM-7; 🅿; **Z** 14839; Ⓟ 898; Ⓒ 849

Greenwood Lake; Inc. Place; ORANGE; ▲ Warwick; **207** SD-5; elev. 624ft./190m.; 🅿; ★ **N.Y.**; **Z** 10925; Ⓟ 3,208; Ⓒ 3,411

Greer Childrens Home; DUTCHESS; see Hope Farm (RMC Place)

Gregorytown; RMC Place; DELAWARE; ▲ Colchester; ***209** NM-15; mail Downsville **Z** 13755; rural

Greig; RMC Place; LEWIS; ▲ Greig; **209** NF-14; 🅿; **Z** 13345; ● 300

Greig; MCD-Town; LEWIS; ***209** NF-14; 🅿; **Z** 13345; Ⓟ 1,323; Ⓒ 1,365

Greigsville; RMC Place; LIVINGSTON; ▲ York; **208** NJ-6; elev. 752ft./229m.; ★ **ROCH**; mail Piffard **Z** 14533; ● 220

Greigsville Station; LIVINGSTON; see Wadsworth (RMC Place)

Grenell; RMC Place; JEFFERSON; ▲ Clayton; ***209** ND-12; elev. 260ft./79m.; 🅿; **Z** 13624; summer pop. 100; ● 40

Greycourt; RMC Place; ORANGE; ***207** SC-5; ★ **N.Y.**; mail Chester **Z** 10918; pop. incl. with Chester (Inc. Place)

Greystone; RMC Place; WESTCHESTER; ***207** SE-7; ★ **N.Y.**; mail Yonkers **Z** 10701-02; pop. incl. with Yonkers (Inc. Place)

Gridleyville; RMC Place; TIOGA; ▲ Candor; ***209** NL-11; mail Willseyville **Z** 13864; rural

Griffins Mills; RMC Place; ERIE; ▲ Aurora; ***208** NJ-4; ★ **BUF**; mail West Falls **Z** 14170; ● 100

Grindstone; RMC Place; JEFFERSON; ▲ Clayton; ***209** ND-12; elev. 291ft./89m.; mail Clayton **Z** 13624; ● 75

Groom Corners (Grooms Corners); RMC Place; SARATOGA; ▲ Clifton Park; **209** NJ-19; ★ **A-S-T**; mail Rexford **Z** 12148; ● 370

Grooms Corners; SARATOGA; see Groom Corners (RMC Place)

Groton; Inc. Place; TOMPKINS; ▲ Groton; **209** NK-11; 🅿; ★ **ITH**; **Z** 13073; Ⓟ 2,398; Ⓒ 2,470

Groton; MCD-Town; TOMPKINS; ***209** NK-11; 🅿; ★ **ITH**; **Z** 13073; Ⓟ 5,483; Ⓒ 5,794

Groton City; RMC Place; TOMPKINS; ▲ Groton; ***209** NK-11; ★ **ITH**; mail Groton **Z** 13073; ● 50

Grove; MCD-Town; ALLEGANY; ***208** NK-6; mail Swain **Z** 14884; Ⓟ 479; Ⓒ 533

Groveland; RMC Place; LIVINGSTON; ▲ Groveland; **208** NK-7; 🅿; ★ **ROCH**; **Z** 14462, **Z** 14545; ● 650

Groveland; MCD-Town; LIVINGSTON; ***208** NJ-7; 🅿; ★ **ROCH**; **Z** 14462, **Z** 14545; Ⓟ 3,190; Ⓒ 3,853

Grover; RMC Place; ERIE; ▲ Amherst; ★ **BUF**; mail Buffalo **Z** 14226

Grover Hills; RMC Place; ESSEX; ▲ Moriah; **209** NE-19; elev. 1,063ft./324m.; mail Mineville **Z** 12956; ● 300

Grovernor Corners; RMC Place; SCHOHARIE; ▲ Carlisle; ***209** NJ-17; mail Central Bridge **Z** 12035; ● 200

Groveville; RMC Place; DUTCHESS; ▲ Fishkill; ***207** SB-6; ★ **POK**; mail Beacon **Z** 12508

Grymes Hill; RMC Place; RICHMOND; **210** K-8; ★ **N.Y.**; mail Staten Island **Z** 10301; pop. incl. with New York (Inc. Place)

Guilderland; RMC Place; ALBANY; ▲ Guilderland; **207** SI-2; 🅿; ★ **A-S-T**; **Z** 12084; ● 1,900

Guilderland; MCD-Town; ALBANY; ***209** NJ-18; 🅿; ★ **A-S-T**; **Z** 12084; Ⓟ 28,764; Ⓒ 32,688; Ⓡ 34,045; ◆ 34,045

Guilderland Center; RMC Place; ALBANY; ▲ Guilderland; **209** NJ-18; 🅿; ★ **A-S-T**; **Z** 12085; ● 860

Guilford; RMC Place; CHENANGO; ▲ Guilford; **209** NL-14; 🅿; **Z** 13780; ● 300

Guilford; MCD-Town; CHENANGO; ***209** NL-14; 🅿; **Z** 13780; Ⓟ 2,875; Ⓒ 3,046

Guilford Center; RMC Place; CHENANGO; ▲ Guilford; ***209** NL-14; mail Guilford **Z** 13780; ● 50

Gulfport; RMC Place; RICHMOND; ***207** SG-6; ★ **N.Y.**; mail Staten Island **Z** 10303; pop. incl. with New York (Inc. Place)

Gulf Summit; RMC Place; BROOME; ▲ Sanford; ***209** NM-14; mail Windsor **Z** 13865; rural

Gunther Park; RMC Place; WESTCHESTER; ***207** SE-7; ★ **N.Y.**; mail Bronxville **Z** 10708; pop. incl. with Yonkers (Inc. Place)

Gurn Spring; RMC Place; SARATOGA; ▲ Wilton; **209** NH-19; ★ **GLFLS**; mail Gansevoort **Z** 12831; ● 145

Guymard; RMC Place; ORANGE; ▲ Mount Hope; ***207** SC-4; ★ **MIDD**; ● 40

Gypsum; RMC Place; ONTARIO; ▲ Phelps, Manchester; ***208** NI-9; mail Clifton Springs **Z** 14432; rural

H

Hadley; RMC Place; SARATOGA; ▲ Hadley; **209** NH-18; 🅿; **Z** 12835; ● 870

Hadley; MCD-Town; SARATOGA; ***209** NH-18; 🅿; **Z** 12835; Ⓟ 1,628; Ⓒ 1,971

Hadley Bay; RMC Place; CHAUTAUQUA; ▲ North Harmony; ***208** NM-2; mail Stow **Z** 14785; ● 260

Hagaman; Inc. Place; MONTGOMERY; ▲ Amsterdam; **209** NI-18; 🅿; ★ **A-S-T**; **Z** 12086; Ⓟ 1,377; Ⓒ 1,357

Hagedorns Mills; RMC Place; SARATOGA; ▲ Providence; ***209** NI-18; mail Galway **Z** 12074; ● 50

Hagerman; RMC Place; SUFFOLK; ▲ Brookhaven; ***207** SF-10; ★ **N.Y.**; mail Bellport **Z** 11713; ● 1,450

Hague; RMC Place; WARREN; ▲ Hague; **209** NF-19; elev. 328ft./100m.; 🅿; **Z** 12836; ● 450

Hague; MCD-Town; WARREN; ***209** NF-19; 🅿; **Z** 12836; Ⓟ 699; Ⓒ 854

Hailesboro; RMC Place; ST. LAWRENCE; ▲ Fowler; **209** ND-14; elev. 487ft./148m.; 🅿; **Z** 13645; ● 400

Haines Falls; RMC Place; GREENE; ▲ Hunter; **209** NL-18; 🅿; **Z** 12436; ● 700

Halcott; GREENE; see Halcott Center (RMC Place)

Halcott; MCD-Town; GREENE; ***209** NL-17; mail Fleischmanns **Z** 12430; Ⓟ 189; Ⓒ 193

Halcott Center (Halcott); RMC Place; GREENE; ▲ Halcott; ***209** NM-17; 🅿; **Z** 12430; ● 60

Halcottsville (Halcottville); RMC Place; DELAWARE; ▲ Middletown; **209** NL-16; 🅿; **Z** 12438; ● 240

Halcottville; DELAWARE; see Halcottsville (RMC Place)

Hale Eddy (Hales Eddy); RMC Place; DELAWARE; ▲ Deposit; ***209** NM-14; mail Hancock **Z** 13783; ● 125

Hales Eddy; DELAWARE; see Hale Eddy (RMC Place)

Halesite; CDP; SUFFOLK; ▲ Huntington; **207** SH-10; 🅿; ★ **N.Y.**; **Z** 11743; Ⓟ 2,687; Ⓒ 2,582

Half Acre; RMC Place; CAYUGA; ▲ Aurelius; ***208** NJ-10; ★ **SYR**; mail Auburn **Z** 13021; ● 25

Half Hollow Hills; RMC Place; SUFFOLK; ▲ Huntington; **207** SI-11; ★ **N.Y.**; mail Huntington Station **Z** 11746; ● 4,950

Halfmoon; RMC Place; SARATOGA; ▲ Halfmoon; **209** NJ-19; ★ **A-S-T**; mail Clifton Park **Z** 12065, Waterford **Z** 12188; ● 500

Halfmoon; MCD-Town; SARATOGA; ***209** NJ-19; ★ **A-S-T**; mail Waterford **Z** 12188; Ⓟ 13,879; Ⓒ 18,474; Ⓡ 18,359; ◆ 21,867

Halfway; RMC Place; ONONDAGA; ▲ Elbridge; ***209** NI-11; ★ **SYR**; mail Elbridge **Z** 13060; rural

Haliham Hill; RMC Place; ULSTER; ▲ Kingston; ***209** NM-18; ★ **KNGST**; mail Kingston **Z** 12401; ● 200

Hall; RMC Place; ONTARIO; ▲ Seneca; **208** NJ-9; 🅿; **Z** 14463; ● 400

Hallow; RMC Place; ONEIDA; ▲ New Hartford; ***209** NI-14; ★ **UT-R**; mail New Hartford **Z** 13413; ● 880

Halls Corners; RMC Place; SENECA; ▲ Covert; ***208** NK-10; elev. 1,127ft./344m.; ★ **ITH**; mail Interlaken **Z** 14847; rural

Halls Corners; RMC Place; WYOMING; ▲ Orangeville; ***208** NJ-5; mail Warsaw **Z** 14569; rural

Halls Mills; RMC Place; SULLIVAN; ▲ Neversink; ***207** SA-4; mail Claryville **Z** 12725; ● 200

Hallsport; RMC Place; ALLEGANY; ▲ Willing; **208** NM-6; elev. 1,768ft./539m.; mail Wellsville **Z** 14895; ● 110

Hallsville; RMC Place; MONTGOMERY; ▲ Minden; ***209** NI-16; mail Fort Plain **Z** 13339; rural

Halsey; RMC Place; KINGS; ★ **N.Y.**; mail Brooklyn **Z** 11233; pop. incl. with New York (Inc. Place)

Halseys; RMC Place; CLINTON; ***209** NB-19; elev. 172ft./52m.; ★ **PLATT**; mail Plattsburgh **Z** 12901

Halsey Valley; RMC Place; TIOGA; ▲ Tioga, Barton; ***209** NM-11; mail Spencer **Z** 14883

Hambletville; RMC Place; DELAWARE; ▲ Deposit; ***209** NM-14; mail Deposit **Z** 13754; rural

Hamburg; Inc. Place; ERIE; ▲ Hamburg; **208** NJ-4; elev. 825ft./251m.; 🅿 🅲 1,064; ★ **BUF**; **Z** 14075 & mail Buffalo **Z** 14219; Ⓟ 10,442; Ⓒ 10,116

Hamburg; MCD-Town; ERIE; ***208** NJ-3; 🅿 🅲 1,064; ★ **BUF**; **Z** 14075 & mail Buffalo **Z** 14219; Ⓟ 53,735; Ⓒ 56,259; ◆ 55,849

Hamburg; RMC Place; GREENE; ▲ Catskill; ***209** NL-19; ★ **KNGST**; mail Catskill **Z** 12414; ● 80

Hamburg-on-the-Lake; RMC Place; ERIE; ▲ Hamburg; ★ **BUF**; mail Hamburg **Z** 14075

Hamden; RMC Place; DELAWARE; ▲ Hamden; **209** NM-15; 🅿; **Z** 13782; ● 250

Hamden; MCD-Town; DELAWARE; ***209** NL-15; 🅿; **Z** 13782; Ⓟ 1,144; Ⓒ 1,280

Hamilton; Inc. Place; MADISON; ▲ Hamilton; **209** NJ-13; elev. 1,126ft./343m.; 🅿 🅷 🅲 2,759; **Z** 13346; Ⓟ 3,790; Ⓒ 3,509

Hamilton; MCD-Town; MADISON; ***209** NJ-14; 🅿 🅲 2,759; **Z** 13346; Ⓟ 6,221; Ⓒ 5,733

HAMILTON; **209** NF-16; Ⓟ 5,279; Ⓒ 5,379; ◆ 5,012

Hamilton Beach; RMC Place; QUEENS; ***207** SG-7; ★ **N.Y.**; mail Howard Beach **Z** 11414; pop. incl. with New York (Inc. Place)

Hamilton Center; RMC Place; MADISON; ▲ Hamilton; ***209** NJ-14; mail Hamilton **Z** 13346; ● 70

Hamilton Grange; RMC Place; NEW YORK; ★ **N.Y.**; mail New York **Z** 10031; pop. incl. with New York (Inc. Place)

Hamlet; RMC Place; CHAUTAUQUA; ▲ Villenova; **208** NL-3; elev. 1,392ft./424m.; mail South Dayton **Z** 14138; ● 80

Hamlin; RMC Place; MONROE; ▲ Hamlin; **208** NH-6; 🅿; ★ **ROCH**; **Z** 14464; ● 700

Hamlin; MCD-Town; MONROE; ***208** NH-6; 🅿; ★ **ROCH**; **Z** 14464; Ⓟ 9,203; Ⓒ 9,355

Hammel; RMC Place; QUEENS; ***207** SG-7; ★ **N.Y.**; mail Far Rockaway **Z** 11693; pop. incl. with New York (Inc. Place)

Hammertown; RMC Place; DUTCHESS; ▲ Pine Plains; ***209** NM-19; mail Pine Plains **Z** 12567; ● 50

Hammond; Inc. Place; ST. LAWRENCE; ▲ Hammond; **209** NC-13; elev. 360ft./110m.; 🅿; **Z** 13646; Ⓟ 270; Ⓒ 302

Hammond; MCD-Town; ST. LAWRENCE; ***209** NC-13; 🅿; **Z** 13646; Ⓟ 1,168; Ⓒ 1,207

Hammondsport; Inc. Place; STEUBEN; ▲ Urbana; **208** NL-8; elev. 743ft./226m.; 🅿; **Z** 14840; Ⓟ 929; Ⓒ 731

Hampton; RMC Place; WASHINGTON; ▲ Hampton; **209** NG-20; elev. 431ft./131m.; 🅿; **Z** 12837; ● 400

Hampton; MCD-Town; WASHINGTON; ***209** NG-20; 🅿; **Z** 12837; Ⓟ 756; Ⓒ 871

Hampton Bays; CDP; SUFFOLK; ▲ Southampton; **207** SE-12; 🅿; **Z** 11946; Ⓟ 7,893; Ⓒ 12,236; Ⓡ 12,240

Hamptonburgh; MCD-Town; ORANGE; ***207** SC-5; ★ **N.Y.**; mail Campbell Hall **Z** 10916; Ⓟ 3,910; Ⓒ 4,686

Hampton Manor; CDP-Census Area Only; RENSSELAER; ▲ East Greenbush; **207** SJ-5; ★ **A-S-T**; mail Rensselaer **Z** 12144; Ⓟ 2,600; Ⓒ 2,525

Hampton Park; RMC Place; SUFFOLK; ▲ Southampton; ***207** SE-12; mail Southampton **Z** 11968; ● 700

Hancock; Inc. Place; DELAWARE; ▲ Hancock; **209** NN-14; 🅿; **Z** 13783; Ⓟ 1,330; Ⓒ 1,189

Hancock; MCD-Town; DELAWARE; ***209** NN-15; 🅿; **Z** 13783; Ⓟ 3,384; Ⓒ 3,449

Handsome Eddy; RMC Place; SULLIVAN; ▲ Lumberland; ***207** SC-3; mail Barryville **Z** 12719; summer pop. 75; ● 15

Hankins; RMC Place; SULLIVAN; ▲ Fremont; **209** NN-15; elev. 807ft./246m.; 🅿; **Z** 12741; ● 400

Hannacroix; RMC Place; GREENE; ▲ New Baltimore; ***209** NK-19; 🅿; ★ **A-S-T**; **Z** 12087; ● 320

Hannawa Falls; RMC Place; ST. LAWRENCE; ▲ Pierrepont; **209** NC-15; 🅿; **Z** 13647; ● 700

Hannibal; Inc. Place; OSWEGO; ▲ Hannibal; **208** NH-10; elev. 327ft./100m.; 🅿; **Z** 13074; Ⓟ 613; Ⓒ 542

Hannibal; MCD-Town; OSWEGO; ***208** NH-10; 🅿; **Z** 13074; Ⓟ 4,616; Ⓒ 4,957

Hannibal Center; RMC Place; OSWEGO; ▲ Hannibal; **208** NH-10; mail Hannibal **Z** 13074; ● 115

Hanover; MCD-Town; CHAUTAUQUA; ***208** NK-3; mail Silver Creek **Z** 14136; Ⓟ 7,380; Ⓒ 7,638

Hanover Center; RMC Place; CHAUTAUQUA; ▲ Hanover; ***208** NK-3; mail Silver Creek **Z** 14136; ● 60

Harbor Acres; RMC Place; NASSAU; ★ **N.Y.**; mail Port Washington **Z** 11050; pop. incl. with Sands Point (Inc. Place)

Harbor Heights Park; RMC Place; SUFFOLK; ▲ Huntington; ★ **N.Y.**; mail Huntington **Z** 11743

Harbor Hills; CDP; NASSAU; ▲ North Hempstead; **211** F-15; ★ **N.Y.**; mail Great Neck **Z** 11023; Ⓒ 563

Harbor Isle; CDP; NASSAU; ▲ Hempstead; **211** K-17; ★ **N.Y.**; mail Island Park **Z** 11558; Ⓒ 1,334

Hardenburgh; MCD-Town; ULSTER; ***209** NM-16; mail Margaretville **Z** 12455; Ⓟ 204; Ⓒ 208

Hardys; RMC Place; WYOMING; ▲ Gainesville; ***208** NK-6; mail Gainesville **Z** 14066; rural

Harford (North Harford); RMC Place; CORTLAND; ▲ Harford; **209** NL-11; 🅿; **Z** 13784; ● 200

Harford; MCD-Town; CORTLAND; ***209** NL-11; 🅿; **Z** 13784; Ⓟ 886; Ⓒ 920

Harford Mills (Mills); RMC Place; CORTLAND; ▲ Harford; **209** NL-12; 🅿; **Z** 13835; ● 180

Harkness; RMC Place; CLINTON; ▲ Au Sable; ***209** NC-19; elev. 379ft./116m.; mail Peru **Z** 12972; ● 60

Harlem; RMC Place; NEW YORK; **211** F-11; ★ **N.Y.**; mail New York **Z** 10030; pop. incl. with New York (Inc. Place)

Harlemville; RMC Place; COLUMBIA; ▲ Hillsdale; ***209** NL-19; elev. 700ft./213m.; mail Ghent **Z** 12075; ● 110

Harmon Park; RMC Place; SCHENECTADY; ▲ Glenville; ***209** NJ-18; ★ **A-S-T**; mail Schenectady **Z** 12302

Harmony; MCD-Town; CHAUTAUQUA; ***208** NM-2; mail Panama **Z** 14767; Ⓟ 2,177; Ⓒ 2,339

Harmony Corners; RMC Place; SARATOGA; ▲ Charlton; ***209** NI-18; elev. 539ft./164m.; ★ **A-S-T**; mail Ballston Spa **Z** 12020; rural

Harpersfield; RMC Place; DELAWARE; ▲ Harpersfield; **209** NL-16; 🅿; **Z** 13786; ● 110

Harpersfield; MCD-Town; DELAWARE; ***209** NK-16; 🅿; **Z** 13786; Ⓟ 1,450; Ⓒ 1,603

Harpursville; RMC Place; BROOME; ▲ Colesville; **209** NM-13; 🅿; ★ **BING**; **Z** 13787, **Z** 13826; ● 500

Harriet; RMC Place; ERIE; ▲ Tonawanda; ★ **BUF**; mail Buffalo **Z** 14223

Harrietstown; MCD-Town; FRANKLIN; ***209** ND-17; mail Saranac Lake **Z** 12983; Ⓟ 5,621; Ⓒ 5,575

Harriman; Inc. Place; ORANGE; ▲ Monroe; **207** SC-6; elev. 542ft./165m.; 🅿; ★ **N.Y.**; **Z** 10926; Ⓟ 2,288; Ⓒ 2,252

Harris; RMC Place; SULLIVAN; ▲ Woodbury; **207** SB-4; 🅿 🅷; **Z** 12742; ● 600

Harrisburg; RMC Place; LEWIS; ▲ Harrisburg; ***209** NF-13; mail Lowville **Z** 13367; ● 25

Harrisburg; MCD-Town; LEWIS; ***209** NF-13; mail Lowville **Z** 13367; Ⓟ 425; Ⓒ 423

Harrisburg; RMC Place; WARREN; ▲ Stony Creek; ***209** NH-18; elev. 1,553ft./473m.; mail Stony Creek **Z** 12878; ● 75

Harris Corners; RMC Place; WYOMING; ***208** NJ-5; elev. 1,313ft./400m.; mail Strykersville **Z** 14145; rural

Harris Hill; CDP; ERIE; ▲ Clarence; **208** NI-4; elev. 727ft./222m.; ★ **BUF**; mail Buffalo **Z** 14221; Ⓟ 4,577; Ⓒ 4,881

Harris Hill Manor; RMC Place; CHEMUNG; ▲ Big Flats; ***208** NM-9; ★ **ELM**; mail Elmira **Z** 14903; ● 200

Harrison; Inc. Place; WESTCHESTER; ▲ Harrison; **207** SE-7; 🅿 🅲 6,872; ★ **N.Y.**; **Z** 10528; Ⓟ 23,308; Ⓒ 24,154; ◆ 25,352

Harrison; MCD-Town; WESTCHESTER; ***207** SE-7; 🅿 🅲 6,872; ★ **N.Y.**; **Z** 10528; coextensive with the Village of Harrison; Ⓟ 23,308; Ⓒ 24,154; ◆ 25,352

Harrisville; Inc. Place; LEWIS; ▲ Diana; **209** NE-14; 🅿; **Z** 13648; Ⓟ 703; Ⓒ 653

Harrower; RMC Place; MONTGOMERY; ▲ Amsterdam; ***209** NI-18; elev. 700ft./213m.; ★ **A-S-T**; mail Amsterdam **Z** 12010; rural

Hartfield; RMC Place; CHAUTAUQUA; ▲ Chautauqua; **208** NL-2; mail Dewittville **Z** 14728; ● 100

Hartford; RMC Place; WASHINGTON; ▲ Hartford; **209** NH-20; elev. 390ft./119m.; 🅿; **Z** 12838; ● 500

Hartford; MCD-Town; WASHINGTON; ***209** NH-20; 🅿; **Z** 12838; Ⓟ 1,989; Ⓒ 2,279

Hartland; RMC Place; NIAGARA; ▲ Hartland; **208** NH-4; ★ **LOCK**; mail Gasport **Z** 14067; ● 200

Hartland; MCD-Town; NIAGARA; ***208** NH-4; ★ **LOCK**; mail Gasport **Z** 14067; Ⓟ 3,911; Ⓒ 4,165

Hart Lot; ONONDAGA; see Skaneateles Junction (RMC Place)

Hartmans Corners; RMC Place; ALBANY; ▲ Guilderland; **207** SH-2; elev. 265ft./81m.; ★ **A-S-T**; mail Altamont **Z** 12009; ● 100

Hartsdale; CDP; WESTCHESTER; ▲ Greenburgh; **207** SI-7; elev. 182ft./55m.; 🅿; ★ **N.Y.**; **Z** 10530; Ⓟ 9,587; Ⓒ 9,830

Harts Hill; RMC Place; ONEIDA; ▲ Whitestown, New Hartford; ***209** NI-14; ★ **UT-R**; mail Whitesboro **Z** 13492; pop. incl. with Whitesboro (Inc. Place)

Hartson Point; RMC Place; LIVINGSTON; ▲ Livonia; ***208** NJ-7; ★ **ROCH**; mail Livonia **Z** 14487; ● 50

Hartsville; RMC Place; STEUBEN; ▲ Hartsville; **208** NL-7; elev. 1,484ft./452m.; mail Hornell **Z** 14843; ● 200

Hartsville; MCD-Town; STEUBEN; ***208** NL-7; mail Hornell **Z** 14843; Ⓟ 546; Ⓒ 585

Hartwick; RMC Place; OTSEGO; ▲ Hartwick; **209** NK-15; 🅿; **Z** 13348; ● 650

Hartwick; MCD-Town; OTSEGO; ***209** NK-15; 🅿; **Z** 13348; Ⓟ 2,045; Ⓒ 2,203

Hartwick Seminary; RMC Place; OTSEGO; ▲ Hartwick; **209** NK-15; elev. 1,266ft./386m.; 🅿; **Z** 13326; ● 100

Hartwood; RMC Place; SULLIVAN; ▲ Forestburgh; **207** SB-4; mail Forestburgh **Z** 12777; ● 50

Harvard; RMC Place; DELAWARE; ▲ Hancock; ***209** NM-15; elev. 1,034ft./315m.; mail East Branch **Z** 13756

Hasbrouck; RMC Place; SULLIVAN; ▲ Fallsburg; **209** NN-16; mail Woodbourne **Z** 12788; ● 220

Haskell Flats; RMC Place; CATTARAUGUS; ▲ Hinsdale; ***208** NM-5; mail Cuba **Z** 14727; ● 60

Haskinville; RMC Place; STEUBEN; ▲ Fremont; **208** NL-7; elev. 1,620ft./494m.; mail Cohocton **Z** 14826; ● 100

Hastings; RMC Place; OSWEGO; ▲ Hastings; **209** NH-12; elev. 474ft./144m.; 🅿; ★ **SYR**; **Z** 13076; ● 350

Hastings; MCD-Town; OSWEGO; ***209** NH-12; 🅿; ★ **SYR**; **Z** 13076; Ⓟ 8,113; Ⓒ 8,803

Hastings Center; RMC Place; OSWEGO; ▲ Hastings; ***209** NH-12; ★ **SYR**; mail Central Square **Z** 13036; rural

Hastings-on-Hudson; Inc. Place; WESTCHESTER; ▲ Greenburgh; **207** SE-7; elev. 199ft./61m.; 🅿; ★ **N.Y.**; **Z** 10706; Ⓟ 8,000; Ⓒ 7,648; Ⓡ 7,715

Hatch's Corner (Owens Corners); RMC Place; ST. LAWRENCE; ▲ Russell; mail Russell **Z** 13684; rural

Hauppauge; CDP; SUFFOLK; ▲ Islip, Smithtown; **207** SH-12; 🅿; ★ **N.Y.**; **Z** 11749, **Z** 11788 & mail Islandia **Z** 11760; Ⓟ 19,750; Ⓒ 20,100; ◆ 20,097

Haven; RMC Place; SULLIVAN; ▲ Mamakating; **207** SB-4; elev. 537ft./164m.; mail Wurtsboro **Z** 12790; ● 70

Haverstraw; Inc. Place; ROCKLAND; ▲ Haverstraw; **207** SD-6; 🅿; ★ **N.Y.**; **Z** 10927; Ⓟ 9,438; Ⓒ 10,117

Haverstraw; MCD-Town; ROCKLAND; ***207** SD-6; 🅿; ★ **N.Y.**; **Z** 10927; Ⓟ 32,712; Ⓒ 33,811; ◆ 35,596

Haviland; CDP-Census Area Only; DUTCHESS; ▲ Hyde Park; ***207** SA-7; ★ **POK**; mail Hyde Park **Z** 12538, Poughkeepsie **Z** 12601; Ⓟ 3,605; Ⓒ 3,710

Hawkeye; RMC Place; CLINTON; ▲ Black Brook; **209** NC-18; mail Au Sable Forks **Z** 12912; ● 100

Hawkins Corner; RMC Place; ONEIDA; ▲ Lee; ***209** NH-14; ★ **UT-R**; mail Lee Center **Z** 13363, Rome **Z** 13440

Hawkinsville; RMC Place; ONEIDA; ▲ Boonville; **209** NG-14; elev. 1,072ft./327m.; mail Boonville **Z** 13309; ● 100

Hawleys; RMC Place; DELAWARE; ▲ Hamden; ***209** NM-15; elev. 1,298ft./396m.; mail Walton **Z** 13856; rural

Hawleyton; RMC Place; BROOME; ▲ Binghamton; ***209** NM-12; ★ **BING**; mail Binghamton **Z** 13903; ● 200

Hawthorne; CDP; WESTCHESTER; ▲ Mount Pleasant; ***207** SD-7; 🅿; ★ **N.Y.**; **Z** 10532; Ⓟ 4,764; Ⓒ 5,083

Hawthorne Hill; RMC Place; SCHENECTADY; ▲ Niskayuna; ***209** NJ-18; ★ **A-S-T**; mail Schenectady **Z** 12309

Hawthorne Park; RMC Place; CHAUTAUQUA; ▲ Westfield; ***208** NL-1; mail Westfield **Z** 14787; rural

Hawversville; RMC Place; SCHOHARIE; ▲ Broome; ***209** NK-17; mail Middleburgh **Z** 12122; rural

Hay Beach Point; RMC Place; SUFFOLK; ▲ Shelter Island; ***207** SD-12; mail Shelter Island **Z** 11964; ● 70

Haydenville; RMC Place; CATTARAUGUS; ▲ Portville; ***208** NM-5; elev. 1,715ft./523m.; mail Olean **Z** 14760; rural

Haynersville; RMC Place; RENSSELAER; ▲ Brunswick; ***209** NJ-19; ★ **A-S-T**; mail Troy **Z** 12180; ● 500

Hayt Corners (Hayts Corners); RMC Place; SENECA; ▲ Romulus; ***208** NK-10; 🅿; **Z** 14521; ● 70

Hayts Corners; SENECA; see Hayt Corners (RMC Place)

Hazel; RMC Place; SULLIVAN; ▲ Rockland; ***207** SA-3; mail Livingston Manor **Z** 12758; rural

Head of the Harbor; Inc. Place; SUFFOLK; ▲ Smithtown; **207** SG-13; ★ **N.Y.**; mail Saint James **Z** 11780; Ⓟ 1,354; Ⓒ 1,447

Heathcote; RMC Place; WESTCHESTER; ***207** SE-7; 🅿; ★ **N.Y.**; **Z** 10583; pop. incl. with Scarsdale (Inc. Place)

Heatherwood North; RMC Place; SUFFOLK; ▲ Brookhaven; ★ **N.Y.**; mail East Setauket **Z** 11733

Heatherwood South; RMC Place; SUFFOLK; ▲ Brookhaven; ★ **N.Y.**; mail Centereach **Z** 11720

Heath Grove; RMC Place; ONONDAGA; ▲ Otisco; ***209** NJ-11; mail Marietta **Z** 13110

Heavenly Valley; RMC Place; ULSTER; ▲ Esopus; ***207** SA-6; ★ **KNGST**; mail Port Ewen **Z** 12466

Hebron; MCD-Town; WASHINGTON; ***209** NH-20; mail Granville **Z** 12832; Ⓟ 1,540; Ⓒ 1,773

Hecla; RMC Place; ONEIDA; ▲ Westmoreland; ***209** NI-14; ★ **UT-R**; mail Westmoreland **Z** 13490; rural

Hector; RMC Place; SCHUYLER; ▲ Hector; **208** NK-9; 🅿; **Z** 14841; ● 300

Hector; MCD-Town; SCHUYLER; ***208** NK-10; 🅿; **Z** 14841; Ⓟ 4,423; Ⓒ 4,854

Hedgesville; RMC Place; STEUBEN; ▲ Woodhull; ***208** NM-8; elev. 1,426ft./435m.; mail Addison **Z** 14801

Helena; RMC Place; ST. LAWRENCE; ▲ Brasher; **209** NA-16; 🅿; **Z** 13649; ● 350

Hell Gate; RMC Place; NEW YORK; ★ **N.Y.**; mail New York **Z** 10029; pop. incl. with New York (Inc. Place)

Hemlock; RMC Place; LIVINGSTON; ▲ Livonia; **208** NJ-7; 🅿; ★ **ROCH**; **Z** 14466; ● 600

Hempstead; Inc. Place; NASSAU; ▲ Hempstead; **207** SF-8; 🅿 🅷 🅲 12,466 ■; ★ **N.Y.**; **Z** 11549-51 & mail East Meadow **Z** 11554, Uniondale **Z** 11553, **Z** 11555-56, West Hempstead **Z** 11552; Ⓟ 49,453; Ⓒ 56,554; Ⓡ 53,127; ◆ 55,658

Hempstead; MCD-Town; NASSAU; ***207** SG-8; 🅿 🅲 24,472; ★ **N.Y.**; **Z** 11549-51; Ⓟ 725,639; Ⓒ 755,924; ◆ 732,355

Hempstead (New Hempstead); Inc. Place; ROCKLAND; ▲ Ramapo; ***207** SD-6; ★ **N.Y.**; mail Spring Valley **Z** 10977; Ⓟ 4,200; Ⓒ 4,767

Hempstead Gardens; RMC Place; NASSAU; ▲ Hempstead; ***207** SF-8; ★ **N.Y.**; mail West Hempstead **Z** 11552

Hemstreet Park; RMC Place; RENSSELAER; ▲ Schaghticoke; ***209** NJ-19; ★ **A-S-T**; mail Mechanicville **Z** 12118; ● 700

Henderson; RMC Place; JEFFERSON; ▲ Henderson; **209** NF-12; 🅿; **Z** 13650; ● 500

Henderson; MCD-Town; JEFFERSON; ***209** NF-12; 🅿; **Z** 13650; Ⓟ 1,268; Ⓒ 1,377

Henderson Harbor; RMC Place; JEFFERSON; ▲ Henderson; **209** NF-12; elev. 257ft./78m.; 🅿; **Z** 13651; ● 350

Hendy Creek; RMC Place; CHEMUNG; ▲ Southport, Big Flats; ★ **ELM**; mail Pine City **Z** 14871; ● 300

Henrietta; RMC Place; MONROE; ▲ Henrietta; **208** NI-7; elev. 596ft./182m.; 🅿; ★ **ROCH**; **Z** 14467; ● 1,200

Henrietta; MCD-Town; MONROE; ***208** NI-7; 🅿; ★ **ROCH**; **Z** 14467; Ⓟ 36,376; Ⓒ 39,028; ◆ 40,445

Hensonville; RMC Place; GREENE; ▲ Windham; **209** NL-18; 🅿; **Z** 12439; ● 600

Heritage; RMC Place; SCHENECTADY; ★ **A-S-T**; mail Schenectady **Z** 12303; pop. incl. with Schenectady (Inc. Place)

Heritage Hills; RMC Place; SARATOGA; ▲ Milton; ***209** NI-19; elev. 420ft./128m.; ★ **A-S-T**; mail Ballston Spa **Z** 12020; ● 700

Heritage Hills; CDP-Census Area Only; WESTCHESTER; ***207** SC-7; ★ **N.Y.**; Ⓒ 3,683

Heritage Knolls; RMC Place; SARATOGA; ▲ Milton; ***209** NI-19; elev. 420ft./128m.; ★ **A-S-T**; mail Ballston Spa **Z** 12020; pop. incl. with Saratoga Springs (Inc. Place)

Herkimer; Inc. Place; ⊡ HERKIMER; ▲ Herkimer; **209** NI-15; elev. 407ft./124m.; 🅿; **Z** 13350; Ⓟ 7,945; Ⓒ 7,498

Herkimer; MCD-Town; HERKIMER; ***209** NI-15; 🅿; **Z** 13350; Ⓟ 10,401; Ⓒ 9,962

HERKIMER; **209** NG-15; Ⓟ 65,797; Ⓒ 64,427; Ⓡ 64,437; ◆ 62,183

Hermitage; RMC Place; STEUBEN; ▲ Urbana; ***208** NL-8; mail Bath **Z** 14810; rural

Hermitage; RMC Place; WYOMING; ▲ Wethersfield; ***208** NK-5; mail Gainesville **Z** 14066; ● 90

Hermon; Inc. Place; ST. LAWRENCE; ▲ Hermon; **209** NC-14; 🅿; **Z** 13652; Ⓟ 407; Ⓒ 402

Hermon; MCD-Town; ST. LAWRENCE; ***209** ND-14; 🅿; **Z** 13652; Ⓟ 1,041; Ⓒ 1,069

Herrick Grove; RMC Place; JEFFERSON; ▲ Lyme; ***209** NE-12; elev. 262ft./80m.; mail Chaumont **Z** 13622

Herricks; CDP; NASSAU; **211** G-17; ★ **N.Y.**; mail New Hyde Park **Z** 11040; Ⓟ 4,097; Ⓒ 4,076

Herrings; Inc. Place; JEFFERSON; ▲ Wilna; ***209** NE-13; mail Carthage **Z** 13619; Ⓟ 140; Ⓒ 129

Hertel; RMC Place; ERIE; ★ **BUF**; mail Buffalo **Z** 14216; pop. incl. with Buffalo (Inc. Place)

Herthum Heights; RMC Place; ONEIDA; ▲ Whitestown; ***209** NI-14; ★ **UT-R**; mail Whitesboro **Z** 13492; ● 500

Hervey Street; RMC Place; GREENE; ▲ Durham; ***209** NL-18; elev. 1,020ft./311m.; mail Cornwallville **Z** 12418; ● 45

Hessville; RMC Place; MONTGOMERY; ▲ Canajoharie; ***209** NJ-16; mail Fort Plain **Z** 13339

Heuvelton; Inc. Place; ST. LAWRENCE; ▲ Oswegatchie; **209** NC-14; elev. 315ft./96m.; 🅿; **Z** 13654; Ⓟ 771; Ⓒ 804

Hewittville; RMC Place; ST. LAWRENCE; ▲ Potsdam; ***209** NB-15; mail Norwood **Z** 13668; ● 60

Hewlett; CDP; NASSAU; ▲ Hempstead; **211** J-16; 🅿; ★ **N.Y.**; **Z** 11557; Ⓟ 6,620; Ⓒ 7,060

Hewlett Bay Park; Inc. Place; NASSAU; ▲ Hempstead; **211** K-16; ★ **N.Y.**; mail Hewlett **Z** 11557; Ⓟ 440; Ⓒ 484

Hewlett Harbor; Inc. Place; NASSAU; ▲ Hempstead; **211** K-17; ★ **N.Y.**; mail Hewlett **Z** 11557; Ⓟ 1,193; Ⓒ 1,271

Hewlett Neck; Inc. Place; NASSAU; ▲ Hempstead; **211** K-16; ★ **N.Y.**; mail Woodmere **Z** 11598; Ⓟ 547; Ⓒ 504

Hickeys Corners; RMC Place; SARATOGA; ***209** NI-19; ★ **A-S-T**; mail Saratoga Springs **Z** 12866; pop. incl. with Saratoga Springs (Inc. Place)

Hickorybush; RMC Place; ULSTER; ▲ Rosendale; ***207** SA-6; ★ **KNGST**; mail Kingston **Z** 12401; ● 250

Hickory Grove; RMC Place; OSWEGO; ▲ New Haven; ***209** NG-11; mail Oswego **Z** 13126; ● 60

Hicks; RMC Place; CHEMUNG; ▲ Baldwin; ***208** NM-10; elev. 1,121ft./342m.; mail Lockwood **Z** 14859; rural

Hicks Corners; RMC Place; WYOMING; ▲ Java; ***208** NK-5; mail Arcade **Z** 14009; rural

Hicksville; CDP; NASSAU; ▲ Oyster Bay; **207** SF-8; elev. 149ft./45m.; 🅿; ★ **N.Y.**; **Z** 11801-02, **Z** 11815, **Z** 11819, **Z** 11854-55 & mail Old Bethpage **Z** 11804, Plainview **Z** 11803; Ⓟ 40,174; Ⓒ 41,260; ◆ 39,183

Higgins; RMC Place; ALLEGANY; ▲ Centerville; ***208** NL-6; elev. 1,429ft./436m.; mail Freedom **Z** 14065; ● 50

Higgins Bay; RMC Place; HAMILTON; ▲ Arietta; **209** NH-16; elev. 1,684ft./513m.; mail Lake Pleasant **Z** 12108; ● 50

Higginsville; RMC Place; ONEIDA; ▲ Verona; **209** NI-13; elev. 431ft./131m.; ★ **UT-R**; mail Durhamville **Z** 13054; ● 50

High Bank; RMC Place; CLINTON; ▲ Saranac; ***209** NC-18; mail Saranac **Z** 12981; ● 85

High Bridge; RMC Place; BRONX; ***207** SF-7; ★ **N.Y.**; mail Bronx **Z** 10452; pop. incl. with New York (Inc. Place)

High Bridge; RMC Place; ONONDAGA; ▲ Manlius; ***209** NI-12; ★ **SYR**; mail Fayetteville **Z** 13066; ● 200

High Falls; CDP; ULSTER; ▲ Rosendale, Marbletown; **209** NN-18; 🅿; ★ **KNGST**; **Z** 12440; Ⓒ 627

High Flats; RMC Place; ST. LAWRENCE; ▲ Parishville; ***209** NC-15; elev. 867ft./264m.; mail Colton **Z** 13625; rural

Highland; MCD-Town; SULLIVAN; ***207** SB-3; mail Eldred **Z** 12732; Ⓟ 2,147; Ⓒ 2,404

Highland; CDP; ULSTER; ▲ Lloyd; **207** SA-6; 🅿; ★ **POK**; **Z** 12528; Ⓟ 4,492; Ⓒ 5,060

Highland Falls; Inc. Place; ORANGE; ▲ Highlands; **207** SC-6; 🅿; ★ **N.Y.**; **Z** 10928; Ⓟ 3,937; Ⓒ 3,678

Highland Lake; RMC Place; SULLIVAN; ▲ Highlands; **207** SB-3; 🅿; **Z** 12743; ● 450

Highland Mills; CDP; ORANGE; ▲ Woodbury; **207** SC-6; 🅿; ★ **N.Y.**; **Z** 10930; Ⓟ 2,576; Ⓒ 3,468

Highland-on-the-Lake; RMC Place; ERIE; ▲ Evans; **208** NJ-3; ★ **BUF**; mail Derby **Z** 14047; ● 1,800

Highlands; MCD-Town; ORANGE; ***207** SC-6; 🅲 4,236; ★ **N.Y.**; mail Highland Falls **Z** 10928; Ⓟ 13,667; Ⓒ 12,484

Highlawn; RMC Place; KINGS; ★ **N.Y.**; mail Brooklyn **Z** 11223; pop. incl. with New York (Inc. Place)

High Mills; RMC Place; SCHENECTADY; ▲ Glenville; ***209** NJ-18; elev. 354ft./108m.; ★ **A-S-T**; mail Burnt Hills **Z** 12027; ● 100

Highmount (Grand Hotel); RMC Place; ULSTER; ▲ Shandaken; **209** NM-17; 🅿; **Z** 12441; ● 300

High View; RMC Place; SULLIVAN; ▲ Mamakating; **207** SB-5; ★ **MIDD**; mail Bloomingburg **Z** 12721; ● 200

High Woods; RMC Place; ULSTER; ▲ Saugerties; ***209** NM-18; ★ **KNGST**; mail Saugerties **Z** 12477; ● 150

Hillburn; Inc. Place; ROCKLAND; ▲ Ramapo; **207** SD-6; 🅿; ★ **N.Y.**; **Z** 10931; Ⓟ 892; Ⓒ 881

Hillcrest; RMC Place; ALLEGANY; ▲ Rushford; ***208** NL-5; mail Caneadea **Z** 14717; rural

Hillcrest; RMC Place; BROOME; ▲ Fenton; ***209** NM-12; ★ **BING**; mail Binghamton **Z** 13901; ● 1,850

Hillcrest; CDP; ROCKLAND; ▲ Ramapo; **207** SD-6; ★ **N.Y.**; mail Spring Valley **Z** 10977; Ⓟ 6,447; Ⓒ 7,106

Hiller Heights; RMC Place; ONONDAGA; ▲ Cicero; ***209** NI-12; ★ **SYR**; mail Clay **Z** 13041, Syracuse **Z** 13212; ● 1,350

Hillis (Hillis Terrace); RMC Place; DUTCHESS; ▲ Poughkeepsie; ***207** SB-7; ★ **POK**; mail Poughkeepsie **Z** 12603; ● 2,000

Hillis Terrace; DUTCHESS; see Hillis (RMC Place)

Hillsboro; RMC Place; ONEIDA; ▲ Camden; ***209** NH-13; elev. 620ft./189m.; mail Camden **Z** 13316; rural

Hillsdale; RMC Place; COLUMBIA; ▲ Hillsdale; ***209** NL-20; 🅿; **Z** 12529; ● 150

Hillsdale; MCD-Town; COLUMBIA; ***209** NL-20; 🅿; **Z** 12529; Ⓟ 1,793; Ⓒ 1,744

Hillside; RMC Place; BRONX; ★ **N.Y.**; mail Bronx **Z** 10469; pop. incl. with New York (Inc. Place)

Hillside; RMC Place; ONEIDA; ▲ Western; ***209** NH-14; mail Westernville **Z** 13486; ● 50

Hillside; RMC Place; QUEENS; **211** H-14; ★ **N.Y.**; mail Jamaica **Z** 11433; pop. incl. with New York (Inc. Place)

Hillside; CDP-Census Area Only; ULSTER; ***209** NN-18; ★ **KNGST**; Ⓒ 882

Hillside Lake; CDP-Census Area Only; DUTCHESS; ▲ East Fishkill; ***207** SB-7; ★ **POK**; mail Wappingers Falls **Z** 12590; Ⓟ 1,692; Ⓒ 2,022

Hillside Manor; RMC Place; NASSAU; ▲ North Hempstead; ***207** SF-8; 🅿; ★ **N.Y.**; **Z** 11040

Hillside Park; RMC Place; FULTON; mail Johnstown **Z** 12095; pop. incl. with Johnstown (Inc. Place)

Hillview; RMC Place; RENSSELAER; ▲ East Greenbush; ***209** NK-19; ★ **A-S-T**; mail Rensselaer **Z** 12144; ● 375

Hilton; Inc. Place; MONROE; ▲ Parma; **208** NH-7; 🅿; ★ **ROCH**; **Z** 14468; Ⓟ 5,216; Ⓒ 5,856

Himrod (Seneca Lake); RMC Place; YATES; ▲ Milo; **208** NK-9; 🅿; **Z** 14842; ● 300

Hinckley; RMC Place; ONEIDA; ▲ Trenton; **209** NH-15; elev. 1,181ft./360m.; 🅿; ★ **UT-R**; **Z** 13352; ● 250

Hinckleyville; RMC Place; MONROE; ▲ Parma; ***208** NH-7; ★ **ROCH**; mail Spencerport **Z** 14559; rural

Hindsburg; RMC Place; ORLEANS; ▲ Murray; ***208** NH-6; ★ **ROCH**; mail Albion **Z** 14411; rural

Hinmans Corners; RMC Place; BROOME; ▲ Chenango; ***209** NM-12; ★ **BING**; mail Binghamton **Z** 13905

Hinmansville; RMC Place; OSWEGO; ▲ Schroeppel; ***209** NH-11; ★ **SYR**; mail Phoenix **Z** 13135; ● 70

Hinsdale; RMC Place; CATTARAUGUS; ▲ Hinsdale; **208** NM-5; elev. 1,489ft./454m.; 🅿; **Z** 14743; ● 900

Hinsdale; MCD-Town; CATTARAUGUS; ***208** NM-5; 🅿; **Z** 14743; Ⓟ 2,095; Ⓒ 2,270

Hitching Corner; RMC Place; HERKIMER; ▲ Winfield; ***209** NJ-16; mail West Winfield **Z** 13491; rural

Hoag Corners; RMC Place; RENSSELAER; ▲ Nassau; **209** NK-20; ★ **A-S-T**; mail East Nassau **Z** 12062; pop. incl. with East Nassau (Inc. Place)

Hobart; Inc. Place; DELAWARE; ▲ Stamford; **209** NL-16; 🅿; **Z** 13788; Ⓟ 385; Ⓒ 390

Hoboken; RMC Place; OTSEGO; ▲ Richfield; ***209** NK-14; mail New Berlin **Z** 13411; rural

Hoffmans; RMC Place; SCHENECTADY; ▲ Glenville; ***209** NJ-18; ★ **A-S-T**; mail Schenectady **Z** 12302; ● 70

Hoffmeister; RMC Place; HAMILTON; ▲ Morehouse; **209** NH-16; elev. 1,857ft./566m.; 🅿; **Z** 13353; ● 45

Hogansburg; RMC Place; FRANKLIN; ▲ Bombay; **209** NA-16; elev. 181ft./55m.; 🅿; **Z** 13655; ● 100

Hogtown; RMC Place; WASHINGTON; ▲ Fort Ann; ***209** NG-19; elev. 1,201ft./366m.; mail Fort Ann **Z** 12827; rural

Holbrook; CDP; SUFFOLK; ▲ Islip, Brookhaven; **207** SH-13; elev. 118ft./36m.; 🅿; ★ **N.Y.**; **Z** 11741; Ⓟ 25,273; Ⓒ 27,512; ◆ 27,506

Holcomb (Bloomfield); Inc. Place; ONTARIO; ▲ East Bloomfield; **208** NJ-8; ★ **ROCH**; mail Bloomfield **Z** 14469; Ⓒ 1,267

Holcombville; RMC Place; WARREN; ▲ Johnsburg; **209** NF-18; mail North Creek **Z** 12853; ● 200

Holiday Manor; RMC Place; ONTARIO; mail Geneva **Z** 14456; pop. incl. with Geneva (Inc. Place)

Holland; CDP; ERIE; ▲ Holland; **208** NK-4; elev. 1,111ft./339m.; 🅿; ★ **BUF**; **Z** 14080; Ⓟ 1,288; Ⓒ 1,261

Holland; MCD-Town; ERIE; ***208** NK-5; 🅿; ★ **BUF**; **Z** 14080; Ⓟ 3,572; Ⓒ 3,603

Holland Cove; RMC Place; WAYNE; ▲ Williamson; ***208** NH-9; ★ **ROCH**; mail Williamson **Z** 14589; rural

Holland Patent; Inc. Place; ONEIDA; ▲ Trenton; **209** NH-14; 🅿; ★ **UT-R**; **Z** 13354; Ⓟ 411; Ⓒ 461

Holley; Inc. Place; ORLEANS; ▲ Murray; **208** NH-6; 🅿; ★ **ROCH**; **Z** 14470; Ⓟ 1,890; Ⓒ 1,802

Hollis; RMC Place; QUEENS; **211** H-15; 🅿; ★ **N.Y.**; **Z** 11423; pop. incl. with New York (Inc. Place)

Holliswood; RMC Place; QUEENS; ★ **N.Y.**; mail Hollis **Z** 11423; pop. incl. with New York (Inc. Place)

Hollowville; RMC Place; COLUMBIA; ▲ Claverack; ***209** NL-19; 🅿; **Z** 12530; ● 280

Holmes; RMC Place; DUTCHESS; ▲ Pawling; **207** SB-8; 🅿; **Z** 12531; ● 460

Holmesville; RMC Place; CHENANGO; ▲ New Berlin; **209** NK-14; mail South New Berlin **Z** 13843; ● 150

Holton Beach; RMC Place; SENECA; ▲ Covert; ***208** NK-10; ★ **ITH**; mail Interlaken **Z** 14847; ● 35

Holtsville; CDP; SUFFOLK; ▲ Islip, Brookhaven; **207** SH-14; 🅿; ★ **N.Y.**; **Z** 00501, **Z** 00544, **Z** 11742; Ⓟ 14,972; Ⓒ 17,006

Homecrest; RMC Place; KINGS; ***207** SG-7; ★ **N.Y.**; mail Brooklyn **Z** 11229; pop. incl. with New York (Inc. Place)

Homer; Inc. Place; CORTLAND; ▲ Homer, Cortlandville; **209** NK-12; elev. 1,133ft./345m.; 🅿; **Z** 13077; Ⓟ 3,476; Ⓒ 3,368

Homer; MCD-Town; CORTLAND; ***209** NK-12; 🅿; **Z** 13077; includes part of the Village of Homer; Ⓟ 6,508; Ⓒ 6,363

Homer Hill; RMC Place; CATTARAUGUS; ***208** NM-5; mail Olean **Z** 14760; pop. incl. with Olean (Inc. Place)

Homestead Park; RMC Place; WESTCHESTER; ***207** SE-7; ★ **N.Y.**; mail New Rochelle **Z** 10801; pop. incl. with New Rochelle (Inc. Place)

Homestead Village; RMC Place; SUFFOLK; ▲ Brookhaven; ***207** SE-10; ★ **N.Y.**; mail Coram **Z** 11727

Homewood; RMC Place; ONONDAGA; ▲ Manlius; **208** NG-10; ★ **SYR**; mail Fayetteville **Z** 13066; ● 1,450

Homewood Park; RMC Place; ERIE; ▲ Cheektowaga; ★ **BUF**; mail Buffalo **Z** 14225

Honeoye; RMC Place; ONTARIO; ▲ Richmond; **208** NJ-8; 🅿; **Z** 14471; ● 1,000

Honeoye Falls; Inc. Place; MONROE; ▲ Mendon; **208** NI-7; 🅿; ★ **ROCH**; **Z** 14472; Ⓟ 2,340; Ⓒ 2,595

Honest Hill; RMC Place; ORLEANS; ▲ Clarendon; ***208** NI-6; elev. 661ft./201m.; ★ **ROCH**; mail Holley **Z** 14470; rural

Honeywell Corners; RMC Place; FULTON; ▲ Broadalbin; ***209** NI-18; ★ **A-S-T**; mail Broadalbin **Z** 12025; rural

Honk Hill; RMC Place; ULSTER; ▲ Wawarsing; ***207** SA-5; mail Napanoch **Z** 12458; ● 100

Honnedaga Lake; RMC Place; ONEIDA; ▲ Forestport; mail Forestport **Z** 13338

Hooper; BROOME; see Endwell (CDP)

Hoosick; RMC Place; RENSSELAER; ▲ Hoosick; **209** NJ-20; 🅿; **Z** 12089; ● 400

Hoosick; MCD-Town; RENSSELAER; ***209** NJ-20; 🅿; **Z** 12089; Ⓟ 6,696; Ⓒ 6,759

Hoosick Falls; Inc. Place; RENSSELAER; ▲ Hoosick; **209** NJ-20; elev. 460ft./140m.; 🅿; **Z** 12090; Ⓟ 3,490; Ⓒ 3,436

Hoosick Junction; RMC Place; RENSSELAER; ▲ Hoosick; ***209** NI-20; mail North Hoosick **Z** 12133; rural

Hope; MCD-Town; HAMILTON; ***209** NH-17; mail Northville **Z** 12134; Ⓟ 358; Ⓒ 392

Hope Falls; RMC Place; HAMILTON; ▲ Hope; **209** NH-18; mail Northville **Z** 12134; ● 80

Hope Farm (Greer Childrens Home); RMC Place; DUTCHESS; ▲ Union Vale; **207** SA-8; mail Millbrook **Z** 12545; ● 300

Hope Valley; RMC Place; HAMILTON; ▲ Hope; ***209** NH-17; mail Northville **Z** 12134; rural

Hopewell; DUTCHESS; see Hopewell Junction (CDP)

Hopewell; MCD-Town; ONTARIO; ***208** NJ-9; mail Canandaigua **Z** 14424; Ⓟ 3,016; Ⓒ 3,346

Hopewell Center; RMC Place; ONTARIO; ▲ Hopewell; ***208** NJ-9; elev. 838ft./255m.; mail Canandaigua **Z** 14424; ● 65

Hopewell Junction (Hopewell); CDP; DUTCHESS; ▲ East Fishkill; **207** SB-7; elev. 257ft./78m.; 🅿; ★ **POK**; **Z** 12533; Ⓟ 1,786; Ⓒ 2,610

Hopkinton; RMC Place; ST. LAWRENCE; ▲ Hopkinton; **209** NB-16; elev. 795ft./242m.; 🅿; **Z** 12965; ● 200

Hopkinton; MCD-Town; ST. LAWRENCE; ***209** NC-16; 🅿; **Z** 12965; Ⓟ 957; Ⓒ 1,020

Horace Harding; RMC Place; QUEENS; ★ **N.Y.**; mail Little Neck **Z** 11362; pop. incl. with New York (Inc. Place)

Horicon; WARREN; see Brant Lake (RMC Place)

Horicon; MCD-Town; WARREN; ***209** NF-19; mail Brant Lake **Z** 12815; Ⓟ 1,269; Ⓒ 1,479

Hornby; RMC Place; STEUBEN; ▲ Hornby; **208** NL-9; elev. 1,516ft./462m.; mail Beaver Dams **Z** 14812; ● 300

Hornby; MCD-Town; STEUBEN; ***208** NL-9; mail Beaver Dams **Z** 14812; Ⓟ 1,655; Ⓒ 1,742

Hornell; Inc. Place; STEUBEN; **208** NL-7; elev. 1,164ft./355m.; 🅿 🅷 ■; **Z** 14843; Ⓟ 9,877; Ⓒ 9,019; ◆ 8,421

Hornellsville; MCD-Town; STEUBEN; ***208** NL-7; mail Arkport **Z** 14807; Ⓟ 4,149; Ⓒ 4,042

Horseheads; Inc. Place; CHEMUNG; **208** NM-10; elev. 898ft./274m.; 🅿; ★ **ELM**; **Z** 14845; Ⓟ 6,802; Ⓒ 6,452; Ⓡ 6,566

Horseheads; MCD-Town; CHEMUNG; ***208** NM-10; 🅿; ★ **ELM**; **Z** 14845; Ⓟ 19,926; Ⓒ 19,561

Horseheads North (Slabtown); CDP-Census Area Only; CHEMUNG; ▲ Horseheads; ***208** NM-10; ★ **ELM**; mail Horseheads **Z** 14845; Ⓟ 3,003; Ⓒ 2,852

Horseshoe Hill; RMC Place; WESTCHESTER; ▲ Pound Ridge; ***207** SD-8; ★ **N.Y.**; mail Pound Ridge **Z** 10576; ● 200

Horton; RMC Place; DELAWARE; ▲ Colchester; ***209** NM-15; mail Roscoe **Z** 12776; rural

Horton Estates; RMC Place; WESTCHESTER; ▲ Somers; ***207** SC-7; ★ **N.Y.**; mail Shenorock **Z** 10587

Hortonville; RMC Place; SULLIVAN; ▲ Delaware; **207** SA-2; 🅿; **Z** 12745; ● 150

Houghton; CDP; ALLEGANY; ▲ Caneadea; **208** NL-6; 🅿 🅲 1,353; **Z** 14744; Ⓟ 1,740; Ⓒ 1,748

Hounsfield; MCD-Town; JEFFERSON; ***209** NF-12; mail Sackets Harbor **Z** 13685; Ⓟ 3,089; Ⓒ 3,323

Houseville; RMC Place; LEWIS; ▲ Turin; ***209** NF-14; mail Turin **Z** 13473; rural

Housons Corners; RMC Place; SCHOHARIE; ▲ Fulton; ***209** NK-17; mail Middleburgh **Z** 12122; rural

Howard; RMC Place; STEUBEN; ▲ Howard; **208** NL-8; elev. 1,650ft./503m.; mail Avoca **Z** 14809; ● 200

Howard; MCD-Town; STEUBEN; ***208** NL-8; mail Avoca **Z** 14809; Ⓟ 1,331; Ⓒ 1,430

Howard Beach; RMC Place; QUEENS; **211** J-13; 🅿; ★ **N.Y.**; **Z** 11414; pop. incl. with New York (Inc. Place)

Howardville; RMC Place; OSWEGO; ▲ Albion; ***209** NG-12; mail Altmar **Z** 13302; rural

Howells; RMC Place; ORANGE; ▲ Wallkill; **207** SC-5; 🅿; ★ **MIDD**; **Z** 10932; ● 500

Howes Cave; RMC Place; SCHOHARIE; ▲ Cobleskill; ***209** NJ-17; elev. 801ft./244m.; 🅿; **Z** 12092; ● 200

Howland Hook; RMC Place; RICHMOND; ★ **N.Y.**; pop. incl. with New York (Inc. Place)

Howlett Hill; RMC Place; ONONDAGA; ▲ Onondaga; **208** NG-6; ★ **SYR**; mail Camillus **Z** 13031; ● 650

Hub; RMC Place; BRONX; ★ **N.Y.**; mail Bronx **Z** 10455; pop. incl. with New York (Inc. Place)

Hubbardsville; RMC Place; MADISON; ▲ Hamilton; **209** NJ-14; elev. 1,218ft./371m.; 🅿; **Z** 13355; ● 250

Hubbardtown; RMC Place; TIOGA; ▲ Candor; ***209** NM-11; mail Candor **Z** 13743; rural

Hudson; Inc. Place; ⊡ COLUMBIA; **209** NL-19; elev. 80ft./24m.; 🅿 🅷; **Z** 12534; Ⓟ 8,034; Ⓒ 7,524

Hudson Falls; Inc. Place; ⊡ WASHINGTON; ▲ Kingsbury; **209** NH-19; elev. 294ft./90m.; 🅿; ★ **GLFLS**; **Z** 12839; Ⓟ 7,651; Ⓒ 6,927

Hudson Upper; RMC Place; COLUMBIA; mail Hudson **Z** 12534; pop. incl. with Hudson (Inc. Place)

Hughsonville; RMC Place; DUTCHESS; ▲ Wappinger; **207** SB-7; 🅿; ★ **POK**; **Z** 12537; ● 1,400

Huguenot; RMC Place; ORANGE; ▲ Deerpark; **207** SC-4; 🅿; **Z** 12746; ● 800

Huguenot; RMC Place; RICHMOND; **210** M-6; ★ **N.Y.**; mail Staten Island **Z** 10312; pop. incl. with New York (Inc. Place)

Huguenot Park; RMC Place; WESTCHESTER; ***207** SE-7; ★ **N.Y.**; mail New Rochelle **Z** 10801; pop. incl. with New Rochelle (Inc. Place)

Hulberton; RMC Place; ORLEANS; ▲ Murray; **208** NH-6; 🅿; ★ **ROCH**; **Z** 14470; ● 100

Huletts Landing; RMC Place; WASHINGTON; ▲ Dresden; **209** NG-19; 🅿; **Z** 12841; ● 200

Hullsville; RMC Place; TIOGA; ▲ Owego; ***209** NM-12; elev. 1,346ft./410m.; ★ **BING**; mail Owego **Z** 13827; rural

Hume; RMC Place; ALLEGANY; ▲ Hume; **208** NK-6; 🅿; **Z** 14745; ● 400

Hume; MCD-Town; ALLEGANY; ***208** NK-6; 🅿; **Z** 14745; Ⓟ 1,970; Ⓒ 1,987

Humphrey; MCD-Town; CATTARAUGUS; ***208** NL-4; mail Great Valley **Z** 14741; Ⓟ 580; Ⓒ 721

Humphrey Center; RMC Place; CATTARAUGUS; ▲ Humphrey; ***208** NL-4; elev. 1,682ft./513m.; mail Great Valley **Z** 14741

Hungary Hill; RMC Place; SCHENECTADY; ★ **A-S-T**; pop. incl. with Schenectady (Inc. Place)

Hungerford Corners; RMC Place; JEFFERSON; ▲ Henderson; ***209** NF-11; elev. 334ft./102m.; mail Henderson **Z** 13650; rural

Hunt; RMC Place; LIVINGSTON; ▲ Portage; **208** NK-6; 🅿; **Z** 14846 & mail Huntington **Z** 11743; ● 150

Hunt Corners; RMC Place; WAYNE; ▲ Galen; ***208** NI-10; mail Clyde **Z** 14433; rural

Hunter; Inc. Place; GREENE; ▲ Hunter; **209** NL-18; 🅿; **Z** 12442; Ⓟ 429; Ⓒ 490

Hunter; MCD-Town; GREENE; ***209** NM-18; 🅿; **Z** 12442; Ⓟ 2,116; Ⓒ 2,721

Hunter Lake; RMC Place; SULLIVAN; ▲ Rockland; ***207** SA-4; mail Parksville **Z** 12768; ● 200

Huntersland; RMC Place; SCHOHARIE; ▲ Middleburgh; ***209** NK-17; mail Middleburgh **Z** 12122; ● 140

Hunters Point; RMC Place; QUEENS; ***207** SF-7; ★ **N.Y.**; mail Long Island City **Z** 11101; pop. incl. with New York (Inc. Place)

Huntington; CDP; SUFFOLK; ▲ Huntington; **207** SF-8; 🅿 🅷; ★ **N.Y.**; **Z** 11743; Ⓟ 18,243; Ⓒ 18,403

Huntington; MCD-Town; SUFFOLK; ***207** SE-9; 🅿 🅲 1,254; ★ **N.Y.**; **Z** 11743; Ⓟ 191,474; Ⓒ 195,289; ◆ 186,959

Huntington Bay; Inc. Place; SUFFOLK; ▲ Huntington; **207** SG-10; ★ **N.Y.**; mail Huntington **Z** 11743; Ⓟ 1,521; Ⓒ 1,496

Huntington Beach; RMC Place; SUFFOLK; ▲ Huntington; ***207** SE-9; ★ **N.Y.**; mail Centerport **Z** 11721; ● 2,700

Huntington Station; CDP; SUFFOLK; ▲ Huntington; **207** SF-9; elev. 216ft./66m.; 🅿; ★ **N.Y.**; **Z** 11746-47, **Z** 11750; Ⓟ 28,247; Ⓒ 29,910; ◆ 29,902

Huntingtonville; RMC Place; JEFFERSON; ▲ Watertown; ***209** NE-12; elev. 518ft./158m.; ★ **WATN**; mail Watertown **Z** 13601; ● 200

Hunts Corners; RMC Place; CORTLAND; ▲ Lapeer; ***209** NL-12; elev. 1,379ft./420m.; mail Marathon **Z** 13803; ● 80

Hunts Corners; RMC Place; ERIE; ▲ Clarence; ***208** NI-4; elev. 621ft./189m.; ★ **BUF**; mail Clarence **Z** 14031; rural

Hunts Corners; RMC Place; SULLIVAN; ▲ Tusten; ***207** SB-2; mail Narrowsburg **Z** 12764; rural

Hunts Point; RMC Place; BRONX; ***207** SF-7; ★ **N.Y.**; pop. incl. with New York (Inc. Place)

Hurd; SULLIVAN; see Swan Lake (RMC Place)

Hurd Corners; RMC Place; DUTCHESS; ▲ Pawling; ***207** SB-8; elev. 495ft./151m.; mail Pawling **Z** 12564; rural

Hurley; CDP; ULSTER; ▲ Ulster, Hurley; **209** NN-18; 🅿; ★ **KNGST**; **Z** 12443; Ⓟ 4,644; Ⓒ 3,561

Hurley; MCD-Town; ULSTER; ***209** NM-18; 🅿; ★ **KNGST**; **Z** 12443; Ⓟ 6,741; Ⓒ 6,564

Hurleyville; RMC Place; SULLIVAN; ▲ Fallsburg; **207** SA-4; elev. 1,318ft./402m.; 🅿; **Z** 12747; ● 750

Huron; MCD-Town; WAYNE; ***208** NH-9; mail Wolcott **Z** 14590; Ⓟ 2,025; Ⓒ 2,117

Hurricane; RMC Place; HERKIMER; ▲ Norway; ***209** NH-15; mail Cold Brook **Z** 13324; ● 90

Hyde Park; RMC Place; DUTCHESS; ▲ Hyde Park; **209** NN-18; elev. 184ft./56m.; 🅿 🅲 2,836; ★ **POK**; **Z** 12538; ● 2,650

Hyde Park; MCD-Town; DUTCHESS; ***207** SA-7; 🅿 🅲 2,836; ★ **POK**; **Z** 12538; Ⓟ 21,230; Ⓒ 20,851; ◆ 19,407

Hyde Park; RMC Place; OTSEGO; ▲ Hartwick; **209** NK-15; elev. 1,212ft./369m.; mail Cooperstown **Z** 13326; ● 100

Hyndsville; RMC Place; SCHOHARIE; ▲ Seward; **209** NJ-16; mail Cobleskill **Z** 12043; ● 200

I

Idle Hour; RMC Place; SUFFOLK; ▲ Islip; ★ **N.Y.**; mail Oakdale **Z** 11769

Idlewood; RMC Place; ERIE; ▲ Hamburg; ★ **BUF**; mail Lake View **Z** 14085

Ilion; Inc. Place; HERKIMER; ▲ German Flatts; **209** NI-15; elev. 410ft./125m.; 🅿; **Z** 13357; Ⓟ 8,888; Ⓒ 8,610

Inavale; RMC Place; ALLEGANY; ▲ Wirt; ***208** NM-6; elev. 1,881ft./573m.; mail Friendship **Z** 14739; rural

Independence; RMC Place; ALLEGANY; ▲ Independence; ***208** NM-7; mail Andover **Z** 14806; ● 40

Independence; MCD-Town; ALLEGANY; ***208** NM-7; mail Andover **Z** 14806; Ⓟ 1,026; Ⓒ 1,074

Index; RMC Place; OTSEGO; ▲ Otsego, Hartwick; ***209** NK-15; mail Cooperstown **Z** 13326; ● 50

Indian Castle; RMC Place; HERKIMER; ▲ Danube; ***209** NI-16; mail Little Falls **Z** 13365; rural

Entries in **UPPERCASE** are counties.
Entries in **bold** have populations of 2,500 or more.
Names in parentheses are alternate names.

Inc. Place	Incorporated Place
RMC Place	Rand McNally Designated Place
CDP	Census Designated Place
MCD	Minor Civil Division

⊡ County Seat
▲ Minor Civil Division
elev. Elevation
🅿 Post Office

🅷 Hospital
🅲 College
■ Principal Business Center
★ Ranally Metro Area (RMA) Abbreviation
Z Zip Code(s)

Ⓟ Previous Census Population
Ⓡ Revised Census Population
Ⓐ Annexation Population
● Rand McNally Population Estimate

Ⓒ Final Census Population
Ⓢ Special Census Population
◆ Estimated Population

For additional definitions see Glossary, Volume 1, and Introduction, Volume 2.

Indian Cove; RMC Place; CAYUGA; ▲ Moravia; ***209** NJ-11; mail Moravia **z** 13118; summer pop. 250; ● 55
Indian Falls; RMC Place; GENESEE; ▲ Pembroke; **208** NI-5; elev. 831ft./253m.; mail Corfu **z** 14036; ● 170
Indian Kettles; RMC Place; WARREN; ▲ Hague; ***209** NF-20; mail Hague **z** 12836; summer pop. 250
Indian Lake; RMC Place; HAMILTON; ▲ Indian Lake; **209** NF-17; elev. 1,752ft./534m.; 🅿; **z** 12842; ● 600
Indian Lake; MCD-Town; HAMILTON; ***209** NF-17; 🅿; **z** 12842; Ⓟ 1,481; Ⓒ 1,471
Indian Neck; RMC Place; SUFFOLK; ▲ Southold; mail Peconic **z** 11958
Indian Park; RMC Place; ORANGE; ▲ Warwick; **207** SD-5; ★ **N.Y.**; mail Greenwood Lake **z** 10925; ● 600
Indian River; RMC Place; LEWIS; ▲ Croghan; **209** NE-14; mail Croghan **z** 13327; ● 45
Indian Springs; RMC Place; ONONDAGA; ▲ Lysander; ***209** NI-11; ★ **SYR**; mail Baldwinsville **z** 13027; ● 600
Indian Village; RMC Place; ONONDAGA; ▲ Onondaga; **209** NI-12; ★ **SYR**; mail Nedrow **z** 13120; ● 700
Ingham Mills; RMC Place; FULTON, HERKIMER; ▲ Manheim, Oppenheim; ***209** NI-16; mail Little Falls **z** 13365; ● 100
Ingleside; RMC Place; STEUBEN; ▲ Prattsburgh; **208** NK-8; mail Naples **z** 14512; ● 90
Ingraham; RMC Place; CLINTON; ▲ Chazy; **209** NB-20; mail West Chazy **z** 12992; ● 110
Inlet; RMC Place; HAMILTON; ▲ Inlet; **209** NF-16; 🅿; **z** 13360; ● 400
Inlet; MCD-Town; HAMILTON; ***209** NF-16; 🅿; **z** 13360; Ⓟ 343; Ⓒ 406
Inman; RMC Place; FRANKLIN; ▲ Franklin; mail Vermontville **z** 12989
Interlaken; Inc. Place; SENECA; ▲ Covert; **208** NK-10; 🅿; ★ **ITH**; **z** 14847; Ⓟ 680; Ⓒ 674
Interlaken Beach; RMC Place; SENECA; ▲ Covert; ***208** NK-10; ★ **ITH**; mail Interlaken **z** 14847; ● 40
International Junction; RMC Place; ERIE; ▲ Tonawanda; ★ **BUF**; mail Buffalo **z** 14223
Inwood; CDP; NASSAU; ▲ Hempstead; **207** SG-7; 🅿; ★ **N.Y.**; **z** 11096; Ⓟ 7,767; Ⓒ 9,325
Inwood; RMC Place; NEW YORK; ***207** SF-7; ★ **N.Y.**; mail New York **z** 10034; pop. incl. with New York (Inc. Place)
Ionia; RMC Place; ONONDAGA; ▲ Van Buren; ***209** NI-11; ★ **SYR**; mail Memphis **z** 13112; rural
Ionia; RMC Place; ONTARIO; ▲ West Bloomfield; **208** NJ-8; 🅿; ★ **ROCH**; **z** 14475; ● 300
Ira; RMC Place; CAYUGA; ▲ Ira; ***208** NH-10; mail Cato **z** 13033; ● 100
Ira; MCD-Town; CAYUGA; ***208** NH-10; mail Cato **z** 13033; Ⓟ 1,990; Ⓒ 2,426
Ireland Corners; RMC Place; ULSTER; ▲ Gardiner; ***207** SB-6; elev. 415ft./126m.; mail Gardiner **z** 12525; ● 100
Irelandville; RMC Place; SCHUYLER; ▲ Reading; ***208** NL-9; elev. 1,024ft./312m.; mail Watkins Glen **z** 14891; rural
Irish Settlement; RMC Place; ST. LAWRENCE; ▲ Colton; ***209** NC-15; mail Colton **z** 13625; rural
Irishtown; RMC Place; ESSEX; ▲ Minerva; ***209** NF-18; mail Olmstedville **z** 12857; rural
Irona; RMC Place; CLINTON; ▲ Altona; **209** NA-19; mail Altona **z** 12910; ● 300
Irondale; RMC Place; DUTCHESS; ▲ North East; ***209** NM-20; mail Millerton **z** 12546; ● 50
Irondale; RMC Place; HERKIMER; ▲ Salisbury; ***209** NI-16; mail Salisbury Center **z** 13454; rural
Irondequoit; CDP; MONROE; ▲ Irondequoit; **208** NH-7; 🅿; ★ **ROCH**; **z** 14617, **z** 14622 & mail Rochester **z** 14621; Ⓟ 52,322; Ⓒ 52,354; ◆ 51,066
Irondequoit; MCD-Town; MONROE; ***208** NH-7; 🅿; ★ **ROCH**; **z** 14617, **z** 14622 & mail Rochester **z** 14621; Ⓟ 52,322; Ⓒ 52,354; ◆ 51,066
Irondequoit Manor; RMC Place; MONROE; ▲ Irondequoit; ★ **ROCH**; mail Rochester **z** 14617
Irongate; RMC Place; ONONDAGA; ▲ Clay; ★ **SYR**; mail Liverpool **z** 13088
Ironville; RMC Place; ESSEX; ▲ Crown Point; **209** NE-19; mail Crown Point **z** 12928; ● 100
Irving; RMC Place; CHAUTAUQUA; ▲ Hanover; **208** NK-3; 🅿 🅷; **z** 14081; ● 600
Irvington; Inc. Place; WESTCHESTER; ▲ Greenburgh; ***207** SE-7; 🅿; ★ **N.Y.**; **z** 10533; Ⓟ 6,348; Ⓒ 6,631
Ischua; RMC Place; CATTARAUGUS; ▲ Ischua; **208** NL-5; 🅿; **z** 14743; ● 200
Ischua; MCD-Town; CATTARAUGUS; ***208** NL-5; 🅿; **z** 14743; Ⓟ 847; Ⓒ 895
Island; RMC Place; NEW YORK; ★ **N.Y.**; mail New York **z** 10044; pop. incl. with New York (Inc. Place)
Island Cottage Beach; RMC Place; MONROE; ▲ Greece; ***208** NH-7; elev. 250ft./76m.; ★ **ROCH**; mail Rochester **z** 14612; ● 350
Islandia; Inc. Place; SUFFOLK; ▲ Smithtown, Islip; ***207** SF-9; 🅿; ★ **N.Y.**; **z** 11749, **z** 11760 & mail Central Islip **z** 11722, Hauppauge **z** 11788, Ronkonkoma **z** 11779; Ⓟ 2,769; Ⓒ 3,057
Island Park; Inc. Place; NASSAU; ▲ Hempstead; **207** SG-8; 🅿; ★ **N.Y.**; **z** 11558; Ⓟ 4,860; Ⓒ 4,732
Isle of San Souci; RMC Place; WESTCHESTER; ***207** SE-7; ★ **N.Y.**; mail New Rochelle **z** 10805; pop. incl. with New Rochelle (Inc. Place)
Islip; CDP; SUFFOLK; ▲ Islip; **207** SF-9; elev. 16ft./5m.; 🅿; ★ **N.Y.**; **z** 11751; Ⓟ 18,924; Ⓒ 20,575; ◆ 20,568
Islip; MCD-Town; SUFFOLK; ***207** SF-9; 🅿 🅲 7,695; ★ **N.Y.**; **z** 11751; Ⓟ 299,587; Ⓒ 322,612; Ⓡ 322,782; ◆ 320,016
Islip Terrace; CDP; SUFFOLK; ▲ Islip; **207** SI-12; 🅿; ★ **N.Y.**; **z** 11752; Ⓟ 5,530; Ⓒ 5,641
Italy; RMC Place; YATES; ▲ Italy; **208** NK-8; elev. 1,121ft./342m.; mail Naples **z** 14512; ● 120
Italy; MCD-Town; YATES; ***208** NK-8; mail Naples **z** 14512; Ⓟ 1,120; Ⓒ 1,087
Itaska; RMC Place; BROOME; ▲ Barker; ***209** NL-12; elev. 935ft./285m.; mail Whitney Point **z** 13862; rural
Ithaca; Inc. Place; ⊡ TOMPKINS; **209** NK-11; 🅿 🅷 🅲 26,048 ■; ★ **ITH**; **z** 14850-53, **z** 14882; Ⓟ 29,541; Ⓒ 29,287; Ⓡ 28,775; ◆ 30,909
Ithaca; MCD-Town; TOMPKINS; ***209** NL-11; 🅿 🅲 26,048; ★ **ITH**; **z** 14850-53, **z** 14882; does not include the City of Ithaca; Ⓟ 17,797; Ⓒ 18,198; Ⓡ 18,710; ◆ 19,322
Ivanhoe; RMC Place; DELAWARE; ▲ Masonville; ***209** NL-14; mail Sidney Center **z** 13839; rural
Ives Corner; RMC Place; RENSSELAER; ▲ Poestenkill; ***209** NJ-20; elev. 946ft./288m.; ★ **A-S-T**; mail Averill Park **z** 12018; rural
Ives Hollow; RMC Place; HERKIMER; ▲ Salisbury; ***209** NI-16; mail Salisbury Center **z** 13454; rural

J

Jackson; MCD-Town; WASHINGTON; ***209** NI-20; mail Cambridge **z** 12816; Ⓟ 1,581; Ⓒ 1,718
Jacksonburg; RMC Place; HERKIMER; ▲ Little Falls; ***209** NI-15; mail Mohawk **z** 13407
Jackson Corners; RMC Place; DUTCHESS; ▲ Milan; ***209** NM-19; mail Red Hook **z** 12571; rural
Jackson Heights; RMC Place; QUEENS; **211** G-12; 🅿; ★ **N.Y.**; **z** 11372; pop. incl. with New York (Inc. Place)
Jackson Summit; RMC Place; FULTON; ▲ Mayfield; ***209** NI-17; ★ **A-S-T**; mail Mayfield **z** 12117; rural
Jacksonville; RMC Place; ONONDAGA; ▲ Lysander; ***209** NH-11; ★ **SYR**; mail Phoenix **z** 13135; rural
Jacksonville; RMC Place; TOMPKINS; ▲ Ulysses; **208** NK-10; 🅿; ★ **ITH**; **z** 14854; ● 670
Jacks Reef; RMC Place; ONONDAGA; ▲ Lysander, Elbridge; **209** NI-11; ★ **SYR**; mail Memphis **z** 13112; ● 500
Jamaica; RMC Place; ⊡ QUEENS; **211** H-14; elev. 60ft./18m.; 🅿; ★ **N.Y.**; **z** 11405, **z** 11411-36, **z** 11439, **z** 11451, **z** 11499; pop. incl. with New York (Inc. Place)
Jamaica Square; NASSAU; see South Floral Park (Inc. Place)
James A Farley; RMC Place; NEW YORK; ★ **N.Y.**; mail New York **z** 10001, **z** 10116; pop. incl. with New York (Inc. Place)
Jamesport; CDP; SUFFOLK; ▲ Riverhead; **207** SE-12; 🅿; **z** 11947 & mail South Jamesport **z** 11970; Ⓟ 1,532; Ⓒ 1,526
Jamestown; Inc. Place; CHAUTAUQUA; ▲ Ellicott; **208** NM-2; 🅿 🅷 ■; ★ **JMST**; **z** 14701-02; Ⓟ 34,681; Ⓒ 31,730; Ⓡ 31,984; ◆ 27,662
Jamestown West (West Ellicott); CDP-Census Area Only; CHAUTAUQUA; ▲ Ellicott; ***208** NM-2; ★ **JMST**; mail Jamestown **z** 14701; Ⓟ 2,633; Ⓒ 2,535
Jamesville; RMC Place; ONONDAGA; ▲ De Witt; **209** NI-12; 🅿; ★ **SYR**; **z** 13078; ● 700
Janesville; RMC Place; SCHOHARIE; ▲ Seward; ***209** NJ-16; mail Cobleskill **z** 12043; ● 100
Jasper; RMC Place; STEUBEN; ▲ Jasper; **208** NM-8; 🅿; **z** 14855; ● 500
Jasper; MCD-Town; STEUBEN; ***208** NM-7; 🅿; **z** 14855; Ⓟ 1,232; Ⓒ 1,270
Java; WYOMING; see Java Center (RMC Place)
Java; MCD-Town; WYOMING; ***208** NK-5; ★ **BUF**; mail Java Center **z** 14082; Ⓟ 2,197; Ⓒ 2,222
Java Center (Java); RMC Place; WYOMING; ▲ Java; **208** NK-5; elev. 1,522ft./464m.; 🅿; **z** 14082; ● 200
Java Lake (East Java); RMC Place; WYOMING; ▲ Java; mail Arcade **z** 14009; summer pop. 300
Java Village; RMC Place; WYOMING; ▲ Java; **208** NK-5; 🅿; **z** 14083; ● 300
Jay; RMC Place; ESSEX; ▲ Jay; ***209** ND-19; 🅿; **z** 12941; ● 500
Jay; MCD-Town; ESSEX; ***209** ND-19; 🅿; **z** 12941; Ⓟ 2,244; Ⓒ 2,306
Jeddo; RMC Place; ORLEANS; ▲ Ridgeway; ***208** NH-5; mail Medina **z** 14103; ● 50
Jefferson; GREENE; see Jefferson Heights (CDP)
Jefferson; RMC Place; SCHOHARIE; ▲ Jefferson; **209** NK-16; elev. 1,873ft./571m.; 🅿; **z** 12093; ● 500
Jefferson; MCD-Town; SCHOHARIE; ***209** NK-16; 🅿; **z** 12093; Ⓟ 1,190; Ⓒ 1,285
JEFFERSON; **209** NE-13; Ⓟ 110,943; Ⓒ 111,738; ◆ 122,928
Jefferson Heights (Jefferson); CDP; GREENE; ▲ Catskill; ***209** NL-19; ★ **KNGST**; mail Catskill **z** 12414; Ⓟ 1,512; Ⓒ 1,104
Jefferson Park; RMC Place; JEFFERSON; ▲ Ellisburg; ***209** NF-11; mail Henderson **z** 13650
Jefferson Valley; RMC Place; WESTCHESTER; ▲ Yorktown; **207** SC-7; 🅿; ★ **N.Y.**; **z** 10535; ● 6,700
Jefferson Valley-Yorktown; CDP-Census Area Only; WESTCHESTER; ▲ Yorktown; ***207** SC-7; ★ **N.Y.**; mail Jefferson Valley **z** 10535; Ⓟ 14,118; Ⓒ 14,891
Jeffersonville; Inc. Place; SULLIVAN; ▲ Callicoon; **209** NN-15; elev. 1,058ft./322m.; 🅿; **z** 12748; Ⓟ 484; Ⓒ 420
Jenksville; RMC Place; TIOGA; ▲ Newark Valley; ***209** NL-11; ★ **BING**; mail Berkshire **z** 13736
Jericho; RMC Place; CLINTON; ▲ Altona; **209** NB-19; elev. 1,393ft./425m.; mail Altona **z** 12910; ● 100
Jericho; CDP; NASSAU; ▲ Oyster Bay; **207** SF-8; 🅿; ★ **N.Y.**; **z** 11753, **z** 11853; Ⓟ 13,141; Ⓒ 13,045
Jericho; RMC Place; SUFFOLK; ▲ East Hampton; ***207** SE-13; mail East Hampton **z** 11937; pop. incl. with East Hampton (Inc. Place)
Jerome Avenue; RMC Place; BRONX; ★ **N.Y.**; mail Bronx **z** 10468; pop. incl. with New York (Inc. Place)
Jersey Colony; SUFFOLK; see Arshamonaque (RMC Place)
Jerusalem; MCD-Town; YATES; ***208** NK-9; 🅲 1,524; mail Branchport **z** 14418; Ⓟ 3,784; Ⓒ 4,525
Jerusalem Corners; RMC Place; ERIE; ▲ Evans; ***208** NJ-3; ★ **BUF**; mail Derby **z** 14047; rural
Jewell (West Vienna); RMC Place; ONEIDA; ▲ Vienna; **209** NH-13; ★ **UT-R**; mail Cleveland **z** 13042; ● 100
Jewel Manor; RMC Place; ONONDAGA; ▲ Salina; ***209** NI-11; ★ **SYR**; mail Liverpool **z** 13088; ● 730
Jewett; RMC Place; GREENE; ▲ Jewett; ***209** NL-17; 🅿; **z** 12444; ● 200
Jewett; MCD-Town; GREENE; ***209** NL-18; 🅿; **z** 12444; Ⓟ 933; Ⓒ 970
Jewett Center; RMC Place; GREENE; ▲ Jewett; ***209** NL-17; elev. 1,405ft./428m.; mail Hunter **z** 12442; rural
Jewettville; RMC Place; ERIE; ▲ Aurora; **208** NJ-4; elev. 1,007ft./307m.; ★ **BUF**; mail West Falls **z** 14170; ● 100
Jewettville; RMC Place; JEFFERSON; ▲ Hounsfield; ***209** NE-12; mail Sackets Harbor **z** 13685; rural
Johnsburg; RMC Place; WARREN; ▲ Johnsburg; **209** NG-18; elev. 1,287ft./392m.; 🅿; **z** 12843; ● 300
Johnsburg; MCD-Town; WARREN; ***209** NG-18; 🅿; **z** 12843; Ⓟ 2,352; Ⓒ 2,450
Johnson; RMC Place; ORANGE; ▲ Minisink; **207** SC-4; 🅿; ★ **MIDD**; **z** 10933; ● 500
Johnsonburg; RMC Place; WYOMING; ▲ Orangeville, Sheldon; **208** NJ-5; mail Varysburg **z** 14167; ● 120
Johnson City; Inc. Place; BROOME; ▲ Union; **209** NM-12; 🅿 ■; ★ **BING**; **z** 13790; Ⓟ 16,890; Ⓒ 15,535; Ⓡ 15,503; ◆ 15,121
Johnson Creek; RMC Place; NIAGARA; ▲ Hartland; **208** NH-5; ★ **LOCK**; mail Gasport **z** 14067; ● 280
Johnsonville; RMC Place; RENSSELAER; ▲ Pittstown; **209** NI-20; elev. 363ft./111m.; 🅿; ★ **A-S-T**; **z** 12094; ● 380
Johnstown; Inc. Place; ⊡ FULTON; **209** NI-17; 🅿; **z** 12095; Ⓟ 9,058; Ⓒ 8,511; Ⓡ 8,610
Johnstown; MCD-Town; FULTON; ***209** NI-17; 🅿; **z** 12095 & mail Gloversville **z** 12078; does not include the City of Johnstown; Ⓟ 6,418; Ⓒ 7,166; Ⓡ 7,067
Jones Point; RMC Place; ROCKLAND; ▲ Stony Point; **207** SD-6; ★ **N.Y.**; mail Tomkins Cove **z** 10986; ● 100
Jonesville; RMC Place; SARATOGA; ▲ Clifton Park; **209** NJ-19; elev. 326ft./99m.; ★ **A-S-T**; mail Clifton Park **z** 12065; ● 420
Jordan; Inc. Place; ONONDAGA; ▲ Elbridge; **209** NI-11; 🅿; ★ **SYR**; **z** 13080; Ⓟ 1,325; Ⓒ 1,314
Jordanville; RMC Place; HERKIMER; ▲ Warren; **209** NJ-15; 🅿; **z** 13361; ● 250
Junction Boulevard; RMC Place; QUEENS; ★ **N.Y.**; mail Jackson Heights **z** 11372; pop. incl. with New York (Inc. Place)
Junius; MCD-Town; SENECA; ***208** NI-9; mail Waterloo **z** 13165; Ⓟ 1,354; Ⓒ 1,362

K

Kabob; RMC Place; CHAUTAUQUA; ▲ Stockton; ***208** NL-2; elev. 1,286ft./392m.; mail Sinclairville **z** 14782; rural
Kaisertown; RMC Place; ORANGE; ▲ Montgomery; ***207** SB-5; mail Montgomery **z** 12549; rural
Kanona; RMC Place; STEUBEN; ▲ Bath; **208** NL-8; elev. 1,142ft./348m.; 🅿; **z** 14856; ● 450
Kaser; Inc. Place; ROCKLAND; ▲ Ramapo; ***207** SD-6; ★ **N.Y.**; mail Spring Valley **z** 10977; Ⓟ 1,730; Ⓒ 3,316
Kasoag; RMC Place; OSWEGO; ▲ Williamstown; ***209** NG-12; elev. 639ft./195m.; mail Altmar **z** 13302; rural
Kast Bridge; RMC Place; HERKIMER; ▲ Herkimer; ***209** NI-15; mail Herkimer **z** 13350; rural
Katonah; RMC Place; WESTCHESTER; ▲ Bedford; **207** SD-7; elev. 226ft./69m.; 🅿 🅷; ★ **N.Y.**; **z** 10536; ● 2,400
Katsbaan; RMC Place; ULSTER; ▲ Saugerties; ***209** NM-18; elev. 79ft./24m.; ★ **KNGST**; mail Saugerties **z** 12477; ● 200
Kattelville; RMC Place; BROOME; ▲ Chenango; **209** NL-13; ★ **BING**; mail Binghamton **z** 13901; ● 800
Kattskill Bay; RMC Place; WARREN; ▲ Queensbury; **209** NG-19; 🅿; ★ **GLFLS**; **z** 12844; ● 500
Kauneonga Lake; RMC Place; SULLIVAN; ▲ Bethel; ***207** SB-3; 🅿; **z** 12749; ● 1,200
Kaydeross Park; RMC Place; SARATOGA; ★ **A-S-T**; mail Saratoga Springs **z** 12866; pop. incl. with Saratoga Springs (Inc. Place)
Kayuta; ONEIDA; see Kayuta Lake (RMC Place)
Kayuta Lake (Kayuta); RMC Place; ONEIDA; ▲ Remsen; ***209** NH-15; mail Forestport **z** 13338; ● 300
Kecks Center; RMC Place; FULTON; ▲ Johnstown; ***209** NI-17; mail Johnstown **z** 12095; ● 45
Keefers Corners; RMC Place; ALBANY; ▲ Coeymans; ***209** NK-18; elev. 688ft./210m.; ★ **A-S-T**; mail Feura Bush **z** 12067
Keene; RMC Place; ESSEX; ▲ Keene; **209** ND-19; elev. 834ft./254m.; 🅿; **z** 12942; ● 450
Keene; MCD-Town; ESSEX; ***209** ND-19; 🅿; **z** 12942; Ⓟ 908; Ⓒ 1,063
Keene Valley; RMC Place; ESSEX; ▲ Keene; **209** ND-19; 🅿; **z** 12943; ● 350
Keeney; RMC Place; CORTLAND; ▲ Cuyler; ***209** NJ-12; mail Truxton **z** 13158; ● 80
Keeseville; Inc. Place; ESSEX, CLINTON; ▲ Au Sable, Chesterfield; **209** NC-19; elev. 503ft./153m.; 🅿; **z** 12911, **z** 12924, **z** 12944; Ⓟ 1,854; Ⓒ 1,850
Kelleys; RMC Place; SCHENECTADY; ▲ Princetown; ***209** NJ-18; ★ **A-S-T**; mail Duanesburg **z** 12056; rural
Kelloggsville; RMC Place; CAYUGA; ▲ Niles; ***209** NJ-11; mail Moravia **z** 13118; ● 35
Kelly Corners; RMC Place; CHAUTAUQUA; ▲ Stockton; ***208** NL-2; mail Stockton **z** 14784; rural
Kelly Corners (Kellys Corners); RMC Place; DELAWARE; ▲ Middletown; ***209** NM-16; mail Margaretville **z** 12455; ● 100
Kellys Corners; DELAWARE; see Kelly Corners (RMC Place)
Kelsey; RMC Place; DELAWARE; ▲ Tompkins; **209** NM-14; mail Hancock **z** 13783; ● 70
Kendaia; RMC Place; SENECA; ▲ Romulus; ***208** NJ-9; mail Romulus **z** 14541; rural
Kendall; RMC Place; ORLEANS; ▲ Kendall; **208** NH-6; elev. 338ft./103m.; 🅿; ★ **ROCH**; **z** 14476; ● 500
Kendall; MCD-Town; ORLEANS; ***208** NH-6; 🅿; ★ **ROCH**; **z** 14476; Ⓟ 2,769; Ⓒ 2,838
Kendall Mills; RMC Place; MONROE, ORLEANS; ▲ Kendall, Hamlin; ***208** NH-6; elev. 354ft./108m.; ★ **ROCH**; mail Holley **z** 14470; ● 150
Kenilworth; RMC Place; NASSAU; ★ **N.Y.**; mail Great Neck **z** 11024; pop. incl. with Kings Point (Inc. Place)
Kenmore; Inc. Place; ERIE; ▲ Tonawanda; **208** NI-4; 🅿 🅷; ★ **BUF**; **z** 14217, **z** 14223; Ⓟ 17,180; Ⓒ 16,426
Kennedy; RMC Place; CHAUTAUQUA; ▲ Poland; **208** NM-3; 🅿; ★ **JMST**; **z** 14747; ● 400
Kenoza Lake; RMC Place; SULLIVAN; ▲ Delaware; **207** SA-3; elev. 1,065ft./325m.; 🅿; **z** 12750; ● 400
Kensington; RMC Place; ERIE; ★ **BUF**; mail Buffalo **z** 14215; pop. incl. with Buffalo (Inc. Place)
Kensington; RMC Place; KINGS; **211** J-11; ★ **N.Y.**; mail Brooklyn **z** 11218; pop. incl. with New York (Inc. Place)
Kensington; Inc. Place; NASSAU; ▲ North Hempstead; **211** F-15; ★ **N.Y.**; mail Great Neck **z** 11021; Ⓟ 1,104; Ⓒ 1,209
Kent; RMC Place; ORLEANS; ▲ Carlton; **208** NH-6; 🅿; **z** 14477; ● 125
Kent; MCD-Town; PUTNAM; ***207** SC-7; ★ **N.Y.**; mail Carmel **z** 10512; Ⓟ 13,183; Ⓒ 14,009
Kent Cliffs; RMC Place; PUTNAM; ▲ Kent; **207** SC-7; elev. 611ft./186m.; ★ **N.Y.**; mail Carmel **z** 10512; ● 110
Kents Corners; RMC Place; ST. LAWRENCE; ▲ Hermon; ***209** NC-14; elev. 622ft./190m.; mail De Kalb Junction **z** 13630; rural
Kenwood; RMC Place; MADISON; ***209** NI-13; mail Oneida **z** 13421; pop. incl. with Oneida (Inc. Place)
Kenwood Estates; RMC Place; PUTNAM; ▲ Kent; ★ **N.Y.**; mail Carmel **z** 10512; ● 200
Kenyonville; RMC Place; ORLEANS; ▲ Carlton; **208** NH-5; elev. 354ft./108m.; mail Waterport **z** 14571; ● 110
Kerhonkson; CDP; ULSTER; ▲ Wawarsing, Rochester; **209** NN-17; elev. 264ft./80m.; 🅿; **z** 12446; Ⓟ 1,629; Ⓒ 1,732
Kerleys Corners; RMC Place; DUTCHESS; ▲ Red Hook; ***209** NM-19; elev. 188ft./57m.; mail Red Hook **z** 12571; rural
Kernan; RMC Place; ONEIDA; ★ **UT-R**; mail Utica **z** 13502; pop. incl. with Utica (Inc. Place)
Kerryville; RMC Place; DELAWARE; ▲ Hancock; ***209** NM-14; mail Hancock **z** 13783; rural
Ketchums Corner; RMC Place; SARATOGA; ▲ Stillwater; ***209** NI-19; ★ **A-S-T**; mail Stillwater **z** 12170; ● 85
Ketchumville; RMC Place; TIOGA; ▲ Newark Valley; ***209** NL-12; elev. 1,252ft./382m.; ★ **BING**; mail Berkshire **z** 13736; rural
Keuka; RMC Place; STEUBEN; ▲ Wayne; **208** NK-9; mail Dundee **z** 14837; ● 150
Keuka Park; RMC Place; YATES; ▲ Jerusalem; **208** NK-9; 🅿 🅲 1,524; **z** 14478 & mail Branchport **z** 14418; ● 1,200
Kew Gardens; RMC Place; QUEENS; **211** I-13; 🅿; ★ **N.Y.**; **z** 11415, **z** 11424 & mail Richmond Hill **z** 11418; pop. incl. with New York (Inc. Place)
Kew Gardens Hills; RMC Place; QUEENS; 🅿; ★ **N.Y.**; **z** 11367 & mail Fresh Meadows **z** 11366; pop. incl. with New York (Inc. Place)
Kiamesha Lake; RMC Place; SULLIVAN; ▲ Thompson; **207** SB-4; elev. 1,417ft./432m.; 🅿; **z** 12751; ● 850
Kiantone; RMC Place; CHAUTAUQUA; ▲ Kiantone; **208** NM-2; elev. 1,505ft./459m.; ★ **JMST**; mail Jamestown **z** 14701; ● 120
Kiantone; MCD-Town; CHAUTAUQUA; ***208** NM-2; ★ **JMST**; mail Jamestown **z** 14701; Ⓟ 1,322; Ⓒ 1,385
Kidders; RMC Place; SENECA; ▲ Ovid; ***208** NK-10; mail Interlaken **z** 14847; ● 50
Killawog; RMC Place; BROOME; ▲ Lisle; **209** NL-12; 🅿; **z** 13794; ● 300
Kill Buck; RMC Place; CATTARAUGUS; ▲ Great Valley; **208** NM-4; 🅿; **z** 14748; ● 650
Kimball Stand; RMC Place; CHAUTAUQUA; ▲ Gerry, Ellicott; ***208** NM-2; elev. 1,290ft./393m.; ★ **JMST**; mail Jamestown **z** 14701; ● 110
Kinderhook; Inc. Place; COLUMBIA; ▲ Kinderhook; **209** NL-19; elev. 256ft./78m.; 🅿; ★ **A-S-T**; **z** 12106; Ⓟ 1,293; Ⓒ 1,275
Kinderhook; MCD-Town; COLUMBIA; ***209** NL-19; 🅿; ★ **A-S-T**; **z** 12106; Ⓟ 8,112; Ⓒ 8,296
King Ferry; RMC Place; CAYUGA; ▲ Genoa; **208** NK-10; elev. 958ft./292m.; 🅿; **z** 13081; ● 300
KINGS; **207** SG-7; Ⓟ 2,300,664; Ⓒ 2,465,326; Ⓡ 2,465,525; ◆ 2,563,161
Kings Bridge; RMC Place; BRONX; ***207** SF-7; ★ **N.Y.**; mail Bronx **z** 10463; pop. incl. with New York (Inc. Place)
Kings Bridge Heights; RMC Place; BRONX; ***207** SF-7; ★ **N.Y.**; mail Bronx **z** 10463; pop. incl. with New York (Inc. Place)
Kingsbury; RMC Place; WASHINGTON; ▲ Kingsbury; **209** NH-19; elev. 305ft./93m.; ★ **GLFLS**; mail Hudson Falls **z** 12839; ● 200
Kingsbury; MCD-Town; WASHINGTON; ***209** NH-19; ★ **GLFLS**; mail Hudson Falls **z** 12839; Ⓟ 11,851; Ⓒ 11,171
Kings Ferry; RMC Place; CAYUGA; ▲ Genoa; ***208** NK-10; mail King Ferry **z** 13081; summer pop. 150
Kings Park; CDP; SUFFOLK; ▲ Smithtown; **207** SE-9; 🅿; ★ **N.Y.**; **z** 11754; Ⓟ 17,773; Ⓒ 16,146; Ⓡ 15,976
Kings Point; Inc. Place; NASSAU; ▲ North Hempstead; **207** SF-7; elev. 26ft./8m.; 🅿 🅲 1,035; ★ **N.Y.**; **z** 11024; Ⓟ 4,843; Ⓒ 5,076
Kings Settlement; RMC Place; CHENANGO; ▲ North Norwich; ***209** NK-14; mail Norwich **z** 13815; rural
Kings Station; RMC Place; SARATOGA; ▲ Wilton; ***209** NI-19; ★ **GLFLS**; mail Gansevoort **z** 12831; rural
Kingston; Inc. Place; ⊡ ULSTER; **209** NN-18; 🅿 🅷 ■; ★ **KNGST**; **z** 12401-02; Ⓟ 23,095; Ⓒ 23,456; ◆ 22,629
Kingston; MCD-Town; ULSTER; ***209** NM-18; 🅿; ★ **KNGST**; **z** 12401-02; does not include the City of Kingston; Ⓟ 864; Ⓒ 908
Kipps; RMC Place; ORANGE; ▲ Hamptonburgh; ***207** SC-5; elev. 389ft./119m.; ★ **N.Y.**; mail Goshen **z** 10924; rural
Kirk; RMC Place; CHENANGO; ▲ Plymouth; ***209** NK-13; mail South Plymouth **z** 13844; ● 200
Kirkland; RMC Place; ONEIDA; ▲ Kirkland; **209** NI-14; ★ **UT-R**; mail Clinton **z** 13323; ● 200
Kirkland; MCD-Town; ONEIDA; ***209** NI-14; 🅲 1,799; ★ **UT-R**; mail Clinton **z** 13323; Ⓟ 10,153; Ⓒ 10,138
Kirkville; RMC Place; ONONDAGA; ▲ Manlius; **209** NI-12; 🅿; ★ **SYR**; **z** 13082; ● 500
Kirkwood; RMC Place; BROOME; ▲ Kirkwood; **209** NM-13; 🅿; ★ **BING**; **z** 13795; ● 600
Kirkwood; MCD-Town; BROOME; ***209** NM-13; 🅿; ★ **BING**; **z** 13795; Ⓟ 6,096; Ⓒ 5,651
Kirkwood; RMC Place; STEUBEN; ▲ Cohocton; ***208** NK-8; mail Cohocton **z** 14826; rural
Kirschnerville; RMC Place; LEWIS; ▲ New Bremen; **209** NF-14; mail Croghan **z** 13327; ● 40
Kiryas Joel; Inc. Place; ORANGE; ▲ Monroe; ***207** SC-6; ★ **N.Y.**; mail Monroe **z** 10950; Ⓟ 7,437; Ⓒ 13,138; ◆ 17,804
Kisco Park; RMC Place; WESTCHESTER; ▲ New Castle; ***207** SD-7; ★ **N.Y.**; mail Mount Kisco **z** 10549; ● 580
Kiskatom; RMC Place; GREENE; ▲ Catskill; ***209** NL-18; ★ **KNGST**; mail Catskill **z** 12414
Kismet; RMC Place; SUFFOLK; ▲ Islip; ***207** SG-9; 🅿; ★ **N.Y.**; **z** 11706; summer pop. 1,000; ● 10
Kitchawan; RMC Place; WESTCHESTER; ▲ Yorktown; ***207** SD-7; ★ **N.Y.**; mail Ossining **z** 10562; rural
Knapp Creek; RMC Place; CATTARAUGUS; ▲ Allegany; **208** NM-5; elev. 2,350ft./716m.; 🅿; **z** 14760; ● 150
Knapps Corner; RMC Place; DUTCHESS; ▲ Poughkeepsie; ***207** SB-7; elev. 172ft./52m.; ★ **POK**; mail Poughkeepsie **z** 12603; rural
Knappville; RMC Place; FULTON; ▲ Stratford; ***209** NH-16; mail Stratford **z** 13470; rural
Knickerbocker; RMC Place; NEW YORK; 🅿; ★ **N.Y.**; **z** 10002; pop. incl. with New York (Inc. Place)
Knight Creek (Knights Creek); RMC Place; ALLEGANY; ▲ Scio; ***208** NM-6; mail Scio **z** 14880; rural
Knights Creek; ALLEGANY; see Knight Creek (RMC Place)
Knights Eddy; RMC Place; SULLIVAN; ▲ Lumberland; ***207** SC-3; mail Sparrow Bush **z** 12780; rural
Knight Settlement; RMC Place; STEUBEN; ▲ Bath; ***208** NL-8; mail Bath **z** 14810; rural
Knowelhurst; RMC Place; WARREN; ▲ Stony Creek; ***209** NG-18; mail Stony Creek **z** 12878; ● 60
Knowlesville; RMC Place; ORLEANS; ▲ Ridgeway; **208** NH-5; 🅿; **z** 14479; ● 300
Knox; RMC Place; ALBANY; ▲ Knox; **209** NK-18; 🅿; **z** 12107; ● 400
Knox; MCD-Town; ALBANY; ***209** NK-18; 🅿; **z** 12107; Ⓟ 2,661; Ⓒ 2,647
Knoxboro; RMC Place; ONEIDA; ▲ Augusta; **209** NI-14; elev. 1,098ft./335m.; 🅿; ★ **UT-R**; **z** 13362; ● 150
Koenig's Point; CAYUGA; see Conklin Cove (RMC Place)
Kohlertown; RMC Place; SULLIVAN; ***207** SA-3; mail Jeffersonville **z** 12748; ● 125
Komar Park; RMC Place; SARATOGA; ▲ Charlton; ***209** NJ-18; ★ **A-S-T**; mail Ballston Lake **z** 12019; ● 800
Kortright; RMC Place; DELAWARE; ▲ Kortright; ***209** NL-16; mail Bloomville **z** 13739; ● 45
Kortright; MCD-Town; DELAWARE; ***209** NL-16; mail Bloomville **z** 13739; Ⓟ 1,410; Ⓒ 1,633
Kossuth; RMC Place; ALLEGANY; ▲ Bolivar; **208** NM-6; elev. 1,703ft./519m.; mail Bolivar **z** 14715; ● 60
Kringsbush; RMC Place; FULTON; ▲ Oppenheim; ***209** NI-16; mail Saint Johnsville **z** 13452; rural
Kripplebush; RMC Place; ULSTER; ▲ Marbletown; ***207** SA-6; ★ **KNGST**; mail Stone Ridge **z** 12484; ● 200
Krumville; RMC Place; ULSTER; ▲ Olive; **209** NN-18; elev. 777ft./237m.; 🅿; **z** 12461; ● 150
Kuckville; RMC Place; ORLEANS; ***208** NH-5; elev. 260ft./79m.; mail Waterport **z** 14571; rural
Kyserike; RMC Place; ULSTER; ▲ Rochester; **207** SA-6; mail High Falls **z** 12440; ● 80

L

Lackawack; RMC Place; ULSTER; ▲ Wawarsing; ***207** SA-5; mail Napanoch **z** 12458; rural
Lackawanna; Inc. Place; ERIE; **208** NJ-4; elev. 620ft./189m.; 🅿 🅷; ★ **BUF**; **z** 14218; Ⓟ 20,585; Ⓒ 19,064
Lackawanna-South Park; RMC Place; ERIE; ***208** NJ-4; ★ **BUF**; pop. incl. with Lackawanna (Inc. Place)
Lacona; Inc. Place; OSWEGO; ▲ Sandy Creek; **209** NG-12; 🅿; **z** 13083; Ⓟ 593; Ⓒ 590
Ladentown; RMC Place; ROCKLAND; ***207** SD-6; ★ **N.Y.**; mail Pomona **z** 10970
La Fargeville; CDP; JEFFERSON; ▲ Orleans; **209** ND-12; elev. 381ft./116m.; 🅿; **z** 13656; Ⓒ 588
LaFayette; RMC Place; ONONDAGA; ▲ LaFayette; **209** NJ-12; 🅿; ★ **SYR**; **z** 13084; ● 600
LaFayette; MCD-Town; ONONDAGA; ***209** NJ-12; ★ **SYR**; mail La Fayette **z** 13084; Ⓟ 5,105; Ⓒ 4,833
Lafayetteville; RMC Place; DUTCHESS; ▲ Milan; ***209** NM-19; mail Red Hook **z** 12571
La Grange; DUTCHESS; see Lagrangeville (RMC Place)
La Grange; MCD-Town; DUTCHESS; ***207** SB-7; ★ **POK**; mail Lagrangeville **z** 12540; Ⓟ 13,274; Ⓒ 14,928
Lagrange; RMC Place; WYOMING; ▲ Perry, Covington; ***208** NJ-6; elev. 1,316ft./401m.; mail Pavilion **z** 14525; ● 80
Lagrangeville (La Grange); RMC Place; DUTCHESS; ▲ La Grange; **207** SB-7; 🅿; ★ **POK**; **z** 12540; ● 500
Lairdsville; RMC Place; ONEIDA; ▲ Westmoreland; ***209** NI-14; ★ **UT-R**; mail Clinton **z** 13323, Vernon **z** 13476; ● 130
Lake; RMC Place; ORANGE; ▲ Warwick; ***207** SD-5; elev. 554ft./169m.; ★ **N.Y.**; mail Warwick **z** 10990
Lake Bluff; RMC Place; WAYNE; ▲ Huron; **208** NH-9; mail Wolcott **z** 14590; ● 50
Lake Bonaparte (Bonaparte); RMC Place; LEWIS; ▲ Diana; **209** NE-14; mail Harrisville **z** 13648
Lake Carmel; CDP; PUTNAM; ▲ Patterson, Kent; **207** SC-7; ★ **N.Y.**; mail Carmel **z** 10512; Ⓟ 8,489; Ⓒ 8,663
Lake Charles; RMC Place; PUTNAM; ▲ Patterson; ***207** SC-8; ★ **N.Y.**; mail Patterson **z** 12563; ● 120
Lake Clear; RMC Place; FRANKLIN; ▲ Harrietstown; **209** ND-17; 🅿; **z** 12945; ● 400
Lake Como; RMC Place; CAYUGA; ▲ Summerhill; mail Cortland **z** 13045; ● 85
Lake Delta; RMC Place; ONEIDA; ▲ Western, Lee; **209** NH-14; ★ **UT-R**; mail Rome **z** 13440; ● 2,020
Lake Desolation; RMC Place; SARATOGA; ▲ Greenfield; ***209** NI-18; ★ **A-S-T**; mail Middle Grove **z** 12850; rural
Lake Erie Beach; CDP; ERIE; ▲ Evans; **208** NK-3; ★ **BUF**; mail Angola **z** 14006; Ⓟ 4,509; Ⓒ 4,499
Lake Gardens; RMC Place; PUTNAM; ▲ Carmel; ***207** SC-7; ★ **N.Y.**; mail Great Neck **z** 11022, Mahopac **z** 10541; ● 350
Lake George; Inc. Place; ⊡ WARREN; ▲ Lake George; **209** NG-19; elev. 353ft./108m.; 🅿; ★ **GLFLS**; **z** 12845; Ⓟ 933; Ⓒ 985
Lake George; MCD-Town; WARREN; ***209** NG-19; 🅿; ★ **GLFLS**; **z** 12845; Ⓟ 3,211; Ⓒ 3,578
Lake Grove; Inc. Place; SUFFOLK; ▲ Brookhaven; **207** SF-10; elev. 119ft./36m.; 🅿; ★ **N.Y.**; **z** 11755; Ⓟ 9,612; Ⓒ 10,250
Lake Hill; RMC Place; ULSTER; ▲ Woodstock; **209** NM-18; 🅿; **z** 12448; ● 400
Lake Huntington; RMC Place; SULLIVAN; ▲ Cochecton; **207** SB-3; 🅿; **z** 12752; ● 600
Lake Katonah; RMC Place; WESTCHESTER; ▲ Lewisboro; ***207** SD-8; ★ **N.Y.**; mail Katonah **z** 10536
Lake Katrine; CDP; ULSTER; ▲ Ulster; **209** NM-18; 🅿; ★ **KNGST**; **z** 12449; Ⓟ 1,998; Ⓒ 2,396
Lake Kitchawan; RMC Place; WESTCHESTER; ▲ Lewisboro; ***207** SD-8; ★ **N.Y.**; mail South Salem **z** 10590; ● 125
Lakeland; CDP; ONONDAGA; ▲ Geddes; **208** NE-7; ★ **SYR**; mail Syracuse **z** 13209; Ⓒ 2,852
Lakeland; RMC Place; SUFFOLK; ▲ Islip; ***207** SF-10; ★ **N.Y.**; mail Ronkonkoma **z** 11779
Lake Lincolndale; RMC Place; WESTCHESTER; ▲ Somers; ***207** SC-7; 🅿; ★ **N.Y.**; **z** 10541; ● 950
Lake Lucille; RMC Place; ROCKLAND; ▲ Clarkstown; ***207** SD-6; ★ **N.Y.**; mail New City **z** 10956
Lake Luzerne; RMC Place; WARREN; ▲ Lake Luzerne; **209** NH-19; 🅿; **z** 12846; ● 1,150
Lake Luzerne; MCD-Town; WARREN; ***209** NH-19; 🅿; **z** 12846; Ⓟ 2,816; Ⓒ 3,219
Lake Luzerne-Hadley; CDP-Census Area Only; WARREN, SARATOGA; ▲ Hadley, Lake Luzerne; ***209** NH-19; mail Hadley **z** 12835, Lake Luzerne **z** 12846; Ⓟ 2,042; Ⓒ 2,240
Lake Mahopac; RMC Place; PUTNAM; ▲ Carmel; ★ **N.Y.**; mail Mahopac **z** 10541
Lake Mohegan; CDP-Census Area Only; WESTCHESTER; ***207** SC-7; ★ **N.Y.**; mail Mohegan Lake **z** 10547; Ⓒ 5,979
Lakemont; RMC Place; YATES; ▲ Starkey; **208** NK-9; 🅿; **z** 14857; ● 250
Lake Moraine; RMC Place; MADISON; ▲ Madison; mail Hamilton **z** 13346
Lake Muskoday; RMC Place; SULLIVAN; ▲ Fremont; ***207** SA-3; mail Roscoe **z** 12776; summer pop. 200
Lake Osceola; RMC Place; WESTCHESTER; ▲ Yorktown; ★ **N.Y.**; mail Jefferson Valley **z** 10535
Lake Osiris Colony; RMC Place; ORANGE; ▲ Montgomery; ***207** SB-6; mail Walden **z** 12586; summer pop. 200; ● 110
Lake Panamoka; RMC Place; SUFFOLK; ▲ Brookhaven; ***207** SE-11; ★ **N.Y.**; mail Ridge **z** 11961; ● 1,850
Lake Peekskill; RMC Place; PUTNAM; ▲ Putnam Valley; **207** SC-7; 🅿; ★ **N.Y.**; **z** 10537; ● 2,150
Lake Placid; Inc. Place; ESSEX; ▲ North Elba; **209** ND-18; 🅿; **z** 12946; Ⓟ 2,485; Ⓒ 2,638
Lake Placid Club Resort; RMC Place; ESSEX; ***209** ND-18; mail Lake Placid **z** 12946
Lake Pleasant; RMC Place; ⊡ HAMILTON; ▲ Lake Pleasant; **209** NG-17; elev. 1,791ft./546m.; 🅿; **z** 12108 & mail Piseco **z** 12139; ● 350
Lake Pleasant; MCD-Town; HAMILTON; ***209** NG-17; 🅿; **z** 12108; Ⓟ 887; Ⓒ 876
Lakeport; RMC Place; MADISON; ▲ Sullivan; **209** NI-12; elev. 394ft./120m.; ★ **SYR**; mail Canastota **z** 13032, Chittenango **z** 13037; ● 500
Lake Purdy; RMC Place; WESTCHESTER; ▲ Somers; ***207** SC-7; ★ **N.Y.**; mail Purdys **z** 10578; ● 650
Lake Ronkonkoma; CDP; SUFFOLK; ▲ Smithtown, Brookhaven, Islip; **207** SH-13; 🅿; ★ **N.Y.**; **z** 11779; Ⓟ 18,997; Ⓒ 19,701
Lake Ronkonkoma Heights; RMC Place; SUFFOLK; ▲ Brookhaven; ★ **N.Y.**; mail Ronkonkoma **z** 11779
Lake Secor; RMC Place; PUTNAM; ▲ Carmel; ***207** SC-7; ★ **N.Y.**; mail Mahopac **z** 10541; ● 1,750
Lake Shenorock; WESTCHESTER; see Shenorock (CDP)
Lakeside; RMC Place; ORANGE; ▲ Woodbury; ★ **N.Y.**; mail Highland Mills **z** 10930
Lakeside; RMC Place; WAYNE; ▲ Ontario; ***208** NH-8; elev. 365ft./111m.; ★ **ROCH**; mail Ontario **z** 14519
Lakeside Park; RMC Place; ALBANY; ▲ Colonie; ★ **A-S-T**; mail Albany **z** 12205
Lakeside Park; RMC Place; ORLEANS; ▲ Carlton; ***208** NH-5; mail Waterport **z** 14571; ● 200
Lake Station; RMC Place; ORANGE; ▲ Warwick; ***207** SD-5; ★ **N.Y.**; mail Warwick **z** 10990
Lake Success; Inc. Place; NASSAU; ▲ North Hempstead; **211** G-16; 🅿; ★ **N.Y.**; **z** 11020 & mail New Hyde Park **z** 11040, **z** 11042; Ⓟ 2,484; Ⓒ 2,797
Lake Sunnyside; RMC Place; WARREN; ▲ Queensbury; ***209** NH-19; elev. 366ft./112m.; ★ **GLFLS**; mail Lake George **z** 12845; ● 400
Lake Vanare; RMC Place; WARREN; ▲ Lake Luzerne; ***209** NH-19; mail Lake Luzerne **z** 12846; ● 550
Lake View; RMC Place; ERIE; ▲ Hamburg; **208** NJ-3; elev. 722ft./220m.; 🅿; ★ **BUF**; **z** 14085 & mail Rockville Centre **z** 11570, West Hempstead **z** 11552; ● 150
Lakeview; CDP; NASSAU; ▲ Hempstead; **211** I-17; ★ **N.Y.**; mail Lake View **z** 14085, Rockville Centre **z** 11570, West Hempstead **z** 11552; Ⓟ 5,476; Ⓒ 5,607
Lakeview; RMC Place; OSWEGO; ▲ Scriba; ***209** NG-11; mail Oswego **z** 13126; ● 50
Lakeville; RMC Place; LIVINGSTON; ▲ Livonia; **208** NJ-7; 🅿; ★ **ROCH**; **z** 14480; ● 1,200
Lakeville; RMC Place; NASSAU; ★ **N.Y.**; mail New Hyde Park **z** 11040; pop. incl. with Lake Success (Inc. Place)
Lakewood; Inc. Place; CHAUTAUQUA; ▲ Busti; **208** NM-2; elev. 1,329ft./405m.; 🅿; ★ **JMST**; **z** 14750; Ⓟ 3,564; Ⓒ 3,258
Lamberton; RMC Place; CHAUTAUQUA; ▲ Pomfret; **208** NL-2; mail Fredonia **z** 14063; ● 130
Lambs Corner (Lambs Corners); RMC Place; ALBANY; ▲ Westerlo; ***209** NK-18; mail Greenville **z** 12083; rural
Lambs Corners; ALBANY; see Lambs Corner (RMC Place)
Lamont; RMC Place; WYOMING; ▲ Pike; ***208** NK-6; elev. 1,532ft./467m.; mail Castile **z** 14427; ● 50
Lamson; RMC Place; ONONDAGA; ▲ Lysander; ***209** NH-11; ★ **SYR**; mail Phoenix **z** 13135; rural
Lancaster; Inc. Place; ERIE; ▲ Lancaster; **208** NJ-4; 🅿; ★ **BUF**; **z** 14086 & mail Depew **z** 14043; Ⓟ 11,940; Ⓒ 11,188
Lancaster; MCD-Town; ERIE; ***208** NJ-4; 🅿; ★ **BUF**; **z** 14086 & mail Depew **z** 14043; Ⓟ 32,181; Ⓒ 39,019; ◆ 38,512
Lane; RMC Place; GENESEE; mail Batavia **z** 14020; pop. incl. with Batavia (Inc. Place)
Lanesville; RMC Place; GREENE; ▲ Hunter; **209** NM-17; 🅿; **z** 12450; ● 350
Langdon; RMC Place; BROOME; ▲ Kirkwood; ***209** NM-13; ★ **BING**; mail Kirkwood **z** 13795
Langdon Corners; RMC Place; ST. LAWRENCE; ▲ Canton; ***209** NC-15; elev. 435ft./133m.; mail Canton **z** 13617
Langford; RMC Place; ERIE; ▲ North Collins; **208** NK-4; elev. 1,296ft./395m.; ★ **BUF**; mail Eden **z** 14057; ● 230
Lansing; RMC Place; OSWEGO; ▲ Scriba; ***209** NG-11; elev. 415ft./126m.; mail Oswego **z** 13126; rural
Lansing (South Lansing); Inc. Place; TOMPKINS; ▲ Lansing; **209** NK-11; 🅿; ★ **ITH**; **z** 14882; Ⓟ 3,281; Ⓒ 3,417
Lansing; MCD-Town; TOMPKINS; ***209** NK-11; 🅿; ★ **ITH**; **z** 14882; Ⓟ 9,296; Ⓒ 10,521
Lansingburg; RMC Place; RENSSELAER; ★ **A-S-T**; mail Troy **z** 12182; pop. incl. with Troy (Inc. Place)
Laona; RMC Place; CHAUTAUQUA; ▲ Pomfret; **208** NL-2; mail Fredonia **z** 14063; ● 250
Lapala; RMC Place; ULSTER; ▲ Kingston; ***207** SA-6; ★ **KNGST**; mail Kingston **z** 12401; ● 250
Lapeer; MCD-Town; CORTLAND; ***209** NL-12; mail Marathon **z** 13803; Ⓟ 613; Ⓒ 686
Laphams Mills; RMC Place; CLINTON; ▲ Peru; **209** NC-19; elev. 273ft./83m.; ★ **PLATT**; mail Peru **z** 12972; ● 120
Larchmont; Inc. Place; WESTCHESTER; ▲ Mamaroneck; **207** SE-7; 🅿; ★ **N.Y.**; **z** 10538; Ⓟ 6,181; Ⓒ 6,485
Larchmont North (North Larchmont); RMC Place; WESTCHESTER; ▲ Mamaroneck; ***207** SE-7; ★ **N.Y.**; mail Larchmont **z** 10538; ● 10,700
La Salle; RMC Place; NIAGARA; ▲ Niagara; ***208** NI-3; ★ **BUF**; mail Niagara Falls **z** 14304; pop. incl. with Niagara Falls (Inc. Place)
Lassellsville; RMC Place; FULTON; ▲ Ephratah; **209** NI-16; elev. 1,154ft./352m.; mail Saint Johnsville **z** 13452; ● 300
Latham; RMC Place; ALBANY; ***209** NJ-19; elev. 356ft./109m.; 🅿; ★ **A-S-T**; **z** 12110, **z** 12128; Ⓟ 10,131; ● 4,200
Lathams Corners; RMC Place; CHENANGO; ▲ Guilford; ***209** NK-14; mail South New Berlin **z** 13843; rural
Lattingtown; Inc. Place; NASSAU; ▲ Oyster Bay; **207** SE-8; elev. 65ft./20m.; ★ **N.Y.**; mail Locust Valley **z** 11560; Ⓟ 1,859; Ⓒ 1,860
Laughing Waters; RMC Place; SUFFOLK; ▲ Southold; ***207** SE-12; mail Southold **z** 11971
Laurel; CDP; SUFFOLK; ▲ Southold; **207** SE-12; elev. 20ft./6m.; 🅿; **z** 11948; Ⓟ 1,094; Ⓒ 1,188
Laurel Hollow; Inc. Place; NASSAU; ▲ Oyster Bay; **207** SH-10; elev. 91ft./28m.; ★ **N.Y.**; mail Oyster Bay **z** 11771, Syosset **z** 11791; Ⓟ 1,748; Ⓒ 1,930
Laurelton; RMC Place; MONROE; ▲ Irondequoit; ★ **ROCH**; mail Rochester **z** 14609
Laurelton; RMC Place; QUEENS; **211** I-15; 🅿; ★ **N.Y.**; **z** 11413; pop. incl. with New York (Inc. Place)
Laurens; Inc. Place; OTSEGO; ▲ Laurens; **209** NK-15; elev. 1,116ft./340m.; 🅿; **z** 13796; Ⓟ 293; Ⓒ 277
Laurens; MCD-Town; OTSEGO; ***209** NK-15; 🅿; **z** 13796; Ⓟ 2,349; Ⓒ 2,402
Lava; RMC Place; SULLIVAN; ▲ Tusten; **207** SB-3; mail Narrowsburg **z** 12764; ● 50
Lawrence; Inc. Place; NASSAU; ▲ Hempstead; **207** SG-7; 🅿; ★ **N.Y.**; **z** 11559; Ⓟ 6,513; Ⓒ 6,522
Lawrence; MCD-Town; ST. LAWRENCE; ***209** NB-16; mail Nicholville **z** 12965; Ⓟ 1,516; Ⓒ 1,545
Lawrence Farms; RMC Place; WESTCHESTER; ▲ New Castle; ***207** SD-7; ★ **N.Y.**; mail Chappaqua **z** 10514; ● 950
Lawrence Park; RMC Place; WESTCHESTER; ***207** SE-7; ★ **N.Y.**; mail Bronxville **z** 10708; pop. incl. with Yonkers (Inc. Place)
Lawrenceville; RMC Place; ST. LAWRENCE; ▲ Lawrence; **209** NB-16; 🅿; **z** 12949 & mail North Lawrence **z** 12967; ● 230
Lawtons; RMC Place; ERIE; ▲ North Collins; **208** NK-3; elev. 849ft./259m.; 🅿; ★ **BUF**; **z** 14091; ● 460
Lawyersville; RMC Place; SCHOHARIE; ▲ Seward, Cobleskill; **209** NJ-17; 🅿; **z** 12043; ● 200
Lebanon; RMC Place; MADISON; ▲ Lebanon; **209** NJ-13; 🅿; **z** 13332; ● 200
Lebanon; MCD-Town; MADISON; ***209** NJ-13; 🅿; **z** 13332; Ⓟ 1,265; Ⓒ 1,329
Lebanon Center; RMC Place; MADISON; ▲ Lebanon; ***209** NJ-13; mail Earlville **z** 13332; rural
Lebanon Springs; RMC Place; COLUMBIA; ▲ New Lebanon; **209** NK-20; 🅿; **z** 12125; ● 500
Ledyard; RMC Place; CAYUGA; ▲ Venice, Ledyard; ***208** NK-10; mail Aurora **z** 13026, King Ferry **z** 13081; ● 45
Ledyard; MCD-Town; CAYUGA; ***208** NJ-10; 🅲 564; mail Aurora **z** 13026; Ⓟ 1,737; Ⓒ 1,832
Lee; RMC Place; ONEIDA; ▲ Lee; **209** NH-13; ★ **UT-R**; mail Rome **z** 13440; ● 200
Lee; MCD-Town; ONEIDA; ***209** NH-14; ★ **UT-R**; mail Rome **z** 13440; Ⓟ 7,115; Ⓒ 6,875
Lee Center; RMC Place; ONEIDA; ▲ Lee; **209** NH-14; 🅿; ★ **UT-R**; **z** 13363; ● 620
Leeds; CDP; GREENE; ▲ Catskill; **209** NL-18; 🅿; ★ **KNGST**; **z** 12451; Ⓒ 369
Leedsville; RMC Place; DUTCHESS; ▲ Amenia; ***207** SA-8; mail Amenia **z** 12501; rural
Leeside; RMC Place; PUTNAM; ▲ Kent; ★ **N.Y.**; mail Carmel **z** 10512
Leesville; RMC Place; SCHOHARIE; ▲ Sharon; ***209** NJ-16; mail Sharon Springs **z** 13459; rural
Lefever Falls; RMC Place; ULSTER; ▲ Rosendale; ***207** SA-6; elev. 70ft./21m.; ★ **KNGST**; mail Rosendale **z** 12472; rural
Lefferts; RMC Place; KINGS; ★ **N.Y.**; mail Brooklyn **z** 11225; pop. incl. with New York (Inc. Place)
Leibhardt; RMC Place; ULSTER; ▲ Rochester; ***207** SA-5; mail Accord **z** 12404; rural
Leicester; Inc. Place; LIVINGSTON; ▲ Leicester; **208** NJ-6; 🅿; **z** 14481; Ⓟ 405; Ⓒ 469
Leicester; MCD-Town; LIVINGSTON; ***208** NJ-6; 🅿; **z** 14481; Ⓟ 2,223; Ⓒ 2,287
LeMarr Estates; RMC Place; COLUMBIA; ▲ Kinderhook; ***209** NK-19; elev. 308ft./94m.; ★ **A-S-T**; mail Valatie **z** 12184; ● 165
Lenox; MCD-Town; MADISON; ***209** NI-13; ★ **SYR**; mail Canastota **z** 13032; Ⓟ 8,621; Ⓒ 8,665
Lenox Furnace; RMC Place; MADISON; ▲ Lincoln; ***209** NI-13; mail Canastota **z** 13032; rural
Lenox Hill; RMC Place; NEW YORK; ★ **N.Y.**; mail New York **z** 10021, **z** 10131; pop. incl. with New York (Inc. Place)
Lenox Park; RMC Place; ONTARIO; ▲ Geneva; ***208** NJ-9; mail Geneva **z** 14456; ● 50
Lent Hill; RMC Place; STEUBEN; ▲ Cohocton; ***208** NK-8; mail Cohocton **z** 14826; rural
Leon; RMC Place; CATTARAUGUS; ▲ Leon; **208** NL-3; elev. 1,378ft./420m.; 🅿; **z** 14751; ● 350
Leon; MCD-Town; CATTARAUGUS; ***208** NL-3; 🅿; **z** 14751; Ⓟ 1,245; Ⓒ 1,380
Leonardsville; RMC Place; MADISON; ▲ Brookfield; **209** NJ-14; 🅿; **z** 13364; ● 500
Leonta; RMC Place; DELAWARE; ▲ Franklin; ***209** NL-15; mail Franklin **z** 13775; rural
Le Ray; MCD-Town; JEFFERSON; ***209** NE-13; ★ **WATN**; mail Evans Mills **z** 13637; Ⓟ 17,973; Ⓒ 19,836; ◆ 21,896
Le Roy; Inc. Place; GENESEE; ▲ Le Roy; **208** NI-6; elev. 869ft./265m.; 🅿; ★ **ROCH**; **z** 14482; Ⓟ 4,974; Ⓒ 4,462
Le Roy; MCD-Town; GENESEE; ***208** NI-6; 🅿; ★ **ROCH**; **z** 14482; Ⓟ 8,176; Ⓒ 7,790
Le Roy Island; RMC Place; WAYNE; ▲ Huron; ***208** NH-9; mail Wolcott **z** 14590; ● 60
Levanna; RMC Place; CAYUGA; ▲ Ledyard; **208** NJ-10; mail Aurora **z** 13026; ● 50
Levant; RMC Place; CHAUTAUQUA; ▲ Poland, Ellicott; ***208** NM-2; ★ **JMST**; mail Falconer **z** 14733; rural
Levittown; CDP; NASSAU; ▲ Hempstead; **207** SF-8; 🅿; ★ **N.Y.**; **z** 11756; Ⓟ 53,286; Ⓒ 53,067; ◆ 50,397
Lewbeach; RMC Place; SULLIVAN; ▲ Rockland; **209** NM-16; 🅿; **z** 12758; ● 200
Lewis; RMC Place; ESSEX; ▲ Lewis; **209** ND-19; 🅿; **z** 12950; ● 450
Lewis; MCD-Town; ESSEX; ***209** ND-19; 🅿; **z** 12950; Ⓟ 1,057; Ⓒ 1,200
Lewis; MCD-Town; LEWIS; ***209** NG-13; mail West Leyden **z** 13489; Ⓟ 858; Ⓒ 857
LEWIS; **209** NF-13; Ⓟ 26,796; Ⓒ 26,944; ◆ 26,430
Lewisboro; MCD-Town; WESTCHESTER; ***207** SD-8; ★ **N.Y.**; mail South Salem **z** 10590; Ⓟ 11,313; Ⓒ 12,324
Lewiston; Inc. Place; NIAGARA; ▲ Lewiston; **208** NH-3; 🅿 🅷; ★ **BUF**; **z** 14092 & mail Stella Niagara **z** 14144; Ⓟ 3,048; Ⓒ 2,781
Lewiston; MCD-Town; NIAGARA; ***208** NH-3; 🅿 🅲 3,881; ★ **BUF**; **z** 14092; Ⓟ 15,453; Ⓒ 16,257
Lewiston Heights; RMC Place; NIAGARA; ***208** NH-3; ★ **BUF**; mail Lewiston **z** 14092; pop. incl. with Lewiston (Inc. Place)
Lewiston Manor; RMC Place; ONONDAGA; ▲ De Witt; ***209** NI-12; ★ **SYR**; mail Syracuse **z** 13224; ● 1,350
Lexington; RMC Place; GREENE; ▲ Lexington; **209** NL-17; elev. 1,331ft./406m.; 🅿; **z** 12452; ● 500
Lexington; MCD-Town; GREENE; ***209** NL-17; 🅿; **z** 12452; Ⓟ 835; Ⓒ 830
Leyden; MCD-Town; LEWIS; ***209** NG-14; mail Port Leyden **z** 13433; Ⓟ 1,796; Ⓒ 1,792
Liberty; Inc. Place; SULLIVAN; ▲ Liberty; **209** NN-16; elev. 1,509ft./460m.; 🅿; **z** 12754; Ⓟ 4,128; Ⓒ 3,975
Liberty; MCD-Town; SULLIVAN; ***207** SA-3; 🅿; **z** 12754; Ⓟ 9,825; Ⓒ 9,632
Liberty Gardens; RMC Place; ONEIDA; ***209** NH-14; ★ **UT-R**; mail Rome **z** 13440; pop. incl. with Rome (Inc. Place)
Libertypole; RMC Place; LIVINGSTON; ▲ Springwater; ***208** NK-7; mail Dansville **z** 14437; rural
Lido Beach; CDP; NASSAU; ▲ Hempstead; **207** SG-8; elev. 8ft./2m.; 🅿; ★ **N.Y.**; **z** 11561; Ⓟ 2,786; Ⓒ 2,825
Lily Dale; RMC Place; CHAUTAUQUA; ▲ Pomfret; **208** NL-2; 🅿; **z** 14752; ● 500
Lima; Inc. Place; LIVINGSTON; ▲ Lima; **208** NJ-7; 🅿; ★ **ROCH**; **z** 14485; Ⓟ 2,165; Ⓒ 2,459
Lima; MCD-Town; LIVINGSTON; ***208** NJ-7; 🅿; ★ **ROCH**; **z** 14485; Ⓟ 4,187; Ⓒ 4,541
Lime Lake; RMC Place; CATTARAUGUS; ▲ Machias; **208** NK-5; mail Delevan **z** 14042, Machias **z** 14101; summer pop. 2,000; ● 400
Lime Lake-Machias; CDP-Census Area Only; CATTARAUGUS; ▲ Machias; ***208** NL-5; mail Delevan **z** 14042, Machias **z** 14101; Ⓟ 1,269; Ⓒ 1,422
Limerick; RMC Place; JEFFERSON; ▲ Brownville; **209** NE-12; elev. 318ft./97m.; 🅿; ★ **WATN**; **z** 13657; ● 170
Lime Rock; RMC Place; GENESEE; ▲ Le Roy; ***208** NI-6; elev. 782ft./238m.; ★ **ROCH**; mail Le Roy **z** 14482; ● 250
Limestone; Inc. Place; CATTARAUGUS; ▲ Carrollton; **208** NM-4; elev. 1,407ft./429m.; 🅿; **z** 14753; Ⓟ 459; Ⓒ 411
Limestreet; RMC Place; GREENE; ▲ Athens; ***209** NL-19; mail Catskill **z** 12414; ● 100
Lincklaen; RMC Place; CHENANGO; ▲ Lincklaen; **209** NK-12; mail De Ruyter **z** 13052; ● 50
Lincklaen; MCD-Town; CHENANGO; ***209** NK-13; mail De Ruyter **z** 13052; Ⓟ 486; Ⓒ 416
Lincoln; MCD-Town; MADISON; ***209** NI-13; mail Clockville **z** 13043; Ⓟ 1,669; Ⓒ 1,818
Lincoln; RMC Place; WAYNE; ▲ Walworth; **208** NH-8; ★ **ROCH**; mail Macedon **z** 14502; ● 140
Lincoln; RMC Place; WESTCHESTER; ***207** SE-7; elev. 207ft./63m.; ★ **N.Y.**; pop. incl. with Yonkers (Inc. Place)
Lincolndale; CDP; WESTCHESTER; ▲ Somers; ***207** SC-7; 🅿; ★ **N.Y.**; **z** 10540; Ⓒ 2,018
Lincoln Park; RMC Place; ERIE; ▲ Tonawanda; ★ **BUF**; mail Buffalo **z** 14222
Lincoln Park; RMC Place; MONROE; ***208** NI-7; ★ **ROCH**; mail Rochester **z** 14611; pop. incl. with Rochester (Inc. Place)
Lincoln Park; CDP; ULSTER; ▲ Ulster; ***209** NM-18; ★ **KNGST**; mail Kingston **z** 12401; Ⓟ 2,457; Ⓒ 2,337
Lincolnshire; RMC Place; TIOGA; ▲ Owego; ***209** NM-11; ★ **BING**; mail Endicott **z** 13760; ● 400
Lincolnton; RMC Place; NEW YORK; ★ **N.Y.**; mail New York **z** 10037; pop. incl. with New York (Inc. Place)
Lincolnwoods; RMC Place; NIAGARA; ▲ Lockport; ***208** NI-4; ★ **LOCK**; mail Lockport **z** 14094; ● 120
Lindbergh Court; RMC Place; ALBANY; ▲ Colonie; ★ **A-S-T**; mail Albany **z** 12204; pop. incl. with Colonie (Inc. Place)
Linden; RMC Place; GENESEE; ▲ Bethany; **208** NJ-6; elev. 1,102ft./336m.; mail East Bethany **z** 14054; ● 110
Linden Acres; RMC Place; DUTCHESS; ▲ Red Hook; ***209** NM-19; mail Red Hook **z** 12571; ● 350
Linden Hill; RMC Place; QUEENS; ★ **N.Y.**; mail Flushing **z** 11354; pop. incl. with New York (Inc. Place)
Lindenhurst; Inc. Place; SUFFOLK; ▲ Babylon; **207** SF-9; elev. 27ft./8m.; 🅿; ★ **N.Y.**; **z** 11757; Ⓟ 26,879; Ⓒ 27,819; ◆ 27,590
Lindley; RMC Place; STEUBEN; ▲ Lindley; **208** NM-9; 🅿; **z** 14858; ● 400
Lindley; MCD-Town; STEUBEN; ***208** NM-9; 🅿; **z** 14858; Ⓟ 1,862; Ⓒ 1,913
Linlithgo; RMC Place; COLUMBIA; ▲ Livingston; ***209** NM-19; elev. 167ft./51m.; mail Germantown **z** 12526; ● 200
Linwood; RMC Place; LIVINGSTON; ▲ York; **208** NJ-6; 🅿; ★ **ROCH**; **z** 14486 & mail Pavilion **z** 14525; ● 120
Lisbon; RMC Place; ST. LAWRENCE; ▲ Lisbon; **209** NB-14; elev. 358ft./109m.; 🅿; **z** 13658; ● 500
Lisbon; MCD-Town; ST. LAWRENCE; ***209** NB-14; 🅿; **z** 13658; Ⓟ 3,746; Ⓒ 4,047
Lisha Kill; RMC Place; ALBANY; ▲ Colonie; ***209** NJ-19; ★ **A-S-T**; mail Albany **z** 12201
Lisle; Inc. Place; BROOME; ▲ Lisle; **209** NL-12; elev. 975ft./297m.; 🅿; **z** 13797; Ⓟ 361; Ⓒ 302
Lisle; MCD-Town; BROOME; ***209** NL-12; 🅿; **z** 13797; Ⓟ 2,486; Ⓒ 2,707
Litchfield; MCD-Town; HERKIMER; ***209** NI-15; mail Sauquoit **z** 13456; Ⓟ 1,414; Ⓒ 1,453
Lithgow; RMC Place; DUTCHESS; ▲ Washington; ***207** SA-8; mail Millbrook **z** 12545; rural
Little America; RMC Place; OSWEGO; ▲ Orwell; ***209** NG-12; elev. 1,108ft./338m.; mail Richland **z** 13144
Little Bow; RMC Place; ST. LAWRENCE; ▲ Gouverneur; ***209** ND-14; mail Gouverneur **z** 13642; rural
Little Britain; RMC Place; ORANGE; ▲ New Windsor; ***207** SC-6; ★ **NWBG**; mail Rock Tavern **z** 12575; rural
Little Canada; RMC Place; GENESEE; ▲ Bethany; ***208** NI-6; elev. 999ft./304m.; mail East Bethany **z** 14054; ● 100
Little Falls; Inc. Place; HERKIMER; **209** NI-16; 🅿 🅷; **z** 13365; Ⓟ 5,829; Ⓒ 5,188
Little Falls; MCD-Town; HERKIMER; ***209** NI-15; 🅿; **z** 13365 & mail Mohawk **z** 13407; does not include the City of Little Falls; Ⓟ 1,635; Ⓒ 1,544
Little Falls Park; RMC Place; DUTCHESS; ▲ Wappinger; ★ **POK**; mail Wappingers Falls **z** 12590; pop. incl. with Wappingers Falls (Inc. Place)
Little France; RMC Place; OSWEGO; ▲ West Monroe, Hastings; ***209** NH-12; elev. 493ft./150m.; ★ **SYR**; mail Central Square **z** 13036
Little Genesee; RMC Place; ALLEGANY; ▲ Genesee; **208** NM-5; 🅿; **z** 14754; ● 270
Little Neck; RMC Place; QUEENS; **211** G-15; 🅿; ★ **N.Y.**; **z** 11362-63; pop. incl. with New York (Inc. Place)
Little Plains; RMC Place; SUFFOLK; ▲ Huntington; ***207** SF-9; elev. 195ft./59m.; ★ **N.Y.**; mail East Northport **z** 11731
Little Ram Island; RMC Place; SUFFOLK; ▲ Shelter Island; ***207** SD-13; mail Shelter Island **z** 11964
Little Utica; RMC Place; ONONDAGA; ▲ Lysander; ***209** NH-11; ★ **SYR**; mail Phoenix **z** 13135; ● 80
Little Valley; Inc. Place; ⊡ CATTARAUGUS; ▲ Little Valley; **208** NL-4; elev. 1,594ft./486m.; 🅿; **z** 14755; Ⓟ 1,188; Ⓒ 1,130
Little Valley; MCD-Town; CATTARAUGUS; ***208** NL-4; 🅿; **z** 14755; Ⓟ 1,881; Ⓒ 1,788
Littleville; RMC Place; LIVINGSTON; ▲ Avon; ***208** NJ-7; ★ **ROCH**; mail Avon **z** 14414; rural
Littleville; RMC Place; ONTARIO; ▲ Manchester, Hopewell; ***208** NI-8; mail Canandaigua **z** 14424; ● 95
Little York; RMC Place; CORTLAND; ▲ Homer; **209** NJ-12; 🅿; **z** 13087; ● 400
Little York; RMC Place; ORANGE; ▲ Warwick; ***207** SD-5; elev. 402ft./123m.; ★ **N.Y.**; mail Pine Island **z** 10969
Liverpool; Inc. Place; ONONDAGA; ▲ Salina; **208** NE-7; 🅿; ★ **SYR**; **z** 13088-90; Ⓟ 2,624; Ⓒ 2,505
Livingston; RMC Place; COLUMBIA; ▲ Livingston; ***209** NM-19; 🅿; **z** 12541; ● 600
Livingston; MCD-Town; COLUMBIA; ***209** NM-19; 🅿; **z** 12541; Ⓟ 3,582; Ⓒ 3,424
LIVINGSTON; **208** NK-7; Ⓟ 62,372; Ⓒ 64,328; ◆ 62,933
Livingston Manor; CDP; SULLIVAN; ▲ Rockland; **209** NN-16; 🅿; **z** 12758; Ⓟ 1,482; Ⓒ 1,355
Livingstonville; RMC Place; SCHOHARIE; ▲ Broome; **209** NK-17; elev. 1,078ft./329m.; mail Middleburgh **z** 12122; ● 110
Livonia; Inc. Place; LIVINGSTON; ▲ Livonia; **208** NJ-7; elev. 1,047ft./319m.; 🅿; ★ **ROCH**; **z** 14487; Ⓟ 1,434; Ⓒ 1,373
Livonia; MCD-Town; LIVINGSTON; ***208** NJ-7; 🅿; ★ **ROCH**; **z** 14487; Ⓟ 6,804; Ⓒ 7,286
Livonia Center; RMC Place; LIVINGSTON; ▲ Livonia; **208** NJ-7; elev. 1,092ft./333m.; 🅿; ★ **ROCH**; **z** 14488; ● 400
Lloyd; MCD-Town; ULSTER; ***207** SA-6; ★ **POK**; mail Highland **z** 12528; Ⓟ 9,231; Ⓒ 9,941
Lloyd Harbor; Inc. Place; SUFFOLK; ▲ Huntington; **207** SE-8; 🅿; ★ **N.Y.**; **z** 11743; Ⓟ 3,343; Ⓒ 3,675
Lochada Lake; RMC Place; SULLIVAN; ▲ Lumberland; ***207** SC-3; mail Barryville **z** 12719
Loch Muller; RMC Place; ESSEX; ▲ Schroon; **209** NF-18; mail Olmstedville **z** 12857; ● 100
Loch Sheldrake; RMC Place; SULLIVAN; ▲ Fallsburg; **209** NN-16; elev. 1,471ft./448m.; 🅿; **z** 12759; ● 1,050
Lock Berlin; RMC Place; WAYNE; ▲ Galen; **208** NI-9; mail Lyons **z** 14489; ● 125
Locke; RMC Place; CAYUGA; ▲ Locke; **209** NK-11; elev. 800ft./244m.; 🅿; **z** 13092; ● 550
Locke; MCD-Town; CAYUGA; ***209** NK-11; 🅿; **z** 13092; Ⓟ 1,917; Ⓒ 1,900
Lockport; Inc. Place; ⊡ NIAGARA; **208** NI-4; 🅿 🅷 ■; ★ **LOCK**; **z** 14094-95; Ⓟ 24,426; Ⓒ 22,279; ◆ 20,807
Lockport; MCD-Town; NIAGARA; ***208** NH-4; 🅿; ★ **LOCK**; **z** 14094-95; does not include the City of Lockport; Ⓟ 16,596; Ⓒ 19,653; ◆ 19,770
Locksley Park; RMC Place; ERIE; ▲ Hamburg; ***208** NJ-3; ★ **BUF**; mail Hamburg **z** 14075; ● 1,000
Lockwood; RMC Place; TIOGA; ▲ Barton; **208** NM-10; 🅿; **z** 14859; ● 300
Locust Grove; RMC Place; LEWIS; ▲ Leyden; ***209** NG-14; mail Boonville **z** 13309; rural
Locust Grove; RMC Place; NASSAU; ▲ Oyster Bay; **211** F-20; ★ **N.Y.**; mail Syosset **z** 11791; ● 9,700
Locust Manor; RMC Place; QUEENS; **211** I-15; ★ **N.Y.**; mail Jamaica **z** 11434; pop. incl. with New York (Inc. Place)
Locust Point; RMC Place; BRONX; ***207** SF-7; ★ **N.Y.**; mail Bronx **z** 10465; pop. incl. with New York (Inc. Place)
Locust Valley; CDP; NASSAU; ▲ Oyster Bay; **207** SF-8; 🅿; ★ **N.Y.**; **z** 11560; Ⓟ 3,963; Ⓒ 3,521
Lodi; Inc. Place; SENECA; ▲ Lodi; **208** NK-10; 🅿; **z** 14860; Ⓟ 364; Ⓒ 338

Entries in **UPPERCASE** are counties.
Entries in **bold** have populations of 2,500 or more.
Names in parentheses are alternate names.
Inc. Place — Incorporated Place
RMC Place — Rand McNally Designated Place
CDP — Census Designated Place
MCD — Minor Civil Division

⊡ County Seat
▲ Minor Civil Division
elev. Elevation
🅿 Post Office
🅷 Hospital
🅲 College
■ Principal Business Center
★ Ranally Metro Area (RMA) Abbreviation
z Zip Code(s)
Ⓟ Previous Census Population
Ⓡ Revised Census Population
Ⓐ Annexation Population
● Rand McNally Population Estimate
Ⓒ Final Census Population
Ⓢ Special Census Population
◆ Estimated Population

For additional definitions see Glossary, Volume 1, and Introduction, Volume 2.

Lodi; MCD-Town; SENECA; *208 NK-10; 🅿; z 14860; Ⓟ 1,429; Ⓒ 1,476
Lodi Center; RMC Place; SENECA; ▲ Lodi; *208 NK-10; elev. 1,286ft./392m.; mail Lodi z 14860; rural
Lodi Point; RMC Place; SENECA; ▲ Lodi; *208 NK-9; mail Lodi z 14860; ● 200
Logan; RMC Place; SCHUYLER; ▲ Hector; *208 NK-10; mail Burdett z 14818; ● 60
Logtown; RMC Place; ORANGE; ▲ Greenville; *207 SC-4; ★ MIDD; mail Port Jervis z 12771; rural
Lomala; RMC Place; DUTCHESS; ▲ East Fishkill; *207 SB-7; ★ POK; mail Hopewell Junction z 12533
Lombard; RMC Place; CHAUTAUQUA; ▲ Westfield; *208 NL-1; elev. 1,560ft./475m.; mail Ripley z 14775; rural
Lomond Shore; RMC Place; ORLEANS; ▲ Kendall; *208 NH-6; ★ ROCH; mail Kendall z 14476; summer pop. 100
Lomontville; RMC Place; ULSTER; ▲ Marbletown; *207 SA-6; ★ KNGST; mail Kingston z 12401; rural
London Terrace; RMC Place; NEW YORK; ★ N.Y.; mail New York z 10011; pop. incl. with New York (Inc. Place)
Lonelyville; RMC Place; SUFFOLK; ▲ Islip; *207 SG-9; elev. 7ft./2m.; ★ N.Y.; mail Bay Shore z 11706; summer pop. 120; ● 10
Long Beach; Inc. Place; NASSAU; 207 SG-8; elev. 9ft./3m.; 🅿 🅷; ★ N.Y.; z 11561; Ⓟ 33,510; Ⓒ 35,462; ◆ 34,250
Long Branch; RMC Place; ONONDAGA; ▲ Salina, Geddes; *209 NI-11; ★ SYR; mail Liverpool z 13088; ● 650
Long Branch Manor; RMC Place; ONONDAGA; ▲ Salina; *209 NI-11; ★ SYR; mail Liverpool z 13088; ● 1,350
Long Bridge; RMC Place; ONONDAGA; ▲ Skaneateles; *209 NI-11; ★ SYR; mail Skaneateles Falls z 13153; ● 50
Long Eddy; RMC Place; SULLIVAN; ▲ Fremont; 209 NN-15; elev. 847ft./258m.; 🅿; z 12760; ● 400
Long Island City; RMC Place; QUEENS; 211 G-11; elev. 15ft./5m.; 🅿; ★ N.Y.; z 11101-06, z 11109, z 11120; pop. incl. with New York (Inc. Place)
Long Lake; RMC Place; HAMILTON; ▲ Long Lake; 209 NE-17; elev. 1,683ft./513m.; 🅿; z 12847; ● 500
Long Lake; MCD-Town; HAMILTON; *209 NE-16; 🅿; z 12847; Ⓟ 930; Ⓒ 852
Long Point; RMC Place; LIVINGSTON; ▲ Geneseo; *208 NJ-7; ★ ROCH; mail Geneseo z 14454; pop. incl. with Long Point (Inc. Place)
Long View; RMC Place; CHAUTAUQUA; ▲ North Harmony; *208 NM-2; mail Ashville z 14710; ● 50
Loomis; RMC Place; SULLIVAN; ▲ Liberty; 207 SA-3; mail Liberty z 12754; ● 200
Loomises; RMC Place; CHAUTAUQUA; ▲ Busti; *208 NM-2; ★ JMST; mail Ashville z 14710; ● 45
Loon Lake; RMC Place; FRANKLIN; ▲ Franklin; 209 NC-18; elev. 1,759ft./536m.; 🅿; z 12989; ● 100
Lordville; RMC Place; DELAWARE; ▲ Hancock; 209 NN-15; mail Hancock z 13783; ● 100
Lorenz Park; CDP-Census Area Only; COLUMBIA; ▲ Greenport; *209 NL-19; mail Hudson z 12534; Ⓟ 1,811; Ⓒ 1,981
Lorings; RMC Place; CORTLAND; ▲ Cortlandville; *209 NK-12; mail Cortland z 13045; rural
Lorraine; RMC Place; JEFFERSON; ▲ Lorraine; 209 NF-12; elev. 998ft./304m.; 🅿; z 13659; ● 200
Lorraine; MCD-Town; JEFFERSON; *209 NF-12; 🅿; z 13659; Ⓟ 766; Ⓒ 930
Lost Valley; RMC Place; MONTGOMERY; ▲ Florida; *209 NJ-17; mail Amsterdam z 12010; ● 55
Loudenville Heights; RMC Place; ALBANY; ▲ Colonie; *209 NJ-19; ★ A-S-T; mail Albany z 12211; pop. incl. with Albany (Inc. Place)
Loudonville; RMC Place; ALBANY; ▲ Colonie; 207 SI-5; elev. 347ft./106m.; 🅿 🅲 3,220; ★ A-S-T; z 12211; Ⓟ 10,822
Louisville; RMC Place; ST. LAWRENCE; ▲ Louisville; 209 NA-15; mail Massena z 13662; ● 500
Louisville; MCD-Town; ST. LAWRENCE; *209 NA-15; mail Massena z 13662; Ⓟ 3,040; Ⓒ 3,195
Lounsberry; RMC Place; TIOGA; ▲ Nichols; *209 NM-11; elev. 801ft./244m.; mail Nichols z 13812; rural
Lowell; RMC Place; ONEIDA; ▲ Westmoreland; *209 NI-14; ★ UT-R; mail Rome z 13440; rural
Lower Chateaugay Lake; RMC Place; FRANKLIN; ▲ Bellmont; *209 NB-18; mail Chateaugay z 12920; ● 400
Lower Cincinnatus; RMC Place; CORTLAND; ▲ Cincinnatus; *209 NK-12; mail Cincinnatus z 13040; ● 130
Lower Genegantslet Corner; RMC Place; CHENANGO; ▲ Greene; *209 NL-13; mail Greene z 13778; rural
Lower Melville; RMC Place; SUFFOLK; ▲ Huntington; *207 SF-9; ★ N.Y.; mail Melville z 11747
Lower Oswegatchie; RMC Place; ST. LAWRENCE; ▲ Fine; *209 ND-15; elev. 1,162ft./354m.; mail Oswegatchie z 13670
Lower Rotterdam; RMC Place; SCHENECTADY; ▲ Rotterdam; *209 NJ-18; ★ A-S-T; mail Schenectady z 12306; ● 200
Lower South Bay (South Bay); RMC Place; ONONDAGA; ▲ Cicero; *209 NH-12; ★ SYR; mail Clay z 13041; summer pop. 1,000; ● 750
Lowertown; RMC Place; NIAGARA; ▲ Lockport; *208 NH-4; ★ LOCK; mail Lockport z 14094; pop. incl. with Lockport (Inc. Place)
Low Hampton; RMC Place; WASHINGTON; ▲ Hampton; *209 NG-20; elev. 360ft./110m.; mail Fair Haven z 05743, Whitehall z 12887; rural
Lowman; RMC Place; CHEMUNG; ▲ Chemung, Ashland; 208 NM-10; 🅿; ★ ELM; z 14861; ● 220
Lowville; Inc. Place; ⊡ LEWIS; ▲ Lowville; 209 NF-14; 🅿 🅷; z 13367; Ⓟ 3,632; Ⓒ 3,476
Lowville; MCD-Town; LEWIS; *209 NF-13; 🅿; z 13367; Ⓟ 4,849; Ⓒ 4,548
Ludingtonville; RMC Place; PUTNAM; ▲ Kent; 207 SB-7; ★ N.Y.; mail Holmes z 12531
Ludlow; RMC Place; WESTCHESTER; *207 SE-7; ★ N.Y.; mail Yonkers z 10705; pop. incl. with Yonkers (Inc. Place)
Ludlowville; RMC Place; TOMPKINS; ▲ Lansing; 209 NK-11; ★ ITH; mail Lansing z 14882; ● 440
Lumberland; MCD-Town; SULLIVAN; *207 SC-3; mail Pond Eddy z 12770; Ⓟ 1,425; Ⓒ 1,939
Luther; RMC Place; RENSSELAER; ▲ East Greenbush; *209 NK-19; ★ A-S-T; mail East Greenbush z 12061; rural
Lutheranville; RMC Place; SCHOHARIE; ▲ Summit; *209 NK-16; mail East Worcester z 12064; rural
Lycoming; RMC Place; OSWEGO; ▲ Scriba; 209 NG-11; elev. 333ft./101m.; 🅿; z 13093; ● 650
Lyell; RMC Place; MONROE; ★ ROCH; mail Rochester z 14606; pop. incl. with Rochester (Inc. Place)
Lykers; RMC Place; MONTGOMERY; ▲ Root; *209 NJ-17; elev. 1,012ft./308m.; mail Sprakers z 12166; ● 100
Lyme; MCD-Town; JEFFERSON; *209 NE-11; mail Three Mile Bay z 13693; Ⓟ 1,701; Ⓒ 2,015
Lynbrook; Inc. Place; NASSAU; ▲ Hempstead; 207 SG-8; elev. 21ft./6m.; 🅿; ★ N.Y.; z 11563; Ⓟ 19,208; Ⓒ 19,911
Lyncourt; CDP-Census Area Only; ONONDAGA; ▲ Salina, De Witt; *209 NI-12; ★ SYR; mail Syracuse z 13208; Ⓟ 4,516; Ⓒ 4,268
Lyndon; MCD-Town; CATTARAUGUS; *208 NL-5; mail Franklinville z 14737; Ⓟ 503; Ⓒ 661
Lyndon; RMC Place; ONONDAGA; ▲ De Witt; 209 NI-12; ★ SYR; mail Fayetteville z 13066; Ⓟ 4,593
Lyndonville; Inc. Place; ORLEANS; ▲ Yates; 208 NH-5; elev. 324ft./99m.; 🅿; z 14098; Ⓟ 953; Ⓒ 862
Lynelle Meadows; RMC Place; ONONDAGA; ▲ Clay; *209 NI-11; ★ SYR; mail Liverpool z 13088; ● 1,300
Lynnwood; RMC Place; SARATOGA; ▲ Hadley; *209 NH-18; mail Hadley z 12835; rural
Lyon Mountain; CDP; CLINTON; ▲ Dannemora; 209 NB-18; 🅿; z 12952, z 12955; Ⓒ 458
Lyons; Inc. Place; ⊡ WAYNE; ▲ Lyons; 208 NI-9; elev. 438ft./134m.; 🅿; z 14489; Ⓟ 4,280; Ⓒ 3,695
Lyons; MCD-Town; WAYNE; *208 NI-9; 🅿; z 14489; Ⓟ 6,315; Ⓒ 5,831
Lyonsdale; RMC Place; LEWIS; ▲ Lyonsdale; 209 NG-14; mail Lyons Falls z 13368; ● 50
Lyonsdale; MCD-Town; LEWIS; *209 NG-14; mail Lyons Falls z 13368; Ⓟ 1,281; Ⓒ 1,273
Lyons Falls; Inc. Place; LEWIS; ▲ West Turin, Lyonsdale; 209 NG-14; 🅿; z 13368; Ⓟ 698; Ⓒ 591
Lyonsville; RMC Place; ULSTER; ▲ Marbletown; *207 SA-5; elev. 716ft./218m.; ★ KNGST; mail Accord z 12404; rural
Lysander; RMC Place; ONONDAGA; ▲ Lysander; 209 NH-11; elev. 418ft./127m.; 🅿; ★ SYR; z 13027; ● 275
Lysander; MCD-Town; ONONDAGA; *209 NI-11; 🅿; ★ SYR; z 13027; Ⓟ 16,346; Ⓒ 19,285; ◆ 19,854
Lysander New Community (Radison); RMC Place; ONONDAGA; ▲ Lysander; *209 NI-11; ★ SYR; mail Baldwinsville z 13027; rural

M

Mabbettsville; RMC Place; DUTCHESS; ▲ Washington; 207 SA-7; elev. 691ft./211m.; mail Millbrook z 12545; ● 65
MacDonnell Heights; RMC Place; DUTCHESS; ▲ Poughkeepsie; *207 SA-7; ★ POK; mail Poughkeepsie z 12603
MacDougall; RMC Place; SENECA; ▲ Fayette; *208 NJ-9; elev. 624ft./190m.; 🅿; z 14541
Macedon; Inc. Place; WAYNE; ▲ Macedon; 208 NI-8; elev. 478ft./146m.; 🅿; ★ ROCH; z 14502; Ⓟ 1,400; Ⓒ 1,496
Macedon; MCD-Town; WAYNE; *208 NI-8; 🅿; ★ ROCH; z 14502; Ⓟ 7,375; Ⓒ 8,688
Macedon Center; RMC Place; WAYNE; ▲ Macedon; 208 NI-8; elev. 554ft./169m.; ★ ROCH; mail Macedon z 14502; ● 200
Machias; RMC Place; CATTARAUGUS; ▲ Machias; 208 NL-5; 🅿; z 14101; ● 900
Machias; MCD-Town; CATTARAUGUS; *208 NL-4; 🅿; z 14101; Ⓟ 2,338; Ⓒ 2,482
Mackey; RMC Place; SCHOHARIE; ▲ Gilboa; *209 NK-17; mail Gilboa z 12076; rural
Macomb; MCD-Town; ST. LAWRENCE; *209 NC-13; mail Gouverneur z 13642; Ⓟ 790; Ⓒ 846
Madison; Inc. Place; MADISON; ▲ Madison; 209 NJ-14; 🅿; z 13402; Ⓟ 316; Ⓒ 315
Madison; MCD-Town; MADISON; *209 NJ-14; 🅿; z 13402; Ⓟ 2,774; Ⓒ 2,801
MADISON; 209 NJ-13; Ⓟ 69,120; Ⓒ 69,441; ◆ 69,060
Madison Park; RMC Place; SUFFOLK; ▲ Huntington; ★ N.Y.; mail East Northport z 11731
Madison Square; RMC Place; NEW YORK; ★ N.Y.; mail New York z 10010, z 10159; pop. incl. with New York (Inc. Place)
Madrid; RMC Place; ST. LAWRENCE; ▲ Madrid; 209 NB-15; 🅿; z 13660; ● 700
Madrid; MCD-Town; ST. LAWRENCE; *209 NB-15; 🅿; z 13660; Ⓟ 1,568; Ⓒ 1,828
Madrid Springs; RMC Place; ST. LAWRENCE; *209 NB-15; mail Madrid z 13660; rural
Magnolia; RMC Place; CHAUTAUQUA; ▲ Chautauqua; *208 NM-2; mail Mayville z 14757; ● 150
Mahopac; CDP; PUTNAM; ▲ Carmel; 207 SC-7; elev. 666ft./203m.; 🅿; ★ N.Y.; z 10541; Ⓟ 7,755; Ⓒ 8,478
Mahopac Falls; RMC Place; PUTNAM; ▲ Carmel; 207 SC-7; 🅿; ★ N.Y.; z 10542; ● 1,200
Mahopac Hills; RMC Place; PUTNAM; ▲ Carmel; ★ N.Y.; mail Mahopac z 10541
Mahopac Point; RMC Place; PUTNAM; ▲ Carmel; ★ N.Y.; mail Mahopac z 10541
Mahopac Ridge; RMC Place; PUTNAM; ▲ Carmel; ★ N.Y.; mail Mahopac z 10541
Maidstone Park; RMC Place; SUFFOLK; ▲ East Hampton; *207 SE-13; mail East Hampton z 11937
Maine; RMC Place; BROOME; ▲ Maine; 209 NM-12; elev. 919ft./280m.; 🅿; ★ BING; z 13802; ● 1,110
Maine; MCD-Town; BROOME; *209 NM-12; 🅿; ★ BING; z 13802; Ⓟ 5,576; Ⓒ 5,459
Main Settlement; RMC Place; CATTARAUGUS; ▲ Portville; *208 NM-5; elev. 1,445ft./440m.; mail Portville z 14770; rural
Main Village; RMC Place; ERIE; ★ BUF; mail Buffalo z 14226; pop. incl. with Williamsville (Inc. Place)
Malba; RMC Place; QUEENS; *207 SF-7; 🅿; ★ N.Y.; z 11357; pop. incl. with New York (Inc. Place)
Malden; CDP-Census Area Only; ULSTER; *209 NM-18; ★ KNGST; mail Malden on Hudson z 12453; Ⓒ 413
Malden Bridge; RMC Place; COLUMBIA; ▲ Chatham; *209 NK-19; 🅿; ★ A-S-T; z 12115; ● 250
Malden-on-Hudson; RMC Place; ULSTER; ▲ Saugerties; 209 NM-18; 🅿; ★ KNGST; z 12453; ● 730
Mallory; RMC Place; OSWEGO; ▲ Hastings; 209 NH-12; 🅿; ★ SYR; z 13103; ● 350
Malone; Inc. Place; ⊡ FRANKLIN; ▲ Malone; 209 NB-17; elev. 722ft./220m.; 🅿 🅷; z 12953; Ⓟ 6,777; Ⓒ 6,075
Malone; MCD-Town; FRANKLIN; *209 NB-17; 🅿; z 12953; Ⓟ 12,982; Ⓒ 14,981
Malta; RMC Place; SARATOGA; ▲ Malta; 209 NI-19; elev. 342ft./104m.; 🅿; ★ A-S-T; z 12020; ● 450
Malta; MCD-Town; SARATOGA; *209 NI-19; 🅿; ★ A-S-T; z 12020; Ⓟ 11,709; Ⓒ 13,005
Malta Ridge; RMC Place; SARATOGA; ▲ Malta; 209 NI-19; ★ A-S-T; mail Ballston Spa z 12020; ● 130
Maltaville; RMC Place; SARATOGA; ▲ Malta; 209 NI-19; ★ A-S-T; mail Ballston Spa z 12020, Mechanicville z 12118; ● 170
Maltbie Heights; RMC Place; CATTARAUGUS; ▲ Persia; mail Gowanda z 14070; ● 70
Malverne; Inc. Place; NASSAU; ▲ Hempstead; 211 I-17; 🅿; ★ N.Y.; z 11565; Ⓟ 9,054; Ⓒ 8,934
Malverne Park Oaks; CDP-Census Area Only; NASSAU; *207 SF-8; ★ N.Y.; Ⓒ 470
Malvic Manor; RMC Place; ONONDAGA; ▲ Salina; *209 NI-12; ★ SYR; mail Liverpool z 13088; ● 1,270
Mamakating; MCD-Town; SULLIVAN; *207 SB-4; mail Wurtsboro z 12790; Ⓟ 9,792; Ⓒ 11,002
Mamakating Park; RMC Place; SULLIVAN; ▲ Mamakating; *207 SB-4; elev. 648ft./198m.; mail Wurtsboro z 12790; ● 50
Mamaroneck; Inc. Place; WESTCHESTER; ▲ Rye, Mamaroneck; 207 SE-7; 🅿; ★ N.Y.; z 10543; Ⓟ 17,325; Ⓒ 18,752
Mamaroneck; MCD-Town; WESTCHESTER; *207 SE-7; 🅿; ★ N.Y.; z 10543; includes part of the Village of Mamaroneck; Ⓟ 27,706; Ⓒ 28,967; ◆ 29,737
Manchester; Inc. Place; ONTARIO; ▲ Manchester; 208 NI-8; 🅿; z 14504; Ⓟ 1,598; Ⓒ 1,475
Manchester; MCD-Town; ONTARIO; *208 NI-9; 🅿; z 14504; Ⓟ 9,351; Ⓒ 9,258
Manchester Bridge; RMC Place; DUTCHESS; ▲ Poughkeepsie, La Grange; *207 SB-7; elev. 181ft./55m.; ★ POK; mail Poughkeepsie z 12603; ● 730
Mandana; RMC Place; ONONDAGA; ▲ Skaneateles; *209 NJ-11; ★ SYR; mail Skaneateles z 13152; rural
Manhasset; CDP; NASSAU; ▲ North Hempstead; 211 F-16; 🅿 🅷; ★ N.Y.; z 11030; Ⓟ 7,718; Ⓒ 8,362
Manhasset Hills; CDP-Census Area Only; NASSAU; ▲ North Hempstead; *207 SF-8; 🅿; ★ N.Y.; z 11040; Ⓟ 3,722; Ⓒ 3,661
Manhattan; RMC Place; NEW YORK; ★ N.Y.; mail New York z 10001-14, z 10016-41, z 10043-46, z 10055, z 10060, z 10069, z 10072, z 10079-82, z 10087, z 10090, z 10094-96, z 10098-99, z 10101, z 10103-08, z 10110-13, z 10116, z 10118-23, z 10128, z 10150-55, z 10158-59, z 10162, z 10165-78, z 10203, z 10211-13, z 10242, z 10249, z 10256-61, z 10265, z 10268-82, z 10286; pop. incl. with New York (Inc. Place)
Manhattan Beach; RMC Place; KINGS; 211 L-11; ★ N.Y.; mail Brooklyn z 11235; pop. incl. with New York (Inc. Place)
Manhattan Park; RMC Place; WESTCHESTER; ★ N.Y.; mail White Plains z 10601
Manhattanville; RMC Place; NEW YORK; ★ N.Y.; mail New York z 10027; pop. incl. with New York (Inc. Place)
Manhattanville College; RMC Place; WESTCHESTER; ★ N.Y.; mail Purchase z 10577; pop. incl. with Harrison (Inc. Place)
Manheim; MCD-Town; HERKIMER; *209 NI-16; mail Dolgeville z 13329; Ⓟ 3,527; Ⓒ 3,171
Manheim Center; RMC Place; HERKIMER; ▲ Manheim; *209 NI-16; mail Little Falls z 13365; rural
Manitou; RMC Place; PUTNAM; ▲ Philipstown; 207 SC-6; ★ N.Y.; mail Garrison z 10524; ● 110
Manitou Beach; RMC Place; MONROE; ▲ Greece; 208 NH-7; elev. 257ft./78m.; ★ ROCH; mail Hilton z 14468; ● 250
Manlius; Inc. Place; ONONDAGA; ▲ Manlius; 209 NI-12; 🅿; ★ SYR; z 13104; Ⓟ 4,764; Ⓒ 4,819
Manlius; MCD-Town; ONONDAGA; *209 NI-12; 🅿; ★ SYR; z 13104; Ⓟ 30,656; Ⓒ 31,872; ◆ 31,742
Manlius Center; RMC Place; ONONDAGA; ▲ Manlius; *209 NI-12; ★ SYR; mail Fayetteville z 13066; rural
Mannetto Hills; RMC Place; SUFFOLK; ▲ Huntington; *207 SF-8; ★ N.Y.; mail Melville z 11747
Manning; RMC Place; ORLEANS; ▲ Clarendon; *208 NH-6; elev. 682ft./208m.; ★ ROCH; mail Holley z 14470; rural
Mannsville; Inc. Place; JEFFERSON; ▲ Ellisburg; 209 NF-12; 🅿; z 13661; Ⓟ 444; Ⓒ 400
Mannville; RMC Place; ALBANY; ▲ Colonie; *209 NJ-19; ★ A-S-T; mail Watervliet z 12189; ● 500
Manny Corners; RMC Place; MONTGOMERY; ▲ Amsterdam; *209 NI-18; elev. 692ft./211m.; ★ A-S-T; mail Amsterdam z 12010; rural
Manor; RMC Place; ONEIDA; ▲ New Hartford; *209 NI-14; ★ UT-R; mail New Hartford z 13413; ● 900
Manorhaven; Inc. Place; NASSAU; ▲ North Hempstead; 211 E-16; ★ N.Y.; mail Port Washington z 11050; Ⓟ 5,672; Ⓒ 6,138
Manorkill; RMC Place; SCHOHARIE; ▲ Conesville; *209 NL-17; elev. 1,515ft./462m.; mail Gilboa z 12076
Manorville; CDP; SUFFOLK; ▲ Brookhaven; 207 SE-11; 🅿; ★ N.Y.; z 11949; Ⓟ 6,198; Ⓒ 11,131
Manorville; RMC Place; ULSTER; ▲ Saugerties; *209 NM-18; ★ KNGST; mail Palenville z 12463, Saugerties z 12477; ● 60
Mansfield; MCD-Town; CATTARAUGUS; *208 NL-4; mail Little Valley z 14755; Ⓟ 724; Ⓒ 800
Maple Bay; RMC Place; CHAUTAUQUA; ▲ Busti; ★ JMST; mail Ashville z 14710; ● 100
Maple Beach; RMC Place; LIVINGSTON; ▲ Groveland; *208 NJ-7; ★ ROCH; mail Geneseo z 14454; ● 100
Maplecrest; RMC Place; GREENE; ▲ Windham; 209 NL-18; 🅿; z 12454; ● 150
Mapledale; RMC Place; ONEIDA; ▲ Trenton; *209 NJ-14; ★ UT-R; mail Barneveld z 13304; ● 25
Mapledale; RMC Place; ULSTER; ▲ Hardenburgh; *209 NM-16; mail Arkville z 12406; ● 100
Maple Grove; RMC Place; HAMILTON, FULTON; ▲ Northampton, Hope; *209 NH-18; elev. 1,132ft./345m.; mail Northville z 12134; ● 80
Maple Grove; RMC Place; OTSEGO; ▲ Morris; *209 NK-14; mail Morris z 13808
Maple Hill; RMC Place; ULSTER; ▲ Rosendale; *207 SA-6; ★ KNGST; mail Kingston z 12401; ● 150
Maplehurst; RMC Place; CATTARAUGUS; ▲ Hinsdale; 208 NM-5; elev. 1,465ft./447m.; mail Hinsdale z 14743; ● 200
Maples; RMC Place; CATTARAUGUS; ▲ Mansfield; 208 NL-4; elev. 1,407ft./429m.; mail Little Valley z 14755; ● 60
Maple Springs; RMC Place; CHAUTAUQUA; ▲ Ellery; 208 NL-2; 🅿; ★ JMST; z 14756; ● 400
Mapleton; RMC Place; CAYUGA; ▲ Fleming; *208 NJ-10; elev. 887ft./270m.; ★ SYR; mail Auburn z 13021; rural
Mapletown; RMC Place; MONTGOMERY; ▲ Canajoharie; *209 NJ-16; mail Canajoharie z 13317; rural
Maple Valley; RMC Place; OTSEGO; ▲ Westford; *209 NK-16; mail Westford z 13488; rural
Maple View; RMC Place; OSWEGO; ▲ Mexico; 209 NG-12; elev. 467ft./142m.; 🅿; z 13107; ● 280
Maplewood; RMC Place; ALBANY; ▲ Colonie; 207 SH-5; ★ A-S-T; mail Watervliet z 12189; ● 800
Maplewood; RMC Place; SULLIVAN; ▲ Thompson; *207 SB-4; elev. 1,240ft./378m.; mail Monticello z 12701; ● 200
Maplewood; RMC Place; WESTCHESTER; *207 SE-7; ★ N.Y.; pop. incl. with New Rochelle (Inc. Place)
Marathon; Inc. Place; CORTLAND; ▲ Marathon; 209 NL-12; elev. 1,020ft./311m.; 🅿; z 13803; Ⓟ 1,107; Ⓒ 1,063
Marathon; MCD-Town; CORTLAND; *209 NL-12; 🅿; z 13803; Ⓟ 2,019; Ⓒ 2,189
Marbletown; RMC Place; ULSTER; ▲ Marbletown; 207 SA-6; ★ KNGST; mail Kingston z 12401; ● 200
Marbletown; MCD-Town; ULSTER; *207 SA-6; ★ KNGST; mail Kingston z 12401; Ⓟ 5,285; Ⓒ 5,854
Marbletown; RMC Place; WAYNE; ▲ Arcadia; *208 NI-9; mail Newark z 14513; rural
Marcellus; Inc. Place; ONONDAGA; ▲ Marcellus; 209 NI-11; 🅿; ★ SYR; z 13108; Ⓟ 1,840; Ⓒ 1,826
Marcellus; MCD-Town; ONONDAGA; *209 NI-11; 🅿; ★ SYR; z 13108; Ⓟ 6,465; Ⓒ 6,319
Marcellus Falls; RMC Place; ONONDAGA; ▲ Marcellus; *209 NI-11; ★ SYR; mail Marcellus z 13108; ● 140
Marcy; MCD-Town; ONEIDA; *209 NI-14; 🅿; ★ UT-R; z 13403 & mail Utica z 13503; Ⓟ 8,685; Ⓒ 9,469; Ⓡ 9,481
Marengo; RMC Place; WAYNE; ▲ Galen; *208 NI-9; mail Clyde z 14433
Margaretville; Inc. Place; DELAWARE; ▲ Middletown; 209 NM-16; 🅿 🅷; z 12455 & mail Watchung z 07069; Ⓟ 639; Ⓒ 643
Mariandale; RMC Place; WESTCHESTER; ▲ Ossining; *207 SD-7; ★ N.Y.; mail Ossining z 10562; pop. incl. with Ossining (Inc. Place)
Mariaville; RMC Place; SCHENECTADY; ▲ Duanesburg; *209 NJ-18; mail Pattersonville z 12137; summer pop. 700; ● 550
Mariaville Lake; CDP-Census Area Only; SCHENECTADY; *209 NJ-18; Ⓒ 710
Marietta; RMC Place; ONONDAGA; ▲ Marcellus; 209 NJ-11; 🅿; ★ SYR; z 13110; ● 80
Marilla; RMC Place; ERIE; ▲ Marilla; 208 NJ-4; elev. 840ft./256m.; 🅿; ★ BUF; z 14102; ● 375
Marilla; MCD-Town; ERIE; *208 NJ-4; 🅿; ★ BUF; z 14102; Ⓟ 5,250; Ⓒ 5,709
Mariners Harbor; RMC Place; RICHMOND; 210 J-6; ★ N.Y.; mail Staten Island z 10303; pop. incl. with New York (Inc. Place)
Marion; RMC Place; WAYNE; ▲ Marion; 208 NI-9; elev. 443ft./135m.; 🅿; ★ ROCH; z 14505; ● 1,100
Marion; MCD-Town; WAYNE; *208 NI-9; 🅿; ★ ROCH; z 14505; Ⓟ 4,901; Ⓒ 4,974
Mariposa; RMC Place; CHENANGO; ▲ Otselic; *209 NJ-13; mail South Otselic z 13155; rural
Markhams; RMC Place; CATTARAUGUS; ▲ Dayton; *208 NL-3; elev. 1,321ft./403m.; mail Gowanda z 14070
Marlboro; CDP; ULSTER; ▲ Marlborough; 207 SB-6; 🅿; ★ POK; z 12542; Ⓟ 2,200; Ⓒ 2,339
Marlborough; MCD-Town; ULSTER; *207 SB-6; ★ POK; mail Marlboro z 12542; partly in ★ NWBG; Ⓟ 7,430; Ⓒ 8,263
Marshall; RMC Place; ALLEGANY; ▲ New Hudson; *208 NL-5; elev. 1,648ft./502m.; mail Belfast z 14711; rural
Marshall; MCD-Town; ONEIDA; *209 NI-14; mail Deansboro z 13328; Ⓟ 2,125; Ⓒ 2,127
Marshfield; RMC Place; ERIE; mail Lawtons z 14091; ● 20
Marshland Heights; RMC Place; TIOGA; ▲ Owego; *209 NM-12; ★ BING; mail Endicott z 13760; ● 425
Marshville; RMC Place; MONTGOMERY; ▲ Canajoharie; *209 NJ-16; mail Canajoharie z 13317; rural
Marshville; RMC Place; ST. LAWRENCE; ▲ Hermon; *209 NC-14; elev. 502ft./153m.; mail Hermon z 13652; rural
Martindale (Martindale Depot); RMC Place; COLUMBIA; ▲ Claverack; *209 NL-19; mail Craryville z 12521; ● 110
Martindale Depot; COLUMBIA; see Martindale (RMC Place)
Martinsburg; RMC Place; LEWIS; ▲ Martinsburg; 209 NF-14; 🅿; z 13404; ● 400
Martinsburg; MCD-Town; LEWIS; *209 NF-13; 🅿; z 13404; Ⓟ 1,358; Ⓒ 1,249
Martisco; RMC Place; ONONDAGA; ▲ Camillus; *209 NI-11; ★ SYR; mail Marcellus z 13108; rural
Martville; RMC Place; CAYUGA; ▲ Sterling; 208 NH-10; 🅿; z 13111; ● 110
Maryknoll; RMC Place; WESTCHESTER; ▲ Ossining; *207 SD-7; 🅿; ★ N.Y.; z 10545; ● 600
Maryland; RMC Place; OTSEGO; ▲ Otsego; 209 NK-15; 🅿; z 12116; ● 165
Maryland; MCD-Town; OTSEGO; *209 NK-16; 🅿; z 12116; Ⓟ 1,716; Ⓒ 1,920
Masonville; RMC Place; DELAWARE; ▲ Masonville; 209 NL-14; elev. 1,294ft./394m.; 🅿; z 13804; ● 600
Masonville; MCD-Town; DELAWARE; *209 NL-14; 🅿; z 13804; Ⓟ 1,352; Ⓒ 1,405
Maspeth; RMC Place; QUEENS; 211 H-12; 🅿; ★ N.Y.; z 11378; pop. incl. with New York (Inc. Place)
Massapequa; CDP; NASSAU; ▲ Oyster Bay; 207 SF-8; elev. 26ft./8m.; 🅿; ★ N.Y.; z 11758; Ⓟ 22,018; Ⓒ 22,652; ◆ 21,520
Massapequa Park; Inc. Place; NASSAU; ▲ Oyster Bay; 207 SJ-10; elev. 24ft./7m.; 🅿; ★ N.Y.; z 11762; Ⓟ 18,044; Ⓒ 17,499
Massawepiee; RMC Place; ST. LAWRENCE; ▲ Piercefield; mail Tupper Lake z 12986
Massena; Inc. Place; ST. LAWRENCE; ▲ Louisville, Massena, Norfolk; 209 NA-15; 🅿 🅷; z 13662; Ⓟ 11,719; Ⓒ 11,209
Massena; MCD-Town; ST. LAWRENCE; *209 NA-15; 🅿; z 13662; includes part of the Village of Massena; Ⓟ 13,826; Ⓒ 13,121
Massena Center; RMC Place; ST. LAWRENCE; ▲ Massena; 209 NA-15; mail Massena z 13662; ● 50
Massena Springs; RMC Place; ST. LAWRENCE; *209 NA-15; elev. 216ft./66m.; mail Massena z 13662; pop. incl. with Massena (Inc. Place)
Masten Lake; RMC Place; SULLIVAN; ▲ Mamakating; *207 SB-4; mail Wurtsboro z 12790; ● 250
Mastic; CDP; SUFFOLK; ▲ Brookhaven; 207 SF-11; elev. 32ft./10m.; 🅿; ★ N.Y.; z 11950; Ⓟ 13,778; Ⓒ 15,436
Mastic Beach; CDP; SUFFOLK; ▲ Brookhaven; 207 SF-11; elev. 9ft./3m.; 🅿; ★ N.Y.; z 11951; Ⓟ 10,293; Ⓒ 11,543
Matinecock; Inc. Place; NASSAU; ▲ Oyster Bay; 211 D-18; ★ N.Y.; mail Locust Valley z 11560; Ⓟ 872; Ⓒ 836
Matteawan; RMC Place; DUTCHESS; ★ POK; mail Beacon z 12508; pop. incl. with Beacon (Inc. Place)
Mattituck; CDP; SUFFOLK; ▲ Southold; 207 SE-12; elev. 16ft./5m.; 🅿; z 11952; Ⓟ 3,902; Ⓒ 4,198
Mattydale; CDP; ONONDAGA; ▲ Salina; 209 NI-12; 🅿; ★ SYR; z 13211; Ⓟ 6,418; Ⓒ 6,367
Maybrook; Inc. Place; ORANGE; ▲ Hamptonburgh, Montgomery; 207 SC-5; 🅿; ★ N.Y.; z 12543; Ⓟ 2,802; Ⓒ 3,084
Mayfair; RMC Place; SCHENECTADY; ▲ Glenville; *209 NJ-18; ★ A-S-T; mail Schenectady z 12302; ● 1,200
Mayfield; Inc. Place; FULTON; ▲ Mayfield; 209 NI-17; 🅿; ★ A-S-T; z 12117; Ⓟ 817; Ⓒ 800
Mayfield; MCD-Town; FULTON; *209 NI-17; 🅿; ★ A-S-T; z 12117; Ⓟ 5,738; Ⓒ 6,432
Mayville; Inc. Place; ⊡ CHAUTAUQUA; ▲ Chautauqua; 208 NL-1; elev. 1,468ft./447m.; 🅿; z 14757; Ⓟ 1,636; Ⓒ 1,756
Maywood; RMC Place; ALBANY; ▲ Colonie; 209 NJ-19; ★ A-S-T; mail Albany z 12205; ● 3,400
Maywood; RMC Place; SUFFOLK; ▲ Babylon; *207 SF-9; ★ N.Y.; mail Amityville z 11701
McClure; RMC Place; BROOME; ▲ Sanford; *209 NM-14; mail Deposit z 13754
McColloms; RMC Place; FRANKLIN; ▲ Brighton; *209 NC-17; mail Paul Smiths z 12970; rural
McConnellsville; RMC Place; ONEIDA; ▲ Annsville, Vienna; 209 NH-13; 🅿; ★ UT-R; z 13401; ● 500
McCormack Corners; ALBANY; see Mohawk Village (RMC Place)
McDonough; RMC Place; CHENANGO; ▲ McDonough; 209 NK-13; 🅿; z 13801; ● 300
McDonough; MCD-Town; CHENANGO; *209 NK-13; mail Mc Donough z 13801; Ⓟ 809; Ⓒ 870
Mc Duffie Town; RMC Place; SENECA; ▲ Varick; *208 NJ-10; mail Romulus z 14541; rural
McGrath Point; RMC Place; SCHUYLER; ▲ Hector; *208 NK-9; mail Hector z 14841; ● 200
McGraw; Inc. Place; CORTLAND; ▲ Cortlandville; 209 NK-12; 🅿; z 13101; Ⓟ 1,074; Ⓒ 1,000
McKeever; RMC Place; HERKIMER; ▲ Webb; 209 NG-15; elev. 1,538ft./469m.; mail Forestport z 13338; rural
McKinley; RMC Place; MONTGOMERY; ▲ Palatine; *209 NJ-17; elev. 723ft./220m.; mail Palatine Bridge z 13428; rural
McKownville; RMC Place; ALBANY; ▲ Guilderland; 207 SI-3; elev. 262ft./80m.; ★ A-S-T; mail Albany z 12203; ● 4,850
McLaughlin Acres; RMC Place; PUTNAM; ▲ Carmel; *207 SC-7; ★ N.Y.; mail Mahopac z 10541; ● 250
McLean; RMC Place; TOMPKINS; ▲ Groton; 209 NK-11; 🅿; ★ ITH; z 13102; ● 600
McMasters Corners; RMC Place; CAYUGA; ▲ Sennett; *208 NI-10; ★ SYR; mail Syracuse z 13201; rural
McNalls; RMC Place; NIAGARA; ▲ Royalton; *208 NI-4; elev. 659ft./201m.; mail Gasport z 14067; ● 80
McPherson Point; RMC Place; LIVINGSTON; ▲ Livonia; *208 NJ-7; ★ ROCH; mail Livonia z 14487; ● 150
Meacham; RMC Place; NASSAU; ▲ Hempstead; 🅿; ★ N.Y.; z 11003
Meadowbrook; RMC Place; ORANGE; ▲ Cornwall; *207 SC-6; ★ NWBG; mail Newburgh z 12550; rural
Meadowdale; RMC Place; ALBANY; ▲ Guilderland; 207 SI-1; ★ A-S-T; mail Altamont z 12009
Meadow Hill; RMC Place; ORANGE; ▲ Newburgh; *207 SB-6; ★ NWBG; mail Newburgh z 12550; ● 4,000
Meadow Lane Estates; RMC Place; COLUMBIA; ▲ Kinderhook; *209 NL-19; ★ A-S-T; mail Valatie z 12184; ● 200
Meadowmere Park; RMC Place; NASSAU; ▲ Hempstead; *207 SG-7; ★ N.Y.; mail Lawrence z 11559, Woodmere z 11598
Meadow Run; RMC Place; ERIE; ★ BUF; mail Hamburg z 14075; pop. incl. with Hamburg (Inc. Place)
Meads; RMC Place; ULSTER; ▲ Woodstock; *209 NM-18; elev. 1,720ft./524m.; mail Woodstock z 12498; rural
Meads Creek; RMC Place; SCHUYLER, STEUBEN; ▲ Campbell, Hornby, Orange; *208 NL-9; mail Painted Post z 14870; rural
Mechanicstown; CDP; ORANGE; ▲ Wallkill; 207 SC-5; ★ MIDD; mail Middletown z 10940; Ⓟ 4,974; Ⓒ 6,061
Mechanicville; Inc. Place; SARATOGA; 209 NJ-19; elev. 104ft./32m.; 🅿; ★ A-S-T; z 12118; Ⓟ 5,249; Ⓒ 5,019
Mecklenburg; RMC Place; SCHUYLER; ▲ Hector; 208 NK-10; 🅿; z 14863; ● 280
Meco; RMC Place; FULTON; ▲ Johnstown; 209 NI-17; mail Gloversville z 12078; ● 150
Medford; CDP; SUFFOLK; ▲ Brookhaven; 207 SF-10; elev. 101ft./31m.; 🅿; ★ N.Y.; z 11763; Ⓟ 21,274; Ⓒ 21,985; ◆ 21,976
Medina; Inc. Place; ORLEANS; ▲ Shelby, Ridgeway; 208 NH-5; elev. 542ft./165m.; 🅿 🅷; z 14103; Ⓟ 6,686; Ⓒ 6,415
Medusa; CDP; ALBANY; ▲ Rensselaerville; 209 NK-18; 🅿; z 12120; Ⓒ 376
Medway; RMC Place; GREENE; ▲ New Baltimore; 209 NL-19; elev. 687ft./209m.; ★ A-S-T; mail Climax z 12042; ● 285
Meekerville; RMC Place; ONEIDA; ▲ Forestport; *209 NG-15; mail Forestport z 13338; rural
Melcourt; RMC Place; BRONX; ★ N.Y.; mail Bronx z 10451; pop. incl. with New York (Inc. Place)
Mellenville; RMC Place; COLUMBIA; ▲ Claverack; *209 NL-19; 🅿; z 12544; ● 350
Melody Lake; RMC Place; SULLIVAN; ▲ Thompson; *207 SB-4; mail Monticello z 12701; ● 30
Melrose; RMC Place; BRONX; *207 SF-7; ★ N.Y.; mail Bronx z 10456; pop. incl. with New York (Inc. Place)
Melrose; RMC Place; RENSSELAER; ▲ Schaghticoke; 209 NJ-19; 🅿; ★ A-S-T; z 12121; ● 350
Melrose Park (Auburn Southeast); CDP; CAYUGA; ▲ Owasco; *208 NJ-10; ★ SYR; mail Auburn z 13021; Ⓟ 2,091; Ⓒ 2,359
Melville; CDP; SUFFOLK; ▲ Huntington; *207 SF-9; 🅿; ★ N.Y.; z 11747, z 11750, z 11775; Ⓟ 12,586; Ⓒ 14,533
Memphis; RMC Place; ONONDAGA; ▲ Camillus, Van Buren; *209 NI-11; 🅿; ★ SYR; z 13112; ● 350
Menands; Inc. Place; ALBANY; ▲ Colonie; 209 NJ-19; 🅿; ★ A-S-T; z 12204; Ⓟ 4,333; Ⓒ 3,910
Mendon; RMC Place; MONROE; ▲ Mendon; 208 NI-8; 🅿; ★ ROCH; z 14506; ● 1,000
Mendon; MCD-Town; MONROE; *208 NI-7; 🅿; ★ ROCH; z 14506; Ⓟ 6,845; Ⓒ 8,370
Mendon Center; RMC Place; MONROE; ▲ Mendon; *208 NI-7; ★ ROCH; mail Honeoye Falls z 14472; ● 40
Menteth Point; RMC Place; ONTARIO; ▲ Canandaigua; *208 NJ-8; mail Canandaigua z 14424
Mentz; MCD-Town; CAYUGA; *208 NI-10; ★ SYR; mail Port Byron z 13140; Ⓟ 2,453; Ⓒ 2,446
Meredith; RMC Place; DELAWARE; ▲ Meredith; *209 NL-15; 🅿; z 13753; ● 40
Meredith; MCD-Town; DELAWARE; *209 NL-15; 🅿; z 13753; Ⓟ 1,513; Ⓒ 1,588
Meridale; RMC Place; DELAWARE; ▲ Meredith; 209 NL-15; elev. 1,800ft./549m.; 🅿; z 13806; ● 250
Meridian; Inc. Place; CAYUGA; ▲ Cato; 209 NI-11; elev. 455ft./139m.; 🅿; ★ SYR; z 13113; Ⓟ 351; Ⓒ 350
Merillon Avenue; RMC Place; NASSAU; ★ N.Y.; mail Garden City z 11530; pop. incl. with Garden City (Inc. Place)
Merrick; CDP; NASSAU; ▲ Hempstead; 207 SG-8; elev. 23ft./7m.; 🅿; ★ N.Y.; z 11566; Ⓟ 23,042; Ⓒ 22,764; ◆ 21,618
Merrickville; RMC Place; DELAWARE; ▲ Franklin; *209 NL-15; mail Sidney Center z 13839; rural
Merriewold; RMC Place; SULLIVAN; ▲ Forestburgh; *207 SB-4; mail Forestburgh z 12777
Merriewold Lake; RMC Place; ORANGE; ▲ Blooming Grove; *207 SC-6; ★ N.Y.; mail Monroe z 10950; ● 3,000
Merrifield; RMC Place; CAYUGA; ▲ Scipio; *208 NJ-10; elev. 1,055ft./322m.; mail Scipio Center z 13147; rural
Merrill; RMC Place; CLINTON; ▲ Dannemora, Ellenburg; 209 NB-18; 🅿; z 12955; ● 450
Merrillsville; RMC Place; MADISON; ▲ Lincoln; *209 NI-13; elev. 690ft./210m.; mail Oneida z 13421; rural
Merrilville; RMC Place; FRANKLIN; ▲ Franklin; *209 NC-18; mail Tupper Lake z 12986; rural
Mertensia; RMC Place; ONTARIO; ▲ Farmington; *208 NI-8; ★ ROCH; mail Victor z 14564; rural
Messengerville; RMC Place; CORTLAND; ▲ Virgil; *209 NK-12; elev. 1,056ft./322m.; mail Marathon z 13803; rural
Metropolitan; RMC Place; KINGS; ★ N.Y.; mail Brooklyn z 11206; pop. incl. with New York (Inc. Place)
Mettacahonts; RMC Place; ULSTER; ▲ Rochester; *207 SA-5; mail Accord z 12404; ● 200
Mews; RMC Place; NASSAU; ▲ North Hempstead; *207 SF-8; ★ N.Y.; mail Albertson z 11507
Mexico; Inc. Place; OSWEGO; ▲ Mexico; 209 NG-11; 🅿; z 13114; Ⓟ 1,555; Ⓒ 1,572
Mexico; MCD-Town; OSWEGO; *209 NG-11; 🅿; z 13114; Ⓟ 5,050; Ⓒ 5,181
Middle Bridge; RMC Place; CHENANGO; ▲ Afton; *209 NL-14; mail Afton z 13730; ● 50
Middleburg; SCHOHARIE; see Middleburgh (Inc. Place)
Middleburgh (Middleburg); Inc. Place; SCHOHARIE; ▲ Middleburgh; 209 NK-17; 🅿; z 12122; Ⓟ 1,436; Ⓒ 1,398
Middleburgh; MCD-Town; SCHOHARIE; *209 NK-17; 🅿; z 12122; Ⓟ 3,296; Ⓒ 3,515
Middlebury; MCD-Town; WYOMING; *208 NJ-6; mail Wyoming z 14591; Ⓟ 1,532; Ⓒ 1,508
Middle Falls; RMC Place; WASHINGTON; ▲ Greenwich; 209 NI-20; 🅿; ★ GLFLS; z 12848; ● 270
Middlefield; RMC Place; OTSEGO; ▲ Middlefield; 209 NK-16; mail Roseboom z 13450; ● 350
Middlefield; MCD-Town; OTSEGO; *209 NJ-16; mail Roseboom z 13450; Ⓟ 2,231; Ⓒ 2,249
Middlefield Center; RMC Place; OTSEGO; ▲ Middlefield; *209 NJ-16; mail Cherry Valley z 13320; ● 85
Middle Granville; RMC Place; WASHINGTON; ▲ Granville; 209 NG-20; 🅿; z 12849; ● 600
Middle Grove; RMC Place; SARATOGA; ▲ Greenfield; 209 NI-18; 🅿; ★ A-S-T; z 12850; ● 620
Middle Hope; RMC Place; ORANGE; ▲ Newburgh; 207 SB-6; ★ NWBG; mail Newburgh z 12550; ● 3,000
Middle Island; CDP; SUFFOLK; ▲ Brookhaven; 207 SE-10; 🅿; ★ N.Y.; z 11953; Ⓟ 7,848; Ⓒ 9,702
Middleport; RMC Place; MADISON; ▲ Lebanon; *209 NJ-13; mail Hamilton z 13346; rural
Middleport; Inc. Place; NIAGARA; ▲ Royalton, Hartland; 208 NH-5; 🅿; ★ LOCK; z 14105; Ⓟ 1,876; Ⓒ 1,917
Middlesex; RMC Place; YATES; ▲ Middlesex; 208 NJ-8; 🅿; z 14507; ● 400
Middlesex; MCD-Town; YATES; *208 NJ-8; 🅿; z 14507; Ⓟ 1,249; Ⓒ 1,345
Middletown; MCD-Town; DELAWARE; *209 NM-16; mail Margaretville z 12455; Ⓟ 3,406; Ⓒ 4,051
Middletown; Inc. Place; ORANGE; 207 SC-5; elev. 500ft./152m.; 🅿 🅷 ■; ★ MIDD; z 10940-41, z 10943; Ⓟ 24,160; Ⓒ 25,388; ◆ 26,780
Middle Village; RMC Place; QUEENS; 211 H-13; 🅿; ★ N.Y.; z 11379; pop. incl. with New York (Inc. Place)
Middleville; Inc. Place; HERKIMER; ▲ Newport, Fairfield; 209 NI-15; 🅿; z 13406; Ⓟ 624; Ⓒ 550
Middleville; RMC Place; SUFFOLK; ▲ Huntington; 207 SG-11; ★ N.Y.; mail Northport z 11768; ● 1,400
Midland Beach; RMC Place; RICHMOND; 210 L-8; ★ N.Y.; mail Staten Island z 10306; pop. incl. with New York (Inc. Place)
Midtown; RMC Place; NEW YORK; ★ N.Y.; mail New York z 10018, z 10138; pop. incl. with New York (Inc. Place)
Midway; RMC Place; CHEMUNG; ▲ Veteran; *208 NL-10; elev. 786ft./240m.; ★ ELM; mail Millport z 14864; rural
Midwood; RMC Place; KINGS; ★ N.Y.; mail Brooklyn z 11230; pop. incl. with New York (Inc. Place)
Milan; MCD-Town; DUTCHESS; *209 NM-19; 🅿; z 12571; Ⓟ 1,895; Ⓒ 4,559; Ⓡ 2,356
Mileses; RMC Place; SULLIVAN; ▲ Fremont; 207 SA-2; elev. 1,074ft./327m.; mail Hankins z 12741; ● 100
Milford; Inc. Place; OTSEGO; ▲ Milford; 209 NK-15; 🅿; z 13807; Ⓟ 462; Ⓒ 511
Milford; MCD-Town; OTSEGO; *209 NK-15; 🅿; z 13807; Ⓟ 2,845; Ⓒ 2,938
Milford Center; RMC Place; OTSEGO; ▲ Milford; *209 NK-15; mail Oneonta z 13820; ● 35
Mill Basin; RMC Place; KINGS; *207 SG-7; ★ N.Y.; mail Brooklyn z 11234; pop. incl. with New York (Inc. Place)
Millbrook; Inc. Place; DUTCHESS; ▲ Washington; 209 NN-19; elev. 569ft./173m.; 🅿; z 12545; Ⓟ 1,339; Ⓒ 1,429
Millen Bay; RMC Place; JEFFERSON; ▲ Cape Vincent; *209 ND-11; mail Cape Vincent z 13618
Miller Place; CDP; SUFFOLK; ▲ Brookhaven; *207 SE-10; 🅿; ★ N.Y.; z 11764; Ⓟ 9,315; Ⓒ 10,580
Millers; RMC Place; ORLEANS; ▲ Yates; 208 NH-5; elev. 346ft./105m.; mail Lyndonville z 14098; ● 150
Millers Mills; RMC Place; HERKIMER; ▲ Columbia; *209 NJ-16; mail West Winfield z 13491; ● 85
Millersport; RMC Place; ERIE; ▲ Clarence, Amherst; 208 NB-6; ★ BUF; mail East Amherst z 14051
Millerton; Inc. Place; DUTCHESS; ▲ North East; 209 NM-20; elev. 701ft./214m.; 🅿; z 12546; Ⓟ 884; Ⓒ 925
Millertown; RMC Place; RENSSELAER; ▲ Pittstown; *209 NJ-20; ★ A-S-T; mail Johnsonville z 12094
Mill Grove; RMC Place; CATTARAUGUS; ▲ Portville; *208 NM-5; mail Portville z 14770; ● 50
Mill Hook; RMC Place; ULSTER; ▲ Rochester; *207 SA-5; mail Accord z 12404; ● 75
Mill Neck; Inc. Place; NASSAU; ▲ Oyster Bay; 211 D-19; 🅿; ★ N.Y.; z 11765; Ⓟ 977; Ⓒ 825
Mill Point; RMC Place; MONTGOMERY; ▲ Florida; *209 NJ-17; mail Amsterdam z 12010; rural
Millport; Inc. Place; CHEMUNG; ▲ Veteran; 208 NL-10; 🅿; ★ ELM; z 14864; Ⓟ 342; Ⓒ 297
Mills; CORTLAND; see Harford Mills (RMC Place)
Millsburgh; RMC Place; ORANGE; ▲ Minisink; *207 SC-4; ★ MIDD; mail Johnson z 10933, Middletown z 10940; ● 120
Mills Mills; RMC Place; ALLEGANY; ▲ Hume; *208 NK-6; elev. 1,375ft./419m.; mail Fillmore z 14735; rural
Millville; RMC Place; ORLEANS; ▲ Shelby; 208 NH-5; elev. 604ft./184m.; mail Medina z 14103; ● 120
Millwood; RMC Place; WESTCHESTER; ▲ New Castle; 207 SD-7; 🅿; ★ N.Y.; z 10546; ● 1,000
Milo; YATES; see Milo Center (RMC Place)
Milo; MCD-Town; YATES; *208 NK-9; mail Penn Yan z 14527; Ⓟ 7,023; Ⓒ 7,026
Milo Center (Milo); RMC Place; YATES; ▲ Milo; *208 NK-9; mail Penn Yan z 14527
Milton; CDP-Census Area Only; SARATOGA; ▲ Milton; *209 NI-19; ★ A-S-T; mail Ballston Spa z 12020; Ⓟ 1,892; Ⓒ 2,692
Milton; MCD-Town; SARATOGA; *209 NI-18; ★ A-S-T; mail Ballston Spa z 12020; Ⓟ 14,658; Ⓒ 17,103
Milton; CDP; ULSTER; ▲ Marlborough; 207 SB-6; 🅿; ★ POK; z 12547; Ⓟ 1,140; Ⓒ 1,251
Milton Point; RMC Place; WESTCHESTER; *207 SE-7; elev. 17ft./5m.; ★ N.Y.; mail Rye z 10580; pop. incl. with Rye (Inc. Place)
Mina; RMC Place; CHAUTAUQUA; ▲ Mina; *208 NM-1; elev. 1,598ft./487m.; mail Sherman z 14781
Mina; MCD-Town; CHAUTAUQUA; *208 NM-1; mail Sherman z 14781; Ⓟ 1,129; Ⓒ 1,176
Minaville; RMC Place; MONTGOMERY; ▲ Florida; 209 NJ-17; mail Amsterdam z 12010; ● 220
Minden; RMC Place; MONTGOMERY; ▲ Minden; *209 NI-16; mail Fort Plain z 13339; ● 150
Minden; MCD-Town; MONTGOMERY; *209 NJ-16; mail Fort Plain z 13339; Ⓟ 4,474; Ⓒ 4,202
Mindenville; RMC Place; MONTGOMERY; ▲ Minden; *209 NI-16; mail Fort Plain z 13339; rural
Mineola; Inc. Place; ⊡ NASSAU; ▲ Hempstead, North Hempstead; 207 SF-8; 🅿 🅷 ■; ★ N.Y.; z 11501; Ⓟ 18,994; Ⓒ 19,234; ◆ 18,143
Mineral Springs; RMC Place; SCHOHARIE; ▲ Cobleskill; *209 NK-17; elev. 1,036ft./316m.; mail Cobleskill z 12043; ● 120
Minerva; RMC Place; ESSEX; ▲ Minerva; 209 NF-18; elev. 1,388ft./423m.; 🅿; z 12851; ● 300
Minerva; MCD-Town; ESSEX; *209 NF-18; 🅿; z 12851; Ⓟ 758; Ⓒ 796
Minetto; CDP; OSWEGO; ▲ Minetto; 209 NH-11; 🅿; z 13115; Ⓟ 1,252; Ⓒ 1,086
Minetto; MCD-Town; OSWEGO; *209 NH-11; 🅿; z 13115; Ⓟ 1,822; Ⓒ 1,663
Mineville; RMC Place; ESSEX; ▲ Moriah; 209 NE-19; 🅿; z 12956 & mail Witherbee z 12998; ● 950
Mineville-Witherbee; CDP-Census Area Only; ESSEX; ▲ Moriah; *209 NE-19; mail Mineville z 12956, Witherbee z 12998; Ⓟ 1,740; Ⓒ 1,747
Minisink; MCD-Town; ORANGE; *207 SC-4; ★ MIDD; mail Westtown z 10998; Ⓟ 2,981; Ⓒ 3,585
Minisink Ford; RMC Place; SULLIVAN; ▲ Highland; 207 SC-3; mail Barryville z 12719; ● 200
Minoa; Inc. Place; ONONDAGA; ▲ Manlius; 209 NI-12; 🅿; ★ SYR; z 13116; Ⓟ 3,745; Ⓒ 3,348
Mitchellsville; RMC Place; STEUBEN; ▲ Wheeler, Urbana; *208 NL-8; elev. 1,357ft./414m.; mail Bath z 14810; ● 150
Model City; RMC Place; NIAGARA; ▲ Lewiston; 208 NH-3; 🅿; ★ BUF; z 14107; ● 300
Modena; RMC Place; ULSTER; ▲ Plattekill; 207 SB-6; elev. 453ft./138m.; 🅿; ★ NWBG; z 12548; ● 900
Moffitsville; RMC Place; CLINTON; ▲ Saranac; *209 NB-19; mail Saranac z 12981; ● 65
Mohawk; Inc. Place; HERKIMER; ▲ German Flatts; 209 NI-15; elev. 407ft./124m.; 🅿; z 13407; Ⓟ 2,986; Ⓒ 2,660
Mohawk; MCD-Town; MONTGOMERY; *209 NI-17; ★ A-S-T; mail Fonda z 12068; Ⓟ 3,976; Ⓒ 3,902
Mohawk Hill; RMC Place; LEWIS; ▲ West Turin; *209 NG-14; mail Boonville z 13309; rural
Mohawk View; RMC Place; ALBANY; ▲ Colonie; 207 SG-4; ★ A-S-T; mail Latham z 12110
Mohawk Village (McCormack Corners); RMC Place; ALBANY; ▲ Guilderland; 207 SH-2; ★ A-S-T; mail Schenectady z 12303; ● 1,300
Mohegan Heights; RMC Place; WESTCHESTER; *207 SE-7; elev. 144ft./44m.; ★ N.Y.; mail Bronxville z 10708; pop. incl. with Yonkers (Inc. Place)
Mohegan Lake; RMC Place; WESTCHESTER; ▲ Yorktown; 207 SC-7; 🅿; ★ N.Y.; z 10547; ● 3,600
Mohonk Lake; RMC Place; ULSTER; ▲ Rochester; 207 SA-6; ★ KNGST; mail New Paltz z 12561; ● 300
Moira; RMC Place; FRANKLIN; ▲ Moira; 209 NB-16; 🅿; z 12957; ● 500
Moira; MCD-Town; FRANKLIN; *209 NB-16; 🅿; z 12957; Ⓟ 2,684; Ⓒ 2,857
Mombaccus; RMC Place; ULSTER; ▲ Rochester; 209 NN-17; elev. 658ft./201m.; mail Kerhonkson z 12446; ● 150
Mongaup; RMC Place; SULLIVAN; ▲ Lumberland; *207 SC-3; mail Sparrow Bush z 12780; rural
Mongaup Valley; RMC Place; SULLIVAN; ▲ Thompson, Bethel; 207 SB-3; elev. 1,113ft./339m.; 🅿; z 12762; ● 750
Monroe; Inc. Place; ORANGE; ▲ Monroe; 207 SC-6; elev. 679ft./207m.; 🅿 🅲 957; ★ N.Y.; z 10949-50; Ⓟ 6,672; Ⓒ 7,780
Monroe; MCD-Town; ORANGE; *207 SC-6; 🅿 🅲 957; ★ N.Y.; z 10949-50; Ⓟ 23,035; Ⓒ 31,407; ◆ 42,080
MONROE; 208 NH-7; Ⓟ 713,968; Ⓒ 735,343; ◆ 726,714
Monsey; CDP; ROCKLAND; ▲ Ramapo; 207 SD-6; 🅿 🅲 407; ★ N.Y.; z 10952; Ⓟ 13,986; Ⓒ 14,504
Monsey Heights; RMC Place; ROCKLAND; ▲ Ramapo; ★ N.Y.; mail Monsey z 10952
Montague; MCD-Town; LEWIS; *209 NF-13; mail Lowville z 13367; Ⓟ 47; Ⓒ 108
Montario Point; RMC Place; JEFFERSON; ▲ Ellisburg; *209 NF-11; mail Mannsville z 13661; ● 50
Montauk; CDP; SUFFOLK; ▲ East Hampton; 207 SD-14; 🅿; z 11954; Ⓟ 3,001; summer pop. 20,000; Ⓒ 3,851
Montauk Beach; RMC Place; SUFFOLK; ▲ East Hampton; *207 SE-14; mail Montauk z 11954
Montclair Colony; RMC Place; SUFFOLK; ▲ Shelter Island; *207 SD-12; mail Shelter Island z 11964
Montebello; Inc. Place; ROCKLAND; ▲ Ramapo; *207 SD-6; 🅿; ★ N.Y.; z 10901; Ⓟ 2,950; Ⓒ 3,688
Monterey; RMC Place; SCHUYLER; ▲ Orange; 208 NL-9; mail Beaver Dams z 14812; ● 215
Montezuma; RMC Place; CAYUGA; ▲ Montezuma; 208 NI-10; 🅿; z 13117; ● 450
Montezuma; MCD-Town; CAYUGA; *208 NI-10; 🅿; z 13117; Ⓟ 1,280; Ⓒ 1,431
Montgomery; Inc. Place; ORANGE; ▲ Montgomery; 207 SB-5; elev. 354ft./108m.; 🅿; z 12549; Ⓟ 2,696; Ⓒ 3,636
Montgomery; MCD-Town; ORANGE; *207 SB-6; 🅿; z 12549; Ⓟ 18,501; Ⓒ 20,891; ◆ 23,636
MONTGOMERY; 209 NJ-16; Ⓟ 51,981; Ⓒ 49,708; ◆ 48,298
Monticello; OTSEGO; see Richfield (RMC Place)
Monticello; Inc. Place; ⊡ SULLIVAN; ▲ Thompson; 207 SB-4; 🅿; z 12701, z 12777; Ⓟ 6,597; Ⓒ 6,512
Montour; MCD-Town; SCHUYLER; *208 NL-10; mail Montour Falls z 14865; Ⓟ 2,528; Ⓒ 2,446
Montour Falls; Inc. Place; SCHUYLER; ▲ Dix, Montour; 208 NL-10; 🅿 🅷; z 14865; Ⓟ 1,845; Ⓒ 1,797
Montrose; RMC Place; WESTCHESTER; ▲ Cortlandt; 207 SD-7; elev. 118ft./36m.; 🅿 🅷; ★ N.Y.; z 10548; ● 2,250
Montville; RMC Place; CAYUGA; ▲ Moravia; *209 NJ-11; mail Moravia z 13118; ● 60
Moody; RMC Place; FRANKLIN; ▲ Tupper Lake; 209 ND-17; mail Tupper Lake z 12986; ● 200
Mooers; CDP; CLINTON; ▲ Mooers; 209 NA-19; 🅿; z 12958; Ⓟ 467; Ⓒ 440
Mooers; MCD-Town; CLINTON; *209 NA-19; 🅿; z 12958; Ⓟ 2,995; Ⓒ 3,404
Mooers Forks; RMC Place; CLINTON; ▲ Mooers; 209 NA-19; 🅿; z 12959; ● 600
Moores Mill; RMC Place; DUTCHESS; ▲ Pleasant Valley; *207 SA-7; elev. 444ft./135m.; ★ POK; mail Pleasant Valley z 12569; ● 120
Moorhouse Corner; RMC Place; COLUMBIA; ▲ Austerlitz; *209 NL-19; elev. 550ft./168m.; mail Chatham z 12037; rural
Moose River; RMC Place; LEWIS; ▲ Lyonsdale; mail Port Leyden z 13433; rural
Moravia; Inc. Place; CAYUGA; ▲ Moravia; 209 NJ-11; 🅿; z 13118; Ⓟ 1,559; Ⓒ 1,363
Moravia; MCD-Town; CAYUGA; *209 NJ-11; 🅿; z 13118; Ⓟ 3,871; Ⓒ 4,040
Moreau; MCD-Town; SARATOGA; *209 NH-19; ★ GLFLS; mail Glens Falls z 12801; Ⓟ 13,022; Ⓒ 13,826; Ⓡ 13,549
Morehouse; MCD-Town; HAMILTON; *209 NG-16; mail Cold Brook z 13324; Ⓟ 106; Ⓒ 151
Morehouseville; RMC Place; HAMILTON; ▲ Morehouse; *209 NH-16; elev. 1,874ft./571m.; mail Cold Brook z 13324; rural
Moreland; RMC Place; SCHUYLER; ▲ Dix; 208 NL-9; mail Beaver Dams z 14812; ● 100
Morey Park; RMC Place; RENSSELAER; ▲ Schodack; *209 NK-19; ★ A-S-T; mail Nassau z 12123
Morgan Hill; RMC Place; ULSTER; ▲ Hurley; *209 NM-18; ★ KNGST; mail Kingston z 12401; rural
Morganville; RMC Place; GENESEE; ▲ Stafford; *208 NI-6; elev. 877ft./267m.; ★ ROCH; mail Stafford z 14143; rural
Moriah; RMC Place; ESSEX; ▲ Moriah; 209 NE-19; elev. 950ft./290m.; 🅿; z 12960; ● 400
Moriah; MCD-Town; ESSEX; *209 NE-19; 🅿; z 12960; Ⓟ 4,884; Ⓒ 4,879
Moriah Center; RMC Place; ESSEX; ▲ Moriah; 209 NE-19; elev. 796ft./243m.; 🅿; z 12961; ● 400
Moriches; CDP; SUFFOLK; ▲ Brookhaven; *207 SF-11; 🅿; ★ N.Y.; z 11955; Ⓒ 2,319
Morley; RMC Place; ST. LAWRENCE; ▲ Canton; 209 NB-14; elev. 341ft./104m.; mail Canton z 13617; ● 120
Morningside; RMC Place; NEW YORK; ★ N.Y.; mail New York z 10026; pop. incl. with New York (Inc. Place)
Morris; Inc. Place; OTSEGO; ▲ Morris; 209 NK-14; 🅿; z 13808; Ⓟ 642; Ⓒ 591
Morris; MCD-Town; OTSEGO; *209 NK-14; 🅿; z 13808; Ⓟ 1,787; Ⓒ 1,867
Morrisania; RMC Place; BRONX; *207 SF-7; ★ N.Y.; mail Bronx z 10456; pop. incl. with New York (Inc. Place)
Morris Heights; RMC Place; BRONX; *207 SF-7; ★ N.Y.; mail Bronx z 10453; pop. incl. with New York (Inc. Place)
Morrison Heights; RMC Place; ORANGE; ▲ Montgomery; *207 SB-6; ★ NWBG; mail Montgomery z 12549; ● 160
Morrisonville; CDP; CLINTON; ▲ Plattsburgh, Schuyler Falls; 209 NB-19; 🅿; ★ PLATT; z 12962; Ⓟ 1,742; Ⓒ 1,702
Morris Park; RMC Place; BRONX; *207 SF-7; ★ N.Y.; mail Bronx z 10461; pop. incl. with New York (Inc. Place)
Morristown; Inc. Place; ST. LAWRENCE; ▲ Morristown; 209 NC-13; 🅿; z 13664; Ⓟ 490; Ⓒ 456
Morristown; MCD-Town; ST. LAWRENCE; *209 NC-13; 🅿; z 13664; Ⓟ 2,019; Ⓒ 2,050
Morrisville; Inc. Place; MADISON; ▲ Eaton; 209 NJ-13; 🅿 🅲 3,048; z 13408; Ⓟ 2,732; Ⓒ 2,148
Morsston; RMC Place; SULLIVAN; ▲ Rockland; *207 SA-3; mail Livingston Manor z 12758
Morton; RMC Place; ORLEANS, MONROE; ▲ Kendall; 208 NH-6; 🅿; ★ ROCH; z 14508; ● 200
Mosherville; RMC Place; SARATOGA; ▲ Galway; *209 NI-18; elev. 887ft./270m.; ★ A-S-T; mail Galway z 12074, Middle Grove z 12850; rural
Mosholu; RMC Place; BRONX; ★ N.Y.; mail Bronx z 10467; pop. incl. with New York (Inc. Place)
Mosquito Point; RMC Place; GREENE; ▲ Lexington; *209 NL-17; mail Prattsville z 12468; rural
Mott Haven; RMC Place; BRONX; *207 SF-7; ★ N.Y.; mail Bronx z 10454; pop. incl. with New York (Inc. Place)
Mottville; RMC Place; ONONDAGA; ▲ Skaneateles; 209 NI-11; 🅿; ★ SYR; z 13119; ● 350
Mountain Dale; RMC Place; SULLIVAN; ▲ Fallsburg; 207 SB-4; 🅿; z 12763; summer pop. 1,000; ● 200
Mountain Lodge; RMC Place; ORANGE; ▲ Blooming Grove; 207 SC-6; ★ N.Y.; mail Monroe z 10950; summer pop. 2,000; ● 1,000
Mountain View; RMC Place; FRANKLIN; ▲ Bellmont; 209 NB-18; elev. 1,501ft./458m.; mail Owls Head z 12969; ● 150
Mountain View; RMC Place; RENSSELAER; ▲ Brunswick; *209 NJ-19; elev. 350ft./107m.; ★ A-S-T; mail Troy z 12180; ● 850
Mountain View East; RMC Place; ROCKLAND; ▲ Clarkstown; ★ N.Y.; mail Valley Cottage z 10989
Mountainville; RMC Place; ORANGE; ▲ Cornwall; 207 SC-6; 🅿; ★ NWBG; z 10953; ● 600
Mount Carmel; RMC Place; BRONX; ★ N.Y.; mail Bronx z 10458; pop. incl. with New York (Inc. Place)
Mount Hope; RMC Place; ORANGE; ▲ Mount Hope; *207 SC-4; elev. 826ft./252m.; ★ MIDD; mail Middletown z 10940; ● 130
Mount Hope; MCD-Town; ORANGE; *207 SC-4; ★ MIDD; mail Middletown z 10940; Ⓟ 5,971; Ⓒ 6,639
Mount Hope; RMC Place; WESTCHESTER; *207 SE-7; ★ N.Y.; mail Hastings On Hudson z 10706; pop. incl. with Hastings-on-Hudson (Inc. Place)
Mount Ivy; CDP; ROCKLAND; ▲ Haverstraw; 207 SD-6; elev. 454ft./138m.; ★ N.Y.; mail Pomona z 10970; Ⓟ 6,013; Ⓒ 6,536
Mount Kisco; Inc. Place; WESTCHESTER; ▲ Mount Kisco; 207 SD-7; elev. 289ft./88m.; 🅿 🅷 ■; ★ N.Y.; z 10549; Ⓟ 9,108; Ⓒ 9,983; ◆ 10,550
Mount Loretto; RMC Place; RICHMOND; *207 SG-6; elev. 48ft./15m.; ★ N.Y.; mail Staten Island z 10309; pop. incl. with New York (Inc. Place)
Mount Marion; RMC Place; ULSTER; ▲ Saugerties; *209 NM-18; 🅿; ★ KNGST; z 12456; ● 130
Mount Merion Park; RMC Place; ULSTER; ▲ Saugerties; *209 NM-18; ★ KNGST; mail Mount Marion z 12456; ● 800

Entries in **UPPERCASE** are counties.
Entries in **bold** have populations of 2,500 or more.
Names in parentheses are alternate names.

Inc. Place	Incorporated Place
RMC Place	Rand McNally Designated Place
CDP	Census Designated Place
MCD	Minor Civil Division
⊡	County Seat
▲	Minor Civil Division
elev.	Elevation
🅿	Post Office
🅷	Hospital
🅲	College
■	Principal Business Center
★	Ranally Metro Area (RMA) Abbreviation
z	Zip Code(s)
Ⓟ	Previous Census Population
Ⓡ	Revised Census Population
Ⓐ	Annexation Population
●	Rand McNally Population Estimate
Ⓒ	Final Census Population
Ⓢ	Special Census Population
◆	Estimated Population

For additional definitions see Glossary, Volume 1, and Introduction, Volume 2.

Mount Morris; Inc. Place; LIVINGSTON; ▲ Mount Morris; **208** NJ-6; elev. 626ft./191m.; [P]; z 14510; Ⓟ 3,102; © 3,266; Ⓡ 3,103

Mount Morris; MCD-Town; LIVINGSTON; ***208** NK-6; [P]; z 14510; Ⓟ 4,633; © 4,567

Mount Pleasant; RMC Place; OSWEGO; ▲ Volney; ***209** NH-11; elev. 431ft./131m.; mail Fulton z 13069; rural

Mount Pleasant; RMC Place; SCHENECTADY; ***209** NJ-18; ★ **A-S-T**; pop. incl. with Schenectady (Inc. Place)

Mount Pleasant; RMC Place; ULSTER; ▲ Shandaken; ***209** NM-17; mail Mount Tremper z 12457; ● 150

Mount Pleasant; MCD-Town; WESTCHESTER; ***207** SD-7; [C] 1,384; ★ **N.Y.**; mail Tarrytown z 10591; Ⓟ 40,590; © 43,221; ◆ 45,143

Mount Prosper; RMC Place; SULLIVAN; ▲ Mamakating; ***207** SB-4; mail Wurtsboro z 12790; ● 100

Mount Riga; RMC Place; DUTCHESS; ▲ North East; ***209** NM-20; mail Millerton z 12546; rural

Mount Ross; RMC Place; DUTCHESS; ▲ Pine Plains; ***209** NM-19; mail Pine Plains z 12567; rural

Mount Sinai; CDP; SUFFOLK; ▲ Brookhaven; ***207** SE-10; [P]; ★ **N.Y.**; z 11766; Ⓟ 8,023; © 8,734

Mount Tremper (The Corner); RMC Place; ULSTER; ▲ Shandaken; **209** NM-17; [P]; z 12457; ● 650

Mount Upton; RMC Place; CHENANGO; ▲ Guilford; **209** NL-14; elev. 1,036ft./316m.; [P]; z 13809; ● 570

Mount Vernon; RMC Place; ERIE; ▲ Hamburg; **208** NJ-3; ★ **BUF**; mail Hamburg z 14075; ● 2,800

Mount Vernon; Inc. Place; WESTCHESTER; **207** SE-7; elev. 136ft./41m.; [P] [H] ■; ★ **N.Y.**; z 10550-53; Ⓟ 67,153; © 68,381; ◆ 69,769

Mount Vernon West; RMC Place; WESTCHESTER; ***207** SE-7; ★ **N.Y.**; pop. incl. with Mount Vernon (Inc. Place)

Mount View Acres; RMC Place; COLUMBIA; ▲ Kinderhook; ***209** NK-19; elev. 308ft./94m.; ★ **A-S-T**; mail Valatie z 12184; ● 265

Mount View Estates; RMC Place; COLUMBIA; ▲ Kinderhook; ***209** NK-19; elev. 308ft./94m.; ★ **A-S-T**; mail Valatie z 12184; ● 170

Mount Vincent; RMC Place; BRONX; ***207** SE-7; elev. 100ft./30m.; ★ **N.Y.**; mail Bronx z 10471; pop. incl. with New York (Inc. Place)

Mount Vision; RMC Place; OTSEGO; ▲ Laurens; **209** NK-15; elev. 1,169ft./356m.; [P]; z 13810; ● 225

Moyers Corners; RMC Place; MONTGOMERY; ▲ Minden; ***209** NI-16; mail Fort Plain z 13339; rural

Mud Mills; RMC Place; WAYNE; ▲ Arcadia; ***208** NI-9; mail Newark z 14513

Muitzeskill; RMC Place; RENSSELAER; ▲ Schodack; ***209** NK-19; ★ **A-S-T**; mail Schodack Landing z 12156; ● 60

Mumford; RMC Place; MONROE; ▲ Wheatland; **208** NI-7; elev. 621ft./189m.; [P]; ★ **ROCH**; z 14511; ● 800

Mungers Corners; RMC Place; OSWEGO; ▲ Palermo; ***209** NH-11; elev. 444ft./135m.; ★ **SYR**; mail Fulton z 13069; rural

Municipal Building; RMC Place; KINGS; ★ **N.Y.**; mail Brooklyn z 11201; pop. incl. with New York (Inc. Place)

Munnsville; Inc. Place; MADISON; ▲ Stockbridge; **209** NI-13; [P]; z 13409; Ⓟ 438; © 437

Munsey Park; Inc. Place; NASSAU; ▲ North Hempstead; **211** F-16; ★ **N.Y.**; mail Manhasset z 11030; Ⓟ 2,692; © 2,632

Munsons Corners; CDP; CORTLAND; ▲ Cortlandville; ***209** NK-11; mail Cortland z 13045; Ⓟ 2,436; © 2,426

Murdochs Crossing; RMC Place; ORLEANS; ▲ Yates; mail Lyndonville z 14098; rural

Murdock Woods; RMC Place; WESTCHESTER; ▲ Mamaroneck; ***207** SE-7; ★ **N.Y.**; mail Scarsdale z 10583; ● 50

Murray; RMC Place; ORLEANS; ▲ Murray; **208** NH-6; elev. 419ft./128m.; ★ **ROCH**; mail Holley z 14470; ● 100

Murray; MCD-Town; ORLEANS; ***208** NH-6; ★ **ROCH**; mail Holley z 14470; Ⓟ 4,921; © 6,259; Ⓡ 4,892

Murray Hill; RMC Place; NEW YORK; ★ **N.Y.**; mail New York z 10016, z 10156; pop. incl. with New York (Inc. Place)

Murray Hill; RMC Place; WESTCHESTER; ***207** SE-7; ★ **N.Y.**; mail Scarsdale z 10583; pop. incl. with Scarsdale (Inc. Place)

Murray Isle; RMC Place; JEFFERSON; ▲ Clayton; ***209** ND-12; elev. 260ft./79m.; [P]; z 13624; summer pop. 150; rural

Muttontown; Inc. Place; NASSAU; ▲ Oyster Bay; **211** E-19; ★ **N.Y.**; mail East Norwich z 11732, Glen Head z 11545, Jericho z 11753, Oyster Bay z 11771, Syosset z 11791; Ⓟ 3,024; © 3,412

Mycenae; RMC Place; ONONDAGA; ▲ Manlius; ***209** NI-12; ★ **SYR**; mail Fayetteville z 13066; ● 40

Myers; RMC Place; TOMPKINS; ▲ Lansing; ***208** NK-10; ★ **ITH**; mail Lansing z 14882

Myers Corner; CDP; DUTCHESS; ▲ Wappinger; ***207** SB-7; elev. 216ft./66m.; ★ **POK**; mail Wappingers Falls z 12590; Ⓟ 5,588; © 5,546

Myers Grove; RMC Place; ORANGE; ▲ Deerpark; ***207** SC-4; ● 200

N

Nanticoke; RMC Place; BROOME; ▲ Nanticoke; ***209** NL-12; elev. 1,101ft./336m.; ★ **BING**; mail Maine z 13802; ● 55

Nanticoke; MCD-Town; BROOME; ***209** NL-12; ★ **BING**; mail Marathon z 13803; Ⓟ 1,846; © 1,790

Nanuet; CDP; ROCKLAND; ▲ Clarkstown; **207** SD-6; [P]; ★ **N.Y.**; z 10954; Ⓟ 14,065; © 16,707

Napanoch; CDP; ULSTER; ▲ Wawarsing; **207** SA-5; [P]; z 12458; Ⓟ 1,068; summer pop. 2,500; © 1,168

Napeague; CDP; SUFFOLK; ***207** SE-13; © 223

Napeaque; RMC Place; SUFFOLK; ▲ East Hampton; ***207** SC-13; mail Amagansett z 11930; pop. incl. with Groton (Inc. Place) summer pop. 2,000

Naples; Inc. Place; ONTARIO; ▲ Naples; **208** NK-8; [P]; z 14512; Ⓟ 1,237; © 1,072

Naples; MCD-Town; ONTARIO; ***208** NK-8; [P]; z 14512; Ⓟ 2,559; © 2,441

Napoli; RMC Place; CATTARAUGUS; ▲ Napoli; ***208** NL-3; elev. 1,735ft./529m.; mail Little Valley z 14755; ● 50

Napoli; MCD-Town; CATTARAUGUS; ***208** NL-3; mail Little Valley z 14755; Ⓟ 1,102; © 1,159

Narrowsburg; CDP; SULLIVAN; ▲ Tusten; **207** SB-2; [P]; z 12764; © 414

Nashville; RMC Place; CHAUTAUQUA; ▲ Hanover; ***208** NK-3; elev. 1,307ft./398m.; mail Forestville z 14062

Nassau; Inc. Place; RENSSELAER; ▲ Nassau; **209** NK-19; [P]; ★ **A-S-T**; z 12123; Ⓟ 1,254; © 1,161

Nassau; MCD-Town; RENSSELAER; ***209** NK-20; [P]; ★ **A-S-T**; z 12123; Ⓟ 4,989; © 4,818

NASSAU; **207** SF-8; Ⓟ 1,287,348; © 1,334,544; ◆ 1,267,444

Nassau Boulevard; RMC Place; NASSAU; ★ **N.Y.**; pop. incl. with Garden City (Inc. Place)

Nassau Lake; RMC Place; RENSSELAER; ▲ Nassau; ***209** NK-19; ★ **A-S-T**; mail Nassau z 12123; ● 400

Nassau Shores; RMC Place; NASSAU; ▲ Oyster Bay; ***207** SG-8; ★ **N.Y.**; mail Massapequa z 11758; ● 8,000

Natural Bridge; CDP; JEFFERSON; ▲ Wilna; **209** NE-14; [P]; z 13665; © 392

Natural Dam; RMC Place; ST. LAWRENCE; ▲ Gouverneur; **209** ND-14; mail Gouverneur z 13642; ● 65

Naumburg; RMC Place; LEWIS; ▲ Croghan; ***209** NF-14; elev. 744ft./227m.; mail Castorland z 13620; rural

Nauraushaun; RMC Place; ROCKLAND; ▲ Orangetown; ***207** SE-6; elev. 113ft./34m.; ★ **N.Y.**; mail Pearl River z 10965

Navarino; RMC Place; ONONDAGA; ▲ Onondaga; ***209** NJ-11; elev. 1,150ft./351m.; ★ **SYR**; mail Marcellus z 13108; ● 200

Nedrow; CDP; ONONDAGA; ▲ Onondaga; **209** NI-12; [P]; ★ **SYR**; z 13120; © 2,265

Nelliston; Inc. Place; MONTGOMERY; ▲ Palatine; **209** NI-16; [P]; z 13410; Ⓟ 569; © 622

Nelson; RMC Place; MADISON; ▲ Nelson; **209** NJ-13; mail Cazenovia z 13035; ● 300

Nelson; MCD-Town; MADISON; ***209** NJ-13; mail Cazenovia z 13035; Ⓟ 1,892; © 1,964

Nelsonville; Inc. Place; PUTNAM; ▲ Philipstown; **207** SC-6; elev. 198ft./60m.; [P]; ★ **N.Y.**; z 10516; Ⓟ 585; © 565

Nepera Park; RMC Place; WESTCHESTER; ***207** SE-7; ★ **N.Y.**; mail Yonkers z 10710; pop. incl. with Yonkers (Inc. Place)

Neponsit; RMC Place; QUEENS; **211** L-13; [P]; ★ **N.Y.**; z 11694; pop. incl. with New York (Inc. Place)

Nepperhan; RMC Place; WESTCHESTER; ★ **N.Y.**; mail Yonkers z 10703; pop. incl. with Yonkers (Inc. Place)

Neptune; RMC Place; KINGS; ★ **N.Y.**; mail Brooklyn z 11224; pop. incl. with New York (Inc. Place)

Nesconset; CDP; SUFFOLK; ▲ Smithtown; **207** SH-13; [P]; ★ **N.Y.**; z 11767; Ⓟ 10,712; © 11,992

Neversink; RMC Place; SULLIVAN; ▲ Neversink; **209** NN-16; elev. 1,633ft./498m.; [P]; z 12765; ● 350

Neversink; MCD-Town; SULLIVAN; ***207** SA-4; [P]; z 12765; Ⓟ 2,951; © 3,553

Nevis; RMC Place; COLUMBIA; ▲ Clermont; ***209** NM-19; elev. 218ft./66m.; mail Tivoli z 12583; ● 400

New Albion; RMC Place; CATTARAUGUS; ▲ New Albion; **208** NL-3; mail Cattaraugus z 14719; ● 200

New Albion; MCD-Town; CATTARAUGUS; ***208** NL-3; mail Cattaraugus z 14719; Ⓟ 1,978; © 2,068

Newark; Inc. Place; WAYNE; ▲ Arcadia; **208** NI-9; elev. 457ft./139m.; [P] [H]; z 14513; Ⓟ 9,849; © 9,682

Newark Valley; Inc. Place; TIOGA; ▲ Newark Valley; **209** NL-12; [P]; ★ **BING**; z 13811; Ⓟ 1,082; © 1,071

Newark Valley; MCD-Town; TIOGA; ***209** NL-12; [P]; ★ **BING**; z 13811; Ⓟ 4,189; © 4,097

New Baltimore; RMC Place; GREENE; ▲ New Baltimore; **209** NK-19; [P]; ★ **A-S-T**; z 12124; ● 960

New Baltimore; MCD-Town; GREENE; ***209** NL-19; [P]; ★ **A-S-T**; z 12124; Ⓟ 3,371; © 3,417

New Berlin; Inc. Place; CHENANGO; ▲ New Berlin; **209** NK-14; [P]; z 13411; Ⓟ 1,220; © 1,129

New Berlin; MCD-Town; CHENANGO; ***209** NK-14; [P]; z 13411; Ⓟ 3,046; © 2,803

New Berlin Junction; CHENANGO; see East Guilford (RMC Place)

New Boston; RMC Place; CORTLAND; ▲ Cuyler; ***209** NK-12; mail Truxton z 13158; rural

New Bremen; RMC Place; LEWIS; ▲ New Bremen; **209** NF-14; mail Lowville z 13367; ● 200

New Bremen; MCD-Town; LEWIS; ***209** NF-14; mail Lowville z 13367; Ⓟ 2,526; © 2,722

New Brighton; RMC Place; RICHMOND; **210** J-8; ★ **N.Y.**; mail Staten Island z 10310; pop. incl. with New York (Inc. Place)

Newburg; RMC Place; WYOMING; ▲ Gainesville; ***208** NJ-6; mail Silver Springs z 14550; rural

Newburgh; Inc. Place; ORANGE; **207** SB-6; elev. 139ft./42m.; [P] [H] [C] 2,601 ■; ★ **NWBG**; z 12550-53, z 12555; Ⓟ 26,454; © 28,259; ◆ 30,198

Newburgh; MCD-Town; ORANGE; ***207** SB-6; [P] [C] 2,601; ★ **NWBG**; z 12550-53, z 12555; does not include the City of Newburgh; Ⓟ 24,058; © 27,568; ◆ 30,639

New Cassel; CDP; NASSAU; ▲ North Hempstead; **211** G-19; ★ **N.Y.**; mail Westbury z 11590; Ⓟ 10,257; © 13,298

New Castle; MCD-Town; WESTCHESTER; ***207** SD-7; ★ **N.Y.**; mail Chappaqua z 10514; Ⓟ 16,648; © 17,491

New City; CDP; ⊡ ROCKLAND; ▲ Clarkstown; **207** SD-6; elev. 163ft./50m.; [P]; ★ **N.Y.**; z 10956; Ⓟ 33,673; © 34,038; ◆ 35,521

New City Park; RMC Place; ROCKLAND; ▲ Clarkstown; ***207** SD-6; ★ **N.Y.**; mail New City z 10956

Newcomb; RMC Place; ESSEX; ▲ Newcomb; **209** NE-18; elev. 1,571ft./479m.; [P]; z 12852, z 12879; ● 300

Newcomb; MCD-Town; ESSEX; ***209** NE-18; [P]; z 12852, z 12879; Ⓟ 544; © 481

New Concord; RMC Place; COLUMBIA; ▲ Chatham; ***209** NL-20; ★ **A-S-T**; mail East Chatham z 12060; ● 200

New Dorp; RMC Place; RICHMOND; **210** L-7; ★ **N.Y.**; mail Staten Island z 10306; pop. incl. with New York (Inc. Place)

New Dorp Beach; RMC Place; RICHMOND; **210** L-8; ★ **N.Y.**; mail Staten Island z 10306; pop. incl. with New York (Inc. Place)

New Ebenezer; RMC Place; ERIE; ***208** NJ-4; ★ **BUF**; mail Buffalo z 14224

New Falconwood; RMC Place; ERIE; ▲ Grand Island; **208** ND-2; ★ **BUF**; mail Grand Island z 14072; ● 1,200

Newfane; CDP; NIAGARA; ▲ Newfane; **208** NH-4; [P] [H]; ★ **LOCK**; z 14108; Ⓟ 3,001; © 3,129

Newfane; MCD-Town; NIAGARA; ***208** NH-4; [P]; ★ **LOCK**; z 14108; Ⓟ 8,996; © 9,657

Newfield; RMC Place; TOMPKINS; ▲ Newfield; ★ **ITH**; ● 530

Newfield; MCD-Town; TOMPKINS; ***208** NL-10; [P]; ★ **ITH**; z 14867; Ⓟ 4,867; © 5,108

Newfield Hamlet; CDP-Census Area Only; TOMPKINS; ▲ Newfield; **208** NL-10; ★ **ITH**; mail Newfield z 14867; Ⓟ 692; © 647

New Hackensack; RMC Place; DUTCHESS; ▲ Wappinger; ***207** SB-7; elev. 185ft./56m.; ★ **POK**; mail Wappingers Falls z 12590; ● 100

New Hamburg; RMC Place; DUTCHESS; ▲ Poughkeepsie; **207** SB-6; [P]; ★ **POK**; z 12590; ● 1,080

New Hampton; RMC Place; ORANGE; ▲ Wawayanda; **207** SC-5; [P]; ★ **MIDD**; z 10958; ● 1,200

New Hartford; Inc. Place; ONEIDA; ▲ New Hartford; **209** NI-14; [P]; ★ **UT-R**; z 13413; Ⓟ 2,111; © 1,886

New Hartford; MCD-Town; ONEIDA; ***209** NI-14; [P]; ★ **UT-R**; z 13413; Ⓟ 21,640; © 21,172; Ⓡ 21,285; ◆ 21,176

New Haven; RMC Place; OSWEGO; ▲ New Haven; **209** NG-11; elev. 418ft./127m.; [P]; z 13121; ● 400

New Haven; MCD-Town; OSWEGO; ***209** NG-11; [P]; z 13121; Ⓟ 2,778; © 2,930

New Hempstead; ROCKLAND; see Hempstead (Inc. Place)

New Hope; RMC Place; CAYUGA; ▲ Niles; **209** NJ-11; mail Moravia z 13118; ● 80

New Hudson; MCD-Town; ALLEGANY; ***208** NL-5; mail Black Creek z 14714; Ⓟ 715; © 736

New Hurley; RMC Place; ULSTER; ▲ Shawangunk; ***207** SB-6; mail Gardiner z 12525; rural

New Hyde Park; Inc. Place; NASSAU; ▲ Hempstead, North Hempstead; **211** H-16; [P]; ★ **N.Y.**; z 11040, z 11042; Ⓟ 9,728; © 9,523

New Ireland; RMC Place; BROOME; ▲ Maine; ***209** NM-12; ★ **BING**; mail Binghamton z 13905; ● 200

New Kingston; RMC Place; DELAWARE; ▲ Middletown; **209** NL-16; elev. 1,689ft./515m.; [P]; z 12459; ● 150

Newkirk; RMC Place; KINGS; ★ **N.Y.**; mail Brooklyn z 11226; pop. incl. with New York (Inc. Place)

New Lebanon; RMC Place; COLUMBIA; ▲ New Lebanon; **209** NK-20; [P]; z 12125; ● 950

New Lebanon; MCD-Town; COLUMBIA; ***209** NK-20; [P]; z 12125; Ⓟ 2,379; © 2,454

New Lebanon Center; RMC Place; COLUMBIA; ▲ New Lebanon; **209** NK-20; mail New Lebanon z 12125; ● 500

New Lisbon; RMC Place; OTSEGO; ▲ New Lisbon; **209** NK-15; elev. 1,234ft./376m.; [P]; z 13415; ● 100

New Lisbon; MCD-Town; OTSEGO; ***209** NK-15; [P]; z 13415; Ⓟ 996; © 1,116

New Lots; RMC Place; KINGS; ★ **N.Y.**; mail Brooklyn z 11208; pop. incl. with New York (Inc. Place)

New Market; RMC Place; NIAGARA; ★ **BUF**; mail Niagara Falls z 14301; pop. incl. with Niagara Falls (Inc. Place)

New Milford; RMC Place; ORANGE; ▲ Warwick; **207** SD-5; [P]; ★ **N.Y.**; z 10959; ● 600

New Oregon; RMC Place; ERIE; ▲ North Collins; ***208** NK-4; elev. 1,075ft./328m.; ★ **BUF**; mail Eden z 14057; ● 100

New Paltz; Inc. Place; ULSTER; ▲ New Paltz; **207** SA-6; elev. 236ft./72m.; [P] [C] 7,699; z 12561; Ⓟ 5,463; © 6,034

New Paltz; MCD-Town; ULSTER; ***207** SA-6; [P] [C] 7,699; z 12561; Ⓟ 11,388; © 12,830

Newport; Inc. Place; HERKIMER; ▲ Newport; **209** NH-15; [P]; z 13416; Ⓟ 676; © 640

Newport; MCD-Town; HERKIMER; ***209** NH-15; [P]; z 13416; Ⓟ 2,148; © 2,192; Ⓡ 2,202

Newport; RMC Place; MONROE; ▲ Irondequoit; ***208** NH-7; ★ **ROCH**; mail Rochester z 14617

Newport; RMC Place; ONONDAGA; ▲ Camillus; ***209** NI-11; ★ **SYR**; mail Warners z 13164

New Rochelle; Inc. Place; WESTCHESTER; **207** SE-7; elev. 94ft./29m.; [P] [H] [C] 10,848 ■; ★ **N.Y.**; z 10801-02, z 10804-05 & mail Pelham z 10803; Ⓟ 67,265; © 72,182; ◆ 74,315

New Russia; RMC Place; ESSEX; ▲ Elizabethtown; **209** ND-19; elev. 628ft./191m.; [P]; z 12964; ● 160

New Salem; RMC Place; ALBANY; ▲ New Scotland; **209** NK-18; elev. 415ft./126m.; ★ **A-S-T**; mail Voorheesville z 12186; ● 450

New Salem; RMC Place; ULSTER; ▲ Esopus; ***207** SA-6; ★ **KNGST**; mail Kingston z 12401; ● 200

New Scotland; RMC Place; ALBANY; ▲ New Scotland; **207** SJ-2; ★ **A-S-T**; mail Slingerlands z 12159; ● 200

New Scotland; MCD-Town; ALBANY; ***209** NK-18; ★ **A-S-T**; mail Slingerlands z 12159; Ⓟ 9,139; © 8,626

Newsday; RMC Place; SUFFOLK; ▲ Huntington; ★ **N.Y.**; mail Melville z 11747

New Springville; RMC Place; RICHMOND; **210** K-6; ★ **N.Y.**; mail Staten Island z 10314; pop. incl. with New York (Inc. Place)

New Square; Inc. Place; ROCKLAND; ▲ Ramapo; ***207** SD-6; ★ **N.Y.**; mail Spring Valley z 10977; Ⓟ 2,605; © 4,624

Newstead; MCD-Town; ERIE; ***208** NI-5; mail Akron z 14001; Ⓟ 7,440; © 8,404

New Suffolk; CDP; SUFFOLK; ▲ Southold; **207** SE-12; [P]; z 11956; summer pop. 2,000; © 337

Newton Falls; RMC Place; ST. LAWRENCE; ▲ Clifton; **209** ND-15; [P]; z 13666; ● 400

Newton Hook; RMC Place; COLUMBIA; ▲ Stuyvesant; ***209** NL-19; ★ **A-S-T**; mail Stuyvesant z 12173; ● 75

Newtonville; RMC Place; ALBANY; ▲ Colonie; **207** SH-4; [P]; ★ **A-S-T**; z 12110, z 12128; ● 2,300

Newtown; RMC Place; SUFFOLK; ▲ Southampton; ***207** SE-12; mail Hampton Bays z 11946

New Utrecht; RMC Place; KINGS; **210** K-10; ★ **N.Y.**; mail Brooklyn z 11204; pop. incl. with New York (Inc. Place)

New Vernon; RMC Place; ORANGE; ▲ Mount Hope; ***207** SC-5; ★ **MIDD**; mail Middletown z 10940; rural

Newville; RMC Place; HERKIMER; ▲ Danube; ***209** NI-16; mail Little Falls z 13365; rural

New Windsor; CDP; ORANGE; ▲ New Windsor; **207** SC-6; [P]; ★ **NWBG**; z 12553; Ⓟ 8,898; © 9,077

New Windsor; MCD-Town; ORANGE; ***207** SC-6; [P]; ★ **NWBG**; z 12553; Ⓟ 22,937; © 22,866; ◆ 23,750

New Woodstock; RMC Place; MADISON; ▲ Cazenovia; **209** NJ-13; [P]; ★ **SYR**; z 13122; ● 500

New York; Inc. Place; ⊡ NEW YORK, BRONX, KINGS, QUEENS, RICHMOND; **207** SG-6; elev. 30ft./9m.; [P] [H] [C] 385,701 ■; ★ **N.Y.**; z 10001-14, z 10016-41, z 10043-46, z 10055, z 10060, z 10065, z 10069, z 10072, z 10075, z 10079-82, z 10087, z 10090, z 10094-96, z 10098-99, z 10101-26, z 10128-33, z 10138, z 10149-79, z 10184-85, z 10196-97, z 10199, z 10203, z 10211-13, z 10242, z 10249, z 10256-61, z 10265, z 10268-82, z 10285-86, z 10292; Ⓟ 7,322,564; © 8,008,278; Ⓡ 8,008,654; ◆ 8,384,203

New York; ONEIDA; see New York Mills (Inc. Place)

NEW YORK; **210** G-10; Ⓟ 1,487,536; © 1,537,195; Ⓡ 1,537,372; ◆ 1,637,583

New York Mills (New York); Inc. Place; ONEIDA; ▲ New Hartford, Whitestown; **209** NI-14; [P]; ★ **UT-R**; z 13417; Ⓟ 3,534; © 3,191

New York Mills Gardens; RMC Place; ONEIDA; ▲ New Hartford, Whitestown; ★ **UT-R**; mail Whitesboro z 13492

Niagara; MCD-Town; NIAGARA; ***208** NI-3; ★ **BUF**; mail Niagara Falls z 14302; Ⓟ 9,880; © 8,978

NIAGARA; **208** NH-4; Ⓟ 220,756; © 219,846; ◆ 212,048

Niagara Falls; Inc. Place; NIAGARA; ▲ Niagara; **208** NI-3; elev. 618ft./188m.; [P] [H] ■; ★ **BUF**; z 14301-05; Ⓟ 61,840; © 55,593; ◆ 51,647

Niagara Square; RMC Place; ERIE; ★ **BUF**; mail Buffalo z 14201-02; pop. incl. with Buffalo (Inc. Place)

Nichols; RMC Place; STEUBEN; ▲ Tuscarora; ***208** NM-8; mail Addison z 14801; rural

Nichols; Inc. Place; TIOGA; ▲ Nichols; **209** NM-11; [P]; z 13812; Ⓟ 573; © 574

Nichols; MCD-Town; TIOGA; ***209** NM-11; [P]; z 13812; Ⓟ 2,525; © 2,584

Nichols Run; RMC Place; CATTARAUGUS; ▲ Allegany; ***208** NM-4; elev. 2,240ft./683m.; mail Limestone z 14753, Olean z 14760; rural

Nichols Siding; RMC Place; QUEENS; ★ **N.Y.**; pop. incl. with New York (Inc. Place)

Nicholville; RMC Place; ST. LAWRENCE; ▲ Hopkinton, Lawrence; **209** NB-16; [P]; z 12965; ● 370

Niets Crest; RMC Place; CHAUTAUQUA; ▲ North Harmony; ***208** NM-2; elev. 1,342ft./409m.; mail Ashville z 14710; rural

Nile; RMC Place; ALLEGANY; ▲ Friendship; **208** NM-6; elev. 1,597ft./487m.; mail Friendship z 14739; ● 250

Niles; RMC Place; CAYUGA; ▲ Niles; ***209** NJ-11; mail Skaneateles z 13152; ● 50

Niles; MCD-Town; CAYUGA; ***209** NJ-11; mail Skaneateles z 13152; Ⓟ 1,194; © 1,208

Nimmonsburg; RMC Place; BROOME; ▲ Chenango; **209** NM-12; ★ **BING**; mail Binghamton z 13901; ● 900

Nineveh; RMC Place; BROOME; ▲ Colesville; **209** NM-13; [P]; ★ **BING**; z 13813; ● 400

Nineveh Junction; RMC Place; CHENANGO; ▲ Afton; ***209** NM-13; mail Afton z 13730; rural

Niobe; RMC Place; CHAUTAUQUA; ▲ Harmony; **208** NM-2; [P]; z 14758; ● 150

Niskayuna; CDP; SCHENECTADY; ▲ Niskayuna; **209** NJ-19; [P]; ★ **A-S-T**; z 12309; Ⓟ 4,942; © 4,892

Niskayuna; MCD-Town; SCHENECTADY; ***209** NJ-19; [P]; ★ **A-S-T**; z 12309; Ⓟ 19,048; © 20,295; ◆ 21,433

Nissequogue; Inc. Place; SUFFOLK; ▲ Smithtown; **207** SE-9; ★ **N.Y.**; mail Saint James z 11780; Ⓟ 1,620; © 1,543

Niverville; CDP; COLUMBIA; ▲ Kinderhook, Chatham; **209** NK-19; [P]; ★ **A-S-T**; z 12130; Ⓟ 1,809; © 1,737

Noblesboro; RMC Place; HERKIMER; ▲ Ohio; ***209** NH-15; mail Cold Brook z 13324; rural

Norfolk; CDP; ST. LAWRENCE; ▲ Norfolk; **209** NB-15; elev. 257ft./78m.; [P]; z 13667; Ⓟ 1,412; © 1,334

Norfolk; MCD-Town; ST. LAWRENCE; ***209** NB-15; [P]; z 13667; Ⓟ 4,258; © 4,565

Normansville; RMC Place; ALBANY; ▲ Bethlehem; **207** SJ-4; ★ **A-S-T**; mail Delmar z 12054; pop. incl. with Albany (Inc. Place)

North; RMC Place; WESTCHESTER; ★ **N.Y.**; mail Yonkers z 10703; pop. incl. with Yonkers (Inc. Place)

North Afton; RMC Place; CHENANGO; ▲ Afton; ***209** NL-14; mail Afton z 13730; rural

North Almond; RMC Place; ALLEGANY; ▲ Almond; ***208** NL-7; mail Arkport z 14807; rural

North Amityville; CDP; SUFFOLK; ▲ Babylon; ***207** SF-9; ★ **N.Y.**; mail Amityville z 11701; Ⓟ 13,849; © 16,572

Northampton; MCD-Town; FULTON; ***209** NH-18; ★ **A-S-T**; mail Northville z 12134; Ⓟ 2,705; © 2,760

Northampton (Wildwood Lake); CDP-Census Area Only; SUFFOLK; ▲ Southampton; ***207** SE-11; ★ **N.Y.**; mail Riverhead z 11901; © 468

North Argyle; RMC Place; WASHINGTON; ▲ Argyle; **209** NH-20; elev. 316ft./96m.; mail Argyle z 12809; ● 250

North Babylon; CDP; SUFFOLK; ▲ Babylon; ***207** SF-9; [P]; ★ **N.Y.**; z 11703; Ⓟ 18,081; © 17,877

North Bailey; RMC Place; ERIE; ▲ Amherst; ***208** NI-4; ★ **BUF**; mail Buffalo z 14226

North Baldwin; RMC Place; NASSAU; ▲ Hempstead; [P]; ★ **N.Y.**; z 11510

North Ballston Spa; CDP-Census Area Only; SARATOGA; ▲ Milton; ***209** NI-19; ★ **A-S-T**; mail Ballston Spa z 12020; Ⓟ 1,362; © 1,237

North Bangor; RMC Place; FRANKLIN; ▲ Bangor; **209** NB-17; [P]; z 12966; ● 600

North Bay; RMC Place; ONEIDA; ▲ Vienna; **209** NH-13; [P]; ★ **UT-R**; z 13123; ● 800

North Bay Shore; CDP; SUFFOLK; ▲ Islip; ***207** SF-9; ★ **N.Y.**; mail Bay Shore z 11706; Ⓟ 12,799; © 14,992

North Beach; RMC Place; QUEENS; ***207** SF-7; ★ **N.Y.**; mail East Elmhurst z 11369; pop. incl. with New York (Inc. Place)

North Bellmore; CDP; NASSAU; ▲ Hempstead; **211** I-19; [P]; ★ **N.Y.**; z 11710; Ⓟ 19,707; © 20,079; ◆ 19,069

North Bellport; CDP; SUFFOLK; ▲ Brookhaven; ***207** SF-10; ★ **N.Y.**; mail Bellport z 11713, Patchogue z 11772; Ⓟ 8,182; © 9,007

North Bergen; RMC Place; GENESEE; ▲ Bergen; ***208** NI-6; elev. 625ft./191m.; ★ **ROCH**; mail Bergen z 14416; ● 100

North Bethlehem; RMC Place; ALBANY; ▲ Bethlehem; **207** SI-3; ★ **A-S-T**; mail Albany z 12203; ● 400

North Blenheim; RMC Place; SCHOHARIE; ▲ Blenheim; **209** NK-17; [P]; z 12131; ● 200

North Bloomfield; RMC Place; ONTARIO; ▲ West Bloomfield; **208** NI-7; ★ **ROCH**; mail Honeoye Falls z 14472; ● 2,260

North Boston; CDP; ERIE; ▲ Boston; **208** NJ-4; [P]; ★ **BUF**; z 14110; Ⓟ 2,581; © 2,680

North Branch; RMC Place; SULLIVAN; ▲ Callicoon; **209** NN-15; elev. 1,036ft./316m.; [P]; z 12766; ● 500

North Bridgewater; RMC Place; ONEIDA; ▲ Bridgewater; ***209** NJ-14; mail Cassville z 13318; ● 100

North Broadalbin; RMC Place; FULTON; ▲ Broadalbin; **209** NI-18; ★ **A-S-T**; mail Broadalbin z 12025; ● 65

North Brookfield; RMC Place; MADISON; ▲ Brookfield; **209** NJ-14; [P]; z 13418; ● 250

North Burke; RMC Place; FRANKLIN; ▲ Burke; ***209** NA-17; elev. 368ft./112m.; mail Burke z 12917; rural

Northbush; RMC Place; FULTON; ▲ Caroga; ***209** NI-17; mail Johnstown z 12095; rural

North Cameron; RMC Place; STEUBEN; ▲ Cameron; ***208** NL-8; elev. 1,631ft./497m.; mail Cameron z 14819; rural

North Castle; MCD-Town; WESTCHESTER; ***207** SD-7; [P]; ★ **N.Y.**; z 10504; Ⓟ 10,061; © 10,849

North Centereach; RMC Place; SUFFOLK; ▲ Brookhaven; ***207** SE-10; ★ **N.Y.**; mail Centereach z 11720

North Chatham; RMC Place; COLUMBIA; ▲ Chatham; ***209** NK-19; [P]; ★ **A-S-T**; z 12132; ● 600

North Chemung; RMC Place; CHEMUNG; ▲ Baldwin; **208** NM-10; mail Lowman z 14861; ● 200

North Chili; RMC Place; MONROE; ▲ Chili; **208** NI-7; elev. 582ft./177m.; [P]; ★ **ROCH**; z 14514; ● 2,300

North Chittenango; RMC Place; MADISON; ▲ Sullivan; **209** NI-13; ★ **SYR**; mail Chittenango z 13037; ● 130

North Clove; RMC Place; DUTCHESS; ▲ Union Vale; ***207** SA-7; mail Millbrook z 12545; rural

North Clymer; RMC Place; CHAUTAUQUA; ▲ Clymer; **208** NM-1; elev. 1,582ft./482m.; mail Panama z 14767; ● 120

North Cohocton; RMC Place; STEUBEN; ▲ Cohocton; **208** NK-8; [P]; z 14808; ● 300

North Collins; Inc. Place; ERIE; ▲ North Collins; **208** NK-3; elev. 847ft./258m.; [P]; ★ **BUF**; z 14111; Ⓟ 1,335; © 1,079

North Collins; MCD-Town; ERIE; ***208** NK-3; [P]; ★ **BUF**; z 14111; Ⓟ 3,502; © 3,376

North Columbia; RMC Place; HERKIMER; ***209** NI-15; mail Ilion z 13357; rural

North Corners; RMC Place; ST. LAWRENCE; ▲ Lisbon; ***209** NB-14; elev. 350ft./107m.; mail Lisbon z 13658; rural

North Creek; RMC Place; WARREN; ▲ Johnsburg; **209** NF-18; elev. 1,028ft./313m.; [P]; z 12853; ● 700

Northcrest; RMC Place; SARATOGA; ▲ Clifton Park; ***209** NJ-19; elev. 250ft./76m.; ★ **A-S-T**; mail Clifton Park z 12065; ● 550

North Cuba; RMC Place; ALLEGANY; ▲ Cuba; **208** NL-5; mail Cuba z 14727; ● 60

North Dansville; MCD-Town; LIVINGSTON; ***208** NK-7; mail Dansville z 14437; Ⓟ 5,783; © 5,738

North Darien; RMC Place; GENESEE; ▲ Darien; mail Corfu z 14036; rural

North East; MCD-Town; DUTCHESS; ***209** NM-20; mail Millerton z 12546; Ⓟ 2,918; © 3,002

Northeast Center; RMC Place; DUTCHESS; ▲ North East; ***209** NM-20; mail Millerton z 12546; rural

Northeast Henrietta; RMC Place; MONROE; ▲ Henrietta; ***208** NI-7; ★ **ROCH**; mail Pittsford z 14534; ● 10,650

Northeast Ithaca; CDP-Census Area Only; TOMPKINS; ▲ Ithaca; ***209** NK-11; elev. 1,000ft./305m.; ★ **ITH**; mail Ithaca z 14850; Ⓟ 2,533; © 2,655

North Easton; RMC Place; WASHINGTON; ▲ Easton; ***209** NI-19; mail Greenwich z 12834; rural

North Elba; MCD-Town; ESSEX; ***209** ND-18; mail Lake Placid z 12946; Ⓟ 7,870; © 8,661

North Evans; RMC Place; ERIE; ▲ Evans; ***208** NJ-3; [P]; ★ **BUF**; z 14112; ● 450

North Fair Haven; RMC Place; CAYUGA; ***208** NH-10; mail Fair Haven z 13064; pop. incl. with Fair Haven (Inc. Place)

North Fenton; RMC Place; BROOME; ▲ Fenton; ***209** NL-13; elev. 972ft./296m.; ★ **BING**; mail Chenango Forks z 13746

Northfield; RMC Place; DELAWARE; ▲ Walton; ***209** NL-15; mail Walton z 13856

North Franklin; RMC Place; DELAWARE; ▲ Franklin; ***209** NL-15; mail Oneonta z 13820; rural

North Gage; RMC Place; ONEIDA; ▲ Deerfield; ***209** NH-15; ★ **UT-R**; mail Utica z 13502; rural

North Gainesville; RMC Place; WYOMING; ▲ Gainesville; ***208** NK-6; elev. 1,444ft./440m.; mail Silver Springs z 14550; rural

Northgate Estates; RMC Place; ONEIDA; ★ **UT-R**; mail Rome z 13440; pop. incl. with Rome (Inc. Place)

North Germantown; RMC Place; COLUMBIA; ▲ Germantown; ***209** NM-19; mail Germantown z 12526; ● 200

North Granville; RMC Place; WASHINGTON; ▲ Granville; **209** NG-20; elev. 335ft./102m.; [P]; z 12854; ● 500

North Great River; CDP; SUFFOLK; ▲ Islip; ***207** SF-9; ★ **N.Y.**; mail Central Islip z 11722; Ⓟ 3,964; © 3,929

North Greece; RMC Place; MONROE; ▲ Greece; **208** NH-7; elev. 335ft./102m.; [P]; ★ **ROCH**; z 14515; ● 500

North Greenbush; MCD-Town; RENSSELAER; ***209** NJ-19; ★ **A-S-T**; mail Wynantskill z 12198; Ⓟ 10,891; © 10,805

North Greenwich; RMC Place; WASHINGTON; ▲ Greenwich; ***209** NH-20; elev. 477ft./145m.; ★ **GLFLS**; mail Greenwich z 12834; rural

North Hannibal; RMC Place; OSWEGO; ▲ Hannibal; ***208** NH-10; elev. 417ft./127m.; mail Hannibal z 13074, Oswego z 13126; rural

North Harford; CORTLAND; see Harford (RMC Place)

North Harmony; MCD-Town; CHAUTAUQUA; ***208** NM-2; mail Stow z 14785; Ⓟ 2,301; © 2,521

North Harpersfield; RMC Place; DELAWARE; ▲ Harpersfield; **209** NK-16; elev. 1,610ft./491m.; mail Jefferson z 12093; ● 100

North Hartland; RMC Place; NIAGARA; ▲ Hartland; ***208** NH-4; elev. 375ft./114m.; ★ **LOCK**; mail Appleton z 14008; rural

North Haven; Inc. Place; SUFFOLK; ▲ Southampton; **207** SE-13; mail Sag Harbor z 11963; Ⓟ 713; © 743

North Hebron; RMC Place; WASHINGTON; ▲ Hebron; ***209** NH-20; elev. 797ft./243m.; mail Granville z 12832; rural

North Hempstead; MCD-Town; NASSAU; ***207** SF-8; [C] 12,157; ★ **N.Y.**; mail New Hyde Park z 11040; Ⓟ 211,393; © 222,611; Ⓡ 220,709; ◆ 217,366

North Highland; RMC Place; PUTNAM; ▲ Philipstown; ***207** SC-7; ★ **N.Y.**; mail Cold Spring z 10516; ● 350

North Hills; Inc. Place; NASSAU; ▲ North Hempstead; ***207** SF-8; [P]; ★ **N.Y.**; z 11040 & mail Manhasset z 11030; Ⓟ 3,453; © 4,301

North Hillsdale; RMC Place; COLUMBIA; ▲ Hillsdale; **209** NL-20; mail Hillsdale z 12529; ● 200

North Hoosick; RMC Place; RENSSELAER; ▲ Hoosick; **209** NI-20; elev. 448ft./137m.; [P]; z 12133; ● 350

North Hornell; Inc. Place; STEUBEN; ▲ Hornellsville; **208** NL-7; mail Hornell z 14843; Ⓟ 822; © 851

North Hudson; RMC Place; ESSEX; ▲ North Hudson; **209** NE-19; elev. 884ft./269m.; [P]; z 12855; ● 100

North Hudson; MCD-Town; ESSEX; ***209** NE-19; [P]; z 12855; Ⓟ 266; © 266

North Huron; RMC Place; WAYNE; ▲ Huron; ***208** NH-9; mail Wolcott z 14590; ● 45

North Ilion; RMC Place; HERKIMER; ▲ Herkimer; ***209** NI-15; mail Frankfort z 13340; rural

North Jasper; RMC Place; STEUBEN; ▲ Jasper; ***208** NM-8; mail Cameron z 14819; rural

North Java; RMC Place; WYOMING; ▲ Sheldon; **208** NK-5; [P]; z 14113; ● 250

North Jay; RMC Place; ESSEX; ▲ Jay; ***209** NC-19; mail Jay z 12941

North Kortright; RMC Place; DELAWARE; ▲ Kortright; ***209** NL-16; mail Bloomville z 13739, Davenport z 13750; rural

North Lansing; RMC Place; TOMPKINS; ▲ Lansing; ***209** NK-11; ★ **ITH**; mail Ithaca z 14852; ● 125

North Larchmont; WESTCHESTER; see Larchmont North (RMC Place)

North Lawrence; RMC Place; ST. LAWRENCE; ▲ Lawrence; **209** NB-16; elev. 340ft./104m.; [P]; z 12967; ● 400

North Lindenhurst; CDP; SUFFOLK; ▲ Babylon; ***207** SF-9; ★ **N.Y.**; mail Lindenhurst z 11757; Ⓟ 10,563; © 11,767

North Litchfield; RMC Place; HERKIMER; ▲ Litchfield; mail Frankfort z 13340; rural

North Long Beach; NASSAU; see Barnum Island (CDP-Census Area Only)

North Lynbrook; CDP-Census Area Only; NASSAU; ▲ Hempstead; **211** I-17; ★ **N.Y.**; mail Lynbrook z 11563; © 742

North Manlius; RMC Place; ONONDAGA; ▲ Manlius; ***209** NI-12; ★ **SYR**; mail Kirkville z 13082; rural

North Massapequa; CDP; NASSAU; ▲ Oyster Bay; **211** H-20; [P]; ★ **N.Y.**; z 11758; Ⓟ 19,365; © 19,152

North Merrick; CDP; NASSAU; ▲ Hempstead; **211** I-19; [P]; ★ **N.Y.**; z 11566; Ⓟ 12,113; © 11,844

North New Hyde Park; CDP; NASSAU; ▲ North Hempstead; **211** G-16; [P]; ★ **N.Y.**; z 11040, z 11042; Ⓟ 14,359; © 14,542

North Norwich (Galena); RMC Place; CHENANGO; ▲ North Norwich; **209** NK-14; [P]; z 13814; ● 600

North Norwich; MCD-Town; CHENANGO; ***209** NK-14; [P]; z 13814; Ⓟ 1,998; © 1,966

North Olean; RMC Place; CATTARAUGUS; ***208** NM-5; mail Olean z 14760; pop. incl. with Olean (Inc. Place)

North Patchogue; CDP; SUFFOLK; ▲ Brookhaven; ***207** SF-10; elev. 49ft./15m.; ★ **N.Y.**; mail Patchogue z 11772; Ⓟ 7,374; © 7,825

North Pembroke; RMC Place; GENESEE; ▲ Pembroke; ***208** NI-5; elev. 851ft./259m.; mail Batavia z 14020; rural

North Petersburg; RMC Place; RENSSELAER; ▲ Petersburgh; **209** NJ-20; mail Petersburg z 12138; ● 250

North Pharsalia; RMC Place; CHENANGO; ▲ Pharsalia; **209** NK-13; mail South Plymouth z 13844; ● 130

North Pitcher; RMC Place; CHENANGO; ▲ Pitcher; **209** NK-13; [P]; z 13124; ● 170

North Pole; RMC Place; ESSEX; ▲ Wilmington; **209** NC-18; mail Lake Placid z 12946; ● 70

Northport; Inc. Place; SUFFOLK; ▲ Huntington; **207** SE-9; [P] [H]; ★ **N.Y.**; z 11768; Ⓟ 7,572; © 7,606

North River; RMC Place; WARREN; ▲ Johnsburg; **209** NF-18; [P]; z 12856; ● 365

North Rockville Centre; RMC Place; NASSAU; ▲ Hempstead; ★ **N.Y.**; mail Rockville Centre z 11570

North Rose; RMC Place; WAYNE; ▲ Rose; **208** NI-9; elev. 388ft./118m.; [P]; z 14516; ● 800

North Roslyn; NASSAU; see Greenvale (CDP)

North Rush; RMC Place; MONROE; ▲ Rush; ***208** NI-7; ★ **ROCH**; mail Rush z 14543; ● 200

North Russell; RMC Place; ST. LAWRENCE; ▲ Russell; ***209** NC-15; elev. 602ft./183m.; mail Canton z 13617; rural

North Salem; RMC Place; WESTCHESTER; ▲ North Salem; **207** SC-8; [P]; ★ **N.Y.**; z 10560; ● 930

North Salem; MCD-Town; WESTCHESTER; ***207** SC-8; [P]; ★ **N.Y.**; z 10560; Ⓟ 4,725; © 5,173

North Sanford; RMC Place; BROOME; ▲ Sanford; ***209** NM-14; mail Deposit z 13754; rural

North Schodack; RMC Place; RENSSELAER; ▲ Schodack; ***209** NK-19; ★ **A-S-T**; mail East Greenbush z 12061; ● 150

North Sea; CDP; SUFFOLK; ▲ Southampton; **207** SE-12; mail Southampton z 11968; Ⓟ 2,530; © 4,493

North Selden; RMC Place; SUFFOLK; ▲ Brookhaven; ***207** SE-10; ★ **N.Y.**; mail Selden z 11784

North Settlement; RMC Place; GREENE; ▲ Ashland; ***209** NL-17; mail Windham z 12496; rural

North Shore Beach; RMC Place; SUFFOLK; ▲ Brookhaven; ★ **N.Y.**; mail Rocky Point z 11778

North Side; RMC Place; ERIE; ★ **BUF**; mail Buffalo z 14207, z 14216; pop. incl. with Buffalo (Inc. Place)

North Spencer; RMC Place; TIOGA; ▲ Spencer; ***209** NL-11; mail Spencer z 14883; rural

North Stephentown; RMC Place; RENSSELAER; ▲ Stephentown; ***209** NK-20; mail Stephentown z 12168

North Sterling; RMC Place; CAYUGA; ▲ Sterling; ***208** NH-10; mail Sterling z 13156; rural

North Stockholm; RMC Place; ST. LAWRENCE; ▲ Stockholm; ***209** NB-15; mail Norwood z 13668; ● 40

North Syracuse; Inc. Place; ONONDAGA; ▲ Cicero, Clay; **209** NI-12; [P]; ★ **SYR**; z 13212; Ⓟ 7,363; © 6,862

North Tarrytown; WESTCHESTER; see Sleepy Hollow (Inc. Place)

North Tonawanda; Inc. Place; NIAGARA; **208** NI-3; elev. 575ft./175m.; [P] [H] ■; ★ **BUF**; z 14120; Ⓟ 34,989; © 33,262; ◆ 32,152

Northumberland; RMC Place; SARATOGA; ▲ Northumberland; **209** NI-19; ★ **GLFLS**; mail Schuylerville z 12871; ● 250

Northumberland; MCD-Town; SARATOGA; ***209** NH-19; ★ **GLFLS**; mail Schuylerville z 12871; Ⓟ 3,645; © 4,603

North Valley Stream; CDP; NASSAU; ▲ Hempstead; **211** I-16; ★ **N.Y.**; mail Valley Stream z 11580; Ⓟ 14,574; © 15,789

North Victory; RMC Place; CAYUGA; ▲ Sterling; ***208** NH-10; elev. 423ft./129m.; mail Martville z 13111; ● 50

Northview Gardens; RMC Place; NIAGARA; ▲ Lockport; ***208** NH-4; ★ **LOCK**; mail Lockport z 14094; ● 550

Northville; Inc. Place; FULTON; ▲ Northampton; **209** NH-18; [P]; ★ **A-S-T**; z 12134; Ⓟ 1,180; © 1,139

Northville; CDP; SUFFOLK; ▲ Riverhead; ***207** SE-11; mail Aquebogue z 11931, Riverhead z 11901; © 801

North Wantagh; CDP; NASSAU; ▲ Hempstead; ***207** SF-8; ★ **N.Y.**; mail Wantagh z 11793; Ⓟ 12,276; © 12,156

North Waverly; RMC Place; TIOGA; ▲ Barton; ***209** NM-11; mail Waverly z 14892; ● 100

North Western; RMC Place; ONEIDA; ▲ Western; **209** NH-14; mail Westernville z 13486; ● 500

Northwest Harbor; CDP-Census Area Only; SUFFOLK; ▲ East Hampton; ***207** SE-13; mail East Hampton z 11937; Ⓟ 2,167; © 3,059

Northwest Ithaca; CDP-Census Area Only; TOMPKINS; ▲ Ithaca; ***208** NK-10; elev. 953ft./290m.; ★ **ITH**; mail Ithaca z 14850; Ⓟ 1,144; © 1,115

North White Plains; RMC Place; WESTCHESTER; ***207** SE-7; ★ **N.Y.**; mail White Plains z 10603

North Wilmurt; RMC Place; HERKIMER; ▲ Ohio; **209** NG-15; elev. 1,610ft./491m.; mail Remsen z 13438; rural

North Winfield; RMC Place; HERKIMER; ▲ Winfield; ***209** NJ-16; elev. 1,278ft./390m.; mail West Winfield z 13491; rural

North Wolcott; RMC Place; WAYNE; ▲ Wolcott; ***208** NH-10; elev. 337ft./103m.; mail Wolcott z 14590; ● 200

Northwood; RMC Place; SARATOGA; ▲ Halfmoon; ***209** NJ-19; elev. 300ft./91m.; ★ **A-S-T**; mail Waterford z 12188; ● 1,030

North Woodmere; RMC Place; NASSAU; ▲ Hempstead; ***207** SG-7; ★ **N.Y.**; mail Valley Stream z 11581

North Yonkers; RMC Place; WESTCHESTER; ★ **N.Y.**; pop. incl. with Yonkers (Inc. Place)

Norton Hill; RMC Place; GREENE; ▲ Greenville; **209** NL-18; elev. 881ft./269m.; [P]; z 12083; ● 385

Norton Summit; RMC Place; ALLEGANY; ▲ Wellsville; ***208** NM-6; mail Wellsville z 14895; rural

Norway; RMC Place; HERKIMER; ▲ Norway; **209** NH-15; mail Newport z 13416; ● 150

Norway; MCD-Town; HERKIMER; ***209** NH-15; mail Newport z 13416; Ⓟ 663; © 711

Norwich; Inc. Place; ⊡ CHENANGO; **209** NK-14; elev. 1,015ft./309m.; [P] [H]; z 13815; Ⓟ 7,613; © 7,355

Norwich; MCD-Town; CHENANGO; ***209** NK-14; [P]; z 13815; does not include the City of Norwich; Ⓟ 4,084; © 3,836

Norwich Corners; RMC Place; HERKIMER; ▲ Litchfield; ***209** NI-14; mail Sauquoit z 13456; rural

Norwood; Inc. Place; ST. LAWRENCE; ▲ Norfolk, Potsdam; **209** NB-15; [P]; z 13668; Ⓟ 1,841; © 1,685

Nostrand; RMC Place; KINGS; ★ **N.Y.**; mail Brooklyn z 11235; pop. incl. with New York (Inc. Place)

Nottingham Estates; RMC Place; NIAGARA; ▲ Lockport; ***208** NH-4; ★ **LOCK**; mail Lockport z 14094; ● 380

Noxon; RMC Place; DUTCHESS; ▲ La Grange; ***207** SB-7; elev. 300ft./91m.; ★ **POK**; mail Poughkeepsie z 12603

Noyack; CDP; SUFFOLK; ▲ Southampton; **207** SE-12; mail Sag Harbor z 11963; Ⓟ 2,059; © 2,696

Number Four; RMC Place; LEWIS; ▲ Watson; ***209** NF-15; elev. 1,583ft./482m.; mail Lowville z 13367; rural

Nunda; Inc. Place; LIVINGSTON; ▲ Nunda; **208** NK-6; elev. 944ft./288m.; [P]; z 14517; Ⓟ 1,347; © 1,330

Nunda; MCD-Town; LIVINGSTON; ***208** NK-6; [P]; z 14517; Ⓟ 2,931; © 3,017

Nyack; Inc. Place; ROCKLAND; ▲ Clarkstown, Orangetown; **207** SD-7; [P] [H] [C] 1,947; ★ **N.Y.**; z 10960; Ⓟ 6,558; © 6,737

O

Oak Beach; RMC Place; SUFFOLK; ▲ Babylon; **207** SG-9; [P]; ★ **N.Y.**; z 11702; ● 100

Oakdale; CDP; SUFFOLK; ▲ Islip; **207** SI-13; [P] [C] 6,304; ★ **N.Y.**; z 11769; Ⓟ 7,875; © 8,075

Oakfield; Inc. Place; GENESEE; **208** NI-5; elev. 753ft./230m.; [P]; z 14125; Ⓟ 1,818; © 1,805

Oakfield; MCD-Town; GENESEE; ***208** NI-5; [P]; z 14125; Ⓟ 3,312; © 3,203

Oak Hill; RMC Place; GREENE; ▲ Durham; **209** NL-18; [P]; z 12460; ● 400

Oakland; RMC Place; LIVINGSTON; ▲ Portage; ***208** NK-6; mail Nunda z 14517

Oakland Gardens; RMC Place; QUEENS; **211** G-15; [P]; ★ **N.Y.**; z 11364; pop. incl. with New York (Inc. Place)

Oakland Valley; RMC Place; SULLIVAN; ▲ Forestburgh; ***207** SC-4; mail Cuddebackville z 12729; ● 50

Oak Orchard; RMC Place; ORLEANS; ▲ Ridgeway; ***208** NH-5; elev. 395ft./120m.; mail Medina z 14103

Oak Point; RMC Place; ST. LAWRENCE; ▲ Hammond; ***209** NC-13; mail Hammond z 13646; rural

Oak Ridge; RMC Place; MONTGOMERY; ▲ Charleston; ***209** NJ-17; mail Esperance z 12066

Oakridge; RMC Place; ONONDAGA; ▲ Clay; ***209** NI-11; ★ **SYR**; mail Liverpool z 13088; ● 300

Oaks Corner; ONTARIO; see Oaks Corners (RMC Place)

Oaks Corners (Oaks Corner); RMC Place; ONTARIO; ▲ Phelps; ***208** NJ-9; elev. 490ft./149m.; [P]; z 14518; ● 120

Oaksville; RMC Place; OTSEGO; ▲ Otsego; ***209** NJ-16; elev. 1,275ft./389m.; mail Fly Creek z 13337; ● 75

Oakwood; RMC Place; CAYUGA; ▲ Springport; ***208** NJ-10; ★ **SYR**; mail Auburn z 13021; rural

Oakwood; RMC Place; RICHMOND; **210** L-7; elev. 18ft./5m.; ★ **N.Y.**; mail Staten Island z 10306; pop. incl. with New York (Inc. Place)

Oakwood Beach; RMC Place; RICHMOND; **210** M-7; ★ **N.Y.**; mail Staten Island z 10306; pop. incl. with New York (Inc. Place)

Oakwood Heights; RMC Place; RICHMOND; ***207** SG-6; elev. 50ft./15m.; ★ **N.Y.**; mail Staten Island z 10301; pop. incl. with New York (Inc. Place)

Obernburg; RMC Place; SULLIVAN; ▲ Fremont; **209** NN-15; elev. 1,656ft./505m.; [P]; z 12767; ● 200

Obi; RMC Place; ALLEGANY; ▲ Clarksville; **208** NM-5; mail Cuba z 14727; ● 45

Occanum; RMC Place; BROOME; ▲ Windsor; ***209** NM-13; ★ **BING**; mail Windsor z 13865; rural

Ocean Bay Park; RMC Place; SUFFOLK; ▲ Islip; ***207** SG-10; ★ **N.Y.**; mail Bay Shore z 11706, Ocean Beach z 11770; summer pop. 1,000; ● 10

Ocean Beach; Inc. Place; SUFFOLK; ▲ Islip; **207** SG-10; [P]; ★ **N.Y.**; z 11770; Ⓟ 131; © 138

Oceanside; CDP; NASSAU; ▲ Hempstead; **207** SG-8; [P] [H]; ★ **N.Y.**; z 11572; Ⓟ 32,423; © 32,733; ◆ 31,086

Odessa; Inc. Place; SCHUYLER; ▲ Montour, Catharine; **208** NL-10; elev. 1,050ft./320m.; [P]; z 14869; Ⓟ 986; © 617

Ogden; MCD-Town; MONROE; ***208** NI-7; ★ **ROCH**; mail Spencerport z 14559; Ⓟ 16,912; © 18,492

Ogden Center; RMC Place; MONROE; ▲ Ogden; ***208** NI-7; elev. 587ft./179m.; ★ **ROCH**; mail Spencerport z 14559

Ogdensburg; Inc. Place; ST. LAWRENCE; ▲ Oswegatchie; **209** NB-14; [P] [H]; z 13669; Ⓟ 13,521; © 12,364

O'Hara Corners; RMC Place; GREENE; ▲ Greenville; ***209** NL-18; elev. 670ft./204m.; mail Greenville z 12083; rural

Ohio; RMC Place; HERKIMER; ▲ Ohio; **209** NH-15; elev. 1,374ft./419m.; [P]; z 13324; ● 70

Ohio; MCD-Town; HERKIMER; ***209** NG-15; [P]; z 13324; Ⓟ 880; © 922

Ohioville; RMC Place; ULSTER; ▲ New Paltz; **207** SA-6; elev. 363ft./111m.; mail New Paltz z 12561; ● 250

Oil Springs Reservation; Indian Reservation; ALLEGANY, CATTARAUGUS; mail Irving z 14081; Ⓟ 6; © 11

Olcott; CDP; NIAGARA; ▲ Newfane; **208** NH-4; elev. 277ft./84m.; [P]; ★ **LOCK**; z 14126; Ⓟ 1,432; © 1,156

Old Bethpage; CDP; NASSAU; ▲ Oyster Bay; ***207** SF-8; [P]; ★ **N.Y.**; z 11804; Ⓟ 5,610; © 5,400

Old Brookville; Inc. Place; NASSAU; ▲ Oyster Bay; **211** E-18; elev. 92ft./28m.; ★ **N.Y.**; mail Glen Head z 11545, Greenvale z 11548; Ⓟ 1,823; © 2,167

Old Central Bridge; RMC Place; SCHOHARIE; ▲ Schoharie; ***209** NJ-17; mail Central Bridge z 12035

Old Chatham; RMC Place; COLUMBIA; ▲ Chatham; ***209** NK-19; [P]; ★ **A-S-T**; z 12136; ● 450

Old Chelsa; RMC Place; NEW YORK; ★ **N.Y.**; mail New York z 10011, z 10113; pop. incl. with New York (Inc. Place)

Old DeKalb; ST. LAWRENCE; see De Kalb (RMC Place)

Old Field; Inc. Place; SUFFOLK; ▲ Brookhaven; **207** SE-10; ★ **N.Y.**; mail East Setauket z 11733; Ⓟ 765; © 947

Old Field South; RMC Place; SUFFOLK; ▲ Brookhaven; ***207** SE-10; ★ **N.Y.**; mail Stony Brook z 11790

Old Forge; RMC Place; HERKIMER; ▲ Webb; **209** NF-15; [P]; z 13420; summer pop. 5,000; ● 1,450

Old Mastic; RMC Place; SUFFOLK; ▲ Brookhaven; ***207** SF-11; ★ **N.Y.**; mail Mastic Beach z 11951

Old Orchard Cove; LIVINGSTON; see Old Orchard Point (RMC Place)

Old Orchard Point (Old Orchard Cove); RMC Place; LIVINGSTON; ▲ Livonia; ***208** NJ-7; ★ **ROCH**; mail Livonia z 14487; summer pop. 300; ● 200

Old Stony Brook; RMC Place; SUFFOLK; ▲ Brookhaven; ***207** SE-10; ★ **N.Y.**; mail Stony Brook z 11790

Old Town; RMC Place; RICHMOND; ***207** SG-6; ★ **N.Y.**; mail Staten Island z 10304; pop. incl. with New York (Inc. Place)

Old Village; RMC Place; NASSAU; ▲ North Hempstead; ***207** SF-7; ★ **N.Y.**; mail Great Neck z 11023; pop. incl. with Great Neck (Inc. Place)

Old Westbury; Inc. Place; NASSAU; ▲ Oyster Bay, North Hempstead; **211** F-18; [P] [C] 11,122; ★ **N.Y.**; z 11568; Ⓟ 3,897; © 4,228

Olean; Inc. Place; CATTARAUGUS; **208** NM-5; elev. 1,451ft./442m.; [P] [H] ■; z 14760; Ⓟ 16,946; © 15,347; ◆ 13,653

Olean; MCD-Town; CATTARAUGUS; ***208** NM-5; [P]; z 14760; does not include the City of Olean; Ⓟ 1,999; © 2,029

Olive; MCD-Town; ULSTER; ***209** NN-17; mail Olivebridge z 12461; Ⓟ 4,086; © 4,579

Olivebridge; RMC Place; ULSTER; ▲ Olive; **209** NN-18; elev. 568ft./173m.; [P]; z 12461; ● 400

Oliverea; RMC Place; ULSTER; ▲ Shandaken; **209** NM-17; [P]; z 12410; ● 150

Olmstedville; RMC Place; ESSEX; ▲ Minerva; **209** NF-18; [P]; z 12857; ● 400

Omar; RMC Place; JEFFERSON; ▲ Orleans; ***209** ND-12; mail Alexandria Bay z 13607, La Fargeville z 13656; ● 90

Omi; RMC Place; COLUMBIA; ▲ Ghent; ***209** NL-19; elev. 299ft./91m.; ★ **A-S-T**; mail Ghent z 12075; rural

Onativia; RMC Place; ONONDAGA; ▲ LaFayette; ***209** NJ-12; ★ **SYR**; mail La Fayette z 13084; rural

Onchiota; RMC Place; FRANKLIN; ▲ Franklin; **209** NC-18; elev. 1,711ft./522m.; [P]; z 12989; ● 85

Oneida; Inc. Place; MADISON; **209** NI-13; elev. 443ft./135m.; [P] [H]; z 13421; Ⓟ 10,850; © 10,987

ONEIDA; **209** NH-13; Ⓟ 250,836; © 235,469; Ⓡ 235,459; ◆ 228,860

Oneida (NY) Reservation; Indian Reservation; MADISON; © 26

Oneida Castle; Inc. Place; ONEIDA; ▲ Vernon; ***209** NI-13; ★ **UT-R**; mail Oneida z 13421; Ⓟ 671; © 627

Oneonta; Inc. Place; OTSEGO; ▲ Oneonta; **209** NK-15; elev. 1,085ft./331m.; [P] [H] [C] 7,266 ■; z 13820; Ⓟ 13,954; © 13,292; ◆ 13,272

Oneonta; MCD-Town; OTSEGO; ***209** NK-15; [P] [C] 7,266; z 13820 & mail West Oneonta z 13861; does not include the City of Oneonta; Ⓟ 4,963; © 4,994

Onesquethaw; ALBANY; see Tarrytown (RMC Place)

Oniontown; RMC Place; DUTCHESS; ▲ Dover; ***207** SA-8; mail Dover Plains z 12522; ● 60

Onleys Station; RMC Place; ORANGE; ▲ Wawayanda; ★ **MIDD**; mail Middletown z 10940; rural

Onondaga; ONONDAGA; see Onondaga Hill (RMC Place)

Onondaga; MCD-Town; ONONDAGA; ***209** NI-11; ★ **SYR**; mail Syracuse z 13215; Ⓟ 18,396; © 21,063; ◆ 21,347

ONONDAGA; **209** NI-12; Ⓟ 468,973; © 458,336; ◆ 448,028

Onondaga Hill (Onondaga); RMC Place; ONONDAGA; ▲ Onondaga; **208** NG-8; ★ **SYR**; mail Syracuse z 13215; ● 2,000

Onondaga Reservation; Indian Reservation; ONONDAGA; ▲ Onondaga; ★ **SYR**; mail Nedrow z 13120; Ⓟ 596; © 1,473

Ontario; RMC Place; WAYNE; ▲ Ontario; **208** NH-8; [P]; ★ **ROCH**; z 14519; ● 1,000

Ontario; MCD-Town; WAYNE; ***208** NH-8; [P]; ★ **ROCH**; z 14519; Ⓟ 8,560; © 9,778

ONTARIO; **208** NJ-8; Ⓟ 95,101; © 100,224; ◆ 103,039

Ontario Center; RMC Place; WAYNE; ▲ Ontario; **208** NH-8; [P]; ★ **ROCH**; z 14520; ● 600

Ontario on the Lake; RMC Place; WAYNE; ▲ Ontario; ***208** NH-8; ★ **ROCH**; mail Ontario z 14519; ● 250

Onteo Beach; RMC Place; MONROE; ▲ Hamlin; ***208** NH-6; ★ **ROCH**; mail Hamlin z 14464; ● 50

Onteora Park; RMC Place; GREENE; ▲ Hunter; ***209** NL-18; mail Tannersville z 12485; ● 100

Oot Park; RMC Place; ONONDAGA; ▲ Manlius; ***209** NI-12; ★ **SYR**; mail East Syracuse z 13057; ● 2,080

Open Meadows; RMC Place; CHAUTAUQUA; ▲ North Harmony; ***208** NM-2; mail Ashville z 14710; rural

Oppenheim; RMC Place; FULTON; ▲ Oppenheim; **209** NI-16; mail Dolgeville z 13329; ● 500

Oppenheim; MCD-Town; FULTON; ***209** NI-16; mail Dolgeville z 13329; Ⓟ 1,848; © 1,774

Oquaga Lake; RMC Place; BROOME; ▲ Sanford; ***209** NM-13; ★ **BING**; mail Deposit z 13754; ● 75

Oramel; RMC Place; ALLEGANY; ▲ Caneadea; **208** NL-6; elev. 1,256ft./383m.; mail Belfast z 14711; ● 150

Oran; RMC Place; ONONDAGA; ▲ Pompey; ***209** NI-12; ★ **SYR**; mail Manlius z 13104; ● 50

Orange; MCD-Town; SCHUYLER; ***208** NL-9; mail Beaver Dams z 14812; Ⓟ 1,561; © 1,752

ORANGE; **207** SD-5; Ⓟ 307,647; © 341,367; ◆ 378,340

Orangeburg; CDP; ROCKLAND; ▲ Orangetown; ***207** SE-7; [P] [H] [C] 2,290; ★ **N.Y.**; z 10962; Ⓟ 3,583; © 3,388; Ⓡ 3,782

Orange Lake; CDP; ORANGE; ▲ Newburgh; **207** SB-6; ★ **NWBG**; mail Newburgh z 12550; Ⓟ 5,196; © 6,085

Orangeport; RMC Place; NIAGARA; ▲ Royalton; ***208** NH-4; mail Gasport z 14067; rural

Orangetown; MCD-Town; ROCKLAND; ***207** SE-7; [C] 6,457; ★ **N.Y.**; mail Nyack z 10960; Ⓟ 46,742; © 47,711; ◆ 49,274

Orangeville; MCD-Town; WYOMING; ***208** NJ-5; mail Warsaw z 14569; Ⓟ 1,115; © 1,301

Orangeville Center; RMC Place; WYOMING; ▲ Orangeville; ***208** NJ-5; mail Attica z 14011; rural

Orchard Knoll; RMC Place; CHEMUNG; ▲ Horseheads; **208** NH-1; ★ **ELM**; mail Horseheads z 14845; ● 250

Orchard Park; Inc. Place; ERIE; ▲ Orchard Park; **208** NJ-4; [P]; ★ **BUF**; z 14127; Ⓟ 3,280; © 3,294

Orchard Park; MCD-Town; ERIE; ***208** NJ-4; [P]; ★ **BUF**; z 14127; Ⓟ 24,632; © 27,637; ◆ 28,255

Orchard Village; RMC Place; ONONDAGA; ▲ Camillus; ***209** NI-11; ★ **SYR**; mail Camillus z 13031; ● 1,400

Oregon; RMC Place; FULTON; ▲ Stratford; ***209** NH-16; mail Stratford z 13470; rural

Oregon; RMC Place; SUFFOLK; ▲ Southold; mail Mattituck z 11952

Orient; CDP; SUFFOLK; ▲ Southold; **207** SD-13; [P]; z 11957; © 709

Entries in **UPPERCASE** are counties.
Entries in **bold** have populations of 2,500 or more.
Names in parentheses are alternate names.

Inc. Place	Incorporated Place
RMC Place	Rand McNally Designated Place
CDP	Census Designated Place
MCD	Minor Civil Division
⊡	County Seat
▲	Minor Civil Division
elev.	Elevation
[P]	Post Office
[H]	Hospital
[C]	College
■	Principal Business Center
★	Ranally Metro Area (RMA) Abbreviation
z	Zip Code(s)
Ⓟ	Previous Census Population
Ⓡ	Revised Census Population
Ⓐ	Annexation Population
●	Rand McNally Population Estimate
©	Final Census Population
Ⓢ	Special Census Population
◆	Estimated Population

For additional definitions see Glossary, Volume 1, and Introduction, Volume 2.

Orienta; RMC Place; WESTCHESTER; *207 SE-7; elev. 17ft./5m.; ★ N.Y.; mail Mamaroneck z 10543; pop. incl. with Mamaroneck (Inc. Place)
Oriental Beach; RMC Place; KINGS; *207 SG-7; ★ N.Y.; mail Brooklyn z 11235; pop. incl. with New York (Inc. Place)
Oriental Park; RMC Place; CHAUTAUQUA; ▲ Ellery; *208 NM-2; ★ JMST; mail Bemus Point z 14712; ● 450
Orient Point; RMC Place; SUFFOLK; ▲ Southold; *207 SD-13; elev. 14ft./4m.; mail Orient z 11957
Oriskany; Inc. Place; ONEIDA; ▲ Whitestown; 209 NI-14; 🅿; ★ UT-R; z 13424; Ⓟ 1,450; © 1,459
Oriskany Falls; Inc. Place; ONEIDA; ▲ Augusta; 209 NJ-14; 🅿; ★ UT-R; z 13425; Ⓟ 795; © 698
Orlando; RMC Place; CATTARAUGUS; ▲ Mansfield; *208 NL-4; elev. 1,613ft./492m.; mail Little Valley z 14755; rural
Orleans; MCD-Town; JEFFERSON; *209 ND-12; mail La Fargeville z 13656; Ⓟ 2,248; © 2,465
Orleans; RMC Place; ONTARIO; ▲ Phelps; *208 NJ-9; mail Clifton Springs z 14432; ● 100
ORLEANS; 208 NH-6; Ⓟ 41,846; © 44,171; ◆ 41,863
Orleans Corners; JEFFERSON; see Orleans Four Corners (RMC Place)
Orleans Four Corners (Orleans Corners); RMC Place; JEFFERSON; ▲ Orleans; *209 ND-12; mail La Fargeville z 13656
Orwell; RMC Place; OSWEGO; ▲ Orwell; 209 NG-12; elev. 808ft./246m.; 🅿; z 13426; ● 400
Orwell; MCD-Town; OSWEGO; *209 NG-12; 🅿; z 13426; Ⓟ 1,171; © 1,254
Oscawana Lake; RMC Place; PUTNAM; ▲ Putnam Valley; *207 SC-7; ★ N.Y.; mail Putnam Valley z 10579
Osceola; RMC Place; LEWIS; ▲ Osceola; 209 NG-13; mail Camden z 13316; ● 200
Osceola; MCD-Town; LEWIS; *209 NG-13; mail Camden z 13316; Ⓟ 239; © 265
Ossian; MCD-Town; LIVINGSTON; *208 NK-7; mail Dansville z 14437; Ⓟ 797; © 751
Ossian Center; RMC Place; LIVINGSTON; ▲ Ossian; *208 NK-7; mail Dansville z 14437; ● 100
Ossining; Inc. Place; WESTCHESTER; ▲ Ossining; 207 SD-7; 🅿 🅷; ★ N.Y.; z 10562; Ⓟ 22,582; © 24,010; ◆ 24,964
Ossining; MCD-Town; WESTCHESTER; *207 SD-7; 🅿; ★ N.Y.; z 10562; Ⓟ 34,124; © 36,534; ◆ 38,054
Oswegatchie; RMC Place; ST. LAWRENCE; ▲ Fine; 209 ND-15; elev. 1,372ft./418m.; 🅿; z 13670 & mail Theresa z 13691; ● 300
Oswegatchie; MCD-Town; ST. LAWRENCE; *209 NC-14; 🅿; z 13670 & mail Heuvelton z 13654, Theresa z 13691; Ⓟ 4,036; © 4,370
Oswego; Inc. Place; ⊡ OSWEGO; 209 NG-11; elev. 298ft./91m.; 🅿 🅷 🅲 8,275 ■; z 13126; Ⓟ 19,195; © 17,954; Ⓡ 18,096; ◆ 17,227
Oswego; MCD-Town; OSWEGO; *208 NH-10; 🅿 🅲 8,275; z 13126; does not include the City of Oswego; Ⓟ 8,027; © 7,287
OSWEGO; 209 NG-12; Ⓟ 121,771; © 122,377; ◆ 118,166
Oswego Bitter; RMC Place; ONONDAGA; ▲ Camillus; *209 NI-11; ★ SYR; mail Camillus z 13031; rural
Oswego Center; RMC Place; OSWEGO; ▲ Oswego; *208 NH-10; elev. 364ft./111m.; mail Oswego z 13126; ● 60
Otego; Inc. Place; OTSEGO; ▲ Otego; 209 NL-15; 🅿; z 13825; Ⓟ 1,068; © 1,052
Otego; MCD-Town; OTSEGO; *209 NL-15; 🅿; z 13825; Ⓟ 3,128; © 3,183
Otisco; RMC Place; ONONDAGA; ▲ Otisco; 209 NJ-11; elev. 1,474ft./449m.; ★ SYR; mail Tully z 13159; ● 250
Otisco; MCD-Town; ONONDAGA; *209 NJ-11; ★ SYR; mail Tully z 13159; Ⓟ 2,255; © 2,561
Otisco Valley; RMC Place; ONONDAGA; ▲ Otisco; *209 NJ-11; ★ SYR; mail Marietta z 13110; rural
Otisville; Inc. Place; ORANGE; ▲ Mount Hope; 207 SC-4; elev. 852ft./260m.; 🅿; ★ MIDD; z 10963; Ⓟ 1,078; © 989
Otsego; MCD-Town; OTSEGO; *209 NJ-16; mail Fly Creek z 13337; Ⓟ 3,932; © 3,904
OTSEGO; 209 NK-15; Ⓟ 60,517; © 61,676; ◆ 61,988
Otselic; RMC Place; CHENANGO; ▲ Otselic; 209 NJ-13; mail Georgetown z 13072; ● 400
Otselic; MCD-Town; CHENANGO; *209 NK-13; mail Georgetown z 13072; Ⓟ 990; © 1,001
Otter Creek; RMC Place; LEWIS; ▲ Greig; *209 NF-14; mail Glenfield z 13343; ● 100
Otter Lake; RMC Place; ONEIDA; ▲ Forestport; 209 NG-15; elev. 1,551ft./473m.; mail Forestport z 13338; ● 460
Ott Meadows; RMC Place; ONONDAGA; ▲ Salina; *209 NI-12; ★ SYR; mail Liverpool z 13088; ● 2,700
Otto; RMC Place; CATTARAUGUS; ▲ Otto; 208 NL-4; elev. 1,266ft./386m.; 🅿; z 14766; ● 550
Otto; MCD-Town; CATTARAUGUS; *208 NL-3; 🅿; z 14766; Ⓟ 777; © 831
Ouaquaga; RMC Place; BROOME; ▲ Colesville; 209 NM-13; elev. 941ft./287m.; 🅿; ★ BING; z 13826; ● 400
Overlook; RMC Place; DUTCHESS; ▲ La Grange; *207 SB-7; ★ POK; mail Poughkeepsie z 12603; rural
Overlook; RMC Place; SARATOGA; ▲ Day; *209 NH-18; mail Corinth z 12822; ● 40
Ovid; Inc. Place; SENECA; ▲ Romulus, Ovid; 208 NK-10; 🅿; z 14521; Ⓟ 660; © 612
Ovid; MCD-Town; SENECA; *208 NK-10; 🅿; z 14521; includes part of the Village of Ovid; Ⓟ 2,306; © 2,757
Ovid Center; SENECA; see Sheldrake Springs (RMC Place)
Ovington; RMC Place; KINGS; ★ N.Y.; mail Brooklyn z 11220; pop. incl. with New York (Inc. Place)
Owasco; RMC Place; CAYUGA; ▲ Owasco; 209 NJ-11; 🅿; ★ SYR; z 13021; ● 400
Owasco; MCD-Town; CAYUGA; *209 NJ-11; 🅿; ★ SYR; z 13021; Ⓟ 3,490; © 3,755
Owego; Inc. Place; ⊡ TIOGA; ▲ Owego; 209 NM-11; elev. 817ft./249m.; 🅿; ★ BING; z 13827; Ⓟ 4,442; © 3,911
Owego; MCD-Town; TIOGA; *209 NM-12; 🅿; ★ BING; z 13827; Ⓟ 21,279; © 20,365; ◆ 19,692
Owens Corners; ST. LAWRENCE; see Hatch's Corner (RMC Place)
Owens Mills; RMC Place; CHEMUNG; ▲ Chemung; *208 NM-10; mail Chemung z 14825; rural
Owls Head; RMC Place; FRANKLIN; ▲ Bellmont; 209 NB-17; elev. 1,526ft./465m.; 🅿; z 12969; ● 350
Oxbow; RMC Place; JEFFERSON; ▲ Antwerp; 209 ND-13; elev. 351ft./107m.; 🅿; z 13608, z 13671; ● 200
Oxford; Inc. Place; CHENANGO; ▲ Oxford; 209 NL-13; elev. 973ft./297m.; 🅿; z 13830; Ⓟ 1,738; © 1,584
Oxford; MCD-Town; CHENANGO; *209 NL-13; 🅿; z 13830; Ⓟ 4,075; © 3,992
Oxford (Oxford Depot); RMC Place; ORANGE; ▲ Blooming Grove; 207 SC-5; elev. 536ft./163m.; ★ N.Y.; mail Chester z 10918; ● 250
Oxford Depot; ORANGE; see Oxford (RMC Place)
Oyster Bay; CDP; NASSAU; ▲ Oyster Bay; 207 SF-8; 🅿; ★ N.Y.; z 11771; Ⓟ 6,687; © 6,826
Oyster Bay; MCD-Town; NASSAU; *207 SF-8; 🅿 🅲 17,937; ★ N.Y.; z 11771; Ⓟ 292,657; © 293,925; Ⓡ 295,827; ◆ 277,530
Oyster Bay Cove; Inc. Place; NASSAU; ▲ Oyster Bay; 211 D-20; ★ N.Y.; mail Oyster Bay z 11771, Syosset z 11791; Ⓟ 2,109; © 2,262
Ozone Park; RMC Place; QUEENS; 211 I-13; 🅿; ★ N.Y.; z 11416-17; pop. incl. with New York (Inc. Place)

P

Pacama; RMC Place; ULSTER; ▲ Marbletown; *209 NN-18; elev. 462ft./141m.; ★ KNGST; mail Kingston z 12401; rural
Paddlefords; RMC Place; ONTARIO; ▲ Canandaigua; *208 NJ-8; mail Canandaigua z 14424; rural
Paddy Hill; RMC Place; JEFFERSON; ▲ Hounsfield; *209 NE-12; mail Brownville z 13615, Dexter z 13634; ● 100
Paines Hollow; RMC Place; HERKIMER; ▲ Little Falls; *209 NI-15; mail Mohawk z 13407; rural
Painted Post; Inc. Place; STEUBEN; ▲ Erwin; 208 NM-9; 🅿; z 14870; Ⓟ 1,950; © 1,842
Palatine; MCD-Town; MONTGOMERY; *209 NI-16; mail Palatine Bridge z 13428; Ⓟ 2,787; © 3,070
Palatine Bridge; Inc. Place; MONTGOMERY; ▲ Palatine; 209 NJ-16; elev. 337ft./103m.; 🅿; z 13428; Ⓟ 520; © 706
Palentown; RMC Place; ULSTER; ▲ Rochester; *207 SA-5; elev. 1,053ft./321m.; mail Kerhonkson z 12446; rural
Palenville; CDP; GREENE; ▲ Catskill; 209 NM-18; 🅿; ★ KNGST; z 12463; © 1,120
Palermo; RMC Place; OSWEGO; ▲ Palermo; 209 NH-11; ★ SYR; mail Fulton z 13069; ● 20
Palermo; MCD-Town; OSWEGO; *209 NH-11; ★ SYR; mail Fulton z 13069; Ⓟ 3,582; © 3,686
Palisades; RMC Place; ROCKLAND; ▲ Orangetown; *207 SE-7; elev. 197ft./60m.; 🅿; ★ N.Y.; z 10964; ● 800
Palmyra; Inc. Place; WAYNE; ▲ Palmyra; 208 NI-8; 🅿; z 14522; Ⓟ 3,566; © 3,490
Palmyra; MCD-Town; WAYNE; *208 NI-9; 🅿; z 14522; Ⓟ 7,690; © 7,672
Pamelia; MCD-Town; JEFFERSON; *209 NE-12; ★ WATN; mail Evans Mills z 13637; Ⓟ 2,811; © 2,897
Pamelia Four Corners; RMC Place; JEFFERSON; ▲ Pamelia; 209 NE-12; elev. 443ft./135m.; ★ WATN; mail Evans Mills z 13637, Watertown z 13601; ● 250
Panama; Inc. Place; CHAUTAUQUA; ▲ Harmony; 208 NM-2; elev. 1,550ft./472m.; 🅿; z 14767; Ⓟ 468; © 491
Panorama; RMC Place; MONROE; ▲ Penfield; *208 NI-8; 🅿; ★ ROCH; z 14625
Panther Lake; RMC Place; OSWEGO; ▲ Constantia, Amboy; 209 NH-12; ★ SYR; mail Bernhards Bay z 13028; ● 50
Pantigo; RMC Place; SUFFOLK; ▲ East Hampton; *207 SE-13; elev. 38ft./12m.; mail East Hampton z 11937
Paradise Hill; RMC Place; GREENE; ▲ New Baltimore; *209 NL-19; elev. 662ft./202m.; ★ A-S-T; mail Coxsackie z 12051; ● 30
Paradox; RMC Place; ESSEX; ▲ Schroon; 209 NF-19; elev. 875ft./267m.; 🅿; z 12858; ● 100
Parc; CDP-Census Area Only; CLINTON; *209 NB-20; ★ PLATT; © 54
Parcells Corner; RMC Place; CHAUTAUQUA; ▲ Hanover; *208 NK-3; mail Forestville z 14062; rural
Paris; RMC Place; ONEIDA; ▲ Paris; 209 NI-14; 🅿; ★ UT-R; z 13456; ● 200
Paris; MCD-Town; ONEIDA; *209 NI-14; 🅿; ★ UT-R; z 13456; Ⓟ 4,414; © 4,609
Parish; Inc. Place; OSWEGO; ▲ Parish; 209 NH-12; 🅿; z 13131 & mail Maple View z 13107; Ⓟ 473; © 512
Parish; MCD-Town; OSWEGO; *209 NH-12; 🅿; z 13131; Ⓟ 2,425; © 2,694
Parishville; RMC Place; ST. LAWRENCE; ▲ Parishville; 209 NC-16; elev. 903ft./275m.; 🅿; z 13672; ● 700
Parishville; MCD-Town; ST. LAWRENCE; *209 NC-15; 🅿; z 13672; Ⓟ 1,901; © 2,049
Parishville Center; RMC Place; ST. LAWRENCE; ▲ Parishville; *209 NC-15; elev. 654ft./199m.; mail Potsdam z 13676
Paris Station; RMC Place; ONEIDA; ▲ Paris; *209 NI-14; elev. 1,419ft./433m.; ★ UT-R; mail Sauquoit z 13456; ● 90
Parkchester; RMC Place; BRONX; 211 E-13; ★ N.Y.; mail Bronx z 10462; pop. incl. with New York (Inc. Place)
Park Hill; RMC Place; ONONDAGA; ▲ De Witt; *209 NI-12; ★ SYR; mail East Syracuse z 13057; ● 2,400
Park Hill; RMC Place; WESTCHESTER; *207 SE-7; ★ N.Y.; mail Yonkers z 10705; pop. incl. with Yonkers (Inc. Place)
Park of Edgewater; RMC Place; BRONX; *207 SF-7; ★ N.Y.; mail Bronx z 10465; pop. incl. with New York (Inc. Place)
Parkside; RMC Place; QUEENS; *207 SF-7; ★ N.Y.; mail Forest Hills z 11375; pop. incl. with New York (Inc. Place)
Parkside; RMC Place; WESTCHESTER; *207 SE-7; ★ N.Y.; pop. incl. with Mount Vernon (Inc. Place)
Park Slope; RMC Place; KINGS; *207 SG-6; ★ N.Y.; mail Brooklyn z 11215; pop. incl. with New York (Inc. Place)
Park Station; RMC Place; CHEMUNG; ▲ Erin; *208 NL-10; mail Erin z 14838; rural
Parkston; RMC Place; SULLIVAN; ▲ Rockland; *207 SA-3; mail Livingston Manor z 12758; rural
Parksville; RMC Place; SULLIVAN; ▲ Liberty; 209 NN-16; elev. 1,673ft./510m.; 🅿; z 12768; ● 700
Park Terrace; RMC Place; BROOME; ▲ Binghamton; 207 SC-11; ★ BING; mail Binghamton z 13903; ● 800
Parkville; RMC Place; KINGS; 210 K-10; ★ N.Y.; mail Brooklyn z 11204; pop. incl. with New York (Inc. Place)
Parkway; RMC Place; BRONX; ★ N.Y.; mail Bronx z 10462; pop. incl. with New York (Inc. Place)
Parma; MONROE; see Parma Center (RMC Place)
Parma; MCD-Town; MONROE; *208 NH-7; ★ ROCH; mail Hilton z 14468; Ⓟ 13,873; © 14,822
Parma Center (Parma); RMC Place; MONROE; ▲ Parma; *208 NH-7; ★ ROCH; mail Hilton z 14468
Parma Corners; RMC Place; MONROE; ▲ Parma; *208 NH-7; ★ ROCH; mail Spencerport z 14559; ● 300
Parson Farms; RMC Place; ONONDAGA; ▲ Camillus; *209 NI-11; ★ SYR; mail Camillus z 13031; ● 2,150
Pastime Park; RMC Place; SENECA; ▲ Fayette; *208 NJ-9; mail Geneva z 14456; ● 45
Pataukunk; RMC Place; ULSTER; ▲ Rochester; *207 SA-5; mail Kerhonkson z 12446
Patchin; RMC Place; NEW YORK; ★ N.Y.; mail New York z 10011; pop. incl. with New York (Inc. Place)
Patchinville; RMC Place; STEUBEN; ▲ Wayland; *208 NK-7; mail Wayland z 14572; rural
Patchogue; Inc. Place; SUFFOLK; ▲ Brookhaven; 207 SF-10; 🅿 🅷 🅲 4,083 ■; ★ N.Y.; z 11772; Ⓟ 11,060; © 11,919; ◆ 11,931
Patchogue Highlands; RMC Place; SUFFOLK; ▲ Brookhaven; *207 SF-10; ★ N.Y.; mail Patchogue z 11772
Patria; RMC Place; SCHOHARIE; ▲ Fulton; *209 NK-17; mail Warnerville z 12187; summer pop. 100
Patroon; RMC Place; ALBANY; ★ A-S-T; mail Albany z 12204; pop. incl. with Albany (Inc. Place)
Patterson; RMC Place; PUTNAM; ▲ Patterson; 207 SB-8; elev. 450ft./137m.; 🅿; ★ N.Y.; z 12563; ● 1,200
Patterson; MCD-Town; PUTNAM; *207 SC-8; 🅿; ★ N.Y.; z 12563; Ⓟ 8,679; © 11,306
Pattersonville; RMC Place; SCHENECTADY; ▲ Rotterdam; 209 NJ-18; 🅿; ★ A-S-T; z 12137; ● 600
Pattersonville-Rotterdam Junction; CDP-Census Area Only; SCHENECTADY; *209 NJ-18; ★ A-S-T; © 918
Paul Smiths; RMC Place; FRANKLIN; ▲ Brighton; 209 NC-17; 🅿 🅲 910; z 12970; ● 500
Pavilion; RMC Place; GENESEE; ▲ Pavilion; 208 NJ-6; 🅿; ★ ROCH; z 14525; ● 600
Pavilion; MCD-Town; GENESEE; *208 NJ-6; 🅿; ★ ROCH; z 14525; Ⓟ 2,327; © 2,467
Pavilion Center; RMC Place; GENESEE; ▲ Pavilion; *208 NJ-6; elev. 954ft./291m.; ★ ROCH; mail Pavilion z 14525; ● 45
Pawling; Inc. Place; DUTCHESS; ▲ Pawling; 207 SB-8; elev. 465ft./142m.; 🅿; z 12564; Ⓟ 1,974; © 2,233
Pawling; MCD-Town; DUTCHESS; *207 SB-8; 🅿; z 12564; Ⓟ 5,947; © 7,521
Payne Beach; RMC Place; MONROE; ▲ Greece; *208 NH-7; ★ ROCH; mail Hilton z 14468; ● 180
Pea Brook; RMC Place; DELAWARE; ▲ Hancock; *207 SA-2; mail Long Eddy z 12760; rural
Peach Lake; CDP-Census Area Only; PUTNAM, WESTCHESTER; ▲ North Salem, Southeast; *207 SC-8; ★ N.Y.; mail Brewster z 10509; Ⓟ 1,499; summer pop. 2,000; © 1,671
Peakville; RMC Place; DELAWARE; ▲ North Salem; *209 NM-15; mail East Branch z 13756; ● 45
Pearl Creek; RMC Place; WYOMING; ▲ Covington; 208 NJ-6; elev. 955ft./291m.; mail Wyoming z 14591; ● 150
Pearl River; CDP; ROCKLAND; ▲ Orangetown; 207 SE-6; 🅿; ★ N.Y.; z 10965; Ⓟ 15,314; © 15,553
Peas Eddy; RMC Place; DELAWARE; ▲ Hancock; *209 NN-14; elev. 940ft./287m.; mail Hancock z 13783; rural
Peasleeville; RMC Place; CLINTON; ▲ Peru; 209 NC-19; elev. 731ft./223m.; ★ PLATT; mail Schuyler Falls z 12985; ● 400
Peat Corners; RMC Place; OSWEGO; ▲ Palermo; *209 NH-11; elev. 482ft./147m.; ★ SYR; mail Central Square z 13036; rural
Pebble Beach; RMC Place; LIVINGSTON; ▲ Livonia; *208 NJ-7; ★ ROCH; mail Lakeville z 14480
Peck Slip; RMC Place; NEW YORK; 🅿; ★ N.Y.; z 10038 & mail New York z 10272; pop. incl. with New York (Inc. Place)
Pecksville; RMC Place; DUTCHESS; mail Holmes z 12531; ● 500
Pecktown; OTSEGO; see Pittsfield (RMC Place)
Peconic; CDP; SUFFOLK; ▲ Southold; 207 SD-12; 🅿; z 11958; Ⓟ 1,100; summer pop. 2,000; © 1,081
Peekskill; Inc. Place; WESTCHESTER; 207 SC-7; elev. 132ft./40m.; 🅿 🅷 ■; ★ N.Y.; z 10566 & mail Cortlandt Manor z 10567; Ⓟ 19,536; © 22,441; ◆ 23,953
Pekin; RMC Place; NIAGARA; ▲ Lewiston, Cambria; 208 NH-3; ★ BUF; mail Sanborn z 14132; ● 250
Pelham; Inc. Place; WESTCHESTER; ▲ Pelham; 211 C-14; 🅿; ★ N.Y.; z 10803; Ⓟ 6,413; © 6,400
Pelham; MCD-Town; WESTCHESTER; *207 SE-7; 🅿; ★ N.Y.; z 10803; Ⓟ 11,903; © 11,866
Pelham Manor; Inc. Place; WESTCHESTER; ▲ Pelham; 211 C-14; ★ N.Y.; mail Pelham z 10803; Ⓟ 5,443; © 5,466
Pellets Island; RMC Place; ORANGE; ▲ Goshen; *207 SC-5; ★ N.Y.; mail New Hampton z 10958; ● 50
Pembroke; RMC Place; GENESEE; ▲ Pembroke; 208 NI-5; elev. 845ft./258m.; mail Corfu z 14036; ● 200
Pembroke; MCD-Town; GENESEE; *208 NI-5; mail Corfu z 14036; Ⓟ 4,232; © 4,530
Penataquit; RMC Place; SUFFOLK; ▲ Islip; *207 SF-9; ★ N.Y.; mail Bay Shore z 11706
Pendleton; RMC Place; NIAGARA; ▲ Pendleton; 208 NI-4; ★ BUF; mail Lockport z 14094, North Tonawanda z 14120, Sanborn z 14132; ● 300
Pendleton; MCD-Town; NIAGARA; *208 NI-4; ★ BUF; mail Lockport z 14094, North Tonawanda z 14120, Sanborn z 14132; Ⓟ 5,010; © 6,050
Pendleton Center; RMC Place; NIAGARA; ▲ Pendleton; 208 NB-5; ★ BUF; mail Lockport z 14094; ● 120
Penfield; RMC Place; MONROE; ▲ Penfield; 208 NI-8; 🅿; ★ ROCH; z 14526; ● 6,300
Penfield; MCD-Town; MONROE; *208 NI-8; 🅿; ★ ROCH; z 14526; Ⓟ 30,219; © 34,645; ◆ 35,845
Pennellville; RMC Place; OSWEGO; ▲ Schroeppel; 209 NH-11; 🅿; ★ SYR; z 13132; ● 400
Penn Yan; Inc. Place; ⊡ YATES; ▲ Jerusalem, Benton, Milo; 208 NK-9; elev. 737ft./225m.; 🅿 🅷; z 14527; Ⓟ 5,248; © 5,219
Peoria; RMC Place; WYOMING; ▲ Covington; *208 NJ-6; elev. 1,148ft./350m.; mail Pavilion z 14525; ● 85
Perch River; RMC Place; JEFFERSON; ▲ Brownville; *209 NE-12; elev. 348ft./106m.; ★ WATN; mail Dexter z 13634, Watertown z 13601
Perinton; MCD-Town; MONROE; *208 NI-8; ★ ROCH; mail Fairport z 14450; Ⓟ 43,015; © 46,090; ◆ 44,939
Perkinsville; RMC Place; STEUBEN; ▲ Wayland; 208 NK-7; 🅿; z 14529; ● 400
Perry; Inc. Place; WYOMING; ▲ Castile, Perry; 208 NJ-6; elev. 1,363ft./415m.; 🅿; z 14530; Ⓟ 4,219; © 3,945
Perry; MCD-Town; WYOMING; *208 NJ-6; 🅿; z 14530; includes part of the Village of Perry; Ⓟ 5,353; © 6,654; Ⓡ 4,876
Perry Center; RMC Place; WYOMING; ▲ Perry; 208 NJ-6; elev. 1,394ft./425m.; mail Perry z 14530; ● 100
Perry City; RMC Place; SCHUYLER; ▲ Hector; *208 NK-10; elev. 1,027ft./313m.; mail Trumansburg z 14886; rural
Perrysburg; Inc. Place; CATTARAUGUS; ▲ Perrysburg; 208 NK-3; 🅿; z 14129; Ⓟ 404; © 408
Perrysburg; MCD-Town; CATTARAUGUS; *208 NK-3; 🅿; z 14129; Ⓟ 1,838; © 1,771
Perrys Mills; RMC Place; CLINTON; ▲ Champlain; *209 NA-19; mail Champlain z 12919; ● 125
Perryville; RMC Place; MADISON; ▲ Fenner, Lincoln, Sullivan; 209 NI-13; 🅿; z 13032; ● 250
Persia; MCD-Town; CATTARAUGUS; *208 NL-3; mail Gowanda z 14070; Ⓟ 2,530; © 2,512
Perth; RMC Place; FULTON; ▲ Perth; 209 NI-18; ★ A-S-T; mail Amsterdam z 12010; ● 400
Perth; MCD-Town; FULTON; *209 NI-17; ★ A-S-T; mail Amsterdam z 12010; Ⓟ 3,377; © 3,638
Peru; CDP; CLINTON; ▲ Peru; 209 NC-19; 🅿; ★ PLATT; z 12972; Ⓟ 1,565; © 1,514
Peru; MCD-Town; CLINTON; *209 NC-19; 🅿; ★ PLATT; z 12972; Ⓟ 6,254; © 6,370
Peru; RMC Place; ONONDAGA; ▲ Elbridge; *209 NI-11; elev. 418ft./127m.; ★ SYR; mail Memphis z 13112; rural
Peruville; RMC Place; TOMPKINS; ▲ Groton; 209 NK-11; ★ ITH; mail Groton z 13073; ● 150
Peterboro; RMC Place; MADISON; ▲ Smithfield; 209 NI-13; 🅿; z 13134; ● 400
Petersburg (Petersburgh); RMC Place; RENSSELAER; ▲ Petersburgh; 209 NJ-20; 🅿; z 12138; ● 600
Petersburgh; RENSSELAER; see Petersburg (RMC Place)
Petersburgh; MCD-Town; RENSSELAER; *209 NJ-20; 🅿; z 12138; Ⓟ 1,461; © 1,563
Peter Stuyvesant; RMC Place; NEW YORK; ★ N.Y.; mail New York z 10009; pop. incl. with New York (Inc. Place)
Peth; RMC Place; CATTARAUGUS; *208 NL-4; elev. 1,443ft./440m.; mail Great Valley z 14741; rural
Petries Corners; RMC Place; LEWIS; ▲ Watson; *209 NF-14; mail Lowville z 13367; rural
Petrolla; RMC Place; ALLEGANY; ▲ Scio; 208 NM-6; mail Wellsville z 14895; ● 70
Pharsalia; MCD-Town; CHENANGO; *209 NK-13; mail East Pharsalia z 13758; Ⓟ 735; © 542
Phelps; Inc. Place; ONTARIO; ▲ Phelps; 208 NI-9; 🅿; z 14532; Ⓟ 1,978; © 1,969
Phelps; MCD-Town; ONTARIO; *208 NI-9; 🅿; z 14532; Ⓟ 6,749; © 7,017
Philadelphia; Inc. Place; JEFFERSON; ▲ Philadelphia; 209 ND-13; elev. 490ft./149m.; 🅿; z 13673; Ⓟ 1,478; © 1,519
Philadelphia; MCD-Town; JEFFERSON; *209 NE-13; 🅿; z 13673; Ⓟ 2,136; © 2,140
Philipse Manor; RMC Place; WESTCHESTER; *207 SD-7; ★ N.Y.; mail Tarrytown z 10591; pop. incl. with Sleepy Hollow (Inc. Place)
Philipstown; MCD-Town; PUTNAM; *207 SC-7; ★ N.Y.; mail Cold Spring z 10516; Ⓟ 9,242; © 9,422
Phillipsburg; RMC Place; ORANGE; ▲ Wallkill; *207 SC-5; elev. 365ft./111m.; ★ MIDD; mail Middletown z 10940; rural
Phillips Creek; RMC Place; ALLEGANY; ▲ Ward; 208 NL-6; elev. 1,855ft./565m.; mail Belmont z 14813; ● 70
Phillips Mills; RMC Place; CHAUTAUQUA; ▲ Ellery; *208 NM-2; ★ JMST; mail Bemus Point z 14712; ● 150
Phillipsport; RMC Place; SULLIVAN; ▲ Mamakating; 207 SB-5; 🅿; z 12769; ● 400
Philmont; Inc. Place; COLUMBIA; ▲ Claverack; 209 NL-19; 🅿; z 12565; Ⓟ 1,623; © 1,480
Phoenicia; CDP; ULSTER; ▲ Shandaken; 209 NM-17; 🅿; z 12464; © 381
Phoenix; Inc. Place; OSWEGO; ▲ Schroeppel; 209 NH-11; 🅿; ★ SYR; z 13135; Ⓟ 2,435; © 2,251
Phoenix Mills; RMC Place; OTSEGO; ▲ Otsego, Middlefield; *209 NK-15; mail Cooperstown z 13326; ● 45
Picketts Corners; RMC Place; CLINTON; ▲ Saranac; 209 NB-19; elev. 776ft./237m.; mail Saranac z 12981; ● 200
Pickettsville; RMC Place; ST. LAWRENCE; ▲ Parishville; *209 NC-16; mail Parishville z 13672; rural
Piercefield; RMC Place; ST. LAWRENCE; ▲ Piercefield; 209 ND-16; elev. 1,580ft./482m.; 🅿; z 12973; ● 200
Piercefield; MCD-Town; ST. LAWRENCE; *209 ND-16; 🅿; z 12973; Ⓟ 285; © 305
Pierces Corner; RMC Place; ST. LAWRENCE; ▲ Macomb; *209 NC-13; mail Gouverneur z 13642; rural
Pierceville; RMC Place; MADISON; ▲ Eaton; *209 NJ-13; mail Eaton z 13334
Piermont; Inc. Place; ROCKLAND; ▲ Orangetown; *207 SE-7; 🅿; ★ N.Y.; z 10968; Ⓟ 2,163; © 2,607
Pierrepont; RMC Place; ST. LAWRENCE; ▲ Pierrepont; 209 NC-15; mail Canton z 13617; ● 100
Pierrepont; MCD-Town; ST. LAWRENCE; *209 NC-15; mail Canton z 13617; Ⓟ 2,375; © 2,674
Pierrepont Manor; RMC Place; JEFFERSON; ▲ Ellisburg; 209 NF-12; 🅿; z 13674; ● 300
Pierstown; RMC Place; OTSEGO; ▲ Otsego; *209 NJ-16; mail Cooperstown z 13326; rural
Piffard; RMC Place; LIVINGSTON; ▲ York; 208 NJ-7; elev. 569ft./173m.; 🅿; ★ ROCH; z 14533; ● 400
Pike; Inc. Place; WYOMING; ▲ Pike; 208 NK-6; elev. 1,551ft./473m.; 🅿; z 14130; Ⓟ 384; © 382
Pike; MCD-Town; WYOMING; *208 NK-6; 🅿; z 14130; Ⓟ 1,081; © 1,086
Pike Five Corners; RMC Place; WYOMING; ▲ Pike; *208 NK-6; elev. 1,595ft./486m.; mail Bliss z 14024; rural
Pilgrim; RMC Place; BRONX; ★ N.Y.; mail Bronx z 10461; pop. incl. with New York (Inc. Place)
Pilgrim Corners; RMC Place; ORANGE; *207 SC-5; ★ MIDD; mail Middletown z 10940
Pilgrimport; RMC Place; WAYNE; ▲ Lyons; *208 NI-9; elev. 422ft./129m.; mail Lyons z 14489; rural
Pilgrim Psychiatric Center; SUFFOLK; see West Brentwood (RMC Place)
Pillar Point; RMC Place; JEFFERSON; ▲ Brownville; *209 NE-12; mail Dexter z 13634
Pilot Knob; RMC Place; WASHINGTON; ▲ Fort Ann; *209 NG-19; 🅿; z 12844; ● 300
Pinckney; MCD-Town; LEWIS; *209 NF-13; mail Copenhagen z 13626; Ⓟ 323; © 319
Pindars Corners; RMC Place; DELAWARE; *209 NL-15; mail West Davenport z 13860; rural
Pine; RMC Place; ALBANY; ★ A-S-T; mail Albany z 12203; pop. incl. with Albany (Inc. Place)
Pine Aire; RMC Place; SUFFOLK; ▲ Islip; *207 SF-9; ★ N.Y.; mail Bay Shore z 11706
Pinebrook; RMC Place; WESTCHESTER; *207 SE-7; ★ N.Y.; mail New Rochelle z 10804; pop. incl. with New Rochelle (Inc. Place)
Pinebrook Heights; RMC Place; WESTCHESTER; *207 SE-7; ★ N.Y.; mail New Rochelle z 10804; pop. incl. with New Rochelle (Inc. Place)
Pine Bush; CDP; ORANGE; ▲ Crawford; 207 SB-5; elev. 396ft./121m.; 🅿; z 12566; Ⓟ 1,445; © 1,539
Pine City; RMC Place; CHEMUNG; ▲ Southport; 208 NM-9; elev. 1,002ft./305m.; 🅿; ★ ELM; z 14871; ● 420
Pine Grove; RMC Place; LEWIS; ▲ Watson; *209 NF-14; mail Glenfield z 13343; rural
Pine Grove; RMC Place; SCHOHARIE; ▲ Middleburgh; *209 NK-17; elev. 1,820ft./555m.; mail Middleburgh z 12122; rural
Pine Grove; RMC Place; ST. LAWRENCE; ▲ Lisbon; *209 NB-14; mail Lisbon z 13658; rural
Pinegrove Park; RMC Place; ALBANY; ▲ Colonie; ★ A-S-T; mail Albany z 12205
Pine Hill; RMC Place; ERIE; ▲ Cheektowaga; *208 NJ-4; ★ BUF; mail Buffalo z 14225
Pine Hill; RMC Place; ONEIDA; ▲ Annsville; *209 NH-13; elev. 718ft./219m.; mail Taberg z 13471; rural
Pine Hill; CDP; ULSTER; ▲ Shandaken; *209 NM-17; 🅿; z 12465; © 308
Pinehill Estates; RMC Place; ALBANY; ▲ Guilderland; *209 NJ-18; elev. 300ft./91m.; ★ A-S-T; mail Schenectady z 12303; ● 850
Pinehurst; RMC Place; ERIE; ▲ Hamburg; *208 NJ-3; ★ BUF; mail Lake View z 14085; ● 1,850
Pine Island; RMC Place; ORANGE; ▲ Warwick; 207 SD-5; elev. 406ft./124m.; 🅿; ★ N.Y.; z 10969; ● 1,500
Pine Knolls; RMC Place; TIOGA; ▲ Owego; *209 NM-12; ★ BING; mail Endicott z 13760
Pine Lake; RMC Place; FULTON; ▲ Caroga; 209 NH-17; mail Caroga Lake z 12032; ● 25
Pine Meadows; RMC Place; OSWEGO; ▲ Albion; *209 NG-12; mail Altmar z 13302; ● 55
Pine Neck; RMC Place; SUFFOLK; ▲ Southampton; *207 SE-12; mail Sag Harbor z 11963
Pine Plains; CDP; DUTCHESS; ▲ Pine Plains; 209 NM-19; elev. 474ft./144m.; 🅿; z 12567; Ⓟ 1,312; © 1,412
Pine Plains; MCD-Town; DUTCHESS; *209 NM-19; 🅿; z 12567; Ⓟ 2,287; © 2,569
Pine Ridge Estates; RMC Place; WESTCHESTER; ▲ Rye; *207 SE-8; ★ N.Y.; mail Port Chester z 10573; pop. incl. with Rye Brook (Inc. Place)
Pinesville; RMC Place; DELAWARE; ▲ Walton; *209 NM-15; mail Walton z 13856; rural
Pine Tavern Corners; RMC Place; LIVINGSTON; ▲ Leicester; *208 NJ-6; mail Leicester z 14481; rural
Pine Valley; RMC Place; CHEMUNG; ▲ Veteran, Catlin; 208 NL-10; 🅿; ★ ELM; z 14872; ● 625
Pine Valley; RMC Place; SUFFOLK; ▲ Southampton; *207 SE-11; mail Riverhead z 11901; ● 1,450
Pineville; RMC Place; OSWEGO; ▲ Albion; *209 NG-12; elev. 545ft./166m.; mail Altmar z 13302, Walton z 13856; rural
Pinewood Estates; RMC Place; ALBANY; ▲ Guilderland; *209 NJ-18; elev. 281ft./86m.; ★ A-S-T; mail Schenectady z 12303; ● 525
Pine Woods; RMC Place; MADISON; ▲ Eaton; *209 NJ-13; mail Bouckville z 13310; ● 60
Pioneer; RMC Place; SARATOGA; ▲ Milton; ★ A-S-T; mail Ballston Spa z 12020; rural
Piseco; RMC Place; HAMILTON; ▲ Arietta; 209 NG-17; 🅿; z 12139; ● 200
Pitcairn; RMC Place; ST. LAWRENCE; ▲ Pitcairn; 209 ND-14; elev. 782ft./238m.; mail Harrisville z 13648; ● 125
Pitcairn; MCD-Town; ST. LAWRENCE; *209 ND-14; mail Harrisville z 13648; Ⓟ 751; © 783
Pitcher; RMC Place; CHENANGO; ▲ Pitcher; 209 NK-13; 🅿; z 13136; ● 200
Pitcher; MCD-Town; CHENANGO; *209 NK-13; 🅿; z 13136; Ⓟ 751; © 848
Pitcher Hill; RMC Place; ONONDAGA; ▲ Salina, Clay; 208 NE-8; ★ SYR; mail Syracuse z 13212; ● 5,000
Pittsfield (Pecktown); RMC Place; OTSEGO; ▲ Pittsfield; 209 NK-14; mail New Berlin z 13411; ● 100
Pittsfield; MCD-Town; OTSEGO; *209 NK-14; mail New Berlin z 13411; Ⓟ 1,116; © 1,295
Pittsford; Inc. Place; MONROE; ▲ Pittsford; 208 NI-8; 🅿; ★ ROCH; z 14534; Ⓟ 1,488; © 1,418
Pittsford; MCD-Town; MONROE; *208 NI-8; 🅿; ★ ROCH; z 14534; Ⓟ 24,497; © 27,219; ◆ 27,623
Pittstown; RMC Place; RENSSELAER; ▲ Pittstown; 209 NJ-20; ★ A-S-T; mail Johnsonville z 12094; ● 100
Pittstown; MCD-Town; RENSSELAER; *209 NJ-20; ★ A-S-T; mail Johnsonville z 12094; Ⓟ 5,468; © 5,644
Place Corners; RMC Place; GREENE; ▲ Greenville; *209 NL-18; elev. 620ft./189m.; mail Freehold z 12431; rural
Plainedge; CDP; NASSAU; ▲ Oyster Bay; *207 SF-8; ★ N.Y.; mail Bethpage z 11714, Levittown z 11756, Seaford z 11783, Shoreham z 11786; Ⓟ 8,739; © 9,195
Plainfield; MCD-Town; OTSEGO; *209 NJ-16; mail West Winfield z 13491; Ⓟ 850; © 986
Plainfield Center; RMC Place; OTSEGO; ▲ Plainfield; *209 NJ-16; elev. 1,756ft./535m.; mail West Winfield z 13491; rural
Plainview; CDP; NASSAU; ▲ Oyster Bay; 207 SF-8; elev. 151ft./46m.; 🅿 🅷; ★ N.Y.; z 11803; Ⓟ 26,207; © 25,637; ◆ 24,347
Plainville; RMC Place; ONONDAGA; ▲ Lysander; *209 NI-11; elev. 486ft./148m.; 🅿; ★ SYR; z 13137; ● 450
Plandome; Inc. Place; NASSAU; ▲ North Hempstead; 211 F-16; 🅿; ★ N.Y.; z 11030; Ⓟ 1,347; © 1,272
Plandome Heights; Inc. Place; NASSAU; ▲ North Hempstead; 211 F-16; elev. 90ft./27m.; ★ N.Y.; mail Manhasset z 11030; Ⓟ 852; © 971
Plandome Manor; Inc. Place; NASSAU; ▲ North Hempstead; 211 F-16; ★ N.Y.; mail Manhasset z 11030; Ⓟ 790; © 838
Planetarium; RMC Place; NEW YORK; ★ N.Y.; mail New York z 10024; pop. incl. with New York (Inc. Place)
Plato; RMC Place; CATTARAUGUS; ▲ Ellicottville, East Otto; *208 NL-4; elev. 1,894ft./577m.; mail West Valley z 14171; ● 30
Platt Clove; GREENE; see Platte Clove (RMC Place)
Platte Clove (Platt Clove); RMC Place; GREENE; ▲ Hunter; *209 NM-18; mail Elka Park z 12427; ● 200
Plattekill; CDP; ULSTER; ▲ Plattekill; 207 SB-6; elev. 566ft./173m.; 🅿; ★ NWBG; z 12568; © 1,050
Plattekill; MCD-Town; ULSTER; *207 SB-6; 🅿; ★ NWBG; z 12568; Ⓟ 8,891; © 9,892
Platten; RMC Place; ORLEANS; ▲ Yates, Carlton; *208 NH-5; elev. 350ft./107m.; mail Lyndonville z 14098; rural
Plattsburgh; Inc. Place; ⊡ CLINTON; 209 NB-20; elev. 135ft./41m.; 🅿 🅷 🅲 6,217 ■; ★ PLATT; z 12901, z 12903; Ⓟ 21,255; © 18,816; ◆ 19,396
Plattsburgh; MCD-Town; CLINTON; *209 NB-19; 🅿 🅲 6,217; ★ PLATT; z 12901, z 12903 & mail Cadyville z 12918; does not include the City of Plattsburgh; Ⓟ 17,231; © 11,190
Plattsburgh West; CDP-Census Area Only; CLINTON; ▲ Plattsburgh; 209 NB-19; ★ PLATT; mail Morrisonville z 12962; Ⓟ 1,274; © 1,289
Pleasantbrook; RMC Place; OTSEGO; ▲ Roseboom; *209 NJ-16; elev. 1,331ft./406m.; mail Cherry Valley z 13320; ● 55
Pleasantdale; RMC Place; RENSSELAER; ▲ Schaghticoke; *209 NJ-19; ★ A-S-T; mail Troy z 12182; ● 1,260
Pleasant Plains; RMC Place; DUTCHESS; ▲ Clinton; *207 SA-7; elev. 375ft./114m.; ★ POK; mail Staatsburg z 12580; ● 200
Pleasant Plains; RMC Place; RICHMOND; 210 M-5; ★ N.Y.; mail Staten Island z 10309; pop. incl. with New York (Inc. Place)
Pleasant Point; RMC Place; OSWEGO; ▲ New Haven; mail Oswego z 13126
Pleasant Ridge; RMC Place; DUTCHESS; *207 SB-8; mail Wingdale z 12594; rural
Pleasantside; RMC Place; WESTCHESTER; ▲ Cortlandt; *207 SD-7; elev. 400ft./122m.; ★ N.Y.; mail Cortlandt Manor z 10567; ● 70
Pleasant Valley; CDP; DUTCHESS; ▲ Pleasant Valley; 207 SA-7; 🅿; ★ POK; z 12569; Ⓟ 1,688; © 1,839
Pleasant Valley; MCD-Town; DUTCHESS; *207 SA-7; 🅿; ★ POK; z 12569; Ⓟ 8,063; © 9,066
Pleasant Valley; RMC Place; ONEIDA; ▲ Sangerfield; *209 NJ-14; mail Waterville z 13480; rural
Pleasant Valley; RMC Place; STEUBEN; ▲ Urbana; *208 NL-8; mail Bath z 14810, Hammondsport z 14840; ● 200
Pleasantville; Inc. Place; WESTCHESTER; ▲ Mount Pleasant; 207 SD-7; elev. 304ft./93m.; 🅿; ★ N.Y.; z 10570-72; Ⓟ 6,592; © 7,172
Plessis; RMC Place; JEFFERSON; ▲ Alexandria; 209 ND-13; elev. 405ft./123m.; 🅿; z 13675; ● 320
Plymouth; RMC Place; CHENANGO; ▲ Plymouth; 209 NK-13; 🅿; z 13832; ● 400
Plymouth; MCD-Town; CHENANGO; *209 NK-13; 🅿; z 13832; Ⓟ 1,704; © 2,049
Pocantico Hills; RMC Place; WESTCHESTER; ▲ Mount Pleasant; *207 SD-7; ★ N.Y.; mail Tarrytown z 10591; ● 300
Podunk; RMC Place; TOMPKINS; ▲ Ulysses; *208 NK-10; ★ ITH; mail Trumansburg z 14886; rural
Poestenkill; CDP; RENSSELAER; ▲ Poestenkill; 209 NJ-19; elev. 484ft./148m.; 🅿; ★ A-S-T; z 12140; Ⓟ 1,000; © 1,024
Poestenkill; MCD-Town; RENSSELAER; *209 NJ-20; 🅿; ★ A-S-T; z 12140; Ⓟ 3,809; © 4,054
Point Au Rouche; RMC Place; CLINTON; ▲ Beekmantown; *209 NB-20; ★ PLATT; mail Plattsburgh z 12901; ● 550
Point Breeze; RMC Place; ORLEANS; ▲ Carlton; *208 NH-6; elev. 261ft./80m.; mail Kent z 14477; ● 150
Point Chautauqua; RMC Place; CHAUTAUQUA; ▲ Chautauqua; 208 NL-2; mail Dewittville z 14728; ● 150
Point Lookout; CDP; NASSAU; ▲ Hempstead; 211 K-19; 🅿; ★ N.Y.; z 11569; © 1,472
Point O'Woods; RMC Place; SUFFOLK; ▲ Islip; *207 SG-10; 🅿; ★ N.Y.; z 11706; summer pop. 600; ● 10
Point Peninsula; RMC Place; JEFFERSON; ▲ Lyme; *209 NE-11; elev. 251ft./77m.; mail Three Mile Bay z 13693; ● 250
Point Pleasant; RMC Place; MONROE; ▲ Irondequoit; ★ ROCH; mail Rochester z 14622
Point Rochester; RMC Place; ONTARIO; ▲ Canandaigua; mail Naples z 14512
Point Rock; RMC Place; ONEIDA; ▲ Lee; *209 NH-13; elev. 1,016ft./310m.; ★ UT-R; mail Taberg z 13471; ● 60
Point Stockholm; RMC Place; CHAUTAUQUA; ▲ Ellery; *208 NM-2; ★ JMST; mail Bemus Point z 14712; rural
Point Vivian; RMC Place; JEFFERSON; ▲ Alexandria; *209 ND-12; 🅿; z 13607; ● 130
Poland; MCD-Town; CHAUTAUQUA; *208 NM-3; ★ JMST; mail Kennedy z 14747; Ⓟ 2,604; © 2,467
Poland; Inc. Place; HERKIMER; ▲ Newport, Russia; 209 NH-15; 🅿; z 13431; Ⓟ 444; © 451; Ⓡ 461
Poland Center; RMC Place; CHAUTAUQUA; ▲ Poland; *208 NM-3; elev. 1,275ft./389m.; ★ JMST; mail Kennedy z 14747
Polkville; RMC Place; CORTLAND; ▲ Cortlandville; mail Mc Graw z 13101; ● 40
Pomfret; MCD-Town; CHAUTAUQUA; *208 NL-2; 🅲 5,406; mail Fredonia z 14063; Ⓟ 14,224; © 14,703
Pomona; Inc. Place; ROCKLAND; ▲ Ramapo; 207 SD-6; 🅿 🅷; ★ N.Y.; z 10970; Ⓟ 2,611; © 2,726
Pomona Heights; RMC Place; ROCKLAND; *207 SD-6; elev. 576ft./176m.; ★ N.Y.; mail Suffern z 10901; pop. incl. with Pomona (Inc. Place)
Pomonok; RMC Place; QUEENS; ★ N.Y.; mail Fresh Meadows z 11365; pop. incl. with New York (Inc. Place)
Pompey; RMC Place; ONONDAGA; ▲ Pompey; 209 NJ-12; elev. 1,673ft./510m.; 🅿; ★ SYR; z 13138; ● 500
Pompey; MCD-Town; ONONDAGA; *209 NJ-12; 🅿; ★ SYR; z 13138; Ⓟ 5,317; © 6,159
Pompey Center; RMC Place; ONONDAGA; ▲ Pompey; *209 NJ-12; elev. 1,241ft./378m.; ★ SYR; mail Manlius z 13104; ● 60
Ponck Hockie; RMC Place; ULSTER; *209 NN-18; ★ KNGST; mail Kingston z 12401; pop. incl. with Kingston (Inc. Place)
Pond Eddy; RMC Place; SULLIVAN; ▲ Lumberland; 207 SC-3; 🅿; z 12770; ● 350
Ponquogue; RMC Place; SUFFOLK; ▲ Southampton; *207 SE-12; mail Hampton Bays z 11946
Poolsburg; RMC Place; COLUMBIA; ▲ Stuyvesant; *209 NK-19; ★ A-S-T; mail Stuyvesant z 12173; rural
Poolville; RMC Place; MADISON; ▲ Hamilton; 209 NJ-14; 🅿; z 13332; ● 250
Poospatuck Reservation; Indian Reservation; SUFFOLK; ★ N.Y.; mail Mastic z 11950; State Reservation; Ⓟ 203; © 283
Pope Mills; RMC Place; ST. LAWRENCE; ▲ Macomb; *209 NC-13; elev. 283ft./86m.; mail Heuvelton z 13654
Popes Ravine; RMC Place; BROOME; *209 NM-13; ★ BING
Poplar Beach; RMC Place; SENECA; ▲ Romulus; *208 NJ-10; mail Romulus z 14541; rural
Poplar Ridge; RMC Place; CAYUGA; ▲ Venice; *208 NJ-10; 🅿; z 13139; ● 180
Poquott; Inc. Place; SUFFOLK; ▲ Brookhaven; 207 SE-10; ★ N.Y.; mail East Setauket z 11733; Ⓟ 770; © 975
Portage; RMC Place; LIVINGSTON; ▲ Portage; *208 NK-6; mail Hunt z 14846; ● 70
Portage; MCD-Town; LIVINGSTON; *208 NK-6; mail Hunt z 14846; Ⓟ 893; © 859
Portageville; RMC Place; WYOMING; ▲ Genesee Falls; 208 NK-6; 🅿; z 14536; ● 300
Port Authority; RMC Place; NEW YORK; ★ N.Y.; mail New York z 10011; pop. incl. with New York (Inc. Place)
Port Ben (East Wawarsing); RMC Place; ULSTER; ▲ Wawarsing; *207 SA-5; mail Wawarsing z 12489; rural
Port Byron; Inc. Place; CAYUGA; ▲ Mentz; 208 NI-10; 🅿; ★ SYR; z 13140; Ⓟ 1,359; © 1,297
Port Chester; Inc. Place; WESTCHESTER; ▲ Rye; 207 SE-8; 🅿 🅷 ■; ★ N.Y.; z 10573; Ⓟ 24,728; © 27,867; ◆ 28,580
Port Crane; RMC Place; BROOME; ▲ Fenton; *209 NM-13; 🅿; ★ BING; z 13833; ● 700
Port Dickinson; Inc. Place; BROOME; ▲ Dickinson; 209 NM-12; ★ BING; mail Binghamton z 13901; Ⓟ 1,785; © 1,697
Port Douglas (Douglass); RMC Place; ESSEX; ▲ Chesterfield; *209 NC-20; mail Keeseville z 12944
Porter; MCD-Town; NIAGARA; *208 NH-3; ★ BUF; mail Ransomville z 14131; Ⓟ 7,110; © 6,920
Porter Center; RMC Place; NIAGARA; ▲ Porter; *208 NH-3; elev. 309ft./94m.; ★ BUF; mail Ransomville z 14131
Porter Corners; RMC Place; SARATOGA; ▲ Greenfield; 209 NI-18; 🅿; ★ A-S-T; z 12859; ● 350
Porterville; RMC Place; ERIE; ▲ Marilla; *208 NJ-4; elev. 940ft./287m.; ★ BUF; mail East Aurora z 14052; rural
Port Ewen; CDP; ULSTER; ▲ Esopus; 209 NN-18; 🅿; ★ KNGST; z 12466; Ⓟ 3,444; © 3,650
Port Gibson; RMC Place; ONTARIO; ▲ Manchester; 208 NI-9; 🅿; z 14537; ● 500
Port Henry; Inc. Place; ESSEX; ▲ Moriah; 209 NE-20; elev. 108ft./33m.; 🅿; z 12974; Ⓟ 1,263; © 1,152
Port Ivory; RMC Place; RICHMOND; *207 SG-6; elev. 14ft./4m.; ★ N.Y.; mail Staten Island z 10303; pop. incl. with New York (Inc. Place)
Port Jefferson; Inc. Place; SUFFOLK; ▲ Brookhaven; 207 SE-10; elev. 12ft./4m.; 🅿 🅷; ★ N.Y.; z 11777 & mail Port Jefferson Station z 11776; Ⓟ 7,455; © 7,837
Port Jefferson; SUFFOLK; see Port Jefferson Station (CDP)
Port Jefferson Station (Port Jefferson); CDP; SUFFOLK; ▲ Brookhaven; *207 SE-10; 🅿; ★ N.Y.; z 11776-77; Ⓟ 7,232; © 7,527
Port Jervis; Inc. Place; ORANGE; 207 SC-4; elev. 442ft./135m.; 🅿 🅷; z 12771, z 12785; Ⓟ 9,060; © 8,860
Port Kent; RMC Place; ESSEX; ▲ Chesterfield; 209 NC-20; elev. 137ft./42m.; 🅿; z 12975; ● 250
Portland; RMC Place; CHAUTAUQUA; ▲ Portland; 208 NL-2; elev. 760ft./232m.; 🅿; z 14769; ● 950
Portland; MCD-Town; CHAUTAUQUA; *208 NL-2; 🅿; z 14769; Ⓟ 4,832; © 5,502
Portlandville; RMC Place; OTSEGO; ▲ Milford; 209 NK-15; 🅿; z 13834; ● 300
Port Leyden; Inc. Place; LEWIS; ▲ Lyonsdale, Leyden; 209 NG-14; 🅿; z 13433; Ⓟ 723; © 665
Port Morris; RMC Place; BRONX; *207 SF-7; ★ N.Y.; mail Bronx z 10454; pop. incl. with New York (Inc. Place)
Port Ontario; RMC Place; OSWEGO; ▲ Richland; *209 NG-12; elev. 265ft./81m.; mail Pulaski z 13142
Port Richmond; RMC Place; RICHMOND; 210 J-7; ★ N.Y.; mail Staten Island z 10302; pop. incl. with New York (Inc. Place)
Portville; Inc. Place; CATTARAUGUS; ▲ Portville; 208 NM-5; 🅿; z 14770; Ⓟ 1,040; © 1,024
Portville; MCD-Town; CATTARAUGUS; *208 NM-5; 🅿; z 14770; Ⓟ 4,397; © 3,952
Port Washington; CDP; NASSAU; ▲ North Hempstead; 207 SF-8; 🅿; ★ N.Y.; z 11050-55; Ⓟ 15,387; © 15,215
Port Washington North; Inc. Place; NASSAU; ▲ North Hempstead; 211 E-16; ■; ★ N.Y.; mail Port Washington z 11050; Ⓟ 2,736; © 2,700; ◆ 2,517
Post Corners; RMC Place; WASHINGTON; ▲ White Creek; *209 NI-20; elev. 528ft./161m.; mail Eagle Bridge z 12057; ● 50
Post Creek; RMC Place; CHEMUNG; ▲ Catlin; 208 NL-9; elev. 1,191ft./363m.; mail Beaver Dams z 14812; ● 100
Potsdam; Inc. Place; ST. LAWRENCE; ▲ Potsdam; 209 NB-15; 🅿 🅷 🅲 7,300; z 13676, z 13699; Ⓟ 10,251; © 9,425; Ⓡ 9,413
Potsdam; MCD-Town; ST. LAWRENCE; *209 NB-15; 🅿 🅲 7,300; z 13676, z 13699; Ⓟ 16,822; © 15,957; Ⓡ 15,945
Potter; RMC Place; YATES; ▲ Potter; 208 NJ-8; mail Penn Yan z 14527; ● 135
Potter; MCD-Town; YATES; *208 NJ-9; mail Penn Yan z 14527; Ⓟ 1,617; © 1,830
Potter Hollow; RMC Place; ALBANY; ▲ Rensselaerville; *209 NL-17; mail Preston Hollow z 12469; ● 65
Pottersville; RMC Place; WARREN; ▲ Chester; 209 NF-19; elev. 822ft./251m.; 🅿; z 12860; ● 750
Poughkeepsie; Inc. Place; ⊡ DUTCHESS; 207 SB-7; elev. 209ft./64m.; 🅿 🅷 🅲 8,239 ■; ★ POK; z 12601-04; Ⓟ 28,844; © 29,871; ◆ 29,870
Poughkeepsie; MCD-Town; DUTCHESS; *207 SB-7; 🅿 🅲 8,239; ★ POK; z 12601-04; does not include the City of Poughkeepsie; Ⓟ 40,143; © 42,777; ◆ 42,330
Poughquag; RMC Place; DUTCHESS; ▲ Beekman; 207 SB-7; elev. 429ft./131m.; 🅿; z 12570; ● 450
Pound Ridge; RMC Place; WESTCHESTER; ▲ Pound Ridge; 207 SD-8; 🅿; ★ N.Y.; z 10576; ● 1,000
Pound Ridge; MCD-Town; WESTCHESTER; *207 SD-8; 🅿; ★ N.Y.; z 10576; Ⓟ 4,550; © 4,726
Pratt; RMC Place; KINGS; ★ N.Y.; mail Brooklyn z 11205; pop. incl. with New York (Inc. Place)
Pratt Corners; RMC Place; CORTLAND; ▲ Homer; *209 NK-12; elev. 1,157ft./353m.; mail Little York z 13087; ● 100
Prattsburg (Prattsburgh); RMC Place; STEUBEN; ▲ Prattsburgh; 208 NK-8; mail Prattsburgh z 14873; ● 950
Prattsburgh; STEUBEN; see Prattsburg (RMC Place)
Prattsburgh; MCD-Town; STEUBEN; *208 NK-8; 🅿; z 14873; Ⓟ 1,894; © 2,064
Pratts Hollow; RMC Place; MADISON; ▲ Eaton; 209 NJ-13; 🅿; z 13409; ● 70
Prattsville; RMC Place; GREENE; ▲ Prattsville; 209 NL-17; elev. 1,165ft./355m.; 🅿; z 12468; ● 600
Prattsville; MCD-Town; GREENE; *209 NL-17; 🅿; z 12468; Ⓟ 774; © 665
Preble; RMC Place; CORTLAND; ▲ Preble; 209 NJ-12; 🅿; z 13141; ● 550
Preble; MCD-Town; CORTLAND; *209 NJ-12; 🅿; ★ SYR; z 13141; Ⓟ 1,577; © 1,582
Prendergast Point; RMC Place; CHAUTAUQUA; ▲ Chautauqua; *208 NL-2; mail Mayville z 14757; ● 150
Presho; RMC Place; STEUBEN; ▲ Lindley; 208 NM-9; elev. 964ft./294m.; mail Lindley z 14858; ● 150
Preston; RMC Place; CHENANGO; ▲ Preston; 209 NK-13; mail Norwich z 13815, Oxford z 13830; ● 125
Preston; MCD-Town; CHENANGO; *209 NK-13; mail Oxford z 13830; Ⓟ 1,100; © 928
Preston Hollow; RMC Place; ALBANY; ▲ Rensselaerville; 209 NK-18; 🅿; z 12469; ● 220
Preston-Potter Hollow; CDP-Census Area Only; ALBANY; *209 NL-17; © 374
Price Corners; RMC Place; CATTARAUGUS; ▲ Coldspring; *208 NM-3; mail Randolph z 14772; rural
Prince; RMC Place; NEW YORK; 🅿; ★ N.Y.; z 10012; pop. incl. with New York (Inc. Place)
Princes Bay; RMC Place; RICHMOND; 210 M-6; ★ N.Y.; mail Staten Island z 10309; pop. incl. with New York (Inc. Place)
Princetown; RMC Place; SCHENECTADY; ▲ Princetown; *209 NJ-18; elev. 380ft./116m.; ★ A-S-T; mail Duanesburg z 12056, Schenectady z 12306; ● 50
Princetown; MCD-Town; SCHENECTADY; *209 NJ-18; ★ A-S-T; mail Duanesburg z 12056; Ⓟ 2,031; © 2,132
Progress; RMC Place; FULTON; ▲ Mayfield, Johnstown; *209 NI-17; ★ A-S-T; mail Gloversville z 12078; rural
Prospect; Inc. Place; ONEIDA; ▲ Trenton; 209 NH-15; 🅿; ★ UT-R; z 13435; Ⓟ 312; © 330
Prospect Heights; RMC Place; RENSSELAER; ▲ East Greenbush; *209 NK-19; ★ A-S-T; mail Rensselaer z 12144; ● 660
Prospect Hill; RMC Place; SARATOGA; ▲ Waterford; *209 NJ-19; ★ A-S-T; mail Waterford z 12188; ● 900
Prospect Park West; RMC Place; KINGS; *207 SG-6; ★ N.Y.; mail Brooklyn z 11215; pop. incl. with New York (Inc. Place)
Providence; MCD-Town; SARATOGA; *209 NI-18; mail Middle Grove z 12850; Ⓟ 1,360; © 1,841
Pulaski; Inc. Place; OSWEGO; ▲ Richland; 209 NG-12; 🅿; z 13142; Ⓟ 2,525; © 2,398
Pulteney; RMC Place; STEUBEN; ▲ Pulteney; 208 NK-9; 🅿; z 14874; ● 400
Pulteney; MCD-Town; STEUBEN; *208 NK-9; 🅿; z 14874; Ⓟ 1,417; © 1,405
Pultneyville; RMC Place; WAYNE; ▲ Williamson; 208 NH-9; 🅿; ★ ROCH; z 14538; ● 400
Pulvers; RMC Place; COLUMBIA; ▲ Ghent; *209 NL-19; elev. 290ft./88m.; ★ A-S-T; mail Ghent z 12075; rural
Pulvers Corners; RMC Place; DUTCHESS; ▲ Pine Plains; *209 NM-19; elev. 803ft./245m.; mail Pine Plains z 12567; rural
Pumpkin Hill; RMC Place; GENESEE; ▲ Byron; *208 NI-6; elev. 642ft./196m.; ★ ROCH; mail Byron z 14422; ● 30
Pumpkin Hollow; RMC Place; COLUMBIA; ▲ Taghkanic; *209 NM-19; elev. 590ft./180m.; mail Hillsdale z 12529; rural
Purchase; RMC Place; WESTCHESTER; *207 SE-7; elev. 355ft./108m.; 🅿; ★ N.Y.; z 10577; pop. incl. with Harrison (Inc. Place)
Purdys (Purdy Station); RMC Place; WESTCHESTER; ▲ North Salem; 207 SC-8; 🅿; ★ N.Y.; z 10578; ● 970
Purdys Mills; RMC Place; CLINTON; ▲ Altona; *209 NB-19; mail Altona z 12910; rural
Purdy Station; WESTCHESTER; see Purdys (RMC Place)
Purling; RMC Place; GREENE; ▲ Cairo; 209 NL-18; elev. 489ft./149m.; 🅿; z 12470; ● 300
Putnam; WASHINGTON; see Putnam Station (RMC Place)
Putnam; MCD-Town; WASHINGTON; *209 NF-20; mail Putnam Station z 12861; Ⓟ 477; © 645
PUTNAM; 207 SC-8; Ⓟ 83,941; © 95,745; ◆ 97,239
Putnam Lake; CDP; PUTNAM; ▲ Patterson; 207 SC-8; ★ N.Y.; mail Brewster z 10509; Ⓟ 3,459; © 3,855
Putnam Station (Putnam); RMC Place; WASHINGTON; ▲ Putnam; 209 NF-20; 🅿; z 12861; ● 300
Putnam Valley; RMC Place; PUTNAM; ▲ Putnam; *207 SC-7; 🅿; ★ N.Y.; z 10579; ● 1,960
Putnam Valley; MCD-Town; PUTNAM; *207 SC-7; 🅿; ★ N.Y.; z 10579; Ⓟ 9,094; © 10,686
Pyrites; RMC Place; ST. LAWRENCE; ▲ Canton; 209 NC-15; elev. 378ft./115m.; 🅿; z 13677; ● 200

Q

Quackenbush Hill; RMC Place; STEUBEN; ▲ Corning; *208 NM-9; mail Corning z 14830; rural
Quackenkill; RMC Place; RENSSELAER; ▲ Grafton; *209 NJ-20; mail Cropseyville z 12052; ● 100
Quail; RMC Place; ALBANY; ★ A-S-T; mail Albany z 12206; pop. incl. with Albany (Inc. Place)
Quaker Basin; RMC Place; MADISON; ▲ DeRuyter; *209 NJ-13; mail De Ruyter z 13052; rural
Quaker Hill; RMC Place; DUTCHESS; ▲ Pawling; 207 SB-8; mail Pawling z 12564; ● 150
Quaker Ridge; RMC Place; WESTCHESTER; *207 SE-7; ★ N.Y.; mail New Rochelle z 10801; pop. incl. with New Rochelle (Inc. Place)
Quaker Springs; RMC Place; SARATOGA; ▲ Saratoga; *209 NI-19; elev. 292ft./89m.; ★ A-S-T; mail Schuylerville z 12871
Quaker Street; RMC Place; SCHENECTADY; ▲ Duanesburg; *209 NJ-18; 🅿; z 12141 & mail Delanson z 12053; ● 150
Quarry Heights; RMC Place; WESTCHESTER; ▲ North Castle; 207 SH-8; ★ N.Y.; mail White Plains z 10603; ● 600
Quarryville; RMC Place; ULSTER; ▲ Saugerties; *209 NM-18; ★ KNGST; mail Saugerties z 12477; ● 500
Queechy; RMC Place; COLUMBIA; ▲ Canaan; *209 NL-20; mail Canaan z 12029; ● 85
Queens; RMC Place; QUEENS; ★ N.Y.; mail Arverne z 11692, Bayside z 11359-61, Bellerose z 11426, Breezy Point z 11697, Cambria Heights z 11411, College Point z 11356, Corona z 11368, East Elmhurst z 11369-70, Elmhurst z 11373, z 11380, Elmont z 11003, Far Rockaway z 11690-91, z 11693, z 11695, Floral Park z 11001-02, z 11005, Flushing z 11351-52, z 11354-55, z 11358, z 11367, z 11371, z 11381, Forest Hills z 11375, Fresh Meadows z 11365-66, Glen Oaks z 11004, Hollis z 11423, Howard Beach z 11414, Jackson Heights z 11372, Jamaica z 11405, z 11424-25, z 11430-36, Kew Gardens z 11415, Little Neck z 11362-63, Maspeth z 11378, Middle Village z 11379, Oakland Gardens z 11364, Ozone Park z 11416-17, Queens Village z 11427-29, Rego Park z 11374, Richmond Hill z 11418, Ridgewood z 11385-86, Rockaway Park z 11694, Rosedale z 11422, Saint Albans z 11412, South Ozone Park z 11420, South Richmond Hill z 11419, Springfield Gardens z 11413, Whitestone z 11357, Woodhaven z 11421, Woodside z 11377; pop. incl. with New York (Inc. Place)
QUEENS; 207 SF-8; Ⓟ 1,951,598; © 2,229,379; ◆ 2,297,507
Queensbury; RMC Place; WARREN; ▲ Queensbury; 209 NH-19; elev. 293ft./89m.; 🅿; ★ GLFLS; z 12801, z 12804; ● 830
Queensbury; MCD-Town; WARREN; *209 NH-19; 🅿; ★ GLFLS; z 12801, z 12804; Ⓟ 22,630; © 25,441; ◆ 27,366
Queens Village; RMC Place; QUEENS; 211 H-15; 🅿; ★ N.Y.; z 11427-29; pop. incl. with New York (Inc. Place)
Quigley Park; RMC Place; CHAUTAUQUA; ▲ Chautauqua; *208 NM-2; mail Ashville z 14710
Quinneville; RMC Place; BROOME, CHENANGO; ▲ Greene, Fenton; *209 NL-13; elev. 995ft./303m.; ★ BING; mail Chenango Forks z 13746; rural
Quioque; CDP; SUFFOLK; ▲ Southampton; *207 SF-11; mail Westhampton Beach z 11978; © 800
Quogue; Inc. Place; SUFFOLK; ▲ Southampton; 207 SF-11; 🅿; z 11959; Ⓟ 898; © 1,018; Ⓡ 1,026

R

Raceville; RMC Place; WASHINGTON; ▲ Granville; *209 NG-20; mail Poultney z 05764; rural
Radio City; RMC Place; NEW YORK; ★ N.Y.; mail New York z 10019, z 10101; pop. incl. with New York (Inc. Place)
Radison; ONONDAGA; see Lysander New Community (RMC Place)
Rainbow Lake; RMC Place; FRANKLIN; ▲ Brighton; 209 NC-17; elev. 1,701ft./518m.; 🅿; z 12976; ● 200
Ralmar Park; RMC Place; SCHENECTADY; ▲ Glenville; *209 NJ-18; ★ A-S-T; mail Schenectady z 12302
Ramapo; RMC Place; ROCKLAND; ▲ Ramapo; 207 SD-6; elev. 314ft./96m.; ★ N.Y.; mail Hillburn z 10931; ● 75
Ramapo; MCD-Town; ROCKLAND; *207 SD-6; 🅲 407; ★ N.Y.; mail Hillburn z 10931; Ⓟ 93,861; © 108,905; ◆ 115,839

Entries in **UPPERCASE** are counties.
Entries in **bold** have populations of 2,500 or more.
Names in parentheses are alternate names.
Inc. Place — Incorporated Place
RMC Place — Rand McNally Designated Place
CDP — Census Designated Place
MCD — Minor Civil Division

⊡ County Seat
▲ Minor Civil Division
elev. Elevation
🅿 Post Office
🅷 Hospital
🅲 College
■ Principal Business Center
★ Ranally Metro Area (RMA) Abbreviation
z Zip Code(s)
Ⓟ Previous Census Population
Ⓡ Revised Census Population
Ⓐ Annexation Population
● Rand McNally Population Estimate
© Final Census Population
Ⓢ Special Census Population
◆ Estimated Population

For additional definitions see Glossary, Volume 1, and Introduction, Volume 2.

Ram Island; RMC Place; SUFFOLK; ▲ Shelter Island; ***207** SD-13; mail Shelter Island z 11964, Shelter Island Heights z 11965; ● 60
Rampasture; RMC Place; SUFFOLK; ▲ Southampton; ***207** SE-12; mail Hampton Bays z 11946; ● 400
Randall; RMC Place; MONTGOMERY; ▲ Root; **209** NJ-17; mail Fultonville z 12072; ● 250
Randallsville; RMC Place; MADISON; ▲ Lebanon; ***209** NJ-13; mail Hamilton z 13346; ● 100
Randelville; RMC Place; ORANGE; ▲ Warwick, Goshen; ***207** SC-5; ★ **N.Y.**; mail Florida z 10921; pop. incl. with Florida (Inc. Place)
Randolph; Inc. Place; CATTARAUGUS; ▲ Randolph; **208** NM-3; elev. 1,278ft./390m.; 🅿; z 14772; Ⓟ 1,298; Ⓒ 1,316
Randolph; MCD-Town; CATTARAUGUS; ***208** NM-3; 🅿; z 14772; Ⓟ 2,613; Ⓒ 2,681
Ransomville; CDP; NIAGARA; ▲ Wilson, Porter; **208** NH-3; elev. 327ft./100m.; 🅿; ★ **BUF**; z 14131; Ⓟ 1,542; Ⓒ 1,488
Rapids; CDP; NIAGARA; ▲ Lockport; **208** NI-4; elev. 591ft./180m.; ★ **LOCK**; mail Lockport z 14094; Ⓟ 1,152; Ⓒ 1,356
Raquette Lake; RMC Place; HAMILTON; ▲ Long Lake; **209** NF-16; 🅿; z 13436; ● 170
Rathbone; RMC Place; STEUBEN; ▲ Rathbone; **208** NM-8; mail Addison z 14801; ● 100
Rathbone; MCD-Town; STEUBEN; ***208** NM-8; mail Addison z 14801; Ⓟ 892; Ⓒ 1,080
Ravena; Inc. Place; ALBANY; ▲ Coeymans; **209** NK-19; elev. 182ft./55m.; 🅿; ★ **A-S-T**; z 12143; Ⓟ 3,547; Ⓒ 3,369
Ravenwood; RMC Place; ALBANY; ***209** NJ-19; ★ **A-S-T**; mail Albany z 12205; pop. incl. with Colonie (Inc. Place)
Rawson; RMC Place; ALLEGANY; ▲ New Hudson; ***208** NL-5; elev. 1,614ft./492m.; mail Cuba z 14727; rural
Ray Brook; RMC Place; ESSEX; ▲ North Elba; **209** ND-18; 🅿; z 12977; ● 400
Raymertown; RMC Place; RENSSELAER; ▲ Pittstown; **209** NJ-20; ★ **A-S-T**; mail Troy z 12180; ● 500
Raymondville; RMC Place; ST. LAWRENCE; ▲ Norfolk; **209** NB-15; 🅿; z 13678; ● 500
Rayville; RMC Place; COLUMBIA; ▲ Chatham; ***209** NK-20; elev. 750ft./229m.; ★ **A-S-T**; mail Old Chatham z 12136; rural
Reading; SCHUYLER; see Reading Center (RMC Place)
Reading; MCD-Town; SCHUYLER; ***208** NL-9; mail Reading Center z 14876; Ⓟ 1,810; Ⓒ 1,786
Reading Center (Reading); RMC Place; SCHUYLER; ▲ Reading; **208** NL-9; elev. 1,245ft./379m.; 🅿; z 14876; ● 175
Reber; RMC Place; ESSEX; ▲ Willsboro; ***209** ND-19; mail Willsboro z 12996; rural
Red Creek; Inc. Place; WAYNE; ▲ Wolcott; **208** NH-10; 🅿; z 13143; Ⓟ 566; Ⓒ 521
Red Falls; RMC Place; GREENE; ▲ Prattsville; ***209** NL-17; mail Prattsville z 12468; rural
Redfield; RMC Place; OSWEGO; ▲ Redfield; **209** NG-13; elev. 951ft./290m.; 🅿; z 13437; ● 250
Redfield; MCD-Town; OSWEGO; ***209** NG-13; 🅿; z 13437; Ⓟ 564; Ⓒ 607
Redford; CDP; CLINTON; ▲ Saranac; **209** NC-19; elev. 1,119ft./341m.; 🅿; z 12978; Ⓒ 512
Red Hook; Inc. Place; DUTCHESS; ▲ Red Hook; **209** NM-19; elev. 218ft./66m.; 🅿; z 12504, z 12507, z 12571; Ⓟ 1,794; Ⓒ 1,805
Red Hook; MCD-Town; DUTCHESS; ***209** NM-19; 🅿 🅲 2,012; z 12504, z 12507, z 12571; Ⓟ 9,565; Ⓒ 10,408
Red Hook; RMC Place; KINGS; ★ **N.Y.**; mail Brooklyn z 11231; pop. incl. with New York (Inc. Place)
Red House; RMC Place; CATTARAUGUS; ▲ Allegany; ***208** NM-4; mail Salamanca z 14779; ● 25
Red House; MCD-Town; CATTARAUGUS; ***208** NM-4; mail Salamanca z 14779; Ⓟ 159; Ⓒ 38
Red Mills; RMC Place; COLUMBIA; ▲ Claverack; ***209** NL-19; elev. 170ft./52m.; mail Claverack z 12513; ● 250
Red Mills; RMC Place; ST. LAWRENCE; ▲ Lisbon; ***209** NB-14; elev. 272ft./83m.; mail Ogdensburg z 13669
Red Oaks Mill; CDP; DUTCHESS; ▲ Poughkeepsie, La Grange; **207** SB-7; ★ **POK**; mail Poughkeepsie z 12603; Ⓟ 4,906; Ⓒ 4,930
Red Rock; RMC Place; COLUMBIA; ▲ Canaan; ***209** NL-20; elev. 852ft./260m.; mail East Chatham z 12060; ● 140
Red Rock; RMC Place; ONONDAGA; ▲ Lysander; ***209** NI-11; ★ **SYR**; mail Baldwinsville z 13027; ● 250
Redwood; CDP; JEFFERSON; ▲ Alexandria; **209** ND-13; elev. 382ft./116m.; 🅿; z 13679; Ⓒ 584
Redwood; RMC Place; SUFFOLK; ***207** SE-13; elev. 17ft./5m.; mail Sag Harbor z 11963; pop. incl. with Sag Harbor (Inc. Place)
Reeds Corner; RMC Place; LIVINGSTON; ▲ Sparta; ***208** NK-7; mail Dansville z 14437; rural
Reeds Corners; RMC Place; ONTARIO; ▲ Gorham; ***208** NJ-8; mail Dansville z 14437; rural
Reeves Park; RMC Place; SUFFOLK; ▲ Riverhead; ***207** SE-11; mail Riverhead z 11901; ● 500
Rego Park; RMC Place; QUEENS; **211** H-13; 🅿; ★ **N.Y.**; z 11374; pop. incl. with New York (Inc. Place)
Reidsville; RMC Place; ALBANY; ▲ Berne; ***209** NK-18; mail Voorheesville z 12186; rural
Remsen; Inc. Place; ONEIDA; ▲ Trenton, Remsen; **209** NH-15; elev. 1,171ft./357m.; 🅿; ★ **UT-R**; z 13438; Ⓟ 518; Ⓒ 531
Remsen; MCD-Town; ONEIDA; ***209** NH-15; 🅿; z 13438; includes part of the Village of Remsen; Ⓟ 1,739; Ⓒ 1,958
Remsenburg; RMC Place; SUFFOLK; ▲ Southampton; ***207** SF-11; 🅿; ★ **N.Y.**; z 11960; ● 850
Remsenburg-Speonk; CDP-Census Area Only; SUFFOLK; ▲ Southampton; ***207** SF-11; ★ **N.Y.**; mail Remsenburg z 11960, Speonk z 11972; Ⓟ 1,851; Ⓒ 2,675; Ⓡ 2,658
Rensselaer; Inc. Place; RENSSELAER; **209** NK-19; elev. 27ft./8m.; 🅿; ★ **A-S-T**; z 12144; Ⓟ 8,255; Ⓒ 7,761
RENSSELAER; **209** NJ-20; Ⓟ 154,429; Ⓒ 152,538; ◆ 155,187
Rensselaer Falls; Inc. Place; ST. LAWRENCE; ▲ Canton; **209** NC-14; elev. 328ft./100m.; 🅿; z 13680; Ⓟ 316; Ⓒ 337
Rensselaerville; RMC Place; ALBANY; ▲ Rensselaerville; **209** NK-18; 🅿; z 12147; ● 350
Rensselaerville; MCD-Town; ALBANY; ***209** NK-18; 🅿; z 12147; Ⓟ 1,990; Ⓒ 1,915
Residence Park; RMC Place; WESTCHESTER; ***207** SE-7; ★ **N.Y.**; mail New Rochelle z 10805; pop. incl. with New Rochelle (Inc. Place)
Retsof; RMC Place; LIVINGSTON; ▲ York; **208** NJ-6; 🅿; ★ **ROCH**; z 14539; ● 500
Rexford; RMC Place; SARATOGA; ▲ Clifton Park; **209** NJ-18; 🅿; ★ **A-S-T**; z 12148; ● 500
Rexville; RMC Place; STEUBEN; ▲ West Union; **208** NM-7; elev. 1,841ft./561m.; 🅿; z 14877; ● 90
Reydon Shores; RMC Place; SUFFOLK; ▲ Southold; ***207** SD-12; mail Southold z 11971
Reynoldsville; RMC Place; SCHUYLER; ▲ Hector; ***208** NK-10; mail Burdett z 14818; ● 150
Rheims; RMC Place; STEUBEN; ▲ Urbana; ***208** NL-8; mail Hammondsport z 14840; rural
Rhinebeck; Inc. Place; DUTCHESS; ▲ Rhinebeck; **209** NN-18; elev. 200ft./61m.; 🅿 🅷; z 12572; Ⓟ 2,725; Ⓒ 3,077
Rhinebeck; MCD-Town; DUTCHESS; ***209** NN-19; 🅿; z 12572; Ⓟ 7,558; Ⓒ 7,762
Rhinecliff; RMC Place; DUTCHESS; ▲ Rhinebeck; **209** NN-18; 🅿; z 12574; ● 600
Rhode Island; RMC Place; CHENANGO; ▲ Otselic; ***209** NK-13; mail South Otselic z 13155; ● 50
Ricard; RMC Place; OSWEGO; ▲ Williamstown; ***209** NG-12; elev. 731ft./223m.; mail Altmar z 13302; rural
Rice Grove; RMC Place; ONONDAGA; ▲ Otisco; ***209** NJ-11; elev. 817ft./249m.; ★ **SYR**; mail Marietta z 13110; ● 80
Riceville; RMC Place; CATTARAUGUS; ▲ Ashford; ***208** NK-4; elev. 1,437ft./438m.; mail West Valley z 14171
Riceville; RMC Place; FULTON; ▲ Mayfield; ***209** NI-17; ★ **A-S-T**; mail Gloversville z 12078
Richburg; Inc. Place; ALLEGANY; ▲ Bolivar, Wirt; **208** NM-6; elev. 1,655ft./504m.; 🅿; z 14774; Ⓟ 494; Ⓒ 448
Riches Corners; ORLEANS; see Richs Corners (RMC Place)
Richfield (Monticello); RMC Place; OTSEGO; ▲ Richfield; ***209** NJ-16; mail Richfield Springs z 13439; ● 80
Richfield; MCD-Town; OTSEGO; ***209** NJ-16; mail Richfield Springs z 13439; Ⓟ 2,711; Ⓒ 2,423
Richfield Junction; ONEIDA; see Cassville (RMC Place)
Richfield Springs; Inc. Place; OTSEGO; ▲ Richfield; **209** NJ-15; elev. 1,315ft./401m.; 🅿; z 13439; Ⓟ 1,565; Ⓒ 1,255
Richford; RMC Place; TIOGA; ▲ Richford; **209** NL-12; 🅿; z 13835 & mail Harford z 13784; ● 500
Richford; MCD-Town; TIOGA; ***209** NL-12; 🅿; z 13835; Ⓟ 1,153; Ⓒ 1,170
Richland; RMC Place; OSWEGO; ▲ Richland; **209** NG-12; elev. 529ft./161m.; 🅿; z 13144; ● 650
Richland; MCD-Town; OSWEGO; ***209** NG-12; 🅿; z 13144; Ⓟ 5,917; Ⓒ 5,824
Richmond; MCD-Town; ONTARIO; ***208** NJ-7; mail Honeoye z 14471; Ⓟ 3,230; Ⓒ 3,452
Richmond; RMC Place; RICHMOND; ***207** SG-6; ★ **N.Y.**; mail Staten Island z 10301-14; pop. incl. with New York (Inc. Place)
RICHMOND; **207** SG-6; Ⓟ 378,977; Ⓒ 443,728; ◆ 489,524
Richmond Hill; RMC Place; QUEENS; **211** I-13; 🅿; ★ **N.Y.**; z 11418; pop. incl. with New York (Inc. Place)
Richmondtown; RMC Place; RICHMOND; ***207** SG-6; elev. 50ft./15m.; ★ **N.Y.**; mail Staten Island z 10314; pop. incl. with New York (Inc. Place)
Richmond Valley; RMC Place; RICHMOND; **210** N-5; ★ **N.Y.**; mail Staten Island z 10309; pop. incl. with New York (Inc. Place)
Richmondville; Inc. Place; SCHOHARIE; ▲ Richmondville; **209** NK-16; elev. 1,148ft./350m.; 🅿; z 12149; Ⓟ 843; Ⓒ 786
Richmondville; MCD-Town; SCHOHARIE; ***209** NK-16; 🅿; z 12149; Ⓟ 2,397; Ⓒ 2,412
Richs Corners (Riches Corners); RMC Place; ORLEANS; ▲ Albion; ***208** NH-6; elev. 611ft./186m.; mail Albion z 14411; rural
Richville; Inc. Place; ST. LAWRENCE; ▲ De Kalb; **209** NC-14; 🅿; z 13681; Ⓟ 311; Ⓒ 274
Riders; COLUMBIA; see Riders Mills (RMC Place)
Riders Mills (Riders); RMC Place; COLUMBIA; ▲ Chatham; ***209** NK-19; ★ **A-S-T**; mail Brainard z 12024; ● 100
Ridge; RMC Place; LIVINGSTON; ▲ Mount Morris; ***208** NK-6; elev. 1,178ft./359m.; mail Mount Morris z 14510; rural
Ridge; CDP; SUFFOLK; ▲ Brookhaven; **207** SE-10; 🅿; ★ **N.Y.**; z 11961; Ⓟ 11,734; Ⓒ 13,380
Ridgebury; RMC Place; ORANGE; ▲ Wawayanda; **207** SC-5; ★ **MIDD**; mail Slate Hill z 10973; ● 550
Ridgelea Heights; RMC Place; NIAGARA; ▲ Lockport; ***208** NH-4; ★ **LOCK**; mail Lockport z 14094; rural
Ridge Mills; RMC Place; ONEIDA; ***209** NH-14; ★ **UT-R**; mail Rome z 13440; pop. incl. with Rome (Inc. Place)
Ridgemont; MONROE; see Greece (CDP)
Ridgeway; RMC Place; ORLEANS; ▲ Ridgeway; **208** NH-5; elev. 420ft./128m.; mail Medina z 14103; ● 100
Ridgeway; MCD-Town; ORLEANS; ***208** NH-5; mail Medina z 14103; Ⓟ 7,341; Ⓒ 6,886
Ridgeway; RMC Place; WESTCHESTER; ***207** SE-7; elev. 253ft./77m.; ★ **N.Y.**; mail White Plains z 10601; pop. incl. with White Plains (Inc. Place)
Ridgewood; RMC Place; NIAGARA; ▲ Newfane; **208** NH-4; ★ **LOCK**; mail Lockport z 14094; ● 210
Ridgewood; RMC Place; ONEIDA; ▲ New Hartford; ***209** NI-14; ★ **UT-R**; mail Utica z 13501; ● 900
Ridgewood; RMC Place; QUEENS; **211** I-12; 🅿; ★ **N.Y.**; z 11385-86; pop. incl. with New York (Inc. Place)
Ridgewood; RMC Place; TIOGA; ▲ Owego; ***209** NM-11; ★ **BING**; mail Owego z 13827
Rifton; CDP; ULSTER; ▲ Esopus; **207** SA-6; 🅿; ★ **KNGST**; z 12471; Ⓒ 501
Riga; MCD-Town; MONROE; ***208** NI-6; ★ **ROCH**; mail Churchville z 14428; Ⓟ 5,114; Ⓒ 5,437
Rigney Bluff; RMC Place; MONROE; ▲ Greece; ***208** NH-7; ★ **ROCH**; mail Rochester z 14612; ● 1,090
Riley Cove; RMC Place; SARATOGA; ▲ Malta; ***209** NI-19; ★ **A-S-T**; mail Ballston Spa z 12020; rural
Ringdahl Court; RMC Place; ONEIDA; ★ **UT-R**; mail Rome z 13440; pop. incl. with Rome (Inc. Place)
Rio; RMC Place; ORANGE; ▲ Deerpark; **207** SC-4; mail Sparrow Bush z 12780; ● 180
Riparius; RMC Place; WARREN; ▲ Chester; **209** NF-18; 🅿; z 12862; ● 200
Ripley; CDP; CHAUTAUQUA; ▲ Ripley; **208** NL-1; 🅿; z 14775; Ⓟ 1,189; Ⓒ 1,030
Ripley; MCD-Town; CHAUTAUQUA; ***208** NL-1; 🅿; z 14775; Ⓟ 2,967; Ⓒ 2,636
Rippleton; RMC Place; MADISON; ▲ Cazenovia; ***209** NJ-12; ★ **SYR**; mail Cazenovia z 13035; rural
Risingville; RMC Place; STEUBEN; ▲ Thurston; ***208** NL-8; mail Cameron Mills z 14820; ● 50
River; RMC Place; MONROE; ★ **ROCH**; mail Rochester z 14627; pop. incl. with Rochester (Inc. Place)
Riverdale; RMC Place; BRONX; ***207** SE-7; ★ **N.Y.**; mail Bronx z 10463, z 10471; pop. incl. with New York (Inc. Place)
Riverhead; CDP; ⊡ SUFFOLK; ▲ Riverhead; **207** SE-11; 🅿 🅷; z 11901; Ⓟ 8,814; Ⓒ 10,513
Riverhead; MCD-Town; SUFFOLK; ***207** SE-11; 🅿; z 11901; Ⓟ 23,011; Ⓒ 27,680; ◆ 30,110
Riverside; RMC Place; BROOME; ▲ Kirkwood; **209** NM-13; ★ **BING**; mail Kirkwood z 13795; ● 250
Riverside; RMC Place; ERIE; ★ **BUF**; mail Buffalo z 14207; pop. incl. with Buffalo (Inc. Place)
Riverside; RMC Place; OTSEGO; ▲ Unadilla; ***209** NL-14; mail Sidney z 13838; ● 170
Riverside; RMC Place; SARATOGA; ▲ Stillwater; ***209** NI-19; ★ **A-S-T**; mail Mechanicville z 12118; ● 620
Riverside; Inc. Place; STEUBEN; ▲ Corning; **208** NM-9; mail Corning z 14830; Ⓟ 585; Ⓒ 594
Riverside; CDP-Census Area Only; SUFFOLK; ▲ Southampton; ***207** SE-11; ★ **N.Y.**; mail Riverhead z 11901; Ⓟ 1,300; Ⓒ 2,875
Riverside Estates; RMC Place; SUFFOLK; ▲ Southampton; mail Riverhead z 11901
Riverside Manors; RMC Place; NIAGARA; ▲ Lewiston; ***208** NH-3; ★ **BUF**; mail Wilson z 14172; ● 950
Riverside Park; RMC Place; ULSTER; ▲ Hurley; ***207** SA-6; ★ **KNGST**; mail Kingston z 12401
Riverview; RMC Place; CLINTON; ▲ Saranac; **209** NC-18; mail Saranac z 12981; ● 200
Roanoke; RMC Place; GENESEE; ▲ Stafford; ***208** NI-6; elev. 932ft./284m.; ★ **ROCH**; mail Stafford z 14143; rural
Robbins Rest; RMC Place; SUFFOLK; ▲ Islip; ***207** SG-9; ★ **N.Y.**; mail Ocean Beach z 11770; ● 30
Roberts Corner; RMC Place; JEFFERSON; ▲ Henderson; ***209** NF-12; elev. 483ft./147m.; mail Henderson z 13650; rural
Rochdale; RMC Place; DUTCHESS; ▲ Poughkeepsie; **207** SA-7; ★ **POK**; mail Jamaica z 11434, Poughkeepsie z 12603; ● 1,800
Rochdale Village; RMC Place; QUEENS; 🅿; ★ **N.Y.**; z 11434; pop. incl. with New York (Inc. Place)
Rochelle Heights; RMC Place; WESTCHESTER; ***207** SE-7; ★ **N.Y.**; mail New Rochelle z 10801; pop. incl. with New Rochelle (Inc. Place)
Rochelle Park; RMC Place; WESTCHESTER; ***207** SE-7; ★ **N.Y.**; mail New Rochelle z 10801; pop. incl. with New Rochelle (Inc. Place)
Rochester; Inc. Place; ⊡ MONROE; **208** NI-7; elev. 515ft./157m.; 🅿 🅷 🅲 33,130 ■; ★ **ROCH**; z 14602-27, z 14638-39, z 14642-44, z 14646-47, z 14649-53, z 14692, z 14694; Ⓟ 231,636; Ⓒ 219,773; ◆ 211,093
Rochester; MCD-Town; ULSTER; ***207** SA-5; mail Accord z 12404; Ⓟ 5,679; Ⓒ 7,018
Rockaway; RMC Place; QUEENS; ★ **N.Y.**; mail Far Rockaway z 11690-91; pop. incl. with New York (Inc. Place)
Rockaway Beach; RMC Place; QUEENS; 🅿; ★ **N.Y.**; z 11693; pop. incl. with New York (Inc. Place)
Rockaway Park; RMC Place; QUEENS; **211** L-13; 🅿; ★ **N.Y.**; z 11694; pop. incl. with New York (Inc. Place)
Rockaway Point; RMC Place; QUEENS; **211** L-12; 🅿; ★ **N.Y.**; z 11697; pop. incl. with New York (Inc. Place)
Rock City; RMC Place; CATTARAUGUS; ▲ Allegany; ***208** NM-5; elev. 2,356ft./718m.; mail Olean z 14760; ● 90
Rock City; RMC Place; DUTCHESS; ▲ Milan, Red Hook, Rhinebeck; ***209** NM-19; elev. 334ft./102m.; mail Red Hook z 12571; rural
Rock City Falls; RMC Place; SARATOGA; ▲ Milton; **209** NI-18; 🅿; ★ **A-S-T**; z 12863; ● 700
Rock Cut; RMC Place; ONONDAGA; ▲ De Witt; ***209** NI-12; ★ **SYR**; mail Jamesville z 13078; ● 200
Rockdale; RMC Place; CHENANGO; ▲ Guilford; **209** NL-14; mail Mount Upton z 13809; ● 150
Rockefeller Center; RMC Place; NEW YORK; ★ **N.Y.**; mail New York z 10020; pop. incl. with New York (Inc. Place)
Rock Glen; RMC Place; WYOMING; ▲ Gainesville; **208** NK-6; 🅿; z 14550; ● 120
Rock Hill; CDP; SULLIVAN; ▲ Thompson; **207** SB-4; 🅿; z 12775; Ⓒ 1,056
Rockhurst; RMC Place; WARREN; ▲ Queensbury; ***209** NG-19; ★ **GLFLS**; mail Cleverdale z 12820, Glens Falls z 12801
Rockland; RMC Place; ROCKLAND; ▲ Orangetown; ★ **N.Y.**; mail Orangeburg z 10962
Rockland; RMC Place; SULLIVAN; ▲ Rockland; **209** NN-15; mail Roscoe z 12776; ● 300
Rockland; MCD-Town; SULLIVAN; ***209** NN-16; mail Roscoe z 12776; Ⓟ 4,096; Ⓒ 3,913
ROCKLAND; **207** SD-6; Ⓟ 265,475; Ⓒ 286,753; ◆ 299,215
Rockland Lake; RMC Place; ROCKLAND; ▲ Clarkstown; ***207** SD-7; ★ **N.Y.**; mail Valley Cottage z 10989; ● 120
Rock Stream; RMC Place; YATES; ▲ Starkey; **208** NK-9; 🅿; z 14878; ● 100
Rock Tavern; RMC Place; ORANGE; ▲ New Windsor; **207** SC-6; 🅿; ★ **NWBG**; z 12575; ● 200
Rockton; RMC Place; MONTGOMERY; ▲ Amsterdam; ***209** NI-18; elev. 650ft./198m.; ★ **A-S-T**; mail Amsterdam z 12010; pop. incl. with Amsterdam (Inc. Place)
Rock Valley; RMC Place; DELAWARE; ▲ Hancock; ***207** SA-2; mail Long Eddy z 12760; rural
Rockville; RMC Place; ALLEGANY; ▲ Belfast; ***208** NL-6; elev. 1,451ft./442m.; mail Belfast z 14711; rural
Rockville; RMC Place; ORANGE; ▲ Wallkill; ***207** SC-5; ★ **MIDD**; mail Middletown z 10940; ● 40
Rockville Centre; Inc. Place; NASSAU; ▲ Hempstead; **207** SG-8; elev. 31ft./9m.; 🅿 🅷 🅲 3,673 ■; ★ **N.Y.**; z 11570-72; Ⓟ 24,727; Ⓒ 24,568; ◆ 22,784
Rockville Lake; RMC Place; ALLEGANY; ▲ Belfast; mail Belfast z 14711; rural
Rockwells Mills; RMC Place; CHENANGO; ▲ Guilford; ***209** NL-14; mail South New Berlin z 13843; rural
Rockwood; RMC Place; FULTON; ▲ Ephratah; **209** NI-17; mail Johnstown z 12095; ● 300
Rocky Point; RMC Place; CLINTON; ▲ Plattsburgh; ***209** NB-20; ★ **PLATT**; mail Plattsburgh z 12901; summer pop. 100
Rocky Point; CDP; SUFFOLK; ▲ Brookhaven; **207** SE-10; 🅿; ★ **N.Y.**; z 11778; Ⓟ 8,596; Ⓒ 10,185
Rodman; RMC Place; JEFFERSON; ▲ Rodman; **209** NF-12; elev. 724ft./221m.; 🅿; z 13682; ● 180
Rodman; MCD-Town; JEFFERSON; ***209** NF-12; 🅿; z 13682; Ⓟ 1,016; Ⓒ 1,147
Roe Park; RMC Place; WESTCHESTER; ▲ Cortlandt; ***207** SC-7; ★ **N.Y.**; mail Cortlandt Manor z 10567; ● 1,200
Roessleville; RMC Place; ALBANY; ▲ Colonie; **207** SI-4; 🅿; ★ **A-S-T**; z 12205; Ⓟ 10,753
Rolling Acres; RMC Place; MONROE; ▲ Ogden; ***208** NH-7; ★ **ROCH**; mail Spencerport z 14559; ● 550
Rolling Hills; RMC Place; MONROE; ▲ Perinton; ***208** NI-8; ★ **ROCH**; mail Fairport z 14450; ● 980
Rolling Meadows; RMC Place; ULSTER; ▲ Hurley; ***209** NN-18; ★ **KNGST**; mail Kingston z 12401
Romanoff; RMC Place; PUTNAM; ▲ Kent; ★ **N.Y.**; mail Carmel z 10512
Rombout Ridge; RMC Place; DUTCHESS; ▲ La Grange; ***207** SB-7; elev. 200ft./61m.; ★ **POK**; mail Poughkeepsie z 12603
Rome; Inc. Place; ONEIDA; **209** NH-14; elev. 462ft./141m.; 🅿 🅷 ■; ★ **UT-R**; z 13440-42, z 13449; Ⓟ 44,350; Ⓒ 34,950; ◆ 33,759
Romulus; RMC Place; SENECA; ▲ Varick, Romulus; **208** NJ-10; 🅿; z 14541; ● 350
Romulus; MCD-Town; SENECA; ***208** NJ-10; 🅿; z 14541; Ⓟ 2,532; Ⓒ 2,036
Rondaxe; RMC Place; HERKIMER; ▲ Webb; mail Old Forge z 13420; summer pop. 150
Rondout; RMC Place; ULSTER; ***209** NN-18; ★ **KNGST**; mail Kingston z 12401; pop. incl. with Kingston (Inc. Place)
Ronkonkoma; CDP; SUFFOLK; ▲ Islip; **207** SH-13; elev. 120ft./37m.; 🅿; ★ **N.Y.**; z 11749, z 11779; Ⓟ 20,391; Ⓒ 20,029; ◆ 20,024
Roosa Gap; RMC Place; SULLIVAN; ▲ Mamakating; ***207** SB-5; elev. 891ft./272m.; ★ **MIDD**; mail Bloomingburg z 12721; ● 200
Roosevelt; CDP; NASSAU; ▲ Hempstead; **211** I-18; 🅿; ★ **N.Y.**; z 11575; Ⓟ 15,030; Ⓒ 15,854
Roosevelt Beach; RMC Place; NIAGARA; ▲ Wilson; **208** NH-4; ★ **BUF**; mail Wilson z 14172; ● 200
Rooseveltown; RMC Place; ST. LAWRENCE; ▲ Massena; ***209** NA-16; 🅿; z 13683; ● 50
Root; MCD-Town; MONTGOMERY; ***209** NJ-17; mail Sprakers z 12166; Ⓟ 1,692; Ⓒ 1,752
Roscoe; CDP; SULLIVAN; ▲ Rockland; **209** NN-15; 🅿; z 12776; Ⓒ 597
Rose; RMC Place; WAYNE; ▲ Rose; **208** NI-9; elev. 418ft./127m.; 🅿; z 14542; ● 400
Rose; MCD-Town; WAYNE; ***208** NI-9; 🅿; z 14542; Ⓟ 2,424; Ⓒ 2,442
Rosebank; RMC Place; RICHMOND; **210** K-8; ★ **N.Y.**; mail Staten Island z 10305; pop. incl. with New York (Inc. Place)
Roseboom; RMC Place; OTSEGO; ▲ Roseboom; **209** NJ-16; 🅿; z 13450; ● 200
Roseboom; MCD-Town; OTSEGO; ***209** NJ-16; 🅿; z 13450; Ⓟ 668; Ⓒ 684
Rosecrans Park; RMC Place; RENSSELAER; ▲ Schodack; ***209** NK-19; ★ **A-S-T**; mail Nassau z 12123
Rosedale; RMC Place; QUEENS; **211** J-15; 🅿; ★ **N.Y.**; z 11422; pop. incl. with New York (Inc. Place)
Rose Grove; RMC Place; SUFFOLK; ▲ Southampton; ***207** SE-12; elev. 24ft./7m.; mail Southampton z 11968
Rose Hill; RMC Place; ONONDAGA; ▲ Marcellus; ***209** NJ-11; ★ **SYR**; mail Marietta z 13110; ● 80
Rosemont Park; RMC Place; RENSSELAER; ***209** NK-19; ★ **A-S-T**; mail Rensselaer z 12144; pop. incl. with Rensselaer (Inc. Place)
Rosendale; ULSTER; see Rosendale Village (CDP)
Rosendale; MCD-Town; ULSTER; ***207** SA-6; 🅿; ★ **KNGST**; z 12472; Ⓟ 6,220; Ⓒ 6,352
Rosendale Village (Rosendale); CDP; ULSTER; ▲ Rosendale; **209** NN-18; ★ **KNGST**; mail Rosendale z 12472; Ⓟ 1,284; Ⓒ 1,374
Roseton; RMC Place; ORANGE; ▲ Newburgh; ***207** SB-6; ★ **NWBG**; mail Newburgh z 12550; ● 100
Rosiere; RMC Place; JEFFERSON; ▲ Cape Vincent; **209** NE-11; mail Cape Vincent z 13618; ● 60
Roslyn; Inc. Place; NASSAU; ▲ North Hempstead; **211** F-17; 🅿 🅷; ★ **N.Y.**; z 11576; Ⓟ 1,965; Ⓒ 2,570
Roslyn Estates; Inc. Place; NASSAU; ▲ North Hempstead; **211** F-17; ★ **N.Y.**; mail Roslyn z 11576; Ⓟ 1,184; Ⓒ 1,210
Roslyn Harbor; Inc. Place; NASSAU; ▲ Oyster Bay, North Hempstead; **211** F-17; ★ **N.Y.**; mail Glen Head z 11545, Greenvale z 11548, Roslyn z 11576; Ⓟ 1,114; Ⓒ 1,023
Roslyn Heights; CDP; NASSAU; ▲ North Hempstead; **211** F-17; 🅿; ★ **N.Y.**; z 11577; Ⓟ 6,405; Ⓒ 6,295
Rossburg; RMC Place; ALLEGANY; ▲ Hume; **208** NK-6; elev. 1,160ft./354m.; 🅿; z 14536; ● 80
Ross Corners; RMC Place; BROOME; ▲ Vestal; **209** NM-12; ★ **BING**; mail Vestal z 13850; ● 800
Rossie; RMC Place; ST. LAWRENCE; ▲ Rossie; **209** ND-13; elev. 283ft./86m.; mail Hammond z 13646; ● 150
Rossie; MCD-Town; ST. LAWRENCE; ***209** ND-13; mail Hammond z 13646; Ⓟ 770; Ⓒ 787
Rossman; RMC Place; COLUMBIA; ▲ Stockport; ***209** NL-19; ★ **A-S-T**; mail Stuyvesant z 12173; ● 200
Ross Mill; RMC Place; CHAUTAUQUA; ▲ Ellicott; ***208** NM-2; ★ **JMST**; mail Falconer z 14733; rural
Rosstown; RMC Place; CHEMUNG; ▲ Southport; ***208** NM-10; elev. 1,155ft./352m.; ★ **ELM**; mail Pine City z 14871; ● 35
Rossville; RMC Place; RICHMOND; **210** M-5; elev. 13ft./4m.; ★ **N.Y.**; mail Staten Island z 10309; pop. incl. with New York (Inc. Place)
Rotterdam; CDP; SCHENECTADY; ▲ Rotterdam; **209** NJ-18; 🅿; ★ **A-S-T**; z 12306 & mail Schenectady z 12303; Ⓟ 21,228; Ⓒ 20,536; ◆ 21,219
Rotterdam; MCD-Town; SCHENECTADY; ***209** NJ-18; 🅿; ★ **A-S-T**; z 12306 & mail Schenectady z 12303; Ⓟ 28,395; Ⓒ 28,316; ◆ 29,748
Rotterdam Junction; RMC Place; SCHENECTADY; ▲ Rotterdam; **209** NJ-18; 🅿; ★ **A-S-T**; z 12150; ● 1,000
Round Lake; Inc. Place; SARATOGA; ▲ Malta; **209** NI-19; elev. 159ft./48m.; 🅿; ★ **A-S-T**; z 12151; Ⓟ 765; Ⓒ 604
Roundout Harbor; RMC Place; ULSTER; ▲ Esopus; ***207** SA-6; ★ **KNGST**; mail Port Ewen z 12466
Round Top; RMC Place; GREENE; ▲ Cairo; **209** NL-18; 🅿; z 12473; ● 600
Rouses Point; Inc. Place; CLINTON; ▲ Champlain; **209** NA-20; 🅿; z 12979; Ⓟ 2,377; Ⓒ 2,277
Roxbury; RMC Place; DELAWARE; ▲ Roxbury; **209** NL-16; 🅿; z 12474; ● 700
Roxbury; MCD-Town; DELAWARE; ***209** NL-17; 🅿; z 12474; Ⓟ 2,388; Ⓒ 2,509
Roxbury; RMC Place; QUEENS; **211** L-12; ★ **N.Y.**; mail Breezy Point z 11697; pop. incl. with New York (Inc. Place)
Royalton; NIAGARA; see Royalton Center (RMC Place)
Royalton; MCD-Town; NIAGARA; ***208** NI-4; mail Gasport z 14067, Middleport z 14105; Ⓟ 7,453; Ⓒ 7,710
Royalton Center (Royalton); RMC Place; NIAGARA; ▲ Royalton; ***208** NI-4; mail Gasport z 14067, Middleport z 14105; ● 150
Ruby; RMC Place; ULSTER; ▲ Ulster; ***209** NM-18; 🅿; ★ **KNGST**; z 12475; ● 900
Ruby Corner; RMC Place; ST. LAWRENCE; ▲ Macomb; ***209** NC-13; elev. 310ft./94m.; mail Hammond z 13646; rural
Rugby; RMC Place; KINGS; ★ **N.Y.**; mail Brooklyn z 11203; pop. incl. with New York (Inc. Place)
Rumsey Ridge; RMC Place; NIAGARA; ▲ Lewiston; ***208** NH-3; elev. 613ft./187m.; ★ **BUF**; mail Lewiston z 14092
Rural Grove; RMC Place; MONTGOMERY; ▲ Root; **209** NJ-17; elev. 929ft./283m.; mail Sprakers z 12166; ● 200
Rural Hill; RMC Place; JEFFERSON; ▲ Ellisburg; ***209** NF-12; elev. 411ft./125m.; mail Henderson z 13650; rural
Rush; RMC Place; MONROE; ▲ Rush; **208** NI-7; 🅿; ★ **ROCH**; z 14543; ● 500
Rush; MCD-Town; MONROE; ***208** NI-7; 🅿; ★ **ROCH**; z 14543; Ⓟ 3,217; Ⓒ 3,603
Rushford; RMC Place; ALLEGANY; ▲ Rushford; **208** NL-5; 🅿; z 14777; ● 700
Rushford; MCD-Town; ALLEGANY; ***208** NL-5; 🅿; z 14777; Ⓟ 1,176; Ⓒ 1,259
Rushford Lake; RMC Place; ALLEGANY; ▲ Rushford; mail Caneadea z 14717, Rushford z 14777; rural
Rushville; Inc. Place; YATES, ONTARIO; ▲ Gorham, Potter; **208** NJ-8; 🅿; z 14544; Ⓟ 609; Ⓒ 621
Russell; RMC Place; ST. LAWRENCE; ▲ North Hempstead; **209** NC-15; elev. 582ft./177m.; 🅿; z 13684; ● 300
Russell; MCD-Town; ST. LAWRENCE; ***209** NC-15; 🅿; z 13684; Ⓟ 1,716; Ⓒ 1,801
Russell Gardens; Inc. Place; NASSAU; ▲ North Hempstead; **211** G-16; ★ **N.Y.**; mail Great Neck z 11021; Ⓟ 1,027; Ⓒ 1,074
Russia; RMC Place; HERKIMER; ▲ Russia; ***209** NH-15; mail Poland z 13431; ● 75
Russia; MCD-Town; HERKIMER; ***209** NH-15; mail Poland z 13431; Ⓟ 2,294; Ⓒ 2,487
Rutland; MCD-Town; JEFFERSON; ***209** NE-13; mail Felts Mills z 13638; Ⓟ 3,023; Ⓒ 2,959
Rutland Center; RMC Place; JEFFERSON; ▲ Rutland; ***209** NE-13; elev. 973ft./297m.; mail Watertown z 13601
Ryder; RMC Place; KINGS; ★ **N.Y.**; mail Brooklyn z 11234; pop. incl. with New York (Inc. Place)
Rye; Inc. Place; WESTCHESTER; **207** SE-7; 🅿 🅷; ★ **N.Y.**; z 10580; Ⓟ 14,936; Ⓒ 14,955
Rye; MCD-Town; WESTCHESTER; ***207** SE-8; 🅿; ★ **N.Y.**; z 10580 & mail Port Chester z 10573; does not include the City of Rye; Ⓟ 39,524; Ⓒ 43,880; ◆ 45,499
Rye Brook; Inc. Place; WESTCHESTER; ▲ Rye; **207** SI-9; 🅿; ★ **N.Y.**; z 10573; Ⓟ 7,765; Ⓒ 8,602
Rye Hills; RMC Place; WESTCHESTER; ▲ Rye; ***207** SE-8; ★ **N.Y.**; mail Port Chester z 10573; pop. incl. with Rye Brook (Inc. Place)

S

Sabael; RMC Place; HAMILTON; ▲ Indian Lake; **209** NF-17; 🅿; z 12864; ● 200
Sabattis; RMC Place; HAMILTON; ▲ Long Lake; **209** NE-16; mail Long Lake z 12847; ● 30
Sabbath Day Point; RMC Place; WARREN; ▲ Hague; **209** NF-19; mail Silver Bay z 12874; ● 160
Sacandaga; FULTON; see Sacandaga Park (RMC Place)
Sacandaga Park (Sacandaga); RMC Place; FULTON; ▲ Northampton; ***209** NH-18; ★ **A-S-T**; mail Northville z 12134; ● 200
Sackets Harbor; Inc. Place; JEFFERSON; ▲ Hounsfield; **209** NE-12; elev. 278ft./85m.; 🅿; z 13685; Ⓟ 1,313; Ⓒ 1,386
Sacketts Lake; RMC Place; SULLIVAN; ▲ Thompson; **207** SB-4; mail Monticello z 12701; summer pop. 1,500; ● 800
Saddle Rock; Inc. Place; NASSAU; ▲ North Hempstead; **211** F-15; ★ **N.Y.**; mail Great Neck z 11023; Ⓟ 832; Ⓒ 791
Saddle Rock Estates; CDP; NASSAU; ***207** SF-7; ★ **N.Y.**; mail Great Neck z 11021; Ⓒ 424
Sagamore; RMC Place; HAMILTON; ▲ Long Lake; ***209** NF-16; mail Raquette Lake z 13436; ● 20
Sagaponack; Inc. Place; SUFFOLK; ▲ Southampton; **207** SE-13; incorporated September 2, 2005; not reported in 2000 Census; ● 350
Sagaponack; CDP-Census Area Only; SUFFOLK; ▲ Southampton; **207** SE-13; 🅿; z 11962; Ⓒ 582; summer pop. 2,000; Ⓡ 587
Sages Cottages; RMC Place; SUFFOLK; ▲ Southold; mail Greenport z 11944; summer pop. 150
Sagetown; RMC Place; CHEMUNG; ▲ Southport; ***208** NM-9; elev. 1,241ft./378m.; ★ **ELM**; mail Pine City z 14871; rural
Sag Harbor; Inc. Place; SUFFOLK; ▲ Southampton, East Hampton; **207** SE-13; 🅿; z 11963; Ⓟ 2,134; Ⓒ 2,313
Sailors Snug Harbor; RMC Place; RICHMOND; ***207** SG-6; elev. 37ft./11m.; ★ **N.Y.**; mail Staten Island z 10301; pop. incl. with New York (Inc. Place)
Saint Albans; RMC Place; QUEENS; **211** I-15; 🅿; ★ **N.Y.**; z 11412; pop. incl. with New York (Inc. Place)
Saint Andrew; RMC Place; ORANGE; ▲ Montgomery; **207** SB-6; ★ **NWBG**; mail Walden z 12586; ● 80
St. Armand; MCD-Town; ESSEX; ***209** ND-18; mail Bloomingdale z 12913; Ⓟ 1,318; Ⓒ 1,321
Saint Bonaventure; CDP; CATTARAUGUS; ▲ Allegany; ***208** NM-5; 🅿 🅲 2,375; z 14778; Ⓟ 2,397; Ⓒ 2,127
Saint Elmo; RMC Place; ULSTER; ▲ Plattekill; ***207** SB-6; mail Modena z 12548; rural
Saint George; RMC Place; ⊡ RICHMOND; **210** J-8; ★ **N.Y.**; mail Staten Island z 10301; pop. incl. with New York (Inc. Place)
Saint Huberts; RMC Place; ESSEX; ▲ Keene; **209** ND-19; 🅿; z 12943; ● 35
Saint James; CDP; SUFFOLK; ▲ Smithtown; **207** SG-13; 🅿; ★ **N.Y.**; z 11780; Ⓟ 12,703; Ⓒ 13,268
Saint James Heights; RMC Place; SUFFOLK; ▲ Smithtown; ★ **N.Y.**; mail Saint James z 11780
Saint Johnsburg; RMC Place; NIAGARA; ▲ Wheatfield; **208** NI-3; ★ **BUF**; mail Niagara Falls z 14302; ● 525
Saint Johns Place; RMC Place; KINGS; ★ **N.Y.**; mail Brooklyn z 11213; pop. incl. with New York (Inc. Place)
Saint Johnsville; Inc. Place; MONTGOMERY; ▲ St. Johnsville; **209** NI-16; 🅿; z 13452; Ⓟ 1,825; Ⓒ 1,685
St. Johnsville; MCD-Town; MONTGOMERY; ***209** NI-16; 🅿; z 13452; Ⓟ 2,773; Ⓒ 2,565
ST. LAWRENCE; **209** ND-15; Ⓟ 111,974; Ⓒ 111,931; Ⓡ 111,919; ◆ 106,906
Saint Lawrence Park; RMC Place; JEFFERSON; ▲ Alexandria; ***209** ND-12; mail Alexandria Bay z 13607; ● 100
Saint Mary's Park; RMC Place; BRONX; ***207** SF-7; ★ **N.Y.**; mail Bronx z 10455; pop. incl. with New York (Inc. Place)
Saint Regis Falls; RMC Place; FRANKLIN; ▲ Waverly; **209** NB-16; elev. 1,291ft./393m.; 🅿; z 12980; ● 950
St. Regis Mohawk Reservation; Indian Reservation; FRANKLIN; mail Hogansburg z 13655; Ⓟ 1,802; Ⓒ 2,699
Saint Remy; RMC Place; ULSTER; ▲ Esopus; ***207** SA-6; 🅿; ★ **KNGST**; z 12401; ● 280
Saintsville; RMC Place; ONONDAGA; ▲ Manlius; ***209** NI-12; ★ **SYR**; mail Kirkville z 13082; rural
Salamanca; Inc. Place; CATTARAUGUS; ▲ Salamanca; **208** NM-4; elev. 1,392ft./424m.; 🅿; z 14779; Ⓟ 6,566; Ⓒ 6,097
Salamanca; MCD-Town; CATTARAUGUS; ***208** NM-4; 🅿; z 14779; Ⓟ 477; Ⓒ 544
Salem; Inc. Place; WASHINGTON; ▲ North Salem; **209** NH-20; 🅿; z 12865; Ⓟ 958; Ⓒ 964
Salem; MCD-Town; WASHINGTON; ***209** NH-20; 🅿; z 12865; Ⓟ 2,608; Ⓒ 2,702
Salem Center; RMC Place; WESTCHESTER; ▲ North Salem; **207** SC-8; elev. 339ft./103m.; ★ **N.Y.**; mail Purdys z 10578; rural
Salina; RMC Place; ONONDAGA; ★ **SYR**; mail Liverpool z 13088, Syracuse z 13208; pop. incl. with Syracuse (Inc. Place)
Salina; MCD-Town; ONONDAGA; ***209** NI-12; ★ **SYR**; mail Liverpool z 13088; Ⓟ 35,145; Ⓒ 33,290; ◆ 32,648
Salisbury; RMC Place; HERKIMER; ▲ Salisbury; **209** NI-16; elev. 1,221ft./372m.; mail Little Falls z 13365; ● 100
Salisbury; MCD-Town; HERKIMER; ***209** NH-16; mail Little Falls z 13365; Ⓟ 1,934; Ⓒ 1,953
Salisbury; CDP-Census Area Only; NASSAU; ▲ Hempstead; ***207** SF-8; elev. 100ft./30m.; ★ **N.Y.**; mail Hicksville z 11801; Ⓟ 12,226; Ⓒ 12,341
Salisbury Center; RMC Place; HERKIMER; ▲ Salisbury; **209** NI-16; 🅿; z 13454; ● 200
Salisbury Mills; RMC Place; ORANGE; ▲ Cornwall, Blooming Grove; **207** SC-6; 🅿; ★ **NWBG**; z 12577
Salmon River; CLINTON; see South Plattsburgh (RMC Place)
Saltaire; Inc. Place; SUFFOLK; ▲ Islip; **207** SG-9; 🅿; ★ **N.Y.**; z 11706; Ⓟ 38; summer pop. 1,000; Ⓒ 43
Salt Point; RMC Place; DUTCHESS; ▲ Pleasant Valley; **209** NN-19; 🅿; ★ **POK**; z 12578; ● 550
Salt Springville; RMC Place; MONTGOMERY, OTSEGO; ▲ Minden; ***209** NJ-16; mail Cherry Valley z 13320; ● 100
Sammonsville; RMC Place; FULTON; ▲ Johnstown; **209** NI-17; mail Fonda z 12068, Johnstown z 12095; ● 95
Samsondale; RMC Place; ROCKLAND; ***207** SD-6; elev. 173ft./53m.; ★ **N.Y.**; mail West Haverstraw z 10993; pop. incl. with West Haverstraw (Inc. Place)
Samsonville; RMC Place; ULSTER; ▲ Olive; **209** NN-17; mail Olivebridge z 12461, Shokan z 12481; ● 150
Sanborn; RMC Place; NIAGARA; ▲ Lewiston; **208** NI-3; elev. 638ft./194m.; 🅿; ★ **BUF**; z 14132; ● 750
Sandford Boulevard; RMC Place; WESTCHESTER; ★ **N.Y.**; mail Mount Vernon z 10550; pop. incl. with Mount Vernon (Inc. Place)
Sandfordville; RMC Place; ST. LAWRENCE; ▲ Stockholm; **209** NB-15; elev. 382ft./116m.; mail Potsdam z 13676; ● 200
Sand Hill; RMC Place; ERIE; ▲ Newstead; ***208** NI-4; elev. 611ft./186m.; mail Akron z 14001; rural
Sand Hill; RMC Place; MONTGOMERY; ▲ Minden; ***209** NI-16; mail Fort Plain z 13339; rural
Sand Hill; RMC Place; OTSEGO; ▲ Unadilla; ***209** NL-14; mail Unadilla z 13849; ● 85
Sand Lake; RMC Place; RENSSELAER; ▲ Sand Lake; **209** NK-20; 🅿; ★ **A-S-T**; z 12153; ● 700
Sand Lake; MCD-Town; RENSSELAER; ***209** NK-20; 🅿; ★ **A-S-T**; z 12153; Ⓟ 7,642; Ⓒ 7,987
Sand Ridge; CDP-Census Area Only; OSWEGO; ▲ Schroeppel; ***209** NH-11; ★ **SYR**; mail Pennellville z 13132; Ⓟ 1,312; Ⓒ 906
Sands Point; Inc. Place; NASSAU; ▲ North Hempstead; **207** SF-7; 🅿; ★ **N.Y.**; z 11050; Ⓟ 2,477; Ⓒ 2,786
Sandusky; RMC Place; CATTARAUGUS; ▲ Freedom; **208** NK-5; 🅿; z 14065, z 14133; ● 450
Sandy Beach; RMC Place; ERIE; ▲ Grand Island; **208** NI-3; ★ **BUF**; mail Grand Island z 14072; ● 2,350
Sandy Creek; Inc. Place; OSWEGO; ▲ Sandy Creek; **209** NG-12; elev. 498ft./152m.; 🅿; z 13145; Ⓟ 793; Ⓒ 789
Sandy Creek; MCD-Town; OSWEGO; ***209** NG-12; 🅿; z 13145; Ⓟ 3,454; Ⓒ 3,863
Sandy Harbour Beach; RMC Place; MONROE; ▲ Hamlin; ***208** NH-6; ★ **ROCH**; mail Hamlin z 14464
Sandy Pond; RMC Place; OSWEGO; **209** NG-12
Sanford; RMC Place; BROOME; mail Deposit z 13754
Sanford; MCD-Town; BROOME; ***209** NM-14; mail Deposit z 13754; Ⓟ 2,576; Ⓒ 2,477
Sangerfield; RMC Place; ONEIDA; ▲ Sangerfield; **209** NJ-14; 🅿; z 13455; ● 400
Sangerfield; MCD-Town; ONEIDA; ***209** NJ-14; 🅿; z 13455; Ⓟ 2,460; Ⓒ 2,610
Sanitaria Springs; RMC Place; BROOME; ▲ Colesville; **209** NM-13; 🅿; ★ **BING**; z 13833; ● 400
San Remo; RMC Place; SUFFOLK; ▲ Smithtown; **207** SH-12; elev. 163ft./50m.; ★ **N.Y.**; mail Kings Park z 11754; ● 8,550
Santa Clara; RMC Place; FRANKLIN; ▲ Santa Clara; **209** NC-17; elev. 1,339ft./408m.; mail Saint Regis Falls z 12980; ● 75
Santa Clara; MCD-Town; FRANKLIN; ***209** NC-17; mail Saint Regis Falls z 12980; Ⓟ 311; Ⓒ 395
Santapoque; RMC Place; SUFFOLK; ▲ Babylon; ***207** SF-9; ★ **N.Y.**; mail West Babylon z 11707
Saranac; RMC Place; CLINTON; ▲ Saranac; **209** NB-19; 🅿; z 12981; ● 400
Saranac; MCD-Town; CLINTON; ***209** NB-18; 🅿; z 12981; Ⓟ 3,710; Ⓒ 4,165
Saranac Inn; RMC Place; FRANKLIN; ▲ Santa Clara; **209** ND-17; mail Saranac Lake z 12983; ● 200
Saranac Lake; Inc. Place; FRANKLIN, ESSEX; ▲ St. Armand, Harrietstown, North Elba; **209** ND-18; elev. 1,547ft./472m.; 🅿 🅷; z 12983; Ⓟ 5,377; Ⓒ 5,041
Saratoga; MCD-Town; SARATOGA; ***209** NI-19; ★ **A-S-T**; mail Schuylerville z 12871; Ⓟ 5,069; Ⓒ 5,141; Ⓡ 5,114
SARATOGA; **209** NH-18; Ⓟ 181,276; Ⓒ 200,635; ◆ 216,338
Saratoga Lake; RMC Place; SARATOGA; ▲ Saratoga; ***209** NI-19; ★ **A-S-T**; mail Saratoga Springs z 12866; ● 500
Saratoga Springs; Inc. Place; SARATOGA; **209** NI-19; 🅿 🅷 🅲 14,623 ■; ★ **A-S-T**; z 12866; Ⓟ 25,001; Ⓒ 26,186; ◆ 28,496
Sardinia; RMC Place; ERIE; ▲ Sardinia; **208** NK-5; elev. 1,398ft./426m.; 🅿; z 14134; ● 550
Sardinia; MCD-Town; ERIE; ***208** NK-4; 🅿; z 14134; Ⓟ 2,667; Ⓒ 2,692
Saugerties; Inc. Place; ULSTER; ▲ Saugerties; **209** NM-18; elev. 155ft./47m.; 🅿; ★ **KNGST**; z 12477; Ⓟ 3,915; Ⓒ 4,955; Ⓡ 3,908
Saugerties; MCD-Town; ULSTER; ***209** NM-18; 🅿; ★ **KNGST**; z 12477; Ⓟ 18,467; Ⓒ 19,868; Ⓡ 18,821
Saugerties South; CDP-Census Area Only; ULSTER; ▲ Saugerties; ***209** NM-18; ★ **KNGST**; mail Saugerties z 12477; Ⓟ 2,346; Ⓒ 2,285
Sauquoit; RMC Place; ONEIDA; ▲ Paris; **209** NI-14; 🅿; ★ **UT-R**; z 13456; ● 930
Savannah; RMC Place; WAYNE; ▲ Savannah; **208** NI-10; elev. 426ft./130m.; 🅿; z 13146; ● 700
Savannah; MCD-Town; WAYNE; ***208** NI-10; 🅿; z 13146; Ⓟ 1,768; Ⓒ 1,838
Savona; Inc. Place; STEUBEN; ▲ Bath; **208** NL-8; 🅿; z 14879; Ⓟ 974; Ⓒ 822
Sawkill; RMC Place; ULSTER; ▲ Kingston; ***209** NM-18; elev. 190ft./58m.; ★ **KNGST**; mail Kingston z 12401; ● 300
Sawyers Corners; RMC Place; CAYUGA; ▲ Throop; ***208** NI-10; ★ **SYR**; mail Auburn z 13021; ● 65
Saxon Park; RMC Place; SUFFOLK; ▲ Islip; ★ **N.Y.**; mail Bay Shore z 11706
Sayville; CDP; SUFFOLK; ▲ Islip; **207** SF-10; 🅿; ★ **N.Y.**; z 11782; Ⓟ 16,550; Ⓒ 16,735
Scarborough; RMC Place; WESTCHESTER; ***207** SD-7; 🅿; ★ **N.Y.**; z 10510; pop. incl. with Briarcliff Manor (Inc. Place)
Scarsdale; Inc. Place; WESTCHESTER; ▲ Scarsdale; **207** SE-7; 🅿; ★ **N.Y.**; z 10583; Ⓟ 16,987; Ⓒ 17,823
Scarsdale Downs; RMC Place; WESTCHESTER; ***207** SE-7; ★ **N.Y.**; pop. incl. with New Rochelle (Inc. Place)
Schaghticoke; Inc. Place; RENSSELAER; ▲ Schaghticoke; **209** NJ-19; 🅿; ★ **A-S-T**; z 12154; Ⓟ 794; Ⓒ 676
Schaghticoke; MCD-Town; RENSSELAER; ***209** NJ-19; 🅿; ★ **A-S-T**; z 12154; Ⓟ 7,574; Ⓒ 7,456
Schaghticoke Hill; RMC Place; RENSSELAER; ▲ Schaghticoke; ***209** NJ-19; ★ **A-S-T**; mail Schaghticoke z 12154; ● 150
Schenectady; Inc. Place; ⊡ SCHENECTADY; **209** NJ-18; elev. 244ft./74m.; 🅿 🅷 🅲 2,624 ■; ★ **A-S-T**; z 12008, z 12301-09, z 12325, z 12345; Ⓟ 65,566; Ⓒ 61,821; ◆ 62,396
SCHENECTADY; **209** NJ-18; Ⓟ 149,285; Ⓒ 146,555; ◆ 151,424
Schenevus; RMC Place; OTSEGO; ▲ Maryland; **209** NK-16; elev. 1,266ft./386m.; 🅿; z 12155; ● 450
Schermerhom Corners; RMC Place; CHAUTAUQUA; ▲ Poland; ***208** NM-3; elev. 1,268ft./386m.; ★ **JMST**; mail Kennedy z 14747; rural
Schodack; RENSSELAER; see Schodack Center (RMC Place)
Schodack; MCD-Town; RENSSELAER; ***209** NK-19; ★ **A-S-T**; mail Castleton On Hudson z 12033; Ⓟ 11,839; Ⓒ 12,536
Schodack Center (Schodack); RMC Place; RENSSELAER; ▲ Schodack; ***209** NK-19; elev. 293ft./89m.; ★ **A-S-T**; mail Castleton On Hudson z 12033; ● 100
Schodack Landing; RMC Place; RENSSELAER; ▲ Schodack; ***209** NK-19; 🅿; ★ **A-S-T**; z 12156; ● 200
Schoharie; Inc. Place; ⊡ SCHOHARIE; ▲ Schoharie; **209** NK-17; elev. 611ft./186m.; 🅿; z 12157; Ⓟ 1,045; Ⓒ 1,030
Schoharie; MCD-Town; SCHOHARIE; ***209** NK-17; 🅿; z 12157; Ⓟ 3,369; Ⓒ 3,299
SCHOHARIE; **209** NK-16; Ⓟ 31,859; Ⓒ 31,582; ◆ 31,949
Schonowe; RMC Place; SCHENECTADY; ▲ Rotterdam; ***209** NJ-18; elev. 300ft./91m.; ★ **A-S-T**; mail Schenectady z 12306; ● 700
Schroeppel; MCD-Town; OSWEGO; ***209** NH-11; ★ **SYR**; mail Phoenix z 13135; Ⓟ 8,931; Ⓒ 8,566
Schroon; MCD-Town; ESSEX; ***209** NF-19; mail Schroon Lake z 12870; Ⓟ 1,721; Ⓒ 1,759
Schroon Falls; RMC Place; ESSEX; ▲ Schroon; ***209** NE-19; mail Schroon Lake z 12870; rural
Schroon Lake; RMC Place; ESSEX; ▲ Schroon; **209** NF-19; elev. 867ft./264m.; 🅿; z 12870; ● 1,100
Schultzville; RMC Place; DUTCHESS; ▲ Clinton; ***207** SA-7; ★ **POK**; mail Rhinebeck z 12572; rural
Schuluski Estates; RMC Place; SARATOGA; ▲ Waterford; ★ **A-S-T**; mail Waterford z 12188; ● 200
Schuyler; MCD-Town; HERKIMER; ***209** NI-15; 🅿; ★ **UT-R**; z 13340 & mail Utica z 13502; Ⓟ 3,508; Ⓒ 3,385
SCHUYLER; **208** NL-9; Ⓟ 18,662; Ⓒ 19,224; ◆ 18,901
Schuyler Falls; RMC Place; CLINTON; ▲ Schuyler Falls; **209** NB-19; elev. 429ft./131m.; 🅿; ★ **PLATT**; z 12985; ● 500
Schuyler Falls; MCD-Town; CLINTON; ***209** NB-19; 🅿; ★ **PLATT**; z 12985; Ⓟ 4,787; Ⓒ 5,128
Schuyler Lake; RMC Place; OTSEGO; ▲ Exeter; **209** NJ-15; 🅿; z 13457; ● 300
Schuylerville; RMC Place; BRONX; ***207** SF-7; elev. 21ft./6m.; ★ **N.Y.**; mail Bronx z 10465; pop. incl. with New York (Inc. Place)
Schuylerville; Inc. Place; SARATOGA; ▲ Saratoga; **209** NI-19; 🅿; ★ **A-S-T**; z 12871; Ⓟ 1,364; Ⓒ 1,197
Scio; RMC Place; ALLEGANY; ▲ Scio; **208** NM-6; 🅿; z 14880; ● 800
Scio; MCD-Town; ALLEGANY; ***208** NM-6; 🅿; z 14880; Ⓟ 1,965; Ⓒ 1,914
Sciota; RMC Place; CLINTON; ▲ Chazy; **209** NA-19; mail Altona z 12910, West Chazy z 12992; ● 180
Scipio; CAYUGA; see Scipio Center (RMC Place)
Scipio; MCD-Town; CAYUGA; ***208** NJ-10; mail Scipio Center z 13147; Ⓟ 1,517; Ⓒ 1,537
Scipio Center (Scipio); RMC Place; CAYUGA; ▲ Scipio; **208** NJ-10; elev. 1,191ft./363m.; 🅿; z 13147; ● 120
Scipioville; RMC Place; CAYUGA; ▲ Scipio; ***208** NJ-10; elev. 987ft./301m.; mail Scipio Center z 13147; ● 65
Scononda; RMC Place; ONEIDA; ▲ Verona; ***209** NI-13; ★ **UT-R**; mail Oneida z 13421; ● 200
Scotchbush; RMC Place; FULTON; ▲ Ephratah; ***209** NI-16; mail Saint Johnsville z 13452; rural
Scotch Bush; RMC Place; MONTGOMERY; ▲ Florida; ***209** NJ-18; mail Amsterdam z 12010; rural
Scotchtown; CDP; ORANGE; ▲ Wallkill; ***207** SC-5; elev. 725ft./221m.; 🅿; ★ **MIDD**; z 10940-41; Ⓟ 8,765; Ⓒ 8,954
Scotia; Inc. Place; SCHENECTADY; ▲ Glenville; **209** NJ-18; 🅿; ★ **A-S-T**; z 12302; Ⓟ 7,359; Ⓒ 7,957
Scott; RMC Place; CORTLAND; ▲ Scott; **209** NJ-11; elev. 1,403ft./428m.; mail Homer z 13077; ● 150
Scott; MCD-Town; CORTLAND; ***209** NJ-11; mail Homer z 13077; Ⓟ 1,167; Ⓒ 1,193
Scottsburg; RMC Place; LIVINGSTON; ▲ Sparta; **208** NK-7; 🅿; z 14462, z 14545; ● 400
Scotts Corner; RMC Place; ORANGE; ▲ Montgomery; ***207** SB-6; mail Montgomery z 12549; rural
Scotts Corners; CDP; WESTCHESTER; ***207** SD-8; ★ **N.Y.**; mail Pound Ridge z 10576; Ⓒ 624
Scottsville; Inc. Place; MONROE; **208** NI-7; elev. 564ft./172m.; 🅿; ★ **ROCH**; z 14546; Ⓟ 1,912; Ⓒ 2,128
Scranton; RMC Place; ERIE; ▲ Hamburg; ***208** NJ-4; ★ **BUF**; mail Hamburg z 14075; ● 1,100
Scriba (Scriba Center); RMC Place; OSWEGO; ▲ Scriba; **209** NG-11; mail Oswego z 13126; ● 160
Scriba; MCD-Town; OSWEGO; ***209** NG-11; mail Oswego z 13126; Ⓟ 6,472; Ⓒ 7,331; Ⓡ 7,189
Scriba Center; OSWEGO; see Scriba (RMC Place)
Scribner Corners; RMC Place; MADISON; ***209** NI-13; elev. 571ft./174m.; mail Oneida z 13421; pop. incl. with Oneida (Inc. Place)
Sea Breeze; RMC Place; MONROE; ▲ Irondequoit; ***208** NH-7; ★ **ROCH**; mail Rochester z 14617
Sea Cliff; Inc. Place; NASSAU; ▲ Oyster Bay; **211** E-17; 🅿; ★ **N.Y.**; z 11579; Ⓟ 5,054; Ⓒ 5,066
Seaford; CDP; NASSAU; ▲ Hempstead; **211** I-20; 🅿 🅷; ★ **N.Y.**; z 11783; Ⓟ 15,597; Ⓒ 15,791
Seagate; RMC Place; KINGS; **210** L-10; ★ **N.Y.**; mail Brooklyn z 11224; pop. incl. with New York (Inc. Place)
Seager; RMC Place; ULSTER; ▲ Hardenburgh; **209** NM-17; mail Arkville z 12406; rural
Searingtown; CDP; NASSAU; ▲ North Hempstead; **211** G-17; ★ **N.Y.**; mail Albertson z 11507; Ⓟ 5,020; Ⓒ 5,034
Searsburg; RMC Place; SCHUYLER; ▲ Hector; ***208** NK-10; mail Trumansburg z 14886; rural
Sears Corners; RMC Place; PUTNAM; ▲ Southeast; ***207** SC-8; elev. 495ft./151m.; ★ **N.Y.**; mail Brewster z 10509; ● 150
Searsville; RMC Place; ORANGE; ▲ Crawford; **207** SB-5; mail Montgomery z 12549
Seaside; RMC Place; QUEENS; ***207** SG-7; ★ **N.Y.**; mail Rockaway Park z 11694; pop. incl. with New York (Inc. Place)
Seaview; RMC Place; SUFFOLK; ▲ Islip; ***207** SG-10; elev. 8ft./2m.; ★ **N.Y.**; mail Ocean Beach z 11770; ● 50
Second Milo; RMC Place; YATES; ▲ Milo; ***208** NK-9; elev. 1,060ft./323m.; mail Penn Yan z 14527
Seeley Creek; RMC Place; CHEMUNG; ▲ Southport; ***208** NM-9; ★ **ELM**; mail Pine City z 14871; ● 40
Selden; CDP; SUFFOLK; ▲ Brookhaven; **207** SE-10; 🅿; ★ **N.Y.**; z 11784; Ⓟ 20,608; Ⓒ 21,861; ◆ 21,860
Selkirk; RMC Place; ALBANY; ▲ Bethlehem; **209** NK-19; 🅿; ★ **A-S-T**; z 12158; ● 700
Selkirk Beach; RMC Place; OSWEGO; ▲ Richland; ***209** NG-11; mail Pulaski z 13142; ● 55
Sellecks Corners; RMC Place; ST. LAWRENCE; ▲ Pierrepont; ***209** NC-15; elev. 1,015ft./309m.; mail Colton z 13625; rural
Semans Corners; RMC Place; ONTARIO; ▲ Naples; ***208** NK-8; mail Naples z 14512; rural
Sempronius; RMC Place; CAYUGA; ▲ Sempronius; **209** NJ-11; mail Moravia z 13118; ● 100
Sempronius; MCD-Town; CAYUGA; ***209** NJ-11; mail Moravia z 13118; Ⓟ 802; Ⓒ 893
Seneca; RMC Place; ERIE
Seneca; MCD-Town; ONTARIO; ***208** NJ-9; mail Stanley z 14561; Ⓟ 2,747; Ⓒ 2,731
SENECA; **208** NJ-10; Ⓟ 33,683; Ⓒ 33,342; ◆ 34,345
Seneca Castle; RMC Place; ONTARIO; ▲ Seneca; **208** NJ-9; 🅿; z 14547; ● 550
Seneca Falls; Inc. Place; SENECA; ▲ Seneca Falls; **208** NJ-10; 🅿 🅲 771; z 13148; Ⓟ 7,370; Ⓒ 6,861
Seneca Falls; MCD-Town; SENECA; ***208** NJ-10; 🅿 🅲 771; z 13148; Ⓟ 9,384; Ⓒ 9,347
Seneca Heights; RMC Place; CATTARAUGUS; ***208** NM-5; elev. 1,423ft./434m.; pop. incl. with Olean (Inc. Place)
Seneca Hill; RMC Place; OSWEGO; ▲ Volney; ***209** NH-11; mail Oswego z 13126; ● 100
Seneca Knolls; CDP-Census Area Only; ONONDAGA; ▲ Van Buren; **208** NE-6; ★ **SYR**; mail Syracuse z 13209; Ⓒ 2,138
Seneca Lake; YATES; see Himrod (RMC Place)
Seneca Point; RMC Place; ONTARIO; ▲ South Bristol; **208** NJ-8; mail Naples z 14512; ● 200
Sennett; RMC Place; CAYUGA; ▲ Sennett; **209** NI-11; elev. 598ft./182m.; ★ **SYR**; mail Auburn z 13021; ● 300
Sennett; MCD-Town; CAYUGA; ***209** NI-11; ★ **SYR**; mail Auburn z 13021; Ⓟ 2,913; Ⓒ 3,244
Sentinel Heights; RMC Place; ONONDAGA; ▲ Onondaga; ***209** NI-12; ★ **SYR**; mail Jamesville z 13078; ● 100
Setauket; RMC Place; SUFFOLK; ▲ Brookhaven; ***207** SE-10; 🅿; ★ **N.Y.**; z 11733; ● 3,300
Setauket; SUFFOLK; see East Setauket (RMC Place)
Setauket-East Setauket; CDP-Census Area Only; SUFFOLK; ▲ Brookhaven; ***207** SE-10; ★ **N.Y.**; mail East Setauket z 11733; Ⓟ 13,634; Ⓒ 15,931
Settlers Hill; RMC Place; PUTNAM; ▲ Southeast; ★ **N.Y.**; mail Brewster z 10509; ● 100
Seven Hills; RMC Place; PUTNAM; ▲ Kent; ★ **N.Y.**; mail Carmel z 10512; ● 250
Seventh Day Hollow; RMC Place; CHENANGO; ▲ Otselic; ***209** NK-13; mail Georgetown z 13072; rural
Severance; RMC Place; ESSEX; ▲ Schroon; **209** NF-19; 🅿; z 12872; ● 200
Seward; RMC Place; SCHOHARIE; ▲ Seward; **209** NJ-16; elev. 1,182ft./360m.; mail Cobleskill z 12043; ● 150
Seward; MCD-Town; SCHOHARIE; ***209** NJ-16; mail Cobleskill z 12043; Ⓟ 1,651; Ⓒ 1,637
Shackport; RMC Place; DELAWARE; ▲ Meredith; ***209** NL-15; mail East Meredith z 13757; rural
Shadigee; RMC Place; ORLEANS; ▲ Yates; **208** NH-5; mail Lyndonville z 14098; ● 100
Shady; RMC Place; ULSTER; ▲ Woodstock; ***209** NM-18; 🅿; z 12409; ● 200
Shandaken; RMC Place; ULSTER; ▲ Shandaken; **209** NM-17; 🅿; z 12480; ● 500
Shandaken; MCD-Town; ULSTER; ***209** NM-17; 🅿; z 12480; Ⓟ 3,013; Ⓒ 3,235
Shandelee; RMC Place; SULLIVAN; ▲ Callicoon; ***207** SA-3; mail Livingston Manor z 12758; rural
Shannon Corners; RMC Place; YATES; ▲ Starkey; ***208** NK-9; mail Dundee z 14837; rural
Sharon; RMC Place; SCHOHARIE; ▲ Sharon; ***209** NJ-17; mail Sharon Springs z 13459; ● 50
Sharon; MCD-Town; SCHOHARIE; ***209** NJ-16; mail Sharon Springs z 13459; Ⓟ 1,892; Ⓒ 1,843
Sharon Center; RMC Place; SCHOHARIE; ***209** NJ-16; elev. 1,443ft./440m.; mail Sharon Springs z 13459; rural
Sharon Springs; Inc. Place; SCHOHARIE; ▲ Sharon; **209** NJ-16; elev. 1,137ft./347m.; 🅿; z 13459; Ⓟ 543; Ⓒ 547
Shawangunk; MCD-Town; ULSTER; ***207** SB-5; ★ **NWBG**; mail Wallkill z 12589; Ⓟ 10,081; Ⓒ 12,022
Shawnee; RMC Place; NIAGARA; ▲ Pendleton; **208** NA-4; ★ **BUF**; mail Sanborn z 14132
Shea Stadium; RMC Place; QUEENS; ***207** SF-7; ★ **N.Y.**; pop. incl. with New York (Inc. Place)
Sheds; RMC Place; MADISON; ▲ DeRuyter; **209** NJ-13; mail New Woodstock z 13122; ● 70
Sheepshead Bay; RMC Place; KINGS; ***207** SG-7; ★ **N.Y.**; mail Brooklyn z 11235; pop. incl. with New York (Inc. Place)
Shekomeko; RMC Place; DUTCHESS; ▲ North East; ***209** NN-19; mail Millerton z 12546, Pine Plains z 12567; rural
Shelby; RMC Place; ORLEANS; ▲ Shelby; **208** NH-5; mail Medina z 14103; ● 300
Shelby; MCD-Town; ORLEANS; ***208** NI-5; mail Medina z 14103; Ⓟ 5,509; Ⓒ 5,420
Shelby Basin; RMC Place; ORLEANS; ▲ Shelby, Ridgeway; ***208** NH-5; elev. 528ft./161m.; mail Medina z 14103; rural
Shelby Center; RMC Place; ORLEANS; ▲ Shelby; ***208** NH-5; elev. 600ft./183m.; mail Medina z 14103; ● 300
Sheldon; RMC Place; WYOMING; ▲ Sheldon; ***208** NJ-5; mail Strykersville z 14145; ● 100
Sheldon; MCD-Town; WYOMING; ***208** NJ-5; mail Strykersville z 14145; Ⓟ 2,487; Ⓒ 2,561
Sheldon Center; RMC Place; WYOMING; ▲ Sheldon; ***208** NJ-5; mail Strykersville z 14145; rural
Sheldrake; RMC Place; SENECA; ▲ Ovid; **208** NK-10; mail Ovid z 14521; ● 110
Sheldrake Springs (Ovid Center); RMC Place; SENECA; ▲ Ovid; **208** NK-10; mail Interlaken z 14847; ● 100
Shelter Island; CDP; SUFFOLK; ▲ Shelter Island; **207** SD-12; 🅿; z 11964; Ⓟ 1,193; summer pop. 4,000; Ⓒ 1,234
Shelter Island; MCD-Town; SUFFOLK; ***207** SD-13; 🅿; z 11964; Ⓟ 2,263; Ⓒ 2,228

Entries in **UPPERCASE** are counties.
Entries in **bold** have populations of 2,500 or more.
Names in parentheses are alternate names.

Inc. Place	Incorporated Place
RMC Place	Rand McNally Designated Place
CDP	Census Designated Place
MCD	Minor Civil Division

⊡ County Seat
▲ Minor Civil Division
elev. Elevation
🅿 Post Office
🅷 Hospital
🅲 College
■ Principal Business Center
★ Ranally Metro Area (RMA) Abbreviation
z Zip Code(s)
Ⓟ Previous Census Population
Ⓡ Revised Census Population
Ⓐ Annexation Population
● Rand McNally Population Estimate
Ⓒ Final Census Population
Ⓢ Special Census Population
◆ Estimated Population

For additional definitions see Glossary, Volume 1, and Introduction, Volume 2.

Shelter Island Heights; CDP; SUFFOLK; ▲ Shelter Island; **207** SD-12; 🄿; z 11965; Ⓟ 1,042; summer pop. 4,000; © 981
Shenandoah; RMC Place; DUTCHESS; ▲ East Fishkill; ***207** SB-7; elev. 400ft./122m.; ★ **POK**; mail Hopewell Junction z 12533; rural
Shenorock (Lake Shenorock); CDP; WESTCHESTER; ▲ Somers; ***207** SC-7; 🄿; ★ **N.Y.**; z 10587; © 1,887
Shepards Corner; RMC Place; WAYNE; ▲ Galen; ***208** NI-10; mail Clyde z 14433; rural
Sherburne; Inc. Place; CHENANGO; ▲ Sherburne; **209** NK-14; elev. 1,055ft./322m.; 🄿; z 13460; Ⓟ 1,531; © 1,455
Sherburne; MCD-Town; CHENANGO; ***209** NK-14; 🄿; z 13460; Ⓟ 3,903; © 3,979
Sheridan; RMC Place; CHAUTAUQUA; ▲ Sheridan; **208** NK-2; 🄿; z 14135; ● 400
Sheridan; MCD-Town; CHAUTAUQUA; ***208** NK-2; 🄿; z 14135; Ⓟ 2,582; © 2,838; Ⓡ 2,584
Sheridan Park; RMC Place; ONTARIO; mail Geneva z 14456; pop. incl. with Geneva (Inc. Place)
Sherman; Inc. Place; CHAUTAUQUA; ▲ Sherman; **208** NM-1; elev. 1,539ft./469m.; 🄿; z 14781; Ⓟ 694; © 714
Sherman; MCD-Town; CHAUTAUQUA; ***208** NM-1; 🄿; z 14781; Ⓟ 1,505; © 1,553
Sherman Park; RMC Place; WESTCHESTER; ▲ Mount Pleasant; ***207** SD-7; ★ **N.Y.**; mail Thornwood z 10594
Shermerhorn Landing; RMC Place; ST. LAWRENCE; ▲ Hammond; ***209** NC-13; mail Hammond z 13646; ● 300
Sherrill; Inc. Place; ONEIDA; ▲ Vernon; **209** NI-13; 🄿; ★ **UT-R**; z 13461; Ⓟ 2,864; © 3,147
Sherwood Forest; RMC Place; SARATOGA; ▲ Clifton Park; ***209** NJ-19; elev. 320ft./98m.; ★ **A-S-T**; mail Clifton Park z 12065; ● 500
Sherwood Knolls; RMC Place; ONONDAGA; ▲ Camillus; ***209** NI-11; ★ **SYR**; mail Camillus z 13031; ● 630
Sherwood Park; RMC Place; RENSSELAER; ▲ East Greenbush; ***209** NK-19; ★ **A-S-T**; mail Rensselaer z 12144; ● 1,230
Shinhopple; RMC Place; DELAWARE; ▲ Colchester; **209** NM-15; 🄿; z 13837 & mail Downsville z 13755; rural
Shinnecock Hills; CDP; SUFFOLK; ▲ Southampton; **207** SE-12; mail Hampton Bays z 11946, Southampton z 11968; Ⓟ 2,847; © 1,749
Shinnecock Reservation; Indian Reservation; SUFFOLK; mail Southampton z 11968; State Reservation; Ⓟ 297; © 504
Shirewood; RMC Place; SARATOGA; ▲ Clifton Park; ***209** NJ-19; ★ **A-S-T**; mail Clifton Park z 12065
Shirley; CDP; SUFFOLK; ▲ Brookhaven; ***207** SF-11; 🄿; ★ **N.Y.**; z 11967; Ⓟ 22,936; © 25,395; ◆ 25,386
Shivers Corners; RMC Place; RENSSELAER; ▲ Schodack; ***209** NK-19; ★ **A-S-T**; mail East Greenbush z 12061; ● 100
Shokan; CDP; ULSTER; ▲ Olive; **209** NM-18; 🄿; z 12481; © 1,252
Sholam; RMC Place; ULSTER; ▲ Wawarsing; ***207** SA-5; mail Napanoch z 12458; rural
Shongo; RMC Place; ALLEGANY; ▲ Willing; **208** NM-6; mail Genesee z 16923; ● 125
Shooktown; RMC Place; NIAGARA; ***208** NI-4; ★ **LOCK**; mail Lockport z 14094; pop. incl. with Lockport (Inc. Place)
Shore Acres; RMC Place; CHAUTAUQUA; ▲ Ellery; ***208** NM-2; ★ **JMST**; mail Bemus Point z 14712; ● 100
Shore Acres; RMC Place; MONROE; ▲ Hamlin; ***208** NH-7; ★ **ROCH**; mail Hilton z 14468; ● 100
Shore Acres; RMC Place; SUFFOLK; ▲ Southold; ***207** SE-12; mail Mattituck z 11952
Shore Acres; RMC Place; WESTCHESTER; ***207** SE-7; ★ **N.Y.**; mail Mamaroneck z 10543; pop. incl. with Mamaroneck (Inc. Place)
Shoreham; Inc. Place; SUFFOLK; ▲ Brookhaven; **207** SE-10; 🄿; ★ **N.Y.**; z 11786; Ⓟ 540; © 417
Shore Haven; RMC Place; CHAUTAUQUA; ▲ Westfield, Ripley; ***208** NL-1; elev. 626ft./191m.; mail Westfield z 14787; summer pop. 300; ● 50
Shorelands; RMC Place; CHAUTAUQUA; ▲ Chautauqua; ***208** NL-2; mail Dewittville z 14728; ● 40
Shore Oaks; RMC Place; OSWEGO; ▲ New Haven; ***209** NG-11; mail Oswego z 13126; ● 65
Shorewood; RMC Place; SUFFOLK; ▲ Huntington; ★ **N.Y.**; mail Centerport z 11721
Shortsville; Inc. Place; ONTARIO; ▲ Manchester; **208** NI-8; 🄿; z 14548; Ⓟ 1,485; © 1,320
Short Tract; RMC Place; ALLEGANY; ▲ Granger; **208** NL-6; elev. 1,621ft./494m.; mail Fillmore z 14735; ● 500
Shrub Oak; CDP; WESTCHESTER; ▲ Yorktown; **207** SC-7; 🄿; ★ **N.Y.**; z 10588; © 1,812
Shumla; RMC Place; CHAUTAUQUA; ▲ Pomfret; ***208** NL-2; mail Fredonia z 14063; ● 120
Shushan; RMC Place; WASHINGTON; ▲ Salem; **209** NI-20; 🄿; z 12873; ● 350
Shutter Corners; RMC Place; SCHOHARIE; ▲ Wright; ***209** NK-17; elev. 671ft./205m.; mail Schoharie z 12157; rural
Shutts Corners; RMC Place; SCHOHARIE; ▲ Cobleskill; ***209** NJ-17; elev. 1,141ft./348m.; mail Cobleskill z 12043; rural
Sibleyville; RMC Place; MONROE; ▲ Mendon; ***208** NI-7; elev. 592ft./180m.; ★ **ROCH**; mail Honeoye Falls z 14472; ● 65
Sidney; Inc. Place; DELAWARE; ▲ Sidney; **209** NL-14; elev. 992ft./302m.; 🄿 🄷; z 13838; Ⓟ 4,720; © 4,068
Sidney; MCD-Town; DELAWARE; ***209** NL-14; 🄿; z 13838; Ⓟ 6,667; © 6,109
Sidney Center; RMC Place; DELAWARE; ▲ Sidney; **209** NL-14; elev. 1,290ft./393m.; 🄿; z 13839; ● 800
Siena; RMC Place; ALBANY; ▲ Colonie; 🄿; ★ **A-S-T**; z 12211
Sillimans Corners; RMC Place; CATTARAUGUS; ▲ Yorkshire; ***208** NK-5; mail Chaffee z 14030; rural
Siloam; RMC Place; MADISON; ▲ Smithfield; ***209** NI-13; mail Munnsville z 13409, Oneida z 13421; rural
Silver Bay; RMC Place; WARREN; ▲ Hague; **209** NF-19; 🄿; z 12874; ● 250
Silver Beach; RMC Place; SUFFOLK; ▲ Shelter Island; ***207** SD-12; mail Shelter Island Heights z 11965
Silver Creek; Inc. Place; CHAUTAUQUA; ▲ Hanover; **208** NK-3; 🄿; z 14136; Ⓟ 2,927; © 2,896
Silver Lake; RMC Place; ORANGE; ▲ Wallkill; ★ **MIDD**; mail Middletown z 10940
Silver Lake (Silver Lake Assembly); RMC Place; WYOMING; ▲ Castile; **208** NJ-6; 🄿; z 14549 & mail Middletown z 10940; ● 600
Silver Lake Assembly; WYOMING; see Silver Lake (RMC Place)
Silver Lake Village; RMC Place; ORANGE; ▲ Wallkill; ***207** SC-5; ★ **MIDD**; mail Middletown z 10940; ● 300
Silver Springs; Inc. Place; WYOMING; ▲ Gainesville; **208** NK-6; 🄿; z 14550; Ⓟ 852; © 844
Simmons Island; RMC Place; ALBANY; ★ **A-S-T**; mail Cohoes z 12047; pop. incl. with Cohoes (Inc. Place)
Simpsonville; RMC Place; DELAWARE; ▲ Davenport; ***209** NK-16; mail Schenevus z 12155; rural
Sinclairville; Inc. Place; CHAUTAUQUA; ▲ Gerry, Charlotte; **208** NL-2; 🄿; z 14782; Ⓟ 708; © 665
Sissonville; RMC Place; ST. LAWRENCE; ▲ Potsdam; ***209** NB-15; mail Potsdam z 13676; rural
Skaneateles; Inc. Place; ONONDAGA; ▲ Skaneateles; **209** NI-11; 🄿; ★ **SYR**; z 13152; Ⓟ 2,724; © 2,616
Skaneateles; MCD-Town; ONONDAGA; ***209** NJ-11; 🄿; ★ **SYR**; z 13152; Ⓟ 7,526; © 7,323
Skaneateles Falls; RMC Place; ONONDAGA; ▲ Skaneateles; **209** NI-11; 🄿; ★ **SYR**; z 13153 & mail Mottville z 13119; ● 850
Skaneateles Junction (Hart Lot); RMC Place; ONONDAGA; ▲ Elbridge; ***209** NI-11; ★ **SYR**; mail Elbridge z 13060; ● 200
Skerry; RMC Place; FRANKLIN; ▲ Brandon; ***209** NB-17; elev. 108ft./33m.; mail North Bangor z 12966
Skinnerville; RMC Place; ST. LAWRENCE; ▲ Stockholm; ***209** NB-16; mail Winthrop z 13697; rural
Sky Meadow Farms; RMC Place; WESTCHESTER; ▲ Harrison; ★ **N.Y.**; mail Port Chester z 10573; ● 50
Slab City; RMC Place; CORTLAND; ▲ Preble; ***209** NJ-12; elev. 1,300ft./396m.; mail Homer z 13077, Preble z 13141; rural
Slab City; RMC Place; ST. LAWRENCE; ▲ Potsdam; ***209** NB-15; elev. 366ft./112m.; mail Potsdam z 13676; ● 45
Slabtown; CHEMUNG; see Horseheads North (CDP-Census Area Only)
Slate Hill; RMC Place; ORANGE; ▲ Wawayanda; **207** SC-5; elev. 505ft./154m.; 🄿; ★ **MIDD**; z 10973; ● 800
Slaterville Springs; RMC Place; TOMPKINS; ▲ Caroline; **209** NL-11; 🄿; z 14881; ● 300
Slateville; RMC Place; WASHINGTON; ▲ Hebron; ***209** NH-20; mail Granville z 12832; rural
Sleepy Hollow (North Tarrytown); Inc. Place; WESTCHESTER; ▲ Mount Pleasant; **207** SD-7; 🄿 🄷; ★ **N.Y.**; z 10591; Ⓟ 8,152; © 9,212
Sleepy Hollow Manor; RMC Place; WESTCHESTER; ***207** SD-7; ★ **N.Y.**; mail Tarrytown z 10591; pop. incl. with Tarrytown (Inc. Place)
Sleightsburg; RMC Place; ULSTER; ▲ Esopus; ***209** NN-18; ★ **KNGST**; mail Kingston z 12401
Slingerlands; RMC Place; ALBANY; ▲ New Scotland, Bethlehem; **207** SJ-3; 🄿; ★ **A-S-T**; z 12159; ● 2,100
Sloan; Inc. Place; ERIE; ▲ Cheektowaga; **208** NE-4; 🄿; ★ **BUF**; z 14212 & mail Buffalo z 14225; Ⓟ 3,830; © 3,775
Sloansville; RMC Place; SCHOHARIE; ▲ Esperance; **209** NJ-17; elev. 683ft./208m.; 🄿; z 12160; ● 200
Sloatsburg; Inc. Place; ROCKLAND; ▲ Ramapo; **207** SD-6; elev. 343ft./105m.; 🄿; ★ **N.Y.**; z 10974; Ⓟ 3,035; © 3,117
Slyboro; RMC Place; WASHINGTON; ▲ Granville; ***209** NG-20; elev. 647ft./197m.; mail Granville z 12832; rural
Smallwood; CDP; SULLIVAN; ▲ Bethel; **207** SB-3; 🄿; z 12778; © 566
Smartville; RMC Place; OSWEGO; ▲ Boylston; **209** NG-12; elev. 1,215ft./370m.; mail Lacona z 13083; rural
Smithboro; RMC Place; TIOGA; ▲ Tioga; **209** NM-11; 🄿; z 13840; ● 375
Smith Corner (Smiths Corner); RMC Place; ALBANY; ▲ Westerlo, Rensselaerville; ***209** NK-18; mail Medusa z 12120; ● 30
Smith Corners; RMC Place; HERKIMER; ▲ Stark; ***209** NI-16; mail Mohawk z 13407; rural
Smithfield; RMC Place; DUTCHESS; ▲ Amenia; ***207** SA-8; elev. 792ft./241m.; mail Amenia z 12501; rural
Smithfield; MCD-Town; MADISON; ***209** NI-13; mail Peterboro z 13134; Ⓟ 1,053; © 1,205
Smith Landing; GREENE; see Cementon (RMC Place)
Smiths Basin; RMC Place; WASHINGTON; ▲ Kingsbury; ***209** NH-20; elev. 142ft./43m.; ★ **GLFLS**; mail Fort Ann z 12827, Hudson Falls z 12839; rural
Smiths Corner; ALBANY; see Smith Corner (RMC Place)
Smiths Mills; RMC Place; CHAUTAUQUA; ▲ Hanover; **208** NK-3; mail Forestville z 14062; ● 70
Smithtown; CDP; SUFFOLK; ▲ Smithtown; **207** SH-12; 🄿 🄷; ★ **N.Y.**; z 11787-88; Ⓟ 25,638; © 26,901; ◆ 26,893
Smithtown; MCD-Town; SUFFOLK; ***207** SE-9; 🄿; ★ **N.Y.**; z 11787-88; Ⓟ 113,406; © 115,715; Ⓡ 115,545; ◆ 111,563
Smithtown Pines; RMC Place; SUFFOLK; ▲ Smithtown; ★ **N.Y.**; mail Smithtown z 11787
Smith Valley; RMC Place; SCHUYLER; ▲ Hector; ***208** NL-10; elev. 1,256ft./383m.; mail Alpine z 14805; rural
Smithville; MCD-Town; CHENANGO; ***209** NL-13; mail Greene z 13778; Ⓟ 1,167; © 1,347
Smithville; RMC Place; JEFFERSON; ▲ Henderson, Adams; **209** NF-12; elev. 354ft./108m.; 🄿; ★ **WATN**; z 13605 & mail Greene z 13778; ● 500
Smithville Center; RMC Place; CHENANGO; ▲ Smithville; ***209** NL-13; mail Greene z 13778; ● 50
Smithville Flats; RMC Place; CHENANGO; ▲ Smithville; **209** NL-13; elev. 1,024ft./312m.; 🄿; z 13841; ● 450
Smyrna; Inc. Place; CHENANGO; ▲ Smyrna; **209** NK-13; 🄿; z 13464; Ⓟ 211; © 241
Smyrna; MCD-Town; CHENANGO; ***209** NK-13; 🄿; z 13464; Ⓟ 1,265; © 1,418
Snooks Corners; RMC Place; MONTGOMERY; ▲ Florida; ***209** NJ-17; elev. 562ft./171m.; mail Amsterdam z 12010; rural
Snufftown; RMC Place; ORANGE; ▲ Warwick; ***207** SC-5; ★ **N.Y.**; mail Goshen z 10924; rural
Snyder; RMC Place; ERIE; ▲ Amherst; **208** ND-5; 🄿; ★ **BUF**; z 14215, z 14226
Snyder Crossing; RMC Place; ONONDAGA; ▲ Manlius; ***209** NI-12; ★ **SYR**; mail Kirkville z 13082; rural
Snyders Corners; RMC Place; ALBANY; ▲ Westerlo; ***209** NK-18; mail Westerlo z 12193; rural
Snyders Corners; RMC Place; RENSSELAER; ▲ North Greenbush, Poestenkill; ***209** NJ-19; ★ **A-S-T**; mail Troy z 12180, Wynantskill z 12198; ● 250
Snyders Lake; RMC Place; RENSSELAER; ▲ North Greenbush; ***209** NK-19; ★ **A-S-T**; mail Troy z 12180, Wynantskill z 12198; ● 650
Sodom; RMC Place; PUTNAM; ▲ Southeast; ***207** SC-8; ★ **N.Y.**; mail Brewster z 10509; ● 40
Sodom; RMC Place; WARREN; ▲ Johnsburg; ***209** NG-18; elev. 1,414ft./431m.; mail North Creek z 12853
Sodus; Inc. Place; WAYNE; ▲ Sodus; **208** NH-9; elev. 432ft./132m.; 🄿 🄷; ★ **ROCH**; z 14551; Ⓟ 1,904; © 1,735
Sodus; MCD-Town; WAYNE; ***208** NH-9; 🄿; ★ **ROCH**; z 14551; Ⓟ 8,877; © 8,949
Sodus Center; RMC Place; WAYNE; ▲ Sodus; **208** NH-9; 🄿; ★ **ROCH**; z 14551; ● 200
Sodus Point; Inc. Place; WAYNE; ▲ Sodus; **208** NH-9; 🄿; ★ **ROCH**; z 14555; Ⓟ 1,190; © 1,160
Solon; RMC Place; CORTLAND; ▲ Solon; **209** NK-12; elev. 1,307ft./398m.; mail Cincinnatus z 13040; ● 50
Solon; MCD-Town; CORTLAND; ***209** NK-12; mail Cincinnatus z 13040; Ⓟ 1,008; © 1,108
Solsville; RMC Place; MADISON; ▲ Madison; **209** NJ-14; 🄿; z 13465; ● 150
Solvay; Inc. Place; ONONDAGA; ▲ Geddes; **209** NI-11; elev. 503ft./153m.; 🄿; ★ **SYR**; z 13209; Ⓟ 6,717; © 6,845
Somers; RMC Place; WESTCHESTER; ▲ Somers; **207** SC-7; 🄿; ★ **N.Y.**; z 10589; ● 620
Somers; MCD-Town; WESTCHESTER; ***207** SC-7; 🄿; ★ **N.Y.**; z 10589; Ⓟ 16,216; © 18,346
Somerset; RMC Place; NIAGARA; ▲ Somerset; **208** NH-5; ★ **LOCK**; mail Barker z 14012; ● 70
Somerset; MCD-Town; NIAGARA; ***208** NH-4; ★ **LOCK**; mail Barker z 14012; Ⓟ 2,655; © 2,865
Somerset Lake; RMC Place; DELAWARE; ▲ Hancock; mail Hancock z 13783; rural
Somerville; RMC Place; ST. LAWRENCE; ▲ Rossie; **209** ND-13; mail Gouverneur z 13642; rural
Sommerville; RMC Place; QUEENS; ***207** SG-7; elev. 25ft./8m.; ★ **N.Y.**; mail Far Rockaway z 11691; pop. incl. with New York (Inc. Place)
Sonora; RMC Place; STEUBEN; ▲ Bath; **208** NL-9; mail Savona z 14879; ● 70
Sonyea; RMC Place; LIVINGSTON; ▲ Groveland; **208** NK-7; 🄿; ★ **ROCH**; z 14556; ● 350
Sound Beach; CDP; SUFFOLK; ▲ Brookhaven; **207** SE-10; 🄿; ★ **N.Y.**; z 11789; Ⓟ 9,102; © 9,807
Soundview; RMC Place; BRONX; ★ **N.Y.**; mail Bronx z 10472; pop. incl. with New York (Inc. Place)
South; RMC Place; WESTCHESTER; ★ **N.Y.**; mail Yonkers z 10705; pop. incl. with Yonkers (Inc. Place)
South Addison; RMC Place; STEUBEN; ▲ Tuscarora; ***208** NM-8; mail Addison z 14801
South Alabama; RMC Place; GENESEE; ▲ Alabama; **208** NI-5; elev. 745ft./227m.; mail Basom z 14013; ● 100
South Albion; RMC Place; OSWEGO; ▲ Albion; ***209** NG-12; mail Altmar z 13302; rural
South Amenia; RMC Place; DUTCHESS; ▲ Amenia; **207** SA-8; mail Wassaic z 12592; ● 100
Southampton; Inc. Place; SUFFOLK; ▲ Southampton; **207** SE-12; 🄿 🄷; z 11968-69; Ⓟ 3,980; © 3,965
Southampton; MCD-Town; SUFFOLK; ***207** SE-12; 🄿; z 11968-69; Ⓟ 44,976; © 54,712; ◆ 58,594
South Amsterdam; RMC Place; MONTGOMERY; ***209** NI-18; ★ **A-S-T**; mail Amsterdam z 12010; pop. incl. with Amsterdam (Inc. Place)
South Apalachin; RMC Place; TIOGA; ▲ Owego; **209** NM-12; elev. 975ft./297m.; ★ **BING**; mail Apalachin z 13732; ● 120
South Argyle; RMC Place; WASHINGTON; ▲ Argyle; **209** NH-20; elev. 431ft./131m.; mail Argyle z 12809; ● 230
South Avon; RMC Place; LIVINGSTON; ▲ Avon; ***208** NJ-7; ★ **ROCH**; mail Avon z 14414; rural
South Bay; RMC Place; MADISON; ▲ Lenox; ***209** NI-13; ★ **SYR**; mail Canastota z 13032; ● 150
South Bay; ONONDAGA; see Lower South Bay (RMC Place)
South Bay Village; RMC Place; WASHINGTON; ▲ Fort Ann; ***209** NG-20; mail Fort Ann z 12827; ● 30
South Beach; RMC Place; RICHMOND; **210** L-8; ★ **N.Y.**; mail Staten Island z 10305; pop. incl. with New York (Inc. Place)
South Berne; RMC Place; ALBANY; **209** NK-18; mail Berne z 12023
South Bethlehem; RMC Place; ALBANY; ▲ Bethlehem; **209** NK-19; elev. 219ft./67m.; 🄿; ★ **A-S-T**; z 12161; ● 550
South Bloomfield; RMC Place; ONTARIO; ▲ East Bloomfield; ***208** NJ-8; elev. 867ft./264m.; ★ **ROCH**; mail Bloomfield z 14469; rural
South Blooming Grove; Inc. Place; ORANGE; ▲ Blooming Grove; ***207** SC-6; ● 3,400
South Bolivar; RMC Place; ALLEGANY; ▲ Bolivar; **208** NM-6; elev. 1,539ft./469m.; mail Bolivar z 14715; ● 75
South Bombay; RMC Place; FRANKLIN; ▲ Bombay; **209** NA-16; elev. 267ft./81m.; mail Moira z 12957
South Bradford; RMC Place; STEUBEN; ▲ Bradford; ***208** NL-9; mail Savona z 14879; ● 85
South Bristol; RMC Place; ONTARIO; ▲ South Bristol; **208** NJ-8; mail Naples z 14512; ● 100
South Bristol; MCD-Town; ONTARIO; ***208** NJ-8; mail Naples z 14512; Ⓟ 1,663; © 1,645
South Brookfield; RMC Place; MADISON; ▲ Brookfield; ***209** NJ-14; mail West Edmeston z 13485; ● 80
South Brooklyn; RMC Place; KINGS; **210** I-10; ★ **N.Y.**; mail Brooklyn z 11231; pop. incl. with New York (Inc. Place)
South Buffalo; RMC Place; ERIE; ★ **BUF**; mail Buffalo z 14210; pop. incl. with Buffalo (Inc. Place)
South Butler; RMC Place; WAYNE; ▲ Savannah, Butler; **208** NI-10; 🄿; z 13154; ● 250
South Byron; RMC Place; GENESEE; ▲ Byron; **208** NI-6; elev. 678ft./207m.; 🄿; ★ **ROCH**; z 14557; ● 300
South Cairo; RMC Place; GREENE; ▲ Cairo; **209** NL-18; 🄿; z 12482; ● 950
South Cambridge; RMC Place; WASHINGTON; ▲ Cambridge; ***209** NI-20; elev. 474ft./144m.; mail Buskirk z 12028; ● 50
South Canisteo; RMC Place; STEUBEN; ▲ Canisteo; **208** NM-7; mail Canisteo z 14823; rural
South Centereach; RMC Place; SUFFOLK; ▲ Brookhaven; ***207** SF-10; ★ **N.Y.**; mail Centereach z 11720
South Centerville; RMC Place; ORANGE; ▲ Wawayanda; ***207** SC-4; ★ **MIDD**; mail Middletown z 10940; ● 75
South Chili; RMC Place; MONROE; ▲ Chili; ***208** NI-7; ★ **ROCH**; mail Scottsville z 14546; ● 1,500
South Colton; RMC Place; ST. LAWRENCE; ▲ Colton; **209** NC-15; elev. 927ft./283m.; 🄿; z 13687; ● 400
South Columbia; RMC Place; HERKIMER; ▲ Columbia; **209** NJ-15; mail Mohawk z 13407; ● 100
South Corinth; RMC Place; SARATOGA; ▲ Corinth; **209** NH-18; ★ **GLFLS**; mail Corinth z 12822; ● 250
South Corning; Inc. Place; STEUBEN; ▲ Corning; **208** NM-9; mail Corning z 14830; Ⓟ 1,025; © 1,147
South Cortland; RMC Place; CORTLAND; ▲ Cortlandville; ***209** NK-11; mail Cortland z 13045; rural
South Danby; RMC Place; TOMPKINS; ▲ Danby; ***209** NL-11; mail Willseyville z 13864; rural
South Dansville; RMC Place; STEUBEN; ▲ Dansville; **208** NK-7; mail Arkport z 14807; ● 125
South Dayton; Inc. Place; CATTARAUGUS; ▲ Dayton; **208** NL-3; elev. 1,303ft./397m.; 🄿; z 14138; Ⓟ 601; © 662
South Dover; RMC Place; DUTCHESS; ▲ Dover; ***207** SB-8; mail Wingdale z 12594; rural
South Durham; RMC Place; GREENE; ▲ Durham; ***209** NL-18; mail Acra z 12405; rural
Southeast; MCD-Town; PUTNAM; ***207** SC-8; ★ **N.Y.**; mail Brewster z 10509; Ⓟ 14,927; © 17,316
Southeast Owasco; RMC Place; CAYUGA; ▲ Moravia; **209** NJ-11; mail Moravia z 13118; ● 50
South Edmeston; RMC Place; OTSEGO; ▲ Edmeston; **209** NK-14; 🄿; z 13411; ● 120
South Edwards; RMC Place; ST. LAWRENCE; ▲ Edwards; ***209** ND-14; mail Edwards z 13635; rural
South Erin; RMC Place; CHEMUNG; ▲ Erin; ***208** NM-10; mail Erin z 14838; rural
South Fallsburg; CDP-Census Area Only; SULLIVAN; ▲ Fallsburg; **207** SB-4; 🄿; z 12779; Ⓟ 2,115; © 2,061
South Farmingdale; CDP; NASSAU; ▲ Oyster Bay; ***207** SF-8; 🄿; ★ **N.Y.**; z 11735; Ⓟ 15,377; © 15,061
Southfields; RMC Place; ORANGE; ▲ Tuxedo; **207** SD-6; 🄿; ★ **N.Y.**; z 10975; ● 500
South Floral Park (Jamaica Square); Inc. Place; NASSAU; ▲ Hempstead; **211** H-16; 🄿; ★ **N.Y.**; z 11001; Ⓟ 1,478; © 1,578
South Flushing; RMC Place; QUEENS; ***207** SF-7; ★ **N.Y.**; mail Fresh Meadows z 11365; pop. incl. with New York (Inc. Place)
South Fort Plain; MONTGOMERY; see Fort Plain (Inc. Place)
South Gilboa; RMC Place; SCHOHARIE; ▲ Gilboa; ***209** NL-17; elev. 2,006ft./611m.; mail Stamford z 12167; ● 50
South Glens Falls; Inc. Place; SARATOGA; ▲ Moreau; **209** NH-19; elev. 345ft./105m.; 🄿; ★ **GLFLS**; z 12803; Ⓟ 3,506; © 3,368
South Glenwood Landing; RMC Place; NASSAU; ▲ North Hempstead; ***207** SF-8; ★ **N.Y.**; mail Glenwood Landing z 11547; ● 700
South Granville; RMC Place; WASHINGTON; ▲ Granville; **209** NH-20; mail Granville z 12832
South Greece; RMC Place; MONROE; ▲ Greece; **208** NB-7; ★ **ROCH**; mail Rochester z 14626; ● 100
South Hamilton; RMC Place; MADISON; ▲ Hamilton; ***209** NJ-14; mail Earlville z 13332; rural
South Hannibal; RMC Place; OSWEGO; ▲ Hannibal; **209** NH-11; mail Hannibal z 13074; ● 35
South Hartford; RMC Place; WASHINGTON; ▲ Hartford; **209** NH-20; elev. 374ft./114m.; mail Hartford z 12838; ● 100
South Hartwick; RMC Place; OTSEGO; ▲ Hartwick; ***209** NK-15; mail Mount Vision z 13810; rural
South Haven; RMC Place; SUFFOLK; ▲ Brookhaven; ***207** SF-10; elev. 30ft./9m.; ★ **N.Y.**; mail Brookhaven z 11719; ● 700
South Hempstead; CDP; NASSAU; ▲ Hempstead; **211** I-18; 🄿; ★ **N.Y.**; z 11550; Ⓟ 3,220; © 3,188
South Highland; RMC Place; PUTNAM; ▲ Philipstown; ***207** SC-7; elev. 615ft./187m.; ★ **N.Y.**; mail Garrison z 10524; ● 100
South Hill; CDP; TOMPKINS; ▲ Ithaca; ***209** NL-11; ★ **ITH**; mail Ithaca z 14850; Ⓟ 5,423; © 6,003
South Holbrook; RMC Place; SUFFOLK; ▲ Islip; ★ **N.Y.**; mail Holbrook z 11741
South Horicon; RMC Place; WARREN; ▲ Horicon; ***209** NF-19; mail Brant Lake z 12815
South Hornell; RMC Place; STEUBEN; ▲ Hornellsville; ***208** NL-7; mail Hornell z 14843; ● 175
South Huntington; CDP; SUFFOLK; ▲ Huntington; **207** SH-10; ★ **N.Y.**; mail Huntington Station z 11746; Ⓟ 9,624; © 9,465
South Ilion; RMC Place; HERKIMER; ▲ German Flatts; ***209** NI-15; mail Ilion z 13357; ● 120
South Jamaica; RMC Place; QUEENS; ***207** SF-7; ★ **N.Y.**; mail Jamaica z 11434; pop. incl. with New York (Inc. Place)
South Jamesport; RMC Place; SUFFOLK; ▲ Riverhead; **207** SE-12; 🄿; z 11970; ● 600
South Jefferson; RMC Place; SCHOHARIE; ▲ Jefferson; ***209** NK-16; mail Stamford z 12167; rural
South Jewett; RMC Place; GREENE; ▲ Jewett; ***209** NL-17; mail Hunter z 12442; rural
South Kortright; RMC Place; DELAWARE; ▲ Kortright; **209** NL-16; 🄿; z 13842; ● 180
South Lake; RMC Place; PUTNAM; ▲ Kent; ***207** SB-7; ★ **N.Y.**; mail Carmel z 10512; ● 300
South Lansing; TOMPKINS; see Lansing (Inc. Place)
South Lebanon; RMC Place; MADISON; ▲ Lebanon; ***209** NJ-13; elev. 1,441ft./439m.; mail Earlville z 13332; rural
South Lima; RMC Place; LIVINGSTON; ▲ Livonia, Lima; ***208** NJ-7; 🄿; ★ **ROCH**; z 14558; ● 350
South Livonia; RMC Place; LIVINGSTON; ▲ Livonia; **208** NJ-7; elev. 1,227ft./374m.; ★ **ROCH**; mail Livonia z 14487; ● 250
South Lockport; CDP; NIAGARA; ▲ Lockport; **208** NI-4; ★ **LOCK**; mail Lockport z 14094; Ⓟ 7,112; © 8,552
South Millbrook; RMC Place; DUTCHESS; ▲ Washington; **209** NN-19; elev. 549ft./167m.; mail Millbrook z 12545; pop. incl. with Millbrook (Inc. Place)
South New Berlin; RMC Place; CHENANGO; ▲ New Berlin; **209** NK-14; elev. 1,058ft./322m.; 🄿; z 13843; ● 570
South Newstead; RMC Place; ERIE; ▲ Newstead; ***208** NI-5; elev. 796ft./243m.; mail Akron z 14001; rural
South Nyack; Inc. Place; ROCKLAND; ▲ Orangetown; ***207** SE-7; ★ **N.Y.**; mail Nyack z 10960; Ⓟ 3,352; © 3,473; Ⓡ 3,480
Southold; CDP; SUFFOLK; ▲ Southold; **207** SD-12; 🄿; z 11971; Ⓟ 5,192; © 5,465
Southold; MCD-Town; SUFFOLK; ***207** SD-13; 🄿; z 11971; Ⓟ 19,836; © 20,599; ◆ 20,120
South Olean; RMC Place; CATTARAUGUS; ***208** NM-5; mail Olean z 14760; pop. incl. with Olean (Inc. Place)
South Onondaga; RMC Place; ONONDAGA; ▲ Onondaga; **209** NJ-11; ★ **SYR**; mail Nedrow z 13120; ● 650
South Otselic; RMC Place; CHENANGO; ▲ Otselic; **209** NK-13; 🄿; z 13155; ● 500
South Owego; RMC Place; TIOGA; ▲ Owego; ***209** NM-11; ★ **BING**; mail Owego z 13827; rural
South Oxford; RMC Place; CHENANGO; ▲ Oxford; ***209** NL-13; mail Oxford z 13830; rural
South Ozone Park; RMC Place; QUEENS; **211** I-14; 🄿; ★ **N.Y.**; z 11420, z 11436; pop. incl. with New York (Inc. Place)
South Park; RMC Place; ERIE; ★ **BUF**; mail Buffalo z 14220; pop. incl. with Buffalo (Inc. Place)
South Plainedge; RMC Place; NASSAU; ▲ Oyster Bay; ★ **N.Y.**; mail Massapequa z 11758
South Plattsburgh (Salmon River); RMC Place; CLINTON; ▲ Plattsburgh; ***209** NB-19; ★ **PLATT**; mail Plattsburgh z 12901; ● 600
South Plymouth; RMC Place; CHENANGO; ▲ Plymouth; ***209** NK-13; 🄿; z 13844; ● 250
South Pole; RMC Place; NEW YORK; ★ **N.Y.**; mail New York z 10090; pop. incl. with New York (Inc. Place)
Southport; CDP; CHEMUNG; ▲ Elmira; **208** NM-10; ★ **ELM**; mail Elmira z 14904; Ⓟ 7,753; © 7,396
Southport; MCD-Town; CHEMUNG; ***208** NM-9; ★ **ELM**; mail Elmira z 14904; Ⓟ 11,571; © 11,185
South Pulteney; RMC Place; STEUBEN; ***208** NK-9; mail Hammondsport z 14840; rural
South Ripley; RMC Place; CHAUTAUQUA; ▲ Ripley; **208** NL-1; elev. 1,407ft./429m.; mail Ripley z 14775
South Russell; RMC Place; ST. LAWRENCE; ▲ Russell; **209** ND-15; elev. 715ft./218m.; mail Russell z 13684; rural
South Rutland; JEFFERSON; see Tylersville (RMC Place)
South Saint Johnsville; RMC Place; MONTGOMERY; ▲ Minden; mail Fort Plain z 13339; rural
South Salem; RMC Place; WESTCHESTER; ▲ Lewisboro; **207** SD-8; 🄿; ★ **N.Y.**; z 10590; ● 12,300
South Schodack; RMC Place; RENSSELAER; ▲ Schodack; ***209** NK-19; 🄿; ★ **A-S-T**; z 12033; ● 200
South Schroon; RMC Place; ESSEX; ▲ Schroon; **209** NF-19; elev. 879ft./268m.; mail Schroon Lake z 12870; ● 200
South Setauket; RMC Place; SUFFOLK; ▲ Brookhaven; ***207** SE-10; 🄿; ★ **N.Y.**; z 11720 & mail East Setauket z 11733; ● 8,000
South Side; RMC Place; CHEMUNG; ★ **ELM**; mail Elmira z 14904; pop. incl. with Elmira (Inc. Place)
South Side; RMC Place; ERIE; ★ **BUF**; mail Buffalo z 14210, z 14220; pop. incl. with Buffalo (Inc. Place)
South Sodus; RMC Place; WAYNE; ▲ Sodus; **208** NI-9; elev. 425ft./130m.; ★ **ROCH**; mail Lyons z 14489; ● 130
South Stockton; RMC Place; CHAUTAUQUA; ▲ Stockton; **208** NL-2; elev. 1,285ft./392m.; mail Sinclairville z 14782
South Stony Brook; RMC Place; SUFFOLK; ▲ Brookhaven; ***207** SE-10; ★ **N.Y.**; mail Stony Brook z 11790; ● 6,200
South Trenton; RMC Place; ONEIDA; ▲ Trenton; ***209** NH-15; ★ **UT-R**; mail Barneveld z 13304; ● 90
South Utica; RMC Place; ONEIDA; ★ **UT-R**; mail Utica z 13501; pop. incl. with Utica (Inc. Place)
South Valley; MCD-Town; CATTARAUGUS; ***208** NM-3; mail Salamanca z 14779; Ⓟ 281; © 302
South Valley; RMC Place; OTSEGO; ▲ Roseboom; **209** NJ-16; mail Cherry Valley z 13320; ● 50
South Valley Stream; CDP-Census Area Only; NASSAU; ▲ Hempstead; **211** J-16; ★ **N.Y.**; mail Valley Stream z 11581; Ⓟ 5,328; © 5,638
South Vandalia; RMC Place; CATTARAUGUS; ▲ Carrollton, Allegany; ***208** NM-4; mail Allegany z 14706; rural
South Vestal; RMC Place; BROOME; ▲ Vestal; ***209** NM-12; ★ **BING**; mail Vestal z 13850; ● 500
Southview; RMC Place; BROOME; ★ **BING**; mail Binghamton z 13903; pop. incl. with Binghamton (Inc. Place)
Southview Gardens; RMC Place; NIAGARA; ▲ Lockport; ★ **LOCK**; mail Lockport z 14094
Southville; RMC Place; ST. LAWRENCE; ▲ Stockholm; ***209** NB-15; mail Parishville z 13672; rural
South Wales; RMC Place; ERIE; ▲ Wales, Aurora; **208** NJ-4; 🄿; ★ **BUF**; z 14139; ● 450
South Warsaw; RMC Place; WYOMING; ▲ Warsaw; **208** NJ-6; mail Warsaw z 14569; ● 200
South Westbury; NASSAU; see Westbury South (RMC Place)
South Westerlo; RMC Place; ALBANY; ▲ Westerlo; **209** NK-18; 🄿; z 12083; ● 200
Southwest Oswego; RMC Place; OSWEGO; ▲ Oswego; ***208** NH-10; elev. 371ft./113m.; mail Oswego z 13126; ● 100
Southwood; RMC Place; ONONDAGA; ▲ Onondaga, De Witt; **208** NG-9; ★ **SYR**; mail Jamesville z 13078; ● 900
South Worcester; RMC Place; OTSEGO; ▲ Worcester; **209** NK-16; mail Worcester z 12197; ● 150
Spackenkill; CDP-Census Area Only; DUTCHESS; ▲ Poughkeepsie; ***207** SB-7; ★ **POK**; mail Poughkeepsie z 12603; Ⓟ 4,660; © 4,756
Spafford; RMC Place; ONONDAGA; ▲ Spafford; **209** NJ-11; mail Homer z 13077; ● 110
Spafford; MCD-Town; ONONDAGA; ***209** NJ-11; mail Homer z 13077; Ⓟ 1,675; © 1,661
Sparkill; RMC Place; ROCKLAND; ▲ Orangetown; ***207** SE-7; 🄿 🄲 2,220; ★ **N.Y.**; z 10976; pop. incl. with Piermont (Inc. Place)
Sparkle Lake; RMC Place; WESTCHESTER; ▲ Yorktown; ***207** SC-7; ★ **N.Y.**; mail Yorktown Heights z 10598; ● 1,750
Sparrow Bush; RMC Place; ORANGE; ▲ Deerpark; **207** SC-4; 🄿; z 12780; ● 1,200
Sparta; MCD-Town; LIVINGSTON; ***208** NK-7; mail Dansville z 14437; Ⓟ 1,578; © 1,627
Sparta; RMC Place; WESTCHESTER; ***207** SD-7; ★ **N.Y.**; mail Ossining z 10562; pop. incl. with Ossining (Inc. Place)
Spawn Hollow; RMC Place; ALBANY; ▲ Bethlehem; ***209** NK-19; elev. 304ft./93m.; ★ **A-S-T**; mail South Bethlehem z 12161; rural
Speculator; Inc. Place; HAMILTON; ▲ Lake Pleasant; **209** NG-17; elev. 1,739ft./530m.; 🄿; z 12164; Ⓟ 400; © 348
Speedsville; RMC Place; TOMPKINS; ▲ Caroline; **209** NL-11; mail Berkshire z 13736; ● 120
Speigletown; RMC Place; RENSSELAER; ▲ Schaghticoke, Brunswick; **209** NJ-19; ★ **A-S-T**; mail Troy z 12180, z 12182; ● 1,200
Spencer; Inc. Place; TIOGA; ▲ Spencer; **209** NL-11; 🄿; z 14883; Ⓟ 815; © 731
Spencer; MCD-Town; TIOGA; ***209** NL-11; 🄿; z 14883; Ⓟ 2,881; © 2,979
Spencerport; Inc. Place; MONROE; ▲ Ogden; **208** NH-7; 🄿; ★ **ROCH**; z 14559; Ⓟ 3,606; © 3,559
Spencers Corner; RMC Place; DUTCHESS; ▲ North East; ***209** NM-20; mail Millerton z 12546; ● 40
Spencer Settlement; RMC Place; ONEIDA; ▲ Westmoreland; ***209** NI-14; ★ **UT-R**; mail Rome z 13440; ● 30
Spencertown; RMC Place; COLUMBIA; ▲ Austerlitz; **209** NL-20; elev. 690ft./210m.; 🄿; z 12165; ● 500
Speonk; RMC Place; SUFFOLK; ▲ Southampton; ***207** SF-11; 🄿; ★ **N.Y.**; z 11972; ● 1,000
Split Rock; RMC Place; ONONDAGA; ▲ Onondaga; **208** NG-7; ★ **SYR**; mail Camillus z 13031; ● 350
Spragueville; RMC Place; ST. LAWRENCE, JEFFERSON; ▲ Antwerp, Rossie; **209** ND-13; mail Gouverneur z 13642; ● 135
Sprakers; RMC Place; MONTGOMERY; ▲ Root; **209** NJ-17; 🄿; z 12166; ● 120
Spring Brook; RMC Place; ERIE; ▲ Elma; **208** NJ-4; 🄿; ★ **BUF**; z 14140; ● 350
Spring Creek; RMC Place; KINGS; ★ **N.Y.**; mail Brooklyn z 11239; pop. incl. with New York (Inc. Place)
Springfield; OTSEGO; see Springfield Center (RMC Place)
Springfield; MCD-Town; OTSEGO; ***209** NJ-16; mail Springfield Center z 13468; Ⓟ 1,267; © 1,350
Springfield Center (Springfield); RMC Place; OTSEGO; ▲ Springfield; **209** NJ-15; elev. 1,258ft./383m.; 🄿; z 13468; ● 400
Springfield Gardens; RMC Place; QUEENS; **211** I-15; 🄿; ★ **N.Y.**; z 11413; pop. incl. with New York (Inc. Place)
Spring Glen; RMC Place; ULSTER; ▲ Wawarsing; **207** SB-5; 🄿; z 12483; ● 650
Spring Lake; RMC Place; CAYUGA; ▲ Conquest; ***208** NI-10; mail Port Byron z 13140; rural
Spring Mills; RMC Place; ALLEGANY; ▲ Independence; ***208** NM-7; elev. 1,999ft./609m.; mail Whitesville z 14897; rural
Springport; MCD-Town; CAYUGA; ***208** NJ-10; ★ **SYR**; mail Union Springs z 13160; Ⓟ 2,198; © 2,256
Springs (The Springs); CDP; SUFFOLK; ▲ East Hampton; **207** SE-13; mail East Hampton z 11937; Ⓟ 4,355; © 4,950
Springtown; RMC Place; ULSTER; ▲ New Paltz; ***207** SA-6; mail New Paltz z 12561; rural
Springvale; RMC Place; CHENANGO; ▲ Norwich; ***209** NK-14; mail Norwich z 13815; rural
Spring Valley; Inc. Place; ROCKLAND; ▲ Clarkstown, Ramapo; **207** SD-6; 🄿; ★ **N.Y.**; z 10977; Ⓟ 21,802; © 25,464; ◆ 26,142
Spring Valley; RMC Place; WESTCHESTER; ***207** SD-7; ★ **N.Y.**; mail Ossining z 10562; pop. incl. with Ossining (Inc. Place)
Springville; Inc. Place; ERIE; ▲ Concord; **208** NK-4; elev. 1,341ft./409m.; 🄿 🄷; ★ **BUF**; z 14141; Ⓟ 4,310; © 4,252
Springville; RMC Place; SUFFOLK; ▲ Southampton; ***207** SE-12; mail Hampton Bays z 11946
Springwater; RMC Place; LIVINGSTON; ▲ Springwater; **208** NK-7; elev. 970ft./296m.; 🄿; z 14560; ● 650
Springwater; MCD-Town; LIVINGSTON; ***208** NK-7; 🄿; z 14560; Ⓟ 2,407; © 2,322
Springwood Village; RMC Place; DUTCHESS; ▲ Hyde Park; ★ **POK**; mail Hyde Park z 12538; ● 300
Sprout Brook; RMC Place; MONTGOMERY; ▲ Canajoharie; ***209** NJ-16; elev. 725ft./221m.; mail Canajoharie z 13317; rural
Spruceton; RMC Place; GREENE; ▲ Lexington; **209** NL-17; mail West Kill z 12492; rural
Spuyten Duyvil; RMC Place; BRONX; ***207** SE-7; ★ **N.Y.**; mail Bronx z 10463; pop. incl. with New York (Inc. Place)
Squiretown; RMC Place; SUFFOLK; ▲ Southampton; ***207** SE-12; elev. 22ft./7m.; mail Hampton Bays z 11946; ● 750
Staatsburg; CDP; DUTCHESS; ▲ Hyde Park; **209** NN-18; elev. 30ft./9m.; 🄿; ★ **POK**; z 12580; © 911
Stacy Basin; RMC Place; ONEIDA; ▲ Verona; ***209** NH-13; ★ **UT-R**; mail Durhamville z 13054
Stadium; RMC Place; BRONX; ★ **N.Y.**; mail Bronx z 10452; pop. incl. with New York (Inc. Place)
Stafford; RMC Place; GENESEE; ▲ Stafford; **208** NI-6; 🄿; ★ **ROCH**; z 14143; ● 500
Stafford; MCD-Town; GENESEE; ***208** NI-6; 🄿; ★ **ROCH**; z 14143; Ⓟ 2,593; © 2,409
Stamford; Inc. Place; DELAWARE; ▲ Harpersfield, Stamford; **209** NL-16; elev. 1,827ft./557m.; 🄿; z 12167; Ⓟ 1,211; © 1,265
Stamford; MCD-Town; DELAWARE; ***209** NL-16; 🄿; z 12167; includes part of the Village of Stamford; Ⓟ 2,047; © 1,943
Standish; RMC Place; CLINTON; ▲ Saranac; **209** NB-18; elev. 1,698ft./518m.; mail Lyon Mountain z 12952; ● 190
Stanford; DUTCHESS; see Stanfordville (RMC Place)
Stanford; MCD-Town; DUTCHESS; ***207** SA-7; mail Stanfordville z 12581; Ⓟ 3,495; © 3,544
Stanford Heights; RMC Place; ALBANY; ▲ Colonie; **209** NJ-18; ★ **A-S-T**; mail Schenectady z 12301; ● 1,050
Stanfordville (Stanford); RMC Place; DUTCHESS; ▲ Stanford; **209** NN-19; elev. 360ft./110m.; 🄿; z 12581; ● 630
Stanley; RMC Place; ONTARIO; ▲ Seneca; **208** NJ-9; elev. 904ft./276m.; 🄿; z 14561; ● 300
Stanley Manor; RMC Place; ONONDAGA; ▲ Camillus; ***209** NI-11; ★ **SYR**; mail Camillus z 13031; ● 1,100
Stannards; CDP; ALLEGANY; ▲ Willing, Wellsville; **208** NM-6; mail Wellsville z 14895; Ⓟ 1,026; © 868
Stanwix; RMC Place; ONEIDA; ***209** NH-14; ★ **UT-R**; mail Rome z 13440; pop. incl. with Rome (Inc. Place)
Stanwix Heights; RMC Place; ONEIDA; ***209** NI-14; ★ **UT-R**; mail Rome z 13440; pop. incl. with Rome (Inc. Place)
Stanwood; RMC Place; WESTCHESTER; ▲ New Castle, Bedford; ***207** SD-7; ★ **N.Y.**; mail Mount Kisco z 10549; ● 470
Stapleton; RMC Place; RICHMOND; ***207** SG-6; ★ **N.Y.**; mail Staten Island z 10304; pop. incl. with New York (Inc. Place)
Star; RMC Place; CLINTON; ▲ Ellenburg; ***209** NA-18; mail Ellenburg z 12933; rural
Starbuckville; RMC Place; WARREN; ▲ Chester; ***209** NF-19; mail Chestertown z 12817; rural
Stark; HERKIMER; see Starkville (RMC Place)
Stark; MCD-Town; HERKIMER; ***209** NJ-16; mail Fort Plain z 13339; Ⓟ 759; © 767
Starkey; RMC Place; YATES; ▲ Starkey; **208** NK-9; elev. 809ft./247m.; mail Dundee z 14837; ● 80
Starkey; MCD-Town; YATES; ***208** NK-9; mail Dundee z 14837; Ⓟ 3,173; © 3,465
Starks Knob; RMC Place; SARATOGA; ▲ Northumberland; ***209** NI-19; ★ **GLFLS**; mail Schuylerville z 12871; rural
Starkville (Stark); RMC Place; HERKIMER; ▲ Stark; **209** NJ-16; elev. 679ft./207m.; mail Fort Plain z 13339; ● 125
Star Lake; CDP; ST. LAWRENCE; ▲ Fine, Clifton; **209** ND-15; 🄿 🄷; z 13690; Ⓟ 1,092; © 860
Starrett City; RMC Place; KINGS; ***207** SG-7; elev. 20ft./6m.; ★ **N.Y.**; mail Brooklyn z 11207; pop. incl. with New York (Inc. Place)
State Bridge; RMC Place; ONEIDA; ▲ Verona; ***209** NI-13; ★ **UT-R**; mail Durhamville z 13054; ● 45
State Line; RMC Place; CHAUTAUQUA; ▲ Ripley; **208** NL-1; mail Ripley z 14775; ● 100
Staten Island; RMC Place; RICHMOND; ***207** SG-6; elev. 30ft./9m.; 🄿; ★ **N.Y.**; z 10301-14; pop. incl. with New York (Inc. Place)
Steamburg; RMC Place; CATTARAUGUS; ▲ Coldspring; **208** NM-3; elev. 1,413ft./431m.; 🄿; z 14783; ● 900
Steam Valley; RMC Place; CATTARAUGUS; ▲ Portville; mail Olean z 14760; ● 100
Stears Corners; RMC Place; JEFFERSON; ▲ Worth; ***209** NF-12; mail Lorraine z 13659; rural
Steelton; RMC Place; ERIE; ▲ Hamburg; ***208** NJ-4; ★ **BUF**; mail Buffalo z 14219; ● 500
Steinway; RMC Place; QUEENS; ***207** SF-7; ★ **N.Y.**; mail Astoria z 11103; pop. incl. with New York (Inc. Place)
Stella; RMC Place; BROOME; ▲ Dickinson; ***209** NM-12; ★ **BING**; mail Binghamton z 13905; ● 1,000
Stella Niagara; RMC Place; NIAGARA; ▲ Lewiston; ***208** NH-3; elev. 320ft./98m.; 🄿; ★ **BUF**; z 14092, z 14144; ● 110
Stephens Mills; RMC Place; STEUBEN; ▲ Fremont; ***208** NL-7; mail Hornell z 14843; ● 250
Stephentown; RMC Place; RENSSELAER; ▲ Stephentown; **209** NK-20; elev. 878ft./268m.; 🄿; z 12168-69; ● 750
Stephentown; MCD-Town; RENSSELAER; ***209** NK-20; 🄿; z 12168-69; Ⓟ 2,521; © 2,873
Stephentown Center; RMC Place; RENSSELAER; ▲ Stephentown; **209** NK-20; mail Stephentown z 12168; ● 370
Sterling (Sterling Center); RMC Place; CAYUGA; ▲ Sterling; **208** NH-10; 🄿; z 13156; ● 300
Sterling; MCD-Town; CAYUGA; ***208** NH-10; 🄿; z 13156; Ⓟ 3,285; © 3,432
Sterling Center; CAYUGA; see Sterling (RMC Place)
Sterling Forest; RMC Place; ORANGE; ▲ Warwick; **207** SD-5; 🄿; ★ **N.Y.**; z 10979; ● 300
Sterlington; RMC Place; ROCKLAND; ▲ Ramapo; ***207** SD-6; ★ **N.Y.**; mail Sloatsburg z 10974; ● 50
Sterling Valley; RMC Place; CAYUGA; ▲ Sterling; ***208** NH-10; mail Sterling z 13156; ● 75
Stetsonville; RMC Place; OTSEGO; ▲ New Lisbon; ***209** NK-15; elev. 1,278ft./390m.; mail New Lisbon z 13415; rural
Steuben; MCD-Town; ONEIDA; ***209** NH-14; mail Holland Patent z 13354; Ⓟ 1,006; © 1,172
STEUBEN; **208** NL-8; Ⓟ 99,088; © 98,726; ◆ 94,074
Steuben Valley; RMC Place; ONEIDA; ▲ Steuben; ***209** NH-14; elev. 816ft./249m.; mail Holland Patent z 13354; rural
Stever Mill; RMC Place; FULTON; ▲ Broadalbin; ***209** NI-18; ★ **A-S-T**; mail Broadalbin z 12025; rural
Stewart Corners (Venice); RMC Place; CAYUGA; ▲ Venice; ***209** NJ-11; mail Scipio Center z 13147; ● 30
Stewart Manor; Inc. Place; NASSAU; ▲ Hempstead; ***207** SF-8; 🄿; ★ **N.Y.**; z 11530; Ⓟ 2,002; © 1,935
Stilesville; RMC Place; DELAWARE; ▲ Deposit; **209** NM-14; mail Deposit z 13754; ● 85
Stillman Village; RMC Place; RENSSELAER; ▲ Petersburgh; ***209** NJ-20; mail Petersburg z 12138; rural
Stillwater; RMC Place; CHAUTAUQUA; ▲ Kiantone; ***208** NM-2; elev. 1,275ft./389m.; ★ **JMST**; mail Jamestown z 14701
Stillwater; RMC Place; PUTNAM; ▲ Carmel; ***207** SC-7; elev. 600ft./183m.; ★ **N.Y.**; mail Mahopac z 10541; ● 250
Stillwater; Inc. Place; SARATOGA; **209** NI-19; elev. 90ft./27m.; 🄿; ★ **A-S-T**; z 12170; Ⓟ 1,531; © 1,644
Stillwater; MCD-Town; SARATOGA; ***209** NI-19; 🄿; ★ **A-S-T**; z 12170; Ⓟ 7,233; © 7,522
Stillwater Hill; RMC Place; WESTCHESTER; ▲ New Castle; ★ **N.Y.**; mail Ossining z 10562; ● 200
Stirling; RMC Place; SUFFOLK; ▲ Southold; ***207** SD-12; mail Greenport z 11944
Stissing; RMC Place; DUTCHESS; ▲ Stanford; ***207** SA-7; mail Stanfordville z 12581; rural
Stittville; RMC Place; ONEIDA; ▲ Marcy; **209** NH-14; 🄿; ★ **UT-R**; z 13469; ● 700
Stockbridge; RMC Place; MADISON; ▲ Stockbridge; **209** NI-13; mail Munnsville z 13409; ● 100
Stockbridge; MCD-Town; MADISON; ***209** NI-13; mail Munnsville z 13409; Ⓟ 1,968; © 2,080
Stockholm; MCD-Town; ST. LAWRENCE; ***209** NB-15; mail Winthrop z 13697; Ⓟ 3,533; © 3,592
Stockholm Center; RMC Place; ST. LAWRENCE; ▲ Stockholm; ***209** NB-15; mail Winthrop z 13697; ● 85
Stockport; RMC Place; COLUMBIA; ▲ Stockport; **209** NL-19; ★ **A-S-T**; mail Hudson z 12534; ● 400
Stockport; MCD-Town; COLUMBIA; ***209** NL-19; ★ **A-S-T**; mail Hudson z 12534, Stuyvesant z 12173; Ⓟ 3,085; © 2,933
Stockport; RMC Place; DELAWARE; ▲ Hancock; mail Hancock z 13783; rural
Stockport Station; RMC Place; COLUMBIA; ▲ Stockport; ***209** NL-19; elev. 20ft./6m.; ★ **A-S-T**; mail Hudson z 12534; rural
Stockton; RMC Place; CHAUTAUQUA; ▲ Stockton; **208** NL-2; elev. 1,328ft./405m.; 🄿; z 14784; ● 450
Stockton; MCD-Town; CHAUTAUQUA; ***208** NL-2; 🄿; z 14784; Ⓟ 2,515; © 2,331
Stockwell; RMC Place; ONEIDA; ▲ Sangerfield; ***209** NJ-14; mail Waterville z 13480
Stokes; ONEIDA; see Stokes Corner (RMC Place)
Stokes Corner (Stokes); RMC Place; ONEIDA; ▲ Lee; ***209** NH-14; ★ **UT-R**; mail Lee Center z 13363; ● 85
Stone Arabia; RMC Place; MONTGOMERY; ▲ Palatine; ***209** NI-16; mail Fort Plain z 13339; rural
Stone Church; RMC Place; GENESEE; ▲ Le Roy, Bergen; ***208** NI-6; elev. 687ft./209m.; ★ **ROCH**; mail Bergen z 14416; ● 65
Stonedam; RMC Place; ALLEGANY; ▲ Willing; ***208** NM-6; elev. 1,576ft./480m.; mail Genesee z 16923; rural
Stone Gate; RMC Place; ORANGE; ▲ Blooming Grove; ★ **N.Y.**; mail Monroe z 10950
Stonehouse; DUTCHESS; see West Pawling (RMC Place)
Stone Mills; RMC Place; JEFFERSON; ▲ Orleans; **209** NE-12; elev. 368ft./112m.; mail La Fargeville z 13656; ● 45
Stone Ridge; RMC Place; MONTGOMERY; ▲ Root; ***209** NJ-17; mail Fultonville z 12072; rural
Stone Ridge; CDP; ULSTER; ▲ Marbletown; **209** NN-18; 🄿; ★ **KNGST**; z 12484; © 1,173
Stony Brook; CDP; SUFFOLK; ▲ Brookhaven; **207** SE-10; 🄿 🄷 🄲 22,524; ★ **N.Y.**; z 11790, z 11794; Ⓟ 13,726; © 13,727
Stony Creek; RMC Place; WARREN; ▲ Stony Creek; **209** NG-18; elev. 835ft./255m.; 🄿; z 12878; ● 250
Stony Creek; MCD-Town; WARREN; ***209** NG-18; 🄿; z 12878; Ⓟ 670; © 743
Stony Creek Estates; RMC Place; SARATOGA; ▲ Clifton Park; ***209** NJ-19; ★ **A-S-T**; mail Clifton Park z 12065; ● 250
Stony Hollow; RMC Place; ULSTER; ▲ Kingston; **209** NM-18; ★ **KNGST**; mail Kingston z 12401; ● 200
Stony Point; RMC Place; RENSSELAER; ▲ Schodack; ***209** NK-19; ★ **A-S-T**; mail Castleton On Hudson z 12033; rural
Stony Point; CDP; ROCKLAND; ▲ Stony Point; **207** SD-6; elev. 116ft./35m.; 🄿; ★ **N.Y.**; z 10980; Ⓟ 10,587; © 11,744
Stony Point; MCD-Town; ROCKLAND; ***207** SD-6; 🄿; ★ **N.Y.**; z 10980; Ⓟ 12,814; © 14,244
Stormville; RMC Place; DUTCHESS; ▲ East Fishkill; **207** SB-7; elev. 317ft./97m.; 🄿; ★ **POK**; z 12582; ● 700
Stottville; CDP; COLUMBIA; ▲ Stockport, Greenport; **209** NL-19; 🄿; ★ **A-S-T**; z 12172; Ⓟ 1,369; © 1,355
Stow; RMC Place; CHAUTAUQUA; ▲ North Harmony; **208** NM-2; 🄿; z 14785; ● 300
Straits Corners; RMC Place; TIOGA; ▲ Tioga; ***209** NM-11; mail Owego z 13827; rural
Stratford; RMC Place; FULTON; ▲ Stratford; **209** NH-16; elev. 1,075ft./328m.; 🄿; z 13470; ● 300
Stratford; MCD-Town; FULTON; ***209** NH-16; 🄿; z 13470; Ⓟ 586; © 640
Strathmore; RMC Place; NASSAU; ▲ North Hempstead; ***207** SF-8; ★ **N.Y.**; mail Manhasset z 11030
Street Road; RMC Place; ESSEX; ▲ Ticonderoga; ***209** NF-20; elev. 322ft./98m.; mail Ticonderoga z 12883
Strykersville; RMC Place; WYOMING; ▲ Java, Sheldon; **208** NJ-5; elev. 1,083ft./330m.; 🄿; z 14145; ● 400
Stuyvesant; RMC Place; COLUMBIA; ▲ Stuyvesant; **209** NL-19; 🄿; ★ **A-S-T**; z 12173; ● 350
Stuyvesant; MCD-Town; COLUMBIA; ***209** NL-19; 🄿; ★ **A-S-T**; z 12173; Ⓟ 2,178; © 2,188
Stuyvesant; RMC Place; KINGS; ***207** SF-7; ★ **N.Y.**; mail Brooklyn z 11233; pop. incl. with New York (Inc. Place)
Stuyvesant Falls; RMC Place; COLUMBIA; ▲ Stuyvesant; **209** NL-19; elev. 212ft./65m.; 🄿; ★ **A-S-T**; z 12174; ● 550
Suffern; Inc. Place; ROCKLAND; ▲ Ramapo; **207** SD-6; elev. 313ft./95m.; 🄿 🄷; ★ **N.Y.**; z 10901 & mail Monsey z 10952; Ⓟ 11,055; © 11,006
Suffern Park; RMC Place; ROCKLAND; ▲ Ramapo; ***207** SD-6; ★ **N.Y.**; mail Suffern z 10901
SUFFOLK; **207** SE-11; Ⓟ 1,321,864; © 1,419,369; ◆ 1,419,046
Sugarbush; RMC Place; FRANKLIN; ▲ Franklin; ***209** NC-18; elev. 1,602ft./488m.; mail Vermontville z 12989; rural
Sugar Loaf; RMC Place; ORANGE; ▲ Chester; **207** SC-5; 🄿; ★ **N.Y.**; z 10981; ● 400
Sugartown; RMC Place; CATTARAUGUS; ▲ Great Valley; ***208** NL-4; elev. 1,531ft./467m.; mail Great Valley z 14741; rural
Sullivan; RMC Place; MADISON; ▲ Sullivan; ***209** NI-13; ★ **SYR**; mail Chittenango z 13037; ● 100
Sullivan; MCD-Town; MADISON; ***209** NI-12; ★ **SYR**; mail Chittenango z 13037; Ⓟ 14,622; © 14,991
SULLIVAN; **207** SA-3; Ⓟ 69,277; © 73,966; ◆ 75,692
Sullivanville; RMC Place; CHEMUNG; ▲ Veteran; **208** NL-10; elev. 1,071ft./326m.; ★ **ELM**; mail Horseheads z 14845; ● 120
Summerdale; RMC Place; CHAUTAUQUA; ▲ Chautauqua; ***208** NL-1; mail Sherman z 14781; rural
Summer Hill; RMC Place; CAYUGA; ▲ Summerhill; **209** NK-11; mail Cortland z 13045, Locke z 13092; ● 110
Summerhill; MCD-Town; CAYUGA; ***209** NK-11; mail Locke z 13092; Ⓟ 1,017; © 1,098
Summerville; RMC Place; MONROE; ***208** NH-7; ★ **ROCH**; mail Rochester z 14617
Summit; RMC Place; SCHOHARIE; ▲ Summit; **209** NK-16; elev. 2,109ft./643m.; 🄿; z 12175; ● 200
Summit; MCD-Town; SCHOHARIE; ***209** NK-16; 🄿; z 12175; Ⓟ 973; © 1,123
Summit Park; RMC Place; ROCKLAND; ▲ Ramapo; ***207** SD-6; ★ **N.Y.**; mail Spring Valley z 10977; pop. incl. with Hempstead (Inc. Place)
Summitville; RMC Place; SULLIVAN; ▲ Mamakating; **207** SB-5; 🄿; z 12781 & mail Wurtsboro z 12790; ● 700
Sun; RMC Place; FRANKLIN; ▲ Burke; ***209** NA-17; elev. 540ft./165m.; mail Burke z 12917; rural
Sundown; RMC Place; ULSTER; ▲ Denning; **209** NN-17; 🄿; z 12740; ● 200
Sun Haven; RMC Place; WESTCHESTER; ***207** SE-7; ★ **N.Y.**; mail New Rochelle z 10801; pop. incl. with New Rochelle (Inc. Place)
Sunmount; RMC Place; FRANKLIN; ***209** ND-17; elev. 1,560ft./475m.; mail Tupper Lake z 12986
Sunny Brae; RMC Place; WESTCHESTER; ***207** SE-7; ★ **N.Y.**; pop. incl. with Mount Vernon (Inc. Place)
Sunny Side; RMC Place; CHAUTAUQUA; ▲ Ellery; ***208** NM-2; ★ **JMST**; mail Jamestown z 14701; ● 125
Sunnyside; RMC Place; COLUMBIA; ▲ Stuyvesant; ***209** NL-19; elev. 224ft./68m.; ★ **A-S-T**; mail Kinderhook z 12106; ● 30
Sunnyside; RMC Place; QUEENS; **211** H-11; 🄿; ★ **N.Y.**; z 11104; pop. incl. with New York (Inc. Place)
Sunrise Terrace; RMC Place; BROOME; ▲ Dickinson; ***209** NM-12; ★ **BING**; mail Binghamton z 13902; ● 950
Sunset; RMC Place; KINGS; ★ **N.Y.**; mail Brooklyn z 11220; pop. incl. with New York (Inc. Place)
Sunset Bay; RMC Place; CHAUTAUQUA; ▲ Hanover; **208** NL-2; mail Irving z 14081; ● 350
Sunset Beach; RMC Place; NIAGARA; ▲ Wilson; ***208** NH-4; ★ **BUF**; mail Wilson z 14172; ● 100
Sunset Beach; RMC Place; ORLEANS; ***208** NH-5; mail Waterport z 14571; rural
Sunset Manor; RMC Place; ONEIDA; ▲ Whitestown; ***209** NI-14; ★ **UT-R**; mail Whitesboro z 13492; ● 800
Sunset Park; RMC Place; KINGS; ***207** SG-6; elev. 100ft./30m.; ★ **N.Y.**; mail Brooklyn z 11220; pop. incl. with New York (Inc. Place)
Sunset View; RMC Place; WAYNE; ▲ Huron; ***208** NH-9; mail Wolcott z 14590; ● 35
Surprise; RMC Place; GREENE; ▲ Greenville; **209** NL-18; 🄿; z 12176; ● 200
Surrey Meadows; RMC Place; ORANGE; ▲ Chester; ***207** SC-5; ★ **N.Y.**; mail Chester z 10918; ● 1,200
Suspension Bridge; NIAGARA; see Bridge (RMC Place)
Swain; RMC Place; ALLEGANY; ▲ Grove; **208** NK-7; 🄿; z 14884; ● 200
Swan Lake (Hurd); RMC Place; SULLIVAN; ▲ Bethel, Liberty; **207** SA-3; elev. 1,341ft./409m.; 🄿; z 12783; ● 1,200
Swartwood; RMC Place; CHEMUNG; ▲ Van Etten; ***208** NL-10; elev. 1,054ft./321m.; mail Van Etten z 14889; ● 100
Swastika; RMC Place; CLINTON; ▲ Black Brook; ***209** NC-19; elev. 1,150ft./351m.; mail Schuyler Falls z 12985; rural
Swazy Acres; RMC Place; SARATOGA; ▲ Waterford; ★ **A-S-T**; mail Waterford z 12188; ● 320
Sweden; MCD-Town; MONROE; ***208** NI-6; 🄲 8,315; ★ **ROCH**; mail Brockport z 14420; Ⓟ 14,181; © 13,716
Sweden Center; RMC Place; MONROE; ▲ Sweden; ***208** NI-6; ★ **ROCH**; mail Brockport z 14420; ● 200
Sweet Meadows; RMC Place; ULSTER; ▲ Kingston; ***209** NM-18; ★ **KNGST**; mail Kingston z 12401; ● 150
Swenson Drive; RMC Place; DUTCHESS; ▲ Poughkeepsie; ★ **POK**; mail Wappingers Falls z 12590; pop. incl. with Wappingers Falls (Inc. Place)
Swifts Mills; RMC Place; ERIE; ▲ Newstead; ***208** NI-5; elev. 610ft./186m.; mail Akron z 14001; rural
Swormville; RMC Place; ERIE; ▲ Amherst, Clarence; **208** NC-6; elev. 587ft./179m.; 🄿; ★ **BUF**; z 14051; ● 550
Sycaway; RMC Place; RENSSELAER; ▲ Brunswick; **207** SH-6; ★ **A-S-T**; mail Troy z 12180; ● 1,950
Sylvan Beach; Inc. Place; ONEIDA; ▲ Vienna; **209** NH-13; 🄿; ★ **UT-R**; z 13157; Ⓟ 1,119; © 1,071

Entries in **UPPERCASE** are counties.
Entries in **bold** have populations of 2,500 or more.
Names in parentheses are alternate names.

Inc. Place	Incorporated Place
RMC Place	Rand McNally Designated Place
CDP	Census Designated Place
MCD	Minor Civil Division

⊡ County Seat
▲ Minor Civil Division
elev. Elevation
🄿 Post Office
🄷 Hospital
🄲 College
■ Principal Business Center
★ Ranally Metro Area (RMA) Abbreviation
z Zip Code(s)
Ⓟ Previous Census Population
Ⓡ Revised Census Population
Ⓐ Annexation Population
● Rand McNally Population Estimate
© Final Census Population
Ⓢ Special Census Population
◆ Estimated Population

For additional definitions see Glossary, Volume 1, and Introduction, Volume 2.

Sylvan Lake; RMC Place; DUTCHESS; ▲ Beekman; *207 SB-7; mail Hopewell Junction z 12533; summer pop. 1,000
Syosset; CDP; NASSAU; ▲ Oyster Bay; 207 SF-8; 🅿 🅷 🅲 827; ★ N.Y.; z 11773, z 11791; Ⓟ 18,967; Ⓒ 18,544
Syracuse; Inc. Place; ⊡ ONONDAGA; 209 NI-12; elev. 406ft./124m.; 🅿 🅷 🅲 25,656 ■; ★ SYR; z 13201-12, z 13214-15, z 13217-21, z 13224-25, z 13235, z 13244, z 13250-52, z 13261, z 13290; Ⓟ 163,860; Ⓒ 147,306; Ⓡ 146,435; ◆ 140,401

T

Taberg; RMC Place; ONEIDA; ▲ Annsville; 209 NH-13; 🅿; z 13471; ● 550
Tabor Corners; RMC Place; LIVINGSTON; ▲ Springwater; *208 NK-7; mail Wayland z 14572; rural
Taborton; RMC Place; RENSSELAER; ▲ Sand Lake; 209 NK-20; elev. 1,427ft./435m.; ★ A-S-T; mail Sand Lake z 12153; ● 200
Taconic Lake; RMC Place; RENSSELAER; ▲ Grafton; *209 NJ-20; 🅿; z 12138; rural
Taghkanic; RMC Place; COLUMBIA; ▲ Taghkanic; 209 NM-19; 🅿; z 12523 & mail Ancram z 12502; ● 120
Taghkanic; MCD-Town; COLUMBIA; *209 NM-19; 🅿; z 12523 & mail Ancram z 12502; Ⓟ 1,111; Ⓒ 1,118
Talcottville; RMC Place; LEWIS; ▲ Leyden; 209 NG-14; mail Boonville z 13309; ● 120
Talcville; RMC Place; ST. LAWRENCE; ▲ Edwards; *209 ND-14; elev. 645ft./197m.; mail Edwards z 13635; ● 100
Tallman (Tallmans); RMC Place; ROCKLAND; ▲ Ramapo; *207 SD-6; 🅿; ★ N.Y.; z 10982; pop. incl. with Airmont (Inc. Place)
Tallmans; ROCKLAND; see Tallman (RMC Place)
Tanglewood Hills; RMC Place; SUFFOLK; ▲ Brookhaven; *207 SE-10; ★ N.Y.; mail Coram z 11727
Tannersville; Inc. Place; GREENE; ▲ Hunter; 209 NL-18; 🅿; z 12424, z 12485; Ⓟ 465; Ⓒ 448
Tappan; CDP; ROCKLAND; ▲ Orangetown; 207 SE-6; 🅿; ★ N.Y.; z 10983 & mail Sparkill z 10976; Ⓟ 6,867; Ⓒ 6,757
Tarrytown (Onesquethaw); RMC Place; ALBANY; ▲ New Scotland; *209 NK-18; ★ A-S-T; mail Feura Bush z 12067; rural
Tarrytown; Inc. Place; WESTCHESTER; 207 SE-7; elev. 118ft./36m.; 🅿; ★ N.Y.; z 10591; Ⓟ 10,739; Ⓒ 11,090
Tarrytown Heights; RMC Place; WESTCHESTER; ★ N.Y.; mail Tarrytown z 10591; pop. incl. with Tarrytown (Inc. Place)
Taunton; RMC Place; ONONDAGA; ▲ Onondaga; 208 NF-7; ★ SYR; mail Syracuse z 13219; ● 1,050
Taylor; RMC Place; CORTLAND; ▲ Taylor; 209 NK-12; mail Cincinnatus z 13040; ● 200
Taylor; MCD-Town; CORTLAND; *209 NK-12; mail Cincinnatus z 13040; Ⓟ 542; Ⓒ 500
Taylor Center; RMC Place; CORTLAND; ▲ Taylor; *209 NK-12; elev. 1,400ft./427m.; mail Cincinnatus z 13040; rural
Taylorshire; RMC Place; ERIE; ▲ Aurora; *208 NJ-4; elev. 856ft./261m.; ★ BUF; mail West Falls z 14170; rural
Teall; RMC Place; ONONDAGA; ★ SYR; mail Syracuse z 13217; pop. incl. with Syracuse (Inc. Place)
Teboville; RMC Place; FRANKLIN; ▲ Malone; *209 NB-17; mail Malone z 12953; rural
Teed Corners; RMC Place; LIVINGSTON; ▲ Leicester; *208 NJ-6; mail Leicester z 14481; rural
Teleport; RMC Place; RICHMOND; ★ N.Y.; mail Staten Island z 10311; pop. incl. with New York (Inc. Place)
Ten Mile River; RMC Place; SULLIVAN; ▲ Tusten; *207 SB-3; mail Narrowsburg z 12764; summer pop. 200; ● 100
Tennanah Lake; RMC Place; SULLIVAN; ▲ Fremont; *207 SA-3; mail Roscoe z 12776; summer pop. 150
Terrace Heights; RMC Place; QUEENS; *207 SF-7; ★ N.Y.; pop. incl. with New York (Inc. Place)
Terrace Park; RMC Place; ST. LAWRENCE; ▲ Morristown; *209 NC-13; mail Ogdensburg z 13669; ● 80
Terry's Corners; RMC Place; NIAGARA; ▲ Royalton; *208 NH-4; elev. 613ft./187m.; mail Gasport z 14067; ● 75
Terryville; CDP; SUFFOLK; ▲ Brookhaven; 207 SG-14; elev. 154ft./47m.; ★ N.Y.; mail Port Jefferson Station z 11776; Ⓟ 10,275; Ⓒ 10,589
Texas; RMC Place; OSWEGO; ▲ Mexico; 209 NG-11; mail Mexico z 13114; ● 175
Texas Valley; RMC Place; CORTLAND; ▲ Marathon; 209 NK-12; mail Marathon z 13803; ● 75
Thayer Corners; RMC Place; FRANKLIN; ▲ Burke; 209 NA-17; elev. 764ft./233m.; mail Burke z 12917
The Bridges; RMC Place; ORLEANS; ▲ Carlton; *208 NH-6; mail Kent z 14477; rural
The Corner; ULSTER; see Mount Tremper (RMC Place)
The Forge; RMC Place; FRANKLIN; ▲ Bellmont; *209 NB-18; mail Chateaugay z 12920; rural
The Forks; RMC Place; CATTARAUGUS; ▲ Yorkshire; *208 NK-5; mail Chaffee z 14030; rural
The Glen; RMC Place; WARREN; ▲ Johnsburg, Chester; *209 NG-18; mail Warrensburg z 12885; rural
The Hook; RMC Place; WASHINGTON; ▲ Salem; *209 NH-20; elev. 430ft./131m.; mail Argyle z 12809; ● 35
The Narrows; RMC Place; CATTARAUGUS; ▲ Franklinville; *208 NL-5; elev. 1,686ft./514m.; mail Franklinville z 14737; rural
Thendara; RMC Place; HERKIMER; ▲ Webb; 209 NF-15; elev. 1,712ft./522m.; 🅿; z 13472; ● 230
Theresa; Inc. Place; JEFFERSON; ▲ Theresa; 209 ND-13; elev. 391ft./119m.; 🅿; z 13691; Ⓟ 889; Ⓒ 812
Theresa; MCD-Town; JEFFERSON; *209 ND-13; 🅿; z 13691; Ⓟ 2,281; Ⓒ 2,414
The Springs; SUFFOLK; see Springs (CDP)
The Terrace; RMC Place; NASSAU; ▲ North Hempstead; *207 SF-7; ★ N.Y.; mail Port Washington z 11050; ● 2,030
The Vly; RMC Place; ULSTER; ▲ Marbletown; *207 SA-5; ★ KNGST; mail Stone Ridge z 12484; ● 110
Thiells; CDP; ROCKLAND; ▲ Haverstraw; *207 SD-6; elev. 301ft./92m.; 🅿; ★ N.Y.; z 10984; Ⓟ 5,204; Ⓒ 4,758
Thomaston; Inc. Place; NASSAU; ▲ North Hempstead; 211 F-16; ★ N.Y.; mail Great Neck z 11021; Ⓟ 2,612; Ⓒ 2,607
Thompson; RMC Place; ONTARIO, SENECA; ▲ Junius, Phelps; *208 NI-9; mail Lyons z 14489; rural
Thompson; MCD-Town; SULLIVAN; *207 SB-4; mail Monticello z 12701; Ⓟ 13,711; Ⓒ 14,189
Thompson Corners; RMC Place; ONEIDA; ▲ Florence; *209 NH-13; ★ UT-R; mail Camden z 13316; rural
Thompson Ridge; RMC Place; ORANGE; ▲ Crawford; 207 SB-5; 🅿; z 10985; ● 450
Thompsons Lake; RMC Place; ALBANY; ▲ Berne; *209 NK-18; mail Altamont z 12009, East Berne z 12059; summer pop. 200
Thompsonville; RMC Place; SULLIVAN; ▲ Thompson; 207 SB-4; elev. 1,176ft./358m.; 🅿; z 12784; ● 400
Thomson; RMC Place; WASHINGTON; ▲ Greenwich; 209 NI-19; 🅿; ★ GLFLS; z 12834; ● 100
Thornton; RMC Place; CHAUTAUQUA; ▲ Cherry Creek; *208 NL-3; mail Cherry Creek z 14723; rural
Thornton Grove; RMC Place; ONONDAGA; ▲ Skaneateles; *209 NJ-11; ★ SYR; mail Skaneateles z 13152; summer pop. 60
Thornton Heights; RMC Place; ONONDAGA; ▲ Skaneateles; *209 NJ-11; ★ SYR; mail Skaneateles z 13152; ● 100
Thornwood; CDP; WESTCHESTER; ▲ Mount Pleasant; *207 SD-7; 🅿; ★ N.Y.; z 10594 & mail Valhalla z 10595; Ⓟ 7,025; Ⓒ 5,980
Thousand Island Park; RMC Place; JEFFERSON; ▲ Orleans; *209 ND-12; 🅿; z 13692; summer pop. 1,000; ● 250
Three Mile Bay; RMC Place; JEFFERSON; ▲ Lyme; 209 NE-12; elev. 265ft./81m.; 🅿; z 13693; ● 600
Three Rivers; RMC Place; ONONDAGA; ▲ Clay; 209 NH-11; ★ SYR; mail Clay z 13041; ● 200
Throg's Neck; RMC Place; BRONX; ★ N.Y.; mail Bronx z 10465; pop. incl. with New York (Inc. Place)
Throop; MCD-Town; CAYUGA; *208 NI-10; ★ SYR; mail Auburn z 13021; Ⓟ 1,792; Ⓒ 1,824
Throopsville; RMC Place; CAYUGA; ▲ Throop; *208 NI-10; ★ SYR; mail Auburn z 13021; ● 200
Thurman; MCD-Town; WARREN; *209 NG-18; 🅿; z 12885; Ⓟ 1,045; Ⓒ 1,199
Thurston; RMC Place; STEUBEN; ▲ Thurston; 208 NL-8; mail Campbell z 14821; ● 100
Thurston; MCD-Town; STEUBEN; *208 NL-8; mail Campbell z 14821; Ⓟ 1,054; Ⓒ 1,309
Thurston Road; RMC Place; MONROE; ★ ROCH; mail Rochester z 14619; pop. incl. with Rochester (Inc. Place)
Tiana; RMC Place; SUFFOLK; ▲ Southampton; *207 SE-12; elev. 17ft./5m.; mail Hampton Bays z 11946; ● 1,150
Tiana Shores; RMC Place; SUFFOLK; ▲ Southampton; *207 SE-12; mail East Quogue z 11942; ● 800
Tiashoke; RENSSELAER; see East Buskirk (RMC Place)
Ticonderoga; RMC Place; ESSEX; ▲ Ticonderoga; 209 NF-20; elev. 154ft./47m.; 🅿 🅷; z 12858, z 12883; ● 2,700
Ticonderoga; MCD-Town; ESSEX; *209 NF-20; 🅿; z 12858, z 12883; Ⓟ 5,149; Ⓒ 5,167
Tillson; CDP; ULSTER; ▲ Rosendale; 209 NN-18; elev. 236ft./72m.; 🅿; ★ KNGST; z 12486; Ⓟ 1,688; Ⓒ 1,709
Tilly Foster; RMC Place; PUTNAM; ▲ Southeast; *207 SC-8; ★ N.Y.; mail Carmel z 10512; rural
Times Plaza; RMC Place; KINGS; *207 SF-6; ★ N.Y.; mail Brooklyn z 11217; pop. incl. with New York (Inc. Place)
Times Square; RMC Place; NEW YORK; ★ N.Y.; mail New York z 10036, z 10108; pop. incl. with New York (Inc. Place)
Timothy Heights; RMC Place; DUTCHESS; ▲ Pleasant Valley; *207 SA-7; ★ POK; mail Pleasant Valley z 12569; ● 580
Tindall Corners; RMC Place; ONEIDA; ▲ Westmoreland; *209 NI-14; ★ UT-R; mail Westmoreland z 13490; ● 125
Tinkertown; RMC Place; ALLEGANY; ▲ Alfred; *208 NL-7; mail Alfred Station z 14803; ● 100
Tioga; TIOGA; see Tioga Center (RMC Place)
Tioga; MCD-Town; TIOGA; *209 NM-11; mail Tioga Center z 13845; Ⓟ 4,772; Ⓒ 4,840
TIOGA; 209 NM-11; Ⓟ 52,337; Ⓒ 51,784; ◆ 50,055
Tioga Center (Tioga); RMC Place; TIOGA; ▲ Tioga; 209 NM-11; 🅿; z 13845; ● 600
Tioga Terrace; RMC Place; TIOGA; ▲ Owego; *209 NM-12; ★ BING; mail Apalachin z 13732; ● 2,500
Tiona; RMC Place; BROOME; ▲ Maine; *209 NL-12; ★ BING; mail Newark Valley z 13811; rural
Titusville; RMC Place; DUTCHESS; ▲ La Grange; *207 SB-7; elev. 220ft./67m.; ★ POK; mail Poughkeepsie z 12603
Tivoli; Inc. Place; DUTCHESS; ▲ Red Hook; 209 NM-18; 🅿; z 12583; Ⓟ 1,035; Ⓒ 1,163
Toddsville; RMC Place; OTSEGO; ▲ Otsego, Hartwick; *209 NK-15; mail Cooperstown z 13326; ● 70
Toddville; RMC Place; WESTCHESTER; ▲ Cortlandt; *207 SC-7; ★ N.Y.; mail Cortlandt Manor z 10567; ● 900
Todt Hill; RMC Place; RICHMOND; 210 K-7; ★ N.Y.; mail Staten Island z 10301; pop. incl. with New York (Inc. Place)
Toll Gate Corner; RMC Place; CATTARAUGUS; ▲ Portville; *208 NM-5; elev. 1,426ft./435m.; mail Portville z 14770; rural
Tomhannock; RMC Place; RENSSELAER; ▲ Pittstown; *209 NJ-19; elev. 422ft./129m.; ★ A-S-T; mail Valley Falls z 12185; ● 75
Tomkins Cove; RMC Place; ROCKLAND; ▲ Stony Point; 207 SD-6; 🅿; ★ N.Y.; z 10986; ● 850
Tompkins; MCD-Town; DELAWARE; *209 NM-14; mail Deposit z 13754; Ⓟ 994; Ⓒ 1,105
TOMPKINS; 208 NL-10; Ⓟ 94,097; Ⓒ 96,501; ◆ 102,342
Tompkins Corners; RMC Place; CHEMUNG; ▲ Catlin; *208 NM-9; elev. 1,048ft./319m.; mail Horseheads z 14845, Putnam Valley z 10579; ● 450
Tompkins Square; RMC Place; NEW YORK; ★ N.Y.; mail New York z 10009; pop. incl. with New York (Inc. Place)
Tompkinsville; RMC Place; RICHMOND; *207 SG-6; ★ N.Y.; mail Staten Island z 10301; pop. incl. with New York (Inc. Place)
Tonawanda; Inc. Place; ERIE; 208 NI-3; 🅿; ★ BUF; z 14150-51, z 14217, z 14223; Ⓟ 17,284; Ⓒ 16,136
Tonawanda; MCD-Town; ERIE; *208 NI-3; 🅿; ★ BUF; z 14150-51, z 14217, z 14223; does not include the City of Tonawanda; Ⓟ 82,464; Ⓒ 78,155; ◆ 70,803
Tonawanda Reservation; Indian Reservation; GENESEE, ERIE, NIAGARA; ▲ Tonawanda; mail Tonawanda z 14150; Ⓟ 467; Ⓒ 543
Tonetta Lake Heights; PUTNAM; see Brewster Hill (CDP-Census Area Only)
Torrey; MCD-Town; YATES; *208 NK-9; mail Dresden z 14441; Ⓟ 1,269; Ⓒ 1,307
Tottenville; RMC Place; RICHMOND; 210 N-5; ★ N.Y.; mail Staten Island z 10307; pop. incl. with New York (Inc. Place)
Towerville Corners; RMC Place; CHAUTAUQUA; ▲ Gerry, Ellery; *208 NL-2; ★ JMST; mail Jamestown z 14701; rural
Towlesville; RMC Place; STEUBEN; ▲ Howard; *208 NL-8; elev. 1,814ft./553m.; mail Bath z 14810
Towners; RMC Place; PUTNAM; ▲ Patterson; 207 SC-8; elev. 459ft./140m.; ★ N.Y.; mail Holmes z 12531; ● 150
Town Line; CDP; ERIE; ▲ Lancaster, Alden; 208 NJ-4; ★ BUF; mail Lancaster z 14086; Ⓟ 2,721; Ⓒ 2,521
Town Of Tonawanda; CDP-Census Area Only; ERIE; ▲ Tonawanda; *208 NI-3; 🅿; ★ BUF; z 14217, z 14223 & mail Buffalo z 14207, Tonawanda z 14150-51; Ⓟ 65,284; Ⓒ 61,729; ◆ 58,230
Town Pump; RMC Place; MONROE; ▲ Ogden; *208 NI-7; ★ ROCH; mail Spencerport z 14559; ● 230
Townsend; RMC Place; SCHUYLER; ▲ Dix; *208 NL-9; elev. 1,313ft./400m.; mail Watkins Glen z 14891
Townsendville; RMC Place; SENECA; ▲ Lodi; *208 NK-10; elev. 1,427ft./435m.; mail Interlaken z 14847; rural
Tracy Creek; RMC Place; BROOME; ▲ Vestal; 209 NM-12; ★ BING; mail Vestal z 13850; ● 200
Trainsmeadow; RMC Place; QUEENS; ★ N.Y.; mail East Elmhurst z 11370; pop. incl. with New York (Inc. Place)
Transit; ERIE; see East Amherst (RMC Place)
Travis; RMC Place; RICHMOND; 210 L-6; ★ N.Y.; mail Staten Island z 10314; pop. incl. with New York (Inc. Place)
Treadwell; RMC Place; DELAWARE; ▲ Franklin; 209 NL-15; elev. 1,530ft./466m.; 🅿; z 13846; ● 200
Tremont; RMC Place; BRONX; *207 SF-7; ★ N.Y.; mail Bronx z 10457; pop. incl. with New York (Inc. Place)
Trenton; ONEIDA; see Barneveld (Inc. Place)
Trenton; MCD-Town; ONEIDA; *209 NH-14; ★ UT-R; mail Barneveld z 13304; Ⓟ 4,682; Ⓒ 4,670
Trenton Assembly Park; RMC Place; ONEIDA; ▲ Trenton; *209 NH-15; ★ UT-R; mail Barneveld z 13304; ● 60
Trenton Falls; RMC Place; ONEIDA; ▲ Trenton; *209 NH-15; ★ UT-R; mail Barneveld z 13304; rural
Triangle; RMC Place; BROOME; ▲ Triangle; 209 NL-12; mail Greene z 13778; ● 350
Triangle; MCD-Town; BROOME; *209 NL-12; mail Greene z 13778; Ⓟ 3,006; Ⓒ 3,032
Triangle Lake; RMC Place; ALBANY; ▲ Rensselaerville; *209 NK-18; mail Middleburgh z 12122; rural
Tribes Hill; CDP; MONTGOMERY; ▲ Amsterdam, Mohawk; *209 NI-17; 🅿; ★ A-S-T; z 12177; Ⓟ 1,060; Ⓒ 1,024
Triborough; RMC Place; NEW YORK; ★ N.Y.; mail New York z 10035; pop. incl. with New York (Inc. Place)
Tripoli; RMC Place; CORTLAND; *209 NJ-12; mail Truxton z 13158; ● 100
Tripoli; RMC Place; WASHINGTON; ▲ Fort Ann; *209 NH-19; mail Fort Ann z 12827; rural
Troupsburg; RMC Place; STEUBEN; ▲ Troupsburg; 208 NM-7; 🅿; z 14885; ● 300
Troupsburg; MCD-Town; STEUBEN; *208 NM-7; 🅿; z 14885; Ⓟ 1,006; Ⓒ 1,126
Troutburg; RMC Place; MONROE; ▲ Hamlin; *208 NH-6; ★ ROCH; mail Hamlin z 14464; ● 100
Trout Creek; RMC Place; DELAWARE; ▲ Tompkins; 209 NL-14; 🅿; z 13847; ● 250
Trout River; RMC Place; FRANKLIN; ▲ Constable; 209 NA-17; mail Constable z 12926; ● 150
Troy; Inc. Place; ⊡ RENSSELAER; 209 NJ-19; elev. 37ft./11m.; 🅿 🅷 🅲 9,224 ■; ★ A-S-T; z 12180-83; Ⓟ 54,269; Ⓒ 49,170; ◆ 48,524
Truesdale Lake; RMC Place; WESTCHESTER; ▲ Lewisboro; ★ N.Y.; mail South Salem z 10590
Trumansburg; Inc. Place; TOMPKINS; ▲ Ulysses; 208 NK-10; 🅿; ★ ITH; z 14886; Ⓟ 1,611; Ⓒ 1,581
Trumbulls Corners; RMC Place; TOMPKINS; ▲ Newfield; 208 NL-10; ★ ITH; mail Newfield z 14867; ● 110
Truthville; RMC Place; WASHINGTON; ▲ Granville; 209 NG-20; elev. 350ft./107m.; mail Granville z 12832, North Granville z 12854; ● 350
Truxton; RMC Place; CORTLAND; ▲ Truxton; 209 NJ-12; 🅿; z 13158 & mail East Homer z 13056; ● 500
Truxton; MCD-Town; CORTLAND; *209 NJ-12; 🅿; z 13158 & mail East Homer z 13056; Ⓟ 1,064; Ⓒ 1,225
Tuckahoe; CDP; SUFFOLK; ▲ Southampton; 207 SE-12; mail Southampton z 11968; Ⓒ 1,741
Tuckahoe; Inc. Place; WESTCHESTER; ▲ Eastchester; 207 SE-12; 🅿; ★ N.Y.; z 10707; Ⓟ 6,302; Ⓒ 6,211
Tucker Heights; RMC Place; SARATOGA; ▲ Charlton; *209 NJ-18; ★ A-S-T; mail Ballston Lake z 12019; ● 375
Tucker Terrace; RMC Place; ST. LAWRENCE; ▲ Louisville; *209 NA-15; mail Massena z 13662; rural
Tully; Inc. Place; ONONDAGA; ▲ Tully; 209 NJ-12; elev. 1,252ft./382m.; 🅿; ★ SYR; z 13159; Ⓟ 911; Ⓒ 924
Tully; MCD-Town; ONONDAGA; *209 NJ-12; 🅿; ★ SYR; z 13159; Ⓟ 2,378; Ⓒ 2,709
Tunnel; RMC Place; BROOME; ▲ Colesville; 209 NL-13; 🅿; ★ BING; z 13848; ● 200
Tupper Lake (Altamont); Inc. Place; FRANKLIN; ▲ Tupper Lake; 209 ND-17; 🅿; z 12986; Ⓟ 4,087; Ⓒ 3,935
Tupper Lake (Altamont); MCD-Town; FRANKLIN; *209 ND-17; mail Tupper Lake z 12986; Ⓟ 6,199; Ⓒ 6,137
Turin; Inc. Place; LEWIS; ▲ Turin; 209 NG-14; elev. 1,264ft./385m.; 🅿; z 13473; Ⓟ 295; Ⓒ 263
Turin; MCD-Town; LEWIS; *209 NG-14; 🅿; z 13473; Ⓟ 873; Ⓒ 793
Turnwood; RMC Place; ULSTER; ▲ Hardenburgh; 209 NM-16; mail Livingston Manor z 12758; rural
Tuscan; RMC Place; OTSEGO; ▲ Worcester; *209 NK-16; mail Worcester z 12197; rural
Tuscarora; RMC Place; LIVINGSTON; ▲ Mount Morris; 208 NK-6; elev. 769ft./234m.; 🅿; z 14510; ● 110
Tuscarora; MCD-Town; STEUBEN; *208 NM-8; mail Addison z 14801; Ⓟ 1,368; Ⓒ 1,400
Tuscarora Reservation; Indian Reservation; NIAGARA; ▲ Niagara; ★ BUF; mail Lewiston z 14092, Sanborn z 14132; Ⓟ 921; Ⓒ 1,138
Tusten; MCD-Town; SULLIVAN; *207 SB-3; mail Narrowsburg z 12764; Ⓟ 1,271; Ⓒ 1,415
Tuthilltown; RMC Place; ULSTER; ▲ Gardiner; *207 SB-6; mail Gardiner z 12525; rural
Tuxedo; MCD-Town; ORANGE; *207 SD-6; ★ N.Y.; mail Tuxedo Park z 10987; Ⓟ 3,023; Ⓒ 3,334
Tuxedo Park; Inc. Place; ORANGE; ▲ Tuxedo; 207 SD-6; elev. 420ft./128m.; 🅿; ★ N.Y.; z 10987; Ⓟ 706; Ⓒ 731
Twilight Park; RMC Place; GREENE; ▲ Hunter; *209 NL-18; mail Haines Falls z 12436; ● 125
Twin Lakes Village; RMC Place; WESTCHESTER; ▲ Lewisboro; *207 SC-8; ★ N.Y.; mail South Salem z 10590; ● 400
Twin Orchards; RMC Place; BROOME; ▲ Vestal; 207 SB-10; ★ BING; mail Vestal z 13850; ● 1,600
Tylersville (South Rutland, Tylerville); RMC Place; JEFFERSON; ▲ Rutland; 209 NF-13; mail Copenhagen z 13626; ● 110
Tylerville; JEFFERSON; see Tylersville (RMC Place)
Tyner; RMC Place; CHENANGO; ▲ Smithville; *209 NL-13; mail Oxford z 13830; ● 100
Tyre; RMC Place; SENECA; ▲ Tyre; 208 NI-10; mail Seneca Falls z 13148; ● 180
Tyre; MCD-Town; SENECA; *208 NI-10; mail Seneca Falls z 13148; Ⓟ 870; Ⓒ 899
Tyrone; RMC Place; SCHUYLER; ▲ Tyrone; 208 NL-9; 🅿; z 14887; ● 500
Tyrone; MCD-Town; SCHUYLER; *208 NL-9; 🅿; z 14887; Ⓟ 1,620; Ⓒ 1,714

U

Ulster; MCD-Town; ULSTER; *209 NM-18; ★ KNGST; mail Kingston z 12401; Ⓟ 12,329; Ⓒ 12,544
ULSTER; 207 SA-6; Ⓟ 165,304; Ⓒ 177,749; ◆ 179,951
Ulster Heights; RMC Place; ULSTER; ▲ Wawarsing; 207 SA-4; mail Ellenville z 12428; ● 150
Ulster Landing; RMC Place; ULSTER; ▲ Ulster; *209 NM-18; ★ KNGST; mail Saugerties z 12477; ● 200
Ulster Park; RMC Place; ULSTER; ▲ Esopus; *207 SA-6; 🅿; ★ KNGST; z 12487; ● 300
Ulsterville; RMC Place; ULSTER; ▲ Shawangunk; *207 SB-5; elev. 421ft./128m.; mail Pine Bush z 12566; ● 150
Ulysses; MCD-Town; TOMPKINS; *208 NK-10; ★ ITH; mail Trumansburg z 14886; Ⓟ 4,906; Ⓒ 4,775
Unadilla; Inc. Place; OTSEGO; ▲ Unadilla; 209 NL-14; elev. 1,024ft./312m.; 🅿; z 13849; Ⓟ 1,265; Ⓒ 1,127
Unadilla; MCD-Town; OTSEGO; *209 NL-14; 🅿; z 13849; Ⓟ 4,343; Ⓒ 4,548
Unadilla Forks; RMC Place; OTSEGO; ▲ Plainfield; 209 NJ-14; mail West Winfield z 13491; ● 150
Underwood; RMC Place; ESSEX; ▲ Elizabethtown; 209 NE-19; mail New Russia z 12964; ● 55
Union; RMC Place; BROOME; ★ BING; mail Endicott z 13760, z 13763; pop. incl. with Endicott (Inc. Place)
Union; MCD-Town; BROOME; *209 NM-12; ★ BING; mail Endicott z 13760; Ⓟ 59,786; Ⓒ 56,298; Ⓡ 56,266; ◆ 55,159
Union Center; RMC Place; BROOME; ▲ Maine, Union; 209 NM-12; ★ BING; mail Endicott z 13760; ● 1,500
Uniondale; CDP; NASSAU; ▲ Hempstead; 211 H-18; 🅿; ★ N.Y.; z 11553, z 11555-56; Ⓟ 20,328; Ⓒ 23,011; ◆ 21,855
Union Falls; RMC Place; CLINTON; ▲ Black Brook; *209 NC-18; mail Au Sable Forks z 12912; rural
Union Hill; RMC Place; WAYNE, MONROE; ▲ Ontario, Webster; 208 NH-8; 🅿; ★ ROCH; z 14563; ● 375
Union Mills; RMC Place; FULTON; ▲ Broadalbin; *209 NI-18; ★ A-S-T; mail Broadalbin z 12025; rural
Union Port; RMC Place; BRONX; 211 E-13; ★ N.Y.; mail Bronx z 10473; pop. incl. with New York (Inc. Place)
Union Settlement; RMC Place; OSWEGO; ▲ West Monroe; *209 NH-12; ★ SYR; mail West Monroe z 13167; ● 150
Union Springs; Inc. Place; CAYUGA; ▲ Springport; 208 NJ-10; 🅿; ★ SYR; z 13160; Ⓟ 1,142; Ⓒ 1,074
Union Vale; MCD-Town; DUTCHESS; *207 SB-7; mail Verbank z 12585; Ⓟ 3,577; Ⓒ 4,546
Union Valley; RMC Place; CHENANGO, CORTLAND; ▲ Taylor, Pitcher; *209 NL-14; mail De Ruyter z 13052; rural
Unionville; RMC Place; ALBANY; ▲ New Scotland; *209 NK-18; ★ A-S-T; mail Delmar z 12054; rural
Unionville; RMC Place; ONTARIO; ▲ Phelps; *208 NI-9; mail Phelps z 14532; rural
Unionville; Inc. Place; ORANGE; ▲ Minisink; 207 SD-4; elev. 1,518ft./463m.; 🅿; ★ MIDD; z 10988; Ⓟ 548; Ⓒ 536
Unionville; RMC Place; ST. LAWRENCE; ▲ Potsdam; 209 NB-15; mail Potsdam z 13676; ● 160
University Gardens; CDP; NASSAU; ▲ North Hempstead; 211 G-16; ★ N.Y.; mail Great Neck z 11020; Ⓟ 4,419; Ⓒ 4,138
University Heights; RMC Place; BRONX; *207 SF-7; ★ N.Y.; mail Bronx z 10452; pop. incl. with New York (Inc. Place)
Upper Benson; RMC Place; HAMILTON; ▲ Benson; *209 NH-17; mail Northville z 12134; rural
Upper Brookville; Inc. Place; NASSAU; ▲ Oyster Bay; 211 E-19; elev. 156ft./48m.; ★ N.Y.; mail East Norwich z 11732, Glen Head z 11545, Oyster Bay z 11771; Ⓟ 1,453; Ⓒ 1,801
Upper Grand View; RMC Place; ROCKLAND; ▲ Orangetown; ★ N.Y.; mail Nyack z 10960; ● 800
Upper Hollowville; RMC Place; COLUMBIA; ▲ Claverack; *209 NL-19; elev. 410ft./125m.; mail Hollowville z 12530; rural
Upper Jay; RMC Place; ESSEX; ▲ Jay; 209 ND-19; elev. 686ft./209m.; 🅿; z 12987; ● 500
Upper Lisle; RMC Place; BROOME; ▲ Triangle; *209 NL-12; elev. 1,031ft./314m.; mail Whitney Point z 13862
Upper Little York; RMC Place; CORTLAND; ▲ Homer; *209 NJ-12; mail Little York z 13087; ● 200
Upper Mongaup; RMC Place; SULLIVAN; ▲ Lumberland; *207 SC-3; mail Glen Spey z 12737; rural
Upper Nyack; Inc. Place; ROCKLAND; ▲ Clarkstown; *207 SD-7; ★ N.Y.; mail Nyack z 10960; Ⓟ 2,084; Ⓒ 1,863
Upper Red Hook; RMC Place; DUTCHESS; ▲ Red Hook; *209 NM-19; mail Red Hook z 12571; ● 235
Upper Saint Regis; RMC Place; FRANKLIN; ▲ Harrietstown; *209 NC-17; 🅿; z 12945; summer pop. 300; ● 100
Upper Union; RMC Place; SCHENECTADY; ▲ Niskayuna; *209 NJ-19; ★ A-S-T; mail Schenectady z 12309
Upperville; RMC Place; CHENANGO; ▲ Smyrna; *209 NJ-13; mail Smyrna z 13464; ● 45
Upton Lake; RMC Place; DUTCHESS; ▲ Stanford; *207 SA-7; mail Clinton Corners z 12514; summer pop. 150
Uptonville; RMC Place; MONROE; *208 NH-7; ★ ROCH; mail Rochester z 14617; pop. incl. with Rochester (Inc. Place)
Uptown; RMC Place; ULSTER; ★ KNGST; mail Kingston z 12401; pop. incl. with Kingston (Inc. Place)
Urbana; RMC Place; STEUBEN
Urbana; MCD-Town; STEUBEN; *208 NL-8; mail Hammondsport z 14840; Ⓟ 2,807; Ⓒ 2,546
Ushers; RMC Place; SARATOGA; ▲ Halfmoon, Clifton Park; *209 NJ-19; ★ A-S-T; mail Round Lake z 12151; ● 125
Utica; Inc. Place; ⊡ ONEIDA; 209 NI-14; elev. 423ft./129m.; 🅿 🅷 🅲 5,528 ■; ★ UT-R; z 13501-05, z 13599; Ⓟ 68,637; Ⓒ 60,651; Ⓡ 60,523; ◆ 59,145
Utopia; RMC Place; QUEENS; 211 H-14; ★ N.Y.; mail Fresh Meadows z 11366; pop. incl. with New York (Inc. Place)

V

Vail Mills; RMC Place; FULTON; ▲ Mayfield; 209 NI-17; ★ A-S-T; mail Broadalbin z 12025; ● 120
Vails Gate; CDP; ORANGE; ▲ New Windsor; 207 SC-6; 🅿; ★ NWBG; z 12584; Ⓟ 3,014; Ⓒ 3,319
Vail's Grove; RMC Place; PUTNAM; ▲ Southeast; ★ N.Y.; mail Brewster z 10509
Valatie; Inc. Place; COLUMBIA; ▲ Kinderhook; 209 NL-19; 🅿; ★ A-S-T; z 12184; Ⓟ 1,487; Ⓒ 1,712
Valcour; RMC Place; CLINTON; ▲ Peru; *209 NC-20; ★ PLATT; mail Peru z 12972; rural
Valhalla; CDP; WESTCHESTER; ▲ Mount Pleasant; 207 SE-7; 🅿 🅷 🅲 1,384; ★ N.Y.; z 10595; Ⓒ 5,379
Valley Brook; RMC Place; MONTGOMERY; ▲ Minden; *209 NJ-16; mail Fort Plain z 13339; ● 100
Valley Cottage; CDP; ROCKLAND; ▲ Clarkstown; 207 SD-7; 🅿; ★ N.Y.; z 10989; Ⓟ 9,007; Ⓒ 9,269
Valley Falls; Inc. Place; RENSSELAER; ▲ Schaghticoke, Pittstown; 209 NJ-19; elev. 330ft./101m.; 🅿; ★ A-S-T; z 12185; Ⓟ 527; Ⓒ 491
Valley Mills; RMC Place; MADISON; ▲ Stockbridge; *209 NI-13; mail Munnsville z 13409; rural
Valley Pond Estates; RMC Place; WESTCHESTER; ▲ Somers; *207 SC-7; ★ N.Y.; mail Katonah z 10536; rural
Valley Stream; Inc. Place; NASSAU; ▲ Hempstead; 207 SG-7; 🅿 🅷 ■; ★ N.Y.; z 11580-82; Ⓟ 33,946; Ⓒ 36,368; ◆ 34,927
Valley View Manor; RMC Place; ONEIDA; ★ UT-R; mail Rome z 13440; pop. incl. with Rome (Inc. Place)
Vallonia Springs; RMC Place; BROOME; ▲ Colesville; *209 NM-14; elev. 1,146ft./349m.; ★ BING; mail Nineveh z 13813; rural
Valois; RMC Place; SCHUYLER; ▲ Hector; 208 NK-9; 🅿; z 14841; ● 350
Van Brunt; RMC Place; KINGS; ★ N.Y.; mail Brooklyn z 11215; pop. incl. with New York (Inc. Place)
Van Buren; MCD-Town; ONONDAGA; *209 NI-11; ★ SYR; mail Baldwinsville z 13027; Ⓟ 13,367; Ⓒ 12,667
Van Buren Bay; RMC Place; CHAUTAUQUA; ▲ Pomfret; *208 NK-2; elev. 586ft./179m.; 🅿; z 14048 & mail Van Buren Point z 14166; ● 350
Van Buren Point; RMC Place; CHAUTAUQUA; ▲ Portland; 208 NK-2; 🅿; z 14166; summer pop. 500; ● 300
Van Burenville; RMC Place; ORANGE; ▲ Wallkill; *207 SC-5; ★ MIDD; mail Middletown z 10940; rural
Van Cortlandt Lake; RMC Place; BRONX; *207 SE-7; ★ N.Y.; pop. incl. with New York (Inc. Place)
Van Cortlandtville (Cortlandt Manor); RMC Place; WESTCHESTER; ▲ Cortlandt; *207 SC-7; ★ N.Y.; mail Cortlandt Manor z 10567; ● 1,400
Van Cott; RMC Place; BRONX; ★ N.Y.; mail Bronx z 10467; pop. incl. with New York (Inc. Place)
Vandalia; RMC Place; CATTARAUGUS; ▲ Allegany; *208 NM-4; mail Allegany z 14706
Van Deusenville; RMC Place; MONTGOMERY; ▲ Canajoharie; *209 NJ-16; elev. 735ft./224m.; mail Canajoharie z 13317; rural
Vandever; RMC Place; KINGS; ★ N.Y.; mail Brooklyn z 11210; pop. incl. with New York (Inc. Place)
Van Etten; Inc. Place; CHEMUNG; ▲ Van Etten; 208 NM-10; 🅿; z 14889; Ⓟ 552; Ⓒ 581
Van Etten; MCD-Town; CHEMUNG; *208 NM-10; 🅿; z 14889; Ⓟ 1,507; Ⓒ 1,518
Van Hornesville; RMC Place; HERKIMER; ▲ Stark; 209 NJ-16; 🅿; z 13475; ● 150
Van Keurens; DUTCHESS; see Crown Heights (CDP-Census Area Only)
Van Nest; RMC Place; BRONX; *207 SF-7; ★ N.Y.; mail Bronx z 10462; pop. incl. with New York (Inc. Place)
Van Riper Tract; RMC Place; TIOGA; ▲ Owego; *209 NM-12; ★ BING; mail Owego z 13827
Van Schaick Island; RMC Place; ALBANY; ★ A-S-T; mail Cohoes z 12047; pop. incl. with Cohoes (Inc. Place)
Van Vleet; RMC Place; STEUBEN; ▲ Tuscarora; *208 NM-8; mail Addison z 14801; rural
Varick; MCD-Town; SENECA; *208 NJ-10; mail Romulus z 14541; Ⓟ 2,161; Ⓒ 1,729
Varna; RMC Place; TOMPKINS; ▲ Dryden; 209 NK-11; ★ ITH; mail Ithaca z 14850; ● 500
Varysburg; RMC Place; WYOMING; ▲ Sheldon; 208 NJ-5; elev. 1,157ft./353m.; 🅿; z 14167; ● 360
Vaughs Corners; RMC Place; WASHINGTON; ▲ Kingsbury; ★ GLFLS; mail Hudson Falls z 12839; rural
Vega; RMC Place; DELAWARE; ▲ Roxbury; *209 NL-17; mail Margaretville z 12455; rural
Venice; CAYUGA; see Stewart Corners (RMC Place)
Venice; MCD-Town; CAYUGA; *208 NJ-10; mail Scipio Center z 13147; Ⓟ 1,315; Ⓒ 1,286
Venice Center; RMC Place; CAYUGA; ▲ Venice; 208 NJ-10; 🅿; z 13147; ● 135
Verbank; RMC Place; DUTCHESS; ▲ Union Vale; 207 SA-7; 🅿; z 12585; ● 400
Verbank Village; RMC Place; DUTCHESS; ▲ Union Vale; *207 SA-7; mail Verbank z 12585; ● 110
Verdoy; RMC Place; ALBANY; ▲ Colonie; 207 SG-4; ★ A-S-T; mail Latham z 12110; ● 1,000
Vermillion; RMC Place; OSWEGO; ▲ Palermo, New Haven; *209 NH-11; ★ SYR; mail Mexico z 13114
Vermontville; RMC Place; FRANKLIN; ▲ Franklin; 209 NC-18; 🅿; z 12989; ● 250
Vernon; Inc. Place; ONEIDA; ▲ Vernon; 209 NI-13; 🅿; ★ UT-R; z 13476; Ⓟ 1,274; Ⓒ 1,155
Vernon; MCD-Town; ONEIDA; *209 NI-14; 🅿; ★ UT-R; z 13476; Ⓟ 5,338; Ⓒ 5,335
Vernon Center; RMC Place; ONEIDA; ▲ Vernon; 209 NI-14; elev. 807ft./246m.; 🅿; ★ UT-R; z 13477; ● 400
Vernon Park; RMC Place; WESTCHESTER; *207 SE-7; ★ N.Y.; pop. incl. with Mount Vernon (Inc. Place)
Vernon Valley; RMC Place; SUFFOLK; ▲ Huntington; *207 SE-9; ★ N.Y.; mail Northport z 11768
Verona; RMC Place; ONEIDA; ▲ Verona; 209 NI-13; 🅿; ★ UT-R; z 13478; ● 600
Verona; MCD-Town; ONEIDA; *209 NI-13; 🅿; ★ UT-R; z 13478; Ⓟ 6,460; Ⓒ 6,425
Verona Beach; RMC Place; ONEIDA; ▲ Verona; 209 NH-13; elev. 377ft./115m.; 🅿; ★ UT-R; z 13162; ● 700
Verona Mills; RMC Place; ONEIDA; ▲ Verona; *209 NH-13; ★ UT-R; mail Rome z 13440; rural
Verplanck; CDP; WESTCHESTER; ▲ Cortlandt; 207 SD-6; 🅿; ★ N.Y.; z 10596; Ⓒ 777
Versailles; RMC Place; CATTARAUGUS; ▲ Perrysburg; 208 NK-3; 🅿; z 14168; ● 280
Vesper; RMC Place; ONONDAGA; ▲ Tully; 209 NJ-12; ★ SYR; mail Tully z 13159; ● 180
Vestal; RMC Place; BROOME; ▲ Vestal; 209 NM-12; 🅿; ★ BING; z 13850-51; ● 5,000
Vestal; MCD-Town; BROOME; *209 NM-12; 🅿; ★ BING; z 13850-51; Ⓟ 26,733; Ⓒ 26,535; Ⓡ 26,567; ◆ 26,358
Vestal Center; RMC Place; BROOME; ▲ Vestal; 209 NM-12; ★ BING; mail Vestal z 13850; ● 800
Vestal Gardens; RMC Place; BROOME; ▲ Vestal; ★ BING; mail Vestal z 13850
Veteran; MCD-Town; CHEMUNG; *208 NL-10; ★ ELM; mail Millport z 14864; Ⓟ 3,468; Ⓒ 3,271
Veteran; RMC Place; ULSTER; ▲ Saugerties; 209 NM-18; ★ KNGST; mail Saugerties z 12477; ● 250
Victor; Inc. Place; ONTARIO; ▲ Victor; 208 NI-8; elev. 586ft./179m.; 🅿; ★ ROCH; z 14564; Ⓟ 2,308; Ⓒ 2,433
Victor; MCD-Town; ONTARIO; *208 NI-8; 🅿; ★ ROCH; z 14564; Ⓟ 7,191; Ⓒ 9,977; Ⓡ 9,823
Victoria; RMC Place; CHAUTAUQUA; ▲ North Harmony; *208 NM-2; mail Ashville z 14710; ● 140
Victory; RMC Place; CAYUGA; ▲ Victory; 208 NH-10; mail Cato z 13033; ● 140
Victory; MCD-Town; CAYUGA; *208 NH-10; mail Cato z 13033; Ⓟ 1,535; Ⓒ 1,838
Victory; SARATOGA; see Victory Mills (Inc. Place)
Victory Mills (Victory); Inc. Place; SARATOGA; ▲ Saratoga; 209 NI-19; 🅿; ★ A-S-T; z 12884; Ⓟ 581; Ⓒ 544
Victory Park; RMC Place; WESTCHESTER; *207 SE-7; ★ N.Y.; mail New Rochelle z 10804; pop. incl. with New Rochelle (Inc. Place)
Vienna; RMC Place; ONEIDA; ▲ Vienna; 209 NH-13; ★ UT-R; mail Blossvale z 13308; ● 600
Vienna; MCD-Town; ONEIDA; *209 NH-13; ★ UT-R; mail Blossvale z 13308; Ⓟ 5,564; Ⓒ 5,819
Viewmonte; RMC Place; COLUMBIA; ▲ Germantown, Clermont; *209 NM-19; mail Germantown z 12526; rural
Village; RMC Place; NEW YORK; ★ N.Y.; mail New York z 10014; pop. incl. with New York (Inc. Place)
Village; RMC Place; NIAGARA; ▲ Lockport; *208 NI-4; ★ LOCK; mail Lockport z 14094; ● 1,110
Village Green; CDP-Census Area Only; ONONDAGA; ▲ Van Buren; 208 NE-6; ★ SYR; mail Baldwinsville z 13027; Ⓟ 4,198; Ⓒ 3,945
Village Green; RMC Place; SARATOGA; ▲ Clifton Park; *209 NJ-19; elev. 302ft./92m.; ★ A-S-T; mail Clifton Park z 12065; ● 100
Village of the Branch; Inc. Place; SUFFOLK; ▲ Smithtown; 207 SH-12; elev. 63ft./19m.; ★ N.Y.; mail Smithtown z 11787; Ⓟ 1,669; Ⓒ 1,895
Villenova; MCD-Town; CHAUTAUQUA; *208 NL-3; mail South Dayton z 14138; Ⓟ 1,065; Ⓒ 1,121
Vincent; RMC Place; ONTARIO; ▲ Bristol; *208 NJ-8; mail Canandaigua z 14424; rural
Vine Valley; RMC Place; YATES; ▲ Middlesex; 208 NJ-8; mail Middlesex z 14507; ● 200
Vintonton; RMC Place; SCHOHARIE; ▲ Fulton; *209 NK-17; mail Warnerville z 12187; rural
Viola; CDP; ROCKLAND; ▲ Ramapo; *207 SD-6; ★ N.Y.; mail Monsey z 10952; Ⓟ 4,504; Ⓒ 5,931
Viola Park; RMC Place; ROCKLAND; ▲ Ramapo; *207 SD-6; ★ N.Y.; mail Monsey z 10952
Virgil; RMC Place; CORTLAND; ▲ Virgil; 209 NK-12; mail Cortland z 13045; ● 200
Virgil; MCD-Town; CORTLAND; *209 NK-12; mail Cortland z 13045; Ⓟ 2,172; Ⓒ 2,287
Vischer Ferry; RMC Place; SARATOGA; ▲ Clifton Park; 207 SG-4; ★ A-S-T; mail Rexford z 12148; ● 330
Vista; RMC Place; WESTCHESTER; ▲ Lewisboro; 207 SD-8; ★ N.Y.; mail New Canaan z 06840; ● 750
Voak; RMC Place; YATES; ▲ Potter; *208 NJ-9; elev. 1,173ft./358m.; mail Penn Yan z 14527; rural
Vollentine; RMC Place; CATTARAUGUS; ▲ Randolph; *208 NM-3; mail Randolph z 14772; rural
Volney; RMC Place; OSWEGO; ▲ Volney; 209 NH-11; mail Fulton z 13069; ● 150
Volney; MCD-Town; OSWEGO; *209 NH-11; mail Fulton z 13069; Ⓟ 5,676; Ⓒ 6,094
Volusia; RMC Place; CHAUTAUQUA; ▲ Westfield; *208 NL-1; elev. 1,556ft./474m.; mail Westfield z 14787; rural
Voorheesville; Inc. Place; ALBANY; ▲ New Scotland; 209 NK-18; elev. 332ft./101m.; 🅿; ★ A-S-T; z 12186; Ⓟ 3,225; Ⓒ 2,705; Ⓡ 2,775
Vukote; RMC Place; CHAUTAUQUA; ▲ Busti; *208 NM-2; ★ JMST; mail Ashville z 14710; ● 300

W

Waccabuc; RMC Place; WESTCHESTER; ▲ Lewisboro; *207 SC-8; elev. 556ft./169m.; 🅿; ★ N.Y.; z 10597; ● 400
Waddington; Inc. Place; ST. LAWRENCE; ▲ Waddington; 209 NB-14; 🅿; z 13694; Ⓟ 944; Ⓒ 923
Waddington; MCD-Town; ST. LAWRENCE; *209 NB-14; 🅿; z 13694; Ⓟ 1,990; Ⓒ 2,212
Wadhams; RMC Place; ESSEX; ▲ Westport; 209 ND-20; 🅿; z 12993; ● 125
Wadhams Park; RMC Place; ST. LAWRENCE; ▲ Morristown; mail Ogdensburg z 13669
Wading River; CDP; SUFFOLK; ▲ Riverhead; 207 SE-11; elev. 200ft./61m.; 🅿; ★ N.Y.; z 11792; Ⓟ 5,317; Ⓒ 6,668
Wadsworth (Greigsville Station); RMC Place; LIVINGSTON; ▲ York; *208 NJ-6; 🅿; ★ ROCH; z 14533; ● 350
Wagners Hollow; RMC Place; MONTGOMERY; ▲ Palatine; *209 NI-16; mail Fort Plain z 13339; rural
Wainscott; CDP; SUFFOLK; ▲ East Hampton; 207 SE-13; 🅿; z 11975; summer pop. 2,200; Ⓒ 628
Waits; RMC Place; TIOGA; ▲ Owego; *209 NM-11; elev. 1,515ft./462m.; ★ BING; mail Owego z 13827; rural
Wakefield; RMC Place; BRONX; 211 C-13; ★ N.Y.; mail Bronx z 10466; pop. incl. with New York (Inc. Place)
Walden; RMC Place; ERIE; ▲ Cheektowaga; *208 NJ-4; elev. 647ft./197m.; ★ BUF; mail Buffalo z 14225
Walden; Inc. Place; ORANGE; ▲ Montgomery; 207 SB-6; 🅿; z 12586; Ⓟ 5,836; Ⓒ 6,164
Waldos Corners; RMC Place; WYOMING; ▲ Java; *208 NK-5; mail Arcade z 14009; rural
Wales; MCD-Town; ERIE; *208 NJ-5; ★ BUF; mail South Wales z 14139; Ⓟ 2,917; Ⓒ 2,960
Wales Center; RMC Place; ERIE; ▲ Wales; 208 NJ-5; elev. 897ft./273m.; 🅿; ★ BUF; z 14169; ● 400
Wales Hollow; RMC Place; ERIE; ▲ Wales; *208 NJ-5; ★ BUF; mail South Wales z 14139; ● 100
Walesville; RMC Place; ONEIDA; ▲ Whitestown; *209 NI-14; ★ UT-R; mail Whitesboro z 13492; rural
Walker; RMC Place; MONROE; ▲ Hamlin; *208 NH-7; elev. 307ft./94m.; ★ ROCH; mail Hilton z 14468; ● 50
Walker Lane; RMC Place; WARREN; ▲ Queensbury; ★ GLFLS; mail Glens Falls z 12801; ● 115
Walker Valley; CDP; ULSTER; ▲ Shawangunk; 207 SB-5; 🅿; z 12588; Ⓒ 758
Wallace; RMC Place; STEUBEN; ▲ Avoca; 208 NL-8; 🅿; z 14809; ● 200
Wallington; RMC Place; WAYNE; ▲ Sodus; 208 NH-9; elev. 405ft./123m.; ★ ROCH; mail Sodus z 14551; ● 110
Wallins Corner; RMC Place; MONTGOMERY; ▲ Amsterdam; *209 NI-18; ★ A-S-T; mail Amsterdam z 12010; rural
Wallkill; MCD-Town; ORANGE; *207 SC-5; ★ MIDD; mail Circleville z 10919; Ⓟ 23,016; Ⓒ 24,659; ◆ 25,798
Wallkill; CDP; ULSTER; ▲ Shawangunk; 207 SB-6; elev. 325ft./99m.; 🅿; z 12589; Ⓟ 2,125; Ⓒ 2,143
Walloomsac; RMC Place; RENSSELAER; ▲ Hoosick; 209 NI-20; elev. 473ft./144m.; mail Hoosick Falls z 12090; ● 150
Wall Street; RMC Place; NEW YORK; 🅿; ★ N.Y.; z 10005 & mail New York z 10268; pop. incl. with New York (Inc. Place)
Walton; Inc. Place; DELAWARE; ▲ Walton; 209 NM-15; elev. 1,226ft./374m.; 🅿 🅷; z 13856; Ⓟ 3,326; Ⓒ 3,070
Walton; MCD-Town; DELAWARE; *209 NM-15; 🅿; z 13856; Ⓟ 5,953; Ⓒ 5,607
Walton Lake; ORANGE; see Walton Park (CDP)
Walton Park (Walton Lake); CDP; ORANGE; ▲ Monroe, Chester; *207 SC-5; ★ N.Y.; mail Monroe z 10950; Ⓒ 2,330
Walworth; RMC Place; WAYNE; ▲ Macedon; 208 NI-8; 🅿; ★ ROCH; z 14568; ● 650
Walworth; MCD-Town; WAYNE; *208 NI-8; 🅿; ★ ROCH; z 14568; Ⓟ 6,945; Ⓒ 8,402
Wampsville; Inc. Place; ⊡ MADISON; ▲ Lenox; 209 NI-13; 🅿; ★ SYR; z 13163; Ⓟ 501; Ⓒ 561
Wanakah; RMC Place; ERIE; ▲ Hamburg; 208 NJ-3; ★ BUF; mail Hamburg z 14075; ● 1,600
Wanakena; RMC Place; ST. LAWRENCE; ▲ Fine; 209 NE-15; elev. 149ft./45m.; 🅿; z 13695; ● 250
Wantagh; CDP; NASSAU; ▲ Hempstead; 211 I-20; 🅿; ★ N.Y.; z 11793; Ⓟ 18,567; Ⓒ 18,971
Wappinger; MCD-Town; DUTCHESS; *207 SB-7; ★ POK; mail Wappingers Falls z 12590; Ⓟ 26,008; Ⓒ 26,274; ◆ 25,467
Wappingers Falls; Inc. Place; DUTCHESS; ▲ Poughkeepsie, Wappinger; 207 SB-7; 🅿; ★ POK; z 12590; Ⓟ 4,605; Ⓒ 4,929
Ward; MCD-Town; ALLEGANY; *208 NL-6; mail Scio z 14880; Ⓟ 334; Ⓒ 390
Wards Island; RMC Place; NEW YORK; ★ N.Y.; mail New York z 10035; pop. incl. with New York (Inc. Place)
Warner; ONONDAGA; see Warners (RMC Place)
Warners (Warner); RMC Place; ONONDAGA; ▲ Camillus, Van Buren; 209 NI-11; elev. 431ft./131m.; 🅿; ★ SYR; z 13164; ● 500
Warnerville; RMC Place; SCHOHARIE; ▲ Richmondville; 209 NK-17; elev. 930ft./283m.; 🅿; z 12187; ● 1,000
Warren; RMC Place; HERKIMER; ▲ Warren; *209 NJ-16; mail Richfield Springs z 13439; ● 70
Warren; MCD-Town; HERKIMER; *209 NJ-16; mail Richfield Springs z 13439; Ⓟ 1,077; Ⓒ 1,136
WARREN; 209 NG-18; Ⓟ 59,209; Ⓒ 63,303; ◆ 66,174
Warrensburg; CDP; WARREN; ▲ Warrensburg; 209 NG-19; elev. 749ft./228m.; 🅿; ★ GLFLS; z 12885; Ⓟ 3,204; Ⓒ 3,208
Warrensburg; MCD-Town; WARREN; *209 NG-19; 🅿; z 12885; Ⓟ 4,174; Ⓒ 4,255
Warrens Corners; RMC Place; NIAGARA; ▲ Cambria; *208 NH-4; ★ BUF; mail Lockport z 14094
Warsaw; Inc. Place; ⊡ WYOMING; ▲ Warsaw; 208 NJ-6; 🅿 🅷; z 14569; Ⓟ 3,830; Ⓒ 3,814
Warsaw; MCD-Town; WYOMING; *208 NJ-6; 🅿; z 14569; Ⓟ 5,342; Ⓒ 5,423
Warwick; Inc. Place; ORANGE; ▲ Warwick; 207 SD-5; elev. 538ft./164m.; 🅿 🅷; ★ N.Y.; z 10990; Ⓟ 5,984; Ⓒ 6,412
Warwick; MCD-Town; ORANGE; *207 SD-5; 🅿; ★ N.Y.; z 10990; partly in ★ MIDD; Ⓟ 27,193; Ⓒ 30,764; ◆ 33,772
Washington; MCD-Town; DUTCHESS; *207 SA-7; mail Millbrook z 12545; Ⓟ 4,479; Ⓒ 4,742
WASHINGTON; 209 NH-20; Ⓟ 59,330; Ⓒ 61,042; ◆ 63,072
Washington Bridge; RMC Place; NEW YORK; ★ N.Y.; mail New York z 10033; pop. incl. with New York (Inc. Place)
Washington Heights; RMC Place; NEW YORK; 211 E-11; ★ N.Y.; mail New York z 10033; pop. incl. with New York (Inc. Place)
Washington Heights; CDP; ORANGE; ▲ Wallkill; *207 SC-5; ★ MIDD; mail Middletown z 10940; Ⓟ 1,159; Ⓒ 1,318
Washington Hollow; RMC Place; DUTCHESS; ▲ Pleasant Valley; *207 SA-7; ★ POK; mail Millbrook z 12545; rural
Washington Lake; RMC Place; ORANGE; ▲ New Windsor; *207 SC-6; ★ NWBG; mail Newburgh z 12550; ● 700
Washington Mills; RMC Place; ONEIDA; ▲ New Hartford; 207 SC-12; 🅿; ★ UT-R; z 13479; ● 1,700
Washingtonville; Inc. Place; ORANGE; ▲ New Windsor, Blooming Grove; 207 SC-6; 🅿; ★ N.Y.; z 10992; Ⓟ 4,906; Ⓒ 5,851
Wassaic; RMC Place; DUTCHESS; ▲ Amenia; 209 NN-20; 🅿; z 12592; ● 700
Waterboro; RMC Place; CHAUTAUQUA; ▲ Poland; *208 NM-3; elev. 1,292ft./394m.; ★ JMST; mail Kennedy z 14747; rural
Waterburg; RMC Place; TOMPKINS; ▲ Ulysses; *208 NK-10; ★ ITH; mail Trumansburg z 14886; rural
Waterford; Inc. Place; SARATOGA; ▲ Waterford; *209 NJ-19; 🅿; ★ A-S-T; z 12188; Ⓟ 2,370; Ⓒ 2,204
Waterford; MCD-Town; SARATOGA; *209 NJ-19; 🅿; ★ A-S-T; z 12188; Ⓟ 8,695; Ⓒ 8,515
Water Island; RMC Place; SUFFOLK; ▲ Brookhaven; 207 SJ-14; ★ N.Y.; mail Patchogue z 11772
Waterloo; Inc. Place; ⊡ SENECA; ▲ Waterloo, Fayette, Seneca Falls; 208 NJ-10; elev. 455ft./139m.; 🅿; z 13165; Ⓟ 5,116; Ⓒ 5,111
Waterloo; MCD-Town; SENECA; *208 NJ-9; 🅿; z 13165; includes part of the Village of Waterloo; Ⓟ 7,765; Ⓒ 7,866
Waterman Corners; RMC Place; CHAUTAUQUA; ▲ Ellery; *208 NL-2; elev. 1,616ft./493m.; ★ JMST; mail Dewittville z 14728; rural
Watermill; CDP-Census Area Only; SUFFOLK; ▲ Southampton; 207 SE-12; elev. 35ft./11m.; 🅿; z 11976; Ⓟ 1,893; Ⓒ 1,724
Waterport; RMC Place; ORLEANS; ▲ Carlton; 208 NH-5; elev. 351ft./107m.; 🅿; z 14571; ● 400
Waterside Park; SUFFOLK; see Crab Meadow (RMC Place)
Watertown; Inc. Place; ⊡ JEFFERSON; 209 NE-12; elev. 478ft./146m.; 🅿 🅷 ■; ★ WATN; z 13601-03; Ⓟ 29,429; Ⓒ 26,705; ◆ 26,808
Watertown; MCD-Town; JEFFERSON; *209 NE-12; 🅿; ★ WATN; z 13601-03; does not include the City of Watertown; Ⓟ 4,341; Ⓒ 4,482
Watertown Center; RMC Place; JEFFERSON; ▲ Watertown; *209 NE-12; ★ WATN; mail Watertown z 13601; rural
Watertown Junction; RMC Place; JEFFERSON; ★ WATN; mail Watertown z 13601; pop. incl. with Watertown (Inc. Place)
Watervale; RMC Place; ONONDAGA; ▲ Pompey; *209 NI-12; ★ SYR; mail Manlius z 13104; rural
Water Valley; RMC Place; ERIE; ▲ Hamburg; *208 NJ-4; elev. 782ft./238m.; ★ BUF; mail Hamburg z 14075; ● 500
Waterville; RMC Place; JEFFERSON; ▲ Lorraine; *209 NF-12; mail Lorraine z 13659; rural
Waterville; Inc. Place; ONEIDA; ▲ Marshall, Sangerfield; 209 NJ-14; elev. 1,237ft./377m.; 🅿; z 13480; Ⓟ 1,664; Ⓒ 1,721
Watervliet; Inc. Place; ALBANY; 209 NJ-19; elev. 50ft./15m.; 🅿; ★ A-S-T; z 12189; Ⓟ 11,061; Ⓒ 10,207
Watkins Glen; Inc. Place; ⊡ SCHUYLER; ▲ Reading, Dix; 208 NL-9; 🅿; z 14891; Ⓟ 2,207; Ⓒ 2,149
Watson; RMC Place; LEWIS; ▲ Watson; 209 NF-14; elev. 749ft./228m.; mail Lowville z 13367; ● 100
Watson; MCD-Town; LEWIS; *209 NF-14; mail Lowville z 13367; Ⓟ 1,613; Ⓒ 1,987
Watsonville; RMC Place; SCHOHARIE; ▲ Fulton; *209 NK-17; elev. 692ft./211m.; mail Middleburgh z 12122; ● 90
Wattlesburg; RMC Place; CHAUTAUQUA; ▲ Ripley; *208 NL-1; mail Ripley z 14775; rural
Watts Flats; RMC Place; CHAUTAUQUA; ▲ Harmony; 208 NM-2; mail Ashville z 14710; ● 100
Wautoma Beach; RMC Place; MONROE; ▲ Hamlin; *208 NH-7; ★ ROCH; mail Hilton z 14468; ● 100
Wave Crest; RMC Place; QUEENS; *207 SG-7; 🅿; ★ N.Y.; z 11690 & mail Far Rockaway z 11691; pop. incl. with New York (Inc. Place)
Waverly; MCD-Town; FRANKLIN; *209 NC-16; mail Saint Regis Falls z 12980; Ⓟ 1,068; Ⓒ 1,118
Waverly; Inc. Place; TIOGA; ▲ Barton; 209 NM-11; 🅿; z 14892; Ⓟ 4,787; Ⓒ 4,607
Wawarsing; RMC Place; ULSTER; ▲ Wawarsing; 207 SA-5; elev. 288ft./88m.; 🅿; z 12489; ● 800
Wawarsing; MCD-Town; ULSTER; *207 SA-5; 🅿; z 12489; Ⓟ 12,348; Ⓒ 12,889; Ⓡ 13,936
Wawayanda; MCD-Town; ORANGE; *207 SC-5; ★ MIDD; mail Slate Hill z 10973; Ⓟ 5,518; Ⓒ 6,273
Wawbeek; RMC Place; FRANKLIN; ▲ Harrietstown; *209 ND-17; mail Tupper Lake z 12986; ● 90
Wayland; Inc. Place; STEUBEN; ▲ Wayland; 208 NK-7; elev. 1,372ft./418m.; 🅿; z 14572; Ⓟ 1,976; Ⓒ 1,893
Wayland; MCD-Town; STEUBEN; *208 NK-7; 🅿; z 14572; Ⓟ 4,311; Ⓒ 4,314
Wayne; RMC Place; SCHUYLER; ▲ Tyrone; 208 NK-9; 🅿; z 14893; ● 550
Wayne; MCD-Town; STEUBEN; *208 NL-9; mail Hammondsport z 14840; Ⓟ 1,029; Ⓒ 1,165
WAYNE; 208 NI-9; Ⓟ 89,123; Ⓒ 93,765; ◆ 88,071
Wayne Center; RMC Place; WAYNE; ▲ Rose; 208 NI-9; elev. 439ft./134m.; mail Lyons z 14489; ● 100
Webatuck; RMC Place; DUTCHESS; *207 SB-8; elev. 403ft./123m.; mail Wingdale z 12594; rural
Webb; MCD-Town; HERKIMER; *209 NF-15; mail Old Forge z 13420; Ⓟ 1,637; Ⓒ 1,912
Webbs Crossing; RMC Place; STEUBEN; ▲ Hornellsville; *208 NL-7; mail Hornell z 14843; rural
Webbs Mills; RMC Place; CHEMUNG; ▲ Southport; 208 NM-9; ★ ELM; mail Pine City z 14871; ● 300
Webster; Inc. Place; MONROE; ▲ Webster; 208 NH-8; 🅿; ★ ROCH; z 14580; Ⓟ 5,464; Ⓒ 5,216
Webster; MCD-Town; MONROE; *208 NH-8; 🅿; ★ ROCH; z 14580; Ⓟ 31,639; Ⓒ 37,926; ◆ 39,974
Webster Crossing; LIVINGSTON; see Websters Crossing (RMC Place)
Websters Corners; RMC Place; ERIE; ▲ Orchard Park; *208 NJ-4; ★ BUF; mail Orchard Park z 14127; rural
Websters Crossing (Webster Crossing); RMC Place; LIVINGSTON; ▲ Springwater; 208 NK-7; mail Springwater z 14560; ● 250
Wedgewood; RMC Place; SCHUYLER; ▲ Dix; *208 NL-9; elev. 1,123ft./342m.; mail Watkins Glen z 14891; rural
Weedsport; Inc. Place; CAYUGA; ▲ Brutus; 208 NI-10; 🅿; ★ SYR; z 13166; Ⓟ 1,996; Ⓒ 2,017
Wegatchie; RMC Place; ST. LAWRENCE; ▲ Rossie; 209 ND-13; mail Antwerp z 13608; ● 65
Welcome; RMC Place; OTSEGO; ▲ New Lisbon; *209 NK-15; mail Mount Vision z 13810; rural
Wells; RMC Place; HAMILTON; ▲ Wells; 209 NH-17; 🅿; z 12190; ● 600
Wells; MCD-Town; HAMILTON; *209 NG-17; 🅿; z 12190; Ⓟ 706; Ⓒ 737
Wells Bridge; RMC Place; OTSEGO; ▲ Unadilla; 209 NL-14; 🅿; z 13859; ● 300
Wellsburg; Inc. Place; CHEMUNG; ▲ Ashland; 208 NM-10; elev. 824ft./251m.; 🅿; ★ ELM; z 14894; Ⓟ 617; Ⓒ 631
Wellsville; Inc. Place; ALLEGANY; ▲ Wellsville; 208 NM-6; elev. 1,517ft./462m.; 🅿 🅷; z 14895; Ⓟ 5,241; Ⓒ 5,171
Wellsville; MCD-Town; ALLEGANY; *208 NM-6; 🅿; z 14895; Ⓟ 8,116; Ⓒ 7,678
Wellsville; RMC Place; MONTGOMERY; ▲ Florida; *209 NJ-17; mail Amsterdam z 12010; ● 85
Weltonville; RMC Place; TIOGA; ▲ Candor; *209 NM-11; mail Newark Valley z 13811; rural
Wendelville; RMC Place; NIAGARA; ▲ Pendleton; 208 NB-5; elev. 583ft./178m.; ★ BUF; mail North Tonawanda z 14120; ● 150
Wesley; RMC Place; CATTARAUGUS; ▲ Dayton; *208 NL-3; elev. 1,317ft./401m.; mail Gowanda z 14070; rural
Wesley Chapel; RMC Place; ROCKLAND; ▲ Ramapo; *207 SD-6; ★ N.Y.; mail Suffern z 10901; pop. incl. with Hillburn (Inc. Place)
Wesley Hills; Inc. Place; ROCKLAND; ▲ Ramapo; *207 SD-6; ★ N.Y.; mail Monsey z 10952, Spring Valley z 10977, Suffern z 10901; Ⓟ 4,305; Ⓒ 4,848
West Albany; RMC Place; ALBANY; *209 NJ-19; ★ A-S-T; pop. incl. with Albany (Inc. Place)
West Almond; RMC Place; ALLEGANY; ▲ West Almond; *208 NL-6; elev. 1,857ft./566m.; mail Almond z 14804; ● 30
West Almond; MCD-Town; ALLEGANY; *208 NL-6; mail Almond z 14804; Ⓟ 277; Ⓒ 353
West Amboy; RMC Place; OSWEGO; ▲ Amboy; 209 NH-12; elev. 588ft./179m.; mail West Monroe z 13167; ● 125
West Babylon; CDP; SUFFOLK; ▲ Babylon; 207 SF-9; 🅿; ★ N.Y.; z 11704, z 11707; Ⓟ 42,410; Ⓒ 43,452; ◆ 43,436
West Bainbridge; RMC Place; CHENANGO; ▲ Bainbridge; *209 NL-14; mail Bainbridge z 13733; ● 50
West Bangor; RMC Place; FRANKLIN; ▲ Bangor; 209 NB-17; 🅿; z 12966; ● 250
West Barre; RMC Place; ORLEANS; ▲ Barre; *208 NI-5; elev. 670ft./204m.; mail Albion z 14411; ● 40

Entries in **UPPERCASE** are counties.
Entries in **bold** have populations of 2,500 or more.
Names in parentheses are alternate names.

Inc. Place	Incorporated Place
RMC Place	Rand McNally Designated Place
CDP	Census Designated Place
MCD	Minor Civil Division
⊡	County Seat
▲	Minor Civil Division
elev.	Elevation
🅿	Post Office
🅷	Hospital
🅲	College
■	Principal Business Center
★	Ranally Metro Area (RMA) Abbreviation
z	Zip Code(s)
Ⓟ	Previous Census Population
Ⓡ	Revised Census Population
Ⓐ	Annexation Population
●	Rand McNally Population Estimate
Ⓒ	Final Census Population
Ⓢ	Special Census Population
◆	Estimated Population

For additional definitions see Glossary, Volume 1, and Introduction, Volume 2.

West Batavia; RMC Place; GENESEE; ▲ Batavia; ***208** NI-5; elev. 893ft./272m.; mail Batavia z 14020; rural
West Bay Shore; CDP; SUFFOLK; ▲ Islip; ***207** SF-9; ★ **N.Y.**; mail Bay Shore z 11706; Ⓟ 4,907; Ⓒ 4,775
West Bellport; RMC Place; SUFFOLK; ▲ Brookhaven; ***207** SF-10; ★ **N.Y.**; mail Patchogue z 11772; ● 5,200
West Berne; RMC Place; ALBANY; ▲ Knox, Berne; **209** NK-18; mail Berne z 12023; ● 200
West Bethany; RMC Place; GENESEE; ▲ Bethany, Alexander; ***208** NJ-6; elev. 995ft./303m.; mail East Bethany z 14054; rural
West Bloomfield; RMC Place; ONTARIO; ▲ West Bloomfield; **208** NJ-8; 🅿; ★ **ROCH**; z 14585; ● 600
West Bloomfield; MCD-Town; ONTARIO; ***208** NJ-8; 🅿; ★ **ROCH**; z 14585; Ⓟ 2,536; Ⓒ 2,549
West Branch; RMC Place; ONEIDA; ▲ Lee; **209** NH-14; ★ **UT-R**; mail Ava z 13303; ● 100
West Brentwood (Pilgrim Psychiatric Center); RMC Place; SUFFOLK; ▲ Islip; 🅿 🄷; ★ **N.Y.**; z 11717
Westbrookville; RMC Place; ORANGE, SULLIVAN; ▲ Mamakating; **207** SC-4; 🅿; ★ **MIDD**; z 12785; ● 500
West Burlington; RMC Place; OTSEGO; ▲ Burlington; **209** NJ-15; 🅿; z 13482; ● 100
Westbury; RMC Place; CAYUGA, WAYNE; ▲ Victory; **208** NH-10; mail Red Creek z 13143; ● 150
Westbury; Inc. Place; NASSAU; ▲ Butler; **207** SF-8; elev. 107ft./33m.; 🅿; ★ **N.Y.**; z 11568, z 11590, z 11594, z 11597; Ⓟ 13,060; Ⓒ 14,263
Westbury South (South Westbury); RMC Place; NASSAU; ▲ Hempstead; **211** G-19; ★ **N.Y.**; mail Westbury z 11590; ● 9,500
West Bush; RMC Place; FULTON; ▲ Johnstown; ***209** NI-17; mail Gloversville z 12078; rural
West Cameron; RMC Place; STEUBEN; ▲ Cameron; ***208** NL-8; elev. 1,058ft./322m.; mail Cameron z 14819; rural
West Camp; RMC Place; ULSTER; ▲ Saugerties; **209** NM-18; 🅿; ★ **KNGST**; z 12490; ● 400
West Candor; RMC Place; TIOGA; ▲ Spencer, Candor; ***209** NL-11; elev. 969ft./295m.; mail Candor z 13743; rural
West Carthage; Inc. Place; JEFFERSON; ▲ Champion; **209** NE-13; mail Carthage z 13619; Ⓟ 2,166; Ⓒ 2,102
West Caton; RMC Place; STEUBEN; ▲ Caton; ***208** NM-9; elev. 1,404ft./428m.; mail Corning z 14830; rural
West Charlton; RMC Place; SARATOGA; ▲ Charlton; ***209** NI-18; elev. 682ft./208m.; 🅿; ★ **A-S-T**; z 12010; ● 100
West Chazy; RMC Place; CLINTON; ▲ Chazy; **209** NB-19; 🅿; z 12992; ● 800
West Chenango; RMC Place; BROOME; ▲ Maine, Chenango; **207** SA-10; ★ **BING**; mail Binghamton z 13905
Westchester; RMC Place; BRONX; ***207** SF-7; ★ **N.Y.**; mail Bronx z 10461; pop. incl. with New York (Inc. Place)
WESTCHESTER; **207** SD-8; Ⓟ 874,866; Ⓒ 923,459; ◆ 954,120
West Chili; RMC Place; MONROE; ▲ Chili; ***208** NI-7; ★ **ROCH**; mail North Chili z 14514; ● 1,000
West Clarksville; RMC Place; ALLEGANY; ▲ Clarksville; **208** NM-5; elev. 1,596ft./486m.; 🅿; z 14786; ● 300
West Colesville; RMC Place; BROOME; ▲ Colesville; ***209** NM-13; ★ **BING**; mail Binghamton z 13904; rural
West Conesville; RMC Place; SCHOHARIE; ▲ Conesville; ***209** NL-17; mail Gilboa z 12076; ● 100
West Constable; FRANKLIN; see Westville (RMC Place)
West Copake; RMC Place; COLUMBIA; ▲ Copake; **209** NM-19; 🅿; z 12593; ● 170
West Corners; RMC Place; BROOME; ▲ Union; **209** NM-12; ★ **BING**; mail Endicott z 13760; ● 1,800
West Coxsackie; RMC Place; GREENE; ***209** NL-19; elev. 130ft./40m.; 🅿; z 12192; pop. incl. with Coxsackie (Inc. Place)
Westdale; RMC Place; ONEIDA; ▲ Camden; **209** NH-13; elev. 550ft./168m.; 🅿; z 13483; ● 400
West Danby; RMC Place; TOMPKINS; ▲ Danby; **209** NL-11; 🅿; z 14883; ● 200
West Davenport; RMC Place; DELAWARE; ▲ Davenport; **209** NK-15; elev. 1,182ft./360m.; 🅿; z 13860; ● 250
West Dryden; RMC Place; TOMPKINS; ▲ Dryden; ***209** NK-11; elev. 1,283ft./391m.; ★ **ITH**; mail Freeville z 13068; rural
West Durham; RMC Place; GREENE; ▲ Durham; ***209** NL-17; mail Durham z 12422; rural
West Eaton; RMC Place; MADISON; ▲ Eaton; **209** NJ-13; 🅿; z 13484; ● 500
West Edmeston; RMC Place; OTSEGO; ▲ Edmeston; **209** NJ-14; elev. 1,138ft./347m.; 🅿; z 13485; ● 125
West Ellicott; CHAUTAUQUA; see Jamestown West (CDP-Census Area Only)
West Elmira; CDP; CHEMUNG; ▲ Elmira; **208** NM-10; elev. 888ft./271m.; ★ **ELM**; mail Elmira z 14905; Ⓟ 5,218; Ⓒ 5,136
West End; CDP-Census Area Only; OTSEGO; ▲ Oneonta; ***209** NK-15; mail Oneonta z 13820; Ⓟ 1,825; Ⓒ 1,813
West Endicott; RMC Place; BROOME; ▲ Union; ***209** NM-12; ★ **BING**; mail Endicott z 13760; ● 2,400
Westerlea; RMC Place; ONONDAGA; ▲ Camillus; ***209** NI-11; ★ **SYR**; mail Camillus z 13031; ● 800
Westerleigh; RMC Place; RICHMOND; **210** K-7; ★ **N.Y.**; mail Staten Island z 10314; pop. incl. with New York (Inc. Place)
Westerlo; RMC Place; ALBANY; ▲ Westerlo; **209** NK-18; 🅿; z 12193 & mail Dormansville z 12055; ● 680
Westerlo; MCD-Town; ALBANY; ***209** NK-18; 🅿; z 12193 & mail Dormansville z 12055; Ⓟ 3,325; Ⓒ 3,466
Western; MCD-Town; ONEIDA; ***209** NH-14; mail Westernville z 13486; Ⓟ 2,057; Ⓒ 2,029
Westernville; RMC Place; ONEIDA; ▲ Western; **209** NH-14; elev. 562ft./171m.; 🅿; z 13486; ● 600
West Exeter; RMC Place; OTSEGO; ▲ Exeter; **209** NJ-15; elev. 1,318ft./402m.; 🅿; z 13491; ● 100
West Falls; RMC Place; ERIE; ▲ Aurora; ***208** NJ-4; elev. 942ft./287m.; 🅿; ★ **BUF**; z 14170; ● 400
West Farms; RMC Place; BRONX; **211** E-13; ★ **N.Y.**; mail Bronx z 10460; pop. incl. with New York (Inc. Place)
Westfield; Inc. Place; CHAUTAUQUA; ▲ Westfield; **208** NL-1; elev. 754ft./230m.; 🅿 🄷; z 14787; Ⓟ 3,451; Ⓒ 3,481
Westfield; MCD-Town; CHAUTAUQUA; ***208** NL-1; 🅿; z 14787; Ⓟ 5,194; Ⓒ 5,232
Westford; RMC Place; OTSEGO; ▲ Westford; **209** NK-16; elev. 1,563ft./476m.; 🅿; z 13488; ● 250
Westford; MCD-Town; OTSEGO; ***209** NK-16; 🅿; z 13488; Ⓟ 634; Ⓒ 784
West Fort Ann; RMC Place; WASHINGTON; ▲ Fort Ann; ***209** NG-19; mail Fort Ann z 12827; rural
West Fort Salonga; RMC Place; SUFFOLK; ▲ Huntington; ***207** SE-9; ★ **N.Y.**; mail Northport z 11768; ● 4,100
West Frankfort; RMC Place; HERKIMER; ▲ Frankfort; ***209** NI-15; ★ **UT-R**; mail Frankfort z 13340; rural
West Fulton; RMC Place; SCHOHARIE; ▲ Schoharie; **209** NK-17; elev. 1,157ft./353m.; 🅿; z 12194; ● 200
West Gaines; RMC Place; ORLEANS; ▲ Ridgeway, Gaines; ***208** NH-5; mail Albion z 14411; ● 100
West Galway; RMC Place; FULTON, SARATOGA; ▲ Broadalbin, Galway, Perth; **209** NI-18; ★ **A-S-T**; mail Amsterdam z 12010; ● 150
West Genesee Terrace; RMC Place; ONONDAGA; ▲ Camillus; ***209** NI-11; ★ **SYR**; mail Camillus z 13031; ● 2,100
West Ghent; RMC Place; COLUMBIA; ▲ Ghent; ***209** NL-19; elev. 250ft./76m.; ★ **A-S-T**; mail Ghent z 12075; rural
West Gilgo Beach; RMC Place; SUFFOLK; ▲ Babylon; ***207** SG-9; 🅿; ★ **N.Y.**; z 11702; ● 120
West Glens Falls; CDP; WARREN; ▲ Queensbury; **209** NH-19; ★ **GLFLS**; mail Glens Falls z 12801; Ⓟ 5,964; Ⓒ 6,721
West Glenville; RMC Place; SCHENECTADY; ▲ Glenville; ***209** NJ-18; ★ **A-S-T**; mail Amsterdam z 12010; ● 60
West Granville Corners; RMC Place; WASHINGTON; ***209** NG-20; mail Granville z 12832; rural
West Greece; RMC Place; MONROE; ▲ Parma, Greece; ***208** NH-7; ★ **ROCH**; mail Rochester z 14626; ● 300
West Greenwood; RMC Place; STEUBEN; ▲ Greenwood; ***208** NM-7; elev. 2,242ft./683m.; mail Greenwood z 14839; rural
West Groton; RMC Place; TOMPKINS; ▲ Groton; **209** NK-11; elev. 1,219ft./372m.; ★ **ITH**; mail Groton z 13073; ● 60
Westhampton; CDP; SUFFOLK; ▲ Southampton; **207** SF-11; 🅿; ★ **N.Y.**; z 11977; Ⓟ 2,129; Ⓒ 2,869; Ⓡ 2,864
Westhampton Beach; Inc. Place; SUFFOLK; ▲ Southampton; **207** SF-11; 🅿; ★ **N.Y.**; z 11978; Ⓟ 1,571; Ⓒ 1,902; Ⓡ 1,893
West Hampton Dunes; Inc. Place; SUFFOLK; ***207** SF-11; ★ **N.Y.**; mail Westhampton Beach z 11978; summer pop. 500; Ⓒ 11
West Harpersfield; RMC Place; DELAWARE; ▲ Harpersfield; ***209** NL-16; mail Harpersfield z 13786; rural
West Harrison; RMC Place; WESTCHESTER; ▲ Harrison; 🅿; z 10604; pop. incl. with Harrison (Inc. Place)
West Haverstraw; Inc. Place; ROCKLAND; ▲ Haverstraw; **207** SD-6; 🅿 🄷; ★ **N.Y.**; z 10993; Ⓟ 9,183; Ⓒ 10,295
West Hebron; RMC Place; WASHINGTON; ▲ Hebron; **209** NH-20; mail Salem z 12865; ● 175
West Hempstead; CDP; NASSAU; ▲ Hempstead; **211** I-17; 🅿; ★ **N.Y.**; z 11552; Ⓟ 17,689; Ⓒ 18,713
West Henrietta; RMC Place; MONROE; ▲ Henrietta; **208** NI-7; 🅿; ★ **ROCH**; z 14586; ● 750
West Hill; RMC Place; SCHENECTADY; ▲ Rotterdam; ***209** NJ-18; ★ **A-S-T**; mail Schenectady z 12301; ● 375
West Hills; CDP; SUFFOLK; ▲ Huntington; **207** SH-10; ★ **N.Y.**; mail Huntington z 11743; Ⓟ 5,849; Ⓒ 5,607
West Hoosick; RMC Place; RENSSELAER; ▲ Hoosick; ***209** NJ-20; mail Buskirk z 12028; rural
West Huntington (West Islip); RMC Place; SUFFOLK; ▲ Huntington; ***207** SF-8; ★ **N.Y.**; mail Huntington z 11743, Huntington Station z 11746; ● 950
West Hurley; CDP; ULSTER; ▲ Woodstock, Hurley; **209** NM-18; 🅿; ★ **KNGST**; z 12491; Ⓟ 2,252; Ⓒ 2,105
West Islip; CDP; SUFFOLK; ▲ Islip; **207** SJ-11; 🅿; ★ **N.Y.**; z 11795; Ⓟ 28,419; Ⓒ 28,907; ◆ 28,897
West Islip; SUFFOLK; see West Huntington (RMC Place)
West Jewett; RMC Place; GREENE; ▲ Jewett; ***209** NL-17; elev. 1,897ft./578m.; mail Jewett z 12444; rural
West Kendall; RMC Place; ORLEANS; ▲ Kendall; ***208** NH-6; elev. 328ft./100m.; ★ **ROCH**; mail Kendall z 14476; rural
West Kill; RMC Place; GREENE; ▲ Lexington; **209** NL-17; 🅿; z 12492; ● 200
West Latham; RMC Place; ALBANY; ▲ Colonie; ★ **A-S-T**; mail Latham z 12110
West Laurens; RMC Place; OTSEGO; ▲ Laurens; **209** NK-15; elev. 1,491ft./454m.; mail Laurens z 13796; ● 150
West Lebanon; RMC Place; COLUMBIA; ▲ New Lebanon; **209** NK-20; 🅿; z 12195; ● 450
West Lee; RMC Place; ONEIDA; ▲ Lee; ***209** NH-13; ★ **UT-R**; mail Lee Center z 13363; rural
West Leyden; RMC Place; LEWIS; ▲ Lewis; **209** NG-14; elev. 1,496ft./456m.; 🅿; z 13489; ● 500
West Lowville; RMC Place; LEWIS; ▲ Lowville; ***209** NF-13; mail Lowville z 13367; rural
West Mahopac; RMC Place; PUTNAM; ▲ Carmel; ***207** SC-7; elev. 561ft./171m.; ★ **N.Y.**; mail Mahopac z 10541; ● 2,000
West Martinsburg; RMC Place; LEWIS; ▲ Martinsburg; **209** NF-14; mail Lowville z 13367; ● 65
Westmere; CDP; ALBANY; ▲ Guilderland; **209** NJ-18; ★ **A-S-T**; mail Albany z 12203; Ⓟ 6,750; Ⓒ 7,188
West Meredith; RMC Place; DELAWARE; ▲ Meredith; ***209** NL-15; mail East Meredith z 13757; rural
West Middleburg; RMC Place; SCHOHARIE; ▲ Middleburgh; ***209** NK-17; mail Middleburgh z 12122; ● 100
West Middlebury; RMC Place; WYOMING; ▲ Middlebury; ***208** NJ-6; elev. 1,136ft./346m.; mail East Bethany z 14054; rural
West Milton; RMC Place; SARATOGA; ▲ Milton; **209** NI-18; ★ **A-S-T**; mail Ballston Spa z 12020; ● 350
Westminster Park; RMC Place; JEFFERSON; ▲ Alexandria; ***209** ND-12; mail Alexandria Bay z 13607; ● 225
West Monroe; RMC Place; OSWEGO; ▲ West Monroe; **209** NH-12; 🅿; ★ **SYR**; z 13167; ● 400
West Monroe; MCD-Town; OSWEGO; ***209** NH-12; 🅿; ★ **SYR**; z 13167; Ⓟ 4,393; Ⓒ 4,428
Westmoreland; RMC Place; ONEIDA; ▲ Westmoreland; **209** NI-14; 🅿; ★ **UT-R**; z 13490; ● 950
Westmoreland; MCD-Town; ONEIDA; ***209** NI-14; 🅿; ★ **UT-R**; z 13490; Ⓟ 5,737; Ⓒ 6,207
Westmoreland; RMC Place; SUFFOLK; ▲ Shelter Island; ***207** SD-12; mail Shelter Island Heights z 11965
West Mount Vernon; RMC Place; WESTCHESTER; ***207** SE-7; ★ **N.Y.**; pop. incl. with Mount Vernon (Inc. Place)
West Newark; RMC Place; TIOGA; ▲ Newark Valley; ***209** NL-11; ★ **BING**; mail Newark Valley z 13811; rural
West New Brighton; RMC Place; RICHMOND; **210** J-8; ★ **N.Y.**; mail Staten Island z 10310; pop. incl. with New York (Inc. Place)
West Newburgh; RMC Place; ORANGE; ★ **NWBG**; mail Newburgh z 12550; pop. incl. with Newburgh (Inc. Place)
West Notch; RMC Place; ALLEGANY; ▲ Wirt; ***208** NM-6; mail Bolivar z 14715; rural
West Nyack; CDP; ROCKLAND; ▲ Clarkstown; ***207** SD-6; 🅿; ★ **N.Y.**; z 10994 & mail Nyack z 10960; Ⓟ 3,437; Ⓒ 3,282
Weston; RMC Place; SCHUYLER; ▲ Tyrone; **208** NL-9; elev. 1,201ft./366m.; mail Dundee z 14837; ● 90
West Oneonta; RMC Place; OTSEGO; ▲ Oneonta; **209** NK-15; elev. 1,144ft./349m.; 🅿; z 13861; ● 600
Weston Mills (Westons Mills); CDP; CATTARAUGUS; ▲ Portville, Olean; **208** NM-5; mail Westons Mills z 14788; Ⓟ 1,750; Ⓒ 1,608
Westons Mills; CATTARAUGUS; see Weston Mills (CDP)
Westover; RMC Place; BROOME; ▲ Union; ***209** NM-12; ★ **BING**; mail Johnson City z 13790; ● 600
West Park; RMC Place; ULSTER; ▲ Esopus; **209** NN-18; elev. 104ft./32m.; 🅿; ★ **KNGST**; z 12493; ● 850
West Pawling (Stonehouse); RMC Place; DUTCHESS; ▲ Pawling; ***207** SB-8; elev. 692ft./211m.; mail Pawling z 12564; rural
West Perrysburg; RMC Place; CATTARAUGUS; ▲ Perrysburg; ***208** NK-3; mail Perrysburg z 14129; rural
West Perth; RMC Place; FULTON; ▲ Perth; ***209** NI-17; ★ **A-S-T**; mail Amsterdam z 12010; rural
West Phoenix; RMC Place; ONONDAGA; ▲ Lysander; ***209** NH-11; ★ **SYR**; mail Phoenix z 13135; ● 260
West Pierrepont; RMC Place; ST. LAWRENCE; ▲ Pierrepont; ***209** NC-15; elev. 749ft./228m.; mail Canton z 13617; rural
West Plattsburgh; RMC Place; CLINTON; ★ **PLATT**; ● 150
West Point; CDP; ORANGE; ▲ Highlands; **207** SC-6; elev. 161ft./49m.; 🅿 🄷 🄲 4,236; ★ **N.Y.**; z 10996-97; Ⓟ 8,024; Ⓒ 7,138
Westport; RMC Place; ESSEX; ▲ Westport; **209** ND-20; 🅿; z 12993; ● 500
Westport; MCD-Town; ESSEX; ***209** ND-20; 🅿; z 12993; Ⓟ 1,446; Ⓒ 1,362
West Portland; RMC Place; CHAUTAUQUA; ▲ Portland; ***208** NL-1; elev. 751ft./229m.; mail Westfield z 14787; rural
West Potsdam; RMC Place; ST. LAWRENCE; ▲ Potsdam; ***209** NB-15; elev. 382ft./116m.; mail Potsdam z 13676; ● 100
West Ridge; RMC Place; MONROE; ★ **ROCH**; mail Rochester z 14615; pop. incl. with Rochester (Inc. Place)
West Rush; RMC Place; MONROE; ▲ Rush; ***208** NI-7; 🅿; ★ **ROCH**; z 14543; ● 250
West Salamanca; RMC Place; CATTARAUGUS; mail Salamanca z 14779; pop. incl. with Salamanca (Inc. Place)
West Sand Lake; CDP; RENSSELAER; ▲ Sand Lake; **209** NK-19; 🅿; ★ **A-S-T**; z 12196; Ⓟ 2,251; Ⓒ 2,439
West Saugerties; RMC Place; ULSTER; ▲ Saugerties; ***209** NM-18; elev. 584ft./178m.; ★ **KNGST**; mail Saugerties z 12477; ● 500
West Sayville; CDP; SUFFOLK; ▲ Islip; **207** SJ-13; 🅿; ★ **N.Y.**; z 11796; Ⓟ 4,680; Ⓒ 5,003
West Schuyler; RMC Place; HERKIMER; ▲ Schuyler; **209** NI-15; ★ **UT-R**; mail Utica z 13502; ● 240
West Seneca; CDP; ERIE; ▲ West Seneca; **208** NJ-4; 🅿 🄷; ★ **BUF**; z 14206, z 14210, z 14218, z 14224 & mail Buffalo z 14220; Ⓟ 47,866; Ⓒ 45,943; ◆ 42,760
West Seneca; MCD-Town; ERIE; ***208** NJ-4; 🅿; ★ **BUF**; z 14206, z 14210, z 14218, z 14224 & mail Buffalo z 14220; Ⓟ 47,866; Ⓒ 45,920; ◆ 42,760
West Shelby; RMC Place; ORLEANS; ▲ Shelby; ***208** NI-5; elev. 675ft./206m.; mail Medina z 14103; ● 65
West Shokan; RMC Place; ULSTER; ▲ Olive; **209** NM-17; 🅿; z 12494; ● 350
West Side; RMC Place; CHEMUNG; ★ **ELM**; mail Elmira z 14905; pop. incl. with Elmira (Inc. Place)
West Side; RMC Place; ERIE; ★ **BUF**; mail Buffalo z 14213, z 14222; pop. incl. with Buffalo (Inc. Place)
West Slaterville; RMC Place; TOMPKINS; ▲ Caroline; ***209** NL-11; elev. 1,058ft./322m.; mail Slaterville Springs z 14881; ● 150
West Smithtown; RMC Place; SUFFOLK; ▲ Smithtown; ★ **N.Y.**; mail Smithtown z 11787
West Somerset; RMC Place; NIAGARA; ▲ Somerset; ***208** NH-4; ★ **LOCK**; mail Appleton z 14008; ● 100
West Sparta; MCD-Town; LIVINGSTON; ***208** NK-7; mail Dansville z 14437; Ⓟ 1,335; Ⓒ 1,244
West Stephentown; RMC Place; RENSSELAER; ▲ Stephentown, Nassau; **209** NK-20; ★ **A-S-T**; mail Stephentown z 12168; ● 330
West Stockholm; RMC Place; ST. LAWRENCE; ▲ Stockholm; **209** NB-15; 🅿; z 13696; ● 300
West Sweden; RMC Place; MONROE; ▲ Sweden; ***208** NI-6; ★ **ROCH**; mail Brockport z 14420; ● 100
West Taghkanic; RMC Place; COLUMBIA; ▲ Taghkanic; **209** NM-19; mail Ancram z 12502; ● 200
West Tiana; RMC Place; SUFFOLK; ▲ Southampton; ***207** SE-12; mail Hampton Bays z 11946; ● 1,050
Westtown; RMC Place; ORANGE; ▲ Minisink; **207** SC-4; 🅿; ★ **MIDD**; z 10998; ● 700
West Turin; MCD-Town; LEWIS; ***209** NG-14; mail Constableville z 13325; Ⓟ 1,753; Ⓒ 1,674
West Union; MCD-Town; STEUBEN; ***208** NM-7; mail Rexville z 14877; Ⓟ 412; Ⓒ 399
West Utica; RMC Place; ONEIDA; ★ **UT-R**; mail Utica z 13502; pop. incl. with Utica (Inc. Place)
Westvale; CDP; ONONDAGA; ▲ Geddes; **209** NI-11; ★ **SYR**; mail Syracuse z 13219; Ⓟ 5,852; Ⓒ 5,166
West Valley; RMC Place; CATTARAUGUS; ▲ Ashford; **208** NL-4; elev. 1,522ft./464m.; 🅿; z 14171; ● 500
West Valley Falls; RMC Place; RENSSELAER; ★ **A-S-T**; mail Valley Falls z 12185; pop. incl. with Valley Falls (Inc. Place)
West Vienna; ONEIDA; see Jewell (RMC Place)
Westview; RMC Place; BROOME; ★ **BING**; mail Binghamton z 13905; pop. incl. with Binghamton (Inc. Place)
Westview; RMC Place; LIVINGSTON; ▲ Ossian; ***208** NK-7; elev. 1,667ft./508m.; mail Dansville z 14437; rural
Westville (West Constable); RMC Place; FRANKLIN; ▲ Westville; **209** NA-17; elev. 205ft./62m.; mail Constable z 12926; ● 100
Westville; MCD-Town; FRANKLIN; ***209** NA-17; mail Constable z 12926; Ⓟ 1,620; Ⓒ 1,823
Westville; RMC Place; OTSEGO; ▲ Westford, Middlefield; ***209** NK-15; mail Schenevus z 12155
Westville Center; RMC Place; FRANKLIN; ▲ Westville; **209** NA-17; elev. 234ft./71m.; mail Constable z 12926; ● 120
West Walworth; RMC Place; WAYNE; ▲ Walworth; **208** NI-8; elev. 544ft./166m.; ★ **ROCH**; mail Macedon z 14502; ● 150
West Waterford; RMC Place; SARATOGA; ★ **A-S-T**; mail Waterford z 12188; pop. incl. with Waterford (Inc. Place)
West Webster; RMC Place; MONROE; ▲ Webster; **208** NH-8; ★ **ROCH**; mail Webster z 14580; ● 8,700
West Windsor; RMC Place; BROOME; ▲ Windsor; **209** NM-13; 🅿; ★ **BING**; z 13865; ● 850
West Winfield; Inc. Place; HERKIMER; ▲ Winfield; **209** NJ-15; elev. 1,220ft./372m.; 🅿; z 13491; Ⓟ 871; Ⓒ 862
West Yaphank; RMC Place; SUFFOLK; ▲ Brookhaven; ***207** SF-10; ★ **N.Y.**; mail Yaphank z 11980; ● 800
Wethersfield; MCD-Town; WYOMING; ***208** NK-5; mail Warsaw z 14569; Ⓟ 794; Ⓒ 891
Wethersfield Springs; RMC Place; WYOMING; ▲ Wethersfield; ***208** NK-5; mail Warsaw z 14569; rural
Wevertown; RMC Place; WARREN; ▲ Johnsburg; **209** NG-18; elev. 1,077ft./328m.; 🅿; z 12886; ● 220
Whaley Lake; RMC Place; DUTCHESS; ▲ Pawling; ***207** SB-7; mail Holmes z 12531; ● 900
Whallonsburg; RMC Place; ESSEX; ▲ Essex; **209** ND-20; elev. 268ft./82m.; 🅿; z 12936; ● 200
Wheatfield; MCD-Town; NIAGARA; ***208** NI-3; ★ **BUF**; mail Niagara Falls z 14304, North Tonawanda z 14120, Tonawanda z 14150; Ⓟ 11,125; Ⓒ 14,086
Wheatland; MCD-Town; MONROE; ***208** NI-7; ★ **ROCH**; mail Scottsville z 14546; Ⓟ 5,093; Ⓒ 5,149
Wheatley; RMC Place; NASSAU; ***207** SF-8; elev. 257ft./78m.; ★ **N.Y.**; mail Old Westbury z 11568; pop. incl. with Old Westbury (Inc. Place)
Wheatley Heights; CDP-Census Area Only; SUFFOLK; ▲ Babylon; **207** SI-10; elev. 100ft./30m.; 🅿; ★ **N.Y.**; z 11798; Ⓟ 5,027; Ⓒ 5,013
Wheatville; RMC Place; GENESEE; ▲ Alabama; **208** NI-5; elev. 673ft./205m.; mail Basom z 14013; ● 150
Wheeler; RMC Place; STEUBEN; ▲ Wheeler; **208** NL-8; mail Bath z 14810; ● 130
Wheeler; MCD-Town; STEUBEN; ***208** NL-8; mail Bath z 14810; Ⓟ 1,084; Ⓒ 1,263
Wheeler Estates; RMC Place; SCHENECTADY; ▲ Glenville; ***209** NJ-18; ★ **A-S-T**; mail Ballston Lake z 12019; ● 650
Wheelerville; RMC Place; FULTON; ▲ Caroga; ***209** NI-17; mail Caroga Lake z 12032
Whig Corners; RMC Place; OTSEGO; ▲ Middlefield; ***209** NJ-16; mail Cooperstown z 13326; rural
Whippleville; RMC Place; FRANKLIN; ▲ Malone; **209** NB-17; 🅿; z 12995; ● 300
Whippoorwill; RMC Place; WESTCHESTER; ▲ North Castle; ***207** SD-7; ★ **N.Y.**; mail Armonk z 10504
White Bay; RMC Place; JEFFERSON; ▲ Henderson; ***209** NF-11; elev. 321ft./98m.; mail Henderson z 13650; summer pop. 300
White Birches; RMC Place; WESTCHESTER; ***207** SE-7; ★ **N.Y.**; pop. incl. with New Rochelle (Inc. Place)
White Creek; RMC Place; WASHINGTON; ▲ White Creek; **209** NI-20; 🅿; z 12057; ● 200
White Creek; MCD-Town; WASHINGTON; ***209** NI-20; 🅿; z 12057; Ⓟ 3,196; Ⓒ 3,411
Whitehall; Inc. Place; WASHINGTON; ▲ Whitehall; **209** NG-20; elev. 125ft./38m.; 🅿; z 12887; Ⓟ 3,071; Ⓒ 2,667
Whitehall; MCD-Town; WASHINGTON; ***209** NG-20; 🅿; z 12887; Ⓟ 4,409; Ⓒ 4,035
Whitehouse Crossing; RMC Place; DUTCHESS; ▲ North East; ***209** NM-20; mail Millerton z 12546; rural
White Lake; RMC Place; ONEIDA; ▲ Forestport; mail Woodgate z 13494
White Lake; RMC Place; SULLIVAN; ▲ Bethel; **207** SB-3; 🅿; z 12786; ● 140
Whitelaw; RMC Place; MADISON; ▲ Lenox; ***209** NI-13; ★ **SYR**; mail Canastota z 13032
White Plains; Inc. Place; ⊡ WESTCHESTER; **207** SE-7; elev. 236ft./72m.; 🅿 🄷 ■; ★ **N.Y.**; z 10601-07, z 10610; Ⓟ 48,718; Ⓒ 53,077; ◆ 55,394
Whiteport; RMC Place; ULSTER; ▲ Rosendale; ***207** SA-6; ★ **KNGST**; mail Kingston z 12401; ● 50
Whitesboro; Inc. Place; ONEIDA; ▲ Whitestown; **207** SA-12; 🅿; ★ **UT-R**; z 13492; Ⓟ 4,195; Ⓒ 3,943
Whites Store; RMC Place; CHENANGO; ▲ Norwich; ***209** NK-14; mail South New Berlin z 13843; rural
Whitestone; RMC Place; QUEENS; **211** F-14; 🅿; ★ **N.Y.**; z 11357; pop. incl. with New York (Inc. Place)
Whitestown; MCD-Town; ONEIDA; ***209** NI-14; ★ **UT-R**; mail Whitesboro z 13492; Ⓟ 18,985; Ⓒ 18,635
White Sulphur Springs; RMC Place; SULLIVAN; ▲ Liberty; **209** NN-16; elev. 1,363ft./415m.; 🅿; z 12787; ● 600
Whitesville; RMC Place; ALLEGANY; ▲ Independence; **208** NM-7; 🅿; z 14897; ● 800
Whitfield; RMC Place; ULSTER; ▲ Rochester; ***207** SA-5; mail Accord z 12404; rural
Whitman; RMC Place; DELAWARE; ▲ Masonville; ***209** NM-14; elev. 1,613ft./492m.; mail Masonville z 13804; rural
Whitney Country; RMC Place; MONROE; ▲ Perinton; ***208** NI-8; ★ **ROCH**; mail Fairport z 14450; pop. incl. with Fairport (Inc. Place)
Whitney Crossings; ALLEGANY; see Garwoods (RMC Place)
Whitney Estates (Burns-Whitney Estates); RMC Place; ALBANY; ▲ Colonie; ***209** NJ-19; ★ **A-S-T**; mail Latham z 12110; ● 2,150
Whitney Highlands; RMC Place; MONROE; ▲ Perinton; ***208** NI-8; ★ **ROCH**; mail Fairport z 14450; ● 1,050
Whitney Point; Inc. Place; BROOME; ▲ Triangle; **209** NL-12; 🅿; z 13862; Ⓟ 1,054; Ⓒ 965
Wiccopee (Wicopee); RMC Place; DUTCHESS; ▲ East Fishkill; ***207** SB-7; 🅿; ★ **POK**; z 12533; ● 500
Wickham Knolls; RMC Place; ORANGE; ▲ Warwick; ***207** SD-5; ★ **N.Y.**; mail Warwick z 10990; ● 200
Wickham Village; RMC Place; ORANGE; ▲ Warwick; ***207** SD-5; ★ **N.Y.**; mail Warwick z 10990; ● 400
Wicopee; DUTCHESS; see Wiccopee (RMC Place)
Wilbur; RMC Place; ULSTER; ***207** SA-6; ★ **KNGST**; mail Kingston z 12401; pop. incl. with Kingston (Inc. Place)
Wildwood; RMC Place; SUFFOLK; ▲ Riverhead; ***207** SE-11; ★ **N.Y.**; mail Wading River z 11792; ● 2,250
Wildwood Lake; SUFFOLK; see Northampton (CDP-Census Area Only)
Wileyville; RMC Place; STEUBEN; ▲ West Union; ***208** NM-7; elev. 2,076ft./633m.; mail Rexville z 14877; rural
Willard; RMC Place; SENECA; ▲ Romulus, Ovid; **208** NK-10; 🅿; z 14588; ● 600
Willet; RMC Place; CORTLAND; ▲ Willet; **209** NK-12; elev. 1,039ft./317m.; 🅿; z 13863; ● 400
Willet; MCD-Town; CORTLAND; ***209** NL-12; 🅿; z 13863; Ⓟ 892; Ⓒ 1,011
Williams Bridge; RMC Place; BRONX; **211** D-13; ★ **N.Y.**; mail Bronx z 10467; pop. incl. with New York (Inc. Place)
Williamsburg; RMC Place; KINGS; **211** I-11; ★ **N.Y.**; mail Brooklyn z 11211; pop. incl. with New York (Inc. Place)
Williams Grove; RMC Place; ONONDAGA; ▲ Otisco; ***209** NJ-11; ★ **SYR**; mail Marietta z 13110; summer pop. 300; ● 75
Williams Lake; RMC Place; ULSTER; ▲ Rosendale; ***207** SA-6; ★ **KNGST**; mail Rosendale z 12472; ● 120
Williamson; RMC Place; WAYNE; ▲ Williamson; **208** NH-9; 🅿; ★ **ROCH**; z 14589; ● 1,850
Williamson; MCD-Town; WAYNE; ***208** NH-9; 🅿; ★ **ROCH**; z 14589; Ⓟ 6,540; Ⓒ 6,777
Williamstown; RMC Place; OSWEGO; ▲ Williamstown; **209** NH-12; 🅿; z 13493; ● 600
Williamstown; MCD-Town; OSWEGO; ***209** NG-12; 🅿; z 13493; Ⓟ 1,279; Ⓒ 1,350
Williamsville; Inc. Place; ERIE; ▲ Amherst; **208** ND-5; elev. 672ft./205m.; 🅿; ★ **BUF**; z 14221, z 14231; Ⓟ 5,583; Ⓒ 5,573
Willing; MCD-Town; ALLEGANY; ***208** NM-6; mail Wellsville z 14895; Ⓟ 1,428; Ⓒ 1,371
Williston Park; Inc. Place; NASSAU; ▲ Hempstead; **211** G-17; elev. 127ft./39m.; 🅿; ★ **N.Y.**; z 11596; Ⓟ 7,516; Ⓒ 7,261
Willoughby; RMC Place; CATTARAUGUS; ▲ Humphrey; ***208** NL-4; elev. 1,519ft./463m.; mail Great Valley z 14741; rural
Willow; RMC Place; ULSTER; ▲ Woodstock; ***209** NM-18; 🅿; z 12495; ● 250
Willow Brook; RMC Place; CHAUTAUQUA; ▲ Ellery; ***208** NL-2; elev. 1,373ft./418m.; ★ **JMST**; mail Bemus Point z 14712; rural
Willowbrook; RMC Place; RICHMOND; ***207** SG-6; ★ **N.Y.**; mail Staten Island z 10314; pop. incl. with New York (Inc. Place)
Willow Brook Estates; RMC Place; ALBANY; ***209** NJ-18; ★ **A-S-T**; mail Schenectady z 12303
Willow Brook Park; RMC Place; SCHENECTADY; ▲ Glenville; ***209** NJ-18; ★ **A-S-T**; mail Schenectady z 12302
Willowemac; RMC Place; SULLIVAN; ▲ Rockland, Neversink; **209** NN-16; mail Livingston Manor z 12758; ● 70
Willow Glen; RMC Place; SARATOGA; ▲ Stillwater; ***209** NI-19; ★ **A-S-T**; mail Mechanicville z 12118; ● 180
Willow Glen; RMC Place; TOMPKINS; ▲ Dryden; ***209** NK-11; ★ **ITH**; mail Dryden z 13053; rural
Willow Grove; RMC Place; CAYUGA; ▲ Montezuma; ***208** NI-10; mail Port Byron z 13140; rural
Willow Grove; RMC Place; ROCKLAND; ▲ Stony Point; ***207** SD-6; ★ **N.Y.**; mail Stony Point z 10980
Willow Point; RMC Place; BROOME; ▲ Vestal; **207** SB-10; ★ **BING**; mail Vestal z 13850; ● 1,700
Willow Ridge Estates; RMC Place; ERIE; ▲ Amherst; ***208** NI-4; ★ **BUF**; mail Buffalo z 14226; ● 4,800
Willsboro; RMC Place; ESSEX; ▲ Willsboro; **209** ND-20; elev. 215ft./66m.; 🅿; z 12996; ● 950
Willsboro; MCD-Town; ESSEX; ***209** NC-20; 🅿; z 12996; Ⓟ 1,736; Ⓒ 1,903
Willsboro Point; RMC Place; ESSEX; ▲ Willsboro; **209** NC-20; mail Willsboro z 12996; ● 500
Willseyville; RMC Place; TIOGA; ▲ Candor; **209** NL-11; 🅿; z 13864; ● 330
Wilmington; RMC Place; ESSEX; ▲ Wilmington; **209** NC-19; 🅿; z 12997; ● 700
Wilmington; MCD-Town; ESSEX; ***209** ND-18; 🅿; z 12997; Ⓟ 1,020; Ⓒ 1,131
Wilmot Woods; RMC Place; WESTCHESTER; ***207** SE-7; ★ **N.Y.**; pop. incl. with New Rochelle (Inc. Place)
Wilna; MCD-Town; JEFFERSON; ***209** NE-13; mail Carthage z 13619; Ⓟ 6,899; Ⓒ 6,235
Wilson; Inc. Place; NIAGARA; ▲ Wilson; **208** NH-4; elev. 290ft./88m.; 🅿; ★ **BUF**; z 14172; Ⓟ 1,307; Ⓒ 1,213
Wilson; MCD-Town; NIAGARA; ***208** NH-4; 🅿; ★ **BUF**; z 14172; Ⓟ 5,761; Ⓒ 5,840
Wilton; RMC Place; SARATOGA; ▲ Wilton; **209** NH-19; 🅿; ★ **GLFLS**; z 12831 & mail Saratoga Springs z 12866; ● 600
Wilton; MCD-Town; SARATOGA; ***209** NI-19; 🅿; ★ **GLFLS**; z 12831 & mail Saratoga Springs z 12866; Ⓟ 10,623; Ⓒ 12,511; Ⓡ 12,541
Winchester; RMC Place; ERIE; ★ **BUF**; mail Buffalo z 14224
Winderest Park; RMC Place; ONONDAGA; ▲ Camillus; ***209** NI-11; ★ **SYR**; mail Camillus z 13031; ● 1,290
Windham; CDP; GREENE; ▲ Windham; **209** NL-17; 🅿; z 12496; Ⓒ 359
Windham; MCD-Town; GREENE; ***209** NL-18; 🅿; z 12496; Ⓟ 1,682; Ⓒ 1,660
Windham Ridge; RMC Place; GREENE; ▲ Windham; ***209** NL-17; mail Windham z 12496; ● 75
Winding Ways; RMC Place; ONONDAGA; ▲ Skaneateles; ***209** NJ-11; ★ **SYR**; mail Skaneateles z 13152; rural
Windmill Farms; RMC Place; WESTCHESTER; ▲ North Castle; ***207** SD-8; ★ **N.Y.**; mail Armonk z 10504
Windom; RMC Place; ERIE; ▲ Orchard Park, Hamburg; **208** NG-4; ★ **BUF**; mail Buffalo z 14219; ● 700
Windsor; Inc. Place; BROOME; ▲ Windsor; **209** NM-13; 🅿; ★ **BING**; z 13865; Ⓟ 1,051; Ⓒ 901
Windsor; MCD-Town; BROOME; ***209** NM-13; 🅿; ★ **BING**; z 13865; Ⓟ 6,440; Ⓒ 6,421
Windsor Beach; RMC Place; MONROE; ▲ Irondequoit; ***208** NH-7; ★ **ROCH**; mail Rochester z 14617
Winebrook Hills; RMC Place; ESSEX; ▲ Newcomb; **209** NE-18; mail Newcomb z 12852; ● 200
Winfield; MCD-Town; HERKIMER; ***209** NJ-16; mail West Winfield z 13491; Ⓟ 2,146; Ⓒ 2,202
Wingdale; RMC Place; DUTCHESS; ▲ Dover; **207** SB-8; 🅿; z 12594; ● 650
Winona; RMC Place; JEFFERSON; ▲ Lorraine; ***209** NF-12; mail Lorraine z 13659; rural
Winona Lake; RMC Place; ORANGE; ▲ Newburgh; ***207** SB-6; ★ **NWBG**; mail Newburgh z 12550; ● 2,150
Winthrop; RMC Place; ST. LAWRENCE; ▲ Stockholm; **209** NB-16; elev. 338ft./103m.; 🅿; z 13697; ● 500
Wirt; MCD-Town; ALLEGANY; ***208** NM-6; mail Richburg z 14774; Ⓟ 1,143; Ⓒ 1,215
Wiscoy; RMC Place; ALLEGANY; ▲ Hume; **208** NK-6; elev. 1,175ft./358m.; mail Portageville z 14536; ● 165
Wisner; RMC Place; ORANGE; ▲ Warwick; ***207** SD-5; elev. 526ft./160m.; ★ **N.Y.**; mail Warwick z 10990; rural
Witherbee; RMC Place; ESSEX; ▲ Moriah; **209** NE-19; 🅿; z 12998; ● 750
Wittenberg; RMC Place; ULSTER; ▲ Woodstock; ***209** NM-18; mail Bearsville z 12409; rural
Wolcott; Inc. Place; WAYNE; ▲ Butler, Wolcott; **208** NH-10; elev. 378ft./115m.; 🅿; z 14590; Ⓟ 1,544; Ⓒ 1,712
Wolcott; MCD-Town; WAYNE; ***208** NH-10; 🅿; z 14590; includes part of the Village of Wolcott; Ⓟ 4,283; Ⓒ 4,692
Wolcottsburg; RMC Place; ERIE; ▲ Clarence; ***208** NI-4; elev. 588ft./179m.; ★ **BUF**; mail Clarence Center z 14032; rural
Wolcottsville; RMC Place; NIAGARA; ▲ Royalton; **208** NI-5; mail Akron z 14001; ● 600
Woodberry Hills; RMC Place; ONEIDA; ▲ New Hartford; ***209** NI-14; ★ **UT-R**; mail New Hartford z 13413; ● 2,500
Woodbourne; RMC Place; SULLIVAN; ▲ Fallsburg; **209** NN-16; 🅿; z 12788; ● 1,200
Woodbury; CDP; NASSAU; ▲ Oyster Bay; **207** SH-10; elev. 186ft./57m.; 🅿; ★ **N.Y.**; z 11797; Ⓟ 8,008; Ⓒ 9,010
Woodbury; Inc. Place; ORANGE; ▲ Woodbury; **207** SH-10; incorporated August 28, 2006; ● 8,900
Woodbury; MCD-Town; ORANGE; ***207** SC-6; ★ **N.Y.**; mail Highland Mills z 10930; Ⓟ 8,236; Ⓒ 9,460
Woodbury Falls; RMC Place; ORANGE; ▲ Woodbury; ★ **N.Y.**; mail Highland Mills z 10930; rural
Woodcliff Park; RMC Place; SUFFOLK; ▲ Riverhead; ***207** SE-11; ★ **N.Y.**; mail Calverton z 11933; ● 450
Woodgate; RMC Place; ONEIDA; ▲ Forestport; **209** NG-15; elev. 1,483ft./452m.; 🅿; z 13494; ● 450
Wood Haven; RMC Place; QUEENS; **211** I-13; 🅿; ★ **N.Y.**; z 11421; pop. incl. with New York (Inc. Place)
Woodhull; RMC Place; ONEIDA; ▲ Forestport; ***209** NG-14; mail Forestport z 13338; ● 55
Woodhull; RMC Place; STEUBEN; ▲ Woodhull; **208** NM-8; 🅿; z 14898; ● 350
Woodhull; MCD-Town; STEUBEN; ***208** NM-8; 🅿; z 14898; Ⓟ 1,518; Ⓒ 1,524
Woodinville; RMC Place; DUTCHESS; ▲ Pawling; **207** SB-8; mail Pawling z 12564; ● 220
Woodland; RMC Place; ULSTER; ▲ Shandaken; **209** NM-17; mail Phoenicia z 12464; ● 125
Woodland Hills; RMC Place; SARATOGA; ▲ Clifton Park; ***209** NJ-19; ★ **A-S-T**; mail Clifton Park z 12065
Woodlands; RMC Place; WESTCHESTER; ▲ Greenburgh; ***207** SE-7; ★ **N.Y.**; mail White Plains z 10607; ● 2,300
Woodlawn; RMC Place; BRONX; **211** C-13; ★ **N.Y.**; mail Bronx z 10470; pop. incl. with New York (Inc. Place)
Woodlawn; RMC Place; CHAUTAUQUA; ▲ North Harmony; ***208** NM-2; mail Ashville z 14710; ● 140
Woodlawn (Woodlawn Beach); RMC Place; ERIE; ▲ Hamburg; **208** NG-4; ★ **BUF**; mail Buffalo z 14219; ● 1,000
Woodlawn; RMC Place; SCHENECTADY; pop. incl. with Schenectady (Inc. Place)
Woodlawn Beach; ERIE; see Woodlawn (RMC Place)
Woodmere; CDP; NASSAU; ▲ Hempstead; **211** J-16; elev. 30ft./9m.; 🅿; ★ **N.Y.**; z 11598; Ⓒ 16,447
Woodridge; Inc. Place; SULLIVAN; ▲ Fallsburg; **207** SB-4; 🅿; z 12789; Ⓟ 783; Ⓒ 902
Woodrow; RMC Place; RICHMOND; **210** M-6; elev. 129ft./39m.; ★ **N.Y.**; mail Staten Island z 10312; pop. incl. with New York (Inc. Place)
Woodruff Heights; RMC Place; SCHENECTADY; ▲ Glenville; ***209** NJ-18; ★ **A-S-T**; mail Schenectady z 12302; ● 615
Woodsburgh; Inc. Place; NASSAU; ▲ Hempstead; **211** K-16; elev. 8ft./2m.; ★ **N.Y.**; mail Woodmere z 11598; Ⓟ 1,190; Ⓒ 831
Woods Corner; RMC Place; STEUBEN; ▲ Tuscarora; ***208** NM-8; mail Addison z 14801; rural
Woods Corners; RMC Place; CHENANGO; ▲ Norwich; ***209** NK-14; elev. 1,026ft./313m.; mail Norwich z 13815; rural
Woods Falls; RMC Place; CLINTON; ▲ Mooers; ***209** NA-19; mail Altona z 12910; rural
Woodside; RMC Place; QUEENS; **211** G-12; 🅿; ★ **N.Y.**; z 11377; pop. incl. with New York (Inc. Place)
Woods Mills; RMC Place; CLINTON; ▲ Plattsburgh; ***209** NB-19; elev. 685ft./209m.; ★ **PLATT**; mail Cadyville z 12918; ● 250
Woodstock; CDP; ULSTER; ▲ Woodstock; **209** NM-18; 🅿; z 12498; Ⓟ 1,870; summer pop. 5,000; Ⓒ 2,187
Woodstock; MCD-Town; ULSTER; ***209** NM-18; 🅿; z 12498; Ⓟ 6,290; Ⓒ 6,241
Woodsville; RMC Place; LIVINGSTON; ▲ West Sparta; ***208** NK-7; mail Dansville z 14437; ● 80
Woodville; RMC Place; JEFFERSON; ▲ Ellisburg; **209** NF-12; elev. 320ft./98m.; 🅿; z 13650; ● 250
Woodville; RMC Place; ONTARIO; ▲ South Bristol; **208** NK-8; mail Naples z 14512; ● 300
Woodwinds; RMC Place; TIOGA; ▲ Owego; ***209** NM-12; ★ **BING**; mail Apalachin z 13732
Wooglin; RMC Place; CHAUTAUQUA; ▲ Chautauqua; ***208** NL-2; mail Dewittville z 14728; summer pop. 100
Woolsey; RMC Place; QUEENS; ★ **N.Y.**; mail Astoria z 11105; pop. incl. with New York (Inc. Place)
Worcester; RMC Place; OTSEGO; ▲ Worcester; **209** NK-16; 🅿; z 12197; ● 900
Worcester; MCD-Town; OTSEGO; ***209** NK-16; 🅿; z 12197; Ⓟ 2,070; Ⓒ 2,207
Worth; RMC Place; JEFFERSON; ▲ Worth; **209** NF-12; mail Lorraine z 13659; ● 25
Worth; MCD-Town; JEFFERSON; ***209** NF-13; mail Lorraine z 13659; Ⓟ 219; Ⓒ 234
Worthington; RMC Place; WESTCHESTER; ***207** SE-7; ★ **N.Y.**; mail White Plains z 10607
Wright; MCD-Town; SCHOHARIE; ***209** NK-17; mail Gallupville z 12073; Ⓟ 1,385; Ⓒ 1,547
Wright Park Manor; RMC Place; ONEIDA; ★ **UT-R**; mail Rome z 13440; pop. incl. with Rome (Inc. Place)
Wrights Corners; RMC Place; NIAGARA; ▲ Newfane, Lockport; **208** NH-4; elev. 398ft./121m.; ★ **LOCK**; mail Lockport z 14094; ● 200
Wurtemburg; RMC Place; DUTCHESS; ▲ Rhinebeck; ***207** SA-7; mail Rhinebeck z 12572; rural
Wurtsboro; Inc. Place; SULLIVAN; ▲ Mamakating; **207** SB-4; 🅿; ★ **MIDD**; z 12790; Ⓟ 1,048; Ⓒ 1,234
Wurtsboro Hills; RMC Place; SULLIVAN; ▲ Mamakating; **207** SB-4; mail Wurtsboro z 12790; ● 500
Wyandanch; CDP; SUFFOLK; ▲ Babylon; **207** SI-11; elev. 56ft./17m.; 🅿; ★ **N.Y.**; z 11798; Ⓟ 8,950; Ⓒ 10,546
Wyatts; RMC Place; SCHENECTADY; ▲ Glenville; ***209** NJ-18; ★ **A-S-T**; mail Schenectady z 12302; ● 150
Wycoff Heights; RMC Place; KINGS; ★ **N.Y.**; mail Brooklyn z 11237; pop. incl. with New York (Inc. Place)
Wykagyl; RMC Place; WESTCHESTER; ***207** SE-7; 🅿; ★ **N.Y.**; z 10804; pop. incl. with New Rochelle (Inc. Place)
Wykagyl Park; RMC Place; WESTCHESTER; ***207** SE-7; ★ **N.Y.**; mail New Rochelle z 10804; pop. incl. with New Rochelle (Inc. Place)
Wynantskill; CDP; RENSSELAER; ▲ North Greenbush; **207** SI-6; 🅿; ★ **A-S-T**; z 12198; Ⓟ 3,329; Ⓒ 3,018
Wyomanock; RMC Place; RENSSELAER; ▲ Stephentown; ***209** NK-20; mail Stephentown z 12168
Wyoming; Inc. Place; WYOMING; ▲ Middlebury; **208** NJ-6; elev. 991ft./302m.; 🅿; z 14591; Ⓟ 478; Ⓒ 513
WYOMING; **208** NJ-5; Ⓟ 42,507; Ⓒ 43,424; ◆ 41,339

Y

Yaddo; RMC Place; SARATOGA; ▲ Malta; ***209** NI-19; ★ **A-S-T**; mail Saratoga Springs z 12866; pop. incl. with Saratoga Springs (Inc. Place)
Yagerville; RMC Place; ULSTER; ▲ Wawarsing; ***207** SA-5; mail Napanoch z 12458; rural
Yaleville; RMC Place; ST. LAWRENCE; ▲ Norfolk; ***209** NB-15; mail Norwood z 13668
Yankee Lake; RMC Place; SULLIVAN; ▲ Mamakating; ***207** SB-4; mail Wurtsboro z 12790; ● 400
Yaphank; CDP; SUFFOLK; ▲ Brookhaven; **207** SF-10; 🅿; ★ **N.Y.**; z 11980; Ⓟ 4,637; Ⓒ 5,025
Yates; ORLEANS; see Yates Center (RMC Place)
Yates; MCD-Town; ORLEANS; ***208** NH-5; mail Lyndonville z 14098; Ⓟ 2,497; Ⓒ 2,510
YATES; **208** NK-8; Ⓟ 22,810; Ⓒ 24,621; ◆ 24,901
Yates Center (Yates); RMC Place; ORLEANS; ▲ Yates; **208** NH-5; elev. 326ft./99m.; mail Lyndonville z 14098; ● 250
Yatesville; RMC Place; YATES; ▲ Potter; ***208** NK-9; mail Penn Yan z 14527; rural
Yonkers; Inc. Place; WESTCHESTER; **207** SE-7; elev. 16ft./5m.; 🅿 🄷 ■; ★ **N.Y.**; z 10701-10; Ⓟ 188,082; Ⓒ 196,086; Ⓡ 196,019; ◆ 203,408
York; RMC Place; LIVINGSTON; ▲ York; **208** NJ-6; elev. 787ft./240m.; 🅿; ★ **ROCH**; z 14592; ● 650
York; MCD-Town; LIVINGSTON; ***208** NJ-6; 🅿; ★ **ROCH**; z 14592; Ⓟ 3,513; Ⓒ 3,219
York Corners; RMC Place; ALLEGANY; ▲ Willing; ***208** NM-6; elev. 1,597ft./487m.; mail Wellsville z 14895; ● 35
Yorkshire; CDP; CATTARAUGUS; ▲ Yorkshire; **208** NK-5; elev. 1,438ft./438m.; 🅿; z 14173; Ⓟ 1,340; Ⓒ 1,403
Yorkshire; MCD-Town; CATTARAUGUS; ***208** NK-4; 🅿; z 14173; Ⓟ 3,905; Ⓒ 4,210
Yorktown; RMC Place; WESTCHESTER; ▲ Yorktown; ***207** SC-7; ★ **N.Y.**; mail Yorktown Heights z 10598; ● 5,500
Yorktown; MCD-Town; WESTCHESTER; ***207** SD-7; ★ **N.Y.**; mail Yorktown Heights z 10598; Ⓟ 33,467; Ⓒ 36,318; ◆ 37,939
Yorktown Heights; CDP; WESTCHESTER; ▲ Yorktown; **207** SD-7; 🅿; ★ **N.Y.**; z 10598; Ⓟ 7,690; Ⓒ 7,972
Yorkville; RMC Place; NEW YORK; ★ **N.Y.**; mail New York z 10128; pop. incl. with New York (Inc. Place)
Yorkville; Inc. Place; ONEIDA; ▲ Whitestown; **209** NI-14; 🅿; ★ **UT-R**; z 13495; Ⓟ 2,972; Ⓒ 2,675
Yosts; RMC Place; MONTGOMERY; ▲ Mohawk; ***209** NJ-17; elev. 300ft./91m.; ★ **A-S-T**; mail Fonda z 12068; rural
Young Corners; RMC Place; MONTGOMERY; ▲ Florida; ***209** NJ-17; mail Amsterdam z 12010; rural
Young Hickory; RMC Place; STEUBEN; ▲ Troupsburg; ***208** NM-7; elev. 1,802ft./549m.; mail Troupsburg z 14885; rural
Youngstown; Inc. Place; NIAGARA; ▲ Porter; **208** NH-3; elev. 301ft./92m.; 🅿; ★ **BUF**; z 14174; Ⓟ 2,075; Ⓒ 1,957
Youngstown Estates; RMC Place; NIAGARA; ▲ Porter; ***208** NH-3; ★ **BUF**; mail Youngstown z 14174; ● 250
Youngsville; RMC Place; SULLIVAN; ▲ Callicoon; **209** NN-16; 🅿; z 12791; ● 850
Yulan; RMC Place; SULLIVAN; ▲ Highland; **207** SB-3; elev. 1,061ft./323m.; 🅿; z 12792; ● 750

Z

Zena; CDP; ULSTER; ▲ Woodstock; ***209** NM-18; ★ **KNGST**; mail Woodstock z 12498; Ⓟ 1,177; Ⓒ 1,119
Zoar; RMC Place; JEFFERSON; ▲ Rodman; ***209** NF-12; elev. 773ft./236m.; mail Rodman z 13682; rural

Entries in **UPPERCASE** are counties.
Entries in **bold** have populations of 2,500 or more.
Names in parentheses are alternate names.

Inc. Place	Incorporated Place
RMC Place	Rand McNally Designated Place
CDP	Census Designated Place
MCD	Minor Civil Division
⊡	County Seat
▲	Minor Civil Division
elev.	Elevation
🅿	Post Office
🄷	Hospital
🄲	College
■	Principal Business Center
★	Ranally Metro Area (RMA) Abbreviation
z	Zip Code(s)
Ⓟ	Previous Census Population
Ⓡ	Revised Census Population
Ⓐ	Annexation Population
●	Rand McNally Population Estimate
Ⓒ	Final Census Population
Ⓢ	Special Census Population
◆	Estimated Population

For additional definitions see Glossary, Volume 1, and Introduction, Volume 2.

NORTH CAROLINA

KY WV VA TN Raleigh GA SC

Statistics

Total area (2000) — 53,819 square miles
Land area (2000) — 48,711 square miles
Water area (2000) — 5,108 square miles
Capital — Raleigh
One of Thirteen Original States

Maps

State maps can be found on pages 142-254 in Vol. 1

Ranally Metro Areas (RMAs) and Abbreviations

Asheville, NC — ASHE
Burlington, NC — BUR
Charlotte, NC-SC — CHRLT
Danville, VA-NC — DANV
Durham, NC — DUR
Fayetteville, NC — FAY
Goldsboro, NC — GLDS
Greensboro-High Point, NC — GRNS-
Greenville, NC — GRNV
Hickory, NC — HICK
Jacksonville, NC — JAX
Martinsville, VA-NC — MRTNV
Myrtle Beach, SC-NC — MYR.B
Raleigh, NC — RAL
Rocky Mount, NC — RKYMT
Salisbury, NC — SLSB
Wilmington, NC — WILM
Winston-Salem, NC — WNS

Principal Places

Place Name	Place Type	County	Population
Charlotte	Inc. Place	MECKLENBURG	◆ 686,952
Raleigh	Inc. Place	WAKE	◆ 396,276
Greensboro	Inc. Place	GUILFORD	◆ 268,704
Durham	Inc. Place	DURHAM	◆ 250,172
Winston-Salem	Inc. Place	FORSYTH	◆ 210,943
Cary	Inc. Place	WAKE	◆ 147,843
Fayetteville	Inc. Place	CUMBERLAND	◆ 137,703
High Point	Inc. Place	GUILFORD	◆ 105,677
Wilmington	Inc. Place	NEW HANOVER	◆ 103,162
Greenville	Inc. Place	PITT	◆ 82,297
Concord	Inc. Place	CABARRUS	◆ 79,253
Jacksonville	Inc. Place	ONSLOW	◆ 76,864
Gastonia	Inc. Place	GASTON	◆ 75,902
Asheville	Inc. Place	BUNCOMBE	◆ 74,365
Rocky Mount	Inc. Place	NASH	◆ 58,485
Chapel Hill	Inc. Place	ORANGE	◆ 55,490
Burlington	Inc. Place	ALAMANCE	◆ 51,830
Wilson	Inc. Place	WILSON	◆ 48,076
Kannapolis	Inc. Place	CABARRUS	◆ 45,968
Hickory	Inc. Place	CATAWBA	◆ 44,615
Huntersville	Inc. Place	MECKLENBURG	◆ 41,986
Monroe	Inc. Place	UNION	◆ 38,626
Apex	Inc. Place	WAKE	◆ 35,741
Goldsboro	Inc. Place	WAYNE	◆ 34,065
Sanford	Inc. Place	LEE	◆ 30,867
Fort Bragg	CDP-Census Area Only	CUMBERLAND	◆ 30,864
Matthews	Inc. Place	MECKLENBURG	◆ 30,388
Statesville	Inc. Place	IREDELL	◆ 28,584
Salisbury	Inc. Place	ROWAN	◆ 28,018
Thomasville	Inc. Place	DAVIDSON	◆ 26,374
New Bern	Inc. Place	CRAVEN	◆ 26,216
Wake Forest	Inc. Place	WAKE	◆ 25,750
Garner	Inc. Place	WAKE	◆ 25,669
Mooresville	Inc. Place	IREDELL	◆ 25,330
Cornelius	Inc. Place	MECKLENBURG	◆ 24,937
Asheboro	Inc. Place	RANDOLPH	◆ 24,119
Havelock	Inc. Place	CRAVEN	◆ 23,822
Mint Hill	Inc. Place	MECKLENBURG	◆ 21,245
Kinston	Inc. Place	LENOIR	◆ 21,023
Elizabeth City	Inc. Place	PASQUOTANK	◆ 21,013
Kernersville	Inc. Place	FORSYTH	◆ 20,975
Lumberton	Inc. Place	ROBESON	◆ 20,227
Lexington	Inc. Place	DAVIDSON	◆ 20,141
Shelby	Inc. Place	CLEVELAND	◆ 19,654
Holly Springs	Inc. Place	WAKE	◆ 18,565
Morganton	Inc. Place	BURKE	◆ 17,053
Roanoke Rapids	Inc. Place	HALIFAX	◆ 16,829
Carrboro	Inc. Place	ORANGE	© 16,782
Lenoir	Inc. Place	CALDWELL	◆ 16,612
Eden	Inc. Place	ROCKINGHAM	◆ 15,878
Laurinburg	Inc. Place	SCOTLAND	© 15,874
Albemarle	Inc. Place	STANLY	© 15,680
Henderson	Inc. Place	VANCE	◆ 15,170
Reidsville	Inc. Place	ROCKINGHAM	© 14,485
Clemmons	Inc. Place	FORSYTH	© 13,827
Boone	Inc. Place	WATAUGA	Ⓡ 13,470
Graham	Inc. Place	ALAMANCE	© 12,833
Newton	Inc. Place	CATAWBA	Ⓡ 12,659
Hendersonville	Inc. Place	HENDERSON	◆ 11,861
Masonboro	CDP	NEW HANOVER	© 11,812
Indian Trail	Inc. Place	UNION	Ⓡ 11,749
Piney Green	CDP	ONSLOW	© 11,658
Hope Mills	Inc. Place	CUMBERLAND	© 11,237
Tarboro	Inc. Place	EDGECOMBE	© 11,138
Southern Pines	Inc. Place	MOORE	© 10,918
Smithfield	Inc. Place	JOHNSTON	Ⓡ 10,867
Dunn	Inc. Place	HARNETT	◆ 10,263
Lincolnton	Inc. Place	LINCOLN	© 9,965
Pinehurst	Inc. Place	MOORE	Ⓡ 9,729
Kings Mountain	Inc. Place	CLEVELAND	© 9,693
Washington	Inc. Place	BEAUFORT	◆ 9,659
Mount Holly	Inc. Place	GASTON	Ⓡ 9,617
Saint Stephens	CDP	CATAWBA	Ⓡ 9,426
Rockingham	Inc. Place	RICHMOND	◆ 9,378
Waynesville	Inc. Place	HAYWOOD	© 9,232
Archdale	Inc. Place	RANDOLPH	Ⓡ 9,007
Lewisville	Inc. Place	FORSYTH	© 8,826
Belmont	Inc. Place	GASTON	Ⓡ 8,794
Roxboro	Inc. Place	PERSON	© 8,696
Mount Airy	Inc. Place	SURRY	◆ 8,542
Clinton	Inc. Place	SAMPSON	◆ 8,503
Oxford	Inc. Place	GRANVILLE	© 8,338
Clayton	Inc. Place	JOHNSTON	Ⓡ 8,126
Spring Lake	Inc. Place	CUMBERLAND	© 8,098
Fuquay-Varina	Inc. Place	WAKE	© 7,898
Kings Grant	CDP	NEW HANOVER	© 7,738
Morehead City	Inc. Place	CARTERET	© 7,691
Black Mountain	Inc. Place	BUNCOMBE	© 7,511
Smith Creek	RMC Place	NEW HANOVER	Ⓟ 7,461
Mebane	Inc. Place	ALAMANCE	Ⓡ 7,367
Murraysville	CDP	NEW HANOVER	© 7,279
Forest City	Inc. Place	RUTHERFORD	◆ 7,178
Davidson	Inc. Place	MECKLENBURG	© 7,139
Myrtle Grove	CDP	NEW HANOVER	Ⓡ 7,123
Summerfield	Inc. Place	GUILFORD	© 7,018
Siler City	Inc. Place	CHATHAM	© 6,966
Brevard	Inc. Place	TRANSYLVANIA	© 6,789
Elon	Inc. Place	ALAMANCE	Ⓡ 6,748
Trinity	Inc. Place	RANDOLPH	Ⓡ 6,714
Weddington	Inc. Place	UNION	© 6,696
Conover	Inc. Place	CATAWBA	Ⓡ 6,667
Half Moon	CDP	ONSLOW	© 6,645
Oak Island	Inc. Place	BRUNSWICK	© 6,571
Butner	Inc. Place	GRANVILLE	● 6,200
Hamlet	Inc. Place	RICHMOND	© 6,018
Knightdale	Inc. Place	WAKE	© 5,958
King	Inc. Place	STOKES	© 5,952
Williamston	Inc. Place	MARTIN	Ⓡ 5,946
Selma	Inc. Place	JOHNSTON	© 5,914
Kill Devil Hills	Inc. Place	DARE	© 5,897
Butner	CDP-Census Area Only	GRANVILLE	© 5,792
Silver Lake	CDP	NEW HANOVER	© 5,788
New Hope	RMC Place	WAKE	Ⓟ 5,694
Ogden	CDP	NEW HANOVER	© 5,481
Hillsborough	Inc. Place	ORANGE	© 5,446
South Gastonia	CDP	GASTON	© 5,433
James City	CDP	CRAVEN	Ⓡ 5,422
Cherryville	Inc. Place	GASTON	© 5,361
Royal Pines	CDP	BUNCOMBE	© 5,334
Morrisville	Inc. Place	WAKE	© 5,208
Whiteville	Inc. Place	COLUMBUS	© 5,148
Bessemer City	Inc. Place	GASTON	© 5,119
Edenton	Inc. Place	CHOWAN	Ⓡ 5,058

County Business Data

County	FIPS Code	County Seat	Land Area (Sq. Mi.)	Census Population			Wholesale Trade		Manufacturing, 2002			
				4/1/2000	4/1/1990	% Change 1990-2000	Sales, 2002 ($1,000)	% Change 1997-2002	Establish-ments	Total Employees	Value Added ($1,000)	Ranally Mfg. Units
Alamance	001	Graham	430	130,800	108,213	20.9	1,222,209	122.0	254	17,381	1,717,939	909
Alexander	003	Taylorsville	260	33,603	27,544	22.0	(d)	(d)	91	4,492	298,373	158
Alleghany	005	Sparta	235	10,677	9,590	11.3	2,018	(d)	20	1,156	112,051	59
Anson	007	Wadesboro	532	25,275	23,474	7.7	(d)	(d)	32	1,947	122,924	65
Ashe	009	Jefferson	426	24,384	22,209	9.8	35,281	-20.2	32	1,177	103,142	55
Avery	011	Newland	247	17,167	14,867	15.5	34,343	-2.1	...	(d)	(d)	...
Beaufort	013	Washington	828	44,958	42,283	6.3	281,195	14.6	62	3,598	356,424	189
Bertie	015	Windsor	699	19,773	20,388	-3.0	107,073	-32.5	18	2,227	172,147	91
Bladen	017	Elizabethtown	875	32,278	28,663	12.6	120,431	-16.8	35	6,217	341,603	181
Brunswick	019	Bolivia	855	73,143	50,985	43.5	68,970	-10.4	68	1,851	263,125	139
Buncombe	021	Asheville	656	206,330	174,821	18.0	1,824,874	(d)	329	14,874	1,385,763	733
Burke	023	Morganton	507	89,148	75,744	17.7	(d)	(d)	160	13,154	1,142,298	604
Cabarrus	025	Concord	364	131,063	98,935	32.5	1,693,297	77.5	166	10,702	9,915,722	5,246
Caldwell	027	Lenoir	472	77,415	70,709	9.5	694,757	-12.2	155	14,128	884,591	468
Camden	029	Camden	241	6,885	5,904	16.6	(d)	(d)	...	(d)	(d)	...
Carteret	031	Beaufort	520	59,383	52,556	13.0	216,132	53.0	77	1,625	100,839	53
Caswell	033	Yanceyville	425	23,501	20,693	13.6	(d)	(d)	...	(d)	(d)	...
Catawba	035	Newton	400	141,685	118,412	19.7	4,226,472	66.2	530	36,044	2,752,999	1,457
Chatham	037	Pittsboro	683	49,329	38,759	27.3	188,876	-28.2	81	6,297	388,053	205
Cherokee	039	Murphy	455	24,298	20,170	20.5	50,506	-1.2	27	1,282	111,118	59
Chowan	041	Edenton	173	14,526	13,506	7.6	62,086	-13.9	18	1,027	75,293	40
Clay	043	Hayesville	215	8,775	7,155	22.6	(d)	(d)	...	(d)	(d)	...
Cleveland	045	Shelby	465	96,287	84,714	13.7	1,266,475	-6.6	175	11,822	1,084,034	574
Columbus	047	Whiteville	937	54,749	49,587	10.4	202,349	-16.1	43	3,067	398,770	211
Craven	049	New Bern	708	91,436	81,613	12.0	397,060	29.1	76	4,361	544,454	288
Cumberland	051	Fayetteville	653	302,963	274,566	10.3	949,293	12.3	117	(d)	(d)	...
Currituck	053	Currituck	262	18,190	13,736	32.4	25,130	(d)	...	(d)	(d)	...
Dare	055	Manteo	384	29,967	22,746	31.7	110,207	6.1	41	577	45,773	24
Davidson	057	Lexington	552	147,246	126,677	16.2	624,861	-21.1	319	(d)	(d)	...
Davie	059	Mocksville	265	34,835	27,859	25.0	134,816	23.4	52	3,374	249,837	132
Duplin	061	Kenansville	818	49,063	39,995	22.7	707,100	(d)	40	3,386	257,534	136
Durham	063	Durham	290	223,314	181,835	22.8	4,119,899	78.6	181	23,482	2,442,681	1,292
Edgecombe	065	Tarboro	505	55,606	56,558	-1.7	(d)	(d)	57	10,667	1,633,173	864
Forsyth	067	Winston Salem	410	306,067	265,878	15.1	5,019,788	38.5	383	23,565	7,970,784	4,217
Franklin	069	Louisburg	492	47,260	36,414	29.8	135,940	-18.1	63	2,340	300,323	159
Gaston	071	Gastonia	356	190,365	175,093	8.7	(d)	(d)	392	17,874	1,528,182	809
Gates	073	Gatesville	341	10,516	9,305	13.0	16,890	1.0	...	(d)	(d)	...
Graham	075	Robbinsville	292	7,993	7,196	11.1	(d)	(d)	6	(d)	(d)	...
Granville	077	Oxford	531	48,498	38,345	26.5	181,769	-17.0	50	6,297	1,480,454	783
Greene	079	Snow Hill	265	18,974	15,384	23.3	17,282	-50.4	...	(d)	(d)	...
Guilford	081	Greensboro	649	421,048	347,420	21.2	12,399,673	-7.8	805	42,727	6,720,318	3,556
Halifax	083	Halifax	725	57,370	55,516	3.3	79,553	-21.7	45	2,483	340,882	180
Harnett	085	Lillington	595	91,025	67,822	34.2	(d)	(d)	64	2,546	155,330	82
Haywood	087	Waynesville	554	54,033	46,942	15.1	(d)	(d)	52	1,907	279,261	148
Henderson	089	Hendersonville	374	89,173	69,285	28.7	465,150	104.0	128	7,137	781,141	413
Hertford	091	Winton	353	22,601	22,523	0.3	167,836	33.2	25	1,113	149,008	79
Hoke	093	Raeford	391	33,646	22,856	47.2	20,153	-33.4	12	(d)	(d)	...
Hyde	095	Swanquarter	613	5,826	5,411	7.7	13,558	-37.7	...	(d)	(d)	...
Iredell	097	Statesville	576	122,660	92,931	32.0	2,370,811	72.6	275	12,879	1,758,357	930
Jackson	099	Sylva	491	33,121	26,846	23.4	26,987	48.5	25	540	56,378	30
Johnston	101	Smithfield	792	121,965	81,306	50.0	1,244,664	48.7	117	6,219	859,371	455
Jones	103	Trenton	472	10,381	9,414	10.3	(d)	(d)	...	(d)	(d)	...
Lee	105	Sanford	257	49,040	41,374	18.5	624,246	20.7	98	8,990	1,081,237	572
Lenoir	107	Kinston	400	59,648	57,274	4.1	500,111	2.8	65	4,916	470,116	249
Lincoln	109	Lincolnton	299	63,780	50,319	26.8	(d)	(d)	112	5,730	487,944	258
Macon	113	Franklin	516	29,811	23,499	26.9	21,749	31.7	37	951	75,781	40
Madison	115	Marshall	449	19,635	16,953	15.8	(d)	(d)	19	797	51,805	27
Martin	117	Williamston	461	25,593	25,078	2.1	61,522	-19.2	20	1,464	132,612	70
McDowell	111	Marion	442	42,151	35,681	18.1	48,609	-17.6	60	7,661	531,220	281
Mecklenburg	119	Charlotte	526	695,454	511,433	36.0	32,743,164	-6.5	939	38,490	4,226,071	2,236
Mitchell	121	Bakersville	221	15,687	14,433	8.7	19,367	(d)	33	1,297	75,170	40
Montgomery	123	Troy	492	26,822	23,346	14.9	126,874	116.4	72	4,739	310,041	164
Moore	125	Carthage	698	74,769	59,013	26.7	165,855	-44.3	89	2,929	251,045	133
Nash	127	Nashville	540	87,420	76,677	14.0	(d)	(d)	94	3,269	226,021	120
New Hanover	129	Wilmington	199	160,307	120,284	33.3	1,229,257	1.0	213	6,848	1,034,150	547
Northampton	131	Jackson	536	22,086	20,798	6.2	176,294	-17.9	...	(d)	(d)	...
Onslow	133	Jacksonville	767	150,355	149,838	0.3	(d)	(d)	41	1,415	46,289	24
Orange	135	Hillsborough	400	118,227	93,851	26.0	252,769	-19.1	66	835	54,252	29
Pamlico	137	Bayboro	337	12,934	11,372	13.7	(d)	(d)	...	(d)	(d)	...
Pasquotank	139	Elizabeth City	227	34,897	31,298	11.5	184,482	22.4	30	(d)	(d)	...
Pender	141	Burgaw	871	41,082	28,855	42.4	289,834	192.5	32	852	50,221	27
Perquimans	143	Hertford	247	11,368	10,447	8.8	(d)	(d)	...	(d)	(d)	...
Person	145	Roxboro	392	35,623	30,180	18.0	(d)	(d)	40	3,818	548,522	290
Pitt	147	Greenville	652	133,798	107,924	24.0	572,727	-54.1	106	(d)	(d)	...
Polk	149	Columbus	238	18,324	14,416	27.1	15,806	-19.7	24	630	32,875	17
Randolph	151	Asheboro	787	130,454	106,546	22.4	710,977	22.2	356	19,460	1,654,711	875

Entries in **UPPERCASE** are counties.
Entries in **bold** have populations of 2,500 or more.
Names in parentheses are alternate names.
Inc. Place — Incorporated Place
RMC Place — Rand McNally Designated Place
CDP — Census Designated Place
MCD — Minor Civil Division

⊡ County Seat
▲ Minor Civil Division
elev. Elevation
🅿 Post Office

Ⓗ Hospital
Ⓒ College
■ Principal Business Center
★ Ranally Metro Area (RMA) Abbreviation
z Zip Code(s)

Ⓟ Previous Census Population
Ⓡ Revised Census Population
Ⓐ Annexation Population
● Rand McNally Population Estimate
© Final Census Population
Ⓢ Special Census Population
◆ Estimated Population

For additional definitions see Glossary, Volume 1, and Introduction, Volume 2.

County	FIPS Code	County Seat	Land Area (Sq. Mi.)	Census Population			Wholesale Trade		Manufacturing, 2002			
				4/1/2000	4/1/1990	% Change 1990-2000	Sales, 2002 ($1,000)	% Change 1997-2002	Establish-ments	Total Employees	Value Added ($1,000)	Ranally Mfg. Units
Richmond	153	Rockingham	474	46,564	44,518	4.6	115,763	19.5	54	3,948	336,256	178
Robeson	155	Lumberton	949	123,339	105,179	17.3	526,823	50.7	89	9,029	1,473,999	780
Rockingham	157	Wentworth	566	91,928	86,064	6.8	169,201	-4.7	125	11,276	1,623,446	859
Rowan	159	Salisbury	511	130,340	110,605	17.8	805,643	46.9	191	12,377	1,009,776	534
Rutherford	161	Rutherfordton	564	62,899	56,918	10.5	(d)	(d)	87	7,350	568,596	301
Sampson	163	Clinton	945	60,161	47,297	27.2	328,493	42.2	56	3,764	300,466	159
Scotland	165	Laurinburg	319	35,998	33,754	6.6	251,941	235.7	42	5,972	643,208	340
Stanly	167	Albemarle	395	58,100	51,765	12.2	(d)	(d)	121	5,663	414,579	219
Stokes	169	Danbury	452	44,711	37,223	20.1	(d)	(d)	38	1,045	75,411	40
Surry	171	Dobson	537	71,219	61,704	15.4	610,757	-5.5	134	9,458	572,000	303
Swain	173	Bryson City	528	12,968	11,268	15.1	16,260	-40.4	...	(d)	(d)	...
Transylvania	175	Brevard	378	29,334	25,520	14.9	(d)	(d)	31	1,231	118,141	63
Tyrrell	177	Columbia	390	4,149	3,856	7.6	(d)	(d)	...	(d)	(d)	...
Union	179	Monroe	637	123,677	84,211	46.9	1,105,261	35.9	245	12,088	979,246	518
Vance	181	Henderson	254	42,954	38,892	10.4	285,218	4.1	47	2,807	297,955	158
Wake	183	Raleigh	832	627,846	423,380	48.3	13,927,454	5.0	687	20,277	7,300,439	3,862
Warren	185	Warrenton	429	19,972	17,265	15.7	5,106	-8.0	11	537	30,167	16
Washington	187	Plymouth	348	13,723	13,997	-2.0	27,325	-24.9	15	(d)	(d)	...
Watauga	189	Boone	313	42,695	36,952	15.5	115,568	-30.4	56	1,066	75,787	40
Wayne	191	Goldsboro	553	113,329	104,666	8.3	946,003	6.2	93	8,764	877,472	464
Wilkes	193	Wilkesboro	757	65,632	59,393	10.5	513,325	19.1	98	6,656	749,974	397
Wilson	195	Wilson	371	73,814	66,061	11.7	900,710	91.2	95	8,861	4,710,766	2,492
Yadkin	197	Yadkinville	336	36,348	30,488	19.2	(d)	(d)	42	2,567	112,655	60
Yancey	199	Burnsville	312	17,774	15,419	15.3	2,420	58.9	19	1,007	50,597	27
The State			**48,711**	**8,049,313**	**6,628,637**	**21.4**	**104,331,152**	**6.4**	**10,762**	**623,333**	**87,355,207**	**46,217**

(d) Data not available. Corresponding percentages or Ranally Manufacturing Units are estimates.
... Represents 0 or amount too minimal to be reported.

Index of Places and Counties

A

Aarons Corner; RMC Place; STOKES; *212 B-7; elev. 1,116ft./340m.; mail Westfield z 27053; rural

Abbottsburg; RMC Place; BLADEN; 213 I-11; elev. 103ft./31m.; mail Bladenboro z 28320; ● 190

Abee; RMC Place; BURKE; *212 E-3; elev. 1,240ft./378m.; ★ HICK; mail Valdese z 28690; rural

Aberdeen; Inc. Place; MOORE; 212 G-9; elev. 339ft./103m.; 🄿; z 28315; Ⓟ 2,700; © 3,400

Abner; RMC Place; MONTGOMERY; *212 F-8; elev. 740ft./226m.; mail Star z 27356; ● 30

Abshers; RMC Place; WILKES; *212 C-5; mail Hays z 28635, Traphill z 28685; rural

Academy Street; RMC Place; WAKE; ★ RAL; mail Cary z 27519; pop. incl. with Cary (Inc. Place)

Acme; RMC Place; COLUMBUS; *213 J-13; elev. 37ft./11m.; mail Riegelwood z 28456; ● 50

Acorn Hill; RMC Place; GATES; *213 B-17; elev. 41ft./12m.; mail Sunbury z 27979; rural

Acorn Woods; RMC Place; UNION; *212 G-6; ★ CHRLT; mail Indian Trail z 28079; pop. incl. with Lake Park (Inc. Place)

Acre; RMC Place; BEAUFORT; *213 E-17; elev. 32ft./10m.; mail Pinetown z 27865; ● 90

Adako; RMC Place; CALDWELL; *212 D-3; elev. 1,200ft./366m.; mail Lenoir z 28645; rural

Addie; RMC Place; JACKSON; *212 L-4; mail Sylva z 28779; ● 360

Addor; RMC Place; MOORE; *212 G-9; elev. 302ft./92m.; mail Aberdeen z 28315, Pinebluff z 28373

Adoniram; RMC Place; GRANVILLE; mail Virgilina z 24598; rural

Advance; RMC Place; DAVIE; 212 D-7; elev. 831ft./253m.; 🄿; z 27006; ● 330

Advent Crossroads; RMC Place; CATAWBA; *212 E-4; elev. 1,262ft./385m.; ★ HICK; mail Hickory z 28601; rural

Afton; RMC Place; WARREN; 213 C-13; elev. 435ft./133m.; mail Warrenton z 27589; ● 60

Aggstone; RMC Place; WAKE; ★ RAL; pop. incl. with Raleigh (Inc. Place)

Aho; RMC Place; WATAUGA; *212 C-3; mail Blowing Rock z 28605, Boone z 28607; ● 200

Ahoskie; Inc. Place; HERTFORD; 213 C-16; elev. 53ft./16m.; 🄿 🄷; z 27910; Ⓟ 4,391; © 4,523

Ai; RMC Place; PERSON; mail Timberlake z 27583; rural

Airboro; RMC Place; WAYNE; *213 F-13; ★ GLDS; mail Goldsboro z 27530; pop. incl. with Goldsboro (Inc. Place)

Airlie; RMC Place; HALIFAX; 213 C-14; mail Littleton z 27850; ● 50

Alamance; Inc. Place; ALAMANCE; *212 D-9; elev. 577ft./176m.; 🄿; ★ BUR; z 27201; Ⓟ 258; © 310

ALAMANCE; 212 D-9; Ⓟ 108,213; © 130,800; ◆ 150,256

Alamance Square; RMC Place; GUILFORD; ★ GRNS-; mail Greensboro z 27406; pop. incl. with Greensboro (Inc. Place)

Alarka; RMC Place; SWAIN; *212 L-3; mail Bryson City z 28713; rural

Albemarle; Inc. Place; ⊡ STANLY; 212 F-7; 🄿 🄷; z 28001-02; Ⓟ 14,939; © 15,680

Albemarle Beach; RMC Place; WASHINGTON; *213 D-17; mail Roper z 27970; ● 100

Albertson; RMC Place; DUPLIN; 213 G-14; elev. 146ft./45m.; 🄿; z 28508; ● 180

Albrittons; RMC Place; LENOIR; *213 G-14; elev. 82ft./25m.; mail Kinston z 28504; rural

Alder Branch; CAMDEN; see Goose Creek (RMC Place)

Alert; RMC Place; FRANKLIN; *213 C-13; elev. 397ft./121m.; mail Warrenton z 27589

Alexander; RMC Place; BUNCOMBE; 212 K-5; elev. 1,792ft./546m.; 🄿; ★ ASHE; z 28701; ● 250

ALEXANDER; 212 D-4; Ⓟ 27,544; © 33,603; ◆ 36,912

Alexander Mills; RMC Place; RUTHERFORD; 212 F-2; elev. 960ft./293m.; 🄿; z 28043; pop. incl. with Forest City (Inc. Place); Ⓟ 662

Alexis; RMC Place; GASTON; 212 F-5; elev. 879ft./268m.; 🄿; ★ CHRLT; z 28006; ● 600

Alfordsville; RMC Place; ROBESON; *212 I-10; elev. 150ft./46m.; mail Rowland z 28383; ● 30

ALLEGHANY; 212 B-4; Ⓟ 9,590; © 10,677; ◆ 10,983

Allen; RMC Place; MECKLENBURG; *212 G-6; elev. 775ft./236m.; ★ CHRLT; mail Charlotte z 28212

Allendale; RMC Place; CLEVELAND; *212 F-3; elev. 900ft./274m.; mail Shelby z 28150; ● 80

Allen Grove; RMC Place; HALIFAX; *213 C-14; elev. 132ft./40m.; mail Halifax z 27839; ● 30

Allen Jay; RMC Place; GUILFORD; *212 D-8; ★ GRNS-; mail High Point z 27263; pop. incl. with High Point (Inc. Place)

Allens Crossroads; RMC Place; UNION; *212 H-7; mail Wingate z 28174; ● 30

Allens Level; RMC Place; PERSON; *212 C-10; elev. 631ft./192m.; mail Roxboro z 27574; rural

Allensville; RMC Place; PERSON; 213 B-11; mail Roxboro z 27574; ● 80

All Healing Springs; RMC Place; ALEXANDER; *212 D-4; mail Taylorsville z 28681; ● 30

Alliance; Inc. Place; PAMLICO; *213 G-17; elev. 11ft./3m.; 🄿; z 28509; Ⓟ 583; © 781; Ⓡ 785

Alligator; RMC Place; TYRRELL; *213 D-19; mail Columbia z 27925; rural

Allison; RMC Place; CASWELL; *212 B-9; elev. 680ft./207m.; mail Ruffin z 27326; rural

Allreds; RMC Place; MONTGOMERY; *212 F-8; mail Star z 27356; rural

Alma; RMC Place; ROBESON; 212 H-10; mail Maxton z 28364; ● 50

Almond; RMC Place; SWAIN; 212 L-3; elev. 2,000ft./610m.; 🄿; z 28702; ● 150

Alspaugh; RMC Place; FORSYTH; *212 C-7; elev. 988ft./301m.; ★ WNS; mail Winston Salem z 27105; pop. incl. with Winston-Salem (Inc. Place)

Altamahaw; RMC Place; ALAMANCE; 212 C-9; elev. 610ft./186m.; 🄿; ★ BUR; z 27202; ● 220

Altamahaw-Ossipee; CDP-Census Area Only; ALAMANCE; *212 C-9; elev. 609ft./186m.; ★ BUR; mail Altamahaw z 27202; Ⓟ 1,076; © 996

Altamont; RMC Place; AVERY; 212 D-2; mail Newland z 28657; ● 50

Altan; RMC Place; UNION; *212 H-6; mail Monroe z 28112; rural

Altapass; RMC Place; MITCHELL; *212 D-2; mail Spruce Pine z 28777; ● 230

Amantha; RMC Place; WATAUGA; 212 C-3; mail Sugar Grove z 28679; ● 50

Amerotron Mill; RMC Place; ROBESON; mail Red Springs z 28377; pop. incl. with Red Springs (Inc. Place)

Amity Gardens; RMC Place; MECKLENBURG; ★ CHRLT; mail Charlotte z 28205; pop. incl. with Charlotte (Inc. Place)

Amity Hill; RMC Place; IREDELL; *212 E-6; mail Cleveland z 27013; ● 30

Ammon; RMC Place; BLADEN; 213 H-12; elev. 98ft./30m.; mail Elizabethtown z 28337; ● 30

Anderson; RMC Place; CASWELL; 212 C-10; elev. 739ft./225m.; mail Burlington z 27215; ● 60

Anderson; RMC Place; DARE; elev. 20ft./6m.; mail Kitty Hawk z 27949; pop. incl. with Kitty Hawk (Inc. Place)

Anderson Creek; RMC Place; HARNETT; *213 F-11; ★ FAY; mail Bunnlevel z 28323, Spring Lake z 28390; ● 200

Anderson Crossroads; RMC Place; HALIFAX; *213 C-14; elev. 207ft./63m.; mail Littleton z 27850; rural

Andrews; Inc. Place; CHEROKEE; 212 M-2; 🄿 🄷; z 28901; Ⓟ 2,551; © 1,602

Angier; Inc. Place; HARNETT; 213 F-11; elev. 301ft./92m.; 🄿; ★ RAL; z 27501; Ⓟ 2,235; © 3,419

Angola; RMC Place; ONSLOW; *213 H-14; elev. 26ft./8m.; mail Maple Hill z 28454; ● 30

ANSON; 212 G-8; Ⓟ 23,474; © 25,275; ◆ 24,992

Ansonville; Inc. Place; ANSON; 212 G-7; elev. 326ft./99m.; 🄿; z 28007; Ⓟ 614; © 636

Antioch; RMC Place; BRUNSWICK; *213 K-13; elev. 38ft./12m.; ★ WILM; mail Bolivia z 28422; ● 100

Antioch; RMC Place; HOKE; *212 H-10; mail Red Springs z 28377; rural

Antioch; RMC Place; MADISON; *212 J-5; mail Marshall z 28753; rural

Apex; Inc. Place; WAKE; 213 E-11; elev. 468ft./143m.; 🄿; ★ RAL; z 27502, z 27523, z 27539 & mail Cary z 27519; Ⓟ 4,968; © 20,212; ◆ 35,741

Appie; RMC Place; GREENE; *213 E-14; elev. 105ft./32m.; mail Walstonburg z 27888; rural

Apple Grove; RMC Place; ASHE; *212 B-3; mail Lansing z 28643; rural

Aquadale; RMC Place; STANLY; 212 G-7; elev. 483ft./147m.; mail Norwood z 28128; ● 210

Aquone; RMC Place; MACON; 212 M-2; elev. 3,200ft./975m.; 🄿; z 28781; ● 220

Arabia; RMC Place; HOKE; 212 H-10; elev. 224ft./68m.; mail Raeford z 28376; ● 110

Arapahoe; Inc. Place; PAMLICO; 213 G-17; elev. 40ft./12m.; 🄿; z 28510; Ⓟ 430; © 436

Ararat; RMC Place; SURRY; 212 B-6; elev. 911ft./278m.; 🄿; z 27007; ● 50

Arba; RMC Place; GREENE; *213 F-14; elev. 116ft./35m.; mail Snow Hill z 28580; ● 60

Arcadia; RMC Place; DAVIDSON; 214 I-8; elev. 826ft./252m.; ★ WNS; mail Lexington z 27292, z 27295; ● 130

Archdale; Inc. Place; RANDOLPH, GUILFORD; 212 D-8; elev. 869ft./265m.; 🄿; ★ GRNS-; z 27263; Ⓟ 6,913; © 9,014; Ⓡ 9,007

Archers Lodge; RMC Place; JOHNSTON; *213 E-12; mail Clayton z 27520; ● 50

Arcola; RMC Place; WARREN; 213 C-13; elev. 319ft./97m.; mail Warrenton z 27589; ● 60

Arden; RMC Place; BUNCOMBE; 212 F-1; elev. 2,225ft./678m.; 🄿; ★ ASHE; z 28704; ● 800

Ardmore; RMC Place; FORSYTH; *212 D-7; ★ WNS; mail Winston Salem z 27103, z 27113; pop. incl. with Winston-Salem (Inc. Place)

Ardulusa; RMC Place; CUMBERLAND; *213 G-11; ★ FAY; mail Fayetteville z 28301

Argura; RMC Place; JACKSON; *212 M-4; mail Tuckasegee z 28783

Arlington; RMC Place; YADKIN; 212 C-5; elev. 1,018ft./310m.; mail Jonesville z 28642; former incorporated place; became part of Jonesville July 1, 2001; pop. incl. with Jonesville (Inc. Place); Ⓟ 795; © 795

Armour; RMC Place; COLUMBUS; *213 J-13; mail Riegelwood z 28456; ● 50

Arnold; RMC Place; DAVIDSON; *212 D-7; mail Lexington z 27292, z 27295

Arran Hills; RMC Place; CUMBERLAND; *213 G-11; elev. 200ft./61m.; ★ FAY; mail Fayetteville z 28304; ● 2,240

Arrowhead Beach; RMC Place; CHOWAN; *213 C-17; elev. 26ft./8m.; mail Edenton z 27932; ● 530

Arrowhead Place; RMC Place; CABARRUS; *212 F-6; elev. 650ft./198m.; ★ CHRLT; mail Concord z 28025; pop. incl. with Concord (Inc. Place)

Arrowood; RMC Place; MECKLENBURG; *212 G-5; elev. 600ft./183m.; ★ CHRLT; mail Charlotte z 28241; pop. incl. with Charlotte (Inc. Place)

Artesia; RMC Place; COLUMBUS; *213 J-12; elev. 65ft./20m.; mail Hallsboro z 28442; ● 40

Arthur; PITT; see Bell Arthur (RMC Place)

Asbury; RMC Place; CHATHAM; *212 E-10; elev. 384ft./117m.; mail Sanford z 27330; ● 70

Ash; RMC Place; BRUNSWICK; 213 K-12; elev. 51ft./16m.; 🄿; z 28420; ● 250

ASHE; 212 B-4; Ⓟ 22,209; © 24,384; ◆ 25,838

Asheboro; Inc. Place; ⊡ RANDOLPH; 212 E-8; elev. 844ft./257m.; 🄿 🄷 ■; z 27203-05; Ⓟ 16,362; © 21,672; ◆ 24,119

Asheville; Inc. Place; ⊡ BUNCOMBE; 212 E-1; elev. 2,134ft./650m.; 🄿 🄷 🄲 4,461 ■; ★ ASHE; z 28801-06, z 28810, z 28813-16; Ⓟ 61,855; © 68,889; ◆ 74,365

Ashford; RMC Place; MCDOWELL; *212 D-2; mail Marion z 28752

Ash Hill; RMC Place; SURRY; *212 B-6; elev. 1,101ft./336m.; mail Ararat z 27007; rural

Ashland; RMC Place; ASHE; *212 B-3; elev. 2,918ft./889m.; mail Creston z 28615

Ashland; RMC Place; BERTIE; *213 C-17; elev. 46ft./14m.; mail Merry Hill z 27957; rural

Ashland; RMC Place; CASWELL; *212 C-9; elev. 772ft./235m.; mail Reidsville z 27320; rural

Ashley Heights; CDP; HOKE; *212 G-10; elev. 439ft./134m.; mail Aberdeen z 28315; © 341

Ashton; RMC Place; PENDER; *213 I-14; mail Burgaw z 28425; rural

Ashton Forrest; RMC Place; CUMBERLAND; *213 G-11; elev. 200ft./61m.; ★ FAY; mail Fayetteville z 28304; ● 1,510

Ashwood; RMC Place; PAMLICO; *213 G-17; mail Oriental z 28571; rural

Askewville; Inc. Place; BERTIE; 213 C-16; mail Windsor z 27983; Ⓟ 201; © 180

Askin; RMC Place; CRAVEN; 213 F-16; elev. 14ft./4m.; mail Ernul z 28527; ● 200

Atkinson; Inc. Place; PENDER; 213 I-13; elev. 63ft./19m.; 🄿; z 28421; Ⓟ 275; © 236

Atlantic; RMC Place; CARTERET; 213 H-18; elev. 7ft./2m.; 🄿; z 28511; ● 1,150

Atlantic Beach; Inc. Place; CARTERET; 213 H-17; elev. 8ft./2m.; 🄿; z 28512; Ⓟ 1,938; © 1,781

Auburn; RMC Place; WAKE; 213 E-12; elev. 336ft./102m.; ★ RAL; mail Raleigh z 27610; ● 350

Audubon; RMC Place; NEW HANOVER; ★ WILM; mail Wilmington z 28403; pop. incl. with Wilmington (Inc. Place)

Aulander; Inc. Place; BERTIE; 213 C-16; elev. 73ft./22m.; 🄿; z 27805; Ⓟ 1,209; © 888; Ⓡ 922

Aurelian Springs; RMC Place; HALIFAX; *213 C-14; elev. 339ft./103m.; mail Littleton z 27850; ● 50

Aurora; Inc. Place; BEAUFORT; 213 F-17; elev. 8ft./2m.; 🄿; z 27806; Ⓟ 654; © 583

Austin; RMC Place; WILKES; *212 C-5; mail Elkin z 28621

Autryville; Inc. Place; SAMPSON; 213 G-12; elev. 113ft./34m.; 🄿; z 28318; Ⓟ 166; © 196

Avalon Valley; RMC Place; ALAMANCE; *212 D-9; elev. 550ft./168m.; ★ BUR; mail Crossville z 38558, Graham z 27253; ● 160

Avent Ferry Road; RMC Place; WAKE; ★ RAL; mail Raleigh z 27606, z 27627; pop. incl. with Raleigh (Inc. Place)

Aventon; RMC Place; NASH; *213 C-13; elev. 287ft./87m.; mail Whitakers z 27891; rural

Averasboro; RMC Place; HARNETT; *213 F-11; elev. 170ft./52m.; mail Dunn z 28334; pop. incl. with Erwin (Inc. Place)

AVERY; 212 D-2; Ⓟ 14,867; © 17,167; ◆ 17,571

Avery Creek; CDP; BUNCOMBE; *212 F-1; ★ ASHE; mail Arden z 28704; Ⓟ 1,144; © 1,405

Avery Shores; RMC Place; CAMDEN; *213 C-19; elev. 1ft./0m.; mail Shiloh z 27974; ● 30

Avon; RMC Place; DARE; 213 F-20; elev. 10ft./3m.; 🄿; z 27915; summer pop. 1,500; ● 630

Axtell; RMC Place; WARREN; *213 C-13; elev. 457ft./139m.; mail Norlina z 27563; rural

Ayden; Inc. Place; PITT; 213 F-15; elev. 63ft./19m.; 🄿; ★ GRNV; z 28513; Ⓟ 4,740; © 4,622

Aydlett; RMC Place; CURRITUCK; 213 B-19; 🄿; z 27916; ● 240

Ayersville; RMC Place; ROCKINGHAM; 212 B-8; elev. 1,018ft./310m.; mail Mayodan z 27027; ● 120

Azalea; RMC Place; BUNCOMBE; *212 E-1; ★ ASHE; mail Asheville z 28805; pop. incl. with Asheville (Inc. Place)

Azalea; RMC Place; NEW HANOVER; ★ WILM; mail Wilmington z 28403, z 28406; pop. incl. with Wilmington (Inc. Place)

B

Bachelor; RMC Place; CRAVEN; *213 G-17; mail Havelock z 28532; ● 50

Badin; Inc. Place; STANLY; 212 F-7; elev. 515ft./157m.; 🄿; z 28009; Ⓟ 1,360; © 1,154

Bagley; RMC Place; JOHNSTON; *213 E-13; elev. 169ft./52m.; mail Kenly z 27542

Bahama; RMC Place; DURHAM; 213 C-11; elev. 505ft./154m.; 🄿; ★ DUR; z 27503; ● 500

Bailey; Inc. Place; NASH; 213 E-13; elev. 233ft./71m.; 🄿; z 27807; Ⓟ 553; © 670

Bailey Camp; RMC Place; CALDWELL; *212 C-3; elev. 2,795ft./852m.; mail Lenoir z 28645; rural

Bailey Town; RMC Place; STOKES; *212 C-7; ★ WNS; mail Walnut Cove z 27052; ● 60

Baker Rhyne Apartments; RMC Place; CLEVELAND; *212 F-3; elev. 857ft./261m.; mail Shelby z 28152; ● 170

Bakers; RMC Place; UNION; *212 G-6; mail Monroe z 28110; pop. incl. with Monroe (Inc. Place)

Bakers Crossroads; RMC Place; ROCKINGHAM; *212 C-8; elev. 845ft./258m.; mail Reidsville z 27320; rural

Bakersville; Inc. Place; ⊡ MITCHELL; 212 D-2; elev. 2,460ft./750m.; 🄿; z 28705; Ⓟ 332; © 357

Bald Creek; RMC Place; YANCEY; 212 D-1; mail Burnsville z 28714; ● 110

Bald Head Island; Inc. Place; BRUNSWICK; *213 K-14; 🄿; z 28461; Ⓟ 78; © 173

Bald Mountain; RMC Place; YANCEY; *212 D-1; mail Burnsville z 28714; rural

Baldwin; RMC Place; ASHE; *212 C-3; elev. 3,095ft./943m.; mail West Jefferson z 28694

Baldwin; RMC Place; MOORE; mail Seagrove z 27341; rural

Baldwin Woods; RMC Place; COLUMBUS; *213 J-11; elev. 80ft./24m.; mail Whiteville z 28472; pop. incl. with Whiteville (Inc. Place)

Balfour (Smyth); CDP; HENDERSON; *212 F-1; elev. 2,104ft./641m.; mail Hendersonville z 28791; © 1,200; Ⓡ 1,212

Ballantree; RMC Place; BUNCOMBE; *212 E-1; ★ ASHE; mail Asheville z 28803; pop. incl. with Asheville (Inc. Place)

Ballard; RMC Place; MARTIN; *213 D-16; mail Hamilton z 27840; rural

Ballards Crossroad; RMC Place; PITT; *213 E-15; ★ GRNV; mail Greenville z 27834; rural

Ballew Store (South Toe Community); RMC Place; YANCEY; *212 D-2; mail Burnsville z 28714; ● 110

Balm; RMC Place; AVERY; *212 C-2; mail Banner Elk z 28604

Balsam; RMC Place; JACKSON; 212 L-4; elev. 3,400ft./1,036m.; 🄿; z 28707; ● 400

Balsam Grove; RMC Place; TRANSYLVANIA; 212 M-4; elev. 2,810ft./856m.; 🄿; z 28708; ● 120

Baltic; RMC Place; DUPLIN, SAMPSON; mail Warsaw z 28398; rural

Baltimore; RMC Place; BLADEN; *213 I-12; elev. 70ft./21m.; mail Council z 28434; ● 50

Bamboo; RMC Place; WATAUGA; *212 C-3; mail Blowing Rock z 28605; ● 250

Bandana; RMC Place; MITCHELL; *212 D-2; mail Bakersville z 28705; ● 30

Bandy; RMC Place; CATAWBA; 212 E-5; elev. 1,037ft./316m.; ★ HICK; mail Catawba z 28609; ● 140

Banks; RMC Place; WAKE; *213 E-11; elev. 290ft./88m.; ★ RAL; mail Raleigh z 27603; rural

Banks Creek; RMC Place; YANCEY; *212 D-1; elev. 2,800ft./853m.; mail Burnsville z 28714; rural

Banner Elk; Inc. Place; AVERY; 212 C-2; elev. 3,739ft./1,140m.; 🄿 🄷 🄲 865; z 28604, z 28691; Ⓟ 933; © 811; Ⓡ 828

Bannertown; RMC Place; SURRY; 212 B-6; elev. 1,062ft./324m.; mail Mount Airy z 27030; pop. incl. with Mount Airy (Inc. Place)

Banoak; RMC Place; CATAWBA; *212 E-4; elev. 1,190ft./363m.; ★ HICK; mail Vale z 28168; rural

Barber; RMC Place; ROWAN; 212 E-6; elev. 758ft./231m.; 🄿; ★ SLSB; z 27013; ● 80

Barclaysville; RMC Place; HARNETT; *213 F-11; elev. 332ft./101m.; ★ RAL; mail Angier z 27501; rural

Barco; RMC Place; CURRITUCK; 213 B-19; 🄿; z 27917; ● 300

Barham; RMC Place; WAKE; *213 D-12; elev. 369ft./112m.; ★ RAL; mail Wake Forest z 27587; ● 30

Barium Springs; RMC Place; IREDELL; *212 E-5; elev. 945ft./288m.; 🄿; z 28010; pop. incl. with Troutman (Inc. Place)

Barker Heights; CDP; HENDERSON; *212 F-1; mail Hendersonville z 28792; Ⓟ 1,137; © 1,237; Ⓡ 1,246

Barkers Creek; RMC Place; JACKSON; 214 J-6; mail Whittier z 28789; ● 50

Barker Ten Mile; CDP-Census Area Only; ROBESON; *213 H-11; elev. 125ft./38m.; mail Lumberton z 28358; Ⓟ 1,087; © 976

Barnard; RMC Place; MADISON; *212 K-5; elev. 1,535ft./468m.; mail Marshall z 28753; ● 90

Barnardsville; RMC Place; BUNCOMBE; 212 E-1; elev. 2,185ft./666m.; 🄿; ★ ASHE; z 28709; ● 550

Barnesfield; RMC Place; CARTERET; *213 H-17; elev. 10ft./3m.; mail Newport z 28570; ● 130

Barnesville; RMC Place; ROBESON; 212 I-10; elev. 103ft./31m.; 🄿; z 28319; ● 130

Barrett; RMC Place; ALLEGHANY; *212 B-5; elev. 2,821ft./860m.; mail Ennice z 28623; rural

Barriers Mill; RMC Place; CABARRUS; 212 F-7; ★ CHRLT; mail Mount Pleasant z 28124; ● 30

Bartlett; RMC Place; CAMDEN; *213 C-19; elev. 2ft./1m.; mail Camden z 27921; rural

Barton College; RMC Place; WILSON; mail Wilson z 27893; pop. incl. with Wilson (Inc. Place)

Bass Crossroads; RMC Place; NASH; *213 D-13; elev. 299ft./91m.; ★ RKYMT; mail Spring Hope z 27882; rural

Basstown; RMC Place; SAMPSON; *213 G-12; mail Clinton z 28328; rural

Bat Cave; RMC Place; HENDERSON; 212 F-1; elev. 1,475ft./450m.; 🄿; z 28710; ● 600

Batchelor Crossroads; RMC Place; NASH; *213 D-13; elev. 206ft./63m.; ★ RKYMT; mail Spring Hope z 27882; rural

Bath; Inc. Place; BEAUFORT; 213 F-17; elev. 6ft./2m.; 🄿; z 27808; Ⓟ 154; © 275

Baton; RMC Place; CALDWELL; 212 D-3; elev. 1,187ft./362m.; ★ HICK; mail Granite Falls z 28630, Lenoir z 28645; ● 500

Battleboro; RMC Place; NASH, EDGECOMBE; 213 D-14; elev. 136ft./41m.; 🄿; ★ RKYMT; z 27809; pop. incl. with Rocky Mount (Inc. Place); Ⓟ 447

Battleground; RMC Place; GUILFORD; ★ GRNS-; mail Greensboro z 27438; pop. incl. with Greensboro (Inc. Place)

Batts Crossroads; RMC Place; BEAUFORT; *213 E-16; elev. 62ft./19m.; mail Washington z 27889; rural

Bay; RMC Place; TYRRELL; *213 D-18; elev. 6ft./2m.; mail Columbia z 27925; rural

Bayboro; Inc. Place; ⊡ PAMLICO; 213 G-17; elev. 12ft./4m.; 🄿; z 28515; Ⓟ 733; © 741

Bayleaf; RMC Place; WAKE; 214 A-6; elev. 426ft./130m.; ★ RAL; mail Raleigh z 27615; ● 800

Baynes; RMC Place; CASWELL; *212 C-10; elev. 738ft./225m.; mail Mebane z 27302; ● 30

Bayshore; CDP-Census Area Only; NEW HANOVER; *213 J-14; elev. 37ft./11m.; ★ WILM; mail Wilmington z 28411; Ⓟ 1,661; © 2,512

Baytree; RMC Place; WAKE; ★ RAL; mail Raleigh z 27613

Bayview; RMC Place; BEAUFORT; 213 F-17; mail Bath z 27808; summer pop. 300; ● 100

Beach Spring; RMC Place; PERQUIMANS; *213 C-18; elev. 3ft./1m.; mail Hertford z 27944; rural

Beaman Crossroads (Beamans Crossroads); RMC Place; SAMPSON; *213 G-12; elev. 180ft./55m.; mail Dunn z 28334, Newton Grove z 28366; rural

Beamans Crossroads; SAMPSON; see Beaman Crossroads (RMC Place)

Bear Creek; RMC Place; CHATHAM; 212 E-9; elev. 473ft./144m.; 🄿; z 27207; ● 130

Bear Creek; RMC Place; ONSLOW; *213 H-16; ★ JAX; mail Hubert z 28539; rural

Beard; RMC Place; CUMBERLAND; *213 G-11; ★ FAY; mail Fayetteville z 28301; ● 170

Bear Grass; Inc. Place; MARTIN; 213 E-16; elev. 47ft./14m.; 🄿; z 27892; Ⓟ 77; © 53; Ⓡ 68

Bear Pond; RMC Place; VANCE; *213 C-12; mail Henderson z 27537

Bear Poplar; RMC Place; ROWAN; *212 E-6; elev. 785ft./239m.; mail Mount Ulla z 28125

Bearskin; RMC Place; SAMPSON; *213 G-12; mail Clinton z 28328; rural

Bearwallow; RMC Place; HENDERSON; *212 F-1; mail Gerton z 28735; ● 40

Beatties Ford; RMC Place; MECKLENBURG; *212 F-5; ★ CHRLT; mail Charlotte z 28216; pop. incl. with Charlotte (Inc. Place)

Beaufort; Inc. Place; ⊡ CARTERET; 213 H-17; 🄿; z 28516; Ⓟ 3,808; © 3,771

BEAUFORT; 213 E-17; Ⓟ 42,283; © 44,958; ◆ 45,308

Beaufort Heights; RMC Place; BEAUFORT; *213 E-16; elev. 15ft./5m.; mail Washington z 27889; ● 200

Beaver Creek; RMC Place; ASHE; *212 C-3; mail West Jefferson z 28694; ● 350

Beaverdam; RMC Place; BUNCOMBE; *212 L-5; ★ ASHE; mail Candler z 28715; rural

Beaver Dam; RMC Place; CLEVELAND; *212 F-3; elev. 800ft./244m.; mail Shelby z 28152; ● 180

Beaver Dam; RMC Place; COLUMBUS; *213 J-11; elev. 104ft./32m.; mail Chadbourn z 28431, Clarendon z 28432; ● 100

Beaverdam; RMC Place; CUMBERLAND; *213 H-12; elev. 114ft./35m.; mail Roseboro z 28382; rural

Beaverdam; RMC Place; HALIFAX; *213 C-14; mail Enfield z 27823; ● 50

Beaverdam; RMC Place; HAYWOOD; *212 L-5; ★ ASHE; mail Canton z 28716; ● 80

Beckwith; RMC Place; BEAUFORT; *213 E-17; mail Pinetown z 27865

Beech; RMC Place; BUNCOMBE; *212 E-1; elev. 2,413ft./735m.; ★ ASHE; mail Weaverville z 28787; ● 380

Beech Bottom; RMC Place; AVERY; *212 D-2; mail Newland z 28657; ● 30

Beechbrook; RMC Place; GASTON; ★ CHRLT; mail Belmont z 28012; pop. incl. with Belmont (Inc. Place)

Beech Creek; RMC Place; AVERY; *212 C-2; mail Elk Park z 28622, Sugar Grove z 28679; rural

Beechertown; RMC Place; MACON; *212 M-2; elev. 2,019ft./615m.; mail Topton z 28781; rural

Beech Mountain; Inc. Place; WATAUGA, AVERY; *212 C-2; 🄿; z 28604; Ⓟ 239; © 310

Beechwood Shores; RMC Place; CURRITUCK; *213 B-19; elev. 3ft./1m.; mail Moyock z 27958; ● 200

Bee Log; RMC Place; YANCEY; *212 D-1; mail Burnsville z 28714; rural

Beesons Crossroads (Matthewstown); RMC Place; FORSYTH; *212 D-7; ★ WNS; mail Kernersville z 27284; ● 160

Belair; RMC Place; CUMBERLAND; *213 G-11; elev. 200ft./61m.; ★ FAY; mail Fayetteville z 28306; ● 1,120

Belcross; RMC Place; CAMDEN; 213 B-19; mail Camden z 27921; ● 140

Belews Creek; RMC Place; FORSYTH; 212 C-7; elev. 872ft./266m.; 🄿; ★ WNS; z 27009; ● 80

Belfast; RMC Place; WAYNE; *213 F-13; ★ GLDS; mail Goldsboro z 27530; ● 550

Belgrade; RMC Place; ONSLOW; 213 H-16; ★ JAX; mail Maysville z 28555; ● 270

Belhaven; Inc. Place; BEAUFORT; 213 E-17; elev. 4ft./1m.; 🄿 🄷; z 27810; Ⓟ 2,269; © 1,968

Bell Arthur (Arthur); RMC Place; PITT; *213 E-15; elev. 74ft./23m.; 🄿; ★ GRNV; z 27811; ● 360

Belle Mead; RMC Place; CATAWBA; ★ HICK; mail Hickory z 28601; ● 400

Bellemont; RMC Place; ALAMANCE; 212 D-9; ★ BUR; mail Burlington z 27216; ● 220

Bell Island; RMC Place; CURRITUCK; *213 B-19; elev. 1ft./0m.; mail Currituck z 27929; ● 250

Bells Crossroads; RMC Place; IREDELL; *212 E-5; elev. 874ft./266m.; ★ HICK; mail Troutman z 28166; rural

Bells Fork; RMC Place; ONSLOW; *213 H-15; elev. 26ft./8m.; ★ JAX; mail Jacksonville z 28546; pop. incl. with Jacksonville (Inc. Place)

Bells Fork; RMC Place; PITT; *213 E-15; ★ GRNV; mail Greenville z 27858; pop. incl. with Greenville (Inc. Place)

Belltown; RMC Place; GRANVILLE; *213 C-12; mail Oxford z 27565; rural

Bell View; RMC Place; CHEROKEE; *212 N-1; mail Murphy z 28906; rural

Belmont; Inc. Place; GASTON; 212 F-5; elev. 685ft./209m.; 🄿 🄲 1,110; ★ CHRLT; z 28012; Ⓟ 8,434; © 8,705; Ⓡ 8,794

Belmont; RMC Place; HALIFAX; *213 B-14; mail Roanoke Rapids z 27870; ● 900

Belmont Junction; GASTON; see North Belmont (RMC Place)

Belmont South; GASTON; see South Belmont (RMC Place)

Belva; RMC Place; MADISON; *212 J-5; elev. 1,693ft./516m.; mail Marshall z 28753; rural

Belvedere; RMC Place; PITT; *213 E-15; elev. 69ft./21m.; ★ GRNV; mail Greenville z 27834; pop. incl. with Greenville (Inc. Place)

Belvidere; RMC Place; PERQUIMANS; 213 C-17; elev. 14ft./4m.; 🄿; z 27919; ● 120

Belville; Inc. Place; BRUNSWICK; *213 J-13; 🄿; ★ WILM; z 28451; Ⓟ 66; © 285; Ⓡ 363

Belvoir; RMC Place; PITT; *213 E-15; elev. 36ft./11m.; ★ GRNV; mail Greenville z 27834; ● 50

Belwood; Inc. Place; CLEVELAND; 212 F-3; elev. 984ft./300m.; mail Lawndale z 28090; Ⓟ 631; © 962

Benham; RMC Place; WILKES; *212 C-5; mail Elkin z 28621; rural

Bennett; RMC Place; CHATHAM; 212 E-9; elev. 488ft./149m.; 🄿; z 27208; ● 300

Benson; Inc. Place; JOHNSTON; 213 F-12; elev. 245ft./75m.; 🄿; z 27504; Ⓟ 2,810; © 2,923; Ⓡ 2,993

Bent Creek; CDP; BUNCOMBE; *212 E-1; ★ ASHE; mail Asheville z 28806; Ⓟ 1,487; © 1,389

Benton Heights; RMC Place; UNION; mail Monroe z 28110; pop. incl. with Monroe (Inc. Place)

Bentons Crossroad; RMC Place; UNION; *212 G-6; ★ CHRLT; mail Monroe z 28110; rural

Berea; RMC Place; GRANVILLE; 213 C-11; elev. 514ft./157m.; mail Oxford z 27565; ● 140

Berkeley; RMC Place; WAYNE; ★ GLDS; mail Goldsboro z 27532, z 27534; pop. incl. with Goldsboro (Inc. Place)

Bermuda Run; Inc. Place; DAVIE; *212 D-6; ★ WNS; mail Advance z 27006; © 1,431

Bertha; RMC Place; CURRITUCK; *213 C-19; mail Poplar Branch z 27965; rural

Bertie; RMC Place; BERTIE; *213 D-16; mail Windsor z 27983

BERTIE; 213 D-16; Ⓟ 20,388; © 19,773; Ⓡ 19,757; ◆ 20,978

Bessemer; RMC Place; GUILFORD; *212 D-8; ★ GRNS-; mail Greensboro z 27405; pop. incl. with Greensboro (Inc. Place)

Bessemer City; Inc. Place; GASTON; 212 F-4; elev. 904ft./276m.; 🄿; ★ CHRLT; z 28016; Ⓟ 4,698; © 5,119

Bests; RMC Place; WAYNE; *213 F-14; ★ GLDS; mail La Grange z 28551; ● 50

Beta; RMC Place; JACKSON; 212 L-4; elev. 2,145ft./654m.; mail Sylva z 28779; ● 130

Bethabara; RMC Place; FORSYTH; ★ WNS; mail Winston Salem z 27106, z 27116; pop. incl. with Winston-Salem (Inc. Place)

Bethania; Inc. Place; FORSYTH; 212 C-7; elev. 817ft./249m.; 🄿; ★ WNS; z 27010; © 354

Bethany; RMC Place; ROCKINGHAM; 212 C-8; elev. 917ft./280m.; mail Reidsville z 27320; ● 100

Bethany Crossroads; RMC Place; CUMBERLAND; *213 G-11; elev. 146ft./45m.; ★ FAY; mail Stedman z 28391; rural

Bethel; RMC Place; CASWELL; 212 B-9; elev. 594ft./181m.; mail Pelham z 27311; ● 60

Bethel; RMC Place; COLUMBUS; *213 J-11; elev. 58ft./18m.; mail Clarendon z 28432

Bethel; RMC Place; HAYWOOD; *212 L-4; ★ ASHE; mail Canton z 28716; ● 100

Bethel; RMC Place; HOKE; *212 G-10; elev. 262ft./80m.; ★ FAY; mail Raeford z 28376; rural

Bethel; RMC Place; PERQUIMANS; *213 C-18; elev. 15ft./5m.; mail Hertford z 27944

Bethel; Inc. Place; PITT; 213 D-15; elev. 65ft./20m.; 🄿; ★ GRNV; z 27812; Ⓟ 1,842; © 1,681; Ⓡ 1,760

Bethel Hill; RMC Place; PERSON; *213 B-11; mail Roxboro z 27574

Bethesda; RMC Place; DAVIDSON; *212 D-7; mail Lexington z 27295; ● 230

Bethesda; RMC Place; DURHAM; 214 B-4; elev. 424ft./129m.; ★ DUR; mail Durham z 27703; pop. incl. with Durham (Inc. Place)

Bethlehem; CDP; ALEXANDER; 212 D-4; elev. 1,100ft./335m.; ★ HICK; mail Hickory z 28601; Ⓟ 3,186; © 3,713

Bettie; RMC Place; CARTERET; 213 H-17; elev. 5ft./2m.; mail Beaufort z 28516; ● 170

Beulah; RMC Place; HYDE; *213 F-18; elev. 4ft./1m.; mail Scranton z 27875; rural

Beulah; RMC Place; POLK; *212 F-2; mail Mill Spring z 28756; rural

Beulahtown; RMC Place; JOHNSTON; *213 E-13; mail Kenly z 27542; rural

Beulaville; Inc. Place; DUPLIN; 213 H-14; elev. 80ft./24m.; 🄿; z 28518; Ⓟ 933; © 1,067

Beverly Hills; RMC Place; BUNCOMBE; *212 E-1; ★ ASHE; pop. incl. with Asheville (Inc. Place)

Beverly Woods; RMC Place; MECKLENBURG; ★ CHRLT; mail Charlotte z 28210; pop. incl. with Charlotte (Inc. Place)

Bexley; RMC Place; NEW HANOVER; mail Wilmington z 28412; pop. incl. with Wilmington (Inc. Place)

Biddleville; RMC Place; MECKLENBURG; ★ CHRLT; mail Charlotte z 28216; pop. incl. with Charlotte (Inc. Place)

Big Cove (Swayney); RMC Place; SWAIN; *212 L-3; elev. 2,417ft./737m.; mail Cherokee z 28719; ● 100

Big Laurel; RMC Place; MADISON; *212 J-5; mail Marshall z 28753; ● 30

Big Lick; RMC Place; STANLY; *212 G-7; mail Oakboro z 28129; pop. incl. with Oakboro (Inc. Place)

Big Pine; RMC Place; MADISON; *212 K-5; mail Marshall z 28753; ● 30

Big Ridge; RMC Place; CARTERET; *213 H-17; elev. 15ft./5m.; mail Newport z 28570

Big Ridge; RMC Place; JACKSON; *212 M-4; mail Glenville z 28736; ● 50

Biltmore; RMC Place; BUNCOMBE; *212 E-1; ★ ASHE; mail Asheville z 28813; pop. incl. with Asheville (Inc. Place)

Biltmore Forest; Inc. Place; BUNCOMBE; 212 E-1; 🄿; ★ ASHE; z 28803; Ⓟ 1,327; © 1,440

Birchwood; RMC Place; ALAMANCE; *212 C-9; elev. 600ft./183m.; ★ BUR; mail Burlington z 27215; ● 50

Bird Cage; RMC Place; COLUMBUS; *213 J-11; elev. 100ft./30m.; mail Chadbourn z 28431; ● 40

Birdtown; RMC Place; SWAIN; 212 L-3; mail Cherokee z 28719; ● 400

Biscoe; Inc. Place; MONTGOMERY; 212 F-8; elev. 610ft./186m.; 🄿; z 27209; Ⓟ 1,484; © 1,700

Bishops Cross; RMC Place; BEAUFORT; *213 E-17; elev. 12ft./4m.; mail Pantego z 27860; rural

Bixby; RMC Place; DAVIE; *212 D-6; elev. 836ft./255m.; mail Advance z 27006

Blackburn; RMC Place; CATAWBA; *212 E-4; elev. 997ft./304m.; ★ HICK; mail Newton z 28658

Black Creek; Inc. Place; WILSON; *213 E-14; elev. 126ft./38m.; 🄿; z 27813; Ⓟ 615; © 714

Black Jack; RMC Place; PITT; *213 E-16; elev. 52ft./16m.; mail Greenville z 27858; ● 50

Blackman; RMC Place; JOHNSTON; *213 F-12; ★ RAL; mail Four Oaks z 27524; rural

Black Mountain; Inc. Place; BUNCOMBE; 212 E-1; elev. 2,400ft./732m.; 🄿 🄷; ★ ASHE; z 28711; Ⓟ 5,533; © 7,511

Blackwell; RMC Place; CASWELL; *212 B-9; elev. 629ft./192m.; mail Pelham z 27311; ● 30

Blackwood; RMC Place; ORANGE; *212 D-10; elev. 487ft./148m.; ★ DUR; mail Chapel Hill z 27514, z 27516; rural

BLADEN; 213 I-12; Ⓟ 28,663; © 32,278; ◆ 31,781

Bladenboro; Inc. Place; BLADEN; 213 I-11; elev. 111ft./34m.; 🄿; z 28320; Ⓟ 1,821; © 1,718

Bladenboro North; RMC Place; BLADEN; *213 I-11; mail Bladenboro z 28320

Bladen Springs; RMC Place; BLADEN; *213 I-12; elev. 87ft./27m.; mail Council z 28434; ● 50

Blaine; RMC Place; MONTGOMERY; *212 F-8; mail Denton z 27239; rural

Blanch; RMC Place; CASWELL; 212 B-10; elev. 387ft./118m.; 🄿; z 27212; ● 100

Blantyre; RMC Place; TRANSYLVANIA; *212 F-1; mail Pisgah Forest z 28768; ● 50

Blevins Crossroads; RMC Place; ALLEGHANY; *212 B-5; elev. 2,598ft./792m.; mail Sparta z 28675; rural

Blevins Store; RMC Place; SURRY; *212 B-5; elev. 1,178ft./359m.; mail Dobson z 27017; rural

Blizzards Crossroads; RMC Place; DUPLIN; *213 G-14; mail Mount Olive z 28365; rural

Bloomingdale; RMC Place; ROBESON; *213 I-11; elev. 108ft./33m.; mail Orrum z 28369; ● 30

Blossomtown; RMC Place; MACON; *212 M-3; mail Franklin z 28734; rural

Blounts Creek; RMC Place; BEAUFORT; 213 F-16; elev. 25ft./8m.; 🄿; z 27814; ● 1,150

Blowing Rock; Inc. Place; WATAUGA, CALDWELL; 212 C-3; elev. 3,579ft./1,091m.; 🄿 🄷; z 28605; Ⓟ 1,257; © 1,418

Blue Ridge; RMC Place; BUNCOMBE; *212 E-1; ★ ASHE; mail Black Mountain z 28711; summer pop. 3,000

Blue Ridge; RMC Place; HENDERSON; *212 F-1; mail Hendersonville z 28792

Bluff; RMC Place; MADISON; *212 K-5; elev. 1,895ft./578m.; mail Hot Springs z 28743

Boardman; Inc. Place; COLUMBUS; 213 I-11; elev. 90ft./27m.; mail Evergreen z 28438; Ⓟ 224; © 202

Boat Club Road; RMC Place; GASTON; *212 G-5; ★ CHRLT; mail Belmont z 28012; ● 60

Bobbitt; RMC Place; VANCE; 213 C-12; elev. 448ft./137m.; mail Kittrell z 27544; ● 100

Boddies Millpond; RMC Place; NASH; *213 D-13; elev. 200ft./61m.; ★ RKYMT; mail Nashville z 27856; rural

Boger City; CDP; LINCOLN; 212 F-4; elev. 960ft./293m.; 🄿; z 28092; Ⓟ 1,373; © 554

Bogue; Inc. Place; CARTERET; 213 H-16; ★ JAX; mail Newport z 28570; Ⓟ 351; © 590

Boiling Spring Lakes; Inc. Place; BRUNSWICK; 213 K-13; elev. 37ft./11m.; mail Southport z 28461; Ⓟ 1,650; © 2,972

Boiling Springs; RMC Place; CHEROKEE; *212 M-1; mail Murphy z 28906; rural

Boiling Springs; Inc. Place; CLEVELAND; 212 F-3; elev. 800ft./244m.; 🄿 🄷 🄲 3,840; z 28017; Ⓟ 2,445; © 3,866

Bolivia; Inc. Place; ⊡ BRUNSWICK; 213 K-13; elev. 40ft./12m.; 🄿; ★ WILM; z 28422; Ⓟ 228; © 148

Bolton; Inc. Place; COLUMBUS; 213 J-12; elev. 66ft./20m.; 🄿; z 28423; Ⓟ 531; © 494

Bolyston Creek; RMC Place; TRANSYLVANIA; *212 M-5; elev. 2,240ft./683m.; mail Pisgah Forest z 28768; ● 30

Bon Air; RMC Place; FORSYTH; *212 C-7; ★ WNS; mail Winston Salem z 27105; pop. incl. with Winston-Salem (Inc. Place)

Bonaparte Landing; RMC Place; BRUNSWICK; *213 K-12; elev. 20ft./6m.; ★ MYR.B; mail Shallotte z 28459; ● 30

Bonlee; RMC Place; CHATHAM; 212 E-9; elev. 526ft./160m.; 🄿; z 27213; ● 320

Bonnerton; RMC Place; BEAUFORT; 213 F-17; elev. 18ft./5m.; mail Aurora z 27806; ● 30

Bonnetsville; CDP; SAMPSON; *213 G-12; mail Clinton z 28328; © 390

Bonnie Doone; RMC Place; CUMBERLAND; *213 G-11; elev. 200ft./61m.; ★ FAY; mail Fayetteville z 28303; pop. incl. with Fayetteville (Inc. Place)

Bonsal; RMC Place; WAKE; *213 E-11; mail New Hill z 27562; rural

Boomer; RMC Place; WILKES; 212 D-4; elev. 1,229ft./375m.; 🄿; z 28606; ● 220

Boone; Inc. Place; ⊡ WATAUGA; 212 C-3; elev. 3,266ft./995m.; 🄿 🄷 🄲 15,117; z 28607-08; Ⓟ 12,915; © 13,472; Ⓡ 13,470

Boones Crossroads; RMC Place; NORTHAMPTON; *213 C-15; mail Jackson z 27845; rural

Boone Trail; RMC Place; HARNETT; *213 F-11; elev. 380ft./116m.; mail Mamers z 27552; rural

Boonford; RMC Place; MITCHELL; *212 D-2; mail Bakersville z 28705; ● 30

Boonville; Inc. Place; YADKIN; 212 C-6; elev. 1,066ft./325m.; 🄿; z 27011; Ⓟ 1,009; © 1,138

Bordeaux; RMC Place; CUMBERLAND; ★ FAY; mail Fayetteville z 28304; pop. incl. with Fayetteville (Inc. Place)

Bosley; GATES; see Wardville (RMC Place)

Bostian Heights; RMC Place; ROWAN; *212 E-6; ★ SLSB; mail China Grove z 28023; ● 220

Bostic; Inc. Place; RUTHERFORD; 212 F-2; elev. 920ft./280m.; 🄿; z 28018; Ⓟ 371; © 328

Bostwood Estates; RMC Place; CABARRUS; *212 F-6; elev. 550ft./168m.; ★ CHRLT; mail Concord z 28027; ● 200

Botany Woods; RMC Place; BUNCOMBE; ★ ASHE; mail Asheville z 28805; ● 550

Bottom; RMC Place; SURRY; *212 B-6; mail Mount Airy z 27030

Boulevard; RMC Place; ROCKINGHAM; *212 B-8; ★ MRTNV; mail Eden z 27288

Bowden; DUPLIN; see Bowdens (RMC Place)

Bowdens (Bowden); RMC Place; DUPLIN; 213 G-13; elev. 166ft./51m.; 🄿; z 28398; ● 270

Bowditch; RMC Place; YANCEY; *212 D-1; mail Burnsville z 28714; rural

Bowmore; CDP; HOKE; *212 H-10; elev. 259ft./79m.; mail Raeford z 28376; © 145

Boyds Crossroads; RMC Place; PITT; *213 E-16; elev. 39ft./12m.; ★ GRNV; mail Grimesland z 27837; rural

Boylan; RMC Place; WAKE; ★ RAL; pop. incl. with Raleigh (Inc. Place)

Boylan Heights; RMC Place; WAKE; ★ RAL; pop. incl. with Raleigh (Inc. Place)

Boyles Chapel; RMC Place; STOKES; *212 C-7; ★ WNS; mail King z 27021; rural

Bradfords Crossroads; RMC Place; IREDELL; *212 E-5; ★ HICK; mail Statesville z 28625; rural

Braggtown; RMC Place; DURHAM; *213 D-11; ★ DUR; mail Durham z 27704; pop. incl. with Durham (Inc. Place)

Branch Village; RMC Place; NASH; *213 D-13; elev. 248ft./76m.; mail Bailey z 27807; ● 50

Branon; RMC Place; YADKIN; *212 C-6; elev. 995ft./303m.; mail Yadkinville z 27055; rural

Brantleys Grove; RMC Place; HERTFORD; *213 C-16; elev. 40ft./12m.; mail Ahoskie z 27910; ● 100

Brasstown; RMC Place; CLAY; 212 M-1; elev. 1,629ft./497m.; 🄿; z 28902; ● 300

Braswell; RMC Place; COLUMBUS; *213 J-11; mail Chadbourn z 28431; rural

Brendletown; RMC Place; MACON; *212 M-3; mail Franklin z 28734; rural

Brentwood; RMC Place; CUMBERLAND; *213 G-11; elev. 200ft./61m.; ★ FAY; mail Fayetteville z 28304; ● 780

Brentwood; RMC Place; WAKE; *213 D-12; 🄿; ★ RAL; z 27604, z 27616 & mail Raleigh z 27629; pop. incl. with Raleigh (Inc. Place)

Brettonwood; RMC Place; CUMBERLAND; *213 G-11; elev. 200ft./61m.; ★ FAY; mail Fayetteville z 28311; ● 280

Brevard; Inc. Place; ⊡ TRANSYLVANIA; 212 M-5; elev. 2,230ft./680m.; 🄿 🄷 🄲 684; z 28712; Ⓟ 5,388; © 6,789

Briarwood Terrace; RMC Place; ROWAN; *212 E-6; ★ SLSB; mail Salisbury z 28147; ● 140

Brices Creek; CDP-Census Area Only; CRAVEN; *213 G-16; © 2,060; Ⓡ 2,052

Brices Crossroads; RMC Place; DUPLIN; *213 H-13; elev. 100ft./30m.; mail Rose Hill z 28458; rural

Brickhaven; RMC Place; CHATHAM; 212 E-10; elev. 247ft./75m.; mail Moncure z 27559; ● 60

Bricks; RMC Place; EDGECOMBE; *213 C-14; elev. 95ft./29m.; mail Whitakers z 27891; ● 30

Brickton; RMC Place; HENDERSON; *212 F-1; ★ ASHE; mail Fletcher z 28732; ● 180

Bridgersville; RMC Place; WILSON; *213 E-14; elev. 126ft./38m.; mail Macclesfield z 27852; rural

Bridgeton; Inc. Place; CRAVEN; 213 G-16; elev. 9ft./3m.; 🄿; z 28519; Ⓟ 453; © 328

Brief; RMC Place; UNION; *212 G-6; elev. 496ft./151m.; ★ CHRLT; mail Midland z 28107; rural

Briertown; RMC Place; MACON; *212 M-2; mail Topton z 28781; rural

Entries in **UPPERCASE** are counties.
Entries in **bold** have populations of 2,500 or more.
Names in parentheses are alternate names.

Inc. Place	Incorporated Place
RMC Place	Rand McNally Designated Place
CDP	Census Designated Place
MCD	Minor Civil Division
⊡	County Seat
▲	Minor Civil Division
elev.	Elevation
🄿	Post Office
🄷	Hospital
🄲	College
■	Principal Business Center
★	Ranally Metro Area (RMA) Abbreviation
z	Zip Code(s)
Ⓟ	Previous Census Population
Ⓡ	Revised Census Population
Ⓐ	Annexation Population
●	Rand McNally Population Estimate
©	Final Census Population
Ⓢ	Special Census Population
◆	Estimated Population

For additional definitions see Glossary, Volume 1, and Introduction, Volume 2.

Brigand Bay; RMC Place; DARE; ***213** F-20; elev. 15ft./5m.; mail Buxton **Z** 27920, Frisco **Z** 27936; ● 170
Brightwood; RMC Place; GUILFORD; ***212** C-8; elev. 801ft./244m.; ★ **GRNS-**; mail Browns Summit **Z** 27214; pop. incl. with Greensboro (Inc. Place)
Brindle Town; RMC Place; BURKE; ***212** E-3; mail Morganton **Z** 28655; ● 30
Brinkleyville; RMC Place; HALIFAX; **213** C-14; elev. 280ft./85m.; mail Enfield **Z** 27823; ● 30
Brinkleyville; RMC Place; HERTFORD; ***213** C-16; elev. 43ft./13m.; mail Ahoskie **Z** 27910; ● 40
British Acres; RMC Place; ALAMANCE; ***212** C-9; elev. 600ft./183m.; ★ **BUR**; mail Burlington **Z** 27215; ● 30
Broad Acres; RMC Place; ALAMANCE; ***212** D-9; elev. 575ft./175m.; ★ **BUR**; mail Graham **Z** 27253; ● 150
Broadacres; RMC Place; CUMBERLAND; ★ **FAY**; pop. incl. with Fayetteville (Inc. Place)
Broad Creek; RMC Place; CARTERET; ***213** H-17; ★ **JAX**; mail Newport **Z** 28570; ● 1,020
Broadway; Inc. Place; LEE, HARNETT; **212** F-10; elev. 472ft./144m.; 🅿; **Z** 27505; Ⓟ 973; Ⓒ 1,015
Brocks; RMC Place; ONSLOW; ***213** H-15; ★ **JAX**; mail Richlands **Z** 28574; rural
Brogden; RMC Place; JOHNSTON; ***213** F-13; elev. 157ft./48m.; mail Smithfield **Z** 27577; rural
Brogden; CDP; WAYNE; ***213** F-13; ★ **GLDS**; mail Goldsboro **Z** 27530; Ⓟ 3,246; Ⓒ 2,907
Brook Cove; RMC Place; STOKES; ***212** C-7; ★ **WNS**; mail Walnut Cove **Z** 27052; rural
Brookdale; RMC Place; HENDERSON; ***212** F-1; mail Hendersonville **Z** 28792; pop. incl. with Hendersonville (Inc. Place)
Brookford; Inc. Place; CATAWBA; **212** E-4; elev. 1,033ft./315m.; ★ **HICK**; mail Hickory **Z** 28601; Ⓟ 451; Ⓒ 434
Brookhaven; RMC Place; WAKE; ***213** D-11; ★ **RAL**; mail Raleigh **Z** 27612; ● 600
Brookland Manor; RMC Place; HENDERSON; ***212** F-1; mail Hendersonville **Z** 28792; pop. incl. with Hendersonville (Inc. Place)
Brooks Crossroads; RMC Place; YADKIN; **212** C-6; elev. 1,072ft./327m.; mail Hamptonville **Z** 27020; ● 320
Brooksdale; RMC Place; PERSON; ***213** C-11; mail Roxboro **Z** 27573; pop. incl. with Roxboro (Inc. Place)
Brookside; RMC Place; WAYNE; ★ **GLDS**; mail Goldsboro **Z** 27530; pop. incl. with Goldsboro (Inc. Place)
Brookston; RMC Place; VANCE; ***213** C-12; elev. 497ft./151m.; mail Henderson **Z** 27537; rural
Brook Valley; RMC Place; PITT; ***213** E-15; elev. 46ft./14m.; ★ **GRNV**; mail Greenville **Z** 27858; pop. incl. with Greenville (Inc. Place)
Brown & Norcott Mills; CABARRUS; see West Concord (RMC Place)
Browns Summit (Brown Summit); RMC Place; GUILFORD; **212** C-8; elev. 805ft./245m.; 🅿; ★ **GRNS-**; **Z** 27214; ● 340
Brown Summit; GUILFORD; see Browns Summit (RMC Place)
Brown Town; RMC Place; GASTON; ***212** F-5; ★ **CHRLT**; mail Belmont **Z** 28012
Brownwood; RMC Place; ASHE; ***212** C-3; elev. 2,319ft./707m.; mail Todd **Z** 28684
Bruce; RMC Place; PITT; ***213** E-15; mail Greenville **Z** 27834; rural
Brunswick; Inc. Place; COLUMBUS; **213** J-11; elev. 68ft./21m.; 🅿; **Z** 28424; Ⓟ 302; Ⓒ 360
BRUNSWICK; **213** J-13; Ⓟ 50,985; Ⓒ 73,143; Ⓡ 73,141; ◆ 107,313
Brutonville; RMC Place; MONTGOMERY; ***212** F-8; mail Candor **Z** 27229; ● 500
Bryantown; RMC Place; NORTHAMPTON; ***213** C-15; elev. 76ft./23m.; mail Rich Square **Z** 27869; rural
Bryantville Park; RMC Place; HERTFORD; ***213** B-16; mail Como **Z** 27818; ● 230
Brynn Marr; RMC Place; ONSLOW; ★ **JAX**; mail Jacksonville **Z** 28546; pop. incl. with Jacksonville (Inc. Place)
Bryson City; Inc. Place; ⊡ SWAIN; **212** L-3; elev. 1,736ft./529m.; 🅿 🅷; **Z** 28713; Ⓟ 1,145; Ⓒ 1,411
Buckhead; RMC Place; COLUMBUS, BRUNSWICK; ***213** I-12; elev. 65ft./20m.; mail Bolton **Z** 28423; ● 100
Buckhorn; RMC Place; ORANGE; ***212** D-10; elev. 687ft./209m.; ★ **DUR**; mail Efland **Z** 27243; rural
Buckhorn Crossroads; RMC Place; WILSON; ***213** E-13; elev. 193ft./59m.; mail Kenly **Z** 27542
Buckland; RMC Place; GATES; ***213** B-17; mail Gates **Z** 27937
Bucklesberry; RMC Place; LENOIR; ***213** F-14; elev. 48ft./15m.; mail La Grange **Z** 28551; ● 50
Buckner; RMC Place; MADISON; ***212** D-1; mail Mars Hill **Z** 28754; rural
Buck Shoals; RMC Place; YADKIN; ***212** D-5; mail Hamptonville **Z** 27020; rural
Buena Vista; RMC Place; BERTIE; **213** C-16; mail Windsor **Z** 27983; ● 30
Buffalo Cove; RMC Place; CALDWELL; ***212** D-3; elev. 1,374ft./419m.; mail Lenoir **Z** 28645; ● 100
Bug Hill; RMC Place; COLUMBUS; ***213** K-12; mail Nakina **Z** 28455; rural
Buie; RMC Place; ROBESON; **212** H-10; elev. 180ft./55m.; mail Red Springs **Z** 28377; ● 110
Buies Creek; CDP; HARNETT; **213** F-11; elev. 213ft./65m.; 🅿 🅲 6,949; ★ **RAL**; **Z** 27506; Ⓟ 2,085; Ⓒ 2,215
Buladean; RMC Place; MITCHELL; **212** C-2; mail Bakersville **Z** 28705; ● 180
Bullhead Crossroads; RMC Place; NASH; ***213** E-13; elev. 208ft./63m.; mail Bailey **Z** 27807; ● 30
Bullock; RMC Place; GRANVILLE; **213** B-12; elev. 440ft./134m.; 🅿; **Z** 27507; ● 250
BUNCOMBE; **212** E-1; Ⓟ 174,821; Ⓒ 206,330; ◆ 235,123
Bunlevel; HARNETT; see Bunnlevel (RMC Place)
Bunn; Inc. Place; FRANKLIN; **213** D-13; elev. 275ft./84m.; 🅿; ★ **RAL**; **Z** 27508; Ⓟ 364; Ⓒ 357
Bunnlevel (Bunlevel); RMC Place; HARNETT; **213** F-11; elev. 146ft./45m.; 🅿; **Z** 28323; ● 600
Bunyan (Bunyon); RMC Place; BEAUFORT; **213** E-16; mail Washington **Z** 27889; ● 40
Bunyon; BEAUFORT; see Bunyan (RMC Place)
Burbage Crossroads; RMC Place; BEAUFORT; ***213** F-17; elev. 9ft./3m.; mail Bath **Z** 27808; rural
Burden; RMC Place; BERTIE; **213** C-16; elev. 66ft./20m.; mail Aulander **Z** 27805; ● 30
Burgaw; Inc. Place; ⊡ PENDER; **213** I-14; elev. 49ft./15m.; 🅿 🅷; **Z** 28425; Ⓟ 1,807; Ⓒ 3,337
Burgess; RMC Place; PERQUIMANS; ***213** C-18; elev. 13ft./4m.; mail Hertford **Z** 27944; rural
BURKE; **212** D-3; Ⓟ 75,744; Ⓒ 89,148; Ⓡ 89,145; ◆ 86,572
Burke Chapel; RMC Place; BURKE; ***212** E-4; ★ **HICK**; mail Hickory **Z** 28601; rural
Burkemont; RMC Place; BURKE; ***212** E-3; elev. 1,256ft./383m.; mail Morganton **Z** 28655; ● 30
Burlington; Inc. Place; ALAMANCE; **212** D-9; elev. 663ft./202m.; 🅿 🅷 ■; ★ **BUR**; **Z** 27215-17; Ⓟ 39,498; Ⓒ 44,917; ◆ 51,830
Burney; RMC Place; BLADEN; **213** H-11; elev. 66ft./20m.; mail White Oak **Z** 28399; ● 70
Burningtown; RMC Place; MACON; ***212** M-3; mail Franklin **Z** 28734; rural
Burnsville; RMC Place; ANSON; **212** G-7; elev. 497ft./151m.; mail Polkton **Z** 28135; ● 50
Burnsville; Inc. Place; ⊡ YANCEY; **212** D-1; elev. 2,814ft./858m.; 🅿; **Z** 28714; Ⓟ 1,482; Ⓒ 1,623
Burnt Mills; RMC Place; CAMDEN; **213** B-18; mail South Mills **Z** 27976; ● 50
Busbee; RMC Place; BUNCOMBE; ***212** F-1; ★ **ASHE**; mail Asheville **Z** 28803; pop. incl. with Asheville (Inc. Place)
Bushy Fork; RMC Place; PERSON; **212** C-10; elev. 680ft./207m.; mail Hurdle Mills **Z** 27541; ● 150
Busick; RMC Place; YANCEY; ***212** E-2; mail Browns Summit **Z** 27214, Burnsville **Z** 28714
Butlers Crossroads; RMC Place; SAMPSON; ***213** H-12; elev. 751ft./229m.; mail Clinton **Z** 28328; rural
Butner; Inc. Place; GRANVILLE; **213** C-11; elev. 394ft./120m.; ★ **DUR**; incorporated November 1, 2007; not reported in 2000 Census; ● 6,200
Butner; CDP-Census Area Only; GRANVILLE; **213** C-11; elev. 394ft./120m.; 🅿 🅷; ★ **DUR**; **Z** 27509; Ⓟ 4,679; Ⓒ 5,792
Butters; CDP; BLADEN; **213** I-11; elev. 111ft./34m.; 🅿; **Z** 28320; Ⓒ 261
Buxton; RMC Place; DARE; **213** F-20; elev. 10ft./3m.; 🅿; **Z** 27920; summer pop. 3,000; ● 1,480
Buzzards Crossroads; RMC Place; BERTIE; ***213** C-16; mail Colerain **Z** 27924; rural
Bynum; RMC Place; CHATHAM; **212** E-10; elev. 350ft./107m.; 🅿; ★ **DUR**; **Z** 27228; ● 490

C

Cabarrus; RMC Place; CABARRUS; ***212** G-6; ★ **CHRLT**; mail Midland **Z** 28107; ● 350
CABARRUS; **212** F-6; Ⓟ 98,935; Ⓒ 131,063; ◆ 176,287
Cabin; RMC Place; DUPLIN; ***213** G-14; mail Pink Hill **Z** 28572; rural
Cairo; RMC Place; ANSON; ***212** H-8; elev. 414ft./126m.; mail Morven **Z** 28119; ● 30
Cajahs Mountain; Inc. Place; CALDWELL; ***212** D-3; ★ **HICK**; mail Granite Falls **Z** 28630, Hudson **Z** 28638, Lenoir **Z** 28645; Ⓟ 2,429; Ⓒ 2,683; Ⓡ 2,694
Calabash; Inc. Place; BRUNSWICK; **213** K-12; elev. 50ft./15m.; 🅿; ★ **MYR.B**; **Z** 28467; Ⓟ 1,210; Ⓒ 711
Calahaln; RMC Place; DAVIE; ***212** D-6; mail Mocksville **Z** 27028
Caldwell; RMC Place; MECKLENBURG; ***212** F-5; elev. 813ft./248m.; ★ **CHRLT**; mail Huntersville **Z** 28078; pop. incl. with Huntersville (Inc. Place)
Caldwell; RMC Place; ORANGE; ***212** C-10; elev. 622ft./190m.; mail Rougemont **Z** 27572
CALDWELL; **212** D-3; Ⓟ 70,709; Ⓒ 77,415; Ⓡ 77,386; ◆ 78,378
California; RMC Place; DARE; ***213** D-20; mail Manteo **Z** 27954; ● 200
California; RMC Place; HERTFORD; ***213** B-16; elev. 50ft./15m.; mail Ahoskie **Z** 27910; ● 50
California; RMC Place; MADISON; ***212** D-1; elev. 2,382ft./726m.; mail Mars Hill **Z** 28754; rural
California; RMC Place; PITT; ***213** E-15; ★ **GRNV**; mail Farmville **Z** 27828; rural
Callisons; RMC Place; PAMLICO; ***213** G-17; mail Oriental **Z** 28571; rural
Calvander; RMC Place; ORANGE; ***212** D-10; elev. 553ft./169m.; ★ **DUR**; mail Chapel Hill **Z** 27516; ● 30
Cal-Vel; RMC Place; PERSON; ***213** B-11; elev. 500ft./152m.; mail Roxboro **Z** 27573; pop. incl. with Roxboro (Inc. Place)
Calvert; RMC Place; TRANSYLVANIA; ***212** M-5; mail Brevard **Z** 28712; rural
Calvin Heights; RMC Place; CARTERET; ***213** H-17; elev. 15ft./5m.; mail Newport **Z** 28570; ● 200
Calypso; Inc. Place; DUPLIN; **213** G-13; elev. 167ft./51m.; 🅿; **Z** 28325; Ⓟ 481; Ⓒ 410
Camden; RMC Place; ⊡ CAMDEN; **213** C-18; 🅿; **Z** 27921; ● 360
CAMDEN; **213** B-18; Ⓟ 5,904; Ⓒ 6,885; ◆ 9,965
Camelot; RMC Place; WAKE; ★ **RAL**; mail Garner **Z** 27529; ● 450
Cameron; Inc. Place; MOORE; **212** F-10; elev. 350ft./107m.; 🅿; **Z** 28326; Ⓟ 215; Ⓒ 151
Campbell Creek; RMC Place; BEAUFORT; **213** F-17; elev. 5ft./2m.; mail Aurora **Z** 27806; ● 100
Camp Glenn; RMC Place; CARTERET; ***213** H-17; mail Morehead City **Z** 28557
Camp Leach; RMC Place; BEAUFORT; ***213** F-17; mail Washington **Z** 27889
Camp Lejeune Junction; RMC Place; ONSLOW; ★ **JAX**; pop. incl. with Jacksonville (Inc. Place)
Camp Springs; RMC Place; CASWELL; **212** C-9; elev. 775ft./236m.; mail Reidsville **Z** 27320; ● 40
Camp Sutton; RMC Place; UNION; mail Monroe **Z** 28110; pop. incl. with Monroe (Inc. Place)
Cana; RMC Place; DAVIE; ***212** D-6; ★ **WNS**; mail Mocksville **Z** 27028; rural
Candler; RMC Place; BUNCOMBE; **212** L-5; elev. 2,107ft./642m.; 🅿; ★ **ASHE**; **Z** 28715; ● 1,100
Candler Heights; RMC Place; BUNCOMBE; ***212** L-5; ★ **ASHE**; mail Candler **Z** 28715; ● 220
Candlewick Estates; RMC Place; PITT; ***213** E-15; elev. 82ft./25m.; ★ **GRNV**; mail Greenville **Z** 27834; ● 150
Candor; Inc. Place; MONTGOMERY; **212** F-8; elev. 730ft./223m.; 🅿; **Z** 27229; Ⓟ 748; Ⓒ 825
Cane Creek (Lanes Store); RMC Place; RUTHERFORD; ***212** F-2; elev. 918ft./280m.; mail Union Mills **Z** 28167; ● 30
Cane Mountain; RMC Place; ALAMANCE; ***212** D-9; elev. 750ft./229m.; mail Snow Camp **Z** 27349; ● 60
Cane River; RMC Place; YANCEY; ***212** D-1; elev. 2,503ft./763m.; mail Burnsville **Z** 28714; ● 160
Cannon Ferry; RMC Place; CHOWAN; ***213** C-17; mail Tyner **Z** 27980; rural
Canto; RMC Place; BUNCOMBE; ***212** K-5; elev. 2,037ft./621m.; ★ **ASHE**; mail Canton **Z** 28716
Canton; Inc. Place; HAYWOOD; **212** L-5; elev. 2,609ft./795m.; 🅿; ★ **ASHE**; **Z** 28716; Ⓟ 3,790; Ⓒ 4,029
Cape Carteret; Inc. Place; CARTERET; **213** H-16; elev. 20ft./6m.; 🅿; ★ **JAX**; **Z** 28584; Ⓟ 1,008; Ⓒ 1,214
Cape Colony; RMC Place; CHOWAN; ***213** D-17; mail Edenton **Z** 27932; ● 630
Cape Fear; RMC Place; CHATHAM; ***212** E-10; elev. 249ft./76m.; 🅿; **Z** 28401 & mail New Hill **Z** 27562; ● 100
Capella; RMC Place; STOKES; ***212** C-7; elev. 1,153ft./351m.; ★ **WNS**; mail King **Z** 27021; rural
Capelsie; RMC Place; MONTGOMERY; ***212** F-8; mail Candor **Z** 27229; rural
Capital Crossings; RMC Place; WAKE; ★ **RAL**; mail Raleigh **Z** 27604; pop. incl. with Raleigh (Inc. Place)
Caraleigh; RMC Place; WAKE; ***213** E-12; ★ **RAL**; pop. incl. with Raleigh (Inc. Place)
Carbonton; RMC Place; CHATHAM; **212** F-10; elev. 256ft./78m.; mail Sanford **Z** 27330; ● 60
Carlos; RMC Place; CUMBERLAND; ***213** G-11; elev. 120ft./37m.; mail Linden **Z** 28356; rural
Carmel Road; RMC Place; MECKLENBURG; ★ **CHRLT**; mail Charlotte **Z** 28226, **Z** 28247, **Z** 28270, **Z** 28277; pop. incl. with Charlotte (Inc. Place)
Caroleen; RMC Place; RUTHERFORD; ***212** F-3; elev. 830ft./253m.; 🅿; **Z** 28019; ● 1,170
Carolina; RMC Place; ALAMANCE; ***212** C-9; ★ **BUR**; mail Burlington **Z** 27217; ● 150
Carolina Beach; Inc. Place; NEW HANOVER; **213** K-14; elev. 5ft./2m.; 🅿; ★ **WILM**; **Z** 28428; Ⓟ 3,630; Ⓒ 4,701; Ⓡ 4,778
Carolina Forest; RMC Place; MONTGOMERY; ***212** F-8; mail Troy **Z** 27371; ● 50
Carolina Pines; RMC Place; CUMBERLAND; ***213** G-11; elev. 232ft./71m.; ★ **FAY**; mail Fayetteville **Z** 28303; pop. incl. with Fayetteville (Inc. Place)
Carolina Pines; RMC Place; WAKE; ***213** E-12; ★ **RAL**; pop. incl. with Raleigh (Inc. Place)
Carolina Shores; Inc. Place; BRUNSWICK; ***213** K-12; 🅿; ★ **MYR.B**; **Z** 28467; Ⓒ 1,482
Carolina Trace; RMC Place; LEE; ***212** F-10; mail Sanford **Z** 27332; ● 300
Carolina Village; RMC Place; HENDERSON; ***212** F-1; mail Hendersonville **Z** 28792; pop. incl. with Hendersonville (Inc. Place)
Carova Beach; RMC Place; CURRITUCK; ***213** B-19; elev. 10ft./3m.; mail Corolla **Z** 27927; ● 100
Carpenter; RMC Place; WAKE; **214** C-4; ★ **RAL**; mail Morrisville **Z** 27560; ● 300
Carpenter Bottom; RMC Place; AVERY; ***212** D-2; mail Minneapolis **Z** 28652, Newland **Z** 28657; ● 30
Carr; RMC Place; ORANGE; **212** C-10; elev. 724ft./221m.; mail Mebane **Z** 27302; ● 50
Carrboro (Venable); Inc. Place; ORANGE; **212** D-10; elev. 465ft./142m.; 🅿; ★ **DUR**; **Z** 27510; Ⓟ 11,553; Ⓒ 16,782
Carr Creek; RMC Place; LEE; ***212** F-10; mail Sanford **Z** 27332; ● 400
Carroll; RMC Place; DUPLIN; ***213** G-13; elev. 139ft./42m.; mail Warsaw **Z** 28398; rural
Carter Cove; RMC Place; CLAY; ***212** M-2; elev. 1,966ft./599m.; mail Hayesville **Z** 28904; rural
CARTERET; **213** H-16; Ⓟ 52,556; Ⓒ 59,383; ◆ 62,826
Carters; RMC Place; GATES; ***213** B-17; elev. 20ft./6m.; mail Gatesville **Z** 27938; rural
Cartersville; RMC Place; DUPLIN; ***213** H-14; mail Wallace **Z** 28466; rural
Carthage; Inc. Place; ⊡ MOORE; **212** F-9; elev. 550ft./168m.; 🅿; **Z** 28327; Ⓟ 976; Ⓒ 1,871; Ⓡ 1,884
Cartoogechaye; MACON; see Wayah Creek (RMC Place)
Carvers; RMC Place; BLADEN; **213** I-12; elev. 71ft./22m.; mail Council **Z** 28434; ● 70
Cary; Inc. Place; WAKE, CHATHAM; **213** E-11; elev. 518ft./158m.; 🅿; ★ **RAL**; **Z** 27511-13, **Z** 27518-19; Ⓟ 43,858; Ⓒ 94,536; ◆ 147,843
Casar; Inc. Place; CLEVELAND; **212** F-3; elev. 1,125ft./343m.; 🅿; **Z** 28020; Ⓟ 328; Ⓒ 308
Cash Corner; PAMLICO; see Hollyville (RMC Place)
Cashiers; CDP; JACKSON; **212** M-4; elev. 3,486ft./1,063m.; 🅿; **Z** 28717; Ⓒ 196
Cason Old Field; RMC Place; ANSON; ***212** H-7; elev. 454ft./138m.; mail Wadesboro **Z** 28170
Castalia; Inc. Place; NASH; **213** D-13; elev. 310ft./94m.; 🅿; **Z** 27816; Ⓟ 261; Ⓒ 340
Castle Hayne; CDP; NEW HANOVER; **213** J-14; elev. 19ft./6m.; 🅿; ★ **WILM**; **Z** 28429; Ⓟ 1,182; Ⓒ 1,116
Castoria; RMC Place; GREENE; ***213** E-14; elev. 107ft./33m.; mail Walstonburg **Z** 27888
Casville; RMC Place; CASWELL; **212** B-9; elev. 693ft./211m.; mail Ruffin **Z** 27326; ● 150
CASWELL; **212** C-9; Ⓟ 20,693; Ⓒ 23,501; ◆ 23,074
Caswell Beach; Inc. Place; BRUNSWICK; **213** K-13; elev. 14ft./4m.; 🅿; **Z** 28465; Ⓟ 175; Ⓒ 370
Catawba; Inc. Place; CATAWBA; **212** E-5; elev. 872ft./266m.; 🅿; ★ **HICK**; **Z** 28609; Ⓟ 467; Ⓒ 698
CATAWBA; **212** E-4; Ⓟ 118,412; Ⓒ 141,685; Ⓡ 141,686; ◆ 158,753
Catawba Heights; RMC Place; GASTON; ***212** F-5; elev. 732ft./223m.; ★ **CHRLT**; mail Belmont **Z** 28012; pop. incl. with Mount Holly (Inc. Place)
Catfish; RMC Place; CATAWBA; ***212** E-5; elev. 990ft./302m.; ★ **HICK**; mail Catawba **Z** 28609, Claremont **Z** 28610; rural
Catharine Lake; ONSLOW; see Catherine Lake (RMC Place)
Catherine Lake (Catharine Lake); RMC Place; ONSLOW; **213** H-15; ★ **JAX**; mail Richlands **Z** 28574; ● 200
Catherine Square; RMC Place; DUPLIN; ***213** H-14; elev. 80ft./24m.; mail Beulaville **Z** 28518; rural
Cat Square; RMC Place; LINCOLN; ***212** E-4; elev. 1,048ft./319m.; ★ **HICK**; mail Vale **Z** 28168
Ca-Vel; RMC Place; PERSON; ***212** B-10; mail Roxboro **Z** 27573
Cayton; RMC Place; CRAVEN; **213** F-16; mail Ernul **Z** 28527; ● 70
Cedar Creek; RMC Place; CUMBERLAND; **213** G-11; ★ **FAY**; mail Fayetteville **Z** 28301; ● 210
Cedar Croft; RMC Place; CABARRUS; ***212** F-6; elev. 812ft./247m.; ★ **CHRLT**; mail Concord **Z** 28025; ● 60
Cedar Falls; RMC Place; RANDOLPH; ***212** E-8; elev. 511ft./156m.; 🅿; **Z** 27230; ● 250
Cedar Fork; RMC Place; DUPLIN; ***213** H-14; mail Beulaville **Z** 28518
Cedar Grove; RMC Place; ORANGE; **212** C-10; elev. 711ft./217m.; 🅿; **Z** 27231; ● 150
Cedar Grove; RMC Place; RANDOLPH; ***212** E-8; elev. 595ft./181m.; mail Asheboro **Z** 27205; ● 100
Cedar Hill; RMC Place; ANSON; ***212** G-7; mail Wadesboro **Z** 28170; rural
Cedar Hill; RMC Place; BRUNSWICK; ***213** J-13; ★ **WILM**; mail Leland **Z** 28451; ● 100
Cedar Island (Roe); RMC Place; CARTERET; **213** G-18; elev. 7ft./2m.; 🅿; **Z** 28520; ● 310
Cedar Lodge; RMC Place; DAVIDSON; ***212** D-7; ★ **GRNS-**; mail Thomasville **Z** 27360
Cedar Mountain; RMC Place; TRANSYLVANIA; **212** M-5; elev. 2,720ft./829m.; 🅿; **Z** 28718; ● 300
Cedar Point; Inc. Place; CARTERET; **213** H-16; elev. 22ft./7m.; 🅿; ★ **JAX**; **Z** 28584; Ⓟ 628; Ⓒ 929
Cedar Rock; Inc. Place; CALDWELL; ***212** D-4; mail Lenoir **Z** 28645; Ⓒ 315
Cedarrock (Stallings); RMC Place; FRANKLIN; ***213** C-13; mail Castalia **Z** 27816; ● 30
Cedar Village; RMC Place; STANLY; ***212** F-7; elev. 555ft./169m.; mail Albemarle **Z** 28001; ● 30
Ceffo; RMC Place; PERSON; ***212** B-10; elev. 583ft./178m.; mail Roxboro **Z** 27574; rural
Celeste Hinkle; RMC Place; IREDELL; ***212** E-5; elev. 950ft./290m.; ★ **HICK**; mail Statesville **Z** 28677; ● 160
Celo; RMC Place; YANCEY; ***212** D-1; mail Burnsville **Z** 28714
Celotex; RMC Place; WAYNE; ★ **GLDS**; mail Dudley **Z** 28333; ● 110
Center; RMC Place; DAVIE; ***212** D-6; mail Mocksville **Z** 27028; ● 30
Center; RMC Place; YADKIN; ***212** C-6; elev. 1,037ft./316m.; mail Yadkinville **Z** 27055
Center City; RMC Place; FORSYTH; ★ **WNS**; mail Winston Salem **Z** 27120; pop. incl. with Winston-Salem (Inc. Place)
Center Hill (Tyner); RMC Place; CHOWAN; **213** C-17; elev. 48ft./15m.; mail Tyner **Z** 27980; ● 350
Center Pigeon; RMC Place; HAYWOOD; ***212** L-5; ★ **ASHE**; mail Canton **Z** 28716; ● 300
Centerview; RMC Place; CABARRUS; ***212** F-6; ★ **CHRLT**; mail Kannapolis **Z** 28081, **Z** 28083; pop. incl. with Kannapolis (Inc. Place)
Centerville; Inc. Place; FRANKLIN; **213** C-13; elev. 340ft./104m.; mail Louisburg **Z** 27549; Ⓟ 115; Ⓒ 99
Central; RMC Place; IREDELL; ***212** D-5; elev. 1,045ft./319m.; mail Statesville **Z** 28625; rural
Central Falls; RMC Place; RANDOLPH; ***212** E-8; elev. 700ft./213m.; mail Asheboro **Z** 27203; pop. incl. with Asheboro (Inc. Place)
Central Heights; RMC Place; CABARRUS; ***212** F-6; elev. 650ft./198m.; ★ **CHRLT**; mail Concord **Z** 28025; pop. incl. with Concord (Inc. Place)
Century; RMC Place; WAKE; ★ **RAL**; mail Raleigh **Z** 27601-02; pop. incl. with Raleigh (Inc. Place)
Cerro Gordo; Inc. Place; COLUMBUS; **213** J-11; elev. 97ft./30m.; 🅿; **Z** 28430; Ⓟ 227; Ⓒ 244
Chadbourn; Inc. Place; COLUMBUS; **213** J-11; elev. 107ft./33m.; 🅿; **Z** 28431; Ⓟ 2,005; Ⓒ 2,129
Chadwick; RMC Place; JONES; ***213** G-16; elev. 40ft./12m.; mail Pollocksville **Z** 28573; ● 30
Chadwick Acres; RMC Place; ONSLOW; ***213** I-15; elev. 9ft./3m.; mail Sneads Ferry **Z** 28460; ● 80
Chalybeate; HARNETT; see Chalybeate Springs (RMC Place)
Chalybeate Springs (Chalybeate); RMC Place; HARNETT; **213** F-11; ★ **RAL**; mail Fuquay Varina **Z** 27526; ● 200
Champion; WILKES; see Mount Pleasant (RMC Place)
Chantilly; RMC Place; CAMDEN; ***213** C-18; elev. 2ft./1m.; mail Camden **Z** 27921; ● 50
Chantilly; RMC Place; MECKLENBURG; ★ **CHRLT**; mail Charlotte **Z** 28205; pop. incl. with Charlotte (Inc. Place)
Chapanoke; RMC Place; PERQUIMANS; ***213** C-18; elev. 14ft./4m.; mail Hertford **Z** 27944
Chapel Hill; Inc. Place; ORANGE, DURHAM; **212** D-10; elev. 487ft./148m.; 🅿 🅷 🅲 27,717 ■; ★ **DUR**; **Z** 27514-17, **Z** 27599; Ⓟ 38,719; Ⓒ 48,715; Ⓡ 46,019; ◆ 55,490
Charity; RMC Place; DUPLIN; ***213** H-14; mail Rose Hill **Z** 28458; ● 30
Charles; RMC Place; IREDELL; ***212** D-5; mail Statesville **Z** 28677
Charleston; RMC Place; HALIFAX; ***213** C-15; elev. 95ft./29m.; mail Scotland Neck **Z** 27874; ● 50
Charlotte; Inc. Place; ⊡ MECKLENBURG; **212** F-5; elev. 700ft./213m.; 🅿 🅷 🅲 28,481 ■; ★ **CHRLT**; **Z** 28201-24, **Z** 28226-37, **Z** 28241-44, **Z** 28246-47, **Z** 28250, **Z** 28253-56, **Z** 28258, **Z** 28260, **Z** 28262-63, **Z** 28265-66, **Z** 28269-75, **Z** 28277-78, **Z** 28280-82, **Z** 28284-85, **Z** 28287-90, **Z** 28296-97, **Z** 28299; Ⓟ 395,934; Ⓒ 540,828; Ⓡ 540,167; ◆ 686,952
Charlotte Junction; RMC Place; MECKLENBURG; ★ **CHRLT**; pop. incl. with Charlotte (Inc. Place)
Chatham; RMC Place; CHATHAM; ***212** D-10; elev. 584ft./178m.; ★ **DUR**; mail Chapel Hill **Z** 27516-17; ● 500
CHATHAM; **212** E-10; Ⓟ 38,759; Ⓒ 49,329; ◆ 63,713
Cheeks; RMC Place; RANDOLPH; ***212** E-9; elev. 410ft./125m.; mail Ramseur **Z** 27316; rural
Chemway; RMC Place; MECKLENBURG; ***212** F-5; ★ **CHRLT**; pop. incl. with Charlotte (Inc. Place)
Cherokee; RMC Place; SWAIN; **212** L-3; located on Eastern Cherokee Ind. Res.; elev. 1,991ft./607m.; 🅿 🅷; **Z** 28719; location of Indian Agency; ● 750
CHEROKEE; **212** M-1; Ⓟ 20,170; Ⓒ 24,298; ◆ 27,020
Cherry; RMC Place; WASHINGTON; **213** D-18; mail Creswell **Z** 27928; ● 50
Cherryfield; RMC Place; TRANSYLVANIA; ***212** M-5; mail Brevard **Z** 28712; rural
Cherry Grove; RMC Place; COLUMBUS; ***213** J-11; elev. 99ft./30m.; mail Cerro Gordo **Z** 28430; ● 30
Cherry Lane; RMC Place; ALLEGHANY; **212** B-5; elev. 2,856ft./871m.; mail Glade Valley **Z** 28627; ● 60
Cherry Oaks; RMC Place; PITT; ***213** E-15; elev. 66ft./20m.; ★ **GRNV**; mail Greenville **Z** 27858; ● 800
Cherry Springs; RMC Place; MCDOWELL; mail Old Fort **Z** 28762; rural
Cherryville; Inc. Place; GASTON; **212** F-4; elev. 960ft./293m.; 🅿; ★ **CHRLT**; **Z** 28021; Ⓟ 4,756; Ⓒ 5,361
Chesterfield; RMC Place; BURKE; ***212** D-3; mail Morganton **Z** 28655; ● 30
Chestnut Dale; RMC Place; AVERY; ***212** D-2; mail Newland **Z** 28657; ● 30
Chestnut Grove; RMC Place; STOKES; ***212** C-7; ★ **WNS**; mail King **Z** 27021
Chestnut Hill; RMC Place; ASHE; ***212** B-4; mail Crumpler **Z** 28617; ● 50
Chestnut Hill; RMC Place; HENDERSON; ***212** F-1; mail Gerton **Z** 28735
Chimney Rock; Inc. Place; RUTHERFORD; **212** F-1; elev. 1,040ft./317m.; 🅿; **Z** 28720; Ⓟ 116; summer pop. 300; Ⓒ 175
China Grove; Inc. Place; ROWAN; **212** E-6; elev. 800ft./244m.; 🅿; ★ **CHRLT**; **Z** 28023; Ⓟ 2,732; Ⓒ 3,616
China Grove Cotton Mill Village; RMC Place; ROWAN; ***212** E-6; ★ **CHRLT**; mail China Grove **Z** 28023; pop. incl. with Landis (Inc. Place)
Chinquapin; RMC Place; DUPLIN; **213** H-14; elev. 40ft./12m.; 🅿; **Z** 28521; ● 350
Chip; RMC Place; CRAVEN; **213** F-16; elev. 10ft./3m.; mail Vanceboro **Z** 28586; ● 180
Chip; RMC Place; MONTGOMERY; ***212** F-8; mail Mount Gilead **Z** 27306; rural
Choco Village; RMC Place; BEAUFORT; ***213** E-16; elev. 35ft./11m.; mail Chocowinity **Z** 27817; ● 90
Chocowinity; Inc. Place; BEAUFORT; **213** E-16; elev. 32ft./10m.; 🅿; **Z** 27817; Ⓟ 624; Ⓒ 733
CHOWAN; **213** C-17; Ⓟ 13,506; Ⓒ 14,526; Ⓡ 14,150; ◆ 14,809
Chowan Beach; RMC Place; CHOWAN; ***213** C-17; elev. 33ft./10m.; mail Edenton **Z** 27932; ● 200
Chowan Beach; RMC Place; HERTFORD; ***213** B-16; elev. 6ft./2m.; mail Murfreesboro **Z** 27855; rural
Chub Lake; RMC Place; PERSON; ***212** B-10; elev. 457ft./139m.; mail Roxboro **Z** 27573; rural
Church Crossroads; RMC Place; MARTIN; ***213** D-16; elev. 59ft./18m.; mail Robersonville **Z** 27871, Williamston **Z** 27892; rural
Church Hill; RMC Place; WARREN; ***213** B-13; mail Macon **Z** 27551; rural
Churchland; RMC Place; DAVIDSON; **212** E-7; elev. 840ft./256m.; mail Lexington **Z** 27292, **Z** 27295; ● 180
Cid; RMC Place; DAVIDSON; **212** E-7; mail Lexington **Z** 27292
Cisco; RMC Place; CHOWAN; ***213** C-17; mail Tyner **Z** 27980
City View; RMC Place; FORSYTH; ***212** D-7; ★ **WNS**; mail Winston Salem **Z** 27101; pop. incl. with Winston-Salem (Inc. Place)
Claremont; Inc. Place; CATAWBA; **212** E-4; elev. 981ft./299m.; 🅿; ★ **HICK**; **Z** 28610; Ⓟ 980; Ⓒ 1,038; Ⓡ 1,060
Clarendon; RMC Place; COLUMBUS; ***213** J-11; elev. 106ft./32m.; 🅿; **Z** 28432; ● 150
Clark; RMC Place; CRAVEN; **213** G-16; mail New Bern **Z** 28562; ● 80
Clarkton; Inc. Place; BLADEN; **213** I-12; elev. 88ft./27m.; 🅿; **Z** 28433; Ⓟ 739; Ⓒ 705
Clarrissa; RMC Place; MITCHELL; ***212** D-2; mail Bakersville **Z** 28705; ● 30
Clay; RMC Place; GRANVILLE; ***213** C-12; mail Oxford **Z** 27565
CLAY; **212** M-2; Ⓟ 7,155; Ⓒ 8,775; ◆ 10,595
Clayroot; RMC Place; PITT; ***213** F-16; mail Ayden **Z** 28513; rural
Clayton; Inc. Place; JOHNSTON; **213** E-12; 🅿; ★ **RAL**; **Z** 27520, **Z** 27527-28; Ⓟ 4,756; Ⓒ 6,973; Ⓡ 8,126
Clear Creek; RMC Place; MECKLENBURG; ***212** G-6; ★ **CHRLT**; mail Charlotte **Z** 28212; rural
Clear Run; RMC Place; SAMPSON; ***213** H-13; elev. 50ft./15m.; mail Garland **Z** 28441; ● 30
Clegg; RMC Place; DURHAM; ***213** D-11; ★ **DUR**; mail Morrisville **Z** 27560; pop. incl. with Durham (Inc. Place)
Clement; RMC Place; SAMPSON; ***213** G-12; elev. 151ft./46m.; mail Autryville **Z** 28318; ● 30
Clemmons; Inc. Place; FORSYTH; **212** D-7; elev. 832ft./254m.; 🅿; ★ **WNS**; **Z** 27012; Ⓟ 6,020; Ⓒ 13,827
Cleveland; Inc. Place; ROWAN; **212** E-6; elev. 819ft./250m.; 🅿; **Z** 27013; Ⓟ 696; Ⓒ 808
CLEVELAND; **212** F-3; Ⓟ 84,714; Ⓒ 96,287; ◆ 98,263
Clifdale; RMC Place; CUMBERLAND; ***213** G-11; elev. 237ft./72m.; ★ **FAY**; mail Fayetteville **Z** 28304; pop. incl. with Fayetteville (Inc. Place)
Cliffside; RMC Place; RUTHERFORD; **212** F-3; elev. 850ft./259m.; 🅿; **Z** 28024; ● 900
Clifton; RMC Place; ASHE; **212** B-3; mail Warrensville **Z** 28693; ● 100
Climax; RMC Place; GUILFORD; **212** D-9; elev. 802ft./244m.; 🅿; ★ **GRNS-**; **Z** 27233; ● 450
Clinchfield; RMC Place; MCDOWELL; ***212** E-2; elev. 142ft./43m.; mail Marion **Z** 28752; pop. incl. with Marion (Inc. Place)
Clingman; RMC Place; WILKES; ***212** C-5; elev. 1,134ft./346m.; mail Ronda **Z** 28670; ● 220
Clinton; Inc. Place; ⊡ SAMPSON; **213** G-13; elev. 152ft./46m.; 🅿 🅷 ■; **Z** 28328-29; Ⓟ 8,204; Ⓒ 8,600; ◆ 8,503
Cloverdale; RMC Place; WAKE; ***213** E-12; ★ **RAL**; mail Garner **Z** 27529; pop. incl. with Garner (Inc. Place)
Clover Garden; RMC Place; ALAMANCE; ***212** C-9; elev. 695ft./212m.; ★ **BUR**; mail Burlington **Z** 27217; ● 170
Cloverleaf; RMC Place; CUMBERLAND; ***213** G-11; elev. 200ft./61m.; ★ **FAY**; mail Fayetteville **Z** 28304; pop. incl. with Fayetteville (Inc. Place)
Club Pines; RMC Place; PITT; ***213** E-15; elev. 69ft./21m.; ★ **GRNV**; mail Greenville **Z** 27834; pop. incl. with Greenville (Inc. Place)
Clyde; Inc. Place; HAYWOOD; **212** L-4; elev. 2,539ft./774m.; 🅿 🅷; ★ **ASHE**; **Z** 28721; Ⓟ 1,041; Ⓒ 1,324
Coakley; RMC Place; EDGECOMBE; ***213** D-15; elev. 81ft./25m.; mail Tarboro **Z** 27886; ● 50
Coalville; RMC Place; CHEROKEE; ***212** M-2; elev. 1,662ft./507m.; mail Andrews **Z** 28901
Coats; Inc. Place; HARNETT; **213** F-11; elev. 314ft./96m.; 🅿; ★ **RAL**; **Z** 27521; Ⓟ 1,493; Ⓒ 1,845
Coats Crossroads; RMC Place; JOHNSTON; ***213** F-12; elev. 252ft./77m.; ★ **RAL**; mail Benson **Z** 27504; ● 30
Cobbs Shop; RMC Place; CASWELL; ***212** C-9; elev. 729ft./222m.; mail Ruffin **Z** 27326; rural
Cobb Town; RMC Place; EDGECOMBE; ***213** E-15; elev. 24ft./7m.; mail Fountain **Z** 27829; rural
Cofield; Inc. Place; HERTFORD; **213** B-16; elev. 43ft./13m.; 🅿; **Z** 27922; Ⓟ 407; Ⓒ 347
Cognac; RMC Place; RICHMOND; ***212** G-9; elev. 399ft./122m.; mail Marston **Z** 28363; ● 30
Coinjock; RMC Place; CURRITUCK; **213** B-19; 🅿; **Z** 27923; ● 400
Cokesbury; RMC Place; HARNETT; ***213** F-11; elev. 405ft./123m.; mail Fuquay Varina **Z** 27526
Cokesbury; RMC Place; VANCE; ***213** C-12; mail Henderson **Z** 27537; rural
Cold Springs; RMC Place; CABARRUS; ***212** F-6; elev. 723ft./220m.; ★ **CHRLT**; mail Concord **Z** 28025; ● 50
Cold Water; RMC Place; CABARRUS; ***212** F-6; elev. 603ft./184m.; ★ **CHRLT**; mail Concord **Z** 28025; ● 50
Cole Park; RMC Place; CHATHAM; ***212** D-10; elev. 553ft./169m.; ★ **DUR**; mail Chapel Hill **Z** 27517; ● 230
Colerain; Inc. Place; BERTIE; **213** C-17; 🅿; **Z** 27924; Ⓟ 139; Ⓒ 221
Coleridge; RMC Place; RANDOLPH; **212** E-9; elev. 424ft./129m.; 🅿; **Z** 27316; ● 230
Colewood Acres; RMC Place; WAKE; ***213** E-12; ★ **RAL**; mail Raleigh **Z** 27604; ● 600
Colfax; RMC Place; GUILFORD; **214** G-11; elev. 972ft./296m.; 🅿; ★ **GRNS-**; **Z** 27235; ● 1,050
Colington (Collington); RMC Place; DARE; ***213** D-20; mail Kitty Hawk **Z** 27949; ● 780
College Downs; RMC Place; MECKLENBURG; ***212** F-6; ★ **CHRLT**; mail Charlotte **Z** 28213; pop. incl. with Charlotte (Inc. Place)
College Lakes; RMC Place; CUMBERLAND; ***213** G-11; elev. 200ft./61m.; ★ **FAY**; mail Fayetteville **Z** 28301; pop. incl. with Fayetteville (Inc. Place)
College Park; RMC Place; CABARRUS; ***212** F-6; elev. 570ft./174m.; ★ **CHRLT**; mail Harrisburg **Z** 28075; pop. incl. with Harrisburg (Inc. Place)
College Park; RMC Place; GUILFORD; ★ **GRNS-**; mail Greensboro **Z** 27403; pop. incl. with Greensboro (Inc. Place)
College Park; RMC Place; RICHMOND; ***212** H-9; mail Hamlet **Z** 28345; pop. incl. with Dobbins Heights (Inc. Place)
College View; RMC Place; WAKE; ★ **RAL**; pop. incl. with Raleigh (Inc. Place)
Collettsville; RMC Place; CALDWELL; **212** D-3; elev. 1,097ft./334m.; 🅿; **Z** 28611; ● 200
Collington; DARE; see Colington (RMC Place)
Collinstown; RMC Place; STOKES; ***212** B-7; elev. 1,228ft./374m.; mail Stuart **Z** 24171; rural
Colly; RMC Place; BLADEN; ***213** I-13; mail Kelly **Z** 28448
Colon; RMC Place; LEE; **212** F-10; elev. 300ft./91m.; 🅿; **Z** 27330; ● 100
Colonial Heights; RMC Place; BEAUFORT; mail Washington **Z** 27889
Colonial Heights; RMC Place; WAKE; ***213** E-11; ★ **RAL**; mail Raleigh **Z** 27603; ● 750
Colony Park; RMC Place; DURHAM; ***213** D-11; ★ **DUR**; mail Durham **Z** 27705; pop. incl. with Durham (Inc. Place)
Columbia; Inc. Place; ⊡ TYRRELL; **213** D-18; elev. 5ft./2m.; 🅿; **Z** 27925; Ⓟ 836; Ⓒ 819
Columbia Heights; RMC Place; FORSYTH; ***212** D-7; elev. 848ft./258m.; ★ **WNS**; mail Winston Salem **Z** 27107; pop. incl. with Winston-Salem (Inc. Place)
Columbus; Inc. Place; ⊡ POLK; **212** F-1; elev. 1,109ft./338m.; 🅿 🅷; **Z** 28722; Ⓟ 812; Ⓒ 992
COLUMBUS; **213** I-11; Ⓟ 49,587; Ⓒ 54,749; ◆ 53,772
Comfort; RMC Place; JONES; **213** G-15; elev. 55ft./17m.; 🅿; **Z** 28522; ● 250
Commodore Peninsula; RMC Place; IREDELL; ***212** E-5; ★ **CHRLT**; mail Mooresville **Z** 28117; ● 200
Como; Inc. Place; HERTFORD; **213** B-16; elev. 74ft./23m.; 🅿; **Z** 27818; Ⓟ 71; Ⓒ 78
Complex; RMC Place; DAVIDSON; ***212** E-8; elev. 700ft./213m.; mail Denton **Z** 27239; rural
Concord; Inc. Place; ⊡ CABARRUS; **212** F-6; elev. 704ft./215m.; 🅿 🅷 🅲 334 ■; ★ **CHRLT**; **Z** 28025-27; Ⓟ 27,347; Ⓒ 55,977; ◆ 79,253
Concord; RMC Place; DUPLIN; ***213** H-13; elev. 110ft./34m.; mail Magnolia **Z** 28453; ● 30
Concord; RMC Place; PERSON; ***212** B-10; elev. 582ft./177m.; mail Roxboro **Z** 27574; rural
Concord; RMC Place; RUTHERFORD; ***212** F-3; mail Bostic **Z** 28018; ● 190
Concord; RMC Place; SAMPSON; ***213** G-12; elev. 168ft./51m.; mail Clinton **Z** 28328, Roseboro **Z** 28382; rural
Conetoe; Inc. Place; EDGECOMBE; **213** D-15; elev. 48ft./15m.; 🅿; **Z** 27819; Ⓟ 292; Ⓒ 365
Congleton; RMC Place; PITT; ***213** E-16; mail Robersonville **Z** 27871; rural
Connarista; RMC Place; BERTIE; **213** C-16; elev. 69ft./21m.; mail Aulander **Z** 27805; ● 20
Connelly Springs (Connellys Springs); Inc. Place; BURKE; **212** E-4; elev. 1,195ft./364m.; mail Connellys Springs **Z** 28612; Ⓟ 1,349; Ⓒ 1,814
Connellys Springs; BURKE; see Connelly Springs (Inc. Place)
Conover; Inc. Place; CATAWBA; **212** E-4; elev. 1,062ft./324m.; 🅿; ★ **HICK**; **Z** 28613; Ⓟ 5,465; Ⓒ 6,604; Ⓡ 6,667
Conway; Inc. Place; NORTHAMPTON; **213** B-15; elev. 105ft./32m.; 🅿; **Z** 27820; Ⓟ 759; Ⓒ 734
Cooksville; RMC Place; CATAWBA; ***212** E-4; elev. 1,232ft./376m.; ★ **HICK**; mail Vale **Z** 28168; rural
Cooktown; RMC Place; MITCHELL; ***212** D-2; mail Bakersville **Z** 28705; ● 30
Cooleemee; Inc. Place; DAVIE; **212** E-6; elev. 663ft./202m.; 🅿; ★ **SLSB**; **Z** 27014; Ⓟ 971; Ⓒ 905
Cool Spring; IREDELL; see Cool Springs (RMC Place)
Cool Springs (Cool Spring); RMC Place; IREDELL; ***212** D-6; mail Cleveland **Z** 27013, Statesville **Z** 28677
Cool Springs; RMC Place; LEE; ***212** F-10; mail Sanford **Z** 27330; pop. incl. with Sanford (Inc. Place)
Cooper Estates; RMC Place; ALAMANCE; ***212** D-9; elev. 550ft./168m.; ★ **BUR**; mail Graham **Z** 27253; pop. incl. with Swepsonville (Inc. Place)
Copeland; RMC Place; SURRY; ***212** C-6; elev. 1,172ft./357m.; mail Dobson **Z** 27017; ● 100
Coral Bay; RMC Place; CARTERET; ***213** H-17; elev. 17ft./5m.; mail Morehead City **Z** 28557; pop. incl. with Morehead City (Inc. Place)
Corapeake; RMC Place; GATES; **213** B-17; elev. 49ft./15m.; 🅿; **Z** 27926; ● 150
Corbett; RMC Place; CASWELL; **212** K-5; elev. 701ft./214m.; mail Mebane **Z** 27302; ● 30
Cordova (Steels Mill); RMC Place; RICHMOND; **212** H-8; elev. 287ft./87m.; 🅿; **Z** 28330; ● 1,300
Core Creek; RMC Place; CARTERET; ***213** H-17; elev. 8ft./2m.; mail Beaufort **Z** 28516; ● 130
Core Point; RMC Place; BEAUFORT; **213** F-17; mail Blounts Creek **Z** 27814; summer pop. 400; ● 120
Corinth; RMC Place; CHATHAM; **213** E-11; elev. 301ft./92m.; mail Moncure **Z** 27559; ● 170
Corinth; RMC Place; NASH; ***213** D-13; ★ **RKYMT**; mail Nashville **Z** 27856; rural
Corinth; RMC Place; RUTHERFORD; ***212** F-3; mail Bostic **Z** 28018, Ellenboro **Z** 28040; ● 100
Cornatzer; RMC Place; DAVIE; ***212** D-6; elev. 799ft./244m.; ★ **WNS**; mail Mocksville **Z** 27028
Cornelius; Inc. Place; MECKLENBURG; **212** F-5; elev. 831ft./253m.; 🅿; ★ **CHRLT**; **Z** 28031; Ⓟ 2,581; Ⓒ 11,969; ◆ 24,937
Corner High; RMC Place; GATES; ***213** B-16; elev. 8ft./2m.; mail Eure **Z** 27935; rural
Cornwall; RMC Place; GRANVILLE; ***213** B-11; mail Oxford **Z** 27565; rural
Corolla; RMC Place; CURRITUCK; **213** B-19; 🅿; **Z** 27927; summer pop. 1,000; ● 150
Correll Park; RMC Place; ROWAN; ***212** E-6; ★ **SLSB**; mail Salisbury **Z** 28144, **Z** 28146; ● 130
Corriher Heights; RMC Place; ROWAN; ***212** E-6; elev. 848ft./258m.; ★ **CHRLT**; mail China Grove **Z** 28023; ● 220
Costin; RMC Place; PENDER; ***213** I-13; mail Atkinson **Z** 28421; rural
Cottonade; RMC Place; CUMBERLAND; ***213** G-11; ★ **FAY**; mail Fayetteville **Z** 28303; pop. incl. with Fayetteville (Inc. Place)
Cotton Grove; RMC Place; DAVIDSON; ***212** E-7; mail Lexington **Z** 27292; rural
Cottonville; RMC Place; STANLY; ***212** G-7; mail Norwood **Z** 28128; rural
Council; RMC Place; BLADEN; **213** I-12; elev. 72ft./22m.; 🅿; **Z** 28434; ● 80
Country Club Estates; RMC Place; COLUMBUS; ***213** J-11; elev. 107ft./33m.; mail Whiteville **Z** 28472; ● 100
Country Hills; RMC Place; JOHNSTON; ***213** E-12; ★ **RAL**; mail Garner **Z** 27529; ● 350
Country Homes Estates; RMC Place; ALAMANCE; ***212** D-10; elev. 550ft./168m.; ★ **BUR**; mail Haw River **Z** 27258; ● 270
Courtney; RMC Place; YADKIN; **212** D-6; elev. 904ft./276m.; mail Yadkinville **Z** 27055; ● 550
Cove; CRAVEN; see Cove City (Inc. Place)
Cove City (Cove); Inc. Place; CRAVEN; **213** G-15; elev. 47ft./14m.; 🅿; **Z** 28523; Ⓟ 497; Ⓒ 433
Cove Creek; RMC Place; HAYWOOD; **212** L-4; elev. 2,480ft./756m.; mail Waynesville **Z** 28785; ● 260
Covington; RMC Place; RICHMOND; ***212** G-8; elev. 566ft./173m.; mail Mount Gilead **Z** 27306; rural
Cowee; RMC Place; MACON; ***212** M-3; mail Franklin **Z** 28734; rural
Cox Crossing; RMC Place; PITT; ***213** E-15; elev. 64ft./20m.; ★ **GRNV**; mail Greenville **Z** 27858; rural
Coxs Crossroad; RMC Place; BEAUFORT; ***213** F-16; elev. 10ft./3m.; mail Blounts Creek **Z** 27814; rural
Coxville; RMC Place; PITT; ***213** F-15; ★ **GRNV**; mail Ayden **Z** 28513; rural
Cozart; RMC Place; GRANVILLE; ***213** C-11; elev. 350ft./107m.; ★ **DUR**; mail Creedmoor **Z** 27522
Crab Point; CARTERET; see Crab Point Village (RMC Place)
Crab Point Village (Crab Point); RMC Place; CARTERET; ***213** H-17; elev. 10ft./3m.; mail Morehead City **Z** 28557; ● 250
Crabtree; RMC Place; HAYWOOD; **212** L-4; mail Clyde **Z** 28721; ● 50
Craggy; RMC Place; BUNCOMBE; ***212** E-1; ★ **ASHE**; mail Asheville **Z** 28804; rural
Cramerton; Inc. Place; GASTON; **212** G-5; elev. 633ft./193m.; 🅿; ★ **CHRLT**; **Z** 28032; Ⓟ 2,371; Ⓒ 2,976
Cranberry; RMC Place; AVERY; **212** C-2; elev. 3,202ft./976m.; mail Elk Park **Z** 28622, Newland **Z** 28657; ● 250
Cranberry Gap; RMC Place; AVERY; ***212** C-2; mail Newland **Z** 28657; ● 50
Crater Park; RMC Place; MECKLENBURG; ***212** F-5; ★ **CHRLT**; mail Charlotte **Z** 28213; pop. incl. with Charlotte (Inc. Place)
CRAVEN; **213** F-16; Ⓟ 81,613; Ⓒ 91,436; Ⓡ 91,523; ◆ 100,296
Creedmoor; Inc. Place; GRANVILLE; **213** C-11; elev. 400ft./122m.; 🅿; ★ **DUR**; **Z** 27522, **Z** 27564; Ⓟ 1,504; Ⓒ 2,232
Creekside Estates; RMC Place; GASTON; ***212** F-4; elev. 1,000ft./305m.; ★ **CHRLT**; mail Bessemer City **Z** 28016; ● 500
Creeksville; RMC Place; NORTHAMPTON; ***213** B-15; elev. 77ft./23m.; mail Conway **Z** 27820; ● 30
Cremo; RMC Place; BERTIE; ***213** C-16; mail Colerain **Z** 27924; rural
Crescent; RMC Place; ROWAN; ***212** E-7; ★ **SLSB**; mail Rockwell **Z** 28138
Crestmont; RMC Place; CATAWBA; ***212** E-4; ★ **HICK**; mail Hickory **Z** 28601; rural
Creston; RMC Place; ASHE; **212** B-3; elev. 2,856ft./871m.; 🅿; **Z** 28615; ● 70
Crestview; RMC Place; CHATHAM; ***212** E-9; elev. 604ft./184m.; mail Siler City **Z** 27344; ● 80
Creswell; Inc. Place; WASHINGTON; **213** D-18; elev. 10ft./3m.; 🅿; **Z** 27928; Ⓟ 361; Ⓒ 278
Cricket; CDP; WILKES; ***212** C-4; mail North Wilkesboro **Z** 28659; Ⓟ 2,015; Ⓒ 2,053
Crisp; RMC Place; EDGECOMBE; **213** E-14; elev. 104ft./32m.; mail Macclesfield **Z** 27852; ● 120
Croatan; RMC Place; CRAVEN; **213** G-16; elev. 29ft./9m.; mail New Bern **Z** 28560; ● 130
Crockers Nub; RMC Place; JOHNSTON; ***213** E-13; elev. 232ft./71m.; mail Middlesex **Z** 27557; rural
Cross Landing; RMC Place; TYRRELL; ***213** D-18; mail Columbia **Z** 27925; rural
Cross Mill; RMC Place; MCDOWELL; ***212** E-2; mail Marion **Z** 28752; ● 650
Crossnore; Inc. Place; AVERY; **212** D-2; elev. 3,360ft./1,024m.; 🅿 🅷; **Z** 28616; Ⓟ 271; Ⓒ 242
Cross Road; RMC Place; SURRY; mail Mount Airy **Z** 27030
Crossway; RMC Place; SCOTLAND; ***212** H-9; mail Laurinburg **Z** 28352; rural
Crosswinds; RMC Place; WAKE; ★ **RAL**; mail Raleigh **Z** 27615
Crouse; RMC Place; LINCOLN; **212** F-4; elev. 860ft./262m.; 🅿; **Z** 28033; ● 900
Crowders; RMC Place; GASTON; ***212** G-4; elev. 776ft./237m.; ★ **CHRLT**; mail Gastonia **Z** 28052
Crowells; RMC Place; HALIFAX; ***213** C-15; mail Halifax **Z** 27839; rural
Crumpler; RMC Place; ASHE; **212** B-4; elev. 2,580ft./786m.; 🅿; **Z** 28617; ● 100
Crump Town; RMC Place; SCOTLAND; ***212** H-10; mail Wagram **Z** 28396; pop. incl. with Wagram (Inc. Place)
Cruso; RMC Place; HAYWOOD; **212** L-5; mail Canton **Z** 28716; ● 200
Crusoe Island; RMC Place; COLUMBUS; **213** J-12; elev. 40ft./12m.; mail Whiteville **Z** 28472; ● 120
Crutchfield Crossroads; RMC Place; CHATHAM; **212** E-9; elev. 619ft./189m.; mail Siler City **Z** 27344; ● 30
Crystal Park; RMC Place; CUMBERLAND; ***213** G-11; elev. 150ft./46m.; ★ **FAY**; mail Fayetteville **Z** 28306; ● 200
Culberson; RMC Place; CHEROKEE; **212** N-1; elev. 1,612ft./491m.; 🅿; **Z** 28903; ● 500
Culbreth; RMC Place; GRANVILLE; ***213** C-11; mail Oxford **Z** 27565; rural
Cullasaja; RMC Place; MACON; ***212** M-3; mail Franklin **Z** 28734
Cullowhee; CDP; JACKSON; **212** L-4; 🅿 🅲 8,861; **Z** 28723; Ⓟ 4,029; Ⓒ 3,579
Cumberland; RMC Place; CUMBERLAND; **213** G-11; elev. 190ft./58m.; 🅿; ★ **FAY**; **Z** 28331; pop. incl. with Hope Mills (Inc. Place)
CUMBERLAND; **213** H-11; Ⓟ 274,566; Ⓒ 302,963; ◆ 320,446
Cumnock; RMC Place; LEE; **212** E-10; elev. 259ft./79m.; 🅿; **Z** 27237; ● 250
Cunningham; RMC Place; PERSON; ***212** B-10; elev. 574ft./175m.; mail Semora **Z** 27343; rural
Currie; RMC Place; PENDER; **213** I-13; elev. 34ft./10m.; 🅿; **Z** 28435; ● 300
Currituck; RMC Place; ⊡ CURRITUCK; **213** B-19; 🅿; **Z** 27929; ● 630
CURRITUCK; **213** B-19; Ⓟ 13,736; Ⓒ 18,190; ◆ 24,583
Currytown; RMC Place; DAVIDSON; ***212** D-7; elev. 848ft./258m.; ★ **WNS**; mail Lexington **Z** 27295; rural
Cutshalltown; RMC Place; MADISON; ***212** J-5; mail Marshall **Z** 28753; rural
Cycle; RMC Place; YADKIN; ***212** C-5; mail Hamptonville **Z** 27020
Cypress Creek; RMC Place; COLUMBUS; ***213** J-12; mail Whiteville **Z** 28472; ● 30
Cypress Creek; RMC Place; DUPLIN; ***213** H-14; elev. 73ft./22m.; mail Wallace **Z** 28466
Cypress Lake; RMC Place; CUMBERLAND; ***213** H-11; elev. 150ft./46m.; ★ **FAY**; mail Hope Mills **Z** 28348; rural

D

Dabney; RMC Place; VANCE; ***213** C-12; elev. 548ft./167m.; mail Henderson **Z** 27536
Dailt Town; RMC Place; EDGECOMBE; ***213** D-15; elev. 16ft./5m.; mail Tarboro **Z** 27886; ● 100
Daisey; FORSYTH; see Daisy (RMC Place)
Daisy (Daisey); RMC Place; FORSYTH; ★ **WNS**; mail Winston Salem **Z** 27101; pop. incl. with Winston-Salem (Inc. Place)
Dallas; Inc. Place; GASTON; **212** F-4; elev. 784ft./239m.; 🅿; ★ **CHRLT**; **Z** 28034; Ⓟ 3,012; Ⓒ 3,402
Dalton; RMC Place; STOKES; ***212** C-7; ★ **WNS**; mail Pinnacle **Z** 27043; rural
Dana; RMC Place; HENDERSON; ***212** F-1; elev. 2,256ft./688m.; 🅿; **Z** 28724; ● 710
Danbury; Inc. Place; ⊡ STOKES; **212** B-7; elev. 825ft./251m.; 🅿 🅷; **Z** 27016; Ⓟ 119; Ⓒ 108
Danieltown; RMC Place; RUTHERFORD; ***212** F-2; mail Forest City **Z** 28043; ● 400
Dan River Shores; RMC Place; STOKES; ***212** B-7; mail Danbury **Z** 27016; rural
Dan Valley; RMC Place; ROCKINGHAM; ***212** B-8; elev. 684ft./208m.; ★ **GRNS-**; mail Stoneville **Z** 27048; rural
Darby; RMC Place; WILKES; ***212** C-3; mail Ferguson **Z** 28624
Darden; MARTIN; see Dardens (RMC Place)
Dardens (Darden); RMC Place; MARTIN; **213** D-17; mail Jamesville **Z** 27846; ● 150
DARE; **213** E-20; Ⓟ 22,746; Ⓒ 29,967; ◆ 33,436
Dark Ridge; RMC Place; AVERY; ***212** C-2; mail Elk Park **Z** 28622; rural
Darlington; RMC Place; HALIFAX; ***213** C-14; elev. 160ft./49m.; mail Halifax **Z** 27839; ● 50
Davenport Forks; RMC Place; WASHINGTON; ***213** D-18; mail Roper **Z** 27970; rural
Davidson; Inc. Place; MECKLENBURG, IREDELL; **212** F-5; elev. 800ft./244m.; 🅿 🅲 1,667; ★ **CHRLT**; **Z** 28035-36; Ⓟ 4,046; Ⓒ 7,139
DAVIDSON; **212** E-7; Ⓟ 126,677; Ⓒ 147,246; ◆ 156,552
Davidson River; RMC Place; TRANSYLVANIA; ***212** M-5; mail Pisgah Forest **Z** 28768; ● 50
DAVIE; **212** D-6; Ⓟ 27,859; Ⓒ 34,835; ◆ 41,757
Davie Crossroads; RMC Place; DAVIE; ***212** D-6; ★ **SLSB**; mail Mocksville **Z** 27028; rural
Davis; RMC Place; CARTERET; **213** H-18; elev. 5ft./2m.; 🅿; **Z** 28524; ● 690
Davistown; RMC Place; EDGECOMBE; ***213** D-14; mail Pinetops **Z** 27864; rural
Davistown; RMC Place; MCDOWELL; ***212** E-2; elev. 1,520ft./463m.; mail Old Fort **Z** 28762, Willow Beach **Z** 86445; rural
Dawson; RMC Place; LENOIR; ***213** F-14; elev. 30ft./9m.; mail Kinston **Z** 28501, **Z** 28504; ● 30
Dawson Crossroads; RMC Place; HALIFAX; ***213** C-15; elev. 124ft./38m.; mail Enfield **Z** 27823; rural
Day Book; RMC Place; YANCEY; ***212** D-1; mail Green Mountain **Z** 28740; rural
Days Crossroads; RMC Place; HALIFAX; ***213** B-14; mail Halifax **Z** 27839; ● 30
Deep Creek; RMC Place; ANSON; ***212** H-7; elev. 459ft./140m.; mail Peachland **Z** 28133; rural
Deep Gap; RMC Place; WATAUGA; **212** C-3; elev. 1,000ft./305m.; 🅿; **Z** 28618; rural
Deep River; RMC Place; GUILFORD; ***212** D-8; elev. 891ft./272m.; ★ **GRNS-**; mail High Point **Z** 27260, **Z** 27265; pop. incl. with High Point (Inc. Place)
Deep Run; RMC Place; LENOIR; **213** G-14; elev. 110ft./34m.; 🅿; **Z** 28525; ● 300
Deerfield; RMC Place; WATAUGA; ***212** C-3; elev. 3,200ft./975m.; mail Boone **Z** 28607; ● 80
Deerwood; RMC Place; CRAVEN; ***213** H-16; elev. 25ft./8m.; mail Havelock **Z** 28532; ● 140
Dehart; RMC Place; WILKES; ***212** C-5; elev. 1,375ft./419m.; mail Hays **Z** 28635; rural
Delco; RMC Place; COLUMBUS; **213** J-13; elev. 50ft./15m.; 🅿; **Z** 28436; ● 670
Delight; RMC Place; CLEVELAND; ***212** F-3; elev. 1,026ft./313m.; mail Lawndale **Z** 28090; rural
Dellview; RMC Place; GASTON; ***212** F-4; elev. 980ft./299m.; ★ **CHRLT**; mail Cherryville **Z** 28021; pop. incl. with Cherryville (Inc. Place)
Dellwood; RMC Place; HAYWOOD; **212** L-4; elev. 2,743ft./836m.; mail Waynesville **Z** 28785; ● 200
Delway; CDP; SAMPSON; ***213** H-13; elev. 129ft./39m.; mail Rose Hill **Z** 28458; Ⓒ 270
Democrat; RMC Place; BUNCOMBE; ***212** E-1; ★ **ASHE**; mail Weaverville **Z** 28787; ● 50
Dennis; RMC Place; FORSYTH; **212** C-7; elev. 861ft./262m.; ★ **WNS**; mail Walnut Cove **Z** 27052; ● 220
Denny Store; RMC Place; PERSON; ***213** C-11; elev. 587ft./179m.; mail Roxboro **Z** 27574; rural
Denton; Inc. Place; DAVIDSON; **212** E-7; elev. 698ft./213m.; 🅿; **Z** 27239; Ⓟ 1,292; Ⓒ 1,450
Denver; RMC Place; LINCOLN; **212** E-5; elev. 902ft./275m.; 🅿; ★ **CHRLT**; **Z** 28037; ● 600
Deppe; RMC Place; ONSLOW; ***213** H-15; elev. 44ft./13m.; ★ **JAX**; mail Maysville **Z** 28555; ● 170
Derby; RMC Place; RICHMOND; ***212** G-9; mail Ellerbe **Z** 28338; ● 30
Derita; RMC Place; MECKLENBURG; ***212** F-5; elev. 812ft./247m.; ★ **CHRLT**; mail Charlotte **Z** 28213, **Z** 28221; pop. incl. with Charlotte (Inc. Place)
Devonshire; RMC Place; CABARRUS; ***212** F-6; elev. 750ft./229m.; ★ **CHRLT**; mail Concord **Z** 28025; ● 40
Devotion; RMC Place; SURRY; ***212** B-5; mail Dobson **Z** 27017; ● 30
Dewey Pier; RMC Place; TYRRELL; ***213** D-18; mail Columbia **Z** 27925; rural
Dexter; RMC Place; GRANVILLE; ***213** B-12; elev. 453ft./138m.; mail Oxford **Z** 27565
Dickens Park; RMC Place; CARTERET; ***213** H-17; elev. 27ft./8m.; mail Newport **Z** 28570; ● 150
Dickerson; RMC Place; GRANVILLE; ***213** C-12; mail Oxford **Z** 27565; rural
Diggs; RMC Place; RICHMOND; ***212** H-8; elev. 360ft./110m.; mail Rockingham **Z** 28379; rural
Dillard; RMC Place; STOKES; **212** B-7; elev. 931ft./284m.; mail Madison **Z** 27025; ● 80
Dillingham; RMC Place; BUNCOMBE
Dillsboro; Inc. Place; JACKSON; **212** L-3; elev. 1,983ft./604m.; 🅿; **Z** 28725; Ⓟ 95; Ⓒ 205
Dilworth; RMC Place; MECKLENBURG; ★ **CHRLT**; mail Charlotte **Z** 28203; pop. incl. with Charlotte (Inc. Place)
Dixie; RMC Place; WILSON; ***213** E-14; elev. 150ft./46m.; mail Wilson **Z** 27893; rural
Dixon; RMC Place; ONSLOW; ***213** I-15; mail Holly Ridge **Z** 28445
Dixon Crossroad; RMC Place; PITT; ***213** E-15; elev. 62ft./19m.; ★ **GRNV**; mail Winterville **Z** 28590; rural
Dobbersville; RMC Place; WAYNE; ***213** G-13; elev. 179ft./55m.; mail Mount Olive **Z** 28365
Dobbins Heights; Inc. Place; RICHMOND; ***212** H-9; mail Hamlet **Z** 28345; Ⓟ 1,144; Ⓒ 936
Dobson; Inc. Place; ⊡ SURRY; **212** C-6; elev. 1,259ft./384m.; 🅿; **Z** 27017; Ⓟ 1,195; Ⓒ 1,457
Dockery; RMC Place; WILKES; ***212** C-5; elev. 1,265ft./386m.; mail Hays **Z** 28635, Traphill **Z** 28685
Dodgetown; RMC Place; STOKES; ***212** B-7; elev. 988ft./301m.; mail Madison **Z** 27025; ● 50
Dodsons Crossroads; RMC Place; ORANGE; ***212** D-10; elev. 644ft./196m.; ★ **DUR**; mail Hillsborough **Z** 27278; ● 50
Dogtown; RMC Place; EDGECOMBE; ***213** D-15; elev. 16ft./5m.; mail Tarboro **Z** 27886; rural
Dogwood Acres; RMC Place; DURHAM; ***213** D-11; ★ **DUR**; mail Durham **Z** 27704; pop. incl. with Durham (Inc. Place)
Dogwood Acres; RMC Place; ORANGE; ***212** D-10; elev. 471ft./144m.; ★ **DUR**; mail Chapel Hill **Z** 27516; ● 100
Dogwood Acres; RMC Place; RANDOLPH; ***212** E-8; mail Asheboro **Z** 27205
Dogwood Park; RMC Place; CABARRUS; ***212** F-6; elev. 692ft./211m.; ★ **CHRLT**; mail Concord **Z** 28027; ● 130
Don Lee Heights; RMC Place; CRAVEN; ***213** H-16; elev. 25ft./8m.; mail Havelock **Z** 28532; pop. incl. with Havelock (Inc. Place)
Donnaha; RMC Place; FORSYTH; ***212** C-6; elev. 757ft./231m.; ★ **WNS**; mail Tobaccoville **Z** 27050; rural
Doolie; RMC Place; IREDELL; ***212** E-5; elev. 869ft./265m.; ★ **CHRLT**; mail Mooresville **Z** 28115, **Z** 28117; ● 100
Dortches; Inc. Place; NASH; **213** D-14; elev. 194ft./59m.; ★ **RKYMT**; mail Rocky Mount **Z** 27801; Ⓟ 840; Ⓒ 809
Dosier; RMC Place; FORSYTH; ***212** C-7; ★ **WNS**; mail Pfafftown **Z** 27040; ● 550
Dothan; RMC Place; COLUMBUS; ***213** K-11; elev. 42ft./13m.; mail Loris **Z** 29569; rural
Double Shoals; RMC Place; CLEVELAND; **212** F-3; mail Lawndale **Z** 28090; ● 300
Douglas Crossroads; RMC Place; BEAUFORT; ***213** E-16; mail Washington **Z** 27889; ● 40
Dover; Inc. Place; CRAVEN; **213** F-15; elev. 63ft./19m.; 🅿; **Z** 28526; Ⓟ 451; Ⓒ 443
Downtown; RMC Place; BUNCOMBE; ★ **ASHE**; mail Asheville **Z** 28802; pop. incl. with Asheville (Inc. Place)
Downtown; RMC Place; CRAVEN; mail New Bern **Z** 28563; pop. incl. with New Bern (Inc. Place)
Downtown; RMC Place; MECKLENBURG; ★ **CHRLT**; mail Charlotte **Z** 28202-04, **Z** 28206, **Z** 28230-37; pop. incl. with Charlotte (Inc. Place)
Downtown; RMC Place; ROWAN; ★ **SLSB**; mail Salisbury **Z** 28145; pop. incl. with Salisbury (Inc. Place)
Downtown; RMC Place; WATAUGA; mail Boone **Z** 28607; pop. incl. with Boone (Inc. Place)
Draco; RMC Place; CALDWELL; ***212** D-4; elev. 1,538ft./469m.; mail Lenoir **Z** 28645; ● 100
Drake; RMC Place; NASH; ***213** D-14; elev. 148ft./45m.; ★ **RKYMT**; mail Battleboro **Z** 27809; ● 200
Drake Park; RMC Place; CUMBERLAND; ***213** G-11; elev. 200ft./61m.; ★ **FAY**; mail Fayetteville **Z** 28304; pop. incl. with Fayetteville (Inc. Place)
Draper; RMC Place; ROCKINGHAM; ***212** B-9; elev. 544ft./166m.; ★ **MRTNV**; mail Eden **Z** 27288; pop. incl. with Eden (Inc. Place)
Draughn; RMC Place; EDGECOMBE; ***213** D-15; elev. 78ft./24m.; mail Whitakers **Z** 27891; rural

Entries in **UPPERCASE** are counties.
Entries in **bold** have populations of 2,500 or more.
Names in parentheses are alternate names.

Inc. Place	Incorporated Place
RMC Place	Rand McNally Designated Place
CDP	Census Designated Place
MCD	Minor Civil Division

⊡ County Seat
▲ Minor Civil Division
elev. Elevation
🅿 Post Office
🅷 Hospital
🅲 College
■ Principal Business Center
★ Ranally Metro Area (RMA) Abbreviation
Z Zip Code(s)
Ⓟ Previous Census Population
Ⓡ Revised Census Population
Ⓐ Annexation Population
● Rand McNally Population Estimate
Ⓒ Final Census Population
Ⓢ Special Census Population
◆ Estimated Population

For additional definitions see Glossary, Volume 1, and Introduction, Volume 2.

Drew; RMC Place; BERTIE; mail Windsor z 27983
Drewry; RMC Place; VANCE, WARREN; ***213** B-12; mail Manson z 27553; ● 110
Drexel; Inc. Place; BURKE; **212** E-3; elev. 1,184ft./361m.; 🄿; z 28619; Ⓟ 1,746; © 1,938
Drivers Store (White Oaks Acres); RMC Place; WILSON; ***213** E-14; mail Wilson z 27893; ● 230
Druid Hills; RMC Place; HENDERSON; ***212** F-1; mail Hendersonville z 28791; pop. incl. with Hendersonville (Inc. Place)
Drum Hill; RMC Place; GATES; ***213** B-17; mail Gates z 27937
Drums Crossroads; RMC Place; CATAWBA; ***212** E-5; elev. 1,064ft./324m.; ★ **HICK**; mail Catawba z 28609, Newton z 28658; ● 30
Dry Creek; RMC Place; MONTGOMERY; ***212** G-8; mail Candor z 27229; ● 70
Duan; RMC Place; CATAWBA; ***212** E-4; elev. 907ft./276m.; ★ **HICK**; mail Newton z 28658; pop. incl. with Maiden (Inc. Place)
Duart; RMC Place; BLADEN; ***213** H-11; mail Saint Pauls z 28384
Dublin; Inc. Place; BLADEN; **213** H-11; elev. 123ft./37m.; 🄿; z 28332; Ⓟ 246; © 250
Duck; Inc. Place; DARE; **213** C-20; 🄿; z 27949; incorporated May 1, 2002; not reported in 2000 Census; ● 500
Dudley; RMC Place; WAYNE; **213** F-13; elev. 188ft./57m.; 🄿; ★ **GLDS**; z 28333; ● 300
Dudley Heights; RMC Place; GUILFORD; ***212** D-8; ★ **GRNS-**; mail Greensboro z 27401; pop. incl. with Greensboro (Inc. Place)
Dudley Shoals; RMC Place; CALDWELL; ***212** D-4; ★ **HICK**; mail Granite Falls z 28630; ● 50
Duff Creek; RMC Place; DUPLIN; ***213** H-13; elev. 75ft./23m.; mail Teachey z 28464; rural
Duffies; RMC Place; HOKE; ***212** H-10; elev. 228ft./69m.; mail Red Springs z 28377; rural
Duke; RMC Place; DURHAM; ★ **DUR**; mail Durham z 27706, z 27708; pop. incl. with Durham (Inc. Place)
Duke Power Village; RMC Place; GASTON; ***212** F-5; elev. 700ft./213m.; ★ **CHRLT**; mail Mount Holly z 28120; rural
Dukes; RMC Place; NASH; ***213** D-13; elev. 280ft./85m.; mail Nashville z 27856; rural
Dulah; RMC Place; COLUMBUS; **213** K-12; elev. 54ft./16m.; mail Tabor City z 28463; ● 30
Dula Springs; RMC Place; BUNCOMBE; ***212** E-1; ★ **ASHE**; mail Weaverville z 28787; ● 190
Duncan; RMC Place; HARNETT; **213** E-11; elev. 468ft./143m.; mail Fuquay Varina z 27526; ● 480
Dundarrach; CDP; HOKE; **212** H-10; elev. 225ft./69m.; mail Shannon z 28386; © 62
Dunn; Inc. Place; HARNETT; **213** F-12; elev. 213ft./65m.; 🄿 🄷 ■; z 28334-35; Ⓟ 8,336; © 9,196; ◆ 10,263
Dunn Crossroads; RMC Place; WILSON; ***213** E-14; elev. 138ft./42m.; ★ **RKYMT**; mail Elm City z 27822; rural
Dunns Rock; RMC Place; TRANSYLVANIA; ***212** M-5; mail Brevard z 28712; rural
Dunns Store; RMC Place; HALIFAX; ***213** C-15; elev. 114ft./35m.; mail Scotland Neck z 27874; rural
Dunnsview Acres; RMC Place; ROWAN; ***212** E-7; elev. 800ft./244m.; ★ **SLSB**; mail Salisbury z 28146; ● 30
DUPLIN; **213** G-14; Ⓟ 39,995; © 49,063; ◆ 53,267
Dupree Crossroads; RMC Place; PITT; ***213** E-15; mail Fountain z 27829; rural
Durant (Durants Neck); RMC Place; PERQUIMANS; **213** C-18; elev. 9ft./3m.; mail Durants Neck z 27930, Hertford z 27944; ● 120
Durants Neck; PERQUIMANS; see Durant (RMC Place)
Durham; Inc. Place; ⊡ DURHAM, ORANGE, WAKE; **213** D-11; elev. 394ft./120m.; 🄿 🄷 🄲 21,416 ■; ★ **DUR**; z 27701-13, z 27715, z 27717, z 27722; Ⓟ 136,612; © 187,035; ◆ 250,172
DURHAM; **213** D-11; Ⓟ 181,835; © 223,314; ◆ 274,839
Dutchess Downs; RMC Place; JOHNSTON; ★ **RAL**; mail Garner z 27529
Dysartsville; RMC Place; MCDOWELL; **212** E-2; mail Nebo z 28761; ● 130

E

Eagle Mills; RMC Place; IREDELL; ***212** D-5; elev. 950ft./290m.; mail Hamptonville z 27020; rural
Eagle Rock; RMC Place; WAKE; **213** E-12; elev. 319ft./97m.; 🄿; ★ **RAL**; z 27591; ● 100
Eagle's Nest; RMC Place; CARTERET; ***213** H-17; elev. 15ft./5m.; mail Newport z 28570; ● 100
Eagle Springs; RMC Place; MOORE; **212** F-9; elev. 653ft./199m.; 🄿; z 27242; ● 350
Eagletown; RMC Place; NORTHAMPTON; ***213** C-16; elev. 73ft./22m.; mail Rich Square z 27869; ● 30
Earl; Inc. Place; CLEVELAND; **212** G-3; elev. 848ft./258m.; 🄿; z 28038; Ⓟ 230; © 234
Earley; RMC Place; HERTFORD; ***213** C-16; mail Ahoskie z 27910
Earpsboro; RMC Place; JOHNSTON; ***213** E-13; elev. 305ft./93m.; mail Zebulon z 27597; rural
Easonburg (Easons Store); RMC Place; NASH; ***213** D-14; ★ **RKYMT**; mail Rocky Mount z 27801; rural
Easons Crossroads; RMC Place; GATES; ***213** B-17; mail Gatesville z 27938; rural
Easons Store; NASH; see Easonburg (RMC Place)
East Arcadia; Inc. Place; BLADEN; **213** I-13; elev. 65ft./20m.; mail Riegelwood z 28456; Ⓟ 468; © 524
East Bend; Inc. Place; YADKIN; **212** C-6; elev. 1,069ft./326m.; 🄿; ★ **WNS**; z 27018; Ⓟ 619; © 659
Eastbrook; RMC Place; ROWAN; ***212** E-7; elev. 800ft./244m.; ★ **SLSB**; mail Salisbury z 28146; ● 80
East Carolina University; RMC Place; PITT; ★ **GRNV**; mail Greenville z 27834-35; pop. incl. with Greenville (Inc. Place)
East Charlotte; RMC Place; MECKLENBURG; ★ **CHRLT**; pop. incl. with Charlotte (Inc. Place)
Eastcrest Ridge; RMC Place; CABARRUS; ***212** F-6; elev. 650ft./198m.; ★ **CHRLT**; mail Concord z 28025; rural
East Durham; RMC Place; DURHAM; ***213** D-11; ★ **DUR**; mail Durham z 27701, z 27703, z 27706; pop. incl. with Durham (Inc. Place)
Eastern Cherokee Reservation; Indian Reservation; SWAIN, CHEROKEE, GRAHAM, HAYWOOD, JACKSON; mail Cherokee z 28719; also location of Indian Agency; Ⓟ 5,717; © 8,092
East Fayetteville; RMC Place; CUMBERLAND; **213** M-16; elev. 90ft./27m.; 🄿; ★ **FAY**; z 28301; pop. incl. with Fayetteville (Inc. Place)
East Flat Rock; CDP; HENDERSON; **212** F-1; elev. 2,207ft./673m.; 🄿; z 28726; Ⓟ 3,218; © 4,151; Ⓡ 4,122
East Franklin; RMC Place; MACON; ***212** M-3; mail Franklin z 28734
East Lake; RMC Place; DARE; **213** D-19; elev. 2ft./1m.; 🄿; z 27953; ● 100
East Laport; RMC Place; JACKSON; **212** M-4; mail Cullowhee z 28723; ● 100
East Laurinburg; Inc. Place; SCOTLAND; ***212** H-9; elev. 220ft./67m.; mail Laurinburg z 28352; Ⓟ 302; © 295
East Lumberton; RMC Place; ROBESON; ***213** I-11; mail Lumberton z 28358; pop. incl. with Lumberton (Inc. Place)
East Marion; RMC Place; MCDOWELL; ***212** E-2; mail Marion z 28752; pop. incl. with Marion (Inc. Place)
East Monbo; RMC Place; IREDELL; ***212** E-5; elev. 886ft./270m.; ★ **HICK**; mail Statesville z 28677; rural
Easton; RMC Place; FORSYTH; ***212** D-7; elev. 923ft./281m.; ★ **WNS**; mail Winston Salem z 27107; pop. incl. with Winston-Salem (Inc. Place)
Eastover; Inc. Place; CUMBERLAND; **213** G-11; ★ **FAY**; incorporated July 26, 2007; not reported in 2000 Census; ● 3,400
Eastover; CDP-Census Area Only; CUMBERLAND; **213** G-11; 🄿; ★ **FAY**; z 28312 & mail Fayetteville z 28301; Ⓟ 1,243; © 1,376
Eastover; RMC Place; MECKLENBURG; ★ **CHRLT**; mail Charlotte z 28207; pop. incl. with Charlotte (Inc. Place)
Eastridge; RMC Place; GASTON; ***212** F-4; ★ **CHRLT**; mail Gastonia z 28054; pop. incl. with Gastonia (Inc. Place)
East Rockingham; CDP; RICHMOND; ***212** H-8; mail Rockingham z 28379; Ⓟ 4,158; © 3,885
East Rocky Mount; RMC Place; EDGECOMBE; ★ **RKYMT**; mail Rocky Mount z 27801; pop. incl. with Rocky Mount (Inc. Place)
East Side Park; RMC Place; RICHMOND; ***212** G-8; mail Rockingham z 28379; pop. incl. with Rockingham (Inc. Place)
East Side Park; RMC Place; ROBESON; ***212** I-10; mail Fairmont z 28340; ● 270
East Spencer; Inc. Place; ROWAN; **212** E-7; elev. 747ft./228m.; 🄿; ★ **SLSB**; z 28039; Ⓟ 2,055; © 1,755
East Tabor; RMC Place; COLUMBUS; ***213** J-11; elev. 91ft./28m.; mail Tabor City z 28463; pop. incl. with Tabor City (Inc. Place)
Eastway; RMC Place; MECKLENBURG; ★ **CHRLT**; mail Charlotte z 28205, z 28218; pop. incl. with Charlotte (Inc. Place)
East Wilmington; RMC Place; NEW HANOVER; ***213** J-14; ★ **WILM**; mail Wilmington z 28405; pop. incl. with Wilmington (Inc. Place)
Eastwood; RMC Place; MOORE; **212** F-9; mail Carthage z 28327; ● 30
Ebenezer; RMC Place; CHEROKEE; ***212** M-1; mail Murphy z 28906; rural
Echo; RMC Place; ROBESON; ***212** I-10; elev. 145ft./44m.; mail Rowland z 28383; rural
Echo Heights; RMC Place; WAKE; ***213** E-12; ★ **RAL**; mail Raleigh z 27603; ● 1,100
Eck Reece; RMC Place; YADKIN; ***212** C-5; mail Jonesville z 28642; ● 180
Eden; Inc. Place; ROCKINGHAM; **212** B-8; elev. 589ft./180m.; 🄿 🄷 ■; ★ **MRTNV**; z 27288-89; Ⓟ 15,238; © 15,908; ◆ 15,878
Edenhouse; RMC Place; BERTIE; ***213** D-17; mail Merry Hill z 27957; ● 60
Edenton; Inc. Place; ⊡ CHOWAN; **213** C-17; 🄿 🄷; z 27932; Ⓟ 5,268; © 5,394; Ⓡ 5,058
Edgar; RMC Place; RANDOLPH; ***212** D-8; ★ **GRNS-**; mail Sophia z 27350; rural
EDGECOMBE; **213** D-14; Ⓟ 56,558; © 55,606; ◆ 51,507
Edgemont; RMC Place; CALDWELL; **212** D-3; elev. 1,800ft./549m.; mail Collettsville z 28611, Lenoir z 28645; ● 50
Edgewood Acres; RMC Place; GASTON; ***212** F-4; ★ **CHRLT**; mail Bessemer City z 28016; pop. incl. with Gastonia (Inc. Place)
Edmonds; RMC Place; ALLEGHANY; **212** B-5; mail Ennice z 28623; ● 80
Edneyville; RMC Place; HENDERSON; **212** F-1; elev. 2,246ft./685m.; 🄿; z 28727; ● 400
Edward; RMC Place; BEAUFORT; **213** F-17; elev. 36ft./11m.; 🄿; z 27821; ● 300
Edwards Crossroads; RMC Place; ALLEGHANY; ***212** B-5; mail Sparta z 28675; ● 60
Edwards Crossroads; RMC Place; NASH; ***213** D-13; elev. 291ft./89m.; mail Spring Hope z 27882; rural
Edwards Crossroads; RMC Place; NORTHAMPTON; ***213** B-15; elev. 88ft./27m.; mail Conway z 27820; rural
Edwards Fork; RMC Place; HALIFAX; ***213** C-15; elev. 96ft./29m.; mail Scotland Neck z 27874; rural
Efland; RMC Place; ORANGE; ***212** D-10; elev. 658ft./201m.; 🄿; ★ **DUR**; z 27243; ● 1,050
Ela; RMC Place; SWAIN; **212** L-3; elev. 1,792ft./546m.; mail Bryson City z 28713; ● 260
Elams; RMC Place; WARREN; ***213** B-13; elev. 310ft./94m.; mail Ebony z 23845; rural
Elberon; RMC Place; WARREN; ***213** C-13; elev. 396ft./121m.; mail Warrenton z 27589; ● 30
Eldorado; RMC Place; MONTGOMERY; **212** F-8; elev. 517ft./158m.; mail Troy z 27371; ● 150
Eleanors Crossroads; RMC Place; GATES; ***213** B-17; mail Gates z 27937; rural
Eleazer; RMC Place; RANDOLPH; ***212** F-8; mail Troy z 27371; rural
Elf; RMC Place; CLAY; ***212** M-2; mail Hayesville z 28904; ● 100
Eli Whitney; RMC Place; ALAMANCE; **212** D-10; mail Graham z 27253; ● 50
Elizabeth; RMC Place; MECKLENBURG; ★ **CHRLT**; mail Charlotte z 28204; pop. incl. with Charlotte (Inc. Place)
Elizabeth City; Inc. Place; ⊡ PASQUOTANK, CAMDEN; **213** C-18; 🄿 🄷 🄲 2,681 ■; z 27906-07, z 27909; Ⓟ 14,292; © 17,188; Ⓡ 17,243; ◆ 21,013
Elizabeth Heights; RMC Place; WILSON; ***213** E-14; mail Wilson z 27896; ● 120
Elizabethtown; Inc. Place; ⊡ BLADEN; **213** I-12; elev. 85ft./26m.; 🄿 🄷; z 28337; Ⓟ 3,704; © 3,698
Elkin; Inc. Place; SURRY, WILKES; **212** C-5; elev. 908ft./277m.; 🄿 🄷; z 28621; Ⓟ 3,790; © 4,109
Elkin Valley; SURRY; see North Elkin (RMC Place)
Elkland; ASHE, WATAUGA; see Todd (RMC Place)
Elk Mountain; RMC Place; BUNCOMBE; ***212** E-1; ★ **ASHE**; mail Asheville z 28804; pop. incl. with Woodfin (Inc. Place)
Elk Park; Inc. Place; AVERY; **212** C-2; elev. 3,182ft./970m.; 🄿; z 28622; Ⓟ 486; © 459
Elk Valley; RMC Place; AVERY; ***212** C-2; mail Banner Elk z 28604; rural
Ellenboro; Inc. Place; RUTHERFORD; **212** F-3; elev. 1,046ft./319m.; 🄿; z 28040; Ⓟ 514; © 479
Ellendale; RMC Place; ALEXANDER; ***212** D-4; ★ **HICK**; mail Taylorsville z 28681; ● 30
Ellendale; RMC Place; WAKE; ***213** E-12; ★ **RAL**; mail Knightdale z 27545; ● 140
Eller; DAVIDSON; see Midway (Inc. Place)
Ellerbe; Inc. Place; RICHMOND; **212** G-8; elev. 540ft./165m.; 🄿; z 28338; Ⓟ 1,132; © 1,021
Ellerbe Grove; RMC Place; RICHMOND; ***212** H-8; elev. 329ft./100m.; mail Rockingham z 28379; rural
Ellijay; RMC Place; MACON; ***212** M-3; mail Franklin z 28734; rural
Elliott; RMC Place; SAMPSON; ***213** G-13; elev. 136ft./41m.; mail Turkey z 28393
Ellisboro (Huntsville); RMC Place; ROCKINGHAM; ***212** C-8; ★ **GRNS-**; mail Madison z 27025; ● 50
Ellis Crossroads; RMC Place; ROWAN; ***212** E-6; ★ **SLSB**; mail Salisbury z 28144; ● 240
Ellis Store; RMC Place; BERTIE; ***213** D-17; mail Windsor z 27983
Elm City; Inc. Place; WILSON; **213** D-14; elev. 143ft./44m.; 🄿; ★ **RKYMT**; z 27822; Ⓟ 1,624; © 1,165; Ⓡ 1,412
Elm Grove; RMC Place; BERTIE; ***213** C-16; elev. 59ft./18m.; mail Colerain z 27924; ● 60
Elm Grove; RMC Place; LENOIR; ***213** G-15; mail Kinston z 28504; rural
Elmore; RMC Place; SCOTLAND; ***212** H-9; mail Laurinburg z 28352; rural
Elmores Crossroads; RMC Place; GASTON; ***212** G-5; elev. 757ft./231m.; ★ **CHRLT**; mail Belmont z 28012, Gastonia z 28054; ● 50
Elmwood; RMC Place; IREDELL; ***212** E-6; elev. 838ft./255m.; mail Statesville z 28625, z 28677
Elon (Elon College); Inc. Place; ALAMANCE; **212** D-9; elev. 710ft./216m.; 🄿 🄲 5,230; ★ **BUR**; z 27244; Ⓟ 4,394; © 6,738; Ⓡ 6,748
Elon College; ALAMANCE; see Elon (Inc. Place)
Elrod (Fairmont Junction); CDP; ROBESON; ***212** I-10; mail Rowland z 28383; © 441
Elroy; CDP; WAYNE; ***213** F-14; ★ **GLDS**; mail Goldsboro z 27534; Ⓟ 4,028; © 3,896; Ⓡ 3,848
Embro; RMC Place; WARREN; ***213** B-13; elev. 387ft./118m.; mail Macon z 27551; rural
Emerald Gardens; RMC Place; CUMBERLAND; ***213** G-11; elev. 200ft./61m.; ★ **FAY**; mail Fayetteville z 28304; ● 670
Emerald Isle; Inc. Place; CARTERET; ***213** H-16; 🄿; ★ **JAX**; z 28594; Ⓟ 2,434; © 3,488
Emerald Village; RMC Place; WAKE; ***213** E-12; ★ **RAL**; mail Raleigh z 27610; ● 180
Emerson (Portersville); RMC Place; BLADEN; **213** J-11; elev. 104ft./32m.; mail Clarkton z 28433; ● 30
Emerson; RMC Place; COLUMBUS; ***213** J-11; elev. 105ft./32m.; mail Tabor City z 28463; ● 30
Emerywood; RMC Place; GUILFORD; ★ **GRNS-**; mail High Point z 27262; pop. incl. with High Point (Inc. Place)
Emit; RMC Place; JOHNSTON; ***213** E-13; elev. 286ft./87m.; mail Middlesex z 27557; rural
Emma; RMC Place; BUNCOMBE; **212** M-7; ★ **ASHE**; mail Asheville z 28806; ● 1,100
Enderly Park; RMC Place; MECKLENBURG; ★ **CHRLT**; mail Charlotte z 28208; pop. incl. with Charlotte (Inc. Place)
Endy; RMC Place; STANLY; ***212** F-7; elev. 450ft./137m.; mail Albemarle z 28001; ● 30
Enfield; Inc. Place; HALIFAX; **213** C-14; elev. 113ft./34m.; 🄿; z 27823; Ⓟ 3,082; © 2,347; Ⓡ 2,370
Engelhard; RMC Place; HYDE; **213** E-19; elev. 3ft./1m.; 🄿; z 27824; ● 600
Englewood; RMC Place; NASH; ★ **RKYMT**; mail Rocky Mount z 27801; pop. incl. with Rocky Mount (Inc. Place)
English Woods; RMC Place; CABARRUS; ***212** F-6; elev. 550ft./168m.; ★ **CHRLT**; mail Concord z 28025; ● 30
Enka; RMC Place; BUNCOMBE; **212** L-5; elev. 2,059ft./628m.; 🄿; ★ **ASHE**; z 28728; pop. incl. with Asheville (Inc. Place)
Enka Village; RMC Place; BUNCOMBE; ***212** E-1; ★ **ASHE**; mail Enka z 28728
Ennice; RMC Place; ALLEGHANY; **212** B-5; elev. 2,538ft./774m.; 🄿; z 28623; ● 60
Eno; RMC Place; ORANGE; ***212** D-10; ★ **DUR**; mail Hillsborough z 27278; rural
Enochville; CDP; ROWAN; ***212** E-6; elev. 847ft./258m.; ★ **CHRLT**; mail China Grove z 28023; Ⓟ 2,901; © 2,851
Enola; RMC Place; BURKE; **212** E-3; mail Morganton z 28655; ● 50
Enon; RMC Place; YADKIN; ***212** C-6; elev. 879ft./268m.; mail East Bend z 27018
Eno Valley; RMC Place; DURHAM; 🄿; ★ **DUR**; z 27712 & mail Durham z 27722; pop. incl. with Durham (Inc. Place)
Enterprise; RMC Place; DAVIDSON; ***212** D-7; elev. 845ft./258m.; ★ **WNS**; mail Lexington z 27292, z 27295; rural
Enterprise; RMC Place; WARREN; **214** I-8; elev. 353ft./108m.; mail Littleton z 27850; ● 70
Ephesus; RMC Place; DAVIE; ***212** D-6; elev. 814ft./248m.; ★ **SLSB**; mail Mocksville z 27028; rural
Epsom; RMC Place; FRANKLIN, VANCE; **213** C-12; mail Henderson z 27536-37; ● 130
Erastus; RMC Place; JACKSON; ***212** M-4; mail Cullowhee z 28723; ● 30
Erect; RMC Place; RANDOLPH; ***212** E-9; elev. 528ft./161m.; mail Seagrove z 27341; rural
Ernul; RMC Place; CRAVEN; **213** F-16; elev. 20ft./6m.; 🄿; z 28527; ● 250
Ervintown; RMC Place; ONSLOW; ***213** H-15; ★ **JAX**; mail Richlands z 28574; ● 50
Erwin; Inc. Place; HARNETT; **213** F-11; elev. 200ft./61m.; 🄿 🄷; ★ **RAL**; z 28339; Ⓟ 4,061; © 4,537
Erwin Heights; RMC Place; DAVIDSON; ***212** D-7; ★ **GRNS-**; mail Thomasville z 27360; pop. incl. with Thomasville (Inc. Place)
Essex; RMC Place; HALIFAX; ***213** C-13; elev. 274ft./84m.; mail Hollister z 27844
Estatoe; RMC Place; MITCHELL; **212** D-2; mail Spruce Pine z 28777; ● 30
Estelle; RMC Place; CASWELL; ***212** B-10; elev. 566ft./173m.; mail Milton z 27305; ● 30
Ether; RMC Place; MONTGOMERY; **212** F-8; elev. 622ft./190m.; 🄿; z 27247; ● 320
Etowah; CDP; HENDERSON; **212** F-1; 🄿; ★ **ASHE**; z 28729; Ⓟ 1,997; © 2,766
Eubanks; RMC Place; ORANGE; ***212** D-10; elev. 490ft./149m.; ★ **DUR**; mail Chapel Hill z 27516; rural
Eufola; RMC Place; IREDELL; ***212** E-5; ★ **HICK**; mail Statesville z 28677; rural
Eure; RMC Place; GATES; **213** B-17; elev. 20ft./6m.; 🄿; z 27935; ● 240
Eureka; Inc. Place; WAYNE; **213** E-14; elev. 126ft./38m.; 🄿; z 27830; Ⓟ 282; © 244
Eureka Springs; RMC Place; CUMBERLAND; ***213** G-11; elev. 260ft./79m.; ★ **FAY**; mail Fayetteville z 28301; ● 2,910
Evansdale; RMC Place; WILSON; ***213** E-14; elev. 119ft./36m.; mail Wilson z 27893; ● 80
Everetts; Inc. Place; MARTIN; **213** D-16; elev. 66ft./20m.; 🄿; z 27825; Ⓟ 143; © 179
Everetts Crossroads; RMC Place; BEAUFORT; ***213** E-17; mail Pinetown z 27865; ● 60
Evergreen; RMC Place; BEAUFORT; ***213** E-16; elev. 34ft./10m.; mail Chocowinity z 27817; pop. incl. with Chocowinity (Inc. Place)
Evergreen; RMC Place; COLUMBUS; **213** I-11; elev. 50ft./15m.; 🄿; z 28438; ● 420
Evergreen Estates; RMC Place; CUMBERLAND; ***213** G-11; elev. 200ft./61m.; ★ **FAY**; mail Fayetteville z 28304; pop. incl. with Fayetteville (Inc. Place)
Exmoor; RMC Place; MECKLENBURG; ★ **CHRLT**; pop. incl. with Charlotte (Inc. Place)
Exum; RMC Place; BRUNSWICK; ***213** J-12; mail Ash z 28420
Exway; RMC Place; MONTGOMERY, RICHMOND; ***212** G-8; mail Mount Gilead z 27306; ● 40

F

Fair Bluff; Inc. Place; COLUMBUS; **212** J-10; elev. 67ft./20m.; 🄿; z 28439; Ⓟ 1,068; © 1,181
Fairfield; RMC Place; HYDE; **213** E-18; elev. 4ft./1m.; 🄿; z 27826; ● 400
Fairfield; RMC Place; UNION; ***212** G-7; elev. 528ft./161m.; mail Marshville z 28103; ● 30
Fairfield; RMC Place; WILSON; ***213** E-14; elev. 108ft./33m.; mail Wilson z 27893; rural
Fairfield Harbour; CDP; CRAVEN; ***213** G-16; elev. 10ft./3m.; mail New Bern z 28560; © 1,983
Fair Field Heights; RMC Place; CLEVELAND; ***212** F-3; elev. 860ft./262m.; mail Shelby z 28152; pop. incl. with Shelby (Inc. Place)
Fairfield Sapphire Valley; RMC Place; JACKSON; ***212** M-4; mail Sapphire z 28774; ● 160
Fair Grove; RMC Place; DAVIDSON; **212** D-7; ★ **GRNS-**; mail Thomasville z 27360; ● 1,680
Fairlane; RMC Place; CUMBERLAND; ***213** G-11; elev. 250ft./76m.; ★ **FAY**; mail Fayetteville z 28303; pop. incl. with Fayetteville (Inc. Place)
Fairmont; Inc. Place; ROBESON; **212** I-10; elev. 125ft./38m.; 🄿; z 28340; Ⓟ 2,489; © 2,604
Fairmont Junction; ROBESON; see Elrod (CDP)
Fairplains; CDP; WILKES; **212** C-4; mail North Wilkesboro z 28659; Ⓟ 2,339; © 2,051
Fairport; RMC Place; GRANVILLE; ***213** C-12; elev. 35ft./11m.; mail Kittrell z 27544; ● 30
Fairview; CDP; BUNCOMBE; **212** E-1; elev. 2,280ft./695m.; 🄿; ★ **ASHE**; z 28730; Ⓟ 1,830; © 2,495
Fairview; RMC Place; ROCKINGHAM; ***212** B-8; elev. 760ft./232m.; ★ **MRTNV**; mail Eden z 27288; rural
Fairview (Fairview Crossroads); RMC Place; SURRY; ***212** C-6; mail Dobson z 27017
Fairview; Inc. Place; UNION; ***212** G-6; elev. 537ft./164m.; ★ **CHRLT**; mail Monroe z 28110; incorporated October 4, 2001; not reported in 2000 Census; ● 3,600
Fairview Crossroads; SURRY; see Fairview (RMC Place)
Fairview Park; RMC Place; ALEXANDER; ***212** D-5; elev. 1,181ft./360m.; mail Hiddenite z 28636; ● 60
Fairway Acres; RMC Place; WAKE; ***213** E-11; ★ **RAL**; pop. incl. with Raleigh (Inc. Place)
Fairway Heights; RMC Place; CLEVELAND; ***212** F-3; elev. 900ft./274m.; mail Shelby z 28150; pop. incl. with Shelby (Inc. Place)
Fairway Hills; RMC Place; HAYWOOD; ***212** L-4; ★ **ASHE**; mail Waynesville z 28786; ● 120
Faison; Inc. Place; DUPLIN; **213** G-13; elev. 166ft./51m.; 🄿; z 28341; Ⓟ 701; © 744
Faisons; RMC Place; NORTHAMPTON; ***213** B-15; elev. 128ft./39m.; mail Seaboard z 27876; ● 80
Faith; Inc. Place; ROWAN; **212** E-6; elev. 860ft./262m.; 🄿; ★ **SLSB**; z 28041; Ⓟ 553; © 695
Falcon; Inc. Place; CUMBERLAND, SAMPSON; **213** G-12; elev. 143ft./44m.; 🄿; z 28342; Ⓟ 216; © 328; Ⓡ 343
Falkland; Inc. Place; PITT; **213** E-15; elev. 76ft./23m.; 🄿; z 27827; Ⓟ 108; © 112
Fall Creek; YADKIN; see Smithtown (RMC Place)
Falling Creek; RMC Place; LENOIR; ***213** F-14; elev. 52ft./16m.; mail Kinston z 28504; rural
Falling Creek Estates; RMC Place; CATAWBA; ***212** E-4; ★ **HICK**; mail Hickory z 28601; pop. incl. with Hickory (Inc. Place)
Falls; RMC Place; WAKE; **214** A-7; ★ **RAL**; mail Raleigh z 27609; ● 110
Fallston; Inc. Place; CLEVELAND; **212** F-3; elev. 1,020ft./311m.; 🄿; z 28042; Ⓟ 498; © 603
Far Away Place; RMC Place; CABARRUS; ***212** F-6; elev. 691ft./211m.; ★ **CHRLT**; mail Concord z 28025; ● 100
Farmer; RMC Place; RANDOLPH; **212** E-8; elev. 545ft./166m.; mail Asheboro z 27205; ● 50
Farmington; RMC Place; DAVIE; **212** D-6; elev. 788ft./240m.; ★ **WNS**; mail Mocksville z 27028; ● 300
Farmville; RMC Place; CHATHAM; ***212** E-10; elev. 280ft./85m.; mail Sanford z 27330; rural
Farmville; Inc. Place; PITT; **213** E-15; elev. 83ft./25m.; 🄿; ★ **GRNV**; z 27828; Ⓟ 4,392; © 4,302; Ⓡ 4,421
Faro; RMC Place; WAYNE; ***213** E-14; elev. 122ft./37m.; mail Stantonsburg z 27883; rural
Farrington; RMC Place; CHATHAM; **212** D-10; elev. 250ft./76m.; ★ **DUR**; mail Chapel Hill z 27517; ● 70
Faust; RMC Place; MADISON; ***212** D-1; elev. 3,108ft./947m.; mail Mars Hill z 28754
Fayblock; RMC Place; CUMBERLAND; ★ **FAY**; mail Fayetteville z 28301; pop. incl. with Fayetteville (Inc. Place)
Fayetteville; Inc. Place; ⊡ CUMBERLAND; **213** G-11; 🄿 🄷 🄲 7,741 ■; ★ **FAY**; z 28301-09, z 28311-12, z 28314 & mail Fort Bragg z 28310; Ⓟ 75,695; © 121,015; ◆ 137,703
Fayetteville North; RMC Place; CUMBERLAND; ★ **FAY**; mail Fayetteville z 28311; pop. incl. with Fayetteville (Inc. Place)
Fearrington (Fearrington Village); CDP-Census Area Only; CHATHAM; **214** D-1; elev. 400ft./122m.; 🄿; ★ **DUR**; z 27312; Ⓟ 1,101; © 903
Fearrington Post; RMC Place; CHATHAM; ***212** E-10; elev. 500ft./152m.; ★ **DUR**; mail Pittsboro z 27312; ● 350
Fearrington Village; CHATHAM; see Fearrington (CDP-Census Area Only)
Federal Building; RMC Place; PASQUOTANK; mail Elizabeth City z 27909; pop. incl. with Elizabeth City (Inc. Place)
Feezor; RMC Place; DAVIDSON; **212** E-7; mail Lexington z 27292; ● 110
Feltonville; RMC Place; WAKE; ***213** E-11; elev. 399ft./122m.; ★ **RAL**; mail Apex z 27539; pop. incl. with Holly Springs (Inc. Place)
Ferguson; RMC Place; WILKES; **212** D-4; elev. 1,080ft./329m.; 🄿; z 28624; ● 170
Ferncliff Estates; RMC Place; CABARRUS; ***212** F-6; elev. 699ft./213m.; ★ **CHRLT**; mail Harrisburg z 28075; ● 30
Fibreville; RMC Place; HAYWOOD; ★ **ASHE**; mail Canton z 28716; pop. incl. with Canton (Inc. Place)
Fields; RMC Place; LENOIR; ***213** F-14; elev. 109ft./33m.; ★ **GLDS**; mail La Grange z 28551; rural
Fillmore; RMC Place; WILSON; ***213** E-13; elev. 146ft./45m.; mail Wilson z 27893; rural
Fines Creek; RMC Place; HAYWOOD; ***212** K-4; mail Clyde z 28721; ● 50
Finger; RMC Place; STANLY; ***212** F-7; mail Mount Pleasant z 28124
Fires Creek; RMC Place; CLAY; ***212** M-2; elev. 1,770ft./539m.; mail Hayesville z 28904; ● 30
First Union; RMC Place; MECKLENBURG; ★ **CHRLT**; mail Charlotte z 28202; pop. incl. with Charlotte (Inc. Place)
Fisher Park; RMC Place; GUILFORD; ***212** D-8; ★ **GRNS-**; mail Greensboro z 27401; pop. incl. with Greensboro (Inc. Place)
Fisher Town; RMC Place; CABARRUS; ***212** F-6; ★ **CHRLT**; mail Concord z 28025, Kannapolis z 28081; ● 600
Fitch; RMC Place; CASWELL; ***212** C-9; elev. 655ft./200m.; mail Yanceyville z 27379
Five Forks; RMC Place; PERSON; ***212** B-10; mail Roxboro z 27573; rural
Five Forks; RMC Place; ROWAN; ***212** E-6; elev. 850ft./259m.; ★ **CHRLT**; mail China Grove z 28023; ● 200
Five Forks; RMC Place; WARREN; ***213** B-13; elev. 298ft./91m.; mail Macon z 27551; rural
Five Point; RMC Place; WAKE; ★ **RAL**; mail Raleigh z 27608, z 27628; pop. incl. with Raleigh (Inc. Place)
Five Points (Jessama); RMC Place; BEAUFORT; ***213** E-17; mail Washington z 27889; ● 50
Five Points; RMC Place; COLUMBUS; ***213** J-11; elev. 100ft./30m.; mail Chadbourn z 28431; ● 80
Five Points; CDP; HOKE; ***212** G-10; elev. 353ft./108m.; mail Raeford z 28376; © 306
Five Points; RMC Place; RICHMOND; ***212** H-8; elev. 311ft./95m.; mail Rockingham z 28379
Flat Branch; RMC Place; GATES; ***213** B-17; mail Gatesville z 27938; rural
Flat Branch; RMC Place; HARNETT; ***213** F-11; elev. 249ft./76m.; mail Bunnlevel z 28323, Lillington z 27546; ● 30
Flat Creek; RMC Place; BUNCOMBE; ***212** E-1; elev. 2,204ft./672m.; ★ **ASHE**; mail Weaverville z 28787
Flat Rock; Inc. Place; HENDERSON; **212** F-1; elev. 2,217ft./676m.; 🄿; z 28731; Ⓟ 1,619; © 2,565
Flat Rock; RMC Place; STOKES; ***212** C-7; elev. 1,185ft./361m.; ★ **WNS**; mail Pinnacle z 27043; ● 30
Flat Rock; CDP; SURRY; ***212** B-6; mail Mount Airy z 27030; Ⓟ 1,812; © 1,690
Flats; RMC Place; MACON; ***212** M-2; mail Topton z 28781; rural
Flat Shoals; RMC Place; STOKES; ***212** C-7; elev. 1,115ft./340m.; ★ **WNS**; mail Germanton z 27019; rural
Flat Springs; RMC Place; AVERY; ***212** C-2; mail Elk Park z 28622; rural
Flay; RMC Place; LINCOLN; **212** F-4; elev. 1,052ft./321m.; mail Cherryville z 28021; ● 50
Fleetwood; RMC Place; ASHE; **212** C-3; elev. 2,874ft./876m.; 🄿; z 28626; ● 220
Fleetwood Acres; RMC Place; GASTON; ***212** G-4; ★ **CHRLT**; mail Gastonia z 28052; ● 920
Fletcher; Inc. Place; HENDERSON; **212** F-1; elev. 2,100ft./640m.; 🄿 🄷; ★ **ASHE**; z 28732; Ⓟ 2,787; © 4,185
Flint Hill; RMC Place; MONTGOMERY; ***212** F-8; elev. 652ft./199m.; mail Troy z 27371; rural
Flint Hill; RMC Place; RANDOLPH; ***212** E-8; elev. 705ft./215m.; ★ **GRNS-**; mail Sophia z 27350
Flint Hill; RMC Place; YADKIN; ***212** C-6; elev. 932ft./284m.; ★ **WNS**; mail East Bend z 27018
Florence; RMC Place; PAMLICO; **213** G-17; mail Merritt z 28556; ● 170
Florence Town; RMC Place; ALAMANCE; ***212** D-10; ★ **BUR**; mail Mebane z 27302; rural
Flowes Store; RMC Place; CABARRUS; ***212** F-6; elev. 678ft./207m.; ★ **CHRLT**; mail Concord z 28025; rural
Floytan Crossroads; RMC Place; VANCE; ***213** C-12; elev. 491ft./150m.; mail Henderson z 27536; rural
Folkstone; RMC Place; ONSLOW; **213** I-15; elev. 65ft./20m.; mail Holly Ridge z 28445; ● 100
Fontana Dam; GRAHAM; see Fontana Village (RMC Place)
Fontana Village (Fontana Dam); RMC Place; GRAHAM; **214** I-2; elev. 2,900ft./884m.; mail Fontana Dam z 28733; summer pop. 500; ● 80
Footsville; RMC Place; YADKIN; ***212** D-6; mail Yadkinville z 27055; rural
Forbes; RMC Place; MITCHELL; ***212** D-1; mail Bakersville z 28705; rural
Forestburg; RMC Place; PERQUIMANS; ***213** C-18; elev. 15ft./5m.; mail Hertford z 27944; rural
Forest City; Inc. Place; RUTHERFORD; **212** F-2; elev. 999ft./304m.; 🄿 ■; z 28043; Ⓟ 7,475; © 7,549; ◆ 7,178
Forest Hills; RMC Place; CUMBERLAND; ★ **FAY**; mail Fayetteville z 28303; pop. incl. with Fayetteville (Inc. Place)
Forest Hills; RMC Place; FORSYTH; ***212** C-7; ★ **WNS**; mail Winston Salem z 27105; pop. incl. with Winston-Salem (Inc. Place)
Forest Hills; RMC Place; GASTON; ★ **CHRLT**; mail Mount Holly z 28120
Forest Hills (Village of Forest Hills); Inc. Place; JACKSON; ***212** M-4; mail Cullowhee z 28723; © 330
Forest Hills; RMC Place; NEW HANOVER; ★ **WILM**; mail Wilmington z 28403; pop. incl. with Wilmington (Inc. Place)
Forest Hills; RMC Place; ROCKINGHAM; ***212** C-9; elev. 796ft./243m.; ★ **GRNS-**; mail Reidsville z 27320; pop. incl. with Reidsville (Inc. Place)
Forest Hills; RMC Place; WILKES; ***212** C-4; pop. incl. with Wilkesboro (Inc. Place)
Forest Oaks; CDP-Census Area Only; GUILFORD; ***212** D-9; elev. 750ft./229m.; ★ **GRNS-**; mail Greensboro z 27406; © 3,241
Forest Ridge; RMC Place; CLEVELAND; ***212** F-3; elev. 800ft./244m.; mail Shelby z 28152; ● 180
Forestville; RMC Place; ANSON; ***212** G-8; elev. 506ft./154m.; mail Lilesville z 28091; ● 100
Forestville; RMC Place; WAKE; **214** A-7; elev. 393ft./120m.; ★ **RAL**; mail Wake Forest z 27587; pop. incl. with Wake Forest (Inc. Place)
Fork Church; RMC Place; DAVIE; **212** D-6; mail Advance z 27006; ● 50
FORSYTH; **212** C-7; Ⓟ 265,878; © 306,067; ◆ 350,443
Fort Barnwell; RMC Place; CRAVEN; **213** F-15; mail Dover z 28526; ● 350
Fort Bragg; CDP-Census Area Only; CUMBERLAND; ***213** G-11; 🄿; ★ **FAY**; z 28307, z 28310; Ⓟ 34,744; © 29,183; ◆ 30,864
Fort Caswell; RMC Place; BRUNSWICK; ***213** K-13; elev. 9ft./3m.; mail Oak Island z 28465; ● 50
Fort Landing; RMC Place; TYRRELL; ***213** D-19; mail Columbia z 27925; rural
Fort Point; RMC Place; BEAUFORT; ***213** E-16; elev. 5ft./2m.; mail Chocowinity z 27817; ● 60
Foscoe; RMC Place; WATAUGA; ***212** C-3; mail Banner Elk z 28604, Boone z 28607; ● 200
Foster Creek; RMC Place; MADISON; ***212** D-1; elev. 2,375ft./724m.; mail Marshall z 28753; rural
Fountain; RMC Place; DUPLIN; **213** H-14; mail Chinquapin z 28521; ● 100
Fountain; Inc. Place; PITT; **213** E-14; elev. 110ft./34m.; 🄿; z 27829; Ⓟ 445; © 533
Fountain Fork; RMC Place; EDGECOMBE; ***213** D-15; elev. 21ft./6m.; mail Tarboro z 27886; ● 30
Fountain Hill; RMC Place; ANSON; **212** G-7; mail Peachland z 28133; ● 30
Four Oaks; Inc. Place; JOHNSTON; **213** F-12; elev. 211ft./64m.; 🄿; ★ **RAL**; z 27524; Ⓟ 1,308; © 1,424; Ⓡ 1,514
Four Seasons; RMC Place; HENDERSON; mail Hendersonville z 28792; pop. incl. with Hendersonville (Inc. Place)
Fourway; RMC Place; GREENE; ***213** F-15; mail Hookerton z 28538; rural
Foxcroft East; RMC Place; MECKLENBURG; mail Charlotte z 28226; pop. incl. with Charlotte (Inc. Place)
Fox Fire; RMC Place; CUMBERLAND; ***213** G-11; elev. 246ft./75m.; ★ **FAY**; mail Fayetteville z 28303; pop. incl. with Fayetteville (Inc. Place)
Foxfire; Inc. Place; MOORE; **212** G-9; mail Jackson Springs z 27281; Ⓟ 334; © 474
Foxlair; RMC Place; CARTERET; ***213** H-17; elev. 25ft./8m.; mail Newport z 28570; ● 100
Foxwood Acres; RMC Place; CABARRUS; ***212** F-6; elev. 549ft./167m.; ★ **CHRLT**; mail Concord z 28025; ● 60
Francisco; RMC Place; STOKES; ***212** B-7; elev. 1,159ft./353m.; mail Westfield z 27053
Francis Mill; RMC Place; BERTIE; ***213** C-16; elev. 66ft./20m.; mail Aulander z 27805; ● 30
Francktown; RMC Place; ONSLOW; ***213** H-15; ★ **JAX**; mail Richlands z 28574; ● 50
Frank; RMC Place; AVERY; ***212** D-2; elev. 3,200ft./975m.; 🄿; z 28657; ● 80
Franklin; Inc. Place; ⊡ MACON; **212** M-3; elev. 2,113ft./644m.; 🄿 🄷; z 28734, z 28744; Ⓟ 2,873; © 3,490
Franklin; RMC Place; ROWAN; **212** E-6; elev. 2,113ft./644m.; ★ **SLSB**; mail Salisbury z 28144; ● 340
FRANKLIN; **213** C-12; Ⓟ 36,414; © 47,260; ◆ 60,313
Franklin Grove; RMC Place; SWAIN; ***212** L-3; mail Bryson City z 28713; ● 160
Franklin Street; RMC Place; ORANGE; ★ **DUR**; mail Chapel Hill z 27514, z 27516; pop. incl. with Chapel Hill (Inc. Place)
Franklinton; Inc. Place; FRANKLIN; **213** C-12; elev. 432ft./132m.; 🄿; ★ **RAL**; z 27525; Ⓟ 1,615; © 1,745
Franklinville; Inc. Place; RANDOLPH; **212** E-9; elev. 500ft./152m.; 🄿; z 27248; Ⓟ 666; © 1,258
Frazier Crossroads; RMC Place; NASH; ***213** D-13; elev. 278ft./85m.; mail Middlesex z 27557; rural
Fraziers Crossroads; RMC Place; HERTFORD; ***213** C-16; mail Ahoskie z 27910; pop. incl. with Ahoskie (Inc. Place)
Frederick; RMC Place; BEAUFORT; **213** F-16; elev. 56ft./17m.; mail Chocowinity z 27817; ● 30
Freedom; RMC Place; MECKLENBURG; ★ **CHRLT**; mail Charlotte z 28208, z 28214, z 28216, z 28266; pop. incl. with Charlotte (Inc. Place)
Freeland; RMC Place; BRUNSWICK; **213** J-12; elev. 43ft./13m.; mail Ash z 28420; ● 60
Freeman; RMC Place; COLUMBUS; **213** J-13; mail Bolton z 28423; ● 150
Fremont; Inc. Place; WAYNE; **213** E-13; elev. 153ft./47m.; 🄿; z 27830; Ⓟ 1,710; © 1,463
Friendly Acres; RMC Place; CABARRUS; ***212** F-6; elev. 672ft./205m.; ★ **CHRLT**; mail Concord z 28027; ● 70
Friendship (Suit); RMC Place; CHEROKEE; ***212** M-1; elev. 1,781ft./543m.; mail Murphy z 28906; rural
Friendship; RMC Place; DUPLIN; ***213** G-13; elev. 148ft./45m.; mail Warsaw z 28398; rural
Friendship; RMC Place; GUILFORD; **212** D-8; ★ **GRNS-**; mail Greensboro z 27410; pop. incl. with Greensboro (Inc. Place)
Friendship; RMC Place; WAKE; ***213** E-11; elev. 390ft./119m.; mail Apex z 27539; rural
Friendship; RMC Place; YADKIN; ***212** C-6; elev. 1,011ft./308m.; mail East Bend z 27018; rural
Frisco; RMC Place; DARE; **213** F-20; elev. 10ft./3m.; 🄿; z 27936; ● 340
Frog Island; RMC Place; PASQUOTANK; ***213** C-19; elev. 1ft./0m.; mail Elizabeth City z 27909; rural
Frog Level; RMC Place; PITT; ***213** E-15; elev. 81ft./25m.; ★ **GRNV**; mail Greenville z 27834; ● 50
Frog Level (Oakland); RMC Place; RUTHERFORD; ***212** F-2; mail Forest City z 28043, Spindale z 28160; ● 210
Frog Pond; RMC Place; STANLY; ***212** F-7; elev. 474ft./144m.; mail Oakboro z 28129; ● 300
Frogsboro; RMC Place; CASWELL; ***212** C-10; elev. 643ft./196m.; mail Leasburg z 27291, Prospect Hill z 27314; rural
Fruitland; RMC Place; HENDERSON; ***212** F-1; elev. 2,217ft./676m.; mail Hendersonville z 28792; ● 170
Frying Pan Landing; RMC Place; TYRRELL; ***213** D-19; mail Columbia z 27925; rural
Fulchers Landing; RMC Place; ONSLOW; ***213** I-15; mail Sneads Ferry z 28460; ● 500
Fullers; RMC Place; RANDOLPH; ***212** D-8; ★ **GRNS-**; mail Thomasville z 27360; rural
Fulp; RMC Place; STOKES; ***212** C-7; ★ **WNS**; mail Walnut Cove z 27052; rural
Funston; RMC Place; BRUNSWICK; ***213** J-13; elev. 47ft./14m.; ★ **WILM**; mail Winnabow z 28479
Fuquay Springs; RMC Place; WAKE; ★ **RAL**; mail Fuquay Varina z 27526; pop. incl. with Fuquay-Varina (Inc. Place)
Fuquay-Varina; Inc. Place; WAKE; **213** E-11; elev. 426ft./130m.; 🄿; ★ **RAL**; z 27526; Ⓟ 4,562; © 7,898
Furches; RMC Place; ALLEGHANY; ***212** B-4; elev. 2,871ft./875m.; mail Laurel Springs z 28644; rural
Furnitureland; RMC Place; GUILFORD; ★ **GRNS-**; mail High Point z 27264; pop. incl. with High Point (Inc. Place)

G

Galatia; RMC Place; NORTHAMPTON; ***213** B-15; elev. 109ft./33m.; mail Seaboard z 27876; ● 50
Gales Creek; RMC Place; CARTERET; ***213** H-17; elev. 10ft./3m.; mail Newport z 28570; ● 150
Galloway Crossroads; RMC Place; PITT; ***213** E-15; elev. 59ft./18m.; ★ **GRNV**; mail Greenville z 27858; rural
Gallup Acres; RMC Place; CUMBERLAND; ***213** G-11; elev. 200ft./61m.; ★ **FAY**; mail Fayetteville z 28304; pop. incl. with Fayetteville (Inc. Place)
Gamble Hill; RMC Place; GASTON; ***212** F-4; ★ **CHRLT**; mail Bessemer City z 28016; ● 100
Gamewell; Inc. Place; CALDWELL; **212** D-3; elev. 1,058ft./322m.; mail Lenoir z 28645; Ⓟ 3,357; © 3,644; Ⓡ 3,721
Garden Homes; RMC Place; GUILFORD; ***212** C-8; ★ **GRNS-**; mail Greensboro z 27408; pop. incl. with Greensboro (Inc. Place)
Gardnerville; RMC Place; PITT; ***213** F-15; elev. 33ft./10m.; ★ **GRNV**; mail Ayden z 28513; rural
Garland; Inc. Place; SAMPSON; **213** H-12; elev. 137ft./42m.; 🄿; z 28441; Ⓟ 746; © 808
Garner; Inc. Place; WAKE; **213** E-12; elev. 370ft./113m.; 🄿; ★ **RAL**; z 27529; Ⓟ 14,967; © 17,757; Ⓡ 17,787; ◆ 25,669
Garysburg; Inc. Place; NORTHAMPTON; **213** B-15; elev. 140ft./43m.; 🄿; z 27831; Ⓟ 1,057; © 1,254
Gaston; Inc. Place; NORTHAMPTON; **213** B-14; elev. 180ft./55m.; 🄿; z 27832; Ⓟ 1,003; © 973
GASTON; **212** F-4; Ⓟ 175,093; © 190,365; Ⓡ 190,304; ◆ 207,989
Gastonia; Inc. Place; ⊡ GASTON; **212** F-4; elev. 816ft./249m.; 🄿 🄷 ■; ★ **CHRLT**; z 28052-56; Ⓟ 54,732; © 66,277; Ⓡ 66,355; ◆ 75,902
Gates; RMC Place; GATES; **213** B-17; elev. 73ft./22m.; 🄿; z 27937; ● 370
GATES; **213** B-17; Ⓟ 9,305; © 10,516; ◆ 12,258
Gates Four; RMC Place; CUMBERLAND; ★ **FAY**; mail Fayetteville z 28306
Gatesville; Inc. Place; ⊡ GATES; **213** B-17; 🄿; z 27938; Ⓟ 308; © 281
Gateway; RMC Place; JACKSON; ***212** L-3; mail Whittier z 28789; rural
Gatewood; RMC Place; CASWELL; ***212** B-9; elev. 600ft./183m.; ★ **DANV**; mail Providence z 27315; ● 90
Gause Landing; RMC Place; BRUNSWICK; **213** K-12; ★ **MYR.B**; mail Ocean Isle Beach z 28469; ● 60
Gay; RMC Place; JACKSON; ***212** M-3; elev. 2,270ft./692m.; mail Sylva z 28779; rural
Gaylord; RMC Place; BEAUFORT; **213** E-17; mail Bath z 27808; ● 120
Gaylord; RMC Place; BEAUFORT; ● 130
Gela; RMC Place; GRANVILLE; **213** B-12; mail Oxford z 27565; ● 500
Gentry Store; RMC Place; PERSON; ***213** B-11; mail Roxboro z 27574; rural
George (Woodland); RMC Place; NORTHAMPTON; **213** C-15; elev. 69ft./21m.; 🄿; z 27897; pop. incl. with Woodland (Inc. Place); ● 90
Georgetown; RMC Place; BUNCOMBE; ***212** K-5; ★ **ASHE**; mail Asheville z 28806; ● 190
Georgetown; RMC Place; DAVIDSON; ***212** D-7; elev. 923ft./281m.; ★ **WNS**; mail Kernersville z 27284; rural
Georgetown; RMC Place; LENOIR; ***213** F-15; elev. 79ft./24m.; mail Kinston z 28501
Georgeville; RMC Place; CABARRUS; ***212** F-6; ★ **CHRLT**; mail Concord z 28025
Germanton; RMC Place; STOKES; **212** C-7; elev. 900ft./274m.; 🄿; ★ **WNS**; z 27019; ● 250
Germantown; RMC Place; HYDE; ***213** F-18; mail Scranton z 27875; rural
Gerton; RMC Place; HENDERSON; ***212** F-1; elev. 2,676ft./816m.; 🄿; z 28735; ● 350
Gethsemane; RMC Place; EDGECOMBE; ***213** D-14; elev. 112ft./34m.; mail Whitakers z 27891
Gibson; Inc. Place; SCOTLAND; **212** H-9; elev. 250ft./76m.; 🄿; z 28343; Ⓟ 532; © 584
Gibsontown; RMC Place; HAYWOOD; ***212** L-5; ★ **ASHE**; mail Canton z 28716; ● 150
Gibsonville; Inc. Place; GUILFORD, ALAMANCE; **212** C-9; elev. 720ft./219m.; 🄿; ★ **BUR**; z 27249; Ⓟ 3,441; © 4,372; Ⓡ 4,418
Giddensville; RMC Place; SAMPSON; ***213** G-13; elev. 172ft./52m.; mail Faison z 28341; rural
Gilkey; RMC Place; RUTHERFORD; **212** F-2; elev. 108ft./33m.; mail Rutherfordton z 28139; ● 190
Gill; RMC Place; VANCE; ***213** C-12; mail Henderson z 27536
Gillburg; RMC Place; VANCE; **213** C-12; elev. 481ft./147m.; mail Henderson z 27537; ● 80
Glade Valley; RMC Place; ALLEGHANY; **212** B-5; elev. 2,770ft./844m.; 🄿; z 28627; ● 150
Glady; RMC Place; BUNCOMBE; ***212** L-5; ★ **ASHE**; mail Candler z 28715; rural
Glass; RMC Place; CABARRUS; ***212** F-6; ★ **CHRLT**; mail Kannapolis z 28081; pop. incl. with Kannapolis (Inc. Place)
Glen Alpine; Inc. Place; BURKE; **212** E-3; elev. 1,206ft./368m.; 🄿; z 28628; Ⓟ 563; © 1,090
Glen Ayre; RMC Place; MITCHELL; **212** D-2; mail Bakersville z 28705; ● 60
Glenbrook; RMC Place; CUMBERLAND; ***213** G-11; elev. 200ft./61m.; ★ **FAY**; mail Fayetteville z 28304; pop. incl. with Fayetteville (Inc. Place)
Glenburnie Gardens; CRAVEN; see Oaks (RMC Place)
Glencoe; RMC Place; ALAMANCE; ***212** C-9; ★ **BUR**; mail Burlington z 27217; ● 30
Glen Cove; RMC Place; PASQUOTANK; ***213** C-19; elev. 1ft./0m.; mail Elizabeth City z 27909; ● 50
Glendale Acres; RMC Place; CUMBERLAND; ★ **FAY**; mail Fayetteville z 28304; pop. incl. with Fayetteville (Inc. Place)
Glendale Springs; RMC Place; ASHE; **212** C-4; elev. 3,060ft./933m.; 🄿; z 28629; ● 250
Glendon; RMC Place; MOORE; **212** F-9; elev. 303ft./92m.; 🄿; z 27325; ● 200
Glen Forest; RMC Place; WAKE; ★ **RAL**; pop. incl. with Raleigh (Inc. Place)
Glenhaven; RMC Place; CUMBERLAND; ***213** G-11; elev. 200ft./61m.; ★ **FAY**; mail Fayetteville z 28304; pop. incl. with Fayetteville (Inc. Place)
Glen Lennox; RMC Place; ORANGE; ***212** D-10; ★ **DUR**; mail Chapel Hill z 27517; pop. incl. with Chapel Hill (Inc. Place)
Glenn; RMC Place; ORANGE; ***212** D-10; ★ **DUR**; mail Durham z 27705; rural
Glenola; RMC Place; RANDOLPH; **212** D-8; ★ **GRNS-**; mail High Point z 27263; ● 160
Glen Raven; CDP; ALAMANCE; ***212** C-9; elev. 694ft./212m.; 🄿; ★ **BUR**; z 27215; Ⓟ 2,616; © 2,750
Glenview; RMC Place; HALIFAX; **213** C-14; elev. 153ft./47m.; mail Enfield z 27823; ● 30
Glenville; RMC Place; JACKSON; **212** M-4; elev. 3,600ft./1,097m.; 🄿; z 28736; ● 680
Glenwood; RMC Place; GUILFORD; ***212** D-8; ★ **GRNS-**; mail Greensboro z 27403; pop. incl. with Greensboro (Inc. Place)
Glenwood; RMC Place; MCDOWELL; **212** E-2; elev. 1,294ft./394m.; 🄿; z 28737; ● 350
Glenwood; RMC Place; RICHMOND; ***212** H-8; mail Rockingham z 28379; pop. incl. with Rockingham (Inc. Place)
Glenwood Hills; RMC Place; WAKE; ★ **RAL**; pop. incl. with Raleigh (Inc. Place)
Glenwood Village; RMC Place; WAKE; ★ **RAL**; pop. incl. with Raleigh (Inc. Place)
Gliden; RMC Place; CHOWAN; elev. 36ft./11m.; mail Belvidere z 27919
Globe; RMC Place; CALDWELL; ***212** D-3; mail Lenoir z 28645; rural
Gloucester; RMC Place; CARTERET; ***213** H-18; elev. 6ft./2m.; 🄿; z 28528; ● 330
Glovers Crossroads (Growers Crossroads); RMC Place; BERTIE; ***213** C-17; mail Colerain z 27924; rural
Gneiss; RMC Place; MACON; ***212** M-3; mail Franklin z 28734
Goat Neck; RMC Place; TYRRELL; **213** D-19; mail Columbia z 27925; ● 80
Godwin; Inc. Place; CUMBERLAND; **213** G-11; elev. 155ft./47m.; 🄿; z 28344; Ⓟ 77; © 112
Golden Forest; RMC Place; WAKE; ***213** E-12; ★ **RAL**; mail Raleigh z 27604; ● 70
Gold Hill; RMC Place; HOKE; ***212** H-10; elev. 224ft./68m.; mail Shannon z 28386; rural
Gold Hill; RMC Place; ROCKINGHAM; ***212** C-8; elev. 800ft./244m.; ★ **GRNS-**; mail Madison z 27025; ● 150
Gold Hill; RMC Place; ROWAN; **212** E-7; elev. 765ft./233m.; 🄿; ★ **SLSB**; z 28071; ● 370
Gold Mine; RMC Place; MACON; ***212** M-3; mail Highlands z 28741; ● 30
Gold Point; RMC Place; MARTIN; **213** D-16; elev. 74ft./23m.; mail Robersonville z 27871; ● 90
Goldrock; RMC Place; NASH; ***213** D-14; ★ **RKYMT**; mail Whitakers z 27891
Goldsboro; Inc. Place; ⊡ WAYNE; **213** F-13; 🄿 🄷 ■; ★ **GLDS**; z 27530-34; Ⓟ 40,709; © 39,043; Ⓡ 39,147; ◆ 34,065
Goldston; Inc. Place; CHATHAM; **212** E-10; elev. 424ft./129m.; 🄿; z 27252; Ⓟ 299; © 319
Gold Valley Crossroads; RMC Place; NASH; ***213** D-13; mail Middlesex z 27557; rural
Goodsonville; RMC Place; LINCOLN; mail Lincolnton z 28092; pop. incl. with Lincolnton (Inc. Place)
Goose Creek (Alder Branch); RMC Place; CAMDEN; ***213** C-19; mail Shiloh z 27974; ● 30
Gooseneck; RMC Place; COLUMBUS; ***213** J-13; mail Riegelwood z 28456; ● 30
Goose Pond; RMC Place; BERTIE; **213** C-17; elev. 19ft./6m.; mail Colerain z 27924; ● 30
Gordonton; RMC Place; PERSON; ***212** C-10; elev. 677ft./206m.; mail Hurdle Mills z 27541; ● 30
Gordontown; RMC Place; DAVIDSON; **212** E-7; elev. 774ft./236m.; mail Lexington z 27292; ● 130
Gorman; CDP; DURHAM; **213** D-11; ★ **DUR**; mail Durham z 27704; Ⓟ 1,090; © 1,002
Goshen; RMC Place; GRANVILLE; ***213** B-11; elev. 556ft./169m.; mail Oxford z 27565; rural
Goshen; RMC Place; WILKES; ***212** C-4; elev. 1,102ft./336m.; mail Wilkesboro z 28697; rural
Governors Island; RMC Place; SWAIN; ***212** L-3; mail Bryson City z 28713; rural
Grabtown; RMC Place; BERTIE; mail Windsor z 27983
Grace; RMC Place; BUNCOMBE; ***212** E-1; ★ **ASHE**; mail Asheville z 28814; pop. incl. with Asheville (Inc. Place)
Grace Chapel; RMC Place; CALDWELL; ***212** D-4; ★ **HICK**; mail Granite Falls z 28630; ● 50
Gradys; RMC Place; WAYNE; ***213** G-14; elev. 132ft./40m.; mail Mount Olive z 28365; rural
Graham; Inc. Place; ⊡ ALAMANCE; **212** D-9; elev. 642ft./196m.; 🄿; ★ **BUR**; z 27253; Ⓟ 10,426; © 12,833
GRAHAM; **212** M-2; Ⓟ 7,196; © 7,993; ◆ 7,610
Graingers; RMC Place; LENOIR; **213** F-15; elev. 74ft./23m.; mail Kinston z 28501; ● 50
Grandfather; Inc. Place; AVERY; ***212** C-2; mail Banner Elk z 28604, Linville z 28646; Ⓟ 34; © 73
Grandin; RMC Place; CALDWELL; ***212** D-4; elev. 1,080ft./329m.; mail Lenoir z 28645; rural
Grandview; RMC Place; CHEROKEE; ***212** M-1; mail Murphy z 28906; rural
Grandview Heights; RMC Place; WATAUGA; ***212** C-3; elev. 3,220ft./981m.; mail Boone z 28607; pop. incl. with Boone (Inc. Place)
Grandy; RMC Place; CURRITUCK; **213** C-19; elev. 5ft./2m.; 🄿; z 27939; ● 950
Granite Falls; Inc. Place; CALDWELL; **212** E-4; elev. 1,214ft./370m.; 🄿; ★ **HICK**; z 28630; Ⓟ 3,253; © 4,612; Ⓡ 4,611
Granite Quarry; Inc. Place; ROWAN; **212** E-6; elev. 802ft./244m.; 🄿; ★ **SLSB**; z 28072, z 28146; Ⓟ 1,646; © 2,175
Grantham; RMC Place; WAYNE; ***213** F-13; elev. 167ft./51m.; mail Goldsboro z 27530
Granthams; RMC Place; CRAVEN; **213** G-16; mail New Bern z 28560, z 28562; ● 950
Grantsboro; Inc. Place; PAMLICO; **213** G-17; elev. 42ft./13m.; 🄿; z 28529; incorporated June 4, 1997; not reported in 2000 Census; Ⓡ 754
Grantville; RMC Place; RANDOLPH; ***212** E-9; elev. 534ft./163m.; mail Asheboro z 27203; rural
GRANVILLE; **213** B-11; Ⓟ 38,345; © 48,498; ◆ 60,088
Grape Creek; RMC Place; CHEROKEE; ***212** M-1; mail Murphy z 28906; rural
Grapevine; RMC Place; MADISON; ***212** D-1; elev. 2,158ft./658m.; mail Marshall z 28753; ● 30
Graphite; RMC Place; MCDOWELL; ***212** E-1; mail Old Fort z 28762; rural
Grassy Creek; RMC Place; ASHE; **212** B-4; elev. 2,654ft./809m.; 🄿; z 28631; ● 60
Grassy Creek; RMC Place; MITCHELL; ***212** D-2; mail Spruce Pine z 28777; ● 30
Grays Chapel; RMC Place; RANDOLPH; ***212** D-9; elev. 741ft./226m.; ★ **GRNS-**; mail Franklinville z 27248
Gray's Creek; RMC Place; CUMBERLAND; ***213** G-11; elev. 83ft./25m.; ★ **FAY**; mail Fayetteville z 28306, Hope Mills z 28348; rural
Grayson; RMC Place; ASHE; ***212** B-3; elev. 3,600ft./1,097m.; mail Creston z 28615; rural
Great Neck Landing; RMC Place; ONSLOW; ***213** H-16; ★ **JAX**; mail Hubert z 28539; ● 200
Green Acres; RMC Place; ALAMANCE; ***212** C-9; elev. 600ft./183m.; ★ **BUR**; mail Burlington z 27217; ● 350
Green Acres; RMC Place; GASTON; ***212** G-5; ★ **CHRLT**; mail Belmont z 28012; ● 110
Green Acres; RMC Place; WAKE; ***213** E-12; ★ **RAL**; mail Raleigh z 27603
Green Acres Park; RMC Place; CABARRUS; ***212** F-6; elev. 600ft./183m.; ★ **CHRLT**; mail Concord z 28025; pop. incl. with Concord (Inc. Place)
Greenbrier Estates; RMC Place; WAKE; ***213** E-12; ★ **RAL**; mail Raleigh z 27603; pop. incl. with Garner (Inc. Place)
GREENE; **213** E-14; Ⓟ 15,384; © 18,974; ◆ 21,573
Greene Cove; RMC Place; MITCHELL; ***212** D-2; mail Bakersville z 28705; rural
Greenevers; Inc. Place; DUPLIN; **213** H-14; elev. 60ft./18m.; mail Rose Hill z 28458; Ⓟ 512; © 560
Green Farm; RMC Place; PITT; ***213** E-15; elev. 82ft./25m.; ★ **GRNV**; mail Greenville z 27834; ● 150
Greenfield; RMC Place; CHOWAN; ***213** C-18; elev. 10ft./3m.; mail Edenton z 27932; rural
Greenhill; RMC Place; HAYWOOD; ***212** L-5; elev. 2,800ft./853m.; ★ **ASHE**; mail Canton z 28716; ● 550
Green Hill; RMC Place; RUTHERFORD; ***212** F-2; elev. 968ft./295m.; mail Rutherfordton z 28139; rural
Greenlee; RMC Place; MCDOWELL; ***212** E-2; elev. 1,288ft./393m.; mail Old Fort z 28762; ● 220
Green Level; Inc. Place; ALAMANCE; ***212** C-10; elev. 600ft./183m.; 🄿; ★ **BUR**; z 27217; Ⓟ 1,548; © 2,042
Green Level; RMC Place; WAKE; ***213** E-11; ★ **RAL**; mail Apex z 27523
Green Mountain; RMC Place; YANCEY; ***212** D-1; elev. 2,154ft./657m.; 🄿; z 28740; ● 150
Green River; RMC Place; POLK; ***212** F-2; mail Columbus z 28722; rural
Greensboro; Inc. Place; ⊡ GUILFORD; **212** D-8; 🄿 🄷 🄲 32,250 ■; ★ **GRNS-**; z 27401-13, z 27415-17, z 27419-20, z 27425, z 27427, z 27429, z 27435, z 27438, z 27455, z 27495, z 27497-99; Ⓟ 183,521; © 223,891; ◆ 268,704
Greens Creek; RMC Place; JACKSON; ***212** L-3; mail Sylva z 28779; rural
Green Valley; RMC Place; ASHE; ***212** B-3; mail Creston z 28615
Green Valley; RMC Place; CLEVELAND; ***212** F-3; elev. 700ft./213m.; mail Shelby z 28152; ● 30
Greenville; RMC Place; MECKLENBURG; ★ **CHRLT**; pop. incl. with Charlotte (Inc. Place)
Greenville; Inc. Place; ⊡ PITT; **213** E-15; 🄿 🄷 🄲 24,351 ■; ★ **GRNV**; z 27833-36, z 27858; Ⓟ 44,972; © 60,476; Ⓡ 61,209; ◆ 82,297
Greenwood Homes; RMC Place; CUMBERLAND; ★ **FAY**; mail Fayetteville z 28303; pop. incl. with Fayetteville (Inc. Place)
Gregory; RMC Place; CURRITUCK; **213** B-19; elev. 11ft./3m.; mail Shawboro z 27973; ● 60
Gregory Crossroads; RMC Place; BERTIE; ***213** D-17; elev. 11ft./3m.; mail Merry Hill z 27957; rural
Gregory Crossroads; ONSLOW; see Gregory Forks (RMC Place)
Gregory Forks (Gregory Crossroads); RMC Place; ONSLOW; ***213** H-15; ★ **JAX**; mail Richlands z 28574; ● 100
Greystone; RMC Place; VANCE; **213** C-12; mail Henderson z 27537; ● 110
Griffins Crossroads; RMC Place; CHATHAM; ***212** E-10; elev. 440ft./134m.; mail Pittsboro z 27312; rural
Griffith; RMC Place; MECKLENBURG; ★ **CHRLT**; pop. incl. with Charlotte (Inc. Place)
Grifton; Inc. Place; PITT, LENOIR; **213** F-15; elev. 28ft./9m.; 🄿; ★ **GRNV**; z 28530; Ⓟ 2,393; © 2,073; Ⓡ 2,123
Grimes Crossroads; RMC Place; FORSYTH; ***212** C-7; elev. 88ft./27m.; ★ **WNS**; mail Belews Creek z 27009; rural
Grimesdale; RMC Place; HENDERSON; ***212** F-1; mail Hendersonville z 28792; ● 350
Grimesland; Inc. Place; PITT; **213** E-16; elev. 44ft./13m.; 🄿; ★ **GRNV**; z 27837; Ⓟ 469; © 440
Grissettown; RMC Place; BRUNSWICK; **213** K-12; mail Shallotte z 28470; ● 50
Grissom; RMC Place; GRANVILLE; ***213** D-12; elev. 475ft./145m.; mail Creedmoor z 27522
Grist; RMC Place; COLUMBUS; ***213** J-11; elev. 104ft./32m.; mail Chadbourn z 28431; ● 50
Grove Hill; RMC Place; WARREN; ***213** C-13; elev. 344ft./105m.; mail Macon z 27551; ● 30
Grovemont; RMC Place; BUNCOMBE; ***212** E-1; ★ **ASHE**; mail Swannanoa z 28778; ● 470
Grove Park; RMC Place; MECKLENBURG; ***212** G-6; elev. 750ft./229m.; ★ **CHRLT**; mail Charlotte z 28215; pop. incl. with Charlotte (Inc. Place)

Entries in **UPPERCASE** are counties.
Entries in **bold** have populations of 2,500 or more.
Names in parentheses are alternate names.
Inc. Place — Incorporated Place
RMC Place — Rand McNally Designated Place
CDP — Census Designated Place
MCD — Minor Civil Division

⊡ County Seat
▲ Minor Civil Division
elev. Elevation
🄿 Post Office

🄷 Hospital
🄲 College
■ Principal Business Center
★ Ranally Metro Area (RMA) Abbreviation
z Zip Code(s)

Ⓟ Previous Census Population
Ⓡ Revised Census Population
Ⓐ Annexation Population
● Rand McNally Population Estimate
© Final Census Population
Ⓢ Special Census Population
◆ Estimated Population

For additional definitions see Glossary, Volume 1, and Introduction, Volume 2.

Grover; Inc. Place; CLEVELAND; **212** G-4; elev. 840ft./256m.; 🅿; ★ **CHRLT**; z 28073; Ⓟ 516; © 698
Grovestone; RMC Place; BUNCOMBE; ***212** E-1; ★ **ASHE**; mail Swannanoa z 28778; pop. incl. with Black Mountain (Inc. Place)
Growers Crossroads; BERTIE; see Glovers Crossroads (RMC Place)
Guide; RMC Place; COLUMBUS; ***213** K-11; elev. 49ft./15m.; mail Tabor City z 28463; rural
Guideway; RMC Place; COLUMBUS; ***213** K-11; elev. 51ft./16m.; mail Tabor City z 28463; ● 30
Guilford; RMC Place; GUILFORD; ***212** D-8; elev. 939ft./286m.; ★ **GRNS-**; mail Greensboro z 27409-10, z 27419; pop. incl. with Greensboro (Inc. Place)
GUILFORD; **212** D-9; Ⓟ 347,420; © 421,048; ◆ 492,400
Guilford Hills; RMC Place; GUILFORD; ★ **GRNS-**; mail Greensboro z 27408; pop. incl. with Greensboro (Inc. Place)
Gulf; RMC Place; CHATHAM; **212** E-10; elev. 270ft./82m.; 🅿; z 27256; ● 330
Gull Rock; HYDE; see Gulrock (RMC Place)
Gulrock (Gull Rock); RMC Place; HYDE; ***213** F-19; mail Engelhard z 27824; rural
Gumberry; RMC Place; NORTHAMPTON; **213** B-15; elev. 146ft./45m.; 🅿; z 27831; ● 140
Gumbranch; RMC Place; ONSLOW; **213** H-15; elev. 48ft./15m.; ★ **JAX**; mail Jacksonville z 28540; ● 230
Gum Neck; RMC Place; TYRRELL; ***213** E-19; mail Columbia z 27925; rural
Gum Springs; RMC Place; CHATHAM; ***212** E-10; elev. 475ft./145m.; mail Pittsboro z 27312; rural
Guntertown; RMC Place; MADISON; ***212** J-5; mail Marshall z 28753; rural
Gupton; RMC Place; FRANKLIN; ***213** C-13; elev. 374ft./114m.; mail Louisburg z 27549
Gurganus; RMC Place; ONSLOW; ***213** H-14; elev. 22ft./7m.; mail Maple Hill z 28454; rural
Guthrie; RMC Place; FORSYTH; **214** G-10; elev. 932ft./284m.; ★ **WNS**; mail Kernersville z 27284; ● 60
Guyton; RMC Place; BLADEN; ***213** I-11; elev. 129ft./39m.; mail Bladenboro z 28320; rural

H

Haddocks Crossroads; RMC Place; PITT; ***213** F-15; ★ **GRNV**; mail Winterville z 28590; rural
Hadley; RMC Place; DUPLIN; ***213** H-14; elev. 27ft./8m.; mail Beulaville z 28518; rural
Hairtown; RMC Place; HARNETT; ***213** F-11; elev. 321ft./98m.; ★ **FAY**; mail Fayetteville z 28302, Linden z 28356; rural
Half Hell; RMC Place; BRUNSWICK; ***213** K-13; elev. 31ft./9m.; ★ **WILM**; mail Bolivia z 28422; ● 50
Half Moon; CDP; ONSLOW; **213** H-15; elev. 30ft./9m.; ★ **JAX**; mail Jacksonville z 28540; Ⓟ 6,306; © 6,645
Halifax; Inc. Place; ⊡ HALIFAX; **213** C-14; elev. 133ft./41m.; 🅿; z 27839; Ⓟ 327; © 344
HALIFAX; **213** C-15; Ⓟ 55,516; © 57,370; ◆ 54,401
Hallison; MOORE; see Parkwood (RMC Place)
Hallsboro; RMC Place; COLUMBUS; **213** J-12; elev. 66ft./20m.; 🅿; z 28442; ● 580
Halls Crossroads; RMC Place; SAMPSON; ***213** G-12; elev. 147ft./45m.; mail Autryville z 28318; rural
Halls Ferry Junction; RMC Place; STANLY; ***212** F-7; mail New London z 28127; rural
Halls Mills; RMC Place; WILKES; ***212** C-4; mail Mc Grady z 28649; rural
Halls Store; RMC Place; SAMPSON; ***213** G-12; elev. 171ft./52m.; mail Salemburg z 28385; ● 30
Hallsville; RMC Place; DUPLIN; ***213** H-14; mail Beulaville z 28518; ● 30
Hamer; RMC Place; CASWELL; ***212** B-10; elev. 566ft./173m.; mail Blanch z 27212; rural
Hamilton; Inc. Place; MARTIN; **213** D-16; elev. 73ft./22m.; 🅿; z 27840; Ⓟ 544; © 516
Hamilton Crossroads; RMC Place; UNION; ***212** G-7; elev. 564ft./172m.; mail Marshville z 28103; rural
Hamilton Lakes; RMC Place; GUILFORD; ***212** D-8; ★ **GRNS-**; mail Greensboro z 27410; pop. incl. with Greensboro (Inc. Place)
Hamlet; Inc. Place; RICHMOND; **212** H-9; 🅿 🅷; z 28345; Ⓟ 6,324; © 6,018
Hampstead; RMC Place; PENDER; **213** I-14; elev. 56ft./17m.; 🅿; z 28443; ● 850
Hamptonville; RMC Place; YADKIN; **212** D-6; elev. 1,026ft./313m.; 🅿; z 27020; ● 200
Hamrick; RMC Place; YANCEY; ***212** D-1; mail Burnsville z 28714; rural
Hams Crossroads; RMC Place; PITT; ***213** E-16; elev. 40ft./12m.; ★ **GRNV**; mail Grimesland z 27837; rural
Hancheys Store; RMC Place; DUPLIN; ***213** H-14; mail Wallace z 28466; rural
Hancock; RMC Place; CHOWAN; ***213** C-17; elev. 14ft./4m.; mail Edenton z 27932
Handy; RMC Place; DAVIDSON; ***212** E-7; mail Denton z 27239
Hanrahan; RMC Place; PITT; ***213** F-15; elev. 20ft./6m.; ★ **GRNV**; mail Grifton z 28530; rural
Happy Valley; RMC Place; BUNCOMBE; ***212** E-1; ★ **ASHE**; mail Asheville z 28805; pop. incl. with Asheville (Inc. Place)
Happy Valley; RMC Place; CALDWELL; ***212** D-3; mail Lenoir z 28645, Patterson z 28661; ● 650
Harbinger; RMC Place; CURRITUCK; **213** C-20; 🅿; z 27941; ● 400
Harbor Island; RMC Place; NEW HANOVER; ***213** J-14; ★ **WILM**; mail Wrightsville Beach z 28480
Hardee Cross Roads (Hardees Cross Road); RMC Place; JOHNSTON; ***213** F-12; ★ **RAL**; mail Benson z 27504; ● 30
Hardees Cross Road; JOHNSTON; see Hardee Cross Roads (RMC Place)
Hardins; RMC Place; GASTON; ***212** F-4; elev. 743ft./226m.; ★ **CHRLT**; mail Dallas z 28034; ● 120
Hare; RMC Place; ALLEGHANY; ***212** B-5; mail Glade Valley z 28627; rural
Hargetts Cross Roads; RMC Place; JONES; ***213** G-14; mail Richlands z 28574; rural
Harkers Island; CDP; CARTERET; **213** H-18; elev. 4ft./1m.; 🅿; z 28531; Ⓟ 1,759; © 1,525
Harlem Heights; RMC Place; ANSON; ***212** H-8; elev. 489ft./149m.; mail Wadesboro z 28170; ● 150
Harlowe; RMC Place; CARTERET; ***213** H-17; elev. 16ft./5m.; mail Newport z 28570; ● 240
Harmony; Inc. Place; IREDELL; **212** D-6; elev. 991ft./302m.; 🅿; z 28634; Ⓟ 431; © 526
Harnett; RMC Place; HARNETT; ***213** F-11; elev. 160ft./49m.; mail Lillington z 27546; ● 80
HARNETT; **213** F-11; Ⓟ 67,822; © 91,025; ◆ 113,225
Harper's Crossroads; RMC Place; CHATHAM; ***212** E-9; elev. 498ft./152m.; mail Bear Creek z 27207; rural
Harrells (Harrells Store); Inc. Place; SAMPSON, DUPLIN; **213** H-13; elev. 88ft./27m.; 🅿; z 28444; Ⓟ 187; © 187; Ⓡ 200
Harrells Store; SAMPSON, DUPLIN; see Harrells (Inc. Place)
Harrellsville; Inc. Place; HERTFORD; **213** C-17; elev. 65ft./20m.; 🅿; z 27942; Ⓟ 106; © 102
Harrelsonville; RMC Place; COLUMBUS; ***213** J-11; elev. 91ft./28m.; mail Whiteville z 28472; rural
Harris; RMC Place; MOORE; ***212** F-9; elev. 528ft./161m.; mail Carthage z 28327; rural
Harris; RMC Place; RUTHERFORD; ***212** F-2; elev. 803ft./245m.; 🅿; z 28074; ● 200
Harrisburg; Inc. Place; CABARRUS; **212** F-6; elev. 676ft./206m.; 🅿; ★ **CHRLT**; z 28075; Ⓟ 1,625; © 4,493
Harrisburg Estates; RMC Place; CABARRUS; ***212** F-6; elev. 570ft./174m.; ★ **CHRLT**; mail Harrisburg z 28075; pop. incl. with Harrisburg (Inc. Place)
Harris Crossroads; RMC Place; FRANKLIN; ***213** D-12; elev. 408ft./124m.; mail Youngsville z 27596; rural
Harris Crossroads; RMC Place; VANCE; ***213** B-12; elev. 383ft./117m.; mail Henderson z 27536; rural
Harris Landing; RMC Place; CHOWAN; ***213** C-17; mail Edenton z 27932; rural
Harrisons Crossroads; RMC Place; ROCKINGHAM; ***212** B-8; mail Reidsville z 27320; ● 50
Harrisville; RMC Place; MONTGOMERY; ***212** G-8; elev. 328ft./100m.; mail Candor z 27229; rural
Hartland; RMC Place; CALDWELL; mail Morganton z 28655; ● 30
Hartman; RMC Place; STOKES; ***212** B-7; elev. 957ft./292m.; mail Danbury z 27016; rural
Hartsease; RMC Place; EDGECOMBE; ***213** D-14; elev. 106ft./32m.; mail Tarboro z 27886; ● 350
Harveytown; RMC Place; LENOIR; ***213** F-15; mail Kinston z 28501; pop. incl. with Kinston (Inc. Place)
Hassell; Inc. Place; MARTIN; **213** D-15; elev. 79ft./24m.; 🅿; z 27841; Ⓟ 95; © 72; Ⓡ 76
Hastings Corner; RMC Place; CAMDEN; ***213** B-18; elev. 2ft./1m.; mail Camden z 27921; ● 50
Hasty; RMC Place; SCOTLAND; **212** H-9; elev. 201ft./61m.; mail Laurinburg z 28352; ● 50
Hatteras; RMC Place; DARE; **213** F-20; elev. 2ft./1m.; 🅿; z 27943; ● 1,150
Havelock; Inc. Place; CRAVEN; **213** H-16; elev. 25ft./8m.; 🅿 🅷; z 28532-33; Ⓟ 20,268; © 22,442; ◆ 23,822
Havelock Station; RMC Place; CRAVEN; mail Havelock z 28532; pop. incl. with Havelock (Inc. Place)
Haw; ONSLOW; see Haws Run (RMC Place)
Haw Branch; RMC Place; MOORE; ***212** F-9; mail Sanford z 27330; rural
Haw Branch; RMC Place; ONSLOW; ***213** G-14; mail Richlands z 28574; ● 30
Haw Creek; RMC Place; BUNCOMBE; ***212** E-1; ★ **ASHE**; mail Asheville z 28805; pop. incl. with Asheville (Inc. Place)
Hawfields; RMC Place; ALAMANCE; ***212** D-10; elev. 650ft./198m.; ★ **BUR**; mail Mebane z 27302; ● 30
Hawk; RMC Place; MITCHELL; ***212** D-2; mail Bakersville z 28705; ● 180
Haw River; Inc. Place; ALAMANCE; **212** D-10; elev. 543ft./166m.; 🅿; ★ **BUR**; z 27258; Ⓟ 1,855; © 1,908
Haws Run (Haw); RMC Place; ONSLOW; **213** H-15; elev. 56ft./17m.; ★ **JAX**; mail Maple Hill z 28454; ● 200
Hayesville; Inc. Place; ⊡ CLAY; **212** M-2; elev. 1,890ft./576m.; 🅿; z 28904; Ⓟ 279; © 297; Ⓡ 458
Haymount; RMC Place; CUMBERLAND; ***213** G-11; ★ **FAY**; mail Fayetteville z 28305; pop. incl. with Fayetteville (Inc. Place)
Hayne; RMC Place; SAMPSON; ***213** G-12; elev. 151ft./46m.; mail Autryville z 28318; ● 30
Hays; CDP; WILKES; **212** C-5; elev. 1,359ft./414m.; 🅿; z 28635; Ⓟ 1,522; © 1,731
Hayti; RMC Place; DURHAM; ★ **DUR**; mail Durham z 27701; pop. incl. with Durham (Inc. Place)
Haywood; RMC Place; CHATHAM; **212** E-10; mail Moncure z 27559; ● 170
HAYWOOD; **212** K-4; Ⓟ 46,942; © 54,033; ◆ 56,817
Haywood Road; RMC Place; BUNCOMBE; ★ **ASHE**; mail Asheville z 28806; pop. incl. with Asheville (Inc. Place)
Hazelwood; RMC Place; HAYWOOD; **212** L-4; elev. 2,724ft./830m.; 🅿; z 28738, z 28786; pop. incl. with Waynesville (Inc. Place); Ⓟ 1,678
Hazelwood Park; RMC Place; EDGECOMBE; ***213** D-14; elev. 105ft./32m.; mail Pinetops z 27864; rural
Healing Springs; RMC Place; DAVIDSON; ***212** E-7; mail Denton z 27239
Heathsville; RMC Place; HALIFAX; ***213** C-14; elev. 207ft./63m.; mail Enfield z 27823; ● 30
Heaton; RMC Place; AVERY; ***212** C-2; elev. 3,036ft./925m.; mail Elk Park z 28622
Hebron; RMC Place; GRANVILLE; ***213** C-11; elev. 572ft./174m.; mail Oxford z 27565; rural
Hedrick Grove; RMC Place; DAVIDSON; ***212** E-7; elev. 829ft./253m.; mail Lexington z 27292; rural
Helens Crossroads; RMC Place; PITT; ***213** F-15; ★ **GRNV**; mail Ayden z 28513; rural
Helton; RMC Place; ASHE; ***212** B-4; mail Grassy Creek z 28631; rural
Hemby Acres; RMC Place; UNION; ***212** G-6; ★ **CHRLT**; mail Indian Trail z 28079; pop. incl. with Lake Park (Inc. Place)
Hemby Bridge; Inc. Place; UNION; ***212** G-6; ★ **CHRLT**; mail Indian Trail z 28079; incorporated November 4, 1998; not reported in 2000 Census
Hemby Bridge; CDP-Census Area Only; UNION; ***212** G-6; ★ **CHRLT**; mail Indian Trail z 28079; Ⓟ 2,876; © 897; Ⓡ 1,414
Henderson; Inc. Place; ⊡ VANCE; **213** C-12; elev. 509ft./155m.; 🅿 🅷 ■; z 27536-37; Ⓟ 15,655; © 16,095; ◆ 15,170
HENDERSON; **212** F-1; Ⓟ 69,285; © 89,173; ◆ 103,957
Hendersonville; Inc. Place; ⊡ HENDERSON; **212** F-1; elev. 2,146ft./654m.; 🅿 🅷 ■; z 28739, z 28791-93; Ⓟ 7,284; © 10,420; Ⓡ 10,569; ◆ 11,861
Hendrix Estates; RMC Place; ROWAN; ***212** E-6; ★ **SLSB**; mail Salisbury z 28147; ● 60
Henrico; RMC Place; NORTHAMPTON; **213** B-14; elev. 272ft./83m.; 🅿; z 27842; ● 150
Henrietta; RMC Place; RUTHERFORD; **212** F-3; elev. 799ft./244m.; 🅿; z 28076; ● 1,000
Henry; RMC Place; LINCOLN; ***212** E-4; elev. 1,068ft./326m.; ★ **HICK**; mail Vale z 28168; rural
Henry River; RMC Place; BURKE; ***212** E-4; ★ **HICK**; mail Hickory z 28602; ● 160
Hepco; RMC Place; HAYWOOD; ***212** K-4; mail Clyde z 28721; rural
Heritage Hill; RMC Place; ORANGE; ***212** D-10; ★ **DUR**; mail Chapel Hill z 27516; ● 850
Heritage Square; RMC Place; DURHAM; ★ **DUR**; mail Durham z 27707; pop. incl. with Durham (Inc. Place)
Heritage Woods; RMC Place; CABARRUS; ***212** F-6; elev. 699ft./213m.; ★ **CHRLT**; mail Concord z 28025; ● 60
Herrings Crossroads; RMC Place; DUPLIN; ***213** G-14; mail Albertson z 28508; rural
Herrings Crossroads; RMC Place; GREENE; ***213** E-14; elev. 112ft./34m.; mail Walstonburg z 27888; rural
Hertford; Inc. Place; ⊡ PERQUIMANS; **213** C-18; elev. 13ft./4m.; 🅿; z 27930, z 27944; Ⓟ 2,105; © 2,070
HERTFORD; **213** C-16; Ⓟ 22,523; © 22,601; Ⓡ 22,977; ◆ 23,354
Hertford Village; RMC Place; WAKE; ***213** E-12; ★ **RAL**; pop. incl. with Raleigh (Inc. Place)
Hester; RMC Place; GRANVILLE; ***213** C-11; elev. 393ft./120m.; ★ **DUR**; mail Stem z 27581
Hesters Store; RMC Place; PERSON; ***212** C-10; elev. 651ft./198m.; mail Hurdle Mills z 27541; ● 50
Hestertown; RMC Place; ROBESON; ***213** I-11; mail Lumberton z 28358; ● 140
Hewitt; RMC Place; SWAIN; ***212** L-2; mail Topton z 28781; rural
Hexlena; RMC Place; BERTIE; ***213** C-16; mail Aulander z 27805; ● 30
Hibbs Acres; RMC Place; CARTERET; ***213** H-17; elev. 29ft./9m.; mail Newport z 28570; ● 190
Hickmans Crossroads; RMC Place; BRUNSWICK; ***213** K-12; ★ **MYR.B**; mail Shallotte z 28470; ● 100
Hickory; Inc. Place; CATAWBA, BURKE; **212** E-4; elev. 1,163ft./354m.; 🅿 🅷 🅲 1,604 ■; ★ **HICK**; z 28601-03; Ⓟ 28,301; © 37,222; ◆ 44,615
Hickory (Pittmans Store); RMC Place; NASH; ***213** C-14; elev. 137ft./42m.; mail Whitakers z 27891; rural
Hickory Crossroads; RMC Place; PERQUIMANS; ***213** C-17; mail Belvidere z 27919; rural
Hickory Grove; RMC Place; CUMBERLAND; ***213** G-11; elev. 200ft./61m.; ★ **FAY**; mail Fayetteville z 28304; ● 280
Hickory Grove; RMC Place; GASTON; ***212** F-5; ★ **CHRLT**; mail Gastonia z 28056; ● 860
Hickory Grove; RMC Place; MECKLENBURG; ***212** G-6; ★ **CHRLT**; mail Charlotte z 28215; pop. incl. with Charlotte (Inc. Place)
Hickory Hill; RMC Place; CLEVELAND; ***212** F-3; elev. 800ft./244m.; mail Shelby z 28152; ● 30
Hickory Knoll; RMC Place; MACON; ***212** M-3; elev. 2,200ft./671m.; mail Franklin z 28734; rural
Hickory Point; RMC Place; BEAUFORT; ***213** F-17; elev. 5ft./2m.; mail Aurora z 27806; ● 80
Hickory Rock; RMC Place; FRANKLIN; ***213** C-13; mail Louisburg z 27549; rural
Hicks Crossroads; RMC Place; MECKLENBURG; ***212** F-5; ★ **CHRLT**; mail Huntersville z 28078; ● 50
Hicks Crossroads; RMC Place; VANCE; ***213** B-12; mail Oxford z 27565; rural
Hidden Hut Farms; RMC Place; ROWAN; ***212** E-6; elev. 750ft./229m.; ★ **SLSB**; mail Salisbury z 28147; ● 50
Hiddenite; RMC Place; ALEXANDER; **212** D-5; elev. 1,166ft./355m.; 🅿; z 28636; ● 880
Higdonville; RMC Place; MACON; ***212** M-3; mail Franklin z 28734; rural
Higgins; RMC Place; YANCEY; ***212** D-1; mail Burnsville z 28714; rural
High Crossroads; RMC Place; NASH; ***213** D-13; elev. 196ft./60m.; mail Bailey z 27807; ● 30
High Falls; RMC Place; MOORE; **212** F-9; elev. 350ft./107m.; 🅿; z 27259; ● 220
High Hampton; RMC Place; JACKSON; **212** M-4; mail Cashiers z 28717; ● 50
Highland Park; RMC Place; RICHMOND; ***212** H-9; mail Hamlet z 28345; pop. incl. with Richmond (Independent City)
Highland Park West; RMC Place; GUILFORD; ***212** D-8; elev. 873ft./266m.; ★ **GRNS-**; mail Greensboro z 27407; pop. incl. with Greensboro (Inc. Place)
Highlands; Inc. Place; MACON, JACKSON; **212** M-4; elev. 3,835ft./1,169m.; 🅿 🅷; z 28741; Ⓟ 948; © 909; Ⓡ 915
Highland Village; RMC Place; CUMBERLAND; ★ **FAY**; pop. incl. with Fayetteville (Inc. Place)
High Point; Inc. Place; GUILFORD, DAVIDSON, FORSYTH, RANDOLPH; **212** D-8; elev. 939ft./286m.; 🅿 🅷 🅲 2,811 ■; ★ **GRNS-**; z 27260-65; Ⓟ 69,496; © 85,839; ◆ 105,677
High Rock; RMC Place; DAVIDSON; **212** E-7; elev. 584ft./178m.; mail Denton z 27239; ● 30
High Shoals; Inc. Place; GASTON, LINCOLN; **212** F-4; elev. 724ft./221m.; 🅿; ★ **CHRLT**; z 28077; Ⓟ 605; © 729
Highsmiths; RMC Place; SAMPSON; ***213** H-12; elev. 148ft./45m.; mail Roseboro z 28382
Hightowers; RMC Place; CASWELL; ***212** C-10; elev. 677ft./206m.; mail Yanceyville z 27379
Hightsville; CDP; NEW HANOVER; ***213** J-14; ★ **WILM**; © 759
Hildebran; Inc. Place; BURKE; **212** E-4; elev. 1,264ft./385m.; 🅿; ★ **HICK**; z 28637; Ⓟ 790; © 1,472
Hillcrest; RMC Place; HOKE; ***212** G-10; elev. 245ft./75m.; ★ **FAY**; mail Boone z 28607, Raeford z 28376; ● 440
Hill Crest; RMC Place; MOORE; ***212** F-9; mail Carthage z 28327
Hillendale; RMC Place; CUMBERLAND; ★ **FAY**; pop. incl. with Fayetteville (Inc. Place)
Hilliardston; RMC Place; NASH; ***213** C-14; mail Nashville z 27856
Hills; RMC Place; STANLY; ***212** F-7; elev. 500ft./152m.; mail Albemarle z 28001; ● 50
Hillsborough; Inc. Place; ⊡ ORANGE; **212** D-10; elev. 624ft./190m.; 🅿; ★ **DUR**; z 27278; Ⓟ 4,263; © 5,446
Hills Crossroads; RMC Place; HALIFAX; ***213** C-15; elev. 120ft./37m.; mail Halifax z 27839; rural
Hillsdale; RMC Place; DAVIE; ***212** D-6; elev. 808ft./246m.; ★ **WNS**; mail Advance z 27006
Hillsdale; RMC Place; GUILFORD; ***212** C-8; elev. 874ft./266m.; ★ **GRNS-**; mail Greensboro z 27405; pop. incl. with Summerfield (Inc. Place)
Hillsville; RMC Place; RANDOLPH; ***212** D-8; ★ **GRNS-**; mail Sophia z 27350; ● 700
Hilltop; RMC Place; GUILFORD; ***212** D-8; ★ **GRNS-**; mail Greensboro z 27407, z 27417; pop. incl. with Greensboro (Inc. Place)
Hilltop; RMC Place; LINCOLN; ***212** F-4; elev. 800ft./244m.; mail Lincolnton z 28092; ● 480
Hilltop Acres; RMC Place; CARTERET; ***213** H-17; elev. 25ft./8m.; mail Newport z 28570; ● 110
Hill View; RMC Place; GREENE; ***213** F-14; mail Snow Hill z 28580; ● 70
Hines Crossroad; RMC Place; PITT; ***213** E-15; elev. 77ft./23m.; ★ **GRNV**; mail Greenville z 27834; rural
Hinsons Crossroads; RMC Place; COLUMBUS; ***213** J-11; elev. 107ft./33m.; mail Fair Bluff z 28439; ● 50
Hiwassee Dam; RMC Place; CHEROKEE; **212** M-1; mail Murphy z 28906; ● 300
Hobbsville; RMC Place; GATES; **213** B-17; elev. 40ft./12m.; 🅿; z 27946; ● 170
Hobbton; RMC Place; SAMPSON; **213** G-12; mail Newton Grove z 28366; ● 40
Hobgood; Inc. Place; HALIFAX; **213** D-15; elev. 95ft./29m.; 🅿; z 27843; Ⓟ 435; © 404
Hobucken; RMC Place; PAMLICO; **213** F-17; elev. 3ft./1m.; 🅿; z 28537; ● 350
Hodges Gap; RMC Place; WATAUGA; ***212** C-3; mail Boone z 28607; pop. incl. with Boone (Inc. Place)
Hodman; RMC Place; DAVIE; ***212** D-6; mail Mocksville z 27028; rural
Hoffman; Inc. Place; RICHMOND; **212** G-9; elev. 380ft./116m.; 🅿; z 28347; Ⓟ 348; © 624
Hog Island; RMC Place; MOORE; ***212** G-10; mail Vass z 28394; rural
Ho-Ho Village; RMC Place; CARTERET; ***213** H-17; elev. 10ft./3m.; mail Newport z 28570
HOKE; **212** G-10; Ⓟ 22,856; © 33,646; ◆ 44,107
Holden Beach; Inc. Place; BRUNSWICK; **213** K-13; elev. 20ft./6m.; 🅿; ★ **MYR.B**; z 28462; Ⓟ 626; © 787
Holdens Crossroads; RMC Place; WILSON; ***213** E-14; mail Wilson z 27893; ● 30
Holiday Island; RMC Place; PERQUIMANS; ***213** C-18; elev. 8ft./2m.; mail Hertford z 27944; ● 280
Holiday Shores; RMC Place; MONTGOMERY; ***212** F-8; elev. 350ft./107m.; mail Troy z 27371; ● 100
Holland; RMC Place; WAKE; ***213** E-11; elev. 406ft./124m.; ★ **RAL**; mail Fuquay Varina z 27526; rural
Hollemans Crossroads; RMC Place; WAKE; ***213** E-11; elev. 285ft./87m.; ★ **RAL**; mail New Hill z 27562; rural
Hollis; RMC Place; RUTHERFORD; **212** F-3; elev. 1,196ft./365m.; mail Ellenboro z 28040; ● 50
Hollister; RMC Place; HALIFAX; **213** C-13; elev. 237ft./72m.; 🅿; z 27844; ● 550
Holly Grove; RMC Place; DAVIDSON; ***212** E-7; elev. 772ft./235m.; ★ **GRNS-**; mail Lexington z 27292; ● 220
Holly Grove; RMC Place; GATES; ***213** B-17; elev. 41ft./12m.; mail Corapeake z 27926; rural
Holly Ridge; Inc. Place; ONSLOW; **213** I-15; elev. 50ft./15m.; 🅿; z 28445; Ⓟ 728; © 831
Holly Spring; RMC Place; RANDOLPH; ***212** E-9; elev. 550ft./168m.; mail Ramseur z 27316; rural
Holly Springs; RMC Place; CUMBERLAND; ★ **FAY**; pop. incl. with Fayetteville (Inc. Place)
Holly Springs; RMC Place; MACON; ***212** M-3; elev. 2,200ft./671m.; mail Franklin z 28734; rural
Holly Springs; Inc. Place; WAKE; **213** E-11; elev. 471ft./144m.; 🅿; ★ **RAL**; z 27540; Ⓟ 908; © 9,192; ◆ 18,565
Hollyville (Cash Corner); RMC Place; PAMLICO; ***213** G-17; mail Bayboro z 28515; ● 100
Hollywood; RMC Place; CUMBERLAND; ***213** G-11; elev. 150ft./46m.; ★ **FAY**; mail Fayetteville z 28304; ● 280
Hollywood Crossroads; RMC Place; PITT; ***213** E-15; elev. 71ft./22m.; ★ **GRNV**; mail Greenville z 27858; rural
Home Acres; RMC Place; WAKE; ***213** E-12; ★ **RAL**; pop. incl. with Raleigh (Inc. Place)
Homestead (Homestead Village); RMC Place; MECKLENBURG; ***212** F-5; ★ **CHRLT**; mail Charlotte z 28214; pop. incl. with Charlotte (Inc. Place)
Homestead Heights; RMC Place; DURHAM; ***213** D-11; ★ **DUR**; mail Durham z 27704; pop. incl. with Durham (Inc. Place)
Homestead Village; MECKLENBURG; see Homestead (RMC Place)
Hominy; RMC Place; BUNCOMBE; ***212** L-5; ★ **ASHE**
Honey Hill; RMC Place; COLUMBUS; ***213** J-12; elev. 63ft./19m.; mail Hallsboro z 28442; ● 70
Honey Island; RMC Place; BRUNSWICK; ***213** J-12; elev. 60ft./18m.; mail Ash z 28420; rural
Honey Town; RMC Place; RICHMOND; ***212** H-8; elev. 301ft./92m.; mail Rockingham z 28379; pop. incl. with Rockingham (Inc. Place)
Honolulu; RMC Place; CRAVEN; ***213** F-15; mail Grifton z 28530; rural
Hood Swamp; RMC Place; WAYNE; ***213** F-14; elev. 125ft./38m.; ★ **GLDS**; mail Goldsboro z 27534; rural
Hookerton; Inc. Place; GREENE; **213** F-15; elev. 60ft./18m.; 🅿; z 28538; Ⓟ 422; © 467
Hooper Hill; RMC Place; BRUNSWICK; ***213** J-13; ★ **WILM**; mail Leland z 28451; ● 100
Hoopers Creek; RMC Place; HENDERSON; ***212** F-1; ★ **ASHE**; mail Fletcher z 28732; pop. incl. with Fletcher (Inc. Place)
Hootentown; RMC Place; BEAUFORT; ***213** E-16; elev. 14ft./4m.; mail Washington z 27889; ● 50
Hopedale; RMC Place; ALAMANCE; ***212** C-9; ★ **BUR**; mail Burlington z 27217; ● 150
Hope Mills; Inc. Place; CUMBERLAND; **213** G-11; elev. 109ft./33m.; 🅿; ★ **FAY**; z 28348; Ⓟ 8,184; © 11,237
Hope Valley; RMC Place; DURHAM; ***213** D-11; ★ **DUR**; mail Durham z 27707; pop. incl. with Durham (Inc. Place)
Hopewell; RMC Place; RUTHERFORD; ***212** F-3; mail Ellenboro z 28040; ● 100
Hopewell; RMC Place; WAYNE; ***213** F-13; elev. 177ft./54m.; mail Mount Olive z 28365; rural
Hopkins; RMC Place; WAKE; ***213** D-12; ★ **RAL**; mail Zebulon z 27597; rural
Horner; RMC Place; GRANVILLE; ***213** C-12; mail Oxford z 27565; rural
Horse Shoe; RMC Place; HENDERSON; ***212** F-1; elev. 2,065ft./629m.; 🅿; z 28742, z 28759; ● 470
Hosiery Mill; RMC Place; ANSON; ***212** G-7; elev. 450ft./137m.; mail Wadesboro z 28170; ● 100
Hoskins; RMC Place; MECKLENBURG; ★ **CHRLT**; mail Charlotte z 28214; pop. incl. with Charlotte (Inc. Place)
Hothouse; RMC Place; CHEROKEE; ***212** M-1; mail Murphy z 28906; rural
Hot Springs; Inc. Place; MADISON; **212** K-5; elev. 1,334ft./407m.; 🅿; z 28743; Ⓟ 478; © 645
Houston; RMC Place; UNION; ***212** G-6; elev. 666ft./203m.; mail Monroe z 28112; rural
Houstonville; RMC Place; IREDELL; ***212** D-6; elev. 915ft./279m.; mail Harmony z 28634
Howland Parkway; RMC Place; CARTERET; ***213** H-17; elev. 11ft./3m.; mail Beaufort z 28516; ● 130
Hubert; RMC Place; ONSLOW; **213** H-16; elev. 40ft./12m.; 🅿; ★ **JAX**; z 28539; ● 330
Hudson; Inc. Place; CALDWELL; **212** D-3; elev. 1,264ft./385m.; 🅿; ★ **HICK**; z 28638; Ⓟ 2,819; © 3,078
Hudsons Crossroads; RMC Place; PITT; ***213** E-15; elev. 53ft./16m.; ★ **GRNV**; mail Greenville z 27858; rural
Huffmantown; RMC Place; ONSLOW; ***213** G-15; mail Richlands z 28574; ● 50
Hughes; RMC Place; AVERY; ***212** D-2; mail Newland z 28657; ● 40
Hugo; RMC Place; LENOIR; ***213** F-15; mail Grifton z 28530; rural
Hulls Crossroads; RMC Place; LINCOLN; ***212** F-4; elev. 1,088ft./332m.; ★ **HICK**; mail Vale z 28168; rural
Huntdale; RMC Place; MITCHELL; ***212** D-1; elev. 2,058ft./627m.; mail Green Mountain z 28740; ● 30
Hunters Bridge; RMC Place; BEAUFORT; ***213** E-17; elev. 16ft./5m.; mail Pinetown z 27865; ● 30
Huntersville; Inc. Place; MECKLENBURG; **212** F-5; elev. 819ft./250m.; 🅿; ★ **CHRLT**; z 28070, z 28078; Ⓟ 3,023; © 24,960; ◆ 41,986
Hunting Creek; RMC Place; WILKES; ***212** C-5; elev. 1,100ft./335m.; mail North Wilkesboro z 28659; rural
Huntley; RMC Place; SAMPSON; ***213** G-12; elev. 159ft./48m.; mail Salemburg z 28385; rural
Huntsboro; RMC Place; GRANVILLE, VANCE; ***213** C-12; mail Oxford z 27565; rural
Huntsville; ROCKINGHAM; see Ellisboro (RMC Place)
Huntsville; RMC Place; YADKIN; ***212** D-6; elev. 880ft./268m.; mail Yadkinville z 27055; ● 30
Hurdle Mills; RMC Place; PERSON; ***212** C-10; elev. 604ft./184m.; 🅿; z 27541
Husk; ASHE; see Nella (RMC Place)
Hyatt Creek; RMC Place; HAYWOOD; ***212** L-4; mail Waynesville z 28786; ● 200
HYDE; **213** E-19; Ⓟ 5,411; © 5,826; ◆ 5,173
Hydeland; RMC Place; HYDE; ***213** F-18; elev. 3ft./1m.; mail Swanquarter z 27885; rural
Hyde Park Estates; RMC Place; MECKLENBURG; ***212** F-5; ★ **CHRLT**; mail Charlotte z 28216; pop. incl. with Charlotte (Inc. Place)
Hymans; RMC Place; CRAVEN; ***213** G-16; elev. 25ft./8m.; mail New Bern z 28562

I

Icard; CDP; BURKE; ***212** E-4; elev. 1,165ft./355m.; 🅿; ★ **HICK**; z 28666; Ⓟ 2,553; © 2,734
Icaria; RMC Place; CHOWAN; ***213** C-17; mail Tyner z 27980; rural
Ida; RMC Place; SCOTLAND; ***212** H-9; mail Laurel Hill z 28351; rural
Idalia; RMC Place; BEAUFORT; ***213** F-17; elev. 8ft./2m.; mail Aurora z 27806; rural
Idlewild; RMC Place; ASHE; ***212** C-4; elev. 2,951ft./899m.; mail West Jefferson z 28694; rural
Idlewild; RMC Place; MECKLENBURG; ***212** G-6; elev. 700ft./213m.; ★ **CHRLT**; mail Charlotte z 28212, z 28229; pop. incl. with Charlotte (Inc. Place)
Idlewild Annex; RMC Place; MECKLENBURG; ★ **CHRLT**; mail Charlotte z 28212, z 28227; pop. incl. with Charlotte (Inc. Place)
Ijames Crossroads; RMC Place; DAVIE; ***212** D-6; elev. 871ft./265m.; mail Mocksville z 27028; rural
Independence; RMC Place; MECKLENBURG; ★ **CHRLT**; mail Charlotte z 28212; pop. incl. with Charlotte (Inc. Place)
Index; RMC Place; ASHE; ***212** B-4; elev. 2,688ft./819m.; mail West Jefferson z 28694; rural
Indian Beach; Inc. Place; CARTERET; ***213** H-17; elev. 5ft./2m.; 🅿; ★ **JAX**; z 28512; Ⓟ 153; © 95
Indian Hills; RMC Place; JACKSON; ***212** L-3; elev. 2,000ft./610m.; mail Whittier z 28789; ● 50
Indian Springs; RMC Place; WAYNE; ***213** F-14; elev. 176ft./54m.; mail Seven Springs z 28578; rural
Indiantown; RMC Place; CAMDEN; ***213** B-19; mail Shawboro z 27973; rural
Indian Trail; Inc. Place; UNION; **212** G-6; elev. 697ft./212m.; 🅿; ★ **CHRLT**; z 28079; Ⓟ 1,942; © 11,905; Ⓡ 11,749
Indian Valley; RMC Place; ALAMANCE; ***212** C-9; elev. 600ft./183m.; ★ **BUR**; mail Burlington z 27217; ● 510
Inez; RMC Place; WARREN; ***213** C-13; elev. 370ft./113m.; mail Warrenton z 27589; rural
Ingalls; RMC Place; AVERY; **212** D-2; elev. 2,775ft./846m.; mail Newland z 28657, Spruce Pine z 28777; ● 200
Ingleside; RMC Place; FRANKLIN; **213** C-13; elev. 398ft./121m.; mail Louisburg z 27549; ● 50
Ingold; CDP; SAMPSON; **213** H-12; elev. 105ft./32m.; 🅿; z 28441; © 484
Institute; RMC Place; LENOIR; ***213** F-14; elev. 117ft./36m.; mail La Grange z 28551; ● 50
Intelligence; RMC Place; ROCKINGHAM; ***212** C-8; mail Madison z 27025; ● 50
Iotla; RMC Place; MACON; ***212** M-3; mail Franklin z 28734; rural
IREDELL; **212** D-5; Ⓟ 92,931; © 122,660; ◆ 161,314
Iris Gardens; RMC Place; CUMBERLAND; ***213** G-11; elev. 153ft./47m.; ★ **FAY**; mail Fayetteville z 28306; ● 450
Iron; LINCOLN; see Iron Station (RMC Place)
Ironduff; RMC Place; HAYWOOD; ***212** L-4; mail Waynesville z 28785; ● 80
Irongate; RMC Place; CUMBERLAND; ***213** G-11; elev. 175ft./53m.; ★ **FAY**; mail Fayetteville z 28306; ● 340
Ironhill; RMC Place; COLUMBUS; ***213** J-11; elev. 81ft./25m.; mail Tabor City z 28463
Iron Station (Iron); RMC Place; LINCOLN; **212** F-4; elev. 886ft./270m.; 🅿; z 28080; ● 500
Irving Park; RMC Place; GUILFORD; ***212** D-8; ★ **GRNS-**; mail Greensboro z 27408; pop. incl. with Greensboro (Inc. Place)
Isenhour; RMC Place; STANLY; ***212** F-7; elev. 30ft./9m.; mail New London z 28127
Island View Shores; RMC Place; BEAUFORT; ***213** F-17; elev. 5ft./2m.; mail Bath z 27808; ● 30
Isle of Pines; RMC Place; IREDELL; ***212** E-5; ★ **CHRLT**; mail Mooresville z 28117; ● 150
Ita; RMC Place; HALIFAX; ***213** C-14; elev. 200ft./61m.; mail Enfield z 27823; ● 30
Ivanhoe; CDP; SAMPSON; **213** I-13; elev. 113ft./34m.; 🅿; z 28447; © 311
Ivy; RMC Place; MADISON; ***212** D-1; elev. 2,073ft./632m.; ★ **ASHE**; mail Mars Hill z 28754; rural
Ivy Hills; RMC Place; HAYWOOD; ***212** L-4; ★ **ASHE**; mail Waynesville z 28785; ● 100

J

JAARS; CDP-Census Area Only; UNION; ***212** H-6; ★ **CHRLT**; © 360
Jackson; Inc. Place; ⊡ NORTHAMPTON; **213** B-15; 🅿; z 27845; Ⓟ 592; © 695
JACKSON; **212** M-4; Ⓟ 26,846; © 33,121; ◆ 36,210
Jackson Hamlet (Vina Vista); RMC Place; MOORE; ***212** G-9; mail Aberdeen z 28315; ● 70
Jackson Hill; RMC Place; DAVIDSON; ***212** E-7; mail Denton z 27239
Jackson Line; RMC Place; SWAIN; ***212** L-3; mail Bryson City z 28713; rural
Jackson Park; RMC Place; CABARRUS; ***212** F-6; elev. 791ft./241m.; ★ **CHRLT**; mail Kannapolis z 28081; pop. incl. with Kannapolis (Inc. Place)
Jacksons Creek; RMC Place; RANDOLPH; ***212** E-8; mail Denton z 27239; rural
Jacksons Crossroads; RMC Place; LENOIR; ***213** F-14; elev. 84ft./26m.; mail Kinston z 28504; rural
Jackson Springs; RMC Place; MOORE; **212** G-9; elev. 445ft./136m.; 🅿; z 27281; ● 300
Jacksons Store; RMC Place; DUPLIN; ***213** H-14; elev. 23ft./7m.; mail Beulaville z 28518; ● 30
Jacksontown; RMC Place; VANCE; ***213** B-12; mail Middleburg z 27556; rural
Jacksonville; Inc. Place; ⊡ ONSLOW; **213** H-15; elev. 15ft./5m.; 🅿 🅷 ■; ★ **JAX**; z 28540-46; Ⓟ 30,398; © 66,715; ◆ 76,864
Jacktown; RMC Place; MCDOWELL; ***212** E-2; mail Marion z 28752; ● 200
Jakesville; RMC Place; DAVIDSON; ***212** D-7; elev. 719ft./219m.; mail Lexington z 27295; rural
James City; CDP; CRAVEN; ***213** G-16; elev. 14ft./4m.; mail New Bern z 28560; Ⓟ 4,279; © 5,420; Ⓡ 5,422
Jamestown; Inc. Place; GUILFORD; **212** D-8; elev. 775ft./236m.; 🅿; ★ **GRNS-**; z 27282; Ⓟ 2,600; © 3,088
Jamesville; Inc. Place; MARTIN; **213** D-16; 🅿; z 27846; Ⓟ 612; © 502
Janeiro; RMC Place; PAMLICO; **213** G-17; mail Arapahoe z 28510; ● 40
Jarmantown; RMC Place; ONSLOW; ***213** G-14; elev. 20ft./6m.; mail Richlands z 28574; rural
Jarvisburg; RMC Place; CURRITUCK; **213** C-19; elev. 6ft./2m.; 🅿; z 27947; ● 450
Jason; RMC Place; GREENE; **213** F-14; elev. 114ft./35m.; mail La Grange z 28551; ● 100
Jasper; RMC Place; CRAVEN; **213** G-16; mail Cove City z 28523, New Bern z 28562; ● 130
Jefferson; Inc. Place; ⊡ ASHE; **212** B-4; 🅿 🅷; z 28640; Ⓟ 1,300; © 1,422
Jefferson Park; RMC Place; RICHMOND; ***212** H-8; elev. 271ft./83m.; mail Rockingham z 28379; ● 150
Jenkins Heights; RMC Place; GASTON; ***212** F-4; ★ **CHRLT**; mail Gastonia z 28052; pop. incl. with Gastonia (Inc. Place)
Jenny Lind; RMC Place; LENOIR; ***213** F-14; elev. 59ft./18m.; ★ **GLDS**; mail La Grange z 28551; rural
Jericho; RMC Place; CASWELL; **212** C-9; elev. 711ft./217m.; mail Yanceyville z 27379; ● 30
Jerome (Live Oak); RMC Place; BLADEN; **213** H-11; elev. 107ft./33m.; mail White Oak z 28399; ● 80
Jerusalem; RMC Place; DAVIE; ***212** E-6; elev. 791ft./241m.; ★ **SLSB**; mail Mocksville z 27028; ● 30
Jessama; BEAUFORT; see Five Points (RMC Place)
Joe; RMC Place; MADISON; ***212** K-4; elev. 2,649ft./807m.; mail Hot Springs z 28743; rural
Johns; RMC Place; SCOTLAND; **212** H-9; elev. 180ft./55m.; mail Laurinburg z 28352; ● 50
Johnson Crossroad; RMC Place; JOHNSTON; ***213** F-12; ★ **RAL**; mail Angier z 27501; rural
Johnsons Corner; RMC Place; CAMDEN; ***213** B-18; mail South Mills z 27976; ● 30
Johnsontown; RMC Place; DAVIDSON; ***212** D-7; elev. 838ft./255m.; ★ **GRNS-**; mail Thomasville z 27360; ● 400
Johnsontown; RMC Place; SAMPSON; ***213** G-12; mail Clinton z 28328; pop. incl. with Clinton (Inc. Place)
Johnsonville; RMC Place; CHEROKEE; ***212** M-1; mail Murphy z 28906; rural
Johnsonville; RMC Place; HARNETT; **212** F-10; elev. 405ft./123m.; mail Cameron z 28326; ● 260
JOHNSTON; **213** F-12; Ⓟ 81,306; © 121,965; Ⓡ 121,900; ◆ 167,367
Johnstown; RMC Place; LINCOLN; ***212** F-4; mail Cherryville z 28021; ● 50
Jonas Ridge; RMC Place; BURKE; ***212** D-2; elev. 3,720ft./1,134m.; 🅿; z 28641; ● 300
Jonathan; RMC Place; HAYWOOD; ***212** L-4; mail Waynesville z 28785; ● 590
Jones; RMC Place; CASWELL; ***212** B-9; elev. 628ft./191m.; mail Pelham z 27311; ● 30
JONES; **213** G-15; Ⓟ 9,414; © 10,381; ◆ 10,200
Jonesboro (Jonesboro Heights); RMC Place; LEE; ***212** F-10; mail Sanford z 27330; pop. incl. with Sanford (Inc. Place)
Jonesboro Heights; LEE; see Jonesboro (RMC Place)
Jones Chapel; RMC Place; WAKE; ***213** D-12; ★ **RAL**; mail Knightdale z 27545; ● 250
Jonestown; RMC Place; LENOIR; **213** G-14; elev. 90ft./27m.; mail Pink Hill z 28572; ● 30
Jonesville; Inc. Place; YADKIN; **212** C-5; elev. 913ft./278m.; 🅿; z 28642; includes Arlington annexed July 1, 2001; Ⓟ 1,549; © 1,464; Ⓐ 2,259
Joppa; RMC Place; CHOWAN, GATES, PERQUIMANS; ***213** C-17; elev. 16ft./5m.; mail Belvidere z 27919
Jordan; RMC Place; JOHNSTON; ***213** E-13; elev. 266ft./81m.; mail Selma z 27576; rural
Joyceton; RMC Place; CALDWELL; ***212** D-3; ★ **HICK**; mail Hudson z 28638, Lenoir z 28645; pop. incl. with Hudson (Inc. Place)
Joyland; RMC Place; DURHAM; ***213** D-11; ★ **DUR**; mail Durham z 27703; pop. incl. with Durham (Inc. Place)
Joyners Crossroads; RMC Place; NASH; ***213** D-14; ★ **RKYMT**; mail Rocky Mount z 27801; rural
Joynes; RMC Place; WILKES; ***212** C-5; elev. 1,269ft./387m.; mail Traphill z 28685
Jubilee; RMC Place; DAVIDSON; ***212** E-6; elev. 798ft./243m.; mail Linwood z 27299; rural
Judges Quarter; RMC Place; HYDE; ***213** F-18; elev. 3ft./1m.; mail Swanquarter z 27885; rural
Jugtown; RMC Place; BUNCOMBE; ***212** L-5; ★ **ASHE**; mail Candler z 28715; rural
Julian; RMC Place; GUILFORD, RANDOLPH; **212** D-9; elev. 750ft./229m.; 🅿; ★ **GRNS-**; z 27283; ● 400
Juno; RMC Place; BUNCOMBE; ***212** E-1; ★ **ASHE**; mail Asheville z 28806; rural
Jupiter; RMC Place; BUNCOMBE; **212** K-5; elev. 2,179ft./664m.; ★ **ASHE**; mail Weaverville z 28787; ● 30
Justice; RMC Place; FRANKLIN; **213** D-13; mail Spring Hope z 27882; ● 30

K

Kalmia; RMC Place; MITCHELL; ***212** D-2; mail Spruce Pine z 28777; rural
Kannapolis; Inc. Place; CABARRUS, ROWAN; **212** F-6; elev. 704ft./215m.; 🅿 ■; ★ **CHRLT**; z 28081-83; Ⓟ 29,709; © 36,910; ◆ 45,968
Kapps Mill; RMC Place; SURRY; ***212** B-5; elev. 1,200ft./366m.; mail Dobson z 27017, State Road z 28676; rural
Katesville; RMC Place; FRANKLIN; ***213** D-12; mail Franklinton z 27525; rural
Kearney; RMC Place; FRANKLIN; ***213** C-13; elev. 398ft./121m.; mail Louisburg z 27549; rural
Keene; RMC Place; DURHAM; ***213** D-11; ★ **DUR**; mail Durham z 27707; pop. incl. with Durham (Inc. Place)
Keener; CDP; SAMPSON; ***213** G-13; mail Clinton z 28328; © 508
Kelford; Inc. Place; BERTIE; **213** C-16; elev. 92ft./28m.; 🅿; z 27847; Ⓟ 204; © 245
Kellersville; RMC Place; WATAUGA; ***212** C-2; mail Banner Elk z 28604; rural
Kellogs Fork; RMC Place; GATES; ***213** B-17; mail Sunbury z 27979; rural
Kellum; RMC Place; ONSLOW; **213** H-15; ★ **JAX**; mail Jacksonville z 28546; ● 30
Kellumtown; RMC Place; ONSLOW; **213** H-16; ★ **JAX**; mail Hubert z 28539; ● 400
Kelly; CDP; BLADEN; **213** I-13; elev. 29ft./9m.; 🅿; z 28448; © 454
Kenansville; Inc. Place; ⊡ DUPLIN; **213** G-14; 🅿 🅷; z 28349; Ⓟ 856; © 1,149
Kenilworth; RMC Place; BUNCOMBE; ***212** E-1; ★ **ASHE**; mail Asheville z 28805; pop. incl. with Asheville (Inc. Place)
Kenly; Inc. Place; JOHNSTON, WILSON; **213** E-13; elev. 204ft./62m.; 🅿; z 27542; Ⓟ 1,549; © 1,569; Ⓡ 1,675
Kenmure; RMC Place; HENDERSON; ***212** F-1; mail Flat Rock z 28731; ● 200
Kennebec; RMC Place; WAKE; ***213** E-11; elev. 341ft./104m.; ★ **RAL**; mail Willow Spring z 27592; rural
Kennells Beach; RMC Place; PAMLICO; ***213** G-17; elev. 5ft./2m.; mail Grantsboro z 28529; summer pop. 1,000; ● 40
Kentwood; RMC Place; CABARRUS; ***212** F-6; elev. 850ft./259m.; ★ **CHRLT**; mail Concord z 28025; ● 70
Kernersville; Inc. Place; FORSYTH, GUILFORD; **212** C-8; elev. 1,023ft./312m.; 🅿; ★ **WNS**; z 27284-85; Ⓟ 10,899; © 17,126; ◆ 20,975
Kerr; RMC Place; SAMPSON; **213** I-13; elev. 91ft./28m.; mail Harrells z 28444; ● 30
Kershaw; RMC Place; PAMLICO; ***213** G-17; mail Oriental z 28571; rural
Keys Crossroads; RMC Place; GATES; ***213** B-17; mail Hobbsville z 27946; rural
Kikers; RMC Place; ANSON; ***212** G-7; elev. 446ft./136m.; mail Peachland z 28133; rural
Kilby Island; RMC Place; BEAUFORT; ***213** F-17; elev. 5ft./2m.; mail Bath z 27808; ● 40
Kilkenny Landing; TYRRELL; see Warbler (RMC Place)
Kill Devil Hills; Inc. Place; DARE; **213** C-20; elev. 20ft./6m.; 🅿; z 27948; Ⓟ 4,238; © 5,897
Kimesville; RMC Place; ALAMANCE, GUILFORD; **212** D-9; ★ **BUR**; mail Liberty z 27298; ● 140
King; Inc. Place; STOKES, FORSYTH; **212** C-7; elev. 1,053ft./321m.; 🅿; ★ **WNS**; z 27021; Ⓟ 4,059; © 5,952
King Charles; RMC Place; WAKE; ★ **RAL**; mail Raleigh z 27610; pop. incl. with Raleigh (Inc. Place)
Kingsboro; RMC Place; EDGECOMBE; ***213** D-14; ★ **RKYMT**; mail Rocky Mount z 27801; rural
Kings Creek; RMC Place; CALDWELL; **212** D-4; elev. 1,284ft./391m.; mail Boomer z 28606, Lenoir z 28645; ● 300
Kings Crossroads; RMC Place; GUILFORD; ***212** C-8; ★ **GRNS-**; mail Kernersville z 27284; pop. incl. with Stokesdale (Inc. Place)
Kings Crossroads; RMC Place; PITT; ***213** E-15; mail Fountain z 27829; rural
Kings Forest; RMC Place; ROWAN; mail Salisbury z 28147
Kings Grant; CDP; NEW HANOVER; ***213** J-14; ★ **WILM**; © 7,738
Kings Mountain; Inc. Place; CLEVELAND, GASTON; **212** F-4; elev. 1,003ft./306m.; 🅿 🅷; ★ **CHRLT**; z 28086; Ⓟ 8,763; © 9,693
Kingstown; Inc. Place; CLEVELAND; ***212** F-3; 🅿; z 28150; Ⓟ 956; © 845
King Whites Fork; RMC Place; HALIFAX; mail Hobgood z 27843; ● 100
Kinston; Inc. Place; ⊡ LENOIR; **213** F-15; elev. 44ft./13m.; 🅿 🅷 ■; z 28501-04; Ⓟ 25,295; © 23,688; ◆ 21,023
Kinton Fork; RMC Place; GRANVILLE; ***213** C-12; mail Oxford z 27565
Kipling; RMC Place; HARNETT; **213** F-11; elev. 309ft./94m.; 🅿; z 27543; ● 200
Kirbys Crossing; RMC Place; WILSON; ***213** E-13; mail Kenly z 27542, Lucama z 27851; ● 50
Kirkland; CDP; NEW HANOVER; ***213** J-14; ★ **WILM**; © 579
Kirkwood; RMC Place; GUILFORD; ***212** D-8; ★ **GRNS-**; mail Greensboro z 27408; pop. incl. with Greensboro (Inc. Place)
Kittrell; Inc. Place; VANCE; **213** C-12; elev. 410ft./125m.; 🅿; z 27544; Ⓟ 228; © 148
Kitty Fork; RMC Place; SAMPSON; **213** G-12; mail Clinton z 28328; ● 50
Kitty Hawk; Inc. Place; DARE; **213** C-20; elev. 20ft./6m.; 🅿; z 27949; Ⓟ 1,937; © 2,991
Knightdale; Inc. Place; WAKE; **213** D-12; elev. 300ft./91m.; 🅿; ★ **RAL**; z 27545; Ⓟ 1,884; © 5,958
Knob Hill; RMC Place; RICHMOND; ***212** H-8; mail Rockingham z 28379; pop. incl. with Rockingham (Inc. Place)
Knollwood; RMC Place; MOORE; ***212** G-9; mail Southern Pines z 28387
Knotts Island; RMC Place; CURRITUCK; **213** B-19; 🅿; z 27950; ● 620
Kona; RMC Place; MITCHELL; **212** D-2; mail Bakersville z 28705; ● 70
Kornbow; RMC Place; CUMBERLAND; ***213** G-11; ★ **FAY**; mail Fayetteville z 28303; pop. incl. with Fayetteville (Inc. Place)
Kornegay; RMC Place; DUPLIN; ***213** G-14; elev. 22ft./7m.; mail Albertson z 28508; rural
Kure Beach; Inc. Place; NEW HANOVER; **213** K-14; elev. 9ft./3m.; 🅿; ★ **WILM**; z 28449; Ⓟ 619; © 1,507; Ⓡ 1,542
Kyle; RMC Place; MACON; ***212** M-2; elev. 3,216ft./980m.; mail Topton z 28781

L

Laboratory; RMC Place; LINCOLN; ***212** F-4; mail Lincolnton z 28092; ● 300
Lackey Hill; RMC Place; SWAIN; ***212** L-3; mail Bryson City z 28713; ● 210
Lackey Town; RMC Place; MCDOWELL; ***212** E-2; mail Old Fort z 28762; ● 110
Ladonia; RMC Place; SURRY; ***212** B-5; elev. 1,247ft./380m.; mail Mount Airy z 27030; rural
Lafayette (Lafayette Village); RMC Place; CUMBERLAND; ***213** G-11; elev. 200ft./61m.; ★ **FAY**; mail Fayetteville z 28304; pop. incl. with Fayetteville (Inc. Place)
Lafayette Village; CUMBERLAND; see Lafayette (RMC Place)
Lagoon; RMC Place; BLADEN; ***213** I-12; mail Kelly z 28448
La Grange; RMC Place; CUMBERLAND; ***213** G-11; elev. 290ft./88m.; ★ **FAY**; mail Fayetteville z 28303; ● 1,570
La Grange; Inc. Place; LENOIR; **213** F-14; elev. 113ft./34m.; 🅿; ★ **GLDS**; z 28551; Ⓟ 2,805; © 2,844
Lake Comfort; RMC Place; HYDE; ***213** F-18; elev. 4ft./1m.; mail Swanquarter z 27885; rural
Lakecrest; RMC Place; CUMBERLAND; ***213** G-11; elev. 200ft./61m.; ★ **FAY**; mail Fayetteville z 28301; pop. incl. with Fayetteville (Inc. Place)
Lakedale; RMC Place; CUMBERLAND; ***213** G-11; ★ **FAY**; mail Fayetteville z 28306; pop. incl. with Fayetteville (Inc. Place)
Lake Daniel; RMC Place; GUILFORD; ***212** D-8; ★ **GRNS-**; mail Greensboro z 27408; pop. incl. with Greensboro (Inc. Place)
Lake Ellsworth; RMC Place; PITT; ***213** E-15; elev. 66ft./20m.; ★ **GRNV**; mail Greenville z 27834; pop. incl. with Greenville (Inc. Place)
Lake Gaston Estates; RMC Place; WARREN; mail Macon z 27551; ● 50
Lake Glenwood; RMC Place; PITT; ***213** E-15; elev. 53ft./16m.; ★ **GRNV**; mail Greenville z 27858; ● 250
Lake in the Pine; RMC Place; MONTGOMERY; ***212** F-8; elev. 350ft./107m.; mail Troy z 27371; ● 100
Lake Junaluska; CDP; HAYWOOD; **212** L-4; elev. 2,562ft./781m.; 🅿; ★ **ASHE**; z 28745; Ⓟ 2,482; © 2,675
Lake Landing; RMC Place; HYDE; ***213** E-19; mail Engelhard z 27824
Lake Lure; Inc. Place; RUTHERFORD; **212** F-1; elev. 1,120ft./341m.; 🅿; z 28746; Ⓟ 691; © 1,027
Lake Lynn; RMC Place; CUMBERLAND; ***213** G-11; elev. 137ft./42m.; ★ **FAY**; mail Fayetteville z 28306; ● 500
Lake Montonia; RMC Place; CLEVELAND; ***212** G-4; elev. 900ft./274m.; ★ **CHRLT**; mail Kings Mountain z 28086; ● 150
Lakemont Park; RMC Place; ALEXANDER; ***212** E-4; ★ **HICK**; mail Hickory z 28601; ● 500
Lake Norman of Catawba; CDP-Census Area Only; CATAWBA; ***212** E-5; ★ **HICK**; © 4,744
Lake Park; Inc. Place; UNION; ***212** G-6; 🅿; ★ **CHRLT**; z 28079; Ⓟ 4; © 2,093
Lake Santeetlah (Santeetlah); Inc. Place; GRAHAM; **212** L-2; 🅿; z 28771; Ⓟ 47; © 67
Lakeside; RMC Place; FORSYTH; ★ **WNS**; mail Winston Salem z 27105; pop. incl. with Winston-Salem (Inc. Place)
Lakeside; RMC Place; STANLY; ***212** F-7; elev. 630ft./192m.; mail Albemarle z 28001; rural
Lake Toxaway; RMC Place; TRANSYLVANIA; **212** M-4; 🅿; z 28747; ● 470
Lakeview; RMC Place; ALAMANCE; ***212** C-9; ★ **BUR**; mail Burlington z 27215; ● 180
Lakeview; RMC Place; DAVIDSON; ***212** E-7; elev. 761ft./232m.; mail Linwood z 27299; rural
Lakeview; RMC Place; MOORE; ***212** F-10; elev. 304ft./93m.; 🅿; z 28350; ● 600
Lakeview Estates; RMC Place; ALAMANCE; ***212** C-9; elev. 600ft./183m.; ★ **BUR**; mail Burlington z 27215; ● 110
Lakeview Estates; RMC Place; HENDERSON; ***212** F-1; mail Hendersonville z 28792; ● 230
Lake View Park; CATAWBA; see Northmoor (RMC Place)
Lake View Park; RMC Place; HALIFAX; ***213** B-14; mail Roanoke Rapids z 27870; ● 200
Lake Waccamaw; Inc. Place; COLUMBUS; **213** J-12; elev. 63ft./19m.; 🅿; z 28450; Ⓟ 954; © 1,411
Lakewood; RMC Place; CABARRUS; ***212** F-6; elev. 650ft./198m.; ★ **CHRLT**; mail Concord z 28025; pop. incl. with Concord (Inc. Place)
Lakewood; RMC Place; HENDERSON; ***212** F-1; mail Hendersonville z 28792; ● 110
Lambert; RMC Place; STANLY; ***212** F-7; elev. 682ft./208m.; mail Mount Pleasant z 28124; ● 50
Lambs Corner; RMC Place; CAMDEN; ***213** B-18; elev. 4ft./1m.; mail Camden z 27921; rural
Lamm; RMC Place; WILSON; ***213** E-13; mail Wilson z 27893; ● 50
Lamm Crossroads; RMC Place; NASH; ***213** D-13; ★ **RKYMT**; mail Spring Hope z 27882; ● 250
Lancaster Crossroads; RMC Place; NASH; ***213** D-13; elev. 280ft./85m.; mail Castalia z 27816; rural
Landis; Inc. Place; ROWAN; **212** E-6; elev. 866ft./264m.; 🅿; ★ **CHRLT**; z 28088; Ⓟ 2,333; © 2,996
Lane; RMC Place; CUMBERLAND; ***213** G-11; elev. 115ft./35m.; mail Linden z 28356; rural
Lanes Store; RUTHERFORD; see Cane Creek (RMC Place)
Langley Crossroads (Langley Store); RMC Place; NASH; ***213** D-14; ★ **RKYMT**; mail Rocky Mount z 27801; rural
Langley Store; NASH; see Langley Crossroads (RMC Place)
Lansdowne; RMC Place; MECKLENBURG; ***212** G-5; ★ **CHRLT**; mail Charlotte z 28226; pop. incl. with Charlotte (Inc. Place)
Lansing; Inc. Place; ASHE; **212** B-3; elev. 2,699ft./823m.; 🅿; z 28643; Ⓟ 171; © 151
Lanvale; RMC Place; BRUNSWICK; ***213** J-13; ★ **WILM**; mail Leland z 28451; ● 150
Lasker; Inc. Place; NORTHAMPTON; **213** C-15; elev. 85ft./26m.; 🅿; z 27845; Ⓟ 139; © 103
Last Chance; RMC Place; HYDE; ***213** F-19; mail Engelhard z 27824; rural
Latham Town; RMC Place; GUILFORD; ***212** D-8; ★ **GRNS-**; mail Greensboro z 27407; pop. incl. with Greensboro (Inc. Place)
Lattimore; Inc. Place; CLEVELAND; **212** F-3; elev. 925ft./282m.; 🅿; z 28089; Ⓟ 183; © 419
Lauada; RMC Place; SWAIN; ***212** L-3; elev. 1,950ft./594m.; mail Bryson City z 28713
Laurel; RMC Place; MADISON; mail Marshall z 28753; ● 50
Laurel Hill; RMC Place; BUNCOMBE; ***212** L-5; ★ **ASHE**; mail Candler z 28715; rural
Laurel Hill; RMC Place; SCOTLAND; **212** H-9; elev. 254ft./77m.; 🅿; z 28351; ● 2,400
Laurel Hills; RMC Place; WAKE; ***213** D-11; ★ **RAL**; mail Raleigh z 27612; ● 650
Laurel Park; Inc. Place; HENDERSON; ***212** F-1; elev. 2,800ft./853m.; 🅿; z 28739 & mail Hendersonville z 28792; Ⓟ 1,322; © 1,835; Ⓡ 2,017
Laurel Springs; RMC Place; ALLEGHANY; **212** B-4; elev. 2,797ft./853m.; 🅿; z 28644; ● 60
Laurinburg; Inc. Place; ⊡ SCOTLAND; **212** H-9; elev. 227ft./69m.; 🅿 🅷 🅲 808; z 28352-53; Ⓟ 11,643; © 15,874
Lawndale; Inc. Place; CLEVELAND; **212** F-3; elev. 817ft./249m.; 🅿; z 28090; Ⓟ 573; © 642
Lawndale; RMC Place; GUILFORD; ***212** C-8; ★ **GRNS-**; mail Greensboro z 27408; pop. incl. with Greensboro (Inc. Place)
Lawrence; RMC Place; EDGECOMBE; **213** D-15; elev. 92ft./28m.; mail Tarboro z 27886; ● 80
Lawsonville; RMC Place; ROCKINGHAM; ***212** B-9; elev. 718ft./219m.; ★ **GRNS-**; mail Reidsville z 27320; rural
Lawsonville; RMC Place; STOKES; **212** B-7; elev. 1,172ft./357m.; 🅿; z 27022; ● 130
Laytown; RMC Place; CALDWELL; ***212** D-4; elev. 1,284ft./391m.; mail Lenoir z 28645; rural
Leaksville; RMC Place; ROCKINGHAM; ***212** B-8; elev. 661ft./201m.; ★ **MRTNV**; mail Eden z 27288; pop. incl. with Eden (Inc. Place)
Leaman; RMC Place; MOORE; mail Robbins z 27325; rural
Leasburg; RMC Place; CASWELL; **212** B-10; elev. 615ft./187m.; 🅿; z 27291; ● 250
Leatherman; RMC Place; MACON; ***212** M-3; elev. 2,192ft./668m.; mail Franklin z 28734
Ledbetter; RMC Place; RICHMOND; ***212** G-9; elev. 295ft./90m.; mail Rockingham z 28379; ● 100
Ledger (Normanville); RMC Place; MITCHELL; **212** D-2; mail Bakersville z 28705; ● 280
LEE; **212** E-10; Ⓟ 41,374; © 49,040; Ⓡ 49,208; ◆ 59,761
Leechville; RMC Place; BEAUFORT; **213** E-18; elev. 4ft./1m.; mail Belhaven z 27810; ● 30
Lee Landing; RMC Place; PAMLICO; ***213** G-16; elev. 10ft./3m.; mail New Bern z 28560; rural
Lee's Ridge; RMC Place; BUNCOMBE; ***212** E-1; ★ **ASHE**; mail Asheville z 28806; ● 220
Leewood Acres; RMC Place; LINCOLN; ***212** F-4; mail Lincolnton z 28092; pop. incl. with Lincolnton (Inc. Place)
Legerwood; RMC Place; CALDWELL; ***212** D-3; elev. 1,165ft./355m.; mail Lenoir z 28645; rural
Leggett; Inc. Place; EDGECOMBE; **213** D-15; elev. 63ft./19m.; mail Tarboro z 27886; Ⓟ 108; © 77
Leggetts Crossroads; RMC Place; BEAUFORT; ***213** E-16; elev. 37ft./11m.; mail Washington z 27889; rural
Leicester; RMC Place; BUNCOMBE; **212** K-5; elev. 2,090ft./637m.; 🅿; ★ **ASHE**; z 28748; ● 600
Leland; Inc. Place; BRUNSWICK; **213** J-13; elev. 25ft./8m.; 🅿; ★ **WILM**; z 28451; Ⓟ 1,801; © 1,938
Lemon Springs; RMC Place; LEE; **212** F-10; elev. 38ft./12m.; 🅿; z 28355; ● 600
Lennon Crossroads; RMC Place; BRUNSWICK; ***213** K-13; elev. 41ft./12m.; mail Bolivia z 28422; rural
Lennons Crossroads; RMC Place; BLADEN, COLUMBUS; ***213** I-11; elev. 110ft./34m.; mail Evergreen z 28438; rural
Lennoxville; CARTERET; see Lenoxville (RMC Place)
Lenoir; Inc. Place; ⊡ CALDWELL; **212** D-3; elev. 1,182ft./360m.; 🅿 🅷 ■; z 28633, z 28645; Ⓟ 14,192; © 16,793; Ⓡ 16,774; ◆ 16,612
LENOIR; **213** G-14; Ⓟ 57,274; © 59,648; Ⓡ 59,636; ◆ 55,852
Lenoir Rhyne; RMC Place; CATAWBA; ★ **HICK**; mail Hickory z 28601; pop. incl. with Hickory (Inc. Place)
Lenoxville (Lennoxville); RMC Place; CARTERET; ***213** H-17; elev. 5ft./2m.; mail Beaufort z 28516; ● 170
Lentzton; RICHMOND; see Mount Pleasant (RMC Place)
Letitia; RMC Place; CHEROKEE; ***212** M-1; elev. 1,820ft./555m.; mail Murphy z 28906; rural
Level Cross; RMC Place; RANDOLPH; **212** D-8; elev. 823ft./251m.; ★ **GRNS-**; mail Randleman z 27317; ● 380
Level Cross; RMC Place; SURRY; ***212** C-6; elev. 1,204ft./367m.; mail Dobson z 27017
Levels; RMC Place; TYRRELL; ***213** D-18; mail Columbia z 27925; rural
Lewarae; RICHMOND; see Midway (RMC Place)

Entries in **UPPERCASE** are counties.
Entries in **bold** have populations of 2,500 or more.
Names in parentheses are alternate names.
Inc. Place — Incorporated Place
RMC Place — Rand McNally Designated Place
CDP — Census Designated Place
MCD — Minor Civil Division

⊡ County Seat
▲ Minor Civil Division
elev. Elevation
🅿 Post Office

🅷 Hospital
🅲 College
■ Principal Business Center
★ Ranally Metro Area (RMA) Abbreviation
z Zip Code(s)

Ⓟ Previous Census Population
Ⓡ Revised Census Population
Ⓐ Annexation Population
● Rand McNally Population Estimate
© Final Census Population
Ⓢ Special Census Population
◆ Estimated Population

For additional definitions see Glossary, Volume 1, and Introduction, Volume 2.

Lewis; RMC Place; GRANVILLE; *213 C-12; mail Oxford z 27565
Lewisburg; RMC Place; YANCEY; *212 D-1; elev. 2,288ft./697m.; mail Burnsville z 28714; rural
Lewiston; BERTIE; see Lewiston Woodville (Inc. Place)
Lewiston Woodville (Lewiston); Inc. Place; BERTIE; 213 C-16; elev. 77ft./23m.; 🅿; z 27849; Ⓟ 788; Ⓒ 613
Lewisville; Inc. Place; FORSYTH; 212 D-7; elev. 973ft./297m.; 🅿; ★ WNS; z 27023; Ⓟ 6,433; Ⓒ 8,826
Lexington; Inc. Place; ⊡ DAVIDSON; 212 D-7; elev. 809ft./247m.; 🅿 🅷 ■; z 27292-95; Ⓟ 16,581; Ⓒ 19,953; ◆ 20,141
Liberia; RMC Place; WARREN; *213 C-13; mail Warrenton z 27589; rural
Liberty; RMC Place; CHEROKEE; *212 M-1; elev. 1,651ft./503m.; mail Turtletown z 37391; ● 50
Liberty; Inc. Place; RANDOLPH; 212 D-9; elev. 790ft./241m.; 🅿; ★ GRNS-; z 27298; Ⓟ 2,047; Ⓒ 2,661
Liberty; RMC Place; ROWAN; 212 E-7; mail Gold Hill z 28071; ● 100
Liberty Hill; RMC Place; MONTGOMERY; *212 F-8; mail Mount Gilead z 27306; ● 30
Liddell; RMC Place; LENOIR; *213 G-14; elev. 158ft./48m.; mail Seven Springs z 28578; rural
Light Oak; CDP-Census Area Only; CLEVELAND; *212 F-3; elev. 800ft./244m.; mail Shelby z 28150; Ⓟ 1,339; Ⓒ 779
Liledoun (Liledown); RMC Place; ALEXANDER; *212 D-4; ★ HICK; mail Taylorsville z 28681; ● 30
Liledown; ALEXANDER; see Liledoun (RMC Place)
Lilesville; Inc. Place; ANSON; 212 G-8; elev. 478ft./146m.; 🅿; z 28091; Ⓟ 468; Ⓒ 459
Lillington; Inc. Place; ⊡ HARNETT; 213 F-11; 🅿; ★ RAL; z 27546; Ⓟ 2,048; Ⓒ 2,915
Lilly; RMC Place; CAMDEN; *213 B-18; elev. 15ft./5m.; mail South Mills z 27976; rural
LINCOLN; 212 F-4; Ⓟ 50,319; Ⓒ 63,780; ◆ 75,240
Lincolnton; Inc. Place; ⊡ LINCOLN; 212 F-4; elev. 873ft./266m.; 🅿 🅷; z 28092-93; Ⓟ 6,847; Ⓒ 9,965
Lindell; RMC Place; GREENE; *213 E-14; elev. 112ft./34m.; mail Stantonsburg z 27883; rural
Linden; Inc. Place; CUMBERLAND; 213 F-11; elev. 116ft./35m.; 🅿; z 28356; Ⓟ 180; Ⓒ 127
Lindley Mill; RMC Place; ALAMANCE; *212 D-10; elev. 500ft./152m.; mail Graham z 27253; rural
Lindley Park; RMC Place; GUILFORD; *212 D-8; ★ GRNS-; mail Greensboro z 27403; pop. incl. with Greensboro (Inc. Place)
Lineberry; RMC Place; RANDOLPH; *212 D-9; ★ GRNS-; mail Climax z 27233; rural
Linville; RMC Place; AVERY; 212 D-2; elev. 3,669ft./1,118m.; 🅿; z 28646; summer pop. 1,500; ● 300
Linville Falls; RMC Place; BURKE; 212 D-2; elev. 3,325ft./1,013m.; 🅿; z 28647; ● 350
Linwood; RMC Place; DAVIDSON; *212 E-7; elev. 659ft./201m.; 🅿; z 27299; ● 900
Lisbon; RMC Place; BLADEN; 213 I-12; elev. 117ft./36m.; mail Council z 28434; ● 100
Little Creek; RMC Place; MADISON; *212 D-1; elev. 2,892ft./881m.; mail Mars Hill z 28754; rural
Littlefield; RMC Place; PITT; *213 F-15; ★ GRNV; mail Ayden z 28513; ● 30
Little Horse Creek; RMC Place; ASHE; *212 B-3; elev. 3,400ft./1,036m.; mail Lansing z 28643; rural
Little Mountain; RMC Place; MCDOWELL; *212 E-2; mail Nebo z 28761; ● 30
Little Pinecreek; RMC Place; MADISON; *212 K-5; mail Marshall z 28753; ● 50
Little Richmond; RMC Place; SURRY; *212 C-6; mail Elkin z 28621; rural
Little River; RMC Place; ALEXANDER; *212 D-4; elev. 1,128ft./344m.; ★ HICK; mail Taylorsville z 28681; ● 30
Little River; RMC Place; TRANSYLVANIA; *212 F-1; mail Penrose z 28766
Littles Mill; RMC Place; RICHMOND; *212 G-8; elev. 276ft./84m.; mail Mount Gilead z 27306; rural
Little Switzerland; RMC Place; MCDOWELL; 212 D-2; elev. 3,500ft./1,067m.; 🅿; z 28749; summer pop. 600; ● 300
Littleton; Inc. Place; HALIFAX; 213 B-14; elev. 376ft./115m.; 🅿; z 27850; Ⓟ 691; Ⓒ 692
Live Oak; BLADEN; see Jerome (RMC Place)
Livingstons Quarters; RMC Place; SCOTLAND; *212 H-9; elev. 225ft./69m.; mail Laurel Hill z 28351; ● 30
Lizard Lick; RMC Place; WAKE; *213 D-12; ★ RAL; mail Wendell z 27591; ● 30
Lizzie; RMC Place; GREENE; 213 E-14; elev. 74ft./23m.; mail Snow Hill z 28580; ● 50
Lloyd Crossroads; RMC Place; HERTFORD; *213 C-17; mail Harrellsville z 27942; rural
Loafers Glory; RMC Place; MITCHELL; *212 D-2; mail Bakersville z 28705; ● 50
Lobelia; RMC Place; MOORE; *212 G-10; mail Vass z 28394; ● 30
Lochlommond; RMC Place; CUMBERLAND; *213 G-11; elev. 200ft./61m.; ★ FAY; mail Fayetteville z 28304; pop. incl. with Fayetteville (Inc. Place)
Locust; Inc. Place; STANLY; 212 F-6; elev. 742ft./226m.; 🅿; z 28097; Ⓟ 1,940; Ⓒ 2,416
Locust Hill; RMC Place; CASWELL; *212 C-9; elev. 603ft./184m.; mail Reidsville z 27320; rural
Loftins Crossroads; RMC Place; LENOIR; *213 G-15; elev. 83ft./25m.; mail Kinston z 28504; rural
Logan; RMC Place; RUTHERFORD; *212 F-2; elev. 912ft./278m.; mail Rutherfordton z 28139
Lola; RMC Place; CARTERET; 213 G-18; mail Cedar Island z 28520; ● 40
Lomax; RMC Place; WILKES; *212 C-5; elev. 1,406ft./429m.; mail Roaring River z 28669; rural
Lone Hickory; RMC Place; YADKIN; *212 D-6; elev. 1,045ft./319m.; mail Yadkinville z 27055; ● 200
Long Acres; RMC Place; ONSLOW; *213 H-15; ★ JAX; mail Jacksonville z 28546; pop. incl. with Jacksonville (Inc. Place)
Long Beach; BRUNSWICK; see Oak Island (Inc. Place)
Longcreek; RMC Place; PENDER; 213 I-13; elev. 21ft./6m.; mail Rocky Point z 28457; ● 220
Longhurst; RMC Place; PERSON; *213 B-11; pop. incl. with Roxboro (Inc. Place)
Longhurst; PERSON; see North Roxboro (RMC Place)
Long Island; RMC Place; CATAWBA; 212 E-5; elev. 856ft./261m.; 🅿; ★ HICK; z 28609; ● 200
Long John Mountain Estates; RMC Place; HENDERSON; *212 F-1; mail Hendersonville z 28791; ● 250
Longleaf; RMC Place; CARTERET; *213 H-17; elev. 10ft./3m.; mail Newport z 28570; ● 80
Long Leaf Park; RMC Place; NEW HANOVER; ★ WILM; mail Wilmington z 28403; pop. incl. with Wilmington (Inc. Place)
Long Pine; RMC Place; ANSON; *212 H-7; elev. 447ft./136m.; mail Peachland z 28133; rural
Long Point; RMC Place; JONES; *213 H-16; elev. 36ft./11m.; mail Maysville z 28555; rural
Long Ridge; RMC Place; MADISON; *212 D-1; ★ ASHE; mail Mars Hill z 28754; ● 100
Long Shoals; RMC Place; LINCOLN; *212 F-4; elev. 732ft./223m.; mail Lincolnton z 28092; ● 500
Longs Store; RMC Place; PERSON; *212 B-10; mail Roxboro z 27574; rural
Longtown; RMC Place; BURKE; *212 E-2; elev. 1,407ft./429m.; mail Nebo z 28761; rural
Longtown; RMC Place; YADKIN; *212 C-6; elev. 1,044ft./318m.; mail Boonville z 27011; ● 130
Long View; RMC Place; BLADEN; *213 I-13; elev. 23ft./7m.; mail Kelly z 28448; rural
Longview; Inc. Place; CATAWBA, BURKE; 212 E-4; elev. 1,152ft./351m.; ★ HICK; mail Hickory z 28601-02; Ⓟ 3,229; Ⓒ 4,722
Longview; RMC Place; CUMBERLAND; *213 G-11; elev. 150ft./46m.; ★ FAY; mail Fayetteville z 28301; pop. incl. with Fayetteville (Inc. Place)
Longwood; RMC Place; BRUNSWICK; 213 K-12; elev. 45ft./14m.; 🅿; z 28452; ● 430
Longwood Park; RMC Place; RICHMOND; 212 H-9; mail Hamlet z 28345; ● 200
Loray; RMC Place; IREDELL; 212 D-5; mail Statesville z 28625, z 28677; ● 190
Louisburg; Inc. Place; ⊡ FRANKLIN; 213 C-13; elev. 224ft./68m.; 🅿 🅷; z 27549; Ⓟ 3,037; Ⓒ 3,111
Love Field; RMC Place; JACKSON; *212 L-4; mail Sylva z 28779; pop. incl. with Sylva (Inc. Place)
Lovejoy; RMC Place; MONTGOMERY; *212 F-8; elev. 732ft./223m.; mail Troy z 27371; ● 30
Love Valley; Inc. Place; IREDELL; 212 D-5; elev. 1,350ft./411m.; mail Statesville z 28625, z 28677; Ⓟ 67; Ⓒ 30
Lowell; Inc. Place; GASTON; 212 F-5; elev. 770ft./235m.; 🅿; ★ CHRLT; z 28098; Ⓟ 2,704; Ⓒ 2,662
Lowes Grove; RMC Place; DURHAM; 213 D-11; ★ DUR; mail Durham z 27713; pop. incl. with Durham (Inc. Place)
Lowesville; CDP; LINCOLN; 212 F-5; elev. 785ft./239m.; ★ CHRLT; mail Stanley z 28164; Ⓟ 1,092; Ⓒ 1,440
Lowgap; RMC Place; SURRY; 212 B-5; elev. 1,457ft./444m.; 🅿; z 27024; ● 380
Lowland; RMC Place; PAMLICO; 213 F-17; elev. 4ft./1m.; 🅿; z 28552; ● 450
Luart; RMC Place; HARNETT; *213 F-11; elev. 350ft./107m.; mail Lillington z 27546; rural
Lucama; Inc. Place; WILSON; 213 E-13; elev. 134ft./41m.; 🅿; z 27851; Ⓟ 933; Ⓒ 847; Ⓡ 876
Lucia; RMC Place; GASTON; 212 F-5; elev. 820ft./250m.; ★ CHRLT; mail Mount Holly z 28120; ● 160
Luck; RMC Place; MADISON; *212 K-5; mail Hot Springs z 28743; rural
Lumber Bridge; Inc. Place; ROBESON; 212 H-10; elev. 193ft./59m.; 🅿; ★ FAY; z 28357; Ⓟ 109; Ⓒ 118
Lumberton; Inc. Place; ⊡ ROBESON; 213 I-11; elev. 137ft./42m.; 🅿 🅷 ■; z 28358-60; Ⓟ 18,601; Ⓒ 20,795; ◆ 20,227
Luther; RMC Place; BUNCOMBE; *212 L-5; ★ ASHE; mail Candler z 28715; ● 50
Lyman; RMC Place; DUPLIN; 213 H-14; mail Chinquapin z 28521; ● 100
Lynchs Corner; RMC Place; PASQUOTANK; *213 B-18; mail Elizabeth City z 27909; ● 30
Lynn; RMC Place; POLK; 212 F-1; elev. 924ft./282m.; 🅿; z 28750; ● 530
Lynndale; RMC Place; PITT; *213 E-15; elev. 69ft./21m.; ★ GRNV; mail Greenville z 27858; pop. incl. with Greenville (Inc. Place)
Lynwood Lakes; RMC Place; GUILFORD; *212 D-8; ★ GRNS-; mail Greensboro z 27406; ● 770

M

Mabel; RMC Place; WATAUGA; 212 C-3; mail Zionville z 28698; ● 90
Macclesfield; Inc. Place; EDGECOMBE; 213 E-14; elev. 100ft./30m.; 🅿; z 27852; Ⓟ 493; Ⓒ 458
Macedonia; CHEROKEE; see Wolf Creek (RMC Place)
Macedonia; RMC Place; WAKE; *213 E-11; elev. 486ft./148m.; ★ RAL; mail Raleigh z 27606
Macedonia; RMC Place; WASHINGTON; *213 D-17; mail Plymouth z 27962; ● 50
MacGee Crossroads; RMC Place; JOHNSTON; *213 F-12; ★ RAL; mail Angier z 27501; rural
Machpelah; RMC Place; LINCOLN; *212 F-5; elev. 840ft./256m.; mail Iron Station z 28080; ● 30
Mackeys; RMC Place; WASHINGTON; 213 D-17; elev. 8ft./2m.; mail Roper z 27970; ● 130
Macks Village; RMC Place; WAKE; *213 E-11; ★ RAL; mail Fuquay Varina z 27526; ● 80
Maco; RMC Place; BRUNSWICK; 213 J-13; ★ WILM; mail Leland z 28451; ● 50
Macon; Inc. Place; WARREN; 213 B-13; elev. 385ft./117m.; 🅿; z 27551; Ⓟ 154; Ⓒ 115
MACON; 212 M-3; Ⓟ 23,499; Ⓒ 29,811; Ⓡ 29,808; ◆ 33,341
Madison; Inc. Place; ROCKINGHAM; 212 C-8; elev. 574ft./175m.; 🅿; ★ GRNS-; z 27025; Ⓟ 2,371; Ⓒ 2,262
MADISON; 212 K-5; Ⓟ 16,953; Ⓒ 19,635; ◆ 20,604
Maggie; HAYWOOD; see Maggie Valley (Inc. Place)
Maggie Valley (Maggie); Inc. Place; HAYWOOD; 212 L-4; 🅿; z 28751; Ⓟ 185; Ⓒ 607
Magnolia; RMC Place; BURKE; *212 E-3; mail Morganton z 28655; pop. incl. with Morganton (Inc. Place)
Magnolia; Inc. Place; DUPLIN; 213 H-13; elev. 139ft./42m.; 🅿; z 28453; Ⓟ 747; Ⓒ 932
Maiden; Inc. Place; CATAWBA, LINCOLN; 212 E-4; elev. 900ft./274m.; 🅿; ★ HICK; z 28650; Ⓟ 2,574; Ⓒ 3,282; Ⓡ 3,177
Maine; RMC Place; DAVIE; *212 D-6; elev. 798ft./243m.; mail Mocksville z 27028
Main Street; RMC Place; WAKE; ★ RAL; mail Garner z 27529; pop. incl. with Garner (Inc. Place)
Makatoka; RMC Place; BRUNSWICK; *213 J-12; mail Ash z 28420; rural
Makleyville; RMC Place; HYDE; *213 F-18; mail Scranton z 27875
Malmo; RMC Place; BRUNSWICK; *213 J-13; ★ WILM; mail Leland z 28451; ● 30
Malpass Corner; RMC Place; PENDER; *213 I-13; mail Burgaw z 28425; rural
Maltby; RMC Place; CHEROKEE; *212 M-1; mail Marble z 28905; ● 180
Malvern Hills; RMC Place; BUNCOMBE; *212 E-1; ★ ASHE; mail Asheville z 28806; pop. incl. with Asheville (Inc. Place)
Mamers; RMC Place; HARNETT; 213 F-11; elev. 110ft./34m.; 🅿; z 27552; ● 400
Mamie; RMC Place; CURRITUCK; 213 C-19; mail Powells Point z 27966; ● 60
Manchester; RMC Place; CUMBERLAND; *213 G-11; ★ FAY; mail Spring Lake z 28390; pop. incl. with Spring Lake (Inc. Place)
Mandale; RMC Place; ALAMANCE; *212 D-10; elev. 533ft./162m.; mail Graham z 27253; rural
Mangum; RMC Place; RICHMOND; *212 G-8; mail Mount Gilead z 27306
Manly; RMC Place; MOORE; *212 G-9; mail Southern Pines z 28387
Manns Harbor; RMC Place; DARE; 213 D-20; elev. 5ft./2m.; 🅿; z 27953; ● 500
Manor; RMC Place; FORSYTH; *212 D-7; ★ WNS; mail Winston Salem z 27103-04, z 27114; pop. incl. with Winston-Salem (Inc. Place)
Mansfield; RMC Place; CARTERET; *213 H-17; mail Morehead City z 28557; pop. incl. with Morehead City (Inc. Place)
Mansfield Park; RMC Place; CARTERET; *213 H-17; elev. 10ft./3m.; mail Morehead City z 28557; pop. incl. with Morehead City (Inc. Place)
Manson; RMC Place; WARREN; 213 B-13; elev. 424ft./129m.; 🅿; z 27553; ● 120
Manteo; Inc. Place; ⊡ DARE; 213 D-20; elev. 5ft./2m.; 🅿; z 27954; Ⓟ 991; Ⓒ 1,052
Maple; RMC Place; CURRITUCK; 213 B-19; 🅿; z 27956; ● 250
Maple Cypress; RMC Place; CRAVEN; *213 F-15; elev. 23ft./7m.; mail Grifton z 28530; rural
Maple Hill; RMC Place; PENDER; 213 H-14; elev. 33ft./10m.; 🅿; z 28454; ● 390
Maple Springs; RMC Place; WILKES; *212 C-4; elev. 1,281ft./390m.; mail Purlear z 28665; ● 30
Mapleton; RMC Place; HERTFORD; *213 B-16; mail Murfreesboro z 27855; ● 150
Mapleville; RMC Place; FRANKLIN; 213 D-13; mail Louisburg z 27549; ● 30
Maplewood; RMC Place; RICHMOND; *212 H-8; mail Rockingham z 28379; pop. incl. with Rockingham (Inc. Place)
Marble; RMC Place; CHEROKEE; 212 M-2; elev. 1,686ft./514m.; 🅿; z 28905; ● 830
Maready; RMC Place; DUPLIN; *213 H-14; mail Chinquapin z 28521
Margaret; RMC Place; FRANKLIN; *213 D-13; elev. 328ft./100m.; mail Louisburg z 27549; rural
Margaretsville; NORTHAMPTON; see Margarettsville (RMC Place)
Margarettsville (Margaretsville); RMC Place; NORTHAMPTON; 213 B-15; elev. 56ft./17m.; 🅿; z 27853; ● 240
Maribel; RMC Place; PAMLICO; *213 G-17; elev. 4ft./1m.; mail Bayboro z 28515; ● 200
Marietta; Inc. Place; ROBESON; 212 J-10; elev. 92ft./28m.; 🅿; z 28362; Ⓟ 206; Ⓒ 164
Marion; Inc. Place; ⊡ MCDOWELL; 212 E-2; elev. 1,395ft./425m.; 🅿 🅷; z 28737, z 28752; Ⓟ 4,765; Ⓒ 4,943
Mariposa; RMC Place; LINCOLN; *212 F-5; mail Stanley z 28164; ● 50
Marko; RMC Place; MECKLENBURG; ★ CHRLT; pop. incl. with Charlotte (Inc. Place)
Marlboro; RMC Place; PITT; *213 E-15; elev. 82ft./25m.; ★ GRNV; mail Farmville z 27828; pop. incl. with Farmville (Inc. Place)
Marler; RMC Place; YADKIN; *212 C-5; mail Hamptonville z 27020
Marlwood Acres; RMC Place; MECKLENBURG; ★ CHRLT; mail Charlotte z 28212; pop. incl. with Charlotte (Inc. Place)
Mar-Mac; CDP-Census Area Only; WAYNE; *213 F-13; ★ GLDS; mail Goldsboro z 27530; Ⓟ 3,282; Ⓒ 3,004
Mar-Man; RMC Place; CRAVEN; *213 H-17; elev. 25ft./8m.; mail Havelock z 28532; pop. incl. with Havelock (Inc. Place)
Marshall; Inc. Place; ⊡ MADISON; 212 K-5; elev. 1,800ft./549m.; 🅿; z 28753; Ⓟ 809; Ⓒ 840
Marshallberg; RMC Place; CARTERET; 213 H-18; elev. 6ft./2m.; 🅿; z 28553; ● 700
Mars Hill; Inc. Place; MADISON; 212 D-1; elev. 2,325ft./709m.; 🅿 🅲 1,251; ★ ASHE; z 28754; Ⓟ 1,611; Ⓒ 1,764
Marshville; Inc. Place; UNION; 212 G-7; elev. 555ft./169m.; 🅿; z 28103; Ⓟ 2,020; Ⓒ 2,360
Marston; RMC Place; RICHMOND; 212 G-9; elev. 442ft./135m.; 🅿; z 28363; ● 260
Martel Village; RMC Place; BUNCOMBE; ★ ASHE; mail Asheville z 28804; pop. incl. with Woodfin (Inc. Place)
MARTIN; 213 D-16; Ⓟ 25,078; Ⓒ 25,593; Ⓡ 25,546; ◆ 22,737
Martins Creek; RMC Place; CHEROKEE; *212 M-1; elev. 1,671ft./509m.; mail Murphy z 28906; rural
Martins Point; RMC Place; DARE; mail Kitty Hawk z 27949; pop. incl. with Kitty Hawk (Inc. Place)
Martins Stores; RMC Place; YADKIN; *212 D-6; elev. 973ft./297m.; mail Yadkinville z 27055; rural
Marvin; Inc. Place; UNION; 212 G-5; elev. 696ft./212m.; 🅿; ★ CHRLT; z 28173; Ⓒ 1,039
Marys Grove; RMC Place; CLEVELAND; *212 F-4; elev. 937ft./286m.; ★ CHRLT; mail Kings Mountain z 28086; ● 150
Mashoes; RMC Place; DARE; *213 D-20; mail Manns Harbor z 27953; ● 50
Masonboro (Masonboro Sound); CDP; NEW HANOVER; *213 J-14; ★ WILM; mail Wilmington z 28403; Ⓟ 7,010; Ⓒ 11,812
Masonboro Sound; NEW HANOVER; see Masonboro (CDP)
Masons Crossroads; RMC Place; SCOTLAND; *212 H-9; elev. 224ft./68m.; mail Gibson z 28343
Mason Store; HARNETT; see Norrington Crossroads (RMC Place)
Masontown; RMC Place; CARTERET; *213 H-18; elev. 3ft./1m.; mail Stacy z 28581
Massapoag; RMC Place; LINCOLN; mail Lincolnton z 28092; pop. incl. with Lincolnton (Inc. Place)
Massey Hill; RMC Place; CUMBERLAND; ★ FAY; pop. incl. with Fayetteville (Inc. Place)
Mast; RMC Place; WATAUGA; *212 C-3; elev. 2,767ft./843m.; mail Vilas z 28692; rural
Mathews Crossroads; NASH; see Matthews Crossroads (RMC Place)
Matkins; RMC Place; CASWELL; *212 C-9; elev. 789ft./240m.; mail Gibsonville z 27249
Matney; RMC Place; WATAUGA; *212 C-3; mail Banner Elk z 28604; rural
Matthews; Inc. Place; MECKLENBURG; 212 G-6; elev. 721ft./220m.; 🅿 🅲 400; ★ CHRLT; z 28104-06; Ⓟ 13,651; Ⓒ 22,127; Ⓡ 22,125; ◆ 30,388
Matthews Crossroads (Mathews Crossroads); RMC Place; NASH; *213 D-13; mail Castalia z 27816; rural
Matthewstown; FORSYTH; see Beesons Crossroads (RMC Place)
Maury; RMC Place; GREENE; 213 F-15; elev. 78ft./24m.; 🅿; z 28554; ● 500
Mavaton; RMC Place; CHOWAN; *213 C-17; elev. 41ft./12m.; mail Edenton z 27932
Maxton; Inc. Place; ROBESON, SCOTLAND; 212 H-10; elev. 196ft./60m.; 🅿; z 28364; Ⓟ 2,373; Ⓒ 2,551
Mayfair; RMC Place; CUMBERLAND; *213 G-11; elev. 200ft./61m.; ★ FAY; mail Fayetteville z 28304; pop. incl. with Fayetteville (Inc. Place)
Mayfield; RMC Place; ROCKINGHAM; 212 B-9; mail Ruffin z 27326; ● 130
Mayhew; RMC Place; IREDELL; *212 E-5; elev. 857ft./261m.; ★ CHRLT; mail Mooresville z 28115, z 28117; ● 100
Mayodan; Inc. Place; ROCKINGHAM; 212 B-8; elev. 580ft./177m.; 🅿; ★ GRNS-; z 27027; Ⓟ 2,471; Ⓒ 2,417
Mayos Crossroads; RMC Place; EDGECOMBE; *213 D-15; elev. 23ft./7m.; mail Bethel z 27812, Tarboro z 27886; rural
Maysville; Inc. Place; JONES; 213 H-16; elev. 40ft./12m.; 🅿; z 28555; Ⓟ 892; Ⓒ 1,002
Mazeppa; RMC Place; IREDELL; *212 E-5; elev. 901ft./275m.; mail Mooresville z 28115; ● 100
McAdenville; Inc. Place; GASTON; 214 B-8; elev. 600ft./183m.; 🅿; ★ CHRLT; z 28101; Ⓟ 830; Ⓒ 619
McAdoo Heights; RMC Place; GUILFORD; *212 D-8; ★ GRNS-; mail Greensboro z 27405; pop. incl. with Greensboro (Inc. Place)
McArthur Crossroads; RMC Place; SCOTLAND; *212 H-9; mail Laurinburg z 28352; rural
McConnell; RMC Place; MOORE; *212 F-9; elev. 387ft./118m.; mail Robbins z 27325
McCray; RMC Place; ALAMANCE; *212 C-9; elev. 659ft./201m.; ★ BUR; mail Burlington z 27215; ● 50
McCullen; RMC Place; SAMPSON; *213 G-13; mail Clinton z 28328; rural
McCullers; RMC Place; WAKE; *213 E-11; ★ RAL; mail Raleigh z 27603
McDade; RMC Place; ORANGE; *212 C-10; elev. 731ft./223m.; mail Cedar Grove z 27231; rural
McDaniel; RMC Place; SAMPSON; *213 H-12; mail Roseboro z 28382; rural
McDonald; Inc. Place; ROBESON; 212 I-10; elev. 145ft./44m.; 🅿; z 28340; Ⓟ 88; Ⓒ 119
MCDOWELL; 212 E-2; Ⓟ 35,681; Ⓒ 42,151; ◆ 43,984
McFarlan; Inc. Place; ANSON; 212 H-8; elev. 304ft./93m.; 🅿; z 28102; Ⓟ 98; Ⓒ 89
McGehees Mill; RMC Place; PERSON; *212 B-10; mail Semora z 27343; rural
McGinnis Crossroads; RMC Place; POLK; *212 G-2; elev. 987ft./301m.; mail Columbus z 28722; rural
McGowans Crossroads; RMC Place; PITT; *213 E-15; elev. 59ft./18m.; ★ GRNV; mail Greenville z 27858; rural
McGrady; RMC Place; WILKES; 212 C-4; elev. 1,457ft./444m.; 🅿; z 28649; ● 220
McLamb Crossroads; RMC Place; SAMPSON; *213 G-12; mail Newton Grove z 28366; ● 30
McLeansville; CDP; GUILFORD; *212 C-9; elev. 763ft./233m.; 🅿; ★ GRNS-; z 27301; Ⓟ 1,154; Ⓒ 1,080
Meadow; JOHNSTON; see Peacocks Crossroads (RMC Place)
Meadow; STOKES; see Peacocks Crossroads (RMC Place)
Meadowbrook; RMC Place; CLEVELAND; *212 F-3; elev. 900ft./274m.; mail Shelby z 28150; rural
Meadowood; RMC Place; RICHMOND; *212 H-8; mail Rockingham z 28379; ● 180
Meadowood Lakes; RMC Place; ALAMANCE; *212 D-10; elev. 600ft./183m.; ★ BUR; mail Mebane z 27302; ● 100
Meadow Summit; RMC Place; ROCKINGHAM; *212 B-8; elev. 648ft./198m.; ★ MRTNV; mail Eden z 27288; pop. incl. with Eden (Inc. Place)
Meadow Wood; RMC Place; CUMBERLAND; *213 G-11; elev. 200ft./61m.; ★ FAY; mail Fayetteville z 28304; ● 560
Meat Camp; RMC Place; WATAUGA; *212 C-3; mail Boone z 28607; ● 50
Mebane; Inc. Place; ALAMANCE, ORANGE; 212 D-10; elev. 674ft./205m.; 🅿; ★ BUR; z 27302; Ⓟ 4,754; Ⓒ 7,284; Ⓡ 7,367
MECKLENBURG; 212 G-5; Ⓟ 511,433; Ⓒ 695,454; Ⓡ 695,370; ◆ 942,785
Medfield; RMC Place; WAKE; *213 E-11; elev. 447ft./136m.; ★ RAL; mail Raleigh z 27607; ● 1,100
Melanchton; RMC Place; RANDOLPH; *212 D-9; elev. 681ft./208m.; ★ GRNS-; mail Liberty z 27298; ● 50
Melrose; RMC Place; POLK; *212 F-1; elev. 1,481ft./451m.; mail Saluda z 28773; rural
Melville; RMC Place; ALAMANCE; *212 D-10; elev. 551ft./168m.; ★ BUR; mail Mebane z 27302; rural
Melvin Hill; RMC Place; POLK; *212 G-2; mail Columbus z 28722; rural
Menola; RMC Place; HERTFORD; *213 C-16; mail Ahoskie z 27910
Meredith College; RMC Place; WAKE; elev. 450ft./137m.; ★ RAL; mail Raleigh z 27601; pop. incl. with Raleigh (Inc. Place)
Merrimon; RMC Place; CARTERET; 213 G-17; elev. 6ft./2m.; mail Beaufort z 28516; ● 130
Merritt; RMC Place; PAMLICO; 213 G-17; elev. 6ft./2m.; 🅿; z 28556; ● 190
Merry Hill; RMC Place; BERTIE; 213 D-17; 🅿; z 27957; ● 80
Merry Oaks; RMC Place; CHATHAM; 213 E-11; mail Moncure z 27559; ● 150
Mesic; Inc. Place; PAMLICO; 213 F-17; elev. 5ft./2m.; 🅿; z 28515; Ⓟ 310; Ⓒ 257
Metcalf; RMC Place; CLEVELAND; mail Shelby z 28150; ● 30
Method; RMC Place; WAKE; *213 E-11; ★ RAL; mail Raleigh z 27606, z 27636; pop. incl. with Raleigh (Inc. Place)
Mewborns Crossroads; RMC Place; LENOIR; *213 F-15; elev. 78ft./24m.; mail Kinston z 28504; rural
Micaville; RMC Place; YANCEY; 212 D-1; 🅿; z 28755; ● 250
Michfield; RMC Place; RANDOLPH; *212 E-8; elev. 700ft./213m.; mail Asheboro z 27205; rural
Micro; Inc. Place; JOHNSTON; 213 E-13; elev. 192ft./59m.; 🅿; ★ RAL; z 27555; Ⓟ 417; Ⓒ 454
Middleburg; Inc. Place; VANCE; 213 B-12; elev. 470ft./143m.; 🅿; z 27556; Ⓟ 131; Ⓒ 162
Middle Fork; RMC Place; TRANSYLVANIA; *212 M-5; mail Brevard z 28712; ● 110
Middlesex; Inc. Place; NASH; 213 E-13; elev. 287ft./87m.; 🅿; z 27557; Ⓟ 730; Ⓒ 838
Middletown; RMC Place; HYDE; *213 E-19; elev. 3ft./1m.; mail Engelhard z 27824; ● 80
Midland; Inc. Place; CABARRUS; 212 G-6; elev. 535ft./163m.; 🅿; ★ CHRLT; z 28107; incorporated November 7 2000; not reported in 2000 Census; ● 2,500
Midpine; RMC Place; CLEVELAND; *212 G-4; elev. 971ft./296m.; ★ CHRLT; mail Kings Mountain z 28086; ● 450
Midway; RMC Place; ALEXANDER; *212 D-5; mail Hiddenite z 28636; ● 330
Midway; RMC Place; BEAUFORT; *213 E-17; elev. 25ft./8m.; mail Washington z 27889; ● 40
Midway; RMC Place; BERTIE; *213 D-17; elev. 40ft./12m.; mail Merry Hill z 27957; ● 30
Midway; RMC Place; BRUNSWICK; *213 K-13; mail Bolivia z 28422; rural
Midway; RMC Place; CABARRUS; *212 F-6; ★ CHRLT; mail Kannapolis z 28081; pop. incl. with Kannapolis (Inc. Place)
Midway (Eller); Inc. Place; DAVIDSON; 212 D-7; ★ WNS; mail Winston Salem z 27107; incorporated June 29, 2006; not reported in 2000 Census; ● 4,500
Midway (Lewarae); RMC Place; RICHMOND; *212 H-8; mail Rockingham z 28379; pop. incl. with Rockingham (Inc. Place)
Midway; RMC Place; ROCKINGHAM; *212 C-8; elev. 851ft./259m.; ★ GRNS-; mail Reidsville z 27320; ● 100
Midway; RMC Place; SAMPSON; *213 G-12; elev. 192ft./59m.; mail Roseboro z 28382; rural
Midway Park; RMC Place; ONSLOW; elev. 30ft./9m.; 🅿; ★ JAX; z 28544; pop. incl. with Jacksonville (Inc. Place)
Midwood; RMC Place; MECKLENBURG; ★ CHRLT; mail Charlotte z 28205; pop. incl. with Charlotte (Inc. Place)
Milburnie; RMC Place; WAKE; *213 E-12; ★ RAL; mail Raleigh z 27604; pop. incl. with Knightdale (Inc. Place)
Mildred; RMC Place; EDGECOMBE; *213 D-15; elev. 48ft./15m.; mail Tarboro z 27886; ● 100
Miles; RMC Place; ORANGE; *212 D-10; elev. 720ft./219m.; ★ DUR; mail Mebane z 27302; ● 200
Millboro; RMC Place; RANDOLPH; *212 E-8; elev. 768ft./234m.; mail Franklinville z 27248; rural
Mill Branch; RMC Place; BRUNSWICK; *213 K-12; elev. 57ft./17m.; mail Ash z 28420; rural
Millbridge; RMC Place; ROWAN; *212 E-6; elev. 785ft./239m.; ★ CHRLT; mail Salisbury z 28147; ● 30
Millbrook; RMC Place; WAKE; *213 D-12; elev. 318ft./97m.; ★ RAL; mail Raleigh z 27609; pop. incl. with Raleigh (Inc. Place)
Mill Creek; RMC Place; ASHE; *212 C-3; elev. 3,151ft./960m.; mail Todd z 28684
Mill Creek; RMC Place; BRUNSWICK; *213 J-13; ★ WILM; mail Winnabow z 28479; rural
Mill Creek; RMC Place; CARTERET; *213 H-17; mail Newport z 28570; ● 350
Mill Crossroads; RMC Place; CHOWAN; *213 C-17; elev. 9ft./3m.; mail Edenton z 27932; rural
Millennium; RMC Place; HERTFORD; *213 C-16; elev. 65ft./20m.; mail Aulander z 27805; ● 300
Millers; RMC Place; WAYNE; pop. incl. with Goldsboro (Inc. Place)
Millers Creek; CDP; WILKES; 212 C-4; elev. 1,409ft./429m.; 🅿; z 28651; Ⓟ 1,787; Ⓒ 2,071
Millersville; RMC Place; ALEXANDER; 212 D-4; ★ HICK; mail Taylorsville z 28681; ● 220
Millingport; RMC Place; STANLY; *212 F-7; elev. 658ft./201m.; mail Albemarle z 28001; ● 30
Mill Neck; RMC Place; HERTFORD; *213 B-16; elev. 48ft./15m.; mail Como z 27818; rural
Mill Spring; RMC Place; POLK; 212 F-2; elev. 1,000ft./305m.; 🅿; z 28756; ● 500
Mills River; Inc. Place; HENDERSON; *212 F-1; 🅿; ★ ASHE; z 28759 & mail Horse Shoe z 28742; incorporated June 24, 2003; not reported in 2000 Census
Milltown; RMC Place; GRAHAM; 212 L-2; mail Robbinsville z 28771; ● 150
Milton; Inc. Place; CASWELL; 212 B-10; elev. 475ft./145m.; 🅿; z 27305; Ⓟ 185; Ⓒ 132
Milwaukee; RMC Place; NORTHAMPTON; 213 B-15; elev. 85ft./26m.; 🅿; z 27820; ● 280
Mimosa Shores; RMC Place; BEAUFORT; *213 E-16; mail Washington z 27889; ● 50
Mineola; BEAUFORT; see Old Ford (RMC Place)
Mineral Springs; RMC Place; ANSON; *212 H-7; mail Polkton z 28135; rural
Mineral Springs; Inc. Place; UNION; 212 H-6; elev. 631ft./192m.; 🅿; ★ CHRLT; z 28108; Ⓒ 1,370
Mingo; RMC Place; SAMPSON; *213 G-12; mail Dunn z 28334; rural
Minneapolis; RMC Place; AVERY; 212 C-2; 🅿; z 28652; ● 250
Minnesott Beach; Inc. Place; PAMLICO; 213 G-17; elev. 26ft./8m.; 🅿; z 28510; Ⓟ 266; Ⓒ 311
Minnie-Bert; RMC Place; PITT; *213 E-15; elev. 12ft./4m.; ★ GRNV; mail Bethel z 27812, Stokes z 27884; rural
Minpro; RMC Place; MITCHELL; *212 D-2; mail Spruce Pine z 28777; ● 120
Mint Hill; Inc. Place; MECKLENBURG; 212 G-6; elev. 780ft./238m.; 🅿; ★ CHRLT; z 28227; Ⓟ 11,615; Ⓒ 14,922; Ⓡ 15,609; ◆ 21,245
Mintons Store; RMC Place; HERTFORD; *213 C-16; elev. 69ft./21m.; mail Woodland z 27897; rural
Mintonsville; RMC Place; GATES; *213 B-17; mail Hobbsville z 27946; rural
Mintz; RMC Place; SAMPSON; *213 H-12; mail Roseboro z 28382; rural
Minuet; RMC Place; MECKLENBURG; ★ CHRLT; mail Charlotte z 28209-10; pop. incl. with Charlotte (Inc. Place)
Mirror Lake; RMC Place; MACON; *212 M-4; mail Highlands z 28741; pop. incl. with Highlands (Inc. Place)
Misenheimer (Misenheimer Springs); Inc. Place; STANLY; 212 F-7; elev. 675ft./206m.; 🅿 🅲 2,119; z 28109; incorporated June 26, 2003; not reported in 2000 Census; ● 1,000
Misenheimer Springs; STANLY; see Misenheimer (Inc. Place)
MITCHELL; 212 D-1; Ⓟ 14,433; Ⓒ 15,687; ◆ 15,918
Mitchells Fork; RMC Place; GATES; *213 B-17; elev. 28ft./9m.; mail Hobbsville z 27946; rural
Mitchell Village; RMC Place; CARTERET; *213 H-17; elev. 25ft./8m.; mail Morehead City z 28557; pop. incl. with Morehead City (Inc. Place)
Mitcheners Crossroads; FRANKLIN; see Mitchiners Crossroads (RMC Place)
Mitchiners Crossroads (Mitcheners Crossroads); RMC Place; FRANKLIN; *213 C-12; mail Franklinton z 27525; rural
Mocksville; Inc. Place; ⊡ DAVIE; 212 D-6; elev. 800ft./244m.; 🅿 🅷; z 27028; Ⓟ 3,399; Ⓒ 4,178
Moffitt Hill; RMC Place; MCDOWELL; 212 E-2; mail Old Fort z 28762; ● 170
Mollie; RMC Place; COLUMBUS; 213 J-11; mail Clarendon z 28432; ● 30
Moltonville; RMC Place; SAMPSON; *213 G-13; elev. 146ft./45m.; mail Clinton z 28328; rural
Momeyer; Inc. Place; NASH; *213 D-13; ★ RKYMT; mail Nashville z 27856; Ⓟ 303; Ⓒ 291
Monbo; RMC Place; CATAWBA; *212 E-5; elev. 892ft./272m.; ★ HICK; mail Catawba z 28609; rural
Moncure; RMC Place; CHATHAM; 212 E-10; elev. 219ft./67m.; 🅿; z 27559; ● 770
Monks Crossroads; RMC Place; SAMPSON; *213 G-12; mail Newton Grove z 28366; ● 30
Monroe; Inc. Place; ⊡ UNION; 212 G-6; elev. 595ft./181m.; 🅿 🅷 ■; z 28110-12; Ⓟ 16,385; Ⓒ 26,228; ◆ 38,626
Monroeton; RMC Place; ROCKINGHAM; *212 C-8; ★ GRNS-; mail Reidsville z 27320; ● 30
Monroetown; RMC Place; MOORE; *212 G-9; mail Southern Pines z 28387; ● 300
Montague; RMC Place; PENDER; *213 I-13; mail Currie z 28435
Montclair; RMC Place; CUMBERLAND; *213 G-11; elev. 200ft./61m.; ★ FAY; mail Fayetteville z 28304; pop. incl. with Fayetteville (Inc. Place)
Montezuma; RMC Place; AVERY; 212 D-2; elev. 3,837ft./1,170m.; 🅿; z 28653; ● 250
MONTGOMERY; 212 F-8; Ⓟ 23,346; Ⓒ 26,822; ◆ 27,521
Monticello; RMC Place; GUILFORD; 212 C-9; elev. 855ft./261m.; ★ GRNS-; mail Browns Summit z 27214; ● 120
Montreat; Inc. Place; BUNCOMBE; 212 E-1; elev. 2,600ft./792m.; 🅿 🅲 1,039; ★ ASHE; z 28757; Ⓟ 693; Ⓒ 630
Montrose; RMC Place; HOKE; *212 G-10; mail Raeford z 28376; rural
MOORE; 212 F-9; Ⓟ 59,013; Ⓒ 74,769; Ⓡ 74,762; ◆ 86,635
Moores Beach; RMC Place; BEAUFORT; *213 F-17; mail Belhaven z 27810; ● 400
Mooresboro; Inc. Place; CLEVELAND; 212 F-3; elev. 902ft./275m.; 🅿; z 28114; Ⓟ 294; Ⓒ 314
Moores School House; RMC Place; JOHNSTON; *213 E-13; mail Kenly z 27542; ● 30
Moores Springs; RMC Place; STOKES; *212 B-7; mail Westfield z 27053
Mooresville; Inc. Place; IREDELL; 212 E-5; elev. 911ft./278m.; 🅿 🅷; ★ CHRLT; z 28115, z 28117; Ⓟ 9,317; Ⓒ 18,823; ◆ 25,330
Moravian Falls; CDP; WILKES; 212 D-4; elev. 1,192ft./363m.; 🅿; z 28654; Ⓟ 1,736; Ⓒ 1,440
Mordecai; RMC Place; WAKE; ★ RAL; mail Raleigh z 27604; pop. incl. with Raleigh (Inc. Place)
Morehead City; Inc. Place; CARTERET; 213 H-17; elev. 16ft./5m.; 🅿 🅷; z 28557; Ⓟ 6,046; Ⓒ 7,691
Morgans Corner (Spences Corner); RMC Place; PASQUOTANK; 213 B-18; mail Elizabeth City z 27909; ● 30
Morganton; Inc. Place; ⊡ BURKE; 212 E-3; elev. 1,182ft./360m.; 🅿 🅷 ■; z 28655, z 28680; Ⓟ 15,085; Ⓒ 17,310; ◆ 17,053
Morgantown; RMC Place; ALAMANCE; 212 C-9; ★ BUR; mail Burlington z 27215; pop. incl. with Burlington (Inc. Place)
Moriah; RMC Place; PERSON; *213 C-11; elev. 592ft./180m.; mail Rougemont z 27572
Morlan Park; RMC Place; ROWAN; *212 E-6; ★ SLSB; mail Salisbury z 28146; pop. incl. with Salisbury (Inc. Place)
Morning Star; RMC Place; HAYWOOD; *212 L-5; ★ ASHE; mail Canton z 28716; ● 200
Morris Landing; RMC Place; ONSLOW; *213 I-15; mail Holly Ridge z 28445; rural
Morrisville; Inc. Place; WAKE, DURHAM; 213 D-11; elev. 300ft./91m.; 🅿; ★ RAL; z 27560 & mail Cary z 27519; Ⓟ 1,022; Ⓒ 5,208
Mortimer; RMC Place; CALDWELL; *212 D-3; mail Collettsville z 28611, Lenoir z 28645; rural
Morven; Inc. Place; ANSON; 212 H-8; elev. 405ft./123m.; 🅿; z 28119; Ⓟ 590; Ⓒ 579
Moss Hill; RMC Place; LENOIR; *213 G-14; elev. 109ft./33m.; mail Kinston z 28504; rural
Mother Vineyard; RMC Place; DARE; *213 D-20; mail Manteo z 27954; ● 150
Motleta; RMC Place; RANDOLPH; *212 E-8; elev. 577ft./176m.; ★ GRNS-; mail Asheboro z 27203; rural
Moulton; RMC Place; FRANKLIN; *213 C-13; elev. 405ft./123m.; mail Louisburg z 27549; rural
Mountain Home; CDP; HENDERSON; 212 F-1; elev. 2,120ft./646m.; 🅿; ★ ASHE; z 28758; Ⓟ 1,898; Ⓒ 2,169
Mountain Island; RMC Place; GASTON; *212 F-5; elev. 730ft./223m.; ★ CHRLT; mail Mount Holly z 28120; ● 80
Mountain Park; RMC Place; SURRY; *212 C-5; mail State Road z 28676; ● 50
Mountain Valley; RMC Place; HENDERSON; *212 F-1; mail Zirconia z 28790; rural
Mountain View; RMC Place; BUNCOMBE; *212 F-1; ★ ASHE; mail Arden z 28704; ● 200
Mountain View; CDP-Census Area Only; CATAWBA; *212 E-4; elev. 1,086ft./331m.; ★ HICK; mail Hickory z 28601-02; Ⓟ 3,697; Ⓒ 3,768
Mountain View; RMC Place; GASTON; *212 F-4; ★ CHRLT; mail Kings Mountain z 28086; ● 110
Mountain View; RMC Place; ORANGE; *212 D-10; ★ DUR; mail Hillsborough z 27278; ● 350
Mountain View; RMC Place; STOKES; *212 C-7; elev. 1,103ft./336m.; ★ WNS; mail King z 27021; rural
Mount Airy; Inc. Place; SURRY; 212 B-6; elev. 1,104ft./336m.; 🅿 🅷 ■; z 27030-31; Ⓟ 7,156; Ⓒ 8,484; ◆ 8,542
Mount Carmel; RMC Place; MONTGOMERY; *212 F-8; elev. 725ft./221m.; mail Troy z 27371; rural
Mount Carmel Acres; RMC Place; BUNCOMBE; *212 E-1; ★ ASHE; mail Asheville z 28806; ● 770
Mount Energy; RMC Place; GRANVILLE; *213 C-12; ★ DUR; mail Creedmoor z 27522; rural
Mount Gilead; RMC Place; AVERY; *212 C-2; mail Elk Park z 28622; rural
Mount Gilead; RMC Place; CABARRUS; *212 F-6; ★ CHRLT; mail Concord z 28025; ● 60
Mount Gilead; Inc. Place; MONTGOMERY; 212 G-8; elev. 433ft./132m.; 🅿; z 27306; Ⓟ 1,336; Ⓒ 1,389
Mount Gould; RMC Place; BERTIE; *213 C-17; elev. 60ft./18m.; mail Merry Hill z 27957; rural
Mount Herman; RMC Place; CALDWELL; *212 D-4; elev. 1,360ft./415m.; mail Hudson z 28638; rural
Mount Holly; Inc. Place; GASTON; 212 F-5; elev. 632ft./193m.; 🅿; ★ CHRLT; z 28120; Ⓟ 7,710; Ⓒ 9,618; Ⓡ 9,617
Mount Mitchell; RMC Place; CABARRUS; *212 F-6; ★ CHRLT; mail Kannapolis z 28083; rural
Mount Mourne; RMC Place; IREDELL; 212 E-5; elev. 875ft./267m.; 🅿; ★ CHRLT; z 28123; ● 580
Mount Olive; RMC Place; BLADEN; *213 I-12; elev. 112ft./34m.; mail Elizabethtown z 28337; ● 320
Mount Olive; RMC Place; COLUMBUS; *213 I-11; elev. 102ft./31m.; mail Whiteville z 28472; ● 80
Mount Olive; RMC Place; HYDE; *213 E-18; mail Belhaven z 27810; rural
Mount Olive; RMC Place; STOKES; *212 C-7; elev. 1,122ft./342m.; ★ WNS; mail King z 27021; rural
Mount Olive; Inc. Place; WAYNE, DUPLIN; 213 G-13; elev. 165ft./50m.; 🅿 🅲 3,155; ★ GLDS; z 28365; Ⓟ 4,582; Ⓒ 4,567
Mount Pleasant; RMC Place; AVERY; *212 D-2; mail Newland z 28657; rural
Mount Pleasant; Inc. Place; CABARRUS; 212 F-6; elev. 629ft./192m.; 🅿; ★ CHRLT; z 28124; Ⓟ 1,027; Ⓒ 1,259
Mount Pleasant; RMC Place; CHEROKEE; mail Murphy z 28906; rural
Mount Pleasant; RMC Place; NASH; *213 D-13; elev. 282ft./86m.; mail Bailey z 27807; ● 50
Mount Pleasant (Lentzton); RMC Place; RICHMOND; *212 G-8; elev. 539ft./164m.; mail Ellerbe z 28338; rural
Mount Pleasant; RMC Place; WAKE; *213 E-11; ★ RAL; mail Willow Spring z 27592; rural
Mount Pleasant (Champion); RMC Place; WILKES; *212 C-4; mail Ferguson z 28624
Mount Pleasant; RMC Place; YADKIN; *212 C-6; elev. 1,045ft./319m.; mail Boonville z 27011; rural
Mount Sterling; RMC Place; HAYWOOD; *212 K-4; elev. 1,557ft./475m.; mail Newport z 37821; rural
Mount Tabor; RMC Place; FORSYTH; *212 C-7; ★ WNS; mail Winston Salem z 27106; pop. incl. with Winston-Salem (Inc. Place)
Mount Tabor; RMC Place; WASHINGTON; *213 D-18; mail Creswell z 27928; rural
Mount Tirzah; RMC Place; PERSON; *213 C-11; elev. 684ft./208m.; mail Rougemont z 27572, Timberlake z 27583; ● 40
Mount Ulla; RMC Place; ROWAN; *212 E-6; elev. 839ft./256m.; 🅿; z 28125; ● 170
Mount Vernon; RMC Place; ROWAN; *212 E-6; elev. 706ft./215m.; mail Cleveland z 27013; rural
Mount Vernon; RMC Place; RUTHERFORD; *212 F-2; elev. 1,058ft./322m.; mail Rutherfordton z 28139; rural
Mount Vernon Springs; RMC Place; CHATHAM; 212 E-9; elev. 500ft./152m.; mail Siler City z 27344; ● 80
Mount Zion; RMC Place; GUILFORD; *212 D-8; ★ GRNS-; mail Greensboro z 27405-06; pop. incl. with Greensboro (Inc. Place)
Mount Zion; RMC Place; WILKES; *212 C-4; elev. 1,337ft./408m.; mail Ferguson z 28624; rural
Moxley; RMC Place; WILKES; *212 C-5; mail Hays z 28635, Traphill z 28685; rural
Moyock; RMC Place; CURRITUCK; 213 B-18; elev. 5ft./2m.; 🅿; z 27958; ● 1,750
Muddy Cross; RMC Place; GATES; *213 B-17; mail Hobbsville z 27946; rural
Mulberry; CDP; WILKES; 212 C-4; mail North Wilkesboro z 28659; Ⓟ 2,339; Ⓒ 2,269
Murdocksville; RMC Place; MOORE; *212 G-9; elev. 452ft./138m.; mail Pinehurst z 28374; ● 300
Murfreesboro; Inc. Place; HERTFORD; 213 B-16; elev. 88ft./27m.; 🅿 🅲 933; z 27855; Ⓟ 2,580; Ⓒ 2,045; Ⓡ 2,421
Murphy; Inc. Place; ⊡ CHEROKEE; 212 M-1; elev. 1,583ft./482m.; 🅿 🅷; z 28906; Ⓟ 1,575; Ⓒ 1,568
Murphy; RMC Place; DUPLIN; *213 H-14; mail Rose Hill z 28458; rural
Murphy Junction; RMC Place; BUNCOMBE; *212 E-1; ★ ASHE; pop. incl. with Asheville (Inc. Place)
Murray Hills; RMC Place; CABARRUS; *212 F-6; elev. 750ft./229m.; ★ CHRLT; mail Concord z 28025; rural
Murray Hills; RMC Place; CUMBERLAND; ★ FAY; pop. incl. with Fayetteville (Inc. Place)
Murrays Mills; RMC Place; CATAWBA; *212 E-5; elev. 900ft./274m.; ★ HICK; mail Catawba z 28609; ● 50
Murraysville; CDP; NEW HANOVER; *213 J-14; ★ WILM; mail Wilmington z 28411; Ⓒ 7,279
Murray Town; RMC Place; PENDER; *213 I-14; mail Burgaw z 28425; rural
Musgraves Crossroads; RMC Place; WAYNE; *213 F-14; ★ GLDS; mail Pikeville z 27863; rural
Myers Park; RMC Place; MECKLENBURG; ★ CHRLT; mail Charlotte z 28207; pop. incl. with Charlotte (Inc. Place)
Myrick Estates; RMC Place; HALIFAX; *213 B-14; mail Littleton z 27850, Scotland Neck z 27874; ● 150
Myrtle Grove; CDP; NEW HANOVER; *213 J-14; elev. 27ft./8m.; ★ WILM; mail Wilmington z 28403; Ⓟ 4,275; Ⓒ 7,125; Ⓡ 7,123

N

Nags Head; Inc. Place; DARE; 213 D-20; elev. 10ft./3m.; 🅿; z 27959; Ⓟ 1,838; Ⓒ 2,700
Nahunta; RMC Place; WAYNE; *213 F-13; elev. 149ft./45m.; ★ GLDS; mail Pikeville z 27863; rural
Nakina; RMC Place; COLUMBUS; 213 J-12; elev. 46ft./14m.; 🅿; z 28455; ● 150
Nantahala; RMC Place; SWAIN; *212 M-2; elev. 1,942ft./592m.; mail Topton z 28781; rural
Naples; RMC Place; HENDERSON; *212 F-1; elev. 2,080ft./634m.; 🅿; ★ ASHE; z 28760; ● 260
NASH; 213 D-13; Ⓟ 76,677; Ⓒ 87,420; Ⓡ 87,385; ◆ 93,889
Nashville; Inc. Place; ⊡ NASH; 213 D-13; 🅿; ★ RKYMT; z 27856; Ⓟ 3,617; Ⓒ 4,309; Ⓡ 4,417
Nathans Creek; RMC Place; ASHE; *212 B-4; elev. 2,973ft./906m.; mail Crumpler z 28617, Jefferson z 28640; ● 50
Navassa; Inc. Place; BRUNSWICK; 213 J-13; elev. 25ft./8m.; 🅿; ★ WILM; z 28451 & mail Wilmington z 28404; Ⓟ 445; Ⓒ 479
Nebo; RMC Place; MCDOWELL; 212 E-2; elev. 1,305ft./398m.; 🅿; z 28761; ● 840
Nebo; RMC Place; YADKIN; *212 C-6; elev. 1,075ft./328m.; mail Boonville z 27011; rural
Nebraska; RMC Place; HYDE; *213 F-19; mail Engelhard z 27824; ● 110
Needmore; RMC Place; ROWAN; 212 E-6; elev. 772ft./235m.; mail Woodleaf z 27054; ● 110
Needmore; RMC Place; SWAIN; *212 L-3; mail Bryson City z 28713; rural
Neel Estates; RMC Place; ROWAN; *212 E-6; ★ SLSB; mail Salisbury z 28147; ● 220
Nella (Husk); RMC Place; ASHE; *212 B-3; elev. 3,000ft./914m.; mail Lansing z 28643; rural
Nelson; RMC Place; DURHAM, WAKE; *213 D-11; ★ DUR; mail Morrisville z 27560; pop. incl. with Durham (Inc. Place)
Neuse; RMC Place; WAKE; 213 D-12; elev. 282ft./86m.; ★ RAL; mail Raleigh z 27604, z 27661; ● 380
Neuse Crossroads; RMC Place; WAKE; *213 D-12; ★ RAL; mail Raleigh z 27616
Neuse Forest; CDP-Census Area Only; CRAVEN; *213 G-16; elev. 29ft./9m.; mail New Bern z 28560, z 28562; Ⓟ 1,110; Ⓒ 1,426
Neverson; RMC Place; WILSON; mail Sims z 27880; rural
New Bern; Inc. Place; ⊡ CRAVEN; 213 G-16; elev. 15ft./5m.; 🅿 🅷 ■; z 28560-64; Ⓟ 17,363; Ⓒ 23,128; Ⓡ 23,111; ◆ 26,216
Newbold; RMC Place; CUMBERLAND; ★ FAY; mail Fayetteville z 28301; pop. incl. with Fayetteville (Inc. Place)
New Bridge; RMC Place; BUNCOMBE; *212 E-1; ★ ASHE; mail Asheville z 28804
Newdale; RMC Place; YANCEY; *212 D-2; elev. 2,491ft./759m.; mail Burnsville z 28714; ● 100
Newell; RMC Place; MECKLENBURG; 214 A-13; elev. 764ft./233m.; 🅿; ★ CHRLT; z 28126; pop. incl. with Charlotte (Inc. Place)
Newfound; RMC Place; BUNCOMBE; *212 L-5; ★ ASHE; mail Leicester z 28748; ● 50
NEW HANOVER; 213 J-14; Ⓟ 120,284; Ⓒ 160,307; Ⓡ 160,327; ◆ 205,372
New Haven; RMC Place; ALLEGHANY; *212 B-4; elev. 2,624ft./800m.; mail Sparta z 28675; ● 30
New Hill; RMC Place; WAKE; 213 E-11; elev. 320ft./98m.; 🅿; z 27562; ● 360
New Holland; RMC Place; HYDE; 213 F-19; mail Swanquarter z 27885; ● 40
New Hope; RMC Place; CHATHAM; *212 E-10; elev. 250ft./76m.; mail Moncure z 27559; ● 50
New Hope; RMC Place; FRANKLIN; *213 D-12; elev. 365ft./111m.; ★ RAL; mail Louisburg z 27549; ● 150
New Hope; RMC Place; GASTON; ★ CHRLT; mail Gastonia z 28054; pop. incl. with Gastonia (Inc. Place)
New Hope; RMC Place; IREDELL; *212 D-5; mail Union Grove z 28689
New Hope; RMC Place; ORANGE; *212 D-10; ★ DUR; mail Chapel Hill z 27514, z 27516; rural
New Hope; RMC Place; RANDOLPH; *212 E-8; elev. 590ft./180m.; mail Denton z 27239
New Hope; RMC Place; WAKE; 214 C-7; ★ RAL; mail Raleigh z 27616; pop. incl. with Raleigh (Inc. Place); Ⓟ 5,694
New Hope; RMC Place; WAYNE; *213 F-14; ★ GLDS; mail Goldsboro z 27534; ● 250
New Hope; RMC Place; WILSON; 213 E-14; mail Wilson z 27896; ● 370
New House; RMC Place; CLEVELAND; *212 F-3; elev. 1,078ft./329m.; mail Shelby z 28150; ● 30
Newland; Inc. Place; ⊡ AVERY; 212 D-2; elev. 3,621ft./1,104m.; 🅿; z 28657; Ⓟ 645; Ⓒ 704
New Lands; RMC Place; TYRRELL; *213 D-18; mail Columbia z 27925; rural
New Life; RMC Place; WILKES; *212 C-4; elev. 1,378ft./420m.; mail Hays z 28635; rural
New London; Inc. Place; STANLY; 212 F-7; elev. 697ft./212m.; 🅿; z 28127; Ⓟ 414; Ⓒ 326
New Market; RMC Place; RANDOLPH; *212 D-8; elev. 801ft./244m.; ★ GRNS-; mail Sophia z 27350
Newport; Inc. Place; CARTERET; 213 H-17; elev. 21ft./6m.; 🅿; z 28570; Ⓟ 2,516; Ⓒ 3,349
New Salem; RANDOLPH; see Salem (RMC Place)
New Salem; RMC Place; UNION; 212 G-7; mail Marshville z 28103; ● 120
Newsom; RMC Place; DAVIDSON; *212 E-7; elev. 559ft./170m.; mail Denton z 27239; rural
Newton; Inc. Place; ⊡ CATAWBA; 212 E-4; elev. 969ft./295m.; 🅿; ★ HICK; z 28658; Ⓟ 9,077; Ⓒ 12,560; Ⓡ 12,659
Newton Grove; Inc. Place; SAMPSON; 213 F-12; elev. 185ft./56m.; 🅿; z 28366; Ⓟ 511; Ⓒ 606
Newton Park; RMC Place; WILSON; *213 E-14; elev. 154ft./47m.; mail Wilson z 27896; pop. incl. with Wilson (Inc. Place)
Newtons Crossroads; RMC Place; SAMPSON; *213 H-13; elev. 76ft./23m.; mail Willard z 28478; rural
New Topsail Beach; PENDER; see Topsail Beach (Inc. Place)
Newtowne; RMC Place; IREDELL; mail Statesville z 28625; pop. incl. with Statesville (Inc. Place)
Niagara; RMC Place; MOORE; 212 G-10; elev. 403ft./123m.; mail Southern Pines z 28387; ● 180
Nicanor; PERQUIMANS; see Whiteston (RMC Place)
Nixons Beach; RMC Place; CHOWAN; *213 D-18; elev. 13ft./4m.; mail Edenton z 27932; ● 60
Nixonton; RMC Place; PASQUOTANK; 213 C-18; mail Elizabeth City z 27909; ● 120
Nobles Crossroads; RMC Place; LENOIR; *213 G-14; elev. 109ft./33m.; mail Deep Run z 28525; rural
Nocarva; RMC Place; WARREN; mail Macon z 27551; ● 30
Nocho Park; RMC Place; GUILFORD; *212 D-8; ★ GRNS-; mail Greensboro z 27406; pop. incl. with Greensboro (Inc. Place)
Norfleet; RMC Place; HALIFAX; *213 C-15; elev. 29ft./9m.; mail Scotland Neck z 27874; rural
Norlina; Inc. Place; WARREN; 213 B-13; elev. 437ft./133m.; 🅿; z 27563; Ⓟ 996; Ⓒ 1,107
Norman; Inc. Place; RICHMOND; 212 G-8; elev. 614ft./187m.; 🅿; z 28367; Ⓟ 105; Ⓒ 72
Normanville; MITCHELL; see Ledger (RMC Place)
Norrington Crossroads (Mason Store); RMC Place; HARNETT; *213 F-11; elev. 213ft./65m.; mail Lillington z 27546; rural
North; RMC Place; FORSYTH; ★ WNS; mail Winston Salem z 27105, z 27115; pop. incl. with Winston-Salem (Inc. Place)
North Albemarle; RMC Place; STANLY; mail Albemarle z 28001; pop. incl. with Albemarle (Inc. Place)
NORTHAMPTON; 213 B-15; Ⓟ 20,798; Ⓒ 22,086; ◆ 20,550
North Asheboro; RMC Place; RANDOLPH; *212 E-8; mail Asheboro z 27203; pop. incl. with Asheboro (Inc. Place)
North Belmont (Belmont Junction); RMC Place; GASTON; *212 F-5; elev. 728ft./222m.; ★ CHRLT; mail Belmont z 28012
North Brevard; RMC Place; TRANSYLVANIA; *212 M-5; mail Brevard z 28712; ● 950
North Burlington; RMC Place; ALAMANCE; ★ BUR; mail Burlington z 27215; pop. incl. with Burlington (Inc. Place)
North Charlotte; RMC Place; MECKLENBURG; *212 F-5; ★ CHRLT; mail Charlotte z 28228; pop. incl. with Charlotte (Inc. Place)
North Chase; RMC Place; NEW HANOVER; mail Wilmington z 28405; pop. incl. with Wilmington (Inc. Place)
North Concord; RMC Place; CABARRUS; *212 F-6; elev. 700ft./213m.; ★ CHRLT; mail Concord z 28025; pop. incl. with Concord (Inc. Place)
North Cooleemee; RMC Place; DAVIE; *212 D-6; ★ SLSB; mail Cooleemee z 27014
North Cove; RMC Place; MCDOWELL; 212 D-2; elev. 1,507ft./459m.; mail Marion z 28752; ● 100
North Durham; RMC Place; DURHAM; *213 D-11; ★ DUR; mail Durham z 27712; pop. incl. with Durham (Inc. Place)
North Elkin (Elkin Valley); RMC Place; SURRY; *212 C-5; mail Elkin z 28621; pop. incl. with Elkin (Inc. Place)
North Gastonia; RMC Place; GASTON; ★ CHRLT; pop. incl. with Gastonia (Inc. Place)
Northgate; RMC Place; DURHAM; *213 D-11; ★ DUR; mail Durham z 27701; pop. incl. with Durham (Inc. Place)
North Harbor; RMC Place; CARTERET; *213 H-17; elev. 4ft./1m.; mail Beaufort z 28516; ● 30
North Harlowe; RMC Place; CRAVEN; 213 H-17; elev. 16ft./5m.; mail Havelock z 28532; ● 100
North Henderson; RMC Place; VANCE; *213 C-12; mail Henderson z 27536
North Hickory; RMC Place; CATAWBA; *212 E-4; elev. 1,040ft./317m.; ★ HICK; mail Hickory z 28601; pop. incl. with Hickory (Inc. Place); Ⓟ 4,299
Northlakes; CDP-Census Area Only; CALDWELL; *212 E-4; elev. 1,000ft./305m.; ★ HICK; mail Granite Falls z 28630; Ⓟ 1,219; Ⓒ 1,390
North Lumberton; RMC Place; ROBESON; mail Lumberton z 28358; pop. incl. with Lumberton (Inc. Place)
Northmoor (Lake View Park); RMC Place; CATAWBA; *212 E-4; ★ HICK; mail Hickory z 28601; ● 200
North Point; RMC Place; FORSYTH; ★ WNS; mail Winston Salem z 27106; pop. incl. with Winston-Salem (Inc. Place)
North Raeford; RMC Place; HOKE; mail Raeford z 28376; rural
North Ridge; RMC Place; WAKE; ★ RAL; mail Raleigh z 27615, z 27624; pop. incl. with Raleigh (Inc. Place)
North River; RMC Place; CARTERET; *213 H-17; elev. 3ft./1m.; mail Beaufort z 28516; ● 150
North River Corner; RMC Place; CARTERET; *213 H-17; elev. 5ft./2m.; mail Beaufort z 28516; ● 60
North Roxboro (Longhurst); RMC Place; PERSON; mail Roxboro z 27573; pop. incl. with Roxboro (Inc. Place)
Northside; RMC Place; GRANVILLE; 213 D-11; elev. 323ft./98m.; ★ DUR; mail Creedmoor z 27522, z 27564; ● 70
Northside; RMC Place; WILSON; ★ RKYMT; mail Elm City z 27822
North Topsail Beach; Inc. Place; ONSLOW; 213 I-15; mail Sneads Ferry z 28460; Ⓒ 843
North Tryon; RMC Place; MECKLENBURG; ★ CHRLT; mail Charlotte z 28213, z 28215, z 28256, z 28262, z 28269; pop. incl. with Charlotte (Inc. Place)
Northview; RMC Place; LEE; *212 E-10; mail Sanford z 27330; rural
Northwest; Inc. Place; BRUNSWICK; *213 J-13; elev. 61ft./19m.; ★ WILM; mail Leland z 28451; Ⓟ 611; Ⓒ 671
Northwest Cabarrus Woods; RMC Place; CABARRUS; *212 F-6; elev. 700ft./213m.; ★ CHRLT; mail Concord z 28025; pop. incl. with Kannapolis (Inc. Place)
North Wilkesboro; Inc. Place; WILKES; 212 C-4; elev. 1,016ft./310m.; 🅿 🅷; z 28656, z 28659; Ⓟ 3,384; Ⓒ 4,116
North Winston; RMC Place; FORSYTH; *212 C-7; elev. 917ft./280m.; ★ WNS; mail Winston Salem z 27105; pop. incl. with Winston-Salem (Inc. Place)
Norton; RMC Place; JACKSON; *212 M-4; mail Cullowhee z 28723; ● 50
Norton; RMC Place; MACON; *212 N-3; mail Otto z 28763; rural
Norwood; RMC Place; ROCKINGHAM; *212 C-9; elev. 813ft./248m.; ★ GRNS-; mail Reidsville z 27320; ● 150
Norwood; Inc. Place; STANLY; 212 G-7; elev. 380ft./116m.; 🅿; z 28128; Ⓟ 1,617; Ⓒ 2,216
Norwood Beach; RMC Place; STANLY; *212 G-7; mail Norwood z 28128; pop. incl. with Norwood (Inc. Place)
Norwood Hollow; RMC Place; AVERY; *212 C-2; mail Banner Elk z 28604; ● 200

O

Oakboro; Inc. Place; STANLY; 212 G-7; elev. 500ft./152m.; 🅿; z 28129; Ⓟ 600; Ⓒ 1,198
Oak City; Inc. Place; MARTIN; 213 D-15; elev. 84ft./26m.; 🅿; z 27857; Ⓟ 389; Ⓒ 339; Ⓡ 376
Oak Crest; RMC Place; CUMBERLAND; ★ FAY; mail Fayetteville z 28301; pop. incl. with Fayetteville (Inc. Place)
Oakdale; RMC Place; GUILFORD; *212 D-8; ★ GRNS-; mail Jamestown z 27282; pop. incl. with Jamestown (Inc. Place)

Entries in **UPPERCASE** are counties.
Entries in **bold** have populations of 2,500 or more.
Names in parentheses are alternate names.
Inc. Place — Incorporated Place
RMC Place — Rand McNally Designated Place
CDP — Census Designated Place
MCD — Minor Civil Division

⊡ County Seat
▲ Minor Civil Division
elev. Elevation
🅿 Post Office

🅷 Hospital
🅲 College
■ Principal Business Center
★ Ranally Metro Area (RMA) Abbreviation
z Zip Code(s)

Ⓟ Previous Census Population
Ⓡ Revised Census Population
Ⓐ Annexation Population
● Rand McNally Population Estimate
Ⓒ Final Census Population
Ⓢ Special Census Population
◆ Estimated Population

For additional definitions see Glossary, Volume 1, and Introduction, Volume 2.

Oakdale; RMC Place; MECKLENBURG; *212 F-5; elev. 806ft./246m.; ★ CHRLT; pop. incl. with Charlotte (Inc. Place)
Oak Forest; RMC Place; BUNCOMBE; *212 F-1; ★ ASHE; mail Asheville z 28803; pop. incl. with Asheville (Inc. Place)
Oak Grove; RMC Place; CLEVELAND; *212 F-4; elev. 809ft./247m.; ★ CHRLT; mail Kings Mountain z 28086; ● 230
Oak Grove; RMC Place; GUILFORD; *212 D-8; ★ GRNS-; mail Greensboro z 27406; pop. incl. with Greensboro (Inc. Place)
Oak Grove; RMC Place; JONES; *213 G-16; elev. 32ft./10m.; mail Pollocksville z 28573; rural
Oak Grove; RMC Place; MACON; *212 M-3; mail Franklin z 28734; rural
Oak Grove; RMC Place; SURRY; *212 B-6; mail Mount Airy z 27030; rural
Oak Grove Inn; RMC Place; JOHNSTON; *213 E-13; elev. 184ft./56m.; mail Selma z 27576; rural
Oak Hill; RMC Place; BURKE; 212 E-3; elev. 1,326ft./404m.; mail Morganton z 28655; ● 120
Oak Hill; RMC Place; CALDWELL; *212 D-4; elev. 1,287ft./392m.; mail Lenoir z 28645; ● 100
Oak Hill; RMC Place; GRANVILLE; *213 B-11; elev. 496ft./151m.; mail Oxford z 27565; rural
Oakhurst; RMC Place; MECKLENBURG; ★ CHRLT; mail Charlotte z 28205; pop. incl. with Charlotte (Inc. Place)
Oak Island (Long Beach); Inc. Place; BRUNSWICK; 213 K-13; 🄿; z 28465 & mail Southport z 28461; Ⓟ 3,816; Ⓒ 6,571
Oakland; RUTHERFORD; see Frog Level (RMC Place)
Oakland; TRANSYLVANIA; see Sapphire (RMC Place)
Oakley; RMC Place; BUNCOMBE; *212 E-1; ★ ASHE; mail Asheville z 28803; pop. incl. with Asheville (Inc. Place)
Oak Park; RMC Place; BUNCOMBE; *212 F-1; ★ ASHE; mail Arden z 28704; ● 150
Oak Park; RMC Place; CHEROKEE; *212 M-1; mail Murphy z 28906
Oak Ridge; Inc. Place; GUILFORD; 212 C-8; elev. 939ft./286m.; 🄿; ★ GRNS-; z 27310; Ⓒ 3,988
Oak Ridge Park; RMC Place; RICHMOND; *212 H-8; mail Rockingham z 28379
Oaks (Glenburnie Gardens); RMC Place; CRAVEN; *213 G-16; elev. 10ft./3m.; mail New Bern z 28560; pop. incl. with New Bern (Inc. Place)
Oaks; RMC Place; ORANGE; *212 D-10; elev. 576ft./176m.; ★ DUR; mail Chapel Hill z 27517; rural
Oaksmith Acres; RMC Place; CARTERET; *213 H-17; elev. 20ft./6m.; mail Morehead City z 28557; ● 260
Oakview; RMC Place; GUILFORD; *212 D-8; ★ GRNS-; mail High Point z 27265; pop. incl. with High Point (Inc. Place)
Oak Villa; RMC Place; HERTFORD; *213 B-16; elev. 47ft./14m.; mail Ahoskie z 27910; ● 30
Oakville; RMC Place; WARREN; *213 B-13; mail Warrenton z 27589
Oakwillow; RMC Place; HERTFORD; *213 B-16; mail Ahoskie z 27910; rural
Oakwood; RMC Place; GUILFORD; *212 D-8; ★ GRNS-; mail Greensboro z 27407; pop. incl. with Greensboro (Inc. Place)
Oakwood Acres; RMC Place; DAVIDSON; *212 E-7; mail Lexington z 27292; ● 180
Occoneechee; RMC Place; ORANGE; *212 D-10; ★ DUR; mail Hillsborough z 27278; pop. incl. with Hillsborough (Inc. Place)
Ocean; RMC Place; CARTERET; *213 H-16; elev. 25ft./8m.; ★ JAX; mail Newport z 28570; ● 150
Ocean Isle Beach; Inc. Place; BRUNSWICK; 213 K-12; elev. 21ft./6m.; 🄿; ★ MYR.B; z 28469; Ⓟ 523; Ⓒ 426
Ochre Hill; JACKSON; see Willits (RMC Place)
Ocracoke; CDP; HYDE; 213 G-19; elev. 6ft./2m.; 🄿; z 27960; Ⓒ 769
Ogburn; RMC Place; FORSYTH; *212 C-7; ★ WNS; mail Winston Salem z 27105; pop. incl. with Winston-Salem (Inc. Place)
Ogden; CDP; NEW HANOVER; 213 L-20; ★ WILM; mail Wilmington z 28411; Ⓟ 3,228; Ⓒ 5,481
Ogreeta; RMC Place; CHEROKEE; *212 M-1; mail Murphy z 28906; rural
Oine; RMC Place; WARREN; *213 B-13; mail Norlina z 27563; rural
Okeewemee; RMC Place; MONTGOMERY; *212 F-8; elev. 630ft./192m.; mail Troy z 27371
Okisko; RMC Place; PASQUOTANK; *213 C-18; elev. 10ft./3m.; mail Elizabeth City z 27909; ● 30
Old Bethlehem; RMC Place; WARREN; *213 C-13; mail Warrenton z 27589; rural
Old Dock; RMC Place; COLUMBUS; 213 J-12; elev. 44ft./13m.; mail Whiteville z 28472; ● 70
Olde Farm; RMC Place; HARNETT; mail Spring Lake z 28390; ● 230
Old Farm; RMC Place; CABARRUS; *212 F-6; elev. 650ft./198m.; ★ CHRLT; mail Concord z 28025; ● 30
Old Ford (Mineola); RMC Place; BEAUFORT; *213 E-16; elev. 25ft./8m.; mail Washington z 27889; ● 50
Old Fort; Inc. Place; MCDOWELL; 212 E-2; elev. 1,438ft./438m.; 🄿; z 28762; Ⓟ 720; Ⓒ 963
Old Fort Shores; RMC Place; BEAUFORT; *213 E-16; elev. 5ft./2m.; mail Chocowinity z 27817; ● 80
Old Hundred; RMC Place; SCOTLAND; 212 H-9; mail Laurel Hill z 28351; ● 260
Old Providence; RMC Place; MECKLENBURG; ★ CHRLT; mail Charlotte z 28226; pop. incl. with Charlotte (Inc. Place)
Old Sparta; RMC Place; EDGECOMBE; 213 E-15; mail Macclesfield z 27852; ● 50
Old Spring Hope; RMC Place; NASH; *213 D-13; elev. 228ft./69m.; ★ RKYMT; mail Spring Hope z 27882; rural
Oldtown; RMC Place; FORSYTH; *212 C-7; ★ WNS; mail Winston Salem z 27106; pop. incl. with Winston-Salem (Inc. Place)
Old Trap; RMC Place; CAMDEN; 213 C-19; mail Shiloh z 27974; ● 150
Olin; RMC Place; IREDELL; 212 D-5; elev. 916ft./279m.; 🄿; z 28660; ● 120
Olive Branch; RMC Place; UNION; 212 G-7; elev. 485ft./148m.; mail Marshville z 28103; ● 100
Olive Hill; RMC Place; PERSON; *212 B-10; elev. 666ft./203m.; mail Roxboro z 27574; rural
Olivers (Olives Crossroads); RMC Place; JONES; *213 G-15; mail Pollocksville z 28573; ● 30
Olivers Crossroads; RMC Place; CATAWBA; *212 E-5; ★ HICK; mail Newton z 28658
Olives Crossroads; JONES; see Olivers (RMC Place)
Olivia; RMC Place; HARNETT; 212 F-10; elev. 334ft./102m.; 🄿; z 28368; ● 600
Olympia; RMC Place; PAMLICO; 213 G-16; elev. 27ft./8m.; mail New Bern z 28560; ● 100
Olyphic; RMC Place; COLUMBUS; *213 K-12; mail Tabor City z 28463
ONSLOW; 213 H-15; Ⓟ 149,838; Ⓒ 150,355; ◆ 187,028
Onvil; RMC Place; MONTGOMERY; *212 F-8; mail Mount Gilead z 27306; ● 30
Ophir; RMC Place; MONTGOMERY; 212 F-8; elev. 522ft./159m.; mail Troy z 27371; ● 30
ORANGE; 212 C-10; Ⓟ 93,851; Ⓒ 118,227; Ⓡ 115,531; ◆ 132,386
Orange Grove; RMC Place; ORANGE; *212 D-10; elev. 556ft./169m.; ★ DUR; mail Hillsborough z 27278; ● 100
Orchard Hills; RMC Place; ROWAN; *212 E-6; elev. 817ft./249m.; ★ SLSB; mail Salisbury z 28146; ● 50
Oregon Hill; RMC Place; ROCKINGHAM; 212 B-9; elev. 790ft./241m.; mail Ruffin z 27326; ● 130
Oriental; Inc. Place; PAMLICO; 213 G-17; elev. 10ft./3m.; 🄿; z 28571; Ⓟ 786; Ⓒ 875
Ormondsville; RMC Place; GREENE; 213 F-15; elev. 72ft./22m.; mail Ayden z 28513; ● 50
Orrum; Inc. Place; ROBESON; 213 I-11; elev. 105ft./32m.; 🄿; z 28369; Ⓟ 103; Ⓒ 79
Osborne; RMC Place; RICHMOND; *212 H-8; elev. 294ft./90m.; mail Hamlet z 28345; rural
Osceola; RMC Place; GUILFORD; *212 C-9; elev. 826ft./252m.; ★ GRNS-; mail Browns Summit z 27214
Osgood; RMC Place; LEE; *212 E-10; elev. 317ft./97m.; mail Sanford z 27330; rural
Osmond; RMC Place; CASWELL; *212 B-10; elev. 570ft./174m.; mail Leasburg z 27291; ● 50
Ossipee; Inc. Place; ALAMANCE; 212 C-9; elev. 609ft./186m.; ★ BUR; mail Elon z 27244; incorporated December 9, 2002; not reported in 2000 Census; ● 150
Ostwalt (Oswalt); RMC Place; IREDELL; *212 E-5; ★ HICK; mail Troutman z 28166
Oswalt; IREDELL; see Ostwalt (RMC Place)
Oteen; RMC Place; BUNCOMBE; 212 E-1; ★ ASHE; mail Asheville z 28805, z 28815; pop. incl. with Asheville (Inc. Place)
Othello; RMC Place; ASHE; *212 C-4; mail West Jefferson z 28694
Otto; RMC Place; MACON; 212 M-3; elev. 2,200ft./671m.; 🄿; z 28763; ● 200
Otway; RMC Place; CARTERET; 213 H-18; elev. 7ft./2m.; mail Beaufort z 28516; ● 260
Outer Banks; RMC Place; DARE; mail Kill Devil Hills z 27948; pop. incl. with Kill Devil Hills (Inc. Place)
Outlaws Bridge; RMC Place; DUPLIN; *213 G-14; elev. 14ft./4m.; mail Albertson z 28508; rural
Overhills (Rockefeller Estates); RMC Place; HARNETT; *212 G-10; ★ FAY; mail Cameron z 28326; ● 30
Overhills Park; RMC Place; CUMBERLAND; *213 G-11; elev. 160ft./49m.; ★ FAY; mail Spring Lake z 28390; ● 730
Owens; RMC Place; CUMBERLAND; *213 G-11; ★ FAY; pop. incl. with Fayetteville (Inc. Place)
Oxford; Inc. Place; ⊡ GRANVILLE; 213 C-12; 🄿 🄷; z 27565; Ⓟ 7,913; Ⓒ 8,338
Oxford Park; RMC Place; CATAWBA; *212 E-4; elev. 993ft./303m.; ★ HICK; mail Claremont z 28610; ● 30
Oyster Creek Landing; RMC Place; HYDE; *213 F-18; elev. 3ft./1m.; mail Swanquarter z 27885; rural

P

Pacolet Valley; RMC Place; POLK; *212 F-1; mail Tryon z 28782; rural
Pactolus; RMC Place; PITT; 213 E-16; mail Greenville z 27834; ● 230
Padgett; RMC Place; ONSLOW; *213 H-15; mail Maple Hill z 28454; rural
Paint Fork; RMC Place; MADISON; *212 D-1; mail Mars Hill z 28754; rural
Paint Rock; RMC Place; MADISON; *212 J-5; mail Hot Springs z 28743
Pala Alto (Palo Alto); RMC Place; ONSLOW; *213 H-16; ★ JAX; mail Maysville z 28555; ● 130
Palestine; RMC Place; STANLY; *212 F-7; mail Albemarle z 28001; ● 150
Palmerville; RMC Place; STANLY; *212 F-7; mail New London z 28127
Palmyra; RMC Place; HALIFAX; 213 C-15; elev. 90ft./27m.; mail Scotland Neck z 27874; ● 30
Palo Alto; ONSLOW; see Pala Alto (RMC Place)
Pamlico; RMC Place; PAMLICO; 213 G-17; mail Oriental z 28571; ● 200
PAMLICO; 213 G-17; Ⓟ 11,372; Ⓒ 12,934; ◆ 12,416
Pamlico Beach; RMC Place; BEAUFORT; 213 F-17; mail Belhaven z 27810; ● 400
Pantego; Inc. Place; BEAUFORT; 213 E-17; elev. 7ft./2m.; 🄿; z 27860; Ⓟ 171; Ⓒ 170
Panther Creek; RMC Place; HAYWOOD; *212 K-4; mail Clyde z 28721; ● 30
Paradise East; RMC Place; CARTERET; *213 H-17; elev. 30ft./9m.; ★ JAX; mail Newport z 28570; ● 150
Paradise Point; RMC Place; GASTON; *212 G-5; ★ CHRLT; mail Belmont z 28012; ● 350
Parkersburg; RMC Place; SAMPSON; 213 H-12; elev. 118ft./36m.; mail Garland z 28441; ● 150
Parkers Fork; RMC Place; GATES; *213 B-17; mail Corapeake z 27926; rural
Parks Crossroads; RMC Place; RANDOLPH; *212 E-9; elev. 557ft./170m.; mail Ramseur z 27316; rural
Park Spring; RMC Place; CASWELL; *212 B-9; elev. 615ft./187m.; mail Providence z 27315; rural
Parkstone; RMC Place; MECKLENBURG; ★ CHRLT; mail Charlotte z 28210; pop. incl. with Charlotte (Inc. Place)
Parkstown; RMC Place; WAYNE; 213 F-14; elev. 104ft./32m.; ★ GLDS; mail La Grange z 28551; ● 50
Parkton; Inc. Place; ROBESON; 212 H-10; elev. 186ft./57m.; 🄿; ★ FAY; z 28371; Ⓟ 367; Ⓒ 428; Ⓡ 429
Parktown; RMC Place; WARREN; *213 C-13; mail Warrenton z 27589; rural
Parkville; RMC Place; PERQUIMANS; *213 C-18; mail Hertford z 27944; rural
Parkway Forest; RMC Place; BUNCOMBE; *212 E-1; ★ ASHE; mail Asheville z 28805; pop. incl. with Asheville (Inc. Place)
Parkwood; RMC Place; CABARRUS; *212 F-6; elev. 700ft./213m.; ★ CHRLT; mail Concord z 28027; pop. incl. with Concord (Inc. Place)
Parkwood (Hallison); RMC Place; MOORE; *212 F-9; mail Carthage z 28327; rural
Parmele; Inc. Place; MARTIN; 213 D-13; elev. 74ft./23m.; 🄿; z 27861; Ⓟ 321; Ⓒ 290
Parrott Fork; RMC Place; LENOIR; *213 F-15; elev. 76ft./23m.; mail Kinston z 28504; rural
Parsonville; RMC Place; WILKES; *212 C-4; elev. 1,373ft./418m.; mail Purlear z 28665; ● 30
Paschall; RMC Place; WARREN; *213 B-13; mail Warrenton z 27589; rural
PASQUOTANK; 213 B-18; Ⓟ 31,298; Ⓒ 34,897; ◆ 43,007
Pates; RMC Place; ROBESON; *212 H-10; mail Pembroke z 28372; rural
Patetown; RMC Place; WAYNE; *213 F-14; ★ GLDS; mail Goldsboro z 27530
Patterson; RMC Place; CALDWELL; 212 D-3; elev. 1,253ft./382m.; 🄿; z 28661; ● 530
Patterson Grove; CLEVELAND; see Sandy Plains (RMC Place)
Patterson Springs; Inc. Place; CLEVELAND; 212 G-3; elev. 897ft./273m.; mail Shelby z 28150, z 28152; Ⓟ 690; Ⓒ 620
Pauls Crossing; RMC Place; STANLY; *212 F-7; mail Richfield z 28137; ● 30
Paw Creek (Thrift); RMC Place; MECKLENBURG; *212 F-5; elev. 783ft./239m.; 🄿; ★ CHRLT; z 28130; pop. incl. with Charlotte (Inc. Place)
Paynes Tavern; RMC Place; PERSON; *212 C-10; elev. 633ft./193m.; mail Roxboro z 27574; rural
Peace Haven Estates; RMC Place; FORSYTH; *212 C-7; ★ WNS; mail Winston Salem z 27104; ● 550
Peachland; Inc. Place; ANSON; 212 G-7; elev. 446ft./136m.; 🄿; z 28133; Ⓟ 384; Ⓒ 554
Peachtree; RMC Place; CHEROKEE; *212 M-1; elev. 1,694ft./516m.; mail Murphy z 28906
Peacock Crossing; RMC Place; COLUMBUS; *213 J-11; elev. 94ft./29m.; mail Chadbourn z 28431; ● 50
Peacocks Crossroads (Meadow); RMC Place; JOHNSTON; *213 F-12; mail Benson z 27504; ● 70
Peacocks Crossroads (Meadow); RMC Place; STOKES; *212 C-7; ★ WNS; mail Walnut Cove z 27052
Pearces; RMC Place; FRANKLIN; *213 D-12; ★ RAL; mail Zebulon z 27597; ● 200
Pea Ridge; RMC Place; POLK; *212 F-2; mail Mill Spring z 28756; rural
Pea Ridge (Pine Ridge); RMC Place; WASHINGTON; *213 D-18; mail Roper z 27970; rural
Pea Ridge; RMC Place; YADKIN; *212 C-5; mail Hamptonville z 27020; rural
Pecan Grove; RMC Place; HALIFAX; mail Scotland Neck z 27874; rural
Peden; RMC Place; ALLEGHANY; *212 B-4; mail Scottville z 28672; rural
Pee Dee; RMC Place; MONTGOMERY; *212 F-8; elev. 412ft./126m.; mail Mount Gilead z 27306; ● 30
Pekin; RMC Place; MONTGOMERY; 212 G-8; elev. 294ft./90m.; mail Mount Gilead z 27306; ● 50
Peletier; Inc. Place; CARTERET; 213 H-16; elev. 29ft./9m.; 🄿; z 28584; Ⓒ 487
Pelham; RMC Place; CASWELL; 212 B-9; elev. 743ft./226m.; 🄿; ★ DANV; z 27311; ● 340
Pembroke; Inc. Place; ROBESON; 212 H-10; elev. 172ft./52m.; 🄿 🄲 5,827; z 28372; Ⓟ 2,241; Ⓒ 2,399; Ⓡ 2,681
PENDER; 213 I-13; Ⓟ 28,855; Ⓒ 41,082; ◆ 53,384
Pender Crossroad; WILSON; see Penders Crossroads (RMC Place)
Penderlea; RMC Place; PENDER; 213 H-13; elev. 66ft./20m.; mail Willard z 28478; ● 220
Penders Crossroads (Pender Crossroad); RMC Place; WILSON; *213 E-14; elev. 120ft./37m.; mail Elm City z 27822; rural
Pendleton; RMC Place; NORTHAMPTON; 213 B-16; elev. 84ft./26m.; 🄿; z 27862; ● 220
Penland; RMC Place; MITCHELL; *212 D-2; elev. 2,600ft./792m.; 🄿; z 28765; ● 300
Penrose; RMC Place; TRANSYLVANIA; 212 M-5; elev. 2,350ft./716m.; 🄿; z 28766; ● 400
Pensacola; RMC Place; YANCEY; 212 D-1; elev. 2,860ft./872m.; mail Burnsville z 28714; ● 60
Perch; RMC Place; SURRY; *212 C-6; elev. 971ft./296m.; mail Pinnacle z 27043; rural
Perfection; RMC Place; CRAVEN; *213 F-16; elev. 14ft./4m.; mail Cove City z 28523
Perkinsville; RMC Place; WATAUGA; *212 C-3; elev. 3,225ft./983m.; mail Boone z 28607; pop. incl. with Boone (Inc. Place)
PERQUIMANS; 213 C-18; Ⓟ 10,447; Ⓒ 11,368; ◆ 13,212
Perry's Beach; RMC Place; BERTIE; *213 C-17; elev. 10ft./3m.; mail Colerain z 27924
Perrytown; RMC Place; BERTIE; *213 C-17; elev. 67ft./20m.; mail Colerain z 27924; ● 70
PERSON; 213 C-11; Ⓟ 30,180; Ⓒ 35,623; ◆ 37,666
Peru; RMC Place; ONSLOW; 213 I-15; mail Sneads Ferry z 28460; ● 250
Petersburg; RMC Place; MADISON; *212 D-1; elev. 1,972ft./601m.; ★ ASHE; mail Marshall z 28753, Morganton z 28655; ● 50
Petersburg; RMC Place; ONSLOW; *213 H-15; ★ JAX; mail Richlands z 28574
Petersville; RMC Place; DAVIDSON; *212 D-7; elev. 745ft./227m.; mail Lexington z 27292, z 27295; rural
Pettys Shore; RMC Place; HERTFORD; *213 B-17; elev. 33ft./10m.; mail Cofield z 27922; rural
Pfafftown; RMC Place; FORSYTH; 212 C-7; elev. 818ft./249m.; 🄿; ★ WNS; z 27040; ● 1,050
Philadelphia; RMC Place; CAMDEN; *213 C-19; elev. 2ft./1m.; mail Shiloh z 27974
Philadelphus; RMC Place; ROBESON; *212 H-10; elev. 188ft./57m.; mail Red Springs z 28377; rural
Phillips Crossroads; RMC Place; JONES; *213 G-15; elev. 49ft./15m.; mail Trenton z 28585; rural
Phoenix; RMC Place; BRUNSWICK; 213 J-13; ★ WILM; mail Leland z 28451; ● 100
Piedmont Heights; RMC Place; GUILFORD; *212 D-8; ★ GRNS-; mail Greensboro z 27403; pop. incl. with Greensboro (Inc. Place)
Pierceville; RMC Place; CAMDEN; *213 B-18; mail South Mills z 27976; ● 30
Pigeon Roost; RMC Place; MITCHELL; *212 D-1; mail Green Mountain z 28740; ● 30
Pike Crossroads; RMC Place; WAYNE; *213 F-13; elev. 148ft./45m.; ★ GLDS; mail Pikeville z 27863; rural
Pike Road; RMC Place; BEAUFORT; 213 E-17; elev. 10ft./3m.; mail Pantego z 27860; ● 100
Pikeville; Inc. Place; WAYNE; 213 F-13; elev. 142ft./43m.; 🄿; ★ GLDS; z 27863; Ⓟ 598; Ⓒ 719
Pilands Crossroads; RMC Place; HERTFORD; *213 C-17; elev. 36ft./11m.; mail Cofield z 27922; rural
Pilot; RMC Place; DAVIDSON; *212 D-7; ★ GRNS-; mail Thomasville z 27360; ● 500
Pilot; RMC Place; FRANKLIN; 213 D-13; elev. 358ft./109m.; ★ RAL; mail Zebulon z 27597; ● 350
Pilot Mountain; Inc. Place; SURRY; 212 C-6; elev. 1,152ft./351m.; 🄿; z 27041; Ⓟ 1,181; Ⓒ 1,281
Pinebluff; Inc. Place; MOORE; 212 G-9; elev. 307ft./94m.; 🄿; z 28373; Ⓟ 876; Ⓒ 1,109
Pine Crest; RMC Place; BEAUFORT; *213 F-17; elev. 5ft./2m.; mail Bath z 27808; ● 30
Pinecrest Acres; RMC Place; CUMBERLAND; *213 G-11; elev. 246ft./75m.; ★ FAY; mail Fayetteville z 28301; ● 340
Pinecroft; RMC Place; GUILFORD; *212 D-8; elev. 832ft./254m.; ★ GRNS-; mail Greensboro z 27407; pop. incl. with Greensboro (Inc. Place)
Pine Hall; RMC Place; STOKES; 212 C-8; elev. 655ft./200m.; 🄿; ★ WNS; z 27042; ● 310
Pine Haven; RMC Place; MONTGOMERY; *212 F-7; mail Denton z 27239; summer pop. 300; ● 150
Pine Hill; RMC Place; HOKE; *212 G-9; elev. 358ft./109m.; mail Aberdeen z 28315; rural
Pine Hill; RMC Place; SURRY; *212 C-6; elev. 1,190ft./363m.; mail Pilot Mountain z 27041; rural
Pinehurst; Inc. Place; MOORE; 212 G-9; elev. 529ft./161m.; 🄿 🄷; z 28370, z 28374; Ⓟ 5,091; Ⓒ 9,706; Ⓡ 9,729
Pinehurst Park; RMC Place; WAKE; *213 E-12; ★ RAL; mail Garner z 27529; ● 280
Pine Knoll; RMC Place; CUMBERLAND; *213 G-11; ★ FAY; mail Hope Mills z 28348
Pine Knoll Shores; Inc. Place; CARTERET; *213 H-17; elev. 15ft./5m.; 🄿; z 28512; Ⓟ 1,360; Ⓒ 1,524
Pine Lakes; RMC Place; SURRY; *212 B-6; mail Mount Airy z 27030; rural
Pine Level; Inc. Place; JOHNSTON; 213 F-13; elev. 172ft./52m.; 🄿; ★ RAL; z 27568; Ⓟ 1,217; Ⓒ 1,313; Ⓡ 1,319
Pinelog; RMC Place; COLUMBUS; *213 J-11; elev. 61ft./19m.; mail Whiteville z 28472; ● 150
Pineola; RMC Place; AVERY; 212 D-2; elev. 3,509ft./1,070m.; 🄿; z 28662; ● 200
Pine Ridge; RMC Place; CABARRUS, MECKLENBURG; *212 F-6; elev. 750ft./229m.; ★ CHRLT; mail Charlotte z 28201; ● 150
Pine Ridge; RMC Place; FRANKLIN; *213 D-13; elev. 310ft./94m.; ★ RAL; mail Zebulon z 27597; rural
Pine Ridge; RMC Place; SURRY; *212 B-6; elev. 1,300ft./396m.; mail Mount Airy z 27030
Pine Ridge; WASHINGTON; see Pea Ridge (RMC Place)
Pinetops; Inc. Place; EDGECOMBE; 213 D-14; elev. 100ft./30m.; 🄿; z 27864; Ⓟ 1,514; Ⓒ 1,419
Pinetown; RMC Place; BEAUFORT; 213 E-17; elev. 43ft./13m.; 🄿; z 27865; ● 250
Pine Valley; RMC Place; NEW HANOVER; *213 J-14; ★ WILM; mail Wilmington z 28412; pop. incl. with Wilmington (Inc. Place)
Pineview; RMC Place; HARNETT; *212 F-10; elev. 321ft./98m.; mail Sanford z 27330
Pineville; Inc. Place; MECKLENBURG; 212 G-5; elev. 550ft./168m.; 🄿 🄷; ★ CHRLT; z 28134; Ⓟ 2,970; Ⓒ 3,449
Piney Creek; RMC Place; ALLEGHANY; 212 B-4; elev. 2,900ft./884m.; 🄿; z 28663; ● 60
Piney Green; CDP; ONSLOW; *213 H-15; ★ JAX; mail Jacksonville z 28540; Ⓟ 8,999; Ⓒ 11,658
Piney Green; RMC Place; SAMPSON; *213 G-12; elev. 188ft./57m.; mail Clinton z 28328
Piney Grove; RMC Place; BRUNSWICK; *213 K-13; ★ WILM; mail Bolivia z 28422; ● 400
Piney Grove; RMC Place; ORANGE; *212 D-10; elev. 661ft./201m.; ★ DUR; mail Hillsborough z 27278; ● 50
Piney Ridge; RMC Place; SAMPSON; *213 G-12; elev. 161ft./49m.; mail Clinton z 28328; rural
Pin Hook; RMC Place; DUPLIN; *213 H-14; mail Wallace z 28466; rural
Pink Hill; Inc. Place; LENOIR; 213 G-14; elev. 120ft./37m.; 🄿; z 28572; Ⓟ 547; Ⓒ 521; Ⓡ 562
Pinkney; RMC Place; WAYNE; 213 E-13; elev. 154ft./47m.; ★ GLDS; mail Fremont z 27830, Gastonia z 28052; ● 110
Pinnacle; RMC Place; STOKES; 212 C-7; elev. 1,079ft./329m.; 🄿; ★ WNS; z 27043; ● 350
Pinoca; RMC Place; MECKLENBURG; ★ CHRLT; pop. incl. with Charlotte (Inc. Place)
Pireway; RMC Place; COLUMBUS; 213 K-12; elev. 42ft./13m.; mail Tabor City z 28463; ● 30
Pisgah; RMC Place; RANDOLPH; *212 E-8; elev. 789ft./240m.; mail Asheboro z 27205; rural
Pisgah Forest; RMC Place; TRANSYLVANIA; 212 M-5; elev. 2,109ft./643m.; 🄿; z 28768; ● 2,150
Pisgah View; RMC Place; BUNCOMBE; *212 E-1; ★ ASHE; mail Asheville z 28806; pop. incl. with Asheville (Inc. Place)
PITT; 213 F-15; Ⓟ 107,924; Ⓒ 133,798; Ⓡ 133,719; ◆ 164,396
Pitt Crossroads; RMC Place; EDGECOMBE; *213 E-14; elev. 33ft./10m.; mail Macclesfield z 27852; rural
Pittmans Store; NASH; see Hickory (RMC Place)
Pittsboro; Inc. Place; ⊡ CHATHAM; 212 E-10; elev. 420ft./128m.; 🄿; z 27228, z 27312; Ⓟ 1,436; Ⓒ 2,226
Plainview; RMC Place; ROBESON; *212 I-10; elev. 144ft./44m.; mail Rowland z 28383; rural
Plain View; CDP-Census Area Only; SAMPSON; *213 F-12; Ⓒ 1,820
Plateau; RMC Place; CATAWBA; *212 E-4; elev. 1,002ft./305m.; ★ HICK; mail Newton z 28658
Pleasant Acres; RMC Place; CUMBERLAND; *213 G-11; elev. 234ft./71m.; ★ FAY; mail Fayetteville z 28301; ● 220
Pleasant Garden; Inc. Place; GUILFORD; 212 D-8; elev. 838ft./255m.; 🄿; ★ GRNS-; z 27313; Ⓟ 2,228; Ⓒ 4,714
Pleasant Gardens; RMC Place; MCDOWELL; 212 E-2; mail Marion z 28752; ● 450
Pleasant Grove; RMC Place; ALAMANCE; *212 C-10; elev. 709ft./216m.; ★ BUR; mail Burlington z 27217; ● 70
Pleasant Grove; RMC Place; BUNCOMBE; *212 E-1; ★ ASHE; mail Weaverville z 28787; ● 110
Pleasant Grove; RMC Place; CASWELL; *212 C-10; mail Yanceyville z 27379
Pleasant Grove; RMC Place; DUPLIN; *213 G-14; elev. 118ft./36m.; mail Mount Olive z 28365; rural
Pleasant Grove; RMC Place; NORTHAMPTON; *213 B-15; mail Garysburg z 27831; rural
Pleasant Grove; RMC Place; WASHINGTON; *213 D-17; mail Roper z 27970
Pleasant Hill; RMC Place; JONES; *213 G-15; elev. 63ft./19m.; mail Pink Hill z 28572
Pleasant Hill; RMC Place; NORTHAMPTON; 213 B-15; elev. 129ft./39m.; 🄿; z 27866; ● 130
Pleasant Hill (West Elkin); CDP; WILKES; *212 C-5; mail Elkin z 28621; Ⓟ 1,114; Ⓒ 1,109
Pleasant Plains; RMC Place; HERTFORD; *213 C-16; mail Ahoskie z 27910; rural
Pleasant Ridge; RMC Place; RANDOLPH; *212 E-9; elev. 562ft./171m.; mail Ramseur z 27316; rural
Pleasant View; RMC Place; TYRRELL; *213 D-18; mail Columbia z 27925; rural
Pleasantville; RMC Place; ROCKINGHAM; *212 C-8; elev. 756ft./230m.; mail Madison z 27025; ● 50
Plott Farm Addition; RMC Place; HAYWOOD; *212 L-5; ★ ASHE; mail Canton z 28716; ● 100
Plumtree; RMC Place; AVERY; 212 D-2; elev. 3,000ft./914m.; 🄿; z 28664; ● 160
Plyer (Plyler); RMC Place; STANLY; *212 F-7; elev. 632ft./193m.; mail Albemarle z 28001; ● 30
Plyler; STANLY; see Plyer (RMC Place)
Plymouth; Inc. Place; ⊡ WASHINGTON; 213 D-17; elev. 6ft./2m.; 🄿 🄷; z 27962; Ⓟ 4,328; Ⓒ 4,107
Pocomoke; RMC Place; FRANKLIN; *213 D-12; ★ RAL; mail Franklinton z 27525; ● 90
Point Caswell; RMC Place; PENDER; *213 I-13; elev. 22ft./7m.; mail Atkinson z 28421; rural
Point Harbor; RMC Place; CURRITUCK; 213 C-20; 🄿; z 27964; ● 370
Pole Creek; RMC Place; BUNCOMBE; *212 L-5; ★ ASHE; mail Candler z 28715; rural
POLK; 212 F-2; Ⓟ 14,416; Ⓒ 18,324; ◆ 18,964
Polks Landing; RMC Place; CHATHAM; *212 D-10; elev. 500ft./152m.; ★ DUR; mail Chapel Hill z 27516; ● 450
Polkton; Inc. Place; ANSON; 212 G-7; elev. 305ft./93m.; 🄿; z 28135; Ⓟ 662; Ⓒ 1,195; Ⓡ 1,916
Polkville; Inc. Place; CLEVELAND; 212 F-3; elev. 1,079ft./329m.; 🄿; z 28136; Ⓟ 1,514; Ⓒ 535
Pollocksville; Inc. Place; JONES; 213 G-16; elev. 23ft./7m.; 🄿; z 28573; Ⓟ 299; Ⓒ 269
Pomona; RMC Place; GUILFORD; *212 D-8; elev. 883ft./269m.; ★ GRNS-; mail Greensboro z 27407; pop. incl. with Greensboro (Inc. Place)
Ponderosa; RMC Place; CUMBERLAND; *213 G-11; elev. 234ft./71m.; ★ FAY; mail Fayetteville z 28303; pop. incl. with Fayetteville (Inc. Place)
Ponderosa; RMC Place; HARNETT; *213 F-12; mail Dunn z 28334; ● 680
Ponzer; RMC Place; HYDE; *213 E-18; mail Belhaven z 27810
Poole Town; RMC Place; ROWAN; 212 E-7; mail Richfield z 28137; ● 130
Poor Town; RMC Place; HERTFORD; *213 C-16; mail Ahoskie z 27910; ● 60
Pope AFB; CDP-Census Area Only; CUMBERLAND; *213 G-11; elev. 250ft./76m.; 🄿; ★ FAY; z 28308; Ⓟ 2,857; Ⓒ 2,583
Poplar; RMC Place; MITCHELL; 212 D-1; mail Green Mountain z 28740; ● 160
Poplar Branch; RMC Place; CURRITUCK; 213 C-19; 🄿; z 27965; ● 550
Poplar Grove; RMC Place; SAMPSON; *213 G-13; mail Faison z 28341; rural
Poplar Springs; RMC Place; STOKES; *212 C-7; ★ WNS; mail King z 27021; rural
Porter; RMC Place; STANLY; 212 F-7; mail Norwood z 28128; ● 30
Portersville; BLADEN; see Emerson (RMC Place)
Portsmouth; RMC Place; CARTERET; *213 G-19; mail Ocracoke z 27960
Postell; RMC Place; CHEROKEE; *212 M-1; mail Murphy z 28906; rural
Potecasi; RMC Place; NORTHAMPTON; 213 B-15; elev. 72ft./22m.; 🄿; z 27867; ● 300
Pot Neck; RMC Place; LENOIR; *213 F-14; elev. 46ft./14m.; ★ GLDS; mail La Grange z 28551; rural
Potters Curve; RMC Place; COLUMBUS; *213 J-11; elev. 103ft./31m.; mail Chadbourn z 28431; rural
Potters Hill; RMC Place; DUPLIN; *213 G-14; mail Pink Hill z 28572
Pottertown; RMC Place; WATAUGA; *212 C-3; elev. 3,480ft./1,061m.; mail Todd z 28684; rural
Powell Crossroads; RMC Place; GATES; *213 C-17; mail Hobbsville z 27946; rural
Powells Point; RMC Place; CURRITUCK; 213 C-19; elev. 7ft./2m.; 🄿; z 27966; ● 470
Powells Store; RMC Place; ROCKINGHAM; *212 B-9; elev. 723ft./220m.; mail Ruffin z 27326; rural
Powellsville; Inc. Place; BERTIE; 213 C-16; 🄿; z 27967; Ⓟ 103; Ⓒ 259
Powhatan; RMC Place; JOHNSTON; *213 E-12; elev. 303ft./92m.; ★ RAL; mail Clayton z 27520; ● 30
Prentiss; RMC Place; MACON; *212 M-3; elev. 2,032ft./619m.; mail Franklin z 28734
Prestonville; RMC Place; STOKES; 212 B-7; elev. 1,096ft./334m.; mail Madison z 27025; ● 30
Price; RMC Place; ROCKINGHAM; *212 B-8; elev. 1,022ft./312m.; mail Stoneville z 27048; rural
Price Creek; RMC Place; YANCEY; *212 D-1; mail Burnsville z 28714; rural
Princeton; Inc. Place; JOHNSTON; 213 F-13; elev. 152ft./46m.; 🄿; z 27569; Ⓟ 1,181; Ⓒ 1,066; Ⓡ 1,090
Princeville; Inc. Place; EDGECOMBE; 213 D-15; elev. 38ft./12m.; 🄿; z 27886; Ⓟ 1,652; Ⓒ 940
Proctors Corner; RMC Place; HERTFORD; *213 C-16; elev. 62ft./19m.; mail Ahoskie z 27910; ● 100
Proctorville; Inc. Place; ROBESON; 212 I-10; elev. 120ft./37m.; 🄿; z 28375; Ⓟ 168; Ⓒ 133
Propst Crossroads; RMC Place; CATAWBA; *212 E-4; ★ HICK; mail Hickory z 28601, Newton z 28658
Prospect; RMC Place; BRUNSWICK; 213 K-13; elev. 48ft./15m.; mail Supply z 28462; ● 50
Prospect; CDP-Census Area Only; ROBESON; *212 H-10; Ⓒ 690
Prospect Hill; RMC Place; CASWELL; 212 C-10; elev. 714ft./218m.; 🄿; z 27314; ● 170
Prosper; RMC Place; COLUMBUS; *213 J-13; elev. 53ft./16m.; mail Delco z 28436; rural
Providence; RMC Place; CASWELL; 212 B-9; elev. 572ft./174m.; 🄿; z 27315; ● 430
Providence; RMC Place; GRANVILLE; 213 C-11; mail Oxford z 27565; ● 160
Providence; RMC Place; MCDOWELL; 212 E-2; mail Marion z 28752; ● 180
Providence; RMC Place; MECKLENBURG; *212 G-5; elev. 10ft./3m.; ★ CHRLT; mail Matthews z 28104; pop. incl. with Charlotte (Inc. Place)
Providence Square; RMC Place; MECKLENBURG; ★ CHRLT; mail Charlotte z 28211; pop. incl. with Charlotte (Inc. Place)
Proximity; RMC Place; GUILFORD; *212 D-8; ★ GRNS-; mail Greensboro z 27405; pop. incl. with Greensboro (Inc. Place)
Pumpkin Center; RMC Place; LINCOLN; *212 F-4; elev. 954ft./291m.; ★ HICK; mail Lincolnton z 28092
Pumpkin Center; CDP; ONSLOW; 213 H-15; ★ JAX; mail Jacksonville z 28540; Ⓟ 2,857; Ⓒ 2,228
Pumpkintown; RMC Place; JACKSON; *212 M-3; mail Sylva z 28779; rural
Pungo; RMC Place; BEAUFORT; *213 E-17; mail Pantego z 27860; ● 30
Pungo Shores; RMC Place; BEAUFORT; *213 E-17; elev. 6ft./2m.; mail Belhaven z 27810; ● 70
Purlear; RMC Place; WILKES; *212 C-4; elev. 1,346ft./410m.; 🄿; z 28665; ● 100
Purley; RMC Place; CASWELL; 212 B-10; mail Yanceyville z 27379; ● 70
Purnell; LEE; see Shallo Well (RMC Place)
Purnell; RMC Place; WAKE; *213 D-12; ★ RAL; mail Wake Forest z 27587; ● 100
Purvis; RMC Place; ROBESON; *212 I-10; mail Rowland z 28383; ● 60
Push; RMC Place; PERSON; *212 C-10; elev. 632ft./193m.; mail Hurdle Mills z 27541; rural
Putnam; RMC Place; MOORE; *212 F-9; mail Carthage z 28327; ● 30
Pyatte; RMC Place; AVERY; *212 D-2; mail Newland z 28657; rural

Q

Quail Corners; RMC Place; MECKLENBURG; ★ CHRLT; mail Charlotte z 28210; pop. incl. with Charlotte (Inc. Place)
Quail Ridge; RMC Place; CRAVEN; *213 H-17; elev. 23ft./7m.; mail Havelock z 28532; pop. incl. with Havelock (Inc. Place)
Quail Ridge; RMC Place; CUMBERLAND; *213 G-11; elev. 200ft./61m.; ★ FAY; mail Fayetteville z 28306; ● 620
Quail Ridge; RMC Place; LEE; *212 F-10; mail Sanford z 27332; ● 110
Qualla (Shoal Creek); RMC Place; JACKSON; *212 L-3; mail Whittier z 28789; ● 30
Quarry Hill Country Club; RMC Place; ALAMANCE; *212 D-10; elev. 550ft./168m.; ★ BUR; mail Graham z 27253; pop. incl. with Swepsonville (Inc. Place)
Quebec; RMC Place; TRANSYLVANIA; *212 M-4; mail Lake Toxaway z 28747; ● 50
Queen; RMC Place; MONTGOMERY; mail Troy z 27371; rural
Quick; RMC Place; CASWELL; 212 B-9; elev. 670ft./204m.; mail Ruffin z 27326; ● 50
Quinerly; RMC Place; PITT; *213 F-15; ★ GRNV; mail Grifton z 28530; rural
Quinns Store; RMC Place; DUPLIN; *213 H-14; elev. 20ft./6m.; mail Beulaville z 28518; rural
Quitsna; RMC Place; BERTIE; *213 D-16; mail Windsor z 27983

R

Rabbit Corner; RMC Place; PASQUOTANK; *213 C-18; elev. 10ft./3m.; mail Elizabeth City z 27909; ● 100
Radical; RMC Place; WILKES; *212 C-4; elev. 1,354ft./413m.; mail Mc Grady z 28649; rural
Radio Island; RMC Place; CARTERET; *213 H-17; elev. 23ft./7m.; mail Beaufort z 28516; ● 50
Raeford; Inc. Place; ⊡ HOKE; 212 G-10; elev. 254ft./77m.; 🄿; ★ FAY; z 28376; Ⓟ 3,469; Ⓒ 3,386
Raemon; CDP; ROBESON; *212 I-10; elev. 168ft./51m.; mail Maxton z 28364; Ⓒ 212
Rainbow Springs; RMC Place; MACON; *212 M-3; mail Franklin z 28734; rural
Raleigh; Inc. Place; **STATE CAPITAL**; ⊡ WAKE; 213 E-12; 🄿 🄷 🄲 38,528 ■; ★ RAL; z 27601-17, z 27619-29, z 27634-36, z 27640, z 27650, z 27656, z 27658, z 27661, z 27668, z 27675-76, z 27690, z 27695, z 27697-99; Ⓟ 207,951; Ⓒ 276,093; Ⓡ 276,094; ◆ 396,276
Rama; RMC Place; MECKLENBURG; *212 G-6; ★ CHRLT; pop. incl. with Charlotte (Inc. Place)
Rama Woods; RMC Place; CABARRUS; *212 F-6; elev. 596ft./182m.; ★ CHRLT; mail Concord z 28025; ● 60
Ramseur; Inc. Place; RANDOLPH; 212 E-9; elev. 527ft./161m.; 🄿; z 27316; Ⓟ 1,186; Ⓒ 1,588
Ramseytown; RMC Place; YANCEY; *212 D-1; mail Burnsville z 28714; rural
Randleman; Inc. Place; RANDOLPH; 212 E-8; elev. 700ft./213m.; 🄿; z 27317; Ⓟ 2,612; Ⓒ 3,557
Randolph; RMC Place; MECKLENBURG; ★ CHRLT; mail Charlotte z 28207, z 28211, z 28222; pop. incl. with Charlotte (Inc. Place)
RANDOLPH; 212 E-8; Ⓟ 106,546; Ⓒ 130,454; Ⓡ 130,471; ◆ 139,065
Ranger; RMC Place; CHEROKEE; *212 M-1; mail Murphy z 28906
Rangewood; RMC Place; WAKE; *213 E-12; ★ RAL; mail Raleigh z 27603
Rankin; RMC Place; GUILFORD; *212 C-8; elev. 806ft./246m.; ★ GRNS-; mail Greensboro z 27405; pop. incl. with Greensboro (Inc. Place)
Ranlo; Inc. Place; GASTON; 212 F-4; elev. 799ft./244m.; ★ CHRLT; mail Gastonia z 28054; Ⓟ 1,650; Ⓒ 2,198
Ransomville; RMC Place; BEAUFORT; 213 F-17; mail Belhaven z 27810; ● 70
Ravenswood; RMC Place; JONES; *213 G-16; elev. 35ft./11m.; mail Pollocksville z 28573; rural
Rawls; RMC Place; HARNETT; *213 E-11; mail Fuquay Varina z 27526
Rayconda; RMC Place; CUMBERLAND; *213 G-11; elev. 200ft./61m.; ★ FAY; mail Fayetteville z 28304; ● 100
Raynham; Inc. Place; ROBESON; 212 I-10; mail Rowland z 28383; Ⓟ 106; Ⓒ 67; Ⓡ 72
Rebel Acres; RMC Place; WAKE; *213 D-12; ★ RAL; mail Raleigh z 27604; ● 140
Rebel City; RMC Place; SAMPSON; *213 G-12; elev. 190ft./58m.; mail Autryville z 28318, Roseboro z 28382, Salemburg z 28385; rural
Red Banks; RMC Place; ROBESON; *212 H-10; mail Maxton z 28364; rural
Redbug; RMC Place; COLUMBUS; *213 J-12; elev. 62ft./19m.; mail Hallsboro z 28442; ● 50
Red Cross; RMC Place; RANDOLPH; *212 D-9; elev. 811ft./247m.; ★ GRNS-; mail Climax z 27233; rural
Red Cross; Inc. Place; STANLY; 212 F-7; elev. 647ft./197m.; mail Oakboro z 28129; incorporated August 1, 2002; not reported in 2000 Census; ● 30
Reddies River; RMC Place; WILKES; *212 C-4; mail Millers Creek z 28651; rural
Red Hill; RMC Place; BLADEN; *213 I-12; mail Clarkton z 28433; ● 30
Red Hill; RMC Place; DUPLIN; *213 G-14; elev. 30ft./9m.; mail Mount Olive z 28365; rural
Red Hill; RMC Place; EDGECOMBE; *213 C-14; mail Whitakers z 27891; rural
Red Hill; RMC Place; MITCHELL; *212 D-1; mail Bakersville z 28705; ● 30
Redland; RMC Place; DAVIE; *212 D-6; elev. 812ft./247m.; ★ WNS; mail Advance z 27006
Red Mountain; DURHAM; see Rougemont (RMC Place)
Red Oak; Inc. Place; NASH; 213 D-14; elev. 212ft./65m.; 🄿; ★ RKYMT; z 27868; Ⓟ 280; Ⓒ 2,723
Red Oak; RMC Place; PITT; *213 E-15; elev. 75ft./23m.; ★ GRNV; mail Greenville z 27834; pop. incl. with Greenville (Inc. Place)
Red Springs; Inc. Place; ROBESON; 212 H-10; elev. 204ft./62m.; 🄿; z 28377; Ⓟ 3,799; Ⓒ 3,493
Reeds Cross Roads; RMC Place; DAVIDSON; 212 D-7; elev. 842ft./257m.; mail Lexington z 27292, z 27295; ● 140
Reedy Creek; RMC Place; DAVIDSON; *212 D-7; ★ WNS; mail Lexington z 27292, z 27295; ● 90
Reelsboro; RMC Place; PAMLICO; *213 G-17; elev. 45ft./14m.; mail New Bern z 28560; ● 150
Reepsville (Reepville); RMC Place; LINCOLN; *212 F-4; elev. 961ft./293m.; mail Vale z 28168; rural
Reepville; LINCOLN; see Reepsville (RMC Place)
Reese; RMC Place; WATAUGA; *212 C-3; elev. 3,026ft./922m.; mail Vilas z 28692; ● 30
Reeves Ferry; RMC Place; COLUMBUS; *213 K-12; elev. 36ft./11m.; mail Nakina z 28455; rural
Regal; RMC Place; CHEROKEE; *212 M-1; mail Murphy z 28906; rural
Regan; RMC Place; BRUNSWICK; *213 K-12; elev. 45ft./14m.; mail Ash z 28420; rural
Register; RMC Place; DUPLIN; *213 H-14; elev. 32ft./10m.; mail Rose Hill z 28458; rural
Rehoboth; RMC Place; NORTHAMPTON; *213 C-15; elev. 79ft./24m.; mail Jackson z 27845; rural
Reidsville; Inc. Place; ROCKINGHAM; 212 C-9; 🄿 🄷; ★ GRNS-; z 27320, z 27323; Ⓟ 12,183; Ⓒ 14,485
Relief; RMC Place; MITCHELL; *212 D-1; elev. 2,092ft./638m.; mail Green Mountain z 28740
Rena; RMC Place; YADKIN; *212 C-5; mail Hamptonville z 27020; rural
Rennert; Inc. Place; ROBESON; 212 H-10; elev. 187ft./57m.; ★ FAY; mail Shannon z 28386; Ⓟ 217; Ⓒ 283
Renston; RMC Place; PITT; *213 E-15; ★ GRNV; mail Ayden z 28513; rural
Republican; RMC Place; BERTIE; 213 C-16; elev. 62ft./19m.; mail Windsor z 27983; ● 30
Research Triangle Park (Triangle); RMC Place; WAKE; 🄿; z 27709, z 27711; rural
Rest Haven; RMC Place; BEAUFORT; *213 F-17; mail Bath z 27808; summer pop. 100; ● 30
Revere (Sodom); RMC Place; MADISON; *212 J-5; mail Marshall z 28753; ● 30
Revolution; RMC Place; GUILFORD; *212 D-8; ★ GRNS-; mail Greensboro z 27405; pop. incl. with Greensboro (Inc. Place)
Rex; RMC Place; GASTON; ★ CHRLT; mail Gastonia z 28054; pop. incl. with Ranlo (Inc. Place)
Rex; CDP; ROBESON; 212 H-10; elev. 185ft./56m.; 🄿; ★ FAY; z 28378; Ⓒ 55
Reynolda; RMC Place; FORSYTH; *212 C-7; ★ WNS; mail Winston Salem z 27109; pop. incl. with Winston-Salem (Inc. Place)
Reynolda Park; RMC Place; FORSYTH; *212 C-7; ★ WNS; mail Winston Salem z 27107; pop. incl. with Winston-Salem (Inc. Place)
Reynolds Crossroads; RMC Place; SAMPSON; *213 G-12; elev. 179ft./55m.; mail Clinton z 28328; rural
Reynoldson; RMC Place; GATES; *213 B-17; mail Gates z 27937; rural
Rheasville; RMC Place; HALIFAX; *213 B-14; mail Roanoke Rapids z 27870; ● 250
Rhems; RMC Place; CRAVEN; *213 G-16; elev. 38ft./12m.; mail New Bern z 28562; ● 50
Rhems Landing; RMC Place; CRAVEN; *213 G-16; mail New Bern z 28562; pop. incl. with River Bend (Inc. Place)
Rhodes; RMC Place; BERTIE; *213 C-16; elev. 72ft./22m.; mail Aulander z 27805; rural
Rhodes-Rhyne; RMC Place; LINCOLN; *212 F-4; elev. 772ft./235m.; mail Lincolnton z 28092; ● 120
Rhodhiss; Inc. Place; CALDWELL, BURKE; *212 E-4; elev. 965ft./294m.; 🄿; ★ HICK; z 28667; Ⓟ 638; Ⓒ 366; Ⓡ 384
Rhodo; RMC Place; CHEROKEE; *212 M-2; mail Andrews z 28901; rural
Rhoney; RMC Place; CATAWBA; *212 E-4; ★ HICK; mail Hickory z 28602; ● 200
Rhyne Crossroads; RMC Place; PENDER; *213 I-13; mail Burgaw z 28425; rural
Riceville; RMC Place; BUNCOMBE; *212 E-1; ★ ASHE; mail Asheville z 28805; rural
Richardson; RMC Place; BLADEN; 213 I-11; elev. 112ft./34m.; mail Bladenboro z 28320; ● 110
Richfield; Inc. Place; STANLY; 212 F-7; elev. 661ft./201m.; 🄿; z 28137; Ⓟ 535; Ⓒ 515
Richlands; Inc. Place; ONSLOW; 213 H-15; elev. 60ft./18m.; 🄿; ★ JAX; z 28574; Ⓟ 996; Ⓒ 928
RICHMOND; 212 G-8; Ⓟ 44,518; Ⓒ 46,564; ◆ 46,003
Richmond Hill; RMC Place; ALAMANCE; *212 D-9; ★ BUR; mail Burlington z 27215; pop. incl. with Burlington (Inc. Place)
Richmond Hill; RMC Place; YADKIN; *212 C-6; mail Boonville z 27011; rural
Richmond Mills; RMC Place; SCOTLAND; *212 H-9; mail Laurel Hill z 28351; ● 30
Rich Square; Inc. Place; NORTHAMPTON; 213 C-15; elev. 78ft./24m.; 🄿; z 27869; Ⓟ 1,058; Ⓒ 931
Rico; RMC Place; COLUMBUS; *213 I-12; elev. 101ft./31m.; mail Whiteville z 28472; ● 50
Riddle; RMC Place; CAMDEN; 213 C-19; mail Shawboro z 27973; ● 180
Ridgecrest; RMC Place; BUNCOMBE; 212 E-1; elev. 2,529ft./771m.; 🄿; ★ ASHE; z 28770; summer pop. 2,000; ● 500
Ridge Haven; RMC Place; WAKE; *213 D-12; ★ RAL; mail Wendell z 27591; ● 170
Ridge Run; RMC Place; CABARRUS; *212 F-6; elev. 600ft./183m.; ★ CHRLT; mail Concord z 28025; ● 30
Ridgeville; RMC Place; CASWELL; *212 C-10; mail Prospect Hill z 27314
Ridgeway; RMC Place; WARREN; 213 B-13; elev. 400ft./122m.; 🄿; z 27570; ● 350
Ridgewood; RMC Place; RICHMOND; *212 H-8; mail Rockingham z 28379; pop. incl. with Rockingham (Inc. Place)
Riegelwood; RMC Place; COLUMBUS; 213 J-13; elev. 30ft./9m.; 🄿; z 28456; ● 1,200
Riley; RMC Place; FRANKLIN; *213 D-12; ★ RAL; mail Youngsville z 27596
Rimer; RMC Place; CABARRUS; *212 F-6; elev. 761ft./232m.; ★ CHRLT; mail Concord z 28025
Ringwood; RMC Place; HALIFAX; 213 C-14; elev. 236ft./72m.; mail Enfield z 27823; ● 40
River Acres; RMC Place; BEAUFORT; *213 E-16; mail Washington z 27889; ● 100
River Bend; Inc. Place; CRAVEN; 213 G-16; mail New Bern z 28562; Ⓟ 2,408; Ⓒ 2,923
Riverdale; RMC Place; CRAVEN; *213 G-16; mail New Bern z 28560, z 28562
River Hills; RMC Place; PITT; *213 E-15; elev. 26ft./8m.; ★ GRNV; mail Greenville z 27858; ● 150
Rivermont; RMC Place; LENOIR; 213 F-15; mail Kinston z 28504; ● 350
River Neck; RMC Place; TYRRELL; *213 D-18; mail Columbia z 27925; rural
River Road; CDP-Census Area Only; BEAUFORT; *213 E-16; elev. 5ft./2m.; mail Washington z 27889; Ⓟ 3,892; Ⓒ 4,094
River Run Plantation; RMC Place; BRUNSWICK; *213 K-13; elev. 25ft./8m.; mail Bolivia z 28422; ● 100
Riverside; RMC Place; CRAVEN; *213 F-15; elev. 10ft./3m.; mail Grifton z 28530; rural
Riverside; RMC Place; YANCEY; *212 D-1; elev. 2,544ft./775m.; mail Burnsville z 28714; rural
Riverton; RMC Place; CHOWAN; *213 C-17; mail Edenton z 27932; ● 120
Roanoke Rapids; Inc. Place; HALIFAX; 213 B-14; elev. 170ft./52m.; 🄿 🄷 ■; z 27870; Ⓟ 15,722; Ⓒ 16,957; ◆ 16,829
Roaring Creek; RMC Place; AVERY; *212 D-2; mail Newland z 28657; rural
Roaring Gap; RMC Place; ALLEGHANY; 212 B-5; elev. 2,852ft./869m.; 🄿; z 28668; summer pop. 1,200; ● 480
Roaring River; RMC Place; WILKES; 212 C-5; elev. 940ft./287m.; 🄿; z 28669; ● 600
Robbins; Inc. Place; MOORE; 212 F-9; elev. 415ft./126m.; 🄿; z 27325; Ⓟ 970; Ⓒ 1,195
Robbinsville; Inc. Place; ⊡ GRAHAM; 212 L-2; elev. 2,064ft./629m.; 🄿; z 28771; Ⓟ 709; Ⓒ 747
Roberdel; RMC Place; RICHMOND; 212 G-8; mail Rockingham z 28379; ● 240
Roberdo; RMC Place; MONTGOMERY; *212 F-8; mail Mount Gilead z 27306; rural
Robersonville; Inc. Place; MARTIN; 213 D-15; elev. 60ft./18m.; 🄿; z 27871 & mail Parmele z 27861; Ⓟ 1,940; Ⓒ 1,731
Roberta Mill (Roberta Mills); RMC Place; CABARRUS; *212 F-6; elev. 600ft./183m.; ★ CHRLT; mail Concord z 28027; pop. incl. with Concord (Inc. Place)
Roberta Mills; CABARRUS; see Roberta Mill (RMC Place)
ROBESON; 212 I-10; Ⓟ 105,179; Ⓒ 123,339; Ⓡ 123,245; ◆ 125,981
Robin Hood Forest; RMC Place; WAKE; *213 E-12; ★ RAL; mail Knightdale z 27545; ● 100
Robinson's; RMC Place; CARTERET; *213 H-17; elev. 25ft./8m.; mail Newport z 28570
Robinwood; RMC Place; GASTON; *212 G-4; ★ CHRLT; mail Gastonia z 28056; pop. incl. with Gastonia (Inc. Place)
Rock Creek; RMC Place; ALAMANCE; *212 D-9; ★ BUR; mail Snow Camp z 27349
Rockdale; RMC Place; CLEVELAND; *212 F-3; elev. 1,005ft./306m.; mail Lawndale z 28090; pop. incl. with Belwood (Inc. Place)
Rockefeller Estates; HARNETT; see Overhills (RMC Place)
Rockfish; CDP; HOKE; 212 G-10; elev. 218ft./66m.; ★ FAY; mail Raeford z 28376; Ⓒ 2,353
Rockford; RMC Place; SURRY; *212 C-6; elev. 854ft./260m.; mail Boonville z 27011, Dobson z 27017
Rockingham; Inc. Place; ⊡ RICHMOND; 212 H-8; elev. 211ft./64m.; 🄿 🄷 ■; z 28379-80; Ⓟ 9,399; Ⓒ 9,672; ◆ 9,378
ROCKINGHAM; 212 C-8; Ⓟ 86,064; Ⓒ 91,928; ◆ 90,810
Rockingham Lake; RMC Place; ROCKINGHAM; *212 C-9; ★ GRNS-; mail Reidsville z 27320; ● 160
Rock Ridge; RMC Place; WILSON; *213 E-13; mail Wilson z 27893; ● 50
Rockwell; Inc. Place; ROWAN; 212 E-7; elev. 786ft./240m.; 🄿; ★ SLSB; z 28138; Ⓟ 1,598; Ⓒ 1,971
Rockwell Park; RMC Place; MECKLENBURG; ★ CHRLT; mail Charlotte z 28213; pop. incl. with Charlotte (Inc. Place)
Rocky Cross; RMC Place; NASH; *213 D-13; elev. 314ft./96m.; mail Middlesex z 27557; rural
Rocky Ford; RMC Place; FRANKLIN; *213 C-12; elev. 398ft./121m.; mail Kittrell z 27544; rural
Rockyhock; RMC Place; CHOWAN; *213 C-17; mail Edenton z 27932
Rocky Mount; Inc. Place; NASH, EDGECOMBE; 213 D-14; elev. 120ft./37m.; 🄿 🄷 🄲 1,629 ■; ★ RKYMT; z 27801-04, z 27815; Ⓟ 48,997; Ⓒ 55,893; Ⓡ 55,977; ◆ 58,485
Rocky Pass; RMC Place; MCDOWELL; *212 E-2; mail Nebo z 28761; rural
Rocky Point; RMC Place; PENDER; 213 I-14; elev. 34ft./10m.; 🄿; z 28457; ● 600
Rocky River; RMC Place; CABARRUS; *212 F-6; elev. 611ft./186m.; ★ CHRLT; mail Concord z 28025
Rocky Springs; RMC Place; ALEXANDER; *212 D-5; elev. 1,191ft./363m.; mail Hiddenite z 28636; rural
Rodanthe; RMC Place; DARE; 213 E-20; elev. 5ft./2m.; 🄿; z 27968; ● 310
Roduco; RMC Place; GATES; 213 B-17; elev. 35ft./11m.; 🄿; z 27969; ● 200
Roe; CARTERET; see Cedar Island (RMC Place)
Rolesville; Inc. Place; WAKE; 213 D-12; elev. 442ft./135m.; 🄿; ★ RAL; z 27571; Ⓟ 572; Ⓒ 907
Rolling Hills; RMC Place; ROWAN; *212 E-6; elev. 750ft./229m.; ★ SLSB; mail Salisbury z 28147; ● 100
Rollingwood; RMC Place; CLEVELAND; *212 F-3; elev. 900ft./274m.; mail Shelby z 28150; ● 60
Rollingwood; RMC Place; CUMBERLAND; *213 G-11; elev. 246ft./75m.; ★ FAY; mail Fayetteville z 28301; ● 560
Rominger; RMC Place; WATAUGA; *212 C-3; elev. 3,379ft./1,030m.; mail Banner Elk z 28604; rural
Ronda; Inc. Place; WILKES; *212 C-5; elev. 935ft./285m.; 🄿; z 28670; Ⓟ 367; Ⓒ 460
Rooks; RMC Place; PENDER; *213 I-13; elev. 58ft./18m.; mail Atkinson z 28421; rural
Roper; Inc. Place; WASHINGTON; 213 D-17; elev. 15ft./5m.; 🄿; z 27970; Ⓟ 669; Ⓒ 613
Rose; WAYNE; see Rosewood (RMC Place)
Rose Bay; RMC Place; HYDE; *213 F-18; mail Swanquarter z 27885; ● 30
Roseboro; Inc. Place; SAMPSON; 213 G-12; elev. 137ft./42m.; 🄿; z 28382; Ⓟ 1,441; Ⓒ 1,267
Rosebud; RMC Place; STOKES; *212 C-7; elev. 788ft./240m.; ★ WNS; mail Walnut Cove z 27052; ● 170
Rosebud; RMC Place; WILSON; *213 E-14; elev. 135ft./41m.; ★ RKYMT; mail Elm City z 27822; rural
Rose Hill; Inc. Place; DUPLIN; 213 H-13; elev. 94ft./29m.; 🄿; z 28458; Ⓟ 1,287; Ⓒ 1,330
Rose Hill; RMC Place; WARREN; *213 B-12; mail Manson z 27553; summer pop. 80
Roseland; RMC Place; COLUMBUS; *213 J-11; elev. 111ft./34m.; mail Chadbourn z 28431, Clarendon z 28432; rural
Roseland; RMC Place; LINCOLN; *212 F-4; mail Lincolnton z 28092; ● 210
Roseland; RMC Place; MOORE; *212 G-9; mail Aberdeen z 28315; rural
Rosemary; HALIFAX; see South Rosemary (CDP-Census Area Only)
Rosemary Park; RMC Place; UNION; *212 G-6; ★ CHRLT; mail Indian Trail z 28079; pop. incl. with Indian Trail (Inc. Place)
Rosemead; RMC Place; BERTIE; 213 C-17; elev. 68ft./21m.; mail Colerain z 27924; ● 30
Rosemont; RMC Place; FORSYTH; *212 D-7; elev. 926ft./282m.; ★ WNS; mail Winston Salem z 27107; pop. incl. with Winston-Salem (Inc. Place)
Roseneath; RMC Place; HALIFAX; *213 D-15; elev. 107ft./33m.; mail Scotland Neck z 27874; rural
Roseville; RMC Place; PERSON; *212 C-10; elev. 683ft./208m.; mail Roxboro z 27574
Rosewood (Rose); RMC Place; WAYNE; 213 F-13; ★ GLDS; mail Goldsboro z 27530; ● 4,300
Rosin; SAMPSON; see Rosin Hill (RMC Place)
Rosindale; RMC Place; BLADEN; *213 I-12; elev. 130ft./40m.; mail Council z 28434; ● 30
Rosin Hill (Rosin); RMC Place; SAMPSON; *213 G-12; elev. 175ft./53m.; mail Newton Grove z 28366; rural
Roslin; RMC Place; CUMBERLAND; *213 H-11; elev. 181ft./55m.; ★ FAY; mail Hope Mills z 28348; ● 30
Rosman; Inc. Place; TRANSYLVANIA; 212 M-5; elev. 2,182ft./665m.; 🄿; z 28772; Ⓟ 385; Ⓒ 490
Ross Store; RMC Place; STOKES; *212 C-7; elev. 1,055ft./322m.; ★ WNS; mail Walnut Cove z 27052; ● 140
Rougemont (Red Mountain); RMC Place; DURHAM; 213 C-11; elev. 549ft./167m.; 🄿; z 27572; ● 600
Roughedge; RMC Place; UNION; *212 H-6; mail Monroe z 28112; rural
Roundtree; RMC Place; PITT; *213 F-15; elev. 67ft./20m.; ★ GRNV; mail Ayden z 28513
ROWAN; 212 E-6; Ⓟ 110,605; Ⓒ 130,340; ◆ 139,188
Rowan Mill; RMC Place; ROWAN; *212 E-6; ★ SLSB; mail Salisbury z 28147
Rowes Corner; RMC Place; CRAVEN; *213 G-16; elev. 25ft./8m.; mail New Bern z 28560
Rowland; Inc. Place; ROBESON; 212 I-10; elev. 151ft./46m.; 🄿; z 28383; Ⓟ 1,139; Ⓒ 1,146
Roxboro; Inc. Place; ⊡ PERSON; 213 C-11; 🄿 🄷; z 27573-74; Ⓟ 7,332; Ⓒ 8,696
Roxobel; Inc. Place; BERTIE; 213 C-15; elev. 97ft./30m.; 🄿; z 27872; Ⓟ 244; Ⓒ 263
Royal; RMC Place; BEAUFORT; 213 F-17; mail Aurora z 27806; ● 70
Royal; RMC Place; FRANKLIN; *213 D-12; elev. 386ft./118m.; mail Louisburg z 27549; rural
Royal Oaks; RMC Place; CABARRUS; *212 F-6; ★ CHRLT; mail Kannapolis z 28081, z 28083; pop. incl. with Kannapolis (Inc. Place)
Royal Pines; CDP; BUNCOMBE; *212 F-1; ★ ASHE; mail Arden z 28704; Ⓟ 4,418; Ⓒ 5,334
Royster; RMC Place; BRUNSWICK; *213 J-13; elev. 4ft./1m.; ★ WILM; mail Leland z 28451; ● 30
Rudd; RMC Place; GUILFORD; *212 C-8; elev. 823ft./251m.; ★ GRNS-; mail Browns Summit z 27214; rural
Ruffin; RMC Place; ROCKINGHAM; 212 B-9; elev. 700ft./213m.; 🄿; z 27326; ● 350
Rufus; RMC Place; CALDWELL; *212 D-3; elev. 1,217ft./371m.; mail Lenoir z 28645; rural
Rural Hall; Inc. Place; FORSYTH; 212 C-7; elev. 998ft./304m.; 🄿; ★ WNS; z 27045, z 27094, z 27098-99; Ⓟ 1,652; Ⓒ 2,464
Ruskin; RMC Place; BLADEN; *213 H-12; elev. 62ft./19m.; mail White Oak z 28399; ● 70
Russtown; RMC Place; BRUNSWICK; *213 K-12; mail Ash z 28420; rural
Ruth; Inc. Place; RUTHERFORD; 212 F-2; elev. 1,034ft./315m.; mail Rutherfordton z 28139; Ⓟ 366; Ⓒ 329
RUTHERFORD; 212 F-2; Ⓟ 56,918; Ⓒ 62,899; Ⓡ 62,901; ◆ 62,746
Rutherford College; Inc. Place; BURKE; 212 E-3; elev. 1,200ft./366m.; 🄿; z 28671; Ⓟ 1,126; Ⓒ 1,293; Ⓡ 1,303
Rutherfordton; Inc. Place; ⊡ RUTHERFORD; 212 F-2; elev. 929ft./283m.; 🄿 🄷; z 28139; Ⓟ 3,617; Ⓒ 4,131
Rutherwood; RMC Place; WATAUGA; *212 C-3; elev. 3,260ft./994m.; mail Boone z 28607; ● 50
Ryland; RMC Place; CHOWAN; 213 C-17; elev. 12ft./4m.; mail Tyner z 27980; ● 40

S

Saddletree; RMC Place; ROBESON; *212 H-10; elev. 155ft./47m.; mail Lumberton z 28358; rural
Sadler; RMC Place; ROCKINGHAM; *212 B-9; mail Reidsville z 27320; ● 30
Safe; RMC Place; DUPLIN; *213 H-13; elev. 49ft./15m.; mail Wallace z 28466; rural
Saint Helena; Inc. Place; PENDER; 213 I-14; mail Burgaw z 28425; Ⓟ 321; Ⓒ 395
Saint James; Inc. Place; BRUNSWICK; *213 K-13; mail Southport z 28461; Ⓒ 804

Entries in **UPPERCASE** are counties.
Entries in **bold** have populations of 2,500 or more.
Names in parentheses are alternate names.
Inc. Place — Incorporated Place
RMC Place — Rand McNally Designated Place
CDP — Census Designated Place
MCD — Minor Civil Division

⊡ County Seat
▲ Minor Civil Division
elev. Elevation
🄿 Post Office
🄷 Hospital
🄲 College
■ Principal Business Center
★ Ranally Metro Area (RMA) Abbreviation
z Zip Code(s)
Ⓟ Previous Census Population
Ⓡ Revised Census Population
Ⓐ Annexation Population
● Rand McNally Population Estimate
Ⓒ Final Census Population
Ⓢ Special Census Population
◆ Estimated Population

For additional definitions see Glossary, Volume 1, and Introduction, Volume 2.

Saint James; RMC Place; COLUMBUS; ***213** I-12; elev. 88ft./27m.; mail Lake Waccamaw z 28450; rural
Saint John; RMC Place; HERTFORD; ***213** C-16; mail Ahoskie z 27910, Aulander z 27805; ● 230
Saint Johns; RMC Place; CHOWAN; ***213** D-18; elev. 15ft./5m.; mail Edenton z 27932; rural
Saint Johns; RMC Place; PITT; ***213** F-15; elev. 8ft./2m.; ★ **GRNV**; mail Grifton z 28530; rural
Saint Lewis; RMC Place; EDGECOMBE; **213** E-14; mail Macclesfield z 27852; ● 70
Saint Martin; RMC Place; STANLY; ***212** F-7; elev. 425ft./130m.; mail Albemarle z 28001; ● 30
Saint Pauls; Inc. Place; ROBESON; **213** H-11; elev. 170ft./52m.; 🅿; ★ **FAY**; z 28384; Ⓟ 1,992; Ⓒ 2,137; Ⓡ 2,247
Saint Stephens; CDP; CATAWBA; ***212** E-4; ★ **HICK**; mail Hickory z 28601; Ⓟ 8,734; Ⓒ 9,439; Ⓡ 9,426
Salem; CDP; BURKE; ***212** E-3; elev. 1,234ft./376m.; mail Morganton z 28655; Ⓟ 2,271; Ⓒ 2,923
Salem; RMC Place; FORSYTH; ***212** D-7; ★ **WNS**; mail Winston Salem z 27108; pop. incl. with Winston-Salem (Inc. Place)
Salem; RMC Place; LINCOLN; ***212** F-4; mail Lincolnton z 28092; rural
Salem; RMC Place; NASH; ***213** C-14; elev. 203ft./62m.; mail Whitakers z 27891; rural
Salem (New Salem); RMC Place; RANDOLPH; ***212** D-8; elev. 760ft./232m.; ★ **GRNS-**; mail Randleman z 27317; ● 290
Salem; RMC Place; SURRY; ***212** B-6; elev. 1,270ft./387m.; mail Mount Airy z 27030; ● 1,500
Salemburg; Inc. Place; SAMPSON; **213** G-12; elev. 164ft./50m.; 🅿; z 28385; Ⓟ 409; Ⓒ 469
Salisbury; Inc. Place; ⊡ ROWAN; **212** E-6; elev. 746ft./227m.; 🅿 🅷 🅲 2,176 ■; ★ **SLSB**; z 28144-47; Ⓟ 23,087; Ⓒ 26,462; ◆ 28,018
Salter Path; RMC Place; CARTERET; **213** H-17; elev. 10ft./3m.; 🅿; z 28575; ● 800
Salty Shores; RMC Place; CARTERET; ***213** H-16; elev. 5ft./2m.; ★ **JAX**; mail Newport z 28570; ● 150
Saluda; Inc. Place; POLK, HENDERSON; **212** F-1; elev. 209ft./64m.; 🅿; z 28773; Ⓟ 488; Ⓒ 575
Salvo; RMC Place; DARE; **213** E-20; elev. 5ft./2m.; 🅿; z 27972; ● 220
Samarcand; RMC Place; MOORE; **212** F-9; elev. 698ft./213m.; mail Eagle Springs z 27242; ● 150
Samaria; RMC Place; NASH; **213** D-13; mail Middlesex z 27557; ● 80
SAMPSON; **213** G-12; Ⓟ 47,297; Ⓒ 60,161; ◆ 64,232
Sanderling; RMC Place; DARE; **213** C-20; mail Kill Devil Hills z 27948; ● 340
Sand Hill; RMC Place; BUNCOMBE; **212** M-6; ★ **ASHE**; mail Asheville z 28806; pop. incl. with Asheville (Inc. Place)
Sandhill; RMC Place; PAMLICO; ***213** G-17; elev. 45ft./14m.; mail New Bern z 28560; ● 30
Sandhill Acres; RMC Place; MONTGOMERY; ***212** G-9; elev. 586ft./179m.; mail Candor z 27229; ● 150
Sands; RMC Place; WATAUGA; ***212** C-3; mail Boone z 28607; ● 100
Sandy Bottom; RMC Place; LENOIR; ***213** G-14; elev. 85ft./26m.; mail Kinston z 28504; rural
Sandy Bottoms; RMC Place; SCOTLAND; ***212** H-9; mail Laurinburg z 28352; rural
Sandy Creek; Inc. Place; BRUNSWICK; ***213** J-13; ★ **WILM**; mail Leland z 28451; Ⓟ 243; Ⓒ 246
Sandy Cross; RMC Place; GATES; ***213** B-17; elev. 52ft./16m.; mail Hobbsville z 27946; ● 30
Sandy Cross; RMC Place; NASH; ***213** D-14; elev. 203ft./62m.; ★ **RKYMT**; mail Nashville z 27856; ● 30
Sandy Cross; RMC Place; ROCKINGHAM; ***212** C-8; elev. 854ft./260m.; ★ **GRNS-**; mail Reidsville z 27320; ● 50
Sandyfield; Inc. Place; COLUMBUS; ***213** I-13; elev. 50ft./15m.; mail Riegelwood z 28456; Ⓒ 340
Sandy Grove; RMC Place; DAVIDSON; ***212** E-7; elev. 782ft./238m.; mail Lexington z 27295; rural
Sandy Grove; RMC Place; HOKE; ***212** H-10; mail Raeford z 28376; ● 60
Sandymush; RMC Place; BUNCOMBE, MADISON; ***212** K-5; mail Marshall z 28753; ● 200
Sandy Mush; RMC Place; RUTHERFORD; ***212** F-2; elev. 921ft./281m.; mail Forest City z 28043, Rutherfordton z 28139; ● 600
Sandy Plain; RMC Place; COLUMBUS; ***213** J-11; elev. 70ft./21m.; mail Tabor City z 28463; rural
Sandy Plain; RMC Place; DUPLIN; mail Pink Hill z 28572; rural
Sandy Plains (Patterson Grove); RMC Place; CLEVELAND; ***212** F-4; elev. 940ft./287m.; ★ **CHRLT**; mail Kings Mountain z 28086; ● 50
Sandy Plains; RMC Place; POLK; ***212** F-2; elev. 101ft./31m.; mail Tryon z 28782; rural
Sandy Ridge; RMC Place; GUILFORD; ***212** D-8; elev. 957ft./292m.; ★ **GRNS-**; mail Colfax z 27235; ● 400
Sandy Ridge; RMC Place; STOKES; **212** B-7; elev. 1,123ft./342m.; 🅿; z 27046; ● 230
Sanford; Inc. Place; ⊡ LEE; **212** F-10; 🅿 🅷 ■; z 27237, z 27330-32; Ⓟ 14,755; Ⓒ 23,220; ◆ 30,867
Sans Souci; RMC Place; BERTIE; ***213** D-17; elev. 29ft./9m.; mail Windsor z 27983; rural
Santeetlah; GRAHAM; see Lake Santeetlah (Inc. Place)
Sapona; RMC Place; CUMBERLAND; ★ **FAY**; mail Fayetteville z 28301
Sapphire (Oakland); RMC Place; TRANSYLVANIA; **212** M-4; elev. 3,200ft./975m.; 🅿; z 28774; ● 150
Saratoga; Inc. Place; WILSON; **213** E-14; elev. 121ft./37m.; 🅿; z 27873; Ⓟ 342; Ⓒ 379
Sardis Village; RMC Place; MECKLENBURG; ★ **CHRLT**; mail Charlotte z 28270; pop. incl. with Charlotte (Inc. Place)
Sarecta; RMC Place; DUPLIN; ***213** G-14; elev. 102ft./31m.; mail Beulaville z 28518, Kenansville z 28349; ● 50
Sarvis Heights; RMC Place; GASTON; ★ **CHRLT**; mail Gastonia z 28052
Sassers Mill; RMC Place; JONES; ***213** G-15; mail Dover z 28526; rural
Satterwhite; RMC Place; GRANVILLE; ***213** B-11; mail Oxford z 27565; rural
Saulston; RMC Place; WAYNE; **213** F-14; elev. 126ft./38m.; ★ **GLDS**; mail Goldsboro z 27530; ● 110
Saunook; RMC Place; HAYWOOD; **212** L-4; mail Waynesville z 28786; ● 120
Savannah; RMC Place; JACKSON; ***212** L-3; mail Sylva z 28779; rural
Savoy Heights; RMC Place; CUMBERLAND; ★ **FAY**; pop. incl. with Fayetteville (Inc. Place)
Saw; RMC Place; ROWAN; ★ **SLSB**; mail China Grove z 28023
Sawmills; Inc. Place; CALDWELL; **212** D-3; 🅿; ★ **HICK**; z 28630 & mail Hudson z 28638; Ⓟ 4,088; Ⓒ 4,921
Saxapahaw; CDP; ALAMANCE; **212** D-10; elev. 539ft./164m.; 🅿; ★ **BUR**; z 27340; Ⓟ 1,178; Ⓒ 1,418
Sayles Village; RMC Place; BUNCOMBE; ***212** E-1; ★ **ASHE**; mail Asheville z 28803; pop. incl. with Asheville (Inc. Place)
Scaly; MACON; see Scaly Mountain (RMC Place)
Scaly Mountain (Scaly); RMC Place; MACON; **212** N-3; elev. 3,505ft./1,068m.; 🅿; z 28775; summer pop. 850; ● 480
Schley; RMC Place; ORANGE; ***212** C-10; elev. 586ft./179m.; mail Hillsborough z 27278; ● 50
Scholl; RMC Place; SCOTLAND; ***212** H-9; elev. 319ft./97m.; mail Hamlet z 28345; rural
Schrams Beach; RMC Place; BEAUFORT; ***213** F-17; elev. 4ft./1m.; mail Belhaven z 27810; ● 100
Scotch Grove; RMC Place; SCOTLAND; ***212** H-9; mail Laurinburg z 28352; rural
SCOTLAND; **212** H-9; Ⓟ 33,754; Ⓒ 35,998; ◆ 36,421
Scotland Neck; Inc. Place; HALIFAX; **213** C-15; elev. 103ft./31m.; 🅿 🅷; z 27874; Ⓟ 2,575; Ⓒ 2,362
Scotsdale; RMC Place; CUMBERLAND; ***213** G-11; elev. 237ft./72m.; ★ **FAY**; mail Fayetteville z 28304; pop. incl. with Fayetteville (Inc. Place)
Scotsdale; RMC Place; SCOTLAND; mail Laurinburg z 28352; pop. incl. with Laurinburg (Inc. Place)
Scott Acres; RMC Place; ALAMANCE; ***212** D-10; elev. 617ft./188m.; ★ **BUR**; mail Mebane z 27302; ● 60
Scott Park; RMC Place; GUILFORD; ***212** D-8; ★ **GRNS-**; mail Greensboro z 27401; pop. incl. with Greensboro (Inc. Place)
Scotts; RMC Place; IREDELL; **212** D-5; elev. 1,031ft./314m.; 🅿; z 28699; ● 190
Scotts; RMC Place; WILSON; ***213** E-13; elev. 155ft./47m.; mail Lucama z 27851; rural
Scotts Crossroads; RMC Place; EDGECOMBE; ***213** D-15; elev. 12ft./4m.; mail Tarboro z 27886; rural
Scotts Hill; RMC Place; PENDER; **213** J-14; mail Wilmington z 28411; ● 140
Scotts Store; RMC Place; DUPLIN; ***213** G-14; elev. 45ft./14m.; mail Mount Olive z 28365; rural
Scotts Store; RMC Place; PAMLICO; ***213** G-17; elev. 26ft./8m.; mail New Bern z 28560; rural
Scottville; RMC Place; ASHE; **212** B-4; elev. 2,858ft./871m.; 🅿; z 28672; ● 50
Scranton; RMC Place; HYDE; **213** E-18; elev. 4ft./1m.; 🅿; z 27875; ● 120
Scuffleton; RMC Place; GREENE; ***213** F-15; elev. 10ft./3m.; mail Ayden z 28513; ● 50
Scuppernong; RMC Place; WASHINGTON; ***213** D-18; elev. 9ft./3m.; mail Creswell z 27928
Seaboard; Inc. Place; NORTHAMPTON; **213** B-15; elev. 130ft./40m.; 🅿; z 27876; Ⓟ 791; Ⓒ 695
Sea Breeze; CDP; NEW HANOVER; **213** K-14; ★ **WILM**; mail Wilmington z 28409; Ⓒ 1,312
Seagate; CDP; NEW HANOVER; **213** M-20; ★ **WILM**; mail Wilmington z 28403; Ⓟ 5,444; Ⓒ 4,590
Seagate IV; RMC Place; CARTERET; ***213** H-17; elev. 5ft./2m.; mail Beaufort z 28516; ● 90
Seagrove; Inc. Place; RANDOLPH; **212** E-8; elev. 763ft./233m.; 🅿; z 27341; Ⓟ 244; Ⓒ 246
Sealevel; RMC Place; CARTERET; **213** H-18; elev. 3ft./1m.; 🅿; z 28577, z 28581; ● 380
Seaside; RMC Place; BRUNSWICK; **213** K-12; ★ **MYR.B**; mail Sunset Beach z 28468; ● 50
Sedalia; Inc. Place; GUILFORD; **212** D-9; elev. 704ft./215m.; 🅿; ★ **BUR**; z 27342; Ⓒ 618
Sedgefield; RMC Place; GUILFORD; **214** H-13; ★ **GRNS-**; mail Greensboro z 27407; ● 1,000
Sedgefield; RMC Place; MECKLENBURG; ★ **CHRLT**; mail Charlotte z 28203; pop. incl. with Charlotte (Inc. Place)
Sedgefield Lakes; RMC Place; GUILFORD; ***212** D-8; ★ **GRNS-**; mail Greensboro z 27407; pop. incl. with Greensboro (Inc. Place)
Sedgefield Park; RMC Place; GUILFORD; ***212** D-8; ★ **GRNS-**; mail Greensboro z 27407; ● 1,000
Sedge Garden; RMC Place; FORSYTH; ***212** D-7; ★ **WNS**; mail Winston Salem z 27105; pop. incl. with Winston-Salem (Inc. Place); Ⓟ 2,784
Selica; RMC Place; TRANSYLVANIA; ***212** M-5; mail Brevard z 28712; rural
Selma; Inc. Place; JOHNSTON; **213** E-13; elev. 179ft./55m.; 🅿; ★ **RAL**; z 27576; Ⓟ 4,600; Ⓒ 5,914
Selwin; RMC Place; GATES; ***213** C-17; mail Hobbsville z 27946; ● 50
Selwyn Park; RMC Place; MECKLENBURG; ★ **CHRLT**; mail Charlotte z 28209; pop. incl. with Charlotte (Inc. Place)
Seminole; RMC Place; HARNETT; ***212** F-10; elev. 462ft./141m.; mail Broadway z 27505
Semora; RMC Place; CASWELL; **212** B-10; elev. 580ft./177m.; 🅿; z 27343; ● 250
Senia; RMC Place; AVERY; ***212** C-2; mail Newland z 28657; rural
Seven Devils; Inc. Place; AVERY, WATAUGA; **212** C-3; 🅿; z 28604; Ⓟ 117; Ⓒ 129
Seven Lakes; CDP; MOORE; **212** F-9; elev. 550ft./168m.; 🅿; z 27376; Ⓟ 2,049; Ⓒ 3,214
Seven Paths; RMC Place; FRANKLIN; ***213** D-13; elev. 313ft./95m.; mail Louisburg z 27549; ● 50
Seven Springs; Inc. Place; WAYNE; **213** F-14; elev. 50ft./15m.; 🅿; z 28578; Ⓟ 163; Ⓒ 86
Severn; Inc. Place; NORTHAMPTON; **213** B-16; elev. 80ft./24m.; 🅿; z 27877; Ⓟ 260; Ⓒ 263
Seversville; RMC Place; MECKLENBURG; ★ **CHRLT**; mail Charlotte z 28208; pop. incl. with Charlotte (Inc. Place)
Sevier; RMC Place; MCDOWELL; ***212** D-2; mail Marion z 28752; rural
Seward; RMC Place; FORSYTH; ***212** C-7; elev. 954ft./291m.; ★ **WNS**; mail Pfafftown z 27040; ● 760
Shacktown; RMC Place; YADKIN; ***212** C-6; elev. 880ft./268m.; mail Yadkinville z 27055; ● 100
Shadey Oaks Acres; RMC Place; CLEVELAND; ***212** F-3; elev. 900ft./274m.; mail Shelby z 28150; ● 100
Shady Banks; RMC Place; BEAUFORT; ***213** E-16; mail Washington z 27889; ● 120
Shady Brook; RMC Place; CABARRUS; ★ **CHRLT**; mail Kannapolis z 28081; pop. incl. with Kannapolis (Inc. Place)
Shady Forest; RMC Place; BRUNSWICK; ***213** K-12; elev. 23ft./7m.; ★ **MYR.B**; mail Calabash z 28467; ● 60
Shady Grove; RMC Place; JONES; ***213** G-15; elev. 71ft./22m.; mail Kinston z 28501; rural
Shallotte; Inc. Place; BRUNSWICK; **213** K-12; elev. 10ft./3m.; 🅿; z 28459, z 28468-70 & mail Calabash z 28467; Ⓟ 965; Ⓒ 1,381
Shallotte Point; RMC Place; BRUNSWICK; ***213** K-12; elev. 20ft./6m.; ★ **MYR.B**; mail Shallotte z 28470; ● 250
Shallo Well (Purnell); RMC Place; LEE; ***212** F-10; elev. 450ft./137m.; mail Sanford z 27332; pop. incl. with Sanford (Inc. Place)
Shanghai; RMC Place; CLEVELAND; ***212** F-3; elev. 864ft./263m.; mail Boiling Springs z 28017; rural
Shanghai; RMC Place; SAMPSON; ***213** H-13; elev. 107ft./33m.; mail Rose Hill z 28458; rural
Shankletown; RMC Place; CABARRUS; ***212** F-6; elev. 650ft./198m.; ★ **CHRLT**; mail Concord z 28025; pop. incl. with Concord (Inc. Place)
Shannon; CDP; ROBESON; **212** H-10; elev. 201ft./61m.; 🅿; z 28386; Ⓒ 197
Sharon; RMC Place; CAMDEN; ***213** B-18; mail South Mills z 27976; ● 30
Sharon; RMC Place; IREDELL; ***212** E-5; elev. 1,004ft./306m.; ★ **HICK**; mail Statesville z 28625, z 28677; rural
Sharonbrook; RMC Place; MECKLENBURG; ***212** G-5; elev. 650ft./198m.; ★ **CHRLT**; mail Charlotte z 28210; pop. incl. with Charlotte (Inc. Place)
Sharp Point; RMC Place; PITT; ***213** F-15; mail Fountain z 27829; rural
Sharpsburg; Inc. Place; NASH, EDGECOMBE, WILSON; **213** D-14; elev. 145ft./44m.; 🅿; ★ **RKYMT**; z 27878; Ⓟ 1,536; Ⓒ 2,421
Shatley Springs; RMC Place; ASHE; ***212** B-4; elev. 2,862ft./872m.; mail Crumpler z 28617; ● 50
Shawboro; RMC Place; CURRITUCK; **213** B-19; elev. 15ft./5m.; 🅿; z 27973; ● 520
Shaw Heights; RMC Place; CUMBERLAND; ***213** G-11; ★ **FAY**; mail Fayetteville z 28303; ● 2,580
Sheb; RMC Place; DURHAM; ★ **DUR**; pop. incl. with Durham (Inc. Place)
Sheffield; RMC Place; DAVIE; ***212** D-6; mail Mocksville z 27028; ● 30
Shelby; Inc. Place; ⊡ CLEVELAND; **212** F-3; elev. 853ft./260m.; 🅿 🅷 ■; z 28150-52; Ⓟ 14,669; Ⓒ 19,477; ◆ 19,654
Shell Rock Landing; RMC Place; ONSLOW; ***213** H-16; ★ **JAX**; mail Hubert z 28539; ● 330
Shelmerdine; RMC Place; PITT; ***213** F-15; mail Ayden z 28513
Shelter Neck; RMC Place; PENDER; ***213** I-14; elev. 18ft./5m.; mail Burgaw z 28425; rural
Shelton; RMC Place; CASWELL; ***212** B-9; elev. 707ft./215m.; ★ **DANV**; mail Pelham z 27311; rural
Shelton Town; RMC Place; SURRY; ***212** B-6; mail Mount Airy z 27030; ● 320
Shepard; RMC Place; DURHAM; ★ **DUR**; mail Durham z 27707; pop. incl. with Durham (Inc. Place)
Shepherds; RMC Place; IREDELL; **212** E-5; elev. 913ft./278m.; ★ **CHRLT**; mail Mooresville z 28115; ● 250
Sherrills Ford; CDP; CATAWBA; **212** E-5; elev. 879ft./268m.; 🅿; ★ **HICK**; z 28673; Ⓟ 3,185; Ⓒ 941
Sherron Acres; RMC Place; DURHAM; ★ **DUR**; mail Durham z 27703; pop. incl. with Durham (Inc. Place)
Sherwood; RMC Place; WATAUGA; ***212** C-3; mail Vilas z 28692
Sherwood Forest; RMC Place; BUNCOMBE; ***212** E-1; ★ **ASHE**; mail Swannanoa z 28778; ● 360
Sherwood Forest; RMC Place; FORSYTH; ***212** D-7; ★ **WNS**; mail Winston Salem z 27104
Sherwood Forest; RMC Place; TRANSYLVANIA; ***212** M-5; mail Brevard z 28712; ● 130
Sherwood Forest; RMC Place; WILKES; ***212** C-4
Sherwood Forest; RMC Place; WILSON; ***213** E-14; mail Wilson z 27896; pop. incl. with Wilson (Inc. Place)
Sherwood Park; RMC Place; CUMBERLAND; ***213** G-11; elev. 150ft./46m.; ★ **FAY**; mail Fayetteville z 28306; ● 560
Sherwood Terrace; RMC Place; TRANSYLVANIA; ***212** M-5; mail Brevard z 28712; ● 80
Sherwood Village; RMC Place; GUILFORD; ***212** D-8; ★ **GRNS-**; mail High Point z 27260; pop. incl. with High Point (Inc. Place)
Shields Commissary; RMC Place; HALIFAX; ***213** C-15; elev. 41ft./12m.; mail Scotland Neck z 27874; rural
Shiloh; RMC Place; BUNCOMBE; ***212** E-1; ★ **ASHE**; mail Asheville z 28803; pop. incl. with Asheville (Inc. Place)
Shiloh; RMC Place; CAMDEN; **213** C-19; elev. 10ft./3m.; 🅿; z 27974; ● 150
Shiloh; RMC Place; RUTHERFORD; ***212** F-2; elev. 1,099ft./335m.; mail Forest City z 28043; ● 100
Shine; RMC Place; GREENE; ***213** F-14; elev. 38ft./12m.; mail Snow Hill z 28580; ● 80
Shingle Hollow; RMC Place; RUTHERFORD; ***212** F-2; elev. 1,185ft./361m.; mail Rutherfordton z 28139; rural
Shinnville; RMC Place; IREDELL; ***212** E-5; elev. 855ft./261m.; mail Mooresville z 28115; ● 100
Shoal; RMC Place; SURRY; ***212** C-6; mail Pinnacle z 27043; ● 30
Shoal Creek; JACKSON; see Qualla (RMC Place)
Shoofly; RMC Place; GRANVILLE; ***213** C-11; mail Stem z 27581; rural
Shooting Creek; RMC Place; CLAY; **212** M-2; mail Hayesville z 28904; ● 100
Shopton; RMC Place; MECKLENBURG; ***212** G-5; elev. 727ft./222m.; ★ **CHRLT**; mail Charlotte z 28210
Short Off; RMC Place; MACON; ***212** M-4; mail Highlands z 28741; ● 30
Shotwell; RMC Place; WAKE; ***213** E-12; elev. 294ft./90m.; ★ **RAL**; mail Knightdale z 27545, Wendell z 27591; rural
Shuffletown; RMC Place; MECKLENBURG; ***212** F-5; elev. 700ft./213m.; ★ **CHRLT**; mail Charlotte z 28214; pop. incl. with Charlotte (Inc. Place)
Shulls Mills; RMC Place; WATAUGA; ***212** C-3; mail Boone z 28607; ● 250
Shupings Mill; RMC Place; ROWAN; ***212** E-6; elev. 859ft./262m.; ★ **SLSB**; mail Rockwell z 28138; rural
Sidestown; RMC Place; CABARRUS; ***212** F-6; elev. 650ft./198m.; ★ **CHRLT**; mail Concord z 28025; pop. incl. with Concord (Inc. Place)
Sidney; RMC Place; BEAUFORT; **213** E-17; mail Belhaven z 27810; ● 100
Sidney; RMC Place; COLUMBUS; **213** J-11; elev. 92ft./28m.; mail Whiteville z 28472; ● 70
Sign Pine; RMC Place; CHOWAN; ***213** C-17; elev. 35ft./11m.; mail Tyner z 27980; ● 30
Siler City; Inc. Place; CHATHAM; **212** E-9; elev. 598ft./182m.; 🅿 🅷; z 27344; Ⓟ 4,808; Ⓒ 6,966
Silk Hope; RMC Place; CHATHAM; ***212** E-9; elev. 654ft./199m.; mail Siler City z 27344; ● 50
Siloam; RMC Place; SURRY; **212** C-6; elev. 834ft./254m.; 🅿; z 27047; ● 60
Silver City; CDP; HOKE; **212** G-10; ★ **FAY**; mail Raeford z 28376; Ⓟ 1,343; Ⓒ 1,146
Silverdale; RMC Place; ONSLOW; ***213** H-16; ★ **JAX**; mail Hubert z 28539; rural
Silver Hill; RMC Place; DAVIDSON; ***212** E-7; elev. 685ft./209m.; mail Lexington z 27295; rural
Silver Hill; RMC Place; PAMLICO; ***213** G-17; elev. 45ft./14m.; mail New Bern z 28560; rural
Silver Lake; CDP; NEW HANOVER; ***213** J-14; ★ **WILM**; mail Wilmington z 28403; Ⓟ 4,071; Ⓒ 5,788
Silverstone; RMC Place; WATAUGA; **212** C-3; mail Zionville z 28698; ● 120
Silver Valley; RMC Place; DAVIDSON; ***212** E-7; elev. 734ft./224m.; mail Lexington z 27292
Simms; WILSON; see Sims (Inc. Place)
Simpson; Inc. Place; PITT; **213** E-16; elev. 70ft./21m.; 🅿; ★ **GRNV**; z 27879; Ⓟ 410; Ⓒ 464
Sims (Simms); Inc. Place; WILSON; **213** E-13; elev. 202ft./62m.; 🅿; z 27880; Ⓟ 124; Ⓒ 128
Sioux; RMC Place; YANCEY; ***212** D-1; mail Green Mountain z 28740; rural
Sivey Town; RMC Place; BRUNSWICK; ***213** K-13; elev. 42ft./13m.; mail Supply z 28462; ● 200
Six Forks; RMC Place; WAKE; ***213** D-12; elev. 498ft./152m.; ★ **RAL**; mail Raleigh z 27615; pop. incl. with Raleigh (Inc. Place)
Six Forks; RMC Place; WAKE; ***213** D-11; ★ **RAL**; mail Raleigh z 27615; pop. incl. with Raleigh (Inc. Place)
Skibo; RMC Place; CUMBERLAND; ***213** G-11; ★ **FAY**; mail Fayetteville z 28304; pop. incl. with Fayetteville (Inc. Place)
Skinnersville; RMC Place; WASHINGTON; ***213** D-17; mail Roper z 27970; rural
Skippers Corner; CDP; NEW HANOVER; ***213** J-14; ★ **WILM**; Ⓒ 1,246
Skyco; RMC Place; DARE; ***213** D-20; mail Manteo z 27954; ● 50
Skycrest Village; RMC Place; WAKE; ***213** D-12; ★ **RAL**; mail Raleigh z 27604; ● 310
Skyland; RMC Place; BUNCOMBE; **212** F-1; 🅿; ★ **ASHE**; z 28776; pop. incl. with Asheville (Inc. Place)
Skyline; RMC Place; MOORE; ***212** G-9; mail Vass z 28394; ● 100
Skyway Terrace; RMC Place; SCOTLAND; mail Maxton z 28364; ● 150
Sladesville; RMC Place; HYDE; ***213** F-18; elev. 3ft./1m.; mail Scranton z 27875
Slatestone Hills; RMC Place; BEAUFORT; ***213** E-16; elev. 26ft./8m.; mail Washington z 27889; pop. incl. with Washington (Inc. Place)
Sligo; RMC Place; CURRITUCK; **213** B-19; mail Moyock z 27958; ● 90
Sloan; RMC Place; DUPLIN; ***213** H-14; mail Wallace z 28466; rural
Slocomb; RMC Place; CUMBERLAND; **213** G-11; ★ **FAY**; mail Fayetteville z 28311, Linden z 28356; ● 60
Slocum; RMC Place; HYDE; ***213** F-19; mail Engelhard z 27824; rural
Small; RMC Place; BEAUFORT; **213** F-17; mail Aurora z 27806; ● 50
Small Crossroads; RMC Place; CHOWAN; ***213** C-17; elev. 10ft./3m.; mail Tyner z 27980
Smallwood; RMC Place; BEAUFORT; mail Washington z 27889; pop. incl. with Washington (Inc. Place)
Smethport; RMC Place; ASHE; **212** B-3; elev. 2,825ft./861m.; mail West Jefferson z 28694; ● 200
Smith Creek; RMC Place; NEW HANOVER; ***213** J-14; ★ **WILM**; mail Wrightsville Beach z 28480; Ⓟ 7,461
Smith Crossing; RMC Place; COLUMBUS; ***213** J-12; elev. 72ft./22m.; mail Hallsboro z 28442; rural
Smithfield; Inc. Place; ⊡ JOHNSTON; **213** F-12; elev. 153ft./47m.; 🅿 🅷; ★ **RAL**; z 27577; Ⓟ 7,540; Ⓒ 11,510; Ⓡ 10,867
Smith Grove; RMC Place; DAVIE; **212** D-6; elev. 807ft./246m.; ★ **WNS**; mail Mocksville z 27028; ● 40
Smith's Corner; RMC Place; CAMDEN; ***213** C-19; elev. 2ft./1m.; mail Camden z 27921; rural
Smithton; RMC Place; BEAUFORT; ***213** E-17; elev. 7ft./2m.; mail Belhaven z 27810; ● 80
Smithtown; RMC Place; PERQUIMANS; ***213** C-18; elev. 7ft./2m.; mail Hertford z 27944; rural
Smithtown (Fall Creek); RMC Place; YADKIN; **212** C-6; elev. 1,104ft./336m.; ★ **WNS**; mail East Bend z 27018; ● 200
Smyre; RMC Place; GASTON; ***212** F-4; ★ **CHRLT**; mail Gastonia z 28052, z 28054; pop. incl. with Gastonia (Inc. Place)
Smyrna; RMC Place; CARTERET; ***213** H-18; elev. 7ft./2m.; 🅿; z 28579; ● 320
Smyth; HENDERSON; see Balfour (CDP)
Sneads Ferry; CDP; ONSLOW; **213** I-15; elev. 28ft./9m.; 🅿; z 28460; Ⓟ 2,031; Ⓒ 2,248
Sneads Grove; RMC Place; SCOTLAND; ***212** H-9; mail Laurinburg z 28352; rural
Snow Camp; RMC Place; ALAMANCE; **212** D-9; elev. 598ft./182m.; 🅿; z 27349; ● 100
Snowden; RMC Place; CURRITUCK; ***213** B-19; mail Moyock z 27958; ● 30
Snow Hill; RMC Place; CHOWAN, PERQUIMANS; ***213** C-17; elev. 50ft./15m.; mail Tyner z 27980; rural
Snow Hill; Inc. Place; ⊡ GREENE; **213** F-14; elev. 64ft./20m.; 🅿; z 28580; Ⓟ 1,378; Ⓒ 1,514
Snow Hill; RMC Place; SAMPSON; ***213** G-12; mail Roseboro z 28382; ● 100
Snug Harbor; RMC Place; PERQUIMANS; ***213** C-18; elev. 8ft./2m.; mail Hertford z 27944; ● 500
Sodom; MADISON; see Revere (RMC Place)
Somerset; RMC Place; CHOWAN; ***213** C-18; elev. 14ft./4m.; mail Edenton z 27932; rural
Somerset; RMC Place; PERSON; ***213** C-11; elev. 650ft./198m.; mail Roxboro z 27573; pop. incl. with Roxboro (Inc. Place)
Somerset Hills; RMC Place; WAKE; ***213** E-12; ★ **RAL**; mail Raleigh z 27604; ● 350
Sophia; RMC Place; RANDOLPH; **212** E-8; elev. 773ft./236m.; 🅿; ★ **GRNS-**; z 27350; ● 400
Soul City; RMC Place; WARREN; ***213** B-13; mail Manson z 27553; ● 100
Sound Side; RMC Place; DARE; ***213** D-20; mail Nags Head z 27959; pop. incl. with Nags Head (Inc. Place)
Sound Side; RMC Place; TYRRELL; ***213** D-18; mail Columbia z 27925; rural
South Albemarle; RMC Place; STANLY; mail Albemarle z 28001; pop. incl. with Albemarle (Inc. Place)
South Ashe; RMC Place; GUILFORD; ★ **GRNS-**; pop. incl. with Greensboro (Inc. Place)
South Aulander; RMC Place; BERTIE; ***213** C-16; elev. 71ft./22m.; mail Aulander z 27805; ● 150
South Belmont (Belmont South); RMC Place; GASTON; ***212** F-4; ★ **CHRLT**; mail Belmont z 28012; pop. incl. with Belmont (Inc. Place)
South Creek; RMC Place; BEAUFORT; **213** F-17; mail Aurora z 27806; ● 130
South Durham; RMC Place; DURHAM; ★ **DUR**; pop. incl. with Durham (Inc. Place)
Southern Hills; RMC Place; CABARRUS; ***212** F-6; elev. 594ft./181m.; ★ **CHRLT**; mail Concord z 28025; ● 150
Southern Pines; Inc. Place; MOORE; **212** G-9; elev. 512ft./156m.; 🅿; z 28387-88; Ⓟ 9,129; Ⓒ 10,918
Southern Shores; Inc. Place; DARE; ***213** C-20; elev. 10ft./3m.; 🅿; z 27949; Ⓟ 1,447; Ⓒ 2,201
Southern Shores; RMC Place; PERQUIMANS; **213** C-20; elev. 13ft./4m.; mail Hertford z 27944; ● 60
South Fork; RMC Place; FORSYTH; ***212** D-7; elev. 898ft./274m.; ★ **WNS**; mail Winston Salem z 27104; pop. incl. with Winston-Salem (Inc. Place)
South Gastonia; CDP; GASTON; **213** K-19; ★ **CHRLT**; mail Gastonia z 28052; Ⓟ 5,487; Ⓒ 5,433
Southgate; RMC Place; CUMBERLAND; ***213** G-11; elev. 200ft./61m.; ★ **FAY**; mail Fayetteville z 28304; ● 1,340
South Henderson; CDP; VANCE; ***213** C-12; mail Henderson z 27536; Ⓟ 1,374; Ⓒ 1,220
South Hills Elizabethtown; RMC Place; BLADEN; ***213** I-12; elev. 100ft./30m.; mail Elizabethtown z 28337; pop. incl. with Elizabethtown (Inc. Place)
South Hominy; RMC Place; BUNCOMBE; ***212** L-5; ★ **ASHE**; mail Candler z 28715; rural
South Lexington; RMC Place; DAVIDSON; mail Lexington z 27292; pop. incl. with Lexington (Inc. Place)
South Lumberton; RMC Place; ROBESON; mail Lumberton z 28358; pop. incl. with Lumberton (Inc. Place)
South Mills; RMC Place; CAMDEN; **213** B-18; elev. 42ft./13m.; 🅿; z 27976; ● 900
Southmont; RMC Place; DAVIDSON; **212** E-7; elev. 669ft./204m.; 🅿; z 27351; ● 900
Southport; Inc. Place; BRUNSWICK; **213** K-13; 🅿 🅷; z 28461, z 28465; Ⓟ 2,369; Ⓒ 2,351
South Raleigh; RMC Place; WAKE; ★ **RAL**; pop. incl. with Raleigh (Inc. Place)
South River; RMC Place; CARTERET; **213** G-17; mail Beaufort z 28516; ● 170
South Rocky Mount; RMC Place; EDGECOMBE; ***213** D-14; ★ **RKYMT**; mail Rocky Mount z 27801; pop. incl. with Rocky Mount (Inc. Place)
South Rosemary (Rosemary); CDP-Census Area Only; HALIFAX; ***213** B-14; mail Roanoke Rapids z 27870; Ⓟ 1,955; Ⓒ 2,843
South Salisbury; RMC Place; ROWAN; ***212** E-6; elev. 789ft./240m.; ★ **SLSB**; mail Salisbury z 28147; pop. incl. with Salisbury (Inc. Place)
Southside; RMC Place; HENDERSON; mail Hendersonville z 28793; pop. incl. with Hendersonville (Inc. Place)
Southside; RMC Place; LINCOLN; ***212** F-4; mail Lincolnton z 28092; ● 210
South Toe Community; YANCEY; see Ballew Store (RMC Place)
South Tunis; RMC Place; HERTFORD; ***213** B-16; mail Winton z 27986; pop. incl. with Cofield (Inc. Place)
South Wadesboro; RMC Place; ANSON; **212** G-7; elev. 497ft./151m.; mail Wadesboro z 28170; ● 160
South Weldon; CDP; HALIFAX; ***213** B-14; mail Weldon z 27890; Ⓟ 1,640; Ⓒ 1,414
Southwest (Waltons Store); RMC Place; ONSLOW; ***213** H-15; ★ **JAX**; mail Jacksonville z 28540; ● 300
South Whiteville; RMC Place; COLUMBUS; ***213** J-11; elev. 72ft./22m.; mail Whiteville z 28472; pop. incl. with Whiteville (Inc. Place)
South Winston-Salem; RMC Place; FORSYTH; ★ **WNS**; pop. incl. with Winston-Salem (Inc. Place)
Southwood; RMC Place; LENOIR; ***213** G-15; mail Kinston z 28504; rural
Southwood Apartments; RMC Place; CUMBERLAND; ***213** G-11; elev. 200ft./61m.; ★ **FAY**; mail Fayetteville z 28304
Sparta; Inc. Place; ⊡ ALLEGHANY; **212** B-5; elev. 2,939ft./896m.; 🅿 🅷; z 28675; Ⓟ 1,957; Ⓒ 1,817
Spear; RMC Place; AVERY; ***212** D-2; mail Newland z 28657; rural
Speed; Inc. Place; EDGECOMBE; **213** D-15; elev. 60ft./18m.; 🅿; z 27881; Ⓟ 88; Ⓒ 70
Speedwell; RMC Place; JACKSON; ***212** M-4; mail Cullowhee z 28723; ● 80
Speights Bridge; RMC Place; GREENE; ***213** E-14; elev. 92ft./28m.; mail Walstonburg z 27888; rural
Spencer; Inc. Place; ROWAN; **212** E-6; elev. 751ft./229m.; 🅿; ★ **SLSB**; z 28159; Ⓟ 3,219; Ⓒ 3,355
Spencer Mountain; Inc. Place; GASTON; **213** I-20; elev. 700ft./213m.; ★ **CHRLT**; mail Gastonia z 28054, z 28056; Ⓟ 135; Ⓒ 51
Spences Corner; RMC Place; CAMDEN; ***213** B-18; elev. 3ft./1m.; mail Camden z 27921; ● 30
Spences Corner; PASQUOTANK; see Morgans Corner (RMC Place)
Spies; RMC Place; MOORE; ***212** F-9; elev. 538ft./164m.; mail Robbins z 27325; rural
Spindale; Inc. Place; RUTHERFORD; **212** F-2; elev. 1,094ft./333m.; 🅿; z 28160; Ⓟ 4,040; Ⓒ 4,022
Spiveys Corner; CDP; SAMPSON; ***213** G-12; mail Dunn z 28334; Ⓒ 448
Spot; RMC Place; CURRITUCK; ***213** C-19; mail Powells Point z 27966
Spout Springs; RMC Place; HARNETT; ***212** F-10; mail Cameron z 28326
Spray; RMC Place; ROCKINGHAM; ***212** B-8; ★ **MRTNV**; mail Eden z 27288; pop. incl. with Eden (Inc. Place)
Spring Creek; RMC Place; BEAUFORT; ***213** F-17; elev. 4ft./1m.; mail Aurora z 27806; rural
Spring Creek; RMC Place; MADISON; ***212** K-5; mail Hot Springs z 28743; ● 10
Springfield; RMC Place; WILKES; ***212** C-4; mail Hays z 28635; rural
Springfield Mills; RMC Place; SCOTLAND; ***212** H-9; elev. 187ft./57m.; mail Laurel Hill z 28351; ● 160
Spring Garden; RMC Place; CRAVEN; ***213** G-16; elev. 27ft./8m.; mail New Bern z 28562; ● 130
Spring Hill; RMC Place; HALIFAX; ***213** C-15; elev. 66ft./20m.; mail Scotland Neck z 27874; rural
Spring Hope; Inc. Place; NASH; **213** D-13; elev. 261ft./80m.; 🅿; z 27882; Ⓟ 1,221; Ⓒ 1,261
Spring Lake; Inc. Place; CUMBERLAND; **213** G-11; elev. 248ft./76m.; 🅿; ★ **FAY**; z 28390; Ⓟ 7,524; Ⓒ 8,098
Spring Road; RMC Place; CATAWBA; ★ **HICK**; mail Hickory z 28601; pop. incl. with Hickory (Inc. Place)
Spring Valley; RMC Place; GUILFORD; ★ **GRNS-**; mail Greensboro z 27406, z 27416; pop. incl. with Greensboro (Inc. Place)
Spring Valley; RMC Place; MECKLENBURG; ★ **CHRLT**; mail Charlotte z 28210; pop. incl. with Charlotte (Inc. Place)
Springwood; RMC Place; GASTON; ***212** F-5; ★ **CHRLT**; mail Gastonia z 28052
Spruce Pine; Inc. Place; MITCHELL; **212** D-2; elev. 2,517ft./767m.; 🅿 🅷; z 28777; Ⓟ 2,010; Ⓒ 2,030
Stackhouse; RMC Place; MADISON; ***212** K-5; elev. 420ft./128m.; mail Marshall z 28753; rural
Stacy; RMC Place; CARTERET; **213** H-18; elev. 4ft./1m.; 🅿; z 28581; ● 280
Stag Park; RMC Place; PENDER; ***213** I-14; mail Burgaw z 28425; rural
Staley; Inc. Place; RANDOLPH; **212** E-9; elev. 700ft./213m.; 🅿; z 27355; Ⓟ 204; Ⓒ 347
Stallings; FRANKLIN; see Cedarrock (RMC Place)
Stallings; Inc. Place; UNION; **212** G-6; elev. 750ft./229m.; 🅿; ★ **CHRLT**; z 28104 & mail Matthews z 28106; Ⓟ 2,132; Ⓒ 3,189; Ⓡ 3,171
Stamey Town; RMC Place; AVERY; ***212** D-2; elev. 3,400ft./1,036m.; mail Newland z 28657; rural
Stanfield; Inc. Place; STANLY; **212** G-7; elev. 628ft./191m.; 🅿; z 28163; Ⓟ 517; Ⓒ 1,113
Stanhope; RMC Place; NASH; **213** D-13; elev. 247ft./75m.; mail Spring Hope z 27882; ● 130
Stanley; Inc. Place; GASTON; **212** F-5; elev. 856ft./261m.; 🅿; ★ **CHRLT**; z 28164; Ⓟ 2,823; Ⓒ 3,053
Stanleyville; RMC Place; FORSYTH; **212** C-7; elev. 941ft./287m.; ★ **WNS**; mail Rural Hall z 27045, Winston Salem z 27105; pop. incl. with Winston-Salem (Inc. Place); Ⓟ 4,779
STANLY; **212** F-7; Ⓟ 51,765; Ⓒ 58,100; ◆ 60,137
Stantonsburg; Inc. Place; WILSON; **213** E-14; elev. 92ft./28m.; 🅿; z 27883; Ⓟ 782; Ⓒ 726
Star; Inc. Place; MONTGOMERY; **212** F-8; elev. 649ft./198m.; 🅿; z 27356; Ⓟ 775; Ⓒ 807
Starmount; RMC Place; MECKLENBURG; ★ **CHRLT**; mail Charlotte z 28210, z 28224; pop. incl. with Charlotte (Inc. Place)
Starmount; RMC Place; WAKE; ***213** D-12; ★ **RAL**; pop. incl. with Raleigh (Inc. Place)
Starmount Forest; RMC Place; GUILFORD; ***212** D-8; ★ **GRNS-**; mail Greensboro z 27403; pop. incl. with Greensboro (Inc. Place)
Startown; RMC Place; CATAWBA; ***212** E-4; elev. 972ft./296m.; ★ **HICK**; mail Newton z 28658; pop. incl. with Newton (Inc. Place)
State Road; RMC Place; SURRY; **212** C-5; elev. 1,333ft./406m.; 🅿; z 28676; ● 480
Statesville; Inc. Place; ⊡ IREDELL; **212** E-5; elev. 923ft./281m.; 🅿 🅷 ■; z 28625, z 28677, z 28687; Ⓟ 17,567; Ⓒ 23,320; ◆ 28,584
Stecoah; RMC Place; GRAHAM; **212** L-2; elev. 2,022ft./616m.; mail Robbinsville z 28771; ● 150
Stedman; Inc. Place; CUMBERLAND; **213** G-11; elev. 129ft./39m.; 🅿; ★ **FAY**; z 28391; Ⓟ 577; Ⓒ 664
Steeds; RMC Place; MONTGOMERY; ***212** F-8; elev. 662ft./202m.; mail Seagrove z 27341
Steels Mill; RICHMOND; see Cordova (RMC Place)
Steen Town; RMC Place; RICHMOND; ***212** H-9; mail Hamlet z 28345; rural
Stella; RMC Place; CARTERET; **213** H-16; elev. 20ft./6m.; 🅿; ★ **JAX**; z 28582; ● 130
Stem; Inc. Place; GRANVILLE; **213** C-11; elev. 476ft./145m.; 🅿; ★ **DUR**; z 27581; Ⓟ 249; Ⓒ 229
Sterling; RMC Place; MECKLENBURG; ***212** G-5; ★ **CHRLT**; mail Pineville z 28134; pop. incl. with Charlotte (Inc. Place)
Stevens Mill; RMC Place; WAYNE; ***213** F-13; elev. 157ft./48m.; ★ **GLDS**; mail Goldsboro z 27533; rural
Stocksville; RMC Place; BUNCOMBE; ***212** E-1; ★ **ASHE**; mail Weaverville z 28787; ● 150
Stokes; RMC Place; PITT; **213** E-15; elev. 56ft./17m.; 🅿; z 27884; ● 450
STOKES; **212** C-7; Ⓟ 37,223; Ⓒ 44,711; ◆ 46,235
Stokesdale; Inc. Place; GUILFORD; **212** C-8; elev. 950ft./290m.; 🅿; ★ **GRNS-**; z 27357; Ⓟ 2,134; Ⓒ 3,267
Stokestown; RMC Place; PITT; ***213** F-15; elev. 12ft./4m.; mail Ayden z 28513; rural
Stonebridge; RMC Place; WAKE; ★ **RAL**; mail Raleigh z 27613
Stonehaven; RMC Place; MECKLENBURG; ***212** G-5; ★ **CHRLT**; mail Charlotte z 28211; pop. incl. with Charlotte (Inc. Place)
Stoneville; Inc. Place; ROCKINGHAM; **212** B-8; elev. 824ft./251m.; 🅿; z 27048; Ⓟ 1,109; Ⓒ 1,002
Stonewall; Inc. Place; PAMLICO; **213** G-17; elev. 9ft./3m.; 🅿; z 28583; Ⓟ 279; Ⓒ 285
Stoneybrook; RMC Place; ROWAN; ***212** E-6; ★ **SLSB**; mail Salisbury z 28147; ● 200
Stoneycrest; RMC Place; HENDERSON; ***212** F-1; mail Hendersonville z 28791; ● 100
Stoney Knob; RMC Place; BUNCOMBE; ***212** E-1; ★ **ASHE**; mail Weaverville z 28787; ● 150
Stonycreek; RMC Place; CASWELL; ***212** C-9; elev. 700ft./213m.; mail Elon z 27244; ● 50
Stony Fork; RMC Place; WATAUGA; ***212** C-4; mail Deep Gap z 28618; rural
Stony Hill; RMC Place; WAKE; ***213** D-12; elev. 400ft./122m.; mail Wake Forest z 27587; ● 50
Stony Knoll; RMC Place; SURRY; ***212** C-6; elev. 1,159ft./353m.; mail Dobson z 27017; ● 30
Stony Point; CDP; ALEXANDER; **212** D-5; elev. 1,060ft./323m.; 🅿; z 28678; Ⓟ 1,286; Ⓒ 1,380
Storys; RMC Place; GATES; ***213** B-16; elev. 33ft./10m.; mail Eure z 27935; rural
Stotts Crossroads; RMC Place; WILSON; ***213** E-13; elev. 223ft./68m.; mail Sims z 27880; rural
Stouts; RMC Place; UNION; ***212** G-6; ★ **CHRLT**; mail Monroe z 28110; pop. incl. with Indian Trail (Inc. Place)
Stovall; Inc. Place; GRANVILLE; **213** B-12; elev. 478ft./146m.; 🅿; z 27582; Ⓟ 409; Ⓒ 376
Strabane; RMC Place; LENOIR; ***213** G-14; elev. 35ft./11m.; mail Kinston z 28504; rural
Straits; RMC Place; CARTERET; ***213** H-18; elev. 6ft./2m.; mail Beaufort z 28516; ● 50
Stratford; RMC Place; ALLEGHANY; ***212** B-4; elev. 2,600ft./792m.; mail Sparta z 28675; ● 30
Strickland Crossroads; RMC Place; NASH; ***213** D-13; mail Spring Hope z 27882; rural
Stubbs; RMC Place; CLEVELAND; **212** F-4; ★ **CHRLT**; mail Waco z 28169; ● 50
Stumpy Point; RMC Place; DARE; **213** E-20; elev. 3ft./1m.; 🅿; z 27953, z 27978; ● 260
Sturdivants; RMC Place; UNION; ***212** H-7; elev. 492ft./150m.; mail Marshville z 28103; rural
Sturgills; RMC Place; ASHE; ***212** B-3; mail Lansing z 28643
Sugar Grove; RMC Place; WATAUGA; **212** C-3; elev. 2,676ft./816m.; 🅿; z 28679; ● 450
Sugar Hill; RMC Place; MCDOWELL; **212** E-2; mail Marion z 28752; ● 70
Sugarloaf Shores; RMC Place; MONTGOMERY; ***212** F-8; elev. 300ft./91m.; mail Troy z 27371; ● 100
Sugar Mountain; Inc. Place; AVERY; **212** C-2; 🅿; z 28604; Ⓟ 132; Ⓒ 226
Sugar Town; RMC Place; ANSON; ***212** G-7; elev. 401ft./122m.; mail Polkton z 28135; rural
Suggs Crossroads; RMC Place; EDGECOMBE; ***213** D-15; elev. 30ft./9m.; mail Pinetops z 27864; rural
Suit; CHEROKEE; see Friendship (RMC Place)
Sulphur Springs (White Sulphur Springs); RMC Place; SURRY; ***212** B-6; mail Mount Airy z 27030; rural
Summerfield; Inc. Place; GUILFORD; **212** C-8; elev. 901ft./275m.; 🅿; ★ **GRNS-**; z 27358; Ⓟ 1,687; Ⓒ 7,018
Summerhaven; RMC Place; BUNCOMBE; ***212** E-1; ★ **ASHE**; mail Swannanoa z 28778; ● 80
Summer Hill; RMC Place; CUMBERLAND; ***213** G-11; elev. 250ft./76m.; ★ **FAY**; mail Fayetteville z 28303; pop. incl. with Fayetteville (Inc. Place)
Summerlins Crossroads; RMC Place; DUPLIN; ***213** G-14; elev. 47ft./14m.; mail Mount Olive z 28365; rural
Summit; RMC Place; GUILFORD; ★ **GRNS-**; mail Greensboro z 27405, z 27419; pop. incl. with Greensboro (Inc. Place)
Summit; RMC Place; HALIFAX; ***213** B-14; mail Littleton z 27850; ● 50
Summit; RMC Place; WILKES; ***212** C-4; elev. 2,535ft./773m.; mail Purlear z 28665; rural
Sunburst; RMC Place; HAYWOOD; ***212** L-4; elev. 2,990ft./911m.; mail Canton z 28716; rural
Sunbury; RMC Place; GATES; **213** B-17; elev. 38ft./12m.; 🅿; z 27979; ● 670
Sunnyside; RMC Place; BURKE; ***212** E-3; mail Morganton z 28655; ● 170
Sunny Side; RMC Place; DARE; ***213** D-20; mail Manteo z 27954; ● 30
Sunnyside; RMC Place; FORSYTH; ***212** D-7; ★ **WNS**; mail Winston Salem z 27107; pop. incl. with Winston-Salem (Inc. Place)
Sunnyside; RMC Place; GASTON; ***212** F-4; ★ **CHRLT**; mail Bessemer City z 28016; ● 50
Sunny Side; RMC Place; HALIFAX; ***213** B-14; mail Littleton z 27850; rural
Sunny View; RMC Place; POLK; **212** F-1; mail Mill Spring z 28756; ● 130
Sunset Beach; Inc. Place; BRUNSWICK; **213** K-12; elev. 20ft./6m.; 🅿; ★ **MYR.B**; z 28468; Ⓟ 311; Ⓒ 1,824
Sunset Harbor; RMC Place; BRUNSWICK; ***213** K-13; elev. 14ft./4m.; mail Bolivia z 28422; summer pop. 600; ● 400
Sunset Hills; RMC Place; CATAWBA; ***212** E-4; ★ **HICK**; mail Hickory z 28601; pop. incl. with Hickory (Inc. Place)
Sunset Hills; RMC Place; GUILFORD; ***212** D-8; ★ **GRNS-**; mail Greensboro z 27403; pop. incl. with Greensboro (Inc. Place)
Sunset Hills; RMC Place; ROCKINGHAM; ***212** B-8; ★ **MRTNV**; mail Eden z 27288; ● 100
Sunshine; RMC Place; RUTHERFORD; ***212** F-3; elev. 1,097ft./334m.; mail Bostic z 28018; ● 100
Supply; RMC Place; BRUNSWICK; **213** K-13; elev. 39ft./12m.; 🅿 🅷; z 28462; ● 550
Surf City; Inc. Place; PENDER, ONSLOW; **213** I-15; elev. 21ft./6m.; 🅿; z 28445; Ⓟ 970; Ⓒ 1,393
Surl; RMC Place; PERSON; ***213** C-11; mail Timberlake z 27583
SURRY; **212** B-6; Ⓟ 61,704; Ⓒ 71,219; ◆ 71,489
Sutherlands; RMC Place; ASHE; ***212** B-3; mail Creston z 28615; rural
Sutton Park; RMC Place; UNION; mail Monroe z 28110; pop. incl. with Monroe (Inc. Place)
Suttontown; RMC Place; SAMPSON; ***213** G-13; elev. 172ft./52m.; mail Faison z 28341
Swain; RMC Place; WASHINGTON; ***213** D-17; mail Roper z 27970; rural
SWAIN; **212** L-3; Ⓟ 11,268; Ⓒ 12,968; ◆ 13,255
Swainsville; RMC Place; CLEVELAND; ***212** F-3; elev. 894ft./272m.; mail Shelby z 28150, z 28152; ● 500
Swan Creek; RMC Place; YADKIN; ***212** C-5; mail Jonesville z 28642; ● 300
Swann; RMC Place; LEE; ***212** F-10; mail Sanford z 27330
Swannanoa; CDP; BUNCOMBE; **212** E-1; 🅿; ★ **ASHE**; z 28778; Ⓟ 3,538; Ⓒ 4,132
Swanns (Swan Station); RMC Place; HARNETT; ***212** F-10; mail Sanford z 27332; ● 200
Swanquarter; RMC Place; ⊡ HYDE; **213** F-18; 🅿; z 27885; ● 600
Swansboro; Inc. Place; ONSLOW; **213** H-16; elev. 25ft./8m.; 🅿; ★ **JAX**; z 28584; Ⓟ 1,165; Ⓒ 1,426; Ⓡ 1,459
Swan Station; HARNETT; see Swanns (RMC Place)
Swayney; SWAIN; see Big Cove (RMC Place)
Sweet Gum; RMC Place; GRAHAM; ***212** M-2; mail Robbinsville z 28771; ● 30
Swepsonville; Inc. Place; ALAMANCE; **212** D-10; elev. 550ft./168m.; 🅿; ★ **BUR**; z 27359; Ⓟ 1,195; Ⓒ 922
Swindell; HYDE; see Tiny Oak Fork (RMC Place)
Swindell's Fork (Swindle Fork); RMC Place; HYDE; ***213** F-18; mail Swanquarter z 27885; ● 30
Swindle Fork; HYDE; see Swindell's Fork (RMC Place)
Swiss; RMC Place; YANCEY; ***212** D-1; mail Burnsville z 28714
Sylva; Inc. Place; ⊡ JACKSON; **212** L-4; elev. 2,036ft./621m.; 🅿 🅷; z 28779; Ⓟ 1,809; Ⓒ 2,435

T

Tabor City; Inc. Place; COLUMBUS; **213** J-11; elev. 106ft./32m.; 🅿; z 28463; Ⓟ 2,330; Ⓒ 2,509
Talleys Crossing; RMC Place; FORSYTH; ***212** C-7; elev. 958ft./292m.; ★ **WNS**; mail Kernersville z 27284; pop. incl. with Kernersville (Inc. Place)
Tallywood; RMC Place; CUMBERLAND; ★ **FAY**; pop. incl. with Fayetteville (Inc. Place)
Tanglewood; RMC Place; CUMBERLAND; ***213** G-11; elev. 175ft./53m.; ★ **FAY**; mail Fayetteville z 28306; ● 160
Tapoco; RMC Place; GRAHAM; **212** L-1; elev. 1,147ft./350m.; 🅿; z 28771; ● 200
Tarawa Terrace (Tarawa Terrace I); RMC Place; ONSLOW; elev. 30ft./9m.; 🅿; ★ **JAX**; z 28543; pop. incl. with Jacksonville (Inc. Place)
Tarawa Terrace I; ONSLOW; see Tarawa Terrace (RMC Place)
Tarboro; Inc. Place; ⊡ EDGECOMBE; **213** D-15; 🅿 🅷; z 27886; Ⓟ 11,037; Ⓒ 11,138
Tar Corner; RMC Place; CAMDEN; ***213** B-18; mail South Mills z 27976; ● 30
Tar Heel; Inc. Place; BLADEN; **213** H-11; elev. 134ft./41m.; 🅿; z 28392; Ⓟ 115; Ⓒ 70
Tarheel; RMC Place; GATES; ***213** B-17; mail Eure z 27935; rural
Tar Landing; RMC Place; ONSLOW; ***213** H-15; elev. 51ft./16m.; ★ **JAX**; mail Jacksonville z 28540; ● 220
Tar River; RMC Place; GRANVILLE; ***213** C-12; mail Oxford z 27565; rural
Tate Street; RMC Place; GUILFORD; ★ **GRNS-**; mail Greensboro z 27403, z 27435; pop. incl. with Greensboro (Inc. Place)
Taylor Crossroads; RMC Place; NASH; ***213** D-13; elev. 200ft./61m.; ★ **RKYMT**; mail Nashville z 27856
Taylor's Beach; RMC Place; CAMDEN; ***213** C-19; elev. 2ft./1m.; mail Camden z 27921; ● 100
Taylors Bridge; RMC Place; SAMPSON; ***213** H-13; elev. 141ft./43m.; mail Clinton z 28328; rural
Taylors Corners; RMC Place; JONES; ***213** G-15; mail Trenton z 28585; rural
Taylors Store; RMC Place; BERTIE; ***213** D-17; elev. 12ft./4m.; mail Merry Hill z 27957
Taylors Store; RMC Place; NASH; ***213** C-13; mail Nashville z 27856
Taylorsville; Inc. Place; ⊡ ALEXANDER; **212** D-4; elev. 1,247ft./380m.; 🅿 🅷; z 28681; Ⓟ 1,566; Ⓒ 1,799; Ⓡ 1,813
Taylorsville Beach; RMC Place; ALEXANDER; ***212** D-4; ★ **HICK**; mail Taylorsville z 28681; ● 150
Taylortown; Inc. Place; MOORE; ***212** G-9; mail Pinehurst z 28374; Ⓟ 543; Ⓒ 845; Ⓡ 875
Teachey; Inc. Place; DUPLIN; **213** H-13; elev. 69ft./21m.; 🅿; z 28464; Ⓟ 244; Ⓒ 245
Teer; RMC Place; ORANGE; ***212** D-10; ★ **DUR**; mail Chapel Hill z 27516; rural
Temple Point; RMC Place; CRAVEN; ***213** G-17; elev. 9ft./3m.; mail Havelock z 28532; ● 50
Temple's; RMC Place; CARTERET; ***213** H-17; elev. 15ft./5m.; mail Newport z 28570
Ten Mile Fork; RMC Place; JONES; ***213** G-16; elev. 35ft./11m.; mail Pollocksville z 28573; rural
Terrace Gardens; RMC Place; HENDERSON; ***212** F-1; mail Hendersonville z 28791; pop. incl. with Hendersonville (Inc. Place)
Terra Ceia; RMC Place; BEAUFORT; ***213** E-17; mail Pantego z 27860; ● 50
Terra Cotta; RMC Place; GUILFORD; ***212** D-8; elev. 889ft./271m.; ★ **GRNS-**; mail Greensboro z 27407; pop. incl. with Greensboro (Inc. Place)
Terrell; RMC Place; CATAWBA; **212** E-5; elev. 841ft./256m.; 🅿; ★ **HICK**; z 28682; ● 650
Texaco Beach; RMC Place; CAMDEN; **213** C-19; mail Shiloh z 27974; ● 170
Texana; RMC Place; CHEROKEE; **212** M-1; mail Murphy z 28906; ● 400
Texas; RMC Place; CAMDEN; ***213** C-19; elev. 1ft./0m.; mail Shiloh z 27974; rural
Thankful; RMC Place; WILKES; ***212** D-4; mail Boomer z 28606; rural
The Black Cat; RMC Place; CARTERET; ***213** H-17; elev. 5ft./2m.; mail Beaufort z 28516; ● 100
The Borough; RMC Place; PENDER; ***213** I-13; elev. 16ft./5m.; mail Currie z 28435; rural
The Bottom; RMC Place; BERTIE; ***213** C-17; elev. 12ft./4m.; mail Colerain z 27924; ● 200
Thelma; RMC Place; HALIFAX; ***213** B-14; mail Littleton z 27850; ● 80
Thomasboro; RMC Place; BRUNSWICK; ***213** K-12; ★ **MYR.B**; mail Shallotte z 28470
Thomas Landing; RMC Place; ONSLOW; ***213** I-15; mail Holly Ridge z 28445; rural
Thomas Valley; RMC Place; JACKSON; ***212** L-3; mail Whittier z 28789; rural
Thomasville; Inc. Place; DAVIDSON, RANDOLPH; **212** D-7; 🅿 🅷 ■; ★ **GRNS-**; z 27360-61; Ⓟ 15,915; Ⓒ 19,788; ◆ 26,374
Thompsonville; ROCKINGHAM; see Williamsburg (RMC Place)
Three Mile; RMC Place; AVERY; ***212** D-2; mail Newland z 28657; rural
Thrift; MECKLENBURG; see Paw Creek (RMC Place)
Thunderbird; RMC Place; GRAHAM; pop. incl. with Lake Santeetlah (Inc. Place)
Thurman; RMC Place; CRAVEN; **213** G-16; mail New Bern z 28560; ● 80
Thurmond; RMC Place; WILKES, SURRY; **212** C-5; elev. 1,402ft./427m.; 🅿; z 28683; ● 220
Tick Bite; RMC Place; LENOIR; ***213** F-15; elev. 6ft./2m.; mail Grifton z 28530; ● 30
Tillery; RMC Place; HALIFAX; **213** C-15; elev. 62ft./19m.; 🅿; z 27887; ● 240
Timberlake; RMC Place; PERSON; **213** C-11; elev. 555ft./169m.; 🅿; z 27583; ● 280
Timberlyne; RMC Place; ORANGE; ★ **DUR**; mail Chapel Hill z 27516; pop. incl. with Chapel Hill (Inc. Place)
Timber Ridge; RMC Place; CABARRUS; ***212** F-6; elev. 800ft./244m.; ★ **CHRLT**; mail Concord z 28025; ● 80
Timothy; RMC Place; SAMPSON; ***213** G-12; elev. 195ft./59m.; mail Dunn z 28334; rural
Tin City; RMC Place; DUPLIN; ***213** H-14; mail Wallace z 28466; pop. incl. with Wallace (Inc. Place)
Tiny Oak Fork (Swindell); RMC Place; HYDE; ***213** F-18; elev. 4ft./1m.; mail Swanquarter z 27885; ● 30
Tipton Hill; RMC Place; MITCHELL; ***212** D-1; mail Green Mountain z 28740; ● 80
Toast; CDP; SURRY; **212** B-6; elev. 1,066ft./325m.; 🅿; z 27049; Ⓟ 2,125; Ⓒ 1,922
Tobaccoville; Inc. Place; FORSYTH, STOKES; **212** C-7; elev. 994ft./303m.; 🅿; ★ **WNS**; z 27050; Ⓟ 914; Ⓒ 2,209
Tobemory; RMC Place; BLADEN; ***213** H-11; mail Saint Pauls z 28384; ● 50
Todd (Elkland); RMC Place; ASHE, WATAUGA; **212** C-3; elev. 2,981ft./909m.; 🅿; z 28684; ● 180
Todds Crossroads; RMC Place; BERTIE; ***213** C-17; elev. 44ft./13m.; mail Windsor z 27983; rural
Toddy; RMC Place; PITT; ***213** E-14; elev. 27ft./8m.; ★ **GRNV**; mail Farmville z 27828; rural
Toecane; RMC Place; MITCHELL; ***212** D-2; mail Bakersville z 28705; ● 30
Tokay Heights; RMC Place; CUMBERLAND; ★ **FAY**; pop. incl. with Fayetteville (Inc. Place)
Tolarsville; RMC Place; ROBESON; ***213** H-11; mail Saint Pauls z 28384; rural
Toledo; RMC Place; YANCEY; ***212** D-1; mail Green Mountain z 28740; rural
Toluca; RMC Place; CLEVELAND, LINCOLN; **212** F-3; elev. 1,094ft./333m.; ★ **CHRLT**; mail Lawndale z 28090; ● 100
Tomahawk; RMC Place; SAMPSON; **213** H-13; elev. 101ft./31m.; mail Harrells z 28444; ● 30
Tom Creek; MCDOWELL; see Toms Creek (RMC Place)
Tomotla; RMC Place; CHEROKEE; **212** M-1; mail Marble z 28905; ● 130
Toms Creek (Tom Creek); RMC Place; MCDOWELL; ***212** E-2; elev. 421ft./128m.; mail Marion z 28752; rural
Topia; RMC Place; ALLEGHANY; ***212** B-4; elev. 2,577ft./785m.; mail Scottville z 28672; rural
Topnot; RMC Place; CASWELL; **212** C-10; elev. 639ft./195m.; mail Yanceyville z 27379; ● 50
Topsail Beach (New Topsail Beach); Inc. Place; PENDER; **213** I-15; elev. 12ft./4m.; 🅿; z 28445; Ⓟ 346; Ⓒ 471
Topton; RMC Place; CHEROKEE; **212** M-2; elev. 2,599ft./792m.; 🅿; z 28781; ● 230
Town and Country Woods; RMC Place; SURRY; ***212** B-6; mail Mount Airy z 27030; ● 320
Town Creek; RMC Place; BRUNSWICK; ***213** J-13; ★ **WILM**; mail Leland z 28451; ● 50
Town Creek; RMC Place; WILSON; ***213** D-14; ★ **RKYMT**; mail Elm City z 27822
Town Forest; RMC Place; HENDERSON; ***212** F-1; mail Hendersonville z 28791; ● 120
Town Mountain Estates; RMC Place; BUNCOMBE; ***212** E-1; ★ **ASHE**; mail Asheville z 28804; ● 200
Townsville; RMC Place; VANCE; **213** B-12; elev. 433ft./132m.; 🅿; z 27584; ● 350
Trading Ford; RMC Place; ROWAN; ***212** E-7; elev. 734ft./224m.; ★ **SLSB**; mail Salisbury z 28146; ● 50
Tramway; RMC Place; LEE; **212** F-10; mail Sanford z 27330, z 27332; ● 250
Tranquility; RMC Place; CABARRUS; ***212** F-6; elev. 700ft./213m.; ★ **CHRLT**; mail Kannapolis z 28081; pop. incl. with Kannapolis (Inc. Place)
TRANSYLVANIA; **212** M-5; Ⓟ 25,520; Ⓒ 29,334; ◆ 30,445
Trap; RMC Place; BERTIE; **213** C-17; mail Colerain z 27924; ● 30
Traphill; RMC Place; WILKES; **212** C-5; elev. 1,292ft./394m.; 🅿; z 28685; ● 220
Travis; RMC Place; TYRRELL; **213** D-18; mail Columbia z 27925; ● 30
Trayton Woods; RMC Place; CABARRUS; ***212** F-6; elev. 600ft./183m.; ★ **CHRLT**; mail Concord z 28025; rural
Tree Haven; RMC Place; HENDERSON; ***212** F-1; mail Hendersonville z 28791; ● 90
Trenholm Woods; RMC Place; HENDERSON; ***212** F-1; mail Hendersonville z 28739; pop. incl. with Flat Rock (Inc. Place)
Trenton; Inc. Place; ⊡ JONES; **213** G-15; elev. 28ft./9m.; 🅿; z 28585; Ⓟ 248; Ⓒ 206
Trent Woods; Inc. Place; CRAVEN; **213** G-16; 🅿; z 28562; Ⓟ 2,366; Ⓒ 4,192; Ⓡ 4,224
Triangle; RMC Place; LINCOLN; **212** F-5; ★ **CHRLT**; mail Denver z 28037; ● 850
Triangle; WAKE; see Research Triangle Park (RMC Place)
Trinity; Inc. Place; RANDOLPH; **212** D-8; elev. 794ft./242m.; 🅿; ★ **GRNS-**; z 27370; Ⓟ 5,469; Ⓒ 6,690; Ⓡ 6,714
Trinity; RMC Place; UNION; ***212** H-6; mail Monroe z 28112; rural
Triple Springs; RMC Place; PERSON; ***213** B-11; elev. 549ft./167m.; mail Roxboro z 27574; rural
Triplett; RMC Place; WATAUGA; ***212** C-3; 🅿; z 28618; rural
Trotville; RMC Place; GATES; ***213** B-17; mail Hobbsville z 27946; rural
Troutman; Inc. Place; IREDELL; **212** E-5; elev. 946ft./288m.; 🅿; ★ **HICK**; z 28166; Ⓟ 1,493; Ⓒ 1,592
Troy; Inc. Place; ⊡ MONTGOMERY; **212** F-8; elev. 664ft./202m.; 🅿 🅷; z 27371; Ⓟ 3,404; Ⓒ 3,430
Trust; RMC Place; MADISON; ***212** K-5; elev. 2,411ft./735m.; mail Hot Springs z 28743; rural
Tryon; RMC Place; GASTON; ***212** F-4; ★ **CHRLT**; mail Bessemer City z 28016; ● 100
Tryon; Inc. Place; POLK; **212** G-1; elev. 1,085ft./331m.; 🅿; z 28782; Ⓟ 1,680; Ⓒ 1,760
Tuckasegee; RMC Place; JACKSON; **212** M-4; elev. 2,158ft./658m.; 🅿; z 28783; ● 420
Tuckerdale; RMC Place; ASHE; ***212** B-3; mail Lansing z 28643; ● 30
Tungsten; RMC Place; VANCE; ***213** B-12; elev. 422ft./129m.; mail Henderson z 27537
Tunis; RMC Place; HERTFORD; **213** B-16; mail Winton z 27986; ● 250
Turkey; Inc. Place; SAMPSON; **213** G-13; elev. 148ft./45m.; 🅿; z 28393; Ⓟ 234; Ⓒ 262
Turkey Knob; RMC Place; ALLEGHANY; ***212** B-4; elev. 272ft./83m.; mail Sparta z 28675; ● 30
Turlington; RMC Place; HARNETT; ***213** F-12; ★ **RAL**; mail Dunn z 28334; rural
Turnersburg; RMC Place; IREDELL; **212** D-5; elev. 791ft./241m.; 🅿; z 28688; ● 50
Turners Crossroads; RMC Place; NORTHAMPTON; ***213** B-15; elev. 90ft./27m.; mail Margarettsville z 27853; rural
Turnpike; RMC Place; BUNCOMBE; ***212** L-5; ★ **ASHE**; mail Candler z 28715; rural
Tuscarora; RMC Place; CRAVEN; **213** G-16; mail New Bern z 28562; ● 50
Tuscarora Beach; RMC Place; HERTFORD; ***213** B-16; elev. 33ft./10m.; mail Winton z 27986; rural
Tusk; RMC Place; CARTERET; ***213** H-18; mail Smyrna z 28579; ● 100
Tuskeegee; RMC Place; GRAHAM; **212** L-2; mail Robbinsville z 28771; ● 50

Entries in **UPPERCASE** are counties.
Entries in **bold** have populations of 2,500 or more.
Names in parentheses are alternate names.

Inc. Place	Incorporated Place
RMC Place	Rand McNally Designated Place
CDP	Census Designated Place
MCD	Minor Civil Division
⊡	County Seat
▲	Minor Civil Division
elev.	Elevation
🅿	Post Office
🅷	Hospital
🅲	College
■	Principal Business Center
★	Ranally Metro Area (RMA) Abbreviation
z	Zip Code(s)
Ⓟ	Previous Census Population
Ⓡ	Revised Census Population
Ⓐ	Annexation Population
●	Rand McNally Population Estimate
Ⓒ	Final Census Population
Ⓢ	Special Census Population
◆	Estimated Population

For additional definitions see Glossary, Volume 1, and Introduction, Volume 2.

Tusquitee; RMC Place; CLAY; 212 M-2; mail Hayesville z 28904; ● 30
Tuxedo; RMC Place; HENDERSON; 212 F-1; elev. 2,057ft./627m.; [P]; z 28784; ● 1,100
Twin Lake; RMC Place; BRUNSWICK; ★ MYR.B; mail Sunset Beach z 28468; pop. incl. with Sunset Beach (Inc. Place)
Twin Oaks; RMC Place; ALLEGHANY; *212 B-4; elev. 2,735ft./834m.; mail Sparta z 28675
Tyner; CHOWAN; see Center Hill (RMC Place)
Tyro; RMC Place; DAVIDSON; *212 E-7; elev. 828ft./252m.; mail Lexington z 27292, z 27295; ● 430
TYRRELL; 213 D-18; Ⓟ 3,856; © 4,149; ◆ 4,212

U

Ulah; RMC Place; RANDOLPH; 212 E-8; elev. 847ft./258m.; mail Asheboro z 27205; ● 200
Unaka; RMC Place; CHEROKEE; *212 M-1; elev. 1,640ft./500m.; [P]; z 28906
Union; RMC Place; HERTFORD; 213 C-16; elev. 65ft./20m.; mail Ahoskie z 27910; ● 300
Union; RMC Place; MACON; *212 M-3; mail Franklin z 28734; rural
Union; RMC Place; RUTHERFORD; *212 F-2; elev. 872ft./266m.; mail Rutherfordton z 28139; rural
UNION; 212 H-6; Ⓟ 84,211; © 123,677; Ⓡ 123,772; ◆ 202,688
Union Cross; RMC Place; FORSYTH; 212 D-7; ★ WNS; mail Kernersville z 27284; ● 330
Union Grove; RMC Place; IREDELL; 212 D-5; elev. 1,122ft./342m.; [P]; z 28689; ● 400
Union Hill; RMC Place; YADKIN; *212 C-6; elev. 983ft./300m.; ★ WNS; mail East Bend z 27018; rural
Union Mills; RMC Place; RUTHERFORD; *212 F-2; elev. 1,100ft./335m.; [P]; z 28167; ● 400
Union Ridge; RMC Place; ALAMANCE; 212 C-9; elev. 674ft./205m.; ★ BUR; mail Burlington z 27215; ● 60
Unionville; Inc. Place; UNION; 212 G-6; elev. 600ft./183m.; ★ CHRLT; mail Monroe z 28110; © 4,797
University Estates; RMC Place; CUMBERLAND; *213 G-11; elev. 200ft./61m.; ★ FAY; mail Fayetteville z 28301; pop. incl. with Fayetteville (Inc. Place)
University Estates; RMC Place; ROCKINGHAM; *212 B-9; mail Reidsville z 27320; pop. incl. with Wentworth (Inc. Place)
University of North Carolina-Charlotte; RMC Place; MECKLENBURG; *212 F-6; ★ CHRLT; mail Charlotte z 28223; pop. incl. with Charlotte (Inc. Place)
University Park; RMC Place; MECKLENBURG; ★ CHRLT; mail Charlotte z 28297; pop. incl. with Charlotte (Inc. Place)
Upchurch; RMC Place; WAKE; *213 E-11; ★ RAL; mail Apex z 27502; pop. incl. with Cary (Inc. Place)
Upton; RMC Place; CALDWELL; *212 D-3; mail Collettsville z 28611, Lenoir z 28645; rural
Upward; RMC Place; HENDERSON; *212 F-1; mail Flat Rock z 28731; ● 400
Uwharie; RMC Place; MONTGOMERY; 212 F-8; mail Troy z 27371; ● 150

V

Valdese; Inc. Place; BURKE; 212 E-3; elev. 1,203ft./367m.; [P] [H]; z 28690; Ⓟ 3,914; © 4,485
Vale; RMC Place; LINCOLN; 212 E-4; elev. 931ft./284m.; [P]; z 28168; ● 100
Valhalla; RMC Place; CHOWAN; 213 C-17; mail Edenton z 27932; ● 30
Valhalla; RMC Place; POLK; *212 F-1; mail Tryon z 28782
Valle Crucis; RMC Place; WATAUGA; 212 C-3; [P]; z 28691; ● 150
Valley; RMC Place; AVERY; *212 D-2; mail Newland z 28657; rural
Valley Hill; CDP; HENDERSON; *212 F-1; mail Hendersonville z 28739; Ⓟ 1,802; © 2,137; Ⓡ 2,008
Valmead; RMC Place; CALDWELL; *212 D-3; mail Lenoir z 28645; pop. incl. with Lenoir (Inc. Place)
VANCE; 213 C-12; Ⓟ 38,892; © 42,954; ◆ 42,560
Vanceboro; Inc. Place; CRAVEN; 213 F-16; elev. 22ft./7m.; [P]; z 28586; Ⓟ 946; © 898
Vandemere; Inc. Place; PAMLICO; 213 G-17; elev. 5ft./2m.; [P]; z 28587; Ⓟ 299; © 289
Vander; CDP; CUMBERLAND; 213 G-11; elev. 126ft./38m.; ★ FAY; mail Fayetteville z 28301; Ⓟ 1,179; © 1,204
Vann Crossroads; CDP; SAMPSON; *213 G-12; elev. 190ft./58m.; mail Clinton z 28328, Newton Grove z 28366; © 324
Vannoy; RMC Place; WILKES; *212 C-4; mail Millers Creek z 28651; rural
Varnamtown; Inc. Place; BRUNSWICK; 213 K-13; mail Supply z 28462; Ⓟ 404; © 481
Varnum; RMC Place; BRUNSWICK; 213 K-13; elev. 26ft./8m.; mail Supply z 28462; pop. incl. with Varnamtown (Inc. Place)
Vashti; RMC Place; ALEXANDER; *212 D-5; mail Hiddenite z 28636
Vass; Inc. Place; MOORE; 212 F-10; elev. 306ft./93m.; [P]; z 28394; Ⓟ 670; © 750
Vaughan; RMC Place; WARREN; 213 B-13; elev. 346ft./105m.; [P]; z 27586; ● 170
Vein Mountain; RMC Place; MCDOWELL; *212 E-2; mail Marion z 28752; rural
Venable; RMC Place; BUNCOMBE; *212 E-1; ★ ASHE; mail Asheville z 28803; ● 330
Venable; ORANGE; see Carrboro (Inc. Place)
Venters; RMC Place; PITT; *213 F-15; ★ GRNV; mail Ayden z 28513; rural
Verona; RMC Place; ONSLOW; 213 H-15; elev. 51ft./16m.; ★ JAX; mail Jacksonville z 28540; ● 870
Vests; RMC Place; CHEROKEE; *212 M-1; mail Murphy z 28906; rural
Vicksboro; RMC Place; WARREN; *213 C-13; elev. 446ft./136m.; mail Henderson z 27536; rural
Victory; RMC Place; CUMBERLAND; ★ FAY; pop. incl. with Fayetteville (Inc. Place)
Vienna; RMC Place; FORSYTH; 212 C-7; elev. 931ft./284m.; ★ WNS; mail Pfafftown z 27040; ● 710
Viewmont; RMC Place; CATAWBA; *212 E-4; ★ HICK; mail Hickory z 28601; pop. incl. with Hickory (Inc. Place)
Vilas; RMC Place; WATAUGA; *212 C-3; elev. 2,761ft./842m.; [P]; z 28692; ● 200
Village; RMC Place; MOORE; mail Pinehurst z 28370; pop. incl. with Pinehurst (Inc. Place)
Village of Forest Hills; JACKSON; see Forest Hills (Inc. Place)
Villa Heights; RMC Place; MECKLENBURG; ★ CHRLT; mail Charlotte z 28205; pop. incl. with Charlotte (Inc. Place)
Vina Vista; MOORE; see Jackson Hamlet (RMC Place)
Vinegar Hill; RMC Place; COLUMBUS; *213 J-11; elev. 108ft./33m.; mail Tabor City z 28463; rural
Vineland Park; RMC Place; CUMBERLAND; *213 G-11; elev. 200ft./61m.; ★ FAY; mail Fayetteville z 28306; ● 150
Vine Swamp; RMC Place; LENOIR; *213 G-15; elev. 20ft./6m.; mail Kinston z 28504; rural
Vinton Woods; RMC Place; GASTON; *212 F-4; ★ CHRLT; mail Dallas z 28034; ● 380
Violet; RMC Place; CHEROKEE; *212 M-1; mail Murphy z 28906; rural
Vista; RMC Place; PENDER; *213 I-15; mail Hampstead z 28443
Vixen; RMC Place; YANCEY; *212 D-1; elev. 2,778ft./847m.; mail Burnsville z 28714; rural
Volunteer; RMC Place; STOKES; *212 C-7; ★ WNS; mail Pinnacle z 27043; ● 50

W

Waccamaw; RMC Place; BRUNSWICK; *213 K-12; mail Ash z 28420; rural
Waco; Inc. Place; CLEVELAND; 212 F-4; elev. 934ft./285m.; [P]; ★ CHRLT; z 28169; Ⓟ 320; © 328
Wade; Inc. Place; CUMBERLAND; 213 G-11; elev. 142ft./43m.; [P]; ★ FAY; z 28395; Ⓟ 238; © 480; Ⓡ 510
Wade Mills; RMC Place; ANSON; *212 G-8; mail Wadesboro z 28170; pop. incl. with Wadesboro (Inc. Place)
Wadesboro; Inc. Place; ⊡ ANSON; 212 G-7; elev. 522ft./159m.; [P] [H]; z 28170; Ⓟ 3,645; © 3,552; Ⓡ 3,568
Wades Point; RMC Place; BEAUFORT; mail Belhaven z 27810
Wadeville; RMC Place; MONTGOMERY; 212 F-8; mail Mount Gilead z 27306; ● 150
Wagoner; RMC Place; ASHE; *212 B-4; mail Jefferson z 28640; ● 30
Wagoner; RMC Place; YADKIN; *212 C-5; elev. 1,074ft./327m.; mail Hamptonville z 27020; rural
Wagram; Inc. Place; SCOTLAND; 212 H-10; elev. 239ft./73m.; [P]; z 28396; Ⓟ 480; © 801
WAKE; 213 D-12; Ⓟ 423,380; © 627,846; Ⓡ 627,866; ◆ 922,543
Wake Crossroads; RMC Place; WAKE; *213 D-12; elev. 248ft./76m.; ★ RAL; mail Raleigh z 27604, z 27616; rural
Wakefield; RMC Place; WAKE; *213 D-12; ★ RAL; mail Zebulon z 27597; ● 50
Wake Forest; Inc. Place; WAKE; 213 D-12; elev. 395ft./120m.; [P] [C] 2,560; ★ RAL; z 27587-88; Ⓟ 5,769; © 12,588; ◆ 25,750
Wakelon; RMC Place; BERTIE; 213 C-17; mail Colerain z 27924; ● 30
Wakulla; RMC Place; ROBESON; 212 H-10; elev. 211ft./64m.; mail Maxton z 28364; ● 50
Walkers Crossroads; RMC Place; WAKE; *213 D-12; elev. 351ft./107m.; ★ RAL; mail Wake Forest z 27587; ● 30
Walkertown; Inc. Place; FORSYTH; 212 C-7; elev. 998ft./304m.; [P]; ★ WNS; z 27051; Ⓟ 1,200; © 4,009
Walkertown; RMC Place; HARNETT; *213 F-11; mail Linden z 28356; rural
Wallace; Inc. Place; DUPLIN, PENDER; 213 H-13; elev. 59ft./18m.; [P]; z 28466; Ⓟ 2,939; © 3,344
Walla Watta; RMC Place; BEAUFORT; *213 E-17; mail Pinetown z 27865; rural
Wallburg; Inc. Place; DAVIDSON; 214 H-10; elev. 920ft./280m.; [P]; ★ GRNS-; z 27373; incorporated June 29, 2004; not reported in 2000 Census; ● 430
Walnut; RMC Place; MADISON; 212 K-5; elev. 1,920ft./585m.; mail Marshall z 28753; ● 600
Walnut Cove; Inc. Place; STOKES; 212 C-7; elev. 689ft./210m.; [P]; ★ WNS; z 27052; Ⓟ 1,088; © 1,465
Walnut Creek; RMC Place; MADISON; *212 K-5; mail Marshall z 28753; ● 50
Walnut Creek; Inc. Place; WAYNE; 213 F-14; elev. 110ft./34m.; ★ GLDS; mail Goldsboro z 27530, z 27534; Ⓟ 623; © 859
Walnut Island; RMC Place; CURRITUCK; *213 C-19; mail Grandy z 27939; ● 300
Walstonburg; Inc. Place; GREENE; 213 E-14; [P]; z 27888; Ⓟ 188; © 224
Waltons Store; ONSLOW; see Southwest (RMC Place)
Wananish; RMC Place; COLUMBUS; *213 J-12; elev. 58ft./18m.; mail Lake Waccamaw z 28450; pop. incl. with Lake Waccamaw (Inc. Place)
Wanchese; CDP; DARE; 213 D-20; elev. 9ft./3m.; [P]; z 27981; Ⓟ 1,380; © 1,527
Warbler (Kilkenny Landing); RMC Place; TYRRELL; 213 E-18; mail Fairfield z 27826; ● 100
Wards; RMC Place; COLUMBUS; 213 J-11; elev. 100ft./30m.; mail Chadbourn z 28431; ● 50
Wards Corner; RMC Place; PENDER; *213 I-13; elev. 57ft./17m.; mail Burgaw z 28425
Wardville (Bosley); RMC Place; GATES; *213 B-17; mail Sunbury z 27979; rural
Warne; RMC Place; CLAY; 212 N-2; elev. 1,736ft./529m.; [P]; z 28909; ● 80
WARREN; 213 C-13; Ⓟ 17,265; © 19,972; ◆ 19,297
Warren Plains; RMC Place; WARREN; *213 B-13; mail Warrenton z 27589; ● 60
Warrensville; RMC Place; ASHE; 212 B-3; elev. 2,800ft./853m.; [P]; z 28693; ● 300
Warrenton; Inc. Place; ⊡ WARREN; 213 B-13; elev. 395ft./120m.; [P]; z 27589; Ⓟ 949; © 811
Warrior; RMC Place; CALDWELL; *212 D-3; mail Lenoir z 28645; ● 100
Warsaw; Inc. Place; DUPLIN; 213 G-13; elev. 160ft./49m.; [P]; z 28398; Ⓟ 2,859; © 3,051
Washburn; RMC Place; CLEVELAND; *212 F-3; elev. 953ft./290m.; mail Boiling Springs z 28017; ● 30
Washburn (Washburn Store); RMC Place; RUTHERFORD; *212 F-3; elev. 1,047ft./319m.; mail Bostic z 28018; ● 50
Washburn Store; RUTHERFORD; see Washburn (RMC Place)
Washington; Inc. Place; ⊡ BEAUFORT; 213 E-16; [P] [H] ■; z 27889; Ⓟ 9,075; © 9,583; Ⓡ 9,619; ◆ 9,659
WASHINGTON; 213 D-17; Ⓟ 13,997; © 13,723; ◆ 12,550
Washington Forks; RMC Place; CRAVEN; *213 G-16; elev. 28ft./9m.; mail New Bern z 28560; pop. incl. with New Bern (Inc. Place)
Washington Park; Inc. Place; BEAUFORT; 213 E-16; elev. 5ft./2m.; mail Washington z 27889; Ⓟ 403; © 440
Watauga; RMC Place; MACON; *212 M-3; elev. 2,200ft./671m.; mail Franklin z 28734; rural
WATAUGA; 212 C-3; Ⓟ 36,952; © 42,695; Ⓡ 42,693; ◆ 45,113
Waterlily; RMC Place; CURRITUCK; 213 B-19; elev. 5ft./2m.; mail Coinjock z 27923; ● 250
Waterville; RMC Place; HAYWOOD; *212 K-4; mail Newport z 37821; rural
Watery Branch; RMC Place; WAYNE; *213 E-14; elev. 112ft./34m.; mail Stantonsburg z 27883; ● 30
Watha; Inc. Place; PENDER; 213 I-14; elev. 60ft./18m.; [P]; z 28478; Ⓟ 99; © 151
Watson Crossroads; RMC Place; WAYNE; *213 E-13; elev. 148ft./45m.; mail Kenly z 27542; rural
Watts Crossroads; RMC Place; CABARRUS; *212 F-6; mail Concord z 28025; rural
Waughtown; RMC Place; FORSYTH; *212 D-7; ★ WNS; mail Winston Salem z 27107, z 27117, z 27127; pop. incl. with Winston-Salem (Inc. Place)
Waverly; RMC Place; MADISON; *212 D-1; mail Mars Hill z 28754; rural
Waves; RMC Place; DARE; 213 E-20; elev. 5ft./2m.; [P]; z 27982; ● 120
Waxhaw; Inc. Place; UNION; 212 H-6; elev. 664ft./202m.; [P]; ★ CHRLT; z 28173; Ⓟ 1,294; © 2,625
Wayah Creek (Cartoogechaye); RMC Place; MACON; *212 M-3; mail Franklin z 28734; rural
Waycross; RMC Place; SAMPSON; *213 H-13; elev. 149ft./45m.; mail Magnolia z 28453; rural
WAYNE; 213 F-14; Ⓟ 104,666; © 113,329; ◆ 112,755
Waynesville; Inc. Place; ⊡ HAYWOOD; 212 L-4; [P]; z 28785-86 & mail Hazelwood z 28738; Ⓟ 6,760; © 9,232
Wayside; RMC Place; HOKE; *212 G-10; ★ FAY; mail Raeford z 28376; rural
Weaversford; RMC Place; ASHE; *212 B-4; mail Crumpler z 28617, Grassy Creek z 28631; ● 30
Weaverville; Inc. Place; BUNCOMBE; 212 E-1; elev. 2,176ft./663m.; [P]; ★ ASHE; z 28787; Ⓟ 2,107; © 2,416
Webster; Inc. Place; JACKSON; 214 J-6; elev. 2,017ft./615m.; [P]; z 28788; Ⓟ 410; © 486
Weddington; Inc. Place; UNION, MECKLENBURG; 212 G-6; elev. 721ft./220m.; [P]; ★ CHRLT; z 28104 & mail Waxhaw z 28173; Ⓟ 3,803; © 6,696
Wedgewood Lakes; RMC Place; CURRITUCK; *213 B-19; elev. 13ft./4m.; mail Moyock z 27958; ● 620
Weeksville; RMC Place; PASQUOTANK; 213 C-19; mail Elizabeth City z 27909; ● 50
Wehutty; RMC Place; CHEROKEE; *212 M-1; elev. 1,600ft./488m.; mail Turtletown z 37391; rural
Welcome; CDP; DAVIDSON; 212 D-7; elev. 859ft./262m.; [P]; z 27374; Ⓟ 3,377; © 3,538
Weldon; Inc. Place; HALIFAX; 213 B-14; elev. 80ft./24m.; [P]; z 27890; Ⓟ 1,392; © 1,374
Wells; RMC Place; CUMBERLAND; *213 G-11; elev. 223ft./68m.; ★ FAY; mail Fayetteville z 28304; ● 70
Welmar Heights; RMC Place; CUMBERLAND; *213 G-11; elev. 150ft./46m.; ★ FAY; mail Fayetteville z 28304; ● 1,290
Wendell; Inc. Place; WAKE; 213 E-12; elev. 333ft./101m.; [P]; ★ RAL; z 27591; Ⓟ 2,822; © 4,247
Wenona; RMC Place; WASHINGTON; *213 E-17; elev. 17ft./5m.; mail Pantego z 27860; rural
Wentworth; Inc. Place; ⊡ ROCKINGHAM; 212 B-8; elev. 700ft./213m.; [P]; z 27375; © 2,779
Wesley Chapel; Inc. Place; UNION; *212 G-6; [P]; ★ CHRLT; z 28104 & mail Monroe z 28110; © 2,549
Wesley Heights; RMC Place; MECKLENBURG; ★ CHRLT; mail Charlotte z 28208; pop. incl. with Charlotte (Inc. Place)
Wesser; RMC Place; SWAIN; *212 L-2; mail Bryson City z 28713; rural
Westarea; RMC Place; CUMBERLAND; ★ FAY; pop. incl. with Fayetteville (Inc. Place)
West Asheville; RMC Place; BUNCOMBE; *212 E-1; ★ ASHE; mail Asheville z 28806, z 28816; pop. incl. with Asheville (Inc. Place)
West Brook; RMC Place; CABARRUS; ★ CHRLT; mail Kannapolis z 28081; pop. incl. with Kannapolis (Inc. Place)
Westbrook Crossroads; RMC Place; DUPLIN; *213 G-14; elev. 38ft./12m.; mail Kenansville z 28349; rural
West Canton; CDP; HAYWOOD; *212 L-5; ★ ASHE; mail Canton z 28716; Ⓟ 1,119; © 1,156
Westcliff; RMC Place; ROWAN; *212 E-6; elev. 750ft./229m.; ★ SLSB; mail Salisbury z 28147; ● 280
West Concord (Brown & Norcott Mills); RMC Place; CABARRUS; *212 F-6; ★ CHRLT; mail Concord z 28027; pop. incl. with Concord (Inc. Place)
West Cramerton; RMC Place; GASTON; *212 F-5; ★ CHRLT; mail Cramerton z 28032
West Durham; RMC Place; DURHAM; *213 D-11; ★ DUR; mail Durham z 27705, z 27715; pop. incl. with Durham (Inc. Place)
West Edgecombe; RMC Place; EDGECOMBE; *213 D-14; elev. 112ft./34m.; ★ RKYMT; mail Rocky Mount z 27801; ● 250
West Elkin; WILKES; see Pleasant Hill (CDP)
Westend; RMC Place; GUILFORD; ★ GRNS-; mail High Point z 27262; pop. incl. with High Point (Inc. Place)
West End; RMC Place; MOORE; 212 G-9; elev. 604ft./184m.; [P]; z 27376; ● 600
Western Prong; RMC Place; COLUMBUS; *213 I-11; elev. 80ft./24m.; mail Whiteville z 28472; ● 70
Westerwood; RMC Place; GUILFORD; *212 D-8; ★ GRNS-; mail Greensboro z 27403; pop. incl. with Greensboro (Inc. Place)
Westfield; RMC Place; SURRY; 212 B-6; elev. 1,262ft./385m.; [P]; z 27053; ● 260
West Gastonia; RMC Place; GASTON; *212 F-4; ★ CHRLT; mail Gastonia z 28052
West Haven; RMC Place; BUNCOMBE; mail Arden z 28704; ● 70
Westhaven; RMC Place; PITT; *213 E-15; elev. 72ft./22m.; ★ GRNV; mail Greenville z 27834; pop. incl. with Greenville (Inc. Place)
West Highlands; RMC Place; FORSYTH; *212 D-7; ★ WNS; mail Winston Salem z 27104; pop. incl. with Winston-Salem (Inc. Place)
West Hillsborough; RMC Place; ORANGE; *212 D-10; ★ DUR; mail Hillsborough z 27278; pop. incl. with Hillsborough (Inc. Place)
West Jefferson; Inc. Place; ASHE; 212 B-4; elev. 3,000ft./914m.; [P]; z 28694; Ⓟ 1,002; © 1,081
West Lake Hills; RMC Place; STANLY; *212 F-7; elev. 550ft./168m.; mail Albemarle z 28001; ● 30
West Lumberton; RMC Place; ROBESON; mail Lumberton z 28358; pop. incl. with Lumberton (Inc. Place)
West Marion; CDP; MCDOWELL; *212 E-2; mail Marion z 28752; Ⓟ 1,291; © 1,556
West Market Street; RMC Place; GUILFORD; ★ GRNS-; mail Greensboro z 27402; pop. incl. with Greensboro (Inc. Place)
Westminster; RMC Place; RUTHERFORD; *212 F-2; mail Rutherfordton z 28139
Westmont; RMC Place; RANDOLPH; mail Asheboro z 27205; pop. incl. with Asheboro (Inc. Place)
Westmore; RMC Place; MOORE; *212 F-9; elev. 580ft./177m.; mail Seagrove z 27341; rural
West New Bern; RMC Place; CRAVEN; mail New Bern z 28562; pop. incl. with New Bern (Inc. Place)
Westover; RMC Place; WAKE; *213 E-11; elev. 472ft./144m.; ★ RAL; mail Raleigh z 27606; pop. incl. with Raleigh (Inc. Place)
Westover; RMC Place; WASHINGTON; *213 D-17; mail Plymouth z 27962, Roper z 27970; rural
West Philadelphia; RMC Place; MOORE; *212 F-9; elev. 512ft./156m.; mail Eagle Springs z 27242; rural
Westport; CDP; LINCOLN; *212 F-5; elev. 800ft./244m.; ★ CHRLT; mail Denver z 28037; Ⓟ 1,280; © 2,006
Westridge; RMC Place; NASH; ★ RKYMT; mail Rocky Mount z 27801; pop. incl. with Rocky Mount (Inc. Place)
West Rockingham; RMC Place; RICHMOND; *212 H-8; mail Rockingham z 28379; ● 2,000
West Rocky Mount; RMC Place; NASH; ★ RKYMT; mail Rocky Mount z 27801; pop. incl. with Rocky Mount (Inc. Place)
Westry; RMC Place; NASH; *213 D-14; ★ RKYMT; mail Rocky Mount z 27801; rural
West Salem; RMC Place; FORSYTH; *212 D-7; ★ WNS; mail Winston Salem z 27101; pop. incl. with Winston-Salem (Inc. Place)
Wests Mill; RMC Place; MACON; 212 M-3; mail Franklin z 28734; ● 30
West Smithfield; CDP; JOHNSTON; *213 E-12; ★ RAL; mail Smithfield z 27577; Ⓟ 2,411; © 59
West Trade Street; RMC Place; MECKLENBURG; ★ CHRLT; mail Charlotte z 28202; pop. incl. with Charlotte (Inc. Place)
Westview; RMC Place; FORSYTH; *212 D-7; elev. 938ft./286m.; ★ WNS; mail Winston Salem z 27114; pop. incl. with Winston-Salem (Inc. Place)
Westwood; RMC Place; SCOTLAND; mail Laurinburg z 28352; pop. incl. with Laurinburg (Inc. Place)
Westwood; RMC Place; SURRY; *212 B-6; mail Toast z 27049; ● 360
Westwood Hills; RMC Place; WILKES; *212 C-4; pop. incl. with Wilkesboro (Inc. Place)
West Yanceyville; RMC Place; CASWELL; *212 B-9; elev. 662ft./202m.; mail Yanceyville z 27379; ● 250
Wexford; RMC Place; MECKLENBURG; *212 F-6; ★ CHRLT; mail Charlotte z 28213; pop. incl. with Charlotte (Inc. Place)
Whalebone; RMC Place; DARE; *213 D-20; mail Nags Head z 27959; pop. incl. with Nags Head (Inc. Place)
Whaley; RMC Place; AVERY; *212 C-2; mail Elk Park z 28622; rural
Wharton; RMC Place; BEAUFORT; *213 E-16; elev. 19ft./6m.; mail Washington z 27889; ● 50
Whichard; RMC Place; PITT; *213 E-15; mail Stokes z 27884; rural
Whichard Beach; RMC Place; BEAUFORT; *213 E-16; elev. 5ft./2m.; mail Chocowinity z 27817
Whispering Pines; Inc. Place; MOORE; 212 F-10; elev. 350ft./107m.; [P]; z 28327; Ⓟ 1,243; © 2,090
Whitakers; Inc. Place; NASH, NASH; 213 C-14; elev. 134ft./41m.; [P]; z 27891; Ⓟ 860; © 799
White Cross; RMC Place; ORANGE; *212 D-10; elev. 560ft./171m.; ★ DUR; mail Chapel Hill z 27516; rural
Whitehall Shores; RMC Place; CAMDEN; *213 C-19; elev. 2ft./1m.; mail Camden z 27921; ● 120
Whitehead; RMC Place; ALLEGHANY; 212 B-4; elev. 3,000ft./914m.; [P]; z 28675; ● 100
White Hill; RMC Place; LEE; *212 F-10; elev. 484ft./148m.; mail Sanford z 27330, z 27332; rural
Whitehouse; RMC Place; RUTHERFORD; *212 E-2; mail Union Mills z 28167; ● 30
Whitehurst; RMC Place; PITT; *213 E-15; elev. 69ft./21m.; ★ GRNV; mail Robersonville z 27871; rural
Whitehurst Park; RMC Place; CABARRUS; *212 F-6; elev. 647ft./197m.; ★ CHRLT; mail Concord z 28025; ● 60
White Lake; Inc. Place; BLADEN; 213 H-12; elev. 70ft./21m.; [P]; z 28337; Ⓟ 390; © 529
White Level; RMC Place; FRANKLIN; *213 C-13; elev. 337ft./103m.; mail Louisburg z 27549; rural
White Oak; CDP; BLADEN; 213 H-11; elev. 58ft./18m.; [P]; z 28399; © 304
White Oak; RMC Place; GATES; *213 B-17; mail Eure z 27935; ● 100
White Oak; RMC Place; GUILFORD; *212 C-8; ★ GRNS-; mail Greensboro z 27405; pop. incl. with Greensboro (Inc. Place)
White Oak; RMC Place; HALIFAX; *213 C-14; elev. 254ft./77m.; mail Enfield z 27823; ● 30
White Oak; RMC Place; NASH; *213 D-13; elev. 216ft./66m.; ★ RKYMT; mail Nashville z 27856; rural
White Oaks Acres; WILSON; see Drivers Store (RMC Place)
White Oaks Acres West; RMC Place; WILSON; mail Wilson z 27893
White Pines; RMC Place; SURRY; *212 B-6; mail Toast z 27049; ● 160
White Plains; RMC Place; HYDE; *213 F-19; mail Engelhard z 27824; rural
White Plains; CDP; SURRY; 212 B-6; elev. 1,150ft./351m.; [P]; z 27031; Ⓟ 1,027; © 1,049
Whitepost; RMC Place; BEAUFORT; *213 E-17; elev. 18ft./5m.; mail Bath z 27808
Whiterock; RMC Place; MADISON; *212 J-5; mail Marshall z 28753; ● 30
White's Beach; RMC Place; BERTIE; *213 C-17; elev. 10ft./3m.; mail Colerain z 27924
Whites Chapel; RMC Place; RANDOLPH; *212 E-9; elev. 581ft./177m.; mail Lexington z 27292; rural
Whites Crossroads; RMC Place; BERTIE; 213 C-17; elev. 20ft./6m.; mail Colerain z 27924; ● 30
Whites Fork; RMC Place; HALIFAX; *213 D-15; elev. 89ft./27m.; mail Hobgood z 27843, Scotland Neck z 27874; rural
White Stocking; RMC Place; PENDER; *213 I-14; elev. 15ft./5m.; mail Burgaw z 28425; rural
Whiteston (Nicanor); RMC Place; PERQUIMANS; *213 C-18; mail Belvidere z 27919; rural
White Store; RMC Place; ANSON; *212 H-7; mail Peachland z 28133; rural
White Sulphur Springs; SURRY; see Sulphur Springs (RMC Place)
Whiteville; Inc. Place; ⊡ COLUMBUS; 213 J-11; elev. 66ft./20m.; [P] [H]; z 28472; Ⓟ 5,078; © 5,148
Whitfield Crossroads; RMC Place; LENOIR; *213 G-14; elev. 30ft./9m.; mail Seven Springs z 28578; rural
Whitley Heights; RMC Place; JOHNSTON; *213 E-12; ★ RAL; mail Clayton z 27520; ● 250
Whitley's Crossroads; RMC Place; NASH; *213 D-13; elev. 212ft./65m.; mail Middlesex z 27557; rural
Whitnel; RMC Place; CALDWELL; *212 D-3; elev. 1,286ft./392m.; mail Lenoir z 28645; pop. incl. with Lenoir (Inc. Place)
Whitsett; Inc. Place; GUILFORD; *212 D-9; elev. 679ft./207m.; [P]; ★ BUR; z 27377; Ⓟ 268; © 686
Whittier; RMC Place; SWAIN, JACKSON; 214 I-5; [P]; z 28789; ● 350
Whitt Town; RMC Place; PERSON; *212 C-10; mail Roxboro z 27574; ● 80
Whortonville; RMC Place; PAMLICO; 213 G-17; mail Merritt z 28556; ● 110
Whynot; RMC Place; RANDOLPH; *212 E-8; elev. 607ft./185m.; mail Seagrove z 27341; rural
Wilbanks; RMC Place; WILSON; *213 E-14; mail Elm City z 27822
Wilbar; RMC Place; WILKES; *212 C-4; elev. 1,245ft./379m.; [P]; z 28651; ● 50
Wilbon; RMC Place; WAKE; *213 E-11; elev. 461ft./141m.; ★ RAL; mail Fuquay Varina z 27526; rural
Wilbourns (Wilbourns Store); RMC Place; GRANVILLE; *213 B-11; mail Virgilina z 24598; rural
Wilbourns Store; GRANVILLE; see Wilbourns (RMC Place)
Wilders Grove; RMC Place; WAKE; *213 E-12; ★ RAL; mail Raleigh z 27604; pop. incl. with Raleigh (Inc. Place)
Wildwood; RMC Place; CARTERET; 213 H-17; elev. 19ft./6m.; mail Morehead City z 28557; ● 100
Wildwood; RMC Place; HENDERSON; *212 F-1; ★ ASHE; mail Fletcher z 28732; pop. incl. with Fletcher (Inc. Place)
Wilgrove; RMC Place; MECKLENBURG; *212 G-6; elev. 80ft./24m.; ★ CHRLT; mail Charlotte z 28212; pop. incl. with Charlotte (Inc. Place)
Wilkerson Crossroads; RMC Place; WILSON; *213 E-13; elev. 186ft./57m.; mail Kenly z 27542; rural
WILKES; 212 C-4; Ⓟ 59,393; © 65,632; ◆ 65,657
Wilkesboro; Inc. Place; ⊡ WILKES; 212 C-4; elev. 1,042ft./318m.; [P]; z 28697; Ⓟ 2,573; © 3,159
Wilkinson; RMC Place; BEAUFORT; 213 E-17; mail Pantego z 27860; ● 30
Willard; RMC Place; PENDER; 213 H-14; elev. 50ft./15m.; [P]; z 28478; ● 350
Willeyton; RMC Place; GATES; *213 B-17; elev. 55ft./17m.; mail Gates z 27937; rural
Williams; RMC Place; COLUMBUS; *213 J-11; elev. 112ft./34m.; mail Whiteville z 28472; ● 120
Williamsboro; RMC Place; VANCE; 213 B-12; elev. 428ft./130m.; mail Henderson z 27536-37; ● 60
Williamsburg; RMC Place; IREDELL; *212 D-5; elev. 1,013ft./309m.; mail Harmony z 28634; rural
Williamsburg (Thompsonville); RMC Place; ROCKINGHAM; 212 C-9; ★ GRNS-; mail Reidsville z 27320; ● 120
Williams Crossroads; RMC Place; WAKE; *213 E-11; elev. 407ft./124m.; ★ RAL; mail Raleigh z 27603; rural
Williamson Crossroads; RMC Place; COLUMBUS; *213 J-11; elev. 96ft./29m.; mail Chadbourn z 28431; ● 80
Williamston; Inc. Place; ⊡ MARTIN; 213 D-16; [P] [H]; z 27892; Ⓟ 5,503; © 5,843; Ⓡ 5,946
Williffordtown; RMC Place; NASH; ★ RKYMT; pop. incl. with Rocky Mount (Inc. Place)
Willis Landing; RMC Place; ONSLOW; *213 H-16; ★ JAX; mail Hubert z 28539; rural
Williston; RMC Place; CARTERET; 213 H-18; elev. 3ft./1m.; [P]; z 28579, z 28589; ● 350
Willits (Ochre Hill); RMC Place; JACKSON; *212 L-4; mail Sylva z 28779; rural
Wil-Lotta Acres; RMC Place; CABARRUS; *212 F-6; elev. 669ft./204m.; ★ CHRLT; mail Concord z 28025; ● 100
Willow; RMC Place; GATES; *213 B-17; elev. 11ft./3m.; mail Hobbsville z 27946; rural
Willow Green; RMC Place; GREENE; *213 E-15; elev. 23ft./7m.; mail Ayden z 28513; rural
Willow Spring; WAKE; see Willow Springs (RMC Place)
Willow Springs (Willow Spring); RMC Place; WAKE; 213 E-11; elev. 356ft./109m.; ★ RAL; mail Willow Spring z 27592; ● 450
Wilmar; RMC Place; BEAUFORT, CRAVEN; 213 F-16; elev. 16ft./5m.; mail Vanceboro z 28586; ● 50
Wil-Mar Park; RMC Place; CABARRUS; *212 F-6; ★ CHRLT; mail Concord z 28025; pop. incl. with Concord (Inc. Place)
Wilmington; Inc. Place; ⊡ NEW HANOVER; 213 J-14; elev. 25ft./8m.; [P] [H] [C] 12,848 ■; ★ WILM; z 28401-12; Ⓟ 55,530; © 75,838; ◆ 103,162
Wilmington Beach; RMC Place; NEW HANOVER; 213 K-14; elev. 12ft./4m.; ★ WILM; mail Carolina Beach z 28428; summer pop. 600; ● 200
Wilmore; RMC Place; MECKLENBURG; ★ CHRLT; mail Charlotte z 28203; pop. incl. with Charlotte (Inc. Place)
Wilmot; RMC Place; JACKSON; *212 L-3; mail Whittier z 28789; rural
Wilshire Park; RMC Place; BUNCOMBE; *212 E-1; ★ ASHE; mail Asheville z 28806; pop. incl. with Asheville (Inc. Place)
Wilson; Inc. Place; ⊡ WILSON; 213 E-14; [P] [H] [C] 1,136 ■; z 27893-96; Ⓟ 36,930; © 44,405; ◆ 48,076
WILSON; 213 E-14; Ⓟ 66,061; © 73,814; Ⓡ 73,811; ◆ 76,766
Wilson's Mill; JOHNSTON; see Wilsons Mills (Inc. Place)
Wilsons Mills (Wilson's Mill); Inc. Place; JOHNSTON; 213 E-12; elev. 228ft./69m.; [P]; ★ RAL; z 27593; © 1,291; Ⓡ 1,296
Wilsonville; RMC Place; CHATHAM; *213 E-11; elev. 291ft./89m.; mail Apex z 27523
Wilton; RMC Place; GRANVILLE; *213 C-12; mail Franklinton z 27525
Wind Blow; RMC Place; MONTGOMERY, RICHMOND; *212 G-9; mail Ellerbe z 28338, Jackson Springs z 27281; rural
Windom; RMC Place; YANCEY; *212 D-1; mail Burnsville z 28714; rural
Windsor; Inc. Place; ⊡ BERTIE; 213 D-16; [P] [H]; z 27983; Ⓟ 2,056; © 2,283; Ⓡ 2,324
Windsors Crossroads; RMC Place; YADKIN; *212 D-5; mail Hamptonville z 27020; rural
Windy Gap; RMC Place; WILKES; *212 C-5; mail North Wilkesboro z 28659; rural
Winfall; Inc. Place; PERQUIMANS; 213 C-18; elev. 15ft./5m.; [P]; z 27985; Ⓟ 501; © 554
Wing; RMC Place; MITCHELL; *212 D-2; mail Bakersville z 28705; rural
Wingate; Inc. Place; UNION; 212 G-6; elev. 576ft./176m.; [P] [C] 1,799; z 28174; Ⓟ 2,821; © 2,406
Winnabow; RMC Place; BRUNSWICK; 213 J-13; elev. 40ft./12m.; [P]; ★ WILM; z 28479; ● 150
Winstead Crossroads; RMC Place; NASH; *213 D-14; elev. 158ft./48m.; ★ RKYMT; mail Elm City z 27822; rural
Winsteadville; RMC Place; BEAUFORT; *213 F-17; mail Belhaven z 27810; ● 50
Winston-Salem; Inc. Place; ⊡ FORSYTH; 212 D-7; elev. 912ft./278m.; [P] [H] [C] 14,632 ■; ★ WNS; z 27101-11, z 27113-17, z 27120, z 27127, z 27130, z 27150, z 27152, z 27155, z 27157, z 27198-99; Ⓟ 143,485; © 185,776; ◆ 210,943
Winston-Salem Junction; RMC Place; FORSYTH; ★ WNS; pop. incl. with Winston-Salem (Inc. Place)
Wintergreen; RMC Place; CRAVEN; *213 F-15; elev. 12ft./4m.; mail Cove City z 28523; rural
Winter Park; RMC Place; CLEVELAND; *212 F-3; elev. 800ft./244m.; mail Shelby z 28152; ● 30
Winterville; Inc. Place; PITT; 213 E-15; elev. 72ft./22m.; [P]; ★ GRNV; z 28590; Ⓟ 2,816; © 4,791; Ⓡ 4,794
Winton; Inc. Place; ⊡ HERTFORD; 213 B-16; elev. 45ft./14m.; [P]; z 27986; Ⓟ 796; © 956
Wise; RMC Place; WARREN; 213 B-13; elev. 390ft./119m.; [P]; z 27594; ● 550
Wise Forks; RMC Place; JONES; *213 F-15; elev. 69ft./21m.; mail Dover z 28526; rural
Witherspoon Crossroads; RMC Place; CATAWBA; *212 E-4; ★ HICK; mail Claremont z 28610; rural
Wittys Crossroads; RMC Place; ROCKINGHAM; *212 C-8; mail Reidsville z 27320; rural
Wolf Creek (Macedonia); RMC Place; CHEROKEE; *212 M-1; mail Copperhill z 37317
Wolf Laurel; RMC Place; MADISON; mail Mars Hill z 28754; summer pop. 600; ● 80
Wolf Mountain; RMC Place; JACKSON; *212 M-4; mail Tuckasegee z 28783; rural
Wood; RMC Place; FRANKLIN; 213 C-13; mail Louisburg z 27549; ● 90
Woodard; RMC Place; BERTIE; 213 D-17; mail Windsor z 27983; ● 40
Woodard; RMC Place; WILSON; mail Wilson z 27893; pop. incl. with Wilson (Inc. Place)
Woodburn; RMC Place; BRUNSWICK; *213 J-13; ★ WILM; mail Leland z 28451; pop. incl. with Belville (Inc. Place)
Wood Crest; RMC Place; CARTERET; *213 H-17; elev. 25ft./8m.; mail Newport z 28570; ● 100
Woodcroft; RMC Place; DURHAM; *213 D-11; elev. 255ft./78m.; ★ DUR; pop. incl. with Durham (Inc. Place)
Woodfin; Inc. Place; BUNCOMBE; 212 K-5; [P]; ★ ASHE; z 28804; Ⓟ 2,736; © 3,162
Woodington; RMC Place; LENOIR; *213 G-14; elev. 96ft./29m.; mail Kinston z 28504; rural
Woodland; NORTHAMPTON; see George (RMC Place)
Woodland; Inc. Place; NORTHAMPTON; 213 C-16; elev. 68ft./21m.; [P]; z 27897; Ⓟ 760; © 833
Woodland Acres; RMC Place; MARTIN; *213 D-16; elev. 66ft./20m.; mail Williamston z 27892; ● 230
Woodland Hills; RMC Place; BUNCOMBE; *212 E-1; elev. 2,100ft./640m.; ★ ASHE; mail Asheville z 28804; ● 660
Woodlawn; CDP; ALAMANCE; *212 C-10; ★ BUR; mail Mebane z 27302; © 1,051
Woodlawn; RMC Place; CLEVELAND; *212 F-3; elev. 900ft./274m.; mail Shelby z 28150; ● 100
Woodlawn; RMC Place; MCDOWELL; *212 E-2; mail Marion z 28752
Woodlea; RMC Place; CUMBERLAND; *213 G-11; elev. 150ft./46m.; ★ FAY; mail Fayetteville z 28304; ● 900
Woodleaf; RMC Place; ROWAN; 212 E-6; elev. 811ft./247m.; [P]; ★ SLSB; z 27054; ● 380
Woodrow; RMC Place; CRAVEN; *213 G-16; mail New Bern z 28560; pop. incl. with New Bern (Inc. Place)
Woodrow; RMC Place; HAYWOOD; 212 L-4; ★ ASHE; mail Canton z 28716; ● 100
Woodrun; RMC Place; MONTGOMERY; *212 F-7; mail Mount Gilead z 27306; rural
Woodsdale; RMC Place; PERSON; *213 B-11; elev. 482ft./147m.; mail Roxboro z 27574
Woodside; RMC Place; CABARRUS; *212 F-6; elev. 800ft./244m.; ★ CHRLT; mail Kannapolis z 28081; ● 80
Woodside Hills; RMC Place; BUNCOMBE; *212 L-5; ★ ASHE; mail Candler z 28715; ● 100
Woodville; RMC Place; BERTIE; *213 C-16; elev. 77ft./23m.; mail Lewiston Woodville z 27849; pop. incl. with Lewiston Woodville (Inc. Place)
Woodville; RMC Place; PERQUIMANS; *213 C-18; elev. 5ft./2m.; mail Hertford z 27944; ● 280
Woodville; RMC Place; SURRY; *212 B-6; mail Mount Airy z 27030; rural
Woodworth; RMC Place; VANCE; *213 B-12; mail Henderson z 27537; rural
Wootens Crossroads; RMC Place; COLUMBUS; *213 I-11; elev. 95ft./29m.; mail Clarkton z 28433; rural
Wootens Crossroads; RMC Place; GREENE; *213 E-14; mail Walstonburg z 27888; rural
Wootens Crossroads; RMC Place; LENOIR; *213 G-14; elev. 40ft./12m.; mail Kinston z 28504
Worley; RMC Place; MADISON; *212 K-5; mail Marshall z 28753; rural
Worth; RMC Place; MECKLENBURG; ★ CHRLT; pop. incl. with Charlotte (Inc. Place)
Worthingtons Crossroads; RMC Place; PITT; *213 E-15; elev. 71ft./22m.; ★ GRNV; mail Greenville z 27858; ● 30
Worthville; RMC Place; RANDOLPH; *212 E-8; elev. 650ft./198m.; mail Randleman z 27317; ● 360
Wrightsboro; CDP; NEW HANOVER; *213 J-14; ★ WILM; mail Wilmington z 28401; Ⓟ 4,752; © 4,496
Wrightsville; RMC Place; NEW HANOVER; 213 M-20; ★ WILM; mail Wrightsville Beach z 28480; pop. incl. with Wilmington (Inc. Place)
Wrightsville Beach; Inc. Place; NEW HANOVER; 213 J-14; elev. 7ft./2m.; [P]; ★ WILM; z 28480; Ⓟ 2,937; © 2,593

Y

Yadkin; RMC Place; ROWAN; *212 E-7; ★ SLSB; mail Salisbury z 28144; ● 220
YADKIN; 212 C-6; Ⓟ 30,488; © 36,348; ◆ 37,851
Yadkin Valley; RMC Place; CALDWELL; *212 D-3; elev. 1,185ft./361m.; mail Ferguson z 28624, Lenoir z 28645; ● 100
Yadkinville; Inc. Place; ⊡ YADKIN; 212 C-6; elev. 962ft./293m.; [P] [H]; z 27055; Ⓟ 2,525; © 2,818
Yamacraw; RMC Place; PENDER; *213 I-13; elev. 51ft./16m.; mail Currie z 28435; rural
YANCEY; 212 D-1; Ⓟ 15,419; © 17,774; ◆ 18,875
Yanceyville; Inc. Place; ⊡ CASWELL; 212 B-10; elev. 619ft./189m.; [P]; z 27379; Ⓟ 1,973; © 2,091
Yaupon Beach; RMC Place; BRUNSWICK; 213 K-13; elev. 14ft./4m.; mail Oak Island z 28465; pop. incl. with Oak Island (Inc. Place); Ⓟ 734
Yeatsville; RMC Place; BEAUFORT; *213 E-17; elev. 12ft./4m.; mail Bath z 27808, Pinetown z 27865; ● 50
Yellow Creek; RMC Place; GRAHAM; 214 J-2; elev. 1,948ft./594m.; mail Robbinsville z 28771; ● 30
Yeopim; RMC Place; CHOWAN; *213 C-18; mail Edenton z 27932; ● 50
Yorick; RMC Place; BLADEN; 213 H-12; elev. 53ft./16m.; mail White Oak z 28399; ● 50
Yorkmont Park; RMC Place; MECKLENBURG; *212 G-5; ★ CHRLT; mail Charlotte z 28217; pop. incl. with Charlotte (Inc. Place)
Yorkwood; RMC Place; GASTON; *212 G-4; ★ CHRLT; mail Gastonia z 28052; ● 1,150
Youngsville; Inc. Place; FRANKLIN; 213 D-12; elev. 462ft./141m.; [P]; ★ RAL; z 27596; Ⓟ 424; © 651

Z

Zebulon; Inc. Place; WAKE; 213 D-12; elev. 327ft./100m.; [P]; ★ RAL; z 27597; Ⓟ 3,173; © 4,046
Zephyr; RMC Place; SURRY; *212 C-5; elev. 1,309ft./399m.; mail Elkin z 28621
Zionville; RMC Place; WATAUGA; 212 C-3; elev. 3,508ft./1,069m.; [P]; z 28698; ● 230
Zirconia; RMC Place; HENDERSON; *212 F-1; elev. 2,187ft./667m.; [P]; z 28790; ● 300

NORTH DAKOTA

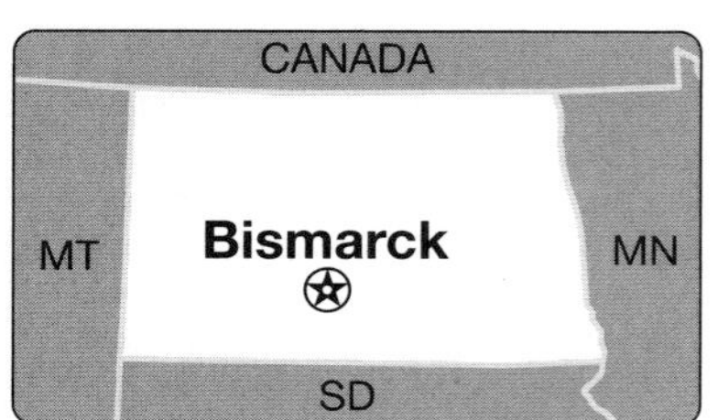

Statistics

Total area (2000) — 70,700 square miles
Land area (2000) — 68,976 square miles
Water area (2000) — 1,724 square miles
Capital — Bismarck
Admitted as state — November, 1889

Maps

State maps can be found on pages 142-254 in Vol. 1

Ranally Metro Areas (RMAs) and Abbreviations

Bismarck, ND — BIS
Fargo-Moorhead, ND-MN — FAR-
Grand Forks, ND-MN — GDFK

Principal Places

Place Name	Place Type	County	Population
Fargo	Inc. Place	CASS	◆ 104,279
Bismarck	Inc. Place	BURLEIGH	◆ 62,026
Grand Forks	Inc. Place	GRAND FORKS	◆ 53,861
Minot	Inc. Place	WARD	◆ 36,764
West Fargo	Inc. Place	CASS	◆ 19,769
Mandan	Inc. Place	MORTON	© 16,718
Dickinson	Inc. Place	STARK	◆ 16,128
Jamestown	Inc. Place	STUTSMAN	◆ 14,019
Williston	Inc. Place	WILLIAMS	◆ 13,266
Wahpeton	Inc. Place	RICHLAND	© 8,586
Minot AFB	CDP-Census Area Only	WARD	© 7,599
Devils Lake	Inc. Place	RAMSEY	© 7,222
Valley City	Inc. Place	BARNES	© 6,826

County Business Data

County	FIPS Code	County Seat	Land Area (Sq. Mi.)	Census Population			Wholesale Trade		Manufacturing, 2002			
				4/1/2000	4/1/1990	% Change 1990-2000	Sales, 2002 ($1,000)	% Change 1997-2002	Establish-ments	Total Employees	Value Added ($1,000)	Ranally Mfg. Units
Adams	001	Hettinger	988	2,593	3,174	-18.3	47,869	-6.2	...	(d)	(d)	...
Barnes	003	Valley City	1,492	11,775	12,545	-6.1	177,770	18.4	...	(d)	(d)	...
Benson	005	Minnewaukan	1,381	6,964	7,198	-3.3	(d)	(d)	...	(d)	(d)	...
Billings	007	Medora	1,151	888	1,108	-19.9	(d)	(d)	...	(d)	(d)	...
Bottineau	009	Bottineau	1,669	7,149	8,011	-10.8	84,790	0.7	...	(d)	(d)	...
Bowman	011	Bowman	1,162	3,242	3,596	-9.8	(d)	(d)	...	(d)	(d)	...
Burke	013	Bowbells	1,104	2,242	3,002	-25.3	28,274	-15.5	...	(d)	(d)	...
Burleigh	015	Bismarck	1,633	69,416	60,131	15.4	646,215	4.3	64	1,343	176,724	93
Cass	017	Fargo	1,765	123,138	102,874	19.7	(d)	(d)	186	7,377	617,756	327
Cavalier	019	Langdon	1,488	4,831	6,064	-20.3	71,066	-24.1	...	(d)	(d)	...
Dickey	021	Ellendale	1,131	5,757	6,107	-5.7	85,286	-8.4	...	(d)	(d)	...
Divide	023	Crosby	1,260	2,283	2,899	-21.2	45,029	-24.7	...	(d)	(d)	...
Dunn	025	Manning	2,010	3,600	4,005	-10.1	16,251	71.6	...	(d)	(d)	...
Eddy	027	New Rockford	630	2,757	2,951	-6.6	(d)	(d)	...	(d)	(d)	...
Emmons	029	Linton	1,510	4,331	4,830	-10.3	27,879	-18.8	...	(d)	(d)	...
Foster	031	Carrington	635	3,759	3,983	-5.6	(d)	(d)	...	(d)	(d)	...
Golden Valley	033	Beach	1,002	1,924	2,108	-8.7	37,349	13.8	...	(d)	(d)	...
Grand Forks	035	Grand Forks	1,438	66,109	70,683	-6.5	658,640	19.2	56	1,765	157,672	83
Grant	037	Carson	1,659	2,841	3,549	-19.9	11,043	-43.0	...	(d)	(d)	...
Griggs	039	Cooperstown	709	2,754	3,303	-16.6	32,803	-10.7	...	(d)	(d)	...
Hettinger	041	Mott	1,132	2,715	3,445	-21.2	20,156	-26.3	...	(d)	(d)	...
Kidder	043	Steele	1,351	2,753	3,332	-17.4	7,847	-20.3	...	(d)	(d)	...
LaMoure	045	Lamoure	1,147	4,701	5,383	-12.7	66,483	-25.0	...	(d)	(d)	...
Logan	047	Napoleon	993	2,308	2,847	-18.9	97,003	0.1	...	(d)	(d)	...
McHenry	049	Towner	1,874	5,987	6,528	-8.3	(d)	(d)	...	(d)	(d)	...
McIntosh	051	Ashley	975	3,390	4,021	-15.7	34,153	53.5	...	(d)	(d)	...
McKenzie	053	Watford City	2,742	5,737	6,383	-10.1	21,657	18.7	...	(d)	(d)	...
McLean	055	Washburn	2,110	9,311	10,457	-11.0	(d)	(d)	...	(d)	(d)	...
Mercer	057	Stanton	1,045	8,644	9,808	-11.9	(d)	(d)	...	(d)	(d)	...
Morton	059	Mandan	1,926	25,303	23,700	6.8	184,503	-4.6	35	1,165	223,507	118
Mountrail	061	Stanley	1,824	6,631	7,021	-5.6	(d)	(d)	...	(d)	(d)	...
Nelson	063	Lakota	982	3,715	4,410	-15.8	76,105	-17.4	...	(d)	(d)	...
Oliver	065	Center	724	2,065	2,381	-13.3	(d)	(d)	...	(d)	(d)	...
Pembina	067	Cavalier	1,119	8,585	9,238	-7.1	250,348	120.2	13	1,281	183,919	97
Pierce	069	Rugby	1,018	4,675	5,052	-7.5	66,440	-26.3	...	(d)	(d)	...
Ramsey	071	Devils Lake	1,185	12,066	12,681	-4.8	138,603	-18.7	...	(d)	(d)	...
Ransom	073	Lisbon	863	5,890	5,921	-0.5	91,457	-29.8	...	(d)	(d)	...
Renville	075	Mohall	875	2,610	3,160	-17.4	(d)	(d)	...	(d)	(d)	...
Richland	077	Wahpeton	1,437	17,998	18,148	-0.8	(d)	(d)	33	2,114	351,285	186
Rolette	079	Rolla	902	13,674	12,772	7.1	101,683	28.1	...	(d)	(d)	...
Sargent	081	Forman	859	4,366	4,549	-4.0	(d)	(d)	7	(d)	(d)	...
Sheridan	083	Mcclusky	972	1,710	2,148	-20.4	12,490	66.2	...	(d)	(d)	...
Sioux	085	Fort Yates	1,094	4,044	3,761	7.5	(d)	(d)	...	(d)	(d)	...
Slope	087	Amidon	1,218	767	907	-15.4	(d)	(d)	...	(d)	(d)	...
Stark	089	Dickinson	1,338	22,636	22,832	-0.9	256,152	-7.4	35	928	55,950	30
Steele	091	Finley	712	2,258	2,420	-6.7	(d)	(d)	...	(d)	(d)	...
Stutsman	093	Jamestown	2,221	21,908	22,241	-1.5	181,822	-22.6	24	1,008	72,541	38
Towner	095	Cando	1,025	2,876	3,627	-20.7	(d)	(d)	...	(d)	(d)	...
Traill	097	Hillsboro	862	8,477	8,752	-3.1	183,998	0.0	...	(d)	(d)	...
Walsh	099	Grafton	1,282	12,389	13,840	-10.5	229,040	50.9	9	623	40,937	22
Ward	101	Minot	2,013	58,795	57,921	1.5	714,078	1.8	44	(d)	(d)	...
Wells	103	Fessenden	1,271	5,102	5,864	-13.0	104,930	15.1	...	(d)	(d)	...
Williams	105	Williston	2,070	19,761	21,129	-6.5	202,435	-38.8	...	(d)	(d)	...
The State			**68,976**	**642,200**	**638,800**	**0.5**	**8,806,340**	**2.2**	**724**	**23,370**	**2,679,559**	**1,418**

(d) Data not available. Corresponding percentages or Ranally Manufacturing Units are estimates.
... Represents 0 or amount too minimal to be reported.

Index of Places and Counties

Entries in **UPPERCASE** are counties.
Entries in **bold** have populations of 2,500 or more.
Names in parentheses are alternate names.

Inc. Place	Incorporated Place
RMC Place	Rand McNally Designated Place
CDP	Census Designated Place
MCD	Minor Civil Division
⊡	County Seat
▲	Minor Civil Division
elev.	Elevation
🅿	Post Office
🅷	Hospital
🅲	College
■	Principal Business Center
★	Ranally Metro Area (RMA) Abbreviation
z	Zip Code(s)
Ⓟ	Previous Census Population
Ⓡ	Revised Census Population
Ⓐ	Annexation Population
●	Rand McNally Population Estimate
©	Final Census Population
Ⓢ	Special Census Population
◆	Estimated Population

For additional definitions see Glossary, Volume 1, and Introduction, Volume 2.

Dickinson; Inc. Place; ⊡ STARK; **215** F-4; elev. 2,417ft./737m.; 🅿 🅷 🅲 2,572 ■; **z** 58601-02; Ⓟ 16,097; Ⓒ 16,010; ◆ 16,128
DIVIDE; **215** A-3; Ⓟ 2,899; Ⓒ 2,283; ◆ 1,898
Dodge; Inc. Place; DUNN; **215** E-5; elev. 1,988ft./606m.; 🅿; **z** 58625; Ⓟ 135; Ⓒ 125
Donnybrook; Inc. Place; WARD; **215** B-5; elev. 1,760ft./536m.; 🅿; **z** 58734; Ⓟ 106; Ⓒ 90
Douglas; Inc. Place; WARD; **215** D-6; elev. 2,055ft./626m.; 🅿; **z** 58735; Ⓟ 93; Ⓒ 64
Downtown; RMC Place; BURLEIGH; ★ **BIS**; mail Bismarck **z** 58501; pop. incl. with Bismarck (Inc. Place)
Doyon; RMC Place; RAMSEY; **215** C-10; elev. 1,510ft./460m.; 🅿; **z** 58327; ● 40
Drake; Inc. Place; MCHENRY; **215** C-7; elev. 1,682ft./513m.; 🅿; **z** 58736; Ⓟ 361; Ⓒ 322
Drayton; Inc. Place; PEMBINA; **215** B-12; elev. 801ft./244m.; 🅿; **z** 58225; Ⓟ 961; Ⓒ 913
Dresden; RMC Place; CAVALIER; ***215** A-10; mail Langdon **z** 58249
Driscoll; RMC Place; BURLEIGH; **215** F-8; elev. 1,867ft./569m.; 🅿; **z** 58532; ● 100
DUNN; **215** E-4; Ⓟ 4,005; Ⓒ 3,600; ◆ 3,238
Dunn Center; Inc. Place; DUNN; **215** E-4; elev. 2,182ft./665m.; 🅿; **z** 58626; Ⓟ 128; Ⓒ 122
Dunning; RMC Place; BOTTINEAU; ***215** B-6; elev. 1,492ft./455m.; mail Maxbass **z** 58760; rural
Dunseith; Inc. Place; ROLETTE; **215** A-8; elev. 1,700ft./518m.; 🅿; **z** 58329; Ⓟ 723; Ⓒ 739
Durbin; RMC Place; CASS; ***215** F-12; elev. 920ft./280m.; 🅿; **z** 58059; rural
Dwight; Inc. Place; RICHLAND; **215** G-13; elev. 955ft./291m.; 🅿; **z** 58075; Ⓟ 83; Ⓒ 75

E

Eagle Bend Estates; RMC Place; RAMSEY; ***215** C-10; elev. 1,425ft./434m.; mail Devils Lake **z** 58301; ● 60
East Dunseith; CDP-Census Area Only; ROLETTE; ***215** A-8; elev. 2,050ft./625m.; mail Dunseith **z** 58329; Ⓟ 260; Ⓒ 219
East Fairview; RMC Place; MCKENZIE; **215** C-2; mail Fairview **z** 59221; ● 50
Eastside Estates; RMC Place; WARD; ***215** C-6; elev. 1,548ft./472m.; mail Minot **z** 58701; ● 120
Eckelson; RMC Place; BARNES; **215** F-11; elev. 1,475ft./450m.; 🅿; **z** 58481; ● 40
Eckman; RMC Place; BOTTINEAU; ***215** B-6; elev. 1,493ft./455m.; mail Maxbass **z** 58760
EDDY; **215** D-9; Ⓟ 2,951; Ⓒ 2,757; ◆ 2,338
Edgeley; Inc. Place; LAMOURE; **215** G-10; elev. 1,565ft./477m.; 🅿; **z** 58433; Ⓟ 680; Ⓒ 637
Edinburg; Inc. Place; WALSH; **215** B-11; elev. 1,187ft./362m.; 🅿; **z** 58227; Ⓟ 284; Ⓒ 252
Edmore; Inc. Place; RAMSEY; **215** B-10; elev. 1,513ft./461m.; 🅿; **z** 58330; Ⓟ 329; Ⓒ 256
Edmunds; RMC Place; STUTSMAN; ***215** E-10; elev. 1,600ft./488m.; 🅿; **z** 58476
Egeland (Olmstead); Inc. Place; TOWNER; **215** B-9; elev. 1,519ft./463m.; 🅿; **z** 58331; Ⓟ 103; Ⓒ 49
El Dorado Acres; RMC Place; STARK; ***215** F-4; elev. 2,550ft./777m.; mail Dickinson **z** 58601; ● 30
Eldridge; RMC Place; STUTSMAN; **215** F-10; elev. 1,545ft./471m.; 🅿; **z** 58401; ● 50
Elgin; Inc. Place; GRANT; **215** G-5; elev. 2,330ft./710m.; 🅿 🅷; **z** 58533; Ⓟ 765; Ⓒ 659
Ellendale; Inc. Place; ⊡ DICKEY; **215** H-10; elev. 1,456ft./444m.; 🅿 🅲 310; **z** 58436; Ⓟ 1,798; Ⓒ 1,559
Elliott; Inc. Place; RANSOM; **215** G-11; 🅿; **z** 58054; Ⓟ 32; Ⓒ 44
Embden; RMC Place; CASS; **215** F-12; 🅿; **z** 58079; ● 60
Emerado; Inc. Place; GRAND FORKS; **215** C-12; 🅿; **z** 58228; Ⓟ 483; Ⓒ 510
Emmet; RMC Place; MCLEAN; ***215** D-5; elev. 2,018ft./615m.; 🅿; **z** 58540; rural
EMMONS; **215** G-8; Ⓟ 4,830; Ⓒ 4,331; ◆ 3,191
Emrick; RMC Place; WELLS; ***215** D-9; elev. 1,598ft./487m.; 🅿; **z** 58422; rural
Enderlin; Inc. Place; RANSOM, CASS; **215** F-12; elev. 1,090ft./332m.; 🅿; **z** 58027; Ⓟ 997; Ⓒ 947
Englevale; RMC Place; RANSOM; **215** G-11; elev. 1,344ft./410m.; 🅿; **z** 58033; ● 40
Epping; Inc. Place; WILLIAMS; **215** B-3; elev. 2,218ft./676m.; 🅿; **z** 58843; Ⓟ 64; Ⓒ 79
Erie; CDP; CASS; **215** E-12; elev. 1,100ft./335m.; 🅿; **z** 58029; Ⓒ 65
Erie Junction; RMC Place; CASS; ***215** E-12; elev. 1,116ft./340m.; mail Erie **z** 58029; ● 50
Esmond; Inc. Place; BENSON; **215** C-8; elev. 1,623ft./495m.; 🅿; **z** 58332; Ⓟ 196; Ⓒ 159
Everest; RMC Place; CASS; ***215** F-12; mail Casselton **z** 58012; ● 20
Evergreen; RMC Place; CASS; ***215** F-13; elev. 940ft./287m.; mail Kindred **z** 58051; ● 30

F

Faiman's Sunrise Addition; RMC Place; BURLEIGH; ***215** F-7; elev. 1,919ft./585m.; mail Bismarck **z** 58504; ● 35
Fairdale; Inc. Place; WALSH; **215** B-11; elev. 1,623ft./495m.; 🅿; **z** 58229; Ⓟ 76; Ⓒ 51
Fairfield; RMC Place; BILLINGS; **215** E-3; elev. 2,752ft./839m.; 🅿; **z** 58627; ● 140
Fairmount; Inc. Place; RICHLAND; **215** H-13; elev. 984ft./300m.; 🅿; **z** 58030; Ⓟ 427; Ⓒ 406
Falconer Estates; RMC Place; BURLEIGH; ***215** F-7; elev. 1,634ft./498m.; ★ **BIS**; mail Bismarck **z** 58504; ● 90
Falkirk; RMC Place; MCLEAN; **215** E-6; elev. 1,851ft./564m.; mail Washburn **z** 58577; ● 20
Fallon; RMC Place; MORTON; ***215** G-6; mail Flasher **z** 58535; rural
Fargo; Inc. Place; ⊡ CASS; **215** F-13; elev. 900ft./274m.; 🅿 🅷 🅲 12,258 ■; ★ **FAR-**; **z** 58102-09, **z** 58121-22, **z** 58124-26; Ⓟ 74,111; Ⓒ 90,599; ◆ 104,279
Fessenden; Inc. Place; ⊡ WELLS; **215** D-9; elev. 1,608ft./490m.; 🅿; **z** 58438; Ⓟ 655; Ⓒ 625
Fillmore; RMC Place; BENSON; **215** C-8; elev. 1,591ft./485m.; 🅿; **z** 58332; ● 30
Fingal; Inc. Place; BARNES; **215** F-11; elev. 1,280ft./390m.; 🅿; **z** 58031; Ⓟ 138; Ⓒ 133
Finley; Inc. Place; ⊡ STEELE; **215** D-11; elev. 1,457ft./444m.; 🅿; **z** 58230; Ⓟ 543; Ⓒ 515
Flasher; Inc. Place; MORTON; **215** G-6; elev. 1,905ft./581m.; 🅿; **z** 58535; Ⓟ 317; Ⓒ 285
Flaxton; Inc. Place; BURKE; **215** A-4; elev. 1,936ft./590m.; 🅿; **z** 58737; Ⓟ 121; Ⓒ 73
Flora; RMC Place; BENSON; **215** C-9; 🅿; **z** 58348; ● 20
Fonda; RMC Place; ROLETTE; ***215** B-8; mail Rolette **z** 58366
Forbes; Inc. Place; DICKEY; **215** H-10; elev. 1,560ft./475m.; 🅿; **z** 58439; Ⓟ 56; Ⓒ 64
Fordville; Inc. Place; WALSH; **215** C-11; elev. 1,144ft./349m.; 🅿; **z** 58231; Ⓟ 299; Ⓒ 266
Forest River; RMC Place; CASS; ***215** F-13; elev. 906ft./276m.; mail Fargo **z** 58104; ● 90
Forest River; Inc. Place; WALSH; **215** C-12; elev. 865ft./264m.; 🅿; **z** 58233; Ⓟ 148; Ⓒ 154
Forest River Colony; RMC Place; GRAND FORKS; ***215** C-12; mail Fordville **z** 58231; ● 85
Forman; Inc. Place; ⊡ SARGENT; **215** H-12; elev. 1,250ft./381m.; 🅿; **z** 58032; Ⓟ 586; Ⓒ 506
Fort Berthold Reservation; Indian Reservation; MCLEAN, DUNN, MCKENZIE, MERCER, MOUNTRAIL, WARD; mail New Town **z** 58763; also location of Indian Agency; Ⓟ 5,577; Ⓒ 5,915
Fort Buford; WILLIAMS; see Buford (RMC Place)
Fort Clark; RMC Place; OLIVER; ***215** E-6; 🅿; **z** 58530
Fort Ransom; Inc. Place; RANSOM; **215** G-11; elev. 1,130ft./344m.; 🅿; **z** 58033; Ⓟ 111; Ⓒ 70
Fort Rice; RMC Place; MORTON; **215** G-7; elev. 1,640ft./500m.; 🅿; **z** 58554; ● 30
Fort Totten; CDP; BENSON; **215** C-10; located on Spirit Lake Ind. Res.; elev. 1,500ft./457m.; 🅿; **z** 58335; location of Indian Agency; Ⓟ 867; Ⓒ 952
Fort Totten Indian Reservation; BENSON, EDDY, NELSON, RAMSEY, WELLS; see Spirit Lake Reservation (Indian Reservation)
Fortuna; Inc. Place; DIVIDE; **215** A-2; elev. 2,190ft./668m.; 🅿; **z** 58844; Ⓟ 53; Ⓒ 31
Fort Yates; Inc. Place; ⊡ SIOUX; **215** H-7; located on Standing Rock Ind. Res.; elev. 1,640ft./500m.; 🅿 🅷 🅲 350; **z** 58538; location of Indian Agency; Ⓟ 183; Ⓒ 228
FOSTER; **215** D-10; Ⓟ 3,983; Ⓒ 3,759; ◆ 3,351
Four Bears Village; CDP; MCKENZIE; ***215** C-4; elev. 1,900ft./579m.; mail New Town **z** 58763; Ⓟ 309; Ⓒ 364
Four K's Estates; RMC Place; BURLEIGH; ***215** F-7; elev. 1,888ft./575m.; mail Bismarck **z** 58503; ● 50
Foxholm; RMC Place; WARD; **215** B-6; elev. 1,654ft./504m.; 🅿; **z** 58718; ● 90
Fox Island; RMC Place; BURLEIGH; ***215** F-7; elev. 1,625ft./495m.; ★ **BIS**; mail Bismarck **z** 58504; ● 80
Fradet (Orchard Park); RMC Place; CASS; ***215** F-13; elev. 915ft./279m.; mail Horace **z** 58047; ● 50
Frazier; RMC Place; BARNES; mail Wimbledon **z** 58492; pop. incl. with Wimbledon (Inc. Place)
Fredonia; Inc. Place; LOGAN; **215** G-9; elev. 2,000ft./610m.; 🅿; **z** 58440; Ⓟ 66; Ⓒ 51
Fried; RMC Place; STUTSMAN; ***215** E-10; elev. 1,521ft./464m.; mail Jamestown **z** 58401; ● 25
Frison; RMC Place; RAMSEY; ***215** C-10; elev. 1,450ft./442m.; mail Devils Lake **z** 58301; ● 220
Frontier; Inc. Place; CASS; **215** F-13; 🅿; ★ **FAR-**; **z** 58104; Ⓟ 218; Ⓒ 273
Fryburg; RMC Place; BILLINGS; **215** F-3; 🅿; **z** 58622; ● 50
Fullerton; Inc. Place; DICKEY; **215** G-10; elev. 1,455ft./443m.; 🅿; **z** 58441; Ⓟ 94; Ⓒ 85

G

Gackle; Inc. Place; LOGAN; **215** F-9; elev. 2,100ft./640m.; 🅿; **z** 58442; Ⓟ 450; Ⓒ 335
Galchutt; RMC Place; RICHLAND; **215** G-13; elev. 950ft./290m.; 🅿; **z** 58075; ● 65
Galesburg; Inc. Place; TRAILL; **215** E-12; elev. 1,080ft./329m.; 🅿; **z** 58035; Ⓟ 161; Ⓒ 157
Gardar; RMC Place; PEMBINA; **215** B-11; elev. 1,165ft./355m.; 🅿; **z** 58227; ● 30
Gardena; Inc. Place; BOTTINEAU; **215** B-7; elev. 1,462ft./446m.; mail Kramer **z** 58748; Ⓟ 41; Ⓒ 38
Gardner; Inc. Place; CASS; **215** E-13; elev. 887ft./270m.; 🅿; **z** 58036; Ⓟ 85; Ⓒ 80
Garrison; Inc. Place; MCLEAN; **215** D-6; elev. 1,920ft./585m.; 🅿 🅷; **z** 58540; Ⓟ 1,530; Ⓒ 1,318
Garske; RMC Place; RAMSEY; **215** B-10; mail Webster **z** 58382; ● 30
Gascoyne; Inc. Place; BOWMAN; **215** G-3; elev. 2,755ft./840m.; 🅿; **z** 58653; Ⓟ 22; Ⓒ 23
Geneseo; RMC Place; SARGENT; **215** H-12; elev. 1,162ft./354m.; 🅿; **z** 58053; ● 60
Gilby; Inc. Place; GRAND FORKS; **215** C-12; elev. 875ft./267m.; 🅿; **z** 58235; Ⓟ 262; Ⓒ 243
Gladstone; Inc. Place; STARK; **215** F-4; elev. 2,354ft./717m.; 🅿; **z** 58630; Ⓟ 224; Ⓒ 248
Glasser; RMC Place; BURLEIGH; ***215** F-7; elev. 1,800ft./549m.; mail Bismarck **z** 58504; rural
Glasston; RMC Place; PEMBINA; **215** B-12; elev. 835ft./255m.; 🅿; **z** 58236; ● 30
Glenburn; Inc. Place; RENVILLE; **215** B-6; elev. 1,565ft./477m.; 🅿; **z** 58740; Ⓟ 439; Ⓒ 374
Glenfield; Inc. Place; FOSTER; **215** E-10; elev. 1,502ft./458m.; 🅿; **z** 58443; Ⓟ 118; Ⓒ 134
Glen Ullin; Inc. Place; MORTON; **215** F-5; elev. 2,072ft./632m.; 🅿; **z** 58631; Ⓟ 927; Ⓒ 865
Glenwood Estates; RMC Place; BURLEIGH; ***215** F-7; elev. 1,635ft./498m.; ★ **BIS**; mail Bismarck **z** 58504; ● 150
Glover; RMC Place; DICKEY; ***215** G-11; elev. 1,373ft./418m.; mail Oakes **z** 58474
Golden Valley; Inc. Place; MERCER; **215** E-5; elev. 1,946ft./593m.; 🅿; **z** 58541; Ⓟ 239; Ⓒ 183
GOLDEN VALLEY; **215** E-2; Ⓟ 2,108; Ⓒ 1,924; ◆ 1,655
Golva; Inc. Place; GOLDEN VALLEY; **215** F-2; elev. 2,800ft./853m.; 🅿; **z** 58632; Ⓟ 101; Ⓒ 106
Goodrich; Inc. Place; SHERIDAN; **215** D-8; elev. 1,977ft./603m.; 🅿; **z** 58444; Ⓟ 192; Ⓒ 163
Gorham; RMC Place; BILLINGS; ***215** E-3; elev. 2,741ft./835m.; 🅿; **z** 58627; rural
Grace City; Inc. Place; FOSTER; **215** D-10; elev. 1,510ft./460m.; 🅿; **z** 58445; Ⓟ 108; Ⓒ 71
Grafton; Inc. Place; ⊡ WALSH; **215** B-12; elev. 826ft./252m.; 🅿 🅷; **z** 58237; Ⓟ 4,840; Ⓒ 4,516
Grandberg; RMC Place; CASS; ***215** F-13; elev. 909ft./277m.; mail Fargo **z** 58104; ● 50
Grand Forks; Inc. Place; ⊡ GRAND FORKS; **215** C-13; elev. 834ft./254m.; 🅿 🅷 🅲 12,834 ■; ★ **GDFK**; **z** 58201-08; Ⓟ 49,425; Ⓒ 49,321; Ⓡ 49,366; ◆ 53,861
GRAND FORKS; **215** D-12; Ⓟ 70,683; Ⓒ 66,109; ◆ 69,413
Grand Forks AFB; CDP-Census Area Only; GRAND FORKS; ***215** C-12; 🅿; **z** 58204-05; Ⓟ 9,343; Ⓒ 4,832
Grandin; Inc. Place; CASS; **215** E-13; elev. 892ft./272m.; 🅿; **z** 58038; Ⓟ 213; Ⓒ 181
Grand Prairie Estates; RMC Place; BURLEIGH; ***215** F-7; elev. 1,800ft./549m.; ★ **BIS**; mail Bismarck **z** 58503; ● 80
Grand Rapids; RMC Place; LAMOURE; **215** G-11; elev. 1,317ft./401m.; 🅿; **z** 58458; ● 25
Grandview; RMC Place; WILLIAMS; ***215** C-2; elev. 1,900ft./579m.; mail Williston **z** 58801; rural
Grano; Inc. Place; RENVILLE; **215** B-6; elev. 1,731ft./528m.; mail Lansford **z** 58750; Ⓟ 9; Ⓒ 9
GRANT; **215** G-5; Ⓟ 3,549; Ⓒ 2,841; ◆ 2,336
Granville; Inc. Place; MCHENRY; **215** C-7; elev. 1,515ft./462m.; 🅿; **z** 58741; Ⓟ 236; Ⓒ 286
Grassna; RMC Place; EMMONS; ***215** H-8; mail Strasburg **z** 58573; rural
Grassy Butte; RMC Place; MCKENZIE; **215** E-3; elev. 2,659ft./810m.; 🅿; **z** 58634; ● 50
Great Bend; Inc. Place; RICHLAND; **215** G-13; elev. 975ft./297m.; 🅿; **z** 58075; Ⓟ 108; Ⓒ 118
Green Acres Estates; RMC Place; BURLEIGH; ***215** F-7; elev. 1,930ft./588m.; ★ **BIS**; mail Bismarck **z** 58503; ● 90
Greene; RMC Place; RENVILLE; ***215** B-5; mail Tolley **z** 58787
Greenvale; RMC Place; STARK; ***215** F-4; elev. 2,449ft./746m.; mail Dickinson **z** 58601; ● 65
Grenora; Inc. Place; WILLIAMS; **215** B-2; elev. 2,105ft./642m.; 🅿; **z** 58845; Ⓟ 261; Ⓒ 202
GRIGGS; **215** D-11; Ⓟ 3,303; Ⓒ 2,754; ◆ 2,339
Guelph; RMC Place; DICKEY; **215** H-11; elev. 1,367ft./417m.; 🅿; **z** 58474; ● 25
Guthrie; RMC Place; MCHENRY; ***215** C-7; mail Drake **z** 58736
Gwinner; Inc. Place; SARGENT; **215** G-12; elev. 1,263ft./385m.; 🅿; **z** 58040; Ⓟ 585; Ⓒ 717

H

Hague; Inc. Place; EMMONS; **215** H-8; elev. 1,900ft./579m.; 🅿; **z** 58542; Ⓟ 109; Ⓒ 91
Halliday; Inc. Place; DUNN; **215** E-4; elev. 2,044ft./623m.; 🅿; **z** 58636; Ⓟ 288; Ⓒ 227
Hallson; RMC Place; PEMBINA; ***215** A-11; mail Cavalier **z** 58220; rural
Hamar; RMC Place; EDDY; **215** D-10; elev. 1,475ft./450m.; 🅿; **z** 58380; ● 20
Hamberg; Inc. Place; WELLS; **215** D-9; elev. 1,547ft./472m.; 🅿; **z** 58341; Ⓟ 19; Ⓒ 28
Hamilton; Inc. Place; PEMBINA; **215** A-12; elev. 825ft./251m.; 🅿; **z** 58238; Ⓟ 74; Ⓒ 73
Hamlet; RMC Place; WILLIAMS; ***215** B-3; elev. 2,276ft./694m.; 🅿; **z** 58795
Hampden; Inc. Place; RAMSEY; **215** B-10; elev. 1,565ft./477m.; 🅿; **z** 58338; Ⓟ 89; Ⓒ 60
Hankinson; Inc. Place; RICHLAND; **215** H-13; elev. 1,067ft./325m.; 🅿; **z** 58041; Ⓟ 1,038; Ⓒ 1,058
Hanks; RMC Place; WILLIAMS; **215** B-2; elev. 2,114ft./644m.; mail Zahl **z** 58856; ● 10
Hanks Corner; RMC Place; CAVALIER; ***215** A-11; elev. 1,250ft./381m.; mail Cavalier **z** 58220; rural
Hannaford; Inc. Place; GRIGGS; **215** E-11; elev. 1,414ft./431m.; 🅿; **z** 58448; Ⓟ 204; Ⓒ 181
Hannah; Inc. Place; CAVALIER; **215** A-10; elev. 1,565ft./477m.; 🅿; **z** 58239; Ⓟ 49; Ⓒ 20
Hannover; RMC Place; OLIVER; **215** E-6; elev. 2,144ft./653m.; 🅿; **z** 58563; ● 30
Hansboro; Inc. Place; TOWNER; **215** A-9; elev. 1,606ft./490m.; 🅿; **z** 58339; Ⓟ 20; Ⓒ 8
Happy Valley; RMC Place; WARD; ***215** C-6; elev. 1,575ft./480m.; mail Minot **z** 58701; ● 50
Harlow; RMC Place; BENSON; **215** C-9; elev. 1,640ft./500m.; 🅿; **z** 58346; ● 50
Hartland; RMC Place; WARD; ***215** B-5; elev. 2,073ft./632m.; mail Carpio **z** 58725
Harvey; Inc. Place; WELLS; **215** D-8; elev. 1,600ft./488m.; 🅿 🅷; **z** 58341; Ⓟ 2,263; Ⓒ 1,989
Harwood; Inc. Place; CASS; **215** F-13; elev. 889ft./271m.; 🅿; ★ **FAR-**; **z** 58042; Ⓟ 590; Ⓒ 607
Hastings; RMC Place; BARNES; **215** F-11; elev. 1,456ft./444m.; 🅿; **z** 58049; ● 40
Hatton; Inc. Place; TRAILL; **215** D-12; elev. 1,081ft./329m.; 🅿; **z** 58240; Ⓟ 800; Ⓒ 707
Havana; Inc. Place; SARGENT; **215** H-12; elev. 1,294ft./394m.; 🅿; **z** 58043; Ⓟ 124; Ⓒ 94
Havelock; RMC Place; HETTINGER; ***215** G-4; elev. 2,566ft./782m.; mail New England **z** 58647
Hay Creek; RMC Place; BURLEIGH; ***215** F-7; elev. 1,750ft./533m.; ★ **BIS**; mail Bismarck **z** 58503; ● 100
Hay Creek Pines; RMC Place; BURLEIGH; ***215** F-7; elev. 1,900ft./579m.; mail Bismarck **z** 58503; ● 25
Haynes; Inc. Place; ADAMS; **215** H-4; elev. 2,540ft./774m.; 🅿; **z** 58639; Ⓟ 37; Ⓒ 19
Hazelton; Inc. Place; EMMONS; **215** G-8; elev. 1,978ft./603m.; 🅿; **z** 58544; Ⓟ 240; Ⓒ 237
Hazen; Inc. Place; MERCER; **215** E-5; elev. 1,743ft./531m.; 🅿 🅷; **z** 58545; Ⓟ 2,818; Ⓒ 2,457
Heaton; RMC Place; WELLS; **215** D-9; elev. 1,705ft./520m.; 🅿; **z** 58418; ● 30
Hebron; Inc. Place; MORTON; **215** F-5; elev. 2,167ft./661m.; 🅿; **z** 58638; Ⓟ 888; Ⓒ 803
Heil; RMC Place; GRANT; **215** G-5; elev. 2,300ft./701m.; 🅿; **z** 58533; ● 50
Heimdal; RMC Place; WELLS; **215** D-9; elev. 1,588ft./484m.; 🅿; **z** 58341; ● 90
Hensel (Canton City); Inc. Place; PEMBINA; **215** B-12; elev. 923ft./281m.; 🅿; **z** 58241; Ⓟ 64; Ⓒ 42
Hensler; RMC Place; OLIVER; **215** E-6; elev. 1,710ft./521m.; 🅿; **z** 58530; ● 30
Heritage Hills Estates; RMC Place; CASS; ***215** F-13; elev. 900ft./274m.; mail Fargo **z** 58104; ● 45
Hesper; RMC Place; BENSON; ***215** C-9; mail Maddock **z** 58348
Hettinger; Inc. Place; ⊡ ADAMS; **215** H-4; elev. 2,668ft./813m.; 🅿 🅷; **z** 58639; Ⓟ 1,574; Ⓒ 1,307
HETTINGER; **215** G-4; Ⓟ 3,445; Ⓒ 2,715; ◆ 2,270
Hickson; RMC Place; CASS; **215** F-13; elev. 918ft./280m.; 🅿; **z** 58047; ● 50
Hi-Land Heights; RMC Place; WILLIAMS; ***215** C-2; elev. 2,000ft./610m.; mail Williston **z** 58801; ● 130
Hillcrest Acres; RMC Place; BURLEIGH; ***215** F-7; elev. 1,680ft./512m.; mail Bismarck **z** 58501; pop. incl. with Bismarck (Inc. Place)
Hillsboro; Inc. Place; ⊡ TRAILL; **215** E-13; elev. 908ft./277m.; 🅿 🅷; **z** 58045; Ⓟ 1,488; Ⓒ 1,563
Holiday Colony; RMC Place; WARD; ***215** C-6; elev. 1,621ft./494m.; mail Minot **z** 58701; ● 150
Holmen's; RMC Place; CASS; ***215** F-13; ★ **FAR-**; mail Fargo **z** 58104; ● 50
Holmes; RMC Place; GRAND FORKS; ***215** D-12; mail Reynolds **z** 58275; rural
Home on the Range for Boys; RMC Place; GOLDEN VALLEY; ***215** F-2; elev. 2,900ft./884m.; mail Sentinel Butte **z** 58654; ● 100
Honeyford; RMC Place; GRAND FORKS; ***215** C-12; elev. 895ft./273m.; 🅿; **z** 58235; rural
Hoople; Inc. Place; WALSH; **215** B-12; elev. 890ft./271m.; 🅿; **z** 58243; Ⓟ 310; Ⓒ 292
Hope; Inc. Place; STEELE; **215** E-12; elev. 1,240ft./378m.; 🅿; **z** 58046; Ⓟ 281; Ⓒ 303
Horace; Inc. Place; CASS; **215** F-13; elev. 910ft./277m.; 🅿; **z** 58047; Ⓟ 662; Ⓒ 915
Horseshoe Bend; RMC Place; CASS; ***215** F-13; elev. 910ft./277m.; mail Fargo **z** 58104; rural
Hove Mobile Park; RMC Place; CAVALIER; ***215** B-11; mail Fairdale **z** 58229; disincorporated July 19, 2002; Ⓒ 2
Huff; RMC Place; MORTON; **215** F-7; elev. 1,655ft./504m.; 🅿; **z** 58554; ● 30
Hull; RMC Place; EMMONS; ***215** H-8; mail Hague **z** 58542
Hunter; Inc. Place; CASS; **215** E-12; elev. 978ft./298m.; 🅿; **z** 58048; Ⓟ 341; Ⓒ 326
Hurdsfield; Inc. Place; WELLS; **215** E-8; elev. 1,906ft./581m.; 🅿; **z** 58451; Ⓟ 92; Ⓒ 91
Hutterite Colony; RMC Place; LAMOURE; ***215** G-11; elev. 1,425ft./434m.; mail Lamoure **z** 58458; ● 40

I

Imperial Manor; RMC Place; WARD; ***215** C-6; elev. 1,600ft./488m.; mail Minot **z** 58701; ● 85
Imperial Valley; RMC Place; BURLEIGH; ***215** F-7; elev. 1,635ft./498m.; ★ **BIS**; mail Bismarck **z** 58504; ● 150
Inkster; Inc. Place; GRAND FORKS; **215** C-12; elev. 1,029ft./314m.; 🅿; **z** 58244; Ⓟ 95; Ⓒ 102

J

Jamestown; Inc. Place; ⊡ STUTSMAN; **215** F-10; elev. 1,413ft./431m.; 🅿 🅷 🅲 996 ■; **z** 58401-02, **z** 58405; Ⓟ 15,571; Ⓒ 15,527; ◆ 14,019
Jessie; RMC Place; GRIGGS; **215** D-11; elev. 1,470ft./448m.; 🅿; **z** 58452; ● 50
Jewett Landing; RMC Place; BARNES; ***215** E-11; elev. 1,273ft./388m.; mail Valley City **z** 58072; summer pop. 100
Jiran; RMC Place; BURLEIGH; ***215** F-7; elev. 1,635ft./498m.; ★ **BIS**; mail Bismarck **z** 58504; ● 20
Johnsons Corner; RMC Place; MCKENZIE; ***215** D-3; elev. 2,344ft./714m.; mail Keene **z** 58847; rural
Johnstown; RMC Place; GRAND FORKS; **215** C-12; elev. 875ft./267m.; 🅿; **z** 58235; ● 40
Joliette; RMC Place; PEMBINA; **215** A-12; elev. 797ft./243m.; 🅿; **z** 58271; ● 25
Juanita; RMC Place; FOSTER; ***215** D-10; elev. 1,500ft./457m.; 🅿; **z** 58443
Jud; Inc. Place; LAMOURE; **215** G-10; elev. 1,738ft./530m.; 🅿; **z** 58454; Ⓟ 84; Ⓒ 76
Judson; RMC Place; MORTON; **215** F-6; elev. 1,951ft./595m.; 🅿; **z** 58563; ● 50

K

Karlsruhe; Inc. Place; MCHENRY; **215** C-7; elev. 1,540ft./469m.; 🅿; **z** 58744; Ⓟ 143; Ⓒ 119
Kathryn; Inc. Place; BARNES; **215** F-11; elev. 1,200ft./366m.; 🅿; **z** 58049; Ⓟ 72; Ⓒ 63
Keene; RMC Place; MCKENZIE; **215** C-3; elev. 2,340ft./713m.; 🅿; **z** 58847; ● 60
Kelso; RMC Place; TRAILL; ***215** E-13; elev. 902ft./275m.; 🅿; **z** 58045
Kelvin; RMC Place; ROLETTE; ***215** A-8; mail Dunseith **z** 58329; rural
Kempton; RMC Place; GRAND FORKS; **215** D-12; elev. 1,124ft./343m.; 🅿; **z** 58267; ● 25
Kenaston; RMC Place; WARD; ***215** B-5; elev. 2,051ft./625m.; mail Kenmare **z** 58746
Kenmare; Inc. Place; WARD; **215** B-5; elev. 1,850ft./564m.; 🅿 🅷; **z** 58746; Ⓟ 1,214; Ⓒ 1,081
Kensal; Inc. Place; STUTSMAN; **215** E-10; elev. 1,540ft./469m.; 🅿; **z** 58455; Ⓟ 191; Ⓒ 161
KIDDER; **215** E-8; Ⓟ 3,332; Ⓒ 2,753; ◆ 2,188
Kief; Inc. Place; MCHENRY; **215** D-7; elev. 1,670ft./509m.; 🅿; **z** 58723; Ⓟ 24; Ⓒ 13
Killdeer; Inc. Place; DUNN; **215** E-4; elev. 2,242ft./683m.; 🅿; **z** 58640; Ⓟ 722; Ⓒ 713
Kindred; Inc. Place; CASS; **215** F-13; elev. 940ft./287m.; 🅿; **z** 58051; Ⓟ 569; Ⓒ 614
Kings Court; RMC Place; WARD; ***215** C-6; elev. 1,570ft./479m.; mail Minot **z** 58701; ● 70
Kintyre; RMC Place; EMMONS; **215** G-8; elev. 1,900ft./579m.; 🅿; **z** 58549; ● 50
Kloten; RMC Place; NELSON; **215** D-11; elev. 1,510ft./460m.; 🅿; **z** 58254; ● 40
KMK Estates; RMC Place; BURLEIGH; ***215** F-7; elev. 1,920ft./585m.; ★ **BIS**; mail Bismarck **z** 58503; ● 70
Knox; Inc. Place; BENSON; **215** B-8; elev. 1,604ft./489m.; 🅿; **z** 58343; Ⓟ 45; Ⓒ 59
Kongsberg; RMC Place; MCHENRY; ***215** D-7; mail Voltaire **z** 58792; rural
Kralicek; RMC Place; STARK; ***215** F-4; elev. 2,550ft./777m.; mail Dickinson **z** 58601; ● 110
Kramer; Inc. Place; BOTTINEAU; **215** B-7; elev. 1,458ft./444m.; 🅿; **z** 58748; Ⓟ 51; Ⓒ 44
Kubishta; RMC Place; STARK; ***215** F-4; elev. 2,458ft./749m.; mail Dickinson **z** 58601; pop. incl. with Dickinson (Inc. Place)
Kulm; Inc. Place; LAMOURE; **215** G-10; elev. 2,000ft./610m.; 🅿; **z** 58456; Ⓟ 514; Ⓒ 422

L

Lake Jessie; RMC Place; WILLIAMS; ***215** C-3; elev. 1,854ft./565m.; mail Williston **z** 58801; ● 30
Lake Metigoshe; RMC Place; BOTTINEAU; ***215** A-7; mail Bottineau **z** 58318; summer pop. 300; rural
Lake Park; RMC Place; WILLIAMS; ***215** C-2; elev. 2,000ft./610m.; mail Williston **z** 58801; ● 35
Lake Shure Estates; RMC Place; CASS; ***215** F-13; ★ **FAR-**; mail Fargo **z** 58102; ● 60
Lake Side Estate; RMC Place; STUTSMAN; ***215** F-10; elev. 1,500ft./457m.; mail Jamestown **z** 58401; ● 150
Lake Traverse Reservation; Indian Reservation; SARGENT, RICHLAND; Reservation extends into SD; Ⓒ 191
Lake Tschida; RMC Place; GRANT; ***215** F-5; elev. 2,137ft./651m.; mail Elgin **z** 58533; summer pop. 300
Lake Williams; RMC Place; KIDDER; **215** E-9; elev. 1,791ft./546m.; 🅿; **z** 58478; ● 25
Lakewood Park; RMC Place; RAMSEY; **215** C-10; elev. 1,452ft./443m.; mail Devils Lake **z** 58301; summer pop. 500; ● 220
Lakota; Inc. Place; ⊡ NELSON; **215** C-11; elev. 1,518ft./463m.; 🅿; **z** 58344; Ⓟ 898; Ⓒ 781
Lamoine Addition; RMC Place; GRAND FORKS; ***215** C-12; elev. 826ft./252m.; mail Grand Forks **z** 58201; ● 110
Lamoure; Inc. Place; ⊡ LAMOURE; **215** G-11; elev. 1,310ft./399m.; 🅿; **z** 58415, **z** 58458 & mail Dickey **z** 58431; Ⓟ 970; Ⓒ 944
LAMOURE; **215** G-10; Ⓟ 5,383; Ⓒ 4,701; ◆ 3,935
Landa; Inc. Place; BOTTINEAU; **215** A-7; elev. 1,480ft./451m.; 🅿; **z** 58783; Ⓟ 38; Ⓒ 28
Langdon; Inc. Place; ⊡ CAVALIER; **215** A-10; elev. 1,617ft./493m.; 🅿 🅷; **z** 58249; Ⓟ 2,241; Ⓒ 2,101
Lankin; Inc. Place; WALSH; **215** C-11; elev. 1,349ft./411m.; 🅿; **z** 58250; Ⓟ 152; Ⓒ 131
Lansford; Inc. Place; BOTTINEAU; **215** B-6; elev. 1,610ft./491m.; 🅿; **z** 58750; Ⓟ 249; Ⓒ 253
Larimore; Inc. Place; GRAND FORKS; **215** C-12; elev. 1,136ft./346m.; 🅿; **z** 58251; Ⓟ 1,464; Ⓒ 1,433
Lark; RMC Place; GRANT; ***215** G-6; elev. 2,100ft./640m.; 🅿; **z** 58535; rural
Larson; RMC Place; BURKE; **215** A-4; elev. 1,925ft./587m.; 🅿; **z** 58727; disincorporated June 30, 2003; Ⓟ 26; Ⓒ 17
Lawton; Inc. Place; RAMSEY; **215** C-10; elev. 1,517ft./462m.; 🅿; **z** 58345; Ⓟ 63; Ⓒ 42
Leal; Inc. Place; BARNES; **215** E-11; elev. 1,465ft./447m.; 🅿; **z** 58479; Ⓟ 35; Ⓒ 36
Leeds; Inc. Place; BENSON; **215** C-9; elev. 1,514ft./461m.; 🅿; **z** 58346; Ⓟ 542; Ⓒ 464
Lefor (Saint Elizabeth); RMC Place; STARK; **215** F-4; elev. 2,592ft./790m.; 🅿; **z** 58641; ● 50
Lehigh; RMC Place; STARK; ***215** F-4; mail Dickinson **z** 58601; ● 40
Lehr (Venturia); Inc. Place; MCINTOSH, LOGAN; **215** G-9; elev. 2,000ft./610m.; 🅿; **z** 58460 & mail Ashley **z** 58413; Ⓟ 191; Ⓒ 114
Leisure World Estates; RMC Place; BURLEIGH; ***215** F-7; elev. 1,700ft./518m.; mail Bismarck **z** 58504; ● 85
Leith; Inc. Place; GRANT; **215** G-5; elev. 2,340ft./713m.; 🅿; **z** 58529; Ⓟ 43; Ⓒ 28
Leonard; Inc. Place; CASS; **215** F-12; elev. 1,050ft./320m.; 🅿; **z** 58052; Ⓟ 310; Ⓒ 255
Leroy; RMC Place; PEMBINA; **215** A-11; elev. 892ft./272m.; 🅿; **z** 58282; ● 50
Lewis and Clark Estates; RMC Place; BURLEIGH; ***215** F-7; elev. 1,750ft./533m.; ★ **BIS**; mail Bismarck **z** 58504; ● 30
Leyden; RMC Place; PEMBINA; ***215** A-11; mail Walhalla **z** 58282; rural
Lidgerwood; Inc. Place; RICHLAND; **215** H-12; elev. 1,114ft./340m.; 🅿; **z** 58053; Ⓟ 799; Ⓒ 738; Ⓡ 781
Lignite; Inc. Place; BURKE; **215** A-4; elev. 1,975ft./602m.; 🅿; **z** 58752; Ⓟ 242; Ⓒ 174
Lincoln; Inc. Place; BURLEIGH; **215** F-7; elev. 1,700ft./518m.; 🅿; ★ **BIS**; **z** 58504; Ⓟ 1,132; Ⓒ 1,730
Lincoln Valley; RMC Place; SHERIDAN; ***215** D-8; elev. 1,788ft./545m.; mail Denhoff **z** 58430; rural
Linha Addition; RMC Place; WARD; ***215** C-6; elev. 1,725ft./526m.; mail Minot **z** 58703; pop. incl. with Minot (Inc. Place)
Linton; Inc. Place; ⊡ EMMONS; **215** G-8; elev. 1,708ft./521m.; 🅿 🅷; **z** 58552; Ⓟ 1,410; Ⓒ 1,321
Lisbon; Inc. Place; ⊡ RANSOM; **215** G-12; elev. 1,091ft./333m.; 🅿 🅷; **z** 58054; Ⓟ 2,177; Ⓒ 2,292
Litchville; Inc. Place; BARNES; **215** F-11; elev. 1,467ft./447m.; 🅿; **z** 58461; Ⓟ 205; Ⓒ 191
Little Ponderosa; RMC Place; WARD; ***215** C-6; elev. 1,675ft./511m.; mail Minot **z** 58703; rural
Livona; RMC Place; EMMONS; ***215** G-7; elev. 1,669ft./509m.; mail Bismarck **z** 58504, Hazelton **z** 58544; rural
Logan; RMC Place; WARD; **215** C-6; mail Minot **z** 58701; ● 70
LOGAN; **215** G-9; Ⓟ 2,847; Ⓒ 2,308; ◆ 1,939
Loma; Inc. Place; CAVALIER; **215** B-10; elev. 1,568ft./478m.; 🅿; **z** 58311; Ⓟ 27; Ⓒ 21
Lone Tree; RMC Place; WARD; ***215** C-5; mail Berthold **z** 58718
Loraine; Inc. Place; RENVILLE; **215** A-6; elev. 1,625ft./495m.; 🅿; **z** 58761; Ⓟ 15; Ⓒ 19
Lostwood; RMC Place; MOUNTRAIL; ***215** B-4; 🅿; **z** 58784; rural
Lucca; RMC Place; BARNES; ***215** F-12; mail Enderlin **z** 58027; rural
Ludden; Inc. Place; DICKEY; **215** H-11; elev. 1,301ft./397m.; 🅿; **z** 58474; Ⓟ 41; Ⓒ 29
Lunds Valley; RMC Place; MOUNTRAIL; ***215** B-4; mail Stanley **z** 58784; rural
Luverne; Inc. Place; STEELE; **215** E-11; elev. 1,430ft./436m.; 🅿; **z** 58056; Ⓟ 41; Ⓒ 44
Lynchburg; RMC Place; CASS; **215** F-12; elev. 953ft./290m.; mail Mapleton **z** 58059; ● 30
Lyons; RMC Place; MORTON; ***215** F-6; mail Mandan **z** 58554; rural

M

Maddock; Inc. Place; BENSON; **215** C-9; elev. 1,580ft./482m.; 🅿; **z** 58348; Ⓟ 559; Ⓒ 498
Maida; RMC Place; CAVALIER; **215** A-10; elev. 1,555ft./474m.; 🅿; **z** 58255; ● 35
Makoti; Inc. Place; WARD; **215** C-5; elev. 2,100ft./640m.; 🅿; **z** 58756; Ⓟ 145; Ⓒ 145
Mandan; Inc. Place; ⊡ MORTON; **215** F-7; elev. 1,651ft./503m.; 🅿 🅷; ★ **BIS**; **z** 58554; Ⓟ 15,177; Ⓒ 16,718
Mandaree; CDP; MCKENZIE; **215** D-4; located on Fort Berthold Ind. Res.; elev. 2,180ft./664m.; 🅿; **z** 58757; Ⓟ 367; Ⓒ 558
Manfred; RMC Place; WELLS; **215** D-8; elev. 1,605ft./489m.; 🅿; **z** 58341; ● 35
Manitou; RMC Place; MOUNTRAIL; ***215** B-4; mail Ross **z** 58776; rural
Manning; RMC Place; ⊡ DUNN; **215** E-4; elev. 2,219ft./676m.; 🅿; **z** 58642; ● 70
Mantador; Inc. Place; RICHLAND; **215** G-13; elev. 1,027ft./313m.; 🅿; **z** 58058; Ⓟ 77; Ⓒ 71
Manvel; Inc. Place; GRAND FORKS; **215** C-12; elev. 826ft./252m.; 🅿; **z** 58256; Ⓟ 333; Ⓒ 370
Mapes; RMC Place; NELSON; **215** C-11; elev. 1,522ft./464m.; 🅿; **z** 58344; ● 20
Mapleton; Inc. Place; CASS; **215** F-13; elev. 908ft./277m.; 🅿; **z** 58059; Ⓟ 682; Ⓒ 606
Marion; Inc. Place; LAMOURE; **215** F-11; elev. 1,460ft./445m.; 🅿; **z** 58466; Ⓟ 169; Ⓒ 146
Marmarth; Inc. Place; SLOPE; **215** G-2; elev. 2,709ft./826m.; 🅿; **z** 58643; Ⓟ 144; Ⓒ 140
Marshall; RMC Place; DUNN; **215** E-4; elev. 1,985ft./605m.; 🅿; **z** 58644; ● 10
Martin; Inc. Place; SHERIDAN; **215** D-8; elev. 1,630ft./497m.; 🅿; **z** 58758; Ⓟ 117; Ⓒ 96
Max; Inc. Place; MCLEAN; **215** D-6; elev. 2,100ft./640m.; 🅿; **z** 58759; Ⓟ 301; Ⓒ 278
Maxbass; Inc. Place; BOTTINEAU; **215** B-6; elev. 1,505ft./459m.; 🅿; **z** 58760; Ⓟ 123; Ⓒ 91
Mayville; Inc. Place; TRAILL; **215** D-12; elev. 976ft./297m.; 🅿 🅷 🅲 832; **z** 58257; Ⓟ 2,092; Ⓒ 1,953
Maza; RMC Place; TOWNER; **215** B-9; elev. 1,463ft./446m.; 🅿; **z** 58324; disincorporated July 1, 2002; Ⓟ 12; Ⓒ 5
McCanna; RMC Place; GRAND FORKS; **215** C-12; elev. 1,141ft./348m.; 🅿; **z** 58251; ● 35
Mcclusky; Inc. Place; ⊡ SHERIDAN; **215** D-7; elev. 1,925ft./587m.; 🅿; **z** 58463; Ⓟ 492; Ⓒ 415
McGregor; RMC Place; WILLIAMS; **215** B-4; elev. 2,222ft./677m.; 🅿; **z** 58755; ● 80
McHenry; Inc. Place; FOSTER; **215** D-10; elev. 1,507ft./459m.; 🅿; **z** 58464; Ⓟ 85; Ⓒ 71
MCHENRY; **215** C-7; Ⓟ 6,528; Ⓒ 5,987; ◆ 4,879
MCINTOSH; **215** H-9; Ⓟ 4,021; Ⓒ 3,390; ◆ 2,441
McKenzie; RMC Place; BURLEIGH; **215** F-7; elev. 1,730ft./527m.; 🅿; **z** 58572; ● 50
MCKENZIE; **215** D-2; Ⓟ 6,383; Ⓒ 5,737; ◆ 5,658
MCLEAN; **215** D-6; Ⓟ 10,457; Ⓒ 9,311; ◆ 8,209
McLeod; RMC Place; RANSOM; **215** G-12; elev. 1,076ft./328m.; 🅿; **z** 58057; ● 50
McVille; Inc. Place; NELSON; **215** D-11; elev. 1,470ft./448m.; 🅿 🅷; **z** 58254; Ⓟ 559; Ⓒ 470
Meadowbrook; RMC Place; WARD; ***215** C-6; elev. 1,541ft./470m.; mail Minot **z** 58701; ● 80
Meadow View; RMC Place; BURLEIGH; ***215** F-7; elev. 1,632ft./497m.; ★ **BIS**; mail Bismarck **z** 58504; pop. incl. with Bismarck (Inc. Place)
Medina; Inc. Place; STUTSMAN; **215** F-9; elev. 1,810ft./552m.; 🅿; **z** 58467; Ⓟ 387; Ⓒ 335
Medora; Inc. Place; ⊡ BILLINGS; **215** F-2; elev. 2,271ft./692m.; 🅿; **z** 58645; Ⓟ 101; Ⓒ 100
Mee's Country Home Estates; RMC Place; BURLEIGH; ***215** F-7; elev. 1,700ft./518m.; mail Menoken **z** 58558; ● 80
Mekinock; RMC Place; GRAND FORKS; **215** C-12; elev. 863ft./263m.; 🅿; **z** 58258; ● 150
Melville; RMC Place; FOSTER; ***215** E-9; elev. 1,603ft./489m.; 🅿; **z** 58421
Menoken (Burleigh); RMC Place; BURLEIGH; **215** F-7; elev. 1,723ft./525m.; 🅿; **z** 58558; ● 30
Mercer; Inc. Place; MCLEAN; **215** D-7; elev. 1,926ft./587m.; 🅿; **z** 58559; Ⓟ 104; Ⓒ 86
MERCER; **215** E-5; Ⓟ 9,808; Ⓒ 8,644; ◆ 7,820
Merricourt; RMC Place; DICKEY; ***215** G-10; elev. 1,644ft./501m.; 🅿; **z** 58433; ● 9
Michigan (Michigan City); Inc. Place; NELSON; **215** C-11; elev. 1,516ft./462m.; 🅿; **z** 58259; Ⓟ 413; Ⓒ 345
Michigan City; NELSON; see Michigan (Inc. Place)
Midway Estates; RMC Place; STUTSMAN; ***215** F-10; mail Jamestown **z** 58401; ● 120
Millarton; RMC Place; STUTSMAN; ***215** F-10; elev. 1,506ft./459m.; 🅿; **z** 58472
Mills; RMC Place; BURLEIGH; ***215** F-7; elev. 1,630ft./497m.; ★ **BIS**; mail Bismarck **z** 58504
Milnor; Inc. Place; SARGENT; **215** G-12; elev. 1,095ft./334m.; 🅿; **z** 58060; Ⓟ 651; Ⓒ 711
Milton; Inc. Place; CAVALIER; **215** B-11; elev. 1,586ft./483m.; 🅿; **z** 58260; Ⓟ 133; Ⓒ 85
Minnewaukan; Inc. Place; ⊡ BENSON; **215** C-9; elev. 1,461ft./445m.; 🅿; **z** 58351; Ⓟ 401; Ⓒ 318
Minot; Inc. Place; ⊡ WARD; **215** C-6; elev. 1,580ft./482m.; 🅿 🅷 🅲 3,712 ■; **z** 58701-05, **z** 58707 & mail Norwich **z** 58768; Ⓟ 34,544; Ⓒ 36,567; ◆ 36,764
Minot AFB; CDP-Census Area Only; WARD; ***215** B-6; elev. 1,625ft./495m.; 🅿; **z** 58704-05; Ⓟ 9,095; Ⓒ 7,599
Minto; Inc. Place; WALSH; **215** C-12; elev. 820ft./250m.; 🅿; **z** 58261; Ⓟ 560; Ⓒ 657
Mirror Lake; RMC Place; ADAMS; ***215** H-4; mail Hettinger **z** 58639; summer pop. 300; rural
Missouri River Estates; RMC Place; BURLEIGH; ***215** F-7; elev. 1,630ft./497m.; ★ **BIS**; mail Bismarck **z** 58504; rural
Moffit (Moffitt); RMC Place; BURLEIGH; **215** F-8; elev. 1,750ft./533m.; 🅿; **z** 58560; ● 75
Moffitt; BURLEIGH; see Moffit (RMC Place)
Mohall; Inc. Place; ⊡ RENVILLE; **215** A-6; elev. 1,639ft./500m.; 🅿; **z** 58761; Ⓟ 931; Ⓒ 812
Monango; Inc. Place; DICKEY; **215** G-10; elev. 1,500ft./457m.; 🅿; **z** 58436; Ⓟ 53; Ⓒ 28
Montair; ROLETTE; see San Haven (RMC Place)
Montpelier; Inc. Place; STUTSMAN; **215** F-10; elev. 1,362ft./415m.; 🅿; **z** 58472; Ⓟ 82; Ⓒ 103
Mooreton; Inc. Place; RICHLAND; **215** G-13; elev. 970ft./296m.; 🅿; **z** 58061; Ⓟ 193; Ⓒ 204
MORTON; **215** F-6; Ⓟ 23,700; Ⓒ 25,303; ◆ 26,352
Mott; Inc. Place; ⊡ HETTINGER; **215** G-4; elev. 2,377ft./725m.; 🅿; **z** 58646; Ⓟ 1,019; Ⓒ 808
Mountain; Inc. Place; PEMBINA; **215** B-11; elev. 1,034ft./315m.; 🅿; **z** 58262; Ⓟ 134; Ⓒ 133
Mount Carmel; RMC Place; CAVALIER; ***215** A-10; mail Langdon **z** 58249
MOUNTRAIL; **215** C-4; Ⓟ 7,021; Ⓒ 6,631; ◆ 6,560
Mouse River Park; RMC Place; RENVILLE; ***215** A-5; elev. 1,600ft./488m.; mail Tolley **z** 58787; summer pop. 300
Mr. B's; RMC Place; BURLEIGH; ***215** F-7; elev. 1,750ft./533m.; ★ **BIS**; mail Bismarck **z** 58503; pop. incl. with Bismarck (Inc. Place)
Munich; Inc. Place; CAVALIER; **215** B-10; elev. 1,590ft./485m.; 🅿; **z** 58352; Ⓟ 310; Ⓒ 268
Murray; RMC Place; TRAILL; ***215** D-12; mail Mayville **z** 58257; rural
Mylo; Inc. Place; ROLETTE; **215** B-9; elev. 1,646ft./502m.; 🅿; **z** 58353; Ⓟ 20; Ⓒ 19

N

Nanson; RMC Place; ROLETTE; ***215** B-8; elev. 1,600ft./488m.; 🅿; **z** 58366; rural
Napoleon; Inc. Place; ⊡ LOGAN; **215** G-8; elev. 1,955ft./596m.; 🅿; **z** 58561; Ⓟ 930; Ⓒ 857
Nash; RMC Place; WALSH; **215** B-12; elev. 853ft./260m.; 🅿; **z** 58237; ● 70
Neche; Inc. Place; PEMBINA; **215** A-12; elev. 830ft./253m.; 🅿; **z** 58265; Ⓟ 434; Ⓒ 437
Nekoma; Inc. Place; CAVALIER; **215** B-10; elev. 1,630ft./497m.; 🅿; **z** 58355; Ⓟ 63; Ⓒ 51
NELSON; **215** C-11; Ⓟ 4,410; Ⓒ 3,715; ◆ 3,102
Newburg; Inc. Place; BOTTINEAU; **215** B-7; elev. 1,461ft./445m.; 🅿; **z** 58762; Ⓟ 104; Ⓒ 88
New England; Inc. Place; HETTINGER; **215** G-3; elev. 2,592ft./790m.; 🅿; **z** 58647; Ⓟ 663; Ⓒ 555
New Hradec; RMC Place; DUNN; **215** E-3; elev. 2,500ft./762m.; 🅿; **z** 58601; ● 130
New Leipzig; Inc. Place; GRANT; **215** G-5; elev. 2,320ft./707m.; 🅿; **z** 58562; Ⓟ 326; Ⓒ 274
Newman; RMC Place; CASS; ***215** E-13; mail Arthur **z** 58006; rural
New Rockford; Inc. Place; ⊡ EDDY; **215** D-9; elev. 1,535ft./468m.; 🅿; **z** 58356; Ⓟ 1,604; Ⓒ 1,463
New Salem; Inc. Place; MORTON; **215** F-6; elev. 2,161ft./659m.; 🅿; **z** 58563; Ⓟ 909; Ⓒ 938
New Town; Inc. Place; MOUNTRAIL; **215** C-4; located on Fort Berthold Ind. Res.; elev. 1,900ft./579m.; 🅿; **z** 58763; location of Indian Agency; Ⓟ 1,388; Ⓒ 1,367
Niagara; Inc. Place; GRAND FORKS; **215** C-11; elev. 1,450ft./442m.; 🅿; **z** 58266; Ⓟ 73; Ⓒ 57
Niobe; RMC Place; WARD; **215** B-5; mail Kenmare **z** 58746; ● 30
Nome; Inc. Place; BARNES; **215** F-11; elev. 1,330ft./405m.; 🅿; **z** 58062; Ⓟ 67; Ⓒ 70
Noonan; Inc. Place; DIVIDE; **215** A-3; elev. 1,965ft./599m.; 🅿; **z** 58765; Ⓟ 231; Ⓒ 154
Norma; RMC Place; RENVILLE; ***215** B-5; elev. 1,885ft./575m.; 🅿; **z** 58746
North Dakota State University; RMC Place; CASS; ★ **FAR-**; mail Fargo **z** 58105; pop. incl. with Fargo (Inc. Place)
North Forty Estates; RMC Place; BURLEIGH; ***215** F-7; elev. 1,907ft./581m.; mail Bismarck **z** 58503; ● 30
Northgate; RMC Place; BURKE; **215** A-5; elev. 1,854ft./565m.; 🅿; **z** 58737; ● 25
North Grand Forks; RMC Place; GRAND FORKS; ***215** C-12; elev. 832ft./254m.; ★ **GDFK**; mail Grand Forks **z** 58203; ● 35
North Lemmon; RMC Place; ADAMS; **215** H-5; mail Lemmon **z** 57638; ● 40
North River; Inc. Place; CASS; ***215** F-13; elev. 893ft./272m.; 🅿; ★ **FAR-**; **z** 58102; Ⓟ 68; Ⓒ 65
North Star Acres; RMC Place; BURLEIGH; ***215** F-7; elev. 1,846ft./563m.; ★ **BIS**; mail Bismarck **z** 58503; ● 30
Northwood; RMC Place; CASS; ***215** F-13; elev. 892ft./272m.; ★ **FAR-**; mail Fargo **z** 58102; ● 30
Northwood; Inc. Place; GRAND FORKS; **215** D-12; elev. 1,113ft./339m.; 🅿 🅷; **z** 58267; Ⓟ 1,166; Ⓒ 959
Northwood Estates; RMC Place; BURLEIGH; ***215** F-7; elev. 1,900ft./579m.; mail Bismarck **z** 58501; ● 35
Nortonville; RMC Place; LAMOURE; **215** G-10; elev. 1,500ft./457m.; 🅿; **z** 58454; ● 50
Norwich; RMC Place; MCHENRY; **215** C-7; elev. 1,545ft./471m.; 🅿; **z** 58768; ● 60

O

Oakes; Inc. Place; DICKEY; **215** G-11; elev. 1,313ft./400m.; 🅿 🅷; **z** 58474; Ⓟ 1,775; Ⓒ 1,979
Oak Ridge; RMC Place; WALSH; ***215** B-11; elev. 950ft./290m.; mail Park River **z** 58270; ● 30
Oakwood; RMC Place; WALSH; **215** B-12; mail Grafton **z** 58237; ● 80
Oberon; Inc. Place; BENSON; **215** C-9; elev. 1,562ft./476m.; 🅿; **z** 58357; Ⓟ 103; Ⓒ 81
Olga; RMC Place; CAVALIER; ***215** A-11; elev. 1,546ft./471m.; mail Langdon **z** 58249
OLIVER; **215** E-6; Ⓟ 2,381; Ⓒ 2,065; ◆ 1,650
Olmstead; TOWNER; see Egeland (Inc. Place)
Omemee; RMC Place; BOTTINEAU; ***215** B-7; elev. 1,505ft./459m.; mail Willow City **z** 58384; rural
Orchard Park; CASS; see Fradet (RMC Place)
Oriska; Inc. Place; BARNES; **215** F-11; elev. 1,265ft./386m.; 🅿; **z** 58063; Ⓟ 103; Ⓒ 128
Orr; RMC Place; GRAND FORKS; **215** C-12; elev. 1,100ft./335m.; 🅿; **z** 58244; ● 30
Orrin; RMC Place; PIERCE; **215** C-8; elev. 1,560ft./475m.; 🅿; **z** 58368; ● 50
Osnabrock; Inc. Place; CAVALIER; **215** B-11; elev. 1,609ft./490m.; 🅿; **z** 58269; Ⓟ 214; Ⓒ 174
Overly; Inc. Place; BOTTINEAU; **215** B-8; elev. 1,538ft./469m.; 🅿; **z** 58384; Ⓟ 25; Ⓒ 19
Oxbow; Inc. Place; CASS; ***215** F-13; 🅿; **z** 58047; Ⓟ 100; Ⓒ 248

P

Page; Inc. Place; CASS; **215** E-12; elev. 1,175ft./358m.; 🅿; **z** 58064; Ⓟ 266; Ⓒ 225
Painted Woods; RMC Place; WILLIAMS; ***215** C-2; mail Williston **z** 58801; rural
Palermo; Inc. Place; MOUNTRAIL; **215** B-5; elev. 2,201ft./671m.; 🅿; **z** 58769; Ⓟ 95; Ⓒ 77
Palm Beach; RMC Place; STARK; ***215** F-4; elev. 2,400ft./732m.; mail Dickinson **z** 58601; ● 130
Park Manor; RMC Place; GRAND FORKS; ***215** C-12; elev. 835ft./255m.; ★ **GDFK**; mail Grand Forks **z** 58201; pop. incl. with Grand Forks (Inc. Place)
Park River; Inc. Place; WALSH; **215** B-11; elev. 1,006ft./307m.; 🅿 🅷; **z** 58270; Ⓟ 1,725; Ⓒ 1,535
Parshall; Inc. Place; MOUNTRAIL; **215** C-5; located on Fort Berthold Ind. Res.; elev. 2,000ft./610m.; 🅿; **z** 58770; Ⓟ 943; Ⓒ 981
Patterson Lake; RMC Place; STARK; ***215** F-4; elev. 2,429ft./740m.; mail Dickinson **z** 58601; ● 100
Pekin; Inc. Place; NELSON; **215** D-11; elev. 1,468ft./447m.; 🅿; **z** 58361; Ⓟ 101; Ⓒ 80
Pembina; Inc. Place; PEMBINA; **215** A-12; elev. 792ft./241m.; 🅿; **z** 58271; Ⓟ 642; Ⓒ 642
PEMBINA; **215** B-11; Ⓟ 9,238; Ⓒ 8,585; ◆ 7,154
Penn; RMC Place; RAMSEY; **215** C-9; elev. 1,465ft./447m.; 🅿; **z** 58362; ● 60
Perth; Inc. Place; TOWNER; **215** B-9; elev. 1,730ft./527m.; 🅿; **z** 58363; Ⓟ 22; Ⓒ 13
Petersburg; Inc. Place; NELSON; **215** C-11; elev. 1,530ft./466m.; 🅿; **z** 58272; Ⓟ 219; Ⓒ 195
Pettibone; Inc. Place; KIDDER; **215** E-9; elev. 1,838ft./560m.; 🅿; **z** 58475; Ⓟ 93; Ⓒ 88
Picardville; RMC Place; SHERIDAN; ***215** D-7; elev. 1,952ft./595m.; mail Mcclusky **z** 58463
Pick City; Inc. Place; MERCER; **215** D-6; elev. 1,920ft./585m.; 🅿; **z** 58545; Ⓟ 203; Ⓒ 166
PIERCE; **215** C-8; Ⓟ 5,052; Ⓒ 4,675; ◆ 3,966
Pillsbury; Inc. Place; BARNES; **215** E-11; elev. 1,280ft./390m.; 🅿; **z** 58065; Ⓟ 31; Ⓒ 24
Pingree; Inc. Place; STUTSMAN; **215** E-10; elev. 1,551ft./473m.; 🅿; **z** 58476; Ⓟ 61; Ⓒ 66
Pisek; Inc. Place; WALSH; **215** B-11; elev. 985ft./300m.; 🅿; **z** 58273; Ⓟ 130; Ⓒ 96
Pitcher Park; RMC Place; RAMSEY; ***215** C-10; elev. 1,450ft./442m.; mail Devils Lake **z** 58301; pop. incl. with Devils Lake (Inc. Place)
Plaza; Inc. Place; MOUNTRAIL; **215** C-5; elev. 2,100ft./640m.; 🅿; **z** 58771; Ⓟ 193; Ⓒ 167
Pleasant Lake; RMC Place; BENSON; ***215** B-8; elev. 1,599ft./487m.; 🅿; **z** 58368; rural
Ponderosa; RMC Place; CASS; ***215** F-13; ★ **FAR-**; mail Fargo **z** 58104; pop. incl. with Fargo (Inc. Place)
Ponderosa Riverside Village; RMC Place; BURLEIGH; ***215** F-7; elev. 1,640ft./500m.; ★ **BIS**; mail Bismarck **z** 58503; ● 100
Porcupine; RMC Place; SIOUX; ***215** G-6; located on Standing Rock Ind. Res.; mail Shields **z** 58569; ● 40
Portal; Inc. Place; BURKE; **215** A-4; elev. 1,960ft./597m.; 🅿; **z** 58772; Ⓟ 192; Ⓒ 131
Portland; Inc. Place; TRAILL; **215** D-12; elev. 984ft./300m.; 🅿; **z** 58274; Ⓟ 602; Ⓒ 604
Powell; RMC Place; GRAND FORKS; ***215** C-12; elev. 849ft./259m.; mail Grand Forks **z** 58201; rural
Powers Lake; Inc. Place; BURKE; **215** B-4; elev. 2,206ft./672m.; 🅿; **z** 58773; Ⓟ 408; Ⓒ 309
Prairie Rose; Inc. Place; CASS; ***215** F-13; elev. 903ft./275m.; 🅿; ★ **FAR-**; **z** 58104; Ⓟ 49; Ⓒ 68
Prairie View Acres; RMC Place; BURLEIGH; ***215** F-7; elev. 1,646ft./502m.; ★ **BIS**; mail Bismarck **z** 58501; ● 100
Price; RMC Place; OLIVER; ***215** E-7; elev. 1,678ft./511m.; mail Center **z** 58530; rural
Prosper; RMC Place; CASS; ***215** F-13; 🅿; **z** 58042; ● 35

R

Raleigh; RMC Place; GRANT; **215** G-6; elev. 2,038ft./621m.; 🅿; **z** 58564; ● 30
RAMSEY; **215** B-10; Ⓟ 12,681; Ⓒ 12,066; ◆ 11,035
RANSOM; **215** G-12; Ⓟ 5,921; Ⓒ 5,890; ◆ 5,711
Raub; RMC Place; MCLEAN; ***215** D-5; located on Fort Berthold Ind. Res.; elev. 1,885ft./575m.; 🅿; **z** 58779; rural
Raulston; RMC Place; WILLIAMS; ***215** C-3; elev. 1,884ft./574m.; mail Williston **z** 58801; rural
Rawson; RMC Place; MCKENZIE; **215** D-3; elev. 2,256ft./688m.; 🅿; **z** 58831; disincorporated March 31, 2002; Ⓟ 9; Ⓒ 6
Ray; Inc. Place; WILLIAMS; **215** B-3; elev. 2,271ft./692m.; 🅿; **z** 58849; Ⓟ 603; Ⓒ 534
Raymond Lee; RMC Place; WILLIAMS; ***215** C-2; elev. 1,900ft./579m.; mail Williston **z** 58801; pop. incl. with Williston (Inc. Place)
Red Willow Lake; RMC Place; GRIGGS; ***215** D-11; elev. 1,474ft./449m.; mail Binford **z** 58416; summer pop. 300; ● 50
Reeder; Inc. Place; ADAMS; **215** H-3; elev. 2,830ft./863m.; 🅿; **z** 58649; Ⓟ 252; Ⓒ 181
Regan; Inc. Place; BURLEIGH; **215** E-7; elev. 2,032ft./619m.; 🅿; **z** 58477; Ⓟ 51; Ⓒ 43
Regent; Inc. Place; HETTINGER; **215** G-4; elev. 2,460ft./750m.; 🅿; **z** 58650; Ⓟ 268; Ⓒ 211
Reiles Acres; Inc. Place; CASS; **215** F-13; elev. 897ft./273m.; 🅿; ★ **FAR-**; **z** 58102; Ⓟ 210; Ⓒ 254
RENVILLE; **215** A-5; Ⓟ 3,160; Ⓒ 2,610; ◆ 2,142
Reynolds; Inc. Place; TRAILL, GRAND FORKS; **215** D-12; elev. 910ft./277m.; 🅿; **z** 58275; Ⓟ 299; Ⓒ 350
Rhame; Inc. Place; BOWMAN; **215** G-2; elev. 3,184ft./970m.; 🅿; **z** 58651; Ⓟ 186; Ⓒ 189
Richards West; RMC Place; GRAND FORKS; ***215** C-12; elev. 835ft./255m.; ★ **GDFK**; mail Grand Forks **z** 58201; pop. incl. with Grand Forks (Inc. Place)
Richardton; Inc. Place; STARK; **215** F-4; elev. 2,470ft./753m.; 🅿 🅷; **z** 58652; Ⓟ 625; Ⓒ 619
RICHLAND; **215** G-12; Ⓟ 18,148; Ⓒ 17,998; ◆ 15,823
Ridgeview Acres; RMC Place; BURLEIGH; ***215** F-7; elev. 1,650ft./503m.; ★ **BIS**; mail Bismarck **z** 58504; ● 35
Rio Vista Heights; RMC Place; WILLIAMS; ***215** C-2; elev. 1,872ft./571m.; mail Williston **z** 58801; ● 30
River Bend; RMC Place; CASS; ***215** F-13; elev. 900ft./274m.; mail Horace **z** 58047; ● 50
Riverdale; RMC Place; CASS; ***215** F-13; ★ **FAR-**; mail Fargo **z** 58104; ● 80
Riverdale; Inc. Place; MCLEAN; **215** D-6; elev. 1,970ft./600m.; 🅿; **z** 58565; Ⓟ 283; Ⓒ 273
Riverside (West Fargo Industrial Park); RMC Place; CASS; ***215** F-13; elev. 895ft./273m.; 🅿; ★ **FAR-**; **z** 58078; pop. incl. with West Fargo (Inc. Place)
River View Acres; RMC Place; BURLEIGH; ***215** F-7; elev. 1,631ft./497m.; ★ **BIS**; mail Bismarck **z** 58504; rural
Riverview Estates; RMC Place; CASS; ***215** F-13; ★ **FAR-**; mail Fargo **z** 58102; ● 30
Riverview Heights; RMC Place; MORTON; ***215** F-7; ★ **BIS**; mail Mandan **z** 58554; ● 130
Robinson; Inc. Place; KIDDER; **215** E-8; elev. 1,776ft./541m.; 🅿; **z** 58478; Ⓟ 87; Ⓒ 71
Rock Haven; RMC Place; MORTON; ***215** F-7; ★ **BIS**; mail Mandan **z** 58554; rural
Rock Lake; Inc. Place; TOWNER; **215** A-9; elev. 1,540ft./469m.; 🅿; **z** 58365; Ⓟ 221; Ⓒ 194
Rogers; Inc. Place; BARNES; **215** E-11; elev. 1,425ft./434m.; 🅿; **z** 58479; Ⓟ 69; Ⓒ 61
Rolette; Inc. Place; ROLETTE; **215** B-8; elev. 1,623ft./495m.; 🅿; **z** 58366; Ⓟ 623; Ⓒ 538
ROLETTE; **215** B-8; Ⓟ 12,772; Ⓒ 13,674; ◆ 13,612
Rolla; Inc. Place; ⊡ ROLETTE; **215** A-9; elev. 1,810ft./552m.; 🅿 🅷; **z** 58367; Ⓟ 1,286; Ⓒ 1,417
Rolling Meadows; RMC Place; BURLEIGH; ***215** F-7; elev. 1,850ft./564m.; ★ **BIS**; mail Bismarck **z** 58503; ● 35
Roseglen; RMC Place; MCLEAN; **215** D-5; located on Fort Berthold Ind. Res.; elev. 2,100ft./640m.; 🅿; **z** 58775; ● 20
Roshau; RMC Place; STARK; ***215** F-4; elev. 2,500ft./762m.; mail Dickinson **z** 58601; ● 90
Ross; Inc. Place; MOUNTRAIL; **215** B-4; elev. 2,287ft./697m.; 🅿; **z** 58776; Ⓟ 61; Ⓒ 48
Roth; RMC Place; BOTTINEAU; ***215** A-7; 🅿; **z** 58783; rural
Round Hill Estates; RMC Place; CASS; ***215** F-13; elev. 908ft./277m.; mail Fargo **z** 58104; ● 50
Rugby; Inc. Place; ⊡ PIERCE; **215** B-8; elev. 1,550ft./472m.; 🅿 🅷; **z** 58368; Ⓟ 2,909; Ⓒ 2,939
Ruso; Inc. Place; MCLEAN; **215** D-7; elev. 2,080ft./634m.; 🅿; **z** 58778; Ⓟ 8; Ⓒ 6
Russell; RMC Place; BOTTINEAU; **215** B-7; elev. 1,465ft./447m.; mail Newburg **z** 58762; Ⓟ 14
Ruthville; RMC Place; WARD; **215** B-6; mail Minot **z** 58701, **z** 58703; ● 70
Rutland; Inc. Place; SARGENT; **215** H-12; elev. 1,224ft./373m.; 🅿; **z** 58067; Ⓟ 212; Ⓒ 220
Ryder; Inc. Place; WARD; **215** C-5; elev. 2,100ft./640m.; 🅿; **z** 58779; Ⓟ 121; Ⓒ 92

S

Sabot's First; RMC Place; BURLEIGH; ***215** F-7; elev. 1,900ft./579m.; ★ **BIS**; mail Bismarck **z** 58503; ● 20
Saint Anthony; RMC Place; MORTON; **215** F-7; elev. 1,783ft./543m.; 🅿; **z** 58554, **z** 58566; ● 50
Saint Benedict; RMC Place; CASS; ***215** F-13; mail Horace **z** 58047; rural
Saint Elizabeth; STARK; see Lefor (RMC Place)
Saint Gertrude; RMC Place; GRANT; ***215** G-6; mail Raleigh **z** 58564; ● 50
Saint John; Inc. Place; ROLETTE; **215** A-8; elev. 1,950ft./594m.; 🅿; **z** 58369; Ⓟ 368; Ⓒ 358
Saint Michael; RMC Place; BENSON; **215** C-10; located on Spirit Lake Ind. Res.; elev. 1,460ft./445m.; 🅿; **z** 58370; ● 30
Saint Thomas; Inc. Place; PEMBINA; **215** B-12; elev. 840ft./256m.; 🅿; **z** 58276; Ⓟ 444; Ⓒ 447
Sanborn; Inc. Place; BARNES; **215** F-11; elev. 1,450ft./442m.; 🅿; **z** 58480; Ⓟ 164; Ⓒ 194
San Haven (Montair); RMC Place; ROLETTE; **215** A-8; 🅿; **z** 58329; ● 70
Sanish; RMC Place; MOUNTRAIL; ***215** C-4; elev. 2,086ft./636m.; 🅿; **z** 58763
SARGENT; **215** G-12; Ⓟ 4,549; Ⓒ 4,366; ◆ 3,999
Sarles; Inc. Place; CAVALIER, TOWNER; **215** A-10; elev. 1,588ft./484m.; 🅿; **z** 58372; Ⓟ 86; Ⓒ 25
Sawdwood; RMC Place; WALSH; ***215** B-11; elev. 1,000ft./305m.; mail Park River **z** 58270; ● 45
Sawyer; Inc. Place; WARD; **215** C-6; elev. 1,542ft./470m.; 🅿; **z** 58781; Ⓟ 319; Ⓒ 377
Scenic East; RMC Place; WILLIAMS; **215** C-3; elev. 2,000ft./610m.; mail Williston **z** 58801; ● 75
Schefield; RMC Place; STARK; ***215** F-4; mail New England **z** 58647; rural
Schmidt; RMC Place; MORTON; ***215** F-7; mail Mandan **z** 58554; rural
Scranton; Inc. Place; BOWMAN; **215** G-3; elev. 2,780ft./847m.; 🅿; **z** 58653; Ⓟ 294; Ⓒ 304
Secluded Acres; RMC Place; BURLEIGH; ***215** F-7; elev. 1,630ft./497m.; ★ **BIS**; mail Bismarck **z** 58504; ● 25
Selfridge; Inc. Place; SIOUX; **215** H-7; located on Standing Rock Ind. Res.; elev. 2,184ft./666m.; 🅿; **z** 58568; Ⓟ 242; Ⓒ 223
Selz; RMC Place; PIERCE; **215** D-8; elev. 1,606ft./490m.; 🅿; **z** 58341; ● 100
Sentinel Butte; Inc. Place; GOLDEN VALLEY; **215** F-2; elev. 2,706ft./825m.; 🅿; **z** 58654; Ⓟ 79; Ⓒ 62
Shady Acres; RMC Place; CASS; ***215** F-13; ★ **FAR-**; mail Fargo **z** 58102; ● 40
Shamrock Acres; RMC Place; BURLEIGH; ***215** F-7; elev. 1,860ft./567m.; mail Bismarck **z** 58503; ● 100
Sharon; Inc. Place; STEELE; **215** D-11; elev. 1,510ft./460m.; 🅿; **z** 58277; Ⓟ 119; Ⓒ 109
Sheldon; Inc. Place; RANSOM; **215** F-12; elev. 1,076ft./328m.; 🅿; **z** 58068; Ⓟ 149; Ⓒ 135
Shell Valley; CDP-Census Area Only; ROLETTE; ***215** A-8; elev. 1,750ft./533m.; mail Belcourt **z** 58316; Ⓟ 343; Ⓒ 395
Shepard; RMC Place; GRIGGS; ***215** E-11; elev. 1,426ft./435m.; mail Cooperstown **z** 58425; rural
SHERIDAN; **215** D-7; Ⓟ 2,148; Ⓒ 1,710; ◆ 1,206
Sherwood; Inc. Place; RENVILLE; **215** A-6; elev. 1,640ft./500m.; 🅿; **z** 58782; Ⓟ 286; Ⓒ 255
Sheyenne; Inc. Place; EDDY; **215** D-9; elev. 1,475ft./450m.; 🅿; **z** 58374; Ⓟ 272; Ⓒ 318

Entries in **UPPERCASE** are counties.
Entries in **bold** have populations of 2,500 or more.
Names in parentheses are alternate names.

Inc. Place	Incorporated Place
RMC Place	Rand McNally Designated Place
CDP	Census Designated Place
MCD	Minor Civil Division
⊡	County Seat
▲	Minor Civil Division
elev.	Elevation
🅿	Post Office
🅷	Hospital
🅲	College
■	Principal Business Center
★	Ranally Metro Area (RMA) Abbreviation
z	Zip Code(s)
Ⓟ	Previous Census Population
Ⓡ	Revised Census Population
Ⓐ	Annexation Population
●	Rand McNally Population Estimate
Ⓒ	Final Census Population
Ⓢ	Special Census Population
◆	Estimated Population

For additional definitions see Glossary, Volume 1, and Introduction, Volume 2.

Sheyenne Valley Addition; RMC Place; BARNES; ***215** F-11; elev. 1,220ft./372m.; mail Valley City **z** 58072; ● 120
Sheyenne Valley Farm; RMC Place; CASS; ***215** F-13; ★ **FAR-**; mail Fargo **z** 58102; ● 25
Shields; RMC Place; GRANT; **215** G-6; elev. 1,820ft./555m.; 🅿; **z** 58569; ● 30
Shryock; RMC Place; WILLIAMS; ***215** C-3; elev. 2,000ft./610m.; mail Williston **z** 58801; ● 30
Sibley; Inc. Place; BARNES; **215** E-11; elev. 1,270ft./387m.; 🅿; **z** 58429; Ⓟ 41; © 46
Sibley Island Estates; RMC Place; BURLEIGH; ***215** F-7; elev. 1,633ft./498m.; ★ **BIS**; mail Bismarck **z** 58504; ● 40
Silva; RMC Place; PIERCE; ***215** C-8; elev. 1,575ft./480m.; 🅿; **z** 58368
Simcoe; RMC Place; MCHENRY; ***215** C-7; elev. 1,586ft./483m.; mail Granville **z** 58741; rural
SIOUX; **215** H-6; Ⓟ 3,761; © 4,044; ◆ 4,187
Sioux Village; RMC Place; SIOUX; ***215** H-7; elev. 1,620ft./494m.; mail Fort Yates **z** 58538; ● 500
Skyline Estates; RMC Place; BURLEIGH; ***215** F-7; elev. 1,950ft./594m.; mail Bismarck **z** 58503; ● 20
Sleepy Hollow; RMC Place; BURLEIGH; ***215** F-7; ★ **BIS**; mail Bismarck **z** 58503; ● 100
Sleepy Hollow; RMC Place; CASS; ***215** F-13; elev. 910ft./277m.; mail Horace **z** 58047; ● 80
SLOPE; **215** G-2; Ⓟ 907; © 767; ◆ 595
Solen; Inc. Place; SIOUX; **215** G-7; located on Standing Rock Ind. Res.; elev. 1,671ft./509m.; 🅿; **z** 58570; Ⓟ 92; © 86
Sorenson Addition; RMC Place; WARD; ***215** C-6; elev. 1,616ft./493m.; mail Minot **z** 58701; ● 50
Souris; Inc. Place; BOTTINEAU; **215** A-7; elev. 1,510ft./460m.; 🅿; **z** 58783; Ⓟ 97; © 83
Southam; RMC Place; RAMSEY; **215** C-10; elev. 1,502ft./458m.; 🅿; **z** 58327; ● 20
South Heart; Inc. Place; STARK; **215** F-3; elev. 2,474ft./754m.; 🅿; **z** 58655; Ⓟ 322; © 307
South Prairie; RMC Place; WARD; ***215** C-6; mail Minot **z** 58701; rural
Southview; RMC Place; WILLIAMS; ***215** C-2; elev. 1,874ft./571m.; mail Williston **z** 58801; rural
Southview Estates; RMC Place; STARK; ***215** F-4; elev. 2,450ft./747m.; mail Dickinson **z** 58601; ● 150
South West Fargo; CASS; see West Fargo (Inc. Place)
Spirit Lake Reservation (Fort Totten Indian Reservation); Indian Reservation; BENSON, EDDY, NELSON, RAMSEY, WELLS; mail Fort Totten **z** 58335; also location of Indian Agency; Ⓟ 3,318; © 4,435
Spiritwood; RMC Place; STUTSMAN; **215** F-10; elev. 1,480ft./451m.; 🅿; **z** 58481; ● 50
Spiritwood Lake; Inc. Place; STUTSMAN; **215** E-10; elev. 1,507ft./459m.; mail Jamestown **z** 58401; Ⓟ 61; © 72
Spring Brook; Inc. Place; WILLIAMS; **215** C-3; elev. 2,066ft./630m.; 🅿; **z** 58843; Ⓟ 29; © 26
Standing Rock Reservation; Indian Reservation; SIOUX; Reservation extends into SD; mail Fort Yates **z** 58538; also location of Indian Agency; Ⓟ 3,620; © 4,044
Stanley; Inc. Place; ⊡ MOUNTRAIL; **215** B-4; elev. 2,260ft./689m.; 🅿 🅷; **z** 58784; Ⓟ 1,371; © 1,279
Stanton; Inc. Place; ⊡ MERCER; **215** E-6; elev. 1,701ft./518m.; 🅿; **z** 58571; Ⓟ 517; © 345
STARK; **215** F-4; Ⓟ 22,832; © 22,636; ◆ 22,860
Starkweather; Inc. Place; RAMSEY; **215** B-10; elev. 1,495ft./456m.; 🅿; **z** 58377; Ⓟ 197; © 157
Steele; Inc. Place; ⊡ KIDDER; **215** F-8; elev. 1,865ft./568m.; 🅿; **z** 58482; Ⓟ 762; © 761
STEELE; **215** D-11; Ⓟ 2,420; © 2,258; ◆ 1,695
Sterling; RMC Place; BURLEIGH; **215** F-8; elev. 1,817ft./554m.; 🅿; **z** 58572; ● 80
Stirum; RMC Place; SARGENT; **215** G-11; elev. 1,355ft./413m.; 🅿; **z** 58069; ● 50
Strasburg; Inc. Place; EMMONS; **215** H-8; elev. 1,804ft./550m.; 🅿; **z** 58573; Ⓟ 553; © 549
Straubville; RMC Place; SARGENT; ***215** H-11; elev. 1,314ft./401m.; 🅿; **z** 58017; rural
Streeter; Inc. Place; STUTSMAN; **215** F-9; elev. 2,000ft./610m.; 🅿; **z** 58483; Ⓟ 161; © 172
Strong; RMC Place; RAMSEY; ***215** C-10; elev. 1,498ft./457m.; mail Devils Lake **z** 58301; ● 60
STUTSMAN; **215** E-9; Ⓟ 22,241; © 21,908; ◆ 19,716
Sunny; RMC Place; MORTON; ***215** F-6; ★ **BIS**; mail Mandan **z** 58554; rural
Sunnyside Addition; RMC Place; CASS; ***215** F-13; elev. 901ft./275m.; mail Fargo **z** 58104; ● 50
Sunny Slope; RMC Place; WARD; ***215** C-6; elev. 1,650ft./503m.; mail Minot **z** 58701; ● 100
Sunrise Acres; RMC Place; CASS; ***215** F-13; ★ **FAR-**; mail Fargo **z** 58102; ● 40
Surrey; Inc. Place; WARD; **215** C-6; elev. 1,625ft./495m.; 🅿; **z** 58785; Ⓟ 856; © 917
Sutton; RMC Place; GRIGGS; **215** E-10; elev. 1,470ft./448m.; 🅿; **z** 58484; ● 50
Swansonville; RMC Place; BURLEIGH; ***215** F-7; elev. 1,693ft./516m.; ★ **BIS**; mail Bismarck **z** 58504; ● 35
Sykeston; Inc. Place; WELLS; **215** D-9; elev. 1,638ft./499m.; 🅿; **z** 58486; Ⓟ 167; © 153

T

Taft; RMC Place; TRAILL; ***215** D-13; elev. 905ft./276m.; mail Hillsboro **z** 58045; rural
Tagus; RMC Place; MOUNTRAIL; ***215** B-5; elev. 2,189ft./667m.; 🅿; **z** 58718
Talbotts; RMC Place; WARD; ***215** C-6; elev. 1,570ft./479m.; mail Minot **z** 58701; ● 40
Tappen; Inc. Place; KIDDER; **215** F-9; elev. 1,770ft./539m.; 🅿; **z** 58487; Ⓟ 239; © 210
Tatley Meadows; RMC Place; BURLEIGH; ***215** F-7; elev. 1,637ft./499m.; ★ **BIS**; mail Bismarck **z** 58504; pop. incl. with Bismarck (Inc. Place)
Taylor; Inc. Place; STARK; **215** F-4; elev. 2,492ft./760m.; 🅿; **z** 58656; Ⓟ 163; © 150
Temvik; RMC Place; EMMONS; ***215** G-8; elev. 1,927ft./587m.; 🅿; **z** 58552
Thompson; Inc. Place; GRAND FORKS; **215** D-12; elev. 865ft./264m.; 🅿; **z** 58278; Ⓟ 930; © 1,006
Thorne; RMC Place; ROLETTE; ***215** B-8; mail Rolette **z** 58366
Tilden; RMC Place; BENSON; ***215** C-9; mail Minnewaukan **z** 58351; rural
Timber Lane Place; RMC Place; BURLEIGH; ***215** F-7; elev. 1,630ft./497m.; ★ **BIS**; mail Bismarck **z** 58504
Tioga; Inc. Place; WILLIAMS; **215** B-3; elev. 2,238ft./682m.; 🅿 🅷; **z** 58852; Ⓟ 1,278; © 1,125
TJ Ranch Estates; RMC Place; BURLEIGH; ***215** F-7; elev. 1,900ft./579m.; mail Bismarck **z** 58503; ● 20
Tokio; RMC Place; BENSON; **215** C-10; located on Spirit Lake Ind. Res.; elev. 1,500ft./457m.; 🅿; **z** 58379; ● 100
Tolley; Inc. Place; RENVILLE; **215** B-5; elev. 1,850ft./564m.; 🅿; **z** 58787; Ⓟ 79; © 63
Tolna; Inc. Place; NELSON; **215** D-10; elev. 1,458ft./444m.; 🅿; **z** 58380; Ⓟ 230; © 202
Tower City; Inc. Place; CASS, BARNES; **215** F-12; elev. 1,172ft./357m.; 🅿; **z** 58071; Ⓟ 233; © 252
Town and Country; RMC Place; WILLIAMS; ***215** C-2; elev. 2,000ft./610m.; mail Williston **z** 58801; ● 35
Town and Country Estates; RMC Place; BURLEIGH; ***215** F-7; elev. 1,710ft./521m.; mail Bismarck **z** 58504; ● 25
Towner; Inc. Place; ⊡ MCHENRY; **215** B-7; elev. 1,486ft./453m.; 🅿; **z** 58788; Ⓟ 669; © 574
TOWNER; **215** B-9; Ⓟ 3,627; © 2,876; ◆ 2,081
TRAILL; **215** D-12; Ⓟ 8,752; © 8,477; ◆ 7,975
Trenton; RMC Place; WILLIAMS; **215** C-2; elev. 1,900ft./579m.; 🅿; **z** 58853; ● 250
Trestle Valley; RMC Place; WARD; ***215** C-6; elev. 1,570ft./479m.; mail Minot **z** 58701; ● 40
Trotters; RMC Place; GOLDEN VALLEY; ***215** E-2; elev. 2,419ft./737m.; 🅿; **z** 58621; rural
Turtle Lake; Inc. Place; MCLEAN; **215** D-7; elev. 1,875ft./572m.; 🅿 🅷; **z** 58575; Ⓟ 681; © 580
Turtle Mountain Reservation; Indian Reservation; ROLETTE; mail Belcourt **z** 58316; also location of Indian Agency; Ⓟ 4,311; © 5,815
Tuttle; Inc. Place; KIDDER; **215** E-8; elev. 1,859ft./567m.; 🅿; **z** 58488; Ⓟ 160; © 106
Twin Butte; RMC Place; BURLEIGH; ***215** F-7; elev. 1,751ft./534m.; mail Bismarck **z** 58504; ● 25
Twin Buttes; RMC Place; DUNN; **215** D-4; located on Fort Berthold Ind. Res.; elev. 2,220ft./677m.; mail Halliday **z** 58636; ● 80
Tyler; RMC Place; RICHLAND; ***215** G-13; mail Wahpeton **z** 58075; rural

U

Underwood; Inc. Place; MCLEAN; **215** D-6; elev. 2,026ft./618m.; 🅿; **z** 58576; Ⓟ 976; © 812
Union; RMC Place; CAVALIER; ***215** B-11; elev. 1,380ft./421m.; 🅿; **z** 58260, **z** 58269; rural
University of North Dakota; RMC Place; GRAND FORKS; ★ **GDFK**; mail Grand Forks **z** 58202; pop. incl. with Grand Forks (Inc. Place)
Upham; Inc. Place; MCHENRY; **215** B-7; elev. 1,445ft./440m.; 🅿; **z** 58789; Ⓟ 205; © 155
Urbana; RMC Place; BARNES; ***215** F-10; mail Spiritwood **z** 58481; rural

V

Valley City; Inc. Place; ⊡ BARNES; **215** F-11; elev. 1,222ft./372m.; 🅿 🅷 🅲 1,037; **z** 58072; Ⓟ 7,163; © 6,826
Velva; Inc. Place; MCHENRY; **215** C-7; elev. 1,510ft./460m.; 🅿; **z** 58790; Ⓟ 968; © 1,049
Venlo; RMC Place; RANSOM; ***215** G-12; mail Mcleod **z** 58057; ● 100
Venturia; Inc. Place; MCINTOSH; **215** H-9; elev. 2,078ft./633m.; 🅿; **z** 58413; Ⓟ 30; © 23
Venturia; MCINTOSH, LOGAN; see Lehr (Inc. Place)
Verona; Inc. Place; LAMOURE; **215** G-11; elev. 1,385ft./422m.; 🅿; **z** 58490; Ⓟ 103; © 108
Veseleyville; RMC Place; WALSH; **215** B-12; elev. 877ft./267m.; mail Grafton **z** 58237; ● 75
Vista South; RMC Place; BURLEIGH; ***215** F-7; elev. 1,800ft./549m.; ★ **BIS**; mail Bismarck **z** 58504; ● 50
Vohs Dapplegrey; RMC Place; WILLIAMS; ***215** C-2; elev. 1,850ft./564m.; mail Williston **z** 58801; rural
Voltaire; Inc. Place; MCHENRY; **215** C-7; elev. 1,588ft./484m.; 🅿; **z** 58792; Ⓟ 63; © 51
Voss; RMC Place; WALSH; **215** C-12; elev. 830ft./253m.; 🅿; **z** 58261; ● 30

W

Wabek; RMC Place; MOUNTRAIL; ***215** C-5; mail Plaza **z** 58771; rural
Wahpeton; Inc. Place; ⊡ RICHLAND; **215** G-13; elev. 963ft./294m.; 🅿; **z** 58074-76; Ⓟ 8,751; © 8,586
Walcott; Inc. Place; RICHLAND; **215** F-13; elev. 955ft./291m.; 🅿; **z** 58077; Ⓟ 178; © 189
Wales; Inc. Place; CAVALIER; **215** A-10; elev. 1,565ft./477m.; 🅿; **z** 58281; Ⓟ 48; © 30
Walhalla; Inc. Place; PEMBINA; **215** A-11; elev. 970ft./296m.; 🅿; **z** 58282; Ⓟ 1,131; © 1,057
WALSH; **215** C-11; Ⓟ 13,840; © 12,389; ◆ 10,555
Walum; RMC Place; GRIGGS; ***215** E-11; elev. 1,433ft./437m.; 🅿; **z** 58448; ● 25
WARD; **215** C-6; Ⓟ 57,921; © 58,795; ◆ 55,296
Warren; RMC Place; CASS; ***215** F-13; elev. 925ft./282m.; mail Davenport **z** 58021; rural
Warsaw; RMC Place; WALSH; **215** C-12; elev. 806ft./246m.; mail Minto **z** 58261; ● 80
Warwick; Inc. Place; BENSON; **215** D-10; elev. 1,471ft./448m.; 🅿; **z** 58381; Ⓟ 80; © 75
Washburn; Inc. Place; ⊡ MCLEAN; **215** E-6; elev. 1,731ft./528m.; 🅿; **z** 58577; Ⓟ 1,506; © 1,389
Watford City; Inc. Place; ⊡ MCKENZIE; **215** D-3; elev. 2,082ft./635m.; 🅿 🅷; **z** 58854; Ⓟ 1,784; © 1,435
Weaver; RMC Place; CAVALIER; ***215** B-10; mail Munich **z** 58352; rural
Webster; RMC Place; RAMSEY; **215** C-10; elev. 1,470ft./448m.; 🅿; **z** 58382; ● 75
Welle; RMC Place; BURLEIGH; ***215** F-7; elev. 1,750ft./533m.; mail Bismarck **z** 58503; ● 25
WELLS; **215** D-8; Ⓟ 5,864; © 5,102; ◆ 4,079
Wellsburg; RMC Place; WELLS; ***215** D-8; elev. 1,597ft./487m.; mail Harvey **z** 58341
West Acres Estates; RMC Place; WILLIAMS; ***215** C-2; elev. 1,935ft./590m.; mail Williston **z** 58801; ● 70
West Bonetrail; RMC Place; WILLIAMS; ***215** B-2; mail Williston **z** 58801; rural
Westbrook; RMC Place; CASS; ***215** F-13; elev. 914ft./279m.; mail Horace **z** 58047; ● 35
West Fargo (South West Fargo); Inc. Place; CASS; **215** F-13; elev. 900ft./274m.; 🅿; ★ **FAR-**; **z** 58078; Ⓟ 12,287; © 14,940; ◆ 19,769
West Fargo Industrial Park; CASS; see Riverside (RMC Place)
Westfield; RMC Place; EMMONS; **215** H-8; elev. 1,997ft./609m.; 🅿; **z** 58542; ● 20
West Heart Estates; RMC Place; BURLEIGH; ***215** F-7; elev. 1,700ft./518m.; mail Bismarck **z** 58504; ● 80
Westhope; Inc. Place; BOTTINEAU; **215** A-6; elev. 1,496ft./456m.; 🅿; **z** 58793; Ⓟ 578; © 533
West Industrial Park; RMC Place; STARK; ***215** F-4; elev. 2,450ft./747m.; mail Dickinson **z** 58601; ● 60
West Jamestown; RMC Place; STUTSMAN; ***215** F-10; mail Jamestown **z** 58401; rural
West Town; RMC Place; STUTSMAN; ***215** F-10; elev. 1,494ft./455m.; mail Jamestown **z** 58401; ● 80
West Williston; RMC Place; WILLIAMS; ***215** C-2; mail Williston **z** 58801; rural
Westwood on the River; RMC Place; BURLEIGH; ***215** F-7; elev. 1,635ft./498m.; ★ **BIS**; mail Bismarck **z** 58503; ● 70
Wheatland; CDP; CASS; **215** F-12; elev. 991ft./302m.; 🅿; **z** 58079; © 60
Wheelock; RMC Place; WILLIAMS; **215** B-3; elev. 2,393ft./729m.; 🅿; **z** 58849; ● 30
White Earth; Inc. Place; MOUNTRAIL; **215** B-4; elev. 2,100ft./640m.; 🅿; **z** 58794; Ⓟ 73; © 63
White Shield; CDP-Census Area Only; MCLEAN; **215** D-5; located on Fort Berthold Ind. Res.; elev. 1,998ft./609m.; 🅿; **z** 58540; Ⓟ 274; © 348
Whitman; RMC Place; NELSON; **215** C-11; elev. 1,526ft./465m.; 🅿; **z** 58259; ● 30
Wild Rice; RMC Place; CASS; ***215** F-13; elev. 909ft./277m.; 🅿; **z** 58047; rural
Wildrose; Inc. Place; WILLIAMS; **215** B-3; elev. 2,254ft./687m.; 🅿; **z** 58795; Ⓟ 193; © 129
WILLIAMS; **215** B-3; Ⓟ 21,129; © 19,761; ◆ 20,017
Williston; Inc. Place; ⊡ WILLIAMS; **215** C-2; elev. 1,882ft./574m.; 🅿 🅷 🅲 955 ■; **z** 58801-02; Ⓟ 13,131; © 12,512; ◆ 13,266
Williston Park; RMC Place; WILLIAMS; ***215** C-2; elev. 1,962ft./598m.; mail Williston **z** 58801; ● 50
Willow City; Inc. Place; BOTTINEAU; **215** B-8; elev. 1,471ft./448m.; 🅿; **z** 58384; Ⓟ 281; © 221
Willow Creek; RMC Place; CASS; ***215** F-13; ★ **FAR-**; mail West Fargo **z** 58078; pop. incl. with Fargo (Inc. Place)
Wilton; Inc. Place; MCLEAN, BURLEIGH; **215** E-7; elev. 2,183ft./665m.; 🅿; **z** 58579; Ⓟ 728; © 807
Wimbledon; Inc. Place; BARNES; **215** E-10; elev. 1,485ft./453m.; 🅿; **z** 58492; Ⓟ 275; © 237
Windsor; RMC Place; STUTSMAN; **215** F-9; elev. 1,841ft./561m.; 🅿; **z** 58424; ● 25
Windsor Green; RMC Place; CASS; ***215** F-13; ★ **FAR-**; mail Fargo **z** 58104; ● 80
Wing; Inc. Place; BURLEIGH; **215** E-8; elev. 1,888ft./575m.; 🅿; **z** 58494; Ⓟ 208; © 124
Wishek; Inc. Place; MCINTOSH; **215** G-9; elev. 2,010ft./613m.; 🅿 🅷; **z** 58495; Ⓟ 1,171; © 1,122
Wolford; Inc. Place; PIERCE; **215** B-8; elev. 1,620ft./494m.; 🅿; **z** 58385; Ⓟ 56; © 50
Wolseth; RMC Place; WARD; ***215** B-6; 🅿; **z** 58740 & mail Deering **z** 58731; rural
Wood Lake; RMC Place; BENSON; ***215** C-10; mail Sheyenne **z** 58374, Tokio **z** 58379; ● 60
Woodland; RMC Place; CASS; ***215** F-13; elev. 950ft./290m.; mail Kindred **z** 58051; ● 35
Woods; RMC Place; CASS; ***215** F-12; elev. 950ft./290m.; mail Leonard **z** 58052; rural
Woodworth; Inc. Place; STUTSMAN; **215** E-9; elev. 2,052ft./625m.; 🅿; **z** 58496; Ⓟ 102; © 80
Wutzke; RMC Place; BURLEIGH; ***215** F-7; elev. 1,850ft./564m.; ★ **BIS**; mail Bismarck **z** 58503; ● 35
Wyndmere; Inc. Place; RICHLAND; **215** G-12; elev. 1,059ft./323m.; 🅿; **z** 58081; Ⓟ 501; © 533

Y

York; Inc. Place; BENSON; **215** C-9; elev. 1,607ft./490m.; 🅿; **z** 58386; Ⓟ 35; © 26
Ypsilanti; RMC Place; STUTSMAN; **215** F-10; elev. 1,383ft./422m.; 🅿; **z** 58497; ● 100

Z

Zahl; RMC Place; WILLIAMS; **215** B-2; elev. 2,000ft./610m.; 🅿; **z** 58856; ● 40
Zap; Inc. Place; MERCER; **215** E-5; elev. 1,845ft./562m.; 🅿; **z** 58580; Ⓟ 287; © 231
Zeeland; Inc. Place; MCINTOSH; **215** H-8; elev. 2,000ft./610m.; 🅿; **z** 58581; Ⓟ 197; © 141

OHIO

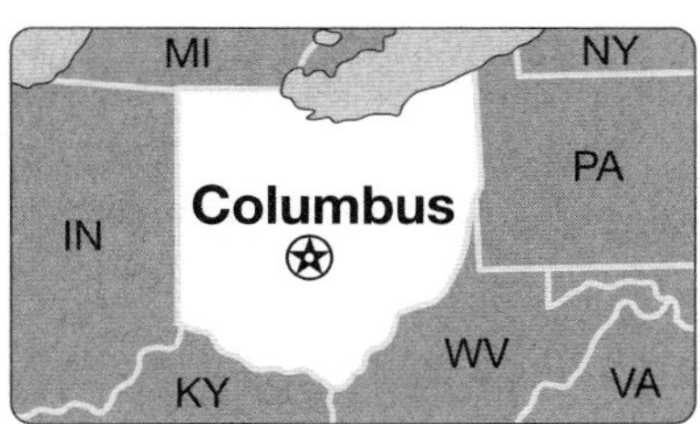

Statistics

Total area (2000) — 44,825 square miles
Land area (2000) — 40,948 square miles
Water area (2000) — 3,877 square miles
Capital — Columbus
Admitted as state — March, 1803

Maps

State maps can be found on pages 142-254 in Vol. 1
County Subdivision maps can be found on pages 255-271 in Vol. 1

Ranally Metro Areas (RMAs) and Abbreviations

Akron, OH — AKR
Alliance, OH — ALLI
Ashtabula, OH — ASHT
Canton , OH — CAN
Cincinnati, OH-KY-IN — CIN
Cleveland, OH — CLEV
Columbus, OH — COL
Dayton, OH — DAY
E. Liverpool, OH — E.LIV
Findlay, OH — FIND
Huntington, WV-KY-OH — HNTG
Lancaster, OH — LANC
Lima, OH — LIMA
Mansfield, OH — MANS
Marion, OH — MRN
Middletown, OH — MIDD
Newark, OH — NWRK
Parkersburg, WV-OH — PRKB
Portsmouth, OH-KY — PTSM
Richmond, IN-OH — RICH
Sandusky, OH — SNDSK
Sharon, PA-OH — SHAR
Springfield, OH — SPR
Steubenville-Weirton, OH-WV — STU-
Toledo, OH-MI — TOL
Wheeling, WV-OH — WHL
Youngstown-Warren, OH-PA — YNGS-
Zanesville, OH — ZAN

Principal Places

Place Name	Place Type	County	Population
Columbus	Inc. Place	FRANKLIN	◆ 796,515
Cleveland	Inc. Place	CUYAHOGA	◆ 401,068
Cincinnati	Inc. Place	HAMILTON	◆ 338,011
Toledo	Inc. Place	LUCAS	◆ 293,189
Akron	Inc. Place	SUMMIT	◆ 210,424
Dayton	Inc. Place	MONTGOMERY	◆ 155,866
Canton	Inc. Place	STARK	◆ 79,526
Parma	Inc. Place	CUYAHOGA	◆ 78,066
Lorain	Inc. Place	LORAIN	◆ 68,632
Youngstown	Inc. Place	MAHONING	◆ 65,949
Hamilton	Inc. Place	BUTLER	◆ 64,014
Springfield	Inc. Place	CLARK	◆ 62,151
Colerain	MCD-Township	HAMILTON	© 60,144
Green	MCD-Township	HAMILTON	© 55,660
West Chester	MCD-Township	BUTLER	© 54,895
Kettering	Inc. Place	MONTGOMERY	◆ 54,823
Elyria	Inc. Place	LORAIN	◆ 54,322
Washington	MCD-Township	MONTGOMERY	© 52,991
Middletown	Inc. Place	BUTLER	◆ 52,589
Plain	MCD-Township	STARK	© 51,997
Mentor	Inc. Place	LAKE	◆ 51,464
Lakewood	Inc. Place	CUYAHOGA	◆ 50,887
Newark	Inc. Place	LICKING	◆ 48,965
Cuyahoga Falls	Inc. Place	SUMMIT	◆ 48,964
Euclid	Inc. Place	CUYAHOGA	◆ 47,835
Miami	MCD-Township	MONTGOMERY	© 45,593
Mansfield	Inc. Place	RICHLAND	◆ 45,487
Marion	MCD-Township	MARION	® 44,900
Sylvania	MCD-Township	LUCAS	© 44,253
Fairfield	Inc. Place	BUTLER	◆ 43,953
Anderson	MCD-Township	HAMILTON	© 43,857
Boardman	MCD-Township	MAHONING	© 42,518
Union	MCD-Township	CLERMONT	© 42,332
Strongsville	Inc. Place	CUYAHOGA	◆ 42,266
Beavercreek	MCD-Township	GREENE	© 41,745
Cleveland Heights	Inc. Place	CUYAHOGA	◆ 41,699
Beavercreek	Inc. Place	GREENE	◆ 41,489
Warren	Inc. Place	TRUMBULL	◆ 41,101
Bath	MCD-Township	GREENE	© 40,231
Westerville	Inc. Place	FRANKLIN	◆ 38,486
Austintown	MCD-Township	MAHONING	© 38,001
Lima	Inc. Place	ALLEN	◆ 37,884
Dublin	Inc. Place	FRANKLIN	◆ 37,759
Jackson	MCD-Township	STARK	© 37,744
Findlay	Inc. Place	HANCOCK	◆ 37,664
Springfield	MCD-Township	HAMILTON	© 37,587
Gahanna	Inc. Place	FRANKLIN	◆ 36,711
Reynoldsburg	Inc. Place	FRANKLIN	◆ 36,695
Miami	MCD-Township	CLERMONT	© 36,632
Upper Arlington	Inc. Place	FRANKLIN	◆ 36,527
Lancaster	Inc. Place	FAIRFIELD	◆ 36,055
Mifflin	MCD-Township	FRANKLIN	© 35,787
Huber Heights	Inc. Place	MONTGOMERY	◆ 35,667
Fairborn	Inc. Place	GREENE	◆ 34,585
Brunswick	Inc. Place	MEDINA	◆ 34,279
Marion	Inc. Place	MARION	◆ 33,245
Jackson	MCD-Township	FRANKLIN	© 32,625
Stow	Inc. Place	SUMMIT	◆ 31,815
Boardman	CDP	MAHONING	◆ 31,779
Massillon	Inc. Place	STARK	◆ 31,717
Bowling Green	Inc. Place	WOOD	◆ 31,454
North Olmsted	Inc. Place	CUYAHOGA	◆ 31,149
Westlake	Inc. Place	CUYAHOGA	◆ 30,361
Grove City	Inc. Place	FRANKLIN	◆ 30,282
Delhi	MCD-Township	HAMILTON	© 30,104
Mason	Inc. Place	WARREN	◆ 29,932
Delaware	Inc. Place	DELAWARE	◆ 29,256
Perry	MCD-Township	STARK	© 29,167
Hilliard	Inc. Place	FRANKLIN	◆ 28,932
North Royalton	Inc. Place	CUYAHOGA	◆ 28,695
Kent	Inc. Place	PORTAGE	◆ 28,067
Garfield Heights	Inc. Place	CUYAHOGA	◆ 27,951
Medina	Inc. Place	MEDINA	◆ 27,908
Franklin	MCD-Township	WARREN	® 27,897
Scioto	MCD-Township	ROSS	© 27,735
Weathersfield	MCD-Township	TRUMBULL	© 27,717
Athens	MCD-Township	ATHENS	© 27,714
Austintown	CDP	MAHONING	◆ 27,669
Norwich	MCD-Township	FRANKLIN	© 27,488
Barberton	Inc. Place	SUMMIT	◆ 27,447
Concord	MCD-Township	MIAMI	© 27,335
Truro	MCD-Township	FRANKLIN	® 27,065
Violet	MCD-Township	FAIRFIELD	® 27,036
Shaker Heights	Inc. Place	CUYAHOGA	◆ 26,379
Delaware	MCD-Township	DELAWARE	© 26,149
Lake	MCD-Township	STARK	© 25,892
Trotwood	Inc. Place	MONTGOMERY	◆ 25,746
Deerfield	MCD-Township	WARREN	© 25,515
Xenia	Inc. Place	GREENE	◆ 25,512
Sandusky	Inc. Place	ERIE	◆ 25,322
Wooster	Inc. Place	WAYNE	◆ 25,215
North Ridgeville	Inc. Place	LORAIN	◆ 24,823
Harrison	MCD-Township	MONTGOMERY	© 24,303
Oxford	MCD-Township	BUTLER	© 24,133
Springfield	MCD-Township	LUCAS	© 24,123
Oxford	Inc. Place	BUTLER	◆ 24,113
Zanesville	Inc. Place	MUSKINGUM	◆ 24,084
Maple Heights	Inc. Place	CUYAHOGA	◆ 23,858
Liberty	MCD-Township	TRUMBULL	© 23,522
Ashtabula	MCD-Township	ASHTABULA	© 23,239
Alliance	Inc. Place	STARK	◆ 23,079
Liberty	MCD-Township	BUTLER	© 22,819
Centerville	Inc. Place	MONTGOMERY	◆ 22,755
Green	Inc. Place	SUMMIT	◆ 22,685
Willoughby	Inc. Place	LAKE	◆ 22,659
East Cleveland	Inc. Place	CUYAHOGA	◆ 22,534
Lebanon	Inc. Place	WARREN	◆ 22,437
Chillicothe	Inc. Place	ROSS	◆ 22,338
Hudson	Inc. Place	SUMMIT	◆ 22,319
Riverside	Inc. Place	MONTGOMERY	◆ 21,919
Ashland	Inc. Place	ASHLAND	◆ 21,902
Troy	Inc. Place	MIAMI	◆ 21,579
Athens	Inc. Place	ATHENS	◆ 21,464
South Euclid	Inc. Place	CUYAHOGA	◆ 21,432
Solon	Inc. Place	CUYAHOGA	◆ 21,354
Madison	MCD-Township	FRANKLIN	® 21,220
Clear Creek	MCD-Township	WARREN	© 20,974
Clinton	MCD-Township	SHELBY	© 20,903
Norwood	Inc. Place	HAMILTON	◆ 20,766
Avon Lake	Inc. Place	LORAIN	◆ 20,435
Sidney	Inc. Place	SHELBY	◆ 20,316
Ashtabula	Inc. Place	ASHTABULA	◆ 20,267
Piqua	Inc. Place	MIAMI	◆ 20,230
Delhi Hills	RMC Place	HAMILTON	● 20,000
Eastlake	Inc. Place	LAKE	◆ 19,910
Parma Heights	Inc. Place	CUYAHOGA	◆ 19,756
Sycamore	MCD-Township	HAMILTON	© 19,675
Wadsworth	Inc. Place	MEDINA	◆ 19,549
Miamisburg	Inc. Place	MONTGOMERY	© 19,489
Forest Park	Inc. Place	HAMILTON	© 19,463
Howland	MCD-Township	TRUMBULL	© 19,451
Oregon	Inc. Place	LUCAS	© 19,355
Whitehall	Inc. Place	FRANKLIN	◆ 19,259
Niles	Inc. Place	TRUMBULL	◆ 19,170
Rocky River	Inc. Place	CUYAHOGA	◆ 19,031
Portsmouth	Inc. Place	SCIOTO	◆ 18,999
Berea	Inc. Place	CUYAHOGA	© 18,970
Bethel	MCD-Township	CLARK	© 18,962
Sylvania	Inc. Place	LUCAS	© 18,670
Painesville	MCD-Township	LAKE	© 18,562
Madison	MCD-Township	LAKE	© 18,428
Greenville	MCD-Township	DARKE	© 18,125
Brook Park	Inc. Place	CUYAHOGA	◆ 18,096
Mayfield Heights	Inc. Place	CUYAHOGA	◆ 17,963
Painesville	Inc. Place	LAKE	◆ 17,814
Tiffin	Inc. Place	SENECA	◆ 17,764
Fairview Park	Inc. Place	CUYAHOGA	© 17,572
Paris	MCD-Township	UNION	© 17,549
Batavia	MCD-Township	CLERMONT	© 17,503
Prairie	MCD-Township	FRANKLIN	© 17,118
Perry	MCD-Township	COLUMBIANA	© 17,049
Twinsburg	Inc. Place	SUMMIT	© 17,006
Perrysburg	Inc. Place	WOOD	© 16,945
Fremont	Inc. Place	SANDUSKY	◆ 16,939
Sharon	MCD-Township	FRANKLIN	© 16,455
New Philadelphia	Inc. Place	TUSCARAWAS	◆ 16,404
Defiance	Inc. Place	DEFIANCE	◆ 16,393
Tallmadge	Inc. Place	SUMMIT	© 16,390
North Canton	Inc. Place	STARK	© 16,369
Steubenville	Inc. Place	JEFFERSON	◆ 16,314
Norwalk	Inc. Place	HURON	© 16,238
Bay Village	Inc. Place	CUYAHOGA	© 16,087
Broadview Heights	Inc. Place	CUYAHOGA	© 15,967
Marysville	Inc. Place	UNION	© 15,942
Upper	MCD-Township	LAWRENCE	© 15,648
Fairfield	MCD-Township	BUTLER	© 15,571
Cambridge	MCD-Township	GUERNSEY	© 15,505
Liberty	MCD-Township	DELAWARE	© 15,429
Monroe	MCD-Township	MIAMI	© 15,339
Concord	MCD-Township	LAKE	© 15,282
Lyndhurst	Inc. Place	CUYAHOGA	© 15,279
Springfield	MCD-Township	SUMMIT	© 15,168
Warrensville Heights	Inc. Place	CUYAHOGA	© 15,109
Urbana	MCD-Township	CHAMPAIGN	© 14,968
Pease	MCD-Township	BELMONT	© 14,961
Middleburg Heights	Inc. Place	CUYAHOGA	◆ 14,944
Symmes	MCD-Township	HAMILTON	© 14,771
Poland	MCD-Township	MAHONING	© 14,711
Canfield	MCD-Township	MAHONING	© 14,624
Vandalia	Inc. Place	MONTGOMERY	© 14,603
Mount Vernon	Inc. Place	KNOX	◆ 14,595
Willowick	Inc. Place	LAKE	© 14,361
Duchouquet	MCD-Township	AUGLAIZE	© 14,329
Hubbard	MCD-Township	TRUMBULL	© 14,304
University Heights	Inc. Place	CUYAHOGA	© 14,146
Worthington	Inc. Place	FRANKLIN	© 14,125
Maumee	Inc. Place	LUCAS	◆ 14,034
American	MCD-Township	ALLEN	® 14,025
Fostoria	Inc. Place	SENECA	© 13,931
Canton	MCD-Township	STARK	© 13,882
West Carrollton City	Inc. Place	MONTGOMERY	© 13,818
Sharonville	Inc. Place	HAMILTON	© 13,804
Goshen	MCD-Township	CLERMONT	© 13,663
Copley	MCD-Township	SUMMIT	© 13,641
Perrysburg	MCD-Township	WOOD	© 13,613
Richland	MCD-Township	BELMONT	© 13,571
Aurora	Inc. Place	PORTAGE	© 13,556
Washington Court House	Inc. Place	FAYETTE	© 13,524
Miami	MCD-Township	HAMILTON	© 13,496
Finneytown	CDP	HAMILTON	© 13,492
Circleville	Inc. Place	PICKAWAY	© 13,485
Wickliffe	Inc. Place	LAKE	© 13,484
Defiance	MCD-Township	DEFIANCE	© 13,461
Marietta	Inc. Place	WASHINGTON	◆ 13,454
Bellefontaine	Inc. Place	LOGAN	◆ 13,414
Brecksville	Inc. Place	CUYAHOGA	© 13,382
Lawrence	MCD-Township	STARK	© 13,382
Clayton	Inc. Place	MONTGOMERY	© 13,347
White Oak	CDP	HAMILTON	© 13,277
Jefferson	MCD-Township	MERCER	© 13,231
Bucyrus	Inc. Place	CRAWFORD	© 13,224
Bexley	Inc. Place	FRANKLIN	© 13,203
Bedford	Inc. Place	CUYAHOGA	◆ 13,078
Greenville	Inc. Place	DARKE	◆ 13,059
Springfield	MCD-Township	CLARK	® 13,045
Landen	CDP	WARREN	© 12,766
Turtlecreek	MCD-Township	WARREN	© 12,617
Perkins	MCD-Township	ERIE	© 12,578
Bridgetown North	CDP-Census Area Only	HAMILTON	© 12,569
Blue Ash	Inc. Place	HAMILTON	© 12,513
East Liverpool	Inc. Place	COLUMBIANA	◆ 12,496
Lake	MCD-Township	LOGAN	© 12,492
Conneaut	Inc. Place	ASHTABULA	© 12,485
Harrison	MCD-Township	HAMILTON	© 12,469
Orange	MCD-Township	DELAWARE	© 12,464
Madison	MCD-Township	RICHLAND	® 12,426
Springboro	Inc. Place	WARREN	© 12,380
Streetsboro	Inc. Place	PORTAGE	© 12,311
Englewood	Inc. Place	MONTGOMERY	© 12,235
Pierce	MCD-Township	CLERMONT	© 12,226
Shawnee	MCD-Township	ALLEN	© 12,220
Green	MCD-Township	WAYNE	© 12,194
Seven Hills	Inc. Place	CUYAHOGA	© 12,080
Salem	Inc. Place	COLUMBIANA	◆ 11,969
Geneva	MCD-Township	ASHTABULA	© 11,954
Wilmington	Inc. Place	CLINTON	® 11,875
Mad River	MCD-Township	CLARK	© 11,828
Franklin	MCD-Township	FRANKLIN	© 11,798
Amherst	Inc. Place	LORAIN	© 11,797
Ravenna	Inc. Place	PORTAGE	◆ 11,785
Dover	Inc. Place	TUSCARAWAS	◆ 11,763
Struthers	Inc. Place	MAHONING	© 11,756
Union	MCD-Township	ROSS	© 11,750
Loveland	Inc. Place	HAMILTON	© 11,677
Urbana	Inc. Place	CHAMPAIGN	© 11,613
St. Marys	MCD-Township	AUGLAIZE	© 11,600
Norton	Inc. Place	SUMMIT	© 11,523
Avon	Inc. Place	LORAIN	© 11,446
Falls	MCD-Township	HOCKING	© 11,409
Moorefield	MCD-Township	CLARK	© 11,402
Franklin	Inc. Place	WARREN	© 11,396
Bedford Heights	Inc. Place	CUYAHOGA	© 11,375
Galion	Inc. Place	CRAWFORD	© 11,341
Cambridge	Inc. Place	GUERNSEY	◆ 11,302
Genoa	MCD-Township	DELAWARE	© 11,293
Reading	Inc. Place	HAMILTON	© 11,292
Shiloh	CDP	MONTGOMERY	© 11,272
Beachwood	Inc. Place	CUYAHOGA	◆ 11,231
Ironton	Inc. Place	LAWRENCE	© 11,211
Coshocton	Inc. Place	COSHOCTON	◆ 11,210
Springdale	Inc. Place	HAMILTON	◆ 11,156
Island Creek	MCD-Township	JEFFERSON	® 11,152
Pleasant	MCD-Township	VAN WERT	© 11,120
Northbrook	CDP	HAMILTON	© 11,076
Forestville	CDP	HAMILTON	© 10,978
Chester	MCD-Township	GEAUGA	© 10,968
Vermilion	Inc. Place	ERIE	© 10,927
Bainbridge	MCD-Township	GEAUGA	© 10,916
Girard	Inc. Place	TRUMBULL	© 10,902
Coventry	MCD-Township	SUMMIT	© 10,900
Van Wert	Inc. Place	VAN WERT	© 10,690
Olmsted	MCD-Township	CUYAHOGA	© 10,575
Huron	MCD-Township	ERIE	© 10,530
Brooklyn	Inc. Place	CUYAHOGA	◆ 10,496
Lake	MCD-Township	WOOD	© 10,350
Napoleon	MCD-Township	HENRY	© 10,331
Unity	MCD-Township	COLUMBIANA	© 10,294
Mill	MCD-Township	TUSCARAWAS	© 10,290
Pataskala	Inc. Place	LICKING	© 10,249
Union	MCD-Township	MIAMI	© 10,222
Richmond Heights	Inc. Place	CUYAHOGA	◆ 10,188
Montgomery	Inc. Place	HAMILTON	© 10,163
Celina	Inc. Place	MERCER	◆ 10,091
Chippewa	MCD-Township	WAYNE	© 10,085
North College Hill	Inc. Place	HAMILTON	© 10,082
Saybrook	MCD-Township	ASHTABULA	© 10,051
Brookfield	MCD-Township	TRUMBULL	© 10,020
Porter	MCD-Township	SCIOTO	© 9,892
Portage Lakes	CDP	SUMMIT	© 9,870
Shelby	Inc. Place	RICHLAND	© 9,821
Bath	MCD-Township	ALLEN	® 9,810
Liberty	MCD-Township	HIGHLAND	© 9,798
Pickerington	Inc. Place	FAIRFIELD	© 9,792
Champion	MCD-Township	TRUMBULL	© 9,762
Sharon	MCD-Township	RICHLAND	© 9,720
Pultney	MCD-Township	BELMONT	© 9,700
Springfield	MCD-Township	RICHLAND	© 9,674
Bath	MCD-Township	SUMMIT	© 9,635
Hamilton	MCD-Township	WARREN	© 9,630
Fairfield	MCD-Township	COLUMBIANA	© 9,583
Vermilion	MCD-Township	ERIE	© 9,575
Green Creek	MCD-Township	SANDUSKY	© 9,527
Newton	MCD-Township	TRUMBULL	© 9,524
Blacklick Estates	CDP-Census Area Only	FRANKLIN	© 9,518
Lincoln Village	CDP-Census Area Only	FRANKLIN	© 9,482
Wapakoneta	Inc. Place	AUGLAIZE	© 9,474
Waterville	MCD-Township	LUCAS	© 9,469
Campbell	Inc. Place	MAHONING	© 9,460
Sheffield Lake	Inc. Place	LORAIN	© 9,371
Sagamore Hills	MCD-Township	SUMMIT	© 9,340
Napoleon	Inc. Place	HENRY	© 9,318
Clinton	MCD-Township	FULTON	© 9,280
Ravenna	MCD-Township	PORTAGE	© 9,270
Milton	MCD-Township	WAYNE	© 9,254
Macedonia	Inc. Place	SUMMIT	© 9,224
Tipp City	Inc. Place	MIAMI	© 9,221
Oakwood	Inc. Place	MONTGOMERY	© 9,215
Blendon	MCD-Township	FRANKLIN	© 9,193
Fayette	MCD-Township	LAWRENCE	© 9,169
Scioto	MCD-Township	PICKAWAY	© 9,165
Nimishillen	MCD-Township	STARK	© 9,098
Cheviot	Inc. Place	HAMILTON	© 9,015
Union	MCD-Township	LAWRENCE	© 9,002
Granville	MCD-Township	LICKING	© 8,994
Tate	MCD-Township	CLERMONT	© 8,935
Madeira	Inc. Place	HAMILTON	© 8,923
Louisville	Inc. Place	STARK	© 8,904
Perry Heights	CDP	STARK	© 8,900
London	Inc. Place	MADISON	© 8,771
Cross Creek	MCD-Township	JEFFERSON	© 8,761
Trenton	Inc. Place	BUTLER	© 8,746
Rome	MCD-Township	LAWRENCE	© 8,694
Beckett Ridge	CDP-Census Area Only	BUTLER	© 8,663
Madison	MCD-Township	BUTLER	© 8,611
Lemon	MCD-Township	BUTLER	® 8,609
Pleasant	MCD-Township	HARDIN	© 8,608
Willoughby Hills	Inc. Place	LAKE	© 8,595
Falls	MCD-Township	MUSKINGUM	© 8,585
Clay	MCD-Township	MONTGOMERY	© 8,566
Orrville	Inc. Place	WAYNE	© 8,551
Heath	Inc. Place	LICKING	© 8,527
Northridge	CDP	MONTGOMERY	© 8,487
Swan Creek	MCD-Township	FULTON	© 8,461
North Madison	CDP	LAKE	© 8,451
Butler	MCD-Township	MONTGOMERY	© 8,382
Saint Marys	Inc. Place	AUGLAIZE	© 8,342
Union	MCD-Township	LICKING	© 8,339
Kenton	Inc. Place	HARDIN	© 8,336
Bryan	Inc. Place	WILLIAMS	© 8,333
Brown	MCD-Township	CARROLL	© 8,300
Hubbard	Inc. Place	TRUMBULL	© 8,284
Wyoming	Inc. Place	HAMILTON	© 8,261
Perry	MCD-Township	LAKE	© 8,240
Monroe	MCD-Township	CLERMONT	© 8,236
Oberlin	Inc. Place	LORAIN	© 8,195
Bellevue	Inc. Place	SANDUSKY	© 8,193
Eaton	Inc. Place	PREBLE	© 8,133
Mentor-on-the-Lake	Inc. Place	LAKE	© 8,127
Highland Heights	Inc. Place	CUYAHOGA	© 8,082
Northgate	CDP-Census Area Only	HAMILTON	© 8,016
Brimfield	MCD-Township	PORTAGE	© 7,963
Olmsted Falls	Inc. Place	CUYAHOGA	© 7,962
Ottawa	MCD-Township	PUTNAM	© 7,961
St. Clair	MCD-Township	COLUMBIANA	© 7,961
Huron	Inc. Place	ERIE	© 7,958
Hamilton	MCD-Township	FRANKLIN	© 7,950
Woodbourne-Hyde Park	CDP-Census Area Only	MONTGOMERY	© 7,910
Hanover	MCD-Township	BUTLER	© 7,878
German	MCD-Township	MONTGOMERY	© 7,830
Bridgetown	RMC Place	HAMILTON	● 7,800
Medina	MCD-Township	MEDINA	© 7,783
Brownhelm	MCD-Township	LORAIN	© 7,782
Pee Pee	MCD-Township	PIKE	© 7,776
York	MCD-Township	ATHENS	© 7,740
German	MCD-Township	CLARK	© 7,663

Entries in **UPPERCASE** are counties.
Entries in **bold** have populations of 2,500 or more.
Names in parentheses are alternate names.

Inc. Place	Incorporated Place
RMC Place	Rand McNally Designated Place
CDP	Census Designated Place
MCD	Minor Civil Division

⊡ County Seat
▲ Minor Civil Division
elev. Elevation
P Post Office

H Hospital
C College
■ Principal Business Center
★ Ranally Metro Area (RMA) Abbreviation
z Zip Code(s)

Ⓟ Previous Census Population
® Revised Census Population
Ⓐ Annexation Population
● Rand McNally Population Estimate
© Final Census Population
Ⓢ Special Census Population
◆ Estimated Population

For additional definitions see Glossary, Volume 1, and Introduction, Volume 2.

Place Name	Place Type	County	Population
Dent	CDP	HAMILTON	© 7,612
Amherst	MCD-Township	LORAIN	© 7,598
Harrison	Inc. Place	HAMILTON	© 7,487
Kenwood	CDP	HAMILTON	© 7,423
Crane	MCD-Township	WYANDOT	© 7,394
Canfield	Inc. Place	MAHONING	© 7,374
Carlisle	MCD-Township	LORAIN	© 7,339
St. Clair	MCD-Township	BUTLER	© 7,336
Liberty	MCD-Township	FAIRFIELD	© 7,265
Wayne	MCD-Township	WARREN	© 7,250
Fairlawn	Inc. Place	SUMMIT	◆ 7,241
Martins Ferry	Inc. Place	BELMONT	© 7,226
Rootstown	MCD-Township	PORTAGE	© 7,212
Groesbeck	CDP	HAMILTON	© 7,202
Liberty	MCD-Township	HARDIN	© 7,149
Mount Healthy	Inc. Place	HAMILTON	© 7,149
Monroe	Inc. Place	BUTLER	® 7,135
Independence	Inc. Place	CUYAHOGA	© 7,109
Wauseon	Inc. Place	FULTON	© 7,091
Pleasant	MCD-Township	FRANKLIN	© 7,030
Bellbrook	Inc. Place	GREENE	© 7,009
Delphos	Inc. Place	ALLEN	© 6,944
Jefferson	MCD-Township	MADISON	© 6,935
Madison	MCD-Township	HIGHLAND	© 6,922
Columbia	MCD-Township	LORAIN	© 6,912
Moraine	Inc. Place	MONTGOMERY	© 6,897
Northridge	CDP	CLARK	© 6,853
Cortland	Inc. Place	TRUMBULL	© 6,830
Perry	MCD-Township	LAWRENCE	© 6,813
Willard	Inc. Place	HURON	© 6,806
Jefferson	MCD-Township	MONTGOMERY	© 6,787
Washington	MCD-Township	RICHLAND	© 6,777
Marion	MCD-Township	ALLEN	© 6,773
Monclova	MCD-Township	LUCAS	© 6,767
Hinckley	MCD-Township	MEDINA	© 6,753
Sugar Creek	MCD-Township	STARK	© 6,740
Logan	Inc. Place	HOCKING	© 6,704
Grandview Heights	Inc. Place	FRANKLIN	© 6,695
Kirtland	Inc. Place	LAKE	© 6,670
Belpre	Inc. Place	WASHINGTON	© 6,660
Wright-Patterson AFB	CDP-Census Area Only	GREENE	© 6,656
Sugarcreek	MCD-Township	GREENE	© 6,629
Sandusky South	CDP-Census Area Only	ERIE	© 6,599
Geneva	Inc. Place	ASHTABULA	© 6,595
Pike	MCD-Township	PERRY	© 6,595
Columbia	MCD-Township	HAMILTON	© 6,557
Dry Run	CDP-Census Area Only	HAMILTON	© 6,553
Upper Sandusky	Inc. Place	WYANDOT	© 6,533
East Union	MCD-Township	WAYNE	© 6,527
Sugar Creek	MCD-Township	WAYNE	© 6,502
Harrison	MCD-Township	LICKING	© 6,494
Newberry	MCD-Township	MIAMI	© 6,490
Howland Center	CDP-Census Area Only	TRUMBULL	© 6,481
Center	MCD-Township	COLUMBIANA	© 6,473
Wheelersburg	CDP	SCIOTO	© 6,471
Liberty	MCD-Township	HANCOCK	© 6,469
Beaver	MCD-Township	MAHONING	© 6,466
Butler	MCD-Township	MERCER	© 6,459
German	MCD-Township	FULTON	© 6,458
Munson	MCD-Township	GEAUGA	© 6,450
Troy	MCD-Township	RICHLAND	© 6,449
Ross	MCD-Township	BUTLER	© 6,448
Salisbury	MCD-Township	MEIGS	© 6,441
Walnut	MCD-Township	FAIRFIELD	© 6,436
Warren	MCD-Township	TRUMBULL	® 6,425
Harrison	MCD-Township	PICKAWAY	© 6,424
Jackson	MCD-Township	MONTGOMERY	© 6,420
Rossford	Inc. Place	WOOD	© 6,406
Ballville	MCD-Township	SANDUSKY	© 6,395
Port Clinton	Inc. Place	OTTAWA	© 6,391
Suffield	MCD-Township	PORTAGE	© 6,383
Bloom	MCD-Township	FAIRFIELD	© 6,374
Hillsboro	Inc. Place	HIGHLAND	© 6,368
Covedale	CDP	HAMILTON	© 6,360
Rittman	Inc. Place	WAYNE	© 6,314
Bazetta	MCD-Township	TRUMBULL	© 6,306
Margaretta	MCD-Township	ERIE	© 6,289
Milford	Inc. Place	CLERMONT	© 6,284
Powell	Inc. Place	DELAWARE	© 6,247
Mifflin	MCD-Township	RICHLAND	© 6,218
Jackson	Inc. Place	JACKSON	© 6,184
Perry	MCD-Township	MONTGOMERY	© 6,184
Noble	MCD-Township	DEFIANCE	© 6,171
Xenia	MCD-Township	GREENE	© 6,117
Tuscarawas	MCD-Township	STARK	© 6,093
Richland	MCD-Township	ALLEN	© 6,090
Wellston	Inc. Place	JACKSON	© 6,078
Clyde	Inc. Place	SANDUSKY	© 6,064
Springfield	MCD-Township	MAHONING	© 6,054
Woodbourne	RMC Place	MONTGOMERY	● 6,050
Pepper Pike	Inc. Place	CUYAHOGA	© 6,040
Mead	MCD-Township	BELMONT	© 6,023
Huntington	MCD-Township	ROSS	© 6,018
Grafton	Inc. Place	LORAIN	® 6,004
Deer Park	Inc. Place	HAMILTON	© 5,982
Shalersville	MCD-Township	PORTAGE	© 5,976
Eaton	MCD-Township	LORAIN	® 5,973
Lagrange	MCD-Township	LORAIN	© 5,972
Washington	MCD-Township	SCIOTO	© 5,971
Paris	MCD-Township	STARK	© 5,969
Plain	MCD-Township	FRANKLIN	© 5,926
The Village of Indian Hill	Inc. Place	HAMILTON	© 5,907
Wellington	MCD-Township	LORAIN	© 5,904
Osnaburg	MCD-Township	STARK	© 5,886
Warren	MCD-Township	BELMONT	© 5,870
Gilead	MCD-Township	MORROW	© 5,868
Mack South	CDP-Census Area Only	HAMILTON	© 5,837
Stonelick	MCD-Township	CLERMONT	© 5,816
Newbury	MCD-Township	GEAUGA	© 5,805
Superior	MCD-Township	WILLIAMS	© 5,769
New Carlisle	Inc. Place	CLARK	© 5,735
Gallipolis	MCD-Township	GALLIA	© 5,707
Salem	MCD-Township	COLUMBIANA	© 5,703
Toronto	Inc. Place	JEFFERSON	© 5,676
Uhrichsville	Inc. Place	TUSCARAWAS	© 5,662
Bethlehem	MCD-Township	STARK	© 5,650
Hardy	MCD-Township	HOLMES	© 5,643
Columbiana	Inc. Place	COLUMBIANA	© 5,635
Lexington	MCD-Township	STARK	© 5,583
Ada	Inc. Place	HARDIN	© 5,582
Union	Inc. Place	MONTGOMERY	© 5,574
Whitewater	MCD-Township	HAMILTON	© 5,564
Jefferson	MCD-Township	ASHTABULA	© 5,559
Pleasant	MCD-Township	FAIRFIELD	© 5,549
Russell	MCD-Township	GEAUGA	© 5,529
Monroe	MCD-Township	LICKING	© 5,523
Summerside	CDP	CLERMONT	© 5,523
Salem	MCD-Township	OTTAWA	© 5,517
Green	MCD-Township	GALLIA	© 5,514
Randolph	MCD-Township	PORTAGE	© 5,504
Brentwood	RMC Place	HAMILTON	● 5,500
Marion	MCD-Township	CLINTON	© 5,489
Jackson	MCD-Township	CRAWFORD	© 5,487
Lafayette	MCD-Township	MEDINA	© 5,476
Northwood	Inc. Place	WOOD	© 5,471
Brunswick Hills	MCD-Township	MEDINA	© 5,469
Guilford	MCD-Township	MEDINA	© 5,447
Union	MCD-Township	MADISON	® 5,447
Springfield	MCD-Township	MUSKINGUM	© 5,433
Richfield	MCD-Township	SUMMIT	© 5,424
Etna	MCD-Township	LICKING	© 5,410
Montville	MCD-Township	MEDINA	© 5,410
Newton	MCD-Township	MUSKINGUM	© 5,402
Harrison	MCD-Township	PERRY	© 5,399
Jackson	MCD-Township	GUERNSEY	© 5,399
Olive	MCD-Township	NOBLE	© 5,395
Stokes	MCD-Township	LOGAN	© 5,367
Morgan	MCD-Township	BUTLER	© 5,328
Jefferson	MCD-Township	FRANKLIN	© 5,322
Munroe Falls	Inc. Place	SUMMIT	© 5,314
Brookville	Inc. Place	MONTGOMERY	© 5,289
Goshen	MCD-Township	TUSCARAWAS	© 5,285
Franklin	MCD-Township	PORTAGE	© 5,276
Pleasant Run	CDP	HAMILTON	© 5,267
Montrose-Ghent	CDP-Census Area Only	SUMMIT	© 5,261
Wooster	MCD-Township	WAYNE	© 5,250
Ohio	MCD-Township	CLERMONT	© 5,245
Lawrence	MCD-Township	TUSCARAWAS	© 5,241
Nelsonville	Inc. Place	ATHENS	© 5,230
Washington	MCD-Township	VAN WERT	© 5,228
Ontario	Inc. Place	RICHLAND	◆ 5,226
Pleasant	MCD-Township	BROWN	© 5,187
Silverton	Inc. Place	HAMILTON	© 5,178
Auburn	MCD-Township	GEAUGA	© 5,158
Chardon	Inc. Place	GEAUGA	© 5,156
Oxford	MCD-Township	TUSCARAWAS	© 5,133
Carlisle	Inc. Place	WARREN	© 5,121
Clay	MCD-Township	OTTAWA	© 5,118
Miami	MCD-Township	GREENE	© 5,106
Granville	Inc. Place	LICKING	® 5,098
Cedarville	MCD-Township	GREENE	© 5,092
Crestline	Inc. Place	CRAWFORD	© 5,088
Crawford	MCD-Township	WYANDOT	© 5,080
Tiffin	MCD-Township	ADAMS	© 5,075
Canal Fulton	Inc. Place	STARK	© 5,061
Wayne	MCD-Township	CLERMONT	© 5,025
Knox	MCD-Township	JEFFERSON	© 5,011
Williamsburg	MCD-Township	CLERMONT	© 5,005
Hicksville	MCD-Township	DEFIANCE	© 5,003
Newton Falls	Inc. Place	TRUMBULL	© 5,002

County Business Data

County	FIPS Code	County Seat	Land Area (Sq. Mi.)	Census Population			Wholesale Trade		Manufacturing, 2002			
				4/1/2000	4/1/1990	% Change 1990-2000	Sales, 2002 ($1,000)	% Change 1997-2002	Establish-ments	Total Employees	Value Added ($1,000)	Ranally Mfg. Units
Adams	001	West Union	584	27,330	25,371	7.7	27,191	-15.2	35	650	40,368	21
Allen	003	Lima	404	108,473	109,755	-1.2	3,619,539	(d)	142	11,742	3,720,876	1,969
Ashland	005	Ashland	424	52,523	47,507	10.6	137,045	13.0	96	5,322	611,651	324
Ashtabula	007	Jefferson	702	102,728	99,821	2.9	162,584	7.0	193	8,883	768,197	406
Athens	009	Athens	507	62,223	59,549	4.5	(d)	(d)	37	(d)	(d)	...
Auglaize	011	Wapakoneta	401	46,611	44,585	4.5	315,789	(d)	97	7,242	734,140	388
Belmont	013	St. Clairsville	537	70,226	71,074	-1.2	(d)	(d)	57	1,727	159,744	85
Brown	015	Georgetown	492	42,285	34,966	20.9	(d)	(d)	23	530	24,621	13
Butler	017	Hamilton	467	332,807	291,479	14.2	7,320,725	(d)	439	20,619	2,471,499	1,308
Carroll	019	Carrollton	395	28,836	26,521	8.7	(d)	(d)	41	1,611	125,550	66
Champaign	021	Urbana	429	38,890	36,019	8.0	105,991	-34.1	49	3,462	579,165	306
Clark	023	Springfield	400	144,742	147,548	-1.9	1,302,839	25.9	204	9,300	1,195,373	632
Clermont	025	Batavia	452	177,977	150,187	18.5	(d)	(d)	176	7,734	877,308	464
Clinton	027	Wilmington	411	40,543	35,415	14.5	114,677	-40.3	47	4,195	367,804	195
Columbiana	029	Lisbon	532	112,075	108,276	3.5	(d)	(d)	210	7,106	520,557	275
Coshocton	031	Coshocton	564	36,655	35,427	3.5	106,940	51.6	54	3,818	400,451	212
Crawford	033	Bucyrus	402	46,966	47,870	-1.9	230,749	31.6	90	5,871	655,104	347
Cuyahoga	035	Cleveland	458	1,393,978	1,412,140	-1.3	23,055,380	-26.0	2,477	97,742	10,396,627	5,501
Darke	037	Greenville	600	53,309	53,619	-0.6	282,876	-42.4	81	5,053	551,743	292
Defiance	039	Defiance	411	39,500	39,350	0.4	(d)	(d)	54	5,764	615,677	326
Delaware	041	Delaware	442	109,989	66,929	64.3	1,231,276	48.6	144	5,564	536,360	284
Erie	043	Sandusky	255	79,551	76,779	3.6	320,233	-19.3	126	8,732	1,198,890	634
Fairfield	045	Lancaster	505	122,759	103,461	18.7	(d)	(d)	128	5,319	424,825	225
Fayette	047	Washington Court House	407	28,433	27,466	3.5	(d)	(d)	40	3,065	295,045	156
Franklin	049	Columbus	540	1,068,978	961,437	11.2	25,947,667	16.3	1,039	45,727	6,996,698	3,702
Fulton	051	Wauseon	407	42,084	38,498	9.3	451,608	23.6	111	9,099	1,157,011	612
Gallia	053	Gallipolis	469	31,069	30,954	0.4	(d)	(d)	21	(d)	(d)	...
Geauga	055	Chardon	404	90,895	81,129	12.0	700,160	1.3	223	9,934	956,420	506
Greene	057	Xenia	415	147,886	136,731	8.2	704,045	-54.3	119	4,461	504,130	267
Guernsey	059	Cambridge	522	40,792	39,024	4.5	100,534	3.3	63	3,257	417,436	221
Hamilton	061	Cincinnati	407	845,303	866,228	-2.4	28,908,517	-11.8	1,308	61,807	10,288,806	5,443
Hancock	063	Findlay	531	71,295	65,536	8.8	(d)	(d)	99	12,406	1,439,857	762
Hardin	065	Kenton	470	31,945	31,111	2.7	59,917	(d)	41	2,234	229,819	122
Harrison	067	Cadiz	404	15,856	16,085	-1.4	52,477	-16.8	20	738	47,854	25
Henry	069	Napoleon	417	29,210	29,108	0.4	(d)	(d)	50	3,703	1,140,575	603
Highland	071	Hillsboro	553	40,875	35,728	14.4	81,542	-62.6	44	3,504	323,711	171
Hocking	073	Logan	423	28,241	25,533	10.6	63,993	(d)	31	1,424	133,794	71
Holmes	075	Millersburg	423	38,943	32,849	18.6	105,795	14.3	206	5,237	474,041	251
Huron	077	Norwalk	493	59,487	56,240	5.8	193,524	-5.3	106	8,553	1,028,262	544
Jackson	079	Jackson	420	32,641	30,230	8.0	92,324	27.4	37	3,296	621,778	329
Jefferson	081	Steubenville	410	73,894	80,298	-8.0	248,141	(d)	42	3,344	437,634	232
Knox	083	Mount Vernon	527	54,500	47,473	14.8	(d)	(d)	75	4,373	423,306	224
Lake	085	Painesville	228	227,511	215,499	5.6	2,153,302	35.3	735	22,002	2,390,248	1,265
Lawrence	087	Ironton	455	62,319	61,834	0.8	66,857	(d)	39	773	64,486	34
Licking	089	Newark	687	145,491	128,300	13.4	583,039	-6.4	158	7,774	1,122,231	594
Logan	091	Bellefontaine	458	46,005	42,310	8.7	(d)	(d)	55	6,188	1,760,650	932
Lorain	093	Elyria	493	284,664	271,126	5.0	1,810,958	81.5	432	24,409	2,884,019	1,526
Lucas	095	Toledo	340	455,054	462,361	-1.6	6,091,272	-3.3	615	31,172	3,724,116	1,970
Madison	097	London	465	40,213	37,068	8.5	(d)	(d)	49	(d)	(d)	...
Mahoning	099	Youngstown	415	257,555	264,806	-2.7	1,850,460	-13.2	398	10,115	942,642	499
Marion	101	Marion	404	66,217	64,274	3.0	(d)	(d)	87	7,166	1,082,747	573
Medina	103	Medina	422	151,095	122,354	23.5	1,355,566	17.3	294	9,537	793,574	420
Meigs	105	Pomeroy	429	23,072	22,987	0.4	26,918	23.9	...	(d)	(d)	...
Mercer	107	Celina	463	40,924	39,443	3.8	422,603	9.9	69	3,250	337,868	179
Miami	109	Troy	407	98,868	93,182	6.1	(d)	(d)	256	13,108	1,358,190	719
Monroe	111	Woodsfield	456	15,180	15,497	-2.0	(d)	(d)	15	(d)	(d)	...
Montgomery	113	Dayton	462	559,062	573,809	-2.6	8,194,550	7.3	900	44,277	8,410,079	4,450
Morgan	115	McConnelsville	418	14,897	14,194	5.0	(d)	(d)	...	(d)	(d)	...
Morrow	117	Mount Gilead	406	31,628	27,749	14.0	(d)	(d)	30	(d)	(d)	...
Muskingum	119	Zanesville	665	84,585	82,068	3.1	492,207	18.4	109	7,530	768,691	407
Noble	121	Caldwell	399	14,058	11,336	24.0	13,550	-52.0	15	619	65,157	34
Ottawa	123	Port Clinton	255	40,985	40,029	2.4	63,483	-26.0	56	2,373	232,483	123
Paulding	125	Paulding	416	20,293	20,488	-1.0	63,747	-8.7	40	1,550	137,518	73
Perry	127	New Lexington	410	34,078	31,557	8.0	38,654	(d)	30	1,486	144,521	76
Pickaway	129	Circleville	502	52,727	48,255	9.3	(d)	(d)	44	3,752	420,631	223
Pike	131	Waverly	441	27,695	24,249	14.2	18,286	-30.0	35	4,683	641,176	339
Portage	133	Ravenna	492	152,061	142,585	6.6	1,734,393	46.9	287	11,178	1,137,665	602
Preble	135	Eaton	425	42,337	40,113	5.5	(d)	(d)	61	3,375	330,929	175
Putnam	137	Ottawa	484	34,726	33,819	2.7	131,680	-18.7	50	3,847	357,607	189
Richland	139	Mansfield	497	128,852	126,137	2.2	788,033	24.4	207	13,896	1,385,581	733
Ross	141	Chillicothe	688	73,345	69,330	5.8	(d)	(d)	45	3,619	699,705	370
Sandusky	143	Fremont	409	61,792	61,963	-0.3	337,794	58.0	119	9,691	1,495,771	791
Scioto	145	Portsmouth	612	79,195	80,327	-1.4	144,297	-34.2	61	2,061	164,463	87
Seneca	147	Tiffin	551	58,683	59,733	-1.8	(d)	(d)	93	4,988	599,210	317
Shelby	149	Sidney	409	47,910	44,915	6.7	355,834	28.8	149	13,685	1,261,874	668
Stark	151	Canton	576	378,098	367,585	2.9	(d)	(d)	604	34,491	4,123,786	2,182
Summit	153	Akron	413	542,899	514,990	5.4	8,400,961	-0.5	1,043	38,394	4,510,125	2,386
Trumbull	155	Warren	616	225,116	227,813	-1.2	1,460,054	20.5	269	24,866	3,484,792	1,844

Entries in UPPERCASE are counties.
Entries in **bold** have populations of 2,500 or more.
Names in parentheses are alternate names.
Inc. Place — Incorporated Place
RMC Place — Rand McNally Designated Place
CDP — Census Designated Place
MCD — Minor Civil Division

⊡ County Seat
▲ Minor Civil Division
elev. Elevation
🅿 Post Office

🄷 Hospital
🄲 College
■ Principal Business Center
★ Ranally Metro Area (RMA) Abbreviation
z Zip Code(s)

Ⓟ Previous Census Population
® Revised Census Population
Ⓐ Annexation Population
● Rand McNally Population Estimate
© Final Census Population
Ⓢ Special Census Population
◆ Estimated Population

For additional definitions see Glossary, Volume 1, and Introduction, Volume 2.

County	FIPS Code	County Seat	Land Area (Sq. Mi.)	Census Population			Wholesale Trade		Manufacturing, 2002			
				4/1/2000	4/1/1990	% Change 1990-2000	Sales, 2002 ($1,000)	% Change 1997-2002	Establish-ments	Total Employees	Value Added ($1,000)	Ranally Mfg. Units
Tuscarawas	157	New Philadelphia	568	90,914	84,090	8.1	295,970	-1.4	232	9,231	850,881	450
Union	159	Marysville	437	40,909	31,969	28.0	(d)	(d)	40	(d)	(d)	...
Van Wert	161	Van Wert	410	29,659	30,464	-2.6	(d)	(d)	46	3,790	323,026	171
Vinton	163	McArthur	414	12,806	11,098	15.4	(d)	(d)	...	(d)	(d)	...
Warren	165	Lebanon	400	158,383	113,909	39.0	7,881,447	30.6	216	12,211	1,093,335	578
Washington	167	Marietta	635	63,251	62,254	1.6	298,791	79.3	110	5,009	756,303	400
Wayne	169	Wooster	555	111,564	101,461	10.0	655,920	0.3	280	14,934	1,609,486	852
Williams	171	Bryan	422	39,188	36,956	6.0	197,237	-42.8	141	7,859	796,555	421
Wood	173	Bowling Green	617	121,065	113,269	6.9	1,456,099	-2.7	226	14,330	1,612,246	853
Wyandot	175	Upper Sandusky	406	22,908	22,254	2.9	172,442	33.1	45	3,683	344,137	182
The State			**40,948**	**11,353,140**	**10,847,115**	**4.7**	**166,446,529**	**3.8**	**17,494**	**868,732**	**113,243,351**	**59,914**

(d) Data not available. Corresponding percentages or Ranally Manufacturing Units are estimates.
... Represents 0 or amount too minimal to be reported.

Administrative Divisions

Townships: All Ohio counties are divided into townships, except as noted below. Although legally incorporated, townships are not treated as incorporated places by the U.S. Census because the population often is scattered among several localities and rural areas rather than being concentrated in a single place. Only townships with an active government recognized by the U.S. Census of Governments are printed in this index.

Cities and Villages: Cities and villages may or may not exist within township areas. Some of the cities form parts of the townships which surround or adjoin them; the remainder are independent of the townships. Most of the incorporated villages, however, form parts of the townships which surround or adjoin them.

Index of Places and Counties

A

Abanaka; RMC Place; VAN WERT; ▲ Willshire; ***216** NJ-1; mail Ohio City z 45874; rural
Abbottsville; RMC Place; DARKE; ▲ Van Buren; ***218** SA-2; mail Arcanum z 45304
Aberdeen; Inc. Place; BROWN; ▲ Huntington; **218** SI-6; [P]; z 45101; Ⓟ 1,329; Ⓒ 1,603
Academia; RMC Place; KNOX; ▲ Morris, Clinton; **217** NL-11; elev. 1,036ft./316m.; mail Mount Vernon z 43050; ● 100
Acme; RMC Place; MEDINA; ▲ Guilford; ***217** NH-14; elev. 1,202ft./366m.; mail Wadsworth z 44281; ● 100
Ada; Inc. Place; HARDIN; ▲ Liberty; **216** NJ-5; [P] [C] 3,620; z 45810; Ⓟ 5,413; Ⓒ 5,582
Adams; MCD-Township; CHAMPAIGN; ***216** NM-4; mail Rosewood z 43070; Ⓟ 1,114; Ⓒ 1,100
Adams; MCD-Township; CLINTON; ***218** SE-5; mail Wilmington z 45177; Ⓟ 1,592; Ⓒ 1,901
Adams; MCD-Township; COSHOCTON; ***217** NL-15; mail Newcomerstown z 43832; Ⓟ 595; Ⓒ 755
Adams; MCD-Township; DARKE; ***216** NN-2; mail Bradford z 45308; Ⓟ 3,477; Ⓒ 3,508
Adams; MCD-Township; DEFIANCE; ***216** NF-3; mail Defiance z 43512; Ⓟ 980; Ⓒ 999
Adams; MCD-Township; GUERNSEY; ***219** SA-15; mail Cambridge z 43725; Ⓟ 1,877; Ⓒ 2,019
Adams; MCD-Township; MONROE; ***219** SC-19; mail Cameron z 43914; Ⓟ 595; Ⓒ 672
Adams; MCD-Township; MUSKINGUM; ***219** SA-14; mail Dresden z 43821; Ⓟ 397; Ⓒ 516
Adams; MCD-Township; SENECA; ***216** NG-9; mail Republic z 44867; Ⓟ 1,285; Ⓒ 1,337
Adams; MCD-Township; WASHINGTON; ***219** SD-16; mail Lowell z 45744; Ⓟ 1,741; Ⓒ 1,830
ADAMS; **218** SH-8; Ⓟ 25,371; Ⓒ 27,330; ◆ 27,858
Adams Mills; RMC Place; MUSKINGUM; ▲ Cass; **217** NN-14; [P]; z 43821; ● 160
Adamsville; RMC Place; GALLIA; ▲ Raccoon; ***219** SH-12; mail Bidwell z 45614
Adamsville; Inc. Place; MUSKINGUM; ▲ Salem; **217** NN-14; [P]; z 43802; Ⓟ 151; Ⓒ 127
Adario; RMC Place; RICHLAND; ▲ Butler; **217** NI-11; elev. 1,153ft./351m.; mail Greenwich z 44837, Shiloh z 44878; ● 120
Addison; RMC Place; GALLIA; ▲ Addison; **219** SH-13; elev. 572ft./174m.; mail Gallipolis z 45631; ● 250
Addison; MCD-Township; GALLIA; ***219** SH-13; mail Gallipolis z 45631; Ⓟ 2,422; Ⓒ 2,366
Addyston; Inc. Place; HAMILTON; ▲ Miami; **218** SG-1; elev. 492ft./150m.; [P]; ★ **CIN**; z 45001; Ⓟ 1,198; Ⓒ 1,010
Adelphi; Inc. Place; ROSS; ▲ Colerain; **218** SE-10; elev. 838ft./255m.; [P]; z 43101; Ⓟ 398; Ⓒ 371
Adena; Inc. Place; JEFFERSON, HARRISON; ▲ Short Creek, Smithfield; **217** NM-19; elev. 884ft./269m.; [P]; z 43901; Ⓟ 842; Ⓒ 815
Adrian; RMC Place; SENECA; ▲ Big Spring; **216** NH-7; [P]; z 43316; ● 100
Africa; RMC Place; DELAWARE; ▲ Orange; **216** NM-9; elev. 865ft./264m.; ★ **COL**; mail Galena z 43021; ● 50
Afton; RMC Place; CLERMONT; ▲ Williamsburg; **218** SG-4; ★ **CIN**; mail Batavia z 45103; ● 200
Agosta; MARION; see New Bloomington (Inc. Place)
Ai; RMC Place; FULTON; ▲ Fulton; ***216** NE-5; ★ **TOL**; mail Swanton z 43558; rural
Aid; RMC Place; LAWRENCE; ▲ Aid; **219** SJ-12; mail Kitts Hill z 45645; ● 150
Aid; MCD-Township; LAWRENCE; ***219** SJ-11; mail Kitts Hill z 45645; Ⓟ 811; Ⓒ 907
Air Line Junction; RMC Place; LUCAS; ***216** NE-6; ★ **TOL**; pop. incl. with Toledo (Inc. Place)
Akron; Inc. Place; ⊡ SUMMIT; **217** NH-16; [P] [H] [C] 23,539 ■; ★ **AKR**; z 44301-17, z 44319-22, z 44325-26, z 44328, z 44333-34, z 44372, z 44393, z 44396, z 44398-99; Ⓟ 223,019; Ⓒ 217,074; ◆ 210,424
Akron Junction; RMC Place; SUMMIT; ★ **AKR**; pop. incl. with Akron (Inc. Place)
Albany; Inc. Place; ATHENS; ▲ Alexander, Lee; **219** SF-13; elev. 755ft./230m.; [P]; z 45710 & mail Shade z 45776; Ⓟ 795; Ⓒ 808
Al Bar Meadows; RMC Place; HAMILTON; ***218** SF-3; ★ **CIN**; mail Cincinnati z 45243; pop. incl. with The Village of Indian Hill (Inc. Place)
Albion; RMC Place; ASHLAND; ▲ Jackson; **217** NI-13; mail West Salem z 44287; ● 70
Alcony; RMC Place; MIAMI; ▲ Elizabeth; **218** SA-4; mail Troy z 45373; ● 150
Alexander; MCD-Township; ATHENS; ***219** SF-13; mail Athens z 45701; Ⓟ 2,366; Ⓒ 2,614
Alexanders; RMC Place; CUYAHOGA; ***217** NF-15; ★ **CLEV**; mail Independence z 44131; pop. incl. with Independence (Inc. Place)
Alexandersville; RMC Place; MONTGOMERY; ★ **DAY**; mail Dayton z 45449; pop. incl. with West Carrollton City (Inc. Place)
Alexandria; Inc. Place; LICKING; ▲ St. Albans; **217** NN-11; [P]; z 43001; Ⓟ 468; Ⓒ 85; Ⓡ 242
Alexis; RMC Place; LUCAS; ***216** ND-6; ★ **TOL**; pop. incl. with Toledo (Inc. Place)
Alexis Place; RMC Place; LUCAS; ▲ Washington; ***216** NF-5; ★ **TOL**; mail Toledo z 43612
Alfred; RMC Place; MEIGS; ▲ Orange; **219** SF-14; elev. 700ft./213m.; mail Coolville z 45723
Alger; Inc. Place; HARDIN; ▲ Marion; **216** NJ-5; elev. 978ft./298m.; [P]; z 45812; Ⓟ 864; Ⓒ 888
Alikanna; RMC Place; JEFFERSON; ▲ Island Creek; ***217** NL-20; ★ **STU-**; mail Steubenville z 43952; ● 110
Alledonia; RMC Place; BELMONT; ▲ Washington; **219** SB-19; [P]; z 43902; ● 60
Allen; MCD-Township; HANCOCK; ***216** NH-6; ★ **FIND**; mail Van Buren z 45889; Ⓟ 1,980; Ⓒ 2,110
Allen; MCD-Township; OTTAWA; ***216** NE-7; ★ **TOL**; mail Curtice z 43412; Ⓟ 3,177; Ⓒ 3,591
Allen; MCD-Township; UNION; ***216** NM-7; mail Rosewood z 43070; Ⓟ 901; Ⓒ 1,518
ALLEN; **216** NJ-4; Ⓟ 109,755; Ⓒ 108,473; ◆ 103,802
Allen Center; RMC Place; UNION; ▲ Allen; ***216** NM-7; mail Marysville z 43040
Allensburg; RMC Place; HIGHLAND; ▲ Dodson; **218** SF-6; mail Hillsboro z 45133; ● 100
Allensville; RMC Place; VINTON; ▲ Richland; **219** SF-11; [P]; z 45651; ● 65
Allentown; RMC Place; ALLEN; ▲ American; **216** NJ-3; elev. 803ft./245m.; ★ **LIMA**; mail Lima z 45807; ● 160
Allentown; RMC Place; SCIOTO; ▲ Porter; **218** SI-10; ★ **PTSM**; mail Wheelersburg z 45694; ● 300
Alliance; Inc. Place; STARK, MAHONING; **217** NI-17; elev. 1,174ft./358m.; [P] [H] [C] 2,193 ■; ★ **ALLI**; z 44601; Ⓟ 23,376; Ⓒ 23,253; ◆ 23,079
Alma; RMC Place; ROSS; ▲ Franklin; **218** SF-9; mail Waverly z 45690; ● 35
Alpha; RMC Place; GREENE; ▲ Beavercreek; **218** SC-4; [P]; ★ **DAY**; z 45301; pop. incl. with Beavercreek (Inc. Place)
Alta; RMC Place; RICHLAND; ▲ Springfield, Madison; ***217** NJ-11; ★ **MANS**; mail Mansfield z 44903
Altamont Hills; RMC Place; JEFFERSON; ▲ Steubenville; ***217** NL-20; ★ **STU-**; mail Mingo Junction z 43938; ● 500
Altamont Park; RMC Place; JEFFERSON; ★ **STU-**; mail Mingo Junction z 43938; pop. incl. with Mingo Junction (Inc. Place)
Alton; RMC Place; FRANKLIN; ▲ Prairie; ***218** SB-8; ★ **COL**; mail Galloway z 43119; ● 100
Alvada; RMC Place; SENECA; ▲ Big Spring; **216** NH-7; [P]; z 44802; ● 100
Alvordton; RMC Place; WILLIAMS; ▲ Mill Creek; **216** ND-2; elev. 847ft./258m.; [P]; z 43501; disincorporated September 1, 2007; Ⓟ 298; Ⓒ 305
Amanda; MCD-Township; ALLEN; ***216** NJ-3; mail Lima z 45807; Ⓟ 1,773; Ⓒ 1,913
Amanda; BUTLER; see Excello (RMC Place)
Amanda; Inc. Place; FAIRFIELD; ▲ Amanda; **218** SC-10; [P]; z 43102; Ⓟ 729; Ⓒ 707
Amanda; MCD-Township; FAIRFIELD; ***218** SC-10; [P]; z 43102; Ⓟ 2,262; Ⓒ 2,429
Amanda; MCD-Township; HANCOCK; ***216** NI-7; mail Mount Blanchard z 45867; Ⓟ 992; Ⓒ 1,045
Amberley; Inc. Place; HAMILTON; **218** SK-4; elev. 803ft./245m.; ★ **CIN**; mail Cincinnati z 45236-37; Ⓟ 3,108; Ⓒ 3,425
Amberly; RMC Place; FRANKLIN; ▲ Madison, Truro; **219** SI-20; ★ **COL**; mail Columbus z 43227; pop. incl. with Columbus (Inc. Place)
Amboy; RMC Place; ASHTABULA; ***217** NC-20; mail Conneaut z 44030; pop. incl. with Conneaut (Inc. Place)
Amboy; MCD-Township; FULTON; ***216** ND-5; mail Metamora z 43540; Ⓟ 1,531; Ⓒ 1,552
Amelia; Inc. Place; CLERMONT; ▲ Pierce, Batavia; **218** SG-3; [P]; ★ **CIN**; z 45102; Ⓟ 1,837; Ⓒ 2,752
American; MCD-Township; ALLEN; ***216** NJ-4; [C] 4,258; ★ **LIMA**; mail Lima z 45807; Ⓟ 12,407; Ⓒ 15,516; Ⓡ 14,025
Ames; MCD-Township; ATHENS; ***219** SE-14; mail Amesville z 45711; Ⓟ 1,128; Ⓒ 1,231
Amesville; Inc. Place; ATHENS; ▲ Ames; **219** SE-14; [P]; z 45711 & mail Sharpsburg z 45777; Ⓟ 250; Ⓒ 184
Amherst; Inc. Place; LORAIN; ▲ New Russia, Amherst; **217** NF-12; [P] [H]; ★ **CLEV**; z 44001; Ⓟ 10,332; Ⓒ 11,797
Amherst; MCD-Township; LORAIN; ***217** NF-12; [P]; ★ **CLEV**; z 44001; Ⓟ 7,060; Ⓒ 7,598
Amity; RMC Place; HAMILTON; ***218** SF-3; elev. 841ft./256m.; ★ **CIN**; mail Cincinnati z 45236; pop. incl. with Deer Park (Inc. Place)
Amity (Democracy); RMC Place; KNOX; ▲ Pike; **217** NL-12; elev. 1,160ft./354m.; mail Mount Vernon z 43050; ● 200
Amity; RMC Place; MADISON; ▲ Canaan; **216** NN-8; mail Plain City z 43064; ● 60
Amity; RMC Place; MONTGOMERY; ▲ Perry; ***218** SC-3; ★ **DAY**; mail Brookville z 45309
Amlin; RMC Place; FRANKLIN; ▲ Washington; **216** NN-8; elev. 944ft./288m.; [P]; ★ **COL**; z 43002; ● 500
Amlin Heights; RMC Place; GREENE; ▲ Xenia; ***218** SC-5; ★ **DAY**; mail Xenia z 45385; ● 1,100
Amsden; RMC Place; SENECA; ▲ Jackson; **216** NG-7; [P]; z 44830; ● 180
Amsterdam; Inc. Place; JEFFERSON; ▲ Smithfield; **217** NL-18; [P]; z 43903; Ⓟ 669; Ⓒ 568
Amsterdam; RMC Place; LICKING; ▲ Franklin; ***219** SB-12; mail Thornville z 43076
Anderson; MCD-Township; HAMILTON; ***218** SG-3; [P]; ★ **CIN**; z 45244, z 45254-55 & mail Cincinnati z 45230, z 45245; Ⓟ 39,939; Ⓒ 43,857
Anderson; RMC Place; ROSS; ▲ Union; ***218** SE-9; mail Chillicothe z 45601; ● 110
Anderson Ferry; RMC Place; HAMILTON; ***218** SG-2; ★ **CIN**; mail Cincinnati z 45238; pop. incl. with Cincinnati (Inc. Place)
Andersonville; RMC Place; ROSS; ▲ Union; **218** SE-9; elev. 653ft./199m.; mail Chillicothe z 45601; ● 200
Andis; RMC Place; LAWRENCE; ▲ Lawrence; **219** SJ-11; elev. 675ft./206m.; ★ **HNTG**; mail Kitts Hill z 45645
Andover; Inc. Place; ASHTABULA; ▲ Andover; **217** NE-20; [P]; z 44003; Ⓟ 1,216; Ⓒ 1,269
Andover; MCD-Township; ASHTABULA; ***217** NE-20; [P]; z 44003; Ⓟ 2,481; Ⓒ 2,672
Angle; RMC Place; GALLIA; ▲ Harrison; ***219** SI-13; mail Gallipolis z 45631; rural
Ankenytown; RMC Place; KNOX; ▲ Berlin; **217** NK-11; elev. 1,127ft./344m.; ★ **MANS**; mail Fredericktown z 43019; ● 60
Anlo; RMC Place; CLARK; ▲ Bethel; ***218** SB-5; ★ **SPR**; mail New Carlisle z 45344; rural
Anna; Inc. Place; SHELBY; ▲ Franklin, Dinsmore; **216** NL-3; [P]; z 45302; Ⓟ 1,164; Ⓒ 1,319
Annapolis; RMC Place; JEFFERSON; ▲ Salem; **217** NL-19; ★ **STU-**; mail Bloomingdale z 43910; ● 90
Ansonia; Inc. Place; DARKE; ▲ Brown; **216** NM-1; elev. 1,009ft./308m.; [P]; z 45303; Ⓟ 1,279; Ⓒ 1,145
Antioch; Inc. Place; MONROE; ▲ Perry; **219** SC-18; [P]; z 43793; Ⓟ 68; Ⓒ 89
Antiquity; RMC Place; MEIGS; ▲ Letart; **219** SH-14; mail Racine z 45771; ● 100
Antrim; RMC Place; GUERNSEY; ▲ Madison; **217** NN-16; mail Quaker City z 43773; ● 100
Antrim; MCD-Township; WYANDOT; ***216** NJ-8; mail Harpster z 43323; Ⓟ 1,322; Ⓒ 1,275
Antwerp; Inc. Place; PAULDING; ▲ Carryall; **216** NG-1; elev. 732ft./223m.; [P]; z 45813; Ⓟ 1,677; Ⓒ 1,740
Apple Creek; Inc. Place; WAYNE; ▲ East Union; **217** NJ-14; [P]; z 44606; Ⓟ 860; Ⓒ 999
Apple Grove; RMC Place; MEIGS; ▲ Letart; **219** SH-14; mail Racine z 45771; ● 90
Appleton; RMC Place; LICKING; ▲ Bennington; ***217** NM-11; elev. 1,147ft./350m.; mail Johnstown z 43031
Aquilla (Lake Aquilla); Inc. Place; GEAUGA; ▲ Claridon; **217** NE-17; ★ **CLEV**; mail Chardon z 44024; Ⓟ 360; Ⓒ 372
Arabia; RMC Place; LAWRENCE; ▲ Mason, Aid; **219** SI-12; elev. 599ft./183m.; mail Pedro z 45659; ● 50
Arcadia; Inc. Place; HANCOCK; ▲ Washington; **216** NH-7; elev. 808ft./246m.; [P]; z 44804; Ⓟ 546; Ⓒ 537
Arcanum; Inc. Place; DARKE; ▲ Twin; **218** SA-2; [P]; ★ **DAY**; z 45304; Ⓟ 1,953; Ⓒ 2,076
Archbold; Inc. Place; FULTON; ▲ German; **216** NE-3; elev. 734ft./224m.; [P]; z 43502, z 43570; Ⓟ 3,440; Ⓒ 4,290
Archer; MCD-Township; HARRISON; ***217** NL-18; mail Jewett z 43986; Ⓟ 299; Ⓒ 306
Archers Fork; RMC Place; WASHINGTON; ▲ Independence; ***219** SD-18; elev. 704ft./215m.; mail New Matamoras z 45767; rural
Arion; RMC Place; SCIOTO; ▲ Union; ***218** SH-9; elev. 588ft./179m.; mail Mc Dermott z 45652; rural
Arkoe; RMC Place; PIKE; ▲ Sunfish; ***218** SG-8; mail Piketon z 45661
Arlington; Inc. Place; HANCOCK; ▲ Madison; **216** NI-6; elev. 869ft./265m.; [P]; z 45814; Ⓟ 1,267; Ⓒ 1,351
Arlington; RMC Place; MONTGOMERY; ▲ Clay; **218** SB-3; ★ **DAY**; mail Brookville z 45309; ● 120
Arlington Heights; Inc. Place; HAMILTON; **218** SK-3; [P]; ★ **CIN**; z 45215; Ⓟ 1,084; Ⓒ 899
Armstrong Mills; BELMONT; see Armstrongs Mills (RMC Place)
Armstrongs Mills (Armstrong Mills); RMC Place; BELMONT; ▲ Washington; **219** SB-19; mail Jacobsburg z 43933; ● 100
Arnheim; RMC Place; BROWN; ▲ Franklin; **218** SH-5; mail Georgetown z 45121; ● 120
Arnold; RMC Place; MIAMI; ▲ Union; ***218** SB-3; ★ **DAY**; mail West Milton z 45383; pop. incl. with West Milton (Inc. Place)
Arnold; RMC Place; UNION; ▲ Jerome; ***216** NN-8; elev. 962ft./293m.; ★ **COL**; mail Plain City z 43064; ● 50
Arrow Head; RMC Place; GREENE; ★ **DAY**; mail Xenia z 45385; pop. incl. with Xenia (Inc. Place)
Artanna; RMC Place; KNOX; ▲ Harrison; ***217** NM-12; mail Gambier z 43022
Arthur; RMC Place; PAULDING; ▲ Auglaize; ***216** NG-3; elev. 720ft./219m.; mail Defiance z 43512
Ashland; Inc. Place; ⊡ ASHLAND; **217** NI-12; [P] [H] [C] 6,459 ■; z 44805; Ⓟ 20,079; Ⓒ 21,249; ◆ 21,902
ASHLAND; **217** NH-12; Ⓟ 47,507; Ⓒ 52,523; ◆ 55,685
Ashley; Inc. Place; DELAWARE; **216** NL-9; elev. 989ft./301m.; [P]; z 43003; Ⓟ 1,059; Ⓒ 1,216
Ashley Corner; RMC Place; SCIOTO; ▲ Vernon, Bloom; ***218** SI-10; mail Wheelersburg z 45694; ● 200
Ash Ridge; RMC Place; BROWN; ▲ Jackson; **218** SH-6; elev. 1,023ft./312m.; mail Georgetown z 45121; ● 50
Ashtabula; Inc. Place; ASHTABULA; ▲ Saybrook, Ashtabula; **217** NC-19; [P] [H] ■; ★ **ASHT**; z 44004-05; Ⓟ 21,633; Ⓒ 20,962; ◆ 20,267
Ashtabula; MCD-Township; ASHTABULA; ***217** NC-19; [P]; ★ **ASHT**; z 44004-05; includes part of the City of Ashtabula; Ⓟ 23,989; Ⓒ 23,239
ASHTABULA; **217** ND-19; Ⓟ 99,821; Ⓒ 102,728; ◆ 97,813
Ashtabula Harbor; ASHTABULA; see Harbor (RMC Place)
Ashtabula Harbor; RMC Place; ASHTABULA; ***217** NC-18; ★ **ASHT**
Ashville; Inc. Place; PICKAWAY; ▲ Harrison; **218** SC-9; elev. 709ft./216m.; [P]; ★ **COL**; z 43103; Ⓟ 2,254; Ⓒ 3,174
Assumption (Caraghar); RMC Place; FULTON; ▲ Amboy; **216** ND-5; mail Swanton z 43558; ● 80
Athalia; Inc. Place; LAWRENCE; ▲ Rome; **219** SJ-12; ★ **HNTG**; mail Proctorville z 45669; Ⓟ 346; Ⓒ 328
Athens; Inc. Place; ⊡ ATHENS; ▲ Athens; **219** SE-13; elev. 723ft./220m.; [P] [H] [C] 20,146 ■; z 45701; Ⓟ 21,265; Ⓒ 21,342; ◆ 21,464
Athens; MCD-Township; ATHENS; ***219** SE-13; [P] [C] 20,146; z 45701; Ⓟ 27,428; Ⓒ 27,714
Athens; MCD-Township; HARRISON; ***217** NM-18; mail New Athens z 43981; Ⓟ 534; Ⓒ 520
ATHENS; **219** SF-14; Ⓟ 59,549; Ⓒ 62,223; ◆ 62,791
Atlanta; RMC Place; PICKAWAY; ▲ Perry; **218** SD-8; elev. 837ft./255m.; mail New Holland z 43145; ● 160
Atlas; BELMONT; see Boston (RMC Place)
Attica; Inc. Place; SENECA; ▲ Venice; **216** NH-9; [P]; z 44807; Ⓟ 944; Ⓒ 955
Attica Junction (Siam); RMC Place; SENECA; ▲ Reed; **216** NH-9; mail Attica z 44807; ● 100
Atwater; RMC Place; PORTAGE; ▲ Atwater; **217** NH-17; [P]; ★ **AKR**; z 44201; ● 850
Atwater; MCD-Township; PORTAGE; ***217** NH-17; [P]; ★ **AKR**; z 44201; Ⓟ 2,663; Ⓒ 2,762
Atwater Center; RMC Place; PORTAGE; ▲ Atwater; ★ **AKR**; mail Atwater z 44201
Auburn; RMC Place; BUTLER; ▲ Hanover, Morgan, Reily, Ross; **218** SE-1; elev. 803ft./245m.; ★ **CIN**; mail Hamilton z 45013; ● 200
Auburn; MCD-Township; CRAWFORD; ***216** NI-10; mail Tiro z 44887; Ⓟ 840; Ⓒ 897
Auburn (Auburn Twp); MCD-Township; GEAUGA; ***217** NF-17; ★ **CLEV**; mail Chagrin Falls z 44023, Mantua z 44255; Ⓟ 3,298; Ⓒ 5,158
Auburn; MCD-Township; TUSCARAWAS; ***217** NL-15; mail Sugarcreek z 44681; Ⓟ 820; Ⓒ 1,078
Auburn Center; RMC Place; GEAUGA; ▲ Auburn; **217** NF-17; ★ **CLEV**; mail Chagrin Falls z 44022; ● 100
Auburn Corners; RMC Place; GEAUGA; ▲ Auburn; **217** NF-17; elev. 1,208ft./368m.; ★ **CLEV**; mail Burton z 44021, Mantua z 44255; ● 260
Auburn Twp; GEAUGA; see Auburn (MCD-Township)
Augersburg; RMC Place; PORTAGE; ▲ Charlestown; ***217** NG-17; ★ **AKR**; mail Ravenna z 44266; rural
Auglaize; MCD-Township; ALLEN; ***216** NJ-5; ★ **LIMA**; mail Harrod z 45850; Ⓟ 2,778; Ⓒ 2,850
Auglaize; MCD-Township; PAULDING; ***216** NG-2; mail Defiance z 43512; Ⓟ 1,521; Ⓒ 1,535
AUGLAIZE; **216** NK-4; Ⓟ 44,585; Ⓒ 46,611; ◆ 46,223
Augusta; RMC Place; CARROLL; ▲ Augusta; **217** NJ-18; [P]; z 44607; ● 270
Augusta; MCD-Township; CARROLL; ***217** NJ-18; [P]; z 44607; Ⓟ 1,369; Ⓒ 1,599
Ault (Aults); RMC Place; BELMONT; ▲ Mead; ***219** SB-19; ★ **WHL**; mail Shadyside z 43947
Aultman; RMC Place; STARK, SUMMIT; ▲ Lake; ***217** NI-16; elev. 1,106ft./337m.; ★ **AKR**; mail Greentown z 44630, North Canton z 44720; ● 200
Aults; BELMONT; see Ault (RMC Place)
Aurelius; MCD-Township; WASHINGTON; ***219** SD-16; mail Macksburg z 45746; Ⓟ 445; Ⓒ 441
Aurora; Inc. Place; PORTAGE; **217** NG-16; elev. 1,130ft./344m.; [P]; ★ **CLEV**; z 44202; Ⓟ 9,192; Ⓒ 13,556
Aurora East; RMC Place; PORTAGE; ▲ Shalersville; ***217** NG-17; ★ **CLEV**; mail Kent z 44240; ● 1,200
Aurora Meadows; RMC Place; PORTAGE; ▲ Mantua; ★ **CLEV**; mail Aurora z 44202; ● 300
Austin; RMC Place; ROSS; ▲ Concord; **218** SE-8; mail Frankfort z 45628; ● 40
Austinburg; RMC Place; ASHTABULA; ▲ Austinburg; **217** ND-19; elev. 817ft./249m.; [P]; z 44010; ● 500
Austinburg; MCD-Township; ASHTABULA; ***217** ND-19; [P]; z 44010; Ⓟ 1,902; Ⓒ 2,234
Austintown; CDP; MAHONING; ▲ Austintown; **217** NH-19; [P]; ★ **YNGS-**; z 44515 & mail Youngstown z 44512; Ⓟ 32,371; Ⓒ 31,627; ◆ 27,669
Austintown; MCD-Township; MAHONING; ***217** NH-19; [P]; ★ **YNGS-**; z 44515; Ⓟ 36,740; Ⓒ 38,001
Austin Village; RMC Place; TRUMBULL; ***217** NG-19; ★ **YNGS-**; mail Warren z 44481; pop. incl. with Warren (Inc. Place)
Autumn Acres; RMC Place; HAMILTON; ▲ Colerain; ***218** SF-2; ★ **CIN**; mail Cincinnati z 45239; ● 700
Ava; RMC Place; NOBLE; ▲ Noble; **219** SB-16; [P]; z 43711; ● 200
Avalon; RMC Place; BUTLER; ***218** SD-3; ★ **MIDD**; mail Middletown z 45042; pop. incl. with Middletown (Inc. Place)
Avalon; RMC Place; PERRY; ▲ Reading; ***219** SC-12; mail Bremen z 43107; rural
Avalon Heights; RMC Place; WARREN; ▲ Turtlecreek; ***218** SE-4; mail Lebanon z 45036; pop. incl. with Lebanon (Inc. Place)
Avon; Inc. Place; LORAIN; **217** NF-13; elev. 670ft./204m.; [P]; ★ **CLEV**; z 44011; Ⓟ 7,337; Ⓒ 11,446
Avondale; RMC Place; BELMONT; ▲ Pultney; ***219** SA-20; ★ **WHL**; mail Shadyside z 43947; ● 80
Avondale; RMC Place; HAMILTON; ***218** SF-2; [P]; ★ **CIN**; z 45229; pop. incl. with Cincinnati (Inc. Place)
Avondale (Avondale Park); RMC Place; LICKING; ▲ Licking; ***219** SB-12; ★ **NWRK**; mail Thornville z 43076; ● 100
Avondale; RMC Place; LOGAN; ▲ Stokes; ***216** NK-5; mail Lakeview z 43331; ● 300
Avondale; RMC Place; MONTGOMERY; **218** SC-4; ★ **DAY**; mail Dayton z 45404; pop. incl. with Riverside (Inc. Place)
Avondale; RMC Place; MUSKINGUM; ▲ Newton; **219** SB-13; ★ **ZAN**; mail Roseville z 43777; ● 400
Avondale; RMC Place; STARK; ▲ Plain; **217** NI-16; ★ **CAN**; mail Canton z 44708; ● 3,050
Avondale Park; LICKING; see Avondale (RMC Place)
Avon Lake; Inc. Place; LORAIN; **217** NE-13; [P]; ★ **CLEV**; z 44012; Ⓟ 15,066; Ⓒ 18,145; ◆ 20,435
Avon Park; RMC Place; TRUMBULL; ★ **YNGS-**; mail Girard z 44420; pop. incl. with Girard (Inc. Place)
Axtel; RMC Place; ERIE; ▲ Vermilion; ***217** NF-12; elev. 763ft./233m.; ★ **CLEV**; mail Vermilion z 44089
Ayersville; RMC Place; DEFIANCE; ▲ Highland; **216** NG-3; elev. 732ft./223m.; mail Defiance z 43512; ● 350

B

Bachman; RMC Place; MONTGOMERY; ▲ Clay; **218** SB-2; ★ **DAY**; mail Brookville z 45309; ● 35
Badgertown; RMC Place; BELMONT; ▲ Goshen; ***219** SA-18; mail Bethesda z 43719; rural
Bailey Lake (Bailey Lakes); Inc. Place; ASHLAND; ▲ Clear Creek; **217** NI-12; mail Ashland z 44805; Ⓟ 367; Ⓒ 397
Bailey Lakes; ASHLAND; see Bailey Lake (Inc. Place)
Baileys Mills; RMC Place; BELMONT; ▲ Warren; **219** SB-17; mail Barnesville z 43713
Bainbridge; CDP; GEAUGA; ▲ Bainbridge; ***217** NF-16; elev. 1,166ft./355m.; ★ **CLEV**; mail Chagrin Falls z 44023; Ⓟ 3,602; Ⓒ 3,417
Bainbridge; MCD-Township; GEAUGA; ***217** NF-16; ★ **CLEV**; mail Chagrin Falls z 44023; Ⓟ 9,694; Ⓒ 10,916
Bainbridge; Inc. Place; ROSS; ▲ Paxton; **218** SF-8; [P]; z 45612; Ⓟ 968; Ⓒ 1,012
Bainbridge Center; RMC Place; GEAUGA; ▲ Bainbridge; ***217** NF-16; ★ **CLEV**; mail Chagrin Falls z 44022; ● 250
Bairdstown; Inc. Place; WOOD; ▲ Bloom; **216** NG-6; [P]; z 45872; Ⓟ 130; Ⓒ 130
Bakersville; RMC Place; COSHOCTON; ▲ Adams; **217** NL-15; [P]; z 43803; ● 150
Ballville; CDP; SANDUSKY; ▲ Ballville; **216** NG-8; mail Fremont z 43420; Ⓟ 3,083; Ⓒ 3,255
Ballville; MCD-Township; SANDUSKY; ***216** NG-8; mail Fremont z 43420; Ⓟ 6,049; Ⓒ 6,395
Baltic; Inc. Place; TUSCARAWAS, COSHOCTON, HOLMES; ▲ Clark, Bucks, Crawford; **217** NL-15; elev. 1,041ft./317m.; [P]; z 43804; Ⓟ 659; Ⓒ 743
Baltimore (Basil); Inc. Place; FAIRFIELD; ▲ Liberty; **219** SB-11; [P]; ★ **COL**; z 43105; Ⓟ 2,971; Ⓒ 2,881
Bangs; RMC Place; KNOX; ▲ Liberty; **217** NL-11; elev. 1,101ft./336m.; mail Mount Vernon z 43050; ● 200
Bannock; RMC Place; BELMONT; ▲ Richland; **217** NN-18; [P]; ★ **WHL**; z 43972; ● 200
Bannon; RMC Place; FRANKLIN; ***218** SB-9; ★ **COL**; mail Columbus z 43207; pop. incl. with Columbus (Inc. Place)
Bantam; RMC Place; CLERMONT; ▲ Tate; **218** SG-4; ★ **CIN**; mail Batavia z 45103; ● 150
Barberton; Inc. Place; SUMMIT; **217** NH-15; elev. 969ft./295m.; [P] [H] ■; ★ **AKR**; z 44203; Ⓟ 27,623; Ⓒ 27,899; ◆ 27,447
Bardwell; RMC Place; BROWN; ▲ Green; **218** SG-5; elev. 941ft./287m.; mail Mount Orab z 45154; ● 100
Barlow; RMC Place; WASHINGTON; ▲ Barlow; **219** SE-15; [P]; z 45712; ● 200
Barlow; MCD-Township; WASHINGTON; ***219** SE-16; [P]; z 45712; Ⓟ 1,982; Ⓒ 2,417
Barnesburg; RMC Place; HAMILTON; ▲ Colerain; ***218** SF-2; ★ **CIN**; mail Cincinnati z 45239; ● 200
Barnesville; Inc. Place; BELMONT; ▲ Warren; **219** SA-18; [P] [H]; z 43713; Ⓟ 4,326; Ⓒ 4,225
Barnhill; Inc. Place; TUSCARAWAS; ▲ Goshen; **217** NL-16; mail New Philadelphia z 44663; Ⓟ 313; Ⓒ 364
Barr; TUSCARAWAS; see Barrs Mills (RMC Place)
Barretts Mills; RMC Place; HIGHLAND; ▲ Paint; **218** SF-7; mail Bainbridge z 45612; rural
Barrs Mills (Barr); RMC Place; TUSCARAWAS; ▲ Sugar Creek; **217** NK-15; mail Sugarcreek z 44681; ● 100
Bartles; RMC Place; LAWRENCE; ▲ Elizabeth; **219** SI-11; mail Pedro z 45659
Bartlett; RMC Place; WASHINGTON; ▲ Wesley; **219** SE-15; elev. 898ft./274m.; [P]; z 45713; ● 200
Bartley Estates; RMC Place; MONTGOMERY; ▲ Harrison; ★ **DAY**; mail Dayton z 45414
Bartlow; MCD-Township; HENRY; ***216** NG-5; mail Deshler z 43516; Ⓟ 2,554; Ⓒ 2,460
Barton; RMC Place; BELMONT; ▲ Colerain; **217** NN-19; [P]; ★ **WHL**; z 43905; ● 465
Bartramville; RMC Place; LAWRENCE; ▲ Union; ***219** SJ-12; ★ **HNTG**; mail Proctorville z 45669
Bascom; RMC Place; SENECA; ▲ Hopewell; **216** NH-8; [P]; z 44809; ● 500
Bashan; RMC Place; MEIGS; ▲ Chester; **219** SG-14; elev. 757ft./231m.; mail Long Bottom z 45743; ● 35
Basil; FAIRFIELD; see Baltimore (Inc. Place)
Bass Lake; RMC Place; GEAUGA; ▲ Munson; ***217** NE-17; ★ **CLEV**; mail Chardon z 44024; ● 500
Batavia; Inc. Place; ⊡ CLERMONT; ▲ Batavia; **218** SG-4; elev. 594ft./181m.; [P] [H]; ★ **CIN**; z 45103; Ⓟ 1,700; Ⓒ 1,617
Batavia; MCD-Township; CLERMONT; ***218** SG-4; [P]; ★ **CIN**; z 45103; Ⓟ 13,673; Ⓒ 17,503
Batemantown; RMC Place; KNOX; ▲ Middlebury; ***217** NK-11; mail Fredericktown z 43019
Batesville; Inc. Place; NOBLE; ▲ Beaver; **219** SB-17; mail Quaker City z 43773; Ⓟ 95; Ⓒ 100
Bath; MCD-Township; ALLEN; ***216** NJ-4; ★ **LIMA**; mail Lima z 45801; Ⓟ 10,105; Ⓒ 9,819; Ⓡ 9,810
Bath; MCD-Township; GREENE; ***218** SC-4; ★ **DAY**; mail Fairborn z 45324; Ⓟ 38,277; Ⓒ 40,231
Bath; RMC Place; SUMMIT; ▲ Bath; **217** NG-15; [P]; ★ **AKR**; z 44210; ● 500
Bath; MCD-Township; SUMMIT; ***217** NG-15; [P]; ★ **AKR**; z 44210; Ⓟ 9,015; Ⓒ 9,635
Battlesburg; RMC Place; STARK; ▲ Pike; ***217** NJ-16; elev. 1,126ft./343m.; ★ **CAN**; mail East Sparta z 44626; rural
Baughman; MCD-Township; WAYNE; ***217** NI-15; ★ **AKR**; mail Orrville z 44667; Ⓟ 4,408; Ⓒ 4,699
Bay; MCD-Township; OTTAWA; ***216** NE-9; ★ **TOL**; mail Port Clinton z 43452; Ⓟ 1,276; Ⓒ 1,294
Bayard; RMC Place; COLUMBIANA; ▲ West; **217** NJ-18; ★ **ALLI**; mail Minerva z 44657; ● 90
Bay Bridge; RMC Place; ERIE; ▲ Margaretta; **216** NF-10; ★ **SNDSK**; mail Sandusky z 44870; ● 100
Bays; RMC Place; WOOD; ▲ Liberty; ***216** NG-6; mail Rudolph z 43462
Bay View; Inc. Place; ERIE; ▲ Margaretta; **216** NF-10; ★ **SNDSK**; mail Sandusky z 44870; Ⓟ 739; Ⓒ 692
Bay Village; Inc. Place; CUYAHOGA; **217** NF-14; [P]; ★ **CLEV**; z 44140; Ⓟ 17,000; Ⓒ 16,087
Bazetta; TRUMBULL; see Klondike (RMC Place)
Bazetta; MCD-Township; TRUMBULL; ***217** NF-19; ★ **YNGS-**; mail Cortland z 44410; Ⓟ 5,414; Ⓒ 6,306
Beach City; Inc. Place; STARK; ▲ Sugar Creek; **217** NK-15; elev. 970ft./296m.; [P]; ★ **CAN**; z 44608; Ⓟ 1,051; Ⓒ 1,137
Beachland; RMC Place; CUYAHOGA; ★ **CLEV**; mail Cleveland z 44119; pop. incl. with Cleveland (Inc. Place)
Beachwood; Inc. Place; CUYAHOGA; **217** NF-16; [P] [C] 1,000 ■; ★ **CLEV**; z 44122; Ⓟ 10,677; Ⓒ 12,186; ◆ 11,231
Beacon Hill; RMC Place; BUTLER; ▲ West Chester; ★ **CIN**; mail Cincinnati z 45241; ● 40
Beallsville; Inc. Place; MONROE; ▲ Sunsbury; **219** SB-18; elev. 1,263ft./385m.; [P]; z 43716; Ⓟ 464; Ⓒ 423
Beals; RMC Place; FAIRFIELD; ▲ Violet; ***218** SB-10; ★ **COL**; mail Pickerington z 43147; pop. incl. with Pickerington (Inc. Place)
Beamsville; RMC Place; DARKE; ▲ Richland; **216** NM-2; mail Greenville z 45331, Versailles z 45380; ● 140
Bear Creek; RMC Place; SCIOTO; ▲ Morgan; ***218** SH-9; mail Lucasville z 45648
Bearfield; MCD-Township; PERRY; ***219** SC-14; mail Corning z 43730; Ⓟ 1,267; Ⓒ 1,412
Beartown; RMC Place; TUSCARAWAS; ▲ Franklin; ***217** NK-16; ★ **CAN**; mail Dover z 44622; ● 50
Beatty; RMC Place; CLARK; ▲ Springfield; **217** NC-16; ★ **SPR**; mail Springfield z 45506; ● 90
Beaumont; RMC Place; ATHENS; ▲ Dover; **219** SE-13; mail Athens z 45701; ● 30
Beaver; MCD-Township; MAHONING; ***217** NI-19; ★ **YNGS-**; mail Columbiana z 44408; Ⓟ 5,433; Ⓒ 6,466
Beaver; MCD-Township; NOBLE; ***219** SB-17; mail Quaker City z 43773; Ⓟ 572; Ⓒ 758
Beaver; Inc. Place; PIKE; ▲ Marion, Beaver; **218** SG-10; [P]; z 45613; Ⓟ 336; Ⓒ 464
Beaver; MCD-Township; PIKE; ***218** SG-10; [P]; z 45613 & mail Waverly z 45690; includes part of the Village of Beaver; Ⓟ 1,335; Ⓒ 1,450
Beavercreek; Inc. Place; GREENE; ▲ Beavercreek; **218** SC-4; [P]; ★ **DAY**; z 45430-32, z 45434 & mail Dayton z 45410, z 45440; Ⓟ 33,626; Ⓒ 37,984; ◆ 41,489
Beavercreek; MCD-Township; GREENE; ***218** SC-4; [P]; ★ **DAY**; z 45430-32, z 45434 & mail Dayton z 45401, z 45410, z 45440; Ⓟ 35,536; Ⓒ 41,745
Beaverdam; Inc. Place; ALLEN; ▲ Richland; **216** NI-4; [P]; z 45808; Ⓟ 467; Ⓒ 356
Beaver Park; RMC Place; LORAIN; ***217** NF-12; ★ **CLEV**; mail Lorain z 44053; pop. incl. with Lorain (Inc. Place)
Beavertown; RMC Place; MONTGOMERY; ★ **DAY**; mail Dayton z 45429; pop. incl. with Kettering (Inc. Place)
Beavertown; RMC Place; WASHINGTON; ▲ Grandview; **219** SD-18; mail New Matamoras z 45767; ● 80
Becker Highlands; RMC Place; JEFFERSON; ★ **STU-**; mail Steubenville z 43952; pop. incl. with Steubenville (Inc. Place)
Beckett Ridge; CDP-Census Area Only; BUTLER; ▲ West Chester; ***218** SE-2; elev. 700ft./213m.; ★ **CIN**; mail West Chester z 45069; Ⓟ 4,505; Ⓒ 8,663
Becks Mills; RMC Place; HOLMES; ▲ Mechanic; ***217** NL-14; mail Millersburg z 44654; rural
Bedford; MCD-Township; COSHOCTON; ***217** NM-13; mail Coshocton z 43812; Ⓟ 499; Ⓒ 601
Bedford; Inc. Place; CUYAHOGA; **217** NF-16; [P] [H] ■; ★ **CLEV**; z 44146; Ⓟ 14,822; Ⓒ 14,214; ◆ 13,078
Bedford; MCD-Township; MEIGS; ***219** SG-14; mail Pomeroy z 45769; Ⓟ 1,097; Ⓒ 1,212
Bedford Heights; Inc. Place; CUYAHOGA; **217** NF-16; [P]; ★ **CLEV**; z 44128, z 44146; Ⓟ 12,131; Ⓒ 11,375
Beebe; RMC Place; ATHENS; ▲ Rome; ***219** SF-14; mail Stewart z 45778; rural
Beechcrest; RMC Place; PORTAGE; ▲ Brimfield; ★ **AKR**; mail Kent z 44240
Beechview Estates; RMC Place; HAMILTON; ***218** SG-3; ★ **CIN**; mail Cincinnati z 45201; pop. incl. with Cincinnati (Inc. Place)
Beechwold; RMC Place; FRANKLIN; ★ **COL**; mail Columbus z 43214; pop. incl. with Columbus (Inc. Place)
Beechwood; RMC Place; JEFFERSON; ★ **STU-**; mail Steubenville z 43953; pop. incl. with Wintersville (Inc. Place)
Beechwood; RMC Place; PREBLE; ▲ Gratis; ***218** SD-2; ★ **MIDD**; mail Camden z 45311, Somerville z 45064; rural
Beechwood; RMC Place; STARK; ▲ Washington; ***217** NI-17; ★ **ALLI**; mail Alliance z 44601; ● 300
Beechwood Trails; CDP-Census Area Only; LICKING; ▲ Harrison; ***219** SA-11; elev. 1,200ft./366m.; ★ **COL**; mail Pataskala z 43062; Ⓟ 1,875; Ⓒ 2,258
Bel-Air Mobile Homes; TRUMBULL; see Belmont Park (RMC Place)
Belden; RMC Place; LORAIN; ▲ Grafton; **217** NG-13; ★ **CLEV**; mail Grafton z 44044; ● 50
Belfast; RMC Place; CLERMONT; ▲ Stonelick; ***218** SF-4; ★ **CIN**; mail Goshen z 45122; ● 300
Belfast; RMC Place; HIGHLAND; ▲ Jackson; **218** SG-7; mail Hillsboro z 45133; ● 120
Belfort; RMC Place; STARK; ▲ Nimishillen; ***217** NJ-17; ★ **CAN**; mail Louisville z 44641
Bellaire; Inc. Place; BELMONT; ▲ Pultney; **217** NN-19; [P] [H]; ★ **WHL**; z 43906; Ⓟ 6,028; Ⓒ 4,892
Bellaire Gardens; RMC Place; MARION; ▲ Marion; **216** NK-8; ★ **MRN**; mail Marion z 43302; ● 100
Bellbrook; Inc. Place; GREENE; **218** SD-4; elev. 796ft./243m.; [P]; ★ **DAY**; z 45305; Ⓟ 6,511; Ⓒ 7,009
Belle Center; Inc. Place; LOGAN; ▲ Richland; **216** NK-5; elev. 1,045ft./319m.; [P]; z 43310; Ⓟ 796; Ⓒ 807
Bellefontaine; Inc. Place; ⊡ LOGAN; ▲ Lake, Harrison, Jefferson; **216** NL-5; elev. 1,251ft./381m.; [P] [H] ■; z 43311; Ⓟ 12,142; Ⓒ 13,069; ◆ 13,414
Bellepoint; RMC Place; DELAWARE; ▲ Concord; **216** NM-8; ★ **COL**; mail Delaware z 43015, Ostrander z 43061; ● 100
Belle Valley; Inc. Place; NOBLE; ▲ Noble; **219** SC-16; [P]; z 43717; Ⓟ 267; Ⓒ 263
Belle Vernon; RMC Place; WYANDOT; ▲ Tymochtee; **216** NI-8; mail Sycamore z 44882; ● 40
Belleview Heights; RMC Place; PREBLE; ▲ Jefferson; ★ **RICH**; mail New Paris z 45347; pop. incl. with New Paris (Inc. Place)
Belleview Heights; RMC Place; ROSS; ***218** SF-9; mail Chillicothe z 45601; pop. incl. with Chillicothe (Inc. Place)
Bellevue; Inc. Place; SANDUSKY, HURON; **216** NG-10; [P] [H]; z 44811; Ⓟ 8,146; Ⓒ 8,193
Bellview; RMC Place; GREENE; ▲ Sugarcreek; ★ **DAY**; mail Bellbrook z 45305; ● 300
Bellview Estates; RMC Place; GREENE; ▲ Sugarcreek; ***218** SD-4; ★ **DAY**; mail Bellbrook z 45305; ● 525
Bellview Heights; RMC Place; BELMONT; ▲ Pultney; ★ **WHL**; mail Bellaire z 43906; ● 150
Bellville; Inc. Place; RICHLAND; ▲ Jefferson; **217** NK-11; [P]; ★ **MANS**; z 44813; Ⓟ 1,568; Ⓒ 1,773
Belmont; RMC Place; ALLEN; ▲ Bath; ***216** NJ-4; ★ **LIMA**; mail Lima z 45801; ● 600
Belmont; Inc. Place; BELMONT; ▲ Goshen; **217** NN-18; [P]; z 43718; Ⓟ 471; Ⓒ 532
Belmont; RMC Place; BUTLER; ▲ Fairfield; ***219** SA-18; mail Hamilton z 45015
Belmont; RMC Place; MONTGOMERY; ★ **DAY**; pop. incl. with Dayton (Inc. Place)
BELMONT; **217** NN-17; Ⓟ 71,074; Ⓒ 70,226; ◆ 65,968
Belmont Meadows; RMC Place; CLARK; ★ **SPR**; mail Springfield z 45505; pop. incl. with Springfield (Inc. Place)
Belmont Park (Bel-Air Mobile Homes); RMC Place; TRUMBULL; ▲ Liberty; ***217** NG-19; ★ **YNGS-**; mail Girard z 44420; ● 300
Belmont Ridge; RMC Place; BELMONT; ▲ Flushing; ***217** NM-17; mail Piedmont z 43983
Belmore; Inc. Place; PUTNAM; ▲ Van Buren; **216** NH-5; elev. 736ft./224m.; [P]; z 45815; Ⓟ 161; Ⓒ 171
Beloit; Inc. Place; MAHONING; ▲ Smith; **217** NI-18; elev. 1,132ft./345m.; [P]; ★ **ALLI**; z 44609; Ⓟ 1,037; Ⓒ 1,024
Belpre; Inc. Place; WASHINGTON; **219** SF-16; [P]; ★ **PRKB**; z 45714; Ⓟ 6,796; Ⓒ 6,660
Belpre; MCD-Township; WASHINGTON; ***219** SF-15; [P]; ★ **PRKB**; z 45714; Ⓟ 4,208; Ⓒ 4,192
Belvedere; RMC Place; JEFFERSON; ▲ Wayne; ***217** NL-19; ★ **STU-**; mail Steubenville z 43952; ● 200
Bennington; MCD-Township; LICKING; ***217** NM-11; mail Centerburg z 43011; Ⓟ 971; Ⓒ 1,265
Bennington; MCD-Township; MORROW; ***216** NL-10; mail Marengo z 43334; Ⓟ 2,377; Ⓒ 2,663
Bentley; RMC Place; MAHONING; ***217** NH-20; ★ **YNGS-**; mail Lowellville z 44436; pop. incl. with Lowellville (Inc. Place)
Bentleyville; Inc. Place; CUYAHOGA; **217** NF-16; elev. 938ft./286m.; [P]; ★ **CLEV**; z 44022; Ⓟ 674; Ⓒ 947
Benton; RMC Place; CRAWFORD; ▲ Texas; **216** NI-8; mail Sycamore z 44882; ● 100
Benton; MCD-Township; HOCKING; ***219** SE-11; mail South Bloomingville z 43152; Ⓟ 763; Ⓒ 814
Benton; RMC Place; HOLMES; ▲ Salt Creek; **217** NK-14; mail Millersburg z 44654
Benton; MCD-Township; MONROE; ***219** SD-18; mail New Matamoras z 45767; Ⓟ 409; Ⓒ 349
Benton; MCD-Township; OTTAWA; ***216** NE-8; mail Graytown z 43432; Ⓟ 2,471; Ⓒ 2,621
Benton; MCD-Township; PAULDING; ***216** NH-1; mail Payne z 45880; Ⓟ 1,054; Ⓒ 1,035
Benton; MCD-Township; PIKE; ***218** SG-8; mail Waverly z 45690; Ⓟ 1,312; Ⓒ 1,520
Benton Ridge; Inc. Place; HANCOCK; ▲ Blanchard; **216** NH-5; elev. 778ft./237m.; [P]; z 45816; Ⓟ 351; Ⓒ 315
Bentonville; RMC Place; ADAMS; ▲ Sprigg; **218** SI-6; [P]; z 45105; ● 150
Berea; Inc. Place; CUYAHOGA; **217** NF-14; [P] [C] 4,365; ★ **CLEV**; z 44017; Ⓟ 19,051; Ⓒ 18,970
Bergholz; Inc. Place; JEFFERSON; ▲ Springfield; **217** NK-19; [P]; z 43908; Ⓟ 713; Ⓒ 769
Berkey; Inc. Place; LUCAS; ▲ Richfield; **216** ND-5; [P]; ★ **TOL**; z 43504; Ⓟ 264; Ⓒ 265
Berkley Heights; RMC Place; MONTGOMERY; ★ **DAY**; mail Dayton z 45429; pop. incl. with Kettering (Inc. Place)
Berkshire; RMC Place; DELAWARE; ▲ Berkshire; **216** NM-9; ★ **COL**; mail Sunbury z 43074; ● 100
Berkshire; MCD-Township; DELAWARE; ***216** NM-9; ★ **COL**; mail Sunbury z 43074; Ⓟ 2,074; Ⓒ 2,251
Berlin; MCD-Township; DELAWARE; ***216** NM-9; mail Delaware z 43015; Ⓟ 1,978; Ⓒ 3,315
Berlin; MCD-Township; ERIE; ***217** NG-11; ★ **CLEV**; mail Berlin Heights z 44814; Ⓟ 3,319; Ⓒ 3,702
Berlin; RMC Place; HOLMES; ▲ Berlin; **217** NK-14; [P]; z 44610; ● 1,000
Berlin; MCD-Township; HOLMES; ***217** NK-14; [P]; z 44610; Ⓟ 3,457; Ⓒ 3,857
Berlin; MCD-Township; KNOX; ***217** NK-11; ★ **MANS**; mail Fredericktown z 43019; Ⓟ 1,388; Ⓒ 1,789
Berlin; MCD-Township; MAHONING; ***217** NH-18; mail Berlin Center z 44401; Ⓟ 2,070; Ⓒ 2,240
Berlin Center; RMC Place; MAHONING; ▲ Berlin; **217** NH-18; [P]; z 44401; ● 250
Berlin Heights; Inc. Place; ERIE; ▲ Berlin; **217** NG-11; [P]; ★ **CLEV**; z 44814; Ⓟ 691; Ⓒ 685
Berlinville; RMC Place; ERIE; ▲ Berlin; **217** NG-11; ★ **CLEV**; mail Berlin Heights z 44814; ● 70
Bern; MCD-Township; ATHENS; ***219** SE-14; mail Portland z 45770; Ⓟ 543; Ⓒ 519
Berne; MCD-Township; FAIRFIELD; ***219** SC-11; ★ **LANC**; mail Sugar Grove z 43155; Ⓟ 4,690; Ⓒ 4,969
Berne; NOBLE; see Carlisle (RMC Place)
Bernice; RMC Place; TUSCARAWAS; ▲ Washington; ***217** NM-16; mail Newcomerstown z 43832; ● 40
Berryman; RMC Place; ALLEN; ▲ Shawnee; ***216** NJ-4; ★ **LIMA**; mail Lima z 45805; ● 650
Berrysville; RMC Place; HIGHLAND; ▲ Washington; **218** SG-7; mail Hillsboro z 45133; ● 100
Berwick; RMC Place; SENECA; ▲ Seneca; **216** NH-8; elev. 843ft./257m.; mail New Riegel z 44853; ● 100
Bessemer; RMC Place; ATHENS; ▲ York; ***219** SE-13; mail Nelsonville z 45764; ● 100
Bethany; RMC Place; BUTLER; ▲ Liberty; **218** SE-3; ★ **CIN**; mail Middletown z 45042; ● 260
Bethel; MCD-Township; CLARK; ***218** SB-4; ★ **SPR**; mail New Carlisle z 45344; Ⓟ 19,580; Ⓒ 18,962
Bethel; Inc. Place; CLERMONT; ▲ Tate; **218** SH-4; elev. 892ft./272m.; [P]; ★ **CIN**; z 45106; Ⓟ 2,407; Ⓒ 2,637
Bethel; MCD-Township; MIAMI; ***218** SB-4; ★ **DAY**; mail Tipp City z 45371; Ⓟ 4,812; Ⓒ 4,927
Bethel; MCD-Township; MONROE; ***219** SD-17; mail Lower Salem z 45745; Ⓟ 433; Ⓒ 357
Bethel; RMC Place; PIKE; ▲ Newton; ***218** SG-9; mail Piketon z 45661; ● 30
Bethesda; Inc. Place; BELMONT; ▲ Goshen; **219** SA-18; [P]; z 43719; Ⓟ 1,161; Ⓒ 1,413
Bethlehem; MCD-Township; COSHOCTON; ***217** NL-14; mail Coshocton z 43812; Ⓟ 1,163; Ⓒ 1,191
Bethlehem; RMC Place; RICHLAND; ▲ Sharon; ***216** NI-10; mail Shelby z 44875; rural
Bethlehem; MCD-Township; STARK; ***217** NJ-16; ★ **CAN**; mail Navarre z 44662; Ⓟ 5,803; Ⓒ 5,650
Bettsville; Inc. Place; SENECA; ▲ Liberty; **216** NG-8; elev. 707ft./215m.; [P]; z 44815; Ⓟ 752; Ⓒ 784
Beulah Beach; RMC Place; ERIE; ▲ Vermilion; ***217** NF-11; ★ **CLEV**; mail Vermilion z 44089; summer pop. 400; ● 120
Beverly; Inc. Place; WASHINGTON; ▲ Waterford; **219** SD-16; [P]; z 45715 & mail Coal Run z 45721; Ⓟ 1,444; Ⓒ 1,282
Beverly Gardens; RMC Place; MONTGOMERY; ***218** SC-4; ★ **DAY**; mail Dayton z 45431; pop. incl. with Riverside (Inc. Place)
Bevis; RMC Place; HAMILTON; ▲ Colerain; **218** SF-2; elev. 874ft./266m.; ★ **CIN**; mail Cincinnati z 45247; ● 1,100
Bexley; Inc. Place; FRANKLIN; **218** SB-9; [P]; ★ **COL**; z 43209; Ⓟ 13,088; Ⓒ 13,203
Bidwell; RMC Place; GALLIA; ▲ Springfield; **219** SH-12; [P]; z 45614; ● 350
Big Island; RMC Place; MARION; ▲ Big Island; **216** NK-8; elev. 933ft./284m.; mail Marion z 43302; ● 200
Big Island; MCD-Township; MARION; ***216** NK-8; mail Marion z 43302; Ⓟ 1,271; Ⓒ 1,223
Biglick; MCD-Township; HANCOCK; ***216** NH-7; mail Alvada z 44802; Ⓟ 933; Ⓒ 955
Big Plain; RMC Place; MADISON; ▲ Fairfield; **218** SB-8; mail London z 43140; ● 150

Entries in **UPPERCASE** are counties.
Entries in **bold** have populations of 2,500 or more.
Names in parentheses are alternate names.
Inc. Place — Incorporated Place
RMC Place — Rand McNally Designated Place
CDP — Census Designated Place
MCD — Minor Civil Division

⊡ County Seat
▲ Minor Civil Division
elev. Elevation
[P] Post Office
[H] Hospital
[C] College
■ Principal Business Center
★ Ranally Metro Area (RMA) Abbreviation
z Zip Code(s)

Ⓟ Previous Census Population
Ⓡ Revised Census Population
Ⓐ Annexation Population
● Rand McNally Population Estimate
Ⓒ Final Census Population
Ⓢ Special Census Population
◆ Estimated Population

For additional definitions see Glossary, Volume 1, and Introduction, Volume 2.

Big Prairie; RMC Place; HOLMES; ▲ Ripley; **217** NJ-13; elev. 947ft./289m.; 🅿; **z** 44611; ● 300
Big Rock; RMC Place; JACKSON; ▲ Liberty; ***218** SG-10; mail Beaver **z** 45613; rural
Big Run; RMC Place; ATHENS; ▲ Rome; ***219** SE-14; mail Cutler **z** 45724, Stewart **z** 45778; rural
Big Spring; MCD-Township; SENECA; ***216** NH-7; mail New Riegel **z** 44853; ℗ 1,746; © 1,791
Big Springs; RMC Place; LOGAN; ▲ Rushcreek; **216** NK-6; mail Rushsylvania **z** 43347; ● 130
Birds Run; RMC Place; GUERNSEY; ▲ Wheeling; **217** NM-15; elev. 812ft./247m.; mail Kimbolton **z** 43749; rural
Birmingham; RMC Place; ERIE; ▲ Florence; **217** NG-12; elev. 782ft./238m.; 🅿; ★ **CLEV**; **z** 44816; ● 500
Birmingham (Milnersville); RMC Place; GUERNSEY; ▲ Monroe; **217** NM-16; mail Kimbolton **z** 43749; ● 45
Bishopville; RMC Place; MORGAN; ▲ Homer; ***219** SD-14; elev. 831ft./253m.; mail Glouster **z** 45732
Bismarck; RMC Place; HURON; ▲ Sherman; ***216** NG-10; elev. 815ft./248m.; mail Bellevue **z** 44811
Blachleyville; RMC Place; WAYNE; ▲ Plain; **217** NJ-13; mail Wooster **z** 44691; ● 120
Black Creek; MCD-Township; MERCER; ***216** NJ-1; mail Rockford **z** 45882; ℗ 619; © 631
Blackfork; RMC Place; LAWRENCE; ▲ Washington; **219** SH-11; mail Oak Hill **z** 45656; ● 250
Black Fork Junction; RMC Place; JACKSON; ▲ Jefferson; ***219** SH-11; mail Oak Hill **z** 45656; rural
Black Horse; RMC Place; PORTAGE; ▲ Ravenna; **217** NG-17; ★ **AKR**; mail Ravenna **z** 44266; ● 500
Blacklick; RMC Place; FRANKLIN; ▲ Jefferson; **218** SA-10; 🅿; ★ **COL**; **z** 43004; ● 300
Blacklick Estates; CDP-Census Area Only; FRANKLIN; ▲ Madison; **218** SB-10; ★ **COL**; mail Columbus **z** 43232; ℗ 10,080; © 9,518
Black Run; RMC Place; MUSKINGUM; ▲ Jackson; ***219** SA-13; mail Nashport **z** 43830
Bladen; RMC Place; GALLIA; ▲ Ohio; **219** SI-13; mail Crown City **z** 45623; ● 50
Bladensburg; RMC Place; KNOX; ▲ Jackson, Clay; **217** NM-12; 🅿; **z** 43005; ● 300
Blaine; RMC Place; BELMONT; ▲ Pease, Colerain; **217** NN-19; 🅿; ★ **WHL**; **z** 43909; ● 500
Blainesville; RMC Place; BELMONT; ▲ Wheeling; ***217** NN-19; mail Maynard **z** 43937, Saint Clairsville **z** 43950; ● 120
Blairmont; RMC Place; HARRISON; ▲ Short Creek; **217** NM-18; mail Adena **z** 43901
Blakeslee (Blakesley); Inc. Place; WILLIAMS; ▲ Florence; **216** NE-1; 🅿; **z** 43505; ℗ 128; © 130
Blakesley; WILLIAMS; see Blakeslee (Inc. Place)
Blanchard; MCD-Township; HANCOCK; ***216** NH-5; mail Benton Ridge **z** 45816; ℗ 1,100; © 1,170
Blanchard; RMC Place; HARDIN; ▲ Pleasant, Blanchard; **216** NJ-6; elev. 953ft./290m.; mail Dunkirk **z** 45836
Blanchard; MCD-Township; HARDIN; ***216** NJ-6; mail Dunkirk **z** 45836; ℗ 1,522; © 1,640
Blanchard; MCD-Township; PUTNAM; ***216** NH-5; mail Ottawa **z** 45875; ℗ 1,344; © 1,232
Blanches Addition; RMC Place; LICKING; ★ **COL**; mail Pataskala **z** 43062; pop. incl. with Pataskala (Inc. Place)
Blanchester; Inc. Place; CLINTON, WARREN; ▲ Marion, Harlan; **218** SF-5; elev. 971ft./296m.; 🅿; **z** 45107; ℗ 4,206; © 4,220
Blendon; MCD-Township; FRANKLIN; ***218** SA-10; ★ **COL**; mail Westerville **z** 43081; ℗ 11,194; © 9,193
Blissfield; RMC Place; COSHOCTON; ▲ Clark; **217** NL-14; elev. 819ft./250m.; 🅿; **z** 43805; ● 100
Bloom; MCD-Township; FAIRFIELD; ***218** SC-10; ★ **COL**; mail Lithopolis **z** 43136; ℗ 5,788; © 6,374
Bloom; MCD-Township; MORGAN; ***219** SC-14; mail McConnelsville **z** 43756; ℗ 1,003; © 1,015
Bloom; MCD-Township; SCIOTO; ***218** SI-10; mail South Webster **z** 45682; ℗ 3,216; © 3,218
Bloom; MCD-Township; SENECA; ***216** NH-9; mail Bloomville **z** 44818; ℗ 1,799; © 1,937
Bloom; MCD-Township; WOOD; ***216** NG-6; mail Bloomdale **z** 44817; ℗ 2,402; © 2,535
Bloom Center; RMC Place; LOGAN; ▲ Bloomfield; **216** NL-5; elev. 1,010ft./308m.; mail De Graff **z** 43318, Lewistown **z** 43333; ● 30
Bloomdale; Inc. Place; WOOD; ▲ Bloom; **216** NG-6; 🅿; **z** 44817; ℗ 632; © 724
Bloomer; RMC Place; MIAMI; ▲ Newberry; **216** NM-2; mail Covington **z** 45318; ● 50
Bloomfield; RMC Place; COLUMBIANA; ▲ Liverpool; mail East Liverpool **z** 43920; ● 150
Bloomfield; MCD-Township; JACKSON; ***219** SG-11; mail Jackson **z** 45640; ℗ 817; © 896
Bloomfield; MCD-Township; LOGAN; ***216** NL-5; mail Lewistown **z** 43333; ℗ 395; © 419
Bloomfield; RMC Place; MORROW; ▲ South Bloomfield; ***216** NL-10; elev. 1,312ft./400m.; mail Centerburg **z** 43011
Bloomfield; RMC Place; MUSKINGUM; ▲ Highland; **217** NN-15; mail New Concord **z** 43762; ● 60
Bloomfield; MCD-Township; TRUMBULL; ***217** NF-19; mail North Bloomfield **z** 44450; ℗ 1,117; © 1,097
Bloomfield; RMC Place; WASHINGTON; ▲ Ludlow; **219** SD-18; mail Graysville **z** 45734; ● 25
Bloomingburg; Inc. Place; FAYETTE; ▲ Union, Paint; **218** SD-7; elev. 998ft./304m.; 🅿; **z** 43106; ℗ 769; © 874
Bloomingdale; Inc. Place; JEFFERSON; ▲ Wayne; **217** NL-19; elev. 1,277ft./389m.; 🅿; ★ **STU-**; **z** 43910; ℗ 227; © 221
Blooming Grove; RMC Place; MORROW; ▲ North Bloomfield; **216** NJ-10; elev. 1,271ft./387m.; mail Galion **z** 44833; ● 80
Bloominggrove; MCD-Township; RICHLAND; ***217** NI-11; mail Shiloh **z** 44878; ℗ 1,061; © 1,157
Bloomington; RMC Place; CLINTON; ▲ Wilson; **218** SD-6; mail Sabina **z** 45169; ● 50
Bloomingville; RMC Place; ERIE; ▲ Perkins; ***216** NF-10; elev. 689ft./210m.; ★ **SNDSK**; mail Sandusky **z** 44870
Bloomville; Inc. Place; SENECA; ▲ Bloom; **216** NH-9; 🅿; **z** 44818; ℗ 949; © 1,045
Blue Ash; Inc. Place; HAMILTON; **218** SF-3; 🅿; ★ **CIN**; **z** 45236, **z** 45241-42; ℗ 11,860; © 12,513
Blue Ball; RMC Place; BUTLER, WARREN; ▲ Franklin, Lemon; **218** SD-3; ★ **MIDD**; mail Franklin **z** 45005, Middletown **z** 45042; pop. incl. with Middletown (Inc. Place)
Bluebell; RMC Place; GUERNSEY; ▲ Valley; ***219** SB-16; mail Cumberland **z** 43732, Pleasant City **z** 43772; rural
Bluebird Beach; RMC Place; ERIE; ★ **CLEV**; mail Vermilion **z** 44089; pop. incl. with Vermilion (Inc. Place)
Blue Creek; RMC Place; ADAMS; ▲ Jefferson; **218** SI-8; 🅿; **z** 45616; ● 25
Blue Creek; MCD-Township; PAULDING; ***216** NH-2; mail Scott **z** 45886; ℗ 828; © 804
Blue Rock (Gaysport); RMC Place; MUSKINGUM; ▲ Blue Rock; **219** SC-14; 🅿; **z** 43720; ● 125
Blue Rock; MCD-Township; MUSKINGUM; ***219** SC-15; 🅿; **z** 43720; ℗ 519; © 641
Blue Valley Acres; RMC Place; FAIRFIELD; ▲ Berne; ***219** SD-11; ★ **LANC**; mail Lancaster **z** 43130; ● 200
Bluffton; Inc. Place; ALLEN, HANCOCK; ▲ Richland; **216** NI-5; elev. 824ft./251m.; 🅿 🅷 🅲 1,158; **z** 45817; ℗ 3,367; © 3,896
Boardman; CDP; MAHONING; ▲ Boardman; **217** NH-19; 🅿; ★ **YNGS-**; **z** 44512-13; ℗ 38,596; © 37,215; ◆ 31,779
Boardman; MCD-Township; MAHONING; ***217** NH-20; 🅿; ★ **YNGS-**; **z** 44512-13; ℗ 41,796; © 42,518
Bobo; RMC Place; PIKE; ▲ Union; ***218** SG-9; mail Beaver **z** 45613; rural
Boden; RMC Place; GUERNSEY; ▲ Knox; ***217** NN-15; mail New Concord **z** 43762; rural
Bogart; RMC Place; ERIE; ▲ Perkins; ***216** NF-10; ★ **SNDSK**; mail Sandusky **z** 44870; ● 120
Bokescreek; MCD-Township; LOGAN; ***216** NL-6; mail West Mansfield **z** 43358; ℗ 1,417; © 1,308
Bolindale; CDP-Census Area Only; TRUMBULL; ▲ Howland; ***217** NG-19; elev. 950ft./290m.; ★ **YNGS-**; mail Warren **z** 44484; ℗ 2,827; © 2,489
Bolivar; Inc. Place; TUSCARAWAS; ▲ Lawrence; **217** NJ-16; 🅿; ★ **CAN**; **z** 44612; ℗ 914; © 894
Bolton; RMC Place; STARK; ▲ Lexington; ***217** NI-17; ★ **ALLI**; mail Alliance **z** 44601; ● 350
Bona Vesta; RMC Place; WILLIAMS; ▲ Pulaski; ***216** NE-2; mail Bryan **z** 43506; ● 220
Bond Hill; RMC Place; HAMILTON; ***218** SF-2; ★ **CIN**; mail Cincinnati **z** 45237; pop. incl. with Cincinnati (Inc. Place)
Boneta; RMC Place; MEDINA; ▲ Sharon; ***217** NH-14; ★ **AKR**; mail Medina **z** 44256; rural
Bonn; RMC Place; WASHINGTON; ▲ Salem; **219** SD-17; elev. 873ft./266m.; mail Whipple **z** 45788; ● 70
Bonnett Lake; ASHLAND, HOLMES; see Long Lake (RMC Place)
Bono; RMC Place; LUCAS; ▲ Jerusalem; **216** NE-8; 🅿; ★ **TOL**; **z** 43445; ● 200
Bookwalter; RMC Place; FAYETTE; ▲ Paint; **218** SC-7; mail Jeffersonville **z** 43128; ● 120
Booth; RMC Place; LUCAS; ***216** NE-7; ★ **TOL**; mail Oregon **z** 43618; pop. incl. with Oregon (Inc. Place)
Boston (Atlas); RMC Place; BELMONT; ▲ Somerset; **219** SB-17; mail Barnesville **z** 43713; ● 30
Boston; RMC Place; HIGHLAND; ▲ Paint, Liberty; **218** SF-7; elev. 1,046ft./319m.; mail Hillsboro **z** 45133; ● 120
Boston; MCD-Township; SUMMIT; ***217** NG-16; ★ **AKR**; mail Peninsula **z** 44264; ℗ 1,879; © 1,664
Boston Heights; Inc. Place; SUMMIT; **217** NG-16; elev. 1,064ft./324m.; ★ **AKR**; mail Hudson **z** 44236; ℗ 733; © 1,186
Boston Mill; RMC Place; SUMMIT; ▲ Boston; ***217** NG-15; ★ **AKR**; mail Peninsula **z** 44264; rural
Botkins; Inc. Place; SHELBY; ▲ Dinsmore; **216** NL-3; elev. 1,011ft./308m.; 🅿; **z** 45306; ℗ 1,340; © 1,205
Boudes Ferry; RMC Place; BROWN; ▲ Lewis; ***218** SI-4; mail Georgetown **z** 45121; rural
Boughtonville; RMC Place; HURON; ▲ Ripley; ***217** NH-11; elev. 985ft./300m.; mail Willard **z** 44890; ● 50
Bourneville; RMC Place; ROSS; ▲ Twin; **218** SF-8; elev. 679ft./207m.; 🅿; **z** 45617; ● 300
Bowerston; Inc. Place; HARRISON; ▲ Monroe; **217** NL-17; 🅿; **z** 44695; ℗ 343; © 414
Bowersville; Inc. Place; GREENE; ▲ Jefferson; **218** SD-6; 🅿; **z** 45307; ℗ 225; © 290
Bowling Green; MCD-Township; LICKING; ***219** SB-12; mail Thornville **z** 43076; ℗ 1,292; © 1,668
Bowling Green; MCD-Township; MARION; ***216** NK-7; mail La Rue **z** 43332; ℗ 699; © 569
Bowling Green; Inc. Place; ⊡ WOOD; **216** NF-6; 🅿 🅷 🅲 21,132 ■; **z** 43402-03; ℗ 28,176; © 29,636; ◆ 31,454
Bowlusville; RMC Place; CHAMPAIGN, CLARK; ▲ Moorefield, Urbana; **218** SA-5; elev. 962ft./293m.; mail Urbana **z** 43078; ● 30
Boydsville; RMC Place; BELMONT; ▲ Pease; ***219** SA-19; ★ **WHL**; mail Bridgeport **z** 43912; ● 50
Braceville; RMC Place; TRUMBULL; ▲ Braceville; **217** NG-18; ★ **YNGS-**; mail Newton Falls **z** 44444; ● 250
Braceville; MCD-Township; TRUMBULL; ***217** NG-18; ★ **YNGS-**; mail Newton Falls **z** 44444; ℗ 2,972; © 2,887
Braceville Ridge; RMC Place; TRUMBULL; ▲ Braceville; ***217** NG-18; ★ **YNGS-**; mail Newton Falls **z** 44444; rural
Bradbury; RMC Place; MEIGS; ▲ Salisbury; ***219** SG-14; mail Middleport **z** 45760; ● 200
Bradford; Inc. Place; MIAMI, DARKE; ▲ Newberry, Adams; **216** NN-2; 🅿; **z** 45308; ℗ 2,005; © 1,859
Bradley; RMC Place; JEFFERSON; ▲ Smithfield; **217** NM-19; mail Dillonvale **z** 43917, Smithfield **z** 43948; ● 90
Bradner; Inc. Place; WOOD; ▲ Montgomery; **216** NF-7; 🅿; **z** 43406; ℗ 1,093; © 1,171
Bradrick; RMC Place; LAWRENCE; ▲ Union; **219** SK-12; ★ **HNTG**; mail Chesapeake **z** 45619; ● 110
Brady; MCD-Township; WILLIAMS; ***216** NE-2; mail West Unity **z** 43570; ℗ 2,582; © 2,822
Brady Lake; Inc. Place; PORTAGE; **217** NH-17; 🅿; ★ **AKR**; **z** 44211; ℗ 490; © 513
Brady Lake Addition; RMC Place; PORTAGE; ▲ Franklin; ***217** NG-17; ★ **AKR**; mail Brady Lake **z** 44211, Kent **z** 44240; ● 850
Bradysville (Bradyville); RMC Place; ADAMS; ▲ Sprigg; ***218** SI-6; mail Manchester **z** 45144; rural
Bradyville; ADAMS; see Bradysville (RMC Place)
Braffettsville; RMC Place; DARKE; ▲ Harrison; **218** SB-1; ★ **RICH**; mail New Paris **z** 45347; ● 70
Brailey; RMC Place; FULTON; ▲ Swan Creek; ***216** NE-5; ★ **TOL**; mail Swanton **z** 43558; ● 25
Branch Hill; RMC Place; CLERMONT; ▲ Miami; **218** SF-3; ★ **CIN**; mail Loveland **z** 45140; ● 370
Brandon; RMC Place; KNOX; ▲ Miller; **217** NM-11; elev. 1,077ft./328m.; mail Mount Vernon **z** 43050; ● 200
Brandt; RMC Place; MIAMI; ▲ Bethel; **218** SB-4; ★ **DAY**; mail Tipp City **z** 45371; ● 320
Brandywine; RMC Place; CRAWFORD; ▲ Liberty; ***216** NI-9; mail Bucyrus **z** 44820
Bratenahl; Inc. Place; CUYAHOGA; **219** SK-18; 🅿; ★ **CLEV**; **z** 44108; ℗ 1,356; © 1,337
Bratton; MCD-Township; ADAMS; ***218** SG-7; mail Peebles **z** 45660; ℗ 862; © 1,412
Brecksville; Inc. Place; CUYAHOGA; **217** NG-15; 🅿; ★ **CLEV**; **z** 44141; ℗ 11,818; © 13,382
Brecon; RMC Place; HAMILTON; ▲ Sycamore; ***218** SF-3; ★ **CIN**; mail Cincinnati **z** 45242
Bremen; Inc. Place; FAIRFIELD; ▲ Rush Creek; **219** SC-12; 🅿; **z** 43107; ℗ 1,386; © 1,265
Brentwood; RMC Place; HAMILTON; ▲ Springfield; **218** SF-2; ★ **CIN**; mail Cincinnati **z** 45231; ● 5,500
Brentwood; RMC Place; LAKE; ***217** NE-16; ★ **CLEV**; mail Mentor **z** 44060; pop. incl. with Mentor (Inc. Place)
Brentwood Estates; RMC Place; JEFFERSON; ▲ Cross Creek; ***217** NL-19; ★ **STU-**; mail Steubenville **z** 43953; ● 1,000
Brentwood Lake; RMC Place; LORAIN; ▲ Carlisle; **217** NG-13; ★ **CLEV**; mail Grafton **z** 44044; ● 650
Brewer Heights; RMC Place; ROSS; ***218** SE-9; pop. incl. with Chillicothe (Inc. Place)
Brewster; Inc. Place; STARK; ▲ Sugar Creek; **217** NJ-15; 🅿; ★ **CAN**; **z** 44613; ℗ 2,307; © 2,324
Briarwood Beach; RMC Place; MEDINA; ▲ Lafayette; **217** NH-14; ★ **CLEV**; mail Chippewa Lake **z** 44215; ℗ 682
Brice; Inc. Place; FRANKLIN; ▲ Truro; **218** SB-10; 🅿; ★ **COL**; **z** 43109; ℗ 109; © 70
Briceton; RMC Place; PAULDING; ▲ Paulding; **216** NH-1; elev. 738ft./225m.; mail Paulding **z** 45879; ● 150
Bridgeport; Inc. Place; BELMONT; ▲ Pease; **217** NN-19; 🅿; ★ **WHL**; **z** 43912; ℗ 2,318; © 2,186
Bridgeport; RMC Place; HARDIN; ▲ Blanchard; ***216** NJ-6; elev. 905ft./276m.; mail Forest **z** 45843; rural
Bridges; RMC Place; HIGHLAND; ▲ Fairfield; **218** SE-7; rural
Bridgetown; RMC Place; HAMILTON; **218** SL-1; ● 7,800
Bridgetown North; CDP-Census Area Only; HAMILTON; ▲ Green; ***218** SF-2; ★ **CIN**; mail Cincinnati **z** 45211; ℗ 11,748; © 12,569
Bridgeville; RMC Place; MUSKINGUM; ▲ Perry; ***219** SB-14; ★ **ZAN**; mail Zanesville **z** 43701; rural
Bridgewater; MCD-Township; WILLIAMS; ***216** ND-2; mail Montpelier **z** 43543; ℗ 1,103; © 1,401
Bridgewater Center; RMC Place; WILLIAMS; ▲ Bridgewater; **216** ND-2; elev. 914ft./279m.; mail Montpelier **z** 43543; ● 70
Brier Hill; RMC Place; MAHONING; ***217** NH-19; elev. 1,051ft./320m.; ★ **YNGS-**; mail Youngstown **z** 44510; pop. incl. with Youngstown (Inc. Place)
Brigglesville; RMC Place; PERRY; ▲ Harrison; ***219** SC-13; ★ **ZAN**; mail Crooksville **z** 43731; ● 120
Briggs; RMC Place; CUYAHOGA; ★ **CLEV**; mail Cleveland **z** 44134; pop. incl. with Parma (Inc. Place)
Briggs (Briggs Station); RMC Place; WASHINGTON; ▲ Dunham; ***219** SE-16; ★ **PRKB**; mail Belpre **z** 45714, Marietta **z** 45750; rural
Briggsdale; RMC Place; FRANKLIN; ▲ Franklin; **218** SB-9; ★ **COL**; mail Columbus **z** 43223; ● 180
Briggs Station; WASHINGTON; see Briggs (RMC Place)
Brighton; RMC Place; CLARK; ▲ Harmony; **218** SB-7; mail South Vienna **z** 45369; ● 50
Brighton; RMC Place; HAMILTON; ***218** SG-2; ★ **CIN**; mail Cincinnati **z** 45214; pop. incl. with Cincinnati (Inc. Place)
Brighton; RMC Place; LORAIN; ▲ Brighton; **217** NG-12; elev. 905ft./276m.; mail Wellington **z** 44090; ● 130
Brighton; MCD-Township; LORAIN; ***217** NG-12; mail Wellington **z** 44090; ℗ 812; © 942
Brightwood; RMC Place; TUSCARAWAS; ▲ Goshen; ***217** NL-16; mail New Philadelphia **z** 44663; ● 500
Brilliant; RMC Place; JEFFERSON; ▲ Wells; **217** NM-20; 🅿; ★ **STU-**; **z** 43913; ● 1,600
Brimfield; CDP; PORTAGE; ▲ Brimfield; **217** NH-16; ★ **AKR**; mail Kent **z** 44240; ℗ 3,223; © 3,248
Brimfield; MCD-Township; PORTAGE; ***217** NH-16; ★ **AKR**; mail Kent **z** 44240; ℗ 8,389; © 7,963
Brinkhaven (Gann); Inc. Place; KNOX; **217** NL-13; 🅿; **z** 43006; ℗ 179; © 143
Bristol; MCD-Township; MORGAN; ***219** SC-15; mail McConnelsville **z** 43756; ℗ 173; © 207
Bristol; RMC Place; PERRY; ▲ Pike; **219** SC-13; mail New Lexington **z** 43764; ● 70
Bristol; MCD-Township; TRUMBULL; ***217** NF-19; ★ **YNGS-**; mail Bristolville **z** 44402; ℗ 3,026; © 3,154
Bristol Village; RMC Place; PIKE; ***218** SG-9; mail Waverly **z** 45690; pop. incl. with Waverly (Inc. Place)
Bristolville; RMC Place; TRUMBULL; ▲ Bristol; **217** NF-19; elev. 902ft./275m.; 🅿; ★ **YNGS-**; **z** 44402; ● 500
Bristolville; TRUMBULL; see Spokane (RMC Place)
Brittain; RMC Place; SUMMIT; ***217** NH-16; ★ **AKR**; pop. incl. with Akron (Inc. Place)
Broadacre; RMC Place; JEFFERSON; ▲ Wayne; ***217** NL-19; ★ **STU-**; mail Bloomingdale **z** 43910; ● 30
Broadview; RMC Place; SUMMIT; ***217** NG-15; ★ **CLEV**; pop. incl. with Richfield (Inc. Place)
Broadview Acres; RMC Place; CLARK; ▲ Bethel; ***218** SB-5; ★ **SPR**; mail Springfield **z** 45504; ● 250
Broadview Acres; RMC Place; MUSKINGUM; ▲ Newton; ***219** SB-14; ★ **ZAN**; mail Zanesville **z** 43701; rural
Broadview Heights; Inc. Place; CUYAHOGA; **217** NG-15; 🅿; ★ **CLEV**; **z** 44147; ℗ 12,219; © 15,967
Broadway; RMC Place; UNION; ▲ Taylor; **216** NL-7; 🅿; **z** 43007; ● 500
Broadwell; RMC Place; ATHENS; ▲ Bern; ***219** SE-14; elev. 629ft./192m.; mail Stewart **z** 45778
Brock; RMC Place; DARKE; ▲ York; **216** NM-2; mail Versailles **z** 45380; ● 50
Brocks Corner; RMC Place; JACKSON; ▲ Jackson; ***218** SF-10; mail Ray **z** 45672; rural
Brokaw; RMC Place; MORGAN; ▲ Windsor; ***219** SD-15; mail Stockport **z** 43787; ● 25
Brokensword; RMC Place; CRAWFORD; ▲ Lykens, Holmes; **216** NI-9; elev. 994ft./303m.; mail Bucyrus **z** 44820; ● 30
Bronson; MCD-Township; HURON; ***217** NG-11; mail Norwalk **z** 44857; ℗ 1,683; © 1,780
Brookfield; MCD-Township; NOBLE; ***219** SC-15; mail Cumberland **z** 43732; ℗ 119; © 119
Brookfield; RMC Place; TRUMBULL; ● 300
Brookfield; MCD-Township; TRUMBULL; ***217** NG-20; 🅿; ★ **SHAR**; **z** 44403; ℗ 10,562; © 10,020
Brookfield Center; CDP-Census Area Only; TRUMBULL; ▲ Brookfield; **217** NG-20; ★ **SHAR**; mail Brookfield **z** 44403; ℗ 1,396; © 1,288
Brookhill; RMC Place; HAMILTON; ▲ Springfield; ***218** SF-2; ★ **CIN**; mail Cincinnati **z** 45224; ● 1,100
Brook Hollow; RMC Place; GREENE; ▲ Beavercreek; ★ **DAY**; mail Fairborn **z** 45324; ● 500
Brooklyn; Inc. Place; CUYAHOGA; **217** NF-15; elev. 765ft./233m.; 🅿 ■; ★ **CLEV**; **z** 44144; ℗ 11,706; © 11,586; ◆ 10,496
Brooklyn Heights; Inc. Place; CUYAHOGA; **219** SM-17; 🅿; ★ **CLEV**; **z** 44131 & mail Cleveland **z** 44109; ℗ 1,450; © 1,558
Brook Park; Inc. Place; CUYAHOGA; **217** NF-14; 🅿; ★ **CLEV**; **z** 44142; ℗ 22,865; © 21,218; ◆ 18,096
Brookside; Inc. Place; BELMONT; ▲ Pease; ***219** SA-20; ★ **WHL**; mail Bridgeport **z** 43912; ℗ 703; © 644
Brookside; RMC Place; SCIOTO; ▲ Union; ***218** SH-9; mail Mc Dermott **z** 45652; rural
Brookside Estates; RMC Place; FRANKLIN; ▲ Perry; **219** SF-18; ★ **COL**; mail Columbus **z** 43235; ● 670
Brookview; RMC Place; BELMONT; ▲ Pease; ★ **WHL**; mail Bridgeport **z** 43912; ● 100
Brookville; Inc. Place; MONTGOMERY; ▲ Perry, Clay; **218** SB-3; elev. 1,033ft./315m.; 🅿; ★ **DAY**; **z** 45309; ℗ 4,621; © 5,289
Brookwood; RMC Place; HAMILTON; ***218** SF-2; ★ **CIN**; mail Cincinnati **z** 45239; pop. incl. with Amberley (Inc. Place)
Broughton; Inc. Place; PAULDING; ▲ Jackson; **216** NH-2; elev. 726ft./221m.; mail Paulding **z** 45879; ℗ 151; © 166
Brown; MCD-Township; CARROLL; ***217** NJ-17; ★ **CAN**; mail Malvern **z** 44644; ℗ 7,958; © 8,300
Brown; MCD-Township; DARKE; ***216** NM-1; mail Ansonia **z** 45303; ℗ 2,211; © 2,046
Brown; MCD-Township; DELAWARE; ***216** NM-9; mail Delaware **z** 43015; ℗ 1,164; © 1,297
Brown; MCD-Township; FRANKLIN; ***218** SA-8; mail Hilliard **z** 43026; ℗ 1,825; © 2,031
Brown; MCD-Township; KNOX; ***217** NK-12; mail Danville **z** 43014; ℗ 1,019; © 1,425
Brown; MCD-Township; MIAMI; ***216** NN-4; mail Conover **z** 45317; ℗ 1,594; © 1,554
Brown; MCD-Township; PAULDING; ***216** NH-3; mail Oakwood **z** 45873; ℗ 2,408; © 2,244
Brown; MCD-Township; VINTON; ***219** SE-12; mail New Plymouth **z** 45654; ℗ 248; © 281
BROWN; **218** SI-5; ℗ 34,966; © 42,285; ◆ 44,029
Brown Heights; RMC Place; GUERNSEY; ▲ Cambridge; **219** SA-16; mail Cambridge **z** 43725; ● 200
Brownhelm; RMC Place; LORAIN; ***217** NF-12; ★ **CLEV**; mail Amherst **z** 44001, Vermilion **z** 44089; pop. incl. with Vermilion (Inc. Place)
Brownhelm; MCD-Township; LORAIN; ***217** NF-12; ★ **CLEV**; mail Amherst **z** 44001; ℗ 7,060; © 7,782
Brownstown (Browntown); RMC Place; BROWN; ▲ Washington; ***218** SH-5; mail Georgetown **z** 45121, Sardinia **z** 45171; ● 45
Brownsville; RMC Place; LICKING; ▲ Bowling Green; **219** SB-13; elev. 948ft./289m.; 🅿; **z** 43721; ● 350
Brownsville; RMC Place; MONROE; ▲ Benton; **219** SD-18; mail New Matamoras **z** 45767; ● 70
Brownsville; RMC Place; ROSS; ▲ Huntington; **218** SF-9; mail Chillicothe **z** 45601; ● 200
Browntown; BROWN; see Brownstown (RMC Place)
Brunersburg; RMC Place; DEFIANCE; ▲ Noble; **216** NG-3; mail Defiance **z** 43512; ● 140
Bruno; RMC Place; PERRY; ▲ Thorn; ***219** SB-12; ★ **COL**; mail Thornville **z** 43076
Brunswick; Inc. Place; MEDINA; **217** NG-14; 🅿; ★ **CLEV**; **z** 44212; ℗ 28,230; © 33,388; ◆ 34,279
Brunswick Hills; MCD-Township; MEDINA; ***217** NG-14; ★ **CLEV**; mail Valley City **z** 44280; ℗ 4,328; © 5,469
Brush Creek; MCD-Township; ADAMS; ***218** SI-7; mail Lynx **z** 45650; ℗ 1,195; © 1,231
Brushcreek; MCD-Township; HIGHLAND; ***218** SG-7; mail Sinking Spring **z** 45172; ℗ 1,103; © 1,308
Brush Creek; MCD-Township; JEFFERSON; ***217** NK-19; mail Salineville **z** 43945; ℗ 461; © 467
Brush Creek; MCD-Township; MUSKINGUM; ***219** SB-14; mail Roseville **z** 43777; ℗ 1,215; © 1,375
Brush Creek; MCD-Township; SCIOTO; ***218** SH-8; mail Otway **z** 45657; ℗ 1,123; © 1,149
Brush Ridge; RMC Place; MARION; ▲ Grand Prairie; ***216** NJ-8; ★ **MRN**; mail Marion **z** 43302
Bryan; Inc. Place; ⊡ WILLIAMS; **216** NF-2; 🅿 🅷; **z** 43506; ℗ 8,348; © 8,333
Buchanan; RMC Place; PIKE; ▲ Pebble; **218** SG-9; elev. 911ft./278m.; mail Waverly **z** 45690; ● 50
Buchtel; Inc. Place; ATHENS, HOCKING; ▲ York; **219** SE-13; 🅿; **z** 45716; ℗ 640; © 574
Buck; MCD-Township; HARDIN; ***216** NK-6; mail Kenton **z** 43326; ℗ 2,776; © 2,441
Buckeye; RMC Place; MUSKINGUM; ▲ Brush Creek; ***219** SB-14; ★ **ZAN**; mail Zanesville **z** 43701
Buckeye Lake; Inc. Place; LICKING, FAIRFIELD; ▲ Licking, Union, Walnut; **219** SB-12; 🅿; ★ **NWRK**; **z** 43008; ℗ 2,986; © 3,049
Buckeyeville (Dogtown); RMC Place; GUERNSEY; ▲ Jackson; **219** SB-16; mail Cambridge **z** 43725; ● 80
Buckhorn; RMC Place; LAWRENCE; ▲ Decatur; ***219** SI-11; mail Pedro **z** 45659
Buckingham; RMC Place; PERRY; ▲ Monroe; **219** SD-13; mail Corning **z** 43730; ● 25
Buckland; Inc. Place; AUGLAIZE; ▲ Logan; **216** NK-3; 🅿; **z** 45819; ℗ 239; © 255
Bucks; MCD-Township; TUSCARAWAS; ***217** NL-15; 🅿; **z** 43804 & mail Fresno **z** 43824; ℗ 1,298; © 1,601
Buckskin; MCD-Township; ROSS; ***218** SE-8; mail Londonderry **z** 45647; ℗ 1,416; © 1,040
Bucyrus; Inc. Place; ⊡ CRAWFORD; **216** NJ-9; 🅿 🅷; **z** 44820; ℗ 13,496; © 13,224
Bucyrus; MCD-Township; CRAWFORD; ***216** NJ-9; 🅿; **z** 44820; ℗ 1,105; © 828
Buena Vista; RMC Place; BUTLER; ▲ Lemon; ***218** SD-3; ★ **MIDD**; mail Middletown **z** 45042; ● 300
Buena Vista (Moons); RMC Place; FAYETTE; ▲ Green; ***218** SE-7; mail Washington Court House **z** 43160; ● 50
Buena Vista; RMC Place; HOCKING; ▲ Perry; ***219** SD-11; elev. 887ft./270m.; mail Rockbridge **z** 43149
Buena Vista; RMC Place; SCIOTO; ▲ Nile; **218** SJ-8; mail Stout **z** 45684; ● 150
Buffalo; RMC Place; GUERNSEY; ▲ Valley; **219** SB-16; 🅿; **z** 43722; ● 200
Buffalo; MCD-Township; NOBLE; ***219** SB-16; mail Pleasant City **z** 43772; ℗ 645; © 782
Buford; RMC Place; HIGHLAND; ▲ Clay; **218** SG-5; elev. 959ft./292m.; 🅿; **z** 45110; ● 245
Bulah; RMC Place; ASHTABULA; ▲ Denmark; ***217** ND-19; mail Jefferson **z** 44047; rural
Bulaville; RMC Place; GALLIA; ▲ Addison; ***219** SH-13; mail Gallipolis **z** 45631; rural
Bundysburg; RMC Place; GEAUGA; ***217** NF-18; mail Middlefield **z** 44062; ● 100
Bunker Hill; RMC Place; BUTLER; ▲ Reily; ***218** SE-1; mail Hamilton **z** 45013
Bunker Hill; RMC Place; HOLMES; ▲ Berlin; ***217** NK-14; mail Millersburg **z** 44654; ● 50
Burbank; Inc. Place; WAYNE; ▲ Congress, Canaan; **217** NI-13; 🅿; ★ **CLEV**; **z** 44214; ℗ 289; © 279
Burghill; RMC Place; TRUMBULL; ▲ Vernon; **217** NF-20; 🅿; **z** 44404; ● 250
Burgoon; Inc. Place; SANDUSKY; ▲ Jackson; **216** NG-8; 🅿; **z** 43407; ℗ 224; © 199
Burkettsville; Inc. Place; MERCER, DARKE; ▲ Granville; **216** NL-1; 🅿; **z** 45310; ℗ 268; © 254
Burkhart; RMC Place; MONROE; ▲ Summit; ***219** SC-17; mail Lewisville **z** 43754; rural
Burlingham; RMC Place; MEIGS; ▲ Bedford; **219** SF-14; mail Shade **z** 45776; ● 50
Burlington; RMC Place; FULTON; ▲ Franklin; **216** NE-3; mail Archbold **z** 43502; ● 130
Burlington; CDP; LAWRENCE; ▲ Fayette; **219** SK-11; ★ **HNTG**; mail South Point **z** 45680; ℗ 3,003; © 2,794
Burlington; MCD-Township; LICKING; ***217** NM-11; mail Homer **z** 43027; ℗ 966; © 1,073
Burnetts Corners; RMC Place; WAYNE; ▲ Wooster; ***217** NJ-14; elev. 1,043ft./318m.; mail Wooster **z** 44691; rural
Burnet Woods; RMC Place; HAMILTON; ★ **CIN**; mail Cincinnati **z** 45220; pop. incl. with Cincinnati (Inc. Place)
Burr Oak; RMC Place; ATHENS; ▲ Trimble; ***219** SD-14; mail Glouster **z** 45732; rural
Burr Oaks; MADISON; see Burr Oaks Heights (RMC Place)
Burr Oaks Heights (Burr Oaks); RMC Place; MADISON; ▲ Pleasant; ***218** SC-8; mail Mount Sterling **z** 43143; ● 150
Burton; Inc. Place; GEAUGA; ▲ Burton; **217** NF-17; 🅿 🅲 1,062; ★ **CLEV**; **z** 44021; ℗ 1,349; © 1,450
Burton; MCD-Township; GEAUGA; ***217** NF-17; 🅿 🅲 1,062; ★ **CLEV**; **z** 44021; ℗ 4,187; © 4,358
Burton City; RMC Place; WAYNE; ▲ Baughman; ***217** NI-15; elev. 1,017ft./310m.; ★ **AKR**; mail Orrville **z** 44667
Burton Lake; RMC Place; GEAUGA; ▲ Burton; ***217** NF-17; ★ **CLEV**; mail Burton **z** 44021; ● 370
Burton Station; RMC Place; GEAUGA; ▲ Burton, Middlefield; **217** NF-17; ★ **CLEV**; mail Middlefield **z** 44062; ● 40
Burtonville; RMC Place; CLINTON; ▲ Union; **218** SE-5; elev. 1,018ft./310m.; mail Wilmington **z** 45177; ● 100
Busenbark; RMC Place; BUTLER; ▲ St. Clair; ***218** SE-2; elev. 644ft./196m.; ★ **MIDD**; mail Hamilton **z** 45011; rural
Bushnell; RMC Place; ASHTABULA; ▲ Monroe; **217** NC-20; elev. 889ft./271m.; mail Conneaut **z** 44030
Businessburg; RMC Place; BELMONT; ▲ Mead; ***219** SB-19; ★ **WHL**; mail Jacobsburg **z** 43933
Business Corners; RMC Place; LUCAS; ▲ Monclova; ***216** NE-6; ★ **TOL**; mail Monclova **z** 43542; rural
Butler; MCD-Township; COLUMBIANA; ***217** NI-18; mail Salem **z** 44460; ℗ 3,265; © 3,444
Butler; MCD-Township; DARKE; ***218** SB-2; mail New Madison **z** 45346; ℗ 1,729; © 1,616
Butler; MCD-Township; KNOX; ***217** NL-12; mail Walhonding **z** 43843; ℗ 504; © 798
Butler; MCD-Township; MERCER; ***216** NL-1; mail Coldwater **z** 45828; ℗ 6,181; © 6,459
Butler; MCD-Township; MONTGOMERY; ***218** SB-4; ★ **DAY**; mail Laura **z** 45337; ℗ 8,634; © 8,382
Butler; Inc. Place; RICHLAND; ▲ Worthington; **217** NK-11; elev. 1,073ft./327m.; 🅿; ★ **MANS**; **z** 44822; ℗ 968; © 921
Butler; MCD-Township; RICHLAND; ***217** NI-11; 🅿; **z** 44822 & mail Greenwich **z** 44837; ℗ 1,122; © 1,386
BUTLER; **218** SE-1; ℗ 291,479; © 332,807; ® 332,705; ◆ 362,394
Butlerville; Inc. Place; WARREN; ▲ Harlan; **218** SF-4; elev. 856ft./261m.; mail Pleasant Plain **z** 45162; ℗ 188; © 231
Byer (Byers Junction); RMC Place; JACKSON; ▲ Washington; ***219** SF-11; mail Wellston **z** 45692; ● 45
Byers Junction; JACKSON; see Byer (RMC Place)
Byesville; Inc. Place; GUERNSEY; ▲ Jackson; **219** SB-16; 🅿; **z** 43723; ℗ 2,435; © 2,574
Byhalia; RMC Place; UNION; ▲ Washington; **216** NL-7; mail Richwood **z** 43344, West Mansfield **z** 43358; ● 130
Byington; RMC Place; PIKE; ▲ Mifflin; **218** SG-8; mail Latham **z** 45646; ● 50
Byrd; MCD-Township; BROWN; ***218** SH-6; mail Decatur **z** 45115; ℗ 697; © 740
Byron; RMC Place; GREENE; ▲ Bath; **218** SC-5; ★ **DAY**; mail Xenia **z** 45385; ● 50

C

Cable; RMC Place; CHAMPAIGN; ▲ Wayne; **216** NM-6; 🅿; **z** 43009; ● 200
Cadiz; Inc. Place; ⊡ HARRISON; ▲ Cadiz; **217** NM-18; elev. 1,280ft./390m.; 🅿 🅷; **z** 43907; ℗ 3,439; © 3,308
Cadiz; MCD-Township; HARRISON; ***217** NM-18; 🅿; **z** 43907; ℗ 3,907; © 3,639
Cadiz Junction (Means); RMC Place; HARRISON; ▲ German; ***217** NL-18; mail Hopedale **z** 43976
Cadmus; RMC Place; GALLIA; ▲ Walnut; **219** SI-12; elev. 622ft./190m.; mail Patriot **z** 45658; ● 60
Caesarscreek; MCD-Township; GREENE; ***218** SD-5; mail Xenia **z** 45385; ℗ 1,170; © 1,225
Cain Heights; RMC Place; COLUMBIANA; ▲ Liverpool; ***217** NJ-20; ★ **E.LIV**; mail East Liverpool **z** 43920
Cairo; Inc. Place; ALLEN; ▲ Monroe; **216** NI-4; elev. 815ft./248m.; 🅿; **z** 45820; ℗ 473; © 499
Cairo; RMC Place; STARK; ▲ Plain, Lake; **217** NI-16; elev. 1,134ft./346m.; ★ **CAN**; mail Canton **z** 44721; ● 120
Calais; RMC Place; MONROE; ▲ Seneca; **219** SB-17; elev. 861ft./262m.; mail Quaker City **z** 43773; ● 25
Calcutta; CDP; COLUMBIANA; ▲ St. Clair; **217** NJ-20; 🅿; ★ **E.LIV**; **z** 43920; ℗ 1,212; © 3,491
Caldwell; Inc. Place; ⊡ NOBLE; ▲ Olive, Center; **219** SC-16; elev. 744ft./227m.; 🅿; **z** 43724; ℗ 1,786; © 1,956
Caledonia; Inc. Place; MARION; ▲ Claridon; **216** NK-9; elev. 998ft./304m.; 🅿; ★ **MRN**; **z** 43314 & mail Martel **z** 43335; ℗ 644; © 578
California; RMC Place; CLARK; ▲ Springfield; ***218** SB-6; ★ **SPR**; mail Springfield **z** 45503; ● 50
California; RMC Place; HAMILTON; ***218** SG-3; ★ **CIN**; mail Cincinnati **z** 45228; pop. incl. with Cincinnati (Inc. Place)
Calla; RMC Place; MAHONING; ▲ Green; ***217** NI-19; elev. 1,153ft./351m.; mail Canfield **z** 44406
Cambridge; Inc. Place; ⊡ GUERNSEY; ▲ Cambridge; **219** SA-16; 🅿 🅷 ■; **z** 43725, **z** 43750; ℗ 11,748; © 11,520; ◆ 11,302
Cambridge; MCD-Township; GUERNSEY; ***219** SA-16; 🅿; **z** 43725, **z** 43750; ℗ 16,126; © 15,505
Camden; MCD-Township; LORAIN; ***217** NG-12; ★ **CLEV**; mail Kipton **z** 44049; ℗ 1,522; © 1,530
Camden; Inc. Place; PREBLE; ▲ Somers; **218** SD-1; 🅿; **z** 45311; ℗ 2,210; © 2,302
Cameron; RMC Place; MONROE; ▲ Adams; **219** SC-19; 🅿; **z** 43914; ● 180
Campbell; Inc. Place; MAHONING; **217** NH-20; 🅿; ★ **YNGS-**; **z** 44405; ℗ 10,038; © 9,460
Campbellsport; RMC Place; PORTAGE; ▲ Ravenna; ***217** NH-17; ★ **AKR**; mail Ravenna **z** 44266
Campbellstown; RMC Place; PREBLE; ▲ Jackson; **218** SC-1; elev. 1,180ft./360m.; mail Eaton **z** 45320; ● 120
Camp Creek; MCD-Township; PIKE; ***218** SH-9; mail Rarden **z** 45671; ℗ 724; © 951
Camp Creek; RMC Place; STARK; ▲ Sugar Creek; ***217** NJ-15; elev. 1,039ft./317m.; ★ **CAN**; mail Navarre **z** 44662; rural
Camp Dennison; RMC Place; HAMILTON; ▲ Symmes; **218** SK-5; 🅿; ★ **CIN**; **z** 45111; ● 600
Camp Ground; RMC Place; FAIRFIELD; ▲ Greenfield; ***219** SC-11; ★ **LANC**; mail Lancaster **z** 43130; pop. incl. with Lancaster (Inc. Place) summer pop. 300
Camp Luther; RMC Place; ASHTABULA; ***217** NC-19; ★ **ASHT**; mail North Kingsville **z** 44068
Canaan; MCD-Township; ATHENS; ***219** SE-14; mail Athens **z** 45701; ℗ 1,568; © 1,780
Canaan; MCD-Township; MADISON; ***218** SA-8; mail Plain City **z** 43064; ℗ 2,309; © 2,496
Canaan; MCD-Township; MORROW; ***216** NK-9; mail Edison **z** 43320; ℗ 844; © 897
Canaan; RMC Place; WAYNE; ▲ Canaan; **217** NI-14; elev. 1,074ft./327m.; ★ **CLEV**; mail Creston **z** 44217
Canaan; MCD-Township; WAYNE; ***217** NI-14; ★ **CLEV**; mail Creston **z** 44217; ℗ 3,996; © 4,736
Canaanville; RMC Place; ATHENS; ▲ Rome; **219** SE-14; mail Athens **z** 45701
Canal Fulton; Inc. Place; STARK; ▲ Lawrence; **217** NI-15; 🅿; ★ **AKR**; **z** 44614; ℗ 4,157; © 5,061
Canal Lewisville; RMC Place; COSHOCTON; ▲ Tuscarawas, Keene; **217** NM-14; mail Coshocton **z** 43812; ● 200
Canal Winchester; Inc. Place; FRANKLIN, FAIRFIELD; ▲ Madison, Bloom, Violet; **218** SB-10; 🅿; ★ **COL**; **z** 43110; ℗ 2,617; © 4,478; ® 4,491
Candle Lite Estates; RMC Place; TRUMBULL; ★ **YNGS-**; mail Warren **z** 44484; pop. incl. with Warren (Inc. Place)
Canfield; Inc. Place; MAHONING; ▲ Canfield; **217** NH-19; elev. 1,161ft./354m.; 🅿; ★ **YNGS-**; **z** 44406; ℗ 5,409; © 7,374
Canfield; MCD-Township; MAHONING; ***217** NH-19; 🅿; ★ **YNGS-**; **z** 44406; ℗ 10,831; © 14,624
Cannelville; RMC Place; MUSKINGUM; ▲ Brush Creek; **219** SC-14; mail Roseville **z** 43777; ● 250
Cannons Creek; RMC Place; LAWRENCE; ▲ Elizabeth; **219** SJ-11; elev. 662ft./202m.; mail Pedro **z** 45659
Cannons Mills; RMC Place; COLUMBIANA; ▲ St. Clair; ***217** NJ-20; ★ **E.LIV**; mail East Liverpool **z** 43920; ● 40
Canton; Inc. Place; ⊡ STARK; **217** NJ-16; 🅿 🅷 🅲 7,613 ■; ★ **CAN**; **z** 44701-11, **z** 44714, **z** 44718, **z** 44720-21, **z** 44730, **z** 44735, **z** 44750, **z** 44767, **z** 44799; ℗ 84,161; © 80,806; ◆ 79,526
Canton; MCD-Township; STARK; ***217** NJ-16; 🅿 🅲 7,613; ★ **CAN**; **z** 44701-11, **z** 44714, **z** 44718, **z** 44720-21, **z** 44730, **z** 44735, **z** 44750, **z** 44767, **z** 44799; ℗ 14,050; © 13,882
Canyon Park; RMC Place; MAHONING; ▲ Milton; ***217** NH-18; elev. 1,000ft./305m.; mail Lake Milton **z** 44429; ● 35
Captina; RMC Place; BELMONT; ▲ York; ***219** SB-19; mail Jacobsburg **z** 43933; rural
Caraghar; FULTON; see Assumption (RMC Place)
Carbondale; RMC Place; ATHENS; ▲ Waterloo; **219** SE-13; elev. 751ft./229m.; 🅿; **z** 45717; ● 120
Carbon Hill; RMC Place; HOCKING; ▲ Ward; **219** SD-13; 🅿; **z** 43111; ● 300
Cardinal Lake; RMC Place; ASHTABULA; ▲ Rome; ***217** NE-18; mail Rome **z** 44085; summer pop. 300; ● 100
Cardington; Inc. Place; MORROW; ▲ Cardington; **216** NK-9; elev. 1,014ft./309m.; 🅿; **z** 43315; ℗ 1,770; © 1,849
Cardington; MCD-Township; MORROW; ***216** NK-9; 🅿; **z** 43315; ℗ 2,651; © 2,790
Carey; Inc. Place; WYANDOT; ▲ Crawford; **216** NI-7; 🅿; **z** 43316; ℗ 3,684; © 3,901
Carlisle; MCD-Township; LORAIN; ***217** NG-13; ★ **CLEV**; mail Elyria **z** 44035; ℗ 7,554; © 7,339
Carlisle (Berne); RMC Place; NOBLE; **219** SC-17; mail Caldwell **z** 43724; ● 50
Carlisle; Inc. Place; WARREN, MONTGOMERY; ▲ Franklin; **218** SD-3; 🅿; ★ **MIDD**; **z** 45005; ℗ 4,872; © 5,121
Carlisle Junction; RMC Place; WARREN; ***218** SD-3; ★ **MIDD**; pop. incl. with Carlisle (Inc. Place)
Carmel; RMC Place; HIGHLAND; ▲ Miami; **218** SF-7; elev. 964ft./294m.; mail Hillsboro **z** 45133; ● 30
Caroline; RMC Place; SENECA; ▲ Venice; **216** NH-9; mail Attica **z** 44807; ● 80
Carpenter; RMC Place; MEIGS; ▲ Columbia; **219** SF-13; elev. 630ft./192m.; mail Albany **z** 45710, Pomeroy **z** 45769; ● 25
Carriage; RMC Place; CLARK; ▲ Springfield; ***218** SB-5; ★ **SPR**; mail Springfield **z** 45502; ● 150
Carroll; Inc. Place; FAIRFIELD; ▲ Greenfield; **219** SC-11; 🅿; ★ **COL**; **z** 43112; ℗ 558; © 488
Carroll; MCD-Township; OTTAWA; ***216** NE-8; mail Oak Harbor **z** 43449; ℗ 1,735; © 1,931
CARROLL; **217** NJ-18; ℗ 26,521; © 28,836; ◆ 28,016
Carrollton; Inc. Place; ⊡ CARROLL; ▲ Center; **217** NK-18; elev. 1,130ft./344m.; 🅿; **z** 44615; ℗ 3,042; © 3,190
Carrothers; RMC Place; SENECA; ▲ Venice; **216** NH-9; 🅿; **z** 44807; ● 60
Carryall; MCD-Township; PAULDING; ***216** NG-1; mail Antwerp **z** 45813; ℗ 3,039; © 3,046
Carthage; MCD-Township; ATHENS; ***219** SF-14; mail Guysville **z** 45735; ℗ 1,360; © 1,467
Carthage; RMC Place; HAMILTON; ***218** SF-2; ★ **CIN**; mail Cincinnati **z** 45216; pop. incl. with Cincinnati (Inc. Place)
Carthagena; RMC Place; MERCER; ▲ Marion; **216** NL-2; 🅿; **z** 45822; ● 40
Carysville; RMC Place; CHAMPAIGN; ▲ Adams; **216** NM-4; elev. 1,131ft./345m.; mail Conover **z** 45317; ● 100
Cass; MCD-Township; HANCOCK; ***216** NH-6; mail Arcadia **z** 44804; ℗ 1,023; © 1,098
Cass; MCD-Township; MUSKINGUM; ***217** NN-13; mail Dresden **z** 43821; ℗ 1,197; © 1,492
Cass; MCD-Township; RICHLAND; ***217** NI-11; mail Shiloh **z** 44878; ℗ 1,626; © 1,735
Cassell; RMC Place; GUERNSEY; ▲ Adams; **219** SA-15; mail Cambridge **z** 43725; ● 100
Cassella; RMC Place; MERCER; ▲ Granville; **216** NL-2; elev. 950ft./290m.; mail Saint Henry **z** 45883; ● 125
Casstown; Inc. Place; MIAMI; ▲ Lostcreek; **216** NN-4; elev. 937ft./286m.; 🅿; **z** 45312; ℗ 246; © 322
Castalia; Inc. Place; ERIE; ▲ Margaretta; **216** NF-10; 🅿; ★ **SNDSK**; **z** 44824; ℗ 915; © 935
Castine; Inc. Place; DARKE; ▲ Butler; **218** SB-2; 🅿; **z** 45304; ℗ 163; © 129
Catawba; CHAMPAIGN; see Catawba Station (RMC Place)
Catawba; Inc. Place; CLARK; ▲ Pleasant; **218** SA-6; 🅿; ★ **SPR**; **z** 43010; ℗ 268; © 312
Catawba Island; RMC Place; OTTAWA; ▲ Catawba Island; **216** NE-10; mail Port Clinton **z** 43452; ● 200
Catawba Island; MCD-Township; OTTAWA; ***216** NE-10; mail Port Clinton **z** 43452; ℗ 3,148; © 3,157
Catawba Station (Catawba); RMC Place; CHAMPAIGN; ▲ Union; ***218** SA-6; mail Mechanicsburg **z** 43044; rural
Causeway Manor; RMC Place; ASHTABULA; ▲ Andover; mail Andover **z** 44003; ● 60
Cavallo; RMC Place; COSHOCTON; ▲ Tiverton; ***217** NL-13; mail Walhonding **z** 43843; ● 20
Cavett; RMC Place; VAN WERT; ▲ Union; **216** NI-2; mail Van Wert **z** 45891
Caywood; RMC Place; WASHINGTON; ▲ Fearing; ***219** SE-17; ★ **PRKB**; mail Marietta **z** 45750
Cecil; Inc. Place; PAULDING; ▲ Crane; **216** NG-2; elev. 725ft./221m.; 🅿; **z** 45821; ℗ 249; © 216
Cedarhill; RMC Place; FAIRFIELD; ▲ Amanda; ***218** SC-10; elev. 881ft./269m.; ★ **LANC**; mail Amanda **z** 43102; ● 25
Cedar Mills; RMC Place; ADAMS; ▲ Brush Creek; **218** SI-7; elev. 565ft./172m.; mail Blue Creek **z** 45616; ● 20
Cedar Point; RMC Place; ERIE; ***216** NF-10; ★ **SNDSK**; mail Sandusky **z** 44870; pop. incl. with Sandusky (Inc. Place)
Cedar Valley; RMC Place; WAYNE; ▲ Chester; ***217** NI-13; mail Burbank **z** 44214; ● 50
Cedarville; Inc. Place; GREENE; ▲ Cedarville; **218** SC-5; elev. 1,055ft./322m.; 🅿 🅲 2,977; **z** 45314; ℗ 3,210; © 3,828
Cedarville; MCD-Township; GREENE; ***218** SC-5; 🅿 🅲 2,977; **z** 45314; ℗ 4,297; © 5,092
Cedron; RMC Place; CLERMONT; ▲ Franklin; ***218** SI-4; mail Georgetown **z** 45121; ● 50
Celeryville; RMC Place; HURON; ▲ Richmond, New Haven; **216** NH-10; mail Willard **z** 44890; ● 360
Celina; Inc. Place; ⊡ MERCER; ▲ Jefferson, Center; **216** NK-2; 🅿 ■; **z** 45822, **z** 45826; ℗ 9,650; © 10,303; ◆ 10,091
Centenary; RMC Place; GALLIA; ▲ Green; ***219** SI-13; mail Gallipolis **z** 45631; ● 200
Center; MCD-Township; CARROLL; ***217** NK-18; mail Carrollton **z** 44615; ℗ 4,434; © 4,412
Center; MCD-Township; COLUMBIANA; ***217** NJ-19; mail Lisbon **z** 44432; ℗ 6,235; © 6,473
Center; RMC Place; GUERNSEY; ▲ Center; **217** NN-16; mail Cambridge **z** 43725; ● 150
Center; MCD-Township; GUERNSEY; ***219** SA-16; mail Cambridge **z** 43725; ℗ 1,597; © 1,779
Center; MCD-Township; MERCER; ***216** NK-2; mail Celina **z** 45822; ℗ 937; © 1,082
Center; MCD-Township; MONROE; ***219** SC-18; mail Woodsfield **z** 43793; ℗ 3,955; © 3,797
Center; MCD-Township; MORGAN; ***219** SD-15; mail Beverly **z** 45715; ℗ 593; © 652
Center; MCD-Township; NOBLE; ***219** SC-16; mail Caldwell **z** 43724; ℗ 993; © 1,027
Center; MCD-Township; WILLIAMS; ***216** NF-2; mail Bryan **z** 43506; ℗ 3,055; © 3,056
Center; MCD-Township; WOOD; ***216** NF-6; mail Bowling Green **z** 43402; ℗ 1,158; © 1,246
Center Belpre; WASHINGTON; see Porterfield (RMC Place)
Centerburg; Inc. Place; KNOX; ▲ Hilliar; **216** NM-10; 🅿; **z** 43011; ℗ 1,323; © 1,432
Centerfield; RMC Place; HIGHLAND; ▲ Fairfield; **218** SE-7; mail Greenfield **z** 45123, Leesburg **z** 45135; ● 60
Centerpoint; RMC Place; GALLIA; ▲ Perry; ***219** SH-12; mail Oak Hill **z** 45656; ● 45
Center Station; RMC Place; LAWRENCE; ▲ Elizabeth, Decatur; **219** SI-11; mail Pedro **z** 45659; ● 30
Centerton; RMC Place; HURON; ▲ Norwich; **216** NH-10; mail Willard **z** 44890; ● 200
Center Village; RMC Place; DELAWARE; ▲ Harlem; **216** NN-10; elev. 1,073ft./327m.; ★ **COL**; mail Galena **z** 43021; ● 280
Centerville; RMC Place; BELMONT; ▲ Smith; **219** SA-19; mail Belmont **z** 43718, Jacobsburg **z** 43933; ● 150
Centerville; RMC Place; BROWN; ▲ Sterling; ***218** SG-5; elev. 948ft./289m.; mail Mount Orab **z** 45154; rural
Centerville; CLINTON; see Lees Creek (RMC Place)
Centerville; GALLIA; see Thurman (Inc. Place)
Centerville; RMC Place; MARION; ▲ Prospect; ***216** NL-8; ★ **MRN**; mail Prospect **z** 43342
Centerville; Inc. Place; MONTGOMERY, GREENE; ▲ Washington; **218** SD-4; elev. 1,020ft./311m.; 🅿; ★ **DAY**; **z** 45440, **z** 45458-59 & mail Dayton **z** 45475; ℗ 21,082; © 23,024; ◆ 22,755
Centerville; RMC Place; WAYNE; ▲ Clinton; ***217** NJ-13; mail Shreve **z** 44676; ● 30
Central; RMC Place; LUCAS; ★ **TOL**; mail Toledo **z** 43603-04; pop. incl. with Toledo (Inc. Place)
Central City; RMC Place; LICKING; ★ **NWRK**; pop. incl. with Newark (Inc. Place)
Cessna; MCD-Township; HARDIN; ***216** NJ-6; mail Kenton **z** 43326; ℗ 430; © 519
Ceylon; RMC Place; ERIE; ▲ Berlin; **217** NF-11; ★ **CLEV**; mail Huron **z** 44839; ● 90
Chagrin Falls; Inc. Place; CUYAHOGA; ▲ Chagrin Falls; **217** NF-16; 🅿 🅷; ★ **CLEV**; **z** 44022-23; ℗ 4,146; © 4,024
Chagrin Falls; MCD-Township; CUYAHOGA; ***217** NF-16; 🅿; ★ **CLEV**; **z** 44022-23; ℗ 4,348; © 4,159
Chagrin Falls Annex; RMC Place; GEAUGA; mail Chagrin Falls **z** 44023
Chagrin Falls Park; RMC Place; GEAUGA; ▲ Bainbridge; ***217** NF-16; ★ **CLEV**; mail Chagrin Falls **z** 44022; ● 270
Chagrin Harbor; RMC Place; LAKE; ★ **CLEV**; mail Willoughby **z** 44094; pop. incl. with Eastlake (Inc. Place)
Chalfants; RMC Place; PERRY; ▲ Hopewell; ***219** SB-12; mail Glenford **z** 43739
Chambersburg; RMC Place; COLUMBIANA; ▲ West; ***217** NJ-18; elev. 1,281ft./390m.; ★ **ALLI**; mail Minerva **z** 44657; rural
Chambersburg; GALLIA; see Eureka (RMC Place)
CHAMPAIGN; **216** NN-4; ℗ 36,019; © 38,890; ◆ 39,427
Champion; TRUMBULL; see Champion Heights (CDP)
Champion; MCD-Township; TRUMBULL; ***217** NG-19; ★ **YNGS-**; mail Warren **z** 44481, **z** 44483; ℗ 9,189; © 9,762
Champion Heights (Champion); CDP; TRUMBULL; ▲ Champion; **217** NG-19; ★ **YNGS-**; mail Warren **z** 44481, **z** 44483; ℗ 4,665; © 4,727
Chandler; RMC Place; JEFFERSON; ▲ Wayne; ***217** NM-19; elev. 1,036ft./316m.; ★ **STU-**; mail Bloomingdale **z** 43910; rural
Chandlersville; RMC Place; MUSKINGUM; ▲ Salt Creek; **219** SB-15; 🅿; **z** 43727; ● 220
Chapmans; RMC Place; JACKSON; ▲ Coal; **219** SG-11; mail Wellston **z** 45692; ● 50
Chardon; Inc. Place; ⊡ GEAUGA; **217** NE-17; 🅿 🅷; ★ **CLEV**; **z** 44024; ℗ 4,446; © 5,156
Chardon; MCD-Township; GEAUGA; ***217** NE-17; 🅿; ★ **CLEV**; **z** 44024; ℗ 4,037; © 4,763
Charity Rotch; RMC Place; STARK; ***217** NI-16; ★ **CAN**; mail Massillon **z** 44646; pop. incl. with Massillon (Inc. Place)
Charlestown; RMC Place; PORTAGE; ▲ Charlestown; **217** NG-17; ★ **AKR**; mail Ravenna **z** 44266; ● 150
Charlestown; MCD-Township; PORTAGE; ***217** NG-17; ★ **AKR**; mail Ravenna **z** 44266; ℗ 1,903; © 2,003
Charloe; RMC Place; PAULDING; ▲ Brown; **216** NH-2; mail Oakwood **z** 45873, Paulding **z** 45879; ● 60
Charm; RMC Place; HOLMES; ▲ Clark; **217** NK-14; elev. 1,032ft./315m.; 🅿; **z** 44617; ● 160
Chase; RMC Place; ATHENS; ▲ Alexander; ***219** SF-13; mail Albany **z** 45710; rural
Chasetown; RMC Place; BROWN; ▲ Perry; ***218** SF-5; mail Fayetteville **z** 45118; ● 40
Chaseville; RMC Place; NOBLE; ▲ Seneca, Buffalo; ***219** SB-16; mail Pleasant City **z** 43772, Senecaville **z** 43780; rural
Chaska Beach; RMC Place; ERIE; ★ **SNDSK**; mail Huron **z** 44839; pop. incl. with Huron (Inc. Place)
Chateau Estates; RMC Place; CLARK; ▲ German; ***218** SB-5; ★ **SPR**; mail Springfield **z** 45502; ● 300
Chateau Ridge; RMC Place; MARION; ▲ Marion; ★ **MRN**; mail Marion **z** 43302; pop. incl. with Marion (Inc. Place)
Chatfield; Inc. Place; CRAWFORD; ▲ Chatfield; **216** NI-9; 🅿; **z** 44825; ℗ 206; © 218
Chatfield; MCD-Township; CRAWFORD; ***216** NI-9; 🅿; **z** 44825; ℗ 796; © 776
Chatham; RMC Place; LICKING; ▲ Newton; ***217** NN-11; ★ **NWRK**; mail Newark **z** 43055; ● 120
Chatham; RMC Place; MEDINA; ▲ Chatham; **217** NH-13; mail Medina **z** 44256, Spencer **z** 44275; ● 220
Chatham; MCD-Township; MEDINA; ***217** NH-13; mail Spencer **z** 44275; ℗ 1,799; © 2,158
Chattanooga; RMC Place; MERCER; ▲ Liberty; **216** NK-1; elev. 836ft./255m.; mail Rockford **z** 45882; ● 120
Chauncey; Inc. Place; ATHENS; ▲ Dover; **219** SE-13; elev. 659ft./201m.; 🅿; **z** 45719; ℗ 980; © 1,067
Chautauqua; RMC Place; MONTGOMERY; ▲ Miami; **218** SD-3; ★ **MIDD**; mail Miamisburg **z** 45342; pop. incl. with Carlisle (Inc. Place)
Chenoweth; RMC Place; MADISON; ▲ Range; **218** SC-8; mail Mount Sterling **z** 43143; rural
Cherokee; RMC Place; LOGAN; ▲ McArthur; ***216** NL-5; mail Huntsville **z** 43324; ● 40
Cherry Fork; Inc. Place; ADAMS; ▲ Wayne; **218** SH-6; 🅿; **z** 45618; ℗ 178; © 127
Cherry Grove; CDP; HAMILTON; ▲ Anderson; **218** SG-3; elev. 850ft./259m.; ★ **CIN**; mail Cincinnati **z** 45230, **z** 45245; ℗ 4,972; © 4,555
Cherry Valley; RMC Place; ASHTABULA; ▲ Cherry Valley; **217** NE-19; elev. 1,050ft./320m.; mail Andover **z** 44003, Dorset **z** 44032; ● 120
Cherry Valley; MCD-Township; ASHTABULA; ***217** NE-19; mail Andover **z** 44003; ℗ 738; © 857
Cherry Valley; RMC Place; HARRISON; ▲ Green; ***217** NM-19; mail Cadiz **z** 43907; rural
Chesapeake; Inc. Place; LAWRENCE; ▲ Union; **219** SK-12; 🅿; ★ **HNTG**; **z** 45619; ℗ 1,073; © 842
Cheshire; RMC Place; DELAWARE; ▲ Berlin; **216** NM-9; elev. 907ft./276m.; mail Galena **z** 43021; ● 100
Cheshire; Inc. Place; GALLIA; ▲ Cheshire; **219** SH-13; elev. 573ft./175m.; 🅿; **z** 45620; ℗ 250; © 221
Cheshire; MCD-Township; GALLIA; ***219** SH-13; 🅿; **z** 45620; ℗ 1,245; © 1,259
Chesswood Acres; RMC Place; HAMILTON; ▲ Colerain; ***218** SF-2; ★ **CIN**; mail Cincinnati **z** 45239; ● 950
Chester; MCD-Township; CLINTON; ***218** SD-5; mail Wilmington **z** 45177; ℗ 1,200; © 1,771
Chester; MCD-Township; GEAUGA; ***217** NE-16; ★ **CLEV**; mail Chesterland **z** 44026; ℗ 11,049; © 10,968
Chester; RMC Place; MEIGS; ▲ Chester; **219** SG-14; 🅿; **z** 45720; ● 260
Chester; MCD-Township; MEIGS; ***219** SG-14; 🅿; **z** 45720; ℗ 2,131; © 2,332
Chester; MCD-Township; MORROW; ***216** NL-10; mail Mount Gilead **z** 43338; ℗ 1,613; © 1,655
Chester; MCD-Township; WAYNE; ***217** NI-13; mail Wooster **z** 44691; ℗ 2,581; © 2,845
Chester Center; RMC Place; GEAUGA; ▲ Chester; ***217** NE-16; ★ **CLEV**; mail Chesterland **z** 44026
Chesterfield; MCD-Township; FULTON; ***216** ND-4; mail Wauseon **z** 43567; ℗ 1,055; © 1,050
Chesterhill; Inc. Place; MORGAN; ▲ Marion; **219** SD-14; 🅿; **z** 43728; ℗ 309; © 305
Chesterland; CDP; GEAUGA; ▲ Chester; **217** NE-16; elev. 1,213ft./370m.; 🅿; ★ **CLEV**; **z** 44026; ℗ 2,078; © 2,646
Chesterville; Inc. Place; MORROW; ▲ Chester; **216** NL-10; elev. 1,142ft./348m.; 🅿; **z** 43317; ℗ 286; © 193
Cheviot; Inc. Place; HAMILTON; **218** SF-2; ★ **CIN**; mail Cincinnati **z** 45211; ℗ 9,616; © 9,015
Cheviot Hills; RMC Place; CLARK; ▲ Springfield; ***218** SB-6; ★ **SPR**; mail Springfield **z** 45505; ● 150
Chevy Chase; RMC Place; CRAWFORD; ▲ Sandusky; mail Galion **z** 44833; ● 200
Chickasaw; Inc. Place; MERCER; ▲ Marion; **216** NL-2; elev. 946ft./288m.; 🅿; **z** 45826; ℗ 378; © 364
Chili (Pearl); RMC Place; COSHOCTON; ▲ White Eyes; ***217** NL-15; mail Fresno **z** 43824
Chillicothe; Inc. Place; ⊡ ROSS; ▲ Scioto; **218** SE-9; 🅿 🅷 🅲 1,983 ■; **z** 45601; ℗ 21,923; © 21,796; ◆ 22,338
Chillicothe Manor; RMC Place; ROSS; ▲ Scioto; mail Chillicothe **z** 45601; ● 500
Chilo; Inc. Place; CLERMONT; ▲ Franklin; **218** SI-4; 🅿; ★ **CIN**; **z** 45112; ℗ 130; © 97
Chipman; RMC Place; ALLEN; ▲ Shawnee; ★ **LIMA**; mail Lima **z** 45805; ● 250
Chippewa; MCD-Township; WAYNE; ***217** NI-15; ★ **AKR**; mail Doylestown **z** 44230; ℗ 9,329; © 10,085
Chippewa Lake (Chippewa-on-the-Lake); Inc. Place; MEDINA; **217** NH-14; 🅿; ★ **CLEV**; **z** 44215; ℗ 271; © 823
Chippewa Lake Park; RMC Place; MEDINA; ▲ Lafayette; ***217** NH-14; elev. 1,005ft./306m.; ★ **CLEV**; mail Chippewa Lake **z** 44215; summer pop. 2,000; ● 500
Chippewa-on-the-Lake; MEDINA; see Chippewa Lake (Inc. Place)
Chockaw Lake; MADISON; see Choctaw Lake (CDP)
Chocktou Lake; MADISON; see Choctaw Lake (CDP)
Choctaw Lake (Chockaw Lake, Chocktou Lake, Choctaw Lake Subdivision); CDP; MADISON; ▲ Stokes; ***218** SB-7; mail London **z** 43140; ℗ 1,234; © 1,562
Choctaw Lake Subdivision; MADISON; see Choctaw Lake (CDP)
Christiansburg; Inc. Place; CHAMPAIGN; ▲ Jackson; **216** NN-4; elev. 1,116ft./340m.; 🅿; **z** 45389; ℗ 599; © 553
Christopher Columbus; RMC Place; FRANKLIN; ★ **COL**; mail Columbus **z** 43215; pop. incl. with Columbus (Inc. Place)
Chuckery; RMC Place; UNION; ▲ Darby; ***218** SA-7; mail Irwin **z** 43029, Milford Center **z** 43045; rural
Churchill; CDP; TRUMBULL; ▲ Liberty; **217** NG-19; elev. 1,050ft./320m.; ★ **YNGS-**; mail Youngstown **z** 44505; ℗ 2,691; © 2,601
Churchills; RMC Place; LUCAS; ★ **TOL**; mail Sylvania **z** 43560; pop. incl. with Sylvania (Inc. Place)

Entries in **UPPERCASE** are counties.
Entries in **bold** have populations of 2,500 or more.
Names in parentheses are alternate names.

Inc. Place	Incorporated Place
RMC Place	Rand McNally Designated Place
CDP	Census Designated Place
MCD	Minor Civil Division

⊡ County Seat
▲ Minor Civil Division
elev. Elevation
🅿 Post Office
🅷 Hospital
🅲 College
■ Principal Business Center
★ Ranally Metro Area (RMA) Abbreviation
z Zip Code(s)
℗ Previous Census Population
® Revised Census Population
Ⓐ Annexation Population
● Rand McNally Population Estimate
© Final Census Population
Ⓢ Special Census Population
◆ Estimated Population

For additional definitions see Glossary, Volume 1, and Introduction, Volume 2.

Churchtown; RMC Place; WASHINGTON; ▲ Watertown; ***219** SE-16; elev. 1,005ft./306m.; mail Marietta **z** 45750; rural
Cincinnati; Inc. Place; ⊡ HAMILTON; **218** SG-2; elev. 683ft./208m.; 🅿 🅷 🅲 47,572 ■; ★ **CIN**; **z** 45201-09, **z** 45211-55, **z** 45258, **z** 45262-64, **z** 45267-71, **z** 45273-75, **z** 45277, **z** 45280, **z** 45296, **z** 45298-99, **z** 45999; Ⓟ 364,040; Ⓒ 331,285; ◆ 338,011
Circle Green; RMC Place; JEFFERSON; ▲ Smithfield; ***217** NK-19; mail Bergholz **z** 43908
Circle Hill; RMC Place; MIAMI; ▲ Newton; ***218** SA-3; mail Bradford **z** 45308
Circleville; Inc. Place; ⊡ PICKAWAY; ▲ Circleville, Washington; **218** SD-9; elev. 702ft./214m.; 🅿 🅲 506; **z** 43113; Ⓟ 11,666; Ⓒ 13,485
Circleville; MCD-Township; PICKAWAY; ***218** SD-9; 🅿 🅷; **z** 43113; Ⓟ 15,154; Ⓒ 2,300
City View Heights; RMC Place; BUTLER; ▲ St. Clair; ***218** SE-2; ★ **CIN**; mail Hamilton **z** 45011; ● 300
Claiborne; RMC Place; UNION; ▲ Claibourne; **216** NL-7; mail Richwood **z** 43344; ● 180
Claibourne; MCD-Township; UNION; ***216** NL-8; mail Richwood **z** 43344; Ⓟ 3,299; Ⓒ 3,421
Claridon; RMC Place; GEAUGA; ▲ Claridon; **217** NE-17; ★ **CLEV**; mail Chardon **z** 44024; ● 170
Claridon; MCD-Township; GEAUGA; ***217** NE-17; ★ **CLEV**; mail Chardon **z** 44024; Ⓟ 3,016; Ⓒ 3,173
Claridon; RMC Place; MARION; ▲ Claridon; **216** NK-9; elev. 984ft./300m.; ★ **MRN**; mail Caledonia **z** 43314; ● 120
Claridon; MCD-Township; MARION; ***216** NK-9; ★ **MRN**; mail Caledonia **z** 43314; Ⓟ 2,498; Ⓒ 2,587
Clarington; Inc. Place; MONROE; ▲ Salem; **219** SC-19; 🅿; **z** 43915; Ⓟ 406; Ⓒ 444
Clark; MCD-Township; BROWN; ***218** SH-5; ★ **CIN**; mail Hamersville **z** 45130; Ⓟ 2,831; Ⓒ 3,165
Clark; MCD-Township; CLINTON; ***218** SF-5; mail Martinsville **z** 45146; Ⓟ 1,581; Ⓒ 1,861
Clark; RMC Place; COSHOCTON, HOLMES; ▲ Mechanic, Clark; **217** NL-14; elev. 831ft./253m.; mail Coshocton **z** 43812; ● 170
Clark; MCD-Township; COSHOCTON; ***217** NL-14; mail Warsaw **z** 43844; Ⓟ 578; Ⓒ 594
Clark; MCD-Township; HOLMES; ***217** NL-15; mail Baltic **z** 43804; Ⓟ 2,940; Ⓒ 3,728
CLARK; **218** SB-6; Ⓟ 147,548; Ⓒ 144,742; Ⓡ 144,741; ◆ 137,356
Clark Corners; RMC Place; ASHTABULA; ***217** NC-20; mail Conneaut **z** 44030
Clark Corners; RMC Place; MEDINA; ▲ Wadsworth; ***217** NH-15; ★ **AKR**; mail Wadsworth **z** 44281; pop. incl. with Wadsworth (Inc. Place)
Clarksburg; RMC Place; BELMONT; ▲ Richland; ★ **WHL**; mail Jacobsburg **z** 43933
Clarksburg; Inc. Place; ROSS; ▲ Deerfield; **218** SD-8; elev. 772ft./235m.; 🅿; **z** 43115; Ⓟ 523; Ⓒ 516
Clarksfield; RMC Place; HURON; ▲ Clarksfield; **217** NG-12; mail Wakeman **z** 44889; ● 200
Clarksfield; MCD-Township; HURON; ***217** NG-12; mail Wakeman **z** 44889; Ⓟ 1,302; Ⓒ 1,518
Clarks Lake; RMC Place; PICKAWAY; ▲ Darby; ***218** SC-8; ★ **COL**; mail Mount Sterling **z** 43143; ● 800
Clarkson; RMC Place; COLUMBIANA; ▲ Middleton; **217** NJ-20; mail Rogers **z** 44455; ● 80
Clarkstown; SCIOTO; see Clarktown (RMC Place)
Clarksville; Inc. Place; CLINTON; ▲ Vernon; **218** SE-5; 🅿; **z** 45113; Ⓟ 485; Ⓒ 497
Clarksville; RMC Place; PERRY; ▲ Jackson; ***219** SC-12; mail Junction City **z** 43748; rural
Clarktown (Clarkstown); RMC Place; SCIOTO; ▲ Jefferson; **218** SH-10; elev. 694ft./212m.; ★ **PTSM**; mail Lucasville **z** 45648; ● 300
Clay; MCD-Township; AUGLAIZE; ***216** NK-4; mail Wapakoneta **z** 45895; Ⓟ 923; Ⓒ 700
Clay; MCD-Township; GALLIA; ***219** SI-13; mail Gallipolis **z** 45631; Ⓟ 1,912; Ⓒ 1,877
Clay; MCD-Township; HIGHLAND; ***218** SG-5; mail Sardinia **z** 45171; Ⓟ 1,219; Ⓒ 1,219
Clay; RMC Place; JACKSON; ▲ Madison, Jefferson, Madison; **219** SH-11; elev. 707ft./215m.; mail Oak Hill **z** 45656; ● 20
Clay; MCD-Township; KNOX; ***217** NM-12; mail Utica **z** 43080; Ⓟ 1,084; Ⓒ 1,328
Clay; MCD-Township; MONTGOMERY; ***218** SB-3; ★ **DAY**; mail Phillipsburg **z** 45354; Ⓟ 8,310; Ⓒ 8,566
Clay; MCD-Township; MUSKINGUM; ***219** SC-14; ★ **ZAN**; mail Roseville **z** 43777; Ⓟ 1,126; Ⓒ 1,038
Clay; MCD-Township; OTTAWA; ***216** NE-7; ★ **TOL**; mail Genoa **z** 43430; Ⓟ 5,267; Ⓒ 5,118
Clay; MCD-Township; SCIOTO; ***218** SI-9; ★ **PTSM**; mail Portsmouth **z** 45662; Ⓟ 4,000; Ⓒ 3,792
Clay; MCD-Township; TUSCARAWAS; ***217** NL-16; mail Gnadenhutten **z** 44629; Ⓟ 1,929; Ⓒ 1,981
Clay Center; Inc. Place; OTTAWA; ▲ Allen; **216** NE-7; 🅿; ★ **TOL**; **z** 43408; Ⓟ 289; Ⓒ 294
Claylick; RMC Place; LICKING; ▲ Madison, Hanover; ***219** SA-12; ★ **NWRK**; mail Newark **z** 43055; rural
Claysville; RMC Place; GUERNSEY; ▲ Westland; **219** SB-15; 🅿; **z** 43725; ● 140
Clayton; RMC Place; ADAMS; ▲ Sprigg; ***218** SI-6; elev. 957ft./292m.; mail Manchester **z** 45144; rural
Clayton; RMC Place; MIAMI; ▲ Newberry; ***216** NN-3; mail Covington **z** 45318
Clayton; Inc. Place; MONTGOMERY; ▲ Clay; **218** SB-3; 🅿; ★ **DAY**; **z** 45315; Ⓟ 713; Ⓒ 13,347
Clayton; MCD-Township; PERRY; ***219** SC-13; mail New Lexington **z** 43764; Ⓟ 1,121; Ⓒ 1,432
Clear Creek; MCD-Township; ASHLAND; ***217** NI-12; mail Savannah **z** 44874; Ⓟ 1,798; Ⓒ 2,069
Clearcreek; MCD-Township; FAIRFIELD; ***218** SD-10; mail Amanda **z** 43102; Ⓟ 3,040; Ⓒ 3,411
Clear Creek; MCD-Township; WARREN; ***218** SD-3; ★ **DAY**; mail Springboro **z** 45066; Ⓟ 13,347; Ⓒ 20,974
Clearport; RMC Place; FAIRFIELD; ▲ Madison; ***219** SD-11; elev. 856ft./261m.; mail Lancaster **z** 43130
Clearview; RMC Place; ATHENS; ▲ Athens; ***219** SF-13; mail Athens **z** 45701; ● 60
Clearview; RMC Place; LORAIN; ▲ Sheffield; **217** NF-13; ★ **CLEV**; mail Lorain **z** 44055; pop. incl. with Lorain (Inc. Place)
Clearview; RMC Place; STARK; ***217** NI-16; ★ **CAN**; mail Massillon **z** 44646; pop. incl. with Massillon (Inc. Place)
CLERMONT; **218** SH-3; Ⓟ 150,187; Ⓒ 177,977; ◆ 194,634
Clermontville; RMC Place; CLERMONT; ▲ Monroe; ***218** SH-3; elev. 520ft./158m.; ★ **CIN**; mail New Richmond **z** 45157; rural
Clertoma; RMC Place; CLERMONT; ***218** SF-3; ★ **CIN**; mail Milford **z** 45150; pop. incl. with Milford (Inc. Place)
Cleveland; Inc. Place; ⊡ CUYAHOGA; **217** NF-15; 🅿 🅷 🅲 33,349 ■; ★ **CLEV**; **z** 44101-47, **z** 44181, **z** 44188, **z** 44190-95, **z** 44197-99 & mail Strongsville **z** 44149; Ⓟ 505,616; Ⓒ 478,403; Ⓡ 477,459; ◆ 401,068
Cleveland Heights; Inc. Place; CUYAHOGA; **217** NE-15; 🅿 ■; ★ **CLEV**; **z** 44106, **z** 44112, **z** 44118, **z** 44121; Ⓟ 54,052; Ⓒ 49,958; Ⓡ 50,769; ◆ 41,699
Cleves; Inc. Place; HAMILTON; ▲ Miami; **218** SF-1; elev. 496ft./151m.; 🅿; ★ **CIN**; **z** 45002; Ⓟ 2,208; Ⓒ 2,790
Clifton; Inc. Place; GREENE, CLARK; **218** SC-5; 🅿; ★ **DAY**; **z** 45316 & mail Cincinnati **z** 45219-20; Ⓟ 165; Ⓒ 179
Clifton; RMC Place; HAMILTON; ***218** SF-2; 🅿; ★ **CIN**; **z** 45316 & mail Cincinnati **z** 45219-20; pop. incl. with Cincinnati (Inc. Place)
Clifton Farms; RMC Place; BUTLER; ★ **MIDD**; mail Middletown **z** 45044; pop. incl. with Middletown (Inc. Place)
Climax; RMC Place; MORROW; ▲ Canaan; ***216** NK-9; elev. 1,033ft./315m.; mail Edison **z** 43320; ● 25
Clinton; MCD-Township; FRANKLIN; ***218** SA-9; ★ **COL**; mail Columbus **z** 43212; Ⓟ 4,579; Ⓒ 4,294
Clinton; MCD-Township; FULTON; ***216** NE-4; mail Wauseon **z** 43567; Ⓟ 8,327; Ⓒ 9,280
Clinton; MCD-Township; KNOX; ***217** NL-11; mail Mount Vernon **z** 43050; Ⓟ 3,502; Ⓒ 3,326; Ⓡ 3,317
Clinton; MCD-Township; SENECA; ***216** NH-8; mail Tiffin **z** 44883; Ⓟ 4,055; Ⓒ 4,188
Clinton; MCD-Township; SHELBY; ***216** NM-4; mail Sidney **z** 45365; Ⓟ 19,755; Ⓒ 20,903
Clinton; Inc. Place; SUMMIT; **217** NI-15; 🅿; ★ **AKR**; **z** 44216; Ⓟ 1,175; Ⓒ 1,337
Clinton; MCD-Township; VINTON; ***219** SF-11; mail Hamden **z** 45634; Ⓟ 1,761; Ⓒ 2,045
Clinton; MCD-Township; WAYNE; ***217** NJ-13; mail Shreve **z** 44676; Ⓟ 3,028; Ⓒ 3,196
CLINTON; **218** SD-6; mail Sabina **z** 45169; Ⓟ 35,415; Ⓒ 40,543; ◆ 43,119
Clintonville; RMC Place; FRANKLIN; ***218** SA-9; ★ **COL**; mail Columbus **z** 43202; pop. incl. with Columbus (Inc. Place)
Clipper Mills; RMC Place; GALLIA; ▲ Clay; ***219** SI-13; mail Gallipolis **z** 45631; rural
Cloverdale; Inc. Place; PUTNAM; ▲ Perry; **216** NH-3; 🅿; **z** 45827; Ⓟ 270; Ⓒ 201
Cloverhill; RMC Place; PERRY; ▲ Clayton; **219** SC-13; mail New Lexington **z** 43764; ● 40
Cluff; RMC Place; HAMILTON; ▲ Anderson; ★ **CIN**; mail Cincinnati **z** 45244; rural
Clyde; Inc. Place; SANDUSKY; ▲ Green Creek, York; **216** NG-9; 🅿; **z** 43410; Ⓟ 5,776; Ⓒ 6,064
Coach Lite Village; RMC Place; LUCAS; ▲ Springfield; ***216** NE-6; ★ **TOL**; mail Holland **z** 43528; ● 2,300
Coal; MCD-Township; JACKSON; ***219** SG-11; mail Coalton **z** 45621; Ⓟ 1,825; Ⓒ 2,078
Coal; MCD-Township; PERRY; ***219** SD-13; mail New Straitsville **z** 43766; Ⓟ 1,156; Ⓒ 1,106
Coalburg; RMC Place; TRUMBULL; ▲ Hubbard; **217** NG-20; ★ **YNGS-**; mail Hubbard **z** 44425; ● 240
Coal Grove; Inc. Place; LAWRENCE; ▲ Upper, Perry; **219** SJ-11; 🅿; ★ **HNTG**; **z** 45638; Ⓟ 2,251; Ⓒ 2,027
Coalport; RMC Place; TUSCARAWAS; ***217** NM-15; mail Newcomerstown **z** 43832; pop. incl. with Newcomerstown (Inc. Place)
Coal Ridge; RMC Place; NOBLE; ▲ Noble; **219** SC-16; mail Ava **z** 43711; ● 100
Coal Run; RMC Place; WASHINGTON; ▲ Waterford, Adams; **219** SD-16; 🅿; **z** 45721 & mail Beverly **z** 45715; ● 200
Coalton; Inc. Place; JACKSON; ▲ Coal; **219** SG-11; 🅿; **z** 45621; Ⓟ 553; Ⓒ 545
Coddingville; RMC Place; MEDINA; ▲ Sharon, Granger; ***217** NH-15; elev. 1,128ft./344m.; ★ **CLEV**; mail Medina **z** 44256
Coffee Corners; RMC Place; TRUMBULL; ▲ Mesopotamia; ***217** NF-18; elev. 972ft./296m.; mail Middlefield **z** 44062
Coitsville; MCD-Township; MAHONING; ***217** NH-20; ★ **YNGS-**; mail Lowellville **z** 44436; Ⓟ 1,841; Ⓒ 1,608
Coitsville Center; RMC Place; MAHONING; ▲ Coitsville; **217** ND-14; elev. 1,073ft./327m.; ★ **YNGS-**; mail Youngstown **z** 44505; pop. incl. with Youngstown (Inc. Place)
Colby; RMC Place; SANDUSKY; ▲ York; **216** NG-9; mail Clyde **z** 43410
Cold Springs; RMC Place; CLARK; ▲ Mad River; ***218** SB-5; ★ **SPR**; mail Springfield **z** 45502; rural
Coldwater; Inc. Place; MERCER; ▲ Butler; **216** NL-1; elev. 912ft./278m.; 🅿 🅷; **z** 45828; Ⓟ 4,335; Ⓒ 4,482
Colebrook; RMC Place; ASHTABULA; ▲ Colebrook; **217** NE-19; elev. 993ft./303m.; mail Orwell **z** 44076, Rome **z** 44085; ● 150
Colebrook; MCD-Township; ASHTABULA; ***217** NE-19; mail Orwell **z** 44076; Ⓟ 747; Ⓒ 887
Colerain; RMC Place; BELMONT; ▲ Colerain; **217** NN-19; 🅿; ★ **WHL**; **z** 43916 & mail Cincinnati **z** 45251-52; ● 450
Colerain; MCD-Township; BELMONT; ***217** NN-19; 🅿; ★ **WHL**; **z** 43916 & mail Cincinnati **z** 45251-52; Ⓟ 4,602; Ⓒ 4,438
Colerain (Colerain Twp); MCD-Township; HAMILTON; ***218** SF-2; ★ **CIN**; mail Cincinnati **z** 45239, **z** 45247, **z** 45251-52; Ⓟ 56,781; Ⓒ 60,144
Colerain; MCD-Township; ROSS; ***218** SE-10; mail Kingston **z** 45644; Ⓟ 1,609; Ⓒ 1,943
Colerain Heights; RMC Place; HAMILTON; ▲ Colerain; **218** SF-2; ★ **CIN**; mail Cincinnati **z** 45239; ● 2,600
Colerain Twp; HAMILTON; see Colerain (MCD-Township)
Coles Park; RMC Place; SCIOTO; ▲ Washington; **218** SI-9; ★ **PTSM**; mail West Portsmouth **z** 45663; ● 300
Coletown; RMC Place; DARKE; ▲ Greenville; **216** NN-1; mail Greenville **z** 45331; ● 90
College; MCD-Township; KNOX; ***217** NL-12; 🅲 1,639; mail Gambier **z** 43022; Ⓟ 2,421; Ⓒ 2,247; Ⓡ 2,388
College Corner; Inc. Place; PREBLE, BUTLER; ▲ Israel, Oxford; **218** SD-1; 🅿; **z** 45003; Ⓟ 379; Ⓒ 424
College Hill; RMC Place; GUERNSEY; ***219** SA-15; mail Cambridge **z** 43725; ● 100
College Hill; RMC Place; HAMILTON; ***218** SF-2; ★ **CIN**; mail Cincinnati **z** 45224; pop. incl. with Cincinnati (Inc. Place)
College Hill Junction; RMC Place; HAMILTON; ★ **CIN**; mail Cincinnati **z** 45224; pop. incl. with Cincinnati (Inc. Place)
Collins; RMC Place; HURON; ▲ Townsend; **217** NG-11; elev. 885ft./270m.; 🅿; **z** 44826; ● 180
Collinsville; RMC Place; BUTLER; ▲ Milford; **218** SD-2; 🅿; ★ **CIN**; **z** 45004; ● 230
Collinwood; RMC Place; CUYAHOGA; ***217** NE-15; ★ **CLEV**; mail Cleveland **z** 44110; pop. incl. with Cleveland (Inc. Place)
Colonial Hills; RMC Place; FRANKLIN; ★ **COL**; mail Columbus **z** 43085; pop. incl. with Worthington (Inc. Place)
Colton; RMC Place; HENRY; ▲ Washington; **216** NF-5; 🅿; **z** 43510; ● 180
Columbia; MCD-Township; HAMILTON; ***218** SF-3; ★ **CIN**; mail Cincinnati **z** 45243; Ⓟ 6,298; Ⓒ 6,557
Columbia; MCD-Township; LORAIN; ***217** NG-14; ★ **CLEV**; mail Columbia Station **z** 44028; Ⓟ 6,594; Ⓒ 6,912
Columbia; MCD-Township; MEIGS; ***219** SF-13; mail Albany **z** 45710; Ⓟ 801; Ⓒ 1,018
Columbia; RMC Place; STARK; ***217** NJ-16; ★ **CAN**; mail Massillon **z** 44646; pop. incl. with Massillon (Inc. Place)
Columbia; RMC Place; TUSCARAWAS; ▲ Franklin, Dover; **217** NK-16; ★ **CAN**; mail Dover **z** 44622; ● 220
Columbia; RMC Place; WILLIAMS; ▲ Northwest; **216** NE-1; mail Edon **z** 43518; ● 100
Columbia Center; RMC Place; LICKING; **219** SA-11; ★ **COL**; mail Pataskala **z** 43062; pop. incl. with Pataskala (Inc. Place)
Columbia Center; RMC Place; LORAIN; ▲ Columbia; ***217** NG-14; ★ **CLEV**; mail Columbia Station **z** 44028; ● 100
Columbia Hills Corners; RMC Place; LORAIN; ▲ Columbia; ***217** NG-14; elev. 788ft./240m.; ★ **CLEV**; mail Columbia Station **z** 44028
Columbiana; Inc. Place; COLUMBIANA, MAHONING; ▲ Fairfield, Beaver, Unity; **217** NI-19; elev. 1,118ft./341m.; 🅿; ★ **YNGS-**; **z** 44408; Ⓟ 4,961; Ⓒ 5,635
COLUMBIANA; **217** NI-18; Ⓟ 108,276; Ⓒ 112,075; ◆ 104,802
Columbia Station; RMC Place; LORAIN; ▲ Columbia; ***217** NG-14; elev. 804ft./245m.; 🅿; ★ **CLEV**; **z** 44028; ● 500
Columbus; Inc. Place; **STATE CAPITAL**; ⊡ FRANKLIN, DELAWARE, FAIRFIELD; **218** SB-9; 🅿 🅷 🅲 70,558 ■; ★ **COL**; **z** 43085, **z** 43201-07, **z** 43209-24, **z** 43226-32, **z** 43234-36, **z** 43240, **z** 43251, **z** 43260, **z** 43266, **z** 43268, **z** 43270-72, **z** 43279, **z** 43287, **z** 43291; Ⓟ 632,910; Ⓒ 711,470; ◆ 796,515
Columbus Circle; RMC Place; ASHLAND; mail Ashland **z** 44805; pop. incl. with Ashland (Inc. Place)
Columbus Grove; Inc. Place; PUTNAM; ▲ Pleasant; **216** NI-4; elev. 773ft./236m.; 🅿; **z** 45830; Ⓟ 2,231; Ⓒ 2,200
Columbus Park; RMC Place; ERIE; ▲ Perkins; **217** NF-11; ★ **SNDSK**; mail Sandusky **z** 44870; ● 500
Comet; RMC Place; SUMMIT; ***217** NI-16; elev. 1,013ft./309m.; ★ **AKR**; mail Clinton **z** 44216; pop. incl. with Green (Inc. Place)
Commercial Point; Inc. Place; PICKAWAY; ▲ Scioto; **218** SC-9; 🅿; ★ **COL**; **z** 43116; Ⓟ 405; Ⓒ 776
Compton Park; RMC Place; HAMILTON; ▲ Springfield; ***218** SF-2; ★ **CIN**; mail Cincinnati **z** 45231
Compton Woods; RMC Place; HAMILTON; ***218** SF-2; ★ **CIN**; mail Cincinnati **z** 45215; pop. incl. with Wyoming (Inc. Place)
Conant; RMC Place; ALLEN; ▲ Amanda; **216** NJ-3; mail Spencerville **z** 45887; ● 50
Concept; RMC Place; ALLEN; ▲ American; ★ **LIMA**; mail Lima **z** 45807; ● 250
Concord; MCD-Township; CHAMPAIGN; ***216** NN-5; mail Saint Paris **z** 43072; Ⓟ 1,122; Ⓒ 1,408
Concord; MCD-Township; DELAWARE; ***216** NM-8; ★ **COL**; mail Delaware **z** 43015; Ⓟ 7,597; Ⓒ 4,507
Concord; MCD-Township; FAYETTE; ***218** SE-7; mail Washington Court House **z** 43160; Ⓟ 1,015; Ⓒ 1,068
Concord; MCD-Township; HIGHLAND; ***218** SG-6; mail Winchester **z** 45697; Ⓟ 995; Ⓒ 1,167
Concord; RMC Place; LAKE; ▲ Concord; ***217** ND-17; ★ **CLEV**; mail Mentor **z** 44060, Painesville **z** 44077; ● 150
Concord; MCD-Township; LAKE; ***217** ND-17; ★ **CLEV**; mail Chardon **z** 44024, Mentor **z** 44060, Painesville **z** 44077; Ⓟ 12,432; Ⓒ 15,282
Concord; RMC Place; LICKING; ▲ Liberty; ***217** NN-11; mail Johnstown **z** 43031
Concord; MCD-Township; MIAMI; ***218** SA-4; mail Troy **z** 45373; Ⓟ 24,392; Ⓒ 27,335
Concord; MCD-Township; ROSS; ***218** SE-8; mail Frankfort **z** 45628; Ⓟ 3,599; Ⓒ 4,107
Condit; RMC Place; DELAWARE; ▲ Trenton; **216** NM-10; mail Sunbury **z** 43074; ● 70
Conesville; Inc. Place; COSHOCTON; ▲ Franklin; **217** NM-14; 🅿; **z** 43811; Ⓟ 420; Ⓒ 364
Congo; RMC Place; PERRY; ▲ Monroe; **219** SD-13; mail Corning **z** 43730; ● 110
Congress; MCD-Township; MORROW; ***216** NK-10; mail Mount Gilead **z** 43338; Ⓟ 1,442; Ⓒ 2,128
Congress; Inc. Place; WAYNE; ▲ Congress; **217** NI-13; 🅿; **z** 44287; Ⓟ 162; Ⓒ 192
Congress; MCD-Township; WAYNE; ***217** NI-13; 🅿; **z** 44287; Ⓟ 4,159; Ⓒ 4,435
Congress Lake; RMC Place; STARK; ▲ Lake; ***217** NI-16; ★ **CAN**; mail Hartville **z** 44632; ● 200
Conneaut; Inc. Place; ASHTABULA; **217** NC-20; elev. 662ft./202m.; 🅿 🅷; **z** 44030; Ⓟ 13,241; Ⓒ 12,485
Conneaut Harbor; RMC Place; ASHTABULA; ***217** NC-20; mail Conneaut **z** 44030; pop. incl. with Conneaut (Inc. Place)
Connett; RMC Place; ATHENS; ▲ York; ***219** SE-13; mail Nelsonville **z** 45764; rural
Connor; JEFFERSON; see Connorville (RMC Place)
Connorville (Connor); RMC Place; JEFFERSON; ▲ Warren; ***217** NM-19; ★ **WHL**; mail Rayland **z** 43943; ● 160
Conotton; RMC Place; HARRISON; ▲ North; **217** NL-17; elev. 955ft./291m.; mail Bowerston **z** 44695; ● 70
Conover; RMC Place; MIAMI; ▲ Brown; **216** NN-4; elev. 1,138ft./347m.; 🅿; **z** 45317; ● 130
Constitution; RMC Place; WASHINGTON; ▲ Warren; **219** SE-16; ★ **PRKB**; mail Marietta **z** 45750; ● 50
Continental; Inc. Place; PUTNAM; ▲ Monroe; **216** NH-3; elev. 723ft./220m.; 🅿; **z** 45831, **z** 45837; Ⓟ 1,214; Ⓒ 1,188
Converse; RMC Place; VAN WERT; ▲ Jennings; **216** NJ-2; elev. 817ft./249m.; mail Spencerville **z** 45887; ● 25
Convoy; Inc. Place; VAN WERT; ▲ Tully; **216** NI-1; elev. 787ft./240m.; 🅿; **z** 45832; Ⓟ 1,200; Ⓒ 1,110
Conway Addition; RMC Place; PERRY; ▲ Harrison; ***219** SC-13; ★ **ZAN**; mail Crooksville **z** 43731; ● 70
Cook (Cooks); RMC Place; FAYETTE; ▲ Madison; ***218** SC-8; mail Mount Sterling **z** 43143
Cooks; FAYETTE; see Cook (RMC Place)
Cool Ridge Heights; RMC Place; RICHLAND; ▲ Madison; ***217** NJ-11; ★ **MANS**; mail Mansfield **z** 44905
Coolville; Inc. Place; ATHENS; ▲ Troy; **219** SF-15; 🅿; **z** 45723; Ⓟ 663; Ⓒ 528
Cooney; RMC Place; WILLIAMS; ▲ Northwest; ***216** ND-1; mail Edon **z** 43518; rural
Coonville; RMC Place; HOCKING; ▲ Starr; ***219** SE-12; mail New Plymouth **z** 45654; ● 35
Cooperdale; RMC Place; COSHOCTON; ▲ Washington; **217** NM-13; mail Dresden **z** 43821, Warsaw **z** 43844; ● 100
Coopersville; RMC Place; PIKE; ▲ Camp Creek; ***218** SH-9; mail Piketon **z** 45661; ● 40
Copley; RMC Place; SUMMIT; ▲ Copley; **217** NH-15; elev. 1,050ft./320m.; 🅿; ★ **AKR**; **z** 44321; ● 750
Copley; MCD-Township; SUMMIT; ***217** NH-15; 🅿; ★ **AKR**; **z** 44321; Ⓟ 11,130; Ⓒ 13,641
Copley Center; RMC Place; SUMMIT; ▲ Copley; ★ **AKR**; mail Akron **z** 44321
Corinth; RMC Place; TRUMBULL; ▲ Johnston; ***217** NF-20; ★ **YNGS-**; mail Farmdale **z** 44417, Kinsman **z** 44428
Cork; RMC Place; ASHTABULA; ▲ Harpersfield; ***217** ND-18; ★ **CLEV**; mail Geneva **z** 44041; ● 40
Corner; RMC Place; WASHINGTON; ▲ Belpre; ***219** SF-15; elev. 686ft./209m.; ★ **PRKB**; mail Belpre **z** 45714; ● 50
Cornersburg; RMC Place; MAHONING; ***217** NH-19; ★ **YNGS-**; mail Youngstown **z** 44511
Cornerville; RMC Place; WASHINGTON; ▲ Marietta; **219** SE-17; ★ **PRKB**; mail Reno **z** 45773; ● 70
Corning; Inc. Place; PERRY; ▲ Monroe; **219** SD-13; elev. 732ft./223m.; 🅿; **z** 43730; Ⓟ 703; Ⓒ 593
Corryville; RMC Place; HAMILTON; ***218** SG-2; ★ **CIN**; mail Cincinnati **z** 45219-20, **z** 45223, **z** 45225; pop. incl. with Cincinnati (Inc. Place)
Corryville; RMC Place; LAWRENCE; ▲ Union; ***219** SK-12; ★ **HNTG**; mail Chesapeake **z** 45619; ● 150
Cortland; Inc. Place; TRUMBULL; **217** NF-19; 🅿; ★ **YNGS-**; **z** 44410; Ⓟ 5,666; Ⓒ 6,830
Cortsville; RMC Place; CLARK; ▲ Green; ***218** SC-6; ★ **SPR**; mail South Charleston **z** 45368
Corwin (Waynesville); Inc. Place; WARREN; ▲ Wayne; **218** SD-4; elev. 732ft./223m.; ★ **DAY**; mail Waynesville **z** 45068; Ⓟ 225; Ⓒ 256
Coryville; RMC Place; LAWRENCE; ▲ Upper; ***219** SJ-11; ★ **HNTG**; mail Ironton **z** 45638; ● 100
Coshocton; Inc. Place; ⊡ COSHOCTON; **217** NM-14; 🅿 🅷 ■; **z** 43812; Ⓟ 12,193; Ⓒ 11,682; ◆ 11,210
COSHOCTON; **217** NM-13; Ⓟ 35,427; Ⓒ 36,655; ◆ 35,706
Cottage Grove; RMC Place; SUMMIT; ▲ Coventry; ***217** NH-16; ★ **AKR**; mail Akron **z** 44319
Country Acres; RMC Place; GREENE; ▲ Bath; ***218** SC-4; ★ **DAY**; mail Fairborn **z** 45324; ● 765
Country Acres; RMC Place; GREENE; ▲ Beavercreek; ***218** SC-4; ★ **DAY**; mail Dayton **z** 45430; pop. incl. with Beavercreek (Inc. Place)
Country Club Estates; RMC Place; JEFFERSON; ★ **STU-**; mail Steubenville **z** 43952; pop. incl. with Steubenville (Inc. Place)
Country Club Hills; RMC Place; ALLEN; ▲ Bath; ★ **LIMA**; mail Lima **z** 45801; ● 600
Country Estates; RMC Place; MIAMI; ▲ Monroe; ***218** SB-4; ★ **DAY**; mail Tipp City **z** 45371; ● 140
Country Fair Station; RMC Place; STARK; ▲ Canton; mail Canton **z** 44708; pop. incl. with Canton (Inc. Place)
Cove; RMC Place; JACKSON; ▲ Scioto; ***218** SG-10; elev. 694ft./212m.; mail Jackson **z** 45640; rural
Covedale; CDP; HAMILTON; ▲ Green; **218** SM-1; ★ **CIN**; mail Cincinnati **z** 45238; Ⓟ 6,669; Ⓒ 6,360
Coventry; MCD-Township; SUMMIT; ***217** NH-16; ★ **AKR**; mail Akron **z** 44319; Ⓟ 11,295; Ⓒ 10,900
Covington; Inc. Place; MIAMI; ▲ Newberry; **216** NN-3; elev. 930ft./283m.; 🅿; **z** 45318; Ⓟ 2,603; Ⓒ 2,559
Cozaddale; RMC Place; WARREN; ▲ Hamilton; **218** SF-4; ★ **CIN**; mail Goshen **z** 45122; ● 250
Crabapple; RMC Place; BELMONT; ▲ Wheeling; ***219** SB-18; mail Saint Clairsville **z** 43950; rural
Craig Beach; Inc. Place; MAHONING; ▲ Milton; **217** NH-18; mail Lake Milton **z** 44429; Ⓟ 1,402; Ⓒ 1,254
Craigton; RMC Place; WAYNE; ▲ Clinton; **217** NJ-13; elev. 958ft./292m.; mail Shreve **z** 44676; ● 25
Cranberry; MCD-Township; CRAWFORD; ***216** NI-10; mail New Washington **z** 44854; Ⓟ 1,714; Ⓒ 1,674
Cranberry Prairie; RMC Place; MERCER; ▲ Granville; **216** NL-2; mail Maria Stein **z** 45860, Saint Henry **z** 45883; ● 100
Crandenbrook; RMC Place; WOOD; ▲ Perrysburg; ***216** NE-6; ★ **TOL**; mail Perrysburg **z** 43551; pop. incl. with Perrysburg (Inc. Place)
Crane; MCD-Township; PAULDING; ***216** NG-1; mail Cecil **z** 45821; Ⓟ 1,527; Ⓒ 1,530
Crane; MCD-Township; WYANDOT; ***216** NI-8; mail Upper Sandusky **z** 43351; Ⓟ 6,935; Ⓒ 7,394
Cranwood; RMC Place; CUYAHOGA; ★ **CLEV**; mail Cleveland **z** 44128; pop. incl. with Cleveland (Inc. Place)
Crawford; MCD-Township; COSHOCTON; ***217** NL-15; mail Baltic **z** 43804; Ⓟ 1,221; Ⓒ 1,594
Crawford; RMC Place; WYANDOT; ▲ Crawford; **216** NI-7; elev. 813ft./248m.; mail Carey **z** 43316; ● 100
Crawford; MCD-Township; WYANDOT; ***216** NI-7; mail Carey **z** 43316; Ⓟ 4,949; Ⓒ 5,080
CRAWFORD; **216** NI-9; Ⓟ 47,870; Ⓒ 46,966; ◆ 43,282
Crawford Corners; RMC Place; MEDINA; ▲ Harrisville; ***217** NH-13; mail Lodi **z** 44254; rural
Cream City; RMC Place; JEFFERSON; ***217** NK-19; mail Irondale **z** 43932; pop. incl. with Irondale (Inc. Place)
Creola; RMC Place; VINTON; ▲ Swan; **219** SF-12; 🅿; **z** 45622; ● 90
Crescent; RMC Place; BELMONT; ▲ Colerain; ***217** NN-19; ★ **WHL**; mail Saint Clairsville **z** 43950; rural
Crescent Gardens; RMC Place; STARK; ▲ Perry; ★ **CAN**; mail Massillon **z** 44646
Crescentville; RMC Place; HAMILTON; ***218** SF-2; ★ **CIN**; mail Cincinnati **z** 45241; pop. incl. with Sharonville (Inc. Place)
Crestline; Inc. Place; CRAWFORD, RICHLAND; ▲ Jackson, Jefferson, Sandusky; **216** NJ-10; 🅿 🅷; ★ **MANS**; **z** 44827; Ⓟ 4,934; Ⓒ 5,088
Creston; Inc. Place; WAYNE; ▲ Canaan; **217** NI-14; elev. 985ft./300m.; 🅿; ★ **CLEV**; **z** 44217; Ⓟ 1,848; Ⓒ 2,161
Crestwood Hills; RMC Place; MONTGOMERY; ▲ Butler; ★ **DAY**; mail Vandalia **z** 45377; pop. incl. with Vandalia (Inc. Place)
Cridersville; Inc. Place; AUGLAIZE; ▲ Duchouquet; **216** NK-4; elev. 890ft./271m.; 🅿; ★ **LIMA**; **z** 45806; Ⓟ 1,885; Ⓒ 1,817
Crissey; RMC Place; LUCAS; ▲ Springfield; **216** NE-5; ★ **TOL**; mail Holland **z** 43528; ● 220
Cromers; RMC Place; SENECA; ▲ Liberty; ***216** NG-8; mail Tiffin **z** 44883; ● 30
Crooked Tree; RMC Place; NOBLE; ▲ Jackson; ***219** SD-16; mail Dexter City **z** 45727; rural
Crooksville; Inc. Place; PERRY; ▲ Harrison; **219** SC-13; 🅿; ★ **ZAN**; **z** 43731; Ⓟ 2,601; Ⓒ 2,483
Crosby; MCD-Township; HAMILTON; ***218** SF-1; ★ **CIN**; mail Harrison **z** 45030; Ⓟ 2,665; Ⓒ 2,748
Cross Creek; MCD-Township; JEFFERSON; ***217** NL-19; ★ **STU-**; mail Steubenville **z** 43952-53; Ⓟ 9,305; Ⓒ 8,761
Crossenville; RMC Place; PERRY; ▲ Jackson; **219** SC-12; mail Bremen **z** 43107; ● 40
Crosstown; RMC Place; BROWN; ▲ Sterling; ***218** SG-4; elev. 913ft./278m.; ★ **CIN**; mail Williamsburg **z** 45176
Crosswick; RMC Place; WARREN; ▲ Wayne; ***218** SD-4; ★ **DAY**; mail Waynesville **z** 45068
Croton (Hartford); Inc. Place; LICKING; ▲ Hartford; **216** NM-10; 🅿; **z** 43013; Ⓟ 418; Ⓒ 412
Crown City; Inc. Place; GALLIA; ▲ Guyan; **219** SJ-13; 🅿; **z** 45623; Ⓟ 445; Ⓒ 411
Crown Point; RMC Place; MONTGOMERY; ***218** SC-3; ★ **DAY**; pop. incl. with Dayton (Inc. Place)
Crystal Lake; RMC Place; ASHTABULA; ▲ Andover; ***217** NE-20; mail Andover **z** 44003; ● 25
Crystal Lakes; CDP; CLARK; ▲ Bethel; **218** SB-4; ★ **DAY**; mail Medway **z** 45341; Ⓟ 1,613; Ⓒ 1,411
Crystal Rock Park; RMC Place; ERIE; ▲ Margaretta; **216** NF-10; ★ **SNDSK**; mail Sandusky **z** 44870; ● 300
Crystal Springs; RMC Place; STARK; ▲ Jackson; **217** NI-16; ★ **CAN**; mail Canal Fulton **z** 44614, Massillon **z** 44646; ● 250
Cuba; RMC Place; CLINTON; ▲ Washington; **218** SE-5; elev. 1,034ft./315m.; 🅿; **z** 45114; ● 160
Cumberland; Inc. Place; GUERNSEY; ▲ Spencer; **219** SB-15; elev. 857ft./261m.; 🅿; **z** 43732; Ⓟ 318; Ⓒ 402
Cumminsville; RMC Place; HAMILTON; ***218** SF-2; ★ **CIN**; mail Cincinnati **z** 45223; pop. incl. with Cincinnati (Inc. Place)
Curtice; RMC Place; OTTAWA, LUCAS; ▲ Jerusalem, Allen; **216** NE-7; 🅿; ★ **TOL**; **z** 43412; ● 800
Custar; Inc. Place; WOOD; ▲ Milton; **216** NG-5; 🅿; **z** 43511; Ⓟ 209; Ⓒ 208
Cutler; RMC Place; WASHINGTON; ▲ Fairfield, Decatur; **219** SE-15; 🅿; **z** 45724; ● 130
CUYAHOGA; **217** NG-15; Ⓟ 1,412,140; Ⓒ 1,393,978; Ⓡ 1,393,845; ◆ 1,256,906
Cuyahoga Falls; Inc. Place; SUMMIT; **217** NH-16; 🅿 🅷 ■; ★ **AKR**; **z** 44221-24; Ⓟ 48,950; Ⓒ 49,374; ◆ 48,964
Cuyahoga Heights; Inc. Place; CUYAHOGA; **219** SM-18; 🅿; ★ **CLEV**; **z** 44127 & mail Cleveland **z** 44105, **z** 44125; Ⓟ 682; Ⓒ 599
Cygnet; Inc. Place; WOOD; ▲ Bloom; **216** NG-6; 🅿; **z** 43413; Ⓟ 560; Ⓒ 564
Cynthian; MCD-Township; SHELBY; ***216** NM-2; mail Fort Loramie **z** 45845; Ⓟ 1,762; Ⓒ 1,972
Cynthiana; RMC Place; PIKE; ▲ Perry; **218** SF-8; elev. 970ft./296m.; 🅿; **z** 45624; ● 200

D

Dabel; RMC Place; MONTGOMERY; ★ **DAY**; mail Dayton **z** 45420; pop. incl. with Dayton (Inc. Place)
Dadsville; RMC Place; PREBLE; ▲ Twin, Lanier; ***218** SC-2; ★ **DAY**; mail West Alexandria **z** 45381; ● 35
Dailyville; RMC Place; PIKE; ▲ Pee Pee; ***218** SG-9; mail Waverly **z** 45690; ● 40
Dale; RMC Place; MORGAN, WASHINGTON; ▲ Wesley, Palmer, Windsor; mail Stockport **z** 43787; rural
Dallas; MCD-Township; CRAWFORD; ***216** NJ-8; mail Nevada **z** 44849; Ⓟ 456; Ⓒ 455
Dallasburg; RMC Place; WARREN; ▲ Hamilton; ***218** SF-4; elev. 806ft./246m.; ★ **CIN**; mail Loveland **z** 45140; rural
Dalton; Inc. Place; WAYNE; ▲ Sugar Creek; **217** NJ-15; 🅿; **z** 44618; Ⓟ 1,377; Ⓒ 1,605
Dalzell; RMC Place; WASHINGTON; ▲ Liberty; **219** SD-17; mail Lower Salem **z** 45745
Daman Park; RMC Place; BUTLER; ▲ Lemon; ***218** SD-1; ★ **CIN**; mail Middletown **z** 45044
Damascus; MCD-Township; HENRY; ***216** NF-5; mail Mc Clure **z** 43534; Ⓟ 1,876; Ⓒ 1,781
Damascus; RMC Place; MAHONING, COLUMBIANA; ▲ Butler, Goshen; **217** NI-18; elev. 1,219ft./372m.; 🅿; **z** 44619; ● 950
Danbury; MCD-Township; OTTAWA; ***216** NE-10; ★ **TOL**; mail Port Clinton **z** 43452; Ⓟ 4,410; Ⓒ 4,631
Danville; RMC Place; HIGHLAND; ▲ Hamer; **218** SG-6; elev. 1,068ft./326m.; mail Hillsboro **z** 45133; ● 120
Danville; Inc. Place; KNOX; ▲ Union; **217** NL-12; elev. 966ft./294m.; 🅿; **z** 43014; Ⓟ 1,001; Ⓒ 1,104
Danville; RMC Place; MEIGS; ▲ Salem; ***219** SG-13; mail Langsville **z** 45741
Darby; MCD-Township; MADISON; ***218** SA-8; mail Plain City **z** 43064; Ⓟ 2,225; Ⓒ 2,872
Darby; MCD-Township; PICKAWAY; ***218** SC-8; ★ **COL**; mail Orient **z** 43146; Ⓟ 3,484; Ⓒ 3,492
Darby; MCD-Township; UNION; ***216** NN-7; mail Plain City **z** 43064; Ⓟ 1,530; Ⓒ 1,934
Darbydale; RMC Place; FRANKLIN; ▲ Pleasant; **218** SB-8; 🅿; ★ **COL**; **z** 43123; ● 600
Darbyville; Inc. Place; PICKAWAY; ▲ Muhlenberg; **218** SC-9; mail Lithopolis **z** 43136, Williamsport **z** 43164; Ⓟ 272; Ⓒ 293
DARKE; **216** NM-1; Ⓟ 53,619; Ⓒ 53,309; ◆ 51,801
Darlington; RMC Place; MUSKINGUM; ▲ Newton; **219** SB-14; ★ **ZAN**; mail Zanesville **z** 43701; ● 35
Darlington; RMC Place; RICHLAND; ▲ Perry; ***217** NK-11; ★ **MANS**; mail Bellville **z** 44813
Darrowville; RMC Place; SUMMIT; ***217** NG-16; ★ **AKR**; mail Stow **z** 44224; pop. incl. with Stow (Inc. Place)
Darrtown; RMC Place; BUTLER; ▲ Milford; **218** SD-1; elev. 742ft./226m.; ★ **CIN**; mail Oxford **z** 45056; ● 400
Dart; RMC Place; WASHINGTON; ▲ Lawrence; **219** SD-17; elev. 640ft./195m.; mail Reno **z** 45773; ● 30
Darwin; RMC Place; MEIGS; ▲ Bedford; ***219** SG-14; elev. 664ft./202m.; mail Pomeroy **z** 45769; rural
Davisville; RMC Place; JACKSON; ▲ Coal; **219** SG-11; mail Wellston **z** 45692; ● 45
Dawn; RMC Place; DARKE; ▲ Richland; **216** NM-2; elev. 1,017ft./310m.; mail Ansonia **z** 45303; ● 170
Dawson; RMC Place; SHELBY; ▲ Loramie; ***216** NM-3; elev. 949ft./289m.; mail Houston **z** 45333; ● 25
Day Heights; CDP-Census Area Only; CLERMONT; ▲ Miami; ***218** SF-3; 🅿; ★ **CIN**; **z** 45150; Ⓟ 2,812; Ⓒ 2,823
Dayton; Inc. Place; ⊡ MONTGOMERY, GREENE; **218** SC-4; 🅿 🅷 🅲 28,210 ■; ★ **DAY**; **z** 45390, **z** 45400-06, **z** 45408-10, **z** 45412-20, **z** 45422-24, **z** 45426-35, **z** 45437, **z** 45439-41, **z** 45448-49, **z** 45454, **z** 45458-59, **z** 45469-70, **z** 45475, **z** 45479, **z** 45481-82, **z** 45490; Ⓟ 182,044; Ⓒ 166,179; ◆ 155,866
Dayton View; RMC Place; MONTGOMERY; ★ **DAY**; mail Dayton **z** 45406; pop. incl. with Dayton (Inc. Place)
Dean Dale; RMC Place; JEFFERSON; ***217** NL-20; ★ **STU-**; mail Mingo Junction **z** 43938; pop. incl. with Mingo Junction (Inc. Place)
Deavertown; RMC Place; MORGAN; ▲ York; **219** SC-14; elev. 946ft./288m.; mail Crooksville **z** 43731; ● 200
Decatur; RMC Place; BROWN; ▲ Byrd; **218** SI-6; elev. 924ft./282m.; 🅿; **z** 45115; ● 250
Decatur; MCD-Township; LAWRENCE; ***219** SI-11; mail Pedro **z** 45659; Ⓟ 870; Ⓒ 839
Decatur; MCD-Township; WASHINGTON; ***219** SE-15; mail Little Hocking **z** 45742; Ⓟ 1,114; Ⓒ 1,181
Decaturville; RMC Place; WASHINGTON; ▲ Decatur; ***219** SE-15; elev. 824ft./251m.; mail Barlow **z** 45712, Cutler **z** 45724, Little Hocking **z** 45742; ● 75
DeCliff; RMC Place; MARION; ▲ Big Island; ***216** NK-7; mail Marion **z** 43302, New Bloomington **z** 43341; rural
Decrow Corners; RMC Place; LICKING; ▲ Bennington, Liberty; ***217** NM-11; mail Johnstown **z** 43031; rural
Deep Run; RMC Place; BELMONT; ▲ Pease; ★ **WHL**; mail Martins Ferry **z** 43935, Yorkville **z** 43971; rural
Deer Creek; MCD-Township; MADISON; ***218** SB-7; mail London **z** 43140; Ⓟ 1,038; Ⓒ 1,030
Deercreek; MCD-Township; PICKAWAY; ***218** SD-9; mail Williamsport **z** 43164; Ⓟ 1,431; Ⓒ 1,644
Deerfield; MCD-Township; MORGAN; ***219** SC-14; mail Malta **z** 43758; Ⓟ 683; Ⓒ 802
Deerfield; RMC Place; PORTAGE; ▲ Deerfield; **217** NH-18; elev. 1,073ft./327m.; 🅿; ★ **AKR**; **z** 44411; ● 520
Deerfield; MCD-Township; PORTAGE; ***217** NH-18; 🅿; ★ **AKR**; **z** 44411; Ⓟ 2,764; Ⓒ 3,211
Deerfield; MCD-Township; ROSS; ***218** SD-8; mail Clarksburg **z** 43115; Ⓟ 1,077; Ⓒ 1,096
Deerfield; MCD-Township; WARREN; ***218** SE-3; ★ **CIN**; mail Mason **z** 45040; Ⓟ 26,359; Ⓒ 25,515
Deering; RMC Place; LAWRENCE; ▲ Perry; **219** SJ-11; ★ **HNTG**; mail Ironton **z** 45638; ● 90
Deer Park; Inc. Place; HAMILTON; **218** SF-3; ★ **CIN**; mail Cincinnati **z** 45236; Ⓟ 6,181; Ⓒ 5,982
Deersville; Inc. Place; HARRISON; ▲ Franklin; **217** NM-17; elev. 1,254ft./382m.; 🅿; **z** 44693; Ⓟ 86; Ⓒ 82
Defiance; Inc. Place; ⊡ DEFIANCE; ▲ Richland, Defiance, Noble; **216** NG-3; 🅿 🅷 🅲 997 ■; **z** 43512; Ⓟ 16,768; Ⓒ 16,465; ◆ 16,393
Defiance; MCD-Township; DEFIANCE; ***216** NG-3; 🅿; **z** 43512; includes part of the City of Defiance; Ⓟ 13,743; Ⓒ 13,461
DEFIANCE; **216** NF-1; Ⓟ 39,350; Ⓒ 39,500; ◆ 38,314
Defiance Junction; RMC Place; DEFIANCE; mail Defiance **z** 43512; pop. incl. with Defiance (Inc. Place)
DeForest; RMC Place; TRUMBULL; ▲ Howland; **217** NB-12; ★ **YNGS-**; mail Warren **z** 44484; ● 1,150
De Graff; Inc. Place; LOGAN; ▲ Pleasant, Miami; **216** NM-5; elev. 1,007ft./307m.; 🅿; **z** 43318; Ⓟ 1,331; Ⓒ 1,212
Dekalb; RMC Place; CRAWFORD; ▲ Vernon; ***216** NI-10; elev. 1,080ft./329m.; mail Tiro **z** 44887
Delaware; MCD-Township; DEFIANCE; ***216** NG-2; mail Sherwood **z** 43556; Ⓟ 2,025; Ⓒ 2,128
Delaware; Inc. Place; ⊡ DELAWARE; ▲ Troy, Brown, Concord, Delaware; **216** NM-8; 🅿 🅷 🅲 1,904 ■; **z** 43015; Ⓟ 20,030; Ⓒ 25,243; ◆ 29,256
Delaware; MCD-Township; DELAWARE; ***216** NM-9; 🅿 🅲 1,904; **z** 43015; includes part of the City of Delaware; Ⓟ 21,028; Ⓒ 26,149
Delaware; MCD-Township; HANCOCK; ***216** NI-6; mail Williamstown **z** 45897; Ⓟ 1,196; Ⓒ 1,229
DELAWARE; **216** NM-10; Ⓟ 66,929; Ⓒ 109,989; ◆ 168,801
Delhi; RMC Place; HAMILTON; ***218** SG-2; ★ **CIN**; mail Cincinnati **z** 45238
Delhi; MCD-Township; HAMILTON; ***218** SG-2; ★ **CIN**; mail Cincinnati **z** 45233, **z** 45238; Ⓟ 30,250; Ⓒ 30,104
Delhi Hills; RMC Place; HAMILTON; ▲ Delhi; **218** SM-2; ★ **CIN**; mail Cincinnati **z** 45238; ● 20,000
Delightful; RMC Place; TRUMBULL; ▲ Southington; **217** NG-18; elev. 942ft./287m.; ★ **YNGS-**; mail Southington **z** 44470; ● 40
Delisle; RMC Place; DARKE; ▲ Van Buren; **218** SA-2; mail Arcanum **z** 45304; ● 50
Dellroy; Inc. Place; CARROLL; ▲ Monroe; **217** NK-17; 🅿; **z** 44620; Ⓟ 314; Ⓒ 294
Delmont; RMC Place; FAIRFIELD; ▲ Hocking; ***219** SC-11; ★ **LANC**; mail Lancaster **z** 43130
Delphi; RMC Place; HURON; ▲ Ripley; **217** NH-11; elev. 1,038ft./316m.; mail Willard **z** 44890; ● 100
Delphos; Inc. Place; ALLEN, VAN WERT; ▲ Washington, Marion; **216** NI-3; 🅿; ★ **LIMA**; **z** 45833; Ⓟ 7,093; Ⓒ 6,944
Delta; Inc. Place; FULTON; ▲ York, Swan Creek; **216** NE-4; 🅿; ★ **TOL**; **z** 43515; Ⓟ 2,849; Ⓒ 2,930
Democracy; KNOX; see Amity (RMC Place)
Denmark; MCD-Township; ASHTABULA; ***217** ND-19; mail Jefferson **z** 44047; Ⓟ 706; Ⓒ 880
Denmark; RMC Place; MORROW; ▲ Canaan; ***216** NK-9; mail Edison **z** 43320
Denmark Center; RMC Place; ASHTABULA; ▲ Denmark; ***217** ND-19; elev. 951ft./290m.; mail Jefferson **z** 44047
Dennison; Inc. Place; TUSCARAWAS; ▲ Union, Mill; **217** NL-17; elev. 862ft./263m.; 🅿 🅷; **z** 44621; Ⓟ 3,282; Ⓒ 2,992
Denson; RMC Place; FULTON; ▲ Chesterfield; ***216** ND-4; mail Lyons **z** 43533, Morenci **z** 49256
Dent; CDP; HAMILTON; ▲ Green; **218** SF-1; elev. 548ft./167m.; ★ **CIN**; mail Cincinnati **z** 45247-48; Ⓟ 6,416; Ⓒ 7,612
Denver; RMC Place; ROSS; ▲ Huntington; **218** SF-9; elev. 836ft./255m.; mail Waverly **z** 45690; ● 25
Derby; RMC Place; PICKAWAY; ▲ Darby; **218** SC-8; 🅿; ★ **COL**; **z** 43117; ● 450
Derwent; RMC Place; GUERNSEY; ▲ Valley; **219** SB-16; 🅿; **z** 43733; ● 250
Deshler; Inc. Place; HENRY; ▲ Bartlow; **216** NG-5; elev. 715ft./218m.; 🅿; **z** 43516; Ⓟ 1,876; Ⓒ 1,831
Deunquat; RMC Place; WYANDOT; ▲ Sycamore; **216** NI-8; mail Sycamore **z** 44882; ● 50
Devil Town; RMC Place; WAYNE; ▲ Wayne; ***217** NI-14; mail Wooster **z** 44691
Devola; CDP; WASHINGTON; ▲ Muskingum; **219** SE-16; ★ **PRKB**; mail Marietta **z** 45750; Ⓟ 2,736; Ⓒ 2,771
Deweyville; RMC Place; HANCOCK; ▲ Pleasant; **216** NH-5; mail Mc Comb **z** 45858; ● 30
Dexter; RMC Place; MEIGS; ▲ Salem; **219** SG-13; elev. 595ft./181m.; 🅿; **z** 45741; ● 70
Dexter City; Inc. Place; NOBLE; ▲ Olive, Enoch, Jackson, Jefferson; **219** SC-16; 🅿; **z** 45727; Ⓟ 161; Ⓒ 166
Deyarmonville; RMC Place; JEFFERSON; ▲ Warren, Smithfield; ***217** NM-19; ★ **WHL**; mail Dillonvale **z** 43917; ● 50
Dialton; RMC Place; CLARK; ▲ Pike; **218** SA-5; elev. 1,150ft./351m.; ★ **SPR**; mail Springfield **z** 45502; ● 60
Diamond; RMC Place; PORTAGE; ▲ Palmyra; **217** NH-18; 🅿; **z** 44412; ● 200
Dicken; RMC Place; HOCKING; ▲ Green, Falls; mail Logan **z** 43138; ● 350
Dille; BELMONT; see Dilles Bottom (RMC Place)
Dilles Bottom (Dille); RMC Place; BELMONT; ▲ Mead; **219** SB-19; ★ **WHL**; mail Shadyside **z** 43947; ● 130
Dillon Falls; RMC Place; MUSKINGUM; ▲ Falls; ***219** SB-14; ★ **ZAN**; mail Zanesville **z** 43701; rural
Dillonvale; CDP-Census Area Only; HAMILTON; ▲ Sycamore; ***218** SF-3; elev. 800ft./244m.; ★ **CIN**; mail Cincinnati **z** 45236; Ⓟ 4,209; Ⓒ 3,716
Dillonvale; Inc. Place; JEFFERSON; ▲ Smithfield, Mount Pleasant; **217** NM-19; 🅿; ★ **WHL**; **z** 43917; Ⓟ 857; Ⓒ 781
Dilworth; RMC Place; TRUMBULL; ▲ Gustavus; ***217** NF-19; mail Farmdale **z** 44417; rural
Dinsmore; MCD-Township; SHELBY; ***216** NL-3; mail Botkins **z** 45306; Ⓟ 3,313; Ⓒ 3,357
Dixie; RMC Place; PERRY; ▲ Pike; ***219** SD-13; mail Shawnee **z** 43782; rural
Dixie Heights; RMC Place; BUTLER; ★ **MIDD**; mail Middletown **z** 45042; pop. incl. with Middletown (Inc. Place)
Dixie Heights; RMC Place; MONTGOMERY; ▲ Harrison; ★ **DAY**; mail Dayton **z** 45414
Dixon; MCD-Township; PREBLE; ***218** SC-1; mail Eaton **z** 45320; Ⓟ 604; Ⓒ 557
Dixon; RMC Place; VAN WERT; ▲ Tully; **216** NI-1; mail Convoy **z** 45832; total pop. including Dixon, IN...200; ● 70
Dixonville; RMC Place; COLUMBIANA; ▲ Liverpool; ***217** NJ-20; ★ **E.LIV**; mail East Liverpool **z** 43920; ● 500
Doanville; RMC Place; ATHENS; ▲ York; **219** SE-13; elev. 671ft./205m.; mail Nelsonville **z** 45764; ● 160
Dobbston; RMC Place; LAWRENCE; ▲ Windsor; ***219** SJ-12; elev. 888ft./271m.; mail Scottown **z** 45678
Dodds; RMC Place; WARREN; ▲ Clear Creek; **218** SD-4; ★ **DAY**; mail Lebanon **z** 45036; ● 80
Dodgeville; RMC Place; ASHTABULA; ▲ New Lyme; **217** NE-19; mail Rome **z** 44085; ● 110
Dodson; MCD-Township; HIGHLAND; ***218** SF-5; mail Lynchburg **z** 45142; Ⓟ 2,304; Ⓒ 2,514
Dodson; RMC Place; MONTGOMERY; ▲ Clay; **218** SB-2; ★ **DAY**; mail Brookville **z** 45309; ● 25
Dodsonville; RMC Place; HIGHLAND; ▲ Dodson; **218** SF-5; mail Lynchburg **z** 45142; ● 70
Dogtown; GUERNSEY; see Buckeyeville (RMC Place)
Dola; RMC Place; HARDIN; ▲ Washington; **216** NJ-6; elev. 948ft./289m.; 🅿; **z** 45835 & mail Cincinnati **z** 45211; ● 200
Dolly Varden; RMC Place; CLARK; ▲ Madison; ***218** SB-6; mail South Charleston **z** 45368
Donald L Marrs; RMC Place; HAMILTON; ***218** SG-2; ★ **CIN**; mail Cincinnati **z** 45258
Doneys; RMC Place; FRANKLIN; ***218** SB-10; ★ **COL**; mail Columbus **z** 43213; pop. incl. with Whitehall (Inc. Place)
Donnelsville; Inc. Place; CLARK; **218** SB-5; 🅿; ★ **SPR**; **z** 45319; Ⓟ 276; Ⓒ 293
Donnersville; RMC Place; BELMONT; ▲ Wheeling; ***217** NN-18; mail Saint Clairsville **z** 43950; rural
Dorcas; RMC Place; MEIGS; ▲ Sutton; ***219** SH-14; mail Racine **z** 45771
Dornbusch; RMC Place; HAMILTON; ▲ Colerain; ***218** SF-2; ★ **CIN**; mail Cincinnati **z** 45239; ● 350
Dorset; RMC Place; ASHTABULA; ▲ Dorset; **217** ND-19; 🅿; **z** 44032; ● 200
Dorset; MCD-Township; ASHTABULA; ***217** ND-19; 🅿; **z** 44032; Ⓟ 850; Ⓒ 892
Dover; MCD-Township; ATHENS; ***219** SE-13; mail Millfield **z** 45761; Ⓟ 3,595; Ⓒ 3,797
Dover; RMC Place; CUYAHOGA; ★ **CLEV**; pop. incl. with Westlake (Inc. Place)
Dover; MCD-Township; FULTON; ***216** NE-3; mail Wauseon **z** 43567; Ⓟ 1,111; Ⓒ 1,468
Dover; Inc. Place; TUSCARAWAS; ▲ Dover; **217** NK-16; elev. 898ft./274m.; 🅿 🅷 ■; **z** 44622; Ⓟ 11,329; Ⓒ 12,210; ◆ 11,763
Dover; MCD-Township; TUSCARAWAS; ***217** NK-16; 🅿; **z** 44622; Ⓟ 4,506; Ⓒ 4,726
Dover; MCD-Township; UNION; ***216** NM-8; mail Marysville **z** 43040; Ⓟ 2,067; Ⓒ 2,331
Dowling; RMC Place; WOOD; ▲ Perrysburg, Middleton; ***216** NF-6; ★ **TOL**; mail Perrysburg **z** 43551; ● 70
Downington; MEIGS; see Pageville (RMC Place)
Downtown; RMC Place; SUMMIT; ★ **AKR**; mail Akron **z** 44308; pop. incl. with Akron (Inc. Place)
Doylestown; Inc. Place; WAYNE; ▲ Chippewa; **217** NI-15; 🅿; ★ **AKR**; **z** 44230; Ⓟ 2,668; Ⓒ 2,799
Drakes; RMC Place; PERRY; ▲ Monroe; **219** SD-13; mail Corning **z** 43730; ● 70
Drakesburg; RMC Place; PORTAGE; ▲ Freedom; **217** NG-17; ★ **AKR**; mail Windham **z** 44288; ● 55
Dresden; Inc. Place; MUSKINGUM; ▲ Cass; **217** NN-13; 🅿; **z** 43821; Ⓟ 1,581; Ⓒ 1,423
Drexel; CDP; MONTGOMERY; **218** SC-3; ★ **DAY**; mail Dayton **z** 45427; Ⓒ 2,057
Driftwood; RMC Place; ASHTABULA, LAKE; ▲ Geneva, Madison; ***217** NC-18; ★ **CLEV**; mail Geneva **z** 44041; ● 150
Drinkle; RMC Place; FAIRFIELD; ▲ Clearcreek; ***218** SD-10; mail Amanda **z** 43102
Dry Run; RMC Place; COLUMBIANA; ***217** NK-20; ★ **E.LIV**; mail East Liverpool **z** 43920; pop. incl. with East Liverpool (Inc. Place)
Dry Run; CDP-Census Area Only; HAMILTON; ▲ Anderson; ***218** SG-3; elev. 900ft./274m.; ★ **CIN**; mail Cincinnati **z** 45244; Ⓟ 5,389; Ⓒ 6,553
Dry Run; RMC Place; SCIOTO; ▲ Washington; **218** SI-9; elev. 559ft./170m.; ★ **PTSM**; mail West Portsmouth **z** 45663; ● 750
Dublin; Inc. Place; FRANKLIN, DELAWARE; ▲ Jerome, Concord, Perry, Washington; **216** NN-8; 🅿; ★ **COL**; **z** 43016-17; Ⓟ 16,366; Ⓒ 31,392; ◆ 37,759
Dublin; MCD-Township; MERCER; ***216** NJ-1; mail Rockford **z** 45882; Ⓟ 2,244; Ⓒ 2,254
Duchouquet; MCD-Township; AUGLAIZE; ***216** NK-3; ★ **LIMA**; mail Wapakoneta **z** 45895; Ⓟ 14,196; Ⓒ 14,329
Dudley; MCD-Township; HARDIN; ***216** NK-7; mail Kenton **z** 43326; Ⓟ 1,092; Ⓒ 1,257
Dudley; RMC Place; NOBLE; ▲ Olive; ***219** SC-16; mail Caldwell **z** 43724; ● 25
Dueber Station; RMC Place; STARK; ▲ Canton; mail Canton **z** 44706; pop. incl. with Canton (Inc. Place)
Duffy; RMC Place; MONROE; ▲ Ohio; **219** SC-19; mail Sardis **z** 43946; ● 230
Dull; RMC Place; VAN WERT; ▲ Liberty; ***216** NJ-1; mail Ohio City **z** 45874
Dumontville; RMC Place; FAIRFIELD; ▲ Greenfield; ***219** SC-11; ★ **COL**; mail Lancaster **z** 43130
Dunbridge; RMC Place; WOOD; ▲ Middleton; **216** NF-6; 🅿; ★ **TOL**; **z** 43414; ● 250
Duncan Falls; RMC Place; MUSKINGUM; ▲ Wayne; **219** SB-14; 🅿; ★ **ZAN**; **z** 43734; ● 600
Dundas; RMC Place; VINTON; ▲ Clinton; **219** SF-12; mail Hamden **z** 45634; ● 220
Dundee; RMC Place; TUSCARAWAS; ▲ Wayne; **217** NK-15; elev. 1,032ft./315m.; 🅿; **z** 44624; ● 250
Dungannon; RMC Place; COLUMBIANA; ▲ Hanover; ***217** NJ-19; mail Hanoverton **z** 44423; ● 50
Dungannon; RMC Place; NOBLE; ▲ Jackson; ***219** SD-16; elev. 994ft./303m.; mail Coal Run **z** 45721
Dunglen; RMC Place; JEFFERSON; ▲ Mount Pleasant; ***217** NM-19; ★ **WHL**; mail Dillonvale **z** 43917; ● 25
Dunham; MCD-Township; WASHINGTON; ***219** SE-15; ★ **PRKB**; mail Vincent **z** 45784; Ⓟ 2,224; Ⓒ 2,505
Dunkinsville; RMC Place; ADAMS; ▲ Oliver; **218** SH-7; mail Peebles **z** 45660, West Union **z** 45693; ● 50
Dunkirk; Inc. Place; HARDIN; ▲ Blanchard; **216** NJ-6; elev. 951ft./290m.; 🅿; **z** 45836; Ⓟ 869; Ⓒ 952
Dunlap; RMC Place; HAMILTON; ▲ Colerain; **218** SF-2; elev. 857ft./261m.; ★ **CIN**; mail Cincinnati **z** 45247; ● 250
Dupont; Inc. Place; PUTNAM; ▲ Perry; **216** NH-3; 🅿; **z** 45837; Ⓟ 279; Ⓒ 268
Durbin; RMC Place; CLARK; ▲ Springfield; **217** NB-15; ★ **SPR**; mail Springfield **z** 45502; ● 25
Durbin; RMC Place; MERCER; ▲ Liberty, Hopewell; ***216** NK-1; elev. 872ft./266m.; mail Celina **z** 45822
Durham Estates; RMC Place; WILLIAMS; ▲ Center; ***216** NF-2; mail Bryan **z** 43506; ● 40
Duvall (Duvalls); RMC Place; PICKAWAY; ▲ Harrison; **218** SC-9; ★ **COL**; mail Lockbourne **z** 43137; ● 50
Duvalls; PICKAWAY; see Duvall (RMC Place)
Dyesville; RMC Place; MEIGS; ▲ Columbia; ***219** SG-13; elev. 614ft./187m.; mail Pomeroy **z** 45769

E

Eagle; MCD-Township; BROWN; ***218** SH-6; mail Sardinia **z** 45171; Ⓟ 1,080; Ⓒ 1,438
Eagle; MCD-Township; HANCOCK; ***216** NI-6; mail Rawson **z** 45881; Ⓟ 1,106; Ⓒ 1,195
Eagle; MCD-Township; VINTON; ***219** SF-11; mail South Bloomingville **z** 43152; Ⓟ 521; Ⓒ 412
Eagle Beach; RMC Place; OTTAWA; ▲ Catawba Island; mail Port Clinton **z** 43452; ● 40
Eagle City; RMC Place; CLARK; ▲ German; **218** SB-5; ★ **SPR**; mail Springfield **z** 45504; ● 70
Eagle Point Colony; RMC Place; WOOD; ***216** NE-6; ★ **TOL**; mail Rossford **z** 43460; pop. incl. with Rossford (Inc. Place)
Eagleport; RMC Place; MORGAN; ▲ Bloom; **219** SC-14; mail McConnelsville **z** 43756; ● 35
Eagleville; RMC Place; ASHTABULA; ▲ Austinburg; ***217** ND-19; elev. 811ft./247m.; mail Jefferson **z** 44047; ● 100
Eagleville; RMC Place; WOOD; ▲ Bloom; **216** NG-6; elev. 738ft./225m.; mail Bloomdale **z** 44817; ● 35
East; MCD-Township; CARROLL; ***217** NJ-18; mail Kensington **z** 44427; Ⓟ 734; Ⓒ 859
East Akron; RMC Place; SUMMIT; ***217** NH-16; ★ **AKR**; mail Akron **z** 44305; pop. incl. with Akron (Inc. Place)
East Alliance; RMC Place; MAHONING; ▲ Smith; **217** NI-18; ★ **ALLI**; mail Alliance **z** 44601; ● 1,175
East Ashtabula; RMC Place; ASHTABULA; ***217** NC-19; ★ **ASHT**; mail Ashtabula **z** 44004; pop. incl. with Ashtabula (Inc. Place)
East Bass Lake; RMC Place; GEAUGA; ▲ Munson; ★ **CLEV**; mail Chardon **z** 44024
East Batavia Heights; RMC Place; CLERMONT; ▲ Batavia; **218** SG-4; elev. 837ft./255m.; ★ **CIN**; mail Batavia **z** 45103; ● 150
East Cadiz; RMC Place; HARRISON; ▲ Green; ***217** NM-18; elev. 1,094ft./333m.; mail Cadiz **z** 43907
East Cambridge; RMC Place; GUERNSEY; ***219** SA-16; mail Cambridge **z** 43725; pop. incl. with Cambridge (Inc. Place)
East Canton; Inc. Place; STARK; ▲ Osnaburg; **217** NJ-17; elev. 1,146ft./349m.; 🅿; ★ **CAN**; **z** 44730; Ⓟ 1,742; Ⓒ 1,629
East Carlisle; RMC Place; LORAIN; ▲ Carlisle; ***217** NF-13; ★ **CLEV**; mail Elyria **z** 44035; ● 480
East Claridon; RMC Place; GEAUGA; ▲ Claridon; **217** NE-17; 🅿; ★ **CLEV**; **z** 44033; ● 260
East Clayton; RMC Place; ATHENS; ▲ York; ***219** SE-13; mail Nelsonville **z** 45764; rural
East Cleveland; Inc. Place; CUYAHOGA; **217** NE-15; 🅿; ★ **CLEV**; **z** 44110, **z** 44112, **z** 44118; Ⓟ 33,096; Ⓒ 27,217; ◆ 22,534
East Columbus; RMC Place; FRANKLIN; ***218** SB-10; ★ **COL**; pop. incl. with Columbus (Inc. Place)
East Conesville; RMC Place; COSHOCTON; ▲ Franklin; mail Conesville **z** 43811; pop. incl. with Conesville (Inc. Place)
East Conneaut; RMC Place; ASHTABULA; mail Conneaut **z** 44030; pop. incl. with Conneaut (Inc. Place)
East Cumminsville; RMC Place; HAMILTON; ★ **CIN**; mail Cincinnati **z** 45223; pop. incl. with Cincinnati (Inc. Place)
East Danville (Winkle); RMC Place; HIGHLAND; ▲ New Market, Hamer; **218** SG-6; mail Hillsboro **z** 45133; ● 100
East End; RMC Place; COLUMBIANA; ***217** NK-20; ★ **E.LIV**; mail East Liverpool **z** 43920; pop. incl. with East Liverpool (Inc. Place)
East End; RMC Place; HAMILTON; ★ **CIN**; mail Cincinnati **z** 45226; pop. incl. with Cincinnati (Inc. Place)
East Fairfield; RMC Place; COLUMBIANA; ▲ Unity, Fairfield; **217** NI-20; ★ **YNGS-**; mail Columbiana **z** 44408; ● 100
East Fultonham; RMC Place; MUSKINGUM; ▲ Newton; **219** SB-13; elev. 763ft./233m.; 🅿; ★ **ZAN**; **z** 43735; ● 460
East Goshen; RMC Place; MAHONING; ▲ Goshen; ***217** NI-18; mail Beloit **z** 44609; rural
East Greenville; RMC Place; STARK; ▲ Tuscarawas; **217** NJ-15; elev. 1,166ft./355m.; ★ **CAN**; mail North Lawrence **z** 44666; ● 180
Eastlake; Inc. Place; LAKE; **217** ND-16; 🅿; ★ **CLEV**; **z** 44095, **z** 44097; Ⓟ 21,161; Ⓒ 20,255; ◆ 19,910
Eastland; RMC Place; FRANKLIN; ★ **COL**; mail Columbus **z** 43232; pop. incl. with Columbus (Inc. Place)
East Lawn; RMC Place; WOOD; ▲ Lake; ***216** NE-7; ★ **TOL**; mail Millbury **z** 43447; ● 650
East Lewistown; RMC Place; MAHONING; ▲ Beaver; ***217** NI-19; elev. 1,121ft./342m.; ★ **YNGS-**; mail Columbiana **z** 44408, North Lima **z** 44452; ● 100
East Liberty; RMC Place; DELAWARE; ▲ Porter; ***216** NM-10; 🅿; **z** 43319; ● 20
East Liberty; RMC Place; LOGAN; ▲ Perry; **216** NL-6; 🅿; **z** 43319 & mail Sunbury **z** 43074; ● 500
East Liberty; RMC Place; SUMMIT; **217** NI-16; elev. 1,098ft./335m.; ★ **AKR**; mail Akron **z** 44319; pop. incl. with Green (Inc. Place)
East Liverpool; Inc. Place; COLUMBIANA; **217** NK-20; elev. 689ft./210m.; 🅿 🅷 ■; ★ **E.LIV**; **z** 43920; Ⓟ 13,654; Ⓒ 13,089; ◆ 12,496
East Mansfield; RMC Place; RICHLAND; ▲ Madison; ***217** NJ-11; ★ **MANS**; mail Mansfield **z** 44905; ● 200
East Mecca; RMC Place; TRUMBULL; ▲ Mecca; ***217** NF-19; ★ **YNGS-**; mail Cortland **z** 44410; ● 150
East Millersport; RMC Place; FAIRFIELD; ▲ Walnut; ***219** SB-11; ★ **COL**; mail Millersport **z** 43046; ● 180
East Millfield; RMC Place; ATHENS; ▲ Dover; ***219** SE-13; mail Millfield **z** 45761; ● 200
East Monroe; RMC Place; HIGHLAND; ▲ Madison, Fairfield; **218** SE-7; mail Leesburg **z** 45135; ● 120
East Norwalk; RMC Place; HURON; ▲ Norwalk; **217** NG-11; elev. 731ft./223m.; ★ **SNDSK**; mail Norwalk **z** 44857; ● 80
East Norwood; RMC Place; HAMILTON; ★ **CIN**; mail Cincinnati **z** 45212; pop. incl. with Norwood (Inc. Place)
East Norwood; RMC Place; WASHINGTON; ***219** SE-16; mail Marietta **z** 45750; pop. incl. with Marietta (Inc. Place)

Entries in **UPPERCASE** are counties.
Entries in **bold** have populations of 2,500 or more.
Names in parentheses are alternate names.
Inc. Place — Incorporated Place
RMC Place — Rand McNally Designated Place
CDP — Census Designated Place
MCD — Minor Civil Division

⊡ County Seat
▲ Minor Civil Division
elev. Elevation
🅿 Post Office
🅷 Hospital
🅲 College
■ Principal Business Center
★ Ranally Metro Area (RMA) Abbreviation
z Zip Code(s)
Ⓟ Previous Census Population
Ⓡ Revised Census Population
Ⓐ Annexation Population
● Rand McNally Population Estimate
Ⓒ Final Census Population
Ⓢ Special Census Population
◆ Estimated Population

For additional definitions see Glossary, Volume 1, and Introduction, Volume 2.

Easton; RMC Place; WAYNE; ▲ Chippewa; **217** NI-15; ★ **AKR**; mail Rittman z 44270; ● 200

East Orwell; RMC Place; ASHTABULA; ***217** NE-19; elev. 939ft./286m.; 🅿; z 44076; pop. incl. with Orwell (Inc. Place)

East Over; RMC Place; BUTLER; ▲ Fairfield; ★ **CIN**; mail Hamilton z 45011; ● 300

East Palestine; Inc. Place; COLUMBIANA; ▲ Unity; **217** NI-20; 🅿; z 44413; Ⓟ 5,168; Ⓒ 4,917

East Plains; RMC Place; BUTLER; ★ **MIDD**; mail Middletown z 45044; pop. incl. with Middletown (Inc. Place)

East Richland; RMC Place; BELMONT; ▲ Richland; **217** NN-18; elev. 1,181ft./360m.; ★ **WHL**; mail Saint Clairsville z 43950; ● 300

East Rochester; RMC Place; COLUMBIANA; ▲ West; **217** NJ-18; elev. 1,094ft./333m.; 🅿; ★ **ALLI**; z 44625; ● 400

East Side; RMC Place; MAHONING; ***217** NH-20; ★ **YNGS-**; mail Youngstown z 44506; pop. incl. with Youngstown (Inc. Place)

East Sparta; Inc. Place; STARK; ▲ Pike; **217** NJ-16; 🅿; ★ **CAN**; z 44626; Ⓟ 771; Ⓒ 806

East Springfield; RMC Place; JEFFERSON; ▲ Salem; **217** NL-19; elev. 1,313ft./400m.; 🅿; ★ **STU-**; z 43925; ● 350

East Steels Corners; RMC Place; SUMMIT; ***217** NG-16; mail Cuyahoga Falls z 44223; pop. incl. with Cuyahoga Falls (Inc. Place)

East Toledo; RMC Place; LUCAS; ★ **TOL**; mail Toledo z 43605; pop. incl. with Toledo (Inc. Place)

East Townsend; RMC Place; HURON; ▲ Townsend; **217** NG-11; elev. 899ft./274m.; mail Collins z 44826; ● 80

East Trumbull; RMC Place; ASHTABULA; ▲ Trumbull; **217** ND-18; elev. 825ft./251m.; mail Rock Creek z 44084; ● 80

East Union; RMC Place; NOBLE; ▲ Stock; **219** SC-17; mail Sarahsville z 43779; ● 30

East Union; MCD-Township; WAYNE; ***217** NJ-14; mail Apple Creek z 44606; Ⓟ 5,833; Ⓒ 6,527

East View; RMC Place; JEFFERSON; ★ **STU-**; mail Mingo Junction z 43938; pop. incl. with Mingo Junction (Inc. Place)

Eastview; RMC Place; MONTGOMERY; **218** SL-9; ★ **DAY**; mail Dayton z 45431; pop. incl. with Riverside (Inc. Place)

Eastwood; RMC Place; BROWN; ▲ Sterling; ***218** SG-5; elev. 931ft./284m.; mail Mount Orab z 45154; rural

Eaton; MCD-Township; LORAIN; ***217** NG-13; ★ **CLEV**; mail Elyria z 44035; Ⓟ 8,821; Ⓒ 9,675; Ⓡ 5,973

Eaton; Inc. Place; ⊡ PREBLE; **218** SC-2; elev. 1,046ft./319m.; 🅿; z 45320; Ⓟ 7,396; Ⓒ 8,133

Eaton Estates; CDP; LORAIN; ▲ Eaton; **217** NG-13; ★ **CLEV**; mail Grafton z 44044; Ⓟ 1,586; Ⓒ 1,409

Eber; RMC Place; FAYETTE; ▲ Union; **218** SD-7; mail Washington Court House z 43160; ● 300

Echo; RMC Place; BELMONT; ▲ Pultney; ***219** SA-19; ★ **WHL**; mail Neffs z 43940

Echo Glen Lake; RMC Place; MEDINA; ▲ Hinckley; ***217** NG-15; ★ **CLEV**; mail Hinckley z 44233; ● 200

Eckmansville; RMC Place; ADAMS; ▲ Wayne; ***218** SH-6; mail Winchester z 45697

Eden; MCD-Township; LICKING; ***217** NM-12; mail Saint Louisville z 43071; Ⓟ 1,135; Ⓒ 1,243

Eden; MCD-Township; SENECA; ***216** NH-8; mail Melmore z 44845; Ⓟ 1,996; Ⓒ 2,020

Eden; MCD-Township; WYANDOT; ***216** NI-8; mail Nevada z 44849; Ⓟ 979; Ⓒ 1,026

Eden Park; RMC Place; HAMILTON; ★ **CIN**; mail Cincinnati z 45202; pop. incl. with Cincinnati (Inc. Place)

Eden Park; RMC Place; SCIOTO; ▲ Clay; **218** SI-9; ★ **PTSM**; mail Portsmouth z 45662; ● 430

Edenton; RMC Place; CLERMONT; ▲ Wayne; **218** SF-4; ★ **CIN**; mail Goshen z 45122, Pleasant Plain z 45162; ● 300

Edenville; RMC Place; WYANDOT; ▲ Eden, Antrim; ***216** NJ-8; mail Nevada z 44849; rural

Edgefield; RMC Place; FAYETTE; ▲ Jefferson; ***218** SD-6; elev. 1,064ft./324m.; mail Jeffersonville z 43128; rural

Edgefield; RMC Place; STARK; ***217** NI-16; ★ **CAN**; mail Canton z 44709; pop. incl. with Canton (Inc. Place)

Edgemont; RMC Place; HAMILTON; ▲ Springfield; ***218** SF-2; ★ **CIN**; mail Cincinnati z 45216; ● 350

Edgemont; RMC Place; MONTGOMERY; ★ **DAY**; pop. incl. with Dayton (Inc. Place)

Edgerton; Inc. Place; WILLIAMS; ▲ St. Joseph; **216** NF-1; 🅿; z 43517; Ⓟ 1,896; Ⓒ 2,117

Edgewater Beach; RMC Place; LICKING; ▲ Licking; ***219** SB-12; ★ **NWRK**; mail Thornville z 43076; ● 500

Edgewater Park; RMC Place; FRANKLIN; ▲ Madison; **218** SB-10; ★ **COL**; mail Columbus z 43232; ● 700

Edgewood; CDP; ASHTABULA; ▲ Ashtabula; **217** NC-19; ★ **ASHT**; mail Ashtabula z 44004; Ⓒ 4,762

Edgewood Farms; RMC Place; CLARK; ★ **SPR**; pop. incl. with Springfield (Inc. Place)

Edgwood Estates; RMC Place; ALLEN; ▲ American; ★ **LIMA**; mail Lima z 45805; ● 650

Edinburg; RMC Place; PORTAGE; ▲ Edinburg; **217** NH-17; elev. 1,181ft./360m.; ★ **AKR**; mail Ravenna z 44266, Rootstown z 44272; ● 250

Edinburg; MCD-Township; PORTAGE; ***217** NH-17; ★ **AKR**; mail Rootstown z 44272; Ⓟ 1,978; Ⓒ 2,344

Edison; Inc. Place; MORROW; ▲ Gilead; **216** NK-10; elev. 1,062ft./324m.; 🅿; z 43320; Ⓟ 488; Ⓒ 437

Edmunds; SCIOTO; see Frederick (RMC Place)

Edmunds Switch; RMC Place; SCIOTO; rural

Edon; Inc. Place; WILLIAMS; ▲ Florence; **216** NE-1; 🅿; z 43518; Ⓟ 880; Ⓒ 898

Egypt; RMC Place; AUGLAIZE; ▲ Jackson; ***216** NL-2; mail Minster z 45865; ● 40

Egypt; RMC Place; BELMONT; ▲ Kirkwood; ***219** SA-18; mail Barnesville z 43713; rural

Eifort; RMC Place; SCIOTO; ▲ Bloom; ***219** SH-11; mail South Webster z 45682; rural

Eileen Gardens; RMC Place; HAMILTON; ▲ Delhi; ***218** SG-2; elev. 880ft./268m.; ★ **CIN**; mail Cincinnati z 45238

Elba; RMC Place; WASHINGTON; ▲ Aurelius; **219** SD-17; 🅿; z 45746; ● 70

Elberta Beach; RMC Place; LORAIN; ***217** NF-12; ★ **CLEV**; mail Vermilion z 44089; pop. incl. with Vermilion (Inc. Place)

Eldean; RMC Place; MIAMI; ▲ Concord; ***218** SA-4; mail Troy z 45373; rural

Eldon (Spencer Station); RMC Place; GUERNSEY; ▲ Millwood; ***219** SB-17; mail Quaker City z 43773; ● 50

Eldorado; RMC Place; BUTLER; ★ **MIDD**; mail Middletown z 45044; pop. incl. with Middletown (Inc. Place)

Eldorado; Inc. Place; PREBLE; ▲ Monroe; **218** SB-1; 🅿; ★ **RICH**; z 45321; Ⓟ 549; Ⓒ 543

Elery; RMC Place; HENRY; ▲ Monroe; **216** NG-4; mail Malinta z 43535; ● 25

Elgin; Inc. Place; VAN WERT; ▲ York; **216** NJ-2; elev. 819ft./250m.; 🅿; z 45838; Ⓟ 71; Ⓒ 50

Elida; Inc. Place; ALLEN; ▲ American; **216** NJ-3; 🅿; ★ **LIMA**; z 45807; Ⓟ 1,486; Ⓒ 1,917

Elizabeth; MCD-Township; LAWRENCE; ***219** SJ-11; mail Pedro z 45659; Ⓟ 2,515; Ⓒ 2,914

Elizabeth; MCD-Township; MIAMI; ***218** SA-4; mail Casstown z 45312; Ⓟ 1,620; Ⓒ 1,620

Elizabethtown; RMC Place; HAMILTON; ▲ Whitewater; **218** SF-1; ★ **CIN**; mail North Bend z 45052; ● 500

Elizabethtown; RMC Place; WARREN; ▲ Franklin; ★ **MIDD**; mail Franklin z 45005; ● 250

Elk; MCD-Township; NOBLE; ***219** SC-17; mail Lower Salem z 45745; Ⓟ 378; Ⓒ 305

Elk; MCD-Township; VINTON; ***219** SF-12; mail Mc Arthur z 45651; Ⓟ 2,684; Ⓒ 3,134

Elkrun; MCD-Township; COLUMBIANA; ***217** NJ-19; mail Elkton z 44415; Ⓟ 2,186; Ⓒ 4,781

Elkton; RMC Place; COLUMBIANA; ▲ Elkrun; **217** NJ-19; elev. 897ft./273m.; 🅿; z 44415; ● 80

Ellerton; RMC Place; MONTGOMERY; ▲ Jefferson; ***218** SC-3; ★ **DAY**; mail Miamisburg z 45342; pop. incl. with Moraine (Inc. Place)

Ellet; RMC Place; SUMMIT; ***217** NH-16; ★ **AKR**; mail Akron z 44312; pop. incl. with Akron (Inc. Place)

Elliot; MORGAN; see Elliot Crossroads (RMC Place)

Elliot Crossroads (Elliot, Elliotts Crossroads); RMC Place; MORGAN; ▲ Homer; ***219** SD-14; mail Chesterhill z 43728

Elliotts Crossroads; MORGAN; see Elliot Crossroads (RMC Place)

Elliottville; RMC Place; ATHENS; ▲ Athens; ***219** SF-13; elev. 754ft./230m.; mail Athens z 45701

Ellis; RMC Place; MUSKINGUM; ▲ Muskingum; ***219** SA-14; elev. 736ft./224m.; ★ **ZAN**; mail Zanesville z 43701; rural

Ellisonville; RMC Place; LAWRENCE; ▲ Elizabeth; **219** SJ-11; mail Ironton z 45638; ● 50

Elliston; RMC Place; OTTAWA; ▲ Benton; ***216** NE-8; 🅿; z 43432; ● 150

Ellsberry (Ellsbury); RMC Place; BROWN; ▲ Huntington; **218** SI-6; mail Aberdeen z 45101; ● 60

Ellsbury; BROWN; see Ellsberry (RMC Place)

Ellsworth; RMC Place; MAHONING; ▲ Ellsworth; **217** NH-19; 🅿; ★ **YNGS-**; z 44416; ● 260

Ellsworth; MCD-Township; MAHONING; ***217** NH-19; 🅿; ★ **YNGS-**; z 44416; Ⓟ 2,103; Ⓒ 2,234

Elm Acres; RMC Place; STARK; ▲ Tuscarawas; ***217** NJ-15; ★ **CAN**; mail Massillon z 44646; ● 250

Elm Center; RMC Place; PUTNAM; ▲ Liberty; ***216** NH-4; mail Miller City z 45864; rural

Elm Grove; RMC Place; PIKE; ▲ Sunfish; **218** SG-8; elev. 618ft./188m.; mail Piketon z 45661; ● 35

Elmira; RMC Place; FULTON; ▲ German; ***216** NE-3; elev. 722ft./220m.; mail Archbold z 43502; ● 100

Elmore; Inc. Place; OTTAWA; ▲ Harris; **216** NF-8; 🅿; ★ **TOL**; z 43416; Ⓟ 1,334; Ⓒ 1,426

Elmville; RMC Place; HIGHLAND; ▲ Brushcreek; ***218** SG-7; mail Hillsboro z 45133, Peebles z 45660; rural

Elmwood Place; Inc. Place; HAMILTON; **218** SL-3; ★ **CIN**; mail Cincinnati z 45216; Ⓟ 2,937; Ⓒ 2,681

Elroy; RMC Place; DARKE; ▲ Jackson, Brown; **216** NM-1; mail Ansonia z 45303; ● 35

Elton; RMC Place; STARK; ▲ Sugar Creek; ***217** NJ-15; elev. 1,030ft./314m.; ★ **CAN**; mail Navarre z 44662; ● 150

Elyria; Inc. Place; ⊡ LORAIN; **217** NF-13; elev. 733ft./223m.; 🅿 🅷 ■; ★ **CLEV**; z 44035-36, z 44039, z 44074; Ⓟ 56,746; Ⓒ 55,953; ◆ 54,322

Elyria; MCD-Township; LORAIN; ***217** NF-13; 🅿; ★ **CLEV**; z 44035-36, z 44039, z 44074; Ⓟ 3,699; Ⓒ 3,520

Emerald; RMC Place; ADAMS; ▲ Winchester; ***218** SG-6; elev. 998ft./304m.; mail Winchester z 45697

Emerald; MCD-Township; PAULDING; ***216** NG-2; mail Paulding z 45879; Ⓟ 766; Ⓒ 824

Emerson (Trenton); RMC Place; JEFFERSON; ▲ Mount Pleasant; ***217** NM-19; ★ **WHL**; mail Dillonvale z 43917; ● 30

Emerson Heights; RMC Place; WASHINGTON; mail Marietta z 45750; pop. incl. with Marietta (Inc. Place)

Emery Chapel; RMC Place; CLARK; ▲ Springfield; ***218** SB-5; ★ **SPR**; mail Springfield z 45502; rural

Empire; Inc. Place; JEFFERSON; ▲ Knox; **217** NK-20; elev. 682ft./208m.; 🅿; ★ **STU-**; z 43926; Ⓟ 364; Ⓒ 300

Enchanted Hills; RMC Place; HIGHLAND; ▲ Paint; ***218** SF-7; mail Hillsboro z 45133; summer pop. 800; ● 400

England Station; RMC Place; ASHLAND; ▲ Montgomery; ***217** NI-12; mail Ashland z 44805; ● 30

Englewood; Inc. Place; MONTGOMERY; **218** SB-3; elev. 920ft./280m.; 🅿; ★ **DAY**; z 45322 & mail Clayton z 45315; Ⓟ 11,432; Ⓒ 12,235

English Woods; RMC Place; HAMILTON; ***218** SG-2; ★ **CIN**; mail Cincinnati z 45225; pop. incl. with Cincinnati (Inc. Place)

Enoch; MCD-Township; NOBLE; ***219** SC-16; mail Caldwell z 43724; Ⓟ 406; Ⓒ 413

Enon; Inc. Place; CLARK; ▲ Mad River; **218** SB-5; 🅿; ★ **SPR**; z 45323; Ⓟ 2,605; Ⓒ 2,638

Enterprise; RMC Place; HOCKING; ▲ Falls; **219** SD-12; elev. 749ft./228m.; mail Logan z 43138; ● 170

Enterprise; RMC Place; PREBLE; ▲ Lanier; ***218** SC-2; ★ **DAY**; mail West Alexandria z 45381; ● 40

Epworth; RMC Place; RICHLAND; ▲ Weller; **217** NI-11; mail Mansfield z 44903

Epworth Heights; RMC Place; CLERMONT; ▲ Miami; **218** SK-5; ★ **CIN**; mail Loveland z 45140; ● 150

Era; RMC Place; PICKAWAY; ▲ Darby; **218** SC-8; ★ **COL**; mail Mount Sterling z 43143; ● 130

Erastus (Murphysburg); RMC Place; MERCER; ▲ Washington; ***216** NK-1; elev. 892ft./272m.; mail Celina z 45822; ● 25

Erhart; RMC Place; MEDINA; ▲ Litchfield, Liverpool, York; ***217** NG-14; ★ **CLEV**; mail Medina z 44256; ● 90

Erie; MCD-Township; OTTAWA; ***216** NE-9; ★ **TOL**; mail Lacarne z 43439; Ⓟ 1,454; Ⓒ 1,328

ERIE; **216** NF-10; Ⓟ 76,779; Ⓒ 79,551; ◆ 75,535

Erieview; RMC Place; CUYAHOGA; ★ **CLEV**; mail Cleveland z 44114; pop. incl. with Cleveland (Inc. Place)

Eris; RMC Place; CHAMPAIGN; ▲ Concord; **216** NN-5; mail Urbana z 43078; ● 25

Erlin; RMC Place; SANDUSKY; ▲ Riley; **216** NF-9; mail Fremont z 43420; ● 80

Espyville; RMC Place; MARION; ▲ Big Island; **216** NK-8; mail Marion z 43302; ● 80

Essex; RMC Place; UNION; ▲ Jackson; ***216** NL-7; mail Richwood z 43344; ● 90

Etna; RMC Place; LICKING; ▲ Etna; **219** SB-11; elev. 1,069ft./326m.; 🅿; ★ **COL**; z 43018; ● 500

Etna; MCD-Township; LICKING; ***218** SB-10; 🅿; ★ **COL**; z 43018; Ⓟ 6,439; Ⓒ 5,410

Euclid; Inc. Place; CUYAHOGA; **217** NE-16; elev. 618ft./188m.; 🅿 🅷 ■; ★ **CLEV**; z 44117, z 44119, z 44123, z 44132, z 44143; Ⓟ 54,875; Ⓒ 52,717; ◆ 47,835

Euclid Heights; RMC Place; BUTLER; ★ **MIDD**; mail Middletown z 45044; pop. incl. with Middletown (Inc. Place)

Eureka (Chambersburg); RMC Place; GALLIA; ▲ Clay; **219** SI-13; mail Gallipolis z 45631; ● 100

Eureka; RMC Place; MAHONING; ▲ Beaver; ***217** NI-19; ★ **YNGS-**; mail Columbiana z 44408; rural

Evansport; RMC Place; DEFIANCE; ▲ Tiffin; **216** NF-3; 🅿; z 43519, z 43557; ● 300

Evanston; RMC Place; HAMILTON; ***218** SG-2; ★ **CIN**; mail Cincinnati z 45207; pop. incl. with Cincinnati (Inc. Place)

Evansville; RMC Place; TRUMBULL; ▲ Weathersfield; **217** NC-12; ★ **YNGS-**; mail Mineral Ridge z 44440, Niles z 44446; ● 200

Evendale; Inc. Place; HAMILTON; **218** SK-4; ★ **CIN**; mail Cincinnati z 45215, z 45241; Ⓟ 3,175; Ⓒ 3,090

Everett; RMC Place; SUMMIT; ▲ Boston; **217** NG-15; elev. 731ft./223m.; ★ **AKR**; mail Peninsula z 44264; ● 25

Evergreen; RMC Place; GALLIA; ▲ Springfield; ***219** SH-13; mail Bidwell z 45614; ● 75

Evergreen; RMC Place; WASHINGTON; ▲ Marietta; mail Marietta z 45750; ● 50

Ewing; RMC Place; HOCKING; ▲ Washington; **219** SE-12; mail Logan z 43138; ● 30

Ewington; RMC Place; GALLIA; ▲ Huntington; **219** SG-12; mail Vinton z 45686; ● 65

Excello (Amanda); RMC Place; BUTLER; ▲ Lemon; **218** SD-3; ★ **MIDD**; mail Middletown z 45044; ● 50

F

Fairborn; Inc. Place; GREENE; ▲ Bath; **218** SB-4; 🅿; ★ **DAY**; z 45324; Ⓟ 31,300; Ⓒ 32,052; ◆ 34,585

Fairbrondt; RMC Place; CRAWFORD; ▲ Jefferson; mail Galion z 44833; ● 400

Fairdale; RMC Place; GUERNSEY; ▲ Cambridge, Adams; ***219** SA-16; mail Cambridge z 43725; ● 660

Fairfax; Inc. Place; HAMILTON; ▲ Columbia; **218** SL-4; ★ **CIN**; mail Cincinnati z 45227, Hillsboro z 45133; Ⓟ 2,029; Ⓒ 1,938

Fairfax; RMC Place; HIGHLAND; ▲ Jackson, Concord; **218** SG-6; elev. 1,129ft./344m.; mail Cincinnati z 45227, Hillsboro z 45133; ● 40

Fairfield; Inc. Place; BUTLER, HAMILTON; **218** SE-2; 🅿 ■; ★ **CIN**; z 45011, z 45014, z 45018; Ⓟ 39,729; Ⓒ 42,097; ◆ 43,953

Fairfield; MCD-Township; BUTLER; ***218** SE-2; 🅿; ★ **CIN**; z 45011, z 45014, z 45018; Ⓟ 9,644; Ⓒ 15,571

Fairfield; MCD-Township; COLUMBIANA; ***217** NI-19; ★ **YNGS-**; mail Columbiana z 44408; Ⓟ 8,981; Ⓒ 9,583

Fairfield; RMC Place; GREENE; ★ **DAY**; mail Fairborn z 45324; pop. incl. with Fairborn (Inc. Place)

Fairfield; MCD-Township; HIGHLAND; ***218** SE-7; mail Leesburg z 45135; Ⓟ 2,616; Ⓒ 3,219

Fairfield; MCD-Township; HURON; ***217** NH-11; mail North Fairfield z 44855; Ⓟ 1,229; Ⓒ 1,284

Fairfield; RMC Place; JEFFERSON; ▲ Salem; **217** NL-19; ★ **STU-**; mail Richmond z 43944; ● 50

Fairfield; MCD-Township; MADISON; ***218** SB-8; mail West Jefferson z 43162; Ⓟ 1,331; Ⓒ 1,333

Fairfield; MCD-Township; TUSCARAWAS; ***217** NK-16; mail Somerdale z 44678; Ⓟ 1,238; Ⓒ 1,487

Fairfield; MCD-Township; WASHINGTON; ***219** SE-15; mail Cutler z 45724; Ⓟ 874; Ⓒ 1,011

FAIRFIELD; **219** SB-11; Ⓟ 103,461; Ⓒ 122,759; Ⓡ 122,881; ◆ 142,445

Fairfield Beach; CDP; FAIRFIELD; ▲ Walnut; ***219** SB-12; ★ **COL**; mail Thornville z 43076; Ⓟ 1,084; Ⓒ 1,163

Fairground Acres; RMC Place; CLINTON; ▲ Marion; ***218** SF-5; mail Blanchester z 45107; pop. incl. with Blanchester (Inc. Place)

Fairhaven; RMC Place; PREBLE; ▲ Israel; **218** SD-1; mail Camden z 45311, College Corner z 45003; ● 200

Fairhope; RMC Place; STARK; ▲ Nimishillen; **217** NJ-17; ★ **CAN**; mail Louisville z 44641; ● 1,720

Fairlawn; Inc. Place; SUMMIT; ▲ Copley; **217** NH-15; 🅿 ■; ★ **AKR**; z 44333-34, z 44398 & mail Akron z 44313; Ⓟ 5,779; Ⓒ 7,307; ◆ 7,241

Fairlawn Heights; RMC Place; TRUMBULL; ▲ Howland; ***217** NG-19; ★ **YNGS-**; mail Warren z 44484; ● 90

Fairmount; RMC Place; HAMILTON; ***218** SG-2; ★ **CIN**; mail Cincinnati z 45211, z 45214; pop. incl. with Cincinnati (Inc. Place)

Fair Oaks; RMC Place; CLERMONT; ▲ Monroe; ***218** SG-4; ★ **CIN**; mail Amelia z 45102; rural

Fairplay; RMC Place; BUTLER; ***218** SE-2; ★ **CIN**; mail Fairfield z 45014; pop. incl. with Fairfield (Inc. Place)

Fairplay; RMC Place; JEFFERSON; ▲ Wayne; ***217** NL-19; ★ **STU-**; mail Bloomingdale z 43910; rural

Fairpoint; RMC Place; BELMONT; ▲ Wheeling; **217** NN-18; elev. 914ft./279m.; 🅿; z 43927; ● 500

Fairport; LAKE; see Fairport Harbor (Inc. Place)

Fairport Harbor (Fairport); Inc. Place; LAKE; ▲ Painesville; **217** ND-17; 🅿; ★ **CLEV**; z 44077; Ⓟ 2,978; Ⓒ 3,180

Fairview; CUYAHOGA; see Fairview Park (Inc. Place)

Fairview; Inc. Place; GUERNSEY, BELMONT; ▲ Kirkwood, Oxford; **217** NN-17; 🅿; z 43736; Ⓟ 79; Ⓒ 81

Fairview; RMC Place; GUERNSEY; ▲ Valley; ***219** SB-16; 🅿; z 43736 & mail Pleasant City z 43772; ● 200

Fairview; RMC Place; HIGHLAND; ▲ Union; **218** SF-6; elev. 1,027ft./313m.; mail Hillsboro z 45133; ● 50

Fairview; RMC Place; MONTGOMERY; ***218** SC-4; ★ **DAY**; pop. incl. with Dayton (Inc. Place)

Fairview Heights; RMC Place; JEFFERSON; ▲ Island Creek; ★ **STU-**; mail Toronto z 43964

Fairview Heights; RMC Place; WASHINGTON; mail Marietta z 45750; pop. incl. with Marietta (Inc. Place)

Fairview Lanes; CDP; ERIE; ▲ Perkins; ***216** NF-10; ★ **SNDSK**; mail Sandusky z 44870; Ⓟ 1,120; Ⓒ 1,015

Fairview Park (Fairview); Inc. Place; CUYAHOGA; **217** NF-14; 🅿; ★ **CLEV**; z 44126; Ⓟ 18,028; Ⓒ 17,572

Fairway Terrace; RMC Place; CLARK; ▲ Bethel; ***218** SB-4; ★ **DAY**; mail Medway z 45341; ● 350

Fairway View Estates; RMC Place; ALLEN; ▲ Shawnee; ***216** NJ-4; ★ **LIMA**; mail Lima z 45805; ● 700

Fairwind Acres; RMC Place; HAMILTON; ***218** SF-3; ★ **CIN**; mail Cincinnati z 45242; pop. incl. with Montgomery (Inc. Place)

Falls; MCD-Township; HOCKING; ***219** SD-12; mail Logan z 43138; Ⓟ 10,878; Ⓒ 11,409

Falls; MCD-Township; MUSKINGUM; ***219** SB-14; ★ **ZAN**; mail Zanesville z 43701; Ⓟ 8,524; Ⓒ 8,585

Fallsburg; RMC Place; LICKING; ▲ Fallsbury; **217** NM-12; elev. 1,006ft./307m.; mail Frazeysburg z 43822; ● 80

Fallsbury; MCD-Township; LICKING; ***217** NM-12; mail Frazeysburg z 43822; Ⓟ 739; Ⓒ 865

Falls Junction; CUYAHOGA; see Glenwillow (Inc. Place)

Fargo; RMC Place; MORROW; ▲ Bennington; ***216** NL-10; elev. 1,081ft./329m.; mail Marengo z 43334, Sunbury z 43074

Farmdale; RMC Place; TRUMBULL; ▲ Kinsman; **217** NF-20; elev. 936ft./285m.; 🅿; z 44417; ● 200

Farmer; RMC Place; DEFIANCE; ▲ Farmer; **216** NF-1; 🅿; z 43520; ● 120

Farmer; MCD-Township; DEFIANCE; ***216** NF-1; 🅿; z 43520; Ⓟ 808; Ⓒ 932

Farmers; RMC Place; CLINTON; ▲ Clark; **218** SE-6; elev. 1,062ft./324m.; mail Martinsville z 45146; ● 45

Farmerstown; RMC Place; HOLMES; ▲ Clark; **217** NL-15; 🅿; z 43804; ● 330

Farmersville; Inc. Place; MONTGOMERY; ▲ Jackson; **218** SC-3; elev. 882ft./269m.; 🅿; ★ **DAY**; z 45325; Ⓟ 932; Ⓒ 980

Farmington; RMC Place; BELMONT; ▲ Colerain; ***217** NN-19; ★ **WHL**; mail Bridgeport z 43912; rural

Farmington; MCD-Township; TRUMBULL; ***217** NF-18; mail West Farmington z 44491; Ⓟ 1,897; Ⓒ 2,353

Farnham; RMC Place; ASHTABULA; ***217** NC-20; mail Conneaut z 44030; pop. incl. with Conneaut (Inc. Place)

Farrington; RMC Place; MIAMI; ▲ Washington; ***218** SA-3; mail Troy z 45373; rural

Fashion Heights; RMC Place; HAMILTON; ▲ Delhi; ***218** SG-2; elev. 850ft./259m.; ★ **CIN**; mail Cincinnati z 45238

Fawcett; RMC Place; ADAMS; ▲ Meigs; ***218** SH-7; elev. 837ft./255m.; mail Blue Creek z 45616, Peebles z 45660

Fayette; Inc. Place; FULTON; ▲ Gorham; **216** ND-3; 🅿; z 43521; Ⓟ 1,248; Ⓒ 1,340

Fayette; MCD-Township; LAWRENCE; ***219** SK-11; ★ **HNTG**; mail South Point z 45680; Ⓟ 9,181; Ⓒ 9,169

FAYETTE; **218** SD-8; Ⓟ 27,466; Ⓒ 28,433; ◆ 28,389

Fayetteville; Inc. Place; BROWN; ▲ Perry; **218** SF-5; elev. 944ft./288m.; 🅿; z 45118; Ⓟ 393; Ⓒ 372

Fay Gardens; RMC Place; CLERMONT; ▲ Wayne; ★ **CIN**; mail Loveland z 45140; ● 250

Fearing; MCD-Township; WASHINGTON; ***219** SD-17; ★ **PRKB**; mail Whipple z 45788; Ⓟ 825; Ⓒ 910

Federal Reserve; RMC Place; CUYAHOGA; ★ **CLEV**; mail Cleveland z 44114; pop. incl. with Cleveland (Inc. Place)

Feed Springs; RMC Place; HARRISON; ▲ Franklin; ***217** NL-17; elev. 882ft./269m.; mail Uhrichsville z 44683; rural

Feesburg; RMC Place; BROWN; ▲ Lewis; **218** SH-4; 🅿; z 45119; ● 500

Felicity; Inc. Place; CLERMONT; ▲ Franklin; **218** SH-4; 🅿; z 45120; Ⓟ 856; Ⓒ 922

Fernald; RMC Place; HAMILTON; ▲ Crosby; **218** SJ-1; ★ **CIN**; mail Harrison z 45030; ● 25

Fernbank; RMC Place; HAMILTON; ***218** SG-1; ★ **CIN**; mail Cincinnati z 45233; pop. incl. with Cincinnati (Inc. Place)

Fernell Heights; RMC Place; CLERMONT; ▲ Union; **218** SM-5; ★ **CIN**; mail Cincinnati z 45244; ● 330

Fernwood; RMC Place; JEFFERSON; ▲ Cross Creek; ***217** NL-19; ★ **STU-**; mail Steubenville z 43952; rural

Ferry; RMC Place; ERIE; ▲ Perkins; ★ **SNDSK**; mail Sandusky z 44870; ● 150

Ferry; RMC Place; GREENE; ▲ Silvercreek; ***218** SD-4; ★ **DAY**; mail Waynesville z 45068; rural

Fields Terrace; RMC Place; LAWRENCE; ▲ Union; ★ **HNTG**; mail Chesapeake z 45619

Filburns Island; RMC Place; SHELBY; ▲ McLean; ***216** NL-3; mail Minster z 45865; ● 100

Fincastle; RMC Place; BROWN; ▲ Eagle; **218** SG-6; mail Sardinia z 45171; ● 85

Findlater Garden; RMC Place; HAMILTON; ***218** SF-2; elev. 570ft./174m.; ★ **CIN**; mail Cincinnati z 45232; pop. incl. with Cincinnati (Inc. Place)

Findlay; Inc. Place; ⊡ HANCOCK; **216** NH-6; 🅿 🅷 🅲 3,900 ■; ★ **FIND**; z 45839-40; Ⓟ 35,703; Ⓒ 38,967; ◆ 37,664

Findley Gardens; RMC Place; JEFFERSON; ▲ Island Creek; ★ **STU-**; mail Toronto z 43964; rural

Finneytown; CDP; HAMILTON; ▲ Springfield; **218** SK-3; ★ **CIN**; mail Cincinnati z 45224, z 45231; Ⓟ 13,096; Ⓒ 13,492

Fire Brick; RMC Place; LAWRENCE; ▲ Washington; ***219** SH-11; mail Oak Hill z 45656; rural

Fireside; RMC Place; SENECA; ▲ Thompson; ***216** NG-9; mail Bellevue z 44811; rural

Firestone Park; RMC Place; SUMMIT; ***217** NH-16; ★ **AKR**; mail Akron z 44301, z 44319; pop. incl. with Akron (Inc. Place)

Fishack; RMC Place; OTTAWA; ▲ Portage; mail Port Clinton z 43452; ● 30

Fitchville; RMC Place; HURON; ▲ Fitchville; **217** NH-11; mail New London z 44851; ● 350

Fitchville; MCD-Township; HURON; ***217** NH-11; mail New London z 44851; Ⓟ 889; Ⓒ 1,012

Five Forks; RMC Place; COLUMBIANA; ▲ Franklin; ***217** NJ-18; mail Salineville z 43945; rural

Fivemile; RMC Place; BROWN; ▲ Green; ***218** SG-5; elev. 953ft./290m.; mail Mount Orab z 45154

Five Points; RMC Place; GREENE; ★ **DAY**; mail Fairborn z 45324; pop. incl. with Fairborn (Inc. Place)

Five Points; RMC Place; MAHONING; ▲ Beaver; ***217** NI-20; elev. 1,111ft./339m.; ★ **YNGS-**; mail North Lima z 44452, Youngstown z 44514; rural

Five Points; RMC Place; PICKAWAY; ▲ Monroe; **218** SC-8; mail Mount Sterling z 43143, Williamsport z 43164; ● 120

Five Points; RMC Place; SUMMIT; ★ **AKR**; mail Akron z 44302; pop. incl. with Akron (Inc. Place)

Five Points; RMC Place; TRUMBULL; ▲ Hartford; ***217** NF-20; elev. 1,034ft./315m.; ★ **YNGS-**; mail Burghill z 44404; ● 25

Five Points; CDP; WARREN; ▲ Clear Creek; ***218** SD-4; elev. 993ft./303m.; ★ **DAY**; mail Springboro z 45066; Ⓟ 1,554; Ⓒ 2,191

Flatiron; RMC Place; PERRY; ▲ Harrison; ***219** SC-13; ★ **ZAN**; mail Crooksville z 43731; rural

Flat Iron; RMC Place; WARREN; ▲ Clear Creek; ***218** SD-3; ★ **DAY**; mail Franklin z 45005; ● 100

Flatrock; MCD-Township; HENRY; ***216** NG-4; mail Napoleon z 43545; Ⓟ 1,370; Ⓒ 1,254

Flat Rock; RMC Place; SENECA; ▲ Thompson; **216** NG-9; 🅿; z 44828; ● 300

Fleatown; RMC Place; LICKING; ▲ Licking; ***219** SA-12; ★ **NWRK**; mail Newark z 43055

Fleetwood Addition; RMC Place; UNION; ▲ Paris; mail Marysville z 43040; pop. incl. with Marysville (Inc. Place)

Fleming; RMC Place; WASHINGTON; ▲ Barlow; **219** SE-16; elev. 797ft./243m.; 🅿; z 45729; ● 40

Fletcher; Inc. Place; MIAMI; ▲ Brown; **216** NN-4; 🅿; z 45326; Ⓟ 545; Ⓒ 510

Flint; RMC Place; FRANKLIN; ▲ Sharon; ***216** NN-9; elev. 937ft./286m.; ★ **COL**

Florence; RMC Place; BELMONT; ▲ Pease; **217** NN-19; ★ **WHL**; mail Martins Ferry z 43935; ● 150

Florence; RMC Place; ERIE; ▲ Florence; **217** NG-12; ★ **CLEV**; mail Berlin Heights z 44814; ● 200

Florence; MCD-Township; ERIE; ***217** NF-12; ★ **CLEV**; mail Berlin Heights z 44814; Ⓟ 2,101; Ⓒ 2,500

Florence; RMC Place; NOBLE; ▲ Noble; **219** SC-16; mail Caldwell z 43724; ● 100

Florence; MCD-Township; WILLIAMS; ***216** NE-1; mail Edon z 43518; Ⓟ 1,956; Ⓒ 2,115

Florida; Inc. Place; HENRY; ▲ Flatrock; **216** NF-3; 🅿; z 43545; Ⓟ 304; Ⓒ 246

Flushing; Inc. Place; BELMONT; ▲ Flushing; **217** NN-18; 🅿; z 43977; Ⓟ 1,042; Ⓒ 900

Flushing; MCD-Township; BELMONT; ***217** NN-18; 🅿; z 43977; Ⓟ 2,081; Ⓒ 1,990

Fly; RMC Place; MONROE; ▲ Jackson; **219** SD-18; 🅿; z 45767; ● 80

Footville; RMC Place; ASHTABULA; ▲ Trumbull; **217** ND-18; mail Rock Creek z 44084

Foraker; RMC Place; HARDIN; ▲ Lynn; **216** NJ-5; elev. 977ft./298m.; mail Alger z 45812, Kenton z 43326; ● 130

Forest; Inc. Place; HARDIN; ▲ Jackson; **216** NJ-7; 🅿; z 45843; Ⓟ 1,594; Ⓒ 1,488

Forestdale; RMC Place; LAWRENCE; ▲ Perry; ***219** SJ-11; ★ **HNTG**; mail Ironton z 45638; rural

Forest Hill; RMC Place; SUMMIT; ***217** NH-16; ★ **AKR**; pop. incl. with Akron (Inc. Place)

Forest Hills; RMC Place; CLARK; ▲ Springfield, German; **217** NA-15; ★ **SPR**; mail Springfield z 45504; ● 200

Forest Hills Estates; RMC Place; HAMILTON; ▲ Anderson; ***218** SG-3; ★ **CIN**; mail Cincinnati z 45230; ● 300

Forest Park; Inc. Place; HAMILTON; **218** SF-2; ★ **CIN**; mail Cincinnati z 45240; Ⓟ 18,609; Ⓒ 19,463

Forest Park; RMC Place; MONTGOMERY; ▲ Harrison; ***218** SC-4; ★ **DAY**; mail Dayton z 45405; pop. incl. with Dayton (Inc. Place)

Forest View; RMC Place; JEFFERSON; ▲ Cross Creek; ***217** NL-19; ★ **STU-**; mail Steubenville z 43952; ● 200

Forestville; CDP; HAMILTON; ▲ Anderson; **218** SG-3; ★ **CIN**; mail Cincinnati z 45230, z 45255; Ⓟ 9,185; Ⓒ 10,978

Fort Jefferson; RMC Place; DARKE; ▲ Neave; **218** SA-2; mail Greenville z 45331; ● 80

Fort Jennings; Inc. Place; PUTNAM; ▲ Jennings; **216** NI-3; 🅿; z 45844; Ⓟ 436; Ⓒ 432

Fort Loramie (Loramie); Inc. Place; SHELBY; ▲ McLean; **216** NL-3; elev. 953ft./290m.; 🅿; z 45845; Ⓟ 1,042; Ⓒ 1,344

Fort McKinley; CDP; MONTGOMERY; ▲ Harrison; ***218** SC-3; ★ **DAY**; mail Dayton z 45426; Ⓟ 4,246; Ⓒ 3,989

Fort Meigs Place; RMC Place; WOOD; ▲ Perrysburg; ***216** NE-6; ★ **TOL**; mail Perrysburg z 43551; ● 250

Fort Miami Addition; RMC Place; LUCAS; ★ **TOL**; mail Maumee z 43537; pop. incl. with Maumee (Inc. Place)

Fort Recovery; Inc. Place; MERCER; ▲ Recovery, Gibson; **216** NL-1; elev. 948ft./289m.; 🅿; z 45846; Ⓟ 1,313; Ⓒ 1,273

Fort Scott Camps; RMC Place; HAMILTON; ▲ Crosby; ★ **CIN**; mail Harrison z 45030; summer pop. 500

Fort Seneca; RMC Place; SENECA; ▲ Pleasant; **216** NG-8; 🅿; z 44883; ● 230

Fort Shawnee; Inc. Place; ALLEN; **216** NJ-4; elev. 866ft./264m.; ★ **LIMA**; mail Lima z 45806; Ⓟ 4,128; Ⓒ 3,855

Foster; RMC Place; WARREN; ▲ Deerfield; ***218** SE-3; ★ **CIN**; mail Maineville z 45039

Fosterville; RMC Place; MAHONING; ***217** NH-19; ★ **YNGS-**; mail Youngstown z 44511; pop. incl. with Youngstown (Inc. Place)

Fostoria; Inc. Place; SENECA, HANCOCK, WOOD; **216** NH-7; elev. 780ft./238m.; 🅿 🅷; z 44830; Ⓟ 14,983; Ⓒ 13,931

Fountain Park; RMC Place; CHAMPAIGN; ▲ Rush; ***216** NM-6; elev. 1,093ft./333m.; mail Woodstock z 43084; ● 30

Fowler; RMC Place; TRUMBULL; ▲ Fowler; **217** NG-19; 🅿; ★ **YNGS-**; z 44418; ● 250

Fowler; MCD-Township; TRUMBULL; ***217** NF-19; 🅿; ★ **YNGS-**; z 44418; Ⓟ 2,868; Ⓒ 2,733

Fowlers Mill; RMC Place; GEAUGA; ▲ Munson; **217** NE-17; ★ **CLEV**; mail Chardon z 44024; ● 320

Fox; MCD-Township; CARROLL; ***217** NK-18; mail Salineville z 43945; Ⓟ 1,033; Ⓒ 1,075

Fox; RMC Place; PICKAWAY; ▲ Jackson; **218** SD-9; mail Circleville z 43113; ● 25

Foxboro Manor; RMC Place; MONTGOMERY; ▲ Butler; ★ **DAY**; mail Vandalia z 45377; pop. incl. with Vandalia (Inc. Place)

Foxborough Commons; RMC Place; ERIE; ▲ Perkins; ***216** NF-10; ★ **SNDSK**; mail Sandusky z 44870; ● 250

Fox Chase; RMC Place; FULTON; ▲ German; ***216** NE-3; mail Archbold z 43502; pop. incl. with Archbold (Inc. Place)

Fox Hollow; RMC Place; LUCAS; ▲ Monclova; ***216** NE-6; ★ **TOL**; mail Monclova z 43542; ● 250

Frank; RMC Place; SENECA; ▲ Thompson; ***216** NG-10; mail Bellevue z 44811; ● 35

Frankfort; Inc. Place; ROSS; ▲ Concord; **218** SE-8; 🅿; z 45628; Ⓟ 1,065; Ⓒ 1,011

Franklin; MCD-Township; ADAMS; ***218** SG-8; mail Peebles z 45660; Ⓟ 1,098; Ⓒ 1,167

Franklin; MCD-Township; BROWN; ***218** SH-5; mail Georgetown z 45121; Ⓟ 1,061; Ⓒ 1,596

Franklin; MCD-Township; CLERMONT; ***218** SH-4; ★ **CIN**; mail Felicity z 45120; Ⓟ 3,803; Ⓒ 4,348

Franklin; MCD-Township; COLUMBIANA; ***217** NJ-19; mail Summitville z 43962; Ⓟ 777; Ⓒ 766

Franklin; MCD-Township; COSHOCTON; ***217** NM-14; mail Conesville z 43811; Ⓟ 1,376; Ⓒ 1,286

Franklin; MCD-Township; DARKE; ***218** SA-2; mail Arcanum z 45304; Ⓟ 1,267; Ⓒ 1,206

Franklin; MCD-Township; FRANKLIN; ***218** SB-9; ★ **COL**; mail Columbus z 43204, z 43223; Ⓟ 14,757; Ⓒ 11,798

Franklin; MCD-Township; FULTON; ***216** NE-3; mail Archbold z 43502; Ⓟ 740; Ⓒ 739

Franklin; MCD-Township; HARRISON; ***217** NL-17; mail Tippecanoe z 44699; Ⓟ 609; Ⓒ 641

Franklin; MCD-Township; JACKSON; ***219** SH-11; mail Jackson z 45640; Ⓟ 1,420; Ⓒ 1,913

Franklin; MCD-Township; LICKING; ***219** SB-12; mail Newark z 43055; Ⓟ 1,349; Ⓒ 1,782

Franklin; MCD-Township; MERCER; ***216** NL-2; mail Montezuma z 45866; Ⓟ 2,126; Ⓒ 2,303

Franklin; MCD-Township; MONROE; ***219** SC-17; mail Lewisville z 43754; Ⓟ 436; Ⓒ 453

Franklin; MCD-Township; MORROW; ***216** NK-10; mail Mount Gilead z 43338; Ⓟ 972; Ⓒ 1,410

Franklin; MCD-Township; PORTAGE; ***217** NG-16; ★ **AKR**; mail Kent z 44240; Ⓟ 34,968; Ⓒ 5,276

Franklin; MCD-Township; RICHLAND; ***217** NI-11; ★ **MANS**; mail Shelby z 44875; Ⓟ 1,713; Ⓒ 1,772

Franklin; MCD-Township; ROSS; ***218** SF-10; mail Chillicothe z 45601; Ⓟ 1,655; Ⓒ 1,671

Franklin; MCD-Township; SHELBY; ***216** NL-4; mail Russia z 45363; Ⓟ 2,375; Ⓒ 2,842

Franklin; MCD-Township; TUSCARAWAS; ***217** NK-16; ★ **CAN**; mail Strasburg z 44680; Ⓟ 3,532; Ⓒ 4,244

Franklin; Inc. Place; WARREN; ▲ Franklin; **218** SD-3; 🅿; ★ **MIDD**; z 45005; Ⓟ 11,026; Ⓒ 11,396

Franklin; MCD-Township; WARREN; ***218** SD-3; 🅿; ★ **MIDD**; z 45005; Ⓟ 27,476; Ⓒ 27,794; Ⓡ 27,897

Franklin; MCD-Township; WAYNE; ***217** NJ-14; mail Fredericksburg z 44627; Ⓟ 2,747; Ⓒ 3,485

FRANKLIN; **218** SB-8; Ⓟ 961,437; Ⓒ 1,068,978; Ⓡ 1,068,869; ◆ 1,160,202

Franklin Furnace; CDP; SCIOTO; ▲ Green; **218** SJ-10; 🅿; ★ **HNTG**; z 45629; Ⓟ 1,212; Ⓒ 1,537

Franklin Square; RMC Place; COLUMBIANA; ▲ Salem; **217** NI-19; mail Leetonia z 44431; ● 240

Frazeysburg; Inc. Place; MUSKINGUM; ▲ Jackson; **217** NN-13; 🅿; z 43822; Ⓟ 1,165; Ⓒ 1,201

Frederick; RMC Place; MIAMI; ▲ Union, Monroe; **218** SB-3; ★ **DAY**; mail Tipp City z 45371; ● 150

Frederick (Edmunds); RMC Place; SCIOTO; ▲ Bloom; ***218** SI-10; elev. 572ft./174m.; mail Wheelersburg z 45694; rural

Fredericksburg; Inc. Place; WAYNE; ▲ Salt Creek; **217** NJ-14; elev. 972ft./296m.; 🅿; z 44627; Ⓟ 502; Ⓒ 487

Fredericksdale; RMC Place; NOBLE; ▲ Center; ***219** SC-16; mail Sarahsville z 43779

Fredericktown; RMC Place; COLUMBIANA; ▲ St. Clair; **217** NJ-20; ★ **E.LIV**; mail East Liverpool z 43920; ● 200

Fredericktown; Inc. Place; KNOX; **217** NL-11; elev. 1,130ft./344m.; 🅿; z 43019; Ⓟ 2,443; Ⓒ 2,428

Fredonia; RMC Place; LICKING; ▲ McKean; ***217** NN-11; elev. 1,245ft./379m.; mail Granville z 43023; ● 70

Freeburg; RMC Place; STARK; ▲ Washington; **217** NI-17; ★ **ALLI**; mail Paris z 44669; ● 90

Freedom; MCD-Township; HENRY; ***216** NF-4; mail Napoleon z 43545; Ⓟ 853; Ⓒ 1,002

Freedom; RMC Place; PORTAGE; ▲ Freedom; **217** NG-17; ★ **AKR**; mail Windham z 44288; ● 90

Freedom; MCD-Township; PORTAGE; ***217** NG-17; ★ **AKR**; mail Windham z 44288; Ⓟ 2,530; Ⓒ 2,751

Freedom; MCD-Township; WOOD; ***216** NF-7; mail Pemberville z 43450; Ⓟ 2,520; Ⓒ 2,695

Freeland; RMC Place; MUSKINGUM; ▲ Rich Hill; **219** SB-15; mail Chandlersville z 43727; rural

Freemans Gardens; RMC Place; LUCAS; ***216** NE-6; ★ **TOL**; pop. incl. with Toledo (Inc. Place)

Freeport; Inc. Place; HARRISON; ▲ Freeport; **217** NM-17; 🅿; z 43973; Ⓟ 475; Ⓒ 398

Freeport; MCD-Township; HARRISON; ***217** NM-17; 🅿; z 43973; Ⓟ 914; Ⓒ 763

Fremont; Inc. Place; ⊡ SANDUSKY; **216** NF-8; 🅿 🅷 ■; z 43420; Ⓟ 17,648; Ⓒ 17,375; ◆ 16,939

Frenchtown; RMC Place; DARKE; ▲ Wayne; **216** NM-2; mail Versailles z 45380; ● 60

Frenchtown; RMC Place; SENECA; ▲ Big Spring; ***216** NH-7; elev. 856ft./261m.; mail Carey z 43316; ● 50

Fresno; RMC Place; COSHOCTON; ▲ White Eyes; **217** NL-15; 🅿; z 43824; ● 180

Friendship; RMC Place; SCIOTO; ▲ Nile; **218** SI-9; 🅿; z 45630; ● 500

Frischkorn Heights; RMC Place; COLUMBIANA; ▲ Yellow Creek; ***217** NK-19; ★ **E.LIV**; mail Wellsville z 43968; rural

Frontier Park; RMC Place; HAMILTON; ▲ Green; ***218** SF-2; ★ **CIN**; mail Cincinnati z 45239; ● 500

Frontier Town; RMC Place; MAHONING; ▲ Poland; ***217** NH-20; ★ **YNGS-**; mail Youngstown z 44514; ● 1,700

Frost; RMC Place; ATHENS; ▲ Rome; **219** SF-15; mail Coolville z 45723; ● 25

Fruitdale; RMC Place; ROSS; ▲ Paint; **218** SF-8; mail Bainbridge z 45612; ● 50

Fruit Hill; CDP; HAMILTON; ▲ Anderson; **218** SG-3; ★ **CIN**; mail Cincinnati z 45230; Ⓟ 4,101; Ⓒ 3,945

Fryburg; RMC Place; AUGLAIZE; ▲ Pusheta; **216** NK-4; mail Wapakoneta z 45895; ● 150

Fryburg; RMC Place; HOLMES; ▲ Salt Creek; ***217** NK-14; elev. 1,087ft./331m.; mail Millersburg z 44654; rural

Frys Corners; RMC Place; DARKE; ▲ Neave; ***218** SA-2; mail Greenville z 45331; rural

Frytown; RMC Place; MONTGOMERY; ▲ Jefferson; **218** SC-3; elev. 851ft./259m.; ★ **DAY**; mail Dayton z 45418; ● 45

Fulda; RMC Place; NOBLE; ▲ Enoch; **219** SC-17; mail Caldwell z 43724; ● 40

Fulton; MCD-Township; FULTON; ***216** NE-5; ★ **TOL**; mail Swanton z 43558; Ⓟ 3,193; Ⓒ 3,261

Fulton; Inc. Place; MORROW; ▲ Lincoln; **216** NL-10; elev. 1,057ft./322m.; 🅿; z 43321; Ⓟ 325; Ⓒ 264

FULTON; **216** NE-4; Ⓟ 38,498; Ⓒ 42,084; ◆ 42,332

Fultonham; Inc. Place; MUSKINGUM; ▲ Newton; **219** SB-13; 🅿; ★ **ZAN**; z 43738; Ⓟ 178; Ⓒ 151

Funk; RMC Place; WAYNE; ▲ Plain; **217** NJ-13; elev. 978ft./298m.; mail Wooster z 44691; ● 110

Fursville; RMC Place; LICKING; ***218** SA-10; ★ **COL**; mail Pataskala z 43062; pop. incl. with Pataskala (Inc. Place)

G

Gabels Corner; RMC Place; SANDUSKY; ▲ Washington; ***216** NG-8; mail Fremont z 43420; rural

Gage; RMC Place; GALLIA; ▲ Perry; ***219** SI-12; elev. 666ft./203m.; mail Patriot z 45658; rural

Gageville; RMC Place; ASHTABULA; ▲ Sheffield; ***217** NC-19; mail Kingsville z 44048; ● 30

Gahanna; Inc. Place; FRANKLIN; ▲ Mifflin; **218** SA-10; 🅿; ★ **COL**; z 43230; Ⓟ 27,791; Ⓒ 32,636; ◆ 36,711

Galatea; RMC Place; WOOD; ▲ Bloom; ***216** NG-6; mail North Baltimore z 45872; ● 40

Galaxy Acres; RMC Place; HAMILTON; ▲ Colerain; ***218** SF-2; ★ **CIN**; mail Cincinnati z 45239; ● 1,000

Galena; Inc. Place; DELAWARE; ▲ Berkshire; **216** NM-9; 🅿; ★ **COL**; z 43021; Ⓟ 361; Ⓒ 305

Galion; Inc. Place; CRAWFORD; **216** NJ-10; elev. 1,166ft./355m.; 🅿 🅷; z 44833; Ⓟ 11,859; Ⓒ 11,341

Gallia; RMC Place; GALLIA; ▲ Greenfield; **219** SI-11; mail Patriot z 45658

GALLIA; **219** SH-13; Ⓟ 30,954; Ⓒ 31,069; ◆ 30,676

Gallipolis; Inc. Place; ⊡ GALLIA; ▲ Gallipolis; **219** SI-13; elev. 576ft./176m.; 🅿 🅷; z 45631; Ⓟ 4,831; Ⓒ 4,180

Gallipolis; MCD-Township; GALLIA; ***219** SH-13; 🅿; z 45631; Ⓟ 6,500; Ⓒ 5,707

Galloway; RMC Place; FRANKLIN; ▲ Prairie; **218** SB-8; 🅿; ★ **COL**; z 43119; ● 250

Gambier; Inc. Place; KNOX; ▲ College; **217** NL-12; 🅿 🅲 1,639; z 43022; Ⓟ 2,073; Ⓒ 1,871; Ⓡ 2,016

Ganges; RMC Place; RICHLAND; ▲ Bloominggrove; **217** NI-11; elev. 1,085ft./331m.; mail Shelby z 44875, Shiloh z 44878; ● 120

Gann; KNOX; see Brinkhaven (Inc. Place)

Gano; RMC Place; BUTLER; ▲ West Chester; **218** SF-3; ★ **CIN**; mail Cincinnati z 45241; ● 200

Garden; RMC Place; ATHENS; ▲ Lodi; ***219** SF-14; mail Guysville z 45735

Garden Acres; RMC Place; CLARK; ▲ Springfield; **217** NB-17; ★ **SPR**; mail Springfield z 45503; ● 250

Garden Acres; RMC Place; JEFFERSON; ★ **STU-**; mail Steubenville z 43952; pop. incl. with Steubenville (Inc. Place)

Garden City; RMC Place; SCIOTO; ▲ Porter; **218** SI-10; ★ **PTSM**; mail Wheelersburg z 45694; ● 300

Garden Hill Top; RMC Place; HAMILTON; ***218** SF-2; ★ **CIN**; mail Cincinnati z 45232; pop. incl. with Cincinnati (Inc. Place)

Garden Isle; RMC Place; MEDINA; ▲ Harrisville; ***217** NH-13; mail Lodi z 44254; rural

Garden Terrace; RMC Place; JEFFERSON; ★ **STU-**; mail Steubenville z 43952; pop. incl. with Steubenville (Inc. Place)

Garfield; RMC Place; MAHONING; ▲ Goshen; **217** NI-18; mail Salem z 44460; ● 120

Garfield Heights; Inc. Place; CUYAHOGA; **217** NF-15; 🅿 🅷; ★ **CLEV**; z 44105, z 44125, z 44128; Ⓟ 31,739; Ⓒ 30,734; ◆ 27,951

Garrettsville; Inc. Place; PORTAGE; **217** NG-17; 🅿; z 44231; Ⓟ 2,014; Ⓒ 2,262

Gaslight Village; RMC Place; CLERMONT; ▲ Goshen; ★ **CIN**; mail Goshen z 45122; ● 500

Gasper; MCD-Township; PREBLE; ***218** SC-1; mail Eaton z 45320; Ⓟ 1,638; Ⓒ 3,229

Gates Mills; Inc. Place; CUYAHOGA; **217** NE-16; 🅿; ★ **CLEV**; z 44040; Ⓟ 2,508; Ⓒ 2,493

Gath; RMC Place; HIGHLAND; ▲ Clay; ***218** SG-5; elev. 978ft./298m.; mail Sardinia z 45171; rural

Gavers; RMC Place; COLUMBIANA; ▲ Wayne; ***217** NJ-19; mail Lisbon z 44432

Gaysport; MUSKINGUM; see Blue Rock (RMC Place)

GEAUGA; **217** NE-17; Ⓟ 81,129; Ⓒ 90,895; ◆ 93,492

Geauga Lake; RMC Place; PORTAGE; ***217** NF-16; ★ **CLEV**; mail Aurora z 44202; pop. incl. with Aurora (Inc. Place)

Geeburg; RMC Place; MAHONING; ▲ Ellsworth; ***217** NH-19; elev. 964ft./294m.; ★ **YNGS-**; mail Canfield z 44406

Geneva; Inc. Place; ASHTABULA; ▲ Geneva; **217** ND-18; elev. 673ft./205m.; 🅿 🅷; ★ **CLEV**; z 44041; Ⓟ 6,597; Ⓒ 6,595

Geneva; MCD-Township; ASHTABULA; ***217** NC-18; 🅿; ★ **CLEV**; z 44041; Ⓟ 11,912; Ⓒ 11,954

Geneva; RMC Place; FAIRFIELD; ▲ Rush Creek, Harpersfield; ***219** SC-12; mail Bremen z 43107

Geneva-on-the-Lake; Inc. Place; ASHTABULA; ▲ Geneva; **217** NC-18; elev. 605ft./184m.; ★ **CLEV**; mail Geneva z 44041; Ⓟ 1,626; Ⓒ 1,545

Genntown (Lelan); RMC Place; WARREN; ▲ Turtlecreek; ***218** SE-4; mail Lebanon z 45036; ● 150

Genoa; MCD-Township; DELAWARE; ***216** NM-9; ★ **COL**; mail Westerville z 43081; Ⓟ 4,053; Ⓒ 11,293

Genoa; Inc. Place; OTTAWA; ▲ Clay; **216** NE-7; 🅿; ★ **TOL**; z 43430; Ⓟ 2,262; Ⓒ 2,230

Genung Corners; RMC Place; LAKE; ▲ Madison; ***217** ND-18; ★ **CLEV**; mail Madison z 44057; rural

Georges Run; RMC Place; JEFFERSON; ▲ Steubenville; **217** NM-20; ★ **STU-**; mail Mingo Junction z 43938; ● 400

Georgesville; RMC Place; FRANKLIN; ▲ Pleasant; **218** SB-8; ★ **COL**; mail Grove City z 43123; ● 160

Georgetown; Inc. Place; ⊡ BROWN; ▲ Pleasant, Franklin; **218** SH-5; elev. 930ft./283m.; 🅿 🅷; z 45121; Ⓟ 3,627; Ⓒ 3,691

Georgetown (Short Creek); RMC Place; HARRISON; ▲ Short Creek; **217** NM-18; mail Cadiz z 43907; ● 150

Gephart (Gepharts); RMC Place; SCIOTO; ▲ Bloom; ***218** SI-10; mail Wheelersburg z 45694

Gepharts; SCIOTO; see Gephart (RMC Place)

Gerald; RMC Place; HENRY; ▲ Freedom; **216** NF-4; elev. 705ft./215m.; mail Napoleon z 43545; ● 50

German; MCD-Township; AUGLAIZE; ***216** NL-3; mail New Bremen z 45869; Ⓟ 3,400; Ⓒ 3,831

German; MCD-Township; CLARK; ***218** SB-5; ★ **SPR**; mail Springfield z 45504; Ⓟ 7,467; Ⓒ 7,663

German; MCD-Township; FULTON; ***216** NE-3; mail Archbold z 43502; Ⓟ 5,477; Ⓒ 6,458

German; MCD-Township; HARRISON; ***217** NL-18; mail Hopedale z 43976; Ⓟ 695; Ⓒ 767

German; MCD-Township; MONTGOMERY; ***218** SD-3; ★ **DAY**; mail Germantown z 45327; Ⓟ 7,712; Ⓒ 7,830

Germano; RMC Place; HARRISON; ▲ German; **217** NL-18; elev. 1,302ft./397m.; mail Jewett z 43986; ● 200

Germantown; Inc. Place; MONTGOMERY; ▲ German; **218** SD-3; 🅿; ★ **DAY**; z 45325, z 45327; Ⓟ 4,916; Ⓒ 4,884

Germantown; RMC Place; WASHINGTON; ▲ Liberty; **219** SD-17; mail Lower Salem z 45745; ● 35

German Village; RMC Place; FRANKLIN; ★ **COL**; mail Columbus z 43206; pop. incl. with Columbus (Inc. Place)

Getaway; RMC Place; LAWRENCE; ▲ Union; **219** SK-12; elev. 560ft./171m.; ★ **HNTG**; mail Chesapeake z 45619; ● 100

Gettysburg; Inc. Place; DARKE; ▲ Adams; **216** NN-2; 🅿; z 45328; Ⓟ 539; Ⓒ 558

Gettysburg; RMC Place; PREBLE; ▲ Jefferson; **218** SB-1; ★ **RICH**; mail New Paris z 45347; ● 80

Geyer; RMC Place; AUGLAIZE; ▲ Clay; **216** NK-4; mail Wapakoneta z 45895; ● 50

Ghent; RMC Place; SUMMIT; ▲ Bath; **217** NG-15; ★ **AKR**; mail Akron z 44333; ● 1,600

Gibisonville; RMC Place; HOCKING; ▲ Laurel; **219** SD-11; mail Rockbridge z 43149; ● 130

Gibson; RMC Place; GUERNSEY; ▲ Richland; ***219** SB-17; mail Salesville z 43778; rural

Gibson; MCD-Township; MERCER; ***216** NL-1; mail Fort Recovery z 45846; Ⓟ 1,855; Ⓒ 1,869

Gibsonburg; Inc. Place; SANDUSKY; ▲ Madison, Washington; **216** NF-7; 🅿; z 43431; Ⓟ 2,579; Ⓒ 2,506

Gilbert; RMC Place; MUSKINGUM; ▲ Washington; ***219** SA-14; ★ **ZAN**; mail Zanesville z 43701

Gilboa; Inc. Place; PUTNAM; ▲ Blanchard; **216** NH-5; 🅿; z 45875; Ⓟ 208; Ⓒ 170

Gilead; MCD-Township; MORROW; ***216** NK-10; mail Mount Gilead z 43338; Ⓟ 5,512; Ⓒ 5,868

Gillivan; RMC Place; MADISON; ▲ Jefferson; ***218** SA-8; ★ **COL**; mail London z 43140, West Jefferson z 43162

Gilmore; RMC Place; TUSCARAWAS; ▲ Washington, Clay; **217** NM-16; mail Port Washington z 43837; ● 85

Ginghamsburg; RMC Place; MIAMI; ▲ Monroe; **218** SB-4; ★ **DAY**; mail Tipp City z 45371; ● 250

Girard; Inc. Place; TRUMBULL; ▲ Liberty, Vienna, Weathersfield; **217** NG-19; 🅿; ★ **YNGS-**; z 44420; Ⓟ 11,304; Ⓒ 10,902

Girton; RMC Place; SANDUSKY; ▲ Scott; **216** NG-7; mail Risingsun z 43457; ● 50

Gist Settlement; RMC Place; HIGHLAND; ▲ Penn; ***218** SF-6; mail New Vienna z 45159; rural

Givens; RMC Place; PIKE; ▲ Beaver; **218** SG-10; mail Waverly z 45690; ● 75

Glade; RMC Place; JACKSON; ▲ Scioto; ***218** SG-10; mail Beaver z 45613; rural

Gladstone; RMC Place; GREENE; ▲ Ross; **218** SC-6; mail Cedarville z 45314; ● 30

Glandorf; Inc. Place; PUTNAM; ▲ Ottawa; **216** NH-4; 🅿; z 45848; Ⓟ 829; Ⓒ 919

Glasgow; RMC Place; COLUMBIANA; ▲ Madison; **217** NJ-19; ★ **E.LIV**; mail Wellsville z 43968; ● 40

Glasgow; RMC Place; TUSCARAWAS; ▲ Salem; **217** NM-16; mail Port Washington z 43837

Glass Rock; RMC Place; PERRY; ▲ Hopewell; ***219** SB-12; mail Glenford z 43739; rural

Glenbrook Acres; RMC Place; GREENE; ▲ Sugarcreek; ★ **DAY**; mail Bellbrook z 45305; ● 215

Glencoe; RMC Place; BELMONT; ▲ Smith; **219** SA-19; 🅿; ★ **WHL**; z 43928; ● 500

Glencoe; RMC Place; HAMILTON; ▲ Springfield; ***218** SF-2; ★ **CIN**; mail Cincinnati z 45231; ● 1,350

Glendale; Inc. Place; HAMILTON; **218** SJ-3; elev. 630ft./192m.; 🅿; ★ **CIN**; z 45246; Ⓟ 2,445; Ⓒ 2,188

Glendwell; RMC Place; JEFFERSON; ★ **STU-**; mail Steubenville z 43952; pop. incl. with Steubenville (Inc. Place)

Glen Este; RMC Place; CLERMONT; ▲ Union; **218** SM-6; ★ **CIN**; mail Batavia z 45103; ● 350

Glenford; Inc. Place; PERRY; ▲ Hopewell; **219** SB-12; elev. 844ft./257m.; 🅿; z 43739; Ⓟ 208; Ⓒ 198

Glengary Heights; RMC Place; FRANKLIN; ▲ Blendon; ★ **COL**; mail Westerville z 43081

Glen Karn; RMC Place; DARKE; ▲ Liberty; **218** SA-1; mail Hollansburg z 45332; ● 40

Glenmary; RMC Place; BUTLER; ***218** SF-2; ★ **CIN**; mail Cincinnati z 45246; pop. incl. with Fairfield (Inc. Place)

Glenmont; Inc. Place; HOLMES; ▲ Richland; **217** NK-13; elev. 881ft./269m.; 🅿; z 44628; Ⓟ 233; Ⓒ 283

Glenmoor; CDP; COLUMBIANA; ▲ St. Clair; **217** NJ-20; elev. 1,127ft./344m.; ★ **E.LIV**; mail East Liverpool z 43920; Ⓟ 2,307; Ⓒ 2,192

Glenmore; RMC Place; VAN WERT; ▲ Willshire; **216** NJ-1; elev. 812ft./247m.; mail Ohio City z 45874; ● 50

Glenns Run; RMC Place; BELMONT; ▲ Pease; ***217** NN-19; ★ **WHL**; mail Martins Ferry z 43935; rural

Glen Robbins; RMC Place; JEFFERSON; ▲ Warren; ***217** NM-19; ★ **WHL**; mail Rayland z 43943; ● 200

Glen Roy; RMC Place; JACKSON; ▲ Coal; **219** SG-11; mail Wellston z 45692; ● 100

Glenville Bratenahl; RMC Place; CUYAHOGA; ★ **CLEV**; mail Cleveland z 44108; pop. incl. with Cleveland (Inc. Place)

Glenwillow (Falls Junction); Inc. Place; CUYAHOGA; **219** SN-20; ★ **CLEV**; mail Solon z 44139; Ⓟ 455; Ⓒ 449

Glenwood; PREBLE; see Sampleville (RMC Place)

Gloria Glens Park; Inc. Place; MEDINA; ▲ Westfield; ***217** NH-14; ★ **CLEV**; mail Chippewa Lake z 44215; Ⓟ 446; Ⓒ 538

Glouster; Inc. Place; ATHENS; ▲ Trimble; **219** SD-13; 🅿; z 45732; Ⓟ 2,001; Ⓒ 1,972

Glynwood; RMC Place; AUGLAIZE; ▲ Moulton; **216** NK-3; elev. 867ft./264m.; mail Saint Marys z 45885; rural

Gnadenhutten; Inc. Place; TUSCARAWAS; ▲ Warwick, Clay; **217** NL-16; 🅿; z 44629; Ⓟ 1,226; Ⓒ 1,280

Goes; RMC Place; GREENE; ▲ Xenia; **218** SC-5; ★ **DAY**; mail Yellow Springs z 45387; ● 100

Golden Corners; RMC Place; WAYNE; ▲ Canaan; ***217** NI-14; elev. 1,202ft./366m.; ★ **CLEV**; mail Burbank z 44214

Goldsboro; RMC Place; JACKSON; ▲ Coal; ***219** SG-11; mail Wellston z 45692; rural

Golf Manor; Inc. Place; HAMILTON; **218** SL-3; ★ **CIN**; mail Cincinnati z 45237; Ⓟ 4,154; Ⓒ 3,999

Golfway Acres; RMC Place; HAMILTON; ▲ Springfield; ***218** SF-2; ★ **CIN**; mail Cincinnati z 45239; ● 280

Gomer; RMC Place; ALLEN; ▲ Sugar Creek; **216** NI-3; 🅿; z 45809; ● 350

Good Hope; RMC Place; FAYETTE; ▲ Wayne; **218** SE-7; elev. 912ft./278m.; mail Washington Court House z 43160; ● 220

Good Hope; MCD-Township; HOCKING; ***219** SD-11; mail Rockbridge z 43149; Ⓟ 1,247; Ⓒ 1,444

Goodland Acres; RMC Place; STARK; ▲ Sandy; ***217** NJ-17; elev. 968ft./295m.; ★ **CAN**; mail Waynesburg z 44688; ● 240

Goodyear Heights; RMC Place; SUMMIT; ***217** NH-16; ★ **AKR**; mail Akron z 44305; pop. incl. with Akron (Inc. Place)

Goose Run; RMC Place; ATHENS; ▲ Trimble; ***219** SD-13; mail Glouster z 45732; rural

Gordon; Inc. Place; DARKE; ▲ Twin; **218** SB-2; 🅿; ★ **DAY**; z 45304; Ⓟ 206; Ⓒ 190

Gore; RMC Place; HOCKING; ▲ Falls; **219** SD-12; elev. 767ft./234m.; mail Logan z 43138, New Plymouth z 45654; ● 240

Gorham; MCD-Township; FULTON; ***216** ND-3; mail Fayette z 43521; Ⓟ 2,248; Ⓒ 2,372

Goshen; MCD-Township; AUGLAIZE; ***216** NK-5; mail Lakeview z 43331; Ⓟ 487; Ⓒ 523

Goshen; MCD-Township; BELMONT; ***219** SA-18; mail Bethesda z 43719; Ⓟ 2,972; Ⓒ 3,252

Goshen; MCD-Township; CHAMPAIGN; ***218** SA-7; mail Mechanicsburg z 43044; Ⓟ 3,172; Ⓒ 3,383

Goshen; RMC Place; CLERMONT; ▲ Goshen; **218** SF-4; 🅿; ★ **CIN**; z 45122; ● 730

Goshen; MCD-Township; CLERMONT; ***218** SF-4; 🅿; ★ **CIN**; z 45122; Ⓟ 12,697; Ⓒ 13,663

Goshen; MCD-Township; HARDIN; ***216** NJ-7; mail Kenton z 43326; Ⓟ 560; Ⓒ 585

Goshen; MCD-Township; MAHONING; ***217** NI-18; mail Salem z 44460; Ⓟ 3,314; Ⓒ 3,281

Goshen; RMC Place; TUSCARAWAS; ▲ Goshen; **217** NL-16; mail New Philadelphia z 44663; ● 200

Goshen; MCD-Township; TUSCARAWAS; ***217** NL-16; mail New Philadelphia z 44663; Ⓟ 5,718; Ⓒ 5,285

Gould (Goulds); RMC Place; JEFFERSON; ▲ Cross Creek; ***217** NL-20; ★ **STU-**; mail Mingo Junction z 43938; ● 50

Gould; RMC Place; LUCAS; ***216** NE-6; ★ **TOL**; pop. incl. with Toledo (Inc. Place)

Gould Park; RMC Place; FRANKLIN; ▲ Blendon; **216** NN-9; ★ **COL**; mail Columbus z 43230; pop. incl. with Columbus (Inc. Place)

Goulds; JEFFERSON; see Gould (RMC Place)

Entries in **UPPERCASE** are counties.
Entries in **bold** have populations of 2,500 or more.
Names in parentheses are alternate names.

Inc. Place	Incorporated Place
RMC Place	Rand McNally Designated Place
CDP	Census Designated Place
MCD	Minor Civil Division
⊡	County Seat
▲	Minor Civil Division
elev.	Elevation
🅿	Post Office
🅷	Hospital
🅲	College
■	Principal Business Center
★	Ranally Metro Area (RMA) Abbreviation
z	Zip Code(s)
Ⓟ	Previous Census Population
Ⓡ	Revised Census Population
Ⓐ	Annexation Population
●	Rand McNally Population Estimate
Ⓒ	Final Census Population
Ⓢ	Special Census Population
◆	Estimated Population

For additional definitions see Glossary, Volume 1, and Introduction, Volume 2.

Grafton; Inc. Place; LORAIN; ▲ Grafton, Eaton; **217** NG-13; elev. 812ft./247m.; 🅿; ★ **CLEV**; z 44044; Ⓟ 3,344; Ⓒ 2,302; Ⓡ 6,004
Grafton; MCD-Township; LORAIN; ***217** NG-13; 🅿; ★ **CLEV**; z 44044; includes part of the Village of Grafton; Ⓟ 3,052; Ⓒ 2,722
Grand; MCD-Township; MARION; ***216** NJ-7; mail Forest z 45843; Ⓟ 340; Ⓒ 385
Grand Prairie; MCD-Township; MARION; ***216** NJ-8; ★ **MRN**; mail Marion z 43302; Ⓟ 1,697; Ⓒ 1,609
Grand Rapids; Inc. Place; WOOD; ▲ Grand Rapids; **216** NF-5; 🅿; ★ **TOL**; z 43522; Ⓟ 955; Ⓒ 1,002
Grand Rapids; MCD-Township; WOOD; ***216** NF-5; elev. 654ft./199m.; 🅿; ★ **TOL**; z 43522; Ⓟ 1,539; Ⓒ 1,631
Grand River (Richmond); Inc. Place; LAKE; ▲ Painesville; **217** ND-17; elev. 600ft./183m.; 🅿; ★ **CLEV**; z 44045; Ⓟ 297; Ⓒ 345
Grandview; CDP-Census Area Only; HAMILTON; ▲ Miami; ***218** SF-1; elev. 776ft./237m.; ★ **CIN**; mail Cleves z 45002; Ⓟ 1,301; Ⓒ 1,391
Grandview; RMC Place; WASHINGTON; ▲ Grandview; **219** SD-18; elev. 628ft./191m.; mail New Matamoras z 45767; ● 60
Grandview; MCD-Township; WASHINGTON; ***219** SD-18; mail New Matamoras z 45767; Ⓟ 1,965; Ⓒ 1,834
Grandview Estates; RMC Place; DELAWARE; mail Delaware z 43015; pop. incl. with Delaware (Inc. Place)
Grandview Estates; RMC Place; MARION; ▲ Marion, Grand Prairie; ***216** NK-9; ★ **MRN**; mail Marion z 43302; ● 500
Grandview Heights; RMC Place; CHAMPAIGN; ▲ Johnson; **216** NM-4; mail Saint Paris z 43072; ● 170
Grandview Heights; Inc. Place; FRANKLIN; **218** SB-9; elev. 770ft./235m.; 🅿; ★ **COL**; z 43212; Ⓟ 7,010; Ⓒ 6,695
Grandview Homes; RMC Place; ALLEN; ▲ Perry; ***216** NJ-4; ★ **LIMA**; mail Lima z 45804; pop. incl. with Lima (Inc. Place)
Grange Hall; RMC Place; PICKAWAY; ▲ Monroe; **218** SD-8; mail Mount Sterling z 43143; ● 20
Granger; RMC Place; MEDINA; ▲ Granger; **217** NH-15; elev. 1,099ft./335m.; ★ **CLEV**; mail Medina z 44256; ● 90
Granger; MCD-Township; MEDINA; ***217** NG-15; ★ **CLEV**; mail Medina z 44256; Ⓟ 2,932; Ⓒ 3,928
Grant (Grants); RMC Place; HARDIN; ▲ Pleasant; **216** NJ-6; mail Forest z 45843; ● 60
Grants; HARDIN; see Grant (RMC Place)
Granville; Inc. Place; LICKING; ▲ Granville; **217** NN-11; elev. 974ft./297m.; 🅿 🅲 2,105; ★ **NWRK**; z 43023; Ⓟ 4,353; Ⓒ 3,167; Ⓡ 5,098
Granville; MCD-Township; LICKING; ***219** SA-11; 🅿 🅲 2,105; ★ **NWRK**; z 43023; Ⓟ 7,819; Ⓒ 8,994
Granville; MCD-Township; MERCER; ***216** NL-1; mail Saint Henry z 45883; Ⓟ 3,615; Ⓒ 3,885
Granville South; CDP-Census Area Only; LICKING; ▲ Granville; ***219** SA-11; elev. 1,041ft./317m.; ★ **NWRK**; mail Granville z 43023; Ⓟ 1,124; Ⓒ 1,194
Grape Grove; RMC Place; GREENE; ▲ Ross; **218** SC-6; mail Jamestown z 45335; ● 35
Gratiot; Inc. Place; LICKING, MUSKINGUM; ▲ Hopewell; **219** SB-13; elev. 988ft./301m.; 🅿; z 43740; Ⓟ 195; Ⓒ 187
Gratis; Inc. Place; PREBLE; ▲ Gratis; **218** SC-2; elev. 870ft./265m.; 🅿; ★ **MIDD**; z 45330; Ⓟ 998; Ⓒ 934
Gratis; MCD-Township; PREBLE; ***218** SD-2; 🅿; ★ **MIDD**; z 45330; Ⓟ 4,474; Ⓒ 4,471
Gravel Bank; WASHINGTON; see Riverview (RMC Place)
Graysville; Inc. Place; MONROE; ▲ Washington; **219** SC-18; 🅿; z 45734; Ⓟ 89; Ⓒ 113
Graytown; RMC Place; OTTAWA; ▲ Benton; **216** NE-8; elev. 599ft./183m.; 🅿; z 43432; ● 180
Greasy Ridge; RMC Place; LAWRENCE; ▲ Mason; ***219** SJ-12; mail Scottown z 45678; rural
Green; MCD-Township; ADAMS; ***218** SI-8; mail Stout z 45684; Ⓟ 704; Ⓒ 782
Green; MCD-Township; ASHLAND; ***217** NK-12; mail Loudonville z 44842; Ⓟ 3,965; Ⓒ 3,887
Green; MCD-Township; BROWN; ***218** SG-5; ★ **CIN**; mail Mount Orab z 45154; Ⓟ 2,860; Ⓒ 3,389
Green; MCD-Township; CLARK; ***218** SB-5; ★ **SPR**; mail Springfield z 45502; Ⓟ 2,861; Ⓒ 2,736
Green; MCD-Township; CLINTON; ***218** SE-6; mail New Vienna z 45159; Ⓟ 2,007; Ⓒ 2,602
Green; MCD-Township; FAYETTE; ***218** SE-7; mail Leesburg z 45135; Ⓟ 451; Ⓒ 499
Green; MCD-Township; GALLIA; ***219** SI-13; mail Patriot z 45658; Ⓟ 5,189; Ⓒ 5,514
Green; MCD-Township; HAMILTON; ***218** SF-2; ★ **CIN**; mail Cincinnati z 45211, z 45247-48; Ⓟ 52,687; Ⓒ 55,660
Green; MCD-Township; HARRISON; ***217** NM-18; mail Hopedale z 43976; Ⓟ 1,723; Ⓒ 1,898
Green; MCD-Township; HOCKING; ***219** SD-12; mail Logan z 43138; Ⓟ 2,217; Ⓒ 2,585
Green; MCD-Township; MAHONING; ***217** NI-19; mail Canfield z 44406; Ⓟ 3,321; Ⓒ 3,450
Green; MCD-Township; MONROE; ***219** SC-18; mail Woodsfield z 43793; Ⓟ 442; Ⓒ 422
Green; MCD-Township; ROSS; ***218** SE-10; mail Kingston z 45644; Ⓟ 3,696; Ⓒ 4,492
Green; MCD-Township; SCIOTO; ***218** SJ-10; ★ **HNTG**; mail Franklin Furnace z 45629; Ⓟ 3,758; Ⓒ 4,079
Green; MCD-Township; SHELBY; ***216** NM-4; mail Sidney z 45365; Ⓟ 973; Ⓒ 927
Green; Inc. Place; SUMMIT; **217** NI-16; 🅿; ★ **AKR**; z 44232; Ⓟ 3,553; Ⓒ 22,817; ◆ 22,685
Green; MCD-Township; WAYNE; ***217** NI-14; mail Orrville z 44667; Ⓟ 11,356; Ⓒ 12,194
Green Acres; RMC Place; BUTLER; ▲ Lemon; ★ **MIDD**; mail Middletown z 45042
Green Acres; JEFFERSON; see Valley View (RMC Place)
Greenbush; RMC Place; BROWN; ***218** SG-5; elev. 946ft./288m.; mail Mount Orab z 45154
Greenbush; RMC Place; PREBLE; ▲ Gratis; ***218** SD-2; elev. 924ft./282m.; ★ **MIDD**; mail Somerville z 45064
Green Camp; Inc. Place; MARION; ▲ Green Camp; **216** NK-8; elev. 930ft./283m.; 🅿; z 43322; Ⓟ 393; Ⓒ 342
Green Camp; MCD-Township; MARION; ***216** NK-8; 🅿; z 43322; Ⓟ 1,188; Ⓒ 1,163
Greencastle; RMC Place; FAIRFIELD; ▲ Bloom; ***218** SC-10; ★ **COL**; mail Carroll z 43112
Green Creek; MCD-Township; SANDUSKY; ***216** NG-9; mail Clyde z 43410; Ⓟ 9,792; Ⓒ 9,527
Greendale; RMC Place; HOCKING; ▲ Ward, Green; **219** SD-12; mail Logan z 43138; ● 30
Greene; MCD-Township; TRUMBULL; ***217** NF-19; mail North Bloomfield z 44450; Ⓟ 940; Ⓒ 986
GREENE; **218** SC-4; Ⓟ 136,731; Ⓒ 147,886; ◆ 158,653
Greenfield; MCD-Township; FAIRFIELD; ***219** SC-11; ★ **COL**; mail Lancaster z 43130; partly in★ LANC; Ⓟ 4,581; Ⓒ 4,944
Greenfield; MCD-Township; GALLIA; ***219** SI-11; mail Patriot z 45658; Ⓟ 437; Ⓒ 498
Greenfield; Inc. Place; HIGHLAND; ▲ Madison; **218** SE-7; elev. 913ft./278m.; 🅿 🅷; z 45123; Ⓟ 5,172; Ⓒ 4,906
Greenfield; MCD-Township; HURON; ***216** NH-10; ★ **SNDSK**; mail North Fairfield z 44855; Ⓟ 1,422; Ⓒ 1,442
Greenfield Village; RMC Place; HAMILTON; ▲ Springfield; ***218** SF-2; ★ **CIN**; mail Cincinnati z 45224
Greenford; RMC Place; MAHONING; ▲ Green; **217** NI-19; elev. 1,236ft./377m.; 🅿; z 44422; ● 700
Greenhills; Inc. Place; HAMILTON; **218** SJ-3; elev. 836ft./255m.; ★ **CIN**; mail Cincinnati z 45218; Ⓟ 4,393; Ⓒ 4,103
Greenland; RMC Place; ROSS; ▲ Concord, Deerfield, Union; **218** SE-9; elev. 821ft./250m.; mail Clarksburg z 43115, Frankfort z 45628
Greenlex; RMC Place; MARION; ▲ Marion; ★ **MRN**; mail Marion z 43302; ● 300
Green Meadows; CDP-Census Area Only; CLARK; ***218** SB-5; ★ **SPR**; mail Enon z 45323; Ⓟ 2,526; Ⓒ 2,318
Greensburg; MCD-Township; PUTNAM; ***216** NH-4; mail Ottawa z 45875; Ⓟ 1,244; Ⓒ 1,425
Greensburg; RMC Place; SUMMIT; **217** NI-16; ● 600
Green Springs; Inc. Place; SENECA, SANDUSKY; **216** NG-9; elev. 700ft./213m.; 🅿 🅷; z 44836; Ⓟ 1,446; Ⓒ 1,247
Greens Run; RMC Place; ATHENS; ▲ Trimble; ***219** SE-13; mail Glouster z 45732; ● 70
Greens Store; RMC Place; JACKSON; ▲ Jackson; ***219** SG-11; mail Jackson z 45640; rural
Greentown; CDP; STARK; ▲ Lake; **217** NI-16; elev. 1,184ft./361m.; 🅿; ★ **CAN**; z 44630; Ⓟ 1,856; Ⓒ 3,154
Greenview; RMC Place; MONTGOMERY; **218** SK-7; ★ **DAY**; mail Dayton z 45415; pop. incl. with Clayton (Inc. Place)
Greenville; Inc. Place; ⊡ DARKE; ▲ Greenville; **216** NN-1; elev. 1,039ft./317m.; 🅿 🅷 ■; z 45331; Ⓟ 12,863; Ⓒ 13,294; ◆ 13,059
Greenville; MCD-Township; DARKE; ***216** NN-1; 🅿; z 45331; Ⓟ 17,302; Ⓒ 18,125
Greenwich; Inc. Place; HURON; **217** NH-11; elev. 1,032ft./315m.; 🅿; z 44837; Ⓟ 1,442; Ⓒ 1,525
Greenwich; MCD-Township; HURON; ***217** NH-11; 🅿; z 44837; Ⓟ 785; Ⓒ 954
Greenwood; RMC Place; GUERNSEY; **219** SB-16; mail Senecaville z 43780; ● 40
Greer; RMC Place; KNOX; ▲ Jefferson; **217** NK-13; mail Glenmont z 44628; ● 50
Gregory; RMC Place; DELAWARE; rural
Grelton; RMC Place; HENRY; ▲ Damascus, Harrison, Monroe, Richfield; **216** NF-4; elev. 683ft./208m.; 🅿; z 43523, z 43534; ● 110
Griffith; RMC Place; HAMILTON; ★ **CIN**; mail North Bend z 45052; pop. incl. with North Bend (Inc. Place)
Griggs (Griggs Corners); RMC Place; ASHTABULA; ▲ Denmark, Jefferson, Plymouth, Sheffield; ***217** ND-19; mail Jefferson z 44047; rural
Griggs Corners; ASHTABULA; see Griggs (RMC Place)
Grimms Bridge (Grim's Bridge); RMC Place; COLUMBIANA; ▲ St. Clair; ***217** NJ-20; ★ **E.LIV**; mail East Liverpool z 43920; rural
Grim's Bridge; COLUMBIANA; see Grimms Bridge (RMC Place)
Groesbeck; CDP; HAMILTON; ▲ Colerain; **218** SF-2; elev. 836ft./255m.; 🅿; ★ **CIN**; z 45239, z 45247, z 45251, z 45253 & mail Cincinnati z 45252; Ⓟ 6,684; Ⓒ 7,202
Groton; MCD-Township; ERIE; ***216** NG-10; mail Huron z 44839; Ⓟ 1,245; Ⓒ 1,384
Grove City; Inc. Place; FRANKLIN; ▲ Jackson; **218** SB-9; elev. 850ft./259m.; 🅿; ★ **COL**; z 43123; Ⓟ 19,661; Ⓒ 27,075; ◆ 30,282
Groveport; Inc. Place; FRANKLIN; ▲ Madison, Hamilton; **218** SB-10; elev. 745ft./227m.; 🅿; ★ **COL**; z 43125, z 43195, z 43199; Ⓟ 2,948; Ⓒ 3,865
Grover Hill; Inc. Place; PAULDING; ▲ Latty; **216** NH-2; elev. 725ft./221m.; 🅿; z 45849; Ⓟ 518; Ⓒ 412
Guerne; RMC Place; WAYNE; ▲ Franklin; **217** NJ-14; mail Wooster z 44691; ● 250
Guernsey; RMC Place; GUERNSEY; ▲ Wheeling; **217** NM-15; elev. 792ft./241m.; 🅿; z 43749; ● 50
GUERNSEY; **217** NM-16; Ⓟ 39,024; Ⓒ 40,792; ◆ 40,218
Guilford; RMC Place; COLUMBIANA; ▲ Hanover; **217** NJ-19; elev. 1,126ft./343m.; mail Lisbon z 44432; ● 320
Guilford; MCD-Township; MEDINA; ***217** NH-14; mail Seville z 44273; Ⓟ 4,773; Ⓒ 5,447
Gunnerville; RMC Place; GREENE; ▲ Jefferson; ***218** SD-6; elev. 1,044ft./318m.; mail Jamestown z 45335; ● 50
Gurneyville; RMC Place; CLINTON; ▲ Union, Liberty; ***218** SD-5; elev. 1,059ft./323m.; mail Wilmington z 45177
Gustavus; RMC Place; TRUMBULL; ▲ Gustavus; ***217** NF-19; elev. 1,074ft./327m.; mail Farmdale z 44417, Kinsman z 44428
Gustavus; MCD-Township; TRUMBULL; ***217** NF-20; mail Farmdale z 44417; Ⓟ 1,031; Ⓒ 948
Gutman; RMC Place; AUGLAIZE; ▲ Clay; **216** NK-4; elev. 1,035ft./315m.; mail Wapakoneta z 45895; ● 35
Guyan; MCD-Township; GALLIA; ***219** SJ-13; mail Crown City z 45623; Ⓟ 1,181; Ⓒ 1,199
Guysville; RMC Place; ATHENS; ▲ Rome; **219** SF-14; elev. 652ft./199m.; 🅿; z 45735; ● 250
Gypsum; RMC Place; OTTAWA; ▲ Portage; **216** NE-9; 🅿; ★ **TOL**; z 43433; ● 200

H

Hackney; RMC Place; MORGAN; ▲ Center; **219** SD-15; mail Beverly z 45715; ● 40
Hagan Addition; RMC Place; HARRISON; ▲ Short Creek; ***217** NM-19; mail Adena z 43901; pop. incl. with Adena (Inc. Place)
Hageman (Hageman Junction); RMC Place; WARREN; ▲ Union; ***218** SE-3; ★ **CIN**; mail Lebanon z 45036; rural
Hageman Junction; WARREN; see Hageman (RMC Place)
Hale; MCD-Township; HARDIN; ***216** NK-6; mail Mount Victory z 43340; Ⓟ 1,371; Ⓒ 1,559
Hallock; RMC Place; WILLIAMS; ▲ Jefferson; **216** NE-2; mail Bryan z 43506; ● 100
Hallsville; RMC Place; ROSS; ▲ Colerain; **218** SE-10; elev. 837ft./255m.; 🅿; z 45633; ● 230
Hambden; RMC Place; GEAUGA; ▲ Hambden; **217** NE-17; ★ **CLEV**; mail Chardon z 44024; ● 180
Hambden; MCD-Township; GEAUGA; ***217** NE-17; ★ **CLEV**; mail Chardon z 44024; Ⓟ 3,311; Ⓒ 4,024
Hamburg; RMC Place; FAIRFIELD; ▲ Hocking; ***219** SC-11; ★ **LANC**; mail Lancaster z 43130
Hamburg; RMC Place; PREBLE; ▲ Monroe; ***218** SB-1; ★ **RICH**; mail Eldorado z 45321
Hamden; Inc. Place; VINTON; ▲ Clinton; **219** SF-11; elev. 707ft./215m.; 🅿; z 45634; Ⓟ 877; Ⓒ 871
Hamer; MCD-Township; HIGHLAND; ***218** SG-6; mail Hillsboro z 45133; Ⓟ 802; Ⓒ 699
Hamersville; Inc. Place; BROWN; ▲ Clark; **218** SH-5; elev. 968ft./295m.; 🅿; ★ **CIN**; z 45130; Ⓟ 586; Ⓒ 515
Hametown; RMC Place; SUMMIT; ★ **AKR**; mail Barberton z 44203; pop. incl. with Norton (Inc. Place)
Hamilton; Inc. Place; ⊡ BUTLER; **218** SE-2; 🅿 🅷 🅲 3,234 ■; ★ **CIN**; z 45011-15, z 45018, z 45025-26; Ⓟ 61,368; Ⓒ 60,690; ◆ 64,014
Hamilton; MCD-Township; FRANKLIN; ***218** SB-9; ★ **COL**; mail Columbus z 43207, Lockbourne z 43137; Ⓟ 9,746; Ⓒ 7,950
Hamilton; MCD-Township; JACKSON; ***218** SH-10; mail Oak Hill z 45656; Ⓟ 453; Ⓒ 513
Hamilton; MCD-Township; LAWRENCE; ***218** SJ-10; ★ **HNTG**; mail Ironton z 45638; Ⓟ 1,899; Ⓒ 1,817
Hamilton; MCD-Township; WARREN; ***218** SE-4; ★ **CIN**; mail Maineville z 45039; Ⓟ 5,900; Ⓒ 9,630
HAMILTON; **218** SF-1; Ⓟ 866,228; Ⓒ 845,303; ◆ 879,761
Hamilton Meadows; RMC Place; FRANKLIN; ▲ Hamilton; **218** SB-9; ★ **COL**; mail Columbus z 43207; ● 2,100
Hamler; Inc. Place; HENRY; ▲ Marion; **216** NG-4; elev. 714ft./218m.; 🅿; z 43524; Ⓟ 623; Ⓒ 650
Hamlet; RMC Place; CLERMONT; ▲ Pierce, Batavia; **218** SG-4; ★ **CIN**; mail Amelia z 45102, Batavia z 45103; ● 160
Hamley Run; RMC Place; ATHENS; ▲ Dover; ***219** SE-13; mail Athens z 45701; ● 25
Hammansburg; RMC Place; WOOD; ▲ Henry; **216** NG-6; elev. 706ft./215m.; mail Cygnet z 43413, North Baltimore z 45872; ● 100
Hammondsville; RMC Place; JEFFERSON; ▲ Saline; **217** NK-19; elev. 687ft./209m.; 🅿; ★ **E.LIV**; z 43930; ● 400
Hampton Woods; RMC Place; CLARK; ▲ Pike; ***218** SB-5; ★ **SPR**; mail Springfield z 45502; ● 100
HANCOCK; **216** NI-5; Ⓟ 65,536; Ⓒ 71,295; ◆ 74,723
Hanersville; RMC Place; GALLIA; ▲ Gallipolis; ***219** SH-13; mail Gallipolis z 45631; ● 40
Hanford; RMC Place; FRANKLIN; ***218** SB-9; ★ **COL**; mail Columbus z 43205; pop. incl. with Columbus (Inc. Place)
Hanging Rock; Inc. Place; LAWRENCE; ▲ Hamilton; **219** SJ-11; elev. 538ft./164m.; 🅿; ★ **HNTG**; z 45638; Ⓟ 306; Ⓒ 279
Hanley Village; RMC Place; RICHLAND; ▲ Washington; **217** NJ-11; ★ **MANS**; mail Mansfield z 44904
Hanna Hills; RMC Place; PORTAGE; ▲ Ravenna; ***217** NG-17; ★ **AKR**; mail Ravenna z 44266; ● 100
Hannibal; RMC Place; MONROE; ▲ Ohio; **219** SC-19; elev. 750ft./229m.; 🅿; z 43931; ● 500
Hanover; MCD-Township; ASHLAND; ***217** NK-12; mail Loudonville z 44842; Ⓟ 2,377; Ⓒ 2,520
Hanover; MCD-Township; BUTLER; ***218** SE-2; ★ **CIN**; mail Hamilton z 45013; Ⓟ 7,653; Ⓒ 7,878
Hanover; MCD-Township; COLUMBIANA; ***217** NJ-18; mail East Rochester z 44625; Ⓟ 3,467; Ⓒ 3,749
Hanover; RMC Place; HARRISON; ▲ North; **217** NL-18; mail Scio z 43988
Hanover; Inc. Place; LICKING; ▲ Hanover; **217** NN-12; elev. 800ft./244m.; ★ **NWRK**; mail Newark z 43055; Ⓟ 803; Ⓒ 885
Hanover; MCD-Township; LICKING; ***219** SA-13; ★ **NWRK**; mail Newark z 43055; Ⓟ 2,551; Ⓒ 2,731
Hanoverton; Inc. Place; COLUMBIANA; ▲ Hanover; **217** NJ-18; elev. 1,137ft./347m.; 🅿; z 44423; Ⓟ 434; Ⓒ 387
Hanville Corners; RMC Place; HURON; ▲ Fairfield; ***217** NH-11; mail North Fairfield z 44855; rural
Harbor (Ashtabula Harbor); RMC Place; ASHTABULA; ***217** NC-19; ★ **ASHT**; mail Ashtabula z 44004; pop. incl. with Ashtabula (Inc. Place)
Harbor Hills; CDP-Census Area Only; LICKING; ▲ Licking; **219** SB-12; ★ **NWRK**; mail Hebron z 43025; Ⓟ 1,372; Ⓒ 1,303
Harbor Point; RMC Place; MERCER; ▲ Jefferson; ***216** NK-2; mail Celina z 45822; ● 100
Harbor View; Inc. Place; LUCAS; **216** ND-7; elev. 581ft./177m.; 🅿; ★ **TOL**; z 43434; Ⓟ 122; Ⓒ 99
Hardin; RMC Place; SHELBY; ▲ Turtle Creek; **216** NM-3; mail Sidney z 45365; ● 80
HARDIN; **216** NJ-6; Ⓟ 31,111; Ⓒ 31,945; ◆ 32,079
Harding; MCD-Township; LUCAS; ***216** NE-5; ★ **TOL**; mail Swanton z 43558; Ⓟ 593; Ⓒ 724
Hardin Station; RMC Place; SHELBY; ▲ Turtle Creek; ***216** NM-3; mail Sidney z 45365; rural
Hardy; MCD-Township; HOLMES; ***217** NK-14; mail Millersburg z 44654; Ⓟ 5,261; Ⓒ 5,643
Harewood Acres; RMC Place; HAMILTON; ▲ Sycamore; ***218** SF-3; elev. 850ft./259m.; ★ **CIN**; mail Cincinnati z 45236
Harlan; MCD-Township; WARREN; ***218** SF-4; mail Pleasant Plain z 45162; Ⓟ 3,268; Ⓒ 3,627
Harlan Park; RMC Place; BUTLER; ***218** SD-3; ★ **MIDD**; mail Middletown z 45042; pop. incl. with Middletown (Inc. Place)
Harlem; RMC Place; DELAWARE; ▲ Harlem; **216** NN-10; elev. 1,007ft./307m.; ★ **COL**; mail Galena z 43021; ● 150
Harlem; MCD-Township; DELAWARE; ***216** NN-10; ★ **COL**; mail Galena z 43021; Ⓟ 3,391; Ⓒ 3,762
Harlem Springs; RMC Place; CARROLL; ▲ Lee; **217** NK-18; elev. 1,246ft./380m.; 🅿; z 44631; ● 300
Harmar; RMC Place; WASHINGTON; mail Marietta z 45750; pop. incl. with Marietta (Inc. Place)
Harmon; RMC Place; STARK; ▲ Sugar Creek; **217** NJ-15; ★ **CAN**; mail Navarre z 44662; ● 50
Harmons Landing; RMC Place; AUGLAIZE; ▲ St. Marys; ***216** NK-2; mail Saint Marys z 45885; ● 50
Harmony; RMC Place; CLARK; ▲ Harmony; **218** SB-6; mail Springfield z 45502; ● 250
Harmony; MCD-Township; CLARK; ***218** SB-6; mail Springfield z 45502; Ⓟ 3,395; Ⓒ 3,548
Harmony; MCD-Township; MORROW; ***216** NL-10; mail Cardington z 43315; Ⓟ 1,594; Ⓒ 2,040
Harper; RMC Place; LOGAN; ▲ Rushcreek; **216** NL-6; mail Bellefontaine z 43311; ● 70
Harpersfield; RMC Place; ASHTABULA; ▲ Harpersfield; **217** ND-18; elev. 850ft./259m.; ★ **CLEV**; mail Geneva z 44041
Harpersfield; MCD-Township; ASHTABULA; ***217** ND-18; ★ **CLEV**; mail Geneva z 44041; Ⓟ 2,496; Ⓒ 2,603
Harpster; Inc. Place; WYANDOT; ▲ Pitt; **216** NJ-8; elev. 904ft./276m.; 🅿; z 43323; Ⓟ 233; Ⓒ 203
Harriett; RMC Place; GUERNSEY; ▲ Jackson; ***218** SG-7; mail Cambridge z 43725; ● 50
Harriett; RMC Place; HIGHLAND; ▲ Marshall; **218** SG-7; elev. 988ft./301m.; mail Hillsboro z 45133; ● 30
Harriettsville; RMC Place; NOBLE; ▲ Elk; **219** SD-17; mail Lower Salem z 45745; ● 60
Harris; MCD-Township; OTTAWA; ***216** NF-8; ★ **TOL**; mail Elmore z 43416; Ⓟ 2,765; Ⓒ 3,009
Harris; RMC Place; ROSS; ▲ Twin; ***218** SF-9; mail Bainbridge z 45612; rural
Harrisburg; Inc. Place; FRANKLIN, PICKAWAY; ▲ Darby, Pleasant; **218** SC-8; elev. 790ft./241m.; 🅿; ★ **COL**; z 43126; Ⓟ 340; Ⓒ 332
Harrisburg; RMC Place; GALLIA; ▲ Raccoon; ***219** SH-12; mail Bidwell z 45614
Harrisburg; RMC Place; STARK; ▲ Nimishillen; **217** NI-17; elev. 1,288ft./393m.; ★ **CAN**; mail Louisville z 44641; ● 100
Harrison; MCD-Township; CARROLL; ***217** NK-17; mail Carrollton z 44615; Ⓟ 2,127; Ⓒ 2,498
Harrison; MCD-Township; CHAMPAIGN; ***216** NM-5; mail West Liberty z 43357; Ⓟ 713; Ⓒ 823
Harrison; MCD-Township; DARKE; ***218** SB-1; ★ **RICH**; mail New Madison z 45346; Ⓟ 2,315; Ⓒ 2,145
Harrison; MCD-Township; GALLIA; ***219** SI-12; mail Gallipolis z 45631; Ⓟ 970; Ⓒ 1,003
Harrison; Inc. Place; HAMILTON; ▲ Harrison; **218** SF-1; elev. 528ft./161m.; 🅿; ★ **CIN**; z 45030; Ⓟ 7,518; Ⓒ 7,487
Harrison; MCD-Township; HAMILTON; ***218** SF-1; 🅿; ★ **CIN**; z 45030; Ⓟ 12,145; Ⓒ 12,469
Harrison; MCD-Township; HENRY; ***216** NF-4; mail Napoleon z 43545; Ⓟ 1,253; Ⓒ 1,232
Harrison; MCD-Township; KNOX; ***217** NL-12; mail Gambier z 43022; Ⓟ 586; Ⓒ 747
Harrison; MCD-Township; LICKING; ***219** SA-11; ★ **COL**; mail Kirkersville z 43033; Ⓟ 5,041; Ⓒ 6,494
Harrison; MCD-Township; LOGAN; ***216** NL-5; mail Bellefontaine z 43311; Ⓟ 2,077; Ⓒ 2,093
Harrison; MCD-Township; MONTGOMERY; ***218** SC-4; ★ **DAY**; mail Dayton z 45415; Ⓟ 26,026; Ⓒ 24,303
Harrison; MCD-Township; MUSKINGUM; ***219** SB-14; ★ **ZAN**; mail Philo z 43771; Ⓟ 1,508; Ⓒ 1,638
Harrison; MCD-Township; PAULDING; ***216** NH-1; mail Payne z 45880; Ⓟ 1,712; Ⓒ 1,566
Harrison; MCD-Township; PERRY; ***219** SC-13; ★ **ZAN**; mail Crooksville z 43731; Ⓟ 5,235; Ⓒ 5,399
Harrison; MCD-Township; PICKAWAY; ***218** SC-9; ★ **COL**; mail Ashville z 43103; Ⓟ 5,292; Ⓒ 6,424
Harrison; PORTAGE; see Hiram Rapids (RMC Place)
Harrison; MCD-Township; PREBLE; ***218** SB-2; ★ **DAY**; mail Lewisburg z 45338; Ⓟ 4,365; Ⓒ 4,601
Harrison; MCD-Township; ROSS; ***218** SE-10; mail Chillicothe z 45601; Ⓟ 1,084; Ⓒ 1,293
Harrison; MCD-Township; SCIOTO; ***218** SI-10; ★ **PTSM**; mail Minford z 45653; Ⓟ 4,316; Ⓒ 4,497
Harrison; MCD-Township; VAN WERT; ***216** NI-1; mail Van Wert z 45891; Ⓟ 1,019; Ⓒ 1,085
Harrison; MCD-Township; VINTON; ***219** SF-11; mail Londonderry z 45647; Ⓟ 938; Ⓒ 1,030
HARRISON; **217** NM-18; Ⓟ 16,085; Ⓒ 15,856; ◆ 15,447
Harrison Furnace (Swauger Valley); RMC Place; SCIOTO; ▲ Harrison; ***218** SH-10; ★ **PTSM**; mail Portsmouth z 45662; rural
Harrison Mills; RMC Place; SCIOTO; ▲ Harrison; ***218** SH-10; ★ **PTSM**; mail South Webster z 45682; rural
Harrisonville; RMC Place; MEIGS; ▲ Scipio; **219** SG-13; mail Pomeroy z 45769; ● 150
Harrisville; Inc. Place; HARRISON; ▲ Short Creek; **217** NM-19; elev. 1,237ft./377m.; 🅿; z 43974; Ⓟ 308; Ⓒ 259
Harrisville; MCD-Township; MEDINA; ***217** NH-13; mail Burbank z 44214; Ⓟ 4,776; Ⓒ 4,914
Harrod; Inc. Place; ALLEN; ▲ Auglaize; **216** NJ-5; elev. 991ft./302m.; 🅿; ★ **LIMA**; z 45850; Ⓟ 537; Ⓒ 491
Harshasville; RMC Place; ADAMS; ▲ Oliver; ***218** SH-7; mail Peebles z 45660
Hartford; LICKING; see Croton (Inc. Place)
Hartford; MCD-Township; LICKING; ***216** NM-10; mail Croton z 43013; Ⓟ 1,197; Ⓒ 1,290
Hartford; RMC Place; TRUMBULL; ▲ Hartford; **217** NG-20; elev. 1,222ft./372m.; 🅿; ★ **YNGS-**; z 44424; ● 350
Hartford; MCD-Township; TRUMBULL; ***217** NF-20; 🅿; ★ **YNGS-**; z 44424; Ⓟ 2,157; Ⓒ 2,104
Hartland (Hartland Station); RMC Place; HURON; ▲ Townsend, Hartland; **217** NG-11; elev. 943ft./287m.; mail Collins z 44826, Norwalk z 44857
Hartland; MCD-Township; HURON; ***217** NG-11; mail Norwalk z 44857; Ⓟ 934; Ⓒ 979
Hartland Center; RMC Place; HURON; ▲ Hartland; ***217** NG-11; mail Collins z 44826; ● 35
Hartland Station; HURON; see Hartland (RMC Place)
Hartleyville; RMC Place; ATHENS; ▲ Trimble; ***219** SD-13; mail Glouster z 45732; rural
Hartsgrove; RMC Place; ASHTABULA; ▲ Hartsgrove; **217** NE-18; mail Rome z 44085, Windsor z 44099; ● 300
Hartsgrove; MCD-Township; ASHTABULA; ***217** NE-18; mail Rome z 44085; Ⓟ 1,157; Ⓒ 1,395
Hartshorn; RMC Place; MONROE; ▲ Wayne; ***219** SC-17; mail Graysville z 45734
Hartville; Inc. Place; STARK; ▲ Lake; **217** NI-16; elev. 1,165ft./355m.; 🅿; ★ **CAN**; z 44632; Ⓟ 2,031; Ⓒ 2,174
Hartwell; RMC Place; HAMILTON; ***218** SF-2; ★ **CIN**; mail Cincinnati z 45216; pop. incl. with Cincinnati (Inc. Place)
Harveysburg; Inc. Place; WARREN; ▲ Massie; **218** SD-4; elev. 904ft./276m.; 🅿; z 45032; Ⓟ 437; Ⓒ 563
Haselton; RMC Place; MAHONING; ***217** NH-20; ★ **YNGS-**; pop. incl. with Youngstown (Inc. Place)
Haskins; Inc. Place; WOOD; ▲ Middleton; **216** NF-6; elev. 663ft./202m.; 🅿; ★ **TOL**; z 43525; Ⓟ 549; Ⓒ 638
Hasting Hill; RMC Place; SCIOTO; ▲ Porter; ***218** SI-10; ★ **PTSM**; mail Portsmouth z 45662; ● 150
Hatch; RMC Place; PIKE; ▲ Sunfish; ***218** SG-8; mail Piketon z 45661; rural
Hatton; RMC Place; WOOD; ▲ Perry; **216** NG-7; mail Risingsun z 43457; ● 50
Havana; RMC Place; HURON; ▲ Norwich; **216** NH-10; mail Willard z 44890; ● 110
Havens Corners; RMC Place; FRANKLIN; ▲ Jefferson; ***218** SA-10; elev. 974ft./297m.; ★ **COL**; mail Blacklick z 43004; ● 140
Havensport; RMC Place; FAIRFIELD; ▲ Greenfield; **219** SC-11; ★ **COL**; mail Carroll z 43112; ● 60
Haven View; RMC Place; MIAMI; ▲ Elizabeth; ***218** SA-4; mail Troy z 45373
Haverhill; RMC Place; SCIOTO; ▲ Green; **218** SJ-10; elev. 542ft./165m.; 🅿; ★ **HNTG**; z 45636; ● 120
Haviland; Inc. Place; PAULDING; ▲ Blue Creek; **216** NH-2; elev. 736ft./224m.; 🅿; z 45851; Ⓟ 210; Ⓒ 180
Hayden; RMC Place; FRANKLIN; ▲ Brown; ***218** SA-8; mail Amlin z 43002
Haydenville; RMC Place; HOCKING; ▲ Starr; **219** SE-12; elev. 725ft./221m.; 🅿; z 43127; ● 450
Hayes Colony; RMC Place; DELAWARE; mail Delaware z 43015; pop. incl. with Delaware (Inc. Place)
Hayes Corners; RMC Place; GEAUGA; ▲ Middlefield; ***217** NF-18; mail Middlefield z 44062; ● 50
Hayesville (Hayesville Siding); Inc. Place; ASHLAND; ▲ Vermillion; **217** NJ-12; elev. 1,244ft./379m.; 🅿; z 44838; Ⓟ 457; Ⓒ 348
Hayesville Siding; ASHLAND; see Hayesville (Inc. Place)
Haynes; RMC Place; HOCKING; ▲ Salt Creek; ***219** SE-11; mail Laurelville z 43135; rural
Hazelwood; RMC Place; HAMILTON; ***218** SF-3; ★ **CIN**; mail Cincinnati z 45242; pop. incl. with Blue Ash (Inc. Place)
Heath; Inc. Place; LICKING; **219** SA-12; elev. 866ft./264m.; 🅿; ★ **NWRK**; z 43056; Ⓟ 7,231; Ⓒ 8,527
Heatherdowns; RMC Place; LUCAS; ★ **TOL**; mail Toledo z 43614; pop. incl. with Toledo (Inc. Place)
Hebbardsville; RMC Place; ATHENS; ▲ Alexander; **219** SF-13; mail Athens z 45701; ● 50
Hebron; Inc. Place; LICKING; ▲ Union; **219** SB-12; elev. 889ft./271m.; 🅿; ★ **NWRK**; z 43025; Ⓟ 2,076; Ⓒ 2,034
Hecla; RMC Place; LAWRENCE; ▲ Upper; **219** SJ-11; elev. 606ft./185m.; ★ **HNTG**; mail Ironton z 45638; ● 200
Hegemans Landing; RMC Place; SHELBY; ▲ McLean; ***216** NL-3; mail Minster z 45865; ● 100
Heidelburg Beach; RMC Place; ERIE; ▲ Vermilion; ***217** NF-11; ★ **CLEV**; mail Vermilion z 44089; summer pop. 160; ● 80
Helena; Inc. Place; SANDUSKY; ▲ Washington, Jackson; **216** NF-8; elev. 699ft./213m.; 🅿; z 43435; Ⓟ 267; Ⓒ 236
Helmick; RMC Place; COSHOCTON; ▲ Clark; ***217** NL-14; elev. 793ft./242m.; mail Warsaw z 43844; rural
Hemlock; Inc. Place; PERRY; ▲ Salt Lick; **219** SD-13; elev. 765ft./233m.; 🅿; z 43730; Ⓟ 203; Ⓒ 142
Hemlock Grove; RMC Place; MEIGS; ▲ Bedford; **219** SG-14; elev. 730ft./223m.; mail Pomeroy z 45769; ● 70
Hempstead; RMC Place; MONTGOMERY; ***218** SC-4; ★ **DAY**; mail Dayton z 45429; pop. incl. with Kettering (Inc. Place)
Hendrysburg; RMC Place; BELMONT; ▲ Kirkwood; **217** NN-17; elev. 1,030ft./314m.; mail Barnesville z 43713; ● 150
Henley; RMC Place; SCIOTO; ▲ Union; ***218** SH-8; elev. 577ft./176m.; mail Mc Dermott z 45652; rural
Henpeck; WARREN; see Wellman (RMC Place)
Henrietta; MCD-Township; LORAIN; ***217** NG-12; ★ **CLEV**; mail Amherst z 44001, Wakeman z 44889; Ⓟ 1,795; Ⓒ 1,873
Henry; MCD-Township; WOOD; ***216** NG-6; mail North Baltimore z 45872; Ⓟ 3,820; Ⓒ 4,070
HENRY; **216** NG-4; Ⓟ 29,108; Ⓒ 29,210; ◆ 28,225
Hepburn; RMC Place; HARDIN; ▲ Dudley; **216** NK-7; mail Kenton z 43326; ● 100
Heritage; RMC Place; ALLEN; ▲ American; ★ **LIMA**; mail Lima z 45805
Heritage Park; RMC Place; MEDINA; ▲ Brunswick Hills; ★ **CLEV**; mail Brunswick z 44212; ● 600
Hessville; RMC Place; SANDUSKY; ▲ Washington; **216** NF-8; mail Gibsonburg z 43431, Lindsey z 43442; ● 125
Hickman (Rocky Fork); RMC Place; LICKING; ▲ Mary Ann; ***217** NN-12; ★ **NWRK**; mail Newark z 43055
Hicksville; Inc. Place; DEFIANCE; **216** NG-1; elev. 766ft./233m.; 🅿 🅷; z 43526; Ⓟ 3,664; Ⓒ 3,649
Hicksville; MCD-Township; DEFIANCE; ***216** NG-1; 🅿; z 43526; Ⓟ 4,923; Ⓒ 5,003
Hideaway Hills; RMC Place; FAIRFIELD; ▲ Rush Creek; ***219** SC-12; elev. 900ft./274m.; mail Bremen z 43107, Sugar Grove z 43155; ● 500
Higginsport; Inc. Place; BROWN; ▲ Lewis; **218** SI-5; elev. 507ft./155m.; 🅿; z 45131; Ⓟ 298; Ⓒ 291
High Hill; RMC Place; MUSKINGUM; ▲ Meigs; **219** SB-15; mail Chandlersville z 43727; rural
Highland; MCD-Township; DEFIANCE; ***216** NG-3; mail Defiance z 43512; Ⓟ 2,612; Ⓒ 2,658
Highland; Inc. Place; HIGHLAND; ▲ Fairfield; **218** SE-6; elev. 1,057ft./322m.; 🅿; z 45132; Ⓟ 275; Ⓒ 283
Highland; MCD-Township; MUSKINGUM; ***219** SA-15; mail New Concord z 43762; Ⓟ 820; Ⓒ 848
HIGHLAND; **218** SF-7; mail Leesburg z 45135; Ⓟ 35,728; Ⓒ 40,875; ◆ 42,655
Highland Heights; Inc. Place; CUYAHOGA; **219** SK-20; elev. 934ft./285m.; 🅿; ★ **CLEV**; z 44143; Ⓟ 6,249; Ⓒ 8,082
Highland Hills; Inc. Place; CUYAHOGA; **219** SM-19; 🅿; ★ **CLEV**; z 44122, z 44128; Ⓒ 1,618
Highland Holliday; RMC Place; HIGHLAND; ▲ Paint; mail Hillsboro z 45133; summer pop. 600; ● 200
Highland Park; RMC Place; HAMILTON; ▲ Delhi; ***218** SG-2; elev. 900ft./274m.; ★ **CIN**; mail Cincinnati z 45238
Highland Park; RMC Place; MERCER; ▲ Jefferson; ***216** NK-2; mail Celina z 45822; ● 200
Highland Park (Hyland Park); RMC Place; SCIOTO; ▲ Union; ***218** SJ-10; ★ **HNTG**; mail Franklin Furnace z 45629; ● 120
Highland Park; RMC Place; STARK; ▲ Jackson; **217** NI-16; ★ **CAN**; mail Massillon z 44646; ● 700
Highland Terrace; RMC Place; BELMONT; ▲ Richland; ***217** NN-19; ★ **WHL**; mail Saint Clairsville z 43950; ● 100
Highlandtown; RMC Place; COLUMBIANA; ▲ Washington; **217** NK-19; elev. 1,187ft./362m.; mail Hammondsville z 43930, Salineville z 43945, Wellsville z 43968; ● 100
Highland Trails; RMC Place; HIGHLAND; ▲ Paint; mail Hillsboro z 45133; ● 400
Highpoint; RMC Place; HAMILTON; ▲ Sycamore; **218** SJ-5; ★ **CIN**; mail Cincinnati z 45242; ● 600
Highview; RMC Place; MONTGOMERY; ★ **DAY**
High Water; RMC Place; LICKING; ▲ McKean; ***217** NM-11; elev. 1,052ft./321m.; mail Newark z 43055; ● 35
Hill Addition; RMC Place; COLUMBIANA; ▲ Liverpool; ***217** NJ-20; ★ **E.LIV**; mail East Liverpool z 43920; pop. incl. with East Liverpool (Inc. Place)
Hill And Hollow; RMC Place; BUTLER; mail Oxford z 45056; pop. incl. with Oxford (Inc. Place)
Hillcrest; RMC Place; COLUMBIANA; ▲ Yellow Creek; ***217** NK-20; ★ **E.LIV**; mail Wellsville z 43968; ● 150
Hillcrest; RMC Place; WARREN; ▲ Union; ***218** SE-3; ★ **CIN**; mail Lebanon z 45036; ● 160
Hill Crest; RMC Place; WAYNE; ▲ Wayne; ***217** NJ-14; mail Wooster z 44691; rural
Hillcrest; RMC Place; WILLIAMS; ▲ Madison; ***216** NE-2; elev. 864ft./263m.; mail Montpelier z 43543; rural
Hill Grove; RMC Place; DARKE; ▲ Washington, Jackson; **216** NM-1; mail Union City z 45390; ● 100
Hilliar; MCD-Township; KNOX; ***216** NM-10; mail Centerburg z 43011; Ⓟ 2,645; Ⓒ 3,080
Hilliard; Inc. Place; FRANKLIN; ▲ Washington, Norwich; **218** SA-8; elev. 935ft./285m.; 🅿; ★ **COL**; z 43026; Ⓟ 11,794; Ⓒ 24,230; ◆ 28,932
Hills and Dales; RMC Place; MONTGOMERY; ★ **DAY**; mail Dayton z 45429; pop. incl. with Kettering (Inc. Place)
Hills and Dales; Inc. Place; STARK; ▲ Jackson; **216** NB-9; elev. 1,091ft./333m.; ★ **CAN**; mail Canton z 44708; Ⓟ 297; Ⓒ 260
Hillsboro; Inc. Place; ⊡ HIGHLAND; ▲ Liberty; **218** SF-6; elev. 1,132ft./345m.; 🅿 🅷; z 45133; Ⓟ 6,235; Ⓒ 6,368
Hillsboro; RMC Place; JEFFERSON; ★ **STU-**; mail Mingo Junction z 43938
Hilltop; RMC Place; FRANKLIN; ★ **COL**; mail Columbus z 43204; pop. incl. with Columbus (Inc. Place)
Hilltop; CDP-Census Area Only; TRUMBULL; ▲ Weathersfield; ***217** NG-19; ★ **YNGS-**; mail Mc Donald z 44437; Ⓒ 534
Hilltop Acres; RMC Place; HAMILTON; ***218** SF-2; ★ **CIN**; mail Cincinnati z 45215; pop. incl. with Wyoming (Inc. Place)
Hinckley; RMC Place; MEDINA; ▲ Hinckley; **217** NG-15; elev. 1,070ft./326m.; 🅿; ★ **CLEV**; z 44233; ● 500
Hinckley; MCD-Township; MEDINA; ***217** NG-15; 🅿; ★ **CLEV**; z 44233; Ⓟ 5,845; Ⓒ 6,753
Hiram; Inc. Place; PORTAGE; **217** NG-17; elev. 1,226ft./374m.; 🅿 🅲 1,205; z 44234; Ⓟ 1,330; Ⓒ 1,242
Hiram; MCD-Township; PORTAGE; ***217** NG-17; 🅿 🅲 1,205; z 44234; Ⓟ 3,218; Ⓒ 2,296
Hiram Rapids (Harrison); RMC Place; PORTAGE; ▲ Hiram; **217** NF-17; mail Hiram z 44234; ● 250
Hiramsburg; RMC Place; NOBLE; ▲ Noble; ***219** SC-16; mail Cumberland z 43732
Hitchcock; RMC Place; JACKSON; ▲ Jefferson; ***219** SH-11; mail Oak Hill z 45656
Hoadley; RMC Place; GALLIA; ▲ Greenfield; ***219** SI-11; mail Patriot z 45658; rural
Hoagland; RMC Place; HIGHLAND; ▲ New Market, Liberty; **218** SF-6; elev. 1,063ft./324m.; mail Hillsboro z 45133; ● 50
Hoaglin; MCD-Township; VAN WERT; ***216** NI-2; mail Van Wert z 45891; Ⓟ 624; Ⓒ 605
Hobson; RMC Place; MEIGS; ▲ Salisbury; **219** SH-13; elev. 579ft./176m.; mail Middleport z 45760; pop. incl. with Middleport (Inc. Place)
Hocking; MCD-Township; FAIRFIELD; ***219** SC-11; ★ **LANC**; mail Lancaster z 43130; Ⓟ 4,331; Ⓒ 4,812
HOCKING; **219** SE-11; Ⓟ 25,533; Ⓒ 28,241; ◆ 29,365
Hockingport; RMC Place; ATHENS; ▲ Troy; **219** SF-15; elev. 605ft./184m.; 🅿; z 45739; ● 300
Hoke; RMC Place; MIAMI; ▲ Union; ***218** SB-3; ★ **DAY**; mail West Milton z 45383; ● 110
Holden; RMC Place; AUGLAIZE, HARDIN; ▲ Roundhead, Wayne; ***216** NK-5; elev. 1,039ft./317m.; mail Waynesfield z 45896
Holgate; Inc. Place; HENRY; ▲ Pleasant, Flatrock; **216** NG-4; elev. 710ft./216m.; 🅿; z 43527; Ⓟ 1,290; Ⓒ 1,194
Holiday Acres; RMC Place; HAMILTON; ▲ Sycamore; ***218** SF-3; elev. 850ft./259m.; ★ **CIN**; mail Cincinnati z 45236
Holiday City; Inc. Place; WILLIAMS; ▲ Jefferson; ***216** NE-2; 🅿; z 43543, z 43554; Ⓒ 49
Holiday Hills; RMC Place; CLARK; ▲ Springfield; ***218** SB-6; ★ **SPR**; mail Springfield z 45502; ● 275
Holiday Lakes; RMC Place; HURON; ▲ Norwich, Greenfield; ***216** NH-10; mail Willard z 44890; ● 500
Holiday Valley; CDP; CLARK; ▲ Mad River; ***218** SB-5; ★ **SPR**; mail Fairborn z 45324; Ⓟ 1,243; Ⓒ 1,712
Holland; Inc. Place; LUCAS; ▲ Springfield; **216** NE-6; elev. 635ft./194m.; 🅿; ★ **TOL**; z 43528; Ⓟ 1,210; Ⓒ 1,306
Hollansburg; Inc. Place; DARKE; ▲ Harrison; **218** SA-1; elev. 1,162ft./354m.; 🅿; ★ **RICH**; z 45332; Ⓟ 300; Ⓒ 214
Hollister; RMC Place; ATHENS; ▲ Trimble; **219** SD-13; mail Glouster z 45732; ● 300
Holloway; Inc. Place; BELMONT; ▲ Flushing; **217** NM-17; elev. 918ft./280m.; 🅿; z 43985; Ⓟ 354; Ⓒ 345
Hollowtown; RMC Place; HIGHLAND; ▲ Salem, Clay; ***218** SG-6; elev. 1,030ft./314m.; mail Sardinia z 45171; ● 30
Holmes; MCD-Township; CRAWFORD; ***216** NI-9; mail Bucyrus z 44820; Ⓟ 1,397; Ⓒ 1,330
HOLMES; **217** NK-14; Ⓟ 32,849; Ⓒ 38,943; ◆ 41,017
Holmesville; Inc. Place; HOLMES; ▲ Prairie; **217** NK-14; elev. 880ft./268m.; 🅿; z 44633; Ⓟ 419; Ⓒ 386
Home Acres; RMC Place; BUTLER; ▲ Lemon; ★ **MIDD**; mail Middletown z 45044
Home Acres; RMC Place; MIAMI; ▲ Concord; mail Troy z 45373; ● 380
Homedale; RMC Place; FRANKLIN; ▲ Sharon; ***218** SA-9; ★ **COL**; mail Columbus z 43085; pop. incl. with Columbus (Inc. Place)
Home Orchards; RMC Place; CLARK; ★ **SPR**; mail Springfield z 45503; pop. incl. with Springfield (Inc. Place)
Homer; RMC Place; LICKING; ▲ Burlington; **217** NM-11; elev. 996ft./304m.; 🅿; z 43027; ● 250
Homer; MCD-Township; MEDINA; ***217** NH-13; mail Homerville z 44235; Ⓟ 1,196; Ⓒ 1,461
Homer; MCD-Township; MORGAN; ***219** SD-14; mail Glouster z 45732; Ⓟ 763; Ⓒ 976
Homerville; RMC Place; MEDINA; ▲ Homer; **217** NH-13; elev. 1,083ft./330m.; 🅿; z 44235; ● 80
Homeside; RMC Place; BELMONT; ▲ Richland; ***219** SA-19; ★ **WHL**; mail Saint Clairsville z 43950; ● 200
Homeville; RMC Place; ERIE; ▲ Perkins; ***216** NF-10; ★ **SNDSK**; mail Sandusky z 44870; ● 1,300
Homewood; RMC Place; BUTLER; ▲ Fairfield; ***218** SE-2; ★ **CIN**; mail Hamilton z 45015; pop. incl. with Hamilton (Inc. Place)
Homeworth; RMC Place; COLUMBIANA; ▲ Knox; **217** NI-18; elev. 1,155ft./352m.; 🅿; ★ **ALLI**; z 44634; ● 400
Honeytown; RMC Place; WAYNE; ▲ Wooster, East Union; **217** NJ-14; mail Wooster z 44691; ● 40
Hooker; RMC Place; FAIRFIELD; ▲ Greenfield; ***219** SC-11; ★ **LANC**; mail Lancaster z 43130
Hooksburg; RMC Place; MORGAN; ▲ Windsor; ***219** SD-15; mail Stockport z 43787; summer pop. 100; ● 40
Hooring; RMC Place; ATHENS; ▲ Waterloo; mail New Marshfield z 45766; rural
Hooven; RMC Place; HAMILTON; ▲ Whitewater; **218** SF-1; elev. 550ft./168m.; 🅿; ★ **CIN**; z 45033; ● 500
Hope; RMC Place; VINTON; ▲ Brown
Hopedale; Inc. Place; HARRISON; ▲ Green; **217** NM-18; elev. 1,290ft./393m.; 🅿; z 43976; Ⓟ 685; Ⓒ 984
Hopetown; RMC Place; ROSS; ▲ Springfield; **218** SE-9; mail Chillicothe z 45601; ● 50
Hopewell; GUERNSEY; see Indian Camp (RMC Place)
Hopewell; RMC Place; JEFFERSON; ▲ Warren; ***217** NM-19; ★ **WHL**; mail Rayland z 43943; ● 60
Hopewell; MCD-Township; LICKING; ***219** SB-13; mail Gratiot z 43740; Ⓟ 1,089; Ⓒ 1,200
Hopewell; MCD-Township; MERCER; ***216** NK-1; mail Celina z 45822; Ⓟ 968; Ⓒ 1,066
Hopewell (Mount Sterling); RMC Place; MUSKINGUM; ▲ Muskingum; **219** SB-13; elev. 1,057ft./322m.; 🅿; z 43746; ● 250
Hopewell; MCD-Township; MUSKINGUM; ***219** SB-13; 🅿; z 43746; Ⓟ 2,648; Ⓒ 3,038
Hopewell; MCD-Township; PERRY; ***219** SB-12; mail Glenford z 43739; Ⓟ 1,724; Ⓒ 2,163
Hopewell; MCD-Township; SENECA; ***216** NH-8; mail Bascom z 44809; Ⓟ 2,976; Ⓒ 2,874
Hopkinsville; RMC Place; WARREN; ▲ Hamilton; ***218** SE-3; elev. 771ft./235m.; ★ **CIN**; mail Maineville z 45039
Horatio; RMC Place; DARKE; ▲ Adams; ***216** NN-2; mail Greenville z 45331; ● 35
Horns Mill; RMC Place; FAIRFIELD; ▲ Berne; ***219** SD-11; ★ **LANC**; mail Lancaster z 43130
Hoskinsville; RMC Place; NOBLE; ▲ Noble; **219** SC-16; mail Caldwell z 43724
Houck Meadows; RMC Place; CLARK; ▲ Mad River; mail Springfield z 45502; pop. incl. with Enon (Inc. Place)
Houcktown; RMC Place; HANCOCK; ▲ Jackson; **216** NI-6; mail Arlington z 45814, Findlay z 45840; ● 180
Houston; RMC Place; SHELBY; ▲ Loramie; **216** NM-3; elev. 952ft./290m.; 🅿; z 45333; ● 220
Howard; RMC Place; KNOX; ▲ Howard; **217** NL-12; elev. 892ft./272m.; 🅿; z 43028; ● 300
Howard; MCD-Township; KNOX; ***217** NL-12; 🅿; z 43028; Ⓟ 2,149; Ⓒ 4,319
Howard Farm Beach; RMC Place; LUCAS; ▲ Jerusalem; ***216** NE-8; ★ **TOL**; mail Curtice z 43412; ● 200
Howenstein; RMC Place; STARK; ▲ Pike; **217** NJ-16; ★ **CAN**; mail East Sparta z 44626; ● 160
Howland; TRUMBULL; see Howland Center (CDP-Census Area Only)
Howland; MCD-Township; TRUMBULL; ***217** NG-19; ★ **YNGS-**; mail Warren z 44484; Ⓟ 20,096; Ⓒ 19,451
Howland Center (Howland); CDP-Census Area Only; TRUMBULL; ▲ Howland; **217** NA-12; ★ **YNGS-**; mail Warren z 44484; Ⓟ 6,732; Ⓒ 6,481
Hoytville; Inc. Place; WOOD; ▲ Jackson; **216** NG-5; elev. 947ft./289m.; 🅿; z 43529; Ⓟ 301; Ⓒ 296
Hubbard; Inc. Place; TRUMBULL; ▲ Hubbard; **217** NG-20; elev. 947ft./289m.; 🅿; ★ **YNGS-**; z 44425; Ⓟ 8,248; Ⓒ 8,284
Hubbard; MCD-Township; TRUMBULL; ***217** NG-20; 🅿; ★ **YNGS-**; z 44425; Ⓟ 14,863; Ⓒ 14,304
Huber Heights; Inc. Place; MONTGOMERY, GREENE, MIAMI; **218** SB-4; elev. 877ft./267m.; 🅿; ★ **DAY**; z 45424; Ⓟ 38,696; Ⓒ 38,212; ◆ 35,667
Huber Ridge; CDP; FRANKLIN; ▲ Blendon; ***218** SA-10; ★ **COL**; mail Westerville z 43081; Ⓟ 5,255; Ⓒ 4,883
Huber South; RMC Place; MONTGOMERY; ▲ Miami; ***218** SC-3; ★ **DAY**; mail Dayton z 45439; pop. incl. with Moraine (Inc. Place)
Hudson (Hudson Village); Inc. Place; SUMMIT; **217** NG-16; elev. 1,100ft./335m.; 🅿; ★ **AKR**; z 44236-37; Ⓟ 5,159; Ⓒ 22,439; ◆ 22,319
Hudson Village; SUMMIT; see Hudson (Inc. Place)
Hue; RMC Place; VINTON; ▲ Swan; ***219** SE-11; elev. 1,054ft./321m.; mail Creola z 45622; rural
Hughes; RMC Place; BUTLER; ▲ Liberty; ***218** SE-3; elev. 709ft./216m.; ★ **CIN**; mail Middletown z 45042; rural
Hulington; RMC Place; CLERMONT; ▲ Monroe; **218** SG-4; elev. 848ft./258m.; ★ **CIN**; mail Bethel z 45106; ● 100
Humboldt; RMC Place; ROSS; ▲ Paint; **218** SF-8; elev. 798ft./243m.; mail Bainbridge z 45612; rural
Hume; RMC Place; ALLEN; ▲ Shawnee; **216** NJ-3; ★ **LIMA**; mail Lima z 45806; ● 135
Hunt (Hunt Station); RMC Place; KNOX; ▲ Pleasant, Miller; ***217** NM-11; elev. 1,042ft./318m.; mail Mount Vernon z 43050
Hunter; RMC Place; BELMONT; ▲ Wayne; **219** SB-18; elev. 1,264ft./385m.; mail Bethesda z 43719
Hunter; CDP-Census Area Only; WARREN; ***218** SD-3; ★ **MIDD**; Ⓒ 1,737
Hunterdon; RMC Place; ATHENS; ▲ Trimble; ***219** SD-13; mail Glouster z 45732; ● 60
Huntington; MCD-Township; BROWN; ***218** SI-6; mail Aberdeen z 45101; Ⓟ 2,704; Ⓒ 2,968
Huntington; MCD-Township; GALLIA; ***219** SH-12; mail Vinton z 45686; Ⓟ 1,445; Ⓒ 1,511
Huntington; RMC Place; LORAIN; ▲ Huntington; **217** NH-12; mail Wellington z 44090; ● 220
Huntington; MCD-Township; LORAIN; ***217** NH-12; mail Wellington z 44090; Ⓟ 1,172; Ⓒ 1,282
Huntington; MCD-Township; ROSS; ***218** SF-9; mail Chillicothe z 45601; Ⓟ 5,102; Ⓒ 6,018
Huntington Hills; RMC Place; FAIRFIELD; ▲ Violet; ***218** SB-10; ★ **COL**; mail Pickerington z 43147; ● 1,050
Huntington Park; RMC Place; BROWN; ***218** SI-6; elev. 539ft./164m.; mail Aberdeen z 45101; pop. incl. with Aberdeen (Inc. Place)
Hunting Valley; Inc. Place; CUYAHOGA, GEAUGA; **217** NE-16; elev. 772ft./235m.; ★ **CLEV**; mail Chagrin Falls z 44022; Ⓟ 799; Ⓒ 735
Huntsburg; RMC Place; GEAUGA; ▲ Huntsburg; **217** NE-18; elev. 1,280ft./390m.; 🅿; ★ **CLEV**; z 44046; ● 300
Huntsburg; MCD-Township; GEAUGA; ***217** NE-18; 🅿; ★ **CLEV**; z 44046; Ⓟ 2,642; Ⓒ 3,297
Hunts Corners; RMC Place; HURON; ▲ Lyme; ***216** NG-10; mail Bellevue z 44811
Hunt Station; KNOX; see Hunt (RMC Place)
Huntsville; RMC Place; BUTLER; ▲ Liberty; ***218** SE-3; elev. 829ft./253m.; ★ **CIN**; mail Middletown z 45042; ● 90
Huntsville; Inc. Place; LOGAN; ▲ McArthur; **216** NL-5; elev. 1,069ft./326m.; 🅿; z 43324; Ⓟ 343; Ⓒ 454
Hurford; RMC Place; HARRISON; ▲ Short Creek; ***217** NM-19; mail Adena z 43901; rural
Huron; Inc. Place; ERIE; ▲ Huron; **217** NF-11; elev. 600ft./183m.; 🅿; ★ **SNDSK**; z 44839; Ⓟ 7,030; Ⓒ 7,958
Huron; MCD-Township; ERIE; ***217** NF-11; 🅿; ★ **SNDSK**; z 44839; Ⓟ 9,297; Ⓒ 10,530
HURON; **217** NG-11; Ⓟ 56,240; Ⓒ 59,487; ◆ 59,445
Huron Junction; RMC Place; HURON; ***217** NG-11; ★ **SNDSK**; pop. incl. with Norwalk (Inc. Place)
Hustead; RMC Place; CLARK; ▲ Mad River, Green; **218** SB-5; ★ **SPR**; mail Springfield z 45502; ● 120
Hyatts; RMC Place; DELAWARE; ▲ Liberty; **216** NM-8; elev. 927ft./283m.; ★ **COL**; mail Powell z 43065; ● 50
Hyde Park; RMC Place; HAMILTON; ***218** SG-2; ★ **CIN**; mail Cincinnati z 45208; pop. incl. with Cincinnati (Inc. Place)
Hyde Park; RMC Place; MONTGOMERY; ▲ Washington; ★ **DAY**; mail Dayton z 45429; ● 1,450
Hyland Park; SCIOTO; see Highland Park (RMC Place)

I

Iberia; RMC Place; MORROW; ▲ Washington; **216** NJ-10; elev. 1,101ft./336m.; 🅿; z 43325; ● 350
Idaho; RMC Place; PIKE; ▲ Pebble; **218** SG-8; elev. 578ft./176m.; 🅿; z 45661; ● 50
Idlewild; RMC Place; HAMILTON; ***218** SG-2; ★ **CIN**; pop. incl. with Cincinnati (Inc. Place)
Iler (Ilers); RMC Place; SENECA; ▲ Jackson; **216** NG-7; mail Fostoria z 44830
Ilers; SENECA; see Iler (RMC Place)
Ilesboro; RMC Place; HOCKING; ▲ Washington; **219** SE-12; elev. 1,058ft./322m.; mail Logan z 43138
Immergrun; RMC Place; LUCAS; ***216** ND-7; ★ **TOL**; mail Oregon z 43618; pop. incl. with Oregon (Inc. Place)
Independence; Inc. Place; CUYAHOGA; **217** NF-15; elev. 855ft./261m.; 🅿; ★ **CLEV**; z 44131; Ⓟ 6,500; Ⓒ 7,109
Independence; RMC Place; DEFIANCE; ▲ Richland; **216** NG-3; mail Defiance z 43512; ● 100
Independence; MCD-Township; WASHINGTON; ***219** SD-17; mail New Matamoras z 45767; Ⓟ 358; Ⓒ 387
Indian Camp (Hopewell); RMC Place; GUERNSEY; ▲ Knox; ***219** SA-15; mail Cambridge z 43725
Indian Hill; HAMILTON; see The Village of Indian Hill (Inc. Place)
Indian Knolls; RMC Place; CLERMONT; ***218** SF-3; ★ **CIN**; mail Milford z 45150; pop. incl. with Milford (Inc. Place)
Indian Ridge; RMC Place; HAMILTON; ▲ Colerain; ***218** SF-2; ★ **CIN**; mail Cincinnati z 45231; ● 85
Indianview; RMC Place; CLERMONT; ▲ Miami; ***218** SF-3; ★ **CIN**; mail Miamiville z 45147; ● 140
Ingle Mann; RMC Place; PREBLE; ▲ Jefferson; ★ **RICH**; mail New Paris z 45347; pop. incl. with New Paris (Inc. Place)
Ingomar; RMC Place; PREBLE; ▲ Lanier; **218** SC-2; ★ **DAY**; mail West Alexandria z 45381; ● 60
Ink; SENECA; see Swander (RMC Place)
Ira; RMC Place; SUMMIT; ▲ Bath; ***217** NG-15; ★ **AKR**; mail Akron z 44333; pop. incl. with Cuyahoga Falls (Inc. Place)
Iradale; RMC Place; SUMMIT; ▲ Bath; ***217** NG-15; ★ **AKR**; mail Akron z 44313; ● 580
Irondale; Inc. Place; JEFFERSON; ▲ Saline; **217** NK-19; elev. 718ft./219m.; 🅿; ★ **E.LIV**; z 43932; Ⓟ 382; Ⓒ 418
Irondale; RMC Place; MUSKINGUM; mail Dresden z 43821; pop. incl. with Dresden (Inc. Place)
Ironspot; RMC Place; MUSKINGUM; ▲ Newton; **219** SB-13; ★ **ZAN**; mail Roseville z 43777; ● 150
Ironton; Inc. Place; ⊡ LAWRENCE; ▲ Upper, Hamilton; **219** SJ-11; elev. 558ft./170m.; 🅿 🅷; ★ **HNTG**; z 45638; Ⓟ 12,751; Ⓒ 11,211
Ironville; RMC Place; LUCAS; ***216** ND-7; ★ **TOL**; pop. incl. with Toledo (Inc. Place)
Irvington; RMC Place; MONTGOMERY; **218** SK-7; ★ **DAY**; mail Dayton z 45414; pop. incl. with Clayton (Inc. Place)
Irwin; RMC Place; UNION; ▲ Union; **216** NN-7; elev. 1,012ft./308m.; 🅿; z 43029; ● 150
Island Creek; MCD-Township; JEFFERSON; ***217** NL-20; ★ **STU-**; mail Toronto z 43964; Ⓟ 11,649; Ⓒ 12,078; Ⓡ 11,152
Island View; RMC Place; LOGAN; ▲ Stokes; **216** NK-5; mail Lakeview z 43331; ● 300
Isle Saint George (North Bass Island); RMC Place; OTTAWA; ▲ Put-in-Bay; **216** ND-10; 🅿; z 43436; ● 50
Isleta; RMC Place; COSHOCTON; ▲ Oxford; **217** NM-15; mail Newcomerstown z 43832, West Lafayette z 43845
Israel; MCD-Township; PREBLE; ***218** SD-1; mail College Corner z 45003; Ⓟ 1,397; Ⓒ 1,273
Ithaca; Inc. Place; DARKE; ▲ Twin; **218** SB-2; elev. 1,028ft./313m.; 🅿; ★ **DAY**; z 45304; Ⓟ 119; Ⓒ 102
Ivorydale; RMC Place; HAMILTON; ***218** SF-2; elev. 528ft./161m.; ★ **CIN**; mail Cincinnati z 45217; pop. incl. with Saint Bernard (Inc. Place)
Ivorydale Junction; RMC Place; HAMILTON; ***218** SF-2; ★ **CIN**; mail Cincinnati z 45217; pop. incl. with Saint Bernard (Inc. Place)

J

Jackson; MCD-Township; ALLEN; ***216** NJ-5; ★ **LIMA**; mail Lafayette z 45854; Ⓟ 2,737; Ⓒ 2,936
Jackson; MCD-Township; ASHLAND; ***217** NI-13; mail West Salem z 44287; Ⓟ 2,439; Ⓒ 3,554
Jackson; MCD-Township; AUGLAIZE; ***216** NL-3; mail Minster z 45865; Ⓟ 3,415; Ⓒ 3,577
Jackson; MCD-Township; BROWN; ***218** SH-6; mail Winchester z 45697; Ⓟ 806; Ⓒ 1,221
Jackson; MCD-Township; CHAMPAIGN; ***218** SA-5; mail Christiansburg z 45389; Ⓟ 2,244; Ⓒ 2,535
Jackson; MCD-Township; CLERMONT; ***218** SG-4; ★ **CIN**; mail Marathon z 45145; Ⓟ 2,461; Ⓒ 2,576
Jackson; MCD-Township; COSHOCTON; ***217** NM-14; mail Coshocton z 43812; Ⓟ 1,947; Ⓒ 2,045
Jackson; MCD-Township; CRAWFORD; ***216** NJ-10; ★ **MANS**; mail Crestline z 44827; Ⓟ 5,392; Ⓒ 5,487
Jackson; MCD-Township; DARKE; ***216** NM-1; mail Union City z 45390; Ⓟ 3,356; Ⓒ 3,057
Jackson; MCD-Township; FRANKLIN; ***218** SB-9; ★ **COL**; mail Grove City z 43123; Ⓟ 25,265; Ⓒ 32,625
Jackson; MCD-Township; GUERNSEY; ***219** SB-16; mail Byesville z 43723; Ⓟ 5,298; Ⓒ 5,399
Jackson; MCD-Township; HANCOCK; ***216** NI-6; mail Arlington z 45814; Ⓟ 971; Ⓒ 1,060
Jackson; MCD-Township; HARDIN; ***216** NJ-6; mail Forest z 45843; Ⓟ 2,210; Ⓒ 2,139
Jackson; MCD-Township; HIGHLAND; ***218** SG-7; mail Hillsboro z 45133; Ⓟ 743; Ⓒ 1,099
Jackson; Inc. Place; ⊡ JACKSON; ▲ Lick, Franklin; **219** SG-11; elev. 680ft./207m.; 🅿; z 45640; Ⓟ 6,144; Ⓒ 6,184

Entries in **UPPERCASE** are counties.
Entries in **bold** have populations of 2,500 or more.
Names in parentheses are alternate names.
Inc. Place — Incorporated Place
RMC Place — Rand McNally Designated Place
CDP — Census Designated Place
MCD — Minor Civil Division

⊡ County Seat
▲ Minor Civil Division
elev. Elevation
🅿 Post Office
🅷 Hospital
🅲 College
■ Principal Business Center
★ Ranally Metro Area (RMA) Abbreviation
z Zip Code(s)
Ⓟ Previous Census Population
Ⓡ Revised Census Population
Ⓐ Annexation Population
● Rand McNally Population Estimate
Ⓒ Final Census Population
Ⓢ Special Census Population
◆ Estimated Population

For additional definitions see Glossary, Volume 1, and Introduction, Volume 2.

Jackson; MCD-Township; JACKSON; *219 SF-11; 🅿; z 45640; Ⓟ 1,113; © 1,296
Jackson; MCD-Township; KNOX; *217 NM-12; mail Bladensburg z 43005; Ⓟ 680; © 878
Jackson; MCD-Township; MAHONING; *217 NH-19; ★ YNGS-; mail North Jackson z 44451; Ⓟ 2,164; © 2,167
Jackson; MCD-Township; MONROE; *219 SD-18; mail New Matamoras z 45767; Ⓟ 388; © 473
Jackson; MCD-Township; MONTGOMERY; *218 SC-3; ★ DAY; mail Farmersville z 45325; Ⓟ 6,390; © 6,420
Jackson; MCD-Township; MUSKINGUM; *217 NN-13; mail Frazeysburg z 43822; Ⓟ 2,076; © 2,221
Jackson; MCD-Township; NOBLE; *219 SD-16; mail Dexter City z 45727; Ⓟ 478; © 536
Jackson; MCD-Township; PAULDING; *216 NH-2; mail Latty z 45855; Ⓟ 1,821; © 1,886
Jackson; MCD-Township; PERRY; *219 SC-12; mail Junction City z 43748; Ⓟ 2,266; © 2,791
Jackson; MCD-Township; PICKAWAY; *218 SC-9; mail Circleville z 43113; Ⓟ 911; © 916
Jackson; MCD-Township; PIKE; *218 SG-10; mail Waverly z 45690; Ⓟ 1,298; © 1,346
Jackson; MCD-Township; PREBLE; *218 SB-1; mail Eaton z 45320; Ⓟ 1,222; © 1,223
Jackson; MCD-Township; PUTNAM; *216 NI-3; mail Fort Jennings z 45844; Ⓟ 974; © 939
Jackson; MCD-Township; RICHLAND; *217 NI-11; ★ MANS; mail Shelby z 44875; Ⓟ 3,602; © 3,861
Jackson; MCD-Township; SANDUSKY; *216 NG-8; mail Burgoon z 43407; Ⓟ 1,614; © 1,609
Jackson; MCD-Township; SENECA; *216 NG-7; mail Fostoria z 44830; Ⓟ 1,747; © 1,640
Jackson; MCD-Township; SHELBY; *216 NL-4; mail Jackson Center z 45334; Ⓟ 2,393; © 2,346
Jackson; MCD-Township; STARK; *217 NI-16; ★ CAN; mail Massillon z 44646; Ⓟ 32,071; © 37,744
Jackson; MCD-Township; UNION; *216 NL-7; mail Richwood z 43344; Ⓟ 757; © 914
Jackson; MCD-Township; VAN WERT; *216 NI-2; mail Middle Point z 45863; Ⓟ 505; © 481
Jackson; MCD-Township; VINTON; *219 SE-11; mail Mc Arthur z 45651; Ⓟ 541; © 714
Jackson; RMC Place; WAYNE; ▲ Canaan; *217 NI-14; ★ CLEV; mail Creston z 44217; pop. incl. with Creston (Inc. Place)
Jackson; MCD-Township; WOOD; *216 NG-5; mail Hoytville z 43529; Ⓟ 765; © 751
Jackson; MCD-Township; WYANDOT; *216 NJ-7; mail Forest z 45843; Ⓟ 586; © 643
JACKSON; 219 SH-11; Ⓟ 30,230; © 32,641; ◆ 33,218
Jackson Belden; RMC Place; STARK; ▲ Jackson; 🅿; ★ CAN; z 44718 & mail Canton z 44735; pop. incl. with Canton (Inc. Place)
Jacksonburg; Inc. Place; BUTLER; ▲ Wayne; 218 SD-2; elev. 955ft./291m.; ★ MIDD; mail Trenton z 45067; Ⓟ 50; © 67
Jackson Center; RMC Place; MAHONING; ▲ Jackson; ★ YNGS-; mail North Jackson z 44451
Jackson Center; Inc. Place; SHELBY; ▲ Jackson; 216 NL-4; elev. 1,025ft./312m.; 🅿; z 45334; Ⓟ 1,398; © 1,369
Jackson Heights; RMC Place; JACKSON; ▲ Lick; *219 SG-11; mail Jackson z 45640; pop. incl. with Jackson (Inc. Place)
Jackson Heights; RMC Place; JEFFERSON; ▲ Warren; *217 NM-19; ★ WHL; mail Rayland z 43943; rural
Jackson Lake; RMC Place; JACKSON; ▲ Jefferson; *219 SH-11; mail Oak Hill z 45656; ● 100
Jacksontown; RMC Place; LICKING; ▲ Licking; 219 SB-12; elev. 1,007ft./307m.; 🅿; ★ NWRK; z 43030; ● 350
Jacksonville; RMC Place; ADAMS; ▲ Meigs; 218 SH-7; mail Peebles z 45660; ● 75
Jacksonville; Inc. Place; ATHENS; ▲ Trimble; 219 SE-13; elev. 683ft./208m.; 🅿; z 45740; Ⓟ 544; © 544
Jacksonville; RMC Place; CLARK; ▲ German; *218 SB-5; ★ SPR; mail Springfield z 45502; ● 100
Jacktown; RMC Place; BUTLER; ▲ Madison; ★ MIDD; mail Middletown z 45042; rural
Jacobsburg; RMC Place; BELMONT; ▲ Smith; 219 SB-19; elev. 1,326ft./404m.; 🅿; z 43933; ● 200
Jamestown; Inc. Place; GREENE; ▲ Silvercreek; 218 SC-6; elev. 1,057ft./322m.; 🅿; z 45335; Ⓟ 1,794; © 1,917
Jasper; MCD-Township; FAYETTE; *218 SD-6; mail Jeffersonville z 43128; Ⓟ 839; © 857
Jasper; RMC Place; PIKE; ▲ Newton; 218 SG-9; elev. 561ft./171m.; 🅿; z 45642; ● 250
Jasper Mills; RMC Place; FAYETTE; ▲ Jasper; 218 SD-7; mail Washington Court House z 43160; ● 40
Jays; DARKE; see Jaysville (RMC Place)
Jaysville (Jays); RMC Place; DARKE; ▲ Van Buren, Neave; 216 NN-1; mail Greenville z 45331; ● 30
Jefferson; MCD-Township; ADAMS; *218 SI-8; mail Stout z 45684; Ⓟ 1,022; © 1,024
Jefferson; Inc. Place; ⊡ ASHTABULA; ▲ Jefferson; 217 ND-19; elev. 967ft./295m.; 🅿; z 44047; Ⓟ 3,331; © 3,572
Jefferson; MCD-Township; ASHTABULA; *217 ND-19; 🅿; z 44047; Ⓟ 5,355; © 5,559
Jefferson; MCD-Township; BROWN; *218 SH-5; mail Russellville z 45168; Ⓟ 1,168; © 1,355
Jefferson; MCD-Township; CLINTON; *218 SF-5; mail Midland z 45148; Ⓟ 1,312; © 1,301
Jefferson; MCD-Township; COSHOCTON; *217 NL-13; mail Warsaw z 43844; Ⓟ 1,383; © 1,549
Jefferson; MCD-Township; CRAWFORD; *216 NJ-10; mail Crestline z 44827; Ⓟ 1,662; © 1,677
Jefferson; RMC Place; FAIRFIELD; ▲ Bloom; *218 SC-10; ★ COL; mail Carroll z 43112; rural
Jefferson; MCD-Township; FAYETTE; *218 SD-7; mail Jeffersonville z 43128; Ⓟ 2,814; © 2,766
Jefferson; MCD-Township; FRANKLIN; *218 SA-10; ★ COL; mail Blacklick z 43004; Ⓟ 3,983; © 5,322
Jefferson; MCD-Township; GREENE; *218 SD-6; mail Jamestown z 45335; Ⓟ 997; © 1,109
Jefferson; MCD-Township; GUERNSEY; *217 NN-16; mail Lore City z 43755; Ⓟ 72; © 94
Jefferson; MCD-Township; JACKSON; *219 SH-11; mail Oak Hill z 45656; Ⓟ 3,132; © 3,508
Jefferson; MCD-Township; KNOX; *217 NK-12; mail Glenmont z 44628; Ⓟ 524; © 604
Jefferson; MCD-Township; LOGAN; *216 NL-6; mail Bellefontaine z 43311; Ⓟ 2,104; © 2,946
Jefferson; MADISON; see West Jefferson (Inc. Place)
Jefferson; MCD-Township; MADISON; *218 SB-8; ★ COL; mail West Jefferson z 43162; Ⓟ 6,987; © 6,935
Jefferson; MCD-Township; MERCER; *216 NK-2; mail Celina z 45822; Ⓟ 12,983; © 13,231
Jefferson; MCD-Township; MONTGOMERY; *218 SC-3; ★ DAY; mail New Lebanon z 45345; Ⓟ 8,652; © 6,787
Jefferson; MCD-Township; MUSKINGUM; *217 NN-13; mail Dresden z 43821; Ⓟ 1,879; © 1,766
Jefferson; MCD-Township; NOBLE; *219 SC-17; mail Caldwell z 43724; Ⓟ 297; © 284
Jefferson; MCD-Township; PREBLE; *218 SB-1; ★ RICH; mail New Paris z 45347; Ⓟ 3,783; © 3,449
Jefferson; MCD-Township; RICHLAND; *217 NK-11; ★ MANS; mail Bellville z 44813; Ⓟ 4,258; © 4,531
Jefferson; MCD-Township; ROSS; *218 SF-10; mail Chillicothe z 45601; Ⓟ 1,026; © 967
Jefferson; MCD-Township; SCIOTO; *218 SH-9; ★ PTSM; mail Lucasville z 45648; Ⓟ 2,536; © 2,751
Jefferson; MCD-Township; TUSCARAWAS; *217 NL-15; mail Stone Creek z 43840; Ⓟ 868; © 976
Jefferson; RMC Place; WAYNE; ▲ Plain; 217 NJ-13; elev. 1,147ft./350m.; mail Wooster z 44691; ● 200
Jefferson; MCD-Township; WILLIAMS; *216 NE-2; mail Montpelier z 43543; Ⓟ 1,795; © 2,021
JEFFERSON; 217 NK-19; Ⓟ 80,298; © 73,894; ◆ 65,797
Jefferson Estates; RMC Place; PICKAWAY; ▲ Pickaway; *218 SD-9; mail Circleville z 43113; ● 300
Jefferson Heights; RMC Place; JEFFERSON; ▲ Steubenville; *217 NL-20; ★ STU-; mail Mingo Junction z 43938; ● 300
Jeffersonville; Inc. Place; FAYETTE; ▲ Jefferson; 218 SD-7; elev. 1,049ft./320m.; 🅿; z 43128; Ⓟ 1,281; © 1,288
Jelloway; RMC Place; KNOX; ▲ Brown; 217 NK-12; elev. 1,047ft./319m.; mail Danville z 43014; ● 90
Jenera; Inc. Place; HANCOCK; ▲ Van Buren; 216 NI-6; elev. 859ft./262m.; 🅿; z 45841; Ⓟ 285; © 235
Jenkins Addition; RMC Place; MUSKINGUM; ▲ Newton; *219 SB-14; ★ ZAN; mail Zanesville z 43701; ● 200
Jennings; MCD-Township; PUTNAM; *216 NI-3; mail Fort Jennings z 45844; Ⓟ 1,806; © 1,968
Jennings; MCD-Township; VAN WERT; *216 NJ-2; mail Venedocia z 45894; Ⓟ 739; © 695
Jep; RMC Place; LAWRENCE; ▲ Decatur; *219 SI-11; mail Pedro z 45659; rural
Jericho; RMC Place; BUTLER; ▲ Liberty; 218 SE-3; elev. 871ft./265m.; ★ CIN; mail Middletown z 45042; ● 200
Jerome; RMC Place; UNION; ▲ Jerome; 216 NN-8; ★ COL; mail Plain City z 43064; ● 200
Jerome; MCD-Township; UNION; *216 NN-8; ★ COL; mail Plain City z 43064; Ⓟ 3,499; © 3,950
Jeromesville; Inc. Place; ASHLAND; ▲ Mohican; 217 NJ-13; elev. 1,012ft./308m.; 🅿; z 44840; Ⓟ 582; © 478
Jerry City; Inc. Place; WOOD; ▲ Portage, Bloom; 216 NG-6; elev. 695ft./212m.; 🅿; z 43437; Ⓟ 517; © 453
Jersey; RMC Place; LICKING; ▲ Jersey; 216 NN-10; ★ COL; mail Pataskala z 43062; ● 250
Jersey; MCD-Township; LICKING; *218 SA-10; ★ COL; mail Pataskala z 43062; Ⓟ 2,432; © 2,841
Jerusalem; MCD-Township; LUCAS; *216 NE-7; ★ TOL; mail Curtice z 43412; Ⓟ 3,253; © 3,181
Jerusalem; Inc. Place; MONROE; ▲ Sunsbury, Malaga; 219 SB-18; elev. 1,268ft./386m.; 🅿; z 43747; Ⓟ 144; © 152
Jesse C Owens; RMC Place; CUYAHOGA; ★ CLEV; mail Cleveland z 44104; pop. incl. with Cleveland (Inc. Place)
Jethro; RMC Place; COLUMBIANA; *217 NK-20; ★ E.LIV; mail East Liverpool z 43920; pop. incl. with East Liverpool (Inc. Place)
Jewell; RMC Place; DEFIANCE; ▲ Richland; 216 NF-3; elev. 720ft./219m.; 🅿; z 43530; ● 160
Jewett; Inc. Place; HARRISON; ▲ Rumley; 217 NL-18; elev. 1,011ft./308m.; 🅿; z 43986; Ⓟ 778; © 784
Jimtown; COLUMBIANA; see New Liberty (RMC Place)
Jobs; RMC Place; HOCKING; ▲ Ward; *219 SD-13; mail Glouster z 45732; rural
Joetown; RMC Place; MORGAN; ▲ Morgan; *219 SC-14; mail Malta z 43758; rural
Johnson; MCD-Township; CHAMPAIGN; *216 NJ-10; mail Saint Paris z 43072; Ⓟ 3,171; © 3,357
Johnsons Corners; RMC Place; SUMMIT; ★ AKR; mail Barberton z 44203; pop. incl. with Barberton (Inc. Place)
Johnston; RMC Place; TRUMBULL; ▲ Johnston; 217 NF-19; elev. 1,081ft./329m.; ★ YNGS-; mail Farmdale z 44417; ● 250
Johnston; MCD-Township; TRUMBULL; *217 NF-19; ★ YNGS-; mail Farmdale z 44417; Ⓟ 1,931; © 2,040
Johnston; RMC Place; TUSCARAWAS; ▲ Fairfield; *217 NK-16; mail Dover z 44622
Johnston Corners; RMC Place; LUCAS; ★ TOL; pop. incl. with Toledo (Inc. Place)
Johnstown; Inc. Place; LICKING; ▲ Monroe; 216 NN-10; elev. 1,155ft./352m.; 🅿; ★ COL; z 43031; Ⓟ 3,237; © 3,440
Johnsville; RMC Place; MONTGOMERY; *218 SC-3; ★ DAY; mail New Lebanon z 45345; pop. incl. with New Lebanon (Inc. Place)
Johnsville; MORROW; see Shauck (RMC Place)
Jonesboro; RMC Place; CLINTON; ▲ Clark; 218 SF-5; mail Martinsville z 45146; rural
Jonesboro; RMC Place; FAYETTE; ▲ Union; *218 SD-7; mail Washington Court House z 43160; ● 20
Jonestown (Tokio); RMC Place; VAN WERT; ▲ York; 216 NJ-2; elev. 798ft./243m.; mail Venedocia z 45894; ● 80
Jordanville; RMC Place; COLUMBIANA; ▲ Center; *217 NJ-19; mail Lisbon z 44432; ● 200
Joy; RMC Place; MORGAN; ▲ Marion, Homer; 219 SE-14; elev. 695ft./212m.; mail Chesterhill z 43728
Joyce Avenue; RMC Place; FRANKLIN; *218 SA-9; ★ COL; mail Columbus z 43219; pop. incl. with Columbus (Inc. Place)
Jug Run; RMC Place; JEFFERSON; ▲ Warren; *217 NM-19; ★ WHL; mail Dillonvale z 43917; ● 30
Jumbo; RMC Place; HARDIN; ▲ McDonald; *216 NK-5; mail Kenton z 43326; rural
Jump; RMC Place; HARDIN; ▲ McDonald; *216 NK-5; mail Kenton z 43326
Junction; RMC Place; PAULDING; ▲ Auglaize; 216 NG-2; elev. 716ft./218m.; mail Defiance z 43512; ● 100
Junction City; Inc. Place; PERRY; ▲ Jackson; 219 SC-12; elev. 900ft./274m.; 🅿; z 43748; Ⓟ 770; © 818
Junior Furnace; RMC Place; SCIOTO; ▲ Green; *218 SJ-10; ★ HNTG; mail Franklin Furnace z 45629; rural
Justus; RMC Place; STARK; ▲ Sugar Creek; 217 NJ-15; ★ CAN; mail Navarre z 44662; ● 100

K

Kalida; Inc. Place; PUTNAM; ▲ Union; 216 NI-3; elev. 727ft./222m.; 🅿; z 45853; Ⓟ 947; © 1,031
Kanauga; RMC Place; GALLIA; ▲ Gallipolis; 219 SH-13; mail Gallipolis z 45631; ● 100
Kansas; RMC Place; SENECA; ▲ Liberty; 216 NG-8; elev. 725ft./221m.; 🅿; z 44841; ● 400
Karen Woods; RMC Place; CLARK; ▲ Mad River; *218 SB-5; ★ SPR; mail Springfield z 45502; rural
Kay; RMC Place; WARREN; ▲ Franklin; *218 SD-3; ★ MIDD; mail Franklin z 45005; ● 200
Keays; RMC Place; BUTLER; ★ MIDD; mail Middletown z 45044; pop. incl. with Middletown (Inc. Place)
Keene; RMC Place; COSHOCTON; ▲ Keene; 217 NL-14; elev. 1,000ft./305m.; 🅿; z 43828; ● 100
Keene; MCD-Township; COSHOCTON; *217 NL-14; 🅿; z 43828; Ⓟ 1,583; © 1,689
Keist Manor; RMC Place; FAIRFIELD; ▲ Pleasant; ★ LANC; mail Lancaster z 43130; ● 200
Keith; RMC Place; NOBLE; ▲ Jackson; *219 SC-16; mail Caldwell z 43724; rural
Kelleys Island; Inc. Place; ERIE; 216 NE-10; elev. 598ft./182m.; 🅿; z 43438; Ⓟ 172; © 367
Kellogg Corners; RMC Place; TRUMBULL; ▲ Fowler; *217 NF-19; elev. 1,102ft./336m.; ★ YNGS-; mail Cortland z 44410; rural
Kelloggsville; RMC Place; ASHTABULA; ▲ Monroe; 217 NC-20; elev. 850ft./259m.; mail Conneaut z 44030; ● 200
Kemp; RMC Place; ALLEN; ▲ Shawnee, Amanda; 216 NJ-3; ★ LIMA; mail Lima z 45806; ● 70
Kendall Heights; RMC Place; STARK; ▲ Jackson; 216 NB-8; ★ CAN; mail Massillon z 44646; ● 850
Kenmore; RMC Place; SUMMIT; ★ AKR; mail Akron z 44314; pop. incl. with Akron (Inc. Place)
Kennard; RMC Place; CHAMPAIGN; ▲ Salem; 216 NM-6; elev. 1,172ft./357m.; mail Cable z 43009; ● 40
Kennedy Heights; RMC Place; HAMILTON; *218 SF-3; elev. 777ft./237m.; ★ CIN; mail Cincinnati z 45213; pop. incl. with Cincinnati (Inc. Place)
Kennonsburg; RMC Place; NOBLE; ▲ Wayne; 219 SB-17; mail Quaker City z 43773; ● 50
Keno; RMC Place; MEIGS; ▲ Chester; *219 SG-14; mail Long Bottom z 45743; rural
Kenridge; RMC Place; HAMILTON; *218 SF-3; ★ CIN; mail Cincinnati z 45242; pop. incl. with Blue Ash (Inc. Place)
Kensington; RMC Place; COLUMBIANA; ▲ Hanover; 217 NJ-18; elev. 1,119ft./341m.; 🅿; z 44427; ● 320
Kensington Park; RMC Place; GREENE; ▲ Sugarcreek; ★ DAY; mail Bellbrook z 45305; ● 170
Kent; Inc. Place; PORTAGE; 217 NH-16; elev. 1,071ft./326m.; 🅿 🅲 22,317 ■; ★ AKR; z 44240, z 44242-43; Ⓟ 28,835; © 27,906; ◆ 28,067
Kenton; Inc. Place; ⊡ HARDIN; ▲ Pleasant, Buck; 216 NK-6; elev. 991ft./302m.; 🅿 🅷; z 43326; Ⓟ 8,356; © 8,336
Kenwood; CDP; HAMILTON; ▲ Sycamore, Columbia; 218 SK-4; ★ CIN; mail Cincinnati z 45236; Ⓟ 7,469; © 7,423
Kenwood (Kenwood Station); RMC Place; HARRISON; ▲ Green; 217 NM-18; mail Adena z 43901; rural
Kenwood; RMC Place; LUCAS; ★ TOL; mail Toledo z 43606; pop. incl. with Toledo (Inc. Place)
Kenwood Gardens; RMC Place; LUCAS; ★ TOL; pop. incl. with Toledo (Inc. Place)
Kenwood Heights; RMC Place; CLARK; ★ SPR; mail Springfield z 45505; pop. incl. with Springfield (Inc. Place)
Kenwood Knolls; RMC Place; HAMILTON; ▲ Sycamore; *218 SF-3; elev. 820ft./250m.; ★ CIN; mail Cincinnati z 45236
Kenwood Station; HARRISON; see Kenwood (RMC Place)
Kerr; RMC Place; GALLIA; ▲ Springfield; 219 SH-13; 🅿; z 45643; ● 90
Kessler; RMC Place; MIAMI; ▲ Union; 218 SA-3; ★ DAY; mail West Milton z 45383; ● 100
Kettering; Inc. Place; MONTGOMERY, GREENE; 218 SC-4; elev. 1,008ft./307m.; 🅿 🅷 🅲 803 ■; ★ DAY; z 45409, z 45419-20, z 45429-30, z 45432, z 45439-40, z 45459; Ⓟ 60,569; © 57,502; ◆ 54,823
Kettlersville; Inc. Place; SHELBY; ▲ Van Buren; 216 NL-3; elev. 980ft./299m.; 🅿; z 45336; Ⓟ 194; © 175
Key; RMC Place; BELMONT; ▲ Mead; 219 SA-19; ★ WHL; mail Jacobsburg z 43933
Kidron; RMC Place; WAYNE; ▲ Sugar Creek; 217 NJ-15; elev. 1,100ft./335m.; 🅿; z 44636; ● 550
Kiefersville; PUTNAM; see Kieferville (RMC Place)
Kieferville (Kiefersville); RMC Place; PUTNAM; ▲ Palmer; 216 NH-3; elev. 721ft./220m.; mail Continental z 45831; ● 40
Kilbourne; RMC Place; DELAWARE; ▲ Brown; 216 NM-9; elev. 916ft./279m.; 🅿; z 43032; ● 200
Kile; MADISON; see Kileville (RMC Place)
Kileville (Kile); RMC Place; MADISON; ▲ Darby; 216 NN-8; ★ COL; mail Plain City z 43064; ● 25
Kilgore; RMC Place; CARROLL; ▲ Loudon; 217 NL-18; mail Carrollton z 44615, Scio z 43988; ● 100
Killbuck; Inc. Place; HOLMES; ▲ Killbuck; 217 NK-14; elev. 800ft./244m.; 🅿; z 44637; Ⓟ 809; © 839
Killbuck; MCD-Township; HOLMES; *217 NL-14; 🅿; z 44637; Ⓟ 1,829; © 1,954
Kilvert; RMC Place; ATHENS; ▲ Rome; *219 SE-14; mail Stewart z 45778
Kimball; RMC Place; ERIE; ▲ Oxford; 216 NG-10; elev. 709ft./216m.; mail Monroeville z 44847; ● 110
Kimberly; RMC Place; ATHENS; ▲ York; 219 SE-13; elev. 676ft./206m.; mail Nelsonville z 45764; ● 40
Kimbolton; RMC Place; GUERNSEY; ▲ Liberty; 217 NN-15; elev. 789ft./240m.; 🅿; z 43749; disincorporated April, 2005; Ⓟ 134; © 190
Kingman (North Kingman); RMC Place; CLINTON; ▲ Chester; 218 SD-5; elev. 989ft./301m.; mail Wilmington z 45177
King Mines; RMC Place; GUERNSEY; ▲ Center; *219 SA-16; mail Lore City z 43755; ● 100
Kings Corners; RMC Place; RICHLAND; ▲ Troy; *217 NK-11; ★ MANS; mail Mansfield z 44904; rural
Kings Creek; RMC Place; CHAMPAIGN; ▲ Salem; 216 NM-6; mail Urbana z 43078; ● 300
Kingsgate; RMC Place; HAMILTON; ▲ Colerain; *218 SF-2; ★ CIN; mail Cincinnati z 45231; ● 1,600
Kings Mills; RMC Place; WARREN; ▲ Deerfield; 218 SE-3; elev. 784ft./239m.; 🅿; ★ CIN; z 45034; ● 500
Kingston; MCD-Township; DELAWARE; *216 NM-9; mail Sunbury z 43074; Ⓟ 1,136; © 1,603
Kingston; Inc. Place; ROSS; ▲ Green; 218 SE-10; elev. 797ft./243m.; 🅿; z 45644; Ⓟ 1,153; © 1,032
Kingsville; RMC Place; ASHTABULA; ▲ Kingsville; 217 NC-19; elev. 750ft./229m.; 🅿; ★ ASHT; z 44048 & mail North Kingsville z 44068; ● 650
Kingsville; ASHTABULA; see North Kingsville (Inc. Place)
Kingsville; MCD-Township; ASHTABULA; *217 NC-19; 🅿; ★ ASHT; z 44048 & mail North Kingsville z 44068; Ⓟ 2,007; © 1,847
Kingsville On-the-Lake; RMC Place; ASHTABULA; *217 NC-19; ★ ASHT; mail North Kingsville z 44068; pop. incl. with North Kingsville (Inc. Place)
Kingsway; RMC Place; SANDUSKY; ▲ Rice; *216 NF-8; mail Fremont z 43420
Kinnickinnick; ROSS; see Kinnikinnick (RMC Place)
Kinnikinnick (Kinnickinnick); RMC Place; ROSS; ▲ Green; 218 SE-9; mail Chillicothe z 45601; ● 65
Kinsman; RMC Place; BELMONT; ▲ Wheeling; *217 NN-19; mail Saint Clairsville z 43950; ● 35
Kinsman; RMC Place; TRUMBULL; ▲ Kinsman; 217 NF-20; elev. 950ft./290m.; 🅿; z 44428; ● 600
Kinsman; MCD-Township; TRUMBULL; *217 NF-20; 🅿; z 44428; Ⓟ 2,099; © 1,943
Kiousville; RMC Place; MADISON; ▲ Pleasant, Fairfield; *218 SC-8; mail Mount Sterling z 43143
Kipling; RMC Place; GUERNSEY; ▲ Center; 219 SA-16; elev. 900ft./274m.; 🅿; z 43750; ● 180
Kipton; Inc. Place; LORAIN; ▲ Camden; 217 NG-12; elev. 857ft./261m.; 🅿; ★ CLEV; z 44049; Ⓟ 283; © 265
Kirby; Inc. Place; WYANDOT; ▲ Mifflin, Jackson; 216 NJ-7; elev. 875ft./267m.; 🅿; z 43330; Ⓟ 155; © 132
Kirkersville; Inc. Place; LICKING; ▲ Harrison; 219 SB-11; elev. 927ft./283m.; 🅿; ★ COL; z 43033; Ⓟ 563; © 520
Kirkpatrick; RMC Place; MARION; ▲ Scott; 216 NJ-9; mail Marion z 43302; ● 80
Kirkwood; MCD-Township; BELMONT; *219 SA-18; mail Barnesville z 43713; Ⓟ 334; © 353
Kirkwood; RMC Place; SHELBY; ▲ Orange; 216 NM-3; elev. 986ft./301m.; mail Sidney z 45365; ● 60
Kirkwood Heights; RMC Place; BELMONT; ▲ Pease; ★ WHL; mail Bridgeport z 43912; ● 400
Kirtland; Inc. Place; LAKE; 217 NE-16; elev. 775ft./236m.; 🅿; ★ CLEV; z 44094 & mail Chardon z 44024, Chesterland z 44026; Ⓟ 5,881; © 6,670
Kirtland Hills; Inc. Place; LAKE; *217 NE-17; elev. 700ft./213m.; ★ CLEV; mail Mentor z 44060, Willoughby z 44094; Ⓟ 628; © 597
Kitchen; RMC Place; JACKSON; ▲ Madison; *219 SH-11; mail Oak Hill z 45656; rural
Kitts Hill; RMC Place; LAWRENCE; ▲ Lawrence; 219 SJ-11; elev. 897ft./273m.; 🅿; ★ HNTG; z 45645; ● 200
Kiwanis Lake; RMC Place; GEAUGA; ▲ Newbury; *217 NF-17; ★ CLEV; mail Newbury z 44065; ● 350
Klondike (Bazetta); RMC Place; TRUMBULL; ▲ Bazetta; *217 NF-19; elev. 942ft./287m.; ★ YNGS-; mail Cortland z 44410; ● 250
Klondyke; RMC Place; COLUMBIANA; ★ E.LIV; mail East Liverpool z 43920; pop. incl. with East Liverpool (Inc. Place)
Knockemstiff (Shady Glen); RMC Place; ROSS; *218 SF-9; elev. 710ft./216m.; mail Chillicothe z 45601
Knollwood; RMC Place; GREENE; ▲ Beavercreek; *218 SC-4; ★ DAY; mail Dayton z 45432; pop. incl. with Beavercreek (Inc. Place)
Knollwood Village; RMC Place; PICKAWAY; ▲ Washington; *218 SD-10; mail Circleville z 43113; ● 150
Knox; MCD-Township; COLUMBIANA; *217 NI-18; ★ ALLI; mail Homeworth z 44634; Ⓟ 4,449; © 4,828
Knox; MCD-Township; GUERNSEY; *219 SA-15; mail Cambridge z 43725; Ⓟ 504; © 532
Knox; MCD-Township; HOLMES; *217 NK-13; mail Lakeville z 44638; Ⓟ 977; © 1,095
Knox; MCD-Township; JEFFERSON; *217 NK-20; ★ STU-; mail Toronto z 43964; Ⓟ 5,506; © 5,011
Knox; MCD-Township; VINTON; *219 SF-12; mail Albany z 45710; Ⓟ 443; © 599
KNOX; 217 NM-12; Ⓟ 47,473; © 54,500; Ⓡ 54,503; ◆ 59,698
Knoxville; RMC Place; JEFFERSON; ▲ Knox; 217 NK-19; elev. 1,289ft./393m.; ★ STU-; mail Toronto z 43964; ● 180
Kolmont; RMC Place; JEFFERSON; ▲ Cross Creek; *217 NL-20; ★ STU-; mail Mingo Junction z 43938; ● 30
Kossuth; RMC Place; AUGLAIZE; ▲ Salem; 216 NJ-3; mail Spencerville z 45887; ● 80
Krohns Acres; RMC Place; WILLIAMS; ▲ Center; *216 NF-2; mail Bryan z 43506; ● 80
Kunkle; RMC Place; WILLIAMS; ▲ Madison; 216 NE-2; elev. 885ft./270m.; 🅿; z 43531; ● 300
Kyger; RMC Place; GALLIA; ▲ Cheshire; 219 SH-13; elev. 602ft./183m.; mail Cheshire z 45620; ● 60
Kylesburg; LICKING; see Union Station (RMC Place)

L

Labelle; LAWRENCE; see Rome (RMC Place)
La Belle View; RMC Place; JEFFERSON; ★ STU-; mail Steubenville z 43952; pop. incl. with Steubenville (Inc. Place)
Lacarne; RMC Place; OTTAWA; ▲ Erie; 216 NE-9; elev. 579ft./176m.; 🅿; z 43439; ● 200
La Croft; CDP; COLUMBIANA; ▲ Liverpool; *217 NJ-20; ★ E.LIV; mail East Liverpool z 43920; Ⓟ 1,427; © 1,307
Lafayette; Inc. Place; ALLEN; ▲ Jackson; 216 NJ-5; elev. 927ft./283m.; 🅿; ★ LIMA; z 45854; Ⓟ 449; © 304
Lafayette; MCD-Township; COSHOCTON; *217 NM-15; mail West Lafayette z 43845; Ⓟ 4,140; © 4,285
Lafayette; RMC Place; MADISON; ▲ Deer Creek; 218 SB-7; mail London z 43140; ● 130
Lafayette; RMC Place; MEDINA; ▲ Lafayette; 217 NH-14; ★ CLEV; mail Medina z 44256; ● 120
Lafayette; MCD-Township; MEDINA; *217 NH-14; ★ CLEV; mail Medina z 44256; Ⓟ 4,804; © 5,476
Lafferty; RMC Place; BELMONT; ▲ Union; 217 NN-18; elev. 1,050ft./320m.; 🅿; z 43951; ● 500
Lagonda; RMC Place; CLARK; ★ SPR; mail Springfield z 45503; pop. incl. with Springfield (Inc. Place)
La Grange; RMC Place; LAWRENCE; ▲ Upper; 219 SJ-11; ★ HNTG; mail Ironton z 45638; ● 70
Lagrange; Inc. Place; LORAIN; ▲ Lagrange; 217 NG-13; elev. 825ft./251m.; 🅿; ★ CLEV; z 44050; Ⓟ 1,199; © 1,815
Lagrange; MCD-Township; LORAIN; *217 NG-13; 🅿; ★ CLEV; z 44050; Ⓟ 4,644; © 5,972
Laings; RMC Place; MONROE; ▲ Green; 219 SC-18; elev. 1,000ft./305m.; 🅿; z 43752; ● 30
Lake; MCD-Township; ASHLAND; *217 NJ-13; mail Glenmont z 44628; Ⓟ 543; © 735
Lake; MCD-Township; LOGAN; *216 NL-5; mail Bellefontaine z 43311; Ⓟ 12,227; © 12,492
Lake; MCD-Township; STARK; *217 NI-16; ★ CAN; mail North Canton z 44720; partly in ★ AKR; Ⓟ 22,343; © 25,892
Lake; MCD-Township; WOOD; *216 NE-7; ★ TOL; mail Millbury z 43447; Ⓟ 10,449; © 10,350
LAKE; 217 ND-17; Ⓟ 215,499; © 227,511; ◆ 233,839
Lake Aquilla; GEAUGA; see Aquilla (Inc. Place)
Lake Cable; RMC Place; STARK; ▲ Jackson; 216 NB-8; ★ CAN; mail Canton z 44718, East Canton z 44730; ● 2,500
Lake Darby; CDP-Census Area Only; FRANKLIN; ▲ Prairie, Brown; *218 SB-8; ★ COL; mail Galloway z 43119; Ⓟ 2,798; © 3,727
Lake Fork; RMC Place; ASHLAND; ▲ Mohican; 217 NJ-13; elev. 1,019ft./311m.; mail Jeromesville z 44840
Lakegrove Estates; RMC Place; ASHTABULA; ▲ Geneva; *217 NC-18; ★ ASHT; mail Geneva z 44041; pop. incl. with Geneva-on-the-Lake (Inc. Place)
Lakeland; RMC Place; LUCAS; ▲ Jerusalem; *216 NE-8; ★ TOL; mail Curtice z 43412; ● 400
Lakeland Beach; RMC Place; HOLMES; ▲ Ripley; *217 NJ-13; mail Lakeville z 44638; ● 50
Lakeline; Inc. Place; LAKE; 217 ND-16; elev. 617ft./188m.; 🅿; ★ CLEV; z 44095 & mail Willoughby z 44094; Ⓟ 210; © 165
Lake Lorelel; RMC Place; BROWN; ▲ Perry; mail Fayetteville z 45118; ● 280
Lake Lucerne; RMC Place; GEAUGA; ▲ Bainbridge; *217 NF-16; ★ CLEV; mail Chagrin Falls z 44022; ● 550
Lake Milton; RMC Place; MAHONING; ▲ Milton; 217 NH-18; elev. 960ft./293m.; 🅿; z 44429; ● 1,100
Lakemore; Inc. Place; SUMMIT; 217 NH-16; elev. 1,100ft./335m.; 🅿; ★ AKR; z 44250; Ⓟ 2,684; © 2,561
Lake of the Woods; RMC Place; DELAWARE; ▲ Harlem; *216 NN-9; ★ COL; mail Galena z 43021; ● 100
Lake O'Springs; RMC Place; STARK; ▲ Jackson; 216 NB-8; ★ CAN; mail Canton z 44718; ● 600
Lake Seneca; RMC Place; WILLIAMS; ▲ Bridgewater; *216 ND-1; mail Montpelier z 43543; ● 110
Lakeside; RMC Place; BUTLER; ★ MIDD; mail Middletown z 45042; pop. incl. with Middletown (Inc. Place)
Lakeside; RMC Place; FAIRFIELD; ▲ Walnut; 219 SB-11; ★ COL; mail Millersport z 43046; ● 200
Lakeside; RMC Place; LICKING; ▲ Union; ★ NWRK; mail Buckeye Lake z 43008; pop. incl. with Buckeye Lake (Inc. Place)
Lakeside; RMC Place; OTTAWA; ▲ Danbury; 216 NE-10; 🅿; z 43440; summer pop. 3,000; ● 950
Lakeside Marblehead; RMC Place; OTTAWA; elev. 600ft./183m.; 🅿; z 43440; pop. incl. with Marblehead (Inc. Place)
Lake Silverstone Mobile Home Park; RMC Place; ASHLAND; *217 NI-12; mail Ashland z 44805; pop. incl. with Ashland (Inc. Place)
Lake Slagle; RMC Place; STARK; ▲ Jackson; 216 NB-8; ★ CAN; mail North Canton z 44720; ● 340
Lake Sylvan; RMC Place; CLARK; ▲ Pleasant, Harmony; *218 SB-6; ★ SPR; mail South Vienna z 45369; ● 150
Lake View; RMC Place; KNOX; ▲ Berlin; *217 NK-11; ★ MANS; mail Fredericktown z 43019; ● 70
Lakeview; Inc. Place; LOGAN; ▲ Stokes; 216 NL-5; elev. 997ft./304m.; 🅿; z 43331; Ⓟ 1,056; © 1,074
Lakeview Heights; RMC Place; PIKE; ▲ Pee Pee; *218 SG-9; mail Waverly z 45690; ● 30
Lakeville; RMC Place; ASHTABULA; *217 NC-20; mail Conneaut z 44030; pop. incl. with Conneaut (Inc. Place)
Lakeville; RMC Place; HOLMES; ▲ Washington; 217 NK-13; elev. 988ft./301m.; 🅿; z 44638; ● 130
Lake Waynoka; RMC Place; BROWN; ▲ Washington; *218 SH-5; mail Sardinia z 45171; ● 400
Lakewood; Inc. Place; CUYAHOGA; 217 NF-14; elev. 670ft./204m.; 🅿 🅷 ■; ★ CLEV; z 44107; Ⓟ 59,718; © 56,646; ◆ 50,887
Lakota Hills; RMC Place; BUTLER; ▲ West Chester; *218 SE-3; ★ CIN; mail West Chester z 45069; ● 700
Lamartine; CARROLL; see Perrysville (RMC Place)
Lamira; RMC Place; BELMONT; ▲ Smith; *219 SA-18; mail Belmont z 43718
Lancaster; Inc. Place; ⊡ FAIRFIELD; 219 SC-11; elev. 860ft./262m.; 🅿 🅷 🅲 1,727 ■; ★ LANC; z 43130; Ⓟ 34,507; © 35,335; ◆ 36,055
Landeck; RMC Place; ALLEN; ▲ Marion; 216 NJ-3; ★ LIMA; mail Delphos z 45833; ● 100
Landen; CDP; WARREN; ▲ Deerfield; *218 SF-3; ★ CIN; mail Maineville z 45039, Mason z 45040; Ⓟ 9,263; © 12,766
Lang; RMC Place; LUCAS; ★ TOL; pop. incl. with Toledo (Inc. Place)
Langsville; RMC Place; MEIGS; ▲ Rutland; 219 SG-13; elev. 600ft./183m.; 🅿; z 45741; ● 80
Lanier; MCD-Township; PREBLE; *218 SC-2; ★ DAY; mail West Alexandria z 45381; Ⓟ 3,734; © 3,931
Lansing; RMC Place; BELMONT; ▲ Pease; 217 NN-19; elev. 700ft./213m.; 🅿; ★ WHL; z 43934; ● 400
LaPorte; RMC Place; LORAIN; ▲ Carlisle; 217 NG-13; ★ CLEV; mail Elyria z 44035; ● 400
La Rue; Inc. Place; MARION; ▲ Montgomery; 216 NK-7; elev. 926ft./282m.; 🅿; z 43332; Ⓟ 802; © 775
Latcha (Latchie); RMC Place; WOOD; ▲ Lake; *216 NE-7; ★ TOL; mail Millbury z 43447, Perrysburg z 43551; ● 200
Latchie; WOOD; see Latcha (RMC Place)
Latham; RMC Place; PIKE; ▲ Mifflin; 218 SG-8; elev. 634ft./193m.; 🅿; z 45646; ● 230
Latimer; RMC Place; TRUMBULL; ▲ Johnston; *217 NF-20; elev. 1,018ft./310m.; ★ YNGS-; mail Kinsman z 44428; ● 50
Lattasburg; RMC Place; WAYNE; ▲ Chester; 217 NI-13; mail West Salem z 44287; ● 100
Lattaville; RMC Place; ROSS; ▲ Concord; 218 SE-8; mail Frankfort z 45628; ● 60
Latty; Inc. Place; PAULDING; ▲ Paulding; 216 NH-2; elev. 730ft./223m.; 🅿; z 45855; Ⓟ 205; © 200
Latty; MCD-Township; PAULDING; *216 NH-2; 🅿; z 45855 & mail Grover Hill z 45849; Ⓟ 1,113; © 1,026
Laura; Inc. Place; MIAMI; ▲ Union; 218 SA-3; elev. 1,000ft./305m.; 🅿; ★ DAY; z 45337; Ⓟ 483; © 487
Laurel; RMC Place; CLERMONT; ▲ Monroe; 218 SH-4; ★ CIN; mail New Richmond z 45157; ● 150
Laurel; MCD-Township; HOCKING; *219 SD-11; mail Rockbridge z 43149; Ⓟ 968; © 1,190
Laurel Ridge; RMC Place; STARK; ▲ Plain; 217 NI-17; ★ CAN; mail Canton z 44721; ● 2,350
Laurelville; Inc. Place; HOCKING; ▲ Perry; 218 SE-10; elev. 741ft./226m.; 🅿; z 43135, z 43152, z 43156; Ⓟ 605; © 533
Lawco Lake; RMC Place; LAWRENCE; ▲ Elizabeth; *219 SJ-11; mail Pedro z 45659; ● 70
Lawndale; RMC Place; STARK; *217 NJ-16; ★ CAN; mail Massillon z 44646; pop. incl. with Massillon (Inc. Place)
Lawrence; RMC Place; LAWRENCE; ▲ Elizabeth; *219 SJ-11; mail Pedro z 45659; ● 40
Lawrence; MCD-Township; LAWRENCE; *219 SJ-11; ★ HNTG; mail Kitts Hill z 45645; Ⓟ 2,484; © 2,574
Lawrence; MCD-Township; STARK; *217 NI-15; ★ AKR; mail Canal Fulton z 44614; Ⓟ 12,047; © 13,382
Lawrence; MCD-Township; TUSCARAWAS; *217 NK-16; ★ CAN; mail Bolivar z 44612; Ⓟ 4,296; © 5,241
Lawrence; MCD-Township; WASHINGTON; *219 SE-17; mail Marietta z 45750; Ⓟ 885; © 956
LAWRENCE; 219 SK-11; Ⓟ 61,834; © 62,319; ◆ 62,371
Lawrenceville; RMC Place; CLARK; ▲ German; 218 SB-5; elev. 1,107ft./337m.; ★ SPR; mail Springfield z 45502; disincorporated August 20, 2005; Ⓟ 304; © 302
Lawshe; RMC Place; ADAMS; ▲ Meigs; 218 SH-7; mail Peebles z 45660; ● 60
Layhigh; RMC Place; BUTLER; ▲ Ross; 218 SE-1; ★ CIN; mail Hamilton z 45013; ● 60
Layland; RMC Place; COSHOCTON; ▲ Clark; 217 NL-14; mail Killbuck z 44637; ● 50
Layman; RMC Place; WASHINGTON; ▲ Fairfield; *219 SE-15; mail Cutler z 45724
Leaper; RMC Place; GALLIA; *219 SI-13; elev. 639ft./195m.; mail Gallipolis z 45631; rural
Leavittsburg; CDP; TRUMBULL; ▲ Warren; 217 NG-18; elev. 900ft./274m.; 🅿; ★ YNGS-; z 44430; © 2,200
Leavittsville; RMC Place; CARROLL; ▲ Monroe; 217 NK-17; mail Sherrodsville z 44675; ● 100
Lebanon; MCD-Township; MEIGS; *219 SG-15; mail Portland z 45770; Ⓟ 905; © 1,029
Lebanon; RMC Place; MONROE; ▲ Bethel; 219 SD-17; elev. 1,069ft./326m.; mail Lower Salem z 45745; ● 50
Lebanon; Inc. Place; ⊡ WARREN; 218 SE-4; elev. 769ft./234m.; 🅿; z 45036; Ⓟ 10,453; © 16,962; ◆ 22,437
Lebanon Junction; RMC Place; MONTGOMERY; *218 SC-4; ★ DAY; pop. incl. with Dayton (Inc. Place)
Lecta; RMC Place; LAWRENCE; ▲ Mason; *219 SI-12; mail Scottown z 45678; rural
Lee; MCD-Township; ATHENS; *219 SF-13; mail Albany z 45710; Ⓟ 2,233; © 2,531
Lee; MCD-Township; CARROLL; *217 NK-18; mail Carrollton z 44615; Ⓟ 1,046; © 1,128
Lee; RMC Place; CUYAHOGA; ★ CLEV; mail Cleveland z 44120; pop. incl. with Shaker Heights (Inc. Place)
Lee; MCD-Township; MONROE; *219 SC-19; mail Sardis z 43946; Ⓟ 1,237; © 1,122
Leesburg; Inc. Place; HIGHLAND; ▲ Fairfield; 218 SE-7; elev. 1,021ft./311m.; 🅿; z 45135; Ⓟ 1,063; © 1,253
Leesburg; MCD-Township; UNION; *216 NM-7; mail Marysville z 43040; Ⓟ 1,373; © 1,438
Lees Creek (Centerville); RMC Place; CLINTON; ▲ Wayne; 218 SE-6; elev. 1,100ft./335m.; 🅿; z 45138; ● 160
Leesville; Inc. Place; CARROLL; ▲ Orange; 217 NL-17; elev. 985ft./300m.; 🅿; z 44639; Ⓟ 156; © 184
Leesville (Leesville Cross Roads); RMC Place; CRAWFORD; 216 NJ-10; mail Crestline z 44827; ● 200
Leesville Cross Roads; CRAWFORD; see Leesville (RMC Place)
Leetonia; Inc. Place; COLUMBIANA; ▲ Salem, Fairfield; 217 NI-19; elev. 1,021ft./311m.; 🅿; z 44431; Ⓟ 2,070; © 2,043
Lehmkuhl Landing; RMC Place; SHELBY; ▲ Van Buren; *216 NL-3; elev. 960ft./293m.; mail Minster z 45865; ● 200
Leipsic; Inc. Place; PUTNAM; ▲ Van Buren, Liberty; 216 NH-4; elev. 765ft./233m.; 🅿; z 45815, z 45856; Ⓟ 2,203; © 2,236
Leipsic Junction; RMC Place; PUTNAM; *216 NH-4; mail Leipsic z 45856; pop. incl. with Leipsic (Inc. Place)
Leistville; RMC Place; PICKAWAY; ▲ Saltcreek; 218 SD-10; mail Circleville z 43113; ● 40
Lelan; WARREN; see Genntown (RMC Place)
Lemert; RMC Place; CRAWFORD; ▲ Holmes; 216 NI-8; mail Sycamore z 44882; ● 30
Lemon; MCD-Township; BUTLER; *218 SE-3; ★ MIDD; mail Monroe z 45050; Ⓟ 12,172; © 8,607; Ⓡ 8,609
Lemoyne; RMC Place; WOOD; ▲ Troy; 216 NE-7; elev. 655ft./200m.; 🅿; ★ TOL; z 43441; ● 300
Lena; RMC Place; MIAMI; ▲ Brown; 216 NN-4; mail Conover z 45317; ● 100
Lenox; ASHTABULA; see Lenox Center (RMC Place)
Lenox; MCD-Township; ASHTABULA; *217 ND-19; mail Jefferson z 44047; Ⓟ 1,266; © 1,388
Lenox Center (Lenox); RMC Place; ASHTABULA; ▲ Lenox; 217 ND-19; mail Jefferson z 44047; ● 60
Leo; RMC Place; JACKSON; ▲ Jackson; 219 SG-11; mail Jackson z 45640
Leon; RMC Place; ASHTABULA; ▲ Richmond; *217 ND-20; elev. 1,101ft./336m.; mail Andover z 44003
Leonardsburg; RMC Place; DELAWARE; ▲ Brown; *216 NL-9; mail Delaware z 43015
Lerado; RMC Place; CLERMONT; ▲ Jackson; *218 SF-4; elev. 941ft./287m.; ★ CIN; mail Williamsburg z 45176; ● 30
Leroy; MCD-Township; LAKE; *217 ND-17; ★ CLEV; mail Painesville z 44077; Ⓟ 2,581; © 3,122
Leroy; MEDINA; see Westfield Center (Inc. Place)
Le Sourdsville; RMC Place; BUTLER; ▲ Lemon; 218 SE-2; elev. 642ft./196m.; ★ MIDD; mail Middletown z 45042; pop. incl. with Monroe (Inc. Place)
Lester; RMC Place; MEDINA; ▲ York; *217 NG-14; elev. 948ft./289m.; ★ CLEV; mail Medina z 44256
Letart; MCD-Township; MEIGS; *219 SH-14; mail Racine z 45771; Ⓟ 689; © 641
Letart Falls; RMC Place; MEIGS; ▲ Letart; 219 SH-14; mail Racine z 45771; ● 180
Levanna; RMC Place; BROWN; ▲ Union; 218 SI-5; elev. 515ft./157m.; mail Ripley z 45167; ● 80
Lewis; MCD-Township; BROWN; *218 SH-5; mail Georgetown z 45121; Ⓟ 1,676; © 2,362
Lewis Addition; RMC Place; JEFFERSON; ▲ Island Creek; *217 NL-20; ★ STU-; mail Steubenville z 43953; ● 200
Lewisburg; Inc. Place; PREBLE; ▲ Harrison; 218 SB-2; elev. 1,000ft./305m.; 🅿; ★ DAY; z 45338; Ⓟ 1,584; © 1,798
Lewis Center; RMC Place; DELAWARE; ▲ Orange; 216 NM-9; elev. 942ft./287m.; 🅿; ★ COL; z 43035; ● 350
Lewistown; RMC Place; LOGAN; ▲ Washington; 216 NL-5; elev. 1,022ft./312m.; 🅿; z 43333; ● 260
Lewisville; Inc. Place; MONROE; ▲ Summit; 219 SC-17; elev. 1,187ft./362m.; 🅿; z 43754; Ⓟ 261; © 233
Lexington; Inc. Place; RICHLAND; ▲ Washington, Troy; 217 NJ-11; elev. 1,200ft./366m.; 🅿; ★ MANS; z 44904; Ⓟ 4,124; © 4,165
Lexington; RMC Place; STARK; ▲ Lexington; *217 NI-18; ★ ALLI; mail Alliance z 44601
Lexington; MCD-Township; STARK; *217 NI-17; ★ ALLI; mail Alliance z 44601; Ⓟ 5,291; © 5,583
Liberty; MCD-Township; ADAMS; *218 SI-6; mail West Union z 45693; Ⓟ 1,400; © 1,816
Liberty (Liberty Township); MCD-Township; BUTLER; *218 SE-3; ★ CIN; mail Hamilton z 45011, Lebanon z 45036, Middletown z 45042, z 45044, Monroe z 45050, West Chester z 45069; Ⓟ 9,249; © 22,819
Liberty; MCD-Township; CLINTON; *218 SD-5; mail Wilmington z 45177; Ⓟ 840; © 1,033
Liberty; MCD-Township; CRAWFORD; *216 NI-9; mail Sulphur Springs z 44881; Ⓟ 1,470; © 1,489
Liberty; MCD-Township; DARKE; *218 SA-1; mail Palestine z 45352; Ⓟ 1,141; © 1,132
Liberty; MCD-Township; DELAWARE; *216 NM-9; ★ COL; mail Powell z 43065; Ⓟ 5,944; © 15,429
Liberty; MCD-Township; FAIRFIELD; *219 SB-11; ★ COL; mail Baltimore z 43105; Ⓟ 6,758; © 7,265
Liberty; MCD-Township; GUERNSEY; *217 NN-15; mail Cambridge z 43725; Ⓟ 1,012; © 1,068
Liberty; MCD-Township; HANCOCK; *216 NH-6; ★ FIND; mail Findlay z 45840; Ⓟ 4,871; © 6,469
Liberty; MCD-Township; HARDIN; *216 NJ-5; 🅲 3,620; mail Ada z 45810; Ⓟ 6,788; © 7,149
Liberty; MCD-Township; HENRY; *216 NF-4; mail Liberty Center z 43532; Ⓟ 2,434; © 2,591
Liberty; MCD-Township; HIGHLAND; *218 SF-6; mail Hillsboro z 45133; Ⓟ 9,184; © 9,798
Liberty; MCD-Township; JACKSON; *218 SG-10; mail Jackson z 45640; Ⓟ 1,431; © 1,672
Liberty; MCD-Township; KNOX; *217 NL-11; mail Mount Vernon z 43050; Ⓟ 1,213; © 1,422
Liberty; MCD-Township; LICKING; *217 NN-11; mail Johnstown z 43031; Ⓟ 1,470; © 1,797
Liberty; MCD-Township; LOGAN; *216 NM-5; mail West Liberty z 43357; Ⓟ 2,999; © 3,126
Liberty; MCD-Township; MERCER; *216 NK-1; mail Rockford z 45882; Ⓟ 964; © 917
Liberty; RMC Place; MONTGOMERY; ▲ Jefferson; 218 SC-3; ★ DAY; mail Dayton z 45418; ● 240
Liberty; MCD-Township; PUTNAM; *216 NH-4; mail Leipsic z 45856; Ⓟ 1,497; © 1,575
Liberty; MCD-Township; ROSS; *218 SF-10; mail Londonderry z 45647; Ⓟ 2,126; © 2,476
Liberty; MCD-Township; SENECA; *216 NG-8; mail Kansas z 44841; Ⓟ 2,358; © 2,340
Liberty; MCD-Township; TRUMBULL; *217 NG-19; ★ YNGS-; mail Girard z 44420; Ⓟ 24,453; © 23,522
Liberty; MCD-Township; UNION; *216 NL-7; mail Marysville z 43040; Ⓟ 1,221; © 1,705
Liberty; MCD-Township; VAN WERT; *216 NJ-1; mail Van Wert z 45891; Ⓟ 2,051; © 1,696
Liberty; MCD-Township; WASHINGTON; *219 SD-17; mail Lower Salem z 45745; Ⓟ 575; © 621
Liberty; MCD-Township; WOOD; *216 NG-6; mail Rudolph z 43462; Ⓟ 1,875; © 1,862
Liberty Center; Inc. Place; HENRY; ▲ Washington, Liberty; 216 NF-4; elev. 675ft./206m.; 🅿; z 43532; Ⓟ 1,084; © 1,109
Liberty Township; BUTLER; see Liberty (MCD-Township)
Lick; MCD-Township; JACKSON; *219 SG-11; mail Jackson z 45640; Ⓟ 8,564; © 2,682
Licking; MCD-Township; LICKING; *219 SB-12; ★ NWRK; mail Thornville z 43076; Ⓟ 3,945; © 3,870
Licking; MCD-Township; MUSKINGUM; *219 SA-13; mail Nashport z 43830; Ⓟ 1,878; © 2,248
LICKING; 217 NN-11; Ⓟ 128,300; © 145,491; Ⓡ 145,621; ◆ 157,974
Licking View; RMC Place; MUSKINGUM; ▲ Falls; *219 SB-14; ★ ZAN; mail Zanesville z 43701; ● 300
Liebs Island; RMC Place; FAIRFIELD; ▲ Walnut; *219 SB-11; ★ COL; mail Millersport z 43046; ● 170
Lightsville; RMC Place; DARKE; ▲ Allen; *216 NM-1; mail Rossburg z 45362; ● 30
Lilly Chapel; RMC Place; MADISON; ▲ Fairfield; 218 SB-8; mail London z 43140, West Jefferson z 43162; ● 200
Lima; Inc. Place; ⊡ ALLEN; ▲ American; 216 NJ-4; elev. 881ft./269m.; 🅿 🅷 🅲 4,258 ■; ★ LIMA; z 45801-02, z 45804-09, z 45819, z 45854; Ⓟ 45,549; © 40,081; Ⓡ 41,581; ◆ 37,884
Limaville; Inc. Place; STARK; ▲ Lexington; 217 NH-17; elev. 1,150ft./351m.; 🅿; ★ ALLI; z 44640; Ⓟ 152; © 193
Lime City; RMC Place; WOOD; ▲ Perrysburg; 216 NC-2; elev. 644ft./196m.; ★ TOL; mail Perrysburg z 43551; ● 120
Limecrest; RMC Place; CLARK; ▲ Springfield; 217 NB-16; ★ SPR; mail Springfield z 45505; ● 400
Limerick; RMC Place; JACKSON; ▲ Jackson; *218 SG-10; elev. 633ft./193m.; mail Chillicothe z 45601, Jackson z 45640
Limestone; RMC Place; OTTAWA; ▲ Benton; 216 NE-8; elev. 593ft./181m.; mail Graytown z 43432; ● 50
Limestone City; RMC Place; CLARK; ▲ Mad River; 217 NB-15; ★ SPR; mail Springfield z 45506; ● 40
Lincoln; MCD-Township; MORROW; *216 NL-10; mail Fulton z 43321; Ⓟ 1,682; © 1,955
Lincoln Heights; Inc. Place; HAMILTON; 218 SK-3; elev. 600ft./183m.; ★ CIN; mail Cincinnati z 45215; Ⓟ 4,805; © 4,113
Lincoln Heights; RMC Place; JEFFERSON; ★ STU-; mail Steubenville z 43952; pop. incl. with Steubenville (Inc. Place)
Lincoln Heights; RMC Place; RICHLAND; ▲ Madison; *217 NJ-11; ★ MANS; mail Mansfield z 44903; ● 1,000
Lincoln Village; CDP-Census Area Only; FRANKLIN; ▲ Prairie; 218 SB-9; elev. 912ft./278m.; ★ COL; mail Columbus z 43228; Ⓟ 9,958; © 9,482
Lindair Estates; RMC Place; CLARK; ▲ Mad River; *218 SB-5; ★ SPR; mail Springfield z 45502; ● 200
Lindale; RMC Place; CLERMONT; ▲ Pierce; 218 SG-3; ★ CIN; mail Amelia z 45102, New Richmond z 45157; ● 200
Linden; RMC Place; FRANKLIN; mail Columbus z 43211; pop. incl. with Columbus (Inc. Place)
Lindentree; RMC Place; CARROLL; ▲ Rose; *217 NK-17; mail Mineral City z 44656
Lindenwald; RMC Place; BUTLER; *218 SE-2; 🅿; ★ CIN; z 45015; pop. incl. with Hamilton (Inc. Place)
Lindsey; Inc. Place; SANDUSKY; ▲ Washington; 216 NF-8; elev. 615ft./187m.; 🅿; z 43442; Ⓟ 529; © 504
Lindsley-Gay; RMC Place; ASHTABULA; ▲ Williamsfield; mail Andover z 44003; ● 80
Linndale; Inc. Place; CUYAHOGA; 219 SM-16; elev. 756ft./230m.; ★ CLEV; mail Cleveland z 44135; Ⓟ 159; © 117
Linneman; RMC Place; ALLEN; ▲ Perry; ★ LIMA; mail Lima z 45804; ● 470
Linnville; RMC Place; LAWRENCE; ▲ Windsor; 219 SJ-12; elev. 586ft./179m.; mail Willow Wood z 45696; ● 90
Linnville; RMC Place; LICKING; ▲ Franklin, Bowling Green; 219 SB-12; mail Thornville z 43076; ● 60
Linton; MCD-Township; COSHOCTON; *217 NM-15; mail Plainfield z 43836; Ⓟ 611; © 632
Linwood; RMC Place; HAMILTON; *218 SG-3; ★ CIN; mail Cincinnati z 45226; pop. incl. with Cincinnati (Inc. Place)
Linworth; RMC Place; FRANKLIN; ▲ Perry; 216 NN-9; ★ COL; mail Columbus z 43085; pop. incl. with Worthington (Inc. Place)
Lippincott; RMC Place; CHAMPAIGN; ▲ Salem; *216 NM-5; mail Urbana z 43078; rural
Lisbon; RMC Place; CLARK; ▲ Harmony; *218 SB-6; mail South Charleston z 45368
Lisbon; Inc. Place; ⊡ COLUMBIANA; ▲ Center; 217 NJ-19; elev. 968ft./295m.; 🅿; z 44432; Ⓟ 3,037; © 2,788
Lisman; RMC Place; LAWRENCE; ▲ Elizabeth; *219 SJ-11; mail Pedro z 45659; rural
Litchfield; RMC Place; MEDINA; ▲ Litchfield; 217 NG-13; elev. 1,010ft./308m.; 🅿; ★ CLEV; z 44253; ● 400
Litchfield; MCD-Township; MEDINA; *217 NG-13; 🅿; ★ CLEV; z 44253; Ⓟ 2,506; © 3,250
Lithopolis; Inc. Place; FAIRFIELD; ▲ Bloom; 218 SC-10; elev. 937ft./286m.; 🅿; ★ COL; z 43136; Ⓟ 563; © 600
Little Hocking; RMC Place; WASHINGTON; ▲ Belpre; 219 SF-15; elev. 626ft./191m.; 🅿; ★ PRKB; z 45742; ● 600
Little Sandusky; RMC Place; WYANDOT; ▲ Pitt; 216 NJ-8; mail Harpster z 43323; ● 50
Little Walnut; RMC Place; PICKAWAY; ▲ Walnut; 218 SC-9; mail Circleville z 43113; ● 80
Little Washington; RMC Place; RICHLAND; ▲ Washington; 217 NJ-11; ★ MANS; mail Mansfield z 44903
Little York; RMC Place; MONTGOMERY; ▲ Butler; *218 SB-3; ★ DAY; mail Dayton z 45414, Nevada z 44849; ● 400
Liverpool; MCD-Township; COLUMBIANA; *217 NJ-20; ★ E.LIV; mail East Liverpool z 43920; Ⓟ 4,746; © 4,374
Liverpool; MCD-Township; MEDINA; *217 NG-14; ★ CLEV; mail Valley City z 44280; Ⓟ 3,713; © 4,329
Livingston; RMC Place; FRANKLIN; ★ COL; mail Columbus z 43227; pop. incl. with Columbus (Inc. Place)
Lloydsville; RMC Place; BELMONT; ▲ Richland; 217 NN-18; ★ WHL; mail Saint Clairsville z 43950; ● 150
Lock; RMC Place; KNOX, LICKING; ▲ Milford; 217 NM-11; mail Centerburg z 43011
Lockbourne; Inc. Place; FRANKLIN; ▲ Bennington; 218 SC-9; elev. 700ft./213m.; 🅿; ★ COL; z 43137, z 43194; Ⓟ 173; © 280
Lockington; Inc. Place; SHELBY; ▲ Washington; 216 NM-3; elev. 949ft./289m.; mail Piqua z 45356; Ⓟ 214; © 208
Lockland; Inc. Place; HAMILTON; 218 SK-3; elev. 575ft./175m.; 🅿; ★ CIN; z 45215; Ⓟ 4,357; © 3,707
Lock Two; RMC Place; AUGLAIZE; ▲ German; *216 NL-3; mail New Bremen z 45869
Lockville; RMC Place; FAIRFIELD; ▲ Violet; 218 SC-10; ★ COL; mail Carroll z 43112; ● 90
Lockwood; RMC Place; TRUMBULL; 217 NF-19; ● 30
Lockwood Corners; RMC Place; SUMMIT; ▲ Coventry; *217 NH-15; ★ AKR; mail Akron z 44319
Lockwoods Crossing; RMC Place; ASHTABULA; ★ ASHT; pop. incl. with Ashtabula (Inc. Place)
Locust Corner; RMC Place; CLERMONT; ▲ Pierce; *218 SG-3; ★ CIN; mail Cincinnati z 45245; ● 150
Locust Grove; RMC Place; ADAMS; ▲ Franklin; 218 SH-7; mail Peebles z 45660; ● 220
Locust Grove; RMC Place; BUTLER; ▲ Lemon; *218 SD-3; ★ MIDD; mail Middletown z 45042; ● 130
Locust Grove; RMC Place; MAHONING; ▲ Green; *217 NI-19; elev. 1,234ft./376m.; mail Salem z 44460; rural
Locust Lake; RMC Place; CLERMONT; ▲ Pierce; *218 SG-3; ★ CIN; mail Amelia z 45102; rural
Locust Point; RMC Place; OTTAWA; ▲ Carroll; *216 NE-8; mail Oak Harbor z 43449; summer pop. 150; ● 80
Locust Ridge; RMC Place; BROWN; ▲ Pike; *218 SG-4; elev. 919ft./280m.; ★ CIN; mail Williamsburg z 45176
Lodi; MCD-Township; ATHENS; *219 SF-14; mail Guysville z 45735; Ⓟ 1,238; © 1,403
Lodi; Inc. Place; MEDINA; ▲ Harrisville; 217 NH-13; elev. 924ft./282m.; 🅿 🅷; z 44254; Ⓟ 3,042; © 3,061
Logan; MCD-Township; AUGLAIZE; *216 NK-3; mail Spencerville z 45887; Ⓟ 1,028; © 1,201
Logan; Inc. Place; ⊡ HOCKING; ▲ Green, Falls; 219 SD-12; elev. 741ft./226m.; 🅿 🅷; z 43138; Ⓟ 6,725; © 6,704
LOGAN; 216 NL-5; Ⓟ 42,310; © 46,005; ◆ 46,604
Logan Elm Village; CDP; PICKAWAY; ▲ Pickaway; *218 SD-9; elev. 700ft./213m.; mail Circleville z 43113; Ⓟ 1,287; © 1,062
Logansville; RMC Place; LOGAN; ▲ Pleasant; 216 NL-5; elev. 1,014ft./309m.; mail De Graff z 43318; ● 55
Logtown; RMC Place; COLUMBIANA; ▲ Center; *217 NJ-19; elev. 964ft./294m.; mail Lisbon z 44432; rural
Lombardsville; RMC Place; SCIOTO; ▲ Union; 218 SI-9; elev. 721ft./220m.; mail Mc Dermott z 45652; ● 40
London; Inc. Place; ⊡ MADISON; 218 SB-7; elev. 1,054ft./321m.; 🅿 🅷; z 43140; Ⓟ 7,807; © 8,771
London; RMC Place; RICHLAND; ▲ Cass; *217 NI-11; elev. 1,088ft./332m.; mail Shelby z 44875
Londonderry; RMC Place; GUERNSEY; ▲ Londonderry; 217 NM-17; mail Freeport z 43973; ● 40
Londonderry; MCD-Township; GUERNSEY; *217 NN-17; mail Freeport z 43973; Ⓟ 653; © 738
Londonderry; RMC Place; ROSS; ▲ Liberty; 218 SF-10; elev. 687ft./209m.; 🅿; z 45647; ● 400
Long; RMC Place; DARKE; ▲ Liberty; *218 SA-1; mail Greenville z 45331; rural
Long Beach; RMC Place; OTTAWA; ▲ Carroll; *216 NE-8; mail Oak Harbor z 43449; ● 100
Long Bottom; RMC Place; MEIGS; ▲ Olive; 219 SG-15; elev. 599ft./183m.; 🅿; z 45743; ● 70

Entries in **UPPERCASE** are counties.
Entries in **bold** have populations of 2,500 or more.
Names in parentheses are alternate names.

Inc. Place	Incorporated Place
RMC Place	Rand McNally Designated Place
CDP	Census Designated Place
MCD	Minor Civil Division

⊡	County Seat
▲	Minor Civil Division
elev.	Elevation
🅿	Post Office
🅷	Hospital
🅲	College
■	Principal Business Center
★	Ranally Metro Area (RMA) Abbreviation
z	Zip Code(s)
Ⓟ	Previous Census Population
Ⓡ	Revised Census Population
Ⓐ	Annexation Population
●	Rand McNally Population Estimate
©	Final Census Population
Ⓢ	Special Census Population
◆	Estimated Population

For additional definitions see Glossary, Volume 1, and Introduction, Volume 2.

Long Lake (Bonnett Lake); RMC Place; ASHLAND, HOLMES; ▲ Washington, Lake; mail Lakeville z 44638; summer pop. 350
Long Run; RMC Place; JEFFERSON; ▲ Mount Pleasant; *217 NM-19; ★ WHL; mail Dillonvale z 43917; rural
Longs Crossing; RMC Place; COLUMBIANA; ▲ Salem; *217 NI-19; mail Leetonia z 44431; rural
Longstreth; RMC Place; HOCKING; ▲ Ward; *219 SD-13; mail Nelsonville z 45764; ● 100
Longview Heights; RMC Place; ATHENS; *219 SF-13; mail Athens z 45701; pop. incl. with Athens (Inc. Place)
Longvue; RMC Place; WASHINGTON; mail Marietta z 45750; pop. incl. with Marietta (Inc. Place)
Loomis; RMC Place; BELMONT; ▲ Goshen; *219 SA-18; mail Belmont z 43718; rural
Lorain; Inc. Place; LORAIN; 217 NF-13; elev. 600ft./183m.; 🅿 🅷 ■; ★ CLEV; z 44052-55; Ⓟ 71,245; Ⓒ 68,652; ◆ 68,632
LORAIN; 217 NG-13; Ⓟ 271,126; Ⓒ 284,664; ◆ 301,905
Loramie; SHELBY; see Fort Loramie (Inc. Place)
Loramie; MCD-Township; SHELBY; *216 NM-2; mail Russia z 45363; Ⓟ 2,190; Ⓒ 2,438
Lordstown; Inc. Place; TRUMBULL; 217 NG-19; elev. 957ft./292m.; ★ YNGS-; mail Warren z 44481; Ⓟ 3,404; Ⓒ 3,633
Lore City; Inc. Place; GUERNSEY; ▲ Wills, Center, Richland; 219 SA-16; elev. 822ft./251m.; 🅿; z 43755; Ⓟ 384; Ⓒ 305
Lostcreek; MCD-Township; MIAMI; *218 SA-4; mail Casstown z 45312; Ⓟ 1,534; Ⓒ 1,633
Lost Creek Addition; RMC Place; ALLEN; ▲ Bath; *216 NJ-4; ★ LIMA; mail Lima z 45804; pop. incl. with Lima (Inc. Place)
Lottridge; RMC Place; ATHENS; ▲ Carthage; 219 SF-14; mail Coolville z 45723
Louden; RMC Place; ADAMS; ▲ Bratton; *218 SG-7; elev. 782ft./238m.; mail Peebles z 45660
Louden; RMC Place; TUSCARAWAS; ▲ Dover; *217 NK-16; mail Dover z 44622; pop. incl. with Dover (Inc. Place)
Loudon; MCD-Township; CARROLL; *217 NL-18; mail Carrollton z 44615; Ⓟ 933; Ⓒ 1,032
Loudon; MCD-Township; SENECA; *216 NH-7; mail Fostoria z 44830; Ⓟ 2,475; Ⓒ 2,395
Loudonville; Inc. Place; ASHLAND, HOLMES; ▲ Washington, Green, Hanover; 217 NK-12; elev. 974ft./297m.; 🅿; z 44842; Ⓟ 2,915; Ⓒ 2,906
Louisville; RMC Place; ADAMS; ▲ Bratton; *218 SG-7; elev. 900ft./274m.; mail Peebles z 45660; rural
Louisville; Inc. Place; STARK; 217 NI-17; 🅿; ★ CAN; z 44641; Ⓟ 8,087; Ⓒ 8,904
Loveland; Inc. Place; HAMILTON, CLERMONT, WARREN; ▲ Hamilton, Hamilton, Miami; 218 SF-3; 🅿; ★ CIN; z 45111, z 45140; Ⓟ 9,990; Ⓒ 11,677
Loveland Park; CDP; WARREN, HAMILTON; ▲ Deerfield, Symmes; 218 SJ-6; ★ CIN; mail Loveland z 45140, Maineville z 45039; Ⓟ 1,357; Ⓒ 1,799
Lovell; RMC Place; WYANDOT; ▲ Salem; *216 NI-7; elev. 817ft./249m.; mail Upper Sandusky z 43351; ● 60
Lowell; Inc. Place; WASHINGTON; ▲ Adams; 219 SD-16; 🅿; z 45744; Ⓟ 617; Ⓒ 628
Lowellville; Inc. Place; MAHONING; 217 NH-20; 🅿; ★ YNGS-; z 44436; Ⓟ 1,349; Ⓒ 1,281
Lowellville Junction; RMC Place; MAHONING; ★ YNGS-; mail Lowellville z 44436; pop. incl. with Lowellville (Inc. Place)
Lower Salem; Inc. Place; WASHINGTON; ▲ Salem; 219 SD-17; elev. 653ft./199m.; 🅿; z 45745; Ⓟ 103; Ⓒ 109
Loyal Oak; RMC Place; SUMMIT; *217 NH-15; ★ AKR; mail Barberton z 44203; pop. incl. with Norton (Inc. Place)
Lucas; Inc. Place; RICHLAND; 217 NJ-12; 🅿; ★ MANS; z 44843; Ⓟ 730; Ⓒ 620
LUCAS; 216 NE-5; Ⓟ 462,361; Ⓒ 455,054; ◆ 434,142
Lucasburg; RMC Place; GUERNSEY; ▲ Jackson; 219 SB-16; mail Byesville z 43723
Lucasville; CDP; SCIOTO; ▲ Valley; 218 SH-9; 🅿; ★ PTSM; z 45648, z 45699; Ⓟ 1,575; Ⓒ 1,588
Lucerne; RMC Place; KNOX; ▲ Wayne; *217 NL-11; mail Fredericktown z 43019
Luckey; Inc. Place; WOOD; ▲ Troy; 216 NF-7; 🅿; ★ TOL; z 43443; Ⓟ 848; Ⓒ 998
Ludington; RMC Place; PERRY; ▲ Salt Lick; *219 SD-13; mail Corning z 43730; rural
Ludlow; MCD-Township; WASHINGTON; *219 SD-17; mail Graysville z 45734; Ⓟ 350; Ⓒ 330
Ludlow Falls; Inc. Place; MIAMI; ▲ Union; 218 SA-3; 🅿; ★ DAY; z 45339; Ⓟ 300; Ⓒ 210
Lugbill Addition; RMC Place; FULTON; mail Archbold z 43502; pop. incl. with Archbold (Inc. Place)
Lumberton; RMC Place; CLINTON; ▲ Liberty; 218 SD-5; elev. 1,014ft./309m.; mail Wilmington z 45177; ● 150
Luray; RMC Place; LICKING; ▲ Union; 219 SB-11; ★ NWRK; mail Hebron z 43025; ● 110
Lush Addition; RMC Place; MARION; ▲ Marion; ★ MRN; mail Marion z 43302; ● 400
Lykens; RMC Place; CRAWFORD; ▲ Lykens; 216 NI-9; elev. 955ft./291m.; mail Bloomville z 44818; ● 70
Lykens; MCD-Township; CRAWFORD; *216 NI-9; mail Bloomville z 44818; Ⓟ 637; Ⓒ 649
Lyme; MCD-Township; HURON; *216 NG-10; mail Bellevue z 44811; Ⓟ 908; Ⓒ 968
Lynchburg; RMC Place; COLUMBIANA; ▲ West; *217 NJ-18; ★ ALLI; mail Kensington z 44427; rural
Lynchburg; Inc. Place; HIGHLAND; ▲ Dodson; 218 SF-5; elev. 1,009ft./308m.; 🅿; z 45142; Ⓟ 1,212; Ⓒ 1,350
Lyndhurst; Inc. Place; CUYAHOGA; 217 NE-16; 🅿; ★ CLEV; z 44124; Ⓟ 15,982; Ⓒ 15,279
Lyndon; RMC Place; ROSS; ▲ Buckskin; 218 SE-8; mail South Salem z 45681; ● 200
Lynn; MCD-Township; HARDIN; *216 NK-6; mail Kenton z 43326; Ⓟ 629; Ⓒ 629
Lynns Corners; RMC Place; MAHONING; ▲ Canfield; *217 NH-19; elev. 1,141ft./348m.; ★ YNGS-; mail Canfield z 44406; rural
Lynx; RMC Place; ADAMS; ▲ Brush Creek; 218 SI-7; elev. 830ft./253m.; 🅿; z 45650 & mail West Union z 45693; ● 220
Lyons; Inc. Place; FULTON; ▲ Royalton; 216 ND-4; elev. 771ft./235m.; 🅿; z 43533; Ⓟ 579; Ⓒ 559
Lyra; RMC Place; SCIOTO; ▲ Vernon; 218 SI-10; mail Wheelersburg z 45694; ● 40
Lytle; RMC Place; WARREN; ▲ Wayne, Clear Creek; 218 SD-4; ★ DAY; mail Waynesville z 45068; ● 200

M

Macedon; RMC Place; MERCER; ▲ Recovery; 216 NK-1; mail Coldwater z 45828, Fort Recovery z 45846; ● 70
Macedonia; Inc. Place; SUMMIT; 217 NG-16; elev. 989ft./301m.; 🅿; ★ CLEV; z 44056, z 44067; Ⓟ 7,509; Ⓒ 9,224
Mack; RMC Place; HAMILTON; ▲ Green; 218 SL-1; elev. 900ft./274m.; ★ CIN; mail Cincinnati z 45211, z 45248; ● 2,000
Mack North; CDP-Census Area Only; HAMILTON; ▲ Green; *218 SF-1; elev. 874ft./266m.; ★ CIN; mail Cincinnati z 45211; Ⓟ 2,816; Ⓒ 3,529
Macksburg; Inc. Place; WASHINGTON; ▲ Aurelius; 219 SD-16; 🅿; z 45746; Ⓟ 218; Ⓒ 202
Mack South; CDP-Census Area Only; HAMILTON; ▲ Green; *218 SG-1; elev. 890ft./271m.; ★ CIN; mail Cincinnati z 45211; Ⓟ 5,767; Ⓒ 5,837
Mackstown (Maxtown); RMC Place; DELAWARE; ▲ Genoa; *216 NN-9; ★ COL; mail Westerville z 43081; rural
Macon; RMC Place; BROWN; ▲ Eagle; 218 SH-6; elev. 1,077ft./328m.; mail Winchester z 45697; ● 140
Madeira; Inc. Place; HAMILTON; 218 SF-3; elev. 772ft./235m.; 🅿; ★ CIN; z 45243; Ⓟ 9,141; Ⓒ 8,923
Madison; MCD-Township; BUTLER; *218 SD-3; ★ MIDD; mail Middletown z 45042; Ⓟ 8,547; Ⓒ 8,611
Madison; MCD-Township; CLARK; *218 SC-6; mail South Charleston z 45368; Ⓟ 2,482; Ⓒ 2,796
Madison; MCD-Township; COLUMBIANA; *217 NJ-20; ★ E.LIV; mail Wellsville z 43968; Ⓟ 3,385; Ⓒ 3,406
Madison; MCD-Township; FAIRFIELD; *219 SD-11; mail Lancaster z 43130; Ⓟ 1,218; Ⓒ 1,385
Madison; MCD-Township; FAYETTE; *218 SC-8; mail Washington Court House z 43160; Ⓟ 1,022; Ⓒ 946
Madison; MCD-Township; FRANKLIN; *218 SB-10; ★ COL; mail Groveport z 43125; Ⓟ 18,749; Ⓒ 21,243; Ⓡ 21,220
Madison; MCD-Township; GUERNSEY; *219 SA-17; mail Quaker City z 43773; Ⓟ 703; Ⓒ 855
Madison; MCD-Township; HANCOCK; *216 NI-6; mail Arlington z 45814; Ⓟ 2,028; Ⓒ 2,156
Madison; MCD-Township; HIGHLAND; *218 SE-7; mail Greenfield z 45123; Ⓟ 6,987; Ⓒ 6,922
Madison; MCD-Township; JACKSON; *219 SH-11; mail Oak Hill z 45656; Ⓟ 2,179; Ⓒ 2,171
Madison; Inc. Place; LAKE; ▲ Madison; 217 ND-18; elev. 744ft./227m.; 🅿; ★ CLEV; z 44057; Ⓟ 2,477; Ⓒ 2,921
Madison; MCD-Township; LAKE; *217 ND-18; 🅿; ★ CLEV; z 44057; Ⓟ 17,954; Ⓒ 18,428
Madison; MCD-Township; LICKING; *219 SA-12; ★ NWRK; mail Newark z 43055; Ⓟ 2,716; Ⓒ 3,061
Madison; MCD-Township; MUSKINGUM; *219 SA-14; mail Dresden z 43821; Ⓟ 388; Ⓒ 487
Madison; MCD-Township; PERRY; *219 SB-13; mail Mount Perry z 43760; Ⓟ 908; Ⓒ 1,229
Madison; MCD-Township; PICKAWAY; *218 SC-10; mail Ashville z 43103; Ⓟ 1,586; Ⓒ 1,461
Madison; MCD-Township; RICHLAND; *217 NJ-11; ★ MANS; mail Mansfield z 44903; Ⓟ 13,286; Ⓒ 14,680; Ⓡ 12,426
Madison; MCD-Township; SANDUSKY; *216 NF-7; mail Helena z 43435; Ⓟ 3,687; Ⓒ 3,721
Madison; MCD-Township; SCIOTO; *218 SH-10; mail Minford z 45653; Ⓟ 3,351; Ⓒ 3,794
Madison; MCD-Township; VINTON; *219 SF-12; mail Zaleski z 45698; Ⓟ 612; Ⓒ 682
Madison; MCD-Township; WILLIAMS; *216 ND-2; mail Pioneer z 43554; Ⓟ 2,350; Ⓒ 2,539
MADISON; 218 SC-7; Ⓟ 37,068; Ⓒ 40,213; ◆ 42,259
Madisonburg; RMC Place; WAYNE; ▲ Wayne; 217 NI-14; elev. 1,150ft./351m.; mail Wooster z 44691; pop. incl. with Wooster (Inc. Place)
Madison Hill; RMC Place; WAYNE; ▲ Wooster; *217 NJ-14; mail Wooster z 44691; pop. incl. with Wooster (Inc. Place)
Madison Lake Area; RMC Place; MADISON; ▲ Union; *218 SB-7; mail London z 43140; ● 300
Madison Mills; RMC Place; FAYETTE; ▲ Madison; 218 SD-8; mail Mount Sterling z 43143; ● 60
Madison-on-the-Lake; RMC Place; LAKE; ▲ Madison; *217 NC-18; ★ CLEV; mail Madison z 44057; ● 950
Madisonville; RMC Place; HAMILTON; *218 SF-3; ★ CIN; mail Cincinnati z 45227; pop. incl. with Cincinnati (Inc. Place)
Mad River; MCD-Township; CHAMPAIGN; *218 SA-5; mail Westville z 43083; Ⓟ 2,353; Ⓒ 2,650
Mad River; MCD-Township; CLARK; *218 SB-5; ★ SPR; mail Fairborn z 45324; Ⓟ 11,819; Ⓒ 11,828
Magnetic Springs; Inc. Place; UNION; ▲ Leesburg; 216 NL-8; elev. 944ft./288m.; 🅿; z 43036; Ⓟ 373; Ⓒ 323
Magnolia; Inc. Place; STARK, CARROLL; ▲ Rose, Sandy; 217 NK-17; 🅿; ★ CAN; z 44643; Ⓟ 937; Ⓒ 931
Mahoning; RMC Place; PORTAGE; ▲ Windham; *217 NG-18; elev. 941ft./287m.; mail Garrettsville z 44231; rural
MAHONING; 217 NH-19; Ⓟ 264,806; Ⓒ 257,555; ◆ 219,901
Maineville; Inc. Place; WARREN; ▲ Hamilton; 218 SF-3; elev. 805ft./245m.; 🅿; ★ CIN; z 45039; Ⓟ 359; Ⓒ 885
Mainsville; RMC Place; PERRY; ▲ Pike; 219 SC-13; mail New Lexington z 43764; ● 30
Malaga; RMC Place; MONROE; ▲ Malaga; 219 SB-18; 🅿; z 43757; ● 180
Malaga; MCD-Township; MONROE; *219 SB-18; 🅿; z 43757; Ⓟ 978; Ⓒ 979
Malinta; Inc. Place; HENRY; ▲ Monroe; 216 NF-4; elev. 686ft./209m.; 🅿; z 43535; Ⓟ 294; Ⓒ 285
Mallet Creek; RMC Place; MEDINA; ▲ York; 217 NG-14; ★ CLEV; mail Medina z 44256; ● 300
Malta; Inc. Place; MORGAN; 219 SC-14; elev. 671ft./205m.; 🅿; z 43758; Ⓟ 802; Ⓒ 696
Malta; MCD-Township; MORGAN; *219 SC-14; 🅿; z 43758; Ⓟ 1,992; Ⓒ 1,964
Malvern; Inc. Place; CARROLL; ▲ Brown; 217 NJ-17; elev. 997ft./304m.; 🅿; ★ CAN; z 44644; Ⓟ 1,112; Ⓒ 1,218
Manchester; Inc. Place; ADAMS; ▲ Manchester; 218 SI-6; 🅿; z 45144; Ⓟ 2,223; Ⓒ 2,043
Manchester; MCD-Township; ADAMS; *218 SI-6; 🅿; z 45144; Ⓟ 2,393; Ⓒ 2,140
Manchester; MCD-Township; MORGAN; *219 SC-15; mail McConnelsville z 43756; Ⓟ 149; Ⓒ 141
Manchester; RMC Place; SUMMIT; ▲ Franklin; 217 NI-15; elev. 1,111ft./339m.; ★ AKR; mail Akron z 44319, Clinton z 44216; ● 4,000
Mandale; RMC Place; PAULDING; ▲ Washington; 216 NH-3; mail Cloverdale z 45827; ● 50
Manhattan; RMC Place; JEFFERSON; ★ STU-; mail Steubenville z 43952; pop. incl. with Steubenville (Inc. Place)
Manhattan Junction; RMC Place; LUCAS; ★ TOL; pop. incl. with Toledo (Inc. Place)
Mannhassett Village; RMC Place; WARREN; ★ CIN; mail Mason z 45040; pop. incl. with Mason (Inc. Place)
Mansfield; Inc. Place; ⊡ RICHLAND; 217 NJ-11; 🅿 🅷 🅲 1,856 ■; ★ MANS; z 44901-07; Ⓟ 50,627; Ⓒ 49,346; Ⓡ 51,600; ◆ 45,487
Mansfield Southeast; RMC Place; RICHLAND; ★ MANS; pop. incl. with Mansfield (Inc. Place)
Mantua; Inc. Place; PORTAGE; 217 NG-17; 🅿; ★ CLEV; z 44021, z 44255; Ⓟ 1,178; Ⓒ 1,046
Mantua; MCD-Township; PORTAGE; *217 NG-17; 🅿; ★ CLEV; z 44021, z 44255; Ⓟ 5,596; Ⓒ 4,661
Mantua Center; RMC Place; PORTAGE; ▲ Mantua; *217 NG-17; elev. 1,180ft./360m.; ★ CLEV; mail Mantua z 44255; ● 80
Mantua Corners; RMC Place; PORTAGE; ▲ Mantua; 217 NG-17; elev. 1,199ft./365m.; ★ CLEV; mail Mantua z 44255; ● 80
Maple (Poetown); RMC Place; BROWN, CLERMONT; ▲ Clark, Tate; *218 SH-4; ★ CIN; mail Hamersville z 45130; ● 60
Maple Corner; RMC Place; GREENE; ▲ Caesarscreek; *218 SD-5; elev. 967ft./295m.; mail Xenia z 45385; rural
Maple Grove; RMC Place; GEAUGA; ▲ Troy; *217 NF-17; elev. 1,110ft./338m.; mail Garrettsville z 44231; rural
Maple Grove; RMC Place; ROSS; ▲ Union; *218 SE-9; mail Chillicothe z 45601; rural
Maple Grove; RMC Place; SENECA; ▲ Liberty; *216 NG-8; mail Tiffin z 44883; rural
Maple Heights; Inc. Place; CUYAHOGA; 217 NF-15; 🅿; ★ CLEV; z 44137; Ⓟ 27,089; Ⓒ 26,156; ◆ 23,858
Maple Heights; RMC Place; NOBLE; ▲ Noble; *219 SC-16; mail Caldwell z 43724; ● 100
Maple Lake; RMC Place; JEFFERSON; ▲ Island Creek; ★ STU-; mail Richmond z 43944; ● 100
Maple Park; RMC Place; WARREN; ▲ Deerfield; ★ CIN; mail Mason z 45040; ● 85
Maple Ridge; CDP; MAHONING; ▲ Smith; *217 NI-18; elev. 1,104ft./336m.; ★ ALLI; mail Alliance z 44601; Ⓟ 1,018; Ⓒ 910
Mapleshade; RMC Place; GALLIA; *219 SH-13; mail Gallipolis z 45631; pop. incl. with Gallipolis (Inc. Place)
Mapleton; RMC Place; STARK; ▲ Osnaburg; 217 NJ-17; elev. 1,024ft./312m.; ★ CAN; mail East Canton z 44730; ● 90
Mapleton Beach; RMC Place; ASHTABULA; ▲ Geneva; *217 NC-18; ★ ASHT
Maple Valley; RMC Place; SUMMIT; *217 NH-15; ★ AKR; mail Akron z 44320; pop. incl. with Akron (Inc. Place)
Maplewood; RMC Place; SHELBY; ▲ Salem; 216 NL-4; 🅿; z 45340; ● 230
Maplewood Park; CDP-Census Area Only; TRUMBULL; *217 NH-20; ★ YNGS-; Ⓒ 321
Marathon; RMC Place; CLERMONT; ▲ Jackson; 218 SG-4; 🅿; ★ CIN; z 45145; ● 300
Marble Cliff; Inc. Place; FRANKLIN; ▲ Franklin; 219 SH-18; 🅿; ★ COL; z 43212; Ⓟ 633; Ⓒ 646
Marble Furnace; RMC Place; ADAMS; ▲ Bratton; *218 SH-7; mail Peebles z 45660; rural
Marblehead; Inc. Place; OTTAWA; ▲ Danbury; 216 NE-10; 🅿; z 43440; Ⓟ 745; Ⓒ 762
Marchand; RMC Place; STARK; ▲ Jackson; *217 NI-16; ★ CAN; mail North Canton z 44720; rural
Marcy; RMC Place; FAIRFIELD; ▲ Bloom; *218 SC-10; ★ COL; mail Canal Winchester z 43110
Marengo; Inc. Place; MORROW; ▲ Bennington; 216 NL-10; elev. 1,119ft./341m.; 🅿; z 43334; Ⓟ 393; Ⓒ 297
Margaretta; MCD-Township; ERIE; *216 NF-10; ★ SNDSK; mail Castalia z 44824; Ⓟ 6,255; Ⓒ 6,289
Maria Stein; RMC Place; MERCER; ▲ Marion; 216 NL-2; 🅿; z 45860; ● 300
Mariemont; Inc. Place; HAMILTON; 218 SG-3; ★ CIN; mail Cincinnati z 45227; Ⓟ 3,118; Ⓒ 3,408
Marietta; Inc. Place; ⊡ WASHINGTON; ▲ Marietta; 219 SE-16; elev. 616ft./188m.; 🅿 🅷 🅲 1,411 ■; ★ PRKB; z 45750; Ⓟ 15,026; Ⓒ 14,515; ◆ 13,454
Marietta; MCD-Township; WASHINGTON; *219 SE-16; 🅿 🅲 1,411; ★ PRKB; z 45750; Ⓟ 4,453; Ⓒ 4,673
Marion; MCD-Township; ALLEN; *216 NI-3; ★ LIMA; mail Delphos z 45833; Ⓟ 6,676; Ⓒ 6,773
Marion; MCD-Township; CLINTON; *218 SF-5; mail Blanchester z 45107; Ⓟ 5,184; Ⓒ 5,489
Marion; MCD-Township; FAYETTE; *218 SC-8; mail New Holland z 43145; Ⓟ 713; Ⓒ 748
Marion; MCD-Township; HANCOCK; *216 NH-6; ★ FIND; mail Findlay z 45840; Ⓟ 2,204; Ⓒ 2,203
Marion; MCD-Township; HARDIN; *216 NJ-5; mail Alger z 45812; Ⓟ 2,357; Ⓒ 2,449
Marion; MCD-Township; HENRY; *216 NG-4; mail Hamler z 43524; Ⓟ 1,439; Ⓒ 1,417
Marion; MCD-Township; HOCKING; *219 SD-12; mail Logan z 43138; Ⓟ 1,950; Ⓒ 2,411
Marion; Inc. Place; ⊡ MARION; ▲ Marion; 216 NK-8; elev. 956ft./291m.; 🅿 🅷 🅲 1,538 ■; ★ MRN; z 43301-02, z 43306-07; Ⓟ 34,075; Ⓒ 35,318; Ⓡ 37,334; ◆ 33,245
Marion; MCD-Township; MARION; *216 NK-8; 🅿 🅲 1,538; ★ MRN; z 43301-02, z 43306-07; includes the City of Marion; Ⓟ 43,564; Ⓒ 44,908; Ⓡ 44,900
Marion; MCD-Township; MERCER; *216 NL-2; mail Saint Henry z 45883; Ⓟ 2,784; Ⓒ 2,969
Marion; MCD-Township; MORGAN; *219 SD-14; mail Chesterhill z 43728; Ⓟ 1,215; Ⓒ 1,336
Marion; MCD-Township; NOBLE; *219 SC-17; mail Summerfield z 43788; Ⓟ 729; Ⓒ 730
Marion; MCD-Township; PIKE; *218 SG-10; mail Beaver z 45613; Ⓟ 1,024; Ⓒ 1,351
MARION; 216 NK-9; Ⓟ 64,274; Ⓒ 66,217; Ⓡ 66,209; ◆ 64,296
Marion East; RMC Place; MARION; ▲ Marion; *216 NK-8; ★ MRN; mail Marion z 43302; ● 200
Mark; MCD-Township; DEFIANCE; *216 NG-2; mail Sherwood z 43556; Ⓟ 963; Ⓒ 968
Mark Center (Mark Centre); RMC Place; DEFIANCE; ▲ Mark; 216 NG-1; elev. 721ft./220m.; 🅿; z 43536; ● 200
Mark Centre; DEFIANCE; see Mark Center (RMC Place)
Marlain Acres; RMC Place; HAMILTON; ▲ Springfield; *218 SF-2; ★ CIN; mail Cincinnati z 45231; ● 350
Marlboro; MCD-Township; DELAWARE; *216 NL-9; mail Delaware z 43015; Ⓟ 213; Ⓒ 227
Marlboro; RMC Place; STARK; ▲ Marlboro; 217 NI-17; elev. 1,174ft./358m.; ★ CAN; mail Alliance z 44601, Homeworth z 44634, Louisville z 44641; ● 500
Marlboro; MCD-Township; STARK; *217 NI-17; ★ CAN; mail Alliance z 44601; Ⓟ 3,687; Ⓒ 4,227
Marne; RMC Place; LICKING; ▲ Madison; 217 NN-12; ★ NWRK; mail Newark z 43055; ● 400
Marquis; RMC Place; MAHONING; ▲ Green, Canfield; *217 NH-19; elev. 1,131ft./345m.; ★ YNGS-; mail Canfield z 44406; rural
Marr; RMC Place; MONROE; ▲ Bethel; *219 SD-17; rural
Marseilles; Inc. Place; WYANDOT; ▲ Marseilles; 216 NJ-7; mail Upper Sandusky z 43351; Ⓟ 130; Ⓒ 124
Marseilles; MCD-Township; WYANDOT; *216 NJ-7; mail Upper Sandusky z 43351; Ⓟ 520; Ⓒ 446
Marshall; RMC Place; HIGHLAND; ▲ Marshall; 218 SG-7; mail Hillsboro z 45133; ● 110
Marshall; MCD-Township; HIGHLAND; *218 SG-7; mail Hillsboro z 45133; Ⓟ 830; Ⓒ 1,008
Marshallville; Inc. Place; WAYNE; ▲ Chippewa, Baughman; 217 NI-15; 🅿; ★ AKR; z 44645; Ⓟ 758; Ⓒ 826
Martel; RMC Place; MARION; ▲ Tully; 216 NJ-9; elev. 1,037ft./316m.; 🅿; z 43335; ● 250
Martin; RMC Place; OTTAWA; ▲ Clay, Allen; *216 NE-7; 🅿; ★ TOL; z 43445; ● 200
Martinsburg; Inc. Place; KNOX; ▲ Clay; 217 NM-12; elev. 1,167ft./356m.; 🅿; z 43037; Ⓟ 213; Ⓒ 185
Martins Ferry; Inc. Place; BELMONT; ▲ Pease; 217 NN-19; 🅿 🅷; ★ WHL; z 43935; Ⓟ 7,990; Ⓒ 7,226
Martinsville; Inc. Place; CLINTON; ▲ Clark; 218 SE-5; elev. 1,087ft./331m.; 🅿; z 45146; Ⓟ 476; Ⓒ 440
Mary Ann; MCD-Township; LICKING; *217 NN-12; ★ NWRK; mail Newark z 43055; Ⓟ 1,927; Ⓒ 2,118
Marygrove; LUCAS; see Raab Corners (RMC Place)
Marysville; Inc. Place; ⊡ UNION; ▲ Paris; 216 NM-7; elev. 991ft./302m.; 🅿 🅷; z 43040-41; Ⓟ 9,656; Ⓒ 15,942
Mason; MCD-Township; LAWRENCE; *219 SJ-12; mail Willow Wood z 45696; Ⓟ 1,036; Ⓒ 1,095
Mason; Inc. Place; WARREN; ▲ Union, Deerfield, Turtlecreek; 218 SE-3; 🅿; ★ CIN; z 45040; Ⓟ 11,452; Ⓒ 22,016; ◆ 29,932
Mason Heights; RMC Place; WARREN; ★ CIN; mail Mason z 45040; pop. incl. with Mason (Inc. Place)
Massie; MCD-Township; WARREN; *218 SD-4; mail Harveysburg z 45032; Ⓟ 885; Ⓒ 1,061
Massieville; RMC Place; ROSS; ▲ Scioto; 218 SF-9; mail Chillicothe z 45601; ● 400
Massillon; Inc. Place; STARK; 217 NJ-16; 🅿 🅷 ■; ★ CAN; z 44646-48; Ⓟ 31,007; Ⓒ 31,325; ◆ 31,717
Masury; CDP; TRUMBULL; ▲ Brookfield; 217 NG-20; 🅿; ★ SHAR; z 44438; Ⓒ 2,618
Matamoras; WASHINGTON; see New Matamoras (Inc. Place)
Matville; RMC Place; PICKAWAY; ▲ Scioto; *218 SC-9; ★ COL; mail Orient z 43146
Maud; RMC Place; BUTLER; ▲ West Chester; 218 SE-3; ★ CIN; mail West Chester z 45069; ● 500
Maumee; Inc. Place; LUCAS; 216 NE-6; 🅿 🅷 ■; ★ TOL; z 43537; Ⓟ 15,561; Ⓒ 15,237; Ⓡ 15,074; ◆ 14,034
Maustown; RMC Place; BUTLER; ▲ Liberty; *218 SE-2; ★ CIN; mail Hamilton z 45011; ● 170
Maximo; RMC Place; STARK; ▲ Washington; 217 NI-17; 🅿; ★ ALLI; z 44650; ● 200
Maxtown; DELAWARE; see Mackstown (RMC Place)
Maxville; RMC Place; PERRY; ▲ Monday Creek; 219 SD-12; elev. 783ft./239m.; mail Logan z 43138; ● 100
Maybee; RMC Place; RICHLAND; *217 NJ-11; ★ MANS; pop. incl. with Ontario (Inc. Place)
Mayfield; RMC Place; BUTLER; *218 SD-3; ★ MIDD; mail Middletown z 45044; pop. incl. with Middletown (Inc. Place)
Mayfield; Inc. Place; CUYAHOGA; 219 SK-20; elev. 927ft./283m.; 🅿; ★ CLEV; z 44143 & mail Cleveland z 44124; Ⓟ 3,462; Ⓒ 3,435
Mayfield Heights; Inc. Place; CUYAHOGA; 217 NE-16; 🅿 ■; ★ CLEV; z 44124 & mail Cleveland z 44143; Ⓟ 19,847; Ⓒ 19,386; ◆ 17,963
Mayflower Village; RMC Place; STARK; *217 NJ-15; ★ CAN; mail Massillon z 44647; pop. incl. with Massillon (Inc. Place)
May Hill; RMC Place; ADAMS; ▲ Scott, Bratton; 218 SG-7; elev. 1,017ft./310m.; mail Seaman z 45679; ● 50
Maynard; RMC Place; BELMONT; ▲ Colerain; 217 NN-19; 🅿; ★ WHL; z 43937; ● 400
Maysville; RMC Place; ALLEN, HARDIN; ▲ Jackson, Auglaize; 216 NJ-5; ★ LIMA; mail Ada z 45810, Lafayette z 45854; ● 50
Maysville; RMC Place; WAYNE; ▲ Salt Creek; 217 NJ-14; elev. 1,146ft./349m.; mail Apple Creek z 44606; ● 100
McArthur; MCD-Township; LOGAN; *216 NL-5; mail Huntsville z 43324; Ⓟ 1,746; Ⓒ 1,949
McArthur; Inc. Place; ⊡ VINTON; ▲ Elk; 219 SF-12; 🅿; z 45651; Ⓟ 1,541; Ⓒ 1,888
McCance; RMC Place; WAYNE; ▲ Franklin; *217 NJ-14; mail Fredericksburg z 44627; rural
Mc Cappin Mill; RMC Place; HIGHLAND; ▲ Paint; *218 SF-7; mail Hillsboro z 45133; summer pop. 250; ● 60
McCartyville; RMC Place; SHELBY; ▲ Van Buren; 216 NL-3; elev. 971ft./296m.; mail Anna z 45302; ● 160
McClainville; RMC Place; BELMONT; ▲ Pultney; *219 SA-19; ★ WHL; mail Bellaire z 43906; rural
McClimansville; RMC Place; MADISON; ▲ Pleasant; 218 SC-8; mail Mount Sterling z 43143; ● 60
McClintocksburg; RMC Place; PORTAGE; ▲ Paris; *217 NG-18; mail Newton Falls z 44444
McClure; Inc. Place; HENRY; ▲ Damascus; 216 NF-5; 🅿; z 43523, z 43534; Ⓟ 781; Ⓒ 761
McComb; Inc. Place; HANCOCK; ▲ Pleasant; 216 NH-5; elev. 778ft./237m.; 🅿; z 45858; Ⓟ 1,544; Ⓒ 1,676
McConnelsville; Inc. Place; ⊡ MORGAN; ▲ Morgan; 219 SC-15; 🅿; z 43756; Ⓟ 1,804; Ⓒ 1,676
McCracken Corners; RMC Place; COLUMBIANA; ▲ Salem; *217 NI-19; elev. 1,195ft./364m.; mail Salem z 44460; rural
McCuneville; RMC Place; PERRY; ▲ Salt Lick; 219 SD-13; mail Shawnee z 43782; ● 90
McCutchenville; RMC Place; WYANDOT, SENECA; ▲ Seneca, Tymochtee; 216 NI-8; 🅿; z 44844; ● 300
McDermott; RMC Place; SCIOTO; ▲ Rush; 218 SH-9; 🅿; ★ PTSM; z 45652; ● 600
McDonald; MCD-Township; HARDIN; *216 NK-5; mail Kenton z 43326; Ⓟ 921; Ⓒ 914
McDonald; Inc. Place; TRUMBULL; 217 NB-13; 🅿; ★ YNGS-; z 44437; Ⓟ 3,526; Ⓒ 3,481
McDonaldsville; RMC Place; STARK; ▲ Jackson; 217 NI-16; elev. 1,184ft./361m.; ★ CAN; mail North Canton z 44720; ● 180
McGill; RMC Place; PAULDING; ▲ Benton; 216 NH-1; elev. 765ft./233m.; mail Payne z 45880; ● 20
McGonigle; RMC Place; BUTLER; ▲ Hanover; 218 SE-1; elev. 912ft./278m.; ★ CIN; mail Hamilton z 45013; ● 130
Mc Gough; RMC Place; KNOX; ▲ Morris; mail Mount Vernon z 43050; ● 150
McGuffey; Inc. Place; HARDIN; ▲ Marion; 216 NJ-5; elev. 973ft./297m.; 🅿; z 45859; Ⓟ 550; Ⓒ 522
McGuffey Heights; RMC Place; MAHONING; *217 NH-20; ★ YNGS-; mail Youngstown z 44505; pop. incl. with Youngstown (Inc. Place)
McIntyre; RMC Place; JEFFERSON; ▲ Wayne; *217 NM-19; ★ STU-; mail Bloomingdale z 43910; ● 25
McKay; RMC Place; ASHLAND; ▲ Green; *217 NJ-12; elev. 1,169ft./356m.; mail Loudonville z 44842; rural
McKean; MCD-Township; LICKING; *217 NN-11; mail Newark z 43055; Ⓟ 1,357; Ⓒ 1,516
McKinley Heights; RMC Place; TRUMBULL; ▲ Weathersfield; 217 NG-19; ★ YNGS-; mail Niles z 44446; ● 700
McLean; MCD-Township; SHELBY; *216 NL-3; mail Fort Loramie z 45845; Ⓟ 2,692; Ⓒ 3,082
McLuney; RMC Place; PERRY; ▲ Harrison; 219 SC-13; ★ ZAN; mail Crooksville z 43731; ● 75
McMorran; RMC Place; LOGAN; ▲ Harrison; *216 NL-5; mail Bellefontaine z 43311
McZena; RMC Place; ASHLAND; ▲ Lake; 217 NJ-13; mail Lakeville z 44638; ● 40
Mead; MCD-Township; BELMONT; *219 SB-19; ★ WHL; mail Shadyside z 43947; Ⓟ 6,166; Ⓒ 6,023
Meade; RMC Place; PICKAWAY; ▲ Pickaway; *218 SD-10; mail Kingston z 45644; ● 70
Meadowbrook; RMC Place; MUSKINGUM; ▲ Falls; *219 SA-14; ★ ZAN; mail Zanesville z 43701; ● 250
Meadowbrook Lake; RMC Place; SUMMIT; ★ AKR; mail Stow z 44224; pop. incl. with Stow (Inc. Place)
Meadowbrook Mobile Home Park; RMC Place; ASHLAND; *217 NI-12; mail Ashland z 44805; pop. incl. with Ashland (Inc. Place)
Meadow Lawn; RMC Place; BUTLER; ★ MIDD; mail Middletown z 45044; pop. incl. with Middletown (Inc. Place)
Means; HARRISON; see Cadiz Junction (RMC Place)
Mecca; RMC Place; TRUMBULL; ▲ Mecca; 217 NF-19; elev. 932ft./284m.; ★ YNGS-; mail Cortland z 44410; ● 60
Mecca; MCD-Township; TRUMBULL; *217 NF-19; ★ YNGS-; mail Cortland z 44410; Ⓟ 2,602; Ⓒ 2,829
Mechanic; MCD-Township; HOLMES; *217 NK-14; 🅿; z 43804; Ⓟ 2,052; Ⓒ 2,652
Mechanicsburg; Inc. Place; CHAMPAIGN; ▲ Goshen; 216 NN-6; 🅿; z 43044; Ⓟ 1,803; Ⓒ 1,744
Mechanicsburg; RMC Place; CRAWFORD; ▲ Auburn; *216 NI-10; mail Tiro z 44887
Mechanicsburg; RMC Place; MONROE; *219 SC-18; mail Woodsfield z 43793; ● 30
Mechanicsburg; RMC Place; WAYNE; ▲ Wayne; *217 NI-14; mail Wooster z 44691
Mechanicstown; RMC Place; CARROLL; ▲ Fox; 217 NK-18; 🅿; z 44651; ● 280
Mechanicsville; RMC Place; ASHTABULA; ▲ Austinburg; *217 ND-18; mail Geneva z 44041; rural
Medina; Inc. Place; ⊡ MEDINA; 217 NH-14; elev. 1,092ft./333m.; 🅿 🅷 ■; ★ CLEV; z 44215, z 44256, z 44258; Ⓟ 19,231; Ⓒ 25,139; ◆ 27,908
Medina; MCD-Township; MEDINA; *217 NG-14; 🅿; ★ CLEV; z 44215, z 44256, z 44258; Ⓟ 4,864; Ⓒ 7,783
MEDINA; 217 NH-14; Ⓟ 122,354; Ⓒ 151,095; ◆ 170,442
Medway; RMC Place; CLARK; ▲ Bethel; 218 SB-4; 🅿; ★ DAY; z 45341; ● 2,000
Meeker; RMC Place; MARION; ▲ Big Island, Grand, Montgomery, Salt Rock; 216 NK-7; mail Marion z 43302; ● 150
Meigs; MCD-Township; ADAMS; *218 SH-7; mail Peebles z 45660; Ⓟ 3,701; Ⓒ 3,753
Meigs; RMC Place; MORGAN; ▲ Bristol; 219 SC-15; mail McConnelsville z 43756; ● 40
Meigs; MCD-Township; MUSKINGUM; *219 SC-15; mail Chandlersville z 43727; Ⓟ 165; Ⓒ 173
MEIGS; 219 SG-14; Ⓟ 22,987; Ⓒ 23,072; ◆ 22,652
Meigsville; MCD-Township; MORGAN; *219 SD-15; mail McConnelsville z 43756; Ⓟ 774; Ⓒ 894
Melbern; RMC Place; WILLIAMS; ▲ Center; 216 NF-1; mail Bryan z 43506; ● 200
Melmore; RMC Place; SENECA; ▲ Eden; 216 NH-8; 🅿; z 44845; ● 220
Melrose; Inc. Place; PAULDING; ▲ Brown; 216 NH-2; 🅿; z 45861, z 45873; Ⓟ 307; Ⓒ 322
Melvin; RMC Place; CLINTON; ▲ Richland; 218 SE-6; mail Wilmington z 45177; ● 90
Memphis; RMC Place; CLINTON; ▲ Wayne; *218 SE-6; elev. 1,104ft./336m.; mail Leesburg z 45135
Mendon; Inc. Place; MERCER; ▲ Union; 216 NJ-2; 🅿; z 45862; Ⓟ 717; Ⓒ 697
Mentor; Inc. Place; LAKE; 217 ND-16; 🅿 ■; ★ CLEV; z 44060-61; Ⓟ 47,358; Ⓒ 50,278; ◆ 51,464
Mentor Headlands; RMC Place; LAKE; *217 ND-16; elev. 609ft./186m.; ★ CLEV; mail Mentor z 44060; pop. incl. with Mentor (Inc. Place)
Mentor-on-the-Lake; Inc. Place; LAKE; 217 ND-16; 🅿; ★ CLEV; z 44060; Ⓟ 8,271; Ⓒ 8,127
Mercer; RMC Place; MERCER; ▲ Dublin; 216 NJ-2; elev. 816ft./249m.; mail Mendon z 45862; ● 50
MERCER; 216 NK-1; Ⓟ 39,443; Ⓒ 40,924; ◆ 40,778
Mercerville; RMC Place; GALLIA; ▲ Guyan; 219 SI-13; mail Gallipolis z 45631; ● 100
Meredith; DELAWARE; see Radnor (RMC Place)
Mermill; RMC Place; WOOD; ▲ Portage; 216 NG-6; mail Portage z 43451
Mesopotamia; RMC Place; TRUMBULL; ▲ Mesopotamia; 217 NF-18; elev. 857ft./261m.; 🅿; z 44439; ● 300
Mesopotamia; MCD-Township; TRUMBULL; *217 NF-18; 🅿; z 44439; Ⓟ 2,533; Ⓒ 3,051
Metamora; Inc. Place; FULTON; ▲ Amboy; 216 ND-5; 🅿; z 43540; Ⓟ 543; Ⓒ 563
Metham; RMC Place; COSHOCTON; ▲ Bethlehem; *217 NL-14; mail Warsaw z 43844; rural
Metzger; RMC Place; ROSS; ▲ Green; 218 SE-9; mail Chillicothe z 45601; ● 200
Mexico; RMC Place; WYANDOT; ▲ Tymochtee, Sycamore; 216 NI-8; mail Sycamore z 44882; ● 60
Meyers Lake (Myers Lake); Inc. Place; STARK; ▲ Plain, Canton; 216 NC-9; ★ CAN; mail East Canton z 44730; Ⓟ 493; Ⓒ 565
Miami; MCD-Township; CLERMONT; *218 SF-3; ★ CIN; mail Miamiville z 45147; Ⓟ 28,199; Ⓒ 36,632
Miami; MCD-Township; GREENE; *218 SC-5; 🅲 4,221; ★ DAY; mail Yellow Springs z 45387; Ⓟ 5,162; Ⓒ 5,106
Miami; RMC Place; HAMILTON; ▲ Colerain; *218 SF-1; ★ CIN; mail Miamitown z 45041
Miami; MCD-Township; HAMILTON; *218 SF-1; ★ CIN; mail Cleves z 45002; Ⓟ 11,552; Ⓒ 13,496
Miami; MCD-Township; LOGAN; *216 NM-5; mail Quincy z 43343; Ⓟ 2,352; Ⓒ 2,352
Miami; MCD-Township; MONTGOMERY; *218 SD-3; ★ DAY; mail Miamisburg z 45342; Ⓟ 40,700; Ⓒ 45,593
MIAMI; 216 NN-3; Ⓟ 93,182; Ⓒ 98,868; ◆ 99,111
Miami Heights; RMC Place; HAMILTON; ▲ Miami; *218 SF-1; ★ CIN; mail Cincinnati z 45248, Cleves z 45002, North Bend z 45052; ● 600
Miamisburg; Inc. Place; MONTGOMERY; ▲ Miami; 218 SD-3; 🅿; ★ DAY; z 45342-43; Ⓟ 17,834; Ⓒ 19,489
Miami Shores; RMC Place; MONTGOMERY; *218 SC-3; ★ DAY; mail Dayton z 45439; pop. incl. with Moraine (Inc. Place)
Miamitown; RMC Place; HAMILTON; 218 SF-1; 🅿; ★ CIN; z 45041; ● 730
Miami University; RMC Place; BUTLER; 🅿; z 45056; pop. incl. with Oxford (Inc. Place)
Miami Villa; RMC Place; MONTGOMERY; *218 SB-4; ★ DAY; mail Dayton z 45424; pop. incl. with Huber Heights (Inc. Place)
Miamiville; RMC Place; CLERMONT; ▲ Miami; 218 SK-5; 🅿; ★ CIN; z 45147; ● 300
Michael Manor; RMC Place; MIAMI; ▲ Monroe; *218 SB-4; ★ DAY; mail Tipp City z 45371; ● 200
Mid City; RMC Place; MONTGOMERY; ★ DAY; mail Dayton z 45402; pop. incl. with Dayton (Inc. Place)
Middle Bass (Middle Bass Island); RMC Place; OTTAWA; ▲ Put-in-Bay; 216 ND-10; 🅿; z 43446 & mail Port Clinton z 43452; summer pop. 350; ● 100
Middle Bass Island; OTTAWA; see Middle Bass (RMC Place)
Middleboro; RMC Place; WARREN; ▲ Harlan; 218 SE-4; elev. 905ft./276m.; ★ CIN; mail Morrow z 45152; ● 50
Middlebourne; RMC Place; GUERNSEY; ▲ Oxford; 217 NN-17; mail Quaker City z 43773; ● 80
Middlebranch; RMC Place; STARK; ▲ Plain; 217 NI-16; 🅿; ★ CAN; z 44652; ● 220
Middleburg; RMC Place; JEFFERSON; ▲ Springfield; *217 NL-19; mail Amsterdam z 43903; ● 25
Middleburg; RMC Place; LOGAN; ▲ Zane; 216 NM-6; 🅿; z 43336; ● 220
Middleburg; RMC Place; NOBLE; ▲ Jefferson, Enoch; 219 SC-17; mail Caldwell z 43724; ● 50
Middleburg Heights (Middleburgh Heights); Inc. Place; CUYAHOGA; 217 NF-14; 🅿 🅷 ■; ★ CLEV; z 44130; Ⓟ 14,702; Ⓒ 15,542; ◆ 14,944
Middleburgh Heights; CUYAHOGA; see Middleburg Heights (Inc. Place)
Middlebury; MCD-Township; KNOX; *217 NK-11; mail Fredericktown z 43019; Ⓟ 849; Ⓒ 1,138
Middlebury; RMC Place; VAN WERT; ▲ Harrison; 216 NI-1; elev. 820ft./250m.; mail Convoy z 45832; ● 30
Middlefield; Inc. Place; GEAUGA; ▲ Middlefield; 217 NF-18; elev. 1,126ft./343m.; 🅿; z 44062; Ⓟ 1,898; Ⓒ 2,233
Middlefield; MCD-Township; GEAUGA; *217 NF-18; 🅿; ★ CLEV; z 44062; Ⓟ 6,009; Ⓒ 4,418
Middle Point; Inc. Place; VAN WERT; ▲ Washington; 216 NI-2; 🅿; z 45863; Ⓟ 639; Ⓒ 593
Middleport; Inc. Place; MEIGS; ▲ Salisbury; 219 SG-14; 🅿; z 45760; Ⓟ 2,725; Ⓒ 2,525
Middleton; RMC Place; COLUMBIANA; ▲ Fairfield; 217 NI-20; elev. 1,251ft./381m.; ★ YNGS-; mail Columbiana z 44408; ● 80
Middleton; MCD-Township; COLUMBIANA; *217 NJ-20; mail Rogers z 44455; Ⓟ 3,422; Ⓒ 3,741
Middleton; RMC Place; JACKSON; ▲ Milton; *219 SG-12; mail Wellston z 45692; rural
Middleton; MCD-Township; WOOD; *216 NF-6; ★ TOL; mail Haskins z 43525; Ⓟ 2,460; Ⓒ 2,598
Middleton Corner; RMC Place; GREENE; ▲ Caesarscreek; *218 SD-5; mail Xenia z 45385
Middletown; Inc. Place; BUTLER, WARREN; 218 SD-3; 🅿 🅷 🅲 2,380 ■; ★ MIDD; z 45042-44; Ⓟ 46,022; Ⓒ 51,605; Ⓡ 51,599; ◆ 52,589
Middletown; RMC Place; CHAMPAIGN; ▲ Wayne; 216 NM-6; mail Cable z 43009; ● 25
Middletown; RMC Place; CRAWFORD; ▲ Jefferson; *216 NJ-10; mail Galion z 44833
Midland (Midland City); Inc. Place; CLINTON; ▲ Jefferson; 218 SF-5; elev. 994ft./303m.; 🅿; z 45148; Ⓟ 319; Ⓒ 265
Midland City; CLINTON; see Midland (Inc. Place)
Midpark; RMC Place; CUYAHOGA; *217 NF-14; ★ CLEV; mail Cleveland z 44130; pop. incl. with Parma Heights (Inc. Place)
Midtown; RMC Place; MUSKINGUM; ★ ZAN; mail Zanesville z 43701-02; pop. incl. with Zanesville (Inc. Place)
Midvale; Inc. Place; TUSCARAWAS; ▲ Warwick, Goshen, Mill; 217 NL-16; 🅿; z 44653; Ⓟ 575; Ⓒ 547
Midway; RMC Place; BELMONT; ▲ Wheeling; *217 NN-19; mail Saint Clairsville z 43950; ● 180
Midway (Sedalia); Inc. Place; MADISON; ▲ Range; 218 SC-7; mail Sedalia z 43151; Ⓟ 289; Ⓒ 274
Mifflin; Inc. Place; ASHLAND; ▲ Mifflin; 217 NJ-12; ★ MANS; mail Ashland z 44805; Ⓟ 162; Ⓒ 144
Mifflin; MCD-Township; ASHLAND; *217 NJ-12; ★ MANS; mail Ashland z 44805; Ⓟ 1,016; Ⓒ 1,083
Mifflin; MCD-Township; FRANKLIN; *218 SA-10; ★ COL; mail Columbus z 43219; Ⓟ 28,449; Ⓒ 35,787
Mifflin; MCD-Township; PIKE; *218 SG-8; mail Latham z 45646; Ⓟ 1,146; Ⓒ 1,194
Mifflin; MCD-Township; RICHLAND; *217 NJ-11; ★ MANS; mail Lucas z 44843; Ⓟ 6,859; Ⓒ 6,218
Mifflin; MCD-Township; WYANDOT; *216 NJ-7; mail Upper Sandusky z 43351; Ⓟ 833; Ⓒ 705
Mifflinville; RMC Place; FRANKLIN; *218 SA-9; ★ COL; mail Columbus z 43224; pop. incl. with Columbus (Inc. Place)
Milan; Inc. Place; ERIE, HURON; ▲ Milan; 217 NG-11; 🅿; ★ SNDSK; z 44846; Ⓟ 1,464; Ⓒ 1,445
Milan; MCD-Township; ERIE; *217 NG-11; 🅿; ★ SNDSK; z 44846; includes part of the Village of Milan; Ⓟ 3,149; Ⓒ 3,686
Milford; MCD-Township; BUTLER; *218 SD-1; ★ CIN; mail Collinsville z 45004; Ⓟ 2,651; Ⓒ 3,254
Milford; Inc. Place; CLERMONT, HAMILTON; 218 SF-3; 🅿; ★ CIN; z 45150; Ⓟ 5,660; Ⓒ 6,284
Milford; MCD-Township; DEFIANCE; *216 NF-1; mail Hicksville z 43526; Ⓟ 947; Ⓒ 1,013
Milford; MCD-Township; KNOX; *217 NM-11; mail Centerburg z 43011; Ⓟ 1,175; Ⓒ 1,422
Milford Center; Inc. Place; UNION; ▲ Union; 216 NM-7; 🅿; z 43045; Ⓟ 651; Ⓒ 626
Mill; MCD-Township; TUSCARAWAS; *217 NL-17; mail Uhrichsville z 44683; Ⓟ 10,315; Ⓒ 10,290
Millbrook; RMC Place; WAYNE; ▲ Plain, Clinton; 217 NJ-13; mail Wooster z 44691; ● 60
Millbury; Inc. Place; WOOD; ▲ Lake; 216 NE-7; 🅿; ★ TOL; z 43447; Ⓟ 1,081; Ⓒ 1,161
Mill Creek; MCD-Township; COSHOCTON; *217 NL-14; mail Millersburg z 44654; Ⓟ 540; Ⓒ 747
Millcreek; MCD-Township; UNION; *216 NM-8; mail Marysville z 43040; Ⓟ 815; Ⓒ 1,261
Mill Creek; MCD-Township; WILLIAMS; *216 ND-2; mail Alvordton z 43501; Ⓟ 954; Ⓒ 935
Milledgeville; Inc. Place; FAYETTE; ▲ Jasper; 218 SD-6; 🅿; z 43142; Ⓟ 120; Ⓒ 122
Miller; MCD-Township; KNOX; *217 NM-11; mail Mount Vernon z 43050; Ⓟ 717; Ⓒ 893
Miller; RMC Place; LAWRENCE; ▲ Rome; 219 SJ-12; ★ HNTG; mail Crown City z 45623; ● 200
Miller City (Millers City); Inc. Place; PUTNAM; ▲ Palmer; 216 NH-4; elev. 732ft./223m.; 🅿; z 45864; Ⓟ 173; Ⓒ 136
Millers; RMC Place; MIAMI; ▲ Union; *218 SB-3; ★ DAY; mail West Milton z 45383; ● 350
Millersburg; Inc. Place; ⊡ HOLMES; 217 NK-14; elev. 906ft./276m.; 🅿 🅷; z 44654; Ⓟ 3,051; Ⓒ 3,326
Millers City; PUTNAM; see Miller City (Inc. Place)
Millersport; Inc. Place; FAIRFIELD; ▲ Walnut; 219 SB-11; elev. 904ft./276m.; 🅿; ★ COL; z 43046; Ⓟ 1,010; Ⓒ 963
Miller Station; RMC Place; HARRISON; ▲ German; *217 NL-19; mail Hopedale z 43976; rural
Millerstown; RMC Place; CHAMPAIGN; ▲ Johnson; 216 NN-5; mail Saint Paris z 43072; ● 90
Millersville; RMC Place; SANDUSKY; ▲ Jackson; 216 NG-8; 🅿; z 43435; ● 150
Millertown; RMC Place; PERRY; ▲ Monroe; *219 SD-13; elev. 910ft./277m.; mail Corning z 43730; ● 40
Millfield; RMC Place; ATHENS; ▲ Dover; 219 SE-13; elev. 678ft./207m.; 🅿; z 45761; ● 500
Milligan; RMC Place; PERRY; ▲ Bearfield; *219 SC-13; mail Crooksville z 43731; ● 30
Millport; RMC Place; COLUMBIANA; ▲ Franklin; 217 NJ-19; mail Kensington z 44427; ● 110
Millport; RMC Place; PICKAWAY; ▲ Harrison; *218 SC-9; ★ COL; mail Ashville z 43103; pop. incl. with Ashville (Inc. Place)
Millville; Inc. Place; BUTLER; ▲ Ross, Hanover; 218 SE-1; ★ CIN; mail Hamilton z 45013; Ⓟ 755; Ⓒ 817
Millville; RMC Place; MAHONING; ▲ Green; *217 NI-19; mail Salem z 44460; rural
Millwood; MCD-Township; GUERNSEY; *219 SA-17; mail Quaker City z 43773; Ⓟ 1,069; Ⓒ 1,318
Millwood; RMC Place; KNOX; ▲ Union; 217 NL-12; mail Howard z 43028; ● 200
Milnersville; GUERNSEY; see Birmingham (RMC Place)
Milton; MCD-Township; ASHLAND; *217 NI-12; mail Ashland z 44805; Ⓟ 2,059; Ⓒ 2,431
Milton; MCD-Township; JACKSON; *219 SG-12; mail Wellston z 45692; Ⓟ 1,090; Ⓒ 1,119
Milton; MCD-Township; MAHONING; *217 NH-18; mail Lake Milton z 44429; Ⓟ 4,068; Ⓒ 4,107
Milton; MCD-Township; WAYNE; *217 NI-14; mail Rittman z 44270; Ⓟ 9,023; Ⓒ 9,254
Milton; WOOD; see Milton Center (Inc. Place)
Milton; MCD-Township; WOOD; *216 NG-5; mail Lemoyne z 43441; Ⓟ 1,297; Ⓒ 1,159
Milton Center (Milton); Inc. Place; WOOD; ▲ Milton; 216 NG-5; 🅿; z 43541; Ⓟ 200; Ⓒ 195
Miltonsburg; Inc. Place; MONROE; ▲ Malaga; 219 SB-18; mail Woodsfield z 43793; Ⓟ 56; Ⓒ 29
Miltonville; RMC Place; BUTLER; ▲ Madison; 218 SD-2; ★ MIDD; mail Middletown z 45042, Trenton z 45067; ● 170
Mineral; RMC Place; ATHENS; ▲ Waterloo; *219 SE-13; mail New Marshfield z 45766
Mineral City; Inc. Place; TUSCARAWAS; ▲ Sandy; 217 NK-16; 🅿; ★ CAN; z 44656; Ⓟ 725; Ⓒ 841
Mineral Ridge; CDP; TRUMBULL, MAHONING; ▲ Austintown, Weathersfield; 217 NH-19; 🅿; ★ YNGS-; z 44440; Ⓟ 3,928; Ⓒ 3,900
Minersville; RMC Place; MEIGS; ▲ Sutton; 219 SG-14; mail Pomeroy z 45769; ● 70
Minerva; Inc. Place; STARK, CARROLL, COLUMBIANA; ▲ West, Brown, Paris; 217 NJ-17; 🅿; ★ CAN; z 44657; Ⓟ 4,318; Ⓒ 3,934
Minerva Park; Inc. Place; FRANKLIN; ▲ Blendon; 216 NN-9; ★ COL; mail Columbus z 43231; Ⓟ 1,463; Ⓒ 1,288
Mineyahta on-The-Bay; RMC Place; OTTAWA; ▲ Danbury; *216 NE-10; elev. 585ft./178m.; ★ TOL; mail Lakeside Marblehead z 43440; ● 200
Minford; RMC Place; SCIOTO; ▲ Madison, Harrison; 218 SH-10; elev. 657ft./200m.; 🅿; ★ PTSM; z 45653; ● 500
Mingo; RMC Place; CHAMPAIGN; ▲ Wayne; 216 NM-6; elev. 1,204ft./367m.; 🅿; z 43047; ● 100
Mingo Junction; Inc. Place; JEFFERSON; ▲ Steubenville; 217 NL-20; elev. 675ft./206m.; 🅿; ★ STU-; z 43938; Ⓟ 4,297; Ⓒ 3,631
Minster; Inc. Place; AUGLAIZE; ▲ Jackson; 216 NL-3; elev. 967ft./295m.; 🅿; z 45865; Ⓟ 2,650; Ⓒ 2,794
Misco; RMC Place; PERRY; ▲ Bearfield; *219 SC-13; mail Crooksville z 43731; rural
Mishler; RMC Place; PORTAGE; ▲ Suffield; *217 NH-16; ★ AKR; mail Mogadore z 44260; rural
Mississinawa; MCD-Township; DARKE; *216 NM-1; mail Union City z 45390; Ⓟ 795; Ⓒ 779
Mitchaw; RMC Place; LUCAS; ▲ Sylvania; *216 ND-5; ★ TOL; mail Temperance z 48182; rural
Mitiwanga; RMC Place; ERIE; ▲ Vermilion; 217 NF-11; ★ CLEV; mail Huron z 44839; summer pop. 300; ● 130
Mizer Addition; TUSCARAWAS; see Mizers (RMC Place)
Mizers (Mizer Addition); RMC Place; TUSCARAWAS; ▲ Oxford; *217 NM-15; mail Newcomerstown z 43832; pop. incl. with Newcomerstown (Inc. Place)
Modest; RMC Place; CLERMONT; ▲ Wayne; 218 SF-4; ★ CIN; mail Goshen z 45122
Modoc; RMC Place; ATHENS; ▲ Trimble; *219 SE-13; elev. 710ft./216m.; mail Glouster z 45732; ● 30
Moffit Heights; RMC Place; STARK; ▲ Tuscarawas; *217 NJ-15; ★ CAN; mail Massillon z 44646; ● 300
Moffitt; RMC Place; HANCOCK; ▲ Blanchard; *216 NH-5; mail Benton Ridge z 45816; rural
Mogadore; Inc. Place; SUMMIT, PORTAGE; 217 NH-16; 🅿; ★ AKR; z 44260; Ⓟ 4,008; Ⓒ 3,893
Mohawk; COSHOCTON; see Mohawk Village (RMC Place)
Mohawk Lake; RMC Place; SENECA; ▲ Eden; *216 NH-8; mail Tiffin z 44883; ● 150
Mohawk Village (Mohawk); RMC Place; COSHOCTON; ▲ Jefferson; *217 NM-13; mail Warsaw z 43844; rural
Mohican; MCD-Township; ASHLAND; *217 NJ-13; mail Jeromesville z 44840; Ⓟ 1,786; Ⓒ 1,857
Mohicanville; RMC Place; ASHLAND; ▲ Mohican; 217 NJ-13; elev. 1,068ft./326m.; mail Jeromesville z 44840; ● 100
Moline; RMC Place; WOOD; ▲ Lake; 216 NC-2; ★ TOL; mail Walbridge z 43465; ● 470
Momeneetown; RMC Place; LUCAS; *216 NE-7; ★ TOL; mail Oregon z 43616; pop. incl. with Oregon (Inc. Place)
Monclova; RMC Place; LUCAS; ▲ Monclova; 216 NE-6; 🅿; ★ TOL; z 43542; ● 120
Monclova; MCD-Township; LUCAS; *216 NE-6; 🅿; ★ TOL; z 43542; Ⓟ 4,547; Ⓒ 6,767
Monclova Gardens; RMC Place; LUCAS; ★ TOL; mail Maumee z 43537; pop. incl. with Maumee (Inc. Place)
Monday Creek; MCD-Township; PERRY; *219 SD-12; mail Logan z 43138; Ⓟ 501; Ⓒ 671
Monfort Heights; RMC Place; HAMILTON; ▲ Green; 218 SL-2; ★ CIN; mail Cincinnati z 45239; ● 2,400
Monfort Heights East; CDP-Census Area Only; HAMILTON; ▲ Green; *218 SF-2; elev. 850ft./259m.; ★ CIN; mail Cincinnati z 45239; Ⓟ 3,661; Ⓒ 3,880
Monfort Heights South; CDP-Census Area Only; HAMILTON; ▲ Green; *218 SF-2; elev. 922ft./281m.; ★ CIN; mail Cincinnati z 45211; Ⓟ 4,587; Ⓒ 4,466
Monnett (Monnette); RMC Place; CRAWFORD; ▲ Dallas; *216 NJ-9; mail Marion z 43302; ● 60
Monnette; CRAWFORD; see Monnett (RMC Place)
Monroe; MCD-Township; ADAMS; *218 SI-7; mail Manchester z 45144; Ⓟ 657; Ⓒ 735
Monroe; MCD-Township; ALLEN; *216 NI-4; mail Lima z 45807; Ⓟ 2,095; Ⓒ 2,219
Monroe; MCD-Township; ASHTABULA; *217 NC-20; mail Conneaut z 44030; Ⓟ 1,883; Ⓒ 2,268
Monroe; Inc. Place; BUTLER, WARREN; ▲ Turtlecreek, Lemon; 218 SE-3; elev. 823ft./251m.; 🅿; ★ MIDD; z 45050; Ⓟ 4,490; Ⓒ 7,133; Ⓡ 7,135
Monroe; MCD-Township; CARROLL; *217 NK-17; mail Dellroy z 44620; Ⓟ 1,755; Ⓒ 1,930
Monroe; MCD-Township; CLERMONT; *218 SH-4; ★ CIN; mail Midland z 45148; Ⓟ 7,762; Ⓒ 8,236
Monroe; MCD-Township; COSHOCTON; *217 NL-13; mail Warsaw z 43844; Ⓟ 399; Ⓒ 452
Monroe; MCD-Township; DARKE; *218 SB-2; ★ DAY; mail Pitsburg z 45358; Ⓟ 1,731; Ⓒ 1,674
Monroe; MCD-Township; GUERNSEY; *217 NM-16; mail Kimbolton z 43749; Ⓟ 614; Ⓒ 598
Monroe; MCD-Township; HARRISON; *217 NL-17; mail Bowerston z 44695; Ⓟ 1,171; Ⓒ 1,241
Monroe; MCD-Township; HENRY; *216 NG-4; mail Malinta z 43535; Ⓟ 1,221; Ⓒ 1,177
Monroe; MCD-Township; HOLMES; *217 NK-13; mail Millersburg z 44654; Ⓟ 1,062; Ⓒ 1,401
Monroe; MCD-Township; KNOX; *217 NL-12; mail Mount Vernon z 43050; Ⓟ 2,062; Ⓒ 2,427; Ⓡ 2,287
Monroe; MCD-Township; LICKING; *216 NN-10; ★ COL; mail Johnstown z 43031; Ⓟ 5,151; Ⓒ 5,523
Monroe; MCD-Township; LOGAN; *216 NM-6; mail Zanesfield z 43360; Ⓟ 1,274; Ⓒ 1,503
Monroe; MCD-Township; MADISON; *218 SA-7; mail London z 43140; Ⓟ 1,467; Ⓒ 1,769
Monroe; MCD-Township; MIAMI; *218 SB-4; ★ DAY; mail Tipp City z 45371; Ⓟ 12,690; Ⓒ 15,339
Monroe; MCD-Township; MUSKINGUM; *217 NN-15; mail New Concord z 43762; Ⓟ 371; Ⓒ 439
Monroe; MCD-Township; PERRY; *219 SD-13; mail Corning z 43730; Ⓟ 1,514; Ⓒ 1,565
Monroe; MCD-Township; PICKAWAY; *219 SC-13; mail Mount Sterling z 43143; Ⓟ 1,124; Ⓒ 1,166
Monroe; MCD-Township; PREBLE; *218 SB-2; ★ RICH; mail Lewisburg z 45338; Ⓟ 2,474; Ⓒ 2,290
Monroe; MCD-Township; PUTNAM; *216 NH-3; mail Continental z 45831; Ⓟ 2,254; Ⓒ 2,234
Monroe; MCD-Township; RICHLAND; *217 NJ-12; ★ MANS; mail Lucas z 44843; Ⓟ 2,646; Ⓒ 2,656
MONROE; 219 SB-17; Ⓟ 15,497; Ⓒ 15,180; ◆ 14,004
Monroe Center; RMC Place; ASHTABULA; ▲ Monroe; 217 NC-20; elev. 905ft./276m.; mail Conneaut z 44030; ● 100
Monroe Mills; RMC Place; KNOX; ▲ Monroe; *217 NL-12; mail Howard z 43028, Mount Vernon z 43050; rural
Monroeville; Inc. Place; HURON; ▲ Ridgefield; 216 NG-10; elev. 723ft./220m.; 🅿; ★ SNDSK; z 44847; Ⓟ 1,381; Ⓒ 1,433
Monroeville; RMC Place; JEFFERSON, COLUMBIANA; ▲ Washington, Brush Creek; 217 NK-19; mail Salineville z 43945; ● 50
Monterey; RMC Place; CLERMONT; ▲ Jackson; 218 SG-4; ★ CIN; mail Batavia z 45103; ● 120
Monterey; MCD-Township; PUTNAM; *216 NI-3; mail Delphos z 45833; Ⓟ 1,972; Ⓒ 2,056
Montezuma; Inc. Place; MERCER; ▲ Franklin; 216 NL-2; elev. 884ft./269m.; 🅿; z 45866; Ⓟ 199; Ⓒ 191
Montgomery; MCD-Township; ASHLAND; *217 NI-12; mail Ashland z 44805; Ⓟ 2,231; Ⓒ 2,412
Montgomery; Inc. Place; HAMILTON; ▲ Symmes, Sycamore; 218 SF-3; 🅿; ★ CIN; z 45242; Ⓟ 9,753; Ⓒ 10,163
Montgomery; MCD-Township; MARION; *216 NK-7; mail La Rue z 43332; Ⓟ 2,316; Ⓒ 2,498
Montgomery; MCD-Township; WOOD; *216 NG-7; mail Wayne z 43466; Ⓟ 4,450; Ⓒ 4,505
MONTGOMERY; 218 SC-2; Ⓟ 573,809; Ⓒ 559,062; ◆ 528,468
Montgomery Heights; RMC Place; HAMILTON; ★ CIN; mail Cincinnati z 45242; pop. incl. with Montgomery (Inc. Place)
Monticello; RMC Place; VAN WERT; ▲ Jennings; 216 NJ-2; elev. 840ft./256m.; mail Spencerville z 45887; ● 40
Montpelier; Inc. Place; WILLIAMS; ▲ Superior, Jefferson; 216 NE-2; 🅿 🅷; z 43543; Ⓟ 4,299; Ⓒ 4,320
Montra; RMC Place; SHELBY; ▲ Jackson; 216 NL-4; mail Anna z 45302; ● 100
Montrose; RMC Place; SUMMIT; ▲ Bath; 217 NH-15; elev. 1,022ft./312m.; ★ AKR; mail Akron z 44333; ● 350
Montrose-Ghent; CDP-Census Area Only; SUMMIT; ▲ Bath; *217 NH-15; elev. 995ft./303m.; ★ AKR; mail Akron z 44333; Ⓟ 4,906; Ⓒ 5,261
Montville; RMC Place; GEAUGA; ▲ Montville; 217 NE-18; 🅿; ★ CLEV; z 44064; ● 330
Montville; MCD-Township; GEAUGA; *217 NE-18; 🅿; ★ CLEV; z 44064; Ⓟ 1,682; Ⓒ 1,984
Montville; MCD-Township; MEDINA; *217 NH-14; ★ CLEV; mail Medina z 44256; Ⓟ 3,371; Ⓒ 5,410
Moons; FAYETTE; see Buena Vista (RMC Place)
Moorefield; CLARK; see New Moorefield (RMC Place)
Moorefield; MCD-Township; CLARK; *218 SA-6; ★ SPR; mail Springfield z 45502; Ⓟ 9,621; Ⓒ 11,402
Moorefield; RMC Place; HARRISON; ▲ Moorefield; 217 NM-17; 🅿; z 43907; ● 100
Moorefield; MCD-Township; HARRISON; *217 NM-17; 🅿; z 43907; Ⓟ 441; Ⓒ 420
Moores Fork; RMC Place; CLERMONT; ▲ Wayne; *218 SF-4; elev. 942ft./287m.; ★ CIN; mail Blanchester z 45107; rural
Moores Junction; RMC Place; PERRY; ▲ Bearfield; *219 SC-13; mail Crooksville z 43731; rural
Mooresville; RMC Place; ROSS; ▲ Harrison; *218 SE-10; mail Chillicothe z 45601
Moraine; Inc. Place; MONTGOMERY; 218 SC-4; 🅿; ★ DAY; z 45409, z 45418, z 45439, z 45459; Ⓟ 5,989; Ⓒ 6,897
Moreland; RMC Place; WAYNE; ▲ Franklin; 217 NJ-14; elev. 1,083ft./330m.; mail Wooster z 44691; ● 100
Moreland Hills; Inc. Place; CUYAHOGA; 219 SM-20; elev. 1,037ft./316m.; 🅿; ★ CLEV; z 44022; Ⓟ 3,354; Ⓒ 3,298
Morgan; MCD-Township; ASHTABULA; *217 ND-19; mail Rock Creek z 44084; Ⓟ 1,593; Ⓒ 1,954
Morgan; MCD-Township; BUTLER; *218 SE-1; ★ CIN; mail Okeana z 45053; Ⓟ 4,972; Ⓒ 5,328
Morgan; MCD-Township; GALLIA; *219 SH-13; mail Vinton z 45686; Ⓟ 1,332; Ⓒ 1,341
Morgan; MCD-Township; KNOX; *217 NM-11; mail Mount Vernon z 43050; Ⓟ 624; Ⓒ 843; Ⓡ 846
Morgan; MCD-Township; MORGAN; *219 SC-15; mail McConnelsville z 43756; Ⓟ 2,646; Ⓒ 2,617
Morgan; MCD-Township; SCIOTO; *218 SH-9; mail Lucasville z 45648; Ⓟ 2,030; Ⓒ 2,297

Entries in **UPPERCASE** are counties.
Entries in **bold** have populations of 2,500 or more.
Names in parentheses are alternate names.

Inc. Place	Incorporated Place
RMC Place	Rand McNally Designated Place
CDP	Census Designated Place
MCD	Minor Civil Division
⊡	County Seat
▲	Minor Civil Division
elev.	Elevation
🅿	Post Office
🅷	Hospital
🅲	College
■	Principal Business Center
★	Ranally Metro Area (RMA) Abbreviation
z	Zip Code(s)
Ⓟ	Previous Census Population
Ⓡ	Revised Census Population
Ⓐ	Annexation Population
●	Rand McNally Population Estimate
Ⓒ	Final Census Population
Ⓢ	Special Census Population
◆	Estimated Population

For additional definitions see Glossary, Volume 1, and Introduction, Volume 2.

MORGAN; 219 SD-14; Ⓟ 14,194; © 14,897; ◆ 14,500
Morgan Center; RMC Place; GALLIA; ▲ Morgan; *219 SH-13; elev. 643ft./196m.; mail Vinton z 45686
Morgandale; RMC Place; TRUMBULL; ▲ Howland; *217 NG-19; elev. 929ft./283m.; ★ YNGS-; mail Warren z 44481; ● 500
Morgan Place; RMC Place; MONTGOMERY; ▲ Butler; *218 SB-3; ★ DAY; mail Englewood z 45322; pop. incl. with Englewood (Inc. Place)
Morgansville; RMC Place; MORGAN; ▲ Union; 219 SD-14; mail Malta z 43758; ● 25
Morgantown; RMC Place; MAHONING; ▲ Springfield; *217 NI-20; ★ YNGS-; mail Youngstown z 44514; ● 100
Morgantown; RMC Place; PIKE; ▲ Benton; 218 SG-8; elev. 627ft./191m.; mail Bainbridge z 45612; ● 50
Morges; RMC Place; CARROLL; ▲ Rose; *217 NK-17; elev. 1,172ft./357m.; mail Magnolia z 44643, Waynesburg z 44688; ● 30
Morning Sun; RMC Place; PREBLE; ▲ Israel; 218 SD-1; mail Camden z 45311; ● 200
Morning View Court; RMC Place; WAYNE; mail Orrville z 44667; pop. incl. with Orrville (Inc. Place)
Morral; Inc. Place; MARION; ▲ Salt Rock; 216 NJ-8; elev. 912ft./278m.; 🅿; z 43337; Ⓟ 373; © 388
Morris; MCD-Township; KNOX; *217 NL-11; mail Fredericktown z 43019; Ⓟ 1,801; © 1,998
Morris Apartments; RMC Place; MONTGOMERY; ▲ Harrison; ★ DAY; mail Dayton z 45414
Morristown; RMC Place; ATHENS; ▲ Dover; *219 SE-13; mail Millfield z 45761; rural
Morristown; Inc. Place; BELMONT; ▲ Union; 217 NN-18; 🅿; z 43759; Ⓟ 296; © 299
Morrisville; RMC Place; CLINTON; ▲ Washington; 218 SE-5; elev. 1,068ft./326m.; mail Martinsville z 45146, Wilmington z 45177; ● 70
Morrow; Inc. Place; WARREN; ▲ Salem; 218 SE-4; 🅿; ★ CIN; z 45152; Ⓟ 1,206; © 1,286
MORROW; 216 NK-9; Ⓟ 27,749; © 31,628; ◆ 34,978
Moscow; Inc. Place; CLERMONT; ▲ Washington; 218 SH-3; 🅿; z 45153; Ⓟ 279; © 244
Moss Run; RMC Place; WASHINGTON; ▲ Lawrence; *219 SE-17; elev. 676ft./206m.; mail Marietta z 45750
Moulton; RMC Place; AUGLAIZE; ▲ Moulton; 216 NK-3; elev. 897ft./273m.; mail Wapakoneta z 45895; ● 130
Moulton; MCD-Township; AUGLAIZE; *216 NK-3; mail Wapakoneta z 45895; Ⓟ 1,618; © 1,704
Moultrie; RMC Place; COLUMBIANA; ▲ West; *217 NJ-18; ★ ALLI; mail Minerva z 44657; rural
Moundbuilders; RMC Place; LICKING; ★ NWRK; mail Newark z 43055; pop. incl. with Newark (Inc. Place)
Moundsville; RMC Place; NOBLE; ▲ Olive; *219 SC-16; mail Caldwell z 43724; rural
Mount Adams; RMC Place; HAMILTON; *218 SG-2; ★ CIN; mail Cincinnati z 45202; pop. incl. with Cincinnati (Inc. Place)
Mount Air; RMC Place; FRANKLIN; ▲ Sharon; 216 NN-9; elev. 794ft./242m.; ★ COL; mail Columbus z 43085; ● 300
Mount Airy; RMC Place; HAMILTON; *218 SF-2; elev. 931ft./284m.; ★ CIN; mail Cincinnati z 45224, z 45239; pop. incl. with Cincinnati (Inc. Place)
Mount Auburn; RMC Place; HAMILTON; *218 SG-2; ★ CIN; mail Cincinnati z 45219; pop. incl. with Cincinnati (Inc. Place)
Mount Blanchard; Inc. Place; HANCOCK; ▲ Delaware; 216 NI-6; elev. 835ft./255m.; 🅿; z 45867; Ⓟ 491; © 484
Mount Carmel; CDP; CLERMONT; ▲ Union; 218 SG-3; ★ CIN; mail Cincinnati z 45244-45; Ⓟ 4,462; © 4,308
Mount Carmel; RMC Place; SANDUSKY; ▲ York; *216 NG-9; mail Clyde z 43410; rural
Mount Carmel Heights; RMC Place; CLERMONT, HAMILTON; ▲ Anderson, Union; 218 SM-5; ★ CIN; mail Cincinnati z 45244; ● 1,200
Mount Cory; Inc. Place; HANCOCK; ▲ Union; 216 NI-5; elev. 820ft./250m.; 🅿; z 45868; Ⓟ 245; © 203
Mount Eaton; Inc. Place; WAYNE; ▲ Paint; 217 NJ-15; 🅿; z 44659; Ⓟ 236; © 246
Mount Ephraim; RMC Place; NOBLE; ▲ Seneca; 219 SB-16; mail Sarahsville z 43779; ● 80
Mount Everett; RMC Place; WASHINGTON; mail Marietta z 45750; pop. incl. with Marietta (Inc. Place)
Mount Forest Trails; RMC Place; CLERMONT; ▲ Union; 218 SM-5; ★ CIN; mail Cincinnati z 45244; ● 450
Mount Gilead; Inc. Place; ⊡ MORROW; ▲ Gilead; 216 NK-10; 🅿 🄷; z 43338; Ⓟ 2,846; © 3,290
Mount Healthy; Inc. Place; HAMILTON; 218 SF-2; elev. 855ft./261m.; 🅿; ★ CIN; z 45231; Ⓟ 7,580; © 7,149
Mount Healthy Heights; CDP-Census Area Only; HAMILTON; ▲ Colerain; *218 SF-2; elev. 850ft./259m.; ★ CIN; mail Cincinnati z 45231; Ⓟ 3,863; © 3,450
Mount Holly; RMC Place; CLERMONT; ▲ Batavia, Monroe, Pierce; 218 SG-4; ★ CIN; mail Amelia z 45102, Batavia z 45103; ● 250
Mount Holly; RMC Place; WARREN; ▲ Wayne; 218 SD-4; ★ DAY; mail Waynesville z 45068
Mount Hope; RMC Place; HOLMES; ▲ Salt Creek; 217 NK-14; 🅿; z 44660; ● 200
Mount Jefferson; RMC Place; SHELBY; ▲ Loramie; 216 NM-3; mail Houston z 45333; ● 100
Mount Joy; RMC Place; SCIOTO; ▲ Rarden; *218 SH-8; mail Otway z 45657; rural
Mount Liberty; RMC Place; KNOX; ▲ Liberty; 217 NL-11; elev. 1,209ft./369m.; 🅿; z 43048; ● 250
Mount Lookout; RMC Place; HAMILTON; *218 SG-2; ★ CIN; mail Cincinnati z 45208, z 45226; pop. incl. with Cincinnati (Inc. Place)
Mount Olive; RMC Place; CLERMONT; ▲ Franklin; *218 SH-4; mail Bethel z 45106
Mount Olivett; BELMONT; see Olivett (RMC Place)
Mount Orab (Mount Oreb); Inc. Place; BROWN; ▲ Pike, Green; 218 SG-5; elev. 922ft./281m.; 🅿; ★ CIN; z 45154; Ⓟ 1,929; © 2,307
Mount Oreb; BROWN; see Mount Orab (Inc. Place)
Mount Perry; RMC Place; PERRY; ▲ Madison; 219 SB-13; 🅿; z 43760; ● 220
Mount Pisgah; RMC Place; CLERMONT; ▲ Ohio; 218 SH-3; elev. 813ft./248m.; ★ CIN; mail New Richmond z 45157; ● 100
Mount Pleasant; RMC Place; HOCKING, VINTON; ▲ Swan, Washington; 219 SE-12; mail Logan z 43138; ● 70
Mount Pleasant; Inc. Place; JEFFERSON; ▲ Mount Pleasant; 217 NM-19; 🅿; ★ WHL; z 43939; Ⓟ 498; © 535
Mount Pleasant; MCD-Township; JEFFERSON; *217 NM-19; 🅿; ★ WHL; z 43939; Ⓟ 2,695; © 2,588
Mount Pleasant; RMC Place; SANDUSKY; ▲ York; *216 NG-10; mail Bellevue z 44811; pop. incl. with Bellevue (Inc. Place)
Mount Pleasant; RMC Place; STARK; ▲ Plain, Lake; *217 NI-16; ★ CAN; mail North Canton z 44720
Mount Repose; CDP; CLERMONT; ▲ Miami; 218 SF-3; ★ CIN; mail Loveland z 45140, Milford z 45150; Ⓟ 3,093; © 4,102
Mount Saint Joseph; RMC Place; HAMILTON; ▲ Delhi; *218 SG-1; 🅿; ★ CIN; z 45051; ● 1,400
Mount Sterling; Inc. Place; MADISON; ▲ Pleasant; 218 SC-8; elev. 906ft./276m.; 🅿; z 43143; Ⓟ 1,647; © 1,865
Mount Sterling; MUSKINGUM; see Hopewell (RMC Place)
Mount Vernon; RMC Place; FRANKLIN; mail Columbus z 43203; pop. incl. with Columbus (Inc. Place)
Mount Vernon; Inc. Place; ⊡ KNOX; 217 NL-11; 🅿 🄷 🄲 2,549 ■; z 43050; Ⓟ 14,550; © 14,375; ® 15,256; ◆ 14,595
Mount Vernon; RMC Place; LUCAS; *216 NE-6; ★ TOL; pop. incl. with Toledo (Inc. Place)
Mount Victory; Inc. Place; HARDIN; ▲ Hale; 216 NK-6; elev. 1,033ft./315m.; 🅿; z 43340; Ⓟ 551; © 600
Mount View; RMC Place; HIGHLAND; ▲ Paint; mail Hillsboro z 45133; ● 60
Mountville; RMC Place; MORGAN; ▲ Homer; *219 SD-14; elev. 1,013ft./309m.; mail Glouster z 45732; rural
Mount Washington; RMC Place; HAMILTON; *218 SG-3; 🅿; ★ CIN; z 45230 & mail Cincinnati z 45228; pop. incl. with Cincinnati (Inc. Place)
Mowrystown; Inc. Place; HIGHLAND; ▲ Whiteoak; 218 SG-6; elev. 997ft./304m.; 🅿; z 45155; Ⓟ 460; © 373
Moxahala; RMC Place; PERRY; ▲ Pleasant; 219 SC-13; 🅿; z 43761; ● 300
Moxahala Park; RMC Place; MUSKINGUM; ▲ Newton; 219 SB-14; ★ ZAN; mail Zanesville z 43701; ● 200
Mudsock; RMC Place; FRANKLIN; ▲ Norwich; 218 SA-8; elev. 937ft./286m.; ★ COL; mail Hilliard z 43026; ● 25
Mudsock; GALLIA; see Sand Fork (RMC Place)
Muhlenberg; MCD-Township; PICKAWAY; *218 SC-9; mail Orient z 43146; Ⓟ 664; © 905
Mulberry; CDP; CLERMONT; ▲ Miami; 218 SF-3; ★ CIN; mail Milford z 45150; Ⓟ 2,856; © 3,139
Mule Town; RMC Place; SCIOTO; ▲ Madison; *218 SH-10; elev. 654ft./199m.; mail Minford z 45653; ● 150
Muncie Hollow; RMC Place; SANDUSKY; ▲ Sandusky; *216 NF-8; mail Fremont z 43420; rural
Munroe Falls; Inc. Place; SUMMIT; 216 NA-6; 🅿; ★ AKR; z 44262; Ⓟ 5,359; © 5,314
Munson; MCD-Township; GEAUGA; *217 NE-17; ★ CLEV; mail Chagrin Falls z 44022, Chardon z 44024; Ⓟ 5,775; © 6,450
Munson Hill; RMC Place; ASHTABULA; ▲ Saybrook; *217 ND-19; ★ ASHT; mail Ashtabula z 44004; rural
Murdock; RMC Place; WARREN; ▲ Hamilton; *218 SF-4; elev. 814ft./248m.; ★ CIN; mail Loveland z 45140
Murlin Heights; RMC Place; MONTGOMERY; ▲ Butler; 218 SB-4; ★ DAY; mail Dayton z 45414; ● 550
Murphysburg; MERCER; see Erastus (RMC Place)
Murray City; Inc. Place; HOCKING; ▲ Ward; 219 SD-13; elev. 712ft./217m.; 🅿; z 43144; Ⓟ 499; © 452
Museville; RMC Place; MUSKINGUM; ▲ Meigs; *219 SC-15; mail Blue Rock z 43720; rural
Muskingum; MCD-Township; MUSKINGUM; *219 SA-14; ★ ZAN; mail Nashport z 43830; Ⓟ 3,343; © 3,813
Muskingum; MCD-Township; WASHINGTON; *219 SE-16; ★ PRKB; mail Lowell z 45744; Ⓟ 4,764; © 4,627
MUSKINGUM; 219 SB-15; Ⓟ 82,068; © 84,585; ◆ 83,601
Mutual; Inc. Place; CHAMPAIGN; ▲ Union; 216 NN-6; mail Mechanicsburg z 43044, Urbana z 43078; Ⓟ 126; © 132
Myers Lake; STARK; see Meyers Lake (Inc. Place)
Myersville; RMC Place; SUMMIT; 217 NI-16; elev. 1,077ft./328m.; ★ AKR; mail Uniontown z 44685; pop. incl. with Green (Inc. Place)
Myrtle Brook; RMC Place; WARREN; ▲ Deerfield; ★ CIN; mail Loveland z 45140; ● 220
Myrtle Village; RMC Place; WARREN; ▲ Deerfield; ★ CIN; mail Loveland z 45140; ● 220

N

Naceville; RMC Place; PIKE; ▲ Mifflin; mail Latham z 45646; rural
Nankin; RMC Place; ASHLAND; ▲ Orange; 217 NI-12; elev. 1,050ft./320m.; 🅿; z 44848; ● 400
Napoleon; Inc. Place; ⊡ HENRY; ▲ Napoleon, Liberty; 216 NF-4; elev. 677ft./206m.; 🅿 🄷; z 43545, z 43550; Ⓟ 8,884; © 9,318
Napoleon; MCD-Township; HENRY; *216 NF-4; 🅿; z 43545, z 43550; includes part of the City of Napoleon; Ⓟ 10,033; © 10,331
Nashport; RMC Place; MUSKINGUM; ▲ Licking; 217 NN-13; 🅿; z 43830; ● 260
Nashville; RMC Place; DARKE; ▲ Washington, Liberty; *218 SA-1; mail Greenville z 45331
Nashville; Inc. Place; HOLMES; ▲ Washington, Knox; 217 NK-13; elev. 1,220ft./372m.; 🅿; z 44661; Ⓟ 181; © 172
Nashville; RMC Place; MIAMI; ▲ Union, Monroe; 218 SB-3; ★ DAY; mail Troy z 45373; ● 100
Navarre; Inc. Place; STARK; ▲ Bethlehem; 217 NJ-16; 🅿; ★ CAN; z 44662; Ⓟ 1,635; © 1,440
Neal; BROWN; see Neel (RMC Place)
Neapolis; RMC Place; LUCAS; ▲ Providence; 216 NF-5; 🅿; ★ TOL; z 43547; ● 260
Neave; MCD-Township; DARKE; *218 SA-2; mail Greenville z 45331; Ⓟ 2,442; © 1,986
Needmore; RMC Place; ALLEN; ▲ Marion; *216 NJ-3; ★ LIMA; mail Delphos z 45833
Neel (Neal); RMC Place; BROWN; ▲ Huntington, Byrd; *218 SI-6; elev. 616ft./188m.; mail Ripley z 45167; rural
Neelysville; RMC Place; MORGAN; ▲ Meigsville; 219 SD-15; mail McConnelsville z 43756; ● 40
Neffs; CDP; BELMONT; ▲ Pultney; 217 NN-19; 🅿; ★ WHL; z 43940; Ⓟ 1,213; © 1,138
Negley; RMC Place; COLUMBIANA; ▲ Middleton; 217 NJ-20; 🅿; z 44441; ● 900
Nellie; Inc. Place; COSHOCTON; ▲ Jefferson; 217 NL-13; elev. 817ft./249m.; mail Warsaw z 43844; Ⓟ 130; © 134
Nelson (Nelson Center); RMC Place; PORTAGE; ▲ Nelson; 217 NG-18; elev. 1,079ft./329m.; mail Garrettsville z 44231; ● 80
Nelson; MCD-Township; PORTAGE; *217 NG-18; mail Garrettsville z 44231; Ⓟ 2,778; © 2,985
Nelson Center; PORTAGE; see Nelson (RMC Place)
Nelsonville; Inc. Place; ATHENS; ▲ York; 219 SE-13; 🅿 🄷; z 45764; Ⓟ 4,563; © 5,230
Neptune; RMC Place; MERCER; ▲ Center; 216 NK-2; elev. 852ft./260m.; mail Celina z 45822; ● 130
Nettle Lake; RMC Place; WILLIAMS; ▲ Northwest; 216 ND-1; mail Montpelier z 43543; ● 200
Nevada; Inc. Place; WYANDOT; ▲ Eden, Antrim; 216 NJ-8; 🅿; z 44849; Ⓟ 849; © 814
Neville; Inc. Place; CLERMONT; ▲ Washington; 218 SI-3; 🅿; z 45156; Ⓟ 226; © 127
New Albany; Inc. Place; FRANKLIN; ▲ Plain; 216 NN-10; 🅿; ★ COL; z 43054; Ⓟ 1,621; © 3,711
New Albany; RMC Place; MAHONING; ▲ Green; 217 NI-19; mail Salem z 44460; ● 75
New Alexander; RMC Place; COLUMBIANA; ▲ West; 217 NJ-18; ★ ALLI; mail East Rochester z 44625; ● 50
New Alexandria; Inc. Place; JEFFERSON; ▲ Wells, Cross Creek; 217 NM-19; elev. 1,250ft./381m.; ★ STU-; mail Mingo Junction z 43938; Ⓟ 257; © 222
New Antioch; RMC Place; CLINTON; ▲ Green; 218 SE-6; elev. 1,069ft./326m.; mail Wilmington z 45177; ● 220
Newark; Inc. Place; ⊡ LICKING; 217 NN-12; 🅿 🄷 🄲 2,310 ■; ★ NWRK; z 43055-56, z 43058, z 43093; Ⓟ 44,389; © 46,279; ® 46,275; ◆ 48,965
Newark; MCD-Township; LICKING; *219 SA-12; 🅿 🄲 2,310; ★ NWRK; z 43055-56, z 43058, z 43093; Ⓟ 2,496; © 1,967
New Athens; Inc. Place; HARRISON; ▲ Athens; 217 NM-18; 🅿; z 43981; Ⓟ 370; © 342
New Baltimore; RMC Place; HAMILTON; ▲ Crosby; 218 SF-1; ★ CIN; mail Harrison z 45030; ● 280
New Baltimore; RMC Place; STARK; ▲ Marlboro; 217 NH-17; ★ CAN; mail Alliance z 44601, Homeworth z 44634; ● 250
New Bavaria; Inc. Place; HENRY; ▲ Pleasant; 216 NG-4; elev. 732ft./223m.; 🅿; z 43548; Ⓟ 92; © 78
New Bedford; RMC Place; COSHOCTON; ▲ Crawford; 217 NL-15; elev. 1,155ft./352m.; 🅿; z 43824 & mail Baltic z 43804; ● 220
Newberry; MCD-Township; MIAMI; *216 NN-3; mail Covington z 45318; Ⓟ 6,460; © 6,490
New Bloomington (Agosta); Inc. Place; MARION; ▲ Montgomery; 216 NK-7; elev. 945ft./288m.; 🅿; z 43341; Ⓟ 282; © 548
New Boston; Inc. Place; SCIOTO; 218 SI-9; 🅿; ★ PTSM; z 45662; Ⓟ 2,717; © 2,340
New Bremen; Inc. Place; AUGLAIZE; ▲ German; 216 NL-3; elev. 941ft./287m.; 🅿; z 45869; Ⓟ 2,558; © 2,909
New Buffalo; RMC Place; MAHONING; ▲ Canfield, Beaver; *217 NH-19; elev. 1,116ft./340m.; ★ YNGS-; mail Canfield z 44406; rural
Newburg; RMC Place; CUYAHOGA; ★ CLEV; mail Cleveland z 44105; pop. incl. with Cleveland (Inc. Place)
Newburg; RMC Place; HAMILTON; ★ CIN; pop. incl. with Cincinnati (Inc. Place)
Newburgh Heights; Inc. Place; CUYAHOGA; 219 SM-18; 🅿; ★ CLEV; z 44105, z 44127; Ⓟ 2,310; © 2,389
New Burlington; RMC Place; HAMILTON; ▲ Springfield; 218 SJ-2; ★ CIN; mail Cincinnati z 45231; ● 400
Newbury; RMC Place; GEAUGA; ▲ Newbury; 217 NF-17; 🅿; ★ CLEV; z 44065; ● 350
Newbury; MCD-Township; GEAUGA; *217 NF-17; 🅿; ★ CLEV; z 44065 & mail Chagrin Falls z 44022; Ⓟ 5,611; © 5,805
New California; RMC Place; UNION; ▲ Jerome; 216 NN-8; elev. 999ft./304m.; ★ COL; mail Plain City z 43064; ● 35
New Carlisle; Inc. Place; CLARK; ▲ Bethel; 218 SB-4; elev. 906ft./276m.; 🅿; ★ DAY; z 45344; Ⓟ 6,049; © 5,735
New Castle; RMC Place; BELMONT; ▲ Wayne; *219 SB-18; elev. 1,272ft./388m.; mail Beallsville z 43716; ● 30
Newcastle; RMC Place; COSHOCTON; ▲ Newcastle; 217 NL-13; mail Walhonding z 43843; ● 100
Newcastle; MCD-Township; COSHOCTON; *217 NL-13; mail Walhonding z 43843; Ⓟ 387; © 441
New Castle; RMC Place; LAWRENCE; ▲ Elizabeth, Hamilton, Upper; *219 SJ-11; ★ HNTG; mail Ironton z 45638
New Cleveland; RMC Place; PUTNAM; ▲ Ottawa; *216 NH-4; mail Ottawa z 45875; ● 40
Newcomerstown; Inc. Place; TUSCARAWAS; ▲ Salem, Oxford; 217 NM-15; elev. 806ft./246m.; 🅿; z 43832; Ⓟ 4,012; © 4,008
New Concord; Inc. Place; MUSKINGUM; ▲ Union; 219 SA-15; 🅿 🄲 2,165; z 43762; Ⓟ 2,086; © 2,651
New Cumberland; RMC Place; TUSCARAWAS; ▲ Warren; 217 NK-17; mail Mineral City z 44656; ● 150
New Dover; RMC Place; UNION; ▲ Dover; 216 NM-7; mail Marysville z 43040; ● 130
Newell; RMC Place; JEFFERSON; ▲ Smithfield; *217 NM-19; ★ STU-; mail Piney Fork z 43941
Newell Run; RMC Place; WASHINGTON; ▲ Newport; 219 SE-17; mail Newport z 45768
New England; RMC Place; ATHENS; ▲ Rome; 219 SE-14; elev. 796ft./243m.; mail Stewart z 45778; ● 50
Newfain; RMC Place; PIKE; ▲ Mifflin; *218 SG-8; mail Peebles z 45660
New Floodwood; RMC Place; ATHENS; ▲ York; *219 SE-13; elev. 670ft./204m.; mail Nelsonville z 45764
New Franklin; RMC Place; STARK; ▲ Paris; 217 NJ-18; ★ CAN; mail Minerva z 44657; ● 230
New Franklin; Inc. Place; SUMMIT; *217 NI-16; ★ AKR; mail Akron z 44319; © 2,191
New Garden; RMC Place; COLUMBIANA; ▲ Hanover; 217 NJ-18; elev. 1,289ft./393m.; mail Hanoverton z 44423; ● 100
New Germany; RMC Place; GREENE; *218 SC-4; ★ DAY; mail Dayton z 45431; pop. incl. with Beavercreek (Inc. Place)
New Guilford; RMC Place; COSHOCTON; ▲ Perry; 217 NM-13; mail Walhonding z 43843; ● 30
New Hagerstown; RMC Place; CARROLL; ▲ Orange; 217 NL-17; elev. 979ft./298m.; mail Bowerston z 44695; ● 40
New Hampshire; RMC Place; AUGLAIZE; ▲ Goshen; 216 NK-5; 🅿; z 45870; ● 200
New Harmony; RMC Place; BROWN; ▲ Pike; *218 SG-4; ★ CIN; mail Mount Orab z 45154, Williamsburg z 45176
New Harrisburg; RMC Place; CARROLL; ▲ Harrison; 217 NK-17; elev. 1,221ft./372m.; mail Carrollton z 44615; ● 100
New Harrison; RMC Place; DARKE; ▲ Adams; 216 NN-2; mail Greenville z 45331; ● 50
New Haven; RMC Place; HAMILTON; ▲ Crosby; 218 SF-1; elev. 561ft./171m.; 🅿; ★ CIN; z 44850 & mail Harrison z 45030; ● 320
New Haven; RMC Place; HURON; ▲ New Haven; 216 NH-10; 🅿; z 44850 & mail Harrison z 45030; ● 450
New Haven; MCD-Township; HURON; *216 NH-10; 🅿; z 44850 & mail Harrison z 45030; Ⓟ 3,049; © 2,860
New Holland; Inc. Place; PICKAWAY, FAYETTE; ▲ Perry; 218 SD-8; elev. 851ft./259m.; 🅿; z 43145; Ⓟ 841; © 785
Newhope; RMC Place; BROWN; ▲ Scott; 218 SC-1; elev. 889ft./271m.; mail Georgetown z 45121; ● 150
New Hope; RMC Place; PREBLE; ▲ Jackson; *218 SC-1; elev. 1,154ft./352m.; mail Eaton z 45320; ● 150
New Jasper; RMC Place; GREENE; ▲ New Jasper; 218 SC-5; ★ DAY; mail Xenia z 45385; ● 100
New Jasper; MCD-Township; GREENE; *218 SC-5; ★ DAY; mail Xenia z 45385; Ⓟ 2,393; © 2,538
New Jerusalem; RMC Place; LOGAN; ▲ Jefferson; *216 NL-6; mail Bellefontaine z 43311; ● 40
New Knoxville; Inc. Place; AUGLAIZE; ▲ Washington; 216 NK-3; elev. 903ft./275m.; 🅿; z 45871; Ⓟ 838; © 891
New Lebanon; Inc. Place; MONTGOMERY; ▲ Perry, Jackson; 218 SC-3; 🅿; ★ DAY; z 45345; Ⓟ 4,323; © 4,231
New Lexington; Inc. Place; ⊡ PERRY; ▲ Pike; 219 SC-13; elev. 958ft./292m.; 🅿; z 43764; Ⓟ 5,117; © 4,689
New Lexington; RMC Place; PREBLE; ▲ Twin; 218 SC-2; ★ DAY; mail West Alexandria z 45381; ● 100
New Liberty (Jimtown); RMC Place; COLUMBIANA; ▲ Unity; *217 NI-20; mail East Palestine z 44413; ● 50
New London; Inc. Place; HURON; ▲ New London; 217 NH-12; 🅿; z 44851; Ⓟ 2,642; © 2,696
New London; MCD-Township; HURON; *217 NH-12; 🅿; z 44851; Ⓟ 3,417; © 3,440
New Lyme; MCD-Township; ASHTABULA; *217 NE-19; 🅿; z 44047 & mail Rome z 44085; Ⓟ 1,015; © 1,072
New Lyme Station; RMC Place; ASHTABULA; ▲ Rome; *217 NE-19; mail Rome z 44085; ● 30
New Madison; Inc. Place; DARKE; ▲ Harrison, Butler; 218 SB-1; 🅿; ★ RICH; z 45346; Ⓟ 928; © 817
Newman; RMC Place; STARK; ▲ Lawrence; *217 NI-15; ★ AKR; mail Massillon z 44646; ● 300
New Market; RMC Place; HIGHLAND; ▲ New Market; 218 SG-6; elev. 1,140ft./347m.; mail Hillsboro z 45133; ● 50
New Market; MCD-Township; HIGHLAND; *218 SG-6; mail Hillsboro z 45133; Ⓟ 1,480; © 1,941
Newmarket Station; RMC Place; STARK; ▲ Canton; mail Canton z 44701-02; pop. incl. with Canton (Inc. Place)
New Marshfield; RMC Place; ATHENS; ▲ Waterloo; 219 SE-13; 🅿; z 45766; ● 400
New Martinsburg; RMC Place; FAYETTE; ▲ Perry; 218 SE-7; mail Greenfield z 45123; ● 150
New Matamoras (Matamoras); Inc. Place; WASHINGTON; 219 SD-18; elev. 637ft./194m.; 🅿; z 45767 & mail Graysville z 45734, Wingett Run z 45789; Ⓟ 1,002; © 957
New Miami; Inc. Place; BUTLER; ▲ St. Clair; 218 SE-2; ★ CIN; mail Hamilton z 45011; Ⓟ 2,555; © 2,469
New Middletown; Inc. Place; MAHONING; 217 NI-20; 🅿; ★ YNGS-; z 44442; Ⓟ 1,912; © 1,682
New Milford (Rootstown); RMC Place; PORTAGE; ▲ Rootstown; *217 NH-17; elev. 1,126ft./343m.; 🅿; ★ AKR; z 44272; ● 100
New Moorefield (Moorefield); RMC Place; CLARK; 218 SA-6; elev. 1,050ft./320m.; ★ SPR; mail Springfield z 45502; ● 300
New Moscow; RMC Place; COSHOCTON; ▲ Virginia; 217 NM-14; mail Coshocton z 43812; ● 35
New Palestine; RMC Place; CLERMONT; ▲ Pierce; *218 SG-3; ★ CIN; mail New Richmond z 45157; ● 30
New Paris; Inc. Place; PREBLE; ▲ Jefferson; 218 SB-1; 🅿; ★ RICH; z 45347; Ⓟ 1,801; © 1,623
New Petersburg; RMC Place; HIGHLAND; ▲ Paint; 218 SF-7; mail Greenfield z 45123, Leesburg z 45135; ● 150
New Philadelphia; Inc. Place; ⊡ TUSCARAWAS; 217 NL-16; 🅿 🄲 1,977 ■; z 44663; Ⓟ 15,698; © 17,056; ◆ 16,404
New Pittsburg; RMC Place; WAYNE; ▲ Chester; 217 NI-13; mail Wooster z 44691; ● 270
New Pittsburgh; RMC Place; CRAWFORD, HURON; ▲ Auburn, New Haven, Richmond; *216 NH-10; mail Plymouth z 44865; ● 30
New Plymouth; RMC Place; VINTON; ▲ Brown; 219 SE-12; elev. 774ft./236m.; 🅿; z 45654; ● 120
New Plymouth Heights; RMC Place; SCIOTO; ▲ Green; mail Franklin Furnace z 45629; ● 275
Newport; RMC Place; MADISON; ▲ Paint; 218 SB-7; mail London z 43140; ● 180
Newport; RMC Place; SHELBY; ▲ Cynthian; 216 NM-3; 🅿; z 45768 & mail Fort Loramie z 45845; ● 220
Newport; RMC Place; TUSCARAWAS; ▲ Mill; *217 NL-16; mail Uhrichsville z 44683; ● 200
Newport; RMC Place; WASHINGTON; ▲ Newport; 219 SE-17; 🅿; z 45768 & mail Fort Loramie z 45845; ● 700
Newport; MCD-Township; WASHINGTON; *219 SE-17; 🅿; z 45768 & mail Fort Loramie z 45845; Ⓟ 2,077; © 2,176
New Princeton; RMC Place; COSHOCTON; *217 NL-13; mail Warsaw z 43844; rural
New Reading; RMC Place; PERRY; ▲ Reading; *219 SC-12; mail Somerset z 43783; ● 120
New Richland; RMC Place; LOGAN; ▲ Richland; 216 NL-5; mail Belle Center z 43310; ● 100
New Richmond; Inc. Place; CLERMONT; ▲ Pierce, Ohio; 218 SH-3; 🅿; ★ CIN; z 45157; Ⓟ 2,408; © 2,219
New Riegel; Inc. Place; SENECA; ▲ Big Spring; 216 NH-7; elev. 824ft./251m.; 🅿; z 44853; Ⓟ 298; © 226
New Rochester; RMC Place; WOOD; ▲ Freedom; 216 NF-7; mail Pemberville z 43450; ● 75
New Rome; RMC Place; FRANKLIN; ▲ Prairie; 218 SB-8; 🅿; ★ COL; z 43228; disincorporated September 11, 2004; Ⓟ 111; © 60
New Rumley; RMC Place; HARRISON; ▲ Rumley; 217 NL-18; 🅿; z 43984; ● 140
New Russia; MCD-Township; LORAIN; *217 NG-12; ★ CLEV; mail Oberlin z 44074; Ⓟ 2,470; © 2,357
New Salem; RMC Place; FAIRFIELD, PERRY; ▲ Thorn, Walnut; 219 SB-12; ★ LANC; mail Pleasantville z 43148; ● 130
New Salisbury; RMC Place; COLUMBIANA; ▲ Yellow Creek; *217 NK-19; ★ E.LIV; mail Hammondsville z 43930; rural
New Somerset; RMC Place; JEFFERSON; ▲ Knox; 217 NK-19; ★ STU-; mail Toronto z 43964; ● 150
New Springfield; RMC Place; MAHONING; ▲ Springfield; 217 NI-20; elev. 1,211ft./369m.; 🅿; ★ YNGS-; z 44443; ● 600
New Stark; RMC Place; HANCOCK; ▲ Van Buren; 216 NI-5; mail Williamstown z 45897; ● 70
New Straitsville; Inc. Place; PERRY; ▲ Coal; 219 SD-13; elev. 862ft./263m.; 🅿; z 43766; Ⓟ 865; © 774
New Strasburg; RMC Place; FAIRFIELD; ▲ Amanda; *218 SD-10; mail Amanda z 43102; rural
Newton; MCD-Township; LICKING; *217 NN-12; ★ NWRK; mail Newark z 43055; Ⓟ 3,092; © 3,111
Newton; MCD-Township; MIAMI; *218 SA-3; mail Ludlow Falls z 45339; Ⓟ 3,221; © 3,354
Newton; MCD-Township; MUSKINGUM; *219 SB-13; ★ ZAN; mail East Fultonham z 43735; Ⓟ 5,205; © 5,402
Newton; MCD-Township; PIKE; *218 SG-9; mail Piketon z 45661; Ⓟ 1,587; © 2,006
Newton; MCD-Township; TRUMBULL; *217 NG-18; ★ YNGS-; mail Newton Falls z 44444; Ⓟ 9,541; © 9,524
Newton Falls; Inc. Place; TRUMBULL; ▲ Braceville, Newton; 217 NG-18; elev. 924ft./282m.; 🅿; ★ YNGS-; z 44444; Ⓟ 4,866; © 5,002
Newtonsville; Inc. Place; CLERMONT; ▲ Wayne; 218 SF-4; 🅿; ★ CIN; z 45158; Ⓟ 427; © 492
Newtown; Inc. Place; HAMILTON; 218 SG-3; 🅿; ★ CIN; z 45244-45 & mail Dillonvale z 43917; Ⓟ 1,589; © 2,420
Newtown; RMC Place; JEFFERSON; ▲ Mount Pleasant; *217 NM-19; 🅿; ★ WHL; z 45244-45 & mail Dillonvale z 43917; pop. incl. with Altheimer (Inc. Place)
Newtown; TUSCARAWAS; see Peoli (RMC Place)
New Vienna; Inc. Place; CLINTON; ▲ Green; 218 SE-6; 🅿; z 45159; Ⓟ 932; © 1,294
Newville; RMC Place; RICHLAND; ▲ Worthington; *217 NK-12; ★ MANS; mail Perrysville z 44864; rural
New Washington; Inc. Place; CRAWFORD; ▲ Cranberry; 216 NI-10; 🅿; z 44854; Ⓟ 1,057; © 987
New Waterford; Inc. Place; COLUMBIANA; ▲ Unity; 217 NI-20; elev. 1,053ft./321m.; 🅿; z 44445; Ⓟ 1,278; © 1,391
New Weston; Inc. Place; DARKE; ▲ Allen; 216 NL-1; 🅿; z 45348; Ⓟ 148; © 135
New Westville; RMC Place; PREBLE; ▲ Jackson; 218 SB-1; elev. 1,188ft./362m.; mail Richmond z 47374; ● 90
New Winchester; RMC Place; CRAWFORD; ▲ Whetstone; 216 NJ-9; mail Bucyrus z 44820; ● 40
New York Central Junction; RMC Place; MAHONING; ★ YNGS-; pop. incl. with Youngstown (Inc. Place)
Ney; Inc. Place; DEFIANCE; ▲ Washington; 216 NF-2; elev. 714ft./218m.; 🅿; z 43549; Ⓟ 331; © 364
Nicholsville; RMC Place; CLERMONT; ▲ Monroe; 218 SH-4; elev. 870ft./265m.; ★ CIN; mail Bethel z 45106; ● 200
Nile; MCD-Township; SCIOTO; *218 SB-8; mail Friendship z 45630; Ⓟ 2,302; © 2,024
Niles; Inc. Place; TRUMBULL; ▲ Weathersfield, Howland; 217 NG-19; 🅿 ■; ★ YNGS-; z 44446; Ⓟ 21,128; © 20,932; ◆ 19,170
Nimishillen; MCD-Township; STARK; *217 NI-17; ★ CAN; mail Louisville z 44641; Ⓟ 9,492; © 9,098
Nimisila; RMC Place; SUMMIT; ★ AKR; mail Clinton z 44216
Nipgen; RMC Place; ROSS; ▲ Twin; 218 SF-8; elev. 1,077ft./328m.; mail Bainbridge z 45612; ● 100
Noble; MCD-Township; AUGLAIZE; *216 NK-3; mail Saint Marys z 45885; Ⓟ 1,070; © 1,439
Noble; MCD-Township; DEFIANCE; *216 NG-3; 🄲 997; mail Defiance z 43512; Ⓟ 6,249; © 6,171
Noble; MCD-Township; NOBLE; *219 SC-16; mail Caldwell z 43724; Ⓟ 1,981; © 2,013
NOBLE; 219 SC-16; Ⓟ 11,336; © 14,058; ◆ 14,190
Norlick Place; RMC Place; WILLIAMS; ▲ Center; *216 NE-2; mail Bryan z 43506; ● 250
Normandy Heights; RMC Place; BUTLER; ▲ Fairfield; *218 SE-2; ★ CIN; mail Hamilton z 45015; pop. incl. with Hamilton (Inc. Place)
Norris; RMC Place; MIAMI; ▲ Union; *218 SB-3; ★ DAY; mail West Milton z 45383; pop. incl. with West Milton (Inc. Place)
North; MCD-Township; HARRISON; *217 NL-18; mail Scio z 43988; Ⓟ 1,822; © 1,652
North Akron; RMC Place; SUMMIT; ★ AKR; mail Akron z 44310; pop. incl. with Akron (Inc. Place)
North Auburn; RMC Place; CRAWFORD; ▲ Auburn; 216 NI-10; mail Tiro z 44887; ● 40
North Baltimore; Inc. Place; WOOD; ▲ Henry; 216 NG-6; 🅿; z 45872; Ⓟ 3,139; © 3,361
North Bass Island; OTTAWA; see Isle Saint George (RMC Place)
North Bend; Inc. Place; HAMILTON; ▲ Miami; 218 SF-1; 🅿; ★ CIN; z 45052 & mail Mount Saint Joseph z 45051; Ⓟ 541; © 603
North Benton; RMC Place; MAHONING; ▲ Smith; 217 NI-18; 🅿; ★ ALLI; z 44449; ● 280
North Benton; PORTAGE; see North Benton Station (RMC Place)
North Benton Station (North Benton); RMC Place; PORTAGE; ▲ Deerfield; *217 NH-18; 🅿; ★ AKR; z 44449; ● 100
North Berne; RMC Place; FAIRFIELD; ▲ Berne; *219 SC-11; ★ LANC; mail Lancaster z 43130; ● 40
North Bloomfield; MCD-Township; MORROW; *216 NK-10; mail Galion z 44833; Ⓟ 1,808; © 1,866
North Bloomfield; RMC Place; TRUMBULL; ▲ Bloomfield; 217 NF-18; 🅿; z 44450; ● 500
North Brewster; RMC Place; STARK; *217 NJ-15; ★ CAN; mail Brewster z 44613; pop. incl. with Brewster (Inc. Place)
North Bristol; RMC Place; TRUMBULL; ▲ Bristol; 217 NF-18; elev. 876ft./267m.; ★ YNGS-; mail Bristolville z 44402; ● 160
Northbrook; CDP; HAMILTON; ▲ Colerain; 218 SF-2; elev. 823ft./251m.; ★ CIN; mail Cincinnati z 45231, z 45251; Ⓟ 11,471; © 11,076
North Canton; Inc. Place; STARK; ▲ Plain; 217 NI-16; 🅿 🄲 1,803; ★ CAN; z 44709, z 44720, z 44799 & mail Canton z 44721; Ⓟ 14,748; © 16,369
North College Hill; Inc. Place; HAMILTON; 218 SF-2; ★ CIN; mail Cincinnati z 45224, z 45231, z 45239; Ⓟ 11,002; © 10,082
North Condit; RMC Place; DELAWARE; ▲ Trenton; *216 NM-10; mail Sunbury z 43074; ● 60
North Creek; RMC Place; PUTNAM; ▲ Palmer; 216 NH-3; elev. 717ft./219m.; mail Continental z 45831; ● 80
North Dayton; RMC Place; DARKE; ▲ Mississinawa; *216 NL-1; mail Union City z 45390; rural
North Dayton; RMC Place; MONTGOMERY; ★ DAY; mail Dayton z 45404; pop. incl. with Dayton (Inc. Place)
North East Waterworks; RMC Place; STARK; ▲ Plain; *217 NI-16; ★ CAN; mail Canton z 44705
North Eaton; RMC Place; LORAIN; ▲ Eaton; *217 NG-13; ★ CLEV; mail Columbia Station z 44028, Grafton z 44044; ● 200
North Fairfield; Inc. Place; HURON; ▲ Fairfield; 217 NH-11; elev. 932ft./284m.; 🅿; z 44855; Ⓟ 504; © 573
Northfield; Inc. Place; SUMMIT; 217 NF-16; 🅿 🄷; ★ CLEV; z 44056, z 44067; Ⓟ 3,624; © 3,827
Northfield Center; RMC Place; SUMMIT; ▲ Northfield Center; 217 NG-16; ★ CLEV; mail Northfield z 44067; ● 2,570
Northfield Center; MCD-Township; SUMMIT; *217 NG-16; ★ CLEV; mail Northfield z 44067; Ⓟ 3,982; © 4,931
North Findlay; RMC Place; HANCOCK; ▲ Allen; *216 NH-6; ★ FIND; mail Findlay z 45840; ● 120
North Fork Village; CDP; ROSS; 218 SE-9; mail Chillicothe z 45601; Ⓟ 1,247; © 1,726
Northgate; CDP-Census Area Only; HAMILTON; ▲ Colerain; *218 SF-2; elev. 900ft./274m.; ★ CIN; mail Cincinnati z 45251; Ⓟ 7,864; © 8,016
North Georgetown; RMC Place; COLUMBIANA; ▲ Knox; 217 NI-18; 🅿; ★ ALLI; z 44665; ● 150
North Greenfield; RMC Place; LOGAN; ▲ Perry; *216 NL-6; mail West Mansfield z 43358; ● 25
North Hampton; Inc. Place; CLARK; ▲ Pike; 218 SA-5; 🅿; ★ SPR; z 45349; Ⓟ 417; © 370
North Hill; RMC Place; SUMMIT; ★ AKR; mail Akron z 44310; pop. incl. with Akron (Inc. Place)
North Hills Estates; RMC Place; HAMILTON; ▲ Springfield; *218 SF-2; ★ CIN; mail Cincinnati z 45224
North Houston; RMC Place; SHELBY; ▲ Loramie; mail Houston z 45333
North Industry; RMC Place; STARK; ▲ Canton; 217 NJ-16; 🅿; ★ CAN; z 44707; ● 2,700
North Jackson; RMC Place; MAHONING; ▲ Jackson; 217 NH-19; 🅿; ★ YNGS-; z 44451; ● 900
North Kenova; RMC Place; LAWRENCE; *219 SK-11; ★ HNTG; mail South Point z 45680; pop. incl. with South Point (Inc. Place)
North Kingman; CLINTON; see Kingman (RMC Place)
North Kingsville (Kingsville); Inc. Place; ASHTABULA; ▲ Kingsville; 217 NC-19; 🅿; ★ ASHT; z 44048, z 44068; Ⓟ 2,672; © 2,658
Northland; RMC Place; FRANKLIN; ★ COL; mail Columbus z 43229; pop. incl. with Columbus (Inc. Place)
North Lawrence; RMC Place; STARK; ▲ Lawrence; 217 NI-15; 🅿; ★ AKR; z 44666; ● 800
North Lewisburg; Inc. Place; CHAMPAIGN; ▲ Rush; 216 NM-6; elev. 1,087ft./331m.; 🅿; z 43060; Ⓟ 1,160; © 1,588
North Liberty; RMC Place; KNOX; ▲ Pike; 217 NK-12; elev. 1,308ft./399m.; mail Butler z 44822; ● 80
North Lima; RMC Place; MAHONING; ▲ Beaver; 217 NI-20; elev. 1,103ft./336m.; 🅿; ★ YNGS-; z 44452; ● 900
North Madison; CDP; LAKE; ▲ Madison; *217 NC-18; ★ CLEV; mail Madison z 44057; Ⓟ 8,699; © 8,451
North Monroeville; RMC Place; ERIE, HURON; ▲ Ridgefield, Oxford; 216 NG-10; ★ SNDSK; mail Monroeville z 44847; ● 40
Northmoor; RMC Place; MONTGOMERY; *218 SB-3; ★ DAY; mail Clayton z 45315, Englewood z 45322; pop. incl. with Englewood (Inc. Place)
North Moreland; RMC Place; SCIOTO; *218 SI-9; elev. 552ft./168m.; ★ PTSM; mail Portsmouth z 45662; pop. incl. with Portsmouth (Inc. Place)
North Mount Vernon; RMC Place; KNOX; ▲ Morris, Clinton; *217 NL-11; mail Mount Vernon z 43050; pop. incl. with Mount Vernon (Inc. Place)
North Olmsted; Inc. Place; CUYAHOGA; ▲ Olmsted; 217 NF-14; 🅿 ■; ★ CLEV; z 44070; Ⓟ 34,204; © 34,113; ◆ 31,149
North Perry; Inc. Place; LAKE; ▲ Perry; 217 ND-17; ★ CLEV; mail Perry z 44081; Ⓟ 824; © 838
North Randall; Inc. Place; CUYAHOGA; 219 SM-19; 🅿; ★ CLEV; z 44128; Ⓟ 977; © 906
North Richmond; RMC Place; ASHTABULA; ▲ Richmond; *217 ND-20; mail Andover z 44003; rural
Northridge; CDP; CLARK; ▲ Moorefield; 218 SA-6; ★ SPR; mail Springfield z 45503; Ⓟ 5,939; © 6,853
Northridge; CDP; MONTGOMERY; ▲ Butler, Harrison; 218 SB-4; ★ DAY; mail Dayton z 45413-14; Ⓟ 9,448; © 8,487
North Ridgeville; Inc. Place; LORAIN; 217 NF-13; 🅿; ★ CLEV; z 44035, z 44039; Ⓟ 21,564; © 22,338; ◆ 24,823
North Robinson (Robinson); Inc. Place; CRAWFORD; ▲ Whetstone, Jefferson; 216 NJ-10; 🅿; z 44856; Ⓟ 216; © 211
North Royalton; Inc. Place; CUYAHOGA; 217 NG-15; elev. 1,197ft./365m.; 🅿; ★ CLEV; z 44133; Ⓟ 23,197; © 28,648; ◆ 28,695
North Sagamore Heights; RMC Place; HAMILTON; *218 SF-3; elev. 820ft./250m.; ★ CIN; mail Cincinnati z 45236
North Salem; RMC Place; GUERNSEY; ▲ Liberty; 217 NN-16; mail Kimbolton z 43749; ● 100
North Side; RMC Place; MAHONING; *217 NH-20; ★ YNGS-; mail Youngstown z 44504; pop. incl. with Youngstown (Inc. Place)
North Star; Inc. Place; DARKE; ▲ Wabash; 216 NL-2; elev. 1,006ft./307m.; 🅿; z 45350; Ⓟ 246; © 209
North Uniontown; RMC Place; HIGHLAND; ▲ Jackson; *218 SG-7; mail Hillsboro z 45133; rural
Northup; RMC Place; GALLIA; ▲ Green; 219 SI-13; mail Patriot z 45658; ● 100
North Warren; RMC Place; TRUMBULL; *217 NG-18; ★ YNGS-
Northwest; RMC Place; FRANKLIN; ★ COL; mail Columbus z 43220; pop. incl. with Columbus (Inc. Place)
Northwest; MCD-Township; WILLIAMS; *216 ND-1; mail Edon z 43518; Ⓟ 1,198; © 1,384
Northwood; RMC Place; LOGAN; ▲ Richland, McArthur; 216 NL-5; mail Belle Center z 43310; ● 80
Northwood; Inc. Place; WOOD; 216 NE-7; 🅿; ★ TOL; z 43605, z 43619; Ⓟ 5,506; © 5,471
North Woodbury; RMC Place; MORROW; ▲ Perry; 216 NK-10; ★ MANS; mail Bellville z 44813; ● 90
North Zanesville; CDP; MUSKINGUM; ▲ Muskingum, Falls; *219 SB-14; ★ ZAN; mail Zanesville z 43701; Ⓟ 2,121; © 3,013
Norton; RMC Place; DELAWARE; ▲ Marlboro; 216 NL-8; elev. 946ft./288m.; mail Waldo z 43356; ● 50
Norton; Inc. Place; SUMMIT; 217 NH-15; 🅿; ★ AKR; z 44203; Ⓟ 11,477; © 11,523
Norwalk; Inc. Place; ⊡ HURON; ▲ Norwalk; 217 NG-11; elev. 731ft./223m.; 🅿 🄷; ★ SNDSK; z 44857; Ⓟ 14,731; © 16,238
Norwalk; MCD-Township; HURON; *217 NG-11; 🅿; ★ SNDSK; z 44857; Ⓟ 3,276; © 3,685
Norwich; MCD-Township; FRANKLIN; *218 SA-9; ★ COL; mail Hilliard z 43026; Ⓟ 15,960; © 27,488
Norwich; MCD-Township; HURON; *216 NH-10; mail Willard z 44890; Ⓟ 958; © 1,072
Norwich; Inc. Place; MUSKINGUM; ▲ Union; 219 SA-15; 🅿; z 43767; Ⓟ 133; © 113
Norwood; Inc. Place; HAMILTON; 218 SF-2; 🅿; ★ CIN; z 45212 & mail Cincinnati z 45207, z 45222, z 45237; Ⓟ 23,674; © 21,675; ◆ 20,766
Norwood; RMC Place; WASHINGTON; *219 SE-16; ★ PRKB; mail Marietta z 45750; pop. incl. with Marietta (Inc. Place)
Norwood Heights; RMC Place; HAMILTON; ★ CIN; mail Cincinnati z 45212; pop. incl. with Cincinnati (Inc. Place)
Nottingham; RMC Place; CUYAHOGA; ★ CLEV; mail Cleveland z 44110; pop. incl. with Cleveland (Inc. Place)
Nottingham; MCD-Township; HARRISON; *217 NM-17; mail Cadiz z 43907; Ⓟ 248; © 392
Nova; RMC Place; ASHLAND; ▲ Troy; 217 NH-12; 🅿; z 44859; ● 430
Novelty; RMC Place; GEAUGA; ▲ Russell, Chester; 217 NE-16; 🅿; ★ CLEV; z 44072-73; ● 500
Nunda; RMC Place; KNOX; ▲ Brown; *217 NK-12; mail Butler z 44822; rural

O

Oakdale; RMC Place; ATHENS; ▲ Trimble; *219 SD-13; elev. 697ft./212m.; mail Glouster z 45732
Oakdale; RMC Place; MONTGOMERY; ★ DAY; mail Dayton z 45429; pop. incl. with Kettering (Inc. Place)
Oakdale; RMC Place; STARK; ▲ Jackson; 216 NB-8; ★ CAN; mail Massillon z 44646; ● 570
Oakfield; RMC Place; PERRY; ▲ Pleasant; 219 SC-13; mail Crooksville z 43731; ● 100
Oakfield; RMC Place; TRUMBULL; ▲ Bristol; 217 NF-19; ★ YNGS-; mail North Bloomfield z 44450; ● 40
Oak Grove; RMC Place; CLARK; ▲ Mad River; *218 SB-5; ★ SPR; mail Springfield z 45502; ● 35
Oak Grove; RMC Place; WASHINGTON; ▲ Muskingum; *219 SE-16; ★ PRKB; mail Marietta z 45750; ● 650
Oak Harbor; Inc. Place; OTTAWA; ▲ Salem; 216 NE-8; 🅿; z 43449; Ⓟ 2,637; © 2,841
Oak Hill; Inc. Place; JACKSON; ▲ Madison, Jefferson; 219 SH-11; 🅿 🄷; z 45656; Ⓟ 1,831; © 1,685
Oakland; RMC Place; BUTLER; *218 SE-3; ★ MIDD; mail Monroe z 45050; pop. incl. with Monroe (Inc. Place)
Oakland; RMC Place; CLINTON; ▲ Chester; *218 SE-5; mail Wilmington z 45177
Oakland; RMC Place; FAIRFIELD; ▲ Clearcreek; 218 SD-10; elev. 1,046ft./319m.; mail Amanda z 43102; ● 120
Oakland Park; RMC Place; FRANKLIN; ▲ Mifflin, Clinton; ★ COL; mail Columbus z 43224; pop. incl. with Columbus (Inc. Place)
Oakley; RMC Place; HAMILTON; *218 SF-3; ★ CIN; mail Cincinnati z 45209; pop. incl. with Cincinnati (Inc. Place)
Oak Meadows; RMC Place; WILLIAMS; ▲ Center; *216 NF-2; mail Bryan z 43506; ● 100
Oakmont; RMC Place; COLUMBIANA; ▲ Liverpool; ★ E.LIV; mail East Liverpool z 43920; rural
Oak Park; RMC Place; HARRISON; ▲ Cadiz; *217 NM-18; mail Cadiz z 43907; pop. incl. with Cadiz (Inc. Place)
Oak Run; MCD-Township; MADISON; *218 SB-7; mail Mount Sterling z 43143; Ⓟ 415; © 514
Oakshade; RMC Place; FULTON; ▲ Chesterfield; 216 ND-4; elev. 806ft./246m.; mail Wauseon z 43567; ● 100
Oakview; RMC Place; ALLEN; ▲ Shawnee; *216 NJ-3; ★ LIMA; mail Lima z 45805; ● 250
Oakwood (Oakwood Village); Inc. Place; CUYAHOGA; 219 SN-20; ★ CLEV; mail Bedford z 44146; Ⓟ 8,957; © 3,667
Oakwood; Inc. Place; MONTGOMERY; 218 SC-4; 🅿; ★ DAY; z 45873 & mail Dayton z 45409, z 45419; Ⓟ 3,392; © 9,215
Oakwood; Inc. Place; PAULDING; ▲ Brown; 216 NH-3; elev. 708ft./216m.; 🅿; z 45873 & mail Dayton z 45409, z 45419; Ⓟ 709; © 607
Oakwood Village; CUYAHOGA; see Oakwood (Inc. Place)
Oberlin; Inc. Place; LORAIN; 217 NG-12; 🅿 🄷 🄲 2,829; ★ CLEV; z 44074; Ⓟ 8,191; © 8,195
Oberlin Beach; RMC Place; ERIE; ▲ Berlin; *217 NF-11; ★ CLEV; mail Huron z 44839; ● 60
Obetz; Inc. Place; FRANKLIN; ▲ Madison, Hamilton; 218 SB-9; 🅿; ★ COL; z 43207; Ⓟ 3,167; © 3,977
Oceola; RMC Place; CRAWFORD; ▲ Tod; 216 NI-8; 🅿; z 44860; ● 280
Oco; RMC Place; BELMONT; ▲ Wheeling; *217 NN-18; mail Saint Clairsville z 43950; rural
O'Connor Landing; RMC Place; LOGAN; ▲ Richland; *216 NK-5; mail Belle Center z 43310; ● 150
Octa; Inc. Place; FAYETTE; ▲ Jasper; 218 SD-6; mail Washington Court House z 43160; Ⓟ 78; © 83
Ogden; RMC Place; CLINTON; ▲ Adams; 218 SE-5; mail Wilmington z 45177; ● 100
Ogontz; RMC Place; ERIE; ▲ Berlin; *217 NF-11; elev. 781ft./238m.; ★ CLEV; mail Berlin Heights z 44814; rural
Ohio; MCD-Township; CLERMONT; *218 SH-3; ★ CIN; mail New Richmond z 45157; Ⓟ 5,310; © 5,245
Ohio; MCD-Township; GALLIA; *219 SJ-13; mail Crown City z 45623; Ⓟ 1,006; © 1,111
Ohio; MCD-Township; MONROE; *219 SC-19; mail Hannibal z 43931; Ⓟ 1,134; © 1,032
Ohio City; Inc. Place; VAN WERT; ▲ Liberty; 216 NJ-1; elev. 822ft./251m.; 🅿; z 45874; Ⓟ 899; © 784
Ohio Furnace; RMC Place; SCIOTO; ▲ Green; 218 SJ-10; ★ HNTG; mail Ironton z 45638; ● 150
Ohio Junction; RMC Place; MAHONING; ★ YNGS-; pop. incl. with Youngstown (Inc. Place)
Ohio Soldiers and Sailors Home; RMC Place; ERIE; ★ SNDSK; mail Sandusky z 44870
Ohmer Park; RMC Place; MONTGOMERY; ★ DAY; pop. incl. with Dayton (Inc. Place)
Okeana; RMC Place; BUTLER; ▲ Morgan; 218 SE-1; elev. 645ft./197m.; 🅿; ★ CIN; z 45053; ● 240
Okolona; RMC Place; HENRY; ▲ Napoleon; 216 NF-3; elev. 700ft./213m.; 🅿; z 43545, z 43550; ● 140
Olde Towne; RMC Place; FRANKLIN; mail Columbus z 43205; pop. incl. with Columbus (Inc. Place)
Olde West Chester; CDP-Census Area Only; BUTLER; *218 SE-3; ★ CIN; © 232
Old Fort; RMC Place; SENECA; ▲ Pleasant; 216 NG-8; 🅿; z 44861; ● 350
Old Gore; RMC Place; HOCKING; ▲ Falls; *219 SD-12; mail Logan z 43138, New Straitsville z 43766; ● 100
Old Mill Creek; RMC Place; MEDINA; ★ CLEV; mail Brunswick z 44212; ● 450
Old Plymouth Heights; RMC Place; SCIOTO; ▲ Green; mail Franklin Furnace z 45629; ● 325
Old Straitsville; RMC Place; PERRY; ▲ Coal; *219 SD-13; mail New Straitsville z 43766; ● 100
Oldtown; RMC Place; GREENE; ▲ Xenia; 218 SC-5; ★ DAY; mail Xenia z 45385; ● 80
Old Washington; Inc. Place; GUERNSEY; ▲ Wills; 217 NN-16; elev. 1,008ft./307m.; 🅿; z 43768; Ⓟ 281; © 265
Old West End; RMC Place; LUCAS; ★ TOL; mail Toledo z 43610; pop. incl. with Toledo (Inc. Place)
Olena; RMC Place; HURON; ▲ Hartland, Bronson; 217 NH-11; elev. 955ft./291m.; mail Norwalk z 44857; ● 350
Olentangy; RMC Place; CRAWFORD; ▲ Whetstone; *216 NJ-9; mail Bucyrus z 44820; rural
Olive; MCD-Township; MEIGS; *219 SG-15; mail Long Bottom z 45743; Ⓟ 1,727; © 1,874
Olive; MCD-Township; NOBLE; *219 SC-16; mail Caldwell z 43724; Ⓟ 3,333; © 5,395
Olive Branch; RMC Place; CLERMONT; ▲ Batavia; 218 SG-3; ★ CIN; mail Batavia z 45103; ● 200
Olive Green; RMC Place; DELAWARE; ▲ Porter; 216 NM-10; elev. 1,097ft./334m.; mail Sunbury z 43074; ● 65
Olive Green; RMC Place; NOBLE; ▲ Sharon; *219 SC-16; mail Caldwell z 43724; rural
Oliver; MCD-Township; ADAMS; *218 SH-7; mail West Union z 45693; Ⓟ 865; © 1,246
Olivesburg; RMC Place; RICHLAND; ▲ Weller; 217 NI-11; elev. 1,076ft./328m.; mail Ashland z 44805; ● 80
Olivett (Mount Olivett); RMC Place; BELMONT; ▲ Warren; 219 SA-18; mail Barnesville z 43713; ● 80
Olmsted; MCD-Township; CUYAHOGA; *217 NF-14; ★ CLEV; mail Olmsted Falls z 44138; Ⓟ 8,380; © 10,575
Olmsted Falls; Inc. Place; CUYAHOGA; 219 SN-14; 🅿; ★ CLEV; z 44138; Ⓟ 6,741; © 7,962
Olszeski; RMC Place; JEFFERSON; ▲ Mount Pleasant; *217 NM-19; ★ WHL; mail Dillonvale z 43917; ● 40
Omega; RMC Place; PIKE; ▲ Jackson; 218 SG-10; mail Waverly z 45690; ● 130
Oneida; RMC Place; BUTLER; ▲ Lemon; 218 SE-3; ★ MIDD; mail Middletown z 45042; pop. incl. with Middletown (Inc. Place)
Oneida; RMC Place; CARROLL; ▲ Brown; 217 NJ-17; elev. 1,014ft./309m.; ★ CAN; mail Malvern z 44644; ● 150
Ontario; Inc. Place; RICHLAND; ▲ Springfield; 216 NJ-10; 🅿 ■; ★ MANS; z 44862, z 44903, z 44906; Ⓟ 4,026; © 5,303; ◆ 5,226
Opperman; RMC Place; GUERNSEY; ▲ Valley; 219 SB-16; mail Cumberland z 43732; ● 30
Oran; RMC Place; SHELBY; ▲ Cynthian; 216 NM-3; elev. 981ft./299m.; mail Sidney z 45365; ● 50
Orange; MCD-Township; ASHLAND; *217 NI-12; mail Ashland z 44805; Ⓟ 2,113; © 2,276
Orange; MCD-Township; CARROLL; *217 NL-17; mail Leesville z 44639; Ⓟ 1,123; © 1,258
Orange; RMC Place; COSHOCTON; ▲ Oxford; 217 NM-15; mail Newcomerstown z 43832, West Lafayette z 43845; ● 35
Orange; Inc. Place; CUYAHOGA; 219 SM-20; elev. 1,158ft./353m.; ★ CLEV; mail Beachwood z 44122, Chagrin Falls z 44022; Ⓟ 2,810; © 3,236
Orange; MCD-Township; DELAWARE; *216 NM-9; ★ COL; mail Galena z 43021; Ⓟ 3,789; © 12,464
Orange; MCD-Township; HANCOCK; *216 NI-5; mail Bluffton z 45817; Ⓟ 1,191; © 1,290
Orange; MCD-Township; MEIGS; *219 SF-14; mail Coolville z 45723; Ⓟ 970; © 934
Orange; MCD-Township; SHELBY; *216 NM-4; mail Sidney z 45365; Ⓟ 1,183; © 1,419
Orangeville; Inc. Place; TRUMBULL; 217 NF-20; 🅿; ★ YNGS-; z 44453; Ⓟ 253; © 189
Orbiston; RMC Place; HOCKING; ▲ Ward; 219 SE-13; mail Glouster z 45732; ● 40
Orchard Beach; RMC Place; ERIE; ▲ Vermilion; *217 NF-12; ★ CLEV; mail Vermilion z 44089; ● 90
Orchard Island; RMC Place; LOGAN; ▲ Stokes; 216 NL-5; mail Lakeview z 43331; summer pop. 1,000; ● 300
Orchard Park Heights; RMC Place; RICHLAND; ▲ Washington; ★ MANS; mail Mansfield z 44904; ● 350
Oregon; Inc. Place; LUCAS; 216 NE-7; 🅿 🄷; ★ TOL; z 43605, z 43616, z 43618; Ⓟ 18,334; © 19,355
Oregonia; RMC Place; WARREN; ▲ Washington; 218 SE-4; 🅿; z 45054; ● 300
Oreville; RMC Place; HOCKING; ▲ Falls; 219 SD-13; mail New Straitsville z 43766; ● 150
Orient; Inc. Place; PICKAWAY; ▲ Scioto; 218 SC-8; elev. 841ft./256m.; 🅿; ★ COL; z 43146; Ⓟ 273; © 269
Orland; RMC Place; VINTON; ▲ Swan; 219 SE-12; elev. 766ft./233m.; mail New Plymouth z 45654; ● 50
Orrville; Inc. Place; WAYNE; ▲ Green, Baughman; 217 NI-14; elev. 1,064ft./324m.; 🅿 🄷; z 44667; Ⓟ 7,712; © 8,551
Orwell; Inc. Place; ASHTABULA; ▲ Orwell; 217 NE-18; elev. 902ft./275m.; 🅿; z 44076; Ⓟ 1,258; © 1,519
Orwell; MCD-Township; ASHTABULA; *217 NE-19; 🅿; z 44076; Ⓟ 2,421; © 2,830
Osage; RMC Place; JEFFERSON; ▲ Knox; *217 NL-19; ★ STU-; mail Toronto z 43964; rural
Osgood; Inc. Place; DARKE; ▲ Patterson; 216 NL-2; elev. 961ft./293m.; 🅿; z 45351; Ⓟ 255; © 255
Osnaburg; MCD-Township; STARK; *217 NJ-17; ★ CAN; mail East Canton z 44730; Ⓟ 5,781; © 5,886
Ostrander; Inc. Place; DELAWARE; ▲ Scioto; 216 NM-8; elev. 937ft./286m.; 🅿; z 43061; Ⓟ 431; © 405
Otsego; RMC Place; MUSKINGUM; ▲ Monroe; 217 NN-15; mail New Concord z 43762; ● 50
Ottawa; Inc. Place; ⊡ PUTNAM; ▲ Ottawa; 216 NH-4; 🅿; z 45875; Ⓟ 3,999; © 4,367
Ottawa; MCD-Township; PUTNAM; *216 NH-4; 🅿; z 45875; Ⓟ 7,589; © 7,961
OTTAWA; 216 NE-7; Ⓟ 40,029; © 40,985; ◆ 40,713
Ottawa Hills; Inc. Place; LUCAS; 216 ND-6; 🅿; ★ TOL; z 43606, z 43615; Ⓟ 4,543; © 4,564
Otterbein Home; WARREN; see Otterbien Home (RMC Place)
Otterbien Home (Otterbein Home); RMC Place; WARREN; ▲ Turtlecreek; 218 SE-3; mail Lebanon z 45036; ● 700
Ottokee; RMC Place; FULTON; ▲ Dover; 216 NE-4; mail Wauseon z 43567; ● 35
Ottoville; Inc. Place; PUTNAM; ▲ Monterey; 216 NI-3; 🅿; z 45876; Ⓟ 842; © 873
Otway; Inc. Place; SCIOTO; ▲ Brush Creek; 218 SH-8; 🅿; z 45657; Ⓟ 105; © 86
Outville; RMC Place; LICKING; ▲ Harrison; 219 SA-11; ★ COL; mail Pataskala z 43062; ● 110
Overlook; RMC Place; MONTGOMERY; 218 SL-9; ★ DAY; mail Dayton z 45431; pop. incl. with Riverside (Inc. Place)
Overlook Court; RMC Place; BELMONT; ▲ Pultney; *219 SA-20; ★ WHL; mail Bellaire z 43906; ● 100
Overlook Hills; RMC Place; JEFFERSON; ▲ Island Creek; *217 NL-19; ★ STU-; mail Steubenville z 43953; ● 500
Overpeck; RMC Place; BUTLER; ▲ St. Clair; 218 SE-2; 🅿; ★ CIN; z 45055; ● 300
Over The Rhine; RMC Place; HAMILTON; ★ CIN; mail Cincinnati z 45202; pop. incl. with Cincinnati (Inc. Place)
Overton; RMC Place; WAYNE; ▲ Chester; 217 NI-13; elev. 884ft./269m.; mail Wooster z 44691; ● 140
Owens Hill; RMC Place; MUSKINGUM; ▲ Springfield; *219 SB-14; ★ ZAN; mail Zanesville z 43701; ● 75
Owensville; Inc. Place; CLERMONT; ▲ Stonelick; 218 SG-4; 🅿; ★ CIN; z 45160; Ⓟ 1,019; © 816
Oxford; Inc. Place; BUTLER; ▲ Oxford; 218 SD-1; elev. 972ft./296m.; 🅿 🄷 🄲 15,657; z 45056; Ⓟ 18,937; © 21,943; ◆ 24,113
Oxford; MCD-Township; BUTLER; *218 SD-1; 🅿 🄲 15,657; z 45056; Ⓟ 23,092; © 24,133
Oxford; MCD-Township; COSHOCTON; *217 NM-15; mail West Lafayette z 43845; Ⓟ 1,512; © 1,560
Oxford; MCD-Township; DELAWARE; *216 NL-9; mail Ashley z 43003; Ⓟ 901; © 854
Oxford; MCD-Township; ERIE; *216 NG-10; mail Sandusky z 44870; Ⓟ 1,150; © 1,096

Entries in **UPPERCASE** are counties.
Entries in **bold** have populations of 2,500 or more.
Names in parentheses are alternate names.

Inc. Place	Incorporated Place
RMC Place	Rand McNally Designated Place
CDP	Census Designated Place
MCD	Minor Civil Division

⊡ County Seat
▲ Minor Civil Division
elev. Elevation
🅿 Post Office
🄷 Hospital
🄲 College
■ Principal Business Center
★ Ranally Metro Area (RMA) Abbreviation
z Zip Code(s)
Ⓟ Previous Census Population
® Revised Census Population
Ⓐ Annexation Population
● Rand McNally Population Estimate
© Final Census Population
Ⓢ Special Census Population
◆ Estimated Population

For additional definitions see Glossary, Volume 1, and Introduction, Volume 2.

Oxford; MCD-Township; GUERNSEY; ***219** SA-17; mail Quaker City z 43773; Ⓟ 512; © 677
Oxford; MCD-Township; TUSCARAWAS; ***217** NM-15; mail Newcomerstown z 43832; Ⓟ 5,149; © 5,133
Ozark; RMC Place; MONROE; ▲ Sunsbury; **219** SB-18; mail Beallsville z 43716; ● 40

P

Padanaram; RMC Place; ASHTABULA; ▲ Richmond; ***217** ND-20; mail Andover z 44003; rural
Padua; RMC Place; MERCER; ▲ Washington; **216** NK-1; mail Fort Recovery z 45846; ● 70
Page Manor; RMC Place; MONTGOMERY; **218** SC-4; ★ **DAY**; mail Dayton z 45431; pop. incl. with Riverside (Inc. Place)
Pagetown; RMC Place; MORROW; ▲ Bennington; **216** NL-10; mail Marengo z 43334; ● 40
Pageville (Downington); RMC Place; MEIGS; ▲ Scipio; ***219** SF-13; mail Albany z 45710; ● 50
Painesville; Inc. Place; ⊡ LAKE; ▲ Painesville; **217** ND-17; elev. 677ft./206m.; 🅿 🅷 🅲 992 ■; ★ **CLEV**; z 44077; Ⓟ 15,699; © 17,503; ◆ 17,814
Painesville; MCD-Township; LAKE; ***217** ND-17; 🅿 🅲 992; ★ **CLEV**; z 44077; Ⓟ 16,493; © 18,562
Painesville on the Lake; RMC Place; LAKE; ▲ Painesville; **217** ND-17; ★ **CLEV**; mail Painesville z 44077; ● 850
Paint; MCD-Township; FAYETTE; ***218** SD-7; mail Bloomingburg z 43106; Ⓟ 1,711; © 1,905
Paint; MCD-Township; HIGHLAND; ***218** SF-7; mail Bainbridge z 45612; Ⓟ 2,908; © 4,112
Paint; MCD-Township; HOLMES; ***217** NK-15; mail Winesburg z 44690; Ⓟ 2,825; © 3,547
Paint; MCD-Township; MADISON; ***218** SB-7; mail London z 43140; Ⓟ 595; © 565
Paint; MCD-Township; ROSS; ***218** SF-8; mail Bainbridge z 45612; Ⓟ 1,125; © 1,169
Paint; MCD-Township; WAYNE; ***217** NJ-15; mail Mount Eaton z 44659; Ⓟ 2,506; © 2,823
Painters Creek; RMC Place; DARKE; ▲ Franklin; **216** NN-2; mail Arcanum z 45304; ● 150
Paintersville; RMC Place; GREENE; ▲ Caesarscreek; **218** SD-5; mail Jamestown z 45335; ● 70
Paint Valley; RMC Place; HOLMES; ▲ Monroe; ***217** NK-13; mail Millersburg z 44654
Palermo; RMC Place; CARROLL; ▲ Perry; ***217** NK-17; elev. 1,237ft./377m.; mail Carrollton z 44615; ● 80
Palestine; Inc. Place; DARKE; ▲ Liberty; **216** NN-1; 🅿; z 45352; Ⓟ 197; © 170
Palmer; MCD-Township; PUTNAM; ***216** NH-4; mail Continental z 45831; Ⓟ 1,264; © 1,143
Palmer; MCD-Township; WASHINGTON; ***219** SE-15; mail Stockport z 43787; Ⓟ 597; © 625
Palmyra; RMC Place; KNOX; ▲ Berlin; ***217** NK-11; ★ **MANS**; mail Fredericktown z 43019
Palmyra; RMC Place; PORTAGE; ▲ Palmyra; **217** NH-18; mail Diamond z 44412; ● 240
Palmyra; MCD-Township; PORTAGE; ***217** NH-18; mail Diamond z 44412; Ⓟ 2,531; © 2,785
Palos; RMC Place; ATHENS; ▲ Trimble; ***219** SD-13; mail Glouster z 45732; rural
Pancoastburg; RMC Place; FAYETTE; ▲ Madison; **218** SD-8; mail Washington Court House z 43160; ● 150
Pandora; Inc. Place; PUTNAM; ▲ Riley; **216** NI-5; elev. 773ft./236m.; 🅿; z 45877; Ⓟ 1,009; © 1,188
Pansy; RMC Place; CLINTON; ▲ Vernon, Marion; ***218** SE-5; elev. 974ft./297m.; mail Blanchester z 45107
Paradise; RMC Place; MAHONING; ▲ Beaver; ***217** NI-19; elev. 1,165ft./355m.; ★ **YNGS-**; mail Canfield z 44406; rural
Paradise Hill; RMC Place; ASHLAND; ▲ Milton; ***217** NI-12; mail Ashland z 44805
Paris; RMC Place; PORTAGE; ▲ Paris; ***217** NG-18; mail Ravenna z 44266; rural
Paris; MCD-Township; PORTAGE; ***217** NG-18; mail Ravenna z 44266; Ⓟ 1,785; © 1,827
Paris; RMC Place; STARK; ▲ Paris; **217** NJ-17; 🅿; ★ **CAN**; z 44669; ● 220
Paris; MCD-Township; STARK; ***217** NJ-13; 🅿; ★ **CAN**; z 44669; Ⓟ 5,907; © 5,969
Paris; MCD-Township; UNION; ***216** NM-7; mail Marysville z 43040; Ⓟ 12,024; © 17,549
Parkdale; RMC Place; HAMILTON; 🅿; ★ **CIN**; z 45218, z 45240, z 45246; pop. incl. with Forest Park (Inc. Place)
Parkdale; RMC Place; JEFFERSON; ★ **STU-**; mail Steubenville z 43952
Parkertown; RMC Place; ERIE; ▲ Groton; **216** NF-10; mail Castalia z 44824; ● 25
Park Layne; CDP-Census Area Only; CLARK; ▲ Bethel; ***218** SB-4; ★ **DAY**; mail New Carlisle z 45344; Ⓟ 4,795; © 4,519
Parkman; RMC Place; GEAUGA; ▲ Parkman; **217** NF-18; elev. 1,091ft./333m.; 🅿; z 44080; ● 600
Parkman; MCD-Township; GEAUGA; ***217** NF-18; 🅿; ★ **CLEV**; z 44080; Ⓟ 3,083; © 3,546
Park Place; RMC Place; HAMILTON; ***218** SF-2; ★ **CIN**; mail Cincinnati z 45215; pop. incl. with Wyoming (Inc. Place)
Park Ridge Acres; RMC Place; CLARK; ▲ Mad River; **217** NB-15; ★ **SPR**; mail Springfield z 45506; ● 300
Parkview; RMC Place; CUYAHOGA; ***217** NF-14; ★ **CLEV**; mail Cleveland z 44126; pop. incl. with Fairview Park (Inc. Place)
Parkview Heights; RMC Place; HAMILTON; ▲ Springfield; ***218** SG-3; ★ **CIN**; mail Cincinnati z 45224; ● 400
Parlett; RMC Place; JEFFERSON; ▲ Wayne; ***217** NM-19; ★ **STU-**; mail Cadiz z 43907
Parma; Inc. Place; CUYAHOGA; **217** NF-15; 🅿 🅷 ■; ★ **CLEV**; z 44129-31, z 44134 & mail North Royalton z 44133; Ⓟ 87,876; © 85,655; ◆ 78,066
Parma Heights; Inc. Place; CUYAHOGA; **217** NF-14; 🅿; ★ **CLEV**; z 44130; Ⓟ 21,448; © 21,659; ◆ 19,756
Parral; Inc. Place; TUSCARAWAS; ▲ Dover; **217** NK-16; mail Dover z 44622; Ⓟ 255; © 241
Parrott (Parrott Station); RMC Place; FAYETTE; ▲ Jefferson; ***218** SD-7; elev. 1,043ft./318m.; mail Washington Court House z 43160
Parrott Station; FAYETTE; see Parrott (RMC Place)
Pasadena; RMC Place; MONTGOMERY; ***218** SC-4; ★ **DAY**; mail Dayton z 45429; pop. incl. with Kettering (Inc. Place)
Pasco; RMC Place; SHELBY; ▲ Perry; **216** NM-4; mail Sidney z 45365; ● 50
Pataskala; Inc. Place; LICKING; **219** SA-11; 🅿; ★ **COL**; z 43062; Ⓟ 3,046; © 10,249
Patmos; RMC Place; MAHONING; ▲ Goshen; ***217** NI-18; elev. 1,213ft./370m.; mail Salem z 44460
Patriot; RMC Place; GALLIA; ▲ Perry; **219** SI-12; 🅿; z 45658; ● 140
Patterson; MCD-Township; DARKE; ***216** NM-2; mail Yorkshire z 45388; Ⓟ 1,394; © 1,308
Patterson; Inc. Place; HARDIN; ▲ Jackson; **216** NJ-6; mail Forest z 45843; Ⓟ 145; © 138
Pattersonville; RMC Place; CARROLL; ▲ Augusta; **217** NJ-18; mail Minerva z 44657; ● 30
Pattin Addition; RMC Place; WASHINGTON; mail Marietta z 45750; pop. incl. with Marietta (Inc. Place)
Pattonsville (Pattonville); RMC Place; JACKSON; ▲ Bloomfield; ***219** SG-12; mail Jackson z 45640
Pattonville; JACKSON; see Pattonsville (RMC Place)
Paulding; Inc. Place; ⊡ PAULDING; ▲ Paulding, Jackson; **216** NH-2; elev. 723ft./220m.; 🅿 🅷; z 45879; Ⓟ 2,605; © 3,595
Paulding; MCD-Township; PAULDING; ***216** NH-2; 🅿; z 45879; includes part of the Village of Paulding; Ⓟ 3,978; © 4,008
PAULDING; **216** NG-1; Ⓟ 20,488; © 20,293; ◆ 18,959
Paul Laurence Dunbar; RMC Place; MONTGOMERY; ★ **DAY**; mail Dayton z 45417; pop. incl. with Dayton (Inc. Place)
Pavonia; RMC Place; RICHLAND; ▲ Weller; **217** NJ-11; mail Mansfield z 44903; ● 100
Pawnee; RMC Place; MEDINA; ▲ Spencer, Chatham; ***217** NH-13; mail Lodi z 44254; rural
Paxton; MCD-Township; ROSS; ***218** SF-8; mail Bainbridge z 45612; Ⓟ 1,962; © 2,165
Payne; Inc. Place; PAULDING; ▲ Harrison, Benton; **216** NH-1; elev. 753ft./230m.; 🅿; z 45880; Ⓟ 1,244; © 1,166
Peacock Acres; RMC Place; CLARK; ▲ Springfield; ***218** SB-5; ★ **SPR**; mail Springfield z 45502; ● 250
Pearl; COSHOCTON; see Chili (RMC Place)
Pearlbrook; RMC Place; CUYAHOGA; ★ **CLEV**; mail Cleveland z 44109; pop. incl. with Cleveland (Inc. Place)
Pease; MCD-Township; BELMONT; ***219** SA-20; ★ **WHL**; mail Martins Ferry z 43935; Ⓟ 16,368; © 14,961
Pebble; MCD-Township; PIKE; ***218** SG-9; mail Waverly z 45690; Ⓟ 1,625; © 2,416
Pedro; RMC Place; LAWRENCE; ▲ Elizabeth; **219** SJ-11; 🅿; z 45659; ● 110
Peebles; Inc. Place; ADAMS; ▲ Meigs; **218** SH-7; elev. 829ft./253m.; 🅿; z 45660; Ⓟ 1,782; © 1,739
Pee Pee; MCD-Township; PIKE; ***218** SG-9; mail Waverly z 45690; Ⓟ 7,481; © 7,776
Pekin; RMC Place; CARROLL; ▲ Brown; **217** NJ-17; ★ **CAN**; mail Minerva z 44657; ● 100
Pekin; RMC Place; JEFFERSON; ▲ Island Creek; ***217** NL-20; elev. 1,153ft./351m.; ★ **STU-**; mail Steubenville z 43952; ● 200
Pekin; RMC Place; WARREN; ▲ Clear Creek; **218** SD-4; elev. 950ft./290m.; ★ **DAY**; mail Lebanon z 45036; ● 250
Pemberton; RMC Place; SHELBY; ▲ Perry; **216** NM-4; 🅿; z 45353; ● 350
Pemberville; Inc. Place; WOOD; ▲ Freedom; **216** NF-7; 🅿; z 43450; Ⓟ 1,279; © 1,365
Penfield; RMC Place; LORAIN; ▲ Penfield; **217** NG-13; elev. 846ft./258m.; mail Lorain z 44052, Wellington z 44090; ● 100
Penfield; MCD-Township; LORAIN; ***217** NG-13; mail Wellington z 44090; Ⓟ 1,312; © 1,690
Peniel; RMC Place; GALLIA; ▲ Greenfield; ***219** SI-11; mail Patriot z 45658; rural
Peninsula; Inc. Place; SUMMIT; ▲ Boston; **217** NG-15; 🅿; ★ **AKR**; z 44264; Ⓟ 562; © 602
Penn; MCD-Township; HIGHLAND; ***218** SF-6; mail Leesburg z 45135; Ⓟ 882; © 1,055
Penn; MCD-Township; MORGAN; ***219** SD-14; mail Stockport z 43787; Ⓟ 784; © 777
Pennsville; RMC Place; MORGAN; ▲ Penn; **219** SD-14; 🅿; z 43787; ● 150
Penn View; RMC Place; ASHTABULA; ▲ Andover; mail Andover z 44003; summer pop. 300; ● 100
Peoli (Newtown); RMC Place; TUSCARAWAS; ▲ Washington, Perry; **217** NM-16; mail Newcomerstown z 43832, Port Washington z 43837; ● 30
Peoria; RMC Place; BUTLER; ▲ Reily; ***218** SE-1; mail Oxford z 45056; rural
Peoria; RMC Place; UNION; ▲ Liberty; **216** NM-7; mail Raymond z 43067; ● 230
Pepper Pike; Inc. Place; CUYAHOGA; **217** NF-16; elev. 1,050ft./320m.; 🅿; ★ **CLEV**; z 44124 & mail Beachwood z 44122; Ⓟ 6,185; © 6,040
Perintown; RMC Place; CLERMONT; ▲ Union, Miami; **218** SG-3; ★ **CIN**; mail Milford z 45150; ● 150
Perkins; MCD-Township; ERIE; ***216** NF-10; ★ **SNDSK**; mail Sandusky z 44870; Ⓟ 10,793; © 12,578
Perry; MCD-Township; ALLEN; ***216** NJ-4; ★ **LIMA**; mail Lima z 45806; Ⓟ 3,577; © 3,620
Perry; MCD-Township; ASHLAND; ***217** NI-13; mail Polk z 44866; Ⓟ 1,791; © 1,927
Perry; MCD-Township; BROWN; ***218** SF-5; mail Fayetteville z 45118; Ⓟ 3,805; © 4,830
Perry; MCD-Township; CARROLL; ***217** NL-18; mail Scio z 43988; Ⓟ 912; © 1,022
Perry; MCD-Township; COLUMBIANA; ***217** NI-19; mail Salem z 44460; Ⓟ 17,215; © 17,049
Perry; MCD-Township; COSHOCTON; ***217** NM-13; mail Walhonding z 43843; Ⓟ 408; © 513
Perry; MCD-Township; FAYETTE; ***218** SE-7; mail Leesburg z 45135; Ⓟ 896; © 945
Perry; MCD-Township; FRANKLIN; ***218** SA-9; ★ **COL**; mail Dublin z 43017; Ⓟ 5,933; © 4,087
Perry; MCD-Township; GALLIA; ***219** SI-12; mail Patriot z 45658; Ⓟ 1,029; © 1,276
Perry; MCD-Township; HOCKING; ***219** SD-11; mail Laurelville z 43135; Ⓟ 2,225; © 2,554
Perry; Inc. Place; LAKE; ▲ Perry; **217** ND-17; elev. 706ft./215m.; 🅿; ★ **CLEV**; z 44081; Ⓟ 1,012; © 1,195
Perry; MCD-Township; LAKE; ***217** ND-17; 🅿; ★ **CLEV**; z 44081; Ⓟ 6,780; © 8,240
Perry; MCD-Township; LAWRENCE; ***219** SK-11; ★ **HNTG**; mail Ironton z 45638; Ⓟ 6,584; © 6,813
Perry; MCD-Township; LICKING; ***217** NN-12; mail Newark z 43055; Ⓟ 1,202; © 1,492
Perry; MCD-Township; LOGAN; ***216** NL-6; mail East Liberty z 43319; Ⓟ 905; © 1,022
Perry; MCD-Township; MONROE; ***219** SC-18; mail Woodsfield z 43793; Ⓟ 496; © 455
Perry; MCD-Township; MONTGOMERY; ***218** SC-3; ★ **DAY**; mail Brookville z 45309; Ⓟ 6,172; © 6,184
Perry; MCD-Township; MORROW; ***216** NK-10; ★ **MANS**; mail Mansfield z 44904; Ⓟ 1,646; © 1,970
Perry; MCD-Township; MUSKINGUM; ***219** SA-14; ★ **ZAN**; mail Zanesville z 43701; Ⓟ 2,086; © 2,420
Perry; MCD-Township; PICKAWAY; ***218** SD-8; mail New Holland z 43145; Ⓟ 1,326; © 1,319
Perry; MCD-Township; PIKE; ***218** SF-8; mail Blue Creek z 45616; Ⓟ 690; © 913
Perry; MCD-Township; PUTNAM; ***216** NH-3; mail Dupont z 45837; Ⓟ 1,225; © 1,206
Perry; MCD-Township; RICHLAND; ***217** NK-11; ★ **MANS**; mail Bellville z 44813; Ⓟ 1,272; © 1,345
Perry; MCD-Township; SHELBY; ***216** NM-4; mail Pemberton z 45353; Ⓟ 1,227; © 1,128
Perry; MCD-Township; STARK; ***217** NJ-16; ★ **CAN**; mail Canton z 44708; Ⓟ 30,307; © 29,167
Perry; MCD-Township; TUSCARAWAS; ***217** NM-16; mail Tippecanoe z 44699; Ⓟ 382; © 462
Perry; MCD-Township; WOOD; ***216** NG-7; mail Bloomdale z 44817; Ⓟ 1,822; © 1,934
PERRY; **219** SC-13; Ⓟ 31,557; © 34,078; ◆ 34,809
Perry Addition; RMC Place; SCIOTO; ▲ Madison; ***218** SH-10; mail Lucasville z 45648; ● 35
Perry Heights; CDP; STARK; ▲ Perry; **216** NC-8; ★ **CAN**; mail Massillon z 44646; Ⓟ 9,055; © 8,900
Perrysburg; Inc. Place; WOOD; **216** NE-6; elev. 632ft./193m.; 🅿; ★ **TOL**; z 43551-52; Ⓟ 12,551; © 16,945
Perrysburg; MCD-Township; WOOD; ***216** NE-6; 🅿; ★ **TOL**; z 43551-52; Ⓟ 13,176; © 13,613
Perrysburg Heights; RMC Place; WOOD; ▲ Perrysburg; ***216** NE-6; ★ **TOL**; mail Perrysburg z 43551; ● 700
Perrysville; Inc. Place; ASHLAND; ▲ Green; **217** NK-12; 🅿; z 44864; Ⓟ 691; © 816
Perrysville (Lamartine); RMC Place; CARROLL; ▲ Perry; **217** NL-18; mail Scio z 43988; ● 60
Perryton; RMC Place; LICKING; ▲ Perry; **217** NN-13; mail Frazeysburg z 43822; ● 100
Peru; RMC Place; HURON; ▲ Peru, Bronson; **216** NH-10; mail Norwalk z 44857; ● 70
Peru; MCD-Township; HURON; ***216** NG-10; mail Monroeville z 44847; Ⓟ 928; © 1,043
Peru; MCD-Township; MORROW; ***216** NL-9; mail Marengo z 43334; Ⓟ 955; © 1,260
Petersburg; RMC Place; CARROLL; ▲ Union; ***217** NK-18; mail Carrollton z 44615; ● 40
Petersburg; RMC Place; JACKSON; ▲ Scioto; ***218** SG-10; elev. 735ft./224m.; mail Jackson z 45640; rural
Petersburg; RMC Place; MAHONING; ▲ Springfield; **217** NI-20; 🅿; ★ **YNGS-**; z 44454; ● 950
Petrea; RMC Place; JACKSON; ▲ Lick; ***219** SG-11; elev. 691ft./211m.; mail Jackson z 45640; rural
Petroleum; RMC Place; TRUMBULL; ▲ Hubbard; ***217** NG-20; ★ **SHAR**; mail Masury z 44438; ● 200
Pettisville; RMC Place; FULTON; ▲ German, Clinton; **216** NE-3; elev. 754ft./230m.; 🅿; z 43553; ● 500
Pfeiffer Station; RMC Place; HARDIN; ▲ Dudley; **216** NK-7; mail Kenton z 43326; ● 30
Phalanx (Phalanx Station); RMC Place; TRUMBULL; ▲ Braceville; **217** NG-18; elev. 917ft./280m.; ★ **YNGS-**; mail Southington z 44470
Phalanx Station; TRUMBULL; see Phalanx (RMC Place)
Pharisburg; RMC Place; UNION; ▲ Leesburg; **216** NL-7; elev. 959ft./292m.; mail Marysville z 43040; ● 50
Phillippstown; RMC Place; FRANKLIN; ★ **COL**; pop. incl. with Columbus (Inc. Place)
Phillipsburg; Inc. Place; MONTGOMERY; ▲ Clay; **218** SB-3; 🅿; ★ **DAY**; z 45354; Ⓟ 644; © 628
Philo (Taylorsville); Inc. Place; MUSKINGUM; ▲ Harrison; **219** SB-14; 🅿; ★ **ZAN**; z 43771; Ⓟ 810; © 769
Philothea; RMC Place; MERCER; ▲ Butler; **216** NL-1; elev. 933ft./284m.; mail Coldwater z 45828; ● 120
Phoneton; RMC Place; MIAMI; ▲ Bethel; **218** SB-4; 🅿; ★ **DAY**; z 45371; ● 220
Pickaway; MCD-Township; PICKAWAY; ***218** SD-10; mail Circleville z 43113; Ⓟ 1,642; © 1,851
PICKAWAY; **218** SD-9; Ⓟ 48,255; © 52,727; ◆ 55,589
Pickerington; Inc. Place; FAIRFIELD, FRANKLIN; ▲ Madison, Violet; **218** SB-10; elev. 842ft./257m.; 🅿; ★ **COL**; z 43147; Ⓟ 5,668; © 9,792
Pickrelltown; RMC Place; LOGAN; ▲ Monroe; **216** NM-6; elev. 1,418ft./432m.; mail West Liberty z 43357; ● 60
Piedmont; RMC Place; HARRISON; ▲ Moorefield; **217** NM-17; 🅿; z 43983; ● 200
Pierce; MCD-Township; CLERMONT; ***218** SG-3; ★ **CIN**; mail Cincinnati z 45245; Ⓟ 9,589; © 12,226
Pierpont; RMC Place; ASHTABULA; ▲ Pierpont; **217** ND-20; 🅿; z 44082; ● 420
Pierpont; MCD-Township; ASHTABULA; ***217** ND-20; 🅿; z 44082; Ⓟ 1,042; © 1,197
Pigeon Creek; CDP-Census Area Only; SUMMIT; ▲ Copley; ***217** NH-15; elev. 1,050ft./320m.; ★ **AKR**; mail Akron z 44321; Ⓟ 1,008; © 945
Pigeon Run; RMC Place; STARK; ▲ Tuscarawas; **217** NJ-15; ★ **CAN**; mail Massillon z 44646; ● 250
Pike; MCD-Township; BROWN; ***218** SG-5; ★ **CIN**; mail Williamsburg z 45176; Ⓟ 2,901; © 3,742
Pike; MCD-Township; CLARK; ***218** SA-5; ★ **SPR**; mail Springfield z 45502; Ⓟ 3,784; © 3,891
Pike; MCD-Township; COSHOCTON; ***217** NM-13; mail Frazeysburg z 43822; Ⓟ 411; © 550
Pike; MCD-Township; FULTON; ***216** NE-4; mail Delta z 43515; Ⓟ 1,542; © 1,738
Pike; MCD-Township; KNOX; ***217** NK-12; mail Butler z 44822; Ⓟ 1,065; © 1,298
Pike; MCD-Township; MADISON; ***218** SA-7; mail Irwin z 43029; Ⓟ 506; © 531
Pike; MCD-Township; PERRY; ***219** SC-13; mail New Lexington z 43764; Ⓟ 6,821; © 6,595
Pike; MCD-Township; STARK; ***217** NJ-16; ★ **CAN**; mail East Sparta z 44626; Ⓟ 3,931; © 4,088
PIKE; **218** SG-9; Ⓟ 24,249; © 27,695; ◆ 27,743
Piketon; Inc. Place; PIKE; ▲ Seal; **218** SG-9; elev. 578ft./176m.; 🅿; z 45661; Ⓟ 1,717; © 1,907
Pikeville; RMC Place; DARKE; ▲ Greenville; **216** NM-1; mail Greenville z 45331; ● 40
Pine Grove; RMC Place; LAWRENCE; ▲ Elizabeth; **219** SJ-11; mail Ironton z 45638; ● 50
Pinehurst; RMC Place; WASHINGTON; ▲ Warren; ***219** SE-16; ★ **PRKB**; mail Marietta z 45750; ● 100
Pine Valley; RMC Place; JEFFERSON; ▲ Smithfield; ***217** NM-19; elev. 729ft./222m.; ★ **WHL**; mail Dillonvale z 43917
Piney Fork; RMC Place; JEFFERSON; ▲ Smithfield; **217** NM-19; 🅿; ★ **STU-**; z 43941; ● 350
Pink; RMC Place; SCIOTO; ▲ Green; ***218** SI-8; mail Friendship z 45630; rural
Pinkerman; RMC Place; SCIOTO; ▲ Bloom; ***218** SH-10; elev. 645ft./197m.; mail South Webster z 45682; rural
Pioneer; Inc. Place; WILLIAMS; ▲ Madison; **216** ND-2; elev. 874ft./266m.; 🅿; z 43554; Ⓟ 1,287; © 1,460
Piqua; Inc. Place; MIAMI; **216** NN-3; elev. 869ft./265m.; 🅿 🅷 ■; z 45356; Ⓟ 20,612; © 20,738; ◆ 20,230
Pisgah; RMC Place; BUTLER; ▲ West Chester; **218** SE-3; ★ **CIN**; mail West Chester z 45069; ● 1,000
Pitchin; RMC Place; CLARK; ▲ Green; **218** SB-6; ★ **SPR**; mail Springfield z 45502; ● 150
Pitsburg; Inc. Place; DARKE; ▲ Monroe; **218** SA-2; 🅿; ★ **DAY**; z 45358; Ⓟ 425; © 392
Pitt; MCD-Township; WYANDOT; ***216** NJ-8; mail Harpster z 43323; Ⓟ 1,009; © 1,036
Pittlime; RMC Place; SUMMIT; ★ **AKR**; mail Barberton z 44203; pop. incl. with Norton (Inc. Place)
Pittsburgh Junction; RMC Place; HARRISON; ▲ Green; ***217** NL-18; mail Jewett z 43986; rural
Pittsfield; RMC Place; LORAIN; ▲ Pittsfield; **217** NG-12; elev. 817ft./249m.; mail Wellington z 44090; ● 200
Pittsfield; MCD-Township; LORAIN; ***217** NG-12; mail Wellington z 44090; Ⓟ 1,546; © 1,549
Placid Meadows; RMC Place; HAMILTON; ▲ Delhi; ***218** SG-2; elev. 900ft./274m.; ★ **CIN**; mail Cincinnati z 45238
Plain; MCD-Township; FRANKLIN; ***218** SA-10; ★ **COL**; mail Westerville z 43081; Ⓟ 4,366; © 5,926
Plain; MCD-Township; STARK; ***217** NI-16; 🅲 1,803; ★ **CAN**; mail Canton z 44708; Ⓟ 49,181; © 51,997
Plain; MCD-Township; WAYNE; ***217** NJ-13; mail Wooster z 44691; Ⓟ 2,499; © 2,894
Plain; MCD-Township; WOOD; ***216** NF-6; mail Bowling Green z 43402; Ⓟ 2,021; © 1,706
Plain City; Inc. Place; MADISON, UNION; ▲ Darby, Jerome; **216** NN-8; elev. 934ft./285m.; 🅿; ★ **COL**; z 43064; Ⓟ 2,278; © 2,832
Plainfield; Inc. Place; COSHOCTON; ▲ Linton; **217** NM-15; 🅿; z 43836; Ⓟ 178; © 158
Plainview; RMC Place; MONROE; ▲ Perry; ***219** SC-18; mail Woodsfield z 43793; rural
Plankton; RMC Place; CRAWFORD; ▲ Texas, Lykens; ***216** NI-8; mail Sycamore z 44882; rural
Planktown; RMC Place; RICHLAND; ▲ Cass; ***217** NI-11; elev. 1,077ft./328m.; mail Shiloh z 44878
Plantation Acres; RMC Place; HAMILTON; ▲ Springfield; ★ **CIN**; mail Cincinnati z 45224
Plants; RMC Place; MEIGS; ▲ Letart; **219** SH-14; mail Racine z 45771; ● 150
Plantsville; RMC Place; MORGAN; ▲ Marion; **219** SE-14; mail Chesterhill z 43728; ● 25
Plattsburg; RMC Place; CLARK; ▲ Harmony; **218** SB-6; mail South Charleston z 45368; ● 160
Plattsville; RMC Place; SHELBY; ▲ Green; **216** NM-4; mail Sidney z 45365; ● 100
Playhouse Square; RMC Place; CUYAHOGA; ★ **CLEV**; mail Cleveland z 44115; pop. incl. with Cleveland (Inc. Place)
Pleasant; MCD-Township; BROWN; ***218** SH-5; mail Georgetown z 45121; Ⓟ 4,819; © 5,187
Pleasant; MCD-Township; CLARK; ***218** SB-6; ★ **SPR**; mail Catawba z 43010; Ⓟ 2,700; © 3,134
Pleasant; MCD-Township; FAIRFIELD; ***219** SC-11; ★ **LANC**; mail Lancaster z 43130; Ⓟ 5,623; © 5,549
Pleasant; MCD-Township; FRANKLIN; ***218** SB-8; ★ **COL**; mail Grove City z 43123; Ⓟ 6,678; © 7,030
Pleasant; MCD-Township; HANCOCK; ***216** NH-5; mail Mc Comb z 45858; Ⓟ 2,298; © 2,473
Pleasant; MCD-Township; HARDIN; ***216** NK-6; mail Kenton z 43326; Ⓟ 8,469; © 8,608
Pleasant; MCD-Township; HENRY; ***216** NG-4; mail Holgate z 43527; Ⓟ 2,399; © 2,158
Pleasant; MCD-Township; KNOX; ***217** NL-12; mail Mount Vernon z 43050; Ⓟ 1,454; © 2,362; Ⓡ 1,489
Pleasant; MCD-Township; LOGAN; ***216** NL-5; mail De Graff z 43318; Ⓟ 889; © 1,082
Pleasant; MCD-Township; MADISON; ***218** SC-8; mail Mount Sterling z 43143; Ⓟ 2,812; © 3,282
Pleasant; MCD-Township; MARION; ***216** NK-8; ★ **MRN**; mail Marion z 43302; Ⓟ 4,107; © 4,368
Pleasant; MCD-Township; PERRY; ***219** SC-13; mail Crooksville z 43731; Ⓟ 782; © 794
Pleasant; MCD-Township; PUTNAM; ***216** NI-4; mail Columbus Grove z 45830; Ⓟ 3,856; © 3,955
Pleasant; MCD-Township; SENECA; ***216** NG-8; mail Old Fort z 44861; Ⓟ 1,594; © 1,685
Pleasant; MCD-Township; VAN WERT; ***216** NI-2; mail Van Wert z 45891; Ⓟ 11,237; © 11,120
Pleasant Bend; RMC Place; HENRY; ▲ Pleasant; **216** NG-3; mail New Bavaria z 43548; ● 50
Pleasant City; Inc. Place; GUERNSEY; ▲ Valley; **219** SB-16; 🅿; z 43772; Ⓟ 419; © 439
Pleasant Corners; RMC Place; FRANKLIN; ▲ Pleasant; **218** SB-9; 🅿; ★ **COL**; z 43146 & mail Grove City z 43123, Lithopolis z 43136; ● 80
Pleasant Grove; RMC Place; BELMONT; ▲ Colerain; **217** NM-19; ★ **WHL**; mail Adena z 43901, Dillonvale z 43917; ● 130
Pleasant Grove; CDP; MUSKINGUM; ▲ Washington; ***219** SB-14; ★ **ZAN**; mail Zanesville z 43701; Ⓟ 2,001; © 2,016
Pleasant Heights; RMC Place; COLUMBIANA; ***217** NK-20; ★ **E.LIV**; mail East Liverpool z 43920; pop. incl. with East Liverpool (Inc. Place)
Pleasant Heights; RMC Place; JEFFERSON; ★ **STU-**; mail Steubenville z 43952; pop. incl. with Steubenville (Inc. Place)
Pleasant Hill; ATHENS; see Pleasanton (RMC Place)
Pleasant Hill; RMC Place; JEFFERSON; ▲ Island Creek; ***217** NL-20; elev. 1,179ft./359m.; ★ **STU-**; mail Steubenville z 43952; ● 150
Pleasant Hill; Inc. Place; MIAMI; ▲ Newton; **216** NN-3; 🅿; z 45359; Ⓟ 1,066; © 1,134
Pleasant Hills; RMC Place; HAMILTON; ▲ Springfield; ***218** SF-2; ★ **CIN**; mail Cincinnati z 45231; ● 750
Pleasant Home; RMC Place; WAYNE; ▲ Congress; **217** NI-13; mail West Salem z 44287; ● 200
Pleasant Lea; RMC Place; FAIRFIELD; ▲ Pleasant; ***219** SC-11; ★ **LANC**; mail Lancaster z 43130; ● 250
Pleasanton (Pleasant Hill); RMC Place; ATHENS; ▲ Alexander; ***219** SF-13; mail Athens z 45701; rural
Pleasant Plain; Inc. Place; WARREN; ▲ Harlan; **218** SF-4; elev. 886ft./270m.; 🅿; z 45162; Ⓟ 138; © 156
Pleasant Ridge; RMC Place; HAMILTON; ***218** SF-3; ★ **CIN**; mail Cincinnati z 45213; pop. incl. with Cincinnati (Inc. Place)
Pleasant Run; CDP; HAMILTON; ▲ Colerain; **218** SJ-2; elev. 744ft./227m.; ★ **CIN**; mail Cincinnati z 45231, z 45251; Ⓟ 4,964; © 5,267
Pleasant Run Farm; CDP-Census Area Only; HAMILTON; ▲ Springfield; **218** SJ-2; ★ **CIN**; mail Cincinnati z 45240; Ⓟ 4,545; © 4,731
Pleasant Valley; RMC Place; COSHOCTON; ▲ Tuscarawas; ***217** NM-14; mail Coshocton z 43812; pop. incl. with Coshocton (Inc. Place)
Pleasant Valley; RMC Place; PIKE; ▲ Newton; ***218** SG-9; mail Piketon z 45661; rural
Pleasant Valley; RMC Place; ROSS; ▲ Union; **218** SE-9; mail Chillicothe z 45601; ● 500
Pleasant Valley; RMC Place; VINTON; ▲ Harrison; mail Chillicothe z 45601; ● 130
Pleasant View; RMC Place; FAYETTE; ▲ Jefferson; **218** SC-6; mail Jeffersonville z 43128; ● 35
Pleasant View; RMC Place; STARK; ▲ Plain; ***217** NI-16; ★ **CAN**; mail Canton z 44705; rural
Pleasantville; Inc. Place; FAIRFIELD; ▲ Walnut, Pleasant; **219** SC-11; elev. 912ft./278m.; 🅿; ★ **LANC**; z 43148; Ⓟ 926; © 877
Plumwood; RMC Place; MADISON; ▲ Monroe; **218** SA-7; elev. 1,012ft./308m.; mail London z 43140; ● 280
Plymouth; RMC Place; ASHTABULA; ▲ Plymouth; ***217** NC-19; ★ **ASHT**; mail Ashtabula z 44004; rural
Plymouth; MCD-Township; ASHTABULA; ***217** NC-19; ★ **ASHT**; mail Ashtabula z 44004; Ⓟ 2,020; © 2,081
Plymouth; Inc. Place; HURON, RICHLAND; ▲ New Haven, Plymouth; **216** NI-10; 🅿; z 44865; Ⓟ 1,942; © 1,852
Plymouth; MCD-Township; RICHLAND; ***216** NI-10; 🅿; z 44865; includes part of the Village of Plymouth; Ⓟ 2,233; © 2,162
Plymouth Center; RMC Place; ASHTABULA; ▲ Plymouth; **217** NC-19; ★ **ASHT**; mail Ashtabula z 44004; ● 50
Poast Town; RMC Place; BUTLER; ▲ Madison; **218** SD-3; elev. 656ft./200m.; ★ **MIDD**; mail Middletown z 45042; ● 150
Poetown; BROWN, CLERMONT; see Maple (RMC Place)
Point Isabel; RMC Place; CLERMONT; ▲ Washington; **218** SH-4; mail Moscow z 45153; ● 45
Point Place; RMC Place; LUCAS; ***216** ND-7; ★ **TOL**; mail Toledo z 43611; pop. incl. with Toledo (Inc. Place)
Point Pleasant; RMC Place; CLERMONT; ▲ Monroe; **218** SH-3; ★ **CIN**; mail Moscow z 45153; ● 35
Point Rock; RMC Place; MEIGS; ▲ Columbia; ***219** SG-12; mail Albany z 45710; rural
Poland; Inc. Place; MAHONING; ▲ Poland; **217** NH-20; 🅿; ★ **YNGS-**; z 44514; Ⓟ 2,992; © 2,866
Poland; MCD-Township; MAHONING; ***217** NH-20; 🅿; ★ **YNGS-**; z 44514; includes the Village of Poland; Ⓟ 13,993; © 14,711
Poland Center; RMC Place; MAHONING; ▲ Poland; **217** NE-14; ★ **YNGS-**; mail Lowellville z 44436, Youngstown z 44514; ● 250
Polaris; RMC Place; FRANKLIN; ★ **COL**; mail Columbus z 43240; pop. incl. with Columbus (Inc. Place)
Polk; Inc. Place; ASHLAND; ▲ Jackson; **217** NI-12; 🅿; z 44866; Ⓟ 355; © 357
Polk; MCD-Township; CRAWFORD; ***216** NJ-10; mail Galion z 44833; Ⓟ 2,321; © 2,334
Pomeroy; Inc. Place; ⊡ MEIGS; ▲ Salisbury; **219** SG-14; 🅿 🅷; z 45769; Ⓟ 2,259; © 1,966
Pond Run; RMC Place; SCIOTO; ▲ Nile; ***218** SI-9; mail Stout z 45684; rural
Poplargrove; RMC Place; PIKE; ▲ Sunfish, Mifflin; ***218** SG-8; elev. 1,133ft./345m.; mail Peebles z 45660; rural
Portage; MCD-Township; HANCOCK; ***216** NH-6; mail North Baltimore z 45872; Ⓟ 555; © 604
Portage; MCD-Township; OTTAWA; ***216** NE-9; ★ **TOL**; mail Port Clinton z 43452; Ⓟ 1,600; © 1,634
Portage; Inc. Place; WOOD; ▲ Portage, Liberty; **216** NF-6; 🅿; z 43451; Ⓟ 469; © 428
Portage; MCD-Township; WOOD; ***216** NG-6; 🅿; z 43451; includes part of the Village of Portage; Ⓟ 1,547; © 1,516
PORTAGE; **217** NG-17; Ⓟ 142,585; © 152,061; ◆ 157,028
Portage Lakes; CDP; SUMMIT; ▲ Coventry, Franklin; **217** NH-16; ★ **AKR**; mail Akron z 44319; Ⓟ 13,373; © 9,870
Port Clinton; Inc. Place; ⊡ OTTAWA; **216** NE-9; 🅿 🅷; ★ **TOL**; z 43452 & mail Middle Bass z 43446; Ⓟ 7,106; © 6,391
Port Columbus; RMC Place; FRANKLIN; ★ **COL**; pop. incl. with Columbus (Inc. Place)
Porter; MCD-Township; DELAWARE; ***216** NM-10; mail Sunbury z 43074; Ⓟ 1,345; © 1,696
Porter; RMC Place; GALLIA; ▲ Springfield; **219** SH-13; mail Bidwell z 45614; ● 150
Porter; MCD-Township; SCIOTO; ***218** SI-10; ★ **PTSM**; mail Wheelersburg z 45694; Ⓟ 9,687; © 9,892
Porterfield (Center Belpre); RMC Place; WASHINGTON; ▲ Belpre; **219** SF-15; ★ **PRKB**; mail Belpre z 45714; ● 130
Portersville; RMC Place; PERRY; ▲ Bearfield; **219** SC-14; mail Corning z 43730; ● 85
Port Homer; RMC Place; JEFFERSON; ▲ Saline; ***217** NK-20; ★ **E.LIV**; mail Toronto z 43964; rural
Port Jefferson; Inc. Place; SHELBY; ▲ Salem; **216** NL-4; elev. 974ft./297m.; 🅿; z 45360; Ⓟ 381; © 321
Portland; RMC Place; MEIGS; ▲ Lebanon; **219** SG-15; 🅿; z 45770; ● 120
Portsmouth; Inc. Place; ⊡ SCIOTO; **218** SI-9; 🅿 🅷 🅲 3,880 ■; ★ **PTSM**; z 45662-63; Ⓟ 22,676; © 20,909; ◆ 18,999
Port Toledo; RMC Place; LUCAS; ★ **TOL**; pop. incl. with Toledo (Inc. Place)
Port Union; RMC Place; BUTLER; ▲ West Chester; **218** SE-2; ★ **CIN**; mail Hamilton z 45015; ● 100
Port Washington; Inc. Place; TUSCARAWAS; ▲ Salem; **217** NL-16; 🅿; z 43837; Ⓟ 513; © 552
Port William; Inc. Place; CLINTON; ▲ Liberty; **218** SD-5; elev. 1,028ft./313m.; 🅿; z 45164; Ⓟ 242; © 258
Possum Woods; RMC Place; CLARK; ▲ Springfield; **217** NC-16; ★ **SPR**; mail Springfield z 45506; ● 200
Poston; ATHENS; see Sugar Creek (RMC Place)
Post Town; RMC Place; MONTGOMERY; ***218** SC-3; ★ **DAY**; mail Dayton z 45426; pop. incl. with Trotwood (Inc. Place)
Post Town Heights; RMC Place; BUTLER; ▲ Madison; ***218** SD-3; ★ **MIDD**; mail Middletown z 45042; ● 600
Potsdam; Inc. Place; MIAMI; ▲ Union; **218** SB-3; 🅿; ★ **DAY**; z 45361; Ⓟ 250; © 203
Pottersburg; RMC Place; UNION; **216** NM-6; mail Marysville z 43040; rural
Pottery Additon; RMC Place; JEFFERSON; ▲ Island Creek; ***217** NL-20; ★ **STU-**; mail Steubenville z 43952; ● 240
Powell; Inc. Place; DELAWARE; ▲ Liberty; **216** NN-8; elev. 922ft./281m.; 🅿; ★ **COL**; z 43065; Ⓟ 2,154; © 6,247
Powellsville; RMC Place; SCIOTO; ▲ Green; **218** SI-10; ★ **HNTG**; mail Franklin Furnace z 45629; ● 50
Powhatan; BELMONT; see Powhatan Point (Inc. Place)
Powhatan Point (Powhatan); Inc. Place; BELMONT; ▲ York; **219** SB-19; 🅿; z 43942; Ⓟ 1,807; © 1,744
Prairie; MCD-Township; FRANKLIN; ***218** SB-8; ★ **COL**; mail Galloway z 43119; Ⓟ 16,945; © 17,118
Prairie; MCD-Township; HOLMES; ***217** NK-14; mail Holmesville z 44633; Ⓟ 2,265; © 2,785
Prairie Meadows; RMC Place; COSHOCTON; ▲ Bethlehem; mail Coshocton z 43812; ● 50
Pratts Fork; RMC Place; ATHENS; ▲ Lodi; ***219** SF-14; elev. 798ft./243m.; mail Shade z 45776
Prattsville; RMC Place; VINTON; ▲ Madison; **219** SF-12; mail Mc Arthur z 45651; ● 30
PREBLE; **218** SC-1; Ⓟ 40,113; © 42,337; ◆ 41,119
Prentiss; RMC Place; PUTNAM; ▲ Liberty; **216** NH-4; elev. 745ft./227m.; mail Leipsic z 45856; ● 20
Presque Isle; LUCAS; see Toledo Yard (RMC Place)
Preston Addition; RMC Place; SCIOTO; ▲ Jefferson; ***218** SH-9; ★ **PTSM**; mail Lucasville z 45648; ● 40
Price Hill; RMC Place; HAMILTON; ***218** SG-2; ★ **CIN**; mail Cincinnati z 45205; pop. incl. with Cincinnati (Inc. Place)
Pricetown; RMC Place; HIGHLAND; ▲ Salem; **218** SG-5; mail Hillsboro z 45133; ● 60
Pricetown; RMC Place; TRUMBULL, MAHONING; ▲ Milton, Newton; **217** NH-18; ★ **YNGS-**; mail Lake Milton z 44429, Newton Falls z 44444; rural
Pride; RMC Place; ROSS; ▲ Franklin; ***218** SF-10; mail Chillicothe z 45601
Princeton; RMC Place; BUTLER; ▲ Liberty; **218** SE-2; elev. 847ft./258m.; ★ **CIN**; mail Hamilton z 45015; ● 120
Proctor; RMC Place; PORTAGE; ▲ Ravenna; ***217** NG-17; ★ **AKR**; mail Ravenna z 44266; ● 50
Proctorville; Inc. Place; LAWRENCE; ▲ Union, Rome; **219** SK-12; 🅿; ★ **HNTG**; z 45669; Ⓟ 765; © 620
Prospect; Inc. Place; MARION; ▲ Prospect; **216** NL-8; 🅿; ★ **MRN**; z 43342; Ⓟ 1,148; © 1,191
Prospect; MCD-Township; MARION; ***216** NK-8; 🅿; ★ **MRN**; z 43342; Ⓟ 2,050; © 2,207
Prout; RMC Place; ERIE; ● 30
Providence; MCD-Township; LUCAS; ***216** NF-5; ★ **TOL**; mail Berkey z 43504; Ⓟ 3,016; © 3,454
Provident; RMC Place; BELMONT; ▲ Richland; ***219** SA-19; ★ **WHL**; mail Saint Clairsville z 43950; pop. incl. with Saint Clairsville (Inc. Place)
Provincial Point; RMC Place; HAMILTON; ▲ Anderson; ***218** SG-3; ★ **CIN**; mail Cincinnati z 45244; ● 200
Public Square; RMC Place; CUYAHOGA; ★ **CLEV**; mail Cleveland z 44114; pop. incl. with Cleveland (Inc. Place)
Pulaski; RMC Place; WILLIAMS; ▲ Pulaski; **216** NE-2; elev. 761ft./232m.; mail Bryan z 43506; ● 220
Pulaski; MCD-Township; WILLIAMS; ***216** NE-2; mail Bryan z 43506; Ⓟ 2,647; © 2,628
Pulaskiville; RMC Place; MORROW; ▲ Franklin; **216** NK-10; mail Mount Gilead z 43338; ● 50
Pulse; RMC Place; HIGHLAND; ▲ Salem; mail Mount Orab z 45154; rural
Pultney; MCD-Township; BELMONT; ***219** SA-19; ★ **WHL**; mail Bellaire z 43906; Ⓟ 11,107; © 9,700
Puritas Park; RMC Place; CUYAHOGA; ★ **CLEV**; mail Cleveland z 44135; pop. incl. with Cleveland (Inc. Place)
Purity; RMC Place; LICKING; ▲ Eden; ***217** NM-12; elev. 1,173ft./358m.; mail Saint Louisville z 43071
Pusheta; MCD-Township; AUGLAIZE; ***216** NK-4; mail Wapakoneta z 45895; Ⓟ 1,175; © 1,346
Put-in-Bay; Inc. Place; OTTAWA; ▲ Put-in-Bay; **216** NE-10; 🅿; z 43456; Ⓟ 141; © 128; Ⓡ 131
Put-in-Bay; MCD-Township; OTTAWA; ***216** ND-10; mail Put In Bay z 43456; Ⓟ 556; © 763
PUTNAM; **216** NI-4; Ⓟ 33,819; © 34,726; ◆ 34,501
Putnam Place; RMC Place; WASHINGTON; mail Marietta z 45750; pop. incl. with Marietta (Inc. Place)
Pymatuning Shores; RMC Place; ASHTABULA; ▲ Andover; mail Andover z 44003; ● 60
Pyrmont; RMC Place; MONTGOMERY; ▲ Perry; **218** SB-2; ★ **DAY**; mail Brookville z 45309; ● 120
Pyro; RMC Place; JACKSON; ▲ Madison; **219** SH-11; elev. 678ft./207m.; mail Oak Hill z 45656; ● 150

Q

Quaker City; Inc. Place; GUERNSEY; ▲ Millwood; **219** SB-17; 🅿; z 43736, z 43773; Ⓟ 560; © 563
Qualey; RMC Place; WASHINGTON; ▲ Fairfield; ***219** SE-15; mail Cutler z 45724
Queen Acres; RMC Place; BUTLER; ▲ Hanover; **218** SE-2; ★ **CIN**; mail Hamilton z 45013; ● 650
Quincy; Inc. Place; LOGAN; ▲ Miami; **216** NM-4; elev. 1,055ft./322m.; 🅿; z 43343; Ⓟ 697; © 734

R

Raab Corners (Marygrove); RMC Place; LUCAS; ▲ Spencer; ***216** NE-5; ★ **TOL**; mail Swanton z 43558; ● 50
Raccoon; MCD-Township; GALLIA; ***219** SH-12; 🅲 2,426; mail Thurman z 45685; Ⓟ 2,247; © 2,302
Raccoon Island; RMC Place; GALLIA; ▲ Clay; **219** SI-13; mail Gallipolis z 45631
Rachel Heights; RMC Place; WILLIAMS; ▲ Springfield; ***216** NF-2; mail Bryan z 43506; pop. incl. with Bryan (Inc. Place)
Racine; Inc. Place; MEIGS; ▲ Sutton; **219** SH-14; elev. 601ft./183m.; 🅿; z 45771; Ⓟ 729; © 746
Radcliff; RMC Place; VINTON; ▲ Vinton; **219** SG-12; 🅿; z 45695; ● 150
Radford Road; RMC Place; ATHENS; ▲ Athens; ***219** SF-13; mail Athens z 45701; ● 350
Radio Heights; RMC Place; COLUMBIANA; ▲ Liverpool; mail East Liverpool z 43920; ● 50
Radnor (Meredith); RMC Place; DELAWARE; ▲ Radnor; **216** NL-8; elev. 938ft./286m.; 🅿; z 43066; ● 250
Radnor; MCD-Township; DELAWARE; ***216** NL-8; 🅿; z 43066; Ⓟ 1,156; © 1,335
Ragersville; RMC Place; TUSCARAWAS; ▲ Auburn; **217** NL-15; elev. 1,016ft./310m.; mail Sugarcreek z 44681; ● 150
Rainsboro; RMC Place; HIGHLAND; ▲ Paint; **218** SF-7; mail Greenfield z 45123; ● 280
Ra-Mar Estates; RMC Place; CLARK; ▲ Springfield; ***218** SB-5; ★ **SPR**; mail Springfield z 45502; ● 125
Ramsey; RMC Place; JEFFERSON; ▲ Mount Pleasant; ***217** NM-19; ★ **WHL**; mail Dillonvale z 43917; ● 60
Ranchwood; RMC Place; ERIE; ▲ Perkins; ***216** NF-10; ★ **SNDSK**; mail Sandusky z 44870; ● 250
Randall Terrace; RMC Place; ROSS; ***218** SE-9; pop. incl. with Chillicothe (Inc. Place)
Randolph; RMC Place; PORTAGE; ▲ Randolph; **217** NH-17; elev. 1,154ft./352m.; 🅿; ★ **AKR**; z 44265; ● 750
Randolph; MCD-Township; PORTAGE; ***217** NH-17; 🅿; ★ **AKR**; z 44265; Ⓟ 4,970; © 5,504
Range; RMC Place; MADISON; ▲ Range; **218** SC-7; mail Mount Sterling z 43143; ● 40
Range; MCD-Township; MADISON; ***218** SC-7; mail Mount Sterling z 43143; Ⓟ 1,082; © 983
Ransom; RMC Place; PREBLE; ▲ Twin, Lanier; ***218** SC-2; ★ **DAY**; mail West Alexandria z 45381
Rarden; Inc. Place; SCIOTO; ▲ Rarden; **218** SH-8; 🅿; z 45671; Ⓟ 184; © 176
Rarden; MCD-Township; SCIOTO; ***218** SH-8; 🅿; z 45671; Ⓟ 948; © 1,122
Rathbone; RMC Place; DELAWARE; ▲ Concord; ***216** NM-8; elev. 904ft./276m.; ★ **COL**; mail Delaware z 43015
Rathbone; RMC Place; WASHINGTON; ***219** SE-16; ★ **PRKB**; mail Marietta z 45750; pop. incl. with Marietta (Inc. Place)
Rathbone Heights; RMC Place; WASHINGTON; mail Marietta z 45750; pop. incl. with Marietta (Inc. Place)
Ravenna; Inc. Place; ⊡ PORTAGE; **217** NG-17; elev. 1,128ft./344m.; 🅿 🅷 ■; ★ **AKR**; z 44266; Ⓟ 12,069; © 11,771; ◆ 11,785
Ravenna; MCD-Township; PORTAGE; ***217** NG-17; 🅿; ★ **AKR**; z 44266; Ⓟ 21,030; © 9,270
Rawson; Inc. Place; HANCOCK; ▲ Union; **216** NI-5; elev. 817ft./249m.; 🅿; z 45881 & mail Jenera z 45841; Ⓟ 482; © 465
Ray; RMC Place; VINTON, JACKSON; ▲ Jackson, Harrison; **219** SF-11; 🅿; z 45672; ● 100
Rayland; Inc. Place; JEFFERSON; ▲ Warren; **217** NM-19; 🅿; ★ **WHL**; z 43943; Ⓟ 490; © 434
Raymond (Raymonds); RMC Place; UNION; ▲ Liberty; **216** NL-7; 🅿; z 43067; ● 300
Raymonds; UNION; see Raymond (RMC Place)
Rays Corners; RMC Place; ASHTABULA; ▲ Lenox; ***217** ND-19; elev. 955ft./291m.; mail Jefferson z 44047; rural
Reading; RMC Place; COLUMBIANA; ▲ Knox; ***217** NI-18; elev. 1,164ft./355m.; ★ **ALLI**; mail Homeworth z 44634
Reading; Inc. Place; HAMILTON; **218** SF-2; 🅿; ★ **CIN**; z 45215, z 45236; Ⓟ 12,038; © 11,292
Reading; MCD-Township; PERRY; ***219** SC-12; mail Somerset z 43783; Ⓟ 3,546; © 3,956
Recovery; MCD-Township; MERCER; ***216** NL-1; mail Fort Recovery z 45846; Ⓟ 1,381; © 1,550
Red Bank; RMC Place; HAMILTON; ***218** SG-3; ★ **CIN**; mail Cincinnati z 45227; pop. incl. with Fairfax (Inc. Place)
Redbird; RMC Place; LAKE; ▲ Madison; ***217** NC-18; ★ **CLEV**; mail Madison z 44057; ● 2,000
Redbush; RMC Place; WASHINGTON; ▲ Belpre; ***219** SF-15; ★ **PRKB**; mail Little Hocking z 45742
Red Coach Farm; RMC Place; MONTGOMERY; ★ **DAY**; mail Dayton z 45429; pop. incl. with Centerville (Inc. Place)
Redfield; RMC Place; PERRY; ▲ Clayton; **219** SC-13; mail New Lexington z 43764; ● 50
Red Fox (Red Fox Estates); RMC Place; PORTAGE; ▲ Shalersville; ***217** NG-17; ★ **CLEV**; mail Kent z 44240; ● 1,000
Red Fox Estates; PORTAGE; see Red Fox (RMC Place)
Redhaw; RMC Place; ASHLAND; ▲ Perry; **217** NI-13; mail Polk z 44866; ● 50
Red Lion; RMC Place; WARREN; ▲ Clear Creek; **218** SD-3; ★ **DAY**; mail Lebanon z 45036; ● 200
Redoak; RMC Place; BROWN; ▲ Jefferson; ***218** SI-5; elev. 894ft./272m.; mail Ripley z 45167
Red River; RMC Place; DARKE; ▲ Franklin; ***218** SA-2; mail Bradford z 45308
Redtown; RMC Place; ATHENS; ▲ Trimble; **219** SE-13; elev. 729ft./222m.; mail Glouster z 45732
Reed; MCD-Township; SENECA; ***216** NH-9; mail Attica z 44807; Ⓟ 966; © 949
Reedsburg; RMC Place; WAYNE; ▲ Plain; **217** NJ-13; mail Wooster z 44691; ● 150
Reeds Mills; RMC Place; JEFFERSON; ▲ Cross Creek; ***217** NL-19; ★ **STU-**; mail Bloomingdale z 43910
Reedsville; RMC Place; MEIGS; ▲ Olive; **219** SG-15; elev. 640ft./195m.; 🅿; z 45772; ● 300
Reedtown; RMC Place; SENECA; ▲ Reed; **216** NH-10; elev. 862ft./263m.; mail Attica z 44807; ● 50
Reedurban; RMC Place; STARK; ▲ Perry; **217** NJ-16; ★ **CAN**; mail Canton z 44710; ● 4,400
Reese (Reese Station); RMC Place; FRANKLIN; ▲ Hamilton; **219** SJ-19; ★ **COL**; mail Columbus z 43207; ● 400
Reese Station; FRANKLIN; see Reese (RMC Place)
Reesville; RMC Place; CLINTON; ▲ Richland; **218** SE-6; 🅿; z 45166; ● 250
Reform; RMC Place; LICKING; ▲ Perry; ***217** NN-12; mail Newark z 43055; ● 70
Rehoboth; RMC Place; PERRY; ▲ Clayton; **219** SC-13; mail New Lexington z 43764; ● 100
Reily; RMC Place; BUTLER; ▲ Reily; **218** SE-1; mail Oxford z 45056; ● 200
Reily; MCD-Township; BUTLER; ***218** SE-1; mail Oxford z 45056; Ⓟ 2,521; © 2,568
Reinersville; RMC Place; MORGAN; ▲ Manchester; **219** SC-15; mail McConnelsville z 43756; ● 100
Reminderville; Inc. Place; SUMMIT; **217** NF-16; 🅿; ★ **CLEV**; z 44202; Ⓟ 2,163; © 2,347
Remington; RMC Place; HAMILTON; ▲ Symmes; **218** SK-5; ★ **CIN**; mail Cincinnati z 45242, Loveland z 45140; ● 300
Remsen Corners; RMC Place; MEDINA; ▲ Granger; **217** NG-15; ★ **CLEV**; mail Medina z 44256; ● 75
Rendville; Inc. Place; PERRY; ▲ Monroe; **219** SD-13; mail Corning z 43730; Ⓟ 32; © 46
Reno; RMC Place; WASHINGTON; ▲ Marietta; **219** SE-17; 🅿; ★ **PRKB**; z 45773; ● 850
Reno Beach; RMC Place; LUCAS; ▲ Jerusalem; **216** ND-8; ★ **TOL**; mail Curtice z 43412; ● 430
Renrock; RMC Place; NOBLE; ▲ Brookfield; **219** SC-15; mail Belle Valley z 43717; rural
Rensselaer Park; RMC Place; HAMILTON; ▲ Springfield; **218** SK-3; ★ **CIN**; mail Cincinnati z 45216; ● 850
Republic; Inc. Place; SENECA; ▲ Scipio; **216** NH-9; elev. 884ft./269m.; 🅿; z 44867; Ⓟ 611; © 614
Resaca; RMC Place; MADISON; ▲ Monroe; **216** NN-7; mail London z 43140, Plain City z 43064; ● 40
Residence Park; RMC Place; MONTGOMERY; ***218** SC-3; ★ **DAY**; mail Dayton z 45417; pop. incl. with Dayton (Inc. Place)
Revenge; RMC Place; FAIRFIELD; ▲ Madison; ***219** SD-11; mail Lancaster z 43130; rural
Reynoldsburg; Inc. Place; FRANKLIN, FAIRFIELD, LICKING; ▲ Etna, Truro, Violet; **218** SB-10; 🅿; ★ **COL**; z 43068-69; Ⓟ 25,748; © 32,069; ◆ 36,695
Reynolds Corner; RMC Place; LUCAS; ★ **TOL**; mail Toledo z 43615, z 43617, z 43635; pop. incl. with Toledo (Inc. Place)
Rialto; RMC Place; BUTLER; ▲ West Chester; ***218** SE-2; ★ **CIN**; mail West Chester z 45069
Rice; RMC Place; LUCAS; ★ **TOL**; pop. incl. with Toledo (Inc. Place)
Rice; RMC Place; PUTNAM; ▲ Monroe; ***216** NH-3; elev. 720ft./219m.; mail Continental z 45831
Rice; MCD-Township; SANDUSKY; ***216** NF-8; mail Fremont z 43420; Ⓟ 1,467; © 1,437
Riceland; RMC Place; WAYNE; ▲ Sugar Creek, East Union; **217** NJ-14; mail Orrville z 44667; ● 200
Richfield; MCD-Township; HENRY; ***216** NG-5; mail Deshler z 43516; Ⓟ 724; © 654
Richfield; MCD-Township; LUCAS; ***216** ND-5; ★ **TOL**; mail Berkey z 43504; Ⓟ 1,442; © 1,573
Richfield; Inc. Place; SUMMIT; ▲ Richfield; **217** NG-15; 🅿; ★ **CLEV**; z 44286; Ⓟ 3,117; © 3,286
Richfield; MCD-Township; SUMMIT; ***217** NG-15; 🅿; ★ **CLEV**; z 44286; Ⓟ 5,010; © 5,424
Richfield Center; RMC Place; LUCAS; ▲ Richfield; **216** ND-5; ★ **TOL**; mail Berkey z 43504; ● 110
Richfield Heights; RMC Place; SUMMIT; ***217** NG-15; ★ **CLEV**; mail Richfield z 44286; pop. incl. with Richfield (Inc. Place)
Rich Hill; RMC Place; KNOX; ▲ Hilliar; **216** NM-10; mail Centerburg z 43011; ● 75
Rich Hill; MCD-Township; MUSKINGUM; ***219** SB-15; mail Chandlersville z 43727; Ⓟ 409; © 385
Richland; MCD-Township; ALLEN; ***216** NI-5; 🅲 1,158; mail Bluffton z 45817; Ⓟ 5,494; © 6,090
Richland; MCD-Township; BELMONT; ***219** SA-19; 🅲 707; ★ **WHL**; mail Saint Clairsville z 43950; Ⓟ 11,318; © 13,571
Richland; MCD-Township; CLINTON; ***218** SE-6; mail Sabina z 45169; Ⓟ 3,626; © 3,758
Richland; MCD-Township; DARKE; ***216** NM-2; mail Versailles z 45380; Ⓟ 906; © 862
Richland; MCD-Township; DEFIANCE; ***216** NG-3; mail Defiance z 43512; Ⓟ 2,791; © 2,941
Richland; MCD-Township; FAIRFIELD; ***219** SC-12; mail Rushville z 43150; Ⓟ 1,840; © 1,940
Richland; MCD-Township; GUERNSEY; ***219** SB-16; mail Senecaville z 43780; Ⓟ 1,525; © 2,033
Richland; MCD-Township; HOLMES; ***217** NK-13; mail Glenmont z 44628; Ⓟ 892; © 1,165
Richland; MCD-Township; LOGAN; ***216** NK-5; mail Belle Center z 43310; Ⓟ 2,132; © 2,455
Richland; MCD-Township; MARION; ***216** NK-9; mail Marion z 43302; Ⓟ 1,531; © 1,663
Richland; MCD-Township; VINTON; ***219** SF-11; mail Mc Arthur z 45651; Ⓟ 1,241; © 1,667
Richland; MCD-Township; WYANDOT; ***216** NI-7; mail Wharton z 43359; Ⓟ 934; © 952
RICHLAND; **217** NI-11; Ⓟ 126,137; © 128,852; ◆ 122,589
Richmond; MCD-Township; ASHTABULA; ***217** ND-20; mail Dorset z 44032; Ⓟ 850; © 937
Richmond; MCD-Township; HURON; ***216** NH-10; mail Willard z 44890; Ⓟ 1,169; © 1,111
Richmond; Inc. Place; JEFFERSON; ▲ Salem; **217** NL-19; 🅿; ★ **STU-**; z 43944; Ⓟ 446; © 471
Richmond; LAKE; see Grand River (Inc. Place)
Richmondale; ROSS; see Richmond Dale (RMC Place)
Richmond Center; RMC Place; ASHTABULA; ▲ Richmond; **217** ND-20; elev. 1,032ft./315m.; mail Andover z 44003; ● 100
Richmond Dale (Richmondale); RMC Place; ROSS; ▲ Jefferson; **218** SF-10; 🅿; z 45673; ● 700
Richmond Heights; Inc. Place; CUYAHOGA; **217** NE-16; 🅿 🅷 ■; ★ **CLEV**; z 44143; Ⓟ 9,611; © 10,944; ◆ 10,188
Richville; RMC Place; STARK; ▲ Perry; **217** NJ-16; elev. 1,063ft./324m.; ★ **CAN**; mail Canton z 44706, Massillon z 44646, Navarre z 44662; ● 1,600
Richwood; Inc. Place; UNION; ▲ Claibourne; **216** NL-7; 🅿; z 43344; Ⓟ 2,186; © 2,156
Rickard Acres; RMC Place; BUTLER; ▲ Madison; ***218** SD-3; ★ **MIDD**; mail Franklin z 45005; ● 250
Ridge; MCD-Township; VAN WERT; ***216** NI-2; mail Van Wert z 45891; Ⓟ 2,964; © 3,114
Ridge; MCD-Township; WYANDOT; ***216** NI-7; mail Carey z 43316; Ⓟ 537; © 512
Ridgefield; MCD-Township; HURON; ***216** NG-10; ★ **SNDSK**; mail Monroeville z 44847; Ⓟ 2,512; © 2,390
Ridgeland; RMC Place; JACKSON; ▲ Bloomfield; **219** SG-11; elev. 657ft./200m.; mail Jackson z 45640; ● 50
Ridgeton; RMC Place; CRAWFORD; ▲ Liberty; **216** NI-9; mail Bucyrus z 44820; ● 20
Ridgeview; RMC Place; LORAIN; mail North Ridgeville z 44039; pop. incl. with North Ridgeville (Inc. Place)
Ridgeville; MCD-Township; HENRY; ***216** NF-3; mail Ridgeville Corners z 43555; Ⓟ 1,129; © 1,132
Ridgeville; RMC Place; WARREN; ▲ Clear Creek; **218** SD-4; ★ **DAY**; mail Lebanon z 45036; ● 200
Ridgeville Corners; RMC Place; HENRY; ▲ Ridgeville; **216** NF-3; elev. 741ft./226m.; 🅿; z 43555; ● 500
Ridgeway; Inc. Place; HARDIN, LOGAN; ▲ Bokescreek, Hale; **216** NK-6; elev. 1,053ft./321m.; 🅿; z 43345; Ⓟ 378; © 354
Ridgewood; RMC Place; ALLEN; ▲ Bath; ★ **LIMA**; mail Zanesville z 43701; ● 400
Ridgewood; RMC Place; MUSKINGUM; ▲ Falls; ★ **ZAN**; mail Dresden z 43821
Ridgewood Heights; RMC Place; MONTGOMERY; ▲ Jefferson; **218** SC-3; ★ **DAY**; mail Dayton z 45427; pop. incl. with Dayton (Inc. Place)
Rigrish; RMC Place; SCIOTO; ▲ Harrison; ***218** SI-10; ★ **PTSM**; mail Portsmouth z 45662; ● 200
Riley; MCD-Township; PUTNAM; ***216** NI-5; mail Pandora z 45877; Ⓟ 2,026; © 2,191
Riley; MCD-Township; SANDUSKY; ***216** NF-9; mail Fremont z 43420; Ⓟ 1,449; © 1,302
Rimer; RMC Place; PUTNAM; ▲ Sugar Creek; **216** NI-3; mail Columbus Grove z 45830; ● 50
Rinard Mills; RMC Place; MONROE; ▲ Washington; **219** SD-18; 🅿; z 45734, z 45767; ● 30
Ringgold; RMC Place; MORGAN; ▲ Union; **219** SD-14; elev. 925ft./282m.; mail Malta z 43758; ● 25
Ringgold; RMC Place; PICKAWAY; **218** SC-10; mail Circleville z 43113; ● 200
Rio Grande; Inc. Place; GALLIA; ▲ Raccoon; **219** SH-12; 🅿 🅲 2,426; z 45674; Ⓟ 995; © 915
Ripley; Inc. Place; BROWN; ▲ Union; **218** SI-5; 🅿; z 45167; Ⓟ 1,816; © 1,745
Ripley; MCD-Township; HOLMES; ***217** NK-13; mail Shreve z 44676; Ⓟ 1,730; © 2,194
Ripley; MCD-Township; HURON; ***217** NH-11; mail Greenwich z 44837; Ⓟ 867; © 943
Risingsun; Inc. Place; WOOD; ▲ Montgomery; **216** NG-7; 🅿; z 43457; Ⓟ 659; © 620
Rittman; Inc. Place; WAYNE, MEDINA; ▲ Guilford, Milton; **217** NI-14; elev. 979ft./298m.; 🅿; ★ **AKR**; z 44270; Ⓟ 6,147; © 6,314
River Corners; RMC Place; MEDINA; ▲ Spencer; **217** NH-13; elev. 870ft./265m.; mail Spencer z 44275; ● 60
Riverdale; RMC Place; PIKE; ▲ Newton; ***218** SG-9; elev. 556ft./169m.; mail Piketon z 45661; rural
Riverlea; Inc. Place; FRANKLIN; ▲ Sharon; **219** SF-18; ★ **COL**; mail Columbus z 43085; Ⓟ 503; © 499
Riverside; RMC Place; HAMILTON; ***218** SG-2; ★ **CIN**; mail Cincinnati z 45238; pop. incl. with Cincinnati (Inc. Place)
Riverside; Inc. Place; MONTGOMERY; **218** SL-9; ★ **DAY**; mail Dayton z 45424, z 45431; Ⓟ 1,471; © 23,545; ◆ 21,919
Riverside; RMC Place; SHELBY; mail Sidney z 45365; pop. incl. with Sidney (Inc. Place)
Riverside Park; RMC Place; TUSCARAWAS; ▲ Warwick; ***217** NL-16; mail Uhrichsville z 44683; pop. incl. with Tuscarawas (Inc. Place)

Entries in **UPPERCASE** are counties.
Entries in **bold** have populations of 2,500 or more.
Names in parentheses are alternate names.

Inc. Place	Incorporated Place
RMC Place	Rand McNally Designated Place
CDP	Census Designated Place
MCD	Minor Civil Division

⊡ County Seat
▲ Minor Civil Division
elev. Elevation
🅿 Post Office
🅷 Hospital
🅲 College
■ Principal Business Center
★ Ranally Metro Area (RMA) Abbreviation
z Zip Code(s)
Ⓟ Previous Census Population
Ⓡ Revised Census Population
Ⓐ Annexation Population
● Rand McNally Population Estimate
© Final Census Population
Ⓢ Special Census Population
◆ Estimated Population

For additional definitions see Glossary, Volume 1, and Introduction, Volume 2.

River Styx; RMC Place; MEDINA; ▲ Guilford; ***217** NH-14; mail Medina z 44256, Wadsworth z 44281; ● 80
Riverview; RMC Place; BELMONT; ▲ Pultney; ***219** SA-20; ★ **WHL**; mail Bellaire z 43906
Riverview (Gravel Bank); RMC Place; WASHINGTON; ▲ Warren; ***219** SE-16; ★ **PRKB**; mail Marietta z 45750; rural
Rix Mills; RMC Place; MUSKINGUM; ▲ Rich Hill; **219** SB-15; mail New Concord z 43762; ● 40
Roachester; RMC Place; WARREN; ▲ Salem; **218** SE-4; elev. 858ft./262m.; ★ **CIN**; mail Morrow z 45152; ● 500
Roads; RMC Place; JACKSON; ▲ Milton; **219** SG-11; mail Jackson z 45640, Wellston z 45692; ● 160
Roaming Shores; Inc. Place; ASHTABULA; **217** NE-19; 🅿; z 44084-85; Ⓟ 775; © 1,239
Roanoke; RMC Place; TUSCARAWAS; ▲ Mill; **217** NL-16; mail Uhrichsville z 44683; pop. incl. with Uhrichsville (Inc. Place)
Robertsville; RMC Place; STARK; ▲ Osnaburg, Paris; **217** NJ-17; 🅿; ★ **CAN**; z 44670; ● 600
Robins; RMC Place; GUERNSEY; ▲ Jackson; **219** SB-16; mail Byesville z 43723; ● 90
Robinson; CRAWFORD; see North Robinson (Inc. Place)
Robtown; RMC Place; PICKAWAY; ▲ Scioto; ***218** SC-9; ★ **COL**; mail Ashville z 43103
Robyville; RMC Place; HARRISON; ▲ Short Creek; **217** NM-19; mail Adena z 43901; ● 70
Rochester; Inc. Place; LORAIN; ▲ Rochester; **217** NH-12; 🅿; z 44090; Ⓟ 206; © 190
Rochester; MCD-Township; LORAIN; ***217** NH-12; 🅿; z 44090; Ⓟ 627; © 752
Rochester Place; RMC Place; WOOD; ★ **TOL**; mail Oregon z 43618; pop. incl. with Northwood (Inc. Place)
Rockbridge; RMC Place; HOCKING; ▲ Good Hope; **219** SD-11; 🅿; z 43149; ● 450
Rock Camp; RMC Place; COLUMBIANA; ▲ Madison; ***217** NJ-20; ★ **E.LIV**; mail Lisbon z 44432; rural
Rock Camp; RMC Place; LAWRENCE; ▲ Perry; **219** SJ-11; elev. 611ft./186m.; 🅿; ★ **HNTG**; z 45675; ● 80
Rock Creek; Inc. Place; ASHTABULA; ▲ Morgan; **217** ND-19; 🅿 🅷; z 44084; Ⓟ 553; © 584
Rockdale; RMC Place; BUTLER; ▲ Liberty, Lemon; ***218** SE-2; ★ **CIN**; mail Hamilton z 45015; ● 220
Rockford; Inc. Place; MERCER; ▲ Dublin; **216** NJ-1; elev. 813ft./248m.; 🅿; z 45882; Ⓟ 1,119; © 1,126
Rockhill; RMC Place; BELMONT; ▲ Flushing; ***217** NN-18; mail Flushing z 43977; ● 30
Rockland; RMC Place; WASHINGTON; ***219** SF-16; ★ **PRKB**; mail Belpre z 45714; pop. incl. with Belpre (Inc. Place)
Rock Mills; RMC Place; FAYETTE; ▲ Wayne, Perry; **218** SE-7; mail Washington Court House z 43160; ● 30
Rockport; RMC Place; ALLEN; ▲ Monroe; **216** NI-4; mail Columbus Grove z 45830; ● 90
Rock Way; RMC Place; CLARK; ▲ Springfield; **217** NB-15; ★ **SPR**; mail Springfield z 45504; ● 160
Rockwood; RMC Place; ERIE; ▲ Margaretta; ★ **SNDSK**; mail Castalia z 44824; ● 100
Rockwood; RMC Place; LAWRENCE; ***219** SK-12; ★ **HNTG**; mail Chesapeake z 45619
Rocky Fall Estates; RMC Place; HIGHLAND; ▲ Paint; mail Hillsboro z 45133; ● 300
Rocky Fork; LICKING; see Hickman (RMC Place)
Rocky Hill; RMC Place; JACKSON; ▲ Bloomfield; ***219** SG-11; elev. 716ft./218m.; mail Jackson z 45640
Rocky Point; RMC Place; CLARK; ▲ Mad River; ***218** SB-5; ★ **SPR**; mail Springfield z 45502; rural
Rocky Ridge; Inc. Place; OTTAWA; ▲ Benton; **216** NE-8; elev. 608ft./185m.; 🅿; z 43458; Ⓟ 425; © 389
Rocky River; Inc. Place; CUYAHOGA; **217** NF-14; 🅿; ★ **CLEV**; z 44116; Ⓟ 20,410; © 20,735; ◆ 19,031
Rodney; RMC Place; GALLIA; ▲ Springfield, Green; **219** SH-12; elev. 681ft./208m.; mail Bidwell z 45614, Gallipolis z 45631; ● 250
Rogers; Inc. Place; COLUMBIANA; ▲ Middleton; **217** NJ-20; elev. 1,023ft./312m.; 🅿; z 44455; Ⓟ 247; © 266
Rokeby Lock; RMC Place; MORGAN; ▲ Bloom; ***219** SC-14; mail McConnelsville z 43756; ● 100
Rolandus; RMC Place; MEIGS; ▲ Lebanon; ***219** SH-15; elev. 579ft./176m.; mail Racine z 45771; rural
Rollersville; RMC Place; SANDUSKY; ▲ Scott, Madison; **216** NF-7; elev. 690ft./210m.; mail Gibsonburg z 43431; ● 40
Rolling Mill Park; RMC Place; BUTLER; ▲ Lemon; ★ **MIDD**; mail Middletown z 45044
Rome; ADAMS; see Stout (Inc. Place)
Rome; RMC Place; ASHTABULA; ▲ Rome; **217** NE-19; elev. 853ft./260m.; 🅿; z 44085; ● 200
Rome; MCD-Township; ASHTABULA; ***217** NE-19; 🅿; z 44085; Ⓟ 1,256; © 1,568
Rome; MCD-Township; ATHENS; ***219** SE-14; mail Coolville z 45723; Ⓟ 1,429; © 1,400
Rome (Labelle); RMC Place; LAWRENCE; ▲ Rome; **219** SK-12; ★ **HNTG**; mail Proctorville z 45669; ● 1,450
Rome; MCD-Township; LAWRENCE; ***219** SK-12; ★ **HNTG**; mail Proctorville z 45669; Ⓟ 7,579; © 8,694
Rome; RMC Place; RICHLAND; ▲ Bloominggrove; **217** NI-11; mail Shiloh z 44878; ● 90
Rome Station; RMC Place; ASHTABULA; ▲ Rome; ***217** NE-19; elev. 885ft./270m.; mail Rome z 44085; ● 50
Romohr Acres; RMC Place; CLERMONT; ▲ Union; **218** SL-5; ★ **CIN**; mail Cincinnati z 45244; ● 300
Rootstown; RMC Place; PORTAGE; ▲ Rootstown; **217** NH-17; 🅿 🅲 459; ★ **AKR**; z 44272; ● 650
Rootstown; PORTAGE; see New Milford (RMC Place)
Rootstown; MCD-Township; PORTAGE; ***217** NH-17; 🅿 🅲 459; ★ **AKR**; z 44272; Ⓟ 6,612; © 7,212
Roscoe; RMC Place; COSHOCTON; ***217** NM-14; mail Coshocton z 43812; pop. incl. with Coshocton (Inc. Place)
Rose; MCD-Township; CARROLL; ***217** NK-17; mail Magnolia z 44643; Ⓟ 1,384; © 1,603
Rosedale; RMC Place; MADISON; ▲ Pike; **216** NN-7; elev. 1,013ft./309m.; mail Irwin z 43029; ● 180
Rose Farm; RMC Place; MORGAN; ▲ York; **219** SC-13; mail Crooksville z 43731; ● 200
Rose Heights; RMC Place; JEFFERSON; ★ **STU-**; mail Steubenville z 43952; pop. incl. with Steubenville (Inc. Place)
Rose Hill; RMC Place; DARKE; ▲ Mississinawa, Allen; ***216** NM-1; elev. 1,078ft./329m.; mail New Weston z 45348
Roseland; RMC Place; RICHLAND; ▲ Madison; **217** NJ-11; ★ **MANS**; mail Mansfield z 44906; ● 2,150
Roselawn; RMC Place; HAMILTON; ***218** SF-2; 🅿; ★ **CIN**; z 45222 & mail Cincinnati z 45237; pop. incl. with Cincinnati (Inc. Place)
Roselms; RMC Place; PAULDING; ▲ Washington; ***216** NH-2; elev. 724ft./221m.; mail Grover Hill z 45849; ● 20
Rosemont; RMC Place; MAHONING; ▲ Jackson, Ellsworth; **217** ND-11; elev. 1,082ft./330m.; ★ **YNGS-**; mail North Jackson z 44451; ● 90
Rosemount; CDP; SCIOTO; ▲ Clay; **218** SI-9; ★ **PTSM**; mail Portsmouth z 45662; Ⓟ 1,926; © 2,043
Roseville; Inc. Place; MUSKINGUM, PERRY; ▲ Harrison, Clay; **219** SC-13; elev. 737ft./225m.; 🅿; ★ **ZAN**; z 43777; Ⓟ 1,847; © 1,936
Rosewood; RMC Place; CHAMPAIGN; ▲ Adams; **216** NM-4; 🅿; z 43070; ● 250
Roslyn; RMC Place; MONTGOMERY; ★ **DAY**; mail Dayton z 45429
Ross (Venice); CDP; BUTLER; ▲ Ross; **218** SF-1; elev. 558ft./170m.; 🅿; ★ **CIN**; z 45061; Ⓟ 2,124; © 1,971
Ross; MCD-Township; BUTLER; ***218** SE-1; 🅿; ★ **CIN**; z 45061; Ⓟ 6,383; © 6,448
Ross; MCD-Township; GREENE; ***218** SC-6; mail South Solon z 43153; Ⓟ 705; © 744
Ross; MCD-Township; JEFFERSON; ***217** NK-19; mail Richmond z 43944; Ⓟ 595; © 655
ROSS; **218** SE-8; Ⓟ 69,330; © 73,345; ◆ 74,732
Rossburg; Inc. Place; DARKE; ▲ Allen; **216** NM-1; elev. 1,036ft./316m.; 🅿; z 45348, z 45362; Ⓟ 250; © 224
Rossford; Inc. Place; WOOD; **216** NE-6; 🅿; ★ **TOL**; z 43460; Ⓟ 5,861; © 6,406
Rossmoyne; RMC Place; HAMILTON; ▲ Sycamore; ***218** SF-3; elev. 831ft./253m.; ★ **CIN**; mail Cincinnati z 45236
Rossville; RMC Place; BUTLER; 🅿; ★ **CIN**; z 45013
Roswell; Inc. Place; TUSCARAWAS; ▲ Union, Goshen; **217** NL-16; mail New Philadelphia z 44663; Ⓟ 257; © 276
Round Bottom; RMC Place; MONROE; ▲ Green; ***219** SC-19; mail Clarington z 43915; rural
Roundhead; RMC Place; HARDIN; ▲ Roundhead; **216** NK-5; elev. 1,007ft./307m.; 🅿; z 43346; ● 300
Roundhead; MCD-Township; HARDIN; ***216** NK-5; 🅿; z 43346; Ⓟ 721; © 752
Rousculp; RMC Place; ALLEN; ▲ Perry; ***216** NJ-4; ★ **LIMA**; mail Lima z 45806; rural
Rowsburg; RMC Place; ASHLAND; ▲ Perry; **217** NI-13; elev. 1,146ft./349m.; mail Polk z 44866; ● 90
Roxabell; RMC Place; ROSS; ▲ Concord; **218** SE-8; elev. 752ft./229m.; mail Frankfort z 45628; ● 200
Roxanna; RMC Place; GREENE; **218** SD-4; elev. 755ft./230m.; ★ **DAY**; rural
Roxbury; RMC Place; MORGAN; ▲ Windsor; ***219** SD-15; mail Stockport z 43787; ● 25
Royalton; RMC Place; FAIRFIELD; ▲ Amanda; **218** SC-10; mail Lancaster z 43130; ● 260
Royalton; MCD-Township; FULTON; ***216** ND-4; mail Lyons z 43533; Ⓟ 1,395; © 1,502
Royersville; RMC Place; LAWRENCE; ▲ Elizabeth; ***219** SJ-11; mail Ironton z 45638; ● 45
Rubyville; RMC Place; SCIOTO; ▲ Clay; **218** SI-9; ★ **PTSM**; mail Portsmouth z 45662
Rudolph; RMC Place; WOOD; ▲ Liberty; **216** NG-6; 🅿; z 43462; ● 500
Ruggles; RMC Place; ASHLAND; ▲ Ruggles; **217** NH-12; mail Greenwich z 44837, New London z 44851; ● 40
Ruggles; MCD-Township; ASHLAND; ***217** NH-12; mail New London z 44851; Ⓟ 678; © 857
Ruggles Beach; RMC Place; ERIE; ▲ Berlin; **217** NF-11; ★ **CLEV**; mail Huron z 44839; summer pop. 300; ● 50
Rumley; MCD-Township; HARRISON; ***217** NL-18; mail Jewett z 43986; Ⓟ 1,530; © 1,575
Rumley; RMC Place; SHELBY; rural
Rural; RMC Place; CLERMONT; ▲ Franklin; ***218** SI-4; elev. 498ft./152m.; mail Felicity z 45120; ● 30
Ruraldale; RMC Place; MUSKINGUM; ▲ Blue Rock; **219** SC-15; mail Blue Rock z 43720; ● 60
Rush; MCD-Township; CHAMPAIGN; ***216** NM-6; mail Woodstock z 43084; Ⓟ 2,248; © 2,779
Rush; MCD-Township; SCIOTO; ***218** SH-9; ★ **PTSM**; mail Mc Dermott z 45652; Ⓟ 2,887; © 3,144
Rush; MCD-Township; TUSCARAWAS; ***217** NL-16; mail Uhrichsville z 44683; Ⓟ 855; © 887
Rush Creek; MCD-Township; FAIRFIELD; ***219** SC-12; mail Bremen z 43107; Ⓟ 3,388; © 3,549
Rushcreek; MCD-Township; LOGAN; ***216** NL-6; mail Rushsylvania z 43347; Ⓟ 1,944; © 2,191
Rushmore; RMC Place; PUTNAM; ▲ Jennings; **216** NI-3; mail Fort Jennings z 45844; ● 50
Rush Run; RMC Place; JEFFERSON; ▲ Wells, Warren; **217** NM-20; ★ **WHL**; mail Rayland z 43943; ● 250
Rushsylvania; Inc. Place; LOGAN; ▲ Rushcreek; **216** NL-6; elev. 1,238ft./377m.; 🅿; z 43347; Ⓟ 573; © 543
Rushtown; RMC Place; SCIOTO; ▲ Rush; ***218** SH-9; elev. 542ft./165m.; ★ **PTSM**; mail Mc Dermott z 45652
Rushville; Inc. Place; FAIRFIELD; ▲ Richland; **219** SC-12; 🅿; z 43150 & mail West Rushville z 43163; Ⓟ 229; © 268
Russell; MCD-Township; GEAUGA; ***217** NF-16; 🅿; ★ **CLEV**; z 44072 & mail Chagrin Falls z 44022; Ⓟ 5,765; © 5,529
Russell; RMC Place; HIGHLAND; ▲ Union; **218** SF-6; mail Hillsboro z 45133; ● 50
Russell Center; RMC Place; GEAUGA; ▲ Russell; **217** NF-16; elev. 1,094ft./333m.; ★ **CLEV**; mail Novelty z 44072; ● 200
Russell Heights; RMC Place; COLUMBIANA; ▲ Yellow Creek; ***217** NK-20; ★ **E.LIV**; mail Wellsville z 43968; ● 400
Russells; RMC Place; MUSKINGUM; ▲ Springfield; ***219** SB-14; ★ **ZAN**; mail Zanesville z 43701; ● 90
Russells Point; Inc. Place; LOGAN; ▲ Washington; **216** NL-5; 🅿; z 43348; Ⓟ 1,504; © 1,619
Russellville; Inc. Place; BROWN; ▲ Jefferson; **218** SH-5; elev. 975ft./297m.; 🅿; z 45168; Ⓟ 459; © 453
Russia; Inc. Place; SHELBY; ▲ Loramie; **216** NM-2; 🅿; z 45363; Ⓟ 442; © 551
Rustic Hills; RMC Place; MEDINA; ▲ Montville; ***217** NH-14; ★ **CLEV**; mail Medina z 44256; ● 375
Rutland; Inc. Place; MEIGS; ▲ Rutland; **219** SG-13; 🅿; z 45775; Ⓟ 469; © 401
Rutland; MCD-Township; MEIGS; ***219** SG-13; 🅿; z 45775; Ⓟ 2,243; © 2,347
Rye Beach; RMC Place; ERIE; ***217** NF-11; ★ **SNDSK**; mail Huron z 44839; pop. incl. with Huron (Inc. Place)

S

Sabina; Inc. Place; CLINTON; ▲ Richland; **218** SD-6; elev. 1,045ft./319m.; 🅿; z 45169; Ⓟ 2,662; © 2,780
Sagamore Hills; RMC Place; SUMMIT; ▲ Sagamore Hills; **217** NG-15; 🅿; ★ **CLEV**; z 44067; ● 1,930
Sagamore Hills; MCD-Township; SUMMIT; ***217** NF-15; 🅿; ★ **CLEV**; z 44067; Ⓟ 6,503; © 9,340
Sahara Sands; RMC Place; STARK; ▲ Jackson; **216** NB-8; ★ **CAN**; mail Massillon z 44646; ● 650
St. Albans; MCD-Township; LICKING; ***219** SA-11; mail Pataskala z 43062; Ⓟ 2,136; © 2,060; Ⓡ 2,197
Saint Anthony; RMC Place; MERCER; ▲ Washington; ***216** NK-1; mail Fort Recovery z 45846; ● 60
Saint Bernard; Inc. Place; HAMILTON; **218** SF-2; elev. 537ft./164m.; 🅿; ★ **CIN**; z 45216-17, z 45232; Ⓟ 5,344; © 4,924
Saint Charles; RMC Place; BUTLER; ***218** SE-1; mail Hamilton z 45013; rural
St. Clair; MCD-Township; BUTLER; ***218** SE-2; ★ **CIN**; mail Hamilton z 45011; Ⓟ 7,718; © 7,336
St. Clair; MCD-Township; COLUMBIANA; ***217** NJ-20; ★ **E.LIV**; mail East Liverpool z 43920; Ⓟ 7,705; © 7,961
Saint Clairsville; Inc. Place; ⊡ BELMONT; ▲ Richland; **217** NN-19; elev. 1,284ft./391m.; 🅿 🅷 🅲 707 ■; ★ **WHL**; z 43950; Ⓟ 5,162; © 5,057; ◆ 4,979
Saint Henry; Inc. Place; MERCER; ▲ Granville; **216** NL-1; elev. 967ft./295m.; 🅿; z 45883; Ⓟ 1,907; © 2,271
Saint Joe; RMC Place; BELMONT; ▲ Pultney; ***219** SA-19; ★ **WHL**; mail Bellaire z 43906; ● 80
Saint Johns; RMC Place; AUGLAIZE; ▲ Union, Clay; **216** NK-4; 🅿; z 45884; ● 200
Saint Joseph (Victoria); RMC Place; MERCER; ▲ Recovery; ***216** NL-1; elev. 976ft./297m.; mail Fort Recovery z 45846; ● 70
Saint Joseph; RMC Place; PORTAGE; ▲ Suffield, Randolph; ***217** NH-17; ★ **AKR**; mail Atwater z 44201
St. Joseph; MCD-Township; WILLIAMS; ***216** NF-1; mail Edgerton z 43517; Ⓟ 2,790; © 2,958
Saint Louisville; Inc. Place; LICKING; ▲ Newton; **217** NM-11; elev. 905ft./276m.; 🅿; ★ **NWRK**; z 43071; Ⓟ 372; © 346
Saint Martin; Inc. Place; BROWN; ▲ Perry; **218** SF-5; elev. 979ft./298m.; mail Fayetteville z 45118; Ⓟ 141; © 91
Saint Marys; Inc. Place; AUGLAIZE; ▲ St. Marys, Noble; **216** NK-2; elev. 871ft./265m.; 🅿 🅷; z 45885; Ⓟ 8,441; © 8,342
St. Marys; MCD-Township; AUGLAIZE; ***216** NK-2; mail Saint Marys z 45885; includes part of the City of Saint Marys; Ⓟ 11,562; © 11,600
Saint Paris; Inc. Place; CHAMPAIGN; ▲ Johnson, Jackson; **216** NN-4; 🅿; z 43072; Ⓟ 1,842; © 1,998
Saint Pauls; RMC Place; PICKAWAY; ▲ Madison; ***218** SC-10; mail Ashville z 43103
Saint Peters; RMC Place; MERCER; ▲ Recovery; ***216** NL-1; mail Fort Recovery z 45846; ● 40
Saint Rosa; RMC Place; MERCER; ▲ Marion; ***216** NL-2; mail Scott z 45886; ● 130
Saint Sebastian; RMC Place; MERCER; ▲ Marion; ***216** NL-2; mail Chickasaw z 45826; ● 80
Saint Stephens; RMC Place; SENECA; ▲ Venice, Bloom; ***216** NH-9; mail Attica z 44807
Saint Wendelin; RMC Place; MERCER; ▲ Granville, Gibson; ***216** NL-1; mail Fort Recovery z 45846, Saint Henry z 45883; ● 100
Salem; MCD-Township; AUGLAIZE; ***216** NK-2; mail Spencerville z 45887; Ⓟ 516; © 580
Salem; MCD-Township; CHAMPAIGN; ***216** NM-6; mail Urbana z 43078; Ⓟ 2,045; © 2,307
Salem; Inc. Place; COLUMBIANA; ▲ Perry; **217** NI-19; elev. 1,226ft./374m.; 🅿 🅷 🅲 1,233 ■; z 44460; Ⓟ 12,233; © 12,197; ◆ 11,969
Salem; MCD-Township; COLUMBIANA; ***217** NI-19; 🅿 🅲 1,233; z 44460 & mail Leetonia z 44431; Ⓟ 5,523; © 5,703
Salem; MCD-Township; HIGHLAND; ***218** SG-5; mail Hillsboro z 45133; Ⓟ 587; © 682
Salem; MCD-Township; JEFFERSON; ***217** NL-19; ★ **STU-**; mail Richmond z 43944; Ⓟ 3,739; © 3,162
Salem; MEIGS; see Salem Center (RMC Place)
Salem; MCD-Township; MEIGS; ***219** SG-13; mail Langsville z 45741; Ⓟ 1,018; © 944
Salem; MCD-Township; MONROE; ***219** SC-19; mail Clarington z 43915; Ⓟ 996; © 1,046
Salem; MCD-Township; MUSKINGUM; ***219** SA-14; mail Adamsville z 43802; Ⓟ 878; © 830
Salem; MCD-Township; OTTAWA; ***216** NE-8; mail Oak Harbor z 43449; Ⓟ 5,064; © 5,517
Salem; MCD-Township; SHELBY; ***216** NL-4; mail Sidney z 45365; Ⓟ 2,080; © 2,231
Salem; MCD-Township; TUSCARAWAS; ***217** NL-16; mail Newcomerstown z 43832; Ⓟ 1,510; © 1,673
Salem; MCD-Township; WARREN; ***218** SE-4; ★ **CIN**; mail Morrow z 45152; Ⓟ 4,038; © 4,133
Salem; MCD-Township; WASHINGTON; ***219** SD-16; mail Lower Salem z 45745; Ⓟ 1,124; © 1,130
Salem; MCD-Township; WYANDOT; ***216** NI-7; mail Upper Sandusky z 43351; Ⓟ 963; © 1,055
Salem Center (Salem); RMC Place; MEIGS; ▲ Salem; **219** SG-13; mail Langsville z 45741; ● 80
Salem Heights; RMC Place; COLUMBIANA; ▲ Perry; ***217** NI-18; mail Salem z 44460; ● 200
Salesville; Inc. Place; GUERNSEY; ▲ Millwood; **219** SB-17; 🅿; z 43778; Ⓟ 84; © 154
Saline; MCD-Township; JEFFERSON; ***217** NK-19; ★ **E.LIV**; mail Irondale z 43932; Ⓟ 1,467; © 1,454
Salineville; Inc. Place; COLUMBIANA, JEFFERSON; ▲ Brush Creek, Washington; **217** NK-19; 🅿; z 43945; Ⓟ 1,474; © 1,397
Salisbury; MCD-Township; MEIGS; ***219** SG-14; mail Pomeroy z 45769; Ⓟ 7,227; © 6,441
Saltair; RMC Place; CLERMONT; ▲ Tate; ***218** SH-4; elev. 901ft./275m.; ★ **CIN**; mail Bethel z 45106
Salt Creek; MCD-Township; HOCKING; ***219** SE-11; mail Laurelville z 43135; Ⓟ 1,172; © 1,260
Salt Creek; MCD-Township; HOLMES; ***217** NK-14; mail Mount Hope z 44660; Ⓟ 3,061; © 3,778
Salt Creek; MCD-Township; MUSKINGUM; ***219** SB-14; mail Chandlersville z 43727; Ⓟ 965; © 1,113
Saltcreek; MCD-Township; PICKAWAY; ***218** SD-10; mail Circleville z 43113; Ⓟ 2,069; © 2,655
Salt Creek; MCD-Township; WAYNE; ***217** NJ-14; mail Fredericksburg z 44627; Ⓟ 3,137; © 3,783
Saltillo; RMC Place; PERRY; ▲ Clayton; **219** SC-13; elev. 855ft./261m.; mail Roseville z 43777; ● 110
Salt Lick; MCD-Township; PERRY; ***219** SD-13; mail Shawnee z 43782; Ⓟ 1,262; © 1,200
Salt Rock; MCD-Township; MARION; ***216** NJ-8; mail Morral z 43337; Ⓟ 706; © 699
Salt Run; RMC Place; JEFFERSON; ▲ Wells; ***217** NM-20; ★ **STU-**; mail Rayland z 43943; rural
Samantha; RMC Place; HIGHLAND; ▲ Penn; **218** SF-6; elev. 1,129ft./344m.; mail Leesburg z 45135; ● 130
Sampleville (Glenwood); RMC Place; PREBLE; ▲ Twin, Lanier; **218** SC-2; ★ **DAY**; mail West Alexandria z 45381; ● 200
Sand Beach; RMC Place; OTTAWA; ▲ Carroll; ***216** NE-8; mail Oak Harbor z 43449; summer pop. 200
Sand Fork (Mudsock); RMC Place; GALLIA; ▲ Walnut; ***219** SI-12; mail Patriot z 45658; rural
Sand Hill; RMC Place; ERIE; ▲ Margaretta; ***216** NF-10; ★ **SNDSK**; mail Sandusky z 44870; rural
Sand Hill; RMC Place; SCIOTO; ▲ Porter; ***218** SI-10; ★ **PTSM**; mail Wheelersburg z 45694
Sandhill; RMC Place; WASHINGTON; ▲ Marietta; ***219** SE-17; ★ **PRKB**; mail Reno z 45773
Sand Ridge; RMC Place; ATHENS; ▲ Dover; ***219** SE-13; mail Millfield z 45761; rural
Sandrun; RMC Place; HOCKING; ▲ Ward; ***219** SD-13; mail Nelsonville z 45764; rural
Sandusky; MCD-Township; CRAWFORD; ***216** NI-10; mail Tiro z 44887; Ⓟ 473; © 475
Sandusky; Inc. Place; ⊡ ERIE; **216** NF-10; 🅿 🅷 ■; ★ **SNDSK**; z 44870-71; Ⓟ 29,764; © 27,844; ◆ 25,322
Sandusky; MCD-Township; RICHLAND; ***216** NJ-10; ★ **MANS**; mail Crestline z 44827; Ⓟ 940; © 856
Sandusky; MCD-Township; SANDUSKY; ***216** NF-8; mail Fremont z 43420; Ⓟ 4,441; © 4,087
SANDUSKY; **216** NF-8; Ⓟ 61,963; © 61,792; ◆ 60,420
Sandusky South; CDP-Census Area Only; ERIE; ▲ Perkins; ***216** NF-10; ★ **SNDSK**; mail Sandusky z 44870; Ⓟ 6,336; © 6,599
Sandy; MCD-Township; STARK; ***217** NJ-17; ★ **CAN**; mail Waynesburg z 44688; Ⓟ 3,630; © 3,679
Sandy; MCD-Township; TUSCARAWAS; ***217** NK-16; ★ **CAN**; mail Mineral City z 44656; Ⓟ 3,162; © 3,354
Sandy Beach; RMC Place; AUGLAIZE, MERCER; ▲ Franklin, St. Marys; ***216** NK-2; mail Saint Marys z 45885; ● 300
Sandy Springs; RMC Place; ADAMS; ▲ Green; ***218** SJ-8; mail Stout z 45684
Sandyville; RMC Place; TUSCARAWAS; ▲ Sandy; **217** NK-16; 🅿; ★ **CAN**; z 44671; ● 420
San Margherita; RMC Place; FRANKLIN; ▲ Franklin; **219** SH-17; elev. 803ft./245m.; ★ **COL**; mail Columbus z 43204; ● 300
Santa Fe; RMC Place; AUGLAIZE, LOGAN; ▲ Stokes, Clay; **216** NL-4; mail Wapakoneta z 45895; ● 100
San Toy; RMC Place; PERRY; ▲ Monroe, Bearfield; **219** SD-14; mail Corning z 43730; rural
Sarahsville; Inc. Place; NOBLE; ▲ Center; **219** SC-16; 🅿; z 43779; Ⓟ 162; © 198
Sardinia; Inc. Place; BROWN, HIGHLAND; ▲ Washington, Whiteoak; **218** SG-5; elev. 962ft./293m.; 🅿; z 45171; Ⓟ 792; © 862
Sardis; RMC Place; MONROE; ▲ Lee; **219** SD-19; elev. 668ft./204m.; 🅿; z 43946; ● 500
Savannah; Inc. Place; ASHLAND; ▲ Clear Creek; **217** NI-12; elev. 1,101ft./336m.; 🅿; z 44874; Ⓟ 363; © 372
Savona; RMC Place; DARKE; ▲ Butler; **218** SB-1; mail Greenville z 45331; ● 50
Sawyerwood; RMC Place; SUMMIT; ▲ Springfield; **216** NC-6; ★ **AKR**; mail Akron z 44312; ● 1,730
Saybrook; RMC Place; ASHTABULA; ▲ Saybrook; **217** ND-18; elev. 681ft./208m.; ★ **ASHT**; mail Ashtabula z 44004
Saybrook; MCD-Township; ASHTABULA; ***217** NC-19; ★ **ASHT**; mail Ashtabula z 44004; Ⓟ 10,164; © 10,051
Saybrook-on-the-Lake; RMC Place; ASHTABULA; ▲ Saybrook; ***217** NC-18; ★ **ASHT**; mail Ashtabula z 44004; summer pop. 150
Sayler Park (Saylor Park); RMC Place; HAMILTON; ***218** SG-1; 🅿; ★ **CIN**; z 45233; pop. incl. with Cincinnati (Inc. Place)
Saylor Park; HAMILTON; see Sayler Park (RMC Place)
Sayre; RMC Place; PERRY; ▲ Bearfield; **219** SC-14; mail Crooksville z 43731
Scenic Hills; RMC Place; MADISON; ▲ Jefferson; ★ **COL**; mail West Jefferson z 43162; ● 200
Schauers Acres; RMC Place; CLARK; ▲ Bethel; ***218** SB-4; ★ **DAY**; mail Medway z 45341; ● 150
Schley; RMC Place; WASHINGTON; ▲ Lawrence, Independence; ***219** SE-17; elev. 1,080ft./329m.; mail Newport z 45768; rural
Schoenbrunn; RMC Place; TUSCARAWAS; ▲ Goshen; **217** NL-16; mail New Philadelphia z 44663; ● 700
Schooleys; RMC Place; ROSS; ▲ Liberty; ***218** SF-10; mail Chillicothe z 45601; rural
Schrader; RMC Place; ROSS; ▲ Springfield; ***218** SF-10; mail Chillicothe z 45601; ● 80
Schumm; RMC Place; VAN WERT; ▲ Willshire; **216** NJ-1; mail Willshire z 45898; ● 25
Scienceville; RMC Place; MAHONING; ***217** NH-20; ★ **YNGS-**; pop. incl. with Youngstown (Inc. Place)
Scio; Inc. Place; HARRISON; ▲ North; **217** NL-18; 🅿; z 43988; Ⓟ 856; © 799
Scioto; MCD-Township; DELAWARE; ***216** NM-8; mail Ostrander z 43061; Ⓟ 2,129; © 2,527
Scioto; MCD-Township; JACKSON; ***218** SG-10; mail Jackson z 45640; Ⓟ 1,432; © 1,788
Scioto; MCD-Township; PICKAWAY; ***218** SC-9; ★ **COL**; mail Ashville z 43103; Ⓟ 8,231; © 9,165
Scioto; MCD-Township; PIKE; ***218** SG-9; mail Wakefield z 45687; Ⓟ 1,170; © 1,232
Scioto; MCD-Township; ROSS; ***218** SE-9; 🅲 1,983; mail Chillicothe z 45601; Ⓟ 30,654; © 27,735
SCIOTO; **218** SI-8; Ⓟ 80,327; © 79,195; ◆ 74,742
Sciotodale; CDP; SCIOTO; ▲ Porter; **218** SI-10; ★ **PTSM**; mail Portsmouth z 45662; Ⓟ 1,128; © 982
Scioto Furnace; RMC Place; SCIOTO; ▲ Bloom; **218** SI-10; elev. 605ft./184m.; 🅿; z 45677; ● 250
Sciotoville; RMC Place; SCIOTO; ***218** SI-10; elev. 545ft./166m.; 🅿; ★ **PTSM**; z 45662; pop. incl. with Portsmouth (Inc. Place)
Scipio; RMC Place; BUTLER; ▲ Reily, Morgan; **218** SE-1; elev. 840ft./256m.; ★ **CIN**; mail Okeana z 45053; ● 40
Scipio; MCD-Township; MEIGS; ***219** SG-13; mail Albany z 45710; Ⓟ 1,094; © 1,050
Scipio; MCD-Township; SENECA; ***216** NH-9; mail Republic z 44867; Ⓟ 1,735; © 1,831
Scotch Ridge; RMC Place; WOOD; ▲ Webster; **216** NF-7; mail Pemberville z 43450; ● 90
Scott; MCD-Township; ADAMS; ***218** SH-7; mail Seaman z 45679; Ⓟ 1,920; © 2,053
Scott; MCD-Township; BROWN; ***218** SH-5; mail Georgetown z 45121; Ⓟ 1,001; © 1,253
Scott; MCD-Township; MARION; ***216** NK-9; mail Marion z 43302; Ⓟ 498; © 521
Scott; MCD-Township; SANDUSKY; ***216** NG-7; mail Helena z 43435; Ⓟ 1,540; © 1,502
Scott; Inc. Place; VAN WERT, PAULDING; ▲ Blue Creek, Union; **216** NI-2; elev. 742ft./226m.; 🅿; z 45886; Ⓟ 339; © 322
Scottown; RMC Place; LAWRENCE; ▲ Windsor; **219** SJ-12; 🅿; z 45678; ● 100
Scotts Crossing; RMC Place; ALLEN; ▲ Marion; ***216** NJ-3; ★ **LIMA**; mail Delphos z 45833; rural
Scotty's Beauty Beach; RMC Place; MERCER; ▲ Jefferson; mail Celina z 45822; ● 130
Scroggsfield; RMC Place; CARROLL; ▲ Fox; ***217** NK-18; mail Carrollton z 44615; rural
Scrub Ridge; RMC Place; ADAMS; ▲ Meigs; ***218** SH-7; elev. 871ft./265m.; mail Blue Creek z 45616; rural
Seal; MCD-Township; PIKE; ***218** SG-9; mail Piketon z 45661; Ⓟ 2,619; © 2,983
Seal; RMC Place; WYANDOT; **216** NI-8; ● 25
Seaman; Inc. Place; ADAMS; ▲ Scott, Wayne; **218** SH-6; 🅿; z 45679; Ⓟ 1,013; © 1,039
Seasons Four; RMC Place; CLERMONT; ▲ Wayne; ★ **CIN**; mail Loveland z 45140; ● 240
Sebring; Inc. Place; MAHONING; ▲ Smith; **217** NI-18; 🅿; ★ **ALLI**; z 44672; Ⓟ 4,848; © 4,912
Secedar Corners; RMC Place; TRUMBULL; ▲ Liberty; **217** NC-14; ★ **YNGS-**; mail Hubbard z 44425; ● 300
Secor Gardens; RMC Place; LUCAS; ★ **TOL**; pop. incl. with Toledo (Inc. Place)
Sedalia; MADISON; see Midway (Inc. Place)
Sedamsville; RMC Place; HAMILTON; ***218** SG-2; ★ **CIN**; mail Cincinnati z 45233; pop. incl. with Cincinnati (Inc. Place)
Seilcrest Acres; RMC Place; WARREN; ▲ Deerfield; ★ **CIN**; mail Loveland z 45140; ● 90
Sellers Point; RMC Place; FAIRFIELD; ▲ Walnut; ***219** SB-11; ★ **COL**; mail Millersport z 43046; ● 200
Selma; RMC Place; CLARK; ▲ Madison; **218** SC-6; 🅿; z 45368; ● 130
Seneca; MCD-Township; MONROE; ***219** SB-17; mail Lewisville z 43754; Ⓟ 386; © 508
Seneca; MCD-Township; NOBLE; ***219** SB-17; mail Sarahsville z 43779; Ⓟ 357; © 453
Seneca; MCD-Township; SENECA; ***216** NH-8; mail New Riegel z 44853; Ⓟ 1,515; © 1,585
SENECA; **216** NH-8; Ⓟ 59,733; © 58,683; ◆ 56,178
Senecaville; Inc. Place; GUERNSEY; ▲ Richland; **219** SB-16; 🅿; z 43780; Ⓟ 434; © 453
Senior; RMC Place; WARREN; ▲ Washington; ***218** SE-4; mail Morrow z 45152
Sentinel; RMC Place; ASHTABULA; ▲ New Lyme; ***217** NE-19; mail Dorset z 44032; rural
Seven Hills; Inc. Place; CUYAHOGA; **217** NF-15; 🅿; ★ **CLEV**; z 44131; Ⓟ 12,339; © 12,080
Seven Hills; RMC Place; HAMILTON; ▲ Springfield; **218** SJ-2; 1 mi. N of New Burlington; ★ **CIN**; mail Cincinnati z 45231; ● 2,000
Seven Mile; Inc. Place; BUTLER; ▲ Wayne, St. Clair; **218** SE-2; elev. 655ft./200m.; 🅿; ★ **CIN**; z 45062; Ⓟ 804; © 678
Seventeen; RMC Place; TUSCARAWAS; ▲ Clay; **217** NL-16; elev. 831ft./253m.; mail Gnadenhutten z 44629; ● 120
Seville; Inc. Place; MEDINA; ▲ Guilford; **217** NH-14; 🅿; z 44273; Ⓟ 1,810; © 2,160
Seward; RMC Place; FULTON; ▲ Royalton; ***216** ND-4; mail Lyons z 43533
Sewellsville; RMC Place; BELMONT; ▲ Kirkwood; **217** NN-17; mail Barnesville z 43713; ● 35
Shade; RMC Place; ATHENS; ▲ Lodi; **219** SF-14; 🅿; z 45776 & mail Athens z 45701; ● 120
Shademore; RMC Place; HAMILTON; ▲ Anderson; **218** SL-4; ★ **CIN**; mail Cincinnati z 45244; ● 40
Shadeville; RMC Place; FRANKLIN; ▲ Hamilton; **218** SB-9; ★ **COL**; mail Lockbourne z 43137; ● 100
Shady Bend; RMC Place; COSHOCTON; ▲ Oxford; ***217** NM-15; mail Newcomerstown z 43832; ● 160
Shady Glen; RMC Place; JEFFERSON; ▲ Knox; ***217** NK-20; elev. 1,049ft./320m.; ★ **STU-**; mail Toronto z 43964; ● 50
Shady Glen; ROSS; see Knockemstiff (RMC Place)
Shady Grove; RMC Place; GREENE; ▲ Beavercreek; ★ **DAY**; mail Fairborn z 45324; rural
Shadyside; Inc. Place; BELMONT; ▲ Pultney, Mead; **219** SA-20; 🅿; ★ **WHL**; z 43947; Ⓟ 3,934; © 3,675
Shadyside; RMC Place; COLUMBIANA; ▲ Liverpool; ***217** NJ-20; ★ **E.LIV**; mail East Liverpool z 43920; pop. incl. with East Liverpool (Inc. Place)
Shaker Crossing; RMC Place; MONTGOMERY; ★ **DAY**; mail Dayton z 45429; pop. incl. with Kettering (Inc. Place)
Shaker Heights; Inc. Place; CUYAHOGA; **217** NF-15; 🅿; ★ **CLEV**; z 44118, z 44120, z 44122; Ⓟ 30,831; © 29,405; ◆ 26,379
Shalersville; RMC Place; PORTAGE; ▲ Shalersville; **217** NG-17; ★ **CLEV**; mail Mantua z 44255, Ravenna z 44266; ● 220
Shalersville; MCD-Township; PORTAGE; ***217** NG-17; ★ **CLEV**; mail Mantua z 44255, Ravenna z 44266; Ⓟ 5,270; © 5,976
Shandon; RMC Place; BUTLER; ▲ Morgan; ***218** SE-1; 🅿; ★ **CIN**; z 45063; ● 400
Shane; RMC Place; JEFFERSON; ***217** NL-19; mail Richmond z 43944; ● 30
Shanesville; RMC Place; TUSCARAWAS; ***217** NK-15; mail Sugarcreek z 44681; pop. incl. with Sugarcreek (Inc. Place)
Shannon; RMC Place; MUSKINGUM; ▲ Muskingum; ***219** SA-13; ★ **ZAN**; mail Dresden z 43821
Sharon; MCD-Township; FRANKLIN; ***218** SA-9; ★ **COL**; mail Westerville z 43081; Ⓟ 17,493; © 16,455
Sharon; MCD-Township; MEDINA; ***217** NH-15; ★ **AKR**; mail Sharon Center z 44274; Ⓟ 3,234; © 4,244
Sharon; RMC Place; NOBLE; ▲ Sharon; **219** SC-16; mail Caldwell z 43724; ● 90
Sharon; MCD-Township; NOBLE; ***219** SC-16; mail Caldwell z 43724; Ⓟ 338; © 353
Sharon; MCD-Township; RICHLAND; ***216** NI-10; mail Shelby z 44875; Ⓟ 9,812; © 9,720
Sharon Center; RMC Place; MEDINA; ▲ Sharon; **217** NH-15; 🅿; ★ **AKR**; z 44274; ● 350
Sharon Hills; RMC Place; FRANKLIN; ▲ Perry; ★ **COL**; mail Columbus z 43085; ● 300
Sharon Park; RMC Place; ALLEN; ▲ American; ***216** NJ-4; ★ **LIMA**; mail Lima z 45805; ● 500
Sharon Park; RMC Place; BUTLER; ▲ St. Clair; ★ **CIN**; mail Hamilton z 45013; ● 800
Sharonville; Inc. Place; HAMILTON, BUTLER; **218** SF-3; elev. 589ft./180m.; 🅿; ★ **CIN**; z 45241 & mail Cincinnati z 45262; Ⓟ 13,153; © 13,804
Sharon West; RMC Place; TRUMBULL; ▲ Brookfield; ★ **SHAR**; mail Masury z 44438
Sharpeye; RMC Place; DARKE; ▲ Greenville; ***216** NN-1; mail Greenville z 45331
Sharpsburg; RMC Place; ATHENS; ▲ Bern; **219** SE-14; 🅿; z 45777; ● 50
Sharpsburg (Zenz City); RMC Place; MERCER; ▲ Gibson; ***216** NL-1; mail Fort Recovery z 45846; ● 65
Shartz Road; RMC Place; WARREN; ▲ Franklin; ***218** SD-4; ★ **DAY**; mail Franklin z 45005, Springboro z 45066; ● 250
Shauck (Johnsville); RMC Place; MORROW; ▲ Perry; **216** NK-10; 🅿; ★ **MANS**; z 43349; ● 200
Shawnee; MCD-Township; ALLEN; ***216** NJ-4; ★ **LIMA**; mail Lima z 45805; Ⓟ 12,133; © 12,220
Shawnee; Inc. Place; PERRY; ▲ Salt Lick; **219** SD-13; 🅿; z 43782; Ⓟ 742; © 608
Shawnee Hills; Inc. Place; DELAWARE; ▲ Concord; **216** NN-8; 🅿; ★ **COL**; z 43065; Ⓟ 423; © 419
Shawnee Hills; CDP; GREENE; ▲ Silvercreek, New Jasper; ***218** SC-6; ★ **DAY**; mail Jamestown z 45335; Ⓟ 2,199; © 2,355
Shawnee Meadows; RMC Place; ALLEN; ▲ Shawnee; ***216** NJ-4; ★ **LIMA**; mail Lima z 45806; ● 700
Shawtown; RMC Place; HANCOCK; ▲ Pleasant; ***216** NH-5; elev. 744ft./227m.; mail Mc Comb z 45858; ● 25
Shawtown; RMC Place; MORROW; ▲ Westfield; ***216** NL-9; mail Cardington z 43315; rural
Shawville; RMC Place; LORAIN; ***217** NF-13; ★ **CLEV**; mail Elyria z 44035; pop. incl. with North Ridgeville (Inc. Place)
Shay; RMC Place; WASHINGTON; ▲ Independence; ***219** SD-17; mail New Matamoras z 45767; rural
Sheffield; MCD-Township; ASHTABULA; ***217** NC-19; mail Kingsville z 44048; Ⓟ 1,362; © 1,491
Sheffield (Sheffield Village); Inc. Place; LORAIN; **217** NF-13; elev. 673ft./205m.; ★ **CLEV**; mail Elyria z 44035, Lorain z 44055, Sheffield Lake z 44054; Ⓟ 1,943; © 2,949
Sheffield; MCD-Township; LORAIN; ***217** NF-13; ★ **CLEV**; mail Lorain z 44053, z 44055, Sheffield Lake z 44054; Ⓟ 3,751; © 4,117
Sheffield Lake; Inc. Place; LORAIN; ▲ Sheffield; **217** NF-13; 🅿; ★ **CLEV**; z 44054; Ⓟ 9,825; © 9,371
Sheffield Village; LORAIN; see Sheffield (Inc. Place)
Shelby; Inc. Place; RICHLAND; ▲ Sharon, Jackson; **216** NI-10; elev. 1,102ft./336m.; 🅿; z 44875; Ⓟ 9,564; © 9,821
SHELBY; **216** NL-4; Ⓟ 44,915; © 47,910; ◆ 49,031
Shelby Junction; RMC Place; RICHLAND; mail Shelby z 44875; pop. incl. with Shelby (Inc. Place)
Shell Beach; RMC Place; FAIRFIELD; ▲ Walnut; ***219** SB-12; ★ **COL**; mail Thornville z 43076
Shenandoah; RMC Place; RICHLAND; ▲ Bloominggrove; **217** NI-11; mail Greenwich z 44837, Shiloh z 44878; ● 100
Shepard; RMC Place; FRANKLIN; mail Columbus z 43219; pop. incl. with Columbus (Inc. Place)
Shepherdstown; RMC Place; BELMONT; ▲ Wheeling; ***217** NM-18; mail Saint Clairsville z 43950; rural
Sherbondy; RMC Place; SUMMIT; ★ **AKR**; pop. incl. with Akron (Inc. Place)
Sheridan; RMC Place; LAWRENCE; ▲ Perry; **219** SK-11; ★ **HNTG**; mail South Point z 45680; ● 500
Sherman; MCD-Township; HURON; ***216** NG-10; mail Monroeville z 44847; Ⓟ 530; © 501
Sherman; RMC Place; RICHLAND; ★ **MANS**; mail Mansfield z 44906; pop. incl. with Mansfield (Inc. Place)
Sherman; RMC Place; SUMMIT; ★ **AKR**; mail Barberton z 44203; pop. incl. with Norton (Inc. Place)
Sherritts; RMC Place; LAWRENCE; ▲ Symmes; ***219** SI-11; mail Waterloo z 45688; rural
Sherrodsville; Inc. Place; CARROLL; ▲ Orange, Monroe; **217** NK-17; 🅿; z 44675; Ⓟ 284; © 316
Sherwood; Inc. Place; DEFIANCE; ▲ Delaware; **216** NG-2; elev. 709ft./216m.; 🅿; z 43556; Ⓟ 828; © 801
Sherwood; CDP-Census Area Only; HAMILTON; ▲ Anderson; ***218** SG-3; elev. 750ft./229m.; ★ **CIN**; mail Cincinnati z 45230; Ⓟ 3,709; © 3,907
Sherwood Park; RMC Place; ALLEN; ▲ American; ***216** NJ-3; ★ **LIMA**; mail Lima z 45805; ● 750
Shillings Mill; RMC Place; MAHONING; ▲ Berlin; ***217** NH-18; elev. 970ft./296m.; mail Lake Milton z 44429; ● 30
Shiloh; RMC Place; CLERMONT; ▲ Wayne, Goshen; ***218** SF-4; ★ **CIN**; mail Goshen z 45122; ● 100
Shiloh; CDP; MONTGOMERY; ▲ Harrison; **218** SB-3; ★ **DAY**; mail Dayton z 45405, z 45415; Ⓟ 11,607; © 11,272
Shiloh; Inc. Place; RICHLAND; ▲ Cass; **217** NI-11; 🅿; z 44878; Ⓟ 778; © 721
Shinrock; RMC Place; ERIE; ▲ Berlin; ***217** NF-11; elev. 627ft./191m.; 🅿; ★ **CLEV**; z 44839
Shore; RMC Place; CUYAHOGA; ***217** NE-15; ★ **CLEV**; mail Euclid z 44123
Short Creek; HARRISON; see Georgetown (RMC Place)
Short Creek; MCD-Township; HARRISON; ***217** NM-19; mail Adena z 43901, Cadiz z 43907; Ⓟ 1,157; © 1,012
Short North; RMC Place; FRANKLIN; mail Columbus z 43201; pop. incl. with Columbus (Inc. Place)
Shreve; Inc. Place; WAYNE; **217** NJ-13; elev. 914ft./279m.; 🅿; z 44676; Ⓟ 1,584; © 1,582
Siam; SENECA; see Attica Junction (RMC Place)
Sidney; Inc. Place; ⊡ SHELBY; ▲ Perry, Clinton, Franklin; **216** NM-4; 🅿 🅷; z 45365, z 45367 & mail Fort Loramie z 45845; Ⓟ 18,710; © 20,211; ◆ 20,316
Signal; RMC Place; COLUMBIANA; ▲ Elkrun; **217** NJ-20; mail Lisbon z 44432; ● 40
Silica; RMC Place; LUCAS; ▲ Sylvania; ***216** ND-6; ★ **TOL**; mail Sylvania z 43560
Silvercreek; MCD-Township; GREENE; ***218** SC-6; mail Jamestown z 45335; Ⓟ 3,373; © 3,688
Silver Creek; RMC Place; MEDINA; ▲ Wadsworth; ***217** NH-15; ★ **AKR**; mail Wadsworth z 44281; pop. incl. with Wadsworth (Inc. Place)
Silver Lake; Inc. Place; SUMMIT; **217** NH-16; 🅿; ★ **AKR**; z 44224 & mail Cuyahoga Falls z 44221; Ⓟ 3,052; © 3,019
Silver Lake Junction; RMC Place; SUMMIT; ★ **AKR**; pop. incl. with Cuyahoga Falls (Inc. Place)
Silverton; Inc. Place; HAMILTON; **218** SL-4; ★ **CIN**; mail Cincinnati z 45236; Ⓟ 5,859; © 5,178
Simons; RMC Place; ASHTABULA; ▲ Williamsfield; **217** NE-20; elev. 1,051ft./320m.; mail Williamsfield z 44093; ● 70
Singing Hills; RMC Place; MONTGOMERY; ▲ Miami; **218** SD-4; ★ **DAY**; mail Dayton z 45449; pop. incl. with West Carrollton City (Inc. Place)
Sinking Spring; Inc. Place; HIGHLAND; ▲ Brushcreek; **218** SG-7; 🅿; z 45172; Ⓟ 189; © 158
Sitka; RMC Place; WASHINGTON; ▲ Lawrence; ***219** SE-17; mail Marietta z 45750; rural
Skyline Acres; RMC Place; HAMILTON; ▲ Springfield, Colerain; **218** SK-2; ★ **CIN**; mail Beachwood z 44122, Cincinnati z 45231; ● 500
Skyview Acres; RMC Place; COLUMBIANA; ▲ Yellow Creek; ***217** NK-19; ★ **E.LIV**; mail Wellsville z 43968; rural
Slabtown; RMC Place; ALLEN; ▲ Bath; ***216** NJ-4; elev. 859ft./262m.; ★ **LIMA**; mail Lima z 45801
Slate Mills; RMC Place; ROSS; ▲ Twin, Scioto; ***218** SE-9; mail Chillicothe z 45601; rural
Slaters; RMC Place; NOBLE; ▲ Noble; ***219** SC-16; mail Caldwell z 43724; rural
Sligo; RMC Place; CLINTON; ▲ Adams; **218** SE-5; elev. 970ft./296m.; mail Wilmington z 45177; ● 300
Slocum (Slocums); RMC Place; SCIOTO; ▲ Porter; **218** SI-10; ★ **PTSM**; mail Portsmouth z 45662
Slocums; SCIOTO; see Slocum (RMC Place)
Smith; MCD-Township; BELMONT; ***219** SA-19; mail Belmont z 43718; Ⓟ 1,624; © 1,445
Smith; MCD-Township; MAHONING; ***217** NI-18; ★ **ALLI**; mail Sebring z 44672; Ⓟ 4,892; © 4,977
Smith Corners; RMC Place; MAHONING; ▲ Austintown; ***217** NH-19; elev. 1,023ft./312m.; ★ **YNGS-**; mail Youngstown z 44515
Smithfield; Inc. Place; JEFFERSON; ▲ Smithfield; **217** NM-19; 🅿; ★ **STU-**; z 43948; Ⓟ 722; © 867
Smithfield; MCD-Township; JEFFERSON; ***217** NM-19; 🅿; ★ **STU-**; z 43948; Ⓟ 3,810; © 3,578
Smithfield Station; JEFFERSON; see Weems (RMC Place)
Smithville; Inc. Place; WAYNE; ▲ Green; **217** NI-14; 🅿; z 44677; Ⓟ 1,354; © 1,333
Smithville; RMC Place; WYANDOT; ▲ Crane; ***216** NI-8; mail Upper Sandusky z 43351
Smyrna; RMC Place; HARRISON; ▲ Freeport; **217** NM-17; mail Freeport z 43973, Piedmont z 43983; ● 40
Snodes; RMC Place; MAHONING; ▲ Smith; ***217** NI-18; elev. 1,122ft./342m.; ★ **ALLI**; mail Beloit z 44609
Snowville; RMC Place; MEIGS; ▲ Scipio; ***219** SF-13; mail Albany z 45710; rural
Snyder Terrace; RMC Place; CLARK; ★ **SPR**; mail Springfield z 45504; pop. incl. with Springfield (Inc. Place)
Snyderville; RMC Place; CLARK; ▲ Mad River; **218** SB-5; ★ **SPR**; mail Springfield z 45502; ● 200
Soaptown; RMC Place; TRUMBULL; ***217** NH-19; ★ **YNGS-**; mail Mineral Ridge z 44440, Warren z 44481; pop. incl. with Lordstown (Inc. Place)
Socialville; RMC Place; WARREN; ▲ Deerfield; ***218** SE-3; elev. 935ft./285m.; ★ **CIN**; mail Monroe z 45050
Solon; Inc. Place; CUYAHOGA; **217** NF-16; elev. 1,036ft./316m.; 🅿; ★ **CLEV**; z 44139; Ⓟ 18,548; © 21,802; ◆ 21,354
Somerdale; RMC Place; TUSCARAWAS; ▲ Fairfield; **217** NK-16; elev. 897ft./273m.; 🅿; z 44678; ● 320
Somerford; MCD-Township; MADISON; ***218** SB-7; mail Mechanicsburg z 43044; Ⓟ 2,544; © 6,975; Ⓡ 2,939
Somers; MCD-Township; PREBLE; ***218** SD-2; mail Camden z 45311; Ⓟ 4,226; © 4,245
Somerset; MCD-Township; BELMONT; ***219** SB-18; mail Barnesville z 43713; Ⓟ 1,029; © 1,186
Somerset; Inc. Place; PERRY; ▲ Reading; **219** SC-12; elev. 1,065ft./325m.; 🅿; z 43783; Ⓟ 1,390; © 1,549
Somersville; UNION; see Summersville (RMC Place)
Somerton; RMC Place; BELMONT; ▲ Somerset; **219** SB-18; 🅿; z 43713; ● 180
Somerville; Inc. Place; BUTLER; ▲ Milford; **218** SD-2; 🅿; ★ **CIN**; z 45064; Ⓟ 279; © 294
Sonora; RMC Place; MUSKINGUM; ▲ Perry; **219** SA-14; 🅿; ★ **ZAN**; z 43701; ● 250
South Akron; RMC Place; SUMMIT; ***217** NH-16; ★ **AKR**; pop. incl. with Akron (Inc. Place)
South Amherst; Inc. Place; LORAIN; ▲ New Russia, Amherst; **217** NF-12; elev. 803ft./245m.; 🅿; ★ **CLEV**; z 44001; Ⓟ 1,765; © 1,863
South Arlington; RMC Place; SUMMIT; ★ **AKR**; mail Akron z 44306; pop. incl. with Akron (Inc. Place)
South Bay; RMC Place; KNOX; ▲ Berlin; ***217** NL-11; ★ **MANS**; mail Fredericktown z 43019; rural
South Bloomfield; MCD-Township; MORROW; ***216** NL-10; mail Mount Vernon z 43050; Ⓟ 1,340; © 1,609
South Bloomfield; Inc. Place; PICKAWAY; ▲ Harrison; **218** SC-9; 🅿; ★ **COL**; z 43103; Ⓟ 900; © 1,179
South Bloomingville; RMC Place; HOCKING; ▲ Benton; **219** SE-11; 🅿; z 43152; ● 40
Southbrook; RMC Place; MONTGOMERY; ▲ Washington; ***218** SC-4; ★ **DAY**; mail Dayton z 45409
South Brooklyn; RMC Place; CUYAHOGA; ★ **CLEV**; mail Cleveland z 44144; pop. incl. with Cleveland (Inc. Place)
South Canal; CDP-Census Area Only; TRUMBULL; ▲ Newton; ***217** NG-18; elev. 940ft./287m.; ★ **YNGS-**; mail Newton Falls z 44444; Ⓟ 1,319; © 1,346
South Charleston; Inc. Place; CLARK; ▲ Madison; **218** SB-6; elev. 1,124ft./343m.; 🅿; z 45368; Ⓟ 1,626; © 1,850
South Columbus; RMC Place; FRANKLIN; ***218** SB-9; ★ **COL**; mail Columbus z 43207; pop. incl. with Columbus (Inc. Place)
South Condit; RMC Place; DELAWARE; ▲ Trenton; **216** NM-10; elev. 1,082ft./330m.; mail Sunbury z 43074; ● 110
Southdale; RMC Place; MONTGOMERY; ★ **DAY**; mail Dayton z 45429; pop. incl. with Kettering (Inc. Place)
South Dayton; RMC Place; MONTGOMERY; ★ **DAY**; pop. incl. with Dayton (Inc. Place)
Southern Hills; RMC Place; CLARK; ★ **SPR**; pop. incl. with Springfield (Inc. Place)
Southern Hills; RMC Place; MONTGOMERY; ★ **DAY**; mail Dayton z 45409; pop. incl. with Kettering (Inc. Place)
Southern Knoll; RMC Place; BUTLER; mail Oxford z 45056; pop. incl. with Oxford (Inc. Place)
South Euclid; Inc. Place; CUYAHOGA; **217** NE-16; 🅿 🅲 1,106; ★ **CLEV**; z 44118, z 44121; Ⓟ 23,866; © 23,537; ◆ 21,432
South Excello; RMC Place; BUTLER; ▲ Lemon; ***218** SE-3; ★ **MIDD**; mail Middletown z 45044; pop. incl. with Middletown (Inc. Place)
Southfield Park; RMC Place; FRANKLIN; ★ **COL**; pop. incl. with Columbus (Inc. Place)
Southgate; RMC Place; CLARK; ★ **SPR**; mail Springfield z 45506; pop. incl. with Springfield (Inc. Place)
Southgate Acres; RMC Place; ERIE; ▲ Perkins; ***216** NF-10; ★ **SNDSK**; mail Sandusky z 44870; ● 700
South Hamilton; RMC Place; BUTLER; ★ **CIN**; pop. incl. with Hamilton (Inc. Place)
South Highlands; RMC Place; BUTLER; ***218** SD-3; ★ **MIDD**; mail Middletown z 45042; pop. incl. with Middletown (Inc. Place)
South Hill Park; RMC Place; LUCAS; ▲ Springfield; **216** NB-1; ★ **TOL**; mail Holland z 43528; ● 1,040
Southington; RMC Place; TRUMBULL; ▲ Southington; **217** NG-18; elev. 891ft./272m.; 🅿; ★ **YNGS-**; z 44470; ● 400
Southington; MCD-Township; TRUMBULL; ***217** NG-18; 🅿; ★ **YNGS-**; z 44470; Ⓟ 3,610; © 3,817
South Kingman; RMC Place; CLINTON; ▲ Chester; ***218** SD-5; mail Wilmington z 45177; rural
South Lebanon; Inc. Place; WARREN; ▲ Union, Hamilton; **218** SE-4; 🅿; ★ **CIN**; z 45065; Ⓟ 2,696; © 2,538
South Logan; RMC Place; HOCKING; ***219** SD-12; mail Logan z 43138; pop. incl. with Logan (Inc. Place)
South Lorain; RMC Place; LORAIN; ***217** NF-13; ★ **CLEV**; mail Lorain z 44055; pop. incl. with Lorain (Inc. Place)
South Madison; RMC Place; LAKE; ▲ Madison; ***217** ND-18; ★ **CLEV**; mail Madison z 44057; ● 200
South Middletown; CDP-Census Area Only; BUTLER; ▲ Lemon; ***218** SD-3; elev. 640ft./195m.; ★ **MIDD**; mail Middletown z 45044; Ⓟ 3,491; © 264
South Milford; RMC Place; CLERMONT; ***218** SF-3; ★ **CIN**; mail Milford z 45150
South Moor Shores; RMC Place; AUGLAIZE; ▲ St. Marys; ***216** NK-2; mail Saint Marys z 45885; ● 300
South Mount Vernon (South Vernon); RMC Place; KNOX; ▲ Clinton; ***217** NL-11; mail Mount Vernon z 43050; ● 1,100
South Newark; RMC Place; LICKING; ★ **NWRK**; pop. incl. with Newark (Inc. Place)
South Newbury; RMC Place; GEAUGA; ▲ Newbury; **217** NF-17; elev. 1,152ft./351m.; ★ **CLEV**; mail Burton z 44021; ● 70
South New Lyme; RMC Place; ASHTABULA; ▲ New Lyme; **217** NE-19; elev. 949ft./289m.; mail Rome z 44085; ● 120
South Olive; RMC Place; NOBLE; ▲ Olive; **219** SC-16; mail Caldwell z 43724; ● 40
South Park; RMC Place; ALLEN; ▲ Perry; ★ **LIMA**; mail Lima z 45804; ● 440
South Park; RMC Place; CUYAHOGA; ***217** NF-15; ★ **CLEV**; mail Independence z 44131; pop. incl. with Independence (Inc. Place)
South Park; RMC Place; WYANDOT; ***216** NJ-8; mail Upper Sandusky z 43351; pop. incl. with Upper Sandusky (Inc. Place)
South Perry; RMC Place; HOCKING; ▲ Perry; **219** SD-11; elev. 804ft./245m.; mail Laurelville z 43135; ● 140
South Plymouth; RMC Place; FAYETTE; ▲ Jasper; **218** SD-6; mail Washington Court House z 43160; ● 20
South Point; Inc. Place; LAWRENCE; ▲ Perry, Fayette; **219** SK-11; 🅿; ★ **HNTG**; z 45680; Ⓟ 3,823; © 3,742
Southridge; RMC Place; CLARK; ▲ Springfield; ***218** SB-6; ★ **SPR**; mail Springfield z 45505; ● 300
South Russell; Inc. Place; GEAUGA; **217** NF-16; ★ **CLEV**; mail Chagrin Falls z 44022; Ⓟ 3,402; © 4,022
South Salem; Inc. Place; ROSS; ▲ Buckskin; **218** SE-8; 🅿; z 45681; Ⓟ 227; © 213
South Shore Acres; RMC Place; AUGLAIZE; ▲ Franklin, St. Marys; ***216** NK-2; mail Saint Marys z 45885; ● 150
South Shore Park; RMC Place; LUCAS; ***216** ND-7; ★ **TOL**; mail Oregon z 43618; pop. incl. with Oregon (Inc. Place)
South Side; RMC Place; MAHONING; ***217** NH-20; ★ **YNGS-**; mail Youngstown z 44507; pop. incl. with Youngstown (Inc. Place)
South Side; RMC Place; TUSCARAWAS; ***217** NL-16; mail New Philadelphia z 44663; pop. incl. with New Philadelphia (Inc. Place)
South Solon; Inc. Place; MADISON; ▲ Stokes; **218** SC-6; 🅿; z 43153; Ⓟ 379; © 405
South Vernon; KNOX; see South Mount Vernon (RMC Place)
South Vienna (Vienna); Inc. Place; CLARK; ▲ Harmony; **218** SB-6; 🅿; z 45369; Ⓟ 550; © 469
South Webster; Inc. Place; SCIOTO; ▲ Bloom; **218** SI-10; elev. 702ft./214m.; 🅿; z 45682; Ⓟ 806; © 764
Southwest; RMC Place; RICHLAND; ★ **MANS**; mail Mansfield z 44907; pop. incl. with Mansfield (Inc. Place)
South West Hubbard; RMC Place; TRUMBULL; ▲ Hubbard; **217** NC-14; ★ **YNGS-**; mail Hubbard z 44425; pop. incl. with Hubbard (Inc. Place)
Southwood; RMC Place; ALLEN; ▲ Shawnee; ★ **LIMA**; mail Lima z 45805; ● 340
South Woodbury; RMC Place; MORROW; ▲ Peru; **216** NL-9; mail Marengo z 43334; ● 30
Southworth; RMC Place; ALLEN; ▲ Spencer, Amanda; ***216** NJ-3; mail Delphos z 45833, Spencerville z 45887
South Zanesville; Inc. Place; MUSKINGUM; ▲ Springfield, Newton; **219** SB-14; 🅿; ★ **ZAN**; z 43701-02; Ⓟ 1,969; © 1,936
Spargursville; RMC Place; ROSS; ▲ Twin; ***218** SF-8; mail Bainbridge z 45612; rural
Sparta; Inc. Place; MORROW; ▲ South Bloomfield; **216** NL-10; 🅿; z 43350; Ⓟ 201; © 191
Speaker's Addition; RMC Place; JEFFERSON; ▲ Island Creek; ★ **STU-**; mail Steubenville z 43952
Speidel; RMC Place; BELMONT; ▲ Goshen; ***219** SA-18; mail Bethesda z 43719; ● 50
Spencer; MCD-Township; ALLEN; ***216** NJ-3; mail Spencerville z 45887; Ⓟ 3,120; © 3,106
Spencer; MCD-Township; GUERNSEY; ***219** SB-15; mail Cumberland z 43732; Ⓟ 929; © 1,058
Spencer; MCD-Township; LUCAS; ***216** NE-5; ★ **TOL**; mail Holland z 43528; Ⓟ 1,665; © 1,708
Spencer; Inc. Place; MEDINA; ▲ Spencer; **217** NH-13; 🅿; z 44275; Ⓟ 726; © 747
Spencer; MCD-Township; MEDINA; ***217** NH-13; 🅿; z 44275; Ⓟ 1,786; © 2,429
Spencer Station; GUERNSEY; see Eldon (RMC Place)
Spencerville; Inc. Place; ALLEN; ▲ Spencer; **216** NJ-3; elev. 833ft./254m.; 🅿; z 45887; Ⓟ 2,288; © 2,235
Spokane (Bristolville); RMC Place; TRUMBULL; ▲ Bristol; ***217** NF-19; ★ **YNGS-**; mail Bristolville z 44402; ● 50
Spreading Oaks; RMC Place; ATHENS; ▲ Alexander; mail Athens z 45701; ● 250
Spreng; RMC Place; ASHLAND; rural
Sprigg; MCD-Township; ADAMS; ***218** SI-6; mail Manchester z 45144; Ⓟ 1,499; © 1,639
Springboro; Inc. Place; WARREN, MONTGOMERY; ▲ Clear Creek; **218** SD-3; 🅿; ★ **DAY**; z 45066; Ⓟ 6,590; © 12,380
Springbrook; RMC Place; ERIE; ▲ Margaretta; ***216** NF-9; ★ **SNDSK**; mail Vickery z 43464; ● 50
Springcreek; MCD-Township; MIAMI; ***216** NM-3; mail Piqua z 45356; Ⓟ 1,883; © 1,826
Springdale; Inc. Place; HAMILTON; **218** SF-2; 🅿 ■; ★ **CIN**; z 45246; Ⓟ 10,621; © 10,563; ◆ 11,156
Springfield; Inc. Place; ⊡ CLARK; **217** NB-17; 🅿 🅷 🅲 1,943 ■; ★ **SPR**; z 45501-06; Ⓟ 70,487; © 65,358; Ⓡ 65,736; ◆ 62,151
Springfield; MCD-Township; CLARK; ***218** SB-6; 🅿 🅲 1,943; ★ **SPR**; z 45501-06; Ⓟ 13,352; © 13,424; Ⓡ 13,045
Springfield; MCD-Township; GALLIA; ***219** SH-13; mail Bidwell z 45614; Ⓟ 3,204; © 3,181
Springfield; MCD-Township; HAMILTON; ***218** SF-2; ★ **CIN**; mail Cincinnati z 45231; Ⓟ 38,509; © 37,587
Springfield; MCD-Township; JEFFERSON; ***217** NK-19; mail Amsterdam z 43903; Ⓟ 2,644; © 2,568
Springfield; MCD-Township; LUCAS; ***216** NE-6; ★ **TOL**; mail Holland z 43528; Ⓟ 20,045; © 24,123
Springfield; MCD-Township; MAHONING; ***217** NI-20; ★ **YNGS-**; mail New Middletown z 44442; Ⓟ 6,031; © 6,054
Springfield; MCD-Township; MUSKINGUM; ***219** SB-14; ★ **ZAN**; mail Zanesville z 43701; Ⓟ 5,290; © 5,433
Springfield; MCD-Township; RICHLAND; ***217** NJ-11; ★ **MANS**; mail Mansfield z 44906; Ⓟ 8,460; © 9,674
Springfield; MCD-Township; ROSS; ***218** SE-10; mail Chillicothe z 45601; Ⓟ 2,284; © 2,277
Springfield; MCD-Township; SUMMIT; ***217** NH-16; ★ **AKR**; mail Akron z 44312; Ⓟ 14,773; © 15,168
Springfield; MCD-Township; WILLIAMS; ***216** NF-3; mail Stryker z 43557; Ⓟ 2,607; © 3,227
Springhills; RMC Place; CHAMPAIGN; ▲ Harrison; **216** NM-5; elev. 1,050ft./320m.; mail West Liberty z 43357; ● 150

Entries in **UPPERCASE** are counties.
Entries in **bold** have populations of 2,500 or more.
Names in parentheses are alternate names.

Inc. Place	Incorporated Place
RMC Place	Rand McNally Designated Place
CDP	Census Designated Place
MCD	Minor Civil Division
⊡	County Seat
▲	Minor Civil Division
elev.	Elevation
🅿	Post Office
🅷	Hospital
🅲	College
■	Principal Business Center
★	Ranally Metro Area (RMA) Abbreviation
z	Zip Code(s)
Ⓟ	Previous Census Population
Ⓡ	Revised Census Population
Ⓐ	Annexation Population
●	Rand McNally Population Estimate
©	Final Census Population
Ⓢ	Special Census Population
◆	Estimated Population

For additional definitions see Glossary, Volume 1, and Introduction, Volume 2.

Spring Meadows; RMC Place; HAMILTON; ▲ Springfield; ***218** SF-2; ★ **CIN**; mail Cincinnati z 45231
Spring Mill; RMC Place; RICHLAND; ▲ Springfield; **217** NJ-11; ★ **MANS**; mail Mansfield z 44903; ● 150
Spring Mountain; RMC Place; COSHOCTON; ▲ Monroe; ***217** NL-13; mail Warsaw z 43844; ● 80
Springvale; RMC Place; CLERMONT; ▲ Goshen; ***218** SF-4; elev. 855ft./261m.; ★ **CIN**; mail Loveland z 45140; ● 100
Spring Valley; Inc. Place; GREENE; ▲ Spring Valley; **218** SD-4; 🅿; ★ **DAY**; z 45370; Ⓟ 507; © 510
Spring Valley; MCD-Township; GREENE; ***218** SD-4; 🅿; ★ **DAY**; z 45370; Ⓟ 2,613; © 2,489
Spring Valley; RMC Place; LORAIN; ★ **CLEV**; mail Elyria z 44035; pop. incl. with Elyria (Inc. Place)
Spring Valley; RMC Place; LUCAS; ▲ Springfield; ***216** NE-6; ★ **TOL**; mail Holland z 43528; ● 350
Springville; RMC Place; SENECA; ▲ Big Spring; ***216** NH-7; mail Carey z 43316; ● 25
Springville; RMC Place; WAYNE; ▲ Plain; **217** NJ-13; elev. 1,011ft./308m.; mail Shreve z 44676, Wooster z 44691; ● 40
Springwood; RMC Place; BUTLER; ▲ Oxford, Milford; ***218** SD-1; mail Oxford z 45056; ● 300
Squirrel Town; RMC Place; ADAMS; ▲ Green; ***218** SI-7; mail Stout z 45684
Stafford; Inc. Place; MONROE; ▲ Franklin; **219** SC-17; 🅿; z 43786; Ⓟ 89; © 86
Standardsburg; RMC Place; HURON; ▲ Ridgefield; ***216** NG-10; elev. 740ft./226m.; ★ **SNDSK**; mail Monroeville z 44847; rural
Standley; RMC Place; HENRY, DEFIANCE; ▲ Flatrock, Richland; **216** NG-3; mail Holgate z 43527
Stanleyville; RMC Place; WASHINGTON; ▲ Fearing; **219** SE-17; ★ **PRKB**; mail Whipple z 45788; ● 40
Stantontown; MORROW; see West Liberty (RMC Place)
Stanwood; RMC Place; STARK; ▲ Tuscarawas; **217** NJ-15; ★ **CAN**; mail Navarre z 44662; ● 30
Starbucktown; RMC Place; CLINTON; ▲ Union; ***218** SE-6; mail Wilmington z 45177; rural
STARK; **217** NI-17; Ⓟ 367,585; © 378,098; ◆ 373,842
Starr; RMC Place; HOCKING; ▲ Starr; **219** SE-12; mail New Plymouth z 45654; ● 25
Starr; MCD-Township; HOCKING; ***219** SE-12; mail Nelsonville z 45764; Ⓟ 1,278; © 1,477
Starrs Corners; RMC Place; MAHONING; ▲ Boardman; ***217** NH-19; elev. 1,019ft./311m.; ★ **YNGS-**; mail Canfield z 44406; rural
State Road; RMC Place; SUMMIT; ***217** NG-16; ★ **AKR**; mail Cuyahoga Falls z 44223; pop. incl. with Cuyahoga Falls (Inc. Place)
Station 15; RMC Place; HARRISON; ▲ Monroe; ***217** NL-17; mail Uhrichsville z 44683; rural
Staunton; RMC Place; FAYETTE; ▲ Concord; **218** SE-7; elev. 983ft./300m.; mail Washington Court House z 43160; ● 100
Staunton; RMC Place; MIAMI; ▲ Staunton; **216** NN-3; mail Troy z 45373; ● 120
Staunton; MCD-Township; MIAMI; ***218** SA-4; mail Troy z 45373; Ⓟ 2,040; © 1,992
Steam Corners; RMC Place; MORROW; ▲ Troy; ***216** NJ-10; elev. 1,416ft./432m.; ★ **MANS**; mail Mansfield z 44904
Steinersville; RMC Place; BELMONT; ▲ York; **219** SB-19; mail Powhatan Point z 43942; ● 200
Stelvideo; RMC Place; DARKE; ▲ Adams; **216** NN-2; mail Greenville z 45331; ● 90
Sterling; MCD-Township; BROWN; ***218** SG-5; ★ **CIN**; mail Mount Orab z 45154; Ⓟ 2,377; © 3,753
Sterling; RMC Place; WAYNE; ▲ Milton; **217** NI-14; 🅿; z 44276; ● 600
Sterling Heights; RMC Place; WARREN; ▲ Franklin; ***218** SD-3; ★ **MIDD**; mail Franklin z 45005; ● 950
Steuben; RMC Place; HURON; ▲ Greenfield; **216** NH-10; mail Monroeville z 44847; ● 60
Steubenville; Inc. Place; ⊡ JEFFERSON; **217** NL-20; 🅿 🅷 🅲 2,387 ■; ★ **STU-**; z 43952-53; Ⓟ 22,125; © 19,015; Ⓡ 19,941; ◆ 16,314
Steubenville; MCD-Township; JEFFERSON; ***217** NL-20; 🅿 🅲 2,387; ★ **STU-**; z 43952-53; Ⓟ 5,513; © 4,695
Stewart; RMC Place; ATHENS; ▲ Rome; **219** SF-14; elev. 667ft./203m.; 🅿; z 45778; ● 250
Stewartsville; RMC Place; BELMONT; ▲ Richland; **219** SA-19; 🅿; ★ **WHL**; z 43933; ● 200
Stillwater; RMC Place; TUSCARAWAS; ▲ Rush; **217** NM-17; 🅿; z 44679; ● 150
Stillwell; RMC Place; HOLMES; ▲ Richland; ***217** NL-13; mail Killbuck z 44637; rural
Stiversville; RMC Place; MEIGS; ▲ Lebanon; ***219** SG-15; mail Portland z 45770; rural
Stock; MCD-Township; HARRISON; ***217** NL-17; mail Scio z 43988; Ⓟ 409; © 432
Stock; MCD-Township; NOBLE; ***219** SC-17; mail Caldwell z 43724; Ⓟ 354; © 383
Stockdale; RMC Place; PIKE; ▲ Marion; **218** SH-10; 🅿; z 45683; ● 200
Stockham; RMC Place; SCIOTO; ▲ Washington; ***218** SI-9; ★ **PTSM**; mail Wheelersburg z 45694; ● 230
Stockport; Inc. Place; MORGAN; ▲ Windsor; **219** SD-15; 🅿; z 43787; Ⓟ 462; © 540
Stockton; RMC Place; BUTLER; ***218** SE-2; ★ **CIN**; mail Fairfield z 45014; pop. incl. with Fairfield (Inc. Place)
Stokes; MCD-Township; LOGAN; ***216** NK-5; mail Lakeview z 43331; Ⓟ 4,991; © 5,367
Stokes; MCD-Township; MADISON; ***218** SC-6; mail South Solon z 43153; Ⓟ 747; © 746
Stone; RMC Place; MUSKINGUM; ▲ Harrison; ***219** SC-14; ★ **ZAN**; mail Blue Rock z 43720
Stone Creek; Inc. Place; TUSCARAWAS; ▲ Jefferson; **217** NL-15; 🅿; z 43840; Ⓟ 181; © 184
Stonelick; RMC Place; CLERMONT; ▲ Stonelick; **218** SG-4; ★ **CIN**; mail Batavia z 45103; ● 100
Stonelick; MCD-Township; CLERMONT; ***218** SF-4; ★ **CIN**; mail Batavia z 45103; Ⓟ 5,597; © 5,816
Stony Lake; RMC Place; CARROLL; ▲ Perry; ***217** NL-18; mail Carrollton z 44615; ● 85
Stony Prairie; CDP-Census Area Only; SANDUSKY; ▲ Sandusky; ***216** NF-8; mail Fremont z 43420; Ⓟ 1,536; © 836
Stony Ridge; RMC Place; WOOD; ▲ Troy; **216** NE-7; 🅿; ★ **TOL**; z 43463; ● 400
Stonyrill; RMC Place; WARREN; ▲ Franklin; ***218** SD-3; ★ **MIDD**; mail Franklin z 45005; ● 185
Storms; RMC Place; ROSS; ▲ Twin; ***218** SF-8; mail Bainbridge z 45612; rural
Story Place; RMC Place; ROSS; mail Chillicothe z 45601; pop. incl. with Chillicothe (Inc. Place)
Stout (Rome); Inc. Place; ADAMS; ▲ Green; **218** SI-7; 🅿; z 45684; Ⓟ 99; © 117
Stoutsville; Inc. Place; FAIRFIELD; ▲ Clearcreek; **218** SD-10; 🅿; z 43154; Ⓟ 518; © 581
Stovertown; RMC Place; MUSKINGUM; ▲ Brush Creek; **219** SB-14; mail Zanesville z 43701; ● 35
Stow; Inc. Place; SUMMIT; **217** NH-16; 🅿; ★ **AKR**; z 44224; Ⓟ 27,702; © 32,139; ◆ 31,815
Strasburg; Inc. Place; TUSCARAWAS; ▲ Franklin; **217** NK-16; 🅿; ★ **CAN**; z 44680; Ⓟ 1,995; © 2,310
Stratford; RMC Place; DELAWARE; ▲ Delaware; **216** NM-9; ★ **COL**; mail Delaware z 43015; ● 80
Stratton; Inc. Place; JEFFERSON; ▲ Saline, Knox; **217** NK-20; elev. 676ft./206m.; 🅿; ★ **STU-**; z 43961; Ⓟ 278; © 277
Streetsboro; Inc. Place; PORTAGE; **217** NG-16; elev. 1,137ft./347m.; 🅿; ★ **CLEV**; z 44241; Ⓟ 9,932; © 12,311
Stringtown; RMC Place; ATHENS; ▲ Canaan; ***219** SF-14; elev. 630ft./192m.; mail Athens z 45701; rural
Stringtown; RMC Place; BROWN; ▲ Union; ***218** SI-5; mail Ripley z 45167
Stringtown; RMC Place; CLERMONT; ▲ Franklin; **218** SH-4; mail Felicity z 45120; ● 50
Stringtown; RMC Place; MUSKINGUM; ***219** SA-14; ★ **ZAN**; mail Zanesville z 43701; ● 50
Stringtown; RMC Place; PERRY; ▲ Harrison; ***219** SC-13; ★ **ZAN**; mail Crooksville z 43731; ● 60
Strongs Ridge; RMC Place; HURON; ▲ Lyme; ***216** NG-10; elev. 760ft./232m.; mail Bellevue z 44811
Strongsville; Inc. Place; CUYAHOGA; **217** NG-14; elev. 932ft./284m.; 🅿; ★ **CLEV**; z 44136, z 44149; Ⓟ 35,308; © 43,858; ◆ 42,266
Struthers; Inc. Place; MAHONING; ▲ Poland, Coitsville; **217** NH-20; 🅿; ★ **YNGS-**; z 44471; Ⓟ 12,284; © 11,756
Stryker; Inc. Place; WILLIAMS; ▲ Springfield; **216** NE-2; 🅿; z 43519, z 43557; Ⓟ 1,468; © 1,406
Stuart Manor; RMC Place; JEFFERSON; ▲ Cross Creek; ***217** NL-19; ★ **STU-**; mail Steubenville z 43952; ● 100
Suffield; RMC Place; PORTAGE; ▲ Suffield; **217** NH-16; ★ **AKR**; mail Mogadore z 44260; ● 500
Suffield; MCD-Township; PORTAGE; ***217** NH-16; ★ **AKR**; mail Mogadore z 44260; Ⓟ 6,312; © 6,383
Sugar Bush Knolls; Inc. Place; PORTAGE; **217** NG-16; ★ **CLEV**; mail Kent z 44240; Ⓟ 211; © 227
Sugar Creek; MCD-Township; ALLEN; ***216** NI-4; mail Lima z 45807; Ⓟ 1,311; © 1,330
Sugar Creek (Poston); RMC Place; ATHENS; ▲ Athens; ***219** SE-13; mail Athens z 45701; ● 130
Sugarcreek; MCD-Township; GREENE; ***218** SD-4; ★ **DAY**; mail Bellbrook z 45305; Ⓟ 3,400; © 6,629
Sugar Creek; MCD-Township; PUTNAM; ***216** NI-4; mail Columbus Grove z 45830; Ⓟ 1,131; © 1,156
Sugar Creek; MCD-Township; STARK; ***217** NJ-15; ★ **CAN**; mail Navarre z 44662; Ⓟ 6,489; © 6,740
Sugarcreek; Inc. Place; TUSCARAWAS; ▲ Sugar Creek; **217** NK-15; 🅿; z 44681; Ⓟ 2,062; © 2,174
Sugar Creek; MCD-Township; TUSCARAWAS; ***217** NK-15; mail Sugarcreek z 44681; Ⓟ 3,666; © 3,894
Sugar Creek; MCD-Township; WAYNE; ***217** NJ-15; mail Dalton z 44618; Ⓟ 5,790; © 6,502
Sugar Grove; CLARK; see Sugar Grove Hill (RMC Place)
Sugar Grove; RMC Place; CRAWFORD; ▲ Whetstone; mail Bucyrus z 44820; rural
Sugar Grove; Inc. Place; FAIRFIELD; ▲ Berne; **219** SD-11; 🅿; ★ **LANC**; z 43155; Ⓟ 465; © 448
Sugar Grove; RMC Place; JEFFERSON; ▲ Knox; **217** NK-20; ★ **STU-**; mail Toronto z 43964; ● 160
Sugar Grove; RMC Place; MIAMI; ▲ Newbury; ***218** SA-3; mail Covington z 45318; rural
Sugar Grove; RMC Place; SCIOTO; ▲ Washington; **218** SI-9; ★ **PTSM**; mail West Portsmouth z 45663; ● 150
Sugar Grove Hill (Sugar Grove); RMC Place; CLARK; ▲ Springfield; **217** NB-14; ★ **SPR**; mail Springfield z 45504; ● 300
Sugar Ridge; RMC Place; WOOD; ▲ Middleton; **216** NF-6; ★ **TOL**; mail Bowling Green z 43402; ● 130
Sugar Tree Ridge; RMC Place; HIGHLAND; ▲ Concord; **218** SG-6; mail Hillsboro z 45133; ● 110
Sugar Valley; RMC Place; PREBLE; ▲ Dixon; **218** SC-1; elev. 1,101ft./336m.; mail Eaton z 45320; ● 25
Sullivan; RMC Place; ASHLAND; ▲ Sullivan; **217** NH-12; elev. 1,126ft./343m.; 🅿; z 44880; ● 450
Sullivan; MCD-Township; ASHLAND; ***217** NH-12; 🅿; z 44880; Ⓟ 1,491; © 2,076
Sulphurgrove; RMC Place; MONTGOMERY; ***218** SB-4; elev. 989ft./301m.; ★ **DAY**; mail Dayton z 45424; pop. incl. with Huber Heights (Inc. Place)
Sulphur Springs; RMC Place; CRAWFORD; ▲ Liberty; **216** NI-9; elev. 1,025ft./312m.; 🅿; z 44881; ● 300
Sulphur Springs; RMC Place; PERRY; ▲ Salt Lick; ***219** SD-13; mail Shawnee z 43782; rural
Summerfield; Inc. Place; NOBLE; ▲ Marion; **219** SC-17; 🅿; z 43788; Ⓟ 295; © 296
Summerford; RMC Place; MADISON; ▲ Somerford; **218** SB-7; 🅿; z 43140; ● 250
Summerside; CDP; CLERMONT; ▲ Union; **218** SM-5; elev. 854ft./260m.; ★ **CIN**; mail Cincinnati z 45244; Ⓟ 4,573; © 5,523
Summerside Estates; RMC Place; CLERMONT; ▲ Union; **218** SM-5; ★ **CIN**; mail Cincinnati z 45244; ● 1,700
Summersville (Somersville); RMC Place; UNION; ▲ York; ***216** NL-7; mail Raymond z 43067, Richwood z 43344; ● 80
Summit; RMC Place; HAMILTON; ***218** SG-2; ★ **CIN**; mail Cincinnati z 45238
Summit; LICKING; see Summit Station (RMC Place)
Summit; MCD-Township; MONROE; ***219** SC-17; mail Lewisville z 43754; Ⓟ 728; © 714
Summit; RMC Place; ROSS; ▲ Huntington; ***218** SF-9; mail Chillicothe z 45601; rural
Summit; RMC Place; TRUMBULL; ▲ Weathersfield; **217** NC-13; elev. 1,005ft./306m.; ★ **YNGS-**; mail Girard z 44420; ● 700
SUMMIT; **217** NH-15; Ⓟ 514,990; © 542,899; ◆ 537,299
Summithill; RMC Place; ROSS; **218** SF-9; mail Chillicothe z 45601; ● 20
Summit Station (Summit); RMC Place; LICKING; ***218** SA-10; 🅿; ★ **COL**; z 43073; pop. incl. with Pataskala (Inc. Place)
Summitville; Inc. Place; COLUMBIANA; ▲ Franklin; **217** NJ-19; 🅿; z 43962; Ⓟ 125; © 108
Sumner; RMC Place; MEIGS; ▲ Orange; ***219** SG-14; mail Chester z 45720
Sunbury; Inc. Place; DELAWARE; **216** NM-9; 🅿; ★ **COL**; z 43074; Ⓟ 2,046; © 2,630
Sunbury (Sunsbury); RMC Place; MONTGOMERY; ▲ German; **218** SD-3; ★ **DAY**; mail Germantown z 45327; ● 110
Sundale; RMC Place; MUSKINGUM; ▲ Union; ***219** SB-15; mail Norwich z 43767
Sunfish; MCD-Township; PIKE; ***218** SG-8; mail Piketon z 45661; Ⓟ 1,091; © 1,317
Sunny Acres; RMC Place; JEFFERSON; ▲ Cross Creek; ★ **STU-**; mail Steubenville z 43952; ● 120
Sunnyland; RMC Place; CLARK; ▲ Springfield; **217** NB-15; ★ **SPR**; mail Springfield z 45506; ● 250
Sunny Meade; RMC Place; GUERNSEY; ▲ Cambridge; ***219** SA-16; mail Cambridge z 43725; ● 50
Sunnyside Beach; RMC Place; LORAIN; ★ **CLEV**; mail Vermilion z 44089; pop. incl. with Vermilion (Inc. Place)
Sunsbury; MCD-Township; MONROE; ***219** SB-18; mail Beallsville z 43716; Ⓟ 1,486; © 1,424
Sunsbury; MONTGOMERY; see Sunbury (RMC Place)
Sunset Beach; RMC Place; MAHONING; ▲ Milton; ***217** NH-18; elev. 960ft./293m.; mail Lake Milton z 44429; ● 130
Sunset Heights; RMC Place; BELMONT; ▲ Pease; ***217** NN-19; ★ **WHL**; mail Bridgeport z 43912; ● 200
Sunset Point; RMC Place; LAKE; ▲ Painesville; ***217** ND-17; ★ **CLEV**; mail Painesville z 44077; ● 320
Sunshine; RMC Place; ADAMS; ▲ Green; ***218** SI-8; mail Stout z 45684; rural
Sunshine Park; RMC Place; JEFFERSON; ▲ Cross Creek; ***217** NL-20; ★ **STU-**; mail Steubenville z 43952; ● 120
Superior; MCD-Township; WILLIAMS; ***216** NE-2; mail Montpelier z 43543; Ⓟ 5,571; © 5,769
Surrey Hill; RMC Place; TRUMBULL; ▲ Howland; **217** NB-12; ★ **YNGS-**; mail Warren z 44484; ● 700
Sutton; MCD-Township; MEIGS; ***219** SG-14; mail Racine z 45771; Ⓟ 3,085; © 3,250
Swan; MCD-Township; VINTON; ***219** SE-12; mail Creola z 45622; Ⓟ 696; © 796
Swan Creek; MCD-Township; FULTON; ***216** NE-5; ★ **TOL**; mail Swanton z 43558; Ⓟ 7,699; © 8,461
Swander (Ink); RMC Place; SENECA; ▲ Clinton; ***216** NH-8; mail Tiffin z 44883
Swanders; RMC Place; SHELBY; ▲ Franklin; **216** NL-3; elev. 1,016ft./310m.; mail South Vienna z 45369; ● 80
Swanktown; RMC Place; MONTGOMERY; ▲ Clay; ***218** SB-3; ★ **DAY**; mail Brookville z 45309
Swanton; Inc. Place; FULTON, LUCAS; ▲ Swanton, Fulton, Swan Creek; **216** NE-5; 🅿; ★ **TOL**; z 43558; Ⓟ 3,557; © 3,307
Swanton; MCD-Township; LUCAS; ***216** NE-5; 🅿; ★ **TOL**; z 43558; Ⓟ 3,508; © 3,354
Swauger Valley; SCIOTO; see Harrison Furnace (RMC Place)
Swickards Additions; RMC Place; JEFFERSON; ▲ Cross Creek; ★ **STU-**; mail Steubenville z 43952
Switzerland; MCD-Township; MONROE; ***219** SB-19; mail Powhatan Point z 43942; Ⓟ 501; © 509
Sybene; RMC Place; LAWRENCE; ▲ Fayette; **219** SK-11; elev. 565ft./172m.; ★ **HNTG**; mail South Point z 45680; ● 200
Sycamore; MCD-Township; HAMILTON; ***218** SF-3; ★ **CIN**; mail Cincinnati z 45236, z 45242, z 45249; Ⓟ 20,074; © 19,675
Sycamore; Inc. Place; WYANDOT; ▲ Sycamore; **216** NI-8; 🅿; z 44882 & mail Cincinnati z 45249; Ⓟ 919; © 914
Sycamore; MCD-Township; WYANDOT; ***216** NI-8; 🅿; z 44882 & mail Cincinnati z 45249; Ⓟ 1,560; © 1,598
Sycamore Valley; RMC Place; MONROE; ▲ Bethel; **219** SC-17; ● 25
Sychar Road; RMC Place; KNOX; ▲ Clinton; mail Mount Vernon z 43050
Sylvania; Inc. Place; LUCAS; ▲ Sylvania; **216** ND-6; 🅿 🅷 🅲 2,035; ★ **TOL**; z 43560; Ⓟ 17,301; © 18,670
Sylvania; MCD-Township; LUCAS; ***216** ND-6; 🅿 🅲 2,035; ★ **TOL**; z 43560 & mail Toledo z 43615, z 43617, z 43623; Ⓟ 39,983; © 44,253
Symmes; RMC Place; BUTLER; ***218** SE-2; elev. 583ft./178m.; ★ **CIN**; mail Fairfield z 45014; pop. incl. with Fairfield (Inc. Place)
Symmes; MCD-Township; HAMILTON; ***218** SF-3; 🅿; ★ **CIN**; z 45249 & mail Loveland z 45140; Ⓟ 11,769; © 14,771
Symmes; MCD-Township; LAWRENCE; ***219** SI-11; mail Waterloo z 45688; Ⓟ 412; © 470
Syracuse; Inc. Place; MEIGS; ▲ Sutton; **219** SG-14; 🅿; z 45779; Ⓟ 827; © 879

T

Taborville; RMC Place; GEAUGA; ▲ Auburn; ***217** NF-17; ★ **CLEV**; mail Chagrin Falls z 44022; ● 270
Tacoma; RMC Place; BELMONT; ▲ Warren; **219** SA-18; mail Barnesville z 43713; ● 100
Taft; RMC Place; HAMILTON; ***218** SF-3; 🅿; ★ **CIN**; z 45213, z 45236; pop. incl. with Silverton (Inc. Place)
Tallmadge; Inc. Place; SUMMIT, PORTAGE; **217** NH-16; 🅿; ★ **AKR**; z 44278; Ⓟ 14,870; © 16,390
Tama; RMC Place; MERCER; ▲ Hopewell; ***216** NK-1; elev. 834ft./254m.; mail Celina z 45822
Tarlton; Inc. Place; PICKAWAY; ▲ Saltcreek; **218** SD-10; elev. 802ft./244m.; 🅿; z 43156; Ⓟ 315; © 298
Tate; MCD-Township; CLERMONT; ***218** SH-4; ★ **CIN**; mail Bethel z 45106; Ⓟ 8,399; © 8,935
Tatmans; RMC Place; PERRY; ▲ Pleasant, Bearfield; ***219** SC-13; mail Corning z 43730; ● 25
Tawawa; RMC Place; SHELBY; ▲ Green; **216** NM-4; mail Sidney z 45365; ● 100
Taylor; RMC Place; FRANKLIN; ***218** SA-10; ★ **COL**; mail Columbus z 43230
Taylor; MCD-Township; UNION; ***216** NM-7; mail Richwood z 43344; Ⓟ 1,266; © 1,444
Taylor Creek; MCD-Township; HARDIN; ***216** NK-6; mail Kenton z 43326; Ⓟ 460; © 517
Taylorsburg; RMC Place; MONTGOMERY; **218** SB-3; ★ **DAY**; mail Clayton z 45315; pop. incl. with Trotwood (Inc. Place)
Taylors Creek; RMC Place; HAMILTON; ▲ Green, Colerain; **218** SK-1; elev. 520ft./158m.; ★ **CIN**; mail Cincinnati z 45239; ● 660
Taylorsville; RMC Place; HIGHLAND; ▲ Whiteoak; ***218** SG-6; mail Hillsboro z 45133
Taylorsville; MUSKINGUM; see Philo (Inc. Place)
Taylortown; RMC Place; JEFFERSON; ▲ Island Creek; ***217** NL-20; ★ **STU-**; mail Toronto z 43964; ● 300
Taylortown; RMC Place; RICHLAND; ▲ Jackson; ***217** NI-11; ★ **MANS**; mail Shelby z 44875
Tedrow; RMC Place; FULTON; ▲ Dover; **216** NE-3; elev. 774ft./236m.; mail Wauseon z 43567; ● 160
Teegarden; RMC Place; COLUMBIANA; ▲ Salem; ***217** NI-19; elev. 991ft./302m.; mail Lisbon z 44432; rural
Temperanceville; RMC Place; BELMONT; ▲ Somerset; **219** SB-17; mail Barnesville z 43713; ● 80
Ten Hills; RMC Place; ALLEN; ▲ Shawnee; ***216** NJ-4; ★ **LIMA**; mail Lima z 45805; ● 135
Tennyson; RMC Place; PIKE; ▲ Newton; ***218** SG-9; mail Piketon z 45661; rural
Terminal Junction; RMC Place; BELMONT; ★ **WHL**; pop. incl. with Martins Ferry (Inc. Place)
Terrace Park; Inc. Place; HAMILTON; **218** SL-5; 🅿; ★ **CIN**; z 45174; Ⓟ 2,133; © 2,273
Terre Haute; RMC Place; CHAMPAIGN; ▲ Mad River; **216** NN-5; elev. 1,084ft./330m.; mail Urbana z 43078; ● 180
Terry Acres; RMC Place; GREENE; ▲ Bath; **218** SL-10; ★ **DAY**; mail Fairborn z 45324; ● 165
Texas; MCD-Township; CRAWFORD; ***216** NI-8; mail Sycamore z 44882; Ⓟ 420; © 409
Texas; RMC Place; HENRY; ▲ Washington; **216** NF-5; mail Liberty Center z 43532; ● 130
Thackery; RMC Place; CHAMPAIGN; ▲ Mad River, Jackson; **216** NN-5; elev. 1,119ft./341m.; mail Springfield z 45502, Urbana z 43078; ● 120
Thatcher; RMC Place; PICKAWAY; ▲ Washington, Pickaway; ***218** SD-10; mail Circleville z 43113
The Avenue; RMC Place; TRUMBULL; ▲ Brookfield; ★ **SHAR**; mail Masury z 44438
The Bend; RMC Place; DEFIANCE; ▲ Delaware; **216** NG-2; mail Defiance z 43512; ● 100
The Eastern; RMC Place; JEFFERSON; ▲ Springfield; ***217** NK-19; mail Bergholz z 43908; rural
The Plains; CDP; ATHENS; ▲ Athens; **219** SE-13; 🅿; z 45780; Ⓟ 2,644; © 2,931
The Village of Indian Hill (Indian Hill); Inc. Place; HAMILTON; **218** SK-5; ★ **CIN**; mail Cincinnati z 45243; Ⓟ 5,383; © 5,907
Thivener; RMC Place; GALLIA; **219** SI-13; rural
Thomastown; RMC Place; SUMMIT; ***217** NH-16; ★ **AKR**; pop. incl. with Akron (Inc. Place)
Thompson; MCD-Township; DELAWARE; ***216** NL-8; mail Radnor z 43066; Ⓟ 582; © 558
Thompson; RMC Place; GEAUGA; ▲ Thompson; **217** ND-18; 🅿; ★ **CLEV**; z 44086; ● 370
Thompson; MCD-Township; GEAUGA; ***217** ND-18; 🅿; ★ **CLEV**; z 44086; Ⓟ 2,219; © 2,383
Thompson; MCD-Township; SENECA; ***216** NG-9; mail Flat Rock z 44828; Ⓟ 1,477; © 1,422
Thorn; MCD-Township; PERRY; ***219** SB-12; ★ **COL**; mail Thornville z 43076; Ⓟ 3,454; © 3,765
Thornport; RMC Place; PERRY; ▲ Thorn; ***219** SB-12; ★ **COL**; mail Thornville z 43076; ● 370
Thornville; Inc. Place; PERRY; ▲ Thorn; **219** SB-12; 🅿; ★ **COL**; z 43076; Ⓟ 758; © 731
Thorny Acres; RMC Place; WARREN; ▲ Franklin; ***218** SD-3; ★ **MIDD**; mail Middletown z 45042; pop. incl. with Middletown (Inc. Place)
Three Locks; RMC Place; ROSS; ▲ Franklin; ***218** SF-10; mail Chillicothe z 45601; rural
Thrifton; RMC Place; ROSS; ▲ Buckskin; **218** SE-7; mail Greenfield z 45123; ● 40
Thurman (Centerville); Inc. Place; GALLIA; ▲ Raccoon; **219** SH-12; 🅿; z 45685; Ⓟ 128; © 134
Thurston; Inc. Place; FAIRFIELD; ▲ Walnut; **219** SB-11; elev. 881ft./269m.; 🅿; ★ **LANC**; z 43157; Ⓟ 539; © 555
Tiffany Acres; RMC Place; CLARK; ▲ Mad River; ***218** SB-5; ★ **SPR**; mail Springfield z 45502; ● 50
Tiffin; MCD-Township; ADAMS; ***218** SI-7; mail West Union z 45693; Ⓟ 5,144; © 5,075
Tiffin; MCD-Township; DEFIANCE; ***216** NF-2; mail Defiance z 43512; Ⓟ 1,772; © 1,705
Tiffin; Inc. Place; ⊡ SENECA; **216** NH-8; 🅿 🅷 🅲 3,560 ■; z 44883; Ⓟ 18,604; © 18,135; ◆ 17,764
Tiltonsville (Tiltonville); Inc. Place; JEFFERSON; ▲ Warren; **217** NM-19; 🅿; ★ **WHL**; z 43963; Ⓟ 1,517; © 1,329
Tiltonville; JEFFERSON; see Tiltonsville (Inc. Place)
Timberlake; Inc. Place; LAKE; **217** ND-16; 🅿; ★ **CLEV**; z 44095 & mail Willoughby z 44094; Ⓟ 833; © 775
Timberview; RMC Place; UNION; ▲ Paris; ***216** NM-7; mail Marysville z 43040; pop. incl. with Marysville (Inc. Place)
Tinney; RMC Place; SANDUSKY; ▲ Scott; ***216** NG-7; mail Helena z 43435; ● 30
Tipp City (Tippecanoe City); Inc. Place; MIAMI; ▲ Monroe; **218** SB-4; 🅿; ★ **DAY**; z 45371; Ⓟ 6,027; © 9,221
Tippecanoe; RMC Place; HARRISON; ▲ Washington; **217** NM-17; 🅿; z 44699; ● 200
Tippecanoe City; MIAMI; see Tipp City (Inc. Place)
Tipton; RMC Place; PAULDING; ▲ Blue Creek; **216** NH-1; elev. 749ft./228m.; mail Haviland z 45851; ● 25
Tiro; Inc. Place; CRAWFORD; ▲ Auburn; **216** NI-10; 🅿; z 44887; Ⓟ 246; © 281
Tiverton; RMC Place; COSHOCTON; ▲ Tiverton; **217** NL-13; mail Brinkhaven z 43006, Walhonding z 43843; ● 80
Tiverton; MCD-Township; COSHOCTON; ***217** NL-13; mail Brinkhaven z 43006; Ⓟ 291; © 348
Toboso; RMC Place; LICKING; ▲ Hanover; **217** NN-12; ★ **NWRK**; mail Newark z 43055; ● 200
Tod; MCD-Township; CRAWFORD; ***216** NI-8; mail Sycamore z 44882; Ⓟ 746; © 739
Todds; RMC Place; MORGAN; ▲ Marion; ***219** SD-15; elev. 983ft./300m.; mail Chesterhill z 43728, Stockport z 43787; rural
Tokio; VAN WERT; see Jonestown (RMC Place)
Toledo; Inc. Place; ⊡ LUCAS; **216** NE-6; 🅿 🅷 🅲 21,369 ■; ★ **TOL**; z 43601, z 43603-15, z 43617, z 43620, z 43623, z 43635, z 43652, z 43654, z 43656-57, z 43659-61, z 43666-67, z 43681-82, z 43697, z 43699; Ⓟ 332,943; © 313,619; Ⓡ 313,782; ◆ 293,189
Toledo Yard (Presque Isle); RMC Place; LUCAS; ★ **TOL**; mail Oregon z 43618; pop. incl. with Oregon (Inc. Place)
Tom Corwin; RMC Place; JACKSON; ▲ Coal; ***219** SG-11; mail Wellston z 45692; rural
Tomlison Addition; RMC Place; SCIOTO; ▲ Valley; ***218** SH-9; ★ **PTSM**; mail Lucasville z 45648; ● 300
Tontogany; Inc. Place; WOOD; ▲ Washington; **216** NF-6; 🅿; ★ **TOL**; z 43565; Ⓟ 364; © 364
Torch; RMC Place; ATHENS; ▲ Troy; **219** SF-15; elev. 730ft./223m.; 🅿; z 45723; ● 300
Toronto; Inc. Place; JEFFERSON; ▲ Knox, Island Creek; **217** NL-20; 🅿; ★ **STU-**; z 43964; Ⓟ 6,127; © 5,676
Town and Country Estates; RMC Place; MONTGOMERY; ▲ Washington; ★ **DAY**; mail Dayton z 45429; pop. incl. with Christiansburg (Inc. Place)
Townsend; MCD-Township; HURON; ***217** NG-11; mail Collins z 44826; Ⓟ 1,571; © 1,567
Townsend; MCD-Township; SANDUSKY; ***216** NF-9; mail Vickery z 43464; Ⓟ 1,528; © 1,670
Townview; RMC Place; MONTGOMERY; ***218** SC-3; ★ **DAY**; mail Dayton z 45427; pop. incl. with Dayton (Inc. Place)
Townwood; RMC Place; PUTNAM; ▲ Van Buren; **216** NH-5; elev. 743ft./226m.; mail Leipsic z 45856; ● 25
Tradersville; RMC Place; MADISON; ▲ Somerford; ***218** SA-7; mail London z 43140, Mechanicsburg z 43044; rural
Trail; RMC Place; HOLMES; ▲ Walnut Creek; **217** NK-15; elev. 1,156ft./352m.; mail Dundee z 44624
Trailerville Mobile Home Park; RMC Place; ASHLAND; ***217** NI-12; mail Ashland z 44805; pop. incl. with Ashland (Inc. Place)
Trail Run; RMC Place; MONROE; ▲ Benton; ***219** SD-18; mail New Matamoras z 45767, Sardis z 43946; rural
Tranquility; RMC Place; ADAMS; ▲ Scott; **218** SH-7; mail Seaman z 45679; ● 30
Traschel; RMC Place; MARION; ▲ Marion; ★ **MRN**; mail Marion z 43302; ● 500
Trebein; RMC Place; GREENE; ▲ Beavercreek; ***218** SC-5; ★ **DAY**; mail Dayton z 45434
Tremont City; Inc. Place; CLARK; ▲ German; **218** SA-5; 🅿; ★ **SPR**; z 45372; Ⓟ 493; © 349
Trenton; Inc. Place; BUTLER; **218** SD-2; 🅿; ★ **MIDD**; z 45067; Ⓟ 6,189; © 8,746
Trenton; MCD-Township; DELAWARE; ***216** NM-10; mail Galena z 43021; Ⓟ 1,906; © 2,137
Trenton; JEFFERSON; see Emerson (RMC Place)
Triadelphia; RMC Place; MORGAN; ▲ Deerfield; **219** SC-14; mail Malta z 43758; ● 40
Trimble; Inc. Place; ATHENS; ▲ Trimble; **219** SE-13; 🅿; z 45782; Ⓟ 441; © 466
Trimble; MCD-Township; ATHENS; ***219** SD-13; 🅿; z 45782; Ⓟ 4,716; © 4,710
Trinway; RMC Place; MUSKINGUM; ▲ Cass; **217** NN-13; 🅿; z 43842; ● 380
Tri-Village; RMC Place; FRANKLIN; ★ **COL**; mail Columbus z 43212; pop. incl. with Columbus (Inc. Place)
Trotwood; Inc. Place; MONTGOMERY; **218** SC-3; 🅿 🅲 303 ■; ★ **DAY**; z 45406, z 45415-16, z 45418, z 45426-27; Ⓟ 8,816; © 27,420; ◆ 25,746
Trowbridge; RMC Place; OTTAWA; ▲ Benton; **216** NE-8; mail Graytown z 43432; ● 50
Troy; MCD-Township; ASHLAND; ***217** NH-12; mail Nova z 44859; Ⓟ 887; © 1,051
Troy; MCD-Township; ATHENS; ***219** SF-15; ★ **PRKB**; mail Coolville z 45723; Ⓟ 2,588; © 2,712
Troy; MCD-Township; DELAWARE; ***216** NL-9; mail Delaware z 43015; Ⓟ 2,261; © 2,665
Troy; MCD-Township; GEAUGA; ***217** NF-17; mail Burton z 44021; Ⓟ 1,903; © 2,567
Troy; Inc. Place; ⊡ MIAMI; ▲ Concord; **216** NN-3; 🅿 🅷 ■; z 45373-74; Ⓟ 19,478; © 21,999; ◆ 21,579
Troy; MCD-Township; MORROW; ***216** NJ-10; ★ **MANS**; mail Mansfield z 44901; Ⓟ 1,096; © 1,190
Troy; MCD-Township; RICHLAND; ***217** NJ-11; ★ **MANS**; mail Mansfield z 44904; Ⓟ 6,179; © 6,449
Troy; MCD-Township; WOOD; ***216** NF-7; ★ **TOL**; mail Luckey z 43443; Ⓟ 3,848; © 4,355
Truetown; RMC Place; ATHENS; ▲ Dover; ***219** SE-13; elev. 701ft./214m.; mail Millfield z 45761; ● 40
Trumbull; RMC Place; ASHTABULA; ▲ Trumbull; **217** ND-18; mail Geneva z 44041, Rock Creek z 44084; ● 200
Trumbull; MCD-Township; ASHTABULA; ***217** ND-18; mail Geneva z 44041; Ⓟ 1,286; © 1,461
TRUMBULL; **217** NF-19; Ⓟ 227,813; © 225,116; ◆ 205,402
Truro; RMC Place; FRANKLIN; ★ **COL**; mail Reynoldsburg z 43068; pop. incl. with Columbus (Inc. Place)
Truro; MCD-Township; FRANKLIN; ***218** SB-10; ★ **COL**; mail Reynoldsburg z 43068; Ⓟ 26,265; © 27,151; Ⓡ 27,065
Tuckaho; RMC Place; ASHTABULA; ▲ Andover; mail Andover z 44003; ● 85
Tucson; RMC Place; ROSS; ▲ Harrison; ***218** SE-10; elev. 719ft./219m.; mail Chillicothe z 45601
Tully; MCD-Township; MARION; ***216** NK-9; mail Caledonia z 43314; Ⓟ 744; © 738
Tully; MCD-Township; VAN WERT; ***216** NI-1; mail Convoy z 45832; Ⓟ 2,134; © 2,119
Tunnel; RMC Place; WASHINGTON; ▲ Warren; ***219** SE-16; elev. 803ft./245m.; ★ **PRKB**; mail Marietta z 45750; rural
Tunnel Hill; RMC Place; COSHOCTON; ▲ Bedford; ***217** NM-13; mail Warsaw z 43844
Tuppers Plains; RMC Place; MEIGS; ▲ Orange; **219** SF-15; elev. 740ft./226m.; 🅿; z 45783; ● 350
Turpin Hills; CDP; HAMILTON; ▲ Anderson; **218** SM-4; ★ **CIN**; mail Cincinnati z 45244; Ⓟ 4,927; © 4,960
Turtle Creek; MCD-Township; SHELBY; ***216** NL-3; mail Sidney z 45365; Ⓟ 1,301; © 1,583
Turtlecreek; MCD-Township; WARREN; ***218** SE-3; mail Lebanon z 45036; partly in ★ MIDD; Ⓟ 10,391; © 12,617
Tuscarawas; MCD-Township; COSHOCTON; ***217** NM-14; mail Coshocton z 43812; Ⓟ 2,151; © 1,798
Tuscarawas; MCD-Township; STARK; ***217** NJ-15; ★ **CAN**; mail Massillon z 44646; Ⓟ 6,251; © 6,093
Tuscarawas; Inc. Place; TUSCARAWAS; ▲ Warwick; **217** NL-16; 🅿; z 44682; Ⓟ 826; © 934
TUSCARAWAS; **217** NM-16; Ⓟ 84,090; © 90,914; ◆ 90,475
Twenty Mile Stand; RMC Place; WARREN; ▲ Deerfield; **218** SJ-5; elev. 831ft./253m.; ★ **CIN**; mail Loveland z 45140, Maineville z 45039; ● 300
Twightwee; RMC Place; HAMILTON; ▲ Symmes; ***218** SF-3; ★ **CIN**; mail Loveland z 45140
Twin; MCD-Township; DARKE; ***218** SB-2; ★ **DAY**; mail Arcanum z 45304; Ⓟ 3,899; © 3,946
Twin; MCD-Township; PREBLE; ***218** SC-2; ★ **DAY**; mail West Alexandria z 45381; Ⓟ 2,826; © 2,831
Twin; MCD-Township; ROSS; ***218** SF-8; mail Bourneville z 45617; Ⓟ 2,755; © 3,146
Twin Lakes; RMC Place; PORTAGE; ▲ Franklin; **217** NG-16; ★ **AKR**; mail Kent z 44240; ● 300
Twin Mobile Home Park; RMC Place; ASHLAND; ***217** NI-12; mail Ashland z 44805; pop. incl. with Ashland (Inc. Place)
Twinsburg; Inc. Place; SUMMIT; **217** NG-16; elev. 1,004ft./306m.; 🅿; ★ **CLEV**; z 44087; Ⓟ 9,606; © 17,006
Twinsburg; MCD-Township; SUMMIT; ***217** NG-16; 🅿; ★ **CLEV**; z 44087; Ⓟ 1,896; © 2,153
Twin Valley; RMC Place; SCIOTO; ▲ Clay; **218** SI-9; elev. 658ft./201m.; ★ **PTSM**; mail Portsmouth z 45662; ● 300
Two Hundred Ten Row; RMC Place; ATHENS; ▲ Athens; ***219** SE-13; mail Athens z 45701; rural
Tymochtee; RMC Place; WYANDOT; ▲ Tymochtee; **216** NI-8; elev. 802ft./244m.; mail Upper Sandusky z 43351; ● 25
Tymochtee; MCD-Township; WYANDOT; ***216** NI-8; mail Sycamore z 44882; Ⓟ 1,127; © 1,186
Tyndall; RMC Place; COSHOCTON; ▲ Franklin; **217** NM-14; elev. 765ft./233m.; mail Coshocton z 43812; ● 150

U

Uhrichsville; Inc. Place; TUSCARAWAS; ▲ Mill; **217** NL-16; 🅿; z 44683; Ⓟ 5,604; © 5,662
Union; RMC Place; ATHENS; ▲ Athens; ***219** SF-13; mail New Marshfield z 45766; ● 200
Union; MCD-Township; AUGLAIZE; ***216** NK-4; mail Wapakoneta z 45895; Ⓟ 1,695; © 1,870
Union; MCD-Township; BELMONT; ***219** SA-18; mail Morristown z 43759; Ⓟ 2,029; © 2,151
Union; MCD-Township; BROWN; ***218** SI-5; mail Ripley z 45167; Ⓟ 3,068; © 3,015
Union; BUTLER; see West Chester (MCD-Township)
Union; MCD-Township; CARROLL; ***217** NK-18; mail Carrollton z 44615; Ⓟ 900; © 1,059
Union; MCD-Township; CHAMPAIGN; ***218** SA-6; mail Cable z 43009; Ⓟ 1,651; © 1,920
Union; MCD-Township; CLERMONT; ***218** SG-3; ★ **CIN**; mail Cincinnati z 45245; Ⓟ 33,368; © 42,332
Union; MCD-Township; CLINTON; ***218** SE-5; 🅲 1,569; mail Wilmington z 45177; Ⓟ 13,379; © 14,929; Ⓡ 3,054
Union; MCD-Township; FAYETTE; ***218** SD-7; mail Washington Court House z 43160; Ⓟ 3,718; © 3,808
Union; MCD-Township; HANCOCK; ***216** NI-5; mail Rawson z 45881; Ⓟ 1,800; © 1,726
Union; MCD-Township; HIGHLAND; ***218** SF-6; mail Hillsboro z 45133; Ⓟ 1,037; © 1,710
Union; MCD-Township; KNOX; ***217** NL-12; mail Danville z 43014; Ⓟ 2,150; © 2,455
Union; LAWRENCE; see Union Landing Siding (RMC Place)
Union; MCD-Township; LAWRENCE; ***219** SK-12; ★ **HNTG**; mail Chesapeake z 45619; Ⓟ 9,139; © 9,002
Union; MCD-Township; LICKING; ***219** SB-11; ★ **NWRK**; mail Hebron z 43025; Ⓟ 7,730; © 8,339
Union; MCD-Township; LOGAN; ***216** NM-5; mail Bellefontaine z 43311; Ⓟ 668; © 787
Union; MCD-Township; MADISON; ***218** SB-7; mail London z 43140; Ⓟ 5,203; © 1,411; Ⓡ 5,447
Union; MCD-Township; MERCER; ***216** NJ-2; mail Mendon z 45862; Ⓟ 1,527; © 1,490
Union; MCD-Township; MIAMI; ***218** SB-3; ★ **DAY**; mail West Milton z 45383; Ⓟ 10,331; © 10,222
Union; Inc. Place; MONTGOMERY, MIAMI; ▲ Butler, Union; **218** SB-3; 🅿; ★ **DAY**; z 45322; Ⓟ 5,501; © 5,574
Union; MCD-Township; MORGAN; ***219** SD-14; mail Malta z 43758; Ⓟ 531; © 607
Union; MCD-Township; MUSKINGUM; ***219** SB-15; 🅲 2,165; mail New Concord z 43762; Ⓟ 3,687; © 4,359
Union; MCD-Township; PIKE; ***218** SG-10; mail Lucasville z 45648; Ⓟ 1,147; © 1,240
Union; MCD-Township; PUTNAM; ***216** NI-3; mail Fort Jennings z 45844; Ⓟ 2,477; © 2,557
Union; MCD-Township; ROSS; ***218** SE-9; mail Frankfort z 45628; Ⓟ 8,160; © 11,750
Union; MCD-Township; SCIOTO; ***218** SI-9; mail Mc Dermott z 45652; Ⓟ 1,960; © 2,105
Union; MCD-Township; TUSCARAWAS; ***217** NL-17; mail Dennison z 44621; Ⓟ 1,207; © 1,599
Union; MCD-Township; UNION; ***216** NM-7; mail Milford Center z 43045; Ⓟ 1,658; © 1,565
Union; MCD-Township; VAN WERT; ***216** NI-2; mail Van Wert z 45891; Ⓟ 1,032; © 1,009
Union; MCD-Township; WARREN; ***218** SE-4; ★ **CIN**; mail Lebanon z 45036; Ⓟ 4,631; © 4,668
UNION; **216** NM-7; Ⓟ 31,969; © 40,909; ◆ 49,417
Union City; Inc. Place; DARKE; ▲ Jackson; **216** NM-1; see also Union City, IN; 🅿; z 45390; Ⓟ 1,984; © 1,767
Union Furnace; RMC Place; HOCKING; ▲ Starr; **219** SE-12; elev. 748ft./228m.; 🅿; z 43158; ● 430
Union Landing Siding (Union); RMC Place; LAWRENCE; ▲ Hamilton; ***218** SJ-10; ★ **HNTG**; mail Ironton z 45638; ● 40
Union Plains; RMC Place; BROWN; ▲ Green; ***218** SG-5; mail Mount Orab z 45154; rural
Unionport; RMC Place; JEFFERSON; ▲ Wayne; **217** NL-19; 🅿; ★ **STU-**; z 43910; ● 150
Union Station (Kylesburg); RMC Place; LICKING; ▲ Union; **219** SA-11; ★ **NWRK**; mail Hebron z 43025
Uniontown; RMC Place; BELMONT; ▲ Wheeling; **217** NN-18; mail Saint Clairsville z 43950; ● 230
Uniontown; CDP; STARK; ▲ Lake; **217** NI-16; 🅿; ★ **AKR**; z 44685; Ⓟ 3,074; © 2,802
Unionvale; RMC Place; HARRISON; ▲ Green; **217** NM-18; elev. 982ft./299m.; mail Cadiz z 43907; ● 90
Unionville; RMC Place; ASHTABULA, LAKE; ▲ Madison, Harpersfield; **217** ND-18; 🅿; ★ **CLEV**; z 44088; ● 500
Unionville; RMC Place; MORGAN; ▲ Meigsville; ***219** SD-15; elev. 666ft./203m.; mail McConnelsville z 43756; ● 30
Unionville; UNION; see Unionville Center (Inc. Place)
Unionville; RMC Place; WASHINGTON; ***219** SE-16; ★ **PRKB**; mail Marietta z 45750
Unionville Center (Unionville); Inc. Place; UNION; ▲ Darby; **216** NN-7; 🅿; z 43077; Ⓟ 238; © 299
Uniopolis; Inc. Place; AUGLAIZE; ▲ Union; **216** NK-4; elev. 935ft./285m.; 🅿; z 45888; Ⓟ 261; © 256
Unity; RMC Place; ADAMS; ▲ Oliver; **218** SH-7; mail West Union z 45693; ● 30
Unity; RMC Place; COLUMBIANA; ▲ Unity; **217** NI-20; mail East Palestine z 44413; ● 100
Unity; MCD-Township; COLUMBIANA; ***217** NI-20; mail East Palestine z 44413; Ⓟ 10,129; © 10,294
University Center; RMC Place; CUYAHOGA; ★ **CLEV**; mail Cleveland z 44106; pop. incl. with Cleveland (Inc. Place)
University Heights; RMC Place; ALLEN; ▲ Bath; ★ **LIMA**; mail Lima z 45804; ● 600
University Heights; Inc. Place; CUYAHOGA; **217** NF-16; 🅿; ★ **CLEV**; z 44118, z 44122; Ⓟ 14,790; © 14,146
University View; RMC Place; FRANKLIN; ▲ Clinton; **219** SH-18; ★ **COL**; mail Columbus z 43212; ● 500
Upland Heights; RMC Place; BELMONT, JEFFERSON; ▲ Warren; ***217** NM-19; ★ **WHL**; mail Rayland z 43943, Yorkville z 43971; ● 200
Upper; MCD-Township; LAWRENCE; ***219** SJ-11; ★ **HNTG**; mail Kitts Hill z 45645; Ⓟ 17,136; © 15,648
Upper Arlington; RMC Place; BUTLER; ***218** SD-3; ★ **MIDD**; mail Middletown z 45042; pop. incl. with Middletown (Inc. Place)
Upper Arlington; Inc. Place; FRANKLIN; **218** SA-9; 🅿 ■; ★ **COL**; z 43212, z 43220-21; Ⓟ 34,128; © 33,686; ◆ 36,527
Upper Five Mile; RMC Place; BROWN; ▲ Green; ***218** SG-5; ★ **CIN**; mail Mount Orab z 45154; rural
Upper Fox Hollow; RMC Place; CLARK; ▲ German; ***218** SB-5; ★ **SPR**; mail Springfield z 45502; ● 100
Upper Lowell; RMC Place; WASHINGTON; ▲ Adams; ***219** SD-16; mail Lowell z 45744; ● 30
Upper Sandusky; Inc. Place; ⊡ WYANDOT; ▲ Crane; **216** NJ-8; elev. 861ft./262m.; 🅿 🅷; z 43351; Ⓟ 5,906; © 6,533
Urbana; Inc. Place; ⊡ CHAMPAIGN; ▲ Urbana; **216** NN-5; 🅿 🅷 🅲 1,571; z 43078; Ⓟ 11,353; © 11,613
Urbana; MCD-Township; CHAMPAIGN; ***218** SA-6; 🅿 🅲 1,571; z 43078; includes the City of Urbana; Ⓟ 14,770; © 14,968
Urbancrest; Inc. Place; FRANKLIN; ▲ Jackson; **218** SB-9; 🅿; ★ **COL**; z 43123; Ⓟ 862; © 868
Utica; Inc. Place; LICKING, KNOX; ▲ Washington; **217** NM-11; elev. 967ft./295m.; 🅿; ★ **NWRK**; z 43080; Ⓟ 1,997; © 2,130; Ⓡ 2,141
Utica; RMC Place; WARREN; ▲ Wayne; ***218** SD-4; ★ **DAY**; mail Lebanon z 45036
Utopia; RMC Place; CLERMONT; ▲ Morgan; **218** SI-4; ★ **CIN**; mail Georgetown z 45121; ● 70

V

Valley; RMC Place; COLUMBIANA; ▲ Butler; ***217** NI-18; elev. 1,158ft./353m.; mail Salem z 44460
Valley; MCD-Township; GUERNSEY; ***219** SB-16; mail Pleasant City z 43772; Ⓟ 2,354; © 2,378
Valley; MCD-Township; SCIOTO; ***218** SH-9; ★ **PTSM**; mail Lucasville z 45648; Ⓟ 4,785; © 4,256
Valley City; RMC Place; MEDINA; ▲ Liverpool; **217** NG-14; elev. 815ft./248m.; 🅿; ★ **CLEV**; z 44280; ● 400
Valley City Station; RMC Place; MEDINA; ▲ Liverpool; ***217** NG-14; ★ **CLEV**; mail Valley City z 44280; ● 100
Valley Crossing; RMC Place; FRANKLIN; ***218** SB-9; ★ **COL**; mail Columbus z 43207; pop. incl. with Columbus (Inc. Place)
Valley Forge; RMC Place; MEDINA; ▲ Brunswick Hills; ★ **CLEV**; mail Brunswick z 44212
Valley Glen; RMC Place; JEFFERSON; ▲ Cross Creek; ***217** NM-20; ★ **STU-**; mail Mingo Junction z 43938; ● 50
Valley Hi; Inc. Place; LOGAN; ▲ Monroe, Jefferson; **216** NM-6; mail Zanesfield z 43360; Ⓟ 217; © 244
Valley Junction; TUSCARAWAS; see Zoarville (RMC Place)
Valley View; Inc. Place; CUYAHOGA; **219** SN-18; 🅿; ★ **CLEV**; z 44125 & mail Independence z 44131; Ⓟ 2,137; © 2,179
Valley View; Inc. Place; FRANKLIN; ▲ Franklin; **219** SH-17; ★ **COL**; mail Columbus z 43204; Ⓟ 604; © 601
Valley View (Green Acres); RMC Place; JEFFERSON; ▲ Wayne; ***217** NL-19; ★ **STU-**; mail Bloomingdale z 43910; ● 120
Valley View; RMC Place; SCIOTO; ▲ Washington; ***218** SI-9; ★ **PTSM**; mail Portsmouth z 45662; ● 110
Valley View Estates; RMC Place; TRUMBULL; ▲ Brookfield; ★ **SHAR**; mail Brookfield z 44403
Valley View Heights; RMC Place; CLERMONT; ▲ Union; ***218** SG-3; ★ **CIN**; mail Cincinnati z 45244; ● 100
Valley View Village; RMC Place; MUSKINGUM; ▲ Falls; ★ **ZAN**; mail Zanesville z 43701
Valleywood; RMC Place; GREENE; ▲ Beavercreek; ***218** SC-4; ★ **DAY**; mail Dayton z 45430; pop. incl. with Beavercreek (Inc. Place)
Vanatta; RMC Place; LICKING; ▲ Newton; **217** NN-11; ★ **NWRK**; mail Newark z 43055; ● 130
Van Buren; MCD-Township; DARKE; ***218** SA-2; mail Arcanum z 45304; Ⓟ 1,652; © 1,573
Van Buren; Inc. Place; HANCOCK; ▲ Allen; **216** NH-6; 🅿; ★ **FIND**; z 45889; Ⓟ 337; © 313
Van Buren; MCD-Township; HANCOCK; ***216** NI-6; 🅿; z 45889 & mail Williamstown z 45897; Ⓟ 910; © 943
Van Buren; RMC Place; LICKING; ▲ Licking; ***219** SA-12; ★ **NWRK**; mail Newark z 43055
Van Buren; MCD-Township; PUTNAM; ***216** NH-4; mail Leipsic z 45856; Ⓟ 3,160; © 3,128
Van Buren; MCD-Township; SHELBY; ***216** NL-3; mail Kettlersville z 45336; Ⓟ 1,816; © 1,599
Vandalia; Inc. Place; MONTGOMERY; **218** SB-4; 🅿; ★ **DAY**; z 45377; Ⓟ 13,882; © 14,603
Vanlue; Inc. Place; HANCOCK; ▲ Amanda; **216** NI-7; 🅿; z 45890; Ⓟ 373; © 371
Van Wert; Inc. Place; ⊡ VAN WERT; ▲ Ridge, Pleasant; **216** NI-2; elev. 788ft./240m.; 🅿 🅷; z 45891; Ⓟ 10,891; © 10,690
VAN WERT; **216** NJ-2; Ⓟ 30,464; © 29,659; ◆ 28,431
Vaughnsville; RMC Place; PUTNAM; ▲ Sugar Creek; **216** NI-4; elev. 768ft./234m.; 🅿; z 45893; ● 350
Vega; RMC Place; JACKSON; ▲ Bloomfield; ***219** SH-12; mail Thurman z 45685; rural
Venedocia; Inc. Place; VAN WERT; ▲ York, Jennings; **216** NJ-2; 🅿; z 45894; Ⓟ 158; © 160
Venice; BUTLER; see Ross (CDP)
Venice; RMC Place; ERIE; ***216** NF-10; ★ **SNDSK**; mail Sandusky z 44870; pop. incl. with Sandusky (Inc. Place)
Venice; MCD-Township; SENECA; ***216** NH-9; mail Attica z 44807; Ⓟ 1,826; © 1,871
Venice Heights; RMC Place; TRUMBULL; ▲ Howland; **217** NA-12; ★ **YNGS-**; mail Warren z 44484; ● 1,300
Vera Cruz; RMC Place; BROWN; ▲ Perry; ***218** SF-5; elev. 936ft./285m.; mail Fayetteville z 45118
Vermilion; Inc. Place; ERIE, LORAIN; ▲ Brownhelm, Vermilion; **217** NF-12; 🅿; ★ **CLEV**; z 44001, z 44089; Ⓟ 11,127; © 10,927
Vermilion; MCD-Township; ERIE; ***217** NF-12; 🅿; ★ **CLEV**; z 44001, z 44089; includes part of the City of Vermilion; Ⓟ 9,534; © 9,575
Vermilion-on-the-Lake; RMC Place; LORAIN; ***217** NF-12; ★ **CLEV**; mail Vermilion z 44089; pop. incl. with Vermilion (Inc. Place)
Vermillion; MCD-Township; ASHLAND; ***217** NJ-12; mail Ashland z 44805; Ⓟ 2,254; © 2,539
Vernon; MCD-Township; CLINTON; ***218** SE-5; mail Clarksville z 45113; Ⓟ 2,015; © 2,685
Vernon; MCD-Township; CRAWFORD; ***216** NI-10; mail Crestline z 44827; Ⓟ 768; © 817
Vernon; RMC Place; LAWRENCE; ▲ Decatur; **219** SI-11; mail Pedro z 45659
Vernon; RICHLAND; see Vernon Junction (RMC Place)
Vernon; MCD-Township; SCIOTO; ***218** SI-10; mail Wheelersburg z 45694; Ⓟ 1,864; © 1,855
Vernon; RMC Place; TRUMBULL; ▲ Vernon; **217** NF-20; mail Kinsman z 44428; ● 100
Vernon; MCD-Township; TRUMBULL; ***217** NF-20; mail Kinsman z 44428; Ⓟ 1,690; © 1,765
Vernon Heights; RMC Place; MARION; ★ **MRN**; mail Marion z 43302
Vernon Junction (Vernon); RMC Place; RICHLAND; ***216** NI-10; elev. 1,135ft./346m.; mail Shelby z 44875
Verona; Inc. Place; PREBLE, MONTGOMERY; ▲ Clay, Harrison; **218** SB-2; 🅿; ★ **DAY**; z 45378; Ⓟ 472; © 430
Versailles; Inc. Place; DARKE; ▲ Wayne; **216** NM-2; elev. 978ft./298m.; 🅿; z 45380; Ⓟ 2,351; © 2,589
Vesuvius; RMC Place; LAWRENCE; ▲ Elizabeth; ***219** SJ-11; mail Pedro z 45659; ● 30
Veto; RMC Place; WASHINGTON; ▲ Dunham; **219** SE-15; elev. 756ft./230m.; ★ **PRKB**; mail Belpre z 45714, Vincent z 45784; ● 110
Vickers; RMC Place; LUCAS; ★ **TOL**; pop. incl. with Toledo (Inc. Place)
Vickery; RMC Place; SANDUSKY; ▲ Townsend; **216** NF-9; 🅿; z 43464; ● 200
Vicksville; RMC Place; MORGAN; ▲ Homer; ***219** SD-14; mail Glouster z 45732; summer pop. 60; rural
Victoria; MERCER; see Saint Joseph (RMC Place)
Victory Camp; RMC Place; DELAWARE; ***216** NM-9; mail Galena z 43021, Westerville z 43082; ● 700
Vienna; CLARK; see South Vienna (Inc. Place)
Vienna; RMC Place; TRUMBULL; ▲ Vienna; **217** NG-19; 🅿; ★ **YNGS-**; z 44473; ● 600
Vienna; MCD-Township; TRUMBULL; ***217** NG-19; 🅿; ★ **YNGS-**; z 44473; Ⓟ 4,180; © 4,021
Vienna Center; CDP-Census Area Only; TRUMBULL; ▲ Vienna; ***217** NG-19; elev. 1,150ft./351m.; ★ **YNGS-**; mail Vienna z 44473; Ⓟ 1,067; © 994
Vigo; RMC Place; ROSS; ▲ Liberty; **218** SF-10; mail Chillicothe z 45601; ● 120
Viking Village; RMC Place; CLERMONT, HAMILTON; ▲ Anderson, Union; **218** SM-5; ★ **CIN**; mail Cincinnati z 45244; ● 1,230
Villa; RMC Place; CLARK; ▲ Moorefield; **218** SB-6; ★ **SPR**; mail Springfield z 45503; ● 120
Villa Nova; RMC Place; AUGLAIZE; ▲ St. Marys; **216** NK-2; elev. 887ft./270m.; mail Saint Marys z 45885; ● 800
Vincent; RMC Place; LORAIN; ▲ Sheffield, Elyria; ***217** NF-13; ★ **CLEV**; mail Elyria z 44035; ● 550
Vincent; RMC Place; WASHINGTON; ▲ Barlow; **219** SE-15; 🅿; z 45784; ● 400
Vinton; Inc. Place; GALLIA; ▲ Huntington; **219** SH-12; 🅿; z 45686; Ⓟ 293; © 324
Vinton; MCD-Township; VINTON; ***219** SF-12; mail Wilkesville z 45695; Ⓟ 512; © 558
VINTON; **219** SF-11; Ⓟ 11,098; © 12,806; ◆ 13,373
Violet; MCD-Township; FAIRFIELD; ***218** SB-10; ★ **COL**; mail Pickerington z 43147; Ⓟ 19,253; © 26,914; Ⓡ 27,036
Virginia; MCD-Township; COSHOCTON; ***217** NM-14; mail Conesville z 43811; Ⓟ 525; © 636
Vo-Ash Lake; RMC Place; CARROLL; ▲ Perry; ***217** NL-18; mail Carrollton z 44615; ● 130
Volunteer Bay; RMC Place; ERIE; ▲ Vermilion; ***217** NF-11; ★ **CLEV**; mail Vermilion z 44089; summer pop. 250; ● 150
Von Willer; RMC Place; CUYAHOGA; ★ **CLEV**; pop. incl. with Cleveland (Inc. Place)
Vulcan; RMC Place; LUCAS; ***216** NE-6; ★ **TOL**; pop. incl. with Toledo (Inc. Place)

W

Wabash; MCD-Township; DARKE; ***216** NL-2; mail Versailles z 45380; Ⓟ 931; © 934
Wabash; RMC Place; MERCER; ▲ Washington; **216** NK-1; mail Celina z 45822; ● 70
Wacker Heights; RMC Place; FAIRFIELD; ▲ Pleasant; ***219** SC-11; ★ **LANC**; mail Lancaster z 43130; ● 750
Waco; RMC Place; STARK; ▲ Canton; **217** NJ-16; ★ **CAN**; mail Canton z 44707; ● 380
Wade; RMC Place; WASHINGTON; ▲ Independence; ***219** SE-18; mail New Matamoras z 45767; rural
Wadsworth; Inc. Place; MEDINA; **217** NH-15; 🅿 🅷; ★ **AKR**; z 44281-82; Ⓟ 15,718; © 18,437; ◆ 19,549
Wadsworth; MCD-Township; MEDINA; ***217** NH-15; 🅿; ★ **AKR**; z 44281-82; Ⓟ 19,093; © 3,996
Waggoner Place; RMC Place; WOOD; ▲ Lake; ★ **TOL**; mail Perrysburg z 43551; ● 100
Wagon Works; RMC Place; LUCAS; ★ **TOL**; pop. incl. with Toledo (Inc. Place)
Wagram; RMC Place; LICKING; ▲ Etna; **218** SB-10; ★ **COL**; mail Pataskala z 43062; ● 125
Wahlsburg; RMC Place; BROWN; ▲ Scott; **218** SH-5; elev. 956ft./291m.; mail Georgetown z 45121; ● 30
Wainwright; RMC Place; JACKSON; ▲ Milton; ***219** SG-12; mail Wellston z 45692; rural
Wainwright; RMC Place; TUSCARAWAS; ▲ Warwick; **217** NL-16; mail New Philadelphia z 44663; ● 250
Waite Hill; Inc. Place; LAKE; **217** NE-16; 🅿; ★ **CLEV**; z 44094; Ⓟ 454; © 446
Wakatomika; RMC Place; COSHOCTON; ▲ Washington; **217** NM-13; mail Dresden z 43821; ● 40
Wakefield; RMC Place; DARKE; ▲ Greenville; ***216** NN-1; mail Greenville z 45331; rural
Wakefield; RMC Place; PIKE; ▲ Scioto; **218** SH-9; 🅿; z 45687; ● 140
Wakeman; Inc. Place; HURON; ▲ Wakeman; **217** NG-12; elev. 856ft./261m.; 🅿; ★ **CLEV**; z 44889; Ⓟ 948; © 951
Wakeman; MCD-Township; HURON; ***217** NG-12; 🅿; ★ **CLEV**; z 44889; Ⓟ 2,518; © 2,528
Walbridge; Inc. Place; WOOD; ▲ Lake; **216** NE-7; 🅿; ★ **TOL**; z 43465; Ⓟ 2,736; © 2,546
Waldo; Inc. Place; MARION; ▲ Waldo; **216** NL-8; 🅿; z 43356; Ⓟ 340; © 332
Waldo; MCD-Township; MARION; ***216** NL-9; 🅿; z 43356; Ⓟ 1,065; © 1,079
Walhonding; RMC Place; COSHOCTON; ▲ Newcastle; **217** NL-13; elev. 897ft./273m.; 🅿; z 43843; ● 90
Walhonding; RMC Place; GUERNSEY; ▲ Valley; **219** SB-16; mail Pleasant City z 43772; ● 100
Wallace Heights; RMC Place; JEFFERSON; ▲ Island Creek; ***217** NL-20; ★ **STU-**; mail Toronto z 43964; ● 200
Walnut; MCD-Township; FAIRFIELD; ***219** SB-11; ★ **COL**; mail Millersport z 43046; Ⓟ 6,182; © 6,436
Walnut; MCD-Township; GALLIA; ***219** SI-12; mail Patriot z 45658; Ⓟ 835; © 924
Walnut; MCD-Township; PICKAWAY; ***218** SC-10; mail Ashville z 43103; Ⓟ 2,179; © 2,428
Walnut Creek; RMC Place; HOLMES; ▲ Walnut Creek; **217** NK-15; 🅿; z 44687; ● 700
Walnut Creek; MCD-Township; HOLMES; ***217** NK-15; 🅿; z 44687; Ⓟ 3,044; © 3,530
Walnut Grove; RMC Place; LOGAN; ***216** NL-6; elev. 1,147ft./350m.; mail West Mansfield z 43358; ● 25
Walnut Hills; RMC Place; HAMILTON; ***218** SG-2; 🅿; ★ **CIN**; z 45206 & mail Cincinnati z 45226; pop. incl. with Cincinnati (Inc. Place)
Walnut Hills; RMC Place; JACKSON; ▲ Lick; mail Jackson z 45640; ● 140
Walnut Hills; RMC Place; MONTGOMERY; ★ **DAY**; pop. incl. with Dayton (Inc. Place)
Walnut Hills; RMC Place; STARK; ★ **CAN**; mail Massillon z 44646; pop. incl. with Massillon (Inc. Place)
Walnutrun; RMC Place; MADISON; ▲ Paint; ***218** SB-7; mail London z 43140; rural
Walton Hills; Inc. Place; CUYAHOGA; **219** SN-19; elev. 989ft./301m.; 🅿; ★ **CLEV**; z 44146; Ⓟ 2,371; © 2,400
Wamsley; RMC Place; ADAMS; ▲ Jefferson; **218** SH-8; elev. 617ft./188m.; mail Otway z 45657; ● 90

Entries in **UPPERCASE** are counties.
Entries in **bold** have populations of 2,500 or more.
Names in parentheses are alternate names.
Inc. Place — Incorporated Place
RMC Place — Rand McNally Designated Place
CDP — Census Designated Place
MCD — Minor Civil Division

⊡ County Seat
▲ Minor Civil Division
elev. Elevation
🅿 Post Office
🅷 Hospital
🅲 College
■ Principal Business Center
★ Ranally Metro Area (RMA) Abbreviation
z Zip Code(s)
Ⓟ Previous Census Population
Ⓡ Revised Census Population
Ⓐ Annexation Population
● Rand McNally Population Estimate
© Final Census Population
Ⓢ Special Census Population
◆ Estimated Population

For additional definitions see Glossary, Volume 1, and Introduction, Volume 2.

Wapakoneta; Inc. Place; ⊡ AUGLAIZE; ▲ Pusheta, Duchouquet, Moulton; **216** NK-3; 🅿; ★ **LIMA**; Z 45895 & mail Buckland Z 45819; Ⓟ 9,214; Ⓒ 9,474
Ward; MCD-Township; HOCKING; ***219** SD-13; mail Murray City Z 43144; Ⓟ 1,857; Ⓒ 1,937
Wardwood Acres; RMC Place; HAMILTON; ▲ Colerain; ***218** SF-2; ★ **CIN**; mail Cincinnati Z 45239; ● 600
Warner; RMC Place; WASHINGTON; ▲ Salem; **219** SD-17; elev. 679ft./207m.; 🅿; Z 45745; ● 130
Warnock; RMC Place; BELMONT; ▲ Smith; **217** NN-18; 🅿; ★ **WHL**; Z 43967; ● 200
Warren; MCD-Township; BELMONT; ***219** SA-18; mail Barnesville Z 43713; Ⓟ 5,887; Ⓒ 5,870
Warren; MCD-Township; JEFFERSON; ***217** NM-19; ★ **WHL**; mail Rayland Z 43943; Ⓟ 4,964; Ⓒ 4,499
Warren; Inc. Place; ⊡ TRUMBULL; ▲ Warren; **217** NG-19; elev. 893ft./272m.; 🅿 🅷 ■; ★ **YNGS-**; Z 44481-86, Z 44488; Ⓟ 50,793; Ⓒ 46,832; Ⓡ 48,224; ◆ 41,101
Warren; MCD-Township; TRUMBULL; ***217** NG-19; 🅿; ★ **YNGS-**; Z 44481-86, Z 44488 & mail Leavittsburg Z 44430; Ⓟ 6,867; Ⓒ 7,817; Ⓡ 6,425
Warren; MCD-Township; TUSCARAWAS; ***217** NK-17; mail Mineral City Z 44656; Ⓟ 1,034; Ⓒ 1,194
Warren; MCD-Township; WASHINGTON; ***219** SE-16; ★ **PRKB**; mail Marietta Z 45750; Ⓟ 3,872; Ⓒ 4,044
WARREN; **218** SE-4; Ⓟ 113,909; Ⓒ 158,383; Ⓡ 158,486; ◆ 208,873
Warrensburg; RMC Place; DELAWARE; ▲ Scioto; ***216** NM-8; mail Ostrander Z 43061
Warrensville Heights; Inc. Place; CUYAHOGA; **217** NF-15; elev. 1,039ft./317m.; 🅿 🅷; ★ **CLEV**; Z 44122, Z 44128; Ⓟ 15,745; Ⓒ 15,109
Warrenton; RMC Place; JEFFERSON; ▲ Warren; **217** NM-19; ★ **WHL**; mail Rayland Z 43943; ● 50
Warsaw; Inc. Place; COSHOCTON; ▲ Jefferson; **217** NL-13; 🅿; Z 43844; Ⓟ 699; Ⓒ 781
Warwick; RMC Place; SUMMIT; ***217** NI-15; ★ **AKR**; mail Clinton Z 44216; pop. incl. with Clinton (Inc. Place)
Warwick; MCD-Township; TUSCARAWAS; ***217** NL-16; mail New Philadelphia Z 44663; Ⓟ 2,532; Ⓒ 2,746
Washington; MCD-Township; AUGLAIZE; ***216** NK-3; mail New Knoxville Z 45871; Ⓟ 1,852; Ⓒ 2,320
Washington; MCD-Township; BELMONT; ***219** SB-19; mail Beallsville Z 43716; Ⓟ 602; Ⓒ 537
Washington; MCD-Township; BROWN; ***218** SG-5; mail Sardinia Z 45171; Ⓟ 2,112; Ⓒ 2,271
Washington; MCD-Township; CARROLL; ***217** NK-18; mail Carrollton Z 44615; Ⓟ 813; Ⓒ 1,061
Washington; MCD-Township; CLERMONT; ***218** SH-4; mail Moscow Z 45153; Ⓟ 2,441; Ⓒ 2,351
Washington; MCD-Township; CLINTON; ***218** SE-5; mail Cuba Z 45114; Ⓟ 1,475; Ⓒ 1,895
Washington; MCD-Township; COLUMBIANA; ***217** NK-19; mail Salineville Z 43945; Ⓟ 2,464; Ⓒ 2,380
Washington; MCD-Township; COSHOCTON; ***217** NM-13; mail Trinway Z 43842; Ⓟ 533; Ⓒ 629
Washington; MCD-Township; DARKE; ***216** NN-1; mail Union City Z 47390; Ⓟ 1,311; Ⓒ 1,382
Washington; MCD-Township; DEFIANCE; ***216** NF-2; mail Ney Z 43549; Ⓟ 1,537; Ⓒ 1,521
Washington; FAYETTE; see Washington Court House (Inc. Place)
Washington; MCD-Township; FRANKLIN; ***218** SA-9; ★ **COL**; mail Dublin Z 43016, Hilliard Z 43026; Ⓟ 13,090; Ⓒ 1,412
Washington; MCD-Township; GUERNSEY; ***217** NM-16; mail Kimbolton Z 43749; Ⓟ 441; Ⓒ 491
Washington; MCD-Township; HANCOCK; ***216** NH-7; mail Columbus Grove Z 45830; Ⓟ 4,675; Ⓒ 4,602
Washington; MCD-Township; HARDIN; ***216** NJ-6; mail Dola Z 45835; Ⓟ 805; Ⓒ 787
Washington; MCD-Township; HARRISON; ***217** NM-17; mail Tippecanoe Z 44699; Ⓟ 626; Ⓒ 598
Washington; MCD-Township; HENRY; ***216** NF-5; mail Liberty Center Z 43532; Ⓟ 1,823; Ⓒ 2,021
Washington; MCD-Township; HIGHLAND; ***218** SG-7; mail Hillsboro Z 45133; Ⓟ 694; Ⓒ 1,048
Washington; MCD-Township; HOCKING; ***219** SE-12; mail Logan Z 43138; Ⓟ 978; Ⓒ 1,160
Washington; MCD-Township; HOLMES; ***217** NK-13; mail Lakeville Z 44638; Ⓟ 1,454; Ⓒ 1,614
Washington; MCD-Township; JACKSON; ***219** SF-11; mail Wellston Z 45692; Ⓟ 725; Ⓒ 743
Washington; MCD-Township; LAWRENCE; ***219** SI-11; mail Oak Hill Z 45656; Ⓟ 302; Ⓒ 250
Washington; MCD-Township; LICKING; ***217** NM-11; ★ **NWRK**; mail Utica Z 43080; Ⓟ 2,984; Ⓒ 3,045; Ⓡ 3,042
Washington; MCD-Township; LOGAN; ***216** NL-5; mail Russells Point Z 43348; Ⓟ 3,486; Ⓒ 3,945
Washington; MCD-Township; LUCAS; ***216** ND-7; ★ **TOL**; mail Toledo Z 43612; Ⓟ 3,803; Ⓒ 3,574
Washington; MCD-Township; MERCER; ***216** NK-1; mail Coldwater Z 45828; Ⓟ 1,259; Ⓒ 1,218
Washington; MCD-Township; MIAMI; ***216** NN-3; mail Piqua Z 45356; Ⓟ 22,595; Ⓒ 1,803
Washington; MCD-Township; MONROE; ***219** SD-18; mail Graysville Z 45734; Ⓟ 518; Ⓒ 520
Washington (Washington Township); MCD-Township; MONTGOMERY; ***218** SD-4; ★ **DAY**; mail Dayton Z 45429, Z 45440, Z 45458-59, Z 45475; Ⓟ 46,609; Ⓒ 52,991
Washington; MCD-Township; MORROW; ***216** NK-10; mail Mount Gilead Z 43338; Ⓟ 1,159; Ⓒ 1,227
Washington; MCD-Township; MUSKINGUM; ***219** SB-14; ★ **ZAN**; mail Zanesville Z 43701; Ⓟ 4,202; Ⓒ 4,284
Washington; MCD-Township; PAULDING; ***216** NH-3; mail Mc Guffey Z 45859; Ⓟ 721; Ⓒ 789
Washington; MCD-Township; PICKAWAY; ***218** SD-10; 🅲 506; mail Circleville Z 43113; Ⓟ 2,662; Ⓒ 2,951
Washington; MCD-Township; PREBLE; ***218** SC-2; mail Eaton Z 45320; Ⓟ 1,974; Ⓒ 2,104
Washington; MCD-Township; RICHLAND; ***217** NJ-11; ★ **MANS**; mail Mansfield Z 44906; Ⓟ 6,474; Ⓒ 6,777
Washington; MCD-Township; SANDUSKY; ***216** NF-8; mail Lindsey Z 43442; Ⓟ 2,308; Ⓒ 2,396
Washington; MCD-Township; SCIOTO; ***218** SI-9; ★ **PTSM**; mail West Portsmouth Z 45663; Ⓟ 6,171; Ⓒ 5,971
Washington; MCD-Township; SHELBY; ***216** NM-3; mail Sidney Z 45365; Ⓟ 1,855; Ⓒ 2,083
Washington; MCD-Township; STARK; ***217** NI-17; ★ **ALLI**; mail Alliance Z 44601; Ⓟ 4,765; Ⓒ 4,791
Washington; MCD-Township; TUSCARAWAS; ***217** NM-16; mail Newcomerstown Z 43832; Ⓟ 612; Ⓒ 762
Washington; MCD-Township; UNION; ***216** NL-7; mail Richwood Z 43344; Ⓟ 634; Ⓒ 705
Washington; MCD-Township; VAN WERT; ***216** NI-3; mail Delphos Z 45833; Ⓟ 5,392; Ⓒ 5,228
Washington; MCD-Township; WARREN; ***218** SE-4; mail Oregonia Z 45054; Ⓟ 1,354; Ⓒ 1,855
Washington; MCD-Township; WOOD; ***216** NF-5; ★ **TOL**; mail Tontogany Z 43565; Ⓟ 1,559; Ⓒ 1,688
WASHINGTON; **219** SD-16; Ⓟ 62,254; Ⓒ 63,251; ◆ 61,352
Washington Court House (Washington); Inc. Place; ⊡ FAYETTE; **218** SD-7; 🅿 🅷; Z 43160; Ⓟ 12,983; Ⓒ 13,524
Washington Township; MONTGOMERY; see Washington (MCD-Township)
Washingtonville; Inc. Place; COLUMBIANA, MAHONING; ▲ Salem, Green; **217** NI-19; elev. 1,069ft./326m.; 🅿; Z 44490; Ⓟ 894; Ⓒ 789
Waterford; RMC Place; KNOX; ▲ Middlebury; **217** NK-11; mail Fredericktown Z 43019; ● 70
Waterford; RMC Place; WASHINGTON; ▲ Waterford; **219** SD-15; 🅿; Z 45786 & mail Watertown Z 45787; ● 600
Waterford; MCD-Township; WASHINGTON; ***219** SD-16; 🅿; Z 45786; Ⓟ 3,701; Ⓒ 3,708
Waterloo; MCD-Township; ATHENS; ***219** SE-13; mail New Marshfield Z 45766; Ⓟ 2,321; Ⓒ 2,605
Waterloo; RMC Place; FAIRFIELD; ▲ Violet; **218** SB-10; ★ **COL**; mail Lithopolis Z 43136; ● 170
Waterloo; RMC Place; LAWRENCE; ▲ Symmes; **219** SI-12; 🅿; Z 45688; ● 150
Watertown; RMC Place; WASHINGTON; ▲ Watertown; **219** SE-16; 🅿; Z 45787; ● 220
Watertown; MCD-Township; WASHINGTON; ***219** SD-16; 🅿; Z 45787; Ⓟ 1,498; Ⓒ 1,563
Waterville; Inc. Place; LUCAS; ▲ Waterville; **216** NE-6; 🅿; ★ **TOL**; Z 43566; Ⓟ 4,517; Ⓒ 4,828
Waterville; MCD-Township; LUCAS; ***216** NE-5; 🅿; ★ **TOL**; Z 43566; Ⓟ 9,003; Ⓒ 9,469
Watkins; RMC Place; UNION; ▲ Millcreek; **216** NM-8; elev. 962ft./293m.; mail Marysville Z 43040; ● 130
Wattsville; RMC Place; CARROLL; ▲ Fox; ***217** NK-18; mail Carrollton Z 44615; rural
Wauseon; Inc. Place; ⊡ FULTON; ▲ Clinton; **216** NE-4; elev. 757ft./231m.; 🅿 🅷; Z 43567; Ⓟ 6,322; Ⓒ 7,091
Waverly (Waverly City); Inc. Place; ⊡ PIKE; ▲ Pee Pee; **218** SG-9; 🅿 🅷; Z 45690; Ⓟ 4,477; Ⓒ 4,433
Waverly City; PIKE; see Waverly (Inc. Place)
Waverly Gables; RMC Place; PIKE; ▲ Pee Pee; ***218** SG-9; mail Waverly Z 45690; ● 200
Way; RMC Place; MONROE; ▲ Washington; ***219** SC-18; mail Graysville Z 45734; rural
Wayland; RMC Place; PORTAGE; ▲ Paris; **217** NG-18; elev. 964ft./294m.; 🅿; Z 44285; ● 200
Wayne; MCD-Township; ADAMS; ***218** SH-6; mail Cherry Fork Z 45618; Ⓟ 1,147; Ⓒ 1,273
Wayne; RMC Place; ASHTABULA; ▲ Wayne; **217** NE-19; elev. 1,091ft./333m.; mail Williamsfield Z 44093; ● 100
Wayne; MCD-Township; ASHTABULA; ***217** NE-19; mail Williamsfield Z 44093; Ⓟ 610; Ⓒ 653
Wayne; MCD-Township; AUGLAIZE; ***216** NK-4; mail Waynesfield Z 45896; Ⓟ 1,648; Ⓒ 1,591
Wayne; MCD-Township; BELMONT; ***219** SB-18; mail Jerusalem Z 43747; Ⓟ 579; Ⓒ 624
Wayne; MCD-Township; BUTLER; ***218** SD-2; ★ **MIDD**; mail Middletown Z 45042; Ⓟ 3,897; Ⓒ 4,252
Wayne; MCD-Township; CHAMPAIGN; ***216** NM-6; mail Cable Z 43009; Ⓟ 1,416; Ⓒ 1,660
Wayne; MCD-Township; CLERMONT; ***218** SF-4; ★ **CIN**; mail Goshen Z 45122; Ⓟ 4,749; Ⓒ 5,025
Wayne; MCD-Township; CLINTON; ***218** SE-6; mail Lees Creek Z 45138; Ⓟ 681; Ⓒ 737
Wayne; MCD-Township; COLUMBIANA; ***217** NJ-19; mail Lisbon Z 44432; Ⓟ 771; Ⓒ 785
Wayne; MCD-Township; DARKE; ***216** NM-2; mail Versailles Z 45380; Ⓟ 3,927; Ⓒ 4,349
Wayne; MCD-Township; FAYETTE; ***218** SE-8; mail Greenfield Z 45123; Ⓟ 1,304; Ⓒ 1,367
Wayne; MCD-Township; JEFFERSON; ***217** NL-19; ★ **STU-**; mail Bloomingdale Z 43910; Ⓟ 2,576; Ⓒ 2,233
Wayne; MCD-Township; KNOX; ***217** NL-11; mail Fredericktown Z 43019; Ⓟ 868; Ⓒ 898
Wayne; MCD-Township; MONROE; ***219** SC-18; mail Graysville Z 45734; Ⓟ 379; Ⓒ 348
Wayne; MCD-Township; MUSKINGUM; ***219** SB-14; ★ **ZAN**; mail Zanesville Z 43701; Ⓟ 4,514; Ⓒ 4,455
Wayne; MCD-Township; NOBLE; ***219** SB-17; mail Quaker City Z 43773; Ⓟ 356; Ⓒ 507
Wayne; MCD-Township; PICKAWAY; ***218** SD-9; mail Circleville Z 43113; Ⓟ 500; Ⓒ 565
Wayne; MCD-Township; TUSCARAWAS; ***217** NK-15; mail Dundee Z 44624; Ⓟ 1,255; Ⓒ 1,743
Wayne; MCD-Township; WARREN; ***218** SD-4; ★ **DAY**; mail Waynesville Z 45068; Ⓟ 5,744; Ⓒ 7,250
Wayne; MCD-Township; WAYNE; ***217** NI-14; mail Wooster Z 44691; Ⓟ 3,958; Ⓒ 4,034
Wayne; Inc. Place; WOOD; ▲ Montgomery; **216** NG-7; 🅿; Z 43466 & mail Williamsfield Z 44093; Ⓟ 803; Ⓒ 842
WAYNE; **217** NI-14; Ⓟ 101,461; Ⓒ 111,564; ◆ 112,464
Wayne Lakes; DARKE; see Wayne Lakes Park (Inc. Place)
Wayne Lakes Park (Wayne Lakes); Inc. Place; DARKE; ▲ Neave; **218** SA-1; mail Greenville Z 45331; Ⓟ 671; Ⓒ 684
Waynesburg; RMC Place; CRAWFORD; ▲ Auburn; ***216** NI-10; elev. 980ft./299m.; mail Tiro Z 44887
Waynesburg; Inc. Place; STARK; ▲ Sandy; **217** NJ-17; 🅿; ★ **CAN**; Z 44688; Ⓟ 1,068; Ⓒ 1,003
Waynesfield; Inc. Place; AUGLAIZE; ▲ Wayne; **216** NK-4; elev. 1,054ft./321m.; 🅿; Z 45896; Ⓟ 831; Ⓒ 803
Waynesville; Inc. Place; WARREN; ▲ Wayne; **218** SD-4; 🅿; ★ **DAY**; Z 45068; Ⓟ 1,949; Ⓒ 2,558
Waynesville; WARREN; see Corwin (Inc. Place)
Weathersfield; MCD-Township; TRUMBULL; ***217** NG-19; ★ **YNGS-**; mail Girard Z 44420; Ⓟ 28,507; Ⓒ 27,717
Weavers (Weaver Station); RMC Place; DARKE; ▲ Neave; ***218** SA-1; mail Greenville Z 45331; ● 80
Weaver Station; DARKE; see Weavers (RMC Place)
Webb; RMC Place; BELMONT; ▲ Mead; ***219** SB-19; ★ **WHL**; mail Shadyside Z 43947; ● 30
Webb Summit; RMC Place; HOCKING; ▲ Falls; **219** SD-12; elev. 794ft./242m.; mail Logan Z 43138
Webster; RMC Place; DARKE; ▲ Wayne; **216** NM-2; mail Bradford Z 45308, Versailles Z 45380; ● 100
Webster; MCD-Township; WOOD; ***216** NF-6; mail Pemberville Z 43450; Ⓟ 1,111; Ⓒ 1,277
Weems (Smithfield Station); RMC Place; JEFFERSON; ▲ Smithfield; ***217** NM-19; ★ **STU-**; mail Rayland Z 43943; ● 30
Wegee; RMC Place; BELMONT; ▲ Mead; **219** SB-19; ★ **WHL**; mail Shadyside Z 43947; ● 160
Welcome; RMC Place; HOLMES; ▲ Monroe; ***217** NK-13; mail Killbuck Z 44637
Weller; MCD-Township; RICHLAND; ***217** NI-11; mail Mansfield Z 44903; Ⓟ 1,462; Ⓒ 1,736
Wellington; Inc. Place; LORAIN; ▲ Wellington; **217** NG-12; elev. 854ft./260m.; 🅿; Z 44090; Ⓟ 4,140; Ⓒ 4,511
Wellington; MCD-Township; LORAIN; ***217** NG-12; 🅿; Z 44090; Ⓟ 5,386; Ⓒ 5,904
Wellington Park; RMC Place; HAMILTON; ▲ Colerain; ***218** SF-2; ★ **CIN**; mail Cincinnati Z 45231; ● 730
Wellman (Henpeck); RMC Place; WARREN; elev. 941ft./287m.; ● 25
Wells; MCD-Township; JEFFERSON; ***217** NM-20; ★ **STU-**; mail Brilliant Z 43913; Ⓟ 3,249; Ⓒ 3,130
Wellston; Inc. Place; JACKSON; **219** SG-11; 🅿; Z 45692; Ⓟ 6,049; Ⓒ 6,078
Wellsville; Inc. Place; COLUMBIANA; **217** NK-20; 🅿; ★ **E.LIV**; Z 43968; Ⓟ 4,532; Ⓒ 4,133
Welshfield; RMC Place; GEAUGA; ▲ Troy; **217** NF-17; elev. 1,222ft./372m.; mail Burton Z 44021; ● 150
Welshtown; RMC Place; MEIGS; ▲ Sutton; ***219** SG-14; mail Pomeroy Z 45769; pop. incl. with Pomeroy (Inc. Place)
Wengerlawn; RMC Place; MONTGOMERY; ▲ Clay; **218** SB-2; ★ **DAY**; mail Brookville Z 45309; ● 85
Wernert (Wernerts Corners); RMC Place; LUCAS; ★ **TOL**; mail Toledo Z 43613; pop. incl. with Toledo (Inc. Place)
Wernerts Corners; RMC Place; LUCAS; ★ **TOL**; pop. incl. with Toledo (Inc. Place)
Wernerts Corners; LUCAS; see Wernert (RMC Place)
Wesley; MCD-Township; WASHINGTON; ***219** SE-15; mail Bartlett Z 45713; Ⓟ 800; Ⓒ 915
Wesleyan Woods; RMC Place; DELAWARE; mail Delaware Z 43015; pop. incl. with Delaware (Inc. Place)
West; MCD-Township; COLUMBIANA; ***217** NJ-18; ★ **ALLI**; mail East Rochester Z 44625; Ⓟ 3,162; Ⓒ 3,351
West Akron; RMC Place; SUMMIT; ***217** NH-15; ★ **AKR**; mail Akron Z 44307; pop. incl. with Akron (Inc. Place)
West Alexandria; Inc. Place; PREBLE; ▲ Twin, Lanier; **218** SC-2; elev. 900ft./274m.; 🅿; ★ **DAY**; Z 45381; Ⓟ 1,460; Ⓒ 1,395
West Andover; RMC Place; ASHTABULA; ▲ Andover; **217** NE-20; elev. 1,052ft./321m.; mail Andover Z 44003; ● 100
West Bass Lake; RMC Place; GEAUGA; ▲ Munson; ★ **CLEV**; mail Chardon Z 44024
West Bedford; RMC Place; COSHOCTON; ▲ Bedford; **217** NM-13; mail Warsaw Z 43844; ● 60
West Bellaire; RMC Place; BELMONT; ★ **WHL**; mail Bellaire Z 43906; pop. incl. with Bellaire (Inc. Place)
West Berlin; RMC Place; DELAWARE; ▲ Berlin; ***216** NM-9; elev. 953ft./290m.; mail Delaware Z 43015; rural
Westboro; RMC Place; CLINTON; ▲ Jefferson; **218** SF-5; elev. 981ft./299m.; mail Midland Z 45148; ● 270
West Brookfield; RMC Place; STARK; ***217** NJ-15; elev. 1,043ft./318m.; ★ **CAN**; mail Massillon Z 44646; pop. incl. with Massillon (Inc. Place)
West Carlisle; RMC Place; COSHOCTON; ▲ Pike; **217** NM-13; mail Frazeysburg Z 43822, Warsaw Z 43844; ● 30
West Carlisle; RMC Place; LORAIN; ▲ Carlisle; ★ **CLEV**; mail Elyria Z 44035; ● 300
West Carrollton; MONTGOMERY; see West Carrollton City (Inc. Place)
West Carrollton City (West Carrollton); Inc. Place; MONTGOMERY; **218** SC-3; ★ **DAY**; mail Dayton Z 45439, Z 45449; Ⓟ 14,403; Ⓒ 13,818
West Charleston; RMC Place; MIAMI; ▲ Bethel; **218** SB-4; ★ **DAY**; mail Tipp City Z 45371; ● 100
West Chesapeake; RMC Place; LAWRENCE; ▲ Union; ***219** SK-12; ★ **HNTG**; mail Chesapeake Z 45619; ● 500
Westchester; RMC Place; BUTLER; ▲ West Chester; **218** SE-3; elev. 661ft./201m.; 🅿; ★ **CIN**; Z 45069, Z 45071; ● 800
West Chester (Union); MCD-Township; BUTLER; ***218** SE-3; 🅿; ★ **CIN**; Z 45069, Z 45071; Ⓟ 39,703; Ⓒ 54,895
West Chester; RMC Place; TUSCARAWAS; ▲ Perry; **217** NM-16; mail Tippecanoe Z 44699; ● 100
West Clarksfield; RMC Place; HURON; ▲ Clarksfield; **217** NG-11; mail Wakeman Z 44889; ● 100
West Conesville; RMC Place; COSHOCTON; ▲ Franklin; mail Conesville Z 43811; pop. incl. with Conesville (Inc. Place)
West Covington; RMC Place; MIAMI; ▲ Newberry; ***216** NN-3; mail Covington Z 45318; ● 130
West Elkton; Inc. Place; PREBLE; ▲ Gratis; **218** SD-2; 🅿; ★ **MIDD**; Z 45070; Ⓟ 208; Ⓒ 194
West End; RMC Place; ASHTABULA; ★ **ASHT**; mail Ashtabula Z 44004; pop. incl. with Ashtabula (Inc. Place)
West Enon; CLARK; see West Enon Estates (RMC Place)
West Enon Estates (West Enon); RMC Place; CLARK; ▲ Mad River; ***218** SB-5; ★ **SPR**; mail Enon Z 45323; ● 500
Westerly Park; RMC Place; ALLEN; ▲ American; ★ **LIMA**; mail Lima Z 45805
Western Hills; RMC Place; HAMILTON; ▲ Green; **181** A-15; 🅿; ★ **CIN**; Z 45238 & mail Cincinnati Z 45233, Z 45258; pop. incl. with Cincinnati (Inc. Place)
Western Reserve Estates; RMC Place; SUMMIT; ***217** NG-16; ★ **AKR**; mail Hudson Z 44236; pop. incl. with Hudson (Inc. Place)
Westerville; Inc. Place; FRANKLIN, DELAWARE; **216** NN-9; 🅿 🅲 3,184; ★ **COL**; Z 43081-82, Z 43086; Ⓟ 30,269; Ⓒ 35,318; ◆ 38,486
West Fairport; RMC Place; LAKE; ***217** ND-17; ★ **CLEV**; mail Grand River Z 44045; pop. incl. with Grand River (Inc. Place)
West Farmington; Inc. Place; TRUMBULL; ▲ Farmington; **217** NF-18; 🅿; Z 44491; Ⓟ 542; Ⓒ 519
Westfield; RMC Place; COLUMBIANA; ▲ Liverpool; ***217** NJ-20; ★ **E.LIV**; mail East Liverpool Z 43920; ● 100
Westfield; MEDINA; see Westfield Center (Inc. Place)
Westfield; MCD-Township; MEDINA; ***217** NH-14; ★ **CLEV**; mail Westfield Center Z 44251; Ⓟ 3,394; Ⓒ 4,172
Westfield; RMC Place; MORROW; ▲ Westfield; **216** NL-9; mail Ashley Z 43003; ● 110
Westfield; MCD-Township; MORROW; ***216** NL-9; mail Ashley Z 43003; Ⓟ 1,058; Ⓒ 1,100
Westfield Center (Leroy, Westfield); Inc. Place; MEDINA; ▲ Westfield; **217** NH-14; 🅿; ★ **CLEV**; Z 44251; Ⓟ 784; Ⓒ 1,054
West Florence; RMC Place; PREBLE; ▲ Jackson, Dixon; **218** SC-1; elev. 1,140ft./347m.; mail Eaton Z 45320; ● 40
West Hill; CDP; TRUMBULL; ▲ Brookfield; ***217** NG-20; elev. 1,088ft./332m.; ★ **SHAR**; mail Brookfield Z 44403; Ⓟ 2,954; Ⓒ 2,523
Westhope; RMC Place; HENRY; ▲ Richfield; **216** NG-5; elev. 692ft./211m.; mail Deshler Z 43516, Mc Clure Z 43534; ● 80
West Independence; RMC Place; HANCOCK; ▲ Biglick; **216** NH-7; elev. 836ft./255m.; mail Alvada Z 44802, Fostoria Z 44830; ● 40
West Jefferson (Jefferson); Inc. Place; MADISON; ▲ Jefferson; **218** SB-8; 🅿; ★ **COL**; Z 43162; Ⓟ 4,504; Ⓒ 4,331
West Jefferson; RMC Place; WILLIAMS; ▲ Jefferson; **216** NE-2; mail Montpelier Z 43543; ● 120
West Lafayette; Inc. Place; COSHOCTON; ▲ Lafayette; **217** NM-15; elev. 807ft./246m.; 🅿; Z 43845; Ⓟ 2,129; Ⓒ 2,313
Westlake; Inc. Place; CUYAHOGA; **217** NF-14; 🅿; ★ **CLEV**; Z 44145; Ⓟ 27,018; Ⓒ 31,719; ◆ 30,361
West Lakeville; RMC Place; ASHTABULA; mail Conneaut Z 44030; pop. incl. with Conneaut (Inc. Place)
West Lancaster; RMC Place; FAYETTE; ▲ Jefferson; **218** SD-6; mail Jeffersonville Z 43128; ● 75
Westland; RMC Place; FRANKLIN; ★ **COL**; mail Columbus Z 43228; pop. incl. with Columbus (Inc. Place)
Westland; MCD-Township; GUERNSEY; ***219** SB-15; mail Cambridge Z 43725; Ⓟ 1,750; Ⓒ 1,931
West Lebanon; RMC Place; WAYNE; ▲ Sugar Creek, Paint; **217** NJ-15; mail Dalton Z 44618; ● 120
West Leipsic; Inc. Place; PUTNAM; ▲ Liberty; **216** NH-4; mail Leipsic Z 45856; Ⓟ 244; Ⓒ 271
West Liberty; RMC Place; CRAWFORD; ▲ Vernon; ***216** NI-10; elev. 1,099ft./335m.; mail Tiro Z 44887; ● 50
West Liberty; Inc. Place; LOGAN; ▲ Liberty; **216** NM-5; elev. 1,111ft./339m.; 🅿; Z 43357; Ⓟ 1,613; Ⓒ 1,813
West Liberty (Stantontown); RMC Place; MORROW; ▲ Peru; **216** NL-9; mail Marengo Z 43334; ● 40
West Lodi; RMC Place; SENECA; ▲ Reed; **216** NG-9; mail Bellevue Z 44811; ● 80
West Logan; RMC Place; HOCKING; ▲ Falls; ***219** SD-12; mail Logan Z 43138; ● 440
West Manchester; Inc. Place; PREBLE; ▲ Monroe; **218** SB-2; elev. 1,093ft./333m.; 🅿; ★ **RICH**; Z 45382; Ⓟ 464; Ⓒ 433
West Mansfield; Inc. Place; LOGAN; ▲ Perry, Bokescreek; **216** NL-6; 🅿; Z 43358; Ⓟ 830; Ⓒ 700
West Marietta; RMC Place; WASHINGTON; ***219** SE-16; ★ **PRKB**; mail Marietta Z 45750; pop. incl. with Marietta (Inc. Place)
West Marysville; RMC Place; UNION; ***216** NM-7; mail Marysville Z 43040; pop. incl. with Marysville (Inc. Place)
West Mecca; RMC Place; TRUMBULL; ▲ Mecca; **217** NF-19; elev. 930ft./283m.; ★ **YNGS-**; mail Cortland Z 44410; ● 120
West Middletown; RMC Place; BUTLER; ▲ Madison; **218** SD-3; elev. 690ft./210m.; ★ **MIDD**; mail Middletown Z 45042; ● 550
West Millgrove; Inc. Place; WOOD; ▲ Perry; **216** NG-7; 🅿; Z 43467; Ⓟ 171; Ⓒ 78
West Milton; Inc. Place; MIAMI; ▲ Union; **218** SB-3; 🅿; ★ **DAY**; Z 45383; Ⓟ 4,348; Ⓒ 4,645
Westminster; RMC Place; ALLEN; ▲ Auglaize; **216** NJ-4; ★ **LIMA**; mail Harrod Z 45850; ● 100
Westmoor; RMC Place; CRAWFORD; ▲ Polk; ***216** NJ-10; mail Galion Z 44833; ● 400
West Newton; RMC Place; ALLEN; ▲ Auglaize; **216** NK-5; elev. 1,047ft./319m.; ★ **LIMA**; mail Harrod Z 45850
Weston; Inc. Place; WOOD; ▲ Weston; **216** NF-5; 🅿; Z 43569; Ⓟ 1,716; Ⓒ 1,659
Weston; MCD-Township; WOOD; ***216** NF-5; 🅿; Z 43569; Ⓟ 2,312; Ⓒ 2,274
Weston Gardens; RMC Place; LUCAS; ★ **TOL**; pop. incl. with Toledo (Inc. Place)
West Park; RMC Place; CUYAHOGA; ★ **CLEV**; mail Cleveland Z 44111; pop. incl. with Cleveland (Inc. Place)
West Park; RMC Place; HANCOCK; ***216** NH-6; ★ **FIND**; mail Findlay Z 45840; pop. incl. with Findlay (Inc. Place)
West Park; RMC Place; JEFFERSON; ▲ Cross Creek; ***217** NL-19; ★ **STU-**; mail Steubenville Z 43952; ● 100
West Park; RMC Place; STARK; ***217** NJ-16; ★ **CAN**; mail Massillon Z 44646; pop. incl. with Massillon (Inc. Place)
West Point; RMC Place; COLUMBIANA; ▲ Madison; **217** NJ-19; 🅿; ★ **E.LIV**; Z 44492; ● 220
West Point; RMC Place; MORROW; ▲ North Bloomfield; ***216** NK-10; mail Galion Z 44833; ● 50
West Portsmouth; CDP; SCIOTO; ▲ Washington; **218** SI-9; 🅿; ★ **PTSM**; Z 45663; Ⓟ 3,551; Ⓒ 3,458
West Richfield; RMC Place; SUMMIT; ***217** NG-15; ★ **CLEV**; mail Richfield Z 44286; pop. incl. with Richfield (Inc. Place)
West Rushville; Inc. Place; FAIRFIELD; ▲ Richland; **219** SC-12; 🅿; Z 43163; Ⓟ 134; Ⓒ 132
West Salem; Inc. Place; WAYNE; ▲ Congress; **217** NI-13; elev. 1,120ft./341m.; 🅿; Z 44287; Ⓟ 1,534; Ⓒ 1,501
West Side; RMC Place; MAHONING; ***217** NH-19; ★ **YNGS-**; mail Youngstown Z 44509; pop. incl. with Youngstown (Inc. Place)
West Sonora; RMC Place; PREBLE; ▲ Harrison; **218** SB-2; ★ **DAY**; mail Lewisburg Z 45338; ● 100
West Steels Corners; RMC Place; SUMMIT; ***217** NG-16; mail Cuyahoga Falls Z 44223; pop. incl. with Cuyahoga Falls (Inc. Place)
West Toledo; RMC Place; LUCAS; ***216** ND-6; ★ **TOL**; mail Toledo Z 43612; pop. incl. with Toledo (Inc. Place)
West Union; Inc. Place; ⊡ ADAMS; ▲ Tiffin, Liberty; **218** SI-7; elev. 967ft./295m.; 🅿 🅷; Z 45693; Ⓟ 3,096; Ⓒ 2,903
West Unity; Inc. Place; WILLIAMS; ▲ Brady; **216** NE-2; elev. 788ft./240m.; 🅿; Z 43570; Ⓟ 1,677; Ⓒ 1,790
West View; RMC Place; CUYAHOGA; ***217** NF-14; ★ **CLEV**; pop. incl. with Olmsted Falls (Inc. Place)
Westview; RMC Place; LORAIN; ▲ Columbia; **217** NF-14; ★ **CLEV**; mail Columbia Station Z 44028; ● 530
Westview Mobile Home Park; RMC Place; ASHLAND; ***217** NI-12; mail Ashland Z 44805; pop. incl. with Ashland (Inc. Place)
Westville; RMC Place; CHAMPAIGN; ▲ Mad River; **217** NI-18; 🅿; Z 43083; ● 200
Westville; RMC Place; COLUMBIANA, MAHONING; ▲ Knox; ***217** NI-18; ★ **ALLI**; mail Beloit Z 44609; ● 250
Westville Lake; RMC Place; COLUMBIANA; ▲ Smith; ***217** NI-18; ★ **ALLI**; mail Beloit Z 44609; summer pop. 700; ● 250
West Warren; RMC Place; TRUMBULL; ★ **YNGS-**; mail Warren Z 44485; pop. incl. with Warren (Inc. Place)
West Wheeling; RMC Place; BELMONT; ▲ Pease; ***219** SA-20; ★ **WHL**; mail Bellaire Z 43906; pop. incl. with Bridgeport (Inc. Place)
West Williamsfield; RMC Place; ASHTABULA; ▲ Williamsfield; **217** NE-20; elev. 1,064ft./324m.; mail Williamsfield Z 44093; ● 110
Westwood; RMC Place; ALLEN; ★ **LIMA**; pop. incl. with Lima (Inc. Place)
Westwood; RMC Place; HAMILTON; ***218** SF-2; 🅿; ★ **CIN**; Z 45248 & mail Cincinnati Z 45211; pop. incl. with Cincinnati (Inc. Place)
Westwood; RMC Place; JEFFERSON; ★ **STU-**; mail Steubenville Z 43952; pop. incl. with Steubenville (Inc. Place)
Westwood; RMC Place; WAYNE; ▲ Wooster; ***217** NJ-14; mail Wooster Z 44691; ● 630
Westwood Estates; RMC Place; JEFFERSON; ★ **STU-**; mail Steubenville Z 43952; pop. incl. with Steubenville (Inc. Place)
West Woodville; RMC Place; CLERMONT; ▲ Wayne; ★ **CIN**; mail Blanchester Z 45107; rural
West Worthington; RMC Place; FRANKLIN; mail Columbus Z 43234-35; pop. incl. with Columbus (Inc. Place)
Wetherington; CDP-Census Area Only; BUTLER; ***218** SE-3; ★ **CIN**; Ⓒ 1,010
Wetsel (Wetzel); RMC Place; VAN WERT; ▲ Jackson; **216** NI-2; mail Middle Point Z 45863
Wetzel; VAN WERT; see Wetsel (RMC Place)
Weymouth; RMC Place; MEDINA; ▲ Medina; **217** NG-14; elev. 1,042ft./318m.; ★ **CLEV**; mail Medina Z 44256; ● 180
Wharton; Inc. Place; WYANDOT; ▲ Richland; **216** NI-7; 🅿; Z 43359 & mail Kirby Z 43330; Ⓟ 378; Ⓒ 409
Wheat Ridge; RMC Place; ADAMS; ▲ Oliver; ***218** SH-7; elev. 953ft./290m.; mail West Union Z 45693; rural
Wheelersburg; CDP; SCIOTO; ▲ Porter; **218** SI-10; 🅿; ★ **PTSM**; Z 45694; Ⓟ 5,113; Ⓒ 6,471
Wheeling; MCD-Township; BELMONT; ***217** NN-18; mail Fairpoint Z 43927; Ⓟ 1,578; Ⓒ 1,477
Wheeling; MCD-Township; GUERNSEY; ***217** NM-15; mail Kimbolton Z 43749; Ⓟ 592; Ⓒ 752
Wheeling Creek; BELMONT; see Wolfhurst (RMC Place)
Whetstone; MCD-Township; CRAWFORD; ***216** NJ-9; mail Bucyrus Z 44820; Ⓟ 2,318; Ⓒ 2,365
Whigville; RMC Place; NOBLE; ▲ Marion; ***219** SB-17; mail Summerfield Z 43788; rural
Whipple; RMC Place; WASHINGTON; ▲ Salem, Fearing; **219** SD-17; elev. 646ft./197m.; 🅿; Z 45788; ● 130
Whisler; RMC Place; PICKAWAY; ▲ Saltcreek; **218** SE-10; mail Kingston Z 45644; ● 120
White Cottage; RMC Place; MUSKINGUM; ▲ Newton; **219** SB-13; 🅿; ★ **ZAN**; Z 43791; ● 300
White Eyes; MCD-Township; COSHOCTON; ***217** NL-15; mail Fresno Z 43824; Ⓟ 981; Ⓒ 1,078
White Hall; RMC Place; ATHENS; ▲ Athens; ***219** SF-13; mail Athens Z 45701; ● 200
Whitehall; Inc. Place; FRANKLIN; **218** SB-10; 🅿 ■; ★ **COL**; Z 43213; Ⓟ 20,572; Ⓒ 19,201; ◆ 19,259
Whitehouse; Inc. Place; LUCAS; ▲ Waterville; **216** NE-5; 🅿; ★ **TOL**; Z 43571; Ⓟ 2,528; Ⓒ 2,733
White Oak; RMC Place; BROWN; ▲ Pike; ***218** SG-5; elev. 950ft./290m.; ★ **CIN**; mail Mount Orab Z 45154
Whiteoak; RMC Place; FAYETTE; ▲ Madison; **218** SC-8; mail Mount Sterling Z 43143; ● 40
White Oak; CDP; HAMILTON; ▲ Green, Colerain; **218** SF-2; ★ **CIN**; mail Cincinnati Z 45239, Z 45247; Ⓟ 12,430; Ⓒ 13,277
Whiteoak; MCD-Township; HIGHLAND; ***218** SG-6; mail Hillsboro Z 45133; Ⓟ 1,357; Ⓒ 1,374
White Oak East; CDP-Census Area Only; HAMILTON; ▲ Green; ***218** SF-2; elev. 922ft./281m.; ★ **CIN**; mail Cincinnati Z 45239; Ⓟ 3,544; Ⓒ 3,508
White Oak Meadows; RMC Place; HAMILTON; ▲ Colerain; ***218** SF-2; ★ **CIN**; mail Cincinnati Z 45239; ● 630
White Oaks; RMC Place; JEFFERSON; ★ **STU-**; mail Steubenville Z 43952
White Oak Valley; RMC Place; BROWN; ▲ Scott; ***218** SH-5; mail Georgetown Z 45121; rural
White Oak West; CDP-Census Area Only; HAMILTON; ▲ Green; ***218** SF-2; elev. 922ft./281m.; ★ **CIN**; mail Cincinnati Z 45247; Ⓟ 2,879; Ⓒ 2,932
White Pond; RMC Place; SUMMIT; ▲ Copley; ★ **AKR**; mail Akron Z 44321
White's Landing; RMC Place; ERIE, SANDUSKY; ▲ Townsend, Margaretta; **216** NF-9; ★ **SNDSK**; mail Vickery Z 43464; ● 300
White Sulphur; RMC Place; DELAWARE; ▲ Scioto; ***216** NM-8; elev. 907ft./276m.; mail Ostrander Z 43061
Whitetree; RMC Place; HAMILTON; ***218** SF-3; elev. 800ft./244m.; ★ **CIN**; mail Cincinnati Z 45236; pop. incl. with Cincinnati (Inc. Place)
Whitewater; RMC Place; HAMILTON; ▲ Harrison; ★ **CIN**; mail Cleves Z 45002; ● 100
Whitewater; MCD-Township; HAMILTON; ***218** SF-1; ★ **CIN**; mail Cleves Z 45002; Ⓟ 5,178; Ⓒ 5,564
Whitfield; RMC Place; MONTGOMERY; ▲ Miami, Jefferson; ***218** SC-3; elev. 715ft./218m.; ★ **DAY**; mail Miamisburg Z 45342; rural
Wick; RMC Place; ASHTABULA; ▲ Wayne; **217** NE-20; elev. 1,002ft./305m.; mail Williamsfield Z 44093; ● 90
Wickliffe; Inc. Place; LAKE; **217** NE-16; 🅿; ★ **CLEV**; Z 44092; Ⓟ 14,558; Ⓒ 13,484
Widowville; RMC Place; ASHLAND; ▲ Vermillion; **217** NJ-12; mail Ashland Z 44805; ● 25
Wiggonsville; RMC Place; CLERMONT; ▲ Tate; **218** SH-4; elev. 920ft./280m.; ★ **CIN**; mail Bethel Z 45106; ● 80
Wightmans Grove; RMC Place; SANDUSKY; ▲ Riley; ***216** NF-9; elev. 575ft./175m.; mail Fremont Z 43420; ● 350
Wilberforce; CDP; GREENE; ▲ Xenia; **218** SC-5; 🅿 🅲 2,629; ★ **DAY**; Z 45384; Ⓟ 2,639; Ⓒ 1,579
Wildare; RMC Place; TRUMBULL; ▲ Bristol, Champion, Mecca; ***217** NF-19; ★ **YNGS-**; mail Cortland Z 44410; rural
Wildbrook Acres; RMC Place; HAMILTON; ▲ Springfield; **218** SK-3; ★ **CIN**; mail Cincinnati Z 45231; ● 1,500
Wildwood; RMC Place; BUTLER; ★ **MIDD**; mail Middletown Z 45042; pop. incl. with Middletown (Inc. Place)
Wilgus; RMC Place; LAWRENCE; ▲ Mason; **219** SJ-12; mail Willow Wood Z 45696; ● 30
Wilkesville; Inc. Place; VINTON; ▲ Wilkesville; **219** SG-12; 🅿; Z 45695; Ⓟ 151; Ⓒ 151
Wilkesville; MCD-Township; VINTON; ***219** SG-12; 🅿; Z 45695; Ⓟ 901; Ⓒ 888
Wilkins Corners; RMC Place; LICKING; ▲ Mary Ann; ***217** NN-12; ★ **NWRK**; mail Newark Z 43055; ● 100
Wilkshire Hills; RMC Place; TUSCARAWAS; ▲ Lawrence; ***217** NK-16; ★ **CAN**; mail Bolivar Z 44612; ● 220
Willard; Inc. Place; HURON; **216** NH-10; 🅿 🅷; Z 44888, Z 44890; Ⓟ 6,210; Ⓒ 6,806
Willetsville; RMC Place; HIGHLAND; ▲ Union; **218** SF-6; mail Hillsboro Z 45133; ● 50
WILLIAMS; **216** NE-1; Ⓟ 36,956; Ⓒ 39,188; ◆ 38,190
Williamsburg; Inc. Place; CLERMONT; ▲ Williamsburg; **218** SG-4; 🅿; ★ **CIN**; Z 45176; Ⓟ 2,322; Ⓒ 2,358
Williamsburg; MCD-Township; CLERMONT; ***218** SG-4; 🅿; ★ **CIN**; Z 45176; Ⓟ 4,789; Ⓒ 5,005
Williams Center; RMC Place; WILLIAMS; ▲ Center; **216** NF-2; elev. 794ft./242m.; mail Bryan Z 43506; ● 300
Williams Corner; RMC Place; CLERMONT; ▲ Stonelick; ***218** SF-4; ★ **CIN**; mail Batavia Z 45103; rural
Williamsdale; RMC Place; BUTLER; ▲ St. Clair; **218** SE-2; ★ **CIN**; mail Hamilton Z 45011; ● 600
Williamsfield; RMC Place; ASHTABULA; ▲ Williamsfield; **217** NE-20; elev. 1,135ft./346m.; 🅿; Z 44093; ● 400
Williamsfield; MCD-Township; ASHTABULA; ***217** NE-20; 🅿; Z 44093; Ⓟ 1,319; Ⓒ 1,683
Williamsport; RMC Place; COLUMBIANA; ▲ Madison; ***217** NJ-20; ★ **E.LIV**; mail Lisbon Z 44432; rural
Williamsport; RMC Place; MORROW; ▲ Congress; **216** NK-10; elev. 1,366ft./416m.; mail Mount Gilead Z 43338; ● 70
Williamsport; Inc. Place; PICKAWAY; ▲ Deercreek; **218** SD-9; elev. 771ft./235m.; 🅿; Z 43164; Ⓟ 851; Ⓒ 1,002
Williamstown; RMC Place; HANCOCK; ▲ Madison; **216** NI-6; 🅿; Z 45897; ● 100
Williston; RMC Place; OTTAWA; ▲ Allen; **216** NE-7; elev. 598ft./182m.; 🅿; ★ **TOL**; Z 43468; ● 600
Willoughby; Inc. Place; LAKE; **217** NE-16; 🅿 🅷 ■; ★ **CLEV**; Z 44094-97; Ⓟ 20,510; Ⓒ 22,621; ◆ 22,659
Willoughby Hills; Inc. Place; LAKE; **217** NE-16; 🅿; ★ **CLEV**; Z 44092, Z 44094; Ⓟ 8,427; Ⓒ 8,595
Willow; RMC Place; CUYAHOGA; ★ **CLEV**; mail Cleveland Z 44127; pop. incl. with Cleveland (Inc. Place)
Willow Brook Heights; RMC Place; STARK; ▲ Plain; ***217** NI-16; ★ **CAN**; mail Canton Z 44721; ● 325
Willowcrest; RMC Place; MAHONING; ▲ Beaver; ***217** NI-20; elev. 1,139ft./347m.; ★ **YNGS-**; mail North Lima Z 44452; rural
Willowdale Lake; RMC Place; STARK; ▲ Jackson; ***217** NI-16; ★ **CAN**; mail North Canton Z 44720; ● 600
Willowdell; RMC Place; DARKE; ▲ Patterson; **216** NM-2; elev. 994ft./303m.; mail Yorkshire Z 45388; ● 75
Willow Grove; RMC Place; BELMONT; ▲ Richland; ★ **WHL**; mail Bellaire Z 43906; rural
Willowick; Inc. Place; LAKE; **217** NE-16; 🅿; ★ **CLEV**; Z 44095 & mail Wickliffe Z 44092, Willoughby Z 44094; Ⓟ 15,269; Ⓒ 14,361
Willow Lakes; RMC Place; MUSKINGUM; ▲ Falls; ★ **ZAN**; mail Zanesville Z 43701
Willowville; RMC Place; CLERMONT; ▲ Williamsburg; **218** SM-6; ★ **CIN**; mail Batavia Z 45103; ● 500
Willow Wood; RMC Place; LAWRENCE; ▲ Windsor; **219** SJ-12; 🅿; Z 45696; ● 20
Wills; MCD-Township; GUERNSEY; ***219** SA-17; mail Lore City Z 43755; Ⓟ 1,396; Ⓒ 1,567
Wills Creek; RMC Place; COSHOCTON; ▲ Franklin; ***217** NM-14; mail Conesville Z 43811, Coshocton Z 43812; ● 100
Willshire; Inc. Place; VAN WERT; ▲ Willshire; **216** NJ-1; elev. 798ft./243m.; 🅿; Z 45898; Ⓟ 541; Ⓒ 463
Willshire; MCD-Township; VAN WERT; ***216** NJ-1; 🅿; Z 45898; Ⓟ 1,807; Ⓒ 1,719
Wilmington; Inc. Place; ⊡ CLINTON; ▲ Union; **218** SE-5; 🅿 🅷 🅲 1,569; Z 45177; Ⓟ 11,199; Ⓒ 11,921; Ⓡ 11,875
Wilmot; Inc. Place; STARK; ▲ Sugar Creek; **217** NK-15; elev. 1,093ft./333m.; 🅿; ★ **CAN**; Z 44689; Ⓟ 261; Ⓒ 335
Wilshire; RMC Place; CLERMONT; ▲ Stonelick; ***218** SF-4; ★ **CIN**; mail Goshen Z 45122; ● 300
Wilshire Heights; RMC Place; WARREN; ▲ Franklin; ***218** SD-3; ★ **MIDD**; mail Franklin Z 45005; ● 1,200
Wilson; MCD-Township; CLINTON; ***218** SD-6; mail Sabina Z 45169; Ⓟ 523; Ⓒ 581
Wilson; Inc. Place; MONROE, BELMONT; ▲ Wayne, Sunsbury; **219** SB-18; elev. 1,247ft./380m.; mail Beallsville Z 43716; Ⓟ 136; Ⓒ 118
Wiltondale; RMC Place; HAMILTON; ▲ Springfield; ★ **CIN**; mail Cincinnati Z 45224
Winameg; RMC Place; FULTON; ▲ Pike; ***216** NE-4; mail Delta Z 43515; ● 60
Winchester; Inc. Place; ADAMS; ▲ Winchester; **218** SH-6; 🅿; Z 45697; Ⓟ 978; Ⓒ 1,025
Winchester; MCD-Township; ADAMS; ***218** SH-6; 🅿; Z 45697; Ⓟ 1,764; Ⓒ 1,984
Winchester; RMC Place; JACKSON; ▲ Bloomfield; **219** SH-11; elev. 752ft./229m.; mail Jackson Z 45640; ● 50
Windfall; RMC Place; MEDINA; ▲ Medina; ***217** NH-14; ★ **CLEV**; mail Medina Z 44256; rural
Windham; Inc. Place; PORTAGE; **217** NG-18; 🅿; Z 44288; Ⓟ 2,943; Ⓒ 2,806
Windham; MCD-Township; PORTAGE; ***217** NG-18; 🅿; Z 44288; Ⓟ 4,898; Ⓒ 2,060
Windor Park; RMC Place; GREENE; ★ **DAY**; mail Xenia Z 45385; pop. incl. with Xenia (Inc. Place)
Windsor; RMC Place; ASHTABULA; ▲ Windsor; **217** NE-18; elev. 834ft./254m.; 🅿; Z 44099; ● 400
Windsor; MCD-Township; ASHTABULA; ***217** NE-18; 🅿; Z 44099; Ⓟ 1,481; Ⓒ 1,932
Windsor; MCD-Township; LAWRENCE; ***219** SJ-12; mail Scottown Z 45678; Ⓟ 1,886; Ⓒ 2,127
Windsor; MCD-Township; MORGAN; ***219** SD-15; mail Stockport Z 43787; Ⓟ 1,939; Ⓒ 1,951
Windsor; RMC Place; RICHLAND; ▲ Mifflin; **217** NJ-11; ★ **MANS**; mail Mansfield Z 44903; ● 120
Windsor; RMC Place; WARREN; ▲ Harlan; ***218** SF-4; elev. 918ft./280m.; mail Pleasant Plain Z 45162
Windsor Mills; RMC Place; ASHTABULA; ▲ Windsor; ***217** NE-18; elev. 1,014ft./309m.; mail Windsor Z 44099
Windy Acres; RMC Place; CLARK; ▲ Pike; ***218** SA-5; ★ **SPR**; mail Springfield Z 45502; ● 30
Winesburg; RMC Place; HOLMES; ▲ Paint; **217** NK-15; elev. 1,312ft./400m.; 🅿; Z 44690; ● 300
Winfield; RMC Place; TUSCARAWAS; ▲ Dover; **217** NK-15; mail Dover Z 44622; ● 200
Wingett Run; RMC Place; WASHINGTON; ▲ Ludlow; **219** SD-17; 🅿; Z 45789; ● 40
Wingston; RMC Place; WOOD; ▲ Liberty; ***216** NG-6; elev. 695ft./212m.; mail Rudolph Z 43462; ● 80
Winkle; HIGHLAND; see East Danville (RMC Place)
Winona; RMC Place; COLUMBIANA; ▲ Butler; **217** NI-18; 🅿; Z 44493; ● 250
Winterdale; RMC Place; JEFFERSON; ★ **STU-**; mail Steubenville Z 43953; pop. incl. with Wintersville (Inc. Place)
Winterhaven; RMC Place; GREENE; ▲ Sugarcreek; ***218** SC-4; ★ **DAY**; mail Bellbrook Z 45305; ● 520
Winterset; RMC Place; GUERNSEY; ▲ Madison; **217** NN-16; mail Lore City Z 43755; ● 150
Wintersville; Inc. Place; JEFFERSON; ▲ Island Creek, Cross Creek; **217** NL-19; 🅿; ★ **STU-**; Z 43952-53; Ⓟ 4,102; Ⓒ 4,067
Wintondale; RMC Place; HAMILTON; ▲ Springfield; ***218** SF-2; elev. 850ft./259m.; ★ **CIN**; mail Cincinnati Z 45231
Winton Place; RMC Place; HAMILTON; ***218** SF-2; ★ **CIN**; mail Cincinnati Z 45232; pop. incl. with Cincinnati (Inc. Place)
Winton Terrace; RMC Place; HAMILTON; ***218** SF-2; elev. 570ft./174m.; ★ **CIN**; mail Cincinnati Z 45232; pop. incl. with Cincinnati (Inc. Place)
Wisterman; RMC Place; PUTNAM; ▲ Monroe; ***216** NH-3; mail Continental Z 45831; rural
Withamsville; CDP; CLERMONT; ▲ Union; **218** SG-3; ★ **CIN**; mail Cincinnati Z 45245; Ⓟ 2,834; Ⓒ 3,145
Wolf; RMC Place; TUSCARAWAS; ▲ Salem; ***217** NM-15; mail Newcomerstown Z 43832; ● 50
Wolfhurst (Wheeling Creek); RMC Place; BELMONT; ▲ Pease; ***219** SA-19; ★ **WHL**; mail Bridgeport Z 43912; ● 600
Wolf Run; RMC Place; JEFFERSON; ▲ Springfield; **217** NL-19; 🅿; Z 43970; ● 120
WOOD; **216** NG-6; Ⓟ 113,269; Ⓒ 121,065; ◆ 127,318
Woodbourne; RMC Place; MONTGOMERY; ▲ Washington; **218** SN-8; ★ **DAY**; mail Dayton Z 45459; ● 6,050
Woodbourne-Hyde Park; CDP-Census Area Only; MONTGOMERY; ▲ Washington; ***218** SC-4; ★ **DAY**; mail Dayton Z 45429, Z 45459; Ⓟ 7,837; Ⓒ 7,910
Woodhaven; RMC Place; WARREN; ▲ Franklin; ★ **MIDD**; mail Franklin Z 45005
Woodington; RMC Place; DARKE; ▲ Greenville; **216** NM-1; mail Greenville Z 45331; ● 100
Woodlawn; Inc. Place; HAMILTON; **218** SK-3; ★ **CIN**; mail Cincinnati Z 45215; Ⓟ 2,674; Ⓒ 2,816
Woodlawn; RMC Place; MIAMI; ▲ Concord; mail Troy Z 45373; ● 180
Woodlawn Village; RMC Place; MIAMI; ▲ Monroe; ***218** SB-4; ★ **DAY**; mail Troy Z 45373; pop. incl. with Tipp City (Inc. Place)
Woodmere; Inc. Place; CUYAHOGA; **219** SL-20; 🅿; ★ **CLEV**; Z 44122; Ⓟ 834; Ⓒ 828
Woods; BUTLER; see Woods Station (RMC Place)
Woodsdale; RMC Place; BUTLER; ▲ St. Clair, Madison; **218** SE-2; elev. 617ft./188m.; ★ **CIN**; mail Trenton Z 45067; ● 200
Woodsfield; Inc. Place; ⊡ MONROE; ▲ Center; **219** SC-18; elev. 1,213ft./370m.; 🅿; Z 43793; Ⓟ 2,832; Ⓒ 2,598
Woodside; RMC Place; WOOD; ▲ Freedom; ***216** NF-7; mail Bradner Z 43406; rural
Woods Station (Woods); RMC Place; BUTLER; ▲ Reily; ***218** SE-1; mail Oxford Z 45056
Woodstock; Inc. Place; CHAMPAIGN; ▲ Rush; **216** NM-6; elev. 1,042ft./318m.; 🅿; Z 43084; Ⓟ 296; Ⓒ 317
Woodville; RMC Place; CLERMONT, WARREN; ▲ Wayne, Harlan; ***218** SF-4; ★ **CIN**; mail Goshen Z 45122
Woodville; Inc. Place; SANDUSKY; ▲ Sandusky; **216** NF-7; 🅿; ★ **TOL**; Z 43469; Ⓟ 1,953; Ⓒ 1,977
Woodville; MCD-Township; SANDUSKY; ***216** NF-7; 🅿; ★ **TOL**; Z 43469; Ⓟ 3,088; Ⓒ 3,304
Woodville Gardens; RMC Place; WOOD; ▲ Lake; ***216** NE-7; ★ **TOL**; mail Oregon Z 43616; ● 350
Woodworth; RMC Place; MAHONING; ▲ Beaver; **217** NI-20; elev. 1,081ft./329m.; ★ **YNGS-**; mail North Lima Z 44452, Youngstown Z 44512, Z 44514; ● 700
Woodworth Corners; RMC Place; TRUMBULL; ▲ Vienna; ***217** NG-20; elev. 1,176ft./358m.; ★ **YNGS-**; mail Vienna Z 44473; rural
Wooster; Inc. Place; ⊡ WAYNE; ▲ Wooster; **217** NJ-14; 🅿 🅷 🅲 1,802 ■; Z 44691; Ⓟ 22,191; Ⓒ 24,811; ◆ 25,215
Wooster; MCD-Township; WAYNE; ***217** NJ-14; 🅿 🅲 1,802; Z 44691; Ⓟ 4,918; Ⓒ 5,250
Wooster Heights; RMC Place; RICHLAND; ▲ Madison; **217** NJ-11; 1 mi. E of Lincoln Heights; ★ **MANS**; mail Mansfield Z 44903; ● 850
Worstville; RMC Place; PAULDING; ▲ Paulding; **216** NH-1; mail Payne Z 45880; ● 25
Worthington; Inc. Place; FRANKLIN; ▲ Sharon; **216** NN-9; 🅿 🅷; ★ **COL**; Z 43085; Ⓟ 14,869; Ⓒ 14,125
Worthington; MCD-Township; RICHLAND; ***217** NK-12; ★ **MANS**; mail Butler Z 44822; Ⓟ 2,505; Ⓒ 2,791
Wren; Inc. Place; VAN WERT; ▲ Willshire; **216** NJ-1; elev. 813ft./248m.; 🅿; Z 45899; Ⓟ 190; Ⓒ 199
Wright Brothers; RMC Place; MONTGOMERY; ★ **DAY**; mail Dayton Z 45409; pop. incl. with Oakwood (Inc. Place)
Wright-Patterson AFB; CDP-Census Area Only; GREENE, MONTGOMERY; ▲ Bath; ***218** SC-4; 🅿; ★ **DAY**; Z 45433 & mail Dayton Z 45431; Ⓟ 8,579; Ⓒ 6,656
Wrightsville; RMC Place; ADAMS; **218** SI-7; mail Manchester Z 45144; ● 30
Wrightsville; RMC Place; FRANKLIN, MADISON; ***218** SB-8; ★ **COL**; mail Grove City Z 43123
Wrightview; RMC Place; GREENE; ***218** SC-4; ★ **DAY**; mail Fairborn Z 45324; pop. incl. with Fairborn (Inc. Place)
Wyandot; RMC Place; WYANDOT; ▲ Antrim; **216** NJ-8; elev. 979ft./298m.; mail Nevada Z 44849; ● 50
WYANDOT; **216** NJ-7; Ⓟ 22,254; Ⓒ 22,908; ◆ 22,152
Wyoming; Inc. Place; HAMILTON; **218** SK-3; 🅿; ★ **CIN**; Z 45215, Z 45231; Ⓟ 8,128; Ⓒ 8,261
Wyoming Meadows; RMC Place; HAMILTON; ▲ Springfield; ***218** SF-2; ★ **CIN**; mail Cincinnati Z 45231; ● 450

X

Xenia; Inc. Place; ⊡ GREENE; **218** SC-5; 🅿 🅷 ■; ★ **DAY**; Z 45385; Ⓟ 24,664; Ⓒ 24,164; ◆ 25,512
Xenia; MCD-Township; GREENE; ***218** SC-5; 🅿 🅲 2,629; ★ **DAY**; Z 45385; Ⓟ 7,633; Ⓒ 6,117

Y

Yale; RMC Place; PORTAGE; ▲ Edinburg, Deerfield; ***217** NH-18; ★ **AKR**; mail Deerfield Z 44411; ● 60
Yankeeburg; RMC Place; WASHINGTON; ▲ Newport; ***219** SE-17; mail Newport Z 45768; rural
Yankee Hills; RMC Place; TRUMBULL; ▲ Brookfield; ***217** NG-20; ★ **SHAR**; mail Brookfield Z 44403
Yankee Lake; Inc. Place; TRUMBULL; ▲ Brookfield; **217** NG-20; ★ **SHAR**; mail Brookfield Z 44403; Ⓟ 88; Ⓒ 99
Yankeetown; RMC Place; BROWN; ▲ Clark; **218** SH-4; elev. 917ft./280m.; ★ **CIN**; mail Hamersville Z 45130; ● 250
Yatesville; RMC Place; FAYETTE; ▲ Paint; **218** SC-7; mail Bloomingburg Z 43106; ● 20
Yellowbud; RMC Place; ROSS; ▲ Union; **218** SD-9; mail Chillicothe Z 45601; ● 120
Yellow Creek; MCD-Township; COLUMBIANA; ***217** NK-19; ★ **E.LIV**; mail Wellsville Z 43968; Ⓟ 2,208; Ⓒ 2,185
Yellow Creek; RMC Place; JEFFERSON; ▲ Saline; ***217** NK-20; ★ **E.LIV**; mail Wellsville Z 43968; rural
Yellow Springs; Inc. Place; GREENE; ▲ Miami; **218** SC-5; 🅿 🅲 4,221; ★ **DAY**; Z 45387; Ⓟ 3,973; Ⓒ 3,761
Yellowtown; RMC Place; PERRY; ▲ Bearfield; ***219** SC-13; mail Crooksville Z 43731; rural
Yelverton; RMC Place; HARDIN; ▲ Taylor Creek; ***216** NK-6; mail Kenton Z 43326; ● 30
Yoder; RMC Place; ALLEN; ▲ Perry; ***216** NJ-4; elev. 964ft./294m.; ★ **LIMA**; mail Lima Z 45806
Yondota; RMC Place; LUCAS; ▲ Jerusalem; ***216** NE-7; ★ **TOL**; mail Curtice Z 43412; rural
York; MCD-Township; ATHENS; ***219** SE-13; mail Nelsonville Z 45764; Ⓟ 7,036; Ⓒ 7,740
York; MCD-Township; BELMONT; ***219** SB-19; mail Powhatan Point Z 43942; Ⓟ 2,798; Ⓒ 2,648
York; MCD-Township; DARKE; ***216** NM-2; mail Versailles Z 45380; Ⓟ 557; Ⓒ 523
York; MCD-Township; FULTON; ***216** NE-4; ★ **TOL**; mail Delta Z 43515; Ⓟ 4,180; Ⓒ 4,203
York; RMC Place; JEFFERSON; ▲ Smithfield; **217** NM-19; ★ **STU-**; mail Adena Z 43901; ● 90
York; MCD-Township; MEDINA; ***217** NG-14; ★ **CLEV**; mail Medina Z 44256; Ⓟ 2,479; Ⓒ 2,912
York; MCD-Township; MORGAN; ***219** SC-14; mail Crooksville Z 43731; Ⓟ 949; Ⓒ 958
York; MCD-Township; SANDUSKY; ***216** NG-9; mail Bellevue Z 44811; Ⓟ 2,401; Ⓒ 2,512
York; MCD-Township; TUSCARAWAS; ***217** NL-16; mail New Philadelphia Z 44663; Ⓟ 1,179; Ⓒ 1,292
York; MCD-Township; UNION; ***216** NL-7; mail Raymond Z 43067; Ⓟ 925; Ⓒ 1,174
York; MCD-Township; VAN WERT; ***216** NJ-2; mail Ohio City Z 45874; Ⓟ 960; Ⓒ 788
York Center; RMC Place; UNION; ▲ York; **216** NL-7; mail Raymond Z 43067; ● 100
Yorkshire; Inc. Place; DARKE; ▲ Patterson; **216** NL-2; elev. 988ft./301m.; 🅿; Z 45388; Ⓟ 126; Ⓒ 110
Yorkshire Estates; RMC Place; MARION; ▲ Marion; ★ **MRN**; mail Marion Z 43302; ● 400
Yorkville; Inc. Place; BELMONT, JEFFERSON; ▲ Warren; **217** NM-19; 🅿; ★ **WHL**; Z 43971; Ⓟ 1,246; Ⓒ 1,230
Young Hickory; RMC Place; MUSKINGUM; ▲ Meigs; ***219** SC-15; mail Cumberland Z 43732; rural
Youngs; RMC Place; SCIOTO; ▲ Rarden, Brush Creek; **218** SH-8; mail Otway Z 45657; ● 110
Youngs Corners; RMC Place; MEDINA; ▲ Sharon, Granger; ***217** NH-15; ★ **CLEV**; mail Medina Z 44256, Wadsworth Z 44281; rural
Youngstown; Inc. Place; ⊡ MAHONING, TRUMBULL; **217** NH-20; elev. 861ft./262m.; 🅿 🅷 🅲 12,812 ■; ★ **YNGS-**; Z 44501-07, Z 44509-15, Z 44555; Ⓟ 95,732; Ⓒ 82,026; ◆ 65,949
Youngsville; RMC Place; ADAMS; ▲ Wayne; **218** SH-6; elev. 884ft./269m.; mail Seaman Z 45679; ● 50

Z

Zahns Corners; RMC Place; PIKE; ▲ Seal; ***218** SG-9; mail Waverly Z 45690
Zaleski; Inc. Place; VINTON; ▲ Madison; **219** SF-12; elev. 713ft./217m.; 🅿; Z 45698; Ⓟ 294; Ⓒ 375
Zane; MCD-Township; LOGAN; ***216** NM-6; mail Middleburg Z 43336; Ⓟ 704; Ⓒ 968
Zane Addition; RMC Place; ROSS; ▲ Scioto; ***218** SE-9; mail Chillicothe Z 45601; pop. incl. with Chillicothe (Inc. Place)
Zanesfield; Inc. Place; LOGAN; ▲ Jefferson; **216** NL-6; 🅿; Z 43360; Ⓟ 183; Ⓒ 220
Zanesville; Inc. Place; ⊡ MUSKINGUM; **219** SB-14; 🅿 🅷 🅲 1,723 ■; ★ **ZAN**; Z 43701-02; Ⓟ 26,778; Ⓒ 25,586; ◆ 24,084
Zenz City; MERCER; see Sharpsburg (RMC Place)
Zimmer Estates; RMC Place; GREENE; ▲ Beavercreek; ★ **DAY**; mail Dayton Z 45431; ● 590
Zimmerman; RMC Place; GREENE; ▲ Beavercreek; ***218** SC-4; ★ **DAY**; mail Dayton Z 45432, Z 45434; pop. incl. with Beavercreek (Inc. Place)
Ziontown; RMC Place; PERRY; ▲ Thorn; ***219** SB-12; ★ **COL**; mail Glenford Z 43739; ● 50
Zoar; Inc. Place; TUSCARAWAS; ▲ Lawrence; **217** NK-16; 🅿; ★ **CAN**; Z 44697; Ⓟ 177; Ⓒ 193
Zoar; RMC Place; WARREN; ▲ Hamilton; ***218** SE-4; elev. 796ft./243m.; ★ **CIN**; mail Morrow Z 45152; ● 40
Zoarville (Valley Junction); RMC Place; TUSCARAWAS; ▲ Sandy; **217** NK-16; 🅿; ★ **CAN**; Z 44656; ● 230
Zone; RMC Place; FULTON; ▲ Franklin; **216** NE-3; mail Fayette Z 43521; ● 30

Entries in **UPPERCASE** are counties.
Entries in **bold** have populations of 2,500 or more.
Names in parentheses are alternate names.
Inc. Place — Incorporated Place
RMC Place — Rand McNally Designated Place
CDP — Census Designated Place
MCD — Minor Civil Division

⊡ County Seat
▲ Minor Civil Division
elev. Elevation
🅿 Post Office
🅷 Hospital
🅲 College
■ Principal Business Center
★ Ranally Metro Area (RMA) Abbreviation
Z Zip Code(s)
Ⓟ Previous Census Population
Ⓡ Revised Census Population
Ⓐ Annexation Population
● Rand McNally Population Estimate
Ⓒ Final Census Population
Ⓢ Special Census Population
◆ Estimated Population

For additional definitions see Glossary, Volume 1, and Introduction, Volume 2.

OKLAHOMA

CO
KS
MO
Oklahoma City
NM
AR
TX

Statistics

Total area (2000) — 69,898 square miles
Land area (2000) — 68,667 square miles
Water area (2000) — 1,231 square miles
Capital — Oklahoma City
Admitted as state — November, 1907

Maps

State maps can be found on pages 142-254 in Vol. 1

Ranally Metro Areas (RMAs) and Abbreviations

Bartlesville, OK — BART
Enid, OK — ENID
Fort Smith, AR-OK — FTSM
Lawton, OK — LAWT
Muskogee, OK — MSKOG
Oklahoma City, OK — O.C.
Tulsa, OK — TUL

Principal Places

Place Name	Place Type	County	Population
Oklahoma City	Inc. Place	OKLAHOMA	◆ 571,899
Tulsa	Inc. Place	TULSA	◆ 409,085
Norman	Inc. Place	CLEVELAND	◆ 113,433
Lawton	Inc. Place	COMANCHE	◆ 112,367
Broken Arrow	Inc. Place	TULSA	◆ 83,383
Edmond	Inc. Place	OKLAHOMA	◆ 77,520
Midwest City	Inc. Place	OKLAHOMA	◆ 55,712
Moore	Inc. Place	CLEVELAND	◆ 51,861
Stillwater	Inc. Place	PAYNE	◆ 50,431
Enid	Inc. Place	GARFIELD	◆ 48,986
Muskogee	Inc. Place	MUSKOGEE	◆ 39,435
Bartlesville	Inc. Place	WASHINGTON	◆ 36,876
Shawnee	Inc. Place	POTTAWATOMIE	◆ 29,911
Ardmore	Inc. Place	CARTER	◆ 25,130
Ponca City	Inc. Place	KAY	◆ 24,068
Duncan	Inc. Place	STEPHENS	◆ 23,586
Yukon	Inc. Place	CANADIAN	◆ 22,543
Owasso	Inc. Place	TULSA	◆ 22,137
Del City	Inc. Place	OKLAHOMA	◆ 21,881
Bethany	Inc. Place	OKLAHOMA	◆ 20,093
Sapulpa	Inc. Place	CREEK	◆ 19,011
Altus	Inc. Place	JACKSON	◆ 18,796
McAlester	Inc. Place	PITTSBURG	◆ 18,323
Sand Springs	Inc. Place	TULSA	© 17,451
Ada	Inc. Place	PONTOTOC	◆ 17,147
Chickasha	Inc. Place	GRADY	◆ 16,585
El Reno	Inc. Place	CANADIAN	© 16,212
Claremore	Inc. Place	ROGERS	© 15,873
Bixby	Inc. Place	TULSA	◆ 15,097
Tahlequah	Inc. Place	CHEROKEE	© 14,458
Durant	Inc. Place	BRYAN	© 13,549
Woodward	Inc. Place	WOODWARD	◆ 13,202
Mustang	Inc. Place	CANADIAN	© 13,156
Elk City	Inc. Place	BECKHAM	◆ 13,024
Okmulgee	Inc. Place	OKMULGEE	© 13,022
Miami	Inc. Place	OTTAWA	◆ 12,087
Guymon	Inc. Place	TEXAS	© 10,472
The Village	Inc. Place	OKLAHOMA	© 10,157
Guthrie	Inc. Place	LOGAN	© 9,925
Weatherford	Inc. Place	CUSTER	© 9,859
Warr Acres	Inc. Place	OKLAHOMA	© 9,735
Jenks	Inc. Place	TULSA	© 9,557
Choctaw	Inc. Place	OKLAHOMA	© 9,377
Clinton	Inc. Place	CUSTER	© 8,833
Pryor	Inc. Place	MAYES	© 8,659
Cushing	Inc. Place	PAYNE	© 8,371
Glenpool	Inc. Place	TULSA	© 8,123
Sallisaw	Inc. Place	SEQUOYAH	© 7,989
Poteau	Inc. Place	LE FLORE	© 7,939
Wagoner	Inc. Place	WAGONER	© 7,669
Blackwell	Inc. Place	KAY	© 7,668
Coweta	Inc. Place	WAGONER	© 7,139
Idabel	Inc. Place	MCCURTAIN	© 6,952
Seminole	Inc. Place	SEMINOLE	© 6,899
Anadarko	Inc. Place	CADDO	© 6,645
Pauls Valley	Inc. Place	GARVIN	© 6,256
Tecumseh	Inc. Place	POTTAWATOMIE	© 6,098
Henryetta	Inc. Place	OKMULGEE	© 6,096
Vinita	Inc. Place	CRAIG	® 6,062
Holdenville	Inc. Place	HUGHES	® 5,700
Purcell	Inc. Place	MCCLAIN	© 5,571
Hugo	Inc. Place	CHOCTAW	© 5,536
Catoosa	Inc. Place	ROGERS	© 5,449
Newcastle	Inc. Place	MCCLAIN	© 5,434
Skiatook	Inc. Place	OSAGE	© 5,396
Alva	Inc. Place	WOODS	© 5,288
Noble	Inc. Place	CLEVELAND	© 5,260
Perry	Inc. Place	NOBLE	© 5,230
Grove	Inc. Place	DELAWARE	© 5,131

County Business Data

County	FIPS Code	County Seat	Land Area (Sq. Mi.)	Census Population			Wholesale Trade		Manufacturing, 2002			
				4/1/2000	4/1/1990	% Change 1990-2000	Sales, 2002 ($1,000)	% Change 1997-2002	Establish-ments	Total Employees	Value Added ($1,000)	Ranally Mfg. Units
Adair	001	Stilwell	576	21,038	18,421	14.2	25,122	349.9	15	1,614	113,434	60
Alfalfa	003	Cherokee	867	6,105	6,416	-4.8	34,278	-34.1	...	(d)	(d)	...
Atoka	005	Atoka	978	13,879	12,778	8.6	(d)	(d)	...	(d)	(d)	...
Beaver	007	Beaver	1,814	5,857	6,023	-2.8	9,202	-10.8	...	(d)	(d)	...
Beckham	009	Sayre	902	19,799	18,812	5.2	82,610	42.4	...	(d)	(d)	...
Blaine	011	Watonga	928	11,976	11,470	4.4	116,247	(d)	...	(d)	(d)	...
Bryan	013	Durant	909	36,534	32,089	13.9	457,360	59.1	43	1,404	89,847	48
Caddo	015	Anadarko	1,278	30,150	29,550	2.0	41,005	-63.2	...	(d)	(d)	...
Canadian	017	El Reno	900	87,697	74,409	17.9	305,336	-62.7	73	3,268	519,573	275
Carter	019	Ardmore	824	45,621	42,919	6.3	(d)	(d)	42	(d)	(d)	...
Cherokee	021	Tahlequah	751	42,521	34,049	24.9	70,704	59.0	...	(d)	(d)	...
Choctaw	023	Hugo	774	15,342	15,302	0.3	29,844	(d)	...	(d)	(d)	...
Cimarron	025	Boise City	1,835	3,148	3,301	-4.6	6,975	-49.2	...	(d)	(d)	...
Cleveland	027	Norman	536	208,016	174,253	19.4	636,786	20.5	144	3,360	441,555	234
Coal	029	Coalgate	518	6,031	5,780	4.3	(d)	(d)	...	(d)	(d)	...
Comanche	031	Lawton	1,069	114,996	111,486	3.1	205,181	2.3	53	3,316	379,997	201
Cotton	033	Walters	637	6,614	6,651	-0.6	10,482	-2.2	...	(d)	(d)	...
Craig	035	Vinita	761	14,950	14,104	6.0	76,268	1.8	18	883	73,734	39
Creek	037	Sapulpa	956	67,367	60,915	10.6	338,061	32.1	105	4,050	475,643	252
Custer	039	Arapaho	987	26,142	26,897	-2.8	197,637	-6.7	31	1,205	157,287	83
Delaware	041	Jay	741	37,077	28,070	32.1	19,220	-29.0	23	534	24,163	13
Dewey	043	Taloga	1,000	4,743	5,551	-14.6	3,169	(d)	...	(d)	(d)	...
Ellis	045	Arnett	1,229	4,075	4,497	-9.4	14,185	-4.8	...	(d)	(d)	...
Garfield	047	Enid	1,058	57,813	56,735	1.9	833,452	46.2	63	1,228	140,901	75
Garvin	049	Pauls Valley	807	27,210	26,605	2.3	66,368	-2.1	25	(d)	(d)	...
Grady	051	Chickasha	1,101	45,516	41,747	9.0	187,006	7.8	65	2,957	285,434	151
Grant	053	Medford	1,001	5,144	5,689	-9.6	20,983	(d)	...	(d)	(d)	...
Greer	055	Mangum	639	6,061	6,559	-7.6	(d)	(d)	...	(d)	(d)	...
Harmon	057	Hollis	538	3,283	3,793	-13.4	(d)	(d)	...	(d)	(d)	...
Harper	059	Buffalo	1,039	3,562	4,063	-12.3	1,900	-85.8	...	(d)	(d)	...
Haskell	061	Stigler	577	11,792	10,940	7.8	9,437	-77.3	...	(d)	(d)	...
Hughes	063	Holdenville	807	14,154	13,023	8.7	7,401	-79.2	...	(d)	(d)	...
Jackson	065	Altus	803	28,439	28,764	-1.1	88,763	33.1	16	872	83,062	44
Jefferson	067	Waurika	759	6,818	7,010	-2.7	(d)	(d)	...	(d)	(d)	...
Johnston	069	Tishomingo	645	10,513	10,032	4.8	45,796	217.7	14	631	59,100	31
Kay	071	Newkirk	919	48,080	48,056	0.0	243,345	15.7	78	3,957	218,623	116
Kingfisher	073	Kingfisher	903	13,926	13,212	5.4	181,422	13.9	...	(d)	(d)	...
Kiowa	075	Hobart	1,015	10,227	11,347	-9.9	32,157	-28.1	...	(d)	(d)	...
Latimer	077	Wilburton	722	10,692	10,333	3.5	20,439	(d)	...	(d)	(d)	...
Le Flore	079	Poteau	1,586	48,109	43,270	11.2	(d)	(d)	27	(d)	(d)	...
Lincoln	081	Chandler	958	32,080	29,216	9.8	(d)	(d)	...	(d)	(d)	...
Logan	083	Guthrie	744	33,924	29,011	16.9	(d)	(d)	...	(d)	(d)	...
Love	085	Marietta	515	8,831	8,157	8.3	(d)	(d)	9	(d)	(d)	...
Major	093	Fairview	957	7,545	8,055	-6.3	60,844	-12.3	...	(d)	(d)	...
Marshall	095	Madill	371	13,184	10,829	21.7	26,482	-45.7	19	909	50,410	27
Mayes	097	Pryor	656	38,369	33,366	15.0	275,138	285.1	68	2,871	395,234	209
McClain	087	Purcell	570	27,740	22,795	21.7	(d)	(d)	...	(d)	(d)	...
McCurtain	089	Idabel	1,852	34,402	33,433	2.9	57,454	-17.6	24	2,861	526,850	279
McIntosh	091	Eufaula	620	19,456	16,779	16.0	2,476	-63.1	...	(d)	(d)	...
Murray	099	Sulphur	418	12,623	12,042	4.8	14,621	-42.7	...	(d)	(d)	...
Muskogee	101	Muskogee	814	69,451	68,078	2.0	332,276	6.1	78	4,867	615,986	326
Noble	103	Perry	732	11,411	11,045	3.3	17,195	-0.1	12	(d)	(d)	...
Nowata	105	Nowata	565	10,569	9,992	5.8	(d)	(d)	...	(d)	(d)	...
Okfuskee	107	Okemah	625	11,814	11,551	2.3	(d)	(d)	...	(d)	(d)	...
Oklahoma	109	Oklahoma City	709	660,448	599,611	10.1	13,436,882	-11.3	793	30,775	4,367,792	2,311
Okmulgee	111	Okmulgee	697	39,685	36,490	8.8	45,382	6.3	40	1,552	225,402	119
Osage	113	Pawhuska	2,251	44,437	41,645	6.7	17,795	-39.7	...	(d)	(d)	...
Ottawa	115	Miami	471	33,194	30,561	8.6	(d)	(d)	55	1,248	109,540	58
Pawnee	117	Pawnee	569	16,612	15,575	6.7	41,666	(d)	...	(d)	(d)	...
Payne	119	Stillwater	686	68,190	61,507	10.9	265,414	25.7	63	2,402	234,565	124
Pittsburg	121	McAlester	1,306	43,953	40,581	8.3	(d)	(d)	26	741	37,159	20
Pontotoc	123	Ada	720	35,143	34,119	3.0	216,201	-16.1	55	1,455	178,117	94
Pottawatomie	125	Shawnee	788	65,521	58,760	11.5	(d)	(d)	63	3,409	286,873	152
Pushmataha	127	Antlers	1,397	11,667	10,997	6.1	2,196	-80.2	...	(d)	(d)	...
Roger Mills	129	Cheyenne	1,142	3,436	4,147	-17.1	6,351	36.7	...	(d)	(d)	...
Rogers	131	Claremore	675	70,641	55,170	28.0	229,095	-36.0	136	4,950	497,670	263
Seminole	133	Wewoka	633	24,894	25,412	-2.0	47,192	-12.3	23	1,465	462,096	244
Sequoyah	135	Sallisaw	674	38,972	33,828	15.2	(d)	(d)	...	(d)	(d)	...
Stephens	137	Duncan	874	43,182	42,299	2.1	83,231	-8.1	53	1,814	121,065	64
Texas	139	Guymon	2,037	20,107	16,419	22.5	112,554	(d)	9	(d)	(d)	...
Tillman	141	Frederick	872	9,287	10,384	-10.6	27,882	-16.5	...	(d)	(d)	...
Tulsa	143	Tulsa	570	563,299	503,341	11.9	9,859,729	4.6	1,103	41,309	4,147,984	2,195
Wagoner	145	Wagoner	563	57,491	47,883	20.1	73,525	-25.2	81	1,661	148,711	79
Washington	147	Bartlesville	417	48,996	48,066	1.9	64,041	23.1	48	1,557	50,022	26
Washita	149	Cordell	1,003	11,508	11,441	0.6	21,910	-34.0	...	(d)	(d)	...
Woods	151	Alva	1,287	9,089	9,103	-0.2	39,858	-16.9	...	(d)	(d)	...
Woodward	153	Woodward	1,242	18,486	18,976	-2.6	77,073	11.9	...	(d)	(d)	...
The State			**68,667**	**3,450,654**	**3,145,585**	**9.7**	**30,799,789**	**-4.1**	**4,027**	**149,983**	**17,005,404**	**8,997**

(d) Data not available. Corresponding percentages or Ranally Manufacturing Units are estimates.
... Represents 0 or amount too minimal to be reported.

Index of Places and Counties

A

Achille; Inc. Place; BRYAN; **221** K-16; elev. 685ft./209m.; 🅿; Z 74720; Ⓟ 491; © 506
Acme; RMC Place; GRADY; ***221** H-12; mail Rush Springs Z 73082; ● 30
Ada; Inc. Place; ⊡ PONTOTOC; **221** H-15; elev. 1,010ft./308m.; 🅿 🅷 🅲 4,506 ■; Z 74820-21; location of Chickasaw Indian Agency; Ⓟ 15,820; © 15,691; ◆ 17,147
Adair; Inc. Place; MAYES; **221** C-18; elev. 680ft./207m.; 🅿; Z 74330; Ⓟ 685; © 704
ADAIR; **221** E-20; Ⓟ 18,421; © 21,038; ◆ 21,712
Adams; RMC Place; TEXAS; **220** B-5; 🅿; Z 73901; ● 200
Adamson; RMC Place; PITTSBURG; **221** H-18; mail Hartshorne Z 74547; ● 150
Addington; Inc. Place; JEFFERSON; **221** J-12; elev. 946ft./288m.; 🅿; Z 73520; Ⓟ 100; © 117
Adel; RMC Place; PUSHMATAHA; ***221** I-18; elev. 708ft./216m.; mail Daisy Z 74540; rural
Afton; Inc. Place; OTTAWA; **221** C-19; elev. 792ft./241m.; 🅿; Z 74331; Ⓟ 915; © 1,118
Agawam; RMC Place; GRADY; **221** H-12; elev. 1,259ft./384m.; mail Ninnekah Z 73067; ● 50
Agnus Valley Acres; RMC Place; TULSA; ***221** D-16; ★ **TUL**; mail Sand Springs Z 74063; pop. incl. with Sand Springs (Inc. Place)
Agra; Inc. Place; LINCOLN; **221** E-15; 🅿; Z 74824; Ⓟ 334; © 356
Ahloso; RMC Place; PONTOTOC; **221** H-15; mail Ada Z 74820; ● 90
Ahpeatone; RMC Place; COTTON; mail Walters Z 73572; rural
Akins; CDP; SEQUOYAH; **221** F-20; mail Sallisaw Z 74955; © 449
Albany; RMC Place; BRYAN; **221** K-16; elev. 585ft./178m.; 🅿; Z 74721; ● 100
Albert (Oney); RMC Place; CADDO; **221** G-11; elev. 1,519ft./463m.; 🅿; Z 73001; ● 120
Albion; Inc. Place; PUSHMATAHA; **221** H-19; 🅿; Z 74521; Ⓟ 88; © 143
Alden; RMC Place; CADDO; ***221** H-11; mail Carnegie Z 73015; rural
Alderson; Inc. Place; PITTSBURG; **221** H-17; 🅿; Z 74522; Ⓟ 395; © 261
Aledo; RMC Place; DEWEY; ***220** E-9; mail Leedey Z 73654; rural
Alex; Inc. Place; GRADY; **221** H-12; elev. 1,048ft./319m.; 🅿; Z 73002; Ⓟ 639; © 635
Alfalfa; RMC Place; CADDO; **221** G-11; elev. 1,458ft./444m.; mail Carnegie Z 73015; ● 100
ALFALFA; **221** C-11; Ⓟ 6,416; © 6,105; ◆ 5,728
Aline; Inc. Place; ALFALFA; **221** C-11; elev. 1,281ft./390m.; 🅿; Z 73716; Ⓟ 295; © 214
Allen; Inc. Place; PONTOTOC, HUGHES; **221** H-16; 🅿; Z 74825; Ⓟ 972; © 951
Allison; RMC Place; BRYAN; ***221** K-16; elev. 639ft./195m.; mail Calera Z 74730; ● 25
Alluwe (New Alluwe); Inc. Place; NOWATA; **221** C-18; mail Chelsea Z 74016; Ⓟ 83; © 95
Alma; RMC Place; STEPHENS; **221** I-13; mail Duncan Z 73533; ● 80
Alpers; RMC Place; CARTER; ***221** I-13; elev. 965ft./294m.; mail Tatums Z 73487; rural
Alsuma; RMC Place; TULSA; ***221** D-17; ★ **TUL**; pop. incl. with Tulsa (Inc. Place)

Entries in **UPPERCASE** are counties.
Entries in **bold** have populations of 2,500 or more.
Names in parentheses are alternate names.

Inc. Place	Incorporated Place
RMC Place	Rand McNally Designated Place
CDP	Census Designated Place
MCD	Minor Civil Division
⊡	County Seat
▲	Minor Civil Division
elev.	Elevation
🅿	Post Office
🅷	Hospital
🅲	College
■	Principal Business Center
★	Ranally Metro Area (RMA) Abbreviation
Z	Zip Code(s)
Ⓟ	Previous Census Population
®	Revised Census Population
Ⓐ	Annexation Population
●	Rand McNally Population Estimate
©	Final Census Population
Ⓢ	Special Census Population
◆	Estimated Population

For additional definitions see Glossary, Volume 1, and Introduction, Volume 2.

Altona; RMC Place; KINGFISHER; ***221** E-12; mail Omega z 73764; rural

Altus; Inc. Place; ⊡ JACKSON; **220** I-9; elev. 1,398ft./426m.; 🅿 🅷 ■; z 73521-23; Ⓟ 21,910; © 21,447; ◆ 18,796

Alva; Inc. Place; ⊡ WOODS; **220** C-10; elev. 1,350ft./411m.; 🅿 🅷 🅲 2,007; z 73717; Ⓟ 5,495; © 5,288

Amber; Inc. Place; GRADY; **221** G-12; 🅿; z 73004; Ⓟ 418; © 490

Ames; Inc. Place; MAJOR; **221** D-12; elev. 1,226ft./374m.; 🅿; z 73718; Ⓟ 268; © 199

Amorita; Inc. Place; ALFALFA; **221** B-11; elev. 1,212ft./369m.; 🅿; z 73719; Ⓟ 56; © 44

Anadarko; Inc. Place; ⊡ CADDO; **221** G-11; 🅿 🅷; z 73005; location of Indian Agency; Ⓟ 6,586; © 6,645

Antioch; RMC Place; GARVIN; **221** H-13; elev. 995ft./303m.; mail Elmore City z 73433; ● 80

Antlers; Inc. Place; ⊡ PUSHMATAHA; **221** J-18; elev. 508ft./155m.; 🅿 🅷; z 74523; Ⓟ 2,524; © 2,552

Apache; Inc. Place; CADDO; **221** H-11; elev. 1,300ft./396m.; 🅿; z 73006; Ⓟ 1,591; © 1,616

Apperson; RMC Place; OSAGE; ***221** C-15; mail Burbank z 74633; ● 30

Apple; RMC Place; CHOCTAW; **221** J-18; elev. 473ft./144m.; mail Spencerville z 74760; ● 40

Aqua Park; RMC Place; SEQUOYAH; ***221** F-19; mail Gore z 74435; pop. incl. with Paradise Hill (Inc. Place)

Arapaho; Inc. Place; ⊡ CUSTER; **220** F-10; elev. 1,669ft./509m.; 🅿; z 73620; Ⓟ 802; © 748

Arcadia; Inc. Place; OKLAHOMA; **221** F-13; elev. 972ft./296m.; 🅿; ★ **O.C.**; z 73007; Ⓟ 320; © 279

Arch; RMC Place; PITTSBURG; ***221** H-17; mail Hartshorne z 74547; rural

Ardmore; Inc. Place; ⊡ CARTER; **221** J-14; elev. 881ft./269m.; 🅿 🅷 ■; z 73401-03; Ⓟ 23,079; © 23,711; ◆ 25,130

Arkoma; Inc. Place; LE FLORE; **221** F-20; 🅿; ★ **FTSM**; z 74901; Ⓟ 2,393; © 2,180

Arlington; RMC Place; LINCOLN; **221** F-15; elev. 908ft./277m.; mail Prague z 74864; ● 25

Armstrong; Inc. Place; BRYAN; **221** J-16; elev. 590ft./180m.; mail Caddo z 74729; Ⓟ 122; © 141

Arnett; Inc. Place; ⊡ ELLIS; **220** D-8; elev. 2,460ft./750m.; 🅿; z 73832; Ⓟ 547; © 520

Arnett; RMC Place; HARMON; ***220** H-7; mail Hollis z 73550; rural

Arpelar; RMC Place; PITTSBURG; **221** H-17; elev. 749ft./228m.; mail McAlester z 74501; ● 600

Arrowhead Estates; RMC Place; PITTSBURG; ***221** G-17; mail Canadian z 74425; pop. incl. with Canadian (Inc. Place)

Artillery Village; RMC Place; COMANCHE; ★ **LAWT**; mail Fort Sill z 73503; pop. incl. with Lawton (Inc. Place)

Asher; Inc. Place; POTTAWATOMIE; **221** H-14; 🅿; z 74826; Ⓟ 449; © 419

Ashland; Inc. Place; PITTSBURG; **221** H-16; mail Stuart z 74570; Ⓟ 56; © 53

Atlee; RMC Place; JEFFERSON; ***221** J-13; mail Ringling z 73456; rural

Atoka; Inc. Place; ⊡ ATOKA; **221** I-16; elev. 583ft./178m.; 🅿 🅷; z 74525, z 74542; Ⓟ 3,298; © 2,988

ATOKA; **221** J-16; Ⓟ 12,778; © 13,879; ◆ 14,874

Atwood; Inc. Place; HUGHES; **221** H-16; elev. 798ft./243m.; 🅿; z 74827; © 113

Avant; Inc. Place; OSAGE; **221** C-16; elev. 681ft./208m.; 🅿; z 74001; Ⓟ 369; © 372

Avard; Inc. Place; WOODS; **220** C-10; elev. 1,481ft./451m.; mail Alva z 73717; Ⓟ 37; © 26

Avery; RMC Place; LINCOLN; **221** E-15; elev. 969ft./295m.; mail Cushing z 74023; ● 60

Aydelotte; RMC Place; POTTAWATOMIE; ***221** F-14; mail Shawnee z 74804

B

Babbs; RMC Place; KIOWA; ***220** H-9; mail Hobart z 73651; rural

Bache; RMC Place; PITTSBURG; ***221** H-17; 🅿; z 74501; ● 150

Bacone; RMC Place; MUSKOGEE; ***221** E-18; ★ **MSKOG**; mail Muskogee z 74401; pop. incl. with Muskogee (Inc. Place)

Bailey; RMC Place; GRADY; ***221** H-12; mail Marlow z 73055; rural

Baker; RMC Place; TEXAS; **220** B-5; 🅿; z 73950; ● 50

Bald Hill; RMC Place; OKMULGEE; ***221** E-17; elev. 730ft./223m.; mail Okmulgee z 74447; rural

Balko; RMC Place; BEAVER; **220** C-6; 🅿; z 73931; ● 100

Ballard; RMC Place; ADAIR; **221** D-20; mail Watts z 74964; ● 120

Ballou; CDP-Census Area Only; MAYES; ***221** D-18; © 142

Banner; RMC Place; CANADIAN; ***221** F-12; elev. 1,287ft./392m.; mail El Reno z 73036

Banty; RMC Place; BRYAN; ***221** J-16; elev. 716ft./218m.; mail Bennington z 74723; rural

Barber; RMC Place; CHEROKEE; ***221** E-19; mail Welling z 74471

Barnes; RMC Place; LOGAN; ***221** E-13; mail Mulhall z 73063; ● 100

Barnsdall; Inc. Place; OSAGE; **221** C-16; elev. 773ft./236m.; 🅿; z 74002; Ⓟ 1,316; © 1,325

Baron; RMC Place; ADAIR; **221** E-20; mail Stilwell z 74960, Westville z 74965; ● 140

Barry; BRYAN; see Platter (RMC Place)

Bartlesville; Inc. Place; ⊡ WASHINGTON, OSAGE; **221** C-17; elev. 715ft./218m.; 🅿 🅷 🅲 1,009 ■; ★ **BART**; z 74003-06; Ⓟ 34,256; © 34,748; ◆ 36,876

Bartlett; OKMULGEE; see Dighton (RMC Place)

Battiest; RMC Place; MCCURTAIN; **221** I-19; 🅿; z 74722; ● 250

Baum; RMC Place; CARTER; ***221** J-14; elev. 717ft./219m.; mail Ardmore z 73401

Beachton; RMC Place; MCCURTAIN; ***221** I-20; mail Smithville z 74957; rural

Bearden; Inc. Place; OKFUSKEE; **221** G-16; elev. 934ft./285m.; 🅿; z 74859; Ⓟ 142; © 140

Beaver (Beaver City); Inc. Place; ⊡ BEAVER; **220** B-6; elev. 2,393ft./729m.; 🅿 🅷; z 73932; Ⓟ 1,584; © 1,570

BEAVER; **220** C-7; Ⓟ 6,023; © 5,857; ◆ 5,345

Beaver City; BEAVER; see Beaver (Inc. Place)

Beckett; STEPHENS; see Sunray (RMC Place)

BECKHAM; **220** G-8; Ⓟ 18,812; © 19,799; ◆ 23,781

Bee; RMC Place; JOHNSTON; **221** J-15; elev. 702ft./214m.; mail Kenefic z 74748; ● 50

Beggs; Inc. Place; OKMULGEE; **221** E-16; elev. 732ft./223m.; 🅿; z 74421; Ⓟ 1,150; © 1,364

Beland; RMC Place; MUSKOGEE; ***221** F-18; mail Muskogee z 74401; ● 30

Belfonte; CDP-Census Area Only; SEQUOYAH; ***221** F-20; © 426

Bell; CDP; ADAIR; ***221** E-20; elev. 858ft./262m.; mail Stilwell z 74960; © 602

Bellemont; RMC Place; POTTAWATOMIE; ***221** F-15; mail Prague z 74864; rural

Bellvue; RMC Place; CREEK; ***221** E-16; mail Bristow z 74010; rural

Belzoni; RMC Place; PUSHMATAHA; ***221** J-18; elev. 459ft./140m.; mail Antlers z 74523; rural

Bengal; RMC Place; LATIMER; **221** H-19; mail Wister z 74966; ● 100

Bennington; Inc. Place; BRYAN; **221** J-17; 🅿; z 74723; Ⓟ 251; © 289

Bentley; RMC Place; ATOKA; **221** J-16; elev. 543ft./166m.; mail Atoka z 74525; ● 100

Berlin; RMC Place; ROGER MILLS; **220** F-8; mail Sayre z 73662; ● 50

Bernice; Inc. Place; DELAWARE; **221** C-19; 🅿; z 74331; Ⓟ 330; © 504

Berwyn; CARTER; see Gene Autry (Inc. Place)

Bessie; Inc. Place; WASHITA; **220** F-10; 🅿; z 73622; Ⓟ 248; © 190

Bethany; Inc. Place; OKLAHOMA; **221** F-13; 🅿 🅷 🅲 2,068; ★ **O.C.**; z 73008; Ⓟ 20,075; © 20,307; ◆ 20,093

Bethel; RMC Place; COMANCHE; ***221** I-12; mail Lawton z 73501

Bethel; RMC Place; MCCURTAIN; **221** I-19; elev. 874ft./266m.; 🅿; z 74724; ● 260

Bethel Acres; Inc. Place; POTTAWATOMIE; **221** G-14; ★ **O.C.**; mail Shawnee z 74801; Ⓟ 2,505; © 2,735

Bidding Springs; ADAIR; see Wauhillau (RMC Place)

Big Cabin; Inc. Place; CRAIG; **221** C-18; 🅿; z 74332; Ⓟ 271; © 293

Big Cedar; RMC Place; LE FLORE; ***221** H-20; elev. 870ft./265m.; mail Hodgen z 74939; rural

Big Creek; RMC Place; LE FLORE; ***221** H-20; mail Heavener z 74937; rural

Big Spring; RMC Place; HUGHES; ***221** G-16; mail Wetumka z 74883; rural

Billings; Inc. Place; NOBLE; **221** C-13; elev. 1,020ft./311m.; 🅿; z 74630; Ⓟ 555; © 436; Ⓡ 579

Binger; Inc. Place; CADDO; **221** G-11; 🅿; z 73009; Ⓟ 724; © 708

Bison; RMC Place; GARFIELD; **221** D-12; 🅿; z 73720; ● 120

Bixby; Inc. Place; TULSA, WAGONER; **221** E-17; 🅿; ★ **TUL**; z 74008; Ⓟ 9,502; © 13,336; ◆ 15,097

Blackburn; Inc. Place; PAWNEE; **221** D-15; elev. 817ft./249m.; mail Pawnee z 74058; Ⓟ 110; © 102

Blackgum; RMC Place; SEQUOYAH; ***221** F-19; mail Vian z 74962; ● 250

Blackwell; Inc. Place; KAY; **221** B-14; elev. 1,014ft./309m.; 🅿 🅷; z 74631; Ⓟ 7,538; © 7,668

BLAINE; **221** E-11; Ⓟ 11,470; © 11,976; ◆ 13,142

Blair; Inc. Place; JACKSON; **220** H-9; 🅿; z 73526; Ⓟ 922; © 894

Blanchard; Inc. Place; MCCLAIN, GRADY; **221** G-13; elev. 1,276ft./389m.; 🅿; z 73010; Ⓟ 1,922; © 2,816

Blanco; RMC Place; PITTSBURG; **221** H-17; elev. 712ft./217m.; 🅿; z 74528; ● 200

Blocker; RMC Place; PITTSBURG; **221** G-18; 🅿; z 74529; ● 200

Blue; RMC Place; BRYAN; **221** J-16; mail Durant z 74701; ● 200

Bluejacket; Inc. Place; CRAIG; **221** B-19; 🅿; z 74333; Ⓟ 175; © 274

Blue Ridge; RMC Place; TULSA; ***221** E-17; ★ **TUL**; mail Bixby z 74008; pop. incl. with Bixby (Inc. Place)

Bluff; RMC Place; CHOCTAW; ***221** J-17; mail Soper z 74759; rural

Boatman; RMC Place; MAYES; **221** D-18; elev. 662ft./202m.; mail Pryor z 74361; ● 100

Boehler; RMC Place; ATOKA; ***221** J-17; elev. 568ft./173m.; mail Boswell z 74727; rural

Boggy Depot; RMC Place; ATOKA; ***221** J-16; mail Atoka z 74525; rural

Bois D'Arc; RMC Place; KAY; ***221** C-14; mail Ponca City z 74601; ● 300

Boise City; Inc. Place; ⊡ CIMARRON; **220** B-2; elev. 4,165ft./1,269m.; 🅿 🅷; z 73933; Ⓟ 1,509; © 1,483; Ⓡ 1,488

Bokchito; Inc. Place; BRYAN; **221** J-16; elev. 637ft./194m.; 🅿; z 74726; Ⓟ 576; © 564

Bokhoma; RMC Place; MCCURTAIN; ***221** K-20; mail Haworth z 74740; rural

Bokoshe; Inc. Place; LE FLORE; **221** G-19; 🅿; z 74930; Ⓟ 403; © 450

Boley; Inc. Place; OKFUSKEE; **221** F-15; 🅿; z 74829; Ⓟ 908; © 1,126

Bond; MCINTOSH; see Onapa (RMC Place)

Boone; RMC Place; CADDO; **221** H-11; mail Apache z 73006; ● 25

Boss; RMC Place; MCCURTAIN; mail Idabel z 74745; rural

Boswell; Inc. Place; CHOCTAW; **221** J-17; elev. 597ft./182m.; 🅿; z 74727; Ⓟ 643; © 703

Boulevard; RMC Place; CLEVELAND; ★ **O.C.**; mail Norman z 73069; pop. incl. with Norman (Inc. Place)

Bowden; RMC Place; CREEK; **220** H-1; ★ **TUL**; mail Sapulpa z 74066

Bowlegs; Inc. Place; SEMINOLE; **221** G-15; 🅿; z 74830; Ⓟ 398; © 371

Bowlin Spring; RMC Place; CRAIG; ***221** C-18; elev. 770ft./235m.; mail Chelsea z 74016; ● 40

Bowring; RMC Place; OSAGE; **221** B-16; located on Osage Ind. Res.; elev. 842ft./257m.; 🅿; z 74056; ● 100

Box; RMC Place; SEQUOYAH; ***221** F-19; elev. 916ft./279m.; mail Vian z 74962; ● 50

Boyd; RMC Place; BEAVER; ***220** C-6; mail Balko z 73931; rural

Boynton; Inc. Place; MUSKOGEE; **221** F-17; 🅿; z 74422; Ⓟ 391; © 274

Braden; RMC Place; LE FLORE; ***221** G-20; elev. 423ft./129m.; mail Spiro z 74959

Bradley; Inc. Place; GRADY; **221** H-13; 🅿; z 73011; Ⓟ 166; © 182

Brady; RMC Place; GARVIN; ***221** I-14; elev. 971ft./296m.; mail Wynnewood z 73098; rural

Braggs; Inc. Place; MUSKOGEE; **221** F-18; elev. 559ft./170m.; 🅿; z 74423, z 74439; Ⓟ 308; © 301

Braman; Inc. Place; KAY; **221** B-13; 🅿; z 74632; Ⓟ 251; © 244

Bray; Inc. Place; STEPHENS; **221** I-12; 🅿; z 73055; Ⓟ 925; © 1,035

Breckenridge; GARFIELD; see Breckinridge (Inc. Place)

Breckinridge (Breckenridge); Inc. Place; GARFIELD; **221** D-13; elev. 1,197ft./365m.; ★ **ENID**; mail Enid z 73701; Ⓟ 251; © 239

Brent; CDP-Census Area Only; SEQUOYAH; ***221** F-19; mail Sallisaw z 74955; © 504

Brentwood; RMC Place; TULSA; ***221** E-17; ★ **TUL**; mail Glenpool z 74033; pop. incl. with Glenpool (Inc. Place)

Briartown; RMC Place; MUSKOGEE; **221** G-18; elev. 561ft./171m.; mail Porum z 74455; ● 150

Bridge Creek; Inc. Place; GRADY; incorporated November 7 2000; not reported in 2000 Census; ● 32

Bridgeport; Inc. Place; CADDO; **221** F-11; elev. 1,428ft./435m.; mail Hinton z 73047; Ⓟ 137; © 109

Briggs; CDP; CHEROKEE; ***221** E-19; mail Tahlequah z 74464; © 358

Brinkman; RMC Place; GREER; ***220** H-8; elev. 1,694ft./516m.; mail Willow z 73673; rural

Bristow; Inc. Place; CREEK; **221** E-16; 🅿 🅷; z 74010; Ⓟ 4,062; © 4,325

Britton; RMC Place; OKLAHOMA; **220** J-4; ★ **O.C.**; mail Oklahoma City z 73113-14, z 73116, z 73131, z 73151, z 73178; pop. incl. with Oklahoma City (Inc. Place)

Brock; RMC Place; CARTER; ***221** J-14; elev. 914ft./279m.; mail Ardmore z 73401; ● 50

Broken Arrow; Inc. Place; TULSA, WAGONER; **220** H-5; elev. 753ft./230m.; 🅿 🅷 ■; ★ **TUL**; z 74011-14; includes New Tulsa annexed February 23, 2001; Ⓟ 58,043; © 74,859; Ⓐ 75,427; ◆ 83,383

Broken Bow; Inc. Place; MCCURTAIN; **221** J-20; 🅿; z 74728; Ⓟ 3,961; © 4,230

Bromide; Inc. Place; JOHNSTON, COAL; **221** I-15; elev. 707ft./215m.; 🅿; z 74530; Ⓟ 162; © 163

Brooken; RMC Place; HASKELL; ***221** G-18; mail Stigler z 74462; ● 120

Brookside; RMC Place; TULSA; ★ **TUL**; mail Tulsa z 74105; pop. incl. with Tulsa (Inc. Place)

Brooksville; Inc. Place; POTTAWATOMIE; ***221** G-14; mail Tecumseh z 74873; Ⓟ 69; © 90

Brown; RMC Place; BRYAN; ***221** J-16; elev. 765ft./233m.; mail Durant z 74701; rural

Broxton; RMC Place; CADDO; ***221** H-11; elev. 1,435ft./437m.; mail Apache z 73006; rural

Bruner; RMC Place; TULSA; ★ **TUL**; mail Tulsa z 74127; pop. incl. with Tulsa (Inc. Place)

Brush Creek; CDP-Census Area Only; DELAWARE; ***221** C-19; © 41

Brush Hill; RMC Place; MCINTOSH; ***221** F-17; elev. 628ft./191m.; mail Checotah z 74426; ● 50

Brushy; CDP; SEQUOYAH; ***221** F-19; mail Sallisaw z 74955; © 787

BRYAN; **221** J-16; Ⓟ 32,089; © 36,534; ◆ 40,026

Bryans Corner; RMC Place; BEAVER; ***220** C-6; mail Balko z 73931; ● 100

Bryant; RMC Place; OKMULGEE; ***221** F-16; mail Weleetka z 74880; ● 60

Buffalo; Inc. Place; ⊡ HARPER; **220** B-8; elev. 1,800ft./549m.; 🅿 🅷; z 73834; Ⓟ 1,312; © 1,200

Buffalo; RMC Place; MCCURTAIN; ***221** I-20; mail Watson z 74963; ● 60

Buffalo Valley; RMC Place; LATIMER; ***221** H-18; mail Tuskahoma z 74574; ● 70

Bull Hollow; CDP-Census Area Only; DELAWARE; ***221** D-19; © 84

Bunch; RMC Place; ADAIR; **221** F-19; elev. 772ft./235m.; 🅿; z 74931; ● 80

Burbank; Inc. Place; OSAGE; **221** C-15; located on Osage Ind. Res.; elev. 1,026ft./313m.; 🅿; z 74633; Ⓟ 165; © 155

Burlington; Inc. Place; ALFALFA; **221** B-11; elev. 1,218ft./371m.; 🅿; z 73722; Ⓟ 169; © 156

Burmah; RMC Place; DEWEY; ***220** E-9; elev. 1,863ft./568m.; mail Putnam z 73659; rural

Burneyville; RMC Place; LOVE; **221** K-14; 🅿; z 73430; ● 60

Burns; WASHITA; see Burns Flat (Inc. Place)

Burns Flat (Burns); Inc. Place; WASHITA; **220** G-9; 🅿; z 73624; Ⓟ 1,027; © 1,782

Burwell; RMC Place; MCCURTAIN; ***221** J-19; mail Ringold z 74754; rural

Bushyhead; CDP; ROGERS; ***221** C-18; mail Chelsea z 74016; © 1,203

Butler; Inc. Place; CUSTER; **220** F-9; 🅿; z 73625; Ⓟ 341; © 345

Butner; RMC Place; SEMINOLE; **221** G-16; elev. 924ft./282m.; mail Wewoka z 74884; ● 100

Byars; Inc. Place; MCCLAIN; **221** H-14; 🅿; z 74831; Ⓟ 263; © 280

Byng; Inc. Place; PONTOTOC; **221** H-15; mail Ada z 74820; Ⓟ 755; © 1,090

Byron; Inc. Place; ALFALFA; **221** B-11; elev. 1,190ft./363m.; 🅿; z 73722; Ⓟ 57; © 45

C

Cache; Inc. Place; COMANCHE; **220** I-10; elev. 1,271ft./387m.; 🅿; z 73527; Ⓟ 2,251; © 2,371

Caddo; Inc. Place; BRYAN; **221** J-16; 🅿; z 74729; Ⓟ 918; © 944

CADDO; **221** G-11; Ⓟ 29,550; © 30,150; ◆ 28,102

Cade; RMC Place; BRYAN; ***221** J-17; mail Bennington z 74723; rural

Cairo; RMC Place; COAL; ***221** I-16; elev. 646ft./197m.; mail Coalgate z 74538; rural

Calera; Inc. Place; BRYAN; **221** K-16; 🅿; z 74730; Ⓟ 1,536; © 1,739

Calhoun; RMC Place; LE FLORE; **221** G-19; mail Shady Point z 74956; ● 50

Calumet; Inc. Place; CANADIAN; **221** F-12; 🅿; z 73014; Ⓟ 560; © 535

Calvin; Inc. Place; HUGHES; **221** H-16; 🅿; z 74531; Ⓟ 251; © 279

Camargo; Inc. Place; DEWEY; **220** E-9; 🅿; z 73835; Ⓟ 185; © 115

Cambria; RMC Place; LATIMER; ***221** H-18; mail Gowen z 74545; ● 60

Cameron; Inc. Place; LE FLORE; **221** G-20; elev. 489ft./149m.; 🅿; z 74932; Ⓟ 327; © 312

Cameron University; RMC Place; COMANCHE; ***221** I-11; ★ **LAWT**; mail Lawton z 73505; pop. incl. with Lawton (Inc. Place)

Camp Houston; RMC Place; WOODS; ***220** B-9; mail Freedom z 73842

Canadian; Inc. Place; PITTSBURG; **221** G-17; 🅿; z 74425; Ⓟ 261; © 239

CANADIAN; **221** F-12; Ⓟ 74,409; © 87,697; ◆ 107,261

Canadian Shores; RMC Place; PITTSBURG; ***221** G-17; mail McAlester z 74501; ● 100

Caney; Inc. Place; ATOKA; **221** J-16; 🅿; z 74533; Ⓟ 184; © 199

Caney Ridge; RMC Place; CHEROKEE; ***221** E-19; mail Welling z 74471; ● 130

Canton; Inc. Place; BLAINE; **221** E-11; elev. 1,591ft./485m.; 🅿; z 73724; Ⓟ 632; © 618

Canute; Inc. Place; WASHITA; **220** F-9; 🅿; z 73626; Ⓟ 538; © 524

Capitol Hill; RMC Place; OKLAHOMA; ***221** F-13; ★ **O.C.**; mail Oklahoma City z 73109; pop. incl. with Oklahoma City (Inc. Place)

Capron; Inc. Place; WOODS; **221** B-11; elev. 1,293ft./394m.; 🅿; z 73717; Ⓟ 38; © 42

Carbondale; RMC Place; TULSA; ***221** D-16; ★ **TUL**; pop. incl. with Tulsa (Inc. Place)

Cardin; Inc. Place; OTTAWA; **221** B-19; elev. 813ft./248m.; 🅿; z 74335; Ⓟ 165; © 150

Carleton; BLAINE; see Carlton (RMC Place)

Carlile; CDP-Census Area Only; SEQUOYAH; ***221** F-19; © 649

Carlton (Carleton); RMC Place; BLAINE; ***221** E-11; mail Watonga z 73772; rural

Carmen; Inc. Place; ALFALFA; **221** C-11; elev. 1,354ft./413m.; 🅿; z 73726; Ⓟ 459; © 411

Carnegie; Inc. Place; CADDO; **221** G-11; elev. 1,309ft./399m.; 🅿 🅷; z 73015; Ⓟ 1,593; © 1,637

Carney; Inc. Place; LINCOLN; **221** E-14; 🅿; z 74832; Ⓟ 558; © 649

Carpenter; RMC Place; ROGER MILLS; ***220** F-9; elev. 1,931ft./589m.; mail Elk City z 73644; rural

Carriage Hills; RMC Place; COMANCHE; ★ **LAWT**; mail Lawton z 73501; pop. incl. with Lawton (Inc. Place)

Carrier; Inc. Place; GARFIELD; **221** C-12; elev. 1,339ft./408m.; 🅿; z 73727; Ⓟ 171; © 77

Carson; RMC Place; HUGHES; ***221** G-16; elev. 743ft./226m.; mail Lamar z 74850; rural

Carter; Inc. Place; BECKHAM; **220** G-8; 🅿; z 73627; Ⓟ 286; © 254

CARTER; **221** J-13; Ⓟ 42,919; © 45,621; ◆ 47,983

Cartersville; RMC Place; HASKELL; ***221** G-19; mail Keota z 74941; ● 70

Cartwright; RMC Place; BRYAN; **221** K-15; 🅿; z 74731; ● 800

Cashion; Inc. Place; KINGFISHER, LOGAN; **221** E-13; 🅿; z 73016; Ⓟ 430; © 635

Castle; Inc. Place; OKFUSKEE; **221** F-16; 🅿; z 74833; Ⓟ 94; © 122

Catale; RMC Place; ROGERS; ***221** C-18; mail Big Cabin z 74332; rural

Catesby; RMC Place; ELLIS; ***220** C-7; elev. 2,399ft./731m.; mail Gage z 73843; rural

Catoosa; Inc. Place; ROGERS, WAGONER; **220** E-6; 🅿; ★ **TUL**; z 74015; Ⓟ 2,954; © 5,449

Cayuga; CDP; DELAWARE; ***221** C-19; mail Grove z 74344; © 105

Cedar Crest; CDP; MAYES; ***221** D-18; mail Locust Grove z 74352; © 308

Cedar Lake; RMC Place; CANADIAN; ***221** F-11; mail Hinton z 73047; ● 250

Cedar Ridge; RMC Place; PAWNEE; mail Cleveland z 74020

Cedar Valley; Inc. Place; LOGAN; ***221** E-13; mail Guthrie z 73044; Ⓟ 61; © 58

Cement; Inc. Place; CADDO; **221** H-12; 🅿; z 73017; Ⓟ 642; © 530

Centennial Station; RMC Place; OKLAHOMA; ★ **O.C.**; mail Edmond z 73013, z 73083; pop. incl. with Edmond (Inc. Place)

Center; RMC Place; PONTOTOC; **221** H-15; mail Ada z 74820; ● 120

Center City; RMC Place; OKLAHOMA; ★ **O.C.**; mail Oklahoma City z 73101-02; pop. incl. with Oklahoma City (Inc. Place)

Center Point; RMC Place; ATOKA; ***221** J-17; mail Atoka z 74525; rural

Centerview; RMC Place; POTTAWATOMIE; ***221** F-15; elev. 990ft./302m.; mail Seminole z 74868

Centrahoma; Inc. Place; COAL; **221** I-16; elev. 711ft./217m.; 🅿; z 74534; Ⓟ 106; © 110

Central High; Inc. Place; STEPHENS; ***221** I-12; © 954

Centralia; RMC Place; CRAIG; **221** B-18; 🅿; z 74301; ● 35

Ceres; RMC Place; NOBLE; ***221** C-14; elev. 972ft./296m.; mail Red Rock z 74651; rural

Cestos; RMC Place; DEWEY; ***220** D-9; elev. 1,878ft./572m.; mail Vici z 73859; rural

Chance; RMC Place; ADAIR; ***221** D-20; mail Watts z 74964; rural

Chandler; Inc. Place; ⊡ LINCOLN; **221** F-15; elev. 940ft./287m.; 🅿; z 74834; Ⓟ 2,596; © 2,842

Chase; RMC Place; MUSKOGEE; mail Muskogee z 74401; rural

Chattanooga; Inc. Place; COMANCHE, TILLMAN; **220** I-10; 🅿; z 73528; Ⓟ 437; © 432

Checotah; Inc. Place; MCINTOSH; **221** F-18; elev. 652ft./199m.; 🅿; z 74426; Ⓟ 3,290; © 3,481

Chelsea; Inc. Place; ROGERS; **221** C-18; 🅿; z 74016; Ⓟ 1,620; © 2,136

Cherokee; Inc. Place; ⊡ ALFALFA; **221** C-11; elev. 1,181ft./360m.; 🅿; z 73728; Ⓟ 1,787; © 1,630

CHEROKEE; **221** E-19; Ⓟ 34,049; © 42,521; ◆ 45,051

Cherry Tree; CDP; ADAIR; ***221** E-20; mail Stilwell z 74960; © 1,202

Chester; RMC Place; MAJOR; **220** D-10; elev. 1,714ft./522m.; 🅿; z 73838; ● 150

Chewey; CDP; ADAIR; ***221** D-19; elev. 871ft./265m.; mail Watts z 74964; © 135

Cheyenne; Inc. Place; ⊡ ROGER MILLS; **220** F-8; elev. 1,933ft./589m.; 🅿 🅷; z 73628; Ⓟ 948; © 778

Cheyenne Valley; RMC Place; MAJOR; ***220** D-10; mail Fairview z 73737; rural

Chickasha; Inc. Place; ⊡ GRADY; **221** G-12; elev. 1,096ft./334m.; 🅿 🅷 🅲 1,492 ■; z 73018, z 73023; Ⓟ 14,988; © 15,850; ◆ 16,585

Chigley; RMC Place; MURRAY; ***221** I-14; mail Davis z 73030; ● 50

Childers; RMC Place; NOWATA; **221** C-18; mail Delaware z 74027; ● 40

Chilli; RMC Place; LATIMER; ***221** H-18; mail Wilburton z 74578; rural

Chilocco; RMC Place; KAY; **221** B-14; mail Newkirk z 74647; ● 30

Chimney Hills; RMC Place; TULSA; ★ **TUL**; mail Tulsa z 74133, z 74137; pop. incl. with Tulsa (Inc. Place)

Chisney (Wye); RMC Place; POTTAWATOMIE; **221** G-14; mail Macomb z 74852; ● 25

Chitwood; RMC Place; GRADY; ***221** H-12; mail Ninnekah z 73067; rural

Chloeta; RMC Place; DELAWARE; ***221** C-19; mail Spavinaw z 74366; ● 50

Choctaw; Inc. Place; OKLAHOMA; **221** F-14; 🅿; ★ **O.C.**; z 73020; Ⓟ 8,545; © 9,377

CHOCTAW; **221** J-17; Ⓟ 15,302; © 15,342; ◆ 14,665

Choska; RMC Place; WAGONER; ***221** E-17; ★ **TUL**; mail Coweta z 74429; rural

Chouteau; Inc. Place; MAYES; **221** D-18; 🅿; z 74337; Ⓟ 1,771; © 1,931

Christie; CDP; ADAIR; **221** E-20; mail Westville z 74965; © 166

Cimarron; RMC Place; OKLAHOMA; ★ **O.C.**; mail Oklahoma City z 73111; pop. incl. with Oklahoma City (Inc. Place)

CIMARRON; **220** B-2; Ⓟ 3,301; © 3,148; ◆ 2,548

Cimarron City; Inc. Place; LOGAN; **221** E-13; mail Crescent z 73028; Ⓟ 71; © 110

Cisco; RMC Place; MCCURTAIN; mail Idabel z 74745; rural

Citra; RMC Place; HUGHES; ***221** H-16; elev. 746ft./227m.; mail Allen z 74825; rural

Claremore; Inc. Place; ⊡ ROGERS; **221** D-17; elev. 600ft./183m.; 🅿 🅷 🅲 3,955; ★ **TUL**; z 74017-19; Ⓟ 13,280; © 15,873

Clarita; RMC Place; COAL; **221** I-16; elev. 682ft./208m.; 🅿; z 74535; ● 150

Clarksville; RMC Place; WAGONER; ***221** E-18; mail Porter z 74454; ● 120

Clayton; Inc. Place; PUSHMATAHA; **221** I-18; 🅿; z 74536; Ⓟ 636; © 719

Clayton Lake; RMC Place; PUSHMATAHA; mail Clayton z 74536; rural

Clear Lake; RMC Place; BEAVER; ***220** C-7; elev. 2,516ft./767m.; mail Beaver z 73932; rural

Clearview; Inc. Place; OKFUSKEE; **221** F-16; 🅿; z 74880; Ⓟ 47; © 56

Clebit; RMC Place; MCCURTAIN; ***221** I-19; elev. 849ft./259m.; mail Broken Bow z 74728

Clemscot; RMC Place; CARTER; **221** I-13; mail Graham z 73437; ● 50

Cleora; CDP; DELAWARE; ***221** C-19; elev. 779ft./237m.; 🅿; z 74331; © 1,113

Cleo Springs; Inc. Place; MAJOR; **221** D-11; 🅿; z 73729; Ⓟ 359; © 326

Cleveland; Inc. Place; PAWNEE; **221** D-15; elev. 777ft./237m.; 🅿 🅷; z 74020; Ⓟ 3,156; © 3,282

CLEVELAND; **221** G-13; Ⓟ 174,253; © 208,016; ◆ 250,863

Clinton; Inc. Place; CUSTER, WASHITA; **220** F-10; elev. 1,592ft./485m.; 🅿 🅷; z 73601; Ⓟ 9,298; © 8,833

Clothier; RMC Place; CLEVELAND; ***221** G-13; elev. 1,227ft./374m.; ★ **O.C.**; mail Oklahoma City z 73160; pop. incl. with Oklahoma City (Inc. Place)

Cloud Chief; RMC Place; WASHITA; **220** G-10; mail Cordell z 73632; ● 50

Cloud Creek; CDP-Census Area Only; DELAWARE; ***221** D-19; © 86

Cloudy; RMC Place; PUSHMATAHA; **221** I-18; mail Rattan z 74562; ● 50

Clyde; RMC Place; GRANT; ***221** B-12; mail Medford z 73759; rural

COAL; **221** I-16; Ⓟ 5,780; © 6,031; ◆ 5,827

Coalgate; Inc. Place; ⊡ COAL; **221** I-16; elev. 623ft./190m.; 🅿 🅷; z 74538; Ⓟ 1,895; © 2,005

Coalton; RMC Place; OKMULGEE; ***221** F-17; mail Henryetta z 74437

Cobb; RMC Place; BRYAN; ***221** J-16; elev. 678ft./207m.; mail Durant z 74701

Cogar; RMC Place; CADDO; **221** G-12; elev. 1,469ft./448m.; mail Minco z 73059; ● 25

Colbert; Inc. Place; BRYAN; **221** K-15; 🅿; z 74733; Ⓟ 1,043; © 1,065

Colcord; Inc. Place; DELAWARE; **221** D-19; 🅿; z 74338; Ⓟ 628; © 819

Cole; Inc. Place; MCCLAIN; **221** G-13; mail Blanchard z 73010; Ⓟ 355; © 473

Coleman; RMC Place; JOHNSTON; **221** J-16; 🅿; z 73432; ● 180

Collinsville; Inc. Place; TULSA, ROGERS; **221** D-17; 🅿; ★ **TUL**; z 74021; Ⓟ 3,612; © 4,077

Colony; Inc. Place; WASHITA; **220** G-10; 🅿; z 73021; Ⓟ 163; © 147

Comanche; Inc. Place; STEPHENS; **221** I-12; elev. 984ft./300m.; 🅿; z 73529; Ⓟ 1,695; © 1,556

COMANCHE; **221** I-11; Ⓟ 111,486; © 114,996; ◆ 123,402

Commerce; Inc. Place; OTTAWA; **221** B-19; 🅿; z 74339; Ⓟ 2,426; © 2,645

Connerville; RMC Place; JOHNSTON; **221** I-15; 🅿; z 74836; ● 250

Conser; RMC Place; LE FLORE; ***221** H-20; elev. 543ft./166m.; mail Heavener z 74937; rural

Cookietown; RMC Place; COTTON; ***221** J-11; elev. 1,031ft./314m.; mail Randlett z 73562

Cookson; RMC Place; CHEROKEE; **221** E-19; elev. 890ft./271m.; 🅿; z 74427; seasonal pop. 1,200; ● 900

Cooperton; Inc. Place; KIOWA; **220** H-10; mail Roosevelt z 73564; Ⓟ 15; © 20

Copan; Inc. Place; WASHINGTON; **221** B-17; 🅿; z 74022; Ⓟ 809; © 796

Copeland; CDP; DELAWARE; ***221** C-19; © 1,448

Corbett; RMC Place; CLEVELAND; ***221** H-14; elev. 1,055ft./322m.; mail Lexington z 73051; ● 60

Cordell (New Cordell); Inc. Place; ⊡ WASHITA; **220** G-10; elev. 1,561ft./476m.; 🅿 🅷; z 73632; Ⓟ 2,903; © 2,867

Corinne; RMC Place; PUSHMATAHA; ***221** J-18; elev. 601ft./183m.; mail Fort Towson z 74735; rural

Corn; Inc. Place; WASHITA; **220** G-10; 🅿; z 73024; Ⓟ 548; © 591

Cornish; Inc. Place; JEFFERSON; **221** J-13; elev. 849ft./259m.; mail Ringling z 73456; Ⓟ 164; © 172

Corum; RMC Place; STEPHENS; **221** I-12; elev. 1,020ft./311m.; mail Comanche z 73529; ● 30

COTTON; **221** J-11; Ⓟ 6,651; © 6,614; ◆ 6,104

Cottonwood; RMC Place; COAL; **221** I-16; elev. 603ft./184m.; mail Coalgate z 74538; ● 160

Council; RMC Place; OKLAHOMA; ★ **O.C.**; pop. incl. with Oklahoma City (Inc. Place)

Council Hill; Inc. Place; MUSKOGEE; **221** F-17; 🅿; z 74428; Ⓟ 139; © 129

Countyline; RMC Place; STEPHENS, CARTER; **221** I-13; 🅿; z 73425; ● 300

Courtney; RMC Place; LOVE; ***221** K-13; elev. 838ft./255m.; mail Ringling z 73456; ● 30

Cove Acres; RMC Place; COMANCHE; ***221** H-11; mail Apache z 73006; ● 50

Covington; Inc. Place; GARFIELD; **221** D-13; 🅿; z 73730; Ⓟ 590; © 553

Cowden; RMC Place; WASHITA; ***220** G-10; elev. 1,482ft./452m.; mail Cordell z 73632; rural

Coweta; Inc. Place; WAGONER; **221** E-17; elev. 654ft./199m.; 🅿; ★ **TUL**; z 74429; Ⓟ 6,159; © 7,139

Cowlington; Inc. Place; LE FLORE; **221** G-19; 🅿; z 74941; Ⓟ 756; © 133

Cox City; RMC Place; GRADY; **221** H-13; elev. 1,195ft./364m.; mail Rush Springs z 73082; ● 100

Coyle; Inc. Place; LOGAN; **221** E-14; 🅿; z 73027; Ⓟ 289; © 337

CRAIG; **221** C-18; Ⓟ 14,104; © 14,950; ◆ 15,429

Cravens; RMC Place; LATIMER; mail Red Oak z 74563; rural

Crawford; RMC Place; ROGER MILLS; **220** E-8; elev. 2,327ft./709m.; 🅿; z 73638; ● 50

CREEK; **221** E-15; Ⓟ 60,915; © 67,367; ◆ 68,265

Crekola; RMC Place; MUSKOGEE; ***221** F-18; mail Muskogee z 74401; ● 40

Creosote; RMC Place; CHOCTAW; mail Hugo z 74743; rural

Crescent; Inc. Place; LOGAN; **221** E-13; 🅿; z 73028; Ⓟ 1,236; © 1,281

Criner; RMC Place; MCCLAIN; **221** H-13; elev. 1,103ft./336m.; mail Lindsay z 73052; ● 50

Cromwell; Inc. Place; SEMINOLE; **221** G-15; 🅿; z 74837; Ⓟ 268; © 265

Crossbow; RMC Place; TULSA; ★ **TUL**; mail Tulsa z 74146; pop. incl. with Tulsa (Inc. Place)

Crowder; Inc. Place; PITTSBURG; **221** G-17; 🅿; z 74430; Ⓟ 339; © 436

Crystal; RMC Place; ATOKA; ***221** J-17; mail Boswell z 74727; rural

Crystal Lakes; RMC Place; MAJOR; ***221** D-11; elev. 1,150ft./351m.; mail Ames z 73718; ● 40

Cumberland; RMC Place; MARSHALL; ***221** J-15; mail Madill z 73446; ● 180

Cushing; Inc. Place; PAYNE; **221** E-15; 🅿 🅷; z 74023; Ⓟ 7,218; © 8,371

CUSTER; **220** F-9; Ⓟ 26,897; © 26,142; ◆ 26,347

Custer City; Inc. Place; CUSTER; **220** F-10; 🅿; z 73639; Ⓟ 443; © 393

Cyril; Inc. Place; CADDO; **221** H-11; 🅿; z 73029; Ⓟ 1,072; © 1,168

D

Dacoma; Inc. Place; WOODS; **221** C-11; elev. 1,366ft./416m.; 🅿; z 73731; Ⓟ 182; © 148

Daisy; RMC Place; ATOKA; **221** I-17; 🅿; z 74540; ● 50

Dale; RMC Place; POTTAWATOMIE; **221** F-14; 🅿; z 74851; ● 100

Damon; RMC Place; LATIMER; ***221** H-18; mail Wilburton z 74578; rural

Dane; RMC Place; MAJOR; ***221** D-11; mail Fairview z 73737; rural

Darwin; RMC Place; PUSHMATAHA; ***221** J-17; mail Antlers z 74523; rural

Davenport; Inc. Place; LINCOLN; **221** F-15; 🅿; z 74026; Ⓟ 979; © 881

Davidson; Inc. Place; TILLMAN; **220** J-9; 🅿; z 73530; Ⓟ 473; © 375

Davis; Inc. Place; MURRAY, GARVIN; **221** I-14; elev. 846ft./258m.; 🅿; z 73030, z 73039; Ⓟ 2,543; © 2,610

Dawson; RMC Place; TULSA; ***221** D-17; ★ **TUL**; mail Tulsa z 74115; pop. incl. with Tulsa (Inc. Place)

Deer Creek; Inc. Place; GRANT; **221** B-13; elev. 1,085ft./331m.; 🅿; z 74636; Ⓟ 124; © 147

Degnan; RMC Place; LATIMER; ***221** H-18; elev. 628ft./191m.; mail Wilburton z 74578; rural

Dela; RMC Place; PUSHMATAHA; ***221** J-18; mail Antlers z 74523; rural

Delaware; Inc. Place; NOWATA; **221** B-17; 🅿; z 74027; Ⓟ 434; © 456

DELAWARE; **221** C-19; Ⓟ 28,070; © 37,077; ◆ 41,214

Del City; Inc. Place; OKLAHOMA; **220** L-5; elev. 1,209ft./369m.; 🅿; ★ **O.C.**; z 73115, z 73135 & mail Oklahoma City z 73155, z 73165; Ⓟ 23,928; © 22,128; ◆ 21,881

Delhi; RMC Place; BECKHAM; **220** G-8; elev. 1,922ft./586m.; mail Sayre z 73662; ● 60

Dempsey; RMC Place; ROGER MILLS; ***220** F-8; elev. 2,413ft./735m.; mail Cheyenne z 73628; rural

Dennis; CDP; DELAWARE; ***221** C-19; mail Vinita z 74301; © 185

Depew; Inc. Place; CREEK; **221** E-15; elev. 870ft./265m.; 🅿; z 74028; Ⓟ 502; © 564

Dereco; RMC Place; OKLAHOMA; ★ **O.C.**; pop. incl. with Oklahoma City (Inc. Place)

Devol; Inc. Place; COTTON; **221** J-11; 🅿; z 73531; Ⓟ 165; © 150

Dewar; Inc. Place; OKMULGEE; **221** F-17; 🅿; z 74431; Ⓟ 921; © 919

Dewey; Inc. Place; WASHINGTON; **221** B-17; 🅿; ★ **BART**; z 74029 & mail Bartlesville z 74006; Ⓟ 3,326; © 3,179

DEWEY; **220** E-9; Ⓟ 5,551; © 4,743; ◆ 4,249

Dewright; SEMINOLE; see Wolf (RMC Place)

Dibble; Inc. Place; MCCLAIN; **221** G-13; 🅿; z 73031; Ⓟ 181; © 289

Dickson; Inc. Place; CARTER; **221** J-14; mail Ardmore z 73401; Ⓟ 942; © 1,139

Dighton (Bartlett); RMC Place; OKMULGEE; ***221** F-17; elev. 654ft./199m.; mail Henryetta z 74437; rural

Dillard; RMC Place; CARTER; ***221** J-13; elev. 908ft./277m.; mail Wilson z 73463; pop. incl. with Wilson (Inc. Place)

Dill City; Inc. Place; WASHITA; **220** G-9; 🅿; z 73641; Ⓟ 622; © 526

Disney; Inc. Place; MAYES; **221** C-19; 🅿; z 74340; Ⓟ 257; © 226

Dixon; RMC Place; SEMINOLE; **221** G-15; mail Wewoka z 74884; ● 250

Dodge; CDP; DELAWARE; ***221** C-20; mail Grove z 74344; © 96

Donaldson; RMC Place; TULSA; ★ **TUL**; mail Tulsa z 74104, z 74114, z 74159; pop. incl. with Tulsa (Inc. Place)

Dotyville; CDP; OTTAWA; **221** B-19; mail Miami z 74354; © 17

Dougherty; Inc. Place; MURRAY; **221** I-14; elev. 773ft./236m.; 🅿; z 73032; Ⓟ 138; © 224

Douglas; Inc. Place; GARFIELD; **221** D-13; 🅿; z 73733; Ⓟ 55; © 32

Dover; Inc. Place; KINGFISHER; **221** E-12; 🅿; z 73734; Ⓟ 376; © 367

Dow; RMC Place; PITTSBURG; **221** H-17; mail McAlester z 74501; ● 100

Drake; RMC Place; MURRAY; ***221** I-14; elev. 940ft./287m.; mail Sulphur z 73086; rural

Driftwood; RMC Place; ALFALFA; **221** B-11; mail Cherokee z 73728; ● 25

Dripping Springs; CDP-Census Area Only; DELAWARE; ***221** D-20; © 41

Drumb; RMC Place; LATIMER; ***221** H-18; mail Wilburton z 74578; rural

Drummond; Inc. Place; GARFIELD; **221** D-12; elev. 1,241ft./378m.; 🅿; z 73735; Ⓟ 408; © 405

Drumright; Inc. Place; CREEK; **221** E-15; 🅿 🅷; z 74030; Ⓟ 2,799; © 2,905

Dry Creek; CDP-Census Area Only; CHEROKEE; ***221** E-19; © 216

Duchess Landing; CDP-Census Area Only; MCINTOSH; ***221** F-18; © 95

Duke (East Duke); Inc. Place; JACKSON; **220** I-8; 🅿; z 73532; Ⓟ 360; © 445

Dunbar; RMC Place; LOVE; ***221** K-14; elev. 756ft./230m.; mail Marietta z 73448; ● 60

Dunbar; RMC Place; PUSHMATAHA; ***221** I-18; elev. 536ft./163m.; mail Moyers z 74557; rural

Duncan; Inc. Place; ⊡ STEPHENS; **221** I-12; elev. 1,126ft./343m.; 🅿 🅷 ■; z 73533-34, z 73536; Ⓟ 21,732; © 22,505; ◆ 23,586

Dunjee Park; RMC Place; OKLAHOMA; **220** K-7; ★ **O.C.**; mail Spencer z 73084; pop. incl. with Oklahoma City (Inc. Place)

Durant; Inc. Place; ⊡ BRYAN; **221** J-16; elev. 657ft./200m.; 🅿 🅷 🅲 3,872; z 74701-02; Ⓟ 12,823; © 13,549

Durham; RMC Place; ROGER MILLS; **220** E-8; elev. 465ft./142m.; 🅿; z 73642; ● 120

Durwood; RMC Place; CARTER; ***221** J-14; mail Ardmore z 73401; pop. incl. with Dickson (Inc. Place)

Dustin; Inc. Place; HUGHES; **221** G-16; elev. 711ft./217m.; 🅿; z 74839; Ⓟ 429; © 452

Dwight Mission; CDP-Census Area Only; SEQUOYAH; ***221** F-19; © 32

E

Eagle City; RMC Place; BLAINE; **221** E-11; 🅿; z 73658; ● 50

Eagletown; RMC Place; MCCURTAIN; **221** J-20; 🅿; z 74734; ● 750

Eakly; Inc. Place; CADDO; **221** G-11; 🅿; z 73033; Ⓟ 277; © 276

Earl; RMC Place; JOHNSTON; ***221** J-15; elev. 751ft./229m.; mail Mannsville z 73447

Earlsboro; Inc. Place; POTTAWATOMIE; **221** G-15; 🅿; z 74840; Ⓟ 535; © 633

Eastborough; RMC Place; WAGONER; ***221** D-17; elev. 700ft./213m.; ★ **TUL**; mail Broken Arrow z 74014; ● 1,000

East Duke; JACKSON; see Duke (Inc. Place)

East Jesse (East Jessie); RMC Place; COAL; ***221** I-15; mail Stonewall z 74871

East Jessie; COAL; see East Jesse (RMC Place)

East Ninnekah; GRADY; see Ninnekah (Inc. Place)

Eastside; RMC Place; CUSTER; mail Weatherford z 73096; pop. incl. with Weatherford (Inc. Place)

Eastside; RMC Place; MUSKOGEE; ★ **MSKOG**; mail Muskogee z 74403; pop. incl. with Muskogee (Inc. Place)

Eastside; RMC Place; OKLAHOMA; ★ **O.C.**; mail Oklahoma City z 73104, z 73111, z 73117, z 73121, z 73141; pop. incl. with Oklahoma City (Inc. Place)

Eastside; RMC Place; TULSA; ★ **TUL**; mail Tulsa z 74108, z 74128-29, z 74134, z 74169; pop. incl. with Tulsa (Inc. Place)

East Side; RMC Place; WASHINGTON; ***221** C-17; mail Bartlesville z 74006

Eddy; RMC Place; KAY; ***221** C-13; elev. 1,062ft./324m.; mail Lamont z 74643; rural

Edgewater Park; RMC Place; COMANCHE; ***221** H-11; mail Apache z 73006; ● 200

Edmond; Inc. Place; OKLAHOMA; **220** I-6; 🅿 🅷 🅲 14,740 ■; ★ **O.C.**; z 73003, z 73012-13, z 73025, z 73034, z 73083; Ⓟ 52,315; © 68,315; ◆ 77,520

Edna; RMC Place; CREEK; ***221** F-16; mail Bristow z 74010; rural

Eighty Ninth Street; RMC Place; OKLAHOMA; ★ **O.C.**; mail Oklahoma City z 73159; pop. incl. with Oklahoma City (Inc. Place)

Eldon; CDP; CHEROKEE; ***221** E-19; mail Tahlequah z 74464; © 991

Eldorado; Inc. Place; JACKSON; **220** I-8; elev. 1,457ft./444m.; 🅿; z 73537; Ⓟ 573; © 527

Electric Park; RMC Place; TULSA; ★ **TUL**; pop. incl. with Tulsa (Inc. Place)

Elgin; Inc. Place; COMANCHE; **221** H-11; 🅿; z 73538; Ⓟ 975; © 1,210

Elk City; Inc. Place; BECKHAM; **220** F-9; elev. 1,928ft./588m.; 🅿 🅷 ■; z 73644, z 73648; Ⓟ 10,428; © 10,510; ◆ 13,024

ELLIS; **220** D-8; Ⓟ 4,497; © 4,075; ◆ 4,036

Elmer; Inc. Place; JACKSON; **220** I-9; elev. 1,308ft./399m.; 🅿; z 73539; Ⓟ 132; © 96

Elmore City; Inc. Place; GARVIN; **221** I-13; 🅿; z 73433; Ⓟ 493; © 756

Elmwood; RMC Place; BEAVER; **220** C-6; 🅿; z 73932; ● 25

El Reno; Inc. Place; ⊡ CANADIAN; **221** F-12; elev. 1,350ft./411m.; 🅿 🅷; ★ **O.C.**; z 73036; location of Concho Indian Agency; Ⓟ 15,414; © 16,212

Emerson Center; RMC Place; COTTON; mail Walters z 73572; rural

Emet; RMC Place; JOHNSTON; ***221** J-15; elev. 814ft./248m.; mail Milburn z 73450; ● 50

Empire City; Inc. Place; STEPHENS; **221** I-12; mail Duncan z 73533; Ⓟ 219; © 734

Enid; Inc. Place; ⊡ GARFIELD; **221** D-12; elev. 1,246ft./380m.; 🅿 🅷 ■; ★ **ENID**; z 73701-03, z 73705-06; Ⓟ 45,309; © 47,045; ◆ 48,986

Enos; RMC Place; MARSHALL; ***221** K-15; mail Kingston z 73439; rural

Enterprise; RMC Place; HASKELL; **221** G-18; elev. 652ft./199m.; mail Quinton z 74561, Stigler z 74462; ● 200

Enville; RMC Place; LOVE; ***221** J-14; mail Marietta z 73448; rural

Eram; RMC Place; OKMULGEE; ***221** F-17; mail Morris z 74445

Erick; Inc. Place; BECKHAM; **220** G-8; 🅿; z 73645; Ⓟ 1,083; © 1,023

Erin Springs; RMC Place; GARVIN; **221** H-13; mail Lindsay z 73052; disincorporated since 2000 Census; Ⓟ 139; © 114

Estella; RMC Place; CRAIG; ***221** C-18; mail Vinita z 74301; ● 70

Ethel; RMC Place; PUSHMATAHA; ***221** J-18; elev. 593ft./181m.; mail Antlers z 74523; rural

Etowah; Inc. Place; CLEVELAND; ***221** G-14; mail Noble z 73068; Ⓟ 33; © 122

Etta; RMC Place; CHEROKEE; mail Welling z 74471; rural

Eucha; RMC Place; DELAWARE; ***221** D-19; elev. 1,121ft./342m.; 🅿; z 74342; ● 150

Euchee Creek; RMC Place; TULSA; ★ **TUL**; mail Sand Springs z 74063; pop. incl. with Sand Springs (Inc. Place)

Eufaula; Inc. Place; ⊡ MCINTOSH; **221** G-18; elev. 617ft./188m.; 🅿 🅷; z 74432 & mail Stidham z 74461; Ⓟ 2,652; © 2,639

Eva; RMC Place; TEXAS; **220** B-3; elev. 3,575ft./1,090m.; mail Goodwell z 73939; rural

Evening Shade; CDP-Census Area Only; SEQUOYAH; ***221** F-19; © 441

Ewing; RMC Place; CUSTER; mail Clinton z 73601; pop. incl. with Clinton (Inc. Place)

F

Fairfax; Inc. Place; OSAGE; **221** C-15; located on Osage Ind. Res.; elev. 842ft./257m.; 🅿 🅷; z 74637; Ⓟ 1,749; © 1,555

Fairfield; CDP-Census Area Only; ADAIR; ***221** E-20; © 367

Fairland; Inc. Place; OTTAWA; **221** C-19; elev. 838ft./255m.; 🅿; z 74343; Ⓟ 916; © 1,025

Fairmont; Inc. Place; GARFIELD; **221** D-13; elev. 1,202ft./366m.; 🅿; ★ **ENID**; z 73736; Ⓟ 129; © 147

Fair Oaks; Inc. Place; WAGONER, ROGERS; **221** D-17; ★ **TUL**; mail Catoosa z 74015; Ⓟ 1,133; © 122

Fairview; Inc. Place; ⊡ MAJOR; **221** D-11; elev. 1,300ft./396m.; 🅿 🅷; z 73737; Ⓟ 2,936; © 2,733

Falconhead; RMC Place; LOVE; ***221** K-14; mail Burneyville z 73430; ● 300

Falfa; RMC Place; LATIMER; ***221** H-19; mail Talihina z 74571; ● 90

Fallis; Inc. Place; LINCOLN; **221** E-14; elev. 970ft./296m.; mail Wellston z 74881; Ⓟ 49; © 28

Fame; RMC Place; MCINTOSH; ***221** F-17; elev. 605ft./184m.; mail Eufaula z 74432; rural

Fanshawe; Inc. Place; LE FLORE, LATIMER; **221** H-19; elev. 545ft./166m.; 🅿; z 74935; Ⓟ 331; © 384

Fargo; Inc. Place; ELLIS; **220** D-8; elev. 2,101ft./640m.; 🅿; z 73840; Ⓟ 299; © 326

Farley; RMC Place; OKLAHOMA; ★ **O.C.**; mail Oklahoma City z 73107, z 73147; pop. incl. with Oklahoma City (Inc. Place)

Farmers Hill; RMC Place; MCCURTAIN; ***221** J-19; mail Garvin z 74736; rural

Farris; RMC Place; ATOKA; **221** J-17; elev. 544ft./166m.; 🅿; z 74542 & mail Atoka z 74525; ● 150

Faxon; Inc. Place; COMANCHE; **221** I-11; 🅿; z 73540; Ⓟ 127; © 134

Fay; RMC Place; DEWEY; **220** E-10; 🅿; z 73646; ● 150

Featherston; RMC Place; PITTSBURG; ***221** G-18; mail Quinton z 74561; ● 90

Felker; RMC Place; MCCURTAIN; **221** J-19; mail Valliant z 74764; ● 100

Felt; RMC Place; CIMARRON; **220** C-1; 🅿; z 73937; ● 100

Fewell; RMC Place; PUSHMATAHA; ***221** I-19; mail Nashoba z 74558; rural

Fillmore; RMC Place; JOHNSTON; **221** J-15; elev. 746ft./227m.; mail Coleman z 73432; ● 45

Finley; RMC Place; PUSHMATAHA; **221** I-18; 🅿; z 74543; ● 150

First National Bank; RMC Place; OKLAHOMA; ★ **O.C.**; mail Oklahoma City z 73102; pop. incl. with Oklahoma City (Inc. Place)

Fisher; RMC Place; TULSA; ***221** D-16; elev. 651ft./198m.; ★ **TUL**; mail Sand Springs z 74063; pop. incl. with Sand Springs (Inc. Place)

Fittstown; RMC Place; PONTOTOC; **221** I-15; elev. 833ft./254m.; 🅿; z 74842; ● 500

Fitzhugh; Inc. Place; PONTOTOC; **221** I-15; elev. 1,250ft./381m.; 🅿; z 74843; Ⓟ 196; © 204

Fleetwood; RMC Place; JEFFERSON; ***221** K-12; mail Terral z 73569; rural

Fletcher; Inc. Place; COMANCHE; **221** H-11; 🅿; z 73541; Ⓟ 1,002; © 1,022

Flint Creek; CDP-Census Area Only; DELAWARE; ***221** D-19; © 580

Floris; RMC Place; BEAVER; ***220** B-6; mail Forgan z 73938, Liberal z 67901, Turpin z 73950; rural

Flute Springs; CDP-Census Area Only; SEQUOYAH; ***221** F-19; © 182

Flynn; RMC Place; OKLAHOMA; ***221** F-13; ★ **O.C.**; mail Oklahoma City z 73107; pop. incl. with Oklahoma City (Inc. Place)

Folsom; RMC Place; JOHNSTON; **221** J-16; mail Coleman z 73432; ● 50

Foraker; Inc. Place; OSAGE; **221** B-15; located on Osage Ind. Res.; elev. 1,271ft./387m.; 🅿; z 74652; Ⓟ 25; © 23

Forest Hill; RMC Place; LE FLORE; ***221** H-20; mail Heavener z 74937; rural

Forest Park; Inc. Place; OKLAHOMA; **220** K-5; ★ **O.C.**; mail Oklahoma City z 73121; Ⓟ 1,249; © 1,066

Forgan; Inc. Place; BEAVER; **220** B-6; 🅿; z 73938; Ⓟ 489; © 532

Forney; RMC Place; CHOCTAW; ***221** J-18; mail Hugo z 74743; rural

Forrester; RMC Place; LE FLORE; ***221** H-20; mail Heavener z 74937; rural

Fort Cobb; Inc. Place; CADDO; **221** G-11; elev. 1,255ft./383m.; 🅿; z 73038; Ⓟ 663; © 667

Fort Coffee; Inc. Place; LE FLORE; ***221** G-20; elev. 465ft./142m.; mail Spiro z 74959; © 412

Fort Gibson; Inc. Place; MUSKOGEE; **221** E-18; 🅿; ★ **MSKOG**; z 74434; Ⓟ 3,359; © 4,054

Fort Reno; RMC Place; CANADIAN; ***221** F-12; ★ **O.C.**; mail El Reno z 73036; pop. incl. with El Reno (Inc. Place)

Fort Supply (Supply); Inc. Place; WOODWARD; **220** C-8; elev. 1,994ft./608m.; 🅿 🅷; z 73841; Ⓟ 369; © 328

Fort Towson; Inc. Place; CHOCTAW; **221** J-18; 🅿; z 74735; Ⓟ 568; © 611

Foss; Inc. Place; WASHITA; **220** F-9; elev. 1,629ft./497m.; 🅿; z 73647; Ⓟ 148; © 127

Foster; Inc. Place; GARVIN; **221** I-13; 🅿; z 73434; incorporated January 8, 2002; not reported in 2000 Census; ● 100

Four Corners; RMC Place; OKMULGEE; ***221** F-17; elev. 633ft./193m.; mail Henryetta z 74437; rural

Four Corners; RMC Place; TEXAS; ***220** B-3; mail Goodwell z 73939; rural

Fox; RMC Place; CARTER; **221** I-13; 🅿; z 73435; ● 300

Fox Run; RMC Place; TULSA; ***221** E-17; ★ **TUL**; mail Jenks z 74037; pop. incl. with Jenks (Inc. Place)

Foyil; Inc. Place; ROGERS; **221** C-18; 🅿; z 74031; Ⓟ 86; © 234

Francis; Inc. Place; PONTOTOC; **221** H-15; 🅿; z 74844; Ⓟ 346; © 332

Franklin; RMC Place; CLEVELAND; ***221** G-13; elev. 1,069ft./326m.; ★ **O.C.**; mail Norman z 73026; pop. incl. with Norman (Inc. Place)

Frederick; Inc. Place; ⊡ TILLMAN; **220** I-10; elev. 1,300ft./396m.; 🅿 🅷; z 73542; Ⓟ 5,221; © 4,637

Freedom; Inc. Place; WOODS; **220** C-9; 🅿; z 73842; Ⓟ 264; © 271

French Market; RMC Place; OKLAHOMA; ★ **O.C.**; mail Oklahoma City z 73116; pop. incl. with Oklahoma City (Inc. Place)

Friendship; Inc. Place; JACKSON; **220** H-9; mail Altus z 73521; incorporated December 8, 1999; not reported in 2000 Census; Ⓡ 17

Frisco; RMC Place; PONTOTOC; ***221** I-15; elev. 719ft./219m.; mail Stonewall z 74871; rural

Frogville; RMC Place; CHOCTAW; ***221** K-18; mail Hugo z 74743; rural

Fugate; RMC Place; ATOKA; ***221** I-17; mail Stringtown z 74569; rural

Fuller; RMC Place; TULSA; ★ **TUL**; pop. incl. with Tulsa (Inc. Place)

G

Gaar Corner; RMC Place; PONTOTOC; ***221** H-15; elev. 1,009ft./308m.; mail Ada z 74820; ● 100

Gage; Inc. Place; ELLIS; **220** D-8; elev. 2,136ft./651m.; 🅿; z 73843; Ⓟ 473; © 429

Gans; Inc. Place; SEQUOYAH; **221** F-20; 🅿; z 74936; Ⓟ 218; © 208

Garber; Inc. Place; GARFIELD; **221** D-13; elev. 1,177ft./359m.; 🅿; z 73738; Ⓟ 959; © 845

Garden City; RMC Place; TULSA; ***221** D-17; ★ **TUL**; pop. incl. with Tulsa (Inc. Place)

Garden Grove; RMC Place; POTTAWATOMIE; ***221** F-15; mail Shawnee z 74804; rural

Gardenview; RMC Place; TULSA; ***221** E-17; ★ **TUL**; mail Bixby z 74008; pop. incl. with Bixby (Inc. Place)

GARFIELD; **221** C-12; Ⓟ 56,735; © 57,813; ◆ 57,723

Garland; RMC Place; HASKELL; ***221** G-19; elev. 522ft./159m.; mail Stigler z 74462; rural

Garnett; RMC Place; TULSA; ***221** D-17; ★ **TUL**; pop. incl. with Tulsa (Inc. Place)

Garvin; Inc. Place; MCCURTAIN; **221** J-19; elev. 494ft./151m.; 🅿; z 74736; Ⓟ 128; © 143

GARVIN; **221** H-13; Ⓟ 26,605; © 27,210; ◆ 27,166

Gate; Inc. Place; BEAVER; **220** B-7; elev. 2,230ft./680m.; 🅿; z 73844; Ⓟ 159; © 112

Gay; RMC Place; CHOCTAW; ***221** J-18; elev. 438ft./134m.; mail Hugo z 74743; rural

Geary (Greenfield); Inc. Place; BLAINE, CANADIAN; **221** F-11; 🅿; z 73040; Ⓟ 1,347; © 1,258

Gene Autry (Berwyn); Inc. Place; CARTER; **221** J-14; 🅿; z 73436; Ⓟ 97; © 99

Georgetown; RMC Place; MUSKOGEE; mail Fort Gibson z 74434; rural

Geronimo; Inc. Place; COMANCHE; **221** I-11; 🅿; ★ **LAWT**; z 73543; Ⓟ 990; © 959

Gerty; Inc. Place; HUGHES; **221** H-16; mail Calvin z 74531; Ⓟ 95; © 101

Gibbon; RMC Place; GRANT; elev. 1,189ft./362m.; mail Manchester z 73758, Wakita z 73771

Gibson; RMC Place; WAGONER; ***221** E-18; mail Wagoner z 74467; ● 100

Gideon; RMC Place; CHEROKEE; ***221** E-19; mail Tahlequah z 74464; rural

Gilcrease; RMC Place; TULSA; ★ **TUL**; mail Tulsa z 74119, z 74127, z 74149; pop. incl. with Tulsa (Inc. Place)

Gilmore; RMC Place; LE FLORE; ***221** G-20; elev. 536ft./163m.; mail Poteau z 74953

Glencoe; Inc. Place; PAYNE; **221** D-14; elev. 1,064ft./324m.; 🅿; z 74032; Ⓟ 473; © 583

Glendale; RMC Place; LE FLORE; ***221** H-20; mail Howe z 74940; ● 200

Glen Pines; RMC Place; TULSA; ***221** E-16; ★ **TUL**; mail Glenpool z 74033; pop. incl. with Glenpool (Inc. Place)

Glenpool; Inc. Place; TULSA; **221** E-17; 🅿; ★ **TUL**; z 74033; Ⓟ 6,688; © 8,123

Glenwood South; RMC Place; TULSA; ***221** E-17; ★ **TUL**; mail Jenks z 74037; pop. incl. with Jenks (Inc. Place)

Glover; RMC Place; MCCURTAIN; **221** J-19; elev. 409ft./125m.; mail Broken Bow z 74728; ● 150

Golden; RMC Place; MCCURTAIN; **221** J-19; 🅿; z 74737; ● 200

Goldsby; Inc. Place; MCCLAIN; **221** G-13; 🅿; z 73093; Ⓟ 816; © 1,204

Goltry; Inc. Place; ALFALFA; **221** C-12; elev. 1,380ft./421m.; 🅿; z 73739; Ⓟ 297; © 268

Goodland; RMC Place; CHOCTAW; **221** J-18; mail Hugo z 74743; ● 50

Goodner; RMC Place; OKLAHOMA; ★ **O.C.**; pop. incl. with Oklahoma City (Inc. Place)

Goodwater; RMC Place; MCCURTAIN; ***221** J-20; mail Haworth z 74740; rural

Goodwell; Inc. Place; TEXAS; **220** C-4; elev. 3,293ft./1,004m.; 🅿 🅲 1,136; z 73939; Ⓟ 1,065; © 1,192

Gore; Inc. Place; SEQUOYAH; **221** F-19; 🅿; z 74435; Ⓟ 690; © 850

Gotebo; Inc. Place; KIOWA; **220** G-10; elev. 1,430ft./436m.; 🅿; z 73041; Ⓟ 370; © 272

Gould; Inc. Place; HARMON; **220** H-8; 🅿; z 73544; Ⓟ 237; © 206

Gowen; RMC Place; LATIMER; **221** H-18; 🅿; z 74545; ● 250

Gracemont; Inc. Place; CADDO; **221** G-11; 🅿; z 73042; Ⓟ 339; © 336

Grady; RMC Place; JEFFERSON; ***221** J-13; 🅿; z 73569; rural

GRADY; **221** H-12; Ⓟ 41,747; © 45,516; ◆ 50,813

Graham; RMC Place; CARTER; **221** I-13; 🅿; z 73437; ● 250

Grainola; Inc. Place; OSAGE; **221** B-15; located on Osage Ind. Res.; mail Shidler z 74652; Ⓟ 58; © 31

Grandfield; Inc. Place; TILLMAN; **220** J-10; 🅿; z 73546 & mail Loveland z 73553; Ⓟ 1,224; © 1,110

Grand Lake Towne; Inc. Place; MAYES; **221** C-19; mail Vinita z 74301; Ⓟ 58; © 65

Grandview Heights; RMC Place; MUSKOGEE; ***221** E-18; ★ **MSKOG**; mail Muskogee z 74403; pop. incl. with Muskogee (Inc. Place)

Granite; Inc. Place; GREER; **220** H-9; 🅿; z 73547; Ⓟ 1,844; © 1,844

Grant; RMC Place; CHOCTAW; **221** J-18; 🅿; z 74738; ● 300

GRANT; **221** B-12; Ⓟ 5,689; © 5,144; ◆ 4,381

Gray; RMC Place; BEAVER; ***220** C-6; elev. 2,917ft./889m.; mail Balko z 73931; rural

Gray Horse; RMC Place; OSAGE; **221** C-15; located on Osage Ind. Res.; elev. 928ft./283m.; mail Fairfax z 74637; ● 60

Grayson; Inc. Place; OKMULGEE; **221** F-17; mail Henryetta z 74437; Ⓟ 66; © 134

Greasy; CDP; ADAIR; ***221** F-20; mail Bunch z 74931; © 387

Greenfield; Inc. Place; BLAINE; **221** F-11; elev. 1,456ft./444m.; 🅿; z 73043; Ⓟ 200; © 123

Greenfield; BLAINE, CANADIAN; see Geary (Inc. Place)

Green Pastures; RMC Place; OKLAHOMA; **220** K-7; elev. 1,238ft./377m.; ★ **O.C.**; mail Spencer z 73084; pop. incl. with Oklahoma City (Inc. Place)

Green Valley Estates; RMC Place; CHEROKEE, SEQUOYAH; mail Vian z 74962; ● 300

Greenville; RMC Place; LOVE; ***221** J-14; mail Marietta z 73448; ● 150

Greenwood; RMC Place; PUSHMATAHA; ***221** J-18; mail Antlers z 74523; rural

GREER; **220** H-8; Ⓟ 6,559; © 6,061; ◆ 5,674

Gregory; CDP-Census Area Only; ROGERS; ***221** D-17; © 150

Griggs; RMC Place; CIMARRON; ***220** C-3; elev. 3,820ft./1,164m.; mail Texhoma z 73949; rural

Grimes; RMC Place; ROGER MILLS; ***220** F-8; mail Cheyenne z 73628

Grove; Inc. Place; DELAWARE; **221** C-19; 🅿 🅷; z 74344-45; Ⓟ 4,020; © 5,131

Gulftown; RMC Place; OKMULGEE; ***221** F-17; mail Henryetta z 74437; rural

Guthrie; Inc. Place; ⊡ LOGAN; **221** E-13; elev. 980ft./299m.; 🅿 🅷; ★ **O.C.**; z 73044; Ⓟ 10,518; © 9,925

Guymon; Inc. Place; ⊡ TEXAS; **220** C-4; elev. 3,121ft./951m.; 🅿 🅷; z 73942; Ⓟ 7,803; © 10,472

Gyp; RMC Place; BLAINE; mail Southard z 73770; rural

Gypsy; RMC Place; CREEK; ***221** F-15; mail Bristow z 74010; rural

H

Haileyville; Inc. Place; PITTSBURG; **221** H-18; 🅿; z 74546; Ⓟ 918; © 891

Hall Addition; RMC Place; TULSA; ★ **TUL**; mail Sand Springs z 74063; pop. incl. with Sand Springs (Inc. Place)

Hallett; Inc. Place; PAWNEE; **221** D-15; 🅿; z 74034; Ⓟ 159; © 168

Hall Park; RMC Place; CLEVELAND; ***221** G-13; ★ **O.C.**; mail Norman z 73071; former incorporated place; became part of Norman October 1, 2003; pop. incl. with Norman (Inc. Place); Ⓟ 1,090; © 1,088

Hammon; Inc. Place; ROGER MILLS, CUSTER; **220** F-9; elev. 1,736ft./529m.; 🅿; z 73650; Ⓟ 611; © 469

Hanna; Inc. Place; MCINTOSH; **221** G-17; elev. 678ft./207m.; 🅿; z 74845; Ⓟ 99; © 133

Hanson; RMC Place; SEQUOYAH; **221** F-20; mail Sallisaw z 74955; ● 150

Happyland; RMC Place; PONTOTOC; ***221** H-15; mail Ada z 74820; rural

Harden City; RMC Place; PONTOTOC; ***221** I-15; elev. 802ft./244m.; 🅿; z 74871 & mail Fittstown z 74842; rural

Hardesty; Inc. Place; TEXAS; **220** C-5; elev. 2,911ft./887m.; 🅿; z 73944; Ⓟ 228; © 277

Hardy; RMC Place; KAY; ***221** B-15; mail Newkirk z 74647; rural

Harjo; RMC Place; POTTAWATOMIE; ***221** G-15; mail Tecumseh z 74873

Harmon; RMC Place; ELLIS; **220** D-8; elev. 2,499ft./762m.; 🅿; z 73832; ● 25

HARMON; **220** H-8; Ⓟ 3,793; © 3,283; ◆ 2,689

Harmony Star; RMC Place; ROGERS; ***221** D-18; mail Claremore z 74017; rural

HARPER; **220** C-8; Ⓟ 4,063; © 3,562; ◆ 3,122

Harrah; Inc. Place; OKLAHOMA; **221** F-14; 🅿; ★ **O.C.**; z 73045; Ⓟ 4,206; © 4,719

Harris; RMC Place; MCCURTAIN; **221** K-20; elev. 346ft./105m.; mail Haworth z 74740; ● 150

Entries in **UPPERCASE** are counties.
Entries in **bold** have populations of 2,500 or more.
Names in parentheses are alternate names.

Inc. Place	Incorporated Place
RMC Place	Rand McNally Designated Place
CDP	Census Designated Place
MCD	Minor Civil Division

⊡	County Seat
▲	Minor Civil Division
elev.	Elevation
🅿	Post Office
🅷	Hospital
🅲	College
■	Principal Business Center
★	Ranally Metro Area (RMA) Abbreviation
z	Zip Code(s)
Ⓟ	Previous Census Population
Ⓡ	Revised Census Population
Ⓐ	Annexation Population
●	Rand McNally Population Estimate
©	Final Census Population
Ⓢ	Special Census Population
◆	Estimated Population

For additional definitions see Glossary, Volume 1, and Introduction, Volume 2.

Harrison; RMC Place; SEQUOYAH; ***221** F-19; mail Sallisaw z 74955; rural
Hartshorne; Inc. Place; PITTSBURG; **221** H-18; elev. 705ft./215m.; 🅿; z 74547; Ⓟ 2,120; Ⓒ 2,102
Haskell; Inc. Place; MUSKOGEE; **221** E-17; 🅿; z 74436; Ⓟ 2,143; Ⓒ 1,765
HASKELL; **221** G-19; Ⓟ 10,940; Ⓒ 11,792; ◆ 11,954
Hastings; Inc. Place; JEFFERSON; **221** J-12; 🅿; z 73548; Ⓟ 164; Ⓒ 155
Haw Creek; RMC Place; LE FLORE; ***221** H-20; elev. 726ft./221m.; mail Heavener z 74937; rural
Hawley; RMC Place; GRANT; ***221** C-12; elev. 1,089ft./332m.; mail Nash z 73761
Haworth; Inc. Place; MCCURTAIN; **221** K-20; 🅿; z 74740; Ⓟ 293; Ⓒ 354
Hayward; RMC Place; GARFIELD; **221** D-13; elev. 1,191ft./363m.; mail Covington z 73730; ● 30
Haywood; RMC Place; PITTSBURG; **221** H-17; elev. 711ft./217m.; 🅿; z 74501; ● 300
Hazel Del; RMC Place; POTTAWATOMIE; ***221** F-14; mail McLoud z 74851; rural
Headrick; Inc. Place; JACKSON; **220** I-9; 🅿; z 73549; Ⓟ 183; Ⓒ 130
Healdton; Inc. Place; CARTER; **221** J-13; 🅿; z 73438; Ⓟ 2,872; Ⓒ 2,786
Heavener; Inc. Place; LE FLORE; **221** H-20; elev. 562ft./171m.; 🅿; z 74937; Ⓟ 2,601; Ⓒ 3,201
Hefner; RMC Place; OKLAHOMA; ★ **O.C.**; mail Oklahoma City z 73142, z 73162, z 73172; pop. incl. with Oklahoma City (Inc. Place)
Helena; Inc. Place; ALFALFA; **221** C-11; elev. 1,397ft./426m.; 🅿; z 73741; Ⓟ 1,043; Ⓒ 443; Ⓡ 1,424
Hendrix (Kemp City); Inc. Place; BRYAN; **221** K-16; 🅿; z 74741; Ⓟ 108; Ⓒ 79
Hennepin; RMC Place; GARVIN; **221** I-14; elev. 940ft./287m.; 🅿; z 73444; ● 250
Hennessey; Inc. Place; KINGFISHER; **221** D-12; 🅿; z 73742; Ⓟ 1,902; Ⓒ 2,058
Henryetta; Inc. Place; OKMULGEE; **221** F-17; 🅿 🄷; z 74437; Ⓟ 5,872; Ⓒ 6,096
Herring; RMC Place; ROGER MILLS; ***220** F-8; elev. 1,803ft./550m.; mail Hammon z 73650; rural
Hess; RMC Place; JACKSON; **220** I-9; elev. 1,328ft./405m.; mail Elmer z 73539; ● 50
Hester; RMC Place; GREER; ***220** H-9; mail Mangum z 73554; rural
Hewitt; RMC Place; CARTER; ***221** J-13; mail Wilson z 73463; pop. incl. with Wilson (Inc. Place)
Hext; RMC Place; BECKHAM; ***220** G-8; elev. 1,923ft./586m.; mail Erick z 73645; rural
Hickory; Inc. Place; MURRAY; **221** I-15; elev. 1,210ft./369m.; mail Roff z 74865; Ⓟ 77; Ⓒ 87
Hicks Addition; RMC Place; OKLAHOMA; **220** K-6; ★ **O.C.**; mail Spencer z 73084
Higgins; RMC Place; LATIMER; ***221** H-18; elev. 668ft./204m.; mail Gowen z 74545, Wilburton z 74578; rural
Highland Park; RMC Place; TULSA; mail Tulsa z 74107; pop. incl. with Tulsa (Inc. Place)
Hill; RMC Place; LE FLORE; ***221** G-20; mail Cameron z 74932; rural
Hillsdale; Inc. Place; GARFIELD; **221** C-12; elev. 1,220ft./372m.; 🅿; z 73743; Ⓟ 96; Ⓒ 101
Hill Top; RMC Place; HUGHES; mail Stuart z 74570; rural
Hinton; Inc. Place; CADDO; **221** F-11; elev. 1,676ft./511m.; 🅿; z 73047; Ⓟ 1,233; Ⓒ 2,175
Hitchcock; Inc. Place; BLAINE; **221** E-11; 🅿; z 73744; Ⓟ 139; Ⓒ 141
Hitchita; Inc. Place; MCINTOSH; **221** F-17; 🅿; z 74438; Ⓟ 118; Ⓒ 113
Hobart; Inc. Place; ⊡ KIOWA; **220** H-9; elev. 1,550ft./472m.; 🅿 🄷; z 73651; Ⓟ 4,305; Ⓒ 3,997
Hockerville; RMC Place; OTTAWA; ***221** B-19; mail Quapaw z 74363; ● 50
Hodgen (Hodgens); RMC Place; LE FLORE; **221** H-20; 🅿; z 74939; ● 260
Hodgens; LE FLORE; see Hodgen (RMC Place)
Hoffman; Inc. Place; OKMULGEE; **221** F-17; 🅿; z 74437; Ⓟ 175; Ⓒ 148
Hog Shooter; RMC Place; WASHINGTON; ***221** C-17; elev. 723ft./220m.; mail Bartlesville z 74003, z 74006; rural
Holdenville; Inc. Place; ⊡ HUGHES; **221** G-16; elev. 910ft./277m.; 🅿 🄷; z 74848; Ⓟ 4,792; Ⓒ 4,732; Ⓡ 5,700
Holley Creek; RMC Place; MCCURTAIN; ***221** J-19; mail Broken Bow z 74728; ● 200
Hollis; Inc. Place; ⊡ HARMON; **220** H-7; elev. 1,620ft./494m.; 🅿 🄷; z 73550; Ⓟ 2,584; Ⓒ 2,264
Hollister; Inc. Place; TILLMAN; **220** I-10; 🅿; z 73551; Ⓟ 59; Ⓒ 60
Hollow; RMC Place; CRAIG; ***221** B-18; mail Welch z 74369; rural
Hollywood Corners; RMC Place; CLEVELAND; ***221** G-13; ★ **O.C.**; mail Norman z 73069, z 73071; pop. incl. with Norman (Inc. Place)
Homer; RMC Place; PONTOTOC; **221** H-15; mail Ada z 74820; ● 100
Homestead; RMC Place; BLAINE; **221** D-11; mail Okeene z 73763; ● 70
Hominy; Inc. Place; OSAGE; **221** D-16; located on Osage Ind. Res.; elev. 792ft./241m.; 🅿; z 74035; Ⓟ 3,229; Ⓒ 2,584; Ⓡ 3,795
Honobia; RMC Place; LE FLORE; **221** I-19; 🅿; z 74549 & mail Clayton z 74536; ● 150
Hontubby; RMC Place; LE FLORE; ***221** H-20; elev. 529ft./161m.; mail Heavener z 74937; ● 50
Hooker; Inc. Place; TEXAS; **220** B-5; 🅿; z 73945; Ⓟ 1,551; Ⓒ 1,788
Hoot Owl; Inc. Place; MAYES; ***221** D-18; mail Salina z 74365; Ⓟ 5; Ⓒ 0
Hopeton; RMC Place; WOODS; **220** C-10; 🅿; z 73746; ● 40
Horntown; Inc. Place; HUGHES; ***221** G-16; mail Holdenville z 74848; Ⓒ 61
Hough; RMC Place; TEXAS; ***220** B-4; elev. 3,284ft./1,001m.; mail Guymon z 73942; ● 100
Howe; Inc. Place; LE FLORE; **221** H-20; 🅿; z 74940; Ⓟ 510; Ⓒ 697
Hoyt; RMC Place; HASKELL; ***221** G-18; 🅿; z 74440, z 74472; ● 100
Hughes; RMC Place; LATIMER; **221** H-19; elev. 549ft./167m.; mail Wister z 74966; rural
HUGHES; **221** G-16; Ⓟ 13,023; Ⓒ 14,154; ◆ 13,510
Hugo; Inc. Place; ⊡ CHOCTAW; **221** J-18; 🅿 🄷; z 74743; Ⓟ 5,978; Ⓒ 5,536
Hulbert; Inc. Place; CHEROKEE; **221** E-19; 🅿; z 74441; Ⓟ 499; Ⓒ 543
Hulen; RMC Place; COTTON; ***221** I-11; mail Walters z 73572; rural
Humphreys; RMC Place; JACKSON; **220** I-9; mail Altus z 73521; ● 150
Hunter; Inc. Place; GARFIELD; **221** C-13; elev. 1,094ft./333m.; 🅿; z 74640; Ⓟ 218; Ⓒ 173
Hyde Park; RMC Place; MUSKOGEE; ***221** E-18; ★ **MSKOG**; mail Muskogee z 74403; pop. incl. with Muskogee (Inc. Place)
Hydro (Lookeba); Inc. Place; CADDO, BLAINE; **221** F-11; 🅿; z 73048; Ⓟ 977; Ⓒ 1,060

I

Idabel; Inc. Place; ⊡ MCCURTAIN; **221** K-19; elev. 489ft./149m.; 🅿 🄷; z 74745; Ⓟ 6,957; Ⓒ 6,952
Independence; RMC Place; LE FLORE; ***221** H-20; elev. 540ft./165m.; mail Heavener z 74937; rural
Indiahoma; Inc. Place; COMANCHE; **220** I-10; elev. 1,335ft./407m.; 🅿; z 73552; Ⓟ 337; Ⓒ 374
Indian Meadows; RMC Place; CHEROKEE; ***221** E-19; mail Tahlequah z 74464; rural
Indianola; Inc. Place; PITTSBURG; **221** G-17; 🅿; z 74442; Ⓟ 171; Ⓒ 191
Ingalls; RMC Place; PAYNE; **221** D-14; elev. 927ft./283m.; mail Stillwater z 74074; ● 60
Ingersoll; RMC Place; ALFALFA; **221** B-11; elev. 1,206ft./368m.; mail Cherokee z 73728; ● 20
Inola; Inc. Place; ROGERS; **221** D-18; elev. 600ft./183m.; 🅿; z 74036; Ⓟ 1,444; Ⓒ 1,589
Iona; RMC Place; MURRAY; ***221** I-14; elev. 1,096ft./334m.; mail Sulphur z 73086; rural
Iron Post; RMC Place; CREEK; ***221** E-16; elev. 845ft./258m.; mail Bristow z 74010; rural
Iron Post; CDP-Census Area Only; MAYES; ***221** D-18; Ⓒ 117
Iron Stob Corner; RMC Place; MCCURTAIN; ***221** K-19; elev. 418ft./127m.; mail Garvin z 74736; rural
Irving; RMC Place; JEFFERSON; ***221** J-12; elev. 957ft./292m.; mail Ryan z 73565; rural
Isabella; RMC Place; MAJOR; **221** D-11; 🅿; z 73747; ● 170
IXL; Inc. Place; OKFUSKEE; incorporated October 24, 2001; not reported in 2000 Census; ● 61

J

Jackson; RMC Place; BRYAN; mail Bennington z 74723; rural
JACKSON; **220** I-8; Ⓟ 28,764; Ⓒ 28,439; ◆ 24,511
Jacktown; RMC Place; LINCOLN; **221** F-14; mail Meeker z 74855; ● 30
Jamestown; RMC Place; ROGERS; ***221** C-17; mail Talala z 74080; disincorporated July 1, 1998; Ⓟ 4; Ⓒ 10
Jay; Inc. Place; ⊡ DELAWARE; **221** C-19; elev. 1,035ft./315m.; 🅿; z 74346; Ⓟ 2,220; Ⓒ 2,482
Jefferson; Inc. Place; GRANT; **221** C-12; elev. 1,041ft./317m.; mail Medford z 73759; Ⓟ 36; Ⓒ 37
JEFFERSON; **221** J-12; Ⓟ 7,010; Ⓒ 6,818; ◆ 6,089
Jenks; Inc. Place; TULSA; **220** H-3; 🅿; ★ **TUL**; z 74037; Ⓟ 7,493; Ⓒ 9,557
Jennings; Inc. Place; PAWNEE; **221** D-15; elev. 932ft./284m.; 🅿; z 74038; Ⓟ 381; Ⓒ 373
Jesse; RMC Place; PONTOTOC; ***221** I-15; mail Stonewall z 74871
Jet; Inc. Place; ALFALFA; **221** C-12; 🅿; z 73749; Ⓟ 272; Ⓒ 230
Jimtown; RMC Place; LOVE; ***221** K-13; mail Burneyville z 73430; ● 40
Johnson; Inc. Place; POTTAWATOMIE; ***221** F-15; mail Shawnee z 74804; Ⓟ 196; Ⓒ 223
JOHNSTON; **221** I-15; Ⓟ 10,032; Ⓒ 10,513; ◆ 10,393
Jollyville; RMC Place; MURRAY; ***221** I-14; mail Davis z 73030; ● 50
Jones; Inc. Place; OKLAHOMA; **220** J-7; 🅿; ★ **O.C.**; z 73049; Ⓟ 2,424; Ⓒ 2,517
Joy; RMC Place; MURRAY; **221** I-14; mail Wynnewood z 73098
Jumbo; RMC Place; PUSHMATAHA; ***221** I-17; mail Moyers z 74557; rural
Justice; CDP-Census Area Only; ROGERS; ***221** D-17; Ⓒ 1,311

K

Kansas; Inc. Place; DELAWARE; **221** D-19; 🅿; z 74347; Ⓟ 556; Ⓒ 685
Katie; Inc. Place; GARVIN; **221** I-13; mail Elmore City z 73433; incorporated July 27, 2004; not reported in 2000 Census; ● 100
Kaw; KAY; see Kaw City (Inc. Place)
Kaw City (Kaw); Inc. Place; KAY; **221** C-15; 🅿; z 74641; Ⓟ 314; Ⓒ 372
KAY; **221** B-14; Ⓟ 48,056; Ⓒ 48,080; ◆ 45,562
Keefeton; MUSKOGEE; see Keefton (RMC Place)
Keefton (Keefeton); RMC Place; MUSKOGEE; **221** F-18; mail Muskogee z 74401, z 74403; ● 100
Keetonville; RMC Place; ROGERS; ***221** D-17; elev. 628ft./191m.; ★ **TUL**; mail Claremore z 74017; ● 200
Kellond; RMC Place; PUSHMATAHA; ***221** J-17; elev. 529ft./161m.; mail Antlers z 74523; rural
Kellyville; Inc. Place; CREEK; **221** E-16; 🅿; ★ **TUL**; z 74039; Ⓟ 984; Ⓒ 906
Kellyville (Sunshine Valley); RMC Place; OTTAWA; ***221** B-19; elev. 760ft./232m.; mail Wyandotte z 74370; ● 50
Kemp; Inc. Place; BRYAN; **221** K-16; 🅿; z 74747; Ⓟ 138; Ⓒ 144
Kemp City; BRYAN; see Hendrix (Inc. Place)
Kendalwood; RMC Place; TULSA; ***221** E-17; ★ **TUL**; mail Glenpool z 74033; pop. incl. with Glenpool (Inc. Place)
Kendrick; Inc. Place; LINCOLN; **221** E-15; 🅿; z 74079; Ⓟ 171; Ⓒ 138
Kenefic; Inc. Place; BRYAN; **221** J-16; 🅿; z 74748; Ⓟ 147; Ⓒ 192
Kent; RMC Place; CHOCTAW; ***221** J-18; mail Soper z 74759; rural
Kenton; RMC Place; CIMARRON; **220** B-1; elev. 4,353ft./1,327m.; 🅿; z 73946; ● 50
Kenwood; RMC Place; DELAWARE; **221** D-19; mail Salina z 74365; ● 120
Keota; Inc. Place; HASKELL; **221** G-19; 🅿; z 74941; Ⓟ 625; Ⓒ 517
Ketchum; Inc. Place; CRAIG; **221** C-19; elev. 772ft./235m.; 🅿; z 74349; Ⓟ 263; Ⓒ 286
Keyes; Inc. Place; CIMARRON; **220** B-2; 🅿; z 73947; Ⓟ 454; Ⓒ 410
Keys; CDP; CHEROKEE; ***221** E-19; mail Park Hill z 74451; Ⓒ 458
Kiamichi; RMC Place; PUSHMATAHA; ***221** H-19; 🅿; z 74549 & mail Tuskahoma z 74574; rural
Kiefer; Inc. Place; CREEK; **221** E-16; 🅿; ★ **TUL**; z 74041; Ⓟ 962; Ⓒ 1,026
Kiersey; RMC Place; BRYAN; ***221** J-16; mail Durant z 74701; rural
Kildare; Inc. Place; KAY; **221** B-14; elev. 1,123ft./342m.; mail Ponca City z 74604; Ⓟ 94; Ⓒ 92
Kingfisher; Inc. Place; ⊡ KINGFISHER; **221** E-12; elev. 1,060ft./323m.; 🅿 🄷; z 73750; Ⓟ 4,095; Ⓒ 4,380
KINGFISHER; **221** E-12; Ⓟ 13,212; Ⓒ 13,926; ◆ 14,602
Kingston; Inc. Place; MARSHALL; **221** J-15; 🅿; z 73439; Ⓟ 1,237; Ⓒ 1,390
Kinta; Inc. Place; HASKELL; **221** G-18; 🅿; z 74552; Ⓟ 233; Ⓒ 243
Kiowa; Inc. Place; PITTSBURG; **221** H-17; elev. 744ft./227m.; 🅿; z 74553; Ⓟ 718; Ⓒ 693
KIOWA; **220** H-10; Ⓟ 11,347; Ⓒ 10,227; ◆ 9,061
Knowles; Inc. Place; BEAVER; **220** B-7; elev. 2,537ft./773m.; 🅿; z 73844; Ⓟ 18; Ⓒ 32
Konawa; Inc. Place; SEMINOLE; **221** H-15; elev. 967ft./295m.; 🅿; z 74849; Ⓟ 1,508; Ⓒ 1,479
Kosoma; RMC Place; PUSHMATAHA; ***221** I-18; mail Moyers z 74557; rural
Krebs; Inc. Place; PITTSBURG; **221** H-17; 🅿; z 74554; Ⓟ 1,955; Ⓒ 2,051
Kremlin; Inc. Place; GARFIELD; **221** C-12; elev. 1,116ft./340m.; 🅿; z 73753; Ⓟ 243; Ⓒ 240
Kulli; MCCURTAIN; see Kullituklo (RMC Place)
Kullituklo (Kulli); RMC Place; MCCURTAIN; ***221** K-20; mail Idabel z 74745; rural
Kusa; RMC Place; OKMULGEE; ***221** F-17; mail Henryetta z 74437; rural

L

Lacey; RMC Place; KINGFISHER; ***221** D-12; elev. 1,184ft./361m.; mail Hennessey z 73742
Lafayette; RMC Place; HASKELL; ***221** G-19; mail Stigler z 74462; ● 40
Lahoma; Inc. Place; GARFIELD; **221** D-12; elev. 1,236ft./377m.; 🅿; z 73754; Ⓟ 645; Ⓒ 577
Lake Aluma; Inc. Place; OKLAHOMA; **220** J-5; elev. 1,148ft./350m.; ★ **O.C.**; mail Oklahoma City z 73121; Ⓟ 96; Ⓒ 97
Lake Creek; RMC Place; GREER; ***220** G-9; mail Granite z 73547; rural
Lake Ellsworth Addition; RMC Place; COMANCHE; ***221** H-11; mail Apache z 73006; ● 100
Lake Hiwasse; RMC Place; OKLAHOMA; ***221** F-14; ★ **O.C.**; mail Arcadia z 73007; ● 200
Lake Humphreys; RMC Place; STEPHENS; ***221** I-12; mail Marlow z 73055; pop. incl. with Duncan (Inc. Place)
Lakeside Village; RMC Place; COMANCHE; ***221** H-11; mail Elgin z 73538; ● 250
Lake Station; RMC Place; TULSA; **220** F-1; ★ **TUL**; mail Tulsa z 74127; pop. incl. with Sand Springs (Inc. Place)
Lake Valley; RMC Place; WASHITA; ***220** G-10; mail Gotebo z 73041; rural
Lake West; RMC Place; BRYAN; ***221** K-17; mail Boswell z 74727; rural
Lamar; Inc. Place; HUGHES; **221** G-16; elev. 763ft./233m.; 🅿; z 74850; Ⓟ 97; Ⓒ 172
Lambert; Inc. Place; ALFALFA; **221** C-11; mail Cherokee z 73728; Ⓟ 11; Ⓒ 9
La Mesa; RMC Place; GARFIELD; ★ **ENID**; mail Enid z 73701; pop. incl. with Enid (Inc. Place)
Lamont; Inc. Place; GRANT; **221** C-13; elev. 1,011ft./308m.; 🅿; z 74643; Ⓟ 454; Ⓒ 465
Lane; RMC Place; ATOKA; **221** J-17; elev. 575ft./175m.; 🅿; z 74555; ● 300
Langley; Inc. Place; MAYES; **221** C-19; 🅿; z 74350; Ⓟ 526; Ⓒ 669
Langston; Inc. Place; LOGAN; **221** E-14; 🅿 🄲 2,943; z 73050; Ⓟ 1,471; Ⓒ 1,670
Lark; RMC Place; MARSHALL; ***221** K-15; mail Kingston z 73439; rural
Last Chance; RMC Place; OKFUSKEE; ***221** F-16; elev. 802ft./244m.; mail Okemah z 74859; rural
LATIMER; **221** H-18; Ⓟ 10,333; Ⓒ 10,692; ◆ 10,335
Latta; RMC Place; PONTOTOC; ***221** H-15; mail Ada z 74820; ● 300
Laverne; Inc. Place; HARPER; **220** C-8; 🅿; z 73848; Ⓟ 1,269; Ⓒ 1,097
Lawrence Creek; Inc. Place; CREEK; ***221** D-16; mail Mannford z 74044; Ⓟ 97; Ⓒ 119
Lawton; Inc. Place; ⊡ COMANCHE; **221** M-17; elev. 1,109ft./338m.; 🅿 🄷 🄲 5,737 ■; ★ **LAWT**; z 73501-03, z 73505-07, z 73558; Ⓟ 80,561; Ⓒ 92,757; ◆ 112,367
Leach; CDP; DELAWARE; **221** D-19; mail Rose z 74364; Ⓒ 220
Lebanon; RMC Place; MARSHALL; **221** J-14; 🅿; z 73440; ● 400
Lecox; RMC Place; OKLAHOMA; ★ **O.C.**; pop. incl. with Oklahoma City (Inc. Place)
Leedey; Inc. Place; DEWEY; **220** E-9; 🅿; z 73654; Ⓟ 468; Ⓒ 345
Leflore; Inc. Place; LE FLORE; **221** H-19; 🅿; z 74942; Ⓟ 119; Ⓒ 168
LE FLORE; **221** I-19; Ⓟ 43,270; Ⓒ 48,109; ◆ 49,958
Lehigh; Inc. Place; COAL; **221** I-16; elev. 611ft./186m.; 🅿; z 74556; Ⓟ 303; Ⓒ 315
Leisure Square; RMC Place; TULSA; ★ **TUL**; mail Tulsa z 74112; pop. incl. with Tulsa (Inc. Place)
Lenapah; Inc. Place; NOWATA; **221** B-17; 🅿; z 74042; Ⓟ 253; Ⓒ 298
Lenna; RMC Place; MCINTOSH; **221** F-17; elev. 630ft./192m.; mail Eufaula z 74432; ● 40
Lenora; RMC Place; DEWEY; ***220** E-10; mail Taloga z 73667
Lenox; RMC Place; LE FLORE; ***221** H-19; mail Muse z 74949, Whitesboro z 74577; rural
Leon; Inc. Place; LOVE; **221** K-13; 🅿; z 73441; Ⓟ 101; Ⓒ 96
Leonard; RMC Place; TULSA; **221** E-17; 🅿; ★ **TUL**; z 74043; ● 550
Lequire; RMC Place; HASKELL; **221** G-19; 🅿; z 74943; ● 250
Lewisville; RMC Place; HASKELL; ***221** G-18; mail Kinta z 74552
Lexington; Inc. Place; CLEVELAND; **221** H-13; elev. 1,034ft./315m.; 🅿; z 73051; Ⓟ 1,776; Ⓒ 2,086
Liberty; RMC Place; BRYAN; ***221** K-16; mail Hendrix z 74741; rural
Liberty; RMC Place; SEQUOYAH; **221** F-20; mail Muldrow z 74948; ● 250
Liberty; Inc. Place; TULSA, OKMULGEE; ***221** E-17; ★ **TUL**; mail Tulsa z 74101; Ⓟ 155; Ⓒ 184
Lighthouse; RMC Place; TULSA; ★ **TUL**; mail Tulsa z 74136; pop. incl. with Tulsa (Inc. Place)
Lillard Park; RMC Place; OKLAHOMA; **220** L-3; ★ **O.C.**; pop. incl. with Oklahoma City (Inc. Place)
Lima; Inc. Place; SEMINOLE; **221** G-15; elev. 881ft./269m.; mail Wewoka z 74884; Ⓟ 133; Ⓒ 74
Limestone; RMC Place; LATIMER; mail Wilburton z 74578; rural
Limestone; CDP-Census Area Only; ROGERS; ***221** D-17; elev. 698ft./213m.; ★ **TUL**; mail Claremore z 74017; Ⓒ 745
LINCOLN; **221** E-14; Ⓟ 29,216; Ⓒ 32,080; ◆ 31,864
Lincolnville; RMC Place; OTTAWA; ***221** B-19; mail Quapaw z 74363; rural
Lindsay; Inc. Place; GARVIN; **221** H-13; elev. 978ft./298m.; 🅿 🄷; z 73052; Ⓟ 2,947; Ⓒ 2,889
Little; RMC Place; SEMINOLE; **221** G-15; elev. 972ft./296m.; mail Seminole z 74868; pop. incl. with Seminole (Inc. Place)
Little Axe; RMC Place; CLEVELAND; ***221** G-14; elev. 1,053ft./321m.; ★ **O.C.**; mail Norman z 73069; pop. incl. with Norman (Inc. Place)
Little Chief; RMC Place; OSAGE; ***221** C-15; mail Fairfax z 74637; ● 30
Little City; RMC Place; MARSHALL; **221** J-15; mail Madill z 73446; ● 150
Little Ponderosa; RMC Place; BEAVER; ***220** B-5; mail Liberal z 67901; rural
Loco; Inc. Place; STEPHENS; **221** I-13; 🅿; z 73442; Ⓟ 160; Ⓒ 150
Locust Grove; Inc. Place; MAYES; **221** D-18; 🅿; z 74352; Ⓟ 1,326; Ⓒ 1,366; Ⓡ 1,412
Lodi; RMC Place; LATIMER; ***221** G-19; elev. 645ft./197m.; mail Red Oak z 74563; rural
Logan; RMC Place; BEAVER; ***220** C-7; elev. 2,381ft./726m.; 🅿; z 73848; rural
LOGAN; **221** E-13; Ⓟ 29,011; Ⓒ 33,924; ◆ 39,715
Lona; RMC Place; HASKELL; mail Kinta z 74552; rural
Lone Grove; Inc. Place; CARTER; **221** J-14; 🅿; z 73443; Ⓟ 4,114; Ⓒ 4,631
Lone Oak; RMC Place; SEQUOYAH; ***221** F-20; elev. 494ft./151m.; ★ **FTSM**; mail Muldrow z 74948; rural
Loneview; RMC Place; OKLAHOMA; ★ **O.C.**; pop. incl. with Oklahoma City (Inc. Place)
Lone Wolf; Inc. Place; KIOWA; **220** H-9; elev. 1,577ft./481m.; 🅿; z 73655; Ⓟ 576; Ⓒ 500
Long; CDP; SEQUOYAH; ***221** F-20; mail Muldrow z 74948; Ⓒ 363
Longdale; Inc. Place; BLAINE; **221** D-11; elev. 1,655ft./504m.; 🅿; z 73755; Ⓟ 281; Ⓒ 310
Longtown; CDP; PITTSBURG; ***221** G-18; elev. 617ft./188m.; mail Quinton z 74561; Ⓟ 1,641; Ⓒ 2,397
Lookeba; Inc. Place; CADDO; **221** G-11; 🅿; z 73053; Ⓟ 141; Ⓒ 131
Lookeba; CADDO, BLAINE; see Hydro (Inc. Place)
Lookout; RMC Place; WOODS; ***220** B-9; mail Freedom z 73842; rural
Lost City; CDP; CHEROKEE; ***221** E-18; Ⓒ 809
Lotsee; Inc. Place; TULSA; ***221** D-16; ★ **TUL**; mail Sand Springs z 74063; Ⓟ 7; Ⓒ 11
LOVE; **221** J-13; Ⓟ 8,157; Ⓒ 8,831; ◆ 9,063
Lovedale; RMC Place; HARPER; ***220** C-9; mail Buffalo z 73834; rural
Loveland; Inc. Place; TILLMAN; **220** J-10; 🅿; z 73553 & mail Grandfield z 73546; Ⓟ 13; Ⓒ 14
Lovell; RMC Place; LOGAN; **221** E-13; mail Crescent z 73028; ● 60
Loving; RMC Place; LE FLORE; ***221** H-20; mail Heavener z 74937; rural
Lowrey; RMC Place; CHEROKEE; ***221** D-19; mail Tahlequah z 74464; rural
Loyal; Inc. Place; KINGFISHER; **221** E-12; elev. 1,115ft./340m.; 🅿; z 73756; Ⓟ 76; Ⓒ 81
Lucien; RMC Place; NOBLE; **221** D-13; 🅿; z 73757; ● 120
Lugert; RMC Place; KIOWA; ***220** H-9; mail Lone Wolf z 73655; rural
Lula; RMC Place; PONTOTOC; **221** H-16; mail Allen z 74825; ● 30
Luther; Inc. Place; OKLAHOMA; **221** F-14; 🅿; ★ **O.C.**; z 73054; Ⓟ 1,560; Ⓒ 612
Lutie; RMC Place; LATIMER; ***221** H-18; mail Wilburton z 74578
Lynn Addition; RMC Place; OSAGE; ***221** C-16; located on Osage Ind. Res.; mail Pawhuska z 74056; ● 350
Lynn Lane; RMC Place; TULSA; **220** F-5; elev. 664ft./202m.; ★ **TUL**; pop. incl. with Tulsa (Inc. Place)
Lyons; RMC Place; ADAIR; ***221** E-19; mail Stilwell z 74960; rural
Lyons Switch; CDP-Census Area Only; ADAIR; ***221** E-20; Ⓒ 227

M

MacArthur Park; RMC Place; COMANCHE; ★ **LAWT**; mail Lawton z 73507; pop. incl. with Lawton (Inc. Place)
Macomb; Inc. Place; POTTAWATOMIE; **221** G-14; 🅿; z 74852; Ⓟ 64; Ⓒ 61
Madge; RMC Place; HARMON; ***220** H-7; mail Vinson z 73571; rural
Madill; Inc. Place; ⊡ MARSHALL; **221** J-15; elev. 789ft./240m.; 🅿 🄷; z 73446; Ⓟ 3,069; Ⓒ 3,410
Maguire; RMC Place; CLEVELAND; ***221** G-14; ★ **O.C.**; mail Noble z 73068; pop. incl. with Slaughterville (Inc. Place)
MAJOR; **220** D-10; Ⓟ 8,055; Ⓒ 7,545; ◆ 7,092
Mallard Bay; RMC Place; WAGONER; ***221** E-18; mail Okay z 74446; rural
Manard; RMC Place; CHEROKEE; mail Fort Gibson z 74434; rural
Manchester; Inc. Place; GRANT; **221** B-12; elev. 1,277ft./389m.; 🅿; z 73758; Ⓟ 106; Ⓒ 104
Mangum; Inc. Place; ⊡ GREER; **220** H-8; elev. 1,606ft./490m.; 🅿 🄷; z 73554; Ⓟ 3,344; Ⓒ 2,924
Manitou; Inc. Place; TILLMAN; **220** I-10; elev. 1,255ft./383m.; 🅿; z 73555; Ⓟ 244; Ⓒ 278
Mannford (New Mannford); Inc. Place; CREEK, PAWNEE, TULSA; **221** D-16; 🅿; ★ **TUL**; z 74044; Ⓟ 1,826; Ⓒ 2,095
Mannsville; Inc. Place; JOHNSTON; **221** J-15; 🅿; z 73447; Ⓟ 396; Ⓒ 587
Maple; RMC Place; SEQUOYAH; ***221** F-20; elev. 681ft./208m.; mail Muldrow z 74948
Maramec; Inc. Place; PAWNEE; **221** D-15; 🅿; z 74045; Ⓟ 110; Ⓒ 104
Marble City; Inc. Place; SEQUOYAH; **221** F-19; 🅿; z 74945; Ⓟ 232; Ⓒ 242
Marble City Community; CDP-Census Area Only; SEQUOYAH; ***221** F-19; Ⓒ 420
Marietta; Inc. Place; ⊡ LOVE; **221** K-14; elev. 850ft./259m.; 🅿 🄷; z 73448; Ⓟ 2,306; Ⓒ 2,445
Marland; Inc. Place; NOBLE; **221** C-14; elev. 1,013ft./309m.; 🅿; z 74644; Ⓟ 280; Ⓒ 280
Marlow; Inc. Place; STEPHENS; **221** I-12; elev. 1,312ft./400m.; 🅿; z 73055; Ⓟ 4,416; Ⓒ 4,592
Marshall; Inc. Place; LOGAN; **221** D-13; 🅿; z 73056; Ⓟ 288; Ⓒ 258
MARSHALL; **221** J-15; Ⓟ 10,829; Ⓒ 13,184; ◆ 15,112
Martha; Inc. Place; JACKSON; **220** H-9; 🅿; z 73556; Ⓟ 217; Ⓒ 205
Martin; RMC Place; MUSKOGEE; ***221** F-18; elev. 533ft./162m.; mail Muskogee z 74401, z 74403
Martin Luther King; RMC Place; OKLAHOMA; ★ **O.C.**; mail Oklahoma City z 73111, z 73136; pop. incl. with Oklahoma City (Inc. Place)
Maryetta; CDP-Census Area Only; ADAIR; ***221** E-20; Ⓒ 138
Mason; RMC Place; OKFUSKEE; **221** F-16; elev. 754ft./230m.; 🅿; z 74859; ● 100
Matoy; RMC Place; BRYAN; ***221** J-16; elev. 574ft./175m.; mail Caddo z 74729
Maud; Inc. Place; SEMINOLE, POTTAWATOMIE; **221** G-15; 🅿; z 74854; Ⓟ 1,204; Ⓒ 1,136
Maxwell; RMC Place; PONTOTOC; ***221** H-15; mail Ada z 74820; rural
May; Inc. Place; HARPER; **220** C-8; elev. 2,039ft./621m.; 🅿; z 73851; Ⓟ 42; Ⓒ 33
MAYES; **221** C-18; Ⓟ 33,366; Ⓒ 38,369; ◆ 39,854
Mayfield; RMC Place; BECKHAM; **220** G-8; mail Sweetwater z 73666; ● 10
Mayhew; RMC Place; CHOCTAW; ***221** J-17; mail Boswell z 74727; rural
May Ridge; RMC Place; OKLAHOMA; ★ **O.C.**; mail Oklahoma City z 73119; pop. incl. with Oklahoma City (Inc. Place)
Maysville; Inc. Place; GARVIN; **221** H-13; elev. 943ft./287m.; 🅿; z 73057; Ⓟ 1,203; Ⓒ 1,313
Mazie; CDP; MAYES; **221** D-18; 🅿; z 74337; Ⓒ 88
McAlester; Inc. Place; ⊡ PITTSBURG; **221** H-17; elev. 740ft./226m.; 🅿 🄷 ■; z 74501-02; Ⓟ 16,370; Ⓒ 17,783; ◆ 18,323
McBride; RMC Place; MARSHALL; **221** K-15; mail Kingston z 73439; ● 80
MCCLAIN; **221** H-13; Ⓟ 22,795; Ⓒ 27,740; ◆ 33,446
McCord; CDP-Census Area Only; OSAGE; ***221** C-14; elev. 1,054ft./321m.; mail Fairfax z 74637; Ⓟ 2,170; Ⓒ 1,711
McCurtain; Inc. Place; HASKELL; **221** G-19; 🅿; z 74944; Ⓟ 465; Ⓒ 466
MCCURTAIN; **221** I-19; Ⓟ 33,433; Ⓒ 34,402; ◆ 33,037
MCINTOSH; **221** G-17; Ⓟ 16,779; Ⓒ 19,456; ◆ 19,873
McKey; CDP; SEQUOYAH; ***221** F-19; elev. 522ft./159m.; mail Vian z 74962; Ⓒ 135
McKiddyville; RMC Place; CLEVELAND; ***221** G-14; elev. 1,178ft./359m.; mail Lexington z 73051; ● 70
McKnight; RMC Place; HARMON; ***220** H-7; mail Hollis z 73550; rural
McLain; RMC Place; MUSKOGEE; ***221** F-18; elev. 535ft./163m.; mail Muskogee z 74401, z 74403
McLoud; Inc. Place; POTTAWATOMIE; **221** F-14; 🅿; ★ **O.C.**; z 74851; Ⓟ 2,493; Ⓒ 3,548
McMillan; RMC Place; MARSHALL; **221** J-14; 🅿; z 73446; ● 25
McWillie; RMC Place; ALFALFA; ***221** C-11; elev. 1,443ft./440m.; mail Aline z 73716; rural
Mead; Inc. Place; BRYAN; **221** J-15; 🅿; z 73449; Ⓟ 109; Ⓒ 123
Medford; Inc. Place; ⊡ GRANT; **221** B-13; elev. 1,090ft./332m.; 🅿; z 73759; Ⓟ 1,172; Ⓒ 1,172
Medicine Park; Inc. Place; COMANCHE; **221** H-11; 🅿; z 73557; Ⓟ 285; Ⓒ 373
Meeker; Inc. Place; LINCOLN; **221** F-14; 🅿; z 74855; Ⓟ 1,003; Ⓒ 978
Meers; RMC Place; COMANCHE; ***221** H-11; 🅿; z 73558 & mail Lawton z 73501; ● 20
Mehan; RMC Place; PAYNE; ***221** E-14; elev. 835ft./255m.; mail Stillwater z 74074; ● 45
Mellette; RMC Place; MCINTOSH; ***221** G-17; elev. 678ft./207m.; mail Eufaula z 74432; rural
Melvin; RMC Place; CHEROKEE; mail Hulbert z 74441; rural
Meno; Inc. Place; MAJOR; **221** D-12; 🅿; z 73760; Ⓟ 155; Ⓒ 195
Meridian; Inc. Place; LOGAN; **221** E-14; 🅿; z 73058; Ⓟ 45; Ⓒ 54
Meridian; CDP-Census Area Only; STEPHENS; ***221** I-12; elev. 1,050ft./320m.; mail Comanche z 73529; Ⓟ 1,471; Ⓒ 1,485
Merritt; RMC Place; BECKHAM; ***220** G-8; elev. 2,055ft./626m.; mail Elk City z 73644; pop. incl. with Elk City (Inc. Place)
Messer; RMC Place; CHOCTAW; ***221** J-18; mail Hugo z 74743
Miami; Inc. Place; ⊡ OTTAWA; **221** B-19; elev. 798ft./243m.; 🅿 🄷 ■; z 74354-55; location of Indian Agency; Ⓟ 13,142; Ⓒ 13,704; ◆ 12,087
Micawber; RMC Place; OKFUSKEE; ***221** F-15; elev. 755ft./230m.; mail Castle z 74833; rural
Middleberg; RMC Place; GRADY; ***221** G-13; elev. 1,323ft./403m.; mail Blanchard z 73010; ● 70
Midland; RMC Place; BRYAN; ***221** K-17; mail Bennington z 74723; rural
Midlothian; RMC Place; LINCOLN; ***221** F-14; mail Chandler z 74834; ● 25
Midway; RMC Place; ATOKA, COAL; mail Coalgate z 74538; rural
Midwest City; Inc. Place; OKLAHOMA; **220** L-6; elev. 1,250ft./381m.; 🅿 🄷 ■; ★ **O.C.**; z 73110, z 73130, z 73140 & mail Oklahoma City z 73145, z 73150; Ⓟ 52,267; Ⓒ 54,088; ◆ 55,712
Milburn; Inc. Place; JOHNSTON; **221** J-15; elev. 721ft./220m.; 🅿; z 73450; Ⓟ 264; Ⓒ 312
Milfay; RMC Place; CREEK; **221** E-15; elev. 810ft./247m.; 🅿; z 74046; ● 170
Mill Creek; Inc. Place; JOHNSTON; **221** I-15; elev. 1,011ft./308m.; 🅿; z 74856; Ⓟ 336; Ⓒ 340
Miller; RMC Place; PUSHMATAHA; ***221** I-17; elev. 511ft./156m.; mail Moyers z 74557; rural
Millerton; Inc. Place; MCCURTAIN; **221** J-19; 🅿; z 74750; Ⓟ 234; Ⓒ 359
Milo; RMC Place; CARTER; ***221** I-13; 🅿; z 73401 & mail Springer z 73458
Milton; RMC Place; LE FLORE; ***221** G-19; mail Bokoshe z 74930; rural
Minco; Inc. Place; GRADY; **221** G-12; 🅿; z 73059; Ⓟ 1,411; Ⓒ 1,672
Mingo; RMC Place; TULSA; ***221** D-17; ★ **TUL**; pop. incl. with Tulsa (Inc. Place)
Mocane; RMC Place; BEAVER; ***220** B-7; mail Forgan z 73938; rural
Moffett; Inc. Place; SEQUOYAH; **221** F-20; 🅿; ★ **FTSM**; z 74946; Ⓟ 219; Ⓒ 179
Monroe; RMC Place; LE FLORE; **221** G-20; 🅿; z 74947; ● 200
Montclair Addition; RMC Place; LE FLORE; ***221** H-20; mail Heavener z 74937; pop. incl. with Heavener (Inc. Place)
Moodys; RMC Place; CHEROKEE; **221** E-19; elev. 932ft./284m.; 🅿; z 74444; ● 170
Moon; RMC Place; MCCURTAIN; ***221** K-20; mail Haworth z 74740; rural
Moore; Inc. Place; CLEVELAND; **220** N-5; elev. 1,250ft./381m.; 🅿 🄲 349; ★ **O.C.**; z 73153, z 73160, z 73170 & mail Oklahoma City z 73165; Ⓟ 40,318; Ⓒ 41,138; ◆ 51,861
Mooreland; Inc. Place; WOODWARD; **220** C-9; 🅿; z 73852; Ⓟ 1,157; Ⓒ 1,226
Moorewood; RMC Place; CUSTER; ***220** E-9; elev. 1,749ft./533m.; mail Hammon z 73650; rural
Morris; Inc. Place; OKMULGEE; **221** F-17; elev. 710ft./216m.; 🅿; z 74445; Ⓟ 1,216; Ⓒ 1,294
Morrison; Inc. Place; NOBLE; **221** D-14; 🅿; z 73061; Ⓟ 640; Ⓒ 636
Mound Grove; RMC Place; MCCURTAIN; ***221** J-19; mail Valliant z 74764; rural
Mounds; Inc. Place; CREEK; **221** E-16; elev. 722ft./220m.; 🅿; ★ **TUL**; z 74047; Ⓟ 980; Ⓒ 1,153
Mountain Park; Inc. Place; KIOWA; **220** H-10; elev. 1,365ft./416m.; 🅿; z 73559; Ⓟ 473; Ⓒ 390
Mountain View; Inc. Place; KIOWA; **220** G-10; elev. 1,336ft./407m.; 🅿; z 73062; Ⓟ 1,086; Ⓒ 880
Mount Herman; RMC Place; MCCURTAIN; ***221** I-19; mail Broken Bow z 74728; ● 150
Mount Zion; RMC Place; MCCURTAIN; ***221** J-19; elev. 469ft./143m.; mail Garvin z 74736; rural
Mouser; RMC Place; TEXAS; ***220** B-4; mail Hooker z 73945; rural
Moyers; RMC Place; PUSHMATAHA; **221** I-17; 🅿; z 74557; ● 100
Mudsand; RMC Place; CHOCTAW; mail Soper z 74759; rural
Muldrow; Inc. Place; SEQUOYAH; **221** F-20; 🅿; ★ **FTSM**; z 74948; Ⓟ 2,889; Ⓒ 3,104
Mule Barn; RMC Place; PAWNEE; ***221** D-16; ★ **TUL**; disincorporated since 2000 Census
Mulhall; Inc. Place; LOGAN; **221** E-13; elev. 945ft./288m.; 🅿; z 73063; Ⓟ 199; Ⓒ 239
Murphy; CDP; MAYES; ***221** D-18; mail Locust Grove z 74352; Ⓒ 231
MURRAY; **221** I-14; Ⓟ 12,042; Ⓒ 12,623; ◆ 12,458
Muse; RMC Place; LE FLORE; **221** H-20; elev. 752ft./229m.; 🅿; z 74949; ● 200
Muskogee; Inc. Place; ⊡ MUSKOGEE; **221** M-19; elev. 600ft./183m.; 🅿 🄷 🄲 958 ■; ★ **MSKOG**; z 74401-03; Ⓟ 37,708; Ⓒ 38,310; ◆ 39,435
MUSKOGEE; **221** F-18; Ⓟ 68,078; Ⓒ 69,451; ◆ 71,176
Mustang; Inc. Place; CANADIAN; **220** M-1; 🅿; ★ **O.C.**; z 73064; Ⓟ 10,434; Ⓒ 13,156
Mutual; Inc. Place; WOODWARD; **220** D-9; elev. 1,873ft./571m.; 🅿; z 73853; Ⓟ 68; Ⓒ 76

N

Nani-Chito; RMC Place; MCCURTAIN; ***221** I-20; mail Smithville z 74957; rural
Narcissa; CDP; OTTAWA; **221** B-19; elev. 844ft./257m.; mail Miami z 74354; Ⓒ 100
Nardin; RMC Place; KAY; **221** B-13; 🅿; z 74646; ● 80
Nash; Inc. Place; GRANT; **221** C-12; 🅿; z 73761; Ⓟ 281; Ⓒ 224
Nashoba; RMC Place; PUSHMATAHA; **221** I-18; 🅿; z 74558; ● 150
Natura; RMC Place; OKMULGEE; ***221** E-17; mail Beggs z 74421; ● 50
Navina; RMC Place; LOGAN; ***221** E-13; elev. 1,054ft./321m.; mail Guthrie z 73044; ● 40
Nebo; RMC Place; MURRAY; ***221** I-14; mail Sulphur z 73086; rural
Needmore; RMC Place; CLEVELAND; ***221** G-14; elev. 1,052ft./321m.; mail Noble z 73068; rural
Neff; RMC Place; LE FLORE; ***221** G-20; mail Poteau z 74953; ● 40
Nelagoney (Nelagony); RMC Place; OSAGE; **221** C-16; mail Pawhuska z 74056; ● 120
Nelagony; OSAGE; see Nelagoney (RMC Place)
Newalla; RMC Place; OKLAHOMA; ***221** F-14; 🅿; ★ **O.C.**; z 74857; pop. incl. with Oklahoma City (Inc. Place)
New Alluwe; NOWATA; see Alluwe (Inc. Place)
Newcastle; Inc. Place; MCCLAIN; **221** G-13; 🅿; ★ **O.C.**; z 73065; Ⓟ 4,214; Ⓒ 5,434
New Cordell; WASHITA; see Cordell (Inc. Place)
New Eucha; CDP-Census Area Only; DELAWARE; ***221** D-19; Ⓒ 300
Newkirk; Inc. Place; ⊡ KAY; **221** B-14; elev. 1,154ft./352m.; 🅿; z 74647; Ⓟ 2,168; Ⓒ 2,243
New Liberty; RMC Place; BECKHAM; ***220** G-8; elev. 2,056ft./627m.; mail Sayre z 73662; rural
New Lima; RMC Place; SEMINOLE; ***221** G-15; 🅿; z 74884; pop. incl. with Lima (Inc. Place)
New Mannford; CREEK, PAWNEE, TULSA; see Mannford (Inc. Place)
New Oberlin; RMC Place; CHOCTAW; ***221** K-17; mail Boswell z 74727; rural
Newport; RMC Place; CARTER; **221** J-14; mail Ardmore z 73401; ● 50
New Prue; OSAGE; see Prue (Inc. Place)
New Ringold; MCCURTAIN; see Ringold (RMC Place)
New Tulsa; RMC Place; WAGONER; **221** E-17; ★ **TUL**; mail Coweta z 74429; former incorporated place; became part of Broken Arrow February 23, 2001; pop. incl. with Broken Arrow (Inc. Place); Ⓟ 272; Ⓒ 568
New Woodville (Woodville); RMC Place; MARSHALL; **221** J-15; mail Kingston z 73439; disincorporated since 2000 Census; Ⓟ 31; Ⓒ 69
Nichols Hills; Inc. Place; OKLAHOMA; **220** J-4; elev. 1,219ft./372m.; 🅿; ★ **O.C.**; z 73116, z 73120; Ⓟ 4,020; Ⓒ 4,056
Nicoma Park; Inc. Place; OKLAHOMA; **220** K-7; 🅿; ★ **O.C.**; z 73066; Ⓟ 2,353; Ⓒ 2,415
Nicut; RMC Place; SEQUOYAH; ***221** F-20; mail Muldrow z 74948; ● 80
Nida; RMC Place; JOHNSTON; **221** J-15; elev. 785ft./239m.; mail Kenefic z 74748; ● 30
Niles; RMC Place; CANADIAN; ***221** F-11; elev. 1,630ft./497m.; mail Hinton z 73047; rural
Ninnekah (East Ninnekah); Inc. Place; GRADY; **221** H-12; 🅿; z 73067; Ⓟ 1,016; Ⓒ 994
Noble; Inc. Place; CLEVELAND; **221** G-13; 🅿; ★ **O.C.**; z 73068; Ⓟ 4,710; Ⓒ 5,260
NOBLE; **221** C-14; Ⓟ 11,045; Ⓒ 11,411; ◆ 11,069
Nobletown; RMC Place; SEMINOLE; ***221** G-15; elev. 835ft./255m.; mail Wewoka z 74884; rural
Non; RMC Place; HUGHES; **221** H-16; mail Calvin z 74531; ● 40
Norge; Inc. Place; GRADY; **221** H-12; mail Chickasha z 73018; Ⓟ 97; Ⓒ 82
Norman; Inc. Place; ⊡ CLEVELAND; **220** N-7; 🅿 🄷 🄲 26,020 ■; ★ **O.C.**; z 73019, z 73026, z 73069-72; includes Hall Park annexed October 1, 2003; Ⓟ 80,071; Ⓒ 95,694; Ⓐ 96,782; ◆ 113,433
Norris; RMC Place; LATIMER; ***221** G-19; mail Red Oak z 74563; rural
Northeast; RMC Place; TULSA; ★ **TUL**; mail Tulsa z 74112, z 74115-17, z 74158; pop. incl. with Tulsa (Inc. Place)
North Enid; Inc. Place; GARFIELD; **221** D-12; elev. 1,260ft./384m.; ★ **ENID**; mail Enid z 73701; Ⓟ 874; Ⓒ 796
North Heights; RMC Place; TULSA; ***221** E-17; ★ **TUL**; mail Bixby z 74008; pop. incl. with Bixby (Inc. Place)
North McAlester; RMC Place; PITTSBURG; ***221** H-17; mail McAlester z 74501; pop. incl. with McAlester (Inc. Place)
North Miami; Inc. Place; OTTAWA; ***221** B-19; 🅿; z 74358; Ⓟ 450; Ⓒ 433
Northside; RMC Place; TULSA; ★ **TUL**; mail Tulsa z 74106, z 74110, z 74126, z 74130, z 74148; pop. incl. with Tulsa (Inc. Place)
Northwest; RMC Place; OKLAHOMA; ★ **O.C.**; mail Oklahoma City z 73103, z 73106, z 73146; pop. incl. with Oklahoma City (Inc. Place)
Notchietown; CDP; SEQUOYAH; ***221** F-19; Ⓒ 430
Nowata; Inc. Place; ⊡ NOWATA; **221** C-17; 🅿 🄷; z 74048; Ⓟ 3,896; Ⓒ 3,971
NOWATA; **221** B-17; Ⓟ 9,992; Ⓒ 10,569; ◆ 10,727
Nowhere; RMC Place; CADDO; ***221** G-11; mail Fort Cobb z 73038; ● 20
Numa; RMC Place; GRANT; elev. 1,120ft./341m.
Nuyaka; RMC Place; OKMULGEE; **221** F-16; elev. 732ft./223m.; mail Okmulgee z 74447; ● 150

O

Oak Grove; RMC Place; MURRAY; ***221** I-14; elev. 1,143ft./348m.; mail Sulphur z 73086
Oak Grove; RMC Place; PAWNEE; ***221** D-16; ★ **TUL**; disincorporated since 2000 Census; Ⓒ 18
Oak Grove; RMC Place; PAYNE; ***221** E-15; mail Drumright z 74030; pop. incl. with Drumright (Inc. Place)
Oak Hill; RMC Place; MCCURTAIN; ***221** J-19; mail Broken Bow z 74728; ● 100
Oakhurst; CDP; TULSA, CREEK; **220** G-1; 🅿; ★ **TUL**; z 74050; Ⓟ 3,030; Ⓒ 2,731
Oakland; Inc. Place; MARSHALL; **221** J-15; 🅿; z 73446; Ⓟ 602; Ⓒ 674
Oakman; RMC Place; PONTOTOC; ***221** H-15; elev. 1,044ft./318m.; mail Ada z 74820; rural
Oak Park; RMC Place; WASHINGTON; mail Bartlesville z 74003; pop. incl. with Bartlesville (Inc. Place)
Oakridge; RMC Place; CREEK; ★ **TUL**
Oaks; Inc. Place; DELAWARE; **221** D-19; 🅿; z 74359; Ⓟ 431; Ⓒ 412
Oakwood; Inc. Place; DEWEY; **220** E-10; 🅿; z 73658; Ⓟ 107; Ⓒ 72
Oakwood; RMC Place; TULSA; ***221** E-17; ★ **TUL**; mail Jenks z 74037; pop. incl. with Jenks (Inc. Place)
Oberlin; RMC Place; BRYAN; ***221** K-17; mail Boswell z 74727; rural
Ochelata; Inc. Place; WASHINGTON; **221** C-17; 🅿; z 74051; Ⓟ 441; Ⓒ 494
Octavia; RMC Place; LE FLORE; **221** I-20; elev. 921ft./281m.; 🅿; z 74957; ● 50
Ogeechee; RMC Place; OTTAWA; ***221** B-19; mail Fairland z 74343; ● 100
Oglesby; RMC Place; WASHINGTON; **221** C-17; elev. 650ft./198m.; mail Ramona z 74061; ● 100
Oil Center; RMC Place; PONTOTOC; ***221** H-15; mail Ada z 74820
Oil City; RMC Place; CARTER; ***221** J-13; mail Wilson z 73463; rural
Oilton; Inc. Place; CREEK; **221** D-15; 🅿; z 74052; Ⓟ 1,060; Ⓒ 1,099
Okarche; Inc. Place; KINGFISHER, CANADIAN; **221** F-12; 🅿; z 73762; Ⓟ 1,160; Ⓒ 1,110
Okay; Inc. Place; WAGONER; **221** E-18; 🅿; ★ **MSKOG**; z 74446; Ⓟ 528; Ⓒ 597
Okeene; Inc. Place; BLAINE; **221** D-11; elev. 1,218ft./371m.; 🅿 🄷; z 73763; Ⓟ 1,343; Ⓒ 1,240
Okemah; Inc. Place; ⊡ OKFUSKEE; **221** F-16; elev. 910ft./277m.; 🅿 🄷; z 74859; Ⓟ 3,085; Ⓒ 3,038
Okesa; RMC Place; OSAGE; **221** C-16; elev. 721ft./220m.; mail Bartlesville z 74003; ● 120
Okfuskee; RMC Place; OKFUSKEE; ***221** F-16; elev. 709ft./216m.; mail Okemah z 74859; rural
OKFUSKEE; **221** F-15; Ⓟ 11,551; Ⓒ 11,814; ◆ 11,206
OKLAHOMA; **221** F-13; Ⓟ 599,611; Ⓒ 660,448; ◆ 716,411
Oklahoma Baptist University; RMC Place; POTTAWATOMIE; mail Shawnee z 74804; pop. incl. with Shawnee (Inc. Place)
Oklahoma City; Inc. Place; **STATE CAPITAL**; ⊡ OKLAHOMA, CANADIAN, CLEVELAND, MCCLAIN, POTTAWATOMIE; **220** J-6; elev. 1,243ft./379m.; 🅿 🄷 🄲 10,800 ■; ★ **O.C.**; z 73101-32, z 73134-37, z 73139-57, z 73159-60, z 73162-65, z 73167, z 73169-70, z 73172-73, z 73178-79, z 73184-85, z 73189-90, z 73194-96, z 73198; Ⓟ 444,719; Ⓒ 506,132; ◆ 571,899
Okmulgee; Inc. Place; ⊡ OKMULGEE; **221** F-17; elev. 670ft./204m.; 🅿 🄷 🄲 2,788; z 74447; location of Indian Agency; Ⓟ 13,441; Ⓒ 13,022
OKMULGEE; **221** E-17; Ⓟ 36,490; Ⓒ 39,685; ◆ 39,504
Oktaha; Inc. Place; MUSKOGEE; **221** F-18; 🅿; z 74450; Ⓟ 266; Ⓒ 327
Old Eucha; CDP-Census Area Only; DELAWARE; ***221** D-19; Ⓒ 46
Oleta; RMC Place; PUSHMATAHA; **221** J-18; elev. 540ft./165m.; mail Fort Towson z 74735; ● 50
Olive; RMC Place; CREEK; **221** E-15; mail Drumright z 74030; ● 200
Olney; RMC Place; COAL; **221** I-16; mail Coalgate z 74538; ● 130
Olustee; Inc. Place; JACKSON; **220** I-9; 🅿; z 73560; Ⓟ 701; Ⓒ 680
Omega; RMC Place; KINGFISHER; ***221** E-11; 🅿; z 73764; ● 200
Onapa (Bond); RMC Place; MCINTOSH; ***221** F-18; mail Checotah z 74426
Oneta; RMC Place; WAGONER; ***221** E-17; elev. 718ft./219m.; ★ **TUL**; mail Broken Arrow z 74012; pop. incl. with Broken Arrow (Inc. Place)
Oney; CADDO; see Albert (RMC Place)
Oolagah; ROGERS; see Oologah (Inc. Place)
Oologah (Oolagah); Inc. Place; ROGERS; **221** C-17; elev. 657ft./200m.; 🅿; z 74053; Ⓟ 828; Ⓒ 883
Oowala; RMC Place; ROGERS; ***221** C-17; mail Claremore z 74017; ● 30
Optima; Inc. Place; TEXAS; **220** B-4; 🅿; z 73945; Ⓟ 92; Ⓒ 266
Ord; RMC Place; CHOCTAW; ***221** K-18; mail Grant z 74738; rural
Orienta; RMC Place; MAJOR; **221** D-11; elev. 1,245ft./379m.; 🅿; z 73737; ● 25
Orion; RMC Place; MAJOR; ***220** D-10; elev. 1,771ft./540m.; mail Fairview z 73737; rural
Orlando; Inc. Place; LOGAN; **221** D-13; 🅿; z 73073; Ⓟ 198; Ⓒ 201
Orr; RMC Place; LOVE; **221** J-13; mail Ringling z 73456; ● 30
Osage; RMC Place; KAY; mail Ponca City z 74604; pop. incl. with Ponca City (Inc. Place)
Osage (Osage City); Inc. Place; OSAGE; **221** D-16; located on Osage Ind. Res.; 🅿; z 74054; Ⓟ 163; Ⓒ 188
OSAGE; **221** C-15; Ⓟ 41,645; Ⓒ 44,437; ◆ 45,919
Osage City; OSAGE; see Osage (Inc. Place)
Osage Hills Estates; RMC Place; TULSA; ★ **TUL**; mail Sand Springs z 74063; pop. incl. with Sand Springs (Inc. Place)
Osage Reservation; Indian Reservation; OSAGE; mail Pawhuska z 74056; also location of Indian Agency; Ⓟ 39,327; Ⓒ 44,437
Oscar; RMC Place; JEFFERSON; **221** J-13; elev. 884ft./269m.; 🅿; z 73561; ● 20
Oswalt; RMC Place; LOVE; ***221** J-14; mail Overbrook z 73453; rural
OTTAWA; **221** B-19; Ⓟ 30,561; Ⓒ 33,194; ◆ 31,203
Overbrook; RMC Place; LOVE; **221** J-14; 🅿; z 73453; ● 100
Owasso; Inc. Place; TULSA, ROGERS; **220** D-4; 🅿; ★ **TUL**; z 74055, z 74073; Ⓟ 11,151; Ⓒ 18,502; ◆ 22,137

P

Paden; Inc. Place; OKFUSKEE; **221** F-15; 🅿; z 74860; Ⓟ 400; Ⓒ 446
Page; RMC Place; LE FLORE; **221** H-20; elev. 918ft./280m.; mail Heavener z 74937; ● 25
Panama; Inc. Place; LE FLORE; **221** G-20; 🅿; z 74951; Ⓟ 1,528; Ⓒ 1,362
Panola; RMC Place; LATIMER; **221** H-18; elev. 640ft./195m.; 🅿; z 74559; ● 300
Paoli; Inc. Place; GARVIN; **221** H-14; elev. 962ft./293m.; 🅿; z 73074; Ⓟ 574; Ⓒ 649
Paradise Hill; Inc. Place; SEQUOYAH; **221** F-19; mail Sallisaw z 74955; Ⓟ 88; Ⓒ 100
Paradise View; RMC Place; MAYES; ***221** D-18; elev. 630ft./192m.; mail Chouteau z 74337; ● 80
Parker; RMC Place; COAL; ***221** H-16; elev. 678ft./207m.; mail Coalgate z 74538; rural
Park Hill; CDP; CHEROKEE; ***221** E-19; 🅿; z 74451; Ⓒ 3,936
Parkland; RMC Place; LINCOLN; **221** E-15; mail Agra z 74824; ● 50
Park Lane; RMC Place; COMANCHE; ★ **LAWT**; mail Lawton z 73501; pop. incl. with Lawton (Inc. Place)
Parkview; RMC Place; TULSA; ★ **TUL**; pop. incl. with Tulsa (Inc. Place)
Patterson; RMC Place; LATIMER; ***221** H-18; mail Wilburton z 74578
Patton; RMC Place; MAYES; ***221** C-18; mail Adair z 74330; ● 100
Pauls Valley; Inc. Place; ⊡ GARVIN; **221** H-14; elev. 876ft./267m.; 🅿 🄷; z 73075; Ⓟ 6,150; Ⓒ 6,256
Pawhuska; Inc. Place; ⊡ OSAGE; **221** C-16; located on Osage Ind. Res.; elev. 818ft./249m.; 🅿 🄷; z 74056; location of Indian Agency; Ⓟ 3,825; Ⓒ 3,629
Pawnee; Inc. Place; ⊡ PAWNEE; **221** D-15; elev. 866ft./264m.; 🅿 🄷; z 74058; location of Indian Agency; Ⓟ 2,197; Ⓒ 2,230
PAWNEE; **221** D-14; Ⓟ 15,575; Ⓒ 16,612; ◆ 16,249
Paw Paw; RMC Place; SEQUOYAH; ***221** F-20; elev. 424ft./129m.; ★ **FTSM**; mail Muldrow z 74948; rural
Payne; RMC Place; MCCLAIN; ***221** H-13; mail Lindsay z 73052; rural
PAYNE; **221** E-14; Ⓟ 61,507; Ⓒ 68,190; ◆ 92,112
Payson; RMC Place; LINCOLN; **221** F-15; elev. 895ft./273m.; mail Meeker z 74855; ● 30
Pearson; RMC Place; POTTAWATOMIE; **221** G-14; mail Asher z 74826; ● 25
Pearsonia; RMC Place; OSAGE; ***221** B-15; mail Pawhuska z 74056; rural
Peavine; CDP-Census Area Only; ADAIR; ***221** E-20; Ⓒ 358
Peckham; RMC Place; KAY; ***221** B-14; elev. 1,116ft./340m.; 🅿; z 74647; ● 75
Peggs; RMC Place; CHEROKEE; **221** D-19; 🅿; z 74452; ● 180
Penn 89th; RMC Place; OKLAHOMA, CLEVELAND; ***221** G-13; ★ **O.C.**; mail Oklahoma City z 73139, z 73159, z 73169, z 73173, z 73189; pop. incl. with Oklahoma City (Inc. Place)
Pensacola; Inc. Place; MAYES; **221** C-18; 🅿; z 74301; Ⓟ 69; Ⓒ 71
Peoria; Inc. Place; OTTAWA; ***221** B-19; 🅿; z 74363; Ⓟ 136; Ⓒ 141
Perkins; Inc. Place; PAYNE; **221** E-14; 🅿; z 74059; Ⓟ 1,925; Ⓒ 2,272
Pernell; RMC Place; GARVIN; **221** I-13; 🅿; z 73433; ● 200
Perry; Inc. Place; ⊡ NOBLE; **221** D-14; elev. 1,000ft./305m.; 🅿 🄷; z 73077; Ⓟ 4,978; Ⓒ 5,230
Pershing; RMC Place; OSAGE; **221** C-16; located on Osage Ind. Res.; mail Barnsdall z 74002; ● 50
Petersburg; RMC Place; JEFFERSON; ***221** K-13; elev. 828ft./252m.; mail Ringling z 73456; rural
Petros; RMC Place; LE FLORE; ***221** H-20; elev. 580ft./177m.; mail Heavener z 74937; pop. incl. with Heavener (Inc. Place)
Pettit; CDP; CHEROKEE; **221** E-19; mail Park Hill z 74451; Ⓒ 771
Pettit Bay; RMC Place; CHEROKEE; ***221** E-19; mail Park Hill z 74451; ● 300
Pharoah; RMC Place; OKFUSKEE; **221** F-16; 🅿; z 74880; pop. incl. with Weleetka (Inc. Place)
Phillips; Inc. Place; COAL; **221** I-16; elev. 591ft./180m.; mail Coalgate z 74538; Ⓟ 161; Ⓒ 150
Picher; Inc. Place; OTTAWA; **221** B-19; 🅿; z 74360; Ⓟ 1,714; Ⓒ 1,640
Pickens; RMC Place; MCCURTAIN; **221** I-19; 🅿; z 74752; ● 170
Pickett; RMC Place; PONTOTOC; ***221** H-15; elev. 975ft./297m.; mail Ada z 74820; ● 400
Piedmont; Inc. Place; CANADIAN, KINGFISHER; **221** F-13; 🅿; z 73078; Ⓟ 2,522; Ⓒ 3,650
Pierce; RMC Place; MCINTOSH; ***221** F-17; elev. 630ft./192m.; mail Checotah z 74426; rural
Piney; RMC Place; ADAIR; ***221** E-20; elev. 1,160ft./354m.; mail Stilwell z 74960; rural
Pinhook Corners; CDP-Census Area Only; SEQUOYAH; ***221** F-19; Ⓒ 161
Pink; Inc. Place; POTTAWATOMIE; **221** G-14; mail Tecumseh z 74873; Ⓟ 1,020; Ⓒ 1,165
Pin Oak Acres; CDP-Census Area Only; MAYES; ***221** D-18; Ⓒ 427
Pin Oaks Acres; RMC Place; MAYES; ***221** D-18; elev. 700ft./213m.; mail Chouteau z 74337; ● 50
Pittsburg; Inc. Place; PITTSBURG; **221** H-17; 🅿; z 74560; Ⓟ 249; Ⓒ 280
PITTSBURG; **221** H-17; Ⓟ 40,581; Ⓒ 43,953; ◆ 45,200
Platter (Barry); RMC Place; BRYAN; ***221** K-15; 🅿; z 74753; ● 200
Pleasant Hill; RMC Place; MCCURTAIN; ***221** K-20; mail Haworth z 74740; ● 50
Plunkettville; RMC Place; MCCURTAIN; **221** I-20; mail Watson z 74963; ● 80
Pocasset; Inc. Place; GRADY; **221** G-12; 🅿; z 73079; Ⓒ 192
Pocola; Inc. Place; LE FLORE; **221** G-20; 🅿; ★ **FTSM**; z 74902; Ⓟ 3,664; Ⓒ 3,994
Pollard; RMC Place; MCCURTAIN; ***221** K-20; mail Haworth z 74740; rural
Ponca City; Inc. Place; KAY, OSAGE; **221** C-14; elev. 1,022ft./312m.; 🅿 🄷 ■; z 74601-02, z 74604; Ⓟ 26,359; Ⓒ 25,919; ◆ 24,068
Pond Creek; Inc. Place; GRANT; **221** C-12; 🅿; z 73766; Ⓟ 982; Ⓒ 896
Pontotoc; RMC Place; JOHNSTON; **221** I-15; 🅿; z 74820; ● 200
PONTOTOC; **221** I-15; Ⓟ 34,119; Ⓒ 35,143; ◆ 37,752
Pooleville; RMC Place; CARTER; **221** I-13; 🅿; z 73401 & mail Springer z 73458; ● 100
Porter; Inc. Place; WAGONER; **221** E-18; 🅿; z 74454; Ⓟ 588; Ⓒ 574
Porter Hill; RMC Place; COMANCHE; ***221** H-11; elev. 1,272ft./388m.; mail Elgin z 73538; ● 25
Porum; Inc. Place; MUSKOGEE; **221** F-18; elev. 582ft./177m.; 🅿; z 74455; Ⓟ 851; Ⓒ 725
Poteau; Inc. Place; ⊡ LE FLORE; **221** G-20; elev. 498ft./152m.; 🅿 🄷; z 74953; Ⓟ 7,210; Ⓒ 7,939
POTTAWATOMIE; **221** G-14; Ⓟ 58,760; Ⓒ 65,521; ◆ 69,493
Powell; RMC Place; MARSHALL; ***221** K-15; elev. 656ft./200m.; mail Kingston z 73439; rural
Prague; Inc. Place; LINCOLN; **221** F-15; 🅿; z 74864; Ⓟ 2,308; Ⓒ 2,138
Prattville; RMC Place; TULSA; ***221** D-16; elev. 778ft./237m.; ★ **TUL**; mail Sand Springs z 74063; pop. incl. with Sand Springs (Inc. Place)
Preston; RMC Place; OKMULGEE; **221** F-17; elev. 777ft./237m.; 🅿; z 74456; ● 500
Proctor; RMC Place; ADAIR; **221** E-19; 🅿; z 74457; ● 130
Prue (New Prue); Inc. Place; OSAGE; **221** D-16; 🅿; z 74060; Ⓟ 346; Ⓒ 433
Pruitt; CARTER; see Pruitt City (RMC Place)
Pruitt City (Pruitt); RMC Place; CARTER; ***221** I-13; elev. 1,075ft./328m.; mail Ratliff City z 73481; ● 100
Pryor (Pryor Creek); Inc. Place; ⊡ MAYES; **221** D-18; elev. 630ft./192m.; 🅿 🄷; z 74361-62; Ⓟ 8,327; Ⓒ 8,659
Pryor Creek; MAYES; see Pryor (Inc. Place)
Pump Back; CDP-Census Area Only; MAYES; ***221** D-19; Ⓒ 155
Pumpkin Center; RMC Place; COMANCHE; ***221** I-11; mail Lawton z 73501
Pumpkin Center; RMC Place; OKMULGEE; ***221** F-17; elev. 659ft./201m.; mail Morris z 74445; rural
Purcell; Inc. Place; ⊡ MCCLAIN; **221** H-13; elev. 1,106ft./337m.; 🅿 🄷; z 73080; Ⓟ 4,784; Ⓒ 5,571
Purdy; RMC Place; GARVIN; **221** H-13; elev. 1,035ft./315m.; mail Lindsay z 73052; ● 45
PUSHMATAHA; **221** I-18; Ⓟ 10,997; Ⓒ 11,667; ◆ 11,824
Putnam; Inc. Place; DEWEY; **220** E-10; elev. 1,971ft./601m.; 🅿; z 73659; Ⓟ 44; Ⓒ 46
Pyramid Corners; RMC Place; CRAIG; **221** B-18; mail Bluejacket z 74333; ● 45

Q

Quail Creek; RMC Place; OKLAHOMA; ★ **O.C.**; mail Oklahoma City z 73120; pop. incl. with Oklahoma City (Inc. Place)
Qualls; RMC Place; CHEROKEE; ***221** E-19; mail Park Hill z 74451; rural
Quapaw; Inc. Place; OTTAWA; **221** B-19; 🅿; z 74363; Ⓟ 928; Ⓒ 984
Quay; RMC Place; PAYNE, PAWNEE; ***221** D-15; mail Yale z 74085; disincorporated August 23, 2000; Ⓟ 59; Ⓒ 47
Quinlan; RMC Place; WOODWARD; ***220** C-10; elev. 1,752ft./534m.; mail Mooreland z 73852
Quinton; Inc. Place; PITTSBURG; **221** G-18; elev. 619ft./189m.; 🅿; z 74561; Ⓟ 1,133; Ⓒ 1,071

R

Raiford; RMC Place; MCINTOSH; ***221** G-17; elev. 644ft./196m.; mail Eufaula z 74432; rural
Ralston; Inc. Place; PAWNEE; **221** C-15; elev. 815ft./248m.; 🅿; z 74650; Ⓟ 405; Ⓒ 355
Ramona; Inc. Place; WASHINGTON; **221** C-17; 🅿; z 74061; Ⓟ 508; Ⓒ 564
Ranchwood Manor; RMC Place; CLEVELAND; ★ **O.C.**; mail Oklahoma City z 73160; pop. incl. with Oklahoma City (Inc. Place)
Randlett; Inc. Place; COTTON; **221** J-11; 🅿; z 73562; Ⓟ 458; Ⓒ 511
Ratliff City; Inc. Place; CARTER; **221** I-13; 🅿; z 73481; Ⓟ 157; Ⓒ 131
Rattan; Inc. Place; PUSHMATAHA; **221** J-18; 🅿; z 74562; Ⓟ 257; Ⓒ 241
Ravia; Inc. Place; JOHNSTON; **221** J-15; elev. 760ft./232m.; 🅿; z 73455; Ⓟ 404; Ⓒ 459
Reagan; RMC Place; JOHNSTON; **221** I-15; elev. 912ft./278m.; mail Tishomingo z 73460; ● 50
Reck; RMC Place; CARTER; ***221** J-13; mail Wilson z 73463; rural
Red Bird; Inc. Place; WAGONER; **221** E-17; 🅿; z 74458; Ⓟ 166; Ⓒ 153
Redbird Smith; CDP-Census Area Only; SEQUOYAH; ***221** F-19; Ⓒ 411
Red Fork; RMC Place; TULSA; ***221** D-16; elev. 677ft./206m.; ★ **TUL**; mail Tulsa z 74107; pop. incl. with Tulsa (Inc. Place)
Red Hill; RMC Place; HASKELL; ***221** F-19; elev. 517ft./158m.; mail Keota z 74941; rural
Red Horse; RMC Place; OKLAHOMA; ★ **O.C.**; mail Oklahoma City z 73110; pop. incl. with Midwest City (Inc. Place)
Redland; RMC Place; SEQUOYAH; ***221** G-20; mail Muldrow z 74948; rural
Red Oak; Inc. Place; LATIMER; **221** H-19; 🅿; z 74563; Ⓟ 602; Ⓒ 581
Red Rock; Inc. Place; NOBLE; ***221** C-14; 🅿; z 74651; Ⓟ 321; Ⓒ 293
Reed; RMC Place; GREER; **220** H-8; elev. 1,744ft./532m.; 🅿; z 73554; ● 40
Regal; RMC Place; COMANCHE; ★ **LAWT**; mail Lawton z 73501; pop. incl. with Lawton (Inc. Place)
Reichert; RMC Place; LE FLORE; ***221** H-19; elev. 512ft./156m.; mail Heavener z 74937; rural
Remus; RMC Place; POTTAWATOMIE, SEMINOLE; **221** G-15; mail Maud z 74854, Tecumseh z 74873; ● 150
Remy; CDP; SEQUOYAH; ***221** F-20; Ⓒ 411
Renfrow; Inc. Place; GRANT; **221** B-13; elev. 1,210ft./369m.; mail Medford z 73759; Ⓟ 19; Ⓒ 16
Reno Meridian; RMC Place; OKLAHOMA; ★ **O.C.**; mail Oklahoma City z 73137; pop. incl. with Oklahoma City (Inc. Place)
Rentiesville; Inc. Place; MCINTOSH; **221** F-18; elev. 589ft./180m.; 🅿; z 74459; Ⓟ 66; Ⓒ 102
Retrop; RMC Place; BECKHAM, WASHITA; ***220** G-9; mail Carter z 73627
Rexroat; RMC Place; CARTER; ***221** J-13; mail Wilson z 73463; rural

Entries in **UPPERCASE** are counties.
Entries in **bold** have populations of 2,500 or more.
Names in parentheses are alternate names.

Inc. Place	Incorporated Place
RMC Place	Rand McNally Designated Place
CDP	Census Designated Place
MCD	Minor Civil Division

⊡ County Seat
▲ Minor Civil Division
elev. Elevation
🅿 Post Office
🄷 Hospital
🄲 College
■ Principal Business Center
★ Ranally Metro Area (RMA) Abbreviation
z Zip Code(s)
Ⓟ Previous Census Population
Ⓡ Revised Census Population
Ⓐ Annexation Population
● Rand McNally Population Estimate
Ⓒ Final Census Population
Ⓢ Special Census Population
◆ Estimated Population

For additional definitions see Glossary, Volume 1, and Introduction, Volume 2.

Reydon; Inc. Place; ROGER MILLS; **220** F-8; 🅿; z 73660; ℗ 200; © 177
Reynolds; RMC Place; ATOKA; ***221** H-17; mail Kiowa z 74553; rural
Rhea; RMC Place; DEWEY; ***220** E-9; elev. 1,961ft./598m.; mail Leedey z 73654; rural
Richards Spur; RMC Place; COMANCHE; ***221** H-11; elev. 1,777ft./542m.; mail Elgin z 73538
Richland; RMC Place; CANADIAN; ***221** F-12; ★ **O.C.**; mail Yukon z 73099; ● 400
Richville; RMC Place; PITTSBURG; ***221** H-17; elev. 637ft./194m.; mail McAlester z 74501; rural
Ringling; Inc. Place; JEFFERSON; **221** J-13; 🅿; z 73456; ℗ 1,250; © 1,135
Ringold (New Ringold); RMC Place; MCCURTAIN; ***221** J-19; 🅿; z 74754; ● 100
Ringwood; Inc. Place; MAJOR; **221** D-11; 🅿; z 73768; ℗ 394; © 424
Ripley; Inc. Place; PAYNE; **221** E-14; 🅿; z 74062; ℗ 376; © 444
River Bottom; CDP-Census Area Only; MUSKOGEE; ***221** F-18; © 265
Roberta; RMC Place; BRYAN; ***221** K-16; elev. 672ft./205m.; mail Durant z 74701; ● 35
Rock Island; Inc. Place; LE FLORE; **221** G-20; ★ **FTSM**; mail Cameron z 74932; ℗ 478; © 709
Rocky; Inc. Place; WASHITA; **220** G-9; 🅿; z 73661; ℗ 181; © 174
Rocky Ford; CDP-Census Area Only; DELAWARE; ***221** D-19; © 60
Rocky Mountain; CDP; ADAIR; ***221** E-19; mail Stilwell z 74960; © 448
Rocky Point; RMC Place; WAGONER; ***221** E-18; mail Wagoner z 74467; ● 370
Roff; Inc. Place; PONTOTOC; **221** I-15; elev. 1,254ft./382m.; 🅿; z 74865; ℗ 717; © 734
ROGER MILLS; **220** E-8; ℗ 4,147; © 3,436; ◆ 3,346
ROGERS; **221** D-17; ℗ 55,170; © 70,641; Ⓡ 70,639; ◆ 83,618
Roland; Inc. Place; SEQUOYAH; **221** F-20; 🅿; ★ **FTSM**; z 74954; ℗ 2,481; © 2,842
Roll; RMC Place; ROGER MILLS; **220** E-8; elev. 2,278ft./694m.; mail Cheyenne z 73628; ● 25
Rolling Meadows; RMC Place; TULSA; ***221** E-16; ★ **TUL**; mail Glenpool z 74033; pop. incl. with Glenpool (Inc. Place)
Roosevelt; Inc. Place; KIOWA; **220** H-10; 🅿; z 73564; ℗ 323; © 280
Rose; RMC Place; MAYES; **221** D-19; elev. 989ft./301m.; 🅿; z 74364; ● 100
Rosedale; Inc. Place; MCCLAIN; **221** H-14; mail Byars z 74831; ℗ 48; © 66
Rosston; Inc. Place; HARPER; **220** B-8; 🅿; z 73855; ℗ 54; © 66
Rossville; RMC Place; LINCOLN; ***221** F-14; elev. 1,032ft./315m.; mail Wellston z 74881
Roxana; RMC Place; LOGAN; ***221** D-13; mail Marshall z 73056; rural
Rubottom; RMC Place; LOVE; **221** K-13; 🅿; z 73463; ● 70
Rufe; RMC Place; MCCURTAIN; **221** J-19; elev. 507ft./155m.; 🅿; z 74755; ● 200
Rush Springs; Inc. Place; GRADY; **221** H-12; 🅿; z 73082; ℗ 1,229; © 1,278
Russell; RMC Place; GREER; **220** H-8; elev. 1,537ft./468m.; mail Mangum z 73554; ● 25
Russellville; RMC Place; PITTSBURG; ***221** G-18; mail Quinton z 74561; rural
Russett; RMC Place; JOHNSTON; ***221** J-15; mail Mannsville z 73447
Ryan; Inc. Place; JEFFERSON; **221** J-12; 🅿; z 73565; ℗ 945; © 894

S

Sacred Heart; RMC Place; POTTAWATOMIE; ***221** H-15; mail Konawa z 74849
Saddle Mountain; RMC Place; KIOWA; ***220** H-10; mail Mountain View z 73062; rural
Sageeyah; RMC Place; ROGERS; ***221** D-17; elev. 647ft./197m.; mail Claremore z 74017; ● 170
Saint Louis; Inc. Place; POTTAWATOMIE; **221** G-15; elev. 1,017ft./310m.; 🅿; z 74866; ℗ 181; © 206
Salem; CDP-Census Area Only; ADAIR; ***221** E-20; © 89
Salem; RMC Place; MCINTOSH, OKMULGEE; ***221** F-17; mail Henryetta z 74437; rural
Salem; RMC Place; OKMULGEE; ***221** F-17; mail Henryetta z 74437; rural
Salina; Inc. Place; MAYES; **221** D-18; 🅿; z 74365; ℗ 1,153; © 1,422
Sallisaw; Inc. Place; ⊡ SEQUOYAH; **221** F-19; elev. 539ft./164m.; 🅿 🅷; z 74955; ℗ 7,122; © 7,989
Salt Fork; RMC Place; GRANT; ***221** C-13; elev. 1,006ft./307m.; mail Hunter z 74640
Sams Corner; CDP-Census Area Only; MAYES; ***221** D-18; © 126
Sams Point; RMC Place; PITTSBURG; ***221** G-17; mail McAlester z 74501; ● 65
Sand Bluff; RMC Place; CHOCTAW; ***221** J-17; elev. 557ft./170m.; mail Soper z 74759; rural
Sand Creek; RMC Place; GRANT; ***221** B-12; mail Wakita z 73771; rural
Sand Hills; CDP-Census Area Only; MUSKOGEE; ***221** F-18; © 422
Sand Point; RMC Place; BRYAN; ***221** J-15; mail Mead z 73449; ● 200
Sand Springs; Inc. Place; TULSA, OSAGE; **220** F-1; 🅿; ★ **TUL**; z 74063; ℗ 15,346; © 17,451
Sansbois; RMC Place; HASKELL; ***221** G-19; elev. 533ft./162m.; mail Kinta z 74552; rural
Santa Fe; RMC Place; STEPHENS; ***221** I-13; mail Loco z 73442, Velma z 73491; rural
Sapulpa; Inc. Place; ⊡ CREEK; **220** I-1; elev. 700ft./213m.; 🅿 🅷; ★ **TUL**; z 74066-67; ℗ 18,074; © 19,166; ◆ 19,011
Sardis; RMC Place; PUSHMATAHA; ***221** H-18; elev. 586ft./179m.; mail Clayton z 74536; rural
Sasakwa; Inc. Place; SEMINOLE; **221** H-15; elev. 839ft./256m.; 🅿; z 74867; ℗ 169; © 150
Savanna; Inc. Place; PITTSBURG; **221** H-17; elev. 729ft./222m.; 🅿; z 74565; ℗ 869; © 730
Sawyer; Inc. Place; CHOCTAW; **221** J-18; 🅿; z 74756; © 274
Sayre; Inc. Place; ⊡ BECKHAM; **220** G-8; 🅿 🅷; z 73662; ℗ 2,881; © 4,114
Schlegal; RMC Place; PAYNE; ***221** E-15; mail Cushing z 74023; rural
Schoolton; RMC Place; SEMINOLE; ***221** F-16; elev. 880ft./268m.; mail Okemah z 74859; pop. incl. with Cromwell (Inc. Place)
Schulter; Inc. Place; OKMULGEE; **221** F-17; 🅿; z 74460; © 600
Scipio; RMC Place; PITTSBURG; **221** G-17; mail McAlester z 74501; ● 50
Scott; RMC Place; CADDO; ***221** G-11; mail Hinton z 73047; rural
Scraper; CDP; CHEROKEE; ***221** E-19; elev. 825ft./251m.; mail Tahlequah z 74464; © 475
Scullin; RMC Place; MURRAY; ***221** I-15; mail Sulphur z 73086; rural
Scullyville; RMC Place; LE FLORE; ***221** G-20; mail Spiro z 74959; ● 40
Sedan; RMC Place; KIOWA; ***220** H-10; mail Mountain View z 73062; rural
Seiling; Inc. Place; DEWEY; **220** D-10; elev. 1,744ft./532m.; 🅿 🅷; z 73663; ℗ 1,031; © 875
Selman; RMC Place; HARPER; **220** B-9; 🅿; z 73834; ● 25
Seminole; Inc. Place; SEMINOLE; **221** G-15; 🅿 🅷; z 74818, z 74868; ℗ 7,071; © 6,899
SEMINOLE; **221** G-15; ℗ 25,412; © 24,894; ◆ 23,851
Sentinel; Inc. Place; WASHITA; **220** G-9; 🅿; z 73664; ℗ 960; © 859
Sequoyah; CDP; ROGERS; **221** D-18; mail Claremore z 74017; © 671
SEQUOYAH; **221** F-20; ℗ 33,828; © 38,972; ◆ 41,013
Seward; RMC Place; LOGAN; **221** E-13; ★ **O.C.**; mail Guthrie z 73044; ● 50
Shady Grove; CDP-Census Area Only; CHEROKEE; ***221** E-19; © 484
Shady Grove; CDP; MCINTOSH; ***221** F-18; mail Checotah z 74426; © 185
Shady Grove; Inc. Place; PAWNEE; ***221** D-16; ★ **TUL**; mail Tulsa z 74112; ℗ 23; © 44
Shady Grove; RMC Place; SEQUOYAH; ***221** F-20; ★ **FTSM**; mail Muldrow z 74948; ● 200
Shady Point; Inc. Place; LE FLORE; **221** G-20; elev. 447ft./136m.; 🅿; z 74956; ℗ 597; © 848
Shamrock; Inc. Place; CREEK; **221** E-15; 🅿; z 74068; ℗ 95; © 125
Sharon; Inc. Place; WOODWARD; **220** D-9; 🅿; z 73857; ℗ 108; © 122
Shartel; RMC Place; OKLAHOMA; ★ **O.C.**; mail Oklahoma City z 73105, z 73118, z 73154; pop. incl. with Oklahoma City (Inc. Place)
Shattuck; Inc. Place; ELLIS; **220** D-8; elev. 2,268ft./691m.; 🅿 🅷; z 73858; ℗ 1,454; © 1,274
Shawnee; Inc. Place; ⊡ POTTAWATOMIE; **221** G-14; elev. 1,055ft./322m.; 🅿 🅷 🅲 2,473 ■; z 74801-02, z 74804; location of Indian Agency; ℗ 26,017; © 28,692; ◆ 29,911
Shay; RMC Place; MARSHALL; ***221** K-15; mail Kingston z 73439
Sheridan; RMC Place; COMANCHE; ★ **LAWT**; mail Lawton z 73505; pop. incl. with Lawton (Inc. Place)
Sheridan; RMC Place; TULSA; ★ **TUL**; mail Tulsa z 74135, z 74153; pop. incl. with Tulsa (Inc. Place)
Sherwood; RMC Place; MCCURTAIN; **221** I-19; mail Broken Bow z 74728; ● 80
Shidler; Inc. Place; OSAGE; **221** C-15; located on Osage Ind. Res.; elev. 1,167ft./356m.; 🅿; z 74652; ℗ 487; © 520
Shinewell; RMC Place; MCCURTAIN; ***221** K-20; mail Haworth z 74740; rural
Short; CDP-Census Area Only; SEQUOYAH; ***221** F-20; mail Muldrow z 74948; © 328
Shults; RMC Place; MCCURTAIN; ***221** K-20; elev. 445ft./136m.; mail Idabel z 74745; rural
Sickles; RMC Place; CADDO; **221** G-11; elev. 1,634ft./498m.; mail Lookeba z 73053; ● 110
Silo; Inc. Place; BRYAN; ***221** J-16; mail Durant z 74701; ℗ 249; © 282
Silver City; RMC Place; CREEK; ***221** D-15; elev. 850ft./259m.; mail Jennings z 74038
Silver Tree; RMC Place; TULSA; ***221** E-17; ★ **TUL**; mail Broken Arrow z 74011; pop. incl. with Broken Arrow (Inc. Place)
Simms; CDP-Census Area Only; MUSKOGEE; ***221** F-18; © 295
Skedee; Inc. Place; PAWNEE; **221** D-15; elev. 834ft./254m.; mail Pawnee z 74058; ℗ 96; © 102
Skiatook; Inc. Place; OSAGE, TULSA; **221** D-17; 🅿; ★ **TUL**; z 74070; ℗ 4,910; © 5,396
Slapout; RMC Place; BEAVER; **220** C-7; elev. 2,454ft./748m.; mail Laverne z 73848; ● 20
Slaughterville; Inc. Place; CLEVELAND; **221** G-13; elev. 1,122ft./342m.; ★ **O.C.**; mail Lexington z 73051; ℗ 1,843; © 3,609
Slick; Inc. Place; CREEK; **221** E-16; elev. 719ft./219m.; 🅿; z 74071; ℗ 124; © 148
Smith Lee; RMC Place; BRYAN; ***221** K-17; elev. 499ft./152m.; mail Bennington z 74723; rural
Smith Village; Inc. Place; OKLAHOMA; **220** L-5; ★ **O.C.**; mail Oklahoma City z 73115; ℗ 34; © 40
Smithville; RMC Place; MCCURTAIN; **221** I-20; 🅿; z 74957; disincorporated since 2000 Census; ℗ 111; © 123
Snake Creek; CDP-Census Area Only; MAYES; ***221** D-19; © 298
Snow; RMC Place; PUSHMATAHA; **221** I-18; 🅿; z 74567; ● 130
Snyder; Inc. Place; KIOWA; **220** I-10; elev. 1,364ft./416m.; 🅿; z 73566; ℗ 1,619; © 1,509
Sobol; RMC Place; PUSHMATAHA; ***221** J-18; mail Fort Towson z 74735; rural
Soper; Inc. Place; CHOCTAW; **221** J-17; 🅿; z 74759; ℗ 305; © 300
Sour John; CDP-Census Area Only; MUSKOGEE; ***221** F-19; © 61
Southard; RMC Place; BLAINE; **221** E-11; elev. 1,553ft./473m.; 🅿; z 73770; ● 80
South Coffeyville; Inc. Place; NOWATA; **221** B-17; mail S Coffeyville z 74072; ℗ 791; © 790
South Country Estate; RMC Place; TULSA; ***221** E-17; ★ **TUL**; mail Bixby z 74008; pop. incl. with Bixby (Inc. Place)
Southeast; RMC Place; OKLAHOMA; ★ **O.C.**; mail Oklahoma City z 73109, z 73129, z 73143, z 73149; pop. incl. with Oklahoma City (Inc. Place)
Southeast; RMC Place; TULSA; ★ **TUL**; mail Tulsa z 74145, z 74147, z 74153; pop. incl. with Tulsa (Inc. Place)
South Heights; RMC Place; TULSA; ***221** D-16; ★ **TUL**; mail Sand Springs z 74063; pop. incl. with Sand Springs (Inc. Place)
South Park; RMC Place; TULSA; ***221** E-17; ★ **TUL**; mail Broken Arrow z 74011
Southside; RMC Place; TULSA; ★ **TUL**; mail Tulsa z 74105, z 74136-37, z 74170; pop. incl. with Tulsa (Inc. Place)
Southwest; RMC Place; OKLAHOMA; ★ **O.C.**; mail Oklahoma City z 73119; pop. incl. with Oklahoma City (Inc. Place)
Southwood East; RMC Place; TULSA; ***221** E-17; ★ **TUL**; mail Bixby z 74008; pop. incl. with Bixby (Inc. Place)
Southwood South; RMC Place; TULSA; ***221** E-17; ★ **TUL**; mail Bixby z 74008; pop. incl. with Bixby (Inc. Place)
Sparks; Inc. Place; LINCOLN; **221** F-15; elev. 846ft./258m.; 🅿; z 74869; ℗ 202; © 137
Spaulding; Inc. Place; HUGHES; **221** G-16; elev. 819ft./250m.; mail Holdenville z 74848; © 62
Spavinaw; Inc. Place; MAYES; **221** D-19; 🅿; z 74366; ℗ 432; © 563
Speer; RMC Place; CHOCTAW; ***221** J-18; elev. 501ft./153m.; mail Hugo z 74743; rural
Spelter City; RMC Place; OKMULGEE; ***221** F-17; elev. 687ft./209m.; mail Henryetta z 74437; pop. incl. with Henryetta (Inc. Place)
Spencer; Inc. Place; OKLAHOMA; **220** J-6; 🅿 🅷; ★ **O.C.**; z 73084; ℗ 3,972; © 3,746
Spencerville; RMC Place; CHOCTAW; **221** J-18; 🅿; z 74760; ● 200
Sperry; Inc. Place; TULSA; **221** D-17; 🅿; ★ **TUL**; z 74073; ℗ 937; © 981
Spiro; Inc. Place; LE FLORE; **221** G-20; 🅿; z 74959; ℗ 2,146; © 2,227
Sportsmen Acres; Inc. Place; MAYES; ***221** D-18; mail Pryor z 74361; ℗ 181; © 204
Sportsmen Acres Community; CDP-Census Area Only; MAYES; ***221** D-18; © 0
Springer; Inc. Place; CARTER; **221** J-14; elev. 917ft./280m.; 🅿; z 73458; ℗ 485; © 577
Springlake Park; RMC Place; OKLAHOMA; ★ **O.C.**; mail Oklahoma City z 73111; pop. incl. with Oklahoma City (Inc. Place)
Stafford; RMC Place; CUSTER; **220** F-9; elev. 1,606ft./490m.; mail Clinton z 73601; ● 25
Stanley; RMC Place; PUSHMATAHA; ***221** I-18; mail Clayton z 74536; rural
Stapp; RMC Place; LE FLORE; ***221** H-20; elev. 660ft./201m.; mail Hodgen z 74939; rural
Star; RMC Place; HASKELL; ***221** G-19; mail Keota z 74941
State Capitol; RMC Place; OKLAHOMA; ★ **O.C.**; mail Oklahoma City z 73105, z 73152; pop. incl. with Oklahoma City (Inc. Place)
Stealy; RMC Place; MCCLAIN; ***221** H-13; mail Wayne z 73095; rural
Stecker; RMC Place; CADDO; ***221** H-11; elev. 1,348ft./411m.; mail Apache z 73006; ● 50
Steedman; RMC Place; PONTOTOC; ***221** H-15; elev. 773ft./236m.; mail Allen z 74825; rural
Steel Junction; RMC Place; MCCURTAIN; ***221** J-20; elev. 504ft./154m.; mail Broken Bow z 74728; ● 40
Steen; RMC Place; GARFIELD; ★ **ENID**; mail Enid z 73701; pop. incl. with Enid (Inc. Place)
Stella; RMC Place; CLEVELAND; ***221** G-14; elev. 1,206ft./368m.; ★ **O.C.**; mail Newalla z 74857; pop. incl. with Oklahoma City (Inc. Place)
STEPHENS; **221** I-13; ℗ 42,299; © 43,182; ◆ 43,831
Sterling; Inc. Place; COMANCHE; **221** H-12; 🅿; z 73567; ℗ 684; © 762
Stidham; Inc. Place; MCINTOSH; **221** F-17; elev. 633ft./193m.; 🅿; z 74461 & mail Eufaula z 74432; ℗ 48; © 23
Stigler; Inc. Place; ⊡ HASKELL; **221** G-19; elev. 583ft./178m.; 🅿 🅷; z 74462, z 74472; ℗ 2,574; © 2,731
Stillwater; Inc. Place; ⊡ PAYNE; **221** D-14; 🅿 🅷 🅲 23,307 ■; z 74074-78; ℗ 36,676; © 39,065; ◆ 50,431
Stilwell; Inc. Place; ⊡ ADAIR; **221** E-20; elev. 1,112ft./339m.; 🅿; z 74960; ℗ 2,663; © 3,276
Stockyards; RMC Place; OKLAHOMA; ★ **O.C.**; mail Oklahoma City z 73108, z 73148; pop. incl. with Oklahoma City (Inc. Place)
Stonebluff; RMC Place; WAGONER; ***221** E-17; mail Haskell z 74436; ● 300
Stones Corner; RMC Place; WAGONER; ***221** E-17; mail Coweta z 74429; rural
Stonewall; Inc. Place; PONTOTOC; **221** I-15; 🅿; z 74871; ℗ 519; © 465
Stony Point; RMC Place; ADAIR; ***221** E-20; mail Stilwell z 74960; rural
Stony Point; RMC Place; LE FLORE; **221** G-20; elev. 468ft./143m.; mail Spiro z 74959; ● 50
Stony Point; CDP-Census Area Only; SEQUOYAH; ***221** F-20; © 177
Story; RMC Place; GARVIN; ***221** H-13; mail Maysville z 73057; rural
Straight; RMC Place; TEXAS; ***220** B-4; mail Guymon z 73942
Strang; Inc. Place; MAYES; ***221** C-18; 🅿; z 74367; ℗ 141; © 100
Stratford; Inc. Place; GARVIN; **221** H-14; elev. 1,110ft./338m.; 🅿; z 74872; ℗ 1,404; © 1,474
Stringtown; Inc. Place; ATOKA; **221** I-16; 🅿; z 74569; ℗ 366; © 396
Strong City; Inc. Place; ROGER MILLS; **220** F-8; 🅿; z 73628; ℗ 49; © 42
Stroud; Inc. Place; LINCOLN, CREEK; **221** E-15; 🅿 🅷; z 74079; ℗ 2,666; © 2,758
Stuart; Inc. Place; HUGHES; **221** H-16; 🅿; z 74570; ℗ 228; © 220
Sugden; Inc. Place; JEFFERSON; **221** J-12; mail Waurika z 73573; ℗ 65; © 59
Sullivan Village; RMC Place; COMANCHE; ★ **LAWT**; mail Lawton z 73501; pop. incl. with Lawton (Inc. Place)
Sulphur; Inc. Place; ⊡ MURRAY; **221** I-14; elev. 950ft./290m.; 🅿 🅷; z 73086; ℗ 4,824; © 4,794
Summerfield; RMC Place; LE FLORE; **221** H-19; elev. 561ft./171m.; mail Wister z 74966; ● 150
Summit; Inc. Place; MUSKOGEE; **221** F-18; elev. 604ft./184m.; ★ **MSKOG**; mail Muskogee z 74401; ℗ 170; © 226
Sumner; RMC Place; NOBLE; ***221** D-14; elev. 951ft./290m.; mail Perry z 73077; ● 230
Sungate; RMC Place; COMANCHE; ★ **LAWT**; mail Lawton z 73501; pop. incl. with Lawton (Inc. Place)
Sunkist; RMC Place; CHOCTAW; ***221** J-17; elev. 564ft./172m.; mail Boswell z 74727; rural
Sunnybrook Estate; RMC Place; TULSA; ***221** E-17; ★ **TUL**; mail Jenks z 74037; pop. incl. with Jenks (Inc. Place)
Sunray (Beckett); RMC Place; STEPHENS; **221** I-12; mail Comanche z 73529; pop. incl. with Empire City (Inc. Place)
Sunshine Valley; OTTAWA; see Kellyville (RMC Place)
Supply; WOODWARD; see Fort Supply (Inc. Place)
Survey Hills; RMC Place; TEXAS; ***220** B-3; mail Keyes z 73947; rural
Sweetwater; Inc. Place; BECKHAM, ROGER MILLS; **220** F-8; 🅿; z 73666; incorporated August 27, 2003; not reported in 2000 Census; ● 68
Swink; RMC Place; CHOCTAW; **221** J-18; 🅿; z 74761; disincorporated December 1, 2000; © 83
Sycamore; CDP; DELAWARE; ***221** C-19; © 183
Sycamore; CDP-Census Area Only; SEQUOYAH; ***221** F-19; © 150

T

Tabler; RMC Place; GRADY; ***221** G-12; elev. 1,081ft./329m.; mail Chickasha z 73018; rural
Tablerville; RMC Place; MCCURTAIN; ***221** J-20; elev. 840ft./256m.; mail Eagletown z 74734; ● 40
Taft; Inc. Place; MUSKOGEE; **221** E-18; 🅿; z 74463; ℗ 400; © 349
Tagg Flats; CDP-Census Area Only; DELAWARE; ***221** D-19; © 11
Tahlequah; Inc. Place; ⊡ CHEROKEE; **221** E-19; elev. 800ft./244m.; 🅿 🅷 🅲 9,540; z 74464-65; location of Indian Agency; ℗ 10,398; © 14,458
Tahona; RMC Place; LE FLORE; ***221** G-20; mail Cameron z 74932; ● 50
Tailholt; RMC Place; CHEROKEE; ***221** E-19; mail Welling z 74471; rural
Taiwah; CDP-Census Area Only; ROGERS; **221** D-17; mail Claremore z 74017; © 166
Talala; Inc. Place; ROGERS; **221** C-17; elev. 685ft./209m.; 🅿; z 74080; ℗ 206; © 270
Talihina; Inc. Place; LE FLORE; **221** H-19; 🅿 🅷; z 74571; location of Indian Agency; ℗ 1,297; © 1,211
Tallant; RMC Place; OSAGE; ***221** C-16; mail Barnsdall z 74002; ● 25
Taloga; Inc. Place; ⊡ DEWEY; **220** E-10; elev. 1,708ft./521m.; 🅿; z 73667; ℗ 415; © 372
Tamaha; Inc. Place; HASKELL; **221** F-19; mail Stigler z 74462; ℗ 188; © 198
Tangier; RMC Place; WOODWARD; ***220** D-8; elev. 2,185ft./666m.; mail Woodward z 73801
Tatums; Inc. Place; CARTER; **221** I-13; 🅿; z 73487; ℗ 176; © 172
Taupa; RMC Place; COMANCHE; ***221** I-11; ★ **LAWT**; pop. incl. with Lawton (Inc. Place)
Taylor; RMC Place; COTTON; ***221** J-11; mail Randlett z 73562; rural
Tecumseh; Inc. Place; POTTAWATOMIE; **221** G-14; 🅿; z 74873; ℗ 5,750; © 6,098
Temple; Inc. Place; COTTON; **221** J-11; elev. 1,007ft./307m.; 🅿; z 73568; ℗ 1,223; © 1,146
Tenkiller; CDP-Census Area Only; CHEROKEE; ***221** E-19; © 549
Teresita; RMC Place; CHEROKEE; ***221** D-19; mail Rose z 74364; rural
Terlton; Inc. Place; PAWNEE; **221** D-15; 🅿; z 74081; ℗ 121; © 85
Terral; Inc. Place; JEFFERSON; **221** K-12; 🅿; z 73561, z 73569; ℗ 469; © 386
Texanna; CDP; MCINTOSH; **221** G-18; mail Checotah z 74426; © 2,083
TEXAS; **220** B-4; ℗ 16,419; © 20,107; ◆ 19,811
Texhoma; Inc. Place; TEXAS; **220** C-3; elev. 3,487ft./1,063m.; 🅿; z 73949; ℗ 746; © 935
Texola; Inc. Place; BECKHAM; **220** G-7; 🅿; z 73668; ℗ 45; © 47
Thackerville; Inc. Place; LOVE; **221** K-14; 🅿; z 73459; ℗ 290; © 404
The Meadows; RMC Place; TULSA; ***221** E-17; ★ **TUL**; mail Broken Arrow z 74011; pop. incl. with Broken Arrow (Inc. Place)
The Village (Village); Inc. Place; OKLAHOMA; **220** J-4; 🅿; ★ **O.C.**; z 73120 & mail Oklahoma City z 73134, z 73156; ℗ 10,353; © 10,157
Thirty-Fourth Street; RMC Place; WOODWARD; mail Woodward z 73801; pop. incl. with Woodward (Inc. Place)
Thirty Ninth Street; RMC Place; OKLAHOMA; ★ **O.C.**; mail Oklahoma City z 73112, z 73157; pop. incl. with Oklahoma City (Inc. Place)
Thomas; Inc. Place; CUSTER; **220** E-10; 🅿; z 73669; ℗ 1,246; © 1,238
Ti; RMC Place; PITTSBURG; **221** H-17; elev. 753ft./230m.; mail Blanco z 74528; rural
Tiajuana; RMC Place; MAYES; ***221** C-19; mail Disney z 74340; rural
Tiawah; RMC Place; ROGERS; ● 150
TILLMAN; **220** I-10; ℗ 10,384; © 9,287; ◆ 7,832
Timber Brook; RMC Place; WAGONER; ***221** E-17; ★ **TUL**; mail Broken Arrow z 74014; ● 1,000
Timberlane; RMC Place; PAWNEE; ***221** D-16; ★ **TUL**; mail Cleveland z 74020; ● 30
Tiner; RMC Place; MCCURTAIN; ***221** J-20; elev. 419ft./128m.; mail Broken Bow z 74728; rural
Tipton; Inc. Place; TILLMAN; **220** I-9; elev. 1,303ft./397m.; 🅿; z 73570; ℗ 1,043; © 916
Tishomingo; Inc. Place; ⊡ JOHNSTON; **221** J-15; elev. 693ft./211m.; 🅿 🅷; z 73460; ℗ 3,116; © 3,162
Titanic; RMC Place; ADAIR; ***221** E-19; elev. 1,061ft./323m.; mail Stilwell z 74960; rural
Tom; RMC Place; MCCURTAIN; **221** K-20; 🅿; z 74740; ● 150
Tonkawa; Inc. Place; KAY; **221** C-14; 🅿; z 74653; ℗ 3,127; © 3,299
Topsy; RMC Place; DELAWARE; ***221** C-19; mail Spavinaw z 74366; rural
Townwest; RMC Place; COMANCHE; ★ **LAWT**; mail Lawton z 73506; pop. incl. with Lawton (Inc. Place)
Tribbey; Inc. Place; POTTAWATOMIE; **221** G-14; elev. 1,006ft./307m.; mail Macomb z 74852; ℗ 288; © 273
Trousdale; RMC Place; POTTAWATOMIE; ***221** G-14; elev. 957ft./292m.; mail Wanette z 74878; rural
Troy; RMC Place; JOHNSTON; **221** I-15; elev. 938ft./286m.; mail Mill Creek z 74856; ● 40
Tryon; Inc. Place; LINCOLN; **221** E-14; 🅿; z 74875; ℗ 514; © 448
Tucker; RMC Place; LE FLORE; ***221** G-19; mail Spiro z 74959; ● 50
Tullahassee; Inc. Place; WAGONER; **221** E-18; 🅿; ★ **MSKOG**; z 74454; ℗ 92; © 106
Tulsa; Inc. Place; ⊡ TULSA, OSAGE; **220** E-1; elev. 711ft./217m.; 🅿 🅷 🅲 10,181 ■; ★ **TUL**; z 74101-08, z 74110, z 74112, z 74114-17, z 74119-21, z 74126-37, z 74141, z 74145-50, z 74152-53, z 74155-59, z 74169-72, z 74182, z 74186-87, z 74192-93; ℗ 367,302; © 393,049; ◆ 409,085
TULSA; **221** E-17; ℗ 503,341; © 563,299; ◆ 594,595
Tupelo; Inc. Place; COAL; **221** I-16; elev. 689ft./210m.; 🅿; z 74572; ℗ 323; © 377
Turkey Ford; RMC Place; DELAWARE; ***221** C-19; mail Grove z 74344; rural
Turley; CDP; TULSA; **220** D-2; elev. 646ft./197m.; ★ **TUL**; mail Tulsa z 74126, z 74156; ℗ 2,930; © 3,231
Turner; RMC Place; LOVE; ***221** K-14; elev. 800ft./244m.; mail Burneyville z 73430; ● 50
Turpin; RMC Place; BEAVER; **220** B-5; 🅿; z 73950; ● 400
Tushka; Inc. Place; ATOKA; **221** I-16; mail Atoka z 74525; ℗ 256; © 345
Tuskahoma; RMC Place; PUSHMATAHA; **221** I-18; 🅿; z 74574; ● 100
Tuskegee; RMC Place; CREEK; ***221** F-16; elev. 766ft./233m.; mail Bristow z 74010; rural
Tussy; RMC Place; CARTER, GARVIN; **221** I-13; 🅿; z 73488; ● 80
Tuttle; Inc. Place; GRADY; **221** G-12; 🅿; ★ **O.C.**; z 73089; ℗ 2,807; © 4,294
Tuxedo; RMC Place; WASHINGTON; ★ **BART**; mail Bartlesville z 74006; pop. incl. with Bartlesville (Inc. Place)
Twin Oaks; CDP; DELAWARE; **221** D-19; elev. 1,132ft./345m.; 🅿; z 74368; © 186
Tyler; RMC Place; MARSHALL; ***221** J-15; mail Madill z 73446; rural
Tyrone; Inc. Place; TEXAS; **220** B-5; elev. 2,921ft./890m.; 🅿; z 73951; ℗ 880; © 880

U

Ulan; RMC Place; PITTSBURG; ***221** G-17; mail Indianola z 74442; rural
Ultima Thule; RMC Place; MCCURTAIN; ***221** J-20; mail Eagletown z 74734; rural
Unger; RMC Place; CHOCTAW; ***221** J-17; mail Boswell z 74727; rural
Union; RMC Place; CLEVELAND; ★ **O.C.**; mail Norman z 73069; pop. incl. with Norman (Inc. Place)
Union; RMC Place; TULSA; ***221** D-17; ★ **TUL**; mail Broken Arrow z 74012; pop. incl. with Tulsa (Inc. Place)
Union City; Inc. Place; CANADIAN; **221** F-12; 🅿; z 73090; ℗ 1,000; © 1,375
Union Valley; RMC Place; PONTOTOC; ***221** H-15; elev. 774ft./236m.; mail Stonewall z 74871; ● 110
Utica; RMC Place; BRYAN; **221** K-16; mail Bokchito z 74726; ● 50

V

Valley Brook; Inc. Place; OKLAHOMA; **220** L-5; ★ **O.C.**; mail Oklahoma City z 73149; ℗ 744; © 817
Valley Park; Inc. Place; ROGERS; ***221** D-17; ★ **TUL**; mail Claremore z 74017; ℗ 1; © 24
Valliant; Inc. Place; MCCURTAIN; **221** J-19; elev. 512ft./156m.; 🅿; z 74764; ℗ 873; © 771
Vamoosa; RMC Place; SEMINOLE; **221** H-15; mail Konawa z 74849; ● 80
Vanoss; RMC Place; PONTOTOC; **221** H-15; mail Ada z 74820; ● 100
Velma; Inc. Place; STEPHENS; **221** I-13; elev. 1,044ft./318m.; 🅿; z 73491; ℗ 661; © 664
Vera; Inc. Place; WASHINGTON; **221** C-17; 🅿; z 74082; ℗ 167; © 188
Verden; Inc. Place; GRADY; **221** G-12; 🅿; z 73092; ℗ 546; © 659
Verdigris; Inc. Place; ROGERS; **221** D-17; ★ **TUL**; mail Claremore z 74017; incorporated June 6, 1980; not reported in 2000 Census; Ⓡ 223
Vernon; RMC Place; MCINTOSH; **221** G-17; elev. 685ft./209m.; 🅿; z 74845; ● 60
Vian; Inc. Place; SEQUOYAH; **221** F-19; 🅿; z 74962; ℗ 1,414; © 1,362
Vici; Inc. Place; DEWEY; **220** D-9; elev. 2,265ft./690m.; 🅿; z 73859; ℗ 751; © 668
Victoria Pond; RMC Place; TULSA; ***221** E-17; ★ **TUL**; mail Jenks z 74037; pop. incl. with Jenks (Inc. Place)
Victory; RMC Place; JACKSON; **220** I-9; elev. 1,390ft./424m.; mail Olustee z 73560; ● 25
Village; OKLAHOMA; see The Village (Inc. Place)
Vinco; RMC Place; PAYNE; ***221** E-14; mail Perkins z 74059; ● 70
Vinita; Inc. Place; ⊡ CRAIG; **221** C-18; 🅿 🅷; z 74301; ℗ 5,804; © 6,472; Ⓡ 6,062
Vinson; RMC Place; HARMON; **220** H-8; elev. 1,883ft./574m.; 🅿; z 73571; ● 50
Virgil; RMC Place; CHOCTAW; ***221** J-18; elev. 462ft./141m.; mail Sawyer z 74756; rural
Vista; RMC Place; POTTAWATOMIE; mail Konawa z 74849; rural
Vivian; RMC Place; MCINTOSH; ***221** G-17; elev. 632ft./193m.; mail Eufaula z 74432

W

Wade; RMC Place; BRYAN; **221** K-16; 🅿; z 74723; ● 70
Wagoner; Inc. Place; ⊡ WAGONER; **221** E-18; elev. 602ft./183m.; 🅿 🅷; z 74467, z 74477; ℗ 6,894; © 7,669
WAGONER; **221** E-18; ℗ 47,883; © 57,491; ◆ 68,307
Wainwright; Inc. Place; MUSKOGEE; **221** F-18; 🅿; z 74468; ℗ 223; © 197
Wakita; Inc. Place; GRANT; **221** B-12; elev. 1,175ft./358m.; 🅿; z 73771; ℗ 453; © 420
Wallville; RMC Place; GARVIN; ***221** H-13; mail Lindsay z 73052; ● 40
Walters; Inc. Place; ⊡ COTTON; **221** I-11; 🅿; z 73572; ℗ 2,519; © 2,657
Wanette; Inc. Place; POTTAWATOMIE; **221** H-14; 🅿; z 74878; ℗ 346; © 402
Wann; Inc. Place; NOWATA; **221** B-17; 🅿; z 74083; ℗ 126; © 132
Wapanucka; Inc. Place; JOHNSTON; **221** I-16; elev. 617ft./188m.; 🅿; z 73461; ℗ 402; © 445
Ward Springs; RMC Place; PITTSBURG; ***221** H-17; mail Stuart z 74570; rural
Wardville; RMC Place; ATOKA; **221** I-17; elev. 682ft./208m.; 🅿; z 74576; ℗ 52
Warner; Inc. Place; MUSKOGEE; **221** F-18; 🅿; z 74469; ℗ 1,479; © 1,430
Warr Acres; Inc. Place; OKLAHOMA; **220** K-3; elev. 1,315ft./401m.; 🅿; ★ **O.C.**; z 73122-23, z 73132; ℗ 9,288; © 9,735
Warren; RMC Place; JACKSON; **220** H-9; elev. 1,553ft./473m.; mail Blair z 73526; ● 80
Warwick; Inc. Place; LINCOLN; **221** F-14; mail Chandler z 74834, Wellston z 74881; ℗ 160; © 235
Washington; Inc. Place; MCCLAIN; **221** G-13; elev. 1,149ft./350m.; 🅿; z 73093; ℗ 279; © 520
WASHINGTON; **221** C-17; ℗ 48,066; © 48,996; ◆ 51,031
Washita; RMC Place; CADDO; **221** G-11; 🅿; z 73094; ● 130
WASHITA; **220** G-9; ℗ 11,441; © 11,508; ◆ 11,953
Waterloo; RMC Place; LOGAN; ***221** F-13; ★ **O.C.**; mail Edmond z 73034; ● 100
Watonga; Inc. Place; ⊡ BLAINE; **221** E-11; 🅿 🅷; z 73772; ℗ 3,408; © 4,658
Watova; RMC Place; NOWATA; **221** C-17; mail Nowata z 74048; ● 150
Watson; RMC Place; MCCURTAIN; **221** I-20; elev. 836ft./255m.; 🅿; z 74963; ● 300
Watts; Inc. Place; ADAIR; **221** D-20; 🅿; z 74964; ℗ 303; © 316
Watts Community; CDP-Census Area Only; ADAIR; ***221** D-20; © 500
Wauhillau (Bidding Springs); RMC Place; ADAIR; ***221** E-19; mail Stilwell z 74960; rural
Waukomis; Inc. Place; GARFIELD; **221** D-12; elev. 1,238ft./377m.; 🅿; ★ **ENID**; z 73773; ℗ 1,322; © 1,261
Waurika; Inc. Place; ⊡ JEFFERSON; **221** J-12; elev. 881ft./269m.; 🅿 🅷; z 73573; ℗ 2,088; © 1,988
Wayne; Inc. Place; MCCLAIN; **221** H-14; 🅿; z 73095; ℗ 519; © 714
Waynoka; Inc. Place; WOODS; **220** C-10; elev. 1,476ft./450m.; 🅿; z 73860; ℗ 947; © 993
Weatherford; Inc. Place; CUSTER; **220** F-10; elev. 1,647ft./502m.; 🅿 🅷 🅲 5,260; z 73096; ℗ 10,124; © 9,859
Weathers; RMC Place; PITTSBURG; ***221** H-18; elev. 710ft./216m.; mail Pittsburg z 74560; rural
Webb; RMC Place; DEWEY; ***220** E-9; elev. 2,092ft./638m.; mail Camargo z 73835
Webb City; Inc. Place; OSAGE; **221** B-15; located on Osage Ind. Res.; elev. 1,096ft./334m.; mail Shidler z 74652; ℗ 99; © 95
Webbers Falls; Inc. Place; MUSKOGEE; **221** F-19; 🅿; z 74470; ℗ 722; © 726
Welch; Inc. Place; CRAIG; **221** B-19; 🅿; z 74369; ℗ 499; © 597
Weleetka; Inc. Place; OKFUSKEE; **221** G-16; 🅿; z 74880; ℗ 1,112; © 1,014
Welling; CDP; CHEROKEE; **221** E-19; 🅿; z 74471; © 669
Wellston; Inc. Place; LINCOLN; **221** F-14; 🅿; z 74881; ℗ 912; © 825
Welon; RMC Place; JACKSON; ***220** I-9; pop. incl. with Altus (Inc. Place)
Welty; RMC Place; OKFUSKEE; **221** F-16; elev. 721ft./220m.; 🅿; z 74833; ● 120
West Nichols Hills; RMC Place; OKLAHOMA; ★ **O.C.**; mail Oklahoma City z 73116; pop. incl. with Oklahoma City (Inc. Place)
West Peavine; CDP-Census Area Only; ADAIR; ***221** E-20; © 225
Westport; Inc. Place; PAWNEE; **221** D-16; ★ **TUL**; mail Cleveland z 74020; ℗ 326; © 264
Westside; RMC Place; MUSKOGEE; ★ **MSKOG**; mail Muskogee z 74401; pop. incl. with Muskogee (Inc. Place)
Westside; RMC Place; OKLAHOMA; ★ **O.C.**; mail Oklahoma City z 73108, z 73127-28; pop. incl. with Oklahoma City (Inc. Place)
West Siloam Springs; Inc. Place; DELAWARE; **221** D-20; elev. 1,138ft./347m.; mail Siloam Springs z 72761; ℗ 539; © 877
West Tulsa; RMC Place; TULSA; ***221** D-17; ★ **TUL**; mail Tulsa z 74107, z 74131-32, z 74157; pop. incl. with Tulsa (Inc. Place)
Westville; Inc. Place; ADAIR; **221** E-20; elev. 1,139ft./347m.; 🅿; z 74965; ℗ 1,374; © 1,596
Wetumka; Inc. Place; HUGHES; **221** G-16; 🅿 🅷; z 74883; ℗ 1,427; © 1,451
Wewoka; Inc. Place; ⊡ SEMINOLE, HUGHES; **221** G-15; elev. 810ft./247m.; 🅿; z 74884; location of Indian Agency; ℗ 4,050; © 3,562
Wheatland; RMC Place; OKLAHOMA; **220** M-2; 🅿; ★ **O.C.**; z 73097; pop. incl. with Oklahoma City (Inc. Place)
Wheeless; RMC Place; CIMARRON; ***220** B-1; elev. 4,672ft./1,424m.; mail Boise City z 73933; rural
Whippoorwill; RMC Place; OSAGE; ***221** B-16; mail Pawhuska z 74056; ● 100
Whispering Creek; RMC Place; TULSA; ***221** D-16; ★ **TUL**; mail Sand Springs z 74063; pop. incl. with Sand Springs (Inc. Place)
White Bead; RMC Place; GARVIN; ***221** H-14; elev. 1,007ft./307m.; mail Pauls Valley z 73075; ● 70
White Eagle; RMC Place; KAY; **221** C-14; elev. 949ft./289m.; mail Ponca City z 74601; ● 100
Whitefield; Inc. Place; HASKELL; **221** G-18; 🅿; z 74472; ℗ 253; © 231
White Oak; RMC Place; CHEROKEE; ***221** E-19; elev. 769ft./234m.; mail Park Hill z 74451; rural
White Oak; RMC Place; CRAIG; **221** C-18; 🅿; z 74301; ● 100
Whitesboro; RMC Place; LE FLORE; **221** H-19; elev. 696ft./212m.; 🅿; z 74577; ● 220
Whittier; RMC Place; TULSA; ★ **TUL**; mail Tulsa z 74120, z 74150; pop. incl. with Tulsa (Inc. Place)
Wichita Mountains Estates; RMC Place; COMANCHE; ***221** H-11; mail Lawton z 73501; ● 600
Wickliffe; CDP-Census Area Only; MAYES; ***221** D-19; © 99
Wilburton; Inc. Place; ⊡ LATIMER; **221** H-18; elev. 660ft./201m.; 🅿 🅷; z 74578; ℗ 3,092; © 2,972
Wildcat Point; RMC Place; CHEROKEE; ***221** E-19; mail Park Hill z 74451; ● 150
Wild Horse; RMC Place; OSAGE; mail Skiatook z 74070; rural
Williams; RMC Place; LE FLORE; **221** G-20; mail Cameron z 74932; ● 120
Willis; RMC Place; MARSHALL; ***221** K-15; elev. 651ft./198m.; mail Kingston z 73439; rural
Willow; Inc. Place; GREER; **220** G-8; 🅿; z 73673; ℗ 142; © 114
Willow Springs; RMC Place; OKLAHOMA; ★ **O.C.**; pop. incl. with Oklahoma City (Inc. Place)
Wilson; Inc. Place; CARTER; **221** J-13; elev. 927ft./283m.; 🅿; z 73463; ℗ 1,639; © 1,584
Wilson; RMC Place; OKMULGEE; ***221** F-16; mail Henryetta z 74437; ● 100
Winchester; Inc. Place; OKMULGEE; **221** E-17; mail Beggs z 74421; ℗ 301; © 424
Winganon; RMC Place; ROGERS; ***221** C-17; elev. 669ft./204m.; mail Chelsea z 74016; rural
Wirt; RMC Place; CARTER; **221** J-13; mail Healdton z 73438; pop. incl. with Healdton (Inc. Place)
Wister; Inc. Place; LE FLORE; **221** H-20; elev. 497ft./151m.; 🅿; z 74966; ℗ 956; © 1,002
Wolco; RMC Place; OSAGE; **221** C-16; mail Barnsdall z 74002; ● 30
Wolf (Dewright); RMC Place; SEMINOLE; **221** G-15; elev. 922ft./281m.; mail Maud z 74854; ● 100
Woodall; CDP-Census Area Only; CHEROKEE; ***221** E-19; © 741
Woodford; RMC Place; CARTER; **221** I-14; mail Springer z 73458; ● 50
Woodland View; RMC Place; TULSA; ★ **TUL**; mail Tulsa z 74145; pop. incl. with Tulsa (Inc. Place)
Woodlawn Park; Inc. Place; OKLAHOMA; **220** K-2; ★ **O.C.**; mail Bethany z 73008; ℗ 170; © 161
Woods; RMC Place; OKLAHOMA; ***221** F-14; elev. 1,212ft./369m.; ★ **O.C.**; mail Choctaw z 73020; pop. incl. with Choctaw (Inc. Place)
WOODS; **220** C-10; ℗ 9,103; © 9,089; ◆ 8,636
Woodville; MARSHALL; see New Woodville (RMC Place)
Woodward; Inc. Place; ⊡ WOODWARD; **220** D-9; elev. 1,910ft./582m.; 🅿 🅷 ■; z 73801-02; ℗ 12,340; © 11,853; ◆ 13,202
WOODWARD; **220** C-9; ℗ 18,976; © 18,486; ◆ 20,844
Woody Chapel; RMC Place; MCCLAIN; ***221** H-13; mail Purcell z 73080; ● 70
Wright City; Inc. Place; MCCURTAIN; **221** J-19; elev. 399ft./122m.; 🅿; z 74766; ℗ 836; © 848
Wyandotte; Inc. Place; OTTAWA; **221** B-19; elev. 761ft./232m.; 🅿; z 74370; ℗ 366; © 363
Wybark; RMC Place; MUSKOGEE, WAGONER; ***221** E-18; ★ **MSKOG**; mail Muskogee z 74401, z 74403; rural
Wye; POTTAWATOMIE; see Chisney (RMC Place)
Wynnewood; Inc. Place; GARVIN; **221** I-14; elev. 896ft./273m.; 🅿; z 73098; ℗ 2,451; © 2,367
Wynona; Inc. Place; OSAGE; **221** C-16; located on Osage Ind. Res.; 🅿; z 74084; ℗ 531; © 531

Y

Yale; Inc. Place; PAYNE; **221** D-15; elev. 814ft./248m.; 🅿; z 74085; ℗ 1,392; © 1,342
Yanush; RMC Place; LATIMER; **221** H-18; elev. 625ft./191m.; mail Tuskahoma z 74574; ● 60
Yarnaby; RMC Place; BRYAN; ***221** K-16; 🅿; z 74741
Yeager; Inc. Place; HUGHES; **221** G-16; elev. 790ft./241m.; mail Holdenville z 74848; ℗ 40; © 67
Yewed; RMC Place; ALFALFA; ***221** C-11; mail Cherokee z 73728; rural
Yost Lake; RMC Place; PAYNE; ***221** D-14; mail Glencoe z 74032; summer pop. 300; ● 10
Yuba; RMC Place; BRYAN; **221** K-16; mail Hendrix z 74741; ● 60
Yukon; Inc. Place; CANADIAN; **220** J-1; 🅿; ★ **O.C.**; z 73085, z 73099; ℗ 20,935; © 21,043; ◆ 22,543

Z

Zafra; RMC Place; LE FLORE; ***221** I-20; mail Smithville z 74957; rural
Zaneis; RMC Place; CARTER; ***221** J-13; mail Wilson z 73463; rural
Zeb; CDP; CHEROKEE; ***221** E-19; mail Tahlequah z 74464; © 498
Zena; CDP; DELAWARE; ***221** C-19; elev. 943ft./287m.; mail Jay z 74346; © 123
Zincville; RMC Place; OTTAWA; ***221** B-19; mail Quapaw z 74363; rural
Zion; CDP; ADAIR; ***221** E-20; mail Stilwell z 74960; © 48
Zoe; RMC Place; LE FLORE; ***221** H-20; mail Hodgen z 74939; rural

OREGON

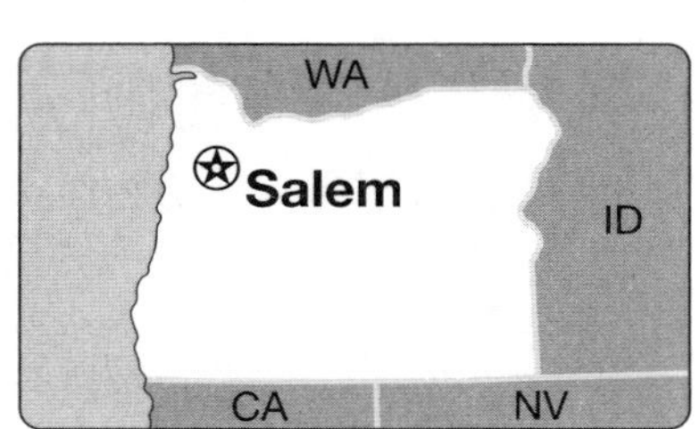

Statistics

Total area (2000) — 98,381 square miles
Land area (2000) — 95,997 square miles
Water area (2000) — 2,384 square miles
Capital — Salem
Admitted as state — February, 1859

Maps

State maps can be found on pages 142-254 in Vol. 1

Ranally Metro Areas (RMAs) and Abbreviations

Corvallis-Albany, OR — CORV-
Eugene, OR — EUG
Longview, WA-OR — LNGV
Medford, OR — MEDF
Portland, OR-WA — POR
Salem, OR — SAL
Walla Walla, WA-OR — WALL

Principal Places

Place Name	Place Type	County	Population
Portland	Inc. Place	MULTNOMAH	◆ 599,642
Eugene	Inc. Place	LANE	◆ 162,084
Salem	Inc. Place	MARION	◆ 153,142
Gresham	Inc. Place	MULTNOMAH	◆ 105,809
Hillsboro	Inc. Place	WASHINGTON	◆ 97,243
Beaverton	Inc. Place	WASHINGTON	◆ 93,873
Bend	Inc. Place	DESCHUTES	◆ 91,597
Medford	Inc. Place	JACKSON	◆ 72,910
Springfield	Inc. Place	LANE	◆ 59,983
Corvallis	Inc. Place	BENTON	◆ 56,396
Tigard	Inc. Place	WASHINGTON	◆ 48,681
Albany	Inc. Place	LINN	◆ 48,667
Aloha	CDP	WASHINGTON	◆ 46,533
Keizer	Inc. Place	MARION	◆ 37,268
Lake Oswego	Inc. Place	CLACKAMAS	◆ 37,107
McMinnville	Inc. Place	YAMHILL	◆ 32,053
Oregon City	Inc. Place	CLACKAMAS	◆ 31,896
Grants Pass	Inc. Place	JOSEPHINE	◆ 29,222
Tualatin	Inc. Place	WASHINGTON	◆ 26,522
West Linn	Inc. Place	CLACKAMAS	◆ 25,105
Woodburn	Inc. Place	MARION	◆ 23,570
Newberg	Inc. Place	YAMHILL	◆ 23,116
Redmond	Inc. Place	DESCHUTES	◆ 22,577
Forest Grove	Inc. Place	WASHINGTON	◆ 21,826
Milwaukie	Inc. Place	CLACKAMAS	◆ 21,452
Ashland	Inc. Place	JACKSON	◆ 21,136
Roseburg	Inc. Place	DOUGLAS	◆ 20,059
Altamont	CDP	KLAMATH	© 19,603
Hayesville	CDP	MARION	© 18,222
Klamath Falls	Inc. Place	KLAMATH	◆ 17,989
Pendleton	Inc. Place	UMATILLA	◆ 16,764

Place Name	Place Type	County	Population
Oatfield	CDP-Census Area Only	CLACKAMAS	© 15,750
Coos Bay	Inc. Place	COOS	◆ 15,284
Wilsonville	Inc. Place	CLACKAMAS	© 13,991
Four Corners	CDP	MARION	© 13,922
Troutdale	Inc. Place	MULTNOMAH	© 13,777
Hermiston	Inc. Place	UMATILLA	© 13,154
Lebanon	Inc. Place	LINN	© 12,950
Santa Clara	RMC Place	LANE	Ⓟ 12,834
Oak Grove	CDP	CLACKAMAS	© 12,808
Canby	Inc. Place	CLACKAMAS	© 12,790
Cedar Mill	CDP	WASHINGTON	© 12,597
Central Point	Inc. Place	JACKSON	© 12,493
Dallas	Inc. Place	POLK	© 12,459
La Grande	Inc. Place	UNION	© 12,327
The Dalles	Inc. Place	WASCO	◆ 12,271
Sherwood	Inc. Place	WASHINGTON	© 11,791
Gladstone	Inc. Place	CLACKAMAS	© 11,438
Ontario	Inc. Place	MALHEUR	◆ 10,048
Saint Helens	Inc. Place	COLUMBIA	© 10,019
Baker City	Inc. Place	BAKER	© 9,860
Astoria	Inc. Place	CLATSOP	© 9,813
Cornelius	Inc. Place	WASHINGTON	© 9,652
Newport	Inc. Place	LINCOLN	© 9,532
River Road	RMC Place	LANE	Ⓟ 9,443
Rockcreek	CDP-Census Area Only	WASHINGTON	© 9,404
North Bend	Inc. Place	COOS	◆ 9,298
Oak Hills	CDP-Census Area Only	WASHINGTON	© 9,050
Cedar Hills	CDP	WASHINGTON	© 8,949
Cottage Grove	Inc. Place	LANE	© 8,445
Sweet Home	Inc. Place	LINN	© 8,016
Monmouth	Inc. Place	POLK	© 7,741

Place Name	Place Type	County	Population
Fairview	Inc. Place	MULTNOMAH	© 7,561
Lincoln City	Inc. Place	LINCOLN	© 7,437
Silverton	Inc. Place	MARION	© 7,414
Prineville	Inc. Place	CROOK	® 7,358
Florence	Inc. Place	LANE	© 7,263
West Haven-Sylvan	CDP-Census Area Only	WASHINGTON	© 7,147
Jennings Lodge	CDP	CLACKAMAS	© 7,036
Garden Home-Whitford	CDP-Census Area Only	WASHINGTON	© 6,931
Stayton	Inc. Place	MARION	© 6,816
Sunnyside	CDP	CLACKAMAS	© 6,791
Sutherlin	Inc. Place	DOUGLAS	© 6,669
Milton-Freewater	Inc. Place	UMATILLA	© 6,470
West Slope	CDP	WASHINGTON	© 6,442
White City	CDP	JACKSON	® 6,199
Green	CDP	DOUGLAS	© 6,174
Independence	Inc. Place	POLK	© 6,035
Seaside	Inc. Place	CLATSOP	© 5,900
Raleigh Hills	CDP	WASHINGTON	© 5,865
Redwood	CDP-Census Area Only	JOSEPHINE	© 5,844
Hood River	Inc. Place	HOOD RIVER	© 5,831
La Pine	CDP-Census Area Only	DESCHUTES	© 5,799
Molalla	Inc. Place	CLACKAMAS	© 5,647
Talent	Inc. Place	JACKSON	© 5,589
Sheridan	Inc. Place	YAMHILL	® 5,561
Roseburg North	CDP-Census Area Only	DOUGLAS	© 5,473
Brookings	Inc. Place	CURRY	© 5,447
Sandy	Inc. Place	CLACKAMAS	© 5,385
Clackamas	CDP	CLACKAMAS	© 5,177
Madras	Inc. Place	JEFFERSON	© 5,078

County Business Data

County	FIPS Code	County Seat	Land Area (Sq. Mi.)	Census Population			Wholesale Trade		Manufacturing, 2002			
				4/1/2000	4/1/1990	% Change 1990-2000	Sales, 2002 ($1,000)	% Change 1997-2002	Establish-ments	Total Employees	Value Added ($1,000)	Ranally Mfg. Units
Baker	001	Baker City	3,068	16,741	15,317	9.3	13,260	0.2	22	560	44,437	24
Benton	003	Corvallis	676	78,153	70,811	10.4	50,392	-55.3	103	5,963	270,924	143
Clackamas	005	Oregon City	1,868	338,391	278,850	21.4	7,427,471	16.4	588	17,809	2,036,297	1,077
Clatsop	007	Astoria	827	35,630	33,301	7.0	74,667	-15.5	48	840	62,620	33
Columbia	009	St. Helens	657	43,560	37,557	16.0	(d)	(d)	51	2,855	510,945	270
Coos	011	Coquille	1,600	62,779	60,273	4.2	210,720	-9.6	76	1,534	116,405	62
Crook	013	Prineville	2,979	19,182	14,111	35.9	58,711	172.8	26	1,393	84,028	44
Curry	015	Gold Beach	1,627	21,137	19,327	9.4	(d)	(d)	29	640	42,566	23
Deschutes	017	Bend	3,018	115,367	74,958	53.9	696,217	21.9	245	5,053	365,085	193
Douglas	019	Roseburg	5,037	100,399	94,649	6.1	455,173	12.6	139	6,070	417,251	221
Gilliam	021	Condon	1,204	1,915	1,717	11.5	(d)	(d)	...	(d)	(d)	...
Grant	023	Canyon City	4,529	7,935	7,853	1.0	5,741	-2.2	...	(d)	(d)	...
Harney	025	Burns	10,134	7,609	7,060	7.8	(d)	(d)	...	(d)	(d)	...
Hood River	027	Hood River	522	20,411	16,903	20.8	128,237	39.1	54	(d)	(d)	...
Jackson	029	Medford	2,785	181,269	146,389	23.8	819,832	-19.8	310	6,552	811,621	429
Jefferson	031	Madras	1,781	19,009	13,676	39.0	61,650	-20.9	22	1,699	60,392	32
Josephine	033	Grants Pass	1,640	75,726	62,649	20.9	237,419	35.2	133	2,831	199,997	106
Klamath	035	Klamath Falls	5,944	63,775	57,702	10.5	212,970	-27.3	71	2,500	293,640	155
Lake	037	Lakeview	8,136	7,422	7,186	3.3	19,746	(d)	...	(d)	(d)	...
Lane	039	Eugene	4,554	322,959	282,912	14.2	2,519,279	0.8	612	19,296	2,393,189	1,266
Lincoln	041	Newport	980	44,479	38,889	14.4	51,517	-29.0	56	949	194,619	103
Linn	043	Albany	2,292	103,069	91,227	13.0	738,430	-3.6	182	8,328	953,390	504
Malheur	045	Vale	9,887	31,615	26,038	21.4	(d)	(d)	28	(d)	(d)	...
Marion	047	Salem	1,184	284,834	228,483	24.7	1,727,477	45.9	378	11,388	1,173,708	621
Morrow	049	Heppner	2,032	10,995	7,625	44.2	63,651	-38.2	8	(d)	(d)	...
Multnomah	051	Portland	435	660,486	583,887	13.1	24,753,892	-1.7	1,220	36,442	4,015,118	2,124
Polk	053	Dallas	741	62,380	49,541	25.9	63,650	-27.1	60	1,812	137,642	73
Sherman	055	Moro	823	1,934	1,918	0.8	5,059	(d)	...	(d)	(d)	...
Tillamook	057	Tillamook	1,102	24,262	21,570	12.5	27,411	45.6	22	1,298	151,736	80
Umatilla	059	Pendleton	3,215	70,548	59,249	19.1	316,460	-4.6	76	(d)	(d)	...
Union	061	La Grande	2,037	24,530	23,598	3.9	95,326	-0.9	31	1,366	97,439	52
Wallowa	063	Enterprise	3,145	7,226	6,911	4.6	(d)	(d)	...	(d)	(d)	...
Wasco	065	The Dalles	2,381	23,791	21,683	9.7	97,104	-16.1	...	(d)	(d)	...
Washington	067	Hillsboro	724	445,342	311,554	42.9	15,387,986	17.0	763	33,506	10,436,863	5,522
Wheeler	069	Fossil	1,715	1,547	1,396	10.8	(d)	(d)	...	(d)	(d)	...
Yamhill	071	McMinnville	716	84,992	65,551	29.7	(d)	(d)	177	5,438	578,773	306
The State			**95,997**	**3,421,399**	**2,842,321**	**20.4**	**56,855,958**	**5.9**	**5,597**	**184,151**	**26,440,699**	**13,989**

(d) Data not available. Corresponding percentages or Ranally Manufacturing Units are estimates.
... Represents 0 or amount too minimal to be reported.

Index of Places and Counties

Entries in **UPPERCASE** are counties.
Entries in **bold** have populations of 2,500 or more.
Names in parentheses are alternate names.

Inc. Place	Incorporated Place
RMC Place	Rand McNally Designated Place
CDP	Census Designated Place
MCD	Minor Civil Division
⊡	County Seat
▲	Minor Civil Division
elev.	Elevation
[P]	Post Office
[H]	Hospital
[C]	College
■	Principal Business Center
★	Ranally Metro Area (RMA) Abbreviation
z	Zip Code(s)
Ⓟ	Previous Census Population
®	Revised Census Population
Ⓐ	Annexation Population
●	Rand McNally Population Estimate
©	Final Census Population
Ⓢ	Special Census Population
◆	Estimated Population

For additional definitions see Glossary, Volume 1, and Introduction, Volume 2.

Canby; Inc. Place; CLACKAMAS; **222** D-5; elev. 153ft./47m.; 🅿; ★ **POR**; **z** 97013; Ⓟ 8,983; © 12,790
Canemah; RMC Place; CLACKAMAS; ***222** D-5; ★ **POR**; mail Oregon City **z** 97045; pop. incl. with Oregon City (Inc. Place)
Cannon Beach; Inc. Place; CLATSOP; **222** B-2; 🅿; **z** 97110 & mail Arch Cape **z** 97102; Ⓟ 1,221; © 1,588
Cannon Beach Junction; RMC Place; CLATSOP; ***222** B-2; elev. 44ft./13m.; mail Seaside **z** 97138
Canyon City; Inc. Place; ⊡ GRANT; **223** G-12; elev. 3,198ft./975m.; 🅿; **z** 97820; Ⓟ 648; © 669
Canyonville; Inc. Place; DOUGLAS; **222** K-3; elev. 785ft./239m.; 🅿; **z** 97417; Ⓟ 1,219; © 1,293
Cape Meares; CDP; TILLAMOOK; **222** C-2; elev. 10ft./3m.; mail Tillamook **z** 97141; © 110
Capitol Hill; RMC Place; MULTNOMAH; **223** L-19; elev. 474ft./144m.; ★ **POR**; mail Portland **z** 97219; pop. incl. with Portland (Inc. Place)
Carlton; Inc. Place; YAMHILL; **222** D-4; 🅿; **z** 97111; Ⓟ 1,289; © 1,514
Carnation; RMC Place; WASHINGTON; ***222** C-4; ★ **POR**; mail Forest Grove **z** 97116; pop. incl. with Forest Grove (Inc. Place)
Carpenterville; RMC Place; CURRY; ***222** M-1; mail Brookings **z** 97415; ● 30
Carson; RMC Place; BAKER; ***223** E-16; elev. 3,341ft./1,018m.; mail Halfway **z** 97834; ● 30
Carus; RMC Place; CLACKAMAS; ***222** D-5; elev. 508ft./155m.; ★ **POR**; mail Oregon City **z** 97045
Carver; RMC Place; CLACKAMAS; **223** M-20; ★ **POR**; mail Clackamas **z** 97015; ● 480
Cascade Gorge; RMC Place; JACKSON; ***222** L-5; mail Prospect **z** 97536, Trail **z** 97541
Cascade Locks; Inc. Place; HOOD RIVER; **222** C-6; 🅿; **z** 97014; Ⓟ 930; © 1,115
Cascade Summit; RMC Place; KLAMATH; **222** I-6; elev. 4,841ft./1,476m.; ● 100
Cascadia; RMC Place; LINN; **222** G-5; elev. 846ft./258m.; 🅿; **z** 97329; ● 240
Cave Junction; Inc. Place; JOSEPHINE; **222** M-2; elev. 1,295ft./395m.; 🅿; **z** 97523, **z** 97531; Ⓟ 1,126; © 1,363
Cayuse; CDP; UMATILLA; **223** C-13; 🅿; **z** 97801; © 59
Cecil; RMC Place; MORROW; ***222** C-10; mail Ione **z** 97843
Cedar Dale; RMC Place; CLACKAMAS; ***222** D-5; ★ **POR**; mail Molalla **z** 97038; ● 30
Cedar Hills; CDP; WASHINGTON; **223** L-17; ★ **POR**; mail Portland **z** 97225; Ⓟ 9,294; © 8,949
Cedarhurst Park; RMC Place; CLACKAMAS; ***222** D-5; ★ **POR**; mail Estacada **z** 97023; ● 120
Cedar Mill; CDP; WASHINGTON; ***222** C-4; elev. 274ft./84m.; ★ **POR**; mail Portland **z** 97229, **z** 97291; Ⓟ 9,697; © 12,597
Celilo; RMC Place; WASCO; **222** C-8; mail The Dalles **z** 97058; ● 80
Celilo Village; Indian Reservation; WASCO; © 44
Central; RMC Place; MULTNOMAH; ★ **POR**; mail Portland **z** 97204, **z** 97240; pop. incl. with Portland (Inc. Place)
Central Point; RMC Place; CLACKAMAS; ***222** D-5; ★ **POR**; mail Oregon City **z** 97045
Central Point; Inc. Place; JACKSON; **222** M-4; elev. 1,278ft./390m.; 🅿; ★ **MEDF**; **z** 97502; Ⓟ 7,509; © 12,493
Central Point West; RMC Place; JACKSON; 1 mi. SW of Central Point; ★ **MEDF**; mail Central Point **z** 97502; ● 1,500
Chapman; RMC Place; COLUMBIA; ***222** B-4; mail Scappoose **z** 97056; ● 30
Charleston; RMC Place; COOS; **222** J-1; 🅿; **z** 97420; ● 700
Charlestown; RMC Place; UMATILLA; ***223** B-12; mail Hermiston **z** 97838; rural
Chemult; RMC Place; KLAMATH; **222** J-6; 🅿; **z** 97731; ● 270
Chenoweth; CDP; WASCO; **222** C-8; mail The Dalles **z** 97058; Ⓟ 3,246; © 3,412
Cherry Grove; RMC Place; WASHINGTON; **222** C-4; elev. 260ft./79m.; ★ **POR**; mail Gaston **z** 97119; ● 300
Cherry Heights; RMC Place; WASCO; ***222** C-8; mail The Dalles **z** 97058; rural
Cherryville; RMC Place; CLACKAMAS; ***222** D-6; elev. 223ft./68m.; mail Sandy **z** 97055; rural
Cheshire; RMC Place; LANE; **222** G-3; 🅿; ★ **EUG**; **z** 97419; ● 350
Chiloquin; Inc. Place; KLAMATH; **222** L-6; elev. 4,179ft./1,274m.; 🅿; **z** 97624, **z** 97639 & mail Crater Lake **z** 97604; Ⓟ 673; © 716
Chitwood; RMC Place; LINCOLN; ***222** F-2; mail Toledo **z** 97391; rural
Christmas Valley; RMC Place; LAKE; **222** J-9; 🅿; **z** 97641; ● 300
Chutes; RMC Place; MULTNOMAH; ***222** C-5; mail Portland **z** 97202; pop. incl. with Portland (Inc. Place)
City of the Dalles; WASCO; see The Dalles (Inc. Place)
Clackamas; CDP; CLACKAMAS; **223** M-20; elev. 151ft./46m.; 🅿 🅷; ★ **POR**; **z** 97015, **z** 97086; Ⓟ 2,578; © 5,177
CLACKAMAS; **222** E-5; Ⓟ 278,850; © 338,391; ◆ 379,594
Clackamas Heights; RMC Place; CLACKAMAS; ***222** D-5; ★ **POR**; mail Oregon City **z** 97045; pop. incl. with Oregon City (Inc. Place)
Clarkes; RMC Place; CLACKAMAS; ***222** D-5; elev. 891ft./272m.; ★ **POR**; mail Beavercreek **z** 97004; rural
Clarno; RMC Place; WASCO, WHEELER; ***222** E-9; mail Antelope **z** 97001, Fossil **z** 97830; rural
Clatskanie; Inc. Place; COLUMBIA; **222** B-4; elev. 33ft./10m.; 🅿; **z** 97016; Ⓟ 1,629; © 1,528
Clatskanie Heights; RMC Place; COLUMBIA; ***222** B-4; mail Clatskanie **z** 97016; rural
CLATSOP; **222** B-3; Ⓟ 33,301; © 35,630; ◆ 37,974
Clear Lake; RMC Place; MARION; ***222** E-4; elev. 182ft./55m.; ★ **SAL**; mail Salem **z** 97303; pop. incl. with Keizer (Inc. Place)
Clearwater; RMC Place; DOUGLAS; ***222** J-5; mail Idleyld Park **z** 97447; rural
Clifton; RMC Place; CLATSOP; ***222** A-3; elev. 15ft./5m.; mail Clatskanie **z** 97016; rural
Cloverdale; RMC Place; DESCHUTES; ***222** G-7; elev. 3,086ft./941m.; mail Redmond **z** 97756; rural
Cloverdale; RMC Place; LANE; ***222** H-4; ★ **EUG**; mail Creswell **z** 97426; rural
Cloverdale; CDP; TILLAMOOK; **222** D-2; elev. 26ft./8m.; 🅿; **z** 97112; © 242
Clow Corner; RMC Place; POLK; ***222** E-3; ★ **SAL**; mail Dallas **z** 97338; rural
Coaledo; RMC Place; COOS; ***222** J-1; elev. 17ft./5m.; mail Coos Bay **z** 97420; rural
Coburg; Inc. Place; LANE; **222** G-4; elev. 400ft./122m.; 🅿; **z** 97408; Ⓟ 763; © 969
Cold Springs Junction; RMC Place; UMATILLA; ***223** B-12; mail Hermiston **z** 97838; rural
College Hill; RMC Place; LANE; ***222** H-4; ★ **EUG**; mail Eugene **z** 97405; pop. incl. with Eugene (Inc. Place)
Colton; RMC Place; CLACKAMAS; **222** D-5; elev. 707ft./215m.; 🅿; **z** 97017; ● 600
COLUMBIA; **222** B-4; Ⓟ 37,557; © 43,560; ◆ 50,232
Columbia City; Inc. Place; COLUMBIA; **222** B-4; elev. 24ft./7m.; 🅿; **z** 97018; Ⓟ 1,003; © 1,571
Concord; RMC Place; CLACKAMAS; ***222** D-5; ★ **POR**; mail Portland **z** 97222; ● 4,000
Condon; Inc. Place; ⊡ GILLIAM; **222** D-10; elev. 2,844ft./867m.; 🅿; **z** 97823; Ⓟ 635; © 759
Cook; RMC Place; CLACKAMAS; ***222** D-5; ★ **POR**; mail Lake Oswego **z** 97034; pop. incl. with Lake Oswego (Inc. Place)
COOS; **222** J-2; Ⓟ 60,273; © 62,779; Ⓡ 62,788; ◆ 62,867
Coos Bay; Inc. Place; COOS; **222** J-1; elev. 11ft./3m.; 🅿 🅷 ■; **z** 97420; Ⓟ 15,076; © 15,374; Ⓡ 15,372; ◆ 15,284
Cooston; RMC Place; COOS; ***222** I-1; mail North Bend **z** 97459; ● 90
Cooswer Umpquad Siuslaw Reservation; Indian Reservation; CURRY, COOS; © 11
Coquille; Inc. Place; ⊡ COOS; **222** J-1; elev. 50ft./15m.; 🅿 🅷; **z** 97423; Ⓟ 4,121; © 4,184
Coquille Reservation; Indian Reservation; © 258
Corbelt Station; RMC Place; MULTNOMAH; ***222** C-5; mail Corbett **z** 97019; rural
Corbett; RMC Place; MULTNOMAH; ***222** C-5; 🅿; ★ **POR**; **z** 97019; ● 460
Cornelius; Inc. Place; WASHINGTON; **222** C-4; elev. 179ft./55m.; 🅿; ★ **POR**; **z** 97113, **z** 97123; Ⓟ 6,148; © 9,652
Cornelius Pass; RMC Place; MULTNOMAH; ***222** C-4; mail Portland **z** 97231; rural
Coronado Shores; RMC Place; LINCOLN; ***222** E-2; mail Gleneden Beach **z** 97388
Corvallis; Inc. Place; ⊡ BENTON; **222** F-3; elev. 225ft./69m.; 🅿 🅷 🅲 19,362 ■; ★ **CORV-**; **z** 97330-31, **z** 97333, **z** 97339; Ⓟ 44,757; © 49,322; ◆ 56,396
Cottage Grove; Inc. Place; LANE; **222** H-4; elev. 641ft./195m.; 🅿 🅷; ★ **EUG**; **z** 97424; Ⓟ 7,402; © 8,445
Cottrell; RMC Place; CLACKAMAS; ***222** C-5; ★ **POR**; mail Boring **z** 97009; ● 50
Council Crest; RMC Place; MULTNOMAH; ***222** C-5; ★ **POR**; mail Portland **z** 97201; pop. incl. with Portland (Inc. Place)
Courtrock; RMC Place; GRANT; ***223** F-12; mail Monument **z** 97864; rural
Cove; Inc. Place; UNION; **223** D-15; 🅿; **z** 97824; Ⓟ 507; © 594
Cove Orchard; RMC Place; YAMHILL; ***222** D-4; mail Yamhill **z** 97148; ● 130
Cow Creek Reservation; Indian Reservation; DOUGLAS; © 22
Crabtree; RMC Place; LINN; **222** F-4; elev. 276ft./84m.; 🅿; **z** 97335; ● 300
Crane; RMC Place; HARNEY; **223** I-13; elev. 4,136ft./1,261m.; 🅿; **z** 97732; ● 160
Crater-Diamond Lake Junction; KLAMATH; see Diamond Lake Junction (RMC Place)
Crawfordsville; RMC Place; LINN; **222** G-4; elev. 461ft./141m.; 🅿; **z** 97336; ● 300
Crescent; RMC Place; KLAMATH; **222** I-7; elev. 4,455ft./1,358m.; 🅿; **z** 97733; ● 770
Crescent Lake; RMC Place; KLAMATH; **222** I-6; elev. 4,775ft./1,455m.; summer pop. 250; ● 150
Crescent Lake Junction; RMC Place; KLAMATH; ***222** I-6; elev. 4,763ft./1,452m.; rural
Creston; RMC Place; MULTNOMAH; ★ **POR**; mail Portland **z** 97206, **z** 97286; pop. incl. with Portland (Inc. Place)
Creswell; Inc. Place; LANE; **222** H-4; elev. 547ft./167m.; 🅿; ★ **EUG**; **z** 97426; Ⓟ 2,431; © 3,579
CROOK; **222** G-9; Ⓟ 14,111; © 19,182; Ⓡ 19,184; ◆ 23,530
Crooked River Ranch; RMC Place; JEFFERSON; ***222** G-8; 🅿; **z** 97760; ● 100
Crow; RMC Place; LANE; **222** H-3; elev. 546ft./166m.; mail Eugene **z** 97401, **z** 97405; ● 100
Crowfoot; RMC Place; LINN; ***222** F-4; mail Lebanon **z** 97355
Culp Creek; RMC Place; LANE; **222** I-4; elev. 969ft./295m.; 🅿; **z** 97427; ● 220
Culver; Inc. Place; JEFFERSON; **222** F-8; elev. 2,636ft./803m.; 🅿; **z** 97734; Ⓟ 570; © 802
Currinsville; RMC Place; CLACKAMAS; ***222** D-5; ★ **POR**; mail Estacada **z** 97023
CURRY; **222** L-1; Ⓟ 19,327; © 21,137; ◆ 21,326
Curtin; RMC Place; DOUGLAS; **222** I-3; elev. 417ft./127m.; 🅿; **z** 97424; ● 270
Cutler City; RMC Place; LINCOLN; ***222** E-2; elev. 34ft./10m.; mail Lincoln City **z** 97367; pop. incl. with Lincoln City (Inc. Place)

D

Dairy; RMC Place; KLAMATH; **222** M-7; elev. 4,137ft./1,261m.; 🅿; **z** 97625; ● 70
Dale; RMC Place; GRANT; **223** E-12; 🅿; **z** 97880; ● 80
Daley; RMC Place; DESCHUTES; mail Bend **z** 97702; rural
Dallas; Inc. Place; ⊡ POLK; **222** E-3; elev. 326ft./99m.; 🅿 🅷; ★ **SAL**; **z** 97338; Ⓟ 9,422; © 12,459
Dalles City; RMC Place; WASCO; pop. incl. with The Dalles (Inc. Place)
Damascus; Inc. Place; CLACKAMAS; **223** M-20; elev. 527ft./161m.; 🅿; ★ **POR**; **z** 97009, **z** 97015, **z** 97089, **z** 97236; incorporated November 2, 2004; not reported in 2000 Census; ● 730
Damascus Heights; RMC Place; CLACKAMAS; ***222** D-5; ★ **POR**; mail Boring **z** 97009; ● 180
Danebo; RMC Place; LANE; ***222** H-4; ★ **EUG**; mail Eugene **z** 97402; pop. incl. with Eugene (Inc. Place)
Danner; RMC Place; MALHEUR; ***223** K-16; mail Jordan Valley **z** 97910; rural
Days Creek; RMC Place; DOUGLAS; **222** K-3; elev. 764ft./233m.; 🅿; **z** 97429; ● 430
Dayton; Inc. Place; YAMHILL; **222** D-4; 🅿; **z** 97114; Ⓟ 1,526; © 2,119
Dayville; Inc. Place; GRANT; **223** F-11; 🅿; **z** 97825; Ⓟ 144; © 138
Deadwood; RMC Place; LANE; **222** G-2; 🅿; **z** 97430; ● 200
Dee; RMC Place; HOOD RIVER; **222** C-7; mail Hood River **z** 97031; ● 200
Deer Island; RMC Place; COLUMBIA; **222** B-4; 🅿; **z** 97054; ● 300
De Lake; RMC Place; LINCOLN; ***222** E-2; elev. 61ft./19m.; mail Lincoln City **z** 97367; pop. incl. with Lincoln City (Inc. Place)
Delena; RMC Place; COLUMBIA; ***222** B-4; elev. 450ft./137m.; mail Clatskanie **z** 97016; rural
Dellmoor; RMC Place; CLATSOP; ***222** B-2; mail Warrenton **z** 97146; rural
Dellwood; RMC Place; COOS; **222** J-2; elev. 42ft./13m.; mail Coos Bay **z** 97420; ● 50
DeMoss Springs; RMC Place; SHERMAN; ***222** C-9; mail Moro **z** 97039; rural
Denmark; RMC Place; CURRY; **222** K-1; elev. 98ft./30m.; mail Langlois **z** 97450; rural
Depoe Bay; Inc. Place; LINCOLN; **222** E-2; elev. 58ft./18m.; 🅿; **z** 97341; Ⓟ 870; © 1,174
DESCHUTES; **222** H-7; Ⓟ 74,958; © 115,367; ◆ 163,509
Deschutes Junction; RMC Place; DESCHUTES; ***222** G-8; elev. 3,261ft./994m.; mail Bend **z** 97701; rural
Deschutes River Woods; CDP-Census Area Only; DESCHUTES; ***222** H-7; mail Bend **z** 97701; Ⓟ 2,373; © 4,631
Detroit; Inc. Place; MARION; **222** F-6; 🅿; **z** 97342; Ⓟ 331; © 262
Dever; RMC Place; LINN; ***222** F-4; mail Albany **z** 97321; rural
Dew Valley; RMC Place; COOS; ***222** J-1; elev. 92ft./28m.; mail Bandon **z** 97411; rural
Dexter; RMC Place; LANE; **222** H-4; elev. 667ft./203m.; 🅿; ★ **EUG**; **z** 97431; ● 300
Diamond; RMC Place; HARNEY; **223** K-13; 🅿; **z** 97722; ● 70
Diamond Lake; RMC Place; DOUGLAS; ***222** J-6; 🅿; **z** 97731; summer pop. 400; ● 110
Diamond Lake Junction (Crater-Diamond Lake Junction); RMC Place; KLAMATH; **222** J-6; elev. 4,609ft./1,405m.; mail Chemult **z** 97731; ● 40
Dickey Prairie; RMC Place; CLACKAMAS; ***222** D-5; elev. 436ft./133m.; ★ **POR**; mail Molalla **z** 97038; ● 30
Dillard; RMC Place; DOUGLAS; **222** J-3; 🅿; **z** 97432; ● 350
Dilley; RMC Place; WASHINGTON; **222** C-4; elev. 193ft./59m.; ★ **POR**; mail Forest Grove **z** 97116; ● 200
Disston; RMC Place; LANE
Dixie; RMC Place; BAKER; ***223** F-16; mail Huntington **z** 97907; rural
Dixonville; RMC Place; DOUGLAS; ***222** J-3; elev. 584ft./178m.; mail Roseburg **z** 97470; ● 100
Dodge; RMC Place; CLACKAMAS; ***222** D-5; elev. 1,378ft./420m.; mail Estacada **z** 97023; rural
Dodson; RMC Place; MULTNOMAH; ***222** C-6; mail Cascade Locks **z** 97014; ● 70
Dolph Corner; RMC Place; POLK; ***222** E-3; elev. 221ft./67m.; mail Dallas **z** 97338; rural
Donald; Inc. Place; MARION; **222** D-4; elev. 195ft./59m.; 🅿; ★ **POR**; **z** 97020; Ⓟ 316; © 608; Ⓡ 625
Dora; RMC Place; COOS; ***222** J-2; mail Myrtle Point **z** 97458; rural
Dorena; RMC Place; LANE; **222** H-4; elev. 911ft./278m.; 🅿; **z** 97434; ● 350
DOUGLAS; **222** J-3; Ⓟ 94,649; © 100,399; ◆ 101,963
Douglas Ridge; RMC Place; CLACKAMAS; ***222** D-5; ★ **POR**; mail Eagle Creek **z** 97022; rural
Dover; RMC Place; CLACKAMAS; ***222** D-6; elev. 1,317ft./401m.; mail Eagle Creek **z** 97022, Sandy **z** 97055; rural
Downing; RMC Place; COLUMBIA; ***222** A-4; ★ **LNGV**; mail Clatskanie **z** 97016; rural
Downs; RMC Place; MARION; ***222** E-4; mail Mount Angel **z** 97362; rural
Downtown; RMC Place; DESCHUTES; mail Bend **z** 97701, **z** 97709; pop. incl. with Bend (Inc. Place)
Drain; Inc. Place; DOUGLAS; **222** I-3; elev. 292ft./89m.; 🅿; **z** 97435; Ⓟ 1,011; © 1,021
Draperville; RMC Place; LINN; ***222** F-4; elev. 228ft./69m.; ★ **CORV-**; mail Albany **z** 97322; pop. incl. with Albany (Inc. Place)
Drew; RMC Place; DOUGLAS; ***222** K-4; elev. 1,345ft./410m.; mail Tiller **z** 97484
Drewsey; RMC Place; HARNEY; **223** H-14; elev. 3,516ft./1,072m.; 🅿; **z** 97904; ● 100
Dufur; Inc. Place; WASCO; **222** D-8; elev. 1,320ft./402m.; 🅿; **z** 97021; Ⓟ 527; © 588
Dukes Valley; RMC Place; HOOD RIVER; ***222** C-7; mail Hood River **z** 97031; rural
Dundee; Inc. Place; YAMHILL; **222** D-4; elev. 190ft./58m.; 🅿; ★ **POR**; **z** 97115; Ⓟ 1,663; © 2,598
Dunes; LANE; see Dunes City (Inc. Place)
Dunes City (Dunes); Inc. Place; LANE; **222** H-2; 🅿; **z** 97439; Ⓟ 1,081; © 1,241
Dunthorpe; RMC Place; MULTNOMAH; ***222** D-5; ★ **POR**; mail Portland **z** 97219; ● 500
Durham; Inc. Place; WASHINGTON; **223** M-18; elev. 142ft./43m.; ★ **POR**; mail Portland **z** 97224; Ⓟ 748; © 1,382
Durkee; RMC Place; BAKER; **223** F-16; 🅿; **z** 97905; ● 160

E

Eagle Creek; RMC Place; CLACKAMAS; **222** D-5; elev. 339ft./103m.; 🅿; ★ **POR**; **z** 97022; ● 430
Eagle Point; Inc. Place; JACKSON; **222** L-4; elev. 1,305ft./398m.; 🅿; ★ **MEDF**; **z** 97524; Ⓟ 3,008; © 4,797
East Gardiner; RMC Place; DOUGLAS; ***222** H-2; mail Reedsport **z** 97467; ● 30
East Lake; RMC Place; DESCHUTES; mail La Pine **z** 97739
East Moreland; RMC Place; MULTNOMAH; ***222** C-5; ★ **POR**; mail Portland **z** 97202; pop. incl. with Portland (Inc. Place)
East Parkrose; RMC Place; MULTNOMAH; ***222** C-5; ★ **POR**; mail Portland **z** 97230; pop. incl. with Portland (Inc. Place)
East Portland; RMC Place; MULTNOMAH; ***222** C-5; ★ **POR**; mail Portland **z** 97214-15, **z** 97232; pop. incl. with Portland (Inc. Place)
East Saint Johns; RMC Place; MULTNOMAH; ★ **POR**; pop. incl. with Portland (Inc. Place)
Eastside; RMC Place; COOS; ***222** J-1; elev. 61ft./19m.; mail Coos Bay **z** 97420; pop. incl. with Coos Bay (Inc. Place)
Eastwood; RMC Place; DOUGLAS; mail Roseburg **z** 97470; pop. incl. with Roseburg (Inc. Place)
Echo; Inc. Place; UMATILLA; **223** C-12; elev. 638ft./194m.; 🅿; **z** 97826; Ⓟ 499; © 650
Echo Dell; RMC Place; CLACKAMAS; ***222** D-5; ★ **POR**; mail Oregon City **z** 97045
Eckman Lake; RMC Place; LINCOLN; ***222** F-2; mail Waldport **z** 97394; ● 80
Eddyville; RMC Place; LINCOLN; **222** F-2; elev. 92ft./28m.; 🅿; **z** 97343; ● 240
Elgarose; RMC Place; DOUGLAS; ***222** J-3; mail Roseburg **z** 97470; rural
Elgin; Inc. Place; UNION; **223** C-15; elev. 2,716ft./828m.; 🅿; **z** 97827; Ⓟ 1,586; © 1,654
Elk City; RMC Place; LINCOLN; **222** F-2; mail Toledo **z** 97391; ● 50
Elkhorn; RMC Place; MARION; ***222** E-5; mail Lyons **z** 97358
Elk Lake; RMC Place; DESCHUTES; ***222** H-6; elev. 4,892ft./1,491m.; mail Bend **z** 97701; summer pop. 200
Elkton; Inc. Place; DOUGLAS; **222** I-3; elev. 149ft./45m.; 🅿; **z** 97436; Ⓟ 172; © 147
Ellendale; RMC Place; POLK; ***222** E-3; ★ **SAL**; mail Dallas **z** 97338; rural
Ellingson Mill; RMC Place; GRANT; ***223** G-11; mail Unity **z** 97884; rural
Elliott Prairie; RMC Place; CLACKAMAS; ***222** D-4; ★ **POR**; mail Woodburn **z** 97071; rural
Elmira; RMC Place; LANE; **222** H-3; 🅿; ★ **EUG**; **z** 97437; ● 600
Elsie; RMC Place; CLATSOP; ***222** B-3; mail Seaside **z** 97138; ● 50
Elwood; RMC Place; CLACKAMAS; ***222** D-5; mail Colton **z** 97017; rural
Emerald Heights; RMC Place; CLATSOP; mail Astoria **z** 97103; pop. incl. with Astoria (Inc. Place)
Emerson; RMC Place; WASCO; ***222** C-8; mail The Dalles **z** 97058; rural
Empire; RMC Place; COOS; ***222** I-1; elev. 9ft./3m.; mail Coos Bay **z** 97420; pop. incl. with Coos Bay (Inc. Place)
Endersby; RMC Place; WASCO; ***222** C-8; mail The Dalles **z** 97058; rural
Englewood; RMC Place; COOS; ***222** J-1; mail Coos Bay **z** 97420; pop. incl. with Coos Bay (Inc. Place)
Englewood; RMC Place; MULTNOMAH; ***222** D-5; ★ **POR**; mail Lake Oswego **z** 97034; ● 30
Enterprise; Inc. Place; ⊡ WALLOWA; **223** C-16; elev. 3,756ft./1,145m.; 🅿 🅷; **z** 97828; Ⓟ 1,905; © 1,895
Eola; CDP; POLK; ***222** E-4; ★ **SAL**; © 49
Eola Village; RMC Place; YAMHILL; ***222** D-4; mail McMinnville **z** 97128; ● 30
Errol Heights; RMC Place; MULTNOMAH; **223** L-19; ★ **POR**; mail Portland **z** 97266; pop. incl. with Portland (Inc. Place)
Estacada; Inc. Place; CLACKAMAS; **222** D-5; 🅿; ★ **POR**; **z** 97023; Ⓟ 2,016; © 2,371
Eugene; Inc. Place; ⊡ LANE; **222** G-4; elev. 419ft./128m.; 🅿 🅷 🅲 20,868 ■; ★ **EUG**; **z** 97401-05, **z** 97408, **z** 97412, **z** 97440, **z** 97455; Ⓟ 112,669; © 137,893; ◆ 162,084

F

Fairbanks; RMC Place; WASCO; ***222** C-8; mail The Dalles **z** 97058; rural
Fairdale; RMC Place; YAMHILL; ***222** D-3; mail Yamhill **z** 97148; rural
Fairfield; RMC Place; MARION; ***222** D-4; elev. 174ft./53m.; mail Gervais **z** 97026; rural
Fair Oaks; RMC Place; CLACKAMAS; ***222** D-5; ★ **POR**; mail Portland **z** 97222
Fair Oaks; RMC Place; DOUGLAS; ***222** I-3; mail Glendale **z** 97442
Fairview; RMC Place; COOS; ***222** J-2; elev. 125ft./38m.; mail Coquille **z** 97423; ● 100
Fairview; Inc. Place; MULTNOMAH; **223** L-11; 🅿; ★ **POR**; **z** 97024; Ⓟ 2,391; © 7,561
Fairview; RMC Place; SHERMAN; ***222** C-9; mail Moro **z** 97039; rural
Fairview; RMC Place; TILLAMOOK; ***222** C-2; mail Tillamook **z** 97141; ● 30
Falcon Heights; RMC Place; KLAMATH; **222** M-6; mail Klamath Falls **z** 97601; ● 800
Fall Creek; RMC Place; LANE; **222** H-4; 🅿; **z** 97438; ● 110
Falls City; Inc. Place; POLK; **222** E-3; elev. 381ft./116m.; 🅿; **z** 97344; Ⓟ 818; © 966
Fargo; RMC Place; MARION; ***222** D-4; ★ **POR**; mail Aurora **z** 97002; rural
Faubion; RMC Place; CLACKAMAS; ***222** D-6; elev. 1,468ft./447m.; mail Rhododendron **z** 97049; ● 30
Fayetteville; RMC Place; LINN; ***222** F-4; mail Shedd **z** 97377; rural
Fern Corner; RMC Place; POLK; ***222** E-3; elev. 290ft./88m.; ★ **SAL**; mail Dallas **z** 97338; rural
Fern Hill; RMC Place; CLATSOP; **222** A-3; mail Astoria **z** 97103; ● 60
Fern Hill; RMC Place; COLUMBIA; ***222** B-4; mail Rainier **z** 97048; rural
Ferns; RMC Place; POLK; ***222** E-3; ★ **SAL**; mail Dallas **z** 97338; rural
Fields; RMC Place; HARNEY; **223** M-13; elev. 4,243ft./1,293m.; 🅿; **z** 97710; ● 30
Fields; RMC Place; LANE; ***222** I-5; mail Oakridge **z** 97463; rural
Finn Rock; RMC Place; LANE; **222** G-5; elev. 997ft./304m.; mail Vida **z** 97488; ● 80
Fir Grove; RMC Place; LANE; ***222** G-4; elev. 376ft./115m.; ★ **EUG**; mail Eugene **z** 97401, **z** 97404
Firlock; RMC Place; WASHINGTON; ***222** C-4; ★ **POR**; mail Portland **z** 97223; ● 800
Fir Villa; RMC Place; POLK; ***222** E-3; ★ **SAL**; mail Dallas **z** 97338; ● 100
Firwood; RMC Place; CLACKAMAS; ***222** D-6; elev. 1,156ft./352m.; mail Sandy **z** 97055; rural
Fisher; RMC Place; LINCOLN; ***222** G-2; mail Tidewater **z** 97390; rural
Fishers Corner; RMC Place; CLACKAMAS; ***222** D-5; ★ **POR**; mail Oregon City **z** 97045
Fish Lake Resort; RMC Place; JACKSON; ***222** L-5; mail Eagle Point **z** 97524
Five Corners; RMC Place; LAKE; ***222** M-9; mail Lakeview **z** 97630
Flora; RMC Place; WALLOWA; ***223** B-16; mail Enterprise **z** 97828
Floras Lake; RMC Place; CURRY; ***222** K-1; mail Langlois **z** 97450; rural
Florence; Inc. Place; LANE; **222** H-2; elev. 23ft./7m.; 🅿 🅷; **z** 97439; Ⓟ 5,162; © 7,263
Flying M Ranch; RMC Place; YAMHILL; ***222** D-3; mail Yamhill **z** 97148; rural
Foley Springs; RMC Place; LANE; ***222** G-6; mail Blue River **z** 97413; rural
Folkenberg; RMC Place; MULTNOMAH; ***222** C-4; mail Portland **z** 97231; rural
Forest Grove; Inc. Place; WASHINGTON; **222** C-4; 🅿 🅷 🅲 2,790; ★ **POR**; **z** 97116 & mail Gales Creek **z** 97117; Ⓟ 13,559; © 17,708; ◆ 21,826
Forest Park; RMC Place; MULTNOMAH; ★ **POR**; mail Portland **z** 97209-10, **z** 97296; pop. incl. with Portland (Inc. Place)
Forfar; RMC Place; LINCOLN; ***222** F-2; mail South Beach **z** 97366; ● 50
Fort Hill; RMC Place; POLK; ***222** E-3; elev. 290ft./88m.; mail Willamina **z** 97396; rural
Fort Klamath; RMC Place; KLAMATH; **222** L-6; elev. 4,175ft./1,273m.; 🅿; **z** 97626; summer pop. 400; ● 250
Fort McDermitt Reservation; Indian Reservation; MALHEUR; Reservation extends into NV; © 0
Fort Rock; RMC Place; LAKE; **222** J-8; 🅿; **z** 97735; ● 50
Fort Rock Junction; RMC Place; LAKE; ***222** J-8; mail Fort Rock **z** 97735; rural
Fort Stevens; RMC Place; CLATSOP; ***222** A-2; mail Hammond **z** 97121
Fortune Branch; RMC Place; DOUGLAS; ***222** K-3; elev. 1,556ft./474m.; mail Glendale **z** 97442; ● 50
Fossil; Inc. Place; ⊡ WHEELER; **222** E-10; elev. 2,654ft./809m.; 🅿; **z** 97830; Ⓟ 399; © 469
Foster; RMC Place; LINN; **222** G-5; 🅿; **z** 97345; pop. incl. with Sweet Home (Inc. Place)
Four Corners; RMC Place; JACKSON; ***222** L-4; ★ **MEDF**; mail Central Point **z** 97502; pop. incl. with Medford (Inc. Place)
Four Corners; CDP; MARION; **223** F-20; ★ **SAL**; mail Salem **z** 97301; Ⓟ 12,156; © 13,922
Fourmile; RMC Place; COOS; ***222** K-1; mail Bandon **z** 97411; ● 30
Fox; RMC Place; GRANT; **223** F-12; 🅿; **z** 97856; ● 50
Franklin (Smithfield); RMC Place; LANE; ***222** G-3; ★ **EUG**; mail Junction City **z** 97448
Freebridge; RMC Place; WASCO; ***222** C-8; rural
Freewater; RMC Place; UMATILLA; mail Milton Freewater **z** 97862; pop. incl. with Milton-Freewater (Inc. Place)
Frenchglen; RMC Place; HARNEY; **223** K-13; 🅿; **z** 97736; ● 30
Friend; RMC Place; WASCO; ***222** D-8; elev. 2,434ft./742m.; 🅿; **z** 97021; rural
Fruitdale; RMC Place; JOSEPHINE; ***222** L-3; mail Grants Pass **z** 97526; ● 1,200
Fruitvale; RMC Place; LINCOLN; ***222** F-2; mail Newport **z** 97365; rural
Fulton (McCommach); RMC Place; UMATILLA; ***223** C-13; mail Pendleton **z** 97801; rural

G

Gales Creek; RMC Place; WASHINGTON; **222** C-4; elev. 287ft./87m.; 🅿; ★ **POR**; **z** 97117; ● 100
Galice; RMC Place; JOSEPHINE; ***222** L-2; elev. 724ft./221m.; mail Merlin **z** 97532
Garden Home; RMC Place; WASHINGTON; **223** L-18; ★ **POR**; mail Portland **z** 97223
Garden Home-Whitford; CDP-Census Area Only; WASHINGTON; ***222** C-4; ★ **POR**; mail Portland **z** 97223; Ⓟ 6,652; © 6,931
Gardiner; RMC Place; DOUGLAS; **222** H-2; elev. 43ft./13m.; 🅿; **z** 97441; ● 540
Garfield; RMC Place; CLACKAMAS; ***222** D-5; mail Estacada **z** 97023; rural
Garibaldi; Inc. Place; TILLAMOOK; **222** C-2; 🅿; **z** 97118; Ⓟ 877; © 899
Gasco; RMC Place; MULTNOMAH; ***222** C-4; elev. 28ft./9m.; ★ **POR**; pop. incl. with Portland (Inc. Place)
Gaston; Inc. Place; WASHINGTON; **222** C-4; 🅿; ★ **POR**; **z** 97119; Ⓟ 563; © 600
Gates; Inc. Place; MARION, LINN; **222** E-5; elev. 942ft./287m.; 🅿; **z** 97346; Ⓟ 499; © 471
Gateway; RMC Place; JEFFERSON; **222** E-8; mail Madras **z** 97741; ● 40
Gaylord; RMC Place; COOS; **222** K-1; mail Myrtle Point **z** 97458; ● 40
Gazley; RMC Place; DOUGLAS; ***222** K-3; mail Myrtle Creek **z** 97457; rural
Gearhart; Inc. Place; CLATSOP; **222** B-2; elev. 16ft./5m.; 🅿; **z** 97138; Ⓟ 1,027; © 995
George; RMC Place; CLACKAMAS; ***222** D-6; elev. 1,286ft./392m.; mail Estacada **z** 97023; rural
Gervais; Inc. Place; MARION; **222** D-4; elev. 184ft./56m.; 🅿; **z** 97026; Ⓟ 992; © 2,009
Gibbon; RMC Place; UMATILLA; ***223** C-14; elev. 1,754ft./535m.; mail Adams **z** 97810
Gilbert; RMC Place; MULTNOMAH; ★ **POR**; mail Portland **z** 97266; pop. incl. with Portland (Inc. Place)
Gilchrist; RMC Place; KLAMATH; **222** I-7; elev. 4,447ft./1,355m.; 🅿; **z** 97737; ● 500
Gillespie Corners; RMC Place; LANE; ***222** H-3; elev. 499ft./152m.; mail Eugene **z** 97405; rural
GILLIAM; **222** D-10; Ⓟ 1,717; © 1,915; ◆ 1,642
Gilliams; RMC Place; POLK; ***222** E-3; ★ **SAL**; mail Dallas **z** 97338; rural
Gladstone; Inc. Place; CLACKAMAS; **223** M-19; 🅿; ★ **POR**; **z** 97027; Ⓟ 10,152; © 11,438
Glasgow; RMC Place; COOS; **222** I-1; mail North Bend **z** 97459; ● 400
Glenada; RMC Place; LANE; **222** H-2; elev. 61ft./19m.; mail Florence **z** 97439; ● 270
Glenbrook; RMC Place; BENTON; ***222** G-3; mail Monroe **z** 97456; rural
Glen Cullen; RMC Place; MULTNOMAH; ***222** C-5; ★ **POR**; mail Portland **z** 97201; pop. incl. with Portland (Inc. Place)
Glendale; Inc. Place; DOUGLAS; **222** K-3; elev. 1,423ft./434m.; 🅿; **z** 97442; Ⓟ 707; © 855
Gleneden Beach; RMC Place; LINCOLN; **222** E-2; elev. 65ft./20m.; 🅿; **z** 97388; summer pop. 3,600; ● 900
Glengary; RMC Place; DOUGLAS; ***222** J-3; mail Roseburg **z** 97470; ● 300
Glenwood; RMC Place; CLATSOP; ***222** A-2; mail Warrenton **z** 97146; ● 140
Glenwood; RMC Place; LANE; ***222** H-4; ★ **EUG**; mail Eugene **z** 97403
Glenwood; RMC Place; WASHINGTON; **222** C-3; 🅿; **z** 97116; ● 80
Glide; CDP; DOUGLAS; **222** J-4; elev. 695ft./212m.; 🅿; **z** 97443; © 1,690
Globe; RMC Place; LANE; ***222** H-3; mail Walton **z** 97490; rural
Goble; RMC Place; COLUMBIA; **222** B-4; mail Rainier **z** 97048; ● 200
Gold Beach; Inc. Place; ⊡ CURRY; **222** L-1; elev. 51ft./16m.; 🅿 🅷; **z** 97444; Ⓟ 1,546; © 1,897
Gold Hill; Inc. Place; JACKSON; **222** L-4; 🅿; **z** 97525; Ⓟ 964; © 1,073
Gooseberry; RMC Place; MORROW; ***222** D-10; mail Ione **z** 97843; rural
Gopher Flats; CDP-Census Area Only; UMATILLA; ***223** C-13; © 401
Goshen; RMC Place; LANE; **222** H-4; ★ **EUG**; mail Eugene **z** 97405; ● 170
Government Camp; RMC Place; CLACKAMAS; **222** D-7; elev. 3,880ft./1,183m.; 🅿; **z** 97028; ● 420
Grand Ronde; CDP; POLK; **222** E-3; 🅿; **z** 97347; © 271
Grand Ronde Agency; RMC Place; YAMHILL; ***222** E-3; elev. 356ft./109m.; mail Grand Ronde **z** 97347; ● 100
Grand Ronde Community; Indian Reservation; YAMHILL; mail Willamina **z** 97396; © 0
Granite; Inc. Place; GRANT; **223** E-14; elev. 4,689ft./1,429m.; 🅿; **z** 97877; Ⓟ 8; © 24
GRANT; **223** F-12; Ⓟ 7,853; © 7,935; ◆ 6,631
Grants Pass; Inc. Place; ⊡ JOSEPHINE; **222** L-3; 🅿 🅷 ■; **z** 97526-28, **z** 97543; Ⓟ 17,488; © 23,003; ◆ 29,222
Grass Valley; Inc. Place; SHERMAN; **222** D-9; elev. 2,252ft./686m.; 🅿; **z** 97029; Ⓟ 160; © 171
Gravelford; RMC Place; COOS; ***222** J-2; mail Myrtle Point **z** 97458; ● 30
Green; CDP; DOUGLAS; **222** J-3; elev. 495ft./151m.; mail Roseburg **z** 97470; Ⓟ 5,076; © 6,174
Green Acres; RMC Place; COOS; **222** J-1; mail Coos Bay **z** 97420; ● 230
Green Acres (Wells Creek); RMC Place; DOUGLAS; ***222** I-2; mail Elkton **z** 97436, Scottsburg **z** 97473; ● 50
Greenberry; RMC Place; BENTON; ***222** F-3; elev. 251ft./77m.; mail Corvallis **z** 97333; ● 50
Green Hills; RMC Place; MULTNOMAH; ***222** C-5; ★ **POR**; mail Portland **z** 97221
Greenhorn; RMC Place; BAKER, GRANT; **223** F-14; mail Sumpter **z** 97877; disincorporated since 2000 Census
Greenleaf; RMC Place; LANE; **222** G-3; 🅿; **z** 97430; ● 100
Greenville; RMC Place; LINN; ***222** G-4; mail Sweet Home **z** 97386; rural
Greenville; RMC Place; WASHINGTON; ***222** C-4; elev. 193ft./59m.; ★ **POR**; mail Forest Grove **z** 97116; pop. incl. with Greenville (Inc. Place)
Greenway; RMC Place; WASHINGTON; ★ **POR**; mail Portland **z** 97223; pop. incl. with Tigard (Inc. Place)
Gresham; Inc. Place; MULTNOMAH; **223** L-11; elev. 323ft./98m.; 🅿 🅷 ■; ★ **POR**; **z** 97030, **z** 97080 & mail Portland **z** 97230, **z** 97233, **z** 97236; Ⓟ 68,235; © 90,205; ◆ 105,809

H

Haines; Inc. Place; BAKER; **223** E-15; elev. 3,333ft./1,016m.; 🅿; **z** 97833; Ⓟ 405; © 426
Halfway; Inc. Place; BAKER; **223** E-16; elev. 2,663ft./812m.; 🅿; **z** 97834; Ⓟ 311; © 337
Halsey; Inc. Place; LINN; **222** G-4; elev. 280ft./85m.; 🅿; **z** 97348; Ⓟ 667; © 724
Hamilton; RMC Place; GRANT; mail Long Creek **z** 97856
Hammond; RMC Place; CLATSOP; ***222** A-2; elev. 9ft./3m.; 🅿; **z** 97121; pop. incl. with Warrenton (Inc. Place)
Hampton; RMC Place; DESCHUTES; **222** I-10; mail Brothers **z** 97712
Happy Valley; Inc. Place; CLACKAMAS; **223** M-20; 🅿; ★ **POR**; **z** 97009, **z** 97015, **z** 97086, **z** 97236, **z** 97266; Ⓟ 1,519; © 4,519
Harbeck-Fruitdale; CDP-Census Area Only; JOSEPHINE; ***222** L-3; mail Grants Pass **z** 97526; Ⓟ 3,982; © 3,780
Harbor; CDP; CURRY; **222** M-1; 🅿; **z** 97415; Ⓟ 2,143; © 2,622
Harbor Track; RMC Place; MULTNOMAH; ★ **POR**; pop. incl. with Portland (Inc. Place)
Hardman; RMC Place; MORROW; **223** D-11; mail Heppner **z** 97836; ● 30
Harlan; RMC Place; LINCOLN; **222** F-2; elev. 242ft./74m.; mail Eddyville **z** 97343; ● 130
Harmony; RMC Place; SHERMAN; ***222** D-9; mail Moro **z** 97039; rural
Harney; RMC Place; HARNEY; ***223** I-13; mail Burns **z** 97720; rural
HARNEY; **223** J-12; Ⓟ 7,060; © 7,609; ◆ 6,704
Harper; RMC Place; MALHEUR; **223** H-15; 🅿; **z** 97906; ● 100
Harrisburg; Inc. Place; LINN; **222** G-4; elev. 309ft./94m.; 🅿; ★ **EUG**; **z** 97446; Ⓟ 1,939; © 2,795
Hauser; RMC Place; COOS; **222** I-1; elev. 8ft./2m.; mail North Bend **z** 97459; ● 700
Havana; RMC Place; UMATILLA; ***223** C-13; mail Adams **z** 97810; rural
Hay Canyon; RMC Place; SHERMAN; ***222** C-9; mail Moro **z** 97039; rural
Hayesville; CDP; MARION; **223** E-20; ★ **SAL**; mail Salem **z** 97303; Ⓟ 14,318; © 18,222
Hebo; CDP; TILLAMOOK; **222** D-2; elev. 77ft./23m.; 🅿; **z** 97122; © 231
Heceta Beach; RMC Place; LANE; ***222** H-1; elev. 40ft./12m.; mail Florence **z** 97439; ● 340
Heceta Junction; RMC Place; LANE; ***222** H-2; mail Florence **z** 97439; ● 40
Helix; Inc. Place; UMATILLA; **223** B-13; elev. 1,754ft./535m.; 🅿; **z** 97835; Ⓟ 150; © 183
Helvetia; RMC Place; WASHINGTON; ***222** C-4; elev. 277ft./84m.; mail Hillsboro **z** 97123-24
Hemlock; RMC Place; LANE; ***222** H-5; elev. 1,075ft./328m.; mail Westfir **z** 97492; pop. incl. with Westfir (Inc. Place)
Hemlock; RMC Place; TILLAMOOK; ***222** D-2; mail Cloverdale **z** 97112; ● 50
Henley; RMC Place; KLAMATH; ***222** M-7; mail Klamath Falls **z** 97603; ● 500
Henrici; RMC Place; CLACKAMAS; ***222** D-5; ★ **POR**; mail Oregon City **z** 97045; ● 50
Heppner; Inc. Place; ⊡ MORROW; **223** D-11; elev. 1,955ft./596m.; 🅿 🅷; **z** 97836; Ⓟ 1,412; © 1,395
Hereford; RMC Place; BAKER; **223** F-14; 🅿; **z** 97837; ● 60
Hermiston; Inc. Place; UMATILLA; **223** B-12; elev. 457ft./139m.; 🅿 🅷; **z** 97838; Ⓟ 10,040; © 13,154
Hidaway Springs; RMC Place; UMATILLA; ***223** D-13; mail Ukiah **z** 97880; rural
Highland; RMC Place; CLACKAMAS; ***222** D-5; ★ **POR**; mail Beavercreek **z** 97004; rural
Hildebrand; RMC Place; KLAMATH; ***222** M-7; elev. 4,189ft./1,277m.; mail Bonanza **z** 97623; rural
Hilgard; RMC Place; UNION; ***223** D-14; mail La Grande **z** 97850
Hillsboro; Inc. Place; ⊡ WASHINGTON; **222** C-4; 🅿 🅷 ■; ★ **POR**; **z** 97006, **z** 97123-24; Ⓟ 37,520; © 70,186; ◆ 97,243
Hillsdale; RMC Place; MULTNOMAH; ***222** C-5; ★ **POR**; mail Portland **z** 97201; pop. incl. with Portland (Inc. Place)
Hines; Inc. Place; HARNEY; **223** I-12; elev. 4,157ft./1,267m.; 🅿; **z** 97738; Ⓟ 1,452; © 1,623
Hobsonville; RMC Place; TILLAMOOK; ***222** C-2; mail Bay City **z** 97107; ● 30
Holbrook; RMC Place; MULTNOMAH; ***222** C-4; mail Portland **z** 97231; rural
Holdman; RMC Place; UMATILLA; ***223** B-12; mail Pendleton **z** 97801; rural
Holladay Park; RMC Place; MULTNOMAH; ★ **POR**; mail Portland **z** 97212, **z** 97227; pop. incl. with Portland (Inc. Place)
Holland; RMC Place; JOSEPHINE; ***222** M-3; mail Cave Junction **z** 97523; rural
Holley (Holly); RMC Place; LINN; ***222** G-4; elev. 638ft./194m.; mail Sweet Home **z** 97386
Holly; LINN; see Holley (RMC Place)
Hollywood; RMC Place; MARION; ★ **SAL**; mail Salem **z** 97303; pop. incl. with Salem (Inc. Place)
Hollywood; RMC Place; MULTNOMAH; ***222** C-5; ★ **POR**; mail Portland **z** 97212-13; pop. incl. with Portland (Inc. Place)
Homestead; RMC Place; BAKER; ***223** E-17; elev. 1,683ft./513m.; mail Oxbow **z** 97840
Homestead; RMC Place; DESCHUTES; mail Bend **z** 97702; rural
Hood River; Inc. Place; ⊡ HOOD RIVER; **222** C-7; 🅿 🅷; **z** 97031; Ⓟ 4,632; © 5,831
HOOD RIVER; **222** C-7; Ⓟ 16,903; © 20,411; ◆ 21,311
Horton; RMC Place; LANE; **222** G-3; mail Blachly **z** 97412; ● 50
Hoskins; RMC Place; BENTON; **222** F-3; mail Blodgett **z** 97326; ● 90
Hot Lake; RMC Place; UNION; ***223** D-14; mail La Grande **z** 97850; rural
Hot Springs; RMC Place; KLAMATH; ***222** M-8; mail Bonanza **z** 97623; ● 50
Hubbard; Inc. Place; MARION; **222** D-4; elev. 182ft./55m.; 🅿; ★ **POR**; **z** 97032; Ⓟ 1,881; © 2,483
Hugo; RMC Place; JOSEPHINE; ***222** L-3; mail Grants Pass **z** 97526; rural
Hunter Creek; RMC Place; CURRY; ***222** L-1; mail Gold Beach **z** 97444; pop. incl. with Gold Beach (Inc. Place)
Huntington; Inc. Place; BAKER; **223** G-16; elev. 2,108ft./643m.; 🅿; **z** 97907; Ⓟ 522; © 515

I

Idanha; Inc. Place; MARION, LINN; **222** F-6; elev. 1,718ft./524m.; 🅿; **z** 97350; Ⓟ 289; © 232
Idaville; RMC Place; TILLAMOOK; ***222** C-2; elev. 20ft./6m.; mail Tillamook **z** 97141; ● 130
Idleyld Park; RMC Place; DOUGLAS; **222** J-4; elev. 781ft./238m.; 🅿; **z** 97447; ● 320
Illahe; RMC Place; CURRY; ***222** L-2; mail Agness **z** 97406; rural
Illinois Valley; RMC Place; JOSEPHINE; **222** M-2; mail Cave Junction **z** 97523; ● 250
Imbler; Inc. Place; UNION; **223** C-14; elev. 2,731ft./832m.; 🅿; **z** 97841; Ⓟ 299; © 284
Imnaha; RMC Place; WALLOWA; **223** C-17; elev. 1,965ft./599m.; 🅿; **z** 97842; ● 90
Independence; Inc. Place; POLK; **222** E-4; elev. 168ft./51m.; 🅿; ★ **SAL**; **z** 97351; Ⓟ 4,425; © 6,035
Indian Ford; RMC Place; DESCHUTES; ***222** G-7; elev. 3,239ft./987m.; mail Sisters **z** 97759; rural
Indian Village; RMC Place; HARNEY; ***223** I-12; mail Burns **z** 97720; pop. incl. with Burns (Inc. Place)
Inglis; RMC Place; COLUMBIA; ***222** A-4; mail Clatskanie **z** 97016; ● 130
Interlachen; RMC Place; MULTNOMAH; ***222** C-5; ★ **POR**; mail Fairview **z** 97024, Government Camp **z** 97028, Troutdale **z** 97060; ● 100
Ione; Inc. Place; MORROW; **223** C-11; 🅿; **z** 97843; Ⓟ 255; © 321
Ironside; RMC Place; MALHEUR; **223** G-15; 🅿; **z** 97908; ● 50
Irrigon; Inc. Place; MORROW; **223** B-11; elev. 297ft./91m.; 🅿; **z** 97844; Ⓟ 737; © 1,702
Irving; RMC Place; LANE; ***222** G-4; ★ **EUG**; mail Eugene **z** 97401-02; ● 450
Irvington; RMC Place; MULTNOMAH; ***222** C-5; ★ **POR**; mail Portland **z** 97212; pop. incl. with Portland (Inc. Place)
Island City; Inc. Place; UNION; **223** D-14; 🅿; **z** 97850; Ⓟ 696; © 916
Ivy Station; RMC Place; CLATSOP; ***222** A-3; elev. 26ft./8m.; mail Astoria **z** 97103; rural
Izee; RMC Place; GRANT; ***223** H-12; mail Canyon City **z** 97820; rural

J

JACKSON; **222** L-4; Ⓟ 146,389; © 181,269; Ⓡ 181,273; ◆ 203,346
Jacksonville; Inc. Place; JACKSON; **222** M-4; elev. 1,569ft./478m.; 🅿; ★ **MEDF**; **z** 97530; Ⓟ 1,896; © 2,235
Jamieson; RMC Place; MALHEUR; **223** G-16; 🅿; **z** 97909; ● 90
Jasper; RMC Place; LANE; **222** H-4; elev. 540ft./165m.; 🅿; ★ **EUG**; **z** 97438; ● 90
Jeffers Garden; RMC Place; CLATSOP; ***222** A-2; mail Astoria **z** 97103; ● 500
Jefferson; Inc. Place; MARION; **222** F-4; elev. 230ft./70m.; 🅿; ★ **SAL**; **z** 97352; Ⓟ 1,805; © 2,487
JEFFERSON; **222** F-7; Ⓟ 13,676; © 19,009; ◆ 21,693
Jennings Lodge; CDP; CLACKAMAS; ***222** D-5; ★ **POR**; mail Portland **z** 97267; Ⓟ 6,530; © 7,036
Jerome Prairie; RMC Place; JOSEPHINE; ***222** L-3; mail Grants Pass **z** 97527; summer pop. 1,500; ● 50
Jewell; RMC Place; CLATSOP; ***222** B-3; mail Seaside **z** 97138; ● 50
Jimtown; RMC Place; BAKER; ***223** E-16; mail Halfway **z** 97834; ● 30
John Day; Inc. Place; GRANT; **223** G-12; 🅿 🅷; **z** 97845; Ⓟ 1,836; © 1,821
Johnson City; Inc. Place; CLACKAMAS; **223** M-19; ★ **POR**; mail Portland **z** 97267; Ⓟ 586; © 634
Jonesboro; RMC Place; MALHEUR; ***223** H-15; mail Juntura **z** 97911; rural
Jordan; RMC Place; LINN; ***222** F-5; elev. 548ft./167m.; mail Scio **z** 97374; rural
Jordan Valley; Inc. Place; MALHEUR; **223** K-17; elev. 4,389ft./1,338m.; 🅿; **z** 97910; Ⓟ 364; © 239
Joseph; Inc. Place; WALLOWA; **223** D-16; elev. 4,190ft./1,277m.; 🅿; **z** 97846; Ⓟ 1,073; © 1,054
JOSEPHINE; **222** L-2; Ⓟ 62,649; © 75,726; ◆ 79,647
Judkins; RMC Place; LANE; ***222** H-4; ★ **EUG**; pop. incl. with Eugene (Inc. Place)
Junction City; Inc. Place; LANE; **222** G-3; elev. 327ft./100m.; 🅿; ★ **EUG**; **z** 97448; Ⓟ 3,670; © 4,721
Juntura; RMC Place; MALHEUR; **223** H-14; 🅿; **z** 97911; ● 60

K

Kahneeta Hot Springs; RMC Place; WASCO; ***222** E-8; mail Warm Springs **z** 97761; summer pop. 100; rural
Kamela; RMC Place; UNION; **223** C-14; mail Pendleton **z** 97801; ● 30
Kansas City; RMC Place; WASHINGTON; ***222** C-4; ★ **POR**; mail Forest Grove **z** 97116; rural
Keasey; RMC Place; COLUMBIA; ***222** B-3; mail Vernonia **z** 97064; summer pop. 130; ● 30
Keating; RMC Place; BAKER; ***223** E-15; elev. 2,720ft./829m.; mail Baker City **z** 97814; rural
Keizer; Inc. Place; MARION; **223** E-19; elev. 134ft./41m.; 🅿; ★ **SAL**; **z** 97303, **z** 97307; Ⓟ 21,884; © 32,203; ◆ 37,268
Kellogg; RMC Place; DOUGLAS; ***222** I-3; elev. 205ft./62m.; mail Elkton **z** 97436, Oakland **z** 97462; rural
Kelso; RMC Place; CLACKAMAS; ***222** D-5; elev. 705ft./215m.; ★ **POR**; mail Boring **z** 97009; ● 50
Kendall; RMC Place; MULTNOMAH; ***222** C-5; ★ **POR**; mail Portland **z** 97206; pop. incl. with Portland (Inc. Place)
Keno; RMC Place; KLAMATH; **222** M-6; elev. 4,094ft./1,248m.; 🅿; **z** 97627; ● 1,100
Kent; RMC Place; SHERMAN; **222** D-9; elev. 2,711ft./826m.; 🅿; **z** 97033; ● 40
Kenton; RMC Place; MULTNOMAH; **223** K-18; ★ **POR**; mail Portland **z** 97217; pop. incl. with Portland (Inc. Place)
Kerby; RMC Place; JOSEPHINE; **222** M-2; 🅿; **z** 97531 & mail Cave Junction **z** 97523; ● 500
Kernville; RMC Place; LINCOLN; **222** E-2; elev. 32ft./10m.; mail Lincoln City **z** 97367; ● 50
Kimberly; RMC Place; GRANT; **223** F-11; elev. 1,828ft./557m.; 🅿; **z** 97848; ● 50
King City; Inc. Place; WASHINGTON; **223** M-17; 🅿; ★ **POR**; **z** 97224; Ⓟ 2,060; © 1,949
Kings Corner; RMC Place; UMATILLA; ***223** B-13; mail Pendleton **z** 97801; rural
Kings Heights; RMC Place; MULTNOMAH; ***222** C-5; elev. 573ft./175m.; ★ **POR**; mail Portland **z** 97210; pop. incl. with Portland (Inc. Place)
Kingston; RMC Place; LINN; ***222** E-4; elev. 531ft./162m.; mail Stayton **z** 97383; rural
Kings Valley; RMC Place; BENTON; **222** F-3; elev. 308ft./94m.; mail Monmouth **z** 97361; ● 200
Kinton; RMC Place; WASHINGTON; ***222** D-4; elev. 264ft./80m.; ★ **POR**; mail Beaverton **z** 97007
Kinzua; RMC Place; WHEELER; ***222** E-10; 🅿; **z** 97830; rural
Kirkpatrick; CDP-Census Area Only; UMATILLA; ***223** C-13; © 172
Kiwanda Beach; RMC Place; TILLAMOOK; mail Neskowin **z** 97149
KLAMATH; **222** L-6; Ⓟ 57,702; © 63,775; ◆ 62,763
Klamath Agency; RMC Place; KLAMATH
Klamath Falls; Inc. Place; ⊡ KLAMATH; **222** M-6; 🅿 🅷 🅲 3,157 ■; **z** 97601-03, **z** 97625; Ⓟ 17,737; © 19,462; Ⓡ 19,460; ◆ 17,989
Klamath Falls Southeast; KLAMATH; see Altamont (CDP)
Klamath Reservation; Indian Reservation; KLAMATH; © 9
Knappa; RMC Place; CLATSOP; **222** A-3; mail Astoria **z** 97103; ● 400
Knoll Heights; RMC Place; DESCHUTES; mail Bend **z** 97702; ● 100

L

Labish Village; CDP; MARION; ***222** E-4; ★ **SAL**; © 376
Lacomb; RMC Place; LINN; **222** F-4; elev. 689ft./210m.; mail Lebanon **z** 97355; ● 230
Lafayette; Inc. Place; YAMHILL; **222** D-4; 🅿; ★ **POR**; **z** 97127; Ⓟ 1,292; © 2,586
La Grande; Inc. Place; ⊡ UNION; **223** D-14; elev. 2,771ft./845m.; 🅿 🅷 🅲 3,425; **z** 97850; Ⓟ 11,766; © 12,327
LAKE; **222** J-9; Ⓟ 7,186; © 7,422; ◆ 7,208
Lakecreek; RMC Place; JACKSON; ***222** L-5; mail Eagle Point **z** 97524; rural
Lake Grove; RMC Place; CLACKAMAS; ***222** D-5; ★ **POR**; mail Lake Oswego **z** 97034-35; pop. incl. with Lake Oswego (Inc. Place)
Lake of the Woods; RMC Place; KLAMATH; ***222** M-5; mail Klamath Falls **z** 97601; summer pop. 1,000
Lake Oswego (Oswego); Inc. Place; CLACKAMAS, MULTNOMAH, WASHINGTON; **223** M-19; elev. 100ft./30m.; 🅿; ★ **POR**; **z** 97034-35; Ⓟ 30,576; © 35,278; ◆ 37,107
Lakeside; Inc. Place; COOS; **222** I-1; elev. 29ft./9m.; 🅿; **z** 97449; Ⓟ 1,437; © 1,371; Ⓡ 1,421
Lakeview; Inc. Place; ⊡ LAKE; **222** M-10; elev. 4,798ft./1,462m.; 🅿 🅷; **z** 97630; Ⓟ 2,526; © 2,474
Lake Yard; RMC Place; MULTNOMAH; ★ **POR**; pop. incl. with Portland (Inc. Place)
Lancaster; RMC Place; LANE; ***222** G-3; elev. 313ft./95m.; ★ **EUG**; mail Junction City **z** 97448; rural
LANE; **222** H-4; Ⓟ 282,912; © 322,959; Ⓡ 322,977; ◆ 354,298
Langell Valley; RMC Place; KLAMATH; ***222** N-8; mail Bonanza **z** 97623; ● 400
Langlois; RMC Place; CURRY; **222** K-1; elev. 99ft./30m.; 🅿; **z** 97450; ● 400
La Pine; Inc. Place; DESCHUTES; **222** I-7; incorporated December 7, 2006; not reported in 2000 Census; ● 900
La Pine; CDP-Census Area Only; DESCHUTES; **222** I-7; elev. 4,233ft./1,290m.; 🅿; **z** 97739; © 5,799
Larwood; RMC Place; LINN; ***222** F-4; mail Scio **z** 97374; rural
Latham; RMC Place; LANE; ***222** H-4; mail Cottage Grove **z** 97424
Latourell Falls; RMC Place; MULTNOMAH; ***222** C-6; mail Cascade Locks **z** 97014, Corbett **z** 97019; ● 70
Laurel; RMC Place; WASHINGTON; ***222** D-4; elev. 194ft./59m.; ★ **POR**; mail Hillsboro **z** 97123
Laurel Grove; RMC Place; COOS; ***222** K-1; elev. 109ft./33m.; mail Bandon **z** 97411; rural
Laurelhurst; RMC Place; MULTNOMAH; ***222** C-5; ★ **POR**; mail Portland **z** 97215; pop. incl. with Portland (Inc. Place)
Laurelwood; RMC Place; WASHINGTON; ***222** D-4; ★ **POR**; mail Gaston **z** 97119; ● 300
Lawen; RMC Place; HARNEY; **223** I-13; 🅿; **z** 97720; ● 60
Leaburg; RMC Place; LANE; **222** G-5; elev. 680ft./207m.; 🅿; **z** 97489; ● 250
Lebanon; Inc. Place; LINN; **222** F-4; elev. 347ft./106m.; 🅿 🅷; **z** 97355; Ⓟ 10,950; © 12,950
Lee's Camp; RMC Place; TILLAMOOK; **222** C-3; mail Tillamook **z** 97141; ● 60
Lehman Springs; RMC Place; UMATILLA; mail Ukiah **z** 97880; rural
Leland; RMC Place; JOSEPHINE; ***222** L-3; mail Wolf Creek **z** 97497
Lents; RMC Place; MULTNOMAH; ***222** C-5; elev. 213ft./65m.; ★ **POR**; mail Portland **z** 97236, **z** 97266; pop. incl. with Portland (Inc. Place)
Leona; RMC Place; DOUGLAS; ***222** I-3; mail Drain **z** 97435; rural
Lewisburg; RMC Place; BENTON; **222** F-3; elev. 241ft./73m.; ★ **CORV-**; mail Corvallis **z** 97330; ● 250
Lexington; Inc. Place; MORROW; **223** D-11; 🅿; **z** 97839; Ⓟ 286; © 263
Libby; RMC Place; COOS; ***222** J-1; mail Coos Bay **z** 97420; ● 30
Liberal; RMC Place; CLACKAMAS; ***222** D-5; elev. 248ft./76m.; ★ **POR**; mail Molalla **z** 97038; ● 30
Liberty; RMC Place; LINN; ***222** F-4; mail Sweet Home **z** 97386; rural
Lime; RMC Place; BAKER; ***223** F-16; mail Huntington **z** 97907; rural
Lincoln; RMC Place; JACKSON; ***222** M-5; mail Ashland **z** 97520; ● 30
LINCOLN; **222** F-2; Ⓟ 38,889; © 44,479; ◆ 46,167
Lincoln Beach; CDP; LINCOLN; **222** E-2; mail Depoe Bay **z** 97341; Ⓟ 1,507; © 2,078
Lincoln City; Inc. Place; LINCOLN; **222** E-2; 🅿 🅷; **z** 97367; Ⓟ 5,892; © 7,437
Lindberg; RMC Place; COLUMBIA; ***222** B-4; ★ **LNGV**; mail Rainier **z** 97048; ● 360
LINN; **222** F-5; Ⓟ 91,227; © 103,069; ◆ 116,585
Linnton; RMC Place; MULTNOMAH; ***222** C-4; ★ **POR**; pop. incl. with Portland (Inc. Place)
Little Albany; RMC Place; LINCOLN; ***222** F-2; mail Tidewater **z** 97390; ● 30
Little Sweden; RMC Place; MARION; ***222** F-5; mail Gates **z** 97346; rural
Little Switzerland; RMC Place; LINCOLN; ***222** F-2; mail Tidewater **z** 97390; rural
Locoda; RMC Place; COLUMBIA; ***222** A-4; mail Clatskanie **z** 97016; rural
Logan; RMC Place; CLACKAMAS; ***222** D-5; ★ **POR**; mail Oregon City **z** 97045; rural
Logsden; RMC Place; LINCOLN; **222** F-2; 🅿; **z** 97357; ● 300
London; RMC Place; LANE; ***222** I-4; mail Cottage Grove **z** 97424; rural
Lone Elder; RMC Place; CLACKAMAS; ***222** D-5; elev. 169ft./52m.; ★ **POR**; mail Canby **z** 97013; rural
Lonerock; Inc. Place; GILLIAM; **222** E-10; mail Condon **z** 97823; Ⓟ 11; © 24
Long Creek; Inc. Place; GRANT; **223** F-12; elev. 3,772ft./1,150m.; 🅿; **z** 97856; Ⓟ 249; © 228
Lookingglass; RMC Place; DOUGLAS; ***222** J-3; mail Roseburg **z** 97470
Looking Glass; UNION; see Palmer Junction (RMC Place)
Lorane; RMC Place; LANE; **222** H-3; 🅿; **z** 97451; ● 220
Lorella; RMC Place; KLAMATH; ***222** M-8; elev. 4,179ft./1,274m.; mail Bonanza **z** 97623
Lostine; Inc. Place; WALLOWA; **223** C-16; 🅿; **z** 97857; Ⓟ 231; © 263
Lowell; Inc. Place; LANE; **222** H-4; elev. 741ft./226m.; 🅿; ★ **EUG**; **z** 97452; Ⓟ 785; © 857; Ⓡ 880
Lynch; RMC Place; MULTNOMAH; ★ **POR**; mail Portland **z** 97236; pop. incl. with Portland (Inc. Place)
Lyons; Inc. Place; LINN; **222** E-5; 🅿; **z** 97358; Ⓟ 938; © 1,008

M

Macksburg; RMC Place; CLACKAMAS; ***222** D-5; elev. 225ft./69m.; ★ **POR**; mail Canby **z** 97013; rural
Madras; Inc. Place; ⊡ JEFFERSON; **222** F-8; elev. 2,283ft./696m.; 🅿 🅷; **z** 97741; Ⓟ 3,443; © 5,078
MALHEUR; **223** J-15; Ⓟ 26,038; © 31,615; ◆ 31,175
Malin; Inc. Place; KLAMATH; **222** N-7; 🅿; **z** 97632; Ⓟ 725; © 638; Ⓡ 640
Manhattan Beach; RMC Place; TILLAMOOK; ***222** C-2; mail Rockaway Beach **z** 97136; pop. incl. with Rockaway Beach (Inc. Place)
Manning; RMC Place; WASHINGTON; **222** C-4; 🅿; **z** 97125; ● 110
Manzanita; Inc. Place; TILLAMOOK; **222** C-2; elev. 111ft./34m.; 🅿; **z** 97130; Ⓟ 513; © 564
Mapleton; RMC Place; LANE; **222** H-2; 🅿; **z** 97453; ● 900
Maplewood; RMC Place; MULTNOMAH; ***222** C-5; ★ **POR**; mail Portland **z** 97219; pop. incl. with Portland (Inc. Place)
Marcola; RMC Place; LANE; **222** G-4; 🅿; **z** 97454; ● 560
Marion; CDP; MARION; **222** F-4; 🅿; ★ **SAL**; **z** 97392; © 274
MARION; **222** E-5; Ⓟ 228,483; © 284,834; Ⓡ 284,838; ◆ 311,069
Marion Forks; RMC Place; LINN; **222** F-6; elev. 2,454ft./748m.; mail Idanha **z** 97350; ● 100
Marlene Village; RMC Place; WASHINGTON; ***222** C-4; ★ **POR**; mail Beaverton **z** 97005; ● 1,800
Marmot; RMC Place; CLACKAMAS; ***222** D-6; mail Sandy **z** 97055; ● 30
Marquam; RMC Place; CLACKAMAS; **222** E-5; elev. 305ft./93m.; mail Mount Angel **z** 97362; ● 60
Marquam Hill; RMC Place; MULTNOMAH; ***222** C-5; ★ **POR**; mail Portland **z** 97201; pop. incl. with Portland (Inc. Place)
Marshland; RMC Place; COLUMBIA; ***222** A-3; elev. 53ft./16m.; mail Clatskanie **z** 97016; ● 80
Martin Manor; RMC Place; WASHINGTON; ★ **POR**; mail Portland **z** 97225
Marylhurst; RMC Place; CLACKAMAS; ***222** D-5; 🅿 🅲 1,258; ★ **POR**; **z** 97036; pop. incl. with Lake Oswego (Inc. Place)
Mason Additions; RMC Place; CROOK; mail Prineville **z** 97754; pop. incl. with Prineville (Inc. Place)
Maupin; Inc. Place; WASCO; **222** D-8; elev. 1,041ft./317m.; 🅿; **z** 97037; Ⓟ 456; © 411
Mayger; RMC Place; COLUMBIA; **222** A-4; elev. 19ft./6m.; mail Clatskanie **z** 97016; ● 120
May Park; RMC Place; UNION; ***223** D-15; mail La Grande **z** 97850; rural
Mayville; RMC Place; GILLIAM; **222** E-10; elev. 2,946ft./898m.; 🅿; **z** 97830; ● 30
Maywood Park; Inc. Place; MULTNOMAH; **223** K-20; ★ **POR**; mail Portland **z** 97220; Ⓟ 781; © 777
McCommach; UMATILLA; see Fulton (RMC Place)
McCoy; RMC Place; POLK; ***222** E-4; ★ **SAL**; mail Rickreall **z** 97371; ● 50
Mc Dermitt; RMC Place; MALHEUR; **223** N-15; mail Jordan Valley **z** 97910; ● 200
McEwen; RMC Place; BAKER; ***223** F-14; mail Baker City **z** 97814; rural
McKee Bridge; RMC Place; JACKSON; ***222** M-4; mail Jacksonville **z** 97530; ● 50
McKenzie Bridge; RMC Place; LANE; **222** G-6; elev. 1,337ft./408m.; 🅿; **z** 97413; ● 400
McKinley; RMC Place; COOS; ***222** J-2; elev. 136ft./41m.; mail Myrtle Point **z** 97458; rural
McMinnville; Inc. Place; ⊡ YAMHILL; **222** D-4; elev. 160ft./49m.; 🅿 🅷 🅲 2,622; **z** 97128; Ⓟ 17,894; © 26,499; ◆ 32,053
McNary; RMC Place; UMATILLA; ***223** B-12; 🅿; **z** 97882; pop. incl. with Umatilla (Inc. Place)
McNulty; RMC Place; COLUMBIA; ***222** B-4; elev. 113ft./34m.; mail Saint Helens **z** 97051; ● 800
Meacham; RMC Place; UMATILLA; **223** C-13; elev. 3,678ft./1,121m.; 🅿; **z** 97859; ● 50
Meadowbrook; RMC Place; CLACKAMAS; ***222** D-5; ★ **POR**; mail Molalla **z** 97038; ● 30
Meadow View; RMC Place; LANE; ***222** G-3; elev. 352ft./107m.; ★ **EUG**; mail Junction City **z** 97448; rural
Meda; RMC Place; TILLAMOOK; ***222** D-2; mail Cloverdale **z** 97112; rural
Medford; Inc. Place; ⊡ JACKSON; **222** M-4; elev. 383ft./117m.; 🅿 🅷 ■; ★ **MEDF**; **z** 97501-04; Ⓟ 46,951; © 63,154; Ⓡ 63,687; ◆ 72,910
Medical Springs; RMC Place; UNION; ***223** E-15; elev. 3,387ft./1,032m.; 🅿; **z** 97814; ● 30
Mehama; CDP; MARION; **222** E-5; elev. 629ft./192m.; 🅿; **z** 97384; © 283
Melrose; RMC Place; DOUGLAS; ***222** J-3; elev. 410ft./125m.; mail Roseburg **z** 97470
Melville; RMC Place; CLATSOP; ***222** B-2; mail Astoria **z** 97103; rural
Menlo Park; RMC Place; MULTNOMAH; ★ **POR**; mail Portland **z** 97230; pop. incl. with Portland (Inc. Place)
Merlin; RMC Place; JOSEPHINE; **222** L-3; elev. 907ft./276m.; 🅿; **z** 97532; ● 600
Merrill; Inc. Place; KLAMATH; **222** N-7; elev. 4,067ft./1,240m.; 🅿; **z** 97633; Ⓟ 837; © 897
Metolius; Inc. Place; JEFFERSON; **222** F-8; elev. 2,530ft./771m.; 🅿; **z** 97741; Ⓟ 450; © 635; Ⓡ 729
Metzger; CDP; WASHINGTON; **223** M-18; ★ **POR**; mail Portland **z** 97223; Ⓟ 3,149; © 3,354
Middle Bridge; RMC Place; BAKER; ***223** E-15; mail Baker City **z** 97814; rural
Midland; RMC Place; KLAMATH; **222** M-6; 🅿; **z** 97634; ● 300
Midway; RMC Place; MULTNOMAH; ★ **POR**; mail Portland **z** 97216, **z** 97233; pop. incl. with Portland (Inc. Place)
Midway; RMC Place; WASHINGTON; ***222** D-4; elev. 195ft./59m.; ★ **POR**; mail Midland **z** 97634
Midway; RMC Place; YAMHILL; ***222** D-3; mail Grand Ronde **z** 97347; rural
Mikkalo; RMC Place; GILLIAM; **222** C-10; elev. 1,468ft./447m.; 🅿; **z** 97861; rural
Miles Crossing; RMC Place; CLATSOP; ***222** A-2; elev. 8ft./2m.; mail Astoria **z** 97103; ● 150
Mill City; Inc. Place; LINN, MARION; **222** F-5; 🅿; **z** 97360; Ⓟ 1,555; © 1,537
Millersburg; Inc. Place; LINN; ***222** F-4; elev. 242ft./74m.; ★ **CORV-**; mail Albany **z** 97321; Ⓟ 715; © 651
Millican; RMC Place; DESCHUTES; ***222** H-8; mail Bend **z** 97701; rural
Millington; RMC Place; COOS; **222** J-1; mail Coos Bay **z** 97420; ● 100
Millwood; RMC Place; DOUGLAS; ***222** J-3; mail Umpqua **z** 97486

Entries in **UPPERCASE** are counties.
Entries in **bold** have populations of 2,500 or more.
Names in parentheses are alternate names.

Inc. Place	Incorporated Place
RMC Place	Rand McNally Designated Place
CDP	Census Designated Place
MCD	Minor Civil Division

⊡ County Seat
▲ Minor Civil Division
elev. Elevation
🅿 Post Office
🅷 Hospital
🅲 College
■ Principal Business Center
★ Ranally Metro Area (RMA) Abbreviation
z Zip Code(s)
Ⓟ Previous Census Population
Ⓡ Revised Census Population
Ⓐ Annexation Population
● Rand McNally Population Estimate
© Final Census Population
Ⓢ Special Census Population
◆ Estimated Population

For additional definitions see Glossary, Volume 1, and Introduction, Volume 2.

Milo; RMC Place; DOUGLAS; **222** K-4; elev. 911ft./278m.; mail Days Creek z 97429; ● 320
Milton; RMC Place; UMATILLA; mail Milton Freewater z 97862; pop. incl. with Milton-Freewater (Inc. Place)
Milton-Freewater; Inc. Place; UMATILLA; **223** B-14; elev. 1,033ft./315m.; 🅿; ★ **WALL**; z 97862; Ⓟ 5,533; © 6,470
Milwaukie; Inc. Place; CLACKAMAS, MULTNOMAH; **223** M-19; 🅿 🅷 ■; ★ **POR**; z 97222, z 97267, z 97269; Ⓟ 18,692; © 20,490; ◆ 21,452
Milwaukie Heights; RMC Place; CLACKAMAS; ***222** D-5; mail Portland z 97222
Minam; RMC Place; WALLOWA; ***223** C-15; mail Elgin z 97827
Mission; CDP; UMATILLA; **223** C-13; located on Umatilla Ind. Res.; elev. 1,215ft./370m.; mail Pendleton z 97801; Ⓟ 664; © 1,019
Mist; RMC Place; COLUMBIA; **222** B-4; mail Clatskanie z 97016; ● 60
Mitchell; Inc. Place; WHEELER; **222** F-10; elev. 2,767ft./843m.; 🅿; z 97750; Ⓟ 163; © 170
Modeville; RMC Place; POLK; ***222** E-4; elev. 171ft./52m.; mail Independence z 97351; rural
Modoc Point; RMC Place; KLAMATH; **222** L-6; mail Chiloquin z 97624; ● 30
Mohawk; RMC Place; LANE; ***222** G-4; ★ **EUG**; mail Springfield z 97477
Mohawk Junction; RMC Place; LANE; ***222** H-4; ★ **EUG**; mail Springfield z 97477; pop. incl. with Springfield (Inc. Place)
Mohler; RMC Place; TILLAMOOK; **222** C-2; elev. 28ft./9m.; mail Nehalem z 97131; ● 60
Molalla; Inc. Place; CLACKAMAS; **222** D-5; elev. 373ft./114m.; 🅿; z 97038; Ⓟ 3,651; © 5,647
Monitor; RMC Place; MARION, CLACKAMAS; ***222** D-4; mail Woodburn z 97071; ● 130
Monkland; RMC Place; SHERMAN; ***222** C-9; mail Moro z 97039; rural
Monmouth; Inc. Place; POLK; **222** E-3; elev. 201ft./61m.; 🅿 🅲 4,889; ★ **SAL**; z 97361; Ⓟ 6,288; © 7,741
Monroe; Inc. Place; BENTON; **222** G-3; elev. 288ft./88m.; 🅿; z 97456; Ⓟ 448; © 607
Montavilla; RMC Place; MULTNOMAH; ***222** C-5; elev. 262ft./80m.; ★ **POR**; mail Portland z 97215; pop. incl. with Portland (Inc. Place)
Monument; Inc. Place; GRANT; **223** E-11; elev. 2,008ft./612m.; 🅿; z 97864; Ⓟ 162; © 151
Moody; RMC Place; LINCOLN; ***222** F-2; mail Toledo z 97391; rural
Morgan; RMC Place; MORROW; ***222** C-10; mail Ione z 97843; rural
Moro; Inc. Place; ⊡ SHERMAN; **222** C-9; elev. 1,808ft./551m.; 🅿; z 97039; Ⓟ 292; © 337
MORROW; **223** D-11; Ⓟ 7,625; © 10,995; ◆ 10,729
Mosier; Inc. Place; WASCO; **222** C-7; elev. 121ft./37m.; 🅿; z 97040; Ⓟ 244; © 410
Mountaindale; RMC Place; WASHINGTON; ***222** C-4; elev. 86ft./26m.; mail North Plains z 97133; rural
Mount Angel; Inc. Place; MARION; **222** E-4; elev. 168ft./51m.; 🅿; z 97362; Ⓟ 2,778; © 3,121
Mount Hebron; RMC Place; UMATILLA; mail Pendleton z 97801; ● 100
Mount Hood; RMC Place; HOOD RIVER; **222** C-7; mail Mount Hood Parkdale z 97041; ● 60
Mount Hood Village; CDP-Census Area Only; CLACKAMAS; ***222** D-6; mail Mount Hood Parkdale z 97041; Ⓟ 2,234; © 3,306
Mount Pleasant; RMC Place; CLACKAMAS; ***222** D-5; ★ **POR**; mail Oregon City z 97045; pop. incl. with Oregon City (Inc. Place)
Mount Vernon; Inc. Place; GRANT; **223** G-12; elev. 2,871ft./875m.; 🅿; z 97865; Ⓟ 538; © 595
Mulino; RMC Place; CLACKAMAS; **222** D-5; elev. 237ft./72m.; 🅿; ★ **POR**; z 97042; ● 350
Mulloy; RMC Place; WASHINGTON; ***222** D-4; ★ **POR**; mail Sherwood z 97140; rural
Multnomah; RMC Place; MULTNOMAH; ***222** C-5; ★ **POR**; mail Portland z 97219, z 97280; pop. incl. with Portland (Inc. Place)
MULTNOMAH; **222** C-6; Ⓟ 583,887; © 660,486; ◆ 741,506
Multnomah Falls; RMC Place; MULTNOMAH; ***222** C-6; mail Bridal Veil z 97010; rural
Murphy; RMC Place; JOSEPHINE; **222** M-3; elev. 1,063ft./324m.; 🅿; z 97533; ● 420
Myrick; RMC Place; UMATILLA; ***223** B-13; mail Adams z 97810; rural
Myrtle Creek; Inc. Place; DOUGLAS; **222** K-3; elev. 640ft./195m.; 🅿; z 97457; Ⓟ 3,063; © 3,419
Myrtle Point; Inc. Place; COOS; **222** J-1; elev. 90ft./27m.; 🅿; z 97458; Ⓟ 2,712; © 2,451

N

Narrows; RMC Place; HARNEY; ***223** J-13; mail Princeton z 97721; rural
Narrows; RMC Place; LINN; ***222** F-4; mail Sweet Home z 97386; rural
Nashville; RMC Place; LINCOLN; ***222** F-3; elev. 239ft./73m.; mail Blodgett z 97326; rural
Natal; RMC Place; COLUMBIA; ***222** B-4; mail Vernonia z 97064
Neahkahnie Beach; RMC Place; TILLAMOOK; ***222** C-2; mail Nehalem z 97131; ● 250
Nedonna; RMC Place; TILLAMOOK; ***222** C-2; mail Rockaway Beach z 97136; ● 450
Needy; RMC Place; CLACKAMAS; ***222** D-5; elev. 176ft./54m.; ★ **POR**; mail Canby z 97013; rural
Nehalem; Inc. Place; TILLAMOOK; **222** C-2; 🅿; z 97131; Ⓟ 232; © 203
Nelscott; RMC Place; LINCOLN; ***222** E-2; elev. 38ft./12m.; mail Lincoln City z 97367; pop. incl. with Lincoln City (Inc. Place)
Neotsu; RMC Place; LINCOLN; **222** E-2; elev. 106ft./32m.; 🅿; z 97364; ● 350
Nesika Beach; RMC Place; CURRY; **222** L-1; mail Gold Beach z 97444; ● 150
Neskowin; CDP; TILLAMOOK; **222** D-2; 🅿; z 97149; summer pop. 750; © 169
Netarts; CDP; TILLAMOOK; **222** C-2; 🅿; z 97143; © 744
Newberg; Inc. Place; YAMHILL; **222** D-4; elev. 176ft./54m.; 🅿 🅷 🅲 3,158; ★ **POR**; z 97132; Ⓟ 13,086; © 18,064; ◆ 23,116
New Bridge; RMC Place; BAKER; **223** E-16; mail Richland z 97870; ● 30
New Era; RMC Place; CLACKAMAS; ***222** D-5; ★ **POR**; mail Canby z 97013; rural
New Hope; RMC Place; JOSEPHINE; ***222** M-3; mail Grants Pass z 97527; ● 700
New Idaho; RMC Place; LAKE; ***222** M-9; mail Lakeview z 97630; rural
New Idanha; RMC Place; LINN; ***222** F-6; mail Idanha z 97350; pop. incl. with Idanha (Inc. Place)
New Pine Creek; RMC Place; LAKE; **222** N-10; 🅿; z 97635; total pop. including New Pine Creek, CA is 400; ● 180
Newport; Inc. Place; ⊡ LINCOLN; **222** F-2; elev. 177ft./54m.; 🅿 🅷; z 97365-66; Ⓟ 8,437; © 9,532
New Princeton (Princeton); RMC Place; HARNEY; **223** J-13; mail Princeton z 97721; ● 150
Newton Creek; RMC Place; DOUGLAS; ***222** J-3; mail Roseburg z 97470; ● 800
Nimrod; RMC Place; LANE; ***222** G-5; mail Vida z 97488
Nonpareil; RMC Place; DOUGLAS; **222** I-4; mail Sutherlin z 97479; ● 70
North Albany; RMC Place; BENTON; ***222** F-4; elev. 200ft./61m.; ★ **CORV-**; mail Albany z 97321; pop. incl. with Albany (Inc. Place); Ⓟ 4,325
North Bend; Inc. Place; COOS; **222** I-1; elev. 23ft./7m.; 🅿 ■; z 97459; Ⓟ 9,614; © 9,544; ◆ 9,298
North Fork; RMC Place; DOUGLAS; ***222** H-2; mail Reedsport z 97467; rural
North Howell; RMC Place; MARION; ***222** E-4; elev. 203ft./62m.; mail Silverton z 97381; rural
North Plains; Inc. Place; WASHINGTON; **222** C-4; 🅿; z 97133; Ⓟ 972; © 1,605
North Powder; Inc. Place; UNION; **223** E-15; elev. 3,256ft./992m.; 🅿; z 97867; Ⓟ 448; © 489
North Roseburg; RMC Place; DOUGLAS; ***222** J-3; mail Roseburg z 97470; pop. incl. with Roseburg (Inc. Place)
North Santiam; RMC Place; MARION; ***222** E-4; ★ **SAL**; mail Aumsville z 97325; ● 80
North Umpqua Village; RMC Place; DOUGLAS; ***222** J-4; mail Idleyld Park z 97447; ● 50
Nortons; RMC Place; LINCOLN; ***222** F-2; mail Blodgett z 97326; ● 30
Norway; RMC Place; COOS; **222** J-1; 🅿; z 97458; ● 150
Norwood; RMC Place; WASHINGTON; ***222** D-4; ★ **POR**; mail Tualatin z 97062; ● 300
Noti; RMC Place; LANE; **222** H-3; 🅿; z 97461; ● 200
Nottingham; RMC Place; DESCHUTES; mail Bend z 97702; ● 150
Nyssa; Inc. Place; MALHEUR; **223** H-17; elev. 2,177ft./664m.; 🅿; z 97913; Ⓟ 2,629; © 3,163
Nyssa Heights; RMC Place; MALHEUR; ***223** H-17; mail Nyssa z 97913; rural

O

Oak Grove; CDP; CLACKAMAS; **223** M-19; 🅿; ★ **POR**; z 97222, z 97267-68; Ⓟ 12,576; © 12,808
Oak Grove; RMC Place; HOOD RIVER; ***222** C-7; elev. 1,032ft./315m.; mail Hood River z 97031; rural
Oak Hills; CDP-Census Area Only; WASHINGTON; ***222** C-4; ★ **POR**; mail Portland z 97225; Ⓟ 6,450; © 9,050
Oakland; Inc. Place; DOUGLAS; **222** I-3; elev. 430ft./131m.; 🅿; z 97462; Ⓟ 844; © 954
Oakridge; Inc. Place; LANE; **222** I-5; elev. 1,209ft./369m.; 🅿; z 97463; Ⓟ 3,063; © 3,148; Ⓡ 3,172
Oak Springs; RMC Place; WASCO; ***222** D-8; mail Maupin z 97037; rural
Oakville; RMC Place; LINN; ***222** F-4; elev. 243ft./74m.; mail Shedd z 97377; rural
Oatfield; CDP-Census Area Only; CLACKAMAS; ***222** D-5; ★ **POR**; mail Portland z 97222; Ⓟ 15,348; © 15,750
O'Brien; RMC Place; JOSEPHINE; **222** M-2; elev. 1,412ft./430m.; 🅿; z 97534; ● 480
Oceanlake; RMC Place; LINCOLN; ***222** E-2; mail Lincoln City z 97367; pop. incl. with Lincoln City (Inc. Place)
Oceanside; CDP; TILLAMOOK; **222** C-2; 🅿; z 97134; summer pop. 400; © 326
Odell; CDP; HOOD RIVER; **222** C-7; elev. 730ft./223m.; 🅿; z 97044; © 1,849
Odessa; RMC Place; KLAMATH; ***222** L-8; mail Klamath Falls z 97601; ● 40
Oklahoma Hill; RMC Place; CLATSOP; ***222** A-3; mail Clatskanie z 97016; rural
Old Colton; RMC Place; CLACKAMAS; ***222** D-5; elev. 828ft./252m.; mail Colton z 97017; rural
Old Town; RMC Place; DOUGLAS; ***222** I-3; mail Oakland z 97462
Olene; RMC Place; KLAMATH; **222** M-7; elev. 4,147ft./1,264m.; mail Klamath Falls z 97601; ● 30
Olex; RMC Place; GILLIAM; ***222** C-10; elev. 1,032ft./315m.; mail Arlington z 97812; rural
Olney; RMC Place; CLATSOP; **222** B-2; mail Astoria z 97103; ● 210
Ontario; Inc. Place; MALHEUR; **223** H-17; elev. 2,154ft./657m.; 🅿 🅷 ■; z 97914; Ⓟ 9,392; © 10,985; ◆ 10,048
Ophir; RMC Place; CURRY; **222** L-1; elev. 28ft./9m.; 🅿; z 97464; ● 220
Orchard View; RMC Place; YAMHILL; ***222** D-3; mail McMinnville z 97128; rural
Oregon City; Inc. Place; ⊡ CLACKAMAS; **223** N-19; 🅿 🅷 ■; ★ **POR**; z 97045; Ⓟ 14,698; © 25,754; ◆ 31,896
Oregon Trunk Junction; RMC Place; WASCO; ***222** C-8; mail The Dalles z 97058; rural
Orenco; RMC Place; WASHINGTON; ***222** C-4; ★ **POR**; mail Hillsboro z 97123-24; pop. incl. with Hillsboro (Inc. Place)
Oretown; RMC Place; TILLAMOOK; ***222** D-2; elev. 48ft./15m.; mail Cloverdale z 97112; rural
Orient; RMC Place; MULTNOMAH; ***222** C-5; ★ **POR**; mail Gresham z 97030; ● 50
Orleans; RMC Place; LINN; ***222** F-4; elev. 230ft./70m.; ★ **CORV-**; mail Albany z 97321; rural
Orrs Corner; RMC Place; POLK; ***222** E-3; ★ **SAL**; mail Dallas z 97338; rural
Oswego; CLACKAMAS, MULTNOMAH, WASHINGTON; see Lake Oswego (Inc. Place)
Otis; RMC Place; LINCOLN; **222** E-2; elev. 33ft./10m.; 🅿; z 97368; ● 230
Otter Rock; RMC Place; LINCOLN; **222** E-2; elev. 132ft./40m.; 🅿; z 97369; ● 200
Outlook; RMC Place; CLACKAMAS; **223** M-20; ★ **POR**; mail Oregon City z 97045; ● 100
Owyhee; RMC Place; MALHEUR; ***223** H-17; mail Nyssa z 97913

P

Pacific City; CDP; TILLAMOOK; **222** D-2; 🅿; z 97135; summer pop. 1,800; © 1,027
Page; RMC Place; LINN; ***222** F-4; ★ **CORV-**; mail Albany z 97321; pop. incl. with Albany (Inc. Place)
Paisley; Inc. Place; LAKE; **222** L-9; elev. 4,369ft./1,332m.; 🅿; z 97636; Ⓟ 350; © 247
Palestine; RMC Place; BENTON; ***222** F-4; ★ **CORV-**; mail Albany z 97321; rural
Palmer Junction (Looking Glass); RMC Place; UNION; ***223** C-15; mail Elgin z 97827; rural
Palmer Junction; RMC Place; UNION; ***223** C-15; mail Elgin z 97827; rural
Paradise Park; RMC Place; CLACKAMAS; ***222** D-5; ★ **POR**; mail Estacada z 97023; ● 120
Parkdale; CDP; HOOD RIVER; **222** C-7; elev. 1,744ft./532m.; mail Mount Hood Parkdale z 97041; © 266
Parker; RMC Place; POLK; ***222** E-4; elev. 213ft./65m.; mail Independence z 97351; rural
Parkersburg; RMC Place; COOS; ***222** J-1; mail Bandon z 97411; rural
Park Place; RMC Place; CLACKAMAS; ***222** D-5; ★ **POR**; mail Oregon City z 97045; pop. incl. with Oregon City (Inc. Place)
Parkrose; RMC Place; MULTNOMAH; **223** K-20; elev. 76ft./23m.; ★ **POR**; mail Portland z 97220, z 97230, z 97294; pop. incl. with Portland (Inc. Place)
Patterson Junction; RMC Place; MORROW; ***223** B-11; mail Irrigon z 97844; ● 80
Paulina; RMC Place; CROOK; **222** G-10; 🅿; z 97751; ● 40
Payette Junction; RMC Place; MALHEUR; ***223** G-17; mail Ontario z 97914; rural
Pedee; RMC Place; POLK; **222** E-3; elev. 267ft./81m.; mail Monmouth z 97361; ● 100
Peel; RMC Place; DOUGLAS; ***222** J-4; mail Glide z 97443; rural
Pelican City; RMC Place; KLAMATH; ***222** M-6; mail Klamath Falls z 97601; pop. incl. with Klamath Falls (Inc. Place)
Pendair Heights; RMC Place; UMATILLA; ***223** C-13; elev. 1,484ft./452m.; mail Pendleton z 97801; pop. incl. with Pendleton (Inc. Place)
Pendleton; Inc. Place; ⊡ UMATILLA; **223** C-13; elev. 1,068ft./326m.; 🅿 🅷 ■; z 97801; location of Umatilla Indian Agency; Ⓟ 15,126; © 16,354; ◆ 16,764
Pendleton Junction; RMC Place; UMATILLA; ***223** C-13; mail Pendleton z 97801; pop. incl. with Pendleton (Inc. Place)
Peoria; RMC Place; LINN; **222** F-4; elev. 258ft./79m.; mail Shedd z 97377; ● 250
Perry; RMC Place; UNION; **223** D-14; mail La Grande z 97850; ● 90
Perrydale; RMC Place; POLK; ***222** E-3; elev. 175ft./53m.; mail Amity z 97101; ● 60
Petersburg; RMC Place; WASCO; ***222** C-8; mail The Dalles z 97058; ● 50
Philomath; Inc. Place; BENTON; **222** F-3; elev. 280ft./85m.; 🅿; ★ **CORV-**; z 97370; Ⓟ 2,983; © 3,838
Phoenix; Inc. Place; JACKSON; **222** M-4; elev. 1,543ft./470m.; 🅿; ★ **MEDF**; z 97535; Ⓟ 3,239; © 4,060
Piedmont; RMC Place; MULTNOMAH; ***222** C-5; ★ **POR**; mail Portland z 97211; pop. incl. with Portland (Inc. Place)
Pike; RMC Place; YAMHILL; ***222** D-3; mail Yamhill z 97148; rural
Pikes Camp; RMC Place; LINCOLN; ***222** E-2; mail Lincoln City z 97367; rural
Pilot Rock; Inc. Place; UMATILLA; **223** C-13; elev. 1,636ft./499m.; 🅿; z 97868; Ⓟ 1,478; © 1,532
Pine; RMC Place; BAKER; ***223** E-16; mail Halfway z 97834; rural
Pine Grove; RMC Place; HOOD RIVER; ***222** C-7; mail Hood River z 97031; rural
Pine Grove; CDP; WASCO; **222** E-7; elev. 2,201ft./671m.; mail Maupin z 97037; © 162
Pine Hollow; CDP-Census Area Only; WASCO; ***222** D-8; © 424
Pinehurst; RMC Place; JACKSON; ***222** M-5; mail Ashland z 97520; ● 40
Pine Ridge; RMC Place; KLAMATH; ***222** L-6; mail Chiloquin z 97624; rural
Pioneer; RMC Place; MULTNOMAH; ★ **POR**; mail Portland z 97204; pop. incl. with Portland (Inc. Place)
Pistol River; RMC Place; CURRY; **222** M-1; elev. 20ft./6m.; 🅿; z 97444; ● 120
Pittsburg; RMC Place; COLUMBIA; **222** B-4; elev. 581ft./177m.; mail Vernonia z 97064; ● 40
Plainview; RMC Place; DESCHUTES; ***222** G-7; elev. 3,233ft./985m.; mail Bend z 97701; rural
Plainview; RMC Place; LINN; ***222** F-4; elev. 278ft./85m.; mail Shedd z 97377; rural
Pleasant Hill; RMC Place; LANE; **222** H-4; elev. 658ft./201m.; 🅿; ★ **EUG**; z 97455 & mail Eugene z 97405; ● 110
Pleasant Valley; RMC Place; BAKER; ***223** F-15; elev. 3,745ft./1,141m.; mail Baker City z 97814; rural
Pleasant Valley; RMC Place; JOSEPHINE; ***222** L-3; elev. 1,092ft./333m.; mail Merlin z 97532
Pleasant Valley; RMC Place; TILLAMOOK; ***222** D-2; elev. 137ft./42m.; mail Tillamook z 97141; ● 30
Plush; RMC Place; LAKE; **223** L-11; 🅿; z 97637; ● 70
Pocahontas; RMC Place; BAKER; ***223** E-15; mail Baker City z 97814; rural
POLK; **222** E-3; Ⓟ 49,541; © 62,380; ◆ 79,048
Polk Station; RMC Place; POLK; ***222** E-3; mail Dallas z 97338; rural
Pondosa; RMC Place; UNION; ***223** E-15; mail Baker City z 97814; rural
Porter Creek; RMC Place; DOUGLAS; ***222** J-3; mail Tenmile z 97481; rural
Portland; Inc. Place; ⊡ MULTNOMAH, CLACKAMAS, WASHINGTON; **223** K-19; 🅿 🅷 🅲 39,551 ■; ★ **POR**; z 97086, z 97201-25, z 97227-33, z 97236, z 97238-40, z 97242, z 97256, z 97258, z 97266-69, z 97280-83, z 97286, z 97290-94, z 97296, z 97298-99; Ⓟ 437,319; © 529,121; ◆ 599,642
Portland Heights; RMC Place; MULTNOMAH; ***222** C-5; ★ **POR**; mail Portland z 97201; pop. incl. with Portland (Inc. Place)
Port Orford; Inc. Place; CURRY; **222** K-1; 🅿; z 97465; Ⓟ 1,025; © 1,153
Post; RMC Place; CROOK; **222** G-9; 🅿; z 97752; ● 40
Powell Butte; RMC Place; CROOK; **222** G-8; 🅿; z 97753; ● 770
Powellhurst; RMC Place; MULTNOMAH; ★ **POR**; mail Portland z 97221, z 97266; pop. incl. with Portland (Inc. Place)
Power City; RMC Place; UMATILLA; ***223** B-12; mail Umatilla z 97882; ● 30
Powers; Inc. Place; COOS; **222** K-2; elev. 286ft./87m.; 🅿; z 97466; Ⓟ 682; © 734
Prairie City; Inc. Place; GRANT; **223** F-13; 🅿; z 97869; Ⓟ 1,117; © 1,080
Pratum; RMC Place; MARION; ***222** E-4; mail Salem z 97301; ● 50
Prescott; Inc. Place; COLUMBIA; **222** B-4; elev. 25ft./8m.; ★ **LNGV**; mail Rainier z 97048; Ⓟ 63; © 72
Princeton; HARNEY; see New Princeton (RMC Place)
Prineville; Inc. Place; ⊡ CROOK; **222** G-8; 🅿 🅷; z 97754; Ⓟ 5,355; © 7,356; Ⓡ 7,358
Prineville Southeast; RMC Place; CROOK; mail Prineville z 97754; pop. incl. with Prineville (Inc. Place)
Progress; RMC Place; WASHINGTON; ***222** C-4; ★ **POR**; mail Beaverton z 97005, z 97008; pop. incl. with Beaverton (Inc. Place)
Prospect; RMC Place; JACKSON; **222** K-5; elev. 2,598ft./792m.; 🅿; z 97536; ● 1,200
Prosper; RMC Place; COOS; ***222** J-1; mail Bandon z 97411; ● 80

Q

Quartz Mountain; RMC Place; LAKE; ***222** M-9; mail Lakeview z 97630; rural
Quinaby; RMC Place; MARION; ***222** E-4; elev. 176ft./54m.; ★ **SAL**; mail Salem z 97303; ● 70
Quincy; RMC Place; COLUMBIA; ***222** A-4; elev. 18ft./5m.; mail Clatskanie z 97016; ● 120
Quines Creek; RMC Place; DOUGLAS; ***222** K-3; elev. 1,562ft./476m.; mail Glendale z 97442

R

Rainbow; RMC Place; LANE; ***222** G-6; mail Blue River z 97413; ● 50
Rainier; Inc. Place; COLUMBIA; **222** B-4; elev. 24ft./7m.; 🅿; ★ **LNGV**; z 97048; Ⓟ 1,674; © 1,687
Raleigh Hills; CDP; WASHINGTON; **223** L-18; ★ **POR**; mail Portland z 97225; Ⓟ 6,066; © 5,865
Ramsey; RMC Place; DESCHUTES; mail Bend z 97701; ● 120
Ramsey Hall; RMC Place; WASCO; ***222** D-8; elev. 1,601ft./488m.; mail Dufur z 97021; rural
Rand; RMC Place; JOSEPHINE; ***222** L-3; mail Merlin z 97532; summer pop. 200; ● 30
Randolph; RMC Place; COOS; ***222** J-1; mail Bandon z 97411; rural
Redland; RMC Place; CLACKAMAS; ***222** D-5; elev. 346ft./105m.; ★ **POR**; mail Oregon City z 97045
Redmond; Inc. Place; DESCHUTES; **222** G-8; elev. 2,997ft./913m.; 🅿 🅷; z 97756; Ⓟ 7,163; © 13,481; ◆ 22,577
Redwood; CDP-Census Area Only; JOSEPHINE; ***222** L-3; mail Grants Pass z 97526; Ⓟ 3,702; © 5,844
Reedsport; Inc. Place; DOUGLAS; **222** I-2; elev. 10ft./3m.; 🅿 🅷; z 97467; Ⓟ 4,796; © 4,378
Remote; RMC Place; COOS; **222** K-2; elev. 239ft./73m.; 🅿; z 97458; ● 30
Reston; RMC Place; DOUGLAS; ***222** J-2; mail Roseburg z 97470; rural
Rhododendron; RMC Place; CLACKAMAS; **222** D-6; elev. 1,623ft./495m.; 🅿; z 97049; ● 800
Rice Hill; RMC Place; DOUGLAS; ***222** I-3; elev. 715ft./218m.; mail Oakland z 97462; rural
Richardson; RMC Place; LANE; ***222** H-2; mail Walton z 97490; rural
Richland; Inc. Place; BAKER; **223** E-16; 🅿; z 97870; Ⓟ 161; © 147
Richmond; RMC Place; WHEELER; ***222** F-10; mail Spray z 97874; rural
Rickreall; CDP; POLK; **222** E-3; elev. 209ft./64m.; 🅿; ★ **SAL**; z 97371; © 57
Riddle; Inc. Place; DOUGLAS; **222** K-3; elev. 705ft./215m.; 🅿; z 97469; Ⓟ 1,143; © 1,014
Rieth; RMC Place; UMATILLA; **223** C-12; mail Pendleton z 97801; ● 70
Riley; RMC Place; HARNEY; **223** I-11; 🅿; z 97758; ● 50
Ripplebrook; RMC Place; CLACKAMAS; ***222** E-6; mail Estacada z 97023; rural
Ritter; RMC Place; GRANT; **223** E-12; 🅿; z 97856; ● 50
Riverdale; RMC Place; MULTNOMAH; ***222** C-5; ★ **POR**; mail Portland z 97219
River Gate; RMC Place; MULTNOMAH; pop. incl. with Portland (Inc. Place)
Rivergrove; Inc. Place; CLACKAMAS, WASHINGTON; **223** M-18; ★ **POR**; mail Lake Oswego z 97035; Ⓟ 294; © 324
River Road; RMC Place; LANE; ***222** G-4; ★ **EUG**; mail Eugene z 97404; Ⓟ 9,443
Riverside; RMC Place; LINN; ***222** F-4; ★ **CORV-**; mail Albany z 97322; ● 100
Riverside; RMC Place; MALHEUR; **223** I-14; 🅿; z 97917; ● 10
Riverside; CDP-Census Area Only; UMATILLA; ***223** C-13; mail Pendleton z 97801; © 189
Riverton; RMC Place; COOS; **222** J-1; mail Coquille z 97423; ● 100
Riverview; RMC Place; COLUMBIA; mail Vernonia z 97064; pop. incl. with Vernonia (Inc. Place)
Riverview; RMC Place; LANE; ***222** G-4; ★ **EUG**; mail Junction City z 97448; rural
Roads End; RMC Place; LINCOLN; ***222** E-2; mail Lincoln City z 97367; summer pop. 400; ● 200
Roaring Springs Ranch; RMC Place; HARNEY; ***223** L-13; mail Frenchglen z 97736; rural
Robinwood; RMC Place; CLACKAMAS; ***222** D-5; ★ **POR**; mail West Linn z 97068; pop. incl. with West Linn (Inc. Place)
Rockaway; TILLAMOOK; see Rockaway Beach (Inc. Place)
Rockaway Beach (Rockaway); Inc. Place; TILLAMOOK; **222** C-2; elev. 16ft./5m.; 🅿; z 97136; Ⓟ 970; © 1,267
Rock Creek; RMC Place; BAKER; ***223** E-14; mail Haines z 97833
Rock Creek; RMC Place; GILLIAM; ***222** C-10; elev. 728ft./222m.; mail Arlington z 97812; rural
Rockcreek; CDP-Census Area Only; WASHINGTON; ***222** C-4; ★ **POR**; mail Portland z 97225, z 97229; Ⓟ 8,282; © 9,404
Rockford; RMC Place; HOOD RIVER; ***222** C-7; mail Hood River z 97031; rural
Rockie Four Corners; RMC Place; MARION; ***222** E-5; mail Scotts Mills z 97375; ● 30
Rock Point; RMC Place; JACKSON; ***222** L-4; elev. 1,051ft./320m.; mail Gold Hill z 97525; rural
Rockville; RMC Place; MALHEUR; ***223** J-17; mail Jordan Valley z 97910; ● 30
Rockwood; RMC Place; MULTNOMAH; **223** L-20; ★ **POR**; mail Portland z 97233; pop. incl. with Gresham (Inc. Place)
Rocky Point; RMC Place; KLAMATH; ***222** L-6; mail Klamath Falls z 97601; ● 110
Rogue River; Inc. Place; JACKSON; **222** L-3; elev. 1,001ft./305m.; 🅿; z 97537; Ⓟ 1,759; © 1,847; Ⓡ 1,851
Rome; RMC Place; MALHEUR; ***223** K-15; elev. 3,391ft./1,034m.; mail Jordan Valley z 97910; rural
Roseburg; Inc. Place; ⊡ DOUGLAS; **222** J-3; elev. 459ft./140m.; 🅿 🅷 ■; z 97470-71; Ⓟ 17,069; © 20,017; ◆ 20,059
Roseburg North; CDP-Census Area Only; DOUGLAS; ***222** J-3; mail Roseburg z 97470; Ⓟ 6,831; © 5,473
Rose City Park; RMC Place; MULTNOMAH; ★ **POR**; mail Portland z 97213, z 97218; pop. incl. with Portland (Inc. Place)
Rose Lodge; CDP; LINCOLN; **222** E-2; elev. 169ft./52m.; 🅿; z 97367; Ⓟ 1,257; © 1,708
Rosemont; RMC Place; CLACKAMAS; ***222** D-5; elev. 669ft./204m.; ★ **POR**; mail West Linn z 97068; pop. incl. with West Linn (Inc. Place)
Rowena; CDP; WASCO; ***222** C-8; mail Mosier z 97040, The Dalles z 97058; © 148
Roy; RMC Place; WASHINGTON; ***222** C-4; elev. 187ft./57m.; mail Banks z 97106; rural
Ruch; RMC Place; JACKSON; **222** M-4; elev. 1,527ft./465m.; mail Jacksonville z 97530; ● 170
Ruckel Junction; RMC Place; UMATILLA; ***223** C-14; mail Meacham z 97859; rural
Rufus; Inc. Place; SHERMAN; **222** C-9; elev. 206ft./63m.; 🅿; z 97050; Ⓟ 295; © 268
Ruggs; RMC Place; MORROW; ***223** D-11; elev. 2,115ft./645m.; mail Heppner z 97836; rural
Rural Dell; RMC Place; CLACKAMAS; ***222** D-5; ★ **POR**; mail Hubbard z 97032; rural
Russellville; RMC Place; MULTNOMAH; elev. 278ft./85m.; ★ **POR**; mail Portland z 97216; pop. incl. with Portland (Inc. Place)
Rye Valley; RMC Place; BAKER; ***223** F-16; mail Huntington z 97907; rural

S

Saginaw; RMC Place; LANE; **222** H-4; elev. 614ft./187m.; 🅿; ★ **EUG**; z 97424; ● 100
Saint Helens; Inc. Place; ⊡ COLUMBIA; **222** B-4; elev. 73ft./22m.; 🅿; z 97051 & mail Deer Island z 97054; Ⓟ 7,535; © 10,019
Saint Johns; RMC Place; MULTNOMAH; ***222** C-4; ★ **POR**; mail Portland z 97203, z 97231, z 97283; pop. incl. with Portland (Inc. Place)
Saint Louis; RMC Place; MARION; ***222** D-4; elev. 181ft./55m.; mail Gervais z 97026, Woodburn z 97071; rural
Saint Paul; Inc. Place; MARION; **222** D-4; elev. 170ft./52m.; 🅿; z 97137; Ⓟ 322; © 354
Salem; Inc. Place; **STATE CAPITAL**; ⊡ MARION, POLK; **223** F-19; elev. 154ft./47m.; 🅿 🅷 🅲 3,565 ■; ★ **SAL**; z 97301-12, z 97314, z 97317; Ⓟ 107,786; © 136,924; ◆ 153,142
Salishan; RMC Place; LINCOLN; ***222** E-2; mail Gleneden Beach z 97388; summer pop. 1,200; ● 200
Salmon Harbor; RMC Place; DOUGLAS; mail Reedsport z 97467
Salt Creek; RMC Place; POLK; ***222** E-3; mail Dallas z 97338; rural
Sams Valley; RMC Place; JACKSON; ***222** L-4; elev. 1,270ft./387m.; mail Gold Hill z 97525
Sand Creek; RMC Place; KLAMATH; ***222** K-6; mail Klamath Falls z 97601; rural
Sand Lake; RMC Place; TILLAMOOK; ***222** D-2; elev. 41ft./12m.; mail Cloverdale z 97112; ● 50
Sandy; Inc. Place; CLACKAMAS; **222** D-6; 🅿; ★ **POR**; z 97055; Ⓟ 4,152; © 5,385
San Marine; RMC Place; LINCOLN; ***222** G-2; mail Yachats z 97498; ● 150
San Rafael; RMC Place; MULTNOMAH; ★ **POR**; pop. incl. with Portland (Inc. Place)
Santa Clara; RMC Place; LANE; **222** A-6; elev. 388ft./118m.; ★ **EUG**; mail Eugene z 97404; Ⓟ 12,834
Santiam Terrace; RMC Place; LINN; ***222** F-4; mail Lebanon z 97355; rural
Saunders Lake; RMC Place; COOS; ***222** I-1; mail North Bend z 97459; ● 80
Sawyers Rapids; RMC Place; DOUGLAS; ***222** I-2; mail Elkton z 97436; rural
Scappoose; Inc. Place; COLUMBIA; **222** C-4; elev. 611ft./186m.; 🅿; z 97056; Ⓟ 3,529; © 4,976
Scholls; RMC Place; WASHINGTON; ***222** D-4; ★ **POR**; mail Hillsboro z 97123; ● 230
Scio; Inc. Place; LINN; **222** F-4; elev. 317ft./97m.; 🅿; z 97374; Ⓟ 623; © 695
Scofield; RMC Place; WASHINGTON; ***222** C-4; mail Buxton z 97109; rural
Scottsburg; RMC Place; DOUGLAS; **222** I-2; elev. 47ft./14m.; 🅿; z 97473; ● 210
Scotts Mills; Inc. Place; MARION; **222** E-5; 🅿; z 97375; Ⓟ 283; © 312
Seal Rock; RMC Place; LINCOLN; **222** F-2; elev. 26ft./8m.; 🅿; z 97376; ● 600
Seaside; Inc. Place; CLATSOP; **222** B-2; 🅿 🅷; z 97138; Ⓟ 5,359; © 5,900
Seekseequa; RMC Place; JEFFERSON; ***222** F-8; mail Warm Springs z 97761; ● 60
Seghers; RMC Place; WASHINGTON; ***222** C-4; elev. 182ft./55m.; ★ **POR**; mail Gaston z 97119; ● 60
Sellwood; RMC Place; MULTNOMAH; ***222** C-5; elev. 115ft./35m.; ★ **POR**; mail Portland z 97202; pop. incl. with Portland (Inc. Place)
Sellwood Moreland; RMC Place; MULTNOMAH; ★ **POR**; mail Portland z 97202, z 97282; pop. incl. with Portland (Inc. Place)
Selma; RMC Place; JOSEPHINE; **222** M-2; elev. 1,325ft./404m.; 🅿; z 97538; ● 840
Seneca; Inc. Place; GRANT; **223** G-12; elev. 4,666ft./1,422m.; 🅿; z 97873; Ⓟ 191; © 223
Service Creek; RMC Place; WHEELER; ***222** E-10; mail Fossil z 97830; rural
Shadowood; RMC Place; CLACKAMAS; ***222** D-5; ★ **POR**; mail West Linn z 97068; ● 50
Shady Cove; Inc. Place; JACKSON; **222** L-4; 🅿; z 97539; Ⓟ 1,351; © 2,307
Shady Dell; RMC Place; CLACKAMAS; ***222** D-5; ★ **POR**; mail Molalla z 97038; rural
Shady Pine; RMC Place; KLAMATH; ***222** M-6; mail Klamath Falls z 97601; rural
Shale City; RMC Place; JACKSON; ***222** M-5; mail Ashland z 97520; rural
Shaniko; Inc. Place; WASCO; **222** E-9; elev. 3,341ft./1,018m.; 🅿; z 97057; Ⓟ 26; © 26
Shaw; RMC Place; MARION; **222** E-4; ★ **SAL**; mail Aumsville z 97325; ● 80
Shedd; RMC Place; LINN; **222** F-4; elev. 264ft./80m.; 🅿; z 97377; ● 250
Shelburn; RMC Place; LINN; ***222** F-4; elev. 352ft./107m.; mail Scio z 97374; ● 40
Sheridan; Inc. Place; YAMHILL; **222** D-3; 🅿; z 97378; Ⓟ 3,979; © 3,570; Ⓡ 5,561
SHERMAN; **222** D-9; Ⓟ 1,918; © 1,934; ◆ 1,707
Sherwood; Inc. Place; WASHINGTON; **223** N-17; elev. 205ft./62m.; 🅿; ★ **POR**; z 97140; Ⓟ 3,093; © 11,791
Shorewood; RMC Place; COOS; ***222** I-1; mail North Bend z 97459; ● 150
Siletz; Inc. Place; LINCOLN; **222** F-2; elev. 131ft./40m.; 🅿; z 97380; location of Indian Agency; Ⓟ 926; © 1,133
Siletz Reservation; LINCOLN; Indian Reservation; © 308
Siltcoos; RMC Place; LANE; **222** H-2; mail Westlake z 97493; ● 30
Silver Lake; RMC Place; LAKE; **222** J-8; elev. 4,345ft./1,324m.; 🅿; z 97638; ● 170
Silverton; Inc. Place; MARION; **222** E-4; elev. 249ft./76m.; 🅿 🅷; z 97381; Ⓟ 5,635; © 7,414
Silvies (Silvies Landing); RMC Place; GRANT; ***223** H-13; mail Burns z 97720; rural
Silvies Landing; GRANT; see Silvies (RMC Place)
Simnasho; RMC Place; WASCO; ***222** E-7; located on Warm Springs Ind. Res.; elev. 2,401ft./732m.; mail Warm Springs z 97761
Sisters; Inc. Place; DESCHUTES; **222** G-7; elev. 3,186ft./971m.; 🅿; z 97759; Ⓟ 679; © 959
Sitkum; RMC Place; COOS; ***222** J-2; elev. 607ft./185m.; mail Myrtle Point z 97458
Six Corners; RMC Place; WASHINGTON; ***222** D-4; ★ **POR**; mail Sherwood z 97140; pop. incl. with Sherwood (Inc. Place)
Sixes; RMC Place; CURRY; **222** K-1; 🅿; z 97476; ● 220
Smithfield; LANE; see Franklin (RMC Place)
Smithfield; RMC Place; POLK; ***222** E-3; mail Dallas z 97338; rural
Sodaville; Inc. Place; LINN; **222** F-4; mail Lebanon z 97355; Ⓟ 192; © 290
South Beach; RMC Place; LINCOLN; **222** F-2; elev. 21ft./6m.; 🅿; z 97366; pop. incl. with Newport (Inc. Place)
South Junction; RMC Place; WASCO; ***222** E-8; elev. 1,263ft./385m.; mail Maupin z 97037; rural
South Lebanon; CDP-Census Area Only; LINN; ***222** F-4; mail Lebanon z 97355; Ⓟ 1,203; © 1,155
South Scappoose; RMC Place; COLUMBIA; ***222** C-4; mail Scappoose z 97056; pop. incl. with Scappoose (Inc. Place)
Southside; RMC Place; LANE; ★ **EUG**; mail Eugene z 97403, z 97405; pop. incl. with Eugene (Inc. Place)
Sparks; RMC Place; UMATILLA; ***223** C-13; mail Pendleton z 97801; rural
Spicer; RMC Place; LINN; ***222** F-4; elev. 296ft./90m.; mail Lebanon z 97355; rural
Sprague River; RMC Place; KLAMATH; **222** L-7; elev. 4,345ft./1,324m.; 🅿; z 97639; ● 350
Spray; Inc. Place; WHEELER; **223** E-11; elev. 1,798ft./548m.; 🅿; z 97874; Ⓟ 149; © 140
Springbrook; RMC Place; YAMHILL; ***222** D-4; elev. 248ft./76m.; ★ **POR**; mail Newberg z 97132; pop. incl. with Newberg (Inc. Place)
Springdale; RMC Place; MULTNOMAH; ***222** C-5; elev. 274ft./84m.; mail Troutdale z 97060; ● 400
Springfield; Inc. Place; LANE; **222** A-8; elev. 456ft./139m.; 🅿 🅷 ■; ★ **EUG**; z 97477-78, z 97482; Ⓟ 44,683; © 52,864; ◆ 59,983
Springwater; RMC Place; CLACKAMAS; ***222** D-5; elev. 1,112ft./339m.; ★ **POR**; mail Estacada z 97023
Stafford (Wankers Corners); RMC Place; CLACKAMAS; ***222** D-5; elev. 413ft./126m.; ★ **POR**; mail West Linn z 97068; ● 30
Staleys Junction; RMC Place; WASHINGTON; ***222** C-4; mail Buxton z 97109; rural
Stanfield; Inc. Place; UMATILLA; **223** B-12; 🅿; z 97875; Ⓟ 1,568; © 1,979
Stapleton; RMC Place; POLK; ***222** E-4; mail Independence z 97351; rural
Starkey; RMC Place; UNION; ***223** D-14; mail La Grande z 97850; rural
Stayton; Inc. Place; MARION; **222** E-4; elev. 457ft./139m.; 🅿 🅷; ★ **SAL**; z 97383; Ⓟ 5,011; © 6,816
Steamboat; RMC Place; DOUGLAS; **222** J-4; mail Idleyld Park z 97447; ● 60
Stewart Lennox Addition; RMC Place; KLAMATH; ***222** M-6; mail Klamath Falls z 97601; pop. incl. with Klamath Falls (Inc. Place)
Stimson Mill; RMC Place; WASHINGTON; ***222** C-4; mail Gaston z 97119; rural
Sublimity; Inc. Place; MARION; **222** E-4; elev. 548ft./167m.; 🅿; ★ **SAL**; z 97385; Ⓟ 1,491; © 2,148
Summer Lake; RMC Place; LAKE; **222** K-9; elev. 4,225ft./1,288m.; 🅿; z 97640; ● 70
Summer Lake Hot Springs; RMC Place; LAKE; ***222** L-9; mail Paisley z 97636; summer pop. 100; ● 10
Summerville; Inc. Place; UNION; **223** C-14; 🅿; z 97876; Ⓟ 111; © 117
Summit; RMC Place; BENTON; ***222** F-3; elev. 729ft./222m.; mail Blodgett z 97326
Sumner; RMC Place; COOS; **222** J-1; mail Coos Bay z 97420; ● 50
Sumpter; Inc. Place; BAKER; **223** E-14; 🅿; z 97877; Ⓟ 119; © 171
Sunnycrest; RMC Place; YAMHILL; ***222** D-4; elev. 285ft./87m.; ★ **POR**; mail Newberg z 97132; rural
Sunnydale; RMC Place; DOUGLAS; ***222** I-3; mail Drain z 97435; rural
Sunnyside; CDP; CLACKAMAS; **223** M-20; ★ **POR**; mail Clackamas z 97015, Portland z 97266, Woodburn z 97071; Ⓟ 4,423; © 6,791
Sunnyside; RMC Place; UMATILLA; ***223** B-14; ★ **WALL**; mail Milton Freewater z 97862
Sunny Valley; RMC Place; JOSEPHINE; **222** L-3; elev. 1,229ft./375m.; mail Wolf Creek z 97497; ● 180
Sunriver; RMC Place; DESCHUTES; **222** H-7; 🅿; z 97707; ● 900
Sunset; RMC Place; CLACKAMAS; ***222** D-5; ★ **POR**; mail West Linn z 97068; pop. incl. with West Linn (Inc. Place)
Sunset Beach; RMC Place; CLATSOP; **222** A-2; mail Warrenton z 97146; ● 320
Sunset Hills; RMC Place; CLATSOP; mail Seaside z 97138; pop. incl. with Seaside (Inc. Place)
Suntex; RMC Place; HARNEY; ***223** I-11; mail Riley z 97758; rural
Suplee; RMC Place; CROOK; ***223** H-11; mail Paulina z 97751; rural
Surf Pines; RMC Place; CLATSOP; ***222** B-2; mail Warrenton z 97146; rural
Surprise Valley; RMC Place; DOUGLAS; ***222** K-3; mail Myrtle Creek z 97457; rural
Sutherlin; Inc. Place; DOUGLAS; **222** J-3; elev. 540ft./165m.; 🅿; z 97479; Ⓟ 5,020; © 6,669
Suver; RMC Place; POLK; **222** F-3; elev. 207ft./63m.; mail Monmouth z 97361; ● 50
Suver Junction; RMC Place; POLK; ***222** F-3; mail Monmouth z 97361; rural
Svensen; RMC Place; CLATSOP; **222** A-3; elev. 9ft./3m.; mail Astoria z 97103; ● 550
Swedetown; RMC Place; COLUMBIA; ***222** B-4; mail Clatskanie z 97016; ● 170
Sweet Home; Inc. Place; LINN; **222** G-4; elev. 525ft./160m.; 🅿; z 97386; Ⓟ 6,850; © 8,016
Swisshome; RMC Place; LANE; **222** H-2; 🅿; z 97480; ● 300
Sylvan; RMC Place; MULTNOMAH; **223** L-18; ★ **POR**; mail Portland z 97221; pop. incl. with Portland (Inc. Place)

T

Table Rock; RMC Place; JACKSON; ***222** L-4; mail Medford z 97501; ● 70
Taft; RMC Place; LINCOLN; ***222** E-2; elev. 36ft./11m.; mail Lincoln City z 97367; pop. incl. with Lincoln City (Inc. Place)
Takilma; RMC Place; JOSEPHINE; **222** M-2; mail Cave Junction z 97523; ● 100
Talbot; RMC Place; MARION; ***222** E-4; ★ **SAL**; mail Jefferson z 97352; rural
Talent; Inc. Place; JACKSON; **222** M-4; elev. 1,635ft./498m.; 🅿; ★ **MEDF**; z 97540; Ⓟ 3,274; © 5,589
Tallman; RMC Place; LINN; ***222** F-4; elev. 307ft./94m.; mail Lebanon z 97355; rural
Tangent; Inc. Place; LINN; **222** F-4; elev. 246ft./75m.; 🅿; ★ **CORV-**; z 97389; Ⓟ 556; © 933
Taylorville; RMC Place; CLATSOP; ***222** A-3; mail Clatskanie z 97016; ● 50
Telocaset; RMC Place; UNION; ***223** D-15; mail Union z 97883
Tenmile; RMC Place; COOS; ***222** I-1; mail Lakeside z 97449; ● 100
Tenmile; RMC Place; DOUGLAS; **222** J-3; elev. 685ft./209m.; 🅿; z 97481; ● 260
Terrebonne; CDP; DESCHUTES; **222** G-8; elev. 2,860ft./872m.; 🅿; z 97760; Ⓟ 1,143; © 1,469
Thatcher; RMC Place; WASHINGTON; ***222** C-4; elev. 172ft./52m.; ★ **POR**; mail Forest Grove z 97116; rural
The Dalles (City of the Dalles); Inc. Place; ⊡ WASCO; **222** C-8; 🅿 🅷 ■; z 97058; Ⓟ 11,060; © 12,156; ◆ 12,271
Thielson; RMC Place; POLK; ***222** E-4; ★ **SAL**; mail Independence z 97351; rural
Thornhollow; RMC Place; UMATILLA; ***223** C-13; located on Umatilla Ind. Res.; mail Adams z 97810
Three Lynx; RMC Place; CLACKAMAS; **222** D-6; elev. 1,487ft./453m.; mail Estacada z 97023; ● 70
Three Rivers; CDP-Census Area Only; DESCHUTES; ***222** H-7; mail Bend z 97701; Ⓟ 1,268; © 2,445
Thurston; RMC Place; LANE; ***222** H-4; elev. 507ft./155m.; 🅿; ★ **EUG**; z 97482; pop. incl. with Springfield (Inc. Place)
Tide; RMC Place; LANE; ***222** G-2; elev. 86ft./26m.; mail Swisshome z 97480; ● 50
Tidewater; RMC Place; LINCOLN; **222** F-2; elev. 32ft./10m.; 🅿; z 97390; ● 300
Tiernan; RMC Place; LANE; ***222** H-2; mail Mapleton z 97453
Tierra Del Mar; RMC Place; TILLAMOOK; **222** D-2; mail Cloverdale z 97112; summer pop. 1,000; ● 220
Tigard; Inc. Place; WASHINGTON; **223** M-17; elev. 166ft./51m.; 🅿; ★ **POR**; z 97223-24, z 97281; Ⓟ 29,344; © 41,223; ◆ 48,681
Tillamook; Inc. Place; ⊡ TILLAMOOK; **222** C-2; elev. 16ft./5m.; 🅿 🅷; z 97141; Ⓟ 4,001; © 4,352
TILLAMOOK; **222** C-2; Ⓟ 21,570; © 24,262; ◆ 24,901
Tiller; RMC Place; DOUGLAS; **222** K-4; elev. 1,043ft./318m.; 🅿; z 97484; ● 210
Tillican; RMC Place; DESCHUTES; mail Bend z 97701; ● 300
Timber; RMC Place; WASHINGTON; **222** C-3; elev. 975ft./297m.; 🅿; z 97144; ● 260
Timber Grove; RMC Place; CLACKAMAS; ***222** D-5; elev. 974ft./297m.; ★ **POR**; mail Beavercreek z 97004; rural
Timberline Lodge; RMC Place; CLACKAMAS; ***222** D-7; 🅿; z 97028; rural
Toketee Falls; RMC Place; DOUGLAS; **222** J-5; mail Idleyld Park z 97447; ● 300
Toledo; Inc. Place; LINCOLN; **222** F-2; elev. 59ft./18m.; 🅿; z 97391; Ⓟ 3,174; © 3,472
Tollgate; RMC Place; UMATILLA; ***223** B-14; mail Sisters z 97759, Weston z 97886
Tolovana Park; RMC Place; CLATSOP; ***222** B-2; elev. 71ft./22m.; 🅿; z 97145; pop. incl. with Cannon Beach (Inc. Place) summer pop. 600
Tongue Point Village; RMC Place; CLATSOP; ***222** A-2; mail Astoria z 97103; pop. incl. with Astoria (Inc. Place)
Top; RMC Place; GRANT; ***223** E-11; mail Monument z 97864; rural
Tophill; RMC Place; WASHINGTON; ***222** C-4; elev. 1,003ft./306m.; mail Buxton z 97109; rural
Trail; RMC Place; JACKSON; **222** L-4; elev. 1,433ft./437m.; 🅿; z 97541; ● 400
Trask; RMC Place; TILLAMOOK; ***222** C-3; mail Tillamook z 97141; ● 30
Treharne; RMC Place; COLUMBIA; ***222** B-4; mail Vernonia z 97064; ● 60
Trent; RMC Place; LANE; ***222** H-4; elev. 611ft./186m.; ★ **EUG**; mail Dexter z 97431; rural
Triangle Lake; RMC Place; LANE; **222** G-3; mail Blachly z 97412; ● 70
Tri-City; CDP; DOUGLAS; **222** K-3; elev. 674ft./205m.; mail Myrtle Creek z 97457; Ⓟ 3,585; © 3,519
Trout Creek; RMC Place; HARNEY; ***223** H-13; mail Fields z 97710; rural
Trout Creek; RMC Place; HOOD RIVER; ***222** C-7; mail Mount Hood Parkdale z 97041; ● 30
Troutdale; Inc. Place; MULTNOMAH; **222** C-5; elev. 73ft./22m.; 🅿; ★ **POR**; z 97060; Ⓟ 7,852; © 13,777
Troy; RMC Place; WALLOWA; **223** B-15; mail Enterprise z 97828; ● 30
Tualatin; Inc. Place; WASHINGTON, CLACKAMAS; **223** N-17; elev. 123ft./37m.; 🅿 🅷 ■; ★ **POR**; z 97062; Ⓟ 15,013; © 22,791; ◆ 26,522
Tumalo; RMC Place; DESCHUTES; **222** G-7; elev. 3,182ft./970m.; mail Bend z 97701; ● 250
Turner; Inc. Place; MARION; **222** E-4; 🅿; ★ **SAL**; z 97392; Ⓟ 1,281; © 1,199
Tutuilla; CDP-Census Area Only; UMATILLA; ***223** C-13; © 460
Twelve Mile (Twelve Mile Corner); RMC Place; MULTNOMAH; ***222** C-5; ★ **POR**; mail Gresham z 97030; pop. incl. with Gresham (Inc. Place)
Twelve Mile Corner; MULTNOMAH; see Twelve Mile (RMC Place)
Twickenham; RMC Place; WHEELER; ***222** F-10; elev. 1,572ft./479m.; mail Mitchell z 97750; rural
Twin Rocks; RMC Place; TILLAMOOK; **222** C-2; mail Rockaway Beach z 97136; ● 510
Twomile; RMC Place; COOS; ***222** J-1; elev. 77ft./23m.; mail Bandon z 97411; rural
Tygh Valley; CDP; WASCO; **222** D-8; 🅿; z 97063; © 224

U

Ukiah; Inc. Place; UMATILLA; **223** D-12; elev. 3,353ft./1,022m.; 🅿; z 97880; Ⓟ 250; © 255
Umapine; RMC Place; UMATILLA; **223** B-13; mail Milton Freewater z 97862; ● 220
Umatilla; Inc. Place; UMATILLA; **223** B-12; elev. 296ft./90m.; 🅿; z 97882; Ⓟ 3,046; © 4,978
UMATILLA; **223** C-13; Ⓟ 59,249; © 70,548; ◆ 74,420
Umatilla Reservation; Indian Reservation; UMATILLA, UNION; mail Pendleton z 97801; Indian Agency located in Pendleton; Ⓟ 2,619; © 2,927
Umpqua; RMC Place; DOUGLAS; **222** J-3; elev. 354ft./108m.; 🅿; z 97486; ● 240
Union; Inc. Place; UNION; **223** D-15; elev. 2,788ft./850m.; 🅿; z 97883; Ⓟ 1,847; © 1,926
UNION; **223** D-14; Ⓟ 23,598; © 24,530; ◆ 25,287
Union Creek; RMC Place; JACKSON; **222** K-5; mail Prospect z 97536; ● 30
Union Gap; RMC Place; DOUGLAS; ***222** I-3; elev. 517ft./158m.; mail Oakland z 97462; rural
Union Mills; RMC Place; CLACKAMAS; ***222** D-5; ★ **POR**; mail Mulino z 97042
Unionvale; RMC Place; YAMHILL; **222** D-4; elev. 163ft./50m.; mail Dayton z 97114
Unity; Inc. Place; BAKER; **223** F-14; 🅿; z 97884; Ⓟ 87; © 131
Unity; RMC Place; LANE; ***222** H-4; mail Fall Creek z 97438; rural
Upper Highland; RMC Place; CLACKAMAS; ***222** D-5; ★ **POR**; mail Beavercreek z 97004; rural
Upper Hood River Valley; RMC Place; HOOD RIVER; ***222** C-7; mail Odell z 97044; rural
Upper Soda; RMC Place; LINN; ***222** G-5; elev. 1,403ft./428m.; mail Foster z 97345; ● 30

V

Vale; Inc. Place; ⊡ MALHEUR; **223** H-16; 🅿; z 97918; Ⓟ 1,491; © 1,976
Valley Falls; RMC Place; LAKE; **222** L-10; elev. 4,324ft./1,318m.; mail Lakeview z 97630
Valley Junction; RMC Place; POLK; ***222** E-3; elev. 294ft./90m.; mail Willamina z 97396
Valley View; RMC Place; BENTON; mail Albany z 97321; ● 200
Valsetz; RMC Place; POLK; ***222** E-3; elev. 1,116ft./340m.; mail Siletz z 97380; ● 430
Van; RMC Place; HARNEY; ***223** H-13; mail Drewsey z 97904; rural
Vaughn; RMC Place; LANE; **222** H-3; mail Veneta z 97487; ● 60
Vaughn Station; RMC Place; LANE; ***222** H-3; mail Veneta z 97487; rural
Veneta; Inc. Place; LANE; **222** H-3; 🅿; ★ **EUG**; z 97487; Ⓟ 2,519; © 2,755; Ⓡ 2,762
Verboort; RMC Place; WASHINGTON; ***222** C-4; ★ **POR**; mail Forest Grove z 97116; ● 250
Vermont Hills; RMC Place; MULTNOMAH; ***222** C-5; ★ **POR**; mail Portland z 97221; pop. incl. with Portland (Inc. Place)
Vernonia; Inc. Place; COLUMBIA; **222** B-4; elev. 621ft./189m.; 🅿; z 97064; Ⓟ 1,808; © 2,228
Vida; RMC Place; LANE; **222** G-5; elev. 780ft./238m.; 🅿; z 97488; ● 450
Viola; RMC Place; CLACKAMAS; ***222** D-5; elev. 376ft./115m.; ★ **POR**; mail Estacada z 97023
Vista; RMC Place; MARION; ★ **SAL**; mail Salem z 97302; pop. incl. with Salem (Inc. Place)

W

Waconda; RMC Place; MARION; ***222** E-4; elev. 174ft./53m.; ★ **SAL**; mail Gervais z 97026; rural
Wagontire; RMC Place; HARNEY; ***223** J-11; mail Hines z 97738; rural
Wagon Trail Ranch; RMC Place; DESCHUTES; mail La Pine z 97739; ● 150
Wakonda Beach; RMC Place; LINCOLN; ***222** G-2; mail Waldport z 97394; ● 70
Walden; RMC Place; LANE; ***222** H-4; ★ **EUG**; mail Cottage Grove z 97424
Waldport; Inc. Place; LINCOLN; **222** F-2; elev. 11ft./3m.; 🅿; z 97394; Ⓟ 1,595; © 2,050
Walker; RMC Place; LANE; ***222** H-4; ★ **EUG**; mail Creswell z 97426
Wallowa; Inc. Place; WALLOWA; **223** C-15; elev. 2,948ft./899m.; 🅿; z 97885; Ⓟ 748; © 869
WALLOWA; **223** C-16; Ⓟ 6,911; © 7,226; ◆ 6,741
Wallowa Lake Resort; RMC Place; WALLOWA; ***223** D-16; mail Joseph z 97846; summer pop. 900; ● 100
Walterville; RMC Place; LANE; **222** H-4; elev. 606ft./185m.; 🅿; z 97489; ● 250
Walton; RMC Place; LANE; **222** H-3; 🅿; z 97490; ● 200
Wamic; CDP; WASCO; **222** D-8; 🅿; z 97063; © 36
Wankers Corners; CLACKAMAS; see Stafford (RMC Place)
Wapato; RMC Place; YAMHILL; ***222** D-4; mail Gaston z 97119
Wapinitia; RMC Place; WASCO; ***222** D-8; mail Maupin z 97037; rural
Warm Springs; CDP; JEFFERSON; **222** F-8; located on Warm Springs Ind. Res.; elev. 1,533ft./467m.; 🅿; z 97761; location of Indian Agency; Ⓟ 2,287; © 2,431
Warm Springs Reservation; Indian Reservation; WASCO, CLACKAMAS, JEFFERSON, MARION; mail Warm Springs z 97761; also location of Indian Agency; Ⓟ 2,244; © 3,311
Warren; RMC Place; COLUMBIA; **222** B-4; elev. 49ft./15m.; 🅿; z 97053; ● 970
Warrendale; RMC Place; MULTNOMAH; ***222** C-6; mail Cascade Locks z 97014; rural
Warrenton; Inc. Place; CLATSOP; **222** A-2; 🅿; z 97146; Ⓟ 2,681; © 4,096
Wasco; Inc. Place; SHERMAN; **222** C-9; elev. 1,270ft./387m.; 🅿; z 97065; Ⓟ 374; © 381
WASCO; **222** E-8; Ⓟ 21,683; © 23,791; ◆ 23,963
WASHINGTON; **222** C-3; Ⓟ 311,554; © 445,342; ◆ 538,010
Washington Park Zoo Railway; RMC Place; MULTNOMAH; ★ **POR**; mail Portland z 97221; pop. incl. with Portland (Inc. Place)
Waterloo; Inc. Place; LINN; **222** F-4; mail Lebanon z 97355; Ⓟ 191; © 239
Watseco; RMC Place; TILLAMOOK; ***222** C-2; mail Rockaway Beach z 97136; ● 120
Weatherby; RMC Place; BAKER; ***223** F-16; mail Durkee z 97905; rural
Wecoma Beach; RMC Place; LINCOLN; ***222** E-2; mail Lincoln City z 97367; pop. incl. with Lincoln City (Inc. Place)
Wedderburn; RMC Place; CURRY; **222** L-1; elev. 62ft./19m.; 🅿; z 97491; ● 330
Welches; RMC Place; CLACKAMAS; ***222** D-6; 🅿; z 97067; summer pop. 1,000; ● 700
Wells Creek; DOUGLAS; see Green Acres (RMC Place)
Wemme; RMC Place; CLACKAMAS; ***222** D-6; elev. 1,337ft./408m.; mail Welches z 97067; rural
Westfall; RMC Place; MALHEUR; **223** H-15; 🅿; z 97920; ● 80
Westfir; Inc. Place; LANE; **222** H-5; 🅿; z 97492; Ⓟ 278; © 276; Ⓡ 280
West Haven-Sylvan; CDP-Census Area Only; WASHINGTON; ***222** C-4; ★ **POR**; mail Portland z 97210, z 97225; Ⓟ 6,009; © 7,147
West Lake; RMC Place; CLATSOP; ***222** B-2; mail Warrenton z 97146; rural
Westlake; RMC Place; LANE; ***222** H-2; 🅿; z 97493; pop. incl. with Dunes City (Inc. Place)
West Linn; Inc. Place; CLACKAMAS; **223** N-19; elev. 128ft./39m.; 🅿; ★ **POR**; z 97068 & mail Lake Oswego z 97034; Ⓟ 16,367; © 22,261; ◆ 25,105
West Moreland; RMC Place; MULTNOMAH; ***222** C-5; elev. 114ft./35m.; ★ **POR**; mail Portland z 97202; pop. incl. with Portland (Inc. Place)
Weston; Inc. Place; UMATILLA; **223** B-13; elev. 1,838ft./560m.; 🅿; z 97886; Ⓟ 606; © 717
Weston Landing; RMC Place; YAMHILL; ***222** D-4; mail McMinnville z 97128; rural
Westport; RMC Place; CLATSOP; **222** A-3; 🅿; z 97016; ● 280
West Portland; RMC Place; MULTNOMAH; **223** M-18; ★ **POR**; mail Portland z 97219; pop. incl. with Portland (Inc. Place)
West Portland Park; RMC Place; MULTNOMAH; ***222** C-5; ★ **POR**; mail Lake Oswego z 97035; pop. incl. with Portland (Inc. Place)
West Saint Helens; RMC Place; COLUMBIA; mail Saint Helens z 97051; pop. incl. with Saint Helens (Inc. Place)
West Salem; RMC Place; POLK; **223** F-19; elev. 150ft./46m.; ★ **SAL**; mail Salem z 97304; pop. incl. with Salem (Inc. Place)
West Scio; RMC Place; LINN; ***222** F-4; mail Scio z 97374; ● 230
West Side; RMC Place; LAKE; ***222** M-9; elev. 4,770ft./1,454m.; mail Lakeview z 97630
West Side; RMC Place; LANE; ★ **EUG**; mail Eugene z 97402; pop. incl. with Eugene (Inc. Place)
West Slope; CDP; WASHINGTON; **223** L-18; elev. 345ft./105m.; ★ **POR**; mail Portland z 97225, z 97298; Ⓟ 7,959; © 6,442
West Stayton; RMC Place; MARION; ***222** E-4; elev. 382ft./116m.; 🅿; ★ **SAL**; z 97325; ● 120
West Union; RMC Place; WASHINGTON; ***222** C-4; ★ **POR**; mail Hillsboro z 97123-24; pop. incl. with Hillsboro (Inc. Place)
Wetmore; RMC Place; WHEELER; **222** E-10; mail Fossil z 97830; rural
Weyerhaeuser Townsite; RMC Place; KLAMATH; ***222** M-6; mail Klamath Falls z 97601; ● 100
Wheeler; Inc. Place; TILLAMOOK; **222** C-2; elev. 18ft./5m.; 🅿; z 97147; Ⓟ 335; © 391
WHEELER; **222** E-10; Ⓟ 1,396; © 1,547; ◆ 1,323
Wheeler Heights; RMC Place; TILLAMOOK; ***222** C-2; mail Wheeler z 97147; pop. incl. with Wheeler (Inc. Place)
Whiskey Hill; RMC Place; CLACKAMAS; ***222** D-4; ★ **POR**; mail Hubbard z 97032; rural
White City; CDP; JACKSON; **222** L-4; elev. 1,305ft./398m.; 🅿; ★ **MEDF**; z 97503; Ⓟ 5,891; © 5,466; Ⓡ 6,199
White Settlement; RMC Place; MALHEUR; ***223** H-16; mail Ontario z 97914; rural
Whiteson; RMC Place; YAMHILL; **222** D-4; mail Amity z 97101; ● 100
Wilbur; RMC Place; DOUGLAS; **222** J-3; 🅿; z 97494; ● 200
Wilcox; RMC Place; SHERMAN; ***222** D-9; mail Kent z 97033; rural
Wilderville; RMC Place; JOSEPHINE; **222** L-3; elev. 938ft./286m.; 🅿; z 97543; ● 380
Wildwood; RMC Place; CLACKAMAS; ***222** D-6; mail Welches z 97067; ● 60
Wilhoit; RMC Place; CLACKAMAS; ***222** E-5; mail Molalla z 97038; ● 40
Willakenzie; RMC Place; LANE; ★ **EUG**; mail Eugene z 97401; pop. incl. with Eugene (Inc. Place)
Willamette; RMC Place; CLACKAMAS; ***222** D-5; ★ **POR**; mail West Linn z 97068; pop. incl. with West Linn (Inc. Place)
Willamette City; RMC Place; LANE; ***222** H-5; elev. 1,821ft./555m.; mail Oakridge z 97463; pop. incl. with Oakridge (Inc. Place)
Willamina; Inc. Place; YAMHILL, POLK; **222** E-3; elev. 225ft./69m.; 🅿; z 97396; Ⓟ 1,717; © 1,844
Willbridge; RMC Place; MULTNOMAH; ***222** C-5; elev. 39ft./12m.; ★ **POR**; mail Portland z 97210; pop. incl. with Portland (Inc. Place)
Williams; RMC Place; JOSEPHINE; **222** M-3; 🅿; z 97544; ● 730
Willowcreek; RMC Place; MALHEUR; ***223** G-16; mail Vale z 97918
Willowdale; RMC Place; JEFFERSON; ***222** E-8; mail Madras z 97741; rural
Willsburg Junction; RMC Place; CLACKAMAS; ***222** C-5; ★ **POR**; mail Portland z 97222; pop. incl. with Milwaukie (Inc. Place)
Wilson Beach; RMC Place; TILLAMOOK; ***222** C-2; mail Tillamook z 97141; ● 80
Wilsonville; Inc. Place; CLACKAMAS, WASHINGTON; **223** N-18; 🅿 🅲 1,095; ★ **POR**; z 97070; Ⓟ 7,106; © 13,991
Wimer; RMC Place; JACKSON; ***222** L-3; elev. 1,134ft./346m.; mail Rogue River z 97537; ● 200
Winchester; RMC Place; DOUGLAS; **222** J-3; elev. 450ft./137m.; 🅿; z 97495; ● 2,700
Winchester Bay; CDP; DOUGLAS; **222** I-1; elev. 17ft./5m.; 🅿; z 97467; © 488
Windmaster Corner; RMC Place; HOOD RIVER; ***222** C-7; mail Hood River z 97031; rural
Winema Beach; RMC Place; TILLAMOOK; ***222** D-2; mail Cloverdale z 97112; ● 50
Wingville; RMC Place; BAKER; ***223** E-15; mail Baker City z 97814; ● 30
Winlock; RMC Place; WHEELER; ***222** E-10; mail Spray z 97874; rural
Winston; Inc. Place; DOUGLAS; **222** J-3; elev. 534ft./163m.; 🅿; z 97496; Ⓟ 3,773; © 4,613
Winterville; RMC Place; COOS; ***222** J-1; elev. 217ft./66m.; mail Bandon z 97411; ● 70
Witch Hazel; RMC Place; WASHINGTON; ***222** C-4; elev. 181ft./55m.; ★ **POR**; mail Hillsboro z 97123; pop. incl. with Hillsboro (Inc. Place)
Wocus; RMC Place; KLAMATH; ***222** M-6; mail Klamath Falls z 97601; ● 50
Wolf Creek; RMC Place; JOSEPHINE; **222** L-3; elev. 1,291ft./393m.; 🅿; z 97497; ● 550
Wonder; RMC Place; JOSEPHINE; ***222** M-3; mail Wilderville z 97543; ● 30
Woodburn; Inc. Place; MARION; **222** D-4; elev. 183ft./56m.; 🅿; z 97071; Ⓟ 13,404; © 20,100; ◆ 23,570
Woods; RMC Place; TILLAMOOK; **222** D-2; mail Cloverdale z 97112; ● 80
Woodson; RMC Place; COLUMBIA; **222** A-3; mail Clatskanie z 97016; ● 60
Woodstock; RMC Place; MULTNOMAH; ***222** C-5; ★ **POR**; mail Portland z 97206; pop. incl. with Portland (Inc. Place)
Wood Village; Inc. Place; MULTNOMAH; ***222** C-5; 🅿; ★ **POR**; z 97060; Ⓟ 2,814; © 2,860
Worden; RMC Place; KLAMATH; **222** M-6; mail Klamath Falls z 97601; ● 30
Wren (Wrens); RMC Place; BENTON; **222** F-3; mail Blodgett z 97326; ● 110
Wrens; BENTON; see Wren (RMC Place)
Wyeth; RMC Place; HOOD RIVER; ***222** C-7; mail Cascade Locks z 97014; rural

Y

Yachats; Inc. Place; LINCOLN; **222** G-2; 🅿; z 97498; Ⓟ 533; © 617
Yamhill; Inc. Place; YAMHILL; **222** D-4; 🅿; z 97148; Ⓟ 867; © 794
YAMHILL; **222** D-3; Ⓟ 65,551; © 84,992; ◆ 100,124
Yankton; RMC Place; COLUMBIA; ***222** B-4; elev. 284ft./87m.; mail Saint Helens z 97051; rural
Yaquina; RMC Place; LINCOLN; ***222** F-2; mail Newport z 97365; rural
Yoakum; RMC Place; UMATILLA; ***223** C-12; mail Pendleton z 97801; rural
Yoder; RMC Place; CLACKAMAS; ***222** D-5; ★ **POR**; mail Hubbard z 97032; rural
Yoncalla; Inc. Place; DOUGLAS; **222** I-3; 🅿; z 97499; Ⓟ 919; © 1,052
Yonna; RMC Place; KLAMATH; ***222** M-7; elev. 4,145ft./1,263m.; mail Bonanza z 97623; rural

Z

Zigzag; RMC Place; CLACKAMAS; **222** D-6; elev. 1,425ft./434m.; 🅿; z 97049; summer pop. 400; ● 300

Entries in **UPPERCASE** are counties.
Entries in **bold** have populations of 2,500 or more.
Names in parentheses are alternate names.
Inc. Place — Incorporated Place
RMC Place — Rand McNally Designated Place
CDP — Census Designated Place
MCD — Minor Civil Division

⊡ County Seat
▲ Minor Civil Division
elev. Elevation
🅿 Post Office

🅷 Hospital
🅲 College
■ Principal Business Center
★ Ranally Metro Area (RMA) Abbreviation
z Zip Code(s)

Ⓟ Previous Census Population
Ⓡ Revised Census Population
Ⓐ Annexation Population
● Rand McNally Population Estimate
© Final Census Population
Ⓢ Special Census Population
◆ Estimated Population

For additional definitions see Glossary, Volume 1, and Introduction, Volume 2.

PENNSYLVANIA

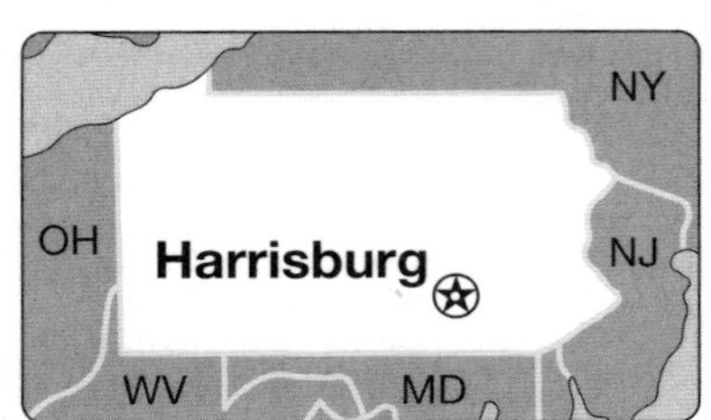

Statistics

Total area (2000) — 46,055 square miles
Land area (2000) — 44,817 square miles
Water area (2000) — 1,238 square miles
Capital — Harrisburg
One of Thirteen Original States

Maps

State maps can be found on pages 142-254 in Vol. 1
County Subdivision maps can be found on pages 255-271 in Vol. 1

Ranally Metro Areas (RMAs) and Abbreviations

Allentown-Bethlehem, PA-NJ — ALL-
Altoona, PA — ALT
Baltimore, MD-PA — BAL
Binghamton, NY-PA — BING
Butler, PA — BUTL
Carlisle, PA — CARL
Erie, PA — ERIE
Hagerstown, MD-PA-WV — HAG
Hanover, PA — HANV
Harrisburg, PA — HRBG
Hazleton, PA — HAZ
Johnstown, PA — JNST
Lancaster, PA — LANC
Latrobe, PA — LTROB
Lebanon, PA — LEB
Morgantown, WV-PA — MORG
New Castle, PA — NWCS
Oil City-Franklin, PA — OILC-F
Philadelphia-Trenton-Wilmington, PA-NJ-DE-MD — PHIL-
Pittsburgh, PA — PGH
Pottstown, PA — PTSTN
Pottsville, PA — PTSVL
Reading, PA — READ
Scranton-Wilkes Barre, PA — SCR-
Sharon, PA-OH — SHAR
State College, PA — STCOL
Uniontown, PA — UNTN
Washington, PA — WASH
Williamsport, PA — WMSPT
York, PA — YORK
Youngstown-Warren, OH-PA — YNGS-

Principal Places

Place Name	Place Type	County	Population
Philadelphia	Inc. Place	PHILADELPHIA	◆ 1,451,149
Pittsburgh	Inc. Place	ALLEGHENY	◆ 302,187
Allentown	Inc. Place	LEHIGH	◆ 109,812
Erie	Inc. Place	ERIE	◆ 103,824
Reading	Inc. Place	BERKS	◆ 81,784
Upper Darby	MCD-Township	DELAWARE	◆ 81,238
Scranton	Inc. Place	LACKAWANNA	◆ 74,340
Bethlehem	Inc. Place	NORTHAMPTON	◆ 73,329
Lower Merion	MCD-Township	MONTGOMERY	◆ 61,080
Bensalem	MCD-Township	BUCKS	◆ 58,810
Lancaster	Inc. Place	LANCASTER	◆ 56,425
Levittown	CDP	BUCKS	◆ 55,660
Abington	MCD-Township	MONTGOMERY	◆ 54,686
Bristol	MCD-Township	BUCKS	◆ 53,533
Millcreek	MCD-Township	ERIE	◆ 51,543
Haverford	MCD-Township	DELAWARE	◆ 47,791
Harrisburg	Inc. Place	DAUPHIN	◆ 47,259
Altoona	Inc. Place	BLAIR	◆ 47,018
Lower Paxton	MCD-Township	DAUPHIN	◆ 46,630
Middletown	MCD-Township	BUCKS	◆ 43,866
Penn Hills	CDP	ALLEGHENY	◆ 43,040
Penn Hills	MCD-Township	ALLEGHENY	◆ 43,040
York	Inc. Place	YORK	◆ 41,662
State College	Inc. Place	CENTRE	◆ 40,580
Northampton	MCD-Township	BUCKS	◆ 40,503
Wilkes-Barre	Inc. Place	LUZERNE	◆ 40,365
Hempfield	MCD-Township	WESTMORELAND	◆ 38,942
Cheltenham	MCD-Township	MONTGOMERY	◆ 37,631
Manheim	MCD-Township	LANCASTER	◆ 36,808
Chester	Inc. Place	DELAWARE	◆ 36,376
Cheltenham	RMC Place	MONTGOMERY	℗ 34,923
Falls	MCD-Township	BUCKS	◆ 34,844
Norristown	Inc. Place	MONTGOMERY	◆ 32,810
Lower Makefield	MCD-Township	BUCKS	◆ 32,759
Warminster	MCD-Township	BUCKS	◆ 32,201
Bethel Park	Inc. Place	ALLEGHENY	◆ 31,914
Warminster	RMC Place	BUCKS	● 31,400
Mount Lebanon	CDP	ALLEGHENY	◆ 31,147
Mount Lebanon	MCD-Township	ALLEGHENY	◆ 31,147
Radnor	MCD-Township	DELAWARE	◆ 30,782
Radnor Township	CDP-Census Area Only	DELAWARE	◆ 30,782
Ross	MCD-Township	ALLEGHENY	◆ 30,781
Ross Township	CDP-Census Area Only	ALLEGHENY	◆ 30,781
Ridley	MCD-Township	DELAWARE	◆ 30,619
Havertown	RMC Place	DELAWARE	● 30,000
Drexel Hill	CDP	DELAWARE	◆ 29,366
Tredyffrin	MCD-Township	CHESTER	◆ 29,135
Williamsport	Inc. Place	LYCOMING	◆ 29,083
North Huntingdon	MCD-Township	WESTMORELAND	◆ 28,795
Monroeville	Inc. Place	ALLEGHENY	◆ 28,357
York	MCD-Township	YORK	◆ 28,109
Shaler	MCD-Township	ALLEGHENY	◆ 28,023
Shaler Township	CDP-Census Area Only	ALLEGHENY	◆ 28,023
Hampden	MCD-Township	CUMBERLAND	◆ 27,214
Whitehall	MCD-Township	LEHIGH	◆ 27,144
McCandless	MCD-Town	ALLEGHENY	◆ 27,084
McCandless Township	CDP-Census Area Only	ALLEGHENY	◆ 27,084
Easton	Inc. Place	NORTHAMPTON	◆ 26,927
Upper Merion	MCD-Township	MONTGOMERY	◆ 26,725
Plum	Inc. Place	ALLEGHENY	◆ 26,362
Cranberry	MCD-Township	BUTLER	◆ 26,334
Upper Dublin	MCD-Township	MONTGOMERY	◆ 26,038
Back Mountain	CDP-Census Area Only	LUZERNE	◆ 25,950
Springettsbury	MCD-Township	YORK	◆ 25,915
Horsham	MCD-Township	MONTGOMERY	◆ 25,265
Lower Providence	MCD-Township	MONTGOMERY	◆ 24,895
Lebanon	Inc. Place	LEBANON	◆ 24,892
New Castle	Inc. Place	LAWRENCE	◆ 24,813
Upper Moreland	MCD-Township	MONTGOMERY	◆ 24,457
Bethlehem	MCD-Township	NORTHAMPTON	◆ 24,444
Exeter	MCD-Township	BERKS	◆ 24,207
Montgomery	MCD-Township	MONTGOMERY	◆ 24,144
Swatara	MCD-Township	DAUPHIN	◆ 23,901
Spring	MCD-Township	BERKS	◆ 23,811
East Hempfield	MCD-Township	LANCASTER	◆ 23,769
Marple	MCD-Township	DELAWARE	◆ 23,731
Susquehanna	MCD-Township	DAUPHIN	◆ 23,537
Springfield	CDP	DELAWARE	◆ 23,525
Springfield	MCD-Township	DELAWARE	◆ 23,525
Moon	MCD-Township	ALLEGHENY	◆ 22,646
McKeesport	Inc. Place	ALLEGHENY	◆ 22,612
Lower Macungie	MCD-Township	LEHIGH	◆ 22,588
Derry	MCD-Township	DAUPHIN	◆ 22,202
West Goshen	MCD-Township	CHESTER	◆ 21,985
Hazleton	Inc. Place	LUZERNE	◆ 21,762
Pottstown	Inc. Place	MONTGOMERY	◆ 21,680
Dover	MCD-Township	YORK	◆ 21,302
West Mifflin	Inc. Place	ALLEGHENY	◆ 20,877
Unity	MCD-Township	WESTMORELAND	◆ 20,402
Johnstown	Inc. Place	CAMBRIA	◆ 20,256
Warrington	MCD-Township	BUCKS	◆ 20,116
Baldwin	Inc. Place	ALLEGHENY	© 19,999
Palmer	MCD-Township	NORTHAMPTON	◆ 19,750
Springfield	MCD-Township	MONTGOMERY	© 19,533
Penn	MCD-Township	WESTMORELAND	◆ 19,286
Upper Saint Clair	CDP	ALLEGHENY	◆ 19,279
Upper St. Clair	MCD-Township	ALLEGHENY	◆ 19,279
Lower Southampton	MCD-Township	BUCKS	© 19,276
Wilkinsburg	Inc. Place	ALLEGHENY	© 19,196
Chambersburg	Inc. Place	FRANKLIN	◆ 19,137
Murrysville	Inc. Place	WESTMORELAND	© 18,872
Peters	MCD-Township	WASHINGTON	◆ 18,846
Carlisle	Inc. Place	CUMBERLAND	◆ 18,667
Whitpain	MCD-Township	MONTGOMERY	© 18,562
King of Prussia	CDP	MONTGOMERY	© 18,511
East Pennsboro	MCD-Township	CUMBERLAND	© 18,254
Newtown	MCD-Township	BUCKS	© 18,206
South Whitehall	MCD-Township	LEHIGH	© 18,028
West Chester	Inc. Place	CHESTER	◆ 17,697
Doylestown	MCD-Township	BUCKS	© 17,619
Towamencin	MCD-Township	MONTGOMERY	© 17,597
Hampton	MCD-Township	ALLEGHENY	© 17,526
Hampton Township	CDP-Census Area Only	ALLEGHENY	© 17,526
Lower Allen	MCD-Township	CUMBERLAND	© 17,437
Scott	MCD-Township	ALLEGHENY	© 17,288
Scott Township	CDP-Census Area Only	ALLEGHENY	© 17,288
Butler	MCD-Township	BUTLER	© 17,185
West Manchester	MCD-Township	YORK	© 17,035
Upper Chichester	MCD-Township	DELAWARE	© 16,842
East Goshen	MCD-Township	CHESTER	© 16,824
Hatfield	MCD-Township	MONTGOMERY	© 16,712
Whitemarsh	MCD-Township	MONTGOMERY	© 16,702
Uwchlan	MCD-Township	CHESTER	© 16,576
West Whiteland	MCD-Township	CHESTER	© 16,499
Manor	MCD-Township	LANCASTER	© 16,498
Buckingham	MCD-Township	BUCKS	© 16,442
Muhlenberg	MCD-Township	BERKS	© 16,305
Harborcreek	MCD-Township	ERIE	® 16,267
Willow Grove	CDP	MONTGOMERY	© 16,234
Aston	MCD-Township	DELAWARE	© 16,203
Middletown	MCD-Township	DELAWARE	◆ 16,153
Plymouth	MCD-Township	MONTGOMERY	◆ 15,930
Hermitage	Inc. Place	MERCER	◆ 15,785
Upper Southampton	MCD-Township	BUCKS	© 15,764
Lansdale	Inc. Place	MONTGOMERY	◆ 15,706
Sharon	Inc. Place	MERCER	◆ 15,486
Warwick	MCD-Township	LANCASTER	© 15,475
Upper Providence	MCD-Township	MONTGOMERY	© 15,398
Upper Allen	MCD-Township	CUMBERLAND	© 15,338
Washington	Inc. Place	WASHINGTON	◆ 15,325
Greensburg	Inc. Place	WESTMORELAND	◆ 15,277
Mountain Top	CDP	LUZERNE	© 15,269
Coolbaugh	MCD-Township	MONROE	© 15,205
West Hempfield	MCD-Township	LANCASTER	© 15,128
West Norriton	CDP-Census Area Only	MONTGOMERY	© 14,901
West Norriton	MCD-Township	MONTGOMERY	© 14,901
Hanover	Inc. Place	YORK	◆ 14,898
Phoenixville	Inc. Place	CHESTER	© 14,788
Horsham	CDP	MONTGOMERY	© 14,779
North Whitehall	MCD-Township	LEHIGH	© 14,731
Derry	MCD-Township	WESTMORELAND	© 14,726
Pottsville	Inc. Place	SCHUYLKILL	◆ 14,596
Penn	MCD-Township	YORK	© 14,592
Indiana	Inc. Place	INDIANA	◆ 14,561
Saint Marys	Inc. Place	ELK	© 14,502
Whitehall	Inc. Place	ALLEGHENY	© 14,444
Chestnuthill	MCD-Township	MONROE	© 14,418
South Park	MCD-Township	ALLEGHENY	© 14,340
South Park Township	CDP-Census Area Only	ALLEGHENY	© 14,340
Newberry	MCD-Township	YORK	© 14,332
Fairview	MCD-Township	YORK	© 14,321
Butler	Inc. Place	BUTLER	◆ 14,283
Fullerton	CDP	LEHIGH	© 14,268
Upper Gwynedd	MCD-Township	MONTGOMERY	© 14,243
North Union	MCD-Township	FAYETTE	© 14,140
New Kensington	Inc. Place	WESTMORELAND	◆ 14,088
Ferguson	MCD-Township	CENTRE	© 14,063
White	MCD-Township	INDIANA	© 14,034
Dunmore	Inc. Place	LACKAWANNA	© 14,018
Stroud	MCD-Township	MONROE	© 13,978
Lancaster	MCD-Township	LANCASTER	© 13,944
Upper Macungie	MCD-Township	LEHIGH	© 13,895
Kingston	Inc. Place	LUZERNE	© 13,855
Elizabeth	MCD-Township	ALLEGHENY	© 13,839
Cumru	MCD-Township	BERKS	© 13,816
East Lampeter	MCD-Township	LANCASTER	© 13,556
Limerick	MCD-Township	MONTGOMERY	© 13,534
Salisbury	MCD-Township	LEHIGH	© 13,498
Nether Providence	MCD-Township	DELAWARE	© 13,456
Nether Providence Township	CDP-Census Area Only	DELAWARE	© 13,456
Colonial Park	CDP	DAUPHIN	© 13,259
Hopewell	MCD-Township	BEAVER	© 13,254
Ephrata	Inc. Place	LANCASTER	© 13,213
East Norriton	CDP-Census Area Only	MONTGOMERY	© 13,211
East Norriton	MCD-Township	MONTGOMERY	© 13,211
West Lampeter	MCD-Township	LANCASTER	© 13,145
Guilford	MCD-Township	FRANKLIN	© 13,100
South Middleton	MCD-Township	CUMBERLAND	© 12,939
Lower Salford	MCD-Township	MONTGOMERY	© 12,893
Windsor	MCD-Township	YORK	© 12,807
Hershey	CDP	DAUPHIN	© 12,771
Manchester	MCD-Township	YORK	© 12,700
Ardmore	CDP	DELAWARE	© 12,616
Lower Burrell	Inc. Place	WESTMORELAND	© 12,608
Richland	MCD-Township	CAMBRIA	© 12,598
Antrim	MCD-Township	FRANKLIN	© 12,504
Meadville	Inc. Place	CRAWFORD	◆ 12,474
Uniontown	Inc. Place	FAYETTE	◆ 12,322
Robinson	MCD-Township	ALLEGHENY	© 12,289
Robinson Township	CDP-Census Area Only	ALLEGHENY	© 12,289
Greene	MCD-Township	FRANKLIN	© 12,284
South Fayette	MCD-Township	ALLEGHENY	© 12,271
Munhall	Inc. Place	ALLEGHENY	© 12,264
North Fayette	MCD-Township	ALLEGHENY	© 12,254
Bloomsburg	Inc. Place	COLUMBIA	◆ 12,220
Fernway	CDP-Census Area Only	BUTLER	© 12,188
Hilltown	MCD-Township	BUCKS	© 12,102
Montgomeryville	CDP	MONTGOMERY	© 12,031
Warwick	MCD-Township	BUCKS	© 11,977
Spring Garden	MCD-Township	YORK	© 11,974
Upper Saucon	MCD-Township	LEHIGH	© 11,939
Logan	MCD-Township	BLAIR	© 11,925
Caln	MCD-Township	CHESTER	© 11,916
Elizabethtown	Inc. Place	LANCASTER	© 11,887
Yeadon	Inc. Place	DELAWARE	© 11,762
Aliquippa	Inc. Place	BEAVER	© 11,734
Newtown	MCD-Township	DELAWARE	© 11,700
Rostraver	MCD-Township	WESTMORELAND	© 11,634
West Deer	MCD-Township	ALLEGHENY	© 11,563
Washington	MCD-Township	FRANKLIN	© 11,559
Sandy	MCD-Township	CLEARFIELD	© 11,556
Franconia	MCD-Township	MONTGOMERY	© 11,523
Southampton	RMC Place	BUCKS	● 11,500
Middle Smithfield	MCD-Township	MONROE	© 11,495
Center	MCD-Township	BEAVER	© 11,492
Hanover	MCD-Township	LUZERNE	© 11,488
Patton	MCD-Township	CENTRE	© 11,420
Plumstead	MCD-Township	BUCKS	© 11,409
Franklin Park	Inc. Place	ALLEGHENY	© 11,364
South Union	MCD-Township	FAYETTE	© 11,337
Emmaus	Inc. Place	LEHIGH	© 11,313
Newtown Square	RMC Place	DELAWARE	● 11,300
Lower Moreland	MCD-Township	MONTGOMERY	© 11,281
Concord	MCD-Township	DELAWARE	® 11,239
Lower Pottsgrove	MCD-Township	MONTGOMERY	© 11,213
Mount Pleasant	MCD-Township	WESTMORELAND	© 11,153
North Versailles	CDP-Census Area Only	ALLEGHENY	© 11,125
North Versailles	MCD-Township	ALLEGHENY	© 11,125
Somerset	MCD-Township	SOMERSET	® 11,088
Broomall	CDP	DELAWARE	© 11,046
Lansdowne	Inc. Place	DELAWARE	© 11,044
Nanticoke	Inc. Place	LUZERNE	© 10,955
Harrison	MCD-Township	ALLEGHENY	© 10,934
Plains	MCD-Township	LUZERNE	© 10,906
Loyalsock	MCD-Township	LYCOMING	© 10,876
Coatesville	Inc. Place	CHESTER	© 10,838
Oil City	Inc. Place	VENANGO	◆ 10,805
West Bradford	MCD-Township	CHESTER	© 10,775
Berwick	Inc. Place	COLUMBIA	© 10,774
New Britain	MCD-Township	BUCKS	© 10,698
Jeannette	Inc. Place	WESTMORELAND	© 10,654
Carnot-Moon	CDP-Census Area Only	ALLEGHENY	© 10,637
North Lebanon	MCD-Township	LEBANON	© 10,629
Coal	MCD-Township	NORTHUMBERLAND	© 10,628
Silver Spring	MCD-Township	CUMBERLAND	© 10,592
Upper Providence	MCD-Township	DELAWARE	© 10,509
Upper Providence Township	CDP-Census Area Only	DELAWARE	© 10,509
Brentwood	Inc. Place	ALLEGHENY	© 10,466
Lower Gwynedd	MCD-Township	MONTGOMERY	© 10,422
Westtown	MCD-Township	CHESTER	© 10,352
Harrison Township	CDP-Census Area Only	ALLEGHENY	◆ 10,315
Columbia	Inc. Place	LANCASTER	© 10,311
Darby	Inc. Place	DELAWARE	© 10,299
Easttown	MCD-Township	CHESTER	© 10,270
Waynesboro	Inc. Place	FRANKLIN	◆ 10,203
North Middleton	MCD-Township	CUMBERLAND	© 10,197
Shiloh	CDP	YORK	© 10,192
Wyomissing	Inc. Place	BERKS	◆ 10,186
Fairview	MCD-Township	ERIE	© 10,140
Weigelstown	CDP	YORK	© 10,117
North Strabane	MCD-Township	WASHINGTON	© 10,057
Woodlyn	CDP	DELAWARE	© 10,036
Morrisville	Inc. Place	BUCKS	© 10,023
Salisbury	MCD-Township	LANCASTER	© 10,012
Willistown	MCD-Township	CHESTER	© 10,011
Abington	RMC Place	MONTGOMERY	● 10,000
Huntingdon Valley	RMC Place	MONTGOMERY	● 10,000
Roslyn	RMC Place	MONTGOMERY	● 10,000
Croydon	CDP	BUCKS	© 9,993
Sunbury	Inc. Place	NORTHUMBERLAND	◆ 9,958
East Cocalico	MCD-Township	LANCASTER	© 9,954
Bristol	Inc. Place	BUCKS	© 9,923
Beaver Falls	Inc. Place	BEAVER	© 9,920
Richland	MCD-Township	BUCKS	© 9,920
Skippack	MCD-Township	MONTGOMERY	® 9,920
East Stroudsburg	Inc. Place	MONROE	© 9,888
Lower Saucon	MCD-Township	NORTHAMPTON	© 9,884
Carbondale	Inc. Place	LACKAWANNA	© 9,804
Cecil	MCD-Township	WASHINGTON	© 9,756
Lehigh	MCD-Township	NORTHAMPTON	© 9,728
Jefferson	Inc. Place	ALLEGHENY	© 9,666
Swissvale	Inc. Place	ALLEGHENY	© 9,653
Progress	CDP	DAUPHIN	© 9,647
Darby	MCD-Township	DELAWARE	© 9,622
Darby Township	CDP-Census Area Only	DELAWARE	© 9,622
Pocono	MCD-Township	MONROE	© 9,607
Hanover	MCD-Township	NORTHAMPTON	© 9,563
Warren	Inc. Place	WARREN	◆ 9,497
East Bradford	MCD-Township	CHESTER	© 9,405
Northampton	Inc. Place	NORTHAMPTON	© 9,405
Economy	Inc. Place	BEAVER	© 9,363
East Whiteland	MCD-Township	CHESTER	© 9,333
Dormont	Inc. Place	ALLEGHENY	© 9,305
Middletown	Inc. Place	DAUPHIN	© 9,242
Richland	MCD-Township	ALLEGHENY	© 9,231
Neshannock	MCD-Township	LAWRENCE	© 9,216
Douglass	MCD-Township	MONTGOMERY	© 9,104
New Garden	MCD-Township	CHESTER	© 9,083
Mechanicsburg	Inc. Place	CUMBERLAND	© 9,042
Lititz	Inc. Place	LANCASTER	© 9,029
Connellsville	Inc. Place	FAYETTE	◆ 9,019
Hazle	MCD-Township	LUZERNE	© 9,000
Hamilton	MCD-Township	FRANKLIN	© 8,949
Quakertown	Inc. Place	BUCKS	© 8,931
Amity	MCD-Township	BERKS	© 8,867
Lewistown	Inc. Place	MIFFLIN	◆ 8,857
O'Hara	MCD-Township	ALLEGHENY	© 8,856
O'Hara Township	CDP-Census Area Only	ALLEGHENY	© 8,856
Park Forest Village	CDP	CENTRE	© 8,830
Perkasie	Inc. Place	BUCKS	© 8,828
Canton	MCD-Township	WASHINGTON	© 8,826
Milford	MCD-Township	BUCKS	© 8,810
Lock Haven	Inc. Place	CLINTON	◆ 8,798
Old Forge	Inc. Place	LACKAWANNA	© 8,798
Harleysville	CDP	MONTGOMERY	© 8,795
Dingman	MCD-Township	PIKE	© 8,788
East York	CDP	YORK	© 8,782
Bellevue	Inc. Place	ALLEGHENY	© 8,770
Ellwood City	Inc. Place	LAWRENCE	© 8,688
Moore	MCD-Township	NORTHAMPTON	© 8,673
Collingdale	Inc. Place	DELAWARE	© 8,664
Northwest Harborcreek	CDP-Census Area Only	ERIE	© 8,658
South Abington	MCD-Township	LACKAWANNA	© 8,638
Canonsburg	Inc. Place	WASHINGTON	© 8,607
Rapho	MCD-Township	LANCASTER	© 8,578
Castle Shannon	Inc. Place	ALLEGHENY	© 8,556
Clairton	Inc. Place	ALLEGHENY	© 8,491
College	MCD-Township	CENTRE	© 8,489
West Goshen	CDP-Census Area Only	CHESTER	© 8,472
White Oak	Inc. Place	ALLEGHENY	© 8,437
Latrobe	Inc. Place	WESTMORELAND	◆ 8,421
Forks	MCD-Township	NORTHAMPTON	© 8,419
Pleasant Hills	Inc. Place	ALLEGHENY	© 8,397
Carnegie	Inc. Place	ALLEGHENY	© 8,389
South Lebanon	MCD-Township	LEBANON	© 8,383
Fairless Hills	CDP	BUCKS	© 8,365
Bradford	Inc. Place	MCKEAN	◆ 8,343
Village Green-Green Ridge	CDP-Census Area Only	DELAWARE	© 8,279
Hamilton	MCD-Township	MONROE	© 8,235
Upper Leacock	MCD-Township	LANCASTER	© 8,229
Center	MCD-Township	BUTLER	© 8,182
Dallas	MCD-Township	LUZERNE	© 8,179
Lower Swatara	MCD-Township	DAUPHIN	© 8,149
Monessen	Inc. Place	WESTMORELAND	◆ 8,127
Pittston	Inc. Place	LUZERNE	© 8,104
Folsom	CDP	DELAWARE	© 8,072
Doylestown	Inc. Place	BUCKS	◆ 8,032
Ephrata	MCD-Township	LANCASTER	© 8,026
Brighton	MCD-Township	BEAVER	© 8,024
Grove City	Inc. Place	MERCER	© 8,024
Kulpsville	CDP	MONTGOMERY	© 8,005
Allegheny	MCD-Township	WESTMORELAND	© 8,002
Bala-Cynwyd	RMC Place	MONTGOMERY	● 8,000
South Strabane	MCD-Township	WASHINGTON	© 7,987
Brookhaven	Inc. Place	DELAWARE	© 7,985
Mount Joy	MCD-Township	LANCASTER	© 7,944
North Codorus	MCD-Township	YORK	© 7,915
Glenside	CDP	MONTGOMERY	© 7,914
Wynnewood	RMC Place	MONTGOMERY	● 7,800
Camp Hill	Inc. Place	CUMBERLAND	◆ 7,797
Worcester	MCD-Township	MONTGOMERY	© 7,789
Bullskin	MCD-Township	FAYETTE	© 7,782
East Huntingdon	MCD-Township	WESTMORELAND	© 7,781
Millersville	Inc. Place	LANCASTER	© 7,774
Ambridge	Inc. Place	BEAVER	© 7,769
Solebury	MCD-Township	BUCKS	© 7,743
Sanatoga	CDP	MONTGOMERY	© 7,734
Lawrence	MCD-Township	CLEARFIELD	© 7,712
Frankstown	MCD-Township	BLAIR	© 7,694
Pine	MCD-Township	ALLEGHENY	© 7,683
Wilson	Inc. Place	NORTHAMPTON	© 7,682
Shenango	MCD-Township	LAWRENCE	© 7,633

Entries in **UPPERCASE** are counties.
Entries in **bold** have populations of 2,500 or more.
Names in parentheses are alternate names.
Inc. Place — Incorporated Place
RMC Place — Rand McNally Designated Place
CDP — Census Designated Place
MCD — Minor Civil Division

⊡ County Seat
▲ Minor Civil Division
elev. Elevation
🅿 Post Office

H Hospital
C College
■ Principal Business Center
★ Ranally Metro Area (RMA) Abbreviation
z Zip Code(s)

℗ Previous Census Population
® Revised Census Population
Ⓐ Annexation Population
● Rand McNally Population Estimate
© Final Census Population
Ⓢ Special Census Population
◆ Estimated Population

For additional definitions see Glossary, Volume 1, and Introduction, Volume 2.

Place Name	Place Type	County	Population
Conshohocken	Inc. Place	MONTGOMERY	© 7,589
Downingtown	Inc. Place	CHESTER	© 7,589
Dunbar	MCD-Township	FAYETTE	© 7,562
Du Bois	Inc. Place	CLEARFIELD	◆ 7,543
Lehman	MCD-Township	PIKE	© 7,515
Kennedy	MCD-Township	ALLEGHENY	© 7,504
Kennedy Township	CDP-Census Area Only	ALLEGHENY	© 7,504
Gettysburg	Inc. Place	ADAMS	© 7,490
Glenolden	Inc. Place	DELAWARE	© 7,476
Conemaugh	MCD-Township	SOMERSET	© 7,452
Lower Windsor	MCD-Township	YORK	© 7,405
Washington	MCD-Township	WESTMORELAND	© 7,384
North Coventry	MCD-Township	CHESTER	© 7,381
Middletown	CDP	NORTHAMPTON	© 7,378
New Hanover	MCD-Township	MONTGOMERY	© 7,369
New Cumberland	Inc. Place	CUMBERLAND	© 7,349
Duquesne	Inc. Place	ALLEGHENY	© 7,332
Penn	MCD-Township	LANCASTER	© 7,312
West View	Inc. Place	ALLEGHENY	© 7,277
Willow Street	CDP	LANCASTER	© 7,258
Derry	MCD-Township	MIFFLIN	© 7,256
Franklin	MCD-Township	GREENE	® 7,224
Shamokin	Inc. Place	NORTHUMBERLAND	◆ 7,202
Ridley Park	Inc. Place	DELAWARE	© 7,196
Upper Makefield	MCD-Township	BUCKS	© 7,180
Tamaqua	Inc. Place	SCHUYLKILL	© 7,174
Butler	MCD-Township	LUZERNE	© 7,166
Hatboro	Inc. Place	MONTGOMERY	◆ 7,158
Chartiers	MCD-Township	WASHINGTON	© 7,154
West Brandywine	MCD-Township	CHESTER	© 7,153
Kingston	MCD-Township	LUZERNE	© 7,145
Palmyra	Inc. Place	LEBANON	© 7,096
Perkiomen	MCD-Township	MONTGOMERY	© 7,093
New Sewickley	MCD-Township	BEAVER	© 7,076
West Caln	MCD-Township	CHESTER	© 7,054
Maple Glen	CDP	MONTGOMERY	© 7,042
Blakely	Inc. Place	LACKAWANNA	© 7,027
Chippewa	MCD-Township	BEAVER	© 7,021
Cranberry	MCD-Township	VENANGO	© 7,014
Warrington	RMC Place	BUCKS	● 7,000
Bushkill	MCD-Township	NORTHAMPTON	© 6,982
Folcroft	Inc. Place	DELAWARE	© 6,978
Ligonier	MCD-Township	WESTMORELAND	© 6,973
West Cocalico	MCD-Township	LANCASTER	© 6,967
Allegheny	MCD-Township	BLAIR	© 6,965
Schuylkill	MCD-Township	CHESTER	© 6,960
Edinboro	Inc. Place	ERIE	© 6,950
Salem	MCD-Township	WESTMORELAND	© 6,939
Huntingdon	Inc. Place	HUNTINGDON	© 6,918
Wilkins	MCD-Township	ALLEGHENY	© 6,917
Wilkins Township	CDP-Census Area Only	ALLEGHENY	© 6,917
Oakmont	Inc. Place	ALLEGHENY	© 6,911
Upper Milford	MCD-Township	LEHIGH	© 6,889
Robeson	MCD-Township	BERKS	© 6,869
Upper Uwchlan	MCD-Township	CHESTER	© 6,850
Corry	Inc. Place	ERIE	© 6,834
Forest Hills	Inc. Place	ALLEGHENY	© 6,831
Buffalo	MCD-Township	BUTLER	© 6,827
Franklin	Inc. Place	VENANGO	◆ 6,822
Indiana	MCD-Township	ALLEGHENY	© 6,809
Clifton Heights	Inc. Place	DELAWARE	© 6,779
Adams	MCD-Township	BUTLER	© 6,774
North Londonderry	MCD-Township	LEBANON	© 6,771
West Earl	MCD-Township	LANCASTER	© 6,766
Mount Joy	Inc. Place	LANCASTER	© 6,765
Somerset	Inc. Place	SOMERSET	© 6,762
Bern	MCD-Township	BERKS	© 6,758
Georges	MCD-Township	FAYETTE	© 6,752
Souderton	Inc. Place	MONTGOMERY	© 6,730
Crafton	Inc. Place	ALLEGHENY	© 6,706
Stowe	MCD-Township	ALLEGHENY	© 6,706
Stowe Township	CDP-Census Area Only	ALLEGHENY	© 6,706
Lafayette Hill	RMC Place	MONTGOMERY	● 6,700
Neshaminy Valley	RMC Place	BUCKS	● 6,700
Brecknock	MCD-Township	LANCASTER	© 6,699
Homeacre-Lyndora	CDP-Census Area Only	BUTLER	© 6,685
Richboro	CDP	BUCKS	© 6,678
Middlesex	MCD-Township	CUMBERLAND	© 6,669
Providence	MCD-Township	LANCASTER	© 6,651
Milton	Inc. Place	NORTHUMBERLAND	© 6,650
New Brighton	Inc. Place	BEAVER	© 6,641
Leacock-Leola-Bareville	CDP-Census Area Only	LANCASTER	© 6,625
McKees Rocks	Inc. Place	ALLEGHENY	© 6,622
Lower Allen	CDP-Census Area Only	CUMBERLAND	© 6,619
North East	MCD-Township	ERIE	® 6,613
Prospect Park	Inc. Place	DELAWARE	© 6,594
Parkville	CDP	YORK	© 6,593
Catasauqua	Inc. Place	LEHIGH	© 6,588
Washington	MCD-Township	LEHIGH	© 6,588
Cumberland	MCD-Township	GREENE	© 6,564
Maidencreek	MCD-Township	BERKS	© 6,553
East Pikeland	MCD-Township	CHESTER	© 6,551
Audubon	CDP	MONTGOMERY	© 6,549
West Donegal	MCD-Township	LANCASTER	© 6,539
Polk	MCD-Township	MONROE	© 6,533
Feasterville-Trevose	CDP-Census Area Only	BUCKS	© 6,525
Plymouth	Inc. Place	LUZERNE	© 6,507
West Hanover	MCD-Township	DAUPHIN	© 6,505
Melrose Park	RMC Place	MONTGOMERY	● 6,500
Adams	MCD-Township	CAMBRIA	© 6,495
Taylor	Inc. Place	LACKAWANNA	© 6,475
Kennett	MCD-Township	CHESTER	© 6,451
Ambler	Inc. Place	MONTGOMERY	© 6,426
Bethel	MCD-Township	DELAWARE	© 6,421
Linglestown	CDP	DAUPHIN	© 6,414
South Williamsport	Inc. Place	LYCOMING	© 6,412
North Braddock	Inc. Place	ALLEGHENY	© 6,410
North Cornwall	MCD-Township	LEBANON	© 6,403
Redstone	MCD-Township	FAYETTE	© 6,397
Bellefonte	Inc. Place	CENTRE	© 6,395
Blue Bell	CDP	MONTGOMERY	© 6,395
Mount Carmel	Inc. Place	NORTHUMBERLAND	© 6,390
Greenville	Inc. Place	MERCER	© 6,380
Jackson	MCD-Township	LEBANON	© 6,338
Antis	MCD-Township	BLAIR	© 6,328
Cambria	MCD-Township	CAMBRIA	© 6,323
Delaware	MCD-Township	PIKE	© 6,319
East Marlborough	MCD-Township	CHESTER	© 6,317
Lionville-Marchwood	CDP-Census Area Only	CHESTER	© 6,298
Monaca	Inc. Place	BEAVER	© 6,286
Honey Brook	MCD-Township	CHESTER	© 6,278
Punxsutawney	Inc. Place	JEFFERSON	© 6,271
Sewickley	MCD-Township	WESTMORELAND	© 6,230
Archbald	Inc. Place	LACKAWANNA	© 6,220
Clearfield	Inc. Place	CLEARFIELD	◆ 6,216
Dickson City	Inc. Place	LACKAWANNA	© 6,205
Clarion	Inc. Place	CLARION	© 6,185
Earl	MCD-Township	LANCASTER	© 6,183
South Huntingdon	MCD-Township	WESTMORELAND	© 6,175
Swarthmore	Inc. Place	DELAWARE	© 6,170
Tobyhanna	MCD-Township	MONROE	© 6,152
Red Lion	Inc. Place	YORK	© 6,149
Titusville	Inc. Place	CRAWFORD	© 6,146
Southampton	MCD-Township	FRANKLIN	© 6,138
Coraopolis	Inc. Place	ALLEGHENY	© 6,131
North Sewickley	MCD-Township	BEAVER	© 6,120
Spring	MCD-Township	CENTRE	© 6,117
Jackson	MCD-Township	YORK	© 6,095
Turtle Creek	Inc. Place	ALLEGHENY	© 6,076
Upper Mount Bethel	MCD-Township	NORTHAMPTON	© 6,063
Trooper	CDP	MONTGOMERY	© 6,061
Farrell	Inc. Place	MERCER	© 6,050
Plymouth Meeting	CDP	MONTGOMERY	® 6,034
Nazareth	Inc. Place	NORTHAMPTON	© 6,023
Allison Park	RMC Place	ALLEGHENY	● 6,000
Haverford	RMC Place	MONTGOMERY	● 6,000
Library	RMC Place	ALLEGHENY	● 6,000
Penn Valley	RMC Place	MONTGOMERY	● 6,000
Marshall	MCD-Township	ALLEGHENY	© 5,996
Norwood	Inc. Place	DELAWARE	© 5,985
Maxatawny	MCD-Township	BERKS	© 5,982
Jackson	MCD-Township	MONROE	© 5,979
Chanceford	MCD-Township	YORK	© 5,973
Exeter	Inc. Place	LUZERNE	© 5,955
Shrewsbury	MCD-Township	YORK	© 5,947
Hellam	MCD-Township	YORK	© 5,930
Upper Yoder	MCD-Township	CAMBRIA	© 5,862
Steelton	Inc. Place	DAUPHIN	© 5,858
Quincy	MCD-Township	FRANKLIN	© 5,846
East Brandywine	MCD-Township	CHESTER	© 5,822
Sayre	Inc. Place	BRADFORD	© 5,813
Thornbury	MCD-Township	DELAWARE	® 5,787
St. Thomas	MCD-Township	FRANKLIN	© 5,775
East Buffalo	MCD-Township	UNION	© 5,730
East Earl	MCD-Township	LANCASTER	© 5,723
Stroudsburg	Inc. Place	MONROE	◆ 5,720
Cumberland	MCD-Township	ADAMS	© 5,718
Conewago	MCD-Township	ADAMS	© 5,709
Jefferson	MCD-Township	BUTLER	© 5,690
Carroll	MCD-Township	WASHINGTON	© 5,677
Smithfield	MCD-Township	MONROE	© 5,672
Plainfield	MCD-Township	NORTHAMPTON	© 5,668
Arnold	Inc. Place	WESTMORELAND	© 5,667
Donora	Inc. Place	WASHINGTON	© 5,653
Enola	CDP	CUMBERLAND	© 5,627
Shenandoah	Inc. Place	SCHUYLKILL	© 5,624
Lewisburg	Inc. Place	UNION	© 5,620
Longswamp	MCD-Township	BERKS	© 5,608
Hellertown	Inc. Place	NORTHAMPTON	© 5,606
Wyndmoor	CDP	MONTGOMERY	© 5,601
Union	MCD-Township	WASHINGTON	© 5,599
German	MCD-Township	FAYETTE	© 5,595
Wright	MCD-Township	LUZERNE	© 5,593
Middlesex	MCD-Township	BUTLER	© 5,586
Shippensburg	Inc. Place	CUMBERLAND	© 5,586
Moosic	Inc. Place	LACKAWANNA	© 5,575
Schuylkill Haven	Inc. Place	SCHUYLKILL	© 5,548
Lehighton	Inc. Place	CARBON	© 5,537
Media	Inc. Place	DELAWARE	© 5,533
Monroe	MCD-Township	CUMBERLAND	© 5,530
Summit	MCD-Township	ERIE	© 5,529
Tyrone	Inc. Place	BLAIR	© 5,528
Westmont	Inc. Place	CAMBRIA	© 5,523
East Nottingham	MCD-Township	CHESTER	© 5,516
Oreland	CDP	MONTGOMERY	© 5,509
Old Lycoming	MCD-Township	LYCOMING	© 5,508
Vernon	MCD-Township	CRAWFORD	© 5,499
East Vincent	MCD-Township	CHESTER	© 5,493
South Heidelberg	MCD-Township	BERKS	© 5,491
Sharon Hill	Inc. Place	DELAWARE	© 5,468
South Londonderry	MCD-Township	LEBANON	© 5,458
Vandergrift	Inc. Place	WESTMORELAND	© 5,455
Penn Forest	MCD-Township	CARBON	© 5,439
Fox Chapel	Inc. Place	ALLEGHENY	© 5,436
Ross	MCD-Township	MONROE	© 5,435
Paoli	CDP	CHESTER	© 5,425
Bedford	MCD-Township	BEDFORD	© 5,417
Stonybrook-Wilshire	CDP-Census Area Only	YORK	© 5,414
East Donegal	MCD-Township	LANCASTER	© 5,405
Selinsgrove	Inc. Place	SNYDER	© 5,383
Penn Wynne	CDP	MONTGOMERY	© 5,382
Hollidaysburg	Inc. Place	BLAIR	© 5,368
Bridgeville	Inc. Place	ALLEGHENY	© 5,341
Sugarcreek	Inc. Place	VENANGO	© 5,331
East Hanover	MCD-Township	DAUPHIN	© 5,322
Bangor	Inc. Place	NORTHAMPTON	© 5,319
Holland	RMC Place	BUCKS	● 5,300
Avalon	Inc. Place	ALLEGHENY	© 5,294
Conewago	MCD-Township	YORK	© 5,278
California	Inc. Place	WASHINGTON	© 5,274
Kennett Square	Inc. Place	CHESTER	© 5,273
Colebrookdale	MCD-Township	BERKS	© 5,270
Collier	MCD-Township	ALLEGHENY	© 5,265
London Grove	MCD-Township	CHESTER	© 5,265
West Pennsboro	MCD-Township	CUMBERLAND	© 5,263
Lower Nazareth	MCD-Township	NORTHAMPTON	© 5,259
Paxtonia	CDP	DAUPHIN	© 5,254
Slippery Rock	MCD-Township	BUTLER	© 5,251
Palmerton	Inc. Place	CARBON	© 5,248
West Mead	MCD-Township	CRAWFORD	© 5,227
Londonderry	MCD-Township	DAUPHIN	© 5,224
Benner	MCD-Township	CENTRE	© 5,217
Penn	MCD-Township	BUTLER	© 5,210
Boothwyn	CDP	DELAWARE	© 5,206
East Rockhill	MCD-Township	BUCKS	© 5,199
Clay	MCD-Township	LANCASTER	© 5,173
East Fallowfield	MCD-Township	CHESTER	© 5,157
Swoyersville	Inc. Place	LUZERNE	© 5,157
Findlay	MCD-Township	ALLEGHENY	© 5,145
Girard	MCD-Township	ERIE	© 5,133
Arlington Heights	CDP	MONROE	© 5,132
Clarks Summit	Inc. Place	LACKAWANNA	© 5,126
Valley	MCD-Township	CHESTER	© 5,116
Reading	MCD-Township	ADAMS	© 5,106
Union	MCD-Township	LAWRENCE	© 5,103
Carroll	MCD-Township	PERRY	© 5,095
New Holland	Inc. Place	LANCASTER	© 5,092
East Manchester	MCD-Township	YORK	© 5,078
West Pittston	Inc. Place	LUZERNE	© 5,072
Devon-Berwyn	CDP-Census Area Only	CHESTER	© 5,067
Kutztown	Inc. Place	BERKS	© 5,067
Birdsboro	Inc. Place	BERKS	© 5,064
Hopewell	MCD-Township	YORK	© 5,062
Shillington	Inc. Place	BERKS	© 5,059
Athens	MCD-Township	BRADFORD	© 5,058
Newport	MCD-Township	LUZERNE	© 5,006
Plymouth Valley	RMC Place	MONTGOMERY	● 5,000
West Bristol	RMC Place	BUCKS	● 5,000

County Business Data

County	FIPS Code	County Seat	Land Area (Sq. Mi.)	Census Population			Wholesale Trade		Manufacturing, 2002			
				4/1/2000	4/1/1990	% Change 1990-2000	Sales, 2002 ($1,000)	% Change 1997-2002	Establish-ments	Total Employees	Value Added ($1,000)	Ranally Mfg. Units
Adams	001	Gettysburg	520	91,292	78,274	16.6	902,741	-0.8	127	6,953	844,564	447
Allegheny	003	Pittsburgh	730	1,281,666	1,336,449	-4.1	29,248,184	3.5	1,355	46,709	5,847,341	3,094
Armstrong	005	Kittanning	654	72,392	73,478	-1.5	(d)	(d)	96	2,725	202,084	107
Beaver	007	Beaver	434	181,412	186,093	-2.5	638,421	11.9	215	9,041	1,058,000	560
Bedford	009	Bedford	1,015	49,984	47,919	4.3	(d)	(d)	72	3,189	221,545	117
Berks	011	Reading	859	373,638	336,523	11.0	2,912,109	-6.7	579	33,203	3,504,867	1,854
Blair	013	Hollidaysburg	526	129,144	130,542	-1.1	1,774,176	8.1	153	7,649	816,174	432
Bradford	015	Towanda	1,151	62,761	60,967	2.9	159,591	-8.9	78	5,162	633,762	335
Bucks	017	Doylestown	607	597,635	541,174	10.4	10,169,570	20.8	1,187	33,458	5,733,332	3,033
Butler	019	Butler	789	174,083	152,013	14.5	4,013,666	-11.6	302	13,697	1,341,354	710
Cambria	021	Ebensburg	688	152,598	163,029	-6.4	516,088	-11.1	151	4,186	355,646	188
Cameron	023	Emporium	397	5,974	5,913	1.0	(d)	(d)	20	1,109	66,693	35
Carbon	025	Jim Thorpe	381	58,802	56,846	3.4	39,546	-56.7	58	2,534	170,190	90
Centre	027	Bellefonte	1,108	135,758	123,786	9.7	189,589	(d)	159	6,350	584,717	309
Chester	029	West Chester	756	433,501	376,396	15.2	11,276,042	-26.9	627	21,440	2,592,519	1,372
Clarion	031	Clarion	602	41,765	41,699	0.2	116,348	-79.5	51	2,718	240,183	127
Clearfield	033	Clearfield	1,147	83,382	78,097	6.8	352,680	25.8	110	3,498	223,518	118
Clinton	035	Lock Haven	891	37,914	37,182	2.0	(d)	(d)	45	2,217	304,970	161
Columbia	037	Bloomsburg	486	64,151	63,202	1.5	(d)	(d)	101	(d)	(d)	...
Crawford	039	Meadville	1,013	90,366	86,169	4.9	111,995	-36.2	323	7,499	735,735	389
Cumberland	041	Carlisle	550	213,674	195,257	9.4	(d)	(d)	207	10,063	1,084,088	574
Dauphin	043	Harrisburg	525	251,798	237,813	5.9	5,638,190	-35.2	222	10,940	1,662,779	880
Delaware	045	Media	184	550,864	547,651	0.6	12,805,645	34.7	466	17,695	2,529,833	1,338
Elk	047	Ridgway	829	35,112	34,878	0.7	(d)	(d)	142	6,434	716,145	379
Erie	049	Erie	802	280,843	275,572	1.9	1,150,933	-9.9	584	27,960	2,873,649	1,520
Fayette	051	Uniontown	790	148,644	145,351	2.3	(d)	(d)	135	3,396	263,593	139
Forest	053	Tionesta	428	4,946	4,802	3.0	(d)	(d)	...	(d)	(d)	...
Franklin	055	Chambersburg	772	129,313	121,082	6.8	676,933	10.9	207	9,620	947,304	501
Fulton	057	McConnellsburg	438	14,261	13,837	3.1	12,158	84.7	19	(d)	(d)	...
Greene	059	Waynesburg	576	40,672	39,550	2.8	92,709	17.5	24	590	55,124	29
Huntingdon	061	Huntingdon	874	45,586	44,164	3.2	53,102	(d)	45	2,184	228,274	121
Indiana	063	Indiana	829	89,605	89,994	-0.4	280,487	-33.0	105	3,392	276,921	147
Jefferson	065	Brookville	655	45,932	46,083	-0.3	151,558	24.8	91	3,986	335,906	178
Juniata	067	Mifflintown	392	22,821	20,625	10.6	60,075	(d)	51	2,153	157,014	83
Lackawanna	069	Scranton	459	213,295	219,039	-2.6	1,553,177	37.9	293	(d)	(d)	...
Lancaster	071	Lancaster	949	470,658	422,822	11.3	11,678,030	6.8	988	47,821	6,541,146	3,461
Lawrence	073	New Castle	360	94,643	96,246	-1.7	(d)	(d)	176	4,798	689,104	365
Lebanon	075	Lebanon	362	120,327	113,744	5.8	(d)	(d)	219	9,613	817,772	433
Lehigh	077	Allentown	347	312,090	291,130	7.2	6,837,435	46.5	458	21,573	3,293,223	1,742
Luzerne	079	Wilkes Barre	891	319,250	328,149	-2.7	3,098,545	44.1	372	20,913	2,278,627	1,206
Lycoming	081	Williamsport	1,235	120,044	118,710	1.1	(d)	(d)	206	11,992	1,306,732	691
McKean	083	Smethport	982	45,936	47,131	-2.5	212,339	-7.3	71	4,629	472,514	250
Mercer	085	Mercer	672	120,293	121,003	-0.6	(d)	(d)	202	8,786	935,301	495
Mifflin	087	Lewistown	412	46,486	46,197	0.6	81,489	-27.1	83	4,497	412,785	218
Monroe	089	Stroudsburg	609	138,687	95,709	44.9	380,789	10.3	122	5,111	948,369	502
Montgomery	091	Norristown	483	750,097	678,111	10.6	35,706,776	56.1	1,280	56,330	14,647,572	7,750
Montour	093	Danville	131	18,236	17,735	2.8	(d)	(d)	23	(d)	(d)	...
Northampton	095	Easton	374	267,066	247,105	8.1	1,544,114	-25.3	363	15,520	1,986,946	1,051
Northumberland	097	Sunbury	460	94,556	96,771	-2.3	489,773	-15.9	111	6,310	463,991	245
Perry	099	New Bloomfield	554	43,602	41,172	5.9	(d)	(d)	42	900	64,851	34
Philadelphia	101	Philadelphia	135	1,517,550	1,585,577	-4.3	12,643,546	5.3	1,142	42,922	4,738,528	2,507
Pike	103	Milford	547	46,302	27,966	65.6	(d)	(d)	...	(d)	(d)	...
Potter	105	Coudersport	1,081	18,080	16,717	8.2	20,190	15.8	26	938	73,088	39
Schuylkill	107	Pottsville	778	150,336	152,585	-1.5	656,216	3.8	202	12,057	1,409,129	746

Entries in **UPPERCASE** are counties.
Entries in **bold** have populations of 2,500 or more.
Names in parentheses are alternate names.
Inc. Place — Incorporated Place
RMC Place — Rand McNally Designated Place
CDP — Census Designated Place
MCD — Minor Civil Division

⊡ County Seat
▲ Minor Civil Division
elev. Elevation
🅿 Post Office

H Hospital
C College
■ Principal Business Center
★ Ranally Metro Area (RMA) Abbreviation
z Zip Code(s)

Ⓟ Previous Census Population
® Revised Census Population
Ⓐ Annexation Population
● Rand McNally Population Estimate
© Final Census Population
Ⓢ Special Census Population
◆ Estimated Population

For additional definitions see Glossary, Volume 1, and Introduction, Volume 2.

County	FIPS Code	County Seat	Land Area (Sq. Mi.)	Census Population 4/1/2000	Census Population 4/1/1990	Census Population % Change 1990-2000	Wholesale Trade Sales, 2002 ($1,000)	Wholesale Trade % Change 1997-2002	Manufacturing, 2002 Establish-ments	Manufacturing, 2002 Total Employees	Manufacturing, 2002 Value Added ($1,000)	Manufacturing, 2002 Ranally Mfg. Units
Snyder	109	Middleburg	331	37,546	36,680	2.4	(d)	(d)	75	5,669	333,861	177
Somerset	111	Somerset	1,075	80,023	78,218	2.3	271,294	-1.2	128	4,623	333,241	176
Sullivan	113	Laporte	450	6,556	6,104	7.4	(d)	(d)	...	(d)	(d)	...
Susquehanna	115	Montrose	823	42,238	40,380	4.6	162,561	(d)	59	827	76,272	40
Tioga	117	Wellsboro	1,134	41,373	41,126	0.6	104,760	12.3	42	2,958	245,697	130
Union	119	Lewisburg	317	41,624	36,176	15.1	(d)	(d)	33	2,988	274,442	145
Venango	121	Franklin	675	57,565	59,381	-3.1	138,221	7.7	90	3,865	342,508	181
Warren	123	Warren	883	43,863	45,050	-2.6	55,689	-17.0	78	3,871	395,007	209
Washington	125	Washington	857	202,897	204,584	-0.8	2,114,225	42.8	268	10,248	1,109,413	587
Wayne	127	Honesdale	729	47,722	39,944	19.5	132,397	96.2	74	783	57,099	30
Westmoreland	129	Greensburg	1,025	369,993	370,321	-0.1	4,443,638	12.0	596	22,021	2,035,002	1,077
Wyoming	131	Tunkhannock	397	28,080	28,076	0.0	73,603	(d)	36	(d)	(d)	...
York	133	York	904	381,751	339,574	12.4	5,025,573	46.6	657	42,586	4,593,119	2,430
The State			**44,817**	**12,281,054**	**11,881,643**	**3.4**	**183,741,873**	**15.3**	**16,665**	**715,453**	**92,319,195**	**48,843**

(d) Data not available. Corresponding percentages or Ranally Manufacturing Units are estimates.
... Represents 0 or amount too minimal to be reported.

Administrative Divisions

Townships: All Pennsylvania counties are divided into townships, except for areas within boroughs, cities or towns. Although legally incorporated, townships are not treated as incorporated places by the U.S. Census because the population often is scattered among several localities and rural areas rather than being concentrated in a single place. Only townships with an active government recognized by the U.S. Census of Governments are printed in this index.

Boroughs, Cities and Towns: Incorporated places do not form part of the townships which adjoin or surround them.

Index of Places and Counties

A

Aaronsburg; CDP; CENTRE; ▲ Haines; **227** EK-2; [P]; z 16820; © 485
Abbott; MCD-Township; POTTER; ***226** EG-1; mail Galeton z 16922; ℗ 173; © 226
Abbottstown; Inc. Place; ADAMS; **227** EQ-4; elev. 549ft./167m.; [P]; ★ **HANV**; z 17301; ℗ 539; © 905
Aberdeen; RMC Place; LACKAWANNA; ▲ Madison; ***226** EH-10; ★ **SCR-**; mail Elizabethtown z 17022, Moscow z 18444; rural
Abington; MCD-Township; LACKAWANNA; ***226** EG-10; ★ **SCR-**; mail Waverly z 18471; ℗ 1,533; © 1,616
Abington; RMC Place; MONTGOMERY; ▲ Abington; **228** A-5; [P] [H] [C] 3,141; ★ **PHIL-**; z 19001; ● 10,000
Abington; MCD-Township; MONTGOMERY; ***227** EO-12; [P] [C] 3,141 ■; ★ **PHIL-**; z 19001; ℗ 56,322; © 56,103; ◆ 54,686
Abrahamsville; RMC Place; WAYNE; ▲ Damascus; ***226** EE-12; elev. 1,101ft./336m.; mail Callicoon z 12723, Damascus z 18415; rural
Abrams; RMC Place; MONTGOMERY; ▲ Upper Merion; ★ **PHIL-**; mail King of Prussia z 19406
Academia; RMC Place; JUNIATA; ▲ Beale; **227** EM-2; mail Port Royal z 17082; ● 30
Academy Corners; RMC Place; TIOGA; ▲ Deerfield; **226** ED-2; elev. 1,219ft./372m.; mail Knoxville z 16928; ● 60
Academy Gardens; RMC Place; PHILADELPHIA; ***227** EO-13; ★ **PHIL-**; mail Philadelphia z 19114; pop. incl. with Philadelphia (Inc. Place)
Accomac; RMC Place; YORK; ▲ Hellam; ***227** EP-6; elev. 271ft./83m.; ★ **YORK**; mail York z 17406; ● 100
Ackermanville; RMC Place; NORTHAMPTON; ▲ Washington; **227** EK-12; [P]; z 18010; ● 325
Acme; RMC Place; WESTMORELAND; ▲ Mount Pleasant; **225** WO-6; [P]; z 15610; ● 180
Acmetonia; RMC Place; ALLEGHENY; ▲ Harmar; **228** H-9; ★ **PGH**; mail Cheswick z 15024; ● 1,500
Acosta; RMC Place; SOMERSET; ▲ Jenner; **225** WO-8; [P]; z 15520; ● 400
Acre Lake; SUSQUEHANNA; see West Lenox (RMC Place)
Adah (Palmer); RMC Place; FAYETTE; ▲ German; **225** WP-4; [P]; ★ **UNTN**; z 15410; ● 450
Adams; RMC Place; ARMSTRONG; ▲ Sugarcreek; ***224** WJ-5; mail East Brady z 16028
Adams; MCD-Township; BUTLER; ***225** WL-4; ★ **PGH**; mail Mars z 16046; ℗ 3,911; © 6,774
Adams; MCD-Township; CAMBRIA; ***225** WN-9; ★ **JNST**; mail Sidman z 15955; ℗ 6,869; © 6,495
Adams; MCD-Township; SNYDER; ***227** EK-3; mail Beavertown z 17813; ℗ 833; © 852
Adams; RMC Place; SOMERSET; ▲ Somerset; mail Friedens z 15541; rural
ADAMS; **227** EP-2; ℗ 78,274; © 91,292; ◆ 100,182
Adamsburg; Inc. Place; WESTMORELAND; **225** WN-5; elev. 1,200ft./366m.; [P]; ★ **PGH**; z 15611; ℗ 257; © 221
Adams Corners; RMC Place; BUTLER; ▲ Slippery Rock; ***224** WI-4; mail Slippery Rock z 16057; rural
Adamsdale; RMC Place; SCHUYLKILL; **227** EL-8; elev. 510ft./155m.; ★ **PTSVL**; mail Schuylkill Haven z 17972; ● 50
Adams Hill; RMC Place; WESTMORELAND; ▲ North Huntingdon; ***225** WN-5; ★ **PGH**; mail Irwin z 15642; ● 200
Adamstown; Inc. Place; LANCASTER, BERKS; **227** EN-8; elev. 500ft./152m.; [P]; z 19501; ℗ 1,108; © 1,203
Adamsville; CDP; CRAWFORD; ▲ West Fallowfield; **224** WG-2; [P]; z 16110; © 117
Adamsville; YORK; see Arbor (RMC Place)
Addingham; RMC Place; DELAWARE; ▲ Upper Darby; ★ **PHIL-**; mail Drexel Hill z 19026
Addison; Inc. Place; SOMERSET; **225** WQ-6; elev. 2,026ft./618m.; [P]; z 15411; ℗ 212; © 214
Addison; MCD-Township; SOMERSET; ***225** WQ-7; [P]; z 15411 & mail Fort Hill z 15540; does not include the Borough of Addison; ℗ 946; © 1,019
Adelaide; RMC Place; FAYETTE; ▲ Dunbar; ***225** WP-5; mail Connellsville z 15425; ● 60
Admire; RMC Place; YORK; ▲ Dover; ***227** EP-4; ★ **YORK**; mail Thomasville z 17364; ● 80
Adrian (Montgomeryville); RMC Place; ARMSTRONG; ▲ East Franklin; **225** WK-6; [P]; ★ **PGH**; z 16210; ● 200
Adrian Furnace; RMC Place; CLEARFIELD; ▲ Sandy; ***224** WI-9; mail Du Bois z 15801; ● 115
Adrian Mines (De Lancey); RMC Place; JEFFERSON; ▲ Young; ***224** WJ-8; mail De Lancey z 15733; ● 200
Advance; RMC Place; INDIANA; ▲ Washington; ***225** WL-7; mail Creekside z 15732; ● 12
Africa; RMC Place; FRANKLIN; ▲ Montgomery; ***225** WQ-13; mail Mercersburg z 17236; rural
Afton Village; RMC Place; LEHIGH; ▲ Upper Saucon; ***227** EM-11; ★ **ALL-**; mail Center Valley z 18034; ● 700
Ahrensville; RMC Place; VENANGO; ▲ President; ***224** WG-5; mail Oil City z 16301; rural
Aiden Lair; RMC Place; MONTGOMERY; ▲ Upper Dublin; ★ **PHIL-**; mail Dresher z 19025
Aiken; RMC Place; MCKEAN; ▲ Keating; ***224** WE-10; elev. 2,210ft./674m.; mail Rew z 16744
Airville; RMC Place; YORK; ▲ Lower Chanceford; **227** EQ-6; elev. 684ft./208m.; [P]; z 17302; ● 100
Airydale; RMC Place; HUNTINGDON; ▲ Brady; ***225** WM-13; mail Mill Creek z 17060; rural
Ajax; RMC Place; VENANGO; ▲ Sandycreek; ***224** WH-5; elev. 980ft./299m.; ★ **OILC-F**; mail Franklin z 16323; rural
Akeley; RMC Place; WARREN; ▲ Pine Grove; ***224** WD-8; elev. 1,242ft./379m.; mail Russell z 16345
Akersville; RMC Place; FULTON; ▲ Brush Creek; ***225** WP-12; mail Crystal Spring z 15536; rural
Akron; Inc. Place; LANCASTER; **227** EO-7; elev. 510ft./155m.; [P]; ★ **LANC**; z 17501; ℗ 3,869; © 4,046
Aladdin; RMC Place; ARMSTRONG; ▲ Gilpin; ***225** WL-5; ★ **PGH**; mail Schenley z 15682; ● 70
Alameda Park; RMC Place; BUTLER; ▲ Butler; ***225** WK-4; ★ **BUTL**; mail Butler z 16001; ● 600
Alaska; RMC Place; JEFFERSON; ▲ Rose; ***224** WI-8; mail Brookville z 15825; ● 85
Alba; Inc. Place; BRADFORD; **226** EF-4; elev. 1,340ft./408m.; [P]; z 16910; ℗ 170; © 186
Albany; RMC Place; BERKS; ▲ Albany; **227** EL-9; mail Kempton z 19529; ● 20
Albany; MCD-Township; BERKS; ***227** EL-9; mail Kempton z 19529; ℗ 1,547; © 1,662
Albany; MCD-Township; BRADFORD; ***226** EF-6; mail New Albany z 18833; ℗ 927; © 927
Albany; RMC Place; FAYETTE; ▲ Jefferson; ***225** WP-4; ★ **PGH**; mail Brownsville z 15417; rural
Albert; RMC Place; LUZERNE; ▲ Wright; **226** EI-9; elev. 1,227ft./374m.; ★ **SCR-**; mail Mountain Top z 18707; ● 60
Albidale; RMC Place; MONTGOMERY; ▲ Lower Moreland; ★ **PHIL-**; mail Huntingdon Valley z 19006
Albion; Inc. Place; ERIE; **224** WE-2; elev. 900ft./274m.; [P]; ★ **ERIE**; z 16401, z 16475; ℗ 1,575; © 1,607
Albion; RMC Place; JEFFERSON; ▲ Bell; ***224** WJ-8; mail Punxsutawney z 15767; ● 120
Albrightsville; RMC Place; CARBON; ▲ Penn Forest, Kidder; **226** EJ-10; [P]; z 18210; ● 600
Alburtis; Inc. Place; LEHIGH; **227** EM-10; elev. 440ft./134m.; [P]; ★ **ALL-**; z 18011; ℗ 1,415; © 2,117
Alcoa Center; RMC Place; WESTMORELAND; ▲ Upper Burrell; ***225** WM-5; ★ **PGH**; mail New Kensington z 15068-69; ● 40
Aldan; Inc. Place; DELAWARE; **228** F-2; elev. 120ft./37m.; [P]; ★ **PHIL-**; z 19018; ℗ 4,549; © 4,313
Alden; RMC Place; LUZERNE; ▲ Newport; **226** EI-8; ★ **SCR-**; mail Nanticoke z 18634; ● 200
Aldenville; RMC Place; WAYNE; ▲ Clinton; **226** EF-11; elev. 1,229ft./375m.; ● 170
Alderson; RMC Place; LUZERNE; ★ **SCR-**; mail Harveys Lake z 18618; pop. incl. with Harveys Lake (Inc. Place)
Aldham; RMC Place; CHESTER; ▲ Charlestown; ***227** EO-10; ★ **PHIL-**; mail Phoenixville z 19460; rural
Aldovin; WYOMING; see Lemon (RMC Place)
Aleppo; MCD-Township; ALLEGHENY; ***225** WM-3; ★ **PGH**; mail Sewickley z 15143; ℗ 1,246; © 1,039
Aleppo; RMC Place; GREENE; ▲ Aleppo; **225** WQ-1; elev. 1,060ft./323m.; [P]; z 15310; ● 60
Aleppo; MCD-Township; GREENE; ***225** WQ-1; [P]; z 15310; ℗ 656; © 597
Alexander Springs; RMC Place; MIFFLIN; ▲ Union; ***227** EL-1; mail Belleville z 17004; rural
Alexandria; Inc. Place; HUNTINGDON; **225** WM-12; elev. 700ft./213m.; [P]; z 16611; ℗ 411; © 401
Alfarata; RMC Place; MIFFLIN; ▲ Decatur; **227** EL-2; mail Mc Clure z 17841; ● 180
Alford; RMC Place; SUSQUEHANNA; ▲ Harford, Brooklyn; **226** EE-9; mail Kingsley z 18826; ● 25
Alicia; RMC Place; FAYETTE; ▲ Luzerne; ***225** WP-4; ★ **UNTN**; mail Brownsville z 15417; ● 50
Alicia; RMC Place; GREENE; ▲ Monongahela; ***225** WQ-4; mail Greensboro z 15338; ● 50
Alinda; RMC Place; PERRY; ▲ Spring; ***227** EN-2; mail Landisburg z 17040
Aline; RMC Place; SNYDER; ▲ Perry; ***227** EL-4; mail Mount Pleasant Mills z 17853; ● 50
Aliquippa; Inc. Place; BEAVER; **225** WL-2; elev. 900ft./274m.; [P] [H]; ★ **PGH**; z 15001; ℗ 13,374; © 11,734
Allandale; RMC Place; CUMBERLAND; ▲ Lower Allen; ***227** EO-4; ★ **HRBG**; mail Camp Hill z 17011; ● 1,000
Allegany; MCD-Township; POTTER; ***224** WE-13; mail Genesee z 16923; ℗ 413; © 402
Allegheny; RMC Place; ALLEGHENY; ***225** WM-4; [P]; ★ **PGH**; z 15212; pop. incl. with Pittsburgh (Inc. Place)
Allegheny; MCD-Township; BLAIR; ***225** WM-10; ★ **ALT**; mail Duncansville z 16635; ℗ 7,023; © 6,965
Allegheny; MCD-Township; BUTLER; ***224** WI-5; mail Parker z 16049; ℗ 504; © 555
Allegheny; MCD-Township; CAMBRIA; ***225** WM-10; mail Loretto z 15940; ℗ 2,075; © 2,498
Allegheny; MCD-Township; SOMERSET; ***225** WP-9; mail Fairhope z 15538; ℗ 695; © 654
Allegheny; MCD-Township; VENANGO; ***224** WG-6; mail Pleasantville z 16341; ℗ 281; © 281
Allegheny; MCD-Township; WESTMORELAND; ***225** WL-5; ★ **PGH**; mail Apollo z 15613; ℗ 7,895; © 8,002
ALLEGHENY; **225** WM-4; ℗ 1,336,449; © 1,281,666; ◆ 1,209,425
Allegheny Acres; RMC Place; ALLEGHENY; ▲ West Deer; ***225** WL-4; ★ **PGH**; mail Cheswick z 15024; ● 150
Allegheny Furnace; RMC Place; BLAIR; ***225** WM-11; ★ **ALT**; mail Altoona z 16602; pop. incl. with Altoona (Inc. Place)
Allegheny Springs; RMC Place; WARREN; ▲ Brokenstraw; ***224** WE-7; elev. 1,450ft./442m.; mail Youngsville z 16371; ● 20
Alleghenyville; RMC Place; BERKS; ▲ Brecknock; ***227** EO-8; ★ **READ**; mail Mohnton z 19540; ● 200
Allemans; RMC Place; CLEARFIELD; ▲ Gulich; **225** WL-11; mail Fallentimber z 16639; ● 60
Allen (Churchtown); RMC Place; CUMBERLAND; ▲ Monroe; **227** EO-3; ★ **HRBG**; mail Boiling Springs z 17007; ● 375
Allen; MCD-Township; NORTHAMPTON; ***227** EL-11; ★ **ALL-**; mail Northampton z 18067; ℗ 2,626; © 2,630
Allen Crest; RMC Place; LEHIGH; ▲ Whitehall; ***227** EL-11; ★ **ALL-**; mail Whitehall z 18052; ● 350
Allendale (Ruthford); RMC Place; CAMBRIA; ▲ Croyle, Adams; ***225** WN-9; ★ **JNST**; mail Sidman z 15955; ● 150
Allen Lane; RMC Place; PHILADELPHIA; ★ **PHIL-**; mail Philadelphia z 19119; pop. incl. with Philadelphia (Inc. Place)
Allenport; RMC Place; HUNTINGDON; ▲ Shirley; **225** WN-13; mail Mount Union z 17066; ● 650
Allenport; Inc. Place; WASHINGTON; ***225** WO-4; elev. 767ft./234m.; [P]; ★ **PGH**; z 15412; ℗ 595; © 549
Allens Mills; RMC Place; JEFFERSON; ▲ Washington, Warsaw; ***224** WI-9; mail Reynoldsville z 15851
Allensville; RMC Place; MIFFLIN; ▲ Menno; **225** WM-13; [P]; z 17002; ● 275
Allentown; Inc. Place; ⊡ LEHIGH; **227** EL-11; elev. 364ft./111m.; [P] [H] [C] 4,165 ■; ★ **ALL-**; z 18101-06, z 18109, z 18195; ℗ 105,090; © 106,632; ◆ 109,812
Allenvale; RMC Place; SOMERSET; ▲ Lincoln, Jefferson; ***225** WO-7; mail Somerset z 15501; rural
Allenwood; RMC Place; UNION; ▲ Gregg; **226** EI-4; elev. 498ft./152m.; [P]; z 17810; ● 145
Allis Hollow; RMC Place; BRADFORD; ▲ Orwell; ***226** EE-7; mail Rome z 18837; ● 200
Allison; MCD-Township; CLINTON; ***226** EI-2; ★ **WMSPT**; mail Mill Hall z 17751; ℗ 191; © 198
Allison; RMC Place; FAYETTE; ▲ Redstone, Luzerne; **225** WP-4; [P]; ★ **UNTN**; z 15413; ● 850
Allison Heights; RMC Place; FAYETTE; ▲ Luzerne; ***225** WP-4; ★ **UNTN**; mail Allison z 15413; ● 100
Allison Park; RMC Place; ALLEGHENY; ▲ Hampton; **225** WM-4; [P]; ★ **PGH**; z 15101; ● 6,000
Allport; RMC Place; CAMBRIA; ▲ Susquehanna; ***225** WL-9; mail Northern Cambria z 15714; ● 400
Allport; RMC Place; CLEARFIELD; ▲ Morris; **224** WJ-12; [P]; z 16821; ● 360
Almaden; RMC Place; CLEARFIELD; ▲ Gulich; ***225** WK-11; mail Smithmill z 16680; rural
Almedia; CDP; COLUMBIA; ▲ South Centre, Scott; **226** EJ-6; elev. 505ft./154m.; mail Bloomsburg z 17815; ℗ 1,116; © 1,056
Almont; RMC Place; BUCKS; ▲ West Rockhill; **227** EN-11; ★ **PHIL-**; mail Sellersville z 18960; ● 75
Alpha; RMC Place; NORTHAMPTON; ***227** EK-11; mail Wind Gap z 18091; pop. incl. with Wind Gap (Inc. Place)
Alpine; RMC Place; YORK; ▲ Warrington; ***227** EP-4; mail Lewisberry z 17339; rural
Alsace; MCD-Township; BERKS; ***227** EN-9; ★ **READ**; mail Reading z 19606; ℗ 3,459; © 3,689
Alsace Manor; RMC Place; BERKS; ▲ Alsace; **227** ES-14; elev. 912ft./278m.; ★ **READ**; mail Temple z 19560; ● 300
Alta Manor; RMC Place; BLAIR; ***225** WM-11; ★ **ALT**; mail Altoona z 16601; pop. incl. with Altoona (Inc. Place)
Altamont; CDP; SCHUYLKILL; ▲ West Mahanoy; ***227** EK-7; mail Frackville z 17931; © 2,689; ® 708
Altenwald; RMC Place; FRANKLIN; ▲ Quincy; **227** EQ-1; mail Waynesboro z 17268; ● 40
Althom; RMC Place; WARREN; ▲ Deerfield; ***224** WF-7; elev. 1,160ft./354m.; mail Tidioute z 16351; summer pop. 200; ● 75
Alton; RMC Place; CHESTER; ▲ East Bradford; ***227** EP-10; ★ **PHIL-**; mail West Chester z 19380; rural
Alton Park; RMC Place; LEHIGH; ***227** EM-11; ★ **ALL-**; mail Allentown z 18103; pop. incl. with Allentown (Inc. Place)
Altoona; Inc. Place; BLAIR; **225** WM-11; elev. 1,170ft./357m.; [P] [H] [C] 3,837 ■; ★ **ALT**; z 16601-03; ℗ 51,881; © 49,523; ◆ 47,018
Alum Bank (Pleasantville); Inc. Place; BEDFORD; **225** WO-10; elev. 1,215ft./370m.; [P]; z 15521; ℗ 215; © 211
Alum Rock; RMC Place; CLARION; ▲ Richland; ***224** WI-5; mail Emlenton z 16373; rural
Aluta; RMC Place; NORTHAMPTON; ▲ Bushkill; ***227** EK-11; ★ **ALL-**; mail Nazareth z 18064; ● 90
Alverda; RMC Place; INDIANA; ▲ Pine; **225** WL-9; [P]; z 15710; ● 400
Alverton; RMC Place; WESTMORELAND; ▲ East Huntingdon; **225** WO-5; [P]; z 15612; ● 350
Amaranth; RMC Place; FULTON; ▲ Union; ***225** WQ-11; elev. 1,020ft./311m.; mail Warfordsburg z 17267; rural
Amasa; RMC Place; LACKAWANNA; ▲ Greenfield, Benton; ***226** EF-10; ★ **SCR-**; mail Jermyn z 18433; rural
Ambau; RMC Place; YORK; ▲ North Codorus; ***227** EQ-4; ★ **YORK**; mail Spring Grove z 17362; ● 50
Amberson; RMC Place; FRANKLIN; ▲ Fannett; ***225** WO-14; [P]; z 17210; ● 100
Ambler; Inc. Place; MONTGOMERY; **227** EO-12; elev. 214ft./65m.; [P] [H]; ★ **PHIL-**; z 19002; ℗ 6,609; © 6,426
Ambler Highlands; RMC Place; MONTGOMERY; ▲ Upper Dublin; ★ **PHIL-**; mail Fort Washington z 19034
Ambridge; Inc. Place; BEAVER; **225** WL-3; elev. 751ft./229m.; [P]; ★ **PGH**; z 15003; ℗ 8,133; © 7,769
Ambridge Heights; RMC Place; BEAVER; ▲ Harmony; ***225** WL-3; ★ **PGH**; mail Ambridge z 15003
Ambrose; RMC Place; INDIANA; ▲ South Mahoning; ***225** WK-8; mail Marion Center z 15759; ● 25
Amend; RMC Place; FAYETTE; ▲ Georges; ***225** WQ-4; ★ **UNTN**; mail Uniontown z 15401; ● 150
American Philatelic Society Building; RMC Place; CENTRE; ★ **STCOL**; mail State College z 16803; pop. incl. with State College (Inc. Place)
Amesville; RMC Place; CLEARFIELD; ▲ Bigler; ***225** WK-11; mail Houtzdale z 16651; rural
Amity; MCD-Township; BERKS; ***227** EN-9; mail Douglassville z 19518; ℗ 6,434; © 8,867
Amity; RMC Place; BUCKS; ▲ Springfield; ***227** EM-11; ★ **ALL-**; mail Coopersburg z 18036; rural
Amity; MCD-Township; ERIE; ***224** WD-5; mail Union City z 16438; ℗ 1,034; © 1,140
Amity; RMC Place; WASHINGTON; ▲ Amwell; **225** WP-3; elev. 1,199ft./365m.; [P]; ★ **WASH**; z 15311; ● 400
Amity Gardens; CDP-Census Area Only; BERKS; ▲ Amity; ***227** EN-9; elev. 200ft./61m.; mail Douglassville z 19518; ℗ 2,714; © 3,370
Amity Hall; RMC Place; PERRY; ▲ Watts; **227** EM-4; ★ **HRBG**; mail Duncannon z 17020; ● 15
Amityville (Athol); RMC Place; BERKS; ▲ Amity; **227** EN-9; mail Douglassville z 19518, Earlville z 19519; ● 250
Amsbry; RMC Place; CAMBRIA; ▲ Gallitzin; **225** WM-10; ★ **ALT**; mail Gallitzin z 16641; ● 65
Amsterdam; RMC Place; MERCER; ▲ Liberty; ***224** WI-3; elev. 1,246ft./380m.; mail Grove City z 16127; rural
Amwell; MCD-Township; WASHINGTON; ***225** WO-3; ★ **WASH**; mail Washington z 15301; ℗ 4,176; © 3,960
Analomink; RMC Place; MONROE; ▲ Stroud; **226** EJ-12; elev. 526ft./160m.; [P]; z 18320; ● 200
Ancient Oaks; CDP; LEHIGH; ▲ Lower Macungie; **227** EM-10; ★ **ALL-**; mail Macungie z 18062; ℗ 2,663; © 3,161
Ancient Oaks West; RMC Place; LEHIGH; ▲ Lower Macungie; ***227** EM-10; elev. 427ft./130m.; ★ **ALL-**; mail Macungie z 18062; ● 500
Andalusia; RMC Place; BUCKS; ▲ Bensalem; **228** B-8; [P]; ★ **PHIL-**; z 19020; ● 3,500
Anderson; RMC Place; MIFFLIN; ▲ Granville; ***227** EM-1; mail Granville z 17029, Lewistown z 17044; rural
Anderson; WASHINGTON; see Venetia (RMC Place)
Andersonburg; RMC Place; PERRY; ▲ Southwest Madison; **227** EN-2; mail Loysville z 17047; ● 50
Andersontown; RMC Place; YORK; ▲ Monaghan; ***227** EO-4; ★ **HRBG**; mail Mechanicsburg z 17055; rural
Andover; RMC Place; FULTON; **225** WP-12; mail Mc Connellsburg z 17233; rural
Andreas; RMC Place; SCHUYLKILL; ▲ West Penn; **227** EK-9; elev. 591ft./180m.; [P]; z 18211; ● 200
Andrews Bridge; RMC Place; LANCASTER; ▲ Colerain; ***227** EQ-8; mail Christiana z 17509; rural
Andrews Plan; RMC Place; BEAVER; ▲ Hopewell; ***225** WL-2; ★ **PGH**; mail Aliquippa z 15001; ● 350
Andrews Settlement; RMC Place; POTTER; ▲ Allegany; **224** WE-13; mail Genesee z 16923; ● 40
Angelica; RMC Place; BERKS; ▲ Cumru; **227** EN-8; elev. 503ft./153m.; ★ **READ**; mail Mohnton z 19540; ● 100
Angels; RMC Place; WAYNE; ▲ Dreher; ***226** EH-11; mail Newfoundland z 18445
Angora; RMC Place; PHILADELPHIA; ★ **PHIL-**; mail Philadelphia z 19143; pop. incl. with Philadelphia (Inc. Place)
Anita; RMC Place; JEFFERSON; ▲ McCalmont; **224** WJ-8; [P]; z 15711; ● 600
Ankeny; RMC Place; SOMERSET; ▲ Jenner; ***225** WO-8; elev. 1,880ft./573m.; mail Jennerstown z 15547; rural
Annaline Village; RMC Place; DELAWARE; ▲ Lower Chichester; ★ **PHIL-**; mail Marcus Hook z 19061
Annandale (Boyers); RMC Place; BUTLER; ▲ Marion; **224** WI-4; [P]; z 16018, z 16020 & mail Boyers z 16016-17; ● 275
Annin; MCD-Township; MCKEAN; ***224** WE-12; mail Port Allegany z 16743; ℗ 805; © 835
Annisville; RMC Place; BUTLER; ▲ Washington; **224** WI-5; mail Parker z 16049; ● 35
Annville; CDP; LEBANON; ▲ Annville; **227** EN-6; [P] [C] 1,961; ★ **LEB**; z 17003; ℗ 4,294; © 4,518
Annville; MCD-Township; LEBANON; ***227** EN-6; [P] [C] 1,961; ★ **LEB**; z 17003; ℗ 4,294; © 4,518
Anselma; RMC Place; CHESTER; ▲ West Pikeland; ***227** EO-10; ★ **PHIL-**; mail Chester Springs z 19425
Ansonia; RMC Place; TIOGA; ▲ Shippen; **226** EF-2; elev. 1,139ft./347m.; mail Wellsboro z 16901; ● 50
Ansonville; RMC Place; CLEARFIELD; ▲ Jordan; **225** WK-10; mail Irvona z 16656; ● 100
Antes Fort; RMC Place; LYCOMING; ▲ Nippenose; **226** EI-3; [P]; ★ **WMSPT**; z 17720; ● 400
Anthony; MCD-Township; LYCOMING; ***226** EH-3; mail Cogan Station z 17728; ℗ 727; © 904
Anthony; MCD-Township; MONTOUR; ***226** EI-5; mail Turbotville z 17772; ℗ 1,287; © 1,388
Anthracite; RMC Place; LEBANON; ***227** EN-6; ★ **LEB**; mail Cornwall z 17016; pop. incl. with Cornwall (Inc. Place)
Antis; MCD-Township; BLAIR; ***225** WL-11; ★ **ALT**; mail Bellwood z 16617; ℗ 6,176; © 6,328
Antrim; MCD-Township; FRANKLIN; ***225** WR-14; ★ **HAG**; mail Greencastle z 17225; ℗ 10,107; © 12,504
Antrim; RMC Place; TIOGA; ▲ Duncan; **226** EF-2; elev. 1,655ft./504m.; mail Wellsboro z 16901; ● 400
Apolacon; MCD-Township; SUSQUEHANNA; ***226** ED-8; mail Little Meadows z 18830; ℗ 493; © 507
Apollo; Inc. Place; ARMSTRONG; **225** WL-6; elev. 820ft./250m.; [P]; ★ **PGH**; z 15613; ℗ 1,895; © 1,765
Appenzell; RMC Place; MONROE; ▲ Jackson; **226** EJ-11; mail Stroudsburg z 18360; ● 150
Applebachsville; RMC Place; BUCKS; ▲ Haycock; **227** EM-12; ★ **PHIL-**; mail Quakertown z 18951; ● 120
Appletree Hill; RMC Place; BUCKS; ▲ Bristol; ***227** EO-14; ★ **PHIL-**; mail Bristol z 19007
Appleville; RMC Place; CHESTER; ▲ West Bradford; ***227** EP-10; elev. 450ft./137m.; ★ **PHIL-**; mail West Chester z 19380; ● 350
Applewold; Inc. Place; ARMSTRONG; **225** WK-6; elev. 800ft./244m.; ★ **PGH**; mail Kittanning z 16201; ℗ 388; © 356
Aquashicola; RMC Place; CARBON; ▲ Lower Towamensing; **227** EK-10; [P]; z 18012; ● 160
Aqueduct; RMC Place; PERRY; ▲ Wheatfield; ***227** EM-4; ★ **HRBG**; mail Duncannon z 17020; ● 25
Aquetong; RMC Place; BUCKS; ▲ Solebury; ***227** EN-13; ★ **PHIL-**; mail New Hope z 18938; ● 55
Ararat; RMC Place; SUSQUEHANNA; ▲ Ararat; ***226** EE-10; elev. 2,009ft./612m.; mail Thompson z 18465
Ararat; MCD-Township; SUSQUEHANNA; ***226** EE-10; mail Thompson z 18465; ℗ 420; © 531
Arbor (Adamsville); RMC Place; YORK; ▲ York; ★ **YORK**; mail Red Lion z 17356; rural
Arbuckle; RMC Place; ERIE; ▲ Amity; **224** WD-4; mail Union City z 16438; ● 50
Arcadia; RMC Place; INDIANA; ▲ Montgomery; **225** WK-9; [P]; z 15712; ● 220
Arcadia; RMC Place; LANCASTER; ▲ Fulton; mail Peach Bottom z 17563; ● 30
Archbald; Inc. Place; LACKAWANNA; **226** EG-10; elev. 920ft./280m.; [P]; ★ **SCR-**; z 18403; ℗ 6,291; © 6,220
Arch Rock; RMC Place; JUNIATA; ▲ Fermanagh; **227** EL-2; mail Mifflintown z 17059; ● 100
Arch Spring; RMC Place; BLAIR; ▲ Tyrone; ***225** WL-12; mail Tyrone z 16686; rural
Arcola; RMC Place; MONTGOMERY; ▲ Upper Providence, Lower Providence; ***227** EO-11; [P]; ★ **PHIL-**; z 19420 & mail Collegeville z 19426; ● 250
Ardara; RMC Place; WESTMORELAND; ▲ North Huntingdon; **228** L-10; [P]; ★ **PGH**; z 15615; ● 300
Arden; RMC Place; WASHINGTON; ▲ South Strabane; ***225** WO-2; ★ **WASH**; mail Washington z 15301; rural
Ardenheim; RMC Place; HUNTINGDON; ▲ Henderson; **225** WM-13; mail Huntingdon z 16652; ● 25
Arden Mines; RMC Place; WASHINGTON; ▲ Chartiers; ***225** WN-2; ★ **WASH**; mail Washington z 15301; ● 60
Ardmore; CDP; DELAWARE, MONTGOMERY; ▲ Haverford, Lower Merion; **228** D-2; [P]; ★ **PHIL-**; z 19003; ℗ 12,646; © 12,616
Ardmore Manor; RMC Place; DELAWARE; ▲ Haverford; ★ **PHIL-**; mail Ardmore z 19003
Ardmore Park; RMC Place; DELAWARE; ▲ Haverford; ***227** EP-12; ★ **PHIL-**; mail Ardmore z 19003
Ardsley; RMC Place; MONTGOMERY; ▲ Upper Dublin, Abington; **228** A-4; ★ **PHIL-**; mail Glenside z 19038; ● 4,500
Arendtsville; Inc. Place; ADAMS; **227** EP-2; elev. 711ft./217m.; [P]; z 17303; ℗ 693; © 848
Arensberg; RMC Place; FAYETTE; ▲ Luzerne; ***225** WP-4; ★ **UNTN**; mail East Millsboro z 15433; rural
Argentine; RMC Place; BUTLER; ▲ Washington; **224** WI-4; mail Hilliards z 16040; ● 60
Argus; RMC Place; BUCKS; ▲ West Rockhill; **227** EN-11; ★ **PHIL-**; mail Sellersville z 18960; ● 60
Ariel; WAYNE; see Lake Ariel (RMC Place)
Aristes; CDP; COLUMBIA; ▲ Conyngham; **227** EK-7; [P]; z 17920; © 230
Arlingham; RMC Place; MONTGOMERY; ▲ Springfield, Whitemarsh; ***227** EO-12; elev. 200ft./61m.; ★ **PHIL-**; mail Flourtown z 19031
Arlingham Hills; RMC Place; MONTGOMERY; ▲ Whitemarsh; ★ **PHIL-**; mail Flourtown z 19031
Arlington; RMC Place; ALLEGHENY; ▲ North Versailles; ***225** WN-4; ★ **PGH**; mail North Versailles z 15137; pop. incl. with Pittsburgh (Inc. Place)
Arlington; RMC Place; WAYNE; ▲ Salem; ***226** EH-11; ★ **SCR-**; mail Lake Ariel z 18436; rural
Arlington Heights; CDP; MONROE; ▲ Stroud; ***226** EJ-12; mail Stroudsburg z 18360; ℗ 4,768; © 5,132
Arlington Knolls; RMC Place; LEHIGH; ▲ Whitehall; ***227** EL-11; ★ **ALL-**; mail Whitehall z 18052
Armagh; Inc. Place; INDIANA; **225** WM-8; elev. 1,531ft./467m.; [P]; ★ **JNST**; z 15920; ℗ 104; © 131
Armagh; MCD-Township; MIFFLIN; ***227** EL-1; mail Milroy z 17063; ℗ 3,627; © 3,988
Armbrust (Weavers Old Stand); RMC Place; WESTMORELAND; ▲ Mount Pleasant, Hempfield; **225** WO-6; [P]; ★ **PGH**; z 15616; ● 230
Armenia; MCD-Township; BRADFORD; ***226** EF-4; mail Troy z 16947; ℗ 134; © 166
Armstrong; MCD-Township; INDIANA; ***225** WL-7; mail Shelocta z 15774; ℗ 3,048; © 3,090
Armstrong; MCD-Township; LYCOMING; ***226** EI-4; [P]; ★ **WMSPT**; z 17702 & mail Williamsport z 17701; ℗ 676; © 717
ARMSTRONG; **225** WK-6; ℗ 73,478; © 72,392; ◆ 66,966
Arndts; RMC Place; NORTHAMPTON; ***227** EK-11; ★ **ALL-**; mail Danielsville z 18038; rural
Arnold; Inc. Place; WESTMORELAND; **225** WL-5; elev. 785ft./239m.; [P]; ★ **PGH**; z 15068; ℗ 6,113; © 5,667
Arnold City; RMC Place; FAYETTE; ▲ Washington; ***225** WO-4; ★ **PGH**; mail Belle Vernon z 15012; ● 350
Arnot; RMC Place; TIOGA; ▲ New Castle, Bloss; **226** EF-3; elev. 1,687ft./514m.; [P]; z 16911; ● 350
Arnots Addition; RMC Place; SCHUYLKILL; ***227** EL-7; ★ **PTSVL**; mail Saint Clair z 17970
Arona; Inc. Place; WESTMORELAND; **225** WN-5; elev. 1,000ft./305m.; [P]; ★ **PGH**; z 15617; ℗ 397; © 407
Aronimink; RMC Place; DELAWARE; ▲ Upper Darby; ***227** EP-11; ★ **PHIL-**; mail Drexel Hill z 19026
Arrowhead Lake; RMC Place; MONROE; ▲ Tobyhanna, Coolbaugh; ***226** EI-10; mail Pocono Lake z 18347; winter pop. 2,000; ● 600
Arsenal; RMC Place; ALLEGHENY; [P]; ★ **PGH**; z 15201; pop. incl. with Pittsburgh (Inc. Place)
Artemas; RMC Place; BEDFORD; ▲ Mann; ***225** WQ-11; [P]; z 17211; ● 40
Arundel Village; RMC Place; MONTGOMERY; ▲ Horsham; ★ **PHIL-**; mail Horsham z 19044
Arwin Acres; RMC Place; DAUPHIN; ▲ South Hanover; ***227** EN-5; elev. 493ft./150m.; ★ **HRBG**; mail Hummelstown z 17036; ● 350
Asaph; RMC Place; TIOGA; ▲ Shippen; **226** EF-2; elev. 1,156ft./352m.; mail Wellsboro z 16901; ● 100
Asbury; RMC Place; COLUMBIA; ▲ Fishing Creek; ***226** EI-7; mail Orangeville z 17859; ● 50
Asbury; RMC Place; ERIE; ▲ Millcreek; ***224** WD-3; ★ **ERIE**; mail Erie z 16509
Ashcom; RMC Place; BEDFORD; ▲ Snake Spring; ***225** WP-11; mail Everett z 15537; rural
Asherton; RMC Place; NORTHUMBERLAND; ▲ Lower Augusta; ***227** EK-5; elev. 600ft./183m.; mail Sunbury z 17801; rural
Ashfield; RMC Place; CARBON; ▲ East Penn; **227** EK-10; elev. 553ft./169m.; [P]; z 18212; ● 300
Ashland; MCD-Township; CLARION; ***224** WH-6; mail Knox z 16232; ℗ 1,019; © 1,081
Ashland; RMC Place; CLEARFIELD; ▲ Decatur; **225** WK-11; mail Osceola Mills z 16666; ● 60
Ashland; Inc. Place; SCHUYLKILL; **227** EK-7; elev. 1,000ft./305m.; [P] [H]; ★ **PTSVL**; z 17921; ℗ 3,859; © 3,283
Ashley; Inc. Place; LUZERNE; **226** EI-9; elev. 640ft./195m.; [P]; ★ **SCR-**; z 18706; ℗ 3,291; © 2,866
Ashtola; RMC Place; SOMERSET; ▲ Paint, Ogle; **225** WO-9; elev. 2,137ft./651m.; mail Windber z 15963; ● 150
Ashville; Inc. Place; CAMBRIA; **225** WM-10; elev. 1,626ft./496m.; [P]; ★ **ALT**; z 16613; ℗ 306; © 279
Askam; RMC Place; LUZERNE; ▲ Hanover; ***226** EI-8; ★ **SCR-**; mail Wilkes Barre z 18706; ● 1,250
Aspers; RMC Place; ADAMS; ▲ Menallen; **227** EP-3; [P]; z 17304; ● 550
Aspinwall; Inc. Place; ALLEGHENY; **228** I-7; elev. 760ft./232m.; [P]; ★ **PGH**; z 15215; ℗ 2,880; © 2,960
Aston; RMC Place; DELAWARE; ▲ Aston; ***227** EQ-11; [P] [C] 2,969; ★ **PHIL-**; z 19014
Aston; MCD-Township; DELAWARE; ***227** EQ-11; [P] [C] 2,969; ★ **PHIL-**; z 19014; ℗ 15,080; © 16,203
Asylum; MCD-Township; BRADFORD; ***226** EF-6; mail Towanda z 18848; ℗ 981; © 1,097
Atco; RMC Place; WAYNE; ▲ Damascus; **226** EF-12; mail Beach Lake z 18405, Narrowsburg z 12764; ● 200
Atglen; Inc. Place; CHESTER; **227** EP-8; elev. 504ft./154m.; [P]; ★ **PHIL-**; z 19310; ℗ 825; © 1,217
Athens; Inc. Place; BRADFORD; **226** ED-6; elev. 760ft./232m.; [P]; z 18810; ℗ 3,468; © 3,415
Athens; MCD-Township; BRADFORD; ***226** ED-6; [P]; z 18810 & mail Sayre z 18840; does not include the Borough of Athens; ℗ 4,755; © 5,058
Athens; MCD-Township; CRAWFORD; ***224** WE-4; mail Centerville z 16404; ℗ 699; © 775
Athol; BERKS; see Amityville (RMC Place)
Atkinsons Mills; RMC Place; MIFFLIN; ▲ Wayne; ***225** WM-13; mail Mc Veytown z 17051; rural
Atlantic; RMC Place; CLEARFIELD; ▲ Bigler; ***225** WK-11; mail Houtzdale z 16651
Atlantic; CDP; CRAWFORD; ▲ East Fallowfield; **224** WG-2; elev. 1,147ft./350m.; [P]; z 16111; © 43
Atlantic; RMC Place; WESTMORELAND; ▲ Derry; ***225** WN-7; ★ **LTROB**; mail New Derry z 15671
Atlas; RMC Place; NORTHUMBERLAND; ▲ Mount Carmel; **227** EK-6; mail Mount Carmel z 17851; ● 1,200
Atlasburg; RMC Place; WASHINGTON; ▲ Smith; **225** WN-2; elev. 1,052ft./321m.; [P]; ★ **PGH**; z 15004; ● 500
Atwood; Inc. Place; ARMSTRONG; **225** WK-7; elev. 1,240ft./378m.; mail Rural Valley z 16249; ℗ 128; © 112
Auburn; Inc. Place; SCHUYLKILL; **227** EL-8; elev. 500ft./152m.; [P]; ★ **PTSVL**; z 17922; ℗ 913; © 839
Auburn; SUSQUEHANNA; see Auburn Center (RMC Place)
Auburn; MCD-Township; SUSQUEHANNA; ***226** EF-8; mail Meshoppen z 18630; ℗ 1,639; © 1,816
Auburn Center (Auburn); RMC Place; SUSQUEHANNA; ▲ Auburn; **226** EF-8; elev. 1,339ft./408m.; mail Laceyville z 18623; ● 50
Auburn Four Corners; RMC Place; SUSQUEHANNA; ▲ Auburn; **226** EF-8; elev. 1,269ft./387m.; mail Meshoppen z 18630; ● 60
Audenried; RMC Place; CARBON; ▲ Banks; **227** EK-8; ★ **HAZ**; mail Hazleton z 18201; ● 130
Audubon; CDP; MONTGOMERY; ▲ Lower Providence; **227** EO-11; elev. 192ft./59m.; [P]; ★ **PHIL-**; z 19403, z 19407; ℗ 6,328; © 6,549
Aughwick; RMC Place; HUNTINGDON; ▲ Shirley; ***225** WN-13; mail Mount Union z 17066; rural
Augustaville; RMC Place; NORTHUMBERLAND; ▲ Rockefeller; ***227** EK-5; elev. 633ft./193m.; mail Sunbury z 17801; ● 110
Aultman; RMC Place; INDIANA; ▲ Center; **225** WM-7; [P]; z 15713; ● 225
Austin; Inc. Place; POTTER; **224** WF-12; elev. 1,352ft./412m.; [P]; z 16720; ℗ 569; © 623
Austinburg; RMC Place; TIOGA; ▲ Brookfield; **226** ED-2; mail Knoxville z 16928; ● 60
Austinville; RMC Place; BRADFORD; ▲ Columbia; **226** EE-4; mail Columbia Cross Roads z 16914, Troy z 16947; ● 150
Avalon; Inc. Place; ALLEGHENY; **225** WM-3; elev. 900ft./274m.; [P]; ★ **PGH**; z 15202; ℗ 5,784; © 5,294
Avella; RMC Place; WASHINGTON; ▲ Independence, Cross Creek; **225** WN-1; [P]; z 15312; ● 500
Avella Highlands (P & W Patch); RMC Place; WASHINGTON; ▲ Independence; ***225** WN-1; elev. 1,223ft./373m.; mail Avella z 15312; ● 100
Avis; Inc. Place; CLINTON; **226** EI-2; elev. 600ft./183m.; [P]; ★ **WMSPT**; z 17721; ℗ 1,506; © 1,492
Avoca; Inc. Place; LUZERNE; **226** EB-10; elev. 700ft./213m.; [P]; ★ **SCR-**; z 18641; ℗ 2,897; © 2,851
Avon; CDP; LEBANON; ▲ South Lebanon, North Lebanon; **227** EN-7; ★ **LEB**; mail Lebanon z 17042; ℗ 2,714; © 2,856
Avondale; Inc. Place; CHESTER; **227** EQ-9; elev. 272ft./83m.; [P]; ★ **PHIL-**; z 19311; ℗ 954; © 1,108
Avondale Knolls; RMC Place; DELAWARE; ▲ Nether Providence; ★ **PHIL-**; mail Wallingford z 19086
Avon Heights; RMC Place; LEBANON; ▲ South Lebanon; ***227** EN-7; ★ **LEB**; mail Lebanon z 17042; ● 200
Avonia; CDP; ERIE; ▲ Fairview; **224** WD-3; ★ **ERIE**; mail Fairview z 16415; ℗ 1,336; © 1,331
Avonmore; Inc. Place; WESTMORELAND; **225** WM-6; elev. 880ft./268m.; [P]; ★ **PGH**; z 15618; ℗ 1,089; © 820
Axemann; RMC Place; CENTRE; ▲ Spring; **225** WK-14; ★ **STCOL**; mail Bellefonte z 16823; ● 150
Ayr; MCD-Township; FULTON; ***225** WQ-12; mail Mc Connellsburg z 17233; ℗ 2,167; © 1,982

B

Bachmanville; RMC Place; DAUPHIN; ▲ Conewago; **227** EO-6; elev. 613ft./187m.; ★ **HRBG**; mail Hershey z 17033; ● 200
Back Mountain; CDP-Census Area Only; LUZERNE; ***226** EH-8; ★ **SCR-**; © 26,690; ◆ 25,950
Baden; Inc. Place; BEAVER; **225** WL-3; elev. 800ft./244m.; [P]; ★ **PGH**; z 15005; ℗ 5,074; © 4,377
Baederwood; RMC Place; MONTGOMERY; ▲ Abington; ***227** EO-12; ★ **PHIL-**; mail Jenkintown z 19046
Bagdad; RMC Place; ARMSTRONG, WESTMORELAND; ▲ Allegheny, Gilpin; ***225** WL-5; ★ **PGH**; mail Leechburg z 15656; rural
Baggaley; RMC Place; WESTMORELAND; ▲ Unity; **225** WN-6; ★ **LTROB**; mail Latrobe z 15650; ● 600
Baidland; CDP; WASHINGTON; ▲ Carroll; ***225** WO-4; ★ **PGH**; mail Monongahela z 15063; ℗ 1,620; © 1,576
Bailey; RMC Place; PERRY; ▲ Miller; ***227** EM-3; ★ **HRBG**; mail Newport z 17074; rural
Baileys Corner; RMC Place; BRADFORD; ▲ Granville; ***226** EF-5; mail Granville Summit z 16926; rural
Baileyville; RMC Place; CENTRE; ▲ Ferguson; ***225** WL-13; ★ **STCOL**; mail Pennsylvania Furnace z 16865; ● 60
Bainbridge; RMC Place; LANCASTER; ▲ Conoy; **227** EO-5; [P]; ★ **HRBG**; z 17502; ● 900
Bair; RMC Place; YORK; ▲ West Manchester; **227** EQ-5; elev. 462ft./141m.; ★ **YORK**; mail York z 17405; ● 400
Bairdford; RMC Place; ALLEGHENY; ▲ West Deer; **225** WL-4; [P]; ★ **PGH**; z 15006; ● 800
Bairdstown; RMC Place; WESTMORELAND; ▲ Derry; ***225** WM-7; elev. 1,100ft./335m.; ★ **LTROB**; mail Blairsville z 15717; ● 80
Bakers Summit; RMC Place; BEDFORD; ▲ Bloomfield; **225** WN-11; [P]; z 16673; ● 110
Baker Station; RMC Place; CHESTER; ▲ London Grove; ***227** EQ-9; ★ **PHIL-**; mail West Grove z 19390; rural
Bakerstown; RMC Place; ALLEGHENY; ▲ Richland; **225** WL-4; elev. 1,107ft./337m.; [P]; ★ **PGH**; z 15007; ● 1,000
Bakerstown Station; RMC Place; ALLEGHENY; ▲ Richland; ***225** WL-4; ★ **PGH**; mail Gibsonia z 15044; ● 400
Bakersville; RMC Place; SOMERSET; ▲ Jefferson; **225** WP-7; elev. 2,093ft./638m.; mail Somerset z 15501; ● 200
Bakerton (Elmora); RMC Place; CAMBRIA; ▲ West Carroll; ***225** WL-9; mail Elmora z 15737; ● 900
Bala; RMC Place; MONTGOMERY; ▲ Lower Merion; ***227** EP-12; ★ **PHIL-**; mail Bala Cynwyd z 19004
Bala-Cynwyd; RMC Place; MONTGOMERY; ▲ Lower Merion; **228** D-3; [P] [H]; ★ **PHIL-**; z 19004; ● 8,000
Bald Eagle; RMC Place; BLAIR; ▲ Snyder; **225** WL-12; ★ **ALT**; mail Tyrone z 16686; ● 250
Bald Eagle; MCD-Township; CLINTON; ***226** EI-2; ★ **WMSPT**; mail Mill Hall z 17751; ℗ 1,809; © 1,898
Bald Hill; RMC Place; CLEARFIELD; ▲ Girard; ***224** WJ-11; mail Lecontes Mills z 16850; ● 120
Bald Hill; RMC Place; GREENE; ▲ Dunkard; ***225** WQ-3; mail Mount Morris z 15349; rural
Baldwin; Inc. Place; ALLEGHENY; **228** L-6; elev. 1,000ft./305m.; ★ **PGH**; mail Pittsburgh z 15227, z 15234, z 15236; ℗ 21,923; © 19,999
Baldwin; MCD-Township; ALLEGHENY; ***225** WN-3; ★ **PGH**; mail Pittsburgh z 15234; does not include the Borough of Baldwin; ℗ 2,479; © 2,244
Baldwin; RMC Place; DELAWARE; ***227** EQ-11; ★ **PHIL-**; mail Chester z 19013; pop. incl. with Eddystone (Inc. Place)
Balliettsville; RMC Place; LEHIGH; ▲ North Whitehall; **226** EA-1; ★ **ALL-**; mail Coplay z 18037; ● 250
Balls Eddy; RMC Place; WAYNE; ▲ Scott; ***226** ED-11; elev. 1,000ft./305m.; mail Starlight z 18461; ● 50
Balls Mills; RMC Place; LYCOMING; ▲ Hepburn; **226** EH-4; ★ **WMSPT**; mail Cogan Station z 17728; ● 60
Balltown; RMC Place; FOREST; ▲ Howe; ***224** WF-7; elev. 1,240ft./378m.; mail Sheffield z 16347; rural
Bally; Inc. Place; BERKS; **227** EN-10; elev. 466ft./142m.; [P]; z 19503; ℗ 973; © 1,062
Balsinger; RMC Place; FAYETTE; ▲ German, Menallen, South Union; ***225** WP-4; ★ **UNTN**; mail Uniontown z 15401; ● 100
Banbury Crossing; RMC Place; DAUPHIN; ▲ South Hanover; ***227** EN-5; ★ **HRBG**; mail Hummelstown z 17036; ● 200
Bandanna (Pleasant Hill); RMC Place; YORK; ▲ West Manheim; **227** ER-4; ★ **HANV**; mail Hanover z 17331; ● 225
Bando; RMC Place; SOMERSET; ▲ Milford; ***225** WP-8; elev. 1,920ft./585m.; mail Somerset z 15501; rural
Banetown; RMC Place; WASHINGTON; ▲ Amwell; **225** WO-2; ★ **WASH**; mail Washington z 15301; ● 100
Baney Settlement; RMC Place; CLEARFIELD; ▲ Lawrence; ***224** WJ-11; elev. 1,220ft./372m.; mail Clearfield z 16830; ● 65
Bangor; Inc. Place; NORTHAMPTON; **227** EK-12; elev. 520ft./158m.; [P]; z 18010, z 18013, z 18050; ℗ 5,383; © 5,319
Banian Junction; RMC Place; CLEARFIELD; ▲ Bigler; ***225** WK-11; mail Madera z 16661; rural
Banks; MCD-Township; CARBON; ***226** EJ-9; ★ **HAZ**; mail Tresckow z 18254; ℗ 1,485; © 1,359
Banks; MCD-Township; INDIANA; ***225** WK-9; mail Glen Campbell z 15742; ℗ 995; © 997
Banksville; RMC Place; ALLEGHENY; ***225** WM-3; ★ **PGH**; mail Pittsburgh z 15216; pop. incl. with Pittsburgh (Inc. Place)
Banner Ridge; RMC Place; CLEARFIELD; ▲ Bell; mail Mahaffey z 15757; rural

Entries in **UPPERCASE** are counties.
Entries in **bold** have populations of 2,500 or more.
Names in parentheses are alternate names.

Inc. Place	Incorporated Place
RMC Place	Rand McNally Designated Place
CDP	Census Designated Place
MCD	Minor Civil Division
⊡	County Seat
▲	Minor Civil Division
elev.	Elevation
[P]	Post Office
[H]	Hospital
[C]	College
■	Principal Business Center
★	Ranally Metro Area (RMA) Abbreviation
z	Zip Code(s)
℗	Previous Census Population
®	Revised Census Population
Ⓐ	Annexation Population
●	Rand McNally Population Estimate
©	Final Census Population
Ⓢ	Special Census Population
◆	Estimated Population

For additional definitions see Glossary, Volume 1, and Introduction, Volume 2.

Bannerville; RMC Place; SNYDER; ▲ West Beaver; **227** EL-2; mail Mc Clure z 17841; ● 110
Banning; RMC Place; FAYETTE; ▲ Perry; ***225** WO-5; ★ **PGH**; mail Dawson z 15428; ● 75
Barbours; RMC Place; LYCOMING; ▲ Plunketts Creek; **226** EH-5; elev. 740ft./226m.; mail Williamsport z 17701; ● 120
Bard; RMC Place; BEDFORD; ▲ Harrison; **225** WP-10; mail Buffalo Mills z 15534; ● 50
Baresville; RMC Place; YORK; ▲ Penn; **227** EQ-4; ★ **HANV**; mail Hanover z 17331; pop. incl. with Hanover (Inc. Place)
Bareville; RMC Place; LANCASTER; ▲ Upper Leacock, West Earl; **227** EO-8; ★ **LANC**; mail Leola z 17540; ● 1,250
Barkeyville; Inc. Place; VENANGO; **224** WI-4; elev. 1,479ft./451m.; mail Harrisville z 16038; Ⓟ 274; © 237
Barlow; RMC Place; ADAMS; ▲ Mount Joy, Cumberland; ***227** EQ-3; mail Gettysburg z 17325; rural
Barnards; RMC Place; ARMSTRONG; ▲ Cowanshannock; ***225** WK-7; mail Dayton z 16222; ● 30
Barnes; RMC Place; CAMBRIA; ▲ West Carroll; ***225** WL-9; mail Elmora z 15737
Barnes; RMC Place; JEFFERSON; ▲ Knox; ***224** WI-8; elev. 1,343ft./409m.; mail Brookville z 15825; rural
Barnes; RMC Place; WARREN; ▲ Sheffield; **224** WF-8; mail Sheffield z 16347; ● 200
Barnesboro; RMC Place; CAMBRIA; ***225** WL-9; pop. incl. with Northern Cambria (Inc. Place)
Barneston; RMC Place; CHESTER; ▲ West Nantmeal; ***227** EO-9; ★ **PHIL-**; mail Honey Brook z 19344; ● 100
Barnesville; RMC Place; SCHUYLKILL; ▲ Rush; **227** EK-8; 🅿; z 18214; ● 300
Barnett; MCD-Township; FOREST; ***224** WH-8; mail Clarington z 15828; Ⓟ 400; © 349
Barnett; MCD-Township; JEFFERSON; ***224** WH-8; mail Sigel z 15860; Ⓟ 269; © 272
Barnettstown; RMC Place; HUNTINGDON; ▲ Carbon; ***225** WO-12; mail Dudley z 16634; ● 80
Barneytown; HUNTINGDON; see Latta Grove (RMC Place)
Barnitz; RMC Place; CUMBERLAND; ▲ Dickinson; ***227** EO-3; ★ **CARL**; mail Carlisle z 17013; ● 100
Barnsley; RMC Place; CHESTER; ▲ East Nottingham; **227** EQ-8; elev. 554ft./169m.; mail Oxford z 19363; ● 100
Barr; MCD-Township; CAMBRIA; ***225** WL-9; mail Nicktown z 15762; Ⓟ 2,260; © 2,175
Barree; RMC Place; HUNTINGDON; ▲ Porter; **225** WM-12; 🅿; z 16611; ● 70
Barree; MCD-Township; HUNTINGDON; ***225** WL-13; 🅿; z 16611 & mail Petersburg z 16669; Ⓟ 450; © 460
Barren Hill; RMC Place; MONTGOMERY; ▲ Whitemarsh; ***227** EO-12; ★ **PHIL-**; mail Lafayette Hill z 19444
Barret Plan; RMC Place; BEAVER; ▲ Hopewell; ***225** WL-2; ★ **PGH**; mail Aliquippa z 15001; ● 400
Barrett; RMC Place; CLEARFIELD; ▲ Bradford; ***224** WJ-11; mail Clearfield z 16830; rural
Barrett; MCD-Township; MONROE; ***226** EI-12; mail Mountainhome z 18342; Ⓟ 3,216; © 3,880
Barronvale; RMC Place; SOMERSET; ▲ Middlecreek; ***225** WP-7; elev. 1,787ft./545m.; mail Rockwood z 15557; rural
Barr Slope; RMC Place; INDIANA; ▲ Green; ***225** WL-8; mail Dixonville z 15734; ● 200
Barrville; RMC Place; MIFFLIN; ▲ Brown; ***225** WL-14; elev. 883ft./269m.; mail Reedsville z 17084; ● 125
Barry; MCD-Township; SCHUYLKILL; ***227** EL-6; mail Ashland z 17921, Hegins z 17938; Ⓟ 845; © 967
Barry Heights; RMC Place; MONTGOMERY; ▲ Lower Providence; ★ **PHIL-**; mail Norristown z 19401; pop. incl. with Norristown (Inc. Place)
Bart; LANCASTER; see Georgetown (RMC Place)
Bart; MCD-Township; LANCASTER; ***227** EP-8; 🅿; z 17503 & mail Paradise z 17562; Ⓟ 2,774; © 3,003
Barto; RMC Place; BERKS; ▲ Washington; **227** EN-10; 🅿; z 19504; ● 180
Bartonsville; RMC Place; MONROE; ▲ Hamilton, Pocono, Stroud; ***226** EJ-11; 🅿; z 18321; ● 500
Bartville; RMC Place; LANCASTER; ▲ Bart; ***227** EQ-8; elev. 681ft./208m.; mail Christiana z 17509
Basket; RMC Place; BERKS; ▲ Ruscombmanor, Alsace; ***227** EN-9; ★ **READ**; mail Oley z 19547; rural
Bassards Corners; RMC Place; NORTHAMPTON; ▲ Lehigh; ***227** EK-10; ★ **ALL-**; mail Danielsville z 18038; rural
Bastress; MCD-Township; LYCOMING; ***226** EI-3; 🅿; ★ **WMSPT**; z 17702 & mail Williamsport z 17701; Ⓟ 513; © 574
Bath; Inc. Place; NORTHAMPTON; **227** EL-11; elev. 432ft./132m.; 🅿; ★ **ALL-**; z 18014; Ⓟ 2,358; © 2,678
Bath Addition; RMC Place; BUCKS; ▲ Bristol; ***227** EO-13; ★ **PHIL-**; mail Bristol z 19007; ● 950
Bath Manor; RMC Place; BUCKS; ▲ Bristol; ★ **PHIL-**; mail Bristol z 19007
Bauerstown; RMC Place; ALLEGHENY; ▲ Shaler; ***225** WM-4; ★ **PGH**; mail Pittsburgh z 15209
Baumgardner; RMC Place; LANCASTER; ▲ Pequea; ***227** EP-7; elev. 382ft./116m.; ★ **LANC**; mail Willow Street z 17584; ● 200
Baumstown; RMC Place; BERKS; ▲ Exeter; **227** EN-9; ★ **READ**; mail Birdsboro z 19508; ● 400
Bausman; RMC Place; LANCASTER; ▲ Lancaster; **227** ET-8; 🅿; ★ **LANC**; z 17504; ● 300
Bavington; RMC Place; WASHINGTON; ▲ Smith, Hanover; **225** WM-2; ★ **PGH**; mail Bulger z 15019; ● 50
Baxter; RMC Place; JEFFERSON; ▲ Clover; ***224** WI-7; mail Corsica z 15829
Beachdale; RMC Place; SOMERSET; ▲ Brothersvalley; ***225** WP-8; mail Berlin z 15530; rural
Beach Haven; RMC Place; LUZERNE; ▲ Salem; **226** EJ-8; 🅿; z 18601; ● 500
Beach Lake; RMC Place; WAYNE; ▲ Berlin; **226** EF-12; 🅿; z 18405; ● 320
Beachly; RMC Place; SOMERSET; ▲ Addison; ***225** WQ-7; elev. 1,640ft./500m.; mail Confluence z 15424; rural
Beadling; RMC Place; ALLEGHENY; ▲ Upper St. Clair; ***225** WN-3; ★ **PGH**; mail Pittsburgh z 15241
Beale; MCD-Township; JUNIATA; ***227** EM-2; mail Port Royal z 17082; Ⓟ 629; © 726
Beallsville; Inc. Place; WASHINGTON; **225** WO-3; elev. 1,136ft./346m.; 🅿; ★ **WASH**; z 15313; Ⓟ 530; © 511
Beans Cove; RMC Place; BEDFORD; ▲ Southampton; ***225** WQ-10; elev. 1,116ft./340m.; mail Clearville z 15535; rural
Bear Creek; MCD-Township; LUZERNE; ***226** EI-9; 🅿; ★ **SCR-**; z 18602 & mail Wilkes Barre z 18702; Ⓟ 2,725; © 2,580
Bear Creek Lake; RMC Place; CARBON; ▲ Penn Forest; ***226** EJ-10; mail Jim Thorpe z 18229; ● 400
Bear Creek Village; Inc. Place; LUZERNE; ▲ Bear Creek; **226** EI-9; ★ **SCR-**; mail Bear Creek z 18602, Wilkes Barre z 18702; Ⓟ 255; © 284
Bear Gap; RMC Place; NORTHUMBERLAND; ▲ Ralpho; ***227** EK-6; mail Elysburg z 17824; ● 65
Bear Lake; Inc. Place; WARREN; **224** WD-6; elev. 1,552ft./473m.; 🅿; z 16402; Ⓟ 193; © 193
Bear Rocks; RMC Place; FAYETTE; ▲ Bullskin; ***225** WO-6; mail Acme z 15610; ● 700
Beartown; RMC Place; FRANKLIN; ▲ Washington; **227** EQ-2; ★ **HAG**; mail Waynesboro z 17268; ● 200
Beartown; RMC Place; LANCASTER; ▲ Caernarvon; ***227** EO-8; mail Narvon z 17555
Bear Valley; RMC Place; NORTHUMBERLAND; ▲ Coal; ***227** EK-6; mail Coal Township z 17866, Shamokin z 17872; rural
Beatty; RMC Place; WESTMORELAND; ▲ Unity; ***225** WN-6; ★ **LTROB**; mail Latrobe z 15650; rural
Beaufort Farms; RMC Place; DAUPHIN; ▲ Susquehanna; ***227** EN-4; ★ **HRBG**; mail Harrisburg z 17110; ● 700
Beaumont; RMC Place; WYOMING; ▲ Monroe; **226** EH-8; elev. 984ft./300m.; mail Dallas z 18612, Harveys Lake z 18618, Noxen z 18636, Tunkhannock z 18657; ● 200
Beautiful; FRANKLIN; see Salem (RMC Place)
Beaver; Inc. Place; ⊡ BEAVER; **225** WL-2; elev. 760ft./232m.; 🅿 🅷 ■; ★ **PGH**; z 15009; Ⓟ 5,028; © 4,775; ◆ 4,372
Beaver; MCD-Township; CLARION; ***224** WI-6; mail Knox z 16232; Ⓟ 1,840; © 1,753
Beaver; MCD-Township; COLUMBIA; ***226** EJ-7; mail Bloomsburg z 17815; Ⓟ 928; © 885
Beaver; MCD-Township; CRAWFORD; ***224** WE-1; mail Conneautville z 16406, Springboro z 16435; Ⓟ 831; © 903
Beaver; MCD-Township; JEFFERSON; ***224** WJ-7; mail Summerville z 15864; Ⓟ 551; © 544
Beaver; MCD-Township; SNYDER; ***227** EL-3; mail Beavertown z 17813; Ⓟ 516; © 527
BEAVER; **225** WL-2; Ⓟ 186,093; © 181,412; ◆ 167,665
Beaver Acres; RMC Place; ALLEGHENY; ▲ Robinson; ★ **PGH**; mail Mc Kees Rocks z 15136; ● 400
Beaver Brook; RMC Place; LUZERNE; ▲ Hazle; **226** EJ-8; ★ **HAZ**; mail Hazleton z 18201; ● 400
Beaver Center; RMC Place; CRAWFORD; ▲ Beaver; **224** WE-2; mail Springboro z 16435; ● 40
Beaverdale; RMC Place; CAMBRIA; ▲ Summerhill; **225** WN-9; elev. 1,929ft./588m.; 🅿; ★ **JNST**; z 15921; ● 800
Beaverdale; RMC Place; NORTHUMBERLAND; ▲ Mount Carmel; ***227** EK-6; mail Mount Carmel z 17851; ● 40
Beaverdale-Lloydell; CDP-Census Area Only; CAMBRIA; ▲ Summerhill; ***225** WN-9; ★ **JNST**; mail Beaverdale z 15921; Ⓟ 1,278; © 1,230
Beaver Dam; RMC Place; ERIE; ▲ Wayne; **224** WD-5; mail Corry z 16407; ● 130
Beaver Falls; Inc. Place; BEAVER; **225** WK-2; elev. 800ft./244m.; 🅿 🅲 1,979; ★ **PGH**; z 15010; Ⓟ 10,687; © 9,920
Beaver Lake; RMC Place; LYCOMING; ▲ Penn; ***226** EH-6; mail Muncy Valley z 17758
Beaver Meadows; Inc. Place; CARBON; **226** EJ-9; elev. 1,559ft./475m.; 🅿; ★ **HAZ**; z 18216; Ⓟ 985; © 968
Beaver Springs; CDP; SNYDER; ▲ Spring; **227** EL-3; elev. 688ft./210m.; 🅿; z 17812, z 17843; © 634
Beavertown; RMC Place; BLAIR; ▲ Huston; **225** WN-11; elev. 1,191ft./363m.; mail Martinsburg z 16662; ● 40
Beavertown; Inc. Place; SNYDER; **227** EL-3; elev. 651ft./198m.; 🅿; z 17813; Ⓟ 877; © 870
Beavertown; RMC Place; YORK; ▲ Carroll; **227** EO-4; ★ **HRBG**; mail Dillsburg z 17019; ● 90
Beaver Valley; RMC Place; CAMBRIA; ▲ White; ***225** WL-10; mail Flinton z 16640; ● 150
Beccaria; RMC Place; CLEARFIELD; ▲ Beccaria; **225** WK-11; 🅿; z 16616; ● 175
Beccaria; MCD-Township; CLEARFIELD; ***225** WL-10; 🅿; z 16616 & mail Coalport z 16627; Ⓟ 1,917; © 1,835
Bechtelsville; Inc. Place; BERKS; **227** EN-10; elev. 420ft./128m.; 🅿; z 19505; Ⓟ 884; © 931
Beckersville; RMC Place; BERKS; ▲ Robeson; **227** EO-9; ★ **READ**; mail Mohnton z 19540; ● 200
Becks; SCHUYLKILL; see Beckville (RMC Place)
Becks Run; RMC Place; ALLEGHENY; ★ **PGH**; pop. incl. with Pittsburgh (Inc. Place)
Beckville (Becks); RMC Place; SCHUYLKILL; ▲ North Manheim; ***227** EL-7; ★ **PTSVL**; mail Cressona z 17929, Pottsville z 17901; rural
Bedford; Inc. Place; ⊡ BEDFORD; **225** WP-10; elev. 1,106ft./337m.; 🅿; z 15522; Ⓟ 3,137; © 3,141
Bedford; MCD-Township; BEDFORD; ***225** WP-10; 🅿; z 15522; does not include the Borough of Bedford; Ⓟ 4,945; © 5,417
BEDFORD; **225** WO-10; Ⓟ 47,919; © 49,984; ◆ 49,319
Bedford Valley; BEDFORD; see Centerville (RMC Place)
Bedminster; RMC Place; BUCKS; ▲ Bedminster; **227** EM-12; 🅿; ★ **PHIL-**; z 18910; ● 500
Bedminster; MCD-Township; BUCKS; ***227** EM-12; 🅿; ★ **PHIL-**; z 18910; Ⓟ 4,602; © 4,804
Beech Creek; Inc. Place; CLINTON; **226** EJ-1; elev. 617ft./188m.; 🅿; z 16822; Ⓟ 716; © 717
Beech Creek; MCD-Township; CLINTON; ***224** WI-14; 🅿; z 16822; does not include the Borough of Beech Creek; Ⓟ 1,007; © 1,010
Beecherstown; RMC Place; ADAMS; ▲ Butler; ***227** EP-2; mail Biglerville z 17307; ● 50
Beech Flats; RMC Place; BRADFORD; ▲ Canton; ***226** EF-5; mail Canton z 17724; rural
Beech Glen; RMC Place; SULLIVAN; ▲ Davidson; ***226** EH-6; mail Muncy Valley z 17758; rural
Beech Grove; RMC Place; ELK; ▲ Horton; ***224** WH-9; elev. 1,760ft./536m.; mail Brandy Camp z 15822; rural
Beech Grove; RMC Place; LYCOMING; ▲ Cogan House; ***226** EG-3; mail Trout Run z 17771; rural
Beechton; RMC Place; JEFFERSON; ▲ Snyder; ***224** WI-9; mail Brockway z 15824; rural
Beechview; RMC Place; ALLEGHENY; ***225** WM-3; ★ **PGH**; mail Pittsburgh z 15216; pop. incl. with Pittsburgh (Inc. Place)
Beechwood; RMC Place; CAMERON; ▲ Shippen; ***224** WG-11; mail Emporium z 15834
Beechwood Park; RMC Place; DELAWARE; ▲ Aston; ***227** EQ-11; ★ **PHIL-**; mail Aston z 19014; ● 100
Beechwoods; RMC Place; JEFFERSON; ▲ Washington; ***224** WI-9; elev. 1,668ft./508m.; mail Falls Creek z 15840; rural
Beeman; RMC Place; TIOGA; ▲ Lawrence; ***226** ED-3; mail Lawrenceville z 16929, Tioga z 16946; rural
Beersville; RMC Place; NORTHAMPTON; ▲ Moore; **227** EK-11; ★ **ALL-**; mail Northampton z 18067; ● 250
Beesons; RMC Place; FAYETTE; ▲ North Union; ★ **UNTN**; mail Hopwood z 15445; rural
Beham; RMC Place; WASHINGTON; ▲ West Finley; ***225** WP-1; mail West Alexander z 15376; rural
Bela; RMC Place; CLARION; ▲ Toby; ***224** WJ-6; mail Parker z 16049; rural
Belair; RMC Place; LANCASTER; ▲ Manheim; ***227** EO-7; ★ **LANC**; mail Lancaster z 17601; ● 1,310
Belair Park; RMC Place; LANCASTER; ▲ Manheim; ★ **LANC**; mail Lancaster z 17601; ● 350
Belardley; RMC Place; BUCKS; ▲ Bristol; ***227** EO-13; ★ **PHIL-**; mail Bristol z 19007
Belden; RMC Place; BEDFORD; ▲ Bedford; ***225** WO-10; mail Bedford z 15522
Belfast; MCD-Township; FULTON; ***225** WQ-12; mail Needmore z 17238; Ⓟ 1,208; © 1,341
Belfast; CDP; NORTHAMPTON; ▲ Plainfield; **227** EK-12; mail Nazareth z 18064; Ⓟ 1,102; © 1,301
Belfast Junction; RMC Place; NORTHAMPTON; ▲ Plainfield; ***227** EK-12; mail Easton z 18040; rural
Belfry; RMC Place; MONTGOMERY; ▲ Whitpain; ***227** EO-11; ★ **PHIL-**; mail Norristown z 19401; rural
Belknap; RMC Place; ARMSTRONG; ▲ Wayne; **225** WK-7; elev. 497ft./151m.; mail Dayton z 16222; ● 40
Bell; MCD-Township; CLEARFIELD; ***225** WK-9; mail Mahaffey z 15757; Ⓟ 925; © 825
Bell; MCD-Township; JEFFERSON; ***224** WJ-8; mail Punxsutawney z 15767; Ⓟ 2,055; © 2,029
Bell; MCD-Township; WESTMORELAND; ***225** WM-6; ★ **PGH**; mail Apollo z 15613; Ⓟ 2,353; © 2,458
Bell Acres; Inc. Place; ALLEGHENY; **225** WL-3; elev. 1,200ft./366m.; ★ **PGH**; mail Sewickley z 15143; Ⓟ 1,436; © 1,382
Bellaire; RMC Place; LANCASTER; ▲ Mount Joy; **227** EO-6; elev. 454ft./138m.; mail Elizabethtown z 17022
Bella Vista; RMC Place; LYCOMING; ▲ Fairfield; ***226** EI-4; ★ **WMSPT**; mail Montoursville z 17754; ● 200
Belle Bridge; RMC Place; ALLEGHENY; ***225** WN-4; ★ **PGH**; mail Elizabeth z 15037; pop. incl. with Lincoln (Inc. Place)
Bellefield; RMC Place; ALLEGHENY; ***225** WM-4; ★ **PGH**; mail Pittsburgh z 15213; pop. incl. with Pittsburgh (Inc. Place)
Bellefonte; Inc. Place; ⊡ CENTRE; **225** WK-14; elev. 809ft./247m.; 🅿; ★ **STCOL**; z 16823; Ⓟ 6,358; © 6,395
Bellegrove; RMC Place; LEBANON; ▲ North Annville; **227** EN-6; ★ **LEB**; mail Annville z 17003; ● 300
Bellemont; RMC Place; LANCASTER; ▲ Paradise; ***227** EP-8; mail Paradise z 17562; rural
Belle Valley; RMC Place; ERIE; ▲ Millcreek; ***224** WC-4; ★ **ERIE**; mail Erie z 16504, z 16509
Belle Vernon; Inc. Place; FAYETTE; **225** WO-4; elev. 903ft./275m.; 🅿; ★ **PGH**; z 15012; Ⓟ 1,213; © 1,211
Belleville; CDP; MIFFLIN; ▲ Union; **225** WL-14; 🅿; z 17004; Ⓟ 1,589; © 1,386
Bellevue; Inc. Place; ALLEGHENY; **225** WM-3; elev. 980ft./299m.; 🅿; ★ **PGH**; z 15202; Ⓟ 9,126; © 8,770
Bell Mountain; RMC Place; LACKAWANNA; ***226** EG-10; ★ **SCR-**; mail Scranton z 18508; pop. incl. with Dickson City (Inc. Place)
Bell Point; RMC Place; WESTMORELAND; ▲ Bell; ***225** WM-6; ★ **PGH**; mail Apollo z 15613; ● 200
Bell Road Station; RMC Place; PHILADELPHIA; ★ **PHIL-**; pop. incl. with Philadelphia (Inc. Place)
Bells Camp; RMC Place; MCKEAN; ▲ Foster; ***224** WD-10; mail Derrick City z 16727; rural
Bells Landing; RMC Place; CLEARFIELD; ▲ Greenwood; **225** WK-10; mail Mahaffey z 15757; ● 75
Bells Mills; RMC Place; JEFFERSON; ▲ Bell; ***224** WJ-8; mail Punxsutawney z 15767; rural
Belltown; RMC Place; ELK; ▲ Millstone; ***224** WH-8; mail Sigel z 15860; ● 50
Belltown; RMC Place; MIFFLIN; ▲ Decatur; **227** EL-2; mail Mc Clure z 17841; ● 60
Bellview; RMC Place; WASHINGTON; ▲ North Franklin; ***225** WO-2; elev. 1,086ft./331m.; ★ **WASH**; mail Washington z 15301; ● 400
Bellwood; Inc. Place; BLAIR; **225** WL-11; elev. 1,060ft./323m.; 🅿; ★ **ALT**; z 16617; Ⓟ 1,976; © 2,016
Belmar; RMC Place; ALLEGHENY; ***225** WM-4; ★ **PGH**; mail Pittsburgh z 15206; pop. incl. with Pittsburgh (Inc. Place)
Belmar; RMC Place; VENANGO; ▲ Sandycreek; ***224** WH-5; elev. 980ft./299m.; ★ **OILC-F**; mail Franklin z 16323; rural
Belmar Park; RMC Place; LAWRENCE; ▲ Union; ***224** WJ-2; elev. 1,034ft./315m.; ★ **NWCS**; mail New Castle z 16101
Belmont; CDP; CAMBRIA; ▲ Stonycreek, Richland; **225** WT-2; ★ **JNST**; mail Johnstown z 15904; Ⓟ 3,184; © 2,846
Belmont; RMC Place; PHILADELPHIA; ★ **PHIL-**; pop. incl. with Philadelphia (Inc. Place)
Belmont Corner; RMC Place; WAYNE; ▲ Mount Pleasant; ***226** EF-11; elev. 2,016ft./614m.; mail Pleasant Mount z 18453; rural
Belmont Hills; RMC Place; BUCKS; ▲ Bensalem; **228** C-3; elev. 117ft./36m.; ★ **PHIL-**; mail Bensalem z 19020; ● 1,500
Belmont Hills; RMC Place; MONTGOMERY; ▲ Lower Merion; ***227** EP-12; 🅿; ★ **PHIL-**; z 19004 & mail Philadelphia z 19151; ● 1,900
Belmont Terrace; RMC Place; MONTGOMERY; ▲ Upper Merion; ***227** EO-11; ★ **PHIL-**; mail King of Prussia z 19406
Belsano; RMC Place; CAMBRIA; ▲ Blacklick; **225** WM-9; elev. 1,829ft./557m.; 🅿; z 15922; ● 400
Belsena (Belsena Mills); RMC Place; CLEARFIELD; ▲ Bigler; ***225** WK-11; mail Madera z 16661; rural
Belsena Mills; CLEARFIELD; see Belsena (RMC Place)
Belton; RMC Place; BEAVER; ▲ North Sewickley; ***225** WK-2; ★ **PGH**; mail Ellwood City z 16117; ● 200
Beltzhoover; RMC Place; ALLEGHENY; ***225** WM-4; ★ **PGH**; mail Pittsburgh z 15210; pop. incl. with Pittsburgh (Inc. Place)
Ben Avon; Inc. Place; ALLEGHENY; **228** I-4; elev. 840ft./256m.; 🅿; ★ **PGH**; z 15202; Ⓟ 2,096; © 1,917
Ben Avon; RMC Place; INDIANA; ▲ White; ***225** WL-7; elev. 1,162ft./354m.; mail Indiana z 15701; ● 200
Ben Avon Heights; Inc. Place; ALLEGHENY; **228** H-4; elev. 1,180ft./360m.; ★ **PGH**; mail Pittsburgh z 15202; Ⓟ 373; © 392
Bencetown; RMC Place; INDIANA; ▲ Green; ***225** WL-8; mail Dixonville z 15734; ● 20
Bendersville; Inc. Place; ADAMS; **227** EP-3; elev. 740ft./226m.; 🅿; z 17306; Ⓟ 560; © 576
Bendersville Station-Aspers; CDP-Census Area Only; ADAMS; ***227** EP-3; © 324
Bendertown; RMC Place; COLUMBIA; ▲ Fishing Creek; **226** EI-7; elev. 956ft./291m.; mail Orangeville z 17859; ● 50
Benedicts; RMC Place; YORK; ▲ Warrington; ***227** EP-4; mail Dover z 17315; rural
Benezett; ELK; see Benezette (RMC Place)
Benezette (Benezett, Bennezette); RMC Place; ELK; ▲ Benezette; **224** WH-11; 🅿; z 15821; ● 200
Benezette; MCD-Township; ELK; ***224** WI-11; 🅿; z 15821; Ⓟ 243; © 227
Benfer; RMC Place; SNYDER; ▲ Spring; **227** EK-3; elev. 607ft./185m.; mail Beaver Springs z 17812; ● 100
Benjamin; RMC Place; BUCKS; ★ **PHIL-**; mail Perkasie z 18944; pop. incl. with Perkasie (Inc. Place)
Benner; MCD-Township; CENTRE; ***225** WK-13; ★ **STCOL**; mail Bellefonte z 16823; Ⓟ 5,085; © 5,217
Bennezette; ELK; see Benezette (RMC Place)
Bensalem (Cornwells Heights); RMC Place; BUCKS; ▲ Bensalem; **228** A-8; 🅿 🅷; ★ **PHIL-**; z 19020-21; ● 3,000
Bensalem; MCD-Township; BUCKS; ***227** EO-13; 🅿 ■; ★ **PHIL-**; z 19020-21; Ⓟ 56,788; © 58,434; ◆ 58,810
Bens Creek; RMC Place; CAMBRIA; ▲ Portage; ***225** WN-10; mail Lilly z 15938; ● 350
Benson (Holsopple); Inc. Place; SOMERSET; **225** WO-8; elev. 1,560ft./475m.; ★ **JNST**; mail Hollsopple z 15935; Ⓟ 277; © 194
Bentley Creek; RMC Place; BRADFORD; ▲ Ridgebury; **226** ED-5; mail Gillett z 16925, Wellsburg z 14894; ● 160
Bentleyville; Inc. Place; WASHINGTON; **225** WO-3; elev. 960ft./293m.; 🅿; z 15314; Ⓟ 2,673; © 2,502
Benton; Inc. Place; COLUMBIA; **226** EI-7; elev. 760ft./232m.; 🅿; z 17814; Ⓟ 958; © 955
Benton; MCD-Township; COLUMBIA; ***226** EI-7; 🅿; z 17814; does not include the Borough of Benton; Ⓟ 1,094; © 1,216
Benton; MCD-Township; LACKAWANNA; ***226** EG-9; ★ **SCR-**; mail Fleetville z 18420; Ⓟ 1,837; © 1,881
Benvenue; RMC Place; DAUPHIN; ▲ Reed; **227** EN-4; ★ **HRBG**; mail Duncannon z 17020; ● 25
Bergey; RMC Place; MONTGOMERY; ▲ Upper Salford; ***227** EN-11; elev. 221ft./67m.; ★ **PHIL-**; mail Harleysville z 19438; ● 30
Berkeley Hills; RMC Place; ALLEGHENY; ▲ Ross; ***225** WM-4; ★ **PGH**; mail Pittsburgh z 15237
Berkley; RMC Place; BERKS; ▲ Maidencreek; **227** EM-9; ★ **READ**; mail Reading z 19605; ● 200
Berkleys Mill; RMC Place; SOMERSET; ▲ Summit; **225** WQ-8; mail Meyersdale z 15552; ● 60
BERKS; **227** EM-8; Ⓟ 336,523; © 373,638; ◆ 403,204
Berkshire Heights; RMC Place; BERKS; ★ **READ**; mail Reading z 19610; pop. incl. with Wyomissing (Inc. Place)
Berlin; Inc. Place; SOMERSET; **225** WP-8; elev. 2,200ft./671m.; 🅿; z 15530; Ⓟ 2,064; © 2,192
Berlin; MCD-Township; WAYNE; ***226** EG-12; mail Honesdale z 18431; Ⓟ 1,777; © 2,188
Berlin Junction; RMC Place; ADAMS; ▲ Oxford; ***227** EQ-4; ★ **HANV**; mail New Oxford z 17350; rural
Berlinsville; RMC Place; NORTHAMPTON; ▲ Lehigh; **227** EK-10; ★ **ALL-**; mail Walnutport z 18088; ● 200
Bermudian; RMC Place; ADAMS, YORK; ▲ Washington, Latimore; **227** EP-4; mail Dillsburg z 17019; ● 40
Bern; MCD-Township; BERKS; ***227** EN-8; ★ **READ**; mail Reading z 19605; Ⓟ 6,303; © 6,758
Berne; RMC Place; BERKS; ▲ Tilden; **227** EM-8; elev. 334ft./102m.; ★ **READ**; mail Hamburg z 19526; ● 130
Bernharts; RMC Place; BERKS; ▲ Muhlenberg; ***227** EN-9; ★ **READ**; mail Reading z 19605
Bernice; RMC Place; SULLIVAN; ▲ Cherry; ***226** EG-6; mail Mildred z 18632
Bernville; Inc. Place; BERKS; **227** EM-8; elev. 322ft./98m.; 🅿; ★ **READ**; z 19506; Ⓟ 789; © 865
Berrysburg; Inc. Place; DAUPHIN; **227** EL-5; elev. 700ft./213m.; 🅿; z 17005; Ⓟ 376; © 354
Berrytown; RMC Place; BRADFORD; ▲ Springfield; ***226** EE-5; mail Gillett z 16925; rural
Berwick; MCD-Township; ADAMS; ***227** EQ-4; ★ **HANV**; mail East Berlin z 17316; Ⓟ 1,831; © 1,818
Berwick; Inc. Place; COLUMBIA; **226** EJ-7; elev. 569ft./173m.; 🅿 🅷; z 18603; Ⓟ 10,976; © 10,774
Berwinsdale; RMC Place; CLEARFIELD; ▲ Jordan; ***225** WK-10; mail Irvona z 16656; ● 30
Berwyn; RMC Place; CHESTER; ▲ Easttown, Tredyffrin; **227** EP-11; 🅿; ★ **PHIL-**; z 19312; ● 3,000
Besco; RMC Place; WASHINGTON; ▲ East Bethlehem; ***225** WP-3; mail Clarksville z 15322; ● 80
Bessemer; RMC Place; ALLEGHENY; ***225** WM-4; ★ **PGH**; mail Braddock z 15104; pop. incl. with North Braddock (Inc. Place)
Bessemer; Inc. Place; LAWRENCE; **224** WJ-1; elev. 1,086ft./331m.; 🅿; ★ **YNGS-**; z 16112; Ⓟ 1,196; © 1,172
Bessemer; RMC Place; WESTMORELAND; ▲ East Huntingdon; ***225** WO-5; mail Mount Pleasant z 15666; rural
Best; RMC Place; ALLEGHENY; mail West Mifflin z 15122; pop. incl. with West Mifflin (Inc. Place)
Best Station; RMC Place; LEHIGH; ▲ Washington; ***227** EL-10; elev. 565ft./172m.; ★ **ALL-**; mail Slatington z 18080; rural
Bethany; Inc. Place; WAYNE; **226** EF-11; elev. 1,420ft./433m.; 🅿; z 18431; Ⓟ 238; © 292
Bethayres; RMC Place; MONTGOMERY; ▲ Lower Moreland; ***227** EO-13; ★ **PHIL-**; mail Huntingdon Valley z 19006
Bethel; MCD-Township; ARMSTRONG; ***225** WL-6; ★ **PGH**; mail Ford City z 16226; Ⓟ 1,261; © 1,290
Bethel; RMC Place; BERKS; ▲ Bethel; **227** EM-7; 🅿; z 19507; ● 700
Bethel; MCD-Township; BERKS; ***227** EM-7; 🅿; z 19507; Ⓟ 3,676; © 4,166
Bethel; MCD-Township; DELAWARE; ***227** EQ-11; ★ **PHIL-**; mail Marcus Hook z 19061; Ⓟ 3,330; © 6,421
Bethel; MCD-Township; FULTON; ***225** WQ-11; mail Warfordsburg z 17267; Ⓟ 1,317; © 1,420
Bethel; MCD-Township; LEBANON; ***227** EM-6; ★ **LEB**; mail Fredericksburg z 17026; Ⓟ 4,343; © 4,526
Bethel; RMC Place; MERCER; ▲ Lackawannock; ***224** WI-2; ★ **SHAR**; mail West Middlesex z 16159; ● 50
Bethel; RMC Place; WESTMORELAND; ▲ Cook; ***225** WO-6; elev. 1,300ft./396m.; mail Ligonier z 15658; ● 120
Bethelboro; RMC Place; FAYETTE; ▲ North Union; ***225** WP-5; elev. 1,100ft./335m.; ★ **UNTN**; mail Uniontown z 15401; ● 70
Bethel Park; Inc. Place; ALLEGHENY; **225** WN-3; elev. 1,200ft./366m.; 🅿; ★ **PGH**; z 15102; Ⓟ 33,823; © 33,556; ◆ 31,914
Bethesda; RMC Place; LANCASTER; ▲ Martic; **227** EQ-7; elev. 664ft./202m.; ★ **LANC**; mail Holtwood z 17532; ● 45
Bethlehem; RMC Place; CLEARFIELD; ▲ Bell; **225** WK-9; mail Mahaffey z 15757; ● 25
Bethlehem; Inc. Place; NORTHAMPTON, LEHIGH; **227** EL-11; elev. 340ft./104m.; 🅿 🅷 🅲 6,485 ■; ★ **ALL-**; z 18015-18, z 18020, z 18025; Ⓟ 71,428; © 71,329; ◆ 73,329
Bethlehem; MCD-Township; NORTHAMPTON; ***227** EL-11; 🅿 🅲 6,485; ★ **ALL-**; z 18015-18, z 18020, z 18025; does not include the City of Bethlehem; Ⓟ 16,425; © 21,171; ◆ 24,444
Bethlehem View; RMC Place; NORTHAMPTON; ***227** EL-11; ★ **ALL-**; pop. incl. with Bethlehem (Inc. Place)
Betula; RMC Place; MCKEAN; ▲ Norwich; ***224** WF-11; elev. 1,594ft./486m.; mail Smethport z 16749
Betz; RMC Place; CLEARFIELD; ▲ Bigler; ***225** WK-11; elev. 1,500ft./457m.; mail Madera z 16661; ● 20
Betzwood; RMC Place; MONTGOMERY; ▲ West Norriton; ***227** EO-11; ★ **PHIL-**; mail Norristown z 19401
Beucher; SCHUYLKILL; see Oak Grove (RMC Place)
Beulah; RMC Place; CLEARFIELD; ▲ Bigler; ***225** WK-11; mail Madera z 16661; ● 65
Beury Lake; SCHUYLKILL; see Mountain Valley Lake (RMC Place)
Beurys Lake; CDP-Census Area Only; SCHUYLKILL; ***227** EL-7; © 133
Beverly Estates; RMC Place; LANCASTER; ▲ Manheim; ***227** EP-7; ★ **LANC**; mail Lancaster z 17601; ● 700
Beverly Heights; RMC Place; LEBANON; ▲ Swatara; ***227** EN-6; ★ **LEB**; mail Lebanon z 17042, z 17046; ● 300
Beverly Hills; RMC Place; BLAIR; ▲ Logan; ***225** WM-11; ★ **ALT**; mail Altoona z 16601; ● 80
Beverly Hills; RMC Place; DELAWARE; ▲ Upper Darby; ***227** EP-12; ★ **PHIL-**; mail Upper Darby z 19082
Beyer; RMC Place; INDIANA; ▲ South Mahoning; **225** WK-7; 🅿; z 16211; ● 100
Biddle; RMC Place; WESTMORELAND; ▲ North Huntingdon; ***225** WN-5; ★ **PGH**; mail Westmoreland City z 15692
Biesecker Gap; RMC Place; FRANKLIN; ▲ Quincy; ***227** EQ-1; mail Waynesboro z 17268; ● 180
Big Beaver; Inc. Place; BEAVER; **225** WK-2; ★ **PGH**; mail Beaver Falls z 15010, Darlington z 16115, Wampum z 16157; Ⓟ 2,298; © 2,186
Big Cove Tannery; RMC Place; FULTON; ▲ Ayr; **225** WQ-12; 🅿; z 17212; ● 200
Biggertown; RMC Place; LYCOMING; ▲ Jordan; ***226** EI-6; mail Unityville z 17774; rural
Bigler; RMC Place; CLEARFIELD; ▲ Bradford; **224** WJ-11; 🅿; z 16825; ● 400
Bigler; MCD-Township; CLEARFIELD; ***225** WK-11; 🅿; z 16825 & mail Madera z 16661; Ⓟ 1,391; © 1,368
Biglerville; Inc. Place; ADAMS; **227** EP-3; elev. 636ft./194m.; 🅿; z 17307; Ⓟ 993; © 1,101
Big Mine Run (Big Mine Run Junction); RMC Place; SCHUYLKILL; ▲ Butler; ***227** EK-7; ★ **PTSVL**; mail Ashland z 17921; ● 100
Big Mine Run Junction; SCHUYLKILL; see Big Mine Run (RMC Place)
Bigmount; RMC Place; YORK; ▲ Paradise; **227** EP-4; mail Dover z 17315; ● 100
Big Pond; RMC Place; BRADFORD; ▲ Springfield; **226** EE-5; mail Columbia Cross Roads z 16914; ● 100
Big Run; Inc. Place; JEFFERSON; **224** WJ-9; elev. 1,283ft./391m.; 🅿; z 15715; Ⓟ 699; © 686
Big Shanty; RMC Place; MCKEAN; ▲ Lafayette; ***224** WE-10; mail Lewis Run z 16738; rural
Big Spring (Springfield); RMC Place; CUMBERLAND; ▲ West Pennsboro; ***227** EO-2; ★ **CARL**; mail Newville z 17241; ● 30
Bimber Corners; RMC Place; WARREN; ▲ Limestone; ***224** WF-7; elev. 1,630ft./497m.; mail Tidioute z 16351; rural
Bingen; RMC Place; NORTHAMPTON; ▲ Lower Saucon; **226** EC-5; ★ **ALL-**; mail Bethlehem z 18015; ● 350
Bingham; RMC Place; MCKEAN; ▲ Lafayette; **224** WE-10; elev. 2,096ft./639m.; mail Cyclone z 16726; ● 40
Bingham; MCD-Township; POTTER; ***224** WD-14; mail Genesee z 16923, Ulysses z 16948; Ⓟ 557; © 687
Bingham Center; RMC Place; POTTER; ▲ Bingham; ***224** WD-14; elev. 1,952ft./595m.; mail Genesee z 16923
Binnstown; RMC Place; WASHINGTON; ***225** WP-4; mail Brownsville z 15417; pop. incl. with Centerville (Inc. Place)
Bino; RMC Place; FRANKLIN; ▲ Montgomery; ***225** WQ-13; mail Greencastle z 17225; rural
Birch Acres; MONROE; see Craigs Meadow (RMC Place)
Birchardville; RMC Place; SUSQUEHANNA; ▲ Forest Lake; **226** EE-8; elev. 1,046ft./319m.; mail Montrose z 18801; ● 40
Birchrunville; RMC Place; CHESTER; ▲ West Vincent; **227** EO-10; 🅿; ★ **PHIL-**; z 19421; ● 300
Birch Valley; RMC Place; BUCKS; ▲ Falls; ***227** EO-14; ★ **PHIL-**; mail Levittown z 19058
Birchwood Lakes; RMC Place; PIKE; ▲ Delaware; ***226** EH-13; elev. 1,100ft./335m.; mail Dingmans Ferry z 18328; ● 700
Birdell; RMC Place; CHESTER; ▲ Honey Brook; ***227** EP-9; elev. 603ft./184m.; ★ **PHIL-**; mail Honey Brook z 19344; ● 30
Bird in Hand; RMC Place; LANCASTER; ▲ East Lampeter; **227** EP-7; elev. 358ft./109m.; 🅿; ★ **LANC**; z 17505; ● 500
Birdsboro (Naomi); Inc. Place; BERKS; **227** EN-9; elev. 163ft./50m.; 🅿; ★ **READ**; z 19508; Ⓟ 4,222; © 5,064
Birdville; RMC Place; HUNTINGDON; ▲ Union; ***225** WN-13; mail Mapleton Depot z 17052; ● 100
Birmingham; RMC Place; CHESTER; ▲ Birmingham; ***227** EP-10; ★ **PHIL-**; mail West Chester z 19380; ● 30
Birmingham; MCD-Township; CHESTER; ***227** EP-10; ★ **PHIL-**; mail West Chester z 19380; Ⓟ 2,636; © 4,221
Birmingham; DELAWARE; see Chadds Ford (MCD-Township)
Birmingham; Inc. Place; HUNTINGDON; **225** WL-12; elev. 960ft./293m.; 🅿; z 16686; Ⓟ 109; © 91
Bishop; RMC Place; WASHINGTON; ▲ Cecil; **225** WN-3; elev. 970ft./296m.; ★ **PGH**; mail Mc Donald z 15057; ● 800
Bismarck; LEBANON; see Quentin (CDP)
Bitner; RMC Place; FAYETTE; ▲ Franklin; ***225** WP-5; ★ **UNTN**; mail Dunbar z 15431; ● 150
Bittersville; RMC Place; YORK; ▲ Windsor, Lower Windsor; **227** EP-6; ★ **YORK**; mail Windsor z 17366; ● 150
Bitumen; RMC Place; CLINTON; ▲ Noyes; ***224** WH-13; mail Westport z 17778; rural
Bixler; RMC Place; PERRY; ▲ Northeast Madison; ***227** EN-2; mail Loysville z 17047
Black; RMC Place; BRADFORD; ▲ Sheshequin; ***226** EE-6; elev. 1,253ft./382m.; mail Towanda z 18848; rural
Black; MCD-Township; SOMERSET; ***225** WQ-7; mail Rockwood z 15557; Ⓟ 942; © 980
Black Ash; RMC Place; CRAWFORD; ▲ Randolph; ***224** WF-4; mail Guys Mills z 16327; ● 20
Black Bear; RMC Place; BERKS; ★ **READ**; mail Reading z 19606; pop. incl. with Saint Lawrence (Inc. Place)
Blackburn; RMC Place; WESTMORELAND; ***225** WN-5; ★ **PGH**; mail Trafford z 15085; pop. incl. with Trafford (Inc. Place)
Black Creek; MCD-Township; LUZERNE; ***226** EJ-7; ★ **HAZ**; mail Rock Glen z 18246; Ⓟ 1,937; © 2,132
Black Diamond; RMC Place; WASHINGTON; ***225** WO-4; ★ **PGH**; mail Monongahela z 15063; pop. incl. with Monongahela (Inc. Place)
Blackfield; RMC Place; SOMERSET; ▲ Black; ***225** WP-8; elev. 2,360ft./719m.; mail Garrett z 15542; rural
Black Gap; RMC Place; FRANKLIN; ▲ Greene; ***227** EQ-1
Blackhawk; RMC Place; BEAVER; ▲ South Beaver; ***225** WL-2; elev. 1,169ft./356m.; ★ **PGH**; mail Beaver Falls z 15010; pop. incl. with Ohioville (Inc. Place)
Blackhorse; RMC Place; CHESTER; ▲ West Sadsbury; ***227** EP-9; elev. 704ft./215m.; ★ **PHIL-**; mail Parkesburg z 19365; rural
Black Horse; RMC Place; DELAWARE; ▲ Middletown; ***227** EP-11; ★ **PHIL-**; mail Media z 19063; ● 70
Black Horse; RMC Place; MONTGOMERY; ▲ Plymouth; ***227** EO-11; 🅿; ★ **PHIL-**; z 19401 & mail Plymouth Meeting z 19462; ● 280
Blacklick; MCD-Township; CAMBRIA; ***225** WM-9; mail Nanty Glo z 15943; Ⓟ 2,206; © 2,200
Black Lick; CDP; INDIANA; ▲ Burrell, Black Lick; **225** WM-7; elev. 998ft./304m.; 🅿; ★ **LTROB**; z 15716 & mail Maytown z 17550; Ⓟ 1,100; © 1,438
Black Lick; MCD-Township; INDIANA; ***225** WM-7; 🅿; z 15716 & mail Blairsville z 15717; Ⓟ 1,225; © 1,317
Blacklog; RMC Place; HUNTINGDON; ▲ Cromwell; ***225** WO-13; mail Orbisonia z 17243; rural
Blackman; RMC Place; LUZERNE; ▲ Wilkes-Barre; ★ **SCR-**; mail Wilkes Barre z 18702
Black Ridge; RMC Place; ALLEGHENY; ▲ Penn Hills; ***225** WM-4; elev. 1,200ft./366m.; ★ **PGH**; mail Pittsburgh z 15235
Blackrock; RMC Place; YORK; ▲ Manheim; ***227** ER-4; ★ **HANV**; mail Lineboro z 21088; ● 80
Blacktown; RMC Place; MERCER; ▲ Springfield; **224** WI-3; mail Mercer z 16137; ● 50
Black Walnut; RMC Place; WYOMING; ▲ Meshoppen, Braintrim; **226** EF-8; mail Laceyville z 18623; ● 150
Blackwell; RMC Place; TIOGA; ▲ Morris; **226** EG-2; elev. 861ft./262m.; mail Morris z 16938; ● 80
Blain; Inc. Place; PERRY; **227** EN-1; elev. 720ft./219m.; 🅿; z 17006; Ⓟ 266; © 252
Blain City; RMC Place; CLEARFIELD; ▲ Beccaria; **225** WL-10; mail Coalport z 16627; ● 250
Blaine; MCD-Township; WASHINGTON; ***225** WO-2; mail Taylorstown z 15365; Ⓟ 682; © 597
Blaine Hill; RMC Place; ALLEGHENY; ▲ Elizabeth; **225** WN-4; ★ **PGH**; mail Elizabeth z 15037; ● 1,100
Blainesburg; RMC Place; WASHINGTON; ★ **PGH**; mail Brownsville z 15417; pop. incl. with West Brownsville (Inc. Place)
Blainsport; RMC Place; LANCASTER; ▲ West Cocalico; **227** EN-8; elev. 493ft./150m.; mail Reinholds z 17569; ● 110
Blair; MCD-Township; BLAIR; ***225** WN-11; ★ **ALT**; mail Duncansville z 16635; Ⓟ 3,994; © 4,587
BLAIR; **225** WN-11; Ⓟ 130,542; © 129,144; ◆ 123,466
Blairs; CLARION; see Blairs Corners (RMC Place)
Blairs Corners (Blairs); RMC Place; CLARION; ***224** WI-6; mail Knox z 16232
Blairs Mills; RMC Place; HUNTINGDON; ▲ Tell; **225** WN-14; 🅿; z 17213; ● 100
Blairsville; Inc. Place; INDIANA; **225** WM-7; elev. 1,015ft./309m.; 🅿; ★ **LTROB**; z 15717; Ⓟ 3,595; © 3,607
Blairtown; RMC Place; GREENE; ▲ Franklin; **225** WQ-3; mail Waynesburg z 15370; ● 60
Blakely; Inc. Place; LACKAWANNA; **226** EG-10; elev. 820ft./250m.; 🅿; ★ **SCR-**; z 18447; Ⓟ 7,222; © 7,027
Blakeslee; RMC Place; MONROE; ▲ Tobyhanna; **226** EI-10; 🅿; z 18610; ● 300
Blanchard; RMC Place; ALLEGHENY; ▲ West Deer; ***225** WL-4; ★ **PGH**; mail Tarentum z 15084; ● 120
Blanchard; CDP; CENTRE; ▲ Liberty; **226** EJ-1; 🅿; z 16826; © 621
Blanco; RMC Place; ARMSTRONG; ▲ Cowanshannock; ***225** WK-6; mail Rural Valley z 16249; rural
Blandburg; RMC Place; CAMBRIA; ▲ Reade; **225** WL-11; elev. 2,105ft./642m.; 🅿; z 16619; ● 550
Blandon; RMC Place; BERKS; ▲ Maidencreek; **227** EM-9; 🅿; ★ **READ**; z 19510; ● 1,200
Blanket Hill; RMC Place; ARMSTRONG; ▲ Kittanning; ***225** WK-6; mail Kittanning z 16201; rural
Blawnox; Inc. Place; ALLEGHENY; **228** I-8; elev. 900ft./274m.; 🅿; ★ **PGH**; z 15238; Ⓟ 1,626; © 1,550
Bloom; MCD-Township; CLEARFIELD; ***224** WJ-10; mail Grampian z 16838; Ⓟ 454; © 412
Bloomfield; RMC Place; ALLEGHENY; ***225** WM-4; 🅿; ★ **PGH**; z 15224; pop. incl. with Pittsburgh (Inc. Place)
Bloomfield; MCD-Township; BEDFORD; ***225** WO-11; mail New Enterprise z 16664; Ⓟ 766; © 973
Bloomfield; MCD-Township; CRAWFORD; ***224** WE-4; mail Union City z 16438; Ⓟ 1,839; © 2,051
Bloomfield; PERRY; see New Bloomfield (Inc. Place)
Bloomingdale; RMC Place; CARBON; ***227** EK-9; mail Summit Hill z 18250; pop. incl. with Summit Hill (Inc. Place)
Bloomingdale; RMC Place; LANCASTER; ▲ Manheim; **227** ES-9; ★ **LANC**; mail Lancaster z 17601; ● 2,100
Bloomingdale; RMC Place; LUZERNE; ▲ Ross; ***226** EI-7; mail Shickshinny z 18655; ● 100
Blooming Glen; RMC Place; BUCKS; ▲ Hilltown; **227** EN-12; 🅿; ★ **PHIL-**; z 18911; ● 650
Blooming Grove; RMC Place; PIKE; ▲ Blooming Grove; **226** EH-12; 🅿; z 18428; ● 200
Blooming Grove; MCD-Township; PIKE; ***226** EH-13; 🅿; z 18428 & mail Tafton z 18464; Ⓟ 2,022; © 3,621
Blooming Grove; RMC Place; YORK; ▲ Penn; **227** EQ-4; elev. 759ft./231m.; ★ **HANV**; mail Hanover z 17331; ● 100
Bloomington; RMC Place; CLEARFIELD; ▲ Pike; **224** WJ-10; mail Curwensville z 16833; ● 80
Bloomington; RMC Place; LACKAWANNA; ▲ Madison; ***226** EH-11; ★ **SCR-**; mail Moscow z 18444; rural
Blooming Valley; Inc. Place; CRAWFORD; **224** WF-4; elev. 1,260ft./384m.; mail Meadville z 16335; Ⓟ 391; © 378
Bloomsburg; Inc. Place; ⊡ COLUMBIA; **226** EJ-6; elev. 530ft./162m.; 🅿 🅷 🅲 8,723 ■; z 17815 & mail Lightstreet z 17839; Ⓟ 12,439; © 12,375; ◆ 12,220
Bloomsdale Gardens; RMC Place; BUCKS; ▲ Bristol; ***227** EO-14; elev. 20ft./6m.; ★ **PHIL-**; mail Levittown z 19058; ● 375
Bloserville; RMC Place; CUMBERLAND; ▲ Upper Frankford; **227** EO-2; mail Newville z 17241; ● 200
Bloss; MCD-Township; TIOGA; ***226** EF-3; mail Arnot z 16911; Ⓟ 388; © 354
Blossburg; Inc. Place; TIOGA; **226** EF-3; elev. 1,332ft./406m.; 🅿; z 16912; Ⓟ 1,571; © 1,480
Blosser Hill; RMC Place; FAYETTE; ▲ Springhill; ***225** WQ-4; ★ **MORG**; mail Point Marion z 15474; ● 120
Blossom Hill; RMC Place; LANCASTER; ▲ Manheim; ***227** EO-7; ★ **LANC**; mail Lancaster z 17601; ● 1,600
Blossom Valley; RMC Place; LANCASTER; ▲ Manheim; ★ **LANC**; mail Lancaster z 17601
Blough; RMC Place; SOMERSET; ▲ Quemahoning; **225** WO-8; mail Hooversville z 15936; ● 80
Blue Ball; CLEARFIELD; see West Decatur (RMC Place)
Blue Ball; RMC Place; LANCASTER; ▲ East Earl; **227** EO-8; 🅿; ★ **LANC**; z 17506; ● 800
Blue Bell; CDP; MONTGOMERY; ▲ Whitpain; **227** EO-12; 🅿; ★ **PHIL-**; z 19422, z 19424; Ⓟ 6,091; © 6,395
Blue Heron Pond; RMC Place; PIKE; ▲ Porter; ***226** EH-12; mail Dingmans Ferry z 18328; summer pop. 150; ● 10
Blue Hill; RMC Place; SNYDER; ▲ Monroe; ***227** EK-5; mail Selinsgrove z 17870; ● 250
Blue Jay; RMC Place; FOREST; ▲ Howe; ***224** WG-8; mail Sheffield z 16347; rural
Blue Knob; RMC Place; BLAIR; ▲ Juniata; ***225** WN-10; elev. 2,375ft./724m.; mail Portage z 15946
Blue Ridge; RMC Place; BUCKS; ▲ Bristol; ***227** EO-13; ★ **PHIL-**; mail Levittown z 19058
Blue Ridge; FRANKLIN; see Blue Ridge Summit (RMC Place)
Blue Ridge Summit (Blue Ridge); RMC Place; FRANKLIN; ▲ Washington; **227** ER-2; 🅿; ★ **HAG**; z 17214; ● 1,500
Bluff; RMC Place; GREENE; ▲ Jackson, Center; ***225** WQ-2; mail Holbrook z 15341
Blythe; MCD-Township; SCHUYLKILL; ***227** EL-8; ★ **PTSVL**; mail Cumbola z 17930; Ⓟ 1,023; © 905
Blytheburn; RMC Place; LUZERNE; ▲ Rice; ***226** EI-8; elev. 1,165ft./355m.; ★ **SCR-**; mail Mountain Top z 18707; ● 300
Blythedale; RMC Place; ALLEGHENY; ▲ Elizabeth; **225** WN-4; ★ **PGH**; mail Buena Vista z 15018; ● 250
Blythewood; RMC Place; BUCKS; ▲ New Britain; ★ **PHIL-**; mail Doylestown z 18901; ● 50
Boaba; RMC Place; PIKE; ▲ Lackawaxen; ***226** EG-12; elev. 900ft./274m.; mail Hawley z 18428; rural
Boalsburg; CDP; CENTRE; ▲ Harris; **225** WK-14; 🅿; ★ **STCOL**; z 16827; Ⓟ 2,206; © 3,578
Boardman; RMC Place; CLEARFIELD; ▲ Knox; **225** WK-11; mail Olanta z 16863; ● 35
Bobbys Corners; RMC Place; MERCER; ***224** WI-2; elev. 950ft./290m.; ★ **SHAR**; mail West Middlesex z 16159; pop. incl. with Hermitage (Inc. Place)
Bobtown; RMC Place; GREENE; ▲ Dunkard; **225** WQ-3; 🅿; z 15315; ● 1,100
Bocktown; RMC Place; BEAVER; ▲ Independence; ***225** WM-2; ★ **PGH**; mail Aliquippa z 15001
Bodines; RMC Place; LYCOMING; ▲ Lewis; **226** EG-4; ● 50
Boeckel Landing; RMC Place; YORK; ▲ Lower Chanceford; ***227** EQ-7; mail Airville z 17302; rural
Boggs; MCD-Township; ARMSTRONG; ***225** WK-6; mail Templeton z 16259; Ⓟ 981; © 979
Boggs; MCD-Township; CENTRE; ***224** WJ-13; mail Bellefonte z 16823; Ⓟ 2,686; © 2,834
Boggs; MCD-Township; CLEARFIELD; ***224** WJ-11; mail West Decatur z 16878; Ⓟ 1,907; © 1,837
Boggsville; RMC Place; ARMSTRONG; ▲ South Buffalo; ***225** WK-5; ★ **PGH**; mail Freeport z 16229, Sarver z 16055
Bohemia; RMC Place; PIKE; ***226** EG-12; mail Hawley z 18428; rural
Bohrmans Mill; RMC Place; SCHUYLKILL; ▲ North Manheim; ***227** EL-8; ★ **PTSVL**; mail Schuylkill Haven z 17972; ● 50
Boiling Springs; CDP; CUMBERLAND; ▲ South Middleton; **227** EO-3; 🅿; ★ **CARL**; z 17007; Ⓟ 1,978; © 2,769
Bolde Point; RMC Place; WAYNE; ▲ Paupack; ***226** EG-12; elev. 1,300ft./396m.; mail Hawley z 18428; ● 120
Bolivar; Inc. Place; WESTMORELAND; **225** WN-7; elev. 1,060ft./323m.; 🅿; z 15923; Ⓟ 544; © 501
Bolivar Run; RMC Place; MCKEAN; ▲ Foster; **224** WD-10; mail Bradford z 16701; ● 350
Boltz; RMC Place; INDIANA; ▲ East Wheatfield; **225** WM-8; ★ **JNST**; mail Seward z 15954; ● 160
Bon Air; RMC Place; CAMBRIA; ▲ Conemaugh; **225** WS-2; ★ **JNST**; mail Johnstown z 15902; ● 600
Bon Air; RMC Place; DELAWARE; ▲ Haverford; ***227** EP-11; ★ **PHIL-**; mail Havertown z 19083
Bon Aire; RMC Place; BUTLER; ▲ Butler; ***225** WK-4; ★ **BUTL**; mail Butler z 16001; ● 700
Bondsville; RMC Place; CHESTER; ▲ East Brandywine; ***227** EP-9; ★ **PHIL-**; mail Downingtown z 19335; ● 45
Bonnair; RMC Place; YORK; ▲ Shrewsbury; ***227** EQ-5; elev. 691ft./211m.; ★ **BAL**; mail Glen Rock z 17327; ● 30
Bonneauville; Inc. Place; ADAMS; **227** EQ-3; elev. 560ft./171m.; ★ **HANV**; mail Gettysburg z 17325; Ⓟ 1,282; © 1,378
Bonnie Brook; RMC Place; BUTLER; ▲ Summit; ***225** WK-4; elev. 1,411ft./430m.; ★ **BUTL**; mail Butler z 16001; rural
Bonus; RMC Place; BUTLER; ▲ Allegheny; ***224** WI-5; mail Parker z 16049; rural
Boone; RMC Place; SOMERSET; ▲ Stonycreek; ***225** WP-9; elev. 2,280ft./695m.; mail Central City z 15926; rural
Booneville; RMC Place; CLINTON; ▲ Logan; **226** EJ-2; mail Loganton z 17747; ● 75
Booths Corner; RMC Place; DELAWARE; ▲ Bethel; **227** EQ-11; elev. 391ft./119m.; ★ **PHIL-**; mail Marcus Hook z 19061; ● 200
Boothwyn; CDP; DELAWARE; ▲ Upper Chichester; ***227** EQ-11; 🅿; ★ **PHIL-**; z 19060-61; Ⓟ 5,069; © 5,206
Boothwyn Highlands; RMC Place; DELAWARE; ▲ Upper Chichester; ★ **PHIL-**; mail Marcus Hook z 19061
Boot Jack; RMC Place; ELK; ▲ Ridgway; ***224** WH-10; elev. 2,169ft./661m.; mail Ridgway z 15853; ● 80
Boquet; RMC Place; WESTMORELAND; ▲ Penn; ***225** WN-5; elev. 1,110ft./338m.; ★ **PGH**; mail Jeannette z 15644; ● 80
Bordnersville; RMC Place; LEBANON; ▲ Union; ***227** EM-6; mail Jonestown z 17038
Borland Manor; RMC Place; WASHINGTON; ▲ North Strabane; ***225** WN-3; ★ **PGH**; mail Canonsburg z 15317; ● 1,750
Bortondale; RMC Place; DELAWARE; ▲ Middletown; ***227** EP-11; ★ **PHIL-**; mail Media z 19063; ● 340
Bossardsville; RMC Place; MONROE; **226** EJ-11; mail Stroudsburg z 18360
Boston; RMC Place; ALLEGHENY; ▲ Elizabeth; **228** N-9; 🅿; ★ **PGH**; z 15135; ● 1,300
Boston Run; RMC Place; SCHUYLKILL; ▲ Mahanoy; ***227** EK-7; mail Mahanoy City z 17948; ● 30
Boswell; Inc. Place; SOMERSET; **225** WO-8; elev. 1,860ft./567m.; 🅿; z 15531; Ⓟ 1,485; © 1,364
Boulevard; RMC Place; PHILADELPHIA; ★ **PHIL-**; mail Philadelphia z 19149; pop. incl. with Philadelphia (Inc. Place)
Bourne; RMC Place; BRADFORD; ▲ West Burlington; ***226** EE-5; mail Ulster z 18850; rural
Bovard; RMC Place; BUTLER; ▲ Cherry; **224** WI-4; mail Boyers z 16020; ● 40
Bovard; RMC Place; WESTMORELAND; ▲ Hempfield; **225** WN-6; 🅿; ★ **PGH**; z 15619; ● 700
Bowdertown; RMC Place; INDIANA; ▲ Montgomery; ***225** WK-9; mail Cherry Tree z 15724; rural
Bower; RMC Place; CLEARFIELD; ▲ Greenwood; ***225** WK-10; elev. 1,220ft./372m.; mail Mahaffey z 15757; rural
Bower Hill; RMC Place; ALLEGHENY; ▲ Scott; ***225** WN-3; ★ **PGH**; mail Carnegie z 15106
Bower Hill; RMC Place; WASHINGTON; ▲ Peters; ***225** WN-3; ★ **PGH**; mail Venetia z 15367; rural
Bowers; RMC Place; BERKS; ▲ Maxatawny; ***227** EM-9; 🅿; z 19511; ● 300
Bowie; RMC Place; MERCER; ▲ Jackson; ***224** WH-3; mail Jackson Center z 16133; rural
Bowling Green; RMC Place; DELAWARE; ▲ Nether Providence; ***227** EP-11; ★ **PHIL-**; mail Media z 19063
Bowman Addition; RMC Place; YORK; ▲ Penn; ★ **HANV**; mail Hanover z 17331; ● 100
Bowman Heights; RMC Place; FRANKLIN; ▲ Hamilton; ***225** WP-14; elev. 700ft./213m.; mail Chambersburg z 17201; ● 100
Bowmans; RMC Place; SCHUYLKILL; ▲ Mahanoy; ***227** EK-8; mail Mahanoy City z 17948; ● 25
Bowmansdale; RMC Place; CUMBERLAND; ▲ Upper Allen; ***227** EO-4; 🅿; ★ **HRBG**; z 17055; ● 275
Bowmans Store; RMC Place; YORK; ▲ Codorus; ***227** EQ-5; ★ **BAL**; mail Glenville z 17329; rural
Bowmanstown; Inc. Place; CARBON; **227** EK-10; elev. 440ft./134m.; 🅿; z 18030; Ⓟ 888; © 895
Bowmansville; RMC Place; LANCASTER; ▲ Brecknock; **227** EO-8; 🅿; z 17507; ● 500
Bowood; RMC Place; FAYETTE; ▲ Nicholson; ***225** WQ-4; mail Smithfield z 15478; rural
Boyce; RMC Place; ALLEGHENY; ▲ Upper St. Clair; ***225** WN-3; ★ **PGH**; mail Pittsburgh z 15241
Boyds Mills; RMC Place; WAYNE; ▲ Damascus; **226** EF-12; elev. 1,110ft./338m.; mail Milanville z 18443; ● 85
Boydstown; RMC Place; BUTLER; ▲ Oakland; **224** WJ-4; ★ **BUTL**; mail Chicora z 16025; ● 50
Boydtown; RMC Place; NORTHUMBERLAND; ▲ Coal; ***227** EK-6; mail Shamokin z 17872; ● 100
Boyers; BUTLER; see Annandale (RMC Place)
Boyers Junction; RMC Place; BERKS; ▲ Rockland; ***227** EM-9; elev. 671ft./205m.; ★ **READ**; mail Fleetwood z 19522; rural
Boyertown; Inc. Place; BERKS; **227** EN-10; elev. 415ft./126m.; 🅿; z 19512; Ⓟ 3,759; © 3,940
Boynton; RMC Place; SOMERSET; ▲ Elk Lick; **225** WQ-8; 🅿; z 15532; ● 200
Brackenridge; Inc. Place; ALLEGHENY; **225** WL-5; elev. 760ft./232m.; 🅿; ★ **PGH**; z 15014; Ⓟ 3,784; © 3,543
Brackney; RMC Place; SUSQUEHANNA; ▲ Silver Lake; **226** ED-8; 🅿; z 18812; ● 200
Bradbury Plan; RMC Place; BEAVER; ▲ Hopewell; ***225** WM-2; ★ **PGH**; mail Aliquippa z 15001; ● 500
Braddock; Inc. Place; ALLEGHENY; **228** K-8; elev. 825ft./251m.; 🅿 🅷; ★ **PGH**; z 15104; Ⓟ 4,682; © 2,912
Braddock; RMC Place; WASHINGTON; ▲ Amwell; ***225** WO-2; elev. 1,342ft./409m.; ★ **WASH**; mail Washington z 15301; ● 50
Braddock Hills; Inc. Place; ALLEGHENY; **228** K-8; ★ **PGH**; mail Pittsburgh z 15221; Ⓟ 2,026; © 1,998
Braden Plan; RMC Place; GREENE; ▲ Jefferson; **225** WP-3; mail Clarksville z 15322; ● 250
Bradenville; RMC Place; WESTMORELAND; ▲ Derry; **225** WN-6; 🅿; ★ **LTROB**; z 15620; ● 1,300
Bradford; MCD-Township; CLEARFIELD; ***224** WJ-11; mail Woodland z 16881; Ⓟ 2,504; © 3,314
Bradford; Inc. Place; MCKEAN; **224** WD-10; elev. 1,442ft./440m.; 🅿 🅷 🅲 1,325 ■; z 16701; Ⓟ 9,625; © 9,175; ◆ 8,343
Bradford; MCD-Township; MCKEAN; ***224** WE-10; 🅿 🅲 1,325; z 16701; does not include the City of Bradford; Ⓟ 5,065; © 4,816
BRADFORD; **226** EE-6; Ⓟ 60,967; © 62,761; ◆ 61,113
Bradford Hills; RMC Place; CHESTER; ▲ West Whiteland; ***227** EP-10; ★ **PHIL-**; mail Downingtown z 19335; ● 170
Bradford Park; RMC Place; BEAVER; ***225** WL-3; elev. 1,274ft./388m.; ★ **PGH**; mail Baden z 15005; pop. incl. with Economy (Inc. Place)
Bradford Woods; Inc. Place; ALLEGHENY; ***225** WL-3; elev. 1,200ft./366m.; 🅿; ★ **PGH**; z 15015; Ⓟ 1,329; © 1,149
Bradley Junction; RMC Place; CAMBRIA; ▲ East Carroll, Allegheny; ***225** WM-10; mail Ebensburg z 15931; rural
Bradleytown; RMC Place; VENANGO; ▲ Plum; **224** WG-4; elev. 1,217ft./371m.; mail Cooperstown z 16317; ● 50
Brady; MCD-Township; BUTLER; ***224** WJ-4; mail Slippery Rock z 16057; Ⓟ 834; © 1,452
Brady; MCD-Township; CLARION; ***224** WJ-5; mail Rimersburg z 16248; Ⓟ 78; © 62
Brady; RMC Place; CLEARFIELD; mail Du Bois z 15801; pop. incl. with Du Bois (Inc. Place)
Brady; MCD-Township; CLEARFIELD; ***224** WJ-9; mail Luthersburg z 15848; Ⓟ 2,023; © 2,010
Brady; MCD-Township; HUNTINGDON; ***225** WM-13; mail Allensville z 17002; Ⓟ 1,053; © 1,035
Brady; MCD-Township; LYCOMING; ***226** EI-4; ★ **WMSPT**; mail Montgomery z 17752; Ⓟ 822; © 494; Ⓡ 1,351
Bradys Bend; RMC Place; ARMSTRONG; ▲ Bradys Bend; **224** WJ-5; mail East Brady z 16028; ● 150
Bradys Bend; MCD-Township; ARMSTRONG; ***224** WJ-5; mail East Brady z 16028; Ⓟ 963; © 939
Braeburn; RMC Place; WESTMORELAND; ***225** WL-5; ★ **PGH**; mail New Kensington z 15068; pop. incl. with Lower Burrell (Inc. Place)
Braintrim; MCD-Township; WYOMING; ***226** EF-8; mail Laceyville z 18623; Ⓟ 465; © 508
Braman; RMC Place; WAYNE; ▲ Manchester; ***226** EE-12; mail Equinunk z 18417; ● 25
Bramcote; RMC Place; MONTGOMERY; ▲ West Pottsgrove; ★ **PTSTN**; mail Pottstown z 19464
Branch; MCD-Township; SCHUYLKILL; ***227** EL-7; ★ **PTSVL**; mail Pottsville z 17901; Ⓟ 2,051; © 1,871
Branchdale; CDP; SCHUYLKILL; ▲ Reilly; **227** EL-7; 🅿; z 17923; © 436
Branchton; RMC Place; BUTLER; ▲ Slippery Rock; **224** WI-4; elev. 1,201ft./366m.; 🅿; z 16021; ● 80
Branchville; RMC Place; ERIE; ▲ McKean; ***224** WD-3; ★ **ERIE**; mail Mc Kean z 16426
Brandamore; RMC Place; CHESTER; ▲ West Brandywine; **227** EP-9; 🅿; ★ **PHIL-**; z 19316; ● 300
Brandon; RMC Place; VENANGO; ▲ Rockland; ***224** WH-4; mail Kennerdell z 16374; ● 25
Brandonville; CDP; SCHUYLKILL; ▲ East Union; **227** EK-7; mail Ringtown z 17967; © 217
Brandt; RMC Place; SUSQUEHANNA; ▲ Harmony; ***226** ED-10; mail Susquehanna z 18847; ● 40
Brandtsville; RMC Place; CUMBERLAND; ▲ Monroe; ***227** EO-3; ★ **HRBG**; mail Mechanicsburg z 17055
Brandy Camp; RMC Place; ELK; ▲ Horton; **224** WH-9; 🅿; z 15822; ● 200

Entries in **UPPERCASE** are counties.
Entries in **bold** have populations of 2,500 or more.
Names in parentheses are alternate names.
Inc. Place — Incorporated Place
RMC Place — Rand McNally Designated Place
CDP — Census Designated Place
MCD — Minor Civil Division

⊡ County Seat
▲ Minor Civil Division
elev. Elevation
🅿 Post Office
🅷 Hospital
🅲 College
■ Principal Business Center
★ Ranally Metro Area (RMA) Abbreviation
z Zip Code(s)
Ⓟ Previous Census Population
Ⓡ Revised Census Population
Ⓐ Annexation Population
● Rand McNally Population Estimate
© Final Census Population
Ⓢ Special Census Population
◆ Estimated Population

For additional definitions see Glossary, Volume 1, and Introduction, Volume 2.

Brandywine Homes; RMC Place; CHESTER; ▲ Caln; ***227** EP-9; ★ **PHIL-**; mail Coatesville z 19320; ● 400
Brandywine Manor; RMC Place; CHESTER; ▲ West Brandywine; **227** EP-9; ★ **PHIL-**; mail Glenmoore z 19343, Honey Brook z 19344; ● 200
Brandywine Summit; RMC Place; DELAWARE; ▲ Concord; ***227** EQ-10; ★ **PHIL-**; mail Glen Mills z 19342; ● 165
Brandywine Village; RMC Place; MONTGOMERY; ▲ Upper Merion; ***227** EO-11; ★ **PHIL-**; mail King of Prussia z 19406
Bratton; MCD-Township; MIFFLIN; ***225** WM-14; mail Lewistown z 17044; Ⓟ 1,427; Ⓒ 1,259
Brave; RMC Place; GREENE; ▲ Wayne; **225** WQ-2; 🅿; z 15316; ● 200
Braznell; RMC Place; FAYETTE; ▲ Redstone; ***225** WP-4; ★ **UNTN**; mail Grindstone z 15442; ● 180
Breakneck; RMC Place; FAYETTE; ▲ Bullskin; ***225** WP-6; mail Connellsville z 15425
Brecknock; MCD-Township; BERKS; ***227** EN-8; ★ **READ**; mail Mohnton z 19540; Ⓟ 3,770; Ⓒ 4,459
Brecknock; MCD-Township; LANCASTER; ***227** EO-8; mail Denver z 17517; Ⓟ 5,197; Ⓒ 6,699
Breezewood; RMC Place; BEDFORD; ▲ East Providence; **225** WP-11; 🅿; z 15533; ● 300
Breezy Corner; RMC Place; BERKS; ▲ Ruscombmanor; ***227** EN-9; ★ **READ**; mail Fleetwood z 19522; rural
Breinigsville; RMC Place; LEHIGH; ▲ Upper Macungie; **227** EM-10; elev. 406ft./124m.; 🅿; ★ **ALL-**; z 18031; ● 500
Brenizer; RMC Place; WESTMORELAND; ▲ Derry; ***225** WN-7; ★ **LTROB**; mail Blairsville z 15717; ● 325
Brent; RMC Place; LAWRENCE; ▲ Plain Grove; **224** WI-3; mail Volant z 16156; ● 90
Brentwood; Inc. Place; ALLEGHENY; **225** WN-4; elev. 1,220ft./372m.; 🅿; ★ **PGH**; z 15227; Ⓟ 10,823; Ⓒ 10,466
Breslau; RMC Place; LUZERNE; ▲ Hanover; **226** EA-7; ★ **SCR-**; mail Wilkes Barre z 18706; ● 500
Bressler; RMC Place; DAUPHIN; ▲ Swatara; **227** ET-4; 🅿; ★ **HRBG**; z 17113; ● 850
Bressler-Enhaut-Oberlin; CDP-Census Area Only; DAUPHIN; ▲ Swatara; ***227** EO-5; elev. 500ft./152m.; ★ **HRBG**; mail Harrisburg z 17113; Ⓟ 2,660; Ⓒ 2,809
Bretonville; RMC Place; CLEARFIELD; ▲ Jordan; ***225** WK-10; mail Irvona z 16656; rural
Briarbrook; RMC Place; LUZERNE; ▲ Fairview; ★ **SCR-**; mail Mountain Top z 18707
Briarcliff; RMC Place; DELAWARE; ▲ Darby; ***227** EP-12; ★ **PHIL-**; mail Glenolden z 19036
Briar Creek; Inc. Place; COLUMBIA; **226** EJ-7; elev. 500ft./152m.; mail Berwick z 18603; Ⓟ 616; Ⓒ 651
Briar Creek; MCD-Township; COLUMBIA; ***226** EI-7; mail Berwick z 18603, Pittsburgh z 15238; does not include the Borough of Briar Creek; Ⓟ 3,010; Ⓒ 3,061
Briar Hill; RMC Place; ARMSTRONG; ▲ East Franklin; ***225** WK-6; elev. 1,200ft./366m.; ★ **PGH**; mail Kittanning z 16201; ● 40
Briar Hill; RMC Place; WAYNE; ▲ Paupack; ***226** EH-11; elev. 1,401ft./427m.; ★ **SCR-**; mail Lakeville z 18438; summer pop. 300; ● 100
Brick Church; RMC Place; ARMSTRONG; ▲ Burrell; ***225** WL-6; mail Ford City z 16226
Brickerville; CDP; LANCASTER; ▲ Elizabeth; **227** EO-7; ★ **LANC**; mail Lititz z 17543; Ⓟ 1,268; Ⓒ 1,287
Brick Tavern; RMC Place; BUCKS; ▲ Milford; ***227** EM-11; ★ **PHIL-**; mail Quakertown z 18951; ● 90
Bridesburg; RMC Place; PHILADELPHIA; ***227** EP-13; ★ **PHIL-**; mail Philadelphia z 19137; pop. incl. with Philadelphia (Inc. Place)
Bridgeburg; RMC Place; ARMSTRONG; ▲ East Franklin; ***225** WK-6; ★ **PGH**; mail Adrian z 16210
Bridgeport; RMC Place; ADAMS; ▲ Franklin; ***227** EP-2; mail Biglerville z 17307; rural
Bridgeport; RMC Place; CARBON; ▲ Kidder; **226** EJ-9; mail White Haven z 18661; ● 25
Bridgeport; RMC Place; CLEARFIELD; ▲ Pike; ***224** WJ-10; mail Curwensville z 16833; rural
Bridgeport; RMC Place; LANCASTER; ▲ East Lampeter; ***227** EP-7; ★ **LANC**; mail Lancaster z 17602; ● 500
Bridgeport; Inc. Place; MONTGOMERY; **227** EO-11; elev. 120ft./37m.; 🅿; ★ **PHIL-**; z 19405; Ⓟ 4,292; Ⓒ 4,371
Bridgeport; RMC Place; PERRY; ▲ Spring; **227** EN-2; mail Landisburg z 17040; ● 40
Bridgeport; RMC Place; WESTMORELAND; ▲ Mount Pleasant; ***225** WO-6; mail Mount Pleasant z 15666; ● 150
Bridgeton; MCD-Township; BUCKS; ***227** EM-12; ★ **PHIL-**; mail Upper Black Eddy z 18972; Ⓟ 1,378; Ⓒ 1,408
Bridgeton; RMC Place; YORK; ▲ Fawn; ***227** EQ-6; elev. 312ft./95m.; ★ **BAL**; mail Fawn Grove z 17321, New Park z 17352
Bridgetown; RMC Place; BUCKS; ▲ Northampton, Middletown; ***227** EO-13; ★ **PHIL-**; mail Langhorne z 19047; ● 600
Bridge Valley; RMC Place; BUCKS; ▲ Warwick, Buckingham; ***227** EN-12; ★ **PHIL-**; mail Furlong z 18925, Jamison z 18929; ● 150
Bridgeville; Inc. Place; ALLEGHENY; **225** WN-3; elev. 825ft./251m.; 🅿 🅷; ★ **PGH**; z 15017; Ⓟ 5,445; Ⓒ 5,341
Bridgewater (West Bridgewater); Inc. Place; BEAVER; **225** WL-2; elev. 720ft./219m.; ★ **PGH**; mail Beaver z 15009; Ⓟ 751; Ⓒ 739
Bridgewater; RMC Place; BUCKS; ▲ Bensalem; **228** B-9; ★ **PHIL-**; mail Bensalem z 19020; ● 250
Bridgewater; MCD-Township; SUSQUEHANNA; ***226** EE-9; mail Montrose z 18801; Ⓟ 2,368; Ⓒ 2,668
Bridgewater Farms; RMC Place; DELAWARE; ▲ Aston; ★ **PHIL-**; mail Aston z 19014
Brier Hill; RMC Place; FAYETTE; ▲ Redstone; ***225** WP-4; 🅿; ★ **UNTN**; z 15415; ● 120
Briggsville; RMC Place; LUZERNE; ▲ Nescopeck; ***226** EJ-8; mail Nescopeck z 18635; rural
Brighton; MCD-Township; BEAVER; ***225** WL-2; ★ **PGH**; mail Beaver z 15009; Ⓟ 7,489; Ⓒ 8,024
Brightwood; RMC Place; ALLEGHENY; ***225** WN-3; ★ **PGH**; mail Bethel Park z 15102; pop. incl. with Bethel Park (Inc. Place)
Brilhart; RMC Place; YORK; ▲ York; ***227** EQ-5; ★ **YORK**; mail York z 17404; rural
Brinker; RMC Place; BUTLER; ▲ Summit; ***225** WK-4; ★ **BUTL**; mail Butler z 16001; rural
Brinkerton; RMC Place; WESTMORELAND; ▲ Mount Pleasant; ***225** WO-6; mail Greensburg z 15601; ● 60
Brintons; RMC Place; CHESTER; ▲ Birmingham; ***227** EQ-10; ★ **PHIL-**; mail West Chester z 19380; rural
Briquette; RMC Place; ALLEGHENY; ★ **PGH**; pop. incl. with Duquesne (Inc. Place)
Brisbin; Inc. Place; CLEARFIELD; **225** WK-11; elev. 1,520ft./463m.; 🅿; z 16620; Ⓟ 369; Ⓒ 413
Briscoe Springs; MERCER; see Perrys Corners (RMC Place)
Bristol; Inc. Place; BUCKS; **227** EO-13; elev. 20ft./6m.; 🅿 🅷; ★ **PHIL-**; z 19007; Ⓟ 10,405; Ⓒ 9,923
Bristol; MCD-Township; BUCKS; ***227** EO-13; 🅿; ★ **PHIL-**; z 19007 & mail Croydon z 19021; does not include the Borough of Bristol; Ⓟ 57,129; Ⓒ 55,521; ◆ 53,533
Bristol Terrace Number 1; BUCKS; see Greenlawn Park (RMC Place)
Bristoria; RMC Place; GREENE; ▲ Richhill; **225** WQ-2; mail Graysville z 15337; ● 40
Brittany Farms; RMC Place; BUCKS; ▲ New Britain; ***227** EN-12; elev. 400ft./122m.; ★ **PHIL-**; mail Chalfont z 18914; ● 2,000
Brittany Farms-Highlands; CDP-Census Area Only; BUCKS; ▲ New Britain; ***227** EN-12; elev. 418ft./127m.; ★ **PHIL-**; mail Chalfont z 18914; Ⓟ 2,747; Ⓒ 3,268
Britton Run; RMC Place; CRAWFORD; ▲ Sparta; ***224** WE-5; mail Spartansburg z 16434
Broad Acres; RMC Place; MERCER; ▲ Pine; ***224** WI-3; mail Grove City z 16127; ● 150
Broad Axe; RMC Place; MONTGOMERY; ▲ Whitpain; ***227** EO-12; elev. 289ft./88m.; ★ **PHIL-**; mail Ambler z 19002; ● 300
Broad Ford; RMC Place; FAYETTE; ▲ Upper Tyrone, Connellsville; ***225** WP-5; elev. 862ft./263m.; mail Connellsville z 15425; rural
Broadlawn Highlands; RMC Place; ALLEGHENY; ▲ Upper St. Clair; ***225** WN-3; ★ **PGH**; mail Pittsburgh z 15241
Broad Street; RMC Place; LUZERNE; ★ **HAZ**; mail Hazleton z 18201-02; pop. incl. with Hazleton (Inc. Place)
Broad Top; MCD-Township; BEDFORD; ***225** WP-11; mail Six Mile Run z 16679; Ⓟ 1,918; Ⓒ 1,827
Broad Top; HUNTINGDON; see Broad Top City (Inc. Place)
Broad Top City (Broad Top); Inc. Place; HUNTINGDON; **225** WO-12; elev. 1,978ft./603m.; mail Broad Top z 16621; Ⓟ 331; Ⓒ 384
Broadview; RMC Place; ALLEGHENY; ▲ Frazer; ***225** WL-5; ★ **PGH**; mail Tarentum z 15084; ● 300
Broadway; RMC Place; LUZERNE; ▲ Ross; ***226** EI-7; elev. 1,150ft./351m.; mail Shickshinny z 18655; ● 120
Broadway Manor; RMC Place; BUCKS; ▲ Bristol; ★ **PHIL-**; mail Bristol z 19007
Brock; RMC Place; GREENE; ▲ Wayne, Perry; ***225** WQ-3; mail Spraggs z 15362; rural
Brockport; RMC Place; ELK; ▲ Horton; **224** WH-9; elev. 1,480ft./451m.; 🅿; z 15823; ● 300
Brockton; RMC Place; SCHUYLKILL; ▲ Schuylkill; **227** EK-8; 🅿; ★ **PTSVL**; z 17925; ● 500
Brockway (Brockwayville); Inc. Place; JEFFERSON; **224** WI-9; elev. 1,441ft./439m.; 🅿; z 15824; Ⓟ 2,207; Ⓒ 2,182
Brockwayville; JEFFERSON; see Brockway (Inc. Place)
Brodbecks; RMC Place; YORK; ▲ Manheim, Codorus; ***227** EQ-5; 🅿; ★ **BAL**; z 17329
Brodhead; RMC Place; NORTHAMPTON; ▲ Bethlehem; **226** EA-5; ★ **ALL-**; mail Bethlehem z 18017, z 18020; ● 100
Brodheadsville; CDP; MONROE; ▲ Chestnuthill; **226** EJ-11; 🅿; ★ **ALL-**; z 18322; Ⓟ 1,389; Ⓒ 1,637
Brogue; RMC Place; YORK; ▲ Chanceford; **227** EQ-6; elev. 803ft./245m.; 🅿; ★ **YORK**; z 17309; ● 200
Brogueville (Parks); RMC Place; YORK; ▲ Chanceford; ***227** EQ-6; elev. 477ft./145m.; ★ **YORK**; mail Felton z 17322; ● 45
Brokenstraw; MCD-Township; WARREN; ***224** WE-7; mail Pittsfield z 16340; Ⓟ 1,962; Ⓒ 2,068
Brommerstown; RMC Place; SCHUYLKILL; ▲ South Manheim; ***227** EL-8; ★ **PTSVL**; mail Auburn z 17922; rural
Brookdale; RMC Place; CAMBRIA; ▲ East Taylor; ***225** WN-9; ★ **JNST**; mail Mineral Point z 15942; ● 50
Brookdale; RMC Place; SUSQUEHANNA; ▲ Liberty; **226** ED-9; mail Hallstead z 18822; ● 60
Brookes Mill; RMC Place; BLAIR; ▲ Blair; ***225** WN-11; ★ **ALT**; mail Duncansville z 16635; rural
Brookfield; MCD-Township; TIOGA; ***226** ED-1; mail Westfield z 16950; Ⓟ 432; Ⓒ 443
Brookhaven; Inc. Place; DELAWARE; **227** EQ-11; elev. 119ft./36m.; 🅿; ★ **PHIL-**; z 19015; Ⓟ 8,567; Ⓒ 7,985
Brookland; RMC Place; POTTER; ▲ Ulysses; **224** WE-13; mail Ulysses z 16948; ● 15
Brookline; RMC Place; ALLEGHENY; ***225** WM-3; 🅿; ★ **PGH**; z 15226 & mail Havertown z 19083; pop. incl. with Pittsburgh (Inc. Place)
Brookline; RMC Place; DELAWARE; ▲ Haverford; ***227** EP-11; ★ **PHIL-**; mail Havertown z 19083
Brooklyn; RMC Place; SUSQUEHANNA; ▲ Brooklyn; **226** EF-9; elev. 1,101ft./336m.; 🅿; z 18813; ● 250
Brooklyn; MCD-Township; SUSQUEHANNA; ***226** EF-9; 🅿; z 18813; Ⓟ 873; Ⓒ 889
Brooklyn (Tioga); RMC Place; TIOGA; ▲ Tioga; ***226** EE-3; 🅿; z 16946
Brookside; RMC Place; CUMBERLAND; ▲ South Newton; ***227** EP-2; mail Shippensburg z 17257; ● 45
Brookside; RMC Place; ERIE; ▲ Harborcreek; **224** WC-4; ★ **ERIE**; mail Erie z 16510; ● 2,200
Brookside; RMC Place; LYCOMING; ▲ Cogan House; ***226** EH-3; elev. 1,267ft./386m.; mail Trout Run z 17771
Brookside; RMC Place; SCHUYLKILL; ▲ Pine Grove; mail Pine Grove z 17963; rural
Brookside; RMC Place; YORK; ▲ Dover; ***227** EQ-4; ★ **YORK**; mail Dover z 17315; ● 220
Brookside Farms; RMC Place; ALLEGHENY; ▲ Upper St. Clair; ★ **PGH**; mail Pittsburgh z 15241
Brookside Villa; RMC Place; LEHIGH; ▲ Lower Macungie; ***227** EM-10; elev. 450ft./137m.; ★ **ALL-**; mail Allentown z 18101; ● 650
Brookston; RMC Place; FOREST; ▲ Howe; **224** WF-8; elev. 1,419ft./433m.; mail Sheffield z 16347; ● 90
Brookthorpe Hills; RMC Place; DELAWARE; ▲ Marple; ***227** EP-11; ★ **PHIL-**; mail Broomall z 19008
Brookville; Inc. Place; ⊡ JEFFERSON; **224** WI-8; elev. 1,269ft./387m.; 🅿 🅷; z 15825; Ⓟ 4,184; Ⓒ 4,230
Brookwater Park; RMC Place; MONTGOMERY; ▲ Perkiomen; ★ **PHIL-**; mail Collegeville z 19426; ● 250
Broomall; CDP; DELAWARE; ▲ Marple; **227** EP-11; 🅿; ★ **PHIL-**; z 19008; Ⓟ 10,930; Ⓒ 11,046
Brothersvalley; MCD-Township; SOMERSET; ***225** WQ-8; mail Berlin z 15530; Ⓟ 2,395; Ⓒ 4,184; Ⓡ 2,415
Brotherton; RMC Place; SOMERSET; ▲ Brothersvalley; **225** WP-8; mail Berlin z 15530; ● 60
Broughton; RMC Place; ALLEGHENY; ▲ South Park; **228** M-6; ★ **PGH**; mail Pittsburgh z 15236; ● 3,000
Brown; MCD-Township; LYCOMING; ***226** EG-1; mail Cedar Run z 17727; Ⓟ 102; Ⓒ 111
Brown; MCD-Township; MIFFLIN; ***227** EL-1; mail Reedsville z 17084; Ⓟ 3,320; Ⓒ 3,852
Brownbacks; RMC Place; CHESTER; ▲ East Coventry; ***227** EO-10; elev. 409ft./125m.; ★ **PTSTN**; mail Spring City z 19475; rural
Browndale; RMC Place; WAYNE; ▲ Clinton; **226** EF-11; 🅿; z 18421; ● 525
Brownfield; RMC Place; FAYETTE; ▲ South Union; **225** WQ-5; 🅿; ★ **UNTN**; z 15416; ● 400
Brown Hill; RMC Place; CRAWFORD; ▲ Rockdale; ***224** WE-4; mail Cambridge Springs z 16403
Browns; RMC Place; LUZERNE; ***226** EH-9; ★ **SCR-**; mail Pittston z 18641; pop. incl. with Avoca (Inc. Place)
Brownsburg; RMC Place; BUCKS; ▲ Upper Makefield; ***227** EN-13; ★ **PHIL-**; mail New Hope z 18938; ● 50
Brownsdale; RMC Place; BUTLER; ▲ Penn; ***225** WK-4; ★ **PGH**; mail Renfrew z 16053; ● 60
Browns Mill; RMC Place; FRANKLIN; ***225** WQ-14; ★ **HAG**; mail Chambersburg z 17201; ● 50
Browns Mill; JUNIATA; see Cocolamus (RMC Place)
Brownstown; RMC Place; ARMSTRONG; ▲ Kiskiminetas; **225** WM-6; elev. 1,358ft./414m.; ★ **PGH**; ● 30
Brownstown; Inc. Place; CAMBRIA; **225** WN-8; elev. 1,443ft./440m.; ★ **JNST**; mail Johnstown z 15906; Ⓟ 937; Ⓒ 883
Brownstown; RMC Place; FAYETTE; ▲ Washington; ***225** WO-4; ★ **PGH**; mail Fayette City z 15438; ● 400
Brownstown; RMC Place; LANCASTER; ▲ West Earl; **227** EO-7; 🅿; ★ **LANC**; z 17508; ● 1,000
Brownsville; RMC Place; BERKS; ▲ Lower Heidelberg; ***227** EN-8; elev. 380ft./116m.; ★ **READ**; mail Wernersville z 19565; ● 65
Brownsville; Inc. Place; FAYETTE; **225** WP-4; elev. 1,100ft./335m.; 🅿 🅷; ★ **UNTN**; z 15417; Ⓟ 3,164; Ⓒ 2,804
Brownsville; MCD-Township; FAYETTE; ***225** WP-4; 🅿; ★ **UNTN**; z 15417; does not include the Borough of Brownsville; Ⓟ 847; Ⓒ 769
Brownsville; RMC Place; FRANKLIN; ▲ Greene; ***227** EQ-1; mail Fayetteville z 17222; ● 60
Brownsville; RMC Place; SCHUYLKILL; ▲ West Mahanoy; mail Shenandoah z 17976; ● 150
Brownsville Junction; RMC Place; FAYETTE; ▲ Brownsville; ★ **UNTN**; mail Brownsville z 15417
Browntown; RMC Place; BRADFORD; ▲ Wyalusing; **226** EF-7; mail Wyalusing z 18853; ● 90
Browntown; RMC Place; LUZERNE; ▲ Pittston; **226** EB-9; ★ **SCR-**; mail Pittston z 18640; ● 900
Bruceton; RMC Place; ALLEGHENY; ▲ South Park; ***225** WN-4; ★ **PGH**; pop. incl. with Jefferson (Inc. Place)
Bruckarts; LANCASTER; see Silver Spring (RMC Place)
Bruin; Inc. Place; BUTLER; **224** WJ-5; elev. 1,094ft./333m.; 🅿; z 16022; Ⓟ 646; Ⓒ 534
Brumfieldville; BERKS; see Weavertown (RMC Place)
Brunnerville; RMC Place; LANCASTER; ▲ Warwick; **227** EO-7; 🅿; ★ **LANC**; z 17543; ● 250
Brunot Island; RMC Place; ALLEGHENY; ***225** WM-3; ★ **PGH**; mail Pittsburgh z 15233; pop. incl. with Pittsburgh (Inc. Place)
Brush Creek; MCD-Township; FULTON; ***225** WP-12; mail Crystal Spring z 15536; Ⓟ 643; Ⓒ 730
Brushtown; RMC Place; ADAMS; ▲ Conewago; **227** EQ-4; ★ **HANV**; mail Hanover z 17331; ● 340
Brushtown; RMC Place; CUMBERLAND; ▲ Penn; ***227** EO-2; mail Newville z 17241
Brush Valley; RMC Place; INDIANA; ▲ Brush Valley; **225** WM-8; 🅿; z 15720; ● 300
Brush Valley; MCD-Township; INDIANA; ***225** WM-8; 🅿; z 15720; Ⓟ 1,811; Ⓒ 1,881
Brushville; RMC Place; SUSQUEHANNA; ▲ Oakland; ***226** EE-10; ★ **BING**; mail Susquehanna z 18847; ● 35
Bryan; RMC Place; ARMSTRONG; ▲ Cowanshannock; **225** WK-7; mail Dayton z 16222; ● 30
Bryan; RMC Place; FAYETTE; ▲ Lower Tyrone; ***225** WO-5; mail Dawson z 15428; ● 50
Bryan Hill Manor; RMC Place; INDIANA; ▲ White; ***225** WL-7; mail Indiana z 15701; ● 150
Bryan Mills; RMC Place; LYCOMING; ▲ Wolf; ***226** EI-5; ★ **WMSPT**; mail Hughesville z 17737; rural
Bryansville; RMC Place; YORK; ▲ Peach Bottom; ***227** EQ-7; ★ **BAL**; mail Delta z 17314; ● 50
Bryant; RMC Place; ALLEGHENY; ★ **PGH**; mail Allison Park z 15101
Bryn Athyn; Inc. Place; MONTGOMERY; **227** EO-13; elev. 200ft./61m.; 🅿; ★ **PHIL-**; z 19009; Ⓟ 1,081; Ⓒ 1,351
Bryn Gweled; RMC Place; BUCKS; ▲ Upper Southampton; ***227** EO-13; elev. 150ft./46m.; ★ **PHIL-**; mail Southampton z 18966; ● 700
Bryn Mawr; RMC Place; ALLEGHENY; ***225** WN-3; ★ **PGH**; mail Pittsburgh z 15241
Bryn Mawr; CDP; MONTGOMERY; ▲ Lower Merion; **228** C-1; 🅿 🅷 🅲 1,799; ★ **PHIL-**; z 19010; Ⓟ 3,271; Ⓒ 4,382; Ⓡ 4,242
Brysonia; RMC Place; ADAMS; ▲ Menallen; ***227** EP-2; mail Biglerville z 17307; rural
Bucher; RMC Place; CLEARFIELD; ▲ Bigler; mail Madera z 16661; rural
Buck; RMC Place; LANCASTER; ▲ East Drumore, Drumore; **227** EQ-7; elev. 715ft./218m.; mail Quarryville z 17566; ● 120
Buck; MCD-Township; LUZERNE; ***226** EI-10; mail Blakeslee z 18610; Ⓟ 375; Ⓒ 396
Buckeye; RMC Place; WESTMORELAND; ▲ East Huntingdon; ***225** WO-6; elev. 1,076ft./328m.; mail Mount Pleasant z 15666; ● 90
Buck Hill Falls; RMC Place; MONROE; ▲ Barrett; **226** EI-11; 🅿; z 18323; ● 950
Buckhorn; RMC Place; CAMBRIA; ▲ Gallitzin; **225** WM-10; ★ **ALT**; mail Ashville z 16613; ● 130
Buckhorn; CDP; COLUMBIA; ▲ Hemlock; **226** EJ-6; elev. 602ft./183m.; mail Bloomsburg z 17815; Ⓒ 176
Buckingham; RMC Place; BUCKS; ▲ Buckingham; **227** EN-13; 🅿; ★ **PHIL-**; z 18912; ● 2,000
Buckingham; MCD-Township; BUCKS; ***227** EN-12; 🅿; ★ **PHIL-**; z 18912; Ⓟ 9,364; Ⓒ 16,442
Buckingham; MCD-Township; WAYNE; ***226** EE-12; mail Lake Como z 18437; Ⓟ 648; Ⓒ 656
Buckingham Valley; RMC Place; BUCKS; ▲ Buckingham; ***227** EN-13; ★ **PHIL-**; mail New Hope z 18938; ● 250
Buckland Valley Farms; RMC Place; BUCKS; ▲ Upper Makefield; ***227** EN-13; ★ **PHIL-**; mail Washington Crossing z 18977; rural
Buckman Village; RMC Place; DELAWARE; ★ **PHIL-**; mail Chester z 19013; pop. incl. with Chester (Inc. Place)
Buckmanville; RMC Place; BUCKS; ▲ Upper Makefield; ***227** EN-13; ★ **PHIL-**; mail New Hope z 18938; ● 85
Buck Mountain; RMC Place; CARBON; ▲ Lausanne; **226** EJ-9; ★ **HAZ**; mail Weatherly z 18255; ● 70
Buck Mountain (Buck Mountain Colliery); RMC Place; SCHUYLKILL; ▲ Mahanoy; ***227** EK-8; mail Barnesville z 18214; ● 100
Buck Mountain Colliery; SCHUYLKILL; see Buck Mountain (RMC Place)
Buck Run; RMC Place; CHESTER; ▲ Highland, East Fallowfield; **227** EP-9; elev. 374ft./114m.; ★ **PHIL-**; mail Coatesville z 19320; ● 150
Buck Run; RMC Place; INDIANA; ▲ Cherryhill; ***225** WL-8; mail Clymer z 15728; rural
Buck Run; CDP; SCHUYLKILL; ▲ Foster; **227** EL-7; mail Pottsville z 17901; Ⓒ 203
BUCKS; **227** EM-12; Ⓟ 541,174; Ⓒ 597,635; ◆ 616,356
Buckstown; RMC Place; SOMERSET; ▲ Stonycreek, Shade; **225** WP-9; elev. 2,431ft./741m.; mail Stoystown z 15563; ● 70
Bucksville; RMC Place; BUCKS; ▲ Nockamixon; ***227** EM-12; ★ **PHIL-**; mail Kintnersville z 18930; ● 60
Bucktown; RMC Place; CHESTER; ▲ South Coventry; **227** EO-10; ★ **PTSTN**; mail Pottstown z 19464; ● 60
Buck Valley; RMC Place; FULTON; ▲ Union; ***225** WQ-11; elev. 1,057ft./322m.; mail Warfordsburg z 17267
Buell Corners; RMC Place; CRAWFORD; ▲ Rome; ***224** WE-5; mail Spartansburg z 16434; rural
Buena Vista; RMC Place; ALLEGHENY; ▲ Elizabeth; **225** WN-4; 🅿; ★ **PGH**; z 15018; ● 600
Buena Vista; RMC Place; BUTLER; ▲ Fairview; **224** WJ-5; mail Chicora z 16025; ● 60
Buena Vista; RMC Place; FAYETTE; ▲ Franklin; ***225** WP-5; ★ **UNTN**; mail Vanderbilt z 15486; rural
Buena Vista; RMC Place; FRANKLIN; ▲ Washington; mail Waynesboro z 17268; ● 75
Buena Vista; RMC Place; LANCASTER; ▲ Salisbury; ***227** EP-8; mail Gap z 17527; ● 180
Buena Vista Springs; RMC Place; FRANKLIN; ▲ Washington; ***227** ER-1; ★ **HAG**; mail Waynesboro z 17268; ● 50
Buffalo; MCD-Township; BUTLER; ***225** WL-5; ★ **PGH**; mail Sarver z 16055; Ⓟ 6,317; Ⓒ 6,827
Buffalo; MCD-Township; PERRY; ***227** EM-4; mail Liverpool z 17045; Ⓟ 1,080; Ⓒ 1,128
Buffalo; MCD-Township; UNION; ***226** EJ-4; mail Lewisburg z 17837; Ⓟ 2,877; Ⓒ 3,207
Buffalo; RMC Place; WASHINGTON; ▲ Hopewell; **225** WN-2; mail Washington z 15301; ● 120
Buffalo; MCD-Township; WASHINGTON; ***225** WO-2; ★ **WASH**; mail Claysville z 15323; Ⓟ 2,148; Ⓒ 2,100
Buffalo Creek; ARMSTRONG; see Buffalo Valley (RMC Place)
Buffalo Cross Roads; RMC Place; UNION; ▲ Buffalo; ***226** EJ-4; mail Lewisburg z 17837; rural
Buffalo Mills; RMC Place; BEDFORD; ▲ Harrison; **225** WP-10; 🅿; z 15534; ● 100
Buffalo Run; RMC Place; CENTRE; **225** WK-13; ★ **STCOL**; mail Port Matilda z 16870; ● 75
Buffalo Springs; RMC Place; LEBANON; ▲ Heidelberg; ***227** EN-7; ★ **LEB**; mail Lebanon z 17042; ● 90
Buffalo Valley (Buffalo Creek); RMC Place; ARMSTRONG; ▲ West Franklin; **225** WK-5; ★ **PGH**; mail Worthington z 16262; ● 120
Buffington; RMC Place; FAYETTE; ▲ Menallen; ***225** WP-4; ★ **UNTN**; mail New Salem z 15468; ● 300
Buffington; MCD-Township; INDIANA; ***225** WM-8; mail Vintondale z 15961; Ⓟ 1,217; Ⓒ 1,275
Buhl; RMC Place; MERCER; ★ **SHAR**; mail Sharon z 16146; pop. incl. with Sharon (Inc. Place)
Buhls; RMC Place; BUTLER; ▲ Forward; ***225** WK-3; ★ **PGH**; mail Evans City z 16033; rural
Bulger; RMC Place; WASHINGTON; ▲ Smith; **225** WN-2; 🅿; ★ **PGH**; z 15019; ● 400
Bullion; RMC Place; VENANGO; ▲ Clinton; **224** WH-4; elev. 1,466ft./447m.; mail Kennerdell z 16374; ● 40
Bullis Mills; RMC Place; MCKEAN; ▲ Eldred; ***224** WD-11; mail Eldred z 16731
Bullskin; MCD-Township; FAYETTE; ***225** WO-6; mail Mount Pleasant z 15666; Ⓟ 7,323; Ⓒ 7,782
Bully Hill; RMC Place; VENANGO; ▲ Sandycreek; **224** WH-4; ★ **OILC-F**; mail Franklin z 16323; ● 150
Bunches; RMC Place; YORK; ▲ Fairview; ***227** EO-4; ★ **HRBG**; mail New Cumberland z 17070; rural
Bungalow Park; RMC Place; LEHIGH; ▲ South Whitehall; **226** EB-2; ★ **ALL-**; mail Allentown z 18104; ● 200
Bunker Hill; RMC Place; CUMBERLAND; ▲ Hampden; ***227** EN-4; ★ **HRBG**; mail Mechanicsburg z 17055; ● 450
Bunker Hill; RMC Place; LEBANON; ▲ Swatara; **227** EN-6; ★ **LEB**; mail Lebanon z 17046; ● 170
Bunkertown; RMC Place; JUNIATA; ▲ Fayette; **227** EL-3; mail Mc Alisterville z 17049; ● 60
Bunola; RMC Place; ALLEGHENY; ▲ Forward; **225** WN-4; 🅿; ★ **PGH**; z 15020; ● 300
Burbank; RMC Place; MCKEAN; ▲ Keating; ***224** WE-11; elev. 1,534ft./468m.; mail Smethport z 16749; rural
Burd Coleman Village; RMC Place; LEBANON; ***227** EN-6; elev. 653ft./199m.; ★ **LEB**; mail Cornwall z 17016; pop. incl. with Cornwall (Inc. Place)
Burgettstown; Inc. Place; WASHINGTON; **225** WN-2; elev. 989ft./301m.; 🅿; ★ **PGH**; z 15021; Ⓟ 1,634; Ⓒ 1,576
Burholme; RMC Place; PHILADELPHIA; ***227** EP-12; ★ **PHIL-**; mail Philadelphia z 19111; pop. incl. with Philadelphia (Inc. Place)
Burlington; Inc. Place; BRADFORD; **226** EE-5; elev. 894ft./272m.; 🅿; z 18814; Ⓟ 479; Ⓒ 182
Burlington; MCD-Township; BRADFORD; ***226** EF-6; 🅿; z 18814 & mail Towanda z 18848; does not include the Borough of Burlington; Ⓟ 705; Ⓒ 799
Burnham; Inc. Place; MIFFLIN; **227** EL-1; elev. 540ft./165m.; 🅿; z 17009; Ⓟ 2,197; Ⓒ 2,144
Burning Well; RMC Place; MCKEAN; ▲ Sergeant; ***224** WF-10; elev. 1,660ft./506m.; mail Kane z 16735
Burnside; MCD-Township; CENTRE; ***224** WJ-13; mail Karthaus z 16845; Ⓟ 390; Ⓒ 410
Burnside; Inc. Place; CLEARFIELD; **225** WK-9; elev. 1,340ft./408m.; 🅿; z 15721; Ⓟ 350; Ⓒ 283
Burnside; MCD-Township; CLEARFIELD; ***225** WK-9; 🅿; z 15721 & mail Westover z 16692; does not include the Borough of Burnside; Ⓟ 1,137; Ⓒ 1,128
Burnside; RMC Place; NORTHUMBERLAND; ▲ Coal; ***227** EK-6; elev. 987ft./301m.; mail Shamokin z 17872; ● 100
Burnstown; RMC Place; LAWRENCE; ▲ Wayne; ***225** WK-2; ★ **PGH**; mail Ellwood City z 16117; ● 60
Burnt Cabins; RMC Place; FULTON; ▲ Dublin; **225** WO-13; 🅿; z 17215; ● 125
Burnwood; RMC Place; SUSQUEHANNA; ▲ Ararat; ***226** EE-10; mail Thompson z 18465; rural
Burrell; MCD-Township; ARMSTRONG; ***225** WL-6; mail Ford City z 16226; Ⓟ 728; Ⓒ 749
Burrell; MCD-Township; INDIANA; ***225** WM-7; ★ **LTROB**; mail Blairsville z 15717; Ⓟ 3,669; Ⓒ 3,746
Burson Plan; RMC Place; GREENE; ▲ Morgan; ***225** WP-3; mail Clarksville z 15322; ● 50
Bursonville; RMC Place; BUCKS; ▲ Springfield; ***227** EM-12; ★ **ALL-**; mail Riegelsville z 18077; ● 30
Burtville; RMC Place; POTTER; ▲ Roulette; ***224** WE-12; elev. 1,528ft./466m.; mail Port Allegany z 16743
Bushkill; MCD-Township; NORTHAMPTON; ***227** EK-11; ★ **ALL-**; mail Nazareth z 18064; Ⓟ 5,512; Ⓒ 6,982
Bushkill; RMC Place; PIKE, MONROE; ▲ Middle Smithfield, Lehman; **226** EI-13; 🅿; z 18324, z 18371, z 18373; summer pop. 1,500; ● 1,200
Bushkill Center; RMC Place; NORTHAMPTON; ▲ Bushkill; ***227** EK-11; elev. 695ft./212m.; ★ **ALL-**; mail Nazareth z 18064; ● 140
Bush Patch; RMC Place; LACKAWANNA; ***226** EH-9; ★ **SCR-**; mail Old Forge z 18518; pop. incl. with Old Forge (Inc. Place)
Bustleton; RMC Place; PHILADELPHIA; ***227** EO-13; ★ **PHIL-**; mail Philadelphia z 19115; pop. incl. with Philadelphia (Inc. Place)
Bute; RMC Place; FAYETTE; ▲ North Union, Franklin; ***225** WP-5; ★ **UNTN**; mail West Leisenring z 15489
Butler; MCD-Township; ADAMS; ***227** EQ-3; mail Biglerville z 17307; Ⓟ 2,514; Ⓒ 2,678
Butler; Inc. Place; ⊡ BUTLER; **225** WK-4; elev. 1,077ft./328m.; 🅿 🅷 ■; ★ **BUTL**; z 16001-03; Ⓟ 15,714; Ⓒ 15,121; ◆ 14,283
Butler; MCD-Township; BUTLER; ***225** WK-4; 🅿; ★ **BUTL**; z 16001-03 & mail Lyndora z 16045; does not include the City of Butler; Ⓟ 17,625; Ⓒ 17,185
Butler; MCD-Township; LUZERNE; ***226** EJ-8; ★ **HAZ**; mail Drums z 18222; Ⓟ 6,020; Ⓒ 7,166
Butler; MCD-Township; SCHUYLKILL; ***227** EK-7; ★ **PTSVL**; mail Ashland z 17921; Ⓟ 4,099; Ⓒ 3,588; Ⓡ 4,987
BUTLER; **224** WJ-4; Ⓟ 152,013; Ⓒ 174,083; ◆ 179,729
Butler Junction; RMC Place; BUTLER; ▲ Buffalo; ***225** WL-5; ★ **PGH**; mail Freeport z 16229; ● 50
Buttonwood; RMC Place; LUZERNE; ▲ Hanover; **226** EA-6; ★ **SCR-**; mail Wilkes Barre z 18706; ● 620
Buttonwood; RMC Place; LYCOMING; ▲ Jackson; ***226** EG-3; mail Trout Run z 17771
Buttonwood Glen; RMC Place; BUCKS; ▲ Doylestown; ***227** EN-12; ★ **PHIL-**; mail Doylestown z 18901; ● 120
Buttonwood Manor; RMC Place; BUCKS; ▲ New Britain; ***227** EN-12; ★ **PHIL-**; mail Doylestown z 18901; ● 130
Butztown; RMC Place; NORTHAMPTON; ▲ Bethlehem; **226** EA-5; 🅿; ★ **ALL-**; z 18017; ● 1,500
Buyerstown (Byerstown); RMC Place; LANCASTER; ▲ Salisbury; ***227** EP-8; mail Kinzers z 17535; ● 60
Buzzingtown; RMC Place; WESTMORELAND; ▲ Hempfield; ***225** WN-5; ★ **PGH**; mail Irwin z 15642; ● 400
Byberry; RMC Place; PHILADELPHIA; ★ **PHIL-**; mail Philadelphia z 19116; pop. incl. with Philadelphia (Inc. Place)
Bycot; RMC Place; BUCKS; ▲ Buckingham; ***227** EN-13; ★ **PHIL-**; mail Holicong z 18928; rural
Byers; RMC Place; CHESTER; ▲ Upper Uwchlan; ***227** EO-10; ★ **PHIL-**; mail Uwchland z 19480; ● 50
Byersdale; RMC Place; BEAVER; ▲ Harmony; ***225** WL-3; ★ **PGH**; mail Baden z 15005
Byerstown; LANCASTER; see Buyerstown (RMC Place)
Byrnedale; RMC Place; ELK; ▲ Jay; **224** WH-10; elev. 1,225ft./373m.; 🅿; z 15827; ● 450
Byrnedale; ELK; see Weedville (RMC Place)
Byrnsville; RMC Place; COLUMBIA; ▲ Conyngham; ***227** EK-7; ● 100
Byromtown; RMC Place; FOREST; ▲ Jenks; ***224** WG-8; mail Marienville z 16239
Bywood; RMC Place; DELAWARE; ▲ Upper Darby; ***227** EP-12; ★ **PHIL-**; mail Upper Darby z 19082
Bywood Heights; RMC Place; DELAWARE; ▲ Upper Darby; ★ **PHIL-**; mail Upper Darby z 19082

C

Cabot; RMC Place; BUTLER; ▲ Winfield; **225** WK-5; 🅿; ★ **PGH**; z 16023; ● 400
Cacoossing; RMC Place; BERKS; ▲ Lower Heidelberg; ***227** EN-8; ★ **READ**; mail Reading z 19608; ● 100
Cadis; RMC Place; BRADFORD; ▲ Warren; ***226** ED-7; mail Rome z 18837; ● 60
Cadogan; RMC Place; ARMSTRONG; ▲ Cadogan; **225** WK-5; 🅿; ★ **PGH**; z 16212; ● 400
Cadogan; MCD-Township; ARMSTRONG; ***225** WK-5; 🅿; ★ **PGH**; z 16212; Ⓟ 427; Ⓒ 390
Caernarvon; MCD-Township; BERKS; ***227** EO-9; mail Morgantown z 19543; Ⓟ 1,951; Ⓒ 2,312
Caernarvon; MCD-Township; LANCASTER; ***227** EO-9; mail Narvon z 17555; Ⓟ 3,946; Ⓒ 4,278
Cains; RMC Place; LANCASTER; ▲ Salisbury; ***227** EP-9; elev. 480ft./146m.; mail Gap z 17527; ● 100
Cairnbrook (Cairnbrook Central City); RMC Place; SOMERSET; ▲ Shade; **225** WO-9; 🅿; z 15924; ● 1,000
Cairnbrook Central City; SOMERSET; see Cairnbrook (RMC Place)
Calder Square; RMC Place; CENTRE; ★ **STCOL**; mail State College z 16805; pop. incl. with State College (Inc. Place)
Caldwell; RMC Place; CLINTON; ▲ Gallagher; ***226** EI-2; mail Lock Haven z 17745; rural
Caledonia; RMC Place; ELK; ▲ Jay; **224** WH-11; mail Weedville z 15868; ● 200
California; RMC Place; BUCKS; ▲ Richland; ***227** EM-11; ★ **PHIL-**; mail Quakertown z 18951; ● 150
California; Inc. Place; WASHINGTON; **225** WO-4; elev. 800ft./244m.; 🅿 🅲 7,720; ★ **PGH**; z 15419; Ⓟ 5,748; Ⓒ 5,274
Calkins; RMC Place; WAYNE; ▲ Damascus; ***226** EF-12; mail Milanville z 18443; rural
Callapoose; RMC Place; WAYNE; ▲ Salem; ***226** EH-11; ★ **SCR-**; mail Moscow z 18444; rural
Callensburg; Inc. Place; CLARION; **224** WI-6; elev. 1,100ft./335m.; 🅿; z 16213; Ⓟ 205; Ⓒ 224
Callery; Inc. Place; BUTLER; **225** WL-3; elev. 974ft./297m.; 🅿; ★ **PGH**; z 16024; Ⓟ 420; Ⓒ 444
Callimont; Inc. Place; SOMERSET; **225** WQ-8; mail Meyersdale z 15552; Ⓟ 55; Ⓒ 51
Caln; RMC Place; CHESTER; ▲ Caln; **227** EP-9; ★ **PHIL-**; mail Coatesville z 19320, Thorndale z 19372; ● 850
Caln; MCD-Township; CHESTER; ***227** EP-9; ★ **PHIL-**; mail Coatesville z 19320; Ⓟ 11,997; Ⓒ 11,916
Calumet; RMC Place; WESTMORELAND; ▲ Mount Pleasant; ***225** WO-6; 🅿; z 15621; ● 300
Calumet-Norvelt; CDP-Census Area Only; WESTMORELAND; ▲ Mount Pleasant; ***225** WO-6; mail Calumet z 15621, Norvelt z 15674; Ⓟ 1,790; Ⓒ 1,682
Calvert; RMC Place; LYCOMING; ▲ Gamble; ***226** EH-4; mail Trout Run z 17771; rural
Calvert Hills; RMC Place; BLAIR; ***225** WM-11; ★ **ALT**; mail Altoona z 16601; pop. incl. with Altoona (Inc. Place)
Calvin; RMC Place; HUNTINGDON; ▲ Union; **225** WN-12; 🅿; z 16622; ● 90
Camargo; RMC Place; LANCASTER; ▲ Eden; ***227** EP-8; elev. 427ft./130m.; mail Quarryville z 17566; ● 65
Cambra; RMC Place; LUZERNE; ▲ Huntington; **226** EI-7; elev. 1,034ft./315m.; 🅿; z 18611; ● 70
Cambria; MCD-Township; CAMBRIA; ***225** WM-9; mail Ebensburg z 15931; Ⓟ 6,357; Ⓒ 6,323
CAMBRIA; **225** WM-10; Ⓟ 163,029; Ⓒ 152,598; ◆ 141,183
Cambria City; RMC Place; CAMBRIA; ***225** WN-8; ★ **JNST**; mail Johnstown z 15906; pop. incl. with Johnstown (Inc. Place)
Cambridge; RMC Place; CHESTER, LANCASTER; ▲ Salisbury, Honey Brook; **227** EO-9; ★ **PHIL-**; mail Honey Brook z 19344; ● 140
Cambridge; MCD-Township; CRAWFORD; ***224** WE-4; ★ **ERIE**; mail Cambridge Springs z 16403; Ⓟ 1,496; Ⓒ 1,486
Cambridge Springs; Inc. Place; CRAWFORD; **224** WE-3; elev. 1,160ft./354m.; 🅿; ★ **ERIE**; z 16403; Ⓟ 1,837; Ⓒ 2,363
Cameron; RMC Place; CAMERON; ▲ Lumber; **224** WG-12; mail Emporium z 15834; ● 50
CAMERON; **224** WG-11; Ⓟ 5,913; Ⓒ 5,974; ◆ 5,224
Cammal; RMC Place; LYCOMING; **226** EH-2; mail Waterville z 17776; ● 25
Camp Akiba; RMC Place; MONROE; ▲ Jackson; ***226** EJ-11; mail Reeders z 18352; summer pop. 1,500
Campbelltown; CDP; LEBANON; ▲ South Londonderry; **227** EN-6; 🅿; z 17010; Ⓟ 1,609; Ⓒ 2,415
Campbelltown; RMC Place; MCKEAN; ▲ Jackson; ***224** WF-10; mail Kane z 16735; rural
Camp Bnai Brith; RMC Place; WAYNE; ▲ Buckingham; ***226** EE-11; elev. 1,559ft./475m.; mail Starlight z 18461; summer pop. 1,400
Camp Curtin; RMC Place; DAUPHIN; ★ **HRBG**; mail Harrisburg z 17110; pop. incl. with Harrisburg (Inc. Place)
Camp Hill; Inc. Place; CUMBERLAND; **227** EO-4; elev. 420ft./128m.; 🅿 🅷 ■; ★ **HRBG**; z 17001, z 17011-12, z 17089; Ⓟ 7,831; Ⓒ 7,636; ◆ 7,797
Camphill; MONTGOMERY; see Fellwick (RMC Place)
Camp Jo-Ann; RMC Place; WESTMORELAND; ▲ Washington; ***225** WM-5; ★ **PGH**; mail Murrysville z 15668; pop. incl. with Murrysville (Inc. Place)
Camp Perry; RMC Place; MERCER; ▲ Perry; ***224** WH-3; elev. 1,238ft./377m.; mail Clarks Mills z 16114; rural
Camp Starlight; RMC Place; WAYNE; ▲ Preston; ***226** EE-11; elev. 1,500ft./457m.; mail Starlight z 18461; summer pop. 1,000; ● 45
Camptown; RMC Place; BRADFORD; ▲ Wyalusing; **226** EF-7; elev. 748ft./228m.; 🅿; z 18815; ● 180
Camp Westmont; RMC Place; WAYNE; ▲ Preston; ***226** EE-11; elev. 2,100ft./640m.; mail Orson z 18449; summer pop. 400
Canaan; RMC Place; WAYNE; ▲ Canaan; ***226** EG-11; elev. 1,497ft./456m.; ★ **SCR-**; mail Waymart z 18472; ● 300
Canaan; MCD-Township; WAYNE; ***226** EG-11; ★ **SCR-**; mail Waymart z 18472; Ⓟ 1,267; Ⓒ 1,916
Canadensis; RMC Place; MONROE; ▲ Barrett; **226** EI-12; 🅿; z 18325; ● 1,200
Canadohta Lake; CDP-Census Area Only; CRAWFORD; ▲ Bloomfield; **224** WE-5; mail Union City z 16438; summer pop. 1,400; Ⓒ 572
Canal; MCD-Township; VENANGO; ***224** WG-4; mail Cochranton z 16314; Ⓟ 1,067; Ⓒ 1,008
Canan; RMC Place; BLAIR; ▲ Allegheny; ***225** WM-11; ★ **ALT**; mail Altoona z 16602; ● 140
Candor; RMC Place; WASHINGTON; ▲ Robinson; **225** WM-2; elev. 1,139ft./347m.; ★ **PGH**; mail Bulger z 15019; ● 60
Cannelton; RMC Place; BEAVER; ▲ Darlington; **225** WK-1; ★ **PGH**; mail Darlington z 16115; ● 100
Canoe; MCD-Township; INDIANA; ***225** WK-8; mail Rossiter z 15772; Ⓟ 1,915; Ⓒ 1,670
Canoe Camp; RMC Place; TIOGA; ▲ Richmond; **226** EE-3; elev. 1,157ft./353m.; mail Mansfield z 16933; ● 150
Canoe Creek; RMC Place; BLAIR; ▲ Frankstown; **225** WM-11; elev. 924ft./282m.; ★ **ALT**; mail Hollidaysburg z 16648; ● 250
Canoe Ridge; RMC Place; INDIANA; ▲ Canoe; ***225** WK-8; mail Rossiter z 15772; rural
Canonsburg; Inc. Place; WASHINGTON; **225** WN-3; elev. 960ft./293m.; 🅿 🅷; ★ **PGH**; z 15317; Ⓟ 9,200; Ⓒ 8,607
Canton; Inc. Place; BRADFORD; **226** EF-4; elev. 1,248ft./380m.; 🅿; z 17724; Ⓟ 1,966; Ⓒ 1,807
Canton; MCD-Township; BRADFORD; ***226** EF-4; 🅿; z 17724; does not include the Borough of Canton; Ⓟ 2,099; Ⓒ 2,084
Canton; MCD-Township; WASHINGTON; ***225** WO-2; ★ **WASH**; mail Washington z 15301; Ⓟ 9,256; Ⓒ 8,826
Caprivi; RMC Place; CUMBERLAND; ▲ North Middleton; ***227** EO-3; ★ **CARL**; mail Carlisle z 17013; ● 75
Carbon; MCD-Township; HUNTINGDON; ***225** WO-12; mail Saxton z 16678; Ⓟ 438; Ⓒ 428
Carbon; RMC Place; MERCER; ▲ Lackawannock; ***224** WI-2; elev. 1,042ft./318m.; ★ **SHAR**; mail Transfer z 16154; rural
Carbon; RMC Place; WESTMORELAND; ▲ Hempfield; ***225** WN-5; ★ **PGH**; mail Greensburg z 15601; ● 275
CARBON; **226** EJ-9; Ⓟ 56,846; Ⓒ 58,802; ◆ 65,144
Carbon Center (Carbon Centre); RMC Place; BUTLER; ▲ Summit; ***225** WK-5; elev. 1,411ft./430m.; ★ **BUTL**; mail Butler z 16001; ● 50
Carbon Centre; BUTLER; see Carbon Center (RMC Place)
Carbondale; Inc. Place; LACKAWANNA; **226** EG-10; elev. 1,070ft./326m.; 🅿 🅷; ★ **SCR-**; z 18407; Ⓟ 10,664; Ⓒ 9,804
Carbondale; MCD-Township; LACKAWANNA; ***226** EG-10; 🅿; ★ **SCR-**; z 18407; does not include the Borough of Carbondale; Ⓟ 907; Ⓒ 1,008
Cardale; RMC Place; FAYETTE; ▲ Redstone; ***225** WP-4; 🅿; ★ **UNTN**; z 15420; ● 200
Cardiff; RMC Place; CAMBRIA; ▲ Blacklick; ***225** WM-9; mail Nanty Glo z 15943; ● 60
Cardington; RMC Place; DELAWARE; ▲ Upper Darby; ★ **PHIL-**; mail Upper Darby z 19082; pop. incl. with Yeadon (Inc. Place)
Carlisle; Inc. Place; ⊡ CUMBERLAND; **227** EO-3; elev. 478ft./146m.; 🅿 🅷 🅲 2,896 ■; ★ **CARL**; z 17013, z 17015; Ⓟ 18,419; Ⓒ 17,970; ◆ 18,667
Carlisle Springs; RMC Place; CUMBERLAND; ▲ Middlesex; ***227** EN-3; ★ **CARL**; mail Carlisle z 17013
Carlson; RMC Place; ELK; ▲ Highland; ***224** WG-9; elev. 2,004ft./611m.; mail Kane z 16735; rural
Carlton; RMC Place; MERCER; ▲ French Creek; **224** WG-4; 🅿; z 16311; ● 80
Carlton Heights; RMC Place; FRANKLIN; ▲ St. Thomas; ***225** WP-14; mail Saint Thomas z 17252; ● 320
Carmichaels; Inc. Place; GREENE; **225** WP-4; elev. 1,000ft./305m.; 🅿; z 15320; Ⓟ 532; Ⓒ 556
Carnegie; Inc. Place; ALLEGHENY; **228** K-4; elev. 773ft./236m.; 🅿; ★ **PGH**; z 15106; Ⓟ 9,278; Ⓒ 8,389
Carnot; RMC Place; ALLEGHENY; ▲ Moon; **225** WM-3; ★ **PGH**; mail Coraopolis z 15108; ● 4,500
Carnot-Moon; CDP-Census Area Only; ALLEGHENY; ▲ Moon; ***225** WM-3; ★ **PGH**; mail Coraopolis z 15108; Ⓟ 10,187; Ⓒ 10,637
Carnwath; RMC Place; CLEARFIELD; ▲ Knox; ***225** WK-10; mail New Millport z 16861; ● 45
Carol Acres; RMC Place; DAUPHIN; ▲ Derry; ***227** EO-5; ★ **HRBG**; mail Hummelstown z 17036; ● 300
Carpenter Corners; RMC Place; MERCER; ▲ New Vernon; ***224** WH-3; mail Stoneboro z 16153; rural
Carpenter Town; RMC Place; LACKAWANNA; ▲ Benton; ***226** EG-9; ★ **SCR-**; mail Dalton z 18414; rural
Carpentertown; RMC Place; WESTMORELAND; ▲ Mount Pleasant; ***225** WO-6; mail Mount Pleasant z 15666; rural
Carriage Hill; RMC Place; BUCKS; ▲ Lower Makefield; ***227** EN-14; ★ **PHIL-**; mail Morrisville z 19067; ● 380
Carrick; RMC Place; ALLEGHENY; ***225** WM-4; ★ **PGH**; mail Pittsburgh z 15210; pop. incl. with Pittsburgh (Inc. Place)
Carrier; RMC Place; JEFFERSON; mail Summerville z 15864; pop. incl. with Summerville (Inc. Place)
Carroll; RMC Place; CLINTON; ▲ Greene; ***226** EJ-3; mail Loganton z 17747
Carroll; MCD-Township; PERRY; ***227** EN-3; ★ **HRBG**; mail Shermans Dale z 17090; Ⓟ 4,597; Ⓒ 5,095
Carroll; MCD-Township; WASHINGTON; ***225** WO-4; ★ **PGH**; mail Monongahela z 15063; Ⓟ 6,210; Ⓒ 5,677
Carroll; MCD-Township; YORK; ***227** EO-4; ★ **HRBG**; mail Dillsburg z 17019; Ⓟ 3,287; Ⓒ 4,715
Carroll Park; RMC Place; COLUMBIA; ▲ Scott; ***226** EJ-6; mail Bloomsburg z 17815; ● 200
Carroll Park; RMC Place; MONTGOMERY; ▲ Lower Merion; ★ **PHIL-**; mail Philadelphia z 19151, Wynnewood z 19096
Carrolltown; Inc. Place; CAMBRIA; **225** WL-9; elev. 2,140ft./652m.; 🅿; z 15722; Ⓟ 1,286; Ⓒ 1,049
Carroll Valley; Inc. Place; ADAMS; **227** EQ-2; mail Fairfield z 17320; Ⓟ 1,457; Ⓒ 3,291
Carson; RMC Place; ALLEGHENY; 🅿; ★ **PGH**; z 15203; pop. incl. with Pittsburgh (Inc. Place)
Carsontown; RMC Place; LYCOMING; ▲ Pine; ***226** EH-2; elev. 797ft./243m.; mail Waterville z 17776; rural
Carson Valley; RMC Place; BLAIR; ▲ Allegheny; ***225** WM-11; ★ **ALT**; mail Duncansville z 16635; ● 300
Carsonville; RMC Place; DAUPHIN; ▲ Jefferson; ***227** EM-5; mail Halifax z 17032
Carter Camp; RMC Place; POTTER; ▲ Abbott; **224** WF-14; mail Galeton z 16922; ● 20
Cartwright; RMC Place; ELK; ▲ Horton; ***224** WH-9; mail Brockport z 15823
Carver Court; RMC Place; CHESTER; ▲ Caln; ***227** EP-9; ★ **PHIL-**; mail Coatesville z 19320; ● 400
Carversville; RMC Place; BUCKS; ▲ Solebury; **227** EN-13; 🅿; ★ **PHIL-**; z 18913; ● 400
Carverton; RMC Place; LUZERNE; ▲ Kingston; **226** EA-9; elev. 874ft./266m.; ★ **SCR-**; mail Wyoming z 18644; ● 500
Casanova; RMC Place; CENTRE; ▲ Rush; **224** WJ-12; elev. 1,413ft./431m.; mail Munson z 16860; ● 90
Cascade; MCD-Township; LYCOMING; ***226** EG-4; mail Trout Run z 17771; Ⓟ 382; Ⓒ 419
Cashtown; RMC Place; ADAMS; ▲ Franklin; **227** EQ-2; 🅿; z 17310; ● 300
Cashtown-McKnightstown; CDP-Census Area Only; ADAMS; ***227** EQ-2; Ⓒ 753
Cass; MCD-Township; HUNTINGDON; ***225** WO-13; mail Cassville z 16623; Ⓟ 998; Ⓒ 1,062
Cass; MCD-Township; SCHUYLKILL; ***227** EL-7; ★ **PTSVL**; mail Pottsville z 17901; Ⓟ 2,088; Ⓒ 2,383; Ⓡ 1,840
Cassandra; Inc. Place; CAMBRIA; **225** WN-10; elev. 1,800ft./549m.; 🅿; z 15925; Ⓟ 192; Ⓒ 136
Casselman; Inc. Place; SOMERSET; **225** WQ-7; elev. 1,742ft./531m.; mail Rockwood z 15557; Ⓟ 89; Ⓒ 99
Cassville; Inc. Place; HUNTINGDON; **225** WN-12; elev. 1,241ft./378m.; 🅿; z 16623; Ⓟ 183; Ⓒ 152
Castanea; CDP; CLINTON; ▲ Castanea; **226** EI-2; 🅿; ★ **WMSPT**; z 17726; Ⓟ 1,123; Ⓒ 1,189
Castanea; MCD-Township; CLINTON; ***226** EI-2; 🅿; ★ **WMSPT**; z 17726; Ⓟ 1,188; Ⓒ 1,233
Castle Garden; RMC Place; CAMERON; ▲ Gibson; **224** WH-12; mail Driftwood z 15832; ● 45
Castle Rock; RMC Place; DELAWARE; ▲ Edgmont; ***227** EP-11; ★ **PHIL-**; mail Newtown Square z 19073; ● 200
Castle Shannon; Inc. Place; ALLEGHENY; **225** WN-3; elev. 1,040ft./317m.; 🅿; ★ **PGH**; z 15234; Ⓟ 9,135; Ⓒ 8,556
Castle Valley; RMC Place; BUCKS; ▲ Doylestown; ***227** EN-12; ★ **PHIL-**; mail Chalfont z 18914; ● 75
Castlewood; RMC Place; LAWRENCE; ▲ Shenango; ***224** WJ-2; ★ **NWCS**; mail New Castle z 16101; rural
Castor; RMC Place; PHILADELPHIA; ★ **PHIL-**; mail Philadelphia z 19149; pop. incl. with Philadelphia (Inc. Place)
Cataract; RMC Place; CLEARFIELD; ▲ Karthaus; ***224** WI-12; mail Pottersdale z 16871; rural
Catasauqua; Inc. Place; LEHIGH; ▲ Whitehall; **227** EL-11; 🅿; ★ **ALL-**; z 18032; Ⓟ 6,662; Ⓒ 6,588
Catawissa; Inc. Place; COLUMBIA; **226** EJ-6; elev. 477ft./145m.; 🅿; z 17820; Ⓟ 1,683; Ⓒ 1,589
Catawissa; MCD-Township; COLUMBIA; ***226** EJ-6; 🅿; z 17820; does not include the Borough of Catawissa; Ⓟ 1,037; Ⓒ 944
Catharine; MCD-Township; BLAIR; ***225** WM-11; mail Williamsburg z 16693; Ⓟ 738; Ⓒ 758
Cavettsville; RMC Place; WESTMORELAND; ▲ North Huntingdon; **228** L-10; ★ **PGH**; mail Trafford z 15085; ● 120
Ceasetown; RMC Place; LUZERNE; ▲ Lehman, Jackson; ***226** EI-8; ★ **SCR-**; mail Dallas z 18612, Hunlock Creek z 18621; ● 300
Cecil; RMC Place; WASHINGTON; ▲ Cecil; **225** WN-3; 🅿; ★ **PGH**; z 15321; ● 900
Cecil; MCD-Township; WASHINGTON; ***225** WN-3; 🅿; ★ **PGH**; z 15321 & mail Mc Donald z 15057; Ⓟ 8,948; Ⓒ 9,756
Cecil-Bishop; CDP-Census Area Only; WASHINGTON; ▲ Cecil; ***225** WN-3; elev. 1,100ft./335m.; ★ **PGH**; mail Cecil z 15321, Mc Donald z 15057; Ⓟ 2,701; Ⓒ 2,585
Cedarbrook; RMC Place; MONTGOMERY; ▲ Cheltenham; ***227** EO-12; ★ **PHIL-**; mail Wyncote z 19095; ● 2,800
Cedarbrook Hills; RMC Place; MONTGOMERY; ▲ Cheltenham; ★ **PHIL-**; mail Wyncote z 19095
Cedar Cliff Manor; RMC Place; CUMBERLAND; ▲ Lower Allen; ***227** EO-4; ★ **HRBG**; mail Camp Hill z 17011; ● 1,200
Cedar Heights; RMC Place; MONTGOMERY; ▲ Whitemarsh; ***227** EO-12; elev. 239ft./73m.; ★ **PHIL-**; mail Conshohocken z 19428; ● 800
Cedar Hollow; RMC Place; CHESTER; ▲ Schuylkill; ***227** EO-10; ★ **PHIL-**; mail Malvern z 19355; rural
Cedar Knoll; RMC Place; CHESTER; ▲ West Brandywine; ***227** EP-9; elev. 635ft./194m.; ★ **PHIL-**; mail Coatesville z 19320; ● 550
Cedar Lane; RMC Place; LANCASTER; ▲ East Earl; ***227** EO-8; ★ **LANC**; mail East Earl z 17519; rural
Cedar Ledge; RMC Place; BRADFORD; ▲ Canton; **226** EF-4; elev. 1,194ft./364m.; mail Canton z 17724; ● 25
Cedar Ridge; RMC Place; ADAMS; ▲ Mount Pleasant; ***227** EQ-3; ★ **HANV**; mail New Oxford z 17350; rural
Cedar Run; RMC Place; LYCOMING; ▲ Brown; **226** EG-2; 🅿; z 17727; ● 100
Cedars; RMC Place; MONTGOMERY; ▲ Worcester; **227** EO-11; 🅿; ★ **PHIL-**; z 19423; ● 270
Cedar Springs; RMC Place; CLINTON; ▲ Lamar; **226** EJ-2; mail Mill Hall z 17751; ● 90
Cedar Top; RMC Place; BERKS; ▲ Cumru; ***227** EN-8; ★ **READ**; mail Reading z 19607; ● 600
Cedarville; RMC Place; CHESTER; ▲ North Coventry; **227** EO-10; ★ **PTSTN**; mail Pottstown z 19464; ● 200
Cementon; RMC Place; LEHIGH; ▲ Whitehall; **227** EL-10; ★ **ALL-**; mail Whitehall z 18052; ● 1,100
Centennial; RMC Place; ADAMS; ▲ Mount Pleasant; ***227** EQ-4; ★ **HANV**; mail Hanover z 17331; ● 350
Centennial; RMC Place; CENTRE; ▲ Worth; ***225** WK-12; elev. 1,249ft./381m.; mail Port Matilda z 16870; ● 25
Centennial Hills; RMC Place; BUCKS; ▲ Warminster; elev. 310ft./94m.; ★ **PHIL-**; mail Warminster z 18974
Center; RMC Place; ALLEGHENY; ***225** WM-5; ★ **PGH**; mail Pittsburgh z 15239; pop. incl. with Plum (Inc. Place)
Center; MCD-Township; BEAVER; ***225** WL-2; ★ **PGH**; mail Aliquippa z 15001; Ⓟ 10,742; Ⓒ 11,492
Center; MCD-Township; BUTLER; ***224** WJ-4; ★ **BUTL**; mail Butler z 16001; Ⓟ 6,239; Ⓒ 8,182
Center; MCD-Township; GREENE; ***225** WQ-2; mail Rogersville z 15359; Ⓟ 1,460; Ⓒ 1,393
Center; MCD-Township; INDIANA; ***225** WM-7; mail Homer City z 15748; Ⓟ 5,257; Ⓒ 4,876
Center; RMC Place; JUNIATA; ▲ Walker; ***227** EM-2; mail Mifflintown z 17059; ● 100
Center; RMC Place; PERRY; ▲ Southwest Madison; mail Millerstown z 17062; rural
Center (Centre); MCD-Township; SNYDER; ***227** EK-3; mail Middleburg z 17842; Ⓟ 1,986; Ⓒ 2,162
Center Bridge; RMC Place; BUCKS; ▲ Solebury; ***227** EM-13; ★ **PHIL-**; mail New Hope z 18938; ● 80
Center City; RMC Place; LYCOMING; ★ **WMSPT**; mail Williamsport z 17701, z 17703; pop. incl. with Williamsport (Inc. Place)
Center Hill; RMC Place; ARMSTRONG; ▲ North Buffalo; ***225** WK-5; ★ **PGH**; mail Kittanning z 16201; ● 100
Center Mills; RMC Place; ADAMS; ▲ Butler; **227** EP-3; mail Aspers z 17304; ● 80
Center Moreland; RMC Place; WYOMING; ▲ Northmoreland; ***226** EH-8; elev. 1,275ft./389m.; mail Tunkhannock z 18657
Center Point; MONTGOMERY; see Worcester (RMC Place)
Centerport; Inc. Place; BERKS; **227** EM-8; elev. 340ft./104m.; 🅿; ★ **READ**; z 19516; Ⓟ 284; Ⓒ 327
Center Road; RMC Place; CRAWFORD; ▲ Conneaut; ***224** WF-2; mail Linesville z 16424
Center Square; RMC Place; MONTGOMERY; ▲ Whitpain; **227** EO-12; elev. 252ft./77m.; 🅿; ★ **PHIL-**; z 19422; ● 700
Centertown; RMC Place; MERCER; ▲ Wolf Creek; ***224** WI-3; mail Grove City z 16127; rural
Center Union; RMC Place; HUNTINGDON; ▲ Oneida; ***225** WM-13; mail Huntingdon z 16652
Center Valley (Centre Valley); RMC Place; LEHIGH; ▲ Upper Saucon; **227** EM-11; 🅿 🅲 2,936; ★ **ALL-**; z 18034; ● 900
Centerville (Bedford Valley); RMC Place; BEDFORD; ▲ Cumberland Valley; **225** WQ-10; mail Bedford z 15522; ● 125
Centerville; BRADFORD; see Ridgebury (RMC Place)
Centerville; Inc. Place; CRAWFORD; **224** WF-5; elev. 1,314ft./401m.; 🅿; z 16404; Ⓟ 249; Ⓒ 247
Centerville; RMC Place; LANCASTER; ▲ East Hempfield; **227** ES-7; ★ **LANC**; mail Lancaster z 17602; ● 1,700
Centerville; NORTHAMPTON; see Stone Church (RMC Place)
Centerville; RMC Place; PERRY; ▲ Liverpool; ***227** EM-4; mail Liverpool z 17045, Millerstown z 17062; rural
Centerville; Inc. Place; WASHINGTON; **225** WP-4; elev. 1,160ft./354m.; mail Brownsville z 15417; Ⓟ 3,842; Ⓒ 3,390
Centerville; RMC Place; YORK; ▲ Shrewsbury; ***227** EQ-5; elev. 980ft./299m.; ★ **BAL**; mail Glen Rock z 17327; ● 25
Central; RMC Place; ALLEGHENY; ★ **PGH**; mail Mckeesport z 15132; pop. incl. with McKeesport (Inc. Place)
Central; RMC Place; COLUMBIA; ▲ Sugarloaf; **226** EH-7; mail Benton z 17814; ● 100
Central; RMC Place; WASHINGTON; ★ **WASH**; mail Washington z 15301
Central; RMC Place; WESTMORELAND; ▲ East Huntingdon; ***225** WO-5; mail Tarrs z 15688; ● 130
Central City; RMC Place; CENTRE; ***224** WJ-13; ★ **STCOL**; mail Milesburg z 16853
Central City; Inc. Place; SOMERSET; **225** WO-9; elev. 2,150ft./655m.; 🅿; z 15926; Ⓟ 1,246; Ⓒ 1,258
Central Highlands; RMC Place; ALLEGHENY; ▲ Elizabeth; ***225** WN-4; ★ **PGH**; mail Elizabeth z 15037; ● 700
Centralia; Inc. Place; COLUMBIA; **227** EK-7; elev. 1,430ft./436m.; 🅿; z 17921; Ⓟ 63; Ⓒ 21
Central Manor; RMC Place; LANCASTER; ▲ Manor; ***227** EP-6; ★ **LANC**; mail Washington Boro z 17582; rural
Central Oak Heights; RMC Place; UNION; ▲ Kelly; ***226** EJ-4; elev. 511ft./156m.; mail West Milton z 17886
Central Square Greens; RMC Place; MONTGOMERY; ▲ Whitpain; ***227** EO-11; ★ **PHIL-**; mail Norristown z 19401; ● 2,500
Central Wharf; RMC Place; ALLEGHENY; ★ **PGH**; pop. incl. with Munhall (Inc. Place)
Centre; MCD-Township; BERKS; ***227** EM-8; ★ **READ**; mail Mohrsville z 19541; Ⓟ 3,154; Ⓒ 3,631
Centre; RMC Place; PERRY; ▲ Southwest Madison; ***227** EN-2; mail Loysville z 17047; ● 50
Centre; MCD-Township; PERRY; ***227** EN-3; ★ **HRBG**; mail New Bloomfield z 17068; Ⓟ 1,974; Ⓒ 2,209
Centre; SNYDER; see Center (MCD-Township)
CENTRE; **224** WJ-13; Ⓟ 123,786; Ⓒ 135,758; ◆ 152,536
Centre Hall; Inc. Place; CENTRE; **225** WK-14; elev. 1,320ft./402m.; 🅿 🅷; ★ **STCOL**; z 16828; Ⓟ 1,203; Ⓒ 1,079
Centre Hill; RMC Place; CENTRE; ▲ Potter; ***227** EK-1; ★ **STCOL**; mail Centre Hall z 16828; rural
Centre Valley; LEHIGH; see Center Valley (RMC Place)
Century; RMC Place; FAYETTE; ▲ Brownsville; ***225** WP-4; ★ **UNTN**; mail Brownsville z 15417; ● 80
Ceres; MCD-Township; MCKEAN; ***224** WD-12; mail Shinglehouse z 16748; Ⓟ 981; Ⓒ 1,003
Cessna; RMC Place; BEDFORD; ▲ Bedford; **225** WO-10; mail Bedford z 15522; ● 60
Cetronia; RMC Place; LEHIGH; ▲ South Whitehall; **226** EB-2; ★ **ALL-**; mail Allentown z 18104
Ceylon; RMC Place; GREENE; ▲ Monongahela; ***225** WQ-4; mail Carmichaels z 15320; rural
Chadds Ford; RMC Place; DELAWARE; ▲ Chadds Ford; **227** EQ-10; 🅿; ★ **PHIL-**; z 19317; ● 1,200
Chadds Ford (Birmingham); MCD-Township; DELAWARE; ***227** EQ-10; 🅿; ★ **PHIL-**; z 19317; Ⓟ 3,118; Ⓒ 3,170
Chadville; RMC Place; FAYETTE; ▲ South Union, Georges; ***225** WQ-5; elev. 1,260ft./384m.; ★ **UNTN**; mail Uniontown z 15401; ● 50
Chain; RMC Place; SCHUYLKILL; ▲ West Penn; ***227** EL-9; elev. 731ft./223m.; mail New Ringgold z 17960; rural

Entries in **UPPERCASE** are counties.
Entries in **bold** have populations of 2,500 or more.
Names in parentheses are alternate names.

Inc. Place	Incorporated Place
RMC Place	Rand McNally Designated Place
CDP	Census Designated Place
MCD	Minor Civil Division

⊡	County Seat
▲	Minor Civil Division
elev.	Elevation
🅿	Post Office
🅷	Hospital
🅲	College
■	Principal Business Center
★	Ranally Metro Area (RMA) Abbreviation
z	Zip Code(s)
Ⓟ	Previous Census Population
Ⓡ	Revised Census Population
Ⓐ	Annexation Population
●	Rand McNally Population Estimate
Ⓒ	Final Census Population
Ⓢ	Special Census Population
◆	Estimated Population

For additional definitions see Glossary, Volume 1, and Introduction, Volume 2.

Chain Bridge; RMC Place; BUCKS; ▲ Northampton; ***227** EN-13; ★ **PHIL-**; mail Newtown z 18940; rural
Chaintown; RMC Place; WESTMORELAND; ▲ Lower Tyrone, East Huntingdon; ***225** WO-5; mail Dawson z 15428; rural
Chalfant; Inc. Place; ALLEGHENY; **228** K-8; elev. 1,140ft./347m.; ★ **PGH**; mail East Pittsburgh z 15112; ℗ 959; © 870
Chalfont; Inc. Place; BUCKS; **227** EN-12; elev. 255ft./78m.; [P]; ★ **PHIL-**; z 18914; ℗ 3,069; © 3,900
Chalkhill; RMC Place; FAYETTE; ▲ Wharton; **225** WQ-5; elev. 2,072ft./632m.; [P]; z 15421; ● 400
Challenge; RMC Place; ELK; ▲ Horton; ***224** WH-10; mail Brockport z 15823
Chalybeate; RMC Place; BEDFORD; ▲ Bedford; ***225** WP-10; mail Bedford z 15522; rural
Chambersburg; Inc. Place; ⊡ FRANKLIN; **225** WP-14; elev. 621ft./189m.; [P] [H] [C] 771 ■; z 17201-02; ℗ 16,647; © 17,862; ◆ 19,137
Chambers Hill; RMC Place; DAUPHIN; ▲ Swatara; ***227** EO-5; elev. 600ft./183m.; ★ **HRBG**; mail Harrisburg z 17111; ● 1,500
Chambers Mill; RMC Place; WASHINGTON; ▲ Amwell; ***225** WO-2; ★ **WASH**; mail Washington z 15301; ● 25
Chambersville; RMC Place; INDIANA; ▲ Rayne; **225** WL-7; [P]; z 15723; ● 100
Champion; RMC Place; FAYETTE, WESTMORELAND; ▲ Saltlick, Donegal; **225** WO-6; [P]; z 15622; ● 300
Chanceford; MCD-Township; YORK; ***227** EP-6; ★ **YORK**; mail Brogue z 17309; ℗ 5,026; © 5,973
Chandlers Valley; RMC Place; WARREN; ▲ Sugar Grove; **224** WD-7; [P]; z 16312; ● 250
Chaneysville; RMC Place; BEDFORD; ▲ Southampton; **225** WQ-10; mail Clearville z 15535; ● 80
Chapel; RMC Place; BERKS; ▲ Hereford; ***227** EM-10; mail Palm z 18070; rural
Chapel Downs; RMC Place; ALLEGHENY; ▲ Harmar; ***225** WM-4; ★ **PGH**; mail Cheswick z 15024; ● 500
Chapel Valley; RMC Place; BEAVER; ▲ Center; ***225** WL-2; ★ **PGH**; mail Aliquippa z 15001; ● 1,000
Chapman; MCD-Township; CLINTON; ***224** WH-14; mail North Bend z 17760; ℗ 978; © 993
Chapman; RMC Place; LEHIGH; ▲ Upper Macungie; ***227** EL-10; ★ **ALL-**; mail Allentown z 18106; ● 300
Chapman (Chapman Quarries); Inc. Place; NORTHAMPTON; **227** EK-11; elev. 700ft./213m.; ★ **ALL-**; mail Bath z 18014; ℗ 254; © 234
Chapman; RMC Place; SNYDER; ▲ Chapman; **227** EL-4; mail Port Trevorton z 17864; ● 35
Chapman; MCD-Township; SNYDER; ***227** EL-4; mail Port Trevorton z 17864; ℗ 1,442; © 1,426
Chapman Lake; RMC Place; LACKAWANNA; ▲ Scott; ***226** EG-10; ★ **SCR-**; mail Jermyn z 18433
Chapman Quarries; NORTHAMPTON; see Chapman (Inc. Place)
Chapmanville (Plum); RMC Place; VENANGO; ***224** WF-4; mail Titusville z 16354; ● 90
Charleroi; Inc. Place; WASHINGTON; **225** WO-4; elev. 765ft./233m.; [P] ■; ★ **PGH**; z 15022; ℗ 5,014; © 4,871; ◆ 4,865
Charleston; RMC Place; MERCER; **224** WH-2; elev. 1,262ft./385m.; mail Hermitage z 16148; ● 100
Charleston; MCD-Township; TIOGA; ***226** EE-3; mail Wellsboro z 16901; ℗ 2,957; © 3,233
Charlestown; RMC Place; CHESTER; ▲ Charlestown; ***227** EO-10; ★ **PHIL-**; mail Phoenixville z 19460; ● 100
Charlestown; MCD-Township; CHESTER; ***227** EO-10; ★ **PHIL-**; mail Phoenixville z 19460; ℗ 2,754; © 4,051
Charlestown; RMC Place; FRANKLIN; ▲ Peters; ***225** WQ-13; mail Mercersburg z 17236; ● 60
Charlesville; RMC Place; BEDFORD; ▲ Colerain; ***225** WP-10; mail Bedford z 15522
Charlottsville; RMC Place; BLAIR; ▲ Antis; ***225** WL-11; ★ **ALT**; mail Tyrone z 16686; rural
Charlton; RMC Place; CLINTON; ▲ Pine Creek; ***226** EI-2; ★ **WMSPT**; mail Lock Haven z 17745; ● 160
Charlton; RMC Place; DAUPHIN; ▲ Lower Paxton; ***227** EN-5; ★ **HRBG**; mail Harrisburg z 17111; ● 700
Charmian; RMC Place; FRANKLIN; ▲ Washington; ***227** ER-2; ★ **HAG**; mail Blue Ridge Summit z 17214; rural
Charming Forge; RMC Place; BERKS; ▲ Marion; ***227** EN-8; elev. 338ft./103m.; mail Geigertown z 19523, Robesonia z 19551; rural
Charteroak; RMC Place; HUNTINGDON; ▲ Barree; ***225** WL-13; mail Petersburg z 16669; rural
Charter Oaks; RMC Place; ERIE; ▲ Millcreek; ***224** WC-3; ★ **ERIE**; mail Erie z 16509
Chartiers; RMC Place; GREENE; ***225** WP-3; mail Clarksville z 15322; ● 150
Chartiers; MCD-Township; WASHINGTON; ***225** WN-2; ★ **WASH**; mail Houston z 15342; ℗ 7,603; © 7,154
Chase; RMC Place; LUZERNE; ▲ Jackson; **226** EA-7; elev. 1,067ft./325m.; ★ **SCR-**; mail Shavertown z 18708; ● 450
Chatham; RMC Place; CHESTER; ▲ London Grove; **227** EQ-9; elev. 449ft./137m.; [P]; ★ **PHIL-**; z 19318; ● 300
Chatham; MCD-Township; TIOGA; ***226** EE-2; mail Middlebury Center z 16935; ℗ 607; © 587
Chatham Park; RMC Place; DELAWARE; ▲ Haverford; ★ **PHIL-**; mail Havertown z 19083
Chatham Village; RMC Place; DELAWARE; ▲ Haverford; ★ **PHIL-**; mail Havertown z 19083
Chatwood; RMC Place; CHESTER; ▲ West Goshen; **227** EP-10; ★ **PHIL-**; mail West Chester z 19380; ● 1,000
Checkerville; RMC Place; BRADFORD; ▲ South Creek; ***226** EE-5; mail Gillett z 16925; rural
Chelsea; RMC Place; DELAWARE; ▲ Bethel; **227** EQ-11; elev. 297ft./91m.; ★ **PHIL-**; mail Chester z 19013; ● 160
Chelten Avenue; RMC Place; PHILADELPHIA; ★ **PHIL-**; mail Philadelphia z 19144; pop. incl. with Philadelphia (Inc. Place)
Cheltenham; RMC Place; MONTGOMERY; ▲ Cheltenham; **228** B-5; [P]; ★ **PHIL-**; z 19012; ℗ 34,923
Cheltenham; MCD-Township; MONTGOMERY; ***227** EO-12; [P] [C] 4,837 ■; ★ **PHIL-**; z 19012; ℗ 34,923; © 36,875; ◆ 37,631
Cherokee Ranch; RMC Place; BERKS; ▲ Muhlenberg; ***227** EN-9; ★ **READ**; mail Temple z 19560; ● 500
Cherry; MCD-Township; BUTLER; ***224** WJ-4; mail Slippery Rock z 16057; ℗ 814; © 1,053
Cherry; MCD-Township; SULLIVAN; ***226** EG-7; mail Dushore z 18614; ℗ 1,481; © 1,718
Cherry City; RMC Place; ALLEGHENY; ▲ Shaler; ***225** WM-4; ★ **PGH**; mail Pittsburgh z 15223
Cherry Flats; RMC Place; TIOGA; ▲ Covington, Charleston; **226** EF-3; elev. 1,475ft./450m.; mail Covington z 16917, Mansfield z 16933; ● 250
Cherry Grove; RMC Place; HUNTINGDON; ▲ Cass; ***225** WN-12; mail Three Springs z 17264; rural
Cherry Grove; RMC Place; WARREN; ▲ Cherry Grove; ***224** WF-8; mail Clarendon z 16313
Cherry Grove; MCD-Township; WARREN; ***224** WF-8; mail Clarendon z 16313; ℗ 155; © 228
Cherry Hill; RMC Place; ERIE; ▲ Conneaut; **224** WD-2; ★ **ERIE**; mail Albion z 16401; ● 60
Cherryhill; MCD-Township; INDIANA; ***225** WL-8; mail Penn Run z 15765; ℗ 2,764; © 2,842
Cherry Hill (McSparren); RMC Place; LANCASTER; ▲ Fulton; **227** EQ-7; mail Peach Bottom z 17563; ● 35
Cherry Hill; RMC Place; NORTHAMPTON; ▲ Bushkill; **227** EK-11; ★ **ALL-**; mail Nazareth z 18064; ● 300
Cherry Hill; RMC Place; YORK; ▲ Fairview; ***227** EO-4; elev. 500ft./152m.; ★ **HRBG**; mail New Cumberland z 17070; ● 100
Cherry Lane; RMC Place; ARMSTRONG; ▲ Kiskiminetas; ***225** WM-6; ★ **PGH**; mail Apollo z 15613; ● 150
Cherry Ridge; MCD-Township; WAYNE; ***226** EG-11; mail Honesdale z 18431; ℗ 1,600; © 1,817
Cherry Run; RMC Place; UNION; ▲ Hartley; ***227** EK-2; mail Weikert z 17885
Cherrytown; RMC Place; HUNTINGDON; ▲ Hopewell; **225** WN-11; mail James Creek z 16657; ● 120
Cherry Tree; Inc. Place; INDIANA; **225** WL-9; [P]; z 15724; ℗ 431; © 443
Cherrytree; RMC Place; VENANGO; ▲ Cherrytree; ***224** WG-5; elev. 1,300ft./396m.; mail Titusville z 16354
Cherrytree; MCD-Township; VENANGO; ***224** WF-5; mail Titusville z 16354; ℗ 1,601; © 1,543
Cherry Valley; Inc. Place; BUTLER; **224** WI-5; elev. 1,320ft./402m.; mail Emlenton z 16373; ℗ 96; © 72
Cherry Valley; RMC Place; WASHINGTON; ▲ Smith; **225** WN-2; elev. 1,028ft./313m.; ★ **PGH**; mail Burgettstown z 15021; ● 200
Cherryville; RMC Place; NORTHAMPTON; ▲ Lehigh; **227** EK-10; [P]; ★ **ALL-**; z 18035; ● 650
Cherryville; RMC Place; SCHUYLKILL; ▲ Pine Grove; mail Ravine z 17966
Chest; MCD-Township; CAMBRIA; ***225** WL-10; mail Patton z 16668; ℗ 312; © 346
Chest; MCD-Township; CLEARFIELD; ***225** WL-10; mail La Jose z 15753; ℗ 565; © 547
Chester; Inc. Place; DELAWARE; **227** EQ-11; elev. 20ft./6m.; [P] [H] [C] 4,745 ■; ★ **PHIL-**; z 19013-16, z 19022; ℗ 41,856; © 36,854; ◆ 36,376
Chester; MCD-Township; DELAWARE; ***227** EQ-11; [P]; ★ **PHIL-**; z 19013-16, z 19022; ℗ 5,399; © 4,604
CHESTER; **227** EP-9; ℗ 376,396; © 433,501; ◆ 494,348
Chesterbrook; CDP-Census Area Only; CHESTER; ▲ Tredyffrin; ***227** EO-11; elev. 300ft./91m.; [P]; ★ **PHIL-**; z 19087; ℗ 4,561; © 4,625
Chesterfield; RMC Place; CLEARFIELD; ▲ Bigler; ***225** WK-10; mail Coalport z 16627; rural
Chester Heights; Inc. Place; DELAWARE; **227** EQ-11; elev. 336ft./102m.; [P]; ★ **PHIL-**; z 19017; ℗ 2,273; © 2,481
Chester Hill; Inc. Place; CLEARFIELD; **225** WK-12; elev. 1,440ft./439m.; mail Philipsburg z 16866; ℗ 945; © 918
Chester Springs (Yellow Springs); RMC Place; CHESTER; ▲ West Pikeland; **227** EO-10; [P]; ★ **PHIL-**; z 19425; ● 450
Chester Township; CDP-Census Area Only; DELAWARE; ▲ Chester; ***227** EQ-11; [P]; ★ **PHIL-**; z 19013; ℗ 5,399; © 4,604
Chester Valley Knoll; RMC Place; CHESTER; ▲ East Whiteland; ***227** EP-10; ★ **PHIL-**; mail Malvern z 19355; ● 400
Chesterville; RMC Place; CHESTER; ▲ Franklin; ***227** EQ-9; ★ **PHIL-**; mail Landenberg z 19350; ● 120
Chestnut Grove; RMC Place; CLEARFIELD; ▲ Bloom; **224** WJ-10; mail Grampian z 16838; ● 100
Chestnut Hill; RMC Place; ERIE; ▲ Millcreek; ***224** WC-3; ★ **ERIE**; mail Erie z 16509
Chestnut Hill; RMC Place; LANCASTER; ▲ West Hempfield; ***227** EP-6; elev. 523ft./159m.; ★ **LANC**; mail Columbia z 17512; ● 50
Chestnut Hill; RMC Place; LEHIGH; ▲ Upper Saucon; ***227** EM-11; ★ **ALL-**; mail Coopersburg z 18036; rural
Chestnuthill; MCD-Township; MONROE; ***226** EJ-11; ★ **ALL-**; mail Gilbert z 18331; ℗ 8,798; © 14,418
Chestnut Hill; RMC Place; NORTHAMPTON; ▲ Forks; ***227** EL-12; ★ **ALL-**; mail Easton z 18042; ● 250
Chestnut Hill; RMC Place; PHILADELPHIA; ***227** EO-12; ★ **PHIL-**; mail Philadelphia z 19118; pop. incl. with Philadelphia (Inc. Place)
Chestnut Level; RMC Place; LANCASTER; ▲ Drumore; **227** EQ-7; mail Quarryville z 17566; ● 200
Chestnut Ridge; RMC Place; FAYETTE; ▲ Redstone; ***225** WP-4; [P]; ★ **UNTN**; z 15422; ● 450
Chestnut Ridge; RMC Place; LANCASTER; ▲ East Hempfield; ***227** EP-7; ★ **LANC**; mail Lancaster z 17603; ● 100
Chestnut View; RMC Place; LANCASTER; ▲ East Hempfield; ***227** EP-7; ★ **LANC**; mail Lancaster z 17603; ● 200
Chest Springs; Inc. Place; CAMBRIA; **225** WM-10; elev. 1,940ft./591m.; [P]; z 16624; ℗ 166; © 110
Cheswick; Inc. Place; ALLEGHENY; **228** H-9; elev. 760ft./232m.; [P]; ★ **PGH**; z 15024; ℗ 1,971; © 1,899
Chevy Chase Heights; CDP; INDIANA; ▲ White; **225** WL-7; mail Indiana z 15701; ℗ 1,535; © 1,511
Chewton; RMC Place; LAWRENCE; ▲ Wayne; **225** WK-2; ★ **PGH**; mail Wampum z 16157; ● 300
Cheyney; RMC Place; DELAWARE, CHESTER; ▲ Westtown, Thornbury; **227** EP-11; [P] [C] 1,667; ★ **PHIL-**; z 19319; ● 150
Chickasaw; RMC Place; ARMSTRONG; ▲ Madison; ***224** WJ-6; mail Templeton z 16259; rural
Chicora; Inc. Place; BUTLER; **224** WJ-5; elev. 1,247ft./380m.; [P]; z 16025; ℗ 1,058; © 1,021
Childs; RMC Place; LACKAWANNA; ▲ Carbondale; **226** EG-10; [P]; ★ **SCR-**; z 18407; ● 450
Chillisquaque; RMC Place; NORTHUMBERLAND; ▲ West Chillisquaque; **226** EJ-4; mail Montandon z 17850; ● 400
Chinchilla; RMC Place; LACKAWANNA; ▲ South Abington; **226** EA-13; [P]; ★ **SCR-**; z 18410; ● 1,300
Chippewa; MCD-Township; BEAVER; ***225** WK-2; ★ **PGH**; mail Beaver Falls z 15010; ℗ 6,988; © 7,021
Choconut; RMC Place; SUSQUEHANNA; ▲ Choconut; **226** ED-8; elev. 1,102ft./336m.; mail Brackney z 18812, Friendsville z 18818; ● 50
Choconut; MCD-Township; SUSQUEHANNA; ***226** ED-8; mail Friendsville z 18818; ℗ 799; © 797
Christiana; Inc. Place; LANCASTER; **227** EP-8; elev. 494ft./151m.; [P]; z 17509; ℗ 1,045; © 1,124
Christian Springs; RMC Place; NORTHAMPTON; ▲ Upper Nazareth; ***227** EL-11; ★ **ALL-**; mail Nazareth z 18064; ● 75
Christmans; RMC Place; CARBON; ▲ Penn Forest; **226** EJ-10; mail Jim Thorpe z 18229; ● 100
Christy Manor; RMC Place; ARMSTRONG; **225** WL-6; mail Ford City z 16226; ● 75
Christy Park; RMC Place; ALLEGHENY; ★ **PGH**; pop. incl. with McKeesport (Inc. Place)
Chrome; RMC Place; CHESTER; ▲ East Nottingham; ***227** ER-8; mail Nottingham z 19362, Oxford z 19363
Chrystal; RMC Place; POTTER; ▲ Oswayo; ***224** WD-12; elev. 1,854ft./565m.; mail Shinglehouse z 16748; rural
Church Hill; RMC Place; FAYETTE; ▲ German; ***225** WQ-4; ★ **UNTN**; mail Mc Clellandtown z 15458; rural
Church Hill; RMC Place; FOREST; ▲ Hickory; ***224** WG-6; mail Tionesta z 16353; summer pop. 100; ● 25
Church Hill; RMC Place; FRANKLIN; ▲ Peters; ***225** WQ-13; mail Mercersburg z 17236; rural
Church Hill; RMC Place; MIFFLIN; ▲ Brown; ***227** EL-1; mail Reedsville z 17084; ● 750
Church Hills; RMC Place; JUNIATA; ▲ Turbett; ***227** EM-2; mail Port Royal z 17082; rural
Churchill; Inc. Place; ALLEGHENY; **228** J-8; elev. 1,100ft./335m.; ★ **PGH**; mail Pittsburgh z 15221, z 15235; ℗ 3,883; © 3,566
Churchill Plan; RMC Place; BEAVER; ▲ Franklin; ***225** WK-2; ★ **PGH**; mail Ellwood City z 16117; ● 150
Churchill Valley; RMC Place; ALLEGHENY; ▲ Penn Hills; ***225** WM-4; elev. 1,200ft./366m.; ★ **PGH**; mail Pittsburgh z 15235
Churchtown; CUMBERLAND; see Allen (RMC Place)
Churchtown; RMC Place; LANCASTER; ▲ Caernarvon; **227** EO-8; mail Narvon z 17555; ● 300
Churchville; RMC Place; BEDFORD; ▲ King, East St. Clair; **225** WO-10; mail Osterburg z 16667; ● 60
Churchville; CDP; BUCKS; ▲ Northampton; **227** EO-13; [P]; ★ **PHIL-**; z 18966; ℗ 4,255; © 4,469
Churchville; RMC Place; CLARION; ▲ Monroe; ***224** WI-6; mail Sligo z 16255; rural
Circleville; RMC Place; WESTMORELAND; ▲ North Huntingdon; **228** M-10; elev. 1,242ft./379m.; ★ **PGH**; mail Irwin z 15642; ● 450
Cisna Run; RMC Place; PERRY; ▲ Southwest Madison; ***227** EN-2; mail Loysville z 17047; ● 35
Cito; RMC Place; FULTON; ▲ Ayr; **225** WQ-13; mail Mc Connellsburg z 17233; ● 20
City View; RMC Place; MIFFLIN; ▲ Derry; ***227** EM-1; elev. 600ft./183m.; mail Lewistown z 17044; rural
Clair Manor; RMC Place; WESTMORELAND; ▲ Rostraver; ***225** WO-4; elev. 1,000ft./305m.; ★ **PGH**; mail Belle Vernon z 15012; ● 300
Clairton; Inc. Place; ALLEGHENY; **228** N-8; elev. 940ft./287m.; [P]; ★ **PGH**; z 15025; ℗ 9,656; © 8,491
Clairton Junction; RMC Place; ALLEGHENY; ★ **PGH**; mail West Mifflin z 15122; pop. incl. with West Mifflin (Inc. Place)
Clamtown; RMC Place; SCHUYLKILL; ▲ West Penn; mail New Ringgold z 17960, Tamaqua z 18252; ● 240
Clappertown; RMC Place; BLAIR; ▲ Huston; **225** WN-11; mail Williamsburg z 16693; ● 110
Clapp Farm; VENANGO; see Clapp Lease (RMC Place)
Clapp Lease (Clapp Farm); RMC Place; VENANGO; ▲ Cornplanter; ***224** WH-6; ★ **OILC-F**; mail Oil City z 16301; rural
Clara; MCD-Township; POTTER; ***224** WE-12; mail Shinglehouse z 16748; ℗ 133; © 168
Clarence; CDP; CENTRE; ▲ Snow Shoe; **224** WJ-13; [P]; z 16829 & mail Snow Shoe z 16874; © 577
Clarendon; Inc. Place; WARREN; **224** WE-8; elev. 1,395ft./425m.; [P]; z 16313; ℗ 650; © 564
Clarendon Heights; RMC Place; WARREN; ▲ Mead; ***224** WE-8; elev. 1,400ft./427m.; mail Clarendon z 16313; ● 170
Claridge; RMC Place; WESTMORELAND; ▲ Penn; **225** WN-5; [P]; ★ **PGH**; z 15623; ● 1,200
Clarington; RMC Place; FOREST; ▲ Barnett; **224** WH-8; [P]; z 15828; ● 125
Clarion; Inc. Place; ⊡ CLARION; **224** WI-6; elev. 1,491ft./454m.; [P] [H] [C] 6,591; z 16214; ℗ 6,457; © 6,185
Clarion; MCD-Township; CLARION; ***224** WI-7; [P] [C] 6,591; z 16214 & mail Strattanville z 16258; does not include the Borough of Clarion; ℗ 3,306; © 3,273
CLARION; **224** WI-6; ℗ 41,699; © 41,765; ◆ 39,624
Clark; Inc. Place; MERCER; **224** WH-2; elev. 900ft./274m.; [P]; ★ **SHAR**; z 16113; ℗ 610; © 633
Clark Manor; RMC Place; BEAVER; ▲ Hopewell; ***225** WL-2; ★ **PGH**; mail Aliquippa z 15001; ● 400
Clarksburg; RMC Place; INDIANA; ▲ Young, Conemaugh; **225** WM-6; [P]; ★ **PGH**; z 15725; ● 180
Clarks Green; Inc. Place; LACKAWANNA; **226** EA-13; elev. 1,302ft./397m.; [P]; ★ **SCR-**; z 18411; ℗ 1,603; © 1,630
Clarks Mills; RMC Place; MERCER; ▲ Perry; **224** WH-3; elev. 1,166ft./355m.; [P]; z 16114; ● 120
Clarks Summit; Inc. Place; LACKAWANNA; **226** EG-10; elev. 1,240ft./378m.; [P] [H] [C] 1,137; ★ **SCR-**; z 18411; ℗ 5,433; © 5,126
Clarkstown; RMC Place; LYCOMING; ▲ Muncy Creek; **226** EI-5; ★ **WMSPT**; mail Muncy z 17756; ● 200
Clarksville; Inc. Place; GREENE; **225** WP-3; elev. 800ft./244m.; [P]; z 15322; ℗ 211; © 234
Clarksville Hill; RMC Place; WASHINGTON; ▲ East Bethlehem; ***225** WP-3; mail Clarksville z 15322; ● 600
Claussville; RMC Place; LEHIGH; ▲ Lowhill; **227** EL-10; ★ **ALL-**; mail Orefield z 18069; ● 40
Clay; MCD-Township; BUTLER; ***224** WJ-4; ★ **BUTL**; mail West Sunbury z 16061; ℗ 2,360; © 2,628
Clay; MCD-Township; HUNTINGDON; ***225** WO-13; mail Three Springs z 17264; ℗ 921; © 920
Clay; RMC Place; LANCASTER; ▲ Clay; **227** EO-7; elev. 363ft./111m.; ★ **LANC**; mail Ephrata z 17522; ● 300
Clay; MCD-Township; LANCASTER; ***227** EN-7; ★ **LANC**; mail Ephrata z 17522, Stevens z 17578; ℗ 5,050; © 5,173
Clay Hill; RMC Place; FRANKLIN; ▲ Antrim; ***225** WQ-14; ★ **HAG**; mail Chambersburg z 17201; ● 75
Claylick; RMC Place; FRANKLIN; ▲ Montgomery; ***225** WQ-13; mail Mercersburg z 17236
Claypoole Heights; RMC Place; INDIANA; ▲ White; ***225** WL-7; mail Indiana z 15701; ● 125
Claysburg; CDP; BLAIR; ▲ Greenfield; **225** WN-10; [P]; ★ **ALT**; z 16625; ℗ 1,399; © 1,503
Claysville; Inc. Place; WASHINGTON; **225** WO-2; elev. 1,140ft./347m.; [P]; z 15323; ℗ 962; © 724
Clayton; RMC Place; BERKS; ▲ Washington, Hereford; ***227** EM-10; elev. 424ft./129m.; mail Bally z 19503; rural
Claytonia; RMC Place; BUTLER; ▲ Clay; ***224** WJ-4; ★ **BUTL**; mail Slippery Rock z 16057; ● 60
Clearbrook Village; RMC Place; MONTGOMERY; ▲ Horsham; ★ **PHIL-**; mail Hatboro z 19040
Clearfield; MCD-Township; BUTLER; ***225** WK-5; ★ **PGH**; mail Fenelton z 16034; ℗ 2,635; © 2,705
Clearfield; MCD-Township; CAMBRIA; ***225** WL-10; mail Patton z 16668; ℗ 1,749; © 1,680
Clearfield; Inc. Place; ⊡ CLEARFIELD; **224** WJ-11; elev. 1,109ft./338m.; [P] [H] ■; z 16830; ℗ 6,633; © 6,631; ◆ 6,216
Clearfield; RMC Place; NORTHAMPTON; ▲ Bushkill; **227** EK-11; ★ **ALL-**; mail Nazareth z 18064; ● 200
CLEARFIELD; **224** WJ-11; ℗ 78,097; © 83,382; ◆ 79,574
Clear Ridge; RMC Place; BEDFORD; ▲ West Providence; ***225** WP-11; mail Everett z 15537; ● 15
Clear Ridge; RMC Place; FULTON; ▲ Taylor, Dublin; **225** WO-13; mail Hustontown z 17229; ● 30
Clear Run; RMC Place; CLEARFIELD; ▲ Sandy; **224** WI-9; mail Du Bois z 15801; ● 350
Clear Spring; RMC Place; YORK; ▲ Franklin; **227** EP-3; ★ **HRBG**; mail Dillsburg z 17019; ● 40
Clearview; RMC Place; LANCASTER; ▲ Manheim; ***227** EP-7; ★ **LANC**; mail Lancaster z 17601; ● 800
Clearview Estates; RMC Place; BEAVER; ▲ Hopewell; ***225** WL-2; ★ **PGH**; mail Aliquippa z 15001; ● 1,800
Clearview Estates; RMC Place; CUMBERLAND; ▲ Hampden; ***227** EO-4; ★ **HRBG**; mail Camp Hill z 17011; ● 2,500
Clearview Manor; RMC Place; LEHIGH; ▲ South Whitehall; ***227** EM-10; elev. 400ft./122m.; ★ **ALL-**; mail Allentown z 18101; ● 450
Clearville; RMC Place; BEDFORD; ▲ Monroe; **225** WP-11; [P]; z 15535; ● 200
Cleona; Inc. Place; LEBANON; **227** EN-6; elev. 460ft./140m.; [P]; ★ **LEB**; z 17042; ℗ 2,322; © 2,148
Clermont; RMC Place; MCKEAN; ▲ Sergeant; **224** WF-10; elev. 2,061ft./628m.; mail Harrisburg z 17112, Mount Jewett z 16740; ● 100
Cleveland; MCD-Township; COLUMBIA; ***227** EK-6; mail Catawissa z 17820; ℗ 997; © 1,004
Cleversburg; RMC Place; CUMBERLAND; ▲ Southampton; **227** EP-2; mail Shippensburg z 17257; ● 100
Cliff Mine; RMC Place; ALLEGHENY; ▲ Findlay; ***225** WM-3; ★ **PGH**; mail Coraopolis z 15108; rural
Clifford; RMC Place; SNYDER; ▲ Penn; ***227** EK-4; mail Selinsgrove z 17870; rural
Clifford; RMC Place; SUSQUEHANNA; ▲ Clifford; **226** EF-10; [P]; z 18413; ● 500
Clifford; MCD-Township; SUSQUEHANNA; ***226** EF-10; [P]; z 18413 & mail Union Dale z 18470; ℗ 2,147; © 2,381
Clifton; RMC Place; DAUPHIN; ▲ Londonderry, Derry; ***227** EO-5; ★ **HRBG**; mail Middletown z 17057; rural
Clifton; RMC Place; LACKAWANNA; ▲ Clifton; **226** EI-10; [P]; z 18424; ● 300
Clifton; MCD-Township; LACKAWANNA; ***226** EI-10; [P]; z 18424; ℗ 1,041; © 1,139
Clifton Heights; Inc. Place; DELAWARE; **228** E-2; elev. 150ft./46m.; [P]; ★ **PHIL-**; z 19018; ℗ 7,111; © 6,779
Climax; RMC Place; ARMSTRONG, CLARION; ▲ Porter, Mahoning; **224** WJ-6; [P]; z 16242; ● 40
Climax; RMC Place; INDIANA; ▲ West Wheatfield; ***225** WN-7; ★ **JNST**; mail New Florence z 15944; ● 50
Clinton; RMC Place; ALLEGHENY; ▲ Findlay; **225** WM-2; [P]; ★ **PGH**; z 15026; ● 600
Clinton; RMC Place; ARMSTRONG; ▲ South Buffalo; **225** WL-5; ★ **PGH**; mail Freeport z 16229; ● 75
Clinton; RMC Place; BUTLER; ▲ Clinton; ***225** WL-5; ★ **PGH**; mail Sarver z 16055; rural
Clinton; MCD-Township; BUTLER; ***225** WL-4; ★ **PGH**; mail Valencia z 16059; ℗ 2,556; © 2,779
Clinton; RMC Place; FAYETTE; ▲ Saltlick; ***225** WP-6; mail Normalville z 15469; ● 200
Clinton; MCD-Township; LYCOMING; ***226** EI-4; ★ **WMSPT**; mail Montgomery z 17752; ℗ 3,086; © 3,947; Ⓡ 3,090
Clinton; MCD-Township; VENANGO; ***224** WH-4; mail Emlenton z 16373; does not include the Borough of Clintonville; ℗ 733; © 758
Clinton; MCD-Township; WAYNE; ***226** EF-11; mail Waymart z 18472; ℗ 1,582; © 1,926
Clinton; MCD-Township; WYOMING; ***226** EG-9; ★ **SCR-**; mail Factoryville z 18419; ℗ 1,063; © 1,343
CLINTON; **226** EI-1; ℗ 37,182; © 37,914; ◆ 36,809
Clintondale; RMC Place; CLINTON; ▲ Porter; **226** EJ-1; mail Mill Hall z 17751; ● 100
Clintonville; Inc. Place; VENANGO; **224** WI-4; elev. 1,473ft./449m.; [P]; z 16372; ℗ 520; © 528
Cloe; RMC Place; JEFFERSON; ▲ Bell; **224** WJ-8; elev. 1,251ft./381m.; mail Punxsutawney z 15767; ● 250
Clonmell; RMC Place; CHESTER; ▲ West Marlborough; ***227** EQ-9; elev. 482ft./147m.; mail West Grove z 19390; rural
Clover; MCD-Township; JEFFERSON; ***224** WI-7; mail Corsica z 15829; ℗ 523; © 474
Clover Creek (Fredericksburg); RMC Place; BLAIR; ▲ North Woodbury; **225** WN-11; mail Martinsburg z 16662; ● 170
Cloverdale Park; RMC Place; MONTGOMERY; ▲ Montgomery; ★ **PHIL-**; mail Colmar z 18915
Clover Hill; RMC Place; WASHINGTON; ▲ West Pike Run; ***225** WO-4; mail Coal Center z 15423; rural
Clover Run; RMC Place; CLEARFIELD; ▲ Bell; ***224** WJ-9; elev. 2,066ft./630m.; mail Mahaffey z 15757; rural
Clune; INDIANA; see Coal Run (RMC Place)
Cly; RMC Place; YORK; ▲ Newberry; **227** EO-5; mail York Haven z 17370; ● 70
Clyde; RMC Place; INDIANA; ▲ West Wheatfield; **225** WM-8; elev. 1,824ft./556m.; ★ **JNST**; mail New Florence z 15944; ● 50
Clyde Number 3; WASHINGTON; see Williamstown (RMC Place)
Clymer; Inc. Place; INDIANA; **225** WL-8; elev. 1,218ft./371m.; [P]; z 15728; ℗ 1,499; © 1,547
Clymer; MCD-Township; TIOGA; ***226** EE-1; mail Sabinsville z 16943; ℗ 597; © 597
Coal; MCD-Township; NORTHUMBERLAND; ***227** EK-6; mail Coal Township z 17866, Shamokin z 17872; ℗ 9,922; © 10,628
Coal Bluff; RMC Place; WASHINGTON; ▲ Union; ***225** WN-4; ★ **PGH**; mail Finleyville z 15332; rural
Coal Cabin Beach; RMC Place; YORK; ▲ Peach Bottom; ***227** EQ-7; ★ **BAL**; mail Delta z 17314; summer pop. 200; ● 25
Coal Castle; RMC Place; SCHUYLKILL; ▲ Cass; ***227** EL-7; ★ **PTSVL**; mail Pottsville z 17901; ● 50
Coal Center; Inc. Place; WASHINGTON; **225** WO-4; elev. 780ft./238m.; [P]; ★ **PGH**; z 15423; ℗ 184; © 134
Coal City; RMC Place; VENANGO; ▲ Rockland; **224** WH-5; mail Kennerdell z 16374; ● 25
Coaldale (Six Mile Run); Inc. Place; BEDFORD; **225** WO-12; elev. 1,200ft./366m.; mail Six Mile Run z 16679; ℗ 143; © 146
Coaldale; RMC Place; DAUPHIN; ▲ Wiconisco; mail Lykens z 17048; ● 150
Coaldale; Inc. Place; SCHUYLKILL; **227** EK-9; elev. 1,040ft./317m.; [P] [H]; z 18218; ℗ 2,531; © 2,295
Coal Glen; RMC Place; JEFFERSON; ▲ Washington; **224** WI-9; mail Brockway z 15824; ● 25
Coal Hill; RMC Place; VENANGO; ▲ Pinegrove; **224** WH-6; mail Oil City z 16301; ● 120
Coal Hollow; RMC Place; ELK; ▲ Fox; ***224** WH-10; mail Kersey z 15846; rural
Coalmont; Inc. Place; HUNTINGDON; **225** WO-12; elev. 1,126ft./343m.; mail Saxton z 16678; ℗ 109; © 128
Coalport; RMC Place; CARBON; mail Jim Thorpe z 18229; pop. incl. with Jim Thorpe (Inc. Place)
Coalport; Inc. Place; CLEARFIELD; **225** WL-10; elev. 1,382ft./421m.; [P]; z 16627; ℗ 578; © 490
Coal Run; RMC Place; CLEARFIELD; ▲ Decatur; ***225** WK-11; mail Osceola Mills z 16666; ● 85
Coal Run (Clune); RMC Place; INDIANA; ▲ Young; **225** WM-7; mail Clune z 15727; ● 310
Coal Run; RMC Place; NORTHUMBERLAND; ▲ Coal; ***227** EK-6; mail Coal Township z 17866, Shamokin z 17872; ● 75
Coal Run; RMC Place; SOMERSET; ▲ Summit; ***225** WQ-8; elev. 2,080ft./634m.; mail Meyersdale z 15552; ● 85
Coaltown; RMC Place; BUTLER; ▲ Cherry; ***224** WJ-4; mail Slippery Rock z 16057; ● 50
Coaltown; RMC Place; LAWRENCE; ▲ Neshannock; **224** WJ-2; ★ **NWCS**; mail New Castle z 16101; ● 1,200
Coal Township; RMC Place; NORTHUMBERLAND; [P] [H]; z 17866; pop. incl. with Shamokin (Inc. Place)
Coatesville; Inc. Place; CHESTER; **227** EP-9; elev. 350ft./107m.; [P] [H]; ★ **PHIL-**; z 19320; ℗ 11,038; © 10,838
Cobalt Ridge; RMC Place; BUCKS; ▲ Middletown; ***227** EO-13; ★ **PHIL-**; mail Levittown z 19058
Cobblerville; RMC Place; CUMBERLAND; ▲ North Newton; ***227** EP-2; mail Newville z 17241; ● 50
Cobbs Corners; RMC Place; WARREN; ▲ Spring Creek; ***224** WE-6; mail Spartansburg z 16434; rural
Cobham; RMC Place; WARREN; ▲ Deerfield; ***224** WF-7; mail Tidioute z 16351
Coburn; RMC Place; BLAIR; ▲ Logan; ***225** WM-11; ★ **ALT**; mail Altoona z 16601; ● 60
Coburn; CDP; CENTRE; ▲ Penn; **227** EK-2; [P]; z 16832; © 145
Cocalico; RMC Place; LANCASTER; ▲ West Cocalico; ***227** EN-7; elev. 550ft./168m.; mail Denver z 17517
Cochran Acres; RMC Place; BEAVER; ▲ Hopewell; ***225** WL-2; ★ **PGH**; mail Aliquippa z 15001; ● 200
Cochrans Mills; RMC Place; ARMSTRONG; ▲ Burrell; ***225** WL-6; mail Ford City z 16226; rural
Cochranton; Inc. Place; CRAWFORD; **224** WG-3; elev. 1,069ft./326m.; [P]; z 16314; ℗ 1,174; © 1,148
Cochranville; RMC Place; CHESTER; ▲ West Fallowfield; **227** EQ-9; elev. 582ft./177m.; [P]; z 19330; ● 400
Cocolamus (Browns Mill); RMC Place; JUNIATA; ▲ Fayette; **227** EL-3; [P]; z 17014; ● 50
Codorus; YORK; see Jefferson (Inc. Place)
Codorus; MCD-Township; YORK; ***227** ER-5; [P]; ★ **BAL**; z 17311 & mail Glen Rock z 17327; does not include the Borough of Jefferson; ℗ 3,653; © 3,646
Codorus Mills; RMC Place; YORK; ★ **YORK**; pop. incl. with York (Inc. Place)
Coffeetown; RMC Place; LEBANON; ▲ North Londonderry; ***227** EN-6; elev. 606ft./185m.; mail Palmyra z 17078; ● 125
Coffeetown; RMC Place; LEHIGH; ▲ North Whitehall; ***227** EL-10; ★ **ALL-**; mail Allentown z 18102, Orefield z 18069; ● 30
Coffeetown; RMC Place; NORTHAMPTON; ▲ Williams; ***227** EL-12; ★ **ALL-**; mail Easton z 18042; ● 50
Cogan House; MCD-Township; LYCOMING; ***226** EH-3; mail Trout Run z 17771; ℗ 807; © 974
Cogan Station; RMC Place; LYCOMING; ▲ Hepburn; **226** EH-3; [P]; ★ **WMSPT**; z 17728; ● 600
Cokeburg; Inc. Place; WASHINGTON; **225** WO-3; elev. 1,040ft./317m.; [P]; ★ **WASH**; z 15324; ℗ 724; © 705
Cokeburg Junction; RMC Place; WASHINGTON; ▲ Somerset; ***225** WO-3; ★ **WASH**; mail Ellsworth z 15331; ● 200
Cold Point; RMC Place; MONTGOMERY; ▲ Whitemarsh, Plymouth; ***227** EO-12; ★ **PHIL-**; mail Plymouth Meeting z 19462
Cold Run; RMC Place; BERKS; ▲ Union; ***227** EO-9; elev. 514ft./157m.; ★ **READ**; mail Birdsboro z 19508, Geigertown z 19523; ● 65
Cold Spring; RMC Place; WAYNE; ▲ Lebanon; ***226** EF-11; mail Honesdale z 18431; rural
Cold Spring; RMC Place; YORK; ▲ North Codorus; ***227** EQ-5; ★ **YORK**; mail Seven Valleys z 17360; rural
Cold Spring Park; RMC Place; CHESTER; ▲ North Coventry; ***227** EO-10; ★ **PTSTN**; mail Pottstown z 19464; rural
Cold Springs Crossing; RMC Place; MONTGOMERY; ▲ Lower Providence; ***227** EO-11; elev. 150ft./46m.; ★ **PHIL-**; mail Collegeville z 19426; ● 500
Colebrook; MCD-Township; CLINTON; ***226** EI-2; ★ **WMSPT**; mail Lock Haven z 17745; ℗ 180; © 179
Colebrook; RMC Place; LEBANON; ▲ South Londonderry; **227** EO-6; elev. 545ft./166m.; [P]; z 17042; ● 150
Colebrookdale; RMC Place; BERKS; ▲ Douglass; **227** EN-10; mail Boyertown z 19512; ● 130
Colebrookdale; MCD-Township; BERKS; ***227** EN-10; mail Boyertown z 19512; ℗ 5,469; © 5,270
Colegrove; RMC Place; MCKEAN; ▲ Norwich; ***224** WF-11; elev. 1,525ft./465m.; mail Smethport z 16749
Coleman; RMC Place; SOMERSET; ▲ Stonycreek, Quemahoning; ***225** WP-8; mail Friedens z 15541; rural
Colemanville; RMC Place; LANCASTER; ▲ Conestoga; ***227** EQ-7; elev. 218ft./66m.; ★ **LANC**; mail Pequea z 17565; rural
Colerain; MCD-Township; BEDFORD; ***225** WP-10; mail Bedford z 15522; ℗ 1,058; © 1,147
Colerain; RMC Place; HUNTINGDON; ▲ Spruce Creek, Franklin; ***225** WL-12; mail Spruce Creek z 16683; rural
Colerain; MCD-Township; LANCASTER; ***227** EQ-8; mail Kirkwood z 17536; ℗ 2,867; © 3,261
Coles; RMC Place; SCHUYLKILL; ▲ Mahanoy; ***227** EK-8; mail Mahanoy City z 17948; ● 35
Colesburg; RMC Place; POTTER; ▲ Allegany; ***224** WE-13; mail Coudersport z 16915
Coles Creek; RMC Place; COLUMBIA; ▲ Sugarloaf; ***226** EI-7; elev. 864ft./263m.; mail Benton z 17814; rural
Colesville; RMC Place; LEHIGH, NORTHAMPTON; ▲ Lower Saucon, Upper Saucon; ***227** EM-11; ★ **ALL-**; mail Bethlehem z 18015; ● 150
Coleville; RMC Place; CENTRE; ▲ Spring; **225** WK-14; ★ **STCOL**; mail Bellefonte z 16823; ● 250
Coleville; RMC Place; MCKEAN; ▲ Keating; ***224** WE-10; mail Smethport z 16749; rural
Colfax; RMC Place; HUNTINGDON; ▲ Union; ***225** WN-13; mail Huntingdon z 16652; rural
College; MCD-Township; CENTRE; ***225** WK-13; ★ **STCOL**; mail State College z 16801; ℗ 6,709; © 8,489
College Heights; RMC Place; BERKS; ▲ Muhlenberg; **227** ES-13; ★ **READ**; mail Reading z 19605; ● 550
College Hill; RMC Place; BEAVER; ***225** WK-2; [P]; ★ **PGH**; z 18042 & mail Beaver Falls z 15010; pop. incl. with Beaver Falls (Inc. Place)
College Manor; RMC Place; LUZERNE; ▲ Dallas; ***226** EH-8; elev. 1,200ft./366m.; ★ **SCR-**; mail Dallas z 18612; ● 300
College Park; RMC Place; MONTGOMERY; ▲ Springfield; ★ **PHIL-**; mail Flourtown z 19031
College Park; RMC Place; UNION; ▲ East Buffalo; **226** EJ-4; mail Lewisburg z 17837; ● 160
College View Heights; RMC Place; NORTHAMPTON; ▲ Bethlehem; ***227** EL-11; elev. 400ft./122m.; ★ **ALL-**; mail Bethlehem z 18016; ● 400
Collegeville; Inc. Place; MONTGOMERY; **227** EO-11; elev. 200ft./61m.; [P] [C] 1,589; ★ **PHIL-**; z 19426, z 19473; ℗ 4,227; © 8,032; Ⓡ 4,628
Colley; MCD-Township; SULLIVAN; ***226** EG-7; mail Dushore z 18614; ℗ 600; © 647
Collier; MCD-Township; ALLEGHENY; ***225** WN-3; ★ **PGH**; mail Carnegie z 15106; ℗ 4,841; © 5,265
Collier; RMC Place; FAYETTE; ▲ Georges; ***225** WQ-4; ★ **UNTN**; mail Uniontown z 15401; ● 200
Collingdale; Inc. Place; DELAWARE; **228** F-2; elev. 120ft./37m.; [P]; ★ **PHIL-**; z 19023; ℗ 9,175; © 8,664
Collins; RMC Place; LANCASTER; ▲ Colerain; ***227** EQ-8; elev. 658ft./201m.; mail Quarryville z 17566
Collinsburg; RMC Place; WESTMORELAND; ▲ Rostraver; ***225** WO-5; ★ **PGH**; mail West Newton z 15089; ● 900
Collinsville; RMC Place; YORK; ▲ Chanceford; **227** EQ-6; elev. 779ft./237m.; ★ **YORK**; mail Airville z 17302, Brogue z 17309; ● 150
Collinswood Acres; RMC Place; WASHINGTON; ▲ Peters; ***225** WN-3; elev. 1,000ft./305m.; ★ **PGH**; mail Canonsburg z 15317; ● 450
Collomsville; RMC Place; LYCOMING; ▲ Limestone; **226** EI-3; [P]; z 17702; ● 200
Colmar; RMC Place; MONTGOMERY; ▲ Hatfield; **227** EN-12; [P]; ★ **PHIL-**; z 18915; ● 800
Colona; RMC Place; BEAVER; ★ **PGH**; mail Monaca z 15061; pop. incl. with Monaca (Inc. Place)
Colonial Crest; RMC Place; DAUPHIN; ▲ Lower Paxton; ***227** EN-5; ★ **HRBG**; mail Harrisburg z 17111-12; ● 500
Colonial Hills; RMC Place; BERKS; ▲ Cumru; ***227** EN-8; ★ **READ**; mail Reading z 19608; ● 200
Colonial Hills; RMC Place; MIFFLIN; ▲ Granville; ***227** EM-1; mail Lewistown z 17044; ● 100
Colonial Manor; RMC Place; LANCASTER; ▲ Manor; ***227** EP-7; ★ **LANC**; mail Lancaster z 17603; ● 550
Colonial Park; CDP; DAUPHIN; ▲ Lower Paxton; **227** EN-5; ★ **HRBG**; mail Harrisburg z 17109; ℗ 13,777; © 13,259
Colonial Park; RMC Place; DELAWARE; ▲ Springfield; ★ **PHIL-**; mail Springfield z 19064
Colonial Park; RMC Place; LANCASTER; ★ **LANC**; mail Leola z 17540
Colonial Park; RMC Place; NORTHUMBERLAND; ▲ West Chillisquaque; ***226** EJ-4; mail Milton z 17847; pop. incl. with Milton (Inc. Place)
Colonial Village; RMC Place; CHESTER, MONTGOMERY; ▲ Tredyffrin; ***227** EO-11; ★ **PHIL-**; mail Wayne z 19087; ● 500
Colonial Village; RMC Place; VENANGO; ▲ Cornplanter; ***224** WG-5; ★ **OILC-F**; mail Oil City z 16301; ● 200
Colony Park; RMC Place; BERKS; ▲ Spring; ***227** EN-8; elev. 380ft./116m.; ★ **READ**; mail Reading z 19608; ● 750
Columbia; MCD-Township; BRADFORD; ***226** EE-4; mail Columbia Cross Roads z 16914; ℗ 1,077; © 1,162
Columbia; Inc. Place; LANCASTER; **227** EP-6; elev. 300ft./91m.; [P] [H]; ★ **LANC**; z 17512; ℗ 10,701; © 10,311
COLUMBIA; **226** EJ-6; ℗ 63,202; © 64,151; ◆ 64,174
Columbia Cross Roads; RMC Place; BRADFORD; ▲ Columbia; **226** EE-5; elev. 130ft./40m.; [P]; z 16914; ● 220
Columbus; RMC Place; WARREN; ▲ Columbus; **224** WD-6; elev. 1,438ft./438m.; [P]; z 16405; ● 1,200
Columbus; MCD-Township; WARREN; ***224** WD-6; [P]; z 16405; ℗ 1,776; © 1,741
Colver; CDP; CAMBRIA; ▲ Cambria; **225** WM-9; [P]; z 15927; ℗ 1,024; © 1,035
Colwyn; Inc. Place; DELAWARE; **228** F-3; elev. 50ft./15m.; ★ **PHIL-**; mail Darby z 19023; ℗ 2,613; © 2,453
Comly; RMC Place; MONTOUR; ▲ Anthony; ***226** EI-5; elev. 599ft./183m.; mail Turbotville z 17772; rural
Commerce; RMC Place; PHILADELPHIA; ★ **PHIL-**; mail Philadelphia z 19108; pop. incl. with Philadelphia (Inc. Place)
Commodore; CDP; INDIANA; ▲ Green; **225** WL-8; [P]; z 15729; © 337
Compass; RMC Place; CHESTER; ▲ West Caln; **227** EP-9; ★ **PHIL-**; mail Gap z 17527; ● 140
Conashaugh Lake; RMC Place; PIKE; ▲ Dingman; ***226** EH-13; elev. 1,400ft./427m.; mail Milford z 18337; ● 900
Concord; MCD-Township; BUTLER; ***224** WJ-4; mail Chicora z 16025; ℗ 1,336; © 1,493
Concord; MCD-Township; DELAWARE; ***227** EQ-11; ★ **PHIL-**; mail Concordville z 19331; ℗ 6,933; © 9,933; Ⓡ 11,239
Concord; MCD-Township; ERIE; ***224** WE-5; mail Corry z 16407; ℗ 1,384; © 1,361
Concord; RMC Place; FRANKLIN; ▲ Fannett; **225** WN-14; [P]; z 17217; ● 135
Concord; RMC Place; WESTMORELAND; ▲ Rostraver; ***225** WO-5; elev. 1,016ft./310m.; ★ **PGH**; mail Belle Vernon z 15012; ● 200
Concord Park; RMC Place; BUCKS; ▲ Bensalem; ★ **PHIL-**; mail Langhorne z 19047
Concordville; RMC Place; DELAWARE; ▲ Concord; **227** EQ-11; [P]; ★ **PHIL-**; z 19331, z 19339-40; ● 600
Conemaugh; MCD-Township; CAMBRIA; ***225** WN-9; [P]; ★ **JNST**; z 15909 & mail Johnstown z 15902; does not include the Borough of East Conemaugh; ℗ 2,399; © 2,145
Conemaugh; MCD-Township; INDIANA; ***225** WM-7; ★ **PGH**; mail Clarksburg z 15725; ℗ 2,448; © 2,437
Conemaugh; MCD-Township; SOMERSET; ***225** WO-8; ★ **JNST**; mail Hollsopple z 15935; ℗ 7,737; © 7,452
Conestoga (Little Conestoga); RMC Place; CHESTER; ▲ West Nantmeal; ***227** EO-9; ★ **PHIL-**; mail Elverson z 19520; rural
Conestoga; RMC Place; LANCASTER; ▲ Conestoga; **227** EP-7; elev. 500ft./152m.; [P]; ★ **LANC**; z 17516; ● 450
Conestoga; MCD-Township; LANCASTER; ***227** EP-7; [P]; ★ **LANC**; z 17516; ℗ 3,470; © 3,749
Conestoga Woods; RMC Place; LANCASTER; ▲ Lancaster; ***227** EP-7; ★ **LANC**; mail Lancaster z 17602; ● 250
Coneville; RMC Place; POTTER; ▲ Hebron; ***224** WE-12; mail Coudersport z 16915
Conewago; MCD-Township; ADAMS; ***227** EQ-4; ★ **HANV**; mail Hanover z 17331; ℗ 4,532; © 5,709
Conewago; MCD-Township; DAUPHIN; ***227** EO-6; ★ **HRBG**; mail Elizabethtown z 17022; ℗ 2,832; © 2,847
Conewago; MCD-Township; YORK; ***227** EO-5; ★ **YORK**; mail Hanover z 17331, York z 17404; ℗ 4,997; © 5,278
Conewago Heights; RMC Place; YORK; ▲ Newberry; **227** EO-5; ★ **HRBG**; mail Manchester z 17345; ● 900
Conewango; MCD-Township; WARREN; ***224** WE-7; mail Warren z 16365; ℗ 4,475; © 3,915
Confluence (Confluence Oakland Junction); Inc. Place; SOMERSET; **225** WQ-6; elev. 1,332ft./406m.; [P]; z 15424; ℗ 873; © 834
Confluence Oakland Junction; SOMERSET; see Confluence (Inc. Place)
Congo; RMC Place; MONTGOMERY; ▲ Douglass; ***227** EN-10; mail Barto z 19504, Schwenksville z 19473; ● 300
Congruity; RMC Place; WESTMORELAND; ▲ Salem; ***225** WN-6; ★ **PGH**; mail Greensburg z 15601; rural
Conifer; RMC Place; JEFFERSON; ▲ Beaver; ***224** WJ-7; mail Summerville z 15864; rural
Connaughton; RMC Place; MONTGOMERY; ▲ Plymouth; ***227** EO-11; elev. 64ft./20m.; ★ **PHIL-**; mail Conshohocken z 19428; ● 250
Conneaut; MCD-Township; CRAWFORD; ***224** WF-2; mail Linesville z 16424; ℗ 1,399; © 1,550
Conneaut; MCD-Township; ERIE; ***224** WE-2; ★ **ERIE**; mail Albion z 16401; ℗ 1,938; © 3,908
Conneaut Lake; Inc. Place; CRAWFORD; **224** WF-2; elev. 1,100ft./335m.; [P]; z 16316; ℗ 699; © 708
Conneaut Lake Park; RMC Place; CRAWFORD; ▲ Summit, Sadsbury; **224** WF-2; mail Conneaut Lake z 16316; ● 200
Conneaut Lakeshore; CDP-Census Area Only; CRAWFORD; ▲ Sadsbury, Summit; ***224** WF-2; elev. 1,080ft./329m.; mail Conneaut Lake z 16316; ℗ 1,852; © 2,502
Conneautville; Inc. Place; CRAWFORD; **224** WE-2; elev. 949ft./289m.; [P]; z 16406; ℗ 822; © 848
Connellsville; Inc. Place; FAYETTE; **225** WP-5; elev. 885ft./270m.; [P] [H] ■; z 15425; ℗ 9,229; © 9,146; ◆ 9,019
Connellsville; MCD-Township; FAYETTE; ***225** WP-5; [P]; z 15425; does not include the City of Connellsville; ℗ 2,553; © 2,483
Connersville; RMC Place; NORTHUMBERLAND; ▲ Mount Carmel; ***227** EK-6; mail Mount Carmel z 17851; ● 75
Connerton; RMC Place; SCHUYLKILL; ▲ Butler; ***227** EK-7; ★ **PTSVL**; mail Girardville z 17935; rural
Connoquenessing; Inc. Place; BUTLER; **225** WK-4; elev. 1,280ft./390m.; [P]; ★ **BUTL**; z 16027; ℗ 507; © 564
Connoquenessing; MCD-Township; BUTLER; ***225** WK-4; [P]; ★ **BUTL**; z 16027 & mail Renfrew z 16053; does not include the Borough of Connoquenessing; ℗ 3,093; © 3,653
Conoy; MCD-Township; LANCASTER; ***227** EO-5; ★ **HRBG**; mail Bainbridge z 17502; ℗ 2,687; © 3,067
Conrad; RMC Place; POTTER; ▲ Eulalia; ***224** WF-13; mail Austin z 16720
Conshohocken; Inc. Place; MONTGOMERY; **227** EO-11; elev. 220ft./67m.; [P]; ★ **PHIL-**; z 19428-29; ℗ 8,064; © 7,589
Continental; RMC Place; PHILADELPHIA; ★ **PHIL-**; mail Philadelphia z 19106; pop. incl. with Philadelphia (Inc. Place)
Conway; Inc. Place; BEAVER; **225** WL-2; elev. 760ft./232m.; [P]; ★ **PGH**; z 15027; ℗ 2,424; © 2,290
Conyngham; MCD-Township; COLUMBIA; ***227** EK-7; mail Mount Carmel z 17851; ℗ 1,038; © 792
Conyngham; Inc. Place; LUZERNE; **226** EJ-8; elev. 948ft./289m.; [P]; ★ **HAZ**; z 18219; ℗ 2,060; © 1,958
Conyngham; MCD-Township; LUZERNE; ***226** EI-8; [P]; z 18219 & mail Shickshinny z 18655; not adjacent to the Borough of Conyngham; ℗ 1,509; © 1,385
Cook; MCD-Township; WESTMORELAND; ***225** WO-7; mail Stahlstown z 15687; ℗ 2,033; © 2,403
Cooke; MCD-Township; CUMBERLAND; ***227** EP-2; mail Carlisle z 17013, Newville z 17241; ℗ 90; © 117
Cookport; RMC Place; INDIANA; ▲ Green; **225** WL-9; mail Commodore z 15729; ● 75
Cooks; RMC Place; HUNTINGDON; ▲ Todd; ***225** WO-12; mail Robertsdale z 16674; rural
Cooksburg; RMC Place; FOREST; **224** WH-7; mail Cooksburg z 16217; ● 20
Cookseytown; RMC Place; LUZERNE; ▲ Wright; ***226** EI-8; ★ **SCR-**; mail Mountain Top z 18707; ● 1,360
Cooks Mill; RMC Place; BEDFORD; ▲ Londonderry; ***225** WQ-9; mail Hyndman z 15545; rural
Cooks Run; RMC Place; CLINTON; ▲ Noyes; ***224** WH-13; mail Westport z 17778; rural
Coolbaugh; MCD-Township; MONROE; ***226** EI-10; mail Tobyhanna z 18466; ℗ 6,756; © 15,205
Coolbaughs; RMC Place; MONROE; ▲ Middle Smithfield; ***226** EJ-12; mail Bushkill z 18324
Coolspring; RMC Place; FAYETTE; ▲ North Union; ***225** WP-5; ★ **UNTN**; mail Hopwood z 15445; ● 300
Coolspring; RMC Place; JEFFERSON; ▲ Oliver; **224** WJ-8; [P]; z 15730; ● 180
Coolspring; MCD-Township; MERCER; ***224** WH-2; mail Mercer z 16137; ℗ 2,140; © 2,287
Cool Valley; RMC Place; WASHINGTON; ▲ Cecil; ***225** WN-3; ★ **PGH**; mail Canonsburg z 15317; rural
Cool Valley; RMC Place; WESTMORELAND; ▲ Hempfield; ***225** WN-5; elev. 1,100ft./335m.; ★ **PGH**; mail Greensburg z 15601; ● 200
Coon Hunter; RMC Place; SNYDER; ▲ Franklin; **227** EK-4; elev. 517ft./158m.; mail Middleburg z 17842; ● 40
Coon Island; RMC Place; WASHINGTON; ***225** WO-1; mail West Alexander z 15376; ● 25
Coontown; RMC Place; MCKEAN; ▲ Wetmore; ***224** WF-9; mail Kane z 16735; ● 20
Cooper; MCD-Township; CLEARFIELD; ***224** WJ-12; mail Grassflat z 16839; ℗ 2,590; © 2,731
Cooper; MCD-Township; MONTOUR; ***226** EJ-6; mail Danville z 17821; ℗ 934; © 966
Coopersburg; Inc. Place; LEHIGH; **227** EM-11; elev. 481ft./147m.; [P]; ★ **ALL-**; z 18036; ℗ 2,599; © 2,582
Cooper Settlement; RMC Place; CLEARFIELD; ▲ Cooper; ***224** WJ-12; mail Drifting z 16834; ● 50
Cooperstown; RMC Place; BUTLER; ▲ Middlesex; **225** WL-4; ★ **PGH**; mail Valencia z 16059; ● 200
Cooperstown; Inc. Place; VENANGO; **224** WG-4; elev. 1,146ft./349m.; [P]; z 16317; ℗ 506; © 460
Cooperstown; RMC Place; WESTMORELAND; ▲ Derry; ***225** WN-6; ★ **LTROB**; mail Latrobe z 15650; ● 1,000
Coopersville; RMC Place; LANCASTER; ▲ Sadsbury; ***227** EP-8; elev. 651ft./198m.; mail Christiana z 17509; rural
Copella; RMC Place; NORTHAMPTON; ▲ Moore; ***227** EK-11; elev. 655ft./200m.; ★ **ALL-**; mail Bath z 18014; ● 200
Copesville; RMC Place; CHESTER; ▲ West Bradford, East Bradford; ***227** EP-10; ★ **PHIL-**; mail West Chester z 19380; rural
Coplay; Inc. Place; LEHIGH; **227** EL-10; elev. 380ft./116m.; [P]; ★ **ALL-**; z 18037; ℗ 3,267; © 3,387
Coppersdale; RMC Place; CAMBRIA; ***225** WN-8; ★ **JNST**; mail Johnstown z 15906; pop. incl. with Johnstown (Inc. Place)
Coral; RMC Place; INDIANA; ▲ Center; **225** WM-7; [P]; z 15731; ● 400
Coraopolis; Inc. Place; ALLEGHENY; **225** WM-3; elev. 720ft./219m.; [P]; ★ **PGH**; z 15108; ℗ 6,747; © 6,131
Coraopolis Heights; RMC Place; ALLEGHENY; ▲ Moon; ***225** WM-3; ★ **PGH**; mail Coraopolis z 15108; ● 1,400
Corinne; RMC Place; CHESTER; ▲ Pocopson; ***227** EP-10; ★ **PHIL-**; mail West Chester z 19380; ● 35
Cork Lane; RMC Place; LUZERNE; ▲ Pittston; **226** EB-10; elev. 681ft./208m.; ★ **SCR-**; mail Pittston z 18640; ● 700
Corliss; RMC Place; ALLEGHENY; ***225** WM-3; [P]; ★ **PGH**; z 15204; pop. incl. with Pittsburgh (Inc. Place)
Corner Ketch; RMC Place; CHESTER; ▲ East Brandywine; ***227** EP-9; elev. 573ft./175m.; ★ **PHIL-**; mail Downingtown z 19335; ● 75
Corner Store; RMC Place; CHESTER; ***227** EO-11; ★ **PHIL-**; mail Phoenixville z 19460; rural
Corning; RMC Place; LEHIGH; ▲ Upper Milford, Lower Milford; ***227** EM-10; ★ **ALL-**; mail Zionsville z 18092; ● 180
Cornish; RMC Place; FAYETTE; ▲ Springhill; ***225** WQ-4; ★ **MORG**; mail Smithfield z 15478; rural
Cornog; RMC Place; CHESTER; ▲ Wallace; ***227** EO-9; ★ **PHIL-**; mail Glenmoore z 19343; ● 100
Cornplanter; MCD-Township; VENANGO; ***224** WG-5; ★ **OILC-F**; mail Oil City z 16301; ℗ 2,968; © 2,687
Cornpropst Mills; RMC Place; HUNTINGDON; ▲ Miller; ***225** WM-13; mail Huntingdon z 16652; rural
Cornwall; Inc. Place; LEBANON; **227** EN-6; elev. 680ft./207m.; [P]; ★ **LEB**; z 17016 & mail Quentin z 17083; ℗ 3,231; © 3,486
Cornwall Center; RMC Place; LEBANON; ***227** EN-6; ★ **LEB**; mail Cornwall z 17016; pop. incl. with Cornwall (Inc. Place)
Cornwells Heights; RMC Place; BUCKS; ▲ Bensalem; ***227** EO-13; [P]; ★ **PHIL-**; z 19020
Cornwells Heights; BUCKS; see Bensalem (RMC Place)
Cornwells Heights-Eddington; CDP-Census Area Only; BUCKS; ▲ Bensalem; ***227** EO-13; elev. 60ft./18m.; ★ **PHIL-**; mail Bensalem z 19020; ℗ 3,621; © 3,406
Corry; Inc. Place; ERIE; **224** WE-5; elev. 1,428ft./435m.; [P] [H]; z 16407; ℗ 7,216; © 6,834
Corsica; Inc. Place; JEFFERSON; **224** WI-7; elev. 1,600ft./488m.; [P]; z 15829; ℗ 337; © 354
Cortez; RMC Place; LACKAWANNA; ▲ Jefferson; **226** EG-11; ★ **SCR-**; mail Lake Ariel z 18436; ● 350
Corwins Corners; RMC Place; MCKEAN; ▲ Foster; ***224** WE-10; mail Bradford z 16701; ● 80
Corydon; MCD-Township; MCKEAN; ***224** WE-9; mail Bradford z 16701; ℗ 319; © 301
Coryville; RMC Place; MCKEAN; ▲ Keating, Eldred; **224** WE-11; elev. 1,444ft./440m.; mail Eldred z 16731; ● 70
Costello; RMC Place; POTTER; ▲ Sylvania, Portage; **224** WG-12; mail Austin z 16720; ● 50
Cosytown; RMC Place; FRANKLIN; ▲ Antrim; ***225** WR-14; ★ **HAG**; mail Greencastle z 17225; rural
Coterell Lake; RMC Place; SUSQUEHANNA; ▲ Clifford; ***226** EF-10; elev. 1,651ft./503m.; mail Union Dale z 18470; summer pop. 200; ● 25
Cottage; RMC Place; HUNTINGDON; ▲ West; ***225** WL-13; mail Petersburg z 16669; ● 40
Cottage Grove; RMC Place; LAWRENCE; ▲ Wilmington; ***224** WI-2; ★ **NWCS**; mail New Castle z 16105; rural
Cottage Hill; RMC Place; CLARION; ▲ Porter; ***224** WJ-7; mail New Bethlehem z 16242; ● 80
Cottageville; RMC Place; BUCKS; ▲ Solebury; ***227** EN-12; ★ **PHIL-**; mail Doylestown z 18901; rural
Cotton Town; RMC Place; BLAIR; ▲ Greenfield; ***225** WN-10; elev. 1,260ft./384m.; ★ **ALT**; mail Claysburg z 16625; ● 40
Couchtown; RMC Place; PERRY; ▲ Southwest Madison; ***227** EN-2; mail Loysville z 17047; rural
Coudersport; Inc. Place; ⊡ POTTER; **224** WE-12; elev. 1,655ft./504m.; [P] [H]; z 16915; ℗ 2,854; © 2,650
Coulter (Coulters); RMC Place; ALLEGHENY; ▲ South Versailles; **228** N-9; ★ **PGH**; mail Coulters z 15028; ● 300
Coulters; ALLEGHENY; see Coulter (RMC Place)
Council Crest; RMC Place; LUZERNE; ▲ Sugarloaf; ★ **HAZ**; mail Hazleton z 18202; rural
Country Club Estates; RMC Place; ARMSTRONG; ▲ East Franklin; ***225** WK-6; elev. 1,160ft./354m.; ★ **PGH**; mail Kittanning z 16201; ● 100
Country Club Estates; RMC Place; LANCASTER; ▲ Manheim; ***227** EP-7; ★ **LANC**; mail Lancaster z 17601; ● 600
Country Club Estates; RMC Place; MONTGOMERY; ▲ Whitemarsh; ★ **PHIL-**; mail Lafayette Hill z 19444
Country Club Heights; RMC Place; LANCASTER; ▲ Manheim; ***227** EP-7; ★ **LANC**; mail Lancaster z 17601
Country Gardens; RMC Place; LANCASTER; ▲ Upper Leacock; ★ **LANC**; mail Leola z 17540
Country Hills; RMC Place; WESTMORELAND; ▲ North Huntingdon; ***225** WN-5; ★ **PGH**; mail Irwin z 15642; ● 1,600
Countryside; RMC Place; CUMBERLAND; ▲ Hampden, East Pennsboro; ***227** EN-4; elev. 360ft./110m.; ★ **HRBG**; mail Camp Hill z 17011; ● 2,500
County Line; RMC Place; BUCKS; ▲ Upper Southampton; ***227** EO-13; elev. 200ft./61m.; ★ **PHIL-**; mail Southampton z 18966; ● 50
County Line Park; RMC Place; BUCKS, MONTGOMERY; ▲ Hatfield, New Britain; ***227** EN-12; elev. 340ft./104m.; ★ **PHIL-**; mail Chalfont z 18914; ● 750
Coupon; RMC Place; CAMBRIA; ▲ Gallitzin; **225** WM-10; elev. 2,341ft./714m.; [P]; ★ **ALT**; z 16629; ● 275
Courtdale; Inc. Place; LUZERNE; **226** EA-8; elev. 740ft./226m.; [P]; ★ **SCR-**; z 18704; ℗ 784; © 791
Courtney; RMC Place; WASHINGTON; ▲ Union; ***225** WO-4; elev. 762ft./232m.; ★ **PGH**; mail New Eagle z 15067; ● 150
Cove; RMC Place; PERRY; ▲ Penn; ***227** EN-4; ★ **HRBG**; mail Duncannon z 17020; ● 60
Covedale; RMC Place; BLAIR; ▲ Woodbury; ***225** WM-12; ★ **ALT**; mail Williamsburg z 16693; ● 65

Entries in **UPPERCASE** are counties.
Entries in **bold** have populations of 2,500 or more.
Names in parentheses are alternate names.

Inc. Place	Incorporated Place
RMC Place	Rand McNally Designated Place
CDP	Census Designated Place
MCD	Minor Civil Division
⊡	County Seat
▲	Minor Civil Division
elev.	Elevation
[P]	Post Office
[H]	Hospital
[C]	College
■	Principal Business Center
★	Ranally Metro Area (RMA) Abbreviation
z	Zip Code(s)
℗	Previous Census Population
Ⓡ	Revised Census Population
Ⓐ	Annexation Population
●	Rand McNally Population Estimate
©	Final Census Population
Ⓢ	Special Census Population
◆	Estimated Population

For additional definitions see Glossary, Volume 1, and Introduction, Volume 2.

Cove Gap (Foltz); RMC Place; FRANKLIN; ▲ Peters; **225** WQ-13; mail Mercersburg z 17236; ● 60
Coventryville; RMC Place; CHESTER; ▲ South Coventry; **227** EO-10; ★ **PTSTN**; mail Pottstown z 19464; ● 350
Coverdale; RMC Place; ALLEGHENY; ***225** WN-3; ★ **PGH**; mail Bethel Park z 15102; pop. incl. with Bethel Park (Inc. Place)
Coveville; RMC Place; MONROE; ▲ Barrett; ***226** EI-11; mail Canadensis z 18325; rural
Coveytown; RMC Place; SULLIVAN; ***226** EG-6; mail Dushore z 18614; rural
Covington; MCD-Township; CLEARFIELD; ***224** WI-12; mail Frenchville z 16836; Ⓟ 648; © 621
Covington; MCD-Township; LACKAWANNA; ***226** EH-11; ★ **SCR-**; mail Gouldsboro z 18424; Ⓟ 2,055; © 1,994
Covington; RMC Place; TIOGA; ▲ Putnam, Covington; **226** EF-3; 🅿; z 16917; ● 650
Covington; MCD-Township; TIOGA; ***226** EF-3; 🅿; z 16917; Ⓟ 918; © 1,047
Covode; RMC Place; INDIANA; ▲ North Mahoning; **225** WK-8; elev. 1,526ft./465m.; mail Punxsutawney z 15767; ● 75
Cowan; ARMSTRONG; see Cowansville (RMC Place)
Cowan; RMC Place; UNION; ▲ Buffalo; ***226** EJ-4; mail Mifflinburg z 17844
Cowanesque; RMC Place; TIOGA; ▲ Westfield; **226** EE-2; 🅿; z 16950; ● 150
Cowansburg; RMC Place; WESTMORELAND; ▲ Sewickley; ***225** WN-5; ★ **PGH**; mail Irwin z 15642; ● 40
Cowanshannock; MCD-Township; ARMSTRONG; ***225** WK-7; mail Rural Valley z 16249; Ⓟ 2,813; © 3,006
Cowans Village; RMC Place; FRANKLIN; ▲ Metal; ***225** WP-13; mail Fort Loudon z 17224; ● 100
Cowansville (Cowan); RMC Place; ARMSTRONG; ▲ East Franklin; **225** WK-5; elev. 1,369ft./417m.; 🅿; ★ **PGH**; z 16218; ● 140
Cowden; RMC Place; WASHINGTON; ▲ Cecil; ***225** WN-3; ★ **PGH**; mail Mc Donald z 15057; ● 200
Cowley; BRADFORD; see Granville Summit (RMC Place)
Coxeville; RMC Place; CARBON; ▲ Banks; ***226** EJ-9; ★ **HAZ**; mail Beaver Meadows z 18216; ● 125
Coy; RMC Place; INDIANA; ▲ Center; ***225** WM-7; mail Homer City z 15748; ● 80
Coy Junction; RMC Place; INDIANA; ▲ Center; ***225** WM-7; elev. 1,147ft./350m.; mail Homer City z 15748; pop. incl. with Homer City (Inc. Place)
Coyleville; RMC Place; BUTLER; ▲ Clearfield; ***225** WK-5; elev. 1,373ft./418m.; ★ **PGH**; mail Fenelton z 16034
Crabapple; RMC Place; GREENE; ▲ Richhill; ***225** WP-1; mail Wind Ridge z 15380; rural
Crabtree; CDP; WESTMORELAND; ▲ Unity, Salem; **225** WN-6; 🅿; ★ **PGH**; z 15624; © 320
Crabtree Hollow; RMC Place; BUCKS; ▲ Bristol; ***227** EO-14; ★ **PHIL-**; mail Feasterville Trevose z 19053
Crackersport; RMC Place; LEHIGH; ▲ South Whitehall; ***227** EL-10; ★ **ALL-**; mail Allentown z 18104; ● 135
Crafton; Inc. Place; ALLEGHENY; **225** WM-3; elev. 880ft./268m.; 🅿; ★ **PGH**; z 15205; Ⓟ 7,188; © 6,706
Craig; RMC Place; LACKAWANNA; ▲ North Abington; ***226** EG-10; ★ **SCR-**; mail Dalton z 18414; ● 100
Craigheads; RMC Place; CUMBERLAND; ▲ South Middleton; ***227** EO-3; ★ **CARL**; mail Carlisle z 17013; rural
Craigs; RMC Place; SCHUYLKILL; ▲ Mahanoy; ***227** EK-8; mail Mahanoy City z 17948; ● 25
Craigs Meadow (Birch Acres); RMC Place; MONROE; ▲ Smithfield; **226** EJ-12; mail East Stroudsburg z 18301; ● 170
Craigsville; RMC Place; ARMSTRONG; ▲ West Franklin; **225** WK-5; elev. 1,020ft./311m.; 🅿; ★ **PGH**; z 16262; ● 150
Craley; RMC Place; YORK; ▲ Lower Windsor; **227** EP-6; 🅿; ★ **YORK**; z 17312; ● 300
Cramer; RMC Place; INDIANA; ▲ East Wheatfield; **225** WM-8; elev. 1,221ft./372m.; ★ **JNST**; mail Seward z 15954; ● 100
Cramer; JEFFERSON; see Stump Creek (RMC Place)
Cramer Heights; RMC Place; WESTMORELAND; ***225** WN-6; ★ **LTROB**; mail Latrobe z 15650
Cranberry (Cranberry Township, Cranberry Twp); MCD-Township; BUTLER; ***225** WL-3; ★ **PGH**; mail Cranberry TWP z 16066; Ⓟ 14,816; © 23,625; ◆ 26,334
Cranberry (New Cranberry); RMC Place; LUZERNE; ▲ Hazle; ***226** EJ-8; ★ **HAZ**; mail Hazleton z 18201; ● 250
Cranberry; RMC Place; VENANGO; ▲ Cranberry; **224** WH-5; 🅿; ★ **OILC-F**; z 16319; ● 300
Cranberry; MCD-Township; VENANGO; ***224** WH-5; 🅿; ★ **OILC-F**; z 16319; Ⓟ 7,256; © 7,014
Cranberry Ridge (Old Cranberry); RMC Place; LUZERNE; ▲ Hazle; ***226** EJ-8; ★ **HAZ**; mail Hazleton z 18202; pop. incl. with Hazleton (Inc. Place)
Cranberry Township; BUTLER; see Cranberry (MCD-Township)
Cranberry Twp; BUTLER; see Cranberry (MCD-Township)
Cranesville; Inc. Place; ERIE; **224** WE-2; elev. 906ft./276m.; 🅿; ★ **ERIE**; z 16410; Ⓟ 598; © 600
Crates; RMC Place; CLARION; ▲ Limestone; ***224** WI-7; mail Mayport z 16240
Crawford; MCD-Township; CLINTON; ***226** EI-3; mail Jersey Shore z 17740; Ⓟ 665; © 848
CRAWFORD; **224** WF-3; Ⓟ 86,169; © 90,366; ◆ 87,179
Crawfordtown; RMC Place; JEFFERSON; ▲ Young; ***224** WJ-8; mail De Lancey z 15733; ● 50
Creamery; RMC Place; MONTGOMERY; ▲ Skippack; ***227** EO-11; 🅿; ★ **PHIL-**; z 19430; ● 200
Creamton; RMC Place; WAYNE; ▲ Clinton; ***226** EF-11; mail Forest City z 18421; rural
Creasy; COLUMBIA; see Mifflinville (CDP)
Creekside; Inc. Place; INDIANA; **225** WL-7; elev. 1,060ft./323m.; 🅿; z 15732; Ⓟ 337; © 323
Creighton; RMC Place; ALLEGHENY; ▲ East Deer; **225** WL-5; 🅿; ★ **PGH**; z 15030; ● 1,500
Crenshaw; RMC Place; JEFFERSON; ▲ Snyder; **224** WI-9; mail Brockway z 15824; ● 80
Crescent; MCD-Township; ALLEGHENY; ***225** WL-3; 🅿; ★ **PGH**; z 15046; Ⓟ 2,490; © 2,314
Crescentdale; RMC Place; LAWRENCE; ★ **PGH**; mail Wampum z 16157; pop. incl. with Wampum (Inc. Place)
Crescent Heights; RMC Place; WASHINGTON; ▲ West Pike Run; ***225** WO-4; mail Daisytown z 15427
Crescent Lake; RMC Place; MONROE; ▲ Pocono; ***226** EJ-11; mail Henryville z 18332; ● 200
Crescent Lake; RMC Place; PIKE; ▲ Dingman; ***226** EH-13; mail Milford z 18337; ● 200
Crescent Township; ALLEGHENY; see Glenwillard (RMC Place)
Cresco; RMC Place; MONROE; ▲ Barrett; **226** EI-11; 🅿; z 18326; ● 500
Cresmont Farms; RMC Place; CHESTER; ▲ West Bradford; ***227** EP-10; elev. 450ft./137m.; ★ **PHIL-**; mail Downingtown z 19335; ● 700
Cress; RMC Place; FRANKLIN; ▲ Washington; ***227** ER-1; ★ **HAG**; mail Waynesboro z 17268; rural
Cressman; BUCKS; see Trumbauersville (Inc. Place)
Cresson; Inc. Place; CAMBRIA; **225** WM-10; elev. 2,100ft./640m.; 🅿 🅲 1,587; z 16630, z 16699; Ⓟ 1,784; © 1,631
Cresson; MCD-Township; CAMBRIA; ***225** WM-10; 🅿 🅲 1,587; z 16630, z 16699; does not include the Borough of Cresson; Ⓟ 3,284; © 4,055
Cressona; Inc. Place; SCHUYLKILL; **227** EL-7; elev. 600ft./183m.; 🅿; ★ **PTSVL**; z 17929; Ⓟ 1,694; © 1,635
Crestmont; RMC Place; CLINTON; ▲ Pine Creek; **226** EI-2; ★ **WMSPT**; mail Lock Haven z 17745; ● 90
Crestmont; RMC Place; MONTGOMERY; ▲ Abington; ***227** EO-12; ★ **PHIL-**; mail Willow Grove z 19090; ● 2,800
Crestmont Village; RMC Place; BEAVER; ▲ Hopewell; ***225** WL-2; ★ **PGH**; mail Aliquippa z 15001; ● 700
Crestview; RMC Place; MONTGOMERY; ▲ Horsham; ★ **PHIL-**; mail Hatboro z 19040
Crestwood; RMC Place; BERKS; ▲ Exeter; ***227** EN-9; ★ **READ**; mail Reading z 19606; ● 800
Crestwood; RMC Place; LACKAWANNA; ▲ Roaring Brook; ***226** EH-10; elev. 1,800ft./549m.; ★ **SCR-**; mail Moscow z 18444; ● 100
Creswell; RMC Place; LANCASTER; ▲ Manor; ***227** EP-6; ★ **LANC**; mail Conestoga z 17516
Crete; RMC Place; INDIANA; ▲ Center; ***225** WL-7; elev. 370ft./113m.; mail Indiana z 15701; rural
Criders Corners; RMC Place; BUTLER; ▲ Cranberry; ***225** WL-3; elev. 1,091ft./333m.; ★ **PGH**; mail Mars z 16046; rural
Crimson Maple; RMC Place; BRADFORD; ▲ Rome; ***226** EE-7; elev. 835ft./255m.; mail Rome z 18837; ● 100
Croft; RMC Place; CLEARFIELD; ▲ Goshen; **224** WJ-11; mail Clearfield z 16830; ● 60
Cromby; RMC Place; CHESTER; ▲ Schuylkill; ***227** EO-10; ★ **PHIL-**; mail Phoenixville z 19460; pop. incl. with Phoenixville (Inc. Place)
Cromwell; MCD-Township; HUNTINGDON; ***225** WO-13; mail Three Springs z 17264; Ⓟ 1,500; © 1,632
Crooked Creek (Holliday); RMC Place; TIOGA; ▲ Middlebury; **226** EE-3; mail Middlebury Center z 16935; ● 50
Crookham; RMC Place; WASHINGTON; ▲ Union; ***225** WO-4; ★ **PGH**; mail Finleyville z 15332; ● 30
Crosby; RMC Place; MCKEAN; ▲ Norwich; **224** WF-11; elev. 1,514ft./461m.; 🅿; z 16724; ● 225
Cross Creek; RMC Place; WASHINGTON; ▲ Cross Creek; **225** WN-2; mail Burgettstown z 15021; ● 180
Cross Creek; MCD-Township; WASHINGTON; ***225** WN-2; mail Avella z 15312; Ⓟ 1,727; © 1,685
Cross Fork; RMC Place; POTTER; ▲ Stewardson; **224** WG-13; elev. 1,056ft./322m.; 🅿; z 17729; ● 60
Crossgrove; RMC Place; SNYDER; ▲ West Beaver; ***227** EL-2; mail Mc Clure z 17841; ● 35
Crossingville; RMC Place; CRAWFORD; ▲ Cussewago; **224** WE-3; elev. 1,133ft./345m.; 🅿; z 16412; ● 60
Cross Keys; RMC Place; ADAMS; ▲ Berwick, Hamilton, Oxford; ***227** EQ-4; ★ **HANV**; mail New Oxford z 17350; rural
Cross Keys; RMC Place; BLAIR; ▲ Allegheny; **225** WM-11; ★ **ALT**; mail Duncansville z 16635; ● 200
Cross Keys; RMC Place; BUCKS; ***227** EN-12; ★ **PHIL-**; mail Doylestown z 18901
Cross Keys; RMC Place; JUNIATA; ▲ Lack; **225** WN-14; mail East Waterford z 17021; ● 70
Crossroads; RMC Place; NORTHAMPTON; ▲ Moore; ***227** EK-11; elev. 822ft./251m.; ★ **ALL-**; mail Bath z 18014; ● 200
Cross Roads; Inc. Place; YORK; **227** EQ-6; elev. 812ft./247m.; ★ **BAL**; mail Felton z 17322; Ⓟ 322; © 518
Crosswicks; RMC Place; MONTGOMERY; ▲ Abington; ***227** EO-12; ★ **PHIL-**; mail Jenkintown z 19046; ● 540
Crown; RMC Place; CLARION; ▲ Farmington; **224** WH-7; 🅿; z 16220; ● 80
Crown Meadows; RMC Place; ALLEGHENY; ▲ O'Hara; ***225** WM-4; ★ **PGH**; mail Pittsburgh z 15238; ● 900
Croydon; CDP; BUCKS; ▲ Bristol; **228** B-9; 🅿; ★ **PHIL-**; z 19021; Ⓟ 9,967; © 9,993
Croydon Acres; RMC Place; BUCKS; ▲ Bristol; ***227** EO-13; ★ **PHIL-**; mail Croydon z 19021
Croydon Heights; RMC Place; BUCKS; ▲ Bristol; ***227** EO-13; ★ **PHIL-**; mail Croydon z 19021
Croydon Manor; RMC Place; BUCKS; ▲ Bristol; ★ **PHIL-**; mail Croydon z 19021
Croyle; MCD-Township; CAMBRIA; ***225** WN-9; ★ **JNST**; mail South Fork z 15956; Ⓟ 2,451; © 2,233
Crozer Park Gardens; RMC Place; DELAWARE; ★ **PHIL-**; mail Chester z 19013; pop. incl. with Chester (Inc. Place)
Crucible; RMC Place; GREENE; ▲ Cumberland; **225** WP-4; 🅿; z 15325; ● 600
Crum Creek Manor; RMC Place; DELAWARE; ▲ Nether Providence; ***227** EQ-11; ★ **PHIL-**; mail Chester z 19013
Crum Lynne (Leiperville); RMC Place; DELAWARE; ***227** EQ-11; elev. 20ft./6m.; 🅿; ★ **PHIL-**; z 19022; pop. incl. with Ridley Park (Inc. Place)
Crystal; RMC Place; FAYETTE; ▲ Springhill; ***225** WQ-4; elev. 1,040ft./317m.; ★ **MORG**; mail Gans z 15439; ● 60
Crystal Lake; RMC Place; SUSQUEHANNA; ▲ Clifford; ***226** EF-10; mail Carbondale z 18407; ● 300
Crystal Spring; RMC Place; FULTON; ▲ Brush Creek; **225** WP-11; 🅿; z 15536; ● 100
Crystal Springs; RMC Place; FOREST; ▲ Kingsley; ***224** WG-7; mail Tionesta z 16353; rural
Cuba Mills; RMC Place; JUNIATA; ▲ Fermanagh; **227** EM-2; mail Mifflintown z 17059; ● 90
Cuddy; ALLEGHENY; see Treveskyn (RMC Place)
Cuddy Hill; RMC Place; ALLEGHENY; ▲ South Fayette; ***225** WN-3; ★ **PGH**; mail Cuddy z 15031
Culbertson; RMC Place; FRANKLIN; ▲ Greene; ***225** WN-14; mail Chambersburg z 17201; ● 100
Cullen Manor; RMC Place; COLUMBIA; ▲ Conyngham; ***227** EK-6; mail Wilburton z 17888; ● 50
Culmerville; RMC Place; ALLEGHENY; ▲ West Deer; **225** WL-4; ★ **PGH**; mail Tarentum z 15084; ● 600
Culp; RMC Place; BLAIR; ▲ Tyrone; ***225** WM-11; elev. 1,053ft./321m.; mail Altoona z 16601; rural
Cumberland; MCD-Township; ADAMS; ***227** ER-3; mail Gettysburg z 17325; Ⓟ 5,431; © 5,718
Cumberland; MCD-Township; GREENE; ***225** WP-3; mail Carmichaels z 15320; Ⓟ 6,742; © 6,564
CUMBERLAND; **227** EO-2; Ⓟ 195,257; © 213,674; ◆ 231,957
Cumberland Park; RMC Place; CUMBERLAND; ▲ Lower Allen; ***227** EO-4; ★ **HRBG**; mail Camp Hill z 17011; ● 140
Cumberland Valley; MCD-Township; BEDFORD; ***225** WQ-10; mail Bedford z 15522; Ⓟ 1,473; © 1,494
Cumberland Village; RMC Place; GREENE; ▲ Cumberland; **225** WP-4; mail Carmichaels z 15320; ● 300
Cumbola; RMC Place; SCHUYLKILL; ▲ Blythe; **227** EL-8; 🅿; ★ **PTSVL**; z 17930; ● 600
Cummings; MCD-Township; LYCOMING; ***226** EH-2; mail Waterville z 17776; Ⓟ 334; © 355
Cumminstown; RMC Place; CUMBERLAND; ▲ Penn; ***227** EO-2; mail Carlisle z 17013; rural
Cumru; MCD-Township; BERKS; ***227** EN-9; ★ **READ**; mail Mohnton z 19540; Ⓟ 13,142; © 13,816
Cupola; RMC Place; CHESTER; ▲ West Nantmeal, Honey Brook; ***227** EO-9; ★ **PHIL-**; mail Honey Brook z 19344; ● 50
Curley Hill; RMC Place; BUCKS; ***227** EN-12; ★ **PHIL-**; mail Doylestown z 18901, Pipersville z 18947; rural
Curllsville; RMC Place; CLARION; ▲ Monroe; **224** WI-6; 🅿; z 16221; ● 110
Curren Terrace; RMC Place; MONTGOMERY; ★ **PHIL-**; mail Norristown z 19401; pop. incl. with Norristown (Inc. Place)
Curry Run; RMC Place; CLEARFIELD; ▲ Greenwood; **225** WK-10; mail Mahaffey z 15757; ● 45
Curryville; RMC Place; BLAIR; ▲ Woodbury; **225** WN-11; 🅿; z 16631; ● 200
Curtin; RMC Place; CENTRE; ▲ Boggs; ***224** WJ-14; ★ **STCOL**; mail Howard z 16841; ● 20
Curtin; MCD-Township; CENTRE; ***224** WJ-14; mail Howard z 16841; Ⓟ 516; © 551
Curtis Hills; RMC Place; MONTGOMERY; ▲ Cheltenham; ★ **PHIL-**; mail Wyncote z 19095
Curtis Park; RMC Place; DELAWARE; ★ **PHIL-**; mail Sharon Hill z 19079; pop. incl. with Sharon Hill (Inc. Place)
Curtisville; CDP; ALLEGHENY; ▲ West Deer; **225** WL-4; 🅿; ★ **PGH**; z 15032; Ⓟ 1,285; © 1,173
Curwensville; Inc. Place; CLEARFIELD; **224** WJ-10; elev. 1,161ft./354m.; 🅿; z 16833; Ⓟ 2,924; © 2,650
Cush Creek; RMC Place; INDIANA; ▲ Montgomery; ***225** WK-9; elev. 1,753ft./534m.; mail Arcadia z 15712; rural
Cussewago; MCD-Township; CRAWFORD; ***224** WE-3; mail Saegertown z 16433; Ⓟ 1,409; © 1,597
Custards; RMC Place; CRAWFORD; ▲ Greenwood, Fairfield; **224** WG-3; elev. 1,079ft./329m.; mail Cochranton z 16314; ● 30
Custer City; RMC Place; MCKEAN; ▲ Bradford; **224** WE-10; elev. 1,516ft./462m.; 🅿; z 16725; ● 300
Custis Woods; RMC Place; MONTGOMERY; ▲ Cheltenham; ★ **PHIL-**; mail Glenside z 19038
Cyclone; RMC Place; MCKEAN; ▲ Keating; **224** WE-10; 🅿; z 16726; ● 450
Cymbria; RMC Place; CAMBRIA; ▲ Susquehanna; ***225** WL-9; mail Northern Cambria z 15714; ● 60
Cypher; RMC Place; BEDFORD; ▲ Hopewell; ***225** WO-11; mail Hopewell z 16650; rural

D

Daggett; RMC Place; TIOGA; ▲ Jackson; **226** EE-4; mail Millerton z 16936; ● 50
Dagus; RMC Place; ELK; ▲ Fox; ***224** WH-10; mail Kersey z 15846
Daguscahonda; RMC Place; ELK; ▲ Ridgway; **224** WH-10; mail Ridgway z 15853; ● 120
Dagus Mines; RMC Place; ELK; ▲ Fox; **224** WH-10; 🅿; z 15831; ● 400
Dahoga; RMC Place; ELK; ***224** WF-9; mail Wilcox z 15870; rural
Daisytown; Inc. Place; CAMBRIA; **225** WS-2; elev. 1,800ft./549m.; ★ **JNST**; mail Johnstown z 15902; Ⓟ 367; © 356
Daisytown; RMC Place; WASHINGTON; ▲ West Pike Run; **225** WP-4; 🅿; ★ **PGH**; z 15427; pop. incl. with California (Inc. Place)
Dale; Inc. Place; CAMBRIA; **225** WN-8; elev. 1,250ft./381m.; ★ **JNST**; mail Johnstown z 15902; Ⓟ 1,642; © 1,503
Dale; RMC Place; CLEARFIELD; ▲ Bradford; ***224** WJ-11; elev. 1,685ft./514m.; mail Woodland z 16881; rural
Dale Summit; RMC Place; CENTRE; ▲ College; **225** WK-13; ★ **STCOL**; mail Bellefonte z 16823; ● 180
Daleville; RMC Place; CHESTER; ▲ Londonderry; ***227** EQ-9; mail Cochranville z 19330; rural
Daleville; RMC Place; LACKAWANNA; ▲ Covington; **226** EH-10; ★ **SCR-**; mail Gouldsboro z 18424; ● 420
Dalevue; RMC Place; CENTRE; ▲ College; ***225** WK-13; ★ **STCOL**; mail State College z 16801; ● 500
Daley; RMC Place; SOMERSET; ▲ Shade; ***225** WO-9; elev. 2,612ft./796m.; mail Cairnbrook z 15924; rural
Dallas; Inc. Place; LUZERNE; **226** EH-8; elev. 1,128ft./344m.; 🅿 🅲 1,858; ★ **SCR-**; z 18612, z 18690; Ⓟ 2,567; © 2,557
Dallas; MCD-Township; LUZERNE; ***226** EH-8; 🅿 🅲 1,858; ★ **SCR-**; z 18612, z 18690; does not include the Borough of Dallas; Ⓟ 7,625; © 8,179
Dallas City; RMC Place; MCKEAN; ▲ Foster; ***224** WD-10; mail Bradford z 16701; rural
Dallastown; Inc. Place; YORK; **227** EQ-5; elev. 880ft./268m.; 🅿; ★ **YORK**; z 17313; Ⓟ 3,974; © 4,087
Dalmatia; RMC Place; NORTHUMBERLAND; ▲ Lower Mahanoy; **227** EL-4; 🅿; z 17017; ● 600
Dalton; Inc. Place; LACKAWANNA; **226** EG-9; elev. 992ft./302m.; 🅿; ★ **SCR-**; z 18414; Ⓟ 1,369; © 1,294
Damascus; RMC Place; WAYNE; ▲ Damascus; **226** EF-12; 🅿; z 18415; ● 365
Damascus; MCD-Township; WAYNE; ***226** EF-12; 🅿; z 18415; Ⓟ 3,081; © 3,662
Danboro; RMC Place; BUCKS; ▲ Plumstead; **227** EN-12; 🅿; ★ **PHIL-**; z 18916; ● 500
D&M Junction; RMC Place; YORK; ▲ Carroll; ***227** EO-4; ★ **HRBG**; mail Dillsburg z 17019; rural
Danielsville; RMC Place; NORTHAMPTON; ▲ Lehigh; **227** EK-10; 🅿; ★ **ALL-**; z 18038; ● 750
Dannersville; RMC Place; NORTHAMPTON; ▲ Moore; ***227** EL-11; elev. 724ft./221m.; ★ **ALL-**; mail Northampton z 18067; rural
Danville; Inc. Place; ⊡ MONTOUR; **226** EJ-5; elev. 490ft./149m.; 🅿 🅷; z 17821-22; Ⓟ 5,165; © 4,897
Darby; Inc. Place; DELAWARE; **227** EP-12; elev. 50ft./15m.; 🅿; ★ **PHIL-**; z 19023; Ⓟ 11,140; © 10,299
Darby; MCD-Township; DELAWARE; ***227** EP-12; 🅿; ★ **PHIL-**; z 19023 & mail Glenolden z 19036; not adjacent to the Borough of Darby; Ⓟ 10,955; © 9,622
Darby Township; CDP-Census Area Only; DELAWARE; ▲ Darby; ***227** EP-12; ★ **PHIL-**; mail Glenolden z 19036; Ⓟ 10,955; © 9,622
Darent; FAYETTE; see Lemont Furnace (RMC Place)
Darling (Darlington); RMC Place; DELAWARE; ▲ Middletown; ***227** EP-11; ★ **PHIL-**; mail Media z 19063; ● 50
Darlington; Inc. Place; BEAVER; **225** WK-2; elev. 912ft./278m.; 🅿; ★ **PGH**; z 16115; Ⓟ 311; © 299
Darlington; MCD-Township; BEAVER; ***225** WK-1; 🅿; ★ **PGH**; z 16115; does not include the Borough of Darlington; Ⓟ 2,040; © 1,974
Darlington; DELAWARE; see Darling (RMC Place)
Darlington; RMC Place; WESTMORELAND; ▲ Ligonier; ***225** WN-7; mail Ligonier z 15658; ● 80
Darlington Corners; RMC Place; CHESTER; ▲ Westtown, Thornbury; ***227** EP-10; elev. 374ft./114m.; ★ **PHIL-**; mail West Chester z 19380
Darragh; RMC Place; WESTMORELAND; ▲ Hempfield; ***225** WN-5; 🅿; ★ **PGH**; z 15625; ● 90
Darthmouth Farms; RMC Place; DAUPHIN; ▲ Derry; ***227** EO-5; elev. 400ft./122m.; ★ **HRBG**; mail Hummelstown z 17036; ● 200
Dauberville; RMC Place; BERKS; ▲ Centre; **227** EM-8; 🅿; ★ **READ**; z 19533; ● 315
Daugherty; MCD-Township; BEAVER; ***225** WK-2; ★ **PGH**; mail New Brighton z 15066; Ⓟ 3,433; © 3,441
Dauphin; Inc. Place; DAUPHIN; **227** EN-4; elev. 340ft./104m.; 🅿; ★ **HRBG**; z 17018; Ⓟ 845; © 773; ® 715
DAUPHIN; **227** EM-5; Ⓟ 237,813; © 251,798; ◆ 258,395
Davidsburg; RMC Place; YORK; ▲ Dover; **227** EP-4; ★ **YORK**; mail Dover z 17315; ● 25
Davidson; MCD-Township; SULLIVAN; ***226** EH-6; mail Muncy Valley z 17758; Ⓟ 597; © 626
Davidson Heights; RMC Place; BEAVER; ▲ Hopewell; ***225** WL-2; ★ **PGH**; mail Aliquippa z 15001; ● 800
Davidsville; CDP; SOMERSET; ▲ Conemaugh; **225** WO-8; 🅿; ★ **JNST**; z 15928; Ⓟ 1,167; © 1,119
Davis Grove; RMC Place; MONTGOMERY; ▲ Horsham; ★ **PHIL-**; mail Horsham z 19044
Davistown; RMC Place; FAYETTE; ▲ Saltlick; **225** WQ-3; mail Indian Head z 15446; ● 60
Davistown; RMC Place; GREENE; ▲ Dunkard; ***225** WQ-3; 🅿; z 15349; ● 60
Dawson; Inc. Place; FAYETTE; **225** WP-5; elev. 849ft./259m.; 🅿; z 15428; Ⓟ 535; © 451
Dawson Manor; RMC Place; MONTGOMERY; ▲ Upper Moreland; ★ **PHIL-**; mail Hatboro z 19040
Dawson Ridge; RMC Place; BEAVER; ▲ Brighton; **225** WL-2; ★ **PGH**; mail Beaver z 15009; ● 1,200
Dawson Run; RMC Place; FOREST; ▲ Harmony; ***224** WG-6; elev. 1,070ft./326m.; mail West Hickory z 16370; rural
Day; RMC Place; CLARION; ▲ Clarion; **224** WI-7; mail Strattanville z 16258; ● 40
Daylesford; RMC Place; CHESTER; ▲ Tredyffrin; ***227** EP-11; ★ **PHIL-**; mail Berwyn z 19312
Dayton; Inc. Place; ARMSTRONG; **225** WK-7; elev. 1,360ft./415m.; 🅿; z 16222; Ⓟ 572; © 543
Dayton; RMC Place; DAUPHIN; ▲ Williams; **227** EM-5; mail Williamstown z 17098; ● 100
Deal; RMC Place; SOMERSET; ▲ Larimer, Greenville; ***225** WQ-8; mail Meyersdale z 15552; ● 25
Dean; RMC Place; CAMBRIA; ▲ Dean; **225** WL-10; elev. 545ft./166m.; mail Dysart z 16636; ● 90
Dean; MCD-Township; CAMBRIA; ***225** WL-10; mail Dysart z 16636; Ⓟ 398; © 408
Deanville; RMC Place; ARMSTRONG; ▲ Madison; **224** WJ-6; mail New Bethlehem z 16242; ● 65
Dearth; RMC Place; FAYETTE; ▲ Menallen; ***225** WP-4; ★ **UNTN**; mail Uniontown z 15401; rural
Decatur; MCD-Township; CLEARFIELD; ***225** WK-11; mail Osceola Mills z 16666; Ⓟ 3,004; © 2,974
Decatur; MCD-Township; MIFFLIN; ***227** EL-2; mail Mc Clure z 17841; Ⓟ 2,735; © 3,021
Deckard; RMC Place; CRAWFORD; ▲ Wayne; ***224** WG-4; elev. 1,250ft./381m.; mail Cochranton z 16314; rural
Deckers Point; RMC Place; INDIANA; ▲ Grant; **225** WK-8; mail Marion Center z 15759; ● 50
Deckertown; RMC Place; SUSQUEHANNA; ▲ Lathrop; ***226** EF-9; elev. 1,225ft./373m.; mail Nicholson z 18446; rural
Deegan (Goff Station); RMC Place; BUTLER; ▲ Venango; ***224** WI-4; mail Boyers z 16020; ● 30
Deemers Cross Roads; RMC Place; JEFFERSON; ▲ Winslow; ***224** WI-8; mail Reynoldsville z 15851; rural
Deemston; Inc. Place; WASHINGTON; **225** WP-3; elev. 920ft./280m.; mail Fredericktown z 15333; Ⓟ 770; © 809
Deep Dale East; RMC Place; BUCKS; ▲ Middletown; ★ **PHIL-**; mail Levittown z 19058
Deep Dale West; RMC Place; BUCKS; ▲ Middletown; ★ **PHIL-**; mail Levittown z 19058
Deep Run; RMC Place; BUCKS; ▲ Bedminster; ***227** EM-12; ★ **PHIL-**; mail Perkasie z 18944; rural
Deep Valley; RMC Place; GREENE; ▲ Springhill; **225** WQ-1; mail New Freeport z 15352; ● 75
Deer Creek; MCD-Township; MERCER; ***224** WG-3; mail Sandy Lake z 16145; Ⓟ 513; © 465
Deerfield; MCD-Township; TIOGA; ***226** ED-2; mail Knoxville z 16928; Ⓟ 647; © 659
Deerfield; MCD-Township; WARREN; ***224** WF-6; mail Tidioute z 16351; Ⓟ 274; © 333
Deer Lake; RMC Place; FAYETTE; ▲ Wharton; ***225** WQ-5; mail Chalk Hill z 15421; ● 325
Deer Lake; Inc. Place; SCHUYLKILL; **227** EL-8; elev. 500ft./152m.; ★ **PTSVL**; mail Orwigsburg z 17961; Ⓟ 550; © 528
Deer Mountain Lake; RMC Place; MONROE; ▲ Pocono; ***226** EI-11; elev. 1,426ft./435m.; mail Scotrun z 18355, Swiftwater z 18370; ● 200
Deer Park; RMC Place; BUCKS; ▲ Solebury; ***227** EN-13; ★ **PHIL-**; mail New Hope z 18938; summer pop. 100
Defiance; RMC Place; BEDFORD; ▲ Broad Top; **225** WO-12; 🅿; z 16633; ● 250
Degolia; RMC Place; MCKEAN; ▲ Bradford; ***224** WE-10; mail Bradford z 16701
Deiblers Station; RMC Place; NORTHUMBERLAND; ▲ Shamokin; ***227** EK-5; mail Danville z 17821; rural
Delabole; RMC Place; NORTHAMPTON; ▲ Plainfield; ***227** EK-12; mail Pen Argyl z 18072; rural
De Lancey; JEFFERSON; see Adrian Mines (RMC Place)
Delano; CDP; SCHUYLKILL; ▲ Delano; **227** EK-8; 🅿; z 18220; © 377
Delano; MCD-Township; SCHUYLKILL; ***227** EK-8; 🅿; z 18220; Ⓟ 573; © 487
Delaware; MCD-Township; JUNIATA; ***227** EM-3; mail Thompsontown z 17094; Ⓟ 1,440; © 1,464
Delaware; MCD-Township; MERCER; ***224** WH-2; mail Fredonia z 16124, Greenville z 16125; Ⓟ 2,064; © 2,159
Delaware; MCD-Township; NORTHUMBERLAND; ***226** EI-4; ★ **WMSPT**; mail Watsontown z 17777; Ⓟ 4,018; © 4,341
Delaware; MCD-Township; PIKE; ***226** EI-13; mail Dingmans Ferry z 18328; Ⓟ 3,527; © 6,319
DELAWARE; **227** EP-11; Ⓟ 547,651; © 550,864; ® 551,974; ◆ 550,957
Delaware Grove; RMC Place; MERCER; ▲ Delaware; **224** WH-2; mail Fredonia z 16124; ● 25
Delaware Run; RMC Place; NORTHUMBERLAND; ***226** EI-4; elev. 535ft./163m.; ★ **WMSPT**; mail Watsontown z 17777; rural
Delaware Water Gap (Water Gap); Inc. Place; MONROE; **226** EJ-12; elev. 400ft./122m.; 🅿; z 18327 & mail Dauphin z 17018; Ⓟ 733; © 744
Dellville; RMC Place; PERRY; ▲ Wheatfield; ***227** EN-3; ★ **HRBG**; mail Duncannon z 17020; ● 30
Delmar; MCD-Township; TIOGA; ***226** EF-2; mail Wellsboro z 16901; Ⓟ 3,048; © 2,893
Delmont; Inc. Place; WESTMORELAND; **225** WM-5; elev. 1,260ft./384m.; 🅿; ★ **PGH**; z 15626; Ⓟ 2,041; © 2,497
Delphi; RMC Place; MONTGOMERY; ▲ Lower Frederick; ***227** EN-11; ★ **PHIL-**; mail Schwenksville z 19473; ● 85
Delps; RMC Place; NORTHAMPTON; ▲ Moore; ***227** EK-11; ★ **ALL-**; mail Danielsville z 18038; ● 120
Delroy; RMC Place; YORK; ▲ Lower Windsor; **227** EP-6; ★ **YORK**; mail York z 17406; ● 200
Delta; Inc. Place; YORK; **227** ER-7; elev. 440ft./134m.; 🅿; ★ **BAL**; z 17314; Ⓟ 761; © 741
Delta Manor; RMC Place; NORTHAMPTON; ▲ Hanover; ***227** EL-11; ★ **ALL-**; mail Bethlehem z 18017; ● 430
Demmler; RMC Place; ALLEGHENY; ▲ North Versailles; ★ **PGH**
Demmler Transfer; RMC Place; ALLEGHENY; ▲ North Versailles; ★ **PGH**
Dempseytown; RMC Place; VENANGO; ▲ Oakland; **224** WG-5; elev. 1,470ft./448m.; mail Cooperstown z 16317; ● 200
Denbeau Heights; RMC Place; WASHINGTON; ***225** WP-4; mail Brownsville z 15417; pop. incl. with Centerville (Inc. Place)
Denbo; RMC Place; WASHINGTON; ***225** WP-4; elev. 800ft./244m.; 🅿; z 15429; pop. incl. with Centerville (Inc. Place)
Denholm; RMC Place; JUNIATA; ▲ Milford; **227** EL-2; mail Mifflintown z 17059; ● 75
Denison; RMC Place; WESTMORELAND; ▲ Unity; ***225** WN-6; ★ **LTROB**; mail Greensburg z 15601; ● 200
Dennison; MCD-Township; LUZERNE; ***226** EJ-9; mail White Haven z 18661; Ⓟ 809; © 908
Dennys Corners; RMC Place; CRAWFORD; ▲ Hayfield; ***224** WF-3; mail Meadville z 16335; rural
Dennys Mill; RMC Place; BUTLER; ▲ Winfield; ***225** WK-5; ★ **PGH**; mail Cabot z 16023; rural
Dents Run; RMC Place; ELK; ▲ Benezette; ***224** WH-11; elev. 919ft./280m.; mail Driftwood z 15832
Denver; Inc. Place; LANCASTER; **227** EO-8; elev. 380ft./116m.; 🅿; z 17517; Ⓟ 2,861; © 3,332
Deodate; RMC Place; DAUPHIN; ▲ Conewago; **227** EO-6; ★ **HRBG**; mail Elizabethtown z 17022; ● 80
Deringer; RMC Place; LUZERNE; ▲ Black Creek; ***226** EJ-8; ★ **HAZ**; mail Nuremberg z 18241; rural
Derrick City; RMC Place; MCKEAN; ▲ Foster; **224** WD-10; elev. 1,566ft./477m.; 🅿; z 16727; ● 1,000
Derrs; RMC Place; COLUMBIA; ▲ Jackson; ***226** EI-6; elev. 1,050ft./320m.; mail Benton z 17814; ● 150
Derry; MCD-Township; DAUPHIN; ***227** EN-5; 🅲 791; ★ **HRBG**; mail Hershey z 17033; Ⓟ 18,408; © 21,273; ◆ 22,202
Derry; MCD-Township; MIFFLIN; ***227** EL-2; mail Lewistown z 17044, Yeagertown z 17099; Ⓟ 7,650; © 7,256
Derry; MCD-Township; MONTOUR; ***226** EJ-5; mail Danville z 17821; Ⓟ 1,272; © 1,215
Derry; Inc. Place; WESTMORELAND; **225** WN-7; elev. 1,175ft./358m.; 🅿; ★ **LTROB**; z 15627; Ⓟ 2,950; © 2,991
Derry; MCD-Township; WESTMORELAND; ***225** WN-7; 🅿; ★ **LTROB**; z 15627; does not include the Borough of Derry; Ⓟ 15,446; © 14,726
Derwood Park; RMC Place; DELAWARE; ▲ Ridley; ★ **PHIL-**; mail Woodlyn z 19094
Derwyn; RMC Place; MONTGOMERY; ▲ Lower Merion; ★ **PHIL-**; mail Bala Cynwyd z 19004
Deshon Manor; RMC Place; BUTLER; ▲ Butler; ***225** WK-4; ★ **BUTL**; mail Butler z 16001; ● 300
Desire; RMC Place; JEFFERSON; ▲ Henderson; **224** WJ-9; mail Reynoldsville z 15851; ● 90
Detters Mill; RMC Place; YORK; ▲ Warrington; ***227** EP-4; elev. 400ft./122m.; ★ **YORK**; mail Dover z 17315; ● 120
De Turksville; RMC Place; SCHUYLKILL; ▲ Washington; ***227** EM-7; mail Pine Grove z 17963; rural
Devault; RMC Place; CHESTER; ▲ East Whiteland, Charlestown; **227** EP-10; 🅿; ★ **PHIL-**; z 19432; ● 100
Devon; RMC Place; CHESTER; ▲ Easttown, Tredyffrin; **227** EP-11; 🅿 🅷; ★ **PHIL-**; z 19333; ● 2,000
Devon-Berwyn; CDP-Census Area Only; CHESTER; ▲ Easttown; ***227** EP-11; ★ **PHIL-**; mail Berwyn z 19312, Devon z 19333; Ⓟ 5,019; © 5,067
Dewart; RMC Place; NORTHUMBERLAND; ▲ Delaware; **226** EI-4; 🅿; ★ **WMSPT**; z 17730; ● 450
Dewey Heights; RMC Place; LEHIGH; ▲ Whitehall; ***227** EL-10; ★ **ALL-**; mail Whitehall z 18052
De Young; ELK; see Russell City (RMC Place)
Diamond; RMC Place; VENANGO; ▲ Plum; **224** WF-5; elev. 1,431ft./436m.; mail Titusville z 16354; ● 50
Diamondtown; RMC Place; NORTHUMBERLAND; ▲ Mount Carmel; ***227** EK-6; mail Mount Carmel z 17851; ● 90
Diamondville; RMC Place; INDIANA; ▲ Cherryhill; **225** WL-8; mail Clymer z 15728; ● 100
Dice; RMC Place; UNION; ▲ Limestone; ***227** EK-4; mail Mifflinburg z 17844
Dickerson Run (Liberty); RMC Place; FAYETTE; ▲ Dunbar; **225** WP-5; 🅿; z 15430; ● 400
Dickeys Mountain; RMC Place; FULTON; ▲ Thompson; ***225** WQ-12; mail Big Cove Tannery z 17212; rural
Dickinson; RMC Place; CUMBERLAND; ▲ Penn; **227** EO-2; mail Newville z 17241; ● 100
Dickinson; MCD-Township; CUMBERLAND; ***227** EP-3; ★ **CARL**; mail Mount Holly Springs z 17065, Newville z 17241; Ⓟ 3,870; © 4,702
Dicksonburg; RMC Place; CRAWFORD; ▲ Summerhill; ***224** WF-2; mail Conneautville z 16406
Dickson City; Inc. Place; LACKAWANNA; **226** EG-10; elev. 783ft./239m.; 🅿; ★ **SCR-**; z 18447, z 18519; Ⓟ 6,276; © 6,205
Dicksonville; CDP-Census Area Only; INDIANA; ***225** WL-8; © 450
Dieners Hall; RMC Place; SCHUYLKILL; ▲ East Norwegian; ***227** EL-7; ★ **PTSVL**; mail Pottsville z 17901; ● 40
Dilliner; RMC Place; GREENE; ▲ Dunkard; **225** WQ-4; 🅿; z 15327; ● 200
Dillinger; RMC Place; LEHIGH; ▲ Upper Milford; ***227** EM-11; ★ **ALL-**; mail Emmaus z 18049; rural
Dillingersville; RMC Place; LEHIGH; ▲ Lower Milford; ***227** EM-11; ★ **ALL-**; mail Zionsville z 18092; ● 135
Dillontown; RMC Place; WAYNE; ▲ Buckingham; ***226** EE-11; mail Equinunk z 18417; rural
Dillsburg; Inc. Place; YORK; **227** EO-4; elev. 580ft./177m.; 🅿; ★ **HRBG**; z 17019; Ⓟ 1,925; © 2,063
Dilltown; RMC Place; INDIANA; ▲ East Wheatfield, Buffington; **225** WM-8; 🅿; ★ **JNST**; z 15929; ● 250
Dilworthtown; RMC Place; CHESTER; ▲ Birmingham; ***227** EQ-10; elev. 471ft./144m.; ★ **PHIL-**; mail West Chester z 19380; ● 200
Dime; RMC Place; ARMSTRONG; ***225** WL-6; ★ **PGH**; mail Vandergrift z 15690
Dimeling; RMC Place; CLEARFIELD; ▲ Boggs; ***224** WJ-11; mail Clearfield z 16830; rural
Dimmsville; RMC Place; JUNIATA; ▲ Greenwood; ***227** EL-3; mail Millerstown z 17062, Thompsontown z 17094; rural
Dimock; RMC Place; SUSQUEHANNA; ▲ Dimock; **226** EF-9; elev. 1,525ft./465m.; 🅿; z 18816; ● 300
Dimock; MCD-Township; SUSQUEHANNA; ***226** EF-9; 🅿; z 18816; Ⓟ 1,226; © 1,398
Dimock Corners; RMC Place; SUSQUEHANNA; ▲ Herrick; ***226** EF-10; elev. 1,990ft./607m.; mail Herrick Center z 18430; rural
Dingman; MCD-Township; PIKE; ***226** EH-13; mail Milford z 18337; Ⓟ 4,591; © 8,788
Dingmans Ferry; RMC Place; PIKE; ▲ Delaware; **226** EI-13; 🅿; z 18328; ● 1,000
Dipple Manor; RMC Place; LUZERNE; ▲ Sugarloaf; ***226** EJ-8; ★ **HAZ**; mail Hazleton z 18202; ● 270
Distant; RMC Place; ARMSTRONG; ▲ Mahoning; **224** WJ-6; elev. 1,391ft./424m.; 🅿; z 16223; ● 750
District; MCD-Township; BERKS; ***227** EM-10; ★ **READ**; mail Boyertown z 19512; Ⓟ 1,211; © 1,449
Divide; RMC Place; COLUMBIA; ▲ Jackson; ***226** EI-6; elev. 1,200ft./366m.; mail Benton z 17814; rural
Dividing Ridge; RMC Place; SOMERSET; ▲ Allegheny; ***225** WP-9; elev. 2,141ft./653m.; mail Berlin z 15530, Fairhope z 15538; rural
Dixmont (Neville Island); RMC Place; ALLEGHENY; ▲ Neville; ***225** WM-3; ★ **PGH**; mail Pittsburgh z 15225; ● 1,273
Dixon; RMC Place; WYOMING; ▲ Tunkhannock; ***226** EG-9; elev. 675ft./206m.; mail Tunkhannock z 18657; ● 300
Dixonville; RMC Place; INDIANA; ▲ Rayne, Green; **225** WL-8; 🅿; z 15734; ● 600
Doe Run; RMC Place; CHESTER; ▲ West Marlborough; **227** EP-9; elev. 306ft./93m.; mail Coatesville z 19320; ● 100
Dogtown; RMC Place; COLUMBIA; ▲ Beaver; ***226** EJ-7; elev. 968ft./295m.; mail Bloomsburg z 17815; ● 100
Dogtown; RMC Place; LUZERNE; ▲ Salem; ***226** EI-8; mail Shickshinny z 18655; ● 50
Dogtown (Penn Avon); RMC Place; SNYDER; ▲ Monroe; ***227** EK-4; mail Selinsgrove z 17870; pop. incl. with Selinsgrove (Inc. Place)
Dogwood Hollow; RMC Place; BUCKS; ▲ Bristol; ***227** EO-14; ★ **PHIL-**; mail Feasterville Trevose z 19053
Dolington; RMC Place; BUCKS; ▲ Upper Makefield; **227** EN-13; ★ **PHIL-**; mail Newtown z 18940; ● 250
Dombach Manor; RMC Place; LANCASTER; ▲ Manheim; ★ **LANC**; mail Lancaster z 17601
Donaldson; CDP; SCHUYLKILL; ▲ Frailey; **227** EL-6; 🅿; z 17981; © 325
Donaldsons Crossroads; RMC Place; WASHINGTON; ▲ Peters; ***225** WN-3; ★ **PGH**; mail Canonsburg z 15317; ● 800
Donation; RMC Place; HUNTINGDON; ▲ Oneida; ***225** WM-13; mail Huntingdon z 16652; rural
Donegal; MCD-Township; BUTLER; ***224** WJ-5; mail Chicora z 16025; Ⓟ 1,563; © 1,722
Donegal; MCD-Township; WASHINGTON; ***225** WO-1; mail Claysville z 15323; Ⓟ 2,347; © 2,428
Donegal; Inc. Place; WESTMORELAND; **225** WO-6; elev. 1,814ft./553m.; 🅿; z 15628; Ⓟ 212; © 165
Donegal; MCD-Township; WESTMORELAND; ***225** WO-6; 🅿; z 15628 & mail Jones Mills z 15646; does not include the Borough of Donegal; Ⓟ 2,419; © 2,442
Donegal Heights; RMC Place; LANCASTER; ▲ East Donegal; ***227** EO-6; mail Mount Joy z 17552; ● 200
Donegal Springs; RMC Place; LANCASTER; ▲ East Donegal; ***227** EO-6; elev. 364ft./111m.; mail Mount Joy z 17552; rural
Donerville; RMC Place; LANCASTER; ▲ Manor, East Hempfield; ***227** EP-6; ★ **LANC**; mail Lancaster z 17603; rural
Donnally Mills; RMC Place; PERRY; ▲ Tuscarora; **227** EM-3; mail Millerstown z 17062; ● 80
Donnelly; RMC Place; WESTMORELAND; ▲ East Huntingdon; ***225** WO-5; mail Alverton z 15612; rural
Donnellytown; RMC Place; CUMBERLAND; ▲ Middlesex; ***227** EN-3; ★ **CARL**; mail Carlisle z 17013; rural
Donohoe; RMC Place; WESTMORELAND; ▲ Unity; ***225** WN-6; ★ **LTROB**; mail Latrobe z 15650; ● 75
Donora; Inc. Place; WASHINGTON; **225** WO-4; elev. 940ft./287m.; 🅿; ★ **PGH**; z 15033; Ⓟ 5,928; © 5,653
Dooleyville; RMC Place; NORTHUMBERLAND; ▲ Mount Carmel; ***227** EK-6; mail Mount Carmel z 17851; ● 50
Dora; RMC Place; GREENE; ▲ Monongahela; ***225** WQ-4; mail Greensboro z 15338; rural
Dora; RMC Place; JEFFERSON; ▲ Ringgold; **224** WJ-7; elev. 1,307ft./398m.; mail Punxsutawney z 15767; ● 50
Dormont; Inc. Place; ALLEGHENY; **225** WN-3; elev. 1,220ft./372m.; ★ **PGH**; mail Pittsburgh z 15216; Ⓟ 9,772; © 9,305
Dorneyville; RMC Place; LEHIGH; ▲ South Whitehall, Salisbury; **226** EC-2; ★ **ALL-**; mail Allentown z 18104; ● 1,450
Dornsife; RMC Place; NORTHUMBERLAND; ▲ Little Mahanoy; **227** EL-5; 🅿; z 17823; ● 100
Dorothy; RMC Place; WESTMORELAND; ▲ Unity; ***225** WN-6; ★ **LTROB**; mail Latrobe z 15650; ● 150
Dorrance; RMC Place; LUZERNE; ▲ Dorrance; **226** EI-8; ★ **SCR-**; mail Mountain Top z 18707; ● 50
Dorrance; MCD-Township; LUZERNE; ***226** EI-8; ★ **SCR-**; mail Mountain Top z 18707; Ⓟ 1,778; © 2,109
Dorset; RMC Place; SCHUYLKILL; ▲ West Penn; ***227** EL-9; elev. 729ft./222m.; mail New Ringgold z 17960; rural
Dorseyville; RMC Place; ALLEGHENY; ▲ Indiana; **225** WL-4; ★ **PGH**; mail Pittsburgh z 15238; ● 650
Dott; RMC Place; FULTON; ▲ Bethel; **225** WQ-12; mail Warfordsburg z 17267; ● 40
Dotters Corners; RMC Place; MONROE; ▲ Polk; ***226** EJ-10; mail Kunkletown z 18058; ● 65
Doubling Gap; RMC Place; CUMBERLAND; ▲ Lower Mifflin; ***227** EN-2; mail Newville z 17241
Douglass; MCD-Township; BERKS; ***227** EN-10; mail Pottstown z 19464; Ⓟ 3,570; © 3,327
Douglass; MCD-Township; MONTGOMERY; ***227** EN-10; mail Gilbertsville z 19525; Ⓟ 7,048; © 9,104
Douglassville; RMC Place; BERKS; ▲ Amity; **227** EN-10; 🅿; z 19518; ● 1,200
Doutyville; RMC Place; NORTHUMBERLAND; ▲ East Cameron; ***227** EL-6; mail Shamokin z 17872; ● 100
Dover; Inc. Place; YORK; **227** EP-4; elev. 431ft./131m.; 🅿; ★ **YORK**; z 17315; Ⓟ 1,884; © 1,815
Dover; MCD-Township; YORK; ***227** EP-4; 🅿; ★ **YORK**; z 17315; does not include the Borough of Dover; Ⓟ 15,668; © 18,074; ◆ 21,302
Down East; RMC Place; CHESTER; ▲ East Whiteland; ***227** EP-10; ★ **PHIL-**; mail Malvern z 19355; ● 450
Downey; RMC Place; SOMERSET; ▲ Stonycreek; ***225** WP-9; mail Berlin z 15530; rural
Downieville; RMC Place; BUTLER; ▲ Adams; ***225** WL-4; ★ **PGH**; mail Valencia z 16059; ● 40
Downingtown; Inc. Place; CHESTER; **227** EP-10; elev. 244ft./74m.; 🅿 🅷; ★ **PHIL-**; z 19335, z 19372; Ⓟ 7,749; © 7,589
Downtown; RMC Place; BERKS; ***227** EN-9; ★ **READ**; mail Reading z 19603; pop. incl. with Reading (Inc. Place)
Downtown; RMC Place; ERIE; ***224** WC-3; ★ **ERIE**; mail Erie z 16501-02, z 16507, z 16512; pop. incl. with Erie (Inc. Place)
Downtown; RMC Place; FAYETTE; ★ **UNTN**; mail Uniontown z 15401; pop. incl. with Uniontown (Inc. Place)
Downtown; RMC Place; LACKAWANNA; ***226** EH-10; ★ **SCR-**; mail Scranton z 18501; pop. incl. with Scranton (Inc. Place)
Downtown; RMC Place; LANCASTER; ★ **LANC**; mail Lancaster z 17603, z 17608; pop. incl. with Lancaster (Inc. Place)
Downtown; RMC Place; LAWRENCE; ★ **NWCS**; mail New Castle z 16103; pop. incl. with New Castle (Inc. Place)
Doylesburg; RMC Place; FRANKLIN; ▲ Fannett; **225** WO-14; elev. 1,042ft./318m.; 🅿; z 17219; ● 150
Doyles Mills; RMC Place; JUNIATA; ▲ Beale; ***227** EM-1; mail Mifflin z 17058; rural
Doylestown; Inc. Place; ⊡ BUCKS; **227** EN-12; elev. 340ft./104m.; 🅿 🅷 🅲 1,605 ■; ★ **PHIL-**; z 18901-02, z 18933; Ⓟ 8,575; © 8,227; ◆ 8,032
Doylestown; MCD-Township; BUCKS; ***227** EN-12; 🅿 🅲 1,605; ★ **PHIL-**; z 18901-02, z 18933; does not include the Borough of Doylestown; Ⓟ 14,510; © 17,619
Drake; RMC Place; MERCER; ▲ Springfield; ***224** WI-3; mail Volant z 16156; ● 60
Drakes Mills; RMC Place; CRAWFORD; ▲ Cambridge; **224** WE-3; ★ **ERIE**; mail Cambridge Springs z 16403; ● 40
Draketown; RMC Place; CLINTON; ▲ Bald Eagle; ***226** EI-2; ★ **WMSPT**; mail Mill Hall z 17751; ● 50
Draketown; RMC Place; SOMERSET; ▲ Lower Turkeyfoot; **225** WQ-6; mail Confluence z 15424; ● 60
Drane; RMC Place; CLEARFIELD; ▲ Decatur; ***225** WK-11; mail Osceola Mills z 16666; ● 55
Draper; RMC Place; TIOGA; ▲ Delmar; ***226** EF-2; mail Wellsboro z 16901
Drauckers (Drauckers Bottom); RMC Place; CLEARFIELD; ▲ Union, Bloom; mail Luthersburg z 15848; rural
Drauckers Bottom; CLEARFIELD; see Drauckers (RMC Place)
Dravosburg; Inc. Place; ALLEGHENY; **228** M-7; elev. 800ft./244m.; 🅿; ★ **PGH**; z 15034; Ⓟ 2,377; © 2,015
Dreher; MCD-Township; WAYNE; ***226** EH-11; mail Newfoundland z 18445; Ⓟ 1,022; © 1,280
Drehersville; RMC Place; SCHUYLKILL; ▲ East Brunswick; **227** EL-8; mail Orwigsburg z 17961; ● 40
Drennen; RMC Place; WESTMORELAND; ***225** WM-5; ★ **PGH**; mail New Kensington z 15068; pop. incl. with Murrysville (Inc. Place)
Dresher; RMC Place; MONTGOMERY; ▲ Upper Dublin; ***227** EO-12; 🅿; ★ **PHIL-**; z 19025; ● 1,500
Drexelbrook; RMC Place; DELAWARE; ▲ Upper Darby; ★ **PHIL-**; mail Drexel Hill z 19026
Drexel Heights; RMC Place; NORTHAMPTON; ▲ Allen; ★ **ALL-**; mail Northampton z 18067; ● 300
Drexel Hill; CDP; DELAWARE; ▲ Upper Darby; **228** E-2; 🅿 🅷; ★ **PHIL-**; z 19026; Ⓟ 29,744; © 29,364; ◆ 29,366
Drexel Hills; RMC Place; CUMBERLAND; ***227** EO-4; ★ **HRBG**; mail New Cumberland z 17070; pop. incl. with New Cumberland (Inc. Place)
Drexlewood; RMC Place; BERKS; ▲ Spring; ***227** EN-8; elev. 340ft./104m.; ★ **READ**; mail Reading z 19610; ● 2,000
Drifting; RMC Place; CLEARFIELD; ▲ Cooper; **224** WJ-12; 🅿; z 16834; ● 150
Drifton; RMC Place; LUZERNE; ▲ Hazle, Foster; **226** EJ-9; 🅿; ★ **HAZ**; z 18221; ● 800
Driftwood; Inc. Place; CAMERON; **224** WH-12; elev. 850ft./259m.; 🅿; z 15832; Ⓟ 116; © 103
Drinker; RMC Place; LACKAWANNA; ▲ Jefferson; ***226** EH-11; ★ **SCR-**; mail Moscow z 18444
Dromgold; RMC Place; PERRY; ▲ Carroll; ***227** EN-3; ★ **HRBG**; mail Shermans Dale z 17090; rural
Druid Hills; RMC Place; LUZERNE; ***226** EH-8; ★ **SCR-**; mail Shavertown z 18708; pop. incl. with Dallas (Inc. Place)
Drummond; RMC Place; ELK; ▲ Horton; ***224** WH-9; mail Brockport z 15823; rural
Drumore (Fishing Creek); RMC Place; LANCASTER; ▲ Drumore; **227** EQ-7; 🅿; z 17518; ● 115
Drumore; MCD-Township; LANCASTER; ***227** EQ-8; 🅿; z 17518 & mail Peach Bottom z 17563; Ⓟ 2,114; © 2,243
Drums; RMC Place; LUZERNE; ▲ Butler; **226** EJ-8; 🅿; ★ **HAZ**; z 18222; ● 600
Drury Run; RMC Place; CLINTON; ▲ Noyes; **224** WH-14; mail Renovo z 17764; ● 100
Dry Hill; RMC Place; FAYETTE; ▲ Upper Tyrone; ***225** WP-5; mail Connellsville z 15425; ● 60
Dry Run; RMC Place; FRANKLIN; ▲ Fannett; **225** WO-14; 🅿; z 17220 & mail Doylesburg z 17219; ● 200
Dry Tavern; RMC Place; GREENE; ▲ Jefferson; **225** WP-3; elev. 1,014ft./309m.; mail Rices Landing z 15357; ● 500
Dry Valley Crossroads; RMC Place; UNION; ▲ Union; ***227** EK-4; mail Winfield z 17889; ● 45
Dryville; RMC Place; BERKS; ▲ Rockland; **227** EM-9; elev. 751ft./229m.; ★ **READ**; mail Mertztown z 19539; ● 75
Dublin; Inc. Place; BUCKS; **227** EN-12; elev. 560ft./171m.; 🅿; ★ **PHIL-**; z 18917; Ⓟ 1,985; © 2,083
Dublin; MCD-Township; FULTON; ***225** WP-13; mail Fort Littleton z 17223; Ⓟ 1,146; © 1,277
Dublin; MCD-Township; HUNTINGDON; ***225** WO-13; mail Neelyton z 17239; Ⓟ 1,119; © 1,280
Dublin Mills; RMC Place; FULTON; ▲ Taylor; ***225** WO-12; mail Hustontown z 17229; ● 40
Du Bois; Inc. Place; CLEARFIELD; **224** WI-9; elev. 1,420ft./433m.; 🅿 🅷 🅲 811 ■; z 15801; Ⓟ 8,286; © 8,123; ◆ 7,543
Duboistown; Inc. Place; LYCOMING; **226** EI-4; elev. 536ft./163m.; 🅿; ★ **WMSPT**; z 17702; Ⓟ 1,201; © 1,280
Dudley; Inc. Place; HUNTINGDON; **225** WO-12; elev. 1,415ft./431m.; 🅿; z 16634; Ⓟ 232; © 192
Duffield; RMC Place; FRANKLIN; ▲ Guilford; ***227** EQ-1; mail Chambersburg z 17201; ● 40
Duffs; RMC Place; ALLEGHENY; ★ **PGH**; pop. incl. with Pittsburgh (Inc. Place)
Duffs Junction; RMC Place; ALLEGHENY; ★ **PGH**; pop. incl. with Pittsburgh (Inc. Place)
Duhring; RMC Place; FOREST; ▲ Jenks; ***224** WG-8; mail Marienville z 16239; ● 10
Duke Center; RMC Place; MCKEAN; ▲ Otto; **224** WD-10; 🅿; z 16729; ● 850
Dumas; RMC Place; SOMERSET; ▲ Addison; ***225** WQ-7; elev. 1,408ft./429m.; mail Confluence z 15424; rural
Dunbar; Inc. Place; FAYETTE; **225** WP-5; elev. 1,000ft./305m.; 🅿; z 15431; Ⓟ 1,213; © 1,219
Dunbar; MCD-Township; FAYETTE; ***225** WP-5; 🅿; z 15431; does not include the Borough of Dunbar; Ⓟ 7,460; © 7,562
Duncan; MCD-Township; TIOGA; ***226** EF-3; mail Wellsboro z 16901; Ⓟ 248; © 213
Duncan Circle; RMC Place; BEAVER; ▲ Brighton; ***225** WL-2; elev. 1,100ft./335m.; ★ **PGH**; mail Beaver z 15009; ● 120
Duncannon; Inc. Place; PERRY; **227** EN-4; elev. 360ft./110m.; 🅿; ★ **HRBG**; z 17020; Ⓟ 1,450; © 1,508
Duncansville; Inc. Place; BLAIR; **225** WM-11; elev. 1,015ft./309m.; 🅿; ★ **ALT**; z 16635; Ⓟ 1,309; © 1,238
Duncott; RMC Place; SCHUYLKILL; ▲ New Castle, Cass; ***227** EL-7; ★ **PTSVL**; mail Pottsville z 17901; ● 100
Dundaff; RMC Place; SUSQUEHANNA; ▲ Clifford; **226** EF-10; elev. 1,599ft./487m.; mail Carbondale z 18407; ● 175
Dundore; RMC Place; SNYDER; ▲ Union; **227** EL-4; mail Port Trevorton z 17864; ● 30
Dungarvin; RMC Place; HUNTINGDON; ▲ Warriors Mark; ***225** WL-12; mail Warriors Mark z 16877; rural
Dunkard (Taylortown); RMC Place; GREENE; ▲ Dunkard; **225** WQ-4; mail Dilliner z 15327; ● 150
Dunkard; MCD-Township; GREENE; ***225** WQ-3; mail Dilliner z 15327; Ⓟ 2,386; © 2,358
Dunkelbergers; RMC Place; NORTHUMBERLAND; ▲ Little Mahanoy; ***227** EK-5; mail Shamokin z 17872; rural
Dunlap Creek Village; RMC Place; FAYETTE; ▲ Redstone; ***225** WP-4; ★ **UNTN**; mail Republic z 15475
Dunlevy; Inc. Place; WASHINGTON; **225** WO-4; elev. 800ft./244m.; 🅿; ★ **PGH**; z 15432; Ⓟ 417; © 397
Dunlo; RMC Place; CAMBRIA; ▲ Adams; **225** WN-9; 🅿; ★ **JNST**; z 15930; ● 750
Dunmore; Inc. Place; LACKAWANNA; **226** EC-13; elev. 940ft./287m.; 🅿 🅲 1,294; ★ **SCR-**; z 18509-10, z 18512; Ⓟ 15,403; © 14,018
Dunningsville; RMC Place; WASHINGTON; ▲ Somerset, Nottingham; ***225** WO-3; ★ **PGH**; mail Eighty Four z 15330; rural
Dunningtown; RMC Place; WESTMORELAND; ***225** WM-5; elev. 1,099ft./335m.; ★ **PGH**; mail Export z 15632; pop. incl. with Murrysville (Inc. Place)
Dunns Eddy; RMC Place; WARREN; ▲ Brokenstraw; mail Youngsville z 16371; rural
Dunnstable; MCD-Township; CLINTON; ***226** EI-2; ★ **WMSPT**; mail Lock Haven z 17745; Ⓟ 846; © 945
Dunnstown; CDP; CLINTON; ▲ Woodward; **226** EI-2; ★ **WMSPT**; mail Lock Haven z 17745; Ⓟ 1,486; © 1,365
Dupont; Inc. Place; LUZERNE; **226** EB-10; elev. 735ft./224m.; 🅿; ★ **SCR-**; z 18641; Ⓟ 2,984; © 2,719
Duquesne; Inc. Place; ALLEGHENY; **225** WN-4; elev. 840ft./256m.; 🅿; ★ **PGH**; z 15110; Ⓟ 8,525; © 7,332
Duquesne Heights; RMC Place; ALLEGHENY; ***225** WM-3; ★ **PGH**; mail Pittsburgh z 15211; pop. incl. with Pittsburgh (Inc. Place)
Duquesne Wharf; RMC Place; ALLEGHENY; ★ **PGH**; mail Duquesne z 15110; pop. incl. with Duquesne (Inc. Place)
Durham; RMC Place; BUCKS; ▲ Durham; **227** EL-12; 🅿; ★ **ALL-**; z 18039; ● 200
Durham; MCD-Township; BUCKS; ***227** EL-12; 🅿; ★ **ALL-**; z 18039; Ⓟ 1,209; © 1,313
Durham Furnace; RMC Place; BUCKS; ▲ Durham; ***227** EL-12; ★ **PHIL-**; mail Kintnersville z 18930; ● 45
Durlach; RMC Place; LANCASTER; ▲ Clay; ***227** EO-7; ★ **LANC**; mail Ephrata z 17522; rural
Durrell; RMC Place; BRADFORD; ▲ Asylum; ***226** EF-7; mail Towanda z 18848; rural
Duryea; Inc. Place; LUZERNE; **226** EH-9; elev. 600ft./183m.; 🅿; ★ **SCR-**; z 18642; Ⓟ 4,869; © 4,634
Dushore; Inc. Place; SULLIVAN; **226** EG-6; elev. 1,500ft./457m.; 🅿; z 18614; Ⓟ 738; © 663
Dutch Hill; RMC Place; CLARION; ▲ Perry; **224** WJ-5; mail Parker z 16049; ● 110
Dutch Hill; RMC Place; FAYETTE; ▲ Luzerne; ***225** WP-4; ★ **UNTN**; mail La Belle z 15450; ● 150
Dutch Hill; RMC Place; MERCER; ***224** WH-2; elev. 1,193ft./364m.; ★ **SHAR**; mail Hermitage z 16148; pop. incl. with Hermitage (Inc. Place)
Dutch Settlement; CAMBRIA; see Germantown (RMC Place)
Dutchtown; RMC Place; CAMBRIA; ▲ Washington; ***225** WM-10; mail Lilly z 15938; rural
Dutchtown; RMC Place; FRANKLIN; ▲ Peters; ***225** WQ-13; mail Mercersburg z 17236; ● 30
Dutton Mill; RMC Place; CHESTER; ▲ East Goshen; ***227** EP-11; ★ **PHIL-**; mail West Chester z 19380; rural
Dyberry; MCD-Township; WAYNE; ***226** EF-12; mail Honesdale z 18431; Ⓟ 1,223; © 1,353
Dysart; RMC Place; CAMBRIA; ▲ Dean; **225** WL-10; 🅿; z 16636; ● 120

E

Eagle (Uwchlan, Uwchland); RMC Place; CHESTER; ▲ Upper Uwchlan; **227** EO-10; ★ **PHIL-**; mail Uwchland z 19480; ● 130
Eagle Foundry; RMC Place; HUNTINGDON; ▲ Todd; ***225** WO-12; mail James Creek z 16657; rural
Eaglehurst; RMC Place; ERIE; ▲ Millcreek; ***224** WC-3; ★ **ERIE**; mail Erie z 16505
Eagle Point; RMC Place; BERKS; ▲ Maxatawny; ***227** EM-9; elev. 460ft./140m.; mail Kutztown z 19530; rural
Eagle Rock; RMC Place; VENANGO; ▲ President; **224** WG-6; elev. 1,068ft./326m.; mail Oil City z 16301; summer pop. 200; ● 60
Eagles Mere; Inc. Place; SULLIVAN; **226** EH-6; elev. 2,000ft./610m.; 🅿; z 17731; Ⓟ 123; © 153
Eagles Mere Park; RMC Place; SULLIVAN; ***226** EH-6; mail Eagles Mere z 17731; pop. incl. with Eagles Mere (Inc. Place)
Eagleville; RMC Place; CENTRE; ▲ Liberty; ***226** EJ-1; mail Blanchard z 16826; ● 80
Eagleville; CDP; MONTGOMERY; ▲ Lower Providence; **227** EO-11; 🅿 🅷; ★ **PHIL-**; z 19403, z 19408, z 19415; Ⓟ 3,637; © 4,458
Earl; MCD-Township; BERKS; ***227** EN-10; mail Boyertown z 19512; Ⓟ 3,016; © 3,050
Earl; MCD-Township; LANCASTER; ***227** EO-8; ★ **LANC**; mail New Holland z 17557; Ⓟ 5,515; © 6,183
Earlington; RMC Place; MONTGOMERY; ▲ Franconia; ***227** EN-11; 🅿; ★ **PHIL-**; z 18918; ● 125
Earlston; RMC Place; BEDFORD; ▲ West Providence; **225** WP-11; mail Everett z 15537; ● 250
Earlville; RMC Place; BERKS; ▲ Earl, Amity; **227** EN-9; 🅿; z 19519; ● 500
Earnest; RMC Place; MONTGOMERY; ▲ Plymouth; ***227** EO-11; ★ **PHIL-**; mail Norristown z 19401; rural
Earnestville; RMC Place; CENTRE; ▲ Rush; ***225** WK-11; mail Osceola Mills z 16666; ● 30
East Allen; MCD-Township; NORTHAMPTON; ***227** EL-11; ★ **ALL-**; mail Northampton z 18067; Ⓟ 4,572; © 4,903
East Altoona; RMC Place; BLAIR; ▲ Logan; **225** WM-11; elev. 1,131ft./345m.; ★ **ALT**; mail Altoona z 16601; ● 200

Entries in **UPPERCASE** are counties.
Entries in **bold** have populations of 2,500 or more.
Names in parentheses are alternate names.

Inc. Place	Incorporated Place
RMC Place	Rand McNally Designated Place
CDP	Census Designated Place
MCD	Minor Civil Division

⊡ County Seat
▲ Minor Civil Division
elev. Elevation
🅿 Post Office
🅷 Hospital
🅲 College
■ Principal Business Center
★ Ranally Metro Area (RMA) Abbreviation
z Zip Code(s)
Ⓟ Previous Census Population
® Revised Census Population
Ⓐ Annexation Population
● Rand McNally Population Estimate
© Final Census Population
Ⓢ Special Census Population
◆ Estimated Population

For additional definitions see Glossary, Volume 1, and Introduction, Volume 2.

East Ararat; RMC Place; SUSQUEHANNA; ▲ Ararat; *226 EE-10; elev. 2,032ft./619m.; mail Union Dale z 18470; rural
East Athens; RMC Place; BRADFORD; ▲ Athens; 226 ED-6; mail Athens z 18810; ● 400
East Bangor; Inc. Place; NORTHAMPTON; 227 EK-12; elev. 572ft./174m.; 🅿; z 18013; Ⓟ 1,006; Ⓒ 979
East Benton (Jordan Hollow); RMC Place; LACKAWANNA; ▲ Scott, Benton; 226 EG-10; ★ SCR-; mail Dalton z 18414; ● 175
East Berlin; Inc. Place; ADAMS; 227 EP-4; elev. 430ft./131m.; 🅿; ★ HANV; z 17316; Ⓟ 1,175; Ⓒ 1,365
East Berwick; CDP; LUZERNE; ▲ Salem; 226 EJ-7; mail Berwick z 18603; Ⓟ 2,128; Ⓒ 1,998
East Bethlehem; MCD-Township; WASHINGTON; *225 WP-3; mail Clarksville z 15322; Ⓟ 2,799; Ⓒ 2,524
East Bradford; MCD-Township; CHESTER; *227 EP-10; ★ PHIL-; mail West Chester z 19380; Ⓟ 6,440; Ⓒ 9,405
East Bradford; RMC Place; MCKEAN; pop. incl. with Bradford (Inc. Place)
East Brady; Inc. Place; CLARION; 224 WJ-5; elev. 855ft./261m.; 🅿; z 16028; Ⓟ 1,047; Ⓒ 1,038
East Branch; RMC Place; WARREN; ▲ Spring Creek; *224 WE-6; elev. 1,566ft./477m.; mail Spartansburg z 16434; rural
East Brandywine; MCD-Township; CHESTER; *227 EP-9; ★ PHIL-; mail Downingtown z 19335; Ⓟ 5,179; Ⓒ 5,822
East Brook; RMC Place; LAWRENCE; ▲ Hickory; 224 WJ-2; ★ NWCS; mail New Castle z 16101; ● 300
East Brunswick; MCD-Township; SCHUYLKILL; *227 EL-8; mail New Ringgold z 17960; Ⓟ 1,506; Ⓒ 1,601
East Buffalo; MCD-Township; UNION; *226 EJ-4; mail Lewisburg z 17837; Ⓟ 5,245; Ⓒ 5,730
East Butler; Inc. Place; BUTLER; 225 WK-4; elev. 1,080ft./329m.; 🅿; ★ BUTL; z 16029; Ⓟ 725; Ⓒ 679
East Caln; MCD-Township; CHESTER; *227 EP-10; ★ PHIL-; mail Exton z 19341; Ⓟ 2,619; Ⓒ 2,857
East Cameron; MCD-Township; NORTHUMBERLAND; *227 EK-6; mail Shamokin z 17872; Ⓟ 646; Ⓒ 686
East Canton; RMC Place; BRADFORD; ▲ Canton; 226 EF-5; elev. 1,111ft./339m.; mail Canton z 17724; ● 25
East Carnegie; RMC Place; ALLEGHENY; *225 WM-3; ★ PGH; mail Pittsburgh z 15230; pop. incl. with Pittsburgh (Inc. Place)
East Carroll; MCD-Township; CAMBRIA; *225 WM-9; mail Carrolltown z 15722; Ⓟ 1,951; Ⓒ 1,798
East Charleston; TIOGA; see Whitneyville (RMC Place)
East Chillisquaque; MCD-Township; NORTHUMBERLAND; *226 EJ-5; mail Milton z 17847; Ⓟ 679; Ⓒ 664
East Cocalico; MCD-Township; LANCASTER; *227 EO-8; mail Denver z 17517; Ⓟ 7,809; Ⓒ 9,954
East Conemaugh; Inc. Place; CAMBRIA; 225 WN-9; elev. 1,240ft./378m.; ★ JNST; mail Johnstown z 15909; Ⓟ 1,470; Ⓒ 1,291
East Connellsville; RMC Place; FAYETTE; ▲ Bullskin; mail Connellsville z 15425; ● 200
East Coventry; MCD-Township; CHESTER; *227 EO-10; ★ PTSTN; mail Parker Ford z 19457; Ⓟ 4,450; Ⓒ 4,566
East Deer; MCD-Township; ALLEGHENY; *225 WL-5; ★ PGH; mail Creighton z 15030; Ⓟ 1,558; Ⓒ 1,362
East Donegal; MCD-Township; LANCASTER; *227 EP-5; mail Marietta z 17547; Ⓟ 4,484; Ⓒ 5,405
East Drumore; MCD-Township; LANCASTER; *227 EQ-8; mail Quarryville z 17566; Ⓟ 3,225; Ⓒ 3,535
East Du Bois; RMC Place; CLEARFIELD; mail Du Bois z 15801; pop. incl. with Du Bois (Inc. Place)
East Earl; RMC Place; LANCASTER; ▲ East Earl; 227 EO-8; 🅿; ★ LANC; z 17519; ● 300
East Earl; MCD-Township; LANCASTER; *227 EO-8; 🅿; ★ LANC; z 17519; Ⓟ 5,491; Ⓒ 5,723
East End; RMC Place; BLAIR; *225 WM-11; ★ ALT; mail Altoona z 16602; pop. incl. with Altoona (Inc. Place)
East End; RMC Place; LUZERNE; ★ SCR-; mail Wilkes Barre z 18702; pop. incl. with Wilkes-Barre (Inc. Place)
East Fairfield; MCD-Township; CRAWFORD; *224 WG-3; mail Cochranton z 16314; Ⓟ 890; Ⓒ 848
East Fallowfield (East Fallowfield Township); MCD-Township; CHESTER; *227 EP-9; ★ PHIL-; mail Coatesville z 19320; Ⓟ 4,433; Ⓒ 5,157
East Fallowfield; MCD-Township; CRAWFORD; *224 WG-2; mail Atlantic z 16111; Ⓟ 1,280; Ⓒ 1,434
East Fallowfield Township; CHESTER; see East Fallowfield (MCD-Township)
East Falls; RMC Place; PHILADELPHIA; *227 EP-12; ★ PHIL-; mail Philadelphia z 19129; pop. incl. with Philadelphia (Inc. Place)
East Faxon; LYCOMING; see Kenmar (RMC Place)
East Finley; RMC Place; WASHINGTON; ▲ East Finley; *225 WP-2; elev. 1,107ft./337m.; mail West Finley z 15377
East Finley; MCD-Township; WASHINGTON; *225 WP-2; mail West Finley z 15377; Ⓟ 1,479; Ⓒ 1,489
East Franklin; MCD-Township; ARMSTRONG; *225 WK-6; ★ PGH; mail Kittanning z 16201; Ⓟ 3,923; Ⓒ 3,900
East Fredericktown; RMC Place; FAYETTE; ▲ Luzerne; *225 WP-3; ★ UNTN; mail La Belle z 15450; ● 30
East Freedom; RMC Place; BLAIR; ▲ Freedom; 225 WN-11; elev. 1,010ft./308m.; 🅿; ★ ALT; z 16637; ● 400
East Germantown; RMC Place; PHILADELPHIA; ★ PHIL-; mail Philadelphia z 19138; pop. incl. with Philadelphia (Inc. Place)
East Goshen; MCD-Township; CHESTER; *227 EP-10; ★ PHIL-; mail West Chester z 19380; Ⓟ 15,138; Ⓒ 16,824
East Greenville; Inc. Place; MONTGOMERY; 227 EM-11; elev. 414ft./126m.; 🅿; ★ PHIL-; z 18041; Ⓟ 3,117; Ⓒ 3,103
East Hanover; MCD-Township; DAUPHIN; *227 EN-5; ★ HRBG; mail Grantville z 17028; Ⓟ 4,569; Ⓒ 5,322
East Hanover; RMC Place; LEBANON; 227 EN-6; mail Annville z 17003; ● 45
East Hanover; MCD-Township; LEBANON; *227 EM-5; mail Annville z 17003; Ⓟ 3,058; Ⓒ 2,858
East Hempfield; MCD-Township; LANCASTER; *227 EO-7; ★ LANC; mail Lancaster z 17603; Ⓟ 18,597; Ⓒ 21,399; ◆ 23,769
East Herrick; RMC Place; BRADFORD; ▲ Herrick; *226 EE-7; elev. 1,275ft./389m.; mail Wyalusing z 18853; rural
East Hickory; RMC Place; FOREST; ▲ Hickory; 224 WG-6; 🅿; z 16321; ● 150
East Hills; RMC Place; CAMBRIA; ▲ Richland; ★ JNST; mail Johnstown z 15904; rural
East Hills; RMC Place; NORTHAMPTON; *227 EL-11; ★ ALL-; pop. incl. with Bethlehem (Inc. Place)
East Honesdale; RMC Place; WAYNE; *226 EG-12; mail Honesdale z 18431; pop. incl. with Honesdale (Inc. Place)
East Hopewell; MCD-Township; YORK; *227 EQ-6; ★ BAL; mail Felton z 17322; Ⓟ 1,929; Ⓒ 2,209
East Huntingdon; MCD-Township; WESTMORELAND; *225 WO-5; mail Ruffs Dale z 15679; Ⓟ 7,708; Ⓒ 7,781
East Kane; RMC Place; MCKEAN; ▲ Wetmore; 224 WF-9; mail Kane z 16735; ● 135
East Keating; MCD-Township; CLINTON; *224 WH-12; mail Westport z 17778; Ⓟ 22; Ⓒ 24
East Kendall; RMC Place; YORK; ▲ Windsor; *227 EP-6; elev. 800ft./244m.; ★ YORK; mail Red Lion z 17356; ● 300
East Kittanning; RMC Place; ARMSTRONG; ▲ Rayburn; *225 WK-6; elev. 880ft./268m.; ★ PGH; mail Kittanning z 16201; pop. incl. with Kittanning (Inc. Place)
East Lackawannock; MCD-Township; MERCER; *224 WI-2; mail Mercer z 16137; Ⓟ 1,606; Ⓒ 1,701
East Lampeter; MCD-Township; LANCASTER; *227 EP-7; ★ LANC; mail Lancaster z 17602; Ⓟ 11,999; Ⓒ 13,556
Eastland; RMC Place; LANCASTER; ▲ Little Britain; *227 EQ-8; mail Nottingham z 19362; rural
Eastland Hills; RMC Place; FRANKLIN; ▲ Washington; *227 EQ-1; ★ HAG; mail Waynesboro z 17268; ● 250
Eastland Hills; RMC Place; LANCASTER; ▲ East Lampeter; *227 EP-7; ★ LANC; mail Lancaster z 17602; ● 550
East Lansdowne; Inc. Place; DELAWARE; 228 E-2; elev. 130ft./40m.; 🅿; ★ PHIL-; z 19050; Ⓟ 2,691; Ⓒ 2,586
East Lawn; RMC Place; NORTHAMPTON; ▲ Upper Nazareth; *227 EK-11; ★ ALL-; mail Nazareth z 18064; ● 900
Eastlawn Gardens; CDP-Census Area Only; NORTHAMPTON; ▲ Upper Nazareth; *227 EK-11; ★ ALL-; mail Nazareth z 18064; Ⓟ 1,794; Ⓒ 2,832
East Lawrence; RMC Place; TIOGA; ▲ Lawrence; *226 ED-3; mail Lawrenceville z 16929; ● 100
East Lemon; RMC Place; WYOMING; ▲ Lemon; 226 EG-9; mail Tunkhannock z 18657; ● 400
East Lenox; RMC Place; SUSQUEHANNA; ▲ Lenox; *226 EF-10; elev. 1,404ft./428m.; mail Union Dale z 18470
East Lewisburg; RMC Place; NORTHUMBERLAND; ▲ East Chillisquaque; *226 EJ-4; mail Milton z 17847; ● 200
East Liberty; RMC Place; ALLEGHENY; *225 WM-4; 🅿; ★ PGH; z 15206; pop. incl. with Pittsburgh (Inc. Place)
East Mahoning; MCD-Township; INDIANA; *225 WK-8; mail Marion Center z 15759; Ⓟ 1,140; Ⓒ 1,196
East Manchester; MCD-Township; YORK; *227 EP-5; ★ YORK; mail Mount Wolf z 17347; Ⓟ 3,714; Ⓒ 5,078
East Marianna; RMC Place; WASHINGTON; ▲ West Bethlehem; *225 WP-3; mail Marianna z 15345; pop. incl. with Marianna (Inc. Place)
East Marlborough; MCD-Township; CHESTER; *227 EQ-10; ★ PHIL-; mail Kennett Square z 19348; Ⓟ 4,781; Ⓒ 6,317
East Mauch Chunk; RMC Place; CARBON; pop. incl. with Jim Thorpe (Inc. Place)
East McKeesport; Inc. Place; ALLEGHENY; 228 L-9; 🅿; ★ PGH; z 15035; Ⓟ 2,678; Ⓒ 2,343
East Mead; MCD-Township; CRAWFORD; *224 WF-3; mail Meadville z 16335; Ⓟ 1,441; Ⓒ 1,485
East Millsboro; RMC Place; FAYETTE; ▲ Luzerne; 225 WP-3; 🅿; ★ UNTN; z 15433; ● 400
East Mines; RMC Place; SCHUYLKILL; *227 EL-7; ★ PTSVL; mail Saint Clair z 17970
Eastmont; RMC Place; ALLEGHENY; ▲ Wilkins; *225 WM-4; ★ PGH; mail Pittsburgh z 15235
Eastmont; RMC Place; YORK; ▲ Dover, Conewago; *227 EP-5; ★ YORK; mail Dover z 17315; ● 100
East Nantmeal; MCD-Township; CHESTER; *227 EO-10; ★ PHIL-; mail Birchrunville z 19421; Ⓟ 1,448; Ⓒ 1,787
East New Castle; RMC Place; LAWRENCE; ▲ Shenango; 224 WJ-2; ★ NWCS; mail New Castle z 16101; ● 250
East Newport; RMC Place; PERRY; ▲ Oliver; ★ HRBG; mail Newport z 17074; ● 250
East Norriton; CDP-Census Area Only; MONTGOMERY; ▲ East Norriton; *227 EO-11; 🅿; ★ PHIL-; z 19401, z 19403; Ⓟ 13,324; Ⓒ 13,211
East Norriton; MCD-Township; MONTGOMERY; *227 EO-11; 🅿; ★ PHIL-; z 19401, z 19403; Ⓟ 13,324; Ⓒ 13,211
East Norwegian; MCD-Township; SCHUYLKILL; *227 EL-8; ★ PTSVL; mail Pottsville z 17901; Ⓟ 991; Ⓒ 864
East Nottingham; MCD-Township; CHESTER; *227 ER-8; mail Oxford z 19363; Ⓟ 3,841; Ⓒ 5,516
East Oakmont; RMC Place; ALLEGHENY; *225 WM-4; ★ PGH; mail Pittsburgh z 15239; pop. incl. with Plum (Inc. Place)
Easton; RMC Place; CLARION; ▲ Licking; *224 WI-6; mail Sligo z 16255; rural
Easton; Inc. Place; ⊡ NORTHAMPTON; 227 EL-12; elev. 300ft./91m.; 🅿 🅷 🅲 2,343 ■; ★ ALL-; z 18040, z 18042-45; Ⓟ 26,276; Ⓒ 26,263; ◆ 26,927
East Oreland; RMC Place; MONTGOMERY; ▲ Upper Dublin; ★ PHIL-; mail Oreland z 19075
East Penn; MCD-Township; CARBON; *227 EL-9; mail Lehighton z 18235; Ⓟ 2,091; Ⓒ 2,461
East Pennsboro; MCD-Township; CUMBERLAND; *227 EO-4; 🅿 🅲 1,115; ★ HRBG; z 17025; Ⓟ 15,185; Ⓒ 18,254
East Petersburg; Inc. Place; LANCASTER; 227 EO-7; elev. 380ft./116m.; 🅿; ★ LANC; z 17520; Ⓟ 4,197; Ⓒ 4,450
East Pike; RMC Place; INDIANA; ▲ White; *225 WL-8; mail Indiana z 15701; ● 150
East Pikeland; MCD-Township; CHESTER; *227 EO-10; ★ PHIL-; mail Phoenixville z 19460; Ⓟ 5,825; Ⓒ 6,551
East Pittsburgh; Inc. Place; ALLEGHENY; 228 L-8; elev. 1,000ft./305m.; 🅿; ★ PGH; z 15112; Ⓟ 2,160; Ⓒ 2,017
East Point; RMC Place; TIOGA; ▲ Liberty; *226 EG-4; mail Roaring Branch z 17765; rural
East Prospect; Inc. Place; YORK; 227 EP-6; elev. 493ft./150m.; 🅿; ★ YORK; z 17317; Ⓟ 558; Ⓒ 678
East Providence; MCD-Township; BEDFORD; *225 WP-11; mail Breezewood z 15533; Ⓟ 1,785; Ⓒ 1,858
East Riverside; RMC Place; FAYETTE; ▲ Luzerne; *225 WP-4; ★ UNTN; mail East Millsboro z 15433; rural
East Rochester; Inc. Place; BEAVER; 225 WL-2; elev. 800ft./244m.; ★ PGH; mail Rochester z 15074; Ⓟ 672; Ⓒ 623
East Rockhill; MCD-Township; BUCKS; *227 EM-12; ★ PHIL-; mail Perkasie z 18944; Ⓟ 3,753; Ⓒ 5,199
East Run; RMC Place; INDIANA; ▲ Grant; *225 WK-8; mail Marion Center z 15759; rural
East Rush; RMC Place; SUSQUEHANNA; ▲ Rush; *226 EF-8; mail Montrose z 18801; ● 80
East Rutherford; CDP-Census Area Only; JUNIATA; *227 EN-1; Ⓒ 185
East St. Clair; MCD-Township; BEDFORD; *225 WO-10; mail Schellsburg z 15559; Ⓟ 2,765; Ⓒ 3,123
East Salem; RMC Place; JUNIATA; ▲ Delaware; 227 EL-3; mail Mifflintown z 17059, Thompsontown z 17094; ● 125
East Saxton; RMC Place; BEDFORD, HUNTINGDON; ▲ Carbon, Liberty; *225 WO-11; elev. 1,000ft./305m.; mail Saxton z 16678; ● 125
East Sharon; RMC Place; POTTER; ▲ Sharon; *224 WD-12; mail Shinglehouse z 16748; rural
East Sharpsburg; RMC Place; BLAIR; ▲ Taylor; 225 WN-11; elev. 1,314ft./401m.; ★ ALT; mail Roaring Spring z 16673; ● 110
East Side; Inc. Place; CARBON; 226 EJ-9; elev. 1,140ft./347m.; mail White Haven z 18661; Ⓟ 330; Ⓒ 290
East Smethport; RMC Place; MCKEAN; ▲ Keating; 224 WE-11; elev. 1,515ft./462m.; 🅿; z 16730; ● 500
East Smithfield; RMC Place; BRADFORD; ▲ Smithfield; 226 EE-5; 🅿; z 18817 & mail Milan z 18831, Ulster z 18850; ● 500
East Springfield; RMC Place; ERIE; 224 WD-2; elev. 700ft./213m.; 🅿; ★ ERIE; z 16411; ● 400
East Stroudsburg; Inc. Place; MONROE; 226 EJ-12; elev. 430ft./131m.; 🅿 🅷 🅲 6,793; z 18301-02; Ⓟ 8,781; Ⓒ 9,888
East Sunbury; NORTHUMBERLAND; see Hamilton (RMC Place)
East Taylor; MCD-Township; CAMBRIA; *225 WN-9; ★ JNST; mail Johnstown z 15909; Ⓟ 3,073; Ⓒ 2,726
East Texas; RMC Place; LEHIGH; ▲ Lower Macungie; 226 EC-2; elev. 437ft./133m.; 🅿; ★ ALL-; z 18046; ● 450
East Titusville (Fieldmore Springs); RMC Place; CRAWFORD; ▲ Oil Creek; 224 WF-5; mail Titusville z 16354; ● 60
East Towanda; RMC Place; BRADFORD; ▲ Wysox; 226 EF-6; mail Towanda z 18848; ● 400
Easttown; MCD-Township; CHESTER; *227 EP-11; ★ PHIL-; mail Berwyn z 19312; Ⓟ 9,570; Ⓒ 10,270
Easttown Woods; RMC Place; CHESTER; ▲ Easttown; ★ PHIL-; mail Berwyn z 19312; ● 300
East Troy; RMC Place; BRADFORD; ▲ Troy; 226 EF-5; mail Troy z 16947; ● 140
East Union; MCD-Township; SCHUYLKILL; *227 EK-8; mail Sheppton z 18248; Ⓟ 1,374; Ⓒ 1,419
East Uniontown; CDP-Census Area Only; FAYETTE; ▲ South Union, North Union; 225 WP-5; ★ UNTN; mail Uniontown z 15401; Ⓟ 2,822; Ⓒ 2,760
Eastvale; Inc. Place; BEAVER; 225 WK-2; elev. 895ft./273m.; ★ PGH; mail Beaver Falls z 15010; Ⓟ 328; Ⓒ 293
East Vandergrift; Inc. Place; WESTMORELAND; 225 WL-5; elev. 800ft./244m.; 🅿; ★ PGH; z 15629; Ⓟ 787; Ⓒ 742
East View; RMC Place; GREENE; ▲ Franklin; *225 WP-2; mail Waynesburg z 15370; ● 90
Eastville; RMC Place; CLINTON; ▲ Greene; 226 EJ-3; elev. 1,313ft./400m.; mail Loganton z 17747; ● 80
East Vincent; MCD-Township; CHESTER; *227 EO-10; ★ PTSTN; mail Spring City z 19475; Ⓟ 4,161; Ⓒ 5,493
East Washington; Inc. Place; WASHINGTON; 225 WO-2; elev. 1,204ft./367m.; ★ WASH; mail Washington z 15301; Ⓟ 2,126; Ⓒ 1,930
East Waterford; RMC Place; JUNIATA; ▲ Tuscarora; 227 EN-1; 🅿; z 17021; ● 190
East Weissport; RMC Place; CARBON; ▲ Franklin; *227 EK-10; elev. 605ft./184m.; mail Lehighton z 18235; ● 400
East Wheatfield; MCD-Township; INDIANA; *225 WM-8; ★ JNST; mail Armagh z 15920; Ⓟ 2,735; Ⓒ 2,607
East Whiteland; MCD-Township; CHESTER; *227 EP-10; 🅲 3,563; ★ PHIL-; mail Malvern z 19355; Ⓟ 8,398; Ⓒ 9,333
Eastwicks; RMC Place; PHILADELPHIA; ★ PHIL-; mail Philadelphia z 19153; pop. incl. with Philadelphia (Inc. Place)
East William Penn; RMC Place; SCHUYLKILL; ▲ West Mahanoy; *227 EK-7; mail Shenandoah z 17976
Eastwood; RMC Place; ALLEGHENY; ▲ Penn Hills; *225 WM-4; elev. 1,200ft./366m.; ★ PGH; mail Pittsburgh z 15235
Eastwood; RMC Place; WESTMORELAND; ▲ Hempfield; *225 WN-6; ★ PGH; mail Greensburg z 15601; ● 450
East Yoe; RMC Place; YORK; ▲ York, Windsor; *227 EP-5; ★ YORK; mail Red Lion z 17356; ● 300
East York; CDP; YORK; ▲ Springettsbury; 225 WS-10; 🅿; ★ YORK; z 17402; Ⓟ 8,487; Ⓒ 8,782
Eaton; MCD-Township; WYOMING; *226 EG-8; mail Tunkhannock z 18657; Ⓟ 1,600; Ⓒ 1,644
Eatonville; RMC Place; WYOMING; ▲ Eaton; 226 EG-8; mail Tunkhannock z 18657; ● 200
Eau Claire; Inc. Place; BUTLER; 224 WI-5; elev. 1,520ft./463m.; 🅿; z 16030; Ⓟ 371; Ⓒ 355
Ebenezer; RMC Place; LEBANON; ▲ North Lebanon; 227 EN-6; ★ LEB; mail Lebanon z 17042, z 17046; ● 200
Ebensburg; Inc. Place; ⊡ CAMBRIA; 225 WM-9; elev. 2,140ft./652m.; 🅿; z 15931; Ⓟ 3,872; Ⓒ 3,091
Eberhardt; RMC Place; ALLEGHENY; ▲ Hampton; ★ PGH
Eberlys Mill; RMC Place; CUMBERLAND; ▲ Lower Allen; *227 EO-4; ★ HRBG; mail Camp Hill z 17011; ● 150
Ebervale; RMC Place; LUZERNE; ▲ Hazle; *226 EJ-8; 🅿; ★ HAZ; z 18223; ● 200
Echo; RMC Place; ARMSTRONG; ▲ Wayne; 225 WK-7; mail Dayton z 16222; ● 30
Echo; RMC Place; CAMBRIA; ▲ East Taylor; 225 WR-3; ★ JNST; mail Mineral Point z 15942; ● 150
Echo Lake; RMC Place; MONROE; ▲ Middle Smithfield; 226 EJ-12; mail East Stroudsburg z 18301; ● 80
Echo Valley; RMC Place; DELAWARE; ▲ Newtown; *227 EP-11; ★ PHIL-; mail Newtown Square z 19073
Echo Valley; RMC Place; SCHUYLKILL; ▲ Tremont; *227 EL-7; mail Tremont z 17981; ● 65
Eckenrode Mill; RMC Place; CAMBRIA; ▲ East Carroll; *225 WL-10; elev. 1,759ft./536m.; mail Patton z 16668; rural
Eckley; RMC Place; LUZERNE; ▲ Foster; 226 EJ-9; ★ HAZ; mail Weatherly z 18255; ● 30
Eckville; RMC Place; BERKS; ▲ Albany; *227 EL-8; elev. 510ft./155m.; mail Kempton z 19529
Economy; Inc. Place; BEAVER; 225 WL-3; elev. 1,180ft./360m.; ★ PGH; mail Baden z 15005; Ⓟ 9,519; Ⓒ 9,363
Eddington; RMC Place; BUCKS; ▲ Bensalem; *227 EO-13; 🅿; ★ PHIL-; z 19020
Eddington Gardens; RMC Place; BUCKS; ▲ Bensalem; *227 EO-13; ★ PHIL-; mail Bensalem z 19020; ● 800
Eddystone; Inc. Place; DELAWARE; 227 EQ-11; elev. 20ft./6m.; 🅿; ★ PHIL-; z 19013, z 19022; Ⓟ 2,446; Ⓒ 2,442
Eddyville; RMC Place; ARMSTRONG; ▲ Redbank, Mahoning; *224 WJ-7; mail New Bethlehem z 16242; ● 40
Edelman; RMC Place; NORTHAMPTON; ▲ Plainfield; 227 EK-12; mail Nazareth z 18064; ● 135
Eden; RMC Place; CLEARFIELD; ▲ Goshen; *224 WI-11; elev. 1,590ft./485m.; mail Frenchville z 16836; rural
Eden; RMC Place; LANCASTER; ▲ Manheim; 227 EP-7; ★ LANC; mail Lancaster z 17601; ● 700
Eden; MCD-Township; LANCASTER; *227 EP-8; mail Quarryville z 17566; Ⓟ 1,857; Ⓒ 1,856
Edenborn; RMC Place; FAYETTE; ▲ German; 225 WQ-4; ★ UNTN; mail Mc Clellandtown z 15458; ● 350
Edenburg; RMC Place; BERKS; ▲ Windsor; 227 EM-8; mail Hamburg z 19526; ● 250
Edendale; RMC Place; CENTRE; ▲ Rush; 225 WK-11; mail Osceola Mills z 16666; ● 100
Eden Heights; RMC Place; LANCASTER; ▲ Manheim; *227 EP-7; ★ LANC; mail Lancaster z 17601
Edenton; RMC Place; CHESTER; ▲ Upper Oxford; *227 EQ-9; mail Cochranville z 19330; rural
Edenville; RMC Place; FRANKLIN; ▲ St. Thomas; 225 WP-13; mail Chambersburg z 17201; ● 150
Edgebrook; RMC Place; ALLEGHENY; *225 WM-3; ★ PGH; mail Pittsburgh z 15226; pop. incl. with Pittsburgh (Inc. Place)
Edgecliff; RMC Place; WESTMORELAND; *225 WL-5; ★ PGH; mail New Kensington z 15068; pop. incl. with Lower Burrell (Inc. Place)
Edgegrove; RMC Place; ADAMS; ▲ Conewago; 227 EQ-4; ★ HANV; mail Hanover z 17331; ● 500
Edge Hill; RMC Place; MONTGOMERY; ▲ Cheltenham; *227 EO-12; ★ PHIL-; mail Glenside z 19038
Edgely; RMC Place; BUCKS; ▲ Bristol; 228 A-10; 🅿; ★ PHIL-; z 19007; ● 500
Edgemere; RMC Place; PIKE; ▲ Delaware; *226 EH-13; mail Dingmans Ferry z 18328
Edgemont; RMC Place; DAUPHIN; ▲ Susquehanna; 227 ES-3; ★ HRBG; mail Harrisburg z 17109; ● 900
Edgemont (Edgmont); RMC Place; DELAWARE; ▲ Edgmont; *227 EP-11; 🅿; ★ PHIL-; z 19028; ● 600
Edgemont; RMC Place; NORTHAMPTON; ▲ Lehigh; *227 EK-10; ★ ALL-; mail Walnutport z 18088; rural
Edgewater Terrace; RMC Place; WESTMORELAND; ▲ Unity; *225 WN-6; ★ LTROB; mail Latrobe z 15650; ● 200
Edgewood; Inc. Place; ALLEGHENY; 228 K-8; elev. 920ft./280m.; ★ PGH; mail Pittsburgh z 15218; Ⓟ 3,581; Ⓒ 3,311
Edgewood; RMC Place; INDIANA; ▲ Center; *225 WL-7; elev. 1,178ft./359m.; mail Indiana z 15701; ● 40
Edgewood; CDP; NORTHUMBERLAND; ▲ Coal; 227 EK-6; mail Shamokin z 17872; Ⓟ 2,719; Ⓒ 2,619
Edgewood Grove; RMC Place; SOMERSET; mail Somerset z 15501; pop. incl. with Somerset (Inc. Place)
Edgewood Park; RMC Place; BUCKS; ▲ Lower Makefield; *227 EO-14; ★ PHIL-; mail Morrisville z 19067; ● 1,300
Edgewood Park; RMC Place; DELAWARE; ▲ Marple; ★ PHIL-; mail Broomall z 19008
Edgeworth; Inc. Place; ALLEGHENY; 225 WM-3; elev. 721ft./220m.; 🅿; ★ PGH; z 15143; Ⓟ 1,670; Ⓒ 1,730
Edgmont; DELAWARE; see Edgemont (RMC Place)
Edgmont; MCD-Township; DELAWARE; *227 EP-11; ★ PHIL-; mail Edgemont z 19028; Ⓟ 2,735; Ⓒ 3,918
Edgmont Park; RMC Place; DELAWARE; ★ PHIL-; pop. incl. with Chester (Inc. Place)
Edie; RMC Place; SOMERSET; ▲ Lincoln; 225 WO-7; elev. 2,002ft./610m.; mail Somerset z 15501; ● 30
Edinboro; Inc. Place; ERIE; 224 WE-3; elev. 1,210ft./369m.; 🅿 🅲 7,579; ★ ERIE; z 16412, z 16444; Ⓟ 7,736; Ⓒ 6,950
Edinburg; RMC Place; LAWRENCE; ▲ Mahoning; 224 WJ-2; 🅿; ★ YNGS-; z 16116; ● 200
Edison; RMC Place; BUCKS; ▲ Doylestown; 227 EN-12; ★ PHIL-; mail Doylestown z 18901; ● 100
Edisonville; RMC Place; LANCASTER; ▲ Strasburg; ★ LANC; mail Strasburg z 17579; rural
Edmon; RMC Place; ARMSTRONG; ▲ Kiskiminetas; 225 WM-6; 🅿; ★ PGH; z 15618; ● 120
Edwardsville; Inc. Place; LUZERNE; 226 EH-9; elev. 700ft./213m.; 🅿; ★ SCR-; z 18704; Ⓟ 5,399; Ⓒ 4,984
Effort; RMC Place; MONROE; ▲ Chestnuthill; 226 EJ-11; 🅿; ★ ALL-; z 18330; ● 1,000
Egypt; RMC Place; CLEARFIELD; ▲ Bradford; *224 WJ-11; elev. 1,320ft./402m.; mail Woodland z 16881; rural
Egypt; RMC Place; JEFFERSON; ▲ Warsaw; *224 WI-8; mail Brockway z 15824; rural
Egypt; RMC Place; LEHIGH; ▲ Whitehall; 226 EA-2; ★ ALL-; mail Whitehall z 18052; ● 1,300
Egypt Corners; RMC Place; VENANGO; ▲ Cranberry; *224 WH-5; ★ OILC-F; mail Franklin z 16323; rural
Ehrenfeld; Inc. Place; CAMBRIA; 225 WR-4; elev. 1,520ft./463m.; ★ JNST; mail South Fork z 15956; Ⓟ 307; Ⓒ 234
Eichelbergertown; RMC Place; BEDFORD; ▲ Hopewell; *225 WO-11; mail Hopewell z 16650; ● 50
Eidenau; RMC Place; BUTLER; ▲ Jackson; *225 WK-3; ★ PGH; mail Harmony z 16037; ● 10
Eighty Four; RMC Place; WASHINGTON; ▲ North Strabane, Somerset; 225 WO-3; 🅿; ★ WASH; z 15330; ● 800
Ekastown; RMC Place; BUTLER; ▲ Buffalo; *225 WL-5; ★ PGH; mail Sarver z 16055
Elam; RMC Place; DELAWARE; ▲ Concord; 227 EQ-10; elev. 393ft./120m.; ★ PHIL-; mail Glen Mills z 19342; ● 200
Elberta; RMC Place; BLAIR; ▲ Tyrone; 225 WM-11; mail Altoona z 16601; ● 180
Elbon; RMC Place; ELK; ▲ Horton; *224 WH-10; mail Brockport z 15823
Elbrook; RMC Place; FRANKLIN; ▲ Quincy; *227 EQ-1; mail Waynesboro z 17268; rural
Elco (Wood Run); Inc. Place; WASHINGTON; 225 WO-4; elev. 765ft./233m.; 🅿; ★ PGH; z 15434; Ⓟ 373; Ⓒ 362
Elder; MCD-Township; CAMBRIA; *225 WL-9; mail Hastings z 16646; Ⓟ 1,185; Ⓒ 990
Elders Ridge; RMC Place; INDIANA; ▲ Young; *225 WL-6; mail Saltsburg z 15681; ● 60
Eldersville; RMC Place; WASHINGTON; ▲ Jefferson; 225 WN-1; elev. 1,319ft./402m.; 🅿; z 15021; ● 200
Elderton; Inc. Place; ARMSTRONG; 225 WL-7; elev. 1,264ft./385m.; 🅿; z 15736; Ⓟ 371; Ⓒ 358
El-Do-Lake; RMC Place; MONROE; *226 EJ-10; elev. 1,139ft./347m.; mail Kunkletown z 18058; ● 100
Eldora; RMC Place; LANCASTER; ▲ Fulton; *227 EQ-8; mail Peach Bottom z 17563; rural
Eldora; RMC Place; WASHINGTON; ▲ Carroll; *225 WO-4; ★ PGH; mail Monongahela z 15063; ● 300
Eldorado; RMC Place; BLAIR; *225 WM-11; ★ ALT; mail Altoona z 16602; pop. incl. with Altoona (Inc. Place)
Eldorado; RMC Place; BUTLER; ▲ Parker; *224 WI-5; mail Parker z 16049; rural
Eldred; MCD-Township; JEFFERSON; *224 WH-8; mail Sigel z 15860; Ⓟ 1,197; Ⓒ 1,277
Eldred; MCD-Township; LYCOMING; *226 EH-4; ★ WMSPT; mail Montoursville z 17754; Ⓟ 2,055; Ⓒ 2,178
Eldred; Inc. Place; MCKEAN; 224 WD-11; elev. 1,500ft./457m.; 🅿; z 16731; Ⓟ 869; Ⓒ 858
Eldred; MCD-Township; MCKEAN; *224 WD-11; 🅿; z 16731; does not include the Borough of Eldred; Ⓟ 1,768; Ⓒ 1,696
Eldred; MCD-Township; MONROE; *227 EK-10; ★ ALL-; mail Kunkletown z 18058; Ⓟ 2,202; Ⓒ 2,665
Eldred; MCD-Township; SCHUYLKILL; *227 EL-6; mail Pitman z 17964; Ⓟ 736; Ⓒ 719
Eldred; MCD-Township; WARREN; *224 WE-6; mail Grand Valley z 16420; Ⓟ 669; Ⓒ 709
Eldredsville; RMC Place; SULLIVAN; ▲ Elkland; *226 EG-5; mail Forksville z 18616; rural
Eleven Mile; RMC Place; POTTER; ▲ Oswayo; *224 WD-13; mail Genesee z 16923; rural
Elfinwild; RMC Place; ALLEGHENY; ▲ Shaler; *225 WM-4; elev. 836ft./255m.; ★ PGH; mail Allison Park z 15101
Elgin; Inc. Place; ERIE; 224 WE-5; elev. 1,388ft./423m.; 🅿; z 16413; Ⓟ 229; Ⓒ 236
Elim; CDP-Census Area Only; CAMBRIA; ▲ Upper Yoder; *225 WN-8; ★ JNST; mail Johnstown z 15905; Ⓟ 3,861; Ⓒ 4,175
Elimsport; RMC Place; LYCOMING; ▲ Washington; 226 EI-4; elev. 548ft./167m.; mail Allenwood z 17810; ● 65
Elizabeth; Inc. Place; ALLEGHENY; 225 WN-4; elev. 760ft./232m.; 🅿; ★ PGH; z 15037; Ⓟ 1,610; Ⓒ 1,609
Elizabeth; MCD-Township; ALLEGHENY; *225 WN-4; 🅿; ★ PGH; z 15037 & mail Buena Vista z 15018; Ⓟ 14,712; Ⓒ 13,839
Elizabeth; MCD-Township; LANCASTER; *227 EN-7; ★ LANC; mail Lititz z 17543; Ⓟ 3,691; Ⓒ 3,833
Elizabethtown; Inc. Place; LANCASTER; 227 EO-6; elev. 456ft./139m.; 🅿 🅲 1,991; z 17022; Ⓟ 9,952; Ⓒ 11,887
Elizabethville; Inc. Place; DAUPHIN; 227 EM-5; elev. 660ft./201m.; 🅿; z 17023; Ⓟ 1,467; Ⓒ 1,344
Elk; MCD-Township; CHESTER; *227 ER-9; ★ PHIL-; mail Lewisville z 19351; Ⓟ 1,129; Ⓒ 1,485
Elk; MCD-Township; CLARION; *224 WH-6; mail Knox z 16232; Ⓟ 1,526; Ⓒ 1,519
Elk; MCD-Township; TIOGA; *226 EG-1; mail Gaines z 16921; Ⓟ 42; Ⓒ 51
Elk; MCD-Township; WARREN; *224 WD-8; mail Russell z 16345; Ⓟ 541; Ⓒ 551
ELK; 224 WG-10; Ⓟ 34,878; Ⓒ 35,112; ◆ 32,033
Elk City; RMC Place; CLARION; ▲ Elk; 224 WI-6; mail Knox z 16232; ● 80
Elk Creek; MCD-Township; ERIE; *224 WE-3; mail Albion z 16401; Ⓟ 1,738; Ⓒ 1,800
Elkdale; RMC Place; CHESTER; ▲ East Nottingham; mail Lincoln University z 19352; rural
Elkdale; RMC Place; SUSQUEHANNA; ▲ Clifford; *226 EF-10; elev. 1,221ft./372m.; mail Union Dale z 18470; rural
Elk Grove; RMC Place; COLUMBIA; ▲ Sugarloaf; 226 EH-6; mail Benton z 17814; ● 45
Elkins Park; RMC Place; MONTGOMERY; ▲ Cheltenham; 228 B-5; 🅿 🅷 🅲 625; ★ PHIL-; z 19027; ● 4,700
Elk Lake; RMC Place; SUSQUEHANNA; ▲ Dimock; *226 EF-8; elev. 1,413ft./431m.; mail Montrose z 18801; ● 100
Elk Lake; RMC Place; WAYNE; ▲ Clinton; 226 EF-8; elev. 1,431ft./436m.; mail Waymart z 18472; summer pop. 800; ● 100
Elkland; MCD-Township; SULLIVAN; *226 EG-5; mail Forksville z 18616; Ⓟ 565; Ⓒ 607
Elkland; Inc. Place; TIOGA; 226 ED-2; elev. 1,135ft./346m.; 🅿; z 16920; Ⓟ 1,849; Ⓒ 1,786
Elk Lick; MCD-Township; SOMERSET; *225 WQ-7; mail Meyersdale z 15552, Salisbury z 15558; Ⓟ 2,313; Ⓒ 2,293
Elk Run Junction; RMC Place; JEFFERSON; mail Punxsutawney z 15767; pop. incl. with Punxsutawney (Inc. Place)
Elkview; RMC Place; CHESTER; ▲ Penn; *227 EQ-9; elev. 469ft./143m.; ★ PHIL-; mail West Grove z 19390; ● 25
Ellen Gowan; RMC Place; SCHUYLKILL; ▲ Mahanoy; *227 EK-7; mail Shenandoah z 17976; rural
Ellenton; RMC Place; LYCOMING; ▲ McNett; 226 EG-5; mail Canton z 17724; ● 25
Ellerslie; RMC Place; BUCKS; ▲ Bensalem; *227 EO-13; ★ PHIL-; mail Bensalem z 19020; ● 550
Elliger Park; RMC Place; MONTGOMERY; ▲ Upper Dublin; ★ PHIL-; mail Fort Washington z 19034
Elliott; RMC Place; ALLEGHENY; *225 WM-3; ★ PGH; mail Pittsburgh z 15205; pop. incl. with Pittsburgh (Inc. Place)
Elliott Heights; RMC Place; LEHIGH; ★ ALL-; mail Bethlehem z 18015; pop. incl. with Bethlehem (Inc. Place)
Elliott Mills; RMC Place; LAWRENCE; ▲ Plain Grove; *224 WJ-3; mail Slippery Rock z 16057
Elliottsburg; RMC Place; PERRY; ▲ Spring; 227 EN-2; 🅿; z 17024; ● 220
Elliottson; RMC Place; CUMBERLAND; ▲ West Pennsboro; *227 EO-3; ★ CARL; mail Carlisle z 17013; ● 150
Elliottsville; RMC Place; FAYETTE; ▲ Wharton; *225 WQ-5; mail Farmington z 15437; rural
Ellisburg; RMC Place; POTTER; ▲ Genesee; 224 WD-13; mail Genesee z 16923; ● 55
Ellport; Inc. Place; LAWRENCE; 225 WK-2; elev. 880ft./268m.; 🅿; ★ PGH; z 16117; Ⓟ 1,243; Ⓒ 1,148
Ellrod; RMC Place; ALLEGHENY; ★ PGH; pop. incl. with Versailles (Inc. Place)
Ellsworth; Inc. Place; WASHINGTON; 225 WO-3; elev. 1,060ft./323m.; 🅿; z 15331; Ⓟ 1,048; Ⓒ 1,083
Ellwood City; Inc. Place; LAWRENCE, BEAVER; 225 WK-2; elev. 900ft./274m.; 🅿 🅷; ★ PGH; z 16117; Ⓟ 8,894; Ⓒ 8,688
Elm; RMC Place; LANCASTER; ▲ Elizabeth, Penn; 227 EO-7; elev. 609ft./186m.; 🅿; ★ LANC; z 17521; ● 150
Elmdale; RMC Place; LACKAWANNA; ▲ Jefferson; *226 EH-11; elev. 1,462ft./446m.; ★ SCR-; mail Lake Ariel z 18436; rural
Elmer; RMC Place; POTTER; ▲ Harrison; *226 EE-1; elev. 1,517ft./462m.; mail Westfield z 16950
Elmhurst; RMC Place; LACKAWANNA; ▲ Elmhurst; 226 EH-10; 🅿; ★ SCR-; z 18416; ● 834
Elmhurst; MCD-Township; LACKAWANNA; *226 EH-10; 🅿; ★ SCR-; z 18416; Ⓟ 834; Ⓒ 838
Elmo; RMC Place; CLARION; ▲ Ashland; *224 WH-6; mail Knox z 16232; rural
Elmora; CAMBRIA; see Bakerton (RMC Place)
Elmwood; RMC Place; PHILADELPHIA; *227 EP-12; ★ PHIL-; mail Philadelphia z 19142; pop. incl. with Philadelphia (Inc. Place)
Elmwood; RMC Place; YORK; ▲ Spring Garden; *227 EP-5; ★ YORK; mail York z 17403
Elmwood Terrace; RMC Place; BUCKS; *227 EO-13; ★ PHIL-; mail Levittown z 19057
Elmwood Terrace; RMC Place; LACKAWANNA; ▲ Roaring Brook; *226 EH-10; elev. 1,100ft./335m.; ★ SCR-; mail Moscow z 18444; ● 350
Elora; RMC Place; BUTLER; ▲ Brady; *224 WJ-4; mail Slippery Rock z 16057; rural
Elrama; RMC Place; WASHINGTON; ▲ Union; 225 WN-4; 🅿; ★ PGH; z 15038; ● 600
Elroy; RMC Place; MONTGOMERY; ▲ Franconia; *227 EN-11; ★ PHIL-; mail Souderton z 18964; ● 300
Elstie; RMC Place; CAMBRIA; ▲ Gallitzin; *225 WM-10; ★ ALT; mail Ashville z 16613; rural
Elstonville; RMC Place; LANCASTER; ▲ Penn; 227 EO-6; elev. 502ft./153m.; ★ LANC; mail Manheim z 17545; ● 60
Elton; RMC Place; CAMBRIA; ▲ Adams; 225 WN-9; elev. 2,064ft./629m.; 🅿; ★ JNST; z 15934; ● 600
Elverson; Inc. Place; CHESTER; 227 EO-9; elev. 660ft./201m.; 🅿; ★ PHIL-; z 19520; Ⓟ 470; Ⓒ 959
Elwood Park; RMC Place; WASHINGTON; ▲ Canton; *225 WO-2; ★ WASH; mail Washington z 15301; ● 500
Elwyn; RMC Place; DELAWARE; ▲ Middletown; *227 EP-11; 🅿; ★ PHIL-; z 19063; ● 1,750
Elwyn Terrace; RMC Place; LANCASTER; ▲ Penn; *227 EO-7; ★ LANC; mail Manheim z 17545; ● 150
Elysburg; CDP; NORTHUMBERLAND; ▲ Ralpho; 227 EK-6; 🅿; z 17824; Ⓟ 1,890; Ⓒ 2,067
Emanuelsville; RMC Place; NORTHAMPTON; ▲ Moore; *227 EK-11; elev. 719ft./219m.; ★ ALL-; mail Bath z 18014; rural
Emaus; LEHIGH; see Emmaus (Inc. Place)
Emblem; RMC Place; ALLEGHENY; *225 WN-4; ★ PGH; mail Mckeesport z 15131; pop. incl. with White Oak (Inc. Place)
Embreeville; RMC Place; CHESTER; ▲ Newlin; 227 EP-10; ★ PHIL-; mail Coatesville z 19320; ● 90
Emeigh; RMC Place; CAMBRIA; ▲ Susquehanna; 225 WL-9; 🅿; z 15738; ● 400
Emerald; RMC Place; LEHIGH; ▲ Washington; 227 EL-10; 🅿; ★ ALL-; z 18080; ● 240
Emerickville; RMC Place; JEFFERSON; ▲ Pine Creek; 224 WI-8; mail Brookville z 15825; ● 150
Emigsville; CDP; YORK; ▲ Manchester; 227 EP-5; 🅿; ★ YORK; z 17318; Ⓟ 2,580; Ⓒ 2,467
Emilie; RMC Place; BUCKS; *227 EO-14; ★ PHIL-; mail Levittown z 19057
Emlenton; Inc. Place; VENANGO, CLARION; 224 WI-5; elev. 902ft./275m.; 🅿; z 16373; Ⓟ 834; Ⓒ 784
Emmaus (Emaus); Inc. Place; LEHIGH; 227 EM-11; elev. 448ft./137m.; 🅿; ★ ALL-; z 18049, z 18098-99; Ⓟ 11,157; Ⓒ 11,313
Emmaus Junction; RMC Place; LEHIGH; *227 EM-11; ★ ALL-; pop. incl. with Emmaus (Inc. Place)
Emmaville; RMC Place; FULTON; ▲ Brush Creek; 225 WP-11; mail Crystal Spring z 15536; ● 40
Emporium; Inc. Place; ⊡ CAMERON; 224 WG-11; elev. 1,075ft./328m.; 🅿; z 15834; Ⓟ 2,513; Ⓒ 2,526
Emsworth; Inc. Place; ALLEGHENY; 225 WM-3; elev. 840ft./256m.; 🅿; ★ PGH; z 15202; Ⓟ 2,892; Ⓒ 2,598
Endeavor; RMC Place; FOREST; ▲ Hickory; 224 WF-6; 🅿; z 16321-22; ● 200
Enders; RMC Place; DAUPHIN; ▲ Jackson; 227 EM-4; mail Halifax z 17032; ● 65
Energy; RMC Place; LAWRENCE; ▲ Shenango; 224 WJ-2; ★ PGH; mail New Castle z 16101; ● 50
Enfield; RMC Place; MONTGOMERY; ▲ Upper Dublin; *227 EO-12; ★ PHIL-; mail Oreland z 19075
Engleside; RMC Place; LANCASTER; *227 EP-7; ★ LANC; mail Lancaster z 17602
Engles Lake; RMC Place; MONROE; ▲ Paradise; mail Swiftwater z 18370
Englesville; RMC Place; BERKS; ▲ Colebrookdale; *227 EN-10; mail Boyertown z 19512; ● 220
Englewood; CDP; SCHUYLKILL; ▲ Butler; *227 EK-7; ★ PTSVL; mail Frackville z 17931; Ⓒ 484
English Center; RMC Place; LYCOMING; ▲ Pine; 226 EG-2; mail Waterville z 17776; ● 60
Enhaut; RMC Place; DAUPHIN; ▲ Swatara; 227 ET-4; ★ HRBG; mail Harrisburg z 17113; ● 950
Enid; RMC Place; FULTON; ▲ Wells; *225 WO-12; mail Wells Tannery z 16691
Enlow; RMC Place; ALLEGHENY; ▲ North Fayette, Findlay; *225 WM-2; elev. 945ft./288m.; ★ PGH; mail Imperial z 15126; ● 1,100
Ennisville; RMC Place; HUNTINGDON; ▲ Jackson; *225 WL-13; elev. 763ft./233m.; mail Huntingdon z 16652
Enola; CDP; CUMBERLAND; ▲ East Pennsboro; 227 EN-4; 🅿; ★ HRBG; z 17025; Ⓟ 5,964; Ⓒ 5,627
Enon; RMC Place; WASHINGTON; ▲ East Finley; *225 WP-2; mail West Finley z 15377; rural
Enon Valley; Inc. Place; LAWRENCE; 225 WK-2; elev. 995ft./303m.; 🅿; z 16120; Ⓟ 355; Ⓒ 387
Enterline; RMC Place; DAUPHIN; ▲ Wayne; *227 EM-4; mail Halifax z 17032; rural
Enterprise; RMC Place; MERCER; ▲ Pine; *224 WI-3; mail Grove City z 16127; rural
Enterprise; RMC Place; WARREN; ▲ Southwest; 224 WF-6; mail Titusville z 16354; ● 50
Entlerville; RMC Place; CUMBERLAND; ▲ Upper Frankford; *227 EN-2; mail Newville z 17241; rural
Entriken; RMC Place; HUNTINGDON; ▲ Lincoln; 225 WN-12; elev. 858ft./262m.; 🅿; z 16638 & mail James Creek z 16657; ● 125
Ephrata; Inc. Place; LANCASTER; 227 EO-7; elev. 380ft./116m.; 🅿 🅷; ★ LANC; z 17522; Ⓟ 12,133; Ⓒ 13,213
Ephrata; MCD-Township; LANCASTER; *227 EO-8; 🅿; ★ LANC; z 17522; does not include the Borough of Ephrata; Ⓟ 7,116; Ⓒ 8,026
Equinunk; RMC Place; WAYNE; ▲ Buckingham; 226 EE-12; elev. 881ft./269m.; 🅿; z 18417; ● 130
Ercildoun; RMC Place; CHESTER; ▲ East Fallowfield; 227 EP-9; ★ PHIL-; mail Coatesville z 19320; ● 100
Erdenheim; RMC Place; MONTGOMERY; ▲ Springfield; *227 EO-12; 🅿; ★ PHIL-; z 19038 & mail Philadelphia z 19118
Erdman; RMC Place; DAUPHIN; ▲ Lykens; 227 EL-5; elev. 553ft./169m.; mail Lykens z 17048; ● 200
Erhard; RMC Place; CLEARFIELD; ▲ Knox; *225 WK-10; mail New Millport z 16861
Erie; Inc. Place; ⊡ ERIE; 224 WC-3; elev. 744ft./227m.; 🅿 🅷 🅲 13,625 ■; ★ ERIE; z 16501-12, z 16514-15, z 16522, z 16530-31, z 16534, z 16538, z 16541, z 16544, z 16546, z 16550, z 16553, z 16563, z 16565; Ⓟ 108,718; Ⓒ 103,717; ◆ 103,824
ERIE; 224 WD-4; Ⓟ 275,572; Ⓒ 280,843; ◆ 277,636
Erie Heights; RMC Place; ERIE; *224 WC-3; ★ ERIE; mail Erie z 16508; pop. incl. with Erie (Inc. Place)
Eriton; RMC Place; CLEARFIELD; *224 WJ-9; mail Du Bois z 15801; ● 80
Erlen; RMC Place; MONTGOMERY; ▲ Cheltenham; *227 EO-12; elev. 240ft./73m.; ★ PHIL-; mail Philadelphia z 19126; ● 800
Erly; RMC Place; PERRY; ▲ Saville; *227 EN-2; mail Elliottsburg z 17024; ● 35
Ernest; Inc. Place; INDIANA; ▲ Rayne; 225 WL-7; 🅿; z 15739; Ⓟ 492; Ⓒ 501
Erney; RMC Place; YORK; ▲ Newberry; *227 EO-5; mail Dover z 17315; ● 200
Erwinna; RMC Place; BUCKS; ▲ Tinicum; 227 EM-12; 🅿; ★ PHIL-; z 18920; ● 140
Eshbach; RMC Place; BERKS; ▲ Washington; *227 EN-10; mail Bechtelsville z 19505; ● 125
Eshcol; RMC Place; PERRY; ▲ Saville; *227 EM-2; mail Millerstown z 17062
Esplen; RMC Place; ALLEGHENY; *225 WM-3; ★ PGH; mail Pittsburgh z 15204; pop. incl. with Pittsburgh (Inc. Place)
Espy; CDP; COLUMBIA; ▲ Scott; 226 EJ-6; mail Bloomsburg z 17815; Ⓟ 1,430; Ⓒ 1,428
Espyville; RMC Place; CRAWFORD; *224 WF-2; 🅿; z 16424; ● 300
Espyville Station; RMC Place; CRAWFORD; ▲ North Shenango; 224 WF-2; elev. 1,094ft./333m.; mail Linesville z 16424; ● 20
Essington; RMC Place; DELAWARE; ▲ Tinicum; *227 EQ-12; 🅿; ★ PHIL-; z 19029
Estella; RMC Place; SULLIVAN; ▲ Elkland; 226 EG-5; mail Forksville z 18616; ● 50
Esterly; RMC Place; BERKS; ★ READ; mail Reading z 19606; pop. incl. with Saint Lawrence (Inc. Place)
Estherton; RMC Place; DAUPHIN; ▲ Susquehanna; 227 ES-3; ★ HRBG; mail Harrisburg z 17110; ● 1,200
Etna; Inc. Place; ALLEGHENY; 225 WM-4; elev. 743ft./226m.; 🅿; ★ PGH; z 15223; Ⓟ 4,200; Ⓒ 3,924
Etters; YORK; see Goldsboro (Inc. Place)
Euclid; RMC Place; BUTLER; ▲ Clay; 224 WJ-4; elev. 1,300ft./396m.; ★ BUTL; mail Butler z 16001; ● 90
Eulalia; MCD-Township; POTTER; *224 WG-13; mail Coudersport z 16915; Ⓟ 701; Ⓒ 941
Eureka; RMC Place; WESTMORELAND; ▲ South Huntingdon; *225 WO-5; ★ PGH; mail Smithton z 15479; rural
Evans; FAYETTE; see Evans Manor (RMC Place)
Evansburg; CDP; MONTGOMERY; ▲ Skippack, Lower Providence; 227 EO-11; ★ PHIL-; mail Collegeville z 19426; Ⓟ 1,047; Ⓒ 1,536
Evans City; Inc. Place; BUTLER; 225 WK-3; elev. 939ft./286m.; 🅿; ★ PGH; z 16033; Ⓟ 2,054; Ⓒ 2,009
Evans Falls; RMC Place; WYOMING; ▲ Monroe; 226 EG-8; mail Tunkhannock z 18657; ● 270
Evans Manor (Evans); RMC Place; FAYETTE; ▲ North Union; *225 WP-5; ★ UNTN; mail Uniontown z 15401; ● 300
Evanston; RMC Place; WESTMORELAND; ▲ Hempfield; *225 WN-5; ★ PGH; mail Darragh z 15625; ● 90
Evansville; RMC Place; BERKS; ▲ Maidencreek; *227 EM-9; 🅿; ★ READ; z 19522; ● 100
Evansville; RMC Place; COLUMBIA; ▲ Briar Creek; *226 EJ-7; elev. 633ft./193m.; mail Berwick z 18603; rural
Evendale; RMC Place; JUNIATA; ▲ Monroe; 227 EL-3; mail Richfield z 17086; ● 165
Everett; Inc. Place; BEDFORD; 225 WP-11; elev. 1,017ft./310m.; 🅿 🅷; z 15537; Ⓟ 1,777; Ⓒ 1,905
Evergreen; RMC Place; BRADFORD; ▲ Albany; 226 EF-6; mail New Albany z 18833; ● 70
Evergreen Park; RMC Place; LEHIGH; ▲ Whitehall; *227 EL-11; ★ ALL-; mail Whitehall z 18052
Everhartville; RMC Place; PERRY; ▲ Oliver; ★ HRBG; mail Newport z 17074; ● 75
Everson; Inc. Place; FAYETTE; 225 WO-5; elev. 1,060ft./323m.; 🅿; z 15631; Ⓟ 939; Ⓒ 842
Ewalt; RMC Place; ALLEGHENY; ★ PGH; mail Pittsburgh z 15212; pop. incl. with Pittsburgh (Inc. Place)
Ewings Mill; RMC Place; INDIANA; ▲ Brush Valley, Buffington, Pine; *225 WM-8; mail Penn Run z 15765; rural
Ewingsville; RMC Place; ALLEGHENY; ▲ Collier; *225 WM-3; ★ PGH; mail Carnegie z 15106; ● 400
Excelsior; RMC Place; NORTHUMBERLAND; ▲ Coal; *227 EK-6; 🅿; z 17866; ● 125
Exchange; RMC Place; MONTOUR; ▲ Anthony; 226 EI-5; elev. 579ft./176m.; mail Danville z 17821, Turbotville z 17772; ● 100
Exeter; MCD-Township; BERKS; *227 EN-9; ★ READ; mail Reading z 19606; Ⓟ 17,260; Ⓒ 21,161; ◆ 24,207
Exeter; Inc. Place; LUZERNE; 226 EB-9; elev. 580ft./177m.; 🅿; ★ SCR-; z 18643; Ⓟ 5,691; Ⓒ 5,955
Exeter; MCD-Township; LUZERNE; *226 EH-9; 🅿; ★ SCR-; z 18643; does not include the Borough of Exeter; Ⓟ 2,457; Ⓒ 2,557
Exeter; MCD-Township; WYOMING; *226 EH-9; ★ SCR-; mail Falls z 18615; Ⓟ 763; Ⓒ 748
Exmoor; RMC Place; SCHUYLKILL; ▲ Pine Grove; *227 EM-6; mail Pine Grove z 17963; rural
Experiment; RMC Place; ALLEGHENY; ▲ South Park; *225 WN-4; ★ PGH; mail Pittsburgh z 15230; pop. incl. with Jefferson (Inc. Place)
Export; Inc. Place; WESTMORELAND; 225 WM-5; elev. 985ft./300m.; 🅿; ★ PGH; z 15632; Ⓟ 981; Ⓒ 895
Exton; CDP; CHESTER; ▲ East Whiteland; 227 EP-10; 🅿; ★ PHIL-; z 19341, z 19353; Ⓟ 2,550; Ⓒ 4,267
Eyers Grove; CDP; COLUMBIA; ▲ Greenwood; 226 EJ-6; elev. 582ft./177m.; mail Millville z 17846; Ⓒ 86
Eynon; RMC Place; LACKAWANNA; *226 EG-10; 🅿; ★ SCR-; z 18403; pop. incl. with Archbald (Inc. Place)

F

Factoryville; RMC Place; NORTHAMPTON; ▲ Washington; *227 EK-12; elev. 423ft./129m.; mail Bangor z 18013; rural
Factoryville; Inc. Place; WYOMING; 226 EG-9; elev. 840ft./256m.; 🅿; ★ SCR-; z 18419; Ⓟ 1,310; Ⓒ 1,144
Faggs Manor; RMC Place; CHESTER; ▲ Londonderry; *227 EQ-9; mail Cochranville z 19330; rural
Fagleysville; RMC Place; MONTGOMERY; ▲ New Hanover; *227 EN-10; mail Gilbertsville z 19525; ● 130
Fagundus; RMC Place; FOREST; ▲ Harmony; *224 WF-6; elev. 1,680ft./512m.; mail Tidioute z 16351; rural
Fair Acres; RMC Place; YORK; ▲ Fairview; 227 ET-3; ★ HRBG; mail New Cumberland z 17070; ● 500
Fairbank; RMC Place; FAYETTE; ▲ Redstone; 225 WP-4; 🅿; ★ UNTN; z 15435; ● 600
Fairbrook; RMC Place; CENTRE; ▲ Ferguson; 225 WL-13; ★ STCOL; mail Pennsylvania Furnace z 16865; ● 225
Fairchance; Inc. Place; FAYETTE; 225 WQ-5; elev. 1,020ft./311m.; 🅿; ★ UNTN; z 15436; Ⓟ 1,918; Ⓒ 2,174
Fairdale; CDP; GREENE; ▲ Cumberland; 225 WQ-4; mail Carmichaels z 15320; Ⓟ 2,049; Ⓒ 1,955
Fairdale; RMC Place; SUSQUEHANNA; ▲ Jessup; 226 EE-8; mail Montrose z 18801; ● 40
Fairfield; Inc. Place; ADAMS; 227 EQ-2; elev. 608ft./185m.; 🅿; z 17320; Ⓟ 524; Ⓒ 486
Fairfield; MCD-Township; CRAWFORD; *224 WG-3; mail Cochranton z 16314; Ⓟ 997; Ⓒ 1,104
Fairfield; RMC Place; ERIE; ▲ Harborcreek; 224 WC-4; ★ ERIE; mail Erie z 16510; ● 1,100
Fairfield; LANCASTER; see Greene (RMC Place)
Fairfield; MCD-Township; LYCOMING; *226 EI-4; ★ WMSPT; mail Montoursville z 17754; Ⓟ 2,580; Ⓒ 2,659
Fairfield; RMC Place; WASHINGTON; ▲ West Bethlehem; *225 WP-3; mail Marianna z 15345; ● 75
Fairfield; MCD-Township; WESTMORELAND; *225 WN-7; mail Bolivar z 15923; Ⓟ 2,276; Ⓒ 2,536
Fair Grounds; RMC Place; GREENE; ▲ Jefferson; mail Jefferson z 15344; ● 40
Fair Haven; RMC Place; ALLEGHENY; ★ PGH; pop. incl. with Pittsburgh (Inc. Place)
Fairhaven Heights; RMC Place; ALLEGHENY; ▲ North Versailles; *225 WN-4; ★ PGH; mail North Versailles z 15137
Fairhill; RMC Place; BUCKS; ▲ Hilltown; *227 EN-12; ★ PHIL-; mail Hatfield z 19440
Fairhill; RMC Place; PHILADELPHIA; ★ PHIL-; mail Philadelphia z 19133; pop. incl. with Philadelphia (Inc. Place)
Fairhope; RMC Place; FAYETTE; ▲ Washington; 225 WO-4; ★ PGH; mail Belle Vernon z 15012; ● 1,800
Fairhope; RMC Place; SOMERSET; ▲ Fairhope; 225 WQ-9; 🅿; z 15538; ● 50
Fairhope; MCD-Township; SOMERSET; *225 WQ-9; 🅿; z 15538; Ⓟ 137; Ⓒ 137
Fairland; RMC Place; LANCASTER; ▲ Penn; *227 EO-7; ★ LANC; mail Lititz z 17543, Manheim z 17545; ● 40
Fairlawn; RMC Place; LYCOMING; ▲ Lycoming; *226 EH-3; ★ WMSPT; mail Cogan Station z 17728; ● 40
Fairless; RMC Place; BUCKS; ▲ Falls; ★ PHIL-; mail Fairless Hills z 19030
Fairless Hills; CDP; BUCKS; ▲ Falls; 227 EO-13; 🅿; ★ PHIL-; z 19030; Ⓟ 9,026; Ⓒ 8,365
Fairmont; RMC Place; WESTMORELAND; ▲ North Huntingdon; *225 WN-5; ★ PGH; mail Irwin z 15642; ● 500
Fairmont City (Fairmount City); RMC Place; CLARION; ▲ Redbank; 224 WJ-7; mail Fairmount City z 16224; ● 300
Fairmount; RMC Place; LANCASTER; ▲ Little Britain; 227 EQ-8; elev. 522ft./159m.; mail Quarryville z 17566; ● 40
Fairmount; MCD-Township; LUZERNE; *226 EH-7; mail Benton z 17814; Ⓟ 1,211; Ⓒ 1,226
Fairmount; RMC Place; PHILADELPHIA; ★ PHIL-; mail Philadelphia z 19121; pop. incl. with Philadelphia (Inc. Place)
Fairmount; RMC Place; WAYNE; ▲ Scott; *226 EE-11; elev. 1,900ft./579m.; mail Starrucca z 18462; rural
Fairmount City; CLARION; see Fairmont City (RMC Place)
Fairmount Springs; RMC Place; LUZERNE; ▲ Fairmount; 226 EI-7; mail Benton z 17814; ● 40
Fairoaks; RMC Place; ALLEGHENY; ▲ Leet; *225 WL-3; 🅿; ★ PGH; z 15003; ● 800
Fairoaks; RMC Place; MONTGOMERY; ▲ Horsham; ★ PHIL-; mail Horsham z 19044
Fairplay; RMC Place; ADAMS; ▲ Freedom; *227 ER-2; mail Gettysburg z 17325
Fairview; RMC Place; BEAVER; *225 WL-1; ★ PGH; mail Industry z 15052; pop. incl. with Ohioville (Inc. Place)
Fairview; RMC Place; BLAIR; *225 WM-11; ★ ALT; mail Altoona z 16601; pop. incl. with Altoona (Inc. Place)
Fairview; Inc. Place; BUTLER; 224 WJ-5; elev. 1,430ft./436m.; mail Petrolia z 16050; Ⓟ 224; Ⓒ 220
Fairview; MCD-Township; BUTLER; *224 WJ-5; mail Chicora z 16025; does not include the Borough of Fairview; Ⓟ 2,009; Ⓒ 2,061
Fairview; RMC Place; CLEARFIELD; ▲ Graham; *224 WJ-12; mail Morrisdale z 16858; rural
Fairview; RMC Place; ELK; ▲ Fox; *224 WH-10; mail Kersey z 15846; ● 120
Fairview; RMC Place; ERIE; 224 WD-3; elev. 790ft./241m.; 🅿; ★ ERIE; z 16415; Ⓟ 1,988
Fairview; MCD-Township; ERIE; *224 WD-3; 🅿; ★ ERIE; z 16415; Ⓟ 7,839; Ⓒ 10,140
Fairview; RMC Place; FRANKLIN; ▲ Quincy; *227 EQ-1; mail Waynesboro z 17268; ● 200
Fairview; RMC Place; JEFFERSON; ▲ Bell; 224 WJ-8; mail Punxsutawney z 15767; ● 250
Fairview; MCD-Township; LUZERNE; *226 EI-9; ★ SCR-; mail Mountain Top z 18707; Ⓟ 3,014; Ⓒ 3,995
Fairview; RMC Place; MERCER; ▲ Fairview; 224 WH-3; mail Fredonia z 16124; ● 50
Fairview; MCD-Township; MERCER; *224 WH-3; mail Mercer z 16137; Ⓟ 910; Ⓒ 1,036
Fairview; RMC Place; MIFFLIN; ▲ Granville; *227 EM-1; mail Lewistown z 17044; ● 200
Fairview; RMC Place; NORTHUMBERLAND; ▲ Coal; *227 EK-6; mail Shamokin z 17872; ● 1,500
Fairview; MCD-Township; YORK; *227 EO-5; ★ HRBG; mail New Cumberland z 17070; Ⓟ 13,258; Ⓒ 14,321
Fairview Drive; RMC Place; YORK; ▲ West Manheim; *227 EQ-4; ★ HANV; mail Hanover z 17331; ● 100
Fairview-Ferndale; CDP-Census Area Only; NORTHUMBERLAND; ▲ Coal; *227 EK-6; mail Shamokin z 17872; Ⓟ 2,895; Ⓒ 2,411
Fairview Heights; RMC Place; ALLEGHENY; ▲ O'Hara; *225 WM-4; ★ PGH; mail Pittsburgh z 15238; ● 600
Fairview Heights; RMC Place; BERKS; ▲ Bern; *227 EM-8; ★ READ; mail Leesport z 19533; ● 125
Fairview Heights; RMC Place; LUZERNE; ▲ Fairview; *226 EI-9; ★ SCR-; mail Mountain Top z 18707; ● 1,100
Fairview Heights; RMC Place; MCKEAN; ▲ Foster; *224 WD-10; elev. 1,500ft./457m.; mail Bradford z 16701; ● 120
Fairview Hills; RMC Place; LUZERNE; ▲ Fairview; ★ SCR-; mail Mountain Top z 18707
Fairview Knolls; RMC Place; NORTHAMPTON; ▲ Palmer; *227 EL-12; ★ ALL-; mail Easton z 18042; ● 800
Fairview Park; RMC Place; CHESTER; ★ PHIL-; mail West Chester z 19380; ● 300
Fairview Park; RMC Place; LUZERNE; ▲ Fairview; ★ SCR-; mail Mountain Top z 18707
Fairview Park (Reesers Summit); RMC Place; YORK; ▲ Fairview; *227 EO-5; elev. 700ft./213m.; ★ HRBG; mail New Cumberland z 17070; ● 1,100
Fairview Village; RMC Place; MONTGOMERY; ▲ Worcester; *227 EO-11; 🅿; ★ PHIL-; z 19409; ● 800
Fairville; RMC Place; CHESTER; ▲ Pennsbury; 227 EQ-10; elev. 384ft./117m.; ★ PHIL-; mail Chadds Ford z 19317; ● 150
Fairville; RMC Place; UNION; ▲ East Buffalo; mail Lewisburg z 17837
Fairway Park; RMC Place; LANCASTER; ▲ Manor; *227 EP-7; ★ LANC; mail Lancaster z 17603; ● 250
Fairways of Brookside; RMC Place; LEHIGH; ▲ Lower Macungie; *227 EM-10; elev. 400ft./122m.; ★ ALL-; mail Macungie z 18062; ● 700
Falconcrest; RMC Place; CHESTER; ▲ West Goshen; ★ PHIL-; mail West Chester z 19380; ● 700
Fall Brook; RMC Place; TIOGA; ▲ Ward; 226 EF-4; mail Morris Run z 16939; ● 200
Fallentimber; RMC Place; CAMBRIA; ▲ Reade; 225 WL-10; elev. 1,432ft./436m.; 🅿; z 16639; ● 150
Falling Spring; RMC Place; FRANKLIN; ▲ Guilford; 227 EQ-1; mail Chambersburg z 17201; ● 200
Falling Spring; RMC Place; PERRY; ▲ Spring; *227 EN-3; mail Landisburg z 17040; rural
Fallowfield; MCD-Township; WASHINGTON; *225 WO-4; ★ PGH; mail Charleroi z 15022; Ⓟ 4,972; Ⓒ 4,461
Falls; MCD-Township; BUCKS; *227 EO-14; ■; ★ PHIL-; mail Levittown z 19054; Ⓟ 34,997; Ⓒ 34,865; ◆ 34,844
Falls; RMC Place; WYOMING; ▲ Falls, Exeter; 226 EG-9; 🅿; ★ SCR-; z 18615 & mail Levittown z 19054; summer pop. 1,500; ● 230

Entries in **UPPERCASE** are counties.
Entries in **bold** have populations of 2,500 or more.
Names in parentheses are alternate names.

Inc. Place	Incorporated Place
RMC Place	Rand McNally Designated Place
CDP	Census Designated Place
MCD	Minor Civil Division

⊡ County Seat
▲ Minor Civil Division
elev. Elevation
🅿 Post Office
🅷 Hospital
🅲 College
■ Principal Business Center
★ Ranally Metro Area (RMA) Abbreviation
z Zip Code(s)
Ⓟ Previous Census Population
Ⓡ Revised Census Population
Ⓐ Annexation Population
● Rand McNally Population Estimate
Ⓒ Final Census Population
Ⓢ Special Census Population
◆ Estimated Population

For additional definitions see Glossary, Volume 1, and Introduction, Volume 2.

Falls; MCD-Township; WYOMING; *226 EG-9; 🅿; ★ SCR-; Z 18615 & mail Levittown Z 19054; Ⓟ 2,055; © 1,997
Falls Creek; Inc. Place; JEFFERSON, CLEARFIELD; 224 WI-9; elev. 1,440ft./439m.; 🅿; Z 15840; Ⓟ 1,087; © 983
Fallsdale; RMC Place; WAYNE; ▲ Damascus; *226 EF-12; mail Honesdale Z 18431; rural
Fallsington; RMC Place; BUCKS; ▲ Falls; 205 T-12; 🅿; ★ PHIL-; Z 19054; ● 1,300
Fallston; Inc. Place; BEAVER; 225 WL-2; elev. 760ft./232m.; ★ PGH; mail New Brighton Z 15066; Ⓟ 392; © 307
Falmouth; RMC Place; LANCASTER; ▲ Conoy; 227 EO-5; ★ HRBG; mail Bainbridge Z 17502; ● 200
Fannett; MCD-Township; FRANKLIN; *227 EO-1; mail Doylesburg Z 17219, Dry Run Z 17220; Ⓟ 2,309; © 2,370
Fannettsburg; RMC Place; FRANKLIN; ▲ Metal; 225 WP-13; 🅿; Z 17221; ● 950
Faraday Park; RMC Place; DELAWARE; ▲ Ridley; *227 EP-11; elev. 130ft./40m.; ★ PHIL-; mail Morton Z 19070; ● 850
Farmbrook; RMC Place; BUCKS; ▲ Bristol; *227 EO-14; ★ PHIL-; mail Bristol Z 19007
Farmdale; RMC Place; LANCASTER; ▲ West Hempfield; *227 EP-6; ★ LANC; mail Mount Joy Z 17552; rural
Farmers; RMC Place; YORK; ▲ Paradise; *227 EP-4; elev. 553ft./169m.; mail Thomasville Z 17364; ● 100
Farmers Mills; RMC Place; CENTRE; ▲ Gregg; *227 EK-1; mail Spring Mills Z 16875
Farmers Valley; RMC Place; BRADFORD; ▲ Troy; *226 EE-4; elev. 1,385ft./422m.; mail Troy Z 16947; rural
Farmers Valley; RMC Place; MCKEAN; ▲ Keating; 224 WE-11; elev. 1,506ft./459m.; mail Smethport Z 16749; ● 120
Farmersville; RMC Place; LANCASTER; ▲ West Earl; 227 EO-8; ★ LANC; mail Ephrata Z 17522; ● 400
Farmersville; RMC Place; NORTHAMPTON; ▲ Bethlehem; 226 EA-6; ★ ALL-; mail Easton Z 18045; ● 50
Farming Ridge; RMC Place; BERKS; ▲ Exeter; *227 EN-9; ★ READ; mail Reading Z 19606; ● 1,500
Farmington; RMC Place; BERKS; ▲ Longswamp; *227 EM-10; mail Mertztown Z 19539; rural
Farmington; MCD-Township; CLARION; *224 WH-7; mail Leeper Z 16233; Ⓟ 1,927; © 1,986
Farmington; RMC Place; FAYETTE; ▲ Wharton; 225 WQ-5; 🅿; Z 15437; ● 250
Farmington; RMC Place; LEHIGH; ▲ Salisbury; 226 EB-4; ★ ALL-; mail Allentown Z 18103; ● 800
Farmington; MCD-Township; TIOGA; *226 EE-3; mail Tioga Z 16946; Ⓟ 644; © 636
Farmington; MCD-Township; WARREN; *224 WD-7; mail Russell Z 16345; Ⓟ 1,287; © 1,353
Farmington Hill; RMC Place; TIOGA; ▲ Farmington; *226 EE-3; mail Tioga Z 16946; ● 200
Farquhar Estates; RMC Place; YORK; ▲ Spring Garden; ★ YORK; mail York Z 17403
Farragut; RMC Place; LYCOMING; ▲ Upper Fairfield; 226 EH-4; ★ WMSPT; mail Montoursville Z 17754; ● 60
Farrandsville; RMC Place; CLINTON; ▲ Colebrook; 226 EI-1; 🅿; ★ WMSPT; Z 17745; ● 120
Farrell; Inc. Place; MERCER; 224 WI-1; elev. 880ft./268m.; 🅿; ★ SHAR; Z 16121 & mail Hermitage Z 16148; Ⓟ 6,841; © 6,050
Farview; RMC Place; BERKS; ▲ Cumru; *227 EM-8; ★ READ; mail Reading Z 19607; ● 600
Farwell; RMC Place; CLINTON; ▲ Chapman; 224 WH-14; mail Renovo Z 17764; ● 350
Fassett; RMC Place; BRADFORD; ▲ South Creek; 226 ED-5; mail Gillett Z 16925; ● 175
Faunce; RMC Place; CLEARFIELD; ▲ Boggs; *225 WK-11; mail Olanta Z 16863
Fawn; MCD-Township; ALLEGHENY; *225 WL-5; ★ PGH; mail Natrona Heights Z 15065, Tarentum Z 15084; Ⓟ 2,712; © 2,504
Fawn; MCD-Township; YORK; *227 ER-6; ★ BAL; mail Fawn Grove Z 17321; Ⓟ 2,175; © 2,727
Fawn Grove; Inc. Place; YORK; 227 ER-6; elev. 732ft./223m.; 🅿; ★ BAL; Z 17321; Ⓟ 489; © 463
Faxon; RMC Place; LYCOMING; ▲ Loyalsock; 226 EI-4; ★ WMSPT; mail Williamsport Z 17701; ● 1,500
Fayette; MCD-Township; JUNIATA; *227 EL-2; mail Mc Alisterville Z 17049; Ⓟ 3,002; © 3,252
Fayette; RMC Place; LAWRENCE; ▲ Wilmington; *224 WI-2; ★ NWCS; mail Volant Z 16156; ● 70
FAYETTE; 225 WP-5; Ⓟ 145,351; © 148,644; ◆ 142,085
Fayette City; Inc. Place; FAYETTE; 225 WO-4; elev. 620ft./189m.; 🅿; ★ PGH; Z 15438; Ⓟ 713; © 714
Fayetteville (Glen Gormely); RMC Place; ALLEGHENY; ▲ North Fayette; *225 WM-3; elev. 1,100ft./335m.; ★ PGH; mail Oakdale Z 15071; ● 300
Fayetteville; CDP; FRANKLIN; ▲ Guilford, Greene; 227 EP-1; 🅿; Z 17222; Ⓟ 3,033; © 2,774
Fayfield; RMC Place; YORK; ▲ Springettsbury; *227 EP-5; ★ YORK; mail York Z 17402
Fay Terrace; RMC Place; MERCER; ▲ Pymatuning; ★ SHAR; mail Greenville Z 16125; ● 200
Fearnot; RMC Place; SCHUYLKILL; ▲ Hubley; *227 EL-5; mail Sacramento Z 17968; ● 130
Feasterville; RMC Place; BUCKS; ▲ Lower Southampton; *227 EO-13; elev. 200ft./61m.; ★ PHIL-; mail Feasterville Trevose Z 19053
Feasterville-Trevose; CDP-Census Area Only; BUCKS; ▲ Lower Southampton; *227 EO-13; 🅿; ★ PHIL-; Z 19053; Ⓟ 6,696; © 6,525
Federal; RMC Place; ALLEGHENY; ▲ South Fayette, Collier; *225 WN-3; ★ PGH; mail Oakdale Z 15071; ● 170
Federal Square; RMC Place; DAUPHIN; ★ HRBG; mail Harrisburg Z 17108; pop. incl. with Harrisburg (Inc. Place)
Fell; MCD-Township; LACKAWANNA; *226 EF-10; ★ SCR-; mail Forest City Z 18421; Ⓟ 2,426; © 2,331
Fellsburg; RMC Place; WESTMORELAND; ▲ Rostraver; 225 WO-4; ★ PGH; mail Belle Vernon Z 15012; ● 1,000
Fellwick (Camphill); RMC Place; MONTGOMERY; ▲ Springfield; *227 EO-12; elev. 300ft./91m.; ★ PHIL-; mail Fort Washington Z 19034; ● 90
Felton; Inc. Place; YORK; 227 EQ-6; elev. 560ft./171m.; 🅿; ★ YORK; Z 17322; Ⓟ 438; © 449
Feltonville; RMC Place; DELAWARE; ▲ Chester; *227 EQ-11; ★ PHIL-; mail Chester Z 19013
Feltonville; RMC Place; PHILADELPHIA; *227 EP-12; ★ PHIL-; pop. incl. with Philadelphia (Inc. Place)
Fenelton; RMC Place; BUTLER; ▲ Clearfield; 225 WK-5; elev. 1,095ft./334m.; 🅿; ★ PGH; Z 16034; ● 110
Ferguson; MCD-Township; CENTRE; *225 WL-13; ★ STCOL; mail State College Z 16801; Ⓟ 9,368; © 14,063
Ferguson; MCD-Township; CLEARFIELD; *225 WK-10; mail Mahaffey Z 15757; Ⓟ 437; © 410
Ferguson; RMC Place; FAYETTE; ▲ Dunbar; *225 WP-5; elev. 1,200ft./366m.; mail Dunbar Z 15431; ● 60
Fergusonville; RMC Place; BUCKS; ▲ Bristol; *227 EO-13; elev. 40ft./12m.; ★ PHIL-; mail Bristol Z 19007; ● 600
Fermanagh; MCD-Township; JUNIATA; *227 EL-2; mail Mifflintown Z 17059; Ⓟ 2,249; © 2,544
Fern; RMC Place; CLARION; ▲ Ashland; *224 WH-6; mail Cranberry Z 16319; rural
Fern Brook; RMC Place; LUZERNE; ▲ Kingston, Dallas; 226 EH-9; elev. 1,031ft./314m.; ★ SCR-; mail Dallas Z 18612; ● 550
Ferndale; RMC Place; BUCKS; ▲ Nockamixon; 227 EM-12; 🅿; ★ PHIL-; Z 18921; ● 400
Ferndale; Inc. Place; CAMBRIA; 225 WN-8; elev. 1,208ft./368m.; ★ JNST; mail Johnstown Z 15905; Ⓟ 2,020; © 1,834
Ferndale; RMC Place; NORTHUMBERLAND; ▲ Coal; *227 EK-6; mail Shamokin Z 17872; ● 1,350
Ferndale; RMC Place; SCHUYLKILL; ▲ Union; *227 EK-7; mail Zion Grove Z 17985; ● 60
Fern Glen; RMC Place; LUZERNE; ▲ Black Creek; 226 EJ-8; 🅿; ★ HAZ; Z 18241; ● 350
Fern Hill; RMC Place; CHESTER; ▲ East Goshen; *227 EP-10; ★ PHIL-; mail West Chester Z 19380; rural
Fernridge; RMC Place; MONROE; ▲ Tunkhannock; *226 EJ-10; mail Blakeslee Z 18610
Fern Village; RMC Place; MONTGOMERY; ▲ Upper Moreland; *227 EO-12; ★ PHIL-; mail Hatboro Z 19040; ● 800
Fernville; CDP; COLUMBIA; ▲ Hemlock; 226 EJ-6; mail Bloomsburg Z 17815; © 488
Fernway; CDP-Census Area Only; BUTLER; ▲ Cranberry; 225 WL-3; ★ PGH; mail Zelienople Z 16063; Ⓟ 9,072; © 12,188
Fernwood; RMC Place; CLEARFIELD; ▲ Gulich; *225 WK-11; elev. 1,611ft./491m.; mail Smithmill Z 16680; rural
Fernwood; RMC Place; DELAWARE; ▲ Upper Darby; *227 EP-12; ★ PHIL-; mail Lansdowne Z 19050; pop. incl. with Yeadon (Inc. Place)
Ferrellton; RMC Place; SOMERSET; ▲ Jenner; *225 WO-8; mail Stoystown Z 15563; ● 120
Fertigs; RMC Place; VENANGO; ▲ Pinegrove; 224 WH-6; mail Venus Z 16364; ● 65
Fertility; RMC Place; LANCASTER; ▲ East Lampeter; *227 EP-7; ★ LANC; mail Lancaster Z 17602; rural
Fetterville; RMC Place; LANCASTER; ▲ East Earl; *227 EO-8; ★ LANC; mail Narvon Z 17555
Fiddle Lake; RMC Place; SUSQUEHANNA; ▲ Ararat; *226 EE-10; elev. 2,045ft./623m.; mail Thompson Z 18465
Fiddlers Green; RMC Place; CAMBRIA; ▲ Portage; *225 WN-10; elev. 1,907ft./581m.; mail Portage Z 15946; ● 90
Fidelity; RMC Place; PHILADELPHIA; ★ PHIL-; mail Philadelphia Z 19109; pop. incl. with Philadelphia (Inc. Place)
Fieldmore Springs; CRAWFORD; see East Titusville (RMC Place)
Fifficktown; RMC Place; CAMBRIA; ▲ Croyle; *225 WN-9; ★ JNST; mail South Fork Z 15956; ● 150
Fiketown; RMC Place; FAYETTE; ▲ Henry Clay; *225 WQ-6; mail Markleysburg Z 15459; rural
Filbert; RMC Place; FAYETTE; ▲ Redstone; 225 WP-4; ★ UNTN; mail Fairbank Z 15435; ● 200
Fillmore; RMC Place; CENTRE; ▲ Patton, Benner; *225 WK-13; ★ STCOL; mail Bellefonte Z 16823; rural
Finch Hill; RMC Place; LACKAWANNA; ▲ Greenfield; *226 EF-10; ★ SCR-; mail Carbondale Z 18407
Findlay; MCD-Township; ALLEGHENY; *225 WM-2; ★ PGH; mail Clinton Z 15026; Ⓟ 4,500; © 5,145
Findley; MCD-Township; MERCER; *224 WI-3; mail Mercer Z 16137; Ⓟ 2,284; © 2,305
Finland; RMC Place; BUCKS; ▲ Milford; *227 EN-11; ★ PHIL-; mail Pennsburg Z 18073; rural
Finleyville; RMC Place; BEDFORD; ▲ Broad Top; *225 WO-12; mail Six Mile Run Z 16679; ● 60
Finleyville; Inc. Place; WASHINGTON; 225 WN-3; elev. 960ft./293m.; 🅿; ★ PGH; Z 15332; Ⓟ 446; © 459
Fireside Terrace; RMC Place; YORK; ★ YORK; mail York Z 17404
Fisher; RMC Place; CLARION; ▲ Millcreek; 224 WH-7; 🅿; Z 16225; ● 130
Fisher; RMC Place; WASHINGTON; ▲ Carroll; *225 WO-4; ★ PGH; mail Monongahela Z 15063; ● 500
Fisherdale; RMC Place; COLUMBIA; ▲ Cleveland; *227 EK-6; mail Elysburg Z 17824; rural
Fisher Heights; RMC Place; BUTLER; ▲ Center; *224 WJ-4; ★ BUTL; mail Butler Z 16001; ● 300
Fishers Corner; RMC Place; DELAWARE; ▲ Aston; ★ PHIL-; mail Chester Z 19013
Fishers Ferry; RMC Place; NORTHUMBERLAND; ▲ Lower Augusta; *227 EK-4; mail Sunbury Z 17801
Fishertown; RMC Place; BEDFORD; ▲ East St. Clair; 225 WO-10; 🅿; Z 15539; ● 400
Fishertown; RMC Place; CAMBRIA; ▲ Croyle; *225 WN-9; ★ JNST; mail South Fork Z 15956; rural
Fisherville; RMC Place; CHESTER; *227 EP-9; ★ PHIL-; mail Downingtown Z 19335; ● 50
Fisherville; RMC Place; DAUPHIN; ▲ Jackson; 227 EM-4; mail Halifax Z 17032; ● 60
Fishing Creek; MCD-Township; COLUMBIA; *226 EI-7; mail Orangeville Z 17859; Ⓟ 1,378; © 1,393
Fishing Creek; LANCASTER; see Drumore (RMC Place)
Fiske; RMC Place; CAMBRIA; ▲ White; *225 WL-10; elev. 1,444ft./440m.; mail Fallentimber Z 16639; rural
Fitch Corner; RMC Place; WYOMING; ▲ Northmoreland; *226 EH-9; mail Falls Z 18615; rural
Fitz Henry; RMC Place; WESTMORELAND; ▲ South Huntingdon; *225 WO-5; ★ PGH; mail Smithton Z 15479; ● 120
Five Corners; RMC Place; CRAWFORD; ▲ Rome; *224 WF-5; mail Centerville Z 16404; rural
Five Forks; RMC Place; FRANKLIN; ▲ Quincy; 227 EQ-1; mail Waynesboro Z 17268; ● 50
Five Points; RMC Place; ADAMS; ▲ Huntington; *227 EP-3; mail New Oxford Z 17350
Five Points; RMC Place; BEAVER; ▲ Hopewell; 225 WL-2; ★ PGH; mail Aliquippa Z 15001; ● 600
Five Points; RMC Place; BERKS; ▲ Exeter, Alsace; 227 ES-14; elev. 719ft./219m.; ★ READ; mail Reading Z 19606; ● 100
Five Points; RMC Place; BUTLER; ▲ Cherry; *224 WJ-4; elev. 1,359ft./414m.; mail West Sunbury Z 16061; rural
Five Points; RMC Place; CHESTER; ▲ Kennett; *227 EQ-10; ★ PHIL-; mail Kennett Square Z 19348; ● 70
Five Points; RMC Place; CLEARFIELD; ▲ Chest; *225 WK-10; mail La Jose Z 15753; rural
Five Points; RMC Place; ERIE; ▲ Summit; *224 WD-3; ★ ERIE; mail Erie Z 16509; rural
Five Points; RMC Place; INDIANA; ▲ Washington; 225 WL-7; mail Creekside Z 15732; ● 20
Five Points; RMC Place; LUZERNE; ▲ Black Creek; *226 EJ-8; ★ HAZ; mail Sugarloaf Z 18249; ● 50
Five Points; RMC Place; MERCER; ▲ Jackson; *224 WH-2; ★ SHAR; mail Jackson Center Z 16133; rural
Five Points; RMC Place; MERCER; ▲ South Pymatuning; ★ SHAR; mail Sharpsville Z 16150; rural
Five Points; RMC Place; NORTHUMBERLAND; ▲ Lewis; *226 EI-5; ★ WMSPT; mail Turbotville Z 17772; rural
Five Points; RMC Place; VENANGO; ▲ Victory; *224 WH-4; elev. 1,503ft./458m.; mail Polk Z 16342; rural
Five Points; RMC Place; WESTMORELAND; ▲ Salem; *225 WM-6; elev. 1,327ft./404m.; ★ PGH; mail Greensburg Z 15601
Fivepointville; RMC Place; LANCASTER; ▲ Brecknock; 227 EO-8; elev. 464ft./141m.; mail Denver Z 17517; ● 120
Fizzleburg; RMC Place; LAWRENCE; ▲ Pulaski; *224 WI-2; ★ YNGS-; mail Pulaski Z 16143; ● 250
Flat Rock; RMC Place; CENTRE; ▲ Worth; *225 WK-12; elev. 1,381ft./421m.; mail Port Matilda Z 16870; ● 35
Flat Rock; RMC Place; FAYETTE; ▲ Henry Clay; 225 WQ-6; mail Markleysburg Z 15459; ● 140
Flatwoods; RMC Place; FAYETTE; ▲ Franklin; *225 WP-5; ★ UNTN; mail Vanderbilt Z 15486; ● 70
Fleetville; RMC Place; LACKAWANNA; ▲ Benton; 226 EF-9; 🅿; ★ SCR-; Z 18420; ● 350
Fleetwing; BUCKS; see Fleetwing Estates (RMC Place)
Fleetwing Estates (Fleetwing); RMC Place; BUCKS; ▲ Bristol; *227 EO-14; elev. 20ft./6m.; ★ PHIL-; mail Levittown Z 19057; ● 200
Fleetwood; Inc. Place; BERKS; 227 EM-9; elev. 440ft./134m.; 🅿; ★ READ; Z 19522; Ⓟ 3,478; © 4,018
Fleming; CENTRE; see Unionville (Inc. Place)
Flemington; Inc. Place; CLINTON; 226 EI-2; elev. 564ft./172m.; 🅿; ★ WMSPT; Z 17745; Ⓟ 1,321; © 1,319
Flicksville; RMC Place; NORTHAMPTON; ▲ Washington; 227 EK-12; 🅿; Z 18050; ● 100
Flinton; RMC Place; CAMBRIA; ▲ Reade; 225 WL-10; 🅿; Z 16640; ● 250
Flintville; RMC Place; LEBANON; ▲ Heidelberg; *227 EN-7; ★ LEB; mail Lebanon Z 17042; ● 120
Floradale; RMC Place; ADAMS; ▲ Menallen; *227 EP-3; mail Biglerville Z 17307
Floreffe; RMC Place; ALLEGHENY; *225 WN-4; elev. 860ft./262m.; 🅿; ★ PGH; Z 15025; pop. incl. with Jefferson (Inc. Place)
Florence; RMC Place; NORTHAMPTON; ★ ALL-; pop. incl. with Bethlehem (Inc. Place)
Florence; RMC Place; WASHINGTON; ▲ Hanover; 225 WM-2; elev. 1,282ft./391m.; mail Burgettstown Z 15021; ● 250
Florida Park; RMC Place; DELAWARE; ▲ Newtown; *227 EP-11; ★ PHIL-; mail Newtown Square Z 19073
Florin; RMC Place; LANCASTER; *227 EO-6; 🅿; ★ LANC; Z 17552
Flourtown; CDP; MONTGOMERY; ▲ Whitemarsh, Springfield; 228 A-3; 🅿; ★ PHIL-; Z 19031; Ⓟ 4,754; © 4,669
Flourtown Gardens; RMC Place; MONTGOMERY; ▲ Springfield; ★ PHIL-; mail Flourtown Z 19031
Flying Hills; CDP-Census Area Only; BERKS; ▲ Cumru; *227 EN-9; elev. 334ft./102m.; ★ READ; mail Reading Z 19607; Ⓟ 1,526; © 1,191
FM Corners; RMC Place; MERCER; *224 WI-2; elev. 1,030ft./314m.; ★ SHAR; mail Hermitage Z 16148; pop. incl. with Hermitage (Inc. Place)
Fogelsville; RMC Place; LEHIGH; ▲ Upper Macungie; 227 EL-10; 🅿 🅲 758; ★ ALL-; Z 18051; ● 950
Folcroft; Inc. Place; DELAWARE; 228 F-2; elev. 70ft./21m.; 🅿; ★ PHIL-; Z 19032; Ⓟ 7,506; © 6,978
Foleys Siding; RMC Place; ALLEGHENY; *225 WN-3; ★ PGH; mail Pittsburgh Z 15234; pop. incl. with Castle Shannon (Inc. Place)
Folsom; CDP; DELAWARE; ▲ Ridley; 228 F-1; 🅿; ★ PHIL-; Z 19033; Ⓟ 8,173; © 8,072
Folstown; RMC Place; LUZERNE; ▲ Slocum; *226 EI-8; ★ SCR-; mail Mountain Top Z 18707; ● 200
Foltz; FRANKLIN; see Cove Gap (RMC Place)
Fombell; RMC Place; BEAVER; ▲ Franklin; 225 WK-3; 🅿; ★ PGH; Z 16123; ● 100
Font; RMC Place; CHESTER; ▲ Upper Uwchlan; *227 EO-10; ★ PHIL-; mail Downingtown Z 19335; ● 100
Fontana; RMC Place; LEBANON; ▲ South Annville; 227 EN-6; ★ LEB; mail Lebanon Z 17042; ● 150
Footedale; RMC Place; FAYETTE; ▲ German; *225 WP-4; ★ UNTN; mail New Salem Z 15468; ● 250
Foot of Ten; RMC Place; BLAIR; ▲ Allegheny; *225 WM-10; ★ ALT; mail Duncansville Z 16635; ● 350
Forbes Road; RMC Place; WESTMORELAND; ▲ Salem, Hempfield; 225 WN-6; 🅿; ★ PGH; Z 15633; ● 650
Force; RMC Place; ELK; ▲ Jay; 224 WH-10; 🅿; Z 15841; ● 350
Ford City; Inc. Place; ARMSTRONG; 225 WK-6; elev. 794ft./242m.; 🅿; ★ PGH; Z 16226; Ⓟ 3,413; © 3,451
Ford Cliff; Inc. Place; ARMSTRONG; *225 WK-6; elev. 840ft./256m.; 🅿; ★ PGH; Z 16228; Ⓟ 450; © 412
Fordham; RMC Place; JEFFERSON; ▲ Perry; *225 WK-8; elev. 1,200ft./366m.; mail Punxsutawney Z 15767; ● 50
Ford View; RMC Place; ARMSTRONG; ▲ Manor; *225 WK-6; ★ PGH; mail Ford City Z 16226; ● 300
Fordville; RMC Place; YORK; ▲ Paradise; *227 EP-4; mail Thomasville Z 17364; rural
Fordyce; RMC Place; GREENE; ▲ Whiteley, Greene; 225 WQ-3; mail Waynesburg Z 15370; ● 20
Forest; RMC Place; CLEARFIELD; ▲ Cooper; *224 WJ-12; mail Winburne Z 16879; rural
FOREST; 224 WG-7; Ⓟ 4,802; © 4,946; ◆ 6,860
Forest Castle; RMC Place; LUZERNE; ★ SCR-; mail Pittston Z 18643; pop. incl. with Exeter (Inc. Place)
Forest City; Inc. Place; SUSQUEHANNA; 226 EF-11; elev. 1,482ft./452m.; 🅿; Z 18421; Ⓟ 1,846; © 1,855
Forest Grove; RMC Place; ALLEGHENY; ▲ Robinson; 228 I-3; ★ PGH; mail Coraopolis Z 15108; ● 2,600
Forest Grove; RMC Place; BUCKS; ▲ Buckingham; *227 EN-13; 🅿; ★ PHIL-; Z 18922; ● 110
Foresthill; RMC Place; UNION; ▲ West Buffalo; *226 EJ-4; mail Mifflinburg Z 17844
Forest Hill; RMC Place; YORK; ▲ Windsor; *227 EQ-6; elev. 936ft./285m.; ★ YORK; mail Red Lion Z 17356; ● 400
Forest Hills; Inc. Place; ALLEGHENY; 228 K-8; elev. 966ft./294m.; ★ PGH; mail Pittsburgh Z 15221; Ⓟ 7,335; © 6,831
Forest Hills; RMC Place; LANCASTER; ▲ Upper Leacock; ★ LANC; mail Leola Z 17540
Forest Inn; RMC Place; CARBON; ▲ Towamensing; *227 EK-10; mail Lehighton Z 18235; rural
Forest Lake; RMC Place; SUSQUEHANNA; ▲ Forest Lake; 226 EE-8; mail Montrose Z 18801; ● 100
Forest Lake; MCD-Township; SUSQUEHANNA; *226 EE-8; mail Montrose Z 18801; Ⓟ 1,229; © 1,194
Forest Park; RMC Place; BUCKS; ★ PHIL-; mail Chalfont Z 18914; pop. incl. with Chalfont (Inc. Place)
Forest Park; RMC Place; LUZERNE; ▲ Bear Creek; 226 EI-9; ★ SCR-; mail Wilkes Barre Z 18702; ● 300
Forest Park (Unity House); RMC Place; PIKE; ▲ Lehman; *226 EI-13; mail Unity House Z 18373; summer pop. 1,000; ● 5
Forestville (Harrisville); RMC Place; BUTLER; ▲ Mercer; ● 100
Forestville; RMC Place; CHESTER; *227 EQ-9; elev. 493ft./150m.; mail West Grove Z 19390; rural
Forestville; RMC Place; SCHUYLKILL; ▲ Cass; 224 WI-4; ★ PTSVL; mail Pottsville Z 17901; ● 200
Forge; BLAIR; see Tyrone Forge (RMC Place)
Forks; RMC Place; COLUMBIA; ▲ Fishing Creek; *226 EI-7; mail Orangeville Z 17859
Forks (Forks Township); MCD-Township; NORTHAMPTON; *227 EK-12; ★ ALL-; mail Easton Z 18040; Ⓟ 5,923; © 8,419
Forks; MCD-Township; SULLIVAN; *226 EG-5; mail Dushore Z 18614; Ⓟ 355; © 407
Forks Church; RMC Place; ARMSTRONG; ▲ Gilpin; *225 WL-5; ★ PGH; mail Leechburg Z 15656; ● 90
Forkston; RMC Place; WYOMING; ▲ Forkston; 226 EG-8; mail Mehoopany Z 18629; ● 70
Forkston; MCD-Township; WYOMING; *226 EG-8; mail Mehoopany Z 18629; Ⓟ 316; © 386
Forks Township; NORTHAMPTON; see Forks (MCD-Township)
Forksville; Inc. Place; SULLIVAN; 226 EG-6; elev. 1,019ft./311m.; 🅿; Z 18616; Ⓟ 160; © 147
Forrestville; CDP-Census Area Only; SCHUYLKILL; *227 EL-7; ★ PTSVL; © 431
Forsythia Gate; RMC Place; BUCKS; ▲ Middletown; ★ PHIL-; mail Levittown Z 19056
Fort Allen Plan; RMC Place; WESTMORELAND; ▲ Hempfield; *225 WN-5; ★ PGH; mail Greensburg Z 15601; ● 1,200
Fortenia; RMC Place; WAYNE; ▲ Texas; *226 EG-11; elev. 1,053ft./321m.; mail Honesdale Z 18431; rural
Fort Fetter; RMC Place; BLAIR; ▲ Blair; *225 WM-11; elev. 965ft./294m.; ★ ALT; mail Hollidaysburg Z 16648; ● 200
Fort Hill; RMC Place; SOMERSET; ▲ Upper Turkeyfoot, Addison; 225 WQ-7; 🅿; Z 15540; ● 35
Fort Hill; RMC Place; WESTMORELAND; *225 WO-6; elev. 1,686ft./514m.; mail Stahlstown Z 15687; ● 80
Fort Hunter; RMC Place; DAUPHIN; ▲ Susquehanna, Middle Paxton; 227 EN-4; ★ HRBG; mail Harrisburg Z 17110; ● 150
Fort Indiantown Gap; CDP-Census Area Only; LEBANON; *227 EM-6; © 85
Fort Littleton; RMC Place; FULTON; ▲ Dublin; 225 WP-13; 🅿; Z 17223; ● 100
Fort Loudon; RMC Place; FRANKLIN; ▲ Peters; 225 WP-13; 🅿; Z 17224; ● 1,200
Fort Mifflin; RMC Place; PHILADELPHIA; ★ PHIL-; pop. incl. with Philadelphia (Inc. Place)
Fortney; RMC Place; YORK; ▲ Warrington; *227 EO-4; mail Lewisberry Z 17339; rural
Fort Roberston; RMC Place; PERRY; ▲ Northeast Madison; *227 EN-2; mail Loysville Z 17047; rural
Fortuna; RMC Place; MONTGOMERY; *227 EN-12; ★ PHIL-; mail Colmar Z 18915; rural
Fort Washington; CDP; MONTGOMERY; ▲ Upper Dublin; 227 EO-12; 🅿 🅷 🅲 935; ★ PHIL-; Z 19034, Z 19048-49; Ⓟ 3,699; © 3,680
Forty Fort (Slocum); Inc. Place; LUZERNE; 226 EH-9; elev. 555ft./169m.; 🅿; ★ SCR-; Z 18704; Ⓟ 5,049; © 4,579
Forward; MCD-Township; ALLEGHENY; *225 WN-4; ★ PGH; mail Monongahela Z 15063; Ⓟ 3,877; © 3,771
Forward; MCD-Township; BUTLER; *225 WK-4; ★ PGH; mail Evans City Z 16033; Ⓟ 2,339; © 2,687
Forwardstown; RMC Place; SOMERSET; ▲ Jenner; *225 WO-8; mail Boswell Z 15531
Fossilville; RMC Place; BEDFORD; ▲ Londonderry; *225 WQ-9; mail Buffalo Mills Z 15534; ● 40
Foster; RMC Place; INDIANA; ▲ Conemaugh; *225 WM-6; ★ PGH; mail Saltsburg Z 15681; rural
Foster; MCD-Township; LUZERNE; *226 EJ-9; ★ HAZ; mail Freeland Z 18224; Ⓟ 3,372; © 3,323
Foster; MCD-Township; MCKEAN; *224 WD-10; mail Bradford Z 16701; Ⓟ 4,691; © 4,566
Foster; MCD-Township; SCHUYLKILL; *227 EL-7; mail Pottsville Z 17901; Ⓟ 298; © 1,124; Ⓡ 268
Foster Brook; RMC Place; MCKEAN; ▲ Foster; 224 WD-10; elev. 1,428ft./435m.; mail Bradford Z 16701; ● 800
Fostoria; RMC Place; BLAIR; ▲ Antis; 225 WL-11; ★ ALT; mail Tyrone Z 16686; ● 40
Foundryville; CDP; COLUMBIA; ▲ Briar Creek; 226 EJ-7; elev. 636ft./194m.; mail Berwick Z 18603; © 265
Fountain; RMC Place; SCHUYLKILL; ▲ Hegins; 227 EL-6; elev. 827ft./252m.; mail Hegins Z 17938; ● 250
Fountain Dale; RMC Place; ADAMS; ▲ Hamiltonban; 227 ER-2; mail Fairfield Z 17320; ● 150
Fountain Hill; Inc. Place; LEHIGH; 227 EL-11; elev. 366ft./112m.; 🅿; ★ ALL-; Z 18015; Ⓟ 4,637; © 4,614
Fountain House Corners; RMC Place; CRAWFORD; ▲ Woodcock; *224 WF-3; mail Saegertown Z 16433; ● 60
Fountain Springs; CDP; SCHUYLKILL; ▲ Butler; 227 EK-7; ★ PTSVL; mail Ashland Z 17921; © 100
Fountainville; RMC Place; BUCKS; ▲ Plumstead, Doylestown; 227 EN-12; 🅿; ★ PHIL-; Z 18923; ● 200
Fourth Avenue; RMC Place; ALLEGHENY; ★ PGH; mail Pittsburgh Z 15222; pop. incl. with Pittsburgh (Inc. Place)
Foustown; RMC Place; YORK; ▲ Manchester; *227 EP-5; ★ YORK; mail York Z 17404; ● 200
Foustwell; RMC Place; SOMERSET; ▲ Conemaugh; *225 WO-8; ★ JNST; mail Hollsopple Z 15935; ● 30
Fowler Heights; RMC Place; INDIANA; ▲ White; *225 WL-7; mail Indiana Z 15701; ● 100
Fowlers; SCHUYLKILL; see Yatesville (RMC Place)
Fowlersville; RMC Place; COLUMBIA; ▲ North Centre; *226 EJ-7; elev. 604ft./184m.; mail Berwick Z 18603; ● 50
Fox; MCD-Township; ELK; *224 WH-10; mail Kersey Z 15846; Ⓟ 3,392; © 3,734
Fox; MCD-Township; SULLIVAN; *226 EG-5; mail Canton Z 17724, Shunk Z 17768; Ⓟ 300; © 332
Foxburg; Inc. Place; CLARION; 224 WI-5; elev. 890ft./271m.; 🅿; Z 16036; Ⓟ 262; © 275
Foxburg; RMC Place; JEFFERSON; ▲ Gaskill; *224 WJ-9; elev. 1,320ft./402m.; mail Punxsutawney Z 15767; ● 60
Fox Chapel; Inc. Place; ALLEGHENY; 228 I-8; elev. 980ft./299m.; ★ PGH; mail Pittsburgh Z 15238; Ⓟ 5,319; © 5,436
Fox Chase; RMC Place; LANCASTER; ▲ Manheim; *227 EO-7; ★ LANC; mail Lancaster Z 17601; ● 200
Fox Chase; RMC Place; PHILADELPHIA; *227 EO-12; ★ PHIL-; mail Philadelphia Z 19111; pop. incl. with Philadelphia (Inc. Place)
Fox Chase Manor; RMC Place; MONTGOMERY; ▲ Abington; ★ PHIL-; mail Elkins Park Z 19027, Jenkintown Z 19046
Foxcroft; RMC Place; DELAWARE; ▲ Marple; *227 EP-11; ★ PHIL-; mail Broomall Z 19008
Foxcroft; RMC Place; MONTGOMERY; ▲ Abington; ★ PHIL-; mail Jenkintown Z 19046
Fox Hill; RMC Place; FRANKLIN; ▲ Quincy; *227 EQ-1; mail Waynesboro Z 17268; ● 75
Fox Hill; RMC Place; LUZERNE; ▲ Plains; *226 EH-9; elev. 710ft./216m.; ★ SCR-; mail Wilkes Barre Z 18702; ● 125
Fox Run; CDP-Census Area Only; BUTLER; ▲ Cranberry; *225 WL-3; elev. 1,182ft./360m.; ★ PGH; mail Evans City Z 16033, Mars Z 16046; Ⓟ 2,384; © 3,044
Foxton Lake; RMC Place; SUSQUEHANNA; ▲ Jackson; *226 EE-10; elev. 1,750ft./533m.; mail Susquehanna Z 18847; ● 25
Foxtown; RMC Place; WESTMORELAND; ▲ Hempfield; *225 WO-5; ★ PGH; mail Hunker Z 15639; ● 150
Foxtown Hill; RMC Place; MONROE; ▲ Stroud; *226 EJ-12; mail Stroudsburg Z 18360; rural
Frackville; Inc. Place; SCHUYLKILL; 227 EK-7; elev. 1,476ft./450m.; 🅿; ★ PTSVL; Z 17931-32; Ⓟ 4,700; © 4,361
Frailey; MCD-Township; SCHUYLKILL; *227 EL-6; mail Tremont Z 17981; Ⓟ 518; © 416
Francis Mine; RMC Place; WASHINGTON; ▲ Smith; *225 WN-2; ★ PGH; mail Burgettstown Z 15021; ● 80
Franconia; RMC Place; MONTGOMERY; ▲ Franconia; 227 EN-11; 🅿; ★ PHIL-; Z 18924; ● 430
Franconia; MCD-Township; MONTGOMERY; *227 EN-11; 🅿; ★ PHIL-; Z 18924; Ⓟ 7,224; © 11,523
Frank; ALLEGHENY; see Industry (RMC Place)
Frankford; RMC Place; PHILADELPHIA; *227 EP-12; ★ PHIL-; mail Philadelphia Z 19124; pop. incl. with Philadelphia (Inc. Place)
Frankfort Springs; Inc. Place; BEAVER; 225 WM-2; elev. 1,186ft./361m.; ★ PGH; mail Hookstown Z 15050; Ⓟ 134; © 130
Franklin; MCD-Township; ADAMS; *227 EQ-2; mail Biglerville Z 17307; Ⓟ 4,126; © 4,590
Franklin; MCD-Township; BEAVER; *225 WK-3; ★ PGH; mail Fombell Z 16123; Ⓟ 3,821; © 4,307
Franklin; MCD-Township; BRADFORD; *226 EF-6; mail Towanda Z 18848; Ⓟ 557; © 698
Franklin; MCD-Township; BUTLER; *224 WJ-4; ★ BUTL; mail Prospect Z 16052; Ⓟ 2,156; © 2,292
Franklin; Inc. Place; CAMBRIA; 225 WN-9; ★ JNST; mail Johnstown Z 15909; Ⓟ 565; © 442
Franklin; MCD-Township; CARBON; *227 EK-10; mail Lehighton Z 18235; Ⓟ 3,706; © 4,243
Franklin; MCD-Township; CHESTER; *227 EQ-9; ★ PHIL-; mail Landenberg Z 19350; Ⓟ 2,779; © 3,850
Franklin; MCD-Township; COLUMBIA; *227 EK-6; mail Catawissa Z 17820; Ⓟ 624; © 597
Franklin; MCD-Township; ERIE; *224 WD-3; mail Edinboro Z 16412; Ⓟ 1,429; © 1,609
Franklin; MCD-Township; FAYETTE; *225 WP-5; ★ UNTN; mail Vanderbilt Z 15486; Ⓟ 2,640; © 2,628
Franklin; MCD-Township; GREENE; *225 WQ-3; mail Waynesburg Z 15370; Ⓟ 5,562; © 7,694; Ⓡ 7,224
Franklin; MCD-Township; HUNTINGDON; *225 WL-13; mail Pennsylvania Furnace Z 16865; Ⓟ 466; © 447
Franklin; MCD-Township; LUZERNE; *226 EH-9; ★ SCR-; mail Pittston Z 18640; Ⓟ 1,414; © 1,601
Franklin; MCD-Township; LYCOMING; *226 EI-6; mail Lairdsville Z 17742; Ⓟ 914; © 915
Franklin; MCD-Township; SNYDER; *227 EL-3; mail Paxtonville Z 17861; Ⓟ 2,158; © 2,094
Franklin; MCD-Township; SUSQUEHANNA; *226 EE-9; mail Montrose Z 18801; Ⓟ 913; © 938
Franklin; Inc. Place; ⊡ VENANGO; 224 WH-4; elev. 1,020ft./311m.; 🅿 🅷 ■; ★ OILC-F; Z 16323; Ⓟ 7,329; © 7,212; ◆ 6,822
Franklin; MCD-Township; YORK; *227 EP-3; ★ HRBG; mail Dillsburg Z 17019; Ⓟ 3,852; © 4,515
FRANKLIN; 225 WP-13; Ⓟ 121,082; © 129,313; ◆ 144,829
Franklin Center; RMC Place; DELAWARE; ▲ Middletown; ★ PHIL-; mail Media Z 19063, Z 19091, Philadelphia Z 19093
Franklin Center; RMC Place; ERIE; ▲ Franklin; 224 WD-3; mail Edinboro Z 16412; ● 30
Franklindale; RMC Place; BRADFORD; ▲ Franklin; 226 EF-6; mail Monroeton Z 18832; ● 100
Franklin Farms; RMC Place; WASHINGTON; ▲ North Franklin; *225 WO-2; ★ WASH; mail Washington Z 15301; ● 300
Franklin Forks; RMC Place; SUSQUEHANNA; ▲ Franklin; 226 EE-9; mail Montrose Z 18801; ● 110
Franklin Hill; SUSQUEHANNA; see Upsonville (RMC Place)
Franklin Park; Inc. Place; ALLEGHENY; 225 WL-3; elev. 1,246ft./380m.; ★ PGH; mail Sewickley Z 15143; Ⓟ 10,109; © 11,364
Franklin Pike Corners (South Meadville); RMC Place; CRAWFORD; *224 WF-3; elev. 1,119ft./341m.; mail Meadville Z 16335; ● 140
Franklintown; Inc. Place; YORK; 227 EP-4; elev. 700ft./213m.; 🅿; ★ HRBG; Z 17323; Ⓟ 373; © 532
Franklinville; RMC Place; HUNTINGDON; ▲ Franklin; 225 WL-12; mail Spruce Creek Z 16683; ● 75
Frankstown; RMC Place; BLAIR; ▲ Frankstown; 225 WM-11; ★ ALT; mail Hollidaysburg Z 16648; ● 200
Frankstown; MCD-Township; BLAIR; *225 WM-11; ★ ALT; mail Hollidaysburg Z 16648; Ⓟ 7,243; © 7,694
Frazer; MCD-Township; ALLEGHENY; *225 WL-4; ★ PGH; mail Tarentum Z 15084; Ⓟ 1,388; © 1,286
Frazer; RMC Place; CHESTER; ▲ East Whiteland; 227 EP-10; 🅿; ★ PHIL-; Z 19355; ● 2,000
Frederick; RMC Place; MONTGOMERY; ▲ Upper Frederick; 227 EN-10; 🅿; ★ PHIL-; Z 19435; ● 120
Fredericksburg; RMC Place; ARMSTRONG; ▲ Perry; *224 WJ-5; elev. 1,299ft./396m.; mail Karns City Z 16041; ● 20
Fredericksburg; RMC Place; BLAIR; ▲ Greenfield; *225 WN-10; ★ ALT; mail Claysburg Z 16625
Fredericksburg; BLAIR; see Clover Creek (RMC Place)
Fredericksburg; CDP; CRAWFORD; ▲ Vernon; 224 WF-3; mail Meadville Z 16335; Ⓟ 1,269; © 1,140
Fredericksburg; CDP; LEBANON; ▲ Bethel; 227 EM-6; 🅿; ★ LEB; Z 17026; Ⓟ 2,338; © 987
Fredericksville (Freemanville); RMC Place; BERKS; ▲ Rockland, District; *227 EM-10; ★ READ; mail Mertztown Z 19539; ● 100
Fredericktown; RMC Place; WASHINGTON; ▲ East Bethlehem; 225 WP-3; 🅿; Z 15333; ● 200
Fredericktown Hill; RMC Place; WASHINGTON; ▲ East Bethlehem; *225 WP-3; mail Fredericktown Z 15333; ● 300
Fredericktown-Millsboro; CDP-Census Area Only; WASHINGTON; ▲ East Bethlehem; *225 WP-3; mail Fredericktown Z 15333, Millsboro Z 15348; Ⓟ 1,237; © 1,094
Fredonia; Inc. Place; MERCER; 224 WH-2; elev. 1,175ft./358m.; 🅿; Z 16124; Ⓟ 683; © 652
Freeburg; Inc. Place; SNYDER; 227 EK-4; elev. 520ft./158m.; 🅿; Z 17827; Ⓟ 640; © 584
Freedom; MCD-Township; ADAMS; *227 EQ-2; mail Biglerville Z 17307; Ⓟ 692; © 844
Freedom; Inc. Place; BEAVER; 225 WL-2; elev. 701ft./214m.; 🅿; ★ PGH; Z 15042; Ⓟ 1,897; © 1,763
Freedom; MCD-Township; BLAIR; *225 WN-10; ★ ALT; mail East Freedom Z 16637; Ⓟ 2,959; © 3,261
Freehold; MCD-Township; WARREN; *224 WD-6; mail Bear Lake Z 16402; Ⓟ 1,318; © 1,402
Freeland; Inc. Place; LUZERNE; 226 EJ-9; elev. 1,880ft./573m.; 🅿; ★ HAZ; Z 18224; Ⓟ 3,909; © 3,643
Freemansburg; Inc. Place; NORTHAMPTON; *227 EL-11; elev. 300ft./91m.; 🅿; ★ ALL-; Z 18017; Ⓟ 1,946; © 1,897
Freemansburg Heights; RMC Place; NORTHAMPTON; ▲ Bethlehem; ★ ALL-; mail Bethlehem Z 18020
Freemansville; RMC Place; BERKS; ▲ Cumru; *227 EN-9; ★ READ; mail Reading Z 19607; rural
Freemanville; BERKS; see Fredericksville (RMC Place)
Freeport; Inc. Place; ARMSTRONG; 225 WL-5; elev. 780ft./238m.; 🅿; ★ PGH; Z 16229; Ⓟ 1,983; © 1,962
Freeport; RMC Place; ERIE; ▲ North East; *224 WC-5; elev. 802ft./244m.; ★ ERIE; mail North East Z 16428; summer pop. 150
Freeport; MCD-Township; GREENE; *225 WQ-2; mail New Freeport Z 15352; Ⓟ 327; © 302
Freeport Junction; RMC Place; ARMSTRONG; ★ PGH; mail Freeport Z 16229; pop. incl. with Freeport (Inc. Place)
Fremont; SNYDER; see Mount Pleasant Mills (CDP)
French Creek; MCD-Township; MERCER; *224 WG-4; mail Carlton Z 16311; Ⓟ 789; © 764
Frenchcreek; MCD-Township; VENANGO; *224 WG-4; ★ OILC-F; mail Franklin Z 16323; Ⓟ 1,676; © 1,605
French Creek Falls; CHESTER; see Saint Peters (RMC Place)
Frenchs Corners; RMC Place; ARMSTRONG; ▲ Washington; *225 WK-6; mail Adrian Z 16210; ● 90
Frenchtown; RMC Place; CRAWFORD; ▲ East Mead; 224 WF-4; elev. 1,417ft./432m.; mail Guys Mills Z 16327; ● 60
Frenchville; RMC Place; CLEARFIELD; ▲ Girard; 224 WI-12; 🅿; Z 16836; ● 200
Freysville; RMC Place; YORK; ▲ Windsor; 227 EP-6; ★ YORK; mail Red Lion Z 17356; ● 400
Fricks; BUCKS; see Leidytown (RMC Place)
Fricks Lock; RMC Place; CHESTER; ▲ East Coventry; *227 EO-10; ★ PTSTN; mail Pottstown Z 19464; ● 150
Friedens; RMC Place; LEHIGH; ▲ Washington; *227 EL-10; ★ ALL-; mail Slatington Z 18080; ● 150
Friedens; CDP; SOMERSET; ▲ Somerset; 225 WP-8; 🅿; Z 15541; Ⓟ 1,576; © 1,673
Friedensburg; CDP; SCHUYLKILL; ▲ Wayne; 227 EL-7; 🅿; ★ PTSVL; Z 17933; © 828
Friedensville; RMC Place; LEHIGH; ▲ Upper Saucon; 226 EC-4; ★ ALL-; mail Bethlehem Z 18020, Center Valley Z 18034; ● 800
Friendship Heights; RMC Place; FAYETTE; ▲ Springhill; *225 WQ-4; ★ MORG; mail New Geneva Z 15467
Friendship Village; RMC Place; CHESTER; ▲ West Brandywine; ★ PHIL-; mail Coatesville Z 19320; ● 500
Friendsville; Inc. Place; SUSQUEHANNA; 226 EE-8; elev. 1,543ft./470m.; 🅿; Z 18818; Ⓟ 102; © 91
Friesville; RMC Place; BLAIR; ▲ Greenfield; *225 WN-10; ★ ALT; mail Claysburg Z 16625; ● 70
Frisbie; RMC Place; SCHUYLKILL; ▲ West Brunswick; *227 EL-8; ★ PTSVL; mail Orwigsburg Z 17961; rural
Frisco; RMC Place; BEAVER; ▲ Franklin; 225 WK-2; ★ PGH; mail Ellwood City Z 16117; ● 850
Fritztown; RMC Place; BERKS; ▲ South Heidelberg, Spring; 227 EN-8; elev. 1,080ft./329m.; ★ READ; mail Reading Z 19608; ● 200
Frogtown; RMC Place; ARMSTRONG; ▲ Sugarcreek; 224 WJ-5; elev. 1,302ft./397m.; mail East Brady Z 16028; ● 70
Frogtown; RMC Place; CLARION; ▲ Limestone; 224 WI-7; mail Fairmount City Z 16224; ● 40
Frogtown; RMC Place; HUNTINGDON; ▲ Warriors Mark; *225 WL-12; mail Warriors Mark Z 16877
Frogtown; RMC Place; YORK; ▲ Fairview; *227 EO-4; ★ HRBG; mail New Cumberland Z 17070; ● 100
Froman; RMC Place; WASHINGTON; *225 WN-4; elev. 1,051ft./320m.; ★ PGH; mail Finleyville Z 15332; rural
Frostburg; RMC Place; JEFFERSON; ▲ Perry; 224 WJ-8; 🅿; Z 15740; ● 120
Frostown; FOREST; see Pigeon (RMC Place)
Frugality; RMC Place; CAMBRIA; ▲ Reade; *225 WL-10; mail Fallentimber Z 16639; rural
Fruitville; RMC Place; LANCASTER; ▲ Manheim; ★ LANC; mail Lancaster Z 17601
Fruitville; RMC Place; MONTGOMERY; ▲ Limerick; *227 EN-10; ★ PHIL-; mail Schwenksville Z 19473; ● 200
Frutcheys; RMC Place; MONROE; ▲ Middle Smithfield; *226 EJ-12; mail East Stroudsburg Z 18301; rural
Fryburg; RMC Place; CLARION; ▲ Washington; 224 WH-6; elev. 1,694ft./516m.; 🅿; Z 16326; ● 375
Frystown; RMC Place; BERKS; ▲ Bethel; 227 EM-7; mail Myerstown Z 17067; ● 150
Fuhrmans Mill; RMC Place; YORK; ▲ West Manheim; *227 EQ-4; elev. 670ft./204m.; ★ HANV; mail Hanover Z 17331; rural
Fullerton (Whitehall); CDP; LEHIGH; ▲ Whitehall; 227 EL-11; ★ ALL-; mail Whitehall Z 18052; Ⓟ 13,127; © 14,268
Fulmor Heights; RMC Place; MONTGOMERY; ▲ Upper Moreland; *227 EO-12; elev. 200ft./61m.; ★ PHIL-; mail Hatboro Z 19040; ● 1,400
Fulton; MCD-Township; LANCASTER; *227 EQ-7; mail Peach Bottom Z 17563; Ⓟ 2,688; © 2,826
FULTON; 225 WP-12; Ⓟ 13,837; © 14,261; ◆ 15,327
Fulton Run; RMC Place; INDIANA; ▲ White; *225 WL-7; mail Indiana Z 15701; ● 40
Furlong; RMC Place; BUCKS; ▲ Doylestown, Buckingham; 227 EN-12; 🅿; ★ PHIL-; Z 18925; ● 700
Furnace Hill; RMC Place; FAYETTE; ▲ Dunbar; *225 WP-5; elev. 1,300ft./396m.; mail Dunbar Z 15431; ● 100
Furnace Hill; RMC Place; MERCER; ▲ Shenango; *224 WI-2; elev. 950ft./290m.; ★ SHAR; mail West Middlesex Z 16159; rural
Furnace Run; RMC Place; ARMSTRONG; ▲ East Franklin; *225 WK-6; ★ PGH; mail Kittanning Z 16201; ● 100
Furniss; RMC Place; LANCASTER; ▲ Drumore; *227 EQ-7; elev. 415ft./126m.; mail Peach Bottom Z 17563; rural

G

Gabby Heights; RMC Place; WASHINGTON; ▲ North Franklin; 225 WO-2; ★ WASH; mail Washington Z 15301; ● 1,200
Gabelsville; RMC Place; BERKS; ▲ Colebrookdale; *227 EN-10; mail Boyertown Z 19512; ● 100
Gahagen; RMC Place; SOMERSET; ▲ Shade; *225 WP-9; mail Central City Z 15926; ● 60
Gaibleton; RMC Place; INDIANA; ▲ Rayne; *225 WL-8; mail Home Z 15747; rural
Gaines; RMC Place; TIOGA; ▲ Gaines; 226 EF-1; 🅿; Z 16921; ● 120
Gaines; MCD-Township; TIOGA; *226 EE-1; 🅿; Z 16921; Ⓟ 601; © 553
Galeton; Inc. Place; POTTER; 224 WF-14; elev. 1,315ft./401m.; 🅿; Z 16922; Ⓟ 1,370; © 1,325
Galilee; RMC Place; WAYNE; ▲ Damascus; 226 EF-12; 🅿; Z 18415; ● 180
Gallagher; MCD-Township; CLINTON; *226 EI-2; mail Lock Haven Z 17745; Ⓟ 213; © 340
Gallagherville; RMC Place; CHESTER; ▲ Caln; *227 EP-10; ★ PHIL-; mail Downingtown Z 19335; pop. incl. with Downingtown (Inc. Place)
Gallatin; RMC Place; ALLEGHENY; ▲ Forward; 225 WO-4; ★ PGH; mail Monongahela Z 15063; ● 250
Gallitzin; Inc. Place; CAMBRIA; 225 WM-10; elev. 2,167ft./661m.; 🅿; ★ ALT; Z 16641; Ⓟ 2,003; © 1,756
Gallitzin; MCD-Township; CAMBRIA; *225 WM-10; 🅿; ★ ALT; Z 16641; does not include the Borough of Gallitzin; Ⓟ 1,289; © 1,310
Galloway; RMC Place; VENANGO; *224 WG-4; elev. 1,454ft./443m.; ★ OILC-F; mail Franklin Z 16323; pop. incl. with Sugarcreek (Inc. Place)
Gamble; MCD-Township; LYCOMING; *226 EH-4; mail Trout Run Z 17771; Ⓟ 744; © 854
Ganister; RMC Place; BLAIR; ▲ Woodbury, Catharine; 225 WM-12; 🅿; ★ ALT; Z 16693; ● 85
Gans; RMC Place; FAYETTE; ▲ Springhill; *225 WQ-4; 🅿; ★ MORG; Z 15439; ● 75
Gap; CDP; LANCASTER; ▲ Salisbury; 227 EP-8; elev. 559ft./170m.; 🅿; Z 17527; Ⓟ 1,226; © 1,611
Gapsville; RMC Place; BEDFORD; ▲ East Providence; *225 WP-11; mail Breezewood Z 15533
Garards Fort; RMC Place; GREENE; ▲ Greene; 225 WQ-3; 🅿; Z 15334; ● 100
Gardeau; RMC Place; MCKEAN; ▲ Norwich; *224 WF-12; mail Austin Z 16720
Garden City; RMC Place; ALLEGHENY; *225 WM-5; ★ PGH; mail Monroeville Z 15146; pop. incl. with Monroeville (Inc. Place)
Garden City; RMC Place; DELAWARE; ▲ Nether Providence; *227 EQ-11; 🅿; ★ PHIL-; Z 19063 & mail Chester Z 19013, Wallingford Z 19086
Gardendale; RMC Place; DELAWARE; ▲ Upper Chichester; *227 EQ-11; ★ PHIL-; mail Marcus Hook Z 19061
Garden Hills; RMC Place; LANCASTER; ▲ Manor; *227 EP-7; ★ LANC; mail Lancaster Z 17603; ● 50
Garden View; CDP; LYCOMING; ▲ Old Lycoming; 226 EI-4; ★ WMSPT; mail Williamsport Z 17701; Ⓟ 2,687; © 2,679
Garden View; RMC Place; MIFFLIN; ▲ Brown; *227 EL-1; mail Reedsville Z 17084; ● 300
Gardenville; RMC Place; BUCKS; ▲ Plumstead; 227 EN-12; 🅿; ★ PHIL-; Z 18926 & mail Danboro Z 18916, Doylestown Z 18901; ● 250
Gardners; RMC Place; ADAMS; ▲ Tyrone; 227 EP-3; 🅿; Z 17324; ● 200
Garfield; RMC Place; BERKS; ▲ Penn, Centre; *227 EM-8; ★ READ; mail Bernville Z 19506; ● 50
Gargol; RMC Place; ADAMS; ▲ Huntington; *227 EP-3; mail Idaville Z 17337; ● 90
Garland; RMC Place; WARREN; ▲ Pittsfield; 224 WE-6; 🅿; Z 16416; ● 300
Garmantown; RMC Place; CAMBRIA; ▲ Susquehanna; *225 WL-9; mail Northern Cambria Z 15714; ● 125
Garrett; Inc. Place; SOMERSET; 225 WQ-8; elev. 1,930ft./588m.; 🅿; Z 15542; Ⓟ 520; © 449
Garrett Hill; RMC Place; DELAWARE; ▲ Radnor; *227 EP-11; ★ PHIL-; mail Bryn Mawr Z 19010
Garretts Run; RMC Place; ARMSTRONG; ▲ Manor; *225 WK-6; ★ PGH; mail Kittanning Z 16201; ● 75
Garrison; RMC Place; GREENE; ▲ Freeport; 225 WQ-1; elev. 1,486ft./453m.; mail New Freeport Z 15352; ● 50
Gas Center; RMC Place; INDIANA; ▲ East Wheatfield; *225 WM-8; ★ JNST; mail Seward Z 15954; ● 40
Gascola; RMC Place; ALLEGHENY; ▲ Penn Hills; *225 WM-4; elev. 1,200ft./366m.; ★ PGH
Gaskill; MCD-Township; JEFFERSON; *224 WJ-9; mail Punxsutawney Z 15767; Ⓟ 675; © 671
Gastonville; CDP; WASHINGTON; ▲ Union; 225 WN-4; 🅿; ★ PGH; Z 15336; Ⓟ 3,090; © 3,002
Gastown; RMC Place; ARMSTRONG; ▲ Plumcreek; 225 WL-7; mail Shelocta Z 15774; ● 150
Gatchellville; RMC Place; YORK; ▲ Fawn; 227 EQ-6; elev. 714ft./218m.; ★ BAL; mail New Park Z 17352; ● 60
Gates; RMC Place; FAYETTE; ▲ German; *225 WP-4; ★ UNTN; mail Adah Z 15410; ● 140
Gatesburg; RMC Place; CENTRE; ▲ Ferguson; 225 WL-13; ★ STCOL; mail Warriors Mark Z 16877; ● 100
Gateway Center; RMC Place; ALLEGHENY; ★ PGH; mail Pittsburgh Z 15222; pop. incl. with Pittsburgh (Inc. Place)
Gauff Hill; RMC Place; LEHIGH; ▲ Salisbury; 226 EB-4; ★ ALL-; mail Bethlehem Z 18017; ● 350
Gayly; RMC Place; ALLEGHENY; ▲ Robinson; 228 J-3; elev. 1,202ft./366m.; ★ PGH; mail Imperial Z 15126; ● 300
Gaysport; RMC Place; BLAIR; *225 WM-11; ★ ALT; mail Hollidaysburg Z 16648; pop. incl. with Hollidaysburg (Inc. Place)
Gay Street; RMC Place; CHESTER; mail West Chester Z 19380-81; pop. incl. with West Chester (Inc. Place)
Gearhartville; RMC Place; CLEARFIELD; ▲ Decatur; *225 WK-11; mail Philipsburg Z 16866; ● 200
Geeseytown; RMC Place; BLAIR; ▲ Frankstown; 225 WM-11; ★ ALT; mail Hollidaysburg Z 16648; ● 100
Geiger; RMC Place; SOMERSET; ▲ Somerset; 225 WP-8; mail Somerset Z 15501; ● 90
Geigertown; RMC Place; BERKS; ▲ Union, Robeson; 227 EO-9; 🅿; ★ READ; Z 19523; ● 500
Geistown; Inc. Place; CAMBRIA; 225 WN-9; elev. 1,900ft./579m.; ★ JNST; mail Johnstown Z 15904; Ⓟ 2,749; © 2,555
Gelatt; RMC Place; SUSQUEHANNA; ▲ Gibson; 226 EE-10; mail Jackson Z 18825; ● 50
General Warren Village; RMC Place; CHESTER; ▲ East Whiteland; *227 EP-10; ★ PHIL-; mail Malvern Z 19355; ● 750
Genesee; RMC Place; POTTER; ▲ Genesee; 224 WD-13; 🅿; Z 16923, Z 16941; ● 300
Genesee; MCD-Township; POTTER; *224 WD-13; 🅿; Z 16923, Z 16941; Ⓟ 803; © 789
Geneva; CDP; CRAWFORD; ▲ Greenwood; 224 WG-3; elev. 1,134ft./346m.; mail Conneaut Lake Z 16316; © 115
Geneva Hill; RMC Place; BEAVER; ▲ White; ★ PGH; mail Beaver Falls Z 15010
Georges; MCD-Township; FAYETTE; *225 WQ-5; ★ UNTN; mail Smithfield Z 15478, Uniontown Z 15401; Ⓟ 6,525; © 6,752
George School; RMC Place; BUCKS; ▲ Middletown; *227 EO-13; 🅿; ★ PHIL-; Z 18940
Georgetown; RMC Place; ADAMS; ▲ Germany; *227 ER-3; mail Littlestown Z 17340; rural
Georgetown; RMC Place; ARMSTRONG; ▲ Gilpin; *225 WL-5; ★ PGH; mail Leechburg Z 15656; ● 220
Georgetown; Inc. Place; BEAVER; 225 WL-1; elev. 760ft./232m.; 🅿; ★ PGH; Z 15043; Ⓟ 194; © 182
Georgetown (Bart); RMC Place; LANCASTER; ▲ Bart; 227 EP-8; mail Bart Z 17503; ● 300
Georgetown; RMC Place; LUZERNE; ▲ Wilkes-Barre; *226 EI-9; ★ SCR-; mail Wilkes Barre Z 18702
Georgetown; RMC Place; NORTHAMPTON; ▲ Upper Nazareth; 227 EL-11; ★ ALL-; mail Nazareth Z 18064; ● 200
Georgeville; RMC Place; INDIANA; ▲ East Mahoning; 225 WK-8; mail Marion Center Z 15759; ● 30
German; MCD-Township; FAYETTE; *225 WP-4; ★ UNTN; mail Mc Clellandtown Z 15458; Ⓟ 5,596; © 5,595
German Corners; RMC Place; LEHIGH; ▲ Heidelberg; *227 EL-9; ★ ALL-; mail Germansville Z 18053; ● 50
Germania; RMC Place; POTTER; ▲ Abbott; 224 WF-14; mail Galeton Z 16922; ● 130
Germans; RMC Place; CARBON; ▲ East Penn; *227 EK-9; mail Lehighton Z 18235; rural
Germansville; RMC Place; LEHIGH; ▲ Heidelberg; 227 EL-10; elev. 606ft./185m.; 🅿; ★ ALL-; Z 18053; ● 250
Germantown; RMC Place; ADAMS; ▲ Mount Joy; *227 EQ-3; mail Littlestown Z 17340; ● 200
Germantown (Dutch Settlement); RMC Place; CAMBRIA; ▲ Portage; *225 WN-10; mail Portage Z 15946; rural
Germantown; RMC Place; FRANKLIN; ▲ Greene; *227 EP-1; mail Fayetteville Z 17222
Germantown; RMC Place; PHILADELPHIA; *227 EP-12; ★ PHIL-; mail Philadelphia Z 19144; pop. incl. with Philadelphia (Inc. Place)
Germantown; RMC Place; PIKE; ▲ Lackawaxen; *226 EG-12; elev. 1,321ft./403m.; mail Hawley Z 18428; rural
Germany; MCD-Township; ADAMS; *227 EQ-3; mail Littlestown Z 17340; Ⓟ 1,949; © 2,269
Geryville; RMC Place; BUCKS; ▲ Milford; *227 EM-11; ★ PHIL-; mail Pennsburg Z 18073
Getty Heights; RMC Place; INDIANA; ▲ White; *225 WL-7; mail Indiana Z 15701; ● 500
Gettysburg; Inc. Place; ⊡ ADAMS; 227 EQ-3; elev. 560ft./171m.; 🅿 🅷 🅲 2,659; Z 17325; Ⓟ 7,025; © 7,490
Ghennes Heights; RMC Place; WASHINGTON; ▲ Fallowfield; 225 WO-4; ★ PGH; mail Monongahela Z 15063; ● 900
Ghent; RMC Place; BRADFORD; ▲ Sheshequin; *226 EE-6; elev. 1,408ft./429m.; mail Ulster Z 18850; rural
Giant Oaks; RMC Place; WASHINGTON; ▲ Peters; *225 WN-3; ★ PGH; mail Canonsburg Z 15317; ● 1,200
Gibbon Glade; RMC Place; FAYETTE; ▲ Wharton; 225 WQ-5; elev. 1,677ft./511m.; 🅿; Z 15440; ● 65
Gibbs Hill; RMC Place; MCKEAN; ▲ Hamilton; *224 WF-9; elev. 2,000ft./610m.; mail Kane Z 16735; rural
Gibraltar; RMC Place; BERKS; ▲ Robeson; 227 EN-9; elev. 190ft./58m.; ★ READ; mail Birdsboro Z 19508; ● 700
Gibson; MCD-Township; CAMERON; *224 WH-12; mail Driftwood Z 15832; Ⓟ 215; © 222
Gibson; RMC Place; SUSQUEHANNA; ▲ Gibson; 226 EE-10; 🅿; Z 18820; ● 200
Gibson; MCD-Township; SUSQUEHANNA; *226 EF-10; 🅿; Z 18820 & mail South Gibson Z 18842; Ⓟ 1,015; © 1,129
Gibson; RMC Place; WASHINGTON; ▲ Fallowfield; *225 WO-3; ★ PGH; mail Bentleyville Z 15314; pop. incl. with Bentleyville (Inc. Place)
Gibsonia; RMC Place; ALLEGHENY; ▲ Richland; 225 WL-4; 🅿; ★ PGH; Z 15044; ● 3,500
Gibsonton; RMC Place; WESTMORELAND; ▲ Rostraver; *225 WO-4; ★ PGH; mail Belle Vernon Z 15012; ● 60
Gifford; RMC Place; MCKEAN; ▲ Keating; 224 WE-10; 🅿; Z 16732; ● 500
Gilbert; RMC Place; MONROE; ▲ Polk, Chestnuthill; 226 EJ-11; 🅿; ★ ALL-; Z 18331; ● 700
Gilberton; Inc. Place; SCHUYLKILL; 227 EK-7; elev. 1,140ft./347m.; 🅿; Z 17934; Ⓟ 953; © 867
Gilbertsville; CDP; MONTGOMERY; ▲ Douglass; 227 EN-10; 🅿; Z 19525; Ⓟ 3,994; © 4,242
Gilfoyl; FOREST; see Gilfoyle (RMC Place)
Gilfoyle (Gilfoyl); RMC Place; FOREST; ▲ Jenks; 224 WG-7; mail Marienville Z 16239; ● 20
Gillespie; RMC Place; FAYETTE; ▲ Washington; *225 WO-4; ★ PGH; mail Fayette City Z 15438; ● 125
Gillett; RMC Place; BRADFORD; ▲ South Creek; 226 ED-5; 🅿; Z 16925; ● 300
Gillingham; RMC Place; CLEARFIELD; ▲ Girard; *224 WI-11; elev. 1,670ft./509m.; mail Frenchville Z 16836; rural
Gillintown; RMC Place; CENTRE; ▲ Snow Shoe; *224 WJ-13; mail Snow Shoe Z 16874; rural
Gilmore; RMC Place; FAYETTE; ▲ Georges; *225 WQ-4; elev. 1,121ft./342m.; ★ UNTN; mail Smithfield Z 15478; ● 15
Gilmore; MCD-Township; GREENE; *225 WQ-2; mail New Freeport Z 15352; Ⓟ 365; © 295
Gilmore; RMC Place; MCKEAN; ▲ Foster; *224 WD-10; mail Derrick City Z 16727
Gilmore; RMC Place; WASHINGTON; ▲ Cecil; *225 WN-2; ★ PGH; mail Mc Donald Z 15057; ● 90
Gilpin; MCD-Township; ARMSTRONG; *225 WL-5; ★ PGH; mail Leechburg Z 15656; Ⓟ 2,804; © 2,587
Ginger Hill; RMC Place; WASHINGTON; ▲ Nottingham, Fallowfield; *225 WO-3; elev. 1,150ft./351m.; ★ PGH; mail Finleyville Z 15332; ● 80
Ginter; RMC Place; CLEARFIELD; ▲ Gulich; 225 WK-11; 🅿; Z 16651; ● 120
Ginther; RMC Place; SCHUYLKILL; ▲ Rush; 227 EK-8; elev. 1,188ft./362m.; mail Tamaqua Z 18252; ● 75
Gipsy; RMC Place; INDIANA; ▲ Montgomery; 225 WK-9; elev. 1,567ft./478m.; 🅿; Z 15741; ● 125
Girard; MCD-Township; CLEARFIELD; *224 WI-11; mail Frenchville Z 16836; Ⓟ 630; © 674
Girard; Inc. Place; ERIE; 224 WD-2; elev. 777ft./237m.; 🅿; ★ ERIE; Z 16417; Ⓟ 2,879; © 3,164
Girard; MCD-Township; ERIE; *224 WD-2; 🅿; ★ ERIE; Z 16417; does not include the Borough of Girard; Ⓟ 4,722; © 5,133
Girard Avenue; RMC Place; PHILADELPHIA; ★ PHIL-; mail Philadelphia Z 19122; pop. incl. with Philadelphia (Inc. Place)
Girardville; Inc. Place; SCHUYLKILL; 227 EK-7; elev. 1,020ft./311m.; 🅿; ★ PTSVL; Z 17935; Ⓟ 1,889; © 1,742

Entries in **UPPERCASE** are counties.
Entries in **bold** have populations of 2,500 or more.
Names in parentheses are alternate names.

Inc. Place	Incorporated Place
RMC Place	Rand McNally Designated Place
CDP	Census Designated Place
MCD	Minor Civil Division
⊡	County Seat
▲	Minor Civil Division
elev.	Elevation
🅿	Post Office
🅷	Hospital
🅲	College
■	Principal Business Center
★	Ranally Metro Area (RMA) Abbreviation
Z	Zip Code(s)
Ⓟ	Previous Census Population
Ⓡ	Revised Census Population
Ⓐ	Annexation Population
●	Rand McNally Population Estimate
©	Final Census Population
Ⓢ	Special Census Population
◆	Estimated Population

For additional definitions see Glossary, Volume 1, and Introduction, Volume 2.

Girty; RMC Place; ARMSTRONG; ▲ South Bend; **225** WL-6; mail Spring Church z 15686; ● 30
Gitts Run; RMC Place; YORK; ▲ Penn; ***227** EQ-4; ★ **HANV**; mail Hanover z 17331; ● 35
Gladden; RMC Place; ALLEGHENY; ▲ South Fayette; ***225** WN-3; elev. 929ft./283m.; ★ **PGH**; mail Mc Donald z 15057; ● 200
Gladden Heights; RMC Place; WASHINGTON; ▲ Cecil; ***225** WN-2; ★ **PGH**; mail Mc Donald z 15057; ● 60
Glade; RMC Place; SOMERSET; ▲ Stonycreek; ***225** WP-9; mail Berlin z 15530; rural
Glade; RMC Place; WARREN; ***224** WE-8; mail Warren z 16365; pop. incl. with Warren (Inc. Place)
Glade; MCD-Township; WARREN; ***224** WE-8; mail Warren z 16365; ℗ 2,372; © 2,319
Glade City; RMC Place; SOMERSET; ▲ Summit; **225** WQ-8; elev. 2,181ft./665m.; mail Meyersdale z 15552; ● 130
Glades; RMC Place; YORK; ▲ Springettsbury; ***227** EP-5; elev. 579ft./176m.; ★ **YORK**; mail York z 17402; ● 50
Gladhill (Greenstone); RMC Place; ADAMS; ▲ Hamiltonban; **227** EQ-2; mail Fairfield z 17320; ● 40
Gladstone; RMC Place; DELAWARE; ★ **PHIL-**; mail Lansdowne z 19050; pop. incl. with Lansdowne (Inc. Place)
Gladwyne; RMC Place; MONTGOMERY; **228** C-2; elev. 350ft./107m.; 🅿; ★ **PHIL-**; z 19035; ● 4,000
Glanford; RMC Place; ALLEGHENY; ★ **PGH**; pop. incl. with Pittsburgh (Inc. Place)
Glasgow; Inc. Place; BEAVER; **225** WL-1; elev. 680ft./207m.; ★ **PGH**; mail Midland z 15059; ℗ 74; © 63
Glasgow; RMC Place; CAMBRIA; ▲ Reade; **225** WL-11; 🅿; z 16644; ● 250
Glasgow; RMC Place; MONTGOMERY; ***227** EN-10; ★ **PTSTN**; mail Pottstown z 19464; pop. incl. with Pottstown (Inc. Place)
Glass City; RMC Place; CENTRE; ▲ Rush; ***225** WK-12; mail Philipsburg z 16866; ● 200
Glassmere; RMC Place; ALLEGHENY; ▲ East Deer; ***225** WL-5; ★ **PGH**; mail Creighton z 15030
Glassport; Inc. Place; ALLEGHENY; **225** WN-4; elev. 800ft./244m.; 🅿; ★ **PGH**; z 15045; ℗ 5,582; © 4,993
Glassworks; RMC Place; GREENE; ▲ Monongahela; ***225** WQ-4; mail Greensboro z 15338; ● 200
Glatfelter; RMC Place; YORK; ▲ North Codorus; ***227** EQ-5; ★ **YORK**; mail Seven Valleys z 17360; rural
Gleason; RMC Place; TIOGA; ▲ Union; ***226** EF-4; mail Canton z 17724
Gleasonton; RMC Place; CLINTON; ▲ Chapman; ***224** WH-14; mail North Bend z 17760
Glen Acres; RMC Place; CHESTER; ▲ West Goshen; ***227** EP-10; ★ **PHIL-**; mail West Chester z 19380; ● 600
Glen Ashton Farms; RMC Place; BUCKS; ▲ Bensalem; ***227** EO-13; ★ **PHIL-**; mail Bensalem z 19020; ● 700
Glenburn; CDP; LACKAWANNA; ▲ Glenburn; **226** EG-9; ★ **SCR-**; mail Clarks Summit z 18411, Dalton z 18414; ℗ 1,242; © 1,212
Glenburn; MCD-Township; LACKAWANNA; ***226** EG-9; ★ **SCR-**; mail Dalton z 18414; ℗ 1,242; © 1,212
Glen Campbell; Inc. Place; INDIANA; **225** WK-9; elev. 1,344ft./410m.; 🅿; z 15742; ℗ 313; © 306
Glen Carbon; RMC Place; SCHUYLKILL; ▲ Foster; ***227** EL-7; ★ **PTSVL**; mail Pottsville z 17901; rural
Glencoe; RMC Place; SOMERSET; ▲ Northampton; **225** WQ-9; 🅿; z 15538; ● 15
Glendale; RMC Place; ALLEGHENY; ▲ Scott; ***225** WM-3; ★ **PGH**; mail Carnegie z 15106
Glendale; RMC Place; LUZERNE; ▲ Pittston; **226** EC-11; ★ **SCR-**; mail Pittston z 18641; ● 75
Glendale Gardens; RMC Place; DELAWARE; ★ **PHIL-**; mail Glenolden z 19036; pop. incl. with Glenolden (Inc. Place)
Glendale Manor; RMC Place; LUZERNE; ▲ Wright, Rice; ***226** EI-9; elev. 1,280ft./390m.; ★ **SCR-**; mail Wilkes Barre z 18701; ● 800
Glendon; Inc. Place; NORTHAMPTON; **227** EL-12; elev. 205ft./62m.; 🅿; ★ **ALL-**; z 18042 & mail Mahanoy City z 17948; ℗ 391; © 367
Glendon; RMC Place; SCHUYLKILL; ▲ Mahanoy; ***227** EK-8; mail Easton z 18042, Mahanoy City z 17948; ● 25
Glendower; RMC Place; SCHUYLKILL; ▲ Foster; ***227** EL-7; mail Pottsville z 17901; rural
Glen Eden; RMC Place; BUTLER; ▲ Cranberry; ***225** WL-3; elev. 1,175ft./358m.; ★ **PGH**; mail Evans City z 16033; rural
Glenfield; Inc. Place; ALLEGHENY; **228** H-3; elev. 720ft./219m.; ★ **PGH**; mail Sewickley z 15143; ℗ 201; © 236
Glen Forney; RMC Place; FRANKLIN; ▲ Washington; **227** EQ-2; ★ **HAG**; mail Waynesboro z 17268; ● 120
Glen Gormely; ALLEGHENY; see Fayetteville (RMC Place)
Glenhall; RMC Place; CHESTER; ▲ Newlin; ***227** EP-10; ★ **PHIL-**; mail West Chester z 19380; rural
Glen Hazel; RMC Place; ELK; ▲ Jones; ***224** WG-10; elev. 1,508ft./460m.; mail Wilcox z 15870
Glen Hope; Inc. Place; CLEARFIELD; **225** WK-10; elev. 1,360ft./415m.; 🅿; z 16645; ℗ 187; © 149
Glenhurst; RMC Place; MONTGOMERY; ★ **PHIL-**; mail Bryn Athyn z 19009; pop. incl. with Bryn Athyn (Inc. Place)
Glen Iron; RMC Place; UNION; ▲ Hartley; **227** EK-3; mail Millmont z 17845; ● 150
Glenloch; RMC Place; CHESTER; ▲ East Whiteland; ***227** EP-10; ★ **PHIL-**; mail West Chester z 19380; rural
Glen Lyon; CDP; LUZERNE; ▲ Newport; **226** EI-8; elev. 742ft./226m.; 🅿; ★ **SCR-**; z 18617; ℗ 2,082; © 1,881
Glenmar Gardens; RMC Place; ERIE; ▲ Summit; **224** WD-4; ★ **ERIE**; mail Erie z 16509; ● 200
Glen Mawr; RMC Place; LYCOMING; ▲ Shrewsbury; **226** EH-5; elev. 716ft./218m.; mail Hughesville z 17737; ● 100
Glen Mills; RMC Place; DELAWARE; ▲ Thornbury; ***227** EP-11; 🅿; ★ **PHIL-**; z 19342; ● 500
Glenmoore; RMC Place; CHESTER; ▲ Wallace; **227** EO-9; 🅿; ★ **PHIL-**; z 19343; ● 900
Glen Moore; RMC Place; LANCASTER; ▲ Manheim; **227** ES-9; ★ **LANC**; mail Lancaster z 17601; ● 1,000
Glenolden; Inc. Place; DELAWARE; **228** F-2; elev. 90ft./27m.; 🅿; ★ **PHIL-**; z 19036; ℗ 7,260; © 7,476
Glen Oley Farms; RMC Place; BERKS; ▲ Exeter; ***227** EN-9; ★ **READ**; mail Reading z 19606; ● 100
Glen Richey; RMC Place; CLEARFIELD; ▲ Lawrence; **224** WJ-10; 🅿; z 16837; ● 270
Glen Riddle; RMC Place; DELAWARE; ▲ Middletown; ***227** EQ-11; 🅿; ★ **PHIL-**; z 19037, z 19063; ● 970
Glen Rock; Inc. Place; YORK; **227** EQ-5; elev. 560ft./171m.; 🅿; ★ **BAL**; z 17327; ℗ 1,688; © 1,809
Glen Rose; RMC Place; CHESTER; ▲ East Fallowfield; ***227** EP-9; ★ **PHIL-**; mail Coatesville z 19320; rural
Glen Roy; RMC Place; CHESTER; ▲ West Nottingham; ***227** EQ-8; elev. 405ft./123m.; mail Nottingham z 19362
Glenruadh; RMC Place; ERIE; ▲ Millcreek; ***224** WC-3; ★ **ERIE**; mail Erie z 16505
Glen Savage; RMC Place; SOMERSET; ▲ Allegheny; ***225** WP-9; elev. 2,310ft./704m.; mail Fairhope z 15538; ● 15
Glenshaw; RMC Place; ALLEGHENY; ▲ Shaler; ***225** WM-4; 🅿; ★ **PGH**; z 15116
Glenside; CDP; MONTGOMERY; ▲ Abington, Cheltenham; **228** A-4; 🅿 🅲 3,592; ★ **PHIL-**; z 19038; ℗ 8,704; © 7,914
Glenside Gardens; RMC Place; MONTGOMERY; ▲ Abington; ★ **PHIL-**; mail Glenside z 19038
Glenside Heights; RMC Place; MONTGOMERY; ▲ Cheltenham; ★ **PHIL-**; mail Glenside z 19038
Glen Summit (Glen Summit Springs); RMC Place; LUZERNE; ▲ Fairview; **226** EI-9; ★ **SCR-**; mail Mountain Top z 18707; ● 250
Glen Summit Springs; LUZERNE; see Glen Summit (RMC Place)
Glenville; RMC Place; YORK; ▲ Manheim, Codorus; **227** EQ-5; 🅿; ★ **BAL**; z 17329; ● 100
Glenwillard (Crescent Township); RMC Place; ALLEGHENY; ▲ Crescent; ***225** WL-3; 🅿; ★ **PGH**; z 15046; ● 1,100
Glenwood; RMC Place; ALLEGHENY; ***225** WM-4; ★ **PGH**; mail Pittsburgh z 15207; pop. incl. with Pittsburgh (Inc. Place)
Glenwood; RMC Place; DAUPHIN; ▲ Susquehanna; **227** ES-3; ★ **HRBG**; mail Harrisburg z 17109; ● 3,000
Glenwood; RMC Place; ERIE; ***224** WC-3; ★ **ERIE**; mail Erie z 16509; pop. incl. with Erie (Inc. Place)
Glenwood; RMC Place; MIFFLIN; ▲ Derry; ***227** EL-1; elev. 655ft./200m.; mail Lewistown z 17044; rural
Glenwood; RMC Place; SUSQUEHANNA; ▲ Lenox; **226** EF-9; elev. 791ft./241m.; mail Nicholson z 18446; ● 50
Glenwood Junction; RMC Place; ALLEGHENY; ★ **PGH**; pop. incl. with Pittsburgh (Inc. Place)
Glenworth; RMC Place; SCHUYLKILL; ▲ North Manheim; ***227** EL-7; ★ **PTSVL**; mail Pottsville z 17901; rural
Globe Mills (Meiser); RMC Place; SNYDER; ▲ Middlecreek; **227** EK-4; mail Middleburg z 17842; ● 45
Glosser View; RMC Place; LYCOMING; ▲ Woodward; ***226** EI-3; ★ **WMSPT**; mail Williamsport z 17701; ● 250
Glyde; RMC Place; WASHINGTON; ▲ Amwell; ***225** WO-3; elev. 1,082ft./330m.; ★ **WASH**; mail Washington z 15301; rural
Glyndon; RMC Place; CRAWFORD; ▲ Sparta; ***224** WE-5; mail Spartansburg z 16434; rural
Gnatstown; RMC Place; YORK; ▲ Jackson; ***227** EQ-4; ★ **YORK**; mail Hanover z 17331; rural
Goat Hill; RMC Place; WASHINGTON; ▲ Canton; ***225** WO-2; elev. 1,200ft./366m.; ★ **WASH**; mail Washington z 15301; ● 1,500
Godfrey; RMC Place; ARMSTRONG; ▲ Gilpin; ***225** WL-5; ★ **PGH**; mail Leechburg z 15656; ● 25
Goff Station; BUTLER; see Deegan (RMC Place)
Goheenville; RMC Place; ARMSTRONG; ▲ Boggs; **225** WK-6; mail Templeton z 16259; ● 50
Gold; RMC Place; POTTER; ▲ Ulysses; **224** WE-13; mail Genesee z 16923; ● 50
Golden Hill; RMC Place; WYOMING; ▲ Windham; ***226** EF-7; mail Laceyville z 18623; rural
Golden Key Lake; RMC Place; PIKE; ▲ Dingman; ***226** EH-13; elev. 1,400ft./427m.; mail Milford z 18337; ● 900
Goldenridge; RMC Place; BUCKS; ▲ Bristol; ***227** EO-14; ★ **PHIL-**; mail Levittown z 19057
Golden Rod Farms; RMC Place; CLEARFIELD; ▲ Bradford; ***224** WJ-11; elev. 1,180ft./360m.; mail Clearfield z 16830; ● 350
Golden Triangle; RMC Place; ALLEGHENY; ***225** WM-3; ★ **PGH**; mail Pittsburgh z 15222; pop. incl. with Pittsburgh (Inc. Place)
Goldsboro (Etters); Inc. Place; YORK; **227** EO-5; elev. 305ft./93m.; mail Etters z 17319; ℗ 458; © 939
Goodhope; RMC Place; CUMBERLAND; ▲ Hampden; ***227** EN-4; ★ **HRBG**; mail Mechanicsburg z 17050, z 17055; rural
Good Hope Farms; RMC Place; CUMBERLAND; ▲ Hampden; ***227** EN-4; ★ **HRBG**; mail Mechanicsburg z 17055; ● 1,200
Good Intent; RMC Place; WASHINGTON; ▲ West Finley; **225** WP-1; mail Claysville z 15323; ● 25
Goodmans Corners; RMC Place; VENANGO; ▲ Pinegrove; ***224** WH-6; mail Venus z 16364; rural
Goods Corner; RMC Place; CAMBRIA; ▲ East Taylor; ***225** WN-9; ★ **JNST**; mail Johnstown z 15901; ● 500
Good Spring; RMC Place; SCHUYLKILL; ▲ Porter; **227** EL-6; 🅿; z 17981; ● 90
Goodtown; RMC Place; SOMERSET; ▲ Brothersvalley; **225** WQ-8; mail Berlin z 15530; ● 20
Goodville; RMC Place; JUNIATA; ***227** EM-3; mail Thompsontown z 17094; rural
Goodville; RMC Place; LANCASTER; ▲ East Earl; **227** EO-8; 🅿; ★ **LANC**; z 17528; ● 300
Goodyear; RMC Place; CUMBERLAND; ▲ Dickinson; **227** EP-3; ★ **CARL**; mail Gardners z 17324; ● 100
Goosetown; RMC Place; CHESTER; ▲ East Fallowfield; ***227** EP-9; ★ **PHIL-**; mail Coatesville z 19320, Watsontown z 17777; ● 200
Gordon; Inc. Place; SCHUYLKILL; **227** EL-7; elev. 860ft./262m.; 🅿; ★ **PTSVL**; z 17936; ℗ 768; © 781
Gordonville; RMC Place; LANCASTER; ▲ Leacock; **227** EP-8; elev. 388ft./118m.; 🅿; ★ **LANC**; z 17529; ● 550
Goshen; RMC Place; CLEARFIELD; ▲ Goshen; ***224** WJ-11; elev. 1,466ft./447m.; mail Clearfield z 16830; rural
Goshen; MCD-Township; CLEARFIELD; ***224** WI-11; mail Clearfield z 16830; ℗ 346; © 496
Goshen; RMC Place; LANCASTER; ▲ Little Britain; ***227** EQ-8; mail Peach Bottom z 17563; rural
Goshenville; RMC Place; CHESTER; ▲ East Goshen; **227** EP-10; ★ **PHIL-**; mail West Chester z 19380; ● 150
Gosser Hill; RMC Place; WESTMORELAND; ▲ Allegheny; ***225** WL-5; ★ **PGH**; mail Leechburg z 15656; ● 200
Gottshalls; RMC Place; NORTHUMBERLAND; ▲ West Cameron; ***227** EL-5; mail Shamokin z 17872
Gouglersville; RMC Place; BERKS; ▲ Cumru; **227** EN-8; elev. 752ft./229m.; ★ **READ**; mail Reading z 19608; ● 200
Gouldsboro; RMC Place; WAYNE; ▲ Lehigh; **226** EI-11; 🅿; z 18424; ● 200
Gourley; RMC Place; BEAVER; ▲ Center; ***225** WL-2; elev. 1,100ft./335m.; ★ **PGH**; mail Monaca z 15061; ● 150
Gowen; RMC Place; LUZERNE; ▲ Black Creek; ***226** EJ-7; ★ **HAZ**; mail Nuremberg z 18241; rural
Gowen City; RMC Place; NORTHUMBERLAND; ▲ East Cameron; **227** EK-6; elev. 976ft./297m.; 🅿; z 17872; ● 220
Gracedale; RMC Place; LUZERNE; ***226** EI-9; ★ **SCR-**; mail Mountain Top z 18707
Graceton; RMC Place; INDIANA; ▲ Center; **225** WM-7; 🅿; z 15748; ● 250
Graceville; RMC Place; BEDFORD; ▲ East Providence; **225** WP-11; mail Everett z 15537; ● 50
Gracey; RMC Place; FULTON; ▲ Taylor; ***225** WO-12; mail Harrisonville z 17228; rural
Gradwohl Terrace; RMC Place; NORTHAMPTON; ▲ Bethlehem; ***227** EL-11; ★ **ALL-**; mail Bethlehem z 18020; ● 370
Gradyville; RMC Place; DELAWARE; ▲ Edgmont; **227** EP-11; 🅿; ★ **PHIL-**; z 19039; ● 500
Grafton; RMC Place; INDIANA; ▲ Black Lick; ***225** WM-7; elev. 980ft./299m.; mail Blairsville z 15717; ● 80
Graham; RMC Place; CLEARFIELD; ▲ Decatur; ***225** WK-11; mail Philipsburg z 16866; ● 80
Graham; MCD-Township; CLEARFIELD; ***224** WJ-12; mail Morrisdale z 16858; ℗ 1,231; © 1,236
Grampian; Inc. Place; CLEARFIELD; **224** WJ-10; elev. 1,560ft./475m.; 🅿; z 16838; ℗ 395; © 441
Grampian Hills; RMC Place; LYCOMING; ***226** EI-4; ★ **WMSPT**; mail Williamsport z 17701; pop. incl. with Williamsport (Inc. Place)
Grand Valley; RMC Place; WARREN; ▲ Eldred; **224** WF-6; 🅿; z 16420; ● 175
Grandview; RMC Place; ARMSTRONG; ▲ Rayburn; ***225** WK-6; ★ **PGH**; mail Kittanning z 16201; ● 80
Grandview; RMC Place; ELK; ***224** WH-10; elev. 1,800ft./549m.; mail Saint Marys z 15857; pop. incl. with Saint Marys (Inc. Place)
Grandview; RMC Place; INDIANA; ▲ White; ***225** WL-7; mail Indiana z 15701; ● 500
Grandview; RMC Place; WASHINGTON; ▲ Carroll; ***225** WO-4; ★ **PGH**; mail Monongahela z 15063; ● 120
Grandview Heights; RMC Place; LANCASTER; ▲ Manheim; ***227** EP-7; ★ **LANC**; mail Lancaster z 17601; ● 2,050
Grand View Heights; RMC Place; MONTGOMERY; ▲ East Norriton; ***227** EO-11; ★ **PHIL-**
Grandview Park; RMC Place; ELK; ***225** WM-10; mail Saint Marys z 15857
Grand View Park; RMC Place; MONTGOMERY; ▲ Lower Providence; ★ **PHIL-**; mail Collegeville z 19426
Grange; RMC Place; JEFFERSON; ▲ Perry; ***224** WJ-8; mail Punxsutawney z 15767; rural
Grange Center; RMC Place; CRAWFORD; ▲ Hayfield; ***224** WE-3; mail Saegertown z 16433; rural
Grangeville; RMC Place; YORK; ▲ Penn; ***227** EQ-4; ★ **HANV**; mail Hanover z 17331; ● 200
Granite (Granite Hill); RMC Place; ADAMS; ▲ Straban; ***227** EQ-3; mail Gettysburg z 17325; ● 25
Granite Hill; ADAMS; see Granite (RMC Place)
Grant; RMC Place; ELK; ▲ Benezette; ***224** WH-11; elev. 970ft./296m.; mail Benezett z 15821
Grant; MCD-Township; INDIANA; ***225** WK-8; mail Marion Center z 15759; ℗ 729; © 696
Grant City; RMC Place; LAWRENCE; ▲ Slippery Rock; ***224** WJ-3; elev. 1,261ft./384m.; ★ **PGH**; mail Portersville z 16051; rural
Grantham; RMC Place; CUMBERLAND; ▲ Upper Allen; **227** EO-4; 🅿 🅲 2,854; ★ **HRBG**; z 17027; ● 500
Grantley; CDP-Census Area Only; YORK; ▲ Spring Garden; ***227** EP-5; elev. 500ft./152m.; ★ **YORK**; mail York z 17403; ℗ 3,069; © 3,580
Grant Street; RMC Place; ALLEGHENY; ★ **PGH**; mail Pittsburgh z 15219; pop. incl. with Pittsburgh (Inc. Place)
Grantville; RMC Place; DAUPHIN; ▲ East Hanover; **227** EN-5; 🅿; ★ **HRBG**; z 17028; ● 230
Granville; MCD-Township; BRADFORD; ***226** EF-5; mail Granville Summit z 16926; ℗ 837; © 873
Granville; RMC Place; MIFFLIN; ▲ Granville; **227** EM-1; 🅿; z 17029; ● 200
Granville; MCD-Township; MIFFLIN; ***227** EM-1; 🅿; z 17029 & mail Lewistown z 17044; ℗ 5,090; © 4,895
Granville Center; RMC Place; BRADFORD; ▲ Granville; **226** EF-5; mail Granville Summit z 16926; ● 110
Granville Summit (Cowley); RMC Place; BRADFORD; ▲ Granville; **226** EF-5; 🅿; z 16926; ● 85
Grapeville; CDP; WESTMORELAND; ▲ Hempfield; ***225** WN-5; 🅿; ★ **PGH**; z 15634; © 676
Grassflat; RMC Place; CLEARFIELD; ▲ Cooper; **224** WJ-12; 🅿; z 16839; ● 700
Grassmere Park; RMC Place; COLUMBIA; ▲ Sugarloaf; **226** EH-7; mail Benton z 17814; ● 50
Grassy; RMC Place; LACKAWANNA; ***226** EG-10; ★ **SCR-**; mail Olyphant z 18447; pop. incl. with Olyphant (Inc. Place)
Graterford (Graters Ford); RMC Place; MONTGOMERY; ▲ Perkiomen; **227** EO-11; ★ **PHIL-**; mail Collegeville z 19426; ● 900
Graters Ford; MONTGOMERY; see Graterford (RMC Place)
Gratz; Inc. Place; DAUPHIN; **227** EL-5; elev. 800ft./244m.; 🅿; z 17030; ℗ 696; © 676
Gratztown; RMC Place; WESTMORELAND; ▲ Sewickley; ***225** WN-4; ★ **PGH**; mail West Newton z 15089; ● 140
Gravity; RMC Place; WAYNE; ▲ Lake; ***226** EG-11; elev. 1,513ft./461m.; ★ **SCR-**; mail Lake Ariel z 18436; ● 200
Gray (Gray Hampton); RMC Place; CLEARFIELD; ▲ Bradford; ***224** WJ-11; mail Woodland z 16881; rural
Gray; MCD-Township; GREENE; ***225** WP-2; mail Graysville z 15337; ℗ 220; © 236
Gray; RMC Place; SOMERSET; ▲ Jenner; **225** WO-8; 🅿; z 15544; ● 275
Graydon; RMC Place; YORK; ▲ North Hopewell; ***227** EQ-5; ★ **YORK**; mail Felton z 17322; ● 30
Gray Hampton; CLEARFIELD; see Gray (RMC Place)
Grays; RMC Place; WESTMORELAND; ▲ Derry; ***225** WN-7; elev. 1,141ft./348m.; ★ **LTROB**; mail Blairsville z 15717; ● 50
Grays Ferry; RMC Place; PHILADELPHIA; ★ **PHIL-**; pop. incl. with Philadelphia (Inc. Place)
Grays Landing; RMC Place; FAYETTE; ▲ Nicholson; ***225** WQ-4; 🅿; z 15461; ● 100
Graysville; RMC Place; GREENE; ▲ Gray; **225** WP-2; elev. 1,092ft./333m.; 🅿; z 15337; ● 160
Graysville; RMC Place; HUNTINGDON; ▲ Franklin; ***225** WL-12; mail Pennsylvania Furnace z 16865; rural
Grazier; RMC Place; SOMERSET; ▲ Conemaugh; ★ **JNST**; mail Hollsopple z 15935; ● 30
Grazierville; RMC Place; BLAIR; ▲ Snyder; **225** WL-11; ★ **ALT**; mail Tyrone z 16686; ● 300
Greason; RMC Place; CUMBERLAND; ▲ West Pennsboro; **227** EO-2; ★ **CARL**; mail Carlisle z 17013; ● 150
Great Belt; RMC Place; BUTLER; ▲ Jefferson; ***225** WK-4; ★ **BUTL**; mail Butler z 16001
Great Bend; Inc. Place; SUSQUEHANNA; **226** ED-9; elev. 881ft./269m.; 🅿; ★ **BING**; z 18821; ℗ 704; © 700
Great Bend; MCD-Township; SUSQUEHANNA; ***226** ED-9; 🅿; ★ **BING**; z 18821 & mail Hallstead z 18822; does not include the Borough of Great Bend; ℗ 1,817; © 1,890
Greater Point Marion; RMC Place; FAYETTE; ▲ Springhill; ***225** WQ-4; ★ **MORG**; mail Point Marion z 15474; ● 120
Greble; RMC Place; LEBANON; ▲ Bethel; **227** EM-7; ★ **LEB**; mail Myerstown z 17067; ● 100
Greece City; RMC Place; BUTLER; ▲ Concord; **224** WJ-4; elev. 1,101ft./336m.; mail Chicora z 16025; ● 40
Greeley; RMC Place; PIKE; ▲ Lackawaxen; **226** EG-13; 🅿; z 18425; ● 1,000
Green; MCD-Township; FOREST; ***224** WG-7; mail Tionesta z 16353; ℗ 335; © 397
Green; MCD-Township; INDIANA; ***225** WL-8; mail Cherry Tree z 15724; ℗ 4,095; © 3,995
Greenawalds; RMC Place; LEHIGH; ▲ South Whitehall; **226** EA-2; elev. 426ft./130m.; ★ **ALL-**; mail Allentown z 18104; ● 1,200
Greenbrae; RMC Place; ARMSTRONG; ▲ Manor; ***225** WK-6; ★ **PGH**; mail Kittanning z 16201; ● 50
Green Briar; RMC Place; JEFFERSON; ▲ Polk; ***224** WH-8; mail Brookville z 15825; rural
Greenbrier; RMC Place; CENTRE; ▲ Penn; ***227** EK-2; mail Spring Mills z 16875; rural
Greenbrier; RMC Place; DAUPHIN; ▲ South Hanover; ***227** EN-5; ★ **HRBG**; mail Hummelstown z 17036; ● 100
Greenbrier; RMC Place; NORTHUMBERLAND; ▲ Upper Mahanoy; ***227** EL-5; mail Rebuck z 17867; rural
Greenbrook; RMC Place; BUCKS; ▲ Bristol; ***227** EO-14; ★ **PHIL-**; mail Bristol z 19007
Greenburr; RMC Place; CLINTON; ▲ Logan; **226** EJ-2; mail Loganton z 17747; ● 130
Greencastle; Inc. Place; FRANKLIN; **225** WQ-14; elev. 595ft./181m.; 🅿; ★ **HAG**; z 17225; ℗ 3,600; © 3,722
Greencrest Park; RMC Place; MERCER; ▲ Pymatuning; ***224** WH-2; ★ **SHAR**; mail Greenville z 16125; ● 900
Greendale; RMC Place; MCKEAN; ▲ Wetmore; ***224** WF-9; mail Kane z 16735
Greendown Acres; RMC Place; BLAIR; ▲ Blair; ***225** WN-11; elev. 1,000ft./305m.; ★ **ALT**; mail Duncansville z 16635; ● 210
Greene; MCD-Township; BEAVER; ***225** WL-1; ★ **PGH**; mail Hookstown z 15050; ℗ 2,573; © 2,705
Greene; MCD-Township; CLINTON; ***226** EJ-2; mail Loganton z 17747; ℗ 1,153; © 1,464
Greene; MCD-Township; ERIE; ***224** WD-4; ★ **ERIE**; mail Erie z 16509; ℗ 4,959; © 4,768
Greene; MCD-Township; FRANKLIN; ***227** EP-1; mail Scotland z 17254; ℗ 11,930; © 12,284
Greene; MCD-Township; GREENE; ***225** WQ-3; mail Carmichaels z 15320; ℗ 494; © 445
Greene (Fairfield); RMC Place; LANCASTER; ▲ Drumore; ***227** EQ-7; mail Drumore z 17518; ● 90
Greene; MCD-Township; MERCER; ***224** WG-1; mail Jamestown z 16134; ℗ 1,247; © 1,153
Greene; MCD-Township; PIKE; ***226** EH-11; mail Greentown z 18426; ℗ 2,097; © 3,149
GREENE; **225** WQ-2; ℗ 39,550; © 40,672; ◆ 39,047
Greene Junction; RMC Place; FAYETTE; mail Connellsville z 15425; pop. incl. with South Connellsville (Inc. Place)
Greenfield; RMC Place; ALLEGHENY; ***225** WM-4; ★ **PGH**; mail Pittsburgh z 15207; pop. incl. with Pittsburgh (Inc. Place)
Greenfield; MCD-Township; BLAIR; ***225** WN-11; ★ **ALT**; mail Claysburg z 16625; ℗ 3,802; © 3,904
Greenfield; RMC Place; CAMBRIA; ▲ Gallitzin; ***225** WM-10; elev. 2,384ft./727m.; ★ **ALT**; mail Ashville z 16613; rural
Greenfield; MCD-Township; ERIE; ***224** WC-5; mail North East z 16428; ℗ 1,770; © 1,909
Greenfield (Greenfield Township); MCD-Township; LACKAWANNA; ***226** EF-10; ★ **SCR-**; mail Carbondale z 18407; ℗ 1,743; © 1,990
Greenfield; RMC Place; MERCER; ▲ Lackawannock; **224** WI-2; ★ **SHAR**; mail Mercer z 16137; ● 40
Greenfields; RMC Place; BERKS; ▲ Bern; ***227** EN-8; ★ **READ**; mail Reading z 19605; ● 1,400
Green Fields; RMC Place; DAUPHIN; ▲ Williams; mail Williamstown z 17098; ● 100
Greenfield Township; LACKAWANNA; see Greenfield (MCD-Township)
Green Garden; RMC Place; BEAVER; ▲ Raccoon; ***225** WL-2; ★ **PGH**; mail Aliquippa z 15001; rural
Green Grove; RMC Place; CENTRE; ▲ Gregg; ***227** EK-1; mail Spring Mills z 16875; rural
Green Grove; RMC Place; LACKAWANNA; ***226** EG-10; ★ **SCR-**; mail Olyphant z 18447; rural
Green Hill; RMC Place; CHESTER; ▲ West Goshen; ***227** EP-10; ★ **PHIL-**; mail West Chester z 19380; ● 200
Green Hill; RMC Place; YORK; ★ **YORK**
Green Hills; RMC Place; BERKS; ▲ Robeson; ***227** EN-9; ★ **READ**; mail Mohnton z 19540, Reading z 19607; rural
Green Hills; RMC Place; DELAWARE; ▲ Upper Darby; ***227** EQ-12; ★ **PHIL-**; mail Sharon Hill z 19079; pop. incl. with Folcroft (Inc. Place)
Green Hills; Inc. Place; WASHINGTON; ***225** WO-2; ★ **WASH**; mail Washington z 15301; ℗ 21; © 18
Green Lane; Inc. Place; MONTGOMERY; **227** EN-11; elev. 240ft./73m.; 🅿; ★ **PHIL-**; z 18054; ℗ 442; © 584
Green Lane Farms; RMC Place; YORK; ▲ Fairview; ***227** EO-4; ★ **HRBG**; mail Camp Hill z 17011; ● 1,100
Greenlawn Park (Bristol Terrace Number 1); RMC Place; BUCKS; ▲ Bristol; ***227** EO-14; ★ **PHIL-**; mail Bristol z 19007; ● 700
Greenmount; RMC Place; ADAMS; ▲ Cumberland; **227** EQ-3; mail Gettysburg z 17325; ● 70
Greenock; RMC Place; ALLEGHENY; ▲ Elizabeth; **228** N-9; 🅿; ★ **PGH**; z 15047; ● 2,400
Green Park; RMC Place; PERRY; ▲ Tyrone; **227** EN-2; 🅿; z 17024; rural
Green Point; RMC Place; LEBANON; ▲ Union; **227** EM-6; mail Jonestown z 17038; ● 75
Green Ridge; RMC Place; DELAWARE; ▲ Aston; ***227** EP-11; ★ **PHIL-**; mail Aston z 19014
Green Ridge; RMC Place; LACKAWANNA; ***226** EG-10; ★ **SCR-**; mail Scranton z 18509; pop. incl. with Scranton (Inc. Place)
Green Ridge; RMC Place; LUZERNE; ▲ Hazle; ***226** EJ-8; ★ **HAZ**; mail Hazleton z 18202; ● 250
Greenridge; RMC Place; WESTMORELAND; ▲ Hempfield; ***225** WN-5; ★ **PGH**; mail Irwin z 15642; ● 1,500
Greensboro; Inc. Place; GREENE; **225** WQ-4; elev. 805ft./245m.; 🅿; z 15338; ℗ 307; © 295
Greensburg; Inc. Place; ⊡ WESTMORELAND; **225** WN-6; elev. 1,099ft./335m.; 🅿 🅷 🅲 3,603 ■; ★ **PGH**; z 15601, z 15605-06; ℗ 16,318; © 15,889; ◆ 15,277
Greens Landing; RMC Place; BRADFORD; ▲ Athens; **226** EE-6; mail Athens z 18810; ● 400
Green Spring; RMC Place; CUMBERLAND; ▲ North Newton; ***227** EO-2; mail Newville z 17241
Green Springs; RMC Place; ADAMS; ▲ Berwick; ***227** EQ-4; ★ **HANV**; mail Hanover z 17331; ● 300
Greenstone; ADAMS; see Gladhill (RMC Place)
Greentown; RMC Place; PIKE; ▲ Greene; **226** EH-11; 🅿; z 18426; summer pop. 3,000; ● 1,000
Green Tree; Inc. Place; ALLEGHENY; **228** K-5; elev. 1,100ft./335m.; 🅿; ★ **PGH**; z 15242; ℗ 4,905; © 4,719
Green Tree; RMC Place; CHESTER; ▲ Willistown; **227** EP-11; ★ **PHIL-**; mail Malvern z 19355; ● 1,350
Green Valley; RMC Place; JEFFERSON; ▲ Knox; ***224** WJ-8; mail Brookville z 15825; rural
Green Village; RMC Place; FRANKLIN; ▲ Greene; **227** EP-1; mail Chambersburg z 17201; ● 400
Greenville; RMC Place; CLEARFIELD; ▲ Bloom; ***224** WJ-10; mail Grampian z 16838; rural
Greenville; Inc. Place; MERCER; **224** WG-2; elev. 940ft./287m.; 🅿 🅷 🅲 1,279; z 16125; ℗ 6,734; © 6,380
Greenville; MCD-Township; SOMERSET; ***225** WQ-8; mail Meyersdale z 15552; ℗ 664; © 718
Greenwald; RMC Place; WESTMORELAND; ▲ Hempfield; ***225** WN-6; ★ **PGH**; mail New Alexandria z 15670; ● 40
Greenwich; MCD-Township; BERKS; ***227** EL-9; mail Kutztown z 19530; ℗ 2,977; © 3,386
Greenwich; RMC Place; CAMBRIA; ▲ Susquehanna; ***225** WL-9; mail Northern Cambria z 15714; ● 80
Greenwich; RMC Place; PHILADELPHIA; pop. incl. with Philadelphia (Inc. Place)
Greenwood; RMC Place; BLAIR; ▲ Logan; **225** WM-11; ★ **ALT**; mail Altoona z 16602; ● 1,600
Greenwood; MCD-Township; CLEARFIELD; ***225** WK-10; mail Mahaffey z 15757; ℗ 415; © 424
Greenwood; RMC Place; COLUMBIA; ▲ Greenwood; **226** EI-6; elev. 796ft./243m.; mail Millville z 17846; ● 30
Greenwood; MCD-Township; COLUMBIA; ***226** EI-6; mail Orangeville z 17859; ℗ 1,972; © 1,932
Greenwood; MCD-Township; CRAWFORD; ***224** WG-3; mail Atlantic z 16111, Conneaut Lake z 16316; ℗ 1,361; © 1,487
Greenwood; RMC Place; FRANKLIN; ***227** EQ-1; mail Fayetteville z 17222; ● 150
Greenwood; MCD-Township; JUNIATA; ***227** EL-3; mail Thompsontown z 17094; ℗ 493; © 548
Greenwood; MCD-Township; PERRY; ***227** EM-3; mail Millerstown z 17062; ℗ 943; © 1,010
Greenwood Hills; RMC Place; DAUPHIN; ▲ Susquehanna; ***227** EO-5; ★ **HRBG**; mail Harrisburg z 17109, Middletown z 17057; ● 300
Greenwood Village; RMC Place; BUTLER; ▲ Butler; ***225** WK-4; ★ **BUTL**; mail Butler z 16001; ● 150
Gregg; RMC Place; ALLEGHENY; ▲ Collier; ***225** WM-3; ★ **PGH**; mail Oakdale z 15071; ● 35
Gregg; MCD-Township; CENTRE; ***227** EK-1; mail Spring Mills z 16875; ℗ 1,805; © 2,119
Gregg; MCD-Township; UNION; ***226** EI-4; mail Allenwood z 17810; ℗ 1,114; © 4,687
Gregory; RMC Place; LUZERNE; ***226** EH-8; ★ **SCR-**; mail Kingston z 18704; pop. incl. with Larksville (Inc. Place)
Grenoble; RMC Place; BUCKS; ▲ Northampton; ***227** EN-13; ★ **PHIL-**; mail Warminster z 18974; rural
Gresham; RMC Place; CRAWFORD; ▲ Oil Creek; **224** WF-5; mail Titusville z 16354; ● 75
Greshville; RMC Place; BERKS; ▲ Douglass; ***227** EN-10; mail Boyertown z 19512; ● 50
Gretna; RMC Place; WASHINGTON; ▲ Chartiers; ***225** WN-2; ★ **WASH**; mail Washington z 15301; rural
Grey Nuns; RMC Place; BUCKS; ▲ Lower Makefield; ***227** EN-13; ★ **PHIL-**; mail Morrisville z 19067; ● 400
Grier City; RMC Place; SCHUYLKILL; ▲ Rush; ***227** EK-8; mail Barnesville z 18214; ● 300
Grier City-Park Crest; CDP-Census Area Only; SCHUYLKILL; ***227** EK-8; ★ **PTSVL**; © 954
Griesemersville; RMC Place; BERKS; ▲ Oley; ***227** EN-9; ★ **READ**; mail Boyertown z 19512; rural
Griffiths; RMC Place; MCKEAN; ▲ Hamlin; ***224** WF-9; mail Kane z 16735; rural
Grill; RMC Place; BERKS; ▲ Cumru; **227** ET-12; ★ **READ**; mail Reading z 19607; ● 750
Grimesville; RMC Place; LYCOMING; ▲ Old Lycoming; ***226** EI-3; ★ **WMSPT**; mail Williamsport z 17701; ● 250
Grimms Crossroads; RMC Place; YORK; ▲ Windsor; ***227** EQ-6; elev. 800ft./244m.; ★ **YORK**; mail Red Lion z 17356; rural
Grimville; RMC Place; BERKS; ▲ Greenwich; **227** EL-9; mail Kutztown z 19530; ● 20
Grindstone; RMC Place; FAYETTE; ▲ Redstone, Jefferson; **225** WP-4; 🅿; ★ **PGH**; z 15442; ● 600
Grindstone-Rowes Run; CDP-Census Area Only; FAYETTE; ▲ Jefferson, Redstone; ***225** WP-4; elev. 1,100ft./335m.; ★ **UNTN**; mail Grindstone z 15442; ℗ 1,041; © 1,141
Gringo; RMC Place; BEAVER; ▲ Hopewell; ***225** WL-2; ★ **PGH**; mail Aliquippa z 15001; ● 600
Grisemore; RMC Place; INDIANA; ▲ Pine, Green; ***225** WL-9; mail Clymer z 15728; rural
Groffdale; RMC Place; LANCASTER; ▲ Leacock, Earl; **227** EO-8; elev. 495ft./151m.; ★ **LANC**; mail New Holland z 17557; ● 125
Grovania; RMC Place; COLUMBIA; ▲ Cooper; ***226** EJ-6; mail Danville z 17821
Grove; MCD-Township; CAMERON; ***224** WH-13; mail Sinnamahoning z 15861; ℗ 168; © 129
Grove; RMC Place; CHESTER; ▲ West Whiteland; ***227** EP-10; elev. 522ft./159m.; ★ **PHIL-**; mail West Chester z 19380; ● 250
Grove Chapel; RMC Place; INDIANA; ▲ Rayne; ***225** WL-8; mail Indiana z 15701; rural
Grove City; Inc. Place; MERCER; **224** WI-3; elev. 1,246ft./380m.; 🅿 🅷 🅲 2,473; z 16127; ℗ 8,240; © 8,024
Grover; RMC Place; BRADFORD; ▲ Canton; **226** EF-4; 🅿; z 17735; ● 200
Groveton; RMC Place; ALLEGHENY; ▲ Robinson; **228** I-3; ★ **PGH**; mail Coraopolis z 15108; ● 500
Grugan; MCD-Township; CLINTON; ***226** EH-1; mail Lock Haven z 17745; ℗ 52; © 52
Gruversville; RMC Place; BUCKS; ▲ Springfield; ***227** EM-11; ★ **ALL-**; mail Coopersburg z 18036; rural
Gruvertown; RMC Place; NORTHAMPTON; ▲ Lower Mount Bethel; ***227** EK-12; elev. 673ft./205m.; ★ **ALL-**; mail Bangor z 18013; rural
Guenot Settlement; RMC Place; CLEARFIELD; ▲ Girard; ***224** WJ-12; elev. 1,262ft./385m.; mail Frenchville z 16836; rural
Guernsey; RMC Place; ADAMS; ▲ Butler; ***227** EP-3; mail Biglerville z 17307; rural
Guffey; RMC Place; MCKEAN; ▲ Lafayette, Hamlin; ***224** WF-10; mail Mount Jewett z 16740; rural
Guffey; RMC Place; WESTMORELAND; ▲ Sewickley; ***225** WN-5; ★ **PGH**; mail Irwin z 15642; ● 100
Guilford; CDP; FRANKLIN; ▲ Guilford, Greene; ***227** EQ-1; mail Chambersburg z 17201; ℗ 1,618; © 1,835
Guilford; MCD-Township; FRANKLIN; ***227** EQ-1; mail Chambersburg z 17201; ℗ 11,893; © 13,100
Guilford Hills; RMC Place; FRANKLIN; ▲ Guilford, Greene; ***227** EP-1; elev. 800ft./244m.; mail Chambersburg z 17201; ● 800
Guilford Springs; RMC Place; FRANKLIN; ▲ Guilford; ***225** WQ-14; mail Chambersburg z 17201; ● 75
Guitonville; RMC Place; FOREST; ▲ Green; **224** WG-7; elev. 1,695ft./517m.; mail Marienville z 16239; ● 50
Guldens; RMC Place; ADAMS; ▲ Straban; ***227** EQ-3; mail Gettysburg z 17325
Gulich; MCD-Township; CLEARFIELD; ***225** WK-11; mail Smithmill z 16680; ℗ 1,192; © 1,275
Gulph; RMC Place; MONTGOMERY; ★ **PHIL-**; mail King of Prussia z 19406
Gulph Mills; RMC Place; MONTGOMERY; ▲ Upper Merion; **228** B-1; 🅿; ★ **PHIL-**; z 19428; ● 450
Gump; RMC Place; GREENE; ▲ Whiteley; ***225** WQ-3; mail Spraggs z 15362; rural
Gum Tree; RMC Place; CHESTER; ▲ Highland; ***227** EP-9; elev. 550ft./168m.; mail Coatesville z 19320
Guth; RMC Place; LEHIGH; ▲ South Whitehall; ***227** EL-10; ★ **ALL-**; mail Allentown z 18104; ● 100
Guthriesville; RMC Place; CHESTER; ▲ East Brandywine; ***227** EP-9; ★ **PHIL-**; mail Downingtown z 19335; ● 120
Guthsville; RMC Place; LEHIGH; ▲ South Whitehall; ***227** EL-10; ★ **ALL-**; mail Orefield z 18069; ● 100
Guys Mills; CDP; CRAWFORD; ▲ Randolph; **224** WF-4; 🅿; z 16327; © 133
Gwynedd; RMC Place; MONTGOMERY; ▲ Lower Gwynedd; **227** EO-12; 🅿; ★ **PHIL-**; z 19436, z 19454; ● 600
Gwynedd Square; RMC Place; MONTGOMERY; ▲ Upper Gwynedd; ***227** EO-11; ★ **PHIL-**; mail Lansdale z 19446; rural
Gwynedd Valley; RMC Place; MONTGOMERY; ▲ Lower Gwynedd; ***227** EO-12; 🅿 🅲 2,727; ★ **PHIL-**; z 19437; ● 650

H

Haafsville; RMC Place; LEHIGH; ▲ Upper Macungie; ***227** EL-10; ★ **ALL-**; mail Breinigsville z 18031; ● 20
Habrenfield Hills; RMC Place; LUZERNE; ▲ Dallas; ***226** EH-8; elev. 1,300ft./396m.; ★ **SCR-**; mail Dallas z 18612; ● 400
Hackelbernie; RMC Place; CARBON; mail Jim Thorpe z 18229; pop. incl. with Jim Thorpe (Inc. Place)
Hackett; RMC Place; WASHINGTON; ▲ Union, Peters; ***225** WN-3; ★ **PGH**; mail Venetia z 15367; ● 300
Haddenville; RMC Place; FAYETTE; ▲ Menallen; ***225** WP-4; elev. 1,230ft./375m.; ★ **UNTN**; mail Uniontown z 15401; ● 60
Haddock; RMC Place; SCHUYLKILL; ▲ Kline; **227** EK-8; ★ **HAZ**; mail Hazleton z 18201, McAdoo z 18237; ● 200
Hadley; RMC Place; MERCER; ▲ Perry; **224** WG-3; 🅿; z 16130; ● 180
Hagersville; RMC Place; BUCKS; ▲ East Rockhill, Bedminster; ***227** EM-12; ★ **PHIL-**; mail Perkasie z 18944
Hahnstown; RMC Place; LANCASTER; ▲ Ephrata; ***227** EO-8; ★ **LANC**; mail Ephrata z 17522; ● 180
Hahntown; RMC Place; WESTMORELAND; ▲ North Huntingdon; ***225** WN-5; ★ **PGH**; mail Irwin z 15642; ● 400
Haines; MCD-Township; CENTRE; ***227** EK-2; mail Woodward z 16882; ℗ 1,315; © 1,479
Haines Acres; RMC Place; YORK; ▲ Springettsbury; ***227** EP-5; ★ **YORK**; mail York z 17402; ● 1,000
Haleeka; RMC Place; LYCOMING; ▲ Hepburn; ***226** EH-3; ★ **WMSPT**; mail Cogan Station z 17728; ● 25
Halfmoon; MCD-Township; CENTRE; ***225** WK-12; mail Warriors Mark z 16877; ℗ 1,469; © 2,357
Halford Hills; RMC Place; MONTGOMERY; ▲ West Norriton; ★ **PHIL-**; mail Norristown z 19401
Halfville; RMC Place; LANCASTER; ▲ Penn, Elizabeth; ***227** EO-7; elev. 565ft./172m.; ★ **LANC**; mail Lititz z 17543; ● 80
Halfway; RMC Place; LEBANON; ▲ North Lebanon; ***227** EN-7; ★ **LEB**; mail Lebanon z 17042; ● 80
Halfway House; CDP-Census Area Only; MONTGOMERY; ▲ Upper Pottsgrove; ***227** EN-10; ★ **PTSTN**; mail Pottstown z 19464; ℗ 1,415; © 1,823
Halifax; Inc. Place; DAUPHIN; **227** EM-4; elev. 380ft./116m.; 🅿; ★ **HRBG**; z 17032; ℗ 911; © 875
Halifax; MCD-Township; DAUPHIN; ***227** EM-4; 🅿; ★ **HRBG**; z 17032; does not include the Borough of Halifax; ℗ 3,449; © 3,329
Hall; RMC Place; ALLEGHENY; ***225** WM-4; ★ **PGH**; pop. incl. with Monroeville (Inc. Place)
Hallam (Hellam); Inc. Place; YORK; **227** EP-6; elev. 380ft./116m.; 🅿; ★ **YORK**; z 17406; ℗ 1,375; © 1,532
Hallowell; RMC Place; MONTGOMERY; ▲ Horsham; ***227** EO-12; ★ **PHIL-**; mail Horsham z 19044
Halls; RMC Place; LYCOMING; ▲ Muncy; ***226** EI-5; ★ **WMSPT**; mail Muncy z 17756; rural
Hallstead; Inc. Place; SUSQUEHANNA; **226** ED-9; elev. 890ft./271m.; 🅿; ★ **BING**; z 18822; ℗ 1,274; © 1,216
Hallston; RMC Place; BUTLER; ▲ Brady; ***224** WJ-4; mail Slippery Rock z 16057; rural
Hallton; RMC Place; ELK; ▲ Spring Creek; **224** WH-8; elev. 1,296ft./395m.; 🅿; z 15860; ● 30
Hallwood; RMC Place; LUZERNE; ▲ Hunlock; ***226** EI-8; elev. 965ft./294m.; ★ **SCR-**; mail Hunlock Creek z 18621; rural
Halsey; RMC Place; MCKEAN; ▲ Sergeant; ***224** WF-10; mail Kane z 16735; rural
Hamburg; Inc. Place; BERKS; **227** EM-8; elev. 373ft./114m.; 🅿; z 19526; ℗ 3,987; © 4,114
Hametown; RMC Place; YORK; ▲ Shrewsbury; **227** EQ-5; elev. 980ft./299m.; ★ **BAL**; mail Glen Rock z 17327; ● 80
Hamilton; MCD-Township; ADAMS; ***227** EQ-4; ★ **HANV**; mail East Berlin z 17316; ℗ 1,760; © 2,044
Hamilton; MCD-Township; FRANKLIN; ***225** WQ-14; mail Chambersburg z 17201; ℗ 7,745; © 8,949
Hamilton; RMC Place; JEFFERSON; ▲ Perry; **224** WJ-8; 🅿; z 15744; ● 125
Hamilton; MCD-Township; MCKEAN; ***224** WE-9; mail Kane z 16735; ℗ 612; © 637
Hamilton; MCD-Township; MONROE; ***227** EK-11; mail Sciota z 18354; ℗ 6,681; © 8,235
Hamilton (East Sunbury); RMC Place; NORTHUMBERLAND; ▲ Upper Augusta; ***227** EK-5; mail Sunbury z 17801; ● 150
Hamilton; MCD-Township; TIOGA; ***226** EF-4; mail Blossburg z 16912; ℗ 496; © 462
Hamiltonban; MCD-Township; ADAMS; ***227** EQ-2; mail Gettysburg z 17325; ℗ 1,872; © 2,216
Hamilton Heights; RMC Place; FRANKLIN; ▲ Hamilton; ***225** WP-14; elev. 700ft./213m.; mail Chambersburg z 17201; ● 350
Hamilton Park; RMC Place; LANCASTER; ▲ Lancaster; **227** ET-8; ★ **LANC**; mail Lancaster z 17603; ● 3,500
Hamlin; RMC Place; LEBANON; ▲ Bethel; **227** EM-7; elev. 549ft./167m.; ★ **LEB**; mail Fredericksburg z 17026; ● 85
Hamlin; MCD-Township; MCKEAN; ***224** WF-10; mail Hazel Hurst z 16733; ℗ 822; © 819
Hamlin; RMC Place; WAYNE; ▲ Salem; **226** EH-11; 🅿; ★ **SCR-**; z 18427; ● 1,100
Hammersley Fork; RMC Place; CLINTON; ▲ Leidy; ***224** WG-13; elev. 923ft./281m.; mail Renovo z 17764; rural
Hammett; RMC Place; ERIE; ▲ Greene; ***224** WD-4; ★ **ERIE**; mail Erie z 16510
Hammond; RMC Place; TIOGA; ▲ Middlebury; ***226** EE-3; mail Tioga z 16946; rural
Hammondville; RMC Place; FAYETTE; ▲ Bullskin; ***225** WO-6; mail Mount Pleasant z 15666; ● 75
Hamorton; RMC Place; CHESTER; ▲ Kennett; **227** EQ-10; ★ **PHIL-**; mail Kennett Square z 19348; ● 100
Hampden; RMC Place; BERKS; ★ **READ**; mail Reading z 19604; pop. incl. with Reading (Inc. Place)
Hampden (Hampden Township); MCD-Township; CUMBERLAND; ***227** EO-4; ★ **HRBG**; mail Mechanicsburg z 17050, z 17055; ℗ 20,384; © 24,135; ◆ 27,214
Hampden Heights; RMC Place; BERKS; ★ **READ**; mail Reading z 19604; pop. incl. with Reading (Inc. Place)
Hampden Township; CUMBERLAND; see Hampden (MCD-Township)
Hampshire Heights; RMC Place; WESTMORELAND; ▲ Hempfield; ***225** WN-6; ★ **PGH**; mail Greensburg z 15601; ● 400
Hampton; CDP; ADAMS; ▲ Reading; **227** EP-4; elev. 550ft./168m.; mail New Oxford z 17350; © 633
Hampton; MCD-Township; ALLEGHENY; ***225** WL-4; ★ **PGH**; mail Allison Park z 15101, Wildwood z 15091; ℗ 15,568; © 17,526
Hampton Station; RMC Place; VENANGO; ▲ Pinegrove; ***224** WH-6; elev. 1,446ft./441m.; mail Oil City z 16301; rural
Hampton Township; CDP-Census Area Only; ALLEGHENY; ▲ Hampton; ***225** WL-4; elev. 1,100ft./335m.; ★ **PGH**; mail Allison Park z 15101, Wildwood z 15091; ℗ 15,568; © 17,526
Hancock; RMC Place; BERKS; ▲ Longswamp; ***227** EM-10; elev. 472ft./144m.; mail Mertztown z 19539; ● 125
Haneyville; RMC Place; CLINTON, LYCOMING; ▲ McHenry, Gallagher; ***226** EH-2; mail Lock Haven z 17745
Hankey Farms; RMC Place; ALLEGHENY; ▲ North Fayette; ***225** WM-3; elev. 1,100ft./335m.; ★ **PGH**; mail Oakdale z 15071; ● 900
Hanlin; RMC Place; WASHINGTON; ▲ Jefferson; ***225** WN-1; mail Burgettstown z 15021; ● 25
Hannah; RMC Place; CENTRE; ▲ Taylor; ***225** WK-12; elev. 1,053ft./321m.; mail Port Matilda z 16870; rural
Hannahstown; RMC Place; BUTLER; ▲ Jefferson; **225** WK-5; ★ **PGH**; mail Cabot z 16023; ● 80
Hannastown; RMC Place; WESTMORELAND; ▲ Hempfield; **225** WN-6; 🅿; ★ **PGH**; z 15635; ● 350
Hannaville; RMC Place; VENANGO; ▲ Canal; **224** WG-4; mail Cochranton z 16314; ● 60
Hann Hill; RMC Place; MERCER; ***224** WI-2; elev. 1,160ft./354m.; ★ **SHAR**; mail West Middlesex z 16159; pop. incl. with Hermitage (Inc. Place)
Hanover; MCD-Township; BEAVER; ***225** WM-2; ★ **PGH**; mail Georgetown z 15043, Hookstown z 15050; ℗ 3,470; © 3,529
Hanover; MCD-Township; LEHIGH; ***227** EL-11; ★ **ALL-**; mail Allentown z 18103; ℗ 2,243; © 1,913
Hanover; RMC Place; LUZERNE; ***226** EI-8; ★ **SCR-**; mail Nanticoke z 18634; pop. incl. with Nanticoke (Inc. Place)
Hanover (Hanover Township); MCD-Township; LUZERNE; ***226** EI-9; ★ **SCR-**; mail Wilkes Barre z 18702, z 18706; ℗ 12,050; © 11,488
Hanover; RMC Place; NORTHAMPTON; ▲ Hanover; **226** EA-4; ★ **ALL-**; mail Bethlehem z 18017; ● 800
Hanover; MCD-Township; NORTHAMPTON; ***227** EL-11; ★ **ALL-**; mail Bethlehem z 18017; ℗ 7,176; © 9,563
Hanover; MCD-Township; WASHINGTON; ***225** WM-2; mail Burgettstown z 15021; ℗ 2,883; © 2,795
Hanover; Inc. Place; YORK; **227** EQ-4; elev. 609ft./186m.; 🅿 🅷 ■; ★ **HANV**; z 17331-33; ℗ 14,399; © 14,535; ◆ 14,898
Hanoverdale; RMC Place; DAUPHIN; ▲ West Hanover; ***227** EN-5; ★ **HRBG**; mail Hummelstown z 17036
Hanover Green; RMC Place; LUZERNE; ▲ Hanover; ***226** EI-8; ★ **SCR-**; mail Wilkes Barre z 18706; ● 700
Hanover Heights; RMC Place; CHESTER; ▲ North Coventry; ***227** EO-10; ★ **PTSTN**; mail Pottstown z 19464; ● 400
Hanover Hills; RMC Place; DAUPHIN; ▲ South Hanover; ***227** EN-5; ★ **HRBG**; mail Hummelstown z 17036; ● 160
Hanover Junction; RMC Place; YORK; ▲ North Codorus; ***227** EQ-5; ★ **YORK**; mail Seven Valleys z 17360; ● 60
Hanover Township; LUZERNE; see Hanover (MCD-Township)
Happy Valley; RMC Place; LUZERNE; ***226** EH-9; ★ **SCR-**; mail Elysburg z 17824, Pittston z 18643; pop. incl. with Exeter (Inc. Place)
Harbor; RMC Place; LAWRENCE; ▲ Union; ***224** WJ-2; ★ **YNGS-**; mail New Castle z 16101; rural
Harborcreek; RMC Place; ERIE; ▲ Harborcreek; **224** WC-4; 🅿; ★ **ERIE**; z 16421; ● 1,500
Harborcreek; MCD-Township; ERIE; ***224** WC-4; 🅿; ★ **ERIE**; z 16421; ℗ 15,108; © 15,178; ® 16,267
Harding; RMC Place; LUZERNE; ▲ Exeter; **226** EA-10; 🅿; ★ **SCR-**; z 18643; ● 400
Hardy Hill; RMC Place; FAYETTE; ▲ Dunbar; ***225** WP-5; elev. 1,200ft./366m.; mail Dunbar z 15431; rural
Harford; RMC Place; SUSQUEHANNA; ▲ Harford; **226** EE-10; 🅿; z 18823; ● 250
Harford; MCD-Township; SUSQUEHANNA; ***226** EF-9; 🅿; z 18823; ℗ 1,100; © 1,301
Harford Heights; RMC Place; WESTMORELAND; ▲ North Huntingdon; ***225** WN-5; ★ **PGH**; mail Irwin z 15642; ● 700
Harkness; RMC Place; BRADFORD; ▲ Springfield; ***226** EE-5; mail Columbia Cross Roads z 16914; rural
Harlan; RMC Place; CLARION, JEFFERSON; ▲ Clover, Limestone; ***224** WI-7; mail Corsica z 15829; rural
Harlansburg; RMC Place; LAWRENCE; ▲ Scott; **224** WJ-3; ★ **PGH**; mail New Castle z 16101; ● 300
Harleigh; RMC Place; LUZERNE; ▲ Hazle; **226** EJ-8; 🅿; ★ **HAZ**; z 18225; ● 275
Harlem; RMC Place; BERKS; ▲ Hereford; ***227** EM-10; elev. 773ft./236m.; mail Barto z 19504, Macungie z 18062; ● 60
Harleysville; CDP; MONTGOMERY; ▲ Lower Salford, Franconia; **227** EN-11; 🅿; ★ **PHIL-**; z 19438, z 19441; ℗ 7,405; © 8,795
Harmar; MCD-Township; ALLEGHENY; ***225** WM-4; ★ **PGH**; mail Cheswick z 15024; ℗ 3,144; © 3,242
Harmar Heights; RMC Place; ALLEGHENY; ▲ Harmar; **228** H-9; ★ **PGH**; mail Cheswick z 15024; ● 1,050
Harmarville; RMC Place; ALLEGHENY; ▲ Harmar; **228** H-8; ★ **PGH**; mail Pittsburgh z 15238; ● 1,100
Harmonsburg; CDP; CRAWFORD; ▲ Summit; **224** WF-2; 🅿; z 16422; © 356
Harmonville; RMC Place; MONTGOMERY; ▲ Whitemarsh; ***227** EO-12; ★ **PHIL-**; mail Conshohocken z 19428; ● 1,500
Harmony; MCD-Township; BEAVER; ***225** WL-3; ★ **PGH**; mail Ambridge z 15003; ℗ 3,694; © 3,373
Harmony; Inc. Place; BUTLER; **225** WK-3; elev. 925ft./282m.; 🅿; ★ **PGH**; z 16037; ℗ 1,054; © 937
Harmony; RMC Place; CLEARFIELD; ▲ Burnside; ***225** WK-9; mail Westover z 16692; rural
Harmony; MCD-Township; FOREST; ***224** WG-6; mail West Hickory z 16370; ℗ 499; © 511
Harmony; RMC Place; JEFFERSON; ▲ Young; ***224** WJ-8; mail Punxsutawney z 15767; ● 40
Harmony; MCD-Township; SUSQUEHANNA; ***226** ED-10; mail Susquehanna z 18847; ℗ 544; © 558
Harmony Grove; RMC Place; YORK; ▲ Dover; ***227** EP-4; ★ **YORK**; mail Dover z 17315; ● 150
Harmony Hill; RMC Place; CHESTER; ▲ East Bradford; ***227** EP-10; ★ **PHIL-**; mail Downingtown z 19335; ● 75
Harmony Junction; RMC Place; BUTLER; ***225** WK-3; ★ **PGH**; mail Harmony z 16037; ● 75
Harmony Township; CDP-Census Area Only; BEAVER; ▲ Harmony; ***225** WL-3; ★ **PGH**; mail Ambridge z 15003, Baden z 15005; ℗ 3,694; © 3,373
Harmonyville; RMC Place; CHESTER; ▲ Warwick; ***227** EO-10; elev. 491ft./150m.; ★ **PHIL-**; mail Pottstown z 19464; ● 110
Harnedsville; RMC Place; SOMERSET; ▲ Lower Turkeyfoot; **225** WQ-6; mail Confluence z 15424; ● 90
Harpers; RMC Place; NORTHAMPTON; ▲ Lehigh; ***227** EK-10; ★ **ALL-**; mail Walnutport z 18088; rural
Harper Tavern; RMC Place; LEBANON; ▲ East Hanover; **227** EN-6; mail Annville z 17003; ● 50
Harper Village; RMC Place; ALLEGHENY; ▲ Crescent; ***225** WL-2; elev. 1,166ft./355m.; ★ **PGH**; mail Aliquippa z 15001; ● 200
Harris; MCD-Township; CENTRE; ***225** WK-14; ★ **STCOL**; mail Boalsburg z 16827; ℗ 4,167; © 4,657
Harris Acres; RMC Place; CENTRE; ▲ Harris, College; ***225** WK-13; ★ **STCOL**; mail State College z 16801; ● 900
Harrisburg; Inc. Place; **STATE CAPITAL**; ⊡ DAUPHIN; **227** EN-4; elev. 360ft./110m.; 🅿 🅷 ■; ★ **HRBG**; z 17101-13, z 17120-30, z 17140, z 17177; ℗ 52,376; © 48,950; ◆ 47,259
Harrison; MCD-Township; ALLEGHENY; ***225** WL-5; ★ **PGH**; mail Natrona Heights z 15065; ℗ 11,763; © 10,934
Harrison; MCD-Township; BEDFORD; ***225** WP-10; mail Buffalo Mills z 15534; ℗ 967; © 1,007
Harrison; MCD-Township; POTTER; ***226** ED-1; mail Harrison Valley z 16927, Westfield z 16950; ℗ 1,129; © 1,093
Harrison City; CDP; WESTMORELAND; ▲ Penn; **225** WN-5; 🅿; ★ **PGH**; z 15636; © 155
Harrison Township; CDP-Census Area Only; ALLEGHENY; ▲ Harrison; **225** WL-5; elev. 985ft./300m.; 🅷 ■; ★ **PGH**; mail Natrona Heights z 15065; ℗ 11,763; © 10,934; ◆ 10,315
Harrison Valley; RMC Place; POTTER; ▲ Harrison; **224** WD-14; elev. 1,622ft./494m.; 🅿; z 16927 & mail Westfield z 16950; ● 250
Harrisonville; RMC Place; FULTON; ▲ Licking Creek; **225** WP-12; 🅿; z 17228; ● 50
Harristown; RMC Place; LANCASTER; ▲ Paradise; ***227** EP-8; mail Paradise z 17562; rural
Harrisville; BUTLER; see Forestville (RMC Place)
Harrisville; Inc. Place; BUTLER; **224** WI-4; elev. 1,313ft./400m.; 🅿; z 16038; ℗ 862; © 883
Harrity; RMC Place; CARBON; ▲ Franklin; ***227** EK-10; elev. 485ft./148m.; mail Lehighton z 18235; rural
Harrow; RMC Place; BUCKS; ▲ Nockamixon; ***227** EM-12; ★ **PHIL-**; mail Ottsville z 18942
Harshaville; RMC Place; BEAVER; ▲ Hanover; ***225** WM-2; elev. 992ft./302m.; ★ **PGH**; mail Clinton z 15026
Hartfield; TIOGA; see Hartsfield (RMC Place)
Hartleton; Inc. Place; UNION; **227** EK-3; elev. 640ft./195m.; 🅿; z 17829; ℗ 246; © 260
Hartley; MCD-Township; UNION; ***227** EK-3; mail Laurelton z 17835; ℗ 1,896; © 1,714
Hartranft; RMC Place; MONTGOMERY; ▲ East Norriton; ★ **PHIL-**; mail Norristown z 19401
Hartsfield (Hartfield); RMC Place; TIOGA; ▲ Liberty; ***226** EG-3; mail Liberty z 16930; rural
Hartstown; CDP; CRAWFORD; ▲ West Fallowfield; **224** WG-2; 🅿; z 16131; © 246
Hartsville; RMC Place; BUCKS; ▲ Warwick; **227** EN-12; 🅿; ★ **PHIL-**; z 18974; ● 700
Harveys Lake; Inc. Place; LUZERNE; **226** EH-8; elev. 1,287ft./392m.; 🅿; ★ **SCR-**; z 18618; ℗ 2,746; © 2,888
Harveyville; CHESTER; see Wilmer (RMC Place)
Harveyville; RMC Place; LUZERNE; ▲ Huntington; **226** EI-7; elev. 794ft./242m.; mail Shickshinny z 18655; ● 50
Harwick; RMC Place; ALLEGHENY; ▲ Springdale; **228** H-9; 🅿; ★ **PGH**; z 15049; ● 1,100
Harwood (Harwood Mines); RMC Place; LUZERNE; ▲ Hazle; **226** EJ-8; ★ **HAZ**; mail Hazleton z 18202; ● 420
Harwood Mines; LUZERNE; see Harwood (RMC Place)
Hasentab's; RMC Place; BLAIR; ▲ Freedom; ***225** WN-10; elev. 1,094ft./333m.; ★ **ALT**; mail Duncansville z 16635; rural
Hasson Heights; CDP-Census Area Only; VENANGO; ▲ Cornplanter; ***224** WG-5; ★ **OILC-F**; mail Oil City z 16301; ℗ 1,610; © 1,495
Hastings; Inc. Place; CAMBRIA; **225** WL-9; elev. 1,840ft./561m.; 🅿; z 16646; ℗ 1,431; © 1,398
Hatboro; Inc. Place; MONTGOMERY; **227** EO-12; elev. 250ft./76m.; 🅿 ■; ★ **PHIL-**; z 19040; ℗ 7,382; © 7,393; ◆ 7,158
Hatfield; RMC Place; FAYETTE; ▲ South Union; ***225** WQ-5; ★ **UNTN**; mail Uniontown z 15401; ● 125
Hatfield; Inc. Place; MONTGOMERY; **227** EN-11; elev. 340ft./104m.; 🅿 🅲 340; ★ **PHIL-**; z 19440; ℗ 2,650; © 2,605
Hatfield; MCD-Township; MONTGOMERY; ***227** EN-12; 🅿 🅲 340; ★ **PHIL-**; z 19440; does not include the Borough of Hatfield; ℗ 15,357; © 16,712
Hauto; RMC Place; CARBON; ***227** EK-9; mail Nesquehoning z 18240; pop. incl. with Nesquehoning (Inc. Place)
Haverford; MCD-Township; DELAWARE; ***227** EP-12; ★ **PHIL-**; mail Havertown z 19083; ℗ 49,848; © 48,498; ® 49,608; ◆ 47,791
Haverford; RMC Place; MONTGOMERY, DELAWARE; ▲ Lower Merion, Haverford; **228** C-2; 🅿 🅷 🅲 1,168; ★ **PHIL-**; z 19041; ● 6,000
Havertown; RMC Place; DELAWARE; ▲ Haverford; **228** D-1; 🅿 🅷; ★ **PHIL-**; z 19083; ● 30,000

Entries in **UPPERCASE** are counties.
Entries in **bold** have populations of 2,500 or more.
Names in parentheses are alternate names.

Inc. Place	Incorporated Place
RMC Place	Rand McNally Designated Place
CDP	Census Designated Place
MCD	Minor Civil Division

⊡	County Seat
▲	Minor Civil Division
elev.	Elevation
🅿	Post Office
🅷	Hospital
🅲	College
■	Principal Business Center
★	Ranally Metro Area (RMA) Abbreviation
z	Zip Code(s)
℗	Previous Census Population
®	Revised Census Population
Ⓐ	Annexation Population
●	Rand McNally Population Estimate
©	Final Census Population
Ⓢ	Special Census Population
◆	Estimated Population

For additional definitions see Glossary, Volume 1, and Introduction, Volume 2.

Hawkeye; RMC Place; WESTMORELAND; ▲ East Huntingdon; ***225** WO-5; mail Scottdale z 15683; ● 40
Hawk Run; RMC Place; CLEARFIELD; ▲ Morris; **224** WJ-12; 🅿; z 16840; ● 900
Hawksville; RMC Place; LANCASTER; ▲ Eden; ***227** EP-8; elev. 529ft./161m.; mail Quarryville z 17566; ● 90
Hawley; Inc. Place; WAYNE; **226** EG-12; elev. 920ft./280m.; 🅿; z 18428, z 18438; Ⓟ 1,244; © 1,303
Hawleywood; RMC Place; WAYNE; ▲ Paupack; ***226** EG-12; elev. 1,300ft./396m.; mail Hawley z 18428; ● 200
Hawstone; RMC Place; MIFFLIN; ▲ Granville; **227** EM-2; mail Lewistown z 17044; ● 60
Hawthorn; Inc. Place; CLARION; **224** WJ-7; elev. 1,000ft./305m.; 🅿; z 16230; Ⓟ 528; © 587
Haycock; MCD-Township; BUCKS; ***227** EM-12; ★ **PHIL-**; mail Quakertown z 18951; Ⓟ 2,165; © 2,191
Haydentown; RMC Place; FAYETTE; ▲ Georges; **225** WQ-4; elev. 1,127ft./344m.; ★ **UNTN**; mail Smithfield z 15478; ● 120
Hayesville; RMC Place; CHESTER; ▲ Lower Oxford; ***227** EQ-9; elev. 582ft./177m.; mail Oxford z 19363; ● 75
Hayfield; MCD-Township; CRAWFORD; ***224** WE-3; mail Saegertown z 16433; Ⓟ 2,937; © 3,092
Haymaker; RMC Place; MCKEAN; ▲ Eldred; ***224** WD-11; elev. 1,517ft./462m.; mail Eldred z 16731; rural
Hays; RMC Place; ALLEGHENY; ***225** WN-4; ★ **PGH**; mail Pittsburgh z 15230; pop. incl. with Pittsburgh (Inc. Place)
Hays; RMC Place; FAYETTE; ▲ Georges; ***225** WQ-4; ★ **UNTN**; mail Uniontown z 15401; ● 40
Hays Grove; RMC Place; CUMBERLAND; ▲ Penn; ***227** EO-2; mail Newville z 17241; rural
Hays Mill; RMC Place; SOMERSET; ▲ Brothersvalley; ***225** WQ-8; mail Meyersdale z 15552; rural
Haysville; Inc. Place; ALLEGHENY; **228** H-2; elev. 724ft./221m.; ★ **PGH**; mail Sewickley z 15143; Ⓟ 100; © 78
Haysville; RMC Place; BUTLER; ▲ Fairview; ***224** WJ-5; mail Karns City z 16041; rural
Hayti; RMC Place; CHESTER; ▲ Valley; **227** EP-9; ★ **PHIL-**; mail Coatesville z 19320; ● 950
Hazel Hurst; RMC Place; MCKEAN; ▲ Hamlin; **224** WF-10; 🅿; z 16733; ● 300
Hazel Kirk; RMC Place; WASHINGTON; ▲ Carroll; ***225** WO-4; ★ **PGH**; mail Monongahela z 15063; ● 80
Hazelwood; RMC Place; ALLEGHENY; ***225** WM-4; 🅿; ★ **PGH**; z 15207; pop. incl. with Pittsburgh (Inc. Place)
Hazen; RMC Place; BEAVER; ▲ North Sewickley; ***225** WK-2; ★ **PGH**; mail Fombell z 16123; ● 100
Hazen; RMC Place; JEFFERSON; ▲ Warsaw; **224** WI-8; 🅿; z 15825; ● 125
Hazle; MCD-Township; LUZERNE; ***226** EJ-9; ★ **HAZ**; mail Hazleton z 18201-02; Ⓟ 9,323; © 9,000
Hazlebrook; RMC Place; LUZERNE; ▲ Foster; ***226** EJ-9; ★ **HAZ**; mail Hazleton z 18201; ● 50
Hazleton; Inc. Place; LUZERNE; **226** EJ-8; elev. 1,660ft./506m.; 🅿 🅷 🅲 1,143 ■; ★ **HAZ**; z 18201-02; Ⓟ 24,730; © 23,329; ◆ 21,762
Hazle Village; RMC Place; LUZERNE; ★ **HAZ**; mail Hazleton z 18201; pop. incl. with Hazleton (Inc. Place)
Hazzard; RMC Place; WASHINGTON; ★ **PGH**; mail Monongahela z 15063; pop. incl. with Monongahela (Inc. Place)
Heacock Meadows; RMC Place; BUCKS; ▲ Lower Makefield; ***227** EO-13; ★ **PHIL-**; mail Morrisville z 19067; ● 1,200
Headlee Heights; RMC Place; GREENE; ▲ Monongahela, Greene; ***225** WQ-4; mail Garards Fort z 15334; rural
Heart Lake; RMC Place; SUSQUEHANNA; ▲ New Milford, Bridgewater; **226** EE-9; mail Montrose z 18801; ● 130
Heath; MCD-Township; JEFFERSON; ***224** WH-8; mail Sigel z 15860; Ⓟ 109; © 160
Heathville; RMC Place; JEFFERSON; ▲ Beaver; **224** WI-7; mail Summerville z 15864; ● 15
Hebe; RMC Place; NORTHUMBERLAND; ▲ Jordan; **227** EL-5; elev. 662ft./202m.; mail Herndon z 17830; ● 70
Heberlig; RMC Place; CUMBERLAND; ▲ Upper Mifflin; ***227** EO-2; mail Newville z 17241; rural
Hebron; RMC Place; LEBANON; ▲ South Lebanon; ***227** EN-6; ★ **LEB**; mail Lebanon z 17042; ● 600
Hebron; MCD-Township; POTTER; ***224** WE-12; mail Coudersport z 16915; Ⓟ 525; © 622
Hebron Center; RMC Place; POTTER; ▲ Hebron; ***224** WE-13; mail Coudersport z 16915
Heckscherville; CDP; SCHUYLKILL; ▲ Cass; **227** EL-7; ★ **PTSVL**; mail Pottsville z 17901; © 76
Hecktown; RMC Place; NORTHAMPTON; ▲ Lower Nazareth; **227** EL-11; ★ **ALL-**; mail Bethlehem z 18020; ● 1,200
Hecla; RMC Place; SCHUYLKILL; ▲ East Brunswick; **227** EL-8; elev. 649ft./198m.; mail New Ringgold z 17960; ● 100
Hecla; WESTMORELAND; see Southwest (RMC Place)
Hector; MCD-Township; POTTER; ***226** EE-1; mail Sabinsville z 16943, Ulysses z 16948; Ⓟ 336; © 453
Hegarty Crossroads; RMC Place; CLEARFIELD; ▲ Beccaria; ***225** WK-10; elev. 1,581ft./482m.; mail Coalport z 16627; rural
Hegins; RMC Place; SCHUYLKILL; ▲ Hegins; **227** EL-6; 🅿; z 17938; ● 1,200
Hegins; MCD-Township; SCHUYLKILL; ***227** EL-6; 🅿; z 17938; Ⓟ 3,561; © 3,519
Heidelberg; Inc. Place; ALLEGHENY; **225** WN-3; elev. 820ft./250m.; 🅿; ★ **PGH**; z 15106; Ⓟ 1,238; © 1,225
Heidelberg; MCD-Township; BERKS; ***227** EN-8; ★ **READ**; mail Womelsdorf z 19567; Ⓟ 1,513; © 1,636
Heidelberg; MCD-Township; LEBANON; ***227** EN-7; ★ **LEB**; mail Schaefferstown z 17088; Ⓟ 3,797; © 3,832
Heidelberg; MCD-Township; LEHIGH; ***227** EL-9; ★ **ALL-**; mail Germansville z 18053; Ⓟ 3,250; © 3,279
Heidelberg; MCD-Township; YORK; ***227** EQ-4; mail Spring Grove z 17362; Ⓟ 2,622; © 2,970
Heidlersburg; RMC Place; ADAMS; ▲ Tyrone; **227** EP-3; mail Gettysburg z 17325, York Springs z 17372; ● 150
Heights; NORTHAMPTON; see Miller Heights (RMC Place)
Heilmandale; RMC Place; LEBANON; ▲ North Lebanon; ***227** EN-6; elev. 519ft./158m.; ★ **LEB**; mail Lebanon z 17042, z 17046; ● 200
Heilwood; CDP; INDIANA; ▲ Pine; **225** WL-8; 🅿; z 15745; © 786
Heise Run; RMC Place; TIOGA; ▲ Delmar; ***226** EF-2; elev. 1,274ft./388m.; mail Wellsboro z 16901; rural
Heistersburg; RMC Place; FAYETTE; ▲ Luzerne; ***225** WP-4; ★ **UNTN**; mail East Millsboro z 15433; rural
Helen Furnace; RMC Place; CLARION; ▲ Highland; ***224** WH-7; elev. 1,420ft./433m.; mail Clarion z 16214; rural
Helen Mills; RMC Place; ELK; ▲ Horton; ***224** WH-9; mail Brockport z 15823; rural
Helfenstein; RMC Place; NORTHUMBERLAND, SCHUYLKILL; ▲ Butler; **227** EL-6; 🅿; ★ **PTSVL**; z 17921; ● 100
Helixville; RMC Place; BEDFORD; ▲ Napier; ***225** WO-9; mail Schellsburg z 15559
Hellam; YORK; see Hallam (Inc. Place)
Hellam; MCD-Township; YORK; ***227** EP-5; 🅿; ★ **YORK**; z 17406 & mail Wrightsville z 17368; does not include the Borough of Hallam; Ⓟ 5,123; © 5,930
Hellertown; Inc. Place; NORTHAMPTON; **227** EL-11; elev. 310ft./94m.; 🅿; ★ **ALL-**; z 18055; Ⓟ 5,662; © 5,606
Helvetia; RMC Place; CLEARFIELD; ▲ Brady; **224** WJ-9; mail Luthersburg z 15848; ● 90
Hemlock; MCD-Township; COLUMBIA; ***226** EJ-6; mail Bloomsburg z 17815; Ⓟ 1,546; © 1,874
Hemlock; RMC Place; WARREN; ▲ Glade; ***224** WE-8; elev. 1,223ft./373m.; mail Warren z 16365
Hemlock Grove; RMC Place; PIKE; ▲ Palmyra; ***226** EH-11; elev. 1,300ft./396m.; mail Greentown z 18426; ● 100
Hemlock Grove; RMC Place; SULLIVAN; ▲ Davidson; ***226** EH-6; elev. 1,211ft./369m.; mail Muncy Valley z 17758; rural
Hempfield; MCD-Township; MERCER; ***224** WG-2; mail Greenville z 16125; Ⓟ 3,826; © 4,004
Hempfield; MCD-Township; WESTMORELAND; ***225** WN-6; ★ **PGH**; mail Greensburg z 15601; Ⓟ 42,609; © 40,721; ® 41,555; ◆ 38,942
Hempfield Manor; RMC Place; WESTMORELAND; ▲ Hempfield; ***225** WN-5; elev. 1,100ft./335m.; ★ **PGH**; mail Greensburg z 15601; ● 250
Henderson; RMC Place; CLEARFIELD; ▲ Woodward; ***225** WK-11; elev. 1,690ft./515m.; mail Houtzdale z 16651; rural
Henderson; MCD-Township; HUNTINGDON; ***225** WM-13; mail Huntingdon z 16652; Ⓟ 933; © 972
Henderson; MCD-Township; JEFFERSON; ***224** WJ-9; mail Punxsutawney z 15767; Ⓟ 1,376; © 1,727
Henderson; MERCER; see Hendersonville (RMC Place)
Henderson Park; RMC Place; MONTGOMERY; ▲ Upper Merion; ***227** EO-11; ★ **PHIL-**; mail King of Prussia z 19406
Hendersonville; RMC Place; BUTLER; ▲ Cranberry; ***225** WL-3; ★ **PGH**; mail Mars z 16046; rural
Hendersonville (Henderson); RMC Place; MERCER; ▲ Worth; ***224** WH-4; mail Stoneboro z 16153
Hendersonville; RMC Place; WASHINGTON; ▲ Cecil; ***225** WN-3; elev. 998ft./304m.; 🅿; ★ **PGH**; z 15339; ● 550
Hendricks; RMC Place; MONTGOMERY; ▲ Upper Salford; ***227** EN-11; ★ **PHIL-**; mail Woxall z 18979; ● 45
Henningsville; RMC Place; BERKS; ▲ Longswamp; ***227** EM-10; mail Alburtis z 18011; rural
Henrietta; RMC Place; BLAIR; ▲ North Woodbury; **225** WN-11; elev. 1,392ft./424m.; mail Martinsburg z 16662; ● 100
Henry Clay; MCD-Township; FAYETTE; ***225** WQ-6; mail Markleysburg z 15459; Ⓟ 1,860; © 1,984
Henrys Bend; RMC Place; VENANGO; ▲ President; **224** WG-5; mail Oil City z 16301; summer pop. 200; ● 60
Henrys Mill; RMC Place; WARREN; ▲ Sheffield; ***224** WF-8; mail Sheffield z 16347
Henryville; RMC Place; MONROE; ▲ Paradise; **226** EI-12; 🅿; z 18332; ● 300
Hensel; RMC Place; LANCASTER; ▲ East Drumore, Drumore; ***227** EQ-7; elev. 622ft./190m.; mail Quarryville z 17566; rural
Hensingerville (New Hensingerville); RMC Place; LEHIGH; ▲ Lower Macungie; ***227** EM-10; ★ **ALL-**; mail Alburtis z 18011; rural
Hepburn; MCD-Township; LYCOMING; ***226** EH-4; ★ **WMSPT**; mail Cogan Station z 17728; Ⓟ 2,834; © 2,836
Hepburn Heights; RMC Place; LYCOMING; ▲ Hepburn; ***226** EH-3; ★ **WMSPT**; mail Cogan Station z 17728
Hepburnia; RMC Place; CLEARFIELD; ▲ Penn; **224** WJ-10; mail Grampian z 16838; ● 140
Hepburnville; RMC Place; LYCOMING; ▲ Hepburn; **226** EH-3; ★ **WMSPT**; mail Cogan Station z 17728; ● 150
Hephzibah; RMC Place; CHESTER; ▲ East Fallowfield; ***227** EP-9; elev. 517ft./158m.; ★ **PHIL-**; mail Coatesville z 19320; ● 90
Hepler; RMC Place; SCHUYLKILL; ▲ Upper Mahantongo; ***227** EL-6; mail Klingerstown z 17941; rural
Herbert; RMC Place; FAYETTE; ▲ Redstone; ***225** WP-4; ★ **UNTN**; mail Fairbank z 15435; ● 100
Hercules; RMC Place; NORTHAMPTON; ★ **ALL-**; mail Stockertown z 18083; pop. incl. with Stockertown (Inc. Place)
Hereford; RMC Place; BERKS; ▲ Hereford; **227** EM-10; 🅿; z 18056; ● 850
Hereford; MCD-Township; BERKS; ***227** EM-10; 🅿; z 18056; Ⓟ 3,026; © 3,174
Heritage Hills; RMC Place; LAWRENCE; ▲ Perry; ***225** WK-2; ★ **PGH**; mail Ellwood City z 16117; ● 200
Herman; RMC Place; BUTLER; ▲ Summit; **225** WK-4; elev. 1,411ft./430m.; 🅿; ★ **BUTL**; z 16039; ● 400
Herminie; CDP; WESTMORELAND; ▲ Sewickley; **225** WN-5; 🅿; ★ **PGH**; z 15637; © 856
Hermitage; Inc. Place; MERCER; **224** WH-2; 🅿 ■; ★ **SHAR**; z 16148 & mail Farrell z 16121, Sharpsville z 16150, West Middlesex z 16159; Ⓟ 15,300; © 16,157; ◆ 15,785
Herndon; Inc. Place; NORTHUMBERLAND; **227** EL-4; elev. 420ft./128m.; 🅿; z 17830; Ⓟ 422; © 383
Hero; RMC Place; GREENE; ▲ Gilmore; ***225** WQ-2; mail Holbrook z 15341; rural
Herrick; MCD-Township; BRADFORD; ***226** EF-7; mail Wyalusing z 18853; Ⓟ 647; © 676
Herrick; MCD-Township; SUSQUEHANNA; ***226** EF-10; mail Herrick Center z 18430; Ⓟ 563; © 599
Herrick Center; RMC Place; SUSQUEHANNA; ▲ Herrick; **226** EF-10; elev. 1,765ft./538m.; 🅿; z 18430; ● 125
Herrick Corner; RMC Place; SUSQUEHANNA; ▲ Herrick; ***226** EF-10; elev. 1,683ft./513m.; mail Herrick Center z 18430; rural
Herrickville; RMC Place; BRADFORD; ▲ Herrick; **226** EE-7; elev. 1,313ft./400m.; mail Wyalusing z 18853; ● 75
Herrs Island; RMC Place; ALLEGHENY; ***225** WM-4; ★ **PGH**; pop. incl. with Pittsburgh (Inc. Place)
Hershey; CDP; DAUPHIN; ▲ Derry; **227** EN-5; 🅿 🅷 🅲 791; ★ **HRBG**; z 17033; Ⓟ 11,860; © 12,771
Hershey Heights; RMC Place; ADAMS; ▲ Berwick; ***227** EQ-4; ★ **HANV**; mail Hanover z 17331; ● 150
Heshbon; RMC Place; INDIANA; ▲ Brush Valley; **225** WM-8; ★ **JNST**; mail Blairsville z 15717; ● 50
Heshbon Park; RMC Place; LYCOMING; ▲ Loyalsock; ***226** EH-3; ★ **WMSPT**; mail Williamsport z 17701; ● 300
Hessdale; RMC Place; LANCASTER; ▲ Strasburg; **227** EP-7; elev. 398ft./121m.; ★ **LANC**; mail New Providence z 17560, Strasburg z 17579; ● 100
Hesston; RMC Place; HUNTINGDON; ▲ Penn; **225** WM-12; 🅿; z 16647; ● 175
Hetlerville; RMC Place; COLUMBIA; ▲ Mifflin; ***226** EJ-7; mail Nescopeck z 18635
Hettesheimer Corners; RMC Place; WYOMING; ▲ Noxen; ***226** EG-8; mail Noxen z 18636
Hiawatha; RMC Place; WAYNE; ▲ Scott; ***226** EE-11; mail Starrucca z 18462; rural
Hibbs; RMC Place; FAYETTE; ▲ German; **225** WP-4; 🅿; ★ **UNTN**; z 15443; ● 200
Hickernell; RMC Place; CRAWFORD; ▲ Spring; **224** WE-2; elev. 1,128ft./344m.; mail Springboro z 16435; ● 50
Hickman; RMC Place; ALLEGHENY; ▲ Collier; ***225** WN-3; ★ **PGH**; mail Oakdale z 15071; ● 40
Hickory; MCD-Township; FOREST; ***224** WF-6; mail Endeavor z 16322; Ⓟ 513; © 525
Hickory; MCD-Township; LAWRENCE; ***224** WJ-2; ★ **NWCS**; mail New Castle z 16105; Ⓟ 2,317; © 2,356
Hickory; RMC Place; WASHINGTON; ▲ Mount Pleasant; **225** WN-2; elev. 1,299ft./396m.; 🅿; ★ **PGH**; z 15340; ● 850
Hickory Corners; RMC Place; MERCER; ***224** WH-2; ★ **SHAR**; mail Sharon z 16146; pop. incl. with Hermitage (Inc. Place)
Hickory Corners; RMC Place; NORTHUMBERLAND; ▲ Lower Mahanoy; **227** EL-4; mail Dalmatia z 17017; ● 60
Hickory Grove; RMC Place; SUSQUEHANNA; ▲ Great Bend; **226** ED-10; elev. 900ft./274m.; ★ **BING**; mail Susquehanna z 18847; ● 30
Hickory Heights; RMC Place; LAWRENCE; ▲ Hickory; ***224** WJ-2; ★ **NWCS**; mail New Castle z 16101; pop. incl. with Lawrenceburg (Inc. Place)
Hickoryhill; RMC Place; CHESTER; ▲ Elk; ***227** EQ-9; ★ **PHIL-**; mail Oxford z 19363; ● 50
Hickory Hills; RMC Place; BUCKS; ▲ Lower Makefield; ***227** EO-14; ★ **PHIL-**; mail Morrisville z 19067; ● 1,300
Hickory Ridge; NORTHUMBERLAND; see Sagon (RMC Place)
Hickory Run Forest; RMC Place; CARBON; ▲ Penn Forest; ***226** EJ-10; elev. 1,700ft./518m.; mail Jim Thorpe z 18229; ● 140
Hickorytown; RMC Place; CUMBERLAND; ▲ Middlesex; ***227** EO-3; ★ **CARL**; mail Carlisle z 17013; ● 50
Hickorytown; RMC Place; MONTGOMERY; ▲ Plymouth; ***227** EO-12; ★ **PHIL-**; mail Plymouth Meeting z 19462
Hickox; RMC Place; POTTER; ▲ Genesee; ***224** WD-13; mail Genesee z 16923; ● 50
Hicksville; RMC Place; ARMSTRONG; ▲ Kiskiminetas; ***225** WM-6; ★ **PGH**; mail Avonmore z 15618; rural
Hidden Valley; RMC Place; MONTGOMERY; ▲ Upper Merion; ★ **PHIL-**; mail King of Prussia z 19406
Hidden Valley Estates; RMC Place; LEHIGH; ▲ Lower Macungie; ***227** EM-10; elev. 368ft./112m.; ★ **ALL-**; mail Macungie z 18062; ● 300
Higgins Corner; RMC Place; BUTLER; ▲ Venango; ***224** WI-4; mail Hilliards z 16040; ● 40
Highcliff; RMC Place; ALLEGHENY; ▲ Ross; ***225** WM-3; ★ **PGH**; mail Pittsburgh z 15229
Highfield; RMC Place; BUTLER; ▲ Butler; ***225** WK-4; ★ **BUTL**; mail Butler z 16001; ● 1,200
High House; RMC Place; FAYETTE; ▲ German, Georges; ***225** WQ-4; elev. 1,214ft./370m.; ★ **UNTN**; mail Smithfield z 15478; rural
Highland; MCD-Township; ADAMS; ***227** EQ-2; mail Gettysburg z 17325; Ⓟ 815; © 825
Highland; RMC Place; ALLEGHENY; ***225** WM-3; ★ **PGH**; mail Pittsburgh z 15237; pop. incl. with Pittsburgh (Inc. Place)
Highland; RMC Place; ALLEGHENY; ***225** WM-4; ★ **PGH**; mail Pittsburgh z 15206
Highland; RMC Place; BEAVER; ★ **PGH**; mail Beaver Falls z 15010; pop. incl. with Big Beaver (Inc. Place)
Highland; MCD-Township; CHESTER; ***227** EP-9; mail Coatesville z 19320; Ⓟ 1,199; © 1,125
Highland; MCD-Township; CLARION; ***224** WH-7; mail Clarion z 16214; Ⓟ 573; © 633
Highland; MCD-Township; ELK; ***224** WG-9; mail Kane z 16735; Ⓟ 551; © 509
Highland; RMC Place; LUZERNE; ▲ Foster; ***226** EJ-9; ★ **HAZ**; mail Freeland z 18224; ● 150
Highland; RMC Place; WESTMORELAND; ▲ Salem; ***225** WN-6; ★ **PGH**; mail Forbes Road z 15633
Highland Acres; RMC Place; LANCASTER; ▲ East Lampeter; ***227** EP-7; ★ **LANC**; mail Lancaster z 17602; ● 450
Highland Corners; RMC Place; ELK; ▲ Highland; ***224** WG-9; elev. 2,042ft./622m.; mail Kane z 16735
Highland Meadows; RMC Place; ALLEGHENY; ▲ Elizabeth; ★ **PGH**; mail Elizabeth z 15037; ● 800
Highland Park; RMC Place; BUCKS; ▲ Middletown; ***227** EN-11; ★ **PHIL-**; mail Sellersville z 18960
Highland Park; RMC Place; CUMBERLAND; ▲ Lower Allen; **227** ET-2; ★ **HRBG**; mail Camp Hill z 17011; ● 1,900
Highland Park; RMC Place; DELAWARE; ▲ Upper Darby; ***227** EP-12; ★ **PHIL-**; mail Upper Darby z 19082
Highland Park; RMC Place; ERIE; ▲ Millcreek; ***224** WC-3; ★ **ERIE**; mail Erie z 16506
Highland Park; CDP; MIFFLIN; ▲ Derry; **227** EL-1; mail Lewistown z 17044; Ⓟ 1,583; © 1,446
Highland Park; RMC Place; NORTHAMPTON; ▲ Palmer; ***227** EL-12; elev. 350ft./107m.; ★ **ALL-**; mail Easton z 18042; ● 900
Highland Woods; RMC Place; LUZERNE; ▲ Fairview; ***226** EI-9; ★ **SCR-**; mail Wilkes Barre z 18701; ● 350
High Meadows; RMC Place; DELAWARE; ▲ Middletown; ***227** EQ-11; elev. 200ft./61m.; ★ **PHIL-**; mail Media z 19063; ● 700
Highmount; RMC Place; YORK; ▲ Hellam; ***227** EP-6; elev. 567ft./173m.; ★ **YORK**; mail York z 17406; ● 150
High Park; RMC Place; MONTGOMERY; ▲ Upper Moreland; ***227** EO-12; elev. 300ft./91m.; ★ **PHIL-**; mail Hatboro z 19040; ● 1,300
Highrock; RMC Place; YORK; ▲ Lower Chanceford, East Hopewell; ***227** EQ-6; mail Airville z 17302; rural
Highspire; Inc. Place; DAUPHIN; **227** EO-5; elev. 340ft./104m.; 🅿; ★ **HRBG**; z 17034; Ⓟ 2,668; © 2,720
Highville; RMC Place; LANCASTER; ▲ Manor; ***227** EP-6; ★ **LANC**; mail Conestoga z 17516; rural
Hileman Heights; RMC Place; BLAIR; ***225** WM-11; ★ **ALT**; mail Altoona z 16602; pop. incl. with Altoona (Inc. Place)
Hillchurch; RMC Place; BERKS; ▲ Pike; ***227** EN-10; ★ **READ**; mail Boyertown z 19512; ● 125
Hill Church; RMC Place; WASHINGTON; ▲ North Strabane; ***225** WN-3; ★ **PGH**; mail Canonsburg z 15317; ● 40
Hill City; RMC Place; VENANGO; ▲ Cranberry; ***224** WH-5; ★ **OILC-F**; mail Cranberry z 16319; rural
Hillcrest; RMC Place; ALLEGHENY; ***225** WN-3; ★ **PGH**; mail Bethel Park z 15102; pop. incl. with Bethel Park (Inc. Place)
Hillcrest; RMC Place; BEAVER; ▲ Hopewell, Center; ***225** WL-2; ★ **PGH**; mail Aliquippa z 15001; ● 300
Hill Crest; RMC Place; FAYETTE; ▲ Connellsville; mail Connellsville z 15425; ● 150
Hill Crest; RMC Place; MONTGOMERY; ▲ Cheltenham; ***227** EO-12; ★ **PHIL-**; mail Philadelphia z 19126
Hillcrest; RMC Place; YORK; ▲ Spring Garden; ***227** EP-5; ★ **YORK**; mail York z 17403
Hillcroft; RMC Place; YORK; ▲ Spring Garden; ***227** EP-5; ★ **YORK**; mail York z 17403
Hilldale; RMC Place; LUZERNE; ▲ Plains; **226** EB-9; 🅿; ★ **SCR-**; z 18702, z 18705; ● 600
Hiller; CDP; FAYETTE; ▲ Luzerne; **225** WP-4; elev. 1,005ft./306m.; 🅿; ★ **UNTN**; z 15444; Ⓟ 1,401; © 1,234
Hilliards; RMC Place; BUTLER; ▲ Washington; **224** WI-4; 🅿; z 16040; ● 120
Hillman; RMC Place; INDIANA; ▲ Banks; ***225** WK-9; mail Punxsutawney z 15767; rural
Hillsboro; RMC Place; SOMERSET; ▲ Paint; ***225** WO-9; ★ **JNST**; mail Windber z 15963; ● 20
Hills Creek Lake; RMC Place; TIOGA; ▲ Charleston; ***226** EE-3; elev. 1,600ft./488m.; mail Wellsboro z 16901; ● 110
Hillsdale; RMC Place; INDIANA; ▲ Montgomery; **225** WK-9; elev. 1,686ft./514m.; 🅿; z 15746; ● 250
Hillsgrove; RMC Place; SULLIVAN; ▲ Hillsgrove; **226** EG-5; 🅿; z 18619; ● 200
Hillsgrove; MCD-Township; SULLIVAN; ***226** EH-5; 🅿; z 18619; Ⓟ 337; © 265
Hillside; RMC Place; LEHIGH; ▲ South Whitehall; ***227** EL-10; ★ **ALL-**; mail Orefield z 18069; ● 35
Hillside; RMC Place; LUZERNE; ▲ Kingston; ***226** EH-9; elev. 813ft./248m.; ★ **SCR-**; mail Shavertown z 18708
Hillside; RMC Place; SCHUYLKILL; ▲ North Manheim; ***227** EL-7; ★ **PTSVL**; mail Pottsville z 17901; ● 100
Hillside; RMC Place; WESTMORELAND; ▲ Derry; **225** WN-7; ★ **LTROB**; mail Derry z 15627; ● 200
Hillside Junction; RMC Place; LACKAWANNA; ***226** EH-9; ★ **SCR-**; mail Moosic z 18507; pop. incl. with Moosic (Inc. Place)
Hills Terrace; RMC Place; SCHUYLKILL; ▲ Mahanoy; ***227** EK-8; mail Mahanoy City z 17948; ● 30
Hillsview; RMC Place; WESTMORELAND; ▲ Fairfield; ***225** WN-7; mail Ligonier z 15658
Hillsville; RMC Place; LAWRENCE; ▲ Mahoning; **224** WJ-1; 🅿; ★ **YNGS-**; z 16132; ● 600
Hilltop; RMC Place; BUCKS; ▲ Springfield; ***227** EM-11; ★ **ALL-**; mail Quakertown z 18951; rural
Hill Top Acres; RMC Place; ARMSTRONG; ▲ Manor; ***225** WK-6; ★ **PGH**; mail Ford City z 16226; ● 90
Hilltop Acres; RMC Place; LANCASTER; ***227** EP-7; ★ **LANC**; mail Lancaster z 17603; pop. incl. with Lancaster (Inc. Place)
Hilltown; RMC Place; ADAMS; ▲ Franklin; ***227** EQ-2; mail Biglerville z 17307
Hilltown; RMC Place; BUCKS; ▲ Hilltown; **227** EN-12; 🅿; ★ **PHIL-**; z 18927; ● 800
Hilltown; MCD-Township; BUCKS; ***227** EN-12; 🅿; ★ **PHIL-**; z 18927 & mail Blooming Glen z 18911; Ⓟ 10,582; © 12,102
Hilltown (Lookout); RMC Place; WAYNE; ▲ Manchester, Damascus; **226** EE-12; mail Equinunk z 18417; ● 60
Hillville; RMC Place; ARMSTRONG; ▲ Perry; ***224** WJ-5; mail Karns City z 16041; ● 90
Hilton; RMC Place; YORK; ▲ Dover; ***227** EP-5; ★ **YORK**; mail Dover z 17315
Hines Corners; RMC Place; WAYNE; ▲ Preston; ***226** EE-11; elev. 2,000ft./610m.; mail Orson z 18449
Hinkle; BUCKS; see Hinkletown (RMC Place)
Hinkletown (Hinkle); RMC Place; BUCKS; ▲ Plumstead; ***227** EM-12; ★ **PHIL-**; mail Pipersville z 18947; rural
Hinkletown; RMC Place; LANCASTER; ▲ Earl; **227** EO-8; ★ **LANC**; mail Ephrata z 17522; ● 175
Hinkson Corner; RMC Place; DELAWARE; ▲ Nether Providence; ★ **PHIL-**; mail Wallingford z 19086
Hiyasota; RMC Place; SOMERSET; ▲ Conemaugh; ***225** WO-8; ★ **JNST**; mail Hollsopple z 15935; rural
Hoadleys; RMC Place; WAYNE; ▲ Cherry Ridge; **226** EG-11; elev. 1,162ft./354m.; mail Honesdale z 18431; ● 110
Hoban Heights (McKune); RMC Place; WYOMING; ▲ Falls; ***226** EG-9; ★ **SCR-**; mail Tunkhannock z 18657; ● 120
Hobart; RMC Place; YORK; ▲ West Manheim; ***227** ER-4; ★ **HANV**; mail Hanover z 17331; ● 40
Hobbie; RMC Place; LUZERNE; ▲ Hollenback; **226** EJ-8; mail Wapwallopen z 18660; ● 350
Hoblitzell; RMC Place; BEDFORD; ▲ Londonderry; ***225** WQ-9; mail Hyndman z 15545; ● 30
Hockersville; RMC Place; CUMBERLAND; ▲ Penn; ***227** EO-2; mail Newville z 17241; rural
Hoernerstown; RMC Place; DAUPHIN; ▲ South Hanover; **227** EN-5; elev. 448ft./137m.; ★ **HRBG**; mail Hummelstown z 17036; ● 50
Hoffer; RMC Place; SNYDER; ▲ Chapman; ***227** EL-4; mail Port Trevorton z 17864; ● 30
Hoffmansville; RMC Place; MONTGOMERY; ▲ New Hanover; ***227** EN-10; elev. 374ft./114m.; mail Frederick z 19435; ● 800
Hogestown; RMC Place; CUMBERLAND; ▲ Silver Spring; **227** EO-4; ★ **HRBG**; mail Mechanicsburg z 17050, z 17055; ● 300
Hog Island; RMC Place; DELAWARE; ***227** EQ-12; ★ **PHIL-**; mail Essington z 19029, Philadelphia z 19113; rural
Hoguetown; RMC Place; CAMBRIA; ▲ Cresson; ***225** WM-10; elev. 2,051ft./625m.; mail Cresson z 16630; ● 100
Hokendauqua; CDP; LEHIGH; ▲ Whitehall; **227** EL-11; 🅿; ★ **ALL-**; z 18052; Ⓟ 3,413; © 3,411
Hokes; RMC Place; YORK; ▲ Manheim; ***227** ER-5; elev. 788ft./240m.; ★ **HANV**; mail Glen Rock z 17327; rural
Holbrook; RMC Place; GREENE; ▲ Center; **225** WQ-2; 🅿; z 15341; ● 40
Holicong; RMC Place; BUCKS; ▲ Buckingham; ***227** EN-13; 🅿; ★ **PHIL-**; z 18928; ● 450
Holiday Hills; RMC Place; LEHIGH; ▲ Upper Macungie; ***227** EM-10; elev. 450ft./137m.; ★ **ALL-**; mail Allentown z 18106; ● 300
Holiday Park; RMC Place; ALLEGHENY; ★ **PGH**; mail Pittsburgh z 15239; pop. incl. with Plum (Inc. Place)
Holiday Pocono; RMC Place; CARBON; ▲ Kidder; ***226** EJ-10; elev. 1,671ft./509m.; mail Albrightsville z 18210; summer pop. 500; ● 100
Holland; RMC Place; BUCKS; ▲ Northampton; **227** EO-13; 🅿; ★ **PHIL-**; z 18966; ● 5,300
Hollenback; MCD-Township; LUZERNE; ***226** EJ-8; mail Wapwallopen z 18660; Ⓟ 1,198; © 1,243
Hollentown; RMC Place; CAMBRIA; ▲ Reade; ***225** WL-10; mail Fallentimber z 16639; ● 160
Hollers Hill; RMC Place; LUZERNE; ▲ Hazle; ***226** EJ-8; ★ **HAZ**; mail Hazleton z 18202; ● 200
Holley Heights; RMC Place; YORK; ▲ West Manchester; ***227** EP-5; ★ **YORK**; mail York z 17404; ● 500
Holliday; TIOGA; see Crooked Creek (RMC Place)
Hollidaysburg; Inc. Place; ⊡ BLAIR; **225** WM-11; elev. 960ft./293m.; 🅿; ★ **ALT**; z 16648; Ⓟ 5,624; © 5,368
Hollinger; RMC Place; LANCASTER; ▲ West Lampeter; ***227** EP-7; ★ **LANC**; mail Lancaster z 17603; ● 200
Hollisterville; RMC Place; WAYNE; ▲ Salem; ***226** EH-11; ★ **SCR-**; mail Moscow z 18444
Hollsopple; RMC Place; SOMERSET; ▲ Conemaugh; **225** WO-8; 🅿; ★ **JNST**; z 15935; ● 500
Holly Hill; RMC Place; BUCKS; ▲ Bristol; ***227** EO-14; ★ **PHIL-**
Hollywood; RMC Place; CLEARFIELD; ▲ Huston; ***224** WI-10; mail Penfield z 15849; ● 100
Hollywood; RMC Place; LUZERNE; ▲ Hazle; ***226** EJ-8; ★ **HAZ**; mail Hazleton z 18202; ● 200
Hollywood; RMC Place; MONTGOMERY; ▲ Abington; **228** B-5; 🅿; ★ **PHIL-**; z 19046 & mail Elkins Park z 19027; ● 800
Hollywood Heights; RMC Place; YORK; ▲ Spring Garden; ***227** EP-5; ★ **YORK**; mail York z 17403
Holmes; RMC Place; DELAWARE; ▲ Ridley; **228** F-2; 🅿; ★ **PHIL-**; z 19043, z 19098; ● 2,800
Holmesburg; RMC Place; PHILADELPHIA; ***227** EP-13; ★ **PHIL-**; mail Philadelphia z 19136; pop. incl. with Philadelphia (Inc. Place)
Holsopple; SOMERSET; see Benson (Inc. Place)
Holt; RMC Place; BEAVER; ▲ Raccoon; ***225** WL-2; ★ **PGH**; mail Aliquippa z 15001; rural
Holtwood; RMC Place; LANCASTER; ▲ Martic; **227** EQ-7; 🅿; ★ **LANC**; z 17532; ● 200
Homans Corner; RMC Place; BEDFORD; ▲ Liberty; ***225** WO-11; mail Saxton z 16678; rural
Home (Kellysburg); RMC Place; INDIANA; ▲ Rayne; **225** WL-8; 🅿; z 15747; ● 400
Homeacre; RMC Place; BUTLER; ***225** WK-4; ★ **BUTL**; mail Butler z 16001; ● 2,000
Homeacre-Lyndora; CDP-Census Area Only; BUTLER; ▲ Butler; ***225** WK-4; ★ **BUTL**; mail Butler z 16001, Lyndora z 16045; Ⓟ 7,511; © 6,685
Home Camp; RMC Place; CLEARFIELD; ▲ Union; ***224** WI-10; mail Rockton z 15856
Homeland; RMC Place; LANCASTER; ▲ Manheim; **227** ES-9; ★ **LANC**; mail Lancaster z 17601; ● 450
Home Park; RMC Place; LEHIGH; ▲ Whitehall; ***227** EL-10; ★ **ALL-**; mail Whitehall z 18052
Homer; MCD-Township; POTTER; ***224** WF-12; mail Coudersport z 16915; Ⓟ 216; © 390
Homer City; Inc. Place; INDIANA; **225** WM-7; elev. 1,062ft./324m.; 🅿; z 15748 & mail Aultman z 15713; Ⓟ 1,809; © 1,844
Homer Gap; RMC Place; BLAIR; ▲ Logan; ***225** WM-11; ★ **ALT**; mail Altoona z 16601; ● 70
Homestead; Inc. Place; ALLEGHENY; **228** K-7; elev. 900ft./274m.; 🅿; ★ **PGH**; z 15120; Ⓟ 4,179; © 3,569
Homestead Transfer; RMC Place; ALLEGHENY; ***225** WM-4; ★ **PGH**; pop. incl. with West Homestead (Inc. Place)
Homesville; RMC Place; SCHUYLKILL; ▲ Butler; ★ **PTSVL**; mail Ashland z 17921; ● 80
Hometown; CDP; SCHUYLKILL; ▲ Rush; **227** EK-8; elev. 1,136ft./346m.; mail Tamaqua z 18252; Ⓟ 1,545; © 1,399
Homets Ferry; RMC Place; BRADFORD; ▲ Wyalusing; ***226** EF-7; mail Wyalusing z 18853; rural
Homeville; RMC Place; CHESTER; ▲ Upper Oxford; **227** EQ-8; elev. 470ft./143m.; mail Cochranville z 19330; ● 50
Homewood; RMC Place; ALLEGHENY; ***225** WM-4; 🅿; ★ **PGH**; z 15208; pop. incl. with Pittsburgh (Inc. Place)
Homewood (Racine); Inc. Place; BEAVER; ***225** WK-2; ★ **PGH**; mail Beaver Falls z 15010; Ⓟ 162; © 147
Homewood; RMC Place; YORK; ▲ Carroll; ***227** EO-4; ★ **HRBG**; mail Dillsburg z 17019; ● 35
Honeoye; RMC Place; POTTER; ▲ Sharon; ***224** WD-12; mail Shinglehouse z 16748; ● 20
Honesdale; Inc. Place; ⊡ WAYNE; **226** EG-12; elev. 980ft./299m.; 🅿 🅷; z 18431; Ⓟ 4,972; © 4,874
Honey Brook; Inc. Place; CHESTER; **227** EO-9; elev. 740ft./226m.; 🅿; ★ **PHIL-**; z 19344; Ⓟ 1,184; © 1,287
Honey Brook; MCD-Township; CHESTER; ***227** EO-9; 🅿; ★ **PHIL-**; z 19344; does not include the Borough of Honey Brook; Ⓟ 5,449; © 6,278
Honey Creek; RMC Place; MIFFLIN; ▲ Armagh; ***227** EL-1; elev. 847ft./258m.; mail Reedsville z 17084; rural
Honey Grove; RMC Place; JUNIATA; ▲ Tuscarora; **227** EN-1; 🅿; z 17035; ● 200
Honey Pot; RMC Place; LUZERNE; ★ **SCR-**; mail Nanticoke z 18634; pop. incl. with Nanticoke (Inc. Place)
Hood; RMC Place; BUCKS; ★ **PHIL-**; pop. incl. with New Hope (Inc. Place)
Hooker; RMC Place; BUTLER; ▲ Concord; **224** WJ-4; mail Karns City z 16041; ● 100
Hookstown; Inc. Place; BEAVER; **225** WL-1; elev. 1,000ft./305m.; 🅿; ★ **PGH**; z 15050; Ⓟ 169; © 152
Hoover; RMC Place; FAYETTE; ▲ German; ***225** WQ-4; ★ **UNTN**; mail Mc Clellandtown z 15458; ● 60
Hooverhurst; RMC Place; INDIANA; ▲ Montgomery; ***225** WK-9; mail Glen Campbell z 15742; ● 25
Hooversville; Inc. Place; SOMERSET; **225** WO-8; elev. 1,730ft./527m.; 🅿; z 15936; Ⓟ 731; © 779
Hop Bottom; Inc. Place; SUSQUEHANNA; **226** EF-9; elev. 880ft./268m.; 🅿; z 18824; Ⓟ 345; © 333
Hopeland; RMC Place; LANCASTER; ▲ Clay; **227** EO-7; 🅿; ★ **LANC**; z 17533; ● 500
Hope Mills; RMC Place; MERCER; ▲ East Lackawannock; ***224** WI-3; elev. 1,080ft./329m.; mail Mercer z 16137; rural
Hopewell; MCD-Township; BEAVER; ***225** WL-2; ★ **PGH**; mail Aliquippa z 15001; Ⓟ 13,274; © 13,254
Hopewell; Inc. Place; BEDFORD; **225** WO-11; elev. 900ft./274m.; 🅿; z 16650; Ⓟ 194; © 222
Hopewell; MCD-Township; BEDFORD; ***225** WO-11; 🅿; z 16650; does not include the Borough of Hopewell; Ⓟ 1,928; © 1,894
Hopewell; RMC Place; CHESTER; ▲ Lower Oxford, East Nottingham; ***227** EQ-8; elev. 345ft./105m.; mail Oxford z 19363; rural
Hopewell; MCD-Township; CUMBERLAND; ***227** EO-1; mail Newburg z 17240; Ⓟ 1,913; © 2,096
Hopewell; MCD-Township; HUNTINGDON; ***225** WO-11; mail James Creek z 16657; Ⓟ 540; © 587
Hopewell; MCD-Township; WASHINGTON; ***225** WN-2; mail Washington z 15301; Ⓟ 942; © 992
Hopewell; MCD-Township; YORK; ***227** ER-6; ★ **BAL**; mail Stewartstown z 17363; Ⓟ 3,177; © 5,062
Hoppenville; RMC Place; MONTGOMERY; ▲ Marlborough; ***227** EN-11; ★ **PHIL-**; mail Pennsburg z 18073; rural
Hopwood; CDP; FAYETTE; ▲ South Union, North Union; **225** WQ-5; 🅿; ★ **UNTN**; z 15445; Ⓟ 2,021; © 2,006
Horatio; RMC Place; JEFFERSON; ▲ Young; ***224** WJ-8; elev. 1,240ft./378m.; mail Punxsutawney z 15767; rural
Hormtown; RMC Place; JEFFERSON; ▲ Washington; ***224** WI-8; mail Reynoldsville z 15851; rural
Horn Brook; RMC Place; BRADFORD; ▲ Sheshequin; ***226** EE-6; mail Towanda z 18848; rural
Hornby; RMC Place; ERIE; ▲ Greenfield; ***224** WC-4; elev. 1,467ft./447m.; mail North East z 16428; rural
Hornerstown; RMC Place; CAMBRIA; ***225** WN-8; ★ **JNST**; mail Johnstown z 15902; pop. incl. with Johnstown (Inc. Place)
Horning; RMC Place; ALLEGHENY; ***225** WN-4; ★ **PGH**; mail Pittsburgh z 15236; pop. incl. with Baldwin (Inc. Place)
Horntown; DELAWARE; see Oakeola (RMC Place)
Horseshoe Heights; RMC Place; LANCASTER; ▲ East Lampeter; ***227** EP-7; ★ **LANC**; mail Lancaster z 17602; ● 500
Horsham; CDP; MONTGOMERY; ▲ Horsham; **227** EO-12; 🅿; ★ **PHIL-**; z 19044; Ⓟ 15,051; © 14,779
Horsham; MCD-Township; MONTGOMERY; ***227** EO-12; 🅿; ★ **PHIL-**; z 19044; Ⓟ 21,896; © 24,232; ◆ 25,265
Horton; MCD-Township; ELK; ***224** WH-9; mail Brockport z 15823; Ⓟ 1,655; © 1,574
Hosensack; RMC Place; LEHIGH; ▲ Lower Milford; ***227** EM-11; ★ **ALL-**; mail Zionsville z 18092
Hosensock; RMC Place; SCHUYLKILL; ▲ Ryan; ***227** EK-8; ★ **PTSVL**; mail Barnesville z 18214; ● 70
Host; RMC Place; BERKS; ▲ Tulpehocken; **227** EN-7; elev. 369ft./112m.; mail Womelsdorf z 19567; ● 25
Hostetter; RMC Place; WESTMORELAND; ▲ Unity; **225** WN-6; 🅿; ★ **LTROB**; z 15638; ● 460
Hottelville; RMC Place; FOREST; ▲ Barnett; ***224** WH-7; mail Marienville z 16239; rural
Houserville; CDP; CENTRE; ▲ College; **225** WK-13; ★ **STCOL**; mail State College z 16801; © 1,809
Houston; Inc. Place; WASHINGTON; **225** WN-3; elev. 960ft./293m.; 🅿; ★ **PGH**; z 15342; Ⓟ 1,445; © 1,314
Houston City; RMC Place; LUZERNE; ▲ Pittston; ***226** EH-9; ★ **SCR-**; mail Pittston z 18641; ● 110
Houtzdale; Inc. Place; CLEARFIELD; **225** WK-11; elev. 1,518ft./463m.; 🅿; z 16651, z 16698; Ⓟ 1,204; © 941
Hovey; MCD-Township; ARMSTRONG; ***224** WI-5; mail Parker z 16049; Ⓟ 99; © 93
Howard; CAMERON; see Howard Siding (RMC Place)
Howard; Inc. Place; CENTRE; **224** WJ-14; elev. 664ft./202m.; 🅿; z 16841; Ⓟ 749; © 699
Howard; MCD-Township; CENTRE; ***224** WJ-14; 🅿; z 16841; does not include the Borough of Howard; Ⓟ 1,004; © 924
Howard Siding (Howard); RMC Place; CAMERON; ▲ Shippen; ***224** WG-11; elev. 1,160ft./354m.; mail Emporium z 15834; rural
Howe; MCD-Township; FOREST; ***224** WG-8; mail Marienville z 16239; Ⓟ 300; © 417
Howe; RMC Place; JEFFERSON; ▲ Eldred; ***224** WI-8; mail Brookville z 15825; rural
Howe; MCD-Township; PERRY; ***227** EM-3; mail Newport z 17074; Ⓟ 459; © 493
Howellville; RMC Place; CHESTER; ▲ Tredyffrin; ***227** EP-11; elev. 203ft./62m.; ★ **PHIL-**; mail Berwyn z 19312; ● 80
Howersville; RMC Place; NORTHAMPTON; ▲ Lehigh; ***227** EK-10; elev. 530ft./162m.; ★ **ALL-**; mail Walnutport z 18088; rural
Howertown; RMC Place; NORTHAMPTON; ▲ Allen; ***227** EL-11; ★ **ALL-**; mail Northampton z 18067; ● 100
Hoytdale; RMC Place; BEAVER; ***225** WK-2; ★ **PGH**; mail Wampum z 16157; pop. incl. with Big Beaver (Inc. Place)
Hoytville; RMC Place; TIOGA; ▲ Morris; **226** EG-2; mail Morris z 16938; ● 40
Hublersburg; RMC Place; CENTRE; ▲ Walker; **226** EJ-1; 🅿; z 16823; ● 150
Hubley; MCD-Township; SCHUYLKILL; ***227** EL-5; mail Sacramento z 17968, Valley View z 17983; Ⓟ 928; © 889
Huckenberry; RMC Place; CLEARFIELD; ▲ Cooper; ***224** WJ-12; mail Lanse z 16849
Hudson; RMC Place; CLEARFIELD; ▲ Decatur; ***225** WK-11; mail Philipsburg z 16866; ● 100
Hudson; RMC Place; LUZERNE; ▲ Wilkes-Barre; **226** EB-8; 🅿; ★ **SCR-**; z 18702, z 18705; ● 1,150
Hudsondale; RMC Place; CARBON; ▲ Packer; **226** EJ-9; ★ **HAZ**; mail Weatherly z 18255; ● 100
Huefner; RMC Place; CLARION; ▲ Knox; ***224** WH-6; mail Lucinda z 16235; ● 50
Huey; RMC Place; CLARION; ▲ Toby; **224** WI-6; elev. 1,241ft./378m.; 🅿; z 16248; ● 125
Huffs Church; RMC Place; BERKS; ▲ Hereford; **227** EM-10; mail Alburtis z 18011, Barto z 19504; ● 150
Hughes Park; RMC Place; MONTGOMERY; ▲ Upper Merion; ***227** EO-11; ★ **PHIL-**; mail King of Prussia z 19406
Hughestown; Inc. Place; LUZERNE; **226** EB-10; elev. 727ft./222m.; 🅿; ★ **SCR-**; z 18640; Ⓟ 1,734; © 1,541
Hughesville; Inc. Place; LYCOMING; **226** EI-5; elev. 580ft./177m.; 🅿; ★ **WMSPT**; z 17737; Ⓟ 2,049; © 2,220
Hughs; RMC Place; LUZERNE; ▲ Plymouth, Hunlock; ***226** EI-8; elev. 987ft./301m.; ★ **SCR-**; mail Hunlock Creek z 18621; rural
Hulltown; RMC Place; FAYETTE; ▲ Lower Tyrone; ***225** WP-5; mail Dawson z 15428; ● 100
Hulmeville; Inc. Place; BUCKS; **227** EO-13; 🅿; ★ **PHIL-**; z 19047; Ⓟ 916; © 893
Humboldt; RMC Place; LUZERNE; ▲ Hazle; **226** EJ-8; ★ **HAZ**; mail Hazleton z 18202; ● 120
Hummelstown; Inc. Place; DAUPHIN; **227** EN-5; elev. 375ft./114m.; 🅿; ★ **HRBG**; z 17036; Ⓟ 3,981; © 4,360
Hummels Wharf; CDP; SNYDER; ▲ Monroe; **227** EK-4; 🅿; z 17831; Ⓟ 1,069; © 641
Humphreys; RMC Place; WESTMORELAND; ▲ Unity; ***225** WN-6; ★ **LTROB**; mail Greensburg z 15601; ● 60
Humphreyville; RMC Place; CHESTER; ▲ East Fallowfield; ***227** EP-9; ★ **PHIL-**; mail Coatesville z 19320; ● 100
Hungerford; RMC Place; YORK; ***227** EQ-5; ★ **BAL**; mail Shrewsbury z 17361; pop. incl. with Shrewsbury (Inc. Place)
Hungerford; YORK; see Turnpike (RMC Place)
Hungry Hollow; RMC Place; ARMSTRONG; ▲ Parks, Gilpin; ***225** WL-6; ★ **PGH**; mail Leechburg z 15656; rural
Hunker; Inc. Place; WESTMORELAND; **225** WO-5; elev. 980ft./299m.; 🅿; ★ **PGH**; z 15639; Ⓟ 328; © 329
Hunlock; MCD-Township; LUZERNE; ***226** EI-8; ★ **SCR-**; mail Hunlock Creek z 18621; Ⓟ 2,496; © 2,568
Hunlock Creek; RMC Place; LUZERNE; ▲ Hunlock; **226** EI-8; 🅿; ★ **SCR-**; z 18621; ● 300
Hunlock Gardens; RMC Place; LUZERNE; ▲ Hunlock; ***226** EI-8; ★ **SCR-**; mail Hunlock Creek z 18621; ● 70
Hunter (Hunter Station, Raker); RMC Place; NORTHUMBERLAND; ▲ Little Mahanoy; ***227** EL-5; mail Shamokin z 17872; ● 40
Hunter Hill; RMC Place; MONTGOMERY; ▲ Whitemarsh; ★ **PHIL-**; mail Plymouth Meeting z 19462
Hunters Run; RMC Place; CUMBERLAND; ▲ Dickinson; **227** EP-3; ★ **CARL**; mail Gardners z 17324; ● 60
Hunter Station; NORTHUMBERLAND; see Hunter (RMC Place)
Hunterstown; RMC Place; ADAMS; ▲ Straban; **227** EQ-3; mail Gettysburg z 17325; ● 160
Huntersville; RMC Place; LYCOMING; ▲ Wolf, Mill Creek; **226** EH-5; ★ **WMSPT**; mail Muncy z 17756; ● 50
Huntingdon; Inc. Place; ⊡ HUNTINGDON; **225** WM-12; elev. 643ft./196m.; 🅿 🅷 🅲 1,460; z 16652, z 16654; Ⓟ 6,843; © 6,918
HUNTINGDON; **225** WN-12; Ⓟ 44,164; © 45,586; ◆ 45,809
Huntingdon Furnace; RMC Place; HUNTINGDON; ▲ Franklin; ***225** WL-12; mail Tyrone z 16686; rural
Huntingdon Heights; RMC Place; WESTMORELAND; ▲ North Huntingdon; ***225** WN-5; ★ **PGH**; mail Irwin z 15642; ● 600
Huntingdon Manor; RMC Place; LANCASTER; ▲ Upper Leacock, West Earl; ★ **LANC**; mail Leola z 17540
Huntingdon Valley; RMC Place; MONTGOMERY; ▲ Lower Moreland; **228** A-6; 🅿; ★ **PHIL-**; z 19006; ● 10,000
Hunting Park; RMC Place; PHILADELPHIA; ★ **PHIL-**; mail Philadelphia z 19140; pop. incl. with Philadelphia (Inc. Place)
Huntington; MCD-Township; ADAMS; ***227** EP-3; mail York Springs z 17372; Ⓟ 1,989; © 2,233
Huntington; MCD-Township; LUZERNE; ***226** EI-7; mail Shickshinny z 18655; Ⓟ 1,905; © 2,104
Huntington Mills; RMC Place; LUZERNE; ▲ Huntington; **226** EI-7; 🅿; z 18622; ● 175
Huntley; RMC Place; CAMERON; ▲ Gibson; ***224** WH-12; mail Driftwood z 15832; rural
Huntsdale; RMC Place; CUMBERLAND; ▲ Penn; **227** EO-2; mail Carlisle z 17013; ● 300
Huntsville; RMC Place; LUZERNE; ▲ Lehman, Jackson; **226** EH-8; ★ **SCR-**; mail Dallas z 18612; ● 100
Husband; RMC Place; SOMERSET; ▲ Somerset; ***225** WP-8; mail Somerset z 15501
Huston; MCD-Township; BLAIR; ***225** WN-11; mail Martinsburg z 16662, Williamsburg z 16693; Ⓟ 1,189; © 1,262
Huston; MCD-Township; CENTRE; ***225** WK-12; mail Julian z 16844; Ⓟ 1,282; © 1,311
Huston; MCD-Township; CLEARFIELD; ***224** WI-10; mail Penfield z 15849; Ⓟ 1,352; © 1,468
Huston Run; RMC Place; WASHINGTON; ▲ Union; ***225** WN-4; elev. 764ft./233m.; ★ **PGH**; mail Finleyville z 15332; rural
Hustontown; RMC Place; FULTON; ▲ Taylor, Dublin; **225** WP-12; 🅿; z 17229 & mail Harrisonville z 17228; ● 450
Hutchins; RMC Place; MCKEAN; ▲ Sergeant; ***224** WF-10; mail Mount Jewett z 16740; rural
Hutchinson; RMC Place; FAYETTE; ▲ South Union; ***225** WQ-5; ★ **UNTN**; mail Uniontown z 15401; ● 250
Hutchinson; RMC Place; WESTMORELAND; ▲ Sewickley; ***225** WO-5; 🅿; ★ **PGH**; z 15640; ● 450
Hyde; CDP; CLEARFIELD; ▲ Lawrence; **224** WJ-10; 🅿; z 16843; Ⓟ 1,643; © 1,491
Hyde Park; RMC Place; BERKS; ▲ Muhlenberg; **227** ES-13; ★ **READ**; mail Reading z 19605; ● 2,200
Hyde Park; RMC Place; LACKAWANNA; ***226** EH-10; ★ **SCR-**; mail Scranton z 18504; pop. incl. with Scranton (Inc. Place)
Hyde Park; Inc. Place; WESTMORELAND; ***225** WL-5; elev. 793ft./242m.; 🅿; ★ **PGH**; z 15641; Ⓟ 542; © 513
Hydetown; Inc. Place; CRAWFORD; **224** WF-5; elev. 1,245ft./379m.; 🅿; z 16328; Ⓟ 681; © 605
Hyde Villa; RMC Place; BERKS; ▲ Muhlenberg; ★ **READ**; mail Reading z 19605
Hyndman; Inc. Place; BEDFORD; **225** WQ-9; elev. 948ft./289m.; 🅿; z 15545; Ⓟ 1,019; © 1,005
Hynemansville; RMC Place; LEHIGH; ▲ Weisenberg; ***227** EL-10; ★ **ALL-**; mail New Tripoli z 18066; rural
Hyner; RMC Place; CLINTON; ▲ Chapman; **224** WH-14; 🅿; z 17738; ● 150

I

Icedale; RMC Place; CHESTER; ▲ West Brandywine; ***227** EP-9; ★ **PHIL-**; mail Honey Brook z 19344; rural
Icedale; CHESTER; see Valley View (RMC Place)
Ickesburg; RMC Place; PERRY; ▲ Saville; **227** EM-2; 🅿; z 17037; ● 280
Idaho; RMC Place; ARMSTRONG; ▲ South Bend; ***225** WL-6; mail Shelocta z 15774; rural
Idamar; RMC Place; INDIANA; ▲ Rayne; **225** WL-8; mail Dixonville z 15734; ● 30
Idaville; RMC Place; ADAMS; ▲ Huntington; **227** EP-3; 🅿; z 17337; ● 200
Idetown; RMC Place; LUZERNE; ***226** EH-8; ★ **SCR-**; mail Dallas z 18612; pop. incl. with Harveys Lake (Inc. Place)
Idlewood; RMC Place; ALLEGHENY; ***225** WM-3; ★ **PGH**; mail Pittsburgh z 15205; pop. incl. with Crafton (Inc. Place)
Imler; RMC Place; BEDFORD; ▲ King; **225** WO-10; 🅿; z 16655; ● 150
Imlertown; RMC Place; BEDFORD; ▲ Bedford; ***225** WO-10; elev. 1,129ft./344m.; mail Bedford z 15522; rural
Immaculata; RMC Place; CHESTER; ▲ East Whiteland; ***227** EP-10; 🅿 🅲 3,563; ★ **PHIL-**; z 19345; ● 1,450
Imperial; RMC Place; ALLEGHENY; ▲ North Fayette, Findlay; **225** WM-2; 🅿; ★ **PGH**; z 15126; ● 2,200
Imperial-Enlow; CDP-Census Area Only; ALLEGHENY; ▲ North Fayette, Findlay; ***225** WM-2; ★ **PGH**; mail Imperial z 15126; Ⓟ 3,449; © 3,514
Independence; RMC Place; BEAVER; ▲ Independence; ***225** WL-2; ★ **PGH**; mail Aliquippa z 15001; ● 100
Independence; MCD-Township; BEAVER; ***225** WM-2; ★ **PGH**; mail Aliquippa z 15001; Ⓟ 2,563; © 2,802
Independence; RMC Place; SNYDER; ▲ Chapman; **227** EL-4; mail Port Trevorton z 17864; ● 70
Independence; RMC Place; WASHINGTON; ▲ Independence; **225** WN-1; mail Avella z 15312; ● 110
Independence; MCD-Township; WASHINGTON; ***225** WN-1; mail Avella z 15312; Ⓟ 1,868; © 1,676
Indiana; MCD-Township; ALLEGHENY; ***225** WL-4; ★ **PGH**; mail Indianola z 15051, Pittsburgh z 15238; Ⓟ 6,024; © 6,809
Indiana; Inc. Place; ⊡ INDIANA; **225** WL-7; elev. 1,310ft./399m.; 🅿 🅷 🅲 14,248 ■; z 15701, z 15705; Ⓟ 15,174; © 14,895; ◆ 14,561
INDIANA; **225** WL-8; Ⓟ 89,994; © 89,605; ◆ 86,678
Indian Creek; RMC Place; BUCKS; ▲ Bristol; ***227** EO-13; ★ **PHIL-**; mail Levittown z 19057
Indian Crossing; RMC Place; MCKEAN; ▲ Ceres; **224** WD-11; elev. 1,444ft./440m.; mail Eldred z 16731; ● 20
Indian Head; RMC Place; ERIE; ▲ LeBoeuf; ***224** WE-4; ★ **ERIE**; mail Waterford z 16441
Indian Head; RMC Place; FAYETTE; ▲ Saltlick; **225** WP-6; 🅿; z 15446; ● 175
Indian Hills; RMC Place; ARMSTRONG; ▲ Manor; ***225** WK-6; elev. 1,223ft./373m.; ★ **PGH**; mail Kittanning z 16201; ● 40
Indian King; RMC Place; CHESTER; ▲ West Whiteland; ***227** EP-10; elev. 512ft./156m.; ★ **PHIL-**; mail West Chester z 19380; ● 900
Indian Lake; RMC Place; LUZERNE; ▲ Buck; ***226** EI-10; elev. 1,889ft./576m.; mail White Haven z 18661; ● 50
Indian Lake; Inc. Place; SOMERSET; ***225** WP-9; elev. 2,300ft./701m.; mail Central City z 15926; Ⓟ 388; © 450
Indianland; RMC Place; NORTHAMPTON; ▲ Lehigh; ***227** EK-10; elev. 596ft./182m.; ★ **ALL-**; mail Walnutport z 18088; rural
Indian Mountain Lake; RMC Place; CARBON; ▲ Tunkhannock, Penn Forest; ***226** EJ-10; mail Albrightsville z 18210; ● 950
Indianola; RMC Place; ALLEGHENY; ▲ Indiana; **225** WM-4; 🅿; ★ **PGH**; z 15051; ● 900
Indian Orchard; RMC Place; WAYNE; ▲ Texas; **226** EG-12; elev. 1,100ft./335m.; mail Honesdale z 18431; ● 300
Indian Springs Estates; RMC Place; INDIANA; ▲ White; ***225** WL-7; elev. 1,322ft./403m.; mail Indiana z 15701; ● 75
Industry (Frank); RMC Place; ALLEGHENY; ▲ Elizabeth; ***225** WN-4; ★ **PGH**; mail Buena Vista z 15018; ● 800
Industry; Inc. Place; BEAVER; **225** WL-2; elev. 700ft./213m.; 🅿; ★ **PGH**; z 15052; Ⓟ 2,124; © 1,921
Inez; RMC Place; POTTER; ▲ Homer; ***224** WF-12; elev. 1,870ft./570m.; mail Coudersport z 16915; rural
Ingleby; RMC Place; CENTRE; ▲ Haines; ***227** EK-2; mail Woodward z 16882; rural
Inglenook; RMC Place; DAUPHIN; ▲ Reed; ***227** EN-4; ★ **HRBG**; mail Halifax z 17032; rural
Inglesmith; RMC Place; BEDFORD; ▲ Mann; ***225** WQ-11; mail Artemas z 17211; rural
Ingomar; RMC Place; ALLEGHENY; ***225** WL-3; elev. 1,200ft./366m.; 🅿; ★ **PGH**; z 15127 & mail Pittsburgh z 15237
Ingram; Inc. Place; ALLEGHENY; **228** J-4; elev. 880ft./268m.; ★ **PGH**; mail Pittsburgh z 15205; Ⓟ 3,901; © 3,712
Inkerman; RMC Place; LUZERNE; ▲ Jackson; **226** EB-9; 🅿; ★ **SCR-**; z 18640; ● 735
Intercourse; RMC Place; LANCASTER; ▲ Leacock; **227** EP-8; 🅿; ★ **LANC**; z 17534; ● 1,200
Iola; CDP; COLUMBIA; ▲ Greenwood; **226** EI-6; mail Millville z 17846; © 129
Iona; RMC Place; LEBANON; ▲ South Lebanon; **227** EN-7; ★ **LEB**; mail Lebanon z 17042; ● 800
Irishtown; RMC Place; ADAMS; ▲ Oxford; **227** EQ-4; ★ **HANV**; mail New Oxford z 17350; ● 430
Irishtown; RMC Place; CLEARFIELD; ▲ Penn; ***224** WJ-10; elev. 1,902ft./580m.; mail Grampian z 16838; rural
Irishtown; RMC Place; MCKEAN; ▲ Lafayette; ***224** WE-10; elev. 2,105ft./642m.; mail Lewis Run z 16738; rural
Irishtown; RMC Place; MERCER; ▲ Findley; ***224** WI-3; mail Mercer z 16137; rural
Ironbridge; MONTGOMERY; see Rahns (RMC Place)
Iron Bridge; RMC Place; WESTMORELAND; ▲ East Huntingdon; ***225** WO-6; mail Mount Pleasant z 15666; ● 300
Iron Springs (Maria Furnace); RMC Place; ADAMS; ▲ Hamiltonban; **227** EQ-2; mail Fairfield z 17320; ● 200
Ironton; RMC Place; LEHIGH; ▲ North Whitehall; **226** EA-1; ★ **ALL-**; mail Coplay z 18037; ● 300
Ironville; RMC Place; BLAIR; ▲ Snyder; ***225** WL-12; ★ **ALT**; mail Tyrone z 16686; ● 125
Ironville; RMC Place; LANCASTER; ▲ West Hempfield; ***227** EP-6; elev. 623ft./190m.; ★ **LANC**; mail Columbia z 17512; ● 100
Irvin; RMC Place; ALLEGHENY; ★ **PGH**; pop. incl. with West Mifflin (Inc. Place)
Irvine; RMC Place; WARREN; ▲ Brokenstraw; **224** WE-7; 🅿; z 16329, z 16368-69; ● 200
Irving; RMC Place; SCHUYLKILL; ▲ Pine Grove; ***227** EM-6; mail Pine Grove z 17963; ● 150
Irvona; Inc. Place; CLEARFIELD; **225** WK-10; elev. 1,379ft./420m.; 🅿; z 16656; Ⓟ 666; © 680
Irwin; MCD-Township; VENANGO; ***224** WH-4; mail Harrisville z 16038; Ⓟ 1,182; © 1,309
Irwin; Inc. Place; WESTMORELAND; **225** WN-5; elev. 960ft./293m.; 🅿; ★ **PGH**; z 15642; Ⓟ 4,604; © 4,366
Isabella; RMC Place; FAYETTE; ▲ Luzerne; **225** WP-4; 🅿; ★ **UNTN**; z 15447; ● 275
Iselin; RMC Place; INDIANA; ▲ Young; **225** WM-6; mail Saltsburg z 15681; ● 275
Iselin Heights; RMC Place; CLEARFIELD; ▲ Sandy; ***224** WI-9; mail Du Bois z 15801; ● 250
Island Lake; RMC Place; WAYNE; ▲ Scott; ***226** EE-11; elev. 1,843ft./562m.; mail Starrucca z 18462; ● 80
Island Park (Packers Island); RMC Place; NORTHUMBERLAND; ▲ Upper Augusta; ***227** EK-5; mail Sunbury z 17801; ● 300
Ithan; RMC Place; DELAWARE; ▲ Radnor; ***227** EP-11; ★ **PHIL-**; mail Villanova z 19085
Iva; RMC Place; LANCASTER; ▲ Paradise; ***227** EP-8; mail Paradise z 17562; rural
Ivarea; RMC Place; ERIE; ▲ Elk Creek; ***224** WE-3; elev. 1,168ft./356m.; mail Cranesville z 16410; rural
Ivyland; Inc. Place; BUCKS; **227** EO-12; 🅿; ★ **PHIL-**; z 18974; Ⓟ 490; © 492
Ivy Mills; RMC Place; DELAWARE; ★ **PHIL-**; mail Glen Mills z 19342
Ivy Ridge; RMC Place; PHILADELPHIA; ★ **PHIL-**; mail Philadelphia z 19101; pop. incl. with Philadelphia (Inc. Place)
Ivywood; RMC Place; BUTLER; ***225** WL-4; ★ **PGH**; mail Saxonburg z 16056; ● 40
Ivywood; RMC Place; PIKE; ▲ Palmyra; ***226** EH-12; mail Paupack z 18451

J

Jacks Creek; RMC Place; MIFFLIN; ▲ Derry; ***227** EL-1; elev. 600ft./183m.; mail Lewistown z 17044; rural
Jacks Mountain; RMC Place; ADAMS; ▲ Hamiltonban; ***227** EQ-2; mail Fairfield z 17320; rural
Jackson; MCD-Township; BUTLER; ***225** WK-3; ★ **PGH**; mail Zelienople z 16063; Ⓟ 3,078; © 3,645
Jackson; MCD-Township; CAMBRIA; ***225** WM-9; ★ **JNST**; mail Johnstown z 15909; Ⓟ 5,213; © 4,925
Jackson; MCD-Township; COLUMBIA; ***226** EH-6; mail Benton z 17814; Ⓟ 508; © 598
Jackson; MCD-Township; DAUPHIN; ***227** EM-4; mail Halifax z 17032; Ⓟ 1,797; © 1,728
Jackson; MCD-Township; GREENE; ***225** WQ-2; mail Holbrook z 15341; Ⓟ 546; © 516
Jackson; MCD-Township; HUNTINGDON; ***225** WL-13; mail Petersburg z 16669; Ⓟ 816; © 882
Jackson; MCD-Township; LEBANON; ***227** EN-7; ★ **LEB**; mail Lebanon z 17042; Ⓟ 5,732; © 6,338
Jackson; MCD-Township; LUZERNE; ***226** EH-8; ★ **SCR-**; mail Shavertown z 18708; Ⓟ 5,336; © 4,453
Jackson; MCD-Township; LYCOMING; ***226** EH-8; mail Roaring Branch z 17765; Ⓟ 421; © 414
Jackson; MCD-Township; MERCER; ***224** WH-3; mail Jackson Center z 16133; does not include the Borough of Jackson Center; Ⓟ 1,089; © 1,206
Jackson; MCD-Township; MONROE; ***226** EJ-11; mail Reeders z 18352; Ⓟ 3,757; © 5,979

Entries in **UPPERCASE** are counties.
Entries in **bold** have populations of 2,500 or more.
Names in parentheses are alternate names.

Inc. Place	Incorporated Place
RMC Place	Rand McNally Designated Place
CDP	Census Designated Place
MCD	Minor Civil Division

⊡ County Seat
▲ Minor Civil Division
elev. Elevation
🅿 Post Office
🅷 Hospital
🅲 College
■ Principal Business Center
★ Ranally Metro Area (RMA) Abbreviation
z Zip Code(s)
Ⓟ Previous Census Population
® Revised Census Population
Ⓐ Annexation Population
● Rand McNally Population Estimate
© Final Census Population
Ⓢ Special Census Population
◆ Estimated Population

For additional definitions see Glossary, Volume 1, and Introduction, Volume 2.

Jackson; MCD-Township; NORTHUMBERLAND; *227 EL-5; mail Herndon z 17830; Ⓟ 845; Ⓒ 928
Jackson; MCD-Township; PERRY; *227 EO-2; mail Blain z 17006; Ⓟ 489; Ⓒ 525
Jackson; MCD-Township; SNYDER; *227 EK-4; mail Winfield z 17889; Ⓟ 1,383; Ⓒ 1,276
Jackson; RMC Place; SUSQUEHANNA; ▲ Jackson; 226 EE-10; elev. 1,355ft./413m.; 🅿; z 18825; ● 90
Jackson; MCD-Township; SUSQUEHANNA; *226 EE-10; 🅿; z 18825; Ⓟ 757; Ⓒ 788
Jackson; MCD-Township; TIOGA; *226 ED-4; mail Millerton z 16936; Ⓟ 2,072; Ⓒ 2,054
Jackson; MCD-Township; VENANGO; *224 WG-4; mail Cooperstown z 16317; Ⓟ 1,089; Ⓒ 1,168
Jackson; MCD-Township; YORK; *227 EQ-4; ★ YORK; mail Spring Grove z 17362; Ⓟ 6,244; Ⓒ 6,095
Jackson Center; Inc. Place; MERCER; 224 WH-3; elev. 1,318ft./402m.; 🅿; z 16133; Ⓟ 244; Ⓒ 221
Jackson Corner; RMC Place; HUNTINGDON; ▲ Miller; *225 WL-13; mail Huntingdon z 16652; rural
Jackson Crossing; RMC Place; WARREN; ▲ Conewango; *224 WE-7; mail Warren z 16365
Jackson Knolls Gardens; RMC Place; LAWRENCE; ▲ North Beaver; *224 WJ-2; ★ YNGS-; mail New Castle z 16101; ● 100
Jackson Summit; RMC Place; TIOGA; ▲ Jackson; *226 EE-4; mail Millerton z 16936
Jackson Valley; RMC Place; SUSQUEHANNA; ▲ Middletown; *226 EE-8; mail Friendsville z 18818, Little Meadows z 18830; rural
Jacksonville (Traymore Manor); RMC Place; BUCKS; ▲ Northampton; *227 EO-13; elev. 309ft./94m.; ★ PHIL-; mail Warminster z 18974; ● 700
Jacksonville; RMC Place; CENTRE; ▲ Marion; 224 WJ-14; mail Howard z 16841; ● 80
Jacksonville (Kent); CDP; INDIANA; ▲ Black Lick; 225 WM-7; elev. 1,063ft./324m.; mail Kent z 15752; Ⓒ 675
Jacksonville; RMC Place; LEHIGH; ▲ Lynn; 227 EL-9; ★ ALL-; mail New Tripoli z 18066; ● 100
Jacksonville; RMC Place; NORTHAMPTON; ▲ East Allen; *227 EL-11; ★ ALL-; mail Bath z 18014; ● 100
Jacksonwald; RMC Place; BERKS; ▲ Exeter; 227 ET-14; elev. 349ft./106m.; ★ READ; mail Reading z 19606; ● 1,100
Jacksville; RMC Place; BUTLER; ▲ Worth; *224 WJ-3; mail Slippery Rock z 16057; ● 20
Jacktown; RMC Place; WESTMORELAND; ▲ North Huntingdon; *225 WN-5; ★ PGH; mail Irwin z 15642; ● 200
Jacktown Acres; RMC Place; WESTMORELAND; ▲ North Huntingdon; *225 WN-5; ★ PGH; mail Irwin z 15642; ● 1,300
Jacobs Creek; RMC Place; WESTMORELAND; ▲ South Huntingdon; 225 WO-5; 🅿; ★ PGH; z 15448; ● 275
Jacobs Mills; RMC Place; YORK; ▲ Heidelberg; *227 EQ-4; mail Hanover z 17331; ● 35
Jacobus; Inc. Place; YORK; 227 EQ-5; elev. 720ft./219m.; 🅿; ★ YORK; z 17407; Ⓟ 1,370; Ⓒ 1,203
Jalappa; RMC Place; BERKS; ▲ Tilden; *227 EM-8; elev. 436ft./133m.; ★ READ; mail Hamburg z 19526; ● 90
James City; RMC Place; ELK; ▲ Highland; 224 WF-9; 🅿; z 16734; ● 400
James Creek; HUNTINGDON; see Marklesburg (Inc. Place)
Jamestown; RMC Place; CAMBRIA; ▲ Portage; 225 WN-10; mail Portage z 15946; ● 400
Jamestown; RMC Place; CARBON; ▲ Mahoning; *227 EK-10; mail Lehighton z 18235; ● 200
Jamestown; Inc. Place; MERCER; 224 WG-2; elev. 982ft./299m.; 🅿; z 16134; Ⓟ 761; Ⓒ 636
Jamesville; RMC Place; NORTHAMPTON; ▲ East Allen; *227 EL-11; elev. 722ft./220m.; ★ ALL-; mail Bath z 18014; ● 200
Jamison; RMC Place; BUCKS; ▲ Warwick; 227 EN-12; 🅿; ★ PHIL-; z 18929; ● 850
Jamison; RMC Place; FAYETTE; ▲ South Union; ★ UNTN; mail Uniontown z 15401
Jamison; RMC Place; FOREST; ▲ Tionesta; *224 WG-6; elev. 1,072ft./327m.; mail West Hickory z 16370; rural
Jamison City; CDP; COLUMBIA; ▲ Sugarloaf; 226 EH-7; mail Benton z 17814; Ⓒ 102
Janesville (Smithmill); RMC Place; CLEARFIELD; ▲ Gulich; 225 WK-11; mail Smithmill z 16680; ● 600
Japan; RMC Place; LUZERNE; ▲ Hazle; *226 EJ-9; ★ HAZ; mail Freeland z 18224; ● 180
Jarrettown; RMC Place; MONTGOMERY; ▲ Upper Dublin; *227 EO-12; ★ PHIL-; mail Dresher z 19025
Jay; MCD-Township; ELK; *224 WH-10; mail Weedville z 15868; Ⓟ 2,087; Ⓒ 2,094
Jeanesville; RMC Place; LUZERNE; ▲ Hazle; *226 EJ-8; ★ HAZ; mail Hazleton z 18201; ● 300
Jeannette; Inc. Place; WESTMORELAND; 225 WN-5; elev. 1,055ft./322m.; 🅿 🅷; ★ PGH; z 15644; Ⓟ 11,221; Ⓒ 10,654
Jeddo; Inc. Place; LUZERNE; 226 EJ-9; elev. 1,603ft./489m.; ★ HAZ; mail Freeland z 18224; Ⓟ 124; Ⓒ 144
Jednota; RMC Place; DAUPHIN; ▲ Lower Swatara; *227 EO-5; ★ HRBG; mail Middletown z 17057; ● 200
Jefferis Crossing; RMC Place; FAYETTE; ▲ German; ★ UNTN; mail Uniontown z 15401; ● 20
Jefferson (Jefferson Hills); Inc. Place; ALLEGHENY; 225 WN-4; elev. 780ft./238m.; ★ PGH; mail Clairton z 15025; Ⓟ 9,533; Ⓒ 9,666
Jefferson; MCD-Township; BERKS; *227 EM-8; mail Bernville z 19506; Ⓟ 1,410; Ⓒ 1,604
Jefferson; MCD-Township; BUTLER; *225 WK-4; ★ PGH; mail Saxonburg z 16056; Ⓟ 4,812; Ⓒ 5,690
Jefferson; MCD-Township; DAUPHIN; *227 EM-5; mail Halifax z 17032; Ⓟ 385; Ⓒ 327
Jefferson; MCD-Township; FAYETTE; *225 WP-4; ★ PGH; mail Grindstone z 15442; Ⓟ 2,047; Ⓒ 2,259
Jefferson; Inc. Place; GREENE; 225 WP-3; elev. 960ft./293m.; 🅿; z 15344; Ⓟ 355; Ⓒ 337
Jefferson; MCD-Township; GREENE; *225 WP-3; 🅿; z 15344; does not include the Borough of Jefferson; Ⓟ 2,536; Ⓒ 2,528
Jefferson; MCD-Township; LACKAWANNA; *226 EG-10; ★ SCR-; mail Lake Ariel z 18436; Ⓟ 3,438; Ⓒ 3,592
Jefferson; MCD-Township; MERCER; *224 WH-2; mail Hermitage z 16148; Ⓟ 1,998; Ⓒ 2,416
Jefferson; RMC Place; SCHUYLKILL; ▲ South Manheim; *227 EM-8; elev. 559ft./170m.; ★ PTSVL; mail Auburn z 17922; ● 30
Jefferson; MCD-Township; SOMERSET; *225 WP-7; mail Somerset z 15501; Ⓟ 1,462; Ⓒ 1,375
Jefferson; RMC Place; WASHINGTON; ▲ Jefferson; *225 WN-1; mail Avella z 15312; ● 40
Jefferson; MCD-Township; WASHINGTON; *225 WN-1; mail Burgettstown z 15021; Ⓟ 1,212; Ⓒ 1,218
Jefferson (Codorus); Inc. Place; YORK; 227 EQ-4; elev. 660ft./201m.; ★ BAL; mail Codorus z 17311; Ⓟ 675; Ⓒ 631
JEFFERSON; 224 WH-8; Ⓟ 46,083; Ⓒ 45,932; ◆ 45,007
Jefferson Center; RMC Place; BUTLER; ▲ Jefferson; 225 WK-4; ★ PGH; mail Saxonburg z 16056; ● 80
Jefferson Hills; ALLEGHENY; see Jefferson (Inc. Place)
Jeffersonville; RMC Place; MONTGOMERY; ▲ West Norriton; *227 EO-11; 🅿; ★ PHIL-; z 19403 & mail Norristown z 19401
Jenkins (Jenkins Township); MCD-Township; LUZERNE; *226 EH-9; ★ SCR-; mail Pittston z 18640; Ⓟ 4,740; Ⓒ 4,584
Jenkins Corner; RMC Place; LANCASTER; ▲ Fulton; *227 ER-8; mail Peach Bottom z 17563; rural
Jenkins Township; LUZERNE; see Jenkins (MCD-Township)
Jenkintown; Inc. Place; MONTGOMERY; 227 EO-12; elev. 250ft./76m.; 🅿 ■; ★ PHIL-; z 19046; Ⓟ 4,574; Ⓒ 4,478; ◆ 4,466
Jenkintown Manor; RMC Place; MONTGOMERY; ▲ Abington; *227 EO-12; elev. 300ft./91m.; ★ PHIL-; mail Elkins Park z 19027; ● 2,100
Jenks; MCD-Township; FOREST; *224 WG-8; mail Marienville z 16239; Ⓟ 1,321; Ⓒ 1,261
Jenner; SOMERSET; see Jenners (RMC Place)
Jenner; MCD-Township; SOMERSET; *225 WO-7; mail Jenners z 15546; Ⓟ 4,147; Ⓒ 4,054
Jenners (Jenner); RMC Place; SOMERSET; ▲ Jenner; 225 WO-8; 🅿; z 15546; ● 250
Jenners Crossroads; RMC Place; SOMERSET; ▲ Jenner; *225 WO-8; elev. 1,930ft./588m.; mail Boswell z 15531; ● 100
Jennerstown; Inc. Place; SOMERSET; 225 WO-8; elev. 1,950ft./594m.; 🅿; z 15547; Ⓟ 635; Ⓒ 714
Jennersville; RMC Place; CHESTER; ▲ Penn; 227 EQ-9; elev. 580ft./177m.; ★ PHIL-; mail West Grove z 19390; ● 45
Jenningsville; RMC Place; WYOMING; ▲ Windham; 226 EG-8; mail Mehoopany z 18629; ● 100
Jericho; RMC Place; CAMERON; ▲ Grove; 224 WH-12; mail Sinnamahoning z 15861; ● 20
Jericho Mills; RMC Place; JUNIATA; ▲ Fermanagh; *227 EL-2; mail Mifflintown z 17059; rural
Jermyn; Inc. Place; LACKAWANNA; 226 EG-10; elev. 956ft./291m.; 🅿; ★ SCR-; z 18433; Ⓟ 2,263; Ⓒ 2,287
Jerome; CDP; SOMERSET; ▲ Conemaugh; 225 WO-8; elev. 1,796ft./547m.; 🅿; ★ JNST; z 15937; Ⓟ 1,074; Ⓒ 1,068
Jerome Junction; RMC Place; SOMERSET; ★ JNST; pop. incl. with Benson (Inc. Place)
Jersey Mills; RMC Place; LYCOMING; ▲ McHenry; 226 EH-2; 🅿; z 17739; ● 55
Jersey Shore; Inc. Place; LYCOMING; 226 EI-3; elev. 610ft./186m.; 🅿 🅷; ★ WMSPT; z 17723, z 17727, z 17740; Ⓟ 4,353; Ⓒ 4,482
Jerseytown; CDP; COLUMBIA; ▲ Madison; 226 EJ-6; elev. 625ft./191m.; mail Bloomsburg z 17815; Ⓒ 150
Jerusalem Corners; RMC Place; VENANGO; ▲ Oilcreek; *224 WF-5; mail Pleasantville z 16341; rural
Jessup; Inc. Place; LACKAWANNA; 226 EG-10; elev. 980ft./299m.; 🅿; ★ SCR-; z 18434; Ⓟ 4,605; Ⓒ 4,718; Ⓡ 4,703
Jessup; MCD-Township; SUSQUEHANNA; *226 EE-8; mail Montrose z 18801; Ⓟ 483; Ⓒ 564
Jim Thorpe (Mauch Chunk); Inc. Place; ⊡ CARBON; 227 EK-9; elev. 600ft./183m.; 🅿; z 18229; Ⓟ 5,048; Ⓒ 4,804
Jimtown; RMC Place; SOMERSET; ▲ Jefferson; *225 WP-7; elev. 2,050ft./625m.; mail Somerset z 15501; rural
Joanna; RMC Place; BERKS; ▲ Caernarvon; 227 EO-9; elev. 627ft./191m.; mail Elverson z 19520, Morgantown z 19543; ● 80
Joanna Heights; RMC Place; BERKS; ▲ Robeson; *227 EO-9; elev. 600ft./183m.; ★ READ; mail Morgantown z 19543
Jobs Corners; RMC Place; TIOGA; ▲ Jackson; *226 EE-4; elev. 1,456ft./444m.; mail Millerton z 16936
Joffre (Raccoon); RMC Place; WASHINGTON; ▲ Smith; 225 WN-2; 🅿; ★ PGH; z 15053; ● 500
Johnsonburg; Inc. Place; ELK; 224 WG-10; elev. 1,455ft./443m.; 🅿; z 15845; Ⓟ 3,350; Ⓒ 3,003
Johnsonburg; RMC Place; INDIANA; ▲ Banks; *225 WK-9; elev. 1,850ft./564m.; mail Rossiter z 15772; rural
Johnsons Corner; RMC Place; DELAWARE; ▲ Concord; *227 EQ-10; elev. 402ft./123m.; ★ PHIL-; mail Chadds Ford z 19317; rural
Johnsonville; NORTHAMPTON; see Stier (RMC Place)
Johnstown; Inc. Place; CAMBRIA; 225 WN-8; elev. 1,180ft./360m.; 🅿 🅷 🅲 3,142 ■; ★ JNST; z 15901-02, z 15904-07, z 15909, z 15915, z 15945; Ⓟ 28,134; Ⓒ 23,906; ◆ 20,256
Johnstown; RMC Place; UNION; ▲ West Buffalo; *226 EJ-4; mail Mifflinburg z 17844; ● 45
Johnsville; RMC Place; BUCKS; ▲ Warminster; *227 EO-13; elev. 310ft./94m.; ★ PHIL-; mail Warminster z 18974
John Wanamaker; RMC Place; PHILADELPHIA; ★ PHIL-; mail Philadelphia z 19107; pop. incl. with Philadelphia (Inc. Place)
Jo Jo; RMC Place; MCKEAN; ▲ Wetmore; *224 WF-9; elev. 1,697ft./517m.; mail Kane z 16735; rural
Joliett; RMC Place; SCHUYLKILL; ▲ Porter; 227 EL-6; 🅿; z 17981; ● 275
Joller; RMC Place; HUNTINGDON; ▲ Todd; *225 WO-12; mail Robertsdale z 16674; rural
Jollytown; RMC Place; GREENE; ▲ Gilmore; 225 WQ-2; mail New Freeport z 15352; ● 25
Jonas; RMC Place; MONROE; ▲ Polk; 226 EJ-10; mail Kunkletown z 18058; ● 60
Jonathan Point; RMC Place; CARBON; ▲ Kidder; *226 EJ-10; elev. 1,541ft./470m.; mail Albrightsville z 18210; rural
Jones; MCD-Township; ELK; *224 WF-10; mail Wilcox z 15870; Ⓟ 1,870; Ⓒ 1,721
Jones Mills; RMC Place; WESTMORELAND; ▲ Donegal; 225 WO-6; 🅿; z 15646; ● 300
Jones Terrace; RMC Place; NORTHAMPTON; ▲ Palmer; *227 EL-12; ★ ALL-; mail Easton z 18042; ● 1,100
Jonestown; CDP; COLUMBIA; ▲ Fishing Creek; 226 EI-7; elev. 696ft./212m.; mail Orangeville z 17859; Ⓒ 34
Jonestown; Inc. Place; LEBANON; 227 EN-6; elev. 475ft./145m.; 🅿; ★ LEB; z 17038; Ⓟ 931; Ⓒ 1,028
Jonestown; RMC Place; SCHUYLKILL; ▲ Cass; *227 EL-7; ★ PTSVL; mail Pottsville z 17901
Jonestown; RMC Place; WASHINGTON; ▲ Fallowfield; *225 WO-4; ★ PGH; mail Charleroi z 15022; rural
Jordan; MCD-Township; CLEARFIELD; *225 WK-10; mail Irvona z 16656; Ⓟ 533; Ⓒ 543
Jordan; LEHIGH; see Pleasant Corners (RMC Place)
Jordan; MCD-Township; LYCOMING; *226 EH-6; mail Unityville z 17774; Ⓟ 871; Ⓒ 878
Jordan; MCD-Township; NORTHUMBERLAND; *227 EL-5; mail Herndon z 17830; Ⓟ 847; Ⓒ 761
Jordan Hollow; LACKAWANNA; see East Benton (RMC Place)
Jordan Valley; RMC Place; LEHIGH; ▲ Heidelberg; *227 EL-10; elev. 639ft./195m.; ★ ALL-; mail Germansville z 18053; ● 40
Josephine; RMC Place; INDIANA; ▲ Burrell; 225 WM-7; 🅿; ★ LTROB; z 15750; ● 300
Joyce; RMC Place; LAWRENCE; *224 WJ-2; ★ NWCS; mail New Castle z 16101; ● 75
J Tower; RMC Place; ALLEGHENY; ★ PGH; pop. incl. with Duquesne (Inc. Place)
Jugtown; RMC Place; BUCKS; ▲ Tinicum; *227 EM-12; elev. 401ft./122m.; ★ PHIL-; mail Upper Black Eddy z 18972; rural
Jugtown; RMC Place; FRANKLIN; ▲ Quincy; *227 EQ-1; mail Waynesboro z 17268; ● 40
Julian; CDP; CENTRE; ▲ Huston; 225 WK-13; 🅿; z 16844; Ⓒ 152
Jumonville; RMC Place; FAYETTE; ▲ North Union; *225 WQ-5; ★ UNTN; mail Hopwood z 15445; rural
Juneau; RMC Place; INDIANA; ▲ Canoe; 225 WK-8; 🅿; z 15767; ● 30
Junedale (Leviston); RMC Place; CARBON; ▲ Banks; 227 EK-8; 🅿; ★ HAZ; z 18230; ● 200
June Meadows; RMC Place; MONTGOMERY; ▲ Abington; ★ PHIL-; mail Huntingdon Valley z 19006
Junewood; RMC Place; BUCKS; ▲ Bristol; ★ PHIL-; mail Levittown z 19055
Juniata; MCD-Township; BEDFORD; *225 WP-9; mail Manns Choice z 15550; Ⓟ 865; Ⓒ 1,016
Juniata; RMC Place; BLAIR; *225 WM-11; ★ ALT; mail Altoona z 16601; pop. incl. with Altoona (Inc. Place)
Juniata; MCD-Township; BLAIR; *225 WN-10; mail Duncansville z 16635; Ⓟ 1,116; Ⓒ 1,115
Juniata; RMC Place; FAYETTE; ▲ Franklin, Dunbar; *225 WP-5; ★ UNTN; mail Dunbar z 15431; ● 100
Juniata; MCD-Township; HUNTINGDON; *225 WN-12; mail Huntingdon z 16652; Ⓟ 429; Ⓒ 553
Juniata; MCD-Township; PERRY; *227 EM-3; mail Newport z 17074; Ⓟ 1,278; Ⓒ 1,359
JUNIATA; 227 EM-2; Ⓟ 20,625; Ⓒ 22,821; ◆ 23,028
Juniata Gap; RMC Place; BLAIR; ▲ Logan; 224 WA-13; elev. 1,421ft./433m.; ★ ALT; mail Altoona z 16601; ● 1,100
Juniata Terrace; Inc. Place; MIFFLIN; 227 EM-1; elev. 560ft./171m.; mail Lewistown z 17044; Ⓟ 556; Ⓒ 502
Just A Farm; RMC Place; MONTGOMERY; ▲ Lower Moreland; ★ PHIL-; mail Huntingdon Valley z 19006
Justus; RMC Place; LACKAWANNA; ▲ Scott; *226 EG-10; ★ SCR-; mail Clarks Summit z 18411, Olyphant z 18447

K

Kaiserville; RMC Place; WYOMING; ▲ Washington; *226 EF-8; mail Meshoppen z 18630, Tunkhannock z 18657; ● 50
Kammerer; RMC Place; WASHINGTON; ▲ Somerset, Nottingham; *225 WO-3; ★ PGH; mail Eighty Four z 15330; rural
Kane; Inc. Place; MCKEAN; 224 WF-9; elev. 2,000ft./610m.; 🅿 🅷; z 16735; Ⓟ 4,590; Ⓒ 4,126
Kanesholm; RMC Place; MCKEAN; ▲ Wetmore; *224 WF-9; mail Kane z 16735
Kaneville; RMC Place; VENANGO; ▲ Cornplanter; *224 WG-5; ★ OILC-F; mail Oil City z 16301
Kantner; RMC Place; SOMERSET; ▲ Quemahoning; 225 WO-8; 🅿; z 15548; ● 80
Kantz; RMC Place; SNYDER; ▲ Washington, Penn; 227 EK-4; mail Selinsgrove z 17870; ● 35
Kaolin; RMC Place; CHESTER; ▲ New Garden; 227 EQ-10; ★ PHIL-; mail Toughkenamon z 19374; ● 150
Kapp Heights; RMC Place; NORTHUMBERLAND; ▲ Point; *227 EK-5; mail Northumberland z 17857; ● 550
Karns City; Inc. Place; BUTLER; 224 WJ-5; elev. 1,220ft./372m.; 🅿; z 16041; Ⓟ 226; Ⓒ 244
Karthaus; RMC Place; CLEARFIELD; ▲ Karthaus; 224 WI-12; 🅿; z 16845; ● 250
Karthaus; MCD-Township; CLEARFIELD; *224 WI-12; 🅿; z 16845; Ⓟ 547; Ⓒ 811
Kaseville; RMC Place; MONTOUR; ▲ Valley; *226 EJ-6; mail Danville z 17821; ● 40
Kasiesville; RMC Place; FRANKLIN; ▲ Montgomery; 225 WQ-13; mail Mercersburg z 17236; ● 30
Kaska; RMC Place; SCHUYLKILL; ▲ Blythe; 227 EL-8; 🅿; ★ PTSVL; z 17959; ● 300
Kasson; RMC Place; MCKEAN; ▲ Hamlin; *224 WF-10; elev. 1,592ft./485m.; mail Smethport z 16749; rural
Kauffman; RMC Place; FRANKLIN; ▲ Antrim; 225 WQ-14; ★ HAG; mail Chambersburg z 17201; ● 150
Kaybrook Manor; RMC Place; LEHIGH; ▲ South Whitehall; *227 EL-10; elev. 550ft./168m.; ★ ALL-; mail Allentown z 18101; ● 240
Kaylor; RMC Place; ARMSTRONG; ▲ Bradys Bend; 224 WJ-5; mail Chicora z 16025; ● 200
Kaywin; RMC Place; LEHIGH; *227 EL-11; ★ ALL-; pop. incl. with Bethlehem (Inc. Place)
Kaywood; RMC Place; CENTRE; ▲ Harris; *224 WJ-13; elev. 1,169ft./356m.; ★ STCOL; mail Boalsburg z 16827; ● 330
Kearney; RMC Place; BEDFORD; ▲ Broad Top; *225 WO-12; mail Six Mile Run z 16679
Kearsarge; RMC Place; ERIE; ▲ Millcreek; *224 WD-3; ★ ERIE; mail Erie z 16509
Keating; RMC Place; CLINTON; ▲ East Keating; *224 WI-13; mail Westport z 17778
Keating; MCD-Township; MCKEAN; *224 WE-10; mail Smethport z 16749; Ⓟ 3,070; Ⓒ 3,087
Keating; MCD-Township; POTTER; *224 WF-12; mail Austin z 16720; Ⓟ 304; Ⓒ 307
Keating Summit; RMC Place; POTTER; ▲ Keating; 224 WF-12; elev. 1,880ft./573m.; mail Austin z 16720, Smethport z 16749; ● 100
Kecksburg; RMC Place; WESTMORELAND; ▲ Mount Pleasant; 225 WO-6; elev. 1,209ft./369m.; mail Mount Pleasant z 15666; ● 140
Kedron Park; RMC Place; DELAWARE; ▲ Ridley; *227 EP-11; elev. 117ft./36m.; ★ PHIL-; mail Morton z 19070; ● 700
Keelersburg; RMC Place; WYOMING; ▲ Northmoreland; *226 EG-9; elev. 611ft./186m.; mail Tunkhannock z 18657; ● 40
Keelersville; RMC Place; BUCKS; ▲ East Rockhill, Bedminster; 227 EM-12; ★ PHIL-; mail Perkasie z 18944; ● 100
Keeneyville; RMC Place; TIOGA; ▲ Middlebury; 226 EE-2; elev. 1,215ft./370m.; mail Middlebury Center z 16935; ● 100
Keepville; RMC Place; ERIE; ▲ Conneaut; *224 WE-2; ★ ERIE; mail Albion z 16401; rural
Keewaydin; RMC Place; CLEARFIELD; ▲ Covington; *224 WI-12; mail Frenchville z 16836
Keffer; RMC Place; SCHUYLKILL; ▲ Porter; *227 EL-6; mail Tremont z 17981
Keifertown; RMC Place; FAYETTE; ▲ Upper Tyrone; *225 WO-5; mail Scottdale z 15683; ● 200
Keiser; NORTHUMBERLAND; see Marion Heights (Inc. Place)
Keisters; RMC Place; BUTLER; ▲ Slippery Rock; *224 WJ-4; mail Slippery Rock z 16057; rural
Keisterville; RMC Place; FAYETTE; ▲ Menallen; 225 WP-4; 🅿; ★ UNTN; z 15449; ● 300
Kelayres; RMC Place; SCHUYLKILL; ▲ Kline; 227 EK-8; 🅿; ★ HAZ; z 18231; ● 600
Kellersburg; RMC Place; ARMSTRONG; ▲ Madison; 224 WJ-6; elev. 1,523ft./464m.; mail Templeton z 16259; ● 100
Kellers Church; RMC Place; BUCKS; ▲ Bedminster; *227 EM-12; ★ PHIL-; mail Perkasie z 18944; rural
Kellersville; RMC Place; MONROE; ▲ Hamilton; *226 EJ-11; mail Stroudsburg z 18360; rural
Kellettville; RMC Place; FOREST; ▲ Kingsley; 224 WG-7; mail Tionesta z 16353; ● 100
Kelley; RMC Place; ALLEGHENY; ★ PGH; pop. incl. with Pittsburgh (Inc. Place)
Kelly; RMC Place; ARMSTRONG; ▲ Bethel; 225 WL-5; ★ PGH; mail Ford City z 16226; ● 70
Kelly; MCD-Township; UNION; *226 EJ-4; mail Lewisburg z 17837; Ⓟ 4,561; Ⓒ 4,502
Kelly Crossroads; RMC Place; UNION; ▲ Kelly; 226 EJ-4; mail Lewisburg z 17837; ● 70
Kelly Point; RMC Place; UNION; ▲ Kelly; *226 EJ-4; mail Lewisburg z 17837; rural
Kellysburg; INDIANA; see Home (RMC Place)
Kellytown; RMC Place; CLEARFIELD; ▲ Knox; *225 WK-11; elev. 1,465ft./447m.; mail Olanta z 16863; ● 35
Kellytown; RMC Place; TIOGA; ▲ Richmond; *226 EE-3; elev. 1,130ft./344m.; mail Mansfield z 16933; ● 20
Kelton; RMC Place; CHESTER; ▲ Penn; 227 EQ-9; elev. 574ft./175m.; 🅿; ★ PHIL-; z 19346; ● 140
Kemblesville; RMC Place; CHESTER; ▲ Franklin; 227 EQ-9; 🅿; ★ PHIL-; z 19347; ● 125
Kempton; RMC Place; BERKS; ▲ Albany; 227 EL-9; 🅿; z 19529; ● 100
Kendall; RMC Place; BEAVER; ▲ Hanover; *225 WM-1; elev. 1,214ft./370m.; ★ PGH; mail Georgetown z 15043
Kendall; RMC Place; YORK; ▲ Windsor; *227 EP-6; elev. 800ft./244m.; ★ YORK; mail Red Lion z 17356; ● 330
Kendrick; RMC Place; CLEARFIELD; ▲ Woodward; *225 WK-11; mail Houtzdale z 16651; rural
Kenhorst; Inc. Place; BERKS; 227 EN-9; elev. 310ft./94m.; ★ READ; mail Reading z 19607; Ⓟ 2,918; Ⓒ 2,679
Kenilworth; CDP; CHESTER; ▲ North Coventry; 227 EO-10; ★ PTSTN; mail Pottstown z 19464; Ⓟ 1,890; Ⓒ 1,576
Kenmar (East Faxon); RMC Place; LYCOMING; ▲ Loyalsock; 226 EI-4; ★ WMSPT; mail Williamsport z 17701; ● 3,000
Kenmawr; RMC Place; ALLEGHENY; ▲ Kennedy; *225 WM-3; ★ PGH; mail Mc Kees Rocks z 15136
Kennard; RMC Place; MERCER; ▲ Sugar Grove; 224 WG-2; mail Greenville z 16125; ● 20
Kennedy; MCD-Township; ALLEGHENY; *225 WM-3; ★ PGH; mail Mc Kees Rocks z 15136; Ⓟ 7,265; Ⓒ 7,504
Kennedy (Kennedyville); RMC Place; TIOGA; ▲ Delmar; *226 EF-2; elev. 1,777ft./542m.; mail Wellsboro z 16901; rural
Kennedy Mill; RMC Place; LAWRENCE; ▲ Slippery Rock; *224 WJ-3; ★ PGH; mail Portersville z 16051; rural
Kennedy's Corner; RMC Place; BEAVER; ▲ Raccoon; ★ PGH; mail Aliquippa z 15001; rural
Kennedy Township; CDP-Census Area Only; ALLEGHENY; ▲ Kennedy; *225 WM-3; ★ PGH; mail Mc Kees Rocks z 15136; Ⓟ 7,152; Ⓒ 7,504
Kennedyville; TIOGA; see Kennedy (RMC Place)
Kennells Mills; RMC Place; SOMERSET; ▲ Southampton; *225 WQ-9; elev. 1,151ft./351m.; mail Hyndman z 15545; rural
Kennerdell; RMC Place; VENANGO; ▲ Rockland; 224 WH-4; 🅿; z 16374; ● 300
Kennett; MCD-Township; CHESTER; *227 EQ-10; ★ PHIL-; mail Kennett Square z 19348; Ⓟ 4,624; Ⓒ 6,451
Kennett Square; Inc. Place; CHESTER; 227 EQ-10; elev. 370ft./113m.; 🅿; ★ PHIL-; z 19348; Ⓟ 5,218; Ⓒ 5,273
Kenney Yard; RMC Place; ALLEGHENY; ★ PGH; pop. incl. with West Mifflin (Inc. Place)
Kenny Row; RMC Place; FAYETTE; ▲ Luzerne; *225 WP-4; ★ UNTN; mail New Salem z 15468; ● 50
Kensington; RMC Place; PHILADELPHIA; *227 EP-12; ★ PHIL-; mail Philadelphia z 19125; pop. incl. with Philadelphia (Inc. Place)
Kensington Heights; RMC Place; FRANKLIN; ▲ Letterkenny, Hamilton; *225 WP-14; elev. 700ft./213m.; mail Chambersburg z 17201; ● 400
Kent; INDIANA; see Jacksonville (CDP)
Kenwick Village; RMC Place; LANCASTER; ▲ Manheim; 227 ES-9; ★ LANC; mail Lancaster z 17601; ● 200
Kenwood; RMC Place; BUCKS; ▲ Bristol; ★ PHIL-; mail Bristol z 19007
Kenwood; RMC Place; INDIANA; ▲ Cherryhill; 225 WL-8; mail Clymer z 15728; ● 25
Kepner; RMC Place; SCHUYLKILL; ▲ West Penn; *227 EL-9; elev. 785ft./239m.; mail New Ringgold z 17960; rural
Kepple Hill; RMC Place; ARMSTRONG; ▲ Parks; *225 WL-5; ★ PGH; mail Vandergrift z 15690; ● 350
Kepples Corner; RMC Place; BUTLER; ▲ Fairview; *224 WJ-5; mail Chicora z 16025; rural
Kernsville; RMC Place; LEHIGH; ▲ North Whitehall; *227 EL-10; ★ ALL-; mail Orefield z 18069; ● 25
Kernville; RMC Place; CAMBRIA; *225 WN-8; ★ JNST; mail Johnstown z 15901; pop. incl. with Johnstown (Inc. Place)
Kerr; RMC Place; CLEARFIELD; ▲ Lawrence; 224 WJ-11; mail Clearfield z 16830; ● 250
Kerrmoor; RMC Place; CLEARFIELD; ▲ Ferguson; 225 WK-10; elev. 1,375ft./419m.; mail Curwensville z 16833; ● 25
Kerrs Corners; RMC Place; MERCER; ▲ Pine; *224 WI-3; elev. 1,344ft./410m.; mail Grove City z 16127; rural
Kerrsville; RMC Place; CUMBERLAND; ▲ West Pennsboro; *227 EO-2; ★ CARL; mail Carlisle z 17013; rural
Kerrtown; RMC Place; CRAWFORD; ▲ Vernon; 224 WF-3; mail Meadville z 16335; ● 200
Kersey; RMC Place; ELK; ▲ Fox; 224 WH-10; 🅿; z 15846; ● 700
Kesslerville; RMC Place; NORTHAMPTON; ▲ Plainfield; *227 EK-12; mail Nazareth z 18064; ● 130
Keys; RMC Place; YORK; ▲ Chanceford; *227 EQ-6; elev. 839ft./256m.; ★ YORK; mail Felton z 17322; ● 25
Keyser Valley; RMC Place; LACKAWANNA; *226 EG-10; ★ SCR-; mail Scranton z 18504; pop. incl. with Scranton (Inc. Place)
Keystone; RMC Place; DAUPHIN; ★ HRBG; mail Harrisburg z 17105; pop. incl. with Harrisburg (Inc. Place)
Keystone; RMC Place; LUZERNE; ▲ Plains; *226 EH-9; elev. 873ft./266m.; ★ SCR-; mail Wilkes Barre z 18702; ● 280
Keystone; RMC Place; SOMERSET; ▲ Larimer; *225 WQ-8; mail Meyersdale z 15552; rural
Keystone; RMC Place; WESTMORELAND; ▲ Sewickley; *225 WN-5; ★ PGH; mail Herminie z 15637; ● 100
Khedive; RMC Place; GREENE; ▲ Cumberland; 225 WQ-3; elev. 1,014ft./309m.; mail Carmichaels z 15320; ● 40
Kidder; MCD-Township; CARBON; *226 EJ-10; mail Lake Harmony z 18624; Ⓟ 1,319; Ⓒ 1,185
Kilbuck; RMC Place; ALLEGHENY; 🅿; ★ PGH; z 15233; pop. incl. with Pittsburgh (Inc. Place)
Kilbuck; MCD-Township; ALLEGHENY; *225 WM-3; 🅿; ★ PGH; z 15233 & mail Sewickley z 15143; Ⓟ 890; Ⓒ 723
Kilgore; RMC Place; MERCER; ▲ Worth; *224 WH-4; mail Stoneboro z 16153; rural
Killinger; RMC Place; DAUPHIN; ▲ Upper Paxton; 227 EM-4; mail Millersburg z 17061; ● 75
Kimberton; RMC Place; CHESTER; ▲ East Pikeland; 227 EO-10; 🅿; ★ PHIL-; z 19442; ● 450
Kimble (Kimbles); RMC Place; PIKE; ▲ Lackawaxen; *226 EG-12; mail Hawley z 18428; rural
Kimbles; PIKE; see Kimble (RMC Place)
Kimmel; MCD-Township; BEDFORD; *225 WO-10; ★ ALT; mail Imler z 16655; Ⓟ 1,605; Ⓒ 1,609
Kimmel; RMC Place; SOMERSET; ▲ Milford; *225 WP-7; mail Rockwood z 15557
Kimmelton; RMC Place; SOMERSET; ▲ Quemahoning; 225 WP-8; mail Stoystown z 15563; ● 80
Kim Plan; RMC Place; WESTMORELAND; ▲ North Huntingdon; *225 WN-5; ★ PGH; mail Irwin z 15642; ● 600
Kinderhook; RMC Place; LANCASTER; ▲ West Hempfield; *227 EP-6; ★ LANC; mail Columbia z 17512; ● 70
Kindts Corner; RMC Place; BERKS; ▲ Ontelaunee; *227 EM-9; elev. 304ft./93m.; ★ READ; mail Shoemakersville z 19555; rural
King; RMC Place; BEDFORD; ▲ Kimmel; *225 WO-10; ★ ALT; mail Imler z 16655
King; MCD-Township; BEDFORD; *225 WO-10; mail Imler z 16655; Ⓟ 1,226; Ⓒ 1,264
King of Prussia; CDP; MONTGOMERY; ▲ Upper Merion; 227 EO-11; 🅿; ★ PHIL-; z 19406; Ⓟ 18,406; Ⓒ 18,511
Kingsdale; RMC Place; ADAMS; ▲ Germany; 227 ER-3; mail Littlestown z 17340; ● 200
Kingsessing; RMC Place; PHILADELPHIA; ★ PHIL-; mail Philadelphia z 19143; pop. incl. with Philadelphia (Inc. Place)
Kingsley; MCD-Township; FOREST; *224 WG-6; mail Tionesta z 16353; Ⓟ 218; Ⓒ 261
Kingsley; RMC Place; SUSQUEHANNA; ▲ Harford; 226 EF-9; 🅿; z 18826; ● 200
Kings Manor; RMC Place; MONTGOMERY; ▲ Upper Merion; 228 B-1; ★ PHIL-; mail King of Prussia z 19406; ● 650
Kingston; Inc. Place; LUZERNE; 226 EH-9; elev. 544ft./166m.; 🅿; ★ SCR-; z 18704; Ⓟ 14,507; Ⓒ 13,855
Kingston; MCD-Township; LUZERNE; *226 EH-9; 🅿; ★ SCR-; z 18704 & mail Shavertown z 18708; not adjacent to the Borough of Kingston; Ⓟ 6,763; Ⓒ 7,145
Kingston; RMC Place; WESTMORELAND; ▲ Unity, Derry; *225 WN-6; ★ LTROB; mail Latrobe z 15650; ● 40
Kingston-Forty Fort; RMC Place; LUZERNE; ★ SCR-; mail Kingston z 18704; pop. incl. with Kingston (Inc. Place)
Kingsville; RMC Place; CLARION; ▲ Limestone; *224 WI-7; mail Summerville z 15864; ● 50
Kingswood Park; RMC Place; BUCKS; ▲ Bristol; *227 EO-14; ★ PHIL-; mail Bristol z 19007; ● 750
Kingview; RMC Place; FAYETTE; ▲ Upper Tyrone; *225 WO-5; mail Scottdale z 15683; ● 225
Kingwood; RMC Place; SOMERSET; ▲ Upper Turkeyfoot; 225 WQ-7; elev. 2,290ft./698m.; mail Markleton z 15551; ● 120
Kinlock; RMC Place; WESTMORELAND; *225 WM-5; ★ PGH; mail New Kensington z 15068; pop. incl. with Lower Burrell (Inc. Place)
Kinney; RMC Place; POTTER; ▲ Genesee; *224 WD-13; mail Genesee z 16923; rural
Kinport; RMC Place; CAMBRIA; ▲ Susquehanna; *225 WL-9; mail Cherry Tree z 15724; ● 35
Kintersburg; RMC Place; INDIANA; ▲ Rayne; *225 WL-8; elev. 1,106ft./337m.; mail Clymer z 15728; rural
Kintigh Plan; RMC Place; WESTMORELAND; ▲ Hempfield; *225 WN-6; elev. 1,200ft./366m.; ★ PGH; mail Greensburg z 15601; ● 100
Kintnersville; RMC Place; BUCKS; ▲ Nockamixon; 227 EM-12; 🅿; ★ PHIL-; z 18930; ● 100
Kinzer; LANCASTER; see Kinzers (RMC Place)
Kinzers (Kinzer); RMC Place; LANCASTER; ▲ Salisbury, Paradise; 227 EP-8; 🅿; z 17535; ● 450
Kipps Run; RMC Place; NORTHUMBERLAND; ▲ Rush; *226 EJ-5; mail Danville z 17821, Riverside z 17868; pop. incl. with Riverside (Inc. Place)
Kirby; RMC Place; GREENE; ▲ Whiteley; 225 WQ-3; mail Waynesburg z 15370; ● 35
Kirbyville; RMC Place; BERKS; ▲ Richmond; *227 EM-9; elev. 420ft./128m.; mail Fleetwood z 19522; rural
Kirks Bridge; RMC Place; LANCASTER; ▲ Little Britain; *227 EQ-8; mail Nottingham z 19362; rural
Kirks Mills; RMC Place; LANCASTER; ▲ Little Britain; *227 EQ-8; mail Nottingham z 19362; rural
Kirkwood; RMC Place; LANCASTER; ▲ Colerain; 227 EQ-8; elev. 536ft./163m.; 🅿; z 17536; ● 250
Kirwan Heights; RMC Place; ALLEGHENY; ▲ Collier; *225 WN-3; ★ PGH; mail Bridgeville z 15017; ● 500
Kiser Corners; RMC Place; FOREST; ▲ Green; *224 WG-6; mail Tionesta z 16353; rural
Kishacoquillas; RMC Place; MIFFLIN; ▲ Brown; *227 EL-1; elev. 840ft./256m.; mail Belleville z 17004; ● 25
Kiskimere; RMC Place; ARMSTRONG; ▲ Parks; *225 WL-5; ★ PGH; mail Vandergrift z 15690; ● 130
Kiskiminetas; MCD-Township; ARMSTRONG; *225 WL-6; ★ PGH; mail Apollo z 15613; Ⓟ 5,456; Ⓒ 4,950
Kissel Hill; RMC Place; LANCASTER; ▲ Warwick; 227 EO-7; ★ LANC; mail Lititz z 17543; ● 750
Kissimmee; RMC Place; SNYDER; ▲ Franklin; 227 EK-3; elev. 632ft./193m.; mail Middleburg z 17842; ● 100
Kissingers Mill; RMC Place; CLARION; ▲ Madison; *224 WJ-6; elev. 1,185ft./361m.; mail Rimersburg z 16248; ● 60
Kistler; Inc. Place; MIFFLIN; 225 WN-13; elev. 660ft./201m.; mail Mount Union z 17066; Ⓟ 314; Ⓒ 344
Kistler; RMC Place; PERRY; ▲ Northeast Madison; 227 EN-2; mail Loysville z 17047; ● 40
Kitches Corners; RMC Place; MERCER; ▲ Otter Creek; *224 WH-2; mail Greenville z 16125; rural
Kittanning; Inc. Place; ⊡ ARMSTRONG; 225 WK-6; elev. 800ft./244m.; 🅿 🅷; ★ PGH; z 16201; Ⓟ 5,120; Ⓒ 4,787
Kittanning; MCD-Township; ARMSTRONG; *225 WK-6; 🅿; z 16201, z 98662 & mail Ford City z 16226; not adjacent to the Borough of Kittanning; Ⓟ 2,310; Ⓒ 2,359
Kittanning Heights; RMC Place; ARMSTRONG; ▲ East Franklin; *225 WK-6; ★ PGH; mail Kittanning z 16201; ● 600
Kladder Station; RMC Place; BLAIR; ▲ Blair; *225 WN-11; elev. 973ft./297m.; ★ ALT; mail Hollidaysburg z 16648; rural
Klahr; RMC Place; BLAIR; ▲ Greenfield; *225 WN-10; elev. 1,628ft./496m.; ★ ALT; mail Claysburg z 16625; ● 100
Klecknersville; RMC Place; NORTHAMPTON; ▲ Moore; 227 EK-11; elev. 806ft./246m.; ★ ALL-; mail Bath z 18014; ● 300
Kleinfeltersville; RMC Place; LEBANON; ▲ Heidelberg; 227 EN-7; 🅿; ★ LEB; z 17039; ● 250
Kline; MCD-Township; SCHUYLKILL; *227 EK-8; ★ HAZ; mail McAdoo z 18237; Ⓟ 1,722; Ⓒ 1,591
Klines Corner; RMC Place; BERKS; ▲ Longswamp; *227 EM-10; mail Mertztown z 19539; rural
Klines Grove; RMC Place; NORTHUMBERLAND; ▲ Upper Augusta, Rush; *227 EK-5; mail Sunbury z 17801; rural
Klinesville; RMC Place; BERKS; ▲ Greenwich; 227 EM-9; mail Lenhartsville z 19534; ● 100
Klinesville; RMC Place; LANCASTER; ▲ West Hempfield; 227 EP-6; ★ LANC; mail Columbia z 17512; ● 60
Kline Village; RMC Place; DAUPHIN; ★ HRBG; mail Harrisburg z 17104; pop. incl. with Harrisburg (Inc. Place)
Klingerstown; CDP; SCHUYLKILL; ▲ Upper Mahantongo; 227 EL-5; 🅿; z 17941; Ⓒ 102
Klondike; RMC Place; MCKEAN; ▲ Corydon; *224 WE-9; mail Lewis Run z 16738; rural
Klondyke; RMC Place; MIFFLIN; ▲ Derry; *227 EL-1; mail Lewistown z 17044; ● 90
Knapp; RMC Place; TIOGA; ▲ Delmar; *226 EF-2; mail Wellsboro z 16901
Knauers; RMC Place; BERKS; ▲ Brecknock; *227 EN-8; ★ READ; mail Mohnton z 19540
Knauertown; RMC Place; CHESTER; ▲ Warwick; *227 EO-10; ★ PHIL-; mail Pottstown z 19464
Kneedler (Wales Junction); RMC Place; MONTGOMERY; ▲ Upper Gwynedd; ★ PHIL-; mail Lansdale z 19446; rural
Knepper; RMC Place; FRANKLIN; ▲ Quincy; *227 EQ-1; mail Waynesboro z 17268; rural
Knightsville; RMC Place; HUNTINGDON; ▲ Cass; *225 WO-12; mail Mapleton Depot z 17052; rural
Knobsville; RMC Place; FULTON; ▲ Todd; 225 WP-13; mail Mc Connellsburg z 17233; ● 100
Knobville; RMC Place; MIFFLIN; ▲ Armagh; *227 EL-1; mail Milroy z 17063; ● 75
Knoebel's Grove; RMC Place; NORTHUMBERLAND; ▲ Ralpho; *227 EK-6; mail Elysburg z 17824; summer pop. 400; ● 25
Knousetown; RMC Place; JUNIATA; ▲ Monroe; *227 EL-3; mail Millerstown z 17062, Mount Pleasant Mills z 17853, Richfield z 17086; ● 40
Knowltonwood; RMC Place; DELAWARE; ▲ Middletown; *227 EQ-11; elev. 200ft./61m.; ★ PHIL-; mail Media z 19065; ● 450
Knox; RMC Place; BEAVER, LAWRENCE; ▲ Perry, Franklin; *225 WK-2; ★ PGH; mail Ellwood City z 16117; ● 600
Knox; Inc. Place; CLARION; 224 WI-6; elev. 1,400ft./427m.; 🅿; z 16232; Ⓟ 1,182; Ⓒ 1,176
Knox; MCD-Township; CLARION; *224 WH-6; 🅿; z 16232 & mail Lucinda z 16235; not adjacent to the Borough of Knox; Ⓟ 1,281; Ⓒ 1,045
Knox; MCD-Township; CLEARFIELD; *225 WK-10; mail Olanta z 16863; Ⓟ 704; Ⓒ 705
Knox; MCD-Township; JEFFERSON; *224 WJ-8; mail Brookville z 15825; Ⓟ 1,014; Ⓒ 1,056
Knox Dale; RMC Place; JEFFERSON; ▲ Knox; 224 WI-8; 🅿; z 15847; ● 300
Knoxlyn; RMC Place; ADAMS; ▲ Highland; *227 EQ-2; mail Gettysburg z 17325; ● 65
Knox Run; RMC Place; CLEARFIELD; ▲ Cooper; mail Morrisdale z 16858; rural
Knoxville; RMC Place; ALLEGHENY; *225 WM-4; ★ PGH; mail Pittsburgh z 15210; pop. incl. with Pittsburgh (Inc. Place)
Knoxville; RMC Place; FAYETTE; ▲ Brownsville; *225 WP-4; ★ UNTN; mail Brownsville z 15417; ● 350
Knoxville; Inc. Place; TIOGA; 226 ED-2; elev. 1,241ft./378m.; 🅿; z 16928; Ⓟ 589; Ⓒ 617
Koonsville; RMC Place; LUZERNE; ▲ Union; 226 EI-7; elev. 631ft./192m.; ★ SCR-; mail Shickshinny z 18655; ● 200
Koppel; Inc. Place; BEAVER; 225 WK-2; elev. 920ft./280m.; 🅿; ★ PGH; z 16136; Ⓟ 1,024; Ⓒ 856
Korn Krest; RMC Place; LUZERNE; ▲ Hanover; 226 EA-6; 🅿; ★ SCR-; z 18702 & mail Wilkes Barre z 18706; ● 850
Kossuth; RMC Place; CLARION; ▲ Ashland; 224 WH-6; 🅿; z 16331; ● 150
Kralltown; RMC Place; YORK; ▲ Washington; 227 EP-4; mail East Berlin z 17316; ● 75
Kratzerville; CDP; SNYDER; ▲ Jackson; 227 EK-4; elev. 664ft./202m.; mail Selinsgrove z 17870; Ⓒ 391
Krayn; RMC Place; CAMBRIA; ▲ Adams; *225 WN-9; ★ JNST; mail Windber z 15963; ● 60
Kreamer; CDP; SNYDER; ▲ Middlecreek; 227 EK-4; 🅿; z 17833; Ⓒ 773
Kregar; RMC Place; WESTMORELAND; ▲ Donegal; *225 WO-7; elev. 1,800ft./549m.; mail Champion z 15622; ● 100
Kreidersville; RMC Place; NORTHAMPTON; ▲ Allen; 227 EL-11; ★ ALL-; mail Northampton z 18067; ● 270
Kremis; RMC Place; MERCER; ▲ Delaware; 224 WH-2; mail Greenville z 16125; ● 20
Kresgeville; RMC Place; MONROE; ▲ Polk; 227 EK-11; 🅿; z 18333; ● 400
Kreutz Creek; RMC Place; YORK; ▲ Hellam; *227 EP-6; ★ YORK; mail York z 17406; ● 150
Kricktown; RMC Place; BERKS; ▲ Spring; ★ READ; mail Reading z 19608; rural
Krings; RMC Place; SOMERSET, CAMBRIA; ▲ Conemaugh, Upper Yoder; *225 WN-8; ★ JNST; mail Johnstown z 15904; ● 150
Krocksville; RMC Place; LEHIGH; ▲ Upper Macungie; *227 EM-10; elev. 462ft./141m.; ★ ALL-; mail Allentown z 18104; ● 150
Krumsville; RMC Place; BERKS; ▲ Greenwich; 227 EL-9; mail Lenhartsville z 19534; ● 140
Kuhn; RMC Place; SOMERSET; ▲ Jefferson; *225 WO-7; elev. 2,642ft./805m.; mail Somerset z 15501; rural
Kuhnsville; RMC Place; LEHIGH; ▲ Upper Macungie; *227 EL-10; ★ ALL-; mail Allentown z 18103; ● 500
Kuhntown; RMC Place; GREENE; ▲ Washington; 225 WQ-2; elev. 1,038ft./316m.; mail Holbrook z 15341; ● 30
Kulp; RMC Place; COLUMBIA; ▲ Roaring Creek; *227 EK-7; elev. 983ft./300m.; mail Catawissa z 17820; rural
Kulpmont; Inc. Place; NORTHUMBERLAND; 227 EK-6; elev. 1,100ft./335m.; 🅿; z 17834; Ⓟ 3,233; Ⓒ 2,985
Kulps Corner; RMC Place; BUCKS; ▲ Hilltown, Bedminster; *227 EN-12; ★ PHIL-; mail Perkasie z 18944; rural
Kulpsville; CDP; MONTGOMERY; ▲ Towamencin; 227 EN-11; 🅿; ★ PHIL-; z 19443; Ⓟ 5,183; Ⓒ 8,005
Kulptown; RMC Place; BERKS; ▲ Union; *227 EN-9; elev. 533ft./162m.; mail Douglassville z 19518; ● 150
Kunkle; RMC Place; LUZERNE; ▲ Dallas; 226 EH-8; elev. 1,073ft./327m.; ★ SCR-; mail Dallas z 18612, Harveys Lake z 18618; ● 150
Kunkletown; RMC Place; MONROE; ▲ Eldred; 227 EK-11; elev. 530ft./162m.; 🅿; ★ ALL-; z 18058; ● 200
Kushequa; RMC Place; MCKEAN; ▲ Hamlin; 224 WF-10; mail Kane z 16735; ● 60
Kutztown; Inc. Place; BERKS; 227 EM-9; elev. 417ft./127m.; 🅿 🅲 9,189; z 19530; Ⓟ 4,704; Ⓒ 5,067
Kutztown; RMC Place; LEBANON; ▲ Jackson; *227 EN-7; ★ LEB; mail Myerstown z 17067; ● 115
Kylers Corners; RMC Place; ELK; ▲ Fox; *224 WH-10; mail Kersey z 15846; ● 75
Kylertown; RMC Place; CLEARFIELD; ▲ Cooper; 224 WJ-12; elev. 1,646ft./502m.; 🅿; z 16847; ● 300
Kyleville; RMC Place; YORK; ▲ Lower Chanceford; 227 EQ-7; elev. 657ft./200m.; mail Airville z 17302; ● 25

L

La Anna; RMC Place; PIKE; ▲ Greene; *226 EI-11; mail Cresco z 18326
La Belle; RMC Place; FAYETTE; ▲ Luzerne; 225 WP-4; elev. 993ft./303m.; 🅿; ★ UNTN; z 15450; ● 350
Laboratory; RMC Place; WASHINGTON; ▲ South Strabane, Amwell; 225 WO-3; elev. 1,355ft./413m.; ★ WASH; mail Washington z 15301; ● 850
Labott; RMC Place; YORK; ▲ Jackson; 227 EP-4; ★ YORK; mail Thomasville z 17364; ● 50
Lacey Park; RMC Place; BUCKS; ▲ Warminster; *227 EO-12; ★ PHIL-; mail Warminster z 18974
Laceyville; Inc. Place; WYOMING; 226 EF-7; elev. 657ft./200m.; 🅿; z 18623; Ⓟ 436; Ⓒ 396
Lack; MCD-Township; JUNIATA; *225 WN-14; mail Blairs Mills z 17213, East Waterford z 17021; Ⓟ 714; Ⓒ 750
LACKAWANNA; 226 EG-9; Ⓟ 219,039; Ⓒ 213,295; ◆ 208,418
Lackawannock; MCD-Township; MERCER; *224 WI-2; ★ SHAR; mail Mercer z 16137; Ⓟ 2,677; Ⓒ 2,561
Lackawaxen; RMC Place; PIKE; ▲ Lackawaxen; 226 EG-13; 🅿; z 18435; ● 600
Lackawaxen; MCD-Township; PIKE; *226 EG-12; 🅿; z 18435 & mail Greeley z 18425; Ⓟ 2,832; Ⓒ 4,154
Lacock; RMC Place; WASHINGTON; ▲ Canton; *225 WO-2; elev. 1,098ft./335m.; ★ WASH; mail Washington z 15301; ● 200
Laddsburg; RMC Place; BRADFORD; ▲ Albany; 226 EG-6; mail New Albany z 18833; ● 60
Lafayette; RMC Place; MCKEAN; ▲ Lafayette; 224 WE-10; mail Lewis Run z 16738; ● 40
Lafayette; MCD-Township; MCKEAN; *224 WE-10; mail Lewis Run z 16738; Ⓟ 2,106; Ⓒ 2,337
Lafayette College; RMC Place; NORTHAMPTON; *227 EL-12; ★ ALL-; mail Easton z 18042; pop. incl. with Easton (Inc. Place)
Lafayette Hill; RMC Place; MONTGOMERY; ▲ Whitemarsh; 228 B-2; 🅿 🅷; ★ PHIL-; z 19444; ● 6,700
Lafayetteville; RMC Place; BEDFORD; ▲ South Woodbury; *225 WO-10; mail New Enterprise z 16664; ● 40
Laflin; Inc. Place; LUZERNE; 226 EB-9; elev. 727ft./222m.; ★ SCR-; mail Wilkes Barre z 18702, z 18705; Ⓟ 1,498; Ⓒ 1,502
La Gonda; RMC Place; WASHINGTON; ▲ South Franklin; 225 WO-2; ★ WASH; mail Washington z 15301; ● 70
Lahaska; RMC Place; BUCKS; ▲ Solebury, Buckingham; 227 EN-13; 🅿; ★ PHIL-; z 18931; ● 200
Lairds Crossing; RMC Place; ARMSTRONG; ▲ West Franklin; *225 WK-5; ★ PGH; mail Worthington z 16262; rural
Lairdsville; RMC Place; LYCOMING; ▲ Franklin; 226 EI-6; elev. 742ft./226m.; 🅿; z 17742; ● 120
La Jose; CLEARFIELD; see Newburg (Inc. Place)
Lake; MCD-Township; LUZERNE; *226 EH-8; ★ SCR-; mail Hunlock Creek z 18621; Ⓟ 1,924; Ⓒ 2,110
Lake; MCD-Township; MERCER; *224 WH-3; mail Stoneboro z 16153; Ⓟ 651; Ⓒ 706
Lake; MCD-Township; WAYNE; *226 EG-11; ★ SCR-; mail Lake Ariel z 18436; Ⓟ 3,287; Ⓒ 4,361
Lake Ariel (Ariel); RMC Place; WAYNE; ▲ Lake; 226 EG-11; 🅿; ★ SCR-; z 18436; ● 1,250
Lake Carey; RMC Place; WYOMING; ▲ Lemon; 226 EF-8; mail Tunkhannock z 18657; ● 400
Lake City; Inc. Place; ERIE; 224 WD-2; elev. 721ft./220m.; 🅿; ★ ERIE; z 16423; Ⓟ 2,519; Ⓒ 2,811
Lake Como; RMC Place; WAYNE; ▲ Preston, Buckingham; 226 EE-11; elev. 1,427ft./435m.; 🅿; z 18437; summer pop. 2,000; ● 280
Lake Donegal; RMC Place; FAYETTE; ▲ Saltlick; *225 WO-6; elev. 1,870ft./570m.; mail Acme z 15610; rural
Lake Harmony; RMC Place; CARBON; ▲ Kidder; 226 EJ-10; 🅿; z 18624; summer pop. 1,000; ● 850
Lake Heritage; CDP-Census Area Only; ADAMS; ▲ Cumberland; *227 EQ-3; elev. 500ft./152m.; mail Gettysburg z 17325; Ⓒ 1,136
Lake Idlewild; RMC Place; SUSQUEHANNA; ▲ Clifford; *226 EF-10; elev. 1,300ft./396m.; mail Union Dale z 18470; ● 25
Lakeland; RMC Place; WAYNE; ▲ Paupack; *226 EH-11; elev. 1,300ft./396m.; mail Lake Ariel z 18436; summer pop. 300; ● 40
Lake Lynn; RMC Place; FAYETTE; ▲ Springhill; *225 WQ-4; 🅿; ★ MORG; z 15439, z 15451; ● 200
Lake Meade; CDP-Census Area Only; ADAMS; ▲ Reading; *227 EP-4; mail East Berlin z 17316; Ⓒ 1,832
Lake Monroe; RMC Place; MONROE; ▲ Middle Smithfield; *226 EI-12; elev. 1,000ft./305m.; mail Marshalls Creek z 18335; ● 500
Lakemont; RMC Place; BLAIR; ▲ Logan; 225 WM-11; ★ ALT; mail Altoona z 16602; ● 500
Lake Naomi; RMC Place; MONROE; *226 EI-11; mail Pocono Pines z 18350
Lake Pleasant; RMC Place; ERIE; ▲ Venango; *224 WD-4; mail Union City z 16438; rural
Lake Quinn; RMC Place; WAYNE; ▲ Canaan; *226 EG-11; elev. 1,334ft./407m.; ★ SCR-; mail Waymart z 18472; ● 25
Lake Sheridan; RMC Place; LACKAWANNA, WYOMING; ▲ Nicholson, Benton; *226 EF-9; ★ SCR-; mail Nicholson z 18446; ● 500
Lakeside; RMC Place; BUCKS; ▲ Falls; *227 EO-14; ★ PHIL-; mail Feasterville Trevose z 19053; pop. incl. with Tullytown (Inc. Place)
Lakeside; RMC Place; SUSQUEHANNA; ▲ New Milford; 226 EE-10; mail New Milford z 18834; ● 200
Lake Stonycreek; RMC Place; SOMERSET; ▲ Stonycreek; *225 WP-9; elev. 2,227ft./679m.; mail Friedens z 15541; summer pop. 300; ● 30
Laketon Heights; RMC Place; ALLEGHENY; ▲ Penn Hills; *225 WM-4; elev. 1,200ft./366m.; ★ PGH; mail Pittsburgh z 15235
Lakeview; RMC Place; SUSQUEHANNA; ▲ Jackson; *226 EE-10; mail Susquehanna z 18847; ● 40
Lakeview Heights; RMC Place; DAUPHIN; ▲ Lower Paxton; *227 EN-5; ★ HRBG; mail Harrisburg z 17111; ● 600
Lakeville; RMC Place; WAYNE; ▲ Paupack; 226 EG-11; 🅿; z 18438; ● 500
Lake Waynewood; RMC Place; WAYNE; ▲ Salem; *226 EH-11; elev. 1,400ft./427m.; ★ SCR-; mail Lake Ariel z 18436; summer pop. 150; rural
Lake Wesauking; RMC Place; BRADFORD; ▲ Wysox; *226 EE-6; elev. 1,185ft./361m.; mail Towanda z 18848; ● 100
Lake Winola; RMC Place; WYOMING; ▲ Overfield; 226 EG-9; 🅿; ★ SCR-; z 18625; summer pop. 2,500; ● 350
Lakewood; RMC Place; ERIE; ▲ Millcreek; *224 WC-3; ★ ERIE; mail Erie z 16505
Lakewood; RMC Place; WAYNE; ▲ Preston; 226 EE-11; 🅿; z 18439; ● 300
Lakewood Park; RMC Place; LAWRENCE; ▲ Hickory; *224 WJ-2; ★ NWCS; mail New Castle z 16101; ● 40
Lake Wynonah; CDP; SCHUYLKILL; ▲ South Manheim, Wayne; *227 EL-8; elev. 642ft./196m.; ★ PTSVL; mail Schuylkill Haven z 17972; Ⓟ 1,055; Ⓒ 1,961
Lamar; RMC Place; CLINTON; ▲ Porter; 226 EJ-1; 🅿; z 16848; ● 900
Lamar; MCD-Township; CLINTON; *226 EJ-2; 🅿; z 16848 & mail Mill Hall z 17751; Ⓟ 2,345; Ⓒ 2,450
Lamartine; RMC Place; CLARION; ▲ Salem; 224 WI-5; 🅿; z 16375; ● 200
Lambert; FAYETTE; see Lamberton (RMC Place)
Lamberton (Lambert); RMC Place; FAYETTE; ▲ German; *225 WP-4; 🅿; ★ UNTN; z 15458; ● 90
Lambertsville; RMC Place; SOMERSET; ▲ Stonycreek; 225 WP-8; mail Stoystown z 15563; ● 70
Lambs Creek; RMC Place; TIOGA; ▲ Richmond; *226 EE-3; mail Mansfield z 16933; rural
Lamokin Street; RMC Place; DELAWARE; ★ PHIL-; pop. incl. with Chester (Inc. Place)
Lamonaville; RMC Place; FOREST; ▲ Jenks; *224 WG-8; mail Marienville z 16239; rural
Lamont (Madge); RMC Place; ELK; ▲ Jones; *224 WF-9; mail Kane z 16735
Lamonts Corners; RMC Place; MERCER; *224 WH-2; elev. 1,012ft./308m.; ★ SHAR; mail Sharpsville z 16150; pop. incl. with Hermitage (Inc. Place)
Lamott; RMC Place; MONTGOMERY; ▲ Cheltenham; 228 B-5; 🅿; ★ PHIL-; z 19027 & mail Cheltenham z 19012; ● 800
Lampeter; RMC Place; LANCASTER; ▲ West Lampeter; 227 EP-7; elev. 407ft./124m.; 🅿; ★ LANC; z 17537; ● 800
Lanark; RMC Place; LEHIGH; ▲ Upper Saucon; 226 EC-4; ★ ALL-; mail Center Valley z 18034; ● 400
Lancaster; MCD-Township; BUTLER; *225 WK-3; ★ PGH; mail Harmony z 16037; Ⓟ 2,268; Ⓒ 2,511
Lancaster; Inc. Place; ⊡ LANCASTER; 227 EP-7; elev. 380ft./116m.; 🅿 🅷 🅲 2,862 ■; ★ LANC; z 17573, z 17601-08, z 17611, z 17622, z 17699; Ⓟ 55,551; Ⓒ 56,348; ◆ 56,425
Lancaster; MCD-Township; LANCASTER; *227 EP-7; 🅿 🅲 2,862; ★ LANC; z 17573, z 17601-08, z 17611, z 17622, z 17699; does not include the Borough of Lancaster; Ⓟ 13,187; Ⓒ 13,944
LANCASTER; 227 EP-7; Ⓟ 422,822; Ⓒ 470,658; ◆ 506,093
Lancaster Avenue; RMC Place; PHILADELPHIA; ★ PHIL-; mail Philadelphia z 19104; pop. incl. with Philadelphia (Inc. Place)
Lancaster Junction; RMC Place; LANCASTER; ▲ Penn; *227 EO-6; elev. 375ft./114m.; ★ LANC; mail Manheim z 17545; ● 140
Landenberg; RMC Place; CHESTER; ▲ New Garden; 227 EQ-9; 🅿; ★ PHIL-; z 19350; ● 100
Lander; RMC Place; WARREN; ▲ Farmington; 224 WD-7; mail Russell z 16345; ● 150
Landingville; Inc. Place; SCHUYLKILL; 227 EL-8; elev. 502ft./153m.; 🅿; ★ PTSVL; z 17942; Ⓟ 192; Ⓒ 175
Landisburg; Inc. Place; PERRY; 227 EN-2; elev. 600ft./183m.; 🅿; z 17040; Ⓟ 178; Ⓒ 195
Landis Farms; RMC Place; LANCASTER; ▲ Manheim; *227 EO-7; ★ LANC; mail Lancaster z 17601; ● 2,000
Landis Store; RMC Place; BERKS; ▲ District; *227 EM-10; ★ READ; mail Boyertown z 19512; ● 80
Landis Valley; RMC Place; LANCASTER; ▲ Manheim; 227 ER-9; ★ LANC; mail Lancaster z 17604; ● 800
Landisville; RMC Place; LANCASTER; ▲ East Hempfield; 227 EO-6; 🅿; ★ LANC; z 17538; ● 1,400
Landreth Manor; RMC Place; BUCKS; ▲ Bristol; *227 EO-14; elev. 20ft./6m.; ★ PHIL-; mail Bristol z 19007; ● 400
Landstreet; RMC Place; SOMERSET; ▲ Paint; *225 WO-8; ★ JNST; mail Hollsopple z 15935; rural
Lanesboro; Inc. Place; SUSQUEHANNA; 226 ED-10; elev. 820ft./250m.; 🅿; ★ BING; z 18827; Ⓟ 659; Ⓒ 588
Lanes Mills; RMC Place; JEFFERSON; ▲ Snyder; 224 WI-9; mail Brockway z 15824; ● 30
Laneville; RMC Place; ARMSTRONG; *225 WL-5; mail Freeport z 16229; pop. incl. with Freeport (Inc. Place)
Langdon; RMC Place; LYCOMING; ▲ McIntyre; mail Ralston z 17763
Langdondale; RMC Place; BEDFORD; ▲ Broad Top; 225 WO-11; mail Hopewell z 16650; ● 100
Langeloth; RMC Place; WASHINGTON; ▲ Smith; 225 WN-2; 🅿; ★ PGH; z 15054; ● 1,500
Langhorne; Inc. Place; BUCKS; 227 EO-13; elev. 220ft./67m.; 🅿 🅷; ★ PHIL-; z 19047, z 19053 & mail Fort Washington z 19048-49; Ⓟ 1,361; Ⓒ 1,981
Langhorne Gardens; RMC Place; BUCKS; ▲ Middletown; *227 EO-13; ★ PHIL-; mail Langhorne z 19047; ● 500
Langhorne Manor; Inc. Place; BUCKS; *227 EO-13; elev. 200ft./61m.; 🅲 1,405; ★ PHIL-; mail Langhorne z 19047; Ⓟ 807; Ⓒ 927
Langhorne Terrace; RMC Place; BUCKS; ▲ Middletown; *227 EO-13; ★ PHIL-; mail Langhorne z 19047; ● 2,800
Lansdale; Inc. Place; MONTGOMERY; 227 EN-12; elev. 360ft./110m.; 🅿 🅷 ■; ★ PHIL-; z 19446; Ⓟ 16,362; Ⓒ 16,071; ◆ 15,706
Lansdowne; Inc. Place; DELAWARE; 227 EP-12; elev. 130ft./40m.; 🅿; ★ PHIL-; z 19050; Ⓟ 11,712; Ⓒ 11,044
Lansdowne Park Gardens; RMC Place; DELAWARE; ★ PHIL-; mail Darby z 19023; pop. incl. with Collingdale (Inc. Place)
Lanse; RMC Place; CLEARFIELD; ▲ Cooper; 224 WJ-12; 🅿; z 16849; ● 450
Lansford; Inc. Place; CARBON; 227 EK-9; elev. 1,134ft./346m.; 🅿; z 18232; Ⓟ 4,583; Ⓒ 4,230
Lantz Corners; RMC Place; MCKEAN; ▲ Hamlin; 224 WF-10; mail Mount Jewett z 16740; ● 40
Lapidea Hills; RMC Place; DELAWARE; ▲ Nether Providence; ★ PHIL-; mail Chester z 19013
La Plume; RMC Place; LACKAWANNA; ▲ La Plume; 226 EG-9; 🅿 🅲 1,820; ★ SCR-; z 18440; ● 400
La Plume; MCD-Township; LACKAWANNA; *226 EG-9; 🅿 🅲 1,820; ★ SCR-; z 18440; Ⓟ 647; Ⓒ 603
Laporte; Inc. Place; ⊡ SULLIVAN; 226 EH-6; elev. 1,966ft./599m.; 🅿; z 18626; Ⓟ 328; Ⓒ 290
Laporte; MCD-Township; SULLIVAN; *226 EH-6; 🅿; z 18626 & mail Muncy Valley z 17758; does not include the Borough of Laporte; Ⓟ 213; Ⓒ 373
Larabee; RMC Place; MCKEAN; ▲ Eldred; *224 WE-11; mail Eldred z 16731
Lardintown; RMC Place; BUTLER; ▲ Clinton; *225 WL-4; ★ PGH; mail Sarver z 16055; rural
Large; RMC Place; ALLEGHENY; *225 WN-4; elev. 780ft./238m.; 🅿; ★ PGH; z 15025; pop. incl. with Jefferson (Inc. Place)
Larimer; MCD-Township; SOMERSET; *225 WQ-8; mail Meyersdale z 15552; Ⓟ 547; Ⓒ 590
Larimer; RMC Place; WESTMORELAND; ▲ North Huntingdon; 225 WN-5; 🅿; ★ PGH; z 15647; ● 750
Larke; RMC Place; BLAIR; ▲ Woodbury; *225 WM-12; elev. 1,027ft./313m.; ★ ALT; mail Williamsburg z 16693; rural
Larksville; Inc. Place; LUZERNE; 226 EI-8; elev. 700ft./213m.; 🅿; ★ SCR-; z 18651, z 18704; Ⓟ 4,700; Ⓒ 4,694
Larrys Creek; RMC Place; LYCOMING; ▲ Piatt; *226 EI-3; ★ WMSPT; mail Jersey Shore z 17740; rural

Entries in **UPPERCASE** are counties.
Entries in **bold** have populations of 2,500 or more.
Names in parentheses are alternate names.

Inc. Place	Incorporated Place
RMC Place	Rand McNally Designated Place
CDP	Census Designated Place
MCD	Minor Civil Division

⊡	County Seat
▲	Minor Civil Division
elev.	Elevation
🅿	Post Office
🅷	Hospital
🅲	College
■	Principal Business Center
★	Ranally Metro Area (RMA) Abbreviation
z	Zip Code(s)
Ⓟ	Previous Census Population
Ⓡ	Revised Census Population
Ⓐ	Annexation Population
●	Rand McNally Population Estimate
Ⓒ	Final Census Population
Ⓢ	Special Census Population
◆	Estimated Population

For additional definitions see Glossary, Volume 1, and Introduction, Volume 2.

Larryville; RMC Place; LYCOMING; ▲ Piatt; *226 EI-3; ★ WMSPT; mail Jersey Shore z 17740; ● 40
Larue; RMC Place; YORK; ▲ Springfield, Codorus; *227 EQ-5; elev. 513ft./156m.; ★ BAL; mail Glen Rock z 17327; ● 50
Lashley; RMC Place; FULTON; ▲ Union; *225 WQ-11; mail Warfordsburg z 17267; rural
Lathrop; MCD-Township; SUSQUEHANNA; *226 EF-9; mail Nicholson z 18446; Ⓟ 794; Ⓒ 835
Latimore; RMC Place; ADAMS; ▲ Latimore; 227 EP-3; mail York Springs z 17372; ● 60
Latimore; MCD-Township; ADAMS; *227 EP-3; mail York Springs z 17372; Ⓟ 2,209; Ⓒ 2,528
Latrobe; Inc. Place; WESTMORELAND; 225 WN-6; elev. 1,020ft./311m.; 🅿 🅷 🅲 1,818 ■; ★ LTROB; z 15650; Ⓟ 9,265; Ⓒ 8,994; ◆ 8,421
Latta Grove (Barneytown); RMC Place; HUNTINGDON; ▲ Cass; *225 WN-13; mail Mapleton Depot z 17052
Lattimer (Lattimer Mines); RMC Place; LUZERNE; ▲ Hazle; 226 EJ-8; ★ HAZ; mail Lattimer Mines z 18234; ● 600
Lattimer Mines; LUZERNE; see Lattimer (RMC Place)
Laughlin Junction; RMC Place; ALLEGHENY; ★ PGH; mail Pittsburgh z 15207; pop. incl. with Pittsburgh (Inc. Place)
Laughlintown; RMC Place; WESTMORELAND; ▲ Ligonier; 225 WO-7; elev. 1,276ft./389m.; 🅿; z 15655; ● 950
Laurel; RMC Place; CUMBERLAND; ▲ Dickinson, Cooke; *227 EP-3; mail Gardners z 17324; summer pop. only; rural
Laurel; RMC Place; YORK; ▲ East Hopewell, Chanceford; 227 EQ-6; elev. 425ft./130m.; ★ YORK; mail Felton z 17322; ● 25
Laurel Bend; RMC Place; BUCKS; ▲ Bristol; *227 EO-13; elev. 40ft./12m.; ★ PHIL-; mail Bristol z 19007; ● 400
Laureldale; Inc. Place; BERKS; 227 EN-9; elev. 380ft./116m.; 🅿; ★ READ; z 19605; Ⓟ 3,726; Ⓒ 3,759
Laurel Falls; RMC Place; SOMERSET; ▲ Summit; *225 WQ-7; elev. 2,250ft./686m.; mail Meyersdale z 15552; ● 50
Laurel Gardens; RMC Place; ALLEGHENY; ▲ Ross; *225 WM-3; ★ PGH; mail Pittsburgh z 15229
Laurel Hill; RMC Place; FAYETTE; ▲ Franklin; *225 WP-5; elev. 973ft./297m.; ★ UNTN; mail Dunbar z 15431; rural
Laurel Hill; RMC Place; WASHINGTON; *225 WN-2; ★ PGH; mail Mc Donald z 15057
Laurel Lake; RMC Place; LUZERNE; ▲ Rice; *226 EI-9; elev. 1,200ft./366m.; ★ SCR-; mail Mountain Top z 18707; ● 150
Laurel Lake; RMC Place; SUSQUEHANNA; ▲ Silver Lake; 226 ED-9; mail Brackney z 18812; ● 300
Laurel Mountain; WESTMORELAND; see Laurel Mountain Park (Inc. Place)
Laurel Mountain Park (Laurel Mountain); Inc. Place; WESTMORELAND; ▲ Ligonier; 225 WO-7; mail Laughlintown z 15655; Ⓟ 195; Ⓒ 185
Laurel Park (Rutherton); RMC Place; UNION; ▲ Hartley; *227 EK-3; mail Millmont z 17845; ● 50
Laurel Ridge; RMC Place; BEAVER; ▲ Brighton; *225 WL-2; elev. 1,100ft./335m.; ★ PGH; mail Beaver z 15009; ● 300
Laurel Run; Inc. Place; LUZERNE; 226 EI-9; elev. 900ft./274m.; 🅿; ★ SCR-; z 18706; Ⓟ 708; Ⓒ 723
Laurelton; RMC Place; UNION; ▲ Hartley; 227 EK-3; 🅿; z 17835; ● 375
Laurelville; RMC Place; FAYETTE, WESTMORELAND; ▲ Bullskin; 225 WO-6; mail Mount Pleasant z 15666; ● 150
Laurelville; RMC Place; LANCASTER; ▲ Earl; *227 EP-8; ★ LANC; mail New Holland z 17557; ● 60
Laurys Station; RMC Place; LEHIGH; ▲ North Whitehall; 227 EL-10; elev. 384ft./117m.; 🅿; ★ ALL-; z 18059; ● 1,100
Lausanne; MCD-Township; CARBON; *226 EJ-9; ★ HAZ; mail Weatherly z 18255; Ⓟ 237; Ⓒ 218
Lavansville; RMC Place; SOMERSET; ▲ Somerset; 225 WP-7; mail Somerset z 15501; ● 150
Lavelle; RMC Place; SCHUYLKILL; ▲ Butler; 227 EK-7; elev. 1,027ft./313m.; 🅿; ★ PTSVL; z 17943; ● 600
Lavelle-Locustdale; CDP-Census Area Only; SCHUYLKILL; *227 EK-7; ★ PTSVL; Ⓒ 649
Laverock; RMC Place; MONTGOMERY; ▲ Springfield, Cheltenham; *227 EO-12; 🅿; ★ PHIL-; z 19038 & mail Philadelphia z 19118; ● 1,100
Lawn; RMC Place; LEBANON; ▲ South Londonderry; 227 EO-6; 🅿; z 17041; ● 300
Lawnherst; RMC Place; NORTHAMPTON; ▲ Palmer; *227 EL-12; ★ ALL-; mail Easton z 18045; ● 150
Lawnton; CDP; DAUPHIN; ▲ Swatara; 227 ET-4; ★ HRBG; mail Harrisburg z 17111; Ⓟ 3,221; Ⓒ 3,787
Lawrence; MCD-Township; CLEARFIELD; *224 WI-11; mail Clearfield z 16830; Ⓟ 8,000; Ⓒ 7,712
Lawrence; MCD-Township; TIOGA; *226 ED-3; mail Tioga z 16946; Ⓟ 1,519; Ⓒ 1,721
Lawrence; RMC Place; WASHINGTON; ▲ Cecil; 225 WN-3; 🅿; ★ PGH; z 15055; ● 1,100
LAWRENCE; 224 WI-2; Ⓟ 96,246; Ⓒ 94,643; ◆ 89,277
Lawrence Park; RMC Place; DELAWARE; ▲ Marple; *227 EP-11; ★ PHIL-; mail Broomall z 19008
Lawrence Park; CDP; ERIE; ▲ Lawrence Park; 224 WC-4; ★ ERIE; mail Erie z 16511; Ⓟ 4,310; Ⓒ 4,048
Lawrence Park; MCD-Township; ERIE; *224 WC-4; ★ ERIE; mail Erie z 16511; Ⓟ 4,310; Ⓒ 4,048
Lawrenceville; RMC Place; ALLEGHENY; *225 WM-4; ★ PGH; mail Pittsburgh z 15201; pop. incl. with Pittsburgh (Inc. Place)
Lawrenceville; RMC Place; LACKAWANNA; *226 EH-9; ★ SCR-; mail Duryea z 18642; pop. incl. with Old Forge (Inc. Place)
Lawrenceville; Inc. Place; TIOGA; 226 ED-3; elev. 996ft./304m.; 🅿; z 16929; Ⓟ 481; Ⓒ 627
Lawsonham; RMC Place; CLARION; ▲ Madison; 224 WJ-6; mail Rimersburg z 16248; ● 50
Lawson Heights; CDP; WESTMORELAND; ▲ Unity; *225 WN-6; ★ LTROB; mail Latrobe z 15650; Ⓟ 2,464; Ⓒ 2,339
Lawsville Center; RMC Place; SUSQUEHANNA; ▲ Liberty; 226 ED-9; elev. 1,082ft./330m.; mail Montrose z 18801; ● 75
Lawton; RMC Place; SUSQUEHANNA; ▲ Rush; 226 EE-8; elev. 934ft./285m.; 🅿; z 18828; ● 85
Layfield; RMC Place; MONTGOMERY; ▲ New Hanover; *227 EN-10; elev. 268ft./82m.; mail Gilbertsville z 19525
Layton; RMC Place; FAYETTE; ▲ Perry; *225 WO-5; elev. 809ft./247m.; 🅿; ★ PGH; z 15473; ● 125
Leacock; RMC Place; LANCASTER; ▲ Upper Leacock; *227 EO-7; ★ LANC; mail Leola z 17540; ● 1,400
Leacock; MCD-Township; LANCASTER; *227 EP-8; ★ LANC; mail Leola z 17540, Ronks z 17572; Ⓟ 4,668; Ⓒ 4,878
Leacock-Leola-Bareville; CDP-Census Area Only; LANCASTER; ▲ Upper Leacock, West Earl; *227 EO-8; elev. 400ft./122m.; ★ LANC; mail Leola z 17540; Ⓟ 5,685; Ⓒ 6,625
Leaders Heights; RMC Place; YORK; ▲ York; 225 WT-10; ★ YORK; mail York z 17403; ● 1,200
Leaf Park; RMC Place; LANCASTER; ▲ Manor; *227 EP-7; ★ LANC; mail Lancaster z 17603; ● 100
Leak Run; RMC Place; ALLEGHENY; *225 WM-4; ★ PGH; pop. incl. with Monroeville (Inc. Place)
Leaman Place; RMC Place; LANCASTER; ▲ Paradise; *227 EP-8; elev. 385ft./117m.; mail Paradise z 17562
Leamersville; RMC Place; BLAIR; ▲ Freedom; 225 WN-11; ★ ALT; mail Duncansville z 16635; ● 80
Learn Settlement; RMC Place; INDIANA; ▲ Green; *225 WL-8; elev. 1,569ft./478m.; mail Commodore z 15729; rural
Leasuresville; RMC Place; BUTLER; ▲ Winfield; *225 WK-5; ★ PGH; mail Sarver z 16055; rural
Leather Corner Post; RMC Place; LEHIGH; ▲ Lowhill; *227 EL-10; elev. 688ft./210m.; ★ ALL-; mail Orefield z 18069; ● 100
Leatherwood; RMC Place; CLARION; ▲ Porter; *224 WJ-6; mail New Bethlehem z 16242; ● 20
Lebanon; Inc. Place; ⊡ LEBANON; 227 EN-6; elev. 460ft./140m.; 🅿 🅷 ■; ★ LEB; z 17042, z 17046; Ⓟ 24,800; Ⓒ 24,461; ◆ 24,892
Lebanon; MCD-Township; WAYNE; *226 EF-12; mail Honesdale z 18431; Ⓟ 479; Ⓒ 645
LEBANON; 227 EN-6; Ⓟ 113,744; Ⓒ 120,327; ◆ 129,771
Lebanon South (South Lebanon); CDP; LEBANON; ▲ South Lebanon; *227 EN-6; ★ LEB; mail Lebanon z 17042; Ⓟ 1,764; Ⓒ 2,145
Lebo; RMC Place; PERRY; ▲ Spring; mail Landisburg z 17040; rural
LeBoeuf; MCD-Township; ERIE; *224 WE-4; ★ ERIE; mail Waterford z 16441; Ⓟ 1,521; Ⓒ 1,680
Le Boeuf Gardens; RMC Place; ERIE; ▲ Waterford; *224 WD-4; ★ ERIE; mail Waterford z 16441; ● 200
Leck Kill; RMC Place; NORTHUMBERLAND; ▲ Upper Mahanoy; 227 EL-5; elev. 759ft./231m.; 🅿; z 17836; ● 200
Leckrone; RMC Place; FAYETTE; ▲ German; 225 WQ-4; 🅿; ★ UNTN; z 15454; ● 250
Lecontes Mills; RMC Place; CLEARFIELD; ▲ Girard; 224 WJ-11; 🅿; z 16850; ● 125
Lederach; RMC Place; MONTGOMERY; ▲ Lower Salford; 227 EN-11; elev. 368ft./112m.; 🅿; ★ PHIL-; z 19450; ● 180
Ledgedale; RMC Place; WAYNE; ▲ Salem; *226 EH-11; ★ SCR-; mail Sterling z 18463; ● 100
Ledger; LANCASTER; see Spring Garden (RMC Place)
Lee; RMC Place; LUZERNE; ▲ Newport; *226 EI-8; ★ SCR-; mail Glen Lyon z 18617; ● 60
Leechburg; Inc. Place; ARMSTRONG; 225 WL-5; elev. 900ft./274m.; 🅿; ★ PGH; z 15656; Ⓟ 2,504; Ⓒ 2,386
Leech Hill; RMC Place; POTTER; ▲ Hector; *226 EE-1; mail Sabinsville z 16943; rural
Leedom Estates; RMC Place; DELAWARE; ▲ Ridley; *227 EQ-11; elev. 50ft./15m.; ★ PHIL-; mail Ridley Park z 19078; pop. incl. with Ridley Park (Inc. Place)
Leedom Gardens; RMC Place; DELAWARE; ▲ Ridley; ★ PHIL-; mail Ridley Park z 19078
Lee Mine; RMC Place; LUZERNE; ▲ Newport; ★ SCR-; mail Nanticoke z 18634
Lee Park; RMC Place; LUZERNE; ▲ Hanover; 226 EI-9; ★ SCR-; mail Wilkes Barre z 18706; ● 3,600
Leeper; RMC Place; CLARION, CLARION; ▲ Farmington; ● 200
Leesburg; RMC Place; MERCER; ▲ Springfield; 224 WI-3; mail Volant z 16156; ● 100
Leesburg Station; RMC Place; MERCER; ▲ Springfield; *224 WI-3; elev. 1,050ft./320m.; mail Volant z 16156; rural
Lees Cross Roads; RMC Place; CUMBERLAND; ▲ Southampton; 227 EP-2; mail Shippensburg z 17257; ● 200
Leesport; Inc. Place; BERKS; 227 EM-8; elev. 340ft./104m.; 🅿; ★ READ; z 19533; Ⓟ 1,270; Ⓒ 1,805
Leet; MCD-Township; ALLEGHENY; *225 WL-3; ★ PGH; mail Sewickley z 15143; Ⓟ 1,731; Ⓒ 1,568
Leetonia; RMC Place; TIOGA; ▲ Elk; *226 EG-2; mail Cedar Run z 17727; summer pop. 100; rural
Leetsdale; Inc. Place; ALLEGHENY; 225 WL-3; elev. 740ft./226m.; 🅿; ★ PGH; z 15056; Ⓟ 1,387; Ⓒ 1,232
Lehigh; MCD-Township; CARBON; *227 EK-9; ★ HAZ; mail Weatherly z 18255; Ⓟ 500; Ⓒ 527
Lehigh; RMC Place; LACKAWANNA; ▲ Covington; 226 EH-11; ★ SCR-; mail Gouldsboro z 18424; ● 100
Lehigh; MCD-Township; NORTHAMPTON; *227 EK-10; ★ ALL-; mail Walnutport z 18088; Ⓟ 9,296; Ⓒ 9,728
Lehigh; MCD-Township; WAYNE; *226 EI-10; mail Gouldsboro z 18424; Ⓟ 1,178; Ⓒ 1,639
LEHIGH; 227 EL-10; Ⓟ 291,130; Ⓒ 312,090; ◆ 340,423
Lehigh Furnace; RMC Place; LEHIGH; ▲ Washington; 227 EL-10; elev. 579ft./176m.; ★ ALL-; mail Slatington z 18080; ● 100
Lehigh Gap; RMC Place; CARBON; ▲ Lower Towamensing; mail Palmerton z 18071; rural
Lehigh Gap; RMC Place; LEHIGH; ▲ Washington; *227 EK-10; ★ ALL-; mail Slatington z 18080; ● 40
Lehigh Tannery; CARBON; see Tannery (RMC Place)
Lehighton; Inc. Place; CARBON; 227 EK-10; elev. 502ft./153m.; 🅿 🅷; z 18235; Ⓟ 5,914; Ⓒ 5,537
Lehigh University; RMC Place; NORTHAMPTON; ★ ALL-; mail Bethlehem z 18015; pop. incl. with Bethlehem (Inc. Place)
Lehman; RMC Place; LUZERNE; ▲ Lehman; 226 EH-8; elev. 1,316ft./401m.; 🅿 🅲 728; ★ SCR-; z 18627; ● 250
Lehman; MCD-Township; LUZERNE; *226 EH-8; 🅿 🅲 728; ★ SCR-; z 18627 & mail Dallas z 18612; Ⓟ 3,076; Ⓒ 3,206
Lehman; MCD-Township; PIKE; *226 EI-13; mail Bushkill z 18324; Ⓟ 3,055; Ⓒ 7,515
Lehman; RMC Place; YORK; ▲ North Codorus; *227 EQ-4; ★ YORK; mail Spring Grove z 17362; ● 150
Leibeyville; RMC Place; SCHUYLKILL; ▲ West Penn; *227 EL-9; elev. 655ft./200m.; mail New Ringgold z 17960; rural
Leidy; MCD-Township; CLINTON; *224 WH-13; mail Renovo z 17764; Ⓟ 214; Ⓒ 229
Leidytown (Fricks); RMC Place; BUCKS; ▲ Hilltown; 227 EN-12; ★ PHIL-; mail Hilltown z 18927, Line Lexington z 18932; ● 130
Leinbachs; RMC Place; BERKS; ▲ Bern; 227 ES-11; elev. 356ft./109m.; ★ READ; mail Reading z 19605; ● 150
Leiperville; DELAWARE; see Crum Lynne (RMC Place)
Leisenring; RMC Place; FAYETTE; ▲ Dunbar; 225 WP-5; 🅿; z 15455; ● 600
Leith; RMC Place; FAYETTE; ▲ South Union; 225 WQ-5; ★ UNTN; mail Uniontown z 15401; ● 900
Leith-Hatfield; CDP-Census Area Only; FAYETTE; ▲ South Union; *225 WQ-5; ★ UNTN; mail Uniontown z 15401; Ⓟ 2,437; Ⓒ 2,820
Leithsville; RMC Place; NORTHAMPTON; ▲ Lower Saucon; 227 EM-11; ★ ALL-; mail Hellertown z 18055; ● 300
Lemasters; RMC Place; FRANKLIN; ▲ Peters; 225 WQ-13; 🅿; z 17231; ● 250
Lemon (Aldovin); RMC Place; WYOMING; ▲ Lemon; *226 EF-8; mail Tunkhannock z 18657
Lemon; MCD-Township; WYOMING; *226 EF-9; mail Tunkhannock z 18657; Ⓟ 1,264; Ⓒ 1,189
Lemont; CDP; CENTRE; ▲ College; 225 WK-13; elev. 1,046ft./319m.; 🅿; ★ STCOL; z 16851; Ⓒ 2,116
Lemont Furnace (Darent); RMC Place; FAYETTE; ▲ North Union; 225 WP-5; 🅿; ★ UNTN; z 15456; ● 800
Lemoyne; Inc. Place; CUMBERLAND; 227 ET-3; elev. 366ft./112m.; 🅿; ★ HRBG; z 17043; Ⓟ 3,959; Ⓒ 3,995
Lemoyne-Camp Hill; RMC Place; CUMBERLAND; ★ HRBG; pop. incl. with Lemoyne (Inc. Place)
Lenape; RMC Place; CHESTER; ▲ Birmingham, East Bradford, Pocopson; 227 EP-10; elev. 184ft./56m.; ★ PHIL-; mail West Chester z 19380; ● 200
Lenape Heights; CDP-Census Area Only; ARMSTRONG; ▲ Manor; *225 WK-6; ★ PGH; mail Ford City z 16226; Ⓟ 1,355; Ⓒ 1,212
Lenhartsville; Inc. Place; BERKS; 227 EM-9; elev. 384ft./117m.; 🅿; z 19534; Ⓟ 195; Ⓒ 173
Lenker Manor; RMC Place; DAUPHIN; ▲ Swatara; *227 EN-5; elev. 400ft./122m.; ★ HRBG; mail Harrisburg z 17109, z 17111; ● 1,500
Lenkerville; RMC Place; DAUPHIN; ▲ Upper Paxton; *227 EM-4; mail Millersburg z 17061; ● 550
Lenni (Lenni Mills); RMC Place; DELAWARE; ▲ Middletown; *227 EQ-11; 🅿; ★ PHIL-; z 19052; ● 775
Lenni Heights; RMC Place; DELAWARE; ▲ Middletown; ★ PHIL-; mail Glen Riddle Lima z 19037
Lenni Mills; DELAWARE; see Lenni (RMC Place)
Lennox Park; RMC Place; DELAWARE; ★ PHIL-; mail Brookhaven z 19015; pop. incl. with Trainer (Inc. Place)
Lenover; RMC Place; CHESTER; ▲ West Sadsbury; *227 EP-9; ★ PHIL-; mail Parkesburg z 19365; rural
Lenox; MCD-Township; SUSQUEHANNA; *226 EF-9; mail Nicholson z 18446; Ⓟ 1,581; Ⓒ 1,832
Lenoxville; RMC Place; SUSQUEHANNA; ▲ Lenox; 226 EF-10; elev. 995ft./303m.; 🅿; z 18441; ● 130
Lenwood Heights; RMC Place; FRANKLIN; ▲ Montgomery; *225 WQ-13; mail Mercersburg z 17236; ● 100
Leola; RMC Place; LANCASTER; ▲ Upper Leacock; 227 EO-7; 🅿; ★ LANC; z 17540; ● 1,100
Leolyn; RMC Place; TIOGA; ▲ Union; mail Roaring Branch z 17765; rural
Leona; RMC Place; BRADFORD; ▲ Springfield; *226 EE-5; mail Columbia Cross Roads z 16914, Troy z 16947; ● 50
Leopard; RMC Place; CHESTER; ▲ Easttown; *227 EP-11; ★ PHIL-; mail Berwyn z 19312
Leopard Lakes; RMC Place; CHESTER; ▲ Easttown; ★ PHIL-; mail Berwyn z 19312
Le Raysville; Inc. Place; BRADFORD; 226 EE-7; elev. 1,423ft./434m.; 🅿; z 18829; Ⓟ 336; Ⓒ 318
Leroy; RMC Place; BRADFORD; ▲ Leroy; 226 EF-5; elev. 1,028ft./313m.; 🅿; z 17724; ● 90
Leroy; MCD-Township; BRADFORD; *226 EF-5; elev. 1,020ft./311m.; 🅿; z 17724; Ⓟ 610; Ⓒ 627
Lester; RMC Place; DELAWARE; ▲ Tinicum; *227 EQ-12; 🅿; ★ PHIL-; z 19029 & mail Philadelphia z 19113
Letort; RMC Place; LANCASTER; ▲ Manor; *227 EP-6; ★ LANC; mail Washington Boro z 17582; ● 350
Letterkenny; MCD-Township; FRANKLIN; *225 WP-14; mail Orrstown z 17244; Ⓟ 2,251; Ⓒ 2,074
Level Corner; RMC Place; LYCOMING; ▲ Woodward, Piatt; *226 EI-3; ★ WMSPT; mail Linden z 17744; rural
Level Green; RMC Place; WESTMORELAND; ▲ Penn; 225 WN-5; ★ PGH; mail Trafford z 15085; ● 2,500
Leviston; CARBON; see Junedale (RMC Place)
Levittown; CDP; BUCKS; ▲ Bristol, Falls, Middletown; 227 EO-14; 🅿 ■; ★ PHIL-; z 19054-58; Ⓟ 55,362; Ⓒ 53,966; ◆ 55,660
Levittown-Tullytown; RMC Place; BUCKS; ▲ Bristol; ★ PHIL-; mail Bristol z 19007
Lewis; MCD-Township; LYCOMING; *226 EH-3; mail Trout Run z 17771; Ⓟ 1,194; Ⓒ 1,139
Lewis; MCD-Township; NORTHUMBERLAND; *226 EI-5; ★ WMSPT; mail Turbotville z 17772; Ⓟ 1,881; Ⓒ 1,862
Lewis; MCD-Township; UNION; *226 EJ-3; mail Swengel z 17880; Ⓟ 1,222; Ⓒ 1,405
Lewisberry; Inc. Place; YORK; 227 EO-4; elev. 422ft./129m.; 🅿; ★ HRBG; z 17339; Ⓟ 314; Ⓒ 385
Lewisburg; Inc. Place; ⊡ UNION; 226 EJ-4; elev. 460ft./140m.; 🅿 🅷 🅲 3,706; z 17837, z 17886; Ⓟ 5,785; Ⓒ 5,620
Lewis Run; Inc. Place; MCKEAN; 224 WE-10; elev. 1,600ft./488m.; 🅿; z 16738; Ⓟ 578; Ⓒ 577
Lewistown; Inc. Place; ⊡ MIFFLIN; 227 EL-1; elev. 520ft./158m.; 🅿 🅷 ■; z 17044; Ⓟ 9,341; Ⓒ 8,998; ◆ 8,857
Lewistown; RMC Place; SCHUYLKILL; ▲ Walker; *227 EL-8; elev. 961ft./293m.; mail Tamaqua z 18252; ● 200
Lewistown Junction; RMC Place; MIFFLIN; ▲ Granville; *227 EM-1; mail Lewistown z 17044; ● 80
Lewisville; RMC Place; CHESTER; ▲ Elk; 227 ER-9; 🅿; ★ PHIL-; z 19351; ● 225
Lewisville; RMC Place; INDIANA; ▲ Conemaugh; *225 WM-7; elev. 1,391ft./424m.; ★ PGH; mail Clarksburg z 15725
Lexington; RMC Place; LANCASTER; ▲ Warwick; *227 EO-7; ★ LANC; mail Lititz z 17543; ● 200
Liberty; MCD-Township; ADAMS; *227 EQ-2; mail Fairfield z 17320; Ⓟ 938; Ⓒ 1,063
Liberty; Inc. Place; ALLEGHENY; 228 M-8; elev. 900ft./274m.; ★ PGH; mail Mckeesport z 15133; Ⓟ 2,744; Ⓒ 2,670
Liberty; MCD-Township; BEDFORD; *225 WN-11; mail Saxton z 16678; Ⓟ 1,478; Ⓒ 1,477
Liberty; MCD-Township; CENTRE; *226 EJ-1; mail Howard z 16841; Ⓟ 1,747; Ⓒ 1,830
Liberty; FAYETTE; see Dickerson Run (RMC Place)
Liberty; RMC Place; MCKEAN; ▲ Liberty; *224 WF-12; mail Port Allegany z 16743; rural
Liberty; MCD-Township; MCKEAN; *224 WE-12; mail Port Allegany z 16743; Ⓟ 1,764; Ⓒ 1,726
Liberty; MCD-Township; MERCER; *224 WI-3; mail Grove City z 16127; Ⓟ 1,223; Ⓒ 1,276
Liberty; MCD-Township; MONTOUR; *226 EJ-5; mail Danville z 17821; Ⓟ 1,309; Ⓒ 1,476
Liberty; MCD-Township; SUSQUEHANNA; *226 ED-9; mail Montrose z 18801; Ⓟ 1,353; Ⓒ 1,266
Liberty; Inc. Place; TIOGA; 226 EG-3; elev. 1,546ft./471m.; 🅿; z 16930; Ⓟ 199; Ⓒ 230
Liberty; MCD-Township; TIOGA; *226 EG-3; 🅿; z 16930; does not include the Borough of Liberty; Ⓟ 930; Ⓒ 868
Liberty Corners; RMC Place; BRADFORD; ▲ Monroe; 226 EF-6; elev. 1,283ft./391m.; mail Towanda z 18848; ● 100
Liberty Square; RMC Place; LANCASTER; ▲ Drumore; *227 EQ-7; mail Drumore z 17518; ● 75
Library; RMC Place; ALLEGHENY; ▲ South Park; 225 WN-3; 🅿; ★ PGH; z 15129; ● 6,000
Lickdale; RMC Place; LEBANON; ▲ Swatara, Union; *227 EM-6; mail Jonestown z 17038; ● 100
Licking; MCD-Township; CLARION; *224 WI-6; mail Parker z 16049, Sligo z 16255; Ⓟ 483; Ⓒ 479
Licking Creek; MCD-Township; FULTON; *225 WP-12; mail Harrisonville z 17228; Ⓟ 1,410; Ⓒ 1,532
Lickingville; RMC Place; CLARION; ▲ Washington; 224 WH-6; elev. 1,587ft./484m.; 🅿; z 16332; ● 60
Lightner; RMC Place; YORK; ▲ Manchester; *227 EP-5; ★ YORK; mail York z 17404; ● 1,400
Lightstreet; CDP; COLUMBIA; ▲ Scott; 226 EJ-6; elev. 548ft./167m.; 🅿; z 17839; Ⓒ 881
Ligonier; Inc. Place; WESTMORELAND; 225 WN-7; elev. 1,200ft./366m.; 🅿; z 15658; Ⓟ 1,638; Ⓒ 1,695
Ligonier; MCD-Township; WESTMORELAND; *225 WO-7; 🅿; z 15658; does not include the Borough of Ligonier; Ⓟ 6,979; Ⓒ 6,973
Lilly; Inc. Place; CAMBRIA; 225 WM-10; elev. 1,904ft./580m.; 🅿; z 15938; Ⓟ 1,162; Ⓒ 948
Lillyville; RMC Place; BEAVER; ▲ Franklin; *225 WK-3; elev. 1,199ft./365m.; ★ PGH; mail Ellwood City z 16117; ● 150
Lima; CDP; DELAWARE; ▲ Middletown; 227 EP-11; 🅿; ★ PHIL-; z 19037; Ⓟ 2,670; Ⓒ 3,225
Limehill; RMC Place; BRADFORD; ▲ Wyalusing; *226 EF-7; mail Wyalusing z 18853
Limekiln; RMC Place; BERKS; ▲ Oley, Exeter; 227 EN-9; 🅿; ★ READ; z 19535; rural
Limeport; RMC Place; LEHIGH; ▲ Lower Milford; 227 EM-11; 🅿; ★ ALL-; z 18060; ● 250
Limerick; RMC Place; MONTGOMERY; ▲ Limerick; 227 EO-10; 🅿; ★ PHIL-; z 19468; ● 800
Limerick; MCD-Township; MONTGOMERY; *227 EO-11; 🅿; ★ PHIL-; z 19468; Ⓟ 6,691; Ⓒ 13,534
Lime Ridge; CDP; COLUMBIA; ▲ South Centre; 226 EJ-7; mail Bloomsburg z 17815; Ⓟ 1,051; Ⓒ 951
Lime Rock; RMC Place; LANCASTER; ▲ Penn; *227 EO-7; ★ LANC; mail Lititz z 17543; rural
Limestone; RMC Place; CLARION; ▲ Limestone; 224 WI-7; 🅿; z 16234; ● 150
Limestone; MCD-Township; CLARION; *224 WI-7; 🅿; z 16234; Ⓟ 1,686; Ⓒ 1,773
Limestone; MCD-Township; LYCOMING; *226 EI-3; mail Jersey Shore z 17740; Ⓟ 1,893; Ⓒ 2,136
Limestone; MCD-Township; MONTOUR; *226 EJ-5; mail Danville z 17821; Ⓟ 787; Ⓒ 1,004
Limestone; MCD-Township; UNION; *227 EK-4; mail Mifflinburg z 17844; Ⓟ 1,346; Ⓒ 1,572
Limestone; MCD-Township; WARREN; *224 WF-6; mail Tidioute z 16351; Ⓟ 359; Ⓒ 418
Limestoneville; RMC Place; MONTOUR; ▲ Limestone; 226 EJ-5; elev. 547ft./167m.; mail Milton z 17847; ● 70
Lime Valley; RMC Place; LANCASTER; ▲ West Lampeter; *227 EP-7; ★ LANC; mail Willow Street z 17584; rural
Limeville; RMC Place; LANCASTER; ▲ Salisbury; *227 EP-8; elev. 500ft./152m.; mail Gap z 17527; ● 35
Lincoln; Inc. Place; ALLEGHENY; 228 N-8; elev. 1,100ft./335m.; ★ PGH; mail Elizabeth z 15037; Ⓟ 1,187; Ⓒ 1,218
Lincoln; MCD-Township; BEDFORD; *225 WO-10; mail Alum Bank z 15521; Ⓟ 394; Ⓒ 380
Lincoln; MCD-Township; HUNTINGDON; *225 WN-12; mail James Creek z 16657; Ⓟ 320; Ⓒ 319
Lincoln; RMC Place; LANCASTER; *227 EO-7; ★ LANC; mail Ephrata z 17522; pop. incl. with Ephrata (Inc. Place)
Lincoln; MCD-Township; SOMERSET; *225 WO-7; mail Somerset z 15501; Ⓟ 1,655; Ⓒ 1,669
Lincoln Acres; RMC Place; WESTMORELAND; ▲ North Huntingdon; *225 WN-5; ★ PGH; mail Irwin z 15642; ● 500
Lincoln Beach; RMC Place; WESTMORELAND; ▲ Upper Burrell; *225 WM-5; elev. 1,000ft./305m.; ★ PGH; mail New Kensington z 15068; ● 200
Lincoln Colliery; RMC Place; SCHUYLKILL; ▲ Tremont; *227 EL-6; mail Pine Grove z 17963; ● 75
Lincoln Falls; RMC Place; SULLIVAN; ▲ Elkland; *226 EG-5; mail Forksville z 18616; rural
Lincoln Heights; RMC Place; BERKS; ★ READ; mail Birdsboro z 19508; pop. incl. with Birdsboro (Inc. Place)
Lincoln Heights; RMC Place; WESTMORELAND; ▲ Hempfield; 225 WN-5; ★ PGH; mail Jeannette z 15644; ● 300
Lincoln Hill; RMC Place; WASHINGTON; ▲ North Franklin; 225 WO-2; ★ WASH; mail Washington z 15301; ● 500
Lincoln Park; RMC Place; ALLEGHENY; ▲ Penn Hills; *225 WM-4; elev. 1,200ft./366m.; ★ PGH; mail Pittsburgh z 15235
Lincoln Park; RMC Place; BERKS; ▲ Cumru, Spring; 227 ET-11; ★ READ; mail Reading z 19609; ● 1,800
Lincoln Park; RMC Place; DELAWARE; ▲ Darby; ★ PHIL-; mail Sharon Hill z 19079
Lincoln Park; RMC Place; NORTHAMPTON; ★ ALL-; pop. incl. with Bethlehem (Inc. Place)
Lincoln Place; RMC Place; ALLEGHENY; *225 WN-4; ★ PGH; mail Pittsburgh z 15207; pop. incl. with Pittsburgh (Inc. Place)
Lincoln Terrace; RMC Place; NORTHAMPTON; ▲ Palmer; *227 EL-12; ★ ALL-; mail Easton z 18042; ● 100
Lincolnville; CDP; CRAWFORD; ▲ Bloomfield; 224 WE-4; mail Centerville z 16404; Ⓒ 112
Lincolnway; RMC Place; YORK; ▲ West Manchester; *227 EP-5; ★ YORK; mail York z 17404; ● 1,900
Linconia; RMC Place; BUCKS; ▲ Bensalem; *227 EO-13; ★ PHIL-; mail Langhorne z 19047; ● 950
Linden; RMC Place; LYCOMING; ▲ Woodward; 226 EI-3; 🅿; ★ WMSPT; z 17744; ● 270
Linden; RMC Place; WASHINGTON; ▲ North Strabane; 225 WN-3; ★ PGH; mail Canonsburg z 15317; ● 100
Linden Hall; RMC Place; CENTRE; ▲ Harris; *225 WK-14; ★ STCOL; mail Centre Hall z 16828; ● 125
Lindenhurst; RMC Place; BUCKS; ▲ Lower Makefield; ★ PHIL-; mail Morrisville z 19067; ● 250
Linds Crossing; RMC Place; BLAIR; ▲ Frankstown; *225 WM-11; ★ ALT; mail Hollidaysburg z 16648; rural
Lindsey; RMC Place; JEFFERSON; elev. 1,255ft./383m.; mail Punxsutawney z 15767; pop. incl. with Punxsutawney (Inc. Place)
Line Lexington; RMC Place; BUCKS; ▲ Hilltown, Hatfield, Montgomery, New Britain; 227 EN-12; 🅿; ★ PHIL-; z 18932; ● 700
Line Mountain; RMC Place; NORTHUMBERLAND; ▲ Upper Mahanoy; *227 EL-6; elev. 765ft./233m.; mail Klingerstown z 17941; rural
Linesville; Inc. Place; CRAWFORD; 224 WF-2; elev. 1,050ft./320m.; 🅿; z 16424; Ⓟ 1,166; Ⓒ 1,155
Linfield; RMC Place; MONTGOMERY; ▲ Limerick; 227 EO-10; 🅿; ★ PHIL-; z 19468; ● 650
Linglestown; CDP; DAUPHIN; ▲ Lower Paxton; 227 EN-5; 🅿; ★ HRBG; z 17112; Ⓟ 5,862; Ⓒ 6,414
Linhart; RMC Place; ALLEGHENY; ▲ Wilkins; *225 WM-4; ★ PGH; mail Turtle Creek z 15145
Linn; RMC Place; FAYETTE; ▲ Jefferson; *225 WP-4; elev. 791ft./241m.; ★ PGH; mail Grindstone z 15442; ● 80
Linntown; CDP; UNION; ▲ East Buffalo; 226 EJ-4; mail Lewisburg z 17837; Ⓟ 1,640; Ⓒ 1,542
Linville Circle; RMC Place; LANCASTER; *227 EP-7; ★ LANC; mail Lancaster z 17602; pop. incl. with Lancaster (Inc. Place)
Linwood; CDP; DELAWARE; ▲ Lower Chichester; 227 EQ-11; 🅿; ★ PHIL-; z 19061; Ⓟ 3,425; Ⓒ 3,374
Linwood Park; RMC Place; DELAWARE; ▲ Upper Chichester; ★ PHIL-; mail Marcus Hook z 19061
Linwood Terrace; RMC Place; DELAWARE; ▲ Lower Chichester; ★ PHIL-; mail Marcus Hook z 19061
Lionville; RMC Place; CHESTER; ▲ Uwchlan; 227 EP-10; 🅿; ★ PHIL-; z 19353; ● 400
Lionville-Marchwood; CDP-Census Area Only; CHESTER; ▲ Uwchlan; *227 EP-10; elev. 600ft./183m.; ★ PHIL-; mail Exton z 19341; Ⓟ 6,468; Ⓒ 6,298
Lippincott; RMC Place; GREENE; ▲ Morgan; 225 WP-3; mail Waynesburg z 15370; ● 40
Lisbon; RMC Place; VENANGO; ▲ Scrubgrass; *224 WI-5; mail Emlenton z 16373; rural
Lisburn; RMC Place; CUMBERLAND; ▲ Lower Allen; 227 EO-4; ★ HRBG; mail Mechanicsburg z 17055; ● 400
Listie; RMC Place; SOMERSET; ▲ Somerset; 225 WP-8; 🅿; z 15549; ● 700
Listonburg; RMC Place; SOMERSET; ▲ Addison; *225 WQ-7; elev. 1,730ft./527m.; 🅿; z 15424
Litchfield; RMC Place; BRADFORD; ▲ Litchfield; 226 ED-6; elev. 1,517ft./462m.; mail Athens z 18810, Sayre z 18840; ● 80
Litchfield; MCD-Township; BRADFORD; *226 ED-6; mail Athens z 18810; Ⓟ 1,296; Ⓒ 1,307
Lithia Springs; RMC Place; NORTHUMBERLAND; ▲ Point; 227 EK-5; mail Northumberland z 17857; ● 90
Lithia Valley; RMC Place; WYOMING; ★ SCR-; mail Factoryville z 18419; pop. incl. with Factoryville (Inc. Place)
Lititz; Inc. Place; LANCASTER; 227 EO-7; elev. 387ft./118m.; 🅿; ★ LANC; z 17543; Ⓟ 8,280; Ⓒ 9,029
Little Beaver; MCD-Township; LAWRENCE; *225 WK-2; mail Enon Valley z 16120; Ⓟ 1,251; Ⓒ 1,310
Little Britain; RMC Place; LANCASTER; 227 EQ-8; mail Quarryville z 17566; ● 45
Little Britain; MCD-Township; LANCASTER; *227 EQ-8; mail Oxford z 19363; Ⓟ 2,701; Ⓒ 3,514
Little Chicago; RMC Place; GREENE; ▲ Cumberland; *225 WQ-4; elev. 927ft./283m.; mail Carmichaels z 15320; ● 60
Little Conestoga; CHESTER; see Conestoga (RMC Place)
Little Cooley; RMC Place; CRAWFORD; ▲ Athens; 224 WF-4; mail Centerville z 16404; ● 50
Little Corners; RMC Place; CRAWFORD; ▲ Hayfield; 224 WF-3; mail Meadville z 16335; ● 45
Little Gap; RMC Place; CARBON; ▲ Lower Towamensing; 227 EK-10; mail Kunkletown z 18058; ● 300
Little Hickory; RMC Place; FOREST; ▲ Hickory; *224 WG-6; mail Tionesta z 16353; rural
Little Hope; RMC Place; ERIE; ▲ Greenfield; 224 WC-5; mail North East z 16428; ● 60
Little Italy; RMC Place; BUCKS; ▲ Wrightstown; *227 EN-13; ★ PHIL-; mail Rushland z 18956; ● 50
Little Kansas; RMC Place; MIFFLIN; ▲ Oliver; *225 WM-13; mail Mc Veytown z 17051; rural
Little Mahanoy; MCD-Township; NORTHUMBERLAND; *227 EK-5; mail Dornsife z 17823; Ⓟ 432; Ⓒ 435
Little Marsh; RMC Place; TIOGA; ▲ Chatham; 226 EE-2; 🅿; z 16950; ● 80
Little Meadows; Inc. Place; SUSQUEHANNA; 226 ED-8; elev. 1,050ft./320m.; 🅿; ★ BING; z 18830; Ⓟ 326; Ⓒ 290
Littlestown; Inc. Place; ADAMS; 227 EQ-3; elev. 635ft./194m.; 🅿; z 17340; Ⓟ 2,974; Ⓒ 3,947
Little Summit; RMC Place; FAYETTE; ▲ Dunbar; *225 WP-5; elev. 1,202ft./366m.; mail Dunbar z 15431; ● 90
Littletown; RMC Place; INDIANA; ▲ Brush Valley; *225 WM-8; mail Homer City z 15748; rural
Little Washington; RMC Place; CHESTER; ▲ East Brandywine; *227 EP-9; elev. 500ft./152m.; ★ PHIL-; mail Downingtown z 19335, Glenmoore z 19343; ● 125
Live Easy; RMC Place; GREENE; ▲ Cumberland; *225 WQ-4; mail Carmichaels z 15320; rural
Liverpool; Inc. Place; PERRY; 227 EM-4; elev. 400ft./122m.; 🅿; z 17045; Ⓟ 934; Ⓒ 876
Liverpool; MCD-Township; PERRY; *227 EM-4; 🅿; z 17045; does not include the Borough of Liverpool; Ⓟ 915; Ⓒ 966
Livonia; RMC Place; CENTRE; ▲ Miles; *226 EJ-2; mail Rebersburg z 16872; rural
Llandrilla; RMC Place; MONTGOMERY; ▲ Lower Merion; ★ PHIL-; mail Bala Cynwyd z 19004
Llanfair; RMC Place; CAMBRIA; ▲ Adams; *225 WN-9; elev. 2,349ft./716m.; ★ JNST; mail Dunlo z 15930; ● 200
Llewellyn; RMC Place; SCHUYLKILL; ▲ Branch; 227 EL-7; 🅿; ★ PTSVL; z 17944; ● 800
Llewellyn Corners (Llewelyn Corners); RMC Place; LUZERNE; ▲ Bear Creek; *226 EI-9; ★ SCR-; mail Bear Creek z 18602
Llewelyn Corners; LUZERNE; see Llewellyn Corners (RMC Place)
Lloydell; RMC Place; CAMBRIA; ▲ Summerhill, Adams; *225 WN-9; elev. 2,022ft./616m.; ★ JNST; mail Beaverdale z 15921; ● 400
Lloydesville; RMC Place; WESTMORELAND; ▲ Unity; *225 WN-6; ★ LTROB; mail Latrobe z 15650; ● 270
Llyswen; RMC Place; BLAIR; *225 WM-11; ★ ALT; mail Altoona z 16602; pop. incl. with Altoona (Inc. Place)
Loag; RMC Place; CHESTER; ▲ West Nantmeal; 227 EO-9; ★ PHIL-; mail Elverson z 19520; ● 200
Lobachsville; RMC Place; BERKS; ▲ Pike; *227 EN-9; ★ READ; mail Oley z 19547
Lochiel; RMC Place; UNION; ▲ East Buffalo; *226 EJ-4; mail Lewisburg z 17837; ● 80
Lochvale; RMC Place; INDIANA; ▲ Banks; *225 WK-9; elev. 1,640ft./500m.; mail Glen Campbell z 15742; rural
Locke Mills; RMC Place; MIFFLIN; ▲ Armagh; *227 EL-1; mail Milroy z 17063
Lock Haven; Inc. Place; ⊡ CLINTON; 226 EI-2; elev. 564ft./172m.; 🅿 🅷 🅲 5,175 ■; ★ WMSPT; z 17745; Ⓟ 9,230; Ⓒ 9,149; ◆ 8,798
Lockport; RMC Place; CLINTON; ▲ Woodward; 226 EI-2; ★ WMSPT; mail Lock Haven z 17745; ● 200
Lockport; RMC Place; MIFFLIN; ▲ Oliver; *227 EM-1; mail Lewistown z 17044; ● 100
Lockport; RMC Place; WESTMORELAND; ▲ Fairfield; *225 WN-7; ★ JNST; mail Bolivar z 15923; ● 30
Locksley; RMC Place; DELAWARE; ▲ Thornbury; *227 EP-11; ★ PHIL-; mail Glen Mills z 19342; ● 125
Lockview; RMC Place; WASHINGTON; ▲ Fallowfield; *225 WO-4; ★ PGH; mail Charleroi z 15022; ● 150
Locust; MCD-Township; COLUMBIA; *227 EK-7; mail Catawissa z 17820; Ⓟ 1,308; Ⓒ 1,410
Locust; RMC Place; INDIANA; ▲ Canoe; *225 WK-8; mail Rochester Mills z 15771
Locustdale; CDP; COLUMBIA, SCHUYLKILL; ▲ Conyngham, Butler; 227 EK-7; 🅿; ★ PTSVL; z 17945; Ⓒ 70
Locust Gap; RMC Place; NORTHUMBERLAND; ▲ Mount Carmel; 227 EK-6; 🅿; z 17840; ● 450
Locust Grove; RMC Place; CENTRE; ▲ Gregg; *227 EK-1; mail Spring Mills z 16875; rural
Locust Grove; RMC Place; YORK; ▲ Windsor; *227 EP-5; ★ YORK; mail York z 17402; ● 150
Locust Grove Gardens; RMC Place; YORK; ▲ Windsor; *227 EP-5; elev. 690ft./210m.; ★ YORK; mail York z 17402; ● 200
Locust Hill; RMC Place; FAYETTE; ▲ Springhill; *225 WQ-4; ★ MORG; mail Point Marion z 15474; rural
Locust Lakes Village; RMC Place; MONROE; ▲ Tobyhanna; *226 EI-10; elev. 1,700ft./518m.; mail Pocono Lake z 18347; summer pop. 1,800; ● 600
Locust Point; RMC Place; CUMBERLAND; ▲ Silver Spring, Monroe; *227 EO-3; ★ HRBG; mail Mechanicsburg z 17055; rural
Locust Run; RMC Place; JUNIATA; ▲ Walker; 227 EM-3; mail Thompsontown z 17094; ● 100
Locust Summit; RMC Place; NORTHUMBERLAND; ▲ Mount Carmel; *227 EK-6; mail Locust Gap z 17840, Locustdale z 17945, Mount Carmel z 17851, Pottsville z 17901; rural
Locust Valley; RMC Place; LEHIGH; ▲ Upper Saucon; *227 EM-11; ★ ALL-; mail Coopersburg z 18036; ● 140
Locust Valley; RMC Place; SCHUYLKILL; ▲ Ryan; *227 EK-8; ★ PTSVL; mail Barnesville z 18214; ● 250
Lofty; RMC Place; SCHUYLKILL; ▲ Kline, Delano; *227 EK-8; ★ HAZ; mail Hazleton z 18201, McAdoo z 18237; ● 45
Logan; MCD-Township; BLAIR; *225 WM-10; ★ ALT; mail Altoona z 16601; Ⓟ 12,381; Ⓒ 11,925
Logan; MCD-Township; CLINTON; *226 EJ-2; mail Loganton z 17747; Ⓟ 730; Ⓒ 773
Logan; MCD-Township; HUNTINGDON; *225 WM-13; mail Petersburg z 16669; Ⓟ 684; Ⓒ 703
Logan; RMC Place; INDIANA; ▲ Banks; *225 WK-9; elev. 1,696ft./517m.; mail Glen Campbell z 15742; rural
Logan; RMC Place; PHILADELPHIA; *227 EP-12; ★ PHIL-; mail Philadelphia z 19141; pop. incl. with Philadelphia (Inc. Place)
Logania; PERRY; see Loshs Run (RMC Place)
Logan Mills; RMC Place; CLINTON; ▲ Logan; *226 EJ-2; mail Loganton z 17747; rural
Logans Ferry; RMC Place; ALLEGHENY; *225 WM-5; ★ PGH; mail Pittsburgh z 15239; pop. incl. with Plum (Inc. Place)
Logans Ferry Heights; RMC Place; ALLEGHENY; *225 WM-5; ★ PGH; mail Pittsburgh z 15239; pop. incl. with Plum (Inc. Place)
Loganton; Inc. Place; CLINTON; 226 EJ-2; elev. 1,297ft./395m.; 🅿; z 17747; Ⓟ 443; Ⓒ 435
Loganville; Inc. Place; YORK; 227 EQ-5; elev. 783ft./239m.; 🅿; ★ YORK; z 17342; Ⓟ 954; Ⓒ 908
Log Pile; RMC Place; WASHINGTON; ▲ Canton; *225 WO-2; ★ WASH; mail Washington z 15301; ● 300
London; RMC Place; MERCER; ▲ Springfield; *224 WI-3; elev. 1,279ft./390m.; mail Grove City z 16127
London Britain; MCD-Township; CHESTER; *227 EQ-9; ★ PHIL-; mail Landenberg z 19350; Ⓟ 2,671; Ⓒ 2,797
Londonderry; MCD-Township; BEDFORD; *225 WQ-9; mail Hyndman z 15545; Ⓟ 1,893; Ⓒ 1,760
Londonderry; MCD-Township; CHESTER; *227 EQ-9; mail Cochranville z 19330; Ⓟ 1,243; Ⓒ 1,632
Londonderry; MCD-Township; DAUPHIN; *227 EO-5; ★ HRBG; mail Middletown z 17057; Ⓟ 4,926; Ⓒ 5,224
London Grove; RMC Place; CHESTER; ▲ West Marlborough; 227 EQ-9; elev. 467ft./142m.; mail Kennett Square z 19348; ● 250
London Grove; MCD-Township; CHESTER; *227 EQ-9; ★ PHIL-; mail West Grove z 19390; Ⓟ 3,922; Ⓒ 5,265
Lone Pine; RMC Place; WASHINGTON; ▲ West Bethlehem, Amwell; 225 WO-3; ★ WASH; mail Washington z 15301; ● 50
Long Acre Park; RMC Place; DELAWARE; ★ PHIL-; mail Lansdowne z 19050; pop. incl. with Yeadon (Inc. Place)
Long Branch; Inc. Place; WASHINGTON; *225 WO-4; elev. 1,095ft./334m.; ★ PGH; mail Charleroi z 15022, Coal Center z 15423; Ⓟ 482; Ⓒ 539
Long Bridge; RMC Place; WESTMORELAND; ▲ Ligonier; *225 WN-7; mail Ligonier z 15658; ● 35
Longbrook; RMC Place; SULLIVAN; ▲ Davidson; *226 EH-6; mail Muncy Valley z 17758; rural
Longfellow; RMC Place; MIFFLIN; ▲ Bratton; 225 WM-14; mail Lewistown z 17044; ● 70
Longlevel; RMC Place; YORK; ▲ Lower Windsor; *227 EP-6; ★ YORK; mail Wrightsville z 17368; ● 275
Long Pond; RMC Place; MONROE; ▲ Tunkhannock; 226 EJ-11; 🅿; z 18334; ● 900
Long Run; RMC Place; CARBON; ▲ Franklin; *227 EK-10; mail Lehighton z 18235; ● 200
Longs Crossroad; RMC Place; CAMBRIA; ▲ White; *225 WL-10; elev. 1,567ft./478m.; mail Patton z 16668; rural
Longsdale; RMC Place; BERKS; ▲ Longswamp; *227 EM-10; elev. 600ft./183m.; mail Mertztown z 19539; rural
Longsdorf; RMC Place; CUMBERLAND; ▲ Penn; *227 EO-2; mail Newville z 17241; rural
Longstown; RMC Place; YORK; ▲ Windsor; 225 WS-11; ★ YORK; mail York z 17402; ● 100
Longswamp; RMC Place; BERKS; ▲ Longswamp; 227 EM-10; mail Mertztown z 19539; ● 300
Longswamp; MCD-Township; BERKS; *227 EM-10; mail Mertztown z 19539; Ⓟ 5,387; Ⓒ 5,608
Longview; RMC Place; ALLEGHENY; *225 WN-3; ★ PGH; mail Bethel Park z 15102; pop. incl. with Bethel Park (Inc. Place)
Longwood Gardens; RMC Place; CHESTER; ▲ East Marlborough; *227 EQ-10; ★ PHIL-; mail Kennett Square z 19348; rural
Lookabough Corners; RMC Place; ARMSTRONG; *225 WL-5; ★ PGH; mail Leechburg z 15656; rural
Lookout; WAYNE; see Hilltown (RMC Place)
Loomis Park; RMC Place; LUZERNE; ▲ Hanover; *226 EI-8; ★ SCR-; mail Wilkes Barre z 18706; ● 150
Loop (Loop Station); RMC Place; BLAIR; ▲ Blair; 224 WC-14; ★ ALT; mail Hollidaysburg z 16648; ● 60
Loop Station; BLAIR; see Loop (RMC Place)
Lopez; RMC Place; SULLIVAN; ▲ Colley; 226 EG-7; 🅿; z 18628; ● 180
Lorain; Inc. Place; CAMBRIA; 225 WN-9; elev. 1,320ft./402m.; ★ JNST; mail Johnstown z 15902; Ⓟ 824; Ⓒ 747
Lorane; CDP; BERKS; ▲ Exeter; 227 EN-9; elev. 192ft./59m.; ★ READ; mail Reading z 19606; Ⓟ 2,580; Ⓒ 2,994
Lorberry; RMC Place; SCHUYLKILL; ▲ Tremont; *227 EL-6; mail Pine Grove z 17963; rural
Lords Valley; RMC Place; PIKE; ▲ Blooming Grove; 226 EH-12; 🅿; z 18428; ● 70
Lorenton; RMC Place; LYCOMING, TIOGA; ▲ Morris, Pine; mail Morris z 16938; rural
Loretto; Inc. Place; CAMBRIA; 225 WM-10; elev. 1,944ft./593m.; 🅿 🅲 2,084; z 15940; Ⓟ 1,072; Ⓒ 1,190
Loretto Road; RMC Place; CAMBRIA; ▲ Allegheny; *225 WM-10; mail Ebensburg z 15931; rural
Loshs Run (Logania); RMC Place; PERRY; ▲ Wheatfield, Miller; *227 EM-4; ★ HRBG; mail Duncannon z 17020; rural
Lost Creek; RMC Place; SCHUYLKILL; ▲ West Mahanoy; 227 EK-7; 🅿; z 17946; ● 500
Lottsville; RMC Place; WARREN; ▲ Freehold; 224 WD-6; elev. 1,417ft./432m.; mail Bear Lake z 16402; ● 100
Loux Corner; RMC Place; BUCKS; ▲ Hilltown; *227 EN-12; elev. 650ft./198m.; ★ PHIL-; mail Hilltown z 18927; rural
Lovedale; RMC Place; ALLEGHENY; ▲ Elizabeth; *225 WN-4; ★ PGH; mail Elizabeth z 15037
Lovejoy; RMC Place; INDIANA; ▲ Green; 225 WL-8; mail Commodore z 15729; ● 50
Lovell; RMC Place; ERIE; ▲ Concord; *224 WE-5; mail Corry z 16407; rural
Lovelton; RMC Place; WYOMING; ▲ North Branch; 226 EG-7; mail Mehoopany z 18629; ● 100
Lovely; RMC Place; BEDFORD; ▲ Lincoln; *225 WO-10; mail Alum Bank z 15521; rural
Lover; RMC Place; WASHINGTON; ▲ Fallowfield; *225 WO-4; ★ PGH; mail Charleroi z 15022
Lovett; CAMBRIA; see Sidman (RMC Place)
Lowber; RMC Place; FAYETTE; ▲ Jefferson; *225 WO-4; ★ PGH; mail Fayette City z 15438; ● 100
Lowber; RMC Place; WESTMORELAND; ▲ Sewickley; *225 WN-5; 🅿; ★ PGH; z 15660; ● 420
Lowe Lake; RMC Place; SUSQUEHANNA; ▲ Herrick; *226 EF-10; elev. 1,867ft./569m.; mail Union Dale z 18470; ● 25
Lower Allen; CDP-Census Area Only; CUMBERLAND; *227 EO-4; elev. 400ft./122m.; ★ HRBG; mail Camp Hill z 17011; Ⓟ 6,329; Ⓒ 6,619
Lower Allen; MCD-Township; CUMBERLAND; *227 EO-4; ★ HRBG; mail Camp Hill z 17011; Ⓟ 15,254; Ⓒ 17,437
Lower Alsace; MCD-Township; BERKS; *227 EN-9; ★ READ; mail Reading z 19606; Ⓟ 4,627; Ⓒ 4,478
Lower Askam; RMC Place; LUZERNE; ▲ Hanover; *226 EI-8; ★ SCR-; mail Wilkes Barre z 18706
Lower Augusta; MCD-Township; NORTHUMBERLAND; *227 EK-5; mail Sunbury z 17801; Ⓟ 1,024; Ⓒ 1,079
Lower Brownville; RMC Place; SCHUYLKILL; ▲ West Mahanoy; *227 EK-7; mail Shenandoah z 17976; ● 80
Lower Burrell; Inc. Place; WESTMORELAND; 225 WL-5; elev. 760ft./232m.; 🅿; ★ PGH; z 15068; Ⓟ 12,251; Ⓒ 12,608
Lower Chanceford; MCD-Township; YORK; *227 EQ-7; mail Airville z 17302; Ⓟ 2,454; Ⓒ 2,899
Lower Chichester; MCD-Township; DELAWARE; *227 EQ-11; ★ PHIL-; mail Marcus Hook z 19061; Ⓟ 3,660; Ⓒ 3,591
Lower Frankford; MCD-Township; CUMBERLAND; *227 EO-3; ★ CARL; mail Carlisle z 17013; Ⓟ 1,491; Ⓒ 1,823
Lower Frederick; MCD-Township; MONTGOMERY; *227 EN-11; ★ PHIL-; mail Zieglerville z 19492; Ⓟ 3,396; Ⓒ 4,795
Lower Gwynedd; MCD-Township; MONTGOMERY; *227 EO-12; 🅿 🅲 2,727; ★ PHIL-; z 19002 & mail Gwynedd Valley z 19437; Ⓟ 9,958; Ⓒ 10,422
Lower Heidelberg; MCD-Township; BERKS; *227 EN-8; ★ READ; mail Reading z 19604; Ⓟ 2,209; Ⓒ 4,150
Lower Longswamp; RMC Place; BERKS; ▲ Longswamp; *227 EM-10; mail Mertztown z 19539; ● 100
Lower Macungie; MCD-Township; LEHIGH; *227 EM-10; ★ ALL-; mail Macungie z 18062; Ⓟ 16,871; Ⓒ 19,220; ◆ 22,588
Lower Mahanoy; MCD-Township; NORTHUMBERLAND; *227 EL-4; mail Dalmatia z 17017; Ⓟ 1,669; Ⓒ 1,586
Lower Makefield; MCD-Township; BUCKS; *227 EN-14; ★ PHIL-; mail Morrisville z 19067; Ⓟ 25,083; Ⓒ 32,681; ◆ 32,759
Lower Merion; MCD-Township; MONTGOMERY; *227 EP-12; 🅲 3,762 ■; ★ PHIL-; mail Ardmore z 19003; Ⓟ 58,003; Ⓒ 59,850; Ⓡ 58,740; ◆ 61,080
Lower Mifflin; MCD-Township; CUMBERLAND; *227 EO-2; mail Newville z 17241; Ⓟ 1,700; Ⓒ 1,620
Lower Milford; MCD-Township; LEHIGH; *227 EM-11; ★ ALL-; mail Coopersburg z 18036; Ⓟ 3,269; Ⓒ 3,617
Lower Mill; NORTHAMPTON; see Walters (RMC Place)
Lower Moreland; MCD-Township; MONTGOMERY; *227 EO-13; ★ PHIL-; mail Huntingdon Valley z 19006; Ⓟ 11,768; Ⓒ 11,281
Lower Mount Bethel; MCD-Township; NORTHAMPTON; *227 EK-12; ★ ALL-; mail Martins Creek z 18063; Ⓟ 3,187; Ⓒ 3,228
Lower Nazareth; MCD-Township; NORTHAMPTON; *227 EL-11; ★ ALL-; mail Bethlehem z 18017; Ⓟ 4,483; Ⓒ 5,259
Lower Orchard; RMC Place; BUCKS; ▲ Middletown; ★ PHIL-; mail Levittown z 19058
Lower Oxford; MCD-Township; CHESTER; *227 EQ-8; mail Oxford z 19363; Ⓟ 3,264; Ⓒ 4,319
Lower Paxton; RMC Place; DAUPHIN; ▲ Lower Paxton; *227 EN-5; 🅿; ★ HRBG; z 17109, z 17112
Lower Paxton; MCD-Township; DAUPHIN; *227 EN-5; 🅿; ★ HRBG; z 17109, z 17112; Ⓟ 39,162; Ⓒ 44,424; ◆ 46,630
Lower Peanut; RMC Place; FAYETTE; ▲ Menallen; *225 WP-5; ★ UNTN; mail Smock z 15480; ● 15
Lower Pottsgrove; MCD-Township; MONTGOMERY; *227 EN-10; ★ PTSTN; mail Pottstown z 19464; Ⓟ 8,808; Ⓒ 11,213
Lower Providence; MCD-Township; MONTGOMERY; *227 EO-11; ★ PHIL-; mail Norristown z 19401; Ⓟ 19,351; Ⓒ 22,390; ◆ 24,895
Lower Sagon; RMC Place; NORTHUMBERLAND; ▲ Coal; mail Snydertown z 17877
Lower Salford; MCD-Township; MONTGOMERY; *227 EN-11; ★ PHIL-; mail Harleysville z 19438; Ⓟ 10,735; Ⓒ 12,893
Lower Saucon; MCD-Township; NORTHAMPTON; *227 EL-11; ★ ALL-; mail Bethlehem z 18015; Ⓟ 8,448; Ⓒ 9,884
Lower Southampton; MCD-Township; BUCKS; *227 EO-13; ★ PHIL-; mail Langhorne z 19047; Ⓟ 19,860; Ⓒ 19,276
Lower Swatara; MCD-Township; DAUPHIN; *227 EO-5; ★ HRBG; mail Middletown z 17057; Ⓟ 7,072; Ⓒ 8,149
Lower Towamensing; MCD-Township; CARBON; *227 EK-10; mail Palmerton z 18071; Ⓟ 2,948; Ⓒ 3,173
Lower Turkeyfoot; MCD-Township; SOMERSET; *225 WQ-6; mail Confluence z 15424; Ⓟ 670; Ⓒ 672
Lower Tyrone; MCD-Township; FAYETTE; *225 WO-5; mail Dawson z 15428; Ⓟ 1,138; Ⓒ 1,171
Lower Wheel; RMC Place; WESTMORELAND; ▲ Sewickley; *225 WO-5; ★ PGH; mail Herminie z 15637; ● 100
Lower Windsor; MCD-Township; YORK; *227 EP-6; ★ YORK; mail Wrightsville z 17368; Ⓟ 7,051; Ⓒ 7,405
Lower Yoder; MCD-Township; CAMBRIA; *225 WN-8; ★ JNST; mail Johnstown z 15905; Ⓟ 3,342; Ⓒ 3,029
Lowhill; MCD-Township; LEHIGH; *227 EL-10; ★ ALL-; mail Orefield z 18069; Ⓟ 1,602; Ⓒ 1,869
Low Hill; RMC Place; WASHINGTON; *225 WP-4; mail Brownsville z 15417; pop. incl. with Centerville (Inc. Place)
Lowville; RMC Place; ERIE; ▲ Venango; 224 WD-5; mail Wattsburg z 16442; ● 130
Loyalhanna; RMC Place; WESTMORELAND; ▲ Derry; *225 WN-6; 🅿; ★ LTROB; z 15661; ● 1,400
Loyalhanna; MCD-Township; WESTMORELAND; *225 WM-6; 🅿; ★ PGH; z 15661 & mail Saltsburg z 15681; Ⓟ 2,171; Ⓒ 2,301
Loyalhanna Woodlands Number 1; RMC Place; WESTMORELAND; ▲ Loyalhanna; *225 WM-6; ★ PGH; mail Saltsburg z 15681; summer pop. 225; ● 40
Loyalsock; MCD-Township; LYCOMING; *226 EI-4; ★ WMSPT; mail Williamsport z 17701; Ⓟ 10,644; Ⓒ 10,876
Loyalsockville; RMC Place; LYCOMING; ▲ Upper Fairfield; 226 EH-4; ★ WMSPT; mail Montoursville z 17754; ● 400
Loyalton; RMC Place; DAUPHIN; ▲ Washington; 227 EM-5; mail Lykens z 17048; ● 450
Loyalville; RMC Place; LUZERNE; ▲ Lake; *226 EH-8; elev. 1,329ft./405m.; ★ SCR-; mail Dallas z 18612, Harveys Lake z 18618; ● 300
Loysburg; RMC Place; BEDFORD; ▲ South Woodbury; 225 WO-11; 🅿; z 16659; ● 330
Loysville; RMC Place; PERRY; ▲ Tyrone; 227 EN-2; 🅿; z 17047; ● 200
Lucas; RMC Place; ALLEGHENY; ★ PGH; pop. incl. with Pittsburgh (Inc. Place)
Lucerne Mines; CDP; INDIANA; ▲ Center; 225 WM-7; 🅿; z 15754; Ⓟ 1,074; Ⓒ 951
Lucinda; RMC Place; CLARION; ▲ Knox; 224 WH-6; 🅿; z 16235; ● 300
Luciusboro; RMC Place; INDIANA; ▲ Center; 225 WM-8; mail Homer City z 15748; ● 100
Lucknow; RMC Place; DAUPHIN; ▲ Susquehanna; *227 EN-4; ★ HRBG; mail Harrisburg z 17110; ● 1,000
Lucky; RMC Place; YORK; ▲ Chanceford; *227 EQ-6; elev. 524ft./160m.; ★ YORK; mail Felton z 17322; rural
Lucon; RMC Place; MONTGOMERY; ▲ Skippack; *227 EO-11; elev. 251ft./77m.; ★ PHIL-; mail Schwenksville z 19473; ● 75
Lucy Crossing; RMC Place; NORTHAMPTON; ★ ALL-; mail Easton z 18042; pop. incl. with Glendon (Inc. Place)
Lucy Furnace; RMC Place; MIFFLIN; ▲ Wayne; *225 WN-13; mail Mount Union z 17066; ● 80
Ludlow; RMC Place; MCKEAN; ▲ Hamilton; 224 WF-8; 🅿; z 16333; ● 500
Ludwigs Corner; RMC Place; CHESTER; ▲ West Vincent; *227 EO-10; elev. 633ft./193m.; ★ PHIL-; mail Glenmoore z 19343; rural
Luke; NORTHUMBERLAND; see Luke Fidler (RMC Place)
Luke Fidler (Luke); RMC Place; NORTHUMBERLAND; ▲ Coal; *227 EK-6; mail Shamokin z 17872; ● 25
Lumber; MCD-Township; CAMERON; *224 WG-12; mail Emporium z 15834; Ⓟ 195; Ⓒ 241
Lumber City; Inc. Place; CLEARFIELD; 224 WJ-10; elev. 1,183ft./361m.; mail Curwensville z 16833; Ⓟ 83; Ⓒ 86
Lumber City; RMC Place; MIFFLIN; ▲ Brown; *227 EL-1; elev. 600ft./183m.; mail Reedsville z 17084; ● 500
Lumberville; RMC Place; BUCKS; ▲ Solebury; 227 EM-13; 🅿; ★ PHIL-; z 18933; ● 200
Lundys Lane (Wellsburg); RMC Place; ERIE; 224 WE-2; 🅿; z 16401; ● 180
Lungerville; RMC Place; LYCOMING; ▲ Jordan; *226 EH-6; elev. 1,387ft./423m.; mail Unityville z 17774; ● 50
Lurgan; RMC Place; FRANKLIN; ▲ Lurgan; 225 WO-14; 🅿; z 17232; ● 90
Lurgan; MCD-Township; FRANKLIN; *227 EP-1; 🅿; z 17232; Ⓟ 2,026; Ⓒ 2,014
Luthersburg; RMC Place; CLEARFIELD; ▲ Brady; 224 WJ-9; 🅿; z 15848; ● 325
Luthers Mills; RMC Place; BRADFORD; ▲ Burlington; *226 EE-6; mail Towanda z 18848
Lutzville; RMC Place; BEDFORD; ▲ Snake Spring; *225 WP-11; mail Everett z 15537; ● 100
Luxor; RMC Place; WESTMORELAND; ▲ Hempfield; 225 WN-6; 🅿; ★ PGH; z 15662; ● 750
Luzerne; RMC Place; FAYETTE; ▲ Luzerne; *225 WP-4; ★ UNTN; mail East Millsboro z 15433; rural
Luzerne; MCD-Township; FAYETTE; *225 WP-4; ★ UNTN; mail Brownsville z 15417; Ⓟ 4,904; Ⓒ 4,683
Luzerne; Inc. Place; LUZERNE; 226 EH-9; elev. 575ft./175m.; 🅿; ★ SCR-; z 18709; Ⓟ 3,206; Ⓒ 2,952
LUZERNE; 226 EI-7; Ⓟ 328,149; Ⓒ 319,250; ◆ 310,426
Lycippus; RMC Place; WESTMORELAND; ▲ Unity, Mount Pleasant; 225 WO-6; ★ LTROB; mail Latrobe z 15650; ● 90
Lycoming; MCD-Township; LYCOMING; *226 EH-3; ★ WMSPT; mail Cogan Station z 17728; Ⓟ 1,748; Ⓒ 1,606
LYCOMING; 226 EH-3; Ⓟ 118,710; Ⓒ 120,044; ◆ 115,055
Lykens; Inc. Place; DAUPHIN; 227 EM-5; elev. 660ft./201m.; 🅿; z 17048; Ⓟ 1,986; Ⓒ 1,937
Lykens; MCD-Township; DAUPHIN; *227 EL-5; 🅿; z 17048; not adjacent to the Borough of Lykens; Ⓟ 1,238; Ⓒ 1,095
Lyleville; RMC Place; CLEARFIELD; ▲ Beccaria; 225 WL-10; mail Coalport z 16627; ● 135
Lynch; RMC Place; FOREST; ▲ Howe; *224 WF-8; elev. 1,269ft./387m.; mail Sheffield z 16347; rural
Lynchville; RMC Place; ELK; *224 WG-10; mail Saint Marys z 15857; pop. incl. with Saint Marys (Inc. Place)
Lyndell; RMC Place; CHESTER; ▲ Upper Uwchlan, East Brandywine; 227 EP-9; 🅿; ★ PHIL-; z 19354; ● 400
Lyndon; RMC Place; LANCASTER; ▲ West Lampeter; 227 EP-7; ★ LANC; mail Lancaster z 17602; ● 750
Lyndora; RMC Place; BUTLER; ▲ Butler; 225 WK-4; 🅿; ★ BUTL; z 16045; ● 1,300
Lynn; MCD-Township; LEHIGH; *227 EL-9; ★ ALL-; mail Kempton z 19529; Ⓟ 3,220; Ⓒ 3,849
Lynn; RMC Place; SUSQUEHANNA; ▲ Springville; 226 EF-8; elev. 1,213ft./370m.; mail Springville z 18844; ● 130
Lynnewood; RMC Place; MONTGOMERY; ▲ Cheltenham; *227 EO-12; elev. 330ft./101m.; ★ PHIL-; mail Philadelphia z 19150
Lynnewood Gardens; RMC Place; MONTGOMERY; ▲ Cheltenham; ★ PHIL-; mail Cheltenham z 19012, Philadelphia z 19150
Lynnport; RMC Place; LEHIGH; ▲ Lynn; 227 EL-9; ★ ALL-; mail New Tripoli z 18066; ● 200

Entries in **UPPERCASE** are counties.
Entries in **bold** have populations of 2,500 or more.
Names in parentheses are alternate names.

Inc. Place	Incorporated Place
RMC Place	Rand McNally Designated Place
CDP	Census Designated Place
MCD	Minor Civil Division

⊡ County Seat
▲ Minor Civil Division
elev. Elevation
🅿 Post Office
🅷 Hospital
🅲 College
■ Principal Business Center
★ Ranally Metro Area (RMA) Abbreviation
z Zip Code(s)
Ⓟ Previous Census Population
Ⓡ Revised Census Population
Ⓐ Annexation Population
● Rand McNally Population Estimate
Ⓒ Final Census Population
Ⓢ Special Census Population
◆ Estimated Population

For additional definitions see Glossary, Volume 1, and Introduction, Volume 2.

Lynnville; RMC Place; LEHIGH; ▲ Lynn; 227 EL-9; elev. 650ft./198m.; ★ ALL-; mail New Tripoli z 18066; ● 55
Lynnwood; RMC Place; FAYETTE, WESTMORELAND; ▲ Rostraver, Washington; 225 WO-4; ★ PGH; mail Belle Vernon z 15012; ● 1,200
Lynnwood; RMC Place; LUZERNE; ▲ Hanover; 226 EA-7; ★ SCR-; mail Wilkes Barre z 18706; ● 1,300
Lynnwood-Pricedale; CDP-Census Area Only; WESTMORELAND, FAYETTE; ▲ Washington, Rostraver; *225 WO-4; ★ PGH; mail Belle Vernon z 15012, Pricedale z 15072; Ⓟ 2,664; Ⓒ 2,168
Lyons (Lyon Station); Inc. Place; BERKS; 227 EM-9; elev. 465ft./142m.; mail Lyon Station z 19536; Ⓟ 499; Ⓒ 504
Lyon Station; BERKS; see Lyons (Inc. Place)
Lyon Valley; RMC Place; LEHIGH; ▲ Lowhill; *227 EL-10; elev. 474ft./144m.; ★ ALL-; mail New Tripoli z 18066; rural

M

Mable; RMC Place; SCHUYLKILL; ▲ Barry; *227 EL-6; mail Ashland z 17921
Mable Hill; RMC Place; GREENE; ▲ Monongahela; *225 WQ-4; mail Dilliner z 15327; ● 50
Macada; RMC Place; NORTHAMPTON; *227 EL-11; ★ ALL-; pop. incl. with Bethlehem (Inc. Place)
MacArthur; RMC Place; BEAVER; 🅿; ★ PGH; z 15001; pop. incl. with Aliquippa (Inc. Place)
Macdonaldton; RMC Place; SOMERSET; ▲ Brothersvalley; 225 WP-8; mail Berlin z 15530; ● 130
Macedonia; RMC Place; BRADFORD; ▲ Asylum; *226 EF-6; mail Towanda z 18848; rural
Macedonia; RMC Place; JUNIATA; ▲ Fermanagh; *227 EL-2; mail Mifflintown z 17059; rural
Mackeyville; RMC Place; CLINTON; ▲ Lamar; 226 EJ-2; elev. 672ft./205m.; 🅿; z 17750; ● 250
Macungie; Inc. Place; LEHIGH; 227 EM-10; elev. 380ft./116m.; 🅿; ★ ALL-; z 18062; Ⓟ 2,597; Ⓒ 3,039
Maddensville; RMC Place; HUNTINGDON; ▲ Springfield; *225 WO-13; mail Hustontown z 17229, Orbisonia z 17243
Madera; RMC Place; CLEARFIELD; ▲ Bigler; 225 WK-11; 🅿; z 16661; ● 1,000
Madge; ELK; see Lamont (RMC Place)
Madison; MCD-Township; ARMSTRONG; *224 WJ-6; mail Templeton z 16259; Ⓟ 941; Ⓒ 943
Madison; MCD-Township; CLARION; *224 WJ-6; mail Rimersburg z 16248; Ⓟ 1,423; Ⓒ 1,442
Madison; MCD-Township; COLUMBIA; *226 EI-6; mail Millville z 17846; Ⓟ 1,565; Ⓒ 1,590
Madison; MCD-Township; LACKAWANNA; *226 EH-11; ★ SCR-; mail Moscow z 18444; Ⓟ 2,207; Ⓒ 2,542
Madison; Inc. Place; WESTMORELAND; 225 WN-5; elev. 1,132ft./345m.; 🅿; ★ PGH; z 15663; Ⓟ 539; Ⓒ 510
Madisonburg; CDP; CENTRE; ▲ Miles; 227 EK-1; 🅿; z 16852; Ⓒ 135
Madisonville; RMC Place; LACKAWANNA; ▲ Madison; 226 EH-11; ★ SCR-; mail Moscow z 18444; ● 150
Madley; RMC Place; BEDFORD; ▲ Londonderry; *225 WQ-9; mail Buffalo Mills z 15534
Magee; RMC Place; WARREN; ▲ Deerfield; *224 WF-7; mail Tidioute z 16351
Magill Heights; RMC Place; ALLEGHENY; ▲ West Deer; *225 WL-4; elev. 1,156ft./352m.; ★ PGH; mail Cheswick z 15024; ● 600
Magnolia Gardens; RMC Place; BUCKS; ▲ Bristol; *227 EO-14; elev. 20ft./6m.; ★ PHIL-; mail Bristol z 19007; rural
Magnolia Hill; RMC Place; BUCKS; ▲ Bristol; *227 EO-14; ★ PHIL-; mail Bristol z 19007
Mahaffey; Inc. Place; CLEARFIELD; 225 WK-9; elev. 1,323ft./403m.; 🅿; z 15757; Ⓟ 341; Ⓒ 402
Mahanoy; MCD-Township; SCHUYLKILL; *227 EK-8; mail Shenandoah z 17976; does not include the Borough of Mahanoy City; Ⓟ 1,273; Ⓒ 1,112; Ⓡ 3,093
Mahanoy City; Inc. Place; SCHUYLKILL; 227 EK-8; elev. 1,256ft./383m.; 🅿; z 17948; Ⓟ 5,209; Ⓒ 4,647
Mahanoy Plane; RMC Place; SCHUYLKILL; *227 EK-7; elev. 1,160ft./354m.; 🅿; z 17949; pop. incl. with Gilberton (Inc. Place)
Mahantango; DAUPHIN; see Paxton (RMC Place)
Mahoning; RMC Place; ARMSTRONG; ▲ Madison; *224 WJ-6; mail Templeton z 16259; ● 35
Mahoning; MCD-Township; ARMSTRONG; *224 WJ-7; mail New Bethlehem z 16242; Ⓟ 1,504; Ⓒ 1,502
Mahoning; MCD-Township; CARBON; *227 EK-9; mail Lehighton z 18235; Ⓟ 4,198; Ⓒ 3,978
Mahoning; MCD-Township; LAWRENCE; *224 WJ-1; ★ YNGS-; mail Hillsville z 16132; Ⓟ 3,560; Ⓒ 3,447
Mahoning; MCD-Township; MONTOUR; *226 EJ-6; mail Danville z 17821; Ⓟ 4,134; Ⓒ 4,263
Mahoning Manor; RMC Place; NORTHUMBERLAND; ▲ Turbot; *226 EJ-4; mail Milton z 17847; ● 550
Mahoningtown; RMC Place; LAWRENCE; *224 WJ-2; elev. 797ft./243m.; ★ NWCS; mail New Castle z 16102; pop. incl. with New Castle (Inc. Place)
Maiden Creek; RMC Place; BERKS; ▲ Maidencreek; 227 EM-9; ★ READ; mail Blandon z 19510; ● 200
Maidencreek; MCD-Township; BERKS; *227 EM-9; ★ READ; mail Reading z 19605; Ⓟ 3,397; Ⓒ 6,553
Main; MCD-Township; COLUMBIA; *226 EJ-7; mail Bloomsburg z 17815; Ⓟ 1,241; Ⓒ 1,289
Mainesburg; RMC Place; TIOGA; ▲ Sullivan; 226 EE-4; elev. 1,398ft./426m.; 🅿; z 16932; ● 200
Mainland; RMC Place; MONTGOMERY; ▲ Lower Salford; 227 EN-11; 🅿; ★ PHIL-; z 19451; ● 2,000
Mainsville; RMC Place; FRANKLIN; ▲ Upper Nazareth; 227 EP-1; mail Shippensburg z 17257; ● 300
Mainville; CDP; COLUMBIA; ▲ Main; 226 EJ-7; elev. 543ft./166m.; mail Bloomsburg z 17815; Ⓒ 83
Maitland; RMC Place; MIFFLIN; ▲ Derry; 227 EL-2; mail Lewistown z 17044; ● 200
Maizeville; RMC Place; SCHUYLKILL; *227 EK-7; mail Gilberton z 17934; pop. incl. with Gilberton (Inc. Place)
Majeriks Corners; RMC Place; ERIE; ▲ Greene; ★ ERIE; mail Waterford z 16441; rural
Malden Place; RMC Place; WASHINGTON; *225 WP-4; mail Brownsville z 15417; pop. incl. with Centerville (Inc. Place)
Malta; RMC Place; NORTHUMBERLAND; ▲ Lower Mahanoy; *227 EL-4; mail Dalmatia z 17017
Malvern; Inc. Place; CHESTER; 227 EP-11; elev. 550ft./168m.; 🅿 🅷 🅲 1,319; ★ PHIL-; z 19355; Ⓟ 2,944; Ⓒ 3,059
Mammoth; RMC Place; WESTMORELAND; ▲ Mount Pleasant; 225 WO-6; 🅿; z 15664; ● 450
Mamont; RMC Place; WESTMORELAND; ▲ Washington; *225 WM-5; elev. 1,190ft./363m.; ★ PGH; mail Export z 15632
Manada Gap; RMC Place; DAUPHIN; ▲ East Hanover; *227 EN-5; ★ HRBG; mail Harrisburg z 17112; rural
Manatawny (Pleasantville); RMC Place; BERKS; ▲ Oley; 227 EN-9; ★ READ; mail Oley z 19547; ● 200
Manayunk; RMC Place; PHILADELPHIA; *227 EP-12; 🅿; ★ PHIL-; z 19127; pop. incl. with Philadelphia (Inc. Place)
Manchester; RMC Place; ALLEGHENY; *225 WM-3; ★ PGH; mail Pittsburgh z 15233; pop. incl. with Pittsburgh (Inc. Place)
Manchester; MCD-Township; WAYNE; *226 EE-12; mail Equinunk z 18417; Ⓟ 663; Ⓒ 888
Manchester; Inc. Place; YORK; 227 EP-5; elev. 500ft./152m.; 🅿; ★ YORK; z 17345; Ⓟ 1,830; Ⓒ 2,350
Manchester; MCD-Township; YORK; *227 EP-5; 🅿; ★ YORK; z 17345 & mail York z 17402; not adjacent to the Borough of Manchester; Ⓟ 7,517; Ⓒ 12,700
Mandata; RMC Place; NORTHUMBERLAND; ▲ Lower Mahanoy, Jordan; 227 EL-5; mail Herndon z 17830; ● 60
Manhattan; RMC Place; TIOGA; ▲ Gaines; *226 EF-1; mail Gaines z 16921; rural
Manheim; Inc. Place; LANCASTER; 227 EO-7; elev. 400ft./122m.; 🅿; ★ LANC; z 17545; Ⓟ 5,011; Ⓒ 4,784
Manheim; MCD-Township; LANCASTER; *227 EO-7; 🅿; ★ LANC; z 17545 & mail Lancaster z 17601; not adjacent to the Borough of Manheim; Ⓟ 28,880; Ⓒ 33,697; ◆ 36,808
Manheim; MCD-Township; YORK; *227 ER-4; ★ HANV; mail Glenville z 17329; Ⓟ 2,692; Ⓒ 3,119
Manifold; RMC Place; WASHINGTON; ▲ South Strabane; *225 WO-2; elev. 1,040ft./317m.; ★ WASH; mail Washington z 15301; rural
Manito; RMC Place; WESTMORELAND; ▲ Unity; *225 WN-6; ★ LTROB; mail Latrobe z 15650; ● 70
Mann; MCD-Township; BEDFORD; *225 WQ-11; mail Artemas z 17211; Ⓟ 481; Ⓒ 481
Mannitto; RMC Place; WESTMORELAND; ▲ Loyalhanna, Derry; *225 WM-6; ★ LTROB; mail New Alexandria z 15670; ● 75
Manns Choice; Inc. Place; BEDFORD; 225 WP-10; elev. 1,136ft./346m.; 🅿; z 15550; Ⓟ 249; Ⓒ 291
Mannsville; RMC Place; PERRY; ▲ Centre; 227 EM-3; ★ HRBG; mail Elliottsburg z 17024, Newport z 17074; ● 25
Manoa; RMC Place; DELAWARE; ▲ Haverford; *227 EP-11; 🅿; ★ PHIL-; z 19083
Manor; MCD-Township; ARMSTRONG; *225 WK-6; ★ PGH; mail Ford City z 16226; Ⓟ 4,482; Ⓒ 4,231
Manor; RMC Place; INDIANA; *225 WL-8; mail Penn Run z 15765; ● 25
Manor; MCD-Township; LANCASTER; *227 EP-6; ★ LANC; mail Lancaster z 17603; Ⓟ 14,130; Ⓒ 16,498
Manor; Inc. Place; WESTMORELAND; 225 WN-5; elev. 1,000ft./305m.; 🅿; ★ PGH; z 15665 & mail Glenolden z 19036; Ⓟ 2,627; Ⓒ 2,796; Ⓡ 2,717
Manor Hill; RMC Place; HUNTINGDON; ▲ Barree; *225 WL-13; mail Huntingdon z 16652; rural
Manor Hills; RMC Place; DELAWARE; ★ PHIL-; mail Lansdowne z 19050; pop. incl. with Yeadon (Inc. Place)
Manor Ridge; RMC Place; LANCASTER; ▲ Manor; 227 ET-8; ★ LANC; mail Lancaster z 17603; ● 1,000
Manorville; Inc. Place; ARMSTRONG; 225 WK-6; elev. 800ft./244m.; 🅿; ★ PGH; z 16238; Ⓟ 418; Ⓒ 401
Manown; RMC Place; ALLEGHENY; ▲ Forward; *225 WO-4; ★ PGH; mail Monongahela z 15063; rural
Mansfield; Inc. Place; TIOGA; 226 EE-3; elev. 1,120ft./341m.; 🅿 🅲 3,360; z 16933; Ⓟ 3,538; Ⓒ 3,411
Mansville; RMC Place; WESTMORELAND; *225 WO-7; mail Elliottsburg z 17024, Ligonier z 15658
Mantua; RMC Place; PHILADELPHIA; ★ PHIL-; pop. incl. with Philadelphia (Inc. Place)
Mantz (Mantzville); RMC Place; SCHUYLKILL; ▲ West Penn; 227 EK-9; elev. 671ft./205m.; mail Tamaqua z 18252; ● 300
Mantzville; SCHUYLKILL; see Mantz (RMC Place)
Maple Beach; RMC Place; BUCKS; ▲ Bristol; *227 EO-13; ★ PHIL-; mail Bristol z 19007; ● 100
Mapledale; RMC Place; VENANGO; ▲ Frenchcreek; 224 WH-4; ★ OILC-F; mail Franklin z 16323; ● 200
Maple Glen; CDP; MONTGOMERY; ▲ Horsham, Upper Dublin; *227 EO-12; elev. 376ft./115m.; 🅿; ★ PHIL-; z 19002; Ⓟ 5,881; Ⓒ 7,042
Maple Glen; RMC Place; WASHINGTON; *225 WP-4; mail Brownsville z 15417; pop. incl. with Centerville (Inc. Place)
Maple Grove; RMC Place; BERKS; ▲ Longswamp; *227 EM-10; elev. 518ft./158m.; mail Alburtis z 18011; ● 40
Maple Grove; RMC Place; CHESTER; ▲ East Nottingham; *227 EQ-9; elev. 425ft./130m.; mail Oxford z 19363; rural
Maple Grove; RMC Place; CLARION; ▲ Madison; 224 WJ-6; mail Rimersburg z 16248; ● 135
Maple Grove; RMC Place; FAYETTE; ▲ Saltlick; *225 WP-6; elev. 1,465ft./447m.; mail Champion z 15622; rural
Maple Grove Park; RMC Place; BERKS; ▲ Brecknock; *227 EO-8; ★ READ; mail Mohnton z 19540; ● 45
Maple Hill; RMC Place; LYCOMING; ▲ Brady; *226 EI-4; ★ WMSPT; mail Montgomery z 17752; ● 75
Maple Hill; RMC Place; MONTGOMERY; ▲ Whitpain; *227 EO-12; ★ PHIL-; mail Blue Bell z 19422; ● 550
Maple Hill; RMC Place; SCHUYLKILL; ▲ Mahanoy; *227 EK-7; mail Shenandoah z 17976; rural
Maple Hills; RMC Place; YORK; ▲ Newberry; *227 EO-5; elev. 437ft./133m.; mail Etters z 17319; ● 100
Maple Hollow; RMC Place; BLAIR; ▲ Allegheny; *225 WM-11; elev. 1,157ft./353m.; ★ ALT; mail Duncansville z 16635; rural
Maple Lake; RMC Place; LACKAWANNA; ▲ Spring Brook; *226 EH-10; mail Moscow z 18444
Maple Manor; RMC Place; LUZERNE; ▲ Hazle; *226 EJ-8; ★ HAZ; mail Hazleton z 18201-02; pop. incl. with Hazleton (Inc. Place)
Maple Ridge; RMC Place; SOMERSET; ▲ Conemaugh; *225 WO-8; ★ JNST; mail Hollsopple z 15935; ● 100
Maple Shade; RMC Place; BUCKS; ▲ Bristol; *227 EO-13; ★ PHIL-; mail Croydon z 19021
Maple Shade; RMC Place; VENANGO; ▲ Cranberry; *224 WH-5; ★ OILC-F; mail Cranberry z 16319
Mapleton (Mapleton Depot); Inc. Place; HUNTINGDON; 225 WN-13; elev. 600ft./183m.; mail Mapleton Depot z 17052; Ⓟ 529; Ⓒ 473
Mapleton Depot; HUNTINGDON; see Mapleton (Inc. Place)
Mapletown; RMC Place; GREENE; ▲ Monongahela; 225 WQ-4; mail Greensboro z 15338; ● 150
Maplewood; RMC Place; WAYNE; ▲ Lake; *226 EG-11; ★ SCR-; mail Lake Ariel z 18436
Maplewood Heights; RMC Place; LUZERNE; ▲ Dallas; *226 EH-8; elev. 1,233ft./376m.; ★ SCR-; mail Dallas z 18612; ● 150
Maplewood Park; RMC Place; DELAWARE; ▲ Ridley; *227 EP-11; elev. 120ft./37m.; ★ PHIL-; mail Clifton Heights z 19018; ● 1,700
Maplewood Terrace; RMC Place; WESTMORELAND; ▲ Hempfield; *225 WN-6; ★ PGH; mail Greensburg z 15601; ● 500
Marble; RMC Place; CLARION; ▲ Washington; 224 WH-6; 🅿; z 16334; ● 130
Marble City; RMC Place; BEDFORD; ▲ Hopewell; *225 WO-11; mail Hopewell z 16650; rural
Marble Hall; RMC Place; MONTGOMERY; ▲ Whitemarsh; *227 EO-12; ★ PHIL-; mail Lafayette Hill z 19444
Marcel Lake Estates; RMC Place; PIKE; ▲ Delaware; *226 EH-13; elev. 1,252ft./382m.; mail Dingmans Ferry z 18328; summer pop. 450; ● 130
Marchand; RMC Place; INDIANA; ▲ North Mahoning; 225 WK-8; 🅿; z 15758; ● 90
Marchwood; RMC Place; CHESTER; *227 EP-10; ★ PHIL-; mail Exton z 19341; ● 4,100
Marcus Hook; Inc. Place; DELAWARE; 227 EQ-11; elev. 40ft./12m.; 🅿; ★ PHIL-; z 19060-61; Ⓟ 2,546; Ⓒ 2,314
Marengo; RMC Place; CENTRE; ▲ Ferguson; *225 WL-12; ★ STCOL; mail Warriors Mark z 16877; rural
Margaret; RMC Place; ARMSTRONG; ▲ Cowanshannock; *225 WK-6; mail Kittanning z 16201; ● 50
Margaretta Furnace; RMC Place; YORK; ▲ Lower Windsor; *227 EP-6; ★ YORK; mail York z 17406; ● 100
Margo Gardens; RMC Place; BUCKS; ▲ Bristol; *227 EO-13; ★ PHIL-; mail Bristol z 19007; ● 300
Marguerite; RMC Place; WESTMORELAND; ▲ Unity; *225 WN-6; ★ LTROB; mail Latrobe z 15650; ● 180
Maria; RMC Place; BEDFORD; ▲ Bloomfield; *225 WO-11; mail New Enterprise z 16664
Maria Furnace; ADAMS; see Iron Springs (RMC Place)
Marianna; Inc. Place; WASHINGTON; 225 WP-3; elev. 1,051ft./320m.; 🅿; z 15345; Ⓟ 616; Ⓒ 626
Mariann Estates; RMC Place; CLARION; ▲ Paint; *224 WI-6; mail Shippenville z 16254; ● 600
Mariasville; RMC Place; VENANGO; ▲ Richland; *224 WI-5; mail Emlenton z 16373
Marienville; RMC Place; FOREST; ▲ Jenks; 224 WG-8; elev. 1,735ft./529m.; 🅿; z 16239; ● 1,325
Marietta; Inc. Place; LANCASTER; 227 EP-6; elev. 280ft./85m.; 🅿; ★ LANC; z 17547; Ⓟ 2,778; Ⓒ 2,689
Marion; MCD-Township; BEAVER; *225 WK-3; ★ PGH; mail New Brighton z 15066; Ⓟ 909; Ⓒ 940
Marion; MCD-Township; BERKS; *227 EN-7; mail Womelsdorf z 19567; Ⓟ 1,415; Ⓒ 1,573
Marion; MCD-Township; BUTLER; *224 WI-4; mail Boyers z 16020; Ⓟ 1,113; Ⓒ 1,330
Marion; MCD-Township; CENTRE; *226 EJ-1; mail Howard z 16841; Ⓟ 730; Ⓒ 978
Marion; RMC Place; FRANKLIN; ▲ Guilford; 225 WQ-14; 🅿; z 17235; ● 800
Marion Acres; RMC Place; COLUMBIA; ▲ Conyngham; *227 EK-6; mail Wilburton z 17888; ● 60
Marion Center; Inc. Place; INDIANA; 225 WK-8; elev. 1,280ft./390m.; 🅿; z 15759; Ⓟ 476; Ⓒ 451
Marion Heights (Keiser); Inc. Place; NORTHUMBERLAND; 227 EK-6; elev. 1,360ft./415m.; 🅿; z 17832; Ⓟ 837; Ⓒ 735
Marion Hill; RMC Place; BEAVER; ▲ Pulaski; *225 WK-2; ★ PGH; mail New Brighton z 15066; ● 1,500
Marion Junction; RMC Place; ALLEGHENY; pop. incl. with Pittsburgh (Inc. Place)
Mark Acres; RMC Place; WESTMORELAND; ▲ North Huntingdon; *225 WN-5; ★ PGH; mail Irwin z 15642; ● 300
Markelsville; RMC Place; PERRY; ▲ Juniata; 227 EM-3; mail Newport z 17074; ● 25
Markes; RMC Place; FRANKLIN; ▲ Peters; 225 WQ-13; mail Mercersburg z 17236; ● 100
Market Square; RMC Place; PHILADELPHIA; ★ PHIL-; mail Philadelphia z 19118; pop. incl. with Philadelphia (Inc. Place)
Market Street; RMC Place; CHESTER; ★ PHIL-; mail West Chester z 19380; pop. incl. with West Chester (Inc. Place)
Markle; RMC Place; WESTMORELAND; ▲ Upper Burrell, Allegheny; *225 WL-5; elev. 1,148ft./350m.; ★ PGH; mail Apollo z 15613; ● 500
Marklesburg (James Creek); Inc. Place; HUNTINGDON; 225 WN-12; elev. 900ft./274m.; mail James Creek z 16657; Ⓟ 165; Ⓒ 216
Markleton; RMC Place; SOMERSET; ▲ Upper Turkeyfoot; 225 WQ-7; 🅿; z 15551; ● 40
Markleysburg; Inc. Place; FAYETTE; 225 WQ-6; elev. 1,985ft./605m.; 🅿; z 15459; Ⓟ 320; Ⓒ 282
Markton; RMC Place; JEFFERSON; ▲ Oliver; *224 WJ-8; mail Oliveburg z 15764
Markvue Manor; RMC Place; WESTMORELAND; ▲ North Huntingdon; *225 WN-5; ★ PGH; mail Irwin z 15642; ● 2,700
Marlboro; RMC Place; CHESTER; ▲ East Marlborough; *227 EQ-10; elev. 429ft./131m.; ★ PHIL-; mail Kennett Square z 19348; ● 100
Marlborough; MCD-Township; MONTGOMERY; *227 EN-11; ★ PHIL-; mail Sumneytown z 18084; Ⓟ 3,116; Ⓒ 3,104
Marlin; CDP; SCHUYLKILL; ▲ Norwegian; 227 EL-7; 🅿; ★ PTSVL; z 17951; Ⓒ 640
Marple; MCD-Township; DELAWARE; *227 EP-11; ■; ★ PHIL-; mail Broomall z 19008; Ⓟ 23,123; Ⓒ 23,737; ◆ 23,731
Marron; RMC Place; CLEARFIELD; ▲ Ferguson; *225 WK-10; mail Curwensville z 16833; rural
Mars; Inc. Place; BUTLER; 225 WL-3; elev. 1,031ft./314m.; 🅿; ★ PGH; z 16046 & mail Cranberry TWP z 16066; Ⓟ 1,713; Ⓒ 1,746
Marsh; RMC Place; CHESTER; ▲ East Nantmeal; *227 EO-9; ★ PHIL-; mail Elverson z 19520
Marshall; MCD-Township; ALLEGHENY; *225 WL-3; ★ PGH; mail Warrendale z 15086; Ⓟ 4,010; Ⓒ 5,996
Marshall Heights; RMC Place; INDIANA; ▲ Burrell; *225 WM-7; ★ LTROB; mail Black Lick z 15716; ● 100
Marshalls Creek; RMC Place; MONROE; ▲ Smithfield; 226 EJ-12; 🅿; z 18335; summer pop. 300; ● 60
Marshall Terrace; RMC Place; DELAWARE; ▲ Lower Chichester; ★ PHIL-; mail Marcus Hook z 19061
Marshallton; RMC Place; CHESTER; ▲ West Bradford; 227 EP-10; elev. 396ft./121m.; ★ PHIL-; mail West Chester z 19380; ● 600
Marshallton; CDP; NORTHUMBERLAND; ▲ Coal; 227 EK-6; mail Shamokin z 17872; Ⓟ 1,482; Ⓒ 1,437
Marshbrook; RMC Place; LACKAWANNA, SUSQUEHANNA; ▲ Benton; *226 EF-10; elev. 1,222ft./372m.; ★ SCR-; mail Dalton z 18414, Factoryville z 18419; ● 100
Marshburg; RMC Place; MCKEAN; ▲ Lenox; 224 WE-9; elev. 2,116ft./645m.; mail Lewis Run z 16738; ● 50
Marsh Hill; RMC Place; LYCOMING; ▲ McIntyre; *226 EG-4; mail Trout Run z 17771
Marshlands; RMC Place; TIOGA; ▲ Gaines; 226 EF-1; elev. 1,283ft./391m.; mail Gaines z 16921; ● 50
Marsh Run; RMC Place; YORK; ▲ Fairview; *227 EO-5; ★ HRBG; mail New Cumberland z 17070; ● 50
Marshview; RMC Place; BRADFORD; ▲ Asylum; *226 EF-6; elev. 1,220ft./372m.; mail Towanda z 18848; rural
Marshwood; RMC Place; LACKAWANNA; *226 EG-10; ★ SCR-; mail Jessup z 18434; pop. incl. with Olyphant (Inc. Place)
Marsteller; RMC Place; CAMBRIA; ▲ Barr; *225 WL-9; 🅿; z 15760; ● 150
Marstown; RMC Place; SCHUYLKILL; ▲ Pine Grove; 227 EM-7; elev. 552ft./168m.; mail Pine Grove z 17963; ● 150
Martha Furnace; RMC Place; CENTRE; ▲ Huston; 225 WK-13; mail Port Matilda z 16870; ● 25
Martic; MCD-Township; LANCASTER; *227 EQ-7; ★ LANC; mail Pequea z 17565; Ⓟ 4,362; Ⓒ 4,990
Martic Forge; RMC Place; LANCASTER; ▲ Martic, Conestoga; *227 EQ-7; ★ LANC; mail Pequea z 17565; rural
Marticville; RMC Place; LANCASTER; ▲ Martic; 227 EP-7; elev. 396ft./121m.; ★ LANC; mail Pequea z 17565; ● 400
Martin; RMC Place; FAYETTE; ▲ Nicholson; 225 WQ-4; 🅿; z 15460; ● 110
Martindale; RMC Place; CAMBRIA; ▲ Portage; 225 WN-10; mail Portage z 15946; ● 140
Martindale; RMC Place; LANCASTER; ▲ Earl; 227 EO-8; 🅿; ★ LANC; z 17549; ● 180
Martinsburg; Inc. Place; BLAIR; 225 WN-11; elev. 1,407ft./429m.; 🅿; z 16662; Ⓟ 2,119; Ⓒ 2,236
Martins Corner; RMC Place; CHESTER; ▲ West Caln; *227 EP-9; ★ PHIL-; mail Coatesville z 19320; ● 200
Martins Creek; RMC Place; NORTHAMPTON; ▲ Lower Mount Bethel; 227 EK-12; elev. 275ft./84m.; 🅿; ★ ALL-; z 18063; ● 1,200
Martinsville; RMC Place; YORK; ▲ Lower Windsor; 227 EP-6; ★ YORK; mail Windsor z 17366; ● 100
Martzville; RMC Place; COLUMBIA; ▲ Briar Creek; *226 EJ-7; elev. 651ft./198m.; mail Berwick z 18603; ● 85
Marvel Gardens; RMC Place; DELAWARE; ▲ Ridley; ★ PHIL-; mail Woodlyn z 19094
Marvindale; RMC Place; MCKEAN; ▲ Hamlin; *224 WF-10; elev. 1,622ft./494m.; mail Smethport z 16749; rural
Marwood; RMC Place; BUTLER; ▲ Winfield; 225 WK-5; 🅿; ★ PGH; z 16023; ● 60
Maryd; RMC Place; SCHUYLKILL; ▲ Schuylkill; *227 EK-8; 🅿; ★ PTSVL; z 17952; ● 350
Marysville; RMC Place; BEDFORD; ▲ Liberty; *225 WO-11; mail Saxton z 16678; rural
Marysville; Inc. Place; PERRY; 227 EN-4; elev. 460ft./140m.; 🅿; ★ HRBG; z 17053; Ⓟ 2,425; Ⓒ 2,306
Mascot; RMC Place; LANCASTER; ▲ Upper Leacock, Leacock; *227 EP-8; elev. 392ft./119m.; ★ LANC; mail Ronks z 17572; rural
Mason-Dixon; RMC Place; FRANKLIN; ▲ Antrim; *225 WR-14; ★ HAG; mail Greencastle z 17225; rural
Masontown; Inc. Place; FAYETTE; 225 WQ-4; elev. 1,050ft./320m.; 🅿; ★ UNTN; z 15461; Ⓟ 3,759; Ⓒ 3,611
Masseyburg; RMC Place; HUNTINGDON; ▲ Barree; *225 WL-13; mail Petersburg z 16669; rural
Mastersonville; RMC Place; LANCASTER; ▲ Rapho; 227 EO-6; elev. 523ft./159m.; mail Manheim z 17545; ● 185
Masthope; RMC Place; PIKE; ▲ Lackawaxen; 226 EG-12; mail Lackawaxen z 18435; ● 50
Matamoras; RMC Place; DAUPHIN; ▲ Halifax; *227 EM-4; ★ HRBG; mail Halifax z 17032
Matamoras; Inc. Place; PIKE; 226 EH-14; elev. 460ft./140m.; 🅿; z 18336; Ⓟ 1,934; Ⓒ 2,312
Mather; RMC Place; GREENE; ▲ Morgan; 225 WP-3; 🅿; z 15346; ● 1,000
Mattawana (McVeytown); RMC Place; MIFFLIN; ▲ Bratton; 225 WM-14; 🅿; z 17054 & mail Mc Veytown z 17051; ● 245
Mattey Plan; RMC Place; WESTMORELAND; ▲ Rostraver; *225 WO-4; ★ PGH; mail Belle Vernon z 15012; ● 120
Matthews Run; RMC Place; WARREN; ▲ Sugar Grove, Brokenstraw; *224 WE-7; mail Youngsville z 16371; ● 60
Mattie; RMC Place; BEDFORD; ▲ East Providence; *225 WP-11; mail Everett z 15537; rural
Mauch Chunk; CARBON; see Jim Thorpe (Inc. Place)
Mausdale; RMC Place; MONTOUR; ▲ Valley; 226 EJ-5; mail Danville z 17821; ● 75
Maxatawny; RMC Place; BERKS; ▲ Maxatawny; 227 EM-10; elev. 480ft./146m.; 🅿; z 19538; ● 250
Maxatawny; MCD-Township; BERKS; *227 EM-9; 🅿; z 19538; Ⓟ 5,724; Ⓒ 5,982
Maxwell; RMC Place; FAYETTE; ▲ Luzerne; *225 WP-4; ★ UNTN; mail La Belle z 15450; ● 170
Mayberry; MCD-Township; MONTOUR; *227 EK-6; mail Catawissa z 17820, Danville z 17821; Ⓟ 207; Ⓒ 244
Mayburg; RMC Place; FOREST; ▲ Kingsley; *224 WF-7; mail Sheffield z 16347
Mayfair; RMC Place; PHILADELPHIA; *227 EP-13; ★ PHIL-; mail Philadelphia z 19136; pop. incl. with Philadelphia (Inc. Place)
Mayfield; Inc. Place; LACKAWANNA; 226 EG-10; elev. 960ft./293m.; 🅿; ★ SCR-; z 18433; Ⓟ 1,890; Ⓒ 1,756
Mayfield East; RMC Place; YORK; ▲ West Manchester; ★ YORK; mail York z 17405
Mayport; RMC Place; CLARION; ▲ Redbank; 224 WJ-7; 🅿; z 16240; ● 80
Maysville; RMC Place; ARMSTRONG; ▲ Kiskiminetas; 225 WM-6; ★ PGH; mail Avonmore z 15618; ● 60
Maysville; RMC Place; MERCER; ▲ West Salem; *224 WG-2; mail Greenville z 16125
Maysville; RMC Place; NORTHUMBERLAND; mail Coal Township z 17866; rural
Maytown; CDP; LANCASTER; ▲ East Donegal; 227 EO-6; 🅿; z 17550; Ⓟ 1,720; Ⓒ 2,604
Maytown; RMC Place; YORK; ▲ Warrington; *227 EO-4; mail Lewisberry z 17339
Mayville; RMC Place; LAWRENCE; ▲ Wilmington; *224 WI-2; ★ NWCS; mail New Castle z 16105; ● 30
Maze; RMC Place; JUNIATA; ▲ Delaware; *227 EL-3; mail Thompsontown z 17094
Mazeppa; RMC Place; UNION; ▲ Buffalo; 226 EJ-4; mail Lewisburg z 17837; ● 225
McAdoo; Inc. Place; SCHUYLKILL; 227 EK-8; elev. 1,808ft./551m.; 🅿; ★ HAZ; z 18237; Ⓟ 2,459; Ⓒ 2,274
McAdoo Heights; RMC Place; SCHUYLKILL; ▲ Kline; *227 EK-8; ★ HAZ; mail McAdoo z 18237; ● 1,100
McAlevys Fort; RMC Place; HUNTINGDON; ▲ Jackson; 225 WL-13; mail Huntingdon z 16652; ● 70
McAlisters Crossroads; RMC Place; ALLEGHENY; ▲ Crescent; *225 WM-2; elev. 1,229ft./375m.; ★ PGH; mail Warrendale z 15086; ● 30
McAlisterville; CDP; JUNIATA; ▲ Fayette; 227 EL-3; 🅿; z 17049; Ⓒ 765
McCalmont; MCD-Township; JEFFERSON; *224 WJ-8; mail Anita z 15711; Ⓟ 1,006; Ⓒ 1,068
McCandless; ALLEGHENY; see McCandless Township (CDP-Census Area Only)
McCandless; MCD-Town; ALLEGHENY; *225 WL-4; ★ PGH; mail Pittsburgh z 15237; Ⓟ 28,781; Ⓒ 29,022; ◆ 27,084
McCandless Township (McCandless); CDP-Census Area Only; ALLEGHENY; 225 WL-3; elev. 1,114ft./340m.; ★ PGH; mail Pittsburgh z 15237; Ⓟ 28,781; Ⓒ 29,022; ◆ 27,084
McCartney; RMC Place; CLEARFIELD; ▲ Jordan; 225 WK-10; mail Madera z 16661; ● 70
McCauley; RMC Place; CLEARFIELD; ▲ Woodward; mail Houtzdale z 16651; rural
McChesneytown; RMC Place; WESTMORELAND; ▲ Derry; *225 WN-6; ★ LTROB; mail Latrobe z 15650; ● 800
McChesneytown-Loyalhanna; CDP-Census Area Only; WESTMORELAND; ▲ Derry; *225 WN-6; ★ LTROB; mail Bradenville z 15620, Latrobe z 15650, Loyalhanna z 15661; Ⓟ 3,708; Ⓒ 3,415
McClarran; RMC Place; WESTMORELAND; ▲ Unity; *225 WN-6; ★ LTROB; mail Latrobe z 15650; rural
McCleary; RMC Place; BEAVER; ▲ Greene; *225 WL-2; elev. 1,100ft./335m.; ★ PGH; mail Hookstown z 15050; rural
McClellan; RMC Place; DAUPHIN; ▲ Halifax; *227 EM-4; ★ HRBG; mail Halifax z 17032; rural
McClellandtown; RMC Place; FAYETTE; ▲ German; 225 WQ-4; 🅿; ★ UNTN; z 15458; ● 500
McClellan Heights; RMC Place; YORK; ▲ Spring Garden; ★ YORK; mail York z 17403
McClintock; RMC Place; VENANGO; ▲ Cornplanter; *224 WG-5; ★ OILC-F; mail Oil City z 16301; ● 40
McClure; RMC Place; FAYETTE; ▲ Upper Tyrone; *225 WO-5; mail Mount Pleasant z 15666; rural
McClure; Inc. Place; SNYDER; 227 EL-2; elev. 689ft./210m.; 🅿; z 17841; Ⓟ 1,070; Ⓒ 975
McConnellsburg; Inc. Place; ⊡ FULTON; 225 WP-13; elev. 890ft./271m.; 🅿 🅷; z 17233 & mail Fort Littleton z 17223; Ⓟ 1,106; Ⓒ 1,073
Mcconnells Mills; RMC Place; WASHINGTON; ▲ Chartiers; *225 WN-2; ★ WASH; mail Canonsburg z 15317, Washington z 15301; ● 60
McConnellstown; RMC Place; HUNTINGDON; ▲ Walker; 225 WM-12; 🅿; z 16660; ● 440
McCoysville; RMC Place; JUNIATA; ▲ Tuscarora; *227 EM-1; mail Mifflin z 17058
McCracken (Sugar Grove); RMC Place; GREENE; ▲ Richhill, Aleppo; 225 WQ-1; elev. 992ft./302m.; mail Wind Ridge z 15380; ● 60
McCrea; RMC Place; CUMBERLAND; ▲ Lower Mifflin; *227 EO-2; mail Newville z 17241
Mccullochs Mills; RMC Place; JUNIATA; ▲ Tuscarora; *227 EN-1; mail Honey Grove z 17035; ● 30
McCullough; RMC Place; WESTMORELAND; ▲ Penn; *225 WN-5; ★ PGH; mail Harrison City z 15636; ● 400
McDonald; Inc. Place; WASHINGTON, ALLEGHENY; 225 WN-2; elev. 1,020ft./311m.; 🅿; ★ PGH; z 15057; Ⓟ 2,252; Ⓒ 2,281
McElhattan; RMC Place; CLINTON; ▲ Wayne; 226 EI-2; 🅿; z 17748; ● 500
McEwensville; Inc. Place; NORTHUMBERLAND; 226 EJ-5; elev. 511ft./156m.; 🅿; ★ WMSPT; z 17749; Ⓟ 273; Ⓒ 314
Mcgarey (McGareys); RMC Place; JEFFERSON; ▲ Rose; *224 WJ-8; mail Brookville z 15825; rural
McGareys; JEFFERSON; see Mcgarey (RMC Place)
McGees; CLEARFIELD; see McGees Mills (RMC Place)
McGees Mills (McGees); RMC Place; CLEARFIELD; ▲ Bell; 225 WK-9; elev. 1,298ft./396m.; 🅿; z 15757; ● 100
McGillstown; RMC Place; LEBANON; ▲ East Hanover; *227 EN-6; elev. 472ft./144m.; mail Annville z 17003, Jonestown z 17038; ● 50
McGovern; CDP; WASHINGTON; ▲ Chartiers; 225 WN-2; ★ WASH; mail Houston z 15342; Ⓟ 2,504; Ⓒ 2,538
McGrann; RMC Place; ARMSTRONG; ▲ Manor; 225 WK-6; 🅿; ★ PGH; z 16236; ● 700
McGraw Corners; WARREN; see New London (RMC Place)
McGregor; RMC Place; ARMSTRONG; ▲ Redbank; *224 WJ-7; mail Dayton z 16222; ● 40
McHenry; MCD-Township; LYCOMING; *226 EH-1; mail Cammal z 17723; Ⓟ 246; Ⓒ 145
McIlhaney; RMC Place; MONROE; ▲ Chestnuthill; *226 EJ-11; ★ ALL-; mail Brodheadsville z 18322, Saylorsburg z 18353; rural
McIntyre; RMC Place; INDIANA; ▲ Young; *225 WM-7; 🅿; z 15756; ● 220
McIntyre; MCD-Township; LYCOMING; *226 EG-4; mail Ralston z 17763; Ⓟ 588; Ⓒ 539
McKean; ERIE; see Middleboro (Inc. Place)
McKean; MCD-Township; ERIE; *224 WD-3; 🅿; ★ ERIE; z 16426; does not include the Borough of McKean; Ⓟ 4,503; Ⓒ 4,619
MCKEAN; 224 WE-11; Ⓟ 47,131; Ⓒ 45,936; ◆ 43,237
McKeansburg; CDP; SCHUYLKILL; ▲ East Brunswick; 227 EL-8; mail New Ringgold z 17960; Ⓒ 155
McKee; RMC Place; BLAIR; ▲ Freedom; 225 WN-11; ★ ALT; mail East Freedom z 16637; ● 200
McKee Half Falls; RMC Place; SNYDER; ▲ Chapman; 227 EL-4; mail Port Trevorton z 17864; ● 130
McKeesport; Inc. Place; ALLEGHENY; 225 WN-4; elev. 950ft./290m.; 🅿 🅷 🅲 761 ■; ★ PGH; z 15131-35; Ⓟ 26,016; Ⓒ 24,040; ◆ 22,612
McKees Rocks; Inc. Place; ALLEGHENY; 225 WM-3; elev. 726ft./221m.; 🅿 🅷; ★ PGH; z 15136; Ⓟ 7,691; Ⓒ 6,622
McKimm; RMC Place; BEAVER; ▲ Franklin; *225 WK-2; ★ PGH; mail Ellwood City z 16117; ● 150
McKinley; RMC Place; MONTGOMERY; ▲ Abington; *227 EO-12; ★ PHIL-; mail Elkins Park z 19027
McKinley Hill; RMC Place; FAYETTE; *225 WQ-4; ★ MORG; mail Point Marion z 15474; pop. incl. with Point Marion (Inc. Place)
McKinney; RMC Place; FRANKLIN; ▲ Lurgan; *227 EO-1; mail Newburg z 17240
McKnight; RMC Place; ALLEGHENY; ▲ Ross; *225 WM-4; 🅿; ★ PGH; z 15237
McKnightstown; RMC Place; ADAMS; ▲ Franklin; 227 EQ-2; 🅿; z 17343; ● 350
McKune; WYOMING; see Hoban Heights (RMC Place)
McLane; RMC Place; ERIE; ▲ Washington; 224 WD-3; ★ ERIE; mail Mc Kean z 16426; ● 75
McMichael (McMichaels); RMC Place; MONROE; 226 EJ-11; mail Inlet z 13360; ● 50
McMichaels; MONROE; see McMichael (RMC Place)
McMurray; CDP; WASHINGTON; ▲ Peters; 225 WN-3; 🅿; ★ PGH; z 15317; Ⓟ 4,082; Ⓒ 4,726
McNett; MCD-Township; LYCOMING; *226 EG-5; mail Roaring Branch z 17765; Ⓟ 200; Ⓒ 211
McPherron; RMC Place; CLEARFIELD; ▲ Chest; *225 WK-10; mail La Jose z 15753; rural
McSherrystown; Inc. Place; ADAMS; 227 EQ-4; elev. 571ft./174m.; 🅿; ★ HANV; z 17344; Ⓟ 2,769; Ⓒ 2,691
McSparren; LANCASTER; see Cherry Hill (RMC Place)
McVeytown; MIFFLIN; see Mattawana (RMC Place)
McVeytown; Inc. Place; MIFFLIN; 225 WM-14; elev. 540ft./165m.; 🅿; z 17051; Ⓟ 408; Ⓒ 405
McVille; RMC Place; ARMSTRONG; ▲ South Buffalo; *225 WL-5; elev. 1,072ft./327m.; ★ PGH; mail Freeport z 16229
Mead; MCD-Township; WARREN; *224 WE-8; mail Clarendon z 16313; Ⓟ 1,579; Ⓒ 1,555
Meade Heights; RMC Place; DAUPHIN; ▲ Lower Swatara; *227 EO-5; ★ HRBG; mail Middletown z 17057; ● 140
Meadia Heights; RMC Place; LANCASTER; ▲ West Lampeter; *227 EP-7; ★ LANC; mail Lancaster z 17602; ● 300
Meadowbrook; RMC Place; FAYETTE; ▲ South Union; *225 WQ-5; ★ UNTN; mail Uniontown z 15401; ● 70
Meadowbrook; RMC Place; MONTGOMERY; ▲ Abington; 228 A-6; 🅿 🅷; ★ PHIL-; z 19046; ● 1,000
Meadowbrook Manor; RMC Place; CHESTER; ▲ West Whiteland; ★ PHIL-; mail Exton z 19341
Meadow Gap; RMC Place; HUNTINGDON; ▲ Springfield; *225 WO-13; mail Orbisonia z 17243; rural
Meadow Lands; RMC Place; WASHINGTON; ▲ Chartiers; 225 WO-2; 🅿; ★ WASH; z 15347; ● 900
Meadowood; CDP-Census Area Only; BUTLER; ▲ Butler; *225 WK-4; ★ BUTL; mail Lyndora z 16045; Ⓟ 3,011; Ⓒ 2,912
Meadowview Estates; RMC Place; LANCASTER; ▲ Upper Leacock; ★ LANC; mail Leola z 17540
Meadville; Inc. Place; ⊡ CRAWFORD; 224 WF-3; elev. 1,100ft./335m.; 🅿 🅷 🅲 2,095 ■; z 16335, z 16388; Ⓟ 14,318; Ⓒ 13,685; ◆ 12,474
Mechanicsburg; Inc. Place; CUMBERLAND; 227 EO-4; elev. 462ft./141m.; 🅿 🅷 ■; ★ HRBG; z 17050, z 17055; Ⓟ 9,452; Ⓒ 9,042; ◆ 9,042
Mechanics Grove; RMC Place; LANCASTER; ▲ East Drumore; 227 EQ-8; mail Quarryville z 17566; ● 120
Mechanics Valley; BUCKS; see Spring Valley (RMC Place)
Mechanicsville; RMC Place; BUCKS; ▲ Buckingham; 227 EN-12; 🅿; ★ PHIL-; z 18934; ● 500
Mechanicsville; RMC Place; CLARION; ▲ Clarion; 224 WI-7; mail Clarion z 16214; ● 35
Mechanicsville; RMC Place; LANCASTER; ▲ East Hempfield; *227 EO-7; elev. 380ft./116m.; ★ LANC; mail Manheim z 17545; rural
Mechanicsville; RMC Place; LEHIGH; ▲ South Whitehall, North Whitehall; 226 EA-2; ★ ALL-; mail Allentown z 18104; ● 120
Mechanicsville; CDP; MONTOUR; ▲ Mahoning; 226 EJ-6; mail Danville z 17821; Ⓟ 2,803; Ⓒ 3,099
Mechanicsville; Inc. Place; SCHUYLKILL; *227 EL-7; elev. 700ft./213m.; ★ PTSVL; mail Pottsville z 17901; Ⓟ 540; Ⓒ 515
Meckesville; RMC Place; CARBON; ▲ Penn Forest; 226 EJ-10; mail Albrightsville z 18210; ● 25
Mecks Corner; RMC Place; PERRY; ▲ Wheatfield; *227 EN-3; ★ HRBG; mail New Bloomfield z 17068
Media; Inc. Place; ⊡ DELAWARE; 227 EP-11; elev. 300ft./91m.; 🅿 🅷 🅲 1,631; ★ PHIL-; z 19063, z 19065, z 19091 & mail Glen Riddle Lima z 19037, Springfield z 19064, Wallingford z 19086; Ⓟ 5,957; Ⓒ 5,533
Media Annex; RMC Place; DELAWARE; *227 EP-11; ★ PHIL-; mail Media z 19063
Medix Run; RMC Place; ELK; ▲ Benezette; *224 WH-11; mail Weedville z 15868; rural
Meeker; RMC Place; LUZERNE; ▲ Lehman; *226 EH-8; elev. 1,161ft./354m.; ★ SCR-; mail Dallas z 18612; ● 100
Megargee; RMC Place; CHESTER; ▲ Caln; *227 EP-9; ★ PHIL-; mail Coatesville z 19320; ● 800
Mehoopany; RMC Place; WYOMING; ▲ Mehoopany; 226 EG-8; 🅿; z 18629; ● 350
Mehoopany; MCD-Township; WYOMING; *226 EG-8; 🅿; z 18629; Ⓟ 888; Ⓒ 993
Meiser; SNYDER; see Globe Mills (RMC Place)
Meiserville; RMC Place; SNYDER; ▲ Chapman; 227 EL-4; mail Mount Pleasant Mills z 17853; ● 100
Melcroft; RMC Place; FAYETTE; ▲ Saltlick; 225 WP-6; 🅿; z 15462; ● 250
Mellingertown; RMC Place; WESTMORELAND; ▲ Mount Pleasant; *225 WO-6; mail Mount Pleasant z 15666; rural
Mellwood Manor; RMC Place; WESTMORELAND; ▲ Allegheny; *225 WL-5; elev. 1,100ft./335m.; ★ PGH; mail New Kensington z 15068; ● 500
Melrose; RMC Place; SUSQUEHANNA; ▲ Harmony; *226 ED-10; 🅿; z 19027 & mail Susquehanna z 18847; rural
Melrose Park; RMC Place; MONTGOMERY; ▲ Cheltenham; 228 B-5; 🅿 🅲 620; ★ PHIL-; z 19027 & mail Cheltenham z 19012; ● 6,500
Menallen; MCD-Township; ADAMS; *227 EP-3; mail Aspers z 17304; Ⓟ 2,700; Ⓒ 2,974
Menallen; MCD-Township; FAYETTE; *225 WP-5; ★ UNTN; mail New Salem z 15468; Ⓟ 4,739; Ⓒ 4,644
Mench; RMC Place; BEDFORD; ▲ West Providence; *225 WP-11; elev. 1,291ft./393m.; mail Everett z 15537
Mendenhall; RMC Place; CHESTER; ▲ Kennett; 227 EQ-10; 🅿; ★ PHIL-; z 19357; ● 600
Mendon; RMC Place; WESTMORELAND; ▲ South Huntingdon; *225 WO-5; ★ PGH; mail Ruffs Dale z 15679; ● 80
Menges Mills; RMC Place; YORK; ▲ Jackson, Heidelberg; 227 EQ-4; 🅿; ★ YORK; z 17362; ● 200
Menno; RMC Place; MIFFLIN; ▲ Menno; 225 WM-14; mail Belleville z 17004; ● 80
Menno; MCD-Township; MIFFLIN; *225 WM-14; mail Belleville z 17004; Ⓟ 1,637; Ⓒ 1,763
Mentcle; RMC Place; INDIANA; ▲ Pine; 225 WL-9; 🅿; z 15761; ● 100
Mercer; MCD-Township; BUTLER; *224 WI-4; mail Harrisville z 16038; Ⓟ 1,110; Ⓒ 1,183
Mercer; Inc. Place; ⊡ MERCER; 224 WI-3; elev. 1,270ft./387m.; 🅿; z 16137; Ⓟ 2,444; Ⓒ 2,391
MERCER; 224 WH-2; Ⓟ 121,003; Ⓒ 120,293; ◆ 113,498
Mercersburg; Inc. Place; FRANKLIN; 225 WQ-13; elev. 560ft./171m.; 🅿; z 17236; Ⓟ 1,640; Ⓒ 1,540
Mercur; RMC Place; BRADFORD; ▲ Wysox; *226 EE-7; elev. 1,385ft./422m.; mail Wysox z 18854; rural
Meredith; RMC Place; ARMSTRONG; ▲ Cowanshannock; *225 WK-7; mail Rural Valley z 16249; ● 50
Meridian; CDP; BUTLER; ▲ Butler; 225 WK-4; 🅿; ★ BUTL; z 16001; Ⓟ 3,473; Ⓒ 3,794
Merion Park; RMC Place; MONTGOMERY; ▲ Lower Merion; ★ PHIL-; mail Merion Station z 19066
Merion Square; RMC Place; MONTGOMERY; ▲ Lower Merion; ★ PHIL-; mail Gladwyne z 19035
Merion Station; RMC Place; MONTGOMERY; ▲ Lower Merion; 228 D-3; 🅿; ★ PHIL-; z 19066; ● 700
Meriwether Farms; RMC Place; CHESTER; ▲ West Goshen; ★ PHIL-; mail West Chester z 19380; ● 600
Merlin; RMC Place; CHESTER; ▲ East Pikeland; *227 EO-10; ★ PHIL-; mail Phoenixville z 19460; rural
Mermaid Estates; RMC Place; MONTGOMERY; ▲ Whitpain; *227 EO-11; ★ PHIL-; mail Norristown z 19401; ● 750
Merrian; RMC Place; NORTHUMBERLAND; ▲ Mount Carmel; *227 EK-6; mail Mount Carmel z 17851; rural
Merrittstown; RMC Place; FAYETTE; ▲ Luzerne; 225 WP-4; 🅿; ★ UNTN; z 15463; ● 200
Merryall; RMC Place; BRADFORD; ▲ Wyalusing; *226 EF-7; elev. 737ft./225m.; mail Wyalusing z 18853; rural
Mertztown; RMC Place; BERKS; ▲ Longswamp; 227 EM-10; 🅿; z 19539; ● 300
Merwinsburg; RMC Place; MONROE; ▲ Chestnuthill; *226 EJ-11; ★ ALL-; mail Effort z 18330; rural
Meshoppen; Inc. Place; WYOMING; 226 EF-8; elev. 640ft./195m.; 🅿; z 18630; Ⓟ 439; Ⓒ 459
Meshoppen; MCD-Township; WYOMING; *226 EF-8; 🅿; z 18630; does not include the Borough of Meshoppen; Ⓟ 879; Ⓒ 877
Messiah College; RMC Place; CUMBERLAND; ▲ Upper Allen; 🅿; ★ HRBG; z 17027
Messmore; RMC Place; FAYETTE; ▲ German; *225 WQ-4; ★ UNTN; mail Mc Clellandtown z 15458; ● 130
Metal; RMC Place; FRANKLIN; ▲ Metal; 225 WP-13; mail Fort Loudon z 17224; ● 100
Metal; MCD-Township; FRANKLIN; *225 WP-13; mail Fort Loudon z 17224; Ⓟ 1,612; Ⓒ 1,721
Metzler; RMC Place; SOMERSET; *225 WP-7; mail Rockwood z 15557; ● 135
Mexico; CDP; JUNIATA; ▲ Walker; 227 EM-2; 🅿; z 17056; Ⓒ 279
Meyersdale; Inc. Place; SOMERSET; 225 WQ-8; elev. 1,975ft./602m.; 🅿 🅷; z 15552; Ⓟ 2,518; Ⓒ 2,473
Meyersville; RMC Place; LEHIGH; ▲ South Whitehall, North Whitehall; *227 EL-10; elev. 470ft./143m.; ★ ALL-; mail Allentown z 18104; rural
Middleboro (McKean); Inc. Place; ERIE; 224 WD-3; elev. 1,040ft./317m.; ★ ERIE; mail Mc Kean z 16426; Ⓟ 418; Ⓒ 389
Middleburg; RMC Place; LUZERNE; ▲ Dennison; 226 EJ-9; mail White Haven z 18661; ● 90
Middleburg; Inc. Place; ⊡ SNYDER; 227 EK-4; elev. 503ft./153m.; 🅿; z 17842; Ⓟ 1,422; Ⓒ 1,382
Middlebury; TIOGA; see Middlebury Center (RMC Place)
Middlebury; MCD-Township; TIOGA; *226 EE-2; mail Middlebury Center z 16935; Ⓟ 1,244; Ⓒ 1,221
Middlebury Center (Middlebury); RMC Place; TIOGA; ▲ Middlebury; 226 EE-3; elev. 1,148ft./350m.; 🅿; z 16935; ● 200
Middle Churches; RMC Place; WESTMORELAND; ▲ Mount Pleasant; mail Mount Pleasant z 15666; rural
Middle City; RMC Place; PHILADELPHIA; ★ PHIL-; mail Philadelphia z 19103; pop. incl. with Philadelphia (Inc. Place)
Middle Creek; RMC Place; SNYDER; ▲ Spring; *227 EL-3; 🅿; z 17812, z 17843 & mail Beavertown z 17813
Middlecreek; MCD-Township; SNYDER; *227 EK-4; mail Kreamer z 17833; Ⓟ 1,791; Ⓒ 1,971
Middlecreek; MCD-Township; SOMERSET; *225 WP-7; mail Rockwood z 15557; Ⓟ 764; Ⓒ 797
Middle Lancaster; RMC Place; BUTLER; ▲ Lancaster; 225 WK-3; ★ PGH; mail Harmony z 16037; ● 100
Middle Paxton; MCD-Township; DAUPHIN; *227 EN-5; ★ HRBG; mail Dauphin z 17018; Ⓟ 5,129; Ⓒ 4,823; Ⓡ 4,881
Middleport; Inc. Place; SCHUYLKILL; 227 EL-8; elev. 740ft./226m.; 🅿; ★ PTSVL; z 17953; Ⓟ 520; Ⓒ 458
Middlesex; MCD-Township; BUTLER; *225 WL-4; ★ PGH; mail Valencia z 16059; Ⓟ 5,578; Ⓒ 5,586
Middlesex; RMC Place; CUMBERLAND; ▲ Middlesex; 227 EO-3; ★ CARL; mail Carlisle z 17013; ● 250
Middlesex; MCD-Township; CUMBERLAND; *227 EO-3; ★ CARL; mail Carlisle z 17013; Ⓟ 5,780; Ⓒ 6,669
Middle Smithfield; MCD-Township; MONROE; *226 EI-13; mail East Stroudsburg z 18301; Ⓟ 6,382; Ⓒ 11,495
Middle Spring; RMC Place; CUMBERLAND; ▲ Southampton; 227 EO-1; mail Shippensburg z 17257; ● 80
Middle Taylor; MCD-Township; CAMBRIA; *225 WN-8; ★ JNST; mail Johnstown z 15906; Ⓟ 802; Ⓒ 792
Middleton; RMC Place; CLEARFIELD; ▲ Bell; *225 WK-9; mail Mahaffey z 15757; ● 35
Middletown; MCD-Township; BUCKS; *227 EO-13; ★ PHIL-; mail Levittown z 19056; Ⓟ 43,063; Ⓒ 44,141; ◆ 43,866
Middletown; Inc. Place; DAUPHIN; 227 EO-5; elev. 360ft./110m.; 🅿 🅲 3,799; ★ HRBG; z 17057 & mail Levittown z 19056; Ⓟ 9,254; Ⓒ 9,242
Middletown; MCD-Township; DELAWARE; *227 EP-11; ■; ★ PHIL-; mail Glen Riddle Lima z 19037; Ⓟ 14,130; Ⓒ 16,064; ◆ 16,153
Middletown; RMC Place; HUNTINGDON; ▲ Carbon; *225 WO-12; mail Saxton z 16678; ● 100
Middletown; RMC Place; MCKEAN; ▲ Bradford; *224 WE-10; elev. 2,210ft./674m.; mail Smethport z 16749; rural
Middletown; CDP; NORTHAMPTON; ▲ Bethlehem; *227 EL-11; ★ ALL-; mail Bethlehem z 18017, z 18020; Ⓟ 6,866; Ⓒ 7,378
Middletown; MCD-Township; SUSQUEHANNA; *226 EE-8; mail Friendsville z 18818; Ⓟ 339; Ⓒ 340
Middletown; RMC Place; WESTMORELAND; ▲ Hempfield; *225 WN-5; elev. 1,298ft./396m.; ★ PGH; mail Greensburg z 15601, New Stanton z 15672; ● 125
Middletown Center; RMC Place; SUSQUEHANNA; ▲ Middletown; *226 EE-8; elev. 975ft./297m.; mail Friendsville z 18818; rural
Middletown Heights; RMC Place; DELAWARE; ▲ Middletown; *227 EQ-11; elev. 200ft./61m.; ★ PHIL-; mail Media z 19063; ● 550
Midland; Inc. Place; BEAVER; 225 WL-2; elev. 800ft./244m.; 🅿; ★ PGH; z 15059; Ⓟ 3,321; Ⓒ 3,137
Midland; RMC Place; WASHINGTON; ▲ Chartiers; *225 WN-3; ★ WASH; mail Houston z 15342; ● 300
Midvale; RMC Place; LUZERNE; ▲ Plains; *226 EH-9; elev. 582ft./177m.; ★ SCR-; mail Wilkes Barre z 18705
Midvale Manor; RMC Place; BERKS; ▲ Spring; *227 EN-8; ★ READ; mail Reading z 19608; ● 700
Midvalley; RMC Place; COLUMBIA; ▲ Conyngham; *227 EK-7; mail Wilburton z 17888; ● 110
Midway; CDP; ADAMS; ▲ Conewago; *227 EQ-4; ★ HANV; mail Hanover z 17331; Ⓟ 2,254; Ⓒ 2,323
Midway; RMC Place; LEBANON; ▲ South Lebanon; *227 EN-6; elev. 638ft./194m.; ★ LEB; mail Lebanon z 17042; ● 75
Midway; Inc. Place; WASHINGTON; 225 WN-2; elev. 1,120ft./341m.; 🅿; ★ PGH; z 15060; Ⓟ 1,043; Ⓒ 982
Midway; RMC Place; WESTMORELAND; ▲ Hempfield; *225 WN-5; ★ PGH; mail Greensburg z 15601; ● 150
Mifflin; MCD-Township; COLUMBIA; *226 EJ-7; mail Mifflinville z 18631; Ⓟ 2,305; Ⓒ 2,251
Mifflin; MCD-Township; DAUPHIN; *227 EL-4; mail Millersburg z 17061; Ⓟ 676; Ⓒ 662
Mifflin; Inc. Place; JUNIATA; 227 EM-2; elev. 500ft./152m.; 🅿; z 17058; Ⓟ 660; Ⓒ 627
Mifflin; MCD-Township; LYCOMING; *226 EI-3; mail Jersey Shore z 17740; Ⓟ 1,110; Ⓒ 1,145
MIFFLIN; 225 WM-14; Ⓟ 46,197; Ⓒ 46,486; ◆ 46,132
Mifflinburg; Inc. Place; UNION; 227 EK-4; elev. 583ft./178m.; 🅿; z 17844; Ⓟ 3,480; Ⓒ 3,594
Mifflin Junction; RMC Place; ALLEGHENY; *225 WN-4; ★ PGH; pop. incl. with West Mifflin (Inc. Place)
Mifflintown; Inc. Place; ⊡ JUNIATA; 227 EM-2; elev. 500ft./152m.; 🅿; z 17059; Ⓟ 866; Ⓒ 861
Mifflinville (Creasy); CDP; COLUMBIA; ▲ Mifflin; 226 EJ-7; 🅿; z 18631; Ⓟ 1,329; Ⓒ 1,213
Milan; RMC Place; BRADFORD; ▲ Ulster; 226 EE-6; 🅿; z 18831; ● 300
Milanville; RMC Place; WAYNE; ▲ Damascus; 226 EF-12; elev. 758ft./231m.; 🅿; z 18443; summer pop. 400; ● 175
Mildred; RMC Place; SULLIVAN; ▲ Cherry; 226 EG-7; 🅿; z 18632; ● 200
Mile Run; RMC Place; NORTHUMBERLAND; ▲ Lower Augusta; *227 EK-5; elev. 628ft./191m.; mail Sunbury z 17801; rural
Miles; MCD-Township; CENTRE; *226 EJ-1; mail Rebersburg z 16872; Ⓟ 1,494; Ⓒ 1,573
Milesburg; Inc. Place; CENTRE; 224 WJ-14; elev. 700ft./213m.; 🅿; ★ STCOL; z 16853; Ⓟ 1,144; Ⓒ 1,187
Milford; MCD-Township; BUCKS; *227 EM-11; ★ PHIL-; mail Spinnerstown z 18968; Ⓟ 7,360; Ⓒ 8,810
Milford; MCD-Township; JUNIATA; *227 EM-2; mail Millerstown z 17062; Ⓟ 1,429; Ⓒ 1,758
Milford; PERRY; see Wila (RMC Place)
Milford; Inc. Place; ⊡ PIKE; 226 EH-14; elev. 503ft./153m.; 🅿; z 18337; Ⓟ 1,064; Ⓒ 1,104
Milford; MCD-Township; PIKE; *226 EH-13; 🅿; z 18337; does not include the Borough of Milford; Ⓟ 1,013; Ⓒ 1,292
Milford; RMC Place; SOMERSET; ▲ Milford; *225 WP-8; elev. 1,940ft./591m.; mail Rockwood z 15557; rural
Milford; MCD-Township; SOMERSET; *225 WP-7; mail Rockwood z 15557; Ⓟ 1,544; Ⓒ 1,561
Milford Manor; RMC Place; BUCKS; ▲ Lower Makefield; *227 EO-14; ★ PHIL-; mail Morrisville z 19067; ● 400
Milford Square; RMC Place; BUCKS; ▲ Milford; 227 EM-11; 🅿; ★ PHIL-; z 18935; ● 700
Milfred Terrace; RMC Place; WASHINGTON; ▲ East Bethlehem; *225 WP-3; mail Millsboro z 15348; ● 250
Militia Hill; RMC Place; MONTGOMERY; ▲ Whitemarsh; *227 EO-12; elev. 166ft./51m.; ★ PHIL-; mail Fort Washington z 19034; ● 400
Millardsville; RMC Place; LEBANON; ▲ Jackson; 227 EN-7; ★ LEB; mail Myerstown z 17067; ● 100
Millbach (Millbach Springs); RMC Place; LEBANON; ▲ Millcreek; *227 EN-7; mail Newmanstown z 17073
Millbach Springs; LEBANON; see Millbach (RMC Place)
Millbank; RMC Place; WESTMORELAND; ▲ Ligonier; *225 WN-7; mail Ligonier z 15658; rural
Millbourne; Inc. Place; DELAWARE; 228 E-3; elev. 100ft./30m.; ★ PHIL-; mail Upper Darby z 19082; Ⓟ 831; Ⓒ 943
Millbrook; RMC Place; CENTRE; ▲ College; *225 WK-13; ★ STCOL; mail State College z 16801; ● 400
Millbrook; RMC Place; MERCER; ▲ Worth; *224 WH-3; mail Jackson Center z 16133; ● 50
Mill Brook; RMC Place; PIKE; ▲ Palmyra; *226 EH-12; elev. 1,300ft./396m.; mail Greentown z 18426; ● 100
Millburn; RMC Place; MERCER; ▲ Springfield; *224 WI-3; elev. 1,090ft./332m.; mail Mercer z 16137; rural
Mill City; RMC Place; WYOMING; ▲ Falls; 226 EG-9; ★ SCR-; mail Dalton z 18414, Falls z 18615; ● 450
Millcreek; MCD-Township; CLARION; *224 WH-7; mail Fisher z 16225; Ⓟ 407; Ⓒ 415
Millcreek; MCD-Township; ERIE; *224 WC-3; ■; ★ ERIE; mail Erie z 16505-06, z 16509; Ⓟ 46,820; Ⓒ 52,129; ◆ 51,543
Mill Creek; Inc. Place; HUNTINGDON; 225 WM-13; elev. 627ft./191m.; 🅿; z 17060; Ⓟ 392; Ⓒ 351
Millcreek; MCD-Township; LEBANON; *227 EN-7; mail Newmanstown z 17073; Ⓟ 2,687; Ⓒ 2,921
Mill Creek; MCD-Township; LYCOMING; *226 EH-5; mail Muncy z 17756; Ⓟ 477; Ⓒ 572
Mill Creek; MCD-Township; MERCER; *224 WG-4; mail Sandy Lake z 16145; Ⓟ 604; Ⓒ 639
Mill Creek; RMC Place; SCHUYLKILL; ▲ Norwegian, East Norwegian; *227 EL-7; ★ PTSVL; mail Pottsville z 17901; ● 150
Mill Creek Falls; RMC Place; BUCKS; ▲ Bristol; *227 EO-13; ★ PHIL-; mail Bristol z 19007
Milledgeville; RMC Place; MERCER; ▲ French Creek; 224 WG-3; mail Carlton z 16311; ● 60
Miller; MCD-Township; HUNTINGDON; *225 WM-13; mail Huntingdon z 16652; Ⓟ 474; Ⓒ 514
Miller; MCD-Township; PERRY; *227 EM-3; ★ HRBG; mail Thompsontown z 17094; Ⓟ 894; Ⓒ 953
Miller Heights (Heights); RMC Place; NORTHAMPTON; ▲ Bethlehem; *227 EL-11; ★ ALL-; mail Bethlehem z 18020; pop. incl. with Bethlehem (Inc. Place)
Miller Manor; RMC Place; NORTHAMPTON; ▲ East Allen; *227 EL-11; ★ ALL-; mail Northampton z 18067; ● 150
Miller Run; RMC Place; SOMERSET; ▲ Shade; *225 WO-9; mail Hooversville z 15936; rural
Millersburg; Inc. Place; DAUPHIN; 227 EM-4; elev. 420ft./128m.; 🅿; z 17061; Ⓟ 2,729; Ⓒ 2,562
Miller Shaft; RMC Place; CAMBRIA; ▲ Portage; *225 WN-10; mail Portage z 15946; ● 100
Millers Station; RMC Place; CRAWFORD; ▲ Rockdale; *224 WE-4; mail Cambridge Springs z 16403; rural
Millerstown; RMC Place; ALLEGHENY; ▲ Fawn; *225 WL-4; ★ PGH; mail Tarentum z 15084; ● 175
Millerstown; RMC Place; BLAIR; ▲ North Woodbury; *225 WN-11; elev. 1,349ft./411m.; mail Martinsburg z 16662; ● 16
Millerstown; RMC Place; CLARION; ▲ Washington; *224 WH-6; elev. 1,554ft./474m.; mail Marble z 16334
Millerstown; Inc. Place; PERRY; 227 EM-3; elev. 420ft./128m.; 🅿; z 17062; Ⓟ 646; Ⓒ 679
Millersville; Inc. Place; LANCASTER; 227 EP-7; elev. 360ft./110m.; 🅿 🅲 8,194; ★ LANC; z 17551; Ⓟ 8,099; Ⓒ 7,774
Millerton; RMC Place; TIOGA; ▲ Jackson; 226 ED-4; 🅿; z 16936; ● 400
Millertown; RMC Place; COLUMBIA; ▲ Mount Pleasant; *226 EJ-6; mail Bloomsburg z 17815; ● 40
Millertown; RMC Place; FAYETTE; ▲ Saltlick; 225 WP-6; mail Indian Head z 15446; ● 200
Mill Grove; RMC Place; COLUMBIA; ▲ Roaring Creek, Locust; 227 EK-7; elev. 926ft./282m.; mail Catawissa z 17820; ● 40
Mill Hall; Inc. Place; CLINTON; 226 EI-2; elev. 580ft./177m.; 🅿; ★ WMSPT; z 17751 & mail Salona z 17767; Ⓟ 1,702; Ⓒ 1,568
Millheim; Inc. Place; CENTRE; 227 EK-2; 🅿; z 16854; Ⓟ 847; Ⓒ 749
Milligantown; RMC Place; WESTMORELAND; ▲ Upper Burrell; *225 WM-5; ★ PGH; mail New Kensington z 15068; ● 150
Millmont; RMC Place; UNION; ▲ Lewis; 227 EK-3; 🅿; z 17845; ● 150
Millport; RMC Place; LANCASTER; ▲ Warwick; *227 EO-7; ★ LANC; mail Leola z 17540, Lititz z 17543; ● 90
Millport; RMC Place; POTTER; ▲ Sharon; 224 WE-12; mail Shinglehouse z 16748; ● 80
Millrift; RMC Place; PIKE; ▲ Westfall; 226 EG-14; 🅿; z 18340; ● 170

Entries in **UPPERCASE** are counties.
Entries in **bold** have populations of 2,500 or more.
Names in parentheses are alternate names.
Inc. Place — Incorporated Place
RMC Place — Rand McNally Designated Place
CDP — Census Designated Place
MCD — Minor Civil Division
⊡ County Seat
▲ Minor Civil Division
elev. Elevation
🅿 Post Office
🅷 Hospital
🅲 College
■ Principal Business Center
★ Ranally Metro Area (RMA) Abbreviation
z Zip Code(s)
Ⓟ Previous Census Population
Ⓡ Revised Census Population
Ⓐ Annexation Population
● Rand McNally Population Estimate
Ⓒ Final Census Population
Ⓢ Special Census Population
◆ Estimated Population

For additional definitions see Glossary, Volume 1, and Introduction, Volume 2.

Mill Run; RMC Place; BLAIR; ▲ Logan; 225 WM-11; ★ ALT; mail Altoona Z 16601; ● 250
Mill Run; RMC Place; CLEARFIELD; *224 WI-10; mail Penfield Z 15849; ● 50
Mill Run; RMC Place; FAYETTE; ▲ Springfield; 225 WP-6; 🅿; Z 15464; ● 400
Mills; RMC Place; POTTER; ▲ Harrison; 224 WD-14; 🅿; Z 16937; ● 125
Millsboro; RMC Place; WASHINGTON; ▲ East Bethlehem; 225 WP-4; 🅿; Z 15348; ● 300
Millstone; MCD-Township; ELK; *224 WH-8; mail Sigel Z 15860; Ⓟ 85; Ⓒ 95
Milltown; RMC Place; ALLEGHENY; ▲ Penn Hills; *225 WM-4; ★ PGH; mail Verona Z 15147
Milltown; RMC Place; BRADFORD; *226 ED-6; mail Sayre Z 18840; pop. incl. with Sayre (Inc. Place)
Milltown; RMC Place; CHESTER; ▲ East Goshen; 227 EP-10; elev. 344ft./105m.; ★ PHIL-; mail West Chester Z 19380; ● 170
Millvale; Inc. Place; ALLEGHENY; 225 WM-4; elev. 800ft./244m.; 🅿; ★ PGH; Z 15209; Ⓟ 4,341; Ⓒ 4,028
Millview; RMC Place; SULLIVAN; ▲ Forks; *226 EG-6; mail Forksville Z 18616
Mill Village; Inc. Place; ERIE; 224 WE-4; elev. 1,206ft./368m.; 🅿; ★ ERIE; Z 16427; Ⓟ 429; Ⓒ 412
Millville; Inc. Place; COLUMBIA; 226 EI-6; elev. 643ft./196m.; 🅿; Z 17846; Ⓟ 969; Ⓒ 991
Millway; RMC Place; LANCASTER; ▲ Warwick; *227 EO-7; ★ LANC; mail Lititz Z 17543; ● 100
Millwood; RMC Place; WESTMORELAND; ▲ Derry; 225 WN-7; ★ LTROB; mail Derry Z 15627; ● 300
Milmont (Milmont Park); RMC Place; DELAWARE; ▲ Ridley; *227 EQ-11; ★ PHIL-; mail Folsom Z 19033
Milmont Park; DELAWARE; see Milmont (RMC Place)
Milnesville; RMC Place; LUZERNE; ▲ Hazle; 226 EJ-8; elev. 1,603ft./489m.; 🅿; ★ HAZ; Z 18239; ● 300
Milnor; RMC Place; FRANKLIN; ▲ Antrim; *225 WQ-14; ★ HAG; mail Greencastle Z 17225; rural
Milroy; CDP; MIFFLIN; ▲ Armagh; 227 EL-1; 🅿; Z 17063; Ⓟ 1,456; Ⓒ 1,386
Milton; RMC Place; ARMSTRONG; ▲ Redbank; *225 WK-7; mail Dayton Z 16222; ● 60
Milton; Inc. Place; NORTHUMBERLAND; 226 EJ-4; elev. 472ft./144m.; 🅿; Z 17847; Ⓟ 6,746; Ⓒ 6,650
Milton Grove; RMC Place; LANCASTER; ▲ Mount Joy; 227 EO-6; mail Mount Joy Z 17552; ● 100
Milwaukee; RMC Place; LACKAWANNA; ▲ Ransom; *226 EH-9; elev. 916ft./279m.; ★ SCR-; mail Clarks Summit Z 18411
Mina; RMC Place; POTTER; ▲ Eulalia; *224 WF-12; elev. 1,601ft./488m.; mail Coudersport Z 16915; rural
Mineral; MCD-Township; VENANGO; *224 WH-4; mail Polk Z 16342; Ⓟ 514; Ⓒ 533
Mineral Point; RMC Place; CAMBRIA; ▲ East Taylor, Conemaugh; 225 WN-9; 🅿; ★ JNST; Z 15942; ● 150
Mineral Springs; RMC Place; CLEARFIELD; ▲ Bradford; 224 WJ-11; 🅿; Z 16855; ● 300
Miners Mill (Miners Mills); RMC Place; LUZERNE; *226 EH-9; 🅿; ★ SCR-; Z 18705; pop. incl. with Wilkes-Barre (Inc. Place)
Miners Mills; LUZERNE; see Miners Mill (RMC Place)
Miners Village; RMC Place; LEBANON; *227 EN-6; ★ LEB; mail Cornwall Z 17016; pop. incl. with Cornwall (Inc. Place)
Minersville; RMC Place; CAMBRIA; *225 WN-8; ★ JNST; mail Johnstown Z 15906; pop. incl. with Johnstown (Inc. Place)
Minersville; Inc. Place; SCHUYLKILL; 227 EL-7; elev. 820ft./250m.; 🅿; ★ PTSVL; Z 17954; Ⓟ 4,877; Ⓒ 4,552
Minesite; RMC Place; LEHIGH; ▲ Lower Macungie; ★ ALL-; mail Allentown Z 18103
Mingo; RMC Place; MONTGOMERY; ▲ Upper Providence; *227 EO-10; ★ PHIL-; mail Royersford Z 19468; ● 300
Mingoville; RMC Place; CENTRE; ▲ Walker; 224 WJ-14; 🅿; Z 16856; ● 300
Minisink Hills; RMC Place; MONROE; ▲ Smithfield; 226 EJ-12; 🅿; Z 18341; ● 350
Minister; RMC Place; FOREST; ▲ Howe; *224 WF-7; elev. 1,228ft./374m.; mail Sheffield Z 16347; rural
Minnequa; RMC Place; BRADFORD; ▲ Canton; *226 EF-4; mail Canton Z 17724; rural
Minooka; RMC Place; LACKAWANNA; *226 EH-10; elev. 890ft./271m.; ★ SCR-; mail Moosic Z 18507; pop. incl. with Scranton (Inc. Place)
Miola; RMC Place; CLARION; ▲ Highland; *224 WH-7; mail Clarion Z 16214; rural
Miquon; RMC Place; MONTGOMERY; ▲ Whitemarsh; *227 EP-12; 🅿; ★ PHIL-; Z 19444; ● 300
Miquon Hills; RMC Place; MONTGOMERY; ▲ Whitemarsh; ★ PHIL-
Mission Hill; RMC Place; LANCASTER; ▲ Manheim; *227 EO-7; ★ LANC; mail Lancaster Z 17601; ● 300
Mitchell Park; RMC Place; MONTGOMERY; ★ PHIL-; mail Hatboro Z 19040; pop. incl. with Hatboro (Inc. Place)
Mix Run; RMC Place; CAMERON; ▲ Gibson; *224 WH-12; mail Driftwood Z 15832; rural
Mocanaqua; RMC Place; LUZERNE; ▲ Conyngham; 226 EI-8; elev. 558ft./170m.; 🅿; Z 18655; ● 1,000
Moc-A-Tek Lake; RMC Place; WAYNE; ▲ Paupack; *226 EG-11; elev. 1,400ft./427m.; mail Lake Ariel Z 18436; summer pop. 300; rural
Mocking Bird Hill; RMC Place; WESTMORELAND; ▲ North Huntingdon; *225 WN-5; ★ PGH; mail Irwin Z 15642; ● 450
Modena; Inc. Place; CHESTER; 227 EP-9; elev. 300ft./91m.; 🅿; ★ PHIL-; Z 19358; Ⓟ 563; Ⓒ 610
Moffit Sterling; RMC Place; GREENE; ▲ Dunkard; *225 WQ-4; mail Dilliner Z 15327; ● 120
Mogees; MONTGOMERY; see Mogeetown (RMC Place)
Mogeetown (Mogees); RMC Place; MONTGOMERY; ▲ Plymouth; *227 EO-11; ★ PHIL-; mail Plymouth Meeting Z 19462; ● 1,400
Mohns Hill; RMC Place; BERKS; ▲ Spring; *227 EN-8; ★ READ; mail Reading Z 19608; ● 200
Mohnton; Inc. Place; BERKS; 227 EN-8; elev. 401ft./122m.; 🅿; ★ READ; Z 19540; Ⓟ 2,484; Ⓒ 2,963
Mohrsville; RMC Place; BERKS; ▲ Perry, Centre; 227 EM-8; 🅿; ★ READ; Z 19541; ● 700
Molino; RMC Place; SCHUYLKILL; ▲ West Brunswick; *227 EL-8; ★ PTSVL; mail Orwigsburg Z 17961; rural
Molltown; RMC Place; BERKS; ▲ Maidencreek; *227 EM-9; ★ READ; mail Fleetwood Z 19522; ● 100
Monaca; Inc. Place; BEAVER; 225 WL-2; elev. 1,000ft./305m.; 🅿 🅲 730; ★ PGH; Z 15061; Ⓟ 6,739; Ⓒ 6,286
Monaghan; MCD-Township; YORK; *227 EO-4; ★ HRBG; mail York Z 17404; Ⓟ 2,009; Ⓒ 2,132
Monarch; RMC Place; FAYETTE; ▲ Dunbar; 225 WP-5; mail Dunbar Z 15431; ● 200
Monessen; Inc. Place; WESTMORELAND; 225 WO-4; elev. 1,020ft./311m.; 🅿 ■; ★ PGH; Z 15062; Ⓟ 9,901; Ⓒ 8,669; ◆ 8,127
Mongul; RMC Place; FRANKLIN; ▲ Southampton; 227 EP-1; mail Shippensburg Z 17257; ● 60
Moninger; RMC Place; WASHINGTON; ▲ Chartiers; *225 WN-3; ★ PGH; mail Houston Z 15342; ● 600
Moniteau; RMC Place; BUTLER; ▲ Cherry; *224 WJ-4; mail West Sunbury Z 16061; rural
Monocacy Station; RMC Place; BERKS; ▲ Union, Amity; 227 EN-9; 🅿; Z 19542; ● 150
Monongahela; MCD-Township; GREENE; *225 WQ-4; mail Greensboro Z 15338; Ⓟ 1,858; Ⓒ 1,714
Monongahela; Inc. Place; WASHINGTON; 225 WO-4; elev. 887ft./270m.; 🅿 🅷; ★ PGH; Z 15063; Ⓟ 4,928; Ⓒ 4,761
Monongahela Junction; RMC Place; ALLEGHENY; ★ PGH; pop. incl. with Duquesne (Inc. Place)
Monroe; MCD-Township; BEDFORD; *225 WQ-11; mail Clearville Z 15535; Ⓟ 1,305; Ⓒ 1,372
Monroe; BRADFORD; see Monroeton (Inc. Place)
Monroe; MCD-Township; BRADFORD; *226 EF-6; mail Towanda Z 18848; does not include the Borough of Monroeton; Ⓟ 1,235; Ⓒ 1,271
Monroe; RMC Place; CLARION; ▲ Beaver; 224 WI-5; mail Knox Z 16232; ● 90
Monroe; MCD-Township; CLARION; *224 WI-6; mail Knox Z 16232; Ⓟ 1,314; Ⓒ 1,587
Monroe; MCD-Township; CUMBERLAND; *227 EO-3; ★ HRBG; mail Mechanicsburg Z 17055; Ⓟ 5,468; Ⓒ 5,530
Monroe; MCD-Township; JUNIATA; *227 EL-3; mail Cocolamus Z 17014, Richfield Z 17086; Ⓟ 1,800; Ⓒ 2,042
Monroe; MCD-Township; SNYDER; *227 EK-4; mail Hummels Wharf Z 17831, Selinsgrove Z 17870; Ⓟ 3,881; Ⓒ 4,012
Monroe; MCD-Township; WYOMING; *226 EH-8; mail Tunkhannock Z 18657; Ⓟ 1,802; Ⓒ 1,836
MONROE; 226 EJ-11; Ⓟ 95,709; Ⓒ 138,687; ◆ 162,648
Monroe Heights; RMC Place; ALLEGHENY; *225 WM-5; elev. 1,188ft./362m.; ★ PGH; mail Monroeville Z 15146; pop. incl. with Monroeville (Inc. Place)
Monroeton (Monroe); Inc. Place; BRADFORD; 226 EF-6; elev. 760ft./232m.; 🅿; Z 18832; Ⓟ 540; Ⓒ 514
Monroeville (Municipality of Monroeville); Inc. Place; ALLEGHENY; 225 WM-5; elev. 1,180ft./360m.; 🅿 🅷 ■; ★ PGH; Z 15140, Z 15146; Ⓟ 29,169; Ⓒ 29,349; ◆ 28,357
Mont Alto; Inc. Place; FRANKLIN; 227 EQ-1; elev. 848ft./258m.; 🅿 🅲 1,032; Z 17237; Ⓟ 1,395; Ⓒ 1,357
Montandon; RMC Place; NORTHUMBERLAND; ▲ West Chillisquaque; 226 EJ-4; 🅿; Z 17850; ● 600
Mont Clare; RMC Place; MONTGOMERY; ▲ Upper Providence; 227 EO-11; 🅿; ★ PHIL-; Z 19453; ● 1,800
Montdale; RMC Place; LACKAWANNA; ▲ Scott; 226 EG-10; ★ SCR-; mail Olyphant Z 18447; ● 400
Montello; RMC Place; BERKS; ▲ Spring; 227 ET-11; ★ READ; mail Reading Z 19608; ● 50
Monterey; RMC Place; BERKS; ▲ Maxatawny; *227 EM-10; mail Kutztown Z 19530
Monterey; RMC Place; FRANKLIN; ▲ Washington; *227 ER-2; ★ HAG; mail Blue Ridge Summit Z 17214
Monterey; RMC Place; LANCASTER; ▲ Upper Leacock; 227 EP-8; elev. 391ft./119m.; ★ LANC; mail Leola Z 17540; ● 100
Montgomery; MCD-Township; FRANKLIN; *225 WR-13; mail Mercersburg Z 17236; Ⓟ 4,558; Ⓒ 4,949
Montgomery; MCD-Township; INDIANA; *225 WK-9; mail Cherry Tree Z 15724; Ⓟ 1,729; Ⓒ 1,706
Montgomery; Inc. Place; LYCOMING; 226 EI-4; elev. 500ft./152m.; 🅿; ★ WMSPT; Z 17752; Ⓟ 1,631; Ⓒ 1,695
Montgomery; MCD-Township; MONTGOMERY; *227 EN-12; ★ PHIL-; mail Montgomeryville Z 18936, North Wales Z 19454; Ⓟ 12,179; Ⓒ 22,025; ◆ 24,144
MONTGOMERY; 227 EN-11; Ⓟ 678,111; Ⓒ 750,097; Ⓡ 748,987; ◆ 776,119
Montgomery Ferry; RMC Place; PERRY; ▲ Buffalo; 227 EM-4; mail Newport Z 17074; ● 50
Montgomery Square; RMC Place; MONTGOMERY; ▲ Montgomery; *227 EN-12; elev. 440ft./134m.; ★ PHIL-; mail Montgomeryville Z 18936
Montgomeryville; ARMSTRONG; see Adrian (RMC Place)
Montgomeryville; CDP; MONTGOMERY; ▲ Montgomery; 227 EN-12; elev. 457ft./139m.; 🅿; ★ PHIL-; Z 18936; Ⓟ 9,114; Ⓒ 12,031
Montmorenci; RMC Place; ELK; *224 WG-9; mail Ridgway Z 15853
Montour; RMC Place; ALLEGHENY; ▲ Kennedy, Robinson; *225 WM-3; 🅿; ★ PGH; Z 15244
Montour; MCD-Township; COLUMBIA; *226 EJ-6; mail Bloomsburg Z 17815; Ⓟ 1,419; Ⓒ 1,437
MONTOUR; 226 EJ-5; Ⓟ 17,735; Ⓒ 18,236; ◆ 17,689
Montour Junction; RMC Place; ALLEGHENY; ★ PGH
Montoursville; Inc. Place; LYCOMING; 226 EI-4; elev. 525ft./160m.; 🅿; ★ WMSPT; Z 17754; Ⓟ 4,983; Ⓒ 4,777
Montrose; RMC Place; BERKS; ▲ Cumru; 227 ET-12; ★ READ; mail Reading Z 19607; ● 1,350
Montrose; Inc. Place; ⊡ SUSQUEHANNA; 226 EE-9; elev. 1,684ft./513m.; 🅿 🅷; Z 18801; Ⓟ 1,982; Ⓒ 1,664
Montrose Hill; RMC Place; ALLEGHENY; ▲ O'Hara; *225 WM-4; ★ PGH; mail Pittsburgh Z 15238; ● 1,600
Montsera; RMC Place; CUMBERLAND; ▲ Dickinson; *227 EO-2; ★ CARL; mail Carlisle Z 17013; rural
Monument; CDP; CENTRE; ▲ Liberty; 224 WI-14; mail Beech Creek Z 16822; Ⓒ 133
Moon; RMC Place; ALLEGHENY; ▲ Moon; 225 WM-2; elev. 1,173ft./358m.; ★ PGH; mail Coraopolis Z 15108; ● 1,000
Moon (Moon Township); MCD-Township; ALLEGHENY; *225 WM-3; 🅲 5,065; ★ PGH; mail Coraopolis Z 15108; Ⓟ 19,631; Ⓒ 22,290; ◆ 22,646
Moon Crest; RMC Place; ALLEGHENY; ▲ Moon; *225 WM-3; ★ PGH; mail Coraopolis Z 15108; ● 2,100
Moon Run; RMC Place; ALLEGHENY; ▲ Robinson; 225 WM-3; ★ PGH; mail Mc Kees Rocks Z 15136; ● 400
Moon Township; ALLEGHENY; see Moon (MCD-Township)
Moore; MCD-Township; NORTHAMPTON; *227 EK-11; ★ ALL-; mail Bath Z 18014; Ⓟ 8,418; Ⓒ 8,673
Mooredale; RMC Place; CUMBERLAND; ▲ Dickinson; *227 EO-2; ★ CARL; mail Carlisle Z 17013; rural
Mooresburg; RMC Place; MONTOUR; ▲ Liberty; 226 EJ-5; elev. 654ft./199m.; mail Danville Z 17821; ● 80
Moores Corners; RMC Place; BUTLER; ▲ Worth; *224 WJ-3; elev. 1,168ft./356m.; mail Slippery Rock Z 16057; rural
Moorestown; RMC Place; NORTHAMPTON; ▲ Moore; 227 EK-11; elev. 772ft./235m.; ★ ALL-; mail Bath Z 18014; ● 250
Moorheadville; RMC Place; ERIE; ▲ Harborcreek; *224 WC-4; ★ ERIE; mail North East Z 16428
Moosic; Inc. Place; LACKAWANNA; 226 EH-9; elev. 647ft./197m.; 🅿; ★ SCR-; Z 18507; Ⓟ 5,339; Ⓒ 5,575
Moosic Lake; RMC Place; LACKAWANNA; ▲ Jefferson; *226 EG-10; ★ SCR-; mail Elmhurst Z 18416; summer pop. 350; ● 200
Morado; RMC Place; BEAVER; *225 WK-2; ★ PGH; mail Beaver Falls Z 15010; pop. incl. with Beaver Falls (Inc. Place)
Morann; RMC Place; CLEARFIELD; ▲ Woodward, Gulich; 225 WK-11; 🅿; Z 16663; ● 400
Moravia; RMC Place; LAWRENCE; ▲ North Beaver; *224 WJ-2; ★ YNGS-; mail Wampum Z 16157
Moravian; RMC Place; NORTHAMPTON; ★ ALL-; mail Bethlehem Z 18018; pop. incl. with Bethlehem (Inc. Place)
Mordansville; RMC Place; COLUMBIA; ▲ Mount Pleasant; *226 EJ-6; mail Bloomsburg Z 17815; rural
Morea (Morea Colliery); RMC Place; SCHUYLKILL; ▲ Mahanoy; *227 EK-8; 🅿; Z 17948; ● 350
Morea Colliery; SCHUYLKILL; see Morea (RMC Place)
Moreland; MCD-Township; LYCOMING; *226 EI-6; mail Muncy Z 17756; Ⓟ 984; Ⓒ 1,036
Moreland Farms; RMC Place; MONTGOMERY; ▲ Upper Moreland; *227 EO-12; elev. 280ft./85m.; ★ PHIL-; mail Hatboro Z 19040; ● 600
Moreland Manor; RMC Place; MONTGOMERY; ▲ Upper Moreland; *227 EO-12; elev. 250ft./76m.; ★ PHIL-; mail Hatboro Z 19040; ● 1,100
Morewood; RMC Place; MONTGOMERY; ▲ Upper Moreland; *227 EO-12; ★ PHIL-; mail Hatboro Z 19040; ● 300
Morgan; RMC Place; ALLEGHENY; ▲ South Fayette; 225 WN-3; 🅿; ★ PGH; Z 15064; ● 800
Morgan; RMC Place; FAYETTE; ▲ North Union; *225 WP-5; ★ UNTN; mail Lemont Furnace Z 15456; ● 175
Morgan; RMC Place; FAYETTE; ▲ Upper Tyrone; *225 WP-5; mail Connellsville Z 15425; rural
Morgan; MCD-Township; GREENE; *225 WP-3; mail Jefferson Z 15344; Ⓟ 2,887; Ⓒ 2,600; Ⓡ 3,070
Morgan Hill; RMC Place; ALLEGHENY; ▲ South Fayette; *225 WN-3; ★ PGH; mail Cuddy Z 15031
Morgans Hill; RMC Place; NORTHAMPTON; ▲ Williams; *227 EL-12; ★ ALL-; mail Easton Z 18042; ● 400
Morgantown; RMC Place; BERKS; ▲ Caernarvon; 227 EO-9; 🅿; Z 19543; ● 700
Morningside; RMC Place; ALLEGHENY; *225 WM-4; ★ PGH; mail Pittsburgh Z 15206; pop. incl. with Pittsburgh (Inc. Place)
Morrellville; RMC Place; CAMBRIA; *225 WN-8; ★ JNST; mail Johnstown Z 15906; pop. incl. with Johnstown (Inc. Place)
Morris; MCD-Township; CLEARFIELD; *224 WJ-12; mail Morrisdale Z 16858; Ⓟ 2,680; Ⓒ 3,063
Morris; MCD-Township; GREENE; *225 WP-2; mail Sycamore Z 15364; Ⓟ 898; Ⓒ 1,040
Morris; MCD-Township; HUNTINGDON; *225 WM-12; mail Alexandria Z 16611; Ⓟ 415; Ⓒ 416
Morris; RMC Place; TIOGA; ▲ Morris; 226 EG-2; 🅿; Z 16938; ● 250
Morris; MCD-Township; TIOGA; *226 EG-3; 🅿; Z 16938; Ⓟ 675; Ⓒ 646
Morris; MCD-Township; WASHINGTON; *225 WP-2; mail Prosperity Z 15329; Ⓟ 1,145; Ⓒ 1,272
Morris Crossroads; RMC Place; FAYETTE; ▲ Springfield; *225 WQ-4; ★ MORG; mail Lake Lynn Z 15451; rural
Morrisdale; RMC Place; CLEARFIELD; ▲ Morris; 224 WJ-12; elev. 1,643ft./501m.; 🅿; Z 16858; ● 600
Morris Run; RMC Place; TIOGA; ▲ Hamilton; 226 EF-4; 🅿; Z 16939; ● 400
Morrisville; Inc. Place; BUCKS; 227 EO-14; elev. 20ft./6m.; 🅿; ★ PHIL-; Z 19067; Ⓟ 9,765; Ⓒ 10,023
Morrisville; CDP; GREENE; ▲ Franklin; 225 WP-3; mail Waynesburg Z 15370; Ⓟ 1,365; Ⓒ 1,443
Morrows Corner; RMC Place; ARMSTRONG; ▲ Washington; *225 WK-6; elev. 1,145ft./349m.; mail Adrian Z 16210; ● 120
Morstein; RMC Place; CHESTER; ▲ West Whiteland; 227 EP-10; ★ PHIL-; mail West Chester Z 19380; ● 200
Morton; Inc. Place; DELAWARE; 228 F-1; elev. 130ft./40m.; 🅿; ★ PHIL-; Z 19070; Ⓟ 2,851; Ⓒ 2,715
Mortonville; RMC Place; CHESTER; ▲ Newlin, East Fallowfield; *227 EP-9; ★ PHIL-; mail Coatesville Z 19320; ● 300
Morwood; RMC Place; MONTGOMERY; ▲ Franconia; *227 EN-11; ★ PHIL-; mail Telford Z 18969; ● 90
Morysville; RMC Place; BERKS; ▲ Colebrookdale; *227 EN-10; mail Boyertown Z 19512; ● 130
Moscow; Inc. Place; LACKAWANNA; 226 EH-10; elev. 1,600ft./488m.; 🅿; ★ SCR-; Z 18444; Ⓟ 1,527; Ⓒ 1,883
Moselem; RMC Place; BERKS; ▲ Richmond; 227 EM-9; mail Hamburg Z 19526; ● 150
Moselem Springs; RMC Place; BERKS; ▲ Richmond; 227 EM-9; elev. 421ft./128m.; mail Fleetwood Z 19522; ● 70
Mosgrove; RMC Place; ARMSTRONG; ▲ Rayburn; *225 WK-6; ★ PGH; mail Templeton Z 16259
Moshannon; RMC Place; CAMBRIA; ▲ Washington; *225 WN-10; mail Lilly Z 15938; rural
Moshannon; RMC Place; CENTRE; ▲ Snow Shoe; 224 WJ-13; 🅿; Z 16859; ● 350
Mosherville; RMC Place; BRADFORD; ▲ Wells; 226 ED-4; mail Gillett Z 16925, Millerton Z 16936; ● 200
Mosiertown; RMC Place; CRAWFORD; ▲ Cussewago; 224 WE-3; mail Saegertown Z 16433; ● 35
Mosserville; RMC Place; LEHIGH; ▲ Lynn; *227 EL-9; elev. 556ft./169m.; ★ ALL-; mail New Tripoli Z 18066; rural
Mostoller; RMC Place; SOMERSET; ▲ Quemahoning; 225 WP-8; mail Stoystown Z 15563; ● 30
Mottarns Mill; RMC Place; INDIANA; ▲ East Mahoning; *225 WK-8; elev. 1,212ft./369m.; mail Rochester Mills Z 15771; rural
Moudy Hill; RMC Place; CAMBRIA; ▲ Portage; *225 WN-9; ★ JNST; mail Portage Z 15946; ● 225
Moulstown; RMC Place; YORK; ▲ Heidelberg; *227 EQ-4; mail Hanover Z 17331; ● 50
Mount Aetna; RMC Place; BERKS; ▲ Tulpehocken; 227 EM-7; elev. 614ft./187m.; 🅿; Z 19544; ● 350
Mountaindale; RMC Place; CAMBRIA; ▲ Reade; *225 WL-11; mail Fallentimber Z 16639; rural
Mountain Dale; RMC Place; DAUPHIN; ▲ Susquehanna; *227 EN-4; ★ HRBG; mail Harrisburg Z 17110; ● 400
Mountain Grove; RMC Place; LUZERNE; ▲ Black Creek; *226 EJ-7; ★ HAZ; mail Bloomsburg Z 17815; ● 100
Mountainhome; CDP; MONROE; ▲ Barrett; 226 EI-12; 🅿; Z 18342; Ⓟ 1,042; summer pop. 3,500; Ⓒ 1,169
Mountain Lake; RMC Place; BRADFORD; ▲ Burlington; *226 EF-6; mail Towanda Z 18848; ● 100
Mountain Top; RMC Place; LANCASTER; ▲ Salisbury; *227 EO-9; elev. 914ft./279m.; ★ LANC; mail Narvon Z 17555; rural
Mountain Top; CDP; LUZERNE; ▲ Fairview; 226 EI-9; 🅿; ★ SCR-; Z 18707; Ⓒ 15,269
Mountain Valley Lake (Beury Lake); RMC Place; SCHUYLKILL; ▲ Barry; *227 EL-7; mail Ashland Z 17921; ● 90
Mountainville; RMC Place; LEHIGH; *227 EM-11; ★ ALL-; pop. incl. with Allentown (Inc. Place)
Mount Airy; BERKS; see West Monocacy (RMC Place)
Mount Airy; RMC Place; LANCASTER; ▲ Salisbury; 227 EP-8; ★ LANC; mail Stevens Z 17578; ● 150
Mount Airy; RMC Place; PHILADELPHIA; *227 EO-12; ★ PHIL-; mail Philadelphia Z 19119; pop. incl. with Philadelphia (Inc. Place)
Mount Airy Terrace; RMC Place; LUZERNE; ▲ Kingston; *226 EH-8; elev. 1,106ft./337m.; ★ SCR-; mail Shavertown Z 18708
Mount Allen; RMC Place; CUMBERLAND; ▲ Upper Allen; 227 EO-4; ★ HRBG; mail Mechanicsburg Z 17055; ● 2,000
Mount Alton; RMC Place; MCKEAN; ▲ Lafayette; *224 WE-10; elev. 2,072ft./632m.; mail Lewis Run Z 16738
Mount Bethel; RMC Place; NORTHAMPTON; ▲ Upper Mount Bethel; 227 EK-12; 🅿; Z 18343; ● 650
Mount Braddock; RMC Place; FAYETTE; ▲ North Union; 225 WP-5; 🅿; ★ UNTN; Z 15465; ● 650
Mount Carbon; Inc. Place; SCHUYLKILL; 227 EL-7; elev. 600ft./183m.; ★ PTSVL; mail Pottsville Z 17901; Ⓟ 132; Ⓒ 87
Mount Carmel; Inc. Place; NORTHUMBERLAND; 227 EK-6; elev. 1,100ft./335m.; 🅿; Z 17851; Ⓟ 7,196; Ⓒ 6,390
Mount Carmel; MCD-Township; NORTHUMBERLAND; *227 EK-6; 🅿; Z 17851; does not include the Borough of Mount Carmel; Ⓟ 2,679; Ⓒ 2,701
Mount Chestnut; RMC Place; BUTLER; ▲ Franklin; 225 WK-4; elev. 1,334ft./407m.; ★ BUTL; mail Butler Z 16001; ● 100
Mount Chestnut Springs; RMC Place; BUTLER; ▲ Franklin; *225 WK-4; ★ BUTL; mail Butler Z 16001; ● 150
Mount Cobb; CDP; LACKAWANNA; ▲ Jefferson; 226 EH-10; elev. 1,668ft./508m.; 🅿; ★ SCR-; Z 18436; Ⓟ 2,043; Ⓒ 2,140
Mount Eagle; RMC Place; CENTRE; ▲ Howard; 224 WJ-14; mail Howard Z 16841; ● 80
Mount Etna; RMC Place; BLAIR; ▲ Catharine; *225 WM-12; mail Williamsburg Z 16693; ● 30
Mount Gretna; Inc. Place; LEBANON; 227 EO-6; elev. 660ft./201m.; 🅿 🅷; ★ LEB; Z 17064; Ⓟ 303; Ⓒ 242
Mount Gretna Heights; CDP; LEBANON; ▲ West Cornwall; *227 EO-6; ★ LEB; mail Mount Gretna Z 17064; Ⓒ 360
Mount Holly Springs; Inc. Place; CUMBERLAND; 227 EO-3; elev. 560ft./171m.; 🅿; ★ CARL; Z 17065; Ⓟ 1,925; Ⓒ 1,925
Mount Hope; RMC Place; ADAMS; ▲ Hamiltonban; *227 EQ-2; mail Fairfield Z 17320
Mount Hope; RMC Place; LANCASTER; *227 EO-6; elev. 498ft./152m.; ★ LANC; mail Manheim Z 17545; rural
Mount Independence; RMC Place; FAYETTE; ▲ North Union; *225 WP-5; ★ UNTN; mail Lemont Furnace Z 15456; ● 150
Mount Jackson; RMC Place; LAWRENCE; ▲ North Beaver; 224 WJ-2; ★ YNGS-; mail New Castle Z 16102; ● 300
Mount Jewett; Inc. Place; MCKEAN; 224 WF-10; elev. 2,230ft./680m.; 🅿; Z 16740; Ⓟ 1,029; Ⓒ 1,070
Mount Joy; MCD-Township; ADAMS; *227 EQ-3; mail Littlestown Z 17340; Ⓟ 2,848; Ⓒ 3,232
Mount Joy; RMC Place; CLEARFIELD; ▲ Lawrence; *224 WJ-11; mail Clearfield Z 16830; rural
Mount Joy; Inc. Place; LANCASTER; 227 EO-6; elev. 380ft./116m.; 🅿; ★ LANC; Z 17552; Ⓟ 6,398; Ⓒ 6,765
Mount Joy; MCD-Township; LANCASTER; *227 EO-6; 🅿; Z 17552 & mail Elizabethtown Z 17022; does not include the Borough of Mount Joy; Ⓟ 6,227; Ⓒ 7,944
Mount Joy; RMC Place; WESTMORELAND; ▲ Mount Pleasant; *225 WO-6; mail Mount Pleasant Z 15666; ● 100
Mount Laffee; RMC Place; SCHUYLKILL; ▲ New Castle; *227 EL-7; ★ PTSVL; mail Pottsville Z 17901; ● 50
Mount Laurel; RMC Place; LUZERNE; ▲ Hazle; *226 EJ-8; ★ HAZ; mail Hazleton Z 18201; ● 100
Mount Lebanon; CDP; ALLEGHENY; ▲ Mount Lebanon; 228 L-4; elev. 1,054ft./321m.; 🅿; ★ PGH; Z 15228; Ⓟ 33,362; Ⓒ 33,017; ◆ 31,147
Mount Lebanon; MCD-Township; ALLEGHENY; *225 WN-3; 🅿; ★ PGH; Z 15228; Ⓟ 33,362; Ⓒ 33,017; ◆ 31,147
Mount Misery; RMC Place; ADAMS; ▲ Oxford; *227 EQ-4; ★ HANV; mail New Oxford Z 17350; ● 100
Mount Morris; RMC Place; GREENE; ▲ Perry; 225 WQ-3; elev. 901ft./275m.; 🅿; Z 15349; ● 1,300
Mount Nebo; RMC Place; ALLEGHENY; ▲ Ohio; 228 H-4; ★ PGH; mail Sewickley Z 15143; ● 1,500
Mount Nebo; RMC Place; LANCASTER; ▲ Martic; 227 EQ-7; elev. 700ft./213m.; ★ LANC; mail Pequea Z 17565; ● 300
Mount Nebo; RMC Place; WESTMORELAND; ▲ East Huntingdon; *225 WO-5; mail Scottdale Z 15683; ● 100
Mount Oliver; Inc. Place; ALLEGHENY; 228 K-6; elev. 1,100ft./335m.; 🅿; ★ PGH; Z 15210; Ⓟ 4,160; Ⓒ 3,970
Mount Patrick; RMC Place; PERRY; ▲ Buffalo; *227 EM-4; mail Liverpool Z 17045; rural
Mount Penn; Inc. Place; BERKS; 227 EN-9; elev. 480ft./146m.; 🅿; ★ READ; Z 19606; Ⓟ 2,883; Ⓒ 3,016
Mount Pleasant; RMC Place; ADAMS; ▲ Conewago; 227 EQ-4; ★ HANV; mail Hanover Z 17331; ● 65
Mount Pleasant; MCD-Township; ADAMS; *227 EQ-3; ★ HANV; mail Gettysburg Z 17325; Ⓟ 4,076; Ⓒ 4,420
Mount Pleasant (Obold); RMC Place; BERKS; ▲ Penn; 227 EN-8; ★ READ; mail Bernville Z 19506; ● 200
Mount Pleasant; MCD-Township; COLUMBIA; *226 EJ-6; mail Bloomsburg Z 17815; Ⓟ 1,383; Ⓒ 1,459
Mount Pleasant; RMC Place; JUNIATA; 227 EM-2; mail Mifflintown Z 17059; ● 100
Mount Pleasant; RMC Place; LEBANON; ▲ South Annville; *227 EN-6; ★ LEB; mail Lebanon Z 17042; ● 300
Mount Pleasant; RMC Place; MIFFLIN; ▲ Armagh; *227 EL-1; mail Milroy Z 17063; ● 180
Mount Pleasant; RMC Place; NORTHAMPTON; ▲ Lower Mount Bethel; *227 EK-12; ★ ALL-; mail Bangor Z 18013; rural
Mount Pleasant; RMC Place; NORTHUMBERLAND; ▲ Upper Augusta; *227 EK-5; mail Sunbury Z 17801; ● 65
Mount Pleasant; RMC Place; PERRY; ▲ Jackson; *227 EN-1; mail Blain Z 17006; rural
Mount Pleasant; RMC Place; SCHUYLKILL; ▲ Foster; *227 EL-7; mail Pottsville Z 17901; ● 30
Mount Pleasant; RMC Place; TIOGA; ▲ Morris; *226 EG-2; mail Morris Z 16938; rural
Mount Pleasant; MCD-Township; WASHINGTON; *225 WN-2; ★ PGH; mail Hickory Z 15340; Ⓟ 3,555; Ⓒ 3,422
Mount Pleasant; MCD-Township; WAYNE; *226 EF-11; mail Waymart Z 18472; Ⓟ 1,271; Ⓒ 1,345
Mount Pleasant; Inc. Place; WESTMORELAND; 225 WO-6; elev. 1,223ft./373m.; 🅿 🅷; Z 15666; Ⓟ 4,787; Ⓒ 4,728
Mount Pleasant; MCD-Township; WESTMORELAND; *225 WO-6; 🅿; Z 15666; does not include the Borough of Mount Pleasant; Ⓟ 11,341; Ⓒ 11,153
Mount Pleasant; RMC Place; YORK; ▲ Monaghan; *227 EO-4; ★ HRBG; mail Dillsburg Z 17019; ● 100
Mount Pleasant Mills (Fremont); CDP; SNYDER; ▲ Perry; 227 EL-4; 🅿; Z 17853; Ⓒ 342
Mount Pocono; Inc. Place; MONROE; 226 EI-11; elev. 1,840ft./561m.; 🅿; Z 18344; Ⓟ 1,795; Ⓒ 2,742
Mountrock; RMC Place; CUMBERLAND; ▲ West Pennsboro; *227 EO-2; ★ CARL; mail Carlisle Z 17013; ● 75
Mount Rock; RMC Place; FRANKLIN; ▲ Southampton; *227 EP-1; mail Shippensburg Z 17257; ● 300
Mount Royal; RMC Place; YORK; ▲ Dover; 227 EP-4; ★ YORK; mail Dover Z 17315; ● 150
Mount Sterling; RMC Place; FAYETTE; ▲ German; *225 WQ-4; ★ UNTN; mail Masontown Z 15461; ● 20
Mount Tabor; RMC Place; ADAMS; ▲ Menallen; *227 EP-3; mail Gardners Z 17324; ● 90
Mount Troy; RMC Place; ALLEGHENY; ▲ Reserve; *225 WM-4; ★ PGH; mail Pittsburgh Z 15212
Mount Union; RMC Place; FRANKLIN; ▲ Greene; 227 EQ-2; mail Fayetteville Z 17222; ● 100
Mount Union; Inc. Place; HUNTINGDON; 225 WN-13; elev. 626ft./191m.; 🅿; Z 17066, Z 17260; Ⓟ 2,878; Ⓒ 2,504
Mount Vernon; RMC Place; ALLEGHENY; ▲ Elizabeth; 228 N-9; ★ PGH; mail Mckeesport Z 15135; ● 2,200
Mount Vernon; RMC Place; CHESTER; ▲ Lower Oxford; *227 EQ-8; mail Oxford Z 19363
Mount Vernon; RMC Place; LANCASTER; ▲ Salisbury; mail Gap Z 17527; rural
Mount Vernon; RMC Place; WESTMORELAND; ▲ Hempfield; *225 WN-6; elev. 1,200ft./366m.; ★ PGH; mail Greensburg Z 15601; pop. incl. with New Kensington (Inc. Place)
Mountville; Inc. Place; LANCASTER; 227 EP-6; elev. 440ft./134m.; 🅿; ★ LANC; Z 17554; Ⓟ 1,977; Ⓒ 2,444
Mount Washington; RMC Place; ALLEGHENY; *225 WM-3; 🅿; ★ PGH; Z 15211; pop. incl. with Pittsburgh (Inc. Place)
Mount Wilson; RMC Place; LEBANON; ▲ South Londonderry, South Annville; 227 EN-6; ★ LEB; mail Lebanon Z 17042; ● 200
Mount Wolf; Inc. Place; YORK; 227 EP-5; elev. 420ft./128m.; 🅿; ★ YORK; Z 17347; Ⓟ 1,365; Ⓒ 1,373
Mount Zion; RMC Place; CUMBERLAND; ▲ Hampden; *227 EO-3; ★ CARL; mail Carlisle Z 17013; ● 100
Mount Zion; RMC Place; CUMBERLAND; ▲ South Middleton; 227 ES-1; ★ HRBG; mail Mechanicsburg Z 17055; ● 100
Mount Zion; RMC Place; LEBANON; ▲ Bethel; 227 EN-7; elev. 539ft./164m.; ★ LEB; mail Lebanon Z 17046; ● 350
Mount Zion; RMC Place; LUZERNE; ▲ Exeter; *226 EH-9; ★ SCR-; mail Pittston Z 18643
Mount Zion; RMC Place; MONROE; ▲ Stroud; *226 EJ-12; mail East Stroudsburg Z 18301, Stroudsburg Z 18360; rural
Mount Zion; RMC Place; YORK; ▲ Springettsbury; *227 EP-5; elev. 761ft./232m.; ★ YORK; mail York Z 17402; rural
Moween; RMC Place; WESTMORELAND; ▲ Loyalhanna; *225 WM-6; ★ PGH; mail Saltsburg Z 15681; ● 170
Mowersville; RMC Place; FRANKLIN; ▲ Lurgan; 227 EO-1; mail Shippensburg Z 17257; ● 40
Mowry; RMC Place; SCHUYLKILL; ▲ Eldred, Barry; 227 EK-6; elev. 1,005ft./306m.; ★ PTSVL; mail Ashland Z 17921; ● 175
Moxham; RMC Place; CAMBRIA; *225 WN-8; ★ JNST; mail Johnstown Z 15902; pop. incl. with Johnstown (Inc. Place)
Moyer; RMC Place; FAYETTE; ▲ Bullskin; *225 WP-5; mail Connellsville Z 15425; ● 30
Moylan; RMC Place; DELAWARE; ▲ Nether Providence; *227 EP-11; 🅿; ★ PHIL-; Z 19065
Mozart; RMC Place; BUCKS; ▲ Buckingham; *227 EN-13; ★ PHIL-; mail Furlong Z 18925; ● 50
Muddy Creek; MCD-Township; BUTLER; *224 WJ-3; ★ PGH; mail Portersville Z 16051; Ⓟ 2,139; Ⓒ 2,267
Muddy Creek Forks; RMC Place; YORK; ▲ Lower Chanceford; 227 EQ-6; mail Airville Z 17302; ● 20
Muff (Snyderville); RMC Place; ARMSTRONG; ▲ Wayne; *225 WK-7; mail Dayton Z 16222; ● 40
Muhlenberg; MCD-Township; BERKS; *227 EN-9; ★ READ; mail Temple Z 19560; Ⓟ 12,636; Ⓒ 16,305
Muhlenberg; RMC Place; LUZERNE; ▲ Union, Hunlock; 226 EI-8; ★ SCR-; mail Hunlock Creek Z 18621; ● 200
Muhlenberg Park; RMC Place; BERKS; ▲ Muhlenberg; 227 ES-12; ★ READ; mail Reading Z 19605; ● 1,300
Muir; RMC Place; SCHUYLKILL; ▲ Porter; 227 EL-6; 🅿; Z 17957; ● 450
Mullertown; RMC Place; YORK; ▲ Penn; ★ HANV; mail Hanover Z 17331; ● 250
Mumbauersville; RMC Place; BUCKS; ▲ Milford; *227 EM-11; ★ PHIL-; mail Pennsburg Z 18073; rural
Mummasburg; RMC Place; ADAMS; ▲ Franklin; 227 EQ-2; mail Gettysburg Z 17325; ● 200
Muncy; Inc. Place; LYCOMING; 226 EI-5; elev. 519ft./158m.; 🅿; ★ WMSPT; Z 17756; Ⓟ 2,702; Ⓒ 2,663
Muncy; MCD-Township; LYCOMING; *226 EI-5; 🅿; ★ WMSPT; Z 17756; not adjacent to the Borough of Muncy; Ⓟ 1,036; Ⓒ 1,059
Muncy Creek; MCD-Township; LYCOMING; *226 EI-5; ★ WMSPT; mail Muncy Z 17756; Ⓟ 3,401; Ⓒ 3,487
Muncy Valley; RMC Place; SULLIVAN; ▲ Shrewsbury; 226 EH-6; elev. 865ft./264m.; 🅿; Z 17758; ● 270
Munderf; RMC Place; JEFFERSON; ▲ Polk; 224 WH-8; mail Brookville Z 15825; ● 30
Mundys Corner; RMC Place; CAMBRIA; ▲ Jackson; 225 WM-9; ★ JNST; mail Johnstown Z 15909; ● 400
Munhall; Inc. Place; ALLEGHENY; 225 WM-4; elev. 1,000ft./305m.; 🅿; ★ PGH; Z 15120; Ⓟ 13,158; Ⓒ 12,264
Municipality of Monroeville; ALLEGHENY; see Monroeville (Inc. Place)
Municipality of Murrysville; WESTMORELAND; see Murrysville (Inc. Place)
Munson; RMC Place; CLEARFIELD; ▲ Morris; 224 WJ-12; 🅿; Z 16860; ● 275
Munster; RMC Place; CAMBRIA; ▲ Munster; 225 WM-10; mail Ebensburg Z 15931, Lilly Z 15938, Loretto Z 15940; ● 300
Munster; MCD-Township; CAMBRIA; *225 WM-10; mail Ebensburg Z 15931, Lilly Z 15938; Ⓟ 688; Ⓒ 675
Murdock; RMC Place; SOMERSET; ▲ Milford, Black; *225 WP-8; mail Somerset Z 15501; ● 50
Murdocksville; RMC Place; BEAVER, WASHINGTON; ▲ Hanover, Independence; 225 WM-2; ● 100
Murraysville; RMC Place; WESTMORELAND; ★ PGH; pop. incl. with Murrysville (Inc. Place)
Murrell; RMC Place; LANCASTER; ▲ Ephrata; 227 EO-8; ★ LANC; mail Ephrata Z 17522
Murrinsville; RMC Place; BUTLER; ▲ Marion; *224 WI-4; mail Boyers Z 16020; rural
Murry Hill; RMC Place; WASHINGTON; ▲ North Strabane; *225 WN-3; ★ PGH; mail Canonsburg Z 15317; ● 90
Murrysville (Municipality of Murrysville); Inc. Place; WESTMORELAND; 225 WM-5; elev. 900ft./274m.; 🅿; ★ PGH; Z 15668; Ⓟ 17,240; Ⓒ 18,872
Muse; RMC Place; WASHINGTON; ▲ Cecil; 225 WN-3; 🅿; ★ PGH; Z 15350; ● 1,000
Mustard; RMC Place; ALLEGHENY; ▲ Elizabeth; *225 WN-4; ★ PGH; mail Elizabeth Z 15037; ● 100
Mutual; RMC Place; WESTMORELAND; ▲ Unity; *225 WN-6; ★ LTROB; mail Greensburg Z 15601; ● 100
Myersburg; RMC Place; BRADFORD; ▲ Wysox; *226 EE-6; mail Wysox Z 18854
Myerstown; RMC Place; CUMBERLAND; ▲ Dickinson; *227 EP-3; ★ CARL; mail Gardners Z 17324; rural
Myerstown; Inc. Place; LEBANON; 227 EN-7; elev. 481ft./147m.; 🅿; ★ LEB; Z 17067; Ⓟ 3,236; Ⓒ 3,171
Mylo Park; RMC Place; CAMBRIA; ▲ Cambria; *225 WM-9; mail Ebensburg Z 15931; ● 400
Myobeach; RMC Place; WYOMING; ▲ Meshoppen; 226 EF-8; mail Meshoppen Z 18630; ● 65
Myoma; RMC Place; BUTLER; ▲ Adams; 225 WL-3; ★ PGH; mail Mars Z 16046; ● 100
Myrtle; RMC Place; MCKEAN; ▲ Ceres; *224 WD-12; elev. 1,462ft./446m.; mail Shinglehouse Z 16748
Mystic Park; RMC Place; CRAWFORD; ▲ Troy; *224 WF-5; elev. 1,302ft./397m.; mail Centerville Z 16404; rural

N

Naces Corner; RMC Place; BUCKS; ▲ Hilltown; *227 EN-12; elev. 640ft./195m.; ★ PHIL-; mail Hilltown Z 18927; rural
Naceville; RMC Place; BUCKS, MONTGOMERY; ▲ Salford, West Rockhill; *227 EN-11; ★ PHIL-; mail Sellersville Z 18960, Telford Z 18969; ● 100
Nadine; RMC Place; ALLEGHENY; ▲ Penn Hills; *225 WM-4; elev. 1,200ft./366m.; ★ PGH; mail Verona Z 15147
Naginey; RMC Place; MIFFLIN; ▲ Armagh; 227 EL-1; mail Milroy Z 17063; ● 120
Nansen; RMC Place; ELK; ▲ Highland; *224 WG-9; mail Kane Z 16735; rural
Nanticoke; Inc. Place; LUZERNE; 226 EI-8; elev. 640ft./195m.; 🅿 🅷; ★ SCR-; Z 18634; Ⓟ 12,267; Ⓒ 10,955
Nantmeal Village; RMC Place; CHESTER; ▲ East Nantmeal; 227 EO-10; ★ PHIL-; mail Glenmoore Z 19343; ● 250
Nanty Glo; Inc. Place; CAMBRIA; 225 WM-9; elev. 1,711ft./522m.; 🅿; ★ JNST; Z 15943; Ⓟ 3,190; Ⓒ 3,054
Naomi; BERKS; see Birdsboro (Inc. Place)
Naomi; RMC Place; FAYETTE; ▲ Washington; *225 WO-4; ★ PGH; mail Fayette City Z 15438; ● 90
Naomi Pines; MONROE; see Pocono Pines (CDP)
Napier; MCD-Township; BEDFORD; *225 WP-10; mail Schellsburg Z 15559; Ⓟ 2,054; Ⓒ 2,145
Napierville; RMC Place; LANCASTER; ▲ East Cocalico; *227 EO-8; mail Ephrata Z 17522; ● 50
Narberth; Inc. Place; MONTGOMERY; 227 EP-12; elev. 285ft./87m.; 🅿; ★ PHIL-; Z 19072; Ⓟ 4,278; Ⓒ 4,233
Narbrook Park; RMC Place; MONTGOMERY; ★ PHIL-; mail Narberth Z 19072; pop. incl. with Narberth (Inc. Place)
Narrows Creek; RMC Place; CLEARFIELD; ▲ Sandy; *224 WI-9; mail Du Bois Z 15801; rural
Narrowsville; RMC Place; BUCKS; ▲ Nockamixon; *227 EL-12; elev. 160ft./49m.; ★ PHIL-; mail Upper Black Eddy Z 18972; rural
Narvon; RMC Place; LANCASTER; ▲ Caernarvon; *227 EO-8; elev. 774ft./236m.; 🅿; Z 17555; ● 950
Nashua; RMC Place; LAWRENCE; ▲ Pulaski; *224 WI-2; elev. 809ft./247m.; ★ YNGS-; mail New Castle Z 16101; rural
Nashville; RMC Place; INDIANA; ▲ Grant; *225 WK-8; mail Rochester Mills Z 15771; rural
Nashville; RMC Place; YORK; ▲ Jackson; 227 EQ-4; ★ YORK; mail Spring Grove Z 17362; ● 200
Nassau Village; RMC Place; DELAWARE; ▲ Ridley; *227 EQ-11; elev. 30ft./9m.; ★ PHIL-; mail Ridley Park Z 19078; ● 1,500
Natalie; RMC Place; NORTHUMBERLAND; ▲ Mount Carmel; *227 EK-6; mail Mount Carmel Z 17851; ● 230
Natrona; RMC Place; ALLEGHENY; ▲ Harrison; *225 WL-5; 🅿; ★ PGH; Z 15065
Natrona Heights; RMC Place; ALLEGHENY; ▲ Harrison; 225 WL-5; ★ PGH; ● 2,800
Nauvoo; RMC Place; TIOGA; ▲ Morris, Liberty; 226 EG-3; mail Morris Z 16938; ● 40
Nazareth; Inc. Place; NORTHAMPTON; 227 EL-11; elev. 540ft./165m.; 🅿; ★ ALL-; Z 18064; Ⓟ 5,713; Ⓒ 6,023
Nealmont; RMC Place; BLAIR; ▲ Snyder; *225 WL-12; ★ ALT; mail Tyrone Z 16686; ● 75
Neason Hill; RMC Place; CRAWFORD; ▲ West Mead; *224 WF-3; mail Meadville Z 16335; pop. incl. with Meadville (Inc. Place)
Neath; RMC Place; BRADFORD; ▲ Pike; *226 EE-8; elev. 1,091ft./333m.; mail Le Raysville Z 18829; rural
Nebo; RMC Place; FAYETTE; ▲ Saltlick; *225 WP-6; elev. 1,460ft./445m.; mail Champion Z 15622; rural
Nectarine; RMC Place; VENANGO; ▲ Irwin; *224 WI-4; mail Harrisville Z 16038
Ned; RMC Place; GREENE; ▲ Springhill; *225 WQ-1; mail New Freeport Z 15352; rural
Needful; RMC Place; CLEARFIELD; ▲ Bradford; *224 WJ-11; mail Woodland Z 16881; rural
Needmore; RMC Place; FULTON; ▲ Belfast; 225 WQ-12; 🅿; Z 17238 & mail Big Cove Tannery Z 17212; ● 300
Neelyton; RMC Place; HUNTINGDON; ▲ Dublin; 225 WO-13; 🅿; Z 17239; ● 80
Neffs; RMC Place; LEHIGH; ▲ North Whitehall; 227 EL-10; 🅿; ★ ALL-; Z 18065; ● 650
Neffs Mills; RMC Place; HUNTINGDON; ▲ West; *225 WL-13; mail Petersburg Z 16669; ● 60
Neffsville; RMC Place; LANCASTER; ▲ Manheim; 227 EO-7; 🅿; ★ LANC; Z 17601 & mail Lancaster Z 17606; ● 1,000
Neiffer; RMC Place; MONTGOMERY; ▲ Limerick; *227 EN-10; ★ PHIL-; mail Schwenksville Z 19473; ● 250
Neiltown; RMC Place; FOREST; ▲ Harmony; 224 WF-6; mail Pleasantville Z 16341; ● 25
Neiman; RMC Place; YORK; ▲ Codorus; *227 EQ-5; ★ BAL; mail Glen Rock Z 17327; ● 90
Nellie; RMC Place; FAYETTE; ▲ Franklin, Dunbar; *225 WP-5; ★ UNTN; mail Vanderbilt Z 15486; rural
Nelson; RMC Place; TIOGA; ▲ Nelson; 226 ED-3; 🅿; Z 16940; ● 300
Nelson; MCD-Township; TIOGA; *226 ED-3; 🅿; Z 16940; Ⓟ 514; Ⓒ 587
Nemacolin; CDP; GREENE; ▲ Cumberland; 225 WQ-4; 🅿; Z 15351; Ⓟ 1,097; Ⓒ 1,034
Nemanie; RMC Place; PIKE; ▲ Palmyra; *226 EG-12; mail Paupack Z 18451
Nescopeck; Inc. Place; LUZERNE; 226 EJ-7; elev. 520ft./158m.; 🅿; Z 18635; Ⓟ 1,651; Ⓒ 1,528
Nescopeck; MCD-Township; LUZERNE; *226 EJ-7; 🅿; Z 18635; does not include the Borough of Nescopeck; Ⓟ 1,072; Ⓒ 1,096
Neshaminy; RMC Place; BUCKS; ▲ Warrington; *227 EO-12; ★ PHIL-; mail Warrington Z 18976
Neshaminy Falls; RMC Place; BUCKS; ▲ Bensalem; *227 EO-13; ★ PHIL-; mail Langhorne Z 19047
Neshaminy Hills; RMC Place; BUCKS; ▲ Lower Southampton; *227 EO-13; ★ PHIL-; mail Langhorne Z 19047; ● 300
Neshaminy Valley; RMC Place; BUCKS; ▲ Bensalem; *227 EO-13; elev. 100ft./30m.; ★ PHIL-; mail Bensalem Z 19020; ● 6,700
Neshaminy Woods; RMC Place; BUCKS; ▲ Lower Southampton; *227 EO-13; ★ PHIL-; mail Langhorne Z 19047; ● 1,200
Neshannock; MCD-Township; LAWRENCE; *224 WJ-2; 🅿; ★ NWCS; Z 16105; Ⓟ 8,373; Ⓒ 9,216
Neshannock; RMC Place; MERCER; *224 WI-2; ★ SHAR; pop. incl. with Hermitage (Inc. Place)
Neshannock Falls; RMC Place; LAWRENCE; ▲ Wilmington; *224 WI-2; ★ NWCS; mail Volant Z 16156; rural
Nesquehoning; Inc. Place; CARBON; 227 EK-9; elev. 820ft./250m.; 🅿; Z 18240; Ⓟ 3,364; Ⓒ 3,288
Nether Providence; MCD-Township; DELAWARE; *227 EQ-11; ★ PHIL-; mail Chester Z 19013, Media Z 19063, Wallingford Z 19086; Ⓟ 13,229; Ⓒ 13,456
Nether Providence Township; CDP-Census Area Only; DELAWARE; ▲ Nether Providence; *227 EP-11; ★ PHIL-; mail Chester Z 19013, Media Z 19063, Wallingford Z 19086; Ⓟ 13,229; Ⓒ 13,456
Neville; MCD-Township; ALLEGHENY; *225 WM-3; ★ PGH; mail Pittsburgh Z 15225; Ⓟ 1,273; Ⓒ 1,232
Neville Island; ALLEGHENY; see Dixmont (RMC Place)
New Albany; Inc. Place; BRADFORD; 226 EG-6; elev. 1,260ft./384m.; 🅿; Z 18833; Ⓟ 306; Ⓒ 306
New Alexandria; Inc. Place; WESTMORELAND; 225 WN-6; elev. 996ft./304m.; 🅿; ★ PGH; Z 15670; Ⓟ 571; Ⓒ 595
New Athens; RMC Place; CLARION; ▲ Madison; *224 WJ-6; elev. 1,400ft./427m.; mail Rimersburg Z 16248; ● 50
New Baltimore; Inc. Place; SOMERSET; 225 WP-9; elev. 1,500ft./457m.; 🅿; Z 15553; Ⓟ 162; Ⓒ 168
New Baltimore; RMC Place; YORK; ★ HANV; mail Hanover Z 17331; pop. incl. with Hanover (Inc. Place)
New Beaver; Inc. Place; LAWRENCE; 225 WK-2; elev. 1,000ft./305m.; ★ PGH; mail New Galilee Z 16141; Ⓟ 1,736; Ⓒ 1,677
New Bedford; RMC Place; LAWRENCE; ▲ Pulaski; 224 WI-1; 🅿; ★ YNGS-; Z 16140; ● 800
New Berlin; Inc. Place; UNION; 227 EK-4; elev. 540ft./165m.; 🅿; Z 17855; Ⓟ 892; Ⓒ 838
New Berlinville; RMC Place; BERKS; ▲ Colebrookdale; 227 EN-10; 🅿; Z 19545; ● 800
Newberry; RMC Place; LYCOMING; *226 EI-4; elev. 533ft./162m.; ★ WMSPT; mail Williamsport Z 17701; pop. incl. with Williamsport (Inc. Place)
Newberry; MCD-Township; YORK; *227 EO-5; mail York Haven Z 17370; Ⓟ 12,003; Ⓒ 14,332
Newberrytown; RMC Place; YORK; ▲ Newberry; 227 EO-5; elev. 577ft./176m.; mail Etters Z 17319; ● 150
New Bethlehem; Inc. Place; CLARION; 224 WJ-7; elev. 1,100ft./335m.; 🅿; Z 16242; Ⓟ 1,151; Ⓒ 1,057
New Bloomfield (Bloomfield); Inc. Place; ⊡ PERRY; 227 EN-3; elev. 700ft./213m.; 🅿; ★ HRBG; Z 17068; Ⓟ 1,092; Ⓒ 1,077
Newboro; RMC Place; FAYETTE; ▲ Menallen; *225 WP-4; ★ UNTN; mail Fairbank Z 15435; ● 200
New Boston; RMC Place; SCHUYLKILL; ▲ Mahanoy; 227 EK-7; 🅿; Z 17948; ● 230
New Boston-Morea; CDP-Census Area Only; SCHUYLKILL; *227 EK-7; Ⓒ 441
New Bridgeville; RMC Place; YORK; ▲ Chanceford; 227 EP-6; elev. 700ft./213m.; ★ YORK; mail Red Lion Z 17356; ● 320
New Brighton; Inc. Place; BEAVER; 225 WK-2; elev. 800ft./244m.; 🅿; ★ PGH; Z 15066; Ⓟ 6,854; Ⓒ 6,641
New Britain; Inc. Place; BUCKS; 227 EN-12; elev. 300ft./91m.; 🅿; ★ PHIL-; Z 18901; Ⓟ 2,174; Ⓒ 3,125
New Britain; MCD-Township; BUCKS; *227 EN-12; 🅿; ★ PHIL-; Z 18901 & mail Chalfont Z 18914; does not include the Borough of New Britain; Ⓟ 9,099; Ⓒ 10,698
New Buena Vista; RMC Place; BEDFORD; ▲ Juniata; 225 WP-9; mail Manns Choice Z 15550; ● 80
New Buffalo; Inc. Place; PERRY; 227 EM-4; elev. 400ft./122m.; 🅿; ★ HRBG; Z 17069; Ⓟ 145; Ⓒ 123
Newburg; RMC Place; BLAIR; ▲ Logan; 225 WM-11; ★ ALT; mail Altoona Z 16601; ● 350
Newburg (La Jose); Inc. Place; CLEARFIELD; 225 WK-10; elev. 1,320ft./402m.; mail La Jose Z 15753; Ⓟ 312; Ⓒ 81
Newburg; Inc. Place; CUMBERLAND; 227 EO-1; elev. 595ft./181m.; 🅿; Z 17240; Ⓟ 117; Ⓒ 372
Newburg; RMC Place; NORTHAMPTON; ▲ Lower Nazareth; 227 EL-11; ★ ALL-; mail Bethlehem Z 18020; ● 250
Newburg Homes; RMC Place; NORTHAMPTON; ▲ Palmer; *227 EL-12; ★ ALL-; mail Easton Z 18045; ● 550
New Castle; Inc. Place; ⊡ LAWRENCE; 224 WJ-2; elev. 860ft./262m.; 🅿 🅷 ■; ★ NWCS; Z 16101-03, Z 16105, Z 16107-08; Ⓟ 28,334; Ⓒ 26,309; ◆ 24,813
New Castle; MCD-Township; SCHUYLKILL; *227 EL-7; ★ PTSVL; mail Saint Clair Z 17970; Ⓟ 567; Ⓒ 395
New Castle Northwest; CDP-Census Area Only; LAWRENCE; ▲ Neshannock; *224 WJ-2; ★ NWCS; mail New Castle Z 16105; Ⓟ 1,515; Ⓒ 1,535
New Castle West; LAWRENCE; see Oakwood (CDP-Census Area Only)
New Centerville; Inc. Place; SOMERSET; 225 WP-7; elev. 2,129ft./649m.; mail Rockwood Z 15557; Ⓟ 211; Ⓒ 193
Newchester; RMC Place; ADAMS; ▲ Straban; 227 EQ-3; mail New Oxford Z 17350; ● 225
New Columbia; RMC Place; UNION; ▲ White Deer; 226 EJ-4; 🅿; Z 17856, Z 17886; ● 435
New Columbus; RMC Place; CARBON; *227 EK-9; mail Nesquehoning Z 18240; pop. incl. with Nesquehoning (Inc. Place)
New Columbus; Inc. Place; LUZERNE; 226 EI-7; elev. 994ft./303m.; mail Stillwater Z 17878; Ⓟ 228; Ⓒ 215
Newcomer; RMC Place; FAYETTE; ▲ Georges; *225 WQ-4; ★ UNTN; mail Uniontown Z 15401
New Cranberry; LUZERNE; see Cranberry (RMC Place)
New Cumberland; Inc. Place; CUMBERLAND; 227 EO-4; elev. 400ft./122m.; 🅿; ★ HRBG; Z 17070; Ⓟ 7,665; Ⓒ 7,349
New Danville; RMC Place; LANCASTER; ▲ Pequea; 227 EP-7; elev. 409ft./125m.; ★ LANC; mail Lancaster Z 17603; ● 500
New Derry; RMC Place; WESTMORELAND; ▲ Derry; 225 WN-7; 🅿; ★ LTROB; Z 15671; ● 800
New Eagle; Inc. Place; WASHINGTON; 225 WO-4; elev. 840ft./256m.; 🅿; ★ PGH; Z 15067; Ⓟ 2,172; Ⓒ 2,262
Newell; Inc. Place; FAYETTE; 225 WO-4; elev. 800ft./244m.; 🅿; ★ PGH; Z 15466; Ⓟ 518; Ⓒ 551
New England; RMC Place; SCHUYLKILL; ▲ Walker; *227 EK-8; elev. 1,066ft./325m.; mail Tamaqua Z 18252; ● 125
New Enterprise; RMC Place; BEDFORD; ▲ South Woodbury; 225 WO-11; 🅿; Z 16664; ● 300
New Era; RMC Place; BRADFORD; ▲ Terry; 226 EF-7; elev. 1,086ft./331m.; mail New Albany Z 18833, Wyalusing Z 18853; ● 35
Newfield; RMC Place; ALLEGHENY; ▲ Penn Hills; *225 WM-4; elev. 1,200ft./366m.; ★ PGH; mail Verona Z 15147
Newfield; RMC Place; POTTER; ▲ Ulysses; *224 WE-13; mail Ulysses Z 16948; rural
New Florence; Inc. Place; WESTMORELAND; 225 WN-8; elev. 1,086ft./331m.; 🅿; ★ JNST; Z 15944; Ⓟ 854; Ⓒ 784
Newfoundland; RMC Place; WAYNE; ▲ Dreher; 226 EH-11; 🅿; Z 18445; ● 650
New Franklin; RMC Place; FRANKLIN; ▲ Guilford; 225 WQ-14; mail Chambersburg Z 17201; ● 275
New Freedom; Inc. Place; YORK; 227 ER-5; elev. 818ft./249m.; 🅿; ★ BAL; Z 17349; Ⓟ 2,920; Ⓒ 3,512
New Freeport; RMC Place; GREENE; ▲ Freeport; 225 WQ-2; elev. 1,070ft./326m.; 🅿; Z 15352; ● 100
New Galena; RMC Place; BUCKS; ▲ New Britain; *227 EN-12; ★ PHIL-; mail Chalfont Z 18914; ● 100
New Galilee; Inc. Place; BEAVER; 225 WK-2; elev. 960ft./293m.; 🅿; ★ PGH; Z 16141; Ⓟ 500; Ⓒ 424
New Garden; RMC Place; CHESTER; ▲ New Garden; 227 EQ-9; ★ PHIL-; mail Avondale Z 19311, Kennett Square Z 19348, Landenberg Z 19350, Toughkenamon Z 19374; ● 300
New Garden; MCD-Township; CHESTER; *227 EQ-9; ★ PHIL-; mail Landenberg Z 19350; Ⓟ 5,430; Ⓒ 9,083
New Geneva; RMC Place; FAYETTE; ▲ Springhill, Nicholson; 225 WQ-4; 🅿; Z 15467; ● 150
New Germantown; RMC Place; PERRY; ▲ Toboyne; 227 EN-1; 🅿; Z 17071; ● 150
New Germany; RMC Place; CAMBRIA; ▲ Croyle; *225 WM-9; ★ JNST; mail Portage Z 15946; rural
New Grass Manor; RMC Place; LUZERNE; ▲ Dallas; *226 EH-8; elev. 1,189ft./362m.; ★ SCR-; mail Dallas Z 18612; ● 760
New Grenada; RMC Place; FULTON; ▲ Wells; 225 WO-12; mail Robertsdale Z 16674; ● 90
New Hamburg; RMC Place; MERCER; ▲ Delaware; 224 WH-2; mail Fredonia Z 16124; ● 75
New Hanover; RMC Place; MONTGOMERY; ▲ New Hanover; 227 EN-10; mail Gilbertsville Z 19525; ● 100
New Hanover; MCD-Township; MONTGOMERY; *227 EN-10; mail Gilbertsville Z 19525; Ⓟ 5,956; Ⓒ 7,369
New Hanover Square; RMC Place; MONTGOMERY; ▲ New Hanover; *227 EN-10; elev. 356ft./109m.; mail Frederick Z 19435; rural
Newhard; RMC Place; LEHIGH; ▲ Washington; *227 EL-10; elev. 725ft./221m.; ★ ALL-; mail Slatington Z 18080; rural
New Hensingerville; LEHIGH; see Hensingerville (RMC Place)
New Holland; Inc. Place; LANCASTER; 227 EO-8; elev. 494ft./151m.; 🅿; ★ LANC; Z 17557; Ⓟ 4,484; Ⓒ 5,092
New Holland; YORK; see Saginaw (RMC Place)
New Hope; Inc. Place; BUCKS; 227 EN-13; elev. 76ft./23m.; 🅿; ★ PHIL-; Z 18938; Ⓟ 1,400; Ⓒ 2,252
New Ireland; RMC Place; ERIE; ▲ LeBoeuf; *224 WE-4; elev. 1,297ft./395m.; ★ ERIE; mail Union City Z 16438
New Jerusalem; RMC Place; BERKS; ▲ Rockland; 227 EM-9; elev. 896ft./273m.; ★ READ; mail Fleetwood Z 19522; ● 100
New Kensington; Inc. Place; WESTMORELAND; 225 WM-5; elev. 780ft./238m.; 🅿 🅷 ■; ★ PGH; Z 15068-69; Ⓟ 15,894; Ⓒ 14,701; ◆ 14,088
New Kingston; CUMBERLAND; see New Kingstown (CDP)
New Kingstown (New Kingston); CDP; CUMBERLAND; ▲ Silver Spring; 227 EO-3; 🅿; ★ HRBG; Z 17072; Ⓒ 539
Newkirk; RMC Place; SCHUYLKILL; ▲ Schuylkill; *227 EK-8; ★ PTSVL; mail Tamaqua Z 18252
New Lebanon; Inc. Place; MERCER; 224 WG-3; elev. 1,400ft./427m.; mail Sandy Lake Z 16145; Ⓟ 209; Ⓒ 205
New Lexington; RMC Place; SOMERSET; ▲ Middlecreek; 225 WP-7; elev. 2,069ft./631m.; mail Rockwood Z 15557; ● 50
Newlin; MCD-Township; CHESTER; *227 EP-10; ★ PHIL-; mail West Chester Z 19380; Ⓟ 1,092; Ⓒ 1,150
Newlin; RMC Place; COLUMBIA; ▲ Locust; *227 EK-7; mail Catawissa Z 17820; ● 100
New London; RMC Place; CHESTER; ▲ New London; 227 EQ-9; elev. 469ft./143m.; 🅿; ★ PHIL-; Z 19360; ● 350
New London; MCD-Township; CHESTER; *227 EQ-9; 🅿 🅲 2,423; ★ PHIL-; Z 19360 & mail Lincoln University Z 19352; Ⓟ 2,721; Ⓒ 4,583
New London (McGraw Corners); RMC Place; WARREN; ▲ Triumph; *224 WF-6; mail Tidioute Z 16351; rural
Newlonsburg; RMC Place; WESTMORELAND; *225 WM-5; ★ PGH; mail Murrysville Z 15668; pop. incl. with Murrysville (Inc. Place)
New Mahoning; RMC Place; CARBON; ▲ Mahoning; 227 EK-9; mail Lehighton Z 18235; ● 170
Newmanstown; CDP; LEBANON; ▲ Millcreek; 227 EN-7; 🅿; Z 17073; Ⓟ 1,410; Ⓒ 1,536
Newmansville; RMC Place; CLARION; ▲ Washington; 224 WG-6; elev. 1,584ft./483m.; mail Tionesta Z 16353; ● 40
New Market; RMC Place; YORK; ▲ Fairview; *227 EO-4; ★ HRBG; mail New Cumberland Z 17070; ● 200
New Milford; Inc. Place; SUSQUEHANNA; 226 EE-9; elev. 1,115ft./340m.; 🅿; Z 18834; Ⓟ 953; Ⓒ 878
New Milford; MCD-Township; SUSQUEHANNA; *226 EE-9; 🅿; Z 18834; does not include the Borough of New Milford; Ⓟ 1,731; Ⓒ 1,859
New Millport; RMC Place; CLEARFIELD; ▲ Knox, Ferguson; 225 WK-10; 🅿; Z 16861; ● 130
New Mines; RMC Place; SCHUYLKILL; ▲ Reilly; *227 EL-7; mail Branchdale Z 17923
New Morgan; Inc. Place; BERKS; *227 EO-9; Ⓒ 35
New Oxford; Inc. Place; ADAMS; 227 EQ-4; elev. 538ft./164m.; 🅿; ★ HANV; Z 17350; Ⓟ 1,617; Ⓒ 1,696
New Paris; Inc. Place; BEDFORD; 225 WO-10; elev. 1,280ft./390m.; 🅿; Z 15554; Ⓟ 223; Ⓒ 214
New Park; RMC Place; YORK; ▲ Fawn; 227 ER-6; elev. 790ft./241m.; 🅿; ★ BAL; Z 17352; ● 300
New Philadelphia; Inc. Place; SCHUYLKILL; 227 EL-8; elev. 700ft./213m.; 🅿; ★ PTSVL; Z 17959; Ⓟ 1,283; Ⓒ 1,149
Newport; RMC Place; LAWRENCE; *224 WJ-2; ★ PGH; mail Wampum Z 16157; pop. incl. with New Beaver (Inc. Place)
Newport; MCD-Township; LUZERNE; *226 EI-8; ★ SCR-; mail Nanticoke Z 18634; Ⓟ 4,593; Ⓒ 5,006

Entries in **UPPERCASE** are counties.
Entries in **bold** have populations of 2,500 or more.
Names in parentheses are alternate names.
Inc. Place — Incorporated Place
RMC Place — Rand McNally Designated Place
CDP — Census Designated Place
MCD — Minor Civil Division

⊡ County Seat
▲ Minor Civil Division
elev. Elevation
🅿 Post Office
🅷 Hospital
🅲 College
■ Principal Business Center
★ Ranally Metro Area (RMA) Abbreviation
Z Zip Code(s)

Ⓟ Previous Census Population
Ⓡ Revised Census Population
Ⓐ Annexation Population
● Rand McNally Population Estimate
Ⓒ Final Census Population
Ⓢ Special Census Population
◆ Estimated Population

For additional definitions see Glossary, Volume 1, and Introduction, Volume 2.

Newport; Inc. Place; PERRY; **227** EM-3; elev. 460ft./140m.; 🅿; ★ **HRBG**; z 17074; Ⓟ 1,568; Ⓒ 1,506
Newportville; RMC Place; BUCKS; ▲ Bristol; **228** A-9; 🅿; ★ **PHIL-**; z 19056; ● 750
Newportville Terrace; RMC Place; BUCKS; ▲ Bensalem; ***227** EO-13; ★ **PHIL-**; mail Bensalem z 19020; ● 700
New Providence; RMC Place; LANCASTER; ▲ Providence; **227** EP-7; 🅿; ★ **LANC**; z 17560; ● 300
New Richmond; RMC Place; CRAWFORD; ▲ Richmond; ***224** WF-4; mail Guys Mills z 16327
New Ringgold; Inc. Place; SCHUYLKILL; **227** EL-8; elev. 560ft./171m.; 🅿; z 17960; Ⓟ 315; Ⓒ 291
Newry; Inc. Place; BLAIR; **225** WN-11; elev. 1,040ft./317m.; 🅿; ★ **ALT**; z 16665; Ⓟ 288; Ⓒ 245
New Salem (Pierce); RMC Place; ARMSTRONG; ▲ Redbank; ***224** WJ-7; mail Mayport z 16240; ● 75
New Salem; RMC Place; FAYETTE; ▲ Menallen; **225** WP-4; 🅿; ★ **UNTN**; z 15468; ● 850
New Salem (York New Salem); Inc. Place; YORK; **227** EQ-5; elev. 620ft./189m.; ★ **YORK**; mail York New Salem z 17371; Ⓟ 669; Ⓒ 648
New Salem-Buffington; CDP-Census Area Only; FAYETTE; ▲ Menallen, German; ***225** WP-4; ★ **UNTN**; mail New Salem z 15468; Ⓟ 1,169; Ⓒ 808
New Schaefferstown (Tulpehocken); RMC Place; BERKS; ▲ Jefferson; **227** EM-8; mail Bernville z 19506, Rehrersburg z 19550; ● 80
New Sewickley; MCD-Township; BEAVER; ***225** WL-3; ★ **PGH**; mail Rochester z 15074; Ⓟ 6,861; Ⓒ 7,076
New Sheffield; RMC Place; BEAVER; ▲ Hopewell; **225** WL-2; ★ **PGH**; mail Aliquippa z 15001; ● 2,000
Newside; RMC Place; LEHIGH; ▲ Washington, Heidelberg; ***227** EL-10; ★ **ALL-**; mail Slatington z 18080; ● 80
New Smithville; RMC Place; LEHIGH; ▲ Weisenberg; ***227** EM-9; ★ **ALL-**; mail Kutztown z 19530; rural
New Stanton; Inc. Place; WESTMORELAND; **225** WO-5; elev. 980ft./299m.; 🅿; ★ **PGH**; z 15672 & mail Hunker z 15639; Ⓟ 2,081; Ⓒ 1,906
New Street; RMC Place; SCHUYLKILL; ▲ Norwegian; ***227** EL-7; ★ **PTSVL**; mail Pottsville z 17901; ● 80
New Texas; RMC Place; ALLEGHENY; ***225** WM-5; ★ **PGH**; mail Pittsburgh z 15239; pop. incl. with Plum (Inc. Place)
New Texas; RMC Place; LANCASTER; ▲ Fulton; ***227** EQ-8; elev. 369ft./112m.; mail Peach Bottom z 17563; ● 100
Newton; MCD-Township; LACKAWANNA; ***226** EG-9; ★ **SCR-**; mail Clarks Summit z 18411; Ⓟ 2,843; Ⓒ 2,699
Newtonburg; RMC Place; CLEARFIELD; ▲ Bell; ***225** WK-9; elev. 1,844ft./562m.; mail Mahaffey z 15757; rural
Newton Hamilton; Inc. Place; MIFFLIN; **225** WN-13; elev. 600ft./183m.; 🅿; z 17075; Ⓟ 287; Ⓒ 272
Newton Lake; RMC Place; LACKAWANNA; ▲ Greenfield; ***226** EF-10; ★ **SCR-**; mail Carbondale z 18407; summer pop. 600; ● 300
Newtown; RMC Place; ALLEGHENY; ***225** WM-4; ★ **PGH**; pop. incl. with Turtle Creek (Inc. Place)
Newtown; Inc. Place; BUCKS; **227** EO-13; elev. 140ft./43m.; 🅿; ★ **PHIL-**; z 18940; Ⓟ 2,565; Ⓒ 2,312
Newtown; MCD-Township; BUCKS; ***227** EN-13; 🅿; ★ **PHIL-**; z 18940; does not include the Borough of Newtown; Ⓟ 13,685; Ⓒ 18,206
New Town; RMC Place; CENTRE; ▲ Rush; ***225** WK-11; mail Osceola Mills z 16666; ● 200
Newtown; RMC Place; CLEARFIELD; ▲ Decatur; ***225** WK-11; mail West Decatur z 16878; ● 40
Newtown; DELAWARE; see Newtown Square (RMC Place)
Newtown; MCD-Township; DELAWARE; ***227** EP-11; ★ **PHIL-**; mail Newtown Square z 19073; Ⓟ 11,366; Ⓒ 11,700
Newtown; RMC Place; GREENE; ***225** WQ-4; mail Dilliner z 15327; ● 40
Newtown; RMC Place; LANCASTER; ▲ Rapho; ***227** EP-6; ★ **LANC**; mail Columbia z 17512; ● 30
Newtown; RMC Place; LEHIGH; ▲ Upper Macungie; ***227** EM-10; elev. 460ft./140m.; ★ **ALL-**; mail Breinigsville z 18031; ● 30
Newtown; RMC Place; LUZERNE; ▲ Hanover; **226** EB-7; ★ **SCR-**; mail Wilkes Barre z 18706; ● 1,400
Newtown (Zerbe); CDP; SCHUYLKILL; ▲ Reilly; **227** EL-7; mail Tremont z 17981; Ⓒ 244
Newtown Grant (Stoopville); CDP-Census Area Only; BUCKS; ▲ Newtown; ***227** EN-13; elev. 297ft./91m.; ★ **PHIL-**; mail Newtown z 18940; Ⓟ 2,141; Ⓒ 3,887
Newtown Square (Newtown); RMC Place; DELAWARE; ▲ Newtown; **227** EP-11; 🅿; ★ **PHIL-**; z 19073; ● 11,300
New Tripoli; RMC Place; LEHIGH; ▲ Lynn; **227** EL-9; elev. 578ft./176m.; 🅿; ★ **ALL-**; z 18066; ● 300
New Vernon; RMC Place; MERCER; ▲ New Vernon; **224** WG-3; mail Sandy Lake z 16145; ● 25
New Vernon; MCD-Township; MERCER; ***224** WG-3; mail Sandy Lake z 16145; Ⓟ 493; Ⓒ 524
Newville; RMC Place; BUCKS; ▲ New Britain; ***227** EN-12; ★ **PHIL-**; mail Chalfont z 18914; rural
Newville; Inc. Place; CUMBERLAND; **227** EO-2; elev. 560ft./171m.; 🅿; ★ **CARL**; z 17241; Ⓟ 1,349; Ⓒ 1,367
Newville; RMC Place; LANCASTER; ▲ West Donegal; **227** EO-5; mail Elizabethville z 17023; ● 350
New Virginia; RMC Place; MERCER; ***224** WI-2; ★ **SHAR**; mail Sharon z 16146; pop. incl. with Hermitage (Inc. Place)
New Washington; Inc. Place; CLEARFIELD; **225** WK-9; elev. 1,660ft./506m.; mail Mahaffey z 15757; Ⓟ 78; Ⓒ 89
New Wilmington; Inc. Place; LAWRENCE; **224** WI-2; elev. 1,050ft./320m.; 🅿 🅲 1,511; ★ **NWCS**; z 16142, z 16172; Ⓟ 2,706; Ⓒ 2,452
Niagara; RMC Place; WAYNE; ▲ Mount Pleasant; ***226** EF-11; mail Pleasant Mount z 18453; rural
Niantic; RMC Place; MONTGOMERY; ▲ Douglass; **227** EN-10; elev. 493ft./150m.; mail Barto z 19504; ● 100
Nicetown; RMC Place; PHILADELPHIA; ***227** EP-12; ★ **PHIL-**; mail Philadelphia z 19140; pop. incl. with Philadelphia (Inc. Place)
Nichola; RMC Place; ARMSTRONG; ▲ West Franklin; ***225** WK-5; ★ **PGH**; mail Worthington z 16262; rural
Nicholson; MCD-Township; FAYETTE; ***225** WQ-4; mail Masontown z 15461; Ⓟ 1,995; Ⓒ 1,989
Nicholson; Inc. Place; WYOMING; **226** EF-9; elev. 740ft./226m.; 🅿; z 18441, z 18446; Ⓟ 857; Ⓒ 713
Nicholson; MCD-Township; WYOMING; ***226** EF-9; 🅿; z 18441, z 18446; does not include the Borough of Nicholson; Ⓟ 1,287; Ⓒ 1,361
Nickel Mines; RMC Place; LANCASTER; ▲ Bart; ***227** EP-8; elev. 713ft./217m.; mail Paradise z 17562
Nickleville; RMC Place; VENANGO; ▲ Richland; ***224** WH-5; mail Emlenton z 16373
Nicklin; RMC Place; VENANGO; ▲ Frenchcreek; ***224** WH-4; elev. 1,442ft./440m.; ★ **OILC-F**; mail Franklin z 16323; ● 100
Nicktown; RMC Place; CAMBRIA; ▲ Barr; **225** WL-9; elev. 1,971ft./601m.; 🅿; z 15762; ● 200
Nilan; RMC Place; FAYETTE; ▲ Springhill; ***225** WQ-4; ★ **MORG**; mail Point Marion z 15474; ● 170
Niles; RMC Place; VENANGO; ▲ Frenchcreek; ***224** WH-4; elev. 1,101ft./336m.; ★ **OILC-F**; mail Franklin z 16323
Niles Valley; RMC Place; TIOGA; ▲ Middlebury; **226** EE-2; mail Middlebury Center z 16935; ● 50
Ninepoints; RMC Place; LANCASTER; ▲ Bart; **227** EP-8; elev. 724ft./221m.; 🅿; z 17509; ● 120
Nine Row; RMC Place; CAMBRIA; ▲ Cambria; ***225** WM-9; mail Colver z 15927
Nineveh; RMC Place; CLARION; ▲ Ashland; **224** WH-5; mail Knox z 16232; ● 100
Nineveh; RMC Place; GREENE; ▲ Morris; **225** WP-2; elev. 1,018ft./310m.; 🅿; z 15353; ● 125
Nippenose; MCD-Township; LYCOMING; ***226** EI-3; ★ **WMSPT**; mail Antes Fort z 17720; Ⓟ 742; Ⓒ 729
Nisbet; RMC Place; LYCOMING; ▲ Susquehanna; **226** EI-3; 🅿; ★ **WMSPT**; z 17702; ● 550
Nittany; RMC Place; CENTRE; ▲ Walker; ***226** EJ-1; elev. 894ft./272m.; mail Howard z 16841
Niverton; RMC Place; SOMERSET; ▲ Elk Lick; ***225** WQ-7; mail Salisbury z 15558; rural
Nixon; CDP-Census Area Only; BUTLER; ▲ Penn; ***225** WK-4; ★ **PGH**; mail Butler z 16001; Ⓟ 1,342; Ⓒ 1,404
Noble; RMC Place; MONTGOMERY; ▲ Abington; ***227** EO-12; ★ **PHIL-**; mail Jenkintown z 19046
Noblestown; RMC Place; ALLEGHENY; ▲ South Fayette, North Fayette; ***225** WM-3; 🅿; ★ **PGH**; z 15071; ● 300
Nockamixon; MCD-Township; BUCKS; ***227** EM-12; ★ **PHIL-**; mail Kintnersville z 18930; Ⓟ 3,329; Ⓒ 3,517
Noll Acres; RMC Place; CUMBERLAND; ▲ Hampden; ***227** EO-4; ★ **HRBG**; mail Mechanicsburg z 17055; ● 1,050
Nolo; RMC Place; INDIANA; ▲ Pine; **225** WM-8; elev. 1,923ft./586m.; mail Penn Run z 15765; ● 40
Nook; RMC Place; JUNIATA; ▲ Beale; ***227** EM-1; mail Mifflin z 17058
Nordmont; RMC Place; SULLIVAN; ▲ Laporte; **226** EH-6; mail Muncy Valley z 17758; ● 35
Normal; CARBON; see Normal Square (RMC Place)
Normal Square (Normal); RMC Place; CARBON; ▲ Mahoning; **227** EK-9; mail Lehighton z 18235; ● 600
Normalville; RMC Place; FAYETTE; ▲ Springfield; **225** WP-6; 🅿; z 15469; ● 700
Norristown; Inc. Place; ⊡ MONTGOMERY; **227** EO-11; elev. 130ft./40m.; 🅿 🅷 ■; ★ **PHIL-**; z 19401, z 19403-09 & mail Plymouth Meeting z 19462; Ⓟ 30,749; Ⓒ 31,282; ◆ 32,810
Norrisville; RMC Place; CRAWFORD; ▲ Summerhill, Hayfield; **224** WF-3; mail Conneautville z 16406; ● 50
North Abington; MCD-Township; LACKAWANNA; ***226** EG-10; ★ **SCR-**; mail Dalton z 18414; Ⓟ 691; Ⓒ 782
Northampton; MCD-Township; BUCKS; ***227** EO-13; ★ **PHIL-**; mail Richboro z 18954; Ⓟ 35,406; Ⓒ 39,384; ◆ 40,503
Northampton; Inc. Place; NORTHAMPTON; **227** EL-11; elev. 320ft./98m.; 🅿; ★ **ALL-**; z 18067 & mail Huntington z 25728; Ⓟ 8,717; Ⓒ 9,405
Northampton; MCD-Township; SOMERSET; ***225** WQ-9; mail Fairhope z 15538; Ⓟ 356; Ⓒ 366
NORTHAMPTON; **227** EK-11; Ⓟ 247,105; Ⓒ 267,066; ◆ 297,816
Northampton Hills; RMC Place; BUCKS; ▲ Northampton; ***227** EO-13; ★ **PHIL-**; mail Southampton z 18966; ● 2,300
North Annville; MCD-Township; LEBANON; ***227** EN-6; ★ **LEB**; mail Jonestown z 17038; Ⓟ 2,441; Ⓒ 2,279
North Apollo; Inc. Place; ARMSTRONG; **225** WL-6; elev. 900ft./274m.; 🅿; ★ **PGH**; z 15673; Ⓟ 1,391; Ⓒ 1,426
North Bangor; RMC Place; NORTHAMPTON; ▲ Upper Mount Bethel; ***227** EK-12; mail Bangor z 18013; ● 120
North Barnesboro; RMC Place; CAMBRIA; ***225** WL-9; mail Northern Cambria z 15714; pop. incl. with Northern Cambria (Inc. Place)
North Beaver; MCD-Township; LAWRENCE; ***224** WJ-1; ★ **YNGS-**; mail New Castle z 16102; Ⓟ 3,982; Ⓒ 4,022
North Belle Vernon; Inc. Place; WESTMORELAND; **225** WO-4; elev. 903ft./275m.; 🅿; ★ **PGH**; z 15012; Ⓟ 2,112; Ⓒ 2,107
North Bend; RMC Place; CLINTON; ▲ Chapman; **224** WH-14; 🅿; z 17738, z 17760; ● 800
North Bessemer; RMC Place; ALLEGHENY; ▲ Penn Hills; ***225** WM-4; elev. 1,200ft./366m.; ★ **PGH**; mail Pittsburgh z 15235
North Bethlehem; MCD-Township; WASHINGTON; ***225** WO-3; ★ **WASH**; mail Scenery Hill z 15360; Ⓟ 1,864; Ⓒ 1,746
North Bingham; RMC Place; POTTER; ▲ Bingham; **224** WD-14; elev. 2,127ft./648m.; 🅿; z 16923, z 16941; ● 50
North Braddock; Inc. Place; ALLEGHENY; **228** K-8; elev. 1,220ft./372m.; ★ **PGH**; mail Braddock z 15104; Ⓟ 7,036; Ⓒ 6,410
North Branch; MCD-Township; WYOMING; ***226** EG-7; mail Mehoopany z 18629; Ⓟ 168; Ⓒ 197
Northbrook; RMC Place; CHESTER; ▲ Pocopson; ***227** EP-10; elev. 207ft./63m.; ★ **PHIL-**; mail West Chester z 19380; ● 200
Northbrook Hills; RMC Place; LANCASTER; ▲ Manheim; ***227** EP-7; ★ **LANC**; mail Lancaster z 17601; ● 700
North Buffalo; MCD-Township; ARMSTRONG; ***225** WK-5; ★ **PGH**; mail Kittanning z 16201; Ⓟ 2,897; Ⓒ 2,942
North Butler; RMC Place; BUTLER; ▲ Butler; ***225** WK-4; ★ **BUTL**; mail Butler z 16001; rural
North Catasauqua; Inc. Place; NORTHAMPTON; **226** EA-3; elev. 400ft./122m.; ★ **ALL-**; mail Catasauqua z 18032; Ⓟ 2,867; Ⓒ 2,814
North Centre; MCD-Township; COLUMBIA; ***226** EJ-7; mail Berwick z 18603; Ⓟ 1,860; Ⓒ 2,009
North Charleroi; Inc. Place; WASHINGTON; **225** WO-4; elev. 1,020ft./311m.; 🅿; ★ **PGH**; z 15022; Ⓟ 1,562; Ⓒ 1,409
North Codorus; MCD-Township; YORK; ***227** EQ-4; ★ **YORK**; mail Spring Grove z 17362; Ⓟ 7,565; Ⓒ 7,915
North Cornwall; RMC Place; LEBANON; ***227** EN-6; ★ **LEB**; mail Cornwall z 17016; pop. incl. with Cornwall (Inc. Place)
North Cornwall; MCD-Township; LEBANON; ***227** EN-6; ★ **LEB**; mail Lebanon z 17042; Ⓟ 4,886; Ⓒ 6,403
North Coventry; MCD-Township; CHESTER; ***227** EO-10; ★ **PTSTN**; mail Pottstown z 19464; Ⓟ 7,506; Ⓒ 7,381
North East; Inc. Place; ERIE; **224** WC-5; elev. 801ft./244m.; 🅿; ★ **ERIE**; z 16428; Ⓟ 4,617; Ⓒ 4,601
North East; MCD-Township; ERIE; ***224** WC-5; elev. 802ft./244m.; 🅿; ★ **ERIE**; z 16428; does not include the Borough of North East; Ⓟ 6,283; Ⓒ 7,702; Ⓡ 6,613
Northeast Madison; MCD-Township; PERRY; ***227** EN-2; mail Loysville z 17047; Ⓟ 674; Ⓒ 856
North Edinburg; RMC Place; LAWRENCE; ▲ Mahoning; ***224** WJ-2; elev. 839ft./256m.; ★ **YNGS-**; mail Edinburg z 16116; ● 80
North End; RMC Place; LUZERNE; ★ **SCR-**; mail Wilkes Barre z 18705; pop. incl. with Wilkes-Barre (Inc. Place)
Northern Cambria; Inc. Place; CAMBRIA; **225** WL-9; elev. 1,500ft./457m.; 🅿; z 15714; Ⓟ 2,530; Ⓒ 4,199
North Essington; RMC Place; DELAWARE; ▲ Tinicum; ★ **PHIL-**; mail Essington z 19029
North Fayette; MCD-Township; ALLEGHENY; ***225** WM-3; ★ **PGH**; mail Imperial z 15126, Oakdale z 15071; Ⓟ 9,537; Ⓒ 12,254
North Fork; RMC Place; POTTER; ▲ Harrison; **224** WD-14; mail Westfield z 16950; ● 30
North Franklin; MCD-Township; WASHINGTON; ***225** WO-2; ★ **WASH**; mail Washington z 15301; Ⓟ 4,997; Ⓒ 4,818
North Fredericktown; RMC Place; WASHINGTON; ▲ East Bethlehem; ***225** WP-3; mail Fredericktown z 15333; ● 200
North Freedom; RMC Place; ARMSTRONG, JEFFERSON; ▲ Ringgold, Redbank; ***224** WJ-7; mail Mayport z 16240; ● 100
North Glenside; MONTGOMERY; see North Hills (RMC Place)
North Heidelberg; MCD-Township; BERKS; ***227** EN-8; ★ **READ**; mail Bernville z 19506; Ⓟ 1,288; Ⓒ 1,325
North Hills (North Glenside); RMC Place; MONTGOMERY; ▲ Abington; **228** A-4; ★ **PHIL-**; mail Glenside z 19038; ● 3,000
North Hills; RMC Place; NORTHUMBERLAND; mail Milton z 17847; pop. incl. with Milton (Inc. Place)
North Hopewell; MCD-Township; YORK; ***227** EQ-5; ★ **YORK**; mail Felton z 17322; Ⓟ 2,205; Ⓒ 2,507
North Huntingdon; MCD-Township; WESTMORELAND; ***225** WN-5; 🅿; ★ **PGH**; z 15642; Ⓟ 28,158; Ⓒ 29,123; ◆ 28,795
North Irwin; Inc. Place; WESTMORELAND; ***225** WN-5; elev. 907ft./276m.; 🅿; ★ **PGH**; z 15642; Ⓟ 956; Ⓒ 879
North Jackson; RMC Place; SUSQUEHANNA; ▲ Jackson; ***226** EE-10; mail Susquehanna z 18847; rural
North Lebanon; MCD-Township; LEBANON; ***227** EN-7; ★ **LEB**; mail Lebanon z 17042, z 17046; Ⓟ 9,741; Ⓒ 10,629
North Liberty; RMC Place; MERCER; ▲ Liberty; **224** WI-3; elev. 1,315ft./401m.; mail Grove City z 16127; ● 100
North Londonderry; MCD-Township; LEBANON; ***227** EN-6; mail Palmyra z 17078; Ⓟ 5,630; Ⓒ 6,771
North Mahoning; MCD-Township; INDIANA; ***225** WK-8; mail Marchand z 15758; Ⓟ 1,254; Ⓒ 1,383
North Manheim; MCD-Township; SCHUYLKILL; ***227** EL-8; ★ **PTSVL**; mail Pottsville z 17901; Ⓟ 3,404; Ⓒ 3,287
North McKees Rocks; RMC Place; ALLEGHENY; ▲ Stowe; ***225** WM-3; ★ **PGH**; pop. incl. with Pittsburgh (Inc. Place)
North Mehoopany; RMC Place; WYOMING; ▲ Mehoopany; ***226** EG-8; mail Mehoopany z 18629
North Middleton; MCD-Township; CUMBERLAND; ***227** EO-3; ★ **CARL**; mail Carlisle z 17013; Ⓟ 9,833; Ⓒ 10,197
Northmoreland; MCD-Township; WYOMING; ***226** EG-9; mail Dallas z 18612; Ⓟ 1,462; Ⓒ 1,463
North Mountain; RMC Place; LYCOMING; ▲ Franklin; **226** EH-6; elev. 1,295ft./395m.; mail Muncy Valley z 17758; ● 500
North Newton; MCD-Township; CUMBERLAND; ***227** EO-2; mail Newville z 17241; Ⓟ 1,779; Ⓒ 2,169
North Oakland; RMC Place; BUTLER; ▲ Donegal; ***224** WJ-5; ★ **BUTL**; mail Chicora z 16025
North Orwell; RMC Place; BRADFORD; ▲ Orwell; **226** EE-7; mail Rome z 18837; ● 100
North Park; RMC Place; BUCKS; ▲ Falls; ***227** EO-14; ★ **PHIL-**
North Philadelphia; RMC Place; PHILADELPHIA; ★ **PHIL-**; mail Philadelphia z 19132; pop. incl. with Philadelphia (Inc. Place)
North Philipsburg; CDP; CENTRE; ▲ Rush; ***225** WK-12; mail Philipsburg z 16866; Ⓒ 697
North Pine Grove; RMC Place; CLARION; ▲ Farmington; ***224** WH-7; elev. 1,634ft./498m.; mail Vowinckel z 16260; ● 80
North Point; RMC Place; BEDFORD; ▲ Broad Top; ***225** WO-12; mail Six Mile Run z 16679; rural
North Point; RMC Place; INDIANA; ▲ West Mahoning; **225** WK-7; 🅿; z 15763; ● 75
North Radcliffe; RMC Place; BUCKS; ▲ Bristol; ***227** EO-14; elev. 20ft./6m.; ★ **PHIL-**; mail Bristol z 19007; ● 600
North Rochester; RMC Place; BEAVER; ▲ Rochester; ***225** WL-2; ★ **PGH**; mail Rochester z 15074
North Rome; RMC Place; BRADFORD; ▲ Rome; **226** EE-6; mail Wysox z 18854; ● 65
North Scottdale; RMC Place; WESTMORELAND; ▲ East Huntingdon; ***225** WO-5; mail Scottdale z 15683; ● 150
North Scranton; RMC Place; LACKAWANNA; ★ **SCR-**; mail Scranton z 18508; pop. incl. with Scranton (Inc. Place)
North Sewickley; RMC Place; BEAVER; ▲ Franklin; ***225** WK-2; ★ **PGH**; mail Ellwood City z 16117; ● 1,100
North Sewickley; MCD-Township; BEAVER; ***225** WK-2; ★ **PGH**; mail Beaver Falls z 15010; Ⓟ 6,178; Ⓒ 6,120
North Shenango; MCD-Township; CRAWFORD; ***224** WF-1; mail Linesville z 16424; Ⓟ 902; Ⓒ 1,387
North Springfield; RMC Place; ERIE; ▲ Springfield; **224** WD-2; elev. 663ft./202m.; 🅿; ★ **ERIE**; z 16430; ● 130
North Strabane; MCD-Township; WASHINGTON; ***225** WN-3; ★ **PGH**; mail Canonsburg z 15317; Ⓟ 8,157; Ⓒ 10,057
North Towanda; RMC Place; BRADFORD; ▲ North Towanda; **226** EE-6; mail Towanda z 18848; ● 400
North Towanda; MCD-Township; BRADFORD; ***226** EE-6; mail Towanda z 18848; Ⓟ 909; Ⓒ 927
Northumberland; Inc. Place; NORTHUMBERLAND; **227** EK-5; elev. 480ft./146m.; 🅿; z 17857; Ⓟ 3,860; Ⓒ 3,714
NORTHUMBERLAND; **227** EK-5; Ⓟ 96,771; Ⓒ 94,556; ◆ 89,623
North Union; MCD-Township; FAYETTE; ***225** WQ-5; ★ **UNTN**; mail Uniontown z 15401; Ⓟ 13,910; Ⓒ 14,140
North Union; MCD-Township; SCHUYLKILL; ***227** EK-7; mail Nuremberg z 18241, Zion Grove z 17985; Ⓟ 1,143; Ⓒ 1,225
North Vandergrift; RMC Place; ARMSTRONG; ▲ Parks; **225** WL-6; ★ **PGH**; mail Vandergrift z 15690; ● 550
North Vandergrift-Pleasant View; CDP-Census Area Only; ARMSTRONG; ▲ Parks; ***225** WL-6; ★ **PGH**; mail Vandergrift z 15690; Ⓟ 1,431; Ⓒ 1,355
North Versailles; CDP-Census Area Only; ALLEGHENY; ▲ North Versailles; ***225** WN-4; 🅿; ★ **PGH**; z 15137; Ⓟ 12,302; Ⓒ 11,125
North Versailles; MCD-Township; ALLEGHENY; ***225** WN-4; 🅿; ★ **PGH**; z 15137; Ⓟ 12,302; Ⓒ 11,125
Northview Eatates; RMC Place; BEAVER; ***225** WL-3; elev. 1,200ft./366m.; ★ **PGH**; mail Baden z 15005; pop. incl. with Economy (Inc. Place)
Northvue; RMC Place; BUTLER; ▲ Center; **224** WJ-4; ★ **BUTL**; mail Butler z 16001; ● 700
North Wales; Inc. Place; MONTGOMERY; **227** EO-12; elev. 380ft./116m.; 🅿 ■; ★ **PHIL-**; z 19436, z 19454-55, z 19477; Ⓟ 3,802; Ⓒ 3,342; ◆ 3,265
North Warren; RMC Place; WARREN; ▲ Conewango; **224** WE-7; 🅿 🅷; z 16365; ● 2,400
North Washington; RMC Place; BUTLER; ▲ Washington; **224** WJ-4; elev. 1,491ft./454m.; 🅿; z 16048; ● 200
North Washington; RMC Place; WESTMORELAND; ▲ Washington; **225** WM-5; ★ **PGH**; mail Apollo z 15613; ● 500
North Weissport; RMC Place; CARBON; ▲ Franklin; **227** EK-10; mail Lehighton z 18235; ● 900
Northwest Harborcreek; CDP-Census Area Only; ERIE; ▲ Harborcreek; ***224** WC-4; ★ **ERIE**; mail Erie z 16510; Ⓟ 6,662; Ⓒ 8,658
North Whitehall; MCD-Township; LEHIGH; ***227** EL-10; ★ **ALL-**; mail Coplay z 18037; Ⓟ 10,827; Ⓒ 14,731
Northwood; RMC Place; BLAIR; ▲ Snyder; **225** WL-12; ★ **ALT**; mail Tyrone z 16686; ● 340
North Woodbury; MCD-Township; BLAIR; ***225** WN-11; mail Martinsburg z 16662; Ⓟ 2,219; Ⓒ 2,276
Northwood Heights; RMC Place; NORTHAMPTON; ▲ Palmer; ***227** EL-12; ★ **ALL-**; mail Easton z 18045; ● 700
North York; Inc. Place; YORK; **227** EP-5; elev. 380ft./116m.; ★ **YORK**; mail York z 17404; Ⓟ 1,689; Ⓒ 1,689
Norvelt; RMC Place; WESTMORELAND; ▲ Mount Pleasant; **225** WO-6; 🅿; z 15674; ● 1,100
Norwegian; MCD-Township; SCHUYLKILL; ***227** EL-7; ★ **PTSVL**; mail Mar Lin z 17951; Ⓟ 1,938; Ⓒ 2,172
Norwich; MCD-Township; MCKEAN; ***224** WF-11; mail Crosby z 16724; Ⓟ 593; Ⓒ 633
Norwin Heights; RMC Place; WESTMORELAND; ▲ North Huntingdon; ***225** WN-5; ★ **PGH**; mail Irwin z 15642; ● 300
Norwood; Inc. Place; DELAWARE; **228** F-2; 🅿; ★ **PHIL-**; z 19074; Ⓟ 6,162; Ⓒ 5,985
Nossville; RMC Place; HUNTINGDON; ▲ Tell; ***225** WO-14; mail Blairs Mills z 17213; rural
Nottingham; RMC Place; BUCKS; ▲ Bensalem; **228** A-8; elev. 100ft./30m.; ★ **PHIL-**; mail Bensalem z 19020; ● 3,000
Nottingham; RMC Place; CHESTER; ▲ West Nottingham, East Nottingham; **227** EQ-8; 🅿; z 19362; ● 200
Nottingham; MCD-Township; WASHINGTON; ***225** WN-4; ★ **PGH**; mail Finleyville z 15332; Ⓟ 2,303; Ⓒ 2,522
Nova; RMC Place; FRANKLIN; ▲ Montgomery; ***225** WR-13; mail Greencastle z 17225; rural
Nowrytown; RMC Place; INDIANA; ▲ Conemaugh; **225** WM-6; ★ **PGH**; mail Saltsburg z 15681; ● 150
Noxen; RMC Place; WYOMING; ▲ Noxen; **226** EH-8; 🅿; z 18636; ● 500
Noxen; MCD-Township; WYOMING; ***226** EH-8; 🅿; z 18636; Ⓟ 944; Ⓒ 951
Noyes; MCD-Township; CLINTON; ***224** WI-14; mail Renovo z 17764; Ⓟ 463; Ⓒ 419
Nuangola; Inc. Place; LUZERNE; **226** EI-8; elev. 1,200ft./366m.; 🅿; ★ **SCR-**; z 18707; Ⓟ 701; Ⓒ 671
Nuangola Station; RMC Place; LUZERNE; ▲ Rice; ***226** EI-8; ★ **SCR-**; mail Mountain Top z 18707; ● 350
Number Five Mine; RMC Place; MERCER; ▲ Springfield; ***224** WI-3; mail Mercer z 16137; ● 70
Number Thirty Seven; RMC Place; CAMBRIA; ▲ Richland; ***225** WN-9; ★ **JNST**; mail Windber z 15963; ● 250
Numidia; CDP; COLUMBIA; ▲ Locust; **227** EK-6; elev. 987ft./301m.; 🅿; z 17858; Ⓒ 254
NuMine; RMC Place; ARMSTRONG; ▲ Cowanshannock; **225** WK-7; 🅿; z 16244; ● 300
Nunnery; RMC Place; FRANKLIN; ▲ Quincy; ***227** EQ-1; mail Waynesboro z 17268; ● 80
Nuremberg; CDP; SCHUYLKILL, LUZERNE; ▲ Black Creek, North Union; **226** EJ-8; 🅿; z 18241; Ⓒ 231
Nutts Corners; RMC Place; MERCER; ▲ Pine; ***224** WI-4; elev. 1,434ft./437m.; mail Grove City z 16127; rural
Nyesville; RMC Place; FRANKLIN; ▲ Greene; **225** WP-14; mail Chambersburg z 17201; ● 75

O

Oak; RMC Place; ALLEGHENY; pop. incl. with Pittsburgh (Inc. Place)
Oakbottom; RMC Place; LANCASTER; ▲ Drumore; ***227** EQ-7; mail Quarryville z 17566; ● 100
Oakdale; Inc. Place; ALLEGHENY; **225** WM-3; elev. 902ft./275m.; 🅿 🅷; ★ **PGH**; z 15071; Ⓟ 1,752; Ⓒ 1,551
Oakdale; RMC Place; LUZERNE; ▲ Hazle; ***226** EJ-9; ★ **HAZ**; mail Freeland z 18224; ● 200
Oakdale Manor; RMC Place; BUCKS; ▲ Lower Makefield; ★ **PHIL-**; mail Morrisville z 19067; ● 300
Oakeola (Horntown); RMC Place; DELAWARE; ▲ Darby; ★ **PHIL-**; mail Glenolden z 19036
Oakford; RMC Place; BUCKS; ▲ Bensalem; ***227** EO-13; 🅿; ★ **PHIL-**; z 19053 & mail Langhorne z 19047; ● 1,100
Oak Forest; RMC Place; GREENE; ▲ Center; **225** WQ-2; elev. 1,008ft./307m.; mail Waynesburg z 15370; ● 60
Oak Grove; RMC Place; CLEARFIELD; ▲ Morris; ***224** WJ-12; mail Morrisdale z 16858; ● 90
Oak Grove (Beucher); RMC Place; SCHUYLKILL; ▲ Pine Grove; mail Pine Grove z 17963; rural
Oak Grove; RMC Place; WESTMORELAND; ▲ Ligonier; **225** WN-7; elev. 1,208ft./368m.; mail Ligonier z 15658; ● 200
Oak Hall; RMC Place; CENTRE; ▲ College; ***225** WK-13; ★ **STCOL**; mail Boalsburg z 16827
Oak Hill; RMC Place; ALLEGHENY; ▲ Wilkins; ***225** WM-4; elev. 1,043ft./318m.; ★ **PGH**; mail Turtle Creek z 15145
Oak Hill; RMC Place; CLEARFIELD; ▲ Karthaus; ***224** WI-12; mail Karthaus z 16845; rural
Oak Hill; RMC Place; LANCASTER; ▲ Little Britain; ***227** EQ-8; mail Nottingham z 19362
Oak Hills; CDP-Census Area Only; BUTLER; ▲ Butler; ***225** WK-4; elev. 1,240ft./378m.; ★ **BUTL**; mail Butler z 16001; Ⓟ 2,245; Ⓒ 2,335
Oakhurst; RMC Place; CAMBRIA; ***225** WN-8; ★ **JNST**; mail Johnstown z 15906; pop. incl. with Johnstown (Inc. Place)
Oakland; RMC Place; ALLEGHENY; ***225** WM-4; 🅿; ★ **PGH**; z 15213; pop. incl. with Pittsburgh (Inc. Place)
Oakland; MCD-Township; BUTLER; ***224** WJ-4; ★ **BUTL**; mail Chicora z 16025; Ⓟ 2,820; Ⓒ 3,074
Oakland; RMC Place; CAMBRIA; ▲ Stonycreek; **225** WT-2; ★ **JNST**; mail Johnstown z 15902; ● 1,600
Oakland; CDP; LAWRENCE; ▲ Taylor, Union; **224** WJ-2; ★ **NWCS**; mail New Castle z 16101; Ⓟ 1,766; Ⓒ 1,516
Oakland; RMC Place; MERCER; ▲ Coolspring; ***224** WH-3; elev. 1,130ft./344m.; mail Mercer z 16137; rural
Oakland; Inc. Place; SUSQUEHANNA; **226** ED-10; elev. 1,000ft./305m.; ★ **BING**; mail Susquehanna z 18847; Ⓟ 641; Ⓒ 622
Oakland; MCD-Township; SUSQUEHANNA; ***226** ED-10; ★ **BING**; mail Susquehanna z 18847; does not include the Borough of Oakland; Ⓟ 544; Ⓒ 550
Oakland; MCD-Township; VENANGO; ***224** WG-5; mail Cooperstown z 16317; Ⓟ 1,527; Ⓒ 1,565
Oakland Hills I; RMC Place; NORTHAMPTON; ▲ Bethlehem; ***227** EL-11; elev. 390ft./119m.; ★ **ALL-**; mail Bethlehem z 18016; ● 250
Oakland Mills; RMC Place; JUNIATA; ▲ Fayette; **227** EL-2; elev. 570ft./174m.; 🅿; z 17076; ● 110
Oakland Park; RMC Place; LEHIGH; ▲ Upper Macungie; ***227** EM-10; elev. 430ft./131m.; ★ **ALL-**; mail Allentown z 18101; ● 450
Oak Lane; RMC Place; PHILADELPHIA; ★ **PHIL-**; mail Philadelphia z 19126; pop. incl. with Philadelphia (Inc. Place)
Oaklane Manor; RMC Place; MONTGOMERY; ▲ Cheltenham; ★ **PHIL-**; mail Cheltenham z 19012
Oakleigh; RMC Place; DAUPHIN; ▲ Swatara; **227** ET-4; ★ **HRBG**; mail Harrisburg z 17111; ● 1,000
Oaklyn; RMC Place; NORTHUMBERLAND; ▲ Upper Augusta; ***227** EK-5; mail Sunbury z 17801; ● 400
Oakmont; Inc. Place; ALLEGHENY; **225** WM-4; elev. 840ft./256m.; 🅿; ★ **PGH**; z 15139; Ⓟ 6,961; Ⓒ 6,911
Oakmont Villa; RMC Place; DAUPHIN; ▲ Derry; ***227** EO-5; ★ **HRBG**; mail Hummelstown z 17036; ● 500
Oak Park; RMC Place; MONTGOMERY; ▲ Hatfield; **227** EO-12; ★ **PHIL-**; mail Lansdale z 19446; ● 700
Oak Park; RMC Place; NORTHUMBERLAND; ▲ Point; ***227** EK-5; mail Northumberland z 17857; ● 150
Oak Ridge; RMC Place; ARMSTRONG, CLARION; ▲ Redbank; ***224** WJ-7; 🅿; z 16245; ● 350
Oak Ridge; RMC Place; CLEARFIELD; ▲ Bigler; ***225** WK-10; elev. 1,774ft./541m.; mail Madera z 16661; rural
Oakryn; RMC Place; LANCASTER; ▲ Little Britain; ***227** EQ-8; elev. 415ft./126m.; mail Peach Bottom z 17563, Quarryville z 17566; ● 40
Oaks; RMC Place; MONTGOMERY; ▲ Upper Providence; **227** EO-11; 🅿; ★ **PHIL-**; z 19456; ● 850
Oak Shade; RMC Place; LANCASTER; ▲ Little Britain; ***227** EQ-8; elev. 476ft./145m.; mail Quarryville z 17566; ● 45
Oaktree Hollow; RMC Place; BUCKS; ▲ Bristol; ***227** EO-14; ★ **PHIL-**; mail Bristol z 19007
Oakville; RMC Place; CUMBERLAND; ▲ North Newton; **227** EO-2; mail Gap z 17527, Shippensburg z 17257; ● 150
Oakwood (New Castle West); CDP-Census Area Only; LAWRENCE; ▲ Union; ***224** WJ-2; ★ **YNGS-**; mail New Castle z 16101; Ⓟ 2,541; Ⓒ 2,249
Oakwood Park; RMC Place; LUZERNE; ★ **SCR-**; mail Wilkes Barre z 18702; pop. incl. with Laflin (Inc. Place)
Obelisk; RMC Place; MONTGOMERY; ▲ Upper Frederick; **227** EN-11; ★ **PHIL-**; mail Zieglerville z 19492; ● 150
Oberlin; RMC Place; DAUPHIN; ▲ Swatara; **227** ET-4; 🅿; ★ **HRBG**; z 17113; ● 850
Oberlin Gardens; RMC Place; DAUPHIN; ▲ Swatara; ***227** EO-5; ★ **HRBG**; mail Harrisburg z 17113
Obold; BERKS; see Mount Pleasant (RMC Place)
Observatory; RMC Place; ALLEGHENY; 🅿; ★ **PGH**; z 15214; pop. incl. with Pittsburgh (Inc. Place)
Odenwelder; RMC Place; NORTHAMPTON; ★ **ALL-**; mail Easton z 18042; pop. incl. with West Easton (Inc. Place)
Odin; RMC Place; POTTER; ▲ Keating; ***224** WF-12; mail Coudersport z 16915; rural
Ogden; RMC Place; DELAWARE; ▲ Upper Chichester; ***227** EQ-11; 🅿; ★ **PHIL-**; z 19061; ● 3,100
Ogdensburg; RMC Place; TIOGA; ▲ Union; **226** EF-4; mail Roaring Branch z 17765; ● 75
Ogle; RMC Place; BUTLER; ▲ Cranberry; ***225** WL-3; elev. 1,061ft./323m.; ★ **PGH**; mail Mars z 16046; rural
Ogle; MCD-Township; SOMERSET; ***225** WO-9; mail Windber z 15963; Ⓟ 597; Ⓒ 588
Ogletown; RMC Place; SOMERSET; ▲ Ogle; **225** WO-9; elev. 2,355ft./718m.; mail Windber z 15963; ● 150
Ogontz; RMC Place; MONTGOMERY; ▲ Cheltenham; ★ **PHIL-**; mail Cheltenham z 19012
O'Hara; MCD-Township; ALLEGHENY; ***225** WM-4; ★ **PGH**; mail Pittsburgh z 15215, z 15238; Ⓟ 9,096; Ⓒ 8,856
O'Hara Township; CDP-Census Area Only; ALLEGHENY; ▲ O'Hara; ***225** WM-4; elev. 1,000ft./305m.; ★ **PGH**; mail Pittsburgh z 15215, z 15238; Ⓟ 9,096; Ⓒ 8,856
Ohio; MCD-Township; ALLEGHENY; ***225** WM-3; ★ **PGH**; mail Sewickley z 15143; Ⓟ 2,459; Ⓒ 3,086
Ohio; FAYETTE; see Ohiopyle (Inc. Place)
Ohiopyle (Ohio); Inc. Place; FAYETTE; **225** WQ-6; elev. 1,217ft./371m.; 🅿; z 15470; Ⓟ 81; Ⓒ 77
Ohioview; RMC Place; BEAVER; ***225** WL-2; ★ **PGH**; mail Industry z 15052; pop. incl. with Industry (Inc. Place)
Ohioville; Inc. Place; BEAVER; **225** WL-1; elev. 1,100ft./335m.; ★ **PGH**; mail Midland z 15059; Ⓟ 3,865; Ⓒ 3,759
Ohl; RMC Place; JEFFERSON; ▲ Beaver; **224** WJ-7; mail Summerville z 15864; ● 75
Oil City; RMC Place; CAMBRIA; ▲ Portage; ***225** WN-10; mail Cassandra z 15925; ● 25
Oil City; Inc. Place; VENANGO; **224** WG-5; elev. 1,000ft./305m.; 🅿 🅲 1,000 ■; ★ **OILC-F**; z 16301; Ⓟ 11,949; Ⓒ 11,504; ◆ 10,805
Oil Creek; MCD-Township; CRAWFORD; ***224** WF-5; mail Titusville z 16354; Ⓟ 2,069; Ⓒ 1,880
Oil Creek; RMC Place; VENANGO; ★ **OILC-F**; mail Oil City z 16301; pop. incl. with Oil City (Inc. Place)
Oilcreek; MCD-Township; VENANGO; ***224** WG-6; mail Pleasantville z 16341; Ⓟ 915; Ⓒ 840
Oklahoma; RMC Place; CLEARFIELD; ▲ Sandy; **224** WI-9; mail Du Bois z 15801; ● 600
Oklahoma; Inc. Place; WESTMORELAND; **225** WL-5; elev. 980ft./299m.; ★ **PGH**; mail Apollo z 15613; Ⓟ 977; Ⓒ 915
Okome; RMC Place; LYCOMING; ▲ McHenry; ***226** EH-2; mail Jersey Mills z 17739; rural
Olanta; RMC Place; CLEARFIELD; ▲ Pine, Knox; **225** WK-10; 🅿; z 16863; ● 100
Old Bethany; WESTMORELAND; see West Bethany (RMC Place)
Old Boston; RMC Place; LUZERNE; ▲ Jenkins; **226** EC-9; ★ **SCR-**; mail Pittston z 18640; ● 200
Old Clarendon; RMC Place; WARREN; ***224** WE-8; mail Clarendon z 16313; ● 100
Old Concord; RMC Place; WASHINGTON; ▲ Morris; **225** WP-2; mail Prosperity z 15329; ● 30
Old Crabtree; RMC Place; WESTMORELAND; ▲ Unity; ***225** WN-6; ★ **LTROB**; mail Latrobe z 15650; ● 70
Old Cranberry; LUZERNE; see Cranberry Ridge (RMC Place)
Old Enon; RMC Place; LAWRENCE; ▲ Little Beaver; ***225** WK-2; mail Enon Valley z 16120; ● 30
Old Forge; Inc. Place; LACKAWANNA; **226** EH-9; elev. 730ft./223m.; 🅿; ★ **SCR-**; z 18518; Ⓟ 8,834; Ⓒ 8,798
Oldframe; RMC Place; FAYETTE; ▲ Nicholson; ***225** WQ-4; mail Smithfield z 15478; rural
Old Line; RMC Place; LANCASTER; ▲ Rapho; ***227** EO-6; mail Manheim z 17545; rural
Old Lycoming; MCD-Township; LYCOMING; ***226** EI-3; ★ **WMSPT**; mail Williamsport z 17701; Ⓟ 5,526; Ⓒ 5,508
Old Meadow; RMC Place; WESTMORELAND; ▲ East Huntingdon; mail Scottdale z 15683; ● 150
Old Orchard; RMC Place; MONROE; ▲ Pocono; ***226** EI-11; mail Swiftwater z 18370; rural
Old Orchard; CDP-Census Area Only; NORTHAMPTON; ▲ Palmer; ***227** EL-12; ★ **ALL-**; mail Easton z 18045; Ⓟ 2,598; Ⓒ 2,443
Old Port; RMC Place; JUNIATA; ▲ Turbett; **227** EM-2; mail Port Royal z 17082; ● 90
Old Stanton; RMC Place; WESTMORELAND; ***225** WO-5; ★ **PGH**; mail New Stanton z 15672; pop. incl. with New Stanton (Inc. Place)
Old Zionsville; RMC Place; LEHIGH; ▲ Upper Milford; **227** EM-10; 🅿; ★ **ALL-**; z 18068; ● 200
Oleona; RMC Place; POTTER; ***224** WG-14; mail Cross Fork z 17729; ● 10
Oleopolis; RMC Place; VENANGO; ▲ Cornplanter; ***224** WG-5; ★ **OILC-F**; mail Oil City z 16301; ● 50
Oley; RMC Place; BERKS; ▲ Oley; **227** EN-9; 🅿; ★ **READ**; z 19547; ● 900
Oley; MCD-Township; BERKS; ***227** EN-9; 🅿; ★ **READ**; z 19547; Ⓟ 3,362; Ⓒ 3,583
Oley Furnace; RMC Place; BERKS; ▲ Oley; ***227** EN-9; ★ **READ**; mail Oley z 19547; rural
Oliphant Furnace; RMC Place; FAYETTE; ▲ Georges; **225** WQ-5; ★ **UNTN**; mail Uniontown z 15401; ● 250
Oliveburg; RMC Place; JEFFERSON; ▲ Oliver; **224** WJ-8; 🅿; z 15764; ● 150
Olive Manor; RMC Place; VENANGO; ***224** WG-5; ★ **OILC-F**; mail Oil City z 16301; pop. incl. with Oil City (Inc. Place)
Oliver; CDP; FAYETTE; ▲ North Union; **225** WP-5; 🅿; ★ **UNTN**; z 15472; Ⓟ 3,271; Ⓒ 2,925
Oliver; MCD-Township; JEFFERSON; ***224** WJ-8; mail Brookville z 15825; Ⓟ 1,119; Ⓒ 1,129
Oliver; MCD-Township; MIFFLIN; ***225** WM-14; mail Mc Veytown z 17051; Ⓟ 1,822; Ⓒ 2,060
Oliver; MCD-Township; PERRY; ***227** EM-3; ★ **HRBG**; mail Newport z 17074; Ⓟ 2,039; Ⓒ 2,061
Olivers Mills; RMC Place; LUZERNE; ★ **SCR-**; mail Wilkes Barre z 18702; pop. incl. with Laurel Run (Inc. Place)
Olivet; RMC Place; ARMSTRONG; ▲ South Bend; ***225** WL-6; mail Avonmore z 15618; rural
Olmsted; RMC Place; POTTER; ▲ Eulalia; ***224** WF-12; mail Coudersport z 16915; rural
Olney; RMC Place; PHILADELPHIA; ***227** EP-12; ★ **PHIL-**; mail Philadelphia z 19120; pop. incl. with Philadelphia (Inc. Place)
Olwen Heights; RMC Place; LACKAWANNA; ▲ Roaring Brook; ***226** EH-10; elev. 1,700ft./518m.; ★ **SCR-**; mail Moscow z 18444; ● 500
Olyphant; Inc. Place; LACKAWANNA; **226** EG-10; elev. 780ft./238m.; 🅿; ★ **SCR-**; z 18447-48; Ⓟ 5,222; Ⓒ 4,978; Ⓡ 4,995
Oneida; RMC Place; BUTLER; ▲ Center; **224** WJ-4; ★ **BUTL**; mail Butler z 16001; ● 100
Oneida; MCD-Township; HUNTINGDON; ***225** WM-13; mail Huntingdon z 16652; Ⓟ 1,085; Ⓒ 1,129
Oneida; CDP; SCHUYLKILL; ▲ East Union; **227** EK-8; 🅿; z 18242; Ⓒ 219
Oniontown; RMC Place; MERCER; ▲ Delaware; ***224** WH-2; mail Greenville z 16125; rural
Onnalinda; RMC Place; CAMBRIA; ▲ Summerhill; ***225** WN-9; ★ **JNST**; mail Sidman z 15955; ● 40
Ono; RMC Place; LEBANON; ▲ East Hanover; **227** EN-6; 🅿; z 17077; ● 300
Ontario; RMC Place; WASHINGTON; ▲ North Bethlehem; ***225** WO-3; ★ **WASH**; mail Eighty Four z 15330; ● 350
Ontelaunee; MCD-Township; BERKS; ***227** EM-9; ★ **READ**; mail Reading z 19605; Ⓟ 1,359; Ⓒ 1,217
Opp; RMC Place; LYCOMING; ▲ Moreland; ***226** EI-5; elev. 638ft./194m.; mail Muncy z 17756
Oppermans Corner; RMC Place; CHESTER; ▲ West Pikeland; ***227** EO-10; elev. 346ft./105m.; ★ **PHIL-**; mail Chester Springs z 19425; rural
Option; RMC Place; ALLEGHENY; ***225** WN-4; ★ **PGH**; mail Pittsburgh z 15236; pop. incl. with Baldwin (Inc. Place)
Orange; MCD-Township; COLUMBIA; ***226** EJ-6; mail Orangeville z 17859; Ⓟ 1,043; Ⓒ 1,148
Orange; RMC Place; LUZERNE; ▲ Franklin; **226** EH-9; elev. 1,130ft./344m.; ★ **SCR-**; mail Dallas z 18612; ● 300
Orangeville; Inc. Place; COLUMBIA; **224** WH-1; elev. 580ft./177m.; 🅿; z 17859; Ⓟ 504; Ⓒ 500
Orbisonia; Inc. Place; HUNTINGDON; **225** WO-13; elev. 640ft./195m.; 🅿; z 17243; Ⓟ 447; Ⓒ 425
Orchard Beach; RMC Place; ERIE; ▲ North East; **224** WC-5; elev. 802ft./244m.; ★ **ERIE**; mail North East z 16428; ● 125
Orchard Crossing; RMC Place; BLAIR; ▲ Snyder; ***225** WL-11; ★ **ALT**; mail Tyrone z 16686; ● 60
Orchard Hill; RMC Place; WESTMORELAND; ***225** WO-6; mail Mount Pleasant z 15666; ● 600
Orchard Hills; CDP; ARMSTRONG; ▲ Kiskiminetas; **225** WL-6; ★ **PGH**; mail Apollo z 15613; Ⓟ 2,019; Ⓒ 2,152
Orefield; RMC Place; LEHIGH; ▲ South Whitehall, North Whitehall; **226** EA-1; elev. 454ft./138m.; 🅿; ★ **ALL-**; z 18069; ● 750
Oregon; RMC Place; LANCASTER; ▲ Manheim; ***227** EP-7; ★ **LANC**; mail Leola z 17540, Lititz z 17543; ● 250
Oregon; MCD-Township; WAYNE; ***226** EF-12; mail Honesdale z 18431; Ⓟ 606; Ⓒ 745
Oregon Hill; RMC Place; LYCOMING; ▲ Pine; **226** EG-2; mail Morris z 16938; ● 100
Ore Hill; RMC Place; BLAIR; ▲ Taylor; **225** WN-11; ★ **ALT**; mail Roaring Spring z 16673; ● 95
Oreland; CDP; MONTGOMERY; ▲ Upper Dublin, Springfield; **228** A-4; 🅿; ★ **PHIL-**; z 19075; Ⓟ 5,695; Ⓒ 5,509
Oreland Gardens; RMC Place; MONTGOMERY; ▲ Upper Dublin; ★ **PHIL-**; mail Oreland z 19075
Oreminea; RMC Place; BLAIR; ▲ Huston; ***225** WN-11; mail Williamsburg z 16693; rural
Ore Valley; RMC Place; YORK; ▲ York; ***227** EP-5; elev. 604ft./184m.; ★ **YORK**; mail York z 17403; ● 200
Oreville; RMC Place; BERKS; ▲ Longswamp; ***227** EM-10; mail Mertztown z 19539; rural
Orient; RMC Place; FAYETTE; ▲ Redstone; ***225** WP-4; elev. 990ft./302m.; ★ **UNTN**; mail Cardale z 15420; ● 60
Oriental; RMC Place; JUNIATA; ▲ Susquehanna; **227** EL-4; mail Liverpool z 17045; ● 100
Oriole; RMC Place; LYCOMING; ▲ Limestone; **226** EI-3; mail Jersey Shore z 17740; ● 100
Ormrod; RMC Place; LEHIGH; ▲ North Whitehall; **226** EA-2; elev. 420ft./128m.; ★ **ALL-**; mail Coplay z 18037; ● 300
Ormsby; RMC Place; MCKEAN; ▲ Keating; **224** WE-10; elev. 2,195ft./669m.; 🅿; z 16726; ● 100
Orners Corner; RMC Place; BLAIR; ▲ Logan; ***225** WM-11; ★ **ALT**; mail Altoona z 16601; rural
Orrstown; Inc. Place; FRANKLIN; **227** EP-1; elev. 620ft./189m.; 🅿; z 17244; Ⓟ 220; Ⓒ 231
Orrtanna; CDP; ADAMS; ▲ Highland, Hamiltonban; **227** EQ-2; elev. 670ft./204m.; 🅿; z 17353; Ⓒ 169
Orrville; RMC Place; ALLEGHENY; ▲ Springdale; ***225** WM-5; ★ **PGH**; mail Springdale z 15144; ● 750
Orson; RMC Place; WAYNE; ▲ Preston; **226** EE-11; 🅿; z 18449; ● 125
Orvilla; RMC Place; MONTGOMERY; ▲ Hatfield; ***227** EN-12; ★ **PHIL-**; mail Hatfield z 19440; ● 900
Orviston; RMC Place; CENTRE; ▲ Curtin; **224** WI-14; 🅿; z 16864; ● 200
Orwell; RMC Place; BRADFORD; ▲ Orwell; **226** EE-7; mail Rome z 18837; ● 100
Orwell; MCD-Township; BRADFORD; ***226** EE-7; mail Rome z 18837; Ⓟ 1,107; Ⓒ 1,097
Orwigsburg; Inc. Place; SCHUYLKILL; **227** EL-8; elev. 640ft./195m.; 🅿; ★ **PTSVL**; z 17961; Ⓟ 2,780; Ⓒ 3,106
Orwin; RMC Place; SCHUYLKILL; ▲ Porter; **227** EM-6; mail Tower City z 17980; ● 300
Osborne; Inc. Place; ALLEGHENY; **228** H-2; elev. 760ft./232m.; ★ **PGH**; mail Sewickley z 15143; Ⓟ 565; Ⓒ 566
Osceola; RMC Place; TIOGA; ▲ Osceola; **226** ED-2; 🅿; z 16942; ● 400
Osceola; MCD-Township; TIOGA; ***226** ED-2; 🅿; z 16942; Ⓟ 772; Ⓒ 700
Osceola Mills; Inc. Place; CLEARFIELD; **225** WK-11; elev. 1,458ft./444m.; 🅿; z 16666; Ⓟ 1,310; Ⓒ 1,249
Osgood; RMC Place; MERCER; ▲ Sugar Grove; **224** WG-2; elev. 990ft./302m.; mail Greenville z 16125; ● 40
Oshanter; RMC Place; CLEARFIELD; ▲ Lawrence; ***224** WJ-10; mail Clearfield z 16830; rural
Ostend; RMC Place; CLEARFIELD; ▲ Bell; ***225** WK-9; mail Mahaffey z 15757; rural
Osterburg; RMC Place; BEDFORD; ▲ King, East St. Clair; **225** WO-10; 🅿; z 16667; ● 250
Osterhout; RMC Place; WYOMING; ▲ Tunkhannock; **226** EG-9; mail Tunkhannock z 18657; ● 30
Oswayo; Inc. Place; POTTER; **224** WE-12; elev. 1,703ft./519m.; 🅿; z 16915; Ⓟ 156; Ⓒ 159
Oswayo; MCD-Township; POTTER; ***224** WD-12; 🅿; z 16915 & mail Shinglehouse z 16748; does not include the Borough of Oswayo; Ⓟ 214; Ⓒ 251
Ottawa; RMC Place; MONTOUR; ▲ Limestone; ***226** EJ-5; mail Danville z 17821; rural
Otter Creek; MCD-Township; MERCER; ***224** WG-2; mail Greenville z 16125; Ⓟ 583; Ⓒ 611
Otto; MCD-Township; MCKEAN; ***224** WD-11; mail Rixford z 16745; Ⓟ 1,820; Ⓒ 1,738
Ottsville; RMC Place; BUCKS; ▲ Tinicum; **227** EM-12; 🅿; ★ **PHIL-**; z 18942; ● 250
Ott Town; RMC Place; BEDFORD; ▲ Colerain; ***225** WP-11; mail Everett z 15537; rural
Outcrop; RMC Place; FAYETTE; ▲ Springhill; ***225** WQ-4; ★ **MORG**; mail Smithfield z 15478; ● 75
Outlet; RMC Place; LUZERNE; ▲ Lehman; ***226** EH-8; ★ **SCR-**; mail Dallas z 18612; ● 150
Outwood; RMC Place; SCHUYLKILL; ▲ Pine Grove; ***227** EM-6; mail Pine Grove z 17963; ● 100
Oval; RMC Place; LYCOMING; ▲ Limestone; **226** EI-3; mail Jersey Shore z 17740, Williamsport z 17702; ● 180
Overbrook; RMC Place; ALLEGHENY; ***225** WN-4; ★ **PGH**; mail Pittsburgh z 15226; pop. incl. with Pittsburgh (Inc. Place)
Overbrook; RMC Place; PHILADELPHIA; ***227** EP-12; ★ **PHIL-**; mail Philadelphia z 19151; pop. incl. with Philadelphia (Inc. Place)
Overbrook Hills; RMC Place; MONTGOMERY; ▲ Lower Merion; 🅿; ★ **PHIL-**; z 19151
Overfield; MCD-Township; WYOMING; ***226** EG-9; ★ **SCR-**; mail Dalton z 18414; Ⓟ 1,466; Ⓒ 1,532
Overholt Acres; RMC Place; WESTMORELAND; ▲ North Huntingdon; ***225** WN-5; ★ **PGH**; mail Irwin z 15642; ● 700
Overlook; RMC Place; LANCASTER; ▲ Manheim; ***227** EP-7; ★ **LANC**; mail Lancaster z 17601; ● 200
Overlook; RMC Place; NORTHUMBERLAND; ▲ Ralpho; **227** ES-9; mail Shamokin z 17872; ● 200
Overlook Heights; RMC Place; CENTRE; ▲ Ferguson; **225** WS-12; ★ **STCOL**; mail State College z 16801; ● 1,200
Overlook Springs; RMC Place; LEHIGH; ▲ Salisbury; ***227** EM-11; elev. 600ft./183m.; ★ **ALL-**; mail Emmaus z 18049; ● 30
Overshot; RMC Place; BRADFORD; ▲ Towanda; ***226** EF-6; mail Towanda z 18848; rural
Overton; RMC Place; BRADFORD; ▲ Overton; **226** EG-6; mail New Albany z 18833; ● 85
Overton; MCD-Township; BRADFORD; ***226** EF-5; mail New Albany z 18833; Ⓟ 157; Ⓒ 187
Overview; RMC Place; CUMBERLAND; ▲ East Pennsboro; **227** ER-2; ★ **HRBG**; mail Marysville z 17053; ● 50
Owensdale; RMC Place; FAYETTE; ▲ Upper Tyrone; ***225** WO-5; mail Connellsville z 15425; ● 400
Oxbow Meadows; RMC Place; BUCKS; ▲ New Britain; ***227** EN-12; elev. 350ft./107m.; ★ **PHIL-**; mail Chalfont z 18914; ● 200
Oxford; MCD-Township; ADAMS; ***227** EQ-4; ★ **HANV**; mail New Oxford z 17350; Ⓟ 3,437; Ⓒ 4,876
Oxford; Inc. Place; CHESTER; **227** EQ-8; elev. 567ft./173m.; 🅿; z 19363; Ⓟ 3,769; Ⓒ 4,315
Oxford Valley; RMC Place; BUCKS; ▲ Falls; ***227** EO-13; elev. 140ft./43m.; ★ **PHIL-**; mail Fairless Hills z 19030
Oyster Point; RMC Place; LANCASTER; ▲ West Hempfield, East Hempfield; ***227** EP-6; elev. 495ft./151m.; ★ **LANC**; mail Lancaster z 17601-02; rural

P

Packer; MCD-Township; CARBON; ***227** EK-9; ★ **HAZ**; mail Weatherly z 18255; Ⓟ 918; Ⓒ 986
Packer; RMC Place; PHILADELPHIA; ★ **PHIL-**; pop. incl. with Philadelphia (Inc. Place)
Packers Island; NORTHUMBERLAND; see Island Park (RMC Place)
Packerton; RMC Place; CARBON; ▲ Mahoning; **227** EK-10; mail Lehighton z 18235; ● 200
Paddytown; RMC Place; SOMERSET; ▲ Upper Turkeyfoot; ***225** WQ-7; elev. 1,950ft./594m.; mail Markleton z 15551; rural
Pageville; RMC Place; ERIE; ▲ Elk Creek; ***224** WE-3; mail Albion z 16401; ● 40
Paint; MCD-Township; CLARION; ***224** WH-6; mail Shippenville z 16254; Ⓟ 1,730; Ⓒ 1,778
Paint; Inc. Place; SOMERSET; **225** WO-9; elev. 1,678ft./511m.; ★ **JNST**; mail Windber z 15963; Ⓟ 1,091; Ⓒ 1,103
Paint; MCD-Township; SOMERSET; ***225** WO-9; ★ **JNST**; mail Windber z 15963; does not include the Borough of Paint; Ⓟ 3,491; Ⓒ 3,300
Paintersville; RMC Place; MIFFLIN; ▲ Decatur; ***227** EL-2; mail Lewistown z 17044
Paintersville; RMC Place; WESTMORELAND; ***225** WO-5; ★ **PGH**; mail Hunker z 15639; pop. incl. with New Stanton (Inc. Place)
Paintertown; RMC Place; WESTMORELAND; ▲ Penn; ***225** WN-5; ★ **PGH**; mail Irwin z 15642; ● 120
Paisley; RMC Place; GREENE; ▲ Cumberland; **225** WQ-4; mail Carmichaels z 15320; ● 100
Paletown; RMC Place; BUCKS; ▲ Richland; ***227** EM-11; ★ **PHIL-**; mail Perkasie z 18944; ● 250
Palm; RMC Place; MONTGOMERY; ▲ Upper Hanover; **227** EM-10; 🅿; ★ **PHIL-**; z 18070; ● 370
Palmdale; RMC Place; DAUPHIN; ▲ Derry; ***227** EN-5; ★ **HRBG**; mail Hershey z 17033
Palmer; RMC Place; CRAWFORD; **224** WE-2; mail Conneautville z 16406; rural
Palmer; FAYETTE; see Adah (RMC Place)
Palmer (Palmer Township); MCD-Township; NORTHAMPTON; ***227** EL-12; 🅿; ★ **ALL-**; z 18043, z 18045; Ⓟ 14,965; Ⓒ 16,809; ◆ 19,750
Palmer Heights; CDP; NORTHAMPTON; ▲ Palmer; **227** EL-12; ★ **ALL-**; mail Easton z 18045; Ⓟ 3,960; Ⓒ 3,612
Palmer Park (Seipsville); RMC Place; NORTHAMPTON; ▲ Palmer; ***227** EL-12; ★ **ALL-**; mail Easton z 18045; ● 1,100
Palmerton; Inc. Place; CARBON; **227** EK-10; elev. 400ft./122m.; 🅿 🅷; z 18071; Ⓟ 5,394; Ⓒ 5,248
Palmerton East; RMC Place; CARBON; mail Palmerton z 18071; pop. incl. with Palmerton (Inc. Place)
Palmertown; RMC Place; INDIANA; ▲ Burrell; ***225** WM-7; ★ **LTROB**; mail Blairsville z 15717; ● 150
Palmer Township; NORTHAMPTON; see Palmer (MCD-Township)
Palmyra; Inc. Place; LEBANON; **227** EN-6; elev. 460ft./140m.; 🅿; z 17078; Ⓟ 6,910; Ⓒ 7,096
Palmyra; MCD-Township; PIKE; ***226** EH-12; mail Paupack z 18451; Ⓟ 1,976; Ⓒ 3,145
Palmyra; MCD-Township; WAYNE; ***226** EG-12; mail Hawley z 18428; Ⓟ 905; Ⓒ 1,127
Palo Alto; RMC Place; BEDFORD; ▲ Londonderry; ***225** WQ-9; mail Hyndman z 15545
Palo Alto; Inc. Place; SCHUYLKILL; **227** EL-7; elev. 680ft./207m.; ★ **PTSVL**; mail Pottsville z 17901; Ⓟ 1,192; Ⓒ 1,052
Palomino Farms; RMC Place; BUCKS; ▲ Warrington; ***227** EN-12; ★ **PHIL-**; mail Warrington z 18976
Pancoast; RMC Place; JEFFERSON; ▲ Winslow; ***224** WI-9; mail Reynoldsville z 15851; rural
P&OV Junction (POV Junction); RMC Place; ALLEGHENY; ▲ Stowe; ★ **PGH**
P & W Patch; WASHINGTON; see Avella Highlands (RMC Place)
Panic; RMC Place; JEFFERSON; ▲ McCalmont; **224** WJ-8; mail Reynoldsville z 15851; ● 80
Panorama Village; RMC Place; CENTRE; ▲ Harris; ***225** WK-13; ★ **STCOL**; mail State College z 16801; ● 500
Pansy; RMC Place; JEFFERSON; ▲ Beaver; ***224** WJ-7; mail Summerville z 15864; rural
Pansy Hill; RMC Place; LEBANON; ▲ North Lebanon; ***227** EN-6; ★ **LEB**; mail Lebanon z 17046; ● 160
Panther; RMC Place; PIKE; ▲ Greene; ***226** EH-11; mail Newfoundland z 18445; rural
Paoli; CDP; CHESTER; ▲ Willistown, Tredyffrin; **227** EP-11; 🅿 🅷; ★ **PHIL-**; z 19301; Ⓟ 5,603; Ⓒ 5,425
Paper Mills; RMC Place; MONTGOMERY; ***227** EO-13; ★ **PHIL-**; mail Bryn Athyn z 19009; pop. incl. with Bryn Athyn (Inc. Place)
Paradise; CDP; LANCASTER; ▲ Paradise; **227** EP-8; 🅿; z 17562; Ⓟ 1,043; Ⓒ 1,028
Paradise; MCD-Township; LANCASTER; ***227** EP-8; 🅿; z 17562; Ⓟ 4,430; Ⓒ 4,698
Paradise; MCD-Township; MONROE; ***226** EI-12; mail Cresco z 18326; Ⓟ 2,251; Ⓒ 2,671
Paradise; RMC Place; SCHUYLKILL; ▲ Pine Grove; **227** EM-7; mail Pine Grove z 17963; ● 250
Paradise; MCD-Township; YORK; ***227** EQ-4; mail Abbottstown z 17301; Ⓟ 3,180; Ⓒ 3,600
Paradise Falls; RMC Place; MONROE; ▲ Paradise; mail Cresco z 18326; summer pop. 200
Paradise Valley; RMC Place; MONROE; ▲ Paradise; ***226** EI-11; 🅿; z 18326
Pardee; RMC Place; CLEARFIELD; ▲ Morris; ***224** WJ-12; mail Philipsburg z 16866; ● 60
Pardeesville; RMC Place; LUZERNE; ▲ Hazle; ***226** EJ-8; 🅿; ★ **HAZ**; z 18202 & mail Hazleton z 18201; ● 500
Pardoe; RMC Place; MERCER; ▲ Findley; **224** WI-3; mail Mercer z 16137; ● 50
Pardus; RMC Place; JEFFERSON; ▲ Washington; ***224** WI-9; mail Reynoldsville z 15851; rural
Paris; RMC Place; WASHINGTON; ▲ Hanover; **225** WM-1; elev. 1,228ft./374m.; 🅿; z 15021; ● 200
Park; RMC Place; WESTMORELAND; 🅿; ★ **PGH**; z 15690; pop. incl. with Vandergrift (Inc. Place)
Parkchester; RMC Place; CHESTER; ▲ West Goshen; ***227** EP-10; ★ **PHIL-**; mail West Chester z 19380; ● 300
Park Crest; RMC Place; SCHUYLKILL; ▲ Delano, Rush, Ryan; ***227** EK-8; elev. 1,131ft./345m.; ★ **PTSVL**; mail Barnesville z 18214; ● 300
Parker; Inc. Place; ARMSTRONG; **224** WI-5; elev. 1,100ft./335m.; 🅿; z 16049; Ⓟ 853; Ⓒ 799
Parker; MCD-Township; BUTLER; ***224** WJ-4; 🅿; z 16049; Ⓟ 601; Ⓒ 700
Parker Ford; RMC Place; CHESTER; ▲ East Coventry; **227** EO-10; 🅿; ★ **PTSTN**; z 19457; ● 800
Parkers Glen; RMC Place; PIKE; ▲ Shohola; ***226** EG-13; mail Shohola z 18458; ● 50
Parkersville; RMC Place; CHESTER; ▲ Pennsbury; ***227** EQ-10; elev. 378ft./115m.; ★ **PHIL-**; mail West Chester z 19380; rural
Parkesburg; Inc. Place; CHESTER; **227** EP-9; elev. 543ft./166m.; 🅿; ★ **PHIL-**; z 19365; Ⓟ 2,981; Ⓒ 3,373
Park Forest Village; CDP; CENTRE; ▲ Patton; **225** WS-11; ★ **STCOL**; mail State College z 16803; Ⓟ 6,703; Ⓒ 8,830
Park Gate; RMC Place; LAWRENCE; ▲ Wayne; ***225** WK-2; ★ **PGH**; mail Ellwood City z 16117; ● 180
Park Heights; RMC Place; YORK; ▲ Penn; ***227** EQ-4; ★ **HANV**; mail Hanover z 17331; ● 100
Parkhill; RMC Place; CAMBRIA; ▲ East Taylor; **225** WS-2; 🅿; ★ **JNST**; z 15945; ● 300
Park Hills; RMC Place; CENTRE; ▲ Ferguson; **225** WT-12; ★ **STCOL**; mail State College z 16803; ● 2,500
Park Hills; RMC Place; YORK; ▲ Penn; ★ **HANV**; mail Hanover z 17331; ● 40
Park Junction; RMC Place; PHILADELPHIA; ★ **PHIL-**; pop. incl. with Philadelphia (Inc. Place)
Parkland; RMC Place; BUCKS; ▲ Middletown; ***227** EO-13; ★ **PHIL-**; mail Langhorne z 19047; ● 1,100
Park Manor; RMC Place; BERKS; ▲ Cumru; ★ **READ**; mail Reading z 19607
Park Meadows; RMC Place; WESTMORELAND; ▲ North Huntingdon; ***225** WN-5; ★ **PGH**; mail Irwin z 15642; ● 200

Entries in **UPPERCASE** are counties.
Entries in **bold** have populations of 2,500 or more.
Names in parentheses are alternate names.

Inc. Place	Incorporated Place
RMC Place	Rand McNally Designated Place
CDP	Census Designated Place
MCD	Minor Civil Division

⊡	County Seat
▲	Minor Civil Division
elev.	Elevation
🅿	Post Office
🅷	Hospital
🅲	College
■	Principal Business Center
★	Ranally Metro Area (RMA) Abbreviation
z	Zip Code(s)
Ⓟ	Previous Census Population
Ⓡ	Revised Census Population
Ⓐ	Annexation Population
●	Rand McNally Population Estimate
Ⓒ	Final Census Population
Ⓢ	Special Census Population
◆	Estimated Population

For additional definitions see Glossary, Volume 1, and Introduction, Volume 2.

Park Place; RMC Place; SCHUYLKILL; ▲ Mahanoy; *227 EK-8; mail Mahanoy City z 17948; ● 135

Parks; MCD-Township; ARMSTRONG; *225 WL-5; ★ PGH; mail Vandergrift z 15690; Ⓟ 2,739; Ⓒ 2,754

Parks; YORK; see Brogueville (RMC Place)

Parkside; Inc. Place; DELAWARE; 227 EQ-11; elev. 100ft./30m.; ★ PHIL-; mail Brookhaven z 19015, Chester z 19013; Ⓟ 2,369; Ⓒ 2,267

Parkside Courts; RMC Place; LEHIGH; ▲ South Whitehall; *227 EL-10; ★ ALL-; mail Allentown z 18104; ● 650

Parkside Manor; RMC Place; DELAWARE; ★ PHIL-; mail Brookhaven z 19015; pop. incl. with Parkside (Inc. Place)

Parkstown; RMC Place; CAMBRIA; ▲ Conemaugh; *225 WN-9; ★ JNST; mail Johnstown z 15902; ● 175

Parkstown; RMC Place; LAWRENCE; ▲ Union; *224 WJ-2; elev. 1,100ft./335m.; ★ YNGS-; mail New Castle z 16101; ● 300

Parktown Estates; RMC Place; BUCKS; ▲ Lower Makefield; *227 EN-14; ★ PHIL-; mail Morrisville z 19067; ● 1,700

Park View; RMC Place; ALLEGHENY; ▲ O'Hara; *225 WM-4; ★ PGH; mail Pittsburgh z 15215; ● 1,300

Parkview Gardens; RMC Place; LEHIGH; ▲ Whitehall; ★ ALL-; mail Whitehall z 18052

Park View Heights; RMC Place; CENTRE; *225 WK-14; ★ STCOL; mail Bellefonte z 16823; pop. incl. with Bellefonte (Inc. Place)

Parkville; CDP; YORK; ▲ Penn; 227 EQ-4; ★ HANV; mail Hanover z 17331; Ⓟ 6,014; Ⓒ 6,593

Park Way Manor; RMC Place; LEHIGH; ▲ South Whitehall; *227 EL-10; ★ ALL-; mail Allentown z 18104; ● 2,000

Parkwood; RMC Place; INDIANA; ▲ Armstrong; *225 WL-7; mail Shelocta z 15774; ● 50

Parnassus; RMC Place; WESTMORELAND; *225 WM-5; 🅿; ★ PGH; z 15068; pop. incl. with New Kensington (Inc. Place)

Parryville; Inc. Place; CARBON; 227 EK-10; elev. 460ft./140m.; 🅿; z 18244; Ⓟ 488; Ⓒ 478

Parsons; RMC Place; LUZERNE; *226 EH-9; 🅿; ★ SCR-; z 18705; pop. incl. with Wilkes-Barre (Inc. Place)

Parsonville; RMC Place; BUTLER; ▲ Washington; *224 WJ-4; mail Petrolia z 16050; rural

Parsonville; RMC Place; CLEARFIELD; ▲ Decatur; *225 WK-11; mail Houtzdale z 16651; ● 40

Parvin; RMC Place; CLINTON; ▲ Porter; *226 EJ-1; mail Mill Hall z 17751; rural

Paschall; RMC Place; PHILADELPHIA; ★ PHIL-; mail Philadelphia z 19142; pop. incl. with Philadelphia (Inc. Place)

Passer; RMC Place; BUCKS; ▲ Springfield; *227 EM-11; elev. 726ft./221m.; ★ ALL-; mail Coopersburg z 18036; ● 150

Patchinville; RMC Place; CLEARFIELD; ▲ Burnside; 225 WK-9; mail Cherry Tree z 15724; ● 30

Patterson; MCD-Township; BEAVER; *225 WK-2; ★ PGH; mail Beaver Falls z 15010; Ⓟ 3,074; Ⓒ 3,197

Patterson; RMC Place; PHILADELPHIA; ★ PHIL-; pop. incl. with Philadelphia (Inc. Place)

Patterson Grove; RMC Place; LUZERNE; ▲ Fairmount; *226 EI-7; mail Shickshinny z 18655; ● 35

Patterson Heights; Inc. Place; BEAVER; 225 WK-2; elev. 1,060ft./323m.; 🅿; ★ PGH; z 15010; Ⓟ 576; Ⓒ 670

Patterson Hill; RMC Place; ALLEGHENY; *225 WN-4; ★ PGH; mail Elizabeth z 15037; pop. incl. with Lincoln (Inc. Place)

Pattersons Mill; RMC Place; WASHINGTON; ▲ Cross Creek; *225 WN-1; elev. 1,019ft./311m.; mail Avella z 15312; rural

Patterson Township; CDP-Census Area Only; BEAVER; ▲ Patterson; *225 WK-2; ★ PGH; mail Beaver Falls z 15010; Ⓟ 3,074; Ⓒ 3,197

Pattersonville; RMC Place; SCHUYLKILL; ▲ Union; *227 EK-7; mail Ringtown z 17967; ● 200

Patton; Inc. Place; CAMBRIA; 225 WL-10; elev. 1,755ft./535m.; 🅿; z 16668; Ⓟ 2,206; Ⓒ 2,023

Patton; MCD-Township; CENTRE; *225 WK-13; ★ STCOL; mail State College z 16803; Ⓟ 9,971; Ⓒ 11,420

Patton; RMC Place; WASHINGTON; ▲ South Strabane; *225 WO-2; elev. 1,100ft./335m.; ★ WASH; mail Washington z 15301; ● 1,300

Pattonville; RMC Place; ARMSTRONG; ▲ Manor; *225 WK-6; ★ PGH; mail Ford City z 16226; ● 300

Paulton; RMC Place; WESTMORELAND; ▲ Washington; *225 WL-5; ★ PGH; mail Apollo z 15613; ● 340

Paupack; RMC Place; PIKE; ▲ Palmyra; 226 EH-12; elev. 1,563ft./476m.; 🅿; z 18451; ● 600

Paupack; MCD-Township; WAYNE; *226 EG-11; mail Hawley z 18428; Ⓟ 1,696; Ⓒ 2,959

Paupack Gardens; RMC Place; PIKE; ▲ Palmyra; *226 EH-12; elev. 1,300ft./396m.; mail Paupack z 18451; ● 250

Pavia; RMC Place; BEDFORD; ▲ Pavia; 225 WN-10; elev. 1,425ft./434m.; mail Imler z 16655; ● 90

Pavia (Union); MCD-Township; BEDFORD; *225 WO-10; mail Imler z 16655; Ⓟ 296; Ⓒ 325

Paxinos; RMC Place; NORTHUMBERLAND; ▲ Shamokin; 227 EK-6; 🅿; z 17860; ● 500

Paxtang; Inc. Place; DAUPHIN; 227 ET-4; 🅿; ★ HRBG; z 17111; Ⓟ 1,599; Ⓒ 1,570

Paxtang Manor; RMC Place; DAUPHIN; ▲ Susquehanna; *227 EN-5; ★ HRBG; mail Harrisburg z 17111; ● 460

Paxton (Mahantango); RMC Place; DAUPHIN; ▲ Upper Paxton; 227 EM-4; mail Dalmatia z 17017; ● 100

Paxtonia; CDP; DAUPHIN; ▲ Lower Paxton; 227 ER-4; 🅿; ★ HRBG; z 17112; Ⓟ 4,862; Ⓒ 5,254

Paxtonville; CDP; SNYDER; ▲ Franklin; 227 EK-3; 🅿; z 17861; Ⓒ 221

Peacedale; RMC Place; CHESTER; ▲ Elk; *227 EQ-9; ★ PHIL-; mail Oxford z 19363; rural

Peach Bottom; LANCASTER; see Wakefield (RMC Place)

Peach Bottom; MCD-Township; YORK; *227 ER-7; ★ BAL; mail Delta z 17314; Ⓟ 3,444; Ⓒ 4,412

Peach Bottom Village; RMC Place; LANCASTER; ▲ Fulton; *227 EQ-7; mail Peach Bottom z 17563; summer pop. 175; ● 100

Peach Glen; RMC Place; ADAMS; ▲ Tyrone; 227 EP-3; 🅿; z 17375; ● 100

Pealertown; RMC Place; COLUMBIA; ▲ Fishing Creek; *226 EI-7; elev. 639ft./195m.; mail Orangeville z 17859; rural

Peanut; RMC Place; LAWRENCE; ▲ Mahoning; *224 WJ-2; ★ YNGS-; mail Edinburg z 16116; ● 160

Peanut; RMC Place; WESTMORELAND; ▲ Derry; *225 WN-7; ★ LTROB; mail Derry z 15627; ● 270

Pearl; RMC Place; VENANGO; ▲ Victory, Irwin; 224 WH-4; mail Polk z 16342; ● 50

Pebble Hill; RMC Place; BUCKS; *227 EN-12; ★ PHIL-; mail Doylestown z 18901; ● 900

Pecan; RMC Place; VENANGO; ▲ Sandycreek; *224 WH-4; ★ OILC-F; mail Polk z 16342; rural

Pechin; RMC Place; FAYETTE; ▲ Dunbar; *225 WP-5; mail Dunbar z 15431; ● 200

Pecks Pond; RMC Place; PIKE; ▲ Porter; *226 EH-12; mail Dingmans Ferry z 18328

Peckville; RMC Place; LACKAWANNA; *226 EG-10; elev. 820ft./250m.; 🅿 🅷; ★ SCR-; z 18452; pop. incl. with Blakely (Inc. Place)

Peely; LUZERNE; see Warrior Run (Inc. Place)

Pemberton; RMC Place; HUNTINGDON; ▲ Spruce Creek; *225 WL-12; mail Spruce Creek z 16683; rural

Pen Argyl; Inc. Place; NORTHAMPTON; 227 EK-12; elev. 847ft./258m.; 🅿; z 18072; Ⓟ 3,492; Ⓒ 3,615

Penarth; RMC Place; MONTGOMERY; ▲ Lower Merion; ★ PHIL-; mail Bala Cynwyd z 19004

Penbrook; Inc. Place; DAUPHIN; 227 ES-3; elev. 486ft./148m.; 🅿; ★ HRBG; z 17103, z 17109; Ⓟ 2,791; Ⓒ 3,044

Penbryn; RMC Place; TIOGA; ▲ Union; *226 EG-4; mail Roaring Branch z 17765; rural

Pendle Hill; RMC Place; DELAWARE; ▲ Nether Providence; *227 EP-11; ★ PHIL-; mail Wallingford z 19086

Penfield; RMC Place; CLEARFIELD; ▲ Huston; 224 WI-10; 🅿; z 15849; ● 650

Penllyn; RMC Place; MONTGOMERY; ▲ Lower Gwynedd; *227 EO-12; 🅿; ★ PHIL-; z 19422; ● 1,200

Pen Mar; RMC Place; FRANKLIN; ▲ Washington; 227 ER-1; elev. 1,246ft./380m.; ★ HAG; mail Waynesboro z 17268; ● 400

Penn; MCD-Township; BERKS; *227 EM-8; ★ READ; mail Bernville z 19506; Ⓟ 1,831; Ⓒ 1,993

Penn; MCD-Township; BUTLER; *225 WK-4; ★ PGH; mail Butler z 16001; Ⓟ 5,080; Ⓒ 5,210

Penn; MCD-Township; CENTRE; *227 EK-1; mail Coburn z 16832; Ⓟ 935; Ⓒ 1,044

Penn; MCD-Township; CHESTER; *227 EQ-9; ★ PHIL-; mail West Grove z 19390; Ⓟ 2,257; Ⓒ 2,812

Penn; MCD-Township; CLEARFIELD; *224 WJ-10; mail Grampian z 16838; Ⓟ 1,372; Ⓒ 1,326

Penn; MCD-Township; CUMBERLAND; *227 EO-2; mail Shippensburg z 17257; Ⓟ 2,425; Ⓒ 2,807

Penn; MCD-Township; HUNTINGDON; *225 WN-12; mail Hesston z 16647; Ⓟ 956; Ⓒ 1,054

Penn; MCD-Township; LANCASTER; *227 EO-7; ★ LANC; mail Manheim z 17545; Ⓟ 6,760; Ⓒ 7,312

Penn; MCD-Township; LYCOMING; *226 EI-5; mail Hughesville z 17737; Ⓟ 788; Ⓒ 900

Penn; MCD-Township; PERRY; *227 EN-4; ★ HRBG; mail Duncannon z 17020; Ⓟ 3,283; Ⓒ 3,013

Penn; MCD-Township; SNYDER; *227 EK-4; mail Selinsgrove z 17870; Ⓟ 3,208; Ⓒ 3,781

Penn; Inc. Place; WESTMORELAND; 225 WN-5; elev. 978ft./298m.; 🅿; ★ PGH; z 15675; Ⓟ 511; Ⓒ 460

Penn; MCD-Township; WESTMORELAND; *225 WN-5; 🅿; ★ PGH; z 15675 & mail Harrison City z 15636; does not include the Borough of Penn; Ⓟ 15,945; Ⓒ 19,591; Ⓡ 19,670; ◆ 19,286

Penn; MCD-Township; YORK; *227 EQ-4; ★ HANV; mail Hanover z 17331; Ⓟ 11,658; Ⓒ 14,592

Penn Allen; RMC Place; NORTHAMPTON; ▲ Upper Nazareth; *227 EL-11; ★ ALL-; mail Nazareth z 18064; ● 50

Penn Avon; SNYDER; see Dogtown (RMC Place)

Pennbrook; RMC Place; MONTGOMERY; ★ PHIL-; mail Lansdale z 19446; pop. incl. with Lansdale (Inc. Place)

Penn Center; RMC Place; PHILADELPHIA; ★ PHIL-; mail Philadelphia z 19102; pop. incl. with Philadelphia (Inc. Place)

Penncraft; RMC Place; FAYETTE; ▲ Luzerne; *225 WP-4; elev. 1,088ft./332m.; ★ UNTN; mail East Millsboro z 15433; ● 200

Penndel; Inc. Place; BUCKS; 227 EO-13; elev. 100ft./30m.; 🅿; ★ PHIL-; z 19047; Ⓟ 2,703; Ⓒ 2,420

Pennersville; RMC Place; FRANKLIN; ▲ Washington; *227 ER-2; ★ HAG; mail Waynesboro z 17268; ● 250

Penn Estates; RMC Place; MONROE; ▲ Stroud; *226 EJ-12; elev. 900ft./274m.; mail East Stroudsburg z 18301; ● 500

Pennfield; RMC Place; BUCKS; ▲ Bristol; ★ PHIL-; mail Bristol z 19007

Penn Five; RMC Place; CENTRE; ▲ Rush; *225 WK-11; mail Osceola Mills z 16666; rural

Penn Forest; MCD-Township; CARBON; *227 EK-10; mail Albrightsville z 18210; Ⓟ 2,895; Ⓒ 5,439

Penn Glyn; RMC Place; WESTMORELAND; *225 WN-5; ★ PGH; mail Irwin z 15642; pop. incl. with Irwin (Inc. Place)

Penn Hall; RMC Place; CENTRE; ▲ Gregg; 227 EK-1; mail Spring Mills z 16875; ● 60

Penn Heights; RMC Place; YORK; ★ HANV; mail Hanover z 17331; pop. incl. with Hanover (Inc. Place)

Penn Hill; RMC Place; LANCASTER; ▲ Fulton; *227 EQ-8; elev. 448ft./137m.; mail Peach Bottom z 17563; ● 35

Penn Hills; CDP; ALLEGHENY; ▲ Penn Hills; 225 WM-4; elev. 1,200ft./366m.; 🅿; ★ PGH; z 15235 & mail Verona z 15147; Ⓟ 51,430; Ⓒ 46,809; ◆ 43,040

Penn Hills; MCD-Township; ALLEGHENY; *225 WM-4; elev. 1,200ft./366m.; 🅿; ★ PGH; z 15235 & mail Verona z 15147; Ⓟ 51,430; Ⓒ 46,809; ◆ 43,040

Penn Lake Park; Inc. Place; LUZERNE; 226 EI-9; mail White Haven z 18661; Ⓟ 242; Ⓒ 269

Pennline; RMC Place; CRAWFORD; ▲ Conneaut; 224 WF-1; elev. 1,156ft./352m.; mail Linesville z 16424; ● 40

Penn Pines; RMC Place; DELAWARE; ▲ Upper Darby; *227 EP-12; elev. 104ft./32m.; ★ PHIL-; mail Clifton Heights z 19018; ● 650

Penn Pitt; RMC Place; GREENE; ▲ Monongahela; *225 WQ-4; mail Greensboro z 15338; ● 100

Penn Rose Park; RMC Place; LANCASTER; ▲ Manheim; *227 EP-7; ★ LANC; mail Lancaster z 17601; ● 450

Penn Run; RMC Place; INDIANA; ▲ Cherryhill; 225 WL-8; elev. 1,474ft./449m.; 🅿; z 15765; ● 250

Pennsburg; Inc. Place; MONTGOMERY; 227 EN-11; elev. 384ft./117m.; 🅿; ★ PHIL-; z 18073; Ⓟ 2,460; Ⓒ 2,732

Pennsbury; MCD-Township; CHESTER; *227 EQ-10; elev. 384ft./117m.; ★ PHIL-; mail Chadds Ford z 19317; Ⓟ 3,326; Ⓒ 3,500

Pennsbury Heights; RMC Place; BUCKS; ▲ Falls; *227 EO-14; elev. 80ft./24m.; ★ PHIL-; mail Morrisville z 19067; ● 1,200

Pennsbury Village; Inc. Place; ALLEGHENY; *225 WM-3; ★ PGH; mail Pittsburgh z 15205; Ⓟ 774; Ⓒ 738

Penns Creek; CDP; SNYDER; ▲ Center; 227 EK-4; 🅿; z 17862; Ⓒ 668

Pennsdale; RMC Place; LYCOMING; ▲ Muncy; 226 EI-5; elev. 536ft./163m.; 🅿; ★ WMSPT; z 17756; ● 110

Pennside; RMC Place; BERKS; ▲ Exeter, Lower Alsace; 227 ET-13; ★ READ; mail Reading z 19606; ● 3,000

Pennside; RMC Place; ERIE; ▲ Conneaut; 224 WE-2; ★ ERIE; mail Albion z 16401; ● 35

Penn's Landing; RMC Place; PHILADELPHIA; ★ PHIL-; pop. incl. with Philadelphia (Inc. Place)

Penns Park; RMC Place; BUCKS; ▲ Wrightstown; 227 EN-13; 🅿; ★ PHIL-; z 18943; ● 500

Penn Square Village; RMC Place; MONTGOMERY; ▲ East Norriton; *227 EO-11; ★ PHIL-; mail Norristown z 19401

Pennsville; RMC Place; FAYETTE; ▲ Bullskin; 225 WO-5; mail Connellsville z 15425; ● 200

Pennsville; RMC Place; NORTHAMPTON; ▲ Lehigh; 227 EK-10; ★ ALL-; mail Northampton z 18067; ● 350

Penns Woods; RMC Place; WESTMORELAND; ▲ North Huntingdon; *225 WN-5; ★ PGH; mail Irwin z 15642; ● 2,600

Pennsylvania Furnace; RMC Place; HUNTINGDON; ▲ Franklin; 225 WL-13; 🅿; z 16865; ● 150

Pennvale; RMC Place; LYCOMING; ▲ Loyalsock; ★ WMSPT; mail Williamsport z 17701

Penn Valley (Penn Valley Terrace); RMC Place; BUCKS; ▲ Bensalem; *227 EO-14; ★ PHIL-; mail Langhorne z 19047; ● 700

Penn Valley; RMC Place; MONTGOMERY; ▲ Lower Merion; 228 C-2; 🅿; ★ PHIL-; z 19072; ● 6,000

Penn Valley Terrace; BUCKS; see Penn Valley (RMC Place)

Penn Village; RMC Place; MONTGOMERY; ★ PTSTN; mail Pottstown z 19464; pop. incl. with Pottstown (Inc. Place)

Pennville; CDP; YORK; ▲ Penn; *227 EQ-4; elev. 663ft./202m.; ★ HANV; mail Hanover z 17331; Ⓟ 1,559; Ⓒ 1,964

Penn Wood; RMC Place; BEDFORD; ▲ Snake Spring; *225 WP-11; mail Everett z 15537; rural

Pennwyn; RMC Place; BERKS; ▲ Cumru; 227 ET-12; ★ READ; mail Reading z 19607; ● 650

Penn Wynne; CDP; MONTGOMERY; ▲ Lower Merion; 228 D-2; ★ PHIL-; mail Philadelphia z 19151, Wynnewood z 19096; Ⓟ 5,807; Ⓒ 5,382

Pennypack Woods; RMC Place; PHILADELPHIA; *227 EP-13; ★ PHIL-; pop. incl. with Philadelphia (Inc. Place)

Penobscot; RMC Place; LUZERNE; ▲ Fairview; *226 EI-9; ★ SCR-; mail Mountain Top z 18707

Penowa; RMC Place; WASHINGTON; ▲ Independence, Jefferson; 225 WN-1; mail Avella z 15312; ● 20

Penryn; RMC Place; LANCASTER; ▲ Penn; 227 EO-7; 🅿; ★ LANC; z 17564; ● 700

Pequea; RMC Place; LANCASTER; ▲ Martic; 227 EQ-7; 🅿; ★ LANC; z 17565; ● 300

Pequea; MCD-Township; LANCASTER; *227 EP-7; 🅿; ★ LANC; z 17565 & mail Willow Street z 17584; Ⓟ 4,512; Ⓒ 4,358

Percy; RMC Place; FAYETTE; ▲ North Union; *225 WP-5; ★ UNTN; mail Lemont Furnace z 15456; ● 70

Perdix; RMC Place; PERRY; ▲ Penn; 227 EN-4; ★ HRBG; mail Duncannon z 17020; ● 90

Perkasie; Inc. Place; BUCKS; 227 EN-11; elev. 400ft./122m.; 🅿; ★ PHIL-; z 18944; Ⓟ 7,878; Ⓒ 8,828

Perkiomen; MCD-Township; MONTGOMERY; *227 EN-11; ★ PHIL-; mail Collegeville z 19426; Ⓟ 3,200; Ⓒ 7,093

Perkiomen Heights; RMC Place; MONTGOMERY; ▲ Upper Hanover; 227 EN-10; ★ PHIL-; mail Pennsburg z 18073; ● 70

Perkiomen Junction; RMC Place; CHESTER; ▲ Schuylkill; *227 EO-11; elev. 155ft./47m.; ★ PHIL-; mail Phoenixville z 19460, Valley Forge z 19481; ● 200

Perkiomen Village; RMC Place; MONTGOMERY; ▲ Perkiomen; ★ PHIL-; mail Collegeville z 19426

Perkiomenville; RMC Place; MONTGOMERY; ▲ Upper Frederick, Marlborough; *227 EN-11; 🅿; ★ PHIL-; z 18074; ● 400

Perrine Corners; RMC Place; MERCER; ▲ Worth; *224 WH-3; mail Stoneboro z 16153

Perry; MCD-Township; ARMSTRONG; *224 WJ-5; mail Karns City z 16041; Ⓟ 322; Ⓒ 404

Perry; MCD-Township; BERKS; *227 EM-9; mail Hamburg z 19526; Ⓟ 2,516; Ⓒ 2,517

Perry; MCD-Township; CLARION; *224 WI-5; mail Parker z 16049; Ⓟ 1,076; Ⓒ 1,064

Perry; MCD-Township; FAYETTE; *225 WO-5; ★ PGH; mail Perryopolis z 15473; does not include the Borough of Perryopolis; Ⓟ 2,817; Ⓒ 2,786

Perry; MCD-Township; GREENE; *225 WQ-3; mail Mount Morris z 15349; Ⓟ 1,719; Ⓒ 1,720

Perry; MCD-Township; JEFFERSON; *224 WJ-8; mail Punxsutawney z 15767; Ⓟ 1,293; Ⓒ 1,289

Perry; MCD-Township; LAWRENCE; *225 WK-3; ★ PGH; mail Ellwood City z 16117; Ⓟ 1,841; Ⓒ 1,930

Perry; MCD-Township; MERCER; *224 WH-3; mail Hadley z 16130; Ⓟ 1,468; Ⓒ 1,471

Perry; MCD-Township; SNYDER; *227 EL-4; mail Mount Pleasant Mills z 17853; Ⓟ 1,873; Ⓒ 1,973

PERRY; 227 EN-3; Ⓟ 41,172; Ⓒ 43,602; ◆ 45,565

Perryopolis; Inc. Place; FAYETTE; 225 WO-5; elev. 980ft./299m.; 🅿; ★ PGH; z 15473; Ⓟ 1,833; Ⓒ 1,764

Perrys Corners (Briscoe Springs); RMC Place; MERCER; ▲ Wolf Creek, Pine; *224 WI-3; mail Grove City z 16127; ● 60

Perry Square; RMC Place; ERIE; *224 WC-3; ★ ERIE; mail Erie z 16507; pop. incl. with Erie (Inc. Place)

Perrysville; RMC Place; ALLEGHENY; ▲ Ross; *225 WM-3; ★ PGH; mail Pittsburgh z 15237

Perryville; RMC Place; CLARION; ▲ Perry; 224 WI-5; mail Parker z 16049; ● 180

Perryville; RMC Place; LYCOMING; ▲ Lycoming; 226 EH-3; ★ WMSPT; mail Cogan Station z 17728; ● 25

Perryville; RMC Place; WESTMORELAND; ▲ Bell; 225 WM-6; ★ PGH; mail Avonmore z 15618; ● 70

Perulack; RMC Place; JUNIATA; ▲ Lack; *227 EN-1; mail East Waterford z 17021; rural

Peters; MCD-Township; FRANKLIN; *225 WQ-13; mail Mercersburg z 17236; Ⓟ 4,090; Ⓒ 4,251

Peters; MCD-Township; WASHINGTON; *225 WN-3; ★ PGH; mail Canonsburg z 15317; Ⓟ 14,467; Ⓒ 17,566; ◆ 18,846

Petersburg; Inc. Place; HUNTINGDON; 225 WM-12; elev. 700ft./213m.; 🅿; z 16669; Ⓟ 469; Ⓒ 455

Peters Corner; RMC Place; BUCKS; ▲ Solebury; *227 EN-13; ★ PHIL-; mail Mechanicsville z 18934; rural

Petersville; RMC Place; NORTHAMPTON; ▲ Lehigh; *227 EK-11; ★ ALL-; mail Northampton z 18067; ● 150

Petrolia; Inc. Place; BUTLER; 224 WJ-5; elev. 1,160ft./354m.; 🅿; z 16050; Ⓟ 292; Ⓒ 218

Pettis Corners; RMC Place; CRAWFORD; ▲ East Mead, East Fairfield; *224 WF-3; mail Meadville z 16335; rural

Pheasant Hill; RMC Place; LANCASTER; ▲ Manheim; ★ LANC; mail Lancaster z 17601; ● 500

Pheasant Ridge; RMC Place; BUCKS; ▲ Buckingham; *227 EN-12; elev. 460ft./140m.; ★ PHIL-; mail Doylestown z 18901; ● 120

Philadelphia; Inc. Place; ⊡ PHILADELPHIA; 227 EP-12; elev. 45ft./14m.; 🅿 🅷 🅲 112,939 ■; ★ PHIL-; z 19019, z 19092-93, z 19099, z 19101-16, z 19118-55, z 19160-62, z 19170-73, z 19175-79, z 19181-85, z 19187-88, z 19190-97, z 19244, z 19255; Ⓟ 1,585,577; Ⓒ 1,517,550; ◆ 1,451,149

PHILADELPHIA; 227 EP-12; Ⓟ 1,585,577; Ⓒ 1,517,550; ◆ 1,451,149

Philipsburg; Inc. Place; CENTRE; 225 WK-12; elev. 1,450ft./442m.; 🅿; z 16866; Ⓟ 3,048; Ⓒ 3,056

Philipsburg; RMC Place; WASHINGTON; *225 WO-4; ★ PGH; mail California z 15419; pop. incl. with California (Inc. Place)

Phillips; RMC Place; FAYETTE; ▲ North Union; 225 WP-5; ★ UNTN; mail Uniontown z 15401; ● 225

Phillips; RMC Place; TIOGA; ▲ Westfield; *226 EE-2; mail Westfield z 16950

Phillipston; RMC Place; CLARION; ▲ Brady; 224 WJ-5; mail Rimersburg z 16248; ● 45

Phillipsville; RMC Place; CHESTER; ▲ West Caln; *227 EP-9; ★ PHIL-; mail Coatesville z 19320; rural

Phillipsville; RMC Place; ERIE; ▲ Venango; *224 WD-4; mail Wattsburg z 16442

Philmont; RMC Place; MONTGOMERY; ▲ Lower Moreland; ★ PHIL-; mail Huntingdon Valley z 19006

Philson; RMC Place; SOMERSET; ▲ Northampton; *225 WQ-8; mail Meyersdale z 15552; rural

Phoenix Park; RMC Place; SCHUYLKILL; ▲ Branch; *227 EL-7; ★ PTSVL; mail Pottsville z 17901; ● 100

Phoenixville; Inc. Place; CHESTER; 227 EO-10; elev. 130ft./40m.; 🅿 🅷 🅲 944; ★ PHIL-; z 19453, z 19460; Ⓟ 15,066; Ⓒ 14,788

Piatt; MCD-Township; LYCOMING; *226 EI-3; ★ WMSPT; mail Jersey Shore z 17740; Ⓟ 1,097; Ⓒ 1,259

Pickering; RMC Place; CHESTER; *227 EO-10; ★ PHIL-

Picture Rocks; Inc. Place; LYCOMING; 226 EH-5; elev. 659ft./201m.; 🅿; ★ WMSPT; z 17762; Ⓟ 660; Ⓒ 693

Pierce; RMC Place; ALLEGHENY; ★ PGH; mail Clairton z 15025; pop. incl. with Jefferson (Inc. Place)

Pierce; ARMSTRONG; see New Salem (RMC Place)

Pierceville; RMC Place; YORK; ▲ Codorus; *227 EQ-5; ★ BAL; mail Glen Rock z 17327; rural

Pigeon (Frostown); RMC Place; FOREST; ▲ Howe; 224 WG-8; mail Marienville z 16239; ● 20

Pike; MCD-Township; BERKS; *227 EN-9; ★ READ; mail Oley z 19547; Ⓟ 1,359; Ⓒ 1,677

Pike; MCD-Township; BRADFORD; *226 EE-7; mail Le Raysville z 18829; Ⓟ 684; Ⓒ 657

Pike; MCD-Township; CLEARFIELD; *224 WJ-10; mail Curwensville z 16833; Ⓟ 2,044; Ⓒ 2,309

Pike; MCD-Township; POTTER; *226 EF-1; mail Galeton z 16922; Ⓟ 252; Ⓒ 292

PIKE; 226 EH-13; Ⓟ 27,966; Ⓒ 46,302; ◆ 61,175

Pikeland; RMC Place; CHESTER; ▲ West Pikeland; *227 EO-10; ★ PHIL-; mail Chester Springs z 19425; ● 50

Pike Mine; RMC Place; FAYETTE; ▲ Brownsville; *225 WP-4; ★ UNTN; mail Brownsville z 15417; ● 300

Pikes Creek; RMC Place; LUZERNE; ▲ Lehman; *226 EH-8; ★ SCR-; mail Hunlock Creek z 18621; rural

Pikes Peak; RMC Place; INDIANA; ▲ Cherryhill; *225 WL-8; elev. 1,500ft./457m.; mail Penn Run z 15765; rural

Piketown; RMC Place; DAUPHIN; ▲ West Hanover; *227 EN-5; ★ HRBG; mail Harrisburg z 17112; rural

Pikeville; RMC Place; BERKS; ▲ Pike; *227 EN-10; ★ READ; mail Oley z 19547; ● 90

Pilgrim Gardens; RMC Place; DELAWARE; ▲ Haverford; 228 E-1; 🅿; ★ PHIL-; z 19026; ● 1,650

Pilgrimham; RMC Place; CLARION; ▲ Salem; *224 WI-5; mail Knox z 16232; rural

Pillow; Inc. Place; DAUPHIN; 227 EL-5; elev. 560ft./171m.; 🅿; z 17080; Ⓟ 341; Ⓒ 304

Pilltown; RMC Place; SOMERSET; ▲ Jenner; *225 WO-8; mail Boswell z 15531; ● 40

Pine; MCD-Township; ALLEGHENY; *225 WL-4; ★ PGH; mail Wexford z 15090; Ⓟ 4,048; Ⓒ 7,683

Pine; MCD-Township; ARMSTRONG; *224 WJ-6; mail Templeton z 16259; Ⓟ 534; Ⓒ 499

Pine; MCD-Township; CLEARFIELD; *224 WI-10; mail Penfield z 15849; Ⓟ 43; Ⓒ 77

Pine; RMC Place; CLINTON; ▲ Wayne; 226 EI-2; mail Mc Elhattan z 17748; ● 80

Pine; MCD-Township; COLUMBIA; *226 EI-6; mail Millville z 17846; Ⓟ 990; Ⓒ 1,092

Pine; MCD-Township; CRAWFORD; *224 WF-2; mail Linesville z 16424; Ⓟ 455; Ⓒ 531

Pine; MCD-Township; INDIANA; *225 WL-9; mail Strongstown z 15957; Ⓟ 2,172; Ⓒ 2,140

Pine; MCD-Township; LYCOMING; *226 EG-3; mail Morris z 16938; Ⓟ 290; Ⓒ 329

Pine; MCD-Township; MERCER; *224 WI-3; mail Grove City z 16127; Ⓟ 4,193; Ⓒ 4,493

Pine Bank; RMC Place; GREENE; ▲ Gilmore; 225 WQ-2; 🅿; z 15352; ● 20

Pine Beach; RMC Place; WAYNE; ▲ Paupack; *226 EG-12; elev. 1,200ft./366m.; mail Hawley z 18428; ● 100

Pinebrook; RMC Place; CUMBERLAND; ▲ Hampden; *227 EN-4; elev. 400ft./122m.; ★ HRBG; mail Camp Hill z 17011; ● 150

Pine City; RMC Place; CLARION; ▲ Elk; *224 WH-6; mail Shippenville z 16254; ● 60

Pine Creek; MCD-Township; CLINTON; *226 EI-2; ★ WMSPT; mail Avis z 17721, Jersey Mills z 17739; Ⓟ 3,188; Ⓒ 3,184

Pinecreek; RMC Place; JEFFERSON; ▲ Pine Creek; *224 WI-8; mail Brookville z 15825; ● 150

Pine Creek; MCD-Township; JEFFERSON; *224 WI-8; mail Brookville z 15825; Ⓟ 1,413; Ⓒ 1,369

Pinecroft; RMC Place; BLAIR; ▲ Antis; 225 WM-11; elev. 1,066ft./325m.; ★ ALT; mail Altoona z 16601; ● 100

Pinedale; RMC Place; SCHUYLKILL; ★ PTSVL; mail Orwigsburg z 17961; pop. incl. with Deer Lake (Inc. Place)

Pine Flats; RMC Place; INDIANA; ▲ Green; 225 WL-8; mail Clymer z 15728; ● 30

Pine Forge; RMC Place; BERKS; ▲ Douglass; 227 EN-10; 🅿; z 19548; ● 200

Pine Glen; CDP; CENTRE; ▲ Burnside; 224 WJ-12; mail Karthaus z 16845; Ⓒ 210

Pine Glen; RMC Place; MIFFLIN; ▲ Bratton; *225 WM-14; mail Lewistown z 17044

Pine Grove; RMC Place; PERRY; ▲ Northeast Madison; *227 EN-2; mail Loysville z 17047; rural

Pine Grove; Inc. Place; SCHUYLKILL; 227 EM-7; elev. 540ft./165m.; 🅿; z 17963; Ⓟ 2,118; Ⓒ 2,154

Pine Grove; MCD-Township; SCHUYLKILL; *227 EM-6; 🅿; z 17963; does not include the Borough of Pine Grove; Ⓟ 3,699; Ⓒ 3,930

Pine Grove; RMC Place; SUSQUEHANNA; ▲ Lathrop; *226 EF-9; elev. 919ft./280m.; mail Nicholson z 18446; rural

Pinegrove; MCD-Township; VENANGO; *224 WH-6; mail Oil City z 16301; Ⓟ 1,395; Ⓒ 1,338

Pine Grove; MCD-Township; WARREN; *224 WD-8; mail Russell z 16345; Ⓟ 2,756; Ⓒ 2,712

Pine Grove Furnace; RMC Place; CUMBERLAND; ▲ Cooke; *227 EP-2; mail Gardners z 17324

Pine Grove Mills; CDP; CENTRE; ▲ Ferguson; 225 WL-13; 🅿; ★ STCOL; z 16868; Ⓟ 1,129; Ⓒ 1,141

Pine Hill; RMC Place; ARMSTRONG; ▲ East Franklin; *225 WK-6; ★ PGH; mail Kittanning z 16201; pop. incl. with West Kittanning (Inc. Place)

Pine Hill; RMC Place; SCHUYLKILL; ▲ Cass; *227 EL-7; ★ PTSVL; mail Pottsville z 17901; ● 35

Pine Hill; RMC Place; SOMERSET; mail Berlin z 15530; ● 30

Pine Ridge; RMC Place; DELAWARE; ▲ Nether Providence; *227 EP-11; ★ PHIL-; mail Media z 19063

Pine Run; RMC Place; BUCKS; ▲ Doylestown; *227 EN-12; ★ PHIL-; mail Doylestown z 18901, Linden z 17744; ● 100

Pine Run; RMC Place; LYCOMING; ▲ Woodward; *226 EI-3; ★ WMSPT; mail Linden z 17744; rural

Pine Summit; RMC Place; COLUMBIA; ▲ Pine; 226 EI-6; mail Millville z 17846; ● 55

Pine Swamp; RMC Place; CHESTER; ▲ Warwick; *227 EO-9; elev. 534ft./163m.; ★ PHIL-; mail Elverson z 19520; rural

Pinetown; RMC Place; YORK; ▲ Fairview; *227 EO-4; ★ HRBG; mail Lewisberry z 17339; rural

Pinetree; RMC Place; WESTMORELAND; *225 WO-5; mail Scottdale z 15683

Pine Valley; RMC Place; WARREN; ▲ Columbus; *224 WD-6; mail Columbus z 16405; rural

Pine Valley Estates; RMC Place; BUCKS; ▲ Doylestown; *227 EN-12; elev. 300ft./91m.; ★ PHIL-; mail Doylestown z 18901; ● 120

Pine View; RMC Place; LUZERNE; ▲ Rice; *226 EI-8; ★ SCR-; mail Mountain Top z 18707; ● 90

Pineville; RMC Place; BUCKS; ▲ Wrightstown, Buckingham; 227 EN-13; 🅿; ★ PHIL-; z 18946; ● 950

Pineville; RMC Place; WARREN; ▲ Southwest; *224 WF-6; mail Grand Valley z 16420; rural

Pinewood; RMC Place; BUCKS; ▲ Falls; *227 EO-14; ★ PHIL-; mail Levittown z 19054

Piney; RMC Place; CLARION; ▲ Piney; *224 WI-6; elev. 1,022ft./312m.; mail Clarion z 16214; rural

Piney; MCD-Township; CLARION; *224 WI-6; mail Sligo z 16255; Ⓟ 515; Ⓒ 516

Piney Fork; RMC Place; ALLEGHENY; ▲ South Park; 228 N-5; ★ PGH; mail South Park z 15129; ● 400

Pinola; RMC Place; FRANKLIN; ▲ Southampton; 227 EP-1; mail Shippensburg z 17257; ● 20

Pipersville; RMC Place; BUCKS; ▲ Bedminster; 227 EM-12; elev. 438ft./134m.; 🅿; ★ PHIL-; z 18947; ● 600

Pitcairn; Inc. Place; ALLEGHENY; 228 K-9; elev. 880ft./268m.; 🅿; ★ PGH; z 15140; Ⓟ 4,087; Ⓒ 3,689

Pitman; RMC Place; SCHUYLKILL; ▲ Eldred; 227 EL-6; 🅿; z 17964; ● 300

Pitt Gas; RMC Place; GREENE; ▲ Jefferson; *225 WP-3; mail Clarksville z 15322; ● 500

Pittock; RMC Place; ALLEGHENY; ▲ Stowe; *225 WM-3; ★ PGH; mail Mc Kees Rocks z 15136

Pitts; RMC Place; TIOGA; ▲ Charleston; *226 EF-3; mail Wellsboro z 16901; ● 100

Pittsburgh; Inc. Place; ⊡ ALLEGHENY; 225 WM-4; elev. 760ft./232m.; 🅿 🅷 🅲 64,213 ■; ★ PGH; z 15122, z 15201-44, z 15250-55, z 15257-62, z 15264-65, z 15267-68, z 15270, z 15272, z 15274-79, z 15281-83, z 15286, z 15289-90, z 15295 & mail West Mifflin z 15123; Ⓟ 369,879; Ⓒ 334,563; ◆ 302,187

Pittsburgh Valley; RMC Place; LANCASTER; ▲ Manor; ★ LANC; mail Conestoga z 17516; rural

Pittsfield; RMC Place; WARREN; ▲ Pittsfield; 224 WE-6; 🅿; z 16340; ● 500

Pittsfield; MCD-Township; WARREN; *224 WE-7; 🅿; z 16340; Ⓟ 1,543; Ⓒ 1,519

Pittston; Inc. Place; LUZERNE; 226 EB-10; elev. 660ft./201m.; 🅿; ★ SCR-; z 18640-44; Ⓟ 9,389; Ⓒ 8,104

Pittston (Pittston Township); MCD-Township; LUZERNE; *226 EH-9; 🅿; ★ SCR-; z 18640-44; does not include the City of Pittston; Ⓟ 2,725; Ⓒ 3,450

Pittston Junction; RMC Place; LUZERNE; *226 EH-9; ★ SCR-; mail Wilkes Barre z 18705; pop. incl. with Wilkes-Barre (Inc. Place)

Pittston Township; LUZERNE; see Pittston (MCD-Township)

Pittsville; RMC Place; VENANGO; ▲ Rockland; 224 WH-5; elev. 1,307ft./398m.; mail Kennerdell z 16374; ● 35

Plainfield; CDP; CUMBERLAND; ▲ West Pennsboro; 227 EO-2; elev. 509ft./155m.; 🅿; ★ CARL; z 17081; Ⓒ 376

Plainfield; MCD-Township; NORTHAMPTON; *227 EK-12; mail Nazareth z 18064; Ⓟ 5,444; Ⓒ 5,668

Plain Grove; RMC Place; LAWRENCE; mail Slippery Rock z 16057; rural

Plain Grove; MCD-Township; LAWRENCE; *224 WI-3; mail Volant z 16156; Ⓟ 791; Ⓒ 854

Plains; RMC Place; LUZERNE; ▲ Plains; 226 EH-9; 🅿; ★ SCR-; z 18702, z 18705; Ⓟ 4,694

Plains (Plains Township); MCD-Township; LUZERNE; *226 EH-9; 🅿; ★ SCR-; z 18702, z 18705; Ⓟ 10,988; Ⓒ 10,906

Plains Junction; RMC Place; LUZERNE; ★ SCR-; pop. incl. with Wilkes-Barre (Inc. Place)

Plains Township; LUZERNE; see Plains (MCD-Township)

Plainsville; RMC Place; LUZERNE; ▲ Wilkes-Barre; 226 EB-8; ★ SCR-; mail Wilkes Barre z 18702; ● 350

Plainview; RMC Place; ADAMS; ▲ Straban; *227 EP-3; mail Gettysburg z 17325; rural

Planebrook; RMC Place; CHESTER; ▲ East Whiteland; *227 EP-10; ★ PHIL-; mail Malvern z 19355

Plank; RMC Place; TIOGA; ▲ Morris; *226 EG-3; mail Morris z 16938; rural

Platea; Inc. Place; ERIE; 224 WD-2; elev. 876ft./267m.; ★ ERIE; mail Girard z 16417; Ⓟ 467; Ⓒ 474

Plateau Heights; RMC Place; CRAWFORD; ▲ West Mead; mail Meadville z 16335

Plattsville; RMC Place; CAMBRIA; ▲ Susquehanna; *225 WL-9; mail Hastings z 16646

Plaza Heights; RMC Place; YORK; ★ HANV; mail Hanover z 17331; pop. incl. with Hanover (Inc. Place)

Pleasant; MCD-Township; WARREN; *224 WF-7; mail Warren z 16365; Ⓟ 2,663; Ⓒ 2,528

Pleasant Acres; RMC Place; MIFFLIN; ▲ Derry; *227 EL-1; mail Lewistown z 17044; ● 900

Pleasant Corners; RMC Place; CARBON; ▲ Mahoning; *227 EK-9; elev. 601ft./183m.; mail Lehighton z 18235; ● 200

Pleasant Corners (Jordan); RMC Place; LEHIGH; ▲ Heidelberg; *227 EL-10; ★ ALL-; mail Germansville z 18053; rural

Pleasant Gap; CDP; CENTRE; ▲ Benner, Spring; 225 WK-14; 🅿 🅷; ★ STCOL; z 16823; Ⓟ 1,699; Ⓒ 1,611

Pleasant Grove; RMC Place; LANCASTER; ▲ Fulton; *227 ER-7; mail Peach Bottom z 17563; ● 35

Pleasant Grove; RMC Place; WASHINGTON; ▲ East Finley; 225 WO-2; mail Claysville z 15323; ● 50

Pleasant Hall; RMC Place; FRANKLIN; ▲ Letterkenny; 225 WP-14; 🅿; z 17246; ● 150

Pleasant Hill (Shazen); RMC Place; CAMBRIA; ▲ Susquehanna; *225 WL-9; elev. 1,690ft./515m.; mail Emeigh z 15738; rural

Pleasant Hill; RMC Place; CLEARFIELD; ▲ Cooper; *225 WK-11; mail Grassflat z 16839; rural

Pleasant Hill; RMC Place; CLEARFIELD; ▲ Decatur; *225 WK-11; mail Philipsburg z 16866; ● 250

Pleasant Hill; RMC Place; DELAWARE; ▲ Nether Providence; ★ PHIL-; mail Media z 19063

Pleasant Hill; RMC Place; FAYETTE; ▲ Springfield; *225 WP-6; elev. 2,195ft./669m.; mail Connellsville z 15425; rural

Pleasant Hill; RMC Place; INDIANA; ▲ White; *225 WL-7; mail Indiana z 15701; ● 50

Pleasant Hill; RMC Place; LAWRENCE; ▲ Perry; *225 WK-3; ★ PGH; mail Fombell z 16123; rural

Pleasant Hill; CDP; LEBANON; ▲ North Lebanon, North Cornwall; *227 EN-6; ★ LEB; mail Lebanon z 17042; Ⓟ 1,659; Ⓒ 2,301

Pleasant Hill; YORK; see Bandanna (RMC Place)

Pleasant Hills; Inc. Place; ALLEGHENY; 225 WN-4; 🅿; ★ PGH; z 15236; Ⓟ 8,884; Ⓒ 8,397

Pleasant Hills; RMC Place; DAUPHIN; ▲ Lower Paxton; 227 ER-4; ★ HRBG; mail Harrisburg z 17112; ● 1,650

Pleasant Mount; RMC Place; WAYNE; ▲ Mount Pleasant; 226 EF-11; elev. 1,981ft./604m.; 🅿; z 18453; ● 125

Pleasant Ridge; RMC Place; FULTON; ▲ Licking Creek; *225 WP-12; mail Harrisonville z 17228; ● 25

Pleasant Union; RMC Place; SOMERSET; ▲ Southampton; *225 WQ-9; elev. 2,441ft./744m.; mail Meyersdale z 15552, Pleasant Unity z 15676

Pleasant Unity; RMC Place; WESTMORELAND; ▲ Unity; 225 WN-6; 🅿; ★ LTROB; z 15676; ● 600

Pleasant Valley; RMC Place; BLAIR; *225 WM-11; ★ ALT; mail Altoona z 16602; pop. incl. with Altoona (Inc. Place)

Pleasant Valley; RMC Place; BUCKS; ▲ Springfield; *227 EM-11; ★ ALL-; mail Quakertown z 18951; ● 200

Pleasant Valley; RMC Place; FAYETTE; ▲ Bullskin; *225 WP-6; mail Connellsville z 15425; rural

Pleasant Valley; RMC Place; LANCASTER; ▲ Manheim; *227 EO-7; ★ LANC; mail Lancaster z 17604; ● 600

Pleasant Valley; MCD-Township; POTTER; *224 WE-12; mail Port Allegany z 16743; Ⓟ 78; Ⓒ 80

Pleasant Valley; RMC Place; SCHUYLKILL; ▲ Pine Grove; 227 EM-11; mail Pine Grove z 17963; ● 200

Pleasant Valley; RMC Place; WESTMORELAND; ▲ Penn; *225 WN-5; ★ PGH; mail Irwin z 15642; rural

Pleasant Valley Estates; RMC Place; MONROE; *226 EJ-10; elev. 1,077ft./328m.; mail Kunkletown z 18058; ● 300

Pleasant View; RMC Place; ARMSTRONG; *225 WL-5; ★ PGH; mail Vandergrift z 15690; ● 250

Pleasant View; RMC Place; FRANKLIN; ▲ Hamilton; *225 WP-14; elev. 700ft./213m.; mail Chambersburg z 17201; ● 500

Pleasantview; RMC Place; JUNIATA; ▲ Spruce Hill; *227 EM-2; mail Port Royal z 17082; rural

Pleasant View; RMC Place; YORK; ▲ Windsor; *227 EQ-6; ★ YORK; mail Red Lion z 17356; ● 200

Pleasantville; BEDFORD; see Alum Bank (Inc. Place)

Pleasantville; BERKS; see Manatawny (RMC Place)

Pleasantville; Inc. Place; VENANGO; 224 WF-6; elev. 1,635ft./498m.; 🅿; z 16341; Ⓟ 215; Ⓒ 850

Pleasureville; RMC Place; YORK; ▲ Springettsbury; 225 WR-10; ★ YORK; mail York z 17402; ● 1,200

Pleasureville Heights; RMC Place; YORK; ▲ Springettsbury; ★ YORK; mail York z 17402

Plowville; RMC Place; BERKS; *227 EO-9; elev. 714ft./218m.; ★ READ; mail Mohnton z 19540; rural

Plum; Inc. Place; ALLEGHENY; 225 WM-5; elev. 1,100ft./335m.; 🅿; ★ PGH; z 15239; Ⓟ 25,609; Ⓒ 26,940; ◆ 26,362

Plum; VENANGO; see Chapmanville (RMC Place)

Plum; MCD-Township; VENANGO; *224 WG-4; mail Titusville z 16354; Ⓟ 1,031; Ⓒ 1,060

Plumbridge; RMC Place; BUCKS; ▲ Middletown; ★ PHIL-; mail Levittown z 19056

Plumbsock; RMC Place; WASHINGTON; ▲ Morris; *225 WP-2; mail Prosperity z 15329; rural

Plumcreek; MCD-Township; ARMSTRONG; *225 WL-6; mail Shelocta z 15774; Ⓟ 2,400; Ⓒ 2,304

Plumer; RMC Place; VENANGO; ▲ Cornplanter; 224 WG-5; elev. 1,308ft./399m.; ★ OILC-F; mail Oil City z 16301; ● 150

Plum Run; RMC Place; FULTON; ▲ Thompson; *225 WQ-12; mail Needmore z 17238; rural

Plumsock; RMC Place; CHESTER; ▲ Willistown; *227 EP-11; elev. 270ft./82m.; ★ PHIL-; mail Newtown Square z 19073; rural

Plumstead; MCD-Township; BUCKS; *227 EN-12; ★ PHIL-; mail Fountainville z 18923; Ⓟ 6,289; Ⓒ 11,409

Plumsteadville; RMC Place; BUCKS; ▲ Plumstead; 227 EN-12; elev. 591ft./180m.; 🅿; ★ PHIL-; z 18949; ● 1,300

Plumville; Inc. Place; INDIANA; 225 WK-7; 🅿; z 16246; Ⓟ 390; Ⓒ 342

Plunketts Creek; MCD-Township; LYCOMING; *226 EH-5; mail Williamsport z 17701; Ⓟ 905; Ⓒ 771

Plymouth; Inc. Place; LUZERNE; 226 EI-8; elev. 538ft./164m.; 🅿; ★ SCR-; z 18651; Ⓟ 7,134; Ⓒ 6,507

Plymouth; MCD-Township; LUZERNE; *226 EI-8; 🅿; ★ SCR-; z 18651; does not include the Borough of Plymouth; Ⓟ 1,773; Ⓒ 2,097

Plymouth; MCD-Township; MONTGOMERY; *227 EO-12; ■; ★ PHIL-; mail Conshohocken z 19428, Norristown z 19401, Plymouth Meeting z 19462; Ⓟ 15,958; Ⓒ 16,045; ◆ 15,930

Plymouth Junction; RMC Place; LUZERNE; *226 EI-9; ★ SCR-; mail Plymouth z 18651; pop. incl. with Larksville (Inc. Place)

Plymouth Meeting; CDP; MONTGOMERY; ▲ Plymouth, Whitemarsh; 228 A-2; 🅿; ★ PHIL-; z 19462; Ⓟ 6,241; Ⓒ 5,593; Ⓡ 6,034

Plymouth Valley; RMC Place; MONTGOMERY; ▲ Plymouth; *227 EO-11; elev. 250ft./76m.; ★ PHIL-; mail Plymouth Meeting z 19462; ● 5,000

Plymptonville; CDP-Census Area Only; CLEARFIELD; ▲ Lawrence; 224 WJ-11; mail Clearfield z 16830; Ⓟ 1,074; Ⓒ 1,040

Pocahontas; RMC Place; SOMERSET; ▲ Greenville; 225 WQ-8; mail Meyersdale z 15552; ● 125

Pocono; MCD-Township; MONROE; *226 EJ-12; mail Tannersville z 18372; Ⓟ 7,529; Ⓒ 9,607

Pocono Country Place; RMC Place; MONROE; ▲ Coolbaugh; *226 EI-11; elev. 2,000ft./610m.; mail Tobyhanna z 18466; ● 1,000

Pocono Farms; RMC Place; MONROE; ▲ Coolbaugh; *226 EI-11; elev. 2,000ft./610m.; mail Tobyhanna z 18466; ● 500

Pocono Farms East; RMC Place; MONROE; ▲ Coolbaugh; *226 EI-11; elev. 940ft./287m.; mail Tobyhanna z 18466; ● 100

Pocono Heights; RMC Place; MONROE; ▲ Middle Smithfield; *226 EI-12; elev. 1,100ft./335m.; mail East Stroudsburg z 18301, Marshalls Creek z 18335; ● 1,100

Pocono Lake; RMC Place; MONROE; ▲ Tobyhanna; 226 EI-11; 🅿; z 18347-48; summer pop. 6,000; ● 750

Pocono Lake Preserve; MONROE; see Preserve (RMC Place)

Pocono Manor; RMC Place; MONROE; ▲ Pocono; 226 EI-11; 🅿; z 18349; summer pop. 1,400; ● 300

Pocono Mount Lake Forest; RMC Place; PIKE; ▲ Delaware; *226 EH-13; elev. 1,200ft./366m.; mail Dingmans Ferry z 18328; ● 200

Pocono Mtn Lake Estate; RMC Place; CARBON; ▲ Kidder; *226 EJ-10; mail White Haven z 18661; ● 350

Pocono Park; RMC Place; MONROE; ▲ Stroud; mail Stroudsburg z 18360

Pocono Pines (Naomi Pines); CDP; MONROE; ▲ Tobyhanna; 226 EI-11; 🅿; z 18350; Ⓟ 824; summer pop. 3,000; Ⓒ 1,013

Pocono Summit; RMC Place; MONROE; ▲ Tobyhanna, Coolbaugh; 226 EI-11; 🅿; z 18346; ● 1,500

Pocono Summit Estates; RMC Place; MONROE; ▲ Coolbaugh; *226 EI-11; mail Pocono Summit z 18346

Pocopson; RMC Place; CHESTER; ▲ Pocopson; *227 EQ-10; 🅿; ★ PHIL-; z 19366; ● 100

Pocopson; MCD-Township; CHESTER; *227 EP-10; 🅿; ★ PHIL-; z 19366; Ⓟ 3,266; Ⓒ 3,350

Pogue; RMC Place; HUNTINGDON; ▲ Cromwell; *225 WO-13; mail Three Springs z 17264; ● 40

Point; RMC Place; BEDFORD; ▲ Napier; *225 WO-10; mail Schellsburg z 15559

Point; MCD-Township; NORTHUMBERLAND; *226 EJ-5; mail Northumberland z 17857; Ⓟ 3,466; Ⓒ 3,722

Point Breeze; RMC Place; ALLEGHENY; ▲ Harrison; *225 WM-4; ★ PGH; mail Pittsburgh z 15208; pop. incl. with Pittsburgh (Inc. Place)

Point Breeze; RMC Place; ALLEGHENY; *225 WM-4; ★ PGH; mail Verona z 15147

Point Breeze; RMC Place; NORTHUMBERLAND; ▲ East Cameron; *227 EL-6; mail Shamokin z 17872; rural

Point Breeze; RMC Place; PHILADELPHIA; ★ PHIL-; mail Philadelphia z 19145; pop. incl. with Philadelphia (Inc. Place)

Point Marion; Inc. Place; FAYETTE; 225 WQ-4; elev. 820ft./250m.; 🅿; ★ MORG; z 15474; Ⓟ 1,344; Ⓒ 1,333

Point Phillip; RMC Place; NORTHAMPTON; ▲ Moore; *227 EK-11; ★ ALL-; mail Bath z 18014; ● 270

Point Pleasant; RMC Place; BUCKS; ▲ Tinicum, Plumstead; 227 EM-12; elev. 106ft./32m.; 🅿; ★ PHIL-; z 18950; ● 800

Point Ridge Farms; RMC Place; CUMBERLAND; ▲ Hampden; *227 EN-4; elev. 400ft./122m.; ★ HRBG; mail Camp Hill z 17011; ● 1,200

Point View; RMC Place; BLAIR; ▲ Catharine; *225 WM-11; mail Williamsburg z 16693; ● 20

Poland (Poland Mines); RMC Place; GREENE; ▲ Monongahela; 225 WQ-4; mail Dilliner z 15327; ● 75

Poland Mines; GREENE; see Poland (RMC Place)

Polk; MCD-Township; JEFFERSON; *224 WH-9; mail Brookville z 15825; Ⓟ 305; Ⓒ 294

Polk; MCD-Township; MONROE; *226 EJ-10; mail Kresgeville z 18333; Ⓟ 4,517; Ⓒ 6,533

Polk; Inc. Place; VENANGO; 224 WH-4; elev. 1,116ft./340m.; 🅿; ★ OILC-F; z 16342; Ⓟ 1,267; Ⓒ 1,031

Polktown; RMC Place; FRANKLIN; ▲ Washington; *227 EQ-1; ★ HAG; mail Waynesboro z 17268; rural

Polk Valley; RMC Place; NORTHAMPTON; ▲ Lower Saucon; *227 EM-11; ★ ALL-; mail Hellertown z 18055; rural

Pomeroy; RMC Place; CHESTER; ▲ Sadsbury; 227 EP-9; elev. 484ft./148m.; 🅿; ★ PHIL-; z 19367; ● 750

Pomeroy Heights; RMC Place; CHESTER; ▲ Sadsbury; *227 EP-9; elev. 643ft./196m.; ★ PHIL-; mail Coatesville z 19320; ● 600

Pond Bank; RMC Place; FRANKLIN; ▲ Guilford; 227 EQ-1; mail Chambersburg z 17201; ● 200

Pond Creek; RMC Place; LUZERNE; ▲ Foster; *226 EJ-9; ★ HAZ; mail White Haven z 18661; ● 35

Pond Eddy; RMC Place; PIKE; ▲ Shohola; 226 EG-13; 🅿; z 12770; ● 50

Pond Hill; RMC Place; LUZERNE; ▲ Conyngham; 226 EI-8; elev. 999ft./304m.; mail Wapwallopen z 18660; ● 200

Pont; RMC Place; ERIE; ▲ Elk Creek; *224 WE-2; elev. 1,090ft./332m.; mail Albion z 16401; rural

Poplar Grove; RMC Place; FAYETTE; ▲ Connellsville; *225 WP-5; mail Connellsville z 15425; ● 500

Poplar Grove; RMC Place; LANCASTER; ▲ Elizabeth; *227 EO-7; ★ LANC; mail Lititz z 17543; ● 100

Porkey; RMC Place; FOREST; ▲ Howe; *224 WF-7; elev. 1,215ft./370m.; mail Sheffield z 16347; rural

Portage; Inc. Place; CAMBRIA; 225 WN-10; elev. 1,700ft./518m.; 🅿; z 15946; Ⓟ 3,105; Ⓒ 2,837

Portage; MCD-Township; CAMBRIA; *225 WN-10; 🅿; z 15946; does not include the Borough of Portage; Ⓟ 4,089; Ⓒ 3,906

Portage; MCD-Township; CAMERON; *224 WG-12; mail Emporium z 15834; Ⓟ 211; Ⓒ 258

Portage; MCD-Township; POTTER; *224 WF-12; mail Austin z 16720; Ⓟ 176; Ⓒ 223

Port Allegany; Inc. Place; MCKEAN; 224 WE-11; elev. 1,481ft./451m.; 🅿; z 16743; Ⓟ 2,391; Ⓒ 2,355

Port Ann; RMC Place; SNYDER; ▲ Adams; *227 EK-3; mail Middleburg z 17842, Troxelville z 17882; ● 60

Port Barnett; RMC Place; JEFFERSON; ▲ Pine Creek; *224 WI-8; mail Brookville z 15825; rural

Port Blanchard; RMC Place; LUZERNE; ▲ Jenkins; *226 EH-9; elev. 555ft./169m.; ★ SCR-; mail Pittston z 18640; ● 260

Port Carbon; Inc. Place; SCHUYLKILL; 227 EL-8; elev. 720ft./219m.; 🅿; ★ PTSVL; z 17965; Ⓟ 2,134; Ⓒ 2,019

Port Clinton; Inc. Place; SCHUYLKILL; 227 EL-8; elev. 406ft./124m.; 🅿; ★ PTSVL; z 19549; Ⓟ 328; Ⓒ 288

Porter; MCD-Township; CLARION; *224 WJ-6; mail New Bethlehem z 16242; Ⓟ 1,564; Ⓒ 1,466

Porter; MCD-Township; CLINTON; *226 EJ-1; mail Mill Hall z 17751; Ⓟ 1,437; Ⓒ 1,419

Porter; MCD-Township; HUNTINGDON; *225 WM-12; mail Alexandria z 16611; Ⓟ 1,942; Ⓒ 1,917

Porter; RMC Place; JEFFERSON; ▲ Porter; 224 WJ-7; elev. 1,572ft./479m.; mail Punxsutawney z 15767; ● 25

Porter; MCD-Township; JEFFERSON; *224 WJ-7; mail Punxsutawney z 15767; Ⓟ 310; Ⓒ 282

Porter; MCD-Township; LYCOMING; *226 EI-3; ★ WMSPT; mail Jersey Shore z 17740; Ⓟ 1,441; Ⓒ 1,633

Porter; MCD-Township; PIKE; *226 EI-12; mail East Stroudsburg z 18301; Ⓟ 163; Ⓒ 385

Porter; MCD-Township; SCHUYLKILL; *227 EL-6; mail Tower City z 17980; Ⓟ 2,560; Ⓒ 2,032

Porters; YORK; see Porters Sideling (RMC Place)

Porters Sideling (Porters); RMC Place; YORK; ▲ Heidelberg; 227 EQ-4; 🅿; z 17354; ● 100

Portersville; Inc. Place; BUTLER; 224 WJ-3; elev. 1,364ft./416m.; 🅿; ★ PGH; z 16051; Ⓟ 307; Ⓒ 268

Port Griffith; RMC Place; LUZERNE; ▲ Jenkins; *226 EH-9; 🅿; ★ SCR-; z 18640; ● 1,350

Port Indian; RMC Place; MONTGOMERY; ▲ West Norriton; *227 EO-11; ★ PHIL-; mail Norristown z 19401

Port Jenkins; RMC Place; LUZERNE; ▲ Dennison; *226 EJ-9; mail White Haven z 18661; rural

Port Kennedy; RMC Place; MONTGOMERY; ▲ Upper Merion; *227 EO-11; ★ PHIL-; mail King of Prussia z 19406

Portland; Inc. Place; NORTHAMPTON; 226 EJ-12; elev. 297ft./91m.; 🅿; z 18351; Ⓟ 516; Ⓒ 579

Portland Mills; RMC Place; ELK; ▲ Spring Creek; 224 WH-9; elev. 1,355ft./413m.; 🅿; z 15853; ● 40

Port Matilda; Inc. Place; CENTRE; 225 WK-12; elev. 1,014ft./309m.; 🅿; z 16870; Ⓟ 669; Ⓒ 638

Port Providence; RMC Place; MONTGOMERY; ▲ Upper Providence; *227 EO-11; ★ PHIL-; mail Mont Clare z 19453, Phoenixville z 19460; ● 300

Port Royal; Inc. Place; JUNIATA; 227 EM-2; elev. 444ft./135m.; 🅿; z 17082; Ⓟ 836; Ⓒ 977

Port Royal; RMC Place; WESTMORELAND; *225 WO-5; ★ PGH; mail Belle Vernon z 15012; rural

Port Trevorton; CDP; SNYDER; ▲ Union; 227 EL-4; 🅿; z 17864; Ⓒ 451

Port Vue; Inc. Place; ALLEGHENY; 228 M-8; elev. 900ft./274m.; ★ PGH; mail Mckeesport z 15133; Ⓟ 4,641; Ⓒ 4,228

Possum Hollow; RMC Place; LAWRENCE; *225 WK-2; ★ PGH; mail Wampum z 16157; pop. incl. with New Beaver (Inc. Place)

Potetown; RMC Place; BLAIR; ▲ Taylor; *225 WN-11; ★ ALT; mail Roaring Spring z 16673; rural

Potosi; RMC Place; YORK; ▲ Springfield; *227 EQ-5; ★ YORK; mail Glen Rock z 17327; ● 25

Potter; MCD-Township; BEAVER; *225 WL-2; ★ PGH; mail Monaca z 15061; Ⓟ 546; Ⓒ 580

Potter; MCD-Township; CENTRE; *227 EK-1; ★ STCOL; mail Centre Hall z 16828, Spring Mills z 16875; Ⓟ 3,020; Ⓒ 3,339

POTTER; 224 WF-13; Ⓟ 16,717; Ⓒ 18,080; ◆ 16,205

Potter Brook; RMC Place; TIOGA; ▲ Westfield; 226 EE-1; mail Westfield z 16950; ● 200

Pottersdale; RMC Place; CLEARFIELD; ▲ Karthaus; 224 WI-12; 🅿; z 16871; ● 20

Potters Mills; RMC Place; CENTRE; ▲ Potter; 227 EK-1; ★ STCOL; mail Spring Mills z 16875; ● 180

Potterville; RMC Place; BRADFORD; ▲ Orwell; 226 EE-7; elev. 1,276ft./389m.; mail Rome z 18837; ● 75

Pottsgrove; CDP-Census Area Only; MONTGOMERY; ▲ Lower Pottsgrove; *227 EN-10; ★ PTSTN; mail Pottstown z 19464; Ⓟ 3,122; Ⓒ 3,266

Potts Grove; RMC Place; NORTHUMBERLAND; ▲ East Chillisquaque; 226 EJ-5; 🅿; z 17865; ● 140

Pottstown; Inc. Place; MONTGOMERY; 227 EN-10; elev. 160ft./49m.; 🅿 🅷 ■; ★ PTSTN; z 19464-65; Ⓟ 21,831; Ⓒ 21,859; ◆ 21,680

Pottstown Landing; RMC Place; CHESTER; ▲ North Coventry; *227 EO-10; ★ PTSTN; mail Pottstown z 19464

Pottsville; Inc. Place; ⊡ SCHUYLKILL; 227 EL-7; elev. 659ft./201m.; 🅿 🅷 ■; ★ PTSVL; z 17901; Ⓟ 16,603; Ⓒ 15,549; ◆ 14,596

POV Junction; ALLEGHENY; see P&OV Junction (RMC Place)

Powder Mill Village; RMC Place; WESTMORELAND; ▲ Cook; *225 WO-7; elev. 1,400ft./427m.; mail Rector z 15677; ● 170

Powder Valley; RMC Place; LEHIGH; ▲ Upper Milford; *227 EM-10; ★ ALL-; mail Zionsville z 18092; rural

Powell; RMC Place; BRADFORD; ▲ Monroe; 226 EF-6; mail Monroeton z 18832; ● 150

Powells Valley; RMC Place; DAUPHIN; ▲ Halifax; 227 EM-4; ★ HRBG; mail Halifax z 17032; ● 600

Powys; RMC Place; LYCOMING; ▲ Lewis; 226 EH-3; ★ WMSPT; mail Cogan Station z 17728; ● 100

Poyntelle; RMC Place; WAYNE; ▲ Preston; *226 EE-11; elev. 2,072ft./632m.; 🅿; z 18454; ● 60

Prentisvale; RMC Place; MCKEAN; ▲ Otto; *224 WE-11; elev. 1,490ft./454m.; mail Eldred z 16731; ● 70

Prescott; RMC Place; LEBANON; ▲ North Lebanon; *227 EN-7; ★ LEB; mail Lebanon z 17042; ● 175

Prescottville; RMC Place; JEFFERSON; ▲ Winslow; 224 WI-9; mail Reynoldsville z 15851; ● 100

Preserve (Pocono Lake Preserve); RMC Place; MONROE; ▲ Tobyhanna; *226 EI-10; mail Pocono Lake Preserve z 18348; summer pop. 1,000

President; RMC Place; VENANGO; ▲ President; 224 WG-6; mail Tionesta z 16353; ● 100

President; MCD-Township; VENANGO; *224 WG-6; mail Oil City z 16301, Tionesta z 16353; Ⓟ 501; Ⓒ 543

Presidential Heights; RMC Place; ALLEGHENY; ★ PGH; mail Pittsburgh z 15237

Presidential Heights; RMC Place; FRANKLIN; ▲ Greene; *227 EP-1; elev. 666ft./203m.; mail Chambersburg z 17201; ● 300

Presque Isle; RMC Place; ERIE; ▲ Millcreek; *224 WC-3; ★ ERIE; mail Erie z 16505-06

Presto; RMC Place; ALLEGHENY; ▲ Collier; *225 WN-3; 🅿; ★ PGH; z 15142; ● 500

Preston; RMC Place; LUZERNE; ▲ Hanover; 226 EB-7; ★ SCR-; mail Wilkes Barre z 18706; ● 240

Preston; MCD-Township; WAYNE; *226 EE-11; mail Preston Park z 18455; Ⓟ 1,044; Ⓒ 1,107

Preston Hill; RMC Place; SCHUYLKILL; ▲ Butler; *227 EK-7; ★ PTSVL; mail Girardville z 17935; ● 30

Preston Park; RMC Place; WAYNE; ▲ Preston; 226 EE-11; 🅿; z 18455; summer pop. 750; ● 200

Pretoria; RMC Place; SOMERSET; ▲ Paint; *225 WO-8; ★ JNST; mail Hollsopple z 15935; ● 50

Price; MCD-Township; MONROE; *226 EI-12; mail East Stroudsburg z 18301; Ⓟ 1,633; Ⓒ 2,649

Priceburg; RMC Place; LACKAWANNA; ★ SCR-; mail Dickson City z 18519; pop. incl. with Dickson City (Inc. Place)

Pricedale; RMC Place; WESTMORELAND; ▲ Rostraver; *225 WO-4; 🅿; ★ PGH; z 15072; ● 800

Pricetown; RMC Place; BERKS; ▲ Ruscombmanor; 227 EM-9; elev. 839ft./256m.; ★ READ; mail Fleetwood z 19522; ● 180

Priceville; RMC Place; WAYNE; ▲ Manchester; *226 EE-12; mail Equinunk z 18417; rural

Primos; RMC Place; DELAWARE; ▲ Upper Darby; 228 F-2; 🅿; ★ PHIL-; z 19018; ● 900

Primos Secane; RMC Place; DELAWARE; ▲ Upper Darby; 🅿; ★ PHIL-; z 19018

Primrose; RMC Place; SCHUYLKILL; ▲ Cass; 227 EL-7; ★ PTSVL; mail Pottsville z 17901; ● 600

Primrose; RMC Place; WASHINGTON; ▲ Mount Pleasant; *225 WN-2; ★ PGH; mail Mc Donald z 15057; ● 150

Princeton; RMC Place; LAWRENCE; ▲ Slippery Rock; 224 WJ-3; ★ PGH; mail New Castle z 16101; ● 150

Pringle; Inc. Place; LUZERNE; 226 EA-8; elev. 660ft./201m.; 🅿; ★ SCR-; z 18704; Ⓟ 1,161; Ⓒ 991

Entries in **UPPERCASE** are counties.
Entries in **bold** have populations of 2,500 or more.
Names in parentheses are alternate names.

Inc. Place	Incorporated Place
RMC Place	Rand McNally Designated Place
CDP	Census Designated Place
MCD	Minor Civil Division
⊡	County Seat
▲	Minor Civil Division
elev.	Elevation
🅿	Post Office
🅷	Hospital
🅲	College
■	Principal Business Center
★	Ranally Metro Area (RMA) Abbreviation
z	Zip Code(s)
Ⓟ	Previous Census Population
Ⓡ	Revised Census Population
Ⓐ	Annexation Population
●	Rand McNally Population Estimate
Ⓒ	Final Census Population
Ⓢ	Special Census Population
◆	Estimated Population

For additional definitions see Glossary, Volume 1, and Introduction, Volume 2.

Pritchard; RMC Place; LUZERNE; ▲ Hunlock; ***226** EI-8; ★ **SCR-**; mail Hunlock Creek **Z** 18621; rural
Pritchards Corner; RMC Place; MERCER; ▲ South Pymatuning; ***224** WH-1; elev. 977ft./298m.; ★ **SHAR**; mail Sharpsville **Z** 16150; ● 100
Prittstown; RMC Place; FAYETTE; ▲ Upper Tyrone, Bullskin; ***225** WO-5; elev. 1,157ft./353m.; mail Mount Pleasant **Z** 15666
Proctor; RMC Place; LYCOMING; ▲ Plunketts Creek; **226** EH-5; elev. 804ft./245m.; mail Williamsport **Z** 17701; ● 50
Progress; CDP; DAUPHIN; ▲ Susquehanna; **227** ES-3; ★ **HRBG**; mail Harrisburg **Z** 17109; Ⓟ 9,654; Ⓒ 9,647
Prompton; Inc. Place; WAYNE; **226** EF-11; elev. 1,093ft./333m.; 🅿; ★ **SCR-**; **Z** 18456; Ⓟ 238; Ⓒ 243
Prospect; Inc. Place; BUTLER; **224** WJ-3; elev. 1,369ft./417m.; 🅿; ★ **BUTL**; **Z** 16052; Ⓟ 1,122; Ⓒ 1,234
Prospect; RMC Place; CAMBRIA; ***225** WN-8; ★ **JNST**; mail Johnstown **Z** 15901; pop. incl. with Johnstown (Inc. Place)
Prospect Gardens; RMC Place; LANCASTER; ▲ East Lampeter; ***227** EP-7; ★ **LANC**; mail Lancaster **Z** 17602; ● 250
Prospect Heights; RMC Place; NORTHAMPTON; ▲ Bethlehem; ***227** EL-11; ★ **ALL-**; mail Bethlehem **Z** 18020; ● 2,300
Prospect Park; RMC Place; CAMERON; ▲ Shippen; **224** WG-12; mail Emporium **Z** 15834; ● 400
Prospect Park; Inc. Place; DELAWARE; **227** EQ-11; elev. 80ft./24m.; 🅿; ★ **PHIL-**; **Z** 19076; Ⓟ 6,764; Ⓒ 6,594
Prospectville; RMC Place; MONTGOMERY; ▲ Horsham; **227** EO-12; ★ **PHIL-**; mail Ambler **Z** 19002; ● 550
Prosperity; RMC Place; WASHINGTON; ▲ Morris; **225** WP-2; elev. 1,045ft./319m.; 🅿; **Z** 15329; ● 175
Providence; RMC Place; LACKAWANNA; ***226** EG-10; ★ **SCR-**; pop. incl. with Scranton (Inc. Place)
Providence; MCD-Township; LANCASTER; ***227** EQ-7; ★ **LANC**; mail New Providence **Z** 17560; Ⓟ 6,071; Ⓒ 6,651
Providence Downe; RMC Place; DELAWARE; ▲ Upper Providence; ★ **PHIL-**; mail Media **Z** 19063
Providence Square; RMC Place; MONTGOMERY; ▲ Lower Providence; ***227** EO-11; ★ **PHIL-**; mail Collegeville **Z** 19426; rural
Provins Works; RMC Place; FAYETTE; ▲ Nicholson; mail Masontown **Z** 15461; ● 20
Pughtown; RMC Place; CHESTER; ▲ South Coventry; **227** EO-10; ★ **PTSTN**; mail Pottstown **Z** 19464; ● 150
Puite; RMC Place; DAUPHIN; ▲ Susquehanna; ***227** EN-4; ★ **HRBG**; mail Harrisburg **Z** 17110; ● 800
Pulaski; MCD-Township; BEAVER; ***225** WK-2; ★ **PGH**; mail New Brighton **Z** 15066; Ⓟ 1,697; Ⓒ 1,674
Pulaski; RMC Place; LAWRENCE; ▲ Pulaski; **224** WI-2; 🅿; ★ **YNGS-**; **Z** 16143; ● 300
Pulaski; MCD-Township; LAWRENCE; ***224** WI-1; 🅿; ★ **YNGS-**; **Z** 16143; Ⓟ 3,469; Ⓒ 3,658
Punxsutawney; Inc. Place; JEFFERSON; **224** WJ-8; elev. 1,238ft./377m.; 🅿 🅷; **Z** 15767; Ⓟ 6,782; Ⓒ 6,271
Purcell; RMC Place; BEDFORD; ▲ Mann; **225** WQ-11; mail Clearville **Z** 15535; ● 25
Purchase Line; RMC Place; INDIANA; ▲ Green; **225** WL-8; mail Commodore **Z** 15729; ● 40
Puritan; RMC Place; CAMBRIA; ▲ Portage; ***225** WN-10; 🅿; **Z** 15946; ● 75
Puritan; RMC Place; FAYETTE; ▲ German; ***225** WQ-4; ★ **UNTN**; mail Mc Clellandtown **Z** 15458; ● 40
Putnam; MCD-Township; TIOGA; ***226** EE-3; mail Covington **Z** 16917; Ⓟ 444; Ⓒ 428
Putneyville; RMC Place; ARMSTRONG; ▲ Mahoning; **224** WJ-7; elev. 943ft./287m.; mail New Bethlehem **Z** 16242; ● 140
Puttstown; RMC Place; BEDFORD, HUNTINGDON; ▲ Carbon, Liberty; ***225** WO-11; elev. 886ft./270m.; mail Saxton **Z** 16678; ● 75
Puzzletown; RMC Place; BLAIR; ▲ Freedom; ***225** WN-10; ★ **ALT**; mail Duncansville **Z** 16635
Pyles Mills; RMC Place; LAWRENCE; ▲ Perry; ***225** WK-3; ★ **PGH**; mail Ellwood City **Z** 16117; rural
Pymatuning; MCD-Township; MERCER; ***224** WH-2; ★ **SHAR**; mail Transfer **Z** 16154; Ⓟ 3,736; Ⓒ 3,782
Pymatuning Central; CDP-Census Area Only; CRAWFORD; ***224** WF-2; Ⓒ 2,216
Pymatuning North; CDP-Census Area Only; CRAWFORD; ***224** WF-2; Ⓒ 325
Pymatuning South; CDP-Census Area Only; CRAWFORD; ***224** WG-2; Ⓒ 467
Pyrra; RMC Place; ARMSTRONG; ▲ Kittanning; ***225** WL-6; mail Ford City **Z** 16226; rural

Q

Quakake; RMC Place; SCHUYLKILL; ▲ Rush; **227** EK-8; 🅿; **Z** 18245; ● 300
Quaker Hills; RMC Place; LANCASTER; ***227** EP-7; ★ **LANC**; mail Millersville **Z** 17551; pop. incl. with Millersville (Inc. Place)
Quaker Lake; RMC Place; SUSQUEHANNA; ▲ Silver Lake; **226** ED-9; mail Brackney **Z** 18812; summer pop. 350; ● 70
Quakertown; Inc. Place; BUCKS; **227** EM-11; elev. 500ft./152m.; 🅿 🅷; ★ **PHIL-**; **Z** 18951; Ⓟ 8,982; Ⓒ 8,931
Quaker Valley; RMC Place; ADAMS; ▲ Menallen; ***227** EP-3; mail Biglerville **Z** 17307; rural
Quarryville; Inc. Place; LANCASTER; **227** EQ-8; elev. 500ft./152m.; 🅿; **Z** 17566; Ⓟ 1,642; Ⓒ 1,994
Quecreek; RMC Place; SOMERSET; ▲ Lincoln; **225** WO-8; 🅿; **Z** 15555; ● 150
Queen; RMC Place; BEDFORD; ▲ Kimmel; **225** WN-10; 🅿; ★ **ALT**; **Z** 16670; ● 100
Queen; RMC Place; FOREST; ▲ Hickory; ***224** WF-7; elev. 1,204ft./367m.; mail Endeavor **Z** 16322, Tidioute **Z** 16351; rural
Queen City; RMC Place; COLUMBIA; ▲ Catawissa; ***227** EK-6; mail Catawissa **Z** 17820
Queens Grant; RMC Place; BUCKS; ▲ Lower Makefield; ★ **PHIL-**; mail Morrisville **Z** 19067; ● 150
Queens Run; RMC Place; CLINTON; ▲ Woodward; **226** EI-2; ★ **WMSPT**; mail Lock Haven **Z** 17745; ● 50
Queenstown; RMC Place; ARMSTRONG; ▲ Perry; ***224** WJ-5; mail Karns City **Z** 16041; ● 60
Quemahoning; MCD-Township; SOMERSET; ***225** WO-8; mail Stoystown **Z** 15563; Ⓟ 2,301; Ⓒ 2,180
Quentin (Bismarck); CDP; LEBANON; ▲ West Cornwall; **227** EN-6; 🅿; ★ **LEB**; **Z** 17083; Ⓒ 529
Quicks Bend; RMC Place; BRADFORD; ▲ Wilmot; ***226** EF-7; mail Sugar Run **Z** 18846; rural
Quicktown; RMC Place; LACKAWANNA; ▲ Madison; **226** EH-11; ★ **SCR-**; mail Moscow **Z** 18444; ● 50
Quiggleville; RMC Place; LYCOMING; ▲ Lycoming; **226** EH-3; ★ **WMSPT**; mail Cogan Station **Z** 17728; ● 50
Quincy; RMC Place; FRANKLIN; ▲ Quincy; **227** EQ-1; 🅿; **Z** 17247; ● 400
Quincy; MCD-Township; FRANKLIN; ***227** EQ-2; 🅿; **Z** 17247 & mail Waynesboro **Z** 17268; Ⓟ 5,704; Ⓒ 5,846
Quincy Hollow; RMC Place; BUCKS; ▲ Middletown; ***227** EO-13; ★ **PHIL-**; mail Levittown **Z** 19057

R

Raccoon; MCD-Township; BEAVER; ***225** WL-2; ★ **PGH**; mail Aliquippa **Z** 15001; Ⓟ 3,426; Ⓒ 3,397
Raccoon; WASHINGTON; see Joffre (RMC Place)
Racine; BEAVER; see Homewood (Inc. Place)
Radebaugh; RMC Place; WESTMORELAND; ▲ Hempfield; ***225** WN-5; ★ **PGH**; mail Greensburg **Z** 15601; ● 130
Radnor; MCD-Township; DELAWARE; ***227** EP-11; 🅿 🅲 16,554 ■; ★ **PHIL-**; **Z** 19008, **Z** 19080, **Z** 19087-89; Ⓟ 28,705; Ⓒ 30,878; ◆ 30,782
Radnor Township; CDP-Census Area Only; DELAWARE; ▲ Radnor; ***227** EP-11; ★ **PHIL-**; mail Wayne **Z** 19087; Ⓟ 28,705; Ⓒ 30,878; ◆ 30,782
Rahn; RMC Place; SCHUYLKILL; pop. incl. with Tamaqua (Inc. Place)
Rahns (Ironbridge); RMC Place; MONTGOMERY; ▲ Perkiomen; **227** EO-11; ★ **PHIL-**; mail Collegeville **Z** 19426; ● 700
Railroad; Inc. Place; YORK; **227** EQ-5; elev. 741ft./226m.; 🅿; ★ **BAL**; **Z** 17355; Ⓟ 317; Ⓒ 300
Raineytown; RMC Place; FAYETTE; ▲ Lower Tyrone; ***225** WP-5; mail Dawson **Z** 15428; rural
Rainsburg; Inc. Place; BEDFORD; **225** WQ-10; elev. 1,398ft./426m.; mail Bedford **Z** 15522; Ⓟ 175; Ⓒ 146
Raker; NORTHUMBERLAND; see Hunter (RMC Place)
Ralph; RMC Place; FAYETTE; ▲ German; ***225** WP-4; ★ **UNTN**; mail Hibbs **Z** 15443; ● 400
Ralpho; MCD-Township; NORTHUMBERLAND; ***227** EK-6; mail Shamokin **Z** 17872; Ⓟ 3,625; Ⓒ 3,764
Ralphton; RMC Place; SOMERSET; ▲ Quemahoning, Jenner; ***225** WO-8; mail Stoystown **Z** 15563; ● 80
Ralston; RMC Place; LYCOMING; ▲ McIntyre; **226** EG-4; 🅿; **Z** 17763; ● 400
Ramblewood; CDP-Census Area Only; CENTRE; ▲ Ferguson; ***225** WL-13; elev. 1,267ft./386m.; ★ **STCOL**; mail Pennsylvania Furnace **Z** 16865; Ⓟ 1,104; Ⓒ 1,054
Ramey; Inc. Place; CLEARFIELD; **225** WK-11; elev. 1,613ft./492m.; 🅿; **Z** 16671; Ⓟ 536; Ⓒ 525
Ramona; RMC Place; LEBANON; ▲ Jackson; ***227** EN-7; ★ **LEB**; mail Myerstown **Z** 17067; ● 100
Ramsay Terrace; RMC Place; WESTMORELAND; ***225** WO-6; mail Mount Pleasant **Z** 15666; pop. incl. with Mount Pleasant (Inc. Place)
Ramsaytown; RMC Place; JEFFERSON; ▲ Knox; ***224** WJ-8; elev. 1,543ft./470m.; mail Brookville **Z** 15825; ● 80
Ramsey; RMC Place; LYCOMING; ▲ Cummings; **226** EH-2; mail Jersey Shore **Z** 17740; ● 45
Ranavilla; RMC Place; CUMBERLAND; ▲ Lower Allen; ***227** EO-4; ★ **HRBG**; mail Camp Hill **Z** 17011; ● 350
Rand; RMC Place; ALLEGHENY; ★ **PGH**; pop. incl. with Baldwin (Inc. Place)
Randolph; MCD-Township; CRAWFORD; ***224** WF-4; mail Guys Mills **Z** 16327; Ⓟ 1,661; Ⓒ 1,838
Rankin; Inc. Place; ALLEGHENY; **228** K-8; elev. 887ft./270m.; 🅿; ★ **PGH**; **Z** 15104; Ⓟ 2,503; Ⓒ 2,315
Ranshaw; RMC Place; NORTHUMBERLAND; ▲ Coal; **227** EK-6; 🅿; **Z** 17866; ● 500
Ransom; RMC Place; LACKAWANNA; ▲ Ransom; **226** EH-9; 🅿; ★ **SCR-**; **Z** 18653; ● 250
Ransom; MCD-Township; LACKAWANNA; ***226** EH-9; 🅿; ★ **SCR-**; **Z** 18653 & mail Clarks Summit **Z** 18411; Ⓟ 1,608; Ⓒ 1,429
Rapho; MCD-Township; LANCASTER; ***227** EO-6; mail Manheim **Z** 17545; Ⓟ 8,211; Ⓒ 8,578
Rasler Run; RMC Place; FAYETTE; ▲ Springfield; ***225** WP-6; elev. 1,652ft./504m.; mail Normalville **Z** 15469; rural
Rasleytown; RMC Place; NORTHAMPTON; ▲ Plainfield; ***227** EK-12; elev. 500ft./152m.; mail Pen Argyl **Z** 18072; rural
Rasselas; RMC Place; ELK; ▲ Jones; ***224** WF-10; elev. 1,928ft./588m.; mail Wilcox **Z** 15870; rural
Rathbun; RMC Place; ELK; ***224** WG-11; mail Saint Marys **Z** 15857; pop. incl. with Saint Marys (Inc. Place)
Rathmel; RMC Place; JEFFERSON; ▲ Winslow; **224** WI-9; mail Reynoldsville **Z** 15851; ● 150
Rattigan; RMC Place; BUTLER; ▲ Donegal; ***225** WK-5; elev. 1,117ft./340m.; mail Chicora **Z** 16025; rural
Raubsville; RMC Place; NORTHAMPTON; ▲ Williams; **227** EL-12; ★ **ALL-**; mail Easton **Z** 18042; ● 200
Rauchtown; RMC Place; CLINTON; ▲ Crawford; **226** EI-3; elev. 889ft./271m.; mail Jersey Shore **Z** 17740; ● 300
Rauschs; RMC Place; SCHUYLKILL; ▲ East Brunswick; ***227** EL-8; mail New Ringgold **Z** 17960; rural
Raven Creek; RMC Place; COLUMBIA; ▲ Benton; mail Benton **Z** 17814; rural
Raven Run; RMC Place; SCHUYLKILL; ▲ West Mahanoy; ***227** EK-7; mail Lost Creek **Z** 17946; ● 50
Ravine; CDP; SCHUYLKILL; ▲ Pine Grove; **227** EM-6; 🅿; **Z** 17966; Ⓒ 629
Rawlinsville; RMC Place; LANCASTER; ▲ Martic; **227** EQ-7; elev. 887ft./270m.; ★ **LANC**; mail Holtwood **Z** 17532; ● 150
Rayburn; MCD-Township; ARMSTRONG; ***225** WK-6; ★ **PGH**; mail Kittanning **Z** 16201; Ⓟ 1,823; Ⓒ 1,811
Raymilton; RMC Place; VENANGO; ▲ Mineral; ***224** WH-4; mail Polk **Z** 16342
Raymond; RMC Place; POTTER; ▲ Allegany; ***224** WE-13; mail Genesee **Z** 16923
Rayne; MCD-Township; INDIANA; ***225** WK-8; mail Home **Z** 15747; Ⓟ 3,339; Ⓒ 3,292
Raytown; RMC Place; INDIANA; ▲ Banks; ***225** WK-9; mail Glen Campbell **Z** 15742; rural
Rea; RMC Place; WASHINGTON; ▲ Cross Creek; **225** WN-2; 🅿; **Z** 15312; ● 50
Reade; MCD-Township; CAMBRIA; ***225** WL-10; mail Blandburg **Z** 16619; Ⓟ 1,716; Ⓒ 1,764
Reading; MCD-Township; ADAMS; ***227** EP-4; mail New Oxford **Z** 17350; Ⓟ 3,828; Ⓒ 5,106
Reading; Inc. Place; ⊡ BERKS; **227** EN-9; elev. 260ft./79m.; 🅿 🅷 🅲 7,734 ■; ★ **READ**; **Z** 19601-12; Ⓟ 78,380; Ⓒ 81,207; ◆ 81,784
Reading Mines; RMC Place; SOMERSET; ▲ Quemahoning; ***225** WO-8; mail Stoystown **Z** 15563; ● 60
Reagantown; RMC Place; WESTMORELAND; ▲ South Huntingdon, East Huntingdon; **225** WO-5; elev. 1,253ft./382m.; ★ **PGH**; mail Ruffs Dale **Z** 15679; ● 70
Reamstown; CDP; LANCASTER; ▲ East Cocalico; **227** EO-8; 🅿; **Z** 17567; Ⓟ 2,649; Ⓒ 3,498
Reamstown Heights; RMC Place; LANCASTER; ▲ East Cocalico; mail Reamstown **Z** 17567
Rebel Hill; RMC Place; MONTGOMERY; ▲ Upper Merion; **228** B-1; elev. 200ft./61m.; ★ **PHIL-**; mail Conshohocken **Z** 19428, King of Prussia **Z** 19406; ● 300
Rebersburg; CDP; CENTRE; ▲ Miles; **226** EJ-2; 🅿; **Z** 16872; Ⓒ 492
Rebuck; RMC Place; NORTHUMBERLAND; ▲ Washington; **227** EL-5; 🅿; **Z** 17867; ● 150
Rector; RMC Place; WESTMORELAND; ▲ Ligonier; **225** WO-7; 🅿; **Z** 15677; ● 400
Redbank; MCD-Township; ARMSTRONG; ***224** WJ-7; mail Mayport **Z** 16240; Ⓟ 1,058; Ⓒ 1,296
Redbank; MCD-Township; CLARION; ***224** WJ-7; mail Fairmount City **Z** 16224; Ⓟ 1,576; Ⓒ 1,502
Red Bank; RMC Place; UNION; ▲ West Buffalo; ***226** EJ-4; mail Mifflinburg **Z** 17844; ● 60
Redbird; RMC Place; CAMBRIA; ▲ Portage; ***225** WN-10; mail Portage **Z** 15946; ● 80
Red Bridge; RMC Place; FRANKLIN; ▲ Greene; **225** WP-14; mail Chambersburg **Z** 17201; ● 200
Red Cedar Hill; RMC Place; BUCKS; ▲ Bristol; ***227** EO-14; ★ **PHIL-**
Redclyffe; RMC Place; FOREST; ▲ Barnett; **224** WH-7; mail Marienville **Z** 16239; ● 20
Red Cross; RMC Place; NORTHUMBERLAND; ▲ Jackson; **227** EL-5; mail Dornsife **Z** 17823; ● 70
Redds Mill; RMC Place; WASHINGTON; ▲ Fallowfield; ***225** WO-4; ★ **PGH**; mail Charleroi **Z** 15022; rural
Red Gate Farms; RMC Place; BUCKS; ▲ Buckingham; ***227** EN-13; elev. 300ft./91m.; ★ **PHIL-**; mail Doylestown **Z** 18901; ● 200
Red Hill; RMC Place; BLAIR; ▲ Logan; **224** WA-12; ★ **ALT**; mail Altoona **Z** 16601; ● 100
Red Hill; Inc. Place; MONTGOMERY; **227** EN-11; elev. 376ft./115m.; 🅿; ★ **PHIL-**; **Z** 18073, **Z** 18076; Ⓟ 1,794; Ⓒ 2,196
Redington; RMC Place; NORTHAMPTON; ▲ Lower Saucon; ***227** EL-11; ★ **ALL-**; mail Hellertown **Z** 18055; rural
Red Lion; RMC Place; BERKS; ▲ Longswamp; ***227** EM-10; mail Macungie **Z** 18062; ● 110
Red Lion; RMC Place; CHESTER; ▲ East Marlborough; **227** EQ-10; ★ **PHIL-**; mail Kennett Square **Z** 19348; ● 200
Red Lion; Inc. Place; YORK; **227** EQ-6; elev. 911ft./278m.; 🅿; ★ **YORK**; **Z** 17356; Ⓟ 6,130; Ⓒ 6,149
Red Mill; RMC Place; JEFFERSON; ▲ Washington; ***224** WI-9; mail Falls Creek **Z** 15840
Red Oak; RMC Place; LACKAWANNA; ▲ Jefferson; ***226** EG-10; ★ **SCR-**; mail Lake Ariel **Z** 18436; ● 100
Red Rock; RMC Place; LUZERNE; ▲ Fairmount; **226** EH-7; elev. 1,243ft./379m.; mail Benton **Z** 17814; ● 30
Red Rock; RMC Place; MCKEAN; ▲ Foster; ***224** WD-10; elev. 1,676ft./511m.; mail Derrick City **Z** 16727; rural
Red Rose Gate; RMC Place; BUCKS; ▲ Middletown; ★ **PHIL-**; mail Levittown **Z** 19056
Redrun; RMC Place; LANCASTER; ▲ Brecknock; ***227** EO-8; mail Denver **Z** 17517, Stevens **Z** 17578; rural
Redstone; RMC Place; FAYETTE; ▲ Jefferson; ***225** WO-4; elev. 900ft./274m.; ★ **PGH**; mail Fayette City **Z** 15438; ● 120
Redstone; MCD-Township; FAYETTE; ***225** WP-4; ★ **UNTN**; mail Grindstone **Z** 15442; Ⓟ 6,459; Ⓒ 6,397
Redstone Junction; RMC Place; FAYETTE; ▲ North Union; ★ **UNTN**; mail Oliver **Z** 15472
Reduction; RMC Place; WESTMORELAND; ▲ South Huntingdon; ***225** WO-5; ★ **PGH**; mail Smithton **Z** 15479; ● 50
Reeceville; RMC Place; CHESTER; ▲ West Brandywine; ***227** EP-9; ★ **PHIL-**; mail Downingtown **Z** 19335; ● 40
Reed; MCD-Township; DAUPHIN; ***227** EN-4; ★ **HRBG**; mail Halifax **Z** 17032; Ⓟ 259; Ⓒ 182
Reed; RMC Place; NORTHUMBERLAND; ▲ Shamokin; ***227** EK-6; mail Paxinos **Z** 17860; rural
Reeder; RMC Place; BUCKS; ▲ Solebury; ***227** EN-13; ★ **PHIL-**; mail New Hope **Z** 18938; rural
Reeders; RMC Place; MONROE; ▲ Jackson; **226** EJ-11; elev. 979ft./298m.; 🅿; **Z** 18352; summer pop. 2,500; ● 350
Reeds Gap; RMC Place; JUNIATA; ▲ Tuscarora; **227** EM-1; mail Honey Grove **Z** 17035; ● 30
Reeds Road; RMC Place; CHESTER; ▲ East Brandywine; ***227** EP-10; ★ **PHIL-**; mail Downingtown **Z** 19335; rural
Reedsville; CDP; MIFFLIN; ▲ Brown; **227** EL-1; 🅿; **Z** 17084; Ⓟ 1,030; Ⓒ 858
Reels Corners; RMC Place; SOMERSET; ▲ Stonycreek, Shade; **225** WP-9; elev. 2,535ft./773m.; mail Central City **Z** 15926; ● 25
Reemersville; RMC Place; PIKE; ▲ Greene; ***226** EH-12; elev. 1,582ft./482m.; mail Greentown **Z** 18426; ● 50
Reese; RMC Place; BLAIR; ▲ Frankstown; **225** WM-11; elev. 914ft./279m.; ★ **ALT**; mail Hollidaysburg **Z** 16648; ● 80
Reesedale; RMC Place; ARMSTRONG; ▲ Washington; **224** WJ-6; mail Adrian **Z** 16210; ● 50
Reesers Summit; YORK; see Fairview Park (RMC Place)
Reevesdale; RMC Place; SCHUYLKILL; ▲ Schuylkill; ***227** EK-8; ★ **PTSVL**; mail Tamaqua **Z** 18252; rural
Reflection Lakes; RMC Place; WAYNE; ▲ Manchester; ***226** EE-12; elev. 1,500ft./457m.; mail Equinunk **Z** 18417; ● 35
Refton; RMC Place; LANCASTER; ▲ Strasburg; **227** EP-7; 🅿; ★ **LANC**; **Z** 17568; ● 250
Regency Park; RMC Place; ALLEGHENY; ***225** WM-5; ★ **PGH**; mail Pittsburgh **Z** 15239; pop. incl. with Plum (Inc. Place)
Register; RMC Place; LUZERNE; ▲ Huntington; ***226** EI-7; mail Cambra **Z** 18611; rural
Rehrersburg; RMC Place; BERKS; ▲ Tulpehocken; **227** EM-7; elev. 587ft./179m.; 🅿; **Z** 19550; ● 600
Reidsburg; RMC Place; CLARION; ▲ Monroe; **224** WI-6; mail Clarion **Z** 16214; ● 40
Reiffton; CDP; BERKS; ▲ Exeter; **227** ET-13; elev. 365ft./111m.; ★ **READ**; mail Reading **Z** 19606; Ⓟ 2,522; Ⓒ 2,888
Reightown; RMC Place; BLAIR; ▲ Antis; **225** WL-11; ★ **ALT**; mail Tyrone **Z** 16686; pop. incl. with Bellwood (Inc. Place)
Reilly; MCD-Township; SCHUYLKILL; ***227** EL-7; mail Branchdale **Z** 17923; Ⓟ 835; Ⓒ 802
Reillys; RMC Place; CAMBRIA; ▲ East Carroll; ***225** WL-10; mail Patton **Z** 16668; ● 200
Reinerton; RMC Place; SCHUYLKILL; ▲ Porter; **227** EL-6; mail Tower City **Z** 17980; ● 500
Reinerton-Orwin-Muir; CDP-Census Area Only; SCHUYLKILL; ▲ Porter; ***227** EM-6; elev. 829ft./253m.; mail Muir **Z** 17957, Tower City **Z** 17980; Ⓟ 1,255; Ⓒ 1,037
Reinholds; RMC Place; LANCASTER; ▲ West Cocalico; **227** EN-8; 🅿; **Z** 17569; ● 500
Reinoeldville; RMC Place; LEBANON; ▲ North Lebanon; ***227** EN-6; ★ **LEB**; mail Lebanon **Z** 17046; ● 350
Reistville; RMC Place; LEBANON; ▲ Heidelberg; **227** EN-7; elev. 550ft./168m.; ★ **LEB**; mail Myerstown **Z** 17067; ● 100
Reitz (Reitz Crossing); RMC Place; JEFFERSON; ▲ Warsaw, Washington; ***224** WI-9; mail Brockway **Z** 15824; rural
Reitz; RMC Place; SOMERSET; ▲ Shade; ***225** WO-9; mail Cairnbrook **Z** 15924; ● 120
Reitz Crossing; JEFFERSON; see Reitz (RMC Place)
Relay; RMC Place; YORK; ▲ York; ***227** EP-5; ★ **YORK**; mail Dallastown **Z** 17313; rural
Reliance; RMC Place; MONTGOMERY; ***227** EN-11; ★ **PHIL-**; mail Souderton **Z** 18964; ● 350
Rembrant; RMC Place; INDIANA; ▲ Cherryhill; ***225** WL-8; elev. 1,300ft./396m.; mail Clymer **Z** 15728; rural
Renfrew; RMC Place; BUTLER; ▲ Penn; **225** WK-4; 🅿; ★ **PGH**; **Z** 16053; ● 350
Rennerdale; RMC Place; ALLEGHENY; ▲ Collier; ***225** WM-3; ★ **PGH**; mail Carnegie **Z** 15106; ● 800
Renningers; CDP-Census Area Only; SCHUYLKILL; ***227** EL-8; ★ **PTSVL**; Ⓒ 380
Reno; RMC Place; VENANGO; ***224** WH-5; 🅿; ★ **OILC-F**; **Z** 16343; pop. incl. with Sugarcreek (Inc. Place)
Renovo; Inc. Place; CLINTON; **224** WH-14; elev. 668ft./204m.; 🅿 🅷; **Z** 17764; Ⓟ 1,526; Ⓒ 1,318
Renton; RMC Place; ALLEGHENY; ***225** WM-5; elev. 1,200ft./366m.; ★ **PGH**; mail Pittsburgh **Z** 15239; pop. incl. with Plum (Inc. Place)
Republic; CDP; FAYETTE; ▲ Redstone, Luzerne; **225** WP-4; 🅿; ★ **UNTN**; **Z** 15475 & mail Merrittstown **Z** 15463; Ⓟ 1,603; Ⓒ 1,396
Reserve; MCD-Township; ALLEGHENY; ***225** WM-4; ★ **PGH**; mail Pittsburgh **Z** 15212; Ⓟ 3,866; Ⓒ 3,856
Reserve Township; CDP-Census Area Only; ALLEGHENY; ▲ Reserve; ***225** WM-4; ★ **PGH**; mail Pittsburgh **Z** 15212; Ⓟ 3,866; Ⓒ 3,856
Reservoir; RMC Place; BLAIR; ▲ Blair; ***225** WN-11; ★ **ALT**; mail Hollidaysburg **Z** 16648; ● 150
Retort; RMC Place; CENTRE; ▲ Rush; mail Sandy Ridge **Z** 16677
Revere; RMC Place; BUCKS; ▲ Nockamixon; **227** EM-12; 🅿; ★ **PHIL-**; **Z** 18953; ● 500
Revere; FAYETTE; see Uledi (RMC Place)
Revloc; RMC Place; CAMBRIA; ▲ Cambria; **225** WM-9; 🅿; **Z** 15948; ● 650
Rew; RMC Place; MCKEAN; ▲ Foster; **224** WE-10; elev. 2,256ft./688m.; 🅿; **Z** 16744; ● 300
Reward; RMC Place; PERRY; ▲ Greenwood; ***227** EM-3; mail Millerstown **Z** 17062; rural
Rexford; RMC Place; TIOGA; ▲ Gaines; **226** EF-2; mail Gaines **Z** 16921; ● 100
Rexis; RMC Place; INDIANA; ▲ Buffington; **225** WM-8; mail Vintondale **Z** 15961; ● 45
Rexmont; RMC Place; LEBANON; ***227** EN-7; elev. 700ft./213m.; 🅿; ★ **LEB**; **Z** 17085; pop. incl. with Cornwall (Inc. Place)
Rextown; RMC Place; LEHIGH; ▲ Washington; ***227** EK-10; ★ **ALL-**; mail Slatington **Z** 18080; ● 80
Reyburn; RMC Place; LUZERNE; ▲ Union; ***226** EI-8; ★ **SCR-**; mail Shickshinny **Z** 18655; rural
Reynolds; RMC Place; SCHUYLKILL; ▲ Walker; ***227** EL-8; mail Tamaqua **Z** 18252; ● 120
Reynoldsdale; RMC Place; BEDFORD; ▲ East St. Clair; ***225** WO-10; mail New Paris **Z** 15554; ● 250
Reynolds Heights; RMC Place; MERCER; ▲ Pymatuning; ***224** WH-2; ★ **SHAR**; mail Greenville **Z** 16125
Reynoldsville; Inc. Place; JEFFERSON; **224** WI-9; elev. 1,400ft./427m.; 🅿; **Z** 15851; Ⓟ 2,818; Ⓒ 2,710
Rhawnhurst; RMC Place; PHILADELPHIA; ***227** EO-13; ★ **PHIL-**; mail Philadelphia **Z** 19111; pop. incl. with Philadelphia (Inc. Place)
Rheems; CDP; LANCASTER; ▲ West Donegal, Mount Joy; **227** EO-6; 🅿; **Z** 17570; Ⓒ 1,557
Ribot; RMC Place; HUNTINGDON; ▲ Logan; ***225** WL-12; mail Petersburg **Z** 16669; rural
Rice; MCD-Township; LUZERNE; ***226** EI-9; ★ **SCR-**; mail Mountain Top **Z** 18707; Ⓟ 1,907; Ⓒ 2,460
Rices Landing; Inc. Place; GREENE; **225** WP-3; elev. 971ft./296m.; 🅿; **Z** 15357; Ⓟ 457; Ⓒ 443
Riceville; CDP; CRAWFORD; ▲ Bloomfield; **224** WE-5; 🅿; **Z** 16432; Ⓒ 82
Richards Grove; RMC Place; LYCOMING; ▲ Jordan; ***226** EI-6; mail Unityville **Z** 17774; rural
Richardsville; RMC Place; JEFFERSON; ▲ Warsaw; **224** WI-8; mail Brookville **Z** 15825; ● 40
Richboro; CDP; BUCKS; ▲ Northampton; **227** EO-13; 🅿; ★ **PHIL-**; **Z** 18954; Ⓟ 5,332; Ⓒ 6,678
Richboro Manor; RMC Place; BUCKS; ▲ Northampton; ★ **PHIL-**; mail Richboro **Z** 18954
Richeyville; RMC Place; WASHINGTON; ***225** WP-3; elev. 1,180ft./360m.; 🅿; **Z** 15358; pop. incl. with Centerville (Inc. Place)
Richfield; CDP; JUNIATA; ▲ Monroe; **227** EL-3; elev. 658ft./201m.; 🅿; **Z** 17086; Ⓒ 459
Rich Hill; RMC Place; BUCKS; ▲ East Rockhill, Richland, West Rockhill; **227** EM-11; ★ **PHIL-**; mail Quakertown **Z** 18951; ● 50
Richhill; MCD-Township; GREENE; ***225** WQ-1; mail West Finley **Z** 15377, Wind Ridge **Z** 15380; Ⓟ 1,102; Ⓒ 1,062
Rich Hill; RMC Place; WASHINGTON; ▲ Chartiers; ***225** WO-2; ★ **WASH**; mail Meadow Lands **Z** 15347
Richland; MCD-Township; ALLEGHENY; ***225** WL-4; ★ **PGH**; mail Gibsonia **Z** 15044; Ⓟ 8,600; Ⓒ 9,231
Richland; MCD-Township; BUCKS; ***227** EM-11; ★ **PHIL-**; mail Quakertown **Z** 18951; does not include the Borough of Richlandtown; Ⓟ 8,560; Ⓒ 9,920
Richland; RMC Place; CAMBRIA; ▲ Dean; ***225** WL-10; elev. 2,224ft./678m.; mail Dysart **Z** 16636; rural
Richland; MCD-Township; CAMBRIA; ***225** WN-9; ★ **JNST**; mail Johnstown **Z** 15904; Ⓟ 12,777; Ⓒ 12,598
Richland; MCD-Township; CLARION; ***224** WI-5; mail Parker **Z** 16049; Ⓟ 490; Ⓒ 553
Richland; Inc. Place; LEBANON; **227** EN-7; elev. 489ft./149m.; 🅿; **Z** 17087; Ⓟ 1,457; Ⓒ 1,508
Richland; MCD-Township; VENANGO; ***224** WH-5; mail Emlenton **Z** 16373; Ⓟ 775; Ⓒ 744
Richlandtown; Inc. Place; BUCKS; **227** EM-11; elev. 520ft./158m.; 🅿; ★ **PHIL-**; **Z** 18955; Ⓟ 1,195; Ⓒ 1,283
Richmond; MCD-Township; BERKS; ***227** EM-9; mail Kutztown **Z** 19530; Ⓟ 3,439; Ⓒ 3,500
Richmond; MCD-Township; CRAWFORD; ***224** WE-4; mail Guys Mills **Z** 16327; Ⓟ 1,370; Ⓒ 1,379
Richmond; INDIANA; see Rochester Mills (RMC Place)
Richmond; RMC Place; NORTHAMPTON; ▲ Washington; **227** EK-12; mail Bangor **Z** 18013; ● 100
Richmond; RMC Place; PHILADELPHIA; ***227** EP-12; ★ **PHIL-**; mail Philadelphia **Z** 19134; pop. incl. with Philadelphia (Inc. Place)
Richmond; MCD-Township; TIOGA; ***226** EE-3; mail Mansfield **Z** 16933; Ⓟ 2,305; Ⓒ 2,475
Richmondale; RMC Place; LACKAWANNA; ▲ Fell; ***226** EF-10; 🅿; ★ **SCR-**; **Z** 18421; ● 160
Richmond Furnace; RMC Place; FRANKLIN; ▲ Metal; **225** WP-13; mail Fort Loudon **Z** 17224; ● 50
Richvale; RMC Place; HUNTINGDON; ▲ Tell; **225** WN-14; mail Blairs Mills **Z** 17213; ● 35
Riddlesburg; RMC Place; BEDFORD; ▲ Broad Top; **225** WO-11; 🅿; **Z** 16672; ● 300
Riddlewood; RMC Place; DELAWARE; ▲ Middletown; ***227** EP-11; ★ **PHIL-**; mail Media **Z** 19063; ● 1,100
Ridgebury (Centerville); RMC Place; BRADFORD; ▲ Ridgebury; **226** ED-5; mail Wellsburg **Z** 14894; ● 170
Ridgebury; MCD-Township; BRADFORD; ***226** ED-5; mail Columbia Cross Roads **Z** 16914; Ⓟ 2,026; Ⓒ 1,982
Ridge Valley; RMC Place; BUCKS; ▲ West Rockhill; ***227** EN-11; ★ **PHIL-**; mail Sellersville **Z** 18960; ● 100
Ridgeview; RMC Place; DAUPHIN; ▲ Lower Paxton; **227** ES-4; ★ **HRBG**; mail Harrisburg **Z** 17112; ● 800
Ridgeville; RMC Place; MONTOUR; ▲ Mahoning, Cooper; ***226** EJ-6; mail Danville **Z** 17821; ● 80
Ridgeway; ELK; see Ridgway (Inc. Place)
Ridgewood; RMC Place; BERKS; ▲ Cumru; ***227** EN-9; elev. 254ft./77m.; ★ **READ**; mail Birdsboro **Z** 19508; ● 75
Ridgewood; RMC Place; LUZERNE; ▲ Plains; **226** EB-9; ★ **SCR-**; mail Wilkes Barre **Z** 18705; ● 300
Ridgewood Farm; RMC Place; CHESTER; ▲ West Goshen; ★ **PHIL-**; mail West Chester **Z** 19380; ● 300
Ridgway (Ridgeway); Inc. Place; ⊡ ELK; **224** WH-9; elev. 1,379ft./420m.; 🅿 🅷; **Z** 15853; Ⓟ 4,793; Ⓒ 4,591
Ridgway; MCD-Township; ELK; ***224** WG-9; 🅿; **Z** 15853; does not include the Borough of Ridgway; Ⓟ 2,617; Ⓒ 2,802
Ridley; MCD-Township; DELAWARE; ***227** EQ-11; 🅿; ★ **PHIL-**; **Z** 19070 & mail Folsom **Z** 19033; Ⓟ 31,169; Ⓒ 30,791; ◆ 30,619
Ridley Farms; RMC Place; DELAWARE; ▲ Ridley; ***227** EP-11; elev. 105ft./32m.; ★ **PHIL-**; mail Morton **Z** 19070; ● 1,500
Ridley Gardens; RMC Place; DELAWARE; ▲ Ridley; ★ **PHIL-**; mail Holmes **Z** 19043
Ridley Park; RMC Place; CUMBERLAND; ▲ East Pennsboro; ***227** EO-4; ★ **HRBG**; mail Camp Hill **Z** 17011; pop. incl. with Camp Hill (Inc. Place)
Ridley Park; Inc. Place; DELAWARE; **228** G-1; elev. 70ft./21m.; 🅿 🅷; ★ **PHIL-**; **Z** 19078; Ⓟ 7,592; Ⓒ 7,196
Riegelsville; Inc. Place; BUCKS; **227** EL-12; elev. 180ft./55m.; 🅿; ★ **ALL-**; **Z** 18077; Ⓟ 912; Ⓒ 863
Rienze; RMC Place; BRADFORD; ▲ Terry; ***226** EF-7; mail Wyalusing **Z** 18853; rural
Rife; RMC Place; DAUPHIN; ▲ Upper Paxton; ***227** EM-4; mail Millersburg **Z** 17061; ● 55
Riggles Gap; RMC Place; BLAIR; ▲ Antis; ***225** WM-11; ★ **ALT**; mail Altoona **Z** 16601; ● 120
Riggs; RMC Place; BRADFORD; ▲ Smithfield; ***226** EE-6; mail Ulster **Z** 18850; rural
Rillton; RMC Place; WESTMORELAND; ▲ Sewickley; **225** WN-5; 🅿; ★ **PGH**; **Z** 15678; ● 900
Rimer; RMC Place; ARMSTRONG; ▲ Madison; **224** WJ-6; elev. 833ft./254m.; mail Templeton **Z** 16259; ● 40
Rimersburg; Inc. Place; CLARION; **224** WJ-6; elev. 1,480ft./451m.; 🅿; **Z** 16248; Ⓟ 1,053; Ⓒ 1,051
Rinely; RMC Place; YORK; ▲ East Hopewell, Hopewell, North Hopewell; ***227** EQ-6; elev. 944ft./288m.; ★ **BAL**; mail Stewartstown **Z** 17363
Ringdale; RMC Place; SULLIVAN; ▲ Laporte; ***226** EG-6; mail Dushore **Z** 18614; rural
Ringertown; RMC Place; WESTMORELAND; ***225** WM-5; ★ **PGH**; mail Export **Z** 15632; pop. incl. with Murrysville (Inc. Place)
Ringgold; RMC Place; JEFFERSON; ▲ Ringgold; ***224** WJ-7; 🅿; **Z** 15770; ● 225
Ringgold; MCD-Township; JEFFERSON; ***224** WJ-7; 🅿; **Z** 15770; Ⓟ 705; Ⓒ 764
Ringing Hill; RMC Place; MONTGOMERY; ▲ Lower Pottsgrove; ***227** EN-10; ★ **PTSTN**; mail Pottstown **Z** 19464; ● 300
Ringtown; RMC Place; BERKS; ▲ Longswamp; ***227** EM-10; mail Mertztown **Z** 19539; ● 100
Ringtown; Inc. Place; SCHUYLKILL; **227** EK-7; elev. 1,140ft./347m.; 🅿; **Z** 17967; Ⓟ 853; Ⓒ 826
Risher Mine Siding; RMC Place; ALLEGHENY; ★ **PGH**; pop. incl. with West Mifflin (Inc. Place)
Rising Sun; RMC Place; LEHIGH; ▲ North Whitehall; ***227** EL-10; elev. 651ft./198m.; ★ **ALL-**; mail Slatington **Z** 18080; ● 120
Riterville; RMC Place; MCKEAN; ▲ Keating; ***224** WE-10; elev. 2,100ft./640m.; mail Lewis Run **Z** 16738; rural
Ritterville; RMC Place; LEHIGH; ***227** EL-11; ★ **ALL-**; pop. incl. with Allentown (Inc. Place)
Ritzie Village; RMC Place; DAUPHIN; ▲ West Hanover; ***227** EN-5; ★ **HRBG**; mail Harrisburg **Z** 17112; ● 100
River Front; RMC Place; PHILADELPHIA; ★ **PHIL-**; pop. incl. with Philadelphia (Inc. Place)
River Hill; RMC Place; ALLEGHENY; ▲ Forward; ***225** WO-4; ★ **PGH**; mail Monongahela **Z** 15063; ● 200
Riverside; RMC Place; CAMBRIA; ▲ Stonycreek; **225** WT-2; ★ **JNST**; mail Johnstown **Z** 15905; ● 700
Riverside; RMC Place; LACKAWANNA; ***226** EG-10; ★ **SCR-**; mail Archbald **Z** 18403; pop. incl. with Archbald (Inc. Place)
Riverside; RMC Place; LEHIGH; ★ **ALL-**; pop. incl. with Bethlehem (Inc. Place)
Riverside (South Danville); Inc. Place; NORTHUMBERLAND; **226** EJ-5; 🅿; **Z** 17868; Ⓟ 1,991; Ⓒ 1,861
Riverton; RMC Place; ALLEGHENY; ★ **PGH**; pop. incl. with McKeesport (Inc. Place)
Riverton; RMC Place; NORTHAMPTON; ***227** EK-12; ★ **ALL-**; mail Bangor **Z** 18013; ● 50
River View; RMC Place; ARMSTRONG; ▲ Parks; ***225** WL-5; ★ **PGH**; mail Vandergrift **Z** 15690; ● 250
Riverview; RMC Place; CLEARFIELD; ▲ Lawrence; ***224** WJ-11; mail Clearfield **Z** 16830; ● 60
River View; RMC Place; WASHINGTON; ***225** WO-4; ★ **PGH**; mail New Eagle **Z** 15067; pop. incl. with New Eagle (Inc. Place)
Riverview Acres; RMC Place; LEHIGH; ▲ Washington; ***227** EL-10; ★ **ALL-**; mail Slatington **Z** 18080; ● 400
Riverview Heights; RMC Place; CUMBERLAND; ▲ East Pennsboro; ***227** EN-4; elev. 450ft./137m.; ★ **HRBG**; mail Camp Hill **Z** 17011; ● 1,500
River View Park; RMC Place; BERKS; ▲ Muhlenberg; **227** ES-12; ★ **READ**; mail Reading **Z** 19605; ● 2,000
Rixford; RMC Place; MCKEAN; ▲ Otto; **224** WE-10; elev. 1,601ft./488m.; 🅿; **Z** 16745; ● 400
Roadside; RMC Place; FRANKLIN; ▲ Washington; ***227** EQ-1; ★ **HAG**; mail Waynesboro **Z** 17268; ● 50
Roaring Branch; RMC Place; TIOGA, LYCOMING; ▲ McNett, Union; **226** EG-4; 🅿; **Z** 17765; ● 100
Roaring Brook; MCD-Township; LACKAWANNA; ***226** EH-10; elev. 1,260ft./384m.; ★ **SCR-**; mail Lake Ariel **Z** 18436, Moscow **Z** 18444; Ⓟ 1,966; Ⓒ 1,637
Roaring Brook Estates; RMC Place; LACKAWANNA; ▲ Roaring Brook; ***226** EH-10; elev. 1,700ft./518m.; ★ **SCR-**; mail Moscow **Z** 18444; ● 350
Roaring Creek; COLUMBIA; see Slabtown (CDP)
Roaring Creek; MCD-Township; COLUMBIA; ***227** EK-7; mail Catawissa **Z** 17820; Ⓟ 478; Ⓒ 495
Roaring Spring; Inc. Place; BLAIR; **225** WN-11; 🅿 🅷; ★ **ALT**; **Z** 16673; Ⓟ 2,615; Ⓒ 2,418
Robb; RMC Place; WESTMORELAND; ▲ St. Clair; ***225** WN-8; ★ **JNST**; mail New Florence **Z** 15944; ● 40
Robert Bruce West; RMC Place; MONTGOMERY; ▲ Upper Moreland; ★ **PHIL-**; mail Hatboro **Z** 19040; pop. incl. with Hatboro (Inc. Place)
Robertsdale; RMC Place; HUNTINGDON; ▲ Wood; **225** WO-12; 🅿; **Z** 16674; ● 240
Robertsville; RMC Place; JEFFERSON; ▲ Bell; ***224** WJ-9; mail Punxsutawney **Z** 15767; rural
Robeson; MCD-Township; BERKS; ***227** EN-9; ★ **READ**; mail Birdsboro **Z** 19508; Ⓟ 5,972; Ⓒ 6,869
Robeson Crossing; RMC Place; BERKS; ▲ Robeson; ***227** EN-9; ★ **READ**; mail Birdsboro **Z** 19508; ● 100
Robeson Extension; RMC Place; BLAIR; ▲ Catharine; ***225** WM-12; mail Williamsburg **Z** 16693; ● 120
Robesonia; Inc. Place; BERKS; **227** EN-8; elev. 420ft./128m.; 🅿; ★ **READ**; **Z** 19551; Ⓟ 1,944; Ⓒ 2,036
Robindale Heights; RMC Place; INDIANA; ***225** WM-8; ★ **JNST**; mail Seward **Z** 15954; ● 95
Robin Hood Lakes; RMC Place; MONROE; ▲ Polk; ***226** EJ-10; mail Kunkletown **Z** 18058; summer pop. 550; ● 250
Robinson; MCD-Township; ALLEGHENY; ***225** WM-3; ★ **PGH**; mail Coraopolis **Z** 15108, Mc Kees Rocks **Z** 15136; Ⓟ 10,830; Ⓒ 12,289
Robinson; RMC Place; INDIANA; ▲ West Wheatfield; **225** WN-7; elev. 1,089ft./332m.; 🅿; ★ **JNST**; **Z** 15949; ● 650
Robinson; RMC Place; LAWRENCE; ▲ Mahoning; ***224** WJ-1; ★ **YNGS-**; mail Hillsville **Z** 16132; rural
Robinson; MCD-Township; WASHINGTON; ***225** WN-2; ★ **PGH**; mail Mc Donald **Z** 15057; Ⓟ 2,160; Ⓒ 2,193
Robinson Township; CDP-Census Area Only; ALLEGHENY; ▲ Robinson; ***225** WM-3; elev. 1,100ft./335m.; ★ **PGH**; mail Coraopolis **Z** 15108, Mc Kees Rocks **Z** 15136; Ⓟ 10,830; Ⓒ 12,289
Rocherty; RMC Place; LEBANON; ▲ North Cornwall; ***227** EN-6; elev. 484ft./148m.; ★ **LEB**; mail Lebanon **Z** 17042; ● 75
Rochester; Inc. Place; BEAVER; **225** WL-2; elev. 800ft./244m.; 🅿; ★ **PGH**; **Z** 15074; Ⓟ 4,156; Ⓒ 4,014
Rochester; MCD-Township; BEAVER; ***225** WL-2; 🅿; ★ **PGH**; **Z** 15074; Ⓟ 3,247; Ⓒ 3,129
Rochester Mills (Richmond); RMC Place; INDIANA; ▲ Grant, East Mahoning; **225** WK-8; 🅿; **Z** 15771; ● 175
Rock; RMC Place; SCHUYLKILL; ▲ Washington; **227** EM-7; mail Pine Grove **Z** 17963; ● 60
Rockdale; RMC Place; BUCKS; ▲ Bristol; ***227** EO-13; ★ **PHIL-**; mail Bristol **Z** 19007
Rockdale; MCD-Township; CRAWFORD; ***224** WE-4; mail Cambridge Springs **Z** 16403; Ⓟ 1,045; Ⓒ 1,343
Rockdale; RMC Place; DELAWARE; ▲ Aston; ***227** EQ-11; ★ **PHIL-**; mail Aston **Z** 19014; ● 200
Rockdale; RMC Place; JEFFERSON; ▲ Washington; ***224** WI-9; mail Falls Creek **Z** 15840; rural
Rockdale; RMC Place; LEHIGH; ▲ North Whitehall; ***227** EL-10; ★ **ALL-**; mail Slatington **Z** 18080; rural
Rockdale Acres; RMC Place; CRAWFORD; ▲ Rockdale; ***224** WE-4; mail Cambridge Springs **Z** 16403; ● 100
Rockefeller; MCD-Township; NORTHUMBERLAND; ***227** EK-5; mail Sunbury **Z** 17801; Ⓟ 2,029; Ⓒ 2,221
Rock Glen; RMC Place; LUZERNE; ▲ Black Creek; **226** EJ-7; 🅿; ★ **HAZ**; **Z** 18246; ● 300
Rock Hill; RMC Place; BUCKS; ▲ East Rockhill; ***227** EM-11; ★ **PHIL-**; mail Sellersville **Z** 18960; ● 100
Rockhill (Rockhill Furnace); Inc. Place; HUNTINGDON; **225** WO-13; elev. 629ft./192m.; mail Rockhill Furnace **Z** 17249; Ⓟ 421; Ⓒ 414
Rockhill; RMC Place; LANCASTER; ▲ Conestoga; ***227** EP-7; ★ **LANC**; mail Conestoga **Z** 17516; rural
Rockhill Furnace; HUNTINGDON; see Rockhill (Inc. Place)
Rockingham; RMC Place; SOMERSET; ▲ Shade; **225** WO-9; mail Cairnbrook **Z** 15924; ● 60
Rock Lake; RMC Place; WAYNE; ▲ Mount Pleasant; mail Pleasant Mount **Z** 18453; rural
Rockland; MCD-Township; BERKS; ***227** EM-9; ★ **READ**; mail Fleetwood **Z** 19522; Ⓟ 2,675; Ⓒ 3,765
Rockland; RMC Place; VENANGO; ▲ Rockland; **224** WH-5; mail Kennerdell **Z** 16374; ● 20
Rockland; RMC Place; VENANGO; ▲ Rockland; ● 30
Rockland; MCD-Township; VENANGO; ***224** WH-5; mail Kennerdell **Z** 16374; Ⓟ 1,320; Ⓒ 1,346
Rockledge; Inc. Place; MONTGOMERY; **228** B-5; 🅿; ★ **PHIL-**; **Z** 19046 & mail Philadelphia **Z** 19111; Ⓟ 2,679; Ⓒ 2,577
Rockport; RMC Place; CARBON; ▲ Lehigh; **226** EJ-9; ★ **HAZ**; mail Weatherly **Z** 18255; ● 85
Rockrimmin Ridge; RMC Place; LANCASTER; ▲ Upper Leacock; ★ **LANC**; mail Leola **Z** 17540
Rock Run; RMC Place; CHESTER; ▲ Valley; ***227** EP-9; ★ **PHIL-**; mail Coatesville **Z** 19320; ● 300
Rockspring; RMC Place; CENTRE; ▲ Ferguson; ***225** WL-13; ★ **STCOL**; mail Pennsylvania Furnace **Z** 16865
Rockton; RMC Place; CLEARFIELD; ▲ Union; **224** WJ-10; 🅿; **Z** 15856; ● 200
Rockton Station; RMC Place; CLEARFIELD; ▲ Union; ***224** WJ-10; mail Rockton **Z** 15856; rural
Rocktown; RMC Place; WESTMORELAND; ▲ East Huntingdon; ***225** WO-5; mail Tarrs **Z** 15688; ● 120
Rockville; RMC Place; ARMSTRONG; ▲ Kittanning; ***225** WL-6; mail Ford City **Z** 16226
Rockville; RMC Place; CAMBRIA; ▲ Croyle; **225** WS-4; ★ **JNST**; mail South Fork **Z** 15956; ● 170
Rockville; RMC Place; CHESTER; ▲ Honey Brook; ***227** EO-9; ★ **PHIL-**; mail Honey Brook **Z** 19344; ● 400
Rockville; RMC Place; CLARION; ▲ Porter; ***224** WJ-6; elev. 1,200ft./366m.; mail New Bethlehem **Z** 16242; rural
Rockville; RMC Place; DAUPHIN; ▲ Susquehanna; **227** EN-4; ★ **HRBG**; mail Harrisburg **Z** 17110; ● 85
Rockville; RMC Place; JUNIATA; ▲ Milford; ***227** EM-2; mail Mifflintown **Z** 17059; ● 200
Rockville; RMC Place; MIFFLIN; ▲ Union; ***225** WL-14; mail Belleville **Z** 17004; ● 90
Rockville; RMC Place; NORTHAMPTON; ▲ Lehigh; ***227** EK-11; ★ **ALL-**; mail Danielsville **Z** 18038; ● 80
Rockwood; RMC Place; LEBANON; ▲ North Lebanon; ***227** EN-6; ★ **LEB**; mail Lebanon **Z** 17046; ● 300
Rockwood; Inc. Place; SOMERSET; **225** WP-7; elev. 1,820ft./555m.; 🅿; **Z** 15557; Ⓟ 1,014; Ⓒ 954
Rock Works; RMC Place; FAYETTE; ▲ Nicholson; ***225** WQ-4; mail Masontown **Z** 15461; ● 15
Rocky Forest; RMC Place; WYOMING; ▲ Windham; ***226** EF-7; mail Laceyville **Z** 18623; rural
Rocky Grove; RMC Place; VENANGO; ***224** WH-4; ★ **OILC-F**; mail Franklin **Z** 16323; pop. incl. with Sugarcreek (Inc. Place)
Rocky Hill; RMC Place; CHESTER; ▲ East Goshen; ***227** EP-10; elev. 478ft./146m.; ★ **PHIL-**; mail West Chester **Z** 19380; ● 300
Rocky Valley; RMC Place; BUCKS; ▲ Springfield; ***227** EM-11; ★ **ALL-**; mail Coopersburg **Z** 18036; rural
Roedersville; RMC Place; SCHUYLKILL; ▲ Washington; **227** EL-7; mail Pine Grove **Z** 17963; ● 200
Rogers Mills; RMC Place; FAYETTE; ▲ Springfield; ***225** WP-6; mail Normalville **Z** 15469; ● 75
Rogers Stop; RMC Place; WASHINGTON; ▲ Fallowfield; ***225** WO-4; ★ **PGH**; mail Charleroi **Z** 15022; ● 40
Rogerstown; RMC Place; FAYETTE; ▲ Dunbar; ***225** WP-5; elev. 992ft./302m.; mail Connellsville **Z** 15425; ● 200
Rogersville; RMC Place; GREENE; ▲ Center; **225** WQ-2; 🅿; **Z** 15359; ● 220
Rogertown; RMC Place; WARREN; ▲ Mead; **224** WE-8; mail Clarendon **Z** 16313; ● 140
Rohrerstown; RMC Place; LANCASTER; ▲ East Hempfield; **227** ES-8; 🅿; ★ **LANC**; **Z** 17603 & mail Lancaster **Z** 17607; ● 1,200
Rohrsburg; CDP; COLUMBIA; ▲ Greenwood; **226** EI-6; elev. 661ft./201m.; mail Orangeville **Z** 17859; Ⓒ 164
Rolling Glen; RMC Place; CHESTER; ▲ Uwchlan; ***227** EP-10; ★ **PHIL-**; mail Exton **Z** 19341; ● 200
Rolling Hills; RMC Place; BERKS; ▲ Cumru; ★ **READ**; mail Reading **Z** 19607
Rolling Hills; RMC Place; LEHIGH; ▲ Whitehall; ★ **ALL-**; mail Whitehall **Z** 18052
Rolling Meadows; RMC Place; GREENE; ▲ Franklin; ***225** WP-3; elev. 1,100ft./335m.; mail Waynesburg **Z** 15370; ● 300
Romansville; RMC Place; CHESTER; ▲ West Bradford; ***227** EP-10; 🅿; ★ **PHIL-**; **Z** 19320; ● 400
Romar; RMC Place; CAMBRIA; ▲ Blacklick; mail Nanty Glo **Z** 15943; rural
Rome; Inc. Place; BRADFORD; **226** EE-7; elev. 830ft./253m.; 🅿; **Z** 18837; Ⓟ 475; Ⓒ 382
Rome; MCD-Township; BRADFORD; ***226** EE-7; 🅿; **Z** 18837 & mail Ulster **Z** 18850; does not include the Borough of Rome; Ⓟ 1,043; Ⓒ 1,221
Rome; MCD-Township; CRAWFORD; ***224** WF-5; mail Titusville **Z** 16354; Ⓟ 1,491; Ⓒ 1,745
Romney; RMC Place; FAYETTE; ▲ Saltlick; ***225** WP-6; elev. 1,408ft./429m.; mail Indian Head **Z** 15446; ● 40
Ronco; RMC Place; FAYETTE; ▲ German; **225** WQ-4; 🅿; ★ **UNTN**; **Z** 15476; ● 300
Ronks; RMC Place; LANCASTER; ▲ East Lampeter; ***227** EP-8; 🅿; ★ **LANC**; **Z** 17572-73; ● 450
Rook; RMC Place; ALLEGHENY; ***225** WM-3; ★ **PGH**; mail Pittsburgh **Z** 15220; pop. incl. with Green Tree (Inc. Place)
Roots (Roots Crossing); RMC Place; BLAIR; ▲ Antis; ***225** WL-11; ★ **ALT**; mail Tyrone **Z** 16686; ● 120
Roots Crossing; BLAIR; see Roots (RMC Place)
Rosas; RMC Place; PIKE; ▲ Westfall; ***226** EG-13; mail Pond Eddy **Z** 12770; rural
Roscoe; Inc. Place; WASHINGTON; **225** WO-4; elev. 870ft./265m.; 🅿; ★ **PGH**; **Z** 15477; Ⓟ 872; Ⓒ 848
Rose; MCD-Township; JEFFERSON; ***224** WI-8; mail Brookville **Z** 15825; Ⓟ 1,198; Ⓒ 1,232
Roseann; RMC Place; MIFFLIN; ▲ Armagh; ***227** EL-1; mail Milroy **Z** 17063; ● 100
Rosebud; RMC Place; CLEARFIELD; ▲ Beccaria; **225** WL-10; mail Coalport **Z** 16627; ● 450
Roseburg; RMC Place; PERRY; ▲ Saville; ***227** EM-2; mail Newport **Z** 17074
Rosecrans; RMC Place; CLINTON; ▲ Greene; ***226** EJ-2; mail Loganton **Z** 17747
Rosedale; RMC Place; ALLEGHENY; ▲ Penn Hills; ***225** WM-4; elev. 1,200ft./366m.; ★ **PGH**; mail Verona **Z** 15147
Rosedale; RMC Place; BUCKS; ***227** EM-11; ★ **PHIL-**; mail Zionhill **Z** 18981; rural
Rosedale; RMC Place; CHESTER; ▲ Kennett; ***227** EQ-10; ★ **PHIL-**; mail Chadds Ford **Z** 19317; ● 50
Rosedale; RMC Place; FAYETTE; ▲ Georges; ★ **UNTN**; mail Uniontown **Z** 15401; pop. incl. with Oak Hill (Inc. Place)
Roseglen; RMC Place; PERRY; ▲ Wheatfield; **227** EN-3; ★ **HRBG**; mail Duncannon **Z** 17020; ● 110
Rosehill; RMC Place; PHILADELPHIA; ★ **PHIL-**; mail Philadelphia **Z** 19140; pop. incl. with Philadelphia (Inc. Place)
Rose Hollow; RMC Place; BUCKS; ▲ Lower Makefield; ***227** EO-13; ★ **PHIL-**; mail Morrisville **Z** 19067; ● 600
Rosemont; RMC Place; DELAWARE; ▲ Radnor; ***227** EP-11; ★ **PHIL-**; mail Bryn Mawr **Z** 19010
Rosemont; RMC Place; MONTGOMERY; ***227** EP-11; elev. 400ft./122m.; 🅲 995; ★ **PHIL-**; mail Bryn Mawr **Z** 19010; ● 1,000
Rose Point; RMC Place; LAWRENCE; ▲ Slippery Rock; **224** WJ-3; ★ **PGH**; mail New Castle **Z** 16101; ● 90
Roses; RMC Place; FOREST; ▲ Jenks; **224** WG-7; elev. 1,678ft./511m.; mail Marienville **Z** 16239; ● 140
Roseto; Inc. Place; NORTHAMPTON; **227** EK-12; elev. 720ft./219m.; 🅿; **Z** 18013; Ⓟ 1,555; Ⓒ 1,653
Rose Valley; Inc. Place; DELAWARE; **227** EP-11; elev. 150ft./46m.; 🅿; ★ **PHIL-**; **Z** 19063, **Z** 19086; Ⓟ 982; Ⓒ 944
Rose Valley; RMC Place; MONTGOMERY; ▲ Upper Dublin; ***227** EO-12; ★ **PHIL-**; mail Ambler **Z** 19002
Rose Valley Acres; RMC Place; DELAWARE; ▲ Upper Providence; ★ **PHIL-**; mail Media **Z** 19063
Roseville; RMC Place; JEFFERSON; ▲ Union; **224** WI-7; mail Brookville **Z** 15825; ● 150
Roseville; Inc. Place; TIOGA; **226** EE-4; elev. 1,355ft./413m.; mail Mansfield **Z** 16933; Ⓟ 230; Ⓒ 207
Roseville (Rossville); RMC Place; YORK; ▲ Warrington; **227** EP-4; mail Rossville **Z** 17358; ● 100
Rosewood Gardens; RMC Place; BUCKS; ▲ Warminster; elev. 310ft./94m.; ★ **PHIL-**; mail Warminster **Z** 18974
Roslyn; RMC Place; CHESTER; ▲ West Goshen; ***227** EP-10; ★ **PHIL-**; mail West Chester **Z** 19380; ● 700
Roslyn; RMC Place; MONTGOMERY; ▲ Abington; **228** A-5; 🅿; ★ **PHIL-**; **Z** 19001; ● 10,000
Ross; MCD-Township; ALLEGHENY; ***225** WM-4; ■; ★ **PGH**; mail Pittsburgh **Z** 15229, **Z** 15237; Ⓟ 33,482; Ⓒ 32,551; ◆ 30,781
Ross; MCD-Township; LUZERNE; ***226** EI-7; mail Sweet Valley **Z** 18656; Ⓟ 2,634; Ⓒ 2,742
Ross; MCD-Township; MONROE; ***227** EK-11; ★ **ALL-**; mail Saylorsburg **Z** 18353; Ⓟ 3,696; Ⓒ 5,435
Ross Common; RMC Place; MONROE; ▲ Ross; ***227** EK-11; ★ **ALL-**; mail Saylorsburg **Z** 18353; rural
Rossford; RMC Place; ARMSTRONG; ▲ Manor; ***225** WK-6; ★ **PGH**; mail Ford City **Z** 16226; ● 140
Rossiter; CDP; INDIANA; ▲ Canoe; **225** WK-8; 🅿; **Z** 15772; Ⓒ 790
Rossland; RMC Place; MONROE; **227** EK-11; ★ **ALL-**; mail Pocono Pines **Z** 18350; ● 60
Rosslyn Farms; Inc. Place; ALLEGHENY; ***225** WM-3; elev. 1,060ft./323m.; ★ **PGH**; mail Carnegie **Z** 15106; Ⓟ 483; Ⓒ 464
Rossmere; RMC Place; LANCASTER; ▲ Manheim; ***227** EP-7; ★ **LANC**; mail Lancaster **Z** 17601; ● 950
Rossmoyne; RMC Place; CUMBERLAND; ▲ Lower Allen; **227** ET-2; ★ **HRBG**; mail Camp Hill **Z** 17011; ● 1,100
Ross Siding (Ross Village); RMC Place; LYCOMING; ▲ McHenry; ***226** EH-2; mail Cammal **Z** 17723; summer pop. 150; rural
Rosston; RMC Place; ARMSTRONG; ▲ Manor; **225** WK-6; ★ **PGH**; mail Ford City **Z** 16226; ● 80
Ross Township; CDP-Census Area Only; ALLEGHENY; ▲ Ross; ***225** WM-3; ★ **PGH**; mail Pittsburgh **Z** 15229, **Z** 15237; Ⓟ 33,482; Ⓒ 32,551; ◆ 30,781
Ross Village; LYCOMING; see Ross Siding (RMC Place)
Rossville; YORK; see Roseville (RMC Place)
Rostraver; MCD-Township; WESTMORELAND; ***225** WO-4; ★ **PGH**; mail Belle Vernon **Z** 15012; Ⓟ 11,224; Ⓒ 11,634
Rote; RMC Place; CLINTON; ▲ Lamar; **226** EJ-2; mail Mill Hall **Z** 17751; ● 250
Rothsville; CDP; LANCASTER; ▲ Warwick; **227** EO-7; ★ **LANC**; mail Lititz **Z** 17543; Ⓟ 2,097; Ⓒ 3,017
Rough and Ready; RMC Place; SCHUYLKILL; ▲ Upper Mahantongo; ***227** EL-5; mail Klingerstown **Z** 17941; rural
Roulette; RMC Place; POTTER; ▲ Roulette; **224** WE-12; elev. 1,528ft./466m.; 🅿; **Z** 16746; ● 1,000
Roulette; MCD-Township; POTTER; ***224** WE-12; elev. 1,528ft./466m.; 🅿; **Z** 16746; Ⓟ 1,266; Ⓒ 1,348
Round Knob; RMC Place; BEDFORD; ▲ Broad Top; ***225** WO-12; elev. 1,657ft./505m.; mail Six Mile Run **Z** 16679; rural
Round Top (Sedgwick); RMC Place; ADAMS; ▲ Cumberland; **225** WT-6; mail Gettysburg **Z** 17325; ● 115
Roundtown; RMC Place; YORK; ▲ Manchester; ***227** EP-5; ★ **YORK**; mail York **Z** 17404; ● 500
Rouseville; Inc. Place; VENANGO; **224** WG-5; elev. 1,035ft./315m.; 🅿; ★ **OILC-F**; **Z** 16344; Ⓟ 583; Ⓒ 472
Rouzerville; CDP; FRANKLIN; ▲ Washington; **227** ER-1; 🅿; ★ **HAG**; **Z** 17250; Ⓟ 1,188; Ⓒ 862
Rowenna (Shocks Mills); RMC Place; LANCASTER; ▲ East Donegal; ***227** EP-6; mail Marietta **Z** 17547
Rowes Run; RMC Place; FAYETTE; ▲ Redstone; **225** WP-4; ★ **UNTN**; mail Grindstone **Z** 15442; ● 400
Rowland; RMC Place; PIKE; ▲ Lackawaxen; **226** EG-12; 🅿; **Z** 18457; ● 200
Rowland Park; RMC Place; MONTGOMERY; ▲ Cheltenham; ★ **PHIL-**; mail Cheltenham **Z** 19012
Rowles; RMC Place; CLEARFIELD; ▲ Penn; mail Mahaffey **Z** 15757; rural
Roxborough; RMC Place; PHILADELPHIA; ***227** EP-12; ★ **PHIL-**; mail Philadelphia **Z** 19128; pop. incl. with Philadelphia (Inc. Place)
Roxbury; RMC Place; CAMBRIA; ***225** WN-8; ★ **JNST**; mail Johnstown **Z** 15905; pop. incl. with Johnstown (Inc. Place)
Roxbury; RMC Place; CUMBERLAND; ▲ Silver Spring, Monroe; ***227** EO-4; ★ **HRBG**; mail Mechanicsburg **Z** 17055; ● 40
Roxbury; RMC Place; FRANKLIN; ▲ Lurgan; **225** WO-14; 🅿; **Z** 17251; ● 275
Roxbury; RMC Place; SOMERSET; ▲ Brothersvalley; **225** WP-8; elev. 2,262ft./689m.; mail Berlin **Z** 15530; ● 50
Royal; RMC Place; SUSQUEHANNA; ▲ Clifford; **226** EF-10; mail Nicholson **Z** 18446; ● 100
Royalton; Inc. Place; DAUPHIN; **227** EO-5; elev. 300ft./91m.; ★ **HRBG**; mail Middletown **Z** 17057; Ⓟ 1,120; Ⓒ 963
Royer; RMC Place; BLAIR; ▲ Woodbury; **225** WM-11; elev. 1,079ft./329m.; ★ **ALT**; mail Williamsburg **Z** 16693; ● 45
Royersford; Inc. Place; MONTGOMERY; **227** EO-10; elev. 180ft./55m.; 🅿; ★ **PHIL-**; **Z** 19468; Ⓟ 4,458; Ⓒ 4,246
Roystone; RMC Place; WARREN; ▲ Sheffield; ***224** WF-8; elev. 1,484ft./452m.; mail Sheffield **Z** 16347; rural
Roytown; RMC Place; SOMERSET; ▲ Lincoln; ***225** WO-7; elev. 2,009ft./612m.; mail Somerset **Z** 15501; ● 30
Rozel Park; RMC Place; BUCKS; ▲ Upper Southampton; ★ **PHIL-**; mail Southampton **Z** 18966
Ruble; RMC Place; FAYETTE; ▲ Georges; ***225** WQ-4; ★ **UNTN**; mail Smithfield **Z** 15478; ● 35
Ruchsville; RMC Place; LEHIGH; ▲ North Whitehall; ***227** EL-10; elev. 411ft./125m.; ★ **ALL-**; mail Coplay **Z** 18037; ● 150
Rudytown; RMC Place; YORK; ▲ Fairview; ***227** EO-4; ★ **HRBG**; mail New Cumberland **Z** 17070; rural
Ruff Creek; RMC Place; GREENE; ▲ Washington; ***225** WP-3; mail Prosperity **Z** 15329
Ruffs Dale; RMC Place; WESTMORELAND; ▲ East Huntingdon; **225** WO-5; 🅿; **Z** 15679; ● 800
Ruggles; RMC Place; WYOMING; ▲ Noxen; ***226** EH-8; mail Harveys Lake **Z** 18618, Noxen **Z** 18636; rural
Rummel; RMC Place; SOMERSET; ▲ Paint; **225** WO-9; ★ **JNST**; mail Windber **Z** 15963; ● 600
Rummerfield; RMC Place; BRADFORD; ▲ Standing Stone; **226** EF-7; mail Wyalusing **Z** 18853; ● 35
Rundell; RMC Place; CRAWFORD; ▲ Spring; ***224** WE-2; mail Conneautville **Z** 16406; rural
Runville; RMC Place; CENTRE; ▲ Boggs; **224** WJ-13; mail Bellefonte **Z** 16823; ● 250
Rupert; CDP; COLUMBIA; ▲ Montour; **226** EJ-6; mail Bloomsburg **Z** 17815; Ⓒ 174
Ruppsville; RMC Place; LEHIGH; ▲ Upper Macungie; ***227** EL-10; ★ **ALL-**; mail Allentown **Z** 18106; ● 400
Rural Ridge; RMC Place; ALLEGHENY; ▲ Indiana; **225** WL-4; 🅿; ★ **PGH**; **Z** 15075; ● 1,000
Rural Valley; Inc. Place; ARMSTRONG; **225** WK-7; elev. 1,112ft./339m.; 🅿; **Z** 16249; Ⓟ 957; Ⓒ 922
Ruscombmanor; MCD-Township; BERKS; ***227** EM-9; ★ **READ**; mail Fleetwood **Z** 19522; Ⓟ 3,129; Ⓒ 3,776
Rush; MCD-Township; CENTRE; ***225** WK-12; mail Philipsburg **Z** 16866; Ⓟ 3,411; Ⓒ 3,466
Rush; MCD-Township; DAUPHIN; ***227** EM-5; mail Tower City **Z** 17980; Ⓟ 201; Ⓒ 180
Rush; MCD-Township; NORTHUMBERLAND; ***227** EK-6; mail Danville **Z** 17821; Ⓟ 1,097; Ⓒ 1,189
Rush; MCD-Township; SCHUYLKILL; ***227** EK-8; mail Tamaqua **Z** 18252, Tower City **Z** 17980; Ⓟ 3,472; Ⓒ 3,957
Rush; RMC Place; SUSQUEHANNA; ▲ Rush; **226** EE-8; mail Montrose **Z** 18801; ● 100
Rush; MCD-Township; SUSQUEHANNA; ***226** EF-8; mail Montrose **Z** 18801; Ⓟ 1,126; Ⓒ 1,290
Rushland; RMC Place; BUCKS; ▲ Wrightstown; **227** EN-13; 🅿; ★ **PHIL-**; **Z** 18956; ● 350
Rushtown; RMC Place; NORTHUMBERLAND; ▲ Rush; ***227** EK-5; elev. 819ft./250m.; mail Danville **Z** 17821; rural
Rushville; RMC Place; SUSQUEHANNA; ▲ Rush; **226** EE-8; elev. 869ft./265m.; 🅿; **Z** 18828; ● 45
Russell; RMC Place; WARREN; ▲ Pine Grove; **224** WD-8; 🅿; **Z** 16345; ● 1,200
Russell City (De Young); RMC Place; ELK; ▲ Highland; **224** WG-9; elev. 1,914ft./583m.; mail De Young **Z** 16728; ● 60

Entries in **UPPERCASE** are counties.
Entries in **bold** have populations of 2,500 or more.
Names in parentheses are alternate names.

Inc. Place	Incorporated Place
RMC Place	Rand McNally Designated Place
CDP	Census Designated Place
MCD	Minor Civil Division
⊡	County Seat
▲	Minor Civil Division
elev.	Elevation
🅿	Post Office
🅷	Hospital
🅲	College
■	Principal Business Center
★	Ranally Metro Area (RMA) Abbreviation
Z	Zip Code(s)
Ⓟ	Previous Census Population
Ⓡ	Revised Census Population
Ⓐ	Annexation Population
●	Rand McNally Population Estimate
Ⓒ	Final Census Population
Ⓢ	Special Census Population
◆	Estimated Population

For additional definitions see Glossary, Volume 1, and Introduction, Volume 2.

Russell Hill; RMC Place; WYOMING; ▲ Washington; ***226** EG-8; mail Tunkhannock **z** 18657
Russellton; CDP; ALLEGHENY; ▲ West Deer; **225** WL-4; 🅿; ★ **PGH**; **z** 15076; Ⓟ 1,691; Ⓒ 1,530
Russellville; RMC Place; CHESTER; ▲ Upper Oxford; **227** EQ-9; mail Oxford **z** 19363; ● 125
Russellville; RMC Place; HUNTINGDON; ▲ Hopewell; ***225** WN-11; mail James Creek **z** 16657
Rutan; RMC Place; GREENE; ▲ Center; ***225** WP-2; mail Holbrook **z** 15341
Rutherford (Rutherford Heights); CDP-Census Area Only; DAUPHIN; ▲ Swatara; **227** ES-4; ★ **HRBG**; mail Harrisburg **z** 17111; Ⓟ 3,481; Ⓒ 3,859
Rutherford Heights; DAUPHIN; see Rutherford (CDP-Census Area Only)
Rutherford Park; RMC Place; DAUPHIN; ▲ South Hanover; ***227** EN-5; ★ **HRBG**; mail Hummelstown **z** 17036; ● 250
Rutherton; UNION; see Laurel Park (RMC Place)
Ruthford; CAMBRIA; see Allendale (RMC Place)
Ruthfred Acres; RMC Place; ALLEGHENY; ***225** WN-3; ★ **PGH**; mail Bethel Park **z** 15102; pop. incl. with Bethel Park (Inc. Place)
Rutland; MCD-Township; TIOGA; ***226** EE-4; mail Mansfield **z** 16933; does not include the Borough of Roseville; Ⓟ 646; Ⓒ 736
Rutledge; Inc. Place; DELAWARE; **228** F-1; elev. 120ft./37m.; 🅿; ★ **PHIL-**; **z** 19070; Ⓟ 843; Ⓒ 860
Rutledgedale; RMC Place; WAYNE; ▲ Damascus; ***226** EF-12; elev. 1,312ft./400m.; mail Tyler Hill **z** 18469; ● 75
Ryan; MCD-Township; SCHUYLKILL; ***227** EK-8; ★ **PTSVL**; mail Barnesville **z** 18214; Ⓟ 1,363; Ⓒ 1,451; Ⓡ 2,461
Ryans Corner; RMC Place; BUCKS; ▲ Wrightstown; ***227** EN-13; ★ **PHIL-**; mail Newtown **z** 18940; ● 70
Rydal; RMC Place; MONTGOMERY; ▲ Abington; **228** A-5; 🅿; ★ **PHIL-**; **z** 19046; ● 1,800
Ryde; RMC Place; MIFFLIN; ▲ Bratton; **225** WM-14; mail Mc Veytown **z** 17051; ● 70
Rye; MCD-Township; PERRY; ***227** EN-4; ★ **HRBG**; mail Marysville **z** 17053; Ⓟ 2,136; Ⓒ 2,327
Rye; RMC Place; YORK; **227** EQ-5; ★ **YORK**; mail Dallastown **z** 17313
Ryerson Station; RMC Place; GREENE; ▲ Richhill; **225** WP-1; mail Wind Ridge **z** 15380; ● 80
Ryot; RMC Place; BEDFORD; ▲ West St. Clair; **225** WO-10; mail Alum Bank **z** 15521; ● 30
Rywal Park; RMC Place; BUCKS; ▲ Bensalem; ★ **PHIL-**; mail Bensalem **z** 19020

S

Sabinsville; RMC Place; TIOGA; ▲ Clymer; **226** EE-1; 🅿; **z** 16943; ● 300
Sabula; RMC Place; CLEARFIELD; ▲ Sandy; **224** WI-9; mail Du Bois **z** 15801; ● 200
Sackett; RMC Place; ELK; ***224** WG-9; mail Kane **z** 16735
Saco; RMC Place; BRADFORD; ▲ Ulster; ***226** EE-6; mail Towanda **z** 18848, Ulster **z** 18850; rural
Saco; RMC Place; LACKAWANNA; ▲ Jefferson; ***226** EH-11; elev. 1,581ft./482m.; ★ **SCR-**; mail Lake Ariel **z** 18436; rural
Sacramento; RMC Place; SCHUYLKILL; ▲ Hubley; **227** EL-6; 🅿; **z** 17968; ● 300
Saddle Brook; RMC Place; LEHIGH; ▲ Salisbury; ***227** EM-10; elev. 420ft./128m.; ★ **ALL-**; mail Allentown **z** 18101; ● 1,160
Saddlebrook Village I and II; RMC Place; BERKS; ▲ Heidelberg; ***227** EN-8; elev. 454ft./138m.; ★ **READ**; mail Wernersville **z** 19565; pop. incl. with Wernersville (Inc. Place)
Sadlers Corner; RMC Place; VENANGO; ▲ Cranberry; ***224** WH-5; elev. 1,440ft./439m.; ★ **OILC-F**; mail Oil City **z** 16301; rural
Sadsbury; MCD-Township; CHESTER; ***227** EP-9; ★ **PHIL-**; mail Sadsburyville **z** 19369; Ⓟ 2,510; Ⓒ 2,582
Sadsbury; MCD-Township; CRAWFORD; ***224** WF-2; mail Conneaut Lake **z** 16316; Ⓟ 2,575; Ⓒ 2,941
Sadsbury; MCD-Township; LANCASTER; ***227** EQ-8; mail Christiana **z** 17509; Ⓟ 2,712; Ⓒ 3,025
Sadsburyville; RMC Place; CHESTER; ▲ Sadsbury; **227** EP-9; 🅿; ★ **PHIL-**; **z** 19369; ● 700
Saegersville; RMC Place; LEHIGH; ▲ Heidelberg; **227** EL-10; elev. 636ft./194m.; ★ **ALL-**; mail Germansville **z** 18053; ● 120
Saegertown; Inc. Place; CRAWFORD; **224** WF-3; elev. 1,120ft./341m.; 🅿; **z** 16433; Ⓟ 1,066; Ⓒ 1,071
Safe Harbor; RMC Place; LANCASTER; ▲ Conestoga; **227** EP-7; ★ **LANC**; mail Conestoga **z** 17516; ● 150
Sagamore; RMC Place; ARMSTRONG; ▲ Cowanshannock; **225** WK-7; 🅿; **z** 16250; ● 450
Sagamore; RMC Place; FAYETTE; ▲ Saltlick; ***225** WP-6; mail Indian Head **z** 15446; rural
Saginaw (New Holland); RMC Place; YORK; ▲ East Manchester; **227** EP-5; ★ **YORK**; mail Mount Wolf **z** 17347; ● 200
Sagon (Hickory Ridge); RMC Place; NORTHUMBERLAND; ▲ Coal; ***227** EK-6; mail Shamokin **z** 17872; ● 80
Saint Augustine; RMC Place; CAMBRIA; ▲ Clearfield; **225** WL-10; elev. 1,645ft./501m.; mail Dysart **z** 16636; ● 20
Saint Benedict; RMC Place; CAMBRIA; ▲ West Carroll; **225** WL-9; 🅿; **z** 15773; ● 450
Saint Boniface; RMC Place; CAMBRIA; ▲ Elder; **225** WL-9; 🅿; **z** 16675; ● 120
Saint Charles; RMC Place; CLARION; ▲ Porter; ***224** WJ-6; elev. 1,024ft./312m.; mail New Bethlehem **z** 16242; rural
Saint Clair; RMC Place; ALLEGHENY; ***225** WM-4; ★ **PGH**; mail Pittsburgh **z** 15210; pop. incl. with Pittsburgh (Inc. Place)
Saint Clair; Inc. Place; SCHUYLKILL; **227** EL-7; elev. 720ft./219m.; 🅿; ★ **PTSVL**; **z** 17970; Ⓟ 3,524; Ⓒ 3,254
Saint Clair; RMC Place; WESTMORELAND; ▲ Hempfield; ***225** WN-6; ★ **PGH**; mail Greensburg **z** 15601; ● 250
St. Clair; MCD-Township; WESTMORELAND; ***225** WN-8; ★ **JNST**; mail Seward **z** 15954; Ⓟ 1,603; Ⓒ 1,398
Saint Clairsville; Inc. Place; BEDFORD; **225** WO-10; elev. 1,240ft./378m.; 🅿; **z** 16667; Ⓟ 88; Ⓒ 86
Saint Davids; RMC Place; DELAWARE; ▲ Radnor; ***227** EP-11; 🅿 🅲 3,918; ★ **PHIL-**; **z** 19087
Saint George; RMC Place; VENANGO; ▲ Rockland; **224** WH-5; mail Kennerdell **z** 16374; summer pop. 200; ● 50
Saint Johns; RMC Place; LUZERNE; ▲ Butler; **226** EJ-8; elev. 970ft./296m.; 🅿; ★ **HAZ**; **z** 18247; ● 300
Saint Joseph; RMC Place; SUSQUEHANNA; ▲ Choconut; **226** EE-8; elev. 1,264ft./385m.; mail Friendsville **z** 18818; ● 150
Saint Lawrence; Inc. Place; BERKS; **227** EN-9; elev. 360ft./110m.; ★ **READ**; mail Reading **z** 19606; Ⓟ 1,542; Ⓒ 1,812
Saint Lawrence; RMC Place; CAMBRIA; ▲ Chest; **225** WL-10; mail Patton **z** 16668; ● 40
Saint Leonard; RMC Place; BUCKS; ▲ Northampton; ***227** EO-13; ★ **PHIL-**; mail Newtown **z** 18940; rural
Saint Marys; CHESTER; see Warwick (RMC Place)
Saint Marys; Inc. Place; ELK; **224** WG-10; elev. 1,667ft./508m.; 🅿 🅷; **z** 15857; Ⓟ 5,511; Ⓒ 14,502
Saint Michael; RMC Place; CAMBRIA; ▲ Croyle, Adams; **225** WN-9; 🅿; ★ **JNST**; **z** 15951; ● 850
Saint Michael-Sidman; CDP-Census Area Only; CAMBRIA; ▲ Croyle, Adams; ***225** WN-9; ★ **JNST**; mail Saint Michael **z** 15951, Sidman **z** 15955; Ⓟ 1,189; Ⓒ 973
Saint Nicholas; RMC Place; SCHUYLKILL; ▲ Mahanoy; ***227** EK-7; mail Mahanoy City **z** 17948; rural
Saint Paul; RMC Place; SOMERSET; ▲ Elk Lick; **225** WQ-7; mail Meyersdale **z** 15552; ● 75
Saint Peters (French Creek Falls); RMC Place; CHESTER; ▲ Warwick; **227** EO-10; 🅿; ★ **PHIL-**; **z** 19470; ● 400
Saint Petersburg; Inc. Place; CLARION; **224** WI-5; elev. 1,400ft./427m.; 🅿; **z** 16054; Ⓟ 349; Ⓒ 405
Saint Thomas; RMC Place; FRANKLIN; ▲ St. Thomas; **225** WP-13; elev. 647ft./197m.; 🅿; **z** 17252; ● 900
St. Thomas; MCD-Township; FRANKLIN; ***225** WQ-14; mail Saint Thomas **z** 17252; Ⓟ 5,861; Ⓒ 5,775
Saint Vincent Shaft; RMC Place; WESTMORELAND; ▲ Unity; ***225** WN-6; ★ **LTROB**; mail Latrobe **z** 15650; ● 70
Salco; RMC Place; SOMERSET; ▲ Brothersvalley; ***225** WQ-8; mail Berlin **z** 15530; rural
Salem; MCD-Township; CLARION; ***224** WI-5; mail Knox **z** 16232; Ⓟ 893; Ⓒ 852
Salem; RMC Place; CLEARFIELD; ▲ Brady; ***224** WJ-9; mail Du Bois **z** 15801; ● 100
Salem (Beautiful); RMC Place; FRANKLIN; ▲ Greene; ***227** EP-1; elev. 783ft./239m.; mail Chambersburg **z** 17201; rural
Salem; MCD-Township; LUZERNE; ***226** EI-7; mail Berwick **z** 18603; Ⓟ 4,503; Ⓒ 4,269
Salem; RMC Place; MERCER; ▲ Sugar Grove; **224** WG-2; mail Greenville **z** 16125; ● 30
Salem; MCD-Township; MERCER; ***224** WG-2; mail Greenville **z** 16125; Ⓟ 678; Ⓒ 769
Salem; RMC Place; SNYDER; ▲ Penn; **227** EK-4; mail Selinsgrove **z** 17870; ● 150
Salem; MCD-Township; WAYNE; ***226** EH-11; ★ **SCR-**; mail Moscow **z** 18444; Ⓟ 2,933; Ⓒ 3,664
Salem; MCD-Township; WESTMORELAND; ***225** WM-6; ★ **PGH**; mail Greensburg **z** 15601; Ⓟ 7,282; Ⓒ 6,939
Salem Harbor; RMC Place; BUCKS; ▲ Bensalem; ★ **PHIL-**; mail Bensalem **z** 19020
Salemville; RMC Place; BEDFORD; ▲ South Woodbury; **225** WO-11; mail New Enterprise **z** 16664; ● 50
Salford; RMC Place; MONTGOMERY; ▲ Upper Salford; **227** EN-11; 🅿; ★ **PHIL-**; **z** 18957; ● 300
Salford; MCD-Township; MONTGOMERY; ***227** EN-11; 🅿; ★ **PHIL-**; **z** 18957 & mail Telford **z** 18969; Ⓟ 2,216; Ⓒ 2,363
Salford Heights; RMC Place; MONTGOMERY; ▲ Lower Salford; ★ **PHIL-**; mail Harleysville **z** 19438
Salfordville; RMC Place; MONTGOMERY; ▲ Upper Salford; ***227** EN-11; 🅿; ★ **PHIL-**; **z** 18958; ● 350
Salida; RMC Place; ALLEGHENY; ▲ Baldwin; ***225** WN-3; ★ **PGH**; mail Pittsburgh **z** 15227; pop. incl. with Baldwin (Inc. Place)
Salina; RMC Place; WESTMORELAND; ▲ Bell; **225** WM-6; 🅿; ★ **PGH**; **z** 15680; ● 500
Salisbury; MCD-Township; LANCASTER; ***227** EP-8; mail Kinzers **z** 17535; Ⓟ 8,527; Ⓒ 10,012
Salisbury; MCD-Township; LEHIGH; ***227** EL-11; ★ **ALL-**; mail Allentown **z** 18103; Ⓟ 13,401; Ⓒ 13,498
Salisbury; Inc. Place; SOMERSET; **225** WQ-8; elev. 2,132ft./650m.; 🅿; **z** 15558; Ⓟ 716; Ⓒ 878
Salisbury Heights; RMC Place; LANCASTER; ▲ Salisbury; ***227** EP-8; mail Gap **z** 17527; ● 80
Salix; RMC Place; CAMBRIA; ▲ Adams; **225** WN-9; elev. 2,052ft./625m.; 🅿; ★ **JNST**; **z** 15952; ● 900
Salix-Beauty Line Park; CDP-Census Area Only; CAMBRIA; ▲ Adams; ***225** WN-9; elev. 2,080ft./634m.; ★ **JNST**; mail Salix **z** 15952; Ⓟ 1,257; Ⓒ 1,259
Salladasburg; Inc. Place; LYCOMING; **226** EH-3; elev. 652ft./199m.; 🅿; **z** 17740; Ⓟ 301; Ⓒ 260
Salona; RMC Place; CLINTON; ▲ Lamar; **226** EJ-2; 🅿; **z** 17767; ● 250
Saltillo; Inc. Place; HUNTINGDON; **225** WO-13; elev. 780ft./238m.; 🅿; **z** 17253; Ⓟ 347; Ⓒ 343
Saltlick; MCD-Township; FAYETTE; ***225** WP-6; mail Normalville **z** 15469; Ⓟ 3,253; Ⓒ 3,715
Saltsburg; Inc. Place; INDIANA; **225** WM-6; elev. 940ft./287m.; 🅿; ★ **PGH**; **z** 15681; Ⓟ 990; Ⓒ 955
Salunga; RMC Place; LANCASTER; ▲ West Hempfield, East Hempfield; **227** EO-6; elev. 405ft./123m.; 🅿; ★ **LANC**; **z** 17538; ● 950
Salunga-Landisville; CDP-Census Area Only; LANCASTER; ▲ East Hempfield, West Hempfield; ***227** EO-6; elev. 433ft./132m.; ★ **LANC**; mail Landisville **z** 17538; Ⓟ 4,239; Ⓒ 4,771
Saluvia; RMC Place; FULTON; ▲ Licking Creek; ***225** WP-12; mail Harrisonville **z** 17228
Sample Run; RMC Place; INDIANA; ***225** WL-8; mail Clymer **z** 15728; pop. incl. with Clymer (Inc. Place)
Sample Spur Junction; RMC Place; LAWRENCE; ★ **NWCS**; pop. incl. with New Castle (Inc. Place)
Sampson; RMC Place; WASHINGTON; ▲ Carroll; ***225** WO-4; ★ **PGH**; mail Monongahela **z** 15063; ● 200
Sanatoga; CDP; MONTGOMERY; ▲ Lower Pottsgrove; **227** EN-10; 🅿; ★ **PTSTN**; **z** 19464; Ⓟ 5,534; Ⓒ 7,734
Sanatoga Park; RMC Place; MONTGOMERY; ▲ Lower Pottsgrove; ★ **PTSTN**; mail Pottstown **z** 19464
Sanbourn; RMC Place; CLEARFIELD; ▲ Woodward; ***225** WK-11; elev. 1,754ft./535m.; mail Houtzdale **z** 16651; rural
Sand Beach; RMC Place; DAUPHIN; ▲ East Hanover; **227** EN-5; ★ **HRBG**; mail Hershey **z** 17033, Hummelstown **z** 17036; ● 300
Sand Hill; CDP; LEBANON; ▲ North Lebanon; **227** EN-6; ★ **LEB**; mail Lebanon **z** 17046; Ⓟ 2,307; Ⓒ 2,345
Sandhill; RMC Place; MONROE; ▲ Hamilton; ***226** EJ-11; mail Sciota **z** 18354; rural
Sand Hill; RMC Place; WESTMORELAND; ▲ Mount Pleasant; ***225** WO-6; mail Mount Pleasant **z** 15666; ● 200
Sand Patch; RMC Place; SOMERSET; ▲ Larimer; ***225** WQ-8; mail Meyersdale **z** 15552; rural
Sand Springs; RMC Place; LUZERNE; ▲ Butler; ***226** EJ-8; ★ **HAZ**; mail Drums **z** 18222; ● 150
Sandts Eddy; RMC Place; NORTHAMPTON; ▲ Lower Mount Bethel; ***227** EK-12; ★ **ALL-**; mail Easton **z** 18040
Sandy; CDP; CLEARFIELD; ▲ Sandy; **224** WI-9; mail Du Bois **z** 15801; Ⓒ 1,687
Sandy; MCD-Township; CLEARFIELD; ***224** WI-9; mail Du Bois **z** 15801; Ⓟ 9,005; Ⓒ 11,556
Sandy Bank; RMC Place; DELAWARE; ▲ Upper Providence; ★ **PHIL-**; mail Media **z** 19063
Sandy Creek; RMC Place; ALLEGHENY; ▲ Penn Hills; ***225** WM-4; elev. 1,200ft./366m.; ★ **PGH**; mail Verona **z** 15147
Sandy Creek; MCD-Township; MERCER; ***224** WG-2; mail Hadley **z** 16130; Ⓟ 806; Ⓒ 848
Sandycreek; MCD-Township; VENANGO; ***224** WH-4; ★ **OILC-F**; mail Franklin **z** 16323; Ⓟ 2,495; Ⓒ 2,406
Sandy Hill; RMC Place; MONTGOMERY; ▲ Plymouth; ★ **PHIL-**; mail Norristown **z** 19401
Sandy Hollow; RMC Place; CLARION; ▲ Madison; **224** WJ-6; mail Rimersburg **z** 16248; ● 55
Sandy Lake; Inc. Place; MERCER; **224** WH-3; elev. 1,160ft./354m.; 🅿; **z** 16145; Ⓟ 722; Ⓒ 743
Sandy Lake; MCD-Township; MERCER; ***224** WH-3; 🅿; **z** 16145; does not include the Borough of Sandy Lake; Ⓟ 1,161; Ⓒ 1,248
Sandy Plains; RMC Place; WASHINGTON; ▲ East Bethlehem; ***225** WP-3; mail Clarksville **z** 15322; ● 120
Sandy Ridge; CDP; CENTRE; ▲ Rush; **225** WK-12; 🅿; **z** 16677; Ⓒ 340
Sandy Ridge Acres; RMC Place; BUCKS; ▲ Doylestown; ***227** EN-12; ★ **PHIL-**; mail Doylestown **z** 18901; pop. incl. with Doylestown (Inc. Place)
Sandy Run; RMC Place; BUCKS; ▲ Lower Makefield; ***227** EN-13; ★ **PHIL-**; mail Morrisville **z** 19067; ● 1,250
Sandy Run; RMC Place; GREENE; ▲ Monongahela; ***225** WQ-4; mail Greensboro **z** 15338; rural
Sandy Run; RMC Place; LUZERNE; ▲ Foster; **226** EJ-9; ★ **HAZ**; mail Freeland **z** 18224; ● 60
Sandy Shore; RMC Place; WAYNE; ▲ Paupack; ***226** EG-12; elev. 1,300ft./396m.; mail Hawley **z** 18428; ● 280
Sandy Valley; RMC Place; JEFFERSON; ▲ Winslow; **224** WI-9; mail Reynoldsville **z** 15851; ● 40
Sandyville; RMC Place; PIKE; ▲ Lehman; **226** EI-13; mail Bushkill **z** 18324; summer pop. 130; ● 25
Sanford; RMC Place; WARREN; ▲ Eldred; ***224** WE-6; mail Pittsfield **z** 16340; rural
Sankertown; Inc. Place; CAMBRIA; **225** WM-10; elev. 2,067ft./630m.; mail Cresson **z** 16630; Ⓟ 770; Ⓒ 680
Santiago (Tyre); RMC Place; ALLEGHENY; ▲ North Fayette; **225** WM-2; ★ **PGH**; mail Imperial **z** 15126; ● 400
Sarah Furnace; RMC Place; CLARION; ▲ Madison; ***224** WJ-5; mail Rimersburg **z** 16248; rural
Sardis; RMC Place; WESTMORELAND; ***225** WM-5; elev. 1,297ft./395m.; ★ **PGH**; mail Murrysville **z** 15668; pop. incl. with Murrysville (Inc. Place)
Sartwell; RMC Place; MCKEAN; ▲ Annin; ***224** WE-11; mail Eldred **z** 16731; rural
Sarver; RMC Place; BUTLER; ▲ Buffalo; **225** WL-5; elev. 1,094ft./333m.; 🅿; ★ **PGH**; **z** 16055; ● 300
Sarverville; RMC Place; BUTLER; ▲ Buffalo; ***225** WL-5; ★ **PGH**; mail Sarver **z** 16055; ● 60
Sassamansville; RMC Place; MONTGOMERY; ▲ New Hanover, Douglass; **227** EN-10; 🅿; **z** 19472; ● 350
Satterfield; RMC Place; SULLIVAN; ▲ Cherry; ***226** EG-6; mail Dushore **z** 18614
Satterfield Junction; RMC Place; SULLIVAN; ▲ Cherry; mail Dushore **z** 18614; rural
Saucon Acres; RMC Place; LEHIGH; ▲ Upper Saucon; ***227** EM-11; ★ **ALL-**; mail Center Valley **z** 18034; ● 250
Saulsburg; RMC Place; HUNTINGDON; ▲ Barree; ***225** WL-13; mail Huntingdon **z** 16652
Saville; RMC Place; PERRY; ▲ Saville; **227** EM-2; mail Newport **z** 17074; ● 20
Saville; MCD-Township; PERRY; ***227** EM-2; mail Ickesburg **z** 17037, Newport **z** 17074; Ⓟ 1,818; Ⓒ 2,204
Sawtown; RMC Place; VENANGO; ▲ Pinegrove; ***224** WH-6; mail Oil City **z** 16301; rural
Sawyer City; RMC Place; MCKEAN; ***224** WD-10; mail Bradford **z** 16701
Saxonburg; Inc. Place; BUTLER; **225** WK-4; elev. 1,288ft./393m.; 🅿; ★ **PGH**; **z** 16056; Ⓟ 1,345; Ⓒ 1,629
Saxton; Inc. Place; BEDFORD; **225** WO-11; elev. 918ft./280m.; 🅿; **z** 16678; Ⓟ 838; Ⓒ 803
Saybrook; RMC Place; WARREN; ▲ Sheffield; ***224** WF-8; elev. 1,349ft./411m.; mail Sheffield **z** 16347
Saylorsburg; RMC Place; MONROE; ▲ Ross, Hamilton; **227** EK-11; 🅿; ★ **ALL-**; **z** 18353; summer pop. 4,000; ● 500
Sayre; Inc. Place; BRADFORD; **226** ED-6; elev. 780ft./238m.; 🅿 🅷; **z** 18840; Ⓟ 5,791; Ⓒ 5,813
Scalp Level; Inc. Place; CAMBRIA; **225** WN-9; elev. 1,840ft./561m.; ★ **JNST**; mail Windber **z** 15963; Ⓟ 1,158; Ⓒ 851
Scammells Corner; RMC Place; BUCKS; ▲ Lower Makefield; ***227** EN-14; elev. 170ft./52m.; ★ **PHIL-**; mail Morrisville **z** 19067; rural
Scandia; RMC Place; WARREN; ▲ Elk; **224** WE-8; elev. 2,100ft./640m.; mail Russell **z** 16345; ● 25
Scanlan Hill; RMC Place; CAMBRIA; ▲ Washington; ***225** WN-10; mail Lilly **z** 15938; ● 75
Scarlets Mill (White Bear); RMC Place; BERKS; ▲ Robeson; **227** EO-9; ★ **READ**; mail Birdsboro **z** 19508; ● 100
Scenery Hill; RMC Place; WASHINGTON; ▲ North Bethlehem; **225** WO-3; 🅿; ★ **WASH**; **z** 15360; ● 600
Schaefferstown; CDP; LEBANON; ▲ Heidelberg; **227** EN-7; 🅿; ★ **LEB**; **z** 17088; Ⓒ 984
Schellsburg; Inc. Place; BEDFORD; **225** WP-10; elev. 1,259ft./384m.; 🅿; **z** 15559; Ⓟ 245; Ⓒ 316
Schenkel; RMC Place; CHESTER; ▲ North Coventry; ***227** EO-10; ★ **PTSTN**; mail Pottstown **z** 19464; ● 500
Schenley; RMC Place; ARMSTRONG; ▲ Gilpin; **225** WL-5; 🅿; ★ **PGH**; **z** 15682; ● 55
Schenley Heights; RMC Place; ALLEGHENY; ***225** WM-4; ★ **PGH**; mail Pittsburgh **z** 15219; pop. incl. with Pittsburgh (Inc. Place)
Scherersville (Sherersville); RMC Place; LEHIGH; **226** EA-2; ★ **ALL-**; mail Allentown **z** 18104; ● 100
Schlusser; CDP-Census Area Only; CUMBERLAND; ▲ Middlesex, North Middleton; **227** EO-3; elev. 450ft./137m.; ★ **CARL**; mail Carlisle **z** 17013; Ⓟ 4,728; Ⓒ 4,750
Schnecksville; CDP; LEHIGH; ▲ North Whitehall; **227** EL-10; elev. 666ft./203m.; 🅿; ★ **ALL-**; **z** 18078; Ⓟ 1,780; Ⓒ 1,989
Schoeneck; RMC Place; LANCASTER; ▲ West Cocalico; **227** EO-7; mail Stevens **z** 17578; ● 650
Schoeneck; RMC Place; NORTHAMPTON; ▲ Upper Nazareth; ***227** EK-11; elev. 564ft./172m.; ★ **ALL-**; mail Nazareth **z** 18064; ● 650
Schoenersville; RMC Place; LEHIGH, NORTHAMPTON; ▲ Hanover; **226** EA-4; ★ **ALL-**; mail Allentown **z** 18103; ● 400
Schoentown; RMC Place; SCHUYLKILL; ★ **PTSVL**; mail Port Carbon **z** 17965; pop. incl. with Port Carbon (Inc. Place)
Schofer; RMC Place; BERKS; ▲ Maxatawny; ***227** EM-10; mail Kutztown **z** 19530; ● 35
Schollard; RMC Place; MERCER; ▲ Springfield; ***224** WI-3; elev. 1,200ft./366m.; mail Mercer **z** 16137; rural
School Lane; RMC Place; LANCASTER; ▲ Manheim; ***227** EP-7; ★ **LANC**; mail Lancaster **z** 17603; ● 450
School Lane Hills; RMC Place; LANCASTER; ▲ Lancaster; **227** ES-8; ★ **LANC**; mail Lancaster **z** 17604; ● 1,840
School Valley Farms; RMC Place; LANCASTER; ▲ Manheim; ***227** EO-7; ★ **LANC**; mail East Petersburg **z** 17520; ● 900
Schubert; RMC Place; BERKS; ▲ Bethel; **227** EM-7; mail Bethel **z** 19507; ● 200
Schultzville; RMC Place; BERKS; ▲ Washington; ***227** EN-10; mail Barto **z** 19504; rural
Schultzville; RMC Place; LACKAWANNA; ▲ Newton; ***226** EG-9; ★ **SCR-**; mail Clarks Summit **z** 18411, Dalton **z** 18414; ● 110
Schuster Heights; RMC Place; BUTLER; ▲ Buffalo; **225** WL-5; ★ **PGH**; mail Freeport **z** 16229; ● 75
Schuyler; RMC Place; MONTOUR, NORTHUMBERLAND; ▲ Lewis, Limestone; ***226** EJ-5; mail Turbotville **z** 17772; ● 40
Schuylkill; MCD-Township; CHESTER; ***227** EO-11; ★ **PHIL-**; mail Phoenixville **z** 19460; Ⓟ 5,538; Ⓒ 6,960
Schuylkill; RMC Place; PHILADELPHIA; ★ **PHIL-**; mail Philadelphia **z** 19146; pop. incl. with Philadelphia (Inc. Place)
Schuylkill; MCD-Township; SCHUYLKILL; ***227** EK-8; ★ **PTSVL**; mail Mary D **z** 17952; Ⓟ 1,230; Ⓒ 1,123
SCHUYLKILL; **227** EL-7; Ⓟ 152,585; Ⓒ 150,336; ◆ 146,970
Schuylkill Haven; Inc. Place; SCHUYLKILL; **227** EL-7; elev. 515ft./157m.; 🅿 🅲 911; ★ **PTSVL**; **z** 17972; Ⓟ 5,610; Ⓒ 5,548
Schuylkill Hills; RMC Place; MONTGOMERY; ▲ West Norriton; ★ **PHIL-**; mail Norristown **z** 19401
Schwenksville; Inc. Place; MONTGOMERY; **227** EN-11; elev. 148ft./45m.; 🅿; ★ **PHIL-**; **z** 19473; Ⓟ 1,326; Ⓒ 1,693
Sciota; RMC Place; MONROE; ▲ Hamilton; **226** EJ-11; 🅿; **z** 18354; ● 700
Sconnelltown; RMC Place; CHESTER; ▲ East Bradford; ***227** EP-10; ★ **PHIL-**; mail West Chester **z** 19380; rural
Scotch Hill; RMC Place; CLARION; ▲ Farmington; ***224** WH-7; mail Leeper **z** 16233
Scotch Hollow; RMC Place; CLEARFIELD; ▲ Decatur; ***225** WK-11; mail Osceola Mills **z** 16666; rural
Scotia; RMC Place; ALLEGHENY; ***225** WN-4; ★ **PGH**; mail Clairton **z** 15025; pop. incl. with Jefferson (Inc. Place)
Scotland; RMC Place; FRANKLIN; ▲ Greene; **227** EP-1; 🅿; **z** 17254; ● 650
Scotrun; RMC Place; MONROE; ▲ Pocono; **226** EJ-11; 🅿; **z** 18355; ● 650
Scott; MCD-Township; ALLEGHENY; ***225** WN-3; ★ **PGH**; mail Carnegie **z** 15106; Ⓟ 17,118; Ⓒ 17,288
Scott; MCD-Township; COLUMBIA; ***226** EJ-6; mail Bloomsburg **z** 17815; Ⓟ 4,423; Ⓒ 4,768
Scott; MCD-Township; LACKAWANNA; ***226** EG-10; ★ **SCR-**; mail Clarks Summit **z** 18411, Dalton **z** 18414, Jermyn **z** 18433, Olyphant **z** 18447; Ⓟ 5,350; Ⓒ 4,931
Scott; MCD-Township; LAWRENCE; ***224** WJ-2; ★ **PGH**; mail New Castle **z** 16101; Ⓟ 2,200; Ⓒ 2,235
Scott; MCD-Township; WAYNE; ***226** ED-11; mail Starrucca **z** 18462; Ⓟ 590; Ⓒ 669
Scott Center; RMC Place; WAYNE; ▲ Scott; ***226** ED-11; mail Starrucca **z** 18462; rural
Scottdale; Inc. Place; WESTMORELAND; **225** WO-5; elev. 1,060ft./323m.; 🅿; **z** 15683; Ⓟ 5,184; Ⓒ 4,772
Scott Haven; RMC Place; WESTMORELAND; ▲ Sewickley; ***225** WN-4; ★ **PGH**; mail Sutersville **z** 15083; rural
Scottsville; RMC Place; BEAVER; ▲ Hopewell; ***225** WL-2; ★ **PGH**; mail Aliquippa **z** 15001; ● 2,400
Scott Township; CDP-Census Area Only; ALLEGHENY; ▲ Scott; ***225** WM-3; ★ **PGH**; mail Carnegie **z** 15106; Ⓟ 17,118; Ⓒ 17,288
Scranton; Inc. Place; ⊡ LACKAWANNA; **226** EH-10; elev. 754ft./230m.; 🅿 🅷 🅲 8,533 ■; ★ **SCR-**; **z** 18501-05, **z** 18507-10, **z** 18512, **z** 18515, **z** 18517-19, **z** 18540, **z** 18577; Ⓟ 81,805; Ⓒ 76,415; ◆ 74,340
Scrubgrass; MCD-Township; VENANGO; ***224** WH-5; mail Emlenton **z** 16373; Ⓟ 673; Ⓒ 799
Scullton; RMC Place; SOMERSET; ▲ Upper Turkeyfoot; ***225** WP-7; mail Rockwood **z** 15557
Scyoc; RMC Place; PERRY; ▲ Toboyne; ***227** EN-1; mail East Waterford **z** 17021; rural
Seamentown; RMC Place; INDIANA; ▲ Green; ***225** WL-8; mail Commodore **z** 15729; rural
Seanor; RMC Place; SOMERSET; ▲ Paint; **225** WO-9; 🅿; ★ **JNST**; **z** 15953; ● 130
Searights; RMC Place; FAYETTE; ▲ Menallen; **225** WP-4; ★ **UNTN**; mail Uniontown **z** 15401; ● 250
Sebring; RMC Place; TIOGA; ▲ Liberty; **226** EG-3; mail Liberty **z** 16930; ● 30
Secane; RMC Place; DELAWARE; ▲ Ridley; **228** F-1; 🅿; ★ **PHIL-**; **z** 19018; ● 1,700
Sedgwick; ADAMS; see Round Top (RMC Place)
Seek; RMC Place; SCHUYLKILL; mail Coaldale **z** 18218; pop. incl. with Coaldale (Inc. Place)
Seelyville; RMC Place; WAYNE; ▲ Texas; **226** EG-11; mail Honesdale **z** 18431; ● 300
Seemsville; RMC Place; NORTHAMPTON; ▲ East Allen, Allen; ***227** EL-11; elev. 669ft./204m.; ★ **ALL-**; mail Northampton **z** 18067; ● 220
Seger; RMC Place; WESTMORELAND; ▲ Derry; ***225** WN-7; ★ **LTROB**; mail Derry **z** 15627; ● 100
Seidersville; RMC Place; NORTHAMPTON; ▲ Lower Saucon; **226** EB-4; ★ **ALL-**; mail Bethlehem **z** 18015; ● 250
Seipstown; RMC Place; LEHIGH; ▲ Weisenberg; **227** EL-10; ★ **ALL-**; mail Breinigsville **z** 18031; ● 30
Seipsville; NORTHAMPTON; see Palmer Park (RMC Place)
Seisholtzville; RMC Place; BERKS; ▲ Hereford; **227** EM-10; elev. 860ft./262m.; mail Macungie **z** 18062; ● 100
Seitzland; RMC Place; YORK; ▲ Shrewsbury; **227** EQ-5; elev. 980ft./299m.; ★ **BAL**; mail Glen Rock **z** 17327; ● 70
Seitzville; RMC Place; YORK; ▲ Codorus; ***227** EQ-5; ★ **BAL**; mail Seven Valleys **z** 17360; ● 20
Selea; RMC Place; HUNTINGDON; ▲ Springfield; ***225** WO-13; mail Three Springs **z** 17264; rural
Selinsgrove; Inc. Place; SNYDER; **227** EK-4; elev. 444ft./135m.; 🅿 🅲 2,009; **z** 17870; Ⓟ 5,384; Ⓒ 5,383
Sellersville; Inc. Place; BUCKS; **227** EN-11; elev. 317ft./97m.; 🅿 🅷; ★ **PHIL-**; **z** 18960; Ⓟ 4,479; Ⓒ 4,564
Seltzer; CDP; SCHUYLKILL; ▲ Norwegian; ***227** EL-7; 🅿; ★ **PTSVL**; **z** 17974; Ⓒ 307
Seminole; RMC Place; ARMSTRONG; ▲ Mahoning; **224** WJ-7; 🅿; **z** 16253; ● 250
Seneca; CDP; VENANGO; ▲ Cranberry; **224** WH-5; elev. 1,444ft./440m.; 🅿; ★ **OILC-F**; **z** 16346; Ⓟ 1,029; Ⓒ 966
Seneca Valley; RMC Place; WESTMORELAND; ▲ North Huntingdon; ***225** WN-5; ★ **PGH**; mail Irwin **z** 15642; ● 150
Sereno; RMC Place; COLUMBIA; ▲ Pine; ***226** EI-6; mail Millville **z** 17846; rural
Sergeant; RMC Place; MCKEAN; ▲ Wetmore; **224** WF-9; elev. 1,716ft./523m.; mail Kane **z** 16735; ● 40
Sergeant; MCD-Township; MCKEAN; ***224** WF-10; mail Mount Jewett **z** 16740; Ⓟ 154; Ⓒ 176
Seven Fields; Inc. Place; BUTLER; ***225** WL-3; 🅿; ★ **PGH**; **z** 16046; Ⓟ 556; Ⓒ 1,986
Seven Hills; RMC Place; BRADFORD; ▲ Rome; ***226** EE-7; elev. 900ft./274m.; mail Rome **z** 18837; ● 140
Seven Pines; RMC Place; JUNIATA; ▲ Spruce Hill; ***227** EM-2; mail Port Royal **z** 17082; ● 25
Seven Points; RMC Place; NORTHUMBERLAND; ▲ Rockefeller; ***227** EK-5; elev. 636ft./194m.; mail Sunbury **z** 17801; ● 45
Seven Springs; Inc. Place; SOMERSET, FAYETTE; **225** WP-7; elev. 2,500ft./762m.; mail Champion **z** 15622; Ⓟ 22; Ⓒ 127
Seven Stars; RMC Place; ADAMS; ▲ Franklin; ***227** EQ-2; mail Gettysburg **z** 17325
Seven Stars; RMC Place; JUNIATA; ▲ Greenwood; ***227** EL-3; mail Millerstown **z** 17062
Seven Valleys (Smyser); Inc. Place; YORK; **227** EQ-5; elev. 688ft./210m.; 🅿; ★ **YORK**; **z** 17360; Ⓟ 483; Ⓒ 492
Seward; Inc. Place; WESTMORELAND; **225** WM-8; elev. 1,140ft./347m.; 🅿; ★ **JNST**; **z** 15954; Ⓟ 522; Ⓒ 484
Sewickley; Inc. Place; ALLEGHENY; **225** WM-3; elev. 720ft./219m.; 🅿 🅷; ★ **PGH**; **z** 15143; Ⓟ 4,134; Ⓒ 3,902
Sewickley; MCD-Township; WESTMORELAND; ***225** WN-5; ★ **PGH**; mail Herminie **z** 15637; Ⓟ 6,642; Ⓒ 6,230
Sewickley Heights; Inc. Place; ALLEGHENY; **228** H-3; elev. 1,100ft./335m.; ★ **PGH**; mail Sewickley **z** 15143; Ⓟ 984; Ⓒ 981
Sewickley Hills; Inc. Place; ALLEGHENY; **225** WL-3; elev. 1,000ft./305m.; ★ **PGH**; mail Sewickley **z** 15143; Ⓟ 622; Ⓒ 652
Seybertown; RMC Place; ARMSTRONG; ▲ Bradys Bend; mail East Brady **z** 16028; rural
Seyfert; RMC Place; BERKS; ▲ Robeson; ***227** EN-9; ★ **READ**; mail Birdsboro **z** 19508; ● 400
Shade; MCD-Township; SOMERSET; ***225** WO-9; mail Central City **z** 15926; Ⓟ 3,177; Ⓒ 2,886
Shade Gap; Inc. Place; HUNTINGDON; **225** WO-13; elev. 1,000ft./305m.; 🅿; **z** 17255; Ⓟ 113; Ⓒ 97
Shadeland; RMC Place; CRAWFORD; ▲ Spring; ***224** WE-2; mail Springboro **z** 16435; rural
Shades Glen; RMC Place; LUZERNE; ▲ Buck; ***226** EI-10; mail White Haven **z** 18661; ● 30
Shade Valley; RMC Place; HUNTINGDON; ▲ Tell; ***225** WN-14; mail Blairs Mills **z** 17213; rural
Shadle; RMC Place; SNYDER; ▲ Perry; ***227** EL-4; mail Mount Pleasant Mills **z** 17853; rural
Shado-wood Village; RMC Place; INDIANA; ▲ White; **225** WL-7; mail Indiana **z** 15701; ● 350
Shady Acres; RMC Place; NORTHUMBERLAND; ▲ Mount Carmel; ***227** EK-6; mail Kulpmont **z** 17834; ● 100
Shady Grove; RMC Place; FRANKLIN; ▲ Antrim; **225** WQ-14; 🅿; ★ **HAG**; **z** 17256; ● 280
Shady Plain; RMC Place; ARMSTRONG; ▲ Kiskiminetas; ***225** WL-6; ★ **PGH**; mail Apollo **z** 15613; ● 200
Shadyside; RMC Place; ALLEGHENY; ***225** WM-4; 🅿; ★ **PGH**; **z** 15232; pop. incl. with Pittsburgh (Inc. Place)
Shaffer; RMC Place; CLEARFIELD; ▲ Sandy; **224** WI-9; mail Du Bois **z** 15801; ● 120
Shaffers Corner; RMC Place; FAYETTE; ▲ South Union; ★ **UNTN**; mail Uniontown **z** 15401; rural
Shaffersville; RMC Place; HUNTINGDON; ▲ Morris; ***225** WM-12; mail Huntingdon **z** 16652; ● 40
Shaft (William Penn); RMC Place; SCHUYLKILL; ▲ West Mahanoy; ***227** EK-7; mail Shenandoah **z** 17976; pop. incl. with Shenandoah (Inc. Place)
Shaft; RMC Place; SOMERSET; ▲ Brothersvalley; ***225** WP-8; elev. 2,100ft./640m.; mail Berlin **z** 15530; rural
Shafton; RMC Place; WESTMORELAND; ▲ North Huntingdon; ***225** WN-5; ★ **PGH**; mail Irwin **z** 15642; ● 250
Shaler; MCD-Township; ALLEGHENY; ***225** WM-4; ★ **PGH**; mail Allison Park **z** 15101, Glenshaw **z** 15116, Pittsburgh **z** 15209, **z** 15215, **z** 15223; Ⓟ 30,533; Ⓒ 29,757; ◆ 28,023
Shaler Township; CDP-Census Area Only; ALLEGHENY; ▲ Shaler; ***225** WM-4; ★ **PGH**; mail Allison Park **z** 15101, Glenshaw **z** 15116, Pittsburgh **z** 15209, **z** 15215, **z** 15223; Ⓟ 30,533; Ⓒ 29,757; ◆ 28,023
Shamokin; Inc. Place; NORTHUMBERLAND; **227** EK-6; elev. 720ft./219m.; 🅿 ■; **z** 17872; Ⓟ 9,184; Ⓒ 8,009; ◆ 7,202
Shamokin; MCD-Township; NORTHUMBERLAND; ***227** EK-5; 🅿; **z** 17872 & mail Paxinos **z** 17860; not adjacent to the City of Shamokin; Ⓟ 1,697; Ⓒ 2,159
Shamokin Dam; Inc. Place; SNYDER; **227** EK-5; elev. 500ft./152m.; 🅿; **z** 17876; Ⓟ 1,690; Ⓒ 1,502
Shamrock; BERKS; see Shamrock Station (RMC Place)
Shamrock; RMC Place; FAYETTE; ▲ Menallen; ***225** WP-4; ★ **UNTN**; mail Uniontown **z** 15401; rural
Shamrock; RMC Place; SOMERSET; ▲ Black; ***225** WP-7; mail Rockwood **z** 15557; rural
Shamrock Station (Shamrock); RMC Place; BERKS; ▲ Longswamp; ***227** EM-10; mail Mertztown **z** 19539; ● 100
Shaner; RMC Place; WESTMORELAND; ▲ Sewickley; ***225** WN-5; ★ **PGH**; mail Irwin **z** 15642; rural
Shanesville; RMC Place; BERKS; ▲ Earl; **227** EN-10; mail Boyertown **z** 19512; ● 70
Shankles; RMC Place; CLEARFIELD; mail Du Bois **z** 15801; pop. incl. with Du Bois (Inc. Place)
Shanksville; Inc. Place; SOMERSET; **225** WP-8; elev. 2,250ft./686m.; 🅿; **z** 15560; Ⓟ 235; Ⓒ 245
Shankweilers; RMC Place; LEHIGH; ***227** EL-10; ★ **ALL-**; mail Orefield **z** 18069
Shannondale; RMC Place; CLARION; ▲ Redbank; **224** WJ-7; mail Mayport **z** 16240; ● 75
Shannon Heights; RMC Place; ALLEGHENY; ▲ Penn Hills; ***225** WM-4; elev. 1,200ft./366m.; ★ **PGH**; mail Verona **z** 15147
Shanor Heights; RMC Place; BUTLER; ▲ Center; ***225** WK-4; ★ **BUTL**; mail Butler **z** 16001; ● 600
Shanor-Northvue; CDP-Census Area Only; BUTLER; ▲ Center; ***224** WJ-4; elev. 1,293ft./394m.; ★ **BUTL**; mail Butler **z** 16001; Ⓟ 3,517; Ⓒ 4,825
Sharon; Inc. Place; MERCER; **224** WH-1; elev. 998ft./304m.; 🅿 🅷 🅲 893 ■; ★ **SHAR**; **z** 16146, **z** 16148 & mail Farrell **z** 16121; Ⓟ 17,493; Ⓒ 16,328; ◆ 15,486
Sharon; MCD-Township; POTTER; ***224** WD-12; mail Shinglehouse **z** 16748; Ⓟ 841; Ⓒ 907
Sharon Center; RMC Place; POTTER; ▲ Sharon; **224** WD-12; mail Shinglehouse **z** 16748; ● 30
Sharon Hill; Inc. Place; DELAWARE; **228** F-2; elev. 70ft./21m.; 🅿; ★ **PHIL-**; **z** 19079; Ⓟ 5,771; Ⓒ 5,468
Sharon Park; RMC Place; DELAWARE; ★ **PHIL-**; mail Sharon Hill **z** 19079; pop. incl. with Sharon Hill (Inc. Place)
Sharpsburg; Inc. Place; ALLEGHENY; **225** WM-4; elev. 740ft./226m.; 🅿; ★ **PGH**; **z** 15215; Ⓟ 3,781; Ⓒ 3,594
Sharpsburg; RMC Place; HUNTINGDON; ▲ Brady; ***225** WM-13; mail Allensville **z** 17002; rural
Sharps Hill; RMC Place; ALLEGHENY; ▲ Shaler; ***225** WM-3; ★ **PGH**; mail Pittsburgh **z** 15215; pop. incl. with Pittsburgh (Inc. Place)
Sharpsville; Inc. Place; MERCER; **224** WH-2; 🅿; ★ **SHAR**; **z** 16150 & mail Hermitage **z** 16148; Ⓟ 4,729; Ⓒ 4,500
Sharrertown; RMC Place; WASHINGTON; ▲ West Pike Run; ***225** WO-4; mail Daisytown **z** 15427; ● 30
Shartlesville; RMC Place; BERKS; ▲ Upper Bern; **227** EM-8; 🅿; **z** 19554; ● 300
Shavertown; RMC Place; DELAWARE; ▲ Concord; ★ **PHIL-**; mail Marcus Hook **z** 19061; rural
Shavertown; RMC Place; LUZERNE; ▲ Dallas, Kingston; **226** EA-8; 🅿; ★ **SCR-**; **z** 18708; ● 2,000
Shawanese; RMC Place; LUZERNE; ***226** EH-8; elev. 1,320ft./402m.; 🅿; ★ **SCR-**; **z** 18654; pop. incl. with Harveys Lake (Inc. Place)
Shaw Mines; RMC Place; SOMERSET; ***225** WQ-8; mail Meyersdale **z** 15552; ● 15
Shawmut; RMC Place; ELK; ▲ Horton; ***224** WH-9; mail Brockport **z** 15823
Shawnee; MONROE; see Shawnee on Delaware (RMC Place)
Shawnee on Delaware (Shawnee); RMC Place; MONROE; ▲ Smithfield; **226** EJ-12; 🅿; **z** 18356; summer pop. 700; ● 400
Shawsville; CLEARFIELD; see Shawville (RMC Place)
Shawtown; RMC Place; WESTMORELAND; ▲ North Huntingdon; ***225** WN-5; ★ **PGH**; mail Irwin **z** 15642; ● 600
Shawville (Shawsville); RMC Place; CLEARFIELD; ▲ Goshen; **224** WJ-11; 🅿; **z** 16873; ● 100
Shay; RMC Place; ARMSTRONG; ▲ Kittanning; ***225** WL-6; mail Ford City **z** 16226
Shazen; CAMBRIA; see Pleasant Hill (RMC Place)
Sheakleyville; Inc. Place; MERCER; **224** WG-3; elev. 1,282ft./391m.; 🅿; **z** 16151; Ⓟ 145; Ⓒ 164
Shearersburg; RMC Place; WESTMORELAND; ▲ Allegheny; ***225** WL-5; ★ **PGH**; mail Apollo **z** 15613; ● 75
Sheatown; RMC Place; LUZERNE; ▲ Newport; ***226** EI-8; elev. 673ft./205m.; ★ **SCR-**; mail Nanticoke **z** 18634
Sheffer; YORK; see Tolna (RMC Place)
Sheffield; CDP; WARREN; ▲ Sheffield; **224** WF-8; elev. 1,340ft./408m.; 🅿; **z** 16347; Ⓟ 1,294; Ⓒ 1,268
Sheffield; MCD-Township; WARREN; ***224** WF-8; 🅿; **z** 16347; Ⓟ 2,382; Ⓒ 2,346
Sheffield Heights; RMC Place; BEAVER; ▲ Hopewell; ***225** WL-2; ★ **PGH**; mail Aliquippa **z** 15001; ● 200
Sheffield Terrace; RMC Place; BEAVER; ▲ Hopewell; ***225** WL-2; ★ **PGH**; mail Aliquippa **z** 15001; ● 150
Sheffield Village; RMC Place; MONTGOMERY; ▲ Whitpain; ***227** EO-12; ★ **PHIL-**; mail Norristown **z** 19401; ● 300
Shehawken; RMC Place; WAYNE; ▲ Preston; **226** EE-11; mail Starrucca **z** 18462; ● 40
Shellsville; RMC Place; DAUPHIN; ▲ East Hanover; **227** EN-5; ★ **HRBG**; mail Grantville **z** 17028; ● 200
Shelly; RMC Place; BUCKS; ▲ Richland; **227** EM-11; ★ **PHIL-**; mail Quakertown **z** 18951; ● 125
Shellytown; RMC Place; BLAIR; ▲ Woodbury; ***225** WN-12; elev. 1,069ft./326m.; ★ **ALT**; mail Williamsburg **z** 16693; ● 18
Shelocta; Inc. Place; INDIANA; **225** WL-7; elev. 992ft./302m.; 🅿; **z** 15774; Ⓟ 108; Ⓒ 127
Shelvey; RMC Place; ELK; ▲ Fox; ***224** WH-10; elev. 1,985ft./605m.; mail Kersey **z** 15846; rural
Shenandoah; Inc. Place; SCHUYLKILL; **227** EK-7; elev. 1,300ft./396m.; 🅿; **z** 17976; Ⓟ 6,221; Ⓒ 5,624
Shenandoah Heights; CDP; SCHUYLKILL; ▲ West Mahanoy; **227** EK-7; mail Shenandoah **z** 17976; Ⓟ 1,386; Ⓒ 1,298
Shenandoah Junction; RMC Place; SCHUYLKILL; ***227** EK-7; mail Mahanoy Plane **z** 17949, Shenandoah **z** 17976; ● 50
Shenango; MCD-Township; LAWRENCE; ***224** WJ-2; ★ **NWCS**; mail New Castle **z** 16101; Ⓟ 7,187; Ⓒ 7,633
Shenango; RMC Place; MERCER; ▲ West Salem; **224** WH-2; 🅿; ★ **SHAR**; **z** 16125; ● 80
Shenango; MCD-Township; MERCER; ***224** WI-1; 🅿; ★ **SHAR**; **z** 16125 & mail West Middlesex **z** 16159; Ⓟ 4,339; Ⓒ 4,037
Shenks Ferry; RMC Place; YORK; ▲ Lower Chanceford, Chanceford; ***227** EQ-7; ★ **YORK**; mail Brogue **z** 17309; ● 50
Shepherd Hills; RMC Place; LEHIGH; ▲ Lower Macungie; ***227** EM-10; elev. 395ft./120m.; ★ **ALL-**; mail Allentown **z** 18101; ● 2,030
Shepherdstown; RMC Place; CUMBERLAND; ▲ Upper Allen; **227** EO-4; ★ **HRBG**; mail Mechanicsburg **z** 17055; ● 200
Sheppton; CDP; SCHUYLKILL; ▲ East Union; **227** EK-8; elev. 1,640ft./500m.; 🅿; **z** 18248; Ⓒ 239
Sheraden; RMC Place; ALLEGHENY; ***225** WM-3; ★ **PGH**; mail Pittsburgh **z** 15204; pop. incl. with Pittsburgh (Inc. Place)
Sherersville; LEHIGH; see Scherersville (RMC Place)
Sheridan; RMC Place; LEBANON; ▲ Millcreek; ***227** EN-7; mail Newmanstown **z** 17073
Sheridan; RMC Place; SCHUYLKILL; ▲ Porter; **227** EM-6; mail Tower City **z** 17980; ● 340
Sherman; RMC Place; WAYNE; ▲ Scott; **226** ED-11; mail Susquehanna **z** 18847; ● 100
Shermans Dale; RMC Place; PERRY; ▲ Carroll; **227** EN-3; 🅿; ★ **HRBG**; **z** 17090; ● 120
Shermansville; RMC Place; CRAWFORD; ▲ Sadsbury; **224** WF-2; mail Conneaut Lake **z** 16316; ● 50
Sherrett; RMC Place; ARMSTRONG; ▲ Washington; **224** WJ-5; elev. 1,236ft./377m.; mail Cowansville **z** 16218; ● 125
Sherwood Acres; RMC Place; BEAVER; ▲ Center; ***225** WL-2; elev. 1,100ft./335m.; ★ **PGH**; mail Monaca **z** 15061; ● 250
Sheshequin; RMC Place; BRADFORD; ▲ Sheshequin; **226** EE-6; mail Ulster **z** 18850; ● 150
Sheshequin; MCD-Township; BRADFORD; ***226** EE-6; mail Towanda **z** 18848; Ⓟ 1,211; Ⓒ 1,300
Shetters Grove; RMC Place; YORK; ▲ West Manchester; ★ **YORK**; mail York **z** 17405
Shickshinny; Inc. Place; LUZERNE; **226** EI-8; elev. 520ft./158m.; 🅿 🅷; **z** 18655; Ⓟ 1,108; Ⓒ 959
Shieldsburg; RMC Place; WESTMORELAND; ▲ Salem; ***225** WN-6; ★ **PGH**; mail New Alexandria **z** 15670; ● 70
Shillington; Inc. Place; BERKS; **227** EN-8; elev. 340ft./104m.; 🅿; ★ **READ**; **z** 19607; Ⓟ 5,062; Ⓒ 5,059
Shiloh; RMC Place; CLEARFIELD; ▲ Bradford; ***224** WJ-11; elev. 1,577ft./481m.; mail Woodland **z** 16881; rural
Shiloh; CDP; YORK; ▲ West Manchester; **227** EP-5; ★ **YORK**; mail York **z** 17404; Ⓟ 8,245; Ⓒ 10,192
Shiloh East; RMC Place; YORK; ▲ West Manchester; ★ **YORK**; mail York **z** 17405
Shimersville; RMC Place; NORTHAMPTON; ***227** EL-11; ★ **ALL-**; pop. incl. with Bethlehem (Inc. Place)
Shimerville; RMC Place; LEHIGH; ▲ Upper Milford; **227** EM-10; ★ **ALL-**; mail Emmaus **z** 18049; ● 130
Shimpstown; RMC Place; FRANKLIN; ▲ Montgomery; **225** WQ-13; mail Mercersburg **z** 17236; ● 80
Shindle; RMC Place; MIFFLIN; ▲ Decatur; **227** EL-2; mail Mc Clure **z** 17841; ● 70
Shinglehouse; Inc. Place; POTTER; **224** WD-12; elev. 1,492ft./455m.; 🅿; **z** 16748; Ⓟ 1,243; Ⓒ 1,250
Shingletown; RMC Place; CENTRE; ▲ Harris; **225** WK-13; ★ **STCOL**; mail State College **z** 16801; ● 150
Shintown; RMC Place; CLINTON; ▲ Noyes; **224** WH-13; mail Renovo **z** 17764; ● 75
Shipmans Eddy; RMC Place; WARREN; ▲ Glade; ***224** WE-8; mail Warren **z** 16365; ● 30
Shippen; MCD-Township; CAMERON; ***224** WG-12; mail Emporium **z** 15834; Ⓟ 2,495; Ⓒ 2,495
Shippen; MCD-Township; TIOGA; ***226** EF-2; mail Wellsboro **z** 16901; Ⓟ 508; Ⓒ 472
Shippensburg; Inc. Place; CUMBERLAND, FRANKLIN; **227** EP-1; elev. 654ft./199m.; 🅿 🅲 7,516; **z** 17257; Ⓟ 5,331; Ⓒ 5,586
Shippensburg; MCD-Township; CUMBERLAND; ***227** EP-1; 🅿 🅲 7,516; **z** 17257; Ⓟ 4,606; Ⓒ 4,504
Shippenville; Inc. Place; CLARION; **224** WH-6; elev. 1,240ft./378m.; 🅿; **z** 16254; Ⓟ 474; Ⓒ 505
Shippingport; Inc. Place; BEAVER; **225** WL-2; elev. 781ft./238m.; 🅿; ★ **PGH**; **z** 15077; Ⓟ 227; Ⓒ 237
Shiremanstown; Inc. Place; CUMBERLAND; **227** EO-4; elev. 421ft./128m.; 🅿; ★ **HRBG**; **z** 17011; Ⓟ 1,567; Ⓒ 1,521
Shirks Corner; RMC Place; MONTGOMERY; ▲ Upper Salford; ***227** EN-11; ★ **PHIL-**; mail Schwenksville **z** 19473; rural
Shirley; MCD-Township; HUNTINGDON; ***225** WN-14; mail Mount Union **z** 17066; Ⓟ 2,494; Ⓒ 2,526
Shirleysburg; Inc. Place; HUNTINGDON; **225** WN-13; elev. 606ft./185m.; 🅿; **z** 17260 & mail Mount Union **z** 17066; Ⓟ 140; Ⓒ 140
Shoaf; RMC Place; FAYETTE; ▲ Georges; ***225** WQ-4; elev. 1,058ft./322m.; ★ **UNTN**; mail Smithfield **z** 15478; ● 140
Shocks Mills; LANCASTER; see Rowenna (RMC Place)
Shoemaker; RMC Place; CAMBRIA; ▲ Portage; ***225** WN-10; mail Portage **z** 15946; rural
Shoemakers; RMC Place; MONROE; ▲ Middle Smithfield; ***226** EI-13; mail East Stroudsburg **z** 18301
Shoemakers; RMC Place; SCHUYLKILL; ▲ Mahanoy; ***227** EK-8; mail Mahanoy City **z** 17948; rural
Shoemakersville; Inc. Place; BERKS; **227** EM-8; elev. 360ft./110m.; 🅿; ★ **READ**; **z** 19555; Ⓟ 1,443; Ⓒ 2,124
Shohola; RMC Place; PIKE; ▲ Shohola; **226** EG-13; 🅿; **z** 18458; ● 160
Shohola; MCD-Township; PIKE; ***226** EG-13; 🅿; **z** 18458; Ⓟ 1,586; Ⓒ 2,088
Shope Gardens; RMC Place; DAUPHIN; ▲ Lower Swatara; ***227** EO-5; ★ **HRBG**; mail Middletown **z** 17057; ● 1,700
Shorbes Hill; RMC Place; YORK; ▲ West Manheim; ★ **HANV**; mail Hanover **z** 17331; rural
Shortsville; RMC Place; TIOGA; ▲ Chatham; ***226** EE-2; mail Middlebury Center **z** 16935; rural
Shrader; RMC Place; MIFFLIN; ▲ Armagh; **227** EL-1; mail Reedsville **z** 17084; ● 100
Shrewsbury; MCD-Township; LYCOMING; ***226** EH-5; mail Hughesville **z** 17737; Ⓟ 402; Ⓒ 433
Shrewsbury; MCD-Township; SULLIVAN; ***226** EH-5; mail Muncy Valley **z** 17758; Ⓟ 307; Ⓒ 328
Shrewsbury; Inc. Place; YORK; **227** EQ-5; 🅿; ★ **BAL**; **z** 17361; Ⓟ 2,672; Ⓒ 3,378
Shrewsbury; MCD-Township; YORK; ***227** EQ-5; elev. 980ft./299m.; 🅿; ★ **BAL**; **z** 17361 & mail Glen Rock **z** 17327; does not include the Borough of Shrewsbury; Ⓟ 5,898; Ⓒ 5,947
Shumans; RMC Place; COLUMBIA; ▲ Beaver; **226** EJ-7; mail Bloomsburg **z** 17815; ● 140
Shunk; RMC Place; SULLIVAN; ▲ Fox; **226** EG-5; 🅿; **z** 17768; ● 45
Sickles Corner; RMC Place; BLAIR; ▲ Tyrone; ***225** WM-11; elev. 1,241ft./378m.; mail Altoona **z** 16601; rural
Siddonsburg; RMC Place; YORK; ▲ Monaghan; **227** EO-4; ★ **HRBG**; mail Dillsburg **z** 17019; ● 110
Sidman (Lovett); RMC Place; CAMBRIA; ▲ Croyle, Adams; **225** WN-9; 🅿; ★ **JNST**; **z** 15955; ● 300
Siegfried; RMC Place; NORTHAMPTON; ★ **ALL-**; mail Northampton **z** 18067; pop. incl. with Northampton (Inc. Place)
Sigel; RMC Place; JEFFERSON; ▲ Eldred; **224** WH-8; 🅿; **z** 15860; ● 250
Siglerville; RMC Place; MIFFLIN; ▲ Armagh; **227** EL-1; mail Milroy **z** 17063; ● 100
Sigmund; RMC Place; LEHIGH; ▲ Upper Milford; ***227** EM-10; ★ **ALL-**; mail Zionsville **z** 18092; rural
Silkworth; RMC Place; LUZERNE; ▲ Lehman; **226** EH-8; ★ **SCR-**; mail Hunlock Creek **z** 18621; ● 100
Silvara; RMC Place; BRADFORD; ▲ Tuscarora; **226** EF-8; elev. 834ft./254m.; mail Laceyville **z** 18623; ● 80
Silver Creek; RMC Place; SCHUYLKILL; ▲ Blythe; ***227** EL-8; ★ **PTSVL**; mail New Philadelphia **z** 17959; ● 40
Silverdale; Inc. Place; BUCKS; **227** EN-12; elev. 440ft./134m.; 🅿; ★ **PHIL-**; **z** 18962; Ⓟ 881; Ⓒ 1,001
Silver Ford Heights; RMC Place; MIFFLIN; ▲ Wayne; ***225** WN-13; mail Mount Union **z** 17066; ● 250
Silver Lake; RMC Place; BUCKS; ▲ Newtown; ***227** EN-13; ★ **PHIL-**; mail Newtown **z** 18940; rural
Silver Lake; RMC Place; SUSQUEHANNA; ▲ Silver Lake; **226** ED-8; mail Brackney **z** 18812; ● 150
Silver Lake; MCD-Township; SUSQUEHANNA; ***226** ED-9; mail Brackney **z** 18812; Ⓟ 1,542; Ⓒ 1,729
Silver Lake; RMC Place; WAYNE; ▲ Damascus; ***226** EF-12; elev. 1,343ft./409m.; mail Tyler Hill **z** 18469; summer pop. 800; ● 370
Silver Lake; RMC Place; YORK; ▲ Fairview; ***227** EO-4; ★ **HRBG**; mail Lewisberry **z** 17339; rural
Silver Spring; MCD-Township; CUMBERLAND; ***227** EO-4; ★ **HRBG**; mail Mechanicsburg **z** 17055; Ⓟ 8,369; Ⓒ 10,592
Silver Spring (Bruckarts); RMC Place; LANCASTER; ▲ West Hempfield; **227** EP-6; 🅿; ★ **LANC**; **z** 17575; ● 300
Silverville; RMC Place; BUTLER; ▲ Buffalo; ***225** WL-5; elev. 1,121ft./342m.; ★ **PGH**; mail Sarver **z** 16055; ● 250
Simmonstown; RMC Place; LANCASTER; ▲ Sadsbury; ***227** EP-8; elev. 636ft./194m.; mail Gap **z** 17527; rural
Simpson; RMC Place; LACKAWANNA; ▲ Fell; **226** EF-10; 🅿; ★ **SCR-**; **z** 18407; ● 1,500
Singersville; RMC Place; DAUPHIN; ▲ Middle Paxton; ***227** EN-4; ★ **HRBG**; mail Dauphin **z** 17018; ● 60
Sinking Spring; Inc. Place; BERKS; **227** EN-8; elev. 347ft./106m.; 🅿; ★ **READ**; **z** 19608; Ⓟ 2,467; Ⓒ 2,639
Sinking Valley; RMC Place; BLAIR; ▲ Tyrone; ***225** WM-11; mail Tyrone **z** 16686; rural
Sinnamahoning; CAMERON; see Sinnemahoning (RMC Place)
Sinnemahoning (Sinnamahoning); RMC Place; CAMERON; ▲ Grove, Gibson; **224** WH-12; mail Sinnamahoning **z** 15861; ● 350
Sinsheim; RMC Place; YORK; ▲ Codorus; ***227** EQ-4; elev. 546ft./166m.; ★ **BAL**; mail Spring Grove **z** 17362; rural
Sipes Mill; RMC Place; FULTON; **255** WQ-12; mail Needmore **z** 17238; rural
Sipesville; RMC Place; SOMERSET; ▲ Lincoln; **225** WO-8; 🅿; **z** 15561; ● 350
Siqusca; RMC Place; CHESTER; ▲ West Brandywine; ***227** EP-9; ★ **PHIL-**; mail Wagontown **z** 19376; rural
Sitka; RMC Place; FAYETTE; ▲ Dunbar; ***225** WP-5; elev. 981ft./299m.; mail Dunbar **z** 15431; ● 250
Siverly; RMC Place; VENANGO; ***224** WG-5; ★ **OILC-F**; mail Oil City **z** 16301; pop. incl. with Oil City (Inc. Place)
Six Mile Run; BEDFORD; see Coaldale (Inc. Place)
Six Points; RMC Place; BUTLER; ▲ Allegheny; ***224** WI-5; elev. 1,529ft./466m.; mail Parker **z** 16049; rural
Sizerville; RMC Place; CAMERON; ▲ Portage; **224** WG-12; mail Emporium **z** 15834; ● 35
Skelp; RMC Place; BLAIR; ▲ Tyrone; **225** WL-11; mail Altoona **z** 16601; ● 60
Skeltontown; RMC Place; CRAWFORD; ▲ Venango; ***224** WE-3; mail Cambridge Springs **z** 16403; ● 25
Skidmore; RMC Place; LAWRENCE; ▲ Hickory; ***224** WJ-2; ★ **NWCS**; mail New Castle **z** 16101; ● 30
Ski Haven Lake Estates; RMC Place; MONROE; ▲ Pocono; ***226** EI-11; elev. 1,100ft./335m.; mail Cresco **z** 18326; ● 100
Skinners Eddy; RMC Place; WYOMING; ▲ Braintrim; **226** EF-8; elev. 647ft./197m.; mail Laceyville **z** 18623; ● 40
Skippack; CDP; MONTGOMERY; ▲ Skippack; **227** EO-11; elev. 190ft./58m.; 🅿; ★ **PHIL-**; **z** 19474; Ⓟ 2,042; Ⓒ 2,889
Skippack; MCD-Township; MONTGOMERY; ***227** EO-11; 🅿; ★ **PHIL-**; **z** 19474; Ⓟ 8,790; Ⓒ 6,516; Ⓡ 9,920
Skyline Heights; RMC Place; YORK; ▲ Springettsbury; ★ **YORK**; mail York **z** 17402
Skyline View; CDP; DAUPHIN; ▲ West Hanover; ***227** EN-5; ★ **HRBG**; mail Harrisburg **z** 17112; Ⓟ 2,370; Ⓒ 2,307
Skytop; RMC Place; MONROE; ▲ Barrett; **226** EI-12; 🅿; **z** 18357; summer pop. 2,000; ● 200
Sky View; RMC Place; PIKE; ▲ Greene; ***226** EH-12; elev. 1,700ft./518m.; mail Greentown **z** 18426; ● 150
Slab; RMC Place; YORK; ▲ Lower Chanceford; ***227** EQ-7; mail Airville **z** 17302; rural
Slabtown (Roaring Creek); CDP; COLUMBIA; ▲ Locust; **227** EK-6; mail Catawissa **z** 17820; Ⓒ 105
Slabtown; RMC Place; FRANKLIN; ▲ Quincy; ***227** EQ-1; mail Waynesboro **z** 17268; rural
Slackwater; RMC Place; LANCASTER; ▲ Conestoga; ***227** EP-7; ★ **LANC**; mail Millersville **z** 17551; rural
Slatedale; RMC Place; LEHIGH; ▲ Washington; **227** EL-10; elev. 501ft./153m.; 🅿; ★ **ALL-**; **z** 18079; ● 600
Slatefield; RMC Place; NORTHAMPTON; ▲ Lehigh; ***227** EK-11; ★ **ALL-**; mail Danielsville **z** 18038; rural
Slateford; RMC Place; NORTHAMPTON; ▲ Upper Mount Bethel; **226** EJ-12; mail Mount Bethel **z** 18343; ● 250
Slate Hill; RMC Place; YORK; ▲ Peach Bottom; ***227** ER-7; elev. 419ft./128m.; ★ **BAL**; mail Delta **z** 17314; rural
Slate Lick; RMC Place; ARMSTRONG; ▲ South Buffalo; **225** WK-5; elev. 1,136ft./346m.; ★ **PGH**; mail Freeport **z** 16229; ● 150
Slate Run; RMC Place; LYCOMING; ▲ Brown; **226** EG-2; 🅿; **z** 17769; ● 60
Slate Valley; RMC Place; NORTHAMPTON; ▲ Lehigh; ***227** EK-10; ★ **ALL-**; mail Danielsville **z** 18038; ● 110
Slateville; RMC Place; LEHIGH; ▲ Lynn; ***227** EL-9; ★ **ALL-**; mail Kempton **z** 19529; rural
Slatington; Inc. Place; LEHIGH; **227** EL-10; elev. 364ft./111m.; 🅿; ★ **ALL-**; **z** 18080; Ⓟ 4,678; Ⓒ 4,434
Slickport; RMC Place; CAMBRIA; ▲ Elder; ***225** WL-9; mail Hastings **z** 16646; ● 100
Slickville; CDP; WESTMORELAND; ▲ Salem, Loyalhanna; **225** WM-6; 🅿; ★ **PGH**; **z** 15684; Ⓒ 372
Sligo; Inc. Place; CLARION; **224** WI-6; elev. 1,200ft./366m.; 🅿; **z** 16255; Ⓟ 706; Ⓒ 728
Slippery Rock; Inc. Place; BUTLER; **224** WJ-3; elev. 1,302ft./397m.; 🅿 🅲 8,230; **z** 16057; Ⓟ 3,008; Ⓒ 3,068
Slippery Rock; MCD-Township; BUTLER; ***224** WJ-3; 🅿 🅲 8,230; **z** 16057; does not include the Borough of Slippery Rock; Ⓟ 4,638; Ⓒ 5,251
Slippery Rock; MCD-Township; LAWRENCE; ***224** WJ-2; ★ **PGH**; mail New Castle **z** 16101; Ⓟ 3,196; Ⓒ 3,179
Slippery Rock Park; RMC Place; BUTLER; ▲ Brady; ***224** WJ-4; mail Slippery Rock **z** 16057; ● 190
Slocum; LUZERNE; see Forty Fort (Inc. Place)
Slocum; MCD-Township; LUZERNE; ***226** EI-8; ★ **SCR-**; mail Wapwallopen **z** 18660; Ⓟ 1,159; Ⓒ 1,112
Slocum Corners; RMC Place; LUZERNE; ▲ Slocum; **226** EI-8; elev. 1,152ft./351m.; ★ **SCR-**; mail Mountain Top **z** 18707, Wapwallopen **z** 18660; ● 150
Slovan; RMC Place; WASHINGTON; ▲ Smith; **225** WN-2; elev. 1,017ft./310m.; 🅿; ★ **PGH**; **z** 15078; ● 1,100
Slovene National Benefit Society; LAWRENCE; see S.N.P.J. (Inc. Place)
Smallwood; RMC Place; WASHINGTON; ***225** WO-4; ★ **PGH**; mail Coal Center **z** 15423; pop. incl. with California (Inc. Place)
Smethport; Inc. Place; ⊡ MCKEAN; **224** WE-11; elev. 1,560ft./475m.; 🅿; **z** 16749; Ⓟ 1,734; Ⓒ 1,684
Smicksburg; Inc. Place; INDIANA; **225** WK-7; 🅿; **z** 16256; Ⓟ 76; Ⓒ 49
Smiley; RMC Place; FAYETTE; ▲ Georges; ***225** WQ-4; ★ **UNTN**; mail Smithfield **z** 15478; ● 20
Smith; RMC Place; INDIANA; ▲ Burrell; ***225** WM-7; elev. 1,072ft./327m.; ★ **LTROB**; mail Blairsville **z** 15717; ● 450
Smith; MCD-Township; WASHINGTON; ***225** WN-2; ★ **PGH**; mail Burgettstown **z** 15021; Ⓟ 4,844; Ⓒ 4,567
Smith Bridge; RMC Place; GREENE; ▲ Richhill; ***225** WQ-1; mail Wind Ridge **z** 15380; rural
Smithdale; RMC Place; ALLEGHENY; ▲ Elizabeth; ***225** WN-4; ★ **PGH**; mail West Newton **z** 15089; ● 160
Smithfield; MCD-Township; BRADFORD; ***226** EE-5; mail Milan **z** 18831; Ⓟ 1,520; Ⓒ 1,538
Smithfield; Inc. Place; FAYETTE; **225** WQ-4; elev. 1,089ft./332m.; 🅿; ★ **UNTN**; **z** 15478; Ⓟ 1,000; Ⓒ 854
Smithfield; RMC Place; HUNTINGDON; ▲ Smithfield; **225** WM-12; mail Huntingdon **z** 16652; ● 4,181
Smithfield; MCD-Township; HUNTINGDON; ***225** WM-13; mail Huntingdon **z** 16652; Ⓟ 4,181; Ⓒ 4,466
Smithfield; MCD-Township; MONROE; ***226** EJ-12; mail Marshalls Creek **z** 18335; Ⓟ 4,692; Ⓒ 5,672
Smith Gardens; RMC Place; YORK; ▲ East Manchester; ★ **YORK**; mail Manchester **z** 17345; ● 200
Smithland; RMC Place; CLARION; ▲ Porter; ***224** WJ-6; mail New Bethlehem **z** 16242; rural
Smithmill; CLEARFIELD; see Janesville (RMC Place)
Smithport; RMC Place; INDIANA; ▲ Banks; **225** WK-9; elev. 1,814ft./553m.; mail Glen Campbell **z** 15742; ● 100
Smiths; YORK; see Smiths Station (RMC Place)
Smiths Corner; RMC Place; BUCKS; ▲ Plumstead; ***227** EM-12; ★ **PHIL-**; mail Point Pleasant **z** 18950; rural

Entries in **UPPERCASE** are counties.
Entries in **bold** have populations of 2,500 or more.
Names in parentheses are alternate names.

Inc. Place	Incorporated Place
RMC Place	Rand McNally Designated Place
CDP	Census Designated Place
MCD	Minor Civil Division

⊡ County Seat
▲ Minor Civil Division
elev. Elevation
🅿 Post Office

🅷 Hospital
🅲 College
■ Principal Business Center
★ Ranally Metro Area (RMA) Abbreviation
z Zip Code(s)

Ⓟ Previous Census Population
Ⓡ Revised Census Population
Ⓐ Annexation Population
● Rand McNally Population Estimate
Ⓒ Final Census Population
Ⓢ Special Census Population
◆ Estimated Population

For additional definitions see Glossary, Volume 1, and Introduction, Volume 2.

Smiths Corners; RMC Place; VENANGO; ▲ Rockland; *224 WH-5; elev. 1,561ft./476m.; mail Kennerdell z 16374; rural
Smiths Ferry; RMC Place; BEAVER; *225 WL-1; ★ PGH; mail Midland z 15059; pop. incl. with Ohioville (Inc. Place)
Smiths Station (Smiths); RMC Place; YORK; ▲ Heidelberg; *227 EQ-4; mail Spring Grove z 17362
Smithton; Inc. Place; WESTMORELAND; 225 WO-5; elev. 820ft./250m.; 🅿; ★ PGH; z 15479; Ⓟ 388; © 444
Smithtown; RMC Place; BUCKS; ▲ Tinicum; *227 EM-12; ★ PHIL-; mail Pipersville z 18947; rural
Smithville; RMC Place; LANCASTER; ▲ Providence; *227 EP-7; ★ LANC; mail New Providence z 17560, Willow Street z 17584
Smock; RMC Place; FAYETTE; ▲ Menallen, Franklin; 225 WP-4; 🅿; ★ UNTN; z 15480; ● 600
Smoke Run; RMC Place; CLEARFIELD; ▲ Bigler; 225 WK-11; 🅿; z 16681; ● 150
Smoketown; RMC Place; BUCKS; ▲ East Rockhill; *227 EN-11; ★ PHIL-; mail Quakertown z 18951; ● 50
Smoketown; RMC Place; FRANKLIN; ▲ Greene; *227 EP-1; mail Fayetteville z 17222; rural
Smoketown; RMC Place; LANCASTER; ▲ East Lampeter; 227 EP-7; 🅿; ★ LANC; z 17576; ● 350
Smullton; RMC Place; CENTRE; ▲ Miles; 226 EJ-2; mail Rebersburg z 16872; ● 125
Smyerstown; RMC Place; INDIANA; ▲ Canoe; mail Rossiter z 15772
Smyrna; RMC Place; LANCASTER; ▲ Sadsbury; *227 EP-8; elev. 653ft./199m.; mail Christiana z 17509
Smyser; YORK; see Seven Valleys (Inc. Place)
Snake Spring; MCD-Township; BEDFORD; *225 WP-11; mail Everett z 15537; Ⓟ 1,511; © 1,482
Snedekerville; RMC Place; BRADFORD; ▲ Columbia; *226 EE-5; mail Columbia Cross Roads z 16914; rural
Snively Corners; RMC Place; CLARION; ▲ Salem; *224 WH-5; mail Knox z 16232; rural
Snowball Gate; RMC Place; BUCKS; ▲ Middletown; ★ PHIL-; mail Levittown z 19056
Snowden; RMC Place; ALLEGHENY; ▲ South Park; *225 WN-4; ★ PGH; mail South Park z 15129; ● 200
Snowdenville; RMC Place; CHESTER; ▲ East Coventry; *227 EO-10; elev. 268ft./82m.; ★ PTSTN; mail Spring City z 19475; ● 100
Snow Shoe; Inc. Place; CENTRE; 224 WJ-13; elev. 1,560ft./475m.; 🅿; z 16874; Ⓟ 800; © 771
Snow Shoe; MCD-Township; CENTRE; *224 WJ-13; 🅿; z 16874 & mail Clarence z 16829; does not include the Borough of Snow Shoe; Ⓟ 1,756; © 1,760
S.N.P.J. (Slovene National Benefit Society); Inc. Place; LAWRENCE; *224 WJ-1; ★ YNGS-; mail Enon Valley z 16120; Ⓟ 12; © 0
Snyder; MCD-Township; BLAIR; *225 WL-11; ★ ALT; mail Tyrone z 16686; Ⓟ 3,163; © 3,358
Snyder; MCD-Township; JEFFERSON; *224 WH-9; mail Brockway z 15824; Ⓟ 2,535; © 2,432
SNYDER; 227 EK-3; Ⓟ 36,680; © 37,546; ◆ 38,354
Snyder Corner; RMC Place; YORK; ▲ Windsor; *227 EP-6; ★ YORK; mail Red Lion z 17356; ● 200
Snyders; RMC Place; SCHUYLKILL; ▲ West Penn; 227 EL-9; mail New Ringgold z 17960; ● 90
Snydersburg; RMC Place; CLARION; ▲ Knox; 224 WH-7; 🅿; z 16257 & mail Lucinda z 16235; ● 100
Snydersville; RMC Place; MONROE; ▲ Hamilton; 226 EJ-11; mail Stroudsburg z 18360; ● 150
Snydertown; RMC Place; CENTRE; ▲ Walker; *226 EJ-1; mail Howard z 16841; rural
Snydertown; Inc. Place; NORTHUMBERLAND; 227 EK-5; elev. 540ft./165m.; 🅿; z 17877; Ⓟ 416; © 357
Snydertown; RMC Place; WESTMORELAND; ▲ Derry; *225 WN-6; ★ LTROB; mail Bradenville z 15620; ● 200
Snyderville; ARMSTRONG; see Muff (RMC Place)
Social Island; RMC Place; FRANKLIN; ▲ Guilford; *225 WQ-14; elev. 800ft./244m.; mail Chambersburg z 17201; rural
Soho; RMC Place; ALLEGHENY; *225 WM-4; ★ PGH; mail Pittsburgh z 15219; pop. incl. with Pittsburgh (Inc. Place)
Soldier; RMC Place; JEFFERSON; ▲ Winslow; *224 WJ-9; mail Reynoldsville z 15851; ● 120
Solebury; RMC Place; BUCKS; ▲ Solebury; *227 EN-13; 🅿; ★ PHIL-; z 18963; ● 600
Solebury; MCD-Township; BUCKS; *227 EN-13; 🅿; ★ PHIL-; z 18963; Ⓟ 5,998; © 7,743
Somerset; Inc. Place; ⊡ SOMERSET; 225 WP-8; elev. 2,190ft./668m.; 🅿 🅷; z 15501, z 15510; Ⓟ 6,454; © 6,762
Somerset; MCD-Township; SOMERSET; *225 WP-8; 🅿; z 15501, z 15510; does not include the Borough of Somerset; Ⓟ 8,732; © 9,319; Ⓡ 11,088
Somerset; MCD-Township; WASHINGTON; *225 WO-4; ★ WASH; mail Eighty Four z 15330; Ⓟ 2,947; © 2,701
SOMERSET; 225 WQ-7; Ⓟ 78,218; © 80,023; ◆ 76,566
Somers Lane; RMC Place; TIOGA; ▲ Lawrence; 226 ED-3; elev. 1,006ft./307m.; mail Lawrenceville z 16929; ● 300
Somerton; RMC Place; PHILADELPHIA; *227 EO-13; ★ PHIL-; mail Philadelphia z 19116; pop. incl. with Philadelphia (Inc. Place)
Somerville; RMC Place; ARMSTRONG; ▲ Sugarcreek; *224 WJ-5; mail East Brady z 16028; rural
Sonestown; RMC Place; SULLIVAN; ▲ Davidson; 226 EH-6; 🅿; z 17758; ● 200
Sonman; RMC Place; CAMBRIA; ▲ Portage; *225 WN-10; mail Portage z 15946; ● 90
Soradoville; RMC Place; MIFFLIN; ▲ Decatur; *227 EL-2; mail Mc Clure z 17841; rural
Soudersburg; RMC Place; LANCASTER; ▲ Leacock; 227 EP-8; elev. 376ft./115m.; 🅿; ★ LANC; z 17572; ● 200
Souderton; Inc. Place; MONTGOMERY; 227 EN-11; elev. 460ft./140m.; 🅿; ★ PHIL-; z 18964; Ⓟ 5,957; © 6,730
Soukesburg; RMC Place; CAMBRIA; ▲ Croyle; *225 WN-9; ★ JNST; mail South Fork z 15956; ● 100
South Abington (South Abington Township); MCD-Township; LACKAWANNA; *226 EG-10; ★ SCR-; mail Chinchilla z 18410, Clarks Summit z 18411; Ⓟ 6,377; © 8,638
South Abington Township; LACKAWANNA; see South Abington (MCD-Township)
South Altoona; RMC Place; BLAIR; *225 WM-11; elev. 1,097ft./334m.; ★ ALT; mail Altoona z 16602; pop. incl. with Altoona (Inc. Place)
Southampton; MCD-Township; BEDFORD; *225 WQ-10; mail Clearville z 15535; Ⓟ 920; © 1,010
Southampton; RMC Place; BUCKS; ▲ Upper Southampton; 227 EO-13; 🅿; ★ PHIL-; z 18954, z 18966; ● 11,500
Southampton; MCD-Township; CUMBERLAND; *227 EP-2; mail Shippensburg z 17257; Ⓟ 3,552; © 4,787
Southampton; MCD-Township; FRANKLIN; *227 EP-1; mail Orrstown z 17244; Ⓟ 5,484; © 6,138
Southampton; MCD-Township; SOMERSET; *225 WQ-9; mail Meyersdale z 15552; Ⓟ 553; © 655
South Annville; MCD-Township; LEBANON; *227 EN-6; ★ LEB; mail Lebanon z 17042; Ⓟ 3,008; © 2,946
South Auburn; RMC Place; SUSQUEHANNA; ▲ Auburn; *226 EF-8; elev. 1,128ft./344m.; mail Meshoppen z 18630; ● 25
South Beaver; MCD-Township; BEAVER; *225 WK-2; ★ PGH; mail Beaver Falls z 15010, Darlington z 16115; Ⓟ 2,942; © 2,974
South Bend; RMC Place; ARMSTRONG; ▲ South Bend; 225 WL-6; mail Spring Church z 15686; ● 40
South Bend; MCD-Township; ARMSTRONG; *225 WL-6; mail Shelocta z 15774; Ⓟ 1,304; © 1,259
South Bethlehem; Inc. Place; ARMSTRONG; 224 WJ-7; elev. 1,080ft./329m.; mail New Bethlehem z 16242; Ⓟ 479; © 444
South Bradford; RMC Place; MCKEAN; ▲ Bradford; 224 WD-10; mail Bradford z 16701; ● 150
South Brownsville; RMC Place; FAYETTE; ★ UNTN; pop. incl. with Brownsville (Inc. Place)
South Buffalo; MCD-Township; ARMSTRONG; *225 WK-5; ★ PGH; mail Freeport z 16229; Ⓟ 2,687; © 2,785
South Canaan; RMC Place; WAYNE; ▲ South Canaan; 226 EG-11; elev. 1,422ft./433m.; 🅿; z 18459; ● 250
South Canaan; MCD-Township; WAYNE; *226 EG-11; 🅿; z 18459 & mail Waymart z 18472; Ⓟ 1,320; © 1,666
South Carnegie; RMC Place; ALLEGHENY; ▲ Scott; ★ PGH; mail Carnegie z 15106
South Centre; MCD-Township; COLUMBIA; *226 EJ-7; mail Bloomsburg z 17815; Ⓟ 1,891; © 1,972
South Clarksville; RMC Place; GREENE; ▲ Morgan; *225 WP-3; mail Clarksville z 15322; ● 50
South Coatesville; Inc. Place; CHESTER; 227 EP-9; elev. 300ft./91m.; ★ PHIL-; mail Coatesville z 19320; Ⓟ 1,026; © 997
South Connellsville; Inc. Place; FAYETTE; 225 WP-5; elev. 1,034ft./315m.; mail Connellsville z 15425; Ⓟ 2,204; © 2,281
South Coventry; MCD-Township; CHESTER; *227 EO-10; ★ PTSTN; mail Pottstown z 19464; Ⓟ 1,682; © 1,895
South Creek; MCD-Township; BRADFORD; *226 ED-5; mail Gillett z 16925; Ⓟ 1,229; © 1,261
Southdale; RMC Place; LUZERNE; ▲ Huntington; *226 EI-7; mail Shickshinny z 18655; rural
South Danville; NORTHUMBERLAND; see Riverside (Inc. Place)
South Duquesne; RMC Place; ALLEGHENY; ★ PGH; mail Duquesne z 15110; pop. incl. with Duquesne (Inc. Place)
South Easton; RMC Place; NORTHAMPTON; *227 EL-12; ★ ALL-; mail Easton z 18042; pop. incl. with Easton (Inc. Place)
South Eaton; RMC Place; WYOMING; ▲ Eaton; *226 EG-9; mail Tunkhannock z 18657; rural
South Enola; RMC Place; CUMBERLAND; ▲ East Pennsboro; ★ HRBG; mail Enola z 17025
South Erie; RMC Place; ERIE; *224 WC-3; ★ ERIE; mail Erie z 16508; pop. incl. with Erie (Inc. Place)
South Fayette; MCD-Township; ALLEGHENY; *225 WN-3; ★ PGH; mail Morgan z 15064; Ⓟ 10,329; © 12,271
South Fork; Inc. Place; CAMBRIA; 225 WN-9; elev. 1,496ft./456m.; 🅿; ★ JNST; z 15956; Ⓟ 1,197; © 1,138
South Franklin; MCD-Township; WASHINGTON; *225 WO-2; ★ WASH; mail Washington z 15301; Ⓟ 3,665; © 3,796
South Gibson; RMC Place; SUSQUEHANNA; ▲ Gibson; 226 EF-10; 🅿; z 18842; ● 175
South Greensburg; Inc. Place; WESTMORELAND; 225 WN-6; ★ PGH; mail Greensburg z 15601; Ⓟ 2,293; © 2,280
South Hanover; MCD-Township; DAUPHIN; *227 EN-5; ★ HRBG; mail Hershey z 17033, Hummelstown z 17036; Ⓟ 4,626; © 4,793
South Heidelberg; MCD-Township; BERKS; *227 EN-8; elev. 1,080ft./329m.; ★ READ; mail Wernersville z 19565; Ⓟ 4,382; © 5,491
South Heights; Inc. Place; BEAVER; 225 WL-2; elev. 745ft./227m.; 🅿; ★ PGH; z 15081; Ⓟ 647; © 542
South Hermitage; RMC Place; LANCASTER; ▲ Salisbury; *227 EP-8; ★ LANC; mail Narvon z 17555; rural
South Hills; RMC Place; ALLEGHENY; *225 WM-3; 🅿; ★ PGH; z 15216; pop. incl. with Dormont (Inc. Place)
South Hills; RMC Place; MIFFLIN; ▲ Derry; *227 EL-1; elev. 600ft./183m.; mail Lewistown z 17044; ● 150
South Hummelstown; RMC Place; DAUPHIN; pop. incl. with Hummelstown (Inc. Place)
South Huntingdon; MCD-Township; WESTMORELAND; *225 WO-5; ★ PGH; mail West Newton z 15089; Ⓟ 6,352; © 6,175
South Lakemont; RMC Place; BLAIR; ▲ Logan; 224 WB-13; ★ ALT; mail Altoona z 16602; ● 1,100
South Langhorne; RMC Place; BUCKS; ★ PHIL-; pop. incl. with Penndel (Inc. Place)
South Lebanon; RMC Place; LEBANON; *227 EN-6; ★ LEB; ● 2,000
South Lebanon; LEBANON; see Lebanon South (CDP)
South Lebanon; MCD-Township; LEBANON; *227 EN-7; ★ LEB; mail Lebanon z 17042; Ⓟ 7,491; © 8,383
South Londonderry; MCD-Township; LEBANON; *227 EN-6; mail Campbelltown z 17010, Hershey z 17033; Ⓟ 4,502; © 5,458
South Mahoning; MCD-Township; INDIANA; *225 WK-8; mail Home z 15747; Ⓟ 1,713; © 1,852
South Manheim; MCD-Township; SCHUYLKILL; *227 EL-8; ★ PTSVL; mail Auburn z 17922, Schuylkill Haven z 17972; Ⓟ 1,558; © 2,191
South Meadville; CRAWFORD; see Franklin Pike Corners (RMC Place)
South Media; RMC Place; DELAWARE; ▲ Nether Providence; *227 EP-11; ★ PHIL-; mail Media z 19063
South Middleton; MCD-Township; CUMBERLAND; *227 EO-3; ★ CARL; mail Boiling Springs z 17007; Ⓟ 10,340; © 12,939
Southmont; Inc. Place; CAMBRIA; 225 WN-8; elev. 1,540ft./469m.; ★ JNST; mail Johnstown z 15905; Ⓟ 2,415; © 2,262
South Montrose; RMC Place; SUSQUEHANNA; ▲ Bridgewater; 226 EE-9; 🅿; z 18843; ● 400
South Mountain; RMC Place; FRANKLIN; ▲ Guilford, Quincy; 227 EQ-2; 🅿; z 17261; ● 600
South New Castle; Inc. Place; LAWRENCE; 224 WJ-2; elev. 1,000ft./305m.; ★ NWCS; mail New Castle z 16101; Ⓟ 805; © 808
South Newton; MCD-Township; CUMBERLAND; *227 EP-2; mail Walnut Bottom z 17266; Ⓟ 1,153; © 1,290
South Park; MCD-Township; ALLEGHENY; *225 WN-4; 🅿; ★ PGH; z 15129; Ⓟ 14,292; © 14,340
South Park Township; CDP-Census Area Only; ALLEGHENY; ▲ South Park; *225 WN-4; elev. 1,200ft./366m.; ★ PGH; mail South Park z 15129; Ⓟ 14,292; © 14,340
South Philipsburg; Inc. Place; CENTRE; 225 WK-12; mail Philipsburg z 16866; Ⓟ 438; © 438
South Pottstown; CDP; CHESTER; ▲ North Coventry; 227 EO-10; ★ PTSTN; mail Pottstown z 19464; Ⓟ 1,966; © 2,135
South Pymatuning; MCD-Township; MERCER; *224 WH-2; ★ SHAR; mail Sharpsville z 16150; Ⓟ 2,775; © 2,857
South Renovo; Inc. Place; CLINTON; 224 WH-14; elev. 720ft./219m.; mail Renovo z 17764; Ⓟ 579; © 557
South Rockwood; RMC Place; SOMERSET; ▲ Black; *225 WP-7; mail Rockwood z 15557; ● 50
South Scranton; RMC Place; LACKAWANNA; ★ SCR-; pop. incl. with Scranton (Inc. Place)
South Shenango; MCD-Township; CRAWFORD; *224 WG-1; mail Jamestown z 16134; Ⓟ 1,560; © 2,047
South Side; RMC Place; ALLEGHENY; *225 WM-4; ★ PGH; mail Pittsburgh z 15203; pop. incl. with Pittsburgh (Inc. Place)
South Side; RMC Place; BUTLER; ▲ Butler; *225 WK-4; ★ BUTL; mail Butler z 16001
South Side; RMC Place; LACKAWANNA; ★ SCR-; mail Scranton z 18505; pop. incl. with Scranton (Inc. Place)
Southside; RMC Place; NORTHAMPTON; *227 EL-11; ★ ALL-; mail Bethlehem z 18015; pop. incl. with Bethlehem (Inc. Place)
South Sterling; RMC Place; WAYNE; ▲ Dreher; 226 EH-11; 🅿; z 18460; ● 150
South Strabane; MCD-Township; WASHINGTON; *225 WO-2; ★ WASH; mail Washington z 15301; Ⓟ 7,676; © 7,987
South Tamaqua; RMC Place; SCHUYLKILL; ▲ West Penn; 227 EK-9; mail Tamaqua z 18252; ● 200
South Temple; RMC Place; BERKS; ▲ Muhlenberg; 227 ER-13; ★ READ; mail Temple z 19560; ● 1,400
South Terrace; RMC Place; NORTHAMPTON; *227 EL-11; ★ ALL-; pop. incl. with Bethlehem (Inc. Place)
South Towanda; RMC Place; BRADFORD; ▲ Towanda; 226 EF-6; mail Towanda z 18848; ● 250
South Union; MCD-Township; FAYETTE; *225 WQ-5; ★ UNTN; mail Uniontown z 15401; Ⓟ 10,223; © 11,337
South Uniontown; RMC Place; FAYETTE; ▲ South Union; 225 WQ-5; ★ UNTN; mail Uniontown z 15401; ● 3,500
South Versailles; MCD-Township; ALLEGHENY; *225 WN-4; ★ PGH; mail Coulters z 15028; Ⓟ 515; © 351
Southview; RMC Place; WASHINGTON; ▲ Mount Pleasant, Cecil; 225 WN-2; elev. 1,099ft./335m.; 🅿; ★ PGH; z 15361; ● 240
Southwark; RMC Place; PHILADELPHIA; ★ PHIL-; mail Philadelphia z 19147; pop. incl. with Philadelphia (Inc. Place)
South Waverly; Inc. Place; BRADFORD; 226 ED-6; elev. 820ft./250m.; 🅿; z 18840 & mail Waverly z 14892; Ⓟ 1,049; © 987
Southwest; MCD-Township; WARREN; *224 WF-6; mail Titusville z 16354; Ⓟ 626; © 561
Southwest (Hecla); RMC Place; WESTMORELAND; ▲ Mount Pleasant; 225 WO-6; 🅿; z 15685; ● 600
Southwest Greensburg; Inc. Place; WESTMORELAND; 225 WN-6; elev. 1,080ft./329m.; ★ PGH; mail Greensburg z 15601; Ⓟ 2,456; © 2,398
Southwest Madison; MCD-Township; PERRY; *227 EN-2; mail Loysville z 17047; Ⓟ 745; © 856
South Whitehall; MCD-Township; LEHIGH; *227 EL-10; ★ ALL-; mail Allentown z 18104; Ⓟ 18,261; © 18,028
South Wilkes-Barre; RMC Place; LUZERNE; ★ SCR-; pop. incl. with Wilkes-Barre (Inc. Place)
South Williamsport; Inc. Place; LYCOMING; 226 EI-4; elev. 540ft./165m.; 🅿; ★ WMSPT; z 17702; Ⓟ 6,496; © 6,412
South Woodbury; MCD-Township; BEDFORD; *225 WO-11; mail New Enterprise z 16664; Ⓟ 1,839; © 2,000
Southwood Hills; RMC Place; YORK; ▲ Spring Garden; ★ YORK; mail York z 17403
Spaces Corners; RMC Place; ARMSTRONG; ▲ Rayburn; *225 WK-6; ★ PGH; mail Kittanning z 16201; ● 50
Spangenberg Lake; RMC Place; LACKAWANNA; ▲ Jefferson; *226 EG-11; elev. 1,579ft./481m.; ★ SCR-; mail Lake Ariel z 18436; summer pop. 300
Spangler; RMC Place; CAMBRIA; *225 WL-9; elev. 1,470ft./448m.; 🅿 🅷; z 15775; pop. incl. with Northern Cambria (Inc. Place); Ⓟ 2,068
Spangsville; RMC Place; BERKS; ▲ Oley; *227 EN-9; ★ READ; mail Boyertown z 19512; ● 60
Sparta; MCD-Township; CRAWFORD; *224 WE-5; mail Spartansburg z 16434; Ⓟ 1,554; © 1,740
Sparta; RMC Place; WASHINGTON; ▲ Morris; *225 WP-2; mail Prosperity z 15329
Spartansburg; Inc. Place; CRAWFORD; 224 WE-5; elev. 1,450ft./442m.; 🅿; z 16434; Ⓟ 403; © 333
Spears Grove; RMC Place; JUNIATA; ▲ Lack; *225 WN-14; mail East Waterford z 17021; rural
Speedwell; RMC Place; LANCASTER; ▲ Elizabeth; *227 EO-7; elev. 525ft./160m.; ★ LANC; mail Lititz z 17543; rural
Speers; Inc. Place; WASHINGTON; 225 WO-4; elev. 860ft./262m.; ★ PGH; mail Belle Vernon z 15012, Charleroi z 15022; Ⓟ 1,284; © 1,241
Spike Island; RMC Place; CENTRE; ▲ Rush; *225 WK-11; mail Osceola Mills z 16666; ● 40
Spillway Lake; RMC Place; FAYETTE; ▲ Franklin; *225 WP-4; ★ UNTN; mail Perryopolis z 15473; ● 25
Spindley City; RMC Place; CAMBRIA; ▲ Gallitzin; *225 WM-10; ★ ALT; mail Gallitzin z 16641; rural
Spinnerstown; RMC Place; BUCKS; ▲ Milford; 227 EM-11; 🅿; ★ PHIL-; z 18968; ● 350
Spinnlers Point; RMC Place; PIKE; ▲ Palmyra; *226 EG-12; elev. 1,300ft./396m.; mail Tafton z 18464; ● 150
Split Rock; RMC Place; CARBON; ▲ Kidder; *226 EJ-10; mail Lake Harmony z 18624; ● 400
Sporting Hill; RMC Place; CUMBERLAND; ▲ Hampden; 227 ET-2; ★ HRBG; mail Mechanicsburg z 17055; ● 200
Sporting Hill; RMC Place; LANCASTER; ▲ Rapho; 227 EO-6; elev. 499ft./152m.; mail Manheim z 17545; ● 300
Sportsburg; RMC Place; JEFFERSON; ▲ Young; *224 WJ-8; mail Punxsutawney z 15767; ● 65
Spraggs; RMC Place; GREENE; ▲ Wayne; 225 WQ-2; 🅿; z 15362; ● 30
Sprankle Mills; RMC Place; JEFFERSON; ▲ Oliver; 224 WJ-8; 🅿; z 15776; ● 60
Spring; MCD-Township; BERKS; *227 EN-8; ★ READ; mail Reading z 19609; Ⓟ 18,899; © 21,805; ◆ 23,811
Spring; MCD-Township; CENTRE; *225 WK-14; ★ STCOL; mail Bellefonte z 16823; Ⓟ 5,344; © 6,117
Spring; MCD-Township; CRAWFORD; *224 WE-2; mail Springboro z 16435; Ⓟ 1,561; © 1,571
Spring; MCD-Township; PERRY; *227 EN-3; mail Landisburg z 17040; Ⓟ 1,665; © 2,021
Spring; MCD-Township; SNYDER; *227 EK-3; mail Beaver Springs z 17812; Ⓟ 1,575; © 1,563
Spring Bank; RMC Place; CENTRE; ▲ Miles; *227 EK-2; mail Rebersburg z 16872; rural
Springboro; Inc. Place; CRAWFORD; 224 WE-2; elev. 910ft./277m.; 🅿; z 16435; Ⓟ 471; © 491
Spring Brook; MCD-Township; LACKAWANNA; *226 EH-10; mail Moscow z 18444; Ⓟ 2,097; © 2,367
Spring Church; RMC Place; ARMSTRONG; ▲ Kiskiminetas; 225 WL-6; 🅿; ★ PGH; z 15686; ● 450
Spring City; Inc. Place; CHESTER; 227 EO-10; elev. 150ft./46m.; 🅿; ★ PTSTN; z 19475; Ⓟ 3,433; © 3,305
Spring Creek; MCD-Township; ELK; *224 WH-9; mail Ridgway z 15853; Ⓟ 215; © 260
Spring Creek; RMC Place; LEHIGH; ▲ Lower Macungie; *227 EM-10; ★ ALL-; mail Alburtis z 18011; ● 80
Spring Creek; RMC Place; WARREN; ▲ Spring Creek; 224 WE-6; elev. 1,405ft./428m.; 🅿; z 16436; ● 100
Spring Creek; MCD-Township; WARREN; *224 WE-6; 🅿; z 16436; Ⓟ 843; © 872
Springdale; Inc. Place; ALLEGHENY; 225 WM-4; elev. 800ft./244m.; 🅿; ★ PGH; z 15144; Ⓟ 3,992; © 3,828
Springdale; MCD-Township; ALLEGHENY; *225 WM-4; 🅿; ★ PGH; z 15144 & mail Harwick z 15049; does not include the Borough of Springdale; Ⓟ 1,777; © 1,802
Springdell; RMC Place; CHESTER; ▲ West Marlborough; *227 EP-9; mail Coatesville z 19320; ● 100
Springettsbury; MCD-Township; YORK; *227 EP-5; ★ YORK; mail York z 17402; Ⓟ 21,564; © 23,883; ◆ 25,915
Springetts Manor-Yorklyn; CDP-Census Area Only; YORK; ▲ Springettsbury; *227 EP-5; elev. 420ft./128m.; ★ YORK; mail York z 17402; Ⓟ 3,433; © 4,156
Springfield; RMC Place; BRADFORD; ▲ Springfield; *226 EE-5; elev. 1,419ft./433m.; mail Columbia Cross Roads z 16914
Springfield; MCD-Township; BRADFORD; *226 EE-5; mail Milan z 18831; Ⓟ 1,118; © 1,167
Springfield; MCD-Township; BUCKS; *227 EM-11; ★ ALL-; mail Quakertown z 18951; Ⓟ 5,177; © 4,963
Springfield; CUMBERLAND; see Big Spring (RMC Place)
Springfield; CDP; DELAWARE; ▲ Springfield; 228 E-1; elev. 246ft./75m.; 🅿 🅷; ★ PHIL-; z 19064 & mail Philadelphia z 19118; Ⓟ 24,160; © 23,677; ◆ 23,525
Springfield; MCD-Township; DELAWARE; *227 EP-11; 🅿 ■; ★ PHIL-; z 19064 & mail Philadelphia z 19118; Ⓟ 24,160; © 23,677; ◆ 23,525
Springfield; MCD-Township; ERIE; *224 WD-2; ★ ERIE; mail East Springfield z 16411, West Springfield z 16443; Ⓟ 3,218; © 3,378
Springfield; MCD-Township; FAYETTE; *225 WP-6; mail Mill Run z 15464; Ⓟ 2,968; © 3,111
Springfield; MCD-Township; HUNTINGDON; *225 WO-12; mail Three Springs z 17264; Ⓟ 507; © 612
Springfield; MCD-Township; MERCER; *224 WI-3; mail Mercer z 16137; Ⓟ 1,892; © 1,972
Springfield; MCD-Township; MONTGOMERY; *227 EO-12; ★ PHIL-; mail Philadelphia z 19118; Ⓟ 19,612; © 19,533
Springfield; MCD-Township; YORK; *227 EQ-5; ★ YORK; mail Glen Rock z 17327; Ⓟ 3,918; © 3,889
Springfield Falls; RMC Place; MERCER; ▲ Springfield; *224 WI-3; elev. 1,210ft./369m.; mail Mercer z 16137; ● 20
Spring Garden; RMC Place; BUCKS; ▲ Northampton; *227 EO-13; ★ PHIL-; mail Newtown z 18940; ● 350
Spring Garden (Ledger); RMC Place; LANCASTER; ▲ Salisbury; *227 EP-8; elev. 445ft./136m.; mail Kinzers z 17535; ● 80
Spring Garden; RMC Place; PHILADELPHIA; ★ PHIL-; mail Philadelphia z 19122; pop. incl. with Philadelphia (Inc. Place)
Spring Garden; RMC Place; UNION; ▲ Gregg; 226 EI-4; mail Allenwood z 17810; ● 45
Spring Garden; RMC Place; WESTMORELAND; mail Mount Pleasant z 15666; pop. incl. with Mount Pleasant (Inc. Place)
Spring Garden; MCD-Township; YORK; *227 EP-5; ★ YORK; mail York z 17403; Ⓟ 11,207; © 11,974
Spring Glen; RMC Place; SCHUYLKILL; ▲ Hubley; 227 EL-5; 🅿; z 17978; ● 300
Spring Grove; Inc. Place; YORK; 227 EQ-4; elev. 467ft./142m.; 🅿; ★ YORK; z 17354, z 17362; Ⓟ 1,863; © 2,050
Spring Hill; RMC Place; ALLEGHENY; *225 WM-4; ★ PGH; mail Pittsburgh z 15212; pop. incl. with Pittsburgh (Inc. Place)
Springhill; RMC Place; BRADFORD; ▲ Tuscarora; *226 EF-7; elev. 1,293ft./394m.; mail Wyalusing z 18853; rural
Spring Hill; CDP; CAMBRIA; ▲ Portage; 225 WN-10; mail Portage z 15946; Ⓟ 1,014; © 970
Spring Hill; RMC Place; DELAWARE; ▲ Ridley; ★ PHIL-; mail Clifton Heights z 19018
Springhill; MCD-Township; FAYETTE; *225 WQ-4; ★ MORG; mail Smithfield z 15478; Ⓟ 2,800; © 2,974
Springhill; MCD-Township; GREENE; *225 WQ-1; mail New Freeport z 15352; Ⓟ 506; © 476
Springhope; RMC Place; BEDFORD; ▲ Napier, East St. Clair; 225 WO-10; mail Schellsburg z 15559; ● 50
Spring House; CDP; MONTGOMERY; ▲ Lower Gwynedd; 227 EO-12; 🅿; ★ PHIL-; z 19477; Ⓟ 2,782; © 3,290
Springhouse Farms; LEHIGH; see Wennersville (RMC Place)
Spring Meadow; RMC Place; BEDFORD; ▲ East St. Clair; *225 WO-10; mail New Paris z 15554; rural
Spring Meadows; RMC Place; BERKS; ▲ South Heidelberg; *227 EN-8; ★ READ; mail Wernersville z 19565; ● 400
Spring Mill; RMC Place; MONTGOMERY; ▲ Whitemarsh; *227 EO-12; ★ PHIL-; mail Conshohocken z 19428
Spring Mills; CDP; CENTRE; ▲ Gregg; 227 EK-1; 🅿; z 16875; © 289
Springmont; RMC Place; BERKS; ▲ Spring; 227 ET-11; ★ READ; mail Reading z 19609; ● 650
Spring Mount; RMC Place; HUNTINGDON; ▲ Warriors Mark; 225 WL-12; mail Warriors Mark z 16877; ● 75
Spring Mount; CDP; MONTGOMERY; ▲ Lower Frederick; 227 EN-11; 🅿; ★ PHIL-; z 19478; Ⓟ 1,365; © 2,205
Spring Ridge; CDP-Census Area Only; BERKS; *227 EN-8; ★ READ; © 786
Spring Run; RMC Place; FRANKLIN; ▲ Fannett; 225 WO-14; 🅿; z 17262; ● 350
Springs; RMC Place; SOMERSET; ▲ Elk Lick; 225 WQ-7; 🅿; z 15562; ● 300
Springtown; RMC Place; BUCKS; ▲ Springfield; 227 EM-12; 🅿; ★ ALL-; z 18081; ● 750
Springtown; RMC Place; FRANKLIN; ▲ Metal; *225 WO-13; mail Fannettsburg z 17221; rural
Springtown; RMC Place; LUZERNE; ▲ Dorrance; *226 EJ-8; ★ SCR-; mail Mountain Top z 18707; rural
Springtown; RMC Place; NORTHUMBERLAND; ▲ Delaware; *226 EI-4; ★ WMSPT; mail Watsontown z 17777; rural
Springvale; RMC Place; YORK; ▲ Windsor; 227 EQ-6; ★ YORK; mail Red Lion z 17356; ● 120
Spring Valley; RMC Place; BERKS; ▲ Muhlenberg; ★ READ; mail Temple z 19560; ● 120
Spring Valley (Mechanics Valley); RMC Place; BUCKS; ▲ Buckingham; *227 EN-12; ★ PHIL-; mail Doylestown z 18901; ● 100
Spring Valley; RMC Place; CLEARFIELD; ▲ Boggs; *224 WJ-11; mail West Decatur z 16878; ● 70
Spring Valley; RMC Place; NORTHAMPTON; ▲ Lower Saucon; *227 EM-11; ★ ALL-; mail Bethlehem z 18015; ● 250
Spring Valley Farms; RMC Place; BUCKS; ▲ Buckingham; *227 EN-12; elev. 400ft./122m.; ★ PHIL-; mail Doylestown z 18901; ● 100
Springville; RMC Place; CUMBERLAND; ▲ South Middleton; ★ CARL; mail Boiling Springs z 17007
Springville; RMC Place; LANCASTER; ▲ Salisbury; *227 EO-7; ★ LANC; mail Kinzers z 17535; ● 45
Springville; RMC Place; SUSQUEHANNA; ▲ Springville; 226 EF-9; elev. 1,265ft./386m.; 🅿; z 18844; ● 400
Springville; MCD-Township; SUSQUEHANNA; *226 EF-9; 🅿; z 18844; Ⓟ 1,424; © 1,555
Springville; RMC Place; VENANGO; ▲ Victory; *224 WH-4; mail Polk z 16342
Sproul; RMC Place; BLAIR; ▲ Greenfield; 225 WN-10; 🅿; ★ ALT; z 16682; ● 250
Spruce Creek; RMC Place; HUNTINGDON; ▲ Spruce Creek; 225 WL-12; 🅿; z 16683; ● 90
Spruce Creek; MCD-Township; HUNTINGDON; *225 WL-12; 🅿; z 16683; Ⓟ 281; © 263
Spruce Hill; RMC Place; JUNIATA; ▲ Spruce Hill; 227 EM-2; mail Port Royal z 17082; ● 40
Spruce Hill; MCD-Township; JUNIATA; *227 EM-1; mail Port Royal z 17082; Ⓟ 694; © 724
Spruces; RMC Place; CHESTER; *227 EP-9; ★ PHIL-; pop. incl. with South Coatesville (Inc. Place)
Sprucetown; RMC Place; FAYETTE; ▲ Springhill; *225 WQ-4; ★ MORG; mail Point Marion z 15474; rural
Spry; CDP; YORK; ▲ York; 225 WT-10; 🅿; ★ YORK; z 17402 & mail York z 17403; Ⓟ 4,271; © 4,903
Squab Hollow; RMC Place; ELK; ▲ Fox; *224 WH-10; elev. 1,743ft./531m.; mail Kersey z 15846; rural
Square Corner; RMC Place; ADAMS; ▲ Mount Pleasant; *227 EQ-3; ★ HANV; mail Gettysburg z 17325; rural
Squirrel Hill; RMC Place; ALLEGHENY; *225 WM-4; 🅿; ★ PGH; z 15217; pop. incl. with Pittsburgh (Inc. Place)
Stack Town; RMC Place; LANCASTER; ▲ Conoy; *227 EO-5; ★ HRBG; mail Bainbridge z 17502; ● 70
Stafore Estates; RMC Place; NORTHAMPTON; ▲ Hanover; 226 EA-4; ★ ALL-; mail Bethlehem z 18017; ● 1,200
Stahlstown; RMC Place; WESTMORELAND; ▲ Donegal, Cook; 225 WO-7; elev. 1,757ft./536m.; 🅿; z 15687; ● 300
Stairville; RMC Place; LUZERNE; ▲ Dorrance; *226 EI-8; elev. 998ft./304m.; ★ SCR-; mail Mountain Top z 18707, Wapwallopen z 18660; ● 100
Stalker; RMC Place; WAYNE; ▲ Manchester; *226 EE-12; elev. 832ft./254m.; mail Hankins z 12741; rural
Stambaugh; FAYETTE; see Youngstown (RMC Place)
Standard; RMC Place; WESTMORELAND; ▲ Mount Pleasant; *225 WO-6; mail Mount Pleasant z 15666
Standard Shaft; RMC Place; WESTMORELAND; ▲ Mount Pleasant; *225 WO-6; mail Mount Pleasant z 15666; ● 300
Standing Stone; RMC Place; BRADFORD; ▲ Standing Stone; 226 EF-7; elev. 704ft./215m.; mail Wysox z 18854; ● 60
Standing Stone; MCD-Township; BRADFORD; *226 EF-7; mail Wyalusing z 18853; Ⓟ 436; © 596
Stanhope; RMC Place; SCHUYLKILL; ▲ Pine Grove; *227 EM-7; mail Pine Grove z 17963; rural
Stanley; RMC Place; CLEARFIELD; ▲ Brady; *224 WJ-9; mail Du Bois z 15801; rural
Stanleys Corner; RMC Place; VENANGO; ▲ Cranberry; *224 WH-5; ★ OILC-F; mail Oil City z 16301; rural
Stanton; RMC Place; JEFFERSON; ▲ Rose; 224 WI-8; mail Brookville z 15825; ● 70
Stanton; RMC Place; LUZERNE; ▲ Exeter; *226 EH-9; ★ SCR-; mail Brookville z 15825; ● 100
Stanton Heights; RMC Place; ALLEGHENY; *225 WM-4; ★ PGH; mail Pittsburgh z 15201; pop. incl. with Pittsburgh (Inc. Place)
Stanton Heights; RMC Place; WESTMORELAND; *225 WO-5; ★ PGH; mail New Stanton z 15672; pop. incl. with New Stanton (Inc. Place)
Stanton Hill; RMC Place; LUZERNE; ▲ Wilkes-Barre; ★ SCR-
Stanwood (Stanwood Gardens); RMC Place; BUCKS; ▲ Bensalem; *227 EO-13; elev. 100ft./30m.; ★ PHIL-; mail Bensalem z 19020; ● 1,550
Stanwood Gardens; BUCKS; see Stanwood (RMC Place)
Starbrick; RMC Place; WARREN; ▲ Conewango; 224 WE-7; mail Warren z 16365; ● 800
Starford; RMC Place; INDIANA; ▲ Green; 225 WL-8; 🅿; z 15777; ● 250
Star Junction; RMC Place; FAYETTE; ▲ Perry; 225 WO-5; 🅿; ★ PGH; z 15482; ● 500
Starks; RMC Place; LACKAWANNA; *226 EH-9; ★ SCR-; pop. incl. with Moosic (Inc. Place)
Starkville; RMC Place; WYOMING; ▲ Nicholson; *226 EF-9; mail Tunkhannock z 18657
Starlight; RMC Place; WAYNE; ▲ Buckingham; 226 EE-11; 🅿; z 18461; ● 135
Starners Station; RMC Place; CUMBERLAND; ▲ Dickinson; *227 EP-3; ★ CARL; mail Gardners z 17324; rural
Starr; RMC Place; FOREST; ▲ Kingsley; *224 WG-7; mail Tionesta z 16353
Starr; RMC Place; WARREN; ▲ Eldred; *224 WF-6; mail Grand Valley z 16420; rural
Starrucca; Inc. Place; WAYNE; 226 EE-11; elev. 1,310ft./399m.; 🅿; z 18462; Ⓟ 199; © 216
Starview; RMC Place; YORK; ▲ East Manchester; 227 EP-5; elev. 588ft./179m.; ★ YORK; mail Mount Wolf z 17347; ● 100
Starview Heights; RMC Place; YORK; ▲ York; *227 EP-5; ★ YORK; mail York z 17402; ● 450
State College; Inc. Place; CENTRE; 225 WK-13; elev. 1,154ft./352m.; 🅿 🅷 🅲 42,039 ■; ★ STCOL; z 16801-05; Ⓟ 38,923; © 38,420; ◆ 40,580
State Hill; RMC Place; BERKS; ▲ Lower Heidelberg; 227 EN-8; ★ READ; mail Reading z 19608; ● 40
State Hill; RMC Place; CHESTER; ▲ West Sadsbury, Sadsbury; *227 EP-9; ★ PHIL-; mail Gap z 17527; rural
State Line; RMC Place; BEDFORD; ▲ Londonderry; 224 WC-5; mail Hyndman z 15545; ● 20
Stateline; RMC Place; ERIE; ▲ North East; *224 WC-5; elev. 802ft./244m.; ★ ERIE; mail North East z 16428; ● 20
State Line; RMC Place; FRANKLIN; ▲ Antrim; 225 WR-14; 🅿; ★ HAG; z 17263; ● 1,100
Steamburg; RMC Place; CRAWFORD; ▲ Conneaut; *224 WE-2; mail Linesville z 16424
Steam Valley; RMC Place; LYCOMING; ▲ Cogan House; *226 EG-3; mail Trout Run z 17771; rural
Steel City; RMC Place; NORTHAMPTON; ▲ Lower Saucon; 226 EA-5; elev. 291ft./89m.; ★ ALL-; mail Bethlehem z 18015; ● 650
Steelstown; RMC Place; LEBANON; ▲ North Annville; 227 EN-6; elev. 536ft./163m.; ★ LEB; mail Annville z 17003; ● 100
Steelton; Inc. Place; DAUPHIN; 227 EO-5; elev. 314ft./96m.; 🅿; ★ HRBG; z 17113; Ⓟ 5,152; © 5,858
Steelville; RMC Place; CHESTER; ▲ West Fallowfield; *227 EQ-8; 🅿; z 19310; ● 35
Steene; RMC Place; WAYNE; ▲ Canaan; *226 EF-11; ★ SCR-; mail Waymart z 18472; rural
Steinbachs Corner; RMC Place; SUSQUEHANNA; ▲ Jackson; *226 EE-10; mail Susquehanna z 18847; rural
Steinsburg; RMC Place; BUCKS; ▲ Milford; 227 EM-11; ★ PHIL-; mail Quakertown z 18951; ● 100
Steinsville; RMC Place; LEHIGH; ▲ Lynn; *227 EL-9; ★ ALL-; mail Kempton z 19529; ● 50
Stemlersville; RMC Place; CARBON; ▲ Towamensing; *227 EK-10; mail Lehighton z 18235; ● 40
Sterling; RMC Place; CLEARFIELD; ▲ Woodward; *225 WK-11; mail Houtzdale z 16651; ● 50
Sterling; RMC Place; WAYNE; ▲ Sterling; 226 EH-11; 🅿; z 18463; ● 150
Sterling; MCD-Township; WAYNE; *226 EH-11; 🅿; z 18463 & mail Newfoundland z 18445; Ⓟ 974; © 1,251
Sterling Run; RMC Place; CAMERON; ▲ Lumber; 224 WH-12; mail Driftwood z 15832; ● 120
Sterlingworth; RMC Place; LEHIGH; ▲ South Whitehall; *227 EL-10; ★ ALL-; mail Allentown z 18104; ● 550
Sterrettania; RMC Place; ERIE; ▲ McKean, Fairview; *224 WD-3; elev. 887ft./270m.; ★ ERIE; mail Fairview z 16415
Stetlersville; RMC Place; LEHIGH; ▲ South Whitehall; *227 EM-10; ★ ALL-; mail Orefield z 18069
Steuben; MCD-Township; CRAWFORD; *224 WF-4; mail Centerville z 16404; Ⓟ 820; © 908
Stevens; MCD-Township; BRADFORD; *226 EF-7; mail Wysox z 18854; Ⓟ 401; © 414
Stevens; RMC Place; LANCASTER; ▲ East Cocalico; 227 EO-8; 🅿; z 17578; ● 400
Stevens Point; RMC Place; SUSQUEHANNA; ▲ Harmony; *226 ED-10; mail Susquehanna z 18847; ● 100
Stevenstown; RMC Place; YORK; ▲ Carroll; *227 EO-4; ★ HRBG; mail Dillsburg z 17019; rural
Stevensville; RMC Place; BRADFORD; ▲ Stevens; 226 EF-7; elev. 865ft./264m.; 🅿; z 18845; ● 250
Stewardson; MCD-Township; POTTER; *224 WG-14; mail Cross Fork z 17729; Ⓟ 66; © 74
Stewart; MCD-Township; FAYETTE; *225 WP-6; mail Ohiopyle z 15470; Ⓟ 734; © 743
Stewart Run; RMC Place; FOREST; ▲ Harmony; *224 WG-6; elev. 1,556ft./474m.; mail Pleasantville z 16341; rural
Stewartstown; Inc. Place; YORK; 227 EQ-6; elev. 860ft./262m.; 🅿; ★ BAL; z 17363; Ⓟ 1,308; © 1,752
Stewartsville; RMC Place; WESTMORELAND; ▲ North Huntingdon; 228 M-10; ★ PGH; mail Irwin z 15642; ● 700
Stickney; RMC Place; MCKEAN; ▲ Corydon; *224 WD-9; mail Bradford z 16701
Sticks; RMC Place; YORK; ▲ Codorus; *227 EQ-5; ★ BAL; mail Glenville z 17329; rural
Stiefler Corner; RMC Place; BEDFORD; ▲ Kimmel; *225 WN-10; elev. 1,460ft./445m.; ★ ALT; mail Queen z 16670; rural
Stier (Johnsonville); RMC Place; NORTHAMPTON; ▲ Upper Mount Bethel; *227 EK-12; mail Bangor z 18013; ● 100
Stifflertown; RMC Place; CLEARFIELD; ▲ Burnside; 225 WL-9; mail Cherry Tree z 15724; ● 120
Stiles (West Coplay); RMC Place; LEHIGH; ▲ Whitehall; 226 EA-2; ★ ALL-; mail Whitehall z 18052; ● 800
Stiles Hill; RMC Place; POTTER; ▲ Hector; *226 EE-1; mail Sabinsville z 16943; rural
Still Creek; RMC Place; SCHUYLKILL; ▲ Rush; *227 EK-8; mail Tamaqua z 18252; ● 180
Stilleys Siding; RMC Place; ALLEGHENY; ★ PGH; pop. incl. with Jefferson (Inc. Place)
Stillwater; Inc. Place; COLUMBIA; 226 EI-7; elev. 700ft./213m.; 🅿; z 17878; Ⓟ 223; © 194
Stillwater Lake Estates; RMC Place; MONROE; ▲ Coolbaugh; *226 EI-11; mail Pocono Summit z 18346; ● 450
Stiltz; RMC Place; YORK; ▲ Codorus; 227 ER-5; elev. 966ft./294m.; ★ BAL; mail Glen Rock z 17327; ● 50
Stines Corner; RMC Place; LEHIGH; ▲ Lynn; *227 EL-9; ★ ALL-; mail New Tripoli z 18066; rural
Stobo; RMC Place; BEAVER; ▲ Center; *225 WL-2; ★ PGH; mail Monaca z 15061; ● 300
Stockdale; Inc. Place; WASHINGTON; 225 WO-4; elev. 765ft./233m.; 🅿; ★ PGH; z 15483; Ⓟ 630; © 555
Stockertown; Inc. Place; NORTHAMPTON; 227 EK-12; elev. 540ft./165m.; 🅿; ★ ALL-; z 18083; Ⓟ 641; © 687
Stockton; RMC Place; LUZERNE; ▲ Hazle; *226 EJ-9; ★ HAZ; mail Hazleton z 18201; ● 150
Stockton Number Eight; RMC Place; LUZERNE; ▲ Hazle; ★ HAZ; mail Hazleton z 18201
Stockton Number Seven; RMC Place; LUZERNE; ▲ Hazle; ★ HAZ; mail Hazleton z 18201; ● 100
Stockton Number Six; RMC Place; LUZERNE; ▲ Hazle; ★ HAZ; mail Hazleton z 18201
Stockyards; RMC Place; PHILADELPHIA; ★ PHIL-; pop. incl. with Philadelphia (Inc. Place)
Stoddartsville; RMC Place; LUZERNE, MONROE; ▲ Tobyhanna, Buck; 226 EI-10; mail Blakeslee z 18610; ● 130
Stokesdale; RMC Place; TIOGA; ▲ Tobyhanna; *226 EE-2; elev. 1,192ft./363m.; mail Wellsboro z 16901
Stoneboro; Inc. Place; MERCER; 224 WH-3; elev. 1,184ft./361m.; 🅿; z 16153; Ⓟ 1,091; © 1,104
Stone Church (Centerville); RMC Place; NORTHAMPTON; ▲ Upper Mount Bethel; 227 EK-12; mail Mount Bethel z 18343; ● 150
Stone Glen; RMC Place; DAUPHIN; ▲ Middle Paxton; *227 EN-4; ★ HRBG; mail Dauphin z 17018
Stoneham; RMC Place; WARREN; ▲ Mead; 224 WE-8; mail Clarendon z 16313; ● 250
Stone Hill; RMC Place; LANCASTER; ▲ Conestoga; *227 EP-7; ★ LANC; mail Conestoga z 17516; rural
Stone House; RMC Place; CLARION; ▲ Clarion; *224 WI-6; elev. 1,402ft./427m.; mail Strattanville z 16258; rural
Stonehurst; RMC Place; BUCKS; ▲ Upper Southampton; ★ PHIL-; mail Huntingdon Valley z 19006
Stonerstown; RMC Place; BEDFORD; ▲ Liberty; 225 WO-11; mail Saxton z 16678; ● 250
Stonersville; RMC Place; BERKS; ▲ Exeter; 227 EN-9; elev. 289ft./88m.; ★ READ; mail Birdsboro z 19508; ● 200
Stonetown; RMC Place; BERKS; ▲ Exeter; *227 EN-9; ★ READ; mail Birdsboro z 19508; ● 120
Stonevilla; RMC Place; WESTMORELAND; ▲ Hempfield; *225 WN-6; ★ PGH; mail Greensburg z 15601; ● 600
Stoneybreak; RMC Place; FULTON; ▲ Bethel; *225 WQ-11; mail Warfordsburg z 17267; rural
Stonington; RMC Place; NORTHUMBERLAND; ▲ Shamokin; 227 EK-5; mail Sunbury z 17801; ● 100
Stonybrook; RMC Place; BUCKS; ▲ Bristol; *227 EO-14; ★ PHIL-
Stonybrook; RMC Place; YORK; ▲ Springettsbury; 227 EP-5; ★ YORK; mail York z 17402; ● 1,500
Stonybrook Heights; RMC Place; YORK; ▲ Springettsbury; ★ YORK; mail York z 17402
Stonybrook-Wilshire; CDP-Census Area Only; YORK; ▲ Springettsbury, Windsor; *227 EP-5; elev. 472ft./144m.; ★ YORK; mail York z 17402; Ⓟ 4,887; © 5,414
Stonycreek; MCD-Township; CAMBRIA; *225 WN-9; ★ JNST; mail Johnstown z 15904; Ⓟ 3,562; © 3,204
Stonycreek; MCD-Township; SOMERSET; *225 WP-9; mail Friedens z 15541; Ⓟ 2,083; © 2,221
Stony Creek Mills; RMC Place; BERKS; ▲ Lower Alsace, Exeter; 227 ET-13; ★ READ; mail Reading z 19606; ● 2,500
Stonyfork; RMC Place; TIOGA; ▲ Delmar; 226 EF-2; mail Wellsboro z 16901; ● 150
Stony Point; RMC Place; BUCKS; ▲ Springfield; ★ ALL-; mail Kintnersville z 18930; ● 30
Stony Point; RMC Place; CRAWFORD; ▲ Sadsbury; *224 WF-2; elev. 1,286ft./392m.; mail Conneaut Lake z 16316; rural
Stony Point; RMC Place; FRANKLIN; ▲ Metal; *225 WO-13; mail Spring Run z 17262; rural
Stony Point; RMC Place; GREENE; ▲ Morgan; *225 WP-3; elev. 985ft./300m.; mail Jefferson z 15344; ● 15
Stony Run; RMC Place; BERKS; ▲ Albany; 227 EL-9; 🅿; z 19529; ● 225
Stoopville; BUCKS; see Newtown Grant (CDP-Census Area Only)
Stormstown; CDP; CENTRE; ▲ Halfmoon; 225 WK-12; elev. 1,329ft./405m.; mail Port Matilda z 16870; © 1,602
Stormville; RMC Place; MONROE; ▲ Hamilton; *226 EJ-12; mail Stroudsburg z 18360
Stouchsburg; RMC Place; BERKS; ▲ Marion; 227 EN-7; 🅿; z 19567; ● 150
Stoufferstown; RMC Place; FRANKLIN; ▲ Guilford; 225 WP-14; mail Chambersburg z 17201; ● 400
Stoughstown; RMC Place; CUMBERLAND; ▲ South Newton, North Newton; 227 EO-2; mail Shippensburg z 17257; ● 75
Stover; RMC Place; HUNTINGDON; ▲ Warriors Mark; *225 WL-12; mail Tyrone z 16686; rural
Stoverdale; RMC Place; DAUPHIN; ▲ Derry; *227 EO-5; ★ HRBG; mail Hummelstown z 17036; ● 100
Stoverstown; RMC Place; YORK; ▲ North Codorus; 227 EQ-5; elev. 607ft./185m.; ★ YORK; mail Spring Grove z 17362; ● 250
Stowe; MCD-Township; ALLEGHENY; *225 WM-3; ★ PGH; mail Mc Kees Rocks z 15136; Ⓟ 7,681; © 6,706
Stowe; CDP; MONTGOMERY; ▲ West Pottsgrove; 227 EN-10; 🅿; ★ PTSTN; z 19464; Ⓟ 3,598; © 3,585
Stowell; RMC Place; WYOMING; ▲ Windham; 226 EG-7; mail Laceyville z 18623; ● 60
Stowe Township; CDP-Census Area Only; ALLEGHENY; ▲ Stowe; *225 WM-3; ★ PGH; mail Mc Kees Rocks z 15136; Ⓟ 7,681; © 6,706
Stoystown; Inc. Place; SOMERSET; 225 WO-8; elev. 2,000ft./610m.; 🅿; z 15563; Ⓟ 389; © 428
Straban; MCD-Township; ADAMS; *227 EQ-3; mail Gettysburg z 17325; Ⓟ 4,565; © 4,539
Strabane; RMC Place; WASHINGTON; ▲ North Strabane; 225 WN-3; 🅿; ★ PGH; z 15363; ● 1,100
Strafford; RMC Place; CHESTER; ▲ Tredyffrin; 227 EP-11; 🅿; ★ PHIL-; z 19087; ● 4,500
Strangford; RMC Place; INDIANA; ▲ Burrell; *225 WM-7; ★ LTROB; mail Blairsville z 15717; ● 120
Strasburg; Inc. Place; LANCASTER; 227 EP-7; elev. 480ft./146m.; 🅿; ★ LANC; z 17579; Ⓟ 2,568; © 2,800
Strasburg; MCD-Township; LANCASTER; *227 EP-7; 🅿; ★ LANC; z 17579 & mail Lancaster z 17602; Ⓟ 3,688; © 4,021
Strattanville (Strattonville); Inc. Place; CLARION; 224 WI-7; elev. 1,531ft./467m.; 🅿; z 16258; Ⓟ 490; © 542
Strattonville; CLARION; see Strattanville (Inc. Place)
Strausstown; Inc. Place; BERKS; 227 EM-7; elev. 560ft./171m.; 🅿; z 19559; Ⓟ 353; © 339
Strawberry Ridge; RMC Place; MONTOUR; ▲ Derry; 226 EJ-5; elev. 539ft./164m.; mail Danville z 17821; ● 30
Strawbridge; RMC Place; LYCOMING; ▲ Penn; *226 EH-5; mail Muncy Valley z 17758; rural
Strickersville; RMC Place; CHESTER; *227 ER-9; ★ PHIL-; mail Landenberg z 19350; ● 35
Strickhousers; RMC Place; YORK; ▲ North Codorus; *227 EQ-5; ★ YORK; mail Seven Valleys z 17360; rural
Stricklerstown; RMC Place; LEBANON; ▲ Millcreek; *227 EN-7; elev. 525ft./160m.; mail Newmanstown z 17073; rural
Strinestown; RMC Place; YORK; ▲ Conewago; 227 EO-5; ★ YORK; mail Manchester z 17345; ● 250
Stringtown; RMC Place; ARMSTRONG; ▲ Manor; *225 WK-6; ★ PGH; mail Ford City z 16226; ● 300
Stringtown; RMC Place; GREENE; ▲ Cumberland; *225 WP-4; mail Carmichaels z 15320; rural
Strobleton; RMC Place; CLARION; ▲ Washington; *224 WH-6; mail Tionesta z 16353; rural
Strodes Mills; RMC Place; MIFFLIN; ▲ Granville; 225 WM-14; mail Lewistown z 17044; ● 350
Stronach; RMC Place; CLEARFIELD; ▲ Penn; *224 WJ-10; mail Curwensville z 16833; ● 50
Strong; RMC Place; NORTHUMBERLAND; ▲ Mount Carmel; *227 EK-6; mail Mount Carmel z 17851; ● 215
Strongstown; RMC Place; INDIANA; ▲ Pine; 225 WM-8; elev. 1,895ft./578m.; 🅿; z 15957; ● 400
Stroud; MCD-Township; MONROE; *226 EJ-12; mail Stroudsburg z 18360; Ⓟ 10,600; © 13,978
Stroudsburg; Inc. Place; ⊡ MONROE; 226 EJ-12; elev. 430ft./131m.; 🅿 ■; z 18360; Ⓟ 5,312; © 5,756; ◆ 5,720
Stroudsburg West; RMC Place; MONROE; ▲ Stroud; *226 EJ-12; mail Stroudsburg z 18360; ● 1,000
Struthers; RMC Place; WARREN; pop. incl. with Warren (Inc. Place)
Studa; RMC Place; WASHINGTON; ▲ Cross Creek; 225 WN-2; elev. 1,004ft./306m.; mail Avella z 15312; ● 100
Stull; RMC Place; WYOMING; ▲ Noxen; *226 EH-8; mail Noxen z 18636; rural
Stump Creek (Cramer); RMC Place; JEFFERSON; ▲ Henderson; 224 WJ-9; 🅿; z 15863; ● 300
Stumptown; RMC Place; CLEARFIELD; ▲ Decatur; *225 WK-11; mail Osceola Mills z 16666; ● 200
Sturgeon; RMC Place; ALLEGHENY; ▲ South Fayette, North Fayette; 225 WN-3; 🅿; ★ PGH; z 15082; ● 1,000
Sturgeon-Noblestown; CDP-Census Area Only; ALLEGHENY; ▲ North Fayette, South Fayette; *225 WM-3; ★ PGH; mail Oakdale z 15071, Sturgeon z 15082; Ⓟ 1,350; © 1,764
Sturges (Sturgis); RMC Place; LACKAWANNA; *226 EG-10; ★ SCR-; mail Olyphant z 18447; pop. incl. with Archbald (Inc. Place)
Sturgis; LACKAWANNA; see Sturges (RMC Place)
Suburban Village; RMC Place; CHESTER; ▲ West Goshen; *227 EP-10; ★ PHIL-; mail West Chester z 19380; ● 700
Suedberg (Suedburg); RMC Place; SCHUYLKILL; ▲ Pine Grove; 227 EM-6; mail Pine Grove z 17963; ● 200
Suedburg; SCHUYLKILL; see Suedberg (RMC Place)
Sugarcreek; MCD-Township; ARMSTRONG; *224 WJ-5; mail Chicora z 16025, East Brady z 16028; Ⓟ 1,496; © 1,557
Sugarcreek; Inc. Place; VENANGO; 224 WG-4; elev. 1,035ft./315m.; ★ OILC-F; mail Franklin z 16323; Ⓟ 5,532; © 5,331
Sugar Grove; GREENE; see McCracken (RMC Place)
Sugar Grove; MCD-Township; MERCER; *224 WG-2; mail Greenville z 16125; Ⓟ 987; © 909
Sugar Grove; Inc. Place; WARREN; 224 WD-7; elev. 1,400ft./427m.; 🅿; z 16350; Ⓟ 604; © 613
Sugar Grove; MCD-Township; WARREN; *224 WD-7; 🅿; z 16350; does not include the Borough of Sugar Grove; Ⓟ 1,745; © 1,870
Sugar Hill; RMC Place; JEFFERSON; ▲ Snyder; 224 WI-9; mail Brockway z 15824; ● 60
Sugarloaf; MCD-Township; COLUMBIA; *226 EH-6; mail Benton z 17814; Ⓟ 730; © 885
Sugarloaf; LUZERNE; see Tomhicken (RMC Place)
Sugarloaf; MCD-Township; LUZERNE; *226 EJ-8; 🅿; ★ HAZ; z 18249 & mail Sybertsville z 18251; Ⓟ 3,534; © 3,652
Sugar Notch; Inc. Place; LUZERNE; 226 EI-9; elev. 740ft./226m.; 🅿; ★ SCR-; z 18706; Ⓟ 1,044; © 1,023
Sugar Run; RMC Place; BRADFORD; ▲ Wilmot; 226 EF-7; elev. 665ft./203m.; 🅿; z 18846; ● 100
Sugartown; RMC Place; CHESTER; ▲ Willistown; *227 EP-11; ★ PHIL-; mail Malvern z 19355
Sullivan; MCD-Township; TIOGA; *226 EF-4; mail Mainesburg z 16932; Ⓟ 1,140; © 1,322
SULLIVAN; 226 EH-6; Ⓟ 6,104; © 6,556; ◆ 6,223
Summerdale; RMC Place; CUMBERLAND; ▲ East Pennsboro; 227 ES-2; 🅿 🅲 1,115; ★ HRBG; z 17093; ● 800
Summerhill; Inc. Place; CAMBRIA; 225 WN-9; elev. 1,540ft./469m.; 🅿; ★ JNST; z 15958; Ⓟ 614; © 521
Summerhill; MCD-Township; CAMBRIA; *225 WM-9; 🅿; ★ JNST; z 15958 & mail Beaverdale z 15921; not adjacent to the Borough of Summerhill; Ⓟ 2,798; © 2,724
Summer Hill; RMC Place; COLUMBIA; ▲ Briar Creek; 226 EI-7; elev. 1,042ft./318m.; mail Berwick z 18603; ● 350
Summerhill; MCD-Township; CRAWFORD; *224 WE-2; mail Conneautville z 16406; Ⓟ 1,264; © 1,350
Summerhill; RMC Place; LANCASTER; ▲ Little Britain; *227 EQ-8; mail Nottingham z 19362; rural
Summerson; RMC Place; ELK; ▲ Benezette; *224 WH-11; elev. 1,000ft./305m.; mail Benezett z 15821; rural
Summersville; SUSQUEHANNA; see Tingley (RMC Place)
Summerville; Inc. Place; JEFFERSON; 224 WI-7; elev. 1,163ft./354m.; 🅿; z 15864; Ⓟ 675; © 525
Summit; MCD-Township; BUTLER; *225 WK-4; elev. 1,411ft./430m.; ★ BUTL; mail Butler z 16001; Ⓟ 4,284; © 4,728
Summit; RMC Place; CAMBRIA; ▲ Cresson; 225 WM-10; mail Cresson z 16630; ● 250
Summit; MCD-Township; CRAWFORD; *224 WF-2; mail Conneaut Lake z 16316; Ⓟ 1,890; © 2,172
Summit; MCD-Township; ERIE; *224 WD-4; ★ ERIE; mail Erie z 16509; Ⓟ 5,284; © 5,529
Summit; RMC Place; MCKEAN; ▲ Otto; *224 WD-10; elev. 2,141ft./653m.; mail Bradford z 16701; rural
Summit; MCD-Township; POTTER; *224 WF-13; mail Austin z 16720, Coudersport z 16915; Ⓟ 115; © 112
Summit; MCD-Township; SOMERSET; *225 WQ-8; mail Meyersdale z 15552; Ⓟ 2,495; © 2,368
Summit Grove Camp; RMC Place; YORK; *227 ER-5; ★ BAL; mail New Freedom z 17349; pop. incl. with New Freedom (Inc. Place)
Summit Hill; Inc. Place; CARBON; 227 EK-9; 🅿; z 18250; Ⓟ 3,332; © 2,974
Summit Lawn; RMC Place; LEHIGH; ▲ Upper Saucon; 226 EC-3; ★ ALL-; mail Allentown z 18103; ● 420
Summit Mills; RMC Place; SOMERSET; ▲ Summit; 225 WQ-8; mail Meyersdale z 15552; ● 175
Summit Station; CDP; SCHUYLKILL; ▲ Wayne; 227 EM-7; 🅿; ★ PTSVL; z 17979; © 208
Sumneytown; RMC Place; MONTGOMERY; ▲ Marlborough; 227 EN-11; 🅿; ★ PHIL-; z 18084; ● 400
Sunbrook; RMC Place; BLAIR; ▲ Allegheny; 224 WB-12; ★ ALT; mail Duncansville z 16635; ● 300
Sunbury; Inc. Place; ⊡ NORTHUMBERLAND; 227 EK-5; elev. 440ft./134m.; 🅿 🅷 ■; z 17801 & mail Snydertown z 17877; Ⓟ 11,591; © 10,610; ◆ 9,958
Suncliff; RMC Place; INDIANA; ▲ Brush Valley; *225 WM-8; elev. 1,340ft./408m.; mail Penn Run z 15765; rural
Sundale; RMC Place; BUCKS; ▲ Tinicum; *227 EM-12; ★ PHIL-; mail Erwinna z 18920; ● 60
Sunderlinville; RMC Place; POTTER; ▲ Hector; 224 WE-14; elev. 1,734ft./529m.; mail Sabinsville z 16943; ● 50
Sunnybrook; RMC Place; MONTGOMERY; ▲ Springfield; *227 EO-12; ★ PHIL-; mail Oreland z 19075; ● 1,300
Sunnyburn; RMC Place; YORK; ▲ Lower Chanceford; 227 EQ-7; mail Airville z 17302; ● 80
Sunny Point; RMC Place; WAYNE; ▲ Paupack; *226 EG-12; elev. 1,200ft./366m.; mail Hawley z 18428; ● 400
Sunny Side; RMC Place; ALLEGHENY; ▲ Forward; *225 WO-4; ★ PGH; mail Monongahela z 15063; ● 200
Sunnyside; RMC Place; ARMSTRONG; ▲ Rayburn; *225 WK-6; ★ PGH; mail Kittanning z 16201; ● 50
Sunny Side; RMC Place; BEDFORD; ▲ Hopewell; *225 WO-11; mail Hopewell z 16650; rural
Sunnyside; RMC Place; LANCASTER; *227 EP-7; ★ LANC; pop. incl. with Lancaster (Inc. Place)
Sunnyside; RMC Place; LAWRENCE; ▲ North Beaver; *224 WJ-2; elev. 1,112ft./339m.; ★ YNGS-; mail New Castle z 16101; ● 125
Sunnyside; RMC Place; LEBANON; ★ LEB; mail Lebanon z 17042; pop. incl. with Cleona (Inc. Place)
Sunnyside; RMC Place; NORTHUMBERLAND; ▲ Ralpho; *227 EK-6; mail Shamokin z 17872; ● 170

Entries in UPPERCASE are counties.
Entries in **bold** have populations of 2,500 or more.
Names in parentheses are alternate names.
Inc. Place — Incorporated Place
RMC Place — Rand McNally Designated Place
CDP — Census Designated Place
MCD — Minor Civil Division

⊡ County Seat
▲ Minor Civil Division
elev. Elevation
🅿 Post Office
🅷 Hospital
🅲 College
■ Principal Business Center
★ Ranally Metro Area (RMA) Abbreviation
z Zip Code(s)
Ⓟ Previous Census Population
Ⓡ Revised Census Population
Ⓐ Annexation Population
● Rand McNally Population Estimate
© Final Census Population
Ⓢ Special Census Population
◆ Estimated Population

For additional definitions see Glossary, Volume 1, and Introduction, Volume 2.

Sunrise Lake; RMC Place; PIKE; ▲ Dingman; ***226** EH-13; elev. 1,400ft./427m.; mail Milford **z** 18337; ● 600
Sunset Acres; RMC Place; INDIANA; ▲ White; ***225** WL-7; mail Indiana **z** 15701; ● 400
Sunset Grove; RMC Place; CHESTER; ▲ West Whiteland; ***227** EP-10; ★ **PHIL-**; mail West Chester **z** 19380; ● 800
Sunset Hills; RMC Place; BEAVER; ***225** WL-2; ★ **PGH**; mail Freedom **z** 15042
Sunset Manor; RMC Place; YORK; ▲ West Manchester; ★ **YORK**; mail York **z** 17405
Sunset Pines; RMC Place; CLINTON; ***226** EI-2; ★ **WMSPT**; mail Lock Haven **z** 17745; pop. incl. with Lock Haven (Inc. Place)
Sunset Valley; RMC Place; WESTMORELAND; ▲ North Huntingdon; **228** N-10; ★ **PGH**; mail Irwin **z** 15642; ● 2,700
Sunset Village; RMC Place; PIKE; ▲ Palmyra; ***226** EH-12; mail Paupack **z** 18451; ● 80
Sunshine; RMC Place; LUZERNE; ▲ Huntington; ***226** EI-7; mail Shickshinny **z** 18655; rural
Sun Valley; RMC Place; MONROE; ▲ Chestnuthill; ***226** EJ-11; ★ **ALL-**; mail Effort **z** 18330; ● 700
Sun Village; RMC Place; DELAWARE; ★ **PHIL-**; mail Chester **z** 19013; pop. incl. with Chester (Inc. Place)
Sunville; RMC Place; VENANGO; ▲ Plum; **224** WG-4; elev. 1,436ft./438m.; mail Cooperstown **z** 16317; ● 30
Superior; RMC Place; FAYETTE; ▲ Luzerne; ***225** WP-4; ★ **UNTN**; mail Brownsville **z** 15417; ● 40
Superior; RMC Place; WESTMORELAND; ▲ Derry; ***225** WN-6; ★ **LTROB**; mail Derry **z** 15627; rural
Suplee; RMC Place; CHESTER; ▲ Honey Brook; ***227** EO-9; 🅿; ★ **PHIL-**; **z** 19371; ● 70
Surveyor (Surveyor Mine); RMC Place; CLEARFIELD; ▲ Girard; **224** WJ-11; mail Clearfield **z** 16830; ● 35
Surveyor Mine; CLEARFIELD; see Surveyor (RMC Place)
Suscon; RMC Place; LUZERNE; ▲ Pittston; **226** EH-9; ★ **SCR-**; mail Pittston **z** 18641; ● 700
Susquehanna; MCD-Township; CAMBRIA; ***225** WL-9; mail Northern Cambria **z** 15714; Ⓟ 2,299; Ⓒ 2,198
Susquehanna; MCD-Township; DAUPHIN; ***227** EN-4; ★ **HRBG**; mail Harrisburg **z** 17109; Ⓟ 18,636; Ⓒ 21,895; ◆ 23,537
Susquehanna; MCD-Township; JUNIATA; ***227** EL-4; mail Liverpool **z** 17045; Ⓟ 1,022; Ⓒ 1,261
Susquehanna; MCD-Township; LYCOMING; ***226** EI-4; ★ **WMSPT**; mail Williamsport **z** 17701; Ⓟ 1,046; Ⓒ 993
Susquehanna (Susquehanna Depot); Inc. Place; SUSQUEHANNA; **226** ED-10; elev. 920ft./280m.; 🅿 🅷; ★ **BING**; **z** 18847; Ⓟ 1,760; Ⓒ 1,690
SUSQUEHANNA; **226** EE-9; Ⓟ 40,380; Ⓒ 42,238; ◆ 40,289
Susquehanna Bridge; RMC Place; CLEARFIELD; ▲ Lawrence; ***224** WJ-10; mail Clearfield **z** 16830; ● 90
Susquehanna Depot; SUSQUEHANNA; see Susquehanna (Inc. Place)
Susquehanna Trails; CDP-Census Area Only; YORK; ▲ Peach Bottom; ***227** EQ-7; elev. 500ft./152m.; ★ **BAL**; mail Delta **z** 17314; Ⓟ 1,419; Ⓒ 2,134
Suter; WESTMORELAND; see Sutersville (Inc. Place)
Sutersville (Suter, Suterville); Inc. Place; WESTMORELAND; **225** WN-4; elev. 800ft./244m.; 🅿; ★ **PGH**; **z** 15083; Ⓟ 755; Ⓒ 636
Suterville; WESTMORELAND; see Sutersville (Inc. Place)
Swales; RMC Place; JUNIATA; ▲ Fayette; ***227** EL-3; mail Mc Alisterville **z** 17049; rural
Swamproot; RMC Place; MERCER; ▲ Pine; ***224** WI-3; elev. 1,282ft./391m.; mail Grove City **z** 16127; rural
Swanville; RMC Place; ERIE; ▲ Fairview; ***224** WD-3; ★ **ERIE**; mail Fairview **z** 16415; ● 150
Swart; RMC Place; GREENE; ▲ Washington; ***225** WP-2; mail Sycamore **z** 15364; ● 30
Swarthmore; Inc. Place; DELAWARE; **228** F-1; elev. 120ft./37m.; 🅿 🅲 1,484; ★ **PHIL-**; **z** 19081; Ⓟ 6,157; Ⓒ 6,170
Swartzville; RMC Place; LANCASTER; ▲ East Cocalico; ***227** EO-8; mail Reinholds **z** 17569; ● 400
Swatara; MCD-Township; DAUPHIN; ***227** EO-5; 🅿 ■; ★ **HRBG**; **z** 17111; Ⓟ 19,661; Ⓒ 22,611; ◆ 23,901
Swatara; MCD-Township; LEBANON; ***227** EM-6; ★ **LEB**; mail Jonestown **z** 17038; Ⓟ 3,318; Ⓒ 3,941
Swatara Station; RMC Place; DAUPHIN; ▲ Derry; ★ **HRBG**; mail Hershey **z** 17033
Swede Hill; RMC Place; WESTMORELAND; ▲ Hempfield; ***225** WN-5; ★ **PGH**; mail Greensburg **z** 15601; ● 150
Swedeland; RMC Place; MONTGOMERY; ▲ Upper Merion; **228** B-1; ★ **PHIL-**; mail Norristown **z** 19401; ● 500
Sweden; MCD-Township; POTTER; ***224** WF-13; mail Coudersport **z** 16915; Ⓟ 581; Ⓒ 775
Sweden Valley; RMC Place; POTTER; ▲ Sweden; **224** WF-13; elev. 1,794ft./547m.; mail Coudersport **z** 16915; ● 100
Swedesburg; RMC Place; MONTGOMERY; ▲ Upper Merion; **228** A-1; ★ **PHIL-**; mail Bridgeport **z** 19405
Swedetown; RMC Place; CAMBRIA; ▲ Elder; ***225** WL-9; mail Hastings **z** 16646; ● 50
Sweeney Plan; RMC Place; WESTMORELAND; ▲ Rostraver; ***225** WO-4; ★ **PGH**; mail Belle Vernon **z** 15012; ● 600
Sweeneys Crossroads; RMC Place; WESTMORELAND; ***225** WO-4; ★ **PGH**; mail Belle Vernon **z** 15012
Sweet Valley; RMC Place; LUZERNE; ▲ Ross; **226** EH-8; 🅿; **z** 18656; ● 500
Swengel; RMC Place; UNION; ▲ Lewis; ***227** EK-3; 🅿; **z** 17880; ● 65
Swiftwater; RMC Place; MONROE; ▲ Pocono; **226** EI-11; 🅿; **z** 18370; ● 600
Swineford; RMC Place; SNYDER; mail Middleburg **z** 17842; pop. incl. with Middleburg (Inc. Place)
Swissdale; RMC Place; CLINTON; ▲ Woodward; ***226** EI-2; ★ **WMSPT**; mail Lock Haven **z** 17745; ● 100
Swissmont; RMC Place; ELK; ***224** WG-10; elev. 1,458ft./444m.; mail Saint Marys **z** 15857; pop. incl. with Saint Marys (Inc. Place)
Swissvale; Inc. Place; ALLEGHENY; **228** K-8; elev. 920ft./280m.; 🅿; ★ **PGH**; **z** 15218; Ⓟ 10,637; Ⓒ 9,653
Switzer; RMC Place; LEHIGH; ▲ Weisenberg; ***227** EL-10; ★ **ALL-**; mail New Tripoli **z** 18066; rural
Swoyersville; Inc. Place; LUZERNE; **226** EH-9; elev. 560ft./171m.; 🅿; ★ **SCR-**; **z** 18704; Ⓟ 5,630; Ⓒ 5,157
Sybertsville; RMC Place; LUZERNE; ▲ Sugarloaf; **226** EJ-8; 🅿; ★ **HAZ**; **z** 18251; ● 300
Sycamore; RMC Place; GREENE; ▲ Washington; **225** WP-2; 🅿; **z** 15364; ● 60
Sygan; RMC Place; ALLEGHENY; ▲ South Fayette; ***225** WN-3; ★ **PGH**; mail Bridgeville **z** 15017; ● 300
Sygan Hill; RMC Place; ALLEGHENY; ▲ South Fayette; ***225** WN-3; ★ **PGH**; mail Bridgeville **z** 15017
Sykesville; Inc. Place; JEFFERSON; **224** WJ-9; elev. 1,340ft./408m.; 🅿; **z** 15865; Ⓟ 1,387; Ⓒ 1,246
Sylmar; RMC Place; CHESTER; ▲ West Nottingham; ***227** ER-8; mail Nottingham **z** 19362; rural
Sylvan; RMC Place; FRANKLIN; ▲ Warren; **225** WQ-12; mail Mercersburg **z** 17236; ● 20
Sylvan Crest; RMC Place; BEAVER; ▲ Center; ***225** WL-2; elev. 900ft./274m.; ★ **PGH**; mail Monaca **z** 15061; pop. incl. with Monaca (Inc. Place)
Sylvan Dell; RMC Place; LYCOMING; ▲ Armstrong; ***226** EI-4; 🅿; ★ **WMSPT**; **z** 17702; ● 150
Sylvan Grove; RMC Place; CLEARFIELD; ▲ Cooper; ***224** WJ-12; mail Morrisdale **z** 16858; rural
Sylvan Hills; RMC Place; BLAIR; ▲ Frankstown; **224** WB-13; ★ **ALT**; mail Hollidaysburg **z** 16648; ● 1,000
Sylvania; Inc. Place; BRADFORD; **226** EE-4; elev. 1,280ft./390m.; 🅿; **z** 16945; Ⓟ 203; Ⓒ 200
Sylvania; MCD-Township; POTTER; ***224** WG-13; mail Austin **z** 16720; Ⓟ 80; Ⓒ 61
Sylvis; RMC Place; CLEARFIELD; ▲ Burnside; ***225** WL-9; elev. 1,700ft./518m.; mail Westover **z** 16692; rural
Syner; RMC Place; LEBANON; ▲ North Annville; ***227** EN-6; ★ **LEB**; mail Annville **z** 17003; rural

T

Table Rock; RMC Place; ADAMS; ▲ Butler; **227** EQ-3; mail Biglerville **z** 17307; ● 45
Tacony; RMC Place; PHILADELPHIA; ***227** EP-13; ★ **PHIL-**; mail Philadelphia **z** 19135; pop. incl. with Philadelphia (Inc. Place)
Tafton; RMC Place; PIKE; ▲ Palmyra; **226** EH-12; 🅿; **z** 18464; summer pop. 1,000; ● 600
Talmage; RMC Place; LANCASTER; ▲ West Earl; **227** EO-7; elev. 314ft./96m.; 🅿; ★ **LANC**; **z** 17580; ● 325
Talmar; RMC Place; COLUMBIA; ▲ Pine; ***226** EI-6; mail Benton **z** 17814; ● 30
Tamanend; RMC Place; SCHUYLKILL; ▲ Rush, Delano; ***227** EK-8; mail Tamaqua **z** 18252; ● 30
Tamaqua; Inc. Place; SCHUYLKILL; **227** EK-8; elev. 807ft./246m.; 🅿; **z** 18252; Ⓟ 7,943; Ⓒ 7,174
Tamarack; RMC Place; CLINTON; ▲ Leidy; ***224** WH-13; mail Renovo **z** 17764; rural
Tamiment; RMC Place; PIKE; ▲ Lehman; **226** EI-13; 🅿; **z** 18371; summer pop. 800; ● 125
Tanglewood Lakes; RMC Place; PIKE; ▲ Noxen; ***226** EH-12; elev. 1,500ft./457m.; mail Greentown **z** 18426; ● 500
Tanguy; RMC Place; CHESTER; ▲ Westtown; ***227** EP-11; ★ **PHIL-**; mail Glen Mills **z** 19342; ● 80
Tank; RMC Place; LUZERNE; ▲ Black Creek; ***226** EJ-7; ★ **HAZ**; mail Sugarloaf **z** 18249; rural
Tanners Falls; RMC Place; WAYNE; ▲ Dyberry; ***226** EF-11; mail Honesdale **z** 18431; rural
Tannersville; RMC Place; MONROE; ▲ Pocono; **226** EJ-11; 🅿; **z** 18372; ● 1,200
Tannery (Lehigh Tannery); RMC Place; CARBON; ▲ Kidder; ***226** EJ-9; mail White Haven **z** 18661; ● 90
Tannery; RMC Place; LUZERNE; ▲ Foster; **226** EJ-9; ★ **HAZ**; mail White Haven **z** 18661; ● 70
Tanoma; RMC Place; INDIANA; ▲ Rayne; ***225** WL-8; mail Clymer **z** 15728; ● 40
Tarentum; Inc. Place; ALLEGHENY; **225** WL-5; elev. 760ft./232m.; 🅿; ★ **PGH**; **z** 15084; Ⓟ 5,674; Ⓒ 4,993
Tarr; WESTMORELAND; see Tarrs (RMC Place)
Tarrs (Tarr); RMC Place; WESTMORELAND; ▲ East Huntingdon; **225** WO-5; 🅿; **z** 15688; ● 600
Tarrtown; RMC Place; ARMSTRONG; ▲ East Franklin; **225** WK-6; ★ **PGH**; mail Adrian **z** 16210; ● 150
Tatamy; Inc. Place; NORTHAMPTON; **227** EL-12; elev. 328ft./100m.; 🅿; ★ **ALL-**; **z** 18085; Ⓟ 873; Ⓒ 930
Tatesville; RMC Place; BEDFORD; ▲ West Providence, Hopewell; **225** WP-11; mail Everett **z** 15537; ● 175
Taylor; MCD-Township; BLAIR; ***225** WN-11; ★ **ALT**; mail Roaring Spring **z** 16673; Ⓟ 2,327; Ⓒ 2,239
Taylor; MCD-Township; CENTRE; ***225** WL-12; mail Tyrone **z** 16686; Ⓟ 714; Ⓒ 741
Taylor; MCD-Township; FULTON; ***225** WP-12; mail Waterfall **z** 16689; Ⓟ 1,172; Ⓒ 1,237
Taylor; Inc. Place; LACKAWANNA; **226** EH-9; elev. 680ft./207m.; 🅿; ★ **SCR-**; **z** 18517; Ⓟ 6,941; Ⓒ 6,475
Taylor; MCD-Township; LAWRENCE; ***224** WJ-2; ★ **NWCS**; mail West Pittsburg **z** 16160; Ⓟ 1,326; Ⓒ 1,198
Taylor Highlands; RMC Place; HUNTINGDON; ***225** WM-12; mail Huntingdon **z** 16652; pop. incl. with Huntingdon (Inc. Place)
Tayloria; RMC Place; LANCASTER; ▲ Little Britain; ***227** EQ-8; mail Oxford **z** 19363; ● 70
Taylorstown; RMC Place; WASHINGTON; ▲ Blaine; **225** WO-2; 🅿; **z** 15365; ● 250
Taylorsville; RMC Place; INDIANA; ▲ Green; ***225** WL-8; mail Commodore **z** 15729; ● 40
Taylortown; GREENE; see Dunkard (RMC Place)
Taylorville; RMC Place; SCHUYLKILL; ▲ Barry; ***227** EL-6; mail Ashland **z** 17921; rural
Teagarden Homes; RMC Place; GREENE; ▲ Morgan; ***225** WP-3; mail Clarksville **z** 15322; ● 400
Tearing Run; RMC Place; INDIANA; ▲ Center; ***225** WM-7; mail Homer City **z** 15748; ● 30
Teedyskung Lake; RMC Place; PIKE; ▲ Lackawaxen; ***226** EG-12; mail Hawley **z** 18428; ● 90
Teepleville; RMC Place; CRAWFORD; ▲ Richmond; **224** WF-4; mail Cambridge Springs **z** 16403; ● 20
Telescope; RMC Place; POTTER; ▲ Ulysses; ***224** WE-14; mail Galeton **z** 16922; rural
Telford; Inc. Place; MONTGOMERY, BUCKS; **227** EN-11; elev. 420ft./128m.; 🅿; ★ **PHIL-**; **z** 18969; Ⓟ 4,238; Ⓒ 4,680
Tell; MCD-Township; HUNTINGDON; ***225** WO-14; mail Blairs Mills **z** 17213; Ⓟ 551; Ⓒ 648
Temple; RMC Place; BERKS; **227** EN-9; elev. 380ft./116m.; 🅿; ★ **READ**; **z** 19560; Ⓟ 1,491
Templeton; RMC Place; ARMSTRONG; ▲ Pine; **224** WJ-6; 🅿; **z** 16259; ● 400
Ten Mile; RMC Place; WASHINGTON; ▲ Amwell; **225** WP-3; ★ **WASH**; mail Amity **z** 15311; ● 60
Tenth Avenue; RMC Place; LEHIGH; ★ **ALL-**; mail Bethlehem **z** 18018; pop. incl. with Bethlehem (Inc. Place)
Terminal; RMC Place; DELAWARE; ▲ Upper Darby; ★ **PHIL-**; mail Upper Darby **z** 19082
Terney Plan; RMC Place; WESTMORELAND; ▲ Unity; ***225** WN-6; ★ **LTROB**; mail Latrobe **z** 15650; ● 300
Terrace Acres; RMC Place; LEHIGH; ▲ Whitehall; ★ **ALL-**; mail Whitehall **z** 18052
Terre Hill; Inc. Place; LANCASTER; **227** EO-8; elev. 540ft./165m.; 🅿; ★ **LANC**; **z** 17581; Ⓟ 1,282; Ⓒ 1,237
Terry; MCD-Township; BRADFORD; ***226** EF-6; mail Wyalusing **z** 18853; Ⓟ 871; Ⓒ 942
Terrytown; RMC Place; BRADFORD; ▲ Terry; **226** EF-7; mail Wyalusing **z** 18853; ● 100
Texas; MCD-Township; WAYNE; ***226** EG-12; mail Honesdale **z** 18431; Ⓟ 2,570; Ⓒ 2,501
Tharptown; NORTHUMBERLAND; see Uniontown (RMC Place)
The Hideout; RMC Place; WAYNE; ▲ Salem, Lake; ***226** EH-11; elev. 1,400ft./427m.; ★ **SCR-**; mail Lake Ariel **z** 18436; summer pop. 1,500; ● 800
The Meadows; RMC Place; CENTRE; ▲ Ferguson; ***225** WL-13; elev. 1,237ft./377m.; ★ **STCOL**; mail Pennsylvania Furnace **z** 16865; ● 300
The Pines; RMC Place; ADAMS; ▲ Straban; ***227** EQ-3; mail New Oxford **z** 17350; rural
The Woodlands; RMC Place; BUTLER; ▲ Cranberry; ***225** WL-3; elev. 1,100ft./335m.; ★ **PGH**; mail Evans City **z** 16033; ● 325
Thieleman Crossroads; RMC Place; BUTLER; ▲ Adams; ***225** WL-3; ★ **PGH**; mail Mars **z** 16046; rural
Thomas; RMC Place; WASHINGTON; ▲ North Strabane; ***225** WN-3; elev. 1,180ft./360m.; ★ **PGH**; mail Eighty Four **z** 15330
Thomasdale; RMC Place; SOMERSET; ▲ Conemaugh, Jenner; ***225** WO-8; elev. 1,501ft./458m.; mail Hollsopple **z** 15935; ● 100
Thomas Mills; RMC Place; SOMERSET; ▲ Conemaugh; **225** WO-8; ★ **JNST**; mail Hollsopple **z** 15935; ● 50
Thomasville; RMC Place; YORK; ▲ Jackson; **227** EP-4; 🅿; ★ **YORK**; **z** 17364; ● 450
Thompson; MCD-Township; FULTON; ***225** WQ-12; mail Mercersburg **z** 17236; Ⓟ 1,048; Ⓒ 998
Thompson; Inc. Place; SUSQUEHANNA; **226** EE-10; elev. 1,640ft./500m.; 🅿; **z** 18465; Ⓟ 291; Ⓒ 299
Thompson; MCD-Township; SUSQUEHANNA; ***226** EE-10; 🅿; **z** 18465 & mail Starrucca **z** 18462; does not include the Borough of Thompson; Ⓟ 374; Ⓒ 440
Thompson Number 1; RMC Place; FAYETTE; ▲ Redstone; ***225** WP-4; elev. 1,001ft./305m.; ★ **UNTN**; mail Republic **z** 15475; ● 175
Thompson Number 2; RMC Place; FAYETTE; ▲ Luzerne; ***225** WP-4; ★ **UNTN**; mail New Salem **z** 15468; ● 40
Thompsontown; RMC Place; CLEARFIELD; ▲ Chest; **225** WK-10; mail La Jose **z** 15753; ● 30
Thompsontown; Inc. Place; JUNIATA; **227** EM-3; elev. 447ft./136m.; 🅿; **z** 17094; Ⓟ 582; Ⓒ 711
Thompsonville; CDP; WASHINGTON; ▲ Peters; ***225** WN-3; elev. 1,100ft./335m.; ★ **PGH**; mail Canonsburg **z** 15317; Ⓟ 3,560; Ⓒ 3,592
Thomson; RMC Place; ALLEGHENY; ★ **PGH**; pop. incl. with Duquesne (Inc. Place)
Thornburg; Inc. Place; ALLEGHENY; ***225** WM-3; elev. 900ft./274m.; ★ **PGH**; mail Pittsburgh **z** 15205; Ⓟ 461; Ⓒ 468
Thornbury; MCD-Township; CHESTER; ***227** EP-10; ★ **PHIL-**; mail Westtown **z** 19395; Ⓟ 1,131; Ⓒ 2,678
Thornbury; MCD-Township; DELAWARE; ***227** EP-11; 🅲 1,667; ★ **PHIL-**; mail Thornton **z** 19373; Ⓟ 5,056; Ⓒ 7,093; Ⓡ 5,787
Thorndale; CDP; CHESTER; ▲ Caln; **227** EP-9; 🅿; ★ **PHIL-**; **z** 19372; Ⓟ 3,518; Ⓒ 3,561
Thorndale Heights; RMC Place; CHESTER; ▲ Caln; ★ **PHIL-**; mail Downingtown **z** 19335
Thornhurst; RMC Place; LACKAWANNA; ▲ Thornhurst; **226** EI-10; 🅿; **z** 18424; ● 250
Thornhurst; MCD-Township; LACKAWANNA; ***226** EI-10; 🅿; **z** 18424; Ⓟ 486; Ⓒ 798
Thornridge; RMC Place; BUCKS; ▲ Falls; ***227** EO-14; ★ **PHIL-**; mail Levittown **z** 19054
Thornton; RMC Place; DELAWARE; ▲ Thornbury; ***227** EP-10; 🅿; ★ **PHIL-**; **z** 19373; ● 1,000
Thornwood; RMC Place; WESTMORELAND; ▲ East Huntingdon; ***225** WO-5; mail Scottdale **z** 15683; ● 120
Three Springs; Inc. Place; HUNTINGDON; **225** WO-13; elev. 742ft./226m.; 🅿; **z** 17264; Ⓟ 422; Ⓒ 445
Three Tuns; RMC Place; MONTGOMERY; ▲ Upper Dublin; ***227** EO-12; elev. 373ft./114m.; ★ **PHIL-**; mail Ambler **z** 19002
Throop; Inc. Place; LACKAWANNA; **226** EB-13; elev. 860ft./262m.; 🅿; ★ **SCR-**; **z** 18512; Ⓟ 4,070; Ⓒ 4,010; Ⓡ 4,008
Thumptown; RMC Place; TIOGA; ▲ Delmar; ***226** EF-2; elev. 1,828ft./557m.; mail Wellsboro **z** 16901; ● 40
Thurston; RMC Place; WYOMING; ▲ Eaton; ***226** EG-8; mail Tunkhannock **z** 18657; rural
Tiadaghton; RMC Place; TIOGA; ***226** EF-2; mail Wellsboro **z** 16901; rural
Tidal; RMC Place; ARMSTRONG; ▲ Madison; **224** WJ-6; mail Templeton **z** 16259; ● 75
Tide; RMC Place; INDIANA; ▲ Center; ***225** WM-7; mail Homer City **z** 15748; ● 40
Tidioute; Inc. Place; WARREN; **224** WF-6; elev. 1,114ft./340m.; 🅿; **z** 16351; Ⓟ 791; Ⓒ 792
Tiffany; RMC Place; SUSQUEHANNA; ▲ Bridgewater; ***226** EE-9; mail Montrose **z** 18801; rural
Tilden; MCD-Township; BERKS; ***227** EM-8; ★ **READ**; mail Hamburg **z** 19526; Ⓟ 2,622; Ⓒ 3,553
Tillotson; RMC Place; CRAWFORD; ▲ Bloomfield; **224** WE-5; elev. 1,561ft./476m.; mail Union City **z** 16438; ● 20
Timber Hills; CDP-Census Area Only; LEBANON; ***227** EO-6; Ⓒ 329
Timber Lakes; RMC Place; BUCKS; ▲ Lower Makefield; ***227** EN-13; ★ **PHIL-**; mail Morrisville **z** 19067; ● 70
Timberly Heights; RMC Place; BUTLER; ▲ Center; **224** WJ-4; ★ **BUTL**; mail Butler **z** 16001; ● 400
Timblin; Inc. Place; JEFFERSON; **224** WJ-7; elev. 1,272ft./388m.; 🅿; **z** 15778; Ⓟ 165; Ⓒ 151
Timbuck; RMC Place; MCKEAN; ▲ Lafayette; ***224** WE-10; elev. 2,081ft./634m.; mail Lewis Run **z** 16738; rural
Time; RMC Place; GREENE; ▲ Richhill; ***225** WP-2; mail Graysville **z** 15337
Tingley (Summersville); RMC Place; SUSQUEHANNA; ▲ New Milford; **226** EE-9; mail Hallstead **z** 18822, New Milford **z** 18834; ● 80
Tinicum; RMC Place; BUCKS; ▲ Tinicum; **227** EM-12; ★ **PHIL-**; mail Pipersville **z** 18947; ● 100
Tinicum; MCD-Township; BUCKS; ***227** EM-12; ★ **PHIL-**; mail Pipersville **z** 18947; Ⓟ 4,167; Ⓒ 4,206
Tinicum; MCD-Township; DELAWARE; ***227** EQ-12; ★ **PHIL-**; mail Essington **z** 19029; Ⓟ 4,440; Ⓒ 4,353
Tinicum Township; CDP-Census Area Only; DELAWARE; ▲ Tinicum; ***227** EQ-12; ★ **PHIL-**; mail Essington **z** 19029; Ⓟ 4,440; Ⓒ 4,353
Tioga; TIOGA; see Brooklyn (RMC Place)
Tioga; Inc. Place; TIOGA; **226** EE-3; elev. 1,039ft./317m.; 🅿; **z** 16946; Ⓟ 638; Ⓒ 622
Tioga; MCD-Township; TIOGA; ***226** EE-3; 🅿; **z** 16946; does not include the Borough of Tioga; Ⓟ 1,019; Ⓒ 995
TIOGA; **226** EF-3; Ⓟ 41,126; Ⓒ 41,373; ◆ 40,451
Tioga Junction; RMC Place; TIOGA; ▲ Lawrence; **226** ED-3; mail Tioga **z** 16946; ● 100
Tiona; RMC Place; WARREN; ▲ Mead; **224** WF-8; elev. 1,363ft./415m.; 🅿; **z** 16352; ● 400
Tionesta; Inc. Place; ⊡ FOREST; **224** WG-6; elev. 1,084ft./330m.; 🅿; **z** 16353; Ⓟ 634; Ⓒ 615
Tionesta; MCD-Township; FOREST; ***224** WG-6; 🅿; **z** 16353; does not include the Borough of Tionesta; Ⓟ 582; Ⓒ 610
Tippecanoe; RMC Place; FAYETTE; ▲ Redstone; ***225** WP-4; ★ **UNTN**; mail Smock **z** 15480; rural
Tippery; RMC Place; VENANGO; ▲ Cranberry; ***224** WH-5; ★ **OILC-F**; mail Oil City **z** 16301; rural
Tipton; CDP; BLAIR; ▲ Antis; **225** WL-11; 🅿; ★ **ALT**; **z** 16684; Ⓟ 1,194; Ⓒ 1,225
Tire Hill; RMC Place; SOMERSET; ▲ Conemaugh; **225** WN-8; 🅿; ★ **JNST**; **z** 15959; ● 900
Titusville; Inc. Place; CRAWFORD; **224** WF-5; elev. 1,199ft./365m.; 🅿 🅷; **z** 16354; Ⓟ 6,434; Ⓒ 6,146
Tivoli; RMC Place; LYCOMING; ▲ Shrewsbury; **226** EH-5; mail Hughesville **z** 17737; ● 25
Toboyne; MCD-Township; PERRY; ***227** EO-1; mail New Germantown **z** 17071; Ⓟ 455; Ⓒ 494
Toby; MCD-Township; CLARION; ***224** WJ-6; mail Rimersburg **z** 16248; Ⓟ 1,153; Ⓒ 1,166
Toby; RMC Place; ELK; ▲ Fox; **224** WH-10; mail Kersey **z** 15846; ● 100
Toby Farms; RMC Place; DELAWARE; ★ **PHIL-**; mail Brookhaven **z** 19015; pop. incl. with Chester (Inc. Place)
Tobyhanna (West Tobyhanna); RMC Place; MONROE; ▲ Coolbaugh; **226** EI-11; 🅿; **z** 18466; ● 1,200
Tobyhanna; MCD-Township; MONROE; ***226** EI-10; 🅿; **z** 18466 & mail Pocono Pines **z** 18350; Ⓟ 4,318; Ⓒ 6,152
Todd; MCD-Township; FULTON; ***225** WP-13; mail Mc Connellsburg **z** 17233; Ⓟ 1,434; Ⓒ 1,488
Todd; RMC Place; HUNTINGDON; ▲ Todd; **225** WN-12; 🅿; **z** 16685; ● 70
Todd; MCD-Township; HUNTINGDON; ***225** WO-12; 🅿; **z** 16685; Ⓟ 889; Ⓒ 1,004
Toddesville; RMC Place; ADAMS; ▲ Cumberland; ***227** EQ-3; elev. 531ft./162m.; mail Gettysburg **z** 17325; ● 300
Toftrees; RMC Place; CENTRE; ▲ Patton; ***225** WK-13; ★ **STCOL**; mail State College **z** 16803; ● 400
Toland; RMC Place; CUMBERLAND; ▲ Dickinson; ***227** EP-3; ★ **CARL**; mail Gardners **z** 17324; ● 80
Tolna (Sheffer); RMC Place; YORK; ▲ Shrewsbury, Hopewell; **227** EQ-5; elev. 744ft./227m.; ★ **BAL**; mail New Freedom **z** 17349; ● 40
Tomb (Tombs Run); RMC Place; LYCOMING; ▲ Watson; mail Jersey Shore **z** 17740; rural
Tombs Run; LYCOMING; see Tomb (RMC Place)
Tomhicken (Sugarloaf); RMC Place; LUZERNE; ▲ Sugarloaf; **226** EJ-8; ★ **HAZ**; mail Sugarloaf **z** 18249; ● 160
Tompkinsville; RMC Place; LACKAWANNA; ▲ Greenfield; **226** EG-10; elev. 1,298ft./396m.; ★ **SCR-**; mail Jermyn **z** 18433; ● 200
Tomstown; RMC Place; FRANKLIN; ▲ Quincy; **227** EQ-1; mail Waynesboro **z** 17268; ● 180
Tooley Corners; RMC Place; LACKAWANNA; ▲ Spring Brook; ***226** EH-10; mail Moscow **z** 18444; rural
Topton; Inc. Place; BERKS; **227** EM-10; elev. 483ft./147m.; 🅿; **z** 19562; Ⓟ 1,987; Ⓒ 1,948
Torpedo; RMC Place; WARREN; ▲ Pittsfield; **224** WE-6; mail Pittsfield **z** 16340; ● 30
Torrance; RMC Place; WESTMORELAND; ▲ Derry; **225** WM-7; 🅿 🅷; ★ **LTROB**; **z** 15779; ● 250
Torresdale; RMC Place; PHILADELPHIA; ***227** EP-13; ★ **PHIL-**; mail Philadelphia **z** 19114; pop. incl. with Philadelphia (Inc. Place)
Torresdale Manor; RMC Place; BUCKS; ▲ Bensalem; ★ **PHIL-**; mail Bensalem **z** 19020
Torrey; RMC Place; WAYNE; ▲ Oregon; ***226** EF-12; elev. 1,479ft./451m.; mail White Mills **z** 18473; rural
Toughkenamon; CDP; CHESTER; ▲ New Garden; **227** EQ-9; elev. 358ft./109m.; 🅿; ★ **PHIL-**; **z** 19374; Ⓟ 1,273; Ⓒ 1,375
Towamencin; MCD-Township; MONTGOMERY; ***227** EN-11; ★ **PHIL-**; mail Kulpsville **z** 19443; Ⓟ 14,167; Ⓒ 17,597
Towamensing; MCD-Township; CARBON; ***227** EK-10; mail Palmerton **z** 18071; Ⓟ 3,111; Ⓒ 3,475
Towamensing Trails; RMC Place; CARBON; ▲ Penn Forest; ***226** EJ-10; elev. 1,860ft./567m.; mail Albrightsville **z** 18210; ● 350
Towanda; Inc. Place; ⊡ BRADFORD; **226** EF-6; elev. 737ft./225m.; 🅿 🅷; **z** 18848; Ⓟ 3,242; Ⓒ 3,024
Towanda; MCD-Township; BRADFORD; ***226** EF-6; 🅿; **z** 18848; does not include the Borough of Towanda; Ⓟ 1,133; Ⓒ 1,131
Tower City; Inc. Place; SCHUYLKILL; **227** EM-6; elev. 803ft./245m.; 🅿; **z** 17980; Ⓟ 1,518; Ⓒ 1,396
Tower Hill; RMC Place; BUCKS; ▲ New Britain; ***227** EN-12; elev. 393ft./120m.; ★ **PHIL-**; mail Chalfont **z** 18914; pop. incl. with Chalfont (Inc. Place)
Tower Hill Number One; RMC Place; FAYETTE; ▲ Redstone; ***225** WP-4; ★ **UNTN**; mail Republic **z** 15475; ● 150
Tower Hill Number Two; RMC Place; FAYETTE; ▲ Luzerne; ***225** WP-4; ★ **UNTN**; mail Brownsville **z** 15417; ● 250
Towerville; RMC Place; CHESTER; ▲ East Fallowfield; ***227** EP-9; elev. 560ft./171m.; ★ **PHIL-**; mail Coatesville **z** 19320; ● 170
Town Hill; RMC Place; LUZERNE; ▲ Huntington; ***226** EI-7; elev. 999ft./304m.; mail Shickshinny **z** 18655; ● 60
Town Line; RMC Place; LUZERNE; ▲ Union, Huntington; ***226** EI-7; elev. 983ft./300m.; mail Shickshinny **z** 18655; rural
Townville; Inc. Place; CRAWFORD; **224** WF-4; elev. 1,411ft./430m.; 🅿; **z** 16360; Ⓟ 358; Ⓒ 306
Traces of Lattimore; RMC Place; PIKE; ▲ Delaware; ***226** EH-13; elev. 1,100ft./335m.; mail Dingmans Ferry **z** 18328; rural
Trachsville; RMC Place; CARBON; ***227** EK-10; mail Palmerton **z** 18071; ● 25
Tracktowne; RMC Place; YORK; ★ **YORK**; pop. incl. with York (Inc. Place)
Trade City; RMC Place; INDIANA; ▲ North Mahoning; **225** WK-8; elev. 1,485ft./453m.; mail Smicksburg **z** 16256; ● 60
Tradesville; RMC Place; BUCKS; ***227** EN-12; ★ **PHIL-**; mail Chalfont **z** 18914; rural
Trafford; Inc. Place; WESTMORELAND, ALLEGHENY; **225** WN-5; elev. 820ft./250m.; 🅿; ★ **PGH**; **z** 15085; Ⓟ 3,345; Ⓒ 3,236
Trailwood; RMC Place; LUZERNE; ▲ Bear Creek; ★ **SCR-**; mail Wilkes Barre **z** 18702; ● 100
Trainer; Inc. Place; DELAWARE; **227** EQ-11; elev. 34ft./10m.; 🅿; ★ **PHIL-**; **z** 19061 & mail Chester **z** 19013; Ⓟ 2,271; Ⓒ 1,901
Transfer; RMC Place; MERCER; ▲ Pymatuning; **224** WH-2; 🅿; ★ **SHAR**; **z** 16154; ● 500
Trappe; Inc. Place; MONTGOMERY; **227** EO-11; elev. 300ft./91m.; 🅿; ★ **PHIL-**; **z** 19426; Ⓟ 2,115; Ⓒ 3,210
Trauger; RMC Place; WESTMORELAND; ▲ Mount Pleasant; **225** WO-6; mail Latrobe **z** 15650; ● 150
Traymore; RMC Place; BUCKS; ▲ Northampton; ***227** EN-13; ★ **PHIL-**; mail Warminster **z** 18974; ● 400
Traymore Manor; BUCKS; see Jacksonville (RMC Place)
Treasure Lake; CDP-Census Area Only; CLEARFIELD; ▲ Sandy; ***224** WI-9; elev. 1,700ft./518m.; mail Du Bois **z** 15801; Ⓟ 2,185; Ⓒ 4,507
Tredyffrin; MCD-Township; CHESTER; ***227** EP-11; 🅿; ★ **PHIL-**; **z** 19312; Ⓟ 28,028; Ⓒ 29,062; ◆ 29,135
Treehaven; RMC Place; ALLEGHENY; ★ **PGH**; mail Bethel Park **z** 15102; pop. incl. with Bethel Park (Inc. Place)
Trees Mills; RMC Place; WESTMORELAND; ▲ Salem; ***225** WM-6; ★ **PGH**; mail Greensburg **z** 15601; rural
Treichler; NORTHAMPTON; see Treichlers (RMC Place)
Treichlers (Treichler); RMC Place; NORTHAMPTON; ▲ Lehigh; **227** EL-10; 🅿; ★ **ALL-**; **z** 18086; ● 600
Tremont; Inc. Place; SCHUYLKILL; **227** EL-7; elev. 760ft./232m.; 🅿; **z** 17981; Ⓟ 1,814; Ⓒ 1,784
Tremont; MCD-Township; SCHUYLKILL; ***227** EL-6; 🅿; **z** 17981 & mail Pine Grove **z** 17963; does not include the Borough of Tremont; Ⓟ 297; Ⓒ 250
Trent; RMC Place; SOMERSET; ▲ Middlecreek; ***225** WP-7; mail Rockwood **z** 15557
Trenton; RMC Place; SCHUYLKILL; ▲ Delano; ***227** EK-8; mail Mahanoy City **z** 17948; ● 90
Tresckow; CDP; CARBON; ▲ Banks; **227** EK-8; 🅿; ★ **HAZ**; **z** 18254; Ⓟ 1,033; Ⓒ 964
Tresslarville; RMC Place; WAYNE; ▲ Lake; ***226** EG-11; ★ **SCR-**; mail Lake Ariel **z** 18436; rural
Treveskyn (Cuddy); RMC Place; ALLEGHENY; ▲ South Fayette; **225** WN-3; ★ **PGH**; mail Cuddy **z** 15031; ● 1,200
Trevorton; CDP; NORTHUMBERLAND; ▲ Zerbe; **227** EK-5; elev. 849ft./259m.; 🅿; **z** 17881; Ⓟ 2,058; Ⓒ 2,010
Trevose; RMC Place; BUCKS; ▲ Lower Southampton; ***227** EO-13; elev. 200ft./61m.; 🅿 🅷; ★ **PHIL-**; **z** 19053 & mail Fort Washington **z** 19048-49
Trevose Heights; RMC Place; BUCKS; ▲ Lower Southampton; ***227** EO-13; ★ **PHIL-**; mail Langhorne **z** 19047
Trexler; RMC Place; BERKS; ▲ Albany; ***227** EL-9; elev. 420ft./128m.; mail Kempton **z** 19529
Trexlertown; RMC Place; LEHIGH; ▲ Upper Macungie; **227** EM-10; elev. 394ft./120m.; 🅿; ★ **ALL-**; **z** 18087; ● 1,000
Trimmer Manor; RMC Place; YORK; ▲ West Manchester; ★ **YORK**; mail York **z** 17405
Trindle Spring; RMC Place; CUMBERLAND; ▲ Silver Spring; ***227** EO-4; ★ **HRBG**; mail Mechanicsburg **z** 17050, **z** 17055; ● 1,000
Trinity Park; RMC Place; WASHINGTON; ▲ North Franklin; ***225** WO-2; elev. 1,100ft./335m.; ★ **WASH**; mail Washington **z** 15301; ● 400
Tripoli; RMC Place; CAMBRIA; ▲ Cambria; ***225** WM-9; mail Colver **z** 15927; ● 100
Triumph; MCD-Township; WARREN; ***224** WF-6; mail Pittsfield **z** 16340; Ⓟ 314; Ⓒ 286
Trooper; CDP; MONTGOMERY; ▲ Lower Providence; **227** EO-11; 🅿; ★ **PHIL-**; **z** 19403 & mail Norristown **z** 19401; Ⓟ 5,137; Ⓒ 6,061
Trotter; RMC Place; FAYETTE; ▲ Dunbar; ***225** WP-5; mail Connellsville **z** 15425; ● 300
Trout Run; RMC Place; LYCOMING; ▲ Lewis; **226** EH-4; elev. 690ft./210m.; 🅿; **z** 17771; ● 350
Trouts Corners; RMC Place; MERCER; ***224** WH-2; elev. 1,145ft./349m.; ★ **SHAR**; mail Hermitage **z** 16148; pop. incl. with Hermitage (Inc. Place)
Trouts Crossing; RMC Place; WESTMORELAND; ▲ Mount Pleasant; mail Mount Pleasant **z** 15666; rural
Troutville; Inc. Place; CLEARFIELD; **224** WJ-9; elev. 1,560ft./475m.; 🅿; **z** 15866; Ⓟ 226; Ⓒ 224
Trowbridge; RMC Place; TIOGA; ▲ Jackson; ***226** ED-4; mail Millerton **z** 16936; rural
Troxelville; CDP; SNYDER; ▲ Adams; **227** EK-3; 🅿; **z** 17882; Ⓒ 192
Troy; Inc. Place; BRADFORD; **226** EE-5; elev. 1,095ft./334m.; 🅿 🅷; **z** 16947; Ⓟ 1,262; Ⓒ 1,508
Troy; MCD-Township; BRADFORD; ***226** EF-5; 🅿; **z** 16947; does not include the Borough of Troy; Ⓟ 1,797; Ⓒ 1,645
Troy; RMC Place; CLEARFIELD; ▲ Morris; ***225** WK-12; mail Philipsburg **z** 16866; ● 100
Troy; MCD-Township; CRAWFORD; ***224** WF-4; mail Centerville **z** 16404; Ⓟ 1,235; Ⓒ 1,339
Troy Center; RMC Place; CRAWFORD; ▲ Troy; ***224** WF-4; mail Centerville **z** 16404
Troy Hill; RMC Place; ARMSTRONG; ▲ Rayburn; ***225** WK-6; ★ **PGH**; mail Kittanning **z** 16201; ● 90
Truce; RMC Place; LANCASTER; ▲ Providence; ***227** EQ-7; elev. 880ft./268m.; ★ **LANC**; mail Quarryville **z** 17566; ● 120
Trucksville; RMC Place; LUZERNE; ▲ Kingston; **226** EA-8; elev. 889ft./271m.; 🅿; ★ **SCR-**; **z** 18708; ● 1,650
Trucksville Gardens; RMC Place; LUZERNE; ▲ Kingston; ***226** EH-9; elev. 1,071ft./326m.; ★ **SCR-**; mail Shavertown **z** 18708; ● 780
Truemans; RMC Place; FOREST; ▲ Howe; ***224** WF-8; mail Sheffield **z** 16347; rural
Truesdale Terrace; RMC Place; LUZERNE; ▲ Hanover; ***226** EI-8; ★ **SCR-**; mail Wilkes Barre **z** 18706; ● 250
Truittsburg; RMC Place; CLARION; ▲ Redbank; **224** WJ-7; mail Fairmount City **z** 16224; ● 15
Truman; RMC Place; CAMERON; ▲ Shippen; **224** WG-11; mail Emporium **z** 15834; ● 75
Trumbauersville (Cressman); Inc. Place; BUCKS; **227** EM-11; elev. 540ft./165m.; 🅿; ★ **PHIL-**; **z** 18970; Ⓟ 894; Ⓒ 1,059
Trunkeyville; RMC Place; FOREST; ▲ Harmony; ***224** WF-6; elev. 1,097ft./334m.; mail Tidioute **z** 16351; ● 40
Truxall; RMC Place; WESTMORELAND; ▲ Bell; ***225** WM-6; ★ **PGH**; mail Apollo **z** 15613; ● 60
Tryonville; RMC Place; CRAWFORD; ▲ Steuben; **224** WF-5; mail Centerville **z** 16404; ● 50
Tuckerton; RMC Place; BERKS; ▲ Muhlenberg; **227** ER-12; elev. 321ft./98m.; ★ **READ**; mail Reading **z** 19605; ● 300
Tullytown; Inc. Place; BUCKS; **227** EO-14; elev. 20ft./6m.; 🅿; ★ **PHIL-**; **z** 19007; Ⓟ 2,339; Ⓒ 2,031
Tulpehocken; BERKS; see New Schaefferstown (RMC Place)
Tulpehocken; MCD-Township; BERKS; ***227** EM-7; mail Rehrersburg **z** 19550; Ⓟ 2,843; Ⓒ 3,290
Tuna; RMC Place; MCKEAN; ▲ Foster; ***224** WD-10; elev. 1,440ft./439m.; mail Bradford **z** 16701; ● 220
Tunkhannock; MCD-Township; MONROE; ***226** EJ-10; mail Blakeslee **z** 18610; Ⓟ 2,060; Ⓒ 4,983
Tunkhannock; Inc. Place; ⊡ WYOMING; **226** EG-8; elev. 660ft./201m.; 🅿 🅷; **z** 18657; Ⓟ 2,251; Ⓒ 1,911
Tunkhannock; MCD-Township; WYOMING; ***226** EG-9; 🅿; **z** 18657; does not include the Borough of Tunkhannock; Ⓟ 4,371; Ⓒ 4,298
Tunnel; RMC Place; LUZERNE; ▲ Dennison; ***226** EI-9; mail White Haven **z** 18661; ● 75
Tunnelhill; Inc. Place; CAMBRIA, BLAIR; **225** WM-10; elev. 2,300ft./701m.; ★ **ALT**; mail Gallitzin **z** 16641; Ⓟ 365; Ⓒ 409
Tunnelton; RMC Place; INDIANA; ▲ Conemaugh; **225** WM-6; elev. 942ft./287m.; ★ **PGH**; mail Saltsburg **z** 15681; ● 110
Turbett; MCD-Township; JUNIATA; ***227** EM-2; mail Port Royal **z** 17082; Ⓟ 779; Ⓒ 819
Turbot; MCD-Township; NORTHUMBERLAND; ***226** EJ-5; mail Milton **z** 17847; Ⓟ 1,846; Ⓒ 1,677
Turbotville; Inc. Place; NORTHUMBERLAND; **226** EI-5; elev. 600ft./183m.; 🅿; ★ **WMSPT**; **z** 17772; Ⓟ 675; Ⓒ 691
Turkey City; RMC Place; CLARION; ▲ Richland; **224** WI-5; 🅿; **z** 16058; ● 100
Turkeyfoot; RMC Place; FRANKLIN; ▲ Hamilton; ***225** WQ-14; mail Chambersburg **z** 17201; rural
Turkeyfoot; RMC Place; WASHINGTON; ▲ Peters; ***225** WN-3; ★ **PGH**; mail Finleyville **z** 15332; rural
Turkey Run; RMC Place; SCHUYLKILL; ***227** EK-7; mail Shenandoah **z** 17976; pop. incl. with Shenandoah (Inc. Place)
Turkeytown; RMC Place; WESTMORELAND; ▲ South Huntingdon; ***225** WO-5; ★ **PGH**; mail West Newton **z** 15089; ● 180
Turnersville; RMC Place; CRAWFORD; ▲ West Shenango; **224** WG-2; mail Jamestown **z** 16134; ● 35
Turnip Hole; RMC Place; CLARION; ▲ Licking; **224** WI-5; mail Emlenton **z** 16373; ● 20
Turnpike (Hungerford); RMC Place; YORK; mail Shrewsbury **z** 17361; pop. incl. with Shrewsbury (Inc. Place)
Turtle Creek (Westinghouse); Inc. Place; ALLEGHENY; **228** K-9; elev. 980ft./299m.; 🅿; ★ **PGH**; **z** 15145; Ⓟ 6,556; Ⓒ 6,076
Turtlepoint; RMC Place; MCKEAN; ▲ Annin; **224** WE-11; 🅿; **z** 16750; ● 90
Tuscarora; MCD-Township; BRADFORD; ***226** EF-8; mail Laceyville **z** 18623; Ⓟ 996; Ⓒ 1,072
Tuscarora; RMC Place; JUNIATA; ▲ Walker, Turbett; **227** EM-2; mail Port Royal **z** 17082; ● 60
Tuscarora; MCD-Township; JUNIATA; ***227** EN-1; mail Honey Grove **z** 17035; Ⓟ 1,099; Ⓒ 1,159
Tuscarora; MCD-Township; PERRY; ***227** EM-3; mail Millerstown **z** 17062; Ⓟ 1,034; Ⓒ 1,122
Tuscarora; CDP; SCHUYLKILL; ▲ Schuylkill; **227** EK-8; 🅿; ★ **PTSVL**; **z** 17982; Ⓟ 1,073; Ⓒ 939
Tusculam; RMC Place; CUMBERLAND, FRANKLIN; ▲ Southampton, Shippensburg; ***227** EP-1; mail Shippensburg **z** 17257; ● 175
Tusseyville; RMC Place; CENTRE; ▲ Potter; **225** WK-14; ★ **STCOL**; mail Centre Hall **z** 16828; ● 30
Twenty Row; RMC Place; CAMBRIA; ▲ Cambria; ***225** WM-9; mail Colver **z** 15927
Twilight; Inc. Place; WASHINGTON; ***225** WO-4; elev. 980ft./299m.; ★ **PGH**; mail Charleroi **z** 15022; Ⓟ 252; Ⓒ 241
Twin Bridge Farm; RMC Place; CHESTER; ▲ West Goshen; ★ **PHIL-**; mail West Chester **z** 19380; ● 400
Twin Bridges; RMC Place; WASHINGTON; ▲ Fallowfield; ***225** WO-4; ★ **PGH**; mail Charleroi **z** 15022; ● 170
Twin Brooks; RMC Place; YORK; ▲ West Manchester; ★ **YORK**; mail York **z** 17405
Twin Lakes; RMC Place; PIKE; ▲ Shohola; **226** EH-13; mail Shohola **z** 18458; ● 125
Twin Oaks; RMC Place; ADAMS; ▲ Cumberland; ***227** EQ-3; elev. 513ft./156m.; mail Gettysburg **z** 17325; ● 500
Twin Oaks; RMC Place; BUCKS; ▲ Middletown; ★ **PHIL-**; mail Levittown **z** 19056
Twin Oaks; RMC Place; DELAWARE; ▲ Upper Chichester; ***227** EQ-11; ★ **PHIL-**; mail Aston **z** 19014; ● 500
Twin Oaks; RMC Place; VENANGO; ▲ Cranberry; ***224** WH-5; ★ **OILC-F**; mail Cranberry **z** 16319; rural
Twin Oaks Farms; RMC Place; DELAWARE; ▲ Upper Chichester; ***227** EQ-11; elev. 100ft./30m.; ★ **PHIL-**; mail Aston **z** 19014; ● 960
Twin Rocks; RMC Place; CAMBRIA; ▲ Blacklick; **225** WM-9; elev. 1,657ft./505m.; 🅿; **z** 15960; ● 600
Two Taverns; RMC Place; ADAMS; ▲ Mount Joy; **227** EQ-3; mail Gettysburg **z** 17325; ● 50
Tyler; RMC Place; CLEARFIELD; ▲ Huston; **224** WI-10; mail Penfield **z** 15849; ● 40
Tylerdale; RMC Place; WASHINGTON; ***225** WO-2; ★ **WASH**; mail Washington **z** 15301; pop. incl. with Washington (Inc. Place)
Tyler Hill; RMC Place; WAYNE; ▲ Damascus; **226** EF-12; elev. 1,200ft./366m.; 🅿; **z** 18469; summer pop. 1,800; ● 450
Tyler Run-Queens Gate; CDP-Census Area Only; YORK; ▲ Spring Garden; ***227** EP-5; elev. 600ft./183m.; ★ **YORK**; mail York **z** 17403; Ⓟ 2,739; Ⓒ 2,926
Tylersburg; RMC Place; CLARION; ▲ Farmington; **224** WH-7; elev. 1,570ft./479m.; 🅿; **z** 16361; ● 310
Tylersburg; CLARION; see Tylersburg Station (RMC Place)
Tylersburg Station (Tylersburg); RMC Place; CLARION; ▲ Farmington; **224** WH-7; elev. 1,644ft./501m.; mail Leeper **z** 16233, Tylersburg **z** 16361; ● 210
Tylersport; RMC Place; MONTGOMERY; ▲ Salford; **227** EN-11; 🅿; ★ **PHIL-**; **z** 18971; ● 320
Tylersville; RMC Place; CLINTON; ▲ Logan; **226** EJ-2; 🅿; **z** 17773; ● 225
Tyre; ALLEGHENY; see Santiago (RMC Place)
Tyrone; MCD-Township; ADAMS; ***227** EP-3; mail Gettysburg **z** 17325; Ⓟ 1,829; Ⓒ 2,273
Tyrone; Inc. Place; BLAIR; **225** WL-11; elev. 896ft./273m.; 🅿 🅷; ★ **ALT**; **z** 16686; Ⓟ 5,743; Ⓒ 5,528
Tyrone; MCD-Township; BLAIR; ***225** WM-11; 🅿; **z** 16686; not adjacent to the Borough of Tyrone; Ⓟ 1,677; Ⓒ 1,800
Tyrone; MCD-Township; PERRY; ***227** EN-2; mail Landisburg **z** 17040; Ⓟ 1,741; Ⓒ 1,863
Tyrone Forge (Forge); RMC Place; BLAIR; ▲ Snyder; ***225** WL-12; ★ **ALT**; mail Tyrone **z** 16686; ● 70

U

Uhlers; NORTHAMPTON; see Ulhers (RMC Place)
Uhlerstown; RMC Place; BUCKS; ▲ Tinicum; **227** EM-12; ★ **PHIL-**; mail Frenchtown **z** 08825, Upper Black Eddy **z** 18972; ● 100
Uledi (Revere); RMC Place; FAYETTE; ▲ South Union, Menallen; **225** WP-4; 🅿; ★ **UNTN**; **z** 15484; ● 250
Ulhers (Uhlers); RMC Place; NORTHAMPTON; ▲ Forks; ***227** EK-12; ★ **ALL-**; mail Easton **z** 18040; rural
Ulrichtown; RMC Place; ADAMS; ▲ Germany; ***227** ER-3; mail Littlestown **z** 17340; ● 100
Ulster; RMC Place; BRADFORD; ▲ Ulster; **226** EE-6; 🅿; **z** 18850; ● 300
Ulster; MCD-Township; BRADFORD; ***226** EE-6; 🅿; **z** 18850; Ⓟ 1,295; Ⓒ 1,340
Ulysses; Inc. Place; POTTER; **224** WE-14; elev. 2,080ft./634m.; 🅿; **z** 16948; Ⓟ 653; Ⓒ 684
Ulysses; MCD-Township; POTTER; ***224** WE-14; 🅿; **z** 16948; does not include the Borough of Ulysses; Ⓟ 557; Ⓒ 691
Unamis; RMC Place; SOMERSET; ▲ Addison; ***225** WQ-7; mail Addison **z** 15411; rural
Unicorn; RMC Place; LANCASTER; ▲ East Drumore; ***227** EQ-8; elev. 588ft./179m.; mail Quarryville **z** 17566
Union; MCD-Township; ADAMS; ***227** EQ-4; ★ **HANV**; mail Hanover **z** 17331; Ⓟ 2,178; Ⓒ 2,989
Union; BEDFORD; see Pavia (MCD-Township)
Union; MCD-Township; BERKS; ***227** EN-9; mail Birdsboro **z** 19508; Ⓟ 3,440; Ⓒ 3,453
Union; MCD-Township; CENTRE; ***224** WJ-13; mail Julian **z** 16844; Ⓟ 895; Ⓒ 1,200
Union; MCD-Township; CLEARFIELD; ***224** WI-10; mail Rockton **z** 15856; Ⓟ 833; Ⓒ 918
Union; MCD-Township; CRAWFORD; ***224** WG-3; mail Meadville **z** 16335; Ⓟ 895; Ⓒ 1,049
Union; MCD-Township; ERIE; ***224** WE-5; mail Union City **z** 16438; does not include the Borough of Union City; Ⓟ 1,735; Ⓒ 1,663
Union; MCD-Township; FULTON; ***225** WQ-11; mail Warfordsburg **z** 17267; Ⓟ 623; Ⓒ 634
Union; MCD-Township; HUNTINGDON; ***225** WN-13; mail Mapleton Depot **z** 17052; Ⓟ 992; Ⓒ 1,005
Union; MCD-Township; JEFFERSON; ***224** WI-7; mail Corsica **z** 15829; Ⓟ 733; Ⓒ 816
Union; RMC Place; LANCASTER; ▲ Colerain; ***227** EQ-8; mail Kirkwood **z** 17536, Oxford **z** 19363; ● 50
Union; RMC Place; LANCASTER; ▲ Providence; ***227** EP-7; elev. 676ft./206m.; ★ **LANC**; mail New Providence **z** 17560; rural
Union; MCD-Township; LAWRENCE; ***224** WJ-2; ★ **YNGS-**; mail New Castle **z** 16101; Ⓟ 5,581; Ⓒ 5,103
Union; MCD-Township; LEBANON; ***227** EN-6; mail Jonestown **z** 17038; Ⓟ 2,755; Ⓒ 2,590
Union; MCD-Township; LUZERNE; ***226** EI-7; ★ **SCR-**; mail Shickshinny **z** 18655; Ⓟ 2,028; Ⓒ 2,100
Union; MCD-Township; MIFFLIN; ***225** WL-14; mail Belleville **z** 17004; Ⓟ 3,265; Ⓒ 3,313
Union; MCD-Township; SCHUYLKILL; ***227** EK-7; mail Ringtown **z** 17967; Ⓟ 1,458; Ⓒ 1,308
Union; MCD-Township; SNYDER; ***227** EL-4; mail Port Trevorton **z** 17864; Ⓟ 1,466; Ⓒ 1,519
Union; MCD-Township; TIOGA; ***226** EG-4; mail Canton **z** 17724; Ⓟ 931; Ⓒ 945
Union; MCD-Township; UNION; ***227** EK-4; mail Winfield **z** 17889; Ⓟ 1,300; Ⓒ 1,427
Union; MCD-Township; WASHINGTON; ***225** WN-4; ★ **PGH**; mail Finleyville **z** 15332; Ⓟ 6,322; Ⓒ 5,599
UNION; **226** EJ-3; Ⓟ 36,176; Ⓒ 41,624; ◆ 43,728
Union Center; RMC Place; TIOGA; ▲ Union; ***226** EF-4; mail Canton **z** 17724; rural
Union City; Inc. Place; ERIE; **224** WE-4; elev. 1,299ft./396m.; 🅿 🅷; **z** 16438; Ⓟ 3,537; Ⓒ 3,463
Union Dale; Inc. Place; SUSQUEHANNA; **226** EF-10; elev. 1,697ft./517m.; 🅿; **z** 18470; Ⓟ 303; Ⓒ 368
Union Deposit; RMC Place; DAUPHIN; ▲ South Hanover; **227** EN-5; ★ **HRBG**; mail Hershey **z** 17033; ● 700
Union Furnace; RMC Place; HUNTINGDON; ▲ Morris; ***225** WL-12; mail Tyrone **z** 16686; rural
Union Grove; RMC Place; LANCASTER; ▲ East Earl; ***227** EO-8; ★ **LANC**; mail East Earl **z** 17519; rural
Union Hill; RMC Place; CARBON; ▲ Franklin; ***227** EK-10; mail Lehighton **z** 18235; ● 500
Union Mills; RMC Place; MIFFLIN; ▲ Union; ***225** WL-14; mail Belleville **z** 17004; rural
Union Square; RMC Place; LANCASTER; ▲ Rapho; ***227** EO-6; elev. 595ft./181m.; mail Manheim **z** 17545; ● 90
Uniontown; Inc. Place; ⊡ FAYETTE; **225** WP-5; elev. 999ft./304m.; 🅿 🅷 🅲 1,139 ■; ★ **UNTN**; **z** 15401; Ⓟ 12,034; Ⓒ 12,422; ◆ 12,322
Uniontown; RMC Place; INDIANA; ▲ Green; **225** WL-9; mail Cherry Tree **z** 15724; ● 100
Uniontown (Tharptown); RMC Place; NORTHUMBERLAND; ▲ Coal; ***227** EK-6; mail Shamokin **z** 17872; ● 360
Uniontown; RMC Place; VENANGO; ▲ Sandycreek, Frenchcreek; ***224** WH-4; ★ **OILC-F**; mail Franklin **z** 16323; ● 300
Uniontown; RMC Place; YORK; ▲ Franklin; ***227** EP-4; ★ **HRBG**; mail Dillsburg **z** 17019; ● 60
Union Valley; RMC Place; LAWRENCE; ▲ Shenango; ***224** WJ-2; elev. 900ft./274m.; ★ **NWCS**; mail Wampum **z** 16157; rural
Union Valley; RMC Place; WASHINGTON; ▲ Union; ***225** WN-3; elev. 1,012ft./308m.; ★ **PGH**; mail Finleyville **z** 15332; ● 1,200
Unionville; RMC Place; BEAVER; ▲ New Sewickley; **225** WK-3; ★ **PGH**; mail New Brighton **z** 15066, Rochester **z** 15074; ● 350
Unionville; RMC Place; BERKS; ▲ Union; ***227** EN-10; mail Douglassville **z** 19518; ● 90
Unionville; RMC Place; BUTLER; ▲ Center; **224** WJ-4; ★ **BUTL**; mail Butler **z** 16001; ● 100
Unionville (Fleming); Inc. Place; CENTRE; **225** WK-13; elev. 800ft./244m.; mail Fleming **z** 16835; Ⓟ 284; Ⓒ 313
Unionville; RMC Place; CHESTER; ▲ East Marlborough; **227** EQ-9; 🅿; ★ **PHIL-**; **z** 19375; ● 900
Union Water Works; RMC Place; LEBANON; ▲ North Annville; ***227** EN-6; ★ **LEB**; mail Annville **z** 17003; rural
United; RMC Place; WESTMORELAND; ▲ Mount Pleasant; ***225** WO-6; 🅿; **z** 15689; ● 1,100
Unity; RMC Place; ALLEGHENY; ***225** WM-5; ★ **PGH**; mail Pittsburgh **z** 15239; pop. incl. with Plum (Inc. Place)
Unity; MCD-Township; WESTMORELAND; ***225** WO-6; ★ **LTROB**; mail Latrobe **z** 15650; Ⓟ 20,109; Ⓒ 21,137; ◆ 20,402
Unity House; PIKE; see Forest Park (RMC Place)
Unity Junction; RMC Place; ALLEGHENY; ***225** WM-4; ★ **PGH**; mail Pittsburgh **z** 15239; pop. incl. with Plum (Inc. Place)
Unityville; RMC Place; LYCOMING; ▲ Jordan; **226** EI-6; elev. 1,236ft./377m.; 🅿; **z** 17774; ● 60
Universal; RMC Place; ALLEGHENY; ▲ Penn Hills; ***225** WM-4; elev. 1,200ft./366m.; ★ **PGH**; mail Pittsburgh **z** 15235
University City; RMC Place; PHILADELPHIA; ***227** EP-12; ★ **PHIL-**; mail Philadelphia **z** 19104; pop. incl. with Philadelphia (Inc. Place)
University Heights; RMC Place; NORTHAMPTON; ▲ Lower Saucon; ***227** EL-11; ★ **ALL-**; mail Bethlehem **z** 18015; ● 300
University Park; RMC Place; CENTRE; ***225** WK-13; 🅿; ★ **STCOL**; **z** 16802; pop. incl. with State College (Inc. Place)
Upland; Inc. Place; DELAWARE; **227** EQ-11; elev. 60ft./18m.; 🅷; ★ **PHIL-**; mail Brookhaven **z** 19015, Chester **z** 19013; Ⓟ 3,334; Ⓒ 2,977
Upland Terrace; RMC Place; MONTGOMERY; ▲ Lower Merion; ★ **PHIL-**; mail Bala Cynwyd **z** 19004
Upper Allen; MCD-Township; CUMBERLAND; ***227** EO-4; 🅲 2,854; ★ **HRBG**; mail Mechanicsburg **z** 17055; Ⓟ 13,347; Ⓒ 15,338
Upper Augusta; MCD-Township; NORTHUMBERLAND; ***227** EK-5; mail Sunbury **z** 17801; Ⓟ 2,681; Ⓒ 2,556
Upper Bern; MCD-Township; BERKS; ***227** EM-8; mail Bernville **z** 19506; Ⓟ 1,458; Ⓒ 1,479
Upper Black Eddy; RMC Place; BUCKS; ▲ Bridgeton; **227** EM-12; 🅿; ★ **PHIL-**; **z** 18972; ● 550
Upper Brownville; RMC Place; SCHUYLKILL; ▲ West Mahanoy; ***227** EK-7; mail Shenandoah **z** 17976; ● 50
Upper Burrell; MCD-Township; WESTMORELAND; ***225** WM-5; 🅲 853; ★ **PGH**; mail New Kensington **z** 15068; Ⓟ 2,258; Ⓒ 2,240
Upper Chichester; MCD-Township; DELAWARE; ***227** EQ-11; 🅿; ★ **PHIL-**; **z** 19013-14, **z** 19061; Ⓟ 15,004; Ⓒ 16,842
Upper Darby; RMC Place; DELAWARE; ▲ Upper Darby; **227** EP-12; 🅿; ★ **PHIL-**; **z** 19082 & mail Clifton Heights **z** 19018, Havertown **z** 19083, Lansdowne **z** 19050
Upper Darby; MCD-Township; DELAWARE; ***227** EP-11; 🅿 ■; ★ **PHIL-**; **z** 19082; Ⓟ 81,177; Ⓒ 81,821; ◆ 81,238
Upper Dublin; MCD-Township; MONTGOMERY; ***227** EO-12; 🅲 935; ★ **PHIL-**; mail Fort Washington **z** 19034; Ⓟ 24,028; Ⓒ 25,878; ◆ 26,038
Upper Exeter; RMC Place; LUZERNE; ▲ Exeter; **226** EH-9; ★ **SCR-**; mail Pittston **z** 18643; ● 150
Upper Fairfield; MCD-Township; LYCOMING; ***226** EH-4; ★ **WMSPT**; mail Montoursville **z** 17754; Ⓟ 1,774; Ⓒ 1,854
Upper Frankford; MCD-Township; CUMBERLAND; ***227** EO-2; mail Newville **z** 17241; Ⓟ 1,703; Ⓒ 1,807
Upper Frederick; MCD-Township; MONTGOMERY; ***227** EN-11; ★ **PHIL-**; mail Perkiomenville **z** 18074; Ⓟ 2,165; Ⓒ 3,141
Upper Glasgow; RMC Place; MONTGOMERY; ▲ West Pottsgrove; ***227** EN-10; ★ **PTSTN**; mail Pottstown **z** 19464
Upper Gwynedd; MCD-Township; MONTGOMERY; ***227** EO-12; 🅿; ★ **PHIL-**; **z** 19446 & mail North Wales **z** 19454; Ⓟ 12,197; Ⓒ 14,243
Upper Hanover; MCD-Township; MONTGOMERY; ***227** EN-11; ★ **PHIL-**; mail East Greenville **z** 18041; Ⓟ 4,604; Ⓒ 4,885
Upper Hillville; RMC Place; CLARION; ▲ Toby; ***224** WJ-5; elev. 880ft./268m.; mail Rimersburg **z** 16248; rural
Upper Lawn; RMC Place; LEBANON; ▲ South Londonderry; ***227** EO-6; mail Palmyra **z** 17078; ● 85
Upper Leacock; MCD-Township; LANCASTER; ***227** EO-8; ★ **LANC**; mail Leola **z** 17540; Ⓟ 7,254; Ⓒ 8,229
Upper Lehigh; RMC Place; LUZERNE; ▲ Butler, Foster; ***226** EJ-9; ★ **HAZ**; mail Freeland **z** 18224; ● 250
Upper Macungie; MCD-Township; LEHIGH; ***227** EL-10; 🅲 758; ★ **ALL-**; mail Trexlertown **z** 18087; Ⓟ 8,757; Ⓒ 13,895
Upper Mahanoy; MCD-Township; NORTHUMBERLAND; ***227** EL-5; mail Leck Kill **z** 17836; Ⓟ 621; Ⓒ 599
Upper Mahantongo; MCD-Township; SCHUYLKILL; ***227** EL-5; mail Klingerstown **z** 17941; Ⓟ 696; Ⓒ 652
Upper Makefield; MCD-Township; BUCKS; ***227** EN-13; 🅿; ★ **PHIL-**; **z** 18940; Ⓟ 5,949; Ⓒ 7,180
Upper Merion; MCD-Township; MONTGOMERY; ***227** EO-11; ■; ★ **PHIL-**; mail King of Prussia **z** 19406; Ⓟ 25,722; Ⓒ 26,863; ◆ 26,725
Upper Middletown; RMC Place; FAYETTE; ▲ Menallen; ***225** WP-5; ★ **UNTN**; mail Smock **z** 15480; ● 70
Upper Mifflin; MCD-Township; CUMBERLAND; ***227** EO-2; mail Newville **z** 17241; Ⓟ 1,013; Ⓒ 1,347
Upper Milford; MCD-Township; LEHIGH; ***227** EM-11; ★ **ALL-**; mail Zionsville **z** 18092; Ⓟ 6,304; Ⓒ 6,889
Upper Mill; RMC Place; CUMBERLAND; ***227** EO-3; ★ **CARL**; mail Mount Holly Springs **z** 17065; pop. incl. with Mount Holly Springs (Inc. Place)
Upper Moreland; MCD-Township; MONTGOMERY; ***227** EO-12; ★ **PHIL-**; mail Willow Grove **z** 19090; Ⓟ 25,313; Ⓒ 24,993; ◆ 24,457
Upper Mount Bethel; MCD-Township; NORTHAMPTON; ***227** EK-12; mail Bangor **z** 18013; Ⓟ 5,476; Ⓒ 6,063
Upper Nazareth; MCD-Township; NORTHAMPTON; ***227** EL-11; ★ **ALL-**; mail Nazareth **z** 18064; Ⓟ 3,413; Ⓒ 4,426
Upper Orchard; RMC Place; BUCKS; ▲ Middletown; ★ **PHIL-**; mail Levittown **z** 19056
Upper Oxford; MCD-Township; CHESTER; ***227** EQ-9; mail Oxford **z** 19363; Ⓟ 1,615; Ⓒ 2,095
Upper Paxton; MCD-Township; DAUPHIN; ***227** EL-4; mail Millersburg **z** 17061; Ⓟ 3,680; Ⓒ 3,930
Upper Peanut; RMC Place; FAYETTE; ▲ Menallen; ***225** WP-4; ★ **UNTN**; mail Smock **z** 15480; ● 12
Upper Pottsgrove; MCD-Township; MONTGOMERY; ***227** EN-10; ★ **PTSTN**; mail Pottstown **z** 19464; Ⓟ 3,315; Ⓒ 4,102
Upper Providence; MCD-Township; DELAWARE; ***227** EP-11; ★ **PHIL-**; mail Media **z** 19063; Ⓟ 9,727; Ⓒ 10,509
Upper Providence; MCD-Township; MONTGOMERY; ***227** EO-11; ★ **PHIL-**; mail Oaks **z** 19456; Ⓟ 9,682; Ⓒ 15,398
Upper Providence Township; CDP-Census Area Only; DELAWARE; ▲ Upper Providence; ***227** EP-11; ★ **PHIL-**; mail Media **z** 19063; Ⓟ 9,727; Ⓒ 10,509
Upper Reese; RMC Place; BLAIR; ▲ Frankstown; ***225** WM-11; ★ **ALT**; mail Hollidaysburg **z** 16648; ● 130
Upper Sagon; RMC Place; NORTHUMBERLAND; ▲ Coal; mail Snydertown **z** 17877
Upper Saint Clair; CDP; ALLEGHENY; ▲ Upper St. Clair; **225** WN-3; 🅿; ★ **PGH**; **z** 15241; Ⓟ 19,692; Ⓒ 20,053; ◆ 19,279
Upper St. Clair; MCD-Township; ALLEGHENY; ***225** WN-3; 🅿 ■; ★ **PGH**; **z** 15241; Ⓟ 19,692; Ⓒ 20,053; ◆ 19,279
Upper Salford; MCD-Township; MONTGOMERY; ***227** EN-11; ★ **PHIL-**; mail Salford **z** 18957; Ⓟ 2,719; Ⓒ 3,024
Upper Saucon; MCD-Township; LEHIGH; ***227** EM-11; 🅲 2,936; ★ **ALL-**; mail Center Valley **z** 18034; Ⓟ 9,775; Ⓒ 11,939
Upper Southampton; MCD-Township; BUCKS; ***227** EO-13; ★ **PHIL-**; mail Southampton **z** 18966; Ⓟ 16,076; Ⓒ 15,764
Upper Strasburg; RMC Place; FRANKLIN; ▲ Letterkenny; **225** WP-14; 🅿; **z** 17265; ● 225
Upper Tulpehocken; MCD-Township; BERKS; ***227** EM-8; mail Strausstown **z** 19559; Ⓟ 1,289; Ⓒ 1,495
Upper Turkeyfoot; MCD-Township; SOMERSET; ***225** WQ-7; mail Rockwood **z** 15557; Ⓟ 1,132; Ⓒ 1,232
Upper Two Lick; RMC Place; INDIANA; ▲ White; ***225** WL-7; elev. 1,080ft./329m.; mail Indiana **z** 15701; rural
Upper Tyrone; MCD-Township; FAYETTE; ***225** WO-5; mail Connellsville **z** 15425, Everson **z** 15631; Ⓟ 1,995; Ⓒ 2,244
Upper Uwchlan; MCD-Township; CHESTER; ***227** EO-10; ★ **PHIL-**; mail Downingtown **z** 19335; Ⓟ 4,396; Ⓒ 6,850
Upper Wheel; RMC Place; WESTMORELAND; ▲ Sewickley; ***225** WN-5; ★ **PGH**; mail Yukon **z** 15698; ● 100
Upper Yoder; MCD-Township; CAMBRIA; ***225** WN-8; ★ **JNST**; mail Johnstown **z** 15905; Ⓟ 5,435; Ⓒ 5,862
Upsonville (Franklin Hill); RMC Place; SUSQUEHANNA; ▲ Franklin; ***226** EE-9; mail Hallstead **z** 18822; ● 120
Upton; RMC Place; FRANKLIN; ▲ Peters; **225** WQ-13; mail Greencastle **z** 17225; ● 100
Uptown; RMC Place; ALLEGHENY; ★ **PGH**; mail Pittsburgh **z** 15219; pop. incl. with Pittsburgh (Inc. Place)
Urban; RMC Place; NORTHUMBERLAND; ▲ Jordan; **227** EL-5; mail Herndon **z** 17830; ● 45
Urey; RMC Place; INDIANA; ▲ Banks; ***225** WK-9; mail Glen Campbell **z** 15742
Uriah; RMC Place; CUMBERLAND; ▲ South Middleton; ***227** EP-3; ★ **CARL**; mail Gardners **z** 17324; rural
Ursina; Inc. Place; SOMERSET; **225** WQ-6; elev. 1,356ft./413m.; 🅿; **z** 15485; Ⓟ 327; Ⓒ 254
Ursina Junction; RMC Place; SOMERSET; mail Confluence **z** 15424; pop. incl. with Confluence (Inc. Place)
Utahville; RMC Place; CLEARFIELD; ▲ Beccaria; **225** WL-10; mail Coalport **z** 16627; ● 160
Utica; Inc. Place; VENANGO; **224** WG-4; elev. 1,054ft./321m.; 🅿; ★ **OILC-F**; **z** 16362; Ⓟ 242; Ⓒ 211
Utopia; RMC Place; WESTMORELAND; ▲ Washington; ***225** WM-5; elev. 1,092ft./333m.; ★ **PGH**; mail Apollo **z** 15613; ● 200
Uwchlan; CHESTER; see Eagle (RMC Place)
Uwchlan (Uwchland); MCD-Township; CHESTER; ***227** EP-10; ★ **PHIL-**; mail Exton **z** 19341, Uwchland **z** 19480; Ⓟ 12,999; Ⓒ 16,576
Uwchland; CHESTER; see Eagle (RMC Place)
Uwchland; CHESTER; see Uwchlan (MCD-Township)

Entries in **UPPERCASE** are counties.
Entries in **bold** have populations of 2,500 or more.
Names in parentheses are alternate names.

Inc. Place	Incorporated Place
RMC Place	Rand McNally Designated Place
CDP	Census Designated Place
MCD	Minor Civil Division

⊡	County Seat
▲	Minor Civil Division
elev.	Elevation
🅿	Post Office
🅷	Hospital
🅲	College
■	Principal Business Center
★	Ranally Metro Area (RMA) Abbreviation
z	Zip Code(s)
Ⓟ	Previous Census Population
Ⓡ	Revised Census Population
Ⓐ	Annexation Population
●	Rand McNally Population Estimate
Ⓒ	Final Census Population
Ⓢ	Special Census Population
◆	Estimated Population

For additional definitions see Glossary, Volume 1, and Introduction, Volume 2.

V

Vail; RMC Place; BLAIR; ▲ Snyder; ***225** WL-12; ★ **ALT**; mail Tyrone z 16686
Valemont Heights; RMC Place; ALLEGHENY; ▲ Penn Hills; ***225** WM-4; ★ **PGH**; mail Verona z 15147
Valencia; Inc. Place; BUTLER; **225** WL-4; elev. 1,100ft./335m.; 🅿; ★ **PGH**; z 16059; Ⓟ 364; Ⓒ 384
Valier; RMC Place; JEFFERSON; ▲ Perry; **225** WK-8; 🅿; z 15780; ● 275
Vallamont Hills; RMC Place; LYCOMING; ***226** EI-4; ★ **WMSPT**; mail Williamsport z 17701; pop. incl. with Williamsport (Inc. Place)
Valley; MCD-Township; ARMSTRONG; ***225** WK-6; mail Kittanning z 16201; Ⓟ 709; Ⓒ 681
Valley (Valley Township); MCD-Township; CHESTER; ***227** EP-9; ★ **PHIL-**; mail Coatesville z 19320; Ⓟ 4,007; Ⓒ 5,116
Valley; MCD-Township; MONTOUR; ***226** EJ-5; mail Danville z 17821; Ⓟ 2,010; Ⓒ 2,093
Valley Camp; RMC Place; WESTMORELAND; ***225** WL-5; ★ **PGH**; mail New Kensington z 15068; pop. incl. with New Kensington (Inc. Place)
Valley Falls; RMC Place; MONTGOMERY; ▲ Lower Moreland; ***227** EO-13; ★ **PHIL-**; mail Huntingdon Valley z 19006
Valley Forge; RMC Place; CHESTER; ▲ Tredyffrin, Schuylkill; **227** EO-11; elev. 237ft./72m.; 🅿; ★ **PHIL-**; z 19481-82, z 19484-85, z 19493-96; ● 1,500
Valley Forge Estates; RMC Place; CHESTER; ▲ Tredyffrin; ***227** EO-11; ★ **PHIL-**; mail Wayne z 19087; ● 3,000
Valley Forge Homes; RMC Place; MONTGOMERY; ▲ Upper Merion; ★ **PHIL-**; mail King of Prussia z 19406
Valley Forge Manor; RMC Place; MONTGOMERY; ▲ Lower Providence; ★ **PHIL-**; mail Phoenixville z 19460; ● 100
Valley Furnace; RMC Place; SCHUYLKILL; ▲ Blythe; ★ **PTSVL**; mail New Philadelphia z 17959; ● 40
Valley Green; CDP-Census Area Only; YORK; ▲ Newberry; ***227** EO-5; elev. 400ft./122m.; mail Etters z 17319; Ⓟ 3,017; Ⓒ 3,550
Valley Green Estates; RMC Place; YORK; ▲ Newberry; ***227** EO-5; elev. 453ft./138m.; mail Etters z 17319; ● 250
Valley Green Heights; RMC Place; YORK; ▲ Newberry; ***227** EO-5; elev. 400ft./122m.; mail Etters z 17319; ● 200
Valley Green West; RMC Place; YORK; ***227** EO-5; elev. 500ft./152m.; mail Etters z 17319; ● 200
Valley-Hi; Inc. Place; FULTON; ▲ Wells, Brush Creek; ***225** WP-12; mail Breezewood z 15533; Ⓟ 19; Ⓒ 20
Valley Stream; RMC Place; LUZERNE; ▲ Wright; ***226** EI-8; elev. 1,090ft./332m.; ★ **SCR-**; mail Mountain Top z 18707; ● 140
Valley Township; CHESTER; see Valley (MCD-Township)
Valley View; RMC Place; CENTRE; ▲ Benner; **225** WK-13; ★ **STCOL**; mail Bellefonte z 16823; ● 150
Valley View (Icedale); RMC Place; CHESTER; ▲ Honey Brook; ***227** EP-9; ★ **PHIL-**; mail Honey Brook z 19344; ● 240
Valley View; RMC Place; LANCASTER; ▲ Penn; **227** EO-7; ★ **LANC**; mail Manheim z 17545; ● 600
Valley View; CDP; SCHUYLKILL; ▲ Hegins; **227** EL-6; 🅿; z 17983; Ⓟ 1,749; Ⓒ 1,677
Valley View; CDP-Census Area Only; YORK; ▲ Spring Garden; ***227** EP-5; elev. 693ft./211m.; ★ **YORK**; mail York z 17403; Ⓟ 2,911; Ⓒ 2,743
Valley View Heights; RMC Place; ARMSTRONG; ▲ Manor; ***225** WK-6; ★ **PGH**; mail Ford City z 16226; ● 100
Van; RMC Place; VENANGO; ▲ Rockland, Cranberry; **224** WH-5; ★ **OILC-F**; mail Cranberry z 16319; ● 60
Van Buren; RMC Place; WASHINGTON; ▲ South Franklin; ***225** WO-2; ★ **WASH**; mail Prosperity z 15329; rural
Vance; RMC Place; WASHINGTON; ▲ South Strabane; ***225** WO-3; ★ **WASH**; mail Washington z 15301; rural
Vances Mill; RMC Place; FAYETTE; ▲ North Union; ***225** WP-5; ★ **UNTN**; mail Uniontown z 15401; ● 20
Vanceville; RMC Place; WASHINGTON; ▲ Somerset; ***225** WO-3; ★ **WASH**; mail Eighty Four z 15330; rural
Vanderbilt; Inc. Place; FAYETTE; **225** WP-5; elev. 900ft./274m.; 🅿; z 15486; Ⓟ 545; Ⓒ 553
Vandergrift; Inc. Place; WESTMORELAND; **225** WL-5; elev. 860ft./262m.; 🅿; ★ **PGH**; z 15690; Ⓟ 5,904; Ⓒ 5,455
Vandling; Inc. Place; LACKAWANNA; **226** EF-11; elev. 1,600ft./488m.; 🅿; ★ **SCR-**; z 18421; Ⓟ 660; Ⓒ 738
Vandyke; RMC Place; JUNIATA; ▲ Walker; **227** EM-3; mail Port Royal z 17082; ● 80
Van Emman; RMC Place; WASHINGTON; ▲ Peters; ***225** WN-3; elev. 918ft./280m.; ★ **PGH**; mail Canonsburg z 15317
Vankirk; RMC Place; WASHINGTON; ▲ South Franklin; ***225** WO-2; ★ **WASH**; mail Washington z 15301
Van Meter; RMC Place; WESTMORELAND; ▲ Rostraver; ***225** WO-5; 🅿; ★ **PGH**; z 15479; ● 160
Van Ormer; RMC Place; CAMBRIA; ▲ Reade; **225** WL-10; mail Fallentimber z 16639; ● 180
Vanport; RMC Place; BEAVER; **225** WL-2; mail Beaver z 15009; ● 1,300
Vanport; MCD-Township; BEAVER; ***225** WL-2; 🅿; ★ **PGH**; z 15009; Ⓟ 1,700; Ⓒ 1,451
Van Voorhis; RMC Place; WASHINGTON; ▲ Fallowfield; **225** WO-3; 🅿; ★ **PGH**; z 15366; ● 400
Van Wert; RMC Place; JUNIATA; ▲ Walker; ***227** EM-2; mail Mifflintown z 17059; ● 35
Varden; RMC Place; WAYNE; ▲ South Canaan; **226** EG-11; mail Lake Ariel z 18436; ● 150
Vawter; RMC Place; BRADFORD; ▲ Litchfield; ***226** EE-6; mail Athens z 18810; ● 100
Venango; MCD-Township; BUTLER; ***224** WI-4; mail Parker z 16049; Ⓟ 707; Ⓒ 732
Venango; Inc. Place; CRAWFORD; **224** WE-3; elev. 1,130ft./344m.; 🅿; z 16440; Ⓟ 289; Ⓒ 288
Venango; MCD-Township; CRAWFORD; ***224** WE-3; 🅿; z 16440; does not include the Borough of Venango; Ⓟ 729; Ⓒ 956
Venango; MCD-Township; ERIE; ***224** WD-5; mail Wattsburg z 16442; Ⓟ 2,235; Ⓒ 2,277
VENANGO; **224** WG-4; Ⓟ 59,381; Ⓒ 57,565; ◆ 53,936
Venetia (Anderson); RMC Place; WASHINGTON; ▲ Peters, Nottingham; **225** WN-3; 🅿; ★ **PGH**; z 15367; ● 450
Venice; RMC Place; WASHINGTON; ▲ Cecil; ***225** WN-3; ★ **PGH**; mail Mc Donald z 15057; ● 90
Venturetown; RMC Place; WARREN; ▲ Conewango; ***224** WE-7; elev. 1,196ft./365m.; mail Warren z 16365
Venus; RMC Place; VENANGO, CLARION; ▲ Washington, Pinegrove; **224** WH-6; 🅿; z 16364; ● 150
Vera Cruz; RMC Place; LEHIGH; ▲ Upper Milford; **227** EM-11; elev. 563ft./172m.; ★ **ALL-**; mail Emmaus z 18049; ● 250
Verdilla; RMC Place; SNYDER; ▲ Union; ***227** EL-4; mail Selinsgrove z 17870; rural
Vere Cruz; RMC Place; LANCASTER; ▲ East Cocalico; ***227** EN-8; mail Reinholds z 17569; ● 60
Vermilion Hill; RMC Place; BUCKS; ▲ Falls; ***227** EO-14; ★ **PHIL-**; mail Levittown z 19054
Vernfield; RMC Place; MONTGOMERY; ▲ Lower Salford; **227** EN-11; ★ **PHIL-**; mail Harleysville z 19438; ● 200
Vernon; MCD-Township; CRAWFORD; ***224** WF-3; mail Meadville z 16335; Ⓟ 5,605; Ⓒ 5,499
Vernon; RMC Place; WYOMING; ▲ Northmoreland; ***226** EG-8; elev. 1,082ft./330m.; mail Tunkhannock z 18657
Vernondale; RMC Place; ERIE; ▲ Millcreek; ***224** WD-3; elev. 739ft./225m.; ★ **ERIE**; mail Erie z 16505
Vernon Park; RMC Place; PHILADELPHIA; ★ **PHIL-**; mail Philadelphia z 19144; pop. incl. with Philadelphia (Inc. Place)
Verona; Inc. Place; ALLEGHENY; **225** WM-4; elev. 860ft./262m.; 🅿; ★ **PGH**; z 15147; Ⓟ 3,260; Ⓒ 3,124
Versailles; Inc. Place; ALLEGHENY; **225** WN-4; elev. 860ft./262m.; ★ **PGH**; mail Mckeesport z 15132; Ⓟ 1,821; Ⓒ 1,724
Vestaburg; RMC Place; WASHINGTON; ▲ East Bethlehem; **225** WP-4; 🅿; z 15368; ● 975
Vesta Heights; RMC Place; WASHINGTON; ▲ East Bethlehem; ***225** WP-3; mail Fredericktown z 15333; ● 75
Vicksburg; RMC Place; BLAIR; ▲ Blair; ***225** WN-11; ★ **ALT**; mail Hollidaysburg z 16648; ● 180
Vicksburg; RMC Place; UNION; ▲ Buffalo; **226** EJ-4; 🅿; z 17883; ● 200
Victory; MCD-Township; VENANGO; ***224** WH-4; mail Polk z 16342; Ⓟ 365; Ⓒ 408
Victory Heights; RMC Place; VENANGO; ▲ Cranberry; **224** WH-5; ★ **OILC-F**; mail Franklin z 16323; ● 250
Victory Hills; RMC Place; WASHINGTON; ▲ Carroll; ***225** WO-4; ★ **PGH**; mail Monongahela z 15063; ● 500
Village; RMC Place; ALLEGHENY; ▲ Upper St. Clair; ***225** WN-3; ★ **PGH**; mail Pittsburgh z 15241; pop. incl. with Bethel Park (Inc. Place)
Village Green; RMC Place; DELAWARE; ▲ Aston; ***227** EQ-11; ★ **PHIL-**; mail Chester z 19013
Village Green-Green Ridge; CDP-Census Area Only; DELAWARE; ▲ Aston; ***227** EQ-11; elev. 200ft./61m.; ★ **PHIL-**; mail Chester z 19013; Ⓟ 9,026; Ⓒ 8,279
Village of Cross Creek; RMC Place; YORK; ▲ Springettsbury; mail York z 17402
Village of Olde Hickory; RMC Place; LANCASTER; ▲ Manheim; ***227** EO-7; ★ **LANC**; mail Lancaster z 17601; ● 900
Village of the Four Seasons; RMC Place; SUSQUEHANNA; ▲ Herrick; ***226** EF-10; elev. 1,625ft./495m.; mail Union Dale z 18470; ● 100
Village of Westover; RMC Place; CUMBERLAND; ▲ Hampden; ***227** EN-4; ★ **HRBG**; mail Mechanicsburg z 17055; ● 1,200
Village Shires; CDP-Census Area Only; BUCKS; ▲ Northampton; ***227** EO-13; elev. 200ft./61m.; ★ **PHIL-**; mail Southampton z 18966; Ⓟ 4,364; Ⓒ 4,137
Villa Green; RMC Place; YORK; ▲ Spring Garden; ***227** EP-5; ★ **YORK**; mail York z 17403
Villa Maria; RMC Place; LAWRENCE; ▲ Pulaski; **224** WI-1; 🅿; ★ **YNGS-**; z 16155; ● 150
Villanova; RMC Place; DELAWARE; ▲ Radnor; ***227** EP-11; elev. 391ft./119m.; 🅿 🅲 10,275; ★ **PHIL-**; z 19085
Vinco (White Hall); CDP; CAMBRIA; ▲ Jackson; **225** WN-9; elev. 1,737ft./529m.; ★ **JNST**; mail Johnstown z 15909; Ⓟ 1,586; Ⓒ 1,429
Vinemont; RMC Place; BERKS; ▲ Spring; **227** EN-8; ★ **READ**; mail Reinholds z 17569; ● 100
Vintage (Williamstown); RMC Place; LANCASTER; ▲ Paradise; **227** EP-8; mail Paradise z 17562; ● 200
Vintondale; Inc. Place; CAMBRIA; **225** WM-8; elev. 1,440ft./439m.; 🅿; ★ **JNST**; z 15961; Ⓟ 582; Ⓒ 528
Violet Hill; RMC Place; YORK; ▲ Spring Garden; ***227** EP-5; ★ **YORK**; mail York z 17403; ● 800
Violet Wood; RMC Place; BUCKS; ▲ Bristol; ***227** EO-14; ★ **PHIL-**; mail Levittown z 19057
Vira; RMC Place; MIFFLIN; ▲ Derry; **227** EL-1; mail Lewistown z 17044; ● 150
Virginia; RMC Place; LACKAWANNA; ★ **SCR-**; pop. incl. with Scranton (Inc. Place)
Virginia Farms; RMC Place; INDIANA; ▲ Black Lick; ***225** WM-7; elev. 1,191ft./363m.; ★ **PGH**; mail Blairsville z 15717; rural
Virginia Hills West; RMC Place; ALLEGHENY; ▲ North Fayette; ***225** WM-2; elev. 1,100ft./335m.; ★ **PGH**; mail Imperial z 15126; ● 380
Virginia Mills; RMC Place; ADAMS; ▲ Hamiltonban; ***227** EQ-2; mail Fairfield z 17320; ● 40
Virginville; RMC Place; BERKS; ▲ Richmond, Perry; **227** EM-9; 🅿; z 19564; ● 300
Voganville; RMC Place; LANCASTER; ▲ Earl; ***227** EO-8; ★ **LANC**; mail Ephrata z 17522; ● 100
Vogleyville; RMC Place; BUTLER; ▲ Summit; ***225** WK-4; elev. 1,411ft./430m.; ★ **BUTL**; mail Butler z 16001
Volant; Inc. Place; LAWRENCE; **224** WI-2; elev. 1,050ft./320m.; 🅿; z 16156; Ⓟ 152; Ⓒ 113
Vosburg; RMC Place; WYOMING; ▲ Washington; ***226** EG-8; mail Tunkhannock z 18657
Vowinckel; RMC Place; CLARION; ▲ Farmington; **224** WH-7; elev. 1,630ft./497m.; 🅿; z 16260; ● 50
Vulcan; RMC Place; SCHUYLKILL; ▲ Mahanoy; ***227** EK-8; mail Barnesville z 18214; ● 30

W

Wadesville; RMC Place; SCHUYLKILL; ▲ New Castle; ***227** EL-7; ★ **PTSVL**; mail Pottsville z 17901; ● 200
Wadsworth; RMC Place; PHILADELPHIA; ★ **PHIL-**; mail Philadelphia z 19150; pop. incl. with Philadelphia (Inc. Place)
Wagner; RMC Place; MIFFLIN; ▲ Decatur; **227** EL-2; mail Mc Clure z 17841; ● 65
Wagnersville; NORTHAMPTON; see Wagnerville (RMC Place)
Wagnerville (Wagnersville); RMC Place; NORTHAMPTON; ▲ Bethlehem; ***227** EL-11; ★ **ALL-**; mail Easton z 18040
Wagontown; RMC Place; CHESTER; ▲ West Caln; **227** EP-9; 🅿; ★ **PHIL-**; z 19376; ● 500
Wahlville; RMC Place; BUTLER; ▲ Forward; ***225** WK-3; ★ **PGH**; mail Evans City z 16033; rural
Wahnetah; RMC Place; CARBON; mail Jim Thorpe z 18229; pop. incl. with Jim Thorpe (Inc. Place)
Wakefield (Peach Bottom); RMC Place; LANCASTER; ▲ Fulton; ***227** EQ-5; mail Peach Bottom z 17563; ● 160
Wakena; RMC Place; WESTMORELAND; ▲ Loyalhanna, Bell; ***225** WM-6; ★ **PGH**; mail Saltsburg z 15681; rural
Walbert; RMC Place; LEHIGH; ▲ South Whitehall; **226** EB-1; elev. 516ft./157m.; ★ **ALL-**; mail Allentown z 18104; ● 200
Walcksville; RMC Place; CARBON; ▲ Franklin; ***227** EK-10; mail Lehighton z 18235; rural
Waldenheim Park; RMC Place; LEHIGH; ★ **ALL-**; pop. incl. with Allentown (Inc. Place)
Walden Woods; RMC Place; ALLEGHENY; ▲ North Fayette; ***225** WM-2; elev. 1,100ft./335m.; ★ **PGH**; mail Imperial z 15126; ● 250
Wales Junction; MONTGOMERY; see Kneedler (RMC Place)
Walkchalk; RMC Place; ARMSTRONG; ▲ East Franklin; ***225** WK-5; ★ **PGH**; mail Kittanning z 16201; ● 100
Walker; MCD-Township; CENTRE; ***227** EK-1; mail Howard z 16841; Ⓟ 2,801; Ⓒ 3,299
Walker; MCD-Township; HUNTINGDON; ***225** WM-12; mail Huntingdon z 16652; Ⓟ 1,515; Ⓒ 1,747
Walker; MCD-Township; JUNIATA; ***227** EM-2; mail Mifflintown z 17059; Ⓟ 2,331; Ⓒ 2,598
Walker; MCD-Township; SCHUYLKILL; ***227** EL-8; mail Tamaqua z 18252; Ⓟ 949; Ⓒ 936
Walkers Mill; RMC Place; ALLEGHENY; ▲ Collier; ***225** WM-3; ★ **PGH**; mail Carnegie z 15106; ● 50
Walkertown; RMC Place; WASHINGTON; ▲ West Pike Run; ***225** WP-4; mail Daisytown z 15427
Wall; Inc. Place; ALLEGHENY; **228** L-9; elev. 800ft./244m.; 🅿; ★ **PGH**; z 15148; Ⓟ 853; Ⓒ 727
Wallace; MCD-Township; CHESTER; ***227** EO-9; ★ **PHIL-**; mail Glenmoore z 19343; Ⓟ 2,541; Ⓒ 3,240
Wallace Junction; RMC Place; ERIE; ***224** WD-2; ★ **ERIE**; mail Girard z 16417; pop. incl. with Girard (Inc. Place)
Wallaceton; Inc. Place; CLEARFIELD; **224** WJ-11; elev. 1,721ft./525m.; 🅿; z 16876; Ⓟ 319; Ⓒ 350
Wallaceville; RMC Place; VENANGO; ▲ Plum; ***224** WG-5; mail Titusville z 16354; rural
Wallenpaupack Lake Estates; RMC Place; WAYNE; ▲ Paupack; ***226** EH-11; elev. 1,400ft./427m.; mail Lake Ariel z 18436; summer pop. 3,000; ● 200
Waller; CDP; COLUMBIA; ▲ Jackson; **226** EI-6; elev. 1,259ft./384m.; mail Benton z 17814; Ⓒ 55
Wallingford; RMC Place; DELAWARE; ▲ Nether Providence; ***227** EQ-11; 🅿; ★ **PHIL-**; z 19086
Wallis Run; RMC Place; LYCOMING; ▲ Cascade; ***226** EH-4; mail Trout Run z 17771; rural
Walls Corners; RMC Place; LACKAWANNA; ▲ West Abington; **226** EG-9; ★ **SCR-**; mail Dalton z 18414; ● 30
Wallsville; RMC Place; LACKAWANNA; ▲ Benton; **226** EG-9; ★ **SCR-**; mail Dalton z 18414; ● 50
Walltown; RMC Place; CLEARFIELD; ▲ Penn; ***224** WJ-10; mail Grampian z 16838; ● 40
Walmo; RMC Place; LAWRENCE; ▲ Neshannock; **224** WJ-2; elev. 1,126ft./343m.; ★ **NWCS**; mail New Castle z 16101; ● 900
Walnut; RMC Place; JUNIATA; ▲ Beale; **227** EM-2; mail Port Royal z 17082; ● 115
Walnut Bend; RMC Place; VENANGO; ▲ President; ***224** WG-5; ★ **OILC-F**; mail Oil City z 16301; ● 60
Walnut Bottom; RMC Place; CUMBERLAND; ▲ South Newton; **227** EO-2; 🅿; z 17266; ● 300
Walnut Gardens; RMC Place; LEHIGH; ▲ Whitehall; ***227** EL-11; ★ **ALL-**; mail Whitehall z 18052; ● 250
Walnut Grove; RMC Place; PERRY; ▲ Juniata; ***227** EM-3; mail Newport z 17074; rural
Walnut Hill; RMC Place; FAYETTE; ▲ South Union, Georges; ***225** WO-5; ★ **UNTN**; mail Uniontown z 15401; ● 60
Walnut Hill; RMC Place; GREENE; ▲ Dunkard; ***225** WQ-4; mail Dilliner z 15327; ● 30
Walnut Hill; RMC Place; MONTGOMERY; ▲ Abington; ***227** EO-13; ★ **PHIL-**; mail Abington z 19001; ● 700
Walnutport; Inc. Place; NORTHAMPTON; **227** EK-10; elev. 380ft./116m.; 🅿; ★ **ALL-**; z 18088; Ⓟ 2,055; Ⓒ 2,043
Walnuttown; RMC Place; BERKS; ▲ Richmond; **227** EM-9; ★ **READ**; mail Fleetwood z 19522; ● 110
Walsall; RMC Place; CAMBRIA; ▲ Richland; ***225** WN-9; ★ **JNST**; mail Johnstown z 15904; rural
Walston; RMC Place; JEFFERSON; ▲ Young; **224** WJ-8; 🅿; z 15781; ● 275
Walston Junction; RMC Place; JEFFERSON; mail Punxsutawney z 15767; pop. incl. with Punxsutawney (Inc. Place)
Walters (Lower Mill); RMC Place; NORTHAMPTON; ▲ Forks; ***227** EL-12; ★ **ALL-**; mail Easton z 18045; ● 20
Waltersburg; RMC Place; FAYETTE; ▲ Franklin, Menallen; **225** WP-5; elev. 898ft./274m.; 🅿; ★ **UNTN**; z 15488; ● 275
Waltonville; RMC Place; DAUPHIN; ▲ Derry; **227** ET-6; ★ **HRBG**; mail Hummelstown z 17036; ● 125
Waltz; WESTMORELAND; see Waltz Mill (RMC Place)
Waltz Landing; RMC Place; WAYNE; ▲ Paupack; ***226** EG-12; mail Hawley z 18428; ● 300
Waltz Mill (Waltz); RMC Place; WESTMORELAND; ▲ South Huntingdon; ***225** WO-5; ★ **PGH**; mail Ruffs Dale z 15679; ● 60
Wampum; Inc. Place; LAWRENCE; **225** WK-2; elev. 880ft./268m.; 🅿; ★ **PGH**; z 16157; Ⓟ 666; Ⓒ 678
Wanamakers; RMC Place; LEHIGH; ▲ Lynn; **227** EL-9; elev. 435ft./133m.; ★ **ALL-**; mail Kempton z 19529; ● 55
Wanamie; RMC Place; LUZERNE; ▲ Newport; **226** EI-8; ★ **SCR-**; mail Nanticoke z 18634; ● 600
Wandin; RMC Place; INDIANA; ▲ Green, Cherryhill; ***225** WL-8; mail Commodore z 15729; ● 20
Wanneta; RMC Place; ERIE; ▲ Conneaut; ★ **ERIE**; mail Albion z 16401; rural
Wapwallopen; RMC Place; LUZERNE; ▲ Conyngham; **226** EJ-8; 🅿; z 18660; ● 150
Ward; RMC Place; DELAWARE; ▲ Concord; ***227** EQ-11; ★ **PHIL-**; mail Concordville z 19331; ● 300
Ward; MCD-Township; TIOGA; ***226** EF-4; mail Canton z 17724; Ⓟ 55; Ⓒ 128
Wardville; RMC Place; PERRY; ▲ Greenwood; ***227** EM-3; mail Millerstown z 17062; rural
Warfordsburg; RMC Place; FULTON; ▲ Bethel; **225** WQ-12; 🅿; z 17267; ● 135
Warminster; RMC Place; BUCKS; ▲ Warminster; **227** EO-12; elev. 310ft./94m.; 🅿 🅷; ★ **PHIL-**; z 18974, z 18991; ● 31,400
Warminster; MCD-Township; BUCKS; ***227** EO-12; elev. 310ft./94m.; 🅿 ■; ★ **PHIL-**; z 18974, z 18991; Ⓒ 31,383; ◆ 32,201
Warminster Heights; CDP; BUCKS; ▲ Warminster; ***227** EO-12; elev. 300ft./91m.; ★ **PHIL-**; mail Warminster z 18974; Ⓟ 4,310; Ⓒ 4,191
Warner; RMC Place; WASHINGTON; ▲ Fallowfield; ***225** WO-4; ★ **PGH**; mail Charleroi z 15022; ● 100
Warren; MCD-Township; BRADFORD; ***226** ED-7; mail Warren Center z 18851; Ⓟ 927; Ⓒ 1,025
Warren; MCD-Township; FRANKLIN; ***225** WQ-13; mail Mercersburg z 17236; Ⓟ 310; Ⓒ 334
Warren; Inc. Place; ⊡ WARREN; **224** WE-7; elev. 1,200ft./366m.; 🅿 🅷 ■; z 16365-69; Ⓟ 11,122; Ⓒ 10,259; ◆ 9,497
WARREN; **224** WF-6; Ⓟ 45,050; Ⓒ 43,863; ◆ 40,569
Warren Center; RMC Place; BRADFORD; ▲ Warren; **226** ED-7; 🅿; z 18851; ● 200
Warrendale; RMC Place; ALLEGHENY; ▲ Marshall; **225** WL-3; 🅿; ★ **PGH**; z 15086, z 15095-96; ● 500
Warren South; CDP-Census Area Only; WARREN; ▲ Pleasant; ***224** WE-7; mail Warren z 16365; Ⓟ 1,780; Ⓒ 1,651
Warrensville; RMC Place; LYCOMING; ▲ Eldred; **226** EH-4; ★ **WMSPT**; mail Williamsport z 17701; ● 300
Warrington; RMC Place; BUCKS; ▲ Warrington; **227** EN-12; 🅿; ★ **PHIL-**; z 18976; ● 7,000
Warrington; MCD-Township; BUCKS; ***227** EN-12; 🅿; ★ **PHIL-**; z 18976; Ⓟ 12,169; Ⓒ 17,580; ◆ 20,116
Warrington; MCD-Township; YORK; ***227** EP-4; mail Dillsburg z 17019; Ⓟ 4,275; Ⓒ 4,435
Warrior Ridge; RMC Place; HUNTINGDON; ▲ Logan; ***225** WM-12; mail Petersburg z 16669
Warrior Run (Peely); Inc. Place; LUZERNE; **226** EI-8; elev. 700ft./213m.; 🅿; ★ **SCR-**; z 18706; Ⓟ 656; Ⓒ 624
Warriors Mark; RMC Place; HUNTINGDON; ▲ Warriors Mark; **225** WL-12; 🅿; z 16877; ● 350
Warriors Mark; MCD-Township; HUNTINGDON; ***225** WL-12; 🅿; z 16877 & mail Tyrone z 16686; Ⓟ 1,375; Ⓒ 1,635
Warsaw; MCD-Township; JEFFERSON; ***224** WI-8; mail Brookville z 15825; Ⓟ 1,213; Ⓒ 1,346
Warsaw; RMC Place; LACKAWANNA; ***226** EG-10; ★ **SCR-**; mail Scranton z 18512; pop. incl. with Throop (Inc. Place)
Warsaw; RMC Place; LUZERNE; ▲ Wilkes-Barre; ★ **SCR-**; mail Wilkes Barre z 18702
Warwick; MCD-Township; BUCKS; ***227** EN-12; 🅿; ★ **PHIL-**; z 18974 & mail Jamison z 18929; Ⓟ 5,915; Ⓒ 11,977
Warwick (Saint Marys); RMC Place; CHESTER; ▲ Warwick; **227** EO-9; ★ **PHIL-**; mail Elverson z 19520; ● 200
Warwick; MCD-Township; CHESTER; ***227** EO-9; ★ **PHIL-**; mail Elverson z 19520; Ⓟ 2,575; Ⓒ 2,556
Warwick; MCD-Township; LANCASTER; ***227** EO-7; ★ **LANC**; mail Lititz z 17543; Ⓟ 11,622; Ⓒ 15,475
Washington; MCD-Township; ARMSTRONG; ***224** WJ-6; mail Cowansville z 16218; Ⓟ 984; Ⓒ 1,029
Washington; MCD-Township; BERKS; ***227** EN-10; mail Boyertown z 19512; Ⓟ 2,799; Ⓒ 3,354
Washington; MCD-Township; BUTLER; ***224** WI-4; mail West Sunbury z 16061; Ⓟ 1,280; Ⓒ 1,419
Washington; MCD-Township; CAMBRIA; ***225** WM-10; mail Lilly z 15938; Ⓟ 929; Ⓒ 921
Washington; MCD-Township; CLARION; ***224** WH-6; mail Fryburg z 16326; Ⓟ 1,925; Ⓒ 2,037
Washington; RMC Place; CUMBERLAND; ▲ Upper Mifflin; ***227** EO-2; mail Newville z 17241
Washington; MCD-Township; DAUPHIN; ***227** EM-5; mail Lykens z 17048; Ⓟ 1,816; Ⓒ 2,047
Washington; MCD-Township; ERIE; ***224** WE-3; ★ **ERIE**; mail Edinboro z 16412; Ⓟ 4,102; Ⓒ 4,526
Washington; MCD-Township; FAYETTE; ***225** WO-4; ★ **PGH**; mail Belle Vernon z 15012; Ⓟ 4,613; Ⓒ 4,461
Washington; MCD-Township; FRANKLIN; ***227** EQ-1; ★ **HAG**; mail Waynesboro z 17268; Ⓟ 11,119; Ⓒ 11,559
Washington; MCD-Township; GREENE; ***225** WP-3; mail Waynesburg z 15370; Ⓟ 1,071; Ⓒ 1,106
Washington; MCD-Township; INDIANA; ***225** WL-7; mail Creekside z 15732; Ⓟ 1,861; Ⓒ 1,805
Washington; MCD-Township; JEFFERSON; ***224** WI-8; mail Falls Creek z 15840; Ⓟ 1,939; Ⓒ 1,931
Washington; MCD-Township; LAWRENCE; ***224** WI-3; mail Volant z 16156; Ⓟ 671; Ⓒ 714
Washington; MCD-Township; LEHIGH; ***227** EK-10; ★ **ALL-**; mail Slatington z 18080; Ⓟ 6,356; Ⓒ 6,588
Washington; MCD-Township; LYCOMING; ***226** EJ-3; mail Allenwood z 17810; Ⓟ 1,552; Ⓒ 1,613
Washington; MCD-Township; NORTHAMPTON; ***227** EK-12; mail Bangor z 18013; Ⓟ 3,759; Ⓒ 4,152
Washington; MCD-Township; NORTHUMBERLAND; ***227** EL-5; mail Rebuck z 17867; Ⓟ 620; Ⓒ 660
Washington; MCD-Township; SCHUYLKILL; ***227** EM-7; mail Pine Grove z 17963; Ⓟ 2,423; Ⓒ 2,750
Washington; MCD-Township; SNYDER; ***227** EL-4; mail Middleburg z 17842; Ⓟ 1,420; Ⓒ 1,532
Washington; Inc. Place; ⊡ WASHINGTON; **225** WO-2; elev. 1,020ft./311m.; 🅿 🅷 🅲 1,515 ■; ★ **WASH**; z 15301; Ⓟ 15,864; Ⓒ 15,268; ◆ 15,325
Washington; MCD-Township; WESTMORELAND; ***225** WM-5; ★ **PGH**; mail Apollo z 15613; Ⓟ 7,725; Ⓒ 7,384
Washington; MCD-Township; WYOMING; ***226** EG-8; mail Tunkhannock z 18657; Ⓟ 1,212; Ⓒ 1,306
Washington; MCD-Township; YORK; ***227** EP-3; mail East Berlin z 17316; Ⓟ 2,291; Ⓒ 2,460
WASHINGTON; **225** WO-3; Ⓟ 204,584; Ⓒ 202,897; ◆ 203,551
Washington Boro; RMC Place; LANCASTER; ▲ Manor; **227** EP-6; 🅿; ★ **LANC**; z 17582; ● 430
Washington Crossing; RMC Place; BUCKS; ▲ Upper Makefield; **227** EN-13; 🅿; ★ **PHIL-**; z 18977; ● 850
Washington Heights; RMC Place; CUMBERLAND; ***227** EO-4; ★ **HRBG**; mail Lemoyne z 17043; pop. incl. with Lemoyne (Inc. Place)
Washington Hill; RMC Place; MONTGOMERY; ***227** EN-10; ★ **PTSTN**; mail Pottstown z 19464; pop. incl. with Pottstown (Inc. Place)
Washington Square Gardens; RMC Place; MONTGOMERY; ▲ East Norriton; ***227** EO-11; ★ **PHIL-**; mail Norristown z 19401
Washingtonville; Inc. Place; MONTOUR; **226** EJ-5; elev. 540ft./165m.; 🅿; z 17884; Ⓟ 228; Ⓒ 201
Wassergass; RMC Place; NORTHAMPTON; ▲ Lower Saucon; **227** EL-11; elev. 549ft./167m.; ★ **ALL-**; mail Hellertown z 18055; ● 200
Waterfall; RMC Place; FULTON; ▲ Taylor; **225** WO-12; 🅿; z 16689; ● 100
Waterford; Inc. Place; ERIE; **224** WD-4; elev. 1,207ft./368m.; 🅿; ★ **ERIE**; z 16441; Ⓟ 1,492; Ⓒ 1,449
Waterford; MCD-Township; ERIE; ***224** WD-4; 🅿; ★ **ERIE**; z 16441; does not include the Borough of Waterford; Ⓟ 3,402; Ⓒ 3,878
Waterford; RMC Place; WESTMORELAND; ▲ Ligonier; **225** WN-7; elev. 1,324ft./404m.; mail Ligonier z 15658; ● 300
Waterford; RMC Place; YORK; ▲ Windsor; ***227** EP-5; elev. 648ft./198m.; ★ **YORK**; mail York z 17402; ● 700
Water Gap; MONROE; see Delaware Water Gap (Inc. Place)
Waterloo; RMC Place; JUNIATA; ▲ Lack; **225** WN-14; mail East Waterford z 17021; ● 50
Waterloo Mills; RMC Place; CHESTER; ▲ Easttown; ***227** EP-11; ★ **PHIL-**; mail Berwyn z 19312, Devon z 19333; rural
Waterman; RMC Place; INDIANA; ▲ Center; **225** WM-7; 🅿; z 15748; ● 140
Waterside; RMC Place; BEDFORD; ▲ South Woodbury; **225** WO-11; mail Woodbury z 16695; ● 50
Waterson; RMC Place; CLARION; ▲ Clarion; ***224** WI-7; mail Strattanville z 16258; ● 50
Water Street; RMC Place; HUNTINGDON; ▲ Morris; **225** WM-12; mail Alexandria z 16611; ● 15
Waterton; RMC Place; LUZERNE; ▲ Huntington; ***226** EI-7; mail Shickshinny z 18655; rural
Waterville; RMC Place; LYCOMING; ▲ Cummings; **226** EH-2; elev. 621ft./189m.; 🅿; z 17776; ● 150
Watkins; RMC Place; CAMBRIA; ▲ West Carroll, Barr; ***225** WL-9; mail Spangler z 15775; ● 150
Watrous; RMC Place; TIOGA; ▲ Gaines; **226** EF-1; mail Gaines z 16921; ● 150
Watrous Corners; RMC Place; SUSQUEHANNA; ▲ Bridgewater; ***226** EE-9; mail Montrose z 18801; rural
Watson; MCD-Township; LYCOMING; ***226** EI-2; mail Jersey Shore z 17740; Ⓟ 565; Ⓒ 550
Watson; MCD-Township; WARREN; ***224** WF-7; mail Tidioute z 16351; Ⓟ 276; Ⓒ 322
Watson Farm; RMC Place; FOREST; ▲ Howe; ***224** WG-8; mail Marienville z 16239; rural
Watson Run; RMC Place; CRAWFORD; ▲ Vernon; ***224** WF-3; elev. 1,079ft./329m.; mail Conneaut Lake z 16316; rural
Watsontown; Inc. Place; NORTHUMBERLAND; **226** EJ-4; elev. 500ft./152m.; 🅿; ★ **WMSPT**; z 17777; Ⓟ 2,310; Ⓒ 2,255
Watters; RMC Place; BUTLER; ▲ Forward; ***225** WK-3; ★ **PGH**; mail Evans City z 16033; rural
Wattersonville; RMC Place; ARMSTRONG; ▲ Washington; **224** WJ-6; mail Cowansville z 16218; ● 150
Watts; MCD-Township; PERRY; ***227** EM-4; ★ **HRBG**; mail Duncannon z 17020; Ⓟ 1,152; Ⓒ 1,196
Wattsburg; Inc. Place; ERIE; **224** WD-5; elev. 1,287ft./392m.; 🅿; z 16442; Ⓟ 486; Ⓒ 378
Waverly; RMC Place; LACKAWANNA; ▲ Abington; **226** EG-10; 🅿; ★ **SCR-**; z 18471; ● 1,000
Wawa; RMC Place; DELAWARE; ***227** EP-11; ★ **PHIL-**; mail Chester Heights z 19017, Media z 19063
Wawaset; RMC Place; CHESTER; ▲ Pocopson, East Bradford; ***227** EP-10; ★ **PHIL-**; mail West Chester z 19380; rural
Wayland; RMC Place; CRAWFORD; ▲ East Mead; ***224** WF-3; elev. 1,350ft./411m.; mail Meadville z 16335; rural
Waymart; Inc. Place; WAYNE; **226** EG-11; elev. 1,400ft./427m.; 🅿; ★ **SCR-**; z 18472; Ⓟ 1,337; Ⓒ 1,429
Wayne; MCD-Township; ARMSTRONG; ***225** WK-7; mail Dayton z 16222; Ⓟ 937; Ⓒ 1,117
Wayne; MCD-Township; CLINTON; ***226** EI-2; mail Mc Elhattan z 17748; Ⓟ 782; Ⓒ 1,363
Wayne; MCD-Township; CRAWFORD; ***224** WG-4; mail Cochranton z 16314; Ⓟ 1,401; Ⓒ 1,558
Wayne; MCD-Township; DAUPHIN; ***227** EM-5; mail Halifax z 17032; Ⓟ 847; Ⓒ 1,184
Wayne; RMC Place; DELAWARE; ▲ Radnor; ***227** EP-11; 🅿; ★ **PHIL-**; z 19080, z 19087-89
Wayne; MCD-Township; ERIE; ***224** WD-5; mail Corry z 16407; Ⓟ 1,679; Ⓒ 1,766
Wayne; MCD-Township; GREENE; ***225** WQ-2; mail Spraggs z 15362; Ⓟ 1,317; Ⓒ 1,223
Wayne; MCD-Township; LAWRENCE; ***225** WK-2; ★ **PGH**; mail Ellwood City z 16117; Ⓟ 2,785; Ⓒ 2,328
Wayne; MCD-Township; MIFFLIN; ***225** WN-13; mail Mc Veytown z 17051; Ⓟ 2,521; Ⓒ 2,414
Wayne; MCD-Township; SCHUYLKILL; ***227** EL-7; ★ **PTSVL**; mail Friedensburg z 17933; Ⓟ 3,929; Ⓒ 4,721
WAYNE; **226** EE-11; Ⓟ 39,944; Ⓒ 47,722; ◆ 52,124
Waynecastle; RMC Place; FRANKLIN; ▲ Washington; ***227** EQ-1; ★ **HAG**; mail Greencastle z 17225; rural
Wayne Heights; CDP; FRANKLIN; ▲ Washington; **227** EQ-1; ★ **HAG**; mail Waynesboro z 17268; Ⓟ 1,683; Ⓒ 1,805
Waynesboro; Inc. Place; FRANKLIN; **227** EQ-1; elev. 713ft./217m.; 🅿 🅷 ■; ★ **HAG**; z 17268; Ⓟ 9,578; Ⓒ 9,614; ◆ 10,203
Waynesburg; Inc. Place; ⊡ GREENE; **225** WP-3; elev. 1,034ft./315m.; 🅿 🅷 🅲 2,323; z 15370; Ⓟ 4,270; Ⓒ 4,184
Waynesburg Lakes; RMC Place; GREENE; ▲ Washington; ***225** WP-3; elev. 1,100ft./335m.; mail Prosperity z 15329; rural
Waynesville; RMC Place; DAUPHIN; ▲ Wayne; ***227** EM-4; mail Halifax z 17032; rural
Weatherly; Inc. Place; CARBON; **226** EJ-9; elev. 1,094ft./333m.; 🅿; ★ **HAZ**; z 18255; Ⓟ 2,640; Ⓒ 2,612
Weaverland; RMC Place; LANCASTER; ▲ East Earl; ***227** EO-8; ★ **LANC**; mail East Earl z 17519; rural
Weavers Old Stand; WESTMORELAND; see Armbrust (RMC Place)
Weaversville; RMC Place; NORTHAMPTON; ▲ East Allen, Allen; ***227** EL-11; ★ **ALL-**; mail Northampton z 18067; ● 125
Weavertown (Brumfieldville); RMC Place; BERKS; ▲ Amity; ***227** EN-9; mail Douglassville z 19518; ● 200
Weavertown; RMC Place; LANCASTER; ▲ Leacock; ***227** EP-8; ★ **LANC**; mail Bird in Hand z 17505; ● 80
Weavertown; RMC Place; LEBANON; ▲ North Lebanon; ***227** EN-7; ★ **LEB**; mail Lebanon z 17046; ● 75
Weavertown; RMC Place; WASHINGTON; ▲ North Strabane; ***225** WN-3; ★ **PGH**; mail Canonsburg z 15317; ● 120
Webster; RMC Place; WESTMORELAND; ▲ Rostraver; **225** WO-4; 🅿; ★ **PGH**; z 15087; ● 400
Webster Mills; RMC Place; FULTON; ▲ Ayr; **225** WQ-12; mail Mc Connellsburg z 17233; ● 25
Wech Corner; LUZERNE; see Wildwood Terrace (RMC Place)
Weedville (Byrnedale); RMC Place; ELK; ▲ Jay; **224** WH-10; 🅿; z 15868; ● 950
Wegley; RMC Place; WESTMORELAND; ▲ Hempfield; ***225** WN-5; ★ **PGH**; mail Irwin z 15642; ● 150
Wehnwood; RMC Place; BLAIR; ***225** WM-11; ★ **ALT**; mail Altoona z 16601; pop. incl. with Altoona (Inc. Place)
Weidasville; RMC Place; LEHIGH; ▲ Lowhill; ***227** EL-10; ★ **ALL-**; mail Schnecksville z 18078; rural
Weidmanville; RMC Place; LANCASTER; ▲ Clay; ***227** EO-7; ★ **LANC**; mail Ephrata z 17522; rural
Weigelstown; CDP; YORK; ▲ Dover; **225** WS-8; ★ **YORK**; mail Dover z 17315; Ⓟ 8,665; Ⓒ 10,117
Weikert; RMC Place; UNION; ▲ Hartley; **227** EK-2; 🅿; z 17885; summer pop. 5,000; ● 215
Weilersville; RMC Place; LEHIGH; ▲ Lower Macungie; ***227** EM-10; ★ **ALL-**; mail Alburtis z 18011; ● 65
Weinel's Crossroads; RMC Place; WESTMORELAND; ▲ Allegheny; ***225** WL-5; ★ **PGH**; mail Leechburg z 15656; ● 200
Weir Lake; RMC Place; MONROE; ▲ Chestnuthill; ***226** EJ-11; ★ **ALL-**; mail Kunkletown z 18058; ● 200
Weisel; RMC Place; BUCKS; ▲ East Rockhill; ***227** EM-12; ★ **PHIL-**; mail Perkasie z 18944; rural
Weisenberg; MCD-Township; LEHIGH; ***227** EL-9; ★ **ALL-**; mail New Tripoli z 18066; Ⓟ 3,246; Ⓒ 4,144
Weishample; RMC Place; SCHUYLKILL; ▲ Barry; **227** EL-6; elev. 910ft./277m.; mail Hegins z 17938; ● 100
Weissport; Inc. Place; CARBON; **227** EK-10; elev. 460ft./140m.; 🅿; z 18235; Ⓟ 472; Ⓒ 434
Weissport East; CDP-Census Area Only; CARBON; ▲ Franklin; ***227** EK-10; mail Lehighton z 18235; Ⓟ 1,843; Ⓒ 1,936
Weldbank; RMC Place; WARREN; ▲ Mead; **224** WE-8; mail Clarendon z 16313; ● 100
Weldon; RMC Place; MONTGOMERY; ▲ Abington; ***227** EO-12; ★ **PHIL-**; mail Huntingdon Valley z 19006; ● 4,300
Wellersburg; Inc. Place; SOMERSET; **225** WR-9; elev. 1,343ft./409m.; 🅿; z 15564; Ⓟ 213; Ⓒ 176
Wellington Estates; RMC Place; BUCKS; ▲ Buckingham; ***227** EN-12; elev. 400ft./122m.; ★ **PHIL-**; mail Doylestown z 18901; ● 165
Welliversville; RMC Place; COLUMBIA; ▲ Mount Pleasant; ***226** EI-6; elev. 907ft./276m.; mail Bloomsburg z 17815; rural
Wells; MCD-Township; BRADFORD; ***226** ED-4; mail Gillett z 16925; Ⓟ 1,018; Ⓒ 1,278
Wells; MCD-Township; FULTON; ***225** WO-12; mail Wells Tannery z 16691; Ⓟ 544; Ⓒ 529
Wellsboro; Inc. Place; ⊡ TIOGA; **226** EF-2; elev. 1,311ft./400m.; 🅿 🅷; z 16901; Ⓟ 3,430; Ⓒ 3,328
Wellsboro Junction; RMC Place; TIOGA; ▲ Delmar; ***226** EE-2; mail Wellsboro z 16901; ● 170
Wellsburg; ERIE; see Lundys Lane (RMC Place)
Wells Creek; RMC Place; SOMERSET; ▲ Somerset; ***225** WP-8; mail Friedens z 15541; ● 40
Wells Tannery; RMC Place; FULTON; ▲ Wells; **225** WO-12; 🅿; z 16691; ● 175
Wellsville; Inc. Place; YORK; **227** EP-4; elev. 500ft./152m.; 🅿; z 17365; Ⓟ 304; Ⓒ 279
Welsh Hill; RMC Place; SUSQUEHANNA; ▲ Clifford; mail Union Dale z 18470; rural
Welsh Run; RMC Place; FRANKLIN; ▲ Montgomery; ***225** WQ-13; mail Greencastle z 17225, Mercersburg z 17236
Welty; WESTMORELAND; see Weltytown (RMC Place)
Weltytown (Welty); RMC Place; WESTMORELAND; ▲ Mount Pleasant; ***225** WO-6; mail Mount Pleasant z 15666; ● 50
Wendel; RMC Place; WESTMORELAND; ▲ Hempfield; ***225** WN-5; 🅿; ★ **PGH**; z 15691; ● 1,500
Wendover; RMC Place; WESTMORELAND; ▲ Hempfield; ***225** WN-6; ★ **PGH**; mail Greensburg z 15601; ● 600
Wenks; ADAMS; see Wenksville (RMC Place)
Wenksville (Wenks); RMC Place; ADAMS; ▲ Menallen; **227** EP-2; mail Aspers z 17304, Biglerville z 17307; ● 120
Wennersville (Springhouse Farms); RMC Place; LEHIGH; ▲ South Whitehall; **226** EB-2; ★ **ALL-**; mail Allentown z 18104; ● 750
Wentlings Corners; RMC Place; CLARION; ▲ Beaver; ***224** WI-6; mail Knox z 16232; ● 175
Werleys Corner; RMC Place; LEHIGH; ▲ Weisenberg; ***227** EL-10; ★ **ALL-**; mail New Tripoli z 18066; ● 75
Wernersville; Inc. Place; BERKS; **227** EN-8; elev. 388ft./118m.; 🅿 🅷; ★ **READ**; z 19565; Ⓟ 1,934; Ⓒ 2,150
Wernersville Heights; RMC Place; BERKS; ▲ South Heidelberg; ***227** EN-8; elev. 440ft./134m.; ★ **READ**; mail Wernersville z 19565; ● 500
Wertz; RMC Place; BLAIR; ▲ Woodbury; ***225** WM-11; ★ **ALT**; mail Williamsburg z 16693; rural
Wertzville; RMC Place; CUMBERLAND; ▲ Silver Spring; **227** EN-4; ★ **HRBG**; mail Mechanicsburg z 17050, z 17055; ● 30
Wescosville; RMC Place; LEHIGH; ▲ Lower Macungie; **226** EC-2; 🅿; ★ **ALL-**; z 18106; ● 1,250
Wesley; RMC Place; VENANGO; ▲ Irwin; **224** WI-4; mail Harrisville z 16038; ● 50
Wesley Chapel; RMC Place; CAMBRIA; ▲ East Taylor; ***225** WN-9; elev. 1,703ft./519m.; ★ **JNST**; mail Johnstown z 15909; ● 250
Wesleyville; Inc. Place; ERIE; **224** WC-4; elev. 720ft./219m.; ★ **ERIE**; mail Erie z 16510; Ⓟ 3,655; Ⓒ 3,617
Wessex Hills; RMC Place; ALLEGHENY; ▲ Moon; ***225** WM-3; ★ **PGH**; mail Coraopolis z 15108; ● 2,000
West; MCD-Township; HUNTINGDON; ***225** WL-13; mail Petersburg z 16669; Ⓟ 572; Ⓒ 528
West Abington; MCD-Township; LACKAWANNA; ***226** EG-9; ★ **SCR-**; mail Factoryville z 18419; Ⓟ 294; Ⓒ 311
West Acres; RMC Place; UNION; ▲ East Buffalo; mail Lewisburg z 17837
West Alexander; Inc. Place; WASHINGTON; **225** WO-1; elev. 1,080ft./329m.; 🅿; z 15376; Ⓟ 301; Ⓒ 320
West Aliquippa; RMC Place; BEAVER; 🅿; ★ **PGH**; z 15001; pop. incl. with Aliquippa (Inc. Place)
West Ambler; RMC Place; MONTGOMERY; ▲ Whitpain; ★ **PHIL-**; mail Ambler z 19002; ● 800
West Annville; RMC Place; LEBANON; ▲ South Annville, North Annville; ★ **LEB**; mail Annville z 17003; rural
West Auburn; RMC Place; SUSQUEHANNA; ▲ Auburn; **226** EF-8; mail Laceyville z 18623; ● 100
West Bangor; RMC Place; NORTHAMPTON; ▲ Washington, Plainfield; ***227** EK-12; mail Pen Argyl z 18072; ● 400
West Bangor; RMC Place; YORK; ▲ Peach Bottom; **227** ER-7; ★ **BAL**; mail Delta z 17314; ● 30
West Beaver; MCD-Township; SNYDER; ***227** EK-2; mail Mc Clure z 17841; Ⓟ 1,096; Ⓒ 1,124
West Belt Junction; RMC Place; ALLEGHENY; ★ **PGH**; mail Pittsburgh z 15230; pop. incl. with Pittsburgh (Inc. Place)
West Bend; RMC Place; FAYETTE; ▲ Luzerne; ***225** WP-4; elev. 1,182ft./360m.; ★ **UNTN**; mail East Millsboro z 15433; rural
West Berwick; RMC Place; COLUMBIA; mail Berwick z 18603; pop. incl. with Berwick (Inc. Place)
West Bethany (Old Bethany); RMC Place; WESTMORELAND; ▲ East Huntingdon; ***225** WO-5; mail Tarrs z 15688; ● 100
West Bethlehem; MCD-Township; WASHINGTON; ***225** WP-3; mail Marianna z 15345; Ⓟ 1,609; Ⓒ 1,432
West Bingham; RMC Place; POTTER; ▲ Bingham; **224** WD-13; mail Genesee z 16923; ● 50
West Bolivar; RMC Place; WESTMORELAND; ▲ Fairfield; ***225** WN-7; mail Bolivar z 15923; ● 400
West Bowmanstown; RMC Place; CARBON; ▲ East Penn; ***227** EK-10; mail Bowmanstown z 18030; ● 220
West Bradford; MCD-Township; CHESTER; ***227** EP-10; 🅿; ★ **PHIL-**; z 19320, z 19335, z 19380; Ⓟ 10,406; Ⓒ 10,775
West Branch; RMC Place; CAMBRIA; ▲ Barr; ***225** WL-9; mail Northern Cambria z 15714; pop. incl. with Northern Cambria (Inc. Place)
West Branch; MCD-Township; POTTER; ***226** EF-1; mail Galeton z 16922; Ⓟ 286; Ⓒ 392
West Brandywine; MCD-Township; CHESTER; ***227** EP-9; 🅿; ★ **PHIL-**; z 19320, z 19343-44; Ⓟ 5,984; Ⓒ 7,153
West Bridgewater; BEAVER; see Bridgewater (Inc. Place)
West Bristol; RMC Place; BUCKS; ▲ Bristol; **228** A-9; 🅿; ★ **PHIL-**; z 19007; ● 5,000
West Brownsville; Inc. Place; WASHINGTON; **225** WP-4; elev. 780ft./238m.; ★ **PGH**; mail Brownsville z 15417; Ⓟ 1,170; Ⓒ 1,075
West Brunswick; MCD-Township; SCHUYLKILL; ***227** EL-8; ★ **PTSVL**; mail Orwigsburg z 17961; Ⓟ 3,227; Ⓒ 3,428
West Buffalo; MCD-Township; UNION; ***226** EJ-3; mail Mifflinburg z 17844; Ⓟ 2,254; Ⓒ 2,795
West Burlington; RMC Place; BRADFORD; ▲ West Burlington; **226** EF-5; elev. 969ft./295m.; mail Troy z 16947; ● 90
West Burlington; MCD-Township; BRADFORD; ***226** EF-5; mail Columbia Cross Roads z 16914; Ⓟ 417; Ⓒ 782
Westbury; RMC Place; ALLEGHENY; ▲ Findlay; ***225** WM-3; elev. 1,100ft./335m.; ★ **PGH**; mail Oakdale z 15071; ● 900
West Caln; MCD-Township; CHESTER; ***227** EP-9; ★ **PHIL-**; mail Wagontown z 19376; Ⓟ 6,143; Ⓒ 7,054
West Cameron; RMC Place; NORTHUMBERLAND; ▲ West Cameron; **227** EL-5; elev. 979ft./298m.; mail Shamokin z 17872; ● 165
West Cameron; MCD-Township; NORTHUMBERLAND; ***227** EL-5; mail Shamokin z 17872; Ⓟ 527; Ⓒ 517
West Carroll; MCD-Township; CAMBRIA; ***225** WL-9; mail Elmora z 15737; Ⓟ 1,524; Ⓒ 1,445
West Catasauqua; RMC Place; LEHIGH; ▲ Whitehall; **226** EA-3; ★ **ALL-**; mail Whitehall z 18052; ● 700
West Chester; Inc. Place; ⊡ CHESTER; **227** EP-10; elev. 459ft./140m.; 🅿 🅷 🅲 12,882 ■; ★ **PHIL-**; z 19380-83, z 19388; Ⓟ 18,041; Ⓒ 17,861; ◆ 17,697
West Chillisquaque; MCD-Township; NORTHUMBERLAND; ***226** EJ-4; mail Montandon z 17850; Ⓟ 3,119; Ⓒ 2,846
West Clifford; RMC Place; SUSQUEHANNA; ▲ Clifford; **226** EF-10; elev. 1,272ft./388m.; mail Union Dale z 18470; ● 50
West Cocalico; MCD-Township; LANCASTER; ***227** EN-8; mail Stevens z 17578; Ⓟ 5,521; Ⓒ 6,967
Westcolang; RMC Place; PIKE; ▲ Lackawaxen; ***226** EG-13; mail Hawley z 18428; ● 50
West Conshohocken; Inc. Place; MONTGOMERY; **228** B-1; elev. 100ft./30m.; 🅿; ★ **PHIL-**; z 19428; Ⓟ 1,294; Ⓒ 1,446
West Coplay; LEHIGH; see Stiles (RMC Place)
West Cornwall; MCD-Township; LEBANON; ***227** EN-6; ★ **LEB**; mail Lebanon z 17042; Ⓟ 1,996; Ⓒ 1,909
West Creek; RMC Place; CAMERON; ▲ Shippen; ***224** WG-11; elev. 1,124ft./343m.; mail Emporium z 15834; rural
West Creek Hills; RMC Place; CUMBERLAND; ▲ East Pennsboro; ***227** EN-4; ★ **HRBG**; mail Camp Hill z 17011; ● 2,100
West Cressona; RMC Place; SCHUYLKILL; ★ **PTSVL**; mail Cressona z 17929; pop. incl. with Cressona (Inc. Place)
West Damascus; RMC Place; WAYNE; ▲ Damascus; ***226** EF-12; mail Tyler Hill z 18469; rural
West Decatur (Blue Ball); RMC Place; CLEARFIELD; ▲ Boggs; **224** WJ-11; 🅿; z 16878; ● 600
West Deer; MCD-Township; ALLEGHENY; ***225** WL-4; ★ **PGH**; mail Cheswick z 15024, Gibsonia z 15044, Russellton z 15076; Ⓟ 11,371; Ⓒ 11,563
West Derry; RMC Place; WESTMORELAND; ▲ Derry; ***225** WN-7; ★ **LTROB**; mail Derry z 15627; ● 800
West Donegal; MCD-Township; LANCASTER; ***227** EO-5; mail Elizabethtown z 17022; Ⓟ 5,605; Ⓒ 6,539
West Earl; MCD-Township; LANCASTER; ***227** EO-8; ★ **LANC**; mail Brownstown z 17508; Ⓟ 6,434; Ⓒ 6,766
West Easton; Inc. Place; NORTHAMPTON; ***227** EL-12; elev. 360ft./110m.; 🅿; ★ **ALL-**; z 18042; Ⓟ 1,163; Ⓒ 1,152
West Eldred; RMC Place; MCKEAN; ▲ Eldred; ***224** WD-11; mail Eldred z 16731; rural
West Elizabeth; Inc. Place; ALLEGHENY; **225** WN-4; elev. 760ft./232m.; 🅿; ★ **PGH**; z 15088; Ⓟ 634; Ⓒ 565
West Elwood Junction; RMC Place; BEAVER; ★ **PGH**; mail Koppel z 16136; pop. incl. with Koppel (Inc. Place)
West End; RMC Place; ALLEGHENY; ***225** WM-3; ★ **PGH**; mail Pittsburgh z 15220; pop. incl. with Pittsburgh (Inc. Place)
West End; RMC Place; DAUPHIN; ★ **HRBG**; mail Harrisburg z 17102; pop. incl. with Harrisburg (Inc. Place)
West End; RMC Place; WASHINGTON; ▲ Canton; ***225** WO-2; elev. 1,018ft./310m.; ★ **WASH**; mail Washington z 15301; ● 1,500
West Enola; RMC Place; CUMBERLAND; ▲ East Pennsboro; **227** ES-2; ★ **HRBG**; mail Enola z 17025; ● 800
West Fairfield; RMC Place; WESTMORELAND; ▲ Fairfield; **225** WN-8; mail New Florence z 15944; ● 60
West Fairview; RMC Place; CUMBERLAND; **227** ES-2; elev. 360ft./110m.; ★ **HRBG**; mail Enola z 17025; Ⓟ 1,403
Westfall; MCD-Township; PIKE; ***226** EG-14; mail Matamoras z 18336; Ⓟ 2,106; Ⓒ 2,430
West Fallowfield; MCD-Township; CHESTER; ***227** EQ-8; mail Cochranville z 19330; Ⓟ 2,342; Ⓒ 2,485
West Fallowfield; MCD-Township; CRAWFORD; ***224** WG-2; mail Hartstown z 16131; Ⓟ 693; Ⓒ 659
West Falls; RMC Place; WYOMING; ▲ Exeter; ***226** EG-9; ★ **SCR-**; mail Falls z 18615
West Fayetteville; RMC Place; FRANKLIN; ▲ Greene, Guilford; ***227** EP-1; mail Fayetteville z 17222
Westfield; Inc. Place; TIOGA; **226** EE-1; elev. 1,374ft./419m.; 🅿; z 16927, z 16950; Ⓟ 1,119; Ⓒ 1,190
Westfield; MCD-Township; TIOGA; ***226** EE-1; 🅿; z 16927, z 16950; does not include the Borough of Westfield; Ⓟ 1,022; Ⓒ 849
Westfield Terrace; RMC Place; YORK; ▲ Fairview; ***227** EO-4; ★ **HRBG**; mail New Cumberland z 17070; ● 100
West Finley; RMC Place; WASHINGTON; ▲ West Finley; **225** WP-1; 🅿; z 15377; ● 100
West Finley; MCD-Township; WASHINGTON; ***225** WP-1; 🅿; z 15377; Ⓟ 972; Ⓒ 951
Westford; RMC Place; CRAWFORD; ▲ South Shenango; **224** WG-2; elev. 1,105ft./337m.; 🅿; z 16134; ● 150
West Franklin; MCD-Township; ARMSTRONG; ***225** WK-5; ★ **PGH**; mail Worthington z 16262; Ⓟ 2,008; Ⓒ 1,935
West Franklin; RMC Place; BRADFORD; ▲ Monroe; **226** EF-5; mail Monroeton z 18832; ● 40
West Freedom; RMC Place; CLARION; ▲ Perry; **224** WI-5; mail Parker z 16049; ● 240
Westgate Hills; RMC Place; NORTHAMPTON; ▲ Hanover; **227** EL-11; ★ **ALL-**; mail Bethlehem z 18017
West Goshen; CDP-Census Area Only; CHESTER; ▲ West Goshen; ***227** EP-10; ★ **PHIL-**; mail West Chester z 19380; Ⓟ 8,948; Ⓒ 8,472
West Goshen; MCD-Township; CHESTER; ***227** EP-10; ★ **PHIL-**; mail West Chester z 19380; Ⓟ 18,082; Ⓒ 20,495; ◆ 21,985
West Goshen Hills; RMC Place; CHESTER; ▲ West Goshen; ★ **PHIL-**; mail West Chester z 19380; ● 300
West Goshen Park; RMC Place; CHESTER; ▲ West Goshen; ***227** EP-10; ★ **PHIL-**; mail West Chester z 19380; ● 300
West Grove; Inc. Place; CHESTER; **227** EQ-9; elev. 400ft./122m.; 🅿 🅷; ★ **PHIL-**; z 19390; Ⓟ 2,128; Ⓒ 2,652
West Hamburg; RMC Place; BERKS; ▲ Tilden; ***227** EM-8; elev. 470ft./143m.; ★ **READ**; mail Hamburg z 19526; ● 240
West Hanover; MCD-Township; DAUPHIN; ***227** EN-5; ★ **HRBG**; mail Harrisburg z 17112; Ⓟ 6,125; Ⓒ 6,505
West Hazleton; Inc. Place; LUZERNE; **226** EJ-8; elev. 1,700ft./518m.; 🅿; ★ **HAZ**; z 18202; Ⓟ 4,136; Ⓒ 3,542
West Hemlock; MCD-Township; MONTOUR; ***226** EJ-6; mail Danville z 17821; Ⓟ 402; Ⓒ 489
West Hempfield; MCD-Township; LANCASTER; ***227** EP-6; ★ **LANC**; mail Lancaster z 17601; Ⓟ 12,942; Ⓒ 15,128
West Hickory; RMC Place; FOREST; ▲ Harmony; **224** WG-6; 🅿; z 16370; ● 300
West Hill; RMC Place; CUMBERLAND; ▲ West Pennsboro; ***227** EO-2; ★ **CARL**; mail Carlisle z 17013; ● 60
West Hills; CDP; ARMSTRONG; ▲ East Franklin; ***225** WK-6; elev. 1,200ft./366m.; ★ **PGH**; mail Kittanning z 16201; Ⓟ 1,240; Ⓒ 1,229
West Hills; RMC Place; MIFFLIN; ▲ Granville; ***227** EM-1; mail Lewistown z 17044; ● 450
West Hills Estates; RMC Place; LYCOMING; ▲ Old Lycoming; ***226** EI-4; ★ **WMSPT**; mail Williamsport z 17701
West Homestead; Inc. Place; ALLEGHENY; **228** K-7; elev. 1,000ft./305m.; 🅿; ★ **PGH**; z 15120; Ⓟ 2,495; Ⓒ 2,197
West Homestead Yard; RMC Place; ALLEGHENY; ***225** WM-4; ★ **PGH**; pop. incl. with West Homestead (Inc. Place)
Westinghouse; ALLEGHENY; see Turtle Creek (Inc. Place)
Westinghouse Village; RMC Place; DELAWARE; ▲ Tinicum; ***227** EQ-12; ★ **PHIL-**; mail Essington z 19029
West Jeannette; RMC Place; WESTMORELAND; ★ **PGH**; mail Jeannette z 15644; pop. incl. with Jeannette (Inc. Place)
West Jonestown; RMC Place; LEBANON; ▲ Union; ***227** EN-6; elev. 475ft./145m.; mail Jonestown z 17038; ● 100
West Keating; MCD-Township; CLINTON; ***224** WI-12; mail Pottersdale z 16871; Ⓟ 34; Ⓒ 42
West Kittanning; Inc. Place; ARMSTRONG; **225** WK-6; elev. 980ft./299m.; ★ **PGH**; mail Kittanning z 16201; Ⓟ 1,253; Ⓒ 1,199
West Lampeter; MCD-Township; LANCASTER; ***227** EP-7; ★ **LANC**; mail Lampeter z 17537; Ⓟ 9,865; Ⓒ 13,145
West Lancaster; RMC Place; LANCASTER; ▲ Manor; **227** ET-8; ★ **LANC**; mail Lancaster z 17603; ● 800
Westland; RMC Place; WASHINGTON; ▲ Mount Pleasant; **225** WN-2; 🅿; ★ **PGH**; z 15378; ● 230
West Lawn; Inc. Place; BERKS; **227** EN-8; elev. 343ft./105m.; 🅿; ★ **READ**; z 19609; Ⓟ 1,606; Ⓒ 1,597
West Lawn; RMC Place; UNION; ▲ East Buffalo; ***226** EJ-4; mail Lewisburg z 17837
West Lebanon; RMC Place; INDIANA; ▲ Young; ***225** WL-6; 🅿; z 15783; ● 125
West Lebanon; RMC Place; LEBANON; ▲ West Lebanon; ***227** EN-6; ★ **LEB**; mail Lebanon z 17046; ● 872
West Lebanon; MCD-Township; LEBANON; ***227** EN-6; ★ **LEB**; mail Lebanon z 17046; Ⓟ 872; Ⓒ 836
West Leechburg; Inc. Place; WESTMORELAND; **225** WL-5; elev. 798ft./243m.; 🅿; ★ **PGH**; z 15656; Ⓟ 1,359; Ⓒ 1,290
West Leesport; RMC Place; BERKS; ★ **READ**; pop. incl. with Leesport (Inc. Place)
West Leisenring; RMC Place; FAYETTE; ▲ North Union, Franklin; **225** WP-5; 🅿; ★ **UNTN**; z 15489; ● 600
West Lenox (Acre Lake); RMC Place; SUSQUEHANNA; ▲ Lenox; ***226** EF-9; elev. 1,219ft./372m.; mail Kingsley z 18826; ● 260
West Leroy; RMC Place; BRADFORD; ▲ Leroy; ***226** EF-5; elev. 1,020ft./311m.; mail Canton z 17724; rural
West Liberty; RMC Place; ALLEGHENY; ***225** WM-3; ★ **PGH**; mail Pittsburgh z 15226; pop. incl. with Pittsburgh (Inc. Place)
West Liberty; Inc. Place; BUTLER; **224** WJ-3; elev. 1,193ft./364m.; mail Slippery Rock z 16057; Ⓟ 282; Ⓒ 325
West Liberty; RMC Place; CLEARFIELD; ▲ Sandy; **224** WJ-9; mail Du Bois z 15801; ● 70
Westline; RMC Place; MCKEAN; ▲ Lafayette; **224** WE-9; elev. 1,464ft./446m.; 🅿; z 16740; ● 75
West Mahanoy; MCD-Township; SCHUYLKILL; ***227** EK-7; mail Shenandoah z 17976; Ⓟ 4,539; Ⓒ 6,166; Ⓡ 3,175
West Mahoning; MCD-Township; INDIANA; ***225** WK-8; mail Smicksburg z 16256; Ⓟ 1,032; Ⓒ 1,128
West Manayunk; RMC Place; MONTGOMERY; ▲ Lower Merion; ***227** EP-12; ★ **PHIL-**; mail Philadelphia z 19151
West Manchester; MCD-Township; YORK; ***227** EP-5; ★ **YORK**; mail York z 17404; Ⓟ 14,369; Ⓒ 17,035
West Manheim; MCD-Township; YORK; ***227** ER-4; ★ **HANV**; mail Hanover z 17331; Ⓟ 4,590; Ⓒ 4,865
West Market; RMC Place; PHILADELPHIA; ★ **PHIL-**; mail Philadelphia z 19139; pop. incl. with Philadelphia (Inc. Place)
West Marlborough; MCD-Township; CHESTER; ***227** EQ-9; mail Kennett Square z 19348; Ⓟ 874; Ⓒ 859
West Mayfield; Inc. Place; BEAVER; **225** WK-2; elev. 1,000ft./305m.; ★ **PGH**; mail Beaver Falls z 15010; Ⓟ 1,312; Ⓒ 1,187
West Mead; MCD-Township; CRAWFORD; ***224** WF-3; mail Meadville z 16335; Ⓟ 5,401; Ⓒ 5,227
West Middlesex; Inc. Place; MERCER; **224** WI-2; elev. 840ft./256m.; 🅿; ★ **SHAR**; z 16159 & mail Hermitage z 16148; Ⓟ 982; Ⓒ 929
West Middletown; RMC Place; DAUPHIN; pop. incl. with Middletown (Inc. Place)
West Middletown; Inc. Place; WASHINGTON; **225** WN-2; elev. 1,333ft./406m.; 🅿; z 15379; Ⓟ 166; Ⓒ 144
West Mifflin; Inc. Place; ALLEGHENY; **228** L-8; elev. 1,000ft./305m.; 🅿 ■; ★ **PGH**; z 15122-23, z 15236 & mail New Columbia z 17856, West Milton z 17886; Ⓟ 23,644; Ⓒ 22,464; ◆ 20,877
West Milton; RMC Place; UNION; ▲ White Deer, Kelly; **226** EJ-4; 🅿; z 17886 & mail New Columbia z 17856; ● 850
Westminster; RMC Place; ERIE; ▲ Millcreek; ***224** WC-3; ★ **ERIE**; mail Erie z 16506
Westminster; RMC Place; LUZERNE; ▲ Jenkins; **226** EC-9; elev. 964ft./294m.; ★ **SCR-**; mail Wilkes Barre z 18702; ● 100
West Monocacy (Mount Airy); RMC Place; BERKS; ▲ Union; ***227** EN-9; mail Douglassville z 19518; ● 100
Westmont; RMC Place; BLAIR; ***225** WM-11; ★ **ALT**; pop. incl. with Altoona (Inc. Place)
Westmont; Inc. Place; CAMBRIA; **225** WN-8; elev. 1,795ft./547m.; ★ **JNST**; mail Johnstown z 15905; Ⓟ 5,789; Ⓒ 5,523

Entries in **UPPERCASE** are counties.
Entries in **bold** have populations of 2,500 or more.
Names in parentheses are alternate names.

Inc. Place	Incorporated Place
RMC Place	Rand McNally Designated Place
CDP	Census Designated Place
MCD	Minor Civil Division

⊡	County Seat
▲	Minor Civil Division
elev.	Elevation
🅿	Post Office
🅷	Hospital
🅲	College
■	Principal Business Center
★	Ranally Metro Area (RMA) Abbreviation
z	Zip Code(s)
Ⓟ	Previous Census Population
Ⓡ	Revised Census Population
Ⓐ	Annexation Population
●	Rand McNally Population Estimate
Ⓒ	Final Census Population
Ⓢ	Special Census Population
◆	Estimated Population

For additional definitions see Glossary, Volume 1, and Introduction, Volume 2.

Westmont; RMC Place; LEBANON; ▲ North Lebanon; *227 EN-6; ★ LEB; mail Lebanon z 17042; rural
West Monterey; RMC Place; CLARION; ▲ Perry; 224 WJ-5; elev. 871ft./265m.; mail Parker z 16049; ● 75
Westmont Plan; RMC Place; ARMSTRONG; ▲ East Franklin; *225 WK-6; elev. 1,200ft./366m.; ★ PGH; mail Kittanning z 16201; ● 40
Westmoreland; RMC Place; PHILADELPHIA; ★ PHIL-; pop. incl. with Philadelphia (Inc. Place)
WESTMORELAND; 225 WM-5; ℗ 370,321; © 369,993; ◆ 353,731
Westmoreland City; RMC Place; WESTMORELAND; ▲ North Huntingdon; 225 WN-5; 🅿; ★ PGH; z 15692; ● 1,400
West Morrisville; RMC Place; BUCKS; ★ PHIL-; pop. incl. with Morrisville (Inc. Place)
West Moshannon; RMC Place; CLEARFIELD; ▲ Woodward; *225 WK-11; mail Houtzdale z 16651; ● 125
West Myerstown; RMC Place; LEBANON; ▲ Jackson; ★ LEB; mail Myerstown z 17067; ● 350
West Nanticoke; RMC Place; LUZERNE; ▲ Plymouth; 226 EI-8; ★ SCR-; mail Nanticoke z 18634; ● 1,200
West Nantmeal; MCD-Township; CHESTER; *227 EO-9; ★ PHIL-; mail Elverson z 19520; ℗ 1,958; © 2,031
West New Kensington; RMC Place; ALLEGHENY; *225 WM-5; ★ PGH; mail Creighton z 15030
West Newton; Inc. Place; WESTMORELAND; 225 WO-5; elev. 769ft./234m.; 🅿; ★ PGH; z 15089; ℗ 3,152; © 3,083
West Nicholson; RMC Place; WYOMING; ▲ Nicholson; *226 EF-9; elev. 1,059ft./323m.; mail Nicholson z 18446; rural
West Norriton; CDP-Census Area Only; MONTGOMERY; ▲ West Norriton; *227 EO-11; ★ PHIL-; mail Norristown z 19401, z 19403; ℗ 15,209; © 14,901
West Norriton; MCD-Township; MONTGOMERY; *227 EO-11; ★ PHIL-; mail Norristown z 19401; ℗ 15,209; © 14,901
West Nottingham; MCD-Township; CHESTER; *227 EQ-8; mail Nottingham z 19362; ℗ 2,183; © 2,634
Weston; RMC Place; LUZERNE; ▲ Black Creek; 226 EJ-8; 🅿; ★ HAZ; z 18256; ● 500
Weston Place; RMC Place; SCHUYLKILL; ▲ West Mahanoy; *227 EK-7; mail Shenandoah z 17976; ● 160
Westover; RMC Place; BUCKS; ▲ Lower Makefield; *227 EO-14; ★ PHIL-; mail Morrisville z 19067; ● 500
Westover; Inc. Place; CLEARFIELD; 225 WL-10; elev. 1,354ft./413m.; 🅿; z 16692; ℗ 446; © 458
West Overton; RMC Place; WESTMORELAND; ▲ East Huntingdon; *225 WO-5; mail Scottdale z 15683; ● 40
Westover Woods; RMC Place; MONTGOMERY; ▲ West Norriton; ★ PHIL-; mail Norristown z 19401
West Park; RMC Place; ALLEGHENY; ▲ Stowe; *225 WM-3; ★ PGH; mail Mc Kees Rocks z 15136
West Park; RMC Place; PHILADELPHIA; ★ PHIL-; mail Philadelphia z 19131; pop. incl. with Philadelphia (Inc. Place)
West Pen Argyl; RMC Place; NORTHAMPTON; ▲ Plainfield; *227 EK-12; mail Pen Argyl z 18072; ● 300
West Penn; MCD-Township; SCHUYLKILL; *227 EL-9; mail New Ringgold z 17960; ℗ 3,693; © 3,852
West Pennsboro; MCD-Township; CUMBERLAND; *227 EO-3; 🅿; ★ CARL; z 17015 & mail Newville z 17241; ℗ 4,945; © 5,263
West Perry; MCD-Township; SNYDER; *227 EL-3; mail Richfield z 17086; ℗ 969; © 1,038
West Philadelphia; RMC Place; PHILADELPHIA; ★ PHIL-; mail Philadelphia z 19104; pop. incl. with Philadelphia (Inc. Place)
West Pike; RMC Place; POTTER; ▲ Pike; 224 WE-14; elev. 1,464ft./446m.; mail Galeton z 16922; ● 20
West Pikeland; MCD-Township; CHESTER; *227 EO-10; ★ PHIL-; mail Chester Springs z 19425; ℗ 2,323; © 3,551
West Pike Run; MCD-Township; WASHINGTON; *225 WO-4; mail Daisytown z 15427; ℗ 1,818; © 1,925
West Pittsburg (West Pittsburgh); RMC Place; LAWRENCE; ▲ Taylor; 224 WJ-2; 🅿; ★ NWCS; z 16160; ● 1,100
West Pittsburgh; LAWRENCE; see West Pittsburg (RMC Place)
West Pittston; Inc. Place; LUZERNE; 226 EH-9; elev. 562ft./171m.; 🅿; ★ SCR-; z 18643; ℗ 5,590; © 5,072
West Pittston Junction; RMC Place; LUZERNE; ★ SCR-; pop. incl. with West Pittston (Inc. Place)
West Point; RMC Place; CAMBRIA; ▲ East Taylor; *225 WN-9; ★ JNST; mail Mineral Point z 15942; ● 60
West Point; RMC Place; MONTGOMERY; ▲ Upper Gwynedd; *227 EO-11; 🅿; ★ PHIL-; z 19486; ● 450
West Point; RMC Place; WESTMORELAND; ▲ Hempfield; *225 WN-7; ★ PGH; mail Greensburg z 15601; ● 800
Westport; RMC Place; CLINTON; ▲ Noyes; 224 WH-13; 🅿; z 17778; ● 80
West Pottsgrove; RMC Place; MONTGOMERY; ▲ West Pottsgrove; *227 EN-10; ★ PTSTN; mail Pottstown z 19464; ● 3,829
West Pottsgrove; MCD-Township; MONTGOMERY; *227 EN-10; ★ PTSTN; mail Pottstown z 19464; ℗ 3,829; © 3,815
West Providence; MCD-Township; BEDFORD; *225 WP-11; mail Everett z 15537; ℗ 3,233; © 3,323
West Reading; Inc. Place; BERKS; 227 ET-12; elev. 320ft./98m.; 🅿; ★ READ; z 19611 & mail Reading z 19602; ℗ 4,142; © 4,049
West Renovo; RMC Place; CLINTON; ▲ Noyes; *224 WH-14; mail Renovo z 17764
West Ridge; RMC Place; LANCASTER; ▲ Manor; *227 EP-7; ★ LANC; mail Lancaster z 17603; ● 430
West Rockhill; MCD-Township; BUCKS; *227 EN-11; ★ PHIL-; mail Sellersville z 18960; ℗ 4,518; © 4,233
West Sadsbury; MCD-Township; CHESTER; *227 EP-9; ★ PHIL-; mail Parkesburg z 19365; ℗ 2,160; © 2,444
West St. Clair; MCD-Township; BEDFORD; *225 WO-10; mail Alum Bank z 15521; ℗ 1,543; © 1,647
West Salem; MCD-Township; MERCER; *224 WG-1; mail Greenville z 16125; ℗ 3,547; © 3,565
West Salisbury; RMC Place; SOMERSET; ▲ Elk Lick; 225 WQ-8; 🅿; z 15565; ● 85
West Scranton; RMC Place; LACKAWANNA; ★ SCR-; mail Scranton z 18504; pop. incl. with Scranton (Inc. Place)
West Shenango; MCD-Township; CRAWFORD; *224 WG-1; mail Jamestown z 16134; ℗ 496; © 541
Westside; RMC Place; NORTHAMPTON; ★ ALL-; mail Bethlehem z 18018; pop. incl. with Bethlehem (Inc. Place)
West Spring Creek; RMC Place; WARREN; ▲ Spring Creek; *224 WE-6; mail Corry z 16407; rural
West Springfield; RMC Place; ERIE; ▲ Springfield; 224 WD-2; 🅿; ★ ERIE; z 16443; ● 300
West Sunbury; Inc. Place; BUTLER; 224 WJ-4; elev. 1,383ft./422m.; 🅿; ★ BUTL; z 16061; ℗ 177; © 104
West Tarentum; RMC Place; ALLEGHENY; *225 WL-5; ★ PGH; mail Tarentum z 15084
West Taylor; MCD-Township; CAMBRIA; *225 WN-9; ★ JNST; mail Johnstown z 15906; ℗ 995; © 862
West Telford; RMC Place; MONTGOMERY; ★ PHIL-; mail Telford z 18969; pop. incl. with Telford (Inc. Place)
West Tobyhanna; MONROE; see Tobyhanna (RMC Place)
Westtown; RMC Place; CHESTER; ▲ Thornbury, Westtown; 227 EP-10; elev. 265ft./81m.; 🅿; ★ PHIL-; z 19395; ● 500
Westtown; MCD-Township; CHESTER; *227 EP-10; 🅿; ★ PHIL-; z 19395; ℗ 9,937; © 10,352
Westtown Acres; RMC Place; CHESTER; ▲ West Goshen; ★ PHIL-; mail West Chester z 19380; ● 300
West Union; RMC Place; GREENE; ▲ Morris; *225 WP-2; mail Sycamore z 15364; ● 50
West Valley; RMC Place; ARMSTRONG; ▲ Valley; *225 WK-6; mail Kittanning z 16201; ● 75
West Vandergrift; RMC Place; WESTMORELAND; *225 WL-5; ★ PGH; mail Vandergrift z 15690; pop. incl. with Vandergrift (Inc. Place)
West View; Inc. Place; ALLEGHENY; 225 WM-3; elev. 1,200ft./366m.; 🅿; ★ PGH; z 15229; ℗ 7,734; © 7,277
Westview; RMC Place; BEAVER; ▲ Brighton; *225 WL-2; ★ PGH; mail Beaver z 15009; ● 750
Westview Heights; RMC Place; LAWRENCE; ▲ Union; *224 WJ-2; ★ NWCS; mail New Castle z 16101
Westville; RMC Place; JEFFERSON; ▲ Washington; 224 WI-9; mail Brockway z 15824; ● 40
West Vincent; MCD-Township; CHESTER; *227 EO-10; ★ PHIL-; mail Chester Springs z 19425; ℗ 2,262; © 3,170
West Warren; RMC Place; BRADFORD; ▲ Warren; 226 ED-7; elev. 1,127ft./344m.; mail Nichols z 13812; ● 50
West Wayne; RMC Place; DELAWARE; ▲ Radnor; *227 EP-11; ★ PHIL-; mail Wayne z 19087
West Waynesburg; RMC Place; GREENE; ▲ Franklin; *225 WP-3; mail Waynesburg z 15370; ● 250
West Wheatfield; MCD-Township; INDIANA; *225 WM-7; ★ JNST; mail New Florence z 15944; ℗ 2,370; © 2,375
West Whiteland; MCD-Township; CHESTER; *227 EP-10; ★ PHIL-; mail Exton z 19341; ℗ 12,403; © 16,499
West William Penn; RMC Place; SCHUYLKILL; ▲ West Mahanoy; *227 EK-7; elev. 1,048ft./319m.; mail Shenandoah z 17976
West Willow; RMC Place; LANCASTER; ▲ Pequea; 227 EP-7; elev. 443ft./135m.; 🅿; ★ LANC; z 17583; ● 300
West Wilmerding; RMC Place; ALLEGHENY; ▲ North Versailles; *225 WM-4; ★ PGH; mail North Versailles z 15137
West Winfield; RMC Place; BUTLER; ▲ Winfield; 225 WK-5; ★ PGH; mail Cabot z 16023; ● 30
Westwood; RMC Place; ALLEGHENY; *225 WM-3; ★ PGH; mail Pittsburgh z 15205; pop. incl. with Pittsburgh (Inc. Place)
Westwood; RMC Place; CAMBRIA; ▲ Lower Yoder; *225 WN-8; ★ JNST; mail Johnstown z 15905; ● 1,000
Westwood; RMC Place; CHESTER; ▲ Valley; *227 EP-9; ★ PHIL-; mail Coatesville z 19320; ● 850
Westwood Park; RMC Place; DELAWARE; ▲ Haverford; ★ PHIL-; mail Havertown z 19083
West Wyoming; Inc. Place; LUZERNE; 226 EA-9; elev. 599ft./183m.; 🅿; ★ SCR-; z 18644; ℗ 3,117; © 2,833
West Wyomissing; CDP; BERKS; ▲ Spring; 227 ET-12; ★ READ; mail Reading z 19609; ℗ 3,097; © 3,016
West York; Inc. Place; YORK; 227 EP-5; elev. 398ft./121m.; 🅿; ★ YORK; z 17404; ℗ 4,283; © 4,321
West Zollarsville; RMC Place; WASHINGTON; ▲ West Bethlehem; *225 WP-3; mail Marianna z 15345; pop. incl. with Marianna (Inc. Place)
Wetherills Corner; RMC Place; MONTGOMERY; ▲ Upper Providence; *227 EO-11; elev. 191ft./58m.; ★ PHIL-; mail Phoenixville z 19460; ● 125
Wetmore; RMC Place; MCKEAN; ▲ Hamilton; *224 WF-9; mail Kane z 16735
Wetmore; MCD-Township; MCKEAN; *224 WF-9; mail Kane z 16735; ℗ 1,745; © 1,721
Wetona; RMC Place; BRADFORD; ▲ Springfield; *226 EE-5; mail Columbia Cross Roads z 16914; rural
Wexford; RMC Place; ALLEGHENY; ▲ Pine; 225 WL-3; 🅿; ★ PGH; z 15090; ● 1,100
Weyant; RMC Place; BEDFORD; ▲ King; *225 WO-10; elev. 257ft./78m.; mail Imler z 16655; rural
Wharton; MCD-Township; FAYETTE; *225 WQ-5; mail Farmington z 15437; ℗ 3,390; © 4,145
Wharton; RMC Place; POTTER; ▲ Wharton; 224 WG-12; elev. 1,095ft./334m.; mail Austin z 16720; ● 25
Wharton; MCD-Township; POTTER; *224 WG-13; mail Austin z 16720; ℗ 70; © 91
Wheatfield; MCD-Township; PERRY; *227 EN-3; ★ HRBG; mail Duncannon z 17020; ℗ 3,097; © 3,329
Wheatland; Inc. Place; MERCER; 224 WI-1; elev. 900ft./274m.; 🅿; ★ SHAR; z 16161; ℗ 760; © 748
Wheatland Hills; RMC Place; LANCASTER; ▲ East Hempfield; *227 EP-7; ★ LANC; mail Lancaster z 17604; ● 700
Wheat Sheaf; RMC Place; BUCKS; ▲ Falls; *227 EO-14; elev. 40ft./12m.; ★ PHIL-; mail Morrisville z 19067; ● 65
Wheeler; RMC Place; FAYETTE; ▲ Dunbar; *225 WP-5; mail Connellsville z 15425; ● 300
Wheelerville; RMC Place; SULLIVAN; ▲ Fox; *226 EG-5; mail Canton z 17724, Shunk z 17768
Whig Hill; RMC Place; FOREST; ▲ Kingsley; *224 WG-7; mail Tionesta z 16353; rural
Whiskerville; RMC Place; BUTLER; ▲ Washington; 224 WI-4; mail Hilliards z 16040; ● 110
Whitaker; Inc. Place; ALLEGHENY; 228 K-7; elev. 1,000ft./305m.; 🅿; ★ PGH; z 15120; ℗ 1,416; © 1,338
White; MCD-Township; BEAVER; *225 WK-2; ★ PGH; mail Beaver Falls z 15010; ℗ 1,610; © 1,434
White; MCD-Township; CAMBRIA; *225 WL-10; mail Fallentimber z 16639; ℗ 553; © 813
White; RMC Place; FAYETTE; ▲ Saltlick; 225 WO-6; 🅿; z 15490; ● 400
White; RMC Place; INDIANA; ▲ Conemaugh; 225 WM-6; ★ PGH; mail Saltsburg z 15681; ● 40
White; MCD-Township; INDIANA; *225 WL-7; mail Indiana z 15701; ℗ 13,788; © 14,034
White Bear; BERKS; see Scarlets Mill (RMC Place)
White Cottage; RMC Place; GREENE; ▲ Jackson; *225 WQ-2; mail Holbrook z 15341; rural
White Deer; RMC Place; UNION; ▲ White Deer; 226 EJ-4; 🅿; z 17887; ● 500
White Deer; MCD-Township; UNION; *226 EJ-4; 🅿; z 17887; ℗ 3,958; © 4,273
Whitehall; RMC Place; ADAMS; ▲ Mount Pleasant; *227 EQ-3; ★ HANV; mail Littlestown z 17340; ● 100
Whitehall; Inc. Place; ALLEGHENY; 228 L-6; elev. 1,200ft./366m.; ★ PGH; mail Pittsburgh z 15227; ℗ 14,451; © 14,444
White Hall; CAMBRIA; see Vinco (CDP)
White Hall; RMC Place; DAUPHIN; ▲ Susquehanna; *227 EN-4; ★ HRBG; mail Harrisburg z 17110; ● 550
Whitehall; LEHIGH; see Fullerton (CDP)
Whitehall; MCD-Township; LEHIGH; *227 EL-11; 🅿; ★ ALL-; z 18052; ℗ 22,779; © 24,896; ◆ 27,144
White Hall; RMC Place; MONTOUR; ▲ Anthony; *226 EI-5; elev. 708ft./216m.; mail Danville z 17821
Whitehall Park; RMC Place; MONTGOMERY; ▲ West Norriton; ★ PHIL-; mail Norristown z 19401
White Haven; Inc. Place; LUZERNE; 226 EJ-9; elev. 1,221ft./372m.; 🅿; ★ HAZ; z 18661; ℗ 1,132; © 1,182
White Hill; RMC Place; CUMBERLAND; ▲ Lower Allen; 227 ET-2; ★ HRBG; mail Camp Hill z 17011; ● 580
White Horse; RMC Place; CHESTER; ▲ Willistown; *227 EP-11; ★ PHIL-; mail Newtown Square z 19073; rural
White Horse; RMC Place; LANCASTER; ▲ Salisbury; 227 EP-8; mail Gap z 17527; ● 130
White House; RMC Place; FAYETTE; ▲ Springhill; 225 WQ-4; ★ MORG; mail Smithfield z 15478; ● 80
Whiteland Crest; RMC Place; CHESTER; ▲ West Whiteland; *227 EP-10; ★ PHIL-; mail Exton z 19341
Whiteland Farms; RMC Place; CHESTER; ▲ East Whiteland; *227 EP-10; ★ PHIL-; mail Malvern z 19355; ● 300
Whiteley; MCD-Township; GREENE; *225 WQ-3; mail Waynesburg z 15370; ℗ 766; © 754
Whitemarsh; MCD-Township; MONTGOMERY; *227 EO-12; ★ PHIL-; mail Conshohocken z 19428; ℗ 14,863; © 16,702
Whitemarsh Downs; RMC Place; MONTGOMERY; ▲ Springfield; ★ PHIL-; mail Oreland z 19075
White Mills; RMC Place; WAYNE; ▲ Texas; 226 EG-12; 🅿; z 18473; ● 500
White Oak; Inc. Place; ALLEGHENY; 225 WN-4; elev. 1,100ft./335m.; 🅿; ★ PGH; z 15131; ℗ 8,761; © 8,437
White Oak; RMC Place; LANCASTER; ▲ Penn; *227 EO-7; elev. 440ft./134m.; ★ LANC; mail Manheim z 17545; ● 50
White Oak; RMC Place; WESTMORELAND; ▲ Allegheny; *225 WL-5; elev. 1,100ft./335m.; ★ PGH; mail New Kensington z 15068; ● 300
White Oak Manor; RMC Place; NORTHAMPTON; ▲ Palmer; *227 EL-12; ★ ALL-; mail Easton z 18040; ● 800
White Oaks; RMC Place; LUZERNE; ▲ Wright, Fairview; *226 EI-9; elev. 1,400ft./427m.; ★ SCR-; mail Wilkes Barre z 18701; ● 450
White Pine; RMC Place; LYCOMING; ▲ Cogan House; *226 EH-3; mail Trout Run z 17771
Whites; LACKAWANNA; see Whites Crossing (RMC Place)
Whitesburg; RMC Place; ARMSTRONG; ▲ Plumcreek; 225 WK-6; mail Kittanning z 16201; ● 90
Whites Corner; RMC Place; POTTER; ▲ Harrison; *224 WD-14; mail Harrison Valley z 16927; rural
Whites Crossing (Whites); RMC Place; LACKAWANNA; ▲ Carbondale; *226 EG-10; ★ SCR-; mail Carbondale z 18407; ● 50
Whites Ferry; RMC Place; WYOMING; ▲ Eaton; *226 EG-9; elev. 584ft./178m.; mail Tunkhannock z 18657; ● 35
Whiteside; RMC Place; CLEARFIELD; ▲ Woodward; *225 WK-11; mail Houtzdale z 16651; ● 50
White Springs; RMC Place; UNION; ▲ Limestone; 227 EK-3; mail Mifflinburg z 17844; ● 550
White Squaw Mission; RMC Place; ADAMS; ▲ Franklin; *227 EP-2; mail Orrtanna z 17353; rural
Whitestown; RMC Place; BUTLER; ▲ Connoquenessing; *225 WK-3; elev. 1,301ft./397m.; ★ BUTL; mail Prospect z 16052; rural
Whites Valley; RMC Place; WAYNE; ▲ Mount Pleasant; 226 EF-11; elev. 1,334ft./407m.; mail Pleasant Mount z 18453; ● 60
White Valley; RMC Place; WESTMORELAND; *225 WM-5; ★ PGH; mail Export z 15632; pop. incl. with Murrysville (Inc. Place)
Whitewood; RMC Place; BUCKS; ▲ Bristol; *227 EO-13; ★ PHIL-; mail Levittown z 19057
Whitfield; CDP-Census Area Only; BERKS; ▲ Spring; *227 EN-8; ★ READ; mail Reading z 19609; ℗ 2,585; © 2,952
Whitford Hills; RMC Place; CHESTER; ▲ West Whiteland, Uwchlan; *227 EP-10; elev. 482ft./147m.; ★ PHIL-; mail Exton z 19341; ● 500
Whitney; RMC Place; WESTMORELAND; ▲ Unity; 225 WN-6; elev. 1,106ft./337m.; 🅿; ★ LTROB; z 15693; ● 400
Whitney Lake; RMC Place; WAYNE; ▲ Paupack; *226 EG-12; elev. 1,362ft./415m.; mail Hawley z 18428; ● 150
Whitneyville (East Charleston); RMC Place; TIOGA; ▲ Charleston; *226 EF-3; mail Mansfield z 16933, Wellsboro z 16901; ● 125
Whitpain; MCD-Township; MONTGOMERY; *227 EO-12; ★ PHIL-; mail Blue Bell z 19422; ℗ 15,673; © 18,562
Whitsett; RMC Place; FAYETTE; ▲ Perry; 225 WO-5; 🅿; ★ PGH; z 15473; ● 200
Wick; RMC Place; BUTLER; ▲ Slippery Rock; *224 WI-4; mail Slippery Rock z 16057; ● 40
Wickerham Manor; RMC Place; WASHINGTON; ▲ Carroll; *225 WO-4; ★ PGH; mail Monongahela z 15063; ● 800
Wickerham Manor-Fisher; CDP-Census Area Only; WASHINGTON; ▲ Carroll; *225 WO-4; elev. 1,100ft./335m.; ★ PGH; mail Monongahela z 15063; ℗ 1,931; © 1,783
Wickerton; RMC Place; CHESTER; ▲ London Grove; *227 EQ-9; ★ PHIL-; mail West Grove z 19390; rural
Wickham Village; RMC Place; BEAVER; ▲ Hopewell; *225 WL-2; ★ PGH; mail Aliquippa z 15001; ● 400
Wickhaven; RMC Place; FAYETTE; ▲ Perry; *225 WO-4; 🅿; ★ PGH; z 15492; ● 250
Wiconisco; RMC Place; DAUPHIN; ▲ Wiconisco; 227 EM-5; 🅿; z 17097; ● 1,300
Wiconisco; MCD-Township; DAUPHIN; *227 EM-5; 🅿; z 17097; ℗ 1,372; © 1,168
Widnoon; RMC Place; ARMSTRONG; ▲ Madison; 224 WJ-6; 🅿; z 16261; ● 90
Wiegletown; RMC Place; LAWRENCE; ▲ Shenango; 224 WJ-2; ★ NWCS; mail New Castle z 16101; ● 100
Wiggans; RMC Place; SCHUYLKILL; ▲ Mahanoy; mail Mahanoy City z 17948; ● 30
Wigwam; RMC Place; MCKEAN; ▲ Eldred; *224 WD-11; elev. 1,661ft./506m.; mail Eldred z 16731; rural
Wila (Milford); RMC Place; PERRY; ▲ Juniata; 227 EM-3; mail Newport z 17074; ● 75
Wilawana; RMC Place; BRADFORD; ▲ Athens; 226 ED-5; mail Sayre z 18840; ● 50
Wilber; SOMERSET; see Wilbur (RMC Place)
Wilbur; RMC Place; LEHIGH; *227 EM-11; ★ ALL-; pop. incl. with Allentown (Inc. Place)
Wilbur (Wilber); RMC Place; SOMERSET; ▲ Shade; 225 WO-8; mail Stoystown z 15563; ● 140
Wilburton; RMC Place; COLUMBIA; ▲ Conyngham; *227 EK-7; 🅿; z 17888; ● 220
Wilburton Number One; CDP; COLUMBIA; *227 EK-6; © 248
Wilburton Number Two; CDP-Census Area Only; COLUMBIA; *227 EK-7; © 77
Wilco Hill; RMC Place; WESTMORELAND; ▲ Rostraver; *225 WO-4; ★ PGH; mail Webster z 15087; ● 15
Wilcox; RMC Place; ELK; ▲ Jones; 224 WG-10; 🅿; z 15870; ● 1,000
Wild Acres Country Club; RMC Place; PIKE; ▲ Delaware; *226 EI-13; mail Dingmans Ferry z 18328; ● 1,000
Wildcat; RMC Place; CLARION; ▲ Madison; *224 WJ-6; mail Rimersburg z 16248; ● 30
Wilden Acres; RMC Place; NORTHAMPTON; ▲ Palmer; ★ ALL-; mail Easton z 18045
Wildwood; RMC Place; ALLEGHENY; ▲ Hampton; *225 WL-4; 🅿; ★ PGH; z 15091; ● 600
Wildwood Terrace (Wech Corner); RMC Place; LUZERNE; ▲ Wright; *226 EI-9; elev. 1,280ft./390m.; ★ SCR-; mail Wilkes Barre z 18701; ● 600
Wiley; RMC Place; YORK; ▲ Hopewell; *227 ER-6; ★ BAL; mail Stewartstown z 17363; rural
Wilgus; RMC Place; INDIANA; ▲ Montgomery; *225 WK-9; mail Glen Campbell z 15742; rural
Wilkes-Barre; Inc. Place; ⊡ LUZERNE; 226 EI-9; elev. 550ft./168m.; 🅿 🅷 🅲 7,180 ■; ★ SCR-; z 18701-11, z 18762, z 18764-67, z 18769, z 18773; ℗ 47,523; © 43,123; ◆ 40,365
Wilkes-Barre (Wilkes Barre Township); MCD-Township; LUZERNE; *226 EI-9; 🅿; ★ SCR-; z 18702, z 18706; ℗ 3,572; © 3,235
Wilkes-Barre Township; CDP-Census Area Only; LUZERNE; ▲ Wilkes-Barre; *226 EI-9; ★ SCR-; mail Wilkes Barre z 18702; ℗ 3,572; © 3,235
Wilkes Barre Township; LUZERNE; see Wilkes-Barre (MCD-Township)
Wilkes Manor; RMC Place; BUCKS; ▲ Upper Makefield; *227 EN-13; ★ PHIL-; mail Washington Crossing z 18977; ● 125
Wilkins; MCD-Township; ALLEGHENY; *225 WM-4; ★ PGH; mail Pittsburgh z 15235, Turtle Creek z 15145; ℗ 7,585; © 6,917
Wilkinsburg; Inc. Place; ALLEGHENY; 225 WM-4; elev. 937ft./286m.; 🅿; ★ PGH; z 15221; ℗ 21,080; © 19,196
Wilkins Township; CDP-Census Area Only; ALLEGHENY; ▲ Wilkins; *225 WM-4; ★ PGH; mail Pittsburgh z 15235, Turtle Creek z 15145; ℗ 7,487; © 6,917
Willet; RMC Place; INDIANA; ▲ Washington; 225 WL-7; mail Creekside z 15732; ● 30
William Penn; SCHUYLKILL; see Shaft (RMC Place)
William Penn Annex; RMC Place; PHILADELPHIA; ★ PHIL-; mail Philadelphia z 19106-07; pop. incl. with Philadelphia (Inc. Place)
William Penn Manor; RMC Place; NORTHAMPTON; ▲ Bethlehem; *227 EL-11; ★ ALL-; mail Bethlehem z 18020; ● 350
Williams; MCD-Township; DAUPHIN; *227 EL-5; mail Williamstown z 17098; ℗ 1,146; © 1,135
Williams (Williams Township); MCD-Township; NORTHAMPTON; *227 EL-12; ★ ALL-; mail Easton z 18042; ℗ 3,982; © 4,470
Williamsburg; Inc. Place; BLAIR; 225 WM-12; elev. 884ft./269m.; 🅿 🅷; ★ ALT; z 16693; ℗ 1,456; © 1,345
Williamsburg; RMC Place; CLARION; ▲ Monroe; *224 WI-6; elev. 1,349ft./411m.; mail Clarion z 16214; ● 60
Williams Grove; RMC Place; CUMBERLAND; ▲ Monroe; 227 EO-4; ★ HRBG; mail Mechanicsburg z 17055; ● 100
Williamson; RMC Place; FRANKLIN; ▲ St. Thomas; 225 WQ-13; 🅿; z 17270; ● 200
Williamsport; Inc. Place; ⊡ LYCOMING; 226 EI-4; elev. 528ft./161m.; 🅿 🅷 🅲 7,968 ■; ★ WMSPT; z 17701-03, z 17705; ℗ 31,933; © 30,706; ◆ 29,083
Williamstown; Inc. Place; DAUPHIN; 227 EM-5; elev. 736ft./224m.; 🅿; z 17098; ℗ 1,509; © 1,433
Williamstown; LANCASTER; see Vintage (RMC Place)
Williamstown (Clyde Number 3); RMC Place; WASHINGTON; ▲ East Bethlehem; *225 WP-3; mail Clarksville z 15322; ● 400
Williams Township; NORTHAMPTON; see Williams (MCD-Township)
Willis Park; RMC Place; YORK; ★ YORK; pop. incl. with York (Inc. Place)
Willistown; MCD-Township; CHESTER; *227 EP-11; ★ PHIL-; mail Malvern z 19355; ℗ 9,380; © 10,011
Willopenn; RMC Place; BUCKS; ▲ Upper Southampton; ★ PHIL-; mail Southampton z 18966
Willowbrook; RMC Place; DELAWARE; ▲ Upper Chichester; ★ PHIL-; mail Marcus Hook z 19061
Willowburn; RMC Place; DELAWARE; ▲ Radnor; *227 EP-11; ★ PHIL-; mail Villanova z 19085
Willowdale; RMC Place; CHESTER; ▲ East Marlborough; *227 EQ-10; ★ PHIL-; mail Kennett Square z 19348
Willow Grove; RMC Place; LAWRENCE; ▲ North Beaver; *224 WJ-2; ★ YNGS-; mail New Castle z 16101; rural
Willow Grove; CDP; MONTGOMERY; ▲ Abington, Upper Moreland; 227 EO-12; 🅿 🅷; ★ PHIL-; z 19090; ℗ 16,325; © 16,234
Willow Hill; RMC Place; FRANKLIN; ▲ Metal; 225 WO-14; 🅿; z 17271; ● 100
Willow Lake; RMC Place; SCHUYLKILL; ▲ North Manheim; *227 EL-7; elev. 800ft./244m.; ★ PTSVL; mail Pottsville z 17901; ● 250
Will-O-Wood; RMC Place; BUCKS; ▲ Falls; *227 EO-14; ★ PHIL-; mail Bristol z 19007
Willow Springs; RMC Place; COLUMBIA; ▲ South Centre; *226 EJ-7; mail Bloomsburg z 17815; rural
Willow Springs; RMC Place; WESTMORELAND; ▲ North Huntingdon; *225 WN-5; ★ PGH; mail Irwin z 15642; ● 1,300
Willow Street; CDP; LANCASTER; ▲ West Lampeter, Pequea; 227 EP-7; elev. 485ft./148m.; 🅿; ★ LANC; z 17584; ℗ 5,817; © 7,258
Willow View Heights; RMC Place; LANCASTER; ▲ West Lampeter; *227 EP-7; ★ LANC; mail Lancaster z 17602, Willow Street z 17584; ● 200
Wills Creek; RMC Place; BEDFORD; ▲ Londonderry; *225 WQ-9; mail Hyndman z 15545; rural
Wilmer (Harveyville); RMC Place; CHESTER; ▲ Schuylkill; *227 EO-10; elev. 205ft./62m.; ★ PHIL-; mail Phoenixville z 19460; pop. incl. with Phoenixville (Inc. Place)
Wilmerding; Inc. Place; ALLEGHENY; 228 L-9; elev. 900ft./274m.; 🅿; ★ PGH; z 15148; ℗ 2,222; © 2,145
Wilmington; MCD-Township; LAWRENCE; *224 WI-2; ★ NWCS; mail New Castle z 16105; ℗ 2,467; © 2,760
Wilmington; MCD-Township; MERCER; *224 WI-2; mail New Wilmington z 16142; ℗ 1,177; © 1,105
Wilmore; Inc. Place; CAMBRIA; 225 WN-9; elev. 1,560ft./475m.; 🅿; ★ JNST; z 15962; ℗ 277; © 252
Wilmore Heights; RMC Place; CAMBRIA; ▲ Summerhill; *225 WN-9; ★ JNST; mail Summerhill z 15958; ● 175
Wilmot; MCD-Township; BRADFORD; *226 EG-7; mail Sugar Run z 18846; ℗ 1,057; © 1,177
Wilpen; RMC Place; WESTMORELAND; ▲ Ligonier; 225 WN-7; 🅿; z 15658; ● 320
Wilshire Hills; RMC Place; LANCASTER; ▲ Manor; *227 EP-7; ★ LANC; mail Lancaster z 17603; ● 600
Wilshire Hills; RMC Place; YORK; ▲ Springettsbury; *227 EP-5; ★ YORK; mail York z 17402; ● 1,600
Wilson; RMC Place; ALLEGHENY; *225 WN-4; elev. 754ft./230m.; ★ PGH; mail Clairton z 15025; pop. incl. with Clairton (Inc. Place)
Wilson; RMC Place; BERKS; ▲ Spring; *227 EN-8; ★ READ; mail Reading z 19608; ● 975
Wilson; Inc. Place; NORTHAMPTON; 227 EL-12; ★ ALL-; mail Easton z 18042; ℗ 7,830; © 7,682
Wilson Creek; RMC Place; SOMERSET; ▲ Black; *225 WP-8; mail Rockwood z 15557; rural
Wilson Heights; RMC Place; PIKE; ▲ Greene; *226 EH-12; elev. 1,810ft./552m.; mail Greentown z 18426; ● 125
Wilsons Corners; RMC Place; CHESTER; ▲ West Vincent; *227 EO-10; ★ PHIL-; mail Kimberton z 19442, Phoenixville z 19460, Pottstown z 19464; rural
Wimmers; RMC Place; LACKAWANNA; ▲ Jefferson; 226 EH-11; elev. 1,573ft./479m.; ★ SCR-; mail Lake Ariel z 18436; ● 250
Winburne; RMC Place; CLEARFIELD; ▲ Cooper; 224 WJ-12; elev. 1,408ft./429m.; 🅿; z 16879; ● 550
Windber; Inc. Place; SOMERSET; 225 WO-9; elev. 1,853ft./565m.; 🅿 🅷; ★ JNST; z 15963; ℗ 4,756; © 4,395
Winder Village; RMC Place; BUCKS; ▲ Bristol; *227 EO-13; ★ PHIL-; mail Bristol z 19007; ● 750
Windfall; RMC Place; BRADFORD; ▲ Granville; 226 EF-5; mail Canton z 17724, Granville Summit z 16926; ● 90
Wind Gap; Inc. Place; NORTHAMPTON; 227 EK-11; elev. 734ft./224m.; 🅿; z 18091; ℗ 2,741; © 2,812
Windham; MCD-Township; BRADFORD; *226 ED-6; mail Rome z 18837; ℗ 862; © 967
Windham; MCD-Township; WYOMING; *226 EF-8; mail Laceyville z 18623; ℗ 778; © 828
Windham Center; RMC Place; BRADFORD; ▲ Windham; *226 ED-7; mail Rome z 18837
Winding Brook Manor; RMC Place; LEHIGH; ▲ Lower Macungie; *227 EM-10; elev. 400ft./122m.; ★ ALL-; mail Macungie z 18062; ● 250
Winding Hill; RMC Place; CUMBERLAND; ▲ Upper Allen; 227 ET-1; ★ HRBG; mail Mechanicsburg z 17055; ● 370
Winding Hill Heights; RMC Place; CUMBERLAND; ▲ Upper Allen; *227 EO-4; ★ HRBG; mail Mechanicsburg z 17055; ● 500
Windom; RMC Place; LANCASTER; ▲ Manor; *227 EP-7; elev. 300ft./91m.; ★ LANC; mail Lancaster z 17603; rural
Wind Ridge; RMC Place; GREENE; ▲ Richhill; 225 WP-1; 🅿; z 15380; ● 200
Windsor; MCD-Township; BERKS; *227 EM-8; mail Hamburg z 19526; ℗ 2,101; © 2,392
Windsor; Inc. Place; YORK; 227 EP-6; elev. 660ft./201m.; 🅿; ★ YORK; z 17366; ℗ 1,355; © 1,331
Windsor; MCD-Township; YORK; *227 EP-6; 🅿; ★ YORK; z 17366 & mail Red Lion z 17356; does not include the Borough of Windsor; ℗ 9,424; © 12,807
Windsor Castle; RMC Place; BERKS; ▲ Windsor; 227 EM-9; mail Hamburg z 19526; ● 100
Windsor Farms; RMC Place; DAUPHIN; ▲ Susquehanna; 227 ER-3; ★ HRBG; mail Harrisburg z 17110; ● 500
Windsor Park; RMC Place; CUMBERLAND; ▲ Lower Allen; 227 ET-1; ★ HRBG; mail Mechanicsburg z 17055; ● 1,100
Windsor Park; RMC Place; YORK; ▲ Spring Garden; ★ YORK; mail York z 17403
Windward Heights; RMC Place; BUTLER; ▲ Center; 224 WJ-4; ★ BUTL; mail Butler z 16001; ● 800
Winfield; MCD-Township; BUTLER; *225 WK-5; ★ PGH; mail Cabot z 16023; ℗ 3,162; © 3,585
Winfield; RMC Place; UNION; ▲ Union; 227 EK-4; 🅿; z 17889; ● 320
Wingate; RMC Place; CENTRE; ▲ Boggs; 224 WJ-13; 🅿; ★ STCOL; z 16823; ● 100
Wingerton; RMC Place; FRANKLIN; ▲ Antrim; *227 ER-1; ★ HAG; mail Waynesboro z 17268; rural
Winslow; RMC Place; JEFFERSON; ▲ Gaskill; *224 WJ-9; elev. 1,707ft./520m.; mail Punxsutawney z 15767; ● 25
Winslow; MCD-Township; JEFFERSON; *224 WI-9; mail Reynoldsville z 15851; ℗ 2,526; © 2,591
Winstead; RMC Place; FAYETTE; ▲ Springhill; *225 WQ-4; ★ MORG; mail Point Marion z 15474; ● 30
Winterburne; RMC Place; CLEARFIELD; ▲ Huston; *224 WI-10; mail Penfield z 15849; rural
Winterdale; RMC Place; WAYNE; ▲ Scott; 226 ED-11; mail Starlight z 18461; ● 250
Winterstown; Inc. Place; YORK; 227 EQ-6; elev. 860ft./262m.; ★ YORK; mail Red Lion z 17356; ℗ 581; © 546
Wintersville; RMC Place; BERKS; ▲ Tulpehocken; *227 EM-7; mail Richland z 17087; rural
Winton; RMC Place; LACKAWANNA; *226 EG-10; ★ SCR-; pop. incl. with Jessup (Inc. Place)
Wireton; RMC Place; ALLEGHENY; ▲ Crescent; *225 WL-3; ★ PGH; mail Aliquippa z 15001; ● 600
Wiscasset; RMC Place; MONROE; ▲ Paradise; *226 EI-11; mail Mount Pocono z 18344
Wishaw; RMC Place; JEFFERSON; ▲ Winslow; *224 WJ-9; mail Reynoldsville z 15851; ● 140
Wismer; RMC Place; BUCKS; ▲ Plumstead; *227 EM-12; ★ PHIL-; mail Pipersville z 18947; rural
Wissahickon Village; RMC Place; MONTGOMERY; ▲ Whitemarsh; ★ PHIL-; mail Lafayette Hill z 19444
Wissingertown; RMC Place; CAMBRIA; ▲ Conemaugh; *225 WN-9; ★ JNST; mail Johnstown z 15902; rural
Wissinoming; RMC Place; PHILADELPHIA; *227 EP-13; elev. 40ft./12m.; ★ PHIL-; mail Philadelphia z 19135; pop. incl. with Philadelphia (Inc. Place)
Witinski Villa; RMC Place; LUZERNE; ▲ Hanover; *226 EI-8; ★ SCR-; mail Wilkes Barre z 18706; ● 50
Witmer; RMC Place; LANCASTER; ▲ East Lampeter; *227 EP-7; 🅿; ★ LANC; z 17585; ● 300
Wittenberg; RMC Place; SOMERSET; ▲ Larimer; *225 WQ-8; mail Meyersdale z 15552; ● 15
Wittmer; RMC Place; ALLEGHENY; ▲ Shaler; *225 WM-4; ★ PGH; mail Glenshaw z 15116
Wolf; MCD-Township; LYCOMING; *226 EI-5; ★ WMSPT; mail Hughesville z 17737; ℗ 2,617; © 2,707
Wolf Creek; MCD-Township; MERCER; *224 WI-3; mail Grove City z 16127; ℗ 653; © 729
Wolfdale; CDP; WASHINGTON; ▲ Canton; 225 WO-2; ★ WASH; mail Washington z 15301; ℗ 2,906; © 2,873
Wolfe Store; RMC Place; CENTRE; ▲ Miles; *226 EJ-2; mail Rebersburg z 16872; rural
Wolf Run; RMC Place; MCKEAN; *224 WE-10; elev. 2,190ft./668m.; mail Smethport z 16749; ● 40
Wolfsburg; RMC Place; BEDFORD; ▲ Bedford; 225 WP-10; mail Bedford z 15522; ● 220
Wolfs Corners; RMC Place; CLARION; ▲ Washington; *224 WH-6; mail Tionesta z 16353; rural
Wolfs Crossroads; RMC Place; NORTHUMBERLAND; ▲ Rockefeller; *227 EK-5; elev. 661ft./201m.; mail Plainfield z 17081, Sunbury z 17801; rural
Womelsdorf; Inc. Place; BERKS; 227 EN-7; elev. 360ft./110m.; 🅿; ★ READ; z 19567; ℗ 2,270; © 2,599
Wood; RMC Place; HUNTINGDON, BEDFORD, FULTON; ▲ Wells, Broad Top, Wood; 225 WO-12; 🅿; z 16694; ● 265
Wood; MCD-Township; HUNTINGDON; *225 WO-12; mail Robertsdale z 16674; ℗ 727; © 713
Woodale; RMC Place; MONROE; ▲ Middle Smithfield; *226 EI-12; mail East Stroudsburg z 18301; ● 650
Woodbine; RMC Place; YORK; ▲ Lower Chanceford, Fawn; 227 EQ-6; ★ BAL; mail Airville z 17302; ● 50
Woodbourne; CDP; BUCKS; ▲ Middletown; *227 EO-13; ★ PHIL-; mail Langhorne z 19047; ℗ 2,953; © 3,512
Woodbridgetown; RMC Place; FAYETTE; ▲ Georges; *225 WQ-4; elev. 1,073ft./327m.; ★ UNTN; mail Smithfield z 15478; rural
Woodbury; Inc. Place; BEDFORD; 225 WO-11; elev. 1,292ft./394m.; 🅿; z 16695; ℗ 239; © 269
Woodbury; MCD-Township; BEDFORD; *225 WO-11; 🅿; z 16695; does not include the Borough of Woodbury; ℗ 1,129; © 1,198
Woodbury; MCD-Township; BLAIR; *225 WM-12; ★ ALT; mail Williamsburg z 16693; ℗ 1,418; © 1,637
Woodchoppertown; RMC Place; BERKS; ▲ Earl; *227 EN-10; mail Boyertown z 19512; ● 110
Woodcock; Inc. Place; CRAWFORD; 224 WE-3; elev. 1,200ft./366m.; mail Saegertown z 16433; ℗ 148; © 146
Woodcock; MCD-Township; CRAWFORD; *224 WF-3; mail Saegertown z 16433; does not include the Borough of Woodcock; ℗ 2,412; © 2,976
Woodcock Grange; RMC Place; CRAWFORD; ▲ Woodcock; *224 WF-3; elev. 1,359ft./414m.; mail Saegertown z 16433; rural
Woodcrest; RMC Place; CHESTER; ▲ West Goshen; *227 EP-10; ★ PHIL-; mail West Chester z 19380; ● 300
Wooddale; RMC Place; FAYETTE; ▲ Bullskin; *225 WO-6; mail Connellsville z 15425; rural
Woodglen; RMC Place; FAYETTE; ▲ Jefferson; *225 WP-4; elev. 1,144ft./349m.; ★ PGH; mail Grindstone z 15442; rural
Woodhaven Estates; RMC Place; BEAVER; ▲ Center; *225 WL-2; ★ PGH; mail Aliquippa z 15001; ● 300
Woodhill; RMC Place; BUCKS; ▲ Upper Makefield; *227 EN-13; ★ PHIL-; mail Newtown z 18940; rural
Woodland; RMC Place; CLEARFIELD; ▲ Bradford; 224 WJ-11; 🅿; z 16881; ● 400
Woodland; RMC Place; MIFFLIN; ▲ Brown; *227 EL-1; mail Reedsville z 17084; ● 120
Woodland Heights; CDP; VENANGO; ▲ Cranberry; 224 WH-5; ★ OILC-F; mail Oil City z 16301; ℗ 1,471; © 1,402
Woodland Park; RMC Place; LYCOMING; ▲ Old Lycoming, Lycoming; 226 EH-4; ★ WMSPT; mail Williamsport z 17701; ● 950
Woodland View; RMC Place; YORK; ▲ Manchester; *227 EP-5; ★ YORK; mail York z 17402; ● 150
Woodlawn; RMC Place; LANCASTER; ▲ Lancaster; *227 EP-7; ★ LANC; mail Lancaster z 17603; ● 550
Woodlawn; RMC Place; LEHIGH; ▲ South Whitehall; 227 EL-10; ★ ALL-; mail Allentown z 18104; ● 1,850
Woodlawn Park; RMC Place; BEAVER; ▲ Hopewell; *225 WL-2; ★ PGH; mail Aliquippa z 15001; ● 425
Woodlyn; CDP; DELAWARE; ▲ Ridley; 228 G-1; 🅿; ★ PHIL-; z 19094; ℗ 10,151; © 10,036
Woodlyn Park; RMC Place; DELAWARE; ▲ Ridley; ★ PHIL-; mail Woodlyn z 19094
Woodrow; RMC Place; WASHINGTON; ▲ Cross Creek; *225 WN-2; mail Hickory z 15340
Woodruff; RMC Place; GREENE; ▲ Jackson; *225 WQ-2; mail Holbrook z 15341; rural
Wood Run; WASHINGTON; see Elco (Inc. Place)
Woodside; CDP; BUCKS; ▲ Lower Makefield; 205 S-11; ★ PHIL-; mail Morrisville z 19067; ℗ 2,947; © 2,575
Woodside; RMC Place; FAYETTE; ▲ Nicholson; *225 WQ-4; elev. 1,022ft./312m.; mail Smithfield z 15478; rural
Woodside; RMC Place; LUZERNE; ▲ Foster; 226 EJ-9; ★ HAZ; mail Freeland z 18224; ● 100
Woods of Sandy Ridge; RMC Place; BUCKS; ▲ Doylestown; *227 EN-12; elev. 353ft./108m.; ★ PHIL-; mail Doylestown z 18901; ● 500
Woodvale; RMC Place; CAMBRIA; *225 WN-8; ★ JNST; mail Johnstown z 15901; pop. incl. with Johnstown (Inc. Place)
Woodvale Heights; RMC Place; CAMBRIA; ▲ East Taylor; *225 WN-9; ★ JNST; mail Johnstown z 15909; ● 250
Woodville; RMC Place; ALLEGHENY; ▲ Scott; *225 WN-3; ★ PGH; mail Carnegie z 15106
Woodville; RMC Place; CHESTER; ▲ London Grove; *227 EQ-9; ★ PHIL-; mail Chatham z 19318; rural
Woodward; CDP; CENTRE; ▲ Haines; 227 EK-2; 🅿; z 16882; © 126
Woodward; MCD-Township; CLEARFIELD; *225 WK-11; mail Houtzdale z 16651; ℗ 1,621; © 3,550
Woodward; MCD-Township; CLINTON; *226 EI-2; ★ WMSPT; mail Lock Haven z 17745; ℗ 2,662; © 2,296
Woodward; MCD-Township; LYCOMING; *226 EI-3; ★ WMSPT; mail Linden z 17744; ℗ 2,267; © 2,397
Woodward Acres; RMC Place; WESTMORELAND; ▲ Hempfield; *225 WN-5; elev. 1,212ft./369m.; ★ PGH; mail Greensburg z 15601; ● 200
Woodycrest; RMC Place; CENTRE; ▲ Patton; 225 WS-12; ★ STCOL; mail State College z 16803; ● 500
Woolrich; RMC Place; CLINTON; ▲ Pine Creek; 226 EI-2; 🅿; ★ WMSPT; z 17779; ● 800
Wopsononock; RMC Place; BLAIR; ▲ Logan; *225 WM-11; ★ ALT; mail Dysart z 16636; rural
Worcester (Center Point); RMC Place; MONTGOMERY; ▲ Worcester; 227 EO-11; elev. 236ft./72m.; 🅿; ★ PHIL-; z 19490; ● 900
Worcester; MCD-Township; MONTGOMERY; *227 EO-11; 🅿; ★ PHIL-; z 19490; ℗ 4,686; © 7,789
Worden Place; RMC Place; LUZERNE; ★ SCR-; mail Harveys Lake z 18618; pop. incl. with Harveys Lake (Inc. Place)
Worleytown; RMC Place; FRANKLIN; ▲ Antrim; *225 WQ-14; ★ HAG; mail Greencastle z 17225
Worman; RMC Place; BERKS; ▲ Earl; *227 EN-10; mail Douglassville z 19518; ● 45
Wormleysburg; Inc. Place; CUMBERLAND; 227 EN-4; elev. 320ft./98m.; 🅿; ★ HRBG; z 17043; ℗ 2,847; © 2,607
Worth; MCD-Township; BUTLER; *224 WJ-3; mail Slippery Rock z 16057; ℗ 955; © 1,331
Worth; MCD-Township; CENTRE; *225 WK-12; mail Port Matilda z 16870; ℗ 709; © 835
Worth; MCD-Township; MERCER; *224 WH-3; mail Jackson Center z 16133; ℗ 906; © 830
Worthington; Inc. Place; ARMSTRONG; 225 WK-5; elev. 1,140ft./347m.; 🅿; ★ PGH; z 16262; ℗ 713; © 778
Worthville; Inc. Place; JEFFERSON; 224 WJ-7; elev. 1,190ft./363m.; 🅿; z 15784; ℗ 65; © 85
Woxall; RMC Place; MONTGOMERY; ▲ Upper Salford; *227 EN-11; elev. 434ft./132m.; 🅿; ★ PHIL-; z 18979; ● 500
Wright; MCD-Township; LUZERNE; *226 EI-9; ★ SCR-; mail Mountain Top z 18707; ℗ 4,685; © 5,593
Wrights; RMC Place; MCKEAN; ▲ Liberty; *224 WF-12; elev. 1,572ft./479m.; mail Port Allegany z 16743
Wrights Corners; RMC Place; MCKEAN; ▲ Keating; *224 WE-10; elev. 1,593ft./486m.; mail Smethport z 16749
Wrightsdale; RMC Place; LANCASTER; ▲ Little Britain, Fulton; 227 EQ-8; elev. 456ft./139m.; mail Peach Bottom z 17563; ● 25
Wrightstown; RMC Place; BUCKS; ▲ Wrightstown; 227 EN-13; ★ PHIL-; mail Newtown z 18940; ● 400
Wrightstown; MCD-Township; BUCKS; *227 EN-13; ★ PHIL-; mail Newtown z 18940, Wycombe z 18980; ℗ 2,426; © 2,839
Wrightsville; RMC Place; WARREN; ▲ Freehold; 224 WE-6; elev. 1,354ft./413m.; mail Pittsfield z 16340; ● 70
Wrightsville; Inc. Place; YORK; 227 EP-6; elev. 306ft./93m.; 🅿; ★ YORK; z 17368; ℗ 2,396; © 2,223
Wurtemburg; RMC Place; LAWRENCE, BEAVER; ▲ Perry, Franklin; 225 WK-2; ★ PGH; mail Ellwood City z 16117; ● 400
Wurtemburg Heights; RMC Place; LAWRENCE, BEAVER; ▲ Perry, Franklin; *225 WK-2; ★ PGH; mail Ellwood City z 16117; ● 200
Wyalusing; Inc. Place; BRADFORD; 226 EF-7; elev. 686ft./209m.; 🅿; z 18853; ℗ 686; © 564
Wyalusing; MCD-Township; BRADFORD; *226 EF-7; 🅿; z 18853; does not include the Borough of Wyalusing; ℗ 1,235; © 1,341
Wyano; RMC Place; WESTMORELAND; ▲ South Huntingdon; 225 WO-5; elev. 981ft./299m.; 🅿; ★ PGH; z 15695; ● 750
Wyattville; RMC Place; VENANGO; *224 WG-4; ★ OILC-F; mail Franklin z 16323; pop. incl. with Sugarcreek (Inc. Place)
Wycombe; RMC Place; BUCKS; ▲ Wrightstown, Buckingham; 227 EN-13; 🅿; ★ PHIL-; z 18980; ● 600
Wydnor; RMC Place; NORTHAMPTON; ▲ Lower Saucon; 226 EB-4; ★ ALL-; mail Bethlehem z 18015; ● 630
Wyebrooke; RMC Place; CHESTER; ▲ West Nantmeal; *227 EO-9; ★ PHIL-; mail Honey Brook z 19344; rural
Wylandville; RMC Place; WASHINGTON; ▲ North Strabane; *225 WO-3; ★ PGH; mail Eighty Four z 15330; rural
Wylie; RMC Place; ALLEGHENY; ▲ Elizabeth; *225 WN-4; ★ PGH; mail Elizabeth z 15037; ● 100
Wyncote; CDP; MONTGOMERY; ▲ Cheltenham; 228 B-5; 🅿; ★ PHIL-; z 19095; ℗ 2,960; © 3,046
Wyncote Hills; RMC Place; MONTGOMERY; ▲ Cheltenham; ★ PHIL-; mail Wyncote z 19095
Wyncroft; RMC Place; DELAWARE; ▲ Middletown; ★ PHIL-; mail Media z 19063
Wyndham Hills; RMC Place; YORK; ▲ Spring Garden; *227 EP-5; ★ YORK; mail York z 17403
Wyndmoor; CDP; MONTGOMERY; ▲ Springfield; *227 EO-12; 🅿; ★ PHIL-; z 19038 & mail Philadelphia z 19118; ℗ 5,682; © 5,601
Wyndmoor Valley; RMC Place; MONTGOMERY; ▲ Springfield; ★ PHIL-; mail Oreland z 19075
Wynnewood; RMC Place; BUCKS; ▲ Lower Makefield; *227 EO-14; ★ PHIL-; mail Morrisville z 19067; ● 300
Wynnewood; RMC Place; MONTGOMERY; ▲ Lower Merion; 228 D-2; 🅿 🅷 🅲 795; ★ PHIL-; z 19096; ● 7,800
Wyoming; Inc. Place; LUZERNE; 226 EH-9; elev. 599ft./183m.; 🅿; ★ SCR-; z 18644; ℗ 3,255; © 3,221
WYOMING; 226 EG-7; ℗ 28,076; © 28,080; ◆ 27,732
Wyoming Camp Ground; RMC Place; LUZERNE; ▲ Exeter; *226 EH-9; elev. 1,216ft./371m.; ★ SCR-; mail Pittston z 18643; summer pop. 100; ● 35
Wyomissing; Inc. Place; BERKS; 227 EN-8; elev. 320ft./98m.; 🅿 ■; ★ READ; z 19610; includes Wyomissing Hills annexed January 7, 2002; ℗ 7,332; © 8,587; Ⓐ 11,155; ◆ 10,186
Wyomissing Hills; RMC Place; BERKS; *227 EN-8; elev. 340ft./104m.; ★ READ; mail Reading z 19609; former incorporated place; became part of Wyomissing January 7, 2002; pop. incl. with West Lawn (Inc. Place); ℗ 2,469; © 2,568
Wyomissing Junction; RMC Place; BERKS; ★ READ; mail Reading z 19610; pop. incl. with Wyomissing (Inc. Place)
Wysox; RMC Place; BRADFORD; ▲ Wysox; 226 EE-6; 🅿; z 18854; ● 400
Wysox; MCD-Township; BRADFORD; *226 EE-6; 🅿; z 18854; ℗ 1,685; © 1,763

Y

Yardley; Inc. Place; BUCKS; 227 EN-14; elev. 40ft./12m.; 🅿; ★ PHIL-; z 19067; ℗ 2,288; © 2,498
Yardley Farms; RMC Place; BUCKS; ▲ Falls; *227 EO-14; elev. 100ft./30m.; ★ PHIL-; mail Morrisville z 19067; ● 125
Yardley Hunt; RMC Place; BUCKS; ▲ Lower Makefield; *227 EN-14; ★ PHIL-; mail Morrisville z 19067; ● 1,200
Yarnell; RMC Place; CENTRE; ▲ Boggs; *224 WJ-13; mail Bellefonte z 16823
Yatesboro; RMC Place; ARMSTRONG; ▲ Cowanshannock; 225 WK-7; 🅿; z 16263; ● 450
Yatesville; Inc. Place; LUZERNE; 226 EH-9; elev. 750ft./229m.; 🅿; ★ SCR-; z 18640 & mail Shenandoah z 17976; ℗ 506; © 649
Yatesville (Fowlers); RMC Place; SCHUYLKILL; ▲ Mahanoy; *227 EK-7; mail Shenandoah z 17976; ● 25
Yeadon; Inc. Place; DELAWARE; 227 EP-12; elev. 100ft./30m.; 🅿; ★ PHIL-; z 19050; ℗ 11,980; © 11,762
Yeagertown; CDP; MIFFLIN; ▲ Derry; 227 EL-1; 🅿; z 17099; ℗ 1,150; © 1,035
Yellow Creek; RMC Place; BEDFORD; ▲ Hopewell; 225 WO-11; mail Hopewell z 16650; ● 60
Yellow Hammer; RMC Place; FOREST; ▲ Hickory; *224 WF-7; mail Tionesta z 16353; rural
Yellow House; RMC Place; BERKS; ▲ Oley, Amity; 227 EN-9; elev. 293ft./89m.; mail Douglassville z 19518; ● 200
Yellow Springs; CHESTER; see Chester Springs (RMC Place)
Yellowwood; RMC Place; BUCKS; ▲ Bristol; ★ PHIL-; mail Bristol z 19007
Yerkes; RMC Place; MONTGOMERY; ▲ Upper Providence, Lower Providence; *227 EO-11; ★ PHIL-; mail Collegeville z 19426; ● 150
Yocumtown; RMC Place; YORK; ▲ Newberry; 227 EO-5; mail Etters z 17319; ● 200
Yoe; Inc. Place; YORK; 227 EP-5; elev. 800ft./244m.; 🅿; ★ YORK; z 17313; ℗ 947; © 1,022
York; Inc. Place; ⊡ YORK; 227 EP-5; elev. 400ft./122m.; 🅿 🅷 🅲 7,336 ■; ★ YORK; z 17315, z 17401-08, z 17415; ℗ 42,192; © 40,862; ◆ 41,662
York; MCD-Township; YORK; *227 EQ-5; 🅿 🅲 7,336; ★ YORK; z 17315, z 17401-08, z 17415; not adjacent to the City of York; ℗ 19,231; © 23,637; ◆ 28,109
YORK; 227 EP-5; ℗ 339,574; © 381,751; ◆ 429,807
Yorkana; Inc. Place; YORK; 227 EP-6; elev. 660ft./201m.; 🅿; ★ YORK; z 17402, z 17406; ℗ 285; © 239
York Haven; Inc. Place; YORK; 227 EO-5; elev. 334ft./102m.; 🅿; ★ YORK; z 17370; ℗ 758; © 809
Yorklyn; RMC Place; YORK; ▲ Springettsbury; ★ YORK; mail York z 17402
York New Salem; YORK; see New Salem (Inc. Place)
York Road; RMC Place; BUCKS; ★ PHIL-; mail Warminster z 18974
York Road; RMC Place; YORK; ▲ Penn, Heidelberg; *227 EQ-4; ★ HANV; mail Hanover z 17331; rural
York Run; RMC Place; FAYETTE; ▲ Georges; *225 WQ-4; ★ UNTN; mail Uniontown z 15401; ● 50
Yorkshire; RMC Place; YORK; ▲ Springettsbury; 225 WS-11; ★ YORK; mail York z 17402; ● 1,700
York Springs; Inc. Place; ADAMS; 227 EP-3; elev. 620ft./189m.; 🅿; z 17372; ℗ 547; © 574
Yostville; RMC Place; LACKAWANNA; ▲ Spring Brook; *226 EH-10; elev. 1,698ft./518m.; mail Moscow z 18444
Young; MCD-Township; INDIANA; *225 WL-7; mail Clarksburg z 15725; ℗ 1,805; © 1,744
Young; MCD-Township; JEFFERSON; *224 WJ-8; mail Punxsutawney z 15767; ℗ 1,667; © 1,800
Youngdale; RMC Place; CLINTON; ▲ Wayne; *226 EI-2; mail Mc Elhattan z 17748
Youngsburg; RMC Place; CHESTER; ▲ East Fallowfield; *227 EP-9; ★ PHIL-; mail Coatesville z 19320; ● 75
Youngstown (Stambaugh); RMC Place; FAYETTE; ▲ North Union; *225 WP-5; ★ UNTN; mail Lemont Furnace z 15456; ● 150
Youngstown; RMC Place; LUZERNE; ▲ Hazle, Foster; *226 EJ-9; ★ HAZ; mail Drifton z 18221
Youngstown; Inc. Place; WESTMORELAND; 225 WN-6; elev. 1,100ft./335m.; 🅿; ★ LTROB; z 15696; ℗ 370; © 400
Youngsville; RMC Place; NORTHAMPTON; ▲ Moore; *227 EK-11; elev. 782ft./238m.; ★ ALL-; mail Danielsville z 18038; rural
Youngsville; Inc. Place; WARREN; 224 WE-7; elev. 1,207ft./368m.; 🅿; z 16371; ℗ 1,775; © 1,834
Youngwood; Inc. Place; WESTMORELAND; 225 WN-5; elev. 980ft./299m.; 🅿; ★ PGH; z 15697; ℗ 3,372; © 4,138; Ⓡ 3,304
Yount; RMC Place; BEDFORD; ▲ Bedford; *225 WP-10; mail Bedford z 15522
Yukon; RMC Place; WESTMORELAND; ▲ South Huntingdon; 225 WO-5; 🅿; ★ PGH; z 15698; ● 1,200

Z

Zebleys Corner; RMC Place; DELAWARE; ▲ Bethel; *227 EQ-11; ★ PHIL-; mail Marcus Hook z 19061; ● 80
Zehners; RMC Place; SCHUYLKILL; ▲ Walker; *227 EK-8; mail New Ringgold z 17960; rural
Zelienople; Inc. Place; BUTLER; 225 WK-3; elev. 911ft./278m.; 🅿; ★ PGH; z 16063; ℗ 4,158; © 4,123
Zerbe; MCD-Township; NORTHUMBERLAND; *227 EK-5; mail Trevorton z 17881; ℗ 2,067; © 2,021
Zerbe; SCHUYLKILL; see Newtown (CDP)
Zieglersville (Zieglerville); RMC Place; MONTGOMERY; ▲ Lower Frederick; 227 EN-11; 🅿; ★ PHIL-; z 19492; ● 900
Zieglerville; MONTGOMERY; see Zieglersville (RMC Place)
Zimmerman; RMC Place; SOMERSET; ▲ Somerset; *225 WP-8; mail Somerset z 15501; rural
Zion; CDP; CENTRE; ▲ Walker; 225 WK-14; mail Bellefonte z 16823; ℗ 1,573; © 2,054
Zion Grove; RMC Place; SCHUYLKILL; ▲ North Union; 227 EK-7; 🅿; z 17985; ● 200
Zionhill; RMC Place; BUCKS; ▲ Springfield; 227 EM-11; 🅿; ★ ALL-; z 18981; ● 100
Zions View; RMC Place; YORK; ▲ Conewago; 227 EP-5; ★ YORK; mail York z 17404; ● 250
Zionsville; RMC Place; LEHIGH; ▲ Upper Milford, Lower Milford; 227 EM-11; 🅿; ★ ALL-; z 18092; ● 300
Zollarsville; RMC Place; WASHINGTON; ▲ West Bethlehem; *225 WP-3; mail Marianna z 15345; ● 35
Zooks Corner; RMC Place; LANCASTER; ▲ East Lampeter; *227 EO-7; ★ LANC; mail Lancaster z 17602; ● 700
Zooks Dam; RMC Place; JUNIATA; ▲ Milford; *227 EM-2; mail Mifflintown z 17059; rural
Zora; RMC Place; ADAMS; ▲ Liberty; 227 ER-2; mail Fairfield z 17320
Zucksville; RMC Place; NORTHAMPTON; ▲ Palmer, Forks; *227 EL-12; ★ ALL-; mail Easton z 18040; rural
Zullinger; RMC Place; FRANKLIN; ▲ Washington; 225 WQ-14; 🅿; ★ HAG; z 17272; ● 250

Entries in are counties.
Entries in **bold** have populations of 2,500 or more.
Names in parentheses are alternate names.
Inc. Place — Incorporated Place
RMC Place — Rand McNally Designated Place
CDP — Census Designated Place
MCD — Minor Civil Division
⊡ County Seat
▲ Minor Civil Division
elev. Elevation
🅿 Post Office
🅷 Hospital
🅲 College
■ Principal Business Center
★ Ranally Metro Area (RMA) Abbreviation
z Zip Code(s)

RHODE ISLAND

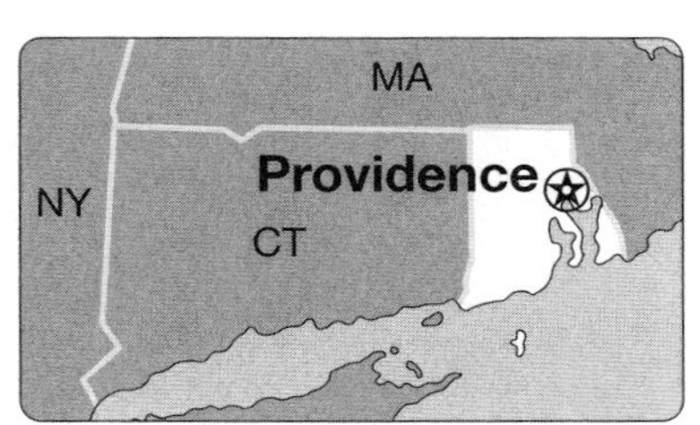

Statistics

Total area (2000) — 1,545 square miles
Land area (2000) — 1,045 square miles
Water area (2000) — 500 square miles
Capital — Providence
One of Thirteen Original States

Maps

State maps can be found on pages 142-254 in Vol. 1
County Subdivision maps can be found on pages 255-271 in Vol. 1

Ranally Metro Areas (RMAs) and Abbreviations

Fall River, MA-RI — F.R.
New London-Norwich, CT-RI — N.LON-
Newport, RI — NWPT
Providence-Warwick, RI-MA — PROV-

Principal Places

Place Name	Place Type	County	Population	Place Name	Place Type	County	Population	Place Name	Place Type	County	Population
Providence	Inc. Place	PROVIDENCE	◆ 180,082	Smithfield	MCD-Town	PROVIDENCE	◆ 21,168	Coventry	RMC Place	KENT	● 8,600
Warwick	Inc. Place	KENT	◆ 83,824	Central Falls	Inc. Place	PROVIDENCE	◆ 19,300	Charlestown	MCD-Town	WASHINGTON	◆ 8,488
Cranston	Inc. Place	PROVIDENCE	◆ 78,264	Westerly	CDP	WASHINGTON	© 17,682	Wakefield-Peacedale	CDP-Census Area Only	WASHINGTON	© 8,468
Pawtucket	Inc. Place	PROVIDENCE	◆ 71,468	Middletown	MCD-Town	NEWPORT	© 17,334	Richmond	MCD-Town	WASHINGTON	◆ 7,860
East Providence	Inc. Place	PROVIDENCE	◆ 47,176	Portsmouth	MCD-Town	NEWPORT	© 17,149	Hopkinton	MCD-Town	WASHINGTON	◆ 7,824
Woonsocket	Inc. Place	PROVIDENCE	◆ 41,492	Barrington	CDP	BRISTOL	© 16,819	Cumberland Hill	CDP	PROVIDENCE	© 7,738
Coventry	MCD-Town	KENT	◆ 34,077	Barrington	MCD-Town	BRISTOL	◆ 16,811	Tiverton	CDP	NEWPORT	© 7,282
Cumberland	MCD-Town	PROVIDENCE	◆ 32,418	Narragansett	MCD-Town	WASHINGTON	◆ 16,569	Exeter	MCD-Town	WASHINGTON	◆ 6,115
North Providence	CDP	PROVIDENCE	◆ 31,779	Burrillville	MCD-Town	PROVIDENCE	◆ 15,880	West Greenwich	MCD-Town	KENT	◆ 5,649
North Providence	MCD-Town	PROVIDENCE	◆ 31,779	Tiverton	MCD-Town	NEWPORT	◆ 15,261	Jamestown	MCD-Town	NEWPORT	◆ 5,549
South Kingstown	MCD-Town	WASHINGTON	◆ 29,384	East Greenwich	MCD-Town	KENT	◆ 13,382	Kingston	CDP	WASHINGTON	© 5,446
West Warwick	CDP	KENT	◆ 28,915	East Greenwich	RMC Place	KENT	● 11,865	Esmond	RMC Place	PROVIDENCE	● 5,000
West Warwick	MCD-Town	KENT	◆ 28,915	Valley Falls	CDP	PROVIDENCE	© 11,599				
Johnston	MCD-Town	PROVIDENCE	◆ 27,876	Newport East	CDP-Census Area Only	NEWPORT	© 11,463				
North Kingstown	MCD-Town	WASHINGTON	◆ 26,268	Warren	RMC Place	BRISTOL	● 11,385				
Newport	Inc. Place	NEWPORT	◆ 25,590	North Smithfield	MCD-Town	PROVIDENCE	◆ 11,101				
Westerly	MCD-Town	WASHINGTON	◆ 22,763	Warren	MCD-Town	BRISTOL	◆ 10,548				
Bristol	CDP	BRISTOL	◆ 22,419	Scituate	MCD-Town	PROVIDENCE	◆ 10,355				
Bristol	MCD-Town	BRISTOL	◆ 22,419	Glocester	MCD-Town	PROVIDENCE	◆ 10,088				
Lincoln	MCD-Town	PROVIDENCE	◆ 21,833	Greenville	CDP	PROVIDENCE	© 8,626				

County Business Data

County	FIPS Code	County Seat †	Land Area (Sq. Mi.)	Census Population 4/1/2000	Census Population 4/1/1990	Census Population % Change 1990-2000	Wholesale Trade Sales, 2002 ($1,000)	Wholesale Trade % Change 1997-2002	Manufacturing, 2002 Establish-ments	Manufacturing, 2002 Total Employees	Manufacturing, 2002 Value Added ($1,000)	Manufacturing, 2002 Ranally Mfg. Units
Bristol	001		25	50,648	48,859	3.7	323,656	198.5	104	2,540	201,122	106
Kent	003		170	167,090	161,135	3.7	1,589,865	-10.6	322	9,707	1,400,994	741
Newport	005		104	85,433	87,194	-2.0	683,719	182.1	97	3,241	454,732	241
Providence	007		413	621,602	596,270	4.2	5,486,325	7.7	1,436	38,583	3,204,400	1,695
Washington	009		333	123,546	110,006	12.3	482,865	27.4	172	8,214	887,386	469
The State			**1,045**	**1,048,319**	**1,003,464**	**4.5**	**8,566,430**	**12.7**	**2,131**	**62,285**	**6,148,634**	**3,253**

(d) Data not available. Corresponding percentages or Ranally Manufacturing Units are estimates.
... Represents 0 or amount too minimal to be reported.
† Not applicable

Administrative Divisions

Counties: Rhode Island's counties are geographic subdivisions for the judicial administration of the state.

Towns: All Rhode Island counties are divided into townships, except for areas within cities. Although legally incorporated, towns are not treated as incorporated places by the U.S. Census because the population often is scattered among several localities and rural areas rather than being concentrated in a single place. Only townships with an active government recognized by the U.S. Census of Governments are printed in this index.

Cities: Incorporated cities do not form part of the townships which adjoin or surround them.

Index of Places and Counties

A

Abbott Run Valley; RMC Place; PROVIDENCE; ▲ Cumberland; **229** B-7; ★ **PROV-**; mail Cumberland z 02864; ● 1,800
Adamsville; RMC Place; NEWPORT; ▲ Little Compton; **229** G-9; elev. 27ft./8m.; [P]; ★ **F.R.**; z 02801 & mail Little Compton z 02837; ● 600
Albion; RMC Place; PROVIDENCE; ▲ Lincoln; **229** B-6; elev. 145ft./44m.; [P]; ★ **PROV-**; z 02802; ● 170
Allendale; RMC Place; PROVIDENCE; ▲ North Providence; ***229** C-6; ★ **PROV-**; mail North Providence z 02911
Allenton; RMC Place; WASHINGTON; ▲ North Kingstown; **229** G-6; ★ **PROV-**; mail North Kingstown z 02852; ● 650
Alton; RMC Place; WASHINGTON; ▲ Hopkinton, Richmond; **229** H-4; ★ **PROV-**; mail Wood River Junction z 02894; ● 400
Annawomscutt; RMC Place; BRISTOL; ▲ Barrington; ***229** E-7; ★ **PROV-**; mail Barrington z 02806
Annex; RMC Place; PROVIDENCE; ★ **PROV-**; mail Providence z 02901, z 02903; pop. incl. with Providence (Inc. Place)
Anthony; RMC Place; KENT; ▲ Coventry; **229** E-5; elev. 225ft./69m.; ★ **PROV-**; mail Coventry z 02816; ● 3,400
Apple Blossom; RMC Place; PROVIDENCE; ★ **PROV-**; mail Cranston z 02920; pop. incl. with Cranston (Inc. Place)
Apponaug; KENT; see Warwick (Inc. Place)
Arcadia; RMC Place; WASHINGTON; ▲ Richmond, Exeter; **229** G-4; ★ **PROV-**; mail Hope Valley z 02832; ● 120
Arctic; RMC Place; KENT; ▲ West Warwick; ***229** E-5; ★ **PROV-**; mail West Warwick z 02893
Arkwright; RMC Place; KENT; ▲ Coventry; **229** E-5; ★ **PROV-**; mail Coventry z 02816; ● 220
Arlington; RMC Place; PROVIDENCE; ★ **PROV-**; mail Cranston z 02920; pop. incl. with Cranston (Inc. Place)
Arnold Mills; RMC Place; PROVIDENCE; ▲ Cumberland; **229** B-7; elev. 161ft./49m.; ★ **PROV-**; mail Cumberland z 02864; ● 640
Arnold's Neck; RMC Place; KENT; ★ **PROV-**; mail Warwick z 02886; pop. incl. with Warwick (Inc. Place)
Ashaway; CDP; WASHINGTON; ▲ Hopkinton; **229** I-3; [P]; ★ **N.LON-**; z 02804; ℗ 1,584; © 1,537
Ashton; RMC Place; PROVIDENCE; ▲ Cumberland; **229** B-6; ★ **PROV-**; mail Cumberland z 02864; ● 910
Auburn; RMC Place; PROVIDENCE; ***229** D-6; ★ **PROV-**; mail Cranston z 02910; pop. incl. with Cranston (Inc. Place)
Austin; RMC Place; WASHINGTON; ▲ Exeter; **229** G-4; ★ **PROV-**; mail Exeter z 02822; ● 150
Avondale; RMC Place; WASHINGTON; ▲ Westerly; **229** J-2; ★ **N.LON-**; mail Westerly z 02891; ● 230

B

Barber Heights; WASHINGTON; see Plum Beach (RMC Place)
Barberville; RMC Place; WASHINGTON; ▲ Hopkinton; ***229** G-4; ★ **N.LON-**; mail Hope Valley z 02832; rural
Barrington; CDP; BRISTOL; ▲ Barrington; **229** E-7; [P]; ★ **PROV-**; z 02806; ℗ 15,849; © 16,819
Barrington; MCD-Town; BRISTOL; ***229** E-7; [P]; ★ **PROV-**; z 02806; ℗ 15,849; © 16,819; ◆ 16,811
Barton's Corner; RMC Place; KENT; ▲ East Greenwich; ***229** F-6; elev. 248ft./76m.; ★ **PROV-**; mail East Greenwich z 02818
Bayridge; RMC Place; KENT; ★ **PROV-**; mail East Greenwich z 02818; pop. incl. with Warwick (Inc. Place)
Bayside; RMC Place; KENT; ***229** E-7; ★ **PROV-**; mail Warwick z 02889; pop. incl. with Warwick (Inc. Place)
Bay Spring; RMC Place; BRISTOL; ▲ Barrington; ***229** E-7; ★ **PROV-**; mail Barrington z 02806
Bay View; RMC Place; PROVIDENCE; ★ **PROV-**; mail East Providence z 02914; pop. incl. with East Providence (Inc. Place)
Beach Terrace; RMC Place; BRISTOL; ▲ Bristol; ***229** E-8; ★ **PROV-**; mail Bristol z 02809
Bellefonte; RMC Place; PROVIDENCE; ★ **PROV-**; mail Cranston z 02920; pop. incl. with Cranston (Inc. Place)
Belleville; RMC Place; WASHINGTON; ▲ North Kingstown; **229** G-6; ★ **PROV-**; mail North Kingstown z 02852; ● 110
Berkeley; RMC Place; PROVIDENCE; ▲ Cumberland; **229** B-6; elev. 139ft./42m.; ★ **PROV-**; mail Cumberland z 02864; ● 910
Beverage Hill; RMC Place; PROVIDENCE; ★ **PROV-**; mail Pawtucket z 02860; pop. incl. with Pawtucket (Inc. Place)
Bishops Heights; RMC Place; PROVIDENCE; ▲ Johnston; ***229** D-5; elev. 446ft./136m.; ★ **PROV-**; mail North Scituate z 02857
Black Plain; RMC Place; WASHINGTON; ▲ Exeter; ***229** G-4; ★ **PROV-**; mail Exeter z 02822; ● 120
Block Island; WASHINGTON; see New Shoreham (RMC Place)
Bonnet Shores; RMC Place; WASHINGTON; ▲ Narragansett; ***229** H-6; ★ **PROV-**; mail Narragansett z 02882; ● 1,500
Boon Lake; RMC Place; WASHINGTON; ▲ Exeter; ***229** G-4; elev. 350ft./107m.; ★ **PROV-**; mail Exeter z 02822; ● 250
Bowdish Lake; RMC Place; PROVIDENCE; ▲ Glocester; ***229** B-3; ★ **PROV-**; mail Chepachet z 02814; ● 100
Bradford; CDP; WASHINGTON; ▲ Westerly; **229** I-3; [P]; ★ **N.LON-**; z 02808; ℗ 1,604; © 1,497
Branch Village; RMC Place; PROVIDENCE; ▲ North Smithfield; ***229** A-5; elev. 235ft./72m.; ★ **PROV-**; mail North Smithfield z 02896; ● 420
Brenton Village; RMC Place; NEWPORT; ***229** H-7; ★ **NWPT**; mail Newport z 02840
Bridgeport; RMC Place; NEWPORT; ▲ Tiverton; ***229** F-8; ★ **F.R.**; mail Tiverton z 02878; ● 50
Bridgetown; RMC Place; WASHINGTON; ▲ Narragansett; ***229** H-6; ★ **PROV-**; mail Saunderstown z 02874; ● 2,200
Briggs Beach; RMC Place; NEWPORT; ▲ Little Compton; ***229** H-9; ★ **F.R.**; mail Little Compton z 02837
Bristol; CDP; BRISTOL; ▲ Bristol; **229** F-8; [P] [C] 5,172; ★ **PROV-**; z 02809; ℗ 21,625; © 22,469; ◆ 22,419
Bristol; MCD-Town; BRISTOL; ***229** E-8; [P] [C] 5,172; ★ **PROV-**; z 02809; ℗ 21,625; © 22,469; ◆ 22,419
BRISTOL; **229** E-8; ℗ 48,859; © 50,648; ◆ 49,225
Bristol Colony; RMC Place; NEWPORT; ▲ Portsmouth; ★ **NWPT**; mail Prudence Island z 02872
Bristol Ferry; RMC Place; NEWPORT; ▲ Portsmouth; **229** F-8; elev. 88ft./27m.; ★ **NWPT**; mail Portsmouth z 02871; ● 180
Bristol Highlands; RMC Place; BRISTOL; ▲ Bristol; ***229** E-8; ★ **PROV-**; mail Bristol z 02809
Bristol Narrows; RMC Place; BRISTOL; ▲ Bristol; ★ **PROV-**; mail Bristol z 02809
Broadway; RMC Place; NEWPORT; ★ **NWPT**; mail Newport z 02840; pop. incl. with Newport (Inc. Place)
Brookfield; RMC Place; PROVIDENCE; ★ **PROV-**; mail Cranston z 02920; pop. incl. with Cranston (Inc. Place)
Brush Neck; RMC Place; KENT; ★ **PROV-**; mail Warwick z 02886; pop. incl. with Warwick (Inc. Place)
Bullocks Point; RMC Place; PROVIDENCE; ★ **PROV-**; mail East Providence z 02914; pop. incl. with East Providence (Inc. Place)
Burdickville; RMC Place; WASHINGTON; ▲ Hopkinton; **229** I-3; ★ **N.LON-**; mail Bradford z 02808; ● 500
Burrillville; MCD-Town; PROVIDENCE; ***229** C-4; [P]; ★ **PROV-**; z 02830 & mail Glendale z 02826, Mapleville z 02839, Oakland z 02858; ℗ 16,230; © 15,796; ◆ 15,880
Buttonwoods; RMC Place; KENT; ***229** E-6; ★ **PROV-**; mail Warwick z 02886; pop. incl. with Warwick (Inc. Place)

C

Canonchet; RMC Place; WASHINGTON; ▲ Hopkinton; **229** H-3; ★ **N.LON-**; mail Hope Valley z 02832; ● 210
Carnegie Heights; RMC Place; PROVIDENCE; ▲ Lincoln; ***229** C-6; ★ **PROV-**; mail Lincoln z 02865
Carolina; RMC Place; WASHINGTON; ▲ Richmond, Charlestown; **229** H-4; [P]; ★ **PROV-**; z 02812; ● 880
Carpenters Beach; RMC Place; WASHINGTON; ▲ South Kingstown; ***229** I-5; elev. 14ft./4m.; ★ **PROV-**; mail Wakefield z 02879; ● 200
Cedar Grove Estates; RMC Place; WASHINGTON; ▲ Exeter; ***229** G-5; elev. 250ft./76m.; ★ **PROV-**; mail Exeter z 02822; ● 200
Cedar Point; RMC Place; NEWPORT; ▲ Jamestown; elev. 8ft./2m.; ★ **PROV-**; mail Jamestown z 02835
Cedar Tree Point; RMC Place; KENT; ★ **PROV-**; mail Warwick z 02886; pop. incl. with Warwick (Inc. Place)
Centerville; RMC Place; KENT; ▲ West Warwick; ***229** E-5; elev. 139ft./42m.; ★ **PROV-**; mail West Warwick z 02893
Centerville; RMC Place; WASHINGTON; ▲ Hopkinton; **229** G-3; ★ **N.LON-**; mail Hope Valley z 02832; ● 80
Central Falls; Inc. Place; PROVIDENCE; **229** C-7; elev. 110ft./34m.; [P]; ★ **PROV-**; z 02863; ℗ 17,637; © 18,928; ◆ 19,300
Centredale; RMC Place; PROVIDENCE; ▲ North Providence; ***229** C-6; elev. 74ft./23m.; ★ **PROV-**; mail North Providence z 02911
Charlestown; RMC Place; WASHINGTON; ▲ Charlestown; **229** I-4; [P]; ★ **PROV-**; z 02813; ● 2,000
Charlestown; MCD-Town; WASHINGTON; ***229** I-4; [P]; ★ **PROV-**; z 02813; ℗ 6,478; © 7,859; ◆ 8,488
Charlestown Beach; RMC Place; WASHINGTON; ▲ Charlestown; ***229** I-4; ★ **PROV-**; mail Charlestown z 02813
Chepachet; RMC Place; PROVIDENCE; ▲ Glocester; **229** C-4; elev. 442ft./135m.; [P]; ★ **PROV-**; z 02814; ● 1,100
Chepiwanoxet; RMC Place; KENT; ***229** F-6; ★ **PROV-**; mail Warwick z 02886; pop. incl. with Warwick (Inc. Place)
Cherry Valley; RMC Place; PROVIDENCE; ▲ Glocester; ***229** C-4; elev. 525ft./160m.; ★ **PROV-**; mail Chepachet z 02814; ● 60
Cherry Valley Beach; RMC Place; PROVIDENCE; ▲ Glocester; ***229** C-4; ★ **PROV-**; mail Chepachet z 02814; ● 60
Chopmist; RMC Place; PROVIDENCE; ▲ Scituate; ***229** D-4; ★ **PROV-**; mail North Scituate z 02857
Clarke's Village; RMC Place; NEWPORT; ▲ Jamestown; elev. 8ft./2m.; ★ **PROV-**; mail Jamestown z 02835
Clayville; RMC Place; PROVIDENCE; ▲ Foster, Scituate; **229** D-4; [P]; ★ **PROV-**; z 02815; ● 200
Clyde; RMC Place; KENT; ▲ West Warwick; ***229** E-5; ★ **PROV-**; mail West Warwick z 02893
Coasters Harbor; RMC Place; NEWPORT; ★ **NWPT**; mail Newport z 02840; pop. incl. with Newport (Inc. Place)
Coggeshall; RMC Place; BRISTOL; ▲ Warren; ***229** E-8; ★ **PROV-**; mail Warren z 02885
Coles; RMC Place; KENT; ***229** E-7; elev. 36ft./11m.; ★ **PROV-**; mail Warwick z 02889; pop. incl. with Warwick (Inc. Place)
Columbia Heights; RMC Place; WASHINGTON; ▲ Charlestown; ***229** H-4; ★ **PROV-**; mail Shannock z 02875; ● 150
Common Fence Point; RMC Place; NEWPORT; ▲ Portsmouth; **229** F-8; ★ **NWPT**; mail Portsmouth z 02871; ● 900
Commons; RMC Place; NEWPORT; ▲ Little Compton; ★ **F.R.**; mail Little Compton z 02837
Comstock Gardens; RMC Place; PROVIDENCE; ***229** D-5; ★ **PROV-**; mail Cranston z 02910; pop. incl. with Cranston (Inc. Place)
Conanicut Park; RMC Place; NEWPORT; ▲ Jamestown; ***229** G-7; elev. 8ft./2m.; ★ **PROV-**; mail Jamestown z 02835
Conimicut; RMC Place; KENT; ***229** E-7; ★ **PROV-**; mail Warwick z 02889; pop. incl. with Warwick (Inc. Place)
Corey's Lane; RMC Place; NEWPORT; ▲ Portsmouth; ★ **NWPT**; mail Portsmouth z 02871
Coventry (Washington); RMC Place; KENT; ▲ Coventry; **229** E-5; [P]; ★ **PROV-**; z 02816, z 02827 & mail West Greenwich z 02817; ● 8,600
Coventry; MCD-Town; KENT; ***229** E-4; [P]; ★ **PROV-**; z 02816, z 02827; ℗ 31,083; © 33,668; ◆ 34,077
Coventry Center; RMC Place; KENT; ▲ Coventry; ***229** E-4; elev. 285ft./87m.; ★ **PROV-**; mail Coventry z 02816
Cowesett; RMC Place; KENT; ***229** E-6; ★ **PROV-**; mail Warwick z 02886; pop. incl. with Warwick (Inc. Place)
Cranston; Inc. Place; PROVIDENCE; **229** D-6; elev. 40ft./12m.; [P] [H] ■; ★ **PROV-**; z 02905, z 02907, z 02910, z 02920-21 & mail Fiskeville z 02823; ℗ 76,060; © 79,269; ◆ 78,264
Crescent Park; RMC Place; PROVIDENCE; ★ **PROV-**; mail East Providence z 02914; pop. incl. with East Providence (Inc. Place)
Crompton; RMC Place; KENT; ▲ West Warwick; ***229** E-5; ★ **PROV-**; mail West Warwick z 02893
Cross Mills; RMC Place; WASHINGTON; ▲ Charlestown; ★ **PROV-**; mail Charlestown z 02813
Cumberland; RMC Place; PROVIDENCE; ▲ Cumberland; ***229** C-7; [P]; ★ **PROV-**; z 02864
Cumberland; MCD-Town; PROVIDENCE; ***229** B-6; [P]; ★ **PROV-**; z 02864; ℗ 29,038; © 31,840; ◆ 32,418
Cumberland Fall; PROVIDENCE; see Cumberland Hill (CDP)
Cumberland Hill (Cumberland Fall); CDP; PROVIDENCE; ▲ Cumberland; **229** B-6; elev. 331ft./101m.; ★ **PROV-**; mail Cumberland z 02864; ℗ 6,379; © 7,738
Curtis Corners; RMC Place; WASHINGTON; ▲ South Kingstown; ***229** H-5; elev. 167ft./51m.; ★ **PROV-**; mail Peace Dale z 02883; ● 180

D

Darlington; RMC Place; PROVIDENCE; ***229** C-7; ★ **PROV-**; mail Pawtucket z 02861; pop. incl. with Pawtucket (Inc. Place)
Davisville; RMC Place; WASHINGTON; ▲ North Kingstown; **229** F-6; elev. 50ft./15m.; ★ **PROV-**; mail North Kingstown z 02854; ● 550
Diamond Hill; RMC Place; PROVIDENCE; ▲ Cumberland; **229** B-6; ★ **PROV-**; mail Woonsocket z 02895; ● 910
Dunns Corners; RMC Place; WASHINGTON; ▲ Westerly; **229** J-3; ★ **N.LON-**; mail Westerly z 02891; ● 170
Durfee Hill; RMC Place; PROVIDENCE; ▲ Glocester; ***229** C-3; elev. 804ft./245m.; ★ **PROV-**; mail Chepachet z 02814; rural

E

Eagleville; RMC Place; NEWPORT; ▲ Tiverton; ***229** F-9; ★ **F.R.**; mail Tiverton z 02878; ● 200
East Greenwich; RMC Place; KENT; ▲ East Greenwich; **229** F-6; [P]; ★ **PROV-**; z 02818; ● 11,865
East Greenwich; MCD-Town; KENT; ***229** F-6; [P]; ★ **PROV-**; z 02818; ℗ 11,865; © 12,948; ◆ 13,382
East Mananuck; WASHINGTON; see Snug Harbor (RMC Place)
East Matunuck; WASHINGTON; see Snug Harbor (RMC Place)
East Natick; RMC Place; KENT; ***229** E-6; ★ **PROV-**; mail West Warwick z 02893; pop. incl. with Warwick (Inc. Place)
East Providence; Inc. Place; PROVIDENCE; **229** D-7; elev. 59ft./18m.; [P] [H] ■; ★ **PROV-**; z 02914 & mail Riverside z 02915, Rumford z 02916; ℗ 50,380; © 48,688; ◆ 47,176
East Providence Wharf; RMC Place; PROVIDENCE; ★ **PROV-**; mail East Providence z 02914; pop. incl. with East Providence (Inc. Place)
East Side; RMC Place; PROVIDENCE; ★ **PROV-**; mail Providence z 02906; pop. incl. with Providence (Inc. Place)
East Warren; RMC Place; BRISTOL; ▲ Warren; ★ **PROV-**; mail Warren z 02885
Echo Lake; RMC Place; PROVIDENCE; ▲ Glocester; ***229** B-4; elev. 500ft./152m.; ★ **PROV-**; mail Chepachet z 02814; ● 300
Eden Park; RMC Place; PROVIDENCE; ★ **PROV-**; mail Cranston z 02920; pop. incl. with Cranston (Inc. Place)
Edgewood; RMC Place; PROVIDENCE; ***229** D-7; ★ **PROV-**; mail Providence z 02905; pop. incl. with Cranston (Inc. Place)
Elmwood; RMC Place; PROVIDENCE; ***229** D-6; ★ **PROV-**; mail Providence z 02907; pop. incl. with Providence (Inc. Place)
Enos; RMC Place; PROVIDENCE; ★ **PROV-**; mail Cranston z 02920; pop. incl. with Cranston (Inc. Place)
Escoheag; RMC Place; WASHINGTON, KENT; ▲ West Greenwich, Exeter; **229** F-3; [P]; ★ **PROV-**; z 02822; ● 120
Esmond; RMC Place; PROVIDENCE; ▲ Smithfield; **229** C-6; elev. 147ft./45m.; ★ **PROV-**; mail Smithfield z 02917; ● 5,000
Exeter; RMC Place; WASHINGTON; ▲ Exeter; **229** G-5; [P]; ★ **PROV-**; z 02822; ● 310
Exeter; MCD-Town; WASHINGTON; ***229** G-5; [P]; ★ **PROV-**; z 02822; ℗ 5,461; © 6,045; ◆ 6,115

F

Fairbanks Corner; RMC Place; KENT; ▲ Coventry; ***229** E-3; elev. 435ft./133m.; ★ **PROV-**; mail Greene z 02827; rural
Fairlawn; RMC Place; PROVIDENCE; ***229** C-6; ★ **PROV-**; pop. incl. with Pawtucket (Inc. Place)
Federal Hill; RMC Place; PROVIDENCE; ★ **PROV-**; pop. incl. with Providence (Inc. Place)
Finast; RMC Place; PROVIDENCE; ★ **PROV-**; mail East Providence z 02914; pop. incl. with East Providence (Inc. Place)
Fiskeville; RMC Place; PROVIDENCE; ***229** E-5; elev. 200ft./61m.; [P]; ★ **PROV-**; z 02823
Fogland Point; RMC Place; NEWPORT; ▲ Tiverton; ★ **F.R.**; mail Tiverton z 02878
Forestdale; RMC Place; PROVIDENCE; ▲ North Smithfield; **229** B-5; [P]; ★ **PROV-**; z 02824; ● 550
Fort Adams; RMC Place; NEWPORT; ★ **NWPT**; mail Newport z 02840; pop. incl. with Newport (Inc. Place)
Foster (Foster Center); RMC Place; PROVIDENCE; ▲ Foster; **229** D-4; elev. 711ft./217m.; [P]; ★ **PROV-**; z 02825; ● 190
Foster; MCD-Town; PROVIDENCE; ***229** D-3; [P]; ★ **PROV-**; z 02825; ℗ 4,316; © 4,274; ◆ 4,325
Foster Center; PROVIDENCE; see Foster (RMC Place)
Fox Point; RMC Place; PROVIDENCE; ★ **PROV-**; mail Providence z 02906; pop. incl. with Providence (Inc. Place)
Frenchtown; RMC Place; KENT; ▲ East Greenwich; ***229** F-6; elev. 109ft./33m.; ★ **PROV-**; mail East Greenwich z 02818
Friar; RMC Place; PROVIDENCE; ★ **PROV-**; mail Providence z 02918; pop. incl. with Providence (Inc. Place)
Fruit Hill; RMC Place; PROVIDENCE; ▲ North Providence; ★ **PROV-**; mail North Providence z 02911

G

Galilee; RMC Place; WASHINGTON; ▲ Narragansett; **229** I-6; ★ **PROV-**; mail Narragansett z 02882; ● 560
Garden City; RMC Place; PROVIDENCE; ***229** D-6; elev. 70ft./21m.; ★ **PROV-**; mail Cranston z 02920; pop. incl. with Cranston (Inc. Place)
Gazzaville; RMC Place; PROVIDENCE; ▲ Burrillville; ***229** B-4; ★ **PROV-**; mail Mapleville z 02839
Geneva; RMC Place; PROVIDENCE; ▲ North Providence; ★ **PROV-**; mail North Providence z 02911
Georgiaville; RMC Place; PROVIDENCE; ▲ Smithfield; ***229** C-6; ★ **PROV-**; mail Smithfield z 02917
Glendale; RMC Place; PROVIDENCE; ▲ Burrillville; **229** B-4; [P]; ★ **PROV-**; z 02826; ● 860
Glocester; MCD-Town; PROVIDENCE; ***229** C-4; ★ **PROV-**; mail Chepachet z 02814, Harmony z 02829, Pascoag z 02859; ℗ 9,227; © 9,948; ◆ 10,088
Goat Island; RMC Place; NEWPORT; ★ **NWPT**; mail Newport z 02840; pop. incl. with Newport (Inc. Place)
Goulds; RMC Place; WASHINGTON; ▲ South Kingstown; ★ **PROV-**; mail Peace Dale z 02883
Graniteville; RMC Place; PROVIDENCE; ▲ Johnston; ***229** B-4; elev. 353ft./108m.; ★ **PROV-**; mail North Providence z 02911
Grants Mills; RMC Place; PROVIDENCE; ▲ Cumberland; ***229** A-6; ★ **PROV-**; mail Manville z 02838
Greene; RMC Place; KENT; ▲ Coventry; **229** E-3; elev. 425ft./130m.; [P]; ★ **PROV-**; z 02827; ● 110
Green Hill; RMC Place; WASHINGTON; ▲ South Kingstown; **229** I-5; ★ **PROV-**; mail Wakefield z 02879; ● 300
Greenville; CDP; PROVIDENCE; ▲ Smithfield; **229** C-5; elev. 322ft./98m.; [P]; ★ **PROV-**; z 02828; ℗ 8,303; © 8,626
Greenwood; RMC Place; KENT; ***229** E-6; ★ **PROV-**; mail Warwick z 02886; pop. incl. with Warwick (Inc. Place)
Greystone; RMC Place; PROVIDENCE; ▲ North Providence; ***229** C-6; elev. 139ft./42m.; ★ **PROV-**; mail North Providence z 02911

H

Hamilton; RMC Place; WASHINGTON; ▲ North Kingstown; **229** G-6; ★ **PROV-**; mail North Kingstown z 02852; ● 270
Hampden Meadows; RMC Place; BRISTOL; ▲ Barrington; ★ **PROV-**; mail Barrington z 02806
Harbor Junction (Harbor Junction Wharf); RMC Place; PROVIDENCE; ★ **PROV-**; pop. incl. with Providence (Inc. Place)
Harbor Junction Wharf; PROVIDENCE; see Harbor Junction (RMC Place)
Harmony; RMC Place; PROVIDENCE; ▲ Glocester; **229** C-5; elev. 409ft./125m.; [P]; ★ **PROV-**; z 02829; ● 1,050
Harris; RMC Place; KENT; ▲ Coventry; **229** E-5; ★ **PROV-**; mail Coventry z 02816; ● 1,250
Harrisville; CDP; PROVIDENCE; ▲ Burrillville; **229** B-4; elev. 336ft./102m.; [P]; ★ **PROV-**; z 02830; ℗ 1,654; © 1,561
Haversham; RMC Place; WASHINGTON; ▲ Westerly; **229** J-3; ★ **N.LON-**; mail Westerly z 02891; ● 170
Highland Beach; RMC Place; KENT; ***229** E-7; ★ **PROV-**; mail Warwick z 02889; pop. incl. with Warwick (Inc. Place)
Hills Grove; RMC Place; KENT; ***229** E-6; ★ **PROV-**; mail Warwick z 02886; pop. incl. with Warwick (Inc. Place)
Hog Island; RMC Place; NEWPORT; ▲ Portsmouth; ★ **NWPT**; mail Bristol z 02809; summer pop. 170
Homestead; RMC Place; NEWPORT; ▲ Portsmouth; ***229** F-7; ★ **NWPT**; mail Prudence Island z 02872
Hope; RMC Place; PROVIDENCE; ▲ Scituate; **229** E-5; [P]; ★ **PROV-**; z 02831; ● 350
Hope Valley; CDP; WASHINGTON; ▲ Hopkinton; **229** H-4; [P]; ★ **N.LON-**; z 02832; ℗ 1,446; © 1,649
Hopkins Hollow; RMC Place; KENT; ▲ Coventry; ***229** F-3; elev. 359ft./109m.; ★ **PROV-**; mail Greene z 02827
Hopkinton; RMC Place; WASHINGTON; ▲ Hopkinton; **229** H-3; [P]; ★ **N.LON-**; z 02833 & mail Ashaway z 02804, Hope Valley z 02832, Rockville z 02873; ● 590
Hopkinton; MCD-Town; WASHINGTON; ***229** H-3; [P]; ★ **N.LON-**; z 02833 & mail Ashaway z 02804, Hope Valley z 02832, Rockville z 02873; ℗ 6,873; © 7,836; ◆ 7,824
Horse Neck; RMC Place; KENT; ***229** E-7; ★ **PROV-**; mail Warwick z 02886; pop. incl. with Warwick (Inc. Place)
Hoxsie; RMC Place; KENT; ***229** E-6; ★ **PROV-**; mail Warwick z 02889; pop. incl. with Warwick (Inc. Place)
Hughesdale; RMC Place; PROVIDENCE; ▲ Johnston; ***229** D-6; elev. 125ft./38m.; ★ **PROV-**; mail Johnston z 02919

Entries in **UPPERCASE** are counties.
Entries in **bold** have populations of 2,500 or more.
Names in parentheses are alternate names.

Inc. Place	Incorporated Place
RMC Place	Rand McNally Designated Place
CDP	Census Designated Place
MCD	Minor Civil Division
⊡	County Seat
▲	Minor Civil Division
elev.	Elevation
[P]	Post Office
[H]	Hospital
[C]	College
■	Principal Business Center
★	Ranally Metro Area (RMA) Abbreviation
z	Zip Code(s)
℗	Previous Census Population
®	Revised Census Population
Ⓐ	Annexation Population
●	Rand McNally Population Estimate
©	Final Census Population
Ⓢ	Special Census Population
◆	Estimated Population

For additional definitions see Glossary, Volume 1, and Introduction, Volume 2.

I

Indian Lake Shores; RMC Place; WASHINGTON; ▲ South Kingstown; **229** H-6; elev. 124ft./38m.; ★ **PROV-**; mail Wakefield **z** 02879; ● 250

India Point; RMC Place; PROVIDENCE; ★ **PROV-**; mail Providence **z** 02903; pop. incl. with Providence (Inc. Place)

Island Park; RMC Place; NEWPORT; ▲ Portsmouth; **229** F-8; ★ **NWPT**; mail Portsmouth **z** 02871; ● 1,550

J

Jackson; RMC Place; PROVIDENCE; ▲ Scituate; **229** E-5; ★ **PROV-**; mail Fiskeville **z** 02823, Hope **z** 02831; ● 200

Jamestown; RMC Place; NEWPORT; ▲ Jamestown; **229** H-7; elev. 8ft./2m.; 🅿; ★ **PROV-**; **z** 02835; ● 4,999

Jamestown; MCD-Town; NEWPORT; ***229** G-7; elev. 8ft./2m.; 🅿; ★ **PROV-**; **z** 02835; Ⓟ 4,999; Ⓒ 5,622; ◆ 5,549

Jamestown Center; RMC Place; NEWPORT; ▲ Jamestown; elev. 8ft./2m.; ★ **PROV-**; mail Jamestown **z** 02835

Jamestown Shores; RMC Place; NEWPORT; ▲ Jamestown; ***229** G-7; elev. 8ft./2m.; ★ **PROV-**; mail Jamestown **z** 02835

Jerusalem; RMC Place; WASHINGTON; ▲ Narragansett; **229** I-5; ★ **PROV-**; mail Wakefield **z** 02879; summer pop. 1,800; ● 100

Johnston; RMC Place; PROVIDENCE; ▲ Johnston; **229** D-6; 🅿; ★ **PROV-**; **z** 02919

Johnston; MCD-Town; PROVIDENCE; ***229** D-5; 🅿; ★ **PROV-**; **z** 02919; Ⓟ 26,542; Ⓒ 28,195; ◆ 27,876

K

KENT; **229** F-4; Ⓟ 161,135; Ⓒ 167,090; ◆ 166,183

Kent Corner; RMC Place; PROVIDENCE; ***229** D-7; ★ **PROV-**; mail East Providence **z** 02914; pop. incl. with East Providence (Inc. Place)

Kent Heights; RMC Place; PROVIDENCE; ★ **PROV-**; mail East Providence **z** 02914; pop. incl. with East Providence (Inc. Place)

Kenyon; RMC Place; WASHINGTON; ▲ Charlestown, Richmond; **229** H-4; 🅿; ★ **PROV-**; **z** 02836; ● 550

Kingston; CDP; WASHINGTON; ▲ South Kingstown; **229** H-5; 🅿 🅲 15,062; ★ **PROV-**; **z** 02881; Ⓟ 6,504; Ⓒ 5,446

Kingston; WASHINGTON; see West Kingston (RMC Place)

Knightsville; RMC Place; PROVIDENCE; ***229** D-6; ★ **PROV-**; mail Cranston **z** 02920; pop. incl. with Cranston (Inc. Place)

L

La Fayette; RMC Place; WASHINGTON; ▲ North Kingstown; **229** G-6; ★ **PROV-**; mail North Kingstown **z** 02852; ● 760

Lake Bel Air; RMC Place; PROVIDENCE; ▲ North Smithfield; ***229** B-5; elev. 300ft./91m.; ★ **PROV-**; mail North Smithfield **z** 02896; ● 100

Lake Mishnock; RMC Place; KENT; ▲ West Greenwich; ***229** F-5; elev. 300ft./91m.; ★ **PROV-**; mail West Greenwich **z** 02817; ● 350

Lakewood; RMC Place; KENT; ***229** E-7; ★ **PROV-**; mail Warwick **z** 02888; pop. incl. with Warwick (Inc. Place)

Langworthy Corner; RMC Place; WASHINGTON; ▲ Westerly; ***229** J-3; ★ **N.LON-**; mail Westerly **z** 02891; rural

Laurel Hill; RMC Place; PROVIDENCE; ▲ Burrillville; ★ **PROV-**; mail Pascoag **z** 02859

Laurel Park; RMC Place; BRISTOL; ▲ Warren; ***229** E-8; ★ **PROV-**; mail Warren **z** 02885

Leonard Corner; RMC Place; PROVIDENCE; ***229** D-7; elev. 90ft./27m.; ★ **PROV-**; mail East Providence **z** 02914; pop. incl. with East Providence (Inc. Place)

Liberty; RMC Place; WASHINGTON; ▲ Exeter; ***229** G-5; ★ **PROV-**; mail Slocum **z** 02877; rural

Lime Rock; RMC Place; PROVIDENCE; ▲ Lincoln; **229** B-6; ★ **PROV-**; mail Lincoln **z** 02865; ● 300

Lincoln; RMC Place; PROVIDENCE; ▲ Lincoln; ***229** C-6; 🅿; ★ **PROV-**; **z** 02865 & mail Albion **z** 02802, Manville **z** 02838

Lincoln; MCD-Town; PROVIDENCE; ***229** C-6; 🅿; ★ **PROV-**; **z** 02865 & mail Albion **z** 02802, Manville **z** 02838, Pawtucket **z** 02860; Ⓟ 18,045; Ⓒ 20,898; ◆ 21,833

Lincoln Park; RMC Place; KENT; ***229** E-6; ★ **PROV-**; mail Warwick **z** 02888; pop. incl. with Warwick (Inc. Place)

Lippit; RMC Place; KENT; ▲ West Warwick; ★ **PROV-**; mail West Warwick **z** 02893

Lippitt Estate; RMC Place; PROVIDENCE; ▲ Cumberland; **229** I-9; ★ **PROV-**; mail Cumberland **z** 02864; ● 380

Little Compton; RMC Place; NEWPORT; ▲ Little Compton; **229** H-9; elev. 104ft./32m.; 🅿; ★ **F.R.**; **z** 02837 & mail Adamsville **z** 02801; ● 550

Little Compton; MCD-Town; NEWPORT; ***229** H-9; 🅿; ★ **F.R.**; **z** 02837 & mail Adamsville **z** 02801; Ⓟ 3,339; Ⓒ 3,593; ◆ 3,560

Lockwood Corner; RMC Place; KENT; ★ **PROV-**; mail Warwick **z** 02889; pop. incl. with Warwick (Inc. Place)

Longmeadow; RMC Place; KENT; ***229** E-7; ★ **PROV-**; mail Warwick **z** 02889; pop. incl. with Warwick (Inc. Place)

Lonsdale; RMC Place; PROVIDENCE; ▲ Cumberland; **229** C-7; ★ **PROV-**; mail Lincoln **z** 02865; ● 4,200

Lymansville; RMC Place; PROVIDENCE; ▲ North Providence; ***229** C-6; ★ **PROV-**; mail North Providence **z** 02911

M

Manton; RMC Place; PROVIDENCE; ***229** D-6; ★ **PROV-**; mail Providence **z** 02909; pop. incl. with Providence (Inc. Place)

Manville; RMC Place; PROVIDENCE; ▲ Lincoln; **229** B-6; 🅿; ★ **PROV-**; **z** 02838; ● 3,200

Maple Root Village; RMC Place; KENT; ▲ Coventry; ***229** F-5; elev. 258ft./79m.; ★ **PROV-**; mail Coventry **z** 02816; ● 570

Mapleville; RMC Place; PROVIDENCE; ▲ Burrillville; **229** B-4; elev. 368ft./112m.; 🅿; ★ **PROV-**; **z** 02839; ● 1,600

Marieville; RMC Place; PROVIDENCE; ▲ North Providence; ***229** C-6; ★ **PROV-**; mail Providence **z** 02904

Matunuck; RMC Place; WASHINGTON; ▲ South Kingstown; **229** I-5; ★ **PROV-**; mail Wakefield **z** 02879; ● 580

Melville; CDP; NEWPORT; ▲ Portsmouth, Middletown; ***229** G-7; ★ **NWPT**; mail Portsmouth **z** 02871; Ⓟ 4,426; Ⓒ 2,325

Meshanticut; RMC Place; PROVIDENCE; ***229** D-6; elev. 86ft./26m.; ★ **PROV-**; mail Cranston **z** 02920; pop. incl. with Cranston (Inc. Place)

Middletown; RMC Place; NEWPORT; ▲ Middletown; **229** G-8; 🅿; ★ **NWPT**; **z** 02842 & mail Newport **z** 02840; ● 3,800

Middletown; MCD-Town; NEWPORT; ***229** H-8; 🅿; ★ **NWPT**; **z** 02842 & mail Newport **z** 02840; Ⓟ 19,460; Ⓒ 17,334

Millville; RMC Place; WASHINGTON; ▲ Exeter; ***229** G-4; elev. 297ft./91m.; ★ **PROV-**; mail Exeter **z** 02822; rural

Misquamicut; RMC Place; WASHINGTON; ▲ Westerly; **229** J-3; ★ **N.LON-**; mail Westerly **z** 02891; ● 60

Mohegan; RMC Place; PROVIDENCE; ▲ Burrillville; **229** B-4; ★ **PROV-**; mail Woonsocket **z** 02895; ● 310

Mohegan Bluffs; RMC Place; WASHINGTON; ▲ New Shoreham; mail Block Island **z** 02807

Mooresfield; RMC Place; WASHINGTON; ▲ South Kingstown; ***229** H-6; ★ **PROV-**; mail Saunderstown **z** 02874; ● 30

Moosup Valley; RMC Place; PROVIDENCE; ▲ Foster; **229** E-3; ★ **PROV-**; mail Greene **z** 02827; ● 220

Moscow; RMC Place; WASHINGTON; ▲ Hopkinton; **229** G-3; ★ **N.LON-**; mail Hope Valley **z** 02832; ● 30

Mount Pleasant; RMC Place; PROVIDENCE; ★ **PROV-**; mail Providence **z** 02908; pop. incl. with Providence (Inc. Place)

Mount View; RMC Place; WASHINGTON; ▲ North Kingstown; **229** F-6; ★ **PROV-**; mail North Kingstown **z** 02852; ● 700

N

Nannaquaket; RMC Place; NEWPORT; ▲ Tiverton; ***229** F-8; ★ **F.R.**; mail Tiverton **z** 02878; ● 300

Narragansett; WASHINGTON; see Narragansett Pier (CDP)

Narragansett; MCD-Town; WASHINGTON; ***229** H-6; 🅿; ★ **PROV-**; **z** 02879, **z** 02882 & mail Saunderstown **z** 02874; Ⓟ 14,985; Ⓒ 16,361; ◆ 16,569

Narragansett Heights; RMC Place; NEWPORT; ▲ Portsmouth; ★ **NWPT**; mail Tiverton **z** 02878

Narragansett Pier (Narragansett); CDP; WASHINGTON; ▲ Narragansett; **229** I-6; ★ **PROV-**; mail Narragansett **z** 02882, Saunderstown **z** 02874, Wakefield **z** 02879; Ⓟ 3,721; Ⓒ 3,671

Narragansett Reservation; Indian Reservation; WASHINGTON; Ⓒ 60

Nasonville; RMC Place; PROVIDENCE; ▲ Burrillville; **229** B-5; ★ **PROV-**; mail Woonsocket **z** 02895; ● 430

Natick; RMC Place; KENT; ***229** E-6; ★ **PROV-**; mail West Warwick **z** 02893

Nausauket; RMC Place; KENT; ***229** E-6; ★ **PROV-**; mail Warwick **z** 02886; pop. incl. with Warwick (Inc. Place)

Nayatt; RMC Place; BRISTOL; ▲ Barrington; ***229** E-7; ★ **PROV-**; mail Barrington **z** 02806

New Harbor; RMC Place; WASHINGTON; ▲ New Shoreham; mail Block Island **z** 02807

Newport; Inc. Place; NEWPORT; **229** H-7; elev. 96ft./29m.; 🅿 🅷 🅲 3,079 ■; ★ **NWPT**; **z** 02840-41; Ⓟ 28,227; Ⓒ 26,475; ◆ 25,590

NEWPORT; **229** G-8; Ⓟ 87,194; Ⓒ 85,433; ◆ 84,005

Newport East; CDP-Census Area Only; NEWPORT; ▲ Middletown; ***229** H-8; ★ **NWPT**; mail Newport **z** 02840; Ⓟ 11,080; Ⓒ 11,463

New Shoreham (Block Island); RMC Place; WASHINGTON; ▲ New Shoreham; **229** L-5; 🅿; **z** 02807; ● 836

New Shoreham; MCD-Town; WASHINGTON; ***229** L-5; 🅿; **z** 02807; Ⓟ 836; Ⓒ 1,010

Nichols Corner; RMC Place; KENT; ▲ East Greenwich; ***229** F-6; elev. 83ft./25m.; ★ **PROV-**; mail East Greenwich **z** 02818

Nooseneck; RMC Place; KENT; ▲ West Greenwich; ***229** F-4; ★ **PROV-**; mail Coventry **z** 02816

North; RMC Place; PROVIDENCE; ★ **PROV-**; mail Providence **z** 02908; pop. incl. with Providence (Inc. Place)

North Foster; RMC Place; PROVIDENCE; ▲ Foster; ***229** D-3; ★ **PROV-**; mail Foster **z** 02825

North Kingstown (Wickford); RMC Place; WASHINGTON; ▲ North Kingstown; **229** G-6; 🅿; ★ **PROV-**; **z** 02852, **z** 02854 & mail Saunderstown **z** 02874; ● 3,000

North Kingstown; MCD-Town; WASHINGTON; ***229** G-6; 🅿; ★ **PROV-**; **z** 02852, **z** 02854 & mail Saunderstown **z** 02874; Ⓟ 23,786; Ⓒ 26,326; ◆ 26,268

North Providence; CDP; PROVIDENCE; ▲ North Providence; **229** C-6; 🅿 🅷; ★ **PROV-**; **z** 02904, **z** 02908, **z** 02911; Ⓟ 32,090; Ⓒ 32,411; ◆ 31,779

North Providence; MCD-Town; PROVIDENCE; ***229** C-6; 🅿; ★ **PROV-**; **z** 02904, **z** 02908, **z** 02911; Ⓟ 32,090; Ⓒ 32,411; ◆ 31,779

North Quidnessett; RMC Place; WASHINGTON; ▲ North Kingstown; ***229** F-6; ★ **PROV-**; mail North Kingstown **z** 02852; ● 330

North Scituate; RMC Place; PROVIDENCE; ▲ Scituate; **229** D-5; elev. 305ft./93m.; 🅿; ★ **PROV-**; **z** 02857; ● 410

North Smithfield; MCD-Town; PROVIDENCE; ***229** B-5; 🅿; ★ **PROV-**; **z** 02896 & mail Forestdale **z** 02824; Ⓟ 10,497; Ⓒ 10,618; ◆ 11,101

North Tiverton; RMC Place; NEWPORT; ▲ Tiverton; ***229** F-9; ★ **F.R.**

Norwood; RMC Place; KENT; ***229** E-6; ★ **PROV-**; mail Warwick **z** 02888; pop. incl. with Warwick (Inc. Place)

O

Oakland; RMC Place; PROVIDENCE; ▲ Burrillville; **229** B-4; 🅿; ★ **PROV-**; **z** 02858; ● 600

Oakland Beach; RMC Place; KENT; ***229** E-7; ★ **PROV-**; mail Warwick **z** 02886; pop. incl. with Warwick (Inc. Place)

Oak Lawn; RMC Place; PROVIDENCE; ***229** E-6; ★ **PROV-**; mail Cranston **z** 02920; pop. incl. with Cranston (Inc. Place)

Old Harbor; RMC Place; WASHINGTON; ▲ New Shoreham; mail Block Island **z** 02807

Old Warwick; RMC Place; KENT; pop. incl. with Warwick (Inc. Place)

Olney Arnold Estates; RMC Place; PROVIDENCE; ★ **PROV-**; mail Cranston **z** 02920; pop. incl. with Cranston (Inc. Place)

Olneyville; RMC Place; PROVIDENCE; ***229** D-6; ★ **PROV-**; mail Providence **z** 02909; pop. incl. with Providence (Inc. Place)

P

Palace Garden; RMC Place; KENT; ***229** E-7; ★ **PROV-**; mail Warwick **z** 02888; pop. incl. with Warwick (Inc. Place)

Parcel Post Annex; RMC Place; WASHINGTON; ▲ Westerly; ★ **N.LON-**; mail Westerly **z** 02891

Pascoag; CDP; PROVIDENCE; ▲ Burrillville; **229** B-4; elev. 422ft./129m.; 🅿; ★ **PROV-**; **z** 02859; Ⓟ 5,011; Ⓒ 4,742

Pawtucket; Inc. Place; PROVIDENCE; **229** C-7; elev. 73ft./22m.; 🅿 🅷 ■; ★ **PROV-**; **z** 02860-62; Ⓟ 72,644; Ⓒ 72,958; ◆ 71,468

Pawtuxet; RMC Place; KENT; ***229** D-7; elev. 50ft./15m.; ★ **PROV-**; mail Warwick **z** 02888; pop. incl. with Warwick (Inc. Place)

Peace Dale; RMC Place; WASHINGTON; ▲ South Kingstown; **229** H-6; 🅿; ★ **PROV-**; **z** 02879, **z** 02883; ● 3,400

Perryville; RMC Place; WASHINGTON; ▲ South Kingstown; **229** I-5; ★ **PROV-**; mail Wakefield **z** 02879; ● 50

Pettaquamscutt Lake Shores; RMC Place; WASHINGTON; ▲ Narragansett; **229** H-6; ★ **PROV-**; mail Saunderstown **z** 02874; ● 750

Phenix; RMC Place; KENT; ▲ West Warwick; ***229** E-5; ★ **PROV-**; mail West Warwick **z** 02893

Phillipsdale; RMC Place; PROVIDENCE; ***229** C-7; ★ **PROV-**; mail East Providence **z** 02914; pop. incl. with East Providence (Inc. Place)

Pilgrim; RMC Place; KENT; ★ **PROV-**; mail Warwick **z** 02888; pop. incl. with Warwick (Inc. Place)

Pine Hill; RMC Place; WASHINGTON; ▲ Exeter; ***229** G-4; ★ **PROV-**; mail Exeter **z** 02822; rural

Pleasant View; RMC Place; PROVIDENCE; ★ **PROV-**; mail Pawtucket **z** 02860; pop. incl. with Pawtucket (Inc. Place)

Plum Beach (Barber Heights); RMC Place; WASHINGTON; ▲ North Kingstown; ***229** G-6; ★ **PROV-**; mail Saunderstown **z** 02874; ● 430

Plum Point; RMC Place; WASHINGTON; ▲ North Kingstown; **229** G-6; ★ **PROV-**; mail Saunderstown **z** 02874; ● 380

Poccasett Heights; RMC Place; NEWPORT; ▲ Portsmouth; ★ **NWPT**; mail Portsmouth **z** 02871

Point Judith; RMC Place; WASHINGTON; ▲ Narragansett; **229** I-6; 🅿; ★ **PROV-**; **z** 02882; ● 430

Pontiac; RMC Place; KENT; ★ **PROV-**; mail Warwick **z** 02886; pop. incl. with Warwick (Inc. Place)

Popasquash Point; RMC Place; BRISTOL; ▲ Bristol; ★ **PROV-**; mail Bristol **z** 02809

Portsmouth; RMC Place; NEWPORT; ▲ Portsmouth; **229** F-8; elev. 122ft./37m.; 🅿; ★ **NWPT**; **z** 02871 & mail Prudence Island **z** 02872; ● 4,200

Portsmouth; MCD-Town; NEWPORT; ***229** G-8; 🅿; ★ **NWPT**; **z** 02871 & mail Prudence Island **z** 02872; Ⓟ 16,857; Ⓒ 17,149

Potowomut; RMC Place; KENT; ***229** F-6; ★ **PROV-**; mail East Greenwich **z** 02818; pop. incl. with Warwick (Inc. Place)

Potter Hill; RMC Place; WASHINGTON; ▲ Westerly, Hopkinton; **229** I-3; ★ **N.LON-**; mail Westerly **z** 02891; ● 300

Primrose; RMC Place; PROVIDENCE; ▲ North Smithfield; **229** B-5; ★ **PROV-**; mail North Smithfield **z** 02896; ● 530

Print Works; RMC Place; PROVIDENCE; ★ **PROV-**; mail Cranston **z** 02920; pop. incl. with Cranston (Inc. Place)

Providence; Inc. Place; **STATE CAPITAL**; PROVIDENCE; **229** D-7; elev. 24ft./7m.; 🅿 🅷 🅲 33,891 ■; ★ **PROV-**; **z** 02901-12, **z** 02918-19, **z** 02940 & mail Hope **z** 02831; Ⓟ 160,728; Ⓒ 173,618; ◆ 180,082

PROVIDENCE; **229** C-4; Ⓟ 596,270; Ⓒ 621,602; ◆ 614,588

Prudence Island; RMC Place; NEWPORT; ▲ Portsmouth; **229** F-7; 🅿; ★ **NWPT**; **z** 02872; summer pop. 400; ● 150

Prudence Park; RMC Place; NEWPORT; ▲ Portsmouth; ***229** F-7; elev. 69ft./21m.; ★ **NWPT**; mail Prudence Island **z** 02872; rural

Q

Quidnessett; RMC Place; WASHINGTON; ▲ North Kingstown; **229** F-6; ★ **PROV-**; mail North Kingstown **z** 02852; ● 2,000

Quidnick; RMC Place; KENT; ▲ Coventry; **229** E-5; ★ **PROV-**; mail Coventry **z** 02816; ● 2,700

Quinnville; RMC Place; PROVIDENCE; ▲ Lincoln; **229** B-6; ★ **PROV-**; mail Lincoln **z** 02865; ● 370

Quonochontaug; RMC Place; WASHINGTON; ▲ Charlestown; **229** J-4; ★ **PROV-**; mail Charlestown **z** 02813; ● 2,000

R

Rice City; RMC Place; KENT; ▲ Coventry; ***229** E-3; ★ **PROV-**; mail Greene **z** 02827; ● 30

Rice Plat; RMC Place; PROVIDENCE; ▲ Scituate; ***229** C-5; ★ **PROV-**; mail North Scituate **z** 02857; ● 700

Richmond; MCD-Town; WASHINGTON; ***229** G-4; 🅿; ★ **PROV-**; **z** 02812, **z** 02832, **z** 02836, **z** 02875, **z** 02892, **z** 02898; Ⓟ 5,351; Ⓒ 7,222; ◆ 7,860

River Point; RMC Place; KENT; ▲ West Warwick; ***229** E-5; ★ **PROV-**; mail West Warwick **z** 02893

Riverside; RMC Place; PROVIDENCE; ***229** D-7; elev. 30ft./9m.; 🅿; ★ **PROV-**; **z** 02915; pop. incl. with East Providence (Inc. Place)

Riverview; RMC Place; KENT; ★ **PROV-**; mail Warwick **z** 02889

Rockville; RMC Place; WASHINGTON; ▲ Hopkinton; **229** G-3; 🅿; ★ **N.LON-**; **z** 02873; ● 320

Rocky Point; RMC Place; KENT; ★ **PROV-**; mail Warwick **z** 02889; pop. incl. with Warwick (Inc. Place)

Rumford; RMC Place; PROVIDENCE; ***229** C-7; elev. 60ft./18m.; 🅿; ★ **PROV-**; **z** 02916; pop. incl. with East Providence (Inc. Place)

Rumstick Point; RMC Place; BRISTOL; ▲ Barrington; ★ **PROV-**; mail Barrington **z** 02806

S

Sakonnet; RMC Place; NEWPORT; ▲ Little Compton; **229** H-8; ★ **F.R.**; mail Little Compton **z** 02837; ● 200

Sandy Point; RMC Place; KENT; ★ **PROV-**; mail East Greenwich **z** 02818; pop. incl. with Warwick (Inc. Place)

Sandy Point; RMC Place; NEWPORT; ▲ Portsmouth; ***229** F-7; ★ **NWPT**; mail Prudence Island **z** 02872

Sandy Point; RMC Place; WASHINGTON; ▲ New Shoreham; mail Block Island **z** 02807

Saunderstown; RMC Place; WASHINGTON; ▲ North Kingstown; **229** H-6; elev. 110ft./34m.; 🅿; ★ **PROV-**; **z** 02874 & mail Narragansett **z** 02882; ● 430

Saundersville; RMC Place; PROVIDENCE; ▲ Scituate; **229** D-5; elev. 390ft./119m.; ★ **PROV-**; mail North Scituate **z** 02857; ● 170

Saylesville; RMC Place; PROVIDENCE; ▲ Lincoln; **229** C-6; ★ **PROV-**; mail Lincoln **z** 02865; ● 3,800

Scituate; MCD-Town; PROVIDENCE; ***229** D-4; 🅿; ★ **PROV-**; **z** 02857 & mail Clayville **z** 02815, Foster **z** 02825, Hope **z** 02831; Ⓟ 9,796; Ⓒ 10,324; ◆ 10,355

Shady Harbor; RMC Place; WASHINGTON; ▲ Charlestown; ***229** J-4; ★ **PROV-**; mail Westerly **z** 02891; ● 200

Shannock; RMC Place; WASHINGTON; ▲ Charlestown, Richmond; **229** H-4; 🅿; ★ **PROV-**; **z** 02875; ● 1,100

Shawomet; RMC Place; KENT; ***229** E-7; ★ **PROV-**; mail Warwick **z** 02889; pop. incl. with Warwick (Inc. Place)

Shelter Harbor; RMC Place; WASHINGTON; ▲ Westerly; **229** J-3; ★ **N.LON-**; mail Westerly **z** 02891; ● 120

Shores Acres; RMC Place; WASHINGTON; ▲ North Kingstown; **229** G-6; ★ **PROV-**; mail North Kingstown **z** 02852; ● 490

Silver Lake; RMC Place; PROVIDENCE; ★ **PROV-**; mail Providence **z** 02909; pop. incl. with Providence (Inc. Place)

Simmonsville; RMC Place; PROVIDENCE; ▲ Johnston; ***229** D-6; ★ **PROV-**; mail Johnston **z** 02919

Slatersville; RMC Place; PROVIDENCE; ▲ North Smithfield; **229** A-5; elev. 269ft./82m.; 🅿; ★ **PROV-**; **z** 02876; ● 2,400

Slocum (Slocums); RMC Place; WASHINGTON; ▲ North Kingstown; **229** G-5; elev. 126ft./38m.; 🅿; ★ **PROV-**; **z** 02877; ● 110

Slocums; WASHINGTON; see Slocum (RMC Place)

Smithfield; MCD-Town; PROVIDENCE; ***229** C-5; 🅿 🅲 3,651; ★ **PROV-**; **z** 02917 & mail Greenville **z** 02828; Ⓟ 19,163; Ⓒ 20,613; ◆ 21,168

Smith Hill; RMC Place; PROVIDENCE; ★ **PROV-**; mail Providence **z** 02908; pop. incl. with Providence (Inc. Place)

Snug Harbor (East Mananuck, East Matunuck); RMC Place; WASHINGTON; ▲ South Kingstown; **229** I-5; ★ **PROV-**; mail Wakefield **z** 02879; summer pop. 2,500; ● 600

Sockannosset; RMC Place; PROVIDENCE; ★ **PROV-**; mail Cranston **z** 02920; pop. incl. with Cranston (Inc. Place)

South Foster; RMC Place; PROVIDENCE; ▲ Foster; **229** D-4; ★ **PROV-**; mail Foster **z** 02825; ● 130

South Hopkinton; RMC Place; WASHINGTON; ▲ Hopkinton; **229** I-3; ★ **N.LON-**; mail Bradford **z** 02808; ● 500

South Kingstown; MCD-Town; WASHINGTON; ***229** I-5; 🅿 🅲 15,062; ★ **PROV-**; **z** 02879, **z** 02883 & mail Saunderstown **z** 02874, West Kingston **z** 02892; Ⓟ 24,631; Ⓒ 27,921; ◆ 29,384

South Providence; RMC Place; PROVIDENCE; ★ **PROV-**; mail Providence **z** 02905; pop. incl. with Providence (Inc. Place)

South Warren; RMC Place; BRISTOL; ▲ Warren; ★ **PROV-**; mail Warren **z** 02885

South Woodlawn; RMC Place; PROVIDENCE; ★ **PROV-**; pop. incl. with Pawtucket (Inc. Place)

Spencer Corner; RMC Place; KENT; ▲ East Greenwich; ***229** F-5; elev. 311ft./95m.; ★ **PROV-**; mail East Greenwich **z** 02818

Spragueville; RMC Place; PROVIDENCE; ▲ Smithfield; **229** J-7; elev. 228ft./69m.; ★ **PROV-**; mail Greenville **z** 02828

Spring Green; RMC Place; KENT; ***229** E-6; ★ **PROV-**; mail Warwick **z** 02888; pop. incl. with Warwick (Inc. Place)

Spring Grove; RMC Place; PROVIDENCE; ▲ Glocester; ***229** C-4; ★ **PROV-**; mail Chepachet **z** 02814

Spring Lake Beach; RMC Place; PROVIDENCE; ▲ Burrillville; ***229** E-4; elev. 400ft./122m.; ★ **PROV-**; mail Glendale **z** 02826; summer pop. 700; ● 370

Squantum; RMC Place; PROVIDENCE; ★ **PROV-**; mail East Providence **z** 02914; pop. incl. with East Providence (Inc. Place)

Stillwater; RMC Place; PROVIDENCE; ▲ Smithfield; ***229** C-5; ★ **PROV-**; mail Smithfield **z** 02917; rural

Summit; RMC Place; KENT; ▲ Coventry; **229** E-4; ★ **PROV-**; mail Greene **z** 02827; ● 100

T

Tarkiln; RMC Place; PROVIDENCE; ▲ Burrillville; **229** B-5; ★ **PROV-**; mail Woonsocket **z** 02895; ● 370

The Anchorage; RMC Place; NEWPORT; ▲ Middletown; ★ **NWPT**; mail Middletown **z** 02842

The Hummocks; RMC Place; NEWPORT; ▲ Portsmouth; **229** F-8; ★ **NWPT**; mail Portsmouth **z** 02871; ● 225

Thornton; RMC Place; PROVIDENCE; ▲ Johnston; ***229** D-6; ★ **PROV-**; mail Johnston **z** 02919; pop. incl. with Cranston (Inc. Place)

Tiverton; CDP; NEWPORT; ▲ Tiverton; **229** F-8; 🅿; ★ **F.R.**; **z** 02878; Ⓟ 7,259; Ⓒ 7,282

Tiverton; MCD-Town; NEWPORT; ***229** F-9; 🅿; ★ **F.R.**; **z** 02878; Ⓟ 14,312; Ⓒ 15,260; ◆ 15,261

Tiverton Four Corners; RMC Place; NEWPORT; ▲ Tiverton; **229** G-9; ★ **F.R.**; mail Tiverton **z** 02878; ● 160

Tockwotten; RMC Place; PROVIDENCE; ★ **PROV-**; mail Providence **z** 02903; pop. incl. with Providence (Inc. Place)

Tonomy Hill; RMC Place; NEWPORT; ★ **NWPT**; mail Newport **z** 02840; pop. incl. with Newport (Inc. Place)

Touisset Highlands; RMC Place; BRISTOL; ▲ Warren; ***229** E-8; ★ **PROV-**; mail Warren **z** 02885

Tuckertown; RMC Place; WASHINGTON; ▲ South Kingstown; ***229** I-5; ★ **PROV-**; mail Wakefield **z** 02879; summer pop. 1,000

Tunipus; RMC Place; NEWPORT; ▲ Little Compton; ***229** H-9; elev. 50ft./15m.; ★ **F.R.**; mail Little Compton **z** 02837; ● 150

U

Union Village; RMC Place; PROVIDENCE; ▲ North Smithfield; **229** B-5; ★ **PROV-**; mail North Smithfield **z** 02896; ● 2,300

Usquepaug; RMC Place; WASHINGTON; ▲ South Kingstown, Richmond; **229** H-5; ★ **PROV-**; mail West Kingston **z** 02892; ● 530

V

Valley Falls; CDP; PROVIDENCE; ▲ Cumberland; **229** C-7; 🅿; ★ **PROV-**; **z** 02864; Ⓟ 11,175; Ⓒ 11,599

Vaughn Hollow; RMC Place; KENT; ▲ Coventry; ***229** E-3; ★ **PROV-**; mail Greene **z** 02827; rural

Vernon; RMC Place; PROVIDENCE; ▲ Foster; ***229** E-4; elev. 597ft./182m.; ★ **PROV-**; mail Foster **z** 02825; rural

W

Wakefield; RMC Place; WASHINGTON; ▲ South Kingstown; **229** H-6; 🅿 🅷; ★ **PROV-**; **z** 02879-80 & mail Kingston **z** 02881, Peace Dale **z** 02883; ● 300

Wakefield-Peacedale; CDP-Census Area Only; WASHINGTON; ▲ South Kingstown; ***229** H-6; ★ **PROV-**; mail Peace Dale **z** 02883, Wakefield **z** 02879; Ⓟ 7,134; Ⓒ 8,468

Warren; RMC Place; BRISTOL; ▲ Warren; **229** E-8; elev. 32ft./10m.; 🅿; ★ **PROV-**; **z** 02885; ● 11,385

Warren; MCD-Town; BRISTOL; ***229** E-8; 🅿; ★ **PROV-**; **z** 02885; Ⓟ 11,385; Ⓒ 11,360; ◆ 10,548

Warren Point; RMC Place; NEWPORT; ▲ Little Compton; ***229** H-9; ★ **F.R.**; mail Little Compton **z** 02837; ● 30

Warwick (Apponaug); Inc. Place; KENT; **229** E-7; elev. 64ft./20m.; 🅿 🅷 🅲 3,075 ■; ★ **PROV-**; **z** 02886-89 & mail East Greenwich **z** 02818; Ⓟ 85,427; Ⓒ 85,808; ◆ 83,824

Warwick Neck; RMC Place; KENT; ★ **PROV-**; mail Warwick **z** 02889; pop. incl. with Warwick (Inc. Place)

Washington; KENT; see Coventry (RMC Place)

WASHINGTON; **229** G-5; Ⓟ 110,006; Ⓒ 123,546; ◆ 125,080

Washington Park; RMC Place; PROVIDENCE; ★ **PROV-**; mail Providence **z** 02905; pop. incl. with Cranston (Inc. Place)

Watch Hill; RMC Place; WASHINGTON; ▲ Westerly; **229** J-2; ★ **N.LON-**; mail Westerly **z** 02891; ● 580

Watchmocket Square; RMC Place; PROVIDENCE; ★ **PROV-**; mail East Providence **z** 02914; pop. incl. with East Providence (Inc. Place)

Waterford; RMC Place; PROVIDENCE; ▲ North Smithfield; ***229** A-5; ★ **PROV-**; mail Blackstone **z** 01504; ● 180

Waterman Four Corners; RMC Place; PROVIDENCE; ▲ Scituate; **229** D-5; elev. 425ft./130m.; ★ **PROV-**; mail North Scituate **z** 02857; ● 120

Weekapaug; RMC Place; WASHINGTON; ▲ Westerly; **229** J-3; ★ **N.LON-**; mail Westerly **z** 02891; ● 290

West Barrington; RMC Place; BRISTOL; ▲ Barrington; ***229** E-7; ★ **PROV-**; mail Barrington **z** 02806

Westcott; RMC Place; KENT; ***229** E-6; elev. 97ft./30m.; ★ **PROV-**; mail West Warwick **z** 02893

Westcott Beach; RMC Place; PROVIDENCE; ▲ Glocester; ***229** C-4; elev. 450ft./137m.; ★ **PROV-**; mail Chepachet **z** 02814; rural

Westerly; CDP; WASHINGTON; ▲ Westerly; **229** I-3; 🅿 🅷; ★ **N.LON-**; **z** 02891 & mail Bradford **z** 02808; Ⓟ 16,477; Ⓒ 17,682

Westerly; MCD-Town; WASHINGTON; ***229** I-2; 🅿 ■; ★ **N.LON-**; **z** 02891 & mail Bradford **z** 02808; Ⓟ 21,605; Ⓒ 22,966; ◆ 22,763

West Glocester; RMC Place; PROVIDENCE; ▲ Glocester; **229** B-3; ★ **PROV-**; mail Putnam **z** 06260; ● 200

West Greenville; RMC Place; PROVIDENCE; ▲ Smithfield; ***229** C-5; ★ **PROV-**; mail Greenville **z** 02828

West Greenwich; RMC Place; KENT; ▲ West Greenwich; ***229** F-4; elev. 527ft./161m.; 🅿; ★ **PROV-**; **z** 02817; rural

West Greenwich; MCD-Town; KENT; ***229** F-5; 🅿; ★ **PROV-**; **z** 02817; Ⓟ 3,492; Ⓒ 5,085; ◆ 5,649

West Greenwich Center; RMC Place; KENT; ▲ West Greenwich; ***229** F-3; elev. 497ft./151m.; ★ **PROV-**; mail West Greenwich **z** 02817

West Kingston (Kingston); RMC Place; WASHINGTON; ▲ South Kingstown; **229** H-5; 🅿; ★ **PROV-**; **z** 02892 & mail Kingston **z** 02881; ● 1,400

West Warwick; CDP; KENT; ▲ West Warwick; **229** E-5; elev. 130ft./40m.; 🅿; ★ **PROV-**; **z** 02893; Ⓟ 29,268; Ⓒ 29,581; ◆ 28,915

West Warwick; MCD-Town; KENT; ***229** E-6; 🅿; ★ **PROV-**; **z** 02893; Ⓟ 29,268; Ⓒ 29,581; ◆ 28,915

Weybosset Hill; RMC Place; PROVIDENCE; ★ **PROV-**; mail Providence **z** 02903; pop. incl. with Providence (Inc. Place)

Whipple; RMC Place; PROVIDENCE; ▲ Burrillville; ***229** B-4; ★ **PROV-**; mail Oakland **z** 02858; ● 100

White Rock; RMC Place; WASHINGTON; ▲ Westerly; **229** I-2; ★ **N.LON-**; mail Westerly **z** 02891; ● 410

Wickford; WASHINGTON; see North Kingstown (RMC Place)

Wickford Junction; RMC Place; WASHINGTON; ▲ North Kingstown; **229** G-6; ★ **PROV-**; mail North Kingstown **z** 02852; ● 100

Wildes Corner; RMC Place; KENT; ***229** E-6; ★ **PROV-**; mail Warwick **z** 02886; pop. incl. with Warwick (Inc. Place)

Wood Estates; RMC Place; KENT; ▲ Coventry; ***229** E-5; elev. 260ft./79m.; ★ **PROV-**; mail Coventry **z** 02816; ● 800

Woodlawn; RMC Place; PROVIDENCE; ***229** C-7; elev. 75ft./23m.; ★ **PROV-**; pop. incl. with Pawtucket (Inc. Place)

Wood River Junction; RMC Place; WASHINGTON; ▲ Richmond; **229** I-4; 🅿; ★ **PROV-**; **z** 02894; ● 270

Woodville; RMC Place; PROVIDENCE; ▲ North Providence; ***229** C-6; ★ **PROV-**; mail North Providence **z** 02911

Woodville; RMC Place; WASHINGTON; ▲ Richmond, Hopkinton; **229** H-4; ★ **N.LON-**; mail Hope Valley **z** 02832; ● 60

Woonsocket; Inc. Place; PROVIDENCE; **229** A-6; elev. 162ft./49m.; 🅿 🅷 ■; ★ **PROV-**; **z** 02895; Ⓟ 43,877; Ⓒ 43,224; ◆ 41,492

Wyoming; RMC Place; WASHINGTON; ▲ Hopkinton, Richmond; **229** H-4; 🅿; ★ **PROV-**; **z** 02898; ● 1,100

Y

Yorktown Manor; RMC Place; WASHINGTON; ▲ North Kingstown; ***229** F-6; ★ **PROV-**; mail North Kingstown **z** 02852; ● 200

Entries in **UPPERCASE** are counties.
Entries in **bold** have populations of 2,500 or more.
Names in parentheses are alternate names.

Inc. Place	Incorporated Place
RMC Place	Rand McNally Designated Place
CDP	Census Designated Place
MCD	Minor Civil Division

⊡	County Seat
▲	Minor Civil Division
elev.	Elevation
🅿	Post Office
🅷	Hospital
🅲	College
■	Principal Business Center
★	Ranally Metro Area (RMA) Abbreviation
z	Zip Code(s)
Ⓟ	Previous Census Population
Ⓡ	Revised Census Population
Ⓐ	Annexation Population
●	Rand McNally Population Estimate
Ⓒ	Final Census Population
Ⓢ	Special Census Population
◆	Estimated Population

For additional definitions see Glossary, Volume 1, and Introduction, Volume 2.

SOUTH CAROLINA

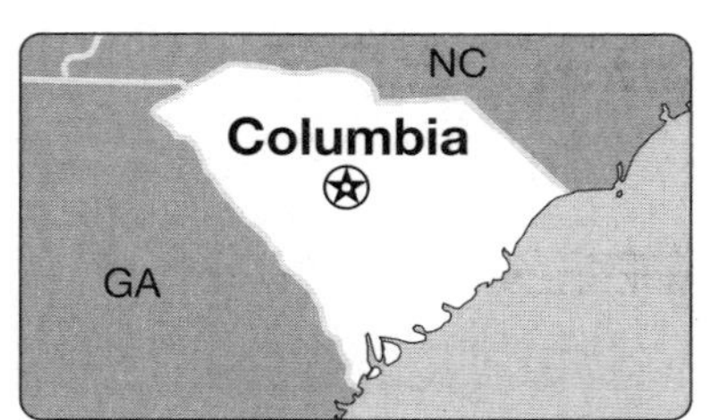

Statistics

Total area (2000) — 32,020 square miles
Land area (2000) — 30,110 square miles
Water area (2000) — 1,910 square miles
Capital — Columbia
One of Thirteen Original States

Maps

State maps can be found on pages 142-254 in Vol. 1

Ranally Metro Areas (RMAs) and Abbreviations

Anderson, SC — AND
Augusta, GA-SC — AUG
Charleston, SC — CHAS
Charlotte, NC-SC — CHRLT
Columbia, SC — COL
Florence, SC — FLO
Greenville, SC — GRNV
Greenwood, SC — GREEN
Myrtle Beach, SC-NC — MYR.B
Spartanburg, SC — SPRT
Sumter, SC — SUMT

Principal Places

Place Name	Place Type	County	Population
Columbia	Inc. Place	RICHLAND	◆ 127,398
Charleston	Inc. Place	CHARLESTON	◆ 118,759
North Charleston	Inc. Place	CHARLESTON	◆ 96,030
Rock Hill	Inc. Place	YORK	◆ 68,901
Greenville	Inc. Place	GREENVILLE	◆ 60,548
Mount Pleasant	Inc. Place	CHARLESTON	◆ 60,161
Summerville	Inc. Place	DORCHESTER	◆ 43,606
Goose Creek	Inc. Place	BERKELEY	◆ 41,468
Spartanburg	Inc. Place	SPARTANBURG	◆ 40,031
Hilton Head Island	Inc. Place	BEAUFORT	◆ 38,582
Sumter	Inc. Place	SUMTER	◆ 36,580
Florence	Inc. Place	FLORENCE	◆ 30,980
Myrtle Beach	Inc. Place	HORRY	◆ 29,359
Aiken	Inc. Place	AIKEN	◆ 28,688
Anderson	Inc. Place	ANDERSON	◆ 25,810
Saint Andrews	CDP-Census Area Only	RICHLAND	◆ 25,669
Wade Hampton	CDP	GREENVILLE	◆ 24,258
Taylors	CDP	GREENVILLE	◆ 23,871
Greer	Inc. Place	GREENVILLE	◆ 23,803
Greenwood	Inc. Place	GREENWOOD	◆ 21,888
Easley	Inc. Place	PICKENS	◆ 20,755
Mauldin	Inc. Place	GREENVILLE	◆ 20,214
North Augusta	Inc. Place	AIKEN	◆ 20,096
Seven Oaks	CDP-Census Area Only	LEXINGTON	Ⓒ 15,755
Socastee	CDP	HORRY	Ⓒ 14,295
Simpsonville	Inc. Place	GREENVILLE	Ⓡ 14,202
Berea	CDP	GREENVILLE	Ⓒ 14,158
Gantt	CDP	GREENVILLE	Ⓒ 13,962
Ladson	CDP	BERKELEY	Ⓒ 13,264
West Columbia	Inc. Place	LEXINGTON	Ⓒ 13,064
Dentsville	CDP	RICHLAND	Ⓡ 13,049
Gaffney	Inc. Place	CHEROKEE	Ⓒ 12,968
Beaufort	Inc. Place	BEAUFORT	Ⓒ 12,950
Hanahan	Inc. Place	BERKELEY	Ⓒ 12,937
Cayce	Inc. Place	LEXINGTON	Ⓒ 12,150
Orangeburg	Inc. Place	ORANGEBURG	◆ 12,050
Clemson	Inc. Place	PICKENS	Ⓒ 11,939
Conway	Inc. Place	HORRY	Ⓒ 11,788
Irmo	Inc. Place	LEXINGTON	Ⓒ 11,039
North Myrtle Beach	Inc. Place	HORRY	Ⓒ 10,974
Parker	CDP-Census Area Only	GREENVILLE	Ⓒ 10,760
Newberry	Inc. Place	NEWBERRY	Ⓒ 10,580
Red Hill	CDP-Census Area Only	HORRY	Ⓒ 10,509
Forest Acres	Inc. Place	RICHLAND	Ⓡ 10,497
Laurens	Inc. Place	LAURENS	Ⓒ 9,916
Lexington	Inc. Place	LEXINGTON	Ⓒ 9,793
Bennettsville	Inc. Place	MARLBORO	Ⓒ 9,425
Garden City	CDP-Census Area Only	HORRY	Ⓒ 9,357
Woodfield	CDP-Census Area Only	RICHLAND	Ⓒ 9,238
Georgetown	Inc. Place	GEORGETOWN	Ⓡ 8,979
Red Bank	CDP	LEXINGTON	Ⓒ 8,811
Union	Inc. Place	UNION	Ⓒ 8,793
Clinton	Inc. Place	LAURENS	Ⓡ 8,545
Oak Grove	CDP-Census Area Only	LEXINGTON	Ⓒ 8,183
Lancaster	Inc. Place	LANCASTER	Ⓒ 8,177
Five Forks	CDP	GREENVILLE	Ⓒ 8,064
Sans Souci	CDP	GREENVILLE	Ⓒ 7,836
Seneca	Inc. Place	OCONEE	Ⓒ 7,652
Fort Mill	Inc. Place	YORK	Ⓒ 7,587
Hartsville	Inc. Place	DARLINGTON	Ⓒ 7,556
Burton	CDP	BEAUFORT	Ⓒ 7,180
Marion	Inc. Place	MARION	Ⓒ 7,042
Little River	CDP	HORRY	Ⓒ 7,027
York	Inc. Place	YORK	Ⓒ 6,985
Darlington	Inc. Place	DARLINGTON	Ⓒ 6,720
Camden	Inc. Place	KERSHAW	Ⓒ 6,682
Laurel Bay	CDP	BEAUFORT	Ⓒ 6,625
Lake City	Inc. Place	FLORENCE	Ⓒ 6,478
Chester	Inc. Place	CHESTER	Ⓒ 6,476
Welcome	CDP	GREENVILLE	Ⓒ 6,390
Homeland Park	CDP	ANDERSON	Ⓒ 6,337
Dillon	Inc. Place	DILLON	Ⓒ 6,316
Lugoff	CDP	KERSHAW	Ⓒ 6,278
Fountain Inn	Inc. Place	GREENVILLE	Ⓒ 6,017
Moncks Corner	Inc. Place	BERKELEY	Ⓒ 5,952
Abbeville	Inc. Place	ABBEVILLE	Ⓒ 5,840
Belvedere	CDP	AIKEN	Ⓒ 5,631
Cheraw	Inc. Place	CHESTERFIELD	Ⓒ 5,524
Murrells Inlet	CDP	GEORGETOWN	Ⓒ 5,519
Batesburg-Leesville	Inc. Place	LEXINGTON	Ⓒ 5,517
Powderville	CDP	ANDERSON	Ⓒ 5,362
Centerville	CDP	ANDERSON	Ⓒ 5,181
Walterboro	Inc. Place	COLLETON	Ⓒ 5,153
Barnwell	Inc. Place	BARNWELL	Ⓒ 5,035
Mullins	Inc. Place	MARION	Ⓒ 5,029
Chaparral Ranches	RMC Place	BERKELEY	● 5,000

County Business Data

County	FIPS Code	County Seat	Land Area (Sq. Mi.)	Census Population 4/1/2000	Census Population 4/1/1990	Census Population % Change 1990-2000	Wholesale Trade Sales, 2002 ($1,000)	Wholesale Trade % Change 1997-2002	Manufacturing, 2002 Establish-ments	Manufacturing, 2002 Total Employees	Manufacturing, 2002 Value Added ($1,000)	Manufacturing, 2002 Ranally Mfg. Units
Abbeville	001	Abbeville	508	26,167	23,862	9.7	25,367	110.5	35	3,236	217,780	115
Aiken	003	Aiken	1,073	142,552	120,940	17.9	(d)	(d)	106	17,813	2,329,321	1,232
Allendale	005	Allendale	408	11,211	11,722	-4.4	17,409	-2.6	10	1,055	128,367	68
Anderson	007	Anderson	718	165,740	145,196	14.1	(d)	(d)	253	17,949	1,666,236	882
Bamberg	009	Bamberg	393	16,658	16,902	-1.4	9,981	(d)	23	1,046	82,870	44
Barnwell	011	Barnwell	548	23,478	20,293	15.7	(d)	(d)	24	2,715	230,671	122
Beaufort	013	Beaufort	587	120,937	86,425	39.9	274,352	62.0	96	851	92,967	49
Berkeley	015	Moncks Corner	1,098	142,651	128,776	10.8	1,106,443	91.5	90	6,461	1,150,795	609
Calhoun	017	St. Matthews	380	15,185	12,753	19.1	(d)	(d)	14	773	64,756	34
Charleston	019	Charleston	919	309,969	295,039	5.1	2,446,472	-34.4	270	10,034	1,529,048	809
Cherokee	021	Gaffney	393	52,537	44,506	18.0	(d)	(d)	64	6,806	1,220,585	646
Chester	023	Chester	581	34,068	32,170	5.9	312,668	-5.7	53	4,320	561,359	297
Chesterfield	025	Chesterfield	799	42,768	38,577	10.9	67,797	-26.2	60	6,182	655,144	347
Clarendon	027	Manning	607	32,502	28,450	14.2	43,926	-21.9	18	1,236	85,459	45
Colleton	029	Walterboro	1,056	38,264	34,377	11.3	291,966	37.4	33	1,340	103,723	55
Darlington	031	Darlington	561	67,394	61,851	9.0	1,062,489	46.0	65	5,299	687,324	364
Dillon	033	Dillon	405	30,722	29,114	5.5	301,659	70.1	27	2,405	129,151	68
Dorchester	035	St. George	575	96,413	83,060	16.1	318,748	227.7	91	3,444	357,009	189
Edgefield	037	Edgefield	502	24,595	18,375	33.9	(d)	(d)	19	1,842	129,574	69
Fairfield	039	Winnsboro	687	23,454	22,295	5.2	(d)	(d)	17	1,818	203,605	108
Florence	041	Florence	800	125,761	114,344	10.0	1,134,711	11.5	128	12,379	1,414,368	748
Georgetown	043	Georgetown	815	55,797	46,302	20.5	166,040	38.8	64	3,026	406,107	215
Greenville	045	Greenville	790	379,616	320,167	18.6	8,963,150	-16.1	607	34,557	9,462,724	5,006
Greenwood	047	Greenwood	456	66,271	59,567	11.3	(d)	(d)	85	9,246	998,856	528
Hampton	049	Hampton	560	21,386	18,191	17.6	(d)	(d)	20	984	65,251	35
Horry	051	Conway	1,134	196,629	144,053	36.5	612,307	27.2	166	4,383	276,715	146
Jasper	053	Ridgeland	656	20,678	15,487	33.5	79,362	21.1	...	(d)	(d)	...
Kershaw	055	Camden	726	52,647	43,599	20.8	37,819	2.4	66	4,138	601,454	318
Lancaster	057	Lancaster	549	61,351	54,516	12.5	169,150	24.1	64	4,677	659,063	349
Laurens	059	Laurens	715	69,567	58,092	19.8	(d)	(d)	69	4,067	378,920	200
Lee	061	Bishopville	410	20,119	18,437	9.1	(d)	(d)	...	(d)	(d)	...
Lexington	063	Lexington	699	216,014	167,611	28.9	3,268,175	43.2	234	10,515	1,043,163	552
Marion	067	Marion	489	35,466	33,899	4.6	142,406	55.5	29	3,048	201,333	107
Marlboro	069	Bennettsville	480	28,818	29,361	-1.8	(d)	(d)	31	3,532	421,550	223
McCormick	065	McCormick	360	9,958	8,868	12.3	(d)	(d)	...	(d)	(d)	...
Newberry	071	Newberry	631	36,108	33,172	8.9	303,136	(d)	46	4,355	262,757	139
Oconee	073	Walhalla	625	66,215	57,494	15.2	(d)	(d)	92	5,901	699,502	370
Orangeburg	075	Orangeburg	1,106	91,582	84,803	8.0	324,816	-14.7	89	7,954	781,738	414
Pickens	077	Pickens	497	110,757	93,894	18.0	(d)	(d)	131	8,491	585,352	310
Richland	079	Columbia	756	320,677	285,720	12.2	3,281,967	9.8	248	13,540	2,408,782	1,274
Saluda	081	Saluda	452	19,181	16,357	17.3	102,930	165.7	8	549	49,272	26
Spartanburg	083	Spartanburg	811	253,791	226,800	11.9	3,127,193	-21.1	521	30,964	3,581,177	1,895
Sumter	085	Sumter	665	104,646	102,637	2.0	236,451	13.3	77	10,353	989,934	524
Union	087	Union	514	29,881	30,337	-1.5	(d)	(d)	35	3,533	232,066	123
Williamsburg	089	Kingstree	934	37,217	36,815	1.1	59,951	-38.8	25	1,518	224,551	119
York	091	York	682	164,614	131,497	25.2	1,928,212	-35.8	230	10,673	1,163,203	615
The State			**30,109**	**4,012,012**	**3,486,703**	**15.1**	**32,988,974**	**-3.5**	**4,457**	**289,933**	**38,611,266**	**20,428**

(d) Data not available. Corresponding percentages or Ranally Manufacturing Units are estimates.
... Represents 0 or amount too minimal to be reported.

Index of Places and Counties

Entries in **UPPERCASE** are counties.
Entries in **bold** have populations of 2,500 or more.
Names in parentheses are alternate names.

Inc. Place	Incorporated Place
RMC Place	Rand McNally Designated Place
CDP	Census Designated Place
MCD	Minor Civil Division
⊡	County Seat
▲	Minor Civil Division
elev.	Elevation
[P]	Post Office
[H]	Hospital
[C]	College
■	Principal Business Center
★	Ranally Metro Area (RMA) Abbreviation
z	Zip Code(s)
Ⓟ	Previous Census Population
Ⓡ	Revised Census Population
Ⓐ	Annexation Population
●	Rand McNally Population Estimate
Ⓒ	Final Census Population
Ⓢ	Special Census Population
◆	Estimated Population

For additional definitions see Glossary, Volume 1, and Introduction, Volume 2.

Belvedere; RMC Place; RICHLAND; ***230** D-7; elev. 300ft./91m.; ★ **COL**; mail Columbia **z** 29204; pop. incl. with Columbia (Inc. Place)
Ben Avon; RMC Place; SPARTANBURG; ***230** B-5; ★ **SPRT**; mail Spartanburg **z** 29302; ● 1,700
Bendale; RMC Place; RICHLAND; ★ **COL**; mail Columbia **z** 29203; pop. incl. with Columbia (Inc. Place)
Beneventum; RMC Place; GEORGETOWN; ***230** F-12; elev. 20ft./6m.; mail Georgetown **z** 29440; ● 120
Bennett; RMC Place; CHARLESTON; ***230** H-10; ★ **CHAS**; mail North Charleston **z** 29405; pop. incl. with North Charleston (Inc. Place)
Bennetts Point; RMC Place; COLLETON; ***230** I-9; mail Green Pond **z** 29446; rural
Bennettsville; Inc. Place; ⊡ MARLBORO; **230** C-11; [P] [H]; **z** 29512; Ⓟ 9,345; © 9,425
Bent Tree; RMC Place; OCONEE; ***230** B-3; elev. 800ft./244m.; mail Seneca **z** 29678; ● 60
Berea; CDP; GREENVILLE; **230** I-4; elev. 315ft./96m.; ★ **GRNV**; mail Greenville **z** 29617; Ⓟ 13,535; © 14,158
BERKELEY; **230** G-10; Ⓟ 128,776; © 142,651; ◆ 186,214
Berlin; RMC Place; AIKEN; ***230** E-7; mail Salley **z** 29137; ● 75
Bethany; RMC Place; YORK; ***230** A-7; elev. 830ft./253m.; mail Clover **z** 29710
Bethera; RMC Place; BERKELEY; **230** G-10; elev. 54ft./16m.; [P]; **z** 29430; ● 100
Bethesda; RMC Place; CHESTERFIELD; ***230** B-10; elev. 248ft./76m.; mail Patrick **z** 29584; rural
Bethune; Inc. Place; KERSHAW; **230** C-9; elev. 283ft./86m.; [P]; **z** 29009; Ⓟ 405; © 352
Beufordtown; RMC Place; BERKELEY; ***230** F-11; elev. 34ft./10m.; mail Jamestown **z** 29453; ● 50
Beverly Hills; RMC Place; BERKELEY; ***230** G-10; elev. 30ft./9m.; ★ **CHAS**; mail Goose Creek **z** 29445; ● 1,500
Beverly Woods; RMC Place; SPARTANBURG; ***230** A-5; elev. 240ft./73m.; ★ **SPRT**; mail Spartanburg **z** 29301; ● 160
Bingham; RMC Place; DILLON; **230** C-11; mail Latta **z** 29565; ● 90
Birdtown Crossroads; RMC Place; DARLINGTON; ***230** C-10; elev. 239ft./73m.; mail Hartsville **z** 29550; rural
Bishopville; Inc. Place; ⊡ LEE; **230** D-9; elev. 226ft./69m.; [P]; **z** 29010; Ⓟ 3,560; © 3,670
Blackjack; RMC Place; FAIRFIELD; ***230** C-7; elev. 546ft./166m.; mail Winnsboro **z** 29180; ● 90
Blacks; RMC Place; SALUDA; ***230** E-6; elev. 563ft./172m.; mail Ward **z** 29166; rural
Blacksburg; Inc. Place; CHEROKEE; **230** A-6; elev. 768ft./234m.; [P]; **z** 29702; Ⓟ 1,907; © 1,880
Blackstock; RMC Place; CHESTER, FAIRFIELD; **230** C-7; elev. 626ft./191m.; [P]; **z** 29014; ● 200
Blackville; Inc. Place; BARNWELL; **230** F-7; [P]; **z** 29817; Ⓟ 2,688; © 2,973
Blair; RMC Place; FAIRFIELD; **230** C-6; elev. 411ft./125m.; [P]; **z** 29015; ● 60
Blairville; RMC Place; YORK; ***230** B-7; mail Sharon **z** 29742; rural
Blakedale; RMC Place; GREENWOOD; ***230** D-4; elev. 655ft./200m.; ★ **GREEN**; mail Greenwood **z** 29649
Blenheim; Inc. Place; MARLBORO; **230** C-11; elev. 120ft./37m.; [P]; **z** 29516; Ⓟ 191; © 137
Bloomingvale; RMC Place; WILLIAMSBURG; **230** F-11; elev. 40ft./12m.; mail Andrews **z** 29510; ● 50
Bloomville; RMC Place; CLARENDON; ***230** E-9; elev. 132ft./40m.; mail Manning **z** 29102; rural
Blossom; RMC Place; FLORENCE; ***230** E-11; elev. 75ft./23m.; mail Pamplico **z** 29583
Blountville; RMC Place; HAMPTON; ***230** H-7; mail Yemassee **z** 29945; pop. incl. with Yemassee (Inc. Place)
Blue Heaven; RMC Place; ABBEVILLE; ***230** C-4; elev. 600ft./183m.; mail Ware Shoals **z** 29692; ● 100
Blue Town; MARLBORO; see Argyle (RMC Place)
Bluff; RMC Place; ORANGEBURG; ***230** F-9; elev. 100ft./30m.; mail Santee **z** 29142; ● 110
Bluff Estates; RMC Place; RICHLAND; ***230** E-7; elev. 152ft./46m.; ★ **COL**; mail Columbia **z** 29209; ● 600
Bluffton; Inc. Place; BEAUFORT; **230** J-8; elev. 25ft./8m.; [P]; **z** 29909-10; Ⓟ 738; © 1,275
Blythewood; Inc. Place; RICHLAND; **230** D-7; elev. 504ft./154m.; [P]; ★ **COL**; **z** 29016; Ⓟ 164; © 170
Boiling Springs (Lyndhurst); RMC Place; BARNWELL; ***230** G-6; mail Barnwell **z** 29812
Boiling Springs; CDP; SPARTANBURG; **230** A-5; elev. 950ft./290m.; [P]; ★ **SPRT**; **z** 29316, **z** 29318; Ⓟ 3,522; © 4,544
Bolentown; RMC Place; ORANGEBURG; ***230** F-7; elev. 297ft./91m.; mail Orangeburg **z** 29115; ● 60
Bon Aire; RMC Place; BEAUFORT; ***230** I-8; elev. 10ft./3m.; mail Beaufort **z** 29906; ● 200
Bon Air Terrace; RMC Place; SUMTER; ***230** E-9; ★ **SUMT**; mail Sumter **z** 29150; pop. incl. with Sumter (Inc. Place)
Bonham; RMC Place; UNION; ***230** B-6; elev. 687ft./209m.; mail Union **z** 29379; ● 90
Bonneau; Inc. Place; BERKELEY; **230** F-10; elev. 62ft./19m.; [P]; **z** 29431; Ⓟ 374; © 354
Bonneau Beach; RMC Place; BERKELEY; **230** F-10; elev. 75ft./23m.; mail Bonneau **z** 29431; ● 200
Bonniview Estates; RMC Place; AIKEN; ***230** F-6; elev. 490ft./149m.; ★ **AUG**; mail Aiken **z** 29803; ● 400
Boones Creek; RMC Place; OCONEE; ***230** B-3; elev. 1,169ft./356m.; mail Salem **z** 29676; ● 50
Bordeaux; RMC Place; MCCORMICK; ***230** E-4; mail Mc Cormick **z** 29835
Borden; RMC Place; SUMTER; **230** D-9; elev. 208ft./63m.; [P]; **z** 29128; ● 80
Boulder Bluff; RMC Place; BERKELEY; ***230** G-10; elev. 40ft./12m.; ★ **CHAS**; mail Goose Creek **z** 29445; pop. incl. with Goose Creek (Inc. Place)
Bounty Land; RMC Place; OCONEE; ***230** B-3; elev. 900ft./274m.; mail Seneca **z** 29672; ● 250
Bowling Green; RMC Place; YORK; **230** A-7; [P]; ★ **CHRLT**; **z** 29703; ● 500
Bowman; Inc. Place; ORANGEBURG; **230** F-8; elev. 39ft./12m.; [P]; **z** 29018; Ⓟ 1,063; © 1,198
Bowyer; RMC Place; ORANGEBURG; ***230** F-9; elev. 92ft./28m.; mail Holly Hill **z** 29059; ● 50
Boyden Arbor; RMC Place; RICHLAND; ***230** D-8; elev. 209ft./64m.; ★ **COL**; mail Columbia **z** 29206; pop. incl. with Columbia (Inc. Place)
Boyd Hill; RMC Place; YORK; ***230** B-7; ★ **CHRLT**; pop. incl. with Rock Hill (Inc. Place)
Boykin; RMC Place; KERSHAW; ***230** D-8; mail Rembert **z** 29128; rural
Boykin; RMC Place; MARLBORO; ***230** B-11; elev. 244ft./74m.; mail Barnwell **z** 29812; rural
Bradley; CDP; GREENWOOD; **230** D-4; [P]; **z** 29819; © 171
Bradleyville; RMC Place; AIKEN; **166** A-13; ★ **AUG**; mail North Augusta **z** 29841
Branchville; Inc. Place; ORANGEBURG; **230** G-8; elev. 125ft./38m.; [P]; **z** 29432; Ⓟ 1,107; © 1,083
Brand; RMC Place; LAURENS; ***230** C-5; elev. 684ft./208m.; mail Laurens **z** 29360; rural
Brandon; RMC Place; GREENVILLE; ***230** B-4; ★ **GRNV**; mail Greenville **z** 29611; ● 1,800
Brandon Acres; RMC Place; RICHLAND; ***230** D-8; ★ **COL**; pop. incl. with Columbia (Inc. Place)
Brandon Hills; RMC Place; RICHLAND; ***230** D-7; ★ **COL**; pop. incl. with Columbia (Inc. Place)
Branwood; RMC Place; GREENVILLE; ★ **GRNV**; mail Greenville **z** 29610; pop. incl. with Greenville (Inc. Place)
Brasstown; RMC Place; OCONEE; ***230** B-2; elev. 1,400ft./427m.; mail Long Creek **z** 29658; ● 40
Brattonsville; RMC Place; YORK; ***230** B-7; elev. 323ft./98m.; ★ **CHRLT**; mail Mc Connells **z** 29726; rural
Breezewood; RMC Place; GREENWOOD; ***230** D-5; elev. 621ft./189m.; mail Bradley **z** 29819; rural
Brentwood; RMC Place; CHARLESTON; ***230** H-10; ★ **CHAS**; mail North Charleston **z** 29405; pop. incl. with North Charleston (Inc. Place)
Brewerton; RMC Place; LAURENS; ***230** C-4; elev. 702ft./214m.; mail Ware Shoals **z** 29692; rural
Briarcliffe Acres; Inc. Place; HORRY; ***230** E-13; elev. 9ft./3m.; ★ **MYR.B**; mail Myrtle Beach **z** 29572; Ⓟ 552; © 470
Briarcreek; RMC Place; CHEROKEE; ***230** A-6; elev. 750ft./229m.; mail Gaffney **z** 29340; ● 120
Brighton; RMC Place; HAMPTON; ***230** H-7; elev. 71ft./22m.; mail Garnett **z** 29922
Brighton Beach; RMC Place; BEAUFORT; ***230** J-8; mail Bluffton **z** 29910; summer pop. 400; ● 150
Brightsville; RMC Place; MARLBORO; ***230** B-11; elev. 250ft./76m.; mail Bennettsville **z** 29512; rural
Bristow; RMC Place; MARLBORO; **230** C-11; mail Blenheim **z** 29516; ● 25
Brittany Park; RMC Place; ANDERSON; ***230** C-3; ★ **AND**; mail Anderson **z** 29621; pop. incl. with Anderson (Inc. Place)
Britton; RMC Place; SUMTER; ***230** E-9; elev. 147ft./45m.; ★ **SUMT**; mail Sumter **z** 29153; rural
Brittons Neck; RMC Place; MARION; **230** E-12; [P]; **z** 29546; ● 600
Broad Street; RMC Place; SUMTER; ★ **SUMT**; mail Sumter **z** 29150; pop. incl. with Sumter (Inc. Place)
Broadway Lake; RMC Place; ANDERSON; ***230** C-4; ★ **AND**; mail Anderson **z** 29621; ● 350
Brock; RMC Place; OCONEE; ***230** B-2; elev. 900ft./274m.; mail Westminster **z** 29693; rural
Brock Circle; RMC Place; ABBEVILLE; ***230** C-4; elev. 746ft./227m.; mail Honea Path **z** 29654; ● 60
Brockington; RMC Place; WILLIAMSBURG; ***230** E-10; mail Kingstree **z** 29556; ● 50
Brocks Mill; RMC Place; CHESTERFIELD; ***230** B-10; mail Cheraw **z** 29520; rural
Brogdon; RMC Place; SUMTER; ***230** E-9; mail Sumter **z** 29150
Brookdale; CDP; ORANGEBURG; ***230** F-8; elev. 82ft./25m.; mail Orangeburg **z** 29115; Ⓟ 5,339; © 4,724
Brook Forest Estates; RMC Place; GREENVILLE; ***230** B-4; elev. 270ft./82m.; ★ **GRNV**; mail Greenville **z** 29605; ● 700
Brookgreen; RMC Place; AIKEN; ***230** F-5; ★ **AUG**; mail North Augusta **z** 29841; pop. incl. with North Augusta (Inc. Place)
Brook Green Park; RMC Place; FLORENCE; ***230** D-10; elev. 42ft./13m.; ★ **FLO**; mail Florence **z** 29501; ● 800
Brookhaven Estates; RMC Place; AIKEN; ***230** F-6; elev. 500ft./152m.; ★ **AUG**; mail Aiken **z** 29801; ● 50
Brooklyn; RMC Place; LANCASTER; ***230** B-8; mail Lancaster **z** 29720; ● 1,850
Brooksville; RMC Place; HORRY; ***230** E-13; elev. 42ft./13m.; ★ **MYR.B**; mail Little River **z** 29566; ● 180
Brownsville; RMC Place; DORCHESTER; ***230** G-9; ★ **CHAS**; mail Summerville **z** 29483; ● 300
Brownsville; RMC Place; MARLBORO; ***230** C-11; elev. 134ft./41m.; mail Blenheim **z** 29516
Brownway; RMC Place; HORRY; ***230** E-12; elev. 37ft./11m.; mail Conway **z** 29526; rural
Bruner; RMC Place; RICHLAND; ***230** E-8; elev. 214ft./65m.; ★ **COL**; mail Hopkins **z** 29061; rural
Brunson; Inc. Place; HAMPTON; **230** H-7; elev. 138ft./42m.; [P]; **z** 29911; Ⓟ 587; © 589
Brunsons Crossroads; RMC Place; WILLIAMSBURG; ***230** E-11; elev. 52ft./16m.; mail Hemingway **z** 29554; ● 50
Bryans Crossroads; RMC Place; WILLIAMSBURG; ***230** F-10; elev. 45ft./14m.; mail Salters **z** 29590; rural
Buckeye Forest; RMC Place; SPARTANBURG; ***230** B-5; elev. 247ft./75m.; ★ **SPRT**; mail Startex **z** 29377; ● 80
Buck Hall; RMC Place; CHARLESTON; ***230** G-11; elev. 20ft./6m.; mail Awendaw **z** 29429, Mc Clellanville **z** 29458; ● 80
Buckingham Landing; RMC Place; BEAUFORT; ***230** J-8; mail Hilton Head Island **z** 29928; ● 100
Bucksport; CDP; HORRY; **230** E-12; [P]; **z** 29527 & mail Conway **z** 29526; Ⓟ 1,022; © 1,117
Bucksville; RMC Place; HORRY; **230** E-12; elev. 23ft./7m.; mail Conway **z** 29527; ● 35
Buffalo; RMC Place; MCCORMICK; ***230** E-4; elev. 475ft./145m.; mail Mc Cormick **z** 29835; rural
Buffalo; CDP; UNION; **230** B-6; [P]; **z** 29321; Ⓟ 1,569; © 1,426
Buford; RMC Place; LANCASTER; ***230** B-8; elev. 650ft./198m.; mail Lancaster **z** 29720; rural
Bufords Bridge; RMC Place; BAMBERG; ***230** G-7; elev. 123ft./37m.; mail Olar **z** 29843; ● 50
Bullock Creek; RMC Place; YORK; ***230** B-6; mail Sharon **z** 29742
Bunker Hill; RMC Place; DILLON; ***230** C-11; elev. 147ft./45m.; mail Dillon **z** 29536; rural
Burgess; RMC Place; HORRY; **230** E-12; elev. 18ft./5m.; ★ **MYR.B**; mail Murrells Inlet **z** 29576; ● 50
Burnettown; Inc. Place; AIKEN; ***230** F-5; ★ **AUG**; mail Langley **z** 29834, Warrenville **z** 29851; Ⓟ 493; © 2,720
Burnt Church Crossroads; RMC Place; COLLETON; ***230** H-9; elev. 33ft./10m.; mail Round O **z** 29474; rural
Burton; CDP; BEAUFORT; **230** I-8; elev. 32ft./10m.; mail Beaufort **z** 29902-03, **z** 29906; Ⓟ 6,917; © 7,180
Bynum; RMC Place; WILLIAMSBURG; ***230** E-10; elev. 75ft./23m.; mail Kingstree **z** 29556; ● 200
Byrd; RMC Place; DORCHESTER; ***230** G-9; elev. 86ft./26m.; mail Saint George **z** 29477
Byrds Crossroads; RMC Place; FLORENCE; ***230** D-10; elev. 107ft./33m.; mail Scranton **z** 29591; rural

C

Cabal; RMC Place; CHESTER; ***230** B-6; mail Sharon **z** 29742; rural
Cades; RMC Place; WILLIAMSBURG; **230** E-10; elev. 68ft./21m.; [P]; **z** 29518; ● 300
Caesars Head; RMC Place; GREENVILLE; ***230** A-3; mail Cedar Mountain **z** 28718
Cainhoy (Wando); RMC Place; BERKELEY; **230** G-10; elev. 19ft./6m.; [P]; **z** 29492; pop. incl. with Charleston (Inc. Place)
Caldwell Street; RMC Place; YORK; ★ **CHRLT**
Calhoun; RMC Place; PICKENS; ***230** B-3; elev. 737ft./225m.; mail Clemson **z** 29631; pop. incl. with Clemson (Inc. Place)
CALHOUN; **230** E-8; Ⓟ 12,753; © 15,185; ◆ 14,664
Calhoun Falls; Inc. Place; ABBEVILLE; **230** D-3; [P]; **z** 29628; Ⓟ 2,328; © 2,303
Callison; RMC Place; GREENWOOD; **230** D-5; mail Bradley **z** 29819; ● 50
Camden; Inc. Place; ⊡ KERSHAW; **230** D-8; [P] [H]; **z** 29020-21; Ⓟ 6,696; © 6,682
Cameron; Inc. Place; CALHOUN; **230** F-8; [P]; **z** 29030; Ⓟ 504; © 449
Camp Creek; RMC Place; LANCASTER; ***230** B-8; mail Lancaster **z** 29720; rural
Camp Croft (Delmar); RMC Place; SPARTANBURG; ***230** B-5; elev. 714ft./218m.; ★ **SPRT**; mail Spartanburg **z** 29302; ● 2,200
Campobello; Inc. Place; SPARTANBURG; **230** A-5; elev. 848ft./258m.; [P]; **z** 29322; Ⓟ 465; © 449
Campton; RMC Place; SPARTANBURG; ***230** A-5; elev. 878ft./268m.; ★ **SPRT**; mail Inman **z** 29349; ● 40
Camp Wadsworth Village; SPARTANBURG; see Wadsworth (RMC Place)
Canaan; RMC Place; ORANGEBURG; ***230** F-8; elev. 158ft./48m.; mail Cope **z** 29038; rural
Canaan; RMC Place; SPARTANBURG; ***230** B-5; elev. 711ft./217m.; ★ **SPRT**; mail Spartanburg **z** 29302; ● 35
Canadys (Cannadys); RMC Place; COLLETON; **230** G-8; [P]; **z** 29433; ● 200
Cane Savannah; CDP; SUMTER; ***230** E-9; elev. 185ft./56m.; ★ **SUMT**; mail Sumter **z** 29154; © 1,452
Cannadys; COLLETON; see Canadys (RMC Place)
Canterbury; RMC Place; CHEROKEE; ***230** A-6; mail Gaffney **z** 29341; pop. incl. with Gaffney (Inc. Place)
Canterbury; RMC Place; GREENVILLE; ***230** B-4; elev. 270ft./82m.; ★ **GRNV**; mail Piedmont **z** 29673; ● 400
Capehart; BEAUFORT; see Laurel Bay (CDP)
Capitol; RMC Place; RICHLAND; ★ **COL**; mail Columbia **z** 29201, **z** 29211; pop. incl. with Columbia (Inc. Place)
Capitol View; RMC Place; RICHLAND; **230** D-8; ★ **COL**; mail Columbia **z** 29209; ● 4,000
Carem; RMC Place; UNION; ***230** B-6; mail Union **z** 29379; rural
Carlisle; Inc. Place; UNION; **230** C-6; [P]; **z** 29031; Ⓟ 470; © 496
Carmel; RMC Place; LANCASTER; ***230** C-8; elev. 596ft./182m.; mail Heath Springs **z** 29058; rural
Carolina Circle; RMC Place; COLLETON; ***230** H-8; elev. 29ft./9m.; mail Walterboro **z** 29488; ● 150
Carolina Forest; RMC Place; HORRY; mail Myrtle Beach **z** 29579; pop. incl. with Myrtle Beach (Inc. Place)
Caroline Terrace; RMC Place; CHARLESTON; ★ **CHAS**; pop. incl. with Charleston (Inc. Place)
Caromi Village; RMC Place; BERKELEY; ***230** G-10; elev. 45ft./14m.; ★ **CHAS**; mail Ladson **z** 29456; ● 150
Carters Crossroads; RMC Place; GEORGETOWN; ***230** E-12; elev. 36ft./11m.; mail Hemingway **z** 29554; ● 25
Cartersville; RMC Place; FLORENCE; **230** D-10; mail Timmonsville **z** 29161; ● 110
Carver Heights; RMC Place; RICHLAND; ***230** D-7; elev. 300ft./91m.; ★ **COL**; mail Columbia **z** 29204; pop. incl. with Columbia (Inc. Place)
Carvers Bay; RMC Place; GEORGETOWN; ***230** E-12; elev. 52ft./16m.; mail Hemingway **z** 29554; ● 30
Cash; RMC Place; CHESTERFIELD; **230** C-10; elev. 145ft./44m.; mail Cheraw **z** 29520; ● 100
Cashville; RMC Place; SPARTANBURG; ***230** B-5; mail Woodruff **z** 29388
Cassatt; RMC Place; KERSHAW; **230** C-9; [P]; **z** 29032; ● 70
Catarrah; RMC Place; CHESTERFIELD; ***230** C-9; elev. 291ft./89m.; mail Jefferson **z** 29718; ● 30
Catawba; RMC Place; YORK; **230** B-8; elev. 570ft./174m.; [P]; ★ **CHRLT**; **z** 29704; ● 400
Catawba Reservation; Indian Reservation; YORK; © 494
Catchall; RMC Place; SUMTER; ***230** D-9; ★ **SUMT**; mail Dalzell **z** 29040; rural
Cateechee; RMC Place; PICKENS; ***230** B-3; [P]; **z** 29667; ● 500
Catholic Hill; RMC Place; COLLETON; ***230** H-8; elev. 75ft./23m.; mail Walterboro **z** 29488; ● 200
Cave; RMC Place; ALLENDALE; ***230** G-7; elev. 267ft./81m.; mail Allendale **z** 29810; rural
Cayce; Inc. Place; LEXINGTON; **230** J-2; [P]; ★ **COL**; **z** 29033; Ⓟ 11,163; © 12,150
Cedar Grove; RMC Place; HORRY; ***230** E-12; elev. 34ft./10m.; ★ **MYR.B**; mail Conway **z** 29527; ● 30
Cedar Hill; RMC Place; MCCORMICK; ***230** E-4; elev. 433ft./132m.; mail Mc Cormick **z** 29835; rural
Cedar Springs; RMC Place; CHARLESTON; ***230** H-10; elev. 10ft./3m.; ★ **CHAS**; mail Johns Island **z** 29455; ● 100
Cedar Terrace; RMC Place; RICHLAND; ***230** E-8; ★ **COL**; mail Columbia **z** 29209; ● 2,000
Celriver; YORK; see Red River (RMC Place)
Cementon; RMC Place; ORANGEBURG; ***230** G-9; elev. 77ft./23m.; mail Holly Hill **z** 29059; rural
Centenary; RMC Place; MARION; **230** D-11; elev. 56ft./17m.; [P]; **z** 29519; ● 500
Center Crossroads; RMC Place; GEORGETOWN; ***230** E-12; elev. 43ft./13m.; mail Hemingway **z** 29554; ● 40
Centerville; CDP; ANDERSON; ***230** C-3; elev. 240ft./73m.; ★ **AND**; mail Anderson **z** 29621; Ⓟ 4,866; © 5,181
Centerville (James Island); RMC Place; CHARLESTON; **230** H-10; elev. 9ft./3m.; ★ **CHAS**; mail Charleston **z** 29412, **z** 29422; ● 4,400
Centerville; RMC Place; DILLON; ***230** C-11; elev. 119ft./36m.; mail Latta **z** 29565; rural
Central; Inc. Place; PICKENS; **230** B-3; elev. 910ft./277m.; [P] [C] 2,586; **z** 29630; Ⓟ 2,438; © 3,522
Central Pacolet; Inc. Place; SPARTANBURG; ***230** B-6; ★ **SPRT**; mail Pacolet **z** 29372; Ⓟ 257; © 267
Central-Shilo; RMC Place; ABBEVILLE; ***230** D-4; mail Abbeville **z** 29620; rural
Challedon; RMC Place; LEXINGTON; ***230** D-7; elev. 250ft./76m.; ★ **COL**; mail Columbia **z** 29210; ● 2,500
Chaparral Ranches; RMC Place; BERKELEY; ***230** G-10; elev. 78ft./24m.; ★ **CHAS**; mail Moncks Corner **z** 29461; ● 5,000
Chapin; Inc. Place; LEXINGTON; **230** D-7; [P]; ★ **COL**; **z** 29036; Ⓟ 282; © 628
Chappell; NEWBERRY; see Chappells (RMC Place)
Chappells (Chappell); RMC Place; NEWBERRY; **230** D-5; [P]; **z** 29037; ● 100
Charleston; Inc. Place; ⊡ CHARLESTON, BERKELEY; **230** H-10; elev. 118ft./36m.; [P] [H] [C] 20,161 ■; ★ **CHAS**; **z** 29401-07, **z** 29409-10, **z** 29412-20, **z** 29422-25, **z** 29492; Ⓟ 80,414; © 96,650; ◆ 118,759
CHARLESTON; **230** H-10; Ⓟ 295,039; © 309,969; Ⓡ 309,960; ◆ 364,915
Charleston Heights; RMC Place; CHARLESTON; ***230** H-10; elev. 20ft./6m.; ★ **CHAS**; mail North Charleston **z** 29405, **z** 29418; pop. incl. with North Charleston (Inc. Place)
Charlestowne Estate; RMC Place; CHARLESTON; ★ **CHAS**; pop. incl. with Charleston (Inc. Place)
Chartwell; RMC Place; RICHLAND; ***230** D-7; elev. 250ft./76m.; ★ **COL**; mail Columbia **z** 29210; ● 500
Cheddar; RMC Place; ANDERSON; ***230** C-4; elev. 876ft./267m.; ★ **GRNV**; mail Belton **z** 29627; ● 250
Cheraw; Inc. Place; CHESTERFIELD; **230** B-10; elev. 157ft./48m.; [P] [H]; **z** 29520; Ⓟ 5,505; © 5,524
Cherokee; SPARTANBURG; see Cherokee Springs (RMC Place)
CHEROKEE; **230** A-6; Ⓟ 44,506; © 52,537; ◆ 54,255
Cherokee Falls; RMC Place; CHEROKEE; ***230** A-6; [P]; **z** 29702; ● 280
Cherokee Forest; RMC Place; GREENVILLE; ***230** B-4; ★ **GRNV**; mail Taylors **z** 29687; ● 2,100
Cherokee Gardens; RMC Place; OCONEE; ***230** B-3; elev. 800ft./244m.; mail Seneca **z** 29672; ● 200
Cherokee Springs (Cherokee); RMC Place; SPARTANBURG; **230** A-5; ★ **SPRT**; mail Spartanburg **z** 29302; ● 110
Cherry Grove Beach; RMC Place; HORRY; ***230** E-13; [P]; ★ **MYR.B**; **z** 29582; pop. incl. with North Myrtle Beach (Inc. Place)
Cherry Hill Estates; RMC Place; BEAUFORT; ***230** I-8; elev. 10ft./3m.; mail Beaufort **z** 29902; ● 70
Cherry Road; RMC Place; YORK; ★ **CHRLT**; mail Rock Hill **z** 29732; pop. incl. with Rock Hill (Inc. Place)
Cherryvale; CDP; SUMTER; ***230** E-9; ★ **SUMT**; mail Sumter **z** 29154; Ⓟ 3,061; © 2,461
Chesnee; Inc. Place; SPARTANBURG, CHEROKEE; **230** A-5; elev. 913ft./278m.; [P]; ★ **SPRT**; **z** 29323; Ⓟ 1,280; © 1,003
Chester; Inc. Place; ⊡ CHESTER; **230** B-7; elev. 549ft./167m.; [P] [H]; **z** 29706; Ⓟ 7,158; © 6,476
CHESTER; **230** C-7; Ⓟ 32,170; © 34,068; ◆ 32,407
Chesterfield; Inc. Place; ⊡ CHESTERFIELD; **230** B-10; [P]; **z** 29709; Ⓟ 1,373; © 1,318; Ⓡ 1,374
CHESTERFIELD; **230** B-9; Ⓟ 38,577; © 42,768; ◆ 43,064
Chestnut Hills; RMC Place; GREENVILLE; ***230** B-4; elev. 276ft./84m.; ★ **GRNV**; mail Greenville **z** 29605; ● 1,400
Chickasaw Point; RMC Place; OCONEE; ***230** C-2; elev. 700ft./213m.; mail Westminster **z** 29693; ● 220
Chicora Place; RMC Place; CHARLESTON; ★ **CHAS**; mail North Charleston **z** 29405; pop. incl. with North Charleston (Inc. Place)
Choppee; RMC Place; GEORGETOWN; ***230** F-11; elev. 48ft./15m.; mail Georgetown **z** 29440; rural
Citadel; RMC Place; CHARLESTON; ★ **CHAS**; mail Charleston **z** 29409; pop. incl. with Charleston (Inc. Place)
City View; CDP; GREENVILLE; **230** I-4; ★ **GRNV**; mail Greenville **z** 29611; © 1,254
Claremont; RMC Place; SUMTER; ***230** D-9; elev. 134ft./41m.; ★ **SUMT**; mail Sumter **z** 29150; rural
CLARENDON; **230** E-9; Ⓟ 28,450; © 32,502; ◆ 32,566
Clark Hill; MCCORMICK; see Clarks Hill (CDP)
Clarks Hill (Clark Hill); CDP; MCCORMICK; **230** E-5; [P]; **z** 29821; © 376
Claussen; RMC Place; FLORENCE; ***230** D-11; elev. 87ft./27m.; ★ **FLO**; mail Florence **z** 29505; rural
Clayton; RMC Place; FAIRFIELD; ***230** C-6; mail Blair **z** 29015; rural
Clearmont; RMC Place; OCONEE; ***230** B-2; mail Westminster **z** 29693; ● 100
Clear Pond; RMC Place; BAMBERG; ***230** G-7; elev. 144ft./44m.; mail Bamberg **z** 29003; ● 50
Clearspring; RMC Place; GREENVILLE; ***230** B-5; elev. 255ft./78m.; ★ **GRNV**; mail Simpsonville **z** 29681; rural
Clearwater; CDP; AIKEN; **166** B-14; [P]; ★ **AUG**; **z** 29822; Ⓟ 4,731; © 4,199
Cleburne; RMC Place; GEORGETOWN; ***230** F-12; elev. 18ft./5m.; mail Georgetown **z** 29440; ● 40
Clemson; Inc. Place; PICKENS, ANDERSON; **230** B-3; [P] [C] 17,309; **z** 29631-34; Ⓟ 11,096; © 11,939
Cleora; RMC Place; EDGEFIELD; ***230** E-5; mail Edgefield **z** 29824; rural
Cleveland; RMC Place; GREENVILLE; **230** A-4; elev. 1,010ft./308m.; [P]; **z** 29635; ● 220
Clifton; RMC Place; SPARTANBURG; ***230** A-5; [P]; ★ **SPRT**; **z** 29324; ● 500
Clinton; Inc. Place; LAURENS; **230** C-5; elev. 676ft./206m.; [P] [H] [C] 1,224; **z** 29325; Ⓟ 7,987; © 8,091; Ⓡ 8,545
Clio; Inc. Place; MARLBORO; **230** C-11; [P]; **z** 29525; Ⓟ 882; © 774
Clover; Inc. Place; YORK; **230** A-7; elev. 814ft./248m.; [P]; **z** 29710; Ⓟ 3,422; © 4,014
Clubhouse Crossroads; RMC Place; DORCHESTER; ***230** H-9; elev. 22ft./7m.; mail Ridgeville **z** 29472; rural
Club House Crossroads; RMC Place; LEXINGTON; ***230** D-6; ★ **COL**; mail Gilbert **z** 29054; ● 50
Clyde; RMC Place; DARLINGTON; ***230** C-9; elev. 243ft./74m.; mail Mc Bee **z** 29101
Coastal; RMC Place; HORRY; ★ **MYR.B**; mail North Myrtle Beach **z** 29582, **z** 29598; pop. incl. with North Myrtle Beach (Inc. Place)
Cochrantown; RMC Place; HORRY; ***230** E-12; elev. 34ft./10m.; ★ **MYR.B**; mail Conway **z** 29526; ● 200
Cokesbury; CDP; GREENWOOD; **230** D-4; ★ **GREEN**; mail Hodges **z** 29653; © 279
Cold Point; RMC Place; LAURENS; ***230** C-5; mail Laurens **z** 29360; ● 40
Coldstream; RMC Place; LEXINGTON; ***230** D-7; elev. 250ft./76m.; ★ **COL**; mail Columbia **z** 29210; ● 1,800
College Acres; RMC Place; AIKEN; ***230** F-6; elev. 450ft./137m.; ★ **AUG**; mail Aiken **z** 29803; ● 1,000
College Heights (East Hartsville); RMC Place; DARLINGTON; ***230** C-10; mail Hartsville **z** 29550; pop. incl. with Hartsville (Inc. Place)
COLLETON; **230** H-9; Ⓟ 34,377; © 38,264; ◆ 39,022
Colliers; RMC Place; EDGEFIELD; ***230** E-5; elev. 430ft./131m.; mail Modoc **z** 29838
Colonial Heights; RMC Place; BEAUFORT; ***230** I-8; elev. 20ft./6m.; mail Beaufort **z** 29906; ● 50
Colonial Heights; RMC Place; RICHLAND; ***230** D-7; ★ **COL**; pop. incl. with Columbia (Inc. Place)
Colonial Village; RMC Place; LANCASTER; ***230** A-8; elev. 650ft./198m.; ★ **CHRLT**; mail Fort Mill **z** 29715; ● 50
Columbia; Inc. Place; **STATE CAPITAL**; ⊡ RICHLAND, LEXINGTON; **230** D-7; [P] [H] [C] 33,564 ■; ★ **COL**; **z** 29201-12, **z** 29214-30, **z** 29240, **z** 29250, **z** 29260, **z** 29290, **z** 29292; Ⓟ 103,477; © 116,278; Ⓡ 115,877; ◆ 127,398
Columbiana Centre; RMC Place; RICHLAND; ***230** D-7; ★ **COL**; mail Columbia **z** 29212; pop. incl. with Columbia (Inc. Place)
Coneross; RMC Place; OCONEE; ***230** B-2; elev. 909ft./277m.; mail Westminster **z** 29693; rural
Conestee; RMC Place; GREENVILLE; **230** B-4; [P]; ★ **GRNV**; **z** 29636; ● 580
Congaree; RMC Place; RICHLAND; ***230** E-8; ★ **COL**; mail Eastover **z** 29044
Connecticut Park; RMC Place; CHEROKEE; ***230** A-6; elev. 650ft./198m.; mail Gaffney **z** 29341; ● 300
Converse; RMC Place; SPARTANBURG; **230** A-5; elev. 713ft./217m.; [P]; ★ **SPRT**; **z** 29329; ● 1,200
Conway; Inc. Place; ⊡ HORRY; **230** E-12; [P] [H] [C] 8,049; ★ **MYR.B**; **z** 29526-28; Ⓟ 9,819; © 11,788
Cooks Crossroads; RMC Place; LAURENS; ***230** B-5; mail Fountain Inn **z** 29644
Cool Branch; RMC Place; FAIRFIELD; ***230** C-6; elev. 544ft./166m.; mail Blair **z** 29015; rural
Cooley Springs; RMC Place; SPARTANBURG; ***230** A-5; elev. 924ft./282m.; ★ **SPRT**; mail Chesnee **z** 29323; rural
Cool Spring; RMC Place; HORRY; ***230** D-12; elev. 102ft./31m.; mail Aynor **z** 29511; ● 100
Coosaw; RMC Place; BEAUFORT; ***230** I-8; elev. 12ft./4m.; mail Seabrook **z** 29940; rural
Coosawatchie; JASPER; see Coosawhatchie (RMC Place)
Coosawhatchie (Coosawatchie); RMC Place; JASPER; **230** I-8; elev. 22ft./7m.; [P]; **z** 29912, **z** 29936; ● 300
Cope; Inc. Place; ORANGEBURG; **230** F-7; [P]; **z** 29038; Ⓟ 124; © 107
Cordesville; RMC Place; BERKELEY; **230** G-10; elev. 53ft./16m.; [P]; **z** 29434; ● 90
Cordova; Inc. Place; ORANGEBURG; **230** F-8; elev. 252ft./77m.; [P]; **z** 29039; Ⓟ 135; © 157
Cornaca; GREENWOOD; see Coronaca (CDP)
Cornwell; RMC Place; CHESTER; **230** C-7; elev. 636ft./194m.; mail Blackstock **z** 29014; ● 50
Coronaca (Cornaca); CDP; GREENWOOD; **230** D-5; elev. 567ft./173m.; ★ **GREEN**; mail Greenwood **z** 29649; © 170
Cottageville; Inc. Place; COLLETON; **230** H-9; [P]; **z** 29435; Ⓟ 572; © 707
Couchton; RMC Place; AIKEN; **230** F-6; elev. 470ft./143m.; ★ **AUG**; mail Aiken **z** 29801; ● 500
Country Club Estates; RMC Place; CHARLESTON; ★ **CHAS**; pop. incl. with Charleston (Inc. Place)
Country Club Estates; RMC Place; YORK; ***230** B-7; elev. 195ft./59m.; ★ **CHRLT**; mail Rock Hill **z** 29730; pop. incl. with Rock Hill (Inc. Place)
Country Homes; RMC Place; GREENWOOD; ***230** D-5; elev. 500ft./152m.; ★ **GREEN**; mail Greenwood **z** 29646; ● 200
Country Place; RMC Place; ANDERSON; ***230** C-3; ★ **AND**; mail Anderson **z** 29621; ● 100
Courtenay; RMC Place; OCONEE; ***230** B-3; elev. 947ft./289m.; mail Seneca **z** 29672; ● 120
Coventry; RMC Place; AIKEN; ***230** F-5; ★ **AUG**; mail North Augusta **z** 29860; ● 80
Coward; Inc. Place; FLORENCE; **230** D-11; [P]; **z** 29530; Ⓟ 532; © 650
Cowpens; Inc. Place; SPARTANBURG; **230** A-5; [P]; ★ **SPRT**; **z** 29330; Ⓟ 2,176; © 2,279
Crane Forest; RMC Place; RICHLAND; ***230** D-7; elev. 250ft./76m.; ★ **COL**; mail Columbia **z** 29203; ● 700
Craytonville; RMC Place; ANDERSON; ***230** C-4; mail Honea Path **z** 29654; rural
Crescent; RMC Place; SPARTANBURG; ***230** B-5; mail Woodruff **z** 29388; ● 110
Crescent Beach; RMC Place; HORRY; ***230** E-13; ★ **MYR.B**; mail North Myrtle Beach **z** 29582; pop. incl. with North Myrtle Beach (Inc. Place)
Creston; RMC Place; CALHOUN; **230** F-8; mail Cameron **z** 29030; ● 60
Crestview; RMC Place; DARLINGTON; ***230** D-10; elev. 129ft./39m.; ★ **FLO**; mail Florence **z** 29501; ● 1,700
Crocketts Crossroads; RMC Place; LANCASTER; ***230** B-8; elev. 535ft./163m.; mail Lancaster **z** 29720; ● 500
Crocketville; RMC Place; HAMPTON; **230** H-7; [P]; **z** 29913; ● 50
Croghan; RMC Place; CHARLESTON; ★ **CHAS**; pop. incl. with Charleston (Inc. Place)
Crooks Crossroads; RMC Place; WILLIAMSBURG; ***230** E-11; elev. 50ft./15m.; mail Hemingway **z** 29554; ● 60
Crosland Park; RMC Place; AIKEN; ***230** F-6; ★ **AUG**; mail Aiken **z** 29801; pop. incl. with Aiken (Inc. Place)
Cross; RMC Place; BERKELEY; **230** F-9; elev. 83ft./25m.; [P]; **z** 29436; ● 300
Cross Anchor; RMC Place; SPARTANBURG; **230** B-5; [P]; **z** 29331; ● 350
Cross County; RMC Place; CHARLESTON; ★ **CHAS**; mail Charleston **z** 29423, **z** 29425, North Charleston **z** 29418, **z** 29420; pop. incl. with North Charleston (Inc. Place)
Cross Hill; Inc. Place; LAURENS; **230** C-5; elev. 587ft./179m.; [P]; **z** 29332; Ⓟ 469; © 601
Cross Keys; RMC Place; UNION; **230** B-6; mail Union **z** 29379; ● 100
Cross Plains; RMC Place; GREENVILLE; ***230** A-4; ★ **GRNV**; mail Tigerville **z** 29688; rural
Crosswell; RMC Place; PICKENS; ***230** B-4; ★ **GRNV**; mail Easley **z** 29640; rural
Cummings; RMC Place; HAMPTON; **230** H-7; elev. 77ft./23m.; mail Varnville **z** 29944; ● 100
Cusaac Crossroads; RMC Place; FLORENCE; ***230** D-10; elev. 33ft./10m.; ★ **FLO**; mail Effingham **z** 29541; rural
Cypress Crossroads; RMC Place; LEE; ***230** D-10; elev. 192ft./59m.; mail Lamar **z** 29069; rural
Cypress Fork; RMC Place; CLARENDON; ***230** E-10; elev. 98ft./30m.; mail Alcolu **z** 29001; rural

D

Dacusville; RMC Place; PICKENS; ***230** B-4; elev. 1,084ft./330m.; ★ **GRNV**; mail Easley **z** 29640
Daisy; RMC Place; HORRY; ***230** D-13; elev. 92ft./28m.; mail Loris **z** 29569; ● 100
Dale; RMC Place; BEAUFORT; **230** I-8; [P]; **z** 29914; ● 150
Dalewood; RMC Place; GREENWOOD; ***230** D-4; elev. 623ft./190m.; ★ **GREEN**; mail Hodges **z** 29653; ● 100
Dalzell; CDP; SUMTER; **230** D-9; elev. 221ft./67m.; [P]; ★ **SUMT**; **z** 29040; © 2,260
Danwood; RMC Place; FLORENCE; ***230** D-10; ★ **FLO**; mail Effingham **z** 29541; ● 100
Darlington; Inc. Place; ⊡ DARLINGTON; **230** C-10; [P]; ★ **FLO**; **z** 29532, **z** 29540; Ⓟ 7,311; © 6,720
DARLINGTON; **230** C-10; Ⓟ 61,851; © 67,394; ◆ 65,351
Daufuskie Island; BEAUFORT; see Daufuskie Landing (RMC Place)
Daufuskie Landing (Daufuskie Island); RMC Place; BEAUFORT; ***230** J-8; elev. 12ft./4m.; mail Daufuskie Island **z** 29915; ● 120
Davis Crossroads; RMC Place; CLARENDON; ***230** F-9; elev. 120ft./37m.; mail Summerton **z** 29148; ● 50
Davis Station; RMC Place; CLARENDON; **230** F-9; [P]; **z** 29041; ● 150
Deans; RMC Place; ANDERSON; ***230** C-3; elev. 791ft./241m.; ★ **AND**; mail Starr **z** 29684
De Bordieu Colony; RMC Place; GEORGETOWN; ***230** F-12; elev. 16ft./5m.; mail Georgetown **z** 29440; ● 3,000
Deer Park; RMC Place; CHARLESTON; ***230** G-10; ★ **CHAS**; mail North Charleston **z** 29405; pop. incl. with North Charleston (Inc. Place)
Dekalb; RMC Place; KERSHAW; ***230** C-8; elev. 423ft./129m.; mail Westville **z** 29175; rural
Delemar Crossroads; RMC Place; CHARLESTON, DORCHESTER; ***230** H-9; elev. 29ft./9m.; mail Ravenel **z** 29470; rural
Delmar; RMC Place; SALUDA; ***230** D-6; mail Leesville **z** 29070; rural
Delmar; SPARTANBURG; see Camp Croft (RMC Place)
Delphia; RMC Place; YORK; ***230** B-7; mail York **z** 29745
Delta; RMC Place; UNION; ***230** C-6; mail Whitmire **z** 29178
Denmark; Inc. Place; BAMBERG; **230** F-7; elev. 244ft./74m.; [P] [C] 703; **z** 29042; Ⓟ 3,762; © 3,328
Denny Terrace; RMC Place; RICHLAND; **230** D-7; ★ **COL**; mail Columbia **z** 29203; ● 1,750
Dentsville; CDP; RICHLAND; **230** H-3; elev. 250ft./76m.; ★ **COL**; mail Columbia **z** 29204; Ⓟ 11,839; © 13,009; Ⓡ 13,049
Denver; RMC Place; ANDERSON; ***230** C-3; elev. 226ft./69m.; ★ **AND**; mail Anderson **z** 29625; ● 40
Deweys Hill; RMC Place; CHARLESTON; ***230** H-10; ★ **CHAS**; mail Charleston **z** 29406; pop. incl. with North Charleston (Inc. Place)
Dillon; Inc. Place; ⊡ DILLON; **230** C-11; elev. 113ft./34m.; [P] [H]; **z** 29536; Ⓟ 6,829; © 6,316
DILLON; **230** C-11; Ⓟ 29,114; © 30,722; ◆ 30,616
Dinkins; RMC Place; SUMTER; ***230** E-9; elev. 180ft./55m.; ★ **SUMT**; mail Sumter **z** 29150; pop. incl. with Sumter (Inc. Place)
Dinkins Mill; RMC Place; SUMTER; ***230** D-9; elev. 145ft./44m.; ★ **SUMT**; mail Rembert **z** 29128; ● 25
Dixiana; RMC Place; LEXINGTON; ***230** E-7; ★ **COL**; mail West Columbia **z** 29169, **z** 29172; ● 50
Docheno; RMC Place; ANDERSON; ***230** C-4; mail Belton **z** 29627; rural
Dog Bluff; RMC Place; HORRY; ***230** D-12; elev. 82ft./25m.; mail Galivants Ferry **z** 29544; rural
Donalds; Inc. Place; ABBEVILLE; **230** C-4; elev. 762ft./232m.; [P]; **z** 29638; Ⓟ 326; © 354
Dongola; RMC Place; HORRY; ***230** E-12; mail Conway **z** 29527; rural
Dorange; RMC Place; DORCHESTER; ***230** G-8; mail Reevesville **z** 29471; rural
Dorchester; RMC Place; DORCHESTER; **230** G-9; elev. 106ft./32m.; [P]; **z** 29437; ● 450
DORCHESTER; **230** G-9; Ⓟ 83,060; © 96,413; Ⓡ 96,361; ◆ 132,453
Dorchester Estates; RMC Place; DORCHESTER; ***230** G-9; elev. 56ft./17m.; ★ **CHAS**; mail Summerville **z** 29485; ● 500
Dorchester Terrace; RMC Place; CHARLESTON; ***230** H-10; elev. 27ft./8m.; ★ **CHAS**; mail North Charleston **z** 29405; pop. incl. with North Charleston (Inc. Place)
Douglass; RMC Place; FAIRFIELD; ***230** C-7; elev. 476ft./145m.; mail Blackstock **z** 29014; rural
Dovesville; RMC Place; DARLINGTON; **230** C-10; elev. 180ft./55m.; mail Darlington **z** 29540; ● 200
Drake; RMC Place; MARLBORO; ***230** C-11; mail Blenheim **z** 29516
Drawdy; RMC Place; COLLETON; ***230** H-8; elev. 14ft./4m.; mail Walterboro **z** 29488; ● 35
Drayton; RMC Place; CHARLESTON; ***230** H-10; elev. 17ft./5m.; ★ **CHAS**; mail Charleston **z** 29407; ● 700
Drayton; RMC Place; SPARTANBURG; **230** G-3; [P]; ★ **SPRT**; **z** 29333; ● 1,400
Draytonville; RMC Place; CHEROKEE; ***230** A-6; elev. 828ft./252m.; mail Gaffney **z** 29340; rural
Drexel Lake Hills; RMC Place; RICHLAND; ***230** D-8; elev. 250ft./76m.; ★ **COL**; mail Columbia **z** 29206; ● 1,200
Dry Branch; RMC Place; AIKEN; ***230** F-6; ★ **AUG**; mail Aiken **z** 29803; ● 350
DuBose; RMC Place; SUMTER; ***230** D-9; mail Sumter **z** 29150; rural
Du Bose Crossroads; RMC Place; LEE; ***230** D-9; elev. 184ft./56m.; mail Sumter **z** 29153; ● 30
Du Bose Park; RMC Place; KERSHAW; ***230** D-8; elev. 183ft./56m.; mail Camden **z** 29020; ● 200
Dudley; RMC Place; CHESTERFIELD; ***230** B-9; elev. 542ft./165m.; mail Pageland **z** 29728; rural
Due West; Inc. Place; ABBEVILLE; **230** C-4; elev. 703ft./214m.; [P] [C] 925; **z** 29639; Ⓟ 1,220; © 1,209
Duford; RMC Place; HORRY; ***230** D-12; mail Nichols **z** 29581; ● 70
Dunbar; RMC Place; GEORGETOWN; ***230** F-11; mail Georgetown **z** 29440; ● 450
Dunbar; RMC Place; MARLBORO; **230** C-11; mail Clio **z** 29525; ● 50
Duncan; Inc. Place; SPARTANBURG; **230** B-5; [P]; **z** 29334, **z** 29390-91; Ⓟ 2,152; © 2,870; Ⓡ 2,861
Dunean; CDP; GREENVILLE; **230** J-4; ★ **GRNV**; mail Greenville **z** 29601; Ⓟ 4,637; © 4,158
Dupont; RMC Place; CHARLESTON; ***230** H-10; ★ **CHAS**; mail Charleston **z** 29407; pop. incl. with Charleston (Inc. Place)
Dusty Bend; RMC Place; KERSHAW; ***230** D-8; mail Camden **z** 29020; pop. incl. with Camden (Inc. Place)
Dutch Fork; RMC Place; RICHLAND; ***230** D-7; ★ **COL**; mail Columbia **z** 29210, **z** 29221
Dutchman; RMC Place; SPARTANBURG; ***230** B-5; elev. 647ft./197m.; mail Pauline **z** 29374; rural
Dutch Village; RMC Place; RICHLAND; ***230** D-7; elev. 250ft./76m.; ★ **COL**; mail Irmo **z** 29063; ● 250
Dyson; RMC Place; GREENWOOD; **230** D-5; elev. 404ft./123m.; mail Ninety Six **z** 29666; rural

E

Eadytown; RMC Place; BERKELEY; **230** F-10; elev. 87ft./27m.; mail Pineville **z** 29468; ● 50
Earle Homes; RMC Place; ANDERSON; ★ **AND**; mail Anderson **z** 29624
Earles; RMC Place; WILLIAMSBURG; **230** F-11; elev. 42ft./13m.; mail Andrews **z** 29510; ● 40
Earles Grove; RMC Place; OCONEE; ***230** C-3; elev. 903ft./275m.; mail Seneca **z** 29678; ● 40
Earlwood Park; RMC Place; DARLINGTON; ***230** C-10; ★ **FLO**; mail Darlington **z** 29532; ● 35
Early Branch; RMC Place; HAMPTON; **230** H-8; [P]; **z** 29916; ● 150
Easley; Inc. Place; PICKENS; **230** B-4; elev. 1,091ft./333m.; [P] [H]; ★ **GRNV**; **z** 29640-42; Ⓟ 15,195; © 17,754; ◆ 20,755
East Bay; RMC Place; CHARLESTON; mail Charleston **z** 29403, **z** 29413; pop. incl. with Charleston (Inc. Place)
East Chester; RMC Place; CHESTER; pop. incl. with Chester (Inc. Place)
East Gaffney; CDP; CHEROKEE; **230** A-6; mail Gaffney **z** 29340; Ⓟ 3,278; © 3,349
East Gantt; RMC Place; GREENVILLE; ***230** B-4; elev. 295ft./90m.; ★ **GRNV**; mail Greenville **z** 29609; ● 1,600
East Greenville; RMC Place; GREENVILLE; pop. incl. with Greenville (Inc. Place)
East Greer; RMC Place; SPARTANBURG; ***230** B-5; ★ **GRNV**; mail Greer **z** 29651; pop. incl. with Greer (Inc. Place)
East Hartsville; DARLINGTON; see College Heights (RMC Place)
Eastmont; RMC Place; RICHLAND; ***230** D-8; elev. 265ft./81m.; ★ **COL**; mail Columbia **z** 29209; ● 500
East Orangeburg; RMC Place; ORANGEBURG; pop. incl. with Orangeburg (Inc. Place)
Eastover; Inc. Place; RICHLAND; **230** E-8; elev. 190ft./58m.; [P]; ★ **COL**; **z** 29044; Ⓟ 1,044; © 830
East Side Acres; RMC Place; COLLETON; ***230** H-8; elev. 17ft./5m.; mail Walterboro **z** 29488; ● 150
East Spartanburg; RMC Place; SPARTANBURG; ***230** B-5; ★ **SPRT**; pop. incl. with Spartanburg (Inc. Place)
East Sumter; CDP-Census Area Only; SUMTER; ***230** E-9; ★ **SUMT**; mail Sumter **z** 29150; Ⓟ 1,590; © 1,220
East View; RMC Place; GREENVILLE; ***230** B-4; elev. 790ft./241m.; ★ **GRNV**; mail Pelzer **z** 29669; rural
Eau Claire; RMC Place; RICHLAND; ***230** D-7; ★ **COL**; mail Columbia **z** 29203, **z** 29230; pop. incl. with Columbia (Inc. Place)
Ebenezer; RMC Place; FLORENCE; ***230** D-10; ★ **FLO**; mail Florence **z** 29501; pop. incl. with Florence (Inc. Place)
Ebenezer; RMC Place; YORK; ***230** B-7; ★ **CHRLT**; mail Rock Hill **z** 29732; pop. incl. with Rock Hill (Inc. Place)
Eden; RMC Place; LAURENS; ***230** C-5; elev. 225ft./69m.; mail Gray Court **z** 29645; rural
Edenwood; RMC Place; LEXINGTON; ***230** E-7; elev. 200ft./61m.; ★ **COL**; mail Cayce **z** 29033; pop. incl. with Cayce (Inc. Place)
Edgefield; Inc. Place; ⊡ EDGEFIELD; **230** E-5; [P] [H]; **z** 29824; Ⓟ 2,563; © 4,449
EDGEFIELD; **230** E-5; Ⓟ 18,375; © 24,595; Ⓡ 24,560; ◆ 25,878
Edgemoor; RMC Place; CHESTER; **230** B-7; [P]; **z** 29712; ● 350
Edgewood; RMC Place; RICHLAND; ★ **COL**; mail Columbia **z** 29204, **z** 29240; pop. incl. with Columbia (Inc. Place)
Edisto; CDP-Census Area Only; ORANGEBURG; ***230** F-8; elev. 200ft./61m.; mail Cope **z** 29038; Ⓟ 2,815; © 2,632
Edisto Beach; Inc. Place; COLLETON; **230** I-9; elev. 10ft./3m.; mail Edisto Island **z** 29438; Ⓟ 340; © 641
Edisto Island; RMC Place; CHARLESTON; **230** I-9; [P]; **z** 29438; summer pop. 2,000; ● 100
Edmund; RMC Place; LEXINGTON; **230** E-7; ★ **COL**; mail Lexington **z** 29072-73; ● 50
Effingham; RMC Place; FLORENCE; **230** D-10; [P]; ★ **FLO**; **z** 29541; ● 230
Ehrhardt; Inc. Place; BAMBERG; **230** G-7; elev. 146ft./45m.; [P]; **z** 29081; Ⓟ 442; © 614
Elgin; Inc. Place; KERSHAW; **230** D-8; elev. 420ft./128m.; [P]; ★ **COL**; **z** 29045; Ⓟ 622; © 806
Elgin; CDP; LANCASTER; **230** B-8; mail Lancaster **z** 29720; Ⓟ 2,196; © 2,426
Elim; RMC Place; FLORENCE; ***230** D-10; ★ **FLO**; mail Effingham **z** 29541; rural
Elko; Inc. Place; BARNWELL; **230** F-6; [P]; **z** 29826; Ⓟ 214; © 212
Elliott; RMC Place; LEE; **230** D-9; elev. 172ft./52m.; [P]; **z** 29046; ● 650
Elloree; Inc. Place; ORANGEBURG; **230** F-8; elev. 174ft./53m.; [P]; **z** 29047; Ⓟ 939; © 742
Elmwood Park; RMC Place; AIKEN; ***230** F-6; elev. 480ft./146m.; ★ **AUG**; mail Aiken **z** 29803; ● 200
Emanuelville; RMC Place; DILLON; ***230** C-11; elev. 116ft./35m.; mail Dillon **z** 29536; ● 150
Emerald Place; RMC Place; GREENWOOD; ***230** D-5; elev. 550ft./168m.; ★ **GREEN**; mail Greenwood **z** 29646; ● 170
Emerald Valley; RMC Place; RICHLAND; ***230** D-7; elev. 250ft./76m.; ★ **COL**; mail Columbia **z** 29210; ● 450
Emory; RMC Place; SALUDA; ***230** D-6; mail Saluda **z** 29138; rural
Enchanted Hills; RMC Place; OCONEE; ***230** B-3; elev. 860ft./262m.; mail Seneca **z** 29672; ● 300
Enola; RMC Place; SPARTANBURG; ***230** A-5; ★ **SPRT**; mail Converse **z** 29329; ● 200
Enoree; RMC Place; SPARTANBURG; **230** B-5; [P]; **z** 29335; ● 1,100
Epworth; RMC Place; GREENWOOD; **230** D-5; mail Ninety Six **z** 29666; ● 70
Equinox Mill; RMC Place; ANDERSON; ***230** C-3; ★ **AND**; mail Anderson **z** 29625; ● 1,500
Erwin; LANCASTER; see Irwin (CDP-Census Area Only)
Estill; Inc. Place; HAMPTON; **230** H-7; elev. 114ft./35m.; [P]; **z** 29918 & mail Scotia **z** 29939; Ⓟ 2,387; © 2,425
Eureka; RMC Place; AIKEN; **230** E-6; elev. 521ft./159m.; ★ **AUG**; mail Trenton **z** 29847; ● 70
Eureka; CHESTER; see Eureka Mill (CDP-Census Area Only)
Eureka Mill (Eureka, Hemlock); CDP-Census Area Only; CHESTER; **230** B-7; elev. 550ft./168m.; mail Chester **z** 29706; Ⓟ 1,738; © 1,737
Eutaw Springs; RMC Place; ORANGEBURG; ***230** F-9; elev. 88ft./27m.; mail Eutawville **z** 29048; ● 200
Eutawville; Inc. Place; ORANGEBURG; **230** F-9; [P]; **z** 29048; Ⓟ 350; © 344
Evergreen (Lucille); RMC Place; FLORENCE; **230** D-11; elev. 104ft./32m.; ★ **FLO**; mail Effingham **z** 29541; ● 120
Evergreen Hills; RMC Place; ANDERSON; ***230** C-3; ★ **AND**; mail Anderson **z** 29625

F

Fair Crossroads; RMC Place; ABBEVILLE; ***230** D-4; mail Due West **z** 29639; rural
Fairfax; Inc. Place; ALLENDALE, HAMPTON; **230** G-7; elev. 136ft./41m.; [P] [H]; **z** 29827; Ⓟ 2,317; © 3,206
Fairfield; RMC Place; BEAUFORT; mail Hilton Head Island **z** 29925, **z** 29928; pop. incl. with Hilton Head Island (Inc. Place)
FAIRFIELD; **230** C-7; Ⓟ 22,295; © 23,454; ◆ 22,635
Fairfield Terrace; RMC Place; RICHLAND; ***230** D-7; elev. 200ft./61m.; ★ **COL**; mail Columbia **z** 29203; ● 200
Fair Forest; RMC Place; GREENWOOD; ***230** D-5; elev. 550ft./168m.; ★ **GREEN**; mail Greenwood **z** 29646; ● 200
Fairforest; RMC Place; SPARTANBURG; **230** G-1; [P]; ★ **SPRT**; **z** 29336; ● 800
Fairmont; RMC Place; SPARTANBURG; **230** B-5; ★ **SPRT**; mail Spartanburg **z** 29301; ● 250
Fair Play; RMC Place; OCONEE; **230** C-3; elev. 816ft./249m.; [P]; **z** 29643; ● 400
Fairview; RMC Place; GREENVILLE; ***230** B-4; ★ **GRNV**; mail Greer **z** 29651; ● 1,200
Fairview; RMC Place; NEWBERRY; ***230** D-6; mail Prosperity **z** 29127; rural
Fairview; RMC Place; OCONEE; ***230** B-3; elev. 900ft./274m.; mail Seneca **z** 29672; rural
Fairview Crossroads; RMC Place; LEXINGTON; ***230** E-7; elev. 486ft./148m.; mail Leesville **z** 29070; ● 60
Farrel Crossroads; RMC Place; BAMBERG; ***230** G-8; elev. 36ft./11m.; mail Branchville **z** 29432; rural
Farrow Terrace; RMC Place; RICHLAND; ***230** D-7; elev. 344ft./105m.; ★ **COL**; mail Columbia **z** 29203; pop. incl. with Columbia (Inc. Place)
Feasterville; RMC Place; FAIRFIELD; ***230** C-7; mail Blair **z** 29015; rural
Fechtig; RMC Place; HAMPTON; ***230** H-8; elev. 87ft./27m.; mail Early Branch **z** 29916; rural
Federal; RMC Place; FLORENCE; ★ **FLO**; mail Florence **z** 29503; pop. incl. with Florence (Inc. Place)
Federal; RMC Place; GREENVILLE; ★ **GRNV**; mail Greenville **z** 29603; pop. incl. with Greenville (Inc. Place)
Felderville; RMC Place; ORANGEBURG; ***230** F-9; mail Elloree **z** 29047; rural
Fenwick Hills; RMC Place; CHARLESTON; ***230** H-10; elev. 20ft./6m.; ★ **CHAS**; mail Johns Island **z** 29455; ● 300
Ferndale; RMC Place; CHARLESTON; ★ **CHAS**; mail Charleston **z** 29406; pop. incl. with North Charleston (Inc. Place)
Ferndale; RMC Place; SPARTANBURG; ***230** A-5; elev. 240ft./73m.; ★ **SPRT**; mail Spartanburg **z** 29303; ● 200
Filbert; RMC Place; YORK; **230** A-7; mail Clover **z** 29710, York **z** 29745; ● 300
Fingerville; RMC Place; SPARTANBURG; **230** A-5; [P]; **z** 29338; ● 380
Finklea; RMC Place; HORRY; ***230** D-12; mail Loris **z** 29569; ● 50
Finland; RMC Place; BAMBERG; ***230** F-7; elev. 222ft./68m.; mail Denmark **z** 29042; rural
Fisher Hill; RMC Place; CHESTERFIELD; ***230** B-10; elev. 185ft./56m.; mail Cheraw **z** 29520; ● 60
Five Forks; RMC Place; ANDERSON; ***230** B-3; elev. 894ft./272m.; ★ **AND**; mail Anderson **z** 29621, Pendleton **z** 29670; ● 80
Five Forks; CDP; GREENVILLE; ***230** B-4; elev. 869ft./265m.; ★ **GRNV**; mail Simpsonville **z** 29681; © 8,064
Five Forks; RMC Place; PICKENS; ***230** B-3; elev. 952ft./290m.; mail Liberty **z** 29657; rural
Five Points; RMC Place; OCONEE; ***230** B-2; elev. 1,006ft./307m.; mail Westminster **z** 29693
Five Points; RMC Place; RICHLAND; ★ **COL**; mail Columbia **z** 29205, **z** 29250
Flamingo Acres; RMC Place; MARLBORO; ***230** C-11; elev. 138ft./42m.; mail Bennettsville **z** 29512; ● 100
Flat Rock; RMC Place; ANDERSON; ***230** C-3; ★ **AND**; mail Anderson **z** 29624; ● 200
Flat Shoals; RMC Place; OCONEE; ***230** B-3; elev. 1,067ft./325m.; mail Walhalla **z** 29691; rural
Fletcher; RMC Place; MARLBORO; ***230** B-11; mail Mc Coll **z** 29570; rural
Florence; Inc. Place; ⊡ FLORENCE; **230** D-10; elev. 149ft./45m.; [P] [H] [C] 4,075 ■; ★ **FLO**; **z** 29501-06; Ⓟ 29,813; © 30,248; ◆ 30,980
FLORENCE; **230** D-11; Ⓟ 114,344; © 125,761; ◆ 133,051
Floydale (Floyd Dale); RMC Place; DILLON; **230** C-11; mail Dillon **z** 29536; ● 250
Floyd Dale; DILLON; see Floydale (RMC Place)
Floyds Crossroads; RMC Place; HORRY; ***230** D-12; elev. 71ft./22m.; mail Nichols **z** 29581; rural
Folly Beach (Folly Island); Inc. Place; CHARLESTON; **230** H-10; [P]; ★ **CHAS**; **z** 29439; Ⓟ 1,398; © 2,116
Folly Field; RMC Place; BEAUFORT; **230** J-11; mail Hilton Head Island **z** 29928; pop. incl. with Hilton Head Island (Inc. Place)
Folly Island; CHARLESTON; see Folly Beach (Inc. Place)
Forest; RMC Place; DORCHESTER; ***230** G-9; elev. 102ft./31m.; mail Dorchester **z** 29437; ● 50
Forest Acres; RMC Place; OCONEE; ***230** B-2; elev. 1,000ft./305m.; mail Walhalla **z** 29691; ● 60
Forest Acres; Inc. Place; RICHLAND; **230** I-3; elev. 248ft./76m.; ★ **COL**; mail Columbia **z** 29206, **z** 29260; Ⓟ 7,197; © 10,558; Ⓡ 10,497
Forest Acres West; RMC Place; CHARLESTON; ★ **CHAS**; pop. incl. with Charleston (Inc. Place)
Forest Beach; RMC Place; BEAUFORT; **230** J-10; mail Hilton Head Island **z** 29928; pop. incl. with Hilton Head Island (Inc. Place)
Forestbrook; CDP; HORRY; **230** J-12; ★ **MYR.B**; mail Myrtle Beach **z** 29579; Ⓟ 2,502; © 3,391
Forest Lake; RMC Place; RICHLAND; ***230** D-8; elev. 200ft./61m.; ★ **COL**; mail Columbia **z** 29206; ● 250
Forest Lake; RMC Place; YORK; ***230** A-8; ★ **CHRLT**; mail Fort Mill **z** 29715
Foreston; RMC Place; CLARENDON; **230** E-10; elev. 95ft./29m.; mail Manning **z** 29102; ● 100
Forest Park; RMC Place; PICKENS; ***230** B-4; elev. 298ft./91m.; ★ **GRNV**; mail Easley **z** 29642; ● 120
Fork; RMC Place; DILLON; **230** C-12; [P]; **z** 29543; ● 280
Fork Shoals; RMC Place; GREENVILLE; **230** C-4; ★ **GRNV**; mail Gray Court **z** 29645; ● 180
Fornance; RMC Place; RICHLAND; ★ **COL**; pop. incl. with Columbia (Inc. Place)
Forrest Hills; RMC Place; DILLON; ***230** C-11; elev. 110ft./34m.; mail Latta **z** 29565; pop. incl. with Latta (Inc. Place)
Fort Lawn; Inc. Place; CHESTER; **230** B-8; elev. 556ft./169m.; [P]; **z** 29714; Ⓟ 718; © 864
Fort Mill; Inc. Place; YORK; **230** A-8; elev. 668ft./204m.; [P]; ★ **CHRLT**; **z** 29707-08, **z** 29715-16; Ⓟ 4,930; © 7,587
Fort Motte; RMC Place; CALHOUN; **230** E-8; elev. 125ft./38m.; [P]; **z** 29135; ● 150
Fountain Inn; Inc. Place; GREENVILLE, LAURENS; **230** B-5; elev. 872ft./266m.; [P]; ★ **GRNV**; **z** 29644; Ⓟ 4,388; © 6,017
Fountain Lake; RMC Place; ORANGEBURG; ***230** F-9; elev. 82ft./25m.; mail Eutawville **z** 29048; ● 150
Four Holes; RMC Place; ORANGEBURG; ***230** G-9; elev. 49ft./15m.; mail Holly Hill **z** 29059; rural
Four Mile; RMC Place; CHARLESTON; ***230** H-10; elev. 18ft./5m.; ★ **CHAS**; mail Mount Pleasant **z** 29464; ● 300
Fowler; RMC Place; WILLIAMSBURG; ***230** E-11; mail Kingstree **z** 29556; rural
Foxtown; RMC Place; AIKEN; ***230** E-6; elev. 483ft./147m.; mail Aiken **z** 29801; rural
Foxwood Hills; RMC Place; OCONEE; ***230** C-2; elev. 823ft./251m.; mail Westminster **z** 29693; ● 500
Fraserville; RMC Place; GEORGETOWN; ***230** F-12; elev. 21ft./6m.; mail Pawleys Island **z** 29585; ● 200
Freemont; RMC Place; HORRY; ***230** D-13; mail Longs **z** 29568; rural
Friarsgate; RMC Place; LEXINGTON; ★ **COL**; mail Irmo **z** 29063; pop. incl. with Irmo (Inc. Place)
Friendfield; RMC Place; FLORENCE; ***230** D-11; mail Scranton **z** 29591; rural

Entries in **UPPERCASE** are counties.
Entries in **bold** have populations of 2,500 or more.
Names in parentheses are alternate names.

Inc. Place	Incorporated Place
RMC Place	Rand McNally Designated Place
CDP	Census Designated Place
MCD	Minor Civil Division

⊡ County Seat
▲ Minor Civil Division
elev. Elevation
[P] Post Office
[H] Hospital
[C] College
■ Principal Business Center
★ Ranally Metro Area (RMA) Abbreviation
z Zip Code(s)
Ⓟ Previous Census Population
Ⓡ Revised Census Population
Ⓐ Annexation Population
● Rand McNally Population Estimate
© Final Census Population
Ⓢ Special Census Population
◆ Estimated Population

For additional definitions see Glossary, Volume 1, and Introduction, Volume 2.

Friendship; RMC Place; OCONEE; *230 B-3; elev. 870ft./265m.; mail Seneca z 29678; ● 45
Fripp Island; RMC Place; BEAUFORT; *230 I-9; elev. 10ft./3m.; [P]; z 29920; summer pop. 500; ● 150
Frogmore (Saint Helena Island); RMC Place; BEAUFORT; 230 I-8; mail Saint Helena Island z 29920; ● 300
Fruit Hill; RMC Place; SALUDA; *230 E-5; elev. 526ft./160m.; mail Saluda z 29138; rural
Furman; Inc. Place; HAMPTON; 230 H-7; elev. 112ft./34m.; [P]; z 29921; Ⓟ 260; © 286

G

Gable; RMC Place; CLARENDON; 230 E-10; elev. 101ft./31m.; [P]; z 29051; ● 200
Gadsden; RMC Place; RICHLAND; 230 E-8; elev. 150ft./46m.; [P]; ★ COL; z 29052; ● 300
Gadsden Village; RMC Place; CHARLESTON; ★ CHAS; pop. incl. with Charleston (Inc. Place)
Gaffney; Inc. Place; ⊡ CHEROKEE; 230 A-6; elev. 769ft./234m.; [P] [H] [C] 3,264; z 29340-42; Ⓟ 13,145; © 12,968
Gaillard Crossroads; RMC Place; SUMTER; *230 D-9; elev. 283ft./86m.; ★ SUMT; mail Dalzell z 29040; rural
Galaxy; RMC Place; RICHLAND; ★ COL; mail Columbia z 29209; pop. incl. with Columbia (Inc. Place)
Galivants Ferry; RMC Place; HORRY; 230 D-12; [P]; z 29544; ● 180
Gantt; CDP; GREENVILLE; 230 J-4; elev. 285ft./87m.; ★ GRNV; mail Greenville z 29605; Ⓟ 13,891; © 13,962
Gapway; RMC Place; MARION; *230 D-12; elev. 96ft./29m.; mail Mullins z 29574
Garden City; CDP-Census Area Only; HORRY; *230 F-12; elev. 20ft./6m.; ★ MYR.B; mail Murrells Inlet z 29576; Ⓟ 6,305; © 9,357
Garden City Beach; RMC Place; HORRY; 230 F-12; ★ MYR.B; mail Murrells Inlet z 29576; summer pop. 2,000; ● 1,100
Gardens Corner; RMC Place; BEAUFORT; *230 I-8; elev. 22ft./7m.; mail Yemassee z 29945
Garnett; RMC Place; HAMPTON; *230 H-7; [P]; z 29922; ● 110
Gaston; Inc. Place; LEXINGTON; 230 E-7; [P]; ★ COL; z 29053; Ⓟ 984; © 1,304
Gatewood; RMC Place; SPARTANBURG; *230 B-5; ★ SPRT; mail Roebuck z 29376; ● 85
Gayle Mill; CDP-Census Area Only; CHESTER; *230 B-7; mail Chester z 29706; Ⓟ 1,037; © 1,094
Gem Lake Estates; RMC Place; AIKEN; *230 F-6; elev. 503ft./153m.; ★ AUG; mail Aiken z 29803; ● 300
Georgetown; Inc. Place; ⊡ GEORGETOWN; 230 F-12; elev. 18ft./5m.; [P] [H]; z 29440, z 29442; Ⓟ 9,517; © 8,950; Ⓡ 8,979
Georgetown; RMC Place; PICKENS; *230 B-4; elev. 285ft./87m.; ★ GRNV; mail Easley z 29640; ● 250
GEORGETOWN; 230 F-11; Ⓟ 46,302; © 55,797; ◆ 61,282
Gifford; Inc. Place; HAMPTON; 230 H-7; elev. 139ft./42m.; [P]; z 29923; Ⓟ 313; © 370
Gilbert; Inc. Place; LEXINGTON; 230 E-7; elev. 529ft./161m.; [P]; ★ COL; z 29054; Ⓟ 324; © 500
Gillisonville; RMC Place; JASPER; 230 H-7; mail Ridgeland z 29936; ● 200
Givhans; RMC Place; DORCHESTER; 230 G-9; elev. 54ft./16m.; mail Ridgeville z 29472; ● 200
Glass Hill; RMC Place; HORRY; *230 E-12; elev. 20ft./6m.; ★ MYR.B; mail Conway z 29526; ● 150
Glendale; RMC Place; SPARTANBURG; 230 B-5; [P]; ★ SPRT; z 29346; ● 1,000
Glenn Springs; RMC Place; SPARTANBURG; 230 B-5; [P]; z 29374; ● 110
Gloverville; CDP; AIKEN; 230 F-5; [P]; ★ AUG; z 29828; Ⓟ 2,753; © 2,805
Gluck; RMC Place; ANDERSON; *230 C-3; ★ AND; mail Anderson z 29624
Glymphville; RMC Place; NEWBERRY; *230 C-6; mail Pomaria z 29126
Godsey; RMC Place; GREENWOOD; *230 D-5; mail Ninety Six z 29666; rural
Golden Grove; CDP; GREENVILLE; 230 B-4; ★ GRNV; mail Piedmont z 29673; Ⓟ 2,055; © 2,348
Golightly; RMC Place; SPARTANBURG; *230 B-5; ★ SPRT; mail Spartanburg z 29302; rural
Gooches; RMC Place; LANCASTER; *230 B-8; mail Lancaster z 29720; ● 350
Good Hope (Mayson); RMC Place; SALUDA; *230 D-5; elev. 521ft./159m.; mail Saluda z 29138
Goodwins Crossroads; RMC Place; LAURENS; *230 C-5; elev. 604ft./184m.; mail Clinton z 29325; rural
Goose Creek; Inc. Place; BERKELEY, CHARLESTON; 230 G-10; [P]; ★ CHAS; z 29445; Ⓟ 24,692; © 29,208; ◆ 41,468
Goretown; RMC Place; HORRY; 230 D-13; mail Loris z 29569; ● 110
Goshen Hill; RMC Place; UNION; *230 C-6; mail Whitmire z 29178; rural
Goucher; RMC Place; CHEROKEE; *230 A-6; mail Gaffney z 29340; rural
Gourdin; RMC Place; WILLIAMSBURG; *230 F-10; elev. 70ft./21m.; mail Lane z 29564
Govan; Inc. Place; BAMBERG; 230 G-7; elev. 244ft./74m.; mail Olar z 29843; Ⓟ 84; © 67
Gowensville; RMC Place; GREENVILLE; *230 A-4; ★ GRNV; mail Campobello z 29322, Landrum z 29356
Grace (Grace Bleachery); RMC Place; LANCASTER; 230 B-8; mail Lancaster z 29720; ● 300
Grace Bleachery; LANCASTER; see Grace (RMC Place)
Grahamville; RMC Place; HORRY; *230 E-13; elev. 43ft./13m.; mail Conway z 29526; rural
Grahamville; RMC Place; JASPER; 230 I-8; elev. 58ft./18m.; mail Ridgeland z 29936; ● 250
Gramling; RMC Place; SPARTANBURG; *230 A-5; elev. 989ft./301m.; [P]; ★ SPRT; z 29348; ● 350
Graniteville; RMC Place; AIKEN; 230 F-5; elev. 227ft./69m.; [P]; ★ AUG; z 29829; ● 1,100
Grassy Pond; RMC Place; CHEROKEE; *230 A-6; mail Gaffney z 29341; rural
Graves; RMC Place; GEORGETOWN; 230 F-11; elev. 21ft./6m.; mail Georgetown z 29440; ● 200
Gray Court; Inc. Place; LAURENS; 230 C-5; [P]; z 29645; Ⓟ 914; © 1,021
Grays; RMC Place; JASPER; *230 H-7; elev. 94ft./29m.; mail Early Branch z 29916
Grays Hill; RMC Place; BEAUFORT; *230 I-8; elev. 40ft./12m.; mail Beaufort z 29906; rural
Great Falls; Inc. Place; CHESTER; 230 C-8; elev. 467ft./142m.; [P]; z 29055; Ⓟ 2,307; © 2,194
Greeleyville; Inc. Place; WILLIAMSBURG; 230 F-10; elev. 79ft./24m.; [P]; z 29056; Ⓟ 464; © 452
Green Acres; RMC Place; ANDERSON; *230 C-3; ★ AND; mail Anderson z 29621; ● 100
Green Bay; RMC Place; BERKELEY; *230 G-11; elev. 32ft./10m.; mail Huger z 29450; ● 40
Greenbriar; RMC Place; OCONEE; *230 B-3; elev. 860ft./262m.; mail Seneca z 29678; rural
Greenbrier; RMC Place; FAIRFIELD; *230 C-7; elev. 550ft./168m.; mail Winnsboro z 29180; rural
Greenlawn; RMC Place; RICHLAND; ★ COL; pop. incl. with Columbia (Inc. Place)
Green Pond; RMC Place; COLLETON; 230 H-8; elev. 31ft./9m.; [P]; z 29446; ● 200
Green Pond; RMC Place; SPARTANBURG; *230 B-5; elev. 794ft./242m.; mail Woodruff z 29388; rural
Green Sea; RMC Place; HORRY; 230 D-12; [P]; z 29545; ● 200
Greenview; RMC Place; RICHLAND; *230 D-7; elev. 300ft./91m.; ★ COL; mail Columbia z 29203; pop. incl. with Columbia (Inc. Place)
Greenville; Inc. Place; ⊡ GREENVILLE; 230 B-4; [P] [H] [C] 6,695 ■; ★ GRNV; z 29601-17, z 29698; Ⓟ 58,282; © 56,002; Ⓡ 55,988; ◆ 60,548
GREENVILLE; 230 B-4; Ⓟ 320,167; © 379,616; Ⓡ 379,612; ◆ 450,222
Greenwood; Inc. Place; ⊡ GREENWOOD; 230 D-5; elev. 665ft./203m.; [P] [H] [C] 2,642 ■; ★ GREEN; z 29646-49; Ⓟ 20,807; © 22,071; Ⓡ 22,228; ◆ 21,888
GREENWOOD; 230 D-5; Ⓟ 59,567; © 66,271; Ⓡ 66,272; ◆ 68,298
Greenwood Shores; RMC Place; GREENWOOD; *230 D-5; mail Ninety Six z 29666; ● 300
Greer; Inc. Place; GREENVILLE, SPARTANBURG; 230 B-4; elev. 1,016ft./310m.; [P] [H]; ★ GRNV; z 29650-52; Ⓟ 10,322; © 16,843; ◆ 23,803
Grenadier; RMC Place; LEXINGTON; *230 D-7; elev. 250ft./76m.; ★ COL; mail Columbia z 29210; ● 2,000
Gresham; RMC Place; MARION; 230 E-11; elev. 51ft./16m.; [P]; z 29546; ● 200
Grice Ferry; RMC Place; MARION; *230 D-12; elev. 40ft./12m.; mail Mullins z 29574; rural
Grove Creek Village; RMC Place; CHARLESTON; *230 H-10; ★ CHAS; pop. incl. with Charleston (Inc. Place)
Grove Park; RMC Place; FLORENCE; *230 D-10; elev. 40ft./12m.; ★ FLO; mail Florence z 29501; ● 550
Grover; RMC Place; DORCHESTER; 230 G-8; elev. 86ft./26m.; [P]; z 29447; ● 180
Guess; RMC Place; CHESTERFIELD; *230 B-9; elev. 536ft./163m.; mail Mount Croghan z 29727; rural
Gurley; RMC Place; HORRY; 230 D-12; elev. 106ft./32m.; mail Loris z 29569; ● 100
Guthries (Guthriesville); RMC Place; YORK; 230 B-7; mail Mc Connells z 29726; ● 50
Guthriesville; YORK; see Guthries (RMC Place)

H

Hagood; RMC Place; SUMTER; 230 D-8; elev. 156ft./48m.; mail Rembert z 29128; ● 50
Hamburg; RMC Place; AIKEN; *230 F-5; ★ AUG; mail North Augusta z 29841; pop. incl. with North Augusta (Inc. Place)
Hamer; RMC Place; DILLON; 230 C-12; elev. 149ft./45m.; [P]; z 29547; ● 500
Hammond; RMC Place; ANDERSON; *230 C-4; elev. 817ft./249m.; ★ AND; mail Belton z 29627; rural
Hammond Crossroads; RMC Place; CALHOUN; *230 E-8; elev. 374ft./114m.; mail Saint Matthews z 29135; rural
Hampton; Inc. Place; ⊡ HAMPTON; 230 H-7; elev. 95ft./29m.; [P]; z 29924 & mail Crocketville z 29913; Ⓟ 2,997; © 2,837
HAMPTON; 230 H-7; Ⓟ 18,191; © 21,386; ◆ 21,379
Hampton Drive; RMC Place; COLLETON; *230 H-8; elev. 15ft./5m.; mail Walterboro z 29488; ● 100
Hampton Heights; RMC Place; GREENVILLE; *230 B-4; ★ GRNV; mail Taylors z 29687; ● 1,600
Hampton Park Terrace; RMC Place; CHARLESTON; ★ CHAS; mail Charleston z 29403; pop. incl. with Charleston (Inc. Place)
Hanahan; Inc. Place; BERKELEY; 230 H-10; elev. 37ft./11m.; [P]; ★ CHAS; z 29406, z 29410, z 29445; Ⓟ 13,176; © 12,937
H & B Village; RMC Place; HAMPTON; *230 H-7; mail Hampton z 29924; pop. incl. with Hampton (Inc. Place)
Hankinson; RMC Place; AIKEN; *230 F-5; mail Jackson z 29831; rural
Hannah; RMC Place; FLORENCE; 230 E-11; mail Pamplico z 29583; ● 50
Hanover Hills; RMC Place; OCONEE; *230 B-3; elev. 900ft./274m.; mail Seneca z 29672; ● 150
Harbison; RMC Place; RICHLAND; *230 D-7; ★ COL; mail Columbia z 29212; pop. incl. with Columbia (Inc. Place)
Harbour Town; RMC Place; BEAUFORT; 230 J-9; mail Hilton Head Island z 29928; pop. incl. with Hilton Head Island (Inc. Place)
Hardeeville; Inc. Place; JASPER; 230 I-7; elev. 20ft./6m.; [P]; z 29927; Ⓟ 1,583; © 1,793
Harleyville; Inc. Place; DORCHESTER; 230 G-9; elev. 92ft./28m.; [P]; z 29448; Ⓟ 633; © 594; Ⓡ 685
Harmony; RMC Place; EDGEFIELD; *230 E-5; elev. 637ft./194m.; mail Johnston z 29832; ● 25
Harmony; RMC Place; YORK; *230 B-8; ★ CHRLT; mail Catawba z 29704; rural
Harmony Hill; RMC Place; CHEROKEE; *230 A-6; elev. 750ft./229m.; mail Gaffney z 29341; ● 100
Harris; RMC Place; GREENWOOD; 230 D-4; elev. 675ft./206m.; ★ GREEN; mail Greenwood z 29646; ● 350
Hartsville; Inc. Place; DARLINGTON; 230 C-10; [P] [H] [C] 1,119; z 29550-51; Ⓟ 8,372; © 7,556
Harveytown; RMC Place; SPARTANBURG; *230 B-5; elev. 924ft./282m.; mail Lyman z 29365; pop. incl. with Duncan (Inc. Place)
Haskell Heights; RMC Place; RICHLAND; *230 D-7; elev. 250ft./76m.; ★ COL; mail Columbia z 29203; ● 1,000
Hayne; RMC Place; SPARTANBURG; *230 A-5; ★ SPRT; mail Spartanburg z 29303; ● 2,200
Hayne Station; RMC Place; SPARTANBURG; *230 B-5; ★ SPRT; mail Spartanburg z 29301
Hazelwood Acres; RMC Place; RICHLAND; *230 D-8; elev. 220ft./67m.; ★ COL; mail Columbia z 29209; ● 1,000
Healing Springs; RMC Place; BARNWELL; *230 F-7; mail Blackville z 29817; ● 120
Heatherwood; RMC Place; PICKENS; *230 B-4; elev. 300ft./91m.; ★ GRNV; mail Easley z 29642; pop. incl. with Clemson (Inc. Place)
Heathley Wood; RMC Place; SUMTER; *230 E-9; elev. 180ft./55m.; ★ SUMT; mail Sumter z 29150; pop. incl. with Sumter (Inc. Place)
Heath Springs; Inc. Place; LANCASTER; 230 C-8; elev. 687ft./209m.; [P]; z 29058; Ⓟ 907; © 864
Heathwood; RMC Place; CHARLESTON; *230 H-10; ★ CHAS; pop. incl. with Charleston (Inc. Place)
Hebron; RMC Place; WILLIAMSBURG; 230 E-10; elev. 81ft./25m.; mail Cades z 29518; ● 90
Helena; RMC Place; NEWBERRY; 230 D-6; mail Newberry z 29108; ● 300
Hemingway; Inc. Place; WILLIAMSBURG; 230 E-11; elev. 53ft./16m.; [P]; z 29554; Ⓟ 829; © 573
Hemlock; CHESTER; see Eureka Mill (CDP-Census Area Only)

Hendersonville; RMC Place; COLLETON; 230 H-8; elev. 44ft./13m.; mail Walterboro z 29488; ● 240
Hendricks Corner; RMC Place; HORRY; *230 E-12; elev. 36ft./11m.; mail Conway z 29526; rural
Hibernia; RMC Place; SALUDA; *230 E-6; mail Monetta z 29105; rural
Hickory Grove; RMC Place; FLORENCE; *230 D-10; elev. 40ft./12m.; ★ FLO; mail Florence z 29501; ● 100
Hickory Grove; RMC Place; HORRY; 230 E-12; mail Conway z 29526; ● 250
Hickory Grove; Inc. Place; YORK; 230 A-6; elev. 685ft./209m.; [P]; z 29717; Ⓟ 287; © 337
Hickory Hill; RMC Place; COLLETON; *230 H-8; elev. 20ft./6m.; mail Green Pond z 29446; ● 50
Hickory Hills; RMC Place; SPARTANBURG; *230 A-5; ★ SPRT; mail Inman z 29349; rural
Hickory Tavern; RMC Place; LAURENS; *230 C-5; elev. 732ft./223m.; mail Gray Court z 29645; ● 300
High Hill Crossroads; RMC Place; DILLON; *230 C-12; mail Lake View z 29563; rural
High Point; RMC Place; ANDERSON; *230 C-4; elev. 800ft./244m.; mail Belton z 29627; ● 50
Hilda; Inc. Place; BARNWELL; 230 F-7; [P]; z 29813; Ⓟ 342; © 436
Hillbrook Forest; RMC Place; SPARTANBURG; *230 B-5; ★ SPRT; mail Spartanburg z 29307; pop. incl. with Spartanburg (Inc. Place)
Hillcrest; RMC Place; SPARTANBURG; *230 B-5; ★ SPRT; mail Boiling Springs z 29318; pop. incl. with Spartanburg (Inc. Place)
Hillcrest Acres; RMC Place; ANDERSON; mail Belton z 29627; pop. incl. with Belton (Inc. Place)
Hillcrest Heights; RMC Place; ANDERSON; ★ GRNV; mail Williamston z 29697; pop. incl. with Williamston (Inc. Place)
Hilton; RMC Place; RICHLAND; *230 D-7; elev. 427ft./130m.; ★ COL; mail Chapin z 29036; rural
Hilton Head Island; Inc. Place; BEAUFORT; 230 J-10; [P] [H]; z 29925-26, z 29928, z 29938 & mail Daufuskie Island z 29915; Ⓟ 23,694; © 33,862; ◆ 38,582
Hobcaw Point; RMC Place; CHARLESTON; *230 H-10; elev. 15ft./5m.; ★ CHAS; mail Mount Pleasant z 29464; pop. incl. with Mount Pleasant (Inc. Place)
Hodges; Inc. Place; GREENWOOD; 230 D-4; [P]; ★ GREEN; z 29653, z 29695; Ⓟ 125; © 158; Ⓡ 165
Hollands Store; RMC Place; ANDERSON; *230 C-3; elev. 690ft./210m.; mail Starr z 29684; rural
Hollow Creek; RMC Place; LEXINGTON; *230 D-6; mail Gilbert z 29054; rural
Holly Hill; Inc. Place; ORANGEBURG; 230 F-9; elev. 108ft./33m.; [P]; z 29059; Ⓟ 1,478; © 1,281; Ⓡ 1,421
Holly Springs; RMC Place; OCONEE; *230 B-2; mail Westminster z 29693; ● 50
Holly Springs; RMC Place; SPARTANBURG; *230 A-5; elev. 928ft./283m.; ★ SPRT; mail Inman z 29349; ● 200
Hollywood; Inc. Place; CHARLESTON; 230 H-9; [P]; ★ CHAS; z 29449; Ⓟ 2,094; © 3,946; Ⓡ 3,879
Hollywood; RMC Place; SALUDA; *230 D-6; elev. 448ft./137m.; mail Saluda z 29138; rural
Hollywood Hills; RMC Place; RICHLAND; *230 D-7; elev. 250ft./76m.; ★ COL; mail Columbia z 29203; ● 950
Holmsville; RMC Place; DILLON; *230 D-12; elev. 92ft./28m.; mail Lake View z 29563; rural
Holtson Crossroads; RMC Place; SALUDA; *230 E-6; elev. 547ft./167m.; mail Batesburg z 29006; ● 40
Homeland Park; CDP; ANDERSON; *230 C-3; ★ AND; mail Anderson z 29621; Ⓟ 6,569; © 6,337
Homewood; RMC Place; HORRY; 230 E-12; elev. 34ft./10m.; ★ MYR.B; mail Conway z 29526; ● 300
Homewood Park; RMC Place; CHESTERFIELD; *230 B-10; elev. 152ft./46m.; mail Cheraw z 29520; ● 100
Honea Path; Inc. Place; ANDERSON, ABBEVILLE; 230 C-4; [P]; z 29654; Ⓟ 3,841; © 3,504
Honey Hill; RMC Place; BERKELEY; 230 G-11; elev. 45ft./14m.; mail Saint Stephen z 29479; ● 110
Hoodtown; RMC Place; YORK; *230 B-6; mail Sharon z 29742; rural
Hopewell; RMC Place; YORK; *230 B-6; elev. 586ft./179m.; mail Hickory Grove z 29717; rural
Hopkins; RMC Place; RICHLAND; 230 E-8; [P]; ★ COL; z 29061; ● 1,600
Horatio; RMC Place; SUMTER; 230 D-8; elev. 144ft./44m.; [P]; ★ SUMT; z 29062; ● 300
Horrel Hill; RMC Place; RICHLAND; 230 E-8; elev. 364ft./111m.; ★ COL; mail Hopkins z 29061; ● 60
Horry; RMC Place; HORRY; *230 E-12; elev. 85ft./26m.; mail Aynor z 29511; ● 40
HORRY; 230 D-12; Ⓟ 144,053; © 196,629; ◆ 272,531
Horsegall; RMC Place; HAMPTON; *230 H-7; elev. 88ft./27m.; mail Varnville z 29944; rural
Howard; RMC Place; HORRY; *230 D-13; mail Loris z 29569
Hudsontown; RMC Place; DORCHESTER; *230 G-8; elev. 98ft./30m.; mail Saint George z 29477; ● 100
Huger; RMC Place; BERKELEY; 230 G-10; elev. 26ft./8m.; [P]; z 29450; ● 40
Hunley Park; RMC Place; CHARLESTON; *230 H-10; ★ CHAS; mail Charleston AFB z 29404; pop. incl. with North Charleston (Inc. Place)
Huntington Estates; RMC Place; EDGEFIELD; *230 F-5; elev. 400ft./122m.; ★ AUG; mail North Augusta z 29860; ● 100
Huntington Woods; RMC Place; CHARLESTON; *230 H-10; ★ CHAS; pop. incl. with Charleston (Inc. Place)
Hyman; RMC Place; FLORENCE; 230 D-11; mail Pamplico z 29583; ● 100

I

Independents; RMC Place; RICHLAND; *230 E-8; elev. 224ft./68m.; ★ COL; mail Columbia z 29209; ● 200
India Hook; CDP; YORK; *230 A-7; elev. 647ft./197m.; ★ CHRLT; mail Rock Hill z 29732; Ⓟ 1,506; © 1,614
Indiantown; RMC Place; WILLIAMSBURG; 230 E-11; elev. 59ft./18m.; mail Hemingway z 29554; ● 30
Industrial; RMC Place; YORK; *230 B-7; ★ CHRLT; mail Rock Hill z 29730; pop. incl. with Rock Hill (Inc. Place)
Ingleside; RMC Place; SPARTANBURG; *230 A-5; elev. 300ft./91m.; ★ SPRT; mail Landrum z 29356; ● 50
Inman; Inc. Place; SPARTANBURG; 230 A-5; elev. 986ft./301m.; [P]; ★ SPRT; z 29349; Ⓟ 1,742; © 1,884
Inman Mills; CDP; SPARTANBURG; 230 A-5; ★ SPRT; mail Inman z 29349; Ⓟ 1,571; © 1,151
Irby; RMC Place; LAURENS; *230 C-5; mail Laurens z 29360; pop. incl. with Laurens (Inc. Place)
Irmo; Inc. Place; LEXINGTON, RICHLAND; 230 D-7; [P]; z 29063; Ⓟ 11,280; © 11,039
Irvines Landing; RMC Place; GREENWOOD; *230 D-5; ★ GREEN; mail Greenwood z 29649; ● 400
Irwin (Erwin); CDP-Census Area Only; LANCASTER; *230 B-8; mail Lancaster z 29720; Ⓟ 1,296; © 1,343
Isgett Circle; RMC Place; CHESTERFIELD; *230 B-10; elev. 171ft./52m.; mail Cheraw z 29520; ● 50
Islandton; RMC Place; COLLETON; 230 H-8; elev. 61ft./19m.; [P]; z 29929; ● 100
Isle of Palms; Inc. Place; CHARLESTON; 230 H-10; [P]; ★ CHAS; z 29451; Ⓟ 3,680; © 4,583
Italy; RMC Place; GEORGETOWN; *230 F-11; elev. 25ft./8m.; mail Andrews z 29510; ● 80
Iva; Inc. Place; ANDERSON; 230 C-3; [P]; z 29655; Ⓟ 1,174; © 1,156

J

Jackson; Inc. Place; AIKEN; 230 F-5; elev. 204ft./62m.; [P]; z 29831; Ⓟ 1,681; © 1,625
Jacksonboro; RMC Place; COLLETON; 230 H-9; [P]; z 29452; ● 500
Jackson Mill; RMC Place; SPARTANBURG; *230 B-5; mail Wellford z 29385; pop. incl. with Wellford (Inc. Place)
Jacksonville; RMC Place; AIKEN; *230 F-5; ★ AUG; mail Langley z 29834; ● 130
Jalapa; RMC Place; NEWBERRY; *230 C-6; elev. 563ft./172m.; mail Newberry z 29108
James Island; CHARLESTON; see Centerville (RMC Place)
Jamestown; Inc. Place; BERKELEY; 230 F-11; elev. 40ft./12m.; [P]; z 29453; Ⓟ 84; © 97
Jamestown; RMC Place; HORRY; *230 E-12; ★ MYR.B; mail Conway z 29526; pop. incl. with Conway (Inc. Place)
Jamison; RMC Place; ORANGEBURG; 230 F-8; mail Orangeburg z 29115, Saint Matthews z 29135; ● 100
JASPER; 230 I-7; Ⓟ 15,487; © 20,678; ◆ 22,739
Jedburg; RMC Place; DORCHESTER; 230 G-9; elev. 63ft./19m.; ★ CHAS; mail Summerville z 29483; ● 200
Jefferson; Inc. Place; CHESTERFIELD; 230 B-9; elev. 454ft./138m.; [P]; z 29718; Ⓟ 745; © 704
Jenkinsville; RMC Place; FAIRFIELD; 230 D-7; [P]; z 29065; ● 250
Jennys; RMC Place; ALLENDALE; *230 G-7; elev. 42ft./13m.; mail Fairfax z 29827; rural
Jericho; RMC Place; CHARLESTON; *230 H-9; elev. 42ft./13m.; [P]; z 29426; ● 60
Joanna; CDP; LAURENS; 230 C-5; elev. 607ft./185m.; [P]; z 29351; Ⓟ 1,735; © 1,609
Jocassee; RMC Place; OCONEE; 230 A-3; elev. 1,100ft./335m.; mail Salem z 29676; ● 60
Johns Island; RMC Place; CHARLESTON; 230 H-10; [P]; ★ CHAS; z 29455, z 29457; pop. incl. with Charleston (Inc. Place)
Johnson City; RMC Place; SPARTANBURG; *230 B-5; elev. 868ft./265m.; ★ SPRT; mail Spartanburg z 29301
Johnson Crossroads; RMC Place; AIKEN; *230 F-6; elev. 415ft./126m.; ★ AUG; mail Williston z 29853; ● 50
Johnsonville; Inc. Place; FLORENCE; 230 E-11; elev. 94ft./29m.; [P]; z 29555; Ⓟ 1,415; © 1,418
Johnston; Inc. Place; EDGEFIELD; 230 E-5; elev. 661ft./201m.; [P]; z 29832; Ⓟ 2,688; © 2,336; Ⓡ 2,400
Johnstown; RMC Place; AIKEN; *230 F-5; ★ AUG; mail Bath z 29816
Johnsville; RMC Place; COLLETON; *230 G-8; elev. 123ft./37m.; mail Smoaks z 29481; rural
Jollystreet; RMC Place; NEWBERRY; *230 D-6; mail Prosperity z 29127; rural
Jones Crossroads; RMC Place; AIKEN; *230 E-6; elev. 591ft./180m.; mail Monetta z 29105; rural
Jones Crossroads; RMC Place; LANCASTER; *230 B-8; mail Lancaster z 29720; ● 50
Jonesville; Inc. Place; UNION; 230 B-6; elev. 682ft./208m.; [P]; z 29353, z 29395; Ⓟ 1,205; © 982
Jordan; RMC Place; CLARENDON; 230 F-9; elev. 125ft./38m.; mail Manning z 29102; ● 50
Jordania; RMC Place; OCONEE; mail Seneca z 29678
Jordanville; RMC Place; HORRY; *230 E-12; elev. 31ft./9m.; mail Galivants Ferry z 29544; ● 40
Judson; CDP-Census Area Only; GREENVILLE; 230 J-4; ★ GRNV; mail Greenville z 29611; Ⓟ 2,859; © 2,456
Judson Number 2; RMC Place; GREENVILLE; *230 B-4; elev. 315ft./96m.; ★ GRNV; mail Greenville z 29611; ● 900
Juniper Bay; RMC Place; HORRY; *230 E-12; elev. 71ft./22m.; mail Conway z 29527; ● 35

K

Kathwood; RMC Place; AIKEN; *230 F-5; mail Jackson z 29831; rural
Kathwood; RMC Place; LEXINGTON; *230 D-7; ★ COL; mail West Columbia z 29169; pop. incl. with West Columbia (Inc. Place)
Kelly; RMC Place; UNION; *230 B-6; elev. 700ft./213m.; mail Union z 29379; rural
Kellytown; RMC Place; DARLINGTON; *230 C-10; mail Hartsville z 29550; ● 200
Kelton; RMC Place; UNION; 230 B-6; [P]; z 29353; ● 150
Kemper; RMC Place; DILLON; 230 C-12; mail Lake View z 29563; ● 60
Kensington; RMC Place; GEORGETOWN; 230 F-12; mail Georgetown z 29440; ● 600
Keowee; RMC Place; ABBEVILLE; *230 C-4; elev. 768ft./234m.; mail Honea Path z 29654; rural
Keowee; RMC Place; OCONEE; *230 B-3; mail Seneca z 29672; ● 65
Kershaw; Inc. Place; LANCASTER; 230 C-8; elev. 522ft./159m.; [P]; z 29067; Ⓟ 1,814; © 1,645
KERSHAW; 230 C-9; Ⓟ 43,599; © 52,647; ◆ 60,335
Ketchuptown; RMC Place; HORRY; *230 D-12; elev. 64ft./20m.; mail Nichols z 29581; ● 30
Keystone Acres; RMC Place; ANDERSON; *230 C-3; ★ AND; mail Anderson z 29621; ● 45
Kiawah Island; Inc. Place; CHARLESTON; 230 I-10; elev. 10ft./3m.; [P]; z 29455; Ⓟ 718; © 1,163
Kilbourn Park; RMC Place; RICHLAND; ★ COL; pop. incl. with Columbia (Inc. Place)
Kilgore; RMC Place; SPARTANBURG; *230 B-5; elev. 697ft./212m.; mail Enoree z 29335
Killian; RMC Place; RICHLAND; *230 D-8; ★ COL; mail Columbia z 29203; rural
Kimberly Woods; RMC Place; YORK; *230 A-7; ★ CHRLT; mail Rock Hill z 29732; ● 110
Kinards; RMC Place; NEWBERRY; 230 C-6; elev. 592ft./180m.; [P]; z 29355; ● 250
King Circle; RMC Place; LANCASTER; *230 B-8; elev. 500ft./152m.; mail Lancaster z 29720; ● 150

Kingsburg; RMC Place; FLORENCE; *230 E-11; elev. 74ft./23m.; mail Johnsonville z 29555; ● 150
Kings Creek; RMC Place; CHEROKEE; 230 A-6; [P]; z 29702; ● 200
Kingstree; Inc. Place; ⊡ WILLIAMSBURG; 230 E-10; [P] [H]; z 29556; Ⓟ 3,858; © 3,496; Ⓡ 3,617
Kingswood; RMC Place; RICHLAND; *230 D-7; elev. 250ft./76m.; ★ COL; mail Columbia z 29210; ● 2,100
Kirkland; RMC Place; KERSHAW; *230 D-8; elev. 295ft./90m.; mail Camden z 29020; ● 100
Kirksey; RMC Place; GREENWOOD; 230 D-5; mail Troy z 29848; ● 60
Kitchings Mill; RMC Place; AIKEN; *230 F-6; mail Salley z 29137; rural
Kline; Inc. Place; BARNWELL; 230 G-7; [P]; z 29812; Ⓟ 285; © 238
Klondike Crossroads; RMC Place; HORRY; *230 E-12; mail Conway z 29526-27; ● 200
Kneece (Baxter); RMC Place; LEXINGTON; *230 E-6; elev. 546ft./166m.; mail Batesburg z 29006; rural
Knightsville; RMC Place; DORCHESTER; *230 G-9; elev. 65ft./20m.; [P]; ★ CHAS; z 29483; ● 800
Knollwood Acres; RMC Place; MARLBORO; *230 B-11; elev. 175ft./53m.; mail Bennettsville z 29512; ● 100
Knox; RMC Place; CHESTER; *230 B-7; elev. 563ft./172m.; mail Chester z 29706; rural

L

Ladson; CDP; BERKELEY, CHARLESTON; 230 G-10; elev. 44ft./13m.; [P]; ★ CHAS; z 29456, z 29485; Ⓟ 13,540; © 13,264
La France; RMC Place; ANDERSON; 230 C-3; elev. 761ft./232m.; [P]; ★ AND; z 29656; ● 900
Lake City; Inc. Place; FLORENCE; 230 E-10; elev. 77ft./23m.; [P] [H]; z 29560; Ⓟ 7,153; © 6,478
Lake Forest; RMC Place; GREENVILLE; 230 I-5; ★ GRNV; mail Greenville z 29606; ● 1,000
Lake Forest; RMC Place; PICKENS; *230 B-4; elev. 285ft./87m.; ★ GRNV; mail Easley z 29642; ● 40
Lake Forest Estates; RMC Place; EDGEFIELD; *230 F-5; elev. 322ft./98m.; ★ AUG; mail North Augusta z 29860; ● 200
Lake Lanier; RMC Place; GREENVILLE; *230 A-4; elev. 360ft./110m.; mail Landrum z 29356; summer pop. 400; ● 200
Lakemont; RMC Place; GREENVILLE; *230 A-3; mail Cleveland z 29635; summer pop. 100; ● 30
Lake Murray of Richland; CDP-Census Area Only; RICHLAND; *230 D-7; ★ COL; © 3,526
Lake Murray Shores; RMC Place; SALUDA; *230 D-6; mail Leesville z 29070; ● 200
Lake Secession; CDP-Census Area Only; ABBEVILLE; *230 D-4; © 928
Lake Shores; RMC Place; GREENWOOD; *230 D-5; ★ GREEN; mail Greenwood z 29649; ● 500
Lakeview; RMC Place; CHESTER; 230 B-8; elev. 479ft./146m.; mail Fort Lawn z 29714; ● 50
Lake View; Inc. Place; DILLON; 230 C-12; [P]; z 29563; Ⓟ 872; © 789
Lakeview Manor; RMC Place; SPARTANBURG; *230 A-5; elev. 240ft./73m.; ★ SPRT; mail Spartanburg z 29303; ● 150
Lakewood; CDP-Census Area Only; SUMTER; *230 E-9; ★ SUMT; © 2,603
Lakewood; RMC Place; YORK; *230 A-7; ★ CHRLT; mail Rock Hill z 29732; ● 500
Lake Wylie; CDP; YORK; 230 A-7; elev. 680ft./207m.; [P]; ★ CHRLT; z 29710; Ⓟ 2,599; © 3,061
Lamar; Inc. Place; DARLINGTON; 230 D-10; [P]; z 29069; Ⓟ 1,125; © 1,015
Lambertown (Saint Delight); RMC Place; GEORGETOWN; *230 F-11; elev. 34ft./10m.; mail Andrews z 29510; ● 300
Lambs; RMC Place; CHARLESTON; *230 H-10; ★ CHAS; mail North Charleston z 29405; pop. incl. with North Charleston (Inc. Place)
Lancaster; Inc. Place; ⊡ LANCASTER; 230 B-8; [P] [H]; z 29720-22; Ⓟ 8,914; © 8,177
LANCASTER; 230 B-8; Ⓟ 54,516; © 61,351; ◆ 77,141
Lancaster Mill; CDP-Census Area Only; LANCASTER; *230 B-8; mail Lancaster z 29720; Ⓟ 2,373; © 2,109
Lando; RMC Place; CHESTER; 230 B-7; [P]; z 29724; ● 300
Landrum; Inc. Place; SPARTANBURG; 230 A-5; [P]; z 29356; Ⓟ 2,347; © 2,472
Lands End; RMC Place; BEAUFORT; *230 I-8; mail Saint Helena Island z 29920
Landsford; RMC Place; CHESTER; *230 B-8; elev. 607ft./185m.; mail Catawba z 29704; rural
Lane; Inc. Place; WILLIAMSBURG; 230 F-10; elev. 70ft./21m.; [P]; z 29564; Ⓟ 523; © 585
Lanford; RMC Place; LAURENS; *230 C-5; elev. 638ft./194m.; mail Enoree z 29335; ● 50
Langley; RMC Place; AIKEN; *230 F-5; elev. 174ft./53m.; [P]; ★ AUG; z 29834; ● 1,700
Larkin; RMC Place; SPARTANBURG; *230 B-5; elev. 225ft./69m.; ★ SPRT; mail Startex z 29377; ● 100
Lathem; RMC Place; PICKENS; *230 B-4; ★ GRNV; mail Easley z 29640
Latimer; RMC Place; ABBEVILLE; *230 D-4; elev. 550ft./168m.; mail Calhoun Falls z 29628; rural
Latta; Inc. Place; DILLON; 230 C-11; [P]; z 29565; Ⓟ 1,565; © 1,410
Laurel Bay (Capehart); CDP; BEAUFORT; 230 I-8; mail Beaufort z 29902, z 29906; Ⓟ 4,972; © 6,625
Laurens; Inc. Place; ⊡ LAURENS; 230 C-5; [P]; z 29360; Ⓟ 9,694; © 9,916
LAURENS; 230 C-5; Ⓟ 58,092; © 69,567; Ⓡ 69,553; ◆ 68,090
Leawood; RMC Place; GREENVILLE; *230 B-4; ★ GRNV; mail Greenville z 29609; ● 700
Lebanon; RMC Place; ANDERSON; *230 C-3; ★ AND; mail Anderson z 29621, Pendleton z 29670; rural
Lebanon; RMC Place; FAIRFIELD; *230 C-7; elev. 524ft./160m.; mail Winnsboro z 29180
LEE; 230 D-9; Ⓟ 18,437; © 20,119; ◆ 19,869
Leeds; RMC Place; CHESTER; 230 C-6; elev. 386ft./118m.; mail Carlisle z 29031; ● 70
Leesburg; RMC Place; RICHLAND; *230 D-8; ★ COL; mail Columbia z 29209, z 29290; pop. incl. with Columbia (Inc. Place)
Leesville; RMC Place; LEXINGTON; *230 E-6; elev. 656ft./200m.; [P]; z 29070; pop. incl. with Batesburg-Leesville (Inc. Place)
Legareville; RMC Place; CHARLESTON; *230 H-10; elev. 15ft./5m.; mail Johns Island z 29455; rural
Lena; RMC Place; HAMPTON; 230 H-7; elev. 111ft./34m.; mail Estill z 29918; ● 100
Leo; RMC Place; FLORENCE; *230 E-11; elev. 62ft./19m.; mail Lake City z 29560; ● 40
Leslie; YORK; see Lesslie (CDP)
Lesslie (Leslie); CDP; YORK; 230 B-8; ★ CHRLT; mail Rock Hill z 29730; © 2,268
Lester; RMC Place; MARLBORO; *230 B-11; mail Bennettsville z 29512; ● 50
Level Land; RMC Place; ABBEVILLE; *230 C-4; mail Iva z 29655
Lewis; RMC Place; CHESTER; 230 B-7; mail Chester z 29706; ● 35
Lewis Crossroads; RMC Place; DARLINGTON; *230 C-10; mail Darlington z 29532; rural
Lexington; Inc. Place; ⊡ LEXINGTON; 230 D-7; elev. 392ft./119m.; [P]; ★ COL; z 29071-73; Ⓟ 3,289; © 9,793
LEXINGTON; 230 E-6; Ⓟ 167,611; © 216,014; ◆ 249,272
Liberty; Inc. Place; PICKENS; 230 B-3; elev. 1,005ft./306m.; [P]; z 29657; Ⓟ 3,228; © 3,009
Liberty Hill; RMC Place; CHARLESTON; *230 H-10; ★ CHAS; mail Charleston z 29406; pop. incl. with North Charleston (Inc. Place)
Liberty Hill; RMC Place; KERSHAW; 230 C-8; elev. 571ft./174m.; [P]; z 29074; ● 160
Liberty Hill; RMC Place; MCCORMICK; *230 E-5; elev. 450ft./137m.; mail Mc Cormick z 29835; rural
Lima; RMC Place; GREENVILLE; *230 A-4; ★ GRNV; mail Tigerville z 29688; rural
Limehouse; RMC Place; JASPER; *230 J-7; mail Hardeeville z 29927; ● 300
Limestone; RMC Place; ORANGEBURG; *230 E-8; elev. 97ft./30m.; mail Orangeburg z 29118; rural
Lincoln Shire; RMC Place; RICHLAND; *230 D-7; elev. 250ft./76m.; ★ COL; mail Columbia z 29203; ● 1,400
Lincolnville; Inc. Place; CHARLESTON; *230 G-10; [P]; ★ CHAS; z 29485; Ⓟ 716; © 904
Lions Beach; RMC Place; BERKELEY; *230 G-10; elev. 80ft./24m.; ★ CHAS; mail Moncks Corner z 29461; ● 500
Litchfield Beach; RMC Place; GEORGETOWN; 230 F-12; elev. 12ft./4m.; mail Pawleys Island z 29585; ● 500
Little Africa; RMC Place; SPARTANBURG; *230 A-5; ★ SPRT; mail Chesnee z 29323; ● 50
Little Camden; RMC Place; RICHLAND; ★ COL; mail Columbia z 29201
Little Chicago; RMC Place; SPARTANBURG; *230 A-5; elev. 330ft./101m.; ★ SPRT; mail Campobello z 29322; rural
Little Eastatoe; RMC Place; PICKENS; *230 B-3; elev. 900ft./274m.; mail Sunset z 29685; rural
Little Mountain; Inc. Place; NEWBERRY; 230 D-6; [P]; z 29075; Ⓟ 235; © 255
Little River; CDP; HORRY; 230 E-13; [P]; ★ MYR.B; z 29566; Ⓟ 3,470; © 7,027
Little Rock; RMC Place; DILLON; 230 C-11; elev. 135ft./41m.; [P]; z 29567; ● 500
Little Texas; RMC Place; GREENVILLE; *230 B-4; elev. 300ft./91m.; ★ GRNV; mail Travelers Rest z 29690; ● 40
Live Oak; RMC Place; HORRY; *230 D-12; mail Myrtle Beach z 29572; rural
Livingston; Inc. Place; ORANGEBURG; 230 F-7; [P]; z 29107; Ⓟ 171; © 148
Lobeco; RMC Place; BEAUFORT; 230 I-8; elev. 23ft./7m.; [P]; z 29931; ● 400
Lockhart; Inc. Place; UNION; 230 B-6; elev. 422ft./129m.; [P] [H]; z 29364; Ⓟ 58; © 39
Lockhart Junction; RMC Place; UNION; *230 B-6; mail Union z 29379; rural
Locust Hill; RMC Place; GREENVILLE; *230 A-4; ★ GRNV; mail Tigerville z 29688; rural
Lodge; Inc. Place; COLLETON; 230 G-8; elev. 111ft./34m.; [P]; z 29082; Ⓟ 147; © 114
Lone Oak; SPARTANBURG; see Southern Shops (CDP-Census Area Only)
Lone Star; RMC Place; CALHOUN; 230 E-8; elev. 171ft./52m.; [P]; z 29030; ● 200
Long Bay Estates; RMC Place; HORRY; *230 E-12; elev. 6ft./2m.; ★ MYR.B; mail Myrtle Beach z 29575; ● 200
Long Branch; RMC Place; BARNWELL; *230 F-6; elev. 260ft./79m.; mail Williston z 29853; rural
Longcreek; RMC Place; OCONEE; *230 B-2; elev. 1,625ft./495m.; mail Long Creek z 29658; ● 200
Longcreek; RMC Place; PICKENS; 230 B-2; elev. 300ft./91m.; [P]; ★ GRNV; z 29658 & mail Easley z 29640; ● 100
Long Leaf; RMC Place; COLLETON; *230 H-8; elev. 20ft./6m.; mail Walterboro z 29488; ● 500
Long Point; RMC Place; HORRY; *230 D-13; elev. 114ft./35m.; mail Loris z 29569; rural
Longs; RMC Place; HORRY; 230 D-13; [P]; z 29568; ● 300
Longtown; RMC Place; FAIRFIELD; *230 C-8; elev. 539ft./164m.; mail Ridgeway z 29130
Lonsdale Mill; OCONEE; see Utica (CDP)
Loris; Inc. Place; HORRY; 230 D-13; elev. 99ft./30m.; [P] [H]; z 29569; Ⓟ 2,067; © 2,079
Lowenstein Mills; RMC Place; ANDERSON; ★ AND; mail Anderson z 29621
Lowndesville; Inc. Place; ABBEVILLE; 230 D-3; [P]; z 29659; Ⓟ 162; © 166
Lowrys; Inc. Place; CHESTER; 230 B-7; elev. 724ft./221m.; mail Chester z 29706; Ⓟ 200; © 207
Lucille; FLORENCE; see Evergreen (RMC Place)
Lucknow; RMC Place; LEE; 230 D-9; elev. 352ft./107m.; mail Bishopville z 29010; ● 50
Lugoff; CDP; KERSHAW; 230 D-8; [P]; ★ COL; z 29078; Ⓟ 3,211; © 6,278
Luray; Inc. Place; HAMPTON; 230 H-7; elev. 140ft./43m.; [P]; z 29932; Ⓟ 102; © 115
Lydia; RMC Place; DARLINGTON; 230 C-10; elev. 213ft./65m.; [P]; z 29079; ● 420
Lydia Mills (South Clinton); RMC Place; LAURENS; *230 C-5; mail Clinton z 29325; ● 1,050
Lykes (Lykesland); RMC Place; RICHLAND; *230 E-8; ★ COL; mail Hopkins z 29061
Lykesland; RICHLAND; see Lykes (RMC Place)
Lyman; Inc. Place; SPARTANBURG; 230 B-5; [P]; z 29365; Ⓟ 2,271; © 2,659
Lynchburg; Inc. Place; LEE; 230 D-10; [P]; z 29080; Ⓟ 475; © 588
Lyndhurst; BARNWELL; see Boiling Springs (RMC Place)
Lynwood; RMC Place; AIKEN; *230 F-5; ★ AUG; mail Bath z 29816; pop. incl. with Burnettown (Inc. Place)

M

Mac Arthurs Junction; RMC Place; ABBEVILLE; *230 C-4; elev. 692ft./211m.; mail Donalds z 29638; ● 110
Macedonia; RMC Place; CHEROKEE; *230 A-6; elev. 270ft./82m.; mail Cowpens z 29330; rural
Macedonia; RMC Place; NEWBERRY; *230 D-6; mail Prosperity z 29127; rural
Maddens; RMC Place; LAURENS; *230 C-5; elev. 706ft./215m.; mail Laurens z 29360; ● 90
Madison; RMC Place; AIKEN; *230 F-5; elev. 221ft./67m.; ★ AUG; mail Graniteville z 29829; ● 1,100
Madison; RMC Place; OCONEE; 230 B-2; [P]; z 29693; ● 100
Magnolia Park; RMC Place; AIKEN; mail Williston z 29853
Mallory; RMC Place; DILLON; *230 C-11; elev. 118ft./36m.; mail Latta z 29565; rural
Manning; Inc. Place; ⊡ CLARENDON; 230 E-9; [P] [H]; z 29102; Ⓟ 4,428; © 4,025
Manning Crossroads; RMC Place; DILLON; *230 C-11; elev. 150ft./46m.; mail Dillon z 29536; rural
Manville; RMC Place; LEE; 230 D-9; mail Bishopville z 29010; ● 90
Maple Crossroads; RMC Place; HORRY; *230 E-12; elev. 46ft./14m.; mail Conway z 29526; rural
Maplewood; RMC Place; CHEROKEE; *230 A-6; elev. 650ft./198m.; mail Gaffney z 29340; ● 120
Marietta; RMC Place; GREENVILLE; 230 A-4; elev. 1,019ft./311m.; [P]; ★ GRNV; z 29661; ● 1,200
Marion; Inc. Place; ⊡ MARION; 230 D-11; elev. 77ft./23m.; [P] [H]; z 29571; Ⓟ 7,658; © 7,042

MARION; 230 D-11; Ⓟ 33,899; © 35,466; ◆ 33,518
Marlboro; RMC Place; MARLBORO; *230 C-11; elev. 87ft./27m.; mail Bennettsville z 29512; ● 250
MARLBORO; 230 C-10; Ⓟ 29,361; © 28,818; ◆ 29,125
Mars Bluff; RMC Place; FLORENCE; *230 D-11; elev. 100ft./30m.; ★ FLO; mail Florence z 29506
Martin; RMC Place; ALLENDALE; 230 G-6; elev. 98ft./30m.; [P]; z 29836; ● 40
Maryville; RMC Place; CHARLESTON; *230 H-10; elev. 16ft./5m.; ★ CHAS; mail Charleston z 29407; pop. incl. with Charleston (Inc. Place)
Maryville; RMC Place; GEORGETOWN; *230 F-12; elev. 10ft./3m.; mail Georgetown z 29440; pop. incl. with Georgetown (Inc. Place)
Masons Crossroads; RMC Place; ANDERSON; *230 C-3; elev. 760ft./232m.; ★ AND; mail Anderson z 29621; rural
Mathews; RMC Place; GREENWOOD; ★ GREEN; mail Greenwood z 29646; pop. incl. with Greenwood (Inc. Place)
Mathews Heights; RMC Place; GREENWOOD; *230 D-5; elev. 609ft./186m.; ★ GREEN; mail Greenwood z 29646; ● 150
Mauldin; Inc. Place; GREENVILLE; 230 B-4; elev. 942ft./287m.; [P]; ★ GRNV; z 29662; Ⓟ 11,587; © 15,224; Ⓡ 15,287; ◆ 20,214
Mayesville; Inc. Place; SUMTER; 230 D-9; [P]; ★ SUMT; z 29104; Ⓟ 694; © 1,001; Ⓡ 1,057
Mayfair Mill; RMC Place; PICKENS; mail Pickens z 29671; pop. incl. with Pickens (Inc. Place)
Mayfair Mill; SPARTANBURG; see Arcadia (RMC Place)
May Hilltop; RMC Place; DILLON; *230 C-12; mail Lake View z 29563; rural
Mayo; CDP; SPARTANBURG; 230 A-5; [P]; ★ SPRT; z 29368; Ⓟ 1,569; © 1,842
Mayo Mills; RMC Place; SPARTANBURG; *230 A-5; elev. 240ft./73m.; ★ SPRT; mail Mayo z 29368; ● 200
Mayson; SALUDA; see Good Hope (RMC Place)
Maysville; RMC Place; CHESTERFIELD; *230 B-9; mail Ruby z 29741; rural
McBee; Inc. Place; CHESTERFIELD; 230 C-9; [P]; z 29101; Ⓟ 715; © 714
McBeth; RMC Place; BERKELEY; *230 G-10; elev. 71ft./22m.; mail Bonneau z 29431; ● 80
McClellanville; Inc. Place; CHARLESTON; 230 G-11; elev. 9ft./3m.; [P]; z 29458; Ⓟ 333; © 459
McColl; Inc. Place; MARLBORO; 230 B-11; elev. 185ft./56m.; [P]; z 29570; Ⓟ 2,685; © 2,498
McConnells; Inc. Place; YORK; 230 B-7; [P]; z 29726; Ⓟ 157; © 287
McCormick; Inc. Place; ⊡ MCCORMICK; 230 E-4; [P]; z 29835, z 29899; Ⓟ 1,659; © 1,489; Ⓡ 2,659
MCCORMICK; 230 D-4; Ⓟ 8,868; © 9,958; ◆ 10,070
McCormick Crossroads; RMC Place; DILLON; *230 C-11; elev. 163ft./50m.; mail Dillon z 29536; rural
McCutchen Crossroads; RMC Place; LEE; *230 D-9; elev. 193ft./59m.; mail Bishopville z 29010; rural
McDonald (Whites Creek); RMC Place; GEORGETOWN; *230 F-12; elev. 16ft./5m.; mail Georgetown z 29440; ● 300
McKellar Farms; RMC Place; GREENWOOD; *230 D-5; elev. 550ft./168m.; ★ GREEN; mail Greenwood z 29646; ● 150
McKenzie Crossroads; RMC Place; FLORENCE; *230 E-10; elev. 109ft./33m.; mail Olanta z 29114; rural
McPhersonville; RMC Place; HAMPTON; *230 H-8; elev. 82ft./25m.; mail Early Branch z 29916
Meadowfield; RMC Place; RICHLAND; ★ COL; pop. incl. with Columbia (Inc. Place)
Meadowlake; RMC Place; RICHLAND; *230 D-7; elev. 300ft./91m.; ★ COL; mail Columbia z 29203; ● 2,700
Meadow Lakes; RMC Place; YORK; *230 B-7; ★ CHRLT; mail Rock Hill z 29732; ● 90
Mechanicsville; RMC Place; DARLINGTON; *230 C-10; mail Bishopville z 29010, Darlington z 29540; ● 80
Meggett; Inc. Place; CHARLESTON; 230 H-9; [P]; ★ CHAS; z 29449; Ⓟ 787; © 1,230
Melrose; RMC Place; AIKEN; *230 F-6; elev. 380ft./116m.; ★ AUG; mail Aiken z 29803; ● 200
Merchant; RMC Place; SALUDA; *230 D-6; elev. 450ft./137m.; mail Saluda z 29138; rural
Middendorf; RMC Place; CHESTERFIELD; 230 C-9; mail Hartsville z 29550; ● 30
Midland Park; RMC Place; CHARLESTON; *230 H-10; ★ CHAS; mail North Charleston z 29405; ● 800
Midland Valley; RMC Place; AIKEN; *230 F-5; elev. 220ft./67m.; ★ AUG; mail Graniteville z 29829; ● 300
Midway; RMC Place; BAMBERG; 230 G-7; elev. 152ft./46m.; mail Bamberg z 29003; ● 50
Midway; RMC Place; KERSHAW; *230 C-9; elev. 250ft./76m.; mail Cassatt z 29032; rural
Midway; RMC Place; LANCASTER; *230 B-8; mail Lancaster z 29720; ● 350
Midway Crossroads; RMC Place; WILLIAMSBURG; *230 E-11; elev. 53ft./16m.; mail Hemingway z 29554; ● 40
Midway Village; RMC Place; HORRY; *230 E-13; elev. 5ft./2m.; ★ MYR.B; mail Myrtle Beach z 29577; ● 200
Miley; RMC Place; HAMPTON; 230 G-7; elev. 82ft./25m.; [P]; z 29933; ● 120
Mill Creek; RMC Place; ORANGEBURG; *230 F-9; elev. 125ft./38m.; mail Vance z 29163; ● 70
Millers Crossroads (Prescott); RMC Place; EDGEFIELD; *230 E-5; elev. 459ft./140m.; mail Modoc z 29838
Millett; RMC Place; ALLENDALE; 230 G-6; mail Martin z 29836; ● 100
Mill Stone Landing (Purysburg Landing); RMC Place; JASPER; 230 I-7; elev. 17ft./5m.; mail Hardeeville z 29927; ● 100
Mill Village; LANCASTER; see Spring Mills (RMC Place)
Mill Village; RMC Place; MARLBORO; mail Bennettsville z 29512; pop. incl. with Bennettsville (Inc. Place)
Millwood; CDP; SUMTER; *230 E-9; ★ SUMT; mail Sumter z 29150; Ⓟ 1,070; © 885
Millwood; RMC Place; WILLIAMSBURG; *230 F-11; mail Kingstree z 29556; ● 100
Millwood Gardens; RMC Place; SUMTER; *230 E-9; elev. 177ft./54m.; ★ SUMT; mail Sumter z 29150; pop. incl. with Sumter (Inc. Place)
Milton; RMC Place; LAURENS; *230 C-5; elev. 509ft./155m.; mail Clinton z 29325; ● 30
Mink Point Plantation; RMC Place; BEAUFORT; *230 I-8; elev. 25ft./8m.; mail Beaufort z 29902; ● 30
Minturn; RMC Place; DILLON; 230 C-11; [P]; z 29573; ● 50
Mitchellville; RMC Place; JASPER; *230 I-7; mail Ridgeland z 29936; pop. incl. with Ridgeland (Inc. Place)
Mitford; RMC Place; FAIRFIELD; *230 C-8; mail Great Falls z 29055; ● 60
Mixville; RMC Place; AIKEN; *230 F-5; elev. 230ft./70m.; ★ AUG; mail Warrenville z 29851
Modoc; CDP; MCCORMICK; 230 E-4; [P]; z 29838; © 256
Monaghan; RMC Place; GREENVILLE; *230 B-4; ★ GRNV; mail Greenville z 29617; ● 1,100
Monarch (Monarch Mills); RMC Place; UNION; *230 C-6; ● 1,200
Monarch Mill; CDP-Census Area Only; UNION; 230 B-6; elev. 628ft./191m.; mail Union z 29379; Ⓟ 2,214; © 1,930
Monarch Mills; UNION; see Monarch (RMC Place)
Moncks Corner; Inc. Place; ⊡ BERKELEY; 230 G-10; elev. 56ft./17m.; [P]; ★ CHAS; z 29430, z 29461; Ⓟ 5,607; © 5,952
Monetta; Inc. Place; AIKEN, SALUDA; 230 E-6; [P]; z 29105; Ⓟ 285; © 220
Monroe Crossroads; RMC Place; MARLBORO; *230 C-11; elev. 129ft./39m.; mail Bennettsville z 29512; rural
Montague; RMC Place; GREENVILLE; *230 B-4; ★ GRNV; mail Greenville z 29617; ● 160
Mont Clare; RMC Place; DARLINGTON; *230 C-10; elev. 176ft./54m.; mail Darlington z 29532; ● 40
Monticello; RMC Place; FAIRFIELD; 230 C-7; [P]; z 29065; ● 70
Montmorenci; RMC Place; AIKEN; 230 F-6; [P]; ★ AUG; z 29839; ● 900
Montrose; RMC Place; CHESTERFIELD; *230 B-10; mail Cheraw z 29520; ● 25
Moore; RMC Place; SPARTANBURG; 230 B-5; [P]; ★ SPRT; z 29369; ● 200
Moores Crossroads; RMC Place; WILLIAMSBURG; *230 E-10; elev. 83ft./25m.; mail Cades z 29518; ● 50
Moreland; RMC Place; CHARLESTON; *230 H-10; elev. 10ft./3m.; ★ CHAS; mail Charleston z 29407; pop. incl. with Charleston (Inc. Place)
Morgan; RMC Place; JASPER; *230 I-7; elev. 25ft./8m.; mail Hardeeville z 29927; ● 35
Morningside; RMC Place; GREENVILLE; *230 B-4; ★ GRNV; mail Greenville z 29607; ● 750
Morris Acres; RMC Place; CHARLESTON; *230 H-10; elev. 19ft./6m.; ★ CHAS; mail Johns Island z 29455; ● 450
Moselle; RMC Place; COLLETON; *230 G-7; elev. 81ft./25m.; mail Islandton z 29929; ● 30
Mountain Brook; RMC Place; RICHLAND; *230 D-8; elev. 300ft./91m.; ★ COL; mail Columbia z 29209; ● 680
Mountain Lake Colony; RMC Place; GREENVILLE; *230 A-3; mail Cleveland z 29635; rural
Mountain Lakes; RMC Place; CHESTER; *230 B-7; elev. 500ft./152m.; mail Chester z 29706; ● 90
Mountain Rest; RMC Place; OCONEE; 230 B-2; [P]; z 29664; ● 100
Mountain View; RMC Place; SPARTANBURG; *230 A-5; elev. 919ft./280m.; ★ SPRT; mail Boiling Springs z 29316; ● 100
Mount Calvary; RMC Place; DILLON; *230 C-12; elev. 125ft./38m.; mail Dillon z 29536; ● 300
Mount Carmel; CDP; MCCORMICK; 230 D-4; elev. 546ft./166m.; [P]; z 29840; © 237
Mount Croghan; Inc. Place; CHESTERFIELD; 230 B-9; elev. 449ft./137m.; [P]; z 29727; Ⓟ 131; © 155
Mount Gallagher; RMC Place; LAURENS; *230 C-5; elev. 641ft./195m.; mail Ware Shoals z 29692; ● 180
Mount Holly; RMC Place; BERKELEY; 230 G-10; ★ CHAS; mail Goose Creek z 29445; ● 150
Mount Olive; RMC Place; HORRY; *230 D-12; elev. 91ft./28m.; mail Nichols z 29581; ● 50
Mount Pleasant; Inc. Place; CHARLESTON; 230 H-10; elev. 24ft./7m.; [P] [H]; ★ CHAS; z 29464-66; Ⓟ 30,108; © 47,609; ◆ 60,161
Mount Tabor; UNION; see Robat (RMC Place)
Mount View; RMC Place; GREENVILLE; *230 A-4; ★ GRNV; mail Taylors z 29687; rural
Mountville; CDP; LAURENS; 230 C-5; [P]; z 29370; © 130
Mulberry; CDP-Census Area Only; SUMTER; *230 E-9; ★ SUMT; mail Sumter z 29150; Ⓟ 1,097; © 841
Mullins; Inc. Place; MARION; 230 D-12; elev. 101ft./31m.; [P] [H]; z 29574; Ⓟ 5,910; © 5,029
Murphy Estates; RMC Place; EDGEFIELD; *230 F-5; elev. 550ft./168m.; ★ AUG; mail North Augusta z 29860; ● 500
Murphys Estates; CDP-Census Area Only; EDGEFIELD; *230 F-5; ★ AUG; © 1,518
Murrells Inlet; CDP; GEORGETOWN; 230 F-12; [P]; ★ MYR.B; z 29576; Ⓟ 3,334; © 5,519
Myers; RMC Place; CHARLESTON; *230 H-10; ★ CHAS; mail Charleston z 29403; pop. incl. with Charleston (Inc. Place)
Myrtle Beach; Inc. Place; HORRY; 230 E-13; elev. 30ft./9m.; [P] [H] ■; ★ MYR.B; z 29572, z 29575, z 29577-79, z 29587-88; Ⓟ 24,848; © 22,759; ◆ 29,359
Myrtle Island; RMC Place; BEAUFORT; *230 J-8; mail Bluffton z 29910; ● 100

N

Neeces; ORANGEBURG; see Neeses (Inc. Place)
Neeses (Neeces); Inc. Place; ORANGEBURG; 230 F-7; [P]; z 29107; Ⓟ 410; © 413
Nesmith; RMC Place; WILLIAMSBURG; 230 E-11; [P]; z 29580; ● 100
Nevitt Forest; RMC Place; ANDERSON; *230 C-4; ★ AND; mail Anderson z 29621; ● 700
Nevitt Woods; RMC Place; ANDERSON; *230 C-4; ★ AND; mail Anderson z 29621; ● 300
Newberry; Inc. Place; ⊡ NEWBERRY; 230 D-6; elev. 503ft./153m.; [P] [H] [C] 841; z 29108; Ⓟ 10,542; © 10,580
NEWBERRY; 230 D-5; Ⓟ 33,172; © 36,108; ◆ 38,190
New Cut; RMC Place; LANCASTER; *230 B-8; elev. 600ft./183m.; mail Lancaster z 29720; rural
New Ellenton; Inc. Place; AIKEN; 230 F-6; [P]; ★ AUG; z 29809; Ⓟ 2,515; © 2,250
New Holland Crossroads; RMC Place; AIKEN; 230 E-6; mail Batesburg z 29006; ● 200
New Hope; RMC Place; FLORENCE; *230 D-10; elev. 79ft./24m.; mail Coward z 29530; rural
New Market; RMC Place; GREENWOOD; *230 D-5; ★ GREEN; mail Greenwood z 29646; pop. incl. with Greenwood (Inc. Place)
Newport; CDP; YORK; 230 A-7; elev. 697ft./212m.; ★ CHRLT; mail Rock Hill z 29732; © 4,033
New Prospect; RMC Place; SPARTANBURG; 230 A-5; elev. 923ft./281m.; ★ SPRT; mail Inman z 29349; ● 100
New Road; RMC Place; BEAUFORT; *230 H-8; elev. 17ft./5m.; mail Yemassee z 29945; ● 30
Newry; RMC Place; OCONEE; 230 B-3; [P]; z 29665; ● 350
Newtonville; RMC Place; MARLBORO; *230 B-11; elev. 220ft./67m.; mail Bennettsville z 29512; rural
New Town; RMC Place; DILLON; *230 C-11; elev. 113ft./34m.; mail Dillon z 29536; ● 1,000
New Zion; RMC Place; CLARENDON; 230 E-10; elev. 99ft./30m.; [P]; z 29111; ● 140
Neyles; RMC Place; COLLETON; *230 H-9; elev. 8ft./2m.; mail Walterboro z 29488; ● 100
Nichols; Inc. Place; MARION; 230 D-12; elev. 61ft./19m.; [P]; z 29581; Ⓟ 528; © 408
Nicholson Village; RMC Place; AIKEN; *230 F-6; ★ AUG; mail Aiken z 29801; ● 220

Entries in **UPPERCASE** are counties.
Entries in **bold** have populations of 2,500 or more.
Names in parentheses are alternate names.

Inc. Place	Incorporated Place
RMC Place	Rand McNally Designated Place
CDP	Census Designated Place
MCD	Minor Civil Division
⊡	County Seat
▲	Minor Civil Division
elev.	Elevation
[P]	Post Office
[H]	Hospital
[C]	College
■	Principal Business Center
★	Ranally Metro Area (RMA) Abbreviation
z	Zip Code(s)
Ⓟ	Previous Census Population
Ⓡ	Revised Census Population
Ⓐ	Annexation Population
●	Rand McNally Population Estimate
©	Final Census Population
Ⓢ	Special Census Population
◆	Estimated Population

For additional definitions see Glossary, Volume 1, and Introduction, Volume 2.

Nimmons; RMC Place; PICKENS; *230 A-3; elev. 927ft./283m.; mail Sunset z 29685; rural
Nine Times; RMC Place; PICKENS; *230 B-3; elev. 999ft./304m.; mail Sunset z 29685
Ninety Six; Inc. Place; GREENWOOD; 230 D-5; 🅿; ★ GREEN; z 29666; ℗ 2,099; © 1,936
Nixons Crossroads; RMC Place; HORRY; 230 E-13; ★ MYR.B; mail Little River z 29566; ● 250
Nixonville; RMC Place; HORRY; 230 E-13; mail Conway z 29526; ● 30
Nixville; RMC Place; HAMPTON; *230 H-7; elev. 106ft./32m.; mail Estill z 29918, Varnville z 29944; rural
Norris; Inc. Place; PICKENS; 230 B-3; elev. 999ft./304m.; 🅿; z 29667; ℗ 884; © 847
North; Inc. Place; ORANGEBURG; 230 F-7; 🅿; z 29112; ℗ 809; © 813
North Aiken; RMC Place; AIKEN; ★ AUG; mail Aiken z 29801; pop. incl. with Aiken (Inc. Place)
North Anderson; RMC Place; ANDERSON; ★ AND; mail Anderson z 29623; pop. incl. with Anderson (Inc. Place)
North Augusta; Inc. Place; AIKEN, EDGEFIELD; 166 B-13; 🅿; ★ AUG; z 29841, z 29860-61 & mail Beech Island z 29842; ℗ 15,351; © 17,574; ◆ 20,096
Northbridge; RMC Place; CHARLESTON; mail Charleston z 29407; pop. incl. with Charleston (Inc. Place)
North Bridge Terrace; RMC Place; CHARLESTON; ★ CHAS; mail North Charleston z 29405; pop. incl. with Charleston (Inc. Place)
North Charleston; Inc. Place; CHARLESTON, BERKELEY, DORCHESTER; 230 H-10; 🅿 ■; ★ CHAS; z 29405-06, z 29410, z 29415, z 29418-20 & mail Charleston AFB z 29404; ℗ 70,218; © 79,641; ◆ 96,030
North Conway; RMC Place; HORRY; *230 E-12; elev. 15ft./5m.; ★ MYR.B; mail Conway z 29526; pop. incl. with Conway (Inc. Place)
North Forest Beach; RMC Place; BEAUFORT; mail Hilton Head Island z 29928; pop. incl. with Hilton Head Island (Inc. Place)
Northgate; RMC Place; CHEROKEE; *230 A-6; elev. 800ft./244m.; mail Gaffney z 29341; ● 100
Northgate; RMC Place; FLORENCE; *230 D-10; elev. 42ft./13m.; ★ FLO; mail Florence z 29501; rural
North Greenville; RMC Place; GREENVILLE; ★ GRNV; pop. incl. with Greenville (Inc. Place)
North Greenwood; RMC Place; GREENWOOD; *230 D-5; elev. 645ft./197m.; ★ GREEN; mail Greenwood z 29649; ● 3,500
North Hartsville; CDP; DARLINGTON; 230 C-10; mail Hartsville z 29550; ℗ 2,906; © 3,136
Northlake; CDP-Census Area Only; ANDERSON; *230 C-3; elev. 232ft./71m.; ★ AND; mail Anderson z 29621; ℗ 3,162; © 3,659
North Litchfield Beach; RMC Place; GEORGETOWN; *230 F-12; elev. 13ft./4m.; mail Pawleys Island z 29585; ● 700
North Mullins; RMC Place; MARION; *230 D-12; mail Mullins z 29574; pop. incl. with Mullins (Inc. Place)
North Myrtle Beach; Inc. Place; HORRY; 230 E-13; 🅿; ★ MYR.B; z 29582, z 29597-98; ℗ 8,636; © 10,974
North Pacolet; RMC Place; SPARTANBURG; *230 A-5; ★ SPRT; mail Campobello z 29322; rural
North Port; RMC Place; CHARLESTON; pop. incl. with Charleston (Inc. Place)
North Santee; RMC Place; GEORGETOWN; 230 G-11; elev. 32ft./10m.; mail Mc Clellanville z 29458; ● 300
North Summerville; RMC Place; DORCHESTER; ★ CHAS; mail Summerville z 29483; pop. incl. with Summerville (Inc. Place)
North Trenholm; RMC Place; RICHLAND; *230 D-7; elev. 300ft./91m.; ★ COL; mail Columbia z 29206; pop. incl. with Forest Acres (Inc. Place)
North Winyah Heights; RMC Place; GEORGETOWN; mail Georgetown z 29440; pop. incl. with Georgetown (Inc. Place)
Northwood Estates; RMC Place; CHARLESTON; *230 G-10; elev. 45ft./14m.; ★ CHAS; mail North Charleston z 29405; pop. incl. with North Charleston (Inc. Place)
Norway; Inc. Place; ORANGEBURG; 230 F-7; elev. 236ft./72m.; 🅿; z 29113; ℗ 401; © 389

O

Oakdale; RMC Place; CHEROKEE; *230 A-6; elev. 240ft./73m.; mail Cowpens z 29330; rural
Oak Dale; RMC Place; CLARENDON; *230 E-10; elev. 80ft./24m.; mail New Zion z 29111; ● 30
Oakdale; RMC Place; FLORENCE; *230 D-10; elev. 43ft./13m.; ★ FLO; mail Florence z 29501; ● 1,500
Oakdale; RMC Place; YORK; *230 B-7; elev. 180ft./55m.; ★ CHRLT; mail Rock Hill z 29730; ● 500
Oak Forest; RMC Place; CHARLESTON; *230 H-10; ★ CHAS; pop. incl. with Charleston (Inc. Place)
Oak Grove; RMC Place; DILLON; 230 C-11; mail Latta z 29565; ● 150
Oak Grove; CDP-Census Area Only; LEXINGTON; 230 E-7; ★ COL; mail Lexington z 29073; ℗ 7,173; © 8,183
Oak Hill; RMC Place; AIKEN; *230 F-6; elev. 450ft./137m.; ★ AUG; mail Aiken z 29803; ● 220
Oakland; RMC Place; BEAUFORT; *230 I-8; elev. 18ft./5m.; mail Beaufort z 29902; ● 180
Oakland; CDP; SUMTER; *230 D-9; ★ SUMT; mail Sumter z 29150; ℗ 1,298; © 1,272
Oakland Crossroads; RMC Place; DILLON; *230 C-11; elev. 162ft./49m.; mail Hamer z 29547; ● 50
Oakland Mill; RMC Place; NEWBERRY; mail Newberry z 29108; pop. incl. with Newberry (Inc. Place)
Oakley; RMC Place; BERKELEY; 230 G-10; elev. 34ft./10m.; ★ CHAS; mail Moncks Corner z 29461; ● 300
Oak Ridge; RMC Place; LANCASTER; *230 B-8; elev. 647ft./197m.; mail Heath Springs z 29058; rural
Oaks Crossroads; RMC Place; ORANGEBURG; *230 F-8; elev. 150ft./46m.; mail Santee z 29142; rural
Oakvale; RMC Place; GREENVILLE; *230 B-4; ★ GRNV; mail Piedmont z 29673; pop. incl. with Greenville (Inc. Place)
Oakway; RMC Place; OCONEE; 230 C-2; mail Westminster z 29693; ● 200
Oakwood; RMC Place; AIKEN; 230 F-6; elev. 452ft./138m.; mail Aiken z 29801; ● 50
Oatland; RMC Place; GEORGETOWN; 230 F-11; mail Georgetown z 29440; ● 150
Oats; RMC Place; DARLINGTON; 230 D-10; elev. 194ft./59m.; mail Lamar z 29069; ● 60
Ocean Drive Beach; RMC Place; HORRY; *230 E-13; ★ MYR.B; mail North Myrtle Beach z 29582; pop. incl. with North Myrtle Beach (Inc. Place)
Ocean Forest; RMC Place; HORRY; *230 E-13; ★ MYR.B; mail Myrtle Beach z 29577; pop. incl. with Myrtle Beach (Inc. Place)
Oceanview; RMC Place; CHARLESTON; *230 H-10; elev. 10ft./3m.; ★ CHAS; mail Charleston z 29412; ● 750
Oceda; RMC Place; GEORGETOWN; *230 F-11; mail Andrews z 29510; rural
OCONEE; 230 B-2; ℗ 57,494; © 66,215; ◆ 71,051
Oconee Estates; RMC Place; OCONEE; *230 B-3; elev. 900ft./274m.; mail Seneca z 29672; ● 90
Oconee Station; RMC Place; OCONEE; *230 B-2; elev. 1,140ft./347m.; mail Walhalla z 29691; rural
Ogden; RMC Place; YORK; *230 B-7; mail Rock Hill z 29730
Olanta; Inc. Place; FLORENCE; 230 E-10; elev. 118ft./36m.; 🅿; z 29114; ℗ 687; © 613
Olar; Inc. Place; BAMBERG; 230 G-7; elev. 206ft./63m.; 🅿; z 29843; ℗ 391; © 237
Old Cordesville; RMC Place; BERKELEY; *230 G-10; mail Cordesville z 29434; rural
Old House; RMC Place; JASPER; 230 I-8; elev. 18ft./5m.; mail Ridgeland z 29936; ● 50
Old Madison; RMC Place; OCONEE; *230 C-2; mail Westminster z 29693; ● 40
Old Town; RMC Place; NEWBERRY; *230 D-6; mail Chappells z 29037; rural
Old Town Acres; RMC Place; CHARLESTON; ★ CHAS; pop. incl. with Charleston (Inc. Place)
Olympia (Olympia Mills); RMC Place; RICHLAND; *230 D-7; ★ COL; mail Columbia z 29201; ● 1,200
Olympia Mills; RICHLAND; see Olympia (RMC Place)
Ora; RMC Place; LAURENS; 230 C-5; mail Laurens z 29360; ● 100
Orangeburg; Inc. Place; ⊡ ORANGEBURG; 230 F-8; elev. 245ft./75m.; 🅿 🅷 🅲 6,142 ■; z 29115-18; ℗ 13,739; © 12,765; ◆ 12,050
ORANGEBURG; 230 F-8; ℗ 84,803; © 91,582; Ⓡ 91,509; ◆ 88,234
Orange Grove Estates; RMC Place; CHARLESTON; *230 H-10; ★ CHAS; pop. incl. with Charleston (Inc. Place)
Orchard Park; RMC Place; GREENVILLE; ★ GRNV; mail Greenville z 29615-16; pop. incl. with Greenville (Inc. Place)
Orr Mill; RMC Place; ANDERSON; *230 C-3; elev. 749ft./228m.; ★ AND; mail Anderson z 29621; ● 2,400
Orrville; RMC Place; ANDERSON; ★ AND; mail Anderson z 29621
Orum; RMC Place; FLORENCE; *230 D-11; elev. 30ft./9m.; mail Pamplico z 29583; rural
Osborn; RMC Place; CHARLESTON; 230 H-9; elev. 30ft./9m.; mail Adams Run z 29426; ● 150
Osceola; RMC Place; LANCASTER; *230 B-8; elev. 603ft./184m.; ★ CHRLT; mail Van Wyck z 29744; rural
Oswego; CDP; SUMTER; 230 D-9; 🅿; z 29150; © 95
Otranto; RMC Place; BERKELEY; *230 G-10; ★ CHAS; mail North Charleston z 29405; pop. incl. with Hanahan (Inc. Place)
Outland; RMC Place; GEORGETOWN, WILLIAMSBURG; *230 E-11; elev. 64ft./20m.; mail Hemingway z 29554; rural
Owdoms; RMC Place; SALUDA; 230 D-5; elev. 548ft./167m.; mail Saluda z 29138; rural
Owings; RMC Place; LAURENS; 230 C-5; mail Gray Court z 29645; ● 100
Oyo Tungi; BEAUFORT; see Yoruba Village (RMC Place)
Oyster Point; RMC Place; CHARLESTON; *230 H-10; elev. 10ft./3m.; ★ CHAS; mail Charleston z 29412; ● 800

P

Pacolet; Inc. Place; SPARTANBURG; 230 B-6; 🅿; ★ SPRT; z 29372; ℗ 1,736; © 2,690
Pacolet Mills; RMC Place; SPARTANBURG; 230 B-6; 🅿; ★ SPRT; z 29373; pop. incl. with Pacolet (Inc. Place)
Pacolet Park; RMC Place; SPARTANBURG; *230 B-6; ★ SPRT; mail Pacolet Mills z 29373
Padgetts; RMC Place; COLLETON; 230 G-8; elev. 34ft./10m.; mail Smoaks z 29481; ● 40
Pageland; Inc. Place; CHESTERFIELD; 230 B-9; elev. 654ft./199m.; 🅿; z 29728; ℗ 2,666; © 2,521
Palmetto; RMC Place; DARLINGTON; *230 D-10; elev. 137ft./42m.; ★ FLO; mail Darlington z 29532
Palmetto Estates; RMC Place; BEAUFORT; *230 I-8; elev. 10ft./3m.; mail Beaufort z 29902; ● 70
Palmetto Fort; RMC Place; CHARLESTON; *230 H-10; elev. 9ft./3m.; ★ CHAS; mail Mount Pleasant z 29466; pop. incl. with Mount Pleasant (Inc. Place)
Pamplico; Inc. Place; FLORENCE; 230 D-11; 🅿; z 29583; ℗ 1,314; © 1,139
Panola; RMC Place; CLARENDON; *230 E-9; mail Pinewood z 29125
Panola; RMC Place; GREENWOOD; *230 D-5; ★ GREEN; mail Greenwood z 29646; pop. incl. with Greenwood (Inc. Place)
Paramount Park; RMC Place; GREENVILLE; *230 B-4; elev. 285ft./87m.; ★ GRNV; mail Greenville z 29605; ● 700
Paris; RMC Place; GREENVILLE; 230 B-4; elev. 330ft./101m.; ★ GRNV; mail Greenville z 29609, Taylors z 29687; ● 1,950
Parker; CDP-Census Area Only; GREENVILLE; *230 B-4; ★ GRNV; mail Greenville z 29611; ℗ 11,072; © 10,760
Parkers Ferry; RMC Place; CHARLESTON; *230 H-9; mail Adams Run z 29426; rural
Parkersville; RMC Place; GEORGETOWN; *230 F-12; mail Pawleys Island z 29585; ● 150
Park Place; RMC Place; GREENVILLE; 230 I-4; ★ GRNV; mail Greenville z 29608-09; ● 1,500
Parksville; Inc. Place; MCCORMICK; 230 E-4; elev. 348ft./106m.; 🅿; z 29844-45; ℗ 193; © 120
Parkwood Estates; RMC Place; CHARLESTON; *230 H-10; ★ CHAS; pop. incl. with Charleston (Inc. Place)
Parler; RMC Place; ORANGEBURG; *230 F-9; elev. 47ft./14m.; mail Santee z 29142
Parr; RMC Place; FAIRFIELD; *230 D-7; mail Jenkinsville z 29065
Parris Island; CDP-Census Area Only; BEAUFORT; *230 I-8; elev. 10ft./3m.; 🅿; z 29905 & mail Beaufort z 29902; ℗ 7,172; © 4,841
Parrot Point; RMC Place; CHARLESTON; *230 H-10; elev. 6ft./2m.; ★ CHAS; mail Charleston z 29412; ● 200
Patrick; Inc. Place; CHESTERFIELD; 230 C-10; elev. 223ft./68m.; 🅿; z 29584; ℗ 368; © 354
Pauline; RMC Place; SPARTANBURG; *230 B-5; 🅿; ★ SPRT; z 29374; ● 500
Pawleys Island; Inc. Place; GEORGETOWN; 230 F-12; 🅿; z 29585; ℗ 176; © 138
Paxville; Inc. Place; CLARENDON; 230 E-9; elev. 182ft./55m.; 🅿; z 29102; ℗ 218; © 248
Peach Valley; RMC Place; SPARTANBURG; *230 A-5; elev. 270ft./82m.; ★ SPRT; mail Spartanburg z 29303; ● 180
Peak; Inc. Place; NEWBERRY; 230 D-7; 🅿; z 29122; ℗ 78; © 61
Pecan Terrace; RMC Place; GREENVILLE; *230 B-4; elev. 292ft./89m.; ★ GRNV; mail Greenville z 29605; ● 1,100
Pecan Way Terrace; RMC Place; ORANGEBURG; mail Orangeburg z 29115; pop. incl. with Orangeburg (Inc. Place)
Pee Dee; RMC Place; MARION; 230 D-11; mail Marion z 29571; ● 250
Pelham; RMC Place; GREENVILLE, SPARTANBURG; 230 B-4; ★ GRNV; mail Greer z 29651; ● 500
Pelion; Inc. Place; LEXINGTON; 230 E-7; elev. 390ft./119m.; 🅿; ★ COL; z 29123; ℗ 336; © 553
Pelzer; Inc. Place; ANDERSON; *230 B-4; 🅿; ★ GRNV; z 29669; ℗ 81; © 97
Pendleton; Inc. Place; ANDERSON; 230 B-3; 🅿; z 29670; ℗ 3,314; © 2,966
Peniel Crossroads; RMC Place; FLORENCE; *230 D-10; elev. 126ft./38m.; ★ FLO; mail Timmonsville z 29161; rural
Pepperhill; RMC Place; CHARLESTON; *230 H-10; ★ CHAS; mail North Charleston z 29418; pop. incl. with North Charleston (Inc. Place)
Percival Crossroads; RMC Place; OCONEE; *230 B-2; elev. 928ft./283m.; mail Westminster z 29693
Perry; Inc. Place; AIKEN; 230 E-7; 🅿; z 29137; ℗ 241; © 237
Philip; RMC Place; CHARLESTON; *230 H-10; ★ CHAS; mail Mount Pleasant z 29464; ● 110
Phoenix; RMC Place; GREENWOOD; *230 D-5; mail Greenwood z 29646
Pickens; Inc. Place; ⊡ PICKENS; 230 B-3; elev. 1,110ft./338m.; 🅿 🅷; z 29671; ℗ 3,042; © 3,012
PICKENS; 230 B-3; ℗ 93,894; © 110,757; ◆ 119,230
Pickett Post; RMC Place; OCONEE; *230 B-2; mail Walhalla z 29691; rural
Piedmont; CDP-Census Area Only; GREENVILLE, ANDERSON; 230 B-4; 🅿; ★ GRNV; z 29673; ℗ 4,143; © 4,684
Piedmont Park; RMC Place; GREENVILLE; *230 B-4; elev. 1,074ft./327m.; ★ GRNV
Piercetown; RMC Place; ANDERSON; *230 B-4; ★ GRNV; mail Williamston z 29697; rural
Pierpont; RMC Place; CHARLESTON; *230 H-10; ★ CHAS; mail Charleston z 29414; ● 2,700
Pimlico; RMC Place; BERKELEY; *230 G-10; elev. 10ft./3m.; ★ CHAS; mail Moncks Corner z 29461; ● 450
Pine Grove; RMC Place; HAMPTON; *230 H-7; elev. 34ft./10m.; mail Hampton z 29924; ● 50
Pinehaven; RMC Place; CHARLESTON; mail North Charleston z 29405, z 29415; pop. incl. with Charleston (Inc. Place)
Pinehurst; RMC Place; DORCHESTER; *230 G-9; elev. 75ft./23m.; ★ CHAS; mail Summerville z 29483; pop. incl. with Summerville (Inc. Place)
Pinehurst; RMC Place; GREENWOOD; *230 D-5; elev. 500ft./152m.; ★ GREEN; mail Greenwood z 29646; ● 200
Pine Island; RMC Place; HORRY; 230 I-12; elev. 26ft./8m.; ★ MYR.B; mail Myrtle Beach z 29577; ● 30
Pineland; RMC Place; CHARLESTON; *230 G-11; elev. 19ft./6m.; mail Awendaw z 29429, Mc Clellanville z 29458; ● 50
Pineland; RMC Place; JASPER; 230 I-7; 🅿; z 29934; ● 200
Pine Ridge; RMC Place; DARLINGTON; *230 C-9; elev. 279ft./85m.; mail Mc Bee z 29101; ● 400
Pineridge; Inc. Place; LEXINGTON; *230 E-7; ★ COL; mail West Columbia z 29169, z 29172; ℗ 1,731; © 1,593
Pine Valley; RMC Place; RICHLAND; *230 D-7; elev. 250ft./76m.; ★ COL; mail Columbia z 29210; ● 1,400
Pineville; RMC Place; BERKELEY; 230 F-10; elev. 81ft./25m.; 🅿; z 29468; ● 500
Pinewood; Inc. Place; SUMTER; 230 E-9; 🅿; ★ SUMT; z 29125; ℗ 600; © 459; Ⓡ 512
Piney Grove; RMC Place; SPARTANBURG; *230 A-5; ★ SPRT; mail Cowpens z 29330; rural
Pinopolis; RMC Place; BERKELEY; 230 G-10; 🅿; z 29469; ● 750
Pisgah; RMC Place; SUMTER; *230 D-9; elev. 316ft./96m.; mail Rembert z 29128; rural
Pittsburg; RMC Place; GREENWOOD; *230 D-5; mail Troy z 29848; rural
Plantation Pines; RMC Place; FAIRFIELD; *230 C-7; elev. 526ft./160m.; mail Winnsboro z 29180; ● 50
Plantersville; RMC Place; GEORGETOWN; 230 F-12; elev. 22ft./7m.; mail Georgetown z 29440; ● 150
Playcards; RMC Place; HORRY; *230 D-12; elev. 78ft./24m.; mail Loris z 29569; rural
Pleasantburg; RMC Place; GREENVILLE; ★ GRNV; mail Greenville z 29606; pop. incl. with Greenville (Inc. Place)
Pleasant Hill; RMC Place; GEORGETOWN; *230 E-11; elev. 45ft./14m.; mail Hemingway z 29554; ● 100
Pleasant Hill; RMC Place; LANCASTER; 230 C-8; mail Heath Springs z 29058, Lancaster z 29720; ● 100
Pleasant Lane; RMC Place; EDGEFIELD; *230 E-5; mail Edgefield z 29824; rural
Pleasant Valley; RMC Place; GREENVILLE; *230 B-4; elev. 270ft./82m.; ★ GRNV; mail Greenville z 29605; ● 1,200
Pleasant View; RMC Place; HORRY; *230 D-12; elev. 81ft./25m.; mail Loris z 29569; rural
Plum Branch; Inc. Place; MCCORMICK; 230 E-4; elev. 471ft./144m.; 🅿; z 29845; ℗ 101; © 98
Pocotaligo; RMC Place; JASPER; 230 H-8; mail Yemassee z 29945; ● 100
Poe; RMC Place; GREENVILLE; ★ GRNV; mail Greenville z 29609
Polk Village; RMC Place; BEAUFORT; *230 I-8; elev. 20ft./6m.; mail Beaufort z 29902; pop. incl. with Beaufort (Inc. Place)
Pomaria; Inc. Place; NEWBERRY; 230 D-6; elev. 404ft./123m.; 🅿; z 29126; ℗ 267; © 177
Pontiac; RMC Place; RICHLAND; 230 D-8; ★ COL; mail Elgin z 29045; ● 250
Poovey Farm; RMC Place; LANCASTER; *230 B-8; elev. 484ft./148m.; mail Lancaster z 29720; ● 500
Poplar Springs; RMC Place; LAURENS; *230 C-4; mail Laurens z 29360; rural
Poplar Springs; RMC Place; SPARTANBURG; *230 B-5; ★ SPRT; mail Moore z 29369; rural
Port Royal; Inc. Place; BEAUFORT; 230 J-12; 🅿; z 29935; ℗ 2,985; © 3,950
Port Royal Plantation; RMC Place; BEAUFORT; *230 J-8; mail Hilton Head Island z 29928; pop. incl. with Hilton Head Island (Inc. Place)
Poston; RMC Place; FLORENCE; 230 E-11; elev. 70ft./21m.; 🅿; z 29555; ● 150
Powdersville; ANDERSON; see Powderville (CDP)
Powderville (Powdersville); CDP; ANDERSON; *230 B-4; ★ GRNV; mail Easley z 29642, Greenville z 29611, Piedmont z 29673; © 5,362
Pregnall; RMC Place; DORCHESTER; 230 G-9; elev. 89ft./27m.; mail Dorchester z 29437
Prescott; EDGEFIELD; see Millers Crossroads (RMC Place)
Priceville; RMC Place; LEXINGTON; *230 D-6; mail Gilbert z 29054; rural
Primus; RMC Place; LANCASTER; *230 B-8; mail Lancaster z 29720; ● 80
Princeton; CDP; LAURENS, GREENVILLE; 230 C-4; ★ GRNV; mail Honea Path z 29654; © 65
Pritchardville; RMC Place; BEAUFORT; 230 J-8; elev. 35ft./11m.; mail Bluffton z 29910; ● 150
Privateer; CDP; SUMTER; *230 E-9; ★ SUMT; © 2,118
Promised Land; CDP; GREENWOOD; *230 D-4; ★ GREEN; mail Bradley z 29819; © 559
Prospect Crossroads; RMC Place; FLORENCE; 230 E-11; mail Lake City z 29560; ● 60
Prosperity; Inc. Place; NEWBERRY; 230 D-6; elev. 541ft./165m.; 🅿; z 29127; ℗ 1,116; © 1,047
Providence; RMC Place; ORANGEBURG; *230 F-9; elev. 114ft./35m.; mail Holly Hill z 29059
Pumpkintown; RMC Place; PICKENS; 230 A-3; elev. 967ft./295m.; mail Pickens z 29671
Puncheon Creek; RMC Place; GEORGETOWN; *230 F-11; elev. 20ft./6m.; mail Andrews z 29510; ● 50
Purysburg Landing; JASPER; see Mill Stone Landing (RMC Place)

Q

Quail Hollow; RMC Place; LEXINGTON; *230 D-7; elev. 300ft./91m.; ★ COL; mail West Columbia z 29169; ● 600
Quinby; Inc. Place; FLORENCE; 230 D-11; elev. 40ft./12m.; 🅿; ★ FLO; z 29506; ℗ 865; © 842
Quinby Estates; RMC Place; FLORENCE; *230 D-11; ★ FLO; mail Florence z 29506; pop. incl. with Quinby (Inc. Place)
Quinby Forest; RMC Place; FLORENCE; *230 D-11; ★ FLO; mail Florence z 29501; pop. incl. with Quinby (Inc. Place)

R

Rabon Crossroads; RMC Place; HORRY; *230 D-12; elev. 100ft./30m.; mail Aynor z 29511; rural
Rains; RMC Place; MARION; 230 D-12; elev. 87ft./27m.; 🅿; z 29589; ● 500
Rantowles; RMC Place; CHARLESTON; 230 H-10; ★ CHAS; mail Hollywood z 29449; pop. incl. with Hollywood (Inc. Place)
Ravenel; Inc. Place; CHARLESTON; 230 H-9; elev. 38ft./12m.; 🅿; ★ CHAS; z 29470; ℗ 2,165; © 2,214; Ⓡ 2,339
Ravenwood; RMC Place; RICHLAND; *230 D-8; ★ COL; mail Columbia z 29206; pop. incl. with Forest Acres (Inc. Place)
Rawlinson Acres; RMC Place; YORK; *230 B-7; ★ CHRLT; mail Rock Hill z 29732; ● 100
Red Bank; CDP; LEXINGTON; *230 E-7; ★ COL; mail Lexington z 29072-73; ℗ 5,950; © 8,811
Red Bank Landing; RMC Place; ORANGEBURG; *230 F-9; elev. 100ft./30m.; mail Eutawville z 29048; ● 90
Red Bluff Crossroads; RMC Place; HORRY; *230 E-13; elev. 10ft./3m.; mail Loris z 29569; ● 90
Red Hill; RMC Place; HORRY; *230 E-12; elev. 33ft./10m.; ★ MYR.B; mail Conway z 29526; ● 600
Red Hill; RMC Place; HORRY; *230 E-12; elev. 43ft./13m.; mail Galivants Ferry z 29544; rural
Red Hill; CDP-Census Area Only; HORRY; *230 E-12; elev. 42ft./13m.; ★ MYR.B; mail Conway z 29526; ℗ 6,112; © 10,509
Red Hill; RMC Place; LEE; *230 D-9; elev. 319ft./97m.; mail Camden z 29020; rural
Red River (Celriver); RMC Place; YORK; *230 B-8; ★ CHRLT; mail Rock Hill z 29730; ● 250
Red Top; RMC Place; CHARLESTON; *230 H-10; ★ CHAS; mail Johns Island z 29455; pop. incl. with Charleston (Inc. Place)
Reevesville; Inc. Place; DORCHESTER; 230 G-8; elev. 12ft./4m.; 🅿; z 29471; ℗ 244; © 207
Regency Woods; RMC Place; ANDERSON; *230 C-3; ★ AND; mail Anderson z 29625; ● 200
Rehobeth; RMC Place; HORRY; *230 D-12; elev. 50ft./15m.; mail Galivants Ferry z 29544; rural
Reid Park; RMC Place; CHESTERFIELD; *230 B-10; elev. 173ft./53m.; mail Cheraw z 29520; ● 200
Reidville; Inc. Place; SPARTANBURG; 230 B-5; 🅿; z 29375; © 478
Rembert; CDP; SUMTER; 230 D-9; 🅿; z 29128; © 406
Remini; CLARENDON, SUMTER; see Rimini (RMC Place)
Remount; RMC Place; CHARLESTON; ★ CHAS; mail Charleston z 29406; pop. incl. with North Charleston (Inc. Place)
Renfrew; RMC Place; GREENVILLE; *230 A-4; ★ GRNV; mail Travelers Rest z 29690; ● 220
Renno; RMC Place; LAURENS; 230 C-6; elev. 504ft./154m.; mail Clinton z 29325; ● 25
Retreat; RMC Place; OCONEE; *230 B-2; elev. 945ft./288m.; mail Westminster z 29693; rural
Return; RMC Place; OCONEE; *230 B-3; elev. 896ft./273m.; mail Seneca z 29678; ● 35
Reynold; RMC Place; BARNWELL; *230 F-7; elev. 310ft./94m.; mail Blackville z 29817; ● 60
Rhems; RMC Place; GEORGETOWN, WILLIAMSBURG; *230 F-11; elev. 36ft./11m.; mail Georgetown z 29440; rural
Ribault Park; RMC Place; BEAUFORT; *230 I-8; mail Beaufort z 29902; pop. incl. with Beaufort (Inc. Place)
Rice Hope; RMC Place; BERKELEY; *230 G-10; mail Cordesville z 29434; ● 80
Richburg; Inc. Place; CHESTER; 230 B-7; elev. 584ft./178m.; 🅿; z 29729 & mail Lancaster z 29720; ℗ 405; © 332
Rich Hill Crossroads; RMC Place; LANCASTER; *230 B-8; elev. 666ft./203m.; mail Heath Springs z 29058, Lancaster z 29720; ● 40
Richland; RMC Place; OCONEE; *230 B-2; 🅿; z 29675; ● 200
RICHLAND; 230 E-8; ℗ 285,720; © 320,677; ◆ 377,295
Richland Springs; RMC Place; SALUDA; *230 E-6; elev. 524ft./160m.; mail Saluda z 29138, Ward z 29166; rural
Richmond Hills; RMC Place; GREENVILLE; *230 B-4; elev. 300ft./91m.; ★ GRNV; mail Greenville z 29617; ● 650
Richtex; RMC Place; FAIRFIELD; *230 D-7; mail Winnsboro z 29180; rural
Ridgecrest; RMC Place; AIKEN; *230 F-6; ★ AUG; mail Aiken z 29801; ● 100
Ridgeland; Inc. Place; ⊡ JASPER; 230 I-7; elev. 62ft./19m.; 🅿 🅷; z 29936 & mail Coosawhatchie z 29912; ℗ 1,071; © 2,518
Ridge Spring; Inc. Place; SALUDA; 230 E-6; 🅿; z 29129; ℗ 861; © 823
Ridgeville; Inc. Place; DORCHESTER; 230 G-9; elev. 75ft./23m.; 🅿; ★ CHAS; z 29472; ℗ 1,625; © 1,690; Ⓡ 1,717
Ridgeway; Inc. Place; FAIRFIELD; 230 C-8; 🅿; z 29130; ℗ 407; © 328
Ridgewood; RMC Place; CHARLESTON; ★ CHAS; mail Ladson z 29456
Ridgewood; RMC Place; OCONEE; *230 B-3; elev. 900ft./274m.; mail Seneca z 29678; ● 100
Ridgewood; RMC Place; RICHLAND; *230 D-7; elev. 300ft./91m.; ★ COL; mail Columbia z 29203; ● 1,600
Rimini (Remini); RMC Place; CLARENDON, SUMTER; 230 E-9; elev. 126ft./38m.; 🅿; z 29125; ● 200
Ringle Heights; RMC Place; GEORGETOWN; *230 F-12; elev. 21ft./6m.; mail Georgetown z 29440; ● 160
Rion; RMC Place; FAIRFIELD; 230 C-7; 🅿; z 29132; ● 80
Ritter; RMC Place; COLLETON; 230 H-8; elev. 7ft./2m.; 🅿; z 29488; ● 80
Riverdale; RMC Place; DILLON; *230 C-12; elev. 128ft./39m.; mail Dillon z 29536; ● 500
Riverdale; RMC Place; SPARTANBURG; *230 A-5; ★ SPRT; mail Inman z 29349; rural
River Falls; RMC Place; GREENVILLE; *230 A-4; elev. 1,109ft./338m.; mail Marietta z 29661; summer pop. 220; ● 150
Riverland; RMC Place; CHARLESTON; *230 H-10; elev. 12ft./4m.; ★ CHAS; mail Charleston z 29412; ● 1,750
Riverland Terrace; RMC Place; CHARLESTON; *230 H-10; ★ CHAS; mail Charleston z 29412; ● 1,750
Rivermont; RMC Place; RICHLAND; ★ COL; mail Columbia z 29210
Riverside; RMC Place; ANDERSON; ★ AND; mail Anderson z 29624; pop. incl. with Anderson (Inc. Place)
Riverside; RMC Place; GREENVILLE; 230 I-4; ★ GRNV; mail Greenville z 29611; ● 2,350
Riverside; RMC Place; LANCASTER; *230 B-8; elev. 602ft./183m.; mail Lancaster z 29720; rural
Riverside Park; RMC Place; RICHLAND; ★ COL; mail Columbia z 29210
Riverview; CDP; YORK; *230 A-7; ★ CHRLT; mail Fort Mill z 29715; © 708
Robat (Mount Tabor); RMC Place; UNION; *230 B-6; elev. 597ft./182m.; mail Union z 29379; rural
Robbins Circle; RMC Place; CHESTER; mail Chester z 29706
Robertville; RMC Place; JASPER; 230 I-7; elev. 69ft./21m.; mail Garnett z 29922; ● 120
Robinson; RMC Place; DARLINGTON; mail Mc Bee z 29101
Rock Bluff; RMC Place; WILLIAMSBURG; *230 F-10; elev. 56ft./17m.; mail Kingstree z 29556; ● 50
Rockbridge; RMC Place; RICHLAND; *230 D-8; elev. 250ft./76m.; ★ COL; mail Columbia z 29206; pop. incl. with Forest Acres (Inc. Place)
Rock Hill; RMC Place; FAIRFIELD; *230 D-7; elev. 457ft./139m.; mail Jenkinsville z 29065; ● 50
Rock Hill; Inc. Place; YORK; 230 B-7; elev. 667ft./203m.; 🅿 🅷 🅲 6,292 ■; ★ CHRLT; z 29730-34; ℗ 41,610; © 49,765; Ⓡ 49,774; ◆ 68,901
Rockton; RMC Place; FAIRFIELD; *230 C-7; elev. 580ft./177m.; mail Winnsboro z 29180
Rockville; Inc. Place; CHARLESTON; 230 H-9; mail Wadmalaw Island z 29487; © 137
Rocky Bottom; RMC Place; PICKENS; *230 A-3; elev. 1,750ft./533m.; mail Sunset z 29685; ● 80
Roddy; RMC Place; YORK; *230 B-8; ★ CHRLT; mail Catawba z 29704; ● 70
Rodman; RMC Place; CHESTER; *230 B-7; mail Chester z 29706; ● 60
Roebuck; CDP; SPARTANBURG; 230 B-5; 🅿; ★ SPRT; z 29376; ℗ 1,966; © 1,725
Rogers Fallout; RMC Place; HORRY; *230 E-12; elev. 60ft./18m.; mail Galivants Ferry z 29544; ● 40
Rosehill Park; RMC Place; CHEROKEE; *230 A-6; elev. 685ft./209m.; mail Gaffney z 29340; ● 100
Roseida; RMC Place; BEAUFORT; *230 I-8; elev. 25ft./8m.; mail Beaufort z 29906; ● 330
Rosewood; RMC Place; RICHLAND; ★ COL; pop. incl. with Columbia (Inc. Place)
Rosinville; RMC Place; DORCHESTER; *230 G-9; elev. 29ft./9m.; mail Saint George z 29477; ● 120
Round O; RMC Place; COLLETON; 230 H-9; elev. 42ft./13m.; 🅿; z 29474; ● 100
Rowell; RMC Place; CHESTER; *230 B-8; elev. 606ft./185m.; mail Catawba z 29704
Rowesville; Inc. Place; ORANGEBURG; 230 F-8; elev. 166ft./51m.; 🅿; z 29133; ℗ 316; © 378
Ruby; Inc. Place; CHESTERFIELD; 230 B-9; elev. 381ft./116m.; 🅿; z 29741; ℗ 300; © 348
Ruffin; RMC Place; COLLETON; 230 G-8; 🅿; z 29475; ● 300
Rushville; RMC Place; GREENWOOD; *230 D-5; mail Bradley z 29819; rural
Russellville; RMC Place; BERKELEY; 230 F-10; elev. 81ft./25m.; 🅿; z 29476; ● 300

S

Saint Andrews; RMC Place; CHARLESTON; 230 B-12; elev. 10ft./3m.; ★ CHAS; mail Charleston z 29407, z 29417; pop. incl. with Charleston (Inc. Place)
Saint Andrews; CDP-Census Area Only; RICHLAND; 230 H-1; elev. 300ft./91m.; ★ COL; mail Columbia z 29210; ℗ 25,692; © 21,814; ◆ 25,669
Saint Andrews Heights; RMC Place; CHARLESTON; ★ CHAS; pop. incl. with Charleston (Inc. Place)
Saint Charles; RMC Place; LEE; 230 D-9; elev. 172ft./52m.; 🅿; z 29104; ● 100
Saint Delight; GEORGETOWN; see Lambertown (RMC Place)
Saint George; Inc. Place; ⊡ DORCHESTER; 230 G-8; elev. 102ft./31m.; 🅿; z 29477; ℗ 2,077; © 2,092
Saint Helena Island; BEAUFORT; see Frogmore (RMC Place)
Saint Julian; RMC Place; ORANGEBURG; *230 F-9; elev. 100ft./30m.; mail Eutawville z 29048; ● 70
Saint Matthews; Inc. Place; ⊡ CALHOUN; 230 E-8; 🅿; z 29135; ℗ 2,345; © 2,107
Saint Paul; RMC Place; CLARENDON; 230 F-9; mail Summerton z 29148; ● 60
Saint Paul Forks; RMC Place; HORRY; *230 E-12; elev. 26ft./8m.; ★ MYR.B; mail Conway z 29526; ● 100
Saint Stephen; Inc. Place; BERKELEY; 230 F-10; 🅿; z 29479; ℗ 1,697; © 1,776
Salak; RMC Place; GREENWOOD; *230 D-4; ★ GREEN; mail Greenwood z 29646
Salem; RMC Place; FLORENCE; 230 E-11; mail Pamplico z 29583; ● 90
Salem; Inc. Place; OCONEE; 230 B-3; 🅿; z 29676; ℗ 192; © 126
Salem Crossroads (Salem Road); RMC Place; FAIRFIELD; 230 C-7; elev. 529ft./161m.; mail Blair z 29015; ● 40
Salem Road; FAIRFIELD; see Salem Crossroads (RMC Place)
Salley; Inc. Place; AIKEN; 230 F-7; 🅿; z 29137; ℗ 451; © 410
Salters; RMC Place; WILLIAMSBURG; 230 F-10; 🅿; z 29590; ● 270
Saluca; RMC Place; GREENWOOD; *230 D-5; elev. 591ft./180m.; ★ GREEN; mail Greenwood z 29646
Saluda; Inc. Place; ⊡ SALUDA; 230 D-6; 🅿; z 29138; ℗ 2,798; © 3,066
SALUDA; 230 D-6; ℗ 16,357; © 19,181; ◆ 18,642
Saluda Gardens; RMC Place; LEXINGTON; *230 D-7; ★ COL; mail West Columbia z 29169; pop. incl. with West Columbia (Inc. Place)
Saluda Terrace; RMC Place; LEXINGTON; ★ COL; mail West Columbia z 29169; pop. incl. with West Columbia (Inc. Place)
Samaria; RMC Place; LEXINGTON; 230 E-6; mail Batesburg z 29006; ● 40
Sampit; RMC Place; GEORGETOWN; 230 F-11; mail Georgetown z 29440; ● 150
Sanders Corner; RMC Place; SUMTER; *230 D-9; ★ SUMT; mail Horatio z 29062; rural
Sandhills; RMC Place; RICHLAND; mail Columbia z 29229; pop. incl. with Columbia (Inc. Place)
Sandhurst; RMC Place; CHARLESTON; ★ CHAS; pop. incl. with Charleston (Inc. Place)
Sandridge; RMC Place; BERKELEY; *230 G-9; elev. 80ft./24m.; mail Holly Hill z 29059; rural
Sand Ridge; RMC Place; HORRY; *230 E-12; elev. 49ft./15m.; ★ MYR.B; mail Conway z 29527; ● 100
Sandwood; RMC Place; RICHLAND; *230 D-8; elev. 2,000ft./610m.; ★ COL; mail Columbia z 29206; ● 2,400
Sandy Flat; RMC Place; GREENVILLE; *230 A-4; ★ GRNV; mail Taylors z 29687; ● 60
Sandy Ridge; RMC Place; GREENWOOD; *230 D-5; elev. 581ft./177m.; mail Ninety Six z 29666; rural
Sandy Springs; RMC Place; ANDERSON; 230 C-3; 🅿; ★ AND; z 29677; ● 1,200
Sans Souci; CDP; GREENVILLE; 230 I-4; ★ GRNV; mail Greenville z 29609; ℗ 7,612; © 7,836
Sans Souci Heights; RMC Place; GREENVILLE; *230 B-4; elev. 300ft./91m.; ★ GRNV; mail Greenville z 29617; ● 2,400
Santee; Inc. Place; ORANGEBURG; 230 F-9; 🅿; z 29142; ℗ 638; © 740
Santee Circle; RMC Place; BERKELEY; 230 G-10; mail Moncks Corner z 29461; ● 350
Santuc; RMC Place; UNION; 230 B-6; mail Union z 29379; ● 50
Sardinia; RMC Place; CLARENDON; 230 E-10; 🅿; z 29143; ● 250
Sardis; RMC Place; FLORENCE; 230 D-10; mail Timmonsville z 29161; ● 100
Satchel Ford Terrace; RMC Place; RICHLAND; *230 D-7; elev. 277ft./84m.; ★ COL; mail Columbia z 29206; pop. incl. with Arcadia Lakes (Inc. Place)
Savannah Bluff; RMC Place; HORRY; *230 E-12; elev. 44ft./13m.; ★ MYR.B; mail Conway z 29526; ● 350
Sawyerdale; RMC Place; ORANGEBURG; *230 F-7; elev. 121ft./37m.; mail North z 29112; rural
Saxon; CDP; SPARTANBURG; *230 B-5; ★ SPRT; mail Spartanburg z 29301; ℗ 4,002; © 3,707
Saylors Crossroads; RMC Place; ANDERSON; *230 C-4; elev. 768ft./234m.; mail Belton z 29627; ● 70
Scanlonville; RMC Place; CHARLESTON; *230 H-10; ★ CHAS; mail Mount Pleasant z 29464; pop. incl. with Mount Pleasant (Inc. Place)
Schofield; RMC Place; BAMBERG; *230 G-7; mail Olar z 29843; rural
Schultz Hill; RMC Place; AIKEN; 166 B-13; ★ AUG; mail North Augusta z 29841
Scotia; Inc. Place; HAMPTON; 230 H-7; elev. 95ft./29m.; 🅿; z 29939; ℗ 182; © 227
Scottsville; RMC Place; SUMTER; *230 E-9; elev. 40ft./12m.; mail Mayesville z 29104; rural
Scranton; Inc. Place; FLORENCE; 230 E-11; elev. 95ft./29m.; 🅿; z 29591; ℗ 802; © 942; Ⓡ 973
Seabrook; RMC Place; BEAUFORT; 230 I-8; 🅿; z 29940 & mail Dale z 29914; ● 100
Seabrook Island; Inc. Place; CHARLESTON; 230 I-10; elev. 10ft./3m.; 🅿; z 29455; ℗ 948; © 1,250
Sea Pines; RMC Place; BEAUFORT; 230 J-10; mail Hilton Head Island z 29928; pop. incl. with Hilton Head Island (Inc. Place)
Seaside; RMC Place; CHARLESTON; *230 H-10; elev. 5ft./2m.; ★ CHAS; mail Charleston z 29412; pop. incl. with Charleston (Inc. Place)
Secessionville; RMC Place; CHARLESTON; *230 H-10; elev. 10ft./3m.; ★ CHAS; mail Charleston z 29412; ● 200
Sedalia; RMC Place; UNION; *230 C-6; mail Union z 29379
Seiglers Crossroads; RMC Place; AIKEN; *230 E-6; elev. 505ft./154m.; mail Aiken z 29801; rural
Seigling; RMC Place; ALLENDALE; *230 G-7; elev. 206ft./63m.; mail Allendale z 29810; rural
Seivern; RMC Place; AIKEN; *230 E-6; elev. 120ft./37m.; mail Wagener z 29164; rural
Sellers; Inc. Place; MARION; 230 D-11; 🅿; z 29592; ℗ 358; © 277
Selma; RMC Place; DILLON; *230 C-11; elev. 140ft./43m.; mail Dillon z 29536; ● 180
Seneca; Inc. Place; OCONEE; 230 B-3; elev. 950ft./290m.; 🅿 🅷; z 29672, z 29678-79; ℗ 7,726; © 7,652
Seneca Landing; RMC Place; OCONEE; *230 B-3; elev. 700ft./213m.; mail Seneca z 29678; rural
Seven Mile; RMC Place; CHARLESTON; *230 H-10; ★ CHAS; mail North Charleston z 29405; pop. incl. with North Charleston (Inc. Place)
Seven Oaks; CDP-Census Area Only; LEXINGTON; *230 D-7; ★ COL; mail Columbia z 29210; ℗ 15,722; © 15,755
Shady Rest; RMC Place; MARLBORO; mail Bennettsville z 29512; pop. incl. with Bennettsville (Inc. Place)
Shalimar; RMC Place; CHEROKEE; *230 A-6; elev. 700ft./213m.; mail Gaffney z 29341; ● 70
Shandon; RMC Place; RICHLAND; ★ COL; pop. incl. with Columbia (Inc. Place)
Shannon Hill; RMC Place; LEE; *230 D-9; elev. 183ft./56m.; mail Bishopville z 29010; rural
Shannontown; RMC Place; SUMTER; 230 E-9; ★ SUMT; mail Sumter z 29150; ● 1,500
Sharon; Inc. Place; YORK; 230 B-7; elev. 652ft./199m.; 🅿; z 29742; ℗ 270; © 421
Sharpes Hill; RMC Place; LEXINGTON; *230 E-7; ★ COL; mail Gaston z 29053; ● 100
Shaw Heights; RMC Place; SUMTER; ★ SUMT; mail Shaw AFB z 29152; pop. incl. with Sumter (Inc. Place)
Sheldon; RMC Place; BEAUFORT; 230 I-8; 🅿; z 29941; ● 200
Shell; RMC Place; HORRY; *230 E-13; elev. 50ft./15m.; mail Conway z 29526; rural
Shell Point; CDP; BEAUFORT; *230 I-8; mail Beaufort z 29906; ℗ 2,885; © 2,856
Shelton; RMC Place; FAIRFIELD; 230 C-6; mail Blair z 29015; rural
Shepard; RMC Place; KERSHAW; 230 C-9; mail Cassatt z 29032; ● 50
Sheppard Crossroads; RMC Place; GREENWOOD; *230 D-5; mail Troy z 29848; rural
Sheppard Park; RMC Place; DORCHESTER; *230 G-9; elev. 80ft./24m.; ★ CHAS; mail Summerville z 29483; pop. incl. with Summerville (Inc. Place)
Sherwood Acres; RMC Place; SPARTANBURG; *230 B-5; ★ SPRT; mail Spartanburg z 29301
Sherwood Forest; RMC Place; CHARLESTON; ★ CHAS; pop. incl. with Charleston (Inc. Place)
Shiloh; RMC Place; OCONEE; *230 B-3; elev. 870ft./265m.; mail Seneca z 29678; ● 50
Shiloh; CDP; SUMTER; *230 E-10; elev. 126ft./38m.; mail Lynchburg z 29080; © 259
Shiloh Estates; RMC Place; OCONEE; *230 B-3; elev. 900ft./274m.; mail Seneca z 29678; ● 90
Shipyard Plantation; RMC Place; BEAUFORT; *230 J-8; mail Hilton Head Island z 29928; pop. incl. with Hilton Head Island (Inc. Place)
Shirley; RMC Place; HAMPTON; 230 H-7; elev. 76ft./23m.; mail Garnett z 29922; ● 50
Shoals Junction; RMC Place; GREENWOOD; 230 C-4; 🅿; z 29638; ● 50
Shulerville; RMC Place; BERKELEY; 230 G-11; elev. 30ft./9m.; 🅿; z 29453 & mail Saint Stephen z 29479; ● 350
Sidney; RMC Place; COLLETON; *230 G-8; mail Round O z 29474; rural
Silver; RMC Place; CLARENDON; *230 E-9; elev. 159ft./48m.; mail Manning z 29102; ● 150
Silver Bluff Estates; RMC Place; AIKEN; *230 F-6; elev. 500ft./152m.; ★ AUG; mail Aiken z 29803; pop. incl. with Aiken (Inc. Place)
Silverstreet; Inc. Place; NEWBERRY; 230 D-6; 🅿; z 29145; ℗ 156; © 216
Simpson; RMC Place; FAIRFIELD; 230 C-7; mail Ridgeway z 29130; ● 150
Simpsonville; Inc. Place; GREENVILLE; 230 B-4; elev. 865ft./264m.; 🅿 🅷; ★ GRNV; z 29680-81; ℗ 11,708; © 14,352; Ⓡ 14,202
Singing Pines; RMC Place; OCONEE; *230 B-3; elev. 920ft./280m.; mail Seneca z 29678; ● 50
Singleton; RMC Place; CALHOUN; *230 E-8; mail Saint Matthews z 29135; rural
Six Mile; Inc. Place; PICKENS; 230 B-3; elev. 1,027ft./313m.; 🅿; z 29682; ℗ 562; © 553
Six Points; RMC Place; AIKEN; *230 F-6; elev. 499ft./152m.; ★ AUG; mail Aiken z 29801
Skyview Terrace; RMC Place; RICHLAND; ★ COL; mail Columbia z 29210
Slandsville; RMC Place; DORCHESTER; *230 G-9; elev. 71ft./22m.; ★ CHAS; mail Summerville z 29483; ● 300
Slater; RMC Place; GREENVILLE; *230 A-4; 🅿; ★ GRNV; z 29683; ● 1,000
Slater-Marietta; CDP-Census Area Only; GREENVILLE; *230 A-4; elev. 304ft./93m.; ★ GRNV; mail Marietta z 29661, Slater z 29683; ℗ 2,245; © 2,228
Slighs; RMC Place; NEWBERRY; 230 D-6; mail Prosperity z 29127; ● 50
Smallwood; RMC Place; FAIRFIELD; 230 D-8; elev. 586ft./179m.; mail Ridgeway z 29130; ● 90
Smallwood; RMC Place; LAURENS; *230 C-5; elev. 600ft./183m.; mail Clinton z 29325; ● 50
Smith; RMC Place; YORK; *230 B-7; mail Rock Hill z 29730; rural
Smithboro; RMC Place; DILLON, MARION; *230 D-12; mail Mullins z 29574
Smith Mills; RMC Place; GEORGETOWN; *230 E-12; elev. 74ft./23m.; mail Hemingway z 29554; rural
Smoaks; Inc. Place; COLLETON; 230 G-8; 🅿; z 29481; ℗ 142; © 140
Smyrna; Inc. Place; YORK, CHEROKEE; 230 A-6; 🅿; z 29743; ℗ 57; © 59
Snelling; Inc. Place; BARNWELL; 230 G-6; elev. 225ft./69m.; mail Barnwell z 29812; ℗ 125; © 246
Sniders Crossroads; RMC Place; COLLETON; *230 H-8; elev. 70ft./21m.; mail Ruffin z 29475
Snowden; RMC Place; CHARLESTON; *230 H-10; elev. 23ft./7m.; ★ CHAS; mail Mount Pleasant z 29464
Socastee; CDP; HORRY; 230 E-12; elev. 14ft./4m.; ★ MYR.B; mail Myrtle Beach z 29577, z 29579, z 29588; ℗ 10,426; © 14,295
Society Hill; Inc. Place; DARLINGTON; 230 C-10; elev. 166ft./51m.; 🅿; z 29593; ℗ 686; © 700
South Anderson; RMC Place; ANDERSON; ★ AND; mail Anderson z 29624; pop. incl. with Anderson (Inc. Place)
South Clinton; LAURENS; see Lydia Mills (RMC Place)
South Congaree; Inc. Place; LEXINGTON; 230 E-7; ★ COL; mail West Columbia z 29169, z 29172; ℗ 2,406; © 2,266
Southern Meadows; RMC Place; OCONEE; *230 B-3; elev. 900ft./274m.; mail Seneca z 29678; ● 160
Southern Shops (Lone Oak); CDP-Census Area Only; SPARTANBURG; *230 A-5; ★ SPRT; mail Spartanburg z 29303; ℗ 3,378; © 3,707
South Florence; RMC Place; FLORENCE; ★ FLO; mail Florence z 29502, z 29504-05; pop. incl. with Florence (Inc. Place)
South Forest Estates; RMC Place; GREENVILLE; *230 B-4; elev. 285ft./87m.; ★ GRNV; mail Greenville z 29605; ● 1,000
South Greenwood; RMC Place; GREENWOOD; *230 D-5; ★ GREEN; mail Greenwood z 29646; pop. incl. with Greenwood (Inc. Place)
South Hartsville; RMC Place; DARLINGTON; *230 C-10; mail Hartsville z 29550; ● 2,400
South Hills; RMC Place; UNION; *230 B-6; elev. 636ft./194m.; mail Union z 29379; ● 110
South Lynchburg; RMC Place; LEE; *230 D-10; elev. 151ft./46m.; mail Lynchburg z 29080; ● 100
South Mullins; RMC Place; MARION; mail Mullins z 29574; pop. incl. with Mullins (Inc. Place)
South Port; RMC Place; CHARLESTON; pop. incl. with Charleston (Inc. Place)
Southside; RMC Place; FLORENCE; *230 D-10; elev. 35ft./11m.; ★ FLO; mail Florence z 29505; ● 1,000
South Sumter; CDP; SUMTER; *230 E-9; elev. 161ft./49m.; ★ SUMT; mail Sumter z 29150; ℗ 4,371; © 3,365
South Union; RMC Place; OCONEE; *230 C-2; elev. 900ft./274m.; mail Westminster z 29693; rural
Spartanburg; Inc. Place; ⊡ SPARTANBURG; 230 B-5; elev. 816ft./249m.; 🅿 🅷 🅲 7,504 ■; ★ SPRT; z 29301-07, z 29316, z 29318-19; ℗ 43,467; © 39,673; ◆ 40,031
SPARTANBURG; 230 B-5; ℗ 226,800; © 253,791; Ⓡ 253,782; ◆ 284,347
Spaulding Heights; RMC Place; FLORENCE; *230 D-10; elev. 40ft./12m.; ★ FLO; mail Florence z 29501; ● 700
Spiderweb; RMC Place; AIKEN; *230 F-5; elev. 300ft./91m.; ★ AUG; mail Beech Island z 29842; rural
Spring Branch; RMC Place; MARION; *230 D-11; elev. 107ft./33m.; mail Marion z 29571; ● 70
Springdale; CDP-Census Area Only; LANCASTER; *230 B-8; elev. 500ft./152m.; mail Lancaster z 29720; ℗ 2,643; © 2,864
Springdale; Inc. Place; LEXINGTON; 230 E-7; ★ COL; mail West Columbia z 29169-70; ℗ 3,226; © 2,877
Springfield; Inc. Place; ORANGEBURG; 230 F-7; elev. 300ft./91m.; 🅿; z 29146; ℗ 523; © 504
Springfield; RMC Place; SPARTANBURG; *230 A-5; ★ SPRT; mail Boiling Springs z 29316; ● 2,000
Spring Hill; RMC Place; LEE; *230 D-9; mail Rembert z 29128; rural
Spring Hill; RMC Place; RICHLAND; *230 D-7; elev. 412ft./126m.; ★ COL; mail White Rock z 29177; rural
Springmaid Beach; RMC Place; HORRY; *230 E-13; ★ MYR.B; mail Myrtle Beach z 29577; rural
Spring Mills (Mill Village); RMC Place; LANCASTER; 230 C-8; mail Kershaw z 29067; ● 1,400
Springtown; RMC Place; COLLETON; *230 G-8; elev. 22ft./7m.; mail Smoaks z 29481; ● 120
Spring Valley; RMC Place; GREENWOOD; *230 D-5; elev. 500ft./152m.; ★ GREEN; mail Greenwood z 29646; ● 200
Springwood; RMC Place; RICHLAND; *230 D-8; elev. 250ft./76m.; ★ COL; mail Columbia z 29204; ● 1,300
Stallsville; RMC Place; DORCHESTER; *230 G-9; elev. 75ft./23m.; ★ CHAS; mail Summerville z 29485; pop. incl. with Summerville (Inc. Place)
Stark Terrace; RMC Place; RICHLAND; *230 D-7; elev. 346ft./105m.; ★ COL; mail Columbia z 29203; ● 370
Starmount; RMC Place; LEXINGTON; *230 E-7; ★ COL; mail West Columbia z 29172; ● 600
Starr; Inc. Place; ANDERSON; 230 C-3; elev. 771ft./235m.; 🅿; z 29684; ℗ 164; © 173
Startex; CDP; SPARTANBURG; *230 B-5; 🅿; z 29377; ℗ 1,162; © 988
Stateburg; CDP; SUMTER; *230 D-9; elev. 349ft./106m.; ★ SUMT; mail Sumter z 29150; © 1,264
State College; RMC Place; ORANGEBURG; mail Orangeburg z 29117; pop. incl. with Orangeburg (Inc. Place)
State Park (State Park Health Center); RMC Place; RICHLAND; *230 D-8; 🅿; ★ COL; z 29147; ● 50
State Park Health Center; RICHLAND; see State Park (RMC Place)
Steedman; RMC Place; LEXINGTON; 230 E-6; elev. 100ft./30m.; mail Leesville z 29070; ● 50
Stiefeltown; RMC Place; AIKEN; *230 F-5; ★ AUG; mail Warrenville z 29851
Stokes; RMC Place; COLLETON; *230 G-8; elev. 87ft./27m.; mail Walterboro z 29488; ● 50
Stokes Bridge; RMC Place; LEE; *230 D-9; elev. 224ft./68m.; mail Bishopville z 29010; rural
Stomp Springs; RMC Place; LAURENS; *230 C-6; elev. 500ft./152m.; mail Clinton z 29325; ● 30
Stoneboro; RMC Place; KERSHAW; *230 C-8; elev. 574ft./175m.; mail Heath Springs z 29058; rural
Stonehaven; RMC Place; ANDERSON; *230 C-3; ★ AND; mail Anderson z 29625; ● 200
Stoney Hill; RMC Place; NEWBERRY; 230 D-6; elev. 587ft./179m.; mail Prosperity z 29127; ● 150
Stono; RMC Place; CHARLESTON; *230 H-10; elev. 10ft./3m.; ★ CHAS; mail Charleston z 29412; pop. incl. with Charleston (Inc. Place)
Stono Park; RMC Place; CHARLESTON; ★ CHAS; pop. incl. with Charleston (Inc. Place)
Stover; RMC Place; FAIRFIELD; *230 C-7; elev. 546ft./166m.; mail Blackstock z 29014; rural
Stratford Hall; RMC Place; AIKEN; ★ AUG; mail Aiken z 29803
Stratton Capers; RMC Place; DORCHESTER; *230 H-10; elev. 29ft./9m.; ★ CHAS; mail North Charleston z 29405; ● 550
Strawberry; RMC Place; BERKELEY; *230 G-10; ★ CHAS; mail Moncks Corner z 29461; rural
Stuart Point; RMC Place; BEAUFORT; *230 I-8; elev. 10ft./3m.; mail Seabrook z 29940; rural
Stuckey; Inc. Place; WILLIAMSBURG; 230 E-11; elev. 54ft./16m.; mail Hemingway z 29554; ℗ 311; © 263
Sullivans Island; Inc. Place; CHARLESTON; 230 H-10; 🅿; ★ CHAS; z 29482; ℗ 1,623; © 1,911
Summer Hill; RMC Place; AIKEN; 166 A-13; ★ AUG; mail North Augusta z 29841; pop. incl. with North Augusta (Inc. Place)
Summerland; RMC Place; LEXINGTON; mail Batesburg z 29006; pop. incl. with Batesburg-Leesville (Inc. Place)
Summerton; Inc. Place; CLARENDON; 230 F-9; 🅿; z 29148; ℗ 975; © 1,061
Summerville; Inc. Place; DORCHESTER, BERKELEY, CHARLESTON; 230 G-9; 🅿 🅷; ★ CHAS; z 29483-85; ℗ 22,519; © 27,752; ◆ 43,606
Summit; Inc. Place; LEXINGTON; 230 E-6; ★ COL; mail Leesville z 29070; ℗ 242; © 219
Sumter; Inc. Place; ⊡ SUMTER; 230 E-9; elev. 169ft./52m.; 🅿 🅷 🅲 824 ■; ★ SUMT; z 29150-51, z 29153-54; ℗ 40,977; © 39,643; ◆ 36,580
SUMTER; 230 E-9; ℗ 102,637; © 104,646; Ⓡ 104,636; ◆ 102,948
Sunnyside; RMC Place; SPARTANBURG; ★ GRNV; mail Greer z 29651; pop. incl. with Greer (Inc. Place)
Sunset; RMC Place; PICKENS; 230 A-3; elev. 1,019ft./311m.; 🅿; z 29685; ● 25
Surfside Beach; Inc. Place; HORRY; 230 E-12; 🅿; ★ MYR.B; z 29575, z 29587; ℗ 3,845; © 4,425
Suttons; RMC Place; WILLIAMSBURG; *230 F-11; mail Andrews z 29510; rural
Swansea; Inc. Place; LEXINGTON; 230 E-7; 🅿; ★ COL; z 29160; ℗ 527; © 533
Sweden; RMC Place; BAMBERG; *230 F-7; mail Denmark z 29042
Sweetwater; RMC Place; AIKEN; *230 F-5; elev. 545ft./166m.; ★ AUG; mail North Augusta z 29860; ● 60
Switzer; RMC Place; SPARTANBURG; *230 B-5; mail Moore z 29369
Switzerland; RMC Place; JASPER; 230 I-7; elev. 50ft./15m.; mail Ridgeland z 29936; ● 50
Sycamore; Inc. Place; ⊡ ALLENDALE; 230 G-7; elev. 153ft./47m.; 🅿; z 29846; ℗ 208; © 185
Syracuse; RMC Place; DARLINGTON; *230 D-10; elev. 172ft./52m.; mail Darlington z 29532; ● 40

T

Talatha; RMC Place; AIKEN; *230 F-6; elev. 406ft./124m.; ★ AUG; mail Aiken z 29803; ● 50
Tall Pines; RMC Place; DILLON; *230 C-11; elev. 123ft./37m.; mail Dillon z 29536; ● 110
Tamassee; RMC Place; OCONEE; 230 B-2; 🅿; z 29686; ● 200
Tanglewood; RMC Place; BEAUFORT; *230 I-8; elev. 25ft./8m.; mail Beaufort z 29902; rural
Tanglewood; RMC Place; GREENVILLE; *230 B-4; elev. 300ft./91m.; ★ GRNV; mail Greenville z 29611; ● 800
Tanglewood; RMC Place; OCONEE; *230 B-3; elev. 900ft./274m.; mail Seneca z 29672; ● 120
Tanglewood; RMC Place; ORANGEBURG; *230 F-8; elev. 82ft./25m.; mail Orangeburg z 29115; ● 80
Tarboro; RMC Place; JASPER; 230 I-7; mail Tillman z 29943; ● 180
Tatum; Inc. Place; MARLBORO; 230 B-11; elev. 199ft./61m.; 🅿; z 29594; ℗ 49; © 69
Taxahaw; RMC Place; LANCASTER; 230 B-9; elev. 661ft./201m.; mail Kershaw z 29067; ● 60
Taylors; CDP; GREENVILLE; 230 B-4; elev. 270ft./82m.; 🅿; ★ GRNV; z 29687; ℗ 19,619; © 20,125; ◆ 23,871
Tega Cay; Inc. Place; YORK; 230 A-7; 🅿; ★ CHRLT; z 29708 & mail Fort Mill z 29715; ℗ 3,016; © 4,044
Temperance Hill; RMC Place; MARION; *230 C-11; elev. 122ft./37m.; mail Marion z 29571; ● 60
Ten Mile; RMC Place; CHARLESTON; *230 H-11; elev. 20ft./6m.; ★ CHAS; mail Awendaw z 29429; ● 1,157
Terrells Crossroads; RMC Place; WILLIAMSBURG; *230 E-10; elev. 88ft./27m.; mail Cades z 29518; rural
Texas; RMC Place; DORCHESTER; *230 G-9; elev. 84ft./26m.; mail Saint George z 29477; rural
The Crescent; RMC Place; CHARLESTON; ★ CHAS; pop. incl. with Charleston (Inc. Place)
The Farms; RMC Place; BERKELEY; *230 H-10; ★ CHAS; mail Hanahan z 29410; pop. incl. with Hanahan (Inc. Place)
The Groves; RMC Place; CHARLESTON; *230 H-10; ★ CHAS; mail Mount Pleasant z 29464; pop. incl. with Mount Pleasant (Inc. Place)
The Meadows; RMC Place; OCONEE; *230 B-3; elev. 800ft./244m.; mail Seneca z 29678; rural
Thicketty; RMC Place; CHEROKEE; *230 A-6; mail Gaffney z 29341; rural
Thor; RMC Place; LEXINGTON; *230 E-7; mail Pelion z 29123; rural

Entries in **UPPERCASE** are counties.
Entries in **bold** have populations of 2,500 or more.
Names in parentheses are alternate names.

Inc. Place	Incorporated Place
RMC Place	Rand McNally Designated Place
CDP	Census Designated Place
MCD	Minor Civil Division

⊡ County Seat
▲ Minor Civil Division
elev. Elevation
🅿 Post Office
🅷 Hospital
🅲 College
■ Principal Business Center
★ Ranally Metro Area (RMA) Abbreviation
z Zip Code(s)
℗ Previous Census Population
Ⓡ Revised Census Population
Ⓐ Annexation Population
● Rand McNally Population Estimate
© Final Census Population
Ⓢ Special Census Population
◆ Estimated Population

For additional definitions see Glossary, Volume 1, and Introduction, Volume 2.

Three Trees; RMC Place; CHARLESTON; ***230** H-10; elev. 15ft./5m.; ★ **CHAS**; mail Charleston z 29412; pop. incl. with Charleston (Inc. Place)
Tibwin; RMC Place; CHARLESTON; ***230** G-11; elev. 11ft./3m.; mail Mc Clellanville z 29458; ● 100
Tifton; RMC Place; DARLINGTON; ***230** D-10; elev. 121ft./37m.; ★ **FLO**; mail Darlington z 29532
Tigerville; RMC Place; GREENVILLE; **230** A-4; elev. 1,025ft./312m.; 🅿 🅲 1,890; ★ **GRNV**; z 29688; ● 200
Tillman; RMC Place; JASPER; **230** I-7; 🅿; z 29943; ● 300
Timberlake; RMC Place; OCONEE; ***230** C-3; elev. 800ft./244m.; mail Seneca z 29678; ● 150
Timmonsville; Inc. Place; FLORENCE; **230** D-10; elev. 150ft./46m.; 🅿; ★ **FLO**; z 29161; Ⓟ 2,182; Ⓒ 2,315
Tina; RMC Place; CALHOUN; ***230** F-8; mail Cameron z 29030; rural
Tirzah; RMC Place; YORK; **230** A-7; elev. 710ft./216m.; ★ **CHRLT**; mail York z 29745; ● 2,150
Toddville; RMC Place; HORRY; **230** E-12; mail Conway z 29526; ● 50
Tokeena Crossroads; RMC Place; OCONEE; **230** C-3; elev. 904ft./276m.; mail Seneca z 29678; ● 100
Toney Creek; RMC Place; ANDERSON; ***230** C-4; elev. 651ft./198m.; mail Belton z 29627; ● 200
Townville; RMC Place; ANDERSON; **230** C-3; 🅿; ★ **AND**; z 29689; ● 500
Toxaway; RMC Place; ANDERSON; ***230** C-3; ★ **AND**; mail Anderson z 29621; pop. incl. with Anderson (Inc. Place)
Tradesville; RMC Place; LANCASTER; ***230** B-9; elev. 531ft./162m.; mail Lancaster z 29720; ● 35
Tranquil Acres; RMC Place; DORCHESTER; ***230** G-10; elev. 20ft./6m.; ★ **CHAS**; mail Ladson z 29456; ● 800
Travelers Rest; Inc. Place; GREENVILLE; **230** A-4; 🅿 🅷; ★ **GRNV**; z 29690; Ⓟ 3,069; Ⓒ 4,099
Trenton; Inc. Place; EDGEFIELD; **230** E-5; elev. 621ft./189m.; 🅿; z 29847; Ⓟ 303; Ⓒ 226; Ⓡ 237
Triangle; RMC Place; ANDERSON; mail Belton z 29627; pop. incl. with Belton (Inc. Place)
Trio; RMC Place; WILLIAMSBURG; **230** F-11; elev. 57ft./17m.; 🅿; z 29590; ● 250
Troy; Inc. Place; GREENWOOD; **230** D-4; 🅿; z 29848; Ⓟ 140; Ⓒ 105
Tuckertown; RMC Place; UNION; ***230** C-6; elev. 440ft./134m.; mail Carlisle z 29031
Tugtown; RMC Place; ORANGEBURG; ***230** F-9; elev. 87ft./27m.; mail Holly Hill z 29059; ● 80
Turbeville; Inc. Place; CLARENDON; **230** E-10; elev. 131ft./40m.; 🅿; z 29162; Ⓟ 698; Ⓒ 602; Ⓡ 720
Twin Lake Hill; RMC Place; RICHLAND; ★ **COL**; mail Columbia z 29209
Tyler; RMC Place; DILLON; ***230** C-11; elev. 116ft./35m.; mail Dillon z 29536; ● 70

U

Ulmer; Inc. Place; ALLENDALE; **230** G-7; 🅿; z 29849; Ⓟ 90; Ⓒ 102
Una; RMC Place; DARLINGTON, LEE; ***230** D-10; mail Lamar z 29069; rural
Una; RMC Place; SPARTANBURG; ***230** B-5; 🅿; ★ **SPRT**; z 29378
Union; Inc. Place; ⊡ UNION; **230** B-6; elev. 641ft./195m.; 🅿 🅷; z 29379; Ⓟ 9,836; Ⓒ 8,793
UNION; **230** B-6; Ⓟ 30,337; Ⓒ 29,881; ◆ 27,227
Union Bleachery; RMC Place; GREENVILLE; ***230** B-4; elev. 300ft./91m.; ★ **GRNV**; mail Greenville z 29617; ● 500
Union Crossroads; RMC Place; CLARENDON; ***230** E-10; mail New Zion z 29111; ● 30
Unity; RMC Place; LANCASTER; ***230** B-8; elev. 628ft./191m.; mail Lancaster z 29720; rural
Utica (Lonsdale Mill); CDP; OCONEE; **230** B-3; mail Seneca z 29678; Ⓟ 1,478; Ⓒ 1,322

V

Valencia Heights; RMC Place; RICHLAND; ***230** D-7; elev. 200ft./61m.; ★ **COL**; mail Columbia z 29205; pop. incl. with Columbia (Inc. Place); Ⓟ 4,122
Valley Falls; CDP; SPARTANBURG; ***230** A-5; ★ **SPRT**; mail Spartanburg z 29303; Ⓟ 3,504; Ⓒ 3,990
Vance; Inc. Place; ORANGEBURG; **230** F-9; 🅿; z 29163; Ⓟ 214; Ⓒ 208
Van Wyck; RMC Place; LANCASTER; **230** B-8; elev. 504ft./154m.; 🅿; ★ **CHRLT**; z 29744; ● 350
Varnville; Inc. Place; HAMPTON; **230** H-7; elev. 111ft./34m.; 🅿 🅷; z 29944; Ⓟ 1,970; Ⓒ 2,074
Vaucluse; RMC Place; AIKEN; **230** F-5; 🅿; ★ **AUG**; z 29850; ● 500
Verdery; RMC Place; GREENWOOD; **230** D-4; mail Bradley z 29819; ● 60
Victor Mills; RMC Place; SPARTANBURG; ★ **GRNV**; mail Greer z 29651; pop. incl. with Greer (Inc. Place)
Village Creek; RMC Place; OCONEE; ***230** B-3; elev. 900ft./274m.; mail Seneca z 29678; ● 50
Virginia Acres; RMC Place; AIKEN; ***230** F-6; elev. 500ft./152m.; ★ **AUG**; mail Aiken z 29803; ● 280

W

Waddell Gardens; RMC Place; BEAUFORT; ***230** I-8; mail Beaufort z 29902; pop. incl. with Beaufort (Inc. Place)
Wade Hampton; CDP; GREENVILLE; ***230** B-4; elev. 300ft./91m.; ★ **GRNV**; mail Greenville z 29607; Ⓟ 20,014; Ⓒ 20,458; Ⓡ 20,461; ◆ 24,258
Wadmalaw Island; RMC Place; CHARLESTON; ***230** H-9; 🅿; z 29487; ● 300
Wadsworth (Camp Wadsworth Village); RMC Place; SPARTANBURG; ***230** B-5; ★ **SPRT**; mail Spartanburg z 29301; ● 150
Wagener; Inc. Place; AIKEN; **230** E-7; 🅿; z 29164; Ⓟ 731; Ⓒ 863
Walhalla; Inc. Place; ⊡ OCONEE; **230** B-2; elev. 1,027ft./313m.; 🅿; z 29691; Ⓟ 3,755; Ⓒ 3,801
Wallace; RMC Place; MARLBORO; **230** B-10; 🅿; z 29596; ● 320
Walnut Grove; RMC Place; SPARTANBURG; ***230** B-5; ★ **SPRT**; mail Pauline z 29374; rural
Walterboro; Inc. Place; ⊡ COLLETON; **230** H-8; elev. 69ft./21m.; 🅿 🅷; z 29488; Ⓟ 5,492; Ⓒ 5,153
Wampee; RMC Place; HORRY; **230** E-13; elev. 37ft./11m.; mail Longs z 29568; ● 200
Wando; BERKELEY; see Cainhoy (RMC Place)
Wando Woods; RMC Place; CHARLESTON; ***230** H-10; ★ **CHAS**; mail North Charleston z 29405; pop. incl. with North Charleston (Inc. Place)
Wappoo Heights; RMC Place; CHARLESTON; ***230** H-10; ★ **CHAS**; pop. incl. with Charleston (Inc. Place)
Wappoo Shores; RMC Place; CHARLESTON; ***230** H-10; ★ **CHAS**; pop. incl. with Charleston (Inc. Place)
Ward; Inc. Place; SALUDA; **230** E-6; elev. 672ft./205m.; 🅿; z 29166; Ⓟ 132; Ⓒ 110
Ware Place; RMC Place; GREENVILLE; ***230** C-4; elev. 884ft./269m.; ★ **GRNV**; mail Pelzer z 29669; ● 120
Ware Shoals; Inc. Place; GREENWOOD, ABBEVILLE, LAURENS; **230** C-4; elev. 642ft./196m.; 🅿; z 29692; Ⓟ 2,497; Ⓒ 2,363
Warren Crossroads; RMC Place; CHARLESTON; ***230** H-9; elev. 34ft./10m.; mail Ravenel z 29470; rural
Warrenville; RMC Place; AIKEN; **230** F-5; 🅿; ★ **AUG**; z 29851; ● 1,000
Warsaw; RMC Place; WILLIAMSBURG; **230** F-11; elev. 37ft./11m.; mail Andrews z 29510; ● 70
Wateree; RMC Place; RICHLAND; ***230** E-8; mail Eastover z 29044
Waterford Estates; RMC Place; GEORGETOWN; ***230** F-12; elev. 8ft./2m.; mail Georgetown z 29440; ● 110
Waterloo; Inc. Place; LAURENS; **230** C-5; 🅿; z 29384; Ⓟ 122; Ⓒ 203
Watkins Store; RMC Place; AIKEN; ***230** F-6; elev. 432ft./132m.; ★ **AUG**; mail Aiken z 29803; ● 100
Watts Mills; CDP-Census Area Only; LAURENS; **230** C-5; mail Laurens z 29360; Ⓟ 1,535; Ⓒ 1,479
Wattsville; RMC Place; LAURENS; ***230** C-5; ● 1,400
Waverly Mills; RMC Place; GEORGETOWN; ***230** F-12; mail Pawleys Island z 29585; ● 50
Waylyn; RMC Place; CHARLESTON; ***230** H-10; ★ **CHAS**; mail North Charleston z 29405; pop. incl. with North Charleston (Inc. Place)
Wedgefield; RMC Place; SUMTER; **230** E-9; elev. 251ft./77m.; 🅿; ★ **SUMT**; z 29168; ● 350
Wedgewood; CDP-Census Area Only; SUMTER; ***230** E-9; Ⓒ 1,544
Welcome; RMC Place; ANDERSON; ***230** C-3; ★ **AND**; mail Pendleton z 29670; rural
Welcome; CDP; GREENVILLE; **230** J-4; ★ **GRNV**; mail Greenville z 29611; Ⓟ 6,560; Ⓒ 6,390
Wellford; Inc. Place; SPARTANBURG; **230** B-5; 🅿; z 29385; Ⓟ 2,511; Ⓒ 2,030
Wells; RMC Place; ORANGEBURG; ***230** F-9; mail Holly Hill z 29059; rural
West Andrews; RMC Place; GEORGETOWN; mail Andrews z 29510; pop. incl. with Andrews (Inc. Place)
West Columbia; Inc. Place; LEXINGTON; **230** J-2; 🅿 🅷; ★ **COL**; z 29033, z 29169-72; Ⓟ 10,588; Ⓒ 13,064
Westerly Park; RMC Place; CHEROKEE; ***230** A-6; mail Gaffney z 29341; pop. incl. with Gaffney (Inc. Place)
West Gantt; RMC Place; GREENVILLE; ***230** B-4; elev. 977ft./298m.; ★ **GRNV**; mail Greenville z 29605; ● 3,050
Westgate; RMC Place; SPARTANBURG; mail Spartanburg z 29301; pop. incl. with Spartanburg (Inc. Place)
West Hartsville; RMC Place; DARLINGTON; ***230** C-10; elev. 230ft./70m.; pop. incl. with Hartsville (Inc. Place)
West Marion; RMC Place; MARION; ***230** D-11; elev. 60ft./18m.; mail Marion z 29571; ● 100
Westminster; Inc. Place; OCONEE; **230** B-2; elev. 935ft./285m.; 🅿; z 29693; Ⓟ 3,120; Ⓒ 2,743
Westover Acres; RMC Place; LEXINGTON; ★ **COL**; mail West Columbia z 29169; pop. incl. with West Columbia (Inc. Place)
West Pelzer; Inc. Place; ANDERSON; **230** B-4; ★ **GRNV**; mail Pelzer z 29669; Ⓟ 989; Ⓒ 879
West Springs; RMC Place; UNION; **230** B-6; elev. 711ft./217m.; mail Jonesville z 29353, Pauline z 29374; ● 160
West Union; Inc. Place; OCONEE; **230** B-2; 🅿; z 29696; Ⓟ 260; Ⓒ 297
Westview; RMC Place; SPARTANBURG; **230** G-1; ★ **SPRT**; mail Spartanburg z 29301; ● 2,000
Westville; RMC Place; GREENVILLE; **230** I-4; ★ **GRNV**; mail Greenville z 29611; ● 2,200
Westville; RMC Place; KERSHAW; **230** C-8; elev. 452ft./138m.; 🅿; z 29175; ● 80
Westwood; RMC Place; CHARLESTON; ★ **CHAS**; pop. incl. with Charleston (Inc. Place)
Wexford; RMC Place; CHESTERFIELD; ***230** B-9; mail Ruby z 29741; rural
Whetstone; RMC Place; OCONEE; ***230** B-2; elev. 690ft./210m.; mail Mountain Rest z 29664
Whipper Barony; RMC Place; CHARLESTON; ★ **CHAS**; mail North Charleston z 29405; pop. incl. with North Charleston (Inc. Place)
White Bluff Crossroads; RMC Place; LANCASTER; ***230** B-8; elev. 605ft./184m.; mail Kershaw z 29067; rural
White Hall; RMC Place; COLLETON; **230** H-8; elev. 12ft./4m.; mail Green Pond z 29446, Yemassee z 29945; ● 40
Whitehall; RMC Place; GREENWOOD; ***230** D-4; mail Greenwood z 29646; rural
Whitehall; RMC Place; LEXINGTON; **230** D-7; ★ **COL**; mail Columbia z 29210; ● 3,600
White Oak; RMC Place; FAIRFIELD; **230** C-7; 🅿; z 29180; ● 50
White Plains; RMC Place; ANDERSON; ***230** B-4; ★ **GRNV**; mail Williamston z 29697; rural
White Plains; RMC Place; CHESTERFIELD; ***230** B-9; elev. 611ft./186m.; mail Jefferson z 29718; rural
White Pond; RMC Place; AIKEN; ***230** F-6; elev. 383ft./117m.; mail Williston z 29853; ● 100
White Rock; RMC Place; RICHLAND; **230** D-7; 🅿; ★ **COL**; z 29177; ● 440
Whites Creek; GEORGETOWN; see McDonald (RMC Place)
White Stone; RMC Place; SPARTANBURG; **230** B-5; elev. 780ft./238m.; 🅿; ★ **SPRT**; z 29386; ● 200
Whitesville; RMC Place; BERKELEY; ***230** G-10; ★ **CHAS**; mail Moncks Corner z 29461; ● 70
Whitetown; RMC Place; MCCORMICK; ***230** E-4; elev. 438ft./134m.; mail Plum Branch z 29845; rural
Whitmire; Inc. Place; NEWBERRY; **230** C-6; 🅿; z 29178; Ⓟ 1,702; Ⓒ 1,512
Whitney; RMC Place; SPARTANBURG; **230** F-2; ★ **SPRT**; mail Spartanburg z 29303; ● 1,500
Wilder; RMC Place; BERKELEY; ***230** F-10; elev. 61ft./19m.; mail Bonneau z 29431
Wilkins; RMC Place; BEAUFORT; **230** I-8; mail Beaufort z 29904
Wilkinson Heights; CDP; ORANGEBURG; ***230** F-8; elev. 60ft./18m.; mail Orangeburg z 29115; Ⓟ 3,394; Ⓒ 3,068
Wilkinsville; RMC Place; CHEROKEE; ***230** B-6; elev. 634ft./193m.; mail Gaffney z 29340
Wilksburg; RMC Place; CHESTER; ***230** B-6; mail Chester z 29706; ● 65
Williams; Inc. Place; COLLETON; **230** G-8; 🅿; z 29493; Ⓟ 188; Ⓒ 116
WILLIAMSBURG; **230** E-11; Ⓟ 36,815; Ⓒ 37,217; ◆ 35,491
Williams Estate; RMC Place; LANCASTER; ***230** B-8; elev. 510ft./155m.; mail Lancaster z 29720; ● 300
Williamston; Inc. Place; ANDERSON; **230** C-4; elev. 826ft./252m.; 🅿; ★ **GRNV**; z 29697; Ⓟ 3,876; Ⓒ 3,791
Willington; CDP; MCCORMICK; **230** D-4; elev. 483ft./147m.; mail Mc Cormick z 29835; Ⓒ 177
Williston; Inc. Place; BARNWELL; **230** F-6; elev. 353ft./108m.; 🅿; z 29853; Ⓟ 3,099; Ⓒ 3,307
Willowbrook; RMC Place; BERKELEY; ***230** G-10; elev. 25ft./8m.; ★ **CHAS**; mail Goose Creek z 29445; ● 1,100
Wilson; RMC Place; CLARENDON; **230** E-10; elev. 119ft./36m.; mail Manning z 29102; ● 25
Wilson Creek; RMC Place; GREENWOOD; ***230** D-5; elev. 500ft./152m.; ★ **GREEN**; mail Greenwood z 29646; ● 50
Wilsons Cross Roads; RMC Place; DARLINGTON; ***230** D-10; elev. 47ft./14m.; mail Darlington z 29532; ● 35
Windsor; Inc. Place; AIKEN; **230** F-6; elev. 391ft./119m.; 🅿; z 29856; Ⓟ 124; Ⓒ 127
Windsor Estates; RMC Place; RICHLAND; ***230** D-8; elev. 300ft./91m.; ★ **COL**; mail Columbia z 29204; ● 2,200
Windsor Forest; RMC Place; FLORENCE; ***230** D-10; elev. 40ft./12m.; ★ **FLO**; mail Florence z 29501; ● 200
Windsor Lake Park; RMC Place; RICHLAND; ***230** D-8; elev. 300ft./91m.; ★ **COL**; mail Columbia z 29206; ● 120
Windsor Park; RMC Place; CHESTERFIELD; ***230** B-10; elev. 173ft./53m.; mail Cheraw z 29520; ● 400
Windsor Plantation; RMC Place; GEORGETOWN; ***230** F-12; elev. 7ft./2m.; mail Georgetown z 29440; ● 50
Windwood; RMC Place; BERKELEY; ***230** G-10; elev. 80ft./24m.; ★ **CHAS**; mail Moncks Corner z 29461; ● 400
Windy Hill; RMC Place; FLORENCE; ***230** D-11; ★ **FLO**; mail Florence z 29506; ● 1,600
Windy Hill Beach; RMC Place; HORRY; ***230** E-13; ★ **MYR.B**; mail North Myrtle Beach z 29582; pop. incl. with North Myrtle Beach (Inc. Place)
Winnsboro; Inc. Place; ⊡ FAIRFIELD; **230** C-7; 🅿 🅷; z 29180; Ⓟ 3,496; Ⓒ 3,599
Winnsboro Mills; CDP; FAIRFIELD; **230** C-7; mail Winnsboro z 29180; Ⓟ 2,275; Ⓒ 2,263
Winona; RMC Place; FLORENCE; ***230** D-11; elev. 99ft./30m.; ★ **FLO**; mail Florence z 29506; rural
Wisacky; RMC Place; LEE; **230** D-9; elev. 189ft./58m.; 🅿; z 29010; ● 80
Wisewood; RMC Place; GREENWOOD; ***230** D-5; ★ **GREEN**; mail Greenwood z 29646
Witherbee; RMC Place; BERKELEY; ***230** G-10; mail Cordesville z 29434; rural
Wolfton; RMC Place; ORANGEBURG; **230** F-7; elev. 302ft./92m.; mail North z 29112; ● 50
Woodburn Hills; RMC Place; SPARTANBURG; ***230** B-5; ★ **SPRT**; mail Spartanburg z 29302; pop. incl. with Spartanburg (Inc. Place)
Woodfield; CDP-Census Area Only; RICHLAND; ***230** D-8; elev. 300ft./91m.; ★ **COL**; mail Columbia z 29206; Ⓟ 8,862; Ⓒ 9,238
Woodfields; RMC Place; GREENVILLE; ***230** B-4; ★ **GRNV**; mail Greenville z 29605; ● 1,600
Woodford; Inc. Place; ORANGEBURG; **230** E-7; mail North z 29112; Ⓟ 200; Ⓒ 196
Woodland Hills; RMC Place; LEXINGTON; ***230** D-7; elev. 250ft./76m.; ★ **COL**; mail Columbia z 29210; ● 2,700
Woodrow; RMC Place; LEE, SUMTER; ***230** D-9; elev. 251ft./77m.; mail Dalzell z 29040
Woodruff; Inc. Place; SPARTANBURG; **230** B-5; elev. 785ft./239m.; 🅿 🅷; z 29388; Ⓟ 4,365; Ⓒ 4,229
Woodside; RMC Place; GREENVILLE; **230** I-4; ★ **GRNV**; mail Greenville z 29610; ● 180
Woodville; RMC Place; GREENVILLE; **230** B-4; ★ **GRNV**; mail Pelzer z 29669; ● 160
Woodward; RMC Place; FAIRFIELD; ***230** C-7; mail Blackstock z 29014
Workman; RMC Place; WILLIAMSBURG; **230** E-10; elev. 72ft./22m.; mail New Zion z 29111; ● 50

Y

Yarn Mill; RMC Place; CHESTERFIELD; ***230** B-10; elev. 175ft./53m.; mail Cheraw z 29520; ● 250
Yauhannah; RMC Place; GEORGETOWN; ***230** E-12; elev. 32ft./10m.; mail Georgetown z 29440
Yeamans Hall; RMC Place; BERKELEY; ★ **CHAS**; mail Hanahan z 29410; pop. incl. with Hanahan (Inc. Place)
Yemassee; Inc. Place; HAMPTON, BEAUFORT; **230** H-8; elev. 25ft./8m.; 🅿; z 29945; Ⓟ 728; Ⓒ 807
Yenome; RMC Place; BARNWELL; ***230** G-7; mail Barnwell z 29812; rural
Yonges Island; RMC Place; CHARLESTON; **230** H-9; 🅿; ★ **CHAS**; z 29449; pop. incl. with Meggett (Inc. Place)
York; Inc. Place; ⊡ YORK; **230** A-7; elev. 756ft./230m.; 🅿; z 29745; Ⓟ 6,709; Ⓒ 6,985
YORK; **230** B-7; Ⓟ 131,497; Ⓒ 164,614; Ⓡ 164,623; ◆ 228,258
York Hills; RMC Place; CHEROKEE; ***230** A-6; mail Gaffney z 29340; pop. incl. with Gaffney (Inc. Place)
Yorkshire; RMC Place; RICHLAND; ***230** D-8; ★ **COL**; mail Columbia z 29209; pop. incl. with Columbia (Inc. Place)
Yoruba Village (Oyo Tungi); RMC Place; BEAUFORT; ***230** H-8; elev. 15ft./5m.; mail Sheldon z 29941; ● 100
Youngs; RMC Place; LAURENS; ***230** B-5; elev. 225ft./69m.; mail Woodruff z 29388; ● 80

Z

Zion; RMC Place; MARION; **230** D-12; elev. 110ft./34m.; mail Mullin z 29574; ● 100

Entries in **UPPERCASE** are counties.
Entries in **bold** have populations of 2,500 or more.
Names in parentheses are alternate names.
Inc. Place — Incorporated Place
RMC Place — Rand McNally Designated Place
CDP — Census Designated Place
MCD — Minor Civil Division

⊡ County Seat
▲ Minor Civil Division
elev. Elevation
🅿 Post Office

🅷 Hospital
🅲 College
■ Principal Business Center
★ Ranally Metro Area (RMA) Abbreviation
z Zip Code(s)

Ⓟ Previous Census Population
Ⓡ Revised Census Population
Ⓐ Annexation Population
● Rand McNally Population Estimate
Ⓒ Final Census Population
Ⓢ Special Census Population
◆ Estimated Population

For additional definitions see Glossary, Volume 1, and Introduction, Volume 2.

SOUTH DAKOTA

MT · ND · MN · WY · NE · IA · ★ Pierre

Statistics

Total area (2000) — 77,117 square miles
Land area (2000) — 75,885 square miles
Water area (2000) — 1,232 square miles
Capital — Pierre
Admitted as state — November, 1869

Maps

State maps can be found on pages 142-254 in Vol. 1

Ranally Metro Areas (RMAs) and Abbreviations

Rapid City, SD — RAP
Sioux City, IA-NE-SD — SXCY
Sioux Falls, SD — SXFL

Principal Places

Place Name	Place Type	County	Population	Place Name	Place Type	County	Population	Place Name	Place Type	County	Population
Sioux Falls	Inc. Place	MINNEHAHA	◆ 168,625	Mitchell	Inc. Place	DAVISON	◆ 13,959	Spearfish	Inc. Place	LAWRENCE	© 8,606
Rapid City	Inc. Place	PENNINGTON	◆ 68,549	Pierre	Inc. Place	HUGHES	© 13,876	Rapid Valley	CDP	PENNINGTON	© 7,043
Aberdeen	Inc. Place	BROWN	◆ 24,798	Yankton	Inc. Place	YANKTON	◆ 12,815	Madison	Inc. Place	LAKE	© 6,540
Watertown	Inc. Place	CODINGTON	◆ 20,534	Huron	Inc. Place	BEADLE	◆ 11,833	Sturgis	Inc. Place	MEADE	© 6,442
Brookings	Inc. Place	BROOKINGS	© 18,504	Vermillion	Inc. Place	CLAY	® 10,276	Brandon	Inc. Place	MINNEHAHA	© 5,693

County Business Data

County	FIPS Code	County Seat	Land Area (Sq. Mi.)	Census Population			Wholesale Trade		Manufacturing, 2002			
				4/1/2000	4/1/1990	% Change 1990-2000	Sales, 2002 ($1,000)	% Change 1997-2002	Establish-ments	Total Employees	Value Added ($1,000)	Ranally Mfg. Units
Aurora	003	Plankinton	708	3,058	3,135	-2.5	7,336	-45.4	...	(d)	(d)	...
Beadle	005	Huron	1,259	17,023	18,253	-6.7	236,931	28.8	28	(d)	(d)	...
Bennett	007	Martin	1,185	3,574	3,206	11.5	(d)	(d)	...	(d)	(d)	...
Bon Homme	009	Tyndall	563	7,260	7,089	2.4	23,045	-55.2	...	(d)	(d)	...
Brookings	011	Brookings	794	28,220	25,207	12.0	63,230	-76.2	33	4,473	724,224	383
Brown	013	Aberdeen	1,713	35,460	35,580	-0.3	693,874	8.9	32	(d)	(d)	...
Brule	015	Chamberlain	819	5,364	5,485	-2.2	32,402	-11.3	...	(d)	(d)	...
Buffalo	017	Gann Valley	471	2,032	1,759	15.5	(d)	(d)	...	(d)	(d)	...
Butte	019	Belle Fourche	2,249	9,094	7,914	14.9	98,659	18.7	...	(d)	(d)	...
Campbell	021	Mound City	736	1,782	1,965	-9.3	(d)	(d)	...	(d)	(d)	...
Charles Mix	023	Lake Andes	1,098	9,350	9,131	2.4	127,219	100.0	...	(d)	(d)	...
Clark	025	Clark	958	4,143	4,403	-5.9	42,220	-47.6	...	(d)	(d)	...
Clay	027	Vermillion	412	13,537	13,186	2.7	(d)	(d)	...	(d)	(d)	...
Codington	029	Watertown	688	25,897	22,698	14.1	355,220	10.8	71	(d)	(d)	...
Corson	031	McIntosh	2,473	4,181	4,195	-0.3	(d)	(d)	...	(d)	(d)	...
Custer	033	Custer	1,558	7,275	6,179	17.7	912	(d)	...	(d)	(d)	...
Davison	035	Mitchell	435	18,741	17,503	7.1	(d)	(d)	35	(d)	(d)	...
Day	037	Webster	1,029	6,267	6,978	-10.2	57,072	7.2	...	(d)	(d)	...
Deuel	039	Clear Lake	624	4,498	4,522	-0.5	5,894	-22.6	...	(d)	(d)	...
Dewey	041	Timber Lake	2,303	5,972	5,523	8.1	10,557	-16.5	...	(d)	(d)	...
Douglas	043	Armour	434	3,458	3,746	-7.7	55,455	219.5	...	(d)	(d)	...
Edmunds	045	Ipswich	1,146	4,367	4,356	0.3	100,483	-1.0	...	(d)	(d)	...
Fall River	047	Hot Springs	1,740	7,453	7,353	1.4	5,311	-2.8	...	(d)	(d)	...
Faulk	049	Faulkton	1,000	2,640	2,744	-3.8	(d)	(d)	...	(d)	(d)	...
Grant	051	Milbank	683	7,847	8,372	-6.3	83,792	-21.1	...	(d)	(d)	...
Gregory	053	Burke	1,016	4,792	5,359	-10.6	46,985	19.8	...	(d)	(d)	...
Haakon	055	Philip	1,813	2,196	2,624	-16.3	18,057	-71.1	...	(d)	(d)	...
Hamlin	057	Hayti	507	5,540	4,974	11.4	35,940	-6.1	...	(d)	(d)	...
Hand	059	Miller	1,437	3,741	4,272	-12.4	38,742	-33.8	...	(d)	(d)	...
Hanson	061	Alexandria	435	3,139	2,994	4.8	(d)	(d)	...	(d)	(d)	...
Harding	063	Buffalo	2,670	1,353	1,669	-18.9	(d)	(d)	...	(d)	(d)	...
Hughes	065	Pierre	741	16,481	14,817	11.2	(d)	(d)	...	(d)	(d)	...
Hutchinson	067	Olivet	813	8,075	8,262	-2.3	87,175	-40.8	...	(d)	(d)	...
Hyde	069	Highmore	861	1,671	1,696	-1.5	(d)	(d)	...	(d)	(d)	...
Jackson	071	Kadoka	1,869	2,930	2,811	4.2	(d)	(d)	...	(d)	(d)	...
Jerauld	073	Wessington Springs	530	2,295	2,425	-5.4	(d)	(d)	...	(d)	(d)	...
Jones	075	Murdo	971	1,193	1,324	-9.9	(d)	(d)	...	(d)	(d)	...
Kingsbury	077	De Smet	838	5,815	5,925	-1.9	67,036	-3.2	...	(d)	(d)	...
Lake	079	Madison	563	11,276	10,550	6.9	94,473	16.7	27	1,012	85,695	45
Lawrence	081	Deadwood	800	21,802	20,655	5.6	18,186	49.8	34	(d)	(d)	...
Lincoln	083	Canton	578	24,131	15,427	56.4	226,791	13.1	37	980	89,731	47
Lyman	085	Kennebec	1,640	3,895	3,638	7.1	(d)	(d)	...	(d)	(d)	...
Marshall	091	Britton	838	4,576	4,844	-5.5	44,179	2.8	...	(d)	(d)	...
McCook	087	Salem	575	5,832	5,688	2.5	(d)	(d)	...	(d)	(d)	...
McPherson	089	Leola	1,137	2,904	3,228	-10.0	(d)	(d)	...	(d)	(d)	...
Meade	093	Sturgis	3,471	24,253	21,878	10.9	115,608	22.0	...	(d)	(d)	...
Mellette	095	White River	1,306	2,083	2,137	-2.5	(d)	(d)	...	(d)	(d)	...
Miner	097	Howard	570	2,884	3,272	-11.9	(d)	(d)	...	(d)	(d)	...
Minnehaha	099	Sioux Falls	810	148,281	123,809	19.8	2,337,275	9.0	173	10,492	902,086	477
Moody	101	Flandreau	520	6,595	6,507	1.4	72,808	454.2	...	(d)	(d)	...
Pennington	103	Rapid City	2,776	88,565	81,343	8.9	833,203	23.3	122	3,337	257,903	136
Perkins	105	Bison	2,872	3,363	3,932	-14.5	14,962	-69.7	...	(d)	(d)	...
Potter	107	Gettysburg	866	2,693	3,190	-15.6	25,617	-55.3	...	(d)	(d)	...
Roberts	109	Sisseton	1,101	10,016	9,914	1.0	152,848	-24.6	...	(d)	(d)	...
Sanborn	111	Woonsocket	569	2,675	2,833	-5.6	5,895	-62.1	...	(d)	(d)	...
Shannon	113	Hot Springs (Fall River County)	2,094	12,466	9,902	25.9	(d)	(d)	...	(d)	(d)	...
Spink	115	Redfield	1,504	7,454	7,981	-6.6	155,155	16.7	...	(d)	(d)	...
Stanley	117	Fort Pierre	1,443	2,772	2,453	13.0	(d)	(d)	...	(d)	(d)	...
Sully	119	Onida	1,007	1,556	1,589	-2.1	(d)	(d)	...	(d)	(d)	...
Todd	121	Winner (Tripp County)	1,388	9,050	8,352	8.4	(d)	(d)	...	(d)	(d)	...
Tripp	123	Winner	1,614	6,430	6,924	-7.1	77,848	-5.6	...	(d)	(d)	...
Turner	125	Parker	617	8,849	8,576	3.2	(d)	(d)	...	(d)	(d)	...
Union	127	Elk Point	460	12,584	10,189	23.5	(d)	(d)	24	(d)	(d)	...
Walworth	129	Selby	708	5,974	6,087	-1.9	97,934	186.2	...	(d)	(d)	...
Yankton	135	Yankton	522	21,652	19,252	12.5	227,700	-21.5	31	2,154	202,926	107
Ziebach	137	Dupree	1,962	2,519	2,220	13.5	(d)	(d)	...	(d)	(d)	...
The State			**75,885**	**754,844**	**696,004**	**8.5**	**7,845,096**	**-0.4**	**926**	**37,019**	**5,176,605**	**2,739**

(d) Data not available. Corresponding percentages or Ranally Manufacturing Units are estimates.
... Represents 0 or amount too minimal to be reported.

Index of Places and Counties

A

Aberdeen; Inc. Place; ⊡ BROWN; **231** B-10; elev. 1,304ft./397m.; 🅿 🅷 🅲 3,105 ■; z 57401-02; Ⓟ 24,927; © 24,658; ◆ 24,798
Academy; RMC Place; CHARLES MIX; **231** F-9; elev. 1,680ft./512m.; 🅿; z 57369; ● 10
Agar; Inc. Place; SULLY; **231** C-8; elev. 1,851ft./564m.; 🅿; z 57520; Ⓟ 82; © 82
Akaska; Inc. Place; WALWORTH; **231** B-8; elev. 1,768ft./539m.; 🅿; z 57420; Ⓟ 52; © 31
Albee; RMC Place; GRANT; **231** C-13; elev. 1,177ft./359m.; 🅿; z 57259; disincorporated July 1, 1996; Ⓟ 15; © 10
Alcester; Inc. Place; UNION; **231** G-13; elev. 1,370ft./418m.; 🅿; z 57001; Ⓟ 843; © 880
Alexandria; Inc. Place; ⊡ HANSON; **231** F-11; elev. 1,350ft./411m.; 🅿; z 57311; Ⓟ 518; © 563
Allen; CDP; BENNETT; **231** F-5; located on Pine Ridge Ind. Res.; elev. 3,400ft./1,036m.; 🅿; z 57714; © 419
Alpena; Inc. Place; JERAULD; **231** E-10; elev. 1,320ft./402m.; 🅿; z 57312; Ⓟ 251; © 265
Altamont; Inc. Place; DEUEL; **231** C-13; elev. 1,834ft./559m.; 🅿; z 57226; Ⓟ 48; © 34
Ames; RMC Place; HAND; ***231** D-9; elev. 1,881ft./573m.; mail Miller z 57362, Pierre z 57501; rural
Amherst; RMC Place; MARSHALL; **231** A-11; elev. 1,310ft./399m.; 🅿; z 57421; ● 70
Andover; Inc. Place; DAY; **231** B-11; elev. 1,482ft./452m.; 🅿; z 57422; Ⓟ 106; © 99
Antelope; CDP; TODD; **231** F-7; located on Rosebud Ind. Res.; mail Mission z 57555; Ⓟ 744; © 867
Ardmore; RMC Place; FALL RIVER; **231** G-2; elev. 3,500ft./1,067m.; 🅿; z 57735
Arlington; Inc. Place; KINGSBURY, BROOKINGS; **231** D-12; elev. 1,842ft./561m.; 🅿; z 57212; Ⓟ 908; © 992
Arlington Beach; RMC Place; BROOKINGS; ***231** D-12; elev. 1,664ft./507m.; mail Arlington z 57212; ● 20
Armour; Inc. Place; ⊡ DOUGLAS; **231** F-10; elev. 1,523ft./464m.; 🅿 🅷; z 57313; Ⓟ 854; © 782
Arpan; RMC Place; BUTTE; ***231** C-2; mail Nisland z 57762; rural
Artas; Inc. Place; CAMPBELL; **231** A-8; elev. 1,813ft./553m.; 🅿; z 57437; Ⓟ 28; © 13
Artesian; Inc. Place; SANBORN; **231** E-11; elev. 1,317ft./401m.; 🅿; z 57314 & mail Fedora z 57337; Ⓟ 217; © 157
Ashland Heights; CDP-Census Area Only; PENNINGTON; ***231** E-3; ★ **RAP**; © 837
Ashton; Inc. Place; SPINK; **231** C-10; elev. 1,291ft./393m.; 🅿; z 57424; Ⓟ 148; © 152
Astoria; Inc. Place; DEUEL; **231** D-13; elev. 1,820ft./555m.; 🅿; z 57213; Ⓟ 155; © 150
Athol; RMC Place; SPINK; **231** C-10; elev. 1,295ft./395m.; 🅿; z 57424; ● 50
Aurora; Inc. Place; BROOKINGS; **231** D-13; elev. 1,624ft./495m.; 🅿; z 57002; Ⓟ 619; © 500
AURORA; **231** F-10; Ⓟ 3,135; © 3,058; ◆ 2,803
Aurora Center; CDP; AURORA; **231** F-10; mail Stickney z 57375; © 7
Avon; Inc. Place; BON HOMME; **231** G-11; elev. 1,608ft./490m.; 🅿; z 57315; Ⓟ 576; © 561

B

Badger; Inc. Place; KINGSBURY; **231** D-12; elev. 1,730ft./527m.; 🅿; z 57214; Ⓟ 114; © 144
Balleyview (Valley View); RMC Place; YANKTON; ***231** G-12; elev. 1,259ft./384m.; mail Volin z 57072
Baltic; Inc. Place; MINNEHAHA; **231** E-13; elev. 1,510ft./460m.; 🅿; z 57003; Ⓟ 666; © 811
Bancroft; Inc. Place; KINGSBURY; **231** D-11; elev. 1,570ft./479m.; 🅿; z 57353; Ⓟ 30; © 37
Barnard; RMC Place; BROWN; **231** A-10; elev. 1,392ft./424m.; 🅿; z 57426; ● 60
Batesland; Inc. Place; SHANNON; **231** G-4; elev. 3,415ft./1,041m.; 🅿; z 57716; Ⓟ 124; © 88
Bath; RMC Place; BROWN; **231** B-10; elev. 1,302ft./397m.; 🅿; z 57427; ● 180
BEADLE; **231** D-10; Ⓟ 18,253; © 17,023; ◆ 16,087
Bear Butte; RMC Place; MEADE; ***231** D-3; elev. 2,853ft./870m.; mail Sturgis z 57785; rural
Bear Creek; RMC Place; DEWEY; ***231** C-6; mail Lantry z 57636; rural
Belle Fourche; Inc. Place; ⊡ BUTTE; **231** D-2; elev. 3,023ft./921m.; 🅿; z 57717; Ⓟ 4,335; © 4,565
Belvidere; Inc. Place; JACKSON; **231** E-6; elev. 2,330ft./710m.; 🅿; z 57521; Ⓟ 63; © 57
Bemis; RMC Place; DEUEL; **231** C-12; elev. 1,940ft./591m.; 🅿; z 57238; ● 35
BENNETT; **231** G-5; Ⓟ 3,206; © 3,574; ◆ 3,374
Beresford; Inc. Place; UNION, LINCOLN; **231** G-13; elev. 1,498ft./457m.; 🅿; z 57004; Ⓟ 1,849; © 2,006
Bethlehem; RMC Place; MEADE; **231** H-3; elev. 3,500ft./1,067m.; 🅿; z 57769; ● 10
Big Bend; RMC Place; PENNINGTON; ***231** E-3; mail Rapid City z 57702; rural
Big Coulee; RMC Place; ROBERTS; ***231** B-12; elev. 1,190ft./363m.; mail Peever z 57257; ● 50
Big Springs; RMC Place; UNION; **231** G-13; elev. 1,381ft./421m.; mail Alcester z 57001; ● 10
Big Stone City; Inc. Place; GRANT; **231** B-13; elev. 977ft./298m.; 🅿; z 57216; Ⓟ 669; © 605
Bijou Hills; RMC Place; BRULE; **231** F-9; mail Chamberlain z 57325, Pukwana z 57370; rural
Billsburg; RMC Place; HAAKON; ***231** D-5; mail Milesville z 57553; rural
Bison; Inc. Place; ⊡ PERKINS; **231** B-4; elev. 2,784ft./849m.; 🅿; z 57620; Ⓟ 451; © 373
Blackhawk; CDP; MEADE; **231** E-3; elev. 3,493ft./1,065m.; 🅿; ★ **RAP**; z 57718; Ⓟ 1,995; © 2,432
Blacktail; RMC Place; LAWRENCE; ***231** D-2; mail Lead z 57754; ● 30
Blumengard Colony; RMC Place; FAULK; ***231** B-9; mail Faulkton z 57438; ● 30
Blunt; Inc. Place; HUGHES; **231** D-8; elev. 1,619ft./493m.; 🅿; z 57522; Ⓟ 342; © 370
Bonesteel; Inc. Place; GREGORY; **231** G-9; elev. 1,963ft./598m.; 🅿; z 57317; Ⓟ 297; © 297
BON HOMME; **231** G-11; Ⓟ 7,089; © 7,260; ◆ 7,028
Bon Homme Colony; RMC Place; BON HOMME; ***231** G-11; mail Tabor z 57063; ● 60
Bonilla; RMC Place; BEADLE; **231** D-10; mail Hitchcock z 57348; ● 30
Bowdle; Inc. Place; EDMUNDS; **231** B-8; elev. 2,004ft./611m.; 🅿 🅷; z 57428; Ⓟ 589; © 571
Box Elder; Inc. Place; PENNINGTON; **231** E-3; elev. 3,030ft./924m.; 🅿; ★ **RAP**; z 57719; Ⓟ 2,680; © 2,841
Bradley; Inc. Place; CLARK; **231** C-11; elev. 1,795ft./547m.; 🅿; z 57217; Ⓟ 117; © 112
Brandon; Inc. Place; MINNEHAHA; **231** F-13; elev. 1,357ft./414m.; 🅿; z 57005; Ⓟ 3,543; © 5,693
Brandt; Inc. Place; DEUEL; **231** D-13; elev. 1,851ft./564m.; 🅿; z 57218; Ⓟ 123; © 113
Brentford; Inc. Place; SPINK; **231** C-10; elev. 1,300ft./396m.; 🅿; z 57429; Ⓟ 69; © 65
Bridger; RMC Place; ZIEBACH; ***231** D-5; located on Cheyenne River Ind. Res.; mail Howes z 57748; ● 50
Bridgewater; Inc. Place; MCCOOK; **231** F-11; elev. 1,420ft./433m.; 🅿; z 57319; Ⓟ 533; © 607
Bristol; Inc. Place; DAY; **231** B-11; elev. 1,790ft./546m.; 🅿; z 57219; Ⓟ 419; © 377
Britton; Inc. Place; ⊡ MARSHALL; **231** A-11; elev. 1,358ft./414m.; 🅿 🅷; z 57430; Ⓟ 1,394; © 1,328
Broadland; Inc. Place; BEADLE; **231** D-10; elev. 1,303ft./397m.; mail Huron z 57350; Ⓟ 40; © 38
Brookings; Inc. Place; ⊡ BROOKINGS; **231** D-12; elev. 1,623ft./495m.; 🅿 🅷 🅲 11,377; z 57006-07; Ⓟ 16,270; © 18,504
BROOKINGS; **231** D-13; Ⓟ 25,207; © 28,220; ◆ 30,134
BROWN; **231** B-10; Ⓟ 35,580; © 35,460; ◆ 35,443
Brownsville; RMC Place; LAWRENCE; ***231** D-2; mail Deadwood z 57732; rural
Bruce; Inc. Place; BROOKINGS; **231** D-12; elev. 1,620ft./494m.; 🅿; z 57220; Ⓟ 235; © 272
BRULE; **231** F-9; Ⓟ 5,485; © 5,364; ◆ 5,335
Bryant; Inc. Place; HAMLIN; **231** D-11; elev. 1,845ft./562m.; 🅿; z 57221; Ⓟ 374; © 396
Buffalo; Inc. Place; ⊡ HARDING; **231** B-3; elev. 2,877ft./877m.; 🅿; z 57720; Ⓟ 488; © 380
BUFFALO; **231** E-9; Ⓟ 1,759; © 2,032; ◆ 2,033
Buffalo Gap; Inc. Place; CUSTER; **231** F-3; elev. 3,260ft./994m.; 🅿; z 57722; Ⓟ 173; © 164
Buffalo Ridge; RMC Place; MINNEHAHA; ***231** F-12; 🅿; z 57107; ● 20
Buffalo Trading Post; RMC Place; MINNEHAHA; ***231** E-12; elev. 1,680ft./512m.; mail Colton z 57018; rural
Bullhead; CDP; CORSON; **231** A-6; located on Standing Rock Ind. Res.; elev. 1,783ft./543m.; 🅿; z 57621; Ⓟ 179; © 308
Burbank; RMC Place; CLAY; **231** H-13; elev. 1,139ft./347m.; 🅿; z 57010; ● 90
Burdock; RMC Place; FALL RIVER; ***231** F-2; 🅿; z 57735; rural
Burke; Inc. Place; ⊡ GREGORY; **231** G-9; located on Rosebud Ind. Res.; elev. 2,213ft./675m.; 🅿 🅷; z 57523; Ⓟ 756; © 676
Bushnell; Inc. Place; BROOKINGS; **231** D-13; elev. 1,693ft./516m.; 🅿; z 57276; Ⓟ 81; © 75
Butler; Inc. Place; DAY; **231** B-11; elev. 1,822ft./555m.; 🅿; z 57219; Ⓟ 17; © 17
BUTTE; **231** C-3; Ⓟ 7,914; © 9,094; ◆ 9,831

C

Cactus Flat; RMC Place; JACKSON; ***231** E-5; elev. 3,100ft./945m.; mail Philip z 57567; rural
CAMPBELL; **231** A-8; Ⓟ 1,965; © 1,782; ◆ 1,253
Camp Crook; Inc. Place; HARDING; **231** B-2; 🅿; z 57724; Ⓟ 146; © 56
Canistota; Inc. Place; MCCOOK; **231** F-12; elev. 1,549ft./472m.; 🅿; z 57012; Ⓟ 608; © 700
Canova; Inc. Place; MINER; **231** E-11; elev. 1,523ft./464m.; 🅿; z 57321; Ⓟ 172; © 140
Canton; Inc. Place; ⊡ LINCOLN; **231** F-13; elev. 1,250ft./381m.; 🅿 🅷; z 57013; Ⓟ 2,787; © 3,110
Capa; RMC Place; JONES; ***231** E-6; elev. 1,771ft./540m.; mail Midland z 57552; rural
Caputa; RMC Place; PENNINGTON; **231** E-3; elev. 2,911ft./887m.; 🅿; z 57725; ● 40
Carpenter; RMC Place; CLARK; **231** D-11; elev. 1,450ft./442m.; 🅿; z 57322; ● 30
Carter; RMC Place; TRIPP; **231** F-7; located on Rosebud Ind. Res.; elev. 2,150ft./655m.; 🅿; z 57580; ● 5
Carthage; Inc. Place; MINER; **231** E-11; elev. 1,430ft./436m.; 🅿; z 57323; Ⓟ 221; © 187
Castle Rock; RMC Place; BUTTE; ***231** C-3; elev. 3,145ft./959m.; mail Newell z 57760; rural
Castlewood; Inc. Place; HAMLIN; **231** C-12; elev. 1,690ft./515m.; 🅿; z 57223; Ⓟ 549; © 666
Cavour; Inc. Place; BEADLE; **231** D-11; elev. 1,310ft./399m.; 🅿; z 57324; Ⓟ 166; © 141
Cedar Butte; RMC Place; MELLETTE; **231** F-6; located on Rosebud Ind. Res.; 🅿; z 57579; rural
Cedar Grove Colony; RMC Place; BRULE; ***231** F-9; elev. 1,610ft./491m.; mail Platte z 57369; ● 80
Center; RMC Place; MCCOOK; ***231** E-12; elev. 1,590ft./485m.; mail Salem z 57058; rural
Center Point; RMC Place; TURNER; **231** G-12; mail Viborg z 57070; ● 20
Centerville; Inc. Place; TURNER; **231** G-12; elev. 1,226ft./374m.; 🅿; z 57014; Ⓟ 887; © 910
Central City; Inc. Place; LAWRENCE; **231** D-2; elev. 5,000ft./1,524m.; 🅿; z 57754; Ⓟ 185; © 149
Chamberlain; Inc. Place; ⊡ BRULE; **231** E-9; elev. 1,465ft./447m.; 🅿 🅷; z 57325-26; Ⓟ 2,347; © 2,338
Chancellor; Inc. Place; TURNER; **231** F-12; elev. 1,367ft./417m.; 🅿; z 57015; Ⓟ 276; © 328
CHARLES MIX; **231** F-10; Ⓟ 9,131; © 9,350; ◆ 8,695
Chautauqua; RMC Place; LAKE; ***231** E-12; elev. 1,624ft./495m.; mail Madison z 57042; ● 60
Chelsea; Inc. Place; FAULK; **231** C-10; elev. 1,344ft./410m.; 🅿; z 57465; Ⓟ 33; © 33
Cherry Creek; RMC Place; ZIEBACH; **231** D-5; elev. 1,724ft./525m.; 🅿; z 57622; ● 300
Chester; RMC Place; LAKE; **231** E-12; elev. 1,600ft./488m.; 🅿; z 57016; ● 250
Cheyenne Crossing; RMC Place; LAWRENCE; ***231** D-2; elev. 5,333ft./1,625m.; mail Lead z 57754
Cheyenne River Reservation; Indian Reservation; DEWEY, ZIEBACH; mail Eagle Butte z 57625; also location of Indian Agency; Ⓟ 1,826; © 8,466
Claire City; Inc. Place; ROBERTS; **231** A-12; located on Lake Traverse Ind. Res.; elev. 1,200ft./366m.; 🅿; z 57224; Ⓟ 85; © 85
Claremont; Inc. Place; BROWN; **231** B-11; elev. 1,300ft./396m.; 🅿; z 57432; Ⓟ 135; © 130
Clark; Inc. Place; ⊡ CLARK; **231** C-11; elev. 1,845ft./562m.; 🅿; z 57225; Ⓟ 1,292; © 1,285
CLARK; **231** C-11; Ⓟ 4,403; © 4,143; ◆ 3,326
Clark Colony; RMC Place; SPINK; ***231** C-11; mail Raymond z 57258; ● 80
CLAY; **231** G-12; Ⓟ 13,186; © 13,537; ◆ 13,984
Clayton; RMC Place; HUTCHINSON; **231** F-11; elev. 1,317ft./401m.; mail Emery z 57332
Clearfield; RMC Place; TRIPP; **231** G-8; located on Rosebud Ind. Res.; elev. 2,320ft./707m.; 🅿; z 57580; ● 10
Clear Lake; Inc. Place; ⊡ DEUEL; **231** C-13; elev. 1,800ft./549m.; 🅿 🅷; z 57226; Ⓟ 1,247; © 1,335
Cliff Avenue; RMC Place; MINNEHAHA; ★ **SXFL**; mail Sioux Falls z 57104; pop. incl. with Sioux Falls (Inc. Place)
CODINGTON; **231** C-12; Ⓟ 22,698; © 25,897; ◆ 26,492
Colman; Inc. Place; MOODY; **231** E-12; 🅿; z 57017; Ⓟ 482; © 572
Colome; Inc. Place; TRIPP; **231** G-8; located on Rosebud Ind. Res.; elev. 2,268ft./691m.; 🅿; z 57528; Ⓟ 309; © 340

Entries in **UPPERCASE** are counties.
Entries in **bold** have populations of 2,500 or more.
Names in parentheses are alternate names.

Inc. Place	Incorporated Place
RMC Place	Rand McNally Designated Place
CDP	Census Designated Place
MCD	Minor Civil Division
⊡	County Seat
▲	Minor Civil Division
elev.	Elevation
🅿	Post Office
🅷	Hospital
🅲	College
■	Principal Business Center
★	Ranally Metro Area (RMA) Abbreviation
z	Zip Code(s)
Ⓟ	Previous Census Population
®	Revised Census Population
Ⓐ	Annexation Population
●	Rand McNally Population Estimate
©	Final Census Population
Ⓢ	Special Census Population
◆	Estimated Population

For additional definitions see Glossary, Volume 1, and Introduction, Volume 2.

Colonial Pine Hills; CDP-Census Area Only; PENNINGTON; ***231** E-3; elev. 4,100ft./1,250m.; mail Rapid City **z** 57701; Ⓟ 1,553; Ⓒ 2,561
Colton; Inc. Place; MINNEHAHA; **231** E-12; elev. 1,605ft./489m.; 🅿; **z** 57018; Ⓟ 657; Ⓒ 662
Columbia; Inc. Place; BROWN; **231** B-10; elev. 1,304ft./397m.; 🅿; **z** 57433 & mail Houghton **z** 57449; Ⓟ 133; Ⓒ 140
Conde; Inc. Place; SPINK; **231** C-10; elev. 1,314ft./401m.; 🅿; **z** 57434; Ⓟ 203; Ⓒ 187
Corn Creek; RMC Place; MELLETTE; ***231** F-6; elev. 2,362ft./720m.; mail Norris **z** 57560; ● 50
Corona; Inc. Place; ROBERTS; **231** B-12; elev. 1,165ft./355m.; 🅿; **z** 57227; Ⓟ 118; Ⓒ 112
Corsica; Inc. Place; DOUGLAS; **231** F-10; 🅿; **z** 57328; Ⓟ 619; Ⓒ 644
Corson; RMC Place; MINNEHAHA; **231** F-13; elev. 1,365ft./416m.; 🅿; **z** 57005; ● 70
CORSON; **231** A-6; Ⓟ 4,195; Ⓒ 4,181; ◆ 4,332
Cottonwood; Inc. Place; JACKSON; **231** E-5; elev. 2,415ft./736m.; 🅿; **z** 57775; Ⓟ 12; Ⓒ 6
Crandall; RMC Place; DAY; **231** C-11; mail Conde **z** 57434
Crazy Horse; RMC Place; CUSTER; ***231** E-2; elev. 5,800ft./1,768m.; 🅿; **z** 57730; rural
Creighton; RMC Place; PENNINGTON; **231** D-4; elev. 2,660ft./811m.; 🅿; **z** 57790; ● 5
Cresbard; Inc. Place; FAULK; **231** C-9; elev. 1,450ft./442m.; 🅿; **z** 57435; Ⓟ 185; Ⓒ 143
Crocker; RMC Place; CLARK; **231** C-11; elev. 1,783ft./543m.; 🅿; **z** 57217; ● 50
Crooks; Inc. Place; MINNEHAHA; **231** F-12; elev. 1,592ft./485m.; 🅿; **z** 57020, **z** 57055; Ⓟ 671; Ⓒ 859
Crow Creek Reservation; Indian Reservation; BUFFALO, HUGHES, HYDE; mail Fort Thompson **z** 57339; also location of Indian Agency; Ⓟ 1,787; Ⓒ 2,225
Crow Lake; RMC Place; JERAULD; ***231** E-10; mail Wessington Springs **z** 57382; rural
Custer; Inc. Place; ⊡ CUSTER; **231** E-2; elev. 5,318ft./1,621m.; 🅿 🄷; **z** 57730; Ⓟ 1,741; Ⓒ 1,860
CUSTER; **231** F-3; Ⓟ 6,179; Ⓒ 7,275; ◆ 7,678

D

Dakota Dunes; RMC Place; UNION; ***231** H-13; 🅿; ★ **SXCY**; **z** 57049; ● 500
Dallas; Inc. Place; GREGORY; **231** G-8; located on Rosebud Ind. Res.; elev. 2,194ft./669m.; 🅿; **z** 57529; Ⓟ 142; Ⓒ 144
Dante; Inc. Place; CHARLES MIX; **231** G-10; located on Yankton Ind. Res.; elev. 1,368ft./417m.; 🅿; **z** 57329; Ⓟ 98; Ⓒ 82
Davis; Inc. Place; TURNER; **231** F-12; elev. 1,250ft./381m.; 🅿; **z** 57021; Ⓟ 87; Ⓒ 104
DAVISON; **231** F-11; Ⓟ 17,503; Ⓒ 18,741; ◆ 18,769
DAY; **231** B-12; Ⓟ 6,978; Ⓒ 6,267; ◆ 5,468
Deadwood; Inc. Place; ⊡ LAWRENCE; **231** D-2; elev. 4,537ft./1,383m.; 🅿 🄷; **z** 57732; Ⓟ 1,830; Ⓒ 1,380
De Grey; RMC Place; HUGHES; ***231** D-8; mail Pierre **z** 57501; rural
Dell Rapids; Inc. Place; MINNEHAHA; **231** E-13; elev. 1,498ft./457m.; 🅿 🄷; **z** 57022; Ⓟ 2,484; Ⓒ 2,980
Delmont; Inc. Place; DOUGLAS; **231** G-10; elev. 1,488ft./454m.; 🅿; **z** 57330; Ⓟ 235; Ⓒ 263
Dempster; RMC Place; HAMLIN; **231** D-12; elev. 1,660ft./506m.; 🅿; **z** 57234; ● 70
Denby; RMC Place; SHANNON; **231** G-4; elev. 3,368ft./1,027m.; 🅿; **z** 57716; rural
De Smet; Inc. Place; ⊡ KINGSBURY; **231** D-11; elev. 1,724ft./525m.; 🅿 🄷; **z** 57231; Ⓟ 1,172; Ⓒ 1,164
DEUEL; **231** C-13; Ⓟ 4,522; Ⓒ 4,498; ◆ 4,118
DEWEY; **231** C-6; Ⓟ 5,523; Ⓒ 5,972; ◆ 5,826
Dimock; Inc. Place; HUTCHINSON; **231** F-11; elev. 1,400ft./427m.; 🅿; **z** 57331; Ⓟ 157; Ⓒ 151
Dixon; RMC Place; GREGORY; ***231** F-8; located on Rosebud Ind. Res.; elev. 1,880ft./573m.; 🅿; **z** 57529, **z** 57533; ● 15
Doland; Inc. Place; SPINK; **231** C-10; elev. 1,358ft./414m.; 🅿; **z** 57436; Ⓟ 306; Ⓒ 297
Dolton; Inc. Place; TURNER; **231** F-12; elev. 1,440ft./439m.; 🅿; **z** 57319; Ⓟ 43; Ⓒ 41
DOUGLAS; **231** F-10; Ⓟ 3,746; Ⓒ 3,458; ◆ 2,874
Downtown; RMC Place; BROWN; mail Aberdeen **z** 57401; pop. incl. with Aberdeen (Inc. Place)
Draper; Inc. Place; JONES; **231** E-7; elev. 2,257ft./688m.; 🅿; **z** 57531; Ⓟ 123; Ⓒ 92
Dupree; Inc. Place; ⊡ ZIEBACH; **231** C-5; located on Cheyenne River Ind. Res.; elev. 2,356ft./718m.; 🅿; **z** 57623; Ⓟ 484; Ⓒ 434

E

Eagle Butte; Inc. Place; DEWEY, ZIEBACH; **231** C-6; located on Cheyenne River Ind. Res.; 🅿 🄷; **z** 57625; location of Indian Agency; Ⓟ 489; Ⓒ 619
East Sioux Falls; RMC Place; MINNEHAHA; ***231** F-13; mail Sioux Falls **z** 57101; ● 80
Eden; Inc. Place; MARSHALL; **231** B-11; elev. 1,836ft./560m.; 🅿; **z** 57232; Ⓟ 97; Ⓒ 97
Edgemont; Inc. Place; FALL RIVER; **231** F-2; elev. 3,459ft./1,054m.; 🅿; **z** 57735; Ⓟ 906; Ⓒ 867
EDMUNDS; **231** B-9; Ⓟ 4,356; Ⓒ 4,367; ◆ 3,953
Egan; Inc. Place; MOODY; **231** E-13; elev. 1,530ft./466m.; 🅿; **z** 57024; Ⓟ 208; Ⓒ 265
Elbon; RMC Place; HAAKON; ***231** D-5; mail Philip **z** 57567; rural
Elevenmile Corner; RMC Place; HAAKON; ***231** E-5; mail Philip **z** 57567; rural
Elk Point; Inc. Place; ⊡ UNION; **231** H-13; elev. 1,127ft./344m.; 🅿; **z** 57025; Ⓟ 1,423; Ⓒ 1,714
Elkton; Inc. Place; BROOKINGS; **231** D-13; elev. 1,751ft./534m.; 🅿; **z** 57026; Ⓟ 602; Ⓒ 677
Ellis; RMC Place; MINNEHAHA; **231** F-12; elev. 1,442ft./440m.; ★ **SXFL**; mail Sioux Falls **z** 57107; ● 90
Ellsworth AFB; CDP-Census Area Only; MEADE; ***231** E-3; 🅿; ★ **RAP**; **z** 57706; Ⓟ 7,017; Ⓒ 4,165
Elmore; RMC Place; LAWRENCE; ***231** D-2; elev. 5,221ft./1,591m.; mail Lead **z** 57754
Elm Springs; RMC Place; MEADE; **231** D-4; elev. 2,680ft./817m.; 🅿; **z** 57791; ● 15
Elm Springs Colony; RMC Place; HUTCHINSON; ***231** F-11; mail Ethan **z** 57334; ● 130
Emery; Inc. Place; HANSON; **231** F-11; elev. 1,382ft./421m.; 🅿; **z** 57332; Ⓟ 417; Ⓒ 439
Empire; RMC Place; BUTTE; ***231** D-3; mail Vale **z** 57788; rural
Enning; RMC Place; MEADE; **231** D-4; elev. 3,039ft./926m.; 🅿; **z** 57737; ● 30
Epiphany; RMC Place; HANSON, MINER; **231** E-11; elev. 1,368ft./417m.; mail Canova **z** 57321; ● 50
Erwin; Inc. Place; KINGSBURY; **231** D-11; elev. 1,862ft./568m.; 🅿; **z** 57233; Ⓟ 42; Ⓒ 58
Esmond; RMC Place; KINGSBURY; ***231** D-11; mail Iroquois **z** 57353
Estelline; Inc. Place; HAMLIN; **231** D-12; 🅿; **z** 57234; Ⓟ 658; Ⓒ 675
Ethan; Inc. Place; DAVISON; **231** F-11; elev. 1,344ft./410m.; 🅿; **z** 57334; Ⓟ 312; Ⓒ 330
Eureka; Inc. Place; MCPHERSON; **231** A-8; elev. 1,891ft./576m.; 🅿 🄷; **z** 57437; Ⓟ 1,197; Ⓒ 1,101

F

Fairburn; Inc. Place; CUSTER; **231** F-3; elev. 3,289ft./1,002m.; 🅿; **z** 57738; Ⓟ 62; Ⓒ 80
Fairfax; Inc. Place; GREGORY; **231** G-9; elev. 1,932ft./589m.; 🅿; **z** 57335; Ⓟ 144; Ⓒ 123
Fairpoint; RMC Place; MEADE; ***231** C-4; elev. 2,934ft./894m.; mail Sturgis **z** 57785, Union Center **z** 57787
Fairview; Inc. Place; LINCOLN; **231** G-13; elev. 1,213ft./370m.; 🅿; **z** 57027; Ⓟ 73; Ⓒ 94
Faith; Inc. Place; MEADE; **231** C-5; elev. 2,600ft./792m.; 🅿; **z** 57626; Ⓟ 548; Ⓒ 489
FALL RIVER; **231** G-3; Ⓟ 7,353; Ⓒ 7,453; ◆ 7,108
Farmer; Inc. Place; HANSON; **231** F-11; elev. 1,394ft./425m.; 🅿; **z** 57311; Ⓟ 23; Ⓒ 18
Farmingdale; RMC Place; PENNINGTON; ***231** E-3; elev. 2,769ft./844m.; mail Caputa **z** 57725
FAULK; **231** C-9; Ⓟ 2,744; Ⓒ 2,640; ◆ 2,208
Faulkton; Inc. Place; ⊡ FAULK; **231** C-9; elev. 1,589ft./484m.; 🅿 🄷; **z** 57438; Ⓟ 809; Ⓒ 785
Fedora; RMC Place; MINER; **231** E-11; elev. 1,370ft./418m.; 🅿; **z** 57337; ● 50
Ferney; RMC Place; BROWN; **231** B-10; elev. 1,304ft./397m.; 🅿; **z** 57439; ● 50
Finley Heights; RMC Place; ROBERTS; ***231** B-12; elev. 1,998ft./609m.; mail Peever **z** 57257; ● 50
Firesteel; RMC Place; DEWEY; **231** B-6; located on Cheyenne River Ind. Res.; elev. 2,340ft./713m.; 🅿; **z** 57633; ● 20
Flandreau; Inc. Place; ⊡ MOODY; **231** E-13; elev. 1,570ft./479m.; 🅿 🄷; **z** 57028; Ⓟ 2,311; Ⓒ 2,376
Flandreau Reservation; Indian Reservation; MOODY; mail Flandreau **z** 57028; Ⓟ 169; Ⓒ 408
Fleetwood; RMC Place; MINNEHAHA; mail Brandon **z** 57005; pop. incl. with Brandon (Inc. Place)
Florence; Inc. Place; CODINGTON; **231** C-12; elev. 1,750ft./533m.; 🅿; **z** 57235; Ⓟ 192; Ⓒ 299
Forestburg; RMC Place; SANBORN; **231** E-11; elev. 1,232ft./376m.; 🅿; **z** 57314; ● 100
Fort Pierre; Inc. Place; ⊡ STANLEY; **231** D-7; elev. 1,441ft./439m.; 🅿; **z** 57532; Ⓟ 1,854; Ⓒ 1,991
Fort Thompson; CDP; BUFFALO; **231** E-9; located on Crow Creek Ind. Res.; elev. 1,444ft./440m.; 🅿; **z** 57339; location of Indian Agency; Ⓟ 1,088; Ⓒ 1,375
Frankfort; Inc. Place; SPINK; **231** C-10; elev. 1,296ft./395m.; 🅿; **z** 57440; Ⓟ 192; Ⓒ 166
Franklin; RMC Place; LAKE; ***231** E-12; elev. 1,665ft./507m.; mail Chester **z** 57016, Madison **z** 57042; rural
Frederick; Inc. Place; BROWN; **231** A-10; elev. 1,375ft./419m.; 🅿; **z** 57441; Ⓟ 241; Ⓒ 255
Freeman; Inc. Place; HUTCHINSON; **231** F-12; elev. 1,514ft./461m.; 🅿 🄷; **z** 57029; Ⓟ 1,293; Ⓒ 1,317
Froehlich Addition; RMC Place; MINNEHAHA; ***231** F-13; ★ **SXFL**; mail Sioux Falls **z** 57104; pop. incl. with Sioux Falls (Inc. Place)
Fruitdale; Inc. Place; BUTTE; **231** D-2; elev. 2,950ft./899m.; 🅿; **z** 57717; Ⓟ 43; Ⓒ 62
Fulton; Inc. Place; HANSON; **231** F-11; elev. 1,328ft./405m.; 🅿; **z** 57340; Ⓟ 70; Ⓒ 86

G

Galena; RMC Place; LAWRENCE; ***231** D-2; elev. 4,790ft./1,460m.; mail Deadwood **z** 57732; rural
Gannvalley; RMC Place; ⊡ BUFFALO; **231** E-9; 🅿; **z** 57341; ● 100
Garden City; Inc. Place; CLARK; **231** C-11; elev. 1,855ft./565m.; 🅿; **z** 57236; Ⓟ 93; Ⓒ 72
Garretson; Inc. Place; MINNEHAHA; **231** E-13; elev. 1,481ft./451m.; 🅿; **z** 57030; Ⓟ 924; Ⓒ 1,165
Gary; Inc. Place; DEUEL; **231** C-13; elev. 1,483ft./452m.; 🅿; **z** 57237; Ⓟ 274; Ⓒ 231
Gayville; Inc. Place; YANKTON; **231** G-12; elev. 1,165ft./355m.; 🅿; **z** 57031; Ⓟ 401; Ⓒ 418
Geddes; Inc. Place; CHARLES MIX; **231** G-10; located on Yankton Ind. Res.; elev. 1,620ft./494m.; 🅿; **z** 57342; Ⓟ 280; Ⓒ 252
Gettysburg; Inc. Place; ⊡ POTTER; **231** C-8; elev. 2,061ft./628m.; 🅿 🄷; **z** 57442; Ⓟ 1,510; Ⓒ 1,352
Glad Valley; RMC Place; ZIEBACH; **231** B-5; located on Cheyenne River Ind. Res.; elev. 2,500ft./762m.; 🅿; **z** 57644; ● 10
Glencross; RMC Place; DEWEY; **231** B-6; located on Cheyenne River Ind. Res.; elev. 2,155ft./657m.; 🅿; **z** 57630; ● 40
Glendale Colony; RMC Place; SPINK; ***231** C-10; mail Frankfort **z** 57440; ● 70
Glenham; Inc. Place; WALWORTH; **231** B-7; elev. 1,709ft./521m.; 🅿; **z** 57631; Ⓟ 134; Ⓒ 139
Goodwin; Inc. Place; DEUEL; **231** C-12; elev. 2,006ft./611m.; 🅿; **z** 57238; Ⓟ 126; Ⓒ 160
Graceville Colony; RMC Place; LAKE; ***231** E-12; mail Winfred **z** 57076; ● 120
GRANT; **231** C-12; Ⓟ 8,372; Ⓒ 7,847; ◆ 6,996
Greenfield; RMC Place; CLAY; ***231** G-12; elev. 1,230ft./375m.; mail Burbank **z** 57010, Vermillion **z** 57069
Green Grass; CDP; DEWEY; **231** C-6; elev. 1,860ft./567m.; mail Eagle Butte **z** 57625; Ⓒ 58
Green Valley; CDP-Census Area Only; PENNINGTON; ***231** E-3; ★ **RAP**; Ⓒ 768
Greenwood; RMC Place; CHARLES MIX; **231** G-10; located on Yankton Ind. Res.; mail Wagner **z** 57380; ● 100
Gregory; Inc. Place; GREGORY; **231** G-9; located on Rosebud Ind. Res.; elev. 2,166ft./660m.; 🅿 🄷; **z** 57533; Ⓟ 1,384; Ⓒ 1,342
GREGORY; **231** F-9; Ⓟ 5,359; Ⓒ 4,792; ◆ 3,966
Grenville; Inc. Place; DAY; **231** B-12; elev. 1,850ft./564m.; 🅿; **z** 57239; Ⓟ 81; Ⓒ 62
Groton; Inc. Place; BROWN; **231** B-10; elev. 1,308ft./399m.; 🅿; **z** 57445; Ⓟ 1,196; Ⓒ 1,356
Grover; RMC Place; CODINGTON; ***231** C-12; elev. 1,740ft./530m.; mail Watertown **z** 57201; rural

H

HAAKON; **231** D-6; Ⓟ 2,624; Ⓒ 2,196; ◆ 1,777
Hamill; CDP; TRIPP; **231** F-8; located on Rosebud Ind. Res.; elev. 1,770ft./539m.; 🅿; **z** 57534; Ⓒ 11
HAMLIN; **231** C-12; Ⓟ 4,974; Ⓒ 5,540; ◆ 5,737
Hammer; RMC Place; ROBERTS; **231** A-12; located on Lake Traverse Ind. Res.; elev. 1,225ft./373m.; mail New Effington **z** 57255
HAND; **231** D-9; Ⓟ 4,272; Ⓒ 3,741; ◆ 3,215
Hanna; RMC Place; LAWRENCE; ***231** D-2; mail Lead **z** 57754; rural
HANSON; **231** E-11; Ⓟ 2,994; Ⓒ 3,139; ◆ 3,609
HARDING; **231** B-3; Ⓟ 1,669; Ⓒ 1,353; ◆ 1,127
Harrington; RMC Place; BENNETT; ***231** G-6; mail Martin **z** 57551; rural
Harrisburg; Inc. Place; LINCOLN; **231** F-13; elev. 1,428ft./435m.; 🅿; **z** 57032; Ⓟ 727; Ⓒ 958
Harrison; CDP; DOUGLAS; **231** F-10; elev. 1,580ft./482m.; 🅿; **z** 57344; Ⓒ 51
Harrold; Inc. Place; HUGHES; **231** D-8; elev. 1,796ft./547m.; 🅿; **z** 57536; Ⓟ 167; Ⓒ 209
Hartford; Inc. Place; MINNEHAHA; **231** F-12; elev. 1,568ft./478m.; 🅿; **z** 57033; Ⓟ 1,262; Ⓒ 1,844
Hartford Beach; RMC Place; ROBERTS; ***231** B-13; mail Corona **z** 57227; ● 20
Hayes; RMC Place; STANLEY; **231** D-6; elev. 2,000ft./610m.; 🅿; **z** 57537; ● 40
Hayti; Inc. Place; ⊡ HAMLIN; **231** D-12; 🅿; **z** 57241; Ⓟ 372; Ⓒ 367
Hayward Addition; RMC Place; MINNEHAHA; ***231** F-13; ★ **SXFL**; mail Sioux Falls **z** 57106; pop. incl. with Sioux Falls (Inc. Place)
Hazel; Inc. Place; HAMLIN; **231** C-12; elev. 1,766ft./538m.; 🅿; **z** 57242; Ⓟ 103; Ⓒ 105
Hecla; Inc. Place; BROWN; **231** A-10; elev. 1,299ft./396m.; 🅿; **z** 57446; Ⓟ 398; Ⓒ 314
Henry; Inc. Place; CODINGTON; **231** C-11; elev. 1,812ft./552m.; 🅿; **z** 57243; Ⓟ 215; Ⓒ 268
Hereford; RMC Place; MEADE; **231** D-3; elev. 2,602ft./793m.; 🅿; **z** 57785; rural
Hermosa; Inc. Place; CUSTER; **231** E-3; elev. 3,303ft./1,007m.; 🅿; **z** 57744; Ⓟ 242; Ⓒ 315
Herreid; Inc. Place; CAMPBELL; **231** A-8; elev. 1,682ft./513m.; 🅿; **z** 57632; Ⓟ 488; Ⓒ 482
Herrick; Inc. Place; GREGORY; **231** G-9; located on Rosebud Ind. Res.; elev. 2,155ft./657m.; 🅿; **z** 57538; Ⓟ 139; Ⓒ 105
Hetland; Inc. Place; KINGSBURY; **231** D-12; elev. 1,733ft./528m.; 🅿; **z** 57212; Ⓟ 53; Ⓒ 43
Hiawatha Beach; RMC Place; ROBERTS; ***231** B-12; mail Wilmot **z** 57279
Hidden Timber; RMC Place; TODD; ***231** G-7; elev. 2,420ft./738m.; mail Mission **z** 57555, Valentine **z** 69201; rural
Highmore; Inc. Place; ⊡ HYDE; **231** D-9; elev. 1,888ft./575m.; 🅿; **z** 57345; Ⓟ 835; Ⓒ 851
Hilland; RMC Place; HAAKON; ***231** D-5; mail Philip **z** 57567; rural
Hill City; Inc. Place; PENNINGTON; **231** E-2; elev. 4,979ft./1,518m.; 🅿; **z** 57745; Ⓟ 650; Ⓒ 780
Hillhead; RMC Place; MARSHALL; ***231** A-11; mail Veblen **z** 57270
Hillside; RMC Place; DOUGLAS; ***231** F-10; elev. 1,636ft./499m.; mail Corsica **z** 57328; rural
Hillside Colony; RMC Place; SPINK; ***231** C-11; mail Doland **z** 57436; ● 60
Hillsview; Inc. Place; MCPHERSON; **231** B-8; elev. 1,851ft./564m.; mail Eureka **z** 57437; Ⓟ 4; Ⓒ 3
Hisega; RMC Place; PENNINGTON; ***231** E-3; elev. 4,022ft./1,226m.; mail Rapid City **z** 57702
Hisle; RMC Place; JACKSON; ***231** F-5; located on Pine Ridge Ind. Res.; mail Wanblee **z** 57577; rural
Hitchcock; Inc. Place; BEADLE; **231** D-10; elev. 1,340ft./408m.; 🅿; **z** 57348; Ⓟ 95; Ⓒ 108
Holabird; RMC Place; HYDE; **231** D-8; elev. 1,788ft./545m.; 🅿; **z** 57540; ● 15
Holmquist; RMC Place; DAY; ***231** B-11; elev. 1,808ft./551m.; mail Webster **z** 57274; rural
Hooker; RMC Place; TURNER; ***231** G-12; elev. 1,279ft./390m.; mail Viborg **z** 57070; ● 15
Hoover; RMC Place; BUTTE; ***231** C-3; elev. 2,775ft./846m.; mail Newell **z** 57760; rural
Hosmer; Inc. Place; EDMUNDS; **231** B-8; elev. 1,906ft./581m.; 🅿; **z** 57448; Ⓟ 310; Ⓒ 287
Hot Springs; Inc. Place; ⊡ FALL RIVER; serves as county seat of Shannon; **231** F-2; elev. 3,464ft./1,056m.; 🅿 🄷; **z** 57747; Ⓟ 4,325; Ⓒ 4,129
Houghton; RMC Place; BROWN; **231** A-10; elev. 1,296ft./395m.; 🅿; **z** 57449; ● 60
Hoven; Inc. Place; POTTER; **231** B-8; elev. 1,902ft./580m.; 🅿 🄷; **z** 57450; Ⓟ 522; Ⓒ 511
Howard; Inc. Place; ⊡ MINER; **231** E-11; elev. 1,572ft./479m.; 🅿; **z** 57349; Ⓟ 1,156; Ⓒ 1,071
Howes; RMC Place; MEADE; **231** D-5; elev. 2,407ft./734m.; 🅿; **z** 57748; ● 20
Hub City; RMC Place; CLAY; ***231** G-12; elev. 1,227ft./374m.; mail Vermillion **z** 57069; rural
Hudson; Inc. Place; LINCOLN; **231** G-13; elev. 1,221ft./372m.; 🅿; **z** 57034; Ⓟ 332; Ⓒ 402
Huffton; RMC Place; BROWN; ***231** B-10; elev. 1,308ft./399m.; mail Claremont **z** 57432; rural
HUGHES; **231** D-8; Ⓟ 14,817; Ⓒ 16,481; ◆ 17,076
Humboldt; Inc. Place; MINNEHAHA; **231** F-12; elev. 1,710ft./521m.; 🅿; **z** 57035; Ⓟ 468; Ⓒ 521; Ⓡ 523
Hurley; Inc. Place; TURNER; **231** F-12; elev. 1,293ft./394m.; 🅿; **z** 57036; Ⓟ 372; Ⓒ 426
Huron; Inc. Place; ⊡ BEADLE; **231** D-10; elev. 1,275ft./389m.; 🅿 🄷 ■; **z** 57350, **z** 57399; Ⓟ 12,448; Ⓒ 11,893; ◆ 11,833
Huron Colony; RMC Place; BEADLE; ***231** D-10; mail Huron **z** 57350; ● 70
HUTCHINSON; **231** F-11; Ⓟ 8,262; Ⓒ 8,075; ◆ 7,188
HYDE; **231** D-9; Ⓟ 1,696; Ⓒ 1,671; ◆ 1,317

I

Ideal; RMC Place; TRIPP; **231** F-8; located on Rosebud Ind. Res.; elev. 1,850ft./564m.; 🅿; **z** 57541; ● 60
Igloo; RMC Place; FALL RIVER; ***231** G-2; elev. 3,690ft./1,125m.; mail Edgemont **z** 57735; rural
Imlay; RMC Place; PENNINGTON; ***231** F-4; elev. 2,616ft./797m.; mail Scenic **z** 57780; rural
Interior; Inc. Place; JACKSON; **231** F-5; elev. 2,378ft./725m.; 🅿; **z** 57750; Ⓟ 67; Ⓒ 77
Iona; RMC Place; LYMAN; **231** F-9; elev. 1,814ft./553m.; 🅿; **z** 57533; ● 10
Ipswich; Inc. Place; ⊡ EDMUNDS; **231** B-9; elev. 1,530ft./466m.; 🅿; **z** 57451; Ⓟ 965; Ⓒ 943
Irene; Inc. Place; YANKTON, CLAY, TURNER; **231** G-12; elev. 1,360ft./415m.; 🅿; **z** 57037; Ⓟ 464; Ⓒ 432
Iron Lightning; RMC Place; ZIEBACH; **231** C-5; mail Dupree **z** 57623; ● 40
Iroquois; Inc. Place; KINGSBURY, BEADLE; **231** D-11; elev. 1,398ft./426m.; 🅿; **z** 57353; Ⓟ 328; Ⓒ 278
Isabel; Inc. Place; DEWEY; **231** B-6; located on Cheyenne River Ind. Res.; elev. 2,402ft./732m.; 🅿; **z** 57633; Ⓟ 319; Ⓒ 239

J

JACKSON; **231** F-5; Ⓟ 2,811; Ⓒ 2,930; ◆ 2,767
James; RMC Place; BROWN; ***231** B-10; elev. 1,303ft./397m.; mail Groton **z** 57445; rural
Java; Inc. Place; WALWORTH; **231** B-8; elev. 2,079ft./634m.; 🅿; **z** 57452; Ⓟ 161; Ⓒ 197
Jefferson; Inc. Place; UNION; **231** H-13; elev. 1,119ft./341m.; 🅿; **z** 57038; Ⓟ 527; Ⓒ 586
JERAULD; **231** E-10; Ⓟ 2,425; Ⓒ 2,295; ◆ 1,867
Jobee Acres; RMC Place; BROWN; ***231** B-10; mail Aberdeen **z** 57401; ● 30
Johnson Siding; RMC Place; PENNINGTON; ***231** E-3; elev. 4,278ft./1,304m.; mail Rapid City **z** 57702; rural
JONES; **231** E-7; Ⓟ 1,324; Ⓒ 1,193; ◆ 993
Joubert; RMC Place; DOUGLAS; ***231** F-10; mail Harrison **z** 57344, New Holland **z** 57364; rural
Junction City; RMC Place; UNION; ***231** G-13; elev. 1,194ft./364m.; mail Burbank **z** 57010, Elk Point **z** 57025; rural
Junius; RMC Place; LAKE; **231** E-12; mail Madison **z** 57042; ● 50

K

Kadoka; Inc. Place; ⊡ JACKSON; **231** E-5; elev. 2,458ft./749m.; 🅿; **z** 57543; Ⓟ 736; Ⓒ 706
Kaylor; CDP; HUTCHINSON; **231** G-11; elev. 1,396ft./426m.; 🅿; **z** 57354; Ⓒ 64
Keldron; RMC Place; CORSON; **231** A-5; located on Standing Rock Ind. Res.; 🅿; **z** 57634; ● 10
Kenel; RMC Place; CORSON; **231** A-7; located on Standing Rock Ind. Res.; mail Mc Laughlin **z** 57642; ● 50
Kennebec; Inc. Place; ⊡ LYMAN; **231** E-8; elev. 1,690ft./515m.; 🅿; **z** 57544; Ⓟ 284; Ⓒ 286
Keyapaha; RMC Place; TRIPP; **231** G-7; elev. 2,375ft./724m.; 🅿; **z** 57580; rural
Keystone; Inc. Place; PENNINGTON; **231** E-3; elev. 4,323ft./1,318m.; 🅿; **z** 57751; Ⓟ 232; Ⓒ 311
Kidder; RMC Place; MARSHALL; **231** A-11; elev. 1,294ft./394m.; mail Britton **z** 57430; ● 100
Kimball; Inc. Place; BRULE; **231** F-9; elev. 1,788ft./545m.; 🅿; **z** 57355; Ⓟ 743; Ⓒ 745
Kingsburg; RMC Place; BON HOMME; **231** G-11; elev. 1,383ft./422m.; mail Springfield **z** 57062; rural
KINGSBURY; **231** D-11; Ⓟ 5,925; Ⓒ 5,815; ◆ 5,350
Kirley; RMC Place; HAAKON; ***231** D-6; mail Midland **z** 57552, Milesville **z** 57553; rural
Kones Corner; RMC Place; HAMLIN; ***231** C-12; elev. 1,787ft./545m.; mail Castlewood **z** 57223; rural
Kranzburg; Inc. Place; CODINGTON; **231** C-12; elev. 1,978ft./603m.; 🅿; **z** 57245; Ⓟ 132; Ⓒ 185
Kyle; CDP; SHANNON; **231** F-4; located on Pine Ridge Ind. Res.; elev. 2,935ft./895m.; 🅿 🄲 1,485; **z** 57752; Ⓟ 914; Ⓒ 970

L

Labolt; Inc. Place; GRANT; **231** C-13; elev. 1,392ft./424m.; 🅿; **z** 57246; Ⓟ 91; Ⓒ 86
Ladner; RMC Place; HARDING; **231** A-2; elev. 3,141ft./957m.; mail Buffalo **z** 57720; rural
LAKE; **231** E-12; Ⓟ 10,550; Ⓒ 11,276; ◆ 11,985
Lake Andes; Inc. Place; ⊡ CHARLES MIX; **231** G-10; located on Yankton Ind. Res.; elev. 1,466ft./447m.; 🅿; **z** 57356; Ⓟ 846; Ⓒ 819
Lake Campbell; RMC Place; MOODY; ***231** E-12; mail Brookings **z** 57006; rural
Lake City; Inc. Place; MARSHALL; **231** A-11; elev. 1,864ft./568m.; 🅿; **z** 57247; Ⓟ 43; Ⓒ 47
Lake Norden; Inc. Place; HAMLIN; **231** D-12; elev. 1,680ft./512m.; 🅿; **z** 57248; Ⓟ 427; Ⓒ 432
Lake Preston; Inc. Place; KINGSBURY; **231** D-12; elev. 1,719ft./524m.; 🅿; **z** 57249 & mail Erwin **z** 57233; Ⓟ 663; Ⓒ 737
Lake Traverse Reservation; Indian Reservation; ROBERTS, CODINGTON, DAY, GRANT, MARSHALL; Reservation extends into ND; Ⓒ 10,217
Lane; Inc. Place; JERAULD; **231** E-10; elev. 1,376ft./419m.; 🅿; **z** 57358; Ⓟ 71; Ⓒ 59
Langford; Inc. Place; MARSHALL; **231** B-11; elev. 1,373ft./418m.; 🅿; **z** 57454; Ⓟ 298; Ⓒ 290
Lantry; RMC Place; DEWEY; **231** C-6; located on Cheyenne River Ind. Res.; elev. 2,400ft./732m.; 🅿; **z** 57636; ● 40
La Plant; CDP; DEWEY; **231** C-7; located on Cheyenne River Ind. Res.; elev. 1,942ft./592m.; 🅿; **z** 57652; Ⓒ 150
LAWRENCE; **231** D-2; Ⓟ 20,655; Ⓒ 21,802; ◆ 24,145
Lead; Inc. Place; LAWRENCE; **231** D-2; elev. 5,400ft./1,646m.; 🅿; **z** 57754; Ⓟ 3,632; Ⓒ 3,027
Lebanon; Inc. Place; POTTER; **231** C-8; elev. 1,953ft./595m.; 🅿; **z** 57455; Ⓟ 115; Ⓒ 86
Lemmon; Inc. Place; PERKINS; **231** A-5; elev. 2,577ft./785m.; 🅿 🄷; **z** 57638; Ⓟ 1,614; Ⓒ 1,398
Lennox; Inc. Place; LINCOLN; **231** F-12; elev. 1,338ft./408m.; 🅿; **z** 57039; Ⓟ 1,767; Ⓒ 2,037
Leola; Inc. Place; ⊡ MCPHERSON; **231** A-9; elev. 1,596ft./486m.; 🅿; **z** 57456; Ⓟ 521; Ⓒ 462
Lesterville; Inc. Place; YANKTON; **231** G-11; elev. 1,380ft./421m.; 🅿; **z** 57040; Ⓟ 168; Ⓒ 158
Letcher; Inc. Place; SANBORN; **231** E-10; elev. 1,308ft./399m.; 🅿; **z** 57359; Ⓟ 164; Ⓒ 177
Lily; Inc. Place; DAY; **231** C-11; elev. 1,845ft./562m.; 🅿; **z** 57274; Ⓟ 26; Ⓒ 21
LINCOLN; **231** G-13; Ⓟ 15,427; Ⓒ 24,131; Ⓡ 24,147; ◆ 41,321
Linden Beach; RMC Place; ROBERTS; ***231** B-13; mail Corona **z** 57227
Littleburg; RMC Place; TODD; ***231** G-7; elev. 2,666ft./813m.; mail Mission **z** 57555; rural
Little Eagle; CDP; CORSON; **231** B-7; located on Standing Rock Ind. Res.; elev. 1,642ft./500m.; 🅿; **z** 57639; Ⓟ 294; Ⓒ 370
Lodgepole; RMC Place; PERKINS; **231** A-4; elev. 2,800ft./853m.; 🅿; **z** 57640; ● 60
Lone Tree; RMC Place; MOODY; ***231** E-13; elev. 1,661ft./506m.; mail Egan **z** 57024
Long Lake; Inc. Place; MCPHERSON; **231** A-9; elev. 1,950ft./594m.; 🅿; **z** 57457; Ⓟ 64; Ⓒ 58
Long Lake Colony; RMC Place; MCPHERSON; ***231** B-9; mail Westport **z** 57481; ● 80
Long Valley; RMC Place; JACKSON; **231** F-5; located on Pine Ridge Ind. Res.; elev. 2,600ft./792m.; 🅿; **z** 57547; ● 20
Loomis; CDP; DAVISON; **231** E-11; elev. 1,304ft./397m.; 🅿; **z** 57301; Ⓒ 47
Lower Brule; CDP; LYMAN; **231** E-8; located on Lower Brule Ind. Res.; elev. 1,443ft./440m.; 🅿; **z** 57548; location of Indian Agency; Ⓟ 655; Ⓒ 599
Lower Brule Reservation; Indian Reservation; LYMAN, STANLEY; mail Lower Brule **z** 57548; also location of Indian Agency; Ⓟ 1,023; Ⓒ 1,353
Lowry; Inc. Place; WALWORTH; **231** B-8; elev. 1,866ft./569m.; 🅿; **z** 57472; Ⓟ 15; Ⓒ 10
Loyalton; RMC Place; EDMUNDS; **231** B-9; elev. 1,685ft./514m.; mail Roscoe **z** 57471
Lucas; RMC Place; GREGORY; **231** F-9; located on Rosebud Ind. Res.; elev. 2,077ft./633m.; 🅿; **z** 57523
Ludlow; RMC Place; HARDING; **231** A-3; elev. 3,075ft./937m.; 🅿; **z** 57755; ● 10
LYMAN; **231** E-8; Ⓟ 3,638; Ⓒ 3,895; ◆ 3,881
Lyons; RMC Place; MINNEHAHA; **231** F-12; elev. 1,540ft./469m.; 🅿; **z** 57041; ● 100

M

Madison; Inc. Place; ⊡ LAKE; **231** E-12; elev. 1,670ft./509m.; 🅿 🄷 🄲 2,439; **z** 57042; Ⓟ 6,257; Ⓒ 6,540
Madsen Beach; RMC Place; ROBERTS; ***231** B-12; mail Wilmot **z** 57279
Mahto; RMC Place; CORSON; **231** A-7; elev. 1,812ft./552m.; mail Wakpala **z** 57658; ● 20
Manchester; RMC Place; KINGSBURY; **231** D-11; elev. 1,536ft./468m.; mail Iroquois **z** 57353; ● 10
Manderson; RMC Place; SHANNON; **231** G-4; located on Pine Ridge Ind. Res.; elev. 3,039ft./926m.; 🅿; **z** 57756; ● 180
Manderson-White Horse Creek; CDP-Census Area Only; SHANNON; ***231** G-4; elev. 3,026ft./922m.; mail Manderson **z** 57756; Ⓟ 243; Ⓒ 626
Mansfield; RMC Place; SPINK, BROWN; **231** B-10; elev. 1,290ft./393m.; 🅿; **z** 57460; ● 100
Marcus; RMC Place; MEADE; **231** D-4; elev. 2,500ft./762m.; 🅿; **z** 57785; rural
Marcy Colony; RMC Place; HUTCHINSON; ***231** F-11; mail Parkston **z** 57366; ● 30
Marion; Inc. Place; TURNER; **231** F-12; elev. 1,450ft./442m.; 🅿; **z** 57043; Ⓟ 831; Ⓒ 892
Marlow; RMC Place; MARSHALL; ***231** A-11; elev. 1,333ft./406m.; mail Veblen **z** 57270; rural
MARSHALL; **231** A-11; Ⓟ 4,844; Ⓒ 4,576; ◆ 4,183
Martin; Inc. Place; ⊡ BENNETT; **231** G-5; located on Pine Ridge Ind. Res.; elev. 3,331ft./1,015m.; 🅿 🄷; **z** 57551 & mail Long Valley **z** 57547; Ⓟ 1,151; Ⓒ 1,106
Marty; CDP; CHARLES MIX; **231** G-10; located on Yankton Ind. Res.; 🅿; **z** 57361; Ⓟ 436; Ⓒ 421
Marvin; Inc. Place; GRANT; **231** B-12; elev. 1,460ft./445m.; 🅿; **z** 57251; Ⓟ 38; Ⓒ 66
Maurine; RMC Place; MEADE; ***231** C-4; elev. 2,876ft./877m.; mail Faith **z** 57626; rural
Maxwell Colony; RMC Place; HUTCHINSON; ***231** G-11; elev. 1,192ft./363m.; mail Scotland **z** 57059; ● 60
Mayfield; RMC Place; YANKTON; **231** G-12; elev. 1,374ft./419m.; mail Irene **z** 57037; ● 20
McCook; UNION; see McCook Lake (RMC Place)
MCCOOK; **231** E-12; Ⓟ 5,688; Ⓒ 5,832; ◆ 5,753
McCook Lake (McCook); RMC Place; UNION; ***231** H-13; 🅿; ★ **SXCY**; **z** 57049; ● 500
McIntosh; Inc. Place; ⊡ CORSON; **231** A-6; located on Standing Rock Ind. Res.; elev. 2,301ft./701m.; 🅿; **z** 57641; Ⓟ 302; Ⓒ 217
McLaughlin; Inc. Place; CORSON; **231** A-7; located on Standing Rock Ind. Res.; elev. 2,001ft./610m.; 🅿; **z** 57642; Ⓟ 780; Ⓒ 775
MCPHERSON; **231** A-9; Ⓟ 3,228; Ⓒ 2,904; ◆ 2,391
MEADE; **231** D-4; Ⓟ 21,878; Ⓒ 24,253; ◆ 23,445
Meadow; RMC Place; PERKINS; **231** B-4; elev. 2,600ft./792m.; 🅿; **z** 57644; ● 30
Meckling; RMC Place; CLAY; **231** G-12; elev. 1,154ft./352m.; 🅿; **z** 57069; ● 90
Mellette; Inc. Place; SPINK; **231** C-10; elev. 1,296ft./395m.; 🅿; **z** 57461; Ⓟ 184; Ⓒ 248
MELLETTE; **231** F-7; Ⓟ 2,137; Ⓒ 2,083; ◆ 2,010
Menno; Inc. Place; HUTCHINSON; **231** G-11; elev. 1,326ft./404m.; 🅿; **z** 57045; Ⓟ 768; Ⓒ 729
Midland; Inc. Place; HAAKON; **231** E-6; elev. 1,879ft./573m.; 🅿; **z** 57552; Ⓟ 233; Ⓒ 179
Midway; RMC Place; YANKTON; **231** G-12; elev. 1,350ft./411m.; mail Irene **z** 57037, Viborg **z** 57070; ● 30
Milbank; Inc. Place; ⊡ GRANT; **231** B-13; elev. 1,150ft./351m.; 🅿 🄷; **z** 57252-53; Ⓟ 3,879; Ⓒ 3,640
Milesville; RMC Place; HAAKON; **231** D-5; elev. 2,350ft./716m.; 🅿; **z** 57553; ● 30
Millboro; RMC Place; TRIPP; **231** G-8; 🅿; **z** 57580; ● 10
Miller; Inc. Place; ⊡ HAND; **231** D-9; elev. 1,578ft./481m.; 🅿 🄷; **z** 57362; Ⓟ 1,678; Ⓒ 1,530
Miller Dale Colony; RMC Place; HAND; ***231** D-9; mail Miller **z** 57362; ● 70
Milltown; CDP; HUTCHINSON; **231** F-11; elev. 1,208ft./368m.; mail Parkston **z** 57366; Ⓒ 8
Mina; RMC Place; EDMUNDS; **231** B-10; elev. 1,436ft./438m.; 🅿; **z** 57451; ● 30
MINER; **231** E-11; Ⓟ 3,272; Ⓒ 2,884; ◆ 2,364
MINNEHAHA; **231** E-12; Ⓟ 123,809; Ⓒ 148,281; Ⓡ 148,265; ◆ 197,613
Miranda; RMC Place; FAULK; **231** C-9; elev. 1,443ft./440m.; 🅿; **z** 57438; ● 20
Mission; Inc. Place; TODD; **231** F-7; located on Rosebud Ind. Res.; elev. 2,581ft./787m.; 🅿 🄲 2,125; **z** 57555; Ⓟ 730; Ⓒ 904
Mission Hill; Inc. Place; YANKTON; **231** G-12; elev. 1,168ft./356m.; 🅿; **z** 57046; Ⓟ 180; Ⓒ 183
Mission Ridge; RMC Place; STANLEY; **231** D-7; elev. 2,000ft./610m.; 🅿; **z** 57532; rural
Mitchell; Inc. Place; ⊡ DAVISON; **231** F-11; elev. 1,293ft./394m.; 🅿 🄷 🄲 777 ■; **z** 57301; Ⓟ 13,798; Ⓒ 14,558; ◆ 13,959
Mobridge; Inc. Place; WALWORTH; **231** B-7; elev. 1,676ft./511m.; 🅿 🄷; **z** 57601 & mail Walker **z** 57659; Ⓟ 3,768; Ⓒ 3,574
Monroe; Inc. Place; TURNER; **231** F-12; elev. 1,500ft./457m.; 🅿; **z** 57047; Ⓟ 151; Ⓒ 163
Montrose; Inc. Place; MCCOOK; **231** F-12; elev. 1,480ft./451m.; 🅿; **z** 57048; Ⓟ 420; Ⓒ 460
MOODY; **231** E-13; Ⓟ 6,507; Ⓒ 6,595; ◆ 6,431
Morningside; RMC Place; BEADLE; **231** D-10; mail Huron **z** 57350; ● 130
Morristown; Inc. Place; CORSON; **231** A-5; located on Standing Rock Ind. Res.; elev. 2,240ft./683m.; 🅿; **z** 57645; Ⓟ 64; Ⓒ 82
Mosher; RMC Place; MELLETTE; **231** F-7; located on Rosebud Ind. Res.; elev. 2,100ft./640m.; mail Winner **z** 57580; rural
Mound City; Inc. Place; ⊡ CAMPBELL; **231** A-8; elev. 1,722ft./525m.; 🅿; **z** 57646; Ⓟ 89; Ⓒ 84
Mount Vernon; Inc. Place; DAVISON; **231** F-10; elev. 1,411ft./430m.; 🅿; **z** 57363; Ⓟ 368; Ⓒ 477
Mud Butte; RMC Place; MEADE; **231** C-3; elev. 2,900ft./884m.; 🅿; **z** 57758; ● 5
Murdo; Inc. Place; ⊡ JONES; **231** E-7; elev. 2,326ft./709m.; 🅿; **z** 57559; Ⓟ 679; Ⓒ 612
Mystic; RMC Place; PENNINGTON; ***231** E-2; elev. 4,868ft./1,484m.; mail Hill City **z** 57745; rural

N

Nahon; RMC Place; BROWN; ***231** B-10; mail Aberdeen **z** 57401; rural
Naples; Inc. Place; CLARK; **231** C-11; elev. 1,789ft./545m.; mail Vienna **z** 57271; Ⓟ 35; Ⓒ 25
Nemo; RMC Place; LAWRENCE; **231** E-2; 🅿; **z** 57759; ● 50
New Effington; Inc. Place; ROBERTS; **231** A-12; located on Lake Traverse Ind. Res.; elev. 1,108ft./338m.; 🅿; **z** 57255; Ⓟ 219; Ⓒ 233
Newell; Inc. Place; BUTTE; **231** C-3; elev. 2,853ft./870m.; 🅿; **z** 57760; Ⓟ 675; Ⓒ 646
New Holland; CDP; DOUGLAS; **231** F-10; elev. 1,600ft./488m.; 🅿; **z** 57364; Ⓒ 78
New Underwood; Inc. Place; PENNINGTON; **231** E-3; elev. 2,839ft./865m.; 🅿; **z** 57761; Ⓟ 553; Ⓒ 616
New Witten; TRIPP; see Witten (Inc. Place)
Nisland; Inc. Place; BUTTE; **231** D-2; elev. 2,857ft./871m.; 🅿; **z** 57762; Ⓟ 174; Ⓒ 204
Nora; RMC Place; UNION; ***231** G-13; elev. 1,389ft./423m.; mail Alcester **z** 57001; rural
Norbeck; RMC Place; FAULK; ***231** C-9; elev. 1,653ft./504m.; 🅿; **z** 57438; rural
Norris; RMC Place; MELLETTE; **231** F-6; located on Rosebud Ind. Res.; elev. 2,500ft./762m.; 🅿; **z** 57560; ● 60
North Eagle Butte; CDP; DEWEY; ***231** C-6; mail Eagle Butte **z** 57625; Ⓟ 1,423; Ⓒ 2,163
North Sioux City; Inc. Place; UNION; **231** H-13; elev. 1,100ft./335m.; 🅿; ★ **SXCY**; **z** 57049; Ⓟ 2,019; Ⓒ 2,288
North Spearfish; CDP-Census Area Only; LAWRENCE; ***231** D-2; elev. 3,573ft./1,089m.; mail Spearfish **z** 57783; Ⓟ 2,274; Ⓒ 2,306
Northville; Inc. Place; SPINK; **231** C-10; elev. 1,279ft./390m.; 🅿; **z** 57465; Ⓟ 105; Ⓒ 124
Norton Acres; RMC Place; MINNEHAHA; ***231** F-13; ★ **SXFL**; mail Sioux Falls **z** 57104; pop. incl. with Sioux Falls (Inc. Place)
Nunda; Inc. Place; LAKE; **231** E-12; elev. 1,760ft./536m.; 🅿; **z** 57050; Ⓟ 45; Ⓒ 47

O

Oacoma; Inc. Place; LYMAN; **231** E-9; elev. 1,390ft./424m.; 🅿; **z** 57365; Ⓟ 367; Ⓒ 390
Oelrichs; Inc. Place; FALL RIVER; **231** G-3; elev. 3,360ft./1,024m.; 🅿; **z** 57763 & mail Smithwick **z** 57782; Ⓟ 138; Ⓒ 145
Oglala; CDP; SHANNON; **231** G-4; elev. 3,000ft./914m.; 🅿; **z** 57764; Ⓟ 618; Ⓒ 1,229
Okaton; CDP; JONES; **231** E-6; elev. 2,250ft./686m.; 🅿; **z** 57562; Ⓒ 29
Okoboto; RMC Place; SULLY; ***231** D-7; mail Pierre **z** 57501; rural
Okreek; RMC Place; TODD; **231** F-7; located on Rosebud Ind. Res.; elev. 2,300ft./701m.; 🅿; **z** 57563; ● 150
Ola; RMC Place; BRULE; ***231** F-9; elev. 1,735ft./529m.; mail Chamberlain **z** 57325; rural
Oldham; Inc. Place; KINGSBURY; **231** D-12; elev. 1,720ft./524m.; 🅿; **z** 57051; Ⓟ 189; Ⓒ 206
Olivet; Inc. Place; ⊡ HUTCHINSON; **231** G-11; elev. 1,220ft./372m.; 🅿; **z** 57052; Ⓟ 74; Ⓒ 70
Olsonville; RMC Place; TODD; ***231** G-7; located on Rosebud Ind. Res.; mail Mission **z** 57555, Valentine **z** 69201; rural
Onaka; Inc. Place; FAULK; **231** C-8; elev. 1,870ft./570m.; 🅿; **z** 57466; Ⓟ 52; Ⓒ 30
Onida; Inc. Place; ⊡ SULLY; **231** D-8; elev. 1,880ft./573m.; 🅿; **z** 57564; Ⓟ 761; Ⓒ 740
Opal; RMC Place; MEADE; **231** C-4; elev. 2,600ft./792m.; 🅿; **z** 57758; ● 30
Oral; RMC Place; FALL RIVER; **231** F-3; elev. 2,960ft./902m.; 🅿; **z** 57766; ● 60
Ordway; RMC Place; BROWN; ***231** B-10; elev. 1,307ft./398m.; mail Aberdeen **z** 57401, Columbia **z** 57433; rural
Orient; Inc. Place; FAULK; **231** C-9; elev. 1,600ft./488m.; 🅿; **z** 57467; Ⓟ 59; Ⓒ 57
Orland; RMC Place; LAKE; ***231** E-12; elev. 1,796ft./547m.; mail Madison **z** 57042; rural
Ortley; Inc. Place; ROBERTS; **231** B-12; located on Lake Traverse Ind. Res.; elev. 1,870ft./570m.; 🅿; **z** 57256; Ⓟ 63; Ⓒ 54
Osceola; RMC Place; KINGSBURY; **231** D-11; mail Iroquois **z** 57353; ● 30
Ottumwa; RMC Place; HAAKON; **231** E-6; elev. 2,200ft./671m.; 🅿; **z** 57552; rural
Owanka; RMC Place; PENNINGTON; **231** E-4; elev. 2,512ft./766m.; 🅿; **z** 57767; ● 20

P

Parade; RMC Place; DEWEY; **231** C-6; elev. 2,400ft./732m.; 🅿; **z** 57625; ● 20
Parker; Inc. Place; ⊡ TURNER; **231** F-12; elev. 1,372ft./418m.; 🅿; **z** 57053; Ⓟ 984; Ⓒ 1,031
Parkston; Inc. Place; HUTCHINSON; **231** F-11; elev. 1,396ft./426m.; 🅿 🄷; **z** 57366; Ⓟ 1,572; Ⓒ 1,674
Parmelee; CDP; TODD; **231** F-6; located on Rosebud Ind. Res.; elev. 2,647ft./807m.; 🅿; **z** 57566; Ⓟ 618; Ⓒ 650
Patricia; RMC Place; BENNETT; ***231** F-5; mail Martin **z** 57551; rural
Pearl Creek Colony; RMC Place; BEADLE; ***231** D-11; mail Iroquois **z** 57353; ● 60
Pearsons Corner; RMC Place; YANKTON; ***231** G-12; elev. 1,638ft./499m.; mail Viborg **z** 57070; rural
Pedro; RMC Place; PENNINGTON; ***231** D-5; elev. 2,024ft./617m.; mail Wall **z** 57790; rural
Peever; Inc. Place; ROBERTS; **231** B-12; located on Lake Traverse Ind. Res.; 🅿; **z** 57257; Ⓟ 195; Ⓒ 209
Peninsula Park; RMC Place; LAKE; ***231** E-12; mail Wentworth **z** 57075
PENNINGTON; **231** E-4; Ⓟ 81,343; Ⓒ 88,565; ◆ 99,085
Perkins; RMC Place; BON HOMME; ***231** G-11; elev. 1,448ft./441m.; mail Springfield **z** 57062
PERKINS; **231** B-4; Ⓟ 3,932; Ⓒ 3,363; ◆ 2,801
Philip; Inc. Place; ⊡ HAAKON; **231** E-5; elev. 2,162ft./659m.; 🅿 🄷; **z** 57567; Ⓟ 1,077; Ⓒ 885
Pickerel (Pickerel Lake); RMC Place; DAY; ***231** B-12; located on Lake Traverse Ind. Res.; mail Grenville **z** 57239; summer pop. 400; ● 30
Pickerel Lake; DAY; see Pickerel (RMC Place)
Pickstown; Inc. Place; CHARLES MIX; **231** G-10; located on Yankton Ind. Res.; elev. 1,462ft./446m.; 🅿; **z** 57367; Ⓟ 95; Ⓒ 168
Piedmont; RMC Place; MEADE; **231** D-3; elev. 3,463ft./1,056m.; 🅿; **z** 57769; ● 350
Pierpont; Inc. Place; DAY; **231** B-11; elev. 1,500ft./457m.; 🅿; **z** 57468; Ⓟ 173; Ⓒ 122
Pierre; Inc. Place; **STATE CAPITAL**; ⊡ HUGHES; **231** D-7; elev. 1,484ft./452m.; 🅿 🄷; **z** 57501; Ⓟ 12,906; Ⓒ 13,876
Pine Ridge; CDP; SHANNON; **231** G-4; located on Pine Ridge Ind. Res.; elev. 3,232ft./985m.; 🅿 🄷; **z** 57770; location of Indian Agency; Ⓟ 2,596; Ⓒ 3,171
Pine Ridge Reservation; Indian Reservation; JACKSON, SHANNON; mail Pine Ridge **z** 57770; also location of Indian Agency; Ⓟ 13,143; Ⓒ 14,068
Plainview; RMC Place; MEADE; **231** D-5; elev. 2,400ft./732m.; 🅿; **z** 57748; ● 20
Plainview Colony; RMC Place; EDMUNDS; ***231** B-9; mail Leola **z** 57456; ● 50
Plana; RMC Place; BROWN; ***231** B-10; mail Aberdeen **z** 57401; rural
Plankinton; Inc. Place; ⊡ AURORA; **231** F-10; elev. 1,525ft./465m.; 🅿; **z** 57368; Ⓟ 604; Ⓒ 601
Plano; RMC Place; HANSON; ***231** E-11; mail Fulton **z** 57340; rural
Platte; Inc. Place; CHARLES MIX; **231** F-9; elev. 1,612ft./491m.; 🅿 🄷; **z** 57369; Ⓟ 1,311; Ⓒ 1,367
Platte Colony; RMC Place; CHARLES MIX; ***231** F-9; mail Platte **z** 57369; ● 80
Pleasant Valley Estates; RMC Place; BROWN; ***231** B-10; mail Aberdeen **z** 57401; ● 30
Pluma; RMC Place; LAWRENCE; **231** D-2; mail Deadwood **z** 57732; pop. incl. with Deadwood (Inc. Place)
Pollock; Inc. Place; CAMPBELL; **231** A-7; elev. 1,665ft./507m.; 🅿; **z** 57648; Ⓟ 379; Ⓒ 339
Polo; RMC Place; HAND; **231** C-9; elev. 1,588ft./484m.; mail Orient **z** 57467; ● 40
Porcupine; CDP; SHANNON; **231** G-4; located on Pine Ridge Ind. Res.; elev. 3,200ft./975m.; 🅿; **z** 57772; Ⓟ 783; Ⓒ 407
Potato Creek; RMC Place; JACKSON; **231** F-5; located on Pine Ridge Ind. Res.; mail Interior **z** 57750; ● 50
POTTER; **231** C-8; Ⓟ 3,190; Ⓒ 2,693; ◆ 2,021
Powell; RMC Place; HAAKON; ***231** E-5; mail Philip **z** 57567; rural
Prairie City; RMC Place; PERKINS; **231** B-4; elev. 2,900ft./884m.; 🅿; **z** 57649; ● 40
Prairie Village; RMC Place; LAKE; ***231** E-12; mail Madison **z** 57042; ● 10
Presho; Inc. Place; LYMAN; **231** E-8; elev. 1,764ft./538m.; 🅿; **z** 57568; Ⓟ 654; Ⓒ 588
Pringle; Inc. Place; CUSTER; **231** F-2; elev. 4,881ft./1,488m.; 🅿; **z** 57773; Ⓟ 96; Ⓒ 125
Promise; RMC Place; DEWEY; ***231** B-7; mail Mobridge **z** 57601; rural
Provo; RMC Place; FALL RIVER; **231** G-2; elev. 3,800ft./1,158m.; 🅿; **z** 57735; ● 80
Pukwana; Inc. Place; BRULE; **231** E-9; elev. 1,549ft./472m.; 🅿; **z** 57370; Ⓟ 263; Ⓒ 287
Putney; RMC Place; BROWN; ***231** B-10; elev. 1,306ft./398m.; mail Groton **z** 57445; rural

Q

Quinn; Inc. Place; PENNINGTON; **231** E-5; elev. 2,606ft./794m.; 🅿; **z** 57775; Ⓟ 72; Ⓒ 44
Quinn Table; RMC Place; PENNINGTON; mail Wall **z** 57790; rural

R

Ralph; RMC Place; HARDING; **231** A-3; elev. 2,726ft./831m.; 🅿; **z** 57650; ● 10
Ramona; Inc. Place; LAKE; **231** E-12; elev. 1,800ft./549m.; 🅿; **z** 57054; Ⓟ 194; Ⓒ 190
Rapid City; Inc. Place; ⊡ PENNINGTON; **231** E-3; elev. 3,247ft./990m.; 🅿 🄷 🄲 7,649 ■; ★ **RAP**; **z** 57701-03, **z** 57709; Ⓟ 54,523; Ⓒ 59,607; Ⓡ 59,573; ◆ 68,549
Rapid Valley; CDP; PENNINGTON; ***231** E-3; ★ **RAP**; mail Rapid City **z** 57703; Ⓟ 5,968; Ⓒ 7,043
Ravinia; Inc. Place; CHARLES MIX; **231** G-10; located on Yankton Ind. Res.; elev. 1,498ft./457m.; 🅿; **z** 57356; Ⓟ 79; Ⓒ 79
Raymond; Inc. Place; CLARK; **231** C-11; elev. 1,456ft./444m.; 🅿; **z** 57258; Ⓟ 96; Ⓒ 86
Red Elm; RMC Place; ZIEBACH; ***231** C-5; mail Dupree **z** 57623; rural
Redfield; Inc. Place; ⊡ SPINK; **231** C-10; elev. 1,303ft./397m.; 🅿 🄷; **z** 57469; Ⓟ 2,770; Ⓒ 2,897; Ⓡ 2,518
Redig; RMC Place; HARDING; **231** B-2; elev. 3,041ft./927m.; 🅿; **z** 57776; ● 10
Redowl; RMC Place; MEADE; **231** D-4; elev. 2,746ft./837m.; 🅿; **z** 57787; ● 10
Red Scaffold; RMC Place; ZIEBACH; **231** C-5; located on Cheyenne River Ind. Res.; mail Faith **z** 57626, Howes **z** 57748; ● 100
Red Shirt; RMC Place; SHANNON; **231** F-3; elev. 2,694ft./821m.; mail Hermosa **z** 57744; ● 40
Ree Heights; Inc. Place; HAND; **231** D-9; elev. 1,729ft./527m.; 🅿; **z** 57371; Ⓟ 91; Ⓒ 85
Reliance; Inc. Place; LYMAN; **231** E-8; elev. 1,796ft./547m.; 🅿; **z** 57569; Ⓟ 169; Ⓒ 206
Renner; RMC Place; MINNEHAHA; **231** F-13; elev. 1,436ft./438m.; 🅿; ★ **SXFL**; **z** 57020, **z** 57055; ● 110
Reva; RMC Place; HARDING; **231** B-3; elev. 3,059ft./932m.; 🅿; **z** 57651; ● 10
Revillo; Inc. Place; GRANT; **231** C-13; elev. 1,215ft./370m.; 🅿; **z** 57259; Ⓟ 152; Ⓒ 147
Richland; RMC Place; UNION; **231** G-13; elev. 1,134ft./346m.; mail Elk Point **z** 57025; ● 80
Ridgeview; RMC Place; DEWEY; **231** C-7; located on Cheyenne River Ind. Res.; elev. 2,300ft./701m.; 🅿; **z** 57652; ● 90
Riverside; RMC Place; HANSON; ***231** F-11; mail Mitchell **z** 57301; ● 30
Riverside Colony; RMC Place; BEADLE; ***231** D-10; mail Huron **z** 57350; ● 50
ROBERTS; **231** B-12; Ⓟ 9,914; Ⓒ 10,016; ◆ 9,678
Rochford; RMC Place; PENNINGTON; **231** E-2; elev. 5,278ft./1,609m.; 🅿; **z** 57745; ● 50
Rockerville; RMC Place; PENNINGTON; ***231** E-3; elev. 4,371ft./1,332m.; 🅿; **z** 57702 & mail Rapid City **z** 57701
Rockham; Inc. Place; FAULK; **231** C-9; elev. 1,396ft./426m.; 🅿; **z** 57470; Ⓟ 48; Ⓒ 53
Rockport; HANSON; see Rockport Colony (RMC Place)
Rockport Colony (Rockport); RMC Place; HANSON; ***231** F-11; mail Alexandria **z** 57311; ● 70
Roscoe; Inc. Place; EDMUNDS; **231** B-9; elev. 1,830ft./558m.; 🅿; **z** 57471; Ⓟ 362; Ⓒ 324
Rosebud; CDP; TODD; **231** G-6; located on Rosebud Ind. Res.; elev. 2,647ft./807m.; 🅿 🄷; **z** 57570; location of Indian Agency; Ⓟ 1,538; Ⓒ 1,557
Rosebud Reservation; Indian Reservation; TODD; mail Rosebud **z** 57570; also location of Indian Agency; Ⓟ 7,328; Ⓒ 9,050
Rosedale Colony; RMC Place; HANSON; ***231** F-11; mail Mitchell **z** 57301; ● 90
Rosholt; Inc. Place; ROBERTS; **231** A-12; located on Lake Traverse Ind. Res.; elev. 1,047ft./319m.; 🅿; **z** 57260; Ⓟ 408; Ⓒ 419
Roslyn; Inc. Place; DAY; **231** B-11; elev. 1,865ft./568m.; 🅿; **z** 57261; Ⓟ 251; Ⓒ 225
Roswell; Inc. Place; MINER; **231** E-11; elev. 1,405ft./428m.; 🅿; **z** 57349; Ⓟ 19; Ⓒ 21
Roubaix; RMC Place; LAWRENCE; ***231** D-2; mail Deadwood **z** 57732; rural
Rowena; RMC Place; MINNEHAHA; ***231** F-13; elev. 1,411ft./430m.; 🅿; **z** 57005; ● 70
Rumford; RMC Place; FALL RIVER; ***231** G-2; elev. 3,517ft./1,072m.
Rumpus Ridge; RMC Place; MCCOOK; ***231** F-12; elev. 1,488ft./454m.; mail Canistota **z** 57012; rural
Running Water; RMC Place; BON HOMME; **231** H-11; elev. 1,251ft./381m.; 🅿; **z** 57062; ● 30
Rutland; RMC Place; LAKE; **231** E-12; elev. 1,660ft./506m.; 🅿; **z** 57057; ● 80

S

Saint Charles; CDP; GREGORY; **231** G-9; located on Rosebud Ind. Res.; elev. 2,065ft./629m.; 🅿; **z** 57571; Ⓒ 19
Saint Francis; Inc. Place; TODD; **231** G-6; located on Rosebud Ind. Res.; elev. 2,980ft./908m.; 🅿; **z** 57572; Ⓟ 815; Ⓒ 675
Saint Lawrence; Inc. Place; HAND; **231** D-9; elev. 1,566ft./477m.; 🅿; **z** 57373; Ⓟ 223; Ⓒ 210
Saint Onge; RMC Place; LAWRENCE; **231** D-2; elev. 3,429ft./1,045m.; 🅿; **z** 57779; ● 130
Salem; Inc. Place; ⊡ MCCOOK; **231** F-12; elev. 1,527ft./465m.; 🅿; **z** 57058; Ⓟ 1,289; Ⓒ 1,371
Sanator; RMC Place; CUSTER; **231** J-2; mail Custer **z** 57730; rural
SANBORN; **231** E-11; Ⓟ 2,833; Ⓒ 2,675; ◆ 2,406
Savoy; RMC Place; LAWRENCE; ***231** D-2; mail Lead **z** 57754; rural
Scenic; RMC Place; PENNINGTON; **231** E-4; elev. 2,809ft./856m.; 🅿; **z** 57780; ● 80
Scotland; Inc. Place; BON HOMME; **231** G-11; elev. 1,348ft./411m.; 🅿 🄷; **z** 57059; Ⓟ 968; Ⓒ 891
Selby; Inc. Place; ⊡ WALWORTH; **231** B-8; elev. 1,912ft./583m.; 🅿; **z** 57472; Ⓟ 707; Ⓒ 736
Seneca; Inc. Place; FAULK; **231** C-8; elev. 1,907ft./581m.; 🅿; **z** 57473; Ⓟ 81; Ⓒ 58
Shadehill; RMC Place; PERKINS; **231** A-5; elev. 2,300ft./701m.; 🅿; **z** 57638; ● 20
Shady Beach; RMC Place; ROBERTS; ***231** B-13; mail Corona **z** 57227; ● 20
SHANNON; **231** F-4; Ⓟ 9,902; Ⓒ 12,466; ◆ 13,360
Sharps Corner; RMC Place; SHANNON; **231** F-4; located on Pine Ridge Ind. Res.; mail Kyle **z** 57752, Porcupine **z** 57772; ● 60
Shelby; RMC Place; BUFFALO; ***231** E-9; mail Fort Thompson **z** 57339, Philip **z** 57567; rural
Sherman; Inc. Place; MINNEHAHA; **231** E-13; elev. 1,500ft./457m.; 🅿; **z** 57030; Ⓟ 66; Ⓒ 87
Silver City; RMC Place; PENNINGTON; **231** E-2; elev. 4,600ft./1,402m.; 🅿; **z** 57702; ● 60
Sinai; Inc. Place; BROOKINGS; **231** D-12; elev. 1,780ft./543m.; 🅿; **z** 57061; Ⓟ 120; Ⓒ 133
Sioux Falls; Inc. Place; ⊡ MINNEHAHA, LINCOLN; **231** F-13; elev. 1,442ft./440m.; 🅿 🄷 🄲 4,543 ■; ★ **SXFL**; **z** 57101, **z** 57103-10, **z** 57117-18, **z** 57186, **z** 57188-89, **z** 57192-94, **z** 57196-98; Ⓟ 100,814; Ⓒ 123,975; Ⓡ 124,158; ◆ 168,625
Sisseton; Inc. Place; ⊡ ROBERTS; **231** A-12; located on Lake Traverse Ind. Res.; elev. 1,204ft./367m.; 🅿 🄷; **z** 57262; Ⓟ 2,181; Ⓒ 2,572
Smiths Park; RMC Place; LAKE; ***231** E-12; mail Wentworth **z** 57075
Smithwick; RMC Place; FALL RIVER; **231** F-3; elev. 3,400ft./1,036m.; 🅿; **z** 57782; ● 30
Snake Creek; RMC Place; CORSON; ***231** B-7; mail Wakpala **z** 57658; rural
So Dak Park; RMC Place; ROBERTS; mail Wilmot **z** 57279
Soldier Creek; RMC Place; TODD; ***231** F-6; located on Rosebud Ind. Res.; mail Mission **z** 57555; ● 200
Sorum; RMC Place; PERKINS; **231** B-3; elev. 2,800ft./853m.; mail Bison **z** 57620
South Shore; Inc. Place; CODINGTON; **231** C-12; elev. 1,862ft./568m.; 🅿; **z** 57263; Ⓟ 260; Ⓒ 270
Spearfish; Inc. Place; LAWRENCE; **231** D-2; elev. 3,643ft./1,110m.; 🅿 🄷 🄲 3,896; **z** 57783, **z** 57799; Ⓟ 6,966; Ⓒ 8,606
Spencer; Inc. Place; MCCOOK; **231** F-11; elev. 1,381ft./421m.; 🅿; **z** 57374; Ⓟ 317; Ⓒ 157
Spink; RMC Place; UNION; **231** G-13; elev. 1,238ft./377m.; mail Elk Point **z** 57025; ● 40
SPINK; **231** C-10; Ⓟ 7,981; Ⓒ 7,454; ◆ 6,523
Spink Colony; RMC Place; SPINK; ***231** C-10; mail Frankfort **z** 57440; ● 100
Spring Creek; CDP; TODD; **231** G-6; located on Rosebud Ind. Res.; elev. 2,648ft./807m.; mail Saint Francis **z** 57572; Ⓟ 112; Ⓒ 136
Spring Creek Colony; RMC Place; MCPHERSON; ***231** A-9; mail Forbes **z** 58439; ● 70
Springfield; Inc. Place; BON HOMME; **231** G-11; elev. 1,275ft./389m.; 🅿; **z** 57062; Ⓟ 834; Ⓒ 792
Spring Valley; RMC Place; TURNER; ***231** G-12; mail Hurley **z** 57036; rural
Spring Valley Colony; RMC Place; JERAULD; ***231** E-9; mail Wessington Springs **z** 57382; ● 100
Standing Rock Reservation; Indian Reservation; CORSON, DEWEY, ZIEBACH; Reservation extends into ND; mail Eagle Butte **z** 57625, Fort Yates **z** 58538; Ⓟ 5,196; Ⓒ 4,206
STANLEY; **231** D-7; Ⓟ 2,453; Ⓒ 2,772; ◆ 2,785
Stephan; RMC Place; HYDE; **231** E-9; located on Crow Creek Ind. Res.; elev. 1,820ft./555m.; 🅿; **z** 57346; ● 30
Stickney; Inc. Place; AURORA; **231** F-10; elev. 1,650ft./503m.; 🅿; **z** 57375; Ⓟ 323; Ⓒ 334
Stockholm; Inc. Place; GRANT; **231** C-12; elev. 1,750ft./533m.; 🅿; **z** 57264; Ⓟ 89; Ⓒ 105
Stone Bridge; RMC Place; HAMLIN; ***231** D-12; mail Castlewood **z** 57223
Stoneville; RMC Place; MEADE; **231** C-4; elev. 2,928ft./892m.; 🅿; **z** 57787; ● 20
Storla; CDP; AURORA; **231** E-10; elev. 1,366ft./416m.; mail Letcher **z** 57359; Ⓒ 15
Strandburg; Inc. Place; GRANT; **231** C-12; elev. 1,650ft./503m.; 🅿; **z** 57265; Ⓟ 74; Ⓒ 69
Stratford; Inc. Place; BROWN; **231** B-10; elev. 1,300ft./396m.; 🅿; **z** 57474; Ⓟ 85; Ⓒ 96
Sturgis; Inc. Place; ⊡ MEADE; **231** D-2; elev. 3,440ft./1,049m.; 🅿 🄷; **z** 57785; Ⓟ 5,330; Ⓒ 6,442
SULLY; **231** C-8; Ⓟ 1,589; Ⓒ 1,556; ◆ 1,384
Summerset; Inc. Place; MEADE; ***231** E-3; 🅿; **z** 57769; incorporated June 7, 2005; not reported in 2000 Census; ● 1,200
Summit; Inc. Place; ROBERTS; **231** B-12; located on Lake Traverse Ind. Res.; elev. 1,999ft./609m.; 🅿; **z** 57266; Ⓟ 267; Ⓒ 281
Sunnyview; RMC Place; BROOKINGS; **231** D-12; mail Brookings **z** 57006; ● 50
Swett; RMC Place; BENNETT; ***231** G-5; mail Martin **z** 57551; rural

T

Tabor; Inc. Place; BON HOMME; **231** G-11; elev. 1,364ft./416m.; 🅿; **z** 57063; Ⓟ 403; Ⓒ 417
Tacoma Park; RMC Place; BROWN; ***231** B-10; elev. 1,302ft./397m.; mail Columbia **z** 57433; rural
Tea; Inc. Place; LINCOLN; **231** F-12; elev. 1,486ft./453m.; 🅿; **z** 57064; Ⓟ 786; Ⓒ 1,742
Thomas; RMC Place; HAMLIN; ***231** C-12; elev. 1,763ft./537m.; mail Hayti **z** 57241
Thunder Butte; RMC Place; ZIEBACH; **231** B-5; located on Cheyenne River Ind. Res.; mail Dupree **z** 57623; ● 70
Thunder Hawk; RMC Place; CORSON; **231** A-5; located on Standing Rock Ind. Res.; 🅿; **z** 57638; ● 30
Tilford; RMC Place; MEADE; **231** D-3; elev. 3,578ft./1,091m.; mail Piedmont **z** 57769; ● 40
Timber Lake; Inc. Place; ⊡ DEWEY; **231** B-6; located on Cheyenne River Ind. Res.; elev. 2,163ft./659m.; 🅿; **z** 57656; Ⓟ 517; Ⓒ 443
TODD; **231** G-7; Ⓟ 8,352; Ⓒ 9,050; ◆ 10,507
Tolstoy; Inc. Place; POTTER; **231** C-8; elev. 1,900ft./579m.; 🅿; **z** 57475; Ⓟ 69; Ⓒ 64

Entries in **UPPERCASE** are counties.
Entries in **bold** have populations of 2,500 or more.
Names in parentheses are alternate names.
Inc. Place — Incorporated Place
RMC Place — Rand McNally Designated Place
CDP — Census Designated Place
MCD — Minor Civil Division

⊡ County Seat
▲ Minor Civil Division
elev. Elevation
🅿 Post Office

🄷 Hospital
🄲 College
■ Principal Business Center
★ Ranally Metro Area (RMA) Abbreviation
z Zip Code(s)

Ⓟ Previous Census Population
Ⓡ Revised Census Population
Ⓐ Annexation Population
● Rand McNally Population Estimate
Ⓒ Final Census Population
Ⓢ Special Census Population
◆ Estimated Population

For additional definitions see Glossary, Volume 1, and Introduction, Volume 2.

Toronto; Inc. Place; DEUEL; **231** D-13; elev. 1,997ft./609m.; 🅿; **z** 57268; Ⓟ 201; © 202
Trail City; RMC Place; DEWEY, CORSON; **231** B-7; elev. 2,131ft./650m.; 🅿; **z** 57657; ● 130
Trail West; RMC Place; MEADE; ***231** D-3; elev. 3,472ft./1,058m.; mail Piedmont **z** 57769; ● 100
Trent; Inc. Place; MOODY; **231** E-13; located on Flandreau Ind. Res.; elev. 1,500ft./457m.; 🅿; **z** 57065; Ⓟ 211; © 254
Tripp; Inc. Place; HUTCHINSON; **231** G-11; elev. 1,531ft./467m.; 🅿; **z** 57376; Ⓟ 664; © 711
TRIPP; **231** G-8; Ⓟ 6,924; © 6,430; ◆ 5,475
Trojan; RMC Place; LAWRENCE; ***231** D-2; mail Lead **z** 57754; rural
Troy; RMC Place; GRANT; **231** C-12; mail Strandburg **z** 57265; ● 10
Tschetter Colony; RMC Place; HUTCHINSON; ***231** F-11; mail Olivet **z** 57052; ● 100
Tulare; Inc. Place; SPINK; **231** C-10; elev. 1,322ft./403m.; 🅿; **z** 57476; Ⓟ 244; © 221
Turkey Ridge; RMC Place; TURNER; **231** G-12; elev. 1,441ft./439m.; mail Hurley **z** 57036; ● 10
TURNER; **231** F-12; Ⓟ 8,576; © 8,849; ◆ 8,349
Turton; Inc. Place; SPINK; **231** C-10; elev. 1,325ft./404m.; 🅿; **z** 57477; Ⓟ 76; © 61
Tuthill; RMC Place; BENNETT; **231** G-5; located on Pine Ridge Ind. Res.; 🅿; **z** 57574; ● 30
Twin Brooks; Inc. Place; GRANT; **231** B-12; elev. 1,260ft./384m.; 🅿; **z** 57269; Ⓟ 54; © 55
Two Strike; CDP-Census Area Only; TODD; ***231** G-6; elev. 2,800ft./853m.; mail Rosebud **z** 57570; Ⓟ 112; © 33
Tyndall; Inc. Place; ⊡ BON HOMME; **231** G-11; elev. 1,422ft./433m.; 🅿 🅷; **z** 57066; Ⓟ 1,201; © 1,239

U

UNION; **231** G-13; Ⓟ 10,189; © 12,584; ◆ 14,454
Union Center; RMC Place; MEADE; **231** D-4; elev. 2,901ft./884m.; 🅿; **z** 57787; ● 80
Unityville; RMC Place; MCCOOK; **231** E-11; elev. 1,528ft./466m.; mail Salem **z** 57058; ● 20
Usta; RMC Place; PERKINS; ***231** B-5; elev. 2,333ft./711m.; mail Faith **z** 57626; rural
Utica; Inc. Place; YANKTON; **231** G-12; elev. 1,400ft./427m.; 🅿; **z** 57067; Ⓟ 115; © 86

V

Vale; RMC Place; BUTTE; **231** D-3; elev. 2,766ft./843m.; 🅿; **z** 57788; ● 140
Valley Springs; Inc. Place; MINNEHAHA; **231** F-13; elev. 1,392ft./424m.; 🅿; **z** 57068; Ⓟ 739; © 792
Valley View; YANKTON; see Balleyview (RMC Place)
Vayland; RMC Place; HAND; ***231** D-9; elev. 1,486ft./453m.; mail Wessington **z** 57381
Veblen; Inc. Place; MARSHALL; **231** A-12; elev. 1,250ft./381m.; 🅿; **z** 57270; Ⓟ 321; © 281
Vedin Corner; RMC Place; YANKTON; ***231** G-12; elev. 1,312ft./400m.; mail Irene **z** 57037; rural
Verdon; Inc. Place; BROWN; **231** B-10; elev. 1,305ft./398m.; 🅿; **z** 57434; Ⓟ 7; © 6
Vermillion; Inc. Place; ⊡ CLAY; **231** G-12; elev. 1,221ft./372m.; 🅿 🅷 🅲 8,746; **z** 57069; Ⓟ 10,034; © 9,765; ® 10,276
Vetal; RMC Place; BENNETT; **231** G-6; located on Pine Ridge Ind. Res.; elev. 3,000ft./914m.; 🅿; **z** 57551
Viborg; Inc. Place; TURNER; **231** G-12; elev. 1,304ft./397m.; 🅿 🅷; **z** 57070; Ⓟ 763; © 832
Victor; RMC Place; ROBERTS; **231** A-12; located on Lake Traverse Ind. Res.; elev. 1,083ft./330m.; mail Rosholt **z** 57260; ● 20
Vienna; Inc. Place; CLARK; **231** D-11; elev. 1,840ft./561m.; 🅿; **z** 57271; Ⓟ 93; © 78
Vilas; Inc. Place; MINER; **231** E-11; elev. 1,478ft./450m.; mail Howard **z** 57349; Ⓟ 28; © 19
Villa Trailer Court; RMC Place; PENNINGTON; ***231** E-3; ★ **RAP**; mail Ellsworth AFB **z** 57706; pop. incl. with Box Elder (Inc. Place)
Virgil; Inc. Place; BEADLE; **231** D-10; elev. 1,300ft./396m.; 🅿; **z** 57379; Ⓟ 33; © 25
Vivian; CDP; LYMAN; **231** E-7; elev. 1,950ft./594m.; 🅿; **z** 57576; © 131
Volga; Inc. Place; BROOKINGS; **231** D-12; elev. 1,634ft./498m.; 🅿; **z** 57071; Ⓟ 1,263; © 1,435
Volin; Inc. Place; YANKTON; **231** G-12; elev. 1,185ft./361m.; 🅿; **z** 57072; Ⓟ 175; © 207

W

Wagner; Inc. Place; CHARLES MIX; **231** G-10; located on Yankton Ind. Res.; elev. 1,448ft./441m.; 🅿 🅷; **z** 57380 & mail Marty **z** 57361; location of Indian Agency; Ⓟ 1,462; © 1,675
Wakonda; Inc. Place; CLAY; **231** G-12; elev. 1,377ft./420m.; 🅿; **z** 57073; Ⓟ 329; © 374
Wakpala; RMC Place; CORSON; **231** B-7; located on Standing Rock Ind. Res.; elev. 1,640ft./500m.; 🅿; **z** 57658; ● 200
Wakpamani; RMC Place; SHANNON; ***231** G-4; elev. 3,477ft./1,060m.; mail Batesland **z** 57716; ● 30
Walker; RMC Place; CORSON; **231** A-6; located on Standing Rock Ind. Res.; elev. 2,200ft./671m.; 🅿; **z** 57659; ● 10
Wall; Inc. Place; PENNINGTON; **231** E-4; elev. 2,818ft./859m.; 🅿; **z** 57790; Ⓟ 834; © 818
Wallace; Inc. Place; CODINGTON; **231** C-11; elev. 1,800ft./549m.; 🅿; **z** 57272; Ⓟ 83; © 86
WALWORTH; **231** B-8; Ⓟ 6,087; © 5,974; ◆ 4,975
Wanblee; CDP; JACKSON; **231** F-5; located on Pine Ridge Ind. Res.; elev. 2,630ft./802m.; 🅿; **z** 57577; Ⓟ 654; © 641
Ward; Inc. Place; MOODY; **231** E-13; elev. 1,750ft./533m.; 🅿; **z** 57026; Ⓟ 35; © 41
Warner; Inc. Place; BROWN; **231** B-10; elev. 1,298ft./396m.; 🅿; **z** 57479; Ⓟ 336; © 419
Wasta; Inc. Place; PENNINGTON; **231** E-4; elev. 2,313ft./705m.; 🅿; **z** 57791 & mail Owanka **z** 57767; Ⓟ 82; © 75
Watauga; RMC Place; CORSON; **231** A-5; located on Standing Rock Ind. Res.; elev. 2,252ft./686m.; 🅿; **z** 57660; ● 30
Watertown; Inc. Place; ⊡ CODINGTON; **231** C-12; elev. 1,739ft./530m.; 🅿 🅷 ■; **z** 57201; Ⓟ 17,592; © 20,237; ◆ 20,534
Waubay; Inc. Place; DAY; **231** B-12; elev. 1,814ft./553m.; 🅿; **z** 57273; Ⓟ 647; © 662
Waverly; RMC Place; CODINGTON; **231** C-12; elev. 1,980ft./604m.; 🅿; **z** 57201; ● 50
Webster; Inc. Place; ⊡ DAY; **231** B-11; elev. 1,847ft./563m.; 🅿 🅷; **z** 57274; Ⓟ 2,017; © 1,952
Webster Grove; RMC Place; MINNEHAHA; ***231** F-12; ★ **SXFL**; mail Sioux Falls **z** 57106; pop. incl. with Sioux Falls (Inc. Place)
Wecota; RMC Place; FAULK; **231** C-9; elev. 1,558ft./475m.; 🅿; **z** 57438; ● 20
Wentworth; Inc. Place; LAKE; **231** E-12; elev. 1,700ft./518m.; 🅿; **z** 57075; Ⓟ 181; © 188
Wessington; Inc. Place; BEADLE, HAND; **231** D-10; elev. 1,415ft./431m.; 🅿; **z** 57381; Ⓟ 265; © 248
Wessington Springs; Inc. Place; ⊡ JERAULD; **231** E-10; elev. 1,687ft./514m.; 🅿 🅷; **z** 57382; Ⓟ 1,083; © 1,011
Westport; Inc. Place; BROWN; **231** B-10; elev. 1,330ft./405m.; 🅿; **z** 57481; Ⓟ 112; © 125
Westreville; RMC Place; CLAY; ***231** G-12; mail Vermillion **z** 57069
West Yard; RMC Place; UNION; ★ **SXCY**; pop. incl. with North Sioux City (Inc. Place)
Wetonka; Inc. Place; MCPHERSON; **231** B-9; elev. 1,471ft./448m.; 🅿; **z** 57481; Ⓟ 12; © 12
Wewela; RMC Place; TRIPP; **231** G-8; located on Rosebud Ind. Res.; elev. 2,200ft./671m.; 🅿; **z** 57580; ● 20
White; Inc. Place; BROOKINGS; **231** D-13; elev. 1,777ft./542m.; 🅿; **z** 57276; Ⓟ 536; © 530
White Butte; RMC Place; PERKINS; ***231** A-4; mail Lemmon **z** 57638; ● 20
Whitehorse; CDP; DEWEY; **231** B-6; located on Cheyenne River Ind. Res.; elev. 1,718ft./524m.; 🅿; **z** 57661; © 141
White Horse; CDP-Census Area Only; TODD; ***231** F-7; elev. 2,558ft./780m.; mail Mission **z** 57555; Ⓟ 152; © 180
White Lake; Inc. Place; AURORA; **231** F-10; elev. 1,640ft./500m.; 🅿; **z** 57383; Ⓟ 419; © 405
White Owl; RMC Place; MEADE; **231** D-4; elev. 2,800ft./853m.; 🅿; **z** 57792; ● 30
White River; Inc. Place; ⊡ MELLETTE; **231** F-7; located on Rosebud Ind. Res.; elev. 2,136ft./651m.; 🅿; **z** 57579; Ⓟ 595; © 598
White Rock; Inc. Place; ROBERTS; **231** A-13; located on Lake Traverse Ind. Res.; elev. 976ft./297m.; mail Rosholt **z** 57260; Ⓟ 7; © 18
Whitewood; Inc. Place; LAWRENCE; **231** D-2; elev. 3,648ft./1,112m.; 🅿; **z** 57793; Ⓟ 891; © 844
Wicksville; RMC Place; PENNINGTON; ***231** E-4; elev. 2,907ft./886m.; mail Owanka **z** 57767; rural
Willow Lake; Inc. Place; CLARK; **231** D-11; elev. 1,785ft./544m.; 🅿; **z** 57278; Ⓟ 317; © 294
Wilmot; Inc. Place; ROBERTS; **231** B-12; elev. 1,200ft./366m.; 🅿; **z** 57279; Ⓟ 566; © 543
Winfred; RMC Place; LAKE; **231** E-12; elev. 1,710ft./521m.; 🅿; **z** 57076; ● 60
Winner; Inc. Place; ⊡ TRIPP; serves as county seat of Todd; **231** F-8; located on Rosebud Ind. Res.; 🅿 🅷; **z** 57580; Ⓟ 3,354; © 3,137
Witten (New Witten); Inc. Place; TRIPP; **231** F-8; located on Rosebud Ind. Res.; elev. 2,000ft./610m.; 🅿; **z** 57584; Ⓟ 87; © 51
Wolf Creek Colony; RMC Place; HUTCHINSON; ***231** F-11; mail Olivet **z** 57052; ● 100
Wolsey; Inc. Place; BEADLE; **231** D-10; elev. 1,353ft./412m.; 🅿; **z** 57384; Ⓟ 442; © 418
Wonder Land Homes; RMC Place; MEADE; ***231** D-3; elev. 3,619ft./1,103m.; mail Black Hawk **z** 57718; ● 100
Wood; Inc. Place; MELLETTE; **231** F-7; located on Rosebud Ind. Res.; elev. 2,100ft./640m.; 🅿; **z** 57585; Ⓟ 73; © 66
Woonsocket; Inc. Place; ⊡ SANBORN; **231** E-10; elev. 1,307ft./398m.; 🅿; **z** 57385; Ⓟ 766; © 720
Worthing; Inc. Place; LINCOLN; **231** F-13; elev. 1,362ft./415m.; 🅿; **z** 57077; Ⓟ 371; © 585
Wounded Knee; CDP; SHANNON; **231** G-4; located on Pine Ridge Ind. Res.; elev. 3,243ft./988m.; 🅿; **z** 57794; Ⓟ 18; © 328

Y

Yale; Inc. Place; BEADLE; **231** D-11; elev. 1,336ft./407m.; 🅿; **z** 57386; Ⓟ 128; © 118
Yankton; Inc. Place; ⊡ YANKTON; **231** G-12; elev. 1,205ft./367m.; 🅿 🅷 🅲 1,220 ■; **z** 57078; Ⓟ 12,703; © 13,528; ◆ 12,815
YANKTON; **231** G-12; Ⓟ 19,252; © 21,652; ◆ 21,808
Yankton Reservation; Indian Reservation; CHARLES MIX; mail Wagner **z** 57380; also location of Indian Agency; Ⓟ 6,541; © 6,500

Z

Zell; RMC Place; FAULK; **231** C-10; elev. 1,364ft./416m.; 🅿; **z** 57469; ● 30
Zeona; RMC Place; PERKINS; **231** B-3; elev. 2,700ft./823m.; 🅿; **z** 57758; rural
ZIEBACH; **231** C-6; Ⓟ 2,220; © 2,519; ◆ 2,537

TENNESSEE

Statistics

Total area (2000) — 42,143 square miles
Land area (2000) — 41,217 square miles
Water area (2000) — 926 square miles
Capital — Nashville
Admitted as state — June, 1796

Ranally Metro Areas (RMAs) and Abbreviations

Chattanooga, TN-GA — CHTN
Clarksville, TN-KY — CLRKV
Cleveland, TN — CLEV
Jackson, TN — JAC
Johnson City-Kingsport-Bristol, TN-VA — JNSC-
Knoxville, TN — KNOX
Memphis, TN-AR-MS — MEM
Morristown, TN — MORR
Murfreesboro, TN — MUR
Nashville, TN — NASH

Maps

State maps can be found on pages 142-254 in Vol. 1

Principal Places

Place Name	Place Type	County	Population
Nashville	Inc. Place	DAVIDSON	◆ 673,012
Memphis	Inc. Place	SHELBY	◆ 659,448
Knoxville	Inc. Place	KNOX	◆ 198,350
Chattanooga	Inc. Place	HAMILTON	◆ 183,424
Clarksville	Inc. Place	MONTGOMERY	◆ 132,794
Murfreesboro	Inc. Place	RUTHERFORD	◆ 114,063
Franklin	Inc. Place	WILLIAMSON	◆ 70,144
Jackson	Inc. Place	MADISON	◆ 65,305
Johnson City	Inc. Place	WASHINGTON	◆ 64,463
Hendersonville	Inc. Place	SUMNER	◆ 48,778
Kingsport	Inc. Place	SULLIVAN	◆ 46,814
Bartlett	Inc. Place	SHELBY	◆ 44,341
Cleveland	Inc. Place	BRADLEY	◆ 42,441
Brentwood	Inc. Place	WILLIAMSON	◆ 37,700
Germantown	Inc. Place	SHELBY	◆ 36,941
Columbia	Inc. Place	MAURY	◆ 36,444
Smyrna	Inc. Place	RUTHERFORD	◆ 35,934
Collierville	Inc. Place	SHELBY	◆ 35,074
La Vergne	Inc. Place	RUTHERFORD	◆ 34,122
Gallatin	Inc. Place	SUMNER	◆ 30,340
Oak Ridge	Inc. Place	ANDERSON	◆ 27,383
Cookeville	Inc. Place	PUTNAM	◆ 27,059
Morristown	Inc. Place	HAMBLEN	◆ 26,995
Maryville	Inc. Place	BLOUNT	◆ 26,359
Bristol	Inc. Place	SULLIVAN	◆ 25,012
Lebanon	Inc. Place	WILSON	◆ 24,732
East Ridge	Inc. Place	HAMILTON	◆ 23,469
Mount Juliet	Inc. Place	WILSON	◆ 21,660
Farragut	Inc. Place	KNOX	◆ 21,030
Tullahoma	Inc. Place	COFFEE	© 17,994
Goodlettsville	Inc. Place	DAVIDSON	◆ 17,482
Dyersburg	Inc. Place	DYER	◆ 17,337
Greeneville	Inc. Place	GREENE	◆ 17,008
Shelbyville	Inc. Place	BEDFORD	© 16,105
Athens	Inc. Place	MCMINN	◆ 14,333
Springfield	Inc. Place	ROBERTSON	© 14,329
East Brainerd	CDP	HAMILTON	© 14,132
Elizabethton	Inc. Place	CARTER	◆ 13,344
McMinnville	Inc. Place	WARREN	© 12,749
Red Bank	Inc. Place	HAMILTON	© 12,418
Dickson	Inc. Place	DICKSON	© 12,244
Middle Valley	CDP	HAMILTON	© 11,854
Sevierville	Inc. Place	SEVIER	© 11,757
Soddy-Daisy	Inc. Place	HAMILTON	© 11,530
Spring Hill	Inc. Place	MAURY	◆ 11,283
Lawrenceburg	Inc. Place	LAWRENCE	© 10,796
Union City	Inc. Place	OBION	◆ 10,760
Brownsville	Inc. Place	HAYWOOD	© 10,748
Martin	Inc. Place	WEAKLEY	© 10,515
Millington	Inc. Place	SHELBY	© 10,433
Lewisburg	Inc. Place	MARSHALL	© 10,413
Bloomingdale	CDP	SULLIVAN	© 10,350
Humboldt	Inc. Place	GIBSON	© 9,467
Clinton	Inc. Place	ANDERSON	© 9,409
Paris	Inc. Place	HENRY	◆ 9,252
Crossville	Inc. Place	CUMBERLAND	© 8,981
Seymour	CDP	SEVIER	© 8,850
Covington	Inc. Place	TIPTON	© 8,463
Portland	Inc. Place	SUMNER	© 8,458
Alcoa	Inc. Place	BLOUNT	◆ 8,295
Manchester	Inc. Place	COFFEE	© 8,294
LaFollette	Inc. Place	CAMPBELL	© 7,926
Pulaski	Inc. Place	GILES	© 7,871
Ripley	Inc. Place	LAUDERDALE	© 7,844
Jefferson City	Inc. Place	JEFFERSON	© 7,760
Milan	Inc. Place	GIBSON	® 7,662
Harrison	CDP	HAMILTON	© 7,630
Powell	RMC Place	KNOX	℗ 7,534
Signal Mountain	Inc. Place	HAMILTON	© 7,429
Lexington	Inc. Place	HENDERSON	© 7,393
Winchester	Inc. Place	FRANKLIN	© 7,329
White House	Inc. Place	SUMNER	® 7,297
Newport	Inc. Place	COCKE	© 7,242
Green Hill	CDP	WILSON	© 7,068
Colonial Heights	CDP	SULLIVAN	© 7,067
Fayetteville	Inc. Place	LINCOLN	© 6,994
Savannah	Inc. Place	HARDIN	© 6,917
Lakeland	Inc. Place	SHELBY	© 6,862
Lenoir City	Inc. Place	LOUDON	© 6,819
Harriman	Inc. Place	ROANE	© 6,744
Collegedale	Inc. Place	HAMILTON	© 6,514
South Cleveland	CDP	BRADLEY	© 6,216
Dayton	Inc. Place	RHEA	© 6,180
Church Hill	Inc. Place	HAWKINS	© 5,916
Bolivar	Inc. Place	HARDEMAN	© 5,802
Fairview	Inc. Place	WILLIAMSON	© 5,800
Rockwood	Inc. Place	ROANE	© 5,774
Lynchburg	Inc. Place	MOORE	© 5,740
Ooltewah	CDP	HAMILTON	© 5,681
Henderson	Inc. Place	CHESTER	© 5,670
Erwin	Inc. Place	UNICOI	© 5,610
Sweetwater	Inc. Place	MONROE	© 5,586
Millersville	Inc. Place	SUMNER	© 5,308
McKenzie	Inc. Place	CARROLL	© 5,295
Kingston	Inc. Place	ROANE	© 5,264
Pigeon Forge	Inc. Place	SEVIER	© 5,083

County Business Data

County	FIPS Code	County Seat	Land Area (Sq. Mi.)	Census Population			Wholesale Trade		Manufacturing, 2002			
				4/1/2000	4/1/1990	% Change 1990-2000	Sales, 2002 ($1,000)	% Change 1997-2002	Establish-ments	Total Employees	Value Added ($1,000)	Ranally Mfg. Units
Anderson	001	Clinton	338	71,330	68,250	4.5	125,092	18.2	118	10,493	1,181,542	625
Bedford	003	Shelbyville	474	37,586	30,411	23.6	104,409	44.4	57	4,477	386,773	205
Benton	005	Camden	395	16,537	14,524	13.9	31,198	-11.5	19	802	64,154	34
Bledsoe	007	Pikeville	406	12,367	9,669	27.9	(d)	(d)	13	(d)	(d)	...
Blount	009	Maryville	559	105,823	85,969	23.1	963,617	47.1	117	8,060	1,391,478	736
Bradley	011	Cleveland	329	87,965	73,712	19.3	(d)	(d)	128	10,765	2,154,458	1,140
Campbell	013	Jacksboro	480	39,854	35,079	13.6	57,235	-51.3	46	1,463	112,290	59
Cannon	015	Woodbury	266	12,826	10,467	22.5	(d)	(d)	...	(d)	(d)	...
Carroll	017	Huntingdon	599	29,475	27,514	7.1	56,813	17.8	44	2,155	144,570	76
Carter	019	Elizabethton	341	56,742	51,505	10.2	(d)	(d)	43	1,812	160,607	85
Cheatham	021	Ashland City	303	35,912	27,140	32.3	19,052	-35.1	39	837	62,729	33
Chester	023	Henderson	289	15,540	12,819	21.2	38,754	12.6	20	534	34,997	19
Claiborne	025	Tazewell	434	29,862	26,137	14.3	20,457	(d)	38	3,268	222,821	118
Clay	027	Celina	236	7,976	7,238	10.2	7,131	(d)	...	(d)	(d)	...
Cocke	029	Newport	434	33,565	29,141	15.2	(d)	(d)	35	2,233	262,813	139
Coffee	031	Manchester	429	48,014	40,339	19.0	(d)	(d)	67	(d)	(d)	...
Crockett	033	Alamo	265	14,532	13,378	8.6	(d)	(d)	21	1,036	142,578	75
Cumberland	035	Crossville	682	46,802	34,736	34.7	(d)	(d)	55	2,094	211,788	112
Davidson	037	Nashville	502	569,891	510,784	11.6	20,032,125	17.8	666	29,151	3,617,798	1,914
Decatur	039	Decaturville	334	11,731	10,472	12.0	(d)	(d)	33	791	69,495	37
DeKalb	041	Smithville	305	17,423	14,360	21.3	(d)	(d)	25	2,640	227,020	120
Dickson	043	Charlotte	490	43,156	35,061	23.1	259,904	-5.4	54	4,022	393,029	208
Dyer	045	Dyersburg	510	37,279	34,854	7.0	172,411	-22.1	42	5,111	615,351	326
Fayette	047	Somerville	704	28,806	25,559	12.7	(d)	(d)	37	1,521	179,384	95
Fentress	049	Jamestown	499	16,625	14,669	13.3	8,631	101.9	...	(d)	(d)	...
Franklin	051	Winchester	555	39,270	34,725	13.1	(d)	(d)	47	(d)	(d)	...
Gibson	053	Trenton	603	48,152	46,315	4.0	(d)	(d)	77	4,988	522,127	276
Giles	055	Pulaski	611	29,447	25,741	14.4	(d)	(d)	43	3,098	362,564	192
Grainger	057	Rutledge	280	20,659	17,095	20.8	(d)	(d)	36	1,092	70,046	37
Greene	059	Greeneville	622	62,909	55,853	12.6	192,262	-32.2	107	7,195	562,812	298
Grundy	061	Altamont	361	14,332	13,362	7.3	1,795	-15.6	...	(d)	(d)	...
Hamblen	063	Morristown	161	58,128	50,480	15.2	482,037	4.8	123	14,715	1,331,027	704
Hamilton	065	Chattanooga	542	307,896	285,536	7.8	2,944,408	(d)	498	30,154	3,175,258	1,680
Hancock	067	Sneedville	222	6,786	6,739	0.7	(d)	(d)	...	(d)	(d)	...
Hardeman	069	Bolivar	668	28,105	23,377	20.2	33,059	(d)	38	1,902	225,551	119
Hardin	071	Savannah	578	25,578	22,633	13.0	68,982	92.1	51	1,984	278,785	147
Hawkins	073	Rogersville	487	53,563	44,565	20.2	(d)	(d)	48	(d)	(d)	...
Haywood	075	Brownsville	533	19,797	19,437	1.9	79,408	-30.7	22	1,979	108,920	58
Henderson	077	Lexington	520	25,522	21,844	16.8	52,412	18.7	42	3,414	242,960	129
Henry	079	Paris	562	31,115	27,888	11.6	235,406	18.9	52	2,644	163,403	86
Hickman	081	Centerville	613	22,295	16,754	33.1	19,449	112.4	32	672	29,589	16
Houston	083	Erin	200	8,088	7,018	15.2	(d)	(d)	...	(d)	(d)	...
Humphreys	085	Waverly	532	17,929	15,795	13.5	42,953	-17.4	30	1,904	363,487	192
Jackson	087	Gainesboro	309	10,984	9,297	18.1	(d)	(d)	8	700	80,065	42
Jefferson	089	Dandridge	274	44,294	33,016	34.2	44,896	-39.1	59	1,991	361,967	192
Johnson	091	Mountain City	298	17,499	13,766	27.1	(d)	(d)	19	849	61,277	32
Knox	093	Knoxville	508	382,032	335,749	13.8	10,700,576	42.5	458	17,135	1,851,301	979
Lake	095	Tiptonville	163	7,954	7,129	11.6	(d)	(d)	...	(d)	(d)	...
Lauderdale	097	Ripley	470	27,101	23,491	15.4	386,242	5.9	16	2,969	219,123	116
Lawrence	099	Lawrenceburg	617	39,926	35,303	13.1	152,428	-12.7	65	3,748	314,037	166
Lewis	101	Hohenwald	282	11,367	9,247	22.9	10,854	-6.5	...	(d)	(d)	...
Lincoln	103	Fayetteville	570	31,340	28,157	11.3	75,904	-26.0	48	2,457	401,844	213
Loudon	105	Loudon	229	39,086	31,255	25.1	348,083	273.9	53	3,505	819,664	434
Macon	111	Lafayette	307	20,386	15,906	28.2	(d)	(d)	38	1,155	34,936	18
Madison	113	Jackson	557	91,837	77,982	17.8	789,495	4.4	127	11,486	1,954,410	1,034
Marion	115	Jasper	498	27,776	24,860	11.7	(d)	(d)	27	1,727	142,684	75
Marshall	117	Lewisburg	375	26,767	21,539	24.3	(d)	(d)	48	4,233	327,109	173
Maury	119	Columbia	613	69,498	54,812	26.8	280,090	11.5	77	9,093	1,659,273	878
McMinn	107	Athens	430	49,015	42,383	15.6	(d)	(d)	65	5,804	777,056	411
McNairy	109	Selmer	560	24,653	22,422	10.0	16,648	(d)	43	2,558	185,946	98
Meigs	121	Decatur	195	11,086	8,033	38.0	(d)	(d)	11	659	48,155	25
Monroe	123	Madisonville	635	38,961	30,541	27.6	37,012	-23.4	73	4,630	380,772	201
Montgomery	125	Clarksville	539	134,768	100,498	34.1	(d)	(d)	75	6,327	931,154	493
Moore	127	Lynchburg	129	5,740	4,721	21.6	(d)	(d)	...	(d)	(d)	...
Morgan	129	Wartburg	522	19,757	17,300	14.2	12,483	(d)	...	(d)	(d)	...
Obion	131	Union City	545	32,450	31,717	2.3	(d)	(d)	40	7,038	611,612	324
Overton	133	Livingston	433	20,118	17,636	14.1	(d)	(d)	27	1,115	101,824	54
Perry	135	Linden	415	7,631	6,612	15.4	(d)	(d)	11	1,392	84,130	45
Pickett	137	Byrdstown	163	4,945	4,548	8.7	(d)	(d)	...	(d)	(d)	...
Polk	139	Benton	435	16,050	13,643	17.6	23,339	(d)	...	(d)	(d)	...
Putnam	141	Cookeville	401	62,315	51,373	21.3	322,938	-24.2	122	7,818	689,023	365
Rhea	143	Dayton	316	28,400	24,344	16.7	16,958	-36.7	38	4,684	342,464	181
Roane	145	Kingston	361	51,910	47,227	9.9	(d)	(d)	32	(d)	(d)	...
Robertson	147	Springfield	476	54,433	41,494	31.2	219,329	-5.9	71	4,907	431,926	229
Rutherford	149	Murfreesboro	619	182,023	118,570	53.5	3,005,986	38.1	190	18,111	1,273,914	674
Scott	151	Huntsville	532	21,127	18,358	15.1	(d)	(d)	46	2,251	145,492	77
Sequatchie	153	Dunlap	266	11,370	8,863	28.3	(d)	(d)	11	610	85,002	45
Sevier	155	Sevierville	592	71,170	51,043	39.4	(d)	(d)	82	1,607	117,345	62
Shelby	157	Memphis	755	897,472	826,330	8.6	37,073,207	4.7	800	33,098	5,264,544	2,785
Smith	159	Carthage	314	17,712	14,143	25.2	36,913	-33.8	24	1,866	220,929	117
Stewart	161	Dover	458	12,370	9,479	30.5	(d)	(d)	13	729	63,607	34
Sullivan	163	Blountville	413	153,048	143,596	6.6	2,207,641	74.0	167	14,070	2,044,917	1,082
Sumner	165	Gallatin	529	130,449	103,281	26.3	1,016,670	103.2	216	8,992	772,203	409
Tipton	167	Covington	459	51,271	37,568	36.5	(d)	(d)	39	2,246	247,166	131
Trousdale	169	Hartsville-Trousdale	114	7,259	5,920	22.6	38,099	-1.4	...	(d)	(d)	...

Entries in **UPPERCASE** are counties.
Entries in **bold** have populations of 2,500 or more.
Names in parentheses are alternate names.
Inc. Place — Incorporated Place
RMC Place — Rand McNally Designated Place
CDP — Census Designated Place
MCD — Minor Civil Division

⊡ County Seat
▲ Minor Civil Division
elev. Elevation
🅿 Post Office

H Hospital
C College
■ Principal Business Center
★ Ranally Metro Area (RMA) Abbreviation
z Zip Code(s)

℗ Previous Census Population
® Revised Census Population
Ⓐ Annexation Population
● Rand McNally Population Estimate
© Final Census Population
Ⓢ Special Census Population
◆ Estimated Population

For additional definitions see Glossary, Volume 1, and Introduction, Volume 2.

County	FIPS Code	County Seat	Land Area (Sq. Mi.)	Census Population 4/1/2000	Census Population 4/1/1990	Census Population % Change 1990-2000	Wholesale Trade Sales, 2002 ($1,000)	Wholesale Trade % Change 1997-2002	Manufacturing, 2002 Establish-ments	Manufacturing, 2002 Total Employees	Manufacturing, 2002 Value Added ($1,000)	Manufacturing, 2002 Ranally Mfg. Units
Unicoi	171	Erwin	186	17,667	16,549	6.8	(d)	(d)	26	1,375	85,291	45
Union	173	Maynardville	224	17,808	13,694	30.0	4,504	(d)	19	938	83,854	44
Van Buren	175	Spencer	273	5,508	4,846	13.7	(d)	(d)	...	(d)	(d)	...
Warren	177	McMinnville	433	38,276	32,992	16.0	80,609	-20.6	65	4,351	418,815	222
Washington	179	Jonesborough	326	107,198	92,315	16.1	(d)	(d)	143	8,142	592,217	313
Wayne	181	Waynesboro	734	16,842	13,935	20.9	(d)	(d)	25	875	50,704	27
Weakley	183	Dresden	580	34,895	31,972	9.1	295,872	-7.6	42	2,311	306,531	162
White	185	Sparta	377	23,102	20,090	15.0	(d)	(d)	50	2,973	260,546	138
Williamson	187	Franklin	583	126,638	81,021	56.3	3,626,037	41.6	121	3,707	289,867	153
Wilson	189	Lebanon	571	88,809	67,675	31.2	2,477,033	308.9	110	7,186	3,194,966	1,690
The State			**41,217**	**5,689,283**	**4,877,185**	**16.7**	**97,792,030**	**18.4**	**6,948**	**411,495**	**49,811,004**	**26,353**

(d) Data not available. Corresponding percentages or Ranally Manufacturing Units are estimates.
... Represents 0 or amount too minimal to be reported.

Index of Places and Counties

A

B

Entries in **UPPERCASE** are counties.
Entries in **bold** have populations of 2,500 or more.
Names in parentheses are alternate names.

Inc. Place	Incorporated Place
RMC Place	Rand McNally Designated Place
CDP	Census Designated Place
MCD	Minor Civil Division
⊡	County Seat
▲	Minor Civil Division
elev.	Elevation
🅿	Post Office
🅷	Hospital
🅲	College
■	Principal Business Center
★	Ranally Metro Area (RMA) Abbreviation
z	Zip Code(s)
Ⓟ	Previous Census Population
Ⓡ	Revised Census Population
Ⓐ	Annexation Population
●	Rand McNally Population Estimate
©	Final Census Population
Ⓢ	Special Census Population
◆	Estimated Population

For additional definitions see Glossary, Volume 1, and Introduction, Volume 2.

Britton Ford; RMC Place; HENRY; *232 B-7; elev. 400ft./122m.; mail Springville z 38256; rural
Brittontown; RMC Place; GREENE; *233 K-17; mail Afton z 37616; rural
Britts Landing; RMC Place; PERRY; *232 D-7; elev. 400ft./122m.; mail Lobelville z 37097; ● 30
Brittsville; RMC Place; MEIGS; *233 F-16; elev. 698ft./213m.; mail Georgetown z 37336; ● 30
Broad Acres; RMC Place; KNOX; *233 C-19; ★ **KNOX**; mail Powell z 37849
Broadmoor; RMC Place; DYER; *232 C-3; elev. 279ft./85m.; mail Dyersburg z 38024; rural
Broadview; RMC Place; CROCKETT; *232 D-4; elev. 453ft./138m.; mail Friendship z 38034; ● 30
Broadview; RMC Place; FRANKLIN; *233 G-13; elev. 960ft./293m.; mail Winchester z 37398; ● 30
Broadway; RMC Place; DAVIDSON; ★ **NASH**; mail Nashville z 37202-03, z 37218; pop. incl. with Nashville (Inc. Place)
Broadway; RMC Place; HENDERSON; *232 E-6; elev. 500ft./152m.; mail Lexington z 38351; ● 30
Brockdell; RMC Place; BLEDSOE; *233 E-15; mail Pikeville z 37367; rural
Brockland Acres; RMC Place; HAMBLEN; *233 K-16; elev. 1,400ft./427m.; ★ **MORR**; mail Morristown z 37813; ● 350
Brock's; RMC Place; WEAKLEY; *232 C-5; mail Greenfield z 38230; rural
Brookhaven; RMC Place; CUMBERLAND; mail Crossville z 38555; pop. incl. with Crossville (Inc. Place)
Brooks; RMC Place; LEWIS; *232 E-9; mail Hohenwald z 38462; pop. incl. with Hohenwald (Inc. Place)
Brookwood; RMC Place; LAWRENCE; *232 F-9; elev. 920ft./280m.; mail Lawrenceburg z 38464; ● 150
Brotherton; RMC Place; PUTNAM; *233 C-15; elev. 1,421ft./433m.; mail Cookeville z 38506
Browder; RMC Place; LOUDON; ★ **KNOX**
Browder; RMC Place; MARION; mail Jasper z 37347; pop. incl. with Jasper (Inc. Place)
Brown Crossroads; RMC Place; LAWRENCE; *232 G-9; mail Loretto z 38469; rural
Brown Ellis; RMC Place; ROANE; *233 D-17; elev. 840ft./256m.; ★ **KNOX**; mail Harriman z 37748; ● 200
Brownington; RMC Place; FRANKLIN; *233 F-12; elev. 1,000ft./305m.; mail Winchester z 37398; rural
Browns; RMC Place; MACON; *233 B-13; elev. 1,023ft./312m.; mail Lafayette z 37083; rural
Browns Chapel; RMC Place; SEQUATCHIE; *233 F-15; elev. 2,159ft./658m.; mail Signal Mountain z 37377; rural
Brownsville; Inc. Place; ⊡ HAYWOOD; 232 E-4; elev. 390ft./119m.; 🅿 🅷; z 38012; Ⓟ 10,019; Ⓒ 10,748
Browntown; RMC Place; CUMBERLAND; *233 D-16; mail Pleasant Hill z 38578; rural
Brownwood Acres; RMC Place; WILLIAMSON; *233 D-11; ★ **NASH**; mail Franklin z 37064
Broylesville; RMC Place; WASHINGTON; *233 K-18; mail Limestone z 37681; rural
Bruceton; Inc. Place; CARROLL; 232 C-7; elev. 412ft./126m.; 🅿; z 38317; Ⓟ 1,586; Ⓒ 1,554
Bruner Grove; RMC Place; COCKE; *233 L-16; mail Bybee z 37713; ● 30
Brunswick; RMC Place; SHELBY; 232 F-2; elev. 260ft./79m.; 🅿; ★ **MEM**; z 38014; ● 240
Brush Creek; RMC Place; SEQUATCHIE; *233 F-15; mail Dunlap z 37327; pop. incl. with Dunlap (Inc. Place)
Brush Creek (North Alexandria); RMC Place; SMITH; 233 C-13; elev. 644ft./196m.; 🅿; z 38547; ● 300
Brush Creek; RMC Place; WILLIAMSON; *232 D-10; elev. 843ft./257m.; ★ **NASH**; mail Fairview z 37062; ● 200
Bruton Branch; RMC Place; HARDIN; *232 G-7; elev. 500ft./152m.; mail Pickwick Dam z 38365; ● 50
Bryan Hill; RMC Place; RHEA; *233 E-16; mail Dayton z 37321; pop. incl. with Dayton (Inc. Place)
Bryant Station; RMC Place; MAURY; *233 E-11; mail Columbia z 38401, Lewisburg z 37091; rural
Bryson; CLAIBORNE; see Bryson Mountain (RMC Place)
Bryson; RMC Place; GILES; 233 G-11; elev. 658ft./201m.; mail Ardmore z 38449; ● 30
Bryson Mountain (Bryson); RMC Place; CLAIBORNE; *233 B-20; mail Middlesboro z 40965; rural
Brysonville (Hardsrabble); RMC Place; CANNON; *233 D-13; mail Woodbury z 37190; rural
Buchanan; RMC Place; HENRY; 232 B-7; elev. 491ft./150m.; 🅿; z 38222; ● 300
Buck Lodge; RMC Place; SUMNER; *233 B-12; elev. 739ft./225m.; mail Portland z 37148; ● 50
Buckner; RMC Place; DEKALB; *233 D-14; elev. 1,045ft./319m.; mail Smithville z 37166; rural
Bucksnort; RMC Place; HICKMAN; *232 D-8; mail Only z 37140; ● 30
Bucktown; RMC Place; HARDIN; *232 F-7; mail Savannah z 38372; rural
Buena Vista; RMC Place; CARROLL; 232 D-7; elev. 507ft./155m.; 🅿; z 38318; ● 150
Buffalo; RMC Place; HUMPHREYS; *232 D-8; mail Hurricane Mills z 37078; ● 100
Buffalo; RMC Place; SCOTT; *233 B-18; mail Huntsville z 37756; pop. incl. with Buffalo (Inc. Place)
Buffalo Springs; RMC Place; GRAINGER; 233 C-20; mail Rutledge z 37861; ● 30
Buffalo Valley; RMC Place; PUTNAM; 233 C-14; elev. 751ft./229m.; 🅿; z 38548; ● 100
Bufords; RMC Place; GILES; *232 F-10; elev. 714ft./218m.; mail Lynnville z 38472; rural
Bugscuffle; RMC Place; BEDFORD; 233 E-12; mail Wartrace z 37183; ● 30
Buladeen; RMC Place; CARTER; *233 J-19; ★ **JNSC-**; mail Elizabethton z 37643
Bullards Creek; RMC Place; JACKSON; *233 B-14; elev. 508ft./155m.; mail Gainesboro z 38562; rural
Bull Creek; RMC Place; SCOTT; *233 C-17; elev. 1,400ft./427m.; mail Huntsville z 37756; rural
Bullet Creek; RMC Place; MONROE; *233 F-18; mail Reliance z 37369; rural
Bull Run; RMC Place; ANDERSON; *233 C-19; ★ **KNOX**; mail Powell z 37849; ● 160
Bull Run; RMC Place; DAVIDSON; ★ **NASH**; mail Ashland City z 37015; pop. incl. with Nashville (Inc. Place)
Bulls Gap; Inc. Place; HAWKINS; 233 K-16; elev. 1,153ft./351m.; 🅿; z 37711; Ⓟ 659; Ⓒ 714
Bumpus Cove; RMC Place; UNICOI, WASHINGTON; *233 K-18; elev. 1,800ft./549m.; mail Erwin z 37650; ● 50
Bumpus Mills; RMC Place; STEWART; 232 A-8; elev. 487ft./148m.; 🅿; z 37028; ● 300
Buncombe; RMC Place; SULLIVAN; *233 J-18; ★ **JNSC-**; mail Blountville z 37617; rural
Bungalow Town; RMC Place; BLOUNT; *233 D-19; ★ **KNOX**; mail Maryville z 37804; ● 500
Bunker Hill; RMC Place; GILES; *233 G-11; mail Pulaski z 38478; ● 80
Buntontown; RMC Place; JOHNSON; *233 K-19; elev. 2,279ft./695m.; mail Butler z 37640; ● 100
Burbank; RMC Place; CARTER; *233 K-19; elev. 2,984ft./910m.; mail Roan Mountain z 37687; ● 50
Burchfield Heights; RMC Place; KNOX; *233 D-19; ★ **KNOX**; mail Oak Ridge z 37830; ● 420
Burem; RMC Place; HAWKINS; *233 K-17; elev. 1,127ft./344m.; mail Rogersville z 37857; rural
Burgen; RMC Place; CANNON; *233 E-13; elev. 725ft./221m.; mail Bradyville z 37026; ● 50
Burgess; RMC Place; PUTNAM; *233 C-15; elev. 1,080ft./329m.; mail Cookeville z 38506; rural
Burke; RMC Place; CUMBERLAND; *233 D-16; elev. 997ft./304m.; mail Pikeville z 37367; rural
Burlington; RMC Place; KNOX; *233 D-19; ★ **KNOX**; mail Knoxville z 37914; pop. incl. with Knoxville (Inc. Place)
Burlington Heights; RMC Place; BRADLEY; *233 F-17; ★ **CLEV**; mail Cleveland z 37312; pop. incl. with Cleveland (Inc. Place)
Burlison; Inc. Place; TIPTON; 232 E-2; elev. 400ft./122m.; 🅿; z 38015; Ⓟ 394; Ⓒ 453
Burnett; RMC Place; PUTNAM; *233 C-15; elev. 1,844ft./562m.; mail Cookeville z 38501; rural
Burns; Inc. Place; DICKSON; 232 C-9; elev. 794ft./242m.; 🅿; z 37029; Ⓟ 1,127; Ⓒ 1,366
Burnt Church; RMC Place; HARDIN; 232 F-7; mail Savannah z 38372; ● 100
Burristown; RMC Place; JACKSON; *233 B-15; elev. 1,013ft./309m.; mail Gainesboro z 38562; ● 30
Burrville; RMC Place; MORGAN; *233 C-17; elev. 1,500ft./457m.; mail Sunbright z 37872
Burt; RMC Place; CANNON; *233 D-13; elev. 730ft./223m.; mail Woodbury z 37190; ● 30
Burton; RMC Place; HAWKINS; mail Rogersville z 37857; pop. incl. with Rogersville (Inc. Place)
Burwood; RMC Place; WILLIAMSON; 232 D-10; mail Thompsons Station z 37179; ● 60
Busby; RMC Place; LAWRENCE; *232 G-9; mail Loretto z 38469; pop. incl. with Loretto (Inc. Place)
Bush Grove; RMC Place; SHELBY; *232 F-2; elev. 335ft./102m.; ★ **MEM**; mail Arlington z 38002; ● 50
Bushtown; RMC Place; HAMILTON; *233 G-15; ★ **CHTN**; pop. incl. with Chattanooga (Inc. Place)
Busselltown; RMC Place; LOUDON; *233 D-18; mail Lenoir City z 37771; rural
Busseltown; RMC Place; DECATUR; *232 E-7; elev. 370ft./113m.; mail Parsons z 38363; rural
Butler; RMC Place; JOHNSON; 233 K-19; elev. 1,974ft./602m.; 🅿; z 37640; ● 500
Butlers Landing; RMC Place; CLAY; 233 B-15; elev. 544ft./166m.; mail Celina z 38551; ● 30
Bybee; RMC Place; COCKE; 233 L-16; elev. 1,100ft./335m.; 🅿; z 37713; ● 450
Bybee; RMC Place; WARREN; 233 E-14; mail Mc Minnville z 37110; ● 300
Byington; RMC Place; KNOX; *233 D-19; elev. 963ft./294m.; ★ **KNOX**
Byrdstown; Inc. Place; ⊡ PICKETT; 233 B-16; elev. 1,037ft./316m.; 🅿; z 38549; Ⓟ 998; Ⓒ 903

C

Cabin Row; RMC Place; MONTGOMERY; *232 B-9; mail Southside z 37171
Cabo; RMC Place; CHESTER; *232 F-6; mail Enville z 38332; rural
Cades; RMC Place; GIBSON; 232 D-5; elev. 368ft./112m.; mail Milan z 38358; ● 50
Cades Cove; RMC Place; BLOUNT; 214 H-2; mail Townsend z 37882; ● 30
Cadet; RMC Place; WILLIAMSON; *233 D-11; elev. 700ft./213m.; ★ **NASH**; mail Franklin z 37064; pop. incl. with Franklin (Inc. Place)
Cagle; RMC Place; SEQUATCHIE; *233 F-15; elev. 2,116ft./645m.; mail Dunlap z 37327; rural
Cain Mill; RMC Place; HAMBLEN; *233 K-16; ★ **MORR**; mail Russellville z 37860; rural
Cainsville; RMC Place; WILSON; 233 D-13; mail Lascassas z 37085; ● 60
Cairo; RMC Place; CROCKETT; 232 D-4; mail Alamo z 38001; ● 60
Cairo; RMC Place; SUMNER; *233 B-12; elev. 460ft./140m.; mail Gallatin z 37066; ● 30
Cairo Bend; RMC Place; WILSON; *233 C-12; elev. 557ft./170m.; ★ **NASH**; mail Lebanon z 37087; pop. incl. with Lebanon (Inc. Place)
Calderwood; RMC Place; BLOUNT; *233 E-19; mail Maryville z 37801; ● 820
Calfkiller; RMC Place; PUTNAM; *233 C-15; mail Monterey z 38574; rural
Calhoun; Inc. Place; MCMINN; 233 F-17; elev. 709ft./216m.; 🅿; z 37309; Ⓟ 552; Ⓒ 496
Calico; RMC Place; MEIGS; *233 E-17; mail Decatur z 37322; ● 30
Calistia; RMC Place; ROBERTSON; 233 B-11; elev. 801ft./244m.; ★ **NASH**; mail Cross Plains z 37049; ● 70
Callins; RMC Place; WEAKLEY; *232 C-5; mail Greenfield z 38230; rural
Calls; RMC Place; COFFEE; *233 F-13; mail Estill Springs z 37330; rural
Calvin Estates; RMC Place; MADISON; *232 E-5; elev. 400ft./122m.; ★ **JAC**; mail Jackson z 38301; ● 80
Camargo; RMC Place; LINCOLN; *233 G-11; mail Fayetteville z 37334; ● 30
Cambria; RMC Place; MCMINN; *233 F-18; mail Delano z 37325, Etowah z 37331; ● 30
Cambridge; RMC Place; WARREN; *233 D-14; mail Rock Island z 38581; rural
Camden; Inc. Place; ⊡ BENTON; 232 C-7; elev. 460ft./140m.; 🅿 🅷; z 38320; Ⓟ 3,643; Ⓒ 3,828
Camelot; RMC Place; CUMBERLAND; mail Crossville z 38555; pop. incl. with Crossville (Inc. Place)
Camelot; RMC Place; HAWKINS; *233 J-16; elev. 1,600ft./488m.; mail Rogersville z 37857; rural
Cameron Hill; RMC Place; HAMILTON; ★ **CHTN**; pop. incl. with Chattanooga (Inc. Place)
Camilla Homes; RMC Place; TIPTON; *232 F-2; ★ **MEM**; mail Atoka z 38004; ● 190
Campaign; RMC Place; WARREN; 233 D-14; elev. 965ft./294m.; 🅿; z 38550; ● 500
Camp Austin; RMC Place; MORGAN; *233 D-17; mail Oakdale z 37829; rural
CAMPBELL; 233 B-19; Ⓟ 35,079; Ⓒ 39,854; ◆ 40,744
Campbell Junction; RMC Place; CUMBERLAND; *233 C-16; elev. 1,959ft./597m.; mail Crossville z 38555; rural
Campbells (Fountain Creek); RMC Place; MAURY; *232 F-10; mail Culleoka z 38451; ● 100
Campbellsville; RMC Place; GILES; 232 F-10; elev. 750ft./229m.; mail Pulaski z 38478; ● 100
Camp Creek; RMC Place; GREENE; *233 L-17; mail Greeneville z 37743; ● 150
Camp Ground; RMC Place; FENTRESS; *233 C-16; elev. 1,800ft./549m.; mail Clarkrange z 38553; ● 70
Camp Ground; RMC Place; WEAKLEY; *232 B-5; mail Martin z 38237; rural
Camp Marymount; RMC Place; WILLIAMSON; *232 D-10; ★ **NASH**; mail Fairview z 37062; pop. incl. with Fairview (Inc. Place) summer pop. 300
Camp Monterey Lake; RMC Place; PUTNAM; mail Monterey z 38574; summer pop. 300
Camp Nakanawa; RMC Place; CUMBERLAND; *233 C-16; elev. 1,940ft./591m.; mail Crossville z 38571; summer pop. 150
Camp Relax; RMC Place; DEKALB; *233 D-14; mail Smithville z 37166; rural
Camps; HANCOCK; see Evanston (RMC Place)
Camp Ta-Pa-Win-Go; RMC Place; CARTER; *233 K-19; ★ **JNSC-**; mail Watauga z 37694
Camp Woodlee; RMC Place; WARREN; *233 E-14; mail Mc Minnville z 37110
Canadaville; RMC Place; FAYETTE; *232 F-3; mail Collierville z 38017, Eads z 38028; rural
Cane Ridge; RMC Place; DAVIDSON; 🅿; ★ **NASH**; z 37013; pop. incl. with Nashville (Inc. Place)
Caney Branch; RMC Place; GREENE; *233 L-16; elev. 1,241ft./378m.; mail Greeneville z 37743
Caney Creek; RMC Place; HAMBLEN; *233 K-16; ★ **MORR**; mail Whitesburg z 37891; rural
Caney Creek; RMC Place; HAWKINS; *233 J-16; elev. 1,201ft./366m.; mail Rogersville z 37857; ● 30
Caney Ford; RMC Place; ROANE; *233 D-17; ★ **KNOX**; mail Harriman z 37748; pop. incl. with Kingston (Inc. Place)
Caney Spring; RMC Place; MARSHALL; *233 E-11; elev. 650ft./198m.; mail Lewisburg z 37091; ● 50
Caney Valley; RMC Place; CLAIBORNE; *233 B-20; mail Tazewell z 37879; ● 150
CANNON; 233 D-13; Ⓟ 10,467; Ⓒ 12,826; ◆ 13,654
Cantrell; RMC Place; WAYNE; *232 F-8; mail Waynesboro z 38485; ● 100
Capitol Hill; RMC Place; FRANKLIN; *233 F-13; mail Estill Springs z 37330; ● 40
Capitol Hill; RMC Place; SCOTT; *233 B-18; elev. 1,485ft./453m.; mail Huntsville z 37756; ● 200
Capleville; RMC Place; SHELBY; 232 G-2; elev. 310ft./94m.; ★ **MEM**; mail Memphis z 38118; pop. incl. with Memphis (Inc. Place)
Caravelle Estates; RMC Place; WILSON; *233 C-12; ★ **NASH**; mail Mount Juliet z 37122; pop. incl. with Mount Juliet (Inc. Place)
Cardiff; RMC Place; ROANE; *233 D-17; ★ **KNOX**; mail Rockwood z 37854; pop. incl. with Rockwood (Inc. Place)
Carlisle; RMC Place; STEWART; 232 B-8; mail Dover z 37058, Tennessee Ridge z 37178; ● 150
Carlock; RMC Place; JACKSON; *233 B-15; elev. 958ft./292m.; mail Gainesboro z 38562; rural
Carlock; RMC Place; MCMINN; 233 F-18; mail Etowah z 37331; ● 200
Carnegie; RMC Place; WASHINGTON; *233 K-18; ★ **JNSC-**; mail Johnson City z 37601; pop. incl. with Johnson City (Inc. Place)
Carpenter Campground; RMC Place; BLOUNT; *233 E-19; elev. 993ft./303m.; mail Maryville z 37804; rural
Carr Branch; RMC Place; CLAIBORNE; *233 B-20; elev. 1,100ft./335m.; mail New Tazewell z 37825; rural
Carroll; RMC Place; WILSON; *233 C-12; mail Lebanon z 37087; ● 60
CARROLL; 232 D-6; Ⓟ 27,514; Ⓒ 29,475; Ⓡ 29,473; ◆ 28,789
Carroll Reece; RMC Place; WASHINGTON; ★ **JNSC-**; mail Johnson City z 37601; pop. incl. with Johnson City (Inc. Place)
Carson Spring; RMC Place; COCKE; 233 L-16; ★ **MORR**; mail Newport z 37821; ● 700
Carter; RMC Place; CARTER; 233 J-19; ★ **JNSC-**; mail Elizabethton z 37643; ● 500
CARTER; 233 K-19; Ⓟ 51,505; Ⓒ 56,742; ◆ 59,116
Carter Chapel; RMC Place; GREENE; *233 K-17; elev. 1,126ft./343m.; mail Mosheim z 37818; ● 30
Carters Creek; RMC Place; MAURY; *232 E-10; mail Columbia z 38401; rural
Carthage; Inc. Place; ⊡ SMITH; 233 C-13; elev. 515ft./157m.; 🅿 🅷; z 37030; Ⓟ 2,386; Ⓒ 2,251
Carthage Junction; RMC Place; SMITH; *233 C-13; mail Hickman z 38567; pop. incl. with Gordonsville (Inc. Place)
Cartwright; RMC Place; SEQUATCHIE; *233 F-15; mail Whitwell z 37397; ● 100
Cartwright; RMC Place; SMITH; *233 B-14; elev. 600ft./183m.; mail Pleasant Shade z 37145; ● 30
Caryville; Inc. Place; CAMPBELL; 233 C-18; elev. 1,095ft./334m.; 🅿; ★ **KNOX**; z 37714; Ⓟ 1,751; Ⓒ 2,243
Cash Point; RMC Place; LINCOLN; 233 G-11; mail Ardmore z 38449; ● 100
Cassville; RMC Place; WHITE; *233 D-14; mail Sparta z 38583; ● 80
Castalian Springs; RMC Place; SUMNER; 233 B-12; elev. 495ft./151m.; 🅿; z 37031; ● 270
Castle Heights; RMC Place; COCKE; *233 L-16; ★ **MORR**; mail Newport z 37821; ● 150
Cataska; RMC Place; MONROE; *233 F-18; elev. 1,600ft./488m.; mail Tellico Plains z 37385; ● 30
Cat Corner; RMC Place; OBION; *232 C-3; elev. 286ft./87m.; mail Obion z 38240; rural
Cates; RMC Place; LAKE; *232 B-3; elev. 305ft./93m.; mail Tiptonville z 38079; rural
Cates Trailor; RMC Place; SEVIER; *233 D-20; ★ **KNOX**; mail Kodak z 37764; rural
Catlettsburg; RMC Place; SEVIER; *233 D-20; elev. 888ft./271m.; ★ **KNOX**; mail Sevierville z 37876; pop. incl. with Sevierville (Inc. Place)
Cato; RMC Place; TROUSDALE; 233 B-13; elev. 514ft./157m.; mail Dixon Springs z 37057; ● 50
Catons Grove; RMC Place; COCKE; *233 M-16; elev. 1,616ft./493m.; mail Cosby z 37722; rural
Catoosa; RMC Place; MORGAN; *233 C-17; elev. 1,300ft./396m.; mail Lancing z 37770; rural
Cave; RMC Place; WHITE; *233 D-15; elev. 929ft./283m.; mail Doyle z 38559; rural
Cave Spring; RMC Place; CLAIBORNE; *233 B-20; mail Tazewell z 37879; ● 30
Cedar Bluff (Cedar Bluff Two); RMC Place; KNOX; *233 D-19; ★ **KNOX**; mail Knoxville z 37922; ● 2,000
Cedar Bluff; RMC Place; SEVIER; *233 D-20; mail Sevierville z 37876; rural
Cedar Bluff Two; KNOX; see Cedar Bluff (RMC Place)
Cedar Chapel; RMC Place; HARDEMAN; *232 F-4; elev. 473ft./144m.; mail Whiteville z 38075; rural
Cedar Creek; RMC Place; GREENE; 233 L-17; mail Greeneville z 37743; ● 300
Cedar Creek Landing; RMC Place; PERRY; *232 E-7; mail Linden z 37096
Cedarcrest; RMC Place; HAWKINS; *233 K-16; elev. 1,120ft./341m.; mail Rogersville z 37857; ● 30
Cedarfork; CLAIBORNE; see Old Cedar Fork (RMC Place)
Cedar Fork; RMC Place; ROANE, LOUDON; *233 E-18; mail Philadelphia z 37846; rural
Cedar Grove; RMC Place; BEDFORD; *233 E-11; elev. 720ft./219m.; mail Chapel Hill z 37034; rural
Cedar Grove; RMC Place; CARROLL; 232 D-6; elev. 493ft./150m.; 🅿; z 38321; ● 115
Cedar Grove; RMC Place; CARTER; *233 K-18; ★ **JNSC-**; mail Johnson City z 37601
Cedar Grove; RMC Place; HENDERSON; *232 E-7; mail Sardis z 38371; rural
Cedar Grove; RMC Place; HUMPHREYS; *232 D-8; mail Hurricane Mills z 37078; ● 30
Cedar Grove; RMC Place; KNOX; ★ **KNOX**
Cedar Grove; RMC Place; PICKETT; *233 B-16; mail Pall Mall z 38577; rural
Cedar Grove; RMC Place; ROANE; *233 D-18; mail Kingston z 37763; ● 100
Cedar Grove; RMC Place; RUTHERFORD; *233 D-11; mail Eagleville z 37060; rural
Cedar Grove; RMC Place; SULLIVAN; *233 J-18; ★ **JNSC-**; mail Kingsport z 37660; ● 650
Cedar Grove; RMC Place; SULLIVAN; 234 K-5; elev. 1,481ft./451m.; ★ **JNSC-**; mail Bluff City z 37618
Cedar Grove; RMC Place; WILSON; *233 C-12; ★ **NASH**; mail Lebanon z 37087; ● 50
Cedar Hill; RMC Place; PUTNAM; *233 C-14; mail Baxter z 38544; rural
Cedar Hill; Inc. Place; ROBERTSON; 232 B-10; elev. 499ft./152m.; 🅿; z 37032; Ⓟ 347; Ⓒ 298
Cedarlane; GREENE; see Bethesda (RMC Place)
Cedar Point; SMITH; see Bluff Creek (RMC Place)
Cedar Springs; RMC Place; MCMINN; *233 F-17; mail Athens z 37303; rural
Cedar Valley; RMC Place; SULLIVAN; *233 J-19; ★ **JNSC-**; mail Bristol z 37620; pop. incl. with Bristol (Inc. Place)
Celina; Inc. Place; ⊡ CLAY; 233 B-15; elev. 562ft./171m.; 🅿 🅷; z 38551; Ⓟ 1,493; Ⓒ 1,379
Center; RMC Place; CROCKETT; *232 D-4; elev. 392ft./119m.; mail Gadsden z 38337; ● 200
Center; RMC Place; LAWRENCE; *232 F-9; mail Lawrenceburg z 38464
Center; RMC Place; MONROE; *233 E-18; mail Tellico Plains z 37385; rural
Center Grove; RMC Place; FRANKLIN; *233 F-13; mail Estill Springs z 37330, Tullahoma z 37388; rural
Center Grove; RMC Place; JACKSON; *233 C-14; mail Gainesboro z 38562; ● 30
Center Hill; RMC Place; CANNON; *233 D-13; elev. 1,230ft./375m.; mail Woodbury z 37190; ● 30
Center Hill; RMC Place; HENDERSON; *232 E-6; elev. 600ft./183m.; mail Reagan z 38368; rural
Center Hill Loop; RMC Place; HENDERSON; *232 E-6; elev. 500ft./152m.; mail Reagan z 38368; ● 50
Center Point; RMC Place; CHESTER; *232 E-6; elev. 500ft./152m.; mail Enville z 38332; rural
Center Point; RMC Place; GILES; *233 F-11; elev. 780ft./238m.; mail Pulaski z 38478; rural
Center Point; RMC Place; HARDEMAN; *232 G-4; mail Grand Junction z 38039, Hickory Valley z 38042; rural
Center Point; RMC Place; LAWRENCE; *232 G-9; mail Leoma z 38468
Center Point; RMC Place; SEQUATCHIE; *233 F-15; elev. 760ft./232m.; mail Dunlap z 37327; rural
Center Point; RMC Place; STEWART; *232 B-8; elev. 400ft./122m.; mail Dover z 37058; rural
Center Point; RMC Place; WHITE; *233 D-14; mail Walling z 38587; ● 30
Center Star; RMC Place; HICKMAN; *232 E-9; elev. 881ft./269m.; mail Duck River z 38454; rural
Centersville; RMC Place; GREENE; *233 K-17; mail Limestone z 37681; rural
Centersville; RMC Place; LOUDON; *233 E-18; elev. 965ft./294m.; mail Greenback z 37742; rural
Centertown; Inc. Place; WARREN; 233 E-13; elev. 1,094ft./333m.; mail Mc Minnville z 37110; Ⓟ 332; Ⓒ 257
Centerville; Inc. Place; ⊡ HICKMAN; 232 D-9; elev. 634ft./193m.; 🅿 🅷; z 37033; Ⓟ 3,616; Ⓒ 3,793
Centerville; RMC Place; WILSON; *233 C-13; mail Lebanon z 37087; ● 50
Central (Central Heights); CDP; CARTER; *233 K-18; ★ **JNSC-**; mail Johnson City z 37601; Ⓟ 2,635; Ⓒ 2,717
Central; RMC Place; GIBSON; 232 D-4; elev. 363ft./111m.; mail Trenton z 38382; ● 50
Central; RMC Place; LAUDERDALE; *232 D-3; mail Ripley z 38063; ● 210
Central; RMC Place; OBION; *232 B-5; elev. 360ft./110m.; mail Rives z 38253; rural
Central Heights; CARTER; see Central (CDP)
Central Heights; SULLIVAN; see Mill Point (RMC Place)
Central Point; RMC Place; GRAINGER; *233 C-20; mail Rutledge z 37861; ● 50
Central View; WHITE; see Yateston (RMC Place)
Cerro Gordo; RMC Place; HARDIN; *232 F-7; elev. 414ft./126m.; mail Savannah z 38372; rural
Chalklevel; RMC Place; BENTON; *232 D-7; mail Camden z 38320; ● 50
Chalk Level; RMC Place; HAWKINS; *233 K-16; mail Rogersville z 37857
Chambers; RMC Place; OBION; *232 B-5; elev. 380ft./116m.; mail Union City z 38261; ● 30
Champ; RMC Place; LINCOLN; *233 G-12; mail Mulberry z 37359; rural
Chanceytown; RMC Place; POLK; *233 G-18; elev. 1,720ft./524m.; mail Turtletown z 37391; rural
Chandler; RMC Place; BLOUNT; *233 D-19; ★ **KNOX**; mail Louisville z 37777; pop. incl. with Alcoa (Inc. Place)
Chantay Acres; RMC Place; MAURY; *232 E-10; mail Columbia z 38401; pop. incl. with Columbia (Inc. Place)
Chanute; RMC Place; PICKETT; *233 A-16; mail Pall Mall z 38577; rural
Chapel Hill; Inc. Place; MARSHALL; 233 E-11; elev. 691ft./211m.; 🅿; z 37034; Ⓟ 833; Ⓒ 943
Chapel Hill; RMC Place; MAURY; 232 E-9; mail Hampshire z 38461; ● 120
Chapman Grove; RMC Place; ROANE; *233 D-17; mail Kingston z 37763; rural
Chapmans; RMC Place; GILES; *232 G-10; elev. 710ft./216m.; mail Pulaski z 38478; ● 80
Chapmansboro (Cheap Hill); RMC Place; CHEATHAM; 232 B-10; elev. 395ft./120m.; 🅿; ★ **NASH**; z 37035; ● 220
Charity; RMC Place; MOORE; mail Fayetteville z 37334; pop. incl. with Lynchburg (Inc. Place)
Charles Creek Estates; RMC Place; WARREN; *233 E-14; mail Mc Minnville z 37110; ● 80
Charleston; Inc. Place; BRADLEY; 233 F-17; elev. 688ft./210m.; 🅿; ★ **CLEV**; z 37310; Ⓟ 653; Ⓒ 630
Charleston (Phelan); RMC Place; TIPTON; *232 E-3; mail Stanton z 38069; ● 150
Charleys Branch; RMC Place; ANDERSON; *233 C-18; mail Briceville z 37710
Charlotte; Inc. Place; ⊡ DICKSON; 232 C-9; elev. 631ft./192m.; 🅿; z 37036; Ⓟ 854; Ⓒ 1,153
Charlotte Park; RMC Place; DAVIDSON; *233 C-11; ★ **NASH**; mail Nashville z 37209; pop. incl. with Nashville (Inc. Place)
Charlton Green; RMC Place; WILLIAMSON; *233 D-11; ★ **NASH**; mail Franklin z 37064; pop. incl. with Franklin (Inc. Place)
Chaska; RMC Place; CAMPBELL; *233 B-19; elev. 1,129ft./344m.; mail La Follette z 37766; rural
Chattanooga; Inc. Place; ⊡ HAMILTON; 233 G-15; elev. 685ft./209m.; 🅿 🅷 🅲 9,351 ■; ★ **CHTN**; z 37401-12, z 37414-16, z 37419, z 37421-22, z 37424, z 37450; Ⓟ 152,466; Ⓒ 155,554; ◆ 183,424
Cheap Hill; CHEATHAM; see Chapmansboro (RMC Place)
CHEATHAM; 232 B-10; Ⓟ 27,140; Ⓒ 35,912; ◆ 39,830
Cherokee; RMC Place; DECATUR; *232 E-7; mail Sugar Tree z 38380; ● 50
Cherokee Harshaw; RMC Place; GREENE; *233 K-17; mail Greeneville z 37743; ● 400
Cherokee Heights; RMC Place; BLOUNT; *233 E-19; ★ **KNOX**; mail Maryville z 37801; ● 220
Cherokee Hills; RMC Place; ROANE; *233 D-18; ★ **KNOX**; mail Kingston z 37763; pop. incl. with Kingston (Inc. Place)
Cherokee Hills; RMC Place; SEVIER; 214 F-4; ★ **KNOX**; mail Seymour z 37865; ● 600
Cherry; RMC Place; LAUDERDALE; 232 E-2; elev. 294ft./90m.; mail Henning z 38041; ● 40
Cherry Acres; RMC Place; GRUNDY; mail Gruetli Laager z 37339; pop. incl. with Gruetli-Laager (Inc. Place)
Cherrybrook; RMC Place; KNOX; *233 D-19; ★ **KNOX**; mail Knoxville z 37912; ● 160
Cherry Chapel; RMC Place; HARDIN; *232 G-7; mail Savannah z 38372; rural
Cherry Creek; RMC Place; WHITE; *233 D-15; elev. 900ft./274m.; mail Sparta z 38583; rural
Cherry Grove; RMC Place; BENTON; *232 C-7; mail Eva z 38333; rural
Cherry Hill; RMC Place; DEKALB; *233 C-14; elev. 1,024ft./312m.; mail Silver Point z 38582; rural
Cherry Valley; RMC Place; WILSON; 233 C-13; elev. 715ft./218m.; mail Watertown z 37184; ● 60
Chesney; RMC Place; UNION; *233 C-20; ★ **KNOX**; mail Powder Springs z 37848; rural
CHESTER; 232 E-5; Ⓟ 12,819; Ⓒ 15,540; ◆ 16,215
Chester Estates; RMC Place; WILLIAMSON; *232 D-10; ★ **NASH**; mail Fairview z 37062; pop. incl. with Fairview (Inc. Place)
Chesterfield; RMC Place; HENDERSON; 232 E-7; elev. 434ft./132m.; mail Lexington z 38351; ● 300
Chestnut Bluff; RMC Place; CROCKETT; 232 D-3; elev. 338ft./103m.; mail Halls z 38040; ● 80
Chestnut Glade; RMC Place; WEAKLEY; *232 B-5; mail Martin z 38237; rural
Chestnut Grove; RMC Place; JEFFERSON; *233 C-20; mail Dandridge z 37725; rural
Chestnut Grove; RMC Place; PERRY; *232 E-8; mail Linden z 37096
Chestnut Grove; RMC Place; ROBERTSON; *233 B-11; elev. 747ft./228m.; ★ **NASH**; mail Greenbrier z 37073; pop. incl. with Coopertown (Inc. Place)
Chestnut Grove; RMC Place; STEWART; *232 B-8; elev. 552ft./168m.; mail Dover z 37058; ● 30
Chestnut Grove; RMC Place; SUMNER; *233 B-12; mail Portland z 37148; rural
Chestnut Grove; RMC Place; UNION; *233 C-20; elev. 1,289ft./393m.; ★ **KNOX**; mail Maynardville z 37807; rural
Chestnut Hill; RMC Place; CUMBERLAND; *233 D-16; mail Crossville z 38555; rural
Chestnut Hill; RMC Place; JEFFERSON; 233 L-15; elev. 1,072ft./327m.; mail Dandridge z 37725; ● 400
Chestnut Hill; RMC Place; SUMNER; *233 B-12; mail Portland z 37148; rural
Chestnut Mound; RMC Place; SMITH; 233 C-14; elev. 992ft./302m.; 🅿; z 38552; ● 150
Chestnut Orchard; RMC Place; ROBERTSON; *233 B-11; ★ **NASH**; mail Springfield z 37172; rural
Chestnut Ridge; RMC Place; GREENE; *233 L-17; elev. 1,460ft./445m.; mail Chuckey z 37641; rural
Chestoa; RMC Place; UNICOI; *233 L-18; mail Erwin z 37650; ● 50
Chestua; RMC Place; MONROE; *233 F-18; elev. 900ft./274m.; mail Madisonville z 37354; rural
Chestuee; RMC Place; BRADLEY; *233 G-17; ★ **CLEV**; mail Cleveland z 37312; rural
Chewalla; RMC Place; MCNAIRY; 232 G-5; elev. 410ft./125m.; 🅿; z 38393; ● 200
Chic; RMC Place; DYER; *232 D-3; mail Finley z 38030; rural
Chickamauga; RMC Place; HAMILTON; ★ **CHTN**; mail Chattanooga z 37421-22, z 37424; pop. incl. with Chattanooga (Inc. Place)
Chickasaw Heights; RMC Place; HENRY; *232 B-7; mail Paris z 38242; pop. incl. with Paris (Inc. Place)
Chickasaw Park; CHESTER; see Lake Placid (RMC Place)
Childers Hill; RMC Place; HARDIN; *232 G-6; mail Counce z 38326
Chilhowee View; RMC Place; BLOUNT; *233 E-19; ★ **KNOX**; mail Maryville z 37803; rural
China Grove; RMC Place; GIBSON; *232 C-5; elev. 342ft./104m.; mail Kenton z 38233; rural
Chinquapin Grove; RMC Place; SULLIVAN; 234 L-5; ★ **JNSC-**; mail Bluff City z 37618; ● 300
Chinubee; RMC Place; LAWRENCE; *232 G-9; mail Westpoint z 38486; ● 30
Chipman; RMC Place; SUMNER; *233 B-12; elev. 592ft./180m.; mail Bethpage z 37022; rural
Chittum; RMC Place; CLAIBORNE; *233 B-20; elev. 1,600ft./488m.; mail Tazewell z 37879; rural
Choptack; RMC Place; HAWKINS; *233 K-16; elev. 1,082ft./330m.; mail Rogersville z 37857; rural
Chota; RMC Place; BLOUNT; *233 E-19; ★ **KNOX**; mail Maryville z 37801; rural
Choto Estates; RMC Place; KNOX; *233 D-19; elev. 900ft./274m.; ★ **KNOX**; mail Knoxville z 37922; ● 100
Choto Hills; RMC Place; BLOUNT; *233 D-19; elev. 900ft./274m.; ★ **KNOX**; mail Louisville z 37777; ● 80
Christiana; RMC Place; RUTHERFORD; 233 E-12; elev. 730ft./223m.; 🅿; z 37037; ● 350
Christian Bend; RMC Place; HAWKINS; *233 J-17; mail Church Hill z 37642; rural
Christianburg; RMC Place; MONROE; *233 E-18; elev. 1,110ft./338m.; mail Sweetwater z 37874; rural
Christian Chapel; RMC Place; GIBSON; *232 D-4; elev. 380ft./116m.; mail Humboldt z 38343; rural
Christie Hill; RMC Place; BLOUNT; *233 E-19; elev. 1,100ft./335m.; mail Maryville z 37801; rural
Christmasville; RMC Place; CARROLL; 232 C-5; mail Mc Kenzie z 38201; ● 100
Christmasville; RMC Place; HAYWOOD; *232 E-4; elev. 330ft./101m.; mail Brownsville z 38012; rural
Chuckey (Fullens); RMC Place; GREENE; 233 K-17; elev. 1,461ft./445m.; 🅿; z 37641; ● 360
Church Hill; Inc. Place; HAWKINS; 233 J-17; elev. 1,249ft./381m.; 🅿; ★ **JNSC-**; z 37642, z 37645; Ⓟ 4,834; Ⓒ 5,916
Churchton; RMC Place; DYER; 232 C-4; mail Newbern z 38059; ● 100
Citico Beach; RMC Place; MONROE; *233 E-19; mail Vonore z 37885; ● 30
Citico Junction; RMC Place; HAMILTON; ★ **CHTN**; pop. incl. with Chattanooga (Inc. Place)
Clacks Gap; RMC Place; ROANE; *233 D-18; ★ **KNOX**; mail Harriman z 37748; ● 50
CLAIBORNE; 233 B-20; Ⓟ 26,137; Ⓒ 29,862; ◆ 31,413
Clairfield; RMC Place; CLAIBORNE; 233 B-19; elev. 1,107ft./337m.; 🅿; z 37715; ● 200
Clark Addition; RMC Place; BLOUNT; ★ **KNOX**; mail Maryville z 37804
Clarkrange; RMC Place; FENTRESS; 233 C-16; elev. 1,801ft./549m.; 🅿; z 38553; ● 280
Clarksburg; Inc. Place; CARROLL; 232 D-6; elev. 545ft./166m.; 🅿; z 38324; Ⓟ 321; Ⓒ 285
Clarksville; Inc. Place; ⊡ MONTGOMERY; 232 B-9; elev. 493ft./150m.; 🅿 🅷 🅲 9,207 ■; ★ **CLRKV**; z 37040-44; Ⓟ 75,494; Ⓒ 103,455; ◆ 132,794
Clarktown; RMC Place; WHITE; *233 D-15; mail Sparta z 38583; ● 30
Claxton; RMC Place; ANDERSON; 233 C-19; ★ **KNOX**; mail Powell z 37849; ● 250
Claxton; RMC Place; MCMINN; *233 F-17; mail Athens z 37303; rural
CLAY; 233 B-14; Ⓟ 7,238; Ⓒ 7,976; ◆ 7,622
Claybrook; RMC Place; MADISON; *232 E-6; mail Jackson z 38301; rural
Clay Hill; RMC Place; SCOTT; *233 B-18; elev. 1,398ft./426m.; mail Winfield z 37892; rural
Claylick; RMC Place; DICKSON; *232 C-10; mail White Bluff z 37187; rural
Clayton; RMC Place; OBION; *232 B-4; mail Troy z 38260; rural
Clearbranch; RMC Place; UNICOI; *233 L-18; mail Erwin z 37650; ● 30
Clear Creek Mill; RMC Place; RHEA; *233 E-16; elev. 750ft./229m.; mail Evensville z 37332; rural
Clearmont; RMC Place; WARREN; *233 E-13; mail Mc Minnville z 37110; rural
Clear Springs; GREENE; see Jockey (RMC Place)
Clear Springs; RMC Place; KNOX; *233 C-19; elev. 1,247ft./380m.; ★ **KNOX**; mail Mascot z 37806; rural
Clear Springs; RMC Place; MCMINN; *233 F-17; mail Calhoun z 37309, Riceville z 37370; rural
Clearview; RMC Place; SUMNER; *233 B-11; elev. 777ft./237m.; ★ **NASH**; mail Cottontown z 37048; rural
Clearwater; RMC Place; MCMINN; 233 E-17; mail Athens z 37303; ● 30
Clements Lake Estates; RMC Place; WILLIAMSON; *232 D-10; ★ **NASH**; mail Fairview z 37062; pop. incl. with Fairview (Inc. Place)
Clementsville; RMC Place; CLAY; *233 A-14; mail Red Boiling Springs z 37150; ● 30
Cleveland; Inc. Place; ⊡ BRADLEY; 233 G-17; elev. 920ft./280m.; 🅿 🅷 🅲 4,367 ■; ★ **CLEV**; z 37311-12, z 37320, z 37323, z 37364; Ⓟ 30,354; Ⓒ 37,192; ◆ 42,441
Clevenger; RMC Place; COCKE; 214 F-6; ★ **MORR**; mail Newport z 37821; ● 50
Cliff Springs; RMC Place; OVERTON; *233 C-16; elev. 1,887ft./575m.; mail Monterey z 38574; rural
Clifftops; RMC Place; MARION; *233 F-14; elev. 1,860ft./567m.; mail Monteagle z 37356; ● 200
Cliffwood; RMC Place; LAWRENCE; *232 F-9; elev. 940ft./287m.; mail Lawrenceburg z 38464; rural
Clifton (Clifton City); Inc. Place; WAYNE; 232 F-7; elev. 403ft./123m.; 🅿; z 38425; Ⓟ 620; Ⓒ 2,699
Clifton City; WAYNE; see Clifton (Inc. Place)
Clifton Hills; RMC Place; HAMILTON; *233 G-15; ★ **CHTN**; pop. incl. with Chattanooga (Inc. Place)
Clifton Junction; RMC Place; WAYNE; *232 F-7; mail Clifton z 38425; ● 220
Clifty; RMC Place; CUMBERLAND, WHITE; *233 D-16; mail Sparta z 38583; ● 30
Clinton; Inc. Place; ⊡ ANDERSON; 233 C-19; elev. 1,070ft./326m.; 🅿; ★ **KNOX**; z 37716-17; Ⓟ 8,972; Ⓒ 9,409
Clopton; RMC Place; TIPTON; *232 E-2; elev. 351ft./107m.; mail Brighton z 38011; rural
Cloud Creek; RMC Place; HAWKINS; *233 K-16; mail Rogersville z 37857; ● 30
Clouds; RMC Place; CLAIBORNE; *233 B-20; elev. 1,332ft./406m.; mail New Tazewell z 37825, Tazewell z 37879; rural
Clouse Hill; RMC Place; GRUNDY; *233 F-14; elev. 2,000ft./610m.; mail Tracy City z 37387; ● 30
Clovercroft; RMC Place; WILLIAMSON; 233 D-11; ★ **NASH**; mail Franklin z 37067; ● 30
Cloverdale; RMC Place; OBION; *232 C-4; elev. 312ft./95m.; mail Obion z 38240; ● 50
Cloverdale; RMC Place; SHELBY; *232 F-2; elev. 283ft./86m.; ★ **MEM**; mail Millington z 38053; ● 300
Cloverdale; RMC Place; WHITE; *233 D-15; mail Sparta z 38583; ● 30
Clover Hill; RMC Place; BLOUNT; *233 E-19; ★ **KNOX**; mail Maryville z 37804; rural
Cloverhill; RMC Place; DAVIDSON; *233 C-11; ★ **NASH**; mail Nashville z 37214; pop. incl. with Nashville (Inc. Place)
Cloverport; RMC Place; HARDEMAN; 232 F-4; mail Mercer z 38392, Toone z 38381; ● 80
Club Springs; RMC Place; SMITH; *233 C-14; mail Elmwood z 38560; rural
Coal Chute; RMC Place; CARTER; *233 K-19; elev. 1,647ft./502m.; ★ **JNSC-**; mail Elizabethton z 37643; ● 500
Coalfield; RMC Place; MORGAN; 233 D-18; elev. 1,034ft./315m.; 🅿; ★ **KNOX**; z 37719; ● 460
Coal Hill; RMC Place; MORGAN; *233 D-18; ★ **KNOX**; mail Sunbright z 37872; rural
Coal Hill; RMC Place; SCOTT; *233 B-17; elev. 1,510ft./460m.; mail Robbins z 37852; rural
Coaling; RMC Place; DICKSON; *232 C-10; mail Charlotte z 37036; rural
Coalmont; Inc. Place; GRUNDY; 233 F-14; elev. 1,900ft./579m.; 🅿; z 37313; Ⓟ 813; Ⓒ 948
Coble; RMC Place; HICKMAN; 232 D-8; mail Centerville z 37033; ● 100
COCKE; 233 L-16; Ⓟ 29,141; Ⓒ 33,565; ◆ 35,768
COFFEE; 233 F-13; Ⓟ 40,339; Ⓒ 48,014; ◆ 52,294
Coffee Landing; RMC Place; HARDIN; *232 F-6; mail Adamsville z 38310; rural
Coffee Ridge; RMC Place; UNICOI; *233 L-18; mail Erwin z 37650; ● 30
Cog Hill; RMC Place; MCMINN; *233 F-17; mail Delano z 37325, Etowah z 37331; ● 200
Coker Creek; RMC Place; MONROE; 233 F-18; elev. 1,600ft./488m.; 🅿; z 37314; ● 130
Cold Spring; RMC Place; BLEDSOE; 233 E-16; mail Pikeville z 37367; ● 200
Cold Spring; RMC Place; JOHNSON; *233 J-20; mail Mountain City z 37683; ● 50
Cold Springs; RMC Place; BLOUNT; *233 D-20; ★ **KNOX**; mail Walland z 37886; ● 130
Cold Springs; RMC Place; HAWKINS; *233 J-17; ★ **JNSC-**; mail Surgoinsville z 37873; rural
Coldwater; RMC Place; LINCOLN; 233 G-11; elev. 632ft./193m.; mail Fayetteville z 37334, Taft z 38488; ● 30
Colesburg; RMC Place; DICKSON; 232 C-9; elev. 871ft./265m.; mail Dickson z 37055; pop. incl. with Burns (Inc. Place)
Coles Ferry; RMC Place; WILSON; *233 C-12; ★ **NASH**; mail Lebanon z 37087; ● 70
Coles Store; RMC Place; PUTNAM; *233 C-14; elev. 1,000ft./305m.; mail Baxter z 38544; rural
Coletown; RMC Place; POLK; *233 G-18; mail Copperhill z 37317; rural
College (College Station); RMC Place; BLEDSOE; 233 E-15; mail Pikeville z 37367; ● 100
Collegedale; Inc. Place; HAMILTON; 233 G-16; elev. 800ft./244m.; 🅿 🅲 2,522; ★ **CHTN**; z 37315, z 37363; Ⓟ 5,048; Ⓒ 6,514
College Grove; RMC Place; WILLIAMSON; 233 D-11; elev. 735ft./224m.; 🅿; z 37046; ● 650
College Grove Estates; RMC Place; ROANE; *233 D-17; elev. 800ft./244m.; ★ **KNOX**; mail Rockwood z 37854; pop. incl. with Rockwood (Inc. Place)
College Heights; RMC Place; WASHINGTON; ★ **JNSC-**; pop. incl. with Johnson City (Inc. Place)
College Hill; RMC Place; RHEA; *233 E-16; mail Dayton z 37321; pop. incl. with Dayton (Inc. Place)
College Park; RMC Place; CARTER; *233 K-18; ★ **JNSC-**; mail Johnson City z 37601
College Park Estates; RMC Place; BLOUNT; *233 E-19; ★ **KNOX**; mail Maryville z 37803; ● 90
College Station; BLEDSOE; see College (RMC Place)
Colliers Corner; RMC Place; JEFFERSON; *233 C-20; ★ **MORR**; mail Jefferson City z 37760; rural
Collierville; Inc. Place; SHELBY; 232 G-2; elev. 387ft./118m.; 🅿; ★ **MEM**; z 38017, z 38027; Ⓟ 14,427; Ⓒ 31,872; ◆ 35,074
Collins (Werner); RMC Place; GRUNDY; *233 F-14; mail Palmer z 37365
Collins; RMC Place; HAWKINS; mail Rogersville z 37857; pop. incl. with Rogersville (Inc. Place)
Collinwood; Inc. Place; WAYNE; 232 G-8; elev. 1,056ft./322m.; 🅿; z 38450; Ⓟ 1,014; Ⓒ 1,024
Colonial; RMC Place; SHELBY; ★ **MEM**; mail Memphis z 38124; pop. incl. with Memphis (Inc. Place)
Colonial Acres; RMC Place; WEAKLEY; *232 B-5; mail Dresden z 38225; ● 100
Colonial Circle; RMC Place; SEVIER; *233 D-20; ★ **KNOX**; mail Seymour z 37865; ● 140
Colonial Heights; CDP; SULLIVAN; 234 K-9; elev. 1,400ft./427m.; 🅿; ★ **JNSC-**; z 37663; Ⓟ 6,716; Ⓒ 7,067
Colonial Village; RMC Place; KNOX; *233 D-19; ★ **KNOX**; mail Knoxville z 37920; pop. incl. with Knoxville (Inc. Place)
Columbia; Inc. Place; ⊡ MAURY; 232 E-10; elev. 637ft./194m.; 🅿 🅷 ■; z 38401-02; Ⓟ 28,583; Ⓒ 33,055; ◆ 36,444
Columbia Hill; RMC Place; OVERTON; *233 C-16; elev. 1,280ft./390m.; mail Monterey z 38574; rural
Columbus Hill; RMC Place; JACKSON; *233 B-14; mail Gainesboro z 38562; rural
Comfort; RMC Place; MARION; *233 G-14; mail South Pittsburg z 37380; rural
Commerce; RMC Place; WILSON; 233 C-13; elev. 620ft./189m.; mail Watertown z 37184; ● 60
Community Acres; RMC Place; BEDFORD; *233 E-12; mail Unionville z 37180; ● 150
Como; RMC Place; HENRY; 232 B-6; elev. 458ft./140m.; 🅿; z 38223; ● 200
Compton; RMC Place; RUTHERFORD; *233 D-12; ★ **MUR**; mail Murfreesboro z 37130; rural
Conasauga; RMC Place; POLK; 233 G-17; elev. 800ft./244m.; 🅿; z 37316; ● 250
Concord; RMC Place; CARROLL; *232 D-6; mail Huntingdon z 38344; ● 80
Concord; RMC Place; GIBSON; *232 D-5; mail Trenton z 38382; ● 30
Concord; RMC Place; HUMPHREYS; *232 C-8; mail Waverly z 37185; rural
Concord; RMC Place; KNOX; *233 D-19; elev. 820ft./250m.; 🅿; ★ **KNOX**; z 37922, z 37934; ● 460
Concord; RMC Place; RHEA; *233 E-16; elev. 820ft./250m.; mail Evensville z 37332; ● 50
Concord; RMC Place; RUTHERFORD; 233 E-12; elev. 776ft./237m.; mail Rockvale z 37153; ● 100
Condon (Plainview); Inc. Place; UNION; 233 C-20; ★ **KNOX**; mail Luttrell z 37779; Ⓟ 1,236; Ⓒ 1,866
Conklin; RMC Place; WASHINGTON; *233 K-18; ★ **JNSC-**; mail Jonesborough z 37659; ● 70
Conner Heights; RMC Place; SEVIER; *233 D-20; mail Pigeon Forge z 37863; pop. incl. with Pigeon Forge (Inc. Place)
Conyersville; RMC Place; HENRY; *232 B-7; mail Puryear z 38251; rural
Cookeville; Inc. Place; ⊡ PUTNAM; 233 C-15; elev. 1,118ft./341m.; 🅿 🅷 🅲 9,733 ■; z 38501-03, z 38505-06; Ⓟ 21,744; Ⓒ 23,923; ◆ 27,059
Cool Springs; RMC Place; GIBSON; *232 C-4; elev. 319ft./97m.; mail Trimble z 38259; rural
Cooper; RMC Place; FENTRESS; *233 B-16; mail Jamestown z 38556; rural
Coopers; RMC Place; CARROLL; *232 D-7; mail Bruceton z 38317; ● 100
Coopertown; Inc. Place; ROBERTSON; 232 B-10; mail Springfield z 37172; Ⓒ 3,027
Copperhill; Inc. Place; POLK; 233 G-18; elev. 1,476ft./450m.; 🅿 🅷; z 37317; Ⓟ 362; Ⓒ 511
Corbin Hill; RMC Place; MORGAN; *233 C-18; ★ **KNOX**; mail Oliver Springs z 37840; rural
Cordell; RMC Place; SCOTT; *233 B-18; elev. 1,191ft./363m.; mail Huntsville z 37756; rural
Corders Crossroads; RMC Place; LINCOLN; *233 G-12; elev. 898ft./274m.; mail Kelso z 37348; rural
Cordova; RMC Place; SHELBY; 232 F-2; elev. 366ft./112m.; 🅿; ★ **MEM**; z 38016, z 38018, z 38088; pop. incl. with Memphis (Inc. Place)
Corinth; RMC Place; KNOX; *233 C-19; ★ **KNOX**; mail Knoxville z 37918; rural
Corinth; RMC Place; SUMNER; *233 B-12; mail Portland z 37148; rural
Cornersville; Inc. Place; MARSHALL; 233 F-11; elev. 893ft./272m.; 🅿; z 37047; Ⓟ 683; Ⓒ 962
Cornpone; SEVIER; see Cove Creek Cascades (RMC Place)
Coro Lake; RMC Place; SHELBY; *232 G-1; ★ **MEM**; mail Memphis z 38109; pop. incl. with Memphis (Inc. Place)
Corona; RMC Place; TIPTON; *232 E-1; elev. 233ft./71m.; mail Frenchmans Bayou z 72338; rural
Corryton; RMC Place; KNOX; 233 C-20; elev. 1,045ft./319m.; 🅿; ★ **KNOX**; z 37721; ● 100
Cortner; RMC Place; BEDFORD; *233 F-12; mail Normandy z 37360; ● 40
Cosby; RMC Place; COCKE; 233 M-16; elev. 1,351ft./412m.; 🅿; z 37722; ● 400
Coster; RMC Place; KNOX; ★ **KNOX**; mail Knoxville z 37917; pop. incl. with Knoxville (Inc. Place)
Cotham; RMC Place; GIBSON; *232 D-5; mail Trenton z 38382; ● 150
Cottage Grove; Inc. Place; HENRY; 232 B-6; elev. 550ft./168m.; 🅿; z 38224; Ⓟ 85; Ⓒ 97
Cottage Home; RMC Place; WILSON; *233 D-13; elev. 658ft./201m.; mail Liberty z 37095; ● 120
Cottonport; RMC Place; MEIGS; *233 E-17; elev. 800ft./244m.; mail Decatur z 37322; rural
Cottontown (Parham); RMC Place; SUMNER; 233 B-12; elev. 571ft./174m.; 🅿; ★ **NASH**; z 37048; ● 250
Cottonwood Estates; RMC Place; WILLIAMSON; *233 D-11; elev. 620ft./189m.; ★ **NASH**; mail Franklin z 37069
Cottonwood Grove; RMC Place; LAKE; *232 C-3; mail Ridgely z 38080; rural
Cotula; RMC Place; CAMPBELL; *233 B-19; mail La Follette z 37766; rural
Couchville; RMC Place; DAVIDSON; ★ **NASH**; mail Nashville z 37214; pop. incl. with Nashville (Inc. Place)
Coulterville; RMC Place; HAMILTON; *233 F-16; ★ **CHTN**; mail Sale Creek z 37373; ● 30
Counce; RMC Place; HARDIN; 232 G-6; elev. 476ft./145m.; 🅿; z 38326; ● 700
Country Club; RMC Place; HARDEMAN; *232 F-4; mail Bolivar z 38008; ● 700
Country Haven Estates; RMC Place; WILLIAMSON; *233 D-11; mail Thompsons Station z 37179; pop. incl. with Thompson's Station (Inc. Place)
Country Roads; RMC Place; WILLIAMSON; *233 D-11; ★ **NASH**; mail Franklin z 37064; pop. incl. with Franklin (Inc. Place)
Countrywood Estates; RMC Place; WILLIAMSON; *233 D-11; ★ **NASH**; mail Franklin z 37064; ● 40
Countyline; RMC Place; MOORE; *233 F-12; elev. 833ft./254m.; mail Lynchburg z 37352; pop. incl. with Lynchburg (Inc. Place)
County Line; RMC Place; SEVIER; *233 D-20; ★ **KNOX**; mail Seymour z 37865; ● 190
Courtland; RMC Place; ROBERTSON; *233 B-11; elev. 741ft./226m.; ★ **NASH**; mail Springfield z 37172; pop. incl. with Springfield (Inc. Place)
Cove Creek; RMC Place; CAMPBELL; *233 C-19; elev. 1,200ft./366m.; mail Caryville z 37714; rural
Cove Creek; RMC Place; CARTER; *233 K-19; elev. 3,161ft./963m.; mail Roan Mountain z 37687; ● 50
Cove Creek Cascades (Cornpone); RMC Place; SEVIER; 214 G-4; mail Sevierville z 37862; ● 90
Cove Lake Estates; RMC Place; CAMPBELL; *233 C-18; elev. 1,200ft./366m.; mail Caryville z 37714; pop. incl. with Caryville (Inc. Place)
Covington; Inc. Place; ⊡ TIPTON; 232 E-2; elev. 339ft./103m.; 🅿 🅷; ★ **MEM**; z 38019; Ⓟ 7,487; Ⓒ 8,463
Cowan; Inc. Place; FRANKLIN; 233 G-13; elev. 980ft./299m.; 🅿; z 37318; Ⓟ 1,738; Ⓒ 1,770
Cowanstown; RMC Place; JOHNSON; *233 K-19; elev. 1,974ft./602m.; mail Butler z 37640; rural
Coxville; RMC Place; CROCKETT; *232 D-4; elev. 363ft./111m.; mail Humboldt z 38343; ● 30
Cozette; RMC Place; DECATUR; *232 D-7; elev. 516ft./157m.; mail Sugar Tree z 38380; ● 30
Crab Orchard; Inc. Place; CUMBERLAND; 233 D-17; elev. 1,671ft./509m.; 🅿; z 37723; Ⓟ 876; Ⓒ 838
Crabtree; RMC Place; CARTER; *233 K-19; mail Roan Mountain z 37687; rural
Crackers Neck; RMC Place; JOHNSON; *233 K-20; mail Mountain City z 37683; ● 30
Craggie Hope; RMC Place; CHEATHAM; *232 C-10; elev. 557ft./170m.; mail Kingston Springs z 37082; ● 150
Craigfield; RMC Place; WILLIAMSON; *232 D-10; mail Bon Aqua z 37025; rural
Crandull; RMC Place; JOHNSON; *233 J-20; elev. 2,631ft./802m.; mail Shady Valley z 37688; rural
Cranmore Cove; RMC Place; RHEA; *233 E-16; mail Dayton z 37321; rural
Cravenstown; RMC Place; OVERTON; *233 C-16; mail Wilder z 38589
Crawfish Valley; RMC Place; LAWRENCE; *232 F-9; mail Lawrenceburg z 38464; rural
Crawford; RMC Place; OVERTON; 233 C-16; elev. 1,878ft./572m.; 🅿; z 38554; ● 100
Creek Store; RMC Place; GREENE; *233 K-16; elev. 1,040ft./317m.; mail Mohawk z 37810; rural
Creekwood; RMC Place; BEDFORD; *233 F-12; elev. 740ft./226m.; mail Shelbyville z 37160; ● 80
Creekwood; RMC Place; WILSON; *233 C-12; ★ **NASH**; mail Mount Juliet z 37122; ● 120
Crenshaw; RMC Place; KNOX; *233 D-19; ★ **KNOX**; mail Knoxville z 37920; rural
Crescent; RMC Place; RUTHERFORD; *233 E-12; elev. 653ft./199m.; mail Murfreesboro z 37128; rural
Creson; RMC Place; LINCOLN; *233 G-12; mail Fayetteville z 37334; pop. incl. with Fayetteville (Inc. Place)
Creston; RMC Place; CUMBERLAND; *233 D-16; elev. 1,699ft./518m.; mail Crossville z 38555; ● 60
Crestwood; RMC Place; ROANE; *233 D-18; ★ **KNOX**; mail Kingston z 37763; ● 380
Crestwood Hills; RMC Place; KNOX; *233 D-19; ★ **KNOX**; mail Knoxville z 37918; ● 1,600
Crewstown; RMC Place; LAWRENCE; *232 G-9; mail Lawrenceburg z 38464; rural
Crieve Hall; RMC Place; DAVIDSON; ★ **NASH**; mail Nashville z 37211; pop. incl. with Nashville (Inc. Place)
Crisp Spring; RMC Place; WARREN; *233 E-14; elev. 950ft./290m.; mail Morrison z 37357; rural
Crockett; RMC Place; OBION; *232 B-4; elev. 295ft./90m.; mail Rives z 38253; rural
CROCKETT; 232 D-4; Ⓟ 13,378; Ⓒ 14,532; ◆ 14,124
Crockett Mills; RMC Place; CROCKETT; 232 D-4; elev. 350ft./107m.; 🅿; z 38021; ● 400
Cromwell Crossroads; RMC Place; WAYNE; *232 G-8; elev. 987ft./301m.; mail Collinwood z 38450; rural
Cronanville; RMC Place; LAKE; *232 B-3; elev. 307ft./94m.; mail Tiptonville z 38079; rural
Crooked Creek; RMC Place; PERRY; *232 D-8; elev. 500ft./152m.; mail Lobelville z 37097; rural
Cross; RMC Place; SULLIVAN; *233 J-18; ★ **JNSC-**; mail Blountville z 37617; rural
Cross Anchor; RMC Place; GREENE; 233 K-17; elev. 1,324ft./404m.; mail Greeneville z 37743; ● 100
Cross Bridges; RMC Place; MAURY; *232 E-10; mail Mount Pleasant z 38474; rural
Cross Keys; RMC Place; WILLIAMSON; *233 E-11; mail College Grove z 37046; rural
Crossland; RMC Place; HENRY; *232 B-6; mail Hazel z 42049; rural
Cross Lanes; RMC Place; MACON; *233 B-13; elev. 1,007ft./307m.; mail Lafayette z 37083, Westmoreland z 37186; rural
Cross Plains; Inc. Place; ROBERTSON; 233 B-11; elev. 749ft./228m.; 🅿; ★ **NASH**; z 37049; Ⓟ 1,025; Ⓒ 1,381
Cross Road; RMC Place; SCOTT; *233 B-17; mail Oneida z 37841; rural
Crossroads; RMC Place; BENTON; 232 F-9; mail Camden z 38320; ● 30
Cross Roads; RMC Place; CANNON; *233 D-13; mail Woodbury z 37190; rural
Crossroads; RMC Place; CROCKETT; *232 D-4; elev. 355ft./108m.; mail Bells z 38006; ● 50
Cross Roads; RMC Place; DEKALB; *233 D-14; mail Dowelltown z 37059, Smithville z 37166; ● 30
Cross Roads; RMC Place; DYER; *232 D-3; mail Friendship z 38034; ● 30
Cross Roads; RMC Place; FENTRESS; *233 B-16; mail Jamestown z 38556; ● 180
Crossroads; RMC Place; HARDIN; *232 F-7; mail Savannah z 38372; rural
Crossroads; RMC Place; LAWRENCE; *232 F-9; mail Leoma z 38468; ● 30
Cross Roads; RMC Place; MACON; *233 A-13; elev. 914ft./279m.; mail Westmoreland z 37186; rural
Crossroads; RMC Place; SHELBY; *232 G-2; ★ **MEM**; mail Collierville z 38017, Memphis z 38174; ● 50
Cross Roads; RMC Place; STEWART; *232 B-8; mail Stewart z 37175; rural
Crossroads; RMC Place; WAYNE; *232 G-8; mail Collinwood z 38450; rural
Crosstown; RMC Place; SHELBY; ★ **MEM**; mail Memphis z 38104; pop. incl. with Memphis (Inc. Place)
Crosstown; RMC Place; TIPTON; *232 E-2; elev. 441ft./134m.; ★ **MEM**; mail Atoka z 38004; pop. incl. with Atoka (Inc. Place)
Crossville; Inc. Place; ⊡ CUMBERLAND; 233 D-16; elev. 1,863ft./568m.; 🅿 🅷; z 38555, z 38557-58, z 38571-72; Ⓟ 6,930; Ⓒ 8,981
Crosswinds; RMC Place; WILSON; *233 C-12; ★ **NASH**; mail Mount Juliet z 37122; ● 200
Crowley Store; RMC Place; WEAKLEY; *232 C-5; elev. 386ft./118m.; mail Greenfield z 38230; rural
Crown Point Estates; RMC Place; WILSON; *233 C-12; ★ **NASH**; mail Mount Juliet z 37122
Crucifer; RMC Place; HENDERSON; *232 E-6; elev. 494ft./151m.; mail Huron z 38345; ● 30
Crump; Inc. Place; HARDIN; 232 F-6; elev. 458ft./140m.; 🅿; z 38327; Ⓟ 2,028; Ⓒ 1,521
Crunk; RMC Place; ROBERTSON; *233 B-11; elev. 680ft./207m.; ★ **NASH**; mail Greenbrier z 37073; rural

Entries in **UPPERCASE** are counties.
Entries in **bold** have populations of 2,500 or more.
Names in parentheses are alternate names.

Inc. Place	Incorporated Place
RMC Place	Rand McNally Designated Place
CDP	Census Designated Place
MCD	Minor Civil Division
⊡	County Seat
▲	Minor Civil Division
elev.	Elevation
🅿	Post Office
🅷	Hospital
🅲	College
■	Principal Business Center
★	Ranally Metro Area (RMA) Abbreviation
z	Zip Code(s)
Ⓟ	Previous Census Population
Ⓡ	Revised Census Population
Ⓐ	Annexation Population
●	Rand McNally Population Estimate
Ⓒ	Final Census Population
Ⓢ	Special Census Population
◆	Estimated Population

For additional definitions see Glossary, Volume 1, and Introduction, Volume 2.

Crystal; RMC Place; OBION; *232 B-4; elev. 478ft./146m.; mail Union City z 38261; rural
Crystal Springs; RMC Place; LINCOLN; *233 G-12; mail Kelso z 37348; rural
Cuba; RMC Place; HAWKINS; *233 K-16; elev. 1,171ft./357m.; mail Mooresburg z 37811; rural
Cuba; RMC Place; SHELBY; 232 F-1; ★ MEM; mail Millington z 38053; ● 50
Cuba Landing; RMC Place; HUMPHREYS; *232 D-8; mail Waverly z 37185; summer pop. 300; ● 100
Cub Creek; RMC Place; JACKSON; *233 B-14; mail Gainesboro z 38562; rural
Culleoka (Pleasant Grove); RMC Place; MAURY; 232 E-10; elev. 715ft./218m.; 🅿; z 38451; ● 360
Culpepper; RMC Place; CANNON; *233 D-13; elev. 640ft./195m.; mail Readyville z 37149; ● 60
CUMBERLAND; 233 D-16; Ⓟ 34,736; Ⓒ 46,802; ◆ 54,558
Cumberland City; Inc. Place; STEWART; 232 B-8; elev. 390ft./119m.; 🅿; z 37050; Ⓟ 319; Ⓒ 316
Cumberland Estates; RMC Place; KNOX; *233 D-19; ★ KNOX; mail Knoxville z 37921; pop. incl. with Knoxville (Inc. Place)
Cumberland Furnace; RMC Place; DICKSON; 232 C-9; elev. 518ft./158m.; 🅿; z 37051; ● 300
Cumberland Gap; Inc. Place; CLAIBORNE; 233 A-20; elev. 1,302ft./397m.; 🅿; z 37724 & mail Harrogate z 37752; Ⓟ 210; Ⓒ 204
Cumberland Heights; RMC Place; DAVIDSON; *233 C-11; ★ NASH; pop. incl. with Nashville (Inc. Place)
Cumberland Heights; RMC Place; GRUNDY; 233 F-14; elev. 1,898ft./579m.; mail Coalmont z 37313; ● 210
Cumberland Heights; RMC Place; MONTGOMERY; *232 B-9; elev. 558ft./170m.; ★ CLRKV; mail Clarksville z 37040; ● 200
Cumberland Springs; RMC Place; RHEA; 233 E-16; mail Dayton z 37321; ● 60
Cumberland View; RMC Place; CAMPBELL; *233 B-19; elev. 1,400ft./427m.; ★ KNOX; mail Jacksboro z 37757; rural
Cumberland View Estates; RMC Place; ANDERSON; *233 C-19; elev. 1,240ft./378m.; ★ KNOX; mail Lake City z 37769; ● 60
Cummings; RMC Place; WHITE; *233 D-15; mail Sparta z 38583; rural
Cummingsville; RMC Place; VAN BUREN; *233 D-15; elev. 907ft./276m.; mail Spencer z 38585; rural
Cunningham (Lone Oak); RMC Place; MONTGOMERY; 232 B-9; elev. 661ft./201m.; 🅿; z 37052; ● 60
Cupp Mill; RMC Place; CLAIBORNE; *233 B-20; mail New Tazewell z 37825; rural
Curlee; RMC Place; CANNON; *233 D-13; mail Woodbury z 37190; ● 30
Curve; RMC Place; LAUDERDALE; 232 D-3; mail Ripley z 38063; ● 350
Cusick; RMC Place; SEVIER; *233 D-20; ★ KNOX; mail Seymour z 37865; rural
Cuzick; RMC Place; LOUDON; *233 D-18; ★ KNOX; mail Lenoir City z 37772; ● 50
Cypress; RMC Place; CROCKETT; *232 D-4; elev. 344ft./105m.; mail Bells z 38006; rural
Cypress Creek; RMC Place; HENRY; mail Buchanan z 38222; summer pop. 175
Cypress Inn; RMC Place; WAYNE; 232 G-8; elev. 721ft./220m.; 🅿; z 38452; ● 350

D

Daisy; RMC Place; HAMILTON; *233 F-16; elev. 734ft./224m.; ★ CHTN; mail Soddy Daisy z 37379; pop. incl. with Soddy-Daisy (Inc. Place)
Dale Hollow; RMC Place; CLAY; 233 B-15; elev. 801ft./244m.; mail Celina z 38551; ● 200
Dalewood; RMC Place; DAVIDSON; *233 C-11; ★ NASH; mail Nashville z 37207; pop. incl. with Nashville (Inc. Place)
Dallas Gardens; RMC Place; HAMILTON; *233 F-16; ★ CHTN; mail Soddy Daisy z 37379; ● 80
Dallas Heights; RMC Place; HAMILTON; ★ CHTN; pop. incl. with Chattanooga (Inc. Place)
Dallas Hills; RMC Place; HAMILTON; *233 F-16; ★ CHTN; mail Soddy Daisy z 37379; rural
Dalton Heights; RMC Place; HAMBLEN; ★ MORR; mail Morristown z 37814; pop. incl. with Morristown (Inc. Place)
Dancyville; RMC Place; HAYWOOD; 232 F-4; mail Stanton z 38069; ● 50
Dandridge; Inc. Place; ⊡ JEFFERSON; 233 C-20; elev. 1,000ft./305m.; 🅿; z 37725; Ⓟ 1,540; Ⓒ 2,078
Danley; RMC Place; DAVIDSON; ★ NASH; pop. incl. with Nashville (Inc. Place)
Dante; RMC Place; KNOX; 233 L-12; ★ KNOX; mail Knoxville z 37921; ● 260
Darden; RMC Place; HENDERSON; 232 E-7; elev. 406ft./124m.; 🅿; z 38328; ● 180
Darks Mill; RMC Place; MAURY; *232 E-10; mail Columbia z 38401; rural
Daugherty Estates; RMC Place; WILLIAMSON; *232 D-10; ★ NASH; mail Fairview z 37062; ● 70
Daus; RMC Place; SEQUATCHIE; *233 F-15; elev. 715ft./218m.; mail Dunlap z 37327; ● 100
Davenport; RMC Place; WARREN; *233 E-13; mail Mc Minnville z 37110
Davidson; RMC Place; FENTRESS; *233 C-16; mail Wilder z 38589
DAVIDSON; 233 C-11; Ⓟ 510,784; Ⓒ 569,891; Ⓡ 569,892; ◆ 697,482
Davidson Chapel; RMC Place; GIBSON; *232 C-5; elev. 400ft./122m.; mail Trenton z 38382; ● 30
Davis Chapel; RMC Place; CAMPBELL; *233 B-19; ★ KNOX; mail La Follette z 37766; rural
Davis Chapel; RMC Place; CARROLL; *232 D-6; elev. 440ft./134m.; mail Huntingdon z 38344; rural
Davis Springs; RMC Place; UNICOI; *233 K-19; mail Unicoi z 37692
Daylight; RMC Place; WARREN; *233 E-14; mail Mc Minnville z 37110; ● 40
Days Crossroads; RMC Place; MACON; *233 B-13; elev. 976ft./297m.; mail Lafayette z 37083; rural
Daysville; RMC Place; CUMBERLAND; *233 D-17; elev. 1,540ft./469m.; mail Rockwood z 37854; ● 150
Dayton; Inc. Place; ⊡ RHEA; 233 E-16; elev. 694ft./212m.; 🅿 🅷 🅲 895; z 37321; Ⓟ 5,671; Ⓒ 6,180
Dayton Spur; RMC Place; CUMBERLAND; *233 D-16; mail Crossville z 38555; pop. incl. with Crossville (Inc. Place)
Deanburg; RMC Place; CHESTER; 232 F-5; elev. 534ft./163m.; mail Pinson z 38366; ● 30
Deane Hill; RMC Place; KNOX; *233 D-19; ★ KNOX; pop. incl. with Knoxville (Inc. Place)
Deans; RMC Place; HICKMAN; *232 E-9; elev. 571ft./174m.; mail Centerville z 37033; ● 30
DeArmond; RMC Place; ROANE; *233 D-18; elev. 818ft./249m.; ★ KNOX; mail Harriman z 37748; rural
Deason; RMC Place; BEDFORD; 233 E-12; mail Bell Buckle z 37020; ● 110
De Busk; RMC Place; GREENE; *233 L-17; mail Greeneville z 37743; ● 200
Decatur; Inc. Place; ⊡ MEIGS; 233 E-17; elev. 788ft./240m.; 🅿; z 37322; Ⓟ 1,361; Ⓒ 1,395
DECATUR; 232 E-7; Ⓟ 10,472; Ⓒ 11,731; ◆ 11,372
Decaturville; Inc. Place; ⊡ DECATUR; 232 E-7; elev. 517ft./158m.; 🅿; z 38329; Ⓟ 879; Ⓒ 859
Decherd; Inc. Place; FRANKLIN; 233 F-13; elev. 960ft./293m.; 🅿; z 37324; Ⓟ 2,196; Ⓒ 2,246
Dedie; RMC Place; KNOX; ★ KNOX; pop. incl. with Knoxville (Inc. Place)
Deep Springs; RMC Place; JEFFERSON; *233 D-20; ★ KNOX; mail Dandridge z 37725; ● 30
Deerfield; RMC Place; LAWRENCE; *232 F-9; elev. 971ft./296m.; mail Lawrenceburg z 38464
Deerfield; RMC Place; WILLIAMSON; *233 D-11; ★ NASH; mail Franklin z 37064; rural
Deerfield Acres; RMC Place; SULLIVAN; *233 J-19; ★ JNSC-; mail Bristol z 37620; ● 160
Deer Lodge; RMC Place; MORGAN; 233 C-17; elev. 1,500ft./457m.; 🅿; z 37726; ● 300
Deermont; RMC Place; MORGAN; *233 D-17; elev. 900ft./274m.; mail Oakdale z 37829; rural
Defeated (Hoggtown); RMC Place; SMITH; *233 B-14; 🅿; z 37030; ● 100
Defense Depot; RMC Place; SHELBY; ★ MEM; mail Memphis z 38114; pop. incl. with Memphis (Inc. Place)
DEKALB; 233 D-14; Ⓟ 14,360; Ⓒ 17,423; ◆ 18,613
Delano; RMC Place; POLK; 233 F-17; elev. 812ft./247m.; 🅿; z 37325; ● 250
Delina; RMC Place; MARSHALL; *233 F-11; mail Cornersville z 37047, Petersburg z 37144; rural
Dellrose (Delrose); RMC Place; LINCOLN; 233 G-11; elev. 622ft./190m.; 🅿; z 38453 & mail Ardmore z 38449; ● 100
Dellwood; RMC Place; BLOUNT; *233 D-19; ★ KNOX; mail Maryville z 37804; ● 130
Del Rio; RMC Place; COCKE; 233 L-16; elev. 1,141ft./348m.; 🅿; z 37727; ● 100
Delrose; LINCOLN; see Dellrose (RMC Place)
Demory; RMC Place; CAMPBELL; *233 B-19; ★ KNOX; mail La Follette z 37766; ● 100
Denmark; RMC Place; MADISON; 232 E-4; elev. 466ft./142m.; 🅿; z 38391; ● 100
Dennis Cove; RMC Place; CARTER; *233 K-19; mail Hampton z 37658; ● 30
Denton; RMC Place; COCKE; *233 M-16; mail Cosby z 37722; rural
Dentville; RMC Place; MCMINN; *233 F-17; mail Delano z 37325, Etowah z 37331; rural
Denver; RMC Place; CANNON; *233 D-13; elev. 662ft./202m.; mail Readyville z 37149; ● 50
Denver; RMC Place; HUMPHREYS; 232 C-8; elev. 372ft./113m.; 🅿; z 37134; ● 150
De Priest Bend; RMC Place; PERRY; *232 E-8; elev. 492ft./150m.; mail Lobelville z 37097; pop. incl. with Lobelville (Inc. Place)
De Rossett; RMC Place; WHITE; 233 D-15; elev. 1,874ft./571m.; mail Sparta z 38583; ● 200
Detroit; RMC Place; TIPTON; *232 E-2; elev. 267ft./81m.; mail Burlison z 38015; rural
Devonia; RMC Place; ANDERSON; *233 C-18; elev. 1,600ft./488m.; 🅿; z 37710; rural
Diana; RMC Place; GILES; *233 F-11; elev. 836ft./255m.; mail Cornersville z 37047; ● 100
Dibrell; RMC Place; WARREN; 233 D-14; elev. 986ft./301m.; mail Mc Minnville z 37110; ● 150
Dickel; RMC Place; COFFEE; 🅿; z 37388; pop. incl. with Tullahoma (Inc. Place)
Dickey Bluff Peninsula; RMC Place; RHEA; *233 E-17; elev. 760ft./232m.; mail Spring City z 37381; rural
Dickey's Landing; HARDIN; see Hookers Bend (RMC Place)
Dickson; Inc. Place; DICKSON; 232 C-9; elev. 794ft./242m.; 🅿 🅷; z 37055-56; Ⓟ 8,791; Ⓒ 12,244
DICKSON; 232 C-9; Ⓟ 35,061; Ⓒ 43,156; ◆ 49,134
Dickson Town; RMC Place; GILES; *233 G-11; elev. 620ft./189m.; mail Elkton z 38455; ● 50
Difficult; RMC Place; SMITH; 233 B-14; elev. 540ft./165m.; mail Pleasant Shade z 37145; ● 120
Dill; RMC Place; BLEDSOE; 233 E-15; mail Pikeville z 37367; ● 150
Dilley; RMC Place; CLAIBORNE; *233 B-19; mail Eagan z 37730; rural
Dillton; RMC Place; RUTHERFORD; *233 D-12; elev. 634ft./193m.; ★ MUR; mail Murfreesboro z 37127; ● 50
Disco; RMC Place; BLOUNT; *233 D-19; elev. 906ft./276m.; ★ KNOX; mail Friendsville z 37737; rural
Dismal; RMC Place; DEKALB; *233 D-13; elev. 614ft./187m.; mail Liberty z 37095; rural
Disney; RMC Place; CAMPBELL; 233 C-19; mail Lake City z 37769; ● 200
Ditty; RMC Place; PUTNAM; *233 C-14; elev. 960ft./293m.; mail Cookeville z 38506; rural
Dixie; RMC Place; OBION; *232 B-4; elev. 487ft./148m.; mail Union City z 38261; rural
Dixie Lee Junction; RMC Place; KNOX, LOUDON; ★ KNOX; mail Knoxville z 37922; pop. incl. with Farragut (Inc. Place)
Dixon Springs; RMC Place; SMITH; 233 B-13; elev. 540ft./165m.; 🅿; z 37057; ● 150
Dixonville; RMC Place; TIPTON; 232 E-2; mail Millington z 38053; ● 170
Doaks Crossroads; RMC Place; WILSON; *233 C-13; elev. 697ft./212m.; mail Lebanon z 37090; ● 30
Dobson Branch; RMC Place; JACKSON; *233 C-15; elev. 982ft./299m.; mail Cookeville z 38501; rural
Dockery; RMC Place; BRADLEY; *233 G-17; ★ CLEV; mail Charleston z 37310
Dodson; RMC Place; ROANE; *233 D-17; mail Harriman z 37748; pop. incl. with Rockwood (Inc. Place)
Dodson; RMC Place; WHITE; *233 D-15; mail Sparta z 38583; rural
Dodson Estates; RMC Place; DAVIDSON; ★ NASH; mail Hermitage z 37076; pop. incl. with Nashville (Inc. Place)
Dodsons; RMC Place; GILES; *232 F-10; elev. 881ft./269m.; mail Lynnville z 38472; rural
Doeville; RMC Place; JOHNSON; 233 K-19; mail Butler z 37640; ● 150
Dog Hill (Siloam); RMC Place; CROCKETT; *232 D-4; mail Friendship z 38034; rural
Dogtown; RMC Place; CARTER; *233 K-19; ★ JNSC-; mail Elizabethton z 37643; ● 50
Dog Town; RMC Place; GRUNDY; *233 F-14; mail Coalmont z 37313; pop. incl. with Coalmont (Inc. Place)
Dogtown; RMC Place; POLK; *233 G-18; mail Turtletown z 37391; rural
Dogwood; RMC Place; ROANE; *233 D-18; mail Kingston z 37763; rural
Dogwood Heights; RMC Place; CLAIBORNE; *233 B-20; mail Tazewell z 37879; ● 300
Dogwood Shores; RMC Place; ROANE; *233 D-18; elev. 800ft./244m.; mail Kingston z 37763; ● 100
Dollar; RMC Place; CARROLL; *232 D-7; elev. 639ft./195m.; mail Buena Vista z 38318; rural
Donelson; RMC Place; DAVIDSON; 232 K-9; elev. 550ft./168m.; ★ NASH; mail Nashville z 37214; pop. incl. with Nashville (Inc. Place)
Donnel Chapel; RMC Place; RUTHERFORD; *233 E-13; elev. 820ft./250m.; mail Readyville z 37149; rural
Donoho; RMC Place; SMITH; *233 C-14; mail Carthage z 37030; rural
Donovan; ANDERSON; see Poplar (RMC Place)
Doran Addition; RMC Place; SULLIVAN; *233 J-18; ★ JNSC-; mail Kingsport z 37660; ● 250
Dorton; RMC Place; CUMBERLAND; *233 D-16; mail Crossville z 38555; ● 300
Dossett; RMC Place; ANDERSON; 233 C-18; ★ KNOX; mail Clinton z 37716; ● 70
Dotson (Dotson's Camp Ground, Red Hill); RMC Place; GRAINGER; *233 B-20; elev. 1,251ft./381m.; mail Washburn z 37888; rural
Dotson's Camp Ground; GRAINGER; see Dotson (RMC Place)
Dotsontown; RMC Place; GREENE; *233 K-17; mail Limestone z 37681; rural
Dotsonville; RMC Place; MONTGOMERY; *232 B-9; elev. 603ft./184m.; ★ CLRKV; mail Clarksville z 37042, Woodlawn z 37191
Doty Chapel; RMC Place; GREENE; *233 K-17; mail Afton z 37616; rural
Double Bridges; RMC Place; LAUDERDALE; 232 D-3; mail Halls z 38040; ● 230
Double Springs; RMC Place; MCMINN; *233 F-17; elev. 750ft./229m.; mail Athens z 37303; rural
Double Springs; RMC Place; PUTNAM; *233 C-14; mail Baxter z 38544; ● 300
Double Springs (Jakestown); RMC Place; RUTHERFORD; 233 D-12; ★ MUR; mail Murfreesboro z 37127; ● 500
Double Top; RMC Place; FENTRESS; *233 B-16; elev. 1,772ft./540m.; mail Jamestown z 38556; rural
Douglas; RMC Place; WILLIAMSON; *233 D-11; ★ NASH; mail Franklin z 37064; rural
Douglas Estates; RMC Place; JEFFERSON; *233 L-15; mail Dandridge z 37725; ● 450
Dover; RMC Place; HAMBLEN; *233 K-16; ★ MORR; mail Morristown z 37813; ● 50
Dover; Inc. Place; ⊡ STEWART; 232 B-8; elev. 400ft./122m.; 🅿; z 37058; Ⓟ 1,341; Ⓒ 1,442
Dowelltown; Inc. Place; DEKALB; 233 D-13; elev. 570ft./174m.; 🅿; z 37059; Ⓟ 308; Ⓒ 302
Dowler Heights; RMC Place; HAMILTON; *233 G-15; ★ CHTN; mail Signal Mountain z 37377; ● 120
Downtown; RMC Place; BLOUNT; ★ KNOX; mail Maryville z 37801; pop. incl. with Maryville (Inc. Place)
Downtown; RMC Place; BRADLEY; ★ CLEV; mail Chattanooga z 37401, z 37403, z 37408, Cleveland z 37311; pop. incl. with Cleveland (Inc. Place)
Downtown; RMC Place; HAMILTON; ★ CHTN; mail Chattanooga z 37401-03, z 37408; pop. incl. with Chattanooga (Inc. Place)
Downtown; RMC Place; KNOX; ★ KNOX; mail Knoxville z 37901; pop. incl. with Knoxville (Inc. Place)
Doyle; Inc. Place; WHITE; 233 D-15; elev. 965ft./294m.; 🅿; z 38559; Ⓟ 345; Ⓒ 525
Drapers Crossroads; RMC Place; MACON; *233 B-13; elev. 1,007ft./307m.; mail Lafayette z 37083; rural
Dresden; Inc. Place; ⊡ WEAKLEY; 232 B-5; elev. 425ft./130m.; 🅿; z 38225; Ⓟ 2,488; Ⓒ 2,855
Driftwood; RMC Place; SULLIVAN; *233 J-19; ★ JNSC-; mail Bristol z 37620; pop. incl. with Bristol (Inc. Place)
Dripping Springs; RMC Place; FRANKLIN; *233 G-13; mail Winchester z 37398; ● 150
Drop; RMC Place; DEKALB; *233 D-14; elev. 971ft./296m.; mail Sparta z 38583; rural
Drummonds (Poplar Grove); RMC Place; TIPTON; 232 E-2; elev. 436ft./133m.; 🅿; z 38023; ● 500
Dry Branch; RMC Place; HANCOCK; *233 J-16; elev. 1,200ft./366m.; mail Sneedville z 37869; rural
Dry Creek; RMC Place; WASHINGTON; *233 K-18; ★ JNSC-; mail Jonesborough z 37659; ● 30
Dry Hill; RMC Place; JOHNSON; *233 K-19; mail Butler z 37640; rural
Dry Hill; RMC Place; LAUDERDALE; *232 D-3; elev. 508ft./155m.; mail Halls z 38040; rural
Dry Hollow; RMC Place; SULLIVAN; ★ JNSC-; mail Kingsport z 37660; pop. incl. with Kingsport (Inc. Place)
Duck Creek; RMC Place; HANCOCK; *233 J-16; elev. 1,534ft./468m.; mail Sneedville z 37869; rural
Duck River; RMC Place; HICKMAN; 232 E-9; elev. 537ft./164m.; 🅿; z 38454; rural
Ducktown; Inc. Place; POLK; 233 G-18; elev. 1,800ft./549m.; 🅿; z 37326; Ⓟ 421; Ⓒ 427
Ducktown; RMC Place; WASHINGTON; *233 K-17; ★ JNSC-; mail Limestone z 37681; ● 60
Dudney Hill; RMC Place; JACKSON; *233 B-14; mail Gainesboro z 38562; rural
Due West; RMC Place; DAVIDSON; ★ NASH; mail Madison z 37115; pop. incl. with Nashville (Inc. Place)
Duff; RMC Place; CAMPBELL; 233 B-19; elev. 1,500ft./457m.; 🅿; z 37729; ● 180
Dukedom; RMC Place; WEAKLEY; 232 B-5; elev. 487ft./148m.; 🅿; z 38226; total pop., including Dukedom, KY, 130; ● 80
Dulaney; RMC Place; GREENE; *233 L-17; elev. 1,358ft./414m.; mail Greeneville z 37743
Dull; RMC Place; DICKSON; *232 C-9; elev. 753ft./230m.; mail Charlotte z 37036; ● 30
Dumplin; RMC Place; JEFFERSON; *233 D-20; elev. 989ft./301m.; ★ KNOX; mail New Market z 37820; rural
Dunbar; RMC Place; DECATUR; *232 F-7; elev. 538ft./164m.; mail Bath Springs z 38311; rural
Duncantown; RMC Place; FRANKLIN; *233 F-13; mail Estill Springs z 37330; rural
Dunlap; Inc. Place; ⊡ SEQUATCHIE; 233 F-15; elev. 722ft./220m.; 🅿; z 37327; Ⓟ 3,731; Ⓒ 4,173
Dunn (Nucarbon); RMC Place; LAWRENCE; *232 G-9; mail Leoma z 38468; pop. incl. with Lawrenceburg (Inc. Place)
Duplex; RMC Place; WILLIAMSON; *233 E-11; mail Franklin z 37064
Dupont; RMC Place; SEVIER; 214 G-3; elev. 1,079ft./329m.; ★ KNOX; mail Seymour z 37865; ● 50
Dupontonia; DAVIDSON; see Lakewood (Inc. Place)
Durhamville; RMC Place; LAUDERDALE; 232 E-3; elev. 334ft./102m.; mail Ripley z 38063; ● 80
Dutch; RMC Place; GRAINGER; *233 B-20; mail Washburn z 37888; ● 30
Dutch Valley; RMC Place; ANDERSON; *233 C-18; ★ KNOX; mail Clinton z 37716; rural
Dycus; JACKSON; see Milltown (RMC Place)
Dyer; Inc. Place; GIBSON; 232 C-4; elev. 360ft./110m.; 🅿; z 38330; Ⓟ 2,204; Ⓒ 2,406
DYER; 232 C-3; Ⓟ 34,854; Ⓒ 37,279; ◆ 37,471
Dyersburg; Inc. Place; ⊡ DYER; 232 C-3; elev. 295ft./90m.; 🅿 🅷 ■; z 38024-25; Ⓟ 16,317; Ⓒ 17,452; ◆ 17,337
Dykes Crossroads; RMC Place; CUMBERLAND; *233 D-16; mail Crossville z 38571; rural
Dyllis; RMC Place; ROANE; 233 D-18; ★ KNOX; mail Harriman z 37748, Oliver Springs z 37840; ● 80
Dyson Grove; RMC Place; JOHNSON; *233 K-20; elev. 2,082ft./635m.; mail Butler z 37640; rural

E

Eads; RMC Place; SHELBY; 232 F-2; elev. 340ft./104m.; 🅿; ★ MEM; z 38028; ● 310
Eagan; RMC Place; CLAIBORNE; 233 B-19; elev. 1,094ft./333m.; 🅿; z 37730; ● 200
Eagle Creek; RMC Place; BENTON; *232 D-7; mail Holladay z 38341; rural
Eagle Furnace; RMC Place; ROANE; *233 D-17; ★ KNOX; mail Rockwood z 37854; rural
Eagleton Village; CDP; BLOUNT; *233 D-19; ★ KNOX; mail Maryville z 37804; Ⓟ 5,169; Ⓒ 4,883
Eagleville; Inc. Place; RUTHERFORD; 233 E-11; elev. 800ft./244m.; 🅿; z 37060; Ⓟ 462; Ⓒ 464
Earleyville; RMC Place; WARREN; *233 E-14; elev. 1,040ft./317m.; mail Mc Minnville z 37110; rural
East; RMC Place; DAVIDSON; ★ NASH; mail Nashville z 37206; pop. incl. with Nashville (Inc. Place)
East; RMC Place; SHELBY; ★ MEM; mail Memphis z 38111, z 38114; pop. incl. with Memphis (Inc. Place)
East Acres; RMC Place; SHELBY; *232 F-2; elev. 300ft./91m.; ★ MEM; mail Millington z 38053; ● 550
East Brainerd; CDP; HAMILTON; *233 G-16; elev. 900ft./274m.; ★ CHTN; mail Chattanooga z 37421; Ⓟ 11,594; Ⓒ 14,132
Eastbrook; RMC Place; FRANKLIN; *233 F-13; mail Estill Springs z 37330
East Chattanooga; RMC Place; HAMILTON; *233 G-15; ★ CHTN; mail Chattanooga z 37406; pop. incl. with Chattanooga (Inc. Place)
East Cleveland; CDP; BRADLEY; *233 G-17; ★ CLEV; mail Cleveland z 37311; Ⓟ 1,249; Ⓒ 1,729
East Cyruston; RMC Place; LINCOLN; *233 G-11; elev. 640ft./195m.; mail Fayetteville z 37334; rural
East Due West; RMC Place; DAVIDSON; ★ NASH; mail Madison z 37115; pop. incl. with Nashville (Inc. Place)
Easter Seal; RMC Place; WILSON; *233 C-12; ★ NASH; mail Mount Juliet z 37122; summer pop. 100
East Etowah; RMC Place; MCMINN; *233 F-18; mail Etowah z 37331; ● 600
East Fork; RMC Place; SEVIER; *233 D-20; mail Sevierville z 37876; rural
East Jamestown; RMC Place; FENTRESS; *233 B-17; elev. 1,720ft./524m.; mail Jamestown z 38556; rural
East Junction; RMC Place; SHELBY; *232 G-1; ★ MEM; mail Memphis z 38101; pop. incl. with Memphis (Inc. Place)
East Lake; RMC Place; HAMILTON; 233 K-12; elev. 694ft./212m.; ★ CHTN; mail Chattanooga z 37407; pop. incl. with Chattanooga (Inc. Place)
Eastland; RMC Place; WHITE; *233 D-15; mail Sparta z 38583; ● 60
East Miller's Cove; RMC Place; BLOUNT; *233 D-20; elev. 1,100ft./335m.; mail Walland z 37886; rural
Eastport; RMC Place; PICKETT; *233 B-16; elev. 689ft./210m.; mail Monroe z 38573; ● 50
East Ridge; Inc. Place; HAMILTON; 233 G-16; elev. 800ft./244m.; 🅿 🅷; ★ CHTN; z 37412; Ⓟ 21,101; Ⓒ 20,640; ◆ 23,469
Eastside; CANNON; see Bluewing (RMC Place)
East Side; RMC Place; CARTER; *233 K-19; ★ JNSC-; mail Elizabethton z 37643; pop. incl. with Elizabethton (Inc. Place)
East Side; RMC Place; DICKSON; *232 C-10; elev. 800ft./244m.; mail Burns z 37029; rural
Eastside; RMC Place; SULLIVAN; ★ JNSC-; mail Kingsport z 37664; pop. incl. with Kingsport (Inc. Place)
Eastside; RMC Place; WARREN; *233 E-14; mail Rock Island z 38581; ● 220
East Springbrook; RMC Place; BLOUNT; *233 D-19; ★ KNOX; mail Alcoa z 37701; pop. incl. with Alcoa (Inc. Place)
East Sweetwater (Pumpkin Center); RMC Place; MONROE; *233 E-18; elev. 1,147ft./350m.; mail Sweetwater z 37874; ● 370
East Union; RMC Place; MADISON; *232 E-5; elev. 426ft./130m.; ★ JAC; mail Jackson z 38301; ● 150
Eastview; RMC Place; GREENE; *233 K-17; mail Greeneville z 37745; pop. incl. with Greeneville (Inc. Place)
Eastview; Inc. Place; MCNAIRY; 232 G-6; elev. 510ft./155m.; mail Ramer z 38367; Ⓟ 563; Ⓒ 618
East View; RMC Place; MEIGS; *233 F-16; mail Georgetown z 37336; ● 50
Eastwood; RMC Place; RUTHERFORD; *233 D-12; ★ NASH; mail La Vergne z 37086; pop. incl. with La Vergne (Inc. Place)
Eaton; RMC Place; GIBSON; 232 D-4; elev. 309ft./94m.; 🅿; z 38331; ● 130
Eaton Crossroad; RMC Place; LOUDON; 233 D-18; ★ KNOX; mail Lenoir City z 37771; ● 350
Eaton Forest; RMC Place; LOUDON; *233 D-18; ★ KNOX; mail Lenoir City z 37771; ● 100
Ebenezer; RMC Place; MARION; *233 G-14; mail Jasper z 37347; ● 30
Ebenezer; RMC Place; MONROE; *233 F-18; elev. 1,100ft./335m.; mail Englewood z 37329; rural
Echo Hills; RMC Place; GREENE; *233 K-17; mail Greeneville z 37743; ● 50
Eddie Hill; RMC Place; SMITH; *233 C-13; mail Lebanon z 37090; ● 100
Edenwold; RMC Place; DAVIDSON; *233 C-11; ★ NASH; mail Madison z 37115; pop. incl. with Nashville (Inc. Place)
Edgefield; RMC Place; SULLIVAN; *233 J-19; ★ JNSC-; mail Bristol z 37620; pop. incl. with Bristol (Inc. Place)
Edgemont; RMC Place; COCKE; 233 L-16; ★ MORR; mail Newport z 37821; ● 500
Edgemont; RMC Place; SULLIVAN; *233 J-19; ★ JNSC-; mail Bristol z 37620; pop. incl. with Bristol (Inc. Place)
Edgemoor; RMC Place; ANDERSON; 233 D-19; ★ KNOX; mail Clinton z 37716; ● 230
Edgewater; RMC Place; RHEA; *233 E-16; mail Dayton z 37321; pop. incl. with Dayton (Inc. Place)
Edgewater; RMC Place; WILSON; *233 C-12; ★ NASH; mail Mount Juliet z 37122; ● 450
Edgewood; RMC Place; DYER; *232 C-4; elev. 338ft./103m.; mail Newbern z 38059; ● 80
Edgewood; RMC Place; SULLIVAN; *233 J-18; ★ JNSC-; mail Kingsport z 37660; pop. incl. with Kingsport (Inc. Place)
Edgewood Acres; RMC Place; BLOUNT; *233 D-19; ★ KNOX; mail Maryville z 37804; ● 100
Edgewood Heights; RMC Place; ANDERSON; *233 C-19; ★ KNOX; mail Powell z 37849; ● 50
Edison; RMC Place; GIBSON; *232 D-5; mail Humboldt z 38343, Trenton z 38382; ● 30
Edith; RMC Place; LAUDERDALE; 232 D-3; elev. 507ft./155m.; mail Ripley z 38063; ● 170
Edward Grove; RMC Place; HAYWOOD; *232 E-3; elev. 390ft./119m.; mail Ripley z 38063; rural
Edwards Point; RMC Place; HAMILTON; *233 G-15; ★ CHTN; mail Signal Mountain z 37377; ● 30
Edwina; RMC Place; COCKE; *233 L-16; ★ MORR; mail Newport z 37821; ● 50
Egam; RMC Place; LINCOLN; *233 G-11; mail Fayetteville z 37334; rural
Egypt; RMC Place; SHELBY; *232 F-2; elev. 306ft./93m.; ★ MEM; mail Memphis z 38128; pop. incl. with Memphis (Inc. Place)
Eidson; RMC Place; HAWKINS; *233 J-16; elev. 1,523ft./464m.; 🅿; z 37731; ● 50
Elba; RMC Place; FAYETTE; *232 G-3; elev. 396ft./121m.; mail Rossville z 38066; rural
Elbethel; RMC Place; BEDFORD; 233 E-12; elev. 758ft./231m.; mail Shelbyville z 37160; ● 200
Elbridge; RMC Place; OBION; 232 C-4; elev. 426ft./130m.; mail Obion z 38240; ● 100
Elgin (Rugby Road); RMC Place; SCOTT; 233 B-17; elev. 1,414ft./431m.; 🅿; z 37732-33; ● 250
Elizabeth; RMC Place; CROCKETT; *232 D-4; mail Friendship z 38034; ● 30
Elizabethton; Inc. Place; ⊡ CARTER; 233 K-19; elev. 1,530ft./466m.; 🅿 🅷 ■; ★ JNSC-; z 37643-44; Ⓟ 11,931; Ⓒ 13,372; ◆ 13,344
Elkhead; RMC Place; GRUNDY; *233 F-14; elev. 1,100ft./335m.; mail Pelham z 37366; ● 30
Elkhorn; RMC Place; HENRY; 232 B-7; mail Paris z 38242, Springville z 38256; ● 30
Elk Mills; RMC Place; CARTER; 233 K-19; elev. 1,994ft./608m.; mail Butler z 37640; ● 30
Elk Mill Village; RMC Place; LINCOLN; *233 G-12; mail Fayetteville z 37334; pop. incl. with Fayetteville (Inc. Place)
Elkmont; RMC Place; SEVIER; 233 E-20; mail Gatlinburg z 37738; ● 100
Elkmont Springs; RMC Place; GILES; *233 G-11; mail Ardmore z 38449; pop. incl. with Ardmore (Inc. Place)
Elkton; Inc. Place; GILES; 233 G-11; elev. 666ft./203m.; 🅿; z 38455; Ⓟ 448; Ⓒ 510
Elk Valley; RMC Place; CAMPBELL; 233 B-18; elev. 1,117ft./340m.; mail Pioneer z 37847; ● 180
Ellejoy; RMC Place; BLOUNT; *233 D-20; ★ KNOX; mail Seymour z 37865; rural
Ellendale; RMC Place; SHELBY; 232 F-2; elev. 321ft./98m.; 🅿; ★ MEM; z 38029; pop. incl. with Bartlett (Inc. Place)
Ellington Park; RMC Place; WILLIAMSON; *233 D-11; elev. 680ft./207m.; ★ NASH; mail Franklin z 37064; ● 200
Ellis Mills; RMC Place; HOUSTON; *232 B-9; elev. 459ft./140m.; mail Cumberland City z 37050; rural
Ellisville; RMC Place; TIPTON; *232 F-2; ★ MEM; mail Atoka z 38004, Trezevant z 38258; rural
Elm Grove; RMC Place; TIPTON; *232 E-2; mail Burlison z 38015; rural
Elmore Park; SHELBY; see Shelby Center (RMC Place)
Elm Springs; RMC Place; GRAINGER; *233 B-20; elev. 1,400ft./427m.; mail Washburn z 37888; rural
Elmwood; RMC Place; SMITH; 233 C-14; elev. 506ft./154m.; 🅿; z 38560; ● 150
Elora; RMC Place; LINCOLN; 233 G-12; elev. 926ft./282m.; 🅿; z 37328; ● 400
Elverton; RMC Place; ROANE; *233 D-18; elev. 835ft./255m.; ★ KNOX; mail Harriman z 37748; rural
Elza; RMC Place; ANDERSON; 233 C-19; ★ KNOX; mail Oak Ridge z 37830; ● 40
Embreeville; RMC Place; WASHINGTON; 233 K-18; ★ JNSC-; mail Erwin z 37650; ● 200
Embreeville Junction; WASHINGTON; see Y Section (RMC Place)
Emerald Acres; RMC Place; HAMBLEN; *233 K-15; ★ MORR; mail Morristown z 37814; ● 400
Emerts Cove; RMC Place; SEVIER; mail Sevierville z 37862; pop. incl. with Pittman Center (Inc. Place)
Emery Mill; RMC Place; BLEDSOE; *233 E-16; elev. 1,599ft./487m.; mail Pikeville z 37367; rural
Emmett; RMC Place; SULLIVAN; 234 K-6; ★ JNSC-; mail Bristol z 37620; ● 30
Emory Gap; RMC Place; ROANE; *233 D-17; ★ KNOX; mail Harriman z 37748; pop. incl. with Harriman (Inc. Place)
Emory Heights; RMC Place; ROANE; *233 D-18; ★ KNOX; mail Harriman z 37748
Englewood; Inc. Place; MCMINN; 233 F-18; elev. 869ft./265m.; 🅿; z 37329; Ⓟ 1,611; Ⓒ 1,590
Englewood; RMC Place; OBION; *232 B-4; elev. 444ft./135m.; mail Troy z 38260; rural
English Mountain Resort; RMC Place; SEVIER; *233 M-15; elev. 2,476ft./755m.; mail Sevierville z 37876; ● 160
Enigma; RMC Place; SMITH; *233 C-14; mail Buffalo Valley z 38548, Elmwood z 38560; rural
Eno; RMC Place; DICKSON; *232 C-9; mail Dickson z 37055; rural
Enon; RMC Place; MACON; *233 A-13; mail Red Boiling Springs z 37150; rural
Ensley; RMC Place; SHELBY; pop. incl. with Memphis (Inc. Place)
Ensor; RMC Place; PUTNAM; *233 C-14; mail Baxter z 38544; pop. incl. with Baxter (Inc. Place)
Enterprise; RMC Place; HAWKINS; *233 K-17; elev. 1,246ft./380m.; mail Rogersville z 37857; rural
Enterprise; RMC Place; MAURY; 232 E-10; mail Mount Pleasant z 38474; ● 75
Enville; Inc. Place; CHESTER, MCNAIRY; 232 F-6; elev. 427ft./130m.; 🅿; z 38332; Ⓟ 211; Ⓒ 230
Epperson; RMC Place; MONROE; *233 F-18; mail Tellico Plains z 37385; rural
Erasmus; RMC Place; CUMBERLAND; *233 D-16; mail Crossville z 38555; rural
Erie; RMC Place; LOUDON; *233 E-17; elev. 935ft./285m.; mail Philadelphia z 37846; ● 50
Erin; Inc. Place; ⊡ HOUSTON; 232 B-8; elev. 492ft./150m.; 🅿 🅷; z 37061; Ⓟ 1,586; Ⓒ 1,490
Erlanger; RMC Place; HAMILTON; ★ CHTN; mail Chattanooga z 37403; pop. incl. with Chattanooga (Inc. Place)
Ernestville; RMC Place; UNICOI; 233 L-18; mail Erwin z 37650; ● 50
Erwin; Inc. Place; ⊡ UNICOI; 233 L-18; elev. 1,675ft./511m.; 🅿 🅷; z 37650; Ⓟ 5,015; Ⓒ 5,610
Essary Springs; RMC Place; HARDEMAN; *232 G-5; mail Pocahontas z 38061; rural
Estes Kefauver; RMC Place; WASHINGTON; ★ JNSC-; mail Johnson City z 37601; pop. incl. with Johnson City (Inc. Place)
Estes Woods; RMC Place; RHEA; *233 E-17; elev. 751ft./229m.; mail Spring City z 37381; rural
Estill Springs; Inc. Place; FRANKLIN; 233 F-13; elev. 945ft./288m.; 🅿; z 37330; Ⓟ 1,408; Ⓒ 2,152
Ethridge; Inc. Place; LAWRENCE; 232 F-9; elev. 995ft./303m.; 🅿; z 38456; Ⓟ 565; Ⓒ 536
Etowah; Inc. Place; MCMINN; 233 F-18; elev. 807ft./246m.; 🅿 🅷; z 37331; Ⓟ 3,815; Ⓒ 3,663
Etter; RMC Place; PICKETT; *233 B-16; mail Byrdstown z 38549; rural
Eucebia; RMC Place; BLOUNT; *233 D-20; elev. 1,000ft./305m.; ★ KNOX; mail Seymour z 37865; rural
Eulia; RMC Place; MACON; *233 B-13; mail Westmoreland z 37186; rural
Eureka; RMC Place; BRADLEY; *233 F-17; ★ CLEV; mail Cleveland z 37323; rural
Eureka; RMC Place; HARDIN; *232 F-7; mail Savannah z 38372; ● 100
Eureka; RMC Place; ROANE; *233 D-17; elev. 760ft./232m.; ★ KNOX; mail Rockwood z 37854; ● 110
Eurekaton; RMC Place; HAYWOOD; *232 F-4; mail Whiteville z 38075; ● 30
Eva; RMC Place; BENTON; 232 C-7; elev. 395ft./120m.; 🅿; z 38333; ● 300
Evanston (Camps); RMC Place; HANCOCK; *233 J-16; mail Sneedville z 37869; ● 90
Evansville; RMC Place; DYER; 232 C-3; elev. 276ft./84m.; mail Dyersburg z 38024; pop. incl. with Dyersburg (Inc. Place)
Evensville; RMC Place; RHEA; 233 E-16; elev. 754ft./230m.; 🅿; z 37332; ● 350
Evergreen; RMC Place; CARTER; *233 K-19; mail Roan Mountain z 37687; rural
Evins Mill; RMC Place; DEKALB; *233 D-14; elev. 913ft./278m.; mail Smithville z 37166; rural
Ewingville; RMC Place; WILLIAMSON; *233 D-11; ★ NASH; mail Franklin z 37064; pop. incl. with Franklin (Inc. Place)
Excell; RMC Place; MONTGOMERY; *232 B-10; elev. 590ft./180m.; ★ CLRKV; mail Clarksville z 37040; rural
Executive Estates; RMC Place; LAWRENCE; *232 F-9; elev. 900ft./274m.; mail Lawrenceburg z 38464; ● 50

F

Factory; RMC Place; WAYNE; *232 F-8; mail Waynesboro z 38485; rural
Fair Acres; RMC Place; HICKMAN; *232 D-10; mail Bon Aqua z 37025; ● 100
Fair Acres; RMC Place; SULLIVAN; *233 J-18; ★ JNSC-; mail Kingsport z 37660; pop. incl. with Kingsport (Inc. Place)
Fairfax Heights; RMC Place; HAMILTON; ★ CHTN; pop. incl. with Chattanooga (Inc. Place)
Fairfield; RMC Place; BEDFORD; 233 E-12; elev. 843ft./257m.; mail Wartrace z 37183; ● 40
Fairfield; RMC Place; HICKMAN; 232 D-9; mail Centerville z 37033, Crossville z 38555, z 38558; pop. incl. with Centerville (Inc. Place)
Fairfield; RMC Place; SUMNER; *233 A-12; elev. 814ft./248m.; mail Westmoreland z 37186; rural
Fairfield Acres; RMC Place; HAMBLEN; ★ MORR; mail Morristown z 37814
Fairfield Glade; CDP; CUMBERLAND; 233 D-17; elev. 1,966ft./599m.; 🅿; z 38555 & mail Crossville z 38558; Ⓟ 2,209; Ⓒ 4,885
Fair Garden; RMC Place; SEVIER; *233 D-20; elev. 1,111ft./339m.; mail Sevierville z 37876; rural
Fairgrounds; RMC Place; BEDFORD; mail Shelbyville z 37160; pop. incl. with Shelbyville (Inc. Place)
Fairlane Estates; RMC Place; BEDFORD; *233 E-12; mail Shelbyville z 37160; pop. incl. with Shelbyville (Inc. Place)
Fairmont; HAMILTON; see Fairmount (CDP)
Fairmont; RMC Place; SULLIVAN; *233 J-19; ★ JNSC-; mail Bristol z 37620; pop. incl. with Bristol (Inc. Place)
Fairmount (Fairmont); CDP; HAMILTON; *233 G-15; elev. 2,000ft./610m.; ★ CHTN; mail Signal Mountain z 37377; Ⓟ 1,578; Ⓒ 2,600
Fairview; RMC Place; BLOUNT; *233 E-19; ★ KNOX; mail Maryville z 37803; pop. incl. with Maryville (Inc. Place)
Fairview; RMC Place; BRADLEY; 233 F-17; ★ CLEV; mail Cleveland z 37312; pop. incl. with Cleveland (Inc. Place)
Fairview; RMC Place; CARROLL; *232 C-6; mail Mc Kenzie z 38201; rural
Fairview; RMC Place; CARTER; *233 K-19; mail Hampton z 37658; pop. incl. with Elizabethton (Inc. Place)
Fairview; RMC Place; CLAY; *233 B-15; elev. 1,002ft./305m.; mail Allons z 38541; rural
Fairview; RMC Place; COFFEE; *233 F-13; mail Normandy z 37360; rural
Fairview; RMC Place; FENTRESS; *233 B-16; elev. 821ft./250m.; mail Jamestown z 38556; rural
Fairview; RMC Place; GREENE; *233 K-17; mail Afton z 37616; rural
Fairview; RMC Place; LAWRENCE; *232 G-9; mail Loretto z 38469; rural
Fair View; RMC Place; LINCOLN; *233 G-11; mail Fayetteville z 37334; rural
Fairview; RMC Place; MACON; *233 B-13; elev. 1,035ft./315m.; mail Hartsville z 37074, Westmoreland z 37186; rural
Fairview; MADISON; see Three Way (Inc. Place)
Fairview; RMC Place; MCMINN; *233 F-17; elev. 1,000ft./305m.; mail Athens z 37303; rural
Fairview; RMC Place; MEIGS; *233 E-17; elev. 788ft./240m.; mail Decatur z 37322; rural
Fairview; RMC Place; PICKETT; *233 B-16; mail Byrdstown z 38549; rural
Fairview; RMC Place; ROANE; 234 N-9; elev. 783ft./239m.; mail Kingston z 37763; ● 30
Fairview; RMC Place; SCOTT; 233 B-18; mail Huntsville z 37756; ● 170
Fairview; RMC Place; STEWART; *232 B-8; mail Dover z 37058; rural
Fairview; RMC Place; WARREN; *233 E-14; elev. 1,002ft./305m.; mail Mc Minnville z 37110; ● 90
Fairview; RMC Place; WASHINGTON; 234 N-1; elev. 1,583ft./482m.; ★ JNSC-; mail Jonesborough z 37659; ● 30
Fairview; RMC Place; WAYNE; *232 G-8; mail Iron City z 38463; ● 400
Fairview; RMC Place; WHITE; *233 D-14; mail Sparta z 38583; ● 90
Fairview (Jingo); Inc. Place; WILLIAMSON; 232 D-10; elev. 821ft./250m.; 🅿; ★ NASH; z 37062; Ⓟ 4,210; Ⓒ 5,800
Fairview Heights; RMC Place; JEFFERSON; *233 D-20; elev. 1,071ft./326m.; ★ KNOX; mail Dandridge z 37725; ● 30
Fairview Heights; RMC Place; WILLIAMSON; *232 D-10; ★ NASH; mail Fairview z 37062; pop. incl. with Fairview (Inc. Place)
Fairyland; RMC Place; CUMBERLAND; *233 D-16; elev. 1,900ft./579m.; mail Crossville z 38572; ● 200
Faix; RMC Place; PICKETT; *233 B-16; mail Byrdstown z 38549; rural
Falcon; RMC Place; MCNAIRY; *232 G-6; elev. 433ft./132m.; mail Selmer z 38375
Fall Branch; CDP; WASHINGTON, GREENE; 233 K-17; elev. 1,499ft./457m.; 🅿; ★ JNSC-; z 37656; Ⓟ 1,203; Ⓒ 1,313
Fall Creek; RMC Place; BEDFORD; *233 E-12; elev. 750ft./229m.; mail Shelbyville z 37160; rural
Falling Water; RMC Place; HAMILTON; *233 F-15; ★ CHTN; mail Hixson z 37343; ● 500
Fall River; RMC Place; LAWRENCE; *232 G-10; mail Leoma z 38468; ● 30
Falls Mill; RMC Place; FRANKLIN; *233 G-12; mail Belvidere z 37306; rural
Fanchers Mills; RMC Place; WHITE; *233 D-14; elev. 877ft./267m.; mail Sparta z 38583; rural
Fancy Meadows; RMC Place; JEFFERSON; *233 C-20; elev. 890ft./271m.; ★ KNOX; mail Strawberry Plains z 37871; ● 90
Farmers Exchange; RMC Place; HICKMAN; *232 E-8; mail Hohenwald z 38462; rural
Farmers Valley; RMC Place; PERRY; *232 E-8; elev. 700ft./213m.; mail Linden z 37096; rural
Farmington; RMC Place; MARSHALL; 233 E-11; mail Lewisburg z 37091; ● 50
Farmington; RMC Place; WILLIAMSON; *233 D-11; ★ NASH; mail Franklin z 37064; ● 100
Farner; RMC Place; POLK; 233 G-18; elev. 1,544ft./471m.; 🅿; z 37333; ● 200
Farragut; Inc. Place; KNOX, LOUDON; 233 D-19; elev. 900ft./274m.; 🅿; ★ KNOX; z 37933-34 & mail Knoxville z 37922; Ⓟ 12,793; Ⓒ 17,720; ◆ 21,030
Farris Chapel; RMC Place; FRANKLIN; *233 G-13; mail Winchester z 37398; rural
Farrport; RMC Place; BLOUNT; *233 D-19; ★ KNOX; mail Alcoa z 37701; pop. incl. with Alcoa (Inc. Place)
Faulkner Springs; RMC Place; WARREN; *233 E-14; mail Mc Minnville z 37110; rural
Faxon; RMC Place; BENTON; 232 C-7; elev. 399ft./122m.; mail Big Sandy z 38221; ● 60
FAYETTE; 232 F-3; Ⓟ 25,559; Ⓒ 28,806; Ⓡ 28,796; ◆ 39,749
Fayette Corners; RMC Place; FAYETTE; *232 F-4; elev. 424ft./129m.; mail Whiteville z 38075; rural
Fayetteville; Inc. Place; ⊡ LINCOLN; 233 G-12; elev. 717ft./219m.; 🅿 🅷; z 37334; Ⓟ 6,921; Ⓒ 6,994
Fellowship; RMC Place; WILSON; *233 C-12; mail Mount Juliet z 37122; rural
FENTRESS; 233 B-16; Ⓟ 14,669; Ⓒ 16,625; ◆ 17,452
Fernvale; RMC Place; WILLIAMSON; *232 D-10; ★ NASH; mail Franklin z 37064; rural
Fernwood; RMC Place; HAMBLEN; *233 L-16; ★ MORR; mail Morristown z 37814; rural
Few Chapel; RMC Place; HUMPHREYS; *232 C-9; mail Mc Ewen z 37101; ● 30
Fielden Store; RMC Place; JEFFERSON; *233 C-20; mail New Market z 37820; rural
Fincastle; RMC Place; CAMPBELL; 233 B-19; ★ KNOX; mail La Follette z 37766; ● 130
Findlay; RMC Place; WHITE; *233 D-15; elev. 971ft./296m.; mail Sparta z 38583; pop. incl. with Sparta (Inc. Place)
Finger; Inc. Place; MCNAIRY; 232 F-6; elev. 431ft./131m.; 🅿; z 38334; Ⓟ 279; Ⓒ 350
Finley; RMC Place; DYER; 232 C-3; elev. 284ft./87m.; 🅿; z 38030; ● 1,000
Fisherville; RMC Place; SHELBY; 232 F-2; 🅿; ★ MEM; z 38017 & mail Collierville z 38027, Eads z 38028; ● 80
Fishery; RMC Place; UNICOI; 233 K-18; mail Erwin z 37650; ● 100
Fish Springs; RMC Place; CARTER; *233 K-19; mail Butler z 37640, Hampton z 37658; ● 30
Fisk University; RMC Place; DAVIDSON; ★ NASH; mail Nashville z 37203; pop. incl. with Nashville (Inc. Place)
Five Points; RMC Place; GILES; *232 G-10; elev. 700ft./213m.; mail Pulaski z 38478; rural
Five Points; RMC Place; LAWRENCE; 232 G-9; elev. 870ft./265m.; 🅿; z 38457; ● 170
Five Points; RMC Place; MADISON; *232 E-5; elev. 422ft./129m.; mail Pinson z 38366; ● 50
Five Points; RMC Place; RHEA; *233 F-16; mail Dayton z 37321; ● 50
Flag Branch; RMC Place; GREENE; *233 L-17; elev. 1,319ft./402m.; mail Greeneville z 37743; rural
Flag Pond; RMC Place; UNICOI; 233 L-18; elev. 2,038ft./621m.; 🅿; z 37657; ● 150
Flat Branch Junction; RMC Place; GRUNDY; *233 F-14; elev. 1,900ft./579m.; mail Tracy City z 37387; rural
Flat Creek; RMC Place; BEDFORD; 233 F-12; mail Shelbyville z 37160; ● 200
Flat Creek; RMC Place; OVERTON; *233 B-15; mail Livingston z 38570; rural
Flat Gap; RMC Place; HANCOCK; *233 K-16; elev. 1,549ft./472m.; mail Thorn Hill z 37881; ● 50
Flatgap; RMC Place; JEFFERSON; *233 C-20; ★ KNOX; mail Jefferson City z 37760; pop. incl. with Jefferson City (Inc. Place)
Flat Hollow; RMC Place; CAMPBELL; *233 B-19; elev. 1,200ft./366m.; mail Speedwell z 37870; rural
Flat Rock; RMC Place; MORGAN; *233 C-17; mail Deer Lodge z 37726; rural
Flat Rock; RMC Place; SMITH; *233 C-13; mail Lebanon z 37090; rural
Flattop; RMC Place; HAMILTON; *233 F-16; elev. 1,914ft./583m.; mail Soddy Daisy z 37379; rural
Flatwood; RMC Place; TIPTON; mail Burlison z 38015; pop. incl. with Gilt Edge (Inc. Place)
Flatwood; RMC Place; WARREN; *233 D-14; mail Mc Minnville z 37110; rural
Flatwoods; RMC Place; LAWRENCE; *232 F-9; mail Ethridge z 38456; rural
Flat Woods; RMC Place; PERRY; 232 E-8; elev. 400ft./122m.; 🅿; z 37096; ● 420
Flewellyn; RMC Place; ROBERTSON; *232 B-10; elev. 673ft./205m.; mail Springfield z 37172; ● 30
Flintville; RMC Place; LINCOLN; 233 G-12; elev. 893ft./272m.; 🅿; z 37335; ● 430
Flippin; RMC Place; LAUDERDALE; 232 D-3; elev. 362ft./110m.; mail Ripley z 38063; ● 50
Floraton; RMC Place; RUTHERFORD; *233 D-12; mail Readyville z 37149; rural
Florence; RMC Place; RUTHERFORD; *233 D-12; elev. 548ft./167m.; ★ NASH; mail Murfreesboro z 37129; rural
Flourville; RMC Place; WASHINGTON; 234 L-3; ★ JNSC-; mail Johnson City z 37601
Flowertown; RMC Place; COFFEE; *233 F-13; mail Normandy z 37360; pop. incl. with Tullahoma (Inc. Place)
Fly (New Flys Village); RMC Place; MAURY; *232 D-10; mail Santa Fe z 38482; ● 50
Flynns Lick; RMC Place; JACKSON; *233 B-14; mail Gainesboro z 38562; rural
Forbus; RMC Place; FENTRESS; 233 B-16; elev. 910ft./277m.; mail Pall Mall z 38577; ● 100
Ford; RMC Place; LOUDON; *233 D-18; elev. 931ft./284m.; ★ KNOX; mail Lenoir City z 37772; ● 400
Ford Chapel; RMC Place; CLAIBORNE; *233 B-20; mail New Tazewell z 37825; rural
Fordtown; RMC Place; CAMPBELL; ★ KNOX; mail La Follette z 37766
Fordtown; RMC Place; SULLIVAN; 233 J-18; elev. 1,469ft./448m.; ★ JNSC-; mail Kingsport z 37663; ● 1,900
Forest Chapel; RMC Place; SUMNER; *233 B-12; elev. 883ft./269m.; mail Westmoreland z 37186; rural
Forest Grove; RMC Place; DAVIDSON; *233 B-11; elev. 772ft./235m.; ★ NASH; mail Joelton z 37080; pop. incl. with Nashville (Inc. Place)
Forest Grove; RMC Place; MEIGS; *233 E-17; elev. 735ft./224m.; mail Decatur z 37322; rural
Forest Hill; RMC Place; BLOUNT; *233 E-19; ★ KNOX; mail Maryville z 37803; rural
Forest Hill; RMC Place; SHELBY; *232 G-2; elev. 366ft./112m.; ★ MEM; mail Germantown z 38139; pop. incl. with Germantown (Inc. Place)
Forest Hills; RMC Place; BEDFORD; *233 F-12; mail Shelbyville z 37160; pop. incl. with Shelbyville (Inc. Place)
Forest Hills; Inc. Place; DAVIDSON; 232 L-7; elev. 659ft./201m.; ★ NASH; mail Nashville z 37215; Ⓟ 4,231; Ⓒ 4,710
Forest Hills; RMC Place; KNOX; *233 D-19; ★ KNOX; mail Knoxville z 37919; pop. incl. with Knoxville (Inc. Place)
Forest Hills; RMC Place; SULLIVAN; *233 J-19; ★ JNSC-; mail Bristol z 37620; pop. incl. with Bristol (Inc. Place)
Forest Home; RMC Place; WILLIAMSON; *233 D-11; elev. 630ft./192m.; ★ NASH; mail Franklin z 37069; rural
Forest Home Farms; RMC Place; WILLIAMSON; *232 D-10; ★ NASH; mail Franklin z 37069; ● 100
Forest Mill; RMC Place; COFFEE; *233 E-13; elev. 1,139ft./347m.; mail Manchester z 37355; rural
Forge Ridge; RMC Place; CLAIBORNE; *233 A-20; mail Harrogate z 37752; ● 30
Forked Deer; RMC Place; HAYWOOD; *232 D-3; mail Gates z 38037; rural
Fork Mountain; RMC Place; ANDERSON; *233 C-18; mail Briceville z 37710; rural
Fork of Pike; RMC Place; DEKALB; *233 D-13; elev. 628ft./191m.; mail Liberty z 37095; rural
Fork Ridge; RMC Place; CLAIBORNE; *233 A-20; mail Middlesboro z 40965; rural
Forrest Park; RMC Place; COFFEE; *233 F-13; mail Tullahoma z 37388; pop. incl. with Tullahoma (Inc. Place)
Forsythe; RMC Place; SHELBY; ★ MEM; mail Memphis z 38101; pop. incl. with Memphis (Inc. Place)
Fort Cheatham; RMC Place; HAMILTON; *233 G-15; ★ CHTN; pop. incl. with Chattanooga (Inc. Place)
Fort Donelson Shores; RMC Place; STEWART; *232 B-8; mail Dover z 37058; ● 120
Fort Loudon Estates; RMC Place; LOUDON; *233 D-18; ★ KNOX; mail Lenoir City z 37772; ● 200
Fort Robinson; RMC Place; SULLIVAN; *233 J-18; ★ JNSC-; mail Kingsport z 37660; pop. incl. with Kingsport (Inc. Place)
Forty Forks; RMC Place; MCNAIRY; *232 F-6; elev. 560ft./171m.; mail Bethel Springs z 38315; ● 30
Fosterville; RMC Place; RUTHERFORD; 233 E-12; elev. 844ft./257m.; 🅿; z 37063; ● 220
Foundry Hill; RMC Place; HENRY; *232 B-6; mail Puryear z 38251; rural
Fountain City; RMC Place; KNOX; 233 L-13; ★ KNOX; mail Knoxville z 37918, z 37928, z 37938; pop. incl. with Knoxville (Inc. Place)
Fountain Creek; MAURY; see Campbells (RMC Place)
Fountain Head; RMC Place; SUMNER; 233 B-12; elev. 807ft./246m.; mail Portland z 37148; ● 380
Fountain Heights; RMC Place; MAURY; *232 E-10; mail Columbia z 38401; rural
Fourmile Board Hill; RMC Place; WAYNE; *232 F-8; mail Waynesboro z 38485; ● 50
Four Points; RMC Place; JEFFERSON; *233 C-20; ★ KNOX; mail New Market z 37820; rural
Fowler Grove; RMC Place; COCKE; *233 L-16; mail Bybee z 37713; rural
Fowlkes; RMC Place; DYER; 232 D-3; elev. 329ft./100m.; mail Dyersburg z 38024; ● 400
Fox Bluff; RMC Place; CHEATHAM; *232 B-10; elev. 406ft./124m.; ★ NASH; mail Ashland City z 37015; rural
Fox Branch; RMC Place; HANCOCK; *233 J-16; elev. 1,300ft./396m.; mail Sneedville z 37869; rural
Foxfire; RMC Place; CUMBERLAND; *233 D-16; elev. 1,900ft./579m.; mail Crossville z 38555; ● 200
Frankewing; RMC Place; GILES; 233 G-11; elev. 668ft./204m.; 🅿; z 38459; ● 100
Frankfort; RMC Place; MORGAN; *233 C-17; mail Lancing z 37770; rural
Franklin; Inc. Place; ⊡ WILLIAMSON; 233 D-11; elev. 648ft./198m.; 🅿 🅷; ★ NASH; z 37064-65, z 37067-69; Ⓟ 20,098; Ⓒ 41,842; ◆ 70,144
FRANKLIN; 233 G-13; Ⓟ 34,725; Ⓒ 39,270; ◆ 41,575
Franklin East; RMC Place; WILLIAMSON; *233 D-11; ★ NASH; mail Franklin z 37064; ● 60
Fraterville; RMC Place; ANDERSON; 233 C-19; ★ KNOX; mail Lake City z 37769; ● 200
Frayser; RMC Place; SHELBY; *232 F-1; ★ MEM; mail Memphis z 38127, z 38167; pop. incl. with Memphis (Inc. Place)
Fredonia; RMC Place; COFFEE; *233 E-13; elev. 1,061ft./323m.; mail Manchester z 37355; rural
Fredonia; RMC Place; HAYWOOD; 232 B-10; elev. 350ft./107m.; mail Mason z 38049, Stanton z 38069; ● 50
Fredonia; RMC Place; MONTGOMERY; *232 B-10; elev. 647ft./197m.; ★ CLRKV; mail Clarksville z 37040, z 37043; ● 50
Free Communion; RMC Place; OVERTON; *233 B-15; mail Monroe z 38573; rural
Free Hill; RMC Place; CLAY; 233 B-15; mail Celina z 38551; ● 120
Freeland; RMC Place; HENRY; *232 B-7; mail Buchanan z 38222; rural
Free State; RMC Place; JACKSON; *233 B-14; elev. 540ft./165m.; mail Gainesboro z 38562; rural
Freewill; RMC Place; JACKSON; *233 C-14; mail Gainesboro z 38562; rural
Fremont; RMC Place; OBION; *232 B-4; mail Union City z 38261; ● 70
French Broad; RMC Place; COCKE; *233 L-16; elev. 1,163ft./354m.; mail Del Rio z 37727; rural
Frettin; RMC Place; HARDEMAN; *232 G-5; elev. 382ft./116m.; mail Middleton z 38052; rural
Friendship; RMC Place; BLEDSOE; *233 E-16; elev. 1,910ft./582m.; mail Spring City z 37381; rural
Friendship; Inc. Place; CROCKETT, DYER; 232 D-4; elev. 403ft./123m.; 🅿; z 38034; Ⓟ 467; Ⓒ 608
Friendship; RMC Place; HAMILTON; ★ CHTN; mail Harrison z 37341
Friendship; RMC Place; HAWKINS; *233 K-16; mail Thorn Hill z 37881; ● 30
Friendship; RMC Place; SULLIVAN; *233 J-19; mail Bristol z 37620; ● 50
Friends Station; RMC Place; JEFFERSON; *233 C-20; mail New Market z 37820
Friendsville; Inc. Place; BLOUNT; 233 D-19; elev. 885ft./270m.; 🅿; ★ KNOX; z 37737; Ⓟ 792; Ⓒ 890
Frisco; RMC Place; HAWKINS; *233 J-17; elev. 1,338ft./408m.; ★ JNSC-; mail Church Hill z 37642; rural
Frog Jump (Gilliland); RMC Place; CROCKETT; *232 D-3; elev. 314ft./96m.; mail Halls z 38040; ● 250
Frog Jump; RMC Place; GIBSON; *232 D-4; mail Trenton z 38382; ● 30
Frog Level; RMC Place; HAWKINS; *233 J-16; mail Eidson z 37731; rural
Frog Pond; RMC Place; MACON; *233 B-13; elev. 948ft./289m.; mail Lafayette z 37083; rural
Front Street; RMC Place; SHELBY; ★ MEM; mail Memphis z 38103, z 38173; pop. incl. with Memphis (Inc. Place)
Frost; ANDERSON; see Frost Bottom (RMC Place)
Frost Bottom (Frost); RMC Place; ANDERSON; *233 C-18; ★ KNOX; mail Oliver Springs z 37840; rural
Fruitland; RMC Place; GIBSON; 232 D-5; elev. 376ft./115m.; mail Humboldt z 38343; ● 180
Fruitvale; RMC Place; CROCKETT; 232 D-4; elev. 353ft./108m.; 🅿; z 38336; ● 110
Fullens; GREENE; see Chuckey (RMC Place)
Fulton; RMC Place; LAUDERDALE; *232 E-2; mail Henning z 38041

G

Gabtown; RMC Place; WASHINGTON; *233 K-18; ★ JNSC-; mail Fall Branch z 37656; rural
Gadsden; Inc. Place; CROCKETT; 232 D-4; elev. 422ft./129m.; 🅿; z 38337; Ⓟ 561; Ⓒ 553
Gainesboro; Inc. Place; ⊡ JACKSON; 233 B-14; elev. 565ft./172m.; 🅿 🅷; z 38562; Ⓟ 1,002; Ⓒ 879
Gainsville; RMC Place; TIPTON; *232 F-3; elev. 350ft./107m.; mail Mason z 38049; rural
Gaitherville; RMC Place; LAWRENCE; 232 F-9; mail Lawrenceburg z 38464; pop. incl. with Lawrenceburg (Inc. Place)
Galaxy Heights; RMC Place; HAMILTON; *233 G-15; ★ CHTN; mail Hixson z 37343; pop. incl. with Chattanooga (Inc. Place)
Galbraith Springs; RMC Place; HAWKINS; *233 K-16; mail Mooresburg z 37811; rural
Galen; RMC Place; MACON; *233 B-13; elev. 930ft./283m.; mail Lafayette z 37083; ● 30
Gallatin; Inc. Place; ⊡ SUMNER; 233 B-12; elev. 526ft./160m.; 🅿 🅷; z 37066; Ⓟ 18,794; Ⓒ 23,230; ◆ 30,340

Entries in **UPPERCASE** are counties.
Entries in **bold** have populations of 2,500 or more.
Names in parentheses are alternate names.
Inc. Place — Incorporated Place
RMC Place — Rand McNally Designated Place
CDP — Census Designated Place
MCD — Minor Civil Division

⊡ County Seat
▲ Minor Civil Division
elev. Elevation
🅿 Post Office
🅷 Hospital
🅲 College
■ Principal Business Center
★ Ranally Metro Area (RMA) Abbreviation
z Zip Code(s)
Ⓟ Previous Census Population
Ⓡ Revised Census Population
Ⓐ Annexation Population
● Rand McNally Population Estimate
Ⓒ Final Census Population
Ⓢ Special Census Population
◆ Estimated Population

For additional definitions see Glossary, Volume 1, and Introduction, Volume 2.

Gallaway; Inc. Place; FAYETTE; 232 F-3; elev. 285ft./87m.; 🅿; ★ MEM; z 38036; Ⓟ 762; Ⓒ 666
Gandy; RMC Place; LAWRENCE; *232 F-9; mail Lawrenceburg z 38464; rural
Gann; RMC Place; GIBSON; *232 C-5; elev. 465ft./142m.; mail Milan z 38358; rural
Gapcreek; RMC Place; CARTER; *233 K-19; ★ JNSC-; mail Elizabethton z 37643; ● 50
Gap of the Ridge; RMC Place; MACON; *233 B-13; elev. 924ft./282m.; mail Lafayette z 37083; rural
Gardner; RMC Place; WEAKLEY; 232 B-5; mail Martin z 38237; ● 200
Garland; Inc. Place; TIPTON; 232 E-2; elev. 358ft./109m.; mail Covington z 38019; Ⓟ 194; Ⓒ 309; Ⓡ 328
Gassaway; RMC Place; CANNON; 233 D-13; 🅿; z 37095; ● 70
Gates; Inc. Place; LAUDERDALE; 232 D-3; elev. 308ft./94m.; 🅿; z 38037; Ⓟ 608; Ⓒ 901
Gath; RMC Place; WARREN; *233 D-14; mail Mc Minnville z 37110; ● 50
Gatlinburg; Inc. Place; SEVIER; 233 E-20; elev. 1,289ft./393m.; 🅿; z 37738; Ⓟ 3,417; Ⓒ 3,382
Gattistown; RMC Place; LINCOLN; *233 F-12; mail Mulberry z 37359; rural
Gause; RMC Place; ROBERTSON; *232 B-10; elev. 708ft./216m.; mail Chapmansboro z 37035; rural
Gay; RMC Place; WARREN; *233 E-14; mail Mc Minnville z 37110; ● 200
Gaylon Heights; RMC Place; HAMILTON; ★ CHTN; pop. incl. with Chattanooga (Inc. Place)
Gentry; RMC Place; PUTNAM; *233 C-14; mail Baxter z 38544; rural
Georgetown; RMC Place; GIBSON; *232 C-5; mail Trenton z 38382; ● 40
Georgetown; RMC Place; HAMILTON; *233 F-16; elev. 802ft./244m.; 🅿; ★ CHTN; z 37336; ● 200
Georgetown; RMC Place; MCMINN; *233 F-17; elev. 900ft./274m.; mail Riceville z 37370; rural
Georgia Crossing; RMC Place; FRANKLIN; *233 G-13; mail Winchester z 37398; rural
Germantown; RMC Place; DAVIDSON; *233 C-11; ★ NASH; mail Whites Creek z 37189; pop. incl. with Nashville (Inc. Place)
Germantown; Inc. Place; SHELBY; 232 G-2; elev. 370ft./113m.; 🅿 🅷 🅲 402; ★ MEM; z 38138-39, z 38183; Ⓟ 32,893; Ⓒ 37,348; ◆ 36,941
Gerren Heights; RMC Place; BLEDSOE; *233 E-16; mail Pikeville z 37367; rural
Gibbs; RMC Place; OBION; *232 B-4; mail Union City z 38261; pop. incl. with Union City (Inc. Place)
Gibbs Crossroads; RMC Place; MACON; *233 B-14; elev. 1,014ft./309m.; mail Pleasant Shade z 37145; rural
Gibson; Inc. Place; GIBSON; 232 D-5; elev. 393ft./120m.; 🅿; z 38338; Ⓟ 281; Ⓒ 305; Ⓡ 414
GIBSON; 232 C-4; Ⓟ 46,315; Ⓒ 48,152; Ⓡ 48,154; ◆ 49,194
Gibson Hall; RMC Place; CLAIBORNE; *233 B-20; mail Tazewell z 37879; ● 200
Gibsontown; RMC Place; SULLIVAN; *233 J-18; ★ JNSC-; mail Kingsport z 37660; pop. incl. with Kingsport (Inc. Place)
Gibson Wells; RMC Place; GIBSON; *232 D-4; mail Humboldt z 38343; ● 150
Gift; RMC Place; TIPTON; 232 E-3; elev. 328ft./100m.; ★ MEM; mail Covington z 38019; ● 100
Gilbreath; RMC Place; GREENE; *233 K-16; elev. 1,160ft./354m.; mail Mosheim z 37818; ● 50
Gilchrist; RMC Place; MCNAIRY; *232 F-6; elev. 480ft./146m.; mail Adamsville z 38310; ● 30
Gildfield; RMC Place; SHELBY; *232 F-2; ★ MEM; mail Arlington z 38002; rural
GILES; 232 F-10; Ⓟ 25,741; Ⓒ 29,447; ◆ 28,683
Gilfield; RMC Place; SULLIVAN; *233 J-18; ★ JNSC-; mail Piney Flats z 37686; ● 400
Gilliland; CROCKETT; see Frog Jump (RMC Place)
Gillises Mills; RMC Place; HARDIN; *232 G-7; mail Savannah z 38372; rural
Gilmore; RMC Place; MADISON; *232 E-5; ★ JAC; mail Jackson z 38301
Gilt Edge; Inc. Place; TIPTON; 232 E-2; elev. 300ft./91m.; 🅿; z 38015; Ⓟ 447; Ⓒ 489
Gin House Lake; RMC Place; TIPTON; *232 E-2; elev. 400ft./122m.; ★ MEM; mail Brighton z 38011; ● 50
Gladdice; RMC Place; JACKSON; *233 B-14; mail Gainesboro z 38562; rural
Glade Creek; RMC Place; PUTNAM; *233 D-15; mail Sparta z 38583; rural
Glades; RMC Place; MORGAN; *233 C-17; mail Deer Lodge z 37726
Glades; RMC Place; SEVIER; mail Gatlinburg z 37738; pop. incl. with Gatlinburg (Inc. Place)
Gladeville; RMC Place; WILSON; 233 C-12; elev. 595ft./181m.; 🅿; z 37071; ● 410
Glass; RMC Place; OBION; *232 C-4; elev. 324ft./99m.; mail Obion z 38240; ● 50
Gleason; Inc. Place; WEAKLEY; 232 C-6; elev. 409ft./125m.; 🅿; z 38229; Ⓟ 1,402; Ⓒ 1,463
Glen; RMC Place; COFFEE; *233 F-13; mail Hillsboro z 37342; rural
Glen Alice; RMC Place; ROANE; 233 D-17; ★ KNOX; mail Rockwood z 37854; ● 110
Glencliff; RMC Place; DAVIDSON; *233 C-11; ★ NASH; mail Nashville z 37211; pop. incl. with Nashville (Inc. Place)
Glendale; RMC Place; HAMILTON; ★ CHTN; mail Chattanooga z 37405; pop. incl. with Chattanooga (Inc. Place)
Glendale; RMC Place; LAWRENCE; *232 G-9; mail Loretto z 38469; rural
Glendale; RMC Place; LOUDON; *233 E-18; mail Greenback z 37742; rural
Glendale; RMC Place; MAURY; 232 E-10; elev. 643ft./196m.; mail Columbia z 38401; ● 70
Glendale; RMC Place; WASHINGTON; *233 K-18; elev. 1,700ft./518m.; ★ JNSC-; mail Limestone z 37681; ● 50
Glendale Estates; RMC Place; GILES; *232 G-10; mail Pulaski z 38478; pop. incl. with Pulaski (Inc. Place)
Glen Del Acres; RMC Place; HAMBLEN; *233 K-16; elev. 1,300ft./396m.; ★ MORR; mail Russellville z 37860; ● 180
Glenhaven; RMC Place; WILLIAMSON; *232 D-10; ★ NASH; mail Fairview z 37062; pop. incl. with Fairview (Inc. Place)
Glen Mary; RMC Place; SCOTT; *233 B-17; elev. 1,277ft./389m.; mail Robbins z 37852; ● 30
Glenmore Estates; RMC Place; BLOUNT; *233 D-19; ★ KNOX; mail Rockford z 37853; ● 300
Glen Oaks; RMC Place; WILSON; *233 C-12; ★ NASH; mail Mount Juliet z 37122; ● 420
Glenobey; RMC Place; FENTRESS; *233 B-16; mail Jamestown z 38556; rural
Glenview; RMC Place; DAVIDSON; *233 C-11; ★ NASH; mail Nashville z 37217; pop. incl. with Nashville (Inc. Place)
Glenwood; RMC Place; HAMILTON; *233 G-15; ★ CHTN; pop. incl. with Chattanooga (Inc. Place)
Glenwood; RMC Place; HUMPHREYS; *232 C-8; mail Waverly z 37185; rural
Glenwylde; RMC Place; DICKSON; *232 C-9; elev. 505ft./154m.; mail Cumberland Furnace z 37051; rural
Glimp; RMC Place; LAUDERDALE; *232 E-3; mail Henning z 38041
Glover; RMC Place; ROBERTSON; *232 B-10; mail Springfield z 37172; rural
Glover Hill; RMC Place; MARION; *233 G-14; mail Jasper z 37347; pop. incl. with Jasper (Inc. Place)
Glynnwood Lake; RMC Place; SHELBY; *232 G-2; ★ MEM; mail Eads z 38028; ● 160
Gnat Hill; RMC Place; COFFEE; *233 E-13; mail Manchester z 37355; rural
Goat City; RMC Place; GIBSON; *232 D-5; elev. 554ft./169m.; mail Medina z 38355; rural
Godwin; RMC Place; MAURY; *232 E-10; mail Columbia z 38401; rural
Goffton; RMC Place; PUTNAM; *233 C-15; mail Cookeville z 38501; rural
Goin; RMC Place; CLAIBORNE; *233 B-20; mail New Tazewell z 37825; rural
Golddust; RMC Place; LAUDERDALE; 232 D-2; elev. 248ft./76m.; mail Ripley z 38063; ● 30
Goldpoint; RMC Place; HAMILTON; ★ CHTN; mail Hixson z 37343; pop. incl. with Chattanooga (Inc. Place)
Goodbars; RMC Place; WARREN; *233 E-14; elev. 915ft./279m.; mail Rock Island z 38581; ● 70
Goodfield; RMC Place; MEIGS; *233 F-17; mail Decatur z 37322
Good Hope; RMC Place; CAMPBELL; *233 B-19; elev. 1,000ft./305m.; mail Jellico z 37762; rural
Good Hope; RMC Place; DYER; *232 C-4; mail Newbern z 38059; ● 100
Goodlettsville; Inc. Place; DAVIDSON, SUMNER; 233 B-11; elev. 509ft./155m.; 🅿 🅲 355 ■; ★ NASH; z 37070, z 37072; Ⓟ 11,219; Ⓒ 13,780; ◆ 17,482
Good Luck; RMC Place; GIBSON; *232 C-5; elev. 357ft./109m.; mail Rutherford z 38369; rural
Goodspring; RMC Place; GILES; 232 G-10; elev. 1,023ft./312m.; 🅿; z 38460; ● 100
Good Springs; RMC Place; MCMINN; 233 F-17; mail Etowah z 37331; ● 60
Goose Horn; RMC Place; MACON; 233 B-14; mail Red Boiling Springs z 37150, Whitleyville z 38588; ● 30
Gooseneck; RMC Place; ANDERSON; *233 C-19; ★ KNOX; mail Andersonville z 37705; rural
Gordon; RMC Place; GILES; *232 F-10; mail Pulaski z 38478; pop. incl. with Pulaski (Inc. Place)
Gordonsburg; RMC Place; LEWIS; *232 E-9; mail Hohenwald z 38462; rural
Gordonsville; Inc. Place; SMITH; 233 C-13; elev. 598ft./182m.; 🅿; z 38563; Ⓟ 891; Ⓒ 1,066
Gorman; RMC Place; HUMPHREYS; 232 C-8; elev. 628ft./191m.; mail Mc Ewen z 37101; ● 80
Goshen; RMC Place; HAWKINS; *233 J-17; mail Church Hill z 37642; ● 30
Gossburg; RMC Place; COFFEE; 233 E-13; mail Beechgrove z 37018; ● 30
Grabal; RMC Place; GIBSON; *232 D-5; mail Milan z 38358; rural
Graball; RMC Place; SUMNER; *233 B-12; mail Portland z 37148; rural
Graham; RMC Place; HICKMAN; *232 D-9; mail Nunnelly z 37137; rural
GRAINGER; 233 C-20; Ⓟ 17,095; Ⓒ 20,659; ◆ 22,801
Grammer Estates; RMC Place; WILLIAMSON; *232 D-10; ★ NASH; mail Fairview z 37062; pop. incl. with Fairview (Inc. Place)
Grand Junction; Inc. Place; HARDEMAN, FAYETTE; 232 G-4; elev. 575ft./175m.; 🅿; z 38039; Ⓟ 365; Ⓒ 301; Ⓡ 321
Grand Valley; RMC Place; HARDEMAN; *232 G-4; elev. 500ft./152m.; mail Saulsbury z 38067; summer pop. 300; ● 100
Grandview; RMC Place; GREENE; *233 K-17; mail Chuckey z 37641; rural
Grandview; RMC Place; KNOX; *233 D-20; ★ KNOX; mail Knoxville z 37920; ● 320
Grandview; RMC Place; RHEA; 233 E-17; 🅿; z 37337; ● 400
Grandview Estates; RMC Place; SEVIER; *233 D-20; ★ KNOX; mail Kodak z 37764; ● 200
Grandview Terrace; RMC Place; SULLIVAN; *233 J-19; ★ JNSC-; mail Bristol z 37620; ● 60
Granite; RMC Place; ANDERSON; *233 C-19; ★ KNOX; mail Clinton z 37716; rural
Grannys Branch; RMC Place; BENTON; *232 B-7; mail Big Sandy z 38221; rural
Grant; RMC Place; SMITH; 233 C-13; mail Gordonsville z 38563; ● 50
Grantsboro; RMC Place; CAMPBELL; *233 B-19; ★ KNOX; mail La Follette z 37766; rural
Granville; RMC Place; JACKSON; 233 C-14; elev. 524ft./160m.; 🅿; z 38564; ● 150
Grasshopper; RMC Place; HAMILTON; *233 F-16; ★ CHTN; mail Birchwood z 37308; rural
Grassland; RMC Place; WILLIAMSON; *233 D-11; elev. 700ft./213m.; ★ NASH; mail Franklin z 37064; ● 100
Grassy Cove; RMC Place; CUMBERLAND; *233 D-16; elev. 1,550ft./472m.; mail Crossville z 38572; ● 100
Grassy Creek; RMC Place; POLK; *233 G-18; mail Copperhill z 37317; rural
Grassy Fork; RMC Place; COCKE; *233 M-16; mail Hartford z 37753; rural
Grassy Valley; RMC Place; GREENE; *233 K-17; mail Greeneville z 37743; rural
Gratio; RMC Place; OBION; *232 C-3; mail Obion z 38240; ● 30
Gravel Hill; RMC Place; MCNAIRY; 232 G-6; mail Guys z 38339, Ramer z 38367, Selmer z 38375; ● 100
Gravel Hill; RMC Place; WASHINGTON; *233 K-18; mail Limestone z 37681; rural
Gravelly Hill; RMC Place; JEFFERSON; *233 C-20; elev. 1,298ft./396m.; mail Jefferson City z 37760; pop. incl. with Jefferson City (Inc. Place)
Graveltown; RMC Place; SMITH; *233 B-13; elev. 515ft./157m.; mail Pleasant Shade z 37145; ● 30
Graveston; RMC Place; KNOX; 233 C-20; ★ KNOX; mail Corryton z 37721; ● 50
Gray; CDP; WASHINGTON; 233 K-18; 🅿; ★ JNSC-; z 37615; Ⓟ 1,071; Ⓒ 1,273
Gray Acres; RMC Place; SULLIVAN; *233 J-19; ★ JNSC-; mail Bristol z 37620; ● 60
Gray's Bend; HICKMAN; see Graytown (RMC Place)
Graysville; Inc. Place; RHEA; 233 F-16; elev. 725ft./221m.; 🅿; z 37338; Ⓟ 1,301; Ⓒ 1,411
Graytown (Gray's Bend); RMC Place; HICKMAN; *232 D-9; mail Centerville z 37033; ● 30
Graywinds; RMC Place; WILSON; *233 C-12; ★ NASH; mail Mount Juliet z 37122; summer pop. 200
Greater Hendersonville; RMC Place; SUMNER; ★ NASH; pop. incl. with Hendersonville (Inc. Place)
Green Ack; RMC Place; ROANE; *233 C-18; ★ KNOX; mail Oliver Springs z 37840; ● 70
Green Acres; RMC Place; GILES; *232 G-10; mail Pulaski z 38478; pop. incl. with Pulaski (Inc. Place)
Green Acres; RMC Place; KNOX; *233 C-20; elev. 1,000ft./305m.; ★ KNOX; mail Knoxville z 37921; ● 120
Green Acres; RMC Place; ROANE; *233 D-18; elev. 780ft./238m.; ★ KNOX; mail Kingston z 37763; rural
Green Acres; RMC Place; SULLIVAN; *233 J-18; ★ JNSC-; mail Kingsport z 37660; pop. incl. with Kingsport (Inc. Place)
Greenback; Inc. Place; LOUDON; 233 E-19; elev. 902ft./275m.; 🅿; z 37742; Ⓟ 611; Ⓒ 954
Greenbriar; RMC Place; HOUSTON; *232 C-8; mail Waverly z 37185; summer pop. 100; ● 30
Greenbriar Village; RMC Place; CUMBERLAND; mail Crossville z 38572; pop. incl. with Crossville (Inc. Place)
Greenbrier; RMC Place; CHEATHAM; 232 C-10; elev. 664ft./202m.; mail Ashland City z 37015; ● 80
Green Brier; RMC Place; PICKETT; *233 A-16; mail Byrdstown z 38549; rural
Greenbrier; Inc. Place; ROBERTSON; 233 B-11; elev. 854ft./260m.; 🅿; ★ NASH; z 37073; Ⓟ 2,873; Ⓒ 4,940
Greenbrier; RMC Place; WILLIAMSON; *232 D-10; elev. 850ft./259m.; mail Franklin z 37064; rural
Greenbrier Lake; RMC Place; WILSON; *233 C-12; mail Lebanon z 37087; ● 50
GREENE; 233 K-17; Ⓟ 55,853; Ⓒ 62,909; ◆ 73,173
Greeneville; Inc. Place; ⊡ GREENE; 233 L-17; elev. 1,531ft./467m.; 🅿 🅷 🅲 2,923 ■; z 37743-45; Ⓟ 13,532; Ⓒ 15,198; ◆ 17,008
Greenfield; Inc. Place; WEAKLEY; 232 C-5; elev. 433ft./132m.; 🅿; z 38230; Ⓟ 2,105; Ⓒ 2,208
Greenfield Bend; RMC Place; MAURY; *232 E-9; elev. 540ft./165m.; mail Williamsport z 38487; rural
Greenfields; RMC Place; SULLIVAN; *233 J-18; ★ JNSC-; mail Kingsport z 37660; pop. incl. with Kingsport (Inc. Place)
Green Grove; RMC Place; MACON; *233 B-13; mail Hartsville z 37074; rural
Green Harbor; RMC Place; WILSON; *233 C-12; ★ NASH; mail Old Hickory z 37138; ● 1,000
Greenhaw; RMC Place; FRANKLIN; *233 F-13; mail Decherd z 37324; ● 30
Green Hill; RMC Place; JEFFERSON; *233 C-20; ★ KNOX; mail Dandridge z 37725; rural
Green Hill; RMC Place; WARREN; *233 D-14; mail Mc Minnville z 37110; ● 50
Green Hill; CDP; WILSON; 233 C-12; elev. 650ft./198m.; ★ NASH; mail Old Hickory z 37138; Ⓟ 6,763; Ⓒ 7,068
Green Hills; RMC Place; DAVIDSON; *233 C-11; ★ NASH; mail Nashville z 37215; pop. incl. with Nashville (Inc. Place)
Greenland; RMC Place; HAWKINS; *233 J-17; ★ JNSC-; mail Church Hill z 37642; pop. incl. with Church Hill (Inc. Place)
Green Meadow; RMC Place; BLOUNT; ★ KNOX; mail Alcoa z 37701; pop. incl. with Alcoa (Inc. Place)
Green Meadow; RMC Place; BRADLEY; *233 G-17; ★ CLEV; mail Cleveland z 37311
Green Meadows; RMC Place; FENTRESS; *233 B-16; mail Jamestown z 38556; ● 100
Green Pond; RMC Place; OVERTON; *233 C-16; mail Crawford z 38554; rural
Greens Crossroads; RMC Place; WARREN; *233 D-14; elev. 980ft./299m.; mail Mc Minnville z 37110; ● 60
Greens Mill; RMC Place; HAMILTON; *233 G-16; elev. 700ft./213m.; ★ CHTN; mail Hixson z 37343; ● 30
Greentown; RMC Place; MARION; *233 F-14; elev. 1,780ft./543m.; mail Tracy City z 37387; rural
Greenvale; RMC Place; WILSON; 233 D-13; elev. 762ft./232m.; mail Watertown z 37184; ● 80
Green Valley; RMC Place; KNOX; *233 D-19; ★ KNOX; mail Knoxville z 37919; pop. incl. with Knoxville (Inc. Place)
Green Valley; RMC Place; MACON; *233 A-13; elev. 740ft./226m.; mail Lafayette z 37083; rural
Green Valley; RMC Place; WILLIAMSON; *233 D-11; ★ NASH; mail Franklin z 37064; pop. incl. with Fairview (Inc. Place)
Green Valley; RMC Place; WILSON; *233 C-12; elev. 600ft./183m.; ★ NASH; mail Mount Juliet z 37122; ● 50
Green Village; RMC Place; HAWKINS; *233 J-17; ★ JNSC-; mail Church Hill z 37642; pop. incl. with Church Hill (Inc. Place)
Greenwood; RMC Place; MACON; *233 B-14; elev. 983ft./300m.; mail Red Boiling Springs z 37150; rural
Greenwood; RMC Place; RUTHERFORD; *233 E-11; elev. 820ft./250m.; mail College Grove z 37046; rural
Greenwood; RMC Place; WASHINGTON; *233 K-18; elev. 1,800ft./549m.; ★ JNSC-; mail Jonesborough z 37659; ● 50
Greenwood; RMC Place; WILSON; *233 C-13; mail Lebanon z 37087; ● 30
Greystone; RMC Place; GREENE; *233 L-17; elev. 1,580ft./482m.; mail Greeneville z 37743; rural
Griffith; RMC Place; BLEDSOE; *233 E-15; elev. 1,830ft./558m.; mail Pikeville z 37367; rural
Griffith Creek; RMC Place; MARION; *233 F-15; elev. 2,230ft./680m.; mail Whitwell z 37397
Grimsley; RMC Place; FENTRESS; 233 C-16; elev. 1,752ft./534m.; 🅿; z 38565; ● 700
Grinders (Grinders Switch); RMC Place; HICKMAN; *232 D-9; elev. 739ft./225m.; mail Centerville z 37033; ● 30
Grinders Switch; HICKMAN; see Grinders (RMC Place)
Gruetli; RMC Place; GRUNDY; *233 F-14; elev. 1,895ft./578m.; mail Gruetli Laager z 37339; pop. incl. with Gruetli-Laager (Inc. Place)
Gruetli-Laager; Inc. Place; GRUNDY; 233 F-14; 🅿; z 37339; Ⓟ 1,810; Ⓒ 1,867
GRUNDY; 233 F-14; Ⓟ 13,362; Ⓒ 14,332; ◆ 14,136
Gudger; RMC Place; MONROE; *233 E-18; mail Madisonville z 37354; rural
Guild; MARION; see Haletown (RMC Place)
Gulf Park; RMC Place; KNOX; *233 D-19; ★ KNOX; mail Knoxville z 37919; ● 1,580
Gum; RMC Place; RUTHERFORD; *233 E-12; ★ MUR; mail Murfreesboro z 37127; rural
Gum Creek; RMC Place; FRANKLIN; *233 F-13; mail Decherd z 37324; ● 50
Gum Flat; RMC Place; CROCKETT; *232 E-4; elev. 381ft./116m.; mail Bells z 38006; rural
Gum Spring; RMC Place; COCKE; *233 L-16; ★ MORR; mail Newport z 37821; rural
Gum Springs; RMC Place; MACON; *233 B-13; mail Pleasant Shade z 37145; rural
Guntown; RMC Place; HAWKINS; *233 K-16; mail Rogersville z 37857; ● 30
Guys; Inc. Place; MCNAIRY; 232 G-6; elev. 447ft./136m.; 🅿; z 38339; Ⓟ 497; Ⓒ 483

H

Habersham; RMC Place; CAMPBELL; 233 B-19; mail La Follette z 37766; ● 150
Hackberry; RMC Place; MONTGOMERY; *232 B-9; elev. 387ft./118m.; ★ CLRKV; mail Palmyra z 37142; rural
Hale; RMC Place; WASHINGTON; 234 M-2; elev. 1,700ft./518m.; ★ JNSC-; mail Jonesborough z 37659; ● 30
Hales Crossroads; RMC Place; HAMBLEN; *233 L-16; elev. 1,099ft./335m.; ★ MORR; mail Morristown z 37813; rural
Hales Point; RMC Place; LAUDERDALE; *232 D-3; elev. 257ft./78m.; mail Halls z 38040; rural
Haletown (Guild); RMC Place; MARION; *233 G-15; elev. 800ft./244m.; mail Guild z 37340; ● 630
Haley; RMC Place; BEDFORD; 233 E-12; mail Wartrace z 37183; ● 40
Half Acre; RMC Place; CANNON; *233 D-13; mail Smithville z 37166; rural
Halls; KNOX; see Halls Crossroads (RMC Place)
Halls; Inc. Place; LAUDERDALE; 232 D-3; elev. 335ft./102m.; 🅿; z 38040; Ⓟ 2,431; Ⓒ 2,311
Halls Creek; RMC Place; HUMPHREYS; *232 C-8; mail Waverly z 37185; rural
Halls Crossroads (Halls); RMC Place; KNOX; 233 C-19; elev. 1,020ft./311m.; ★ KNOX; mail Knoxville z 37918; ● 1,250
Hallshare Estates; RMC Place; BENTON; *232 C-7; mail Camden z 38320; ● 80
Halls Hill; RMC Place; RUTHERFORD; *233 D-13; mail Milton z 37118, Murfreesboro z 37130; rural
Halls Mill; RMC Place; BEDFORD; *233 E-12; elev. 689ft./210m.; mail Shelbyville z 37160; ● 50
Hall Town; RMC Place; SUMNER; *233 B-12; elev. 830ft./253m.; ★ NASH; mail Portland z 37148; rural
Halltown; RMC Place; TROUSDALE; *233 B-13; mail Hartsville z 37074; rural
Hallview Meadows; RMC Place; WILLIAMSON; *232 D-10; ★ NASH; mail Fairview z 37062; pop. incl. with Fairview (Inc. Place)
HAMBLEN; 233 K-16; Ⓟ 50,480; Ⓒ 58,128; ◆ 63,301
Hamburg; RMC Place; HARDIN; *232 G-6; elev. 398ft./121m.; mail Shiloh z 38376; rural
Hamillville; RMC Place; HAMILTON; *233 G-16; ★ CHTN; mail Hixson z 37343; pop. incl. with Chattanooga (Inc. Place)
HAMILTON; 233 F-16; Ⓟ 285,536; Ⓒ 307,896; ◆ 362,632
Hamilton Mill; RMC Place; LINCOLN; *233 G-11; mail Ardmore z 38449; rural
Hamilton Village; RMC Place; HAMILTON; *233 G-16; ★ CHTN; mail Chattanooga z 37421; pop. incl. with Chattanooga (Inc. Place)
Hamlin Town; RMC Place; CLAIBORNE; 233 B-19; mail Clairfield z 37715; ● 350
Hammon Chapel; RMC Place; JOHNSON; *233 J-20; mail Mountain City z 37683; rural
Hampshire; RMC Place; MAURY; 232 E-9; elev. 700ft./213m.; 🅿; z 38461; ● 200
Hampton; RMC Place; CARTER; 233 K-19; elev. 1,784ft./544m.; 🅿; z 37658; ● 2,000
Hamptons Crossroads; RMC Place; WHITE; *233 C-15; mail Sparta z 38583; ● 100
Hampton Station (Beldon); RMC Place; MONTGOMERY; *232 A-10; elev. 543ft./166m.; ★ CLRKV; mail Clarksville z 37040; ● 30
HANCOCK; 233 J-16; Ⓟ 6,739; Ⓒ 6,786; Ⓡ 6,780; ◆ 6,838
Handleyton; RMC Place; ROBERTSON; *233 A-11; elev. 661ft./201m.; mail Portland z 37148; pop. incl. with Orlinda (Inc. Place)
Hanging Limb; RMC Place; OVERTON; 233 C-16; mail Crawford z 38554; ● 180
Happy Hill; RMC Place; GILES; *232 F-10; elev. 800ft./244m.; mail Pulaski z 38478; rural
Happy Valley (Rasar); RMC Place; BLOUNT; *233 E-19; elev. 1,333ft./406m.; mail Tallassee z 37878; ● 40
Harbin; RMC Place; ROANE; *233 D-17; mail Rockwood z 37854; ● 80
Harbison; RMC Place; KNOX; *233 C-20; ★ KNOX; mail Corryton z 37721; ● 30
Harbor Town; RMC Place; BENTON; *232 C-7; mail Big Sandy z 38221; ● 30
Harbour Island; RMC Place; WILSON; *233 C-12; ★ NASH; mail Old Hickory z 37138; ● 60
Harbuck; RMC Place; POLK; *233 G-18; mail Turtletown z 37391
HARDEMAN; 232 G-4; Ⓟ 23,377; Ⓒ 28,105; ◆ 27,685
HARDIN; 232 G-7; Ⓟ 22,633; Ⓒ 25,578; ◆ 26,242
Hardin Estates; RMC Place; LOUDON; *233 D-18; ★ KNOX; mail Lenoir City z 37772; ● 450
Hardsrabble; CANNON; see Brysonville (RMC Place)
Hardy; RMC Place; OVERTON; *233 B-15; elev. 1,048ft./319m.; mail Cookeville z 38506; rural
Harmon; RMC Place; JOHNSON; *233 J-20; mail Shady Valley z 37688; rural
Harmony; RMC Place; FRANKLIN; *233 G-12; mail Winchester z 37398; rural
Harmony; RMC Place; JACKSON; *233 B-14; elev. 880ft./268m.; mail Gainesboro z 38562; rural
Harmony; RMC Place; WASHINGTON; 234 L-8; ★ JNSC-; mail Jonesborough z 37659; ● 30
Harmony Grove; RMC Place; COCKE; *233 L-16; mail Del Rio z 37727; rural
Harmony Hills; RMC Place; SULLIVAN; *233 J-18; ★ JNSC-; mail Kingsport z 37660; ● 350
Harms; RMC Place; LINCOLN; 233 G-11; mail Fayetteville z 37334; ● 60
Harpeth; RMC Place; WILLIAMSON; *233 D-11; ★ NASH; mail Franklin z 37064; rural
Harpeth Estates; RMC Place; WILLIAMSON; *232 D-10; ★ NASH; mail Franklin z 37064; ● 40
Harpeth Hills; RMC Place; WILLIAMSON; *233 D-11; ★ NASH; mail Franklin z 37064; ● 100
Harpeth Meadows; RMC Place; WILLIAMSON; *233 D-11; ★ NASH; mail Franklin z 37064; pop. incl. with Franklin (Inc. Place)
Harpeth Valley; RMC Place; DICKSON; *232 C-10; mail White Bluff z 37187; rural
Harpeth Valley Park; RMC Place; DAVIDSON; ★ NASH; mail Nashville z 37221; pop. incl. with Nashville (Inc. Place)
Harrill Hills; RMC Place; KNOX; *233 C-19; ★ KNOX; mail Knoxville z 37918; pop. incl. with Knoxville (Inc. Place)
Harriman; Inc. Place; ROANE, MORGAN; 233 D-18; elev. 798ft./243m.; 🅿 🅷; ★ KNOX; z 37748; Ⓟ 7,119; Ⓒ 6,744
Harriman Junction; RMC Place; ROANE; *233 D-17; elev. 789ft./240m.; ★ KNOX; mail Harriman z 37748; pop. incl. with Harriman (Inc. Place)
Harris; RMC Place; OBION; 232 B-5; elev. 325ft./99m.; mail Union City z 38261; ● 100
Harrisburg; RMC Place; SEVIER; 233 D-20; elev. 964ft./294m.; mail Sevierville z 37876; ● 60
Harrison; CDP; HAMILTON; 233 I-14; elev. 730ft./223m.; 🅿; ★ CHTN; z 37341; Ⓟ 7,191; Ⓒ 7,630
Harrison Hills; RMC Place; LOUDON; *233 D-18; ★ KNOX; mail Lenoir City z 37771; ● 450
Harrogate; Inc. Place; CLAIBORNE; 233 B-20; elev. 1,300ft./396m.; 🅿 🅲 2,981; z 37752 & mail Arthur z 37707; incorporated November 3, 1992; not reported in 2000 Census; Ⓡ 4,073
Harrogate-Shawanee; CDP-Census Area Only; CLAIBORNE; *233 A-20; mail Harrogate z 37752; Ⓟ 2,657; Ⓒ 2,865
Harrtown; RMC Place; SULLIVAN; *233 J-18; ★ JNSC-; mail Blountville z 37617; rural
Hartford; RMC Place; COCKE; 233 M-16; elev. 1,260ft./384m.; 🅿; z 37753; ● 200
Hartmantown; RMC Place; WASHINGTON; 234 M-8; ★ JNSC-; mail Jonesborough z 37659; ● 30
Hartsville (Hartsville-Trousdale, Hartsville-Trousdale County); Inc. Place; ⊡ TROUSDALE; 233 B-13; elev. 474ft./144m.; 🅿 🅷; z 37074; formed from the consolidation of Hartsville and Trousedale county on March 21, 2001; Ⓟ 2,188; Ⓒ 2,395
Hartsville-Trousdale; TROUSDALE; see Hartsville (Inc. Place)
Hartsville-Trousdale County; TROUSDALE; see Hartsville (Inc. Place)
Haskins Chapel; RMC Place; BEDFORD; *233 E-11; mail Lewisburg z 37091; ● 30
Hatchertown; RMC Place; SEVIER; *233 E-20; mail Sevierville z 37862; rural
Hatchie; RMC Place; MADISON; *232 F-4; elev. 324ft./99m.; mail Mercer z 38392
Havley Springs; RMC Place; HAMBLEN; *233 K-16; ★ MORR; mail Morristown z 37814; pop. incl. with Morristown (Inc. Place)
Havron Chapel; RMC Place; MARION; *233 G-14; elev. 700ft./213m.; mail Jasper z 37347; rural
HAWKINS; 233 J-17; Ⓟ 44,565; Ⓒ 53,563; ◆ 57,585
Hawkinsville; RMC Place; DYER; *232 D-4; mail Friendship z 38034; rural
Hawthorne; RMC Place; BEDFORD; *233 F-12; mail Shelbyville z 37160; rural
Haydenburg; RMC Place; JACKSON; *233 B-14; elev. 997ft./304m.; mail Whitleyville z 38588
Hayes; RMC Place; WHITE; *233 D-15; mail Sparta z 38583; ● 100
Hayes Fork; RMC Place; STEWART; *232 B-8; elev. 440ft./134m.; mail Dover z 37058; rural
Haynes; RMC Place; LAKE; *232 B-3; elev. 284ft./87m.; mail Wynnburg z 38077; rural
Haynesfield; RMC Place; SULLIVAN; *233 J-19; ★ JNSC-; mail Bristol z 37620; pop. incl. with Bristol (Inc. Place)
Hays; RMC Place; FAYETTE; *232 G-3; elev. 354ft./108m.; mail Moscow z 38057; rural
Haysboro; RMC Place; DAVIDSON; *233 C-11; ★ NASH; mail Nashville z 37216; pop. incl. with Nashville (Inc. Place)
Haysville; RMC Place; MACON; 233 A-13; elev. 860ft./262m.; mail Lafayette z 37083; ● 30
HAYWOOD; 232 E-3; Ⓟ 19,437; Ⓒ 19,797; ◆ 18,783
Head of Barren; RMC Place; CLAIBORNE; *233 B-20; elev. 1,369ft./417m.; mail New Tazewell z 37825; rural
Heatherwood Hill; RMC Place; WILLIAMSON; *233 D-11; ★ NASH; mail Franklin z 37064; ● 300
Heatoncreek; RMC Place; CARTER; *233 K-19; elev. 3,000ft./914m.; mail Roan Mountain z 37687; rural
Hebbertsburg; RMC Place; CUMBERLAND; *233 D-17; mail Crab Orchard z 37723; rural
Hebron; RMC Place; HARDEMAN; *232 G-5; elev. 451ft./137m.; mail Middleton z 38052
Heiskell; RMC Place; KNOX; *233 C-19; elev. 900ft./274m.; 🅿; ★ KNOX; z 37754; ● 250
Helena; RMC Place; FENTRESS; *233 B-16; elev. 850ft./259m.; mail Jamestown z 38556; rural
Helenwood; RMC Place; SCOTT; 233 B-18; elev. 1,395ft./425m.; 🅿; z 37755; disincorporated sometime after October 4, 1999; Ⓒ 846
Heloise; RMC Place; DYER; *232 C-3; elev. 269ft./82m.; mail Finley z 38030; rural
Helton; RMC Place; DEKALB; *233 C-13; mail Alexandria z 37012; rural
Helton Springs; RMC Place; GRAINGER; *233 C-20; mail Rutledge z 37861; rural
Heltonville; RMC Place; GRAINGER; *233 B-20; elev. 1,274ft./388m.; ★ MORR; mail Bean Station z 37708; rural
Hemlock Hills; RMC Place; UNICOI; *233 K-18; mail Erwin z 37650; ● 80
Henard Mill; RMC Place; HAWKINS; *233 J-16; mail Rogersville z 37857; rural
Henardtown; RMC Place; HAWKINS; *233 K-16; mail Rogersville z 37857; ● 100
Henderson; Inc. Place; ⊡ CHESTER; 232 F-5; elev. 462ft./141m.; 🅿 🅲 1,969; z 38340; Ⓟ 4,760; Ⓒ 5,670
HENDERSON; 232 E-6; Ⓟ 21,844; Ⓒ 25,522; ◆ 26,981
Hendersonville; Inc. Place; SUMNER; 233 C-11; elev. 459ft./140m.; 🅿 🅷; ★ NASH; z 37075, z 37077; Ⓟ 32,188; Ⓒ 40,620; ◆ 48,778
Hendon; RMC Place; BLEDSOE; *233 F-15; mail Graysville z 37338; rural
Hendron; RMC Place; KNOX; *233 D-20; elev. 1,000ft./305m.; ★ KNOX; mail Knoxville z 37920; ● 100
Henley; RMC Place; FRANKLIN; *233 F-13; mail Decherd z 37324; pop. incl. with Decherd (Inc. Place)
Henning; Inc. Place; LAUDERDALE; 232 E-3; elev. 293ft./89m.; 🅿; z 38041; Ⓟ 802; Ⓒ 970; Ⓡ 1,033
Henrietta; RMC Place; CHEATHAM; 232 B-10; ★ NASH; mail Ashland City z 37015; ● 150
Henry; Inc. Place; HENRY; 232 C-6; elev. 547ft./167m.; 🅿; z 38231; Ⓟ 317; Ⓒ 520
HENRY; 232 C-7; Ⓟ 27,888; Ⓒ 31,115; ◆ 31,590
Henrys Crossroads; RMC Place; SEVIER; *233 D-20; elev. 1,100ft./335m.; ★ KNOX; mail Kodak z 37764; pop. incl. with Sevierville (Inc. Place)
Henry Street; RMC Place; HAMBLEN; ★ MORR; mail Morristown z 37814; pop. incl. with Morristown (Inc. Place)
Henryville; RMC Place; LAWRENCE; 232 F-9; mail Summertown z 38483; ● 70
Hensley Chapel; RMC Place; WHITE; *233 D-15; elev. 1,314ft./401m.; mail Sparta z 38583; ● 70
Herbert Domain; RMC Place; BLEDSOE; *233 D-15; mail Pikeville z 37367; rural
Heritage Estates; RMC Place; CUMBERLAND; *233 D-16; elev. 1,900ft./579m.; mail Crossville z 38572; ● 250
Heritage Hills; RMC Place; BLOUNT; *233 E-19; ★ KNOX; mail Maryville z 37803; pop. incl. with Maryville (Inc. Place)
Hermitage; RMC Place; DAVIDSON; *233 C-11; 🅿 🅷; ★ NASH; z 37076; pop. incl. with Nashville (Inc. Place)
Hermitage Hills; RMC Place; DAVIDSON; *233 C-11; ★ NASH; mail Hermitage z 37076; pop. incl. with Nashville (Inc. Place)
Hermitage Springs; RMC Place; CLAY; 233 B-14; elev. 758ft./231m.; mail Red Boiling Springs z 37150; ● 250
Hermon; RMC Place; GREENE; *233 L-17; elev. 1,400ft./427m.; mail Afton z 37616; rural
Herrens Chapel; PUTNAM; see Roberts (RMC Place)
Hiawassee; RMC Place; WARREN; *233 E-14; mail Morrison z 37357; pop. incl. with Morrison (Inc. Place)
Hickerson Station; RMC Place; COFFEE; *233 F-13; elev. 1,044ft./318m.; mail Tullahoma z 37388; rural
Hickey; RMC Place; PUTNAM; *233 C-14; elev. 1,027ft./313m.; mail Silver Point z 38582; ● 50
Hickman; RMC Place; SMITH; 233 C-13; elev. 507ft./155m.; 🅿; z 38567; ● 250
HICKMAN; 232 E-9; Ⓟ 16,754; Ⓒ 22,295; ◆ 24,076
Hickory Bend; RMC Place; DAVIDSON; ★ NASH; mail Nashville z 37214; pop. incl. with Nashville (Inc. Place)
Hickory Flat; RMC Place; CARROLL; *232 D-6; mail Cedar Grove z 38321
Hickory Flats; RMC Place; HENDERSON; *232 E-6; elev. 460ft./140m.; mail Reagan z 38368; rural
Hickory Flats; RMC Place; MCNAIRY; 232 F-6; mail Adamsville z 38310; ● 150
Hickory Grove; RMC Place; FRANKLIN; *233 G-13; elev. 960ft./293m.; mail Huntland z 37345; rural
Hickory Grove; RMC Place; GIBSON; *232 D-4; elev. 365ft./111m.; mail Trenton z 38382; rural
Hickory Grove; RMC Place; SUMNER; *233 B-12; mail Castalian Springs z 37031; ● 220
Hickory Hill; RMC Place; MOORE; *233 F-12; mail Lynchburg z 37352; pop. incl. with Lynchburg (Inc. Place)
Hickory Hill Estates; RMC Place; COFFEE; mail Tullahoma z 37388; pop. incl. with Tullahoma (Inc. Place)
Hickory Hills; RMC Place; WILLIAMSON; *233 D-11; ★ NASH; mail Franklin z 37064; rural
Hickory Point; RMC Place; MONTGOMERY; *232 B-10; elev. 641ft./195m.; ★ CLRKV; mail Clarksville z 37040, z 37043; rural
Hickory Star Landing; RMC Place; UNION; 233 C-19; ★ KNOX; mail Maynardville z 37807; ● 130
Hickory Tree; RMC Place; SULLIVAN; 234 K-5; ★ JNSC-; mail Bluff City z 37618; ● 80
Hickory Valley; Inc. Place; HARDEMAN; 232 G-4; elev. 564ft./172m.; 🅿; z 38042; Ⓟ 159; Ⓒ 136
Hickory Valley; RMC Place; UNION; *233 C-19; elev. 1,300ft./396m.; ★ KNOX; mail Maynardville z 37807; rural
Hickory Withe; RMC Place; FAYETTE; 232 F-3; elev. 423ft./129m.; former incorporated place; disincorporated September 9, 2002; Ⓒ 2,574
Hicks Chapel; RMC Place; MARION; *233 F-15; elev. 760ft./232m.; mail Whitwell z 37397; rural
Hicksville; RMC Place; MADISON; *232 E-5; ★ JAC; mail Jackson z 38301; pop. incl. with Jackson (Inc. Place)
Hico; RMC Place; CARROLL; *232 C-6; mail Huntingdon z 38344; rural
Hico Station; RMC Place; CARROLL; *232 C-6; elev. 420ft./128m.; mail Huntingdon z 38344; rural
Hide-A-Way Hills; RMC Place; CUMBERLAND; *233 D-16; elev. 1,840ft./561m.; mail Crossville z 38555; ● 50
Highcliff; RMC Place; CAMPBELL; *233 A-19; mail Jellico z 37762; ● 60
Highgate; RMC Place; WILLIAMSON; *233 D-11; ★ NASH; mail Franklin z 37064; ● 30
Highland; RMC Place; DEKALB; *233 D-14; elev. 1,060ft./323m.; mail Smithville z 37166; ● 80
Highland; RMC Place; JACKSON; *233 B-14; mail Gainesboro z 38562; rural
Highland; RMC Place; OVERTON; *233 C-15; mail Livingston z 38570; rural
Highland; RMC Place; WAYNE; *232 F-9; elev. 1,023ft./312m.; mail Collinwood z 38450; rural
Highland Academy; RMC Place; SUMNER; *233 B-12; mail Portland z 37148; ● 250
Highland Acres; RMC Place; BLOUNT; *233 E-19; ★ KNOX; mail Maryville z 37804; pop. incl. with Maryville (Inc. Place)
Highland Forest; RMC Place; ROANE; *233 D-17; mail Rockwood z 37854; pop. incl. with Rockwood (Inc. Place)
Highland Heights; RMC Place; DAVIDSON; ★ NASH; mail Nashville z 37207; pop. incl. with Nashville (Inc. Place)
Highland Heights; RMC Place; GILES; *232 G-10; mail Pulaski z 38478; pop. incl. with Pulaski (Inc. Place)
Highland Heights; RMC Place; SHELBY; ★ MEM; mail Memphis z 38122; pop. incl. with Memphis (Inc. Place)
Highland Junction; RMC Place; FENTRESS; mail Wilder z 38589
Highland Manor; RMC Place; HAMILTON; *233 G-16; elev. 900ft./274m.; ★ CHTN; mail Harrison z 37341
Highland Park; RMC Place; CAMPBELL; *233 B-19; elev. 1,080ft./329m.; ★ KNOX; mail La Follette z 37766
Highland Park; RMC Place; HAMILTON; *233 G-15; ★ CHTN; mail Chattanooga z 37404; pop. incl. with Chattanooga (Inc. Place)
Highland Park; RMC Place; LOUDON; *233 D-18; elev. 845ft./258m.; ★ KNOX; mail Lenoir City z 37771; ● 600
Highland Park; RMC Place; SULLIVAN; *233 J-18; ★ JNSC-; mail Kingsport z 37660; pop. incl. with Kingsport (Inc. Place)
Highland Springs; RMC Place; GRAINGER; *233 C-20; mail Blaine z 37709; rural
Highlandview; RMC Place; KNOX; *233 C-19; ★ KNOX; mail Knoxville z 37920; ● 570
High Point; RMC Place; CAMPBELL; *233 B-18; ★ KNOX; mail Caryville z 37714; rural
High Point; RMC Place; SCOTT; *233 B-17; mail Oneida z 37841; ● 50
Hilham; RMC Place; OVERTON; 233 B-15; elev. 1,094ft./333m.; 🅿; z 38568; ● 110
Hillcrest; RMC Place; CUMBERLAND; mail Crossville z 38555; pop. incl. with Crossville (Inc. Place)
Hillcrest; RMC Place; HAMBLEN; *233 K-16; ★ MORR; mail Morristown z 37814; pop. incl. with Morristown (Inc. Place)
Hillcrest; RMC Place; SULLIVAN; *233 J-18; elev. 1,364ft./416m.; ★ JNSC-; mail Kingsport z 37660; pop. incl. with Kingsport (Inc. Place)
Hilldale; RMC Place; MONTGOMERY; ★ CLRKV; mail Clarksville z 37043; pop. incl. with Clarksville (Inc. Place)
Hill Estates; RMC Place; WILLIAMSON; *233 D-11; elev. 700ft./213m.; ★ NASH; mail Franklin z 37064; pop. incl. with Franklin (Inc. Place)
Hilliard; RMC Place; CARROLL; *232 D-6; elev. 400ft./122m.; mail Westport z 38387; rural
Hillsboro; RMC Place; COFFEE; 233 F-13; elev. 1,080ft./329m.; 🅿; z 37342; ● 380
Hillsboro; WILLIAMSON; see Leipers Fork (RMC Place)
Hillsboro Acres; RMC Place; WILLIAMSON; *233 D-11; elev. 660ft./201m.; ★ NASH; mail Franklin z 37069
Hillsdale; RMC Place; MACON; 233 B-13; elev. 549ft./167m.; mail Dixon Springs z 37057; ● 90
Hillside; RMC Place; WEAKLEY; *232 B-5; mail Martin z 38237; rural
Hills View; RMC Place; MCMINN; *233 F-17; mail Riceville z 37370; ● 30
Hilltop; RMC Place; BEDFORD; *233 F-12; mail Shelbyville z 37160; ● 50
Hilltop; RMC Place; MONTGOMERY; *232 B-9; elev. 605ft./184m.; ★ CLRKV; mail Clarksville z 37040; rural
Hilltop; RMC Place; RUTHERFORD; *233 D-12; ★ NASH; mail Smyrna z 37167; pop. incl. with Smyrna (Inc. Place)
Hill Top; RMC Place; WASHINGTON; ★ JNSC-; mail Johnson City z 37601; pop. incl. with Johnson City (Inc. Place)
Hill Town; RMC Place; MAURY; *232 D-10; elev. 930ft./283m.; mail Santa Fe z 38482; ● 30
Hillvale; RMC Place; ANDERSON; *233 C-19; ★ KNOX; mail Clinton z 37716; rural
Hillville (Mount Pleasant); RMC Place; HAYWOOD; 232 E-4; mail Whiteville z 38075; ● 50
Hillwood; RMC Place; DAVIDSON; ★ NASH; mail Nashville z 37205; pop. incl. with Nashville (Inc. Place)
Himesville; RMC Place; BEDFORD; *233 F-12; elev. 810ft./247m.; mail Shelbyville z 37160; rural
Hindscreek; RMC Place; ANDERSON; *233 C-19; ★ KNOX; mail Clinton z 37716; rural
Hinds Creek Valley; RMC Place; UNION; *233 C-19; elev. 1,184ft./361m.; ★ KNOX; mail Maynardville z 37807; rural
Hinkle; RMC Place; HARDIN; *232 F-6; mail Sardis z 38371; rural
Hinkledale; RMC Place; CARROLL; *232 C-6; elev. 381ft./116m.; mail Mc Kenzie z 38201; rural
Hitchcox; RMC Place; BLEDSOE; *233 E-15; mail Pikeville z 37367
Hiwassee Hills; RMC Place; MONROE; *233 E-18; mail Madisonville z 37354; ● 150
Hixon; RMC Place; GRUNDY; *233 F-14; mail Altamont z 37301; rural
Hixson; RMC Place; HAMILTON; 233 I-13; elev. 672ft./205m.; 🅿; ★ CHTN; z 37343; pop. incl. with Chattanooga (Inc. Place)
Hobbs Hill; RMC Place; GRUNDY; *233 F-14; mail Tracy City z 37387; rural
Hodges; RMC Place; JEFFERSON; *233 C-20; ★ KNOX; mail New Market z 37820; ● 150
Hodson (McLin's Corner); RMC Place; CROCKETT; *232 D-4; elev. 315ft./96m.; mail Friendship z 38034; rural
Hoggtown; SMITH; see Defeated (RMC Place)
Hohenwald; Inc. Place; ⊡ LEWIS; 232 E-9; elev. 976ft./297m.; 🅿; z 38462; Ⓟ 3,760; Ⓒ 3,754
Holiday City; RMC Place; SHELBY; ★ MEM; mail Memphis z 38118, z 38181; pop. incl. with Memphis (Inc. Place)
Holiday Hills; RMC Place; CUMBERLAND; *233 D-16; elev. 1,840ft./561m.; mail Crossville z 38555; ● 50
Holiday Hills; RMC Place; ROANE; *233 D-17; mail Kingston z 37763; ● 30
Holiday Shores; RMC Place; STEWART; *232 A-8; mail Bumpus Mills z 37028; ● 100
Holladay; RMC Place; BENTON; 232 D-7; elev. 420ft./128m.; 🅿; z 38341; ● 200
Holladay; RMC Place; PUTNAM; *233 C-15; elev. 1,100ft./335m.; mail Cookeville z 38506; rural
Holland Mill; RMC Place; GREENE; *233 K-17; elev. 1,212ft./369m.; mail Afton z 37616; rural
Hollow Rock; Inc. Place; CARROLL; 232 C-7; elev. 424ft./129m.; 🅿; z 38342; Ⓟ 902; Ⓒ 963
Hollow Springs; RMC Place; CANNON; *233 E-13; mail Bradyville z 37026; ● 50
Holly Grove; RMC Place; HAYWOOD; *232 E-4; mail Bells z 38006; rural
Holly Grove; RMC Place; MARSHALL; *233 F-11; mail Lewisburg z 37091; rural
Holly Grove; RMC Place; TIPTON; *232 E-2; elev. 394ft./120m.; ★ MEM; mail Brighton z 38011; rural
Holly Leaf; RMC Place; GIBSON; *232 C-5; elev. 344ft./105m.; mail Atwood z 38220, Trezevant z 38258; rural
Holly Springs; RMC Place; MONROE; *233 F-18; elev. 1,195ft./364m.; mail Tellico Plains z 37385; rural
Holly Springs; RMC Place; OVERTON; *233 B-15; mail Livingston z 38570; rural
Hollywood; RMC Place; MAURY; *232 E-10; mail Culleoka z 38451; rural
Hollywood; RMC Place; SHELBY; ★ MEM; mail Memphis z 38108, z 38112; pop. incl. with Memphis (Inc. Place)
Hollywood Hills; RMC Place; SUMNER; *233 B-12; mail Gallatin z 37066; ● 500
Holston Heights; RMC Place; SULLIVAN; *233 J-18; ★ JNSC-; mail Kingsport z 37660; pop. incl. with Kingsport (Inc. Place)
Holston Hills; RMC Place; KNOX; *233 D-20; ★ KNOX; mail Knoxville z 37914; pop. incl. with Knoxville (Inc. Place)
Holston Hills; RMC Place; SULLIVAN; *233 J-19; ★ JNSC-; mail Bristol z 37620; pop. incl. with Bristol (Inc. Place)
Holston Terrace; RMC Place; HAWKINS; *233 K-16; elev. 1,200ft./366m.; mail Rogersville z 37857; ● 30
Holston Valley; RMC Place; SULLIVAN; *233 J-19; ★ JNSC-; mail Bristol z 37620; rural
Holtland; MARSHALL; see Holts Corner (RMC Place)
Holts Corner (Holtland); RMC Place; MARSHALL; 233 E-11; mail Chapel Hill z 37034; ● 200
Holttown; RMC Place; COCKE; *233 L-16; mail Newport z 37821; ● 30
Holy Hill; RMC Place; JOHNSON; *233 J-20; mail Mountain City z 37683; rural
Homestead; RMC Place; CUMBERLAND; 233 D-16; mail Crossville z 38555; ● 350
Honeycutt; RMC Place; HAWKINS; *233 K-17; mail Rogersville z 37857; rural
Hood Lake; RMC Place; LAWRENCE; *232 F-9; mail Lawrenceburg z 38464; pop. incl. with Lawrenceburg (Inc. Place)
Hoodoo; RMC Place; COFFEE; *233 E-13; mail Beechgrove z 37018; ● 50
Hookers Bend (Dickey's Landing); RMC Place; HARDIN; *232 F-7; elev. 416ft./127m.; mail Morris Chapel z 38361; ● 30
Hoop; RMC Place; CLAIBORNE; *233 B-20; elev. 1,600ft./488m.; mail Tazewell z 37879; rural
Hoovers Gap; RMC Place; RUTHERFORD; *233 E-12; mail Christiana z 37037; rural
Hopewell; CDP; BRADLEY; *233 F-16; ★ CLEV; mail Cleveland z 37312; Ⓟ 2,569; Ⓒ 1,815
Hopewell; RMC Place; CARROLL; *232 D-6; elev. 506ft./154m.; mail Lavinia z 38348; rural
Hopewell; RMC Place; CLAIBORNE; *233 B-20; mail Tazewell z 37879; ● 30
Hopewell; RMC Place; DAVIDSON; *233 C-11; ★ NASH; mail Old Hickory z 37138; pop. incl. with Nashville (Inc. Place)
Hopewell; RMC Place; GIBSON; *232 C-4; elev. 335ft./102m.; mail Yorkville z 38389; rural
Hopewell; RMC Place; TIPTON; 232 E-2; ★ MEM; mail Brighton z 38011; ● 120
Hopewell Springs; RMC Place; MONROE; *233 E-18; elev. 848ft./258m.; mail Madisonville z 37354; rural
Hopper Bluff; RMC Place; GRAINGER; *233 C-20; elev. 1,100ft./335m.; mail Rutledge z 37861; rural
Hopson; RMC Place; CARTER; *233 K-19; mail Roan Mountain z 37687; rural
Hornbeak; Inc. Place; OBION; 232 B-4; elev. 474ft./144m.; 🅿; z 38232; Ⓟ 445; Ⓒ 435
Horner; RMC Place; PERRY; *232 E-8; mail Linden z 37096; rural
Hornertown; RMC Place; HICKMAN; *232 E-9; rural
Hornsby; Inc. Place; HARDEMAN; 232 F-5; elev. 384ft./117m.; 🅿; z 38044; Ⓟ 313; Ⓒ 306
Horn Springs; RMC Place; WILSON; *233 C-12; ★ NASH; mail Lebanon z 37087; ● 80
Horse Creek; RMC Place; GREENE; *233 K-17; mail Chuckey z 37641; rural
Horse Creek; RMC Place; SULLIVAN; *233 J-17; ★ JNSC-; mail Kingsport z 37660; rural
Horseshoe; RMC Place; CARTER; *233 K-19; ★ JNSC-; mail Elizabethton z 37643; rural
Horseshoe Bend; RMC Place; SMITH; *233 C-14; mail Elmwood z 38560; rural
Horsleys; RMC Place; MACON; *233 B-13; mail Hartsville z 37074; rural
Housley Addition; RMC Place; MCMINN; *233 F-17; mail Athens z 37303; pop. incl. with Athens (Inc. Place)
Houston; RMC Place; WAYNE; 232 F-8; mail Waynesboro z 38485; ● 110
HOUSTON; 232 C-8; Ⓟ 7,018; Ⓒ 8,088; ◆ 8,321
Houston Valley; RMC Place; GREENE; *233 L-17; mail Greeneville z 37743; rural
Howard; RMC Place; MONROE; *233 E-19; elev. 1,000ft./305m.; mail Vonore z 37885; rural
Howard; RMC Place; SEVIER; *233 D-20; ★ KNOX; mail Seymour z 37865; ● 250
Howard Chapel; RMC Place; OVERTON; *233 B-15; mail Livingston z 38570; rural
Howard Hill; RMC Place; SULLIVAN; *233 J-18; elev. 1,203ft./367m.; ★ JNSC-; mail Kingsport z 37660; pop. incl. with Kingsport (Inc. Place)
Howard Quarter; RMC Place; CLAIBORNE; *233 B-20; mail Tazewell z 37879; ● 50
Howard Springs; RMC Place; CUMBERLAND; *233 D-16; mail Crossville z 38571; rural
Howell; RMC Place; LINCOLN; 233 F-11; elev. 752ft./229m.; mail Fayetteville z 37334, Petersburg z 37144; ● 90
Howell; RMC Place; WHITE; *233 D-15; mail Sparta z 38583; ● 40
Howell Hill; RMC Place; LINCOLN; *233 G-12; elev. 932ft./284m.; mail Fayetteville z 37334; rural
Howley; RMC Place; CARROLL; *232 D-6; elev. 596ft./182m.; mail Cedar Grove z 38321; ● 60
Hubbard; RMC Place; BLOUNT; *233 D-19; ★ KNOX; mail Maryville z 37801; rural
Hubertville; RMC Place; ROBERTSON; *233 B-11; mail Springfield z 37172; rural
Huckleberry; HAMILTON; see Mowbray (RMC Place)
Hudson; RMC Place; LAWRENCE; *232 F-9; mail Lawrenceburg z 38464, Summertown z 38483; rural
Hugarth; RMC Place; FENTRESS; 233 B-16; mail Jamestown z 38556; pop. incl. with Jamestown (Inc. Place)
Hughes Loop; RMC Place; GIBSON; *232 D-5; elev. 400ft./122m.; mail Milan z 38358; rural
Hughett; RMC Place; SCOTT; *233 B-18; elev. 1,150ft./351m.; mail Robbins z 37852; rural
Hughey; RMC Place; LINCOLN; *233 F-11; mail Fayetteville z 37334; rural
Hulan Hollow; RMC Place; UNICOI; *233 L-18; mail Erwin z 37650; pop. incl. with Erwin (Inc. Place)
Humboldt; Inc. Place; GIBSON, MADISON; 232 D-5; elev. 357ft./109m.; 🅿 🅷; z 38343; Ⓟ 9,651; Ⓒ 9,467
Humphrey; RMC Place; SEVIER; *233 D-20; ★ KNOX; mail Seymour z 37865
HUMPHREYS; 232 C-8; Ⓟ 15,795; Ⓒ 17,929; ◆ 18,248
Hunter (Watuaga Valley); CDP; CARTER; 234 M-5; elev. 1,577ft./481m.; ★ JNSC-; mail Elizabethton z 37643; Ⓟ 1,250; Ⓒ 1,566
Hunter Hills; RMC Place; HAMILTON; *233 F-16; elev. 720ft./219m.; ★ CHTN; mail Soddy Daisy z 37379; ● 30
Hunters Point; RMC Place; WILSON; *233 C-12; mail Lebanon z 37087; ● 80
Hunters Ridge; RMC Place; WILLIAMSON; *233 C-11; ★ NASH; mail Franklin z 37064; ● 40
Huntersville; RMC Place; MADISON; 232 E-4; elev. 433ft./132m.; mail Jackson z 38301; ● 50
Hunting Creek Farms; RMC Place; WILLIAMSON; *232 D-10; ★ NASH; mail Franklin z 37064; ● 60
Huntingdon; Inc. Place; ⊡ CARROLL; 232 D-6; elev. 419ft./128m.; 🅿 🅷; z 38344; Ⓟ 4,180; Ⓒ 4,349
Huntland; Inc. Place; FRANKLIN; 233 G-12; elev. 940ft./287m.; 🅿; z 37345; Ⓟ 885; Ⓒ 916
Huntsville; RMC Place; LOUDON; *233 D-18; ★ KNOX; mail Lenoir City z 37771; ● 200
Huntsville; Inc. Place; ⊡ SCOTT; 233 B-18; elev. 1,332ft./406m.; 🅿; z 37756; Ⓟ 660; Ⓒ 981
Hurdlow; RMC Place; MOORE; *233 G-12; mail Belvidere z 37306; pop. incl. with Lynchburg (Inc. Place)
Hurley; RMC Place; HARDIN; *232 G-6; mail Michie z 38357
Hurley Acres; RMC Place; HAMBLEN; *233 K-16; elev. 1,400ft./427m.; ★ MORR; mail Morristown z 37813; ● 300
Huron; RMC Place; HENDERSON; 232 E-6; elev. 415ft./126m.; 🅿; z 38345; ● 50
Hurricane; RMC Place; HOUSTON; *232 B-8; mail Stewart z 37175; summer pop. 150; ● 60
Hurricane; RMC Place; JACKSON; *233 B-14; mail Gainesboro z 38562; rural
Hurricane; RMC Place; WILSON; *233 C-12; mail Lebanon z 37090; rural
Hurricane Hill; RMC Place; LAUDERDALE; *232 E-3; elev. 419ft./128m.; mail Ripley z 38063; rural
Hurricane Mills; RMC Place; HUMPHREYS; 232 D-8; elev. 400ft./122m.; 🅿; z 37078; ● 50
Hustburg; RMC Place; HUMPHREYS; 232 D-8; elev. 404ft./123m.; mail New Johnsonville z 37134; ● 150
Hutsell; RMC Place; MCMINN; *233 F-17; elev. 953ft./290m.; mail Athens z 37303; pop. incl. with Athens (Inc. Place)
Hygeia Springs; RMC Place; ROBERTSON; *233 B-11; elev. 800ft./244m.; ★ NASH; mail Greenbrier z 37073; pop. incl. with Greenbrier (Inc. Place)
Hyndsver; RMC Place; WEAKLEY; *232 B-5; elev. 413ft./126m.; mail Martin z 38237; rural

I

Iconium; RMC Place; CANNON; *233 D-13; mail Woodbury z 37190; ● 30
Idaho; RMC Place; LAWRENCE; *232 G-9; mail Leoma z 38468; rural
Idaville; RMC Place; TIPTON; *232 E-2; elev. 395ft./120m.; ★ MEM; mail Atoka z 38004; rural
Ideal Valley; RMC Place; RHEA; *233 E-17; mail Spring City z 37381; pop. incl. with Spring City (Inc. Place)
Idlewild; RMC Place; GIBSON; 232 C-5; elev. 373ft./114m.; 🅿; z 38346; ● 150
Idlewild; RMC Place; MCMINN; *233 E-17; mail Athens z 37303
Idlewood; RMC Place; WILLIAMSON; *233 D-11; ★ NASH; mail Franklin z 37064; pop. incl. with Franklin (Inc. Place)
Idol; GRAINGER; see Thorn Hill (RMC Place)
Ilemar; RMC Place; WILSON; *233 C-12; ★ NASH; mail Mount Juliet z 37122; ● 170
Imperial Estates; RMC Place; KNOX; *233 D-19; ★ KNOX; mail Knoxville z 37921; ● 110
Independence; RMC Place; HANCOCK; *233 J-17; elev. 1,400ft./427m.; mail Eidson z 37731; rural
Independence; RMC Place; OVERTON; *233 B-15; elev. 1,051ft./320m.; mail Monroe z 38573; rural
Independence Estates; RMC Place; WILSON; *233 C-12; mail Lebanon z 37087; ● 60
India; RMC Place; HENRY; 232 B-7; mail Paris z 38242; ● 30
Indian Bluff (Braden); RMC Place; ANDERSON; *233 C-18; elev. 2,000ft./610m.; ★ KNOX; mail Briceville z 37710; rural
Indian Cave; RMC Place; GRAINGER; *233 C-20; mail Blaine z 37709; rural
Indian Creek; RMC Place; CAMPBELL; *233 C-19; ★ KNOX; mail Jacksboro z 37757; rural
Indian Fork; ANDERSON; see Braytown (RMC Place)
Indian Hills; RMC Place; HAMILTON; *233 G-16; ★ CHTN; pop. incl. with Chattanooga (Inc. Place)
Indian Hills; RMC Place; WILSON; *233 C-12; mail Lebanon z 37087; pop. incl. with Lebanon (Inc. Place)
Indian Mound; RMC Place; DEKALB; *233 D-14; mail Sparta z 38583; rural
Indian Mound; RMC Place; STEWART; 232 B-8; elev. 384ft./117m.; 🅿; z 37079; ● 400
Indian Ridge; RMC Place; GRAINGER; *233 C-20; elev. 1,258ft./383m.; mail Blaine z 37709; rural
Indian Ridge; RMC Place; WASHINGTON; *233 K-18; ★ JNSC-; mail Johnson City z 37601; pop. incl. with Johnson City (Inc. Place)
Indian Springs; RMC Place; SULLIVAN; 234 J-10; elev. 1,610ft./491m.; ★ JNSC-; mail Blountville z 37617, Kingsport z 37663; ● 2,200
Ingleside Hill; RMC Place; MCMINN; *233 F-17; mail Athens z 37303; pop. incl. with Athens (Inc. Place)
Inglewood; RMC Place; DAVIDSON; 232 J-8; elev. 518ft./158m.; ★ NASH; mail Nashville z 37216; pop. incl. with Nashville (Inc. Place)
Inskip; RMC Place; KNOX; 233 L-12; ★ KNOX; mail Knoxville z 37912; pop. incl. with Knoxville (Inc. Place)
Interstate Park; RMC Place; ROBERTSON; *232 B-10; mail Cedar Hill z 37032; ● 80
Irish Cut; RMC Place; COCKE; *233 L-16; ★ MORR; mail Newport z 37821; ● 330
Iron City; Inc. Place; LAWRENCE, WAYNE; 232 G-9; elev. 559ft./170m.; 🅿; z 38463; Ⓟ 402; Ⓒ 368
Ironsburg; RMC Place; MONROE; *233 F-18; mail Tellico Plains z 37385; rural
Irving College; RMC Place; WARREN; 233 E-14; mail Mc Minnville z 37110; ● 40
Irwinton Shores; RMC Place; ROANE; *233 D-17; elev. 800ft./244m.; mail Ten Mile z 37880; ● 40

Entries in **UPPERCASE** are counties.
Entries in **bold** have populations of 2,500 or more.
Names in parentheses are alternate names.

Inc. Place	Incorporated Place
RMC Place	Rand McNally Designated Place
CDP	Census Designated Place
MCD	Minor Civil Division
⊡	County Seat
▲	Minor Civil Division
elev.	Elevation
🅿	Post Office
🅷	Hospital
🅲	College
■	Principal Business Center
★	Ranally Metro Area (RMA) Abbreviation
z	Zip Code(s)
Ⓟ	Previous Census Population
Ⓡ	Revised Census Population
Ⓐ	Annexation Population
●	Rand McNally Population Estimate
Ⓒ	Final Census Population
Ⓢ	Special Census Population
◆	Estimated Population

For additional definitions see Glossary, Volume 1, and Introduction, Volume 2.

Isabella; RMC Place; POLK; **233** G-18; elev. 1,720ft./524m.; mail Copperhill z 37317; ● 180
Isham; RMC Place; SCOTT; ***233** A-18; mail Winfield z 37892
Island Home; RMC Place; KNOX; ***233** D-19; ★ **KNOX**; mail Knoxville z 37920; pop. incl. with Knoxville (Inc. Place)
Island Park; RMC Place; SULLIVAN; ***233** J-19; ★ **JNSC-**; mail Bluff City z 37618; ● 30
Isoline; RMC Place; CUMBERLAND; ***233** C-16; elev. 1,835ft./559m.; mail Crossville z 38571
Isom; RMC Place; MAURY; ***232** E-9; mail Hampshire z 38461; rural
Ivy; RMC Place; MONROE; ***233** F-18; mail Reliance z 37369; rural
Ivy Bluff; RMC Place; CANNON; ***233** E-13; elev. 1,100ft./335m.; mail Mc Minnville z 37110; rural
Ivydell; RMC Place; CAMPBELL; ***233** B-19; ★ **KNOX**; mail La Follette z 37766; rural
Ivy Point; RMC Place; DAVIDSON; ***233** B-11; ★ **NASH**; mail Goodlettsville z 37072; pop. incl. with Nashville (Inc. Place)
Ivyton; RMC Place; OVERTON; ***233** B-16; mail Alpine z 38543; ● 30

J

Jacksboro; Inc. Place; ⊡ CAMPBELL; **233** B-19; elev. 1,070ft./326m.; 🅿; ★ **KNOX**; z 37757; Ⓟ 1,568; Ⓒ 1,887
Jacks Creek; RMC Place; CHESTER; **232** E-6; elev. 465ft./142m.; 🅿; z 38347; ● 300
Jackson; Inc. Place; ⊡ MADISON; **232** E-5; elev. 401ft./122m.; 🅿 🅷 🅲 5,331 ■; ★ **JAC**; z 38301-03, z 38305, z 38308, z 38314; Ⓟ 48,949; Ⓒ 59,643; ◆ 65,305
JACKSON; **233** C-14; Ⓟ 9,297; Ⓒ 10,984; ◆ 10,677
Jackson Heights; RMC Place; RUTHERFORD; ★ **MUR**; mail Murfreesboro z 37129; pop. incl. with Murfreesboro (Inc. Place)
Jackson Ridge; RMC Place; RUTHERFORD; ***233** D-12; mail Eagleville z 37060, Rockvale z 37153; rural
Jacksons Chapel; RMC Place; DICKSON; ***232** C-10; mail Charlotte z 37036; ● 50
Jackson Square; RMC Place; ANDERSON; ***233** D-18; ★ **KNOX**; mail Oak Ridge z 37830; pop. incl. with Oak Ridge (Inc. Place)
Jacobs Hill; RMC Place; WILSON; ***233** C-12; mail Lebanon z 37090; rural
Jakestown; RUTHERFORD; see Double Springs (RMC Place)
Jamestown; Inc. Place; ⊡ FENTRESS; **233** B-16; elev. 1,716ft./523m.; 🅿 🅷; z 38556; Ⓟ 1,862; Ⓒ 1,839
Jamestown; RMC Place; TIPTON; ***232** E-2; mail Burlison z 38015; rural
Jarrell; RMC Place; CARROLL; ***232** C-6; mail Mc Kenzie z 38201; ● 80
Jasper; Inc. Place; ⊡ MARION; **233** G-14; elev. 622ft./190m.; 🅿; z 37347; Ⓟ 2,780; Ⓒ 3,214
Jaybird; RMC Place; COCKE; ***233** L-16; ★ **MORR**; mail Newport z 37821; pop. incl. with Newport (Inc. Place)
Jaybird; RMC Place; HAMBLEN; ***233** K-16; ★ **MORR**; mail Morristown z 37814; ● 100
Jeannette; RMC Place; DECATUR; ***232** D-7; mail Parsons z 38363; ● 30
Jearoldstown; RMC Place; GREENE; ***233** K-17; mail Chuckey z 37641; rural
Jefferson; RMC Place; DEKALB; ***233** D-14; mail Smithville z 37166; ● 30
JEFFERSON; **233** C-20; Ⓟ 33,016; Ⓒ 44,294; ◆ 52,085
Jefferson City; Inc. Place; JEFFERSON; **233** C-20; elev. 1,205ft./367m.; 🅿 🅷 🅲 1,949; z 37760; Ⓟ 5,522; Ⓒ 7,760
Jefferson Estates; RMC Place; JEFFERSON; ***233** C-20; ★ **MORR**; mail Talbott z 37877; pop. incl. with Jefferson City (Inc. Place)
Jefferson Springs; RMC Place; RUTHERFORD; ***233** D-12; ★ **NASH**; mail Smyrna z 37167; ● 150
Jellico; Inc. Place; CAMPBELL; **233** A-19; elev. 982ft./299m.; 🅿 🅷; z 37762; Ⓟ 2,447; Ⓒ 2,448
Jena; RMC Place; LOUDON; ***233** E-19; elev. 847ft./258m.; mail Greenback z 37742; pop. incl. with Greenback (Inc. Place)
Jenkins Hill; RMC Place; SEVIER; ★ **KNOX**; mail Sevierville z 37862; pop. incl. with Sevierville (Inc. Place)
Jenkinsville; RMC Place; DYER; ***232** C-3; mail Dyersburg z 38024; ● 150
Jere Baxter; RMC Place; DAVIDSON; ***233** C-11; ★ **NASH**; mail Nashville z 37216; pop. incl. with Nashville (Inc. Place)
Jernigan Town; RMC Place; ROBERTSON; ***233** B-11; elev. 740ft./226m.; ★ **NASH**; mail White House z 37188; rural
Jersey; RMC Place; HAMILTON; ***233** G-16; ★ **CHTN**; mail Chattanooga z 37416; pop. incl. with Chattanooga (Inc. Place)
Jessie; RMC Place; WARREN; ***233** E-14; mail Mc Minnville z 37110; rural
Jewell; RMC Place; WEAKLEY; ***232** B-6; mail Dresden z 38225
Jewett; RMC Place; CUMBERLAND; ***233** D-16; mail Grandview z 37337; ● 30
Jimtown; RMC Place; COCKE; ***233** L-16; ★ **MORR**; mail Newport z 37821; pop. incl. with Newport (Inc. Place)
Jingo; WILLIAMSON; see Fairview (Inc. Place)
Jockey (Clear Springs); RMC Place; GREENE; ***233** K-17; mail Limestone z 37681; rural
Joelton; RMC Place; DAVIDSON; ***233** B-11; 🅿; ★ **NASH**; z 37080; pop. incl. with Nashville (Inc. Place)
John Sevier; RMC Place; KNOX; **233** L-14; ★ **KNOX**; mail Knoxville z 37914; ● 800
JOHNSON; **233** K-20; Ⓟ 13,766; Ⓒ 17,499; ◆ 18,151
Johnson City; Inc. Place; WASHINGTON, CARTER, SULLIVAN; **233** K-18; elev. 1,635ft./498m.; 🅿 🅷 🅲 13,108 ■; ★ **JNSC-**; z 37601-02, z 37604-05, z 37614-15; Ⓟ 49,479; Ⓒ 55,469; ◆ 64,463
Johnsons; RMC Place; SUMNER; ***233** B-12; ★ **NASH**; mail Cottontown z 37048; pop. incl. with Walnut Grove (RMC Place)
Johnsons Chapel; RMC Place; DEKALB; ***233** D-14; elev. 1,000ft./305m.; mail Sparta z 38583; rural
Johnsons Grove; RMC Place; CROCKETT; **232** D-4; elev. 357ft./109m.; mail Bells z 38006; ● 60
Johnsonville; HUMPHREYS; see New Johnsonville (Inc. Place)
Johntown; RMC Place; TROUSDALE; ***233** B-13; mail Hartsville z 37074; rural
Jones; RMC Place; HAYWOOD; ***232** E-4; mail Bells z 38006; rural
Jonesborough; Inc. Place; ⊡ WASHINGTON; **233** K-18; elev. 1,692ft./516m.; 🅿; ★ **JNSC-**; z 37659; Ⓟ 3,091; Ⓒ 4,168
Jones Chapel; RMC Place; PICKETT; ***233** A-16; elev. 1,008ft./307m.; mail Byrdstown z 38549; rural
Jones Cove; RMC Place; SEVIER; **214** G-5; mail Sevierville z 37876; ● 50
Jones Mill; RMC Place; HENRY; **232** B-6; mail Cottage Grove z 38224; ● 30
Jones Valley; RMC Place; HICKMAN; ***232** D-10; elev. 545ft./166m.; mail Santa Fe z 38482; ● 30
Jonesville; RMC Place; FENTRESS; ***233** C-16; elev. 1,700ft./518m.; mail Clarkrange z 38553; ● 50
Jonesville; RMC Place; ROANE; **233** D-18; ★ **KNOX**; mail Oliver Springs z 37840; ● 50
Joppa; RMC Place; GRAINGER; **233** C-20; mail Rutledge z 37861; ● 30
Joppa; RMC Place; WHITE; ***233** D-14; elev. 970ft./296m.; mail Walling z 38587; rural
Jordonia; RMC Place; DAVIDSON; ***233** C-11; ★ **NASH**; mail Nashville z 37218; pop. incl. with Nashville (Inc. Place)
Jug Town; RMC Place; RUTHERFORD; ***233** D-12; elev. 626ft./191m.; ★ **MUR**; mail Murfreesboro z 37130; pop. incl. with Murfreesboro (Inc. Place)
Juno; RMC Place; HENDERSON; **232** E-6; mail Lexington z 38351; ● 50

K

Kagley; RMC Place; BLOUNT; ***233** E-19; mail Maryville z 37801; rural
K and A Junction; RMC Place; KNOX; ★ **KNOX**; pop. incl. with Knoxville (Inc. Place)
Kansas; RMC Place; JEFFERSON; ***233** L-15; ★ **MORR**; mail Jefferson City z 37760, Talbott z 37877; rural
Kansas; RMC Place; SUMNER; ***233** B-12; mail Gallatin z 37066; rural
Karns; RMC Place; KNOX; **233** D-19; elev. 963ft./294m.; 🅿; ★ **KNOX**; z 37921; Ⓟ 1,458
Kaywood; RMC Place; COFFEE; mail Tullahoma z 37388; pop. incl. with Tullahoma (Inc. Place)
Kedron; RMC Place; GILES; ***232** G-10; mail Prospect z 38477; ● 30
Kedron; RMC Place; MAURY; ***233** E-11; mail Spring Hill z 37174; pop. incl. with Spring Hill (Inc. Place)
Keefe; RMC Place; LAKE; ***232** B-3; elev. 293ft./89m.; mail Ridgely z 38080; ● 30
Keeling; RMC Place; HAYWOOD, TIPTON; ***232** E-3; mail Stanton z 38069
Keenburg; RMC Place; CARTER; ***233** K-19; ★ **JNSC-**; mail Elizabethton z 37643; ● 80
Keese; RMC Place; FRANKLIN; ***233** F-13; mail Decherd z 37324; pop. incl. with Decherd (Inc. Place)
Keith Springs; RMC Place; FRANKLIN; ***233** G-13; elev. 1,860ft./567m.; mail Winchester z 37398; rural
Kellertown; RMC Place; BEDFORD; ***233** E-12; elev. 860ft./262m.; mail Wartrace z 37183; rural
Kelley Town; RMC Place; ROANE; ***233** C-18; ★ **KNOX**; mail Oliver Springs z 37840; pop. incl. with Oliver Springs (Inc. Place)
Kelso; RMC Place; LINCOLN; **233** G-12; elev. 949ft./289m.; 🅿; z 37348; ● 130
Keltonburg; RMC Place; DEKALB; ***233** D-14; elev. 960ft./293m.; mail Smithville z 37166; ● 30
Kemmer Hill; RMC Place; RHEA; ***233** E-17; mail Spring City z 37381; pop. incl. with Spring City (Inc. Place)
Kempville; RMC Place; SMITH; ***233** B-14; elev. 625ft./191m.; mail Carthage z 37030; ● 90
Kendricks Creek; RMC Place; SULLIVAN; ***233** J-18; ★ **JNSC-**; mail Kingsport z 37663
Kennedy Creek; RMC Place; WILSON; ***233** D-13; mail Auburntown z 37016; rural
Kenneytown; RMC Place; GREENE; ***233** K-17; mail Greeneville z 37745; rural
Kenton; Inc. Place; OBION, GIBSON; **232** C-4; elev. 308ft./94m.; 🅿; z 38233; Ⓟ 1,366; Ⓒ 1,306
Kepler; RMC Place; HAWKINS; ***233** K-17; mail Rogersville z 37857; rural
Kerrville; RMC Place; SHELBY; **232** F-2; ★ **MEM**; mail Millington z 38053; ● 210
Kettle Mills; RMC Place; MAURY; ***232** E-9; mail Hampshire z 38461; rural
Key; RMC Place; WHITE; ***233** C-15; mail Sparta z 38583; ● 30
Key Corner; RMC Place; LAUDERDALE; ***232** D-3; elev. 297ft./91m.; mail Halls z 38040; rural
Keystone; RMC Place; WASHINGTON; ***233** K-18; ★ **JNSC-**; mail Johnson City z 37601; pop. incl. with Johnson City (Inc. Place)
Killians Chapel; RMC Place; GRUNDY; mail Altamont z 37301; pop. incl. with Altamont (Inc. Place)
Kilsyth; RMC Place; CAMPBELL; ***233** B-19; mail La Follette z 37766; rural
Kimball; Inc. Place; MARION; **233** G-14; elev. 672ft./205m.; 🅿; z 37347; Ⓟ 1,243; Ⓒ 1,312
Kimberlin Heights; RMC Place; KNOX; **233** D-20; elev. 992ft./302m.; 🅿; ★ **KNOX**; z 37920; ● 680
Kimberly Acres; RMC Place; WILSON; ***233** C-12; mail Mount Juliet z 37122; ● 230
Kimbrough Crossroad; RMC Place; JEFFERSON; ***233** L-15; ★ **MORR**; mail White Pine z 37890; pop. incl. with White Pine (Inc. Place)
Kimery; RMC Place; WEAKLEY; ***232** C-5; elev. 341ft./104m.; mail Greenfield z 38230; rural
Kimmins; RMC Place; LEWIS; **232** E-9; elev. 935ft./285m.; 🅿; z 38462; ● 130
Kimsey; RMC Place; POLK; ***233** G-18; mail Turtletown z 37391; rural
Kin Cove; RMC Place; WILSON; ***233** C-12; elev. 500ft./152m.; ★ **NASH**; mail Mount Juliet z 37122; ● 80
Kinderhook; RMC Place; MAURY; ***232** D-10; elev. 820ft./250m.; mail Primm Springs z 38476; ● 30
Kingfield; RMC Place; WILLIAMSON; ***232** D-10; elev. 936ft./285m.; mail Franklin z 37064
Kings Point; RMC Place; HAMILTON; ***233** G-16; ★ **CHTN**; pop. incl. with Chattanooga (Inc. Place)
Kingsport; Inc. Place; SULLIVAN, HAWKINS; **233** J-18; elev. 1,208ft./368m.; 🅿 🅷 ■; ★ **JNSC-**; z 37660, z 37662-65, z 37669; Ⓟ 36,353; Ⓒ 44,905; ◆ 46,814
King Springs; RMC Place; WASHINGTON; ★ **JNSC-**; mail Johnson City z 37601; pop. incl. with Johnson City (Inc. Place)
Kings Ridge; RMC Place; HAMILTON; ★ **CHTN**; mail Hixson z 37343; pop. incl. with Chattanooga (Inc. Place)
Kingston; Inc. Place; ⊡ ROANE; **233** D-18; elev. 233ft./71m.; 🅿; ★ **KNOX**; z 37763; Ⓟ 4,552; Ⓒ 5,264
Kingston Heights; RMC Place; ROANE; ***233** D-18; ★ **KNOX**; mail Kingston z 37763; ● 180
Kingston Hills; RMC Place; KNOX; ***233** D-19; ★ **KNOX**; mail Knoxville z 37919; pop. incl. with Knoxville (Inc. Place)
Kingston Mill; BEDFORD; see Anchor Mill (RMC Place)
Kingston Springs; Inc. Place; CHEATHAM; **232** C-10; elev. 512ft./156m.; 🅿; ★ **NASH**; z 37082; Ⓟ 1,529; Ⓒ 2,773
Kingston Woods; RMC Place; KNOX; ***233** D-19; elev. 964ft./294m.; ★ **KNOX**; mail Knoxville z 37919; ● 840
Kinneys; RMC Place; ROBERTSON; ***232** B-10; elev. 650ft./198m.; mail Springfield z 37172; rural
Kinzel Springs; RMC Place; BLOUNT; ***233** E-20; mail Townsend z 37882; summer pop. 500; ● 180
Kirk; RMC Place; FAYETTE; ***232** G-3; elev. 357ft./109m.; mail Collierville z 38017; rural
Kirkland; RMC Place; LINCOLN; ***233** G-11; elev. 938ft./286m.; mail Fayetteville z 37334, Taft z 38488; rural
Kirkland; RMC Place; WILLIAMSON; **233** D-11; elev. 760ft./232m.; mail College Grove z 37046; ● 80
Kirkwood; RMC Place; MONTGOMERY; ***232** A-10; elev. 559ft./170m.; ★ **CLRKV**; mail Clarksville z 37040; ● 30
Kite; RMC Place; HAWKINS; ***233** K-16; elev. 1,094ft./333m.; mail Rogersville z 37857; rural
Kittrell; RMC Place; RUTHERFORD; **233** D-13; mail Readyville z 37149; ● 120
Kleburne; RMC Place; MAURY; ***232** E-10; elev. 690ft./210m.; mail Spring Hill z 37174; pop. incl. with Spring Hill (Inc. Place)
Klondike; RMC Place; HAWKINS; ***233** K-16; mail Rogersville z 37857; rural
Knapp; RMC Place; ANDERSON; ***233** C-19; ★ **KNOX**; mail Lake City z 37769; rural
Knob Creek; RMC Place; LAUDERDALE; ***232** D-3; mail Ripley z 38063; rural
Knob Creek; RMC Place; SEVIER; **214** G-3; ★ **KNOX**; mail Seymour z 37865; ● 70
KNOX; **233** C-20; Ⓟ 335,749; Ⓒ 382,032; ◆ 445,260
Knoxville; Inc. Place; ⊡ KNOX; **233** D-19; elev. 889ft./271m.; 🅿 🅷 🅲 28,075 ■; ★ **KNOX**; z 37901-02, z 37909, z 37912, z 37914-24, z 37927-34, z 37938-40, z 37950, z 37995-98; Ⓟ 165,039; Ⓒ 173,890; ◆ 198,350
Kodak; RMC Place; SEVIER; **214** F-4; elev. 893ft./272m.; 🅿; ★ **KNOX**; z 37764; ● 350
Kodak Estates; RMC Place; SEVIER; ***233** D-20; ★ **KNOX**; mail Kodak z 37764; rural
KoKo; RMC Place; HAYWOOD; ***232** E-4; elev. 311ft./95m.; mail Stanton z 38069; rural
Kontika; RMC Place; WILSON; ***233** C-12; mail Lebanon z 37087; pop. incl. with Lebanon (Inc. Place)
Kyles Ford; RMC Place; HANCOCK; **233** J-16; elev. 1,173ft./358m.; 🅿; z 37765; ● 90

L

Laager; RMC Place; GRUNDY; ***233** F-14; elev. 1,901ft./579m.; mail Gruetli Laager z 37339; pop. incl. with Gruetli-Laager (Inc. Place)
Laconia; RMC Place; FAYETTE; **232** F-4; elev. 437ft./133m.; 🅿; z 38045; ● 60
Lacy; RMC Place; HARDEMAN; ***232** G-5; elev. 416ft./127m.; mail Middleton z 38052
Lafayette; Inc. Place; ⊡ MACON; **233** B-13; elev. 963ft./294m.; 🅿 🅷; z 37083; Ⓟ 3,641; Ⓒ 3,885
LaFollette; Inc. Place; CAMPBELL; **233** B-19; elev. 1,226ft./374m.; 🅿 🅷; ★ **KNOX**; z 37729, z 37766; Ⓟ 7,192; Ⓒ 7,926
La Grange; Inc. Place; FAYETTE; **232** G-4; elev. 554ft./169m.; 🅿; z 38046; Ⓟ 167; Ⓒ 136
Laguardo; RMC Place; WILSON; **233** C-12; ★ **NASH**; mail Lebanon z 37087; ● 170
LAKE; **232** B-3; Ⓟ 7,129; Ⓒ 7,954; ◆ 7,238
Lake City; Inc. Place; ANDERSON; **233** C-19; elev. 855ft./261m.; 🅿; ★ **KNOX**; z 37769; Ⓟ 2,166; Ⓒ 1,888
Lake Colonial Estates; RMC Place; WILLIAMSON; ***233** D-11; ★ **NASH**; mail Arrington z 37014; rural
Lake Crest; RMC Place; SULLIVAN; ***233** J-18; ★ **JNSC-**; mail Kingsport z 37663
Lake Drive; RMC Place; LAKE; ***232** B-3; elev. 290ft./88m.; mail Tiptonville z 38079; ● 50
Lake Farm Estates; RMC Place; RUTHERFORD; ***233** D-12; ★ **NASH**; mail Smyrna z 37167; ● 200
Lake Forest; RMC Place; GRAINGER; ***233** C-20; mail Rutledge z 37861; rural
Lake Forest; RMC Place; HAMILTON; ★ **CHTN**; mail Hixson z 37343; pop. incl. with Chattanooga (Inc. Place)
Lake Forest; RMC Place; KNOX; **233** N-14; ★ **KNOX**; mail Knoxville z 37920; pop. incl. with Knoxville (Inc. Place)
Lakeharbor; RMC Place; ROANE; ***233** D-17; elev. 760ft./232m.; mail Kingston z 37763; rural
Lake Harbor Estates; RMC Place; HAMILTON; ***233** G-16; ★ **CHTN**; mail Chattanooga z 37416
Lake Haven; RMC Place; WILSON; ***233** C-12; ★ **NASH**; mail Lebanon z 37087
Lake Hills; RMC Place; COFFEE; mail Tullahoma z 37388; pop. incl. with Tullahoma (Inc. Place)
Lake Hills; RMC Place; HAMILTON; **233** J-13; ★ **CHTN**; pop. incl. with Chattanooga (Inc. Place)
Lakeland; Inc. Place; SHELBY; **232** F-2; 🅿; ★ **MEM**; z 38002; Ⓟ 1,204; Ⓒ 6,862
Lakemont; RMC Place; BLOUNT; ***233** D-19; ★ **KNOX**; mail Louisville z 37777; ● 380
Lakemont Cabin Area; RMC Place; HAWKINS; ***233** K-16; elev. 1,096ft./334m.; mail Mooresburg z 37811; ● 70
Lakemont Heights; RMC Place; ROANE; ***233** D-17; mail Rockwood z 37854; pop. incl. with Rockwood (Inc. Place)
Lakemoor; RMC Place; KNOX; ***233** D-19; elev. 900ft./274m.; ★ **KNOX**; mail Knoxville z 37920; ● 450
Lakemoore; RMC Place; HAMBLEN; ***233** K-16; elev. 1,173ft./358m.; ★ **MORR**; mail Morristown z 37814
Lake Placid (Chickasaw Park); RMC Place; CHESTER; mail Henderson z 38340; summer pop. 200
Lake Road; RMC Place; WILLIAMSON; ***232** D-10; ★ **NASH**; mail Fairview z 37062; pop. incl. with Fairview (Inc. Place)
Lakeshore Estates; RMC Place; HAMILTON; ***233** G-16; ★ **CHTN**; mail Chattanooga z 37416
Lake Side; RMC Place; JEFFERSON; ***233** L-15; elev. 1,022ft./312m.; ★ **MORR**; mail White Pine z 37890; ● 30
Lakeside; RMC Place; MONROE; ***233** E-18; mail Vonore z 37885; rural
Lakeside Estates; RMC Place; FRANKLIN; mail Estill Springs z 37330
Lakeside Heights; RMC Place; JEFFERSON; ***233** L-15; ★ **MORR**; mail White Pine z 37890; ● 50
Lakeside Park; RMC Place; HAMILTON; ***233** G-16; elev. 709ft./216m.; ★ **CHTN**; mail Hixson z 37343; ● 300
Lakesite; Inc. Place; HAMILTON; **233** F-16; elev. 780ft./238m.; 🅿; ★ **CHTN**; z 37379; Ⓟ 732; Ⓒ 1,845
Lake Tansi Village; CDP; CUMBERLAND; **233** D-16; elev. 1,880ft./573m.; mail Crossville z 38572; Ⓒ 2,621
Lake Tullahoma Estates; RMC Place; COFFEE; ***233** F-13; mail Tullahoma z 37388; pop. incl. with Tullahoma (Inc. Place)
Lakeview; RMC Place; BLOUNT; ***233** D-19; elev. 860ft./262m.; ★ **KNOX**; mail Louisville z 37777; pop. incl. with Louisville (Inc. Place)
Lakeview; RMC Place; CLAIBORNE; ***233** B-20; mail New Tazewell z 37825; rural
Lakeview; RMC Place; ROANE; ***233** D-17; ★ **KNOX**; mail Kingston z 37763; ● 100
Lakeview; RMC Place; ROBERTSON; ***233** B-11; elev. 740ft./226m.; mail Springfield z 37172; rural
Lakeview Commercial Park; RMC Place; WILLIAMSON; ***233** D-11; ★ **NASH**; mail Franklin z 37064; pop. incl. with Franklin (Inc. Place)
Lakeview Estates; RMC Place; BLOUNT; ***233** D-19; elev. 860ft./262m.; ★ **KNOX**; mail Louisville z 37777; ● 160
Lake View Heights; RMC Place; ROANE; ★ **KNOX**; mail Harriman z 37748; pop. incl. with Harriman (Inc. Place)
Lakeview Manor; RMC Place; HENRY; ***232** C-7; mail Springville z 38256; ● 100
Lakeview Park; RMC Place; JEFFERSON; ***233** C-20; mail Dandridge z 37725; pop. incl. with Dandridge (Inc. Place)
Lake Vista; RMC Place; HAMILTON; ***233** G-16; ★ **CHTN**; pop. incl. with Chattanooga (Inc. Place)
Lakewood (Dupontonia); Inc. Place; DAVIDSON; **233** C-11; elev. 476ft./145m.; ★ **NASH**; mail Old Hickory z 37138; Ⓟ 2,009; Ⓒ 2,341
Lakewood Village; RMC Place; RHEA; ***233** E-17; elev. 760ft./232m.; mail Spring City z 37381; ● 90
Lamar; RMC Place; SHELBY; ★ **MEM**; mail Memphis z 38114; pop. incl. with Memphis (Inc. Place)
Lamar; RMC Place; WASHINGTON; ***233** K-18; elev. 1,568ft./478m.; ★ **JNSC-**; mail Jonesborough z 37659; ● 50
Lambert; RMC Place; FAYETTE; ***232** F-3; elev. 313ft./95m.; mail Somerville z 38068; rural
Lamont; RMC Place; ROBERTSON; **233** A-11; elev. 678ft./207m.; mail Springfield z 37172; ● 90
Lamontville; RMC Place; MCMINN; ***233** F-17; elev. 704ft./215m.; mail Calhoun z 37309; rural
Lancaster; RMC Place; SMITH; **233** C-14; elev. 630ft./192m.; 🅿; z 38569; ● 180
Lancaster Hill; RMC Place; SMITH; ***233** C-14; mail Hickman z 38567; ● 50
Lancelot Acres; RMC Place; GILES; ***232** G-10; mail Pulaski z 38478; pop. incl. with Pulaski (Inc. Place)
Lancing; RMC Place; MORGAN; **233** C-17; elev. 1,189ft./362m.; 🅿; z 37770; ● 200
Lane; RMC Place; DYER; **232** C-3; elev. 273ft./83m.; mail Obion z 38240; ● 50
Laneview; RMC Place; GIBSON; **232** C-5; elev. 429ft./131m.; mail Trenton z 38382; ● 130
Langford Farms; RMC Place; WILSON; ***233** C-12; ★ **NASH**; mail Old Hickory z 37138; ● 800
Lanier; RMC Place; BLOUNT; ***233** E-19; elev. 1,000ft./305m.; mail Maryville z 37801; rural
Lantana; RMC Place; CUMBERLAND; ***233** D-16; elev. 2,054ft./626m.; mail Crossville z 38572
Lapata (Laplata); RMC Place; DYER; ***232** C-4; elev. 356ft./109m.; mail Newbern z 38059; ● 60
Laplata; DYER; see Lapata (RMC Place)
Lascassas; RMC Place; RUTHERFORD; **233** D-12; elev. 585ft./178m.; 🅿; z 37085; ● 120
Lassiter Corner; RMC Place; OBION; ***232** B-3; elev. 311ft./95m.; mail Hornbeak z 38232; rural
Latham; RMC Place; WEAKLEY; **232** B-5; mail Dresden z 38225; ● 130
LAUDERDALE; **232** D-2; Ⓟ 23,491; Ⓒ 27,101; ◆ 26,681
Laurel; RMC Place; ANDERSON; ***233** C-19; ★ **KNOX**; mail Clinton z 37716; rural
Laurel; RMC Place; SEVIER; ***233** D-20; mail Sevierville z 37876; rural
Laurel Bloomery; RMC Place; JOHNSON; **233** J-20; elev. 2,412ft./735m.; 🅿; z 37680; ● 200
Laurel Bluff; RMC Place; ROANE; ***233** D-18; mail Kingston z 37763; rural
Laurel Brook; RMC Place; RHEA; ***233** E-16; mail Dayton z 37321; ● 180
Laurelburg; RMC Place; VAN BUREN; ***233** E-14; mail Rock Island z 38581; rural
Laurel Cove; RMC Place; VAN BUREN; ***233** E-15; elev. 965ft./294m.; mail Rock Island z 38581; ● 30
Laurel Grove; RMC Place; ANDERSON; ***233** C-18; elev. 969ft./295m.; ★ **KNOX**; mail Briceville z 37710; rural
Laurel Hill (Wolf Creek); RMC Place; DEKALB; ***233** C-14; elev. 535ft./163m.; mail Silver Point z 38582; rural
La Vergne; Inc. Place; RUTHERFORD; **233** D-12; elev. 672ft./205m.; 🅿; ★ **NASH**; z 37086, z 37089; Ⓟ 7,499; Ⓒ 18,687; ◆ 34,122
Lavinia; RMC Place; CARROLL; **232** D-5; elev. 528ft./161m.; 🅿; z 38348; ● 150
Law; RMC Place; HENDERSON; ***232** D-6; elev. 502ft./153m.; mail Lexington z 38351; rural
Law Chapel; RMC Place; BLOUNT; ***233** E-19; elev. 1,019ft./311m.; ★ **KNOX**; mail Maryville z 37801; rural
Lawnville; RMC Place; ROANE; ***233** D-18; elev. 798ft./243m.; mail Kingston z 37763; ● 120
LAWRENCE; **232** F-9; Ⓟ 35,303; Ⓒ 39,926; ◆ 41,255
Lawrenceburg; Inc. Place; ⊡ LAWRENCE; **232** F-9; elev. 890ft./271m.; 🅿 🅷; z 38464; Ⓟ 10,412; Ⓒ 10,796
Lawson Crossroad; RMC Place; BLOUNT; ***233** E-20; elev. 1,227ft./374m.; mail Townsend z 37882; rural
Lawton; MCNAIRY; see New Lawton (RMC Place)
Leach; RMC Place; CARROLL; **232** D-6; mail Huntingdon z 38344; ● 80
Leadvale; RMC Place; COCKE; ***233** L-16; elev. 1,005ft./306m.; ★ **MORR**; mail White Pine z 37890; rural
Leadvale; RMC Place; JEFFERSON; ***233** L-16; elev. 1,070ft./326m.; ★ **MORR**; mail White Pine z 37890; ● 50
Leana; RMC Place; RUTHERFORD; ***233** D-12; elev. 550ft./168m.; ★ **MUR**; mail Murfreesboro z 37129; rural
Leapwood; RMC Place; MCNAIRY; **232** F-6; mail Adamsville z 38310; ● 40
Lea Springs; RMC Place; GRAINGER; ***233** C-20; elev. 965ft./294m.; ★ **KNOX**; mail Blaine z 37709; rural
Leatherwood; RMC Place; WAYNE; ***232** F-8; mail Waynesboro z 38485; ● 30
Lebanon; Inc. Place; ⊡ WILSON; **233** C-12; elev. 531ft./162m.; 🅿 🅷 🅲 1,526 ■; z 37087-88, z 37090 & mail La Vergne z 37089; Ⓟ 15,208; Ⓒ 20,235; Ⓡ 20,195; ◆ 24,732
Ledgemere; RMC Place; BEDFORD; ***233** E-12; mail Shelbyville z 37160; pop. incl. with Shelbyville (Inc. Place)
Lee; BLEDSOE; see Lees Station (RMC Place)
Leeland; RMC Place; WILLIAMSON; ***233** D-11; ★ **NASH**; mail Franklin z 37064; rural
Leemans Corner; RMC Place; WILSON; ***233** C-13; mail Lebanon z 37090; rural
Leesburg; RMC Place; WASHINGTON; **233** K-18; ★ **JNSC-**; mail Jonesborough z 37659; ● 80
Lees Station (Lee); RMC Place; BLEDSOE; **233** E-15; mail Pikeville z 37367; ● 80
Lee Valley; RMC Place; HAWKINS; ***233** J-16; mail Sneedville z 37869; ● 30
Leeville; RMC Place; WILSON; ***233** C-12; elev. 581ft./177m.; ★ **NASH**; mail Lebanon z 37090; ● 90
Leewood; RMC Place; SHELBY; ★ **MEM**; mail Memphis z 38101; pop. incl. with Memphis (Inc. Place)
Leftwich; RMC Place; MAURY; ***233** E-11; mail Columbia z 38401; rural
Legate; RMC Place; STEWART; ***232** B-8; mail Indian Mound z 37079; ● 30
Leighs; RMC Place; TIPTON; ***232** E-2; elev. 300ft./91m.; ★ **MEM**; mail Covington z 38019; rural
Leighton; RMC Place; MADISON; **232** E-4; elev. 415ft./126m.; mail Denmark z 38391; ● 50
Leinart; RMC Place; ANDERSON; ***233** C-19; elev. 900ft./274m.; ★ **KNOX**; mail Clinton z 37716; rural
Leipers Fork (Hillsboro); RMC Place; WILLIAMSON; **232** D-10; mail Franklin z 37064; ● 510
Lenoir City; Inc. Place; LOUDON; **233** D-18; elev. 798ft./243m.; 🅿; ★ **KNOX**; z 37771-72; Ⓟ 6,147; Ⓒ 6,819
Lenow; RMC Place; SHELBY; ***232** F-2; ★ **MEM**; mail Cordova z 38018; rural
Lenox; RMC Place; DYER; **232** C-3; elev. 304ft./93m.; 🅿; z 38047; ● 250
Leoma; RMC Place; LAWRENCE; **232** G-9; elev. 900ft./274m.; 🅿; z 38468; ● 390
Leonardtown; RMC Place; SULLIVAN; ***233** J-18; ★ **JNSC-**; mail Bristol z 37620; ● 100
Leoni; RMC Place; CANNON; ***233** D-13; elev. 1,146ft./349m.; mail Woodbury z 37190; ● 30
LEWIS; **232** E-9; Ⓟ 9,247; Ⓒ 11,367; ◆ 11,710
Lewisburg; Inc. Place; ⊡ MARSHALL; **233** F-11; elev. 734ft./224m.; 🅿 🅷; z 37091; Ⓟ 9,879; Ⓒ 10,413
Lewis Chapel; RMC Place; SEQUATCHIE; **233** F-15; mail Dunlap z 37327; ● 80
Lexie; RMC Place; FRANKLIN; ***233** G-12; mail Belvidere z 37306; rural
Lexie Crossroads; RMC Place; FRANKLIN; ***233** G-12; mail Belvidere z 37306
Lexington; Inc. Place; ⊡ HENDERSON; **232** E-6; elev. 503ft./153m.; 🅿 🅷; z 38351; Ⓟ 5,810; Ⓒ 7,393
Liberty; RMC Place; BENTON; ***232** C-7; elev. 551ft./168m.; mail Camden z 38320; ● 50
Liberty; Inc. Place; DEKALB; **233** D-13; elev. 616ft./188m.; 🅿; z 37095; Ⓟ 391; Ⓒ 367
Liberty; RMC Place; DECATUR; ***232** F-7; elev. 530ft./162m.; mail Scotts Hill z 38374; rural
Liberty; RMC Place; FRANKLIN; ***233** G-13; mail Winchester z 37398; rural
Liberty; RMC Place; GILES; ***232** G-10; mail Prospect z 38477; ● 30
Liberty; RMC Place; JACKSON; ***233** C-14; mail Granville z 38564; rural
Liberty; RMC Place; LINCOLN; ***233** G-12; elev. 714ft./218m.; mail Fayetteville z 37334; rural
Liberty; RMC Place; MORGAN; ***233** C-17; elev. 1,303ft./397m.; mail Wartburg z 37887; rural
Liberty; RMC Place; SEQUATCHIE; ***233** F-15; elev. 700ft./213m.; mail Whitwell z 37397; ● 50
Liberty; RMC Place; SUMNER; ***233** B-12; elev. 736ft./224m.; mail Bethpage z 37022; rural
Liberty; RMC Place; WASHINGTON; **233** L-17; mail Chuckey z 37641; ● 130
Liberty; RMC Place; WEAKLEY; ***232** C-5; mail Gleason z 38229; rural
Liberty Grove; RMC Place; LAWRENCE; **232** G-9; mail Loretto z 38469; ● 30
Liberty Hill; RMC Place; GILES; ***232** F-10; elev. 1,000ft./305m.; mail Ethridge z 38456; rural
Liberty Hill; RMC Place; GRAINGER; ***233** B-20; elev. 1,253ft./382m.; mail Washburn z 37888; ● 50
Liberty Hill; RMC Place; GREENE; ***233** K-17; elev. 1,795ft./547m.; mail Chuckey z 37641; rural
Liberty Hill; RMC Place; MCMINN; ***233** F-18; elev. 912ft./278m.; mail Englewood z 37329; rural
Liberty Hill; RMC Place; WILLIAMSON; ***232** D-10; ★ **NASH**; mail Bon Aqua z 37025; rural
Liberty Hill; RMC Place; WILSON; ***233** C-13; elev. 820ft./250m.; mail Alexandria z 37012; rural
Lick Creek; RMC Place; BENTON; ***232** B-7; mail Big Sandy z 38221; rural
Lick Creek; RMC Place; DECATUR; ***232** E-7; elev. 400ft./122m.; mail Parsons z 38363; ● 50
Lickskillet; RMC Place; UNION; ***233** C-20; elev. 1,064ft./324m.; ★ **KNOX**; mail Maynardville z 37807; rural
Lickton; RMC Place; DAVIDSON; ***233** C-11; elev. 523ft./159m.; ★ **NASH**; mail Whites Creek z 37189; pop. incl. with Nashville (Inc. Place)
Lightfoot; RMC Place; LAUDERDALE; ***232** D-3; elev. 315ft./96m.; mail Ripley z 38063; rural
Lillamay; RMC Place; CHEATHAM; ***232** C-10; mail Ashland City z 37015; ● 50
Lillydale; RMC Place; UNICOI; ***233** L-18; mail Erwin z 37650; ● 600
Lily Grove; RMC Place; CLAIBORNE; ***233** B-20; mail New Tazewell z 37825; rural
Limestone; RMC Place; WASHINGTON; **233** K-17; elev. 1,394ft./425m.; 🅿; z 37681; ● 550
Limestone Cove; RMC Place; UNICOI; ***233** K-19; mail Unicoi z 37692; ● 200
Linary; RMC Place; CUMBERLAND; ***233** D-16; mail Crossville z 38572; rural
Lincoln; RMC Place; LINCOLN; **233** G-12; elev. 826ft./252m.; mail Fayetteville z 37334; ● 160
LINCOLN; **233** G-11; Ⓟ 28,157; Ⓒ 31,340; ◆ 33,083
Lincoln Park; RMC Place; KNOX; ***233** D-19; ★ **KNOX**; mail Knoxville z 37917; pop. incl. with Knoxville (Inc. Place)
Lincoya Hills; RMC Place; DAVIDSON; ***233** C-11; ★ **NASH**; mail Nashville z 37214; pop. incl. with Nashville (Inc. Place)
Linde; RMC Place; KNOX; ★ **KNOX**; pop. incl. with Knoxville (Inc. Place)
Linden; Inc. Place; ⊡ PERRY; **232** E-8; elev. 567ft./173m.; 🅿 🅷; z 37096; Ⓟ 1,099; Ⓒ 1,015
Lindsay Mill; RMC Place; CAMPBELL; ***233** C-19; elev. 1,060ft./323m.; ★ **KNOX**; mail Lake City z 37769; ● 30
Link; RMC Place; RUTHERFORD; ***233** E-12; mail Christiana z 37037; rural
Linsdale; RMC Place; POLK; ***233** F-17; elev. 740ft./226m.; mail Delano z 37325; ● 30
Linton; RMC Place; DAVIDSON; ***232** D-10; elev. 620ft./189m.; ★ **NASH**; mail Nashville z 37216; pop. incl. with Nashville (Inc. Place)
Linwood; RMC Place; WILSON; ***233** C-13; mail Lebanon z 37090; rural
Lisbon; RMC Place; HARDEMAN; ***232** G-5; mail Middleton z 38052; rural
Little Barren; RMC Place; CLAIBORNE, UNION; ***233** B-20; mail New Tazewell z 37825; rural
Littlebrook; RMC Place; BLOUNT; ***233** D-19; elev. 860ft./262m.; ★ **KNOX**; mail Rockford z 37853; pop. incl. with Rockford (Inc. Place)
Littlecrab; RMC Place; FENTRESS; ***233** B-16; elev. 940ft./287m.; mail Jamestown z 38556; ● 30
Little Creek; RMC Place; CLAIBORNE; ***233** B-20; mail Harrogate z 37752; ● 30
Little Doe; RMC Place; JOHNSON; ***233** J-20; mail Butler z 37640; rural
Little Emory; RMC Place; ROANE; ***233** D-18; elev. 752ft./229m.; ★ **KNOX**; mail Harriman z 37748; ● 70
Little Hope; RMC Place; RUTHERFORD; ***233** D-12; ★ **NASH**; mail Murfreesboro z 37129; ● 150
Little Hope; RMC Place; WAYNE; ***232** F-8; elev. 700ft./213m.; mail Waynesboro z 38485; rural
Littlelot; RMC Place; HICKMAN; **232** D-9; mail Duck River z 38454; ● 120
Little Milligan; RMC Place; CARTER; ***233** K-19; mail Butler z 37640; ● 30
Little River; RMC Place; BLOUNT; ***233** D-19; ★ **KNOX**; mail Maryville z 37804; pop. incl. with Rockford (Inc. Place)
Little Texas; WILLIAMSON; see Peytonsville (RMC Place)
Little White Oak; RMC Place; CAMPBELL; ***233** B-19; mail La Follette z 37766; rural
Litton; RMC Place; BLEDSOE; ***233** E-16; mail Pikeville z 37367; ● 50
Litz Manor; RMC Place; SULLIVAN; ***233** J-18; ★ **JNSC-**; mail Kingsport z 37660; pop. incl. with Kingsport (Inc. Place)
Liverwort; RMC Place; MONTGOMERY; ***232** B-9; elev. 630ft./192m.; mail Clarksville z 37040; rural
Livesay Mill; RMC Place; HANCOCK; ***233** J-16; elev. 1,157ft./353m.; mail Eidson z 37731; rural
Livingston; Inc. Place; ⊡ OVERTON; **233** B-15; elev. 1,038ft./316m.; 🅿 🅷; z 38570; Ⓟ 3,809; Ⓒ 3,498
Lobelville; Inc. Place; PERRY; **232** D-8; elev. 501ft./153m.; 🅿; z 37097; Ⓟ 830; Ⓒ 915
Locke; RMC Place; SHELBY; **232** F-1; elev. 394ft./120m.; ★ **MEM**; mail Millington z 38053; ● 110
Lockertsville; RMC Place; CHEATHAM; ***232** B-10; elev. 687ft./209m.; ★ **NASH**; mail Ashland City z 37015; rural
Lockmiller Addition; RMC Place; MCMINN; ***233** F-17; mail Athens z 37303; pop. incl. with Athens (Inc. Place)
Locust Grove; RMC Place; DYER; ***232** C-4; mail Newbern z 38059; ● 50
Locust Mount; RMC Place; WASHINGTON; ***233** K-18; ★ **JNSC-**; mail Jonesborough z 37659; rural
Locust Springs; RMC Place; GREENE; ***233** K-17; elev. 1,210ft./369m.; mail Afton z 37616; rural
Lodge; RMC Place; MARION; ***233** G-14; mail South Pittsburg z 37380; rural
Lodi; RMC Place; LAWRENCE; ***232** F-9; mail Westpoint z 38486; rural
Logans Lake; RMC Place; MCNAIRY; ***232** F-5; elev. 465ft./142m.; mail Finger z 38334; rural
Lois; RMC Place; MOORE; ***233** F-12; mail Mulberry z 37359; pop. incl. with Lynchburg (Inc. Place)
Lomax Crossroads; RMC Place; LEWIS; ***232** E-9; mail Hohenwald z 38462; pop. incl. with Hohenwald (Inc. Place)
Lone Mountain; RMC Place; CLAIBORNE; **233** B-20; elev. 1,126ft./343m.; 🅿; z 37773 & mail New Tazewell z 37825; ● 220
Lone Mountain; RMC Place; SCOTT; ***233** C-18; mail Robbins z 37852; rural
Lone Oak; MONTGOMERY; see Cunningham (RMC Place)
Lone Oak; RMC Place; SEQUATCHIE; **233** G-15; mail Signal Mountain z 37377; ● 400
Lone Oaks; RMC Place; TIPTON; ***232** E-2; ★ **MEM**; mail Atoka z 38004; pop. incl. with Atoka (Inc. Place)
Lone Star; RMC Place; SULLIVAN; ***233** J-17; ★ **JNSC-**; mail Kingsport z 37660; rural
Lonewood; RMC Place; VAN BUREN; ***233** D-15; elev. 1,691ft./515m.; mail Spencer z 38585; rural
Long Branch; RMC Place; HAMILTON; ★ **CHTN**; mail Hixson z 37343; pop. incl. with Chattanooga (Inc. Place)
Long Branch; RMC Place; LAWRENCE; ***232** G-9; mail Lawrenceburg z 38464; rural
Long Creek; RMC Place; COCKE; ***233** L-16; mail Del Rio z 37727, Parrottsville z 37843; ● 50
Long Hollow; RMC Place; CAMPBELL; ★ **KNOX**; mail La Follette z 37766
Long Island; RMC Place; SULLIVAN; ***233** J-18; elev. 1,194ft./364m.; ★ **JNSC-**; mail Kingsport z 37660
Long Rock; RMC Place; CARROLL; ***232** C-6; elev. 467ft./142m.; mail Huntingdon z 38344; ● 30
Longs Mills; RMC Place; MCMINN; mail Athens z 37303; pop. incl. with Athens (Inc. Place)
Longtown; RMC Place; FAYETTE; ***232** F-3; mail Mason z 38049
Longview; RMC Place; BEDFORD; ***233** E-12; elev. 745ft./227m.; mail Bell Buckle z 37020; ● 50
Longwood; RMC Place; WILLIAMSON; ***232** D-10; ★ **NASH**; mail Franklin z 37064; ● 50
Lonsdale; RMC Place; KNOX; ***233** D-19; ★ **KNOX**; mail Knoxville z 37921; pop. incl. with Knoxville (Inc. Place)
Lookout Mountain; Inc. Place; HAMILTON; **233** K-11; elev. 2,100ft./640m.; 🅿; ★ **CHTN**; z 37350; Ⓟ 1,901; Ⓒ 2,000
Lookout Valley; RMC Place; HAMILTON; **233** J-11; elev. 700ft./213m.; ★ **CHTN**; mail Chattanooga z 37419; pop. incl. with Chattanooga (Inc. Place)
Loon Bay; RMC Place; STEWART; ***232** A-8; mail Bumpus Mills z 37028
Loretto; Inc. Place; LAWRENCE; **232** G-9; elev. 833ft./254m.; 🅿; z 38469; Ⓟ 1,515; Ⓒ 1,665
Lorraine; RMC Place; RHEA; ***233** E-17; mail Spring City z 37381; rural
Lost Creek; RMC Place; DECATUR; ***232** E-7; elev. 400ft./122m.; mail Decaturville z 38329; ● 100
Lost Creek; RMC Place; WHITE; ***233** D-15; elev. 1,291ft./393m.; mail Sparta z 38583; ● 50
Lost Mountain; RMC Place; GREENE; ***233** K-17; elev. 1,300ft./396m.; mail Greeneville z 37745; rural
Loudon; Inc. Place; ⊡ LOUDON; **233** E-18; elev. 900ft./274m.; 🅿 🅷; ★ **KNOX**; z 37774; Ⓟ 4,026; Ⓒ 4,476
LOUDON; **233** E-18; Ⓟ 31,255; Ⓒ 39,086; ◆ 47,294
Louise; RMC Place; MONTGOMERY; ***232** B-9; elev. 600ft./183m.; mail Cumberland Furnace z 37051; rural
Louisville; Inc. Place; BLOUNT; **233** D-19; elev. 819ft./250m.; 🅿 🅷; ★ **KNOX**; z 37777; Ⓟ 866; Ⓒ 2,001
Lovejoy; RMC Place; OVERTON; ***233** C-16; mail Monterey z 38574; rural
Lovelace; RMC Place; GREENE; ***233** K-17; ★ **JNSC-**; mail Chuckey z 37641; rural
Love Lady; RMC Place; PICKETT; ***233** B-16; elev. 1,032ft./315m.; mail Byrdstown z 38549; rural
Loveland; RMC Place; KNOX; ***233** D-19; ★ **KNOX**; mail Knoxville z 37924; pop. incl. with Knoxville (Inc. Place)
Lovell Heights; RMC Place; KNOX; ***233** D-19; ★ **KNOX**; mail Knoxville z 37922; ● 500
Love Station; RMC Place; UNICOI; ***233** L-18; mail Erwin z 37650; ● 300
Lovetown; RMC Place; MAURY; ***232** E-10; mail Mount Pleasant z 38474; rural
Lower Mill; RMC Place; HAMILTON; ***233** G-16; elev. 680ft./207m.; ★ **CHTN**; mail Hixson z 37343
Lower Mockeson; RMC Place; LAWRENCE; ***232** G-9; mail Leoma z 38468; rural
Lowland; RMC Place; HAMBLEN; **233** L-16; elev. 1,050ft./320m.; 🅿; ★ **MORR**; z 37778; ● 130
Lowryville; RMC Place; HARDIN; ***232** G-7; mail Savannah z 38372; rural
Luckett; RMC Place; LAUDERDALE; ***232** D-2; mail Ripley z 38063; rural
Lucky; RMC Place; WARREN; ***233** D-14; elev. 1,049ft./320m.; mail Mc Minnville z 37110; rural
Lucy; RMC Place; SHELBY; ***232** F-2; elev. 277ft./84m.; ★ **MEM**; mail Millington z 38053; ● 170
Luna; RMC Place; MARSHALL; ***233** F-11; elev. 960ft./293m.; mail Belfast z 37019; rural
Lunns Store; RMC Place; MARSHALL; ***233** E-11; mail Chapel Hill z 37034; rural
Lupton City; RMC Place; HAMILTON; ***233** G-15; elev. 800ft./244m.; 🅿; ★ **CHTN**; z 37351; pop. incl. with Chattanooga (Inc. Place)
Luray; RMC Place; HENDERSON; **232** E-6; elev. 400ft./122m.; 🅿; z 38352; ● 140
Lusk (Atpontley); RMC Place; BLEDSOE; **233** E-15; mail Dunlap z 37327; ● 170
Luskville; RMC Place; MCMINN; ***233** F-17; mail Calhoun z 37309; rural
Luther; RMC Place; HANCOCK; ***233** J-16; mail Sneedville z 37869; rural
Luttrell; RMC Place; LOUDON; ***233** E-18; elev. 1,065ft./325m.; mail Philadelphia z 37846; ● 30
Luttrell; Inc. Place; UNION; **233** C-20; elev. 1,080ft./329m.; 🅿; ★ **KNOX**; z 37779; Ⓟ 812; Ⓒ 915
Lutts; RMC Place; WAYNE; **232** G-8; elev. 580ft./177m.; 🅿; z 38471; ● 300
Lyles; RMC Place; HICKMAN; **232** D-9; elev. 800ft./244m.; 🅿; z 37098; ● 450
Lynchburg (Lynchburg, Moore County); Inc. Place; ⊡ MOORE; **233** F-12; elev. 798ft./243m.; 🅿; z 37352; the governments of Lynchburg and Moore county are consolidated as Lynchburg, Moore County; Ⓟ 4,721; Ⓒ 5,740
Lynchburg, Moore County; MOORE; see Lynchburg (Inc. Place)
Lynn Garden; RMC Place; SULLIVAN; **234** J-8; elev. 1,400ft./427m.; ★ **JNSC-**; mail Kingsport z 37665; pop. incl. with Kingsport (Inc. Place)
Lynn Point; RMC Place; GIBSON; ***232** C-5; elev. 346ft./105m.; mail Bradford z 38316; rural
Lynnville; Inc. Place; GILES; **232** F-10; elev. 755ft./230m.; 🅿; z 38472; Ⓟ 344; Ⓒ 345
Lyons View; RMC Place; KNOX; ***233** D-19; ★ **KNOX**; mail Knoxville z 37919; pop. incl. with Knoxville (Inc. Place)

M

Macedonia; RMC Place; CARROLL; ***232** C-6; mail Mc Kenzie z 38201; ● 60
Macedonia; RMC Place; MCMINN; ***233** F-18; mail Englewood z 37329; rural
Macedonia; RMC Place; OBION; ***232** C-5; elev. 356ft./109m.; mail Kenton z 38233; rural
Macedonia; RMC Place; WHITE; ***233** D-15; elev. 1,034ft./315m.; mail Sparta z 38583; ● 30
Mace's Hill; RMC Place; SMITH; ***233** B-13; elev. 849ft./259m.; mail Dixon Springs z 37057, Pleasant Shade z 37145; rural
Macon; RMC Place; FAYETTE; **232** F-3; elev. 396ft./121m.; 🅿; z 38048; ● 250
MACON; **233** A-13; Ⓟ 15,906; Ⓒ 20,386; ◆ 21,728
Maddox; RMC Place; HARDIN; ***232** G-7; mail Savannah z 38372; rural
Madge; RMC Place; SHELBY; ***232** F-2; ★ **MEM**; mail Arlington z 38002; rural
Madie; RMC Place; LAKE; ***232** B-3; elev. 298ft./91m.; mail Ridgely z 38080; ● 40
Madison; RMC Place; DAVIDSON; **232** I-9; elev. 487ft./148m.; 🅿 🅷; ★ **NASH**; z 37115-16; pop. incl. with Nashville (Inc. Place)
MADISON; **232** E-5; Ⓟ 77,982; Ⓒ 91,837; ◆ 97,201
Madison Hall; RMC Place; MADISON; ***232** E-5; elev. 528ft./161m.; ★ **JAC**; mail Jackson z 38301
Madisonville; Inc. Place; ⊡ MONROE; **233** E-18; elev. 968ft./295m.; 🅿; z 37354; Ⓟ 3,033; Ⓒ 3,939
Maggart; RMC Place; SMITH; ***233** C-14; elev. 516ft./157m.; mail Elmwood z 38560; rural
Magnolia; RMC Place; HOUSTON; ***232** C-8; mail Stewart z 37175; ● 30
Magnolia Place; RMC Place; WILLIAMSON; ***233** D-11; ★ **NASH**; mail Franklin z 37064; pop. incl. with Franklin (Inc. Place)
Major; RMC Place; WILSON; ***233** C-12; elev. 626ft./191m.; mail Lebanon z 37090; rural
Malesus; RMC Place; MADISON; ***232** E-5; elev. 452ft./138m.; ★ **JAC**; mail Jackson z 38301; pop. incl. with Jackson (Inc. Place)
Mallorys; RMC Place; WILLIAMSON; ★ **NASH**; mail Franklin z 37067; pop. incl. with Franklin (Inc. Place)
Maloney Heights; RMC Place; KNOX; ***233** D-19; elev. 900ft./274m.; ★ **KNOX**; mail Knoxville z 37920; ● 340
Maloneyville; RMC Place; KNOX; ***233** C-20; elev. 1,058ft./322m.; ★ **KNOX**; mail Knoxville z 37918; ● 30
Manchester; Inc. Place; ⊡ COFFEE; **233** F-13; elev. 1,063ft./324m.; 🅿 🅷; z 37349, z 37355; Ⓟ 7,709; Ⓒ 8,294
Manchester Park; RMC Place; HAMILTON; ★ **CHTN**; pop. incl. with Chattanooga (Inc. Place)
Manila; RMC Place; MCMINN; ***233** F-18; elev. 840ft./256m.; mail Englewood z 37329; rural
Mankinville; RMC Place; RUTHERFORD; ***233** D-12; elev. 632ft./193m.; ★ **MUR**; mail Murfreesboro z 37127; rural
Manlyville; RMC Place; HENRY; **232** C-7; mail Springville z 38256; ● 30
Mansfield; RMC Place; HENRY; **232** C-7; elev. 463ft./141m.; 🅿; z 38236; ● 200
Mansfield Gap; RMC Place; JEFFERSON; ***233** C-20; ★ **MORR**; mail Talbott z 37877; rural
Manson; RMC Place; FENTRESS; ***233** B-16; elev. 826ft./252m.; mail Jamestown z 38556; rural
Maple Grove; RMC Place; CLAY; ***233** B-15; elev. 1,012ft./308m.; mail Allons z 38541; rural
Maple Grove; RMC Place; MACON; **233** B-13; elev. 925ft./282m.; mail Lafayette z 37083; ● 30
Maple Grove; RMC Place; MEIGS; ***233** E-17; mail Ten Mile z 37880; rural
Maple Hill; RMC Place; SULLIVAN; **234** J-4; ★ **JNSC-**; mail Bristol z 37620; ● 410
Maplehurst; RMC Place; SULLIVAN; ***233** J-19; ★ **JNSC-**; mail Bluff City z 37618; pop. incl. with Bristol (Inc. Place)
Maplewood; RMC Place; DAVIDSON; ***233** C-11; ★ **NASH**; mail Nashville z 37216; pop. incl. with Nashville (Inc. Place)
Marble City; RMC Place; KNOX; ***233** D-19; ★ **KNOX**; mail Knoxville z 37919; pop. incl. with Knoxville (Inc. Place)
Marbledale; RMC Place; KNOX; **214** F-2; ★ **KNOX**; mail Knoxville z 37914; ● 500
Marble Hall; RMC Place; HAWKINS; ***233** K-16; mail Rogersville z 37857; rural
Marble Hill; RMC Place; BLOUNT; ***233** E-19; ★ **KNOX**; mail Friendsville z 37737; rural
Marble Hill; RMC Place; MOORE; ***233** G-12; mail Winchester z 37398; pop. incl. with Lynchburg (Inc. Place)
Marble Plains; RMC Place; FRANKLIN; ***233** F-12; elev. 969ft./295m.; mail Winchester z 37398; rural
Marbleton (Shadtown); RMC Place; UNICOI; ***233** K-18; mail Unicoi z 37692; pop. incl. with Unicoi (Inc. Place)
Marguerite; RMC Place; HAMBLEN; ***233** K-16; ★ **MORR**; mail Morristown z 37814; rural
Marion; RMC Place; CLAIBORNE; ***233** B-19; mail Clairfield z 37715; rural
Marion; RMC Place; MONTGOMERY; **232** B-9; mail Cumberland Furnace z 37051; ● 130
MARION; **233** G-14; Ⓟ 24,860; Ⓒ 27,776; ◆ 28,271
Markham; RMC Place; LAKE; ***232** B-3; mail Tiptonville z 38079; rural
Marlborough; RMC Place; CARROLL; ***232** C-7; mail Bruceton z 38317, Hollow Rock z 38342; rural
Marlow; RMC Place; ANDERSON; ***233** C-18; elev. 846ft./258m.; ★ **KNOX**; mail Clinton z 37716; ● 100
Marlyn Hills; RMC Place; SULLIVAN; ***233** J-19; ★ **JNSC-**; mail Bristol z 37620; pop. incl. with Bristol (Inc. Place)
Marrowbone; RMC Place; CHEATHAM; ***232** C-10; elev. 445ft./136m.; ★ **NASH**; mail Ashland City z 37015; rural
MARSHALL; **233** F-11; Ⓟ 21,539; Ⓒ 26,767; ◆ 30,136
Mars Hill; RMC Place; LAWRENCE; ***232** F-9; mail Lawrenceburg z 38464; ● 30
Mars Hill; RMC Place; RHEA; ***233** E-17; elev. 800ft./244m.; mail Spring City z 37381; rural
Martel Estates; RMC Place; LOUDON; ***233** D-18; ★ **KNOX**; mail Lenoir City z 37772; ● 150
Martha; RMC Place; WILSON; **233** C-12; ★ **NASH**; mail Lebanon z 37090; pop. incl. with Lebanon (Inc. Place)
Marthas Chapel; RMC Place; MONTGOMERY; ***232** B-9; elev. 604ft./184m.; ★ **CLRKV**; mail Clarksville z 37040; ● 30
Martin; Inc. Place; WEAKLEY; **232** B-5; elev. 413ft./126m.; 🅿 🅷 🅲 6,888; z 38237-38; Ⓟ 8,600; Ⓒ 10,515
Martin Creek; RMC Place; HANCOCK; ***233** J-15; elev. 1,400ft./427m.; mail Tazewell z 37879; ● 30
Martin Creek; RMC Place; PUTNAM; ***233** C-14; elev. 600ft./183m.; mail Baxter z 38544; rural
Martin Springs; RMC Place; MARION; ***233** G-14; elev. 680ft./207m.; mail South Pittsburg z 37380; rural
Marvin; RMC Place; GREENE; ***233** K-16; mail Mosheim z 37818; rural
Marys Grove; RMC Place; LINCOLN; ***233** G-11; elev. 940ft./287m.; mail Taft z 38488; rural
Maryville; Inc. Place; ⊡ BLOUNT; **233** D-19; elev. 940ft./287m.; 🅿 🅷 🅲 1,155 ■; ★ **KNOX**; z 37801-04; Ⓟ 19,208; Ⓒ 23,120; ◆ 26,359
Mascot; CDP; KNOX; **233** C-20; elev. 953ft./290m.; 🅿; ★ **KNOX**; z 37806; Ⓟ 2,138; Ⓒ 2,119
Masomhall; OBION; see Mason Hall (RMC Place)
Mason; Inc. Place; TIPTON; **232** F-3; elev. 305ft./93m.; 🅿; z 38049, z 38068; Ⓟ 337; Ⓒ 1,089
Mason Grove; RMC Place; CROCKETT; ***232** D-5; elev. 418ft./127m.; mail Humboldt z 38343; rural
Mason Hall (Masomhall); RMC Place; OBION; **232** C-4; elev. 354ft./108m.; mail Kenton z 38233; ● 270
Masseyville; RMC Place; CHESTER; **232** F-5; mail Bethel Springs z 38315; ● 100
Matheny Grove; RMC Place; WEAKLEY; ***232** B-6; elev. 481ft./147m.; mail Dresden z 38225; rural
Maupin Row; RMC Place; WASHINGTON; ★ **JNSC-**; mail Johnson City z 37601; pop. incl. with Johnson City (Inc. Place)
MAURY; **232** E-10; Ⓟ 54,812; Ⓒ 69,498; ◆ 82,817
Maury City; Inc. Place; CROCKETT; **232** D-4; elev. 346ft./105m.; 🅿; z 38050; Ⓟ 782; Ⓒ 704
Maxey; RMC Place; DYER; ***232** C-4; elev. 328ft./100m.; mail Newbern z 38059; ● 50
Maxwell; RMC Place; FRANKLIN; **233** G-13; elev. 934ft./285m.; mail Belvidere z 37306; ● 150
Maxwell Chapel; RMC Place; OVERTON; ***233** B-15; mail Hilham z 38568; rural
May Acres; RMC Place; JEFFERSON; ★ **MORR**; mail Talbott z 37877
Mayhome; RMC Place; WILSON; ***233** C-13; mail Watertown z 37184; ● 30
Mayland; RMC Place; CUMBERLAND; **233** C-16; elev. 1,972ft./601m.; mail Crossville z 38571; ● 440
Maymead; RMC Place; JOHNSON; ***233** J-20; elev. 2,215ft./675m.; mail Mountain City z 37683; ● 100
Maynardville; Inc. Place; ⊡ UNION; **233** C-20; elev. 1,217ft./371m.; 🅿; ★ **KNOX**; z 37807; Ⓟ 1,298; Ⓒ 1,782
Mayview Heights; RMC Place; KNOX; ***233** C-19; ★ **KNOX**; mail Powell z 37849
McAllister Hill; RMC Place; POLK; ***233** G-18; elev. 1,720ft./524m.; mail Copperhill z 37317; rural
McAllisters Crossroads; RMC Place; MONTGOMERY; ***232** B-9; mail Southside z 37171; rural
McAnna; RMC Place; OBION; ***232** B-4; elev. 440ft./134m.; mail Troy z 38260; rural
McBurg; RMC Place; LINCOLN; **233** G-11; mail Frankewing z 38459; ● 100
McCains; RMC Place; MAURY; ***232** E-10; mail Columbia z 38401; ● 30
McClamerys Stand; RMC Place; WAYNE; ***232** G-8; mail Collinwood z 38450
McCloud; RMC Place; HAWKINS; **233** K-16; mail Rogersville z 37857; ● 30
McClures Bend; RMC Place; SMITH; ***233** C-14; elev. 532ft./162m.; mail Carthage z 37030; ● 70
McCoinsville; RMC Place; JACKSON; ***233** B-14; mail Gainesboro z 38562; rural
McConnell; RMC Place; OBION; **232** B-5; elev. 351ft./107m.; mail Martin z 38237; ● 100
McCullough; RMC Place; DYER; ***232** C-3; elev. 400ft./122m.; mail Dyersburg z 38024; rural
McCutchen Heights; RMC Place; OBION; ***232** B-4; elev. 320ft./98m.; mail Union City z 38261; ● 50
McDonald; RMC Place; BRADLEY; **233** G-16; elev. 869ft./265m.; 🅿; ★ **CLEV**; z 37353; ● 350
Mc Donald; RMC Place; GREENE; ***233** L-16; elev. 1,069ft./326m.; mail Mohawk z 37810; rural
McDonald Hill; RMC Place; HAWKINS; ***233** K-16; mail Rogersville z 37857; ● 120
McDowell; RMC Place; HAMILTON; ★ **CHTN**; pop. incl. with Chattanooga (Inc. Place)
McElroy; RMC Place; VAN BUREN; ***233** D-15; elev. 904ft./276m.; mail Doyle z 38559; rural
McEwen; Inc. Place; HUMPHREYS; **232** C-8; elev. 836ft./255m.; 🅿; z 37101; Ⓟ 1,442; Ⓒ 1,702
McGeetown; RMC Place; POLK; ***233** G-18; elev. 1,720ft./524m.; mail Copperhill z 37317; rural
McIllwain; RMC Place; BENTON; ***232** D-7; mail Holladay z 38341; ● 30
McKenzie; Inc. Place; CARROLL, HENRY, WEAKLEY; **232** C-6; elev. 495ft./151m.; 🅿 🅷 🅲 2,080; z 38201; Ⓟ 5,168; Ⓒ 5,295
McKinley; RMC Place; WASHINGTON; ***233** K-18; ★ **JNSC-**; mail Johnson City z 37601; ● 250
McKinnon; RMC Place; HOUSTON; **232** B-8; elev. 380ft./116m.; mail Stewart z 37175; ● 200
McLemoresville; Inc. Place; CARROLL; **232** D-6; elev. 413ft./126m.; 🅿; z 38235; Ⓟ 280; Ⓒ 259
McLin's Corner; CROCKETT; see Hodson (RMC Place)
McMahan; RMC Place; SEVIER; ***233** D-20; ★ **KNOX**; mail Sevierville z 37862
McMillan; RMC Place; KNOX; ***233** C-20; ★ **KNOX**; mail Knoxville z 37914; rural
MCMINN; **233** F-17; Ⓟ 42,383; Ⓒ 49,015; ◆ 52,737
McMinnville; Inc. Place; ⊡ WARREN; **233** E-14; elev. 976ft./297m.; 🅿 🅷; z 37110-11; Ⓟ 11,194; Ⓒ 12,749
McNairy; RMC Place; MCNAIRY; **232** F-5; elev. 457ft./139m.; mail Bethel Springs z 38315; ● 100
MCNAIRY; **232** F-6; Ⓟ 22,422; Ⓒ 24,653; ◆ 25,698
McPheeter Bend; RMC Place; HAWKINS; ***233** J-17; mail Church Hill z 37642; ● 30
Meacham; RMC Place; DYER; ***232** C-3; elev. 444ft./135m.; mail Dyersburg z 38024; rural
Meades Quarry; RMC Place; KNOX; ★ **KNOX**; mail Knoxville z 37920; pop. incl. with Knoxville (Inc. Place)
Meadorville; RMC Place; MACON; ***233** B-13; mail Lafayette z 37083; rural
Meadow; RMC Place; LOUDON; ***233** E-19; elev. 898ft./274m.; mail Greenback z 37742; rural

Entries in **UPPERCASE** are counties.
Entries in **bold** have populations of 2,500 or more.
Names in parentheses are alternate names.
Inc. Place — Incorporated Place
RMC Place — Rand McNally Designated Place
CDP — Census Designated Place
MCD — Minor Civil Division
⊡ County Seat
▲ Minor Civil Division
elev. Elevation
🅿 Post Office
🅷 Hospital
🅲 College
■ Principal Business Center
★ Ranally Metro Area (RMA) Abbreviation
z Zip Code(s)
Ⓟ Previous Census Population
Ⓡ Revised Census Population
Ⓐ Annexation Population
● Rand McNally Population Estimate
Ⓒ Final Census Population
Ⓢ Special Census Population
◆ Estimated Population

For additional definitions see Glossary, Volume 1, and Introduction, Volume 2.

Meadowbrook; RMC Place; BLOUNT; *233 D-19; ★ **KNOX**; mail Maryville z 37804; pop. incl. with Maryville (Inc. Place)
Meadowbrook; RMC Place; GREENE; *233 K-17; mail Afton z 37616; ● 200
Meadow Brook; RMC Place; WARREN; *233 E-14; mail Mc Minnville z 37110; ● 300
Meadow Green Acres; RMC Place; WILLIAMSON; *233 D-11; ★ **NASH**; mail Franklin z 37064
Meadow Mead; RMC Place; HENRY; *232 B-7; mail Paris z 38242; pop. incl. with Paris (Inc. Place)
Meadow View; RMC Place; HAMILTON; *233 F-16; ★ **CHTN**; mail Georgetown z 37336; rural
Meadowview; RMC Place; LAWRENCE; *232 F-9; mail Lawrenceburg z 38464; pop. incl. with Lawrenceburg (Inc. Place)
Meadowview Gardens; RMC Place; ROANE; ★ **KNOX**; mail Harriman z 37748; pop. incl. with Harriman (Inc. Place)
Meadowwood Acres; RMC Place; WILLIAMSON; *232 D-10; ★ **NASH**; mail Fairview z 37062; pop. incl. with Fairview (Inc. Place)
Medford; RMC Place; ANDERSON; *233 C-19; ★ **KNOX**; mail Lake City z 37769; ● 180
Medina; Inc. Place; GIBSON; 232 D-5; elev. 505ft./154m.; 🅿; z 38355; Ⓟ 658; © 969
Medon; Inc. Place; MADISON; 232 E-5; elev. 478ft./146m.; 🅿; z 38356; Ⓟ 137; © 191
MEIGS; 233 E-17; Ⓟ 8,033; © 11,086; ◆ 11,784
Melrose; RMC Place; BLOUNT; *233 D-20; ★ **KNOX**; mail Walland z 37886; rural
Melrose; RMC Place; DAVIDSON; 🅿; ★ **NASH**; z 37204 & mail Nashville z 37220; pop. incl. with Nashville (Inc. Place)
Melville Hill; RMC Place; HAMILTON; ★ **CHTN**; mail Soddy Daisy z 37379; pop. incl. with Soddy-Daisy (Inc. Place)
Melvine (Patton); RMC Place; BLEDSOE; 233 E-16; elev. 965ft./294m.; mail Pikeville z 37367; ● 60
Melwood; CHESTER; see Robertson (RMC Place)
Memphis; Inc. Place; ⊡ SHELBY; 232 F-1; elev. 264ft./80m.; 🅿 🅷 🅲 30,964 ■; ★ **MEM**; z 37501, z 37544, z 38101, z 38103-09, z 38111-20, z 38122, z 38124-28, z 38130-39, z 38141, z 38145, z 38147-48, z 38150-52, z 38157, z 38159, z 38161, z 38163, z 38166-68, z 38173-75, z 38177, z 38181-82, z 38184, z 38186-88, z 38190, z 38193-94, z 38197 & mail Germantown z 38183; Ⓟ 610,337; © 650,100; ◆ 659,448
Memphis Hub; RMC Place; SHELBY; ★ **MEM**; pop. incl. with Memphis (Inc. Place)
Mendenhall; RMC Place; SHELBY; ★ **MEM**; mail Memphis z 38117, z 38177; pop. incl. with Memphis (Inc. Place)
Mengelwood; RMC Place; DYER; *232 C-3; elev. 266ft./81m.; mail Lenox z 38047; ● 30
Mentor; RMC Place; BLOUNT; *233 D-19; ★ **KNOX**; mail Louisville z 37777; ● 500
Mercer; RMC Place; MADISON; 232 E-4; elev. 343ft./105m.; 🅿; z 38392; ● 210
Meredith Cave; RMC Place; CAMPBELL; *233 B-19; elev. 1,200ft./366m.; ★ **KNOX**; mail La Follette z 37766; rural
Merry Oaks; RMC Place; DAVIDSON; *233 C-11; ★ **NASH**; mail Nashville z 37214; pop. incl. with Nashville (Inc. Place)
Michie; Inc. Place; MCNAIRY; 232 G-6; elev. 600ft./183m.; 🅿; z 38357; Ⓟ 677; © 647
Middlebrook Heights; RMC Place; KNOX; *233 D-19; ★ **KNOX**; mail Knoxville z 37919; pop. incl. with Knoxville (Inc. Place)
Middleburg; RMC Place; HARDEMAN; *232 F-4; elev. 537ft./164m.; mail Bolivar z 38008
Middleburg; RMC Place; HENDERSON; 232 E-7; elev. 462ft./141m.; mail Scotts Hill z 38374; ● 100
Middle City; RMC Place; DYER; *232 C-3; elev. 276ft./84m.; mail Dyersburg z 38024; ● 120
Middle Creek; RMC Place; SEVIER; *233 D-20; mail Sevierville z 37862; pop. incl. with Pigeon Forge (Inc. Place)
Middle Fork; RMC Place; HENDERSON; 232 E-6; mail Huron z 38345; ● 50
Middle Settlement; RMC Place; BLOUNT; *233 D-19; elev. 835ft./255m.; ★ **KNOX**; mail Louisville z 37777; rural
Middleton; Inc. Place; HARDEMAN; 232 G-5; elev. 409ft./125m.; 🅿; z 38052; Ⓟ 536; © 602
Middle Valley; CDP; HAMILTON; 233 G-16; elev. 700ft./213m.; ★ **CHTN**; mail Hixson z 37343; Ⓟ 12,255; © 11,854
Middle Valley Estates; RMC Place; HAMILTON; *233 G-16; ★ **CHTN**; mail Hixson z 37343; ● 400
Midfields; RMC Place; SULLIVAN; *233 J-18; ★ **JNSC-**; mail Kingsport z 37665; pop. incl. with Kingsport (Inc. Place)
Midland; RMC Place; RUTHERFORD; *233 E-12; mail Bell Buckle z 37020; ● 30
Midtown (Pine Grove); RMC Place; ROANE; 233 D-18; elev. 1,000ft./305m.; ★ **KNOX**; mail Harriman z 37748; former incorporated place; disincorporated January 1, 2005; © 1,306
Midtown Heights; RMC Place; ROANE; *233 D-17; elev. 1,000ft./305m.; ★ **KNOX**; mail Harriman z 37748; ● 300
Midway; RMC Place; CANNON; *233 E-13; mail Bradyville z 37026; ● 50
Midway; RMC Place; COCKE; *233 M-16; mail Del Rio z 37727; rural
Midway; RMC Place; CUMBERLAND; *233 D-16; mail Crossville z 38572; rural
Midway; RMC Place; DEKALB; *233 D-14; mail Smithville z 37166; ● 50
Midway; RMC Place; DYER; *232 C-2; elev. 263ft./80m.; mail Finley z 38030; rural
Midway; RMC Place; FRANKLIN; *233 F-14; elev. 1,940ft./591m.; mail Sewanee z 37375; ● 80
Midway; RMC Place; GREENE; 233 K-16; elev. 253ft./77m.; 🅿; z 37809; ● 420
Midway; RMC Place; JOHNSON; *233 J-20; mail Butler z 37640; rural
Midway; RMC Place; KNOX; *233 D-20; elev. 900ft./274m.; ★ **KNOX**; mail Strawberry Plains z 37871; rural
Midway; RMC Place; OBION; 232 B-4; elev. 332ft./101m.; mail Union City z 38261; ● 130
Midway; RMC Place; ROANE; *233 D-17; mail Kingston z 37763; rural
Midway; RMC Place; WARREN; *233 D-14; elev. 1,000ft./305m.; mail Mc Minnville z 37110; ● 50
Midway; CDP; WASHINGTON; *233 K-18; elev. 1,800ft./549m.; ★ **JNSC-**; mail Johnson City z 37601, Jonesborough z 37659; Ⓟ 2,953; © 2,491
Mifflin; RMC Place; CHESTER; 232 E-6; elev. 483ft./147m.; mail Luray z 38352; ● 80
Milan; Inc. Place; GIBSON; 232 D-5; elev. 420ft./128m.; 🅿 🅷; z 38358; Ⓟ 7,512; © 7,664; Ⓡ 7,662
Milburnton; RMC Place; GREENE; *233 K-17; mail Limestone z 37681; rural
Miles Crossroads; RMC Place; CLAY; *233 B-14; mail Red Boiling Springs z 37150; ● 90
Mile Straight; RMC Place; HAMILTON; *233 F-16; ★ **CHTN**; mail Soddy Daisy z 37379; pop. incl. with Soddy-Daisy (Inc. Place)
Milky Way; RMC Place; GILES; *232 F-10; mail Pulaski z 38478; rural
Mill Brook; RMC Place; WASHINGTON; *233 K-17; mail Limestone z 37681; rural
Mill Creek; RMC Place; ANDERSON; *233 C-19; ★ **KNOX**; mail Andersonville z 37705; rural
Mill Creek; RMC Place; MORGAN; *233 C-17; elev. 1,518ft./463m.; mail Sunbright z 37872; rural
Mill Creek; RMC Place; PUTNAM; *233 C-15; elev. 1,516ft./462m.; mail Cookeville z 38506; rural
Milldale; RMC Place; ROBERTSON; 233 B-11; ★ **NASH**; mail Springfield z 37172; ● 50
Milledgeville; Inc. Place; MCNAIRY, CHESTER, HARDIN; 232 F-6; elev. 418ft./127m.; 🅿; z 38359; Ⓟ 279; © 287
Miller's Store; RMC Place; WEAKLEY; *232 B-6; mail Dresden z 38225; rural
Millersville; Inc. Place; SUMNER, ROBERTSON; 233 B-11; ★ **NASH**; mail Goodlettsville z 37072; Ⓟ 2,575; © 5,308
Millertown; RMC Place; KNOX; 233 L-14; ★ **KNOX**; mail Knoxville z 37914; ● 130
Millican Grove; RMC Place; SEVIER; 214 F-4; elev. 996ft./304m.; mail Sevierville z 37876; ● 50
Milligan; RMC Place; CARTER; mail Johnson City z 37601; pop. incl. with Elizabethton (Inc. Place)
Millington; Inc. Place; SHELBY; 232 F-2; elev. 270ft./82m.; 🅿 🅷; ★ **MEM**; z 38053-55, z 38083; Ⓟ 17,866; © 10,433
Mill Point (Central Heights); RMC Place; SULLIVAN; *233 J-18; ★ **JNSC-**; mail Blountville z 37617; rural
Millsfield; RMC Place; DYER; *232 C-3; elev. 507ft./155m.; mail Dyersburg z 38024; ● 80
Mill Spring; RMC Place; JEFFERSON; *233 C-20; mail New Market z 37820; rural
Milltown; RMC Place; HUMPHREYS; *232 D-9; mail Mc Ewen z 37101; rural
Milltown (Dycus); RMC Place; JACKSON; *233 B-14; elev. 532ft./162m.; mail Whitleyville z 38588
Milltown; RMC Place; MACON; *233 B-14; mail Red Boiling Springs z 37150; ● 30
Milltown; RMC Place; MARSHALL; *233 E-11; mail Lewisburg z 37091; rural
Millview; RMC Place; WILLIAMSON; *233 D-11; elev. 640ft./195m.; ★ **NASH**; mail Franklin z 37067; ● 50
Milo; RMC Place; BLEDSOE; *233 E-16; mail Spring City z 37381; rural
Milton; RMC Place; RUTHERFORD; 233 D-13; elev. 760ft./232m.; 🅿; z 37118; ● 130
Mimms; RMC Place; DAVIDSON; ★ **NASH**; mail Nashville z 37211; pop. incl. with Nashville (Inc. Place)
Mimosa; RMC Place; LINCOLN; *233 F-12; mail Fayetteville z 37334; rural
Mimosa Estates; RMC Place; BLOUNT; *233 D-19; ★ **KNOX**; mail Louisville z 37777; ● 250
Mimosa Heights; RMC Place; BLOUNT; *233 D-19; elev. 940ft./287m.; ★ **KNOX**; mail Louisville z 37777; ● 100
Mineral Park; RMC Place; BRADLEY; *233 G-16; ★ **CLEV**; mail Mc Donald z 37353; ● 110
Mineral Springs; RMC Place; OVERTON; *233 C-15; mail Monterey z 38574; rural
Mink; RMC Place; WAYNE; *232 F-8; mail Waynesboro z 38485; pop. incl. with Waynesboro (Inc. Place)
Minnick; RMC Place; OBION; *232 B-3; elev. 460ft./140m.; mail Obion z 38240; rural
Minor Hill; Inc. Place; GILES; 232 G-10; elev. 895ft./273m.; 🅿; z 38473; Ⓟ 372; © 437
Mint; RMC Place; BLOUNT; *233 E-19; mail Maryville z 37803; rural
Miser Station; RMC Place; BLOUNT; 233 D-19; ★ **KNOX**; mail Friendsville z 37737, Louisville z 37777; ● 50
Miston; RMC Place; DYER; 232 C-3; elev. 274ft./84m.; ● 180
Mitchell; RMC Place; ROBERTSON; *233 A-12; elev. 740ft./226m.; mail Portland z 37148; ● 30
Mitchellville; Inc. Place; SUMNER; 233 A-12; elev. 777ft./237m.; 🅿; z 37119; Ⓟ 193; © 207
Mixie; RMC Place; CARROLL; *232 C-6; mail Hollow Rock z 38342; ● 30
Moberry; WHITE; see Mourberry (RMC Place)
Moccasin; RMC Place; WAYNE; *232 F-8; elev. 680ft./207m.; mail Waynesboro z 38485; ● 30
Mohawk; RMC Place; GREENE; 233 K-16; elev. 1,086ft./331m.; 🅿; z 37810; ● 100
Mohawk Crossroad; RMC Place; GREENE; *233 K-16; mail Bulls Gap z 37711; pop. incl. with Mosheim (Inc. Place)
Molino; RMC Place; LINCOLN; *233 G-11; mail Fayetteville z 37334; rural
Mon; RMC Place; WILSON; *233 C-12; mail Lebanon z 37087; ● 120
Mona; RMC Place; RUTHERFORD; *233 D-12; elev. 531ft./162m.; mail Murfreesboro z 37129; rural
Monoville; RMC Place; SMITH; 233 C-13; elev. 485ft./148m.; mail Carthage z 37030; ● 70
Monroe; RMC Place; OVERTON; 233 B-15; elev. 1,020ft./311m.; 🅿; z 38573; ● 50
MONROE; 233 E-18; Ⓟ 30,541; © 38,961; ◆ 46,480
Montague; RMC Place; DAVIDSON; *233 C-11; elev. 506ft./154m.; ★ **NASH**; mail Nashville z 37216; pop. incl. with Nashville (Inc. Place)
Montague; RMC Place; RHEA; *233 F-16; mail Dayton z 37321, Graysville z 37338; ● 100
Monteagle; Inc. Place; MARION, GRUNDY; 233 F-14; elev. 1,927ft./587m.; 🅿; z 37356; Ⓟ 1,138; © 1,238
Monterey; Inc. Place; PUTNAM; 233 C-15; elev. 1,875ft./572m.; 🅿; z 38574; Ⓟ 2,559; © 2,717
Montezuma; RMC Place; CHESTER; 232 F-5; mail Henderson z 38340; ● 50
MONTGOMERY; 232 B-9; Ⓟ 100,498; © 134,768; ◆ 168,217
Montgomery Junction; RMC Place; SCOTT; *233 B-18; elev. 1,200ft./366m.; mail Huntsville z 37756; ● 30
Monticello; RMC Place; WILLIAMSON; *233 D-11; elev. 640ft./195m.; ★ **NASH**; mail Franklin z 37069
Monticello; RMC Place; WILSON; *233 C-12; ★ **NASH**; mail Mount Juliet z 37122; pop. incl. with Mount Juliet (Inc. Place)
Montpier Farms; RMC Place; WILLIAMSON; *232 D-10; elev. 700ft./213m.; ★ **NASH**; mail Franklin z 37069; ● 320
Montvale; RMC Place; BLOUNT; *233 E-19; mail Maryville z 37803; ● 250
Moodyville; RMC Place; PICKETT; *233 B-16; mail Byrdstown z 38549; ● 30
Mooneyham; RMC Place; VAN BUREN; *233 E-15; mail Spencer z 38585; rural
Moons; RMC Place; HENRY; *232 B-7; elev. 400ft./122m.; mail Springville z 38256; ● 50
Moon Shadows; RMC Place; HAMILTON; *233 G-16; elev. 860ft./262m.; ★ **CHTN**; mail Harrison z 37341; ● 500
MOORE; 233 F-12; Ⓟ 4,721; © 5,740; ◆ 6,281
Mooreland Heights; RMC Place; KNOX; 233 N-13; elev. 947ft./289m.; ★ **KNOX**; mail Knoxville z 37920; pop. incl. with Knoxville (Inc. Place)
Mooresburg; RMC Place; HAWKINS; 233 K-16; elev. 1,100ft./335m.; 🅿; z 37811; ● 170
Mooresburg Springs; RMC Place; HAWKINS; *233 K-16; mail Mooresburg z 37811; ● 30
Moores Chapel; RMC Place; GIBSON; *232 D-5; elev. 385ft./117m.; mail Milan z 38358; rural
Mooresville; RMC Place; MARSHALL; 233 F-11; mail Lewisburg z 37091; ● 80
Mooretown; RMC Place; CANNON; *233 E-13; mail Woodbury z 37190; ● 50
Mooring; RMC Place; LAKE; *232 B-3; elev. 281ft./86m.; mail Tiptonville z 38079; rural
MORGAN; 233 C-17; Ⓟ 17,300; © 19,757; ◆ 20,736
Morgan Springs; RMC Place; RHEA; 233 E-16; mail Dayton z 37321; ● 140
Morganton; RMC Place; LOUDON; *233 E-18; elev. 791ft./241m.; mail Greenback z 37742; rural
Morgantown; RMC Place; RHEA; 233 E-16; mail Dayton z 37321; ● 600
Morganville; RMC Place; MARION; mail Whitwell z 37397; rural
Morley; RMC Place; CAMPBELL; 233 B-19; elev. 1,058ft./322m.; 🅿; z 37766; ● 180
Morny; RMC Place; DAVIDSON; *233 C-11; ★ **NASH**; mail Joelton z 37080; pop. incl. with Nashville (Inc. Place)
Morris Chapel; RMC Place; BENTON; *232 C-7; elev. 452ft./138m.; mail Camden z 38320; pop. incl. with Camden (Inc. Place)
Morris Chapel; RMC Place; HARDIN; 232 F-6; elev. 450ft./137m.; 🅿; z 38361; ● 220
Morrison; Inc. Place; WARREN; 233 E-13; elev. 1,076ft./328m.; 🅿; z 37357; Ⓟ 570; © 684
Morrison City; RMC Place; SULLIVAN; 234 J-8; ★ **JNSC-**; mail Kingsport z 37665; pop. incl. with Kingsport (Inc. Place)
Morrison Creek; RMC Place; JACKSON; *233 B-14; elev. 569ft./173m.; mail Gainesboro z 38562; rural
Morristown; Inc. Place; ⊡ HAMBLEN, JEFFERSON; 233 K-16; elev. 1,350ft./411m.; 🅿 🅷 ■; ★ **MORR**; z 37813-16; Ⓟ 21,385; © 24,965; ◆ 26,995
Moscow; Inc. Place; FAYETTE; 232 G-3; elev. 356ft./109m.; 🅿; z 38057, z 38076; Ⓟ 384; © 422; Ⓡ 460
Mosheim; Inc. Place; GREENE; 233 K-17; elev. 1,298ft./396m.; 🅿; z 37818; Ⓟ 1,451; © 1,749
Moss; RMC Place; CLAY; 233 B-14; elev. 1,057ft./322m.; 🅿; z 38575; ● 230
Mossy Grove; RMC Place; MORGAN; *233 C-18; elev. 1,200ft./366m.; ★ **KNOX**; mail Harriman z 37748, Wartburg z 37887; rural
Mountain City; Inc. Place; ⊡ JOHNSON; 233 J-20; elev. 2,429ft./740m.; 🅿; z 37683; Ⓟ 2,169; © 2,383; Ⓡ 2,500
Mountain Dale; RMC Place; UNICOI; *233 L-18; mail Erwin z 37650; rural
Mountain Home; RMC Place; WASHINGTON; *233 K-18; elev. 1,738ft./530m.; 🅿 🅷; ★ **JNSC-**; z 37684; pop. incl. with Johnson City (Inc. Place)
Mountain View; RMC Place; RHEA; *233 E-16; mail Dayton z 37321; pop. incl. with Dayton (Inc. Place)
Mountain View; RMC Place; SCOTT; *233 B-17; elev. 1,488ft./454m.; mail Robbins z 37852; ● 150
Mountain View; RMC Place; SULLIVAN; ★ **JNSC-**; pop. incl. with Kingsport (Inc. Place)
Mountain View Acres; RMC Place; FRANKLIN; *233 G-13; mail Winchester z 37398; pop. incl. with Winchester (Inc. Place)
Mount Airy; RMC Place; SEQUATCHIE; *233 F-15; mail Dunlap z 37327; rural
Mount Ararat; RMC Place; CANNON; *233 D-13; mail Liberty z 37095; rural
Mount Carmel; RMC Place; DECATUR; *232 E-7; mail Decaturville z 38329; rural
Mount Carmel; RMC Place; FRANKLIN; *233 G-12; elev. 936ft./285m.; mail Huntland z 37345; rural
Mount Carmel; RMC Place; GREENE; *233 K-17; elev. 1,192ft./363m.; mail Bulls Gap z 37711, Mosheim z 37818; ● 100
Mount Carmel; Inc. Place; HAWKINS; 233 J-17; elev. 1,300ft./396m.; 🅿; ★ **JNSC-**; z 37645; Ⓟ 4,082; © 4,795
Mount Carmel; RMC Place; TIPTON; *232 E-3; ★ **MEM**; mail Covington z 38019; ● 30
Mount Carmel; RMC Place; WASHINGTON; *233 L-18; mail Chuckey z 37641; ● 200
Mount Crest; RMC Place; BLEDSOE; 233 E-15; elev. 1,722ft./525m.; mail Pikeville z 37367; ● 50
Mount Cumberland; RMC Place; MCMINN; *233 F-18; elev. 860ft./262m.; mail Englewood z 37329; rural
Mount Denson; RMC Place; ROBERTSON; *233 B-11; mail Springfield z 37172; rural
Mount Gilead; RMC Place; HENDERSON; *232 D-6; mail Cedar Grove z 38321; ● 30
Mount Gilead; RMC Place; WHITE; *233 D-15; mail Sparta z 38583; ● 50
Mount Harmony; RMC Place; MCMINN; *233 E-18; elev. 962ft./293m.; mail Niota z 37826; rural
Mount Harmony; RMC Place; MONROE; *233 F-18; mail Tellico Plains z 37385; rural
Mount Helen; RMC Place; FENTRESS; *233 B-17; mail Allardt z 38504; ● 100
Mount Herman; RMC Place; BEDFORD, MOORE; *233 F-12; elev. 1,200ft./366m.; mail Shelbyville z 37160; ● 30
Mount Herman; RMC Place; WEAKLEY; *232 C-5; elev. 406ft./124m.; mail Greenfield z 38230; rural
Mount Hope; RMC Place; WAYNE; *232 F-8; mail Waynesboro z 38485; ● 50
Mount Horeb; RMC Place; JEFFERSON; *233 C-20; ★ **MORR**; mail Jefferson City z 37760; rural
Mount Joy; RMC Place; MAURY; 232 E-9; mail Mount Pleasant z 38474; ● 200
Mount Juliet; Inc. Place; WILSON; 233 C-12; elev. 550ft./168m.; 🅿; ★ **NASH**; z 37121-22; Ⓟ 5,389; © 12,366; Ⓡ 12,390; ◆ 21,660
Mount Lebanon; RMC Place; DECATUR; *232 E-7; elev. 400ft./122m.; mail Decaturville z 38329; rural
Mount Lebanon; RMC Place; LAWRENCE; *232 F-9; mail Lawrenceburg z 38464; rural
Mount Lebanon; RMC Place; TIPTON; *232 E-2; elev. 339ft./103m.; ★ **MEM**; mail Covington z 38019; ● 30
Mount Leo; RMC Place; WARREN; *233 E-14; mail Mc Minnville z 37110; pop. incl. with McMinnville (Inc. Place)
Mount Moriah; RMC Place; BENTON; 232 D-7; elev. 415ft./126m.; mail Camden z 38320; ● 150
Mount Moriah; DEKALB; see Pea Ridge (RMC Place)
Mount Nebo; RMC Place; LAWRENCE; *232 G-9; elev. 860ft./262m.; mail Iron City z 38463; ● 30
Mount Olive; RMC Place; GRUNDY; *233 E-14; elev. 900ft./274m.; mail Mc Minnville z 37110
Mount Olive; RMC Place; KNOX; 233 N-13; ★ **KNOX**; mail Knoxville z 37920; ● 720
Mount Olive; RMC Place; MARION; *233 G-15; mail Whitwell z 37397; rural
Mount Olive; RMC Place; RUTHERFORD; *233 D-12; ★ **MUR**; mail Murfreesboro z 37129; ● 100
Mount Pelia; RMC Place; WEAKLEY; 232 B-5; elev. 385ft./117m.; mail Martin z 38237; ● 200
Mount Pisgah; RMC Place; WHITE; *233 D-14; elev. 1,002ft./305m.; mail Walling z 38587; ● 40
Mount Pleasant; RMC Place; GREENE; *233 K-17; mail Greeneville z 37743; ● 150
Mount Pleasant; HAYWOOD; see Hillville (RMC Place)
Mount Pleasant; RMC Place; HENRY; *232 B-7; mail Buchanan z 38222; rural
Mount Pleasant; Inc. Place; MAURY; 232 E-10; elev. 675ft./206m.; 🅿; z 38474; Ⓟ 4,278; © 4,491
Mount Pleasant; RMC Place; PUTNAM; *233 C-15; elev. 1,451ft./442m.; mail Cookeville z 38506; rural
Mount Pleasant; RMC Place; SCOTT; *233 B-17; elev. 1,137ft./347m.; mail Robbins z 37852; rural
Mount Tabor; RMC Place; BLOUNT; *233 D-19; elev. 880ft./268m.; ★ **KNOX**; mail Maryville z 37804; rural
Mount Tucker Addition; RMC Place; SULLIVAN; *233 J-18; ★ **JNSC-**; mail Blountville z 37617; ● 180
Mount Union (Union Hill); RMC Place; JACKSON; *233 C-14; mail Granville z 38564; rural
Mount Union; RMC Place; PICKETT; *233 B-16; elev. 292ft./89m.; mail Byrdstown z 38549; rural
Mount Vernon; RMC Place; COFFEE; *233 F-13; elev. 1,058ft./322m.; mail Tullahoma z 37388; rural
Mount Vernon; RMC Place; MONROE; 233 F-18; elev. 1,058ft./322m.; mail Tellico Plains z 37385; ● 200
Mount Vernon; RMC Place; RUTHERFORD; *233 E-11; mail Rockvale z 37153; ● 50
Mount Vernon; RMC Place; SUMNER; *233 B-12; mail Bethpage z 37022; rural
Mount View; RMC Place; DAVIDSON; *233 C-11; elev. 618ft./188m.; ★ **NASH**; mail Nashville z 37211; pop. incl. with Nashville (Inc. Place)
Mount View; RMC Place; GRUNDY; *233 F-14; mail Pelham z 37366; ● 120
Mount Vinson; RMC Place; MCNAIRY; *232 F-6; mail Stantonville z 38379; ● 50
Mount Zion; RMC Place; CHEATHAM; *232 B-10; elev. 724ft./221m.; ★ **NASH**; mail Ashland City z 37015; rural
Mount Zion; RMC Place; MONROE; *233 E-19; mail Vonore z 37885; rural
Mount Zion; RMC Place; MONTGOMERY; *232 B-9; mail Cumberland Furnace z 37051; rural
Mount Zion; RMC Place; OBION; *232 B-4; mail Hornbeak z 38232; rural
Mount Zion (Thaxton); RMC Place; WARREN; *233 E-14; elev. 1,062ft./324m.; mail Mc Minnville z 37110; rural
Mourberry (Moberry); RMC Place; WHITE; *233 D-15; elev. 1,710ft./521m.; mail Sparta z 38583; rural
Mowbray (Huckleberry); RMC Place; HAMILTON; *233 F-16; ★ **CHTN**; mail Soddy Daisy z 37379; ● 170
Mud Creek; RMC Place; MCNAIRY; *232 F-6; mail Adamsville z 38310; pop. incl. with Adamsville (Inc. Place)
Mud Creek; RMC Place; WARREN; *233 E-14; mail Rock Island z 38581; ● 200
Muddy Pond; RMC Place; OVERTON; *233 C-16; mail Monterey z 38574; rural
Mudsink; RMC Place; WILLIAMSON; *233 D-11; elev. 720ft./219m.; ★ **NASH**; mail Franklin z 37067; ● 80
Mulberry; RMC Place; LINCOLN; 233 F-12; elev. 741ft./226m.; 🅿; z 37359; ● 200
Mulberry Gap; RMC Place; HANCOCK; *233 J-16; mail Sneedville z 37869; rural
Mulberry Hill; RMC Place; STEWART; *232 B-7; elev. 400ft./122m.; mail Dover z 37058; rural
Mulloy; RMC Place; SUMNER; *233 B-11; elev. 774ft./236m.; mail Cottontown z 37048; rural
Munford; Inc. Place; TIPTON; 232 E-2; elev. 445ft./136m.; 🅿; ★ **MEM**; z 38058; Ⓟ 2,326; © 4,708
Murfreesboro; Inc. Place; ⊡ RUTHERFORD; 233 D-12; elev. 619ft./189m.; 🅿 🅷 🅲 22,863 ■; ★ **MUR**; z 37127-33; Ⓟ 44,922; © 68,816; ◆ 114,063
Murphy Hill; RMC Place; KNOX; ★ **KNOX**
Murray Hills; RMC Place; HAMILTON; *233 G-16; ★ **CHTN**; pop. incl. with Chattanooga (Inc. Place)
Murray-Lake Hills; RMC Place; HAMILTON; ★ **CHTN**; mail Chattanooga z 37416; pop. incl. with Chattanooga (Inc. Place)
Murray Store; RMC Place; MCMINN; *233 E-17; elev. 938ft./286m.; mail Niota z 37826; rural
Myers; RMC Place; FRANKLIN; mail Winchester z 37398; pop. incl. with Winchester (Inc. Place)

N

Nacome; HICKMAN; see Beaverdam Springs (RMC Place)
Nameless; RMC Place; JACKSON; *233 C-14; mail Bloomington Springs z 38545; rural
Nance; RMC Place; CROCKETT; *232 D-4; mail Alamo z 38001; rural
Nance Ferry; RMC Place; GRAINGER; *233 C-20; mail Blaine z 37709; rural
Nances Grove; RMC Place; JEFFERSON; *233 C-20; mail New Market z 37820; rural
Nankipoo; RMC Place; LAUDERDALE; 232 D-3; mail Halls z 38040; ● 30
Napier; RMC Place; LEWIS; *232 F-9; elev. 800ft./244m.; mail Hohenwald z 38462; rural
Narrows of the Harpeth; RMC Place; CHEATHAM; *232 C-10; elev. 585ft./178m.; ★ **NASH**; mail Kingston Springs z 37082; rural
Narrow Valley; RMC Place; GRAINGER; *233 C-20; mail Rutledge z 37861; rural
Nash; RMC Place; PUTNAM; *233 C-14; mail Baxter z 38544; ● 30
Nashville (Nashville-Davidson); Inc. Place; **STATE CAPITAL**; ⊡ DAVIDSON; 233 C-11; elev. 440ft./134m.; 🅿 🅷 🅲 33,275 ■; ★ **NASH**; z 37201-22, z 37224, z 37227-30, z 37232, z 37234-36, z 37238, z 37240-44, z 37246, z 37249-50; Ⓟ 488,374; © 545,524; Ⓡ 545,535; ◆ 673,012
Nashville-Davidson; DAVIDSON; see Nashville (Inc. Place)
Natco; RMC Place; MAURY; *232 E-10; mail Columbia z 38401
National Cemetery; RMC Place; SHELBY; ★ **MEM**; mail Memphis z 38122; pop. incl. with Memphis (Inc. Place)
Natural Bridge; RMC Place; COCKE; *233 L-16; elev. 1,154ft./352m.; mail Parrottsville z 37843; ● 50
Nauvoo; RMC Place; DYER; *232 C-3; elev. 363ft./111m.; mail Dyersburg z 38024; ● 130
Neapolis; RMC Place; MAURY; *232 E-10; mail Columbia z 38401; pop. incl. with Columbia (Inc. Place)
Neboville; RMC Place; GIBSON; *232 C-4; mail Newbern z 38059; ● 50
Needmore; RMC Place; HAMBLEN; *233 K-16; elev. 1,123ft./342m.; ★ **MORR**; mail Whitesburg z 37891
Needmore; RMC Place; MARSHALL; *233 F-11; mail Lewisburg z 37091; pop. incl. with Lewisburg (Inc. Place)
Needmore; RMC Place; MAURY; *232 E-10; mail Mount Pleasant z 38474; pop. incl. with Mount Pleasant (Inc. Place)
Needmore; RMC Place; MONTGOMERY; *232 B-9; elev. 690ft./210m.; mail Indian Mound z 37079; ● 30
Needmore; RMC Place; WILSON; *233 C-12; ★ **NASH**; mail Old Hickory z 37138; ● 200
Neely; RMC Place; MADISON; *232 E-5; mail Denmark z 38391; rural
Neely Crossroads; RMC Place; CLAY; *233 B-15; mail Celina z 38551; ● 30
Nelsontown; RMC Place; SULLIVAN; *233 J-18; ★ **JNSC-**; mail Kingsport z 37660; pop. incl. with Kingsport (Inc. Place)
Nemo; RMC Place; MORGAN; *233 C-17; mail Wartburg z 37887; rural
Nenny; RMC Place; HAMBLEN; *233 K-16; ★ **MORR**; mail Whitesburg z 37891; rural
Neptune; RMC Place; CHEATHAM; *232 B-10; elev. 612ft./187m.; ★ **NASH**; mail Ashland City z 37015; rural
Neubert; RMC Place; KNOX; *233 D-20; ★ **KNOX**; mail Knoxville z 37920; rural
Neva; RMC Place; JOHNSON; 233 K-20; mail Mountain City z 37683; ● 30
Newbern; Inc. Place; DYER; 232 C-4; elev. 376ft./115m.; 🅿; z 38059; Ⓟ 2,515; © 2,988
New Bethel; RMC Place; MCMINN; *233 F-17; mail Etowah z 37331; rural
New Canton; RMC Place; HAWKINS; *233 J-17; ★ **JNSC-**; mail Church Hill z 37642; ● 150
Newcastle; RMC Place; HARDEMAN; 232 F-4; elev. 539ft./164m.; mail Whiteville z 38075; ● 30
Newcomb; RMC Place; CAMPBELL; 233 B-19; elev. 977ft./298m.; 🅿; z 37819; ● 350
New Corinth; RMC Place; GRAINGER; *233 C-20; mail Rutledge z 37861; rural
New Deal; RMC Place; SUMNER; 233 B-12; elev. 924ft./282m.; ★ **NASH**; mail Cottontown z 37048; ● 470
New Dellrose; RMC Place; LINCOLN; *233 G-11; mail Dellrose z 38453
New Due West; RMC Place; DAVIDSON; ★ **NASH**; mail Madison z 37115; pop. incl. with Nashville (Inc. Place)
Newell Station; RMC Place; SEVIER; 233 D-20; elev. 1,114ft./340m.; ★ **KNOX**; mail Seymour z 37865; ● 360
New Enterprise; RMC Place; GIBSON; *232 D-5; elev. 376ft./115m.; mail Gibson z 38338; rural
New Era; RMC Place; CUMBERLAND; *233 D-16; mail Crossville z 38555; rural
New Flys Village; MAURY; see Fly (RMC Place)
New Harmony; RMC Place; BLEDSOE; 233 E-16; mail Pikeville z 37367; ● 100
New Harmony; RMC Place; MACON; *233 B-13; mail Hartsville z 37074; rural
New Haven; RMC Place; LAWRENCE; *232 F-9; mail Lawrenceburg z 38464; rural
New Haven; RMC Place; SCOTT; *233 B-17; mail Oneida z 37841; rural
New Herman; RMC Place; BEDFORD; *233 F-12; mail Shelbyville z 37160; rural
New Hope; RMC Place; CHEATHAM; *232 B-10; ★ **NASH**; mail Joelton z 37080; ● 30
New Hope; RMC Place; HANCOCK; *233 J-16; mail Sneedville z 37869; rural
New Hope; RMC Place; HARDIN; *232 F-6; mail Adamsville z 38310; pop. incl. with Crump (Inc. Place)
New Hope; RMC Place; HAWKINS; *233 K-17; mail Rogersville z 37857; rural
New Hope; RMC Place; HOUSTON; *232 C-8; elev. 391ft./119m.; mail Stewart z 37175; ● 30
New Hope; RMC Place; HUMPHREYS; *232 C-8; mail Mc Ewen z 37101; rural
New Hope; RMC Place; JACKSON; *233 B-15; elev. 983ft./300m.; mail Hilham z 38568; rural
New Hope; RMC Place; LINCOLN; *233 G-12; mail Fayetteville z 37334; rural
New Hope; Inc. Place; MARION; 233 G-14; elev. 700ft./213m.; mail South Pittsburg z 37380; Ⓟ 854; © 1,043
New Hope; RMC Place; MCNAIRY; *232 G-6; mail Guys z 38339, Michie z 38357; rural
New Hope; RMC Place; ROANE; *233 D-17; ★ **KNOX**; mail Rockwood z 37854; rural
New Hope; RMC Place; WILLIAMSON; *232 D-10; elev. 726ft./221m.; ★ **NASH**; mail Fairview z 37062; pop. incl. with Fairview (Inc. Place)
New Hope; RMC Place; WILSON; *233 C-12; ★ **NASH**; mail Lebanon z 37087; ● 50
New Johnsonville (Johnsonville); Inc. Place; HUMPHREYS; 232 D-7; elev. 429ft./131m.; 🅿; z 37134; Ⓟ 1,643; © 1,905
New Lawton (Lawton); RMC Place; MCNAIRY; *232 F-6; mail Selmer z 38375; ● 30
New Line; RMC Place; HAMBLEN; *233 K-15; ★ **MORR**; mail Morristown z 37814; rural
New Loyston; RMC Place; UNION; 233 C-19; ★ **KNOX**; mail Maynardville z 37807; ● 30
Newmansville; RMC Place; GREENE; *233 K-17; mail Afton z 37616; rural
New Market; Inc. Place; JEFFERSON; 233 C-20; elev. 1,100ft./335m.; 🅿; z 37820; Ⓟ 1,086; © 1,234
New Markham; RMC Place; LAKE; *232 B-3; elev. 290ft./88m.; mail Tiptonville z 38079; ● 40
New Middleton; RMC Place; SMITH; *233 C-13; elev. 576ft./176m.; mail Gordonsville z 38563
New Midway; RMC Place; ROANE; *233 D-18; mail Kingston z 37763; rural
Newport; Inc. Place; ⊡ COCKE; 233 L-16; elev. 1,055ft./322m.; 🅿 🅷; ★ **MORR**; z 37821-22; Ⓟ 7,123; © 7,242
Newport Camp; RHEA; see White's Creek (RMC Place)
New Prospect; RMC Place; LAWRENCE; *232 F-10; mail Lawrenceburg z 38464; ● 50
New Providence; RMC Place; LOUDON; *233 D-18; ★ **KNOX**; mail Loudon z 37774; rural
New Providence; RMC Place; MONTGOMERY; *232 B-9; elev. 549ft./167m.; ★ **CLRKV**; mail Clarksville z 37042; pop. incl. with Clarksville (Inc. Place)
New River; RMC Place; SCOTT; *233 B-17; elev. 1,206ft./368m.; mail Helenwood z 37755; ● 200
New Safford; RMC Place; HENDERSON; *232 E-7; elev. 500ft./152m.; mail Darden z 38328; ● 50
New Salem; RMC Place; HAMILTON; *233 F-16; ★ **CHTN**; mail Soddy Daisy z 37379
New Salem; RMC Place; JACKSON; *233 C-14; mail Gainesboro z 38562; rural
New Salem; RMC Place; SCOTT; *233 B-18; mail Oneida z 37841; rural
New Tazewell (Tazewell); Inc. Place; CLAIBORNE; 233 B-20; elev. 1,472ft./449m.; 🅿; z 37824-25 & mail Tazewell z 37879; Ⓟ 1,864; © 2,871
Newton; RMC Place; CUMBERLAND; *233 D-16; mail Crossville z 38572; rural
New Town; RMC Place; MARSHALL; *233 F-11; mail Cornersville z 37047; pop. incl. with Cornersville (Inc. Place)
New Town; RMC Place; MAURY; *233 D-11; elev. 720ft./219m.; mail Spring Hill z 37174; pop. incl. with Spring Hill (Inc. Place)
Newtown; RMC Place; POLK; *233 G-18; mail Copperhill z 37317; pop. incl. with Copperhill (Inc. Place)
Newtown; RMC Place; RUTHERFORD; *233 E-12; elev. 770ft./235m.; mail Rockvale z 37153; rural
New Union; RMC Place; COFFEE; *233 E-13; elev. 1,093ft./333m.; mail Manchester z 37355; ● 160
New Victory; RMC Place; WASHINGTON; *233 K-18; elev. 1,660ft./506m.; ★ **JNSC-**; mail Jonesborough z 37659; ● 50
New Zion; RMC Place; CARROLL; *232 C-6; mail Huntingdon z 38344; ● 30
New Zion; RMC Place; MACON; *233 B-13; elev. 944ft./288m.; mail Westmoreland z 37186; rural
Nickletown; RMC Place; MARION; *233 G-14; mail Jasper z 37347; rural
Nicks Creek; RMC Place; CAMPBELL; *233 C-18; elev. 1,250ft./381m.; mail Huntsville z 37756; rural
Ninemile; RMC Place; BLEDSOE; *233 E-16; mail Pikeville z 37367
Ninth Model; RMC Place; COFFEE; *233 E-13; mail Morrison z 37357; ● 30
Niota; Inc. Place; MCMINN; 233 E-18; elev. 978ft./298m.; 🅿; z 37826; Ⓟ 745; © 781
Nixon; RMC Place; HARDIN; 232 G-7; mail Savannah z 38372; ● 240
Noah; RMC Place; COFFEE; *233 E-13; mail Manchester z 37355, Wartrace z 37183; rural
Nobles; RMC Place; HENRY; *232 B-7; elev. 399ft./122m.; mail Paris z 38242
Nolensville; Inc. Place; WILLIAMSON; 233 D-11; elev. 620ft./189m.; 🅿; ★ **NASH**; z 37135; Ⓟ 1,570; © 3,099
Nonaburg; RMC Place; MCMINN; *233 F-18; mail Englewood z 37329; rural
Nonaville; RMC Place; WILSON; *233 C-12; ★ **NASH**; mail Mount Juliet z 37122; rural
Nonconnah; RMC Place; SHELBY; ★ **MEM**; mail Memphis z 38116; pop. incl. with Memphis (Inc. Place)
Norene; RMC Place; WILSON; 233 C-13; elev. 742ft./226m.; 🅿; z 37136; ● 100
Norma; RMC Place; SCOTT; 233 B-18; mail Huntsville z 37756; ● 120
Normandy; Inc. Place; BEDFORD; 233 F-12; elev. 825ft./251m.; 🅿; z 37360; Ⓟ 118; © 141
Norris; Inc. Place; ANDERSON; 233 C-19; elev. 1,042ft./318m.; 🅿; ★ **KNOX**; z 37828; Ⓟ 1,303; © 1,446
North; RMC Place; DAVIDSON; ★ **NASH**; mail Nashville z 37208; pop. incl. with Nashville (Inc. Place)
North; RMC Place; SHELBY; ★ **MEM**; mail Memphis z 38107; pop. incl. with Memphis (Inc. Place)
North Alexandria; SMITH; see Brush Creek (RMC Place)
Northaven; RMC Place; SHELBY; 232 I-2; elev. 240ft./73m.; rural
North Chattanooga; RMC Place; HAMILTON; *233 G-15; elev. 673ft./205m.; ★ **CHTN**; mail Chattanooga z 37405; pop. incl. with Chattanooga (Inc. Place)
Northcott; RMC Place; SULLIVAN; *233 J-18; ★ **JNSC-**; mail Kingsport z 37660; ● 800
Northcutts Cove; RMC Place; GRUNDY; *233 E-14; elev. 1,156ft./352m.; mail Mc Minnville z 37110; rural
Northcutt's Cove; RMC Place; WARREN; *233 E-14; mail Mc Minnville z 37110; ● 80
Northeast; RMC Place; DAVIDSON; ★ **NASH**; mail Nashville z 37207; pop. incl. with Nashville (Inc. Place)
Northern Hills; RMC Place; HAMILTON; *233 G-15; ★ **CHTN**; mail Hixson z 37343; pop. incl. with Chattanooga (Inc. Place)
North Glen Estates; RMC Place; HAMILTON; *233 G-15; ★ **CHTN**; mail Hixson z 37343; pop. incl. with Chattanooga (Inc. Place)
North Hills; RMC Place; KNOX; *233 D-19; ★ **KNOX**; mail Knoxville z 37917; pop. incl. with Knoxville (Inc. Place)
North Johnson City; RMC Place; WASHINGTON; *233 K-18; ★ **JNSC-**; mail Johnson City z 37601; pop. incl. with Johnson City (Inc. Place)
North Knoxville; RMC Place; KNOX; *233 D-19; ★ **KNOX**; mail Knoxville z 37917, z 37927; pop. incl. with Knoxville (Inc. Place)
Northpoint; RMC Place; MONROE; *233 E-18; mail Sweetwater z 37874; ● 50
North Riverside; RMC Place; LEWIS; mail Hohenwald z 38462; rural
Northside; RMC Place; MADISON; ★ **JAC**; mail Jackson z 38301; pop. incl. with Jackson (Inc. Place)
North Springs; RMC Place; JACKSON; 233 B-14; elev. 604ft./184m.; mail Whitleyville z 38588; ● 40
Norwood; RMC Place; ANDERSON; *233 C-18; ★ **KNOX**; mail Oliver Springs z 37840; pop. incl. with Oliver Springs (Inc. Place)
Norwood; RMC Place; KNOX; *233 D-19; ★ **KNOX**; mail Knoxville z 37912; pop. incl. with Knoxville (Inc. Place)
Notchy Creek; RMC Place; MONROE; *233 F-18; elev. 1,000ft./305m.; mail Madisonville z 37354; rural
Nough; RMC Place; COCKE; *233 M-16; mail Del Rio z 37727; rural
Nubia; RMC Place; SUMNER; *233 A-12; elev. 852ft./260m.; mail Westmoreland z 37186; rural
Nucarbon; LAWRENCE; see Dunn (RMC Place)
Number One; RMC Place; SUMNER; *233 B-12; elev. 458ft./140m.; mail Gallatin z 37066; pop. incl. with Gallatin (Inc. Place)
Nunnelly; RMC Place; HICKMAN; 232 D-9; elev. 700ft./213m.; 🅿; z 37137; ● 350
Nutbush; RMC Place; HAYWOOD; *232 E-3; mail Brownsville z 38012

O

Oak City; RMC Place; SEVIER; 233 D-20; elev. 938ft./286m.; ★ **KNOX**; mail Seymour z 37865; ● 120
Oakdale; RMC Place; HAWKINS; *233 J-17; elev. 1,400ft./427m.; ★ **JNSC-**; mail Surgoinsville z 37873; ● 30
Oakdale; RMC Place; MACON; *233 B-13; mail Westmoreland z 37186; rural
Oakdale; Inc. Place; MORGAN; 233 D-17; elev. 803ft./245m.; 🅿; z 37829; Ⓟ 268; © 244
Oak Dale; RMC Place; OVERTON; *233 B-16; mail Monroe z 38573; rural
Oakdale; RMC Place; WHITE; *233 D-15; elev. 900ft./274m.; mail Sparta z 38583; ● 200
Oakfield; RMC Place; MADISON; 232 D-5; elev. 444ft./135m.; 🅿; ★ **JAC**; z 38362; ● 100
Oak Grove; RMC Place; CAMPBELL; *233 C-19; mail Lake City z 37769; ● 300
Oak Grove; RMC Place; CARTER; *233 K-19; ★ **JNSC-**; mail Elizabethton z 37643; rural
Oak Grove; RMC Place; CLAIBORNE; *233 B-20; mail Harrogate z 37752; ● 30
Oak Grove; RMC Place; CLAY; *233 A-14; mail Moss z 38575
Oak Grove; RMC Place; DICKSON; *232 D-9; mail Dickson z 37055; rural
Oak Grove; RMC Place; FRANKLIN; *233 F-13; elev. 1,070ft./326m.; mail Decherd z 37324; ● 50
Oak Grove; RMC Place; GILES; *232 G-10; mail Goodspring z 38460; ● 30
Oak Grove; RMC Place; HARDIN; *232 F-7; elev. 411ft./125m.; mail Savannah z 38372; rural
Oak Grove; RMC Place; HENRY; *232 B-7; mail Buchanan z 38222; rural
Oak Grove; RMC Place; JEFFERSON; *233 L-15; ★ **MORR**; mail Dandridge z 37725; rural
Oak Grove; RMC Place; LEWIS; *232 F-9; mail Hohenwald z 38462; rural
Oak Grove; RMC Place; MADISON; ★ **JAC**; mail Jackson z 38301
Oak Grove; RMC Place; MARION; *233 G-15; mail Whitwell z 37397; rural
Oak Grove; RMC Place; MONROE; *233 E-18; mail Madisonville z 37354; rural
Oak Grove; RMC Place; OVERTON; *233 B-15; mail Hilham z 38568; rural
Oak Grove; RMC Place; PICKETT; *233 B-16; elev. 951ft./290m.; mail Monroe z 38573; rural
Oak Grove; RMC Place; POLK; *233 G-17; mail Benton z 37307; rural
Oak Grove; RMC Place; SUMNER; 233 B-12; elev. 886ft./270m.; mail Bethpage z 37022; ● 150
Oak Grove; RMC Place; TIPTON; *232 E-2; elev. 350ft./107m.; mail Covington z 38019; rural
Oak Grove; RMC Place; UNION; *233 B-20; mail Sharps Chapel z 37866; rural
Oak Grove; RMC Place; WARREN; *233 E-13; mail Morrison z 37357; rural
Oak Grove; CDP; WASHINGTON; 234 L-2; ★ **JNSC-**; mail Johnson City z 37615; Ⓟ 3,498; © 4,072
Oak Grove; RMC Place; WEAKLEY; *232 B-5; mail Martin z 38237; ● 250
Oak Grove Heights; RMC Place; KNOX; *233 D-19; ★ **KNOX**; mail Knoxville z 37921; ● 180
Oakhaven; RMC Place; SHELBY; ★ **MEM**; mail Memphis z 38116; pop. incl. with Memphis (Inc. Place)
Oak Hill; RMC Place; CARTER; *233 K-19; mail Hampton z 37658; ● 80
Oak Hill; RMC Place; COCKE; *233 L-16; elev. 1,450ft./442m.; mail Parrottsville z 37843; rural
Oak Hill; RMC Place; CUMBERLAND; *233 D-16; mail Crossville z 38571; rural
Oak Hill; Inc. Place; DAVIDSON; 232 L-8; elev. 600ft./183m.; ★ **NASH**; mail Nashville z 37220; Ⓟ 4,301; © 4,493
Oak Hill; RMC Place; OVERTON; *233 C-15; elev. 1,020ft./311m.; mail Rickman z 38580; rural
Oak Hill; RMC Place; PICKETT; *233 A-15; elev. 972ft./296m.; mail Byrdstown z 38549; rural
Oak Hill; RMC Place; SULLIVAN; *233 J-19; ★ **JNSC-**; mail Bristol z 37620; pop. incl. with Bristol (Inc. Place)
Oak Hill; RMC Place; WASHINGTON; *233 K-18; ★ **JNSC-**; mail Jonesborough z 37659; rural
Oakhurst; RMC Place; BLOUNT; ★ **KNOX**; mail Maryville z 37803; pop. incl. with Maryville (Inc. Place)
Oakland; Inc. Place; FAYETTE; 232 F-3; elev. 382ft./116m.; 🅿; z 38060, z 38076; Ⓟ 392; © 1,279
Oakland; RMC Place; GRAINGER; *233 C-20; mail Rutledge z 37861; rural
Oakland; RMC Place; HENRY; *232 C-7; mail Paris z 38242; ● 30
Oakland; RMC Place; JEFFERSON; *233 C-20; ★ **KNOX**; mail Jefferson City z 37760; pop. incl. with Dandridge (Inc. Place)
Oakland; RMC Place; KNOX; *233 C-19; ★ **KNOX**; mail Knoxville z 37918; pop. incl. with Knoxville (Inc. Place)
Oakland; RMC Place; ROBERTSON; *233 B-11; elev. 669ft./204m.; mail Springfield z 37172; rural
Oakland; RMC Place; WARREN; *233 E-14; elev. 964ft./294m.; mail Mc Minnville z 37110; rural
Oakland; RMC Place; WASHINGTON; *233 K-18; mail Telford z 37690; ● 50
Oaklawn; RMC Place; DEKALB; *233 D-14; elev. 1,080ft./329m.; mail Smithville z 37166; ● 100
Oakleigh Estates; RMC Place; SULLIVAN; *233 J-19; ★ **JNSC-**; mail Bristol z 37620
Oakley; RMC Place; OVERTON; *233 B-15; elev. 1,045ft./319m.; mail Allons z 38541; rural
Oaklyn; RMC Place; CUMBERLAND; *233 D-16; elev. 1,800ft./549m.; mail Crossville z 38555; ● 330
Oak Park; RMC Place; COFFEE; mail Tullahoma z 37388
Oak Plains; RMC Place; MONTGOMERY; *232 B-10; elev. 673ft./205m.; ★ **CLRKV**; mail Clarksville z 37040; ● 30
Oak Ridge; Inc. Place; ANDERSON, ROANE; 233 D-18; elev. 900ft./274m.; 🅿 🅷 ■; ★ **KNOX**; z 37830-31; Ⓟ 27,310; © 27,387; ◆ 27,383
Oak Tree; RMC Place; WILLIAMSON; *232 D-10; ★ **NASH**; mail Fairview z 37062; pop. incl. with Fairview (Inc. Place)
Oak View; RMC Place; BLOUNT; *233 D-20; ★ **KNOX**; mail Walland z 37886; rural
Oakville; RMC Place; SHELBY; *232 G-2; ★ **MEM**; mail Memphis z 38118; pop. incl. with Memphis (Inc. Place)
Oakwood; RMC Place; KNOX; ★ **KNOX**; mail Knoxville z 37917; pop. incl. with Knoxville (Inc. Place)
Oakwood; RMC Place; MONTGOMERY; 232 B-9; elev. 624ft./190m.; ★ **CLRKV**; mail Woodlawn z 37191; ● 150
Oakwood Estates; RMC Place; WILLIAMSON; *233 D-11; elev. 700ft./213m.; ★ **NASH**; mail Franklin z 37064; ● 600
Obion; Inc. Place; OBION; 232 C-4; elev. 290ft./88m.; 🅿; z 38240; Ⓟ 1,241; © 1,134
OBION; 232 B-4; Ⓟ 31,717; © 32,450; ◆ 31,192
Ocana; RMC Place; SUMNER; *233 B-12; ★ **NASH**; mail Hendersonville z 37075; rural
Ocoee; RMC Place; POLK; 233 G-17; elev. 788ft./240m.; 🅿; z 37361; ● 300
O'Connors; RMC Place; WHITE; *233 D-15; elev. 1,048ft./319m.; mail Sparta z 38583; ● 70
Odd Fellows Hall; RMC Place; GILES; *232 F-10; mail Pulaski z 38478; rural
Officers Chapel; RMC Place; PUTNAM; *233 C-15; elev. 1,000ft./305m.; mail Cookeville z 38506; rural
Offutt; RMC Place; ANDERSON; *233 C-19; ★ **KNOX**; mail Clinton z 37716; rural
Ogden; RMC Place; RHEA; *233 E-16; mail Dayton z 37321; rural
Okalona; RMC Place; OVERTON; *233 B-15; elev. 1,004ft./306m.; mail Livingston z 38570; rural
Okolona; RMC Place; CARTER; *233 K-18; ★ **JNSC-**; mail Johnson City z 37601; pop. incl. with Johnson City (Inc. Place)
Okolona; RMC Place; HAWKINS; *233 J-17; ★ **JNSC-**; mail Church Hill z 37642; rural
Old Antioch; RMC Place; JACKSON; *233 B-15; elev. 1,031ft./314m.; mail Gainesboro z 38562; rural
Old Cedar Fork (Cedarfork); RMC Place; CLAIBORNE; *233 B-20; elev. 1,300ft./396m.; mail Tazewell z 37879; ● 30
Old Chihowee; RMC Place; BLOUNT; *233 D-20; ★ **KNOX**; mail Seymour z 37865; rural
Olde Mill; RMC Place; HAMILTON; *233 G-16; ★ **CHTN**; mail Hixson z 37343; ● 200
Oldfort; RMC Place; POLK; 233 G-17; elev. 857ft./261m.; 🅿; z 37362; ● 150
Old Glory; RMC Place; BLOUNT; *233 D-19; ★ **KNOX**; mail Maryville z 37804; pop. incl. with Alcoa (Inc. Place)
Old Hickory; RMC Place; DAVIDSON; *233 C-11; 🅿; ★ **NASH**; z 37138; pop. incl. with Nashville (Inc. Place)
Old Kingsport; RMC Place; SULLIVAN; *233 J-18; ★ **JNSC-**; mail Kingsport z 37660; pop. incl. with Kingsport (Inc. Place)
Old Laguardo; RMC Place; WILSON; *233 C-12; ★ **NASH**; mail Mount Juliet z 37122; pop. incl. with Mount Juliet (Inc. Place)
Old Lawton; RMC Place; MCNAIRY; *232 F-6; elev. 505ft./154m.; mail Selmer z 38375; rural
Old Salem; RMC Place; FRANKLIN; *233 G-12; elev. 922ft./281m.; mail Huntland z 37345; rural
Old Springville; RMC Place; HENRY; *232 C-7; mail Springville z 38256; ● 30
Old Sweetwater; RMC Place; MONROE; *233 E-18; mail Sweetwater z 37874; rural
Old Washington; RMC Place; RHEA; 233 E-16; elev. 700ft./213m.; mail Dayton z 37321; ● 180
Old Winesap; RMC Place; CUMBERLAND; *233 D-16; elev. 1,740ft./530m.; mail Crossville z 38572; rural
Old Zion; RMC Place; WHITE; *233 D-15; mail Sparta z 38583; ● 100
Olivehill; RMC Place; HARDIN; 232 F-7; elev. 463ft./141m.; 🅿; z 38475; ● 160
Oliver Springs; Inc. Place; ROANE, ANDERSON, MORGAN; 233 C-18; elev. 785ft./239m.; 🅿; ★ **KNOX**; z 37840; Ⓟ 3,433; © 3,303
Olivet; RMC Place; HARDIN; 232 F-7; mail Savannah z 38372; ● 180
Oneida; Inc. Place; SCOTT; 233 B-18; elev. 1,456ft./444m.; 🅿 🅷; z 37841; Ⓟ 3,502; © 3,615
Only; RMC Place; HICKMAN; 232 D-8; elev. 600ft./183m.; 🅿; z 37140; ● 120
Ooltewah; CDP; HAMILTON; 233 G-16; elev. 900ft./274m.; 🅿; ★ **CHTN**; z 37363; Ⓟ 4,903; © 5,681
Opossum; RMC Place; LAUDERDALE; *232 D-3; mail Ripley z 38063; pop. incl. with Ripley (Inc. Place)
Opossum Creek Pines; RMC Place; HAMILTON; *233 F-16; elev. 740ft./226m.; ★ **CHTN**; mail Soddy Daisy z 37379; ● 300
Oral; RMC Place; ROANE; *233 D-18; mail Lenoir City z 37771; rural
Orchard Knob; RMC Place; HAMILTON; ★ **CHTN**; pop. incl. with Chattanooga (Inc. Place)
Orchard View; RMC Place; ROANE; *233 D-18; ★ **KNOX**; mail Oliver Springs z 37840; ● 50
Orebank; RMC Place; SULLIVAN; 234 J-9; elev. 1,385ft./422m.; ★ **JNSC-**; mail Kingsport z 37664; ● 1,300
Ore Spring; RMC Place; WEAKLEY; *232 B-6; elev. 379ft./116m.; mail Dresden z 38225; rural
Orgains Crossroads; RMC Place; MONTGOMERY; *232 B-9; elev. 638ft./194m.; ★ **CLRKV**; mail Clarksville z 37040; ● 30
Orlinda; Inc. Place; ROBERTSON; 233 B-11; elev. 720ft./219m.; 🅿; ★ **NASH**; z 37141; Ⓟ 469; © 594
Orme; Inc. Place; MARION; 233 G-14; elev. 1,500ft./457m.; mail South Pittsburg z 37380; Ⓟ 150; © 124
Orysa; RMC Place; LAUDERDALE; *232 E-3; elev. 315ft./96m.; mail Ripley z 38063
Osage; RMC Place; HENRY; *232 B-6; mail Paris z 38242; rural
Osemont Chapel; RMC Place; CANNON; *233 D-13; mail Woodbury z 37190; rural
Ostella; RMC Place; MARSHALL; 233 F-11; mail Cornersville z 37047, Lewisburg z 37091; ● 40
Oswego; RMC Place; CAMPBELL; *233 B-19; mail Jellico z 37762; ● 30
Otes; RMC Place; HAWKINS; *233 K-16; mail Rogersville z 37857; rural
Otter Creek Junction; RMC Place; CUMBERLAND; *233 D-16; elev. 1,688ft./515m.; mail Crossville z 38572; rural
Ottway; RMC Place; GREENE; *233 K-17; elev. 1,164ft./355m.; mail Greeneville z 37745; rural
Overall; RMC Place; RUTHERFORD; 233 D-12; ★ **MUR**; mail Murfreesboro z 37127; ● 60
Overlook; RMC Place; BLOUNT; ★ **KNOX**; mail Maryville z 37804
OVERTON; 233 B-15; Ⓟ 17,636; © 20,118; ◆ 21,316
Ovilla; RMC Place; LAWRENCE; *232 F-9; mail Lawrenceburg z 38464; rural
Ovoca; RMC Place; COFFEE; *233 F-13; mail Tullahoma z 37388; rural
Owens Chapel; RMC Place; ROBERTSON; *233 B-11; ★ **NASH**; mail Springfield z 37172; rural
Owl City; RMC Place; LAKE; 232 B-3; elev. 298ft./91m.; mail Tiptonville z 38079; ● 30
Owl Hoot; RMC Place; LAKE; *232 C-3; elev. 271ft./83m.; mail Ridgely z 38080; rural
Ozone; RMC Place; CUMBERLAND; 233 D-17; elev. 1,648ft./502m.; ● 150
Ozone; RMC Place; OVERTON; *233 B-15; elev. 1,034ft./315m.; mail Monroe z 38573; rural

P

Pactolus; RMC Place; SULLIVAN; *233 J-18; ★ **JNSC-**; mail Kingsport z 37663; rural
Pailo; RMC Place; BLEDSOE; *233 F-15; mail Dunlap z 37327
Paint Rock; RMC Place; ROANE; *233 E-18; mail Philadelphia z 37846; ● 300
Palestine; RMC Place; HENDERSON; *232 E-6; mail Lexington z 38351
Palestine; RMC Place; ROBERTSON; *233 B-11; elev. 708ft./216m.; ★ **NASH**; mail Springfield z 37172; ● 30
Pall Mall; RMC Place; FENTRESS; 233 B-16; elev. 900ft./274m.; 🅿; z 38577; ● 140
Palmer; Inc. Place; GRUNDY; 233 F-15; elev. 1,810ft./552m.; 🅿; z 37365; Ⓟ 769; © 726
Palmersville; RMC Place; WEAKLEY; 232 B-6; elev. 450ft./137m.; 🅿; z 38241; ● 100
Palmyra; RMC Place; MONTGOMERY; 232 B-9; elev. 338ft./103m.; 🅿; ★ **CLRKV**; z 37142; ● 160
Pandora; RMC Place; JOHNSON; *233 J-19; mail Butler z 37640
Paperville; RMC Place; SULLIVAN; *233 J-19; ★ **JNSC-**; mail Bristol z 37620; pop. incl. with Bristol (Inc. Place)
Paradise Acres; RMC Place; WILSON; *233 C-12; ★ **NASH**; mail Mount Juliet z 37122; pop. incl. with Mount Juliet (Inc. Place)
Paragon Mills; RMC Place; DAVIDSON; ★ **NASH**; mail Nashville z 37211; pop. incl. with Nashville (Inc. Place)
Parham; SUMNER; see Cottontown (RMC Place)
Paris; Inc. Place; ⊡ HENRY; 232 B-6; elev. 519ft./158m.; 🅿 🅷 ■; z 38242; Ⓟ 9,332; © 9,763; ◆ 9,252
Parkburg; RMC Place; MADISON; *232 E-5; elev. 504ft./154m.; mail Pinson z 38366; ● 50
Park City; RMC Place; KNOX; *233 D-19; ★ **KNOX**; mail Knoxville z 37914; pop. incl. with Knoxville (Inc. Place)
Park City; RMC Place; LINCOLN; *233 G-12; elev. 1,000ft./305m.; mail Fayetteville z 37334; ● 500
Parker; RMC Place; PICKETT; *233 B-16; elev. 982ft./299m.; mail Pall Mall z 38577; rural
Parker Crossroads (Parkers Crossroads); Inc. Place; HENDERSON; 232 D-6; 🅿; z 38388; Ⓟ 161; © 241
Parkers Crossroads; HENDERSON; see Parker Crossroads (Inc. Place)
Park Grove; RMC Place; LAWRENCE; *232 F-9; mail Ethridge z 38456, Lawrenceburg z 38464; rural
Park Settlement; RMC Place; SEVIER; *233 E-20; mail Sevierville z 37862; rural
Park Shore; HAMILTON; see Parkshore Estates (RMC Place)
Parkshore Estates (Park Shore); RMC Place; HAMILTON; *233 G-16; elev. 700ft./213m.; ★ **CHTN**; mail Hixson z 37343; ● 200
Parksville; RMC Place; POLK; 233 G-17; mail Benton z 37307; ● 30
Parkview; RMC Place; ROANE; *233 D-17; ★ **KNOX**; mail Rockwood z 37854; ● 180
Parkway; RMC Place; BLOUNT; ★ **KNOX**; mail Maryville z 37801; pop. incl. with Maryville (Inc. Place)
Parragon; RMC Place; PUTNAM; *233 C-15; elev. 1,422ft./433m.; mail Cookeville z 38506; rural
Parrottsville; Inc. Place; COCKE; 233 L-16; elev. 1,170ft./357m.; 🅿; z 37843; Ⓟ 121; © 207
Parsons; Inc. Place; DECATUR; 232 E-7; elev. 497ft./151m.; 🅿 🅷; z 38363; Ⓟ 2,033; © 2,452
Pasquo; RMC Place; DAVIDSON; *232 D-10; elev. 646ft./197m.; ★ **NASH**; mail Nashville z 37221; pop. incl. with Nashville (Inc. Place)
Pate Hill; RMC Place; GREENE; *233 L-16; elev. 1,112ft./339m.; mail Mosheim z 37818; rural
Patterson; RMC Place; RUTHERFORD; *233 D-11; ★ **NASH**; mail Rockvale z 37153; rural
Patterson Crossroads; RMC Place; CLAIBORNE; *233 B-20; mail Harrogate z 37752; ● 130
Pattie Gap; RMC Place; ROANE; *233 E-18; elev. 818ft./249m.; mail Philadelphia z 37846; rural
Patton; BLEDSOE; see Melvine (RMC Place)
Patty; RMC Place; POLK; *233 F-17; elev. 760ft./232m.; mail Delano z 37325; rural
Paulette; RMC Place; UNION; 233 C-19; elev. 1,029ft./314m.; ★ **KNOX**; mail Maynardville z 37807; ● 160
Paw Paw Ridge; RMC Place; DYER; *232 D-3; elev. 259ft./79m.; mail Finley z 38030; rural
Payne Cove; RMC Place; GRUNDY; *233 F-14; mail Pelham z 37366; rural
Paynes Store; RMC Place; TROUSDALE; *233 B-12; elev. 594ft./181m.; mail Bethpage z 37022, Castalian Springs z 37031, Hartsville z 37074; rural
Peabody; RMC Place; CAMPBELL; *233 B-19; mail La Follette z 37766; ● 50
Peak; RMC Place; ANDERSON; *233 C-19; ★ **KNOX**; mail Clinton z 37716; ● 150
Peakland; RMC Place; MEIGS; 233 E-17; elev. 720ft./219m.; mail Decatur z 37322; ● 50
Peanut; RMC Place; COCKE; *233 L-16; elev. 1,400ft./427m.; mail Parrottsville z 37843; rural

Entries in **UPPERCASE** are counties.
Entries in **bold** have populations of 2,500 or more.
Names in parentheses are alternate names.
Inc. Place — Incorporated Place
RMC Place — Rand McNally Designated Place
CDP — Census Designated Place
MCD — Minor Civil Division

⊡ County Seat
▲ Minor Civil Division
elev. Elevation
🅿 Post Office
🅷 Hospital
🅲 College
■ Principal Business Center
★ Ranally Metro Area (RMA) Abbreviation
z Zip Code(s)

Ⓟ Previous Census Population
Ⓡ Revised Census Population
Ⓐ Annexation Population
● Rand McNally Population Estimate
© Final Census Population
Ⓢ Special Census Population
◆ Estimated Population

For additional definitions see Glossary, Volume 1, and Introduction, Volume 2.

Pea Ridge (Mount Moriah); RMC Place; DEKALB; *233 D-13; elev. 1,144ft./349m.; mail Liberty z 37095; ● 50
Pea Ridge; RMC Place; LAWRENCE; *232 F-9; mail Lawrenceburg z 38464; rural
Pearl City; RMC Place; LINCOLN; *233 G-11; mail Fayetteville z 37334; rural
Peavine; RMC Place; CUMBERLAND; *233 D-16; mail Crossville z 38558, z 38571; rural
Pebble Hill; RMC Place; MCNAIRY; *232 G-6; mail Michie z 38357; rural
Peckerwood Point; RMC Place; TIPTON; *232 E-2; ★ MEM; mail Atoka z 38004, Munford z 38058; rural
Peeled Chestnut; RMC Place; WHITE; *233 D-14; mail Sparta z 38583; ● 50
Pegram; Inc. Place; CHEATHAM; 232 C-10; elev. 549ft./167m.; 🅿; ★ NASH; z 37143; Ⓟ 1,371; © 2,146
Pelham; RMC Place; GRUNDY; 233 F-14; elev. 1,025ft./312m.; 🅿; z 37366; ● 370
Penile Hill; RMC Place; FRANKLIN; *233 F-13; mail Decherd z 37324; rural
Pennine; RMC Place; RHEA; 233 E-16; mail Spring City z 37381; ● 70
Pennington Bend; RMC Place; DAVIDSON; ★ NASH; mail Nashville z 37214; pop. incl. with Nashville (Inc. Place)
Pennington Chapel; RMC Place; UNION; *233 B-20; elev. 1,034ft./315m.; ★ KNOX; mail Washburn z 37888; rural
Peppertown; RMC Place; LAWRENCE; *232 G-9; elev. 800ft./244m.; mail Loretto z 38469; rural
Perrin Hollow; RMC Place; GRAINGER; *233 C-20; mail Blaine z 37709; rural
PERRY; 232 E-8; Ⓟ 6,612; © 7,631; ◆ 7,803
Perryville; RMC Place; DECATUR; 232 E-7; elev. 377ft./115m.; mail Parsons z 38363; ● 270
Persia; RMC Place; HAWKINS; *233 K-16; elev. 1,134ft./346m.; mail Rogersville z 37857; ● 30
Petersburg; RMC Place; HAWKINS; *233 K-16; mail Rogersville z 37857; rural
Petersburg; Inc. Place; LINCOLN, MARSHALL; 233 F-11; elev. 747ft./228m.; 🅿; z 37144; Ⓟ 514; © 580
Peters Landing; RMC Place; PERRY; *232 E-7; mail Clifton z 38425
Petros; RMC Place; MORGAN; 233 C-18; elev. 1,370ft./418m.; 🅿; ★ KNOX; z 37845; ● 1,350
Petway; RMC Place; CHEATHAM; *232 C-10; mail Ashland City z 37015; ● 50
Peytonsville (Little Texas); RMC Place; WILLIAMSON; 233 D-11; ★ NASH; mail Franklin z 37064; ● 100
Phelan; TIPTON; see Charleston (RMC Place)
Philadelphia; RMC Place; JACKSON; *233 C-14; elev. 1,027ft./313m.; mail Bloomington Springs z 38545; rural
Philadelphia; Inc. Place; LOUDON; 233 E-18; elev. 863ft./263m.; 🅿; z 37846; Ⓟ 463; © 533
Philadelphia; RMC Place; WASHINGTON; *233 K-17; mail Chuckey z 37641; ● 45
Philippi; RMC Place; DEKALB; *233 D-14; mail Smithville z 37166; ● 30
Phillippy; RMC Place; LAKE; *232 B-3; elev. 290ft./88m.; mail Tiptonville z 38079; rural
PICKETT; 233 A-16; Ⓟ 4,548; © 4,945; ◆ 4,717
Pickwatina Place; RMC Place; MCMINN; *233 F-17; mail Athens z 37303; pop. incl. with Athens (Inc. Place)
Pickwick; HARDIN; see Pickwick Dam (RMC Place)
Pickwick Dam (Pickwick); RMC Place; HARDIN; 232 G-7; elev. 466ft./142m.; 🅿; z 38365; summer pop. 200; ● 100
Piedmont; RMC Place; JEFFERSON; 233 C-20; ★ KNOX; mail Dandridge z 37725; ● 200
Pierce; OBION; see Pierce Station (RMC Place)
Pierce Station (Pierce); RMC Place; OBION; *232 B-5; mail South Fulton z 38257; rural
Pierce Town; RMC Place; CARTER; *233 K-19; elev. 2,004ft./611m.; mail Butler z 37640; ● 50
Pigeon Forge; Inc. Place; SEVIER; 233 D-20; elev. 1,031ft./314m.; 🅿; z 37862-64, z 37868, z 37876; Ⓟ 3,027; © 5,083
Pigeon River Estates; RMC Place; SEVIER; ★ KNOX; mail Sevierville z 37862; pop. incl. with Sevierville (Inc. Place)
Pigeon Roost; RMC Place; HUMPHREYS; *232 C-8; mail Waverly z 37185; ● 100
Pikeville; Inc. Place; ⊡ BLEDSOE; 233 E-16; elev. 865ft./264m.; 🅿 🅷; z 37367; Ⓟ 1,771; © 1,781
Pillowville; RMC Place; WEAKLEY; *232 C-5; elev. 355ft./108m.; mail Mc Kenzie z 38201; ● 60
Pilot Knob; RMC Place; GREENE; *233 K-16; mail Bulls Gap z 37711; rural
Pilot Mountain; RMC Place; MORGAN; 233 C-17; mail Lancing z 37770; ● 80
Pine Bluff; RMC Place; FRANKLIN; *233 F-13; mail Winchester z 37398; ● 80
Pinebrook Estates; RMC Place; HAMILTON; *233 G-16; elev. 840ft./256m.; ★ CHTN; mail Harrison z 37341; ● 160
Pine Crest; RMC Place; CAMPBELL; *233 C-19; ★ KNOX; mail Jacksboro z 37757; rural
Pine Crest; CDP; CARTER; *233 K-18; ★ JNSC-; mail Johnson City z 37601; Ⓟ 3,821; © 2,872
Pine Grove; RMC Place; GREENE; *233 K-17; mail Greeneville z 37743; rural
Pine Grove; RMC Place; LOUDON; *233 D-18; elev. 861ft./262m.; ★ KNOX; mail Loudon z 37774; rural
Pine Grove; RMC Place; RHEA; *233 E-17; elev. 786ft./240m.; mail Spring City z 37381; rural
Pine Grove; ROANE; see Midtown (RMC Place)
Pine Grove; RMC Place; SEVIER; *233 D-20; mail Pigeon Forge z 37863; pop. incl. with Pigeon Forge (Inc. Place)
Pine Grove; RMC Place; VAN BUREN; *233 E-15; elev. 1,700ft./518m.; mail Spencer z 38585; rural
Pine Haven; RMC Place; FENTRESS; *233 B-16; elev. 1,775ft./541m.; mail Jamestown z 38556; ● 150
Pinehaven; RMC Place; SHELBY; *232 F-2; elev. 300ft./91m.; ★ MEM; mail Millington z 38053; ● 110
Pine Hill; RMC Place; BRADLEY; *233 G-16; ★ CLEV; mail Mc Donald z 37353; rural
Pine Hill; RMC Place; CLAY; *233 B-14; mail Moss z 38575; rural
Pine Hill; RMC Place; MARION; *233 F-15; elev. 1,800ft./549m.; mail Whitwell z 37397
Pine Hill; RMC Place; SCOTT; *233 B-18; elev. 1,610ft./491m.; mail Oneida z 37841; ● 200
Pine Lake; RMC Place; FAYETTE; *232 F-3; elev. 350ft./107m.; mail Arlington z 38002; ● 100
Pineland; RMC Place; MEIGS; *233 F-17; elev. 299ft./91m.; mail Decatur z 37322; rural
Pine Orchard; RMC Place; MORGAN; *233 D-17; mail Oakdale z 37829; rural
Pine Point; RMC Place; HENRY; *232 B-7; elev. 400ft./122m.; mail Springville z 38256; ● 180
Pine Ridge; RMC Place; JEFFERSON; mail White Pine z 37890; rural
Pine Ridge; RMC Place; POLK; *233 G-18; mail Farner z 37333; rural
Pine Top; RMC Place; LOUDON; 233 D-18; ★ KNOX; mail Lenoir City z 37772; ● 330
Pine Tree Estates; RMC Place; HAMILTON; *233 G-16; ★ CHTN; mail Hixson z 37343
Pineview; RMC Place; PERRY; *232 E-8; mail Linden z 37096; ● 210
Pineville; RMC Place; HAMBLEN; *233 K-16; ★ MORR; mail Morristown z 37814
Pinewood; RMC Place; CHEATHAM; *232 B-10; elev. 600ft./183m.; ★ NASH; mail Ashland City z 37015; ● 50
Pinewood; RMC Place; HICKMAN; *232 D-9; mail Nunnelly z 37137; ● 30
Piney; RMC Place; LOUDON; *233 E-18; elev. 1,000ft./305m.; ★ KNOX; mail Loudon z 37774; rural
Piney; RMC Place; VAN BUREN; *233 E-14; elev. 1,755ft./535m.; mail Spencer z 38585; rural
Piney Flats; RMC Place; SULLIVAN; 233 J-18; elev. 1,560ft./475m.; 🅿; ★ JNSC-; z 37686, z 37699; ● 500
Piney Grove; RMC Place; MCMINN; *233 F-17; mail Athens z 37303; rural
Piney Grove; RMC Place; SCOTT; *233 B-18; elev. 1,350ft./411m.; mail Winfield z 37892; rural
Piney Grove; RMC Place; WASHINGTON; *233 K-18; ★ JNSC-; mail Johnson City z 37601; pop. incl. with Johnson City (Inc. Place)
Piney Shores Estates; RMC Place; RHEA; *233 E-17; elev. 740ft./226m.; mail Spring City z 37381; rural
Pinhook; RMC Place; PUTNAM; *233 C-15; elev. 1,837ft./560m.; mail Monterey z 38574; rural
Pinhook; RMC Place; UNION; *233 C-20; elev. 1,032ft./315m.; ★ KNOX; mail Maynardville z 37807; rural
Pinnacle; RMC Place; SEVIER; *233 D-20; mail Sevierville z 37876; pop. incl. with Pittman Center (Inc. Place)
Pinson; RMC Place; MADISON; 232 E-5; elev. 385ft./117m.; 🅿; z 38366; ● 330
Pioneer; RMC Place; CAMPBELL; 233 B-18; elev. 1,545ft./471m.; 🅿; z 37847; ● 30
Pipers Chapel; RMC Place; SUMNER; *233 B-12; mail Portland z 37148; pop. incl. with Portland (Inc. Place)
Piperton; Inc. Place; FAYETTE; 232 G-3; elev. 363ft./111m.; 🅿; ★ MEM; z 38017 & mail Collierville z 38027; Ⓟ 612; © 589
Pisgah; RMC Place; DEKALB; *233 D-14; elev. 1,116ft./340m.; mail Smithville z 37166; rural
Pisgah; RMC Place; GILES; *233 G-11; mail Pulaski z 38478; rural
Pisgah; RMC Place; SHELBY; *232 F-2; elev. 399ft./122m.; ★ MEM; mail Cordova z 38018, Eads z 38028; rural
Pisgah; RMC Place; WEAKLEY; *232 B-5; elev. 408ft./124m.; mail Dresden z 38225; rural
Pittman Center; Inc. Place; SEVIER; 233 D-20; elev. 1,281ft./390m.; mail Sevierville z 37862; Ⓟ 478; © 477
Pittsburg Landing; HARDIN; see Shiloh (RMC Place)
Plainfield; RMC Place; BLOUNT; *233 D-19; ★ KNOX; mail Maryville z 37804; pop. incl. with Maryville (Inc. Place)
Plain Grove; RMC Place; PICKETT; *233 B-15; mail Monroe z 38573; rural
Plainview; RMC Place; RUTHERFORD; *233 E-12; mail Christiana z 37037; rural
Plainview; UNION; see Condon (Inc. Place)
Plant; RMC Place; HUMPHREYS; 232 D-8; elev. 419ft./128m.; mail New Johnsonville z 37134; ● 450
Plantation Hills; RMC Place; KNOX; *233 D-19; ★ KNOX; mail Knoxville z 37917; pop. incl. with Knoxville (Inc. Place)
Plateau; RMC Place; CUMBERLAND; *233 C-16; mail Crossville z 38571; rural
Pleasant Green; RMC Place; MORGAN; *233 C-17; elev. 1,600ft./488m.; mail Deer Lodge z 37726; rural
Pleasant Grove; RMC Place; BEDFORD; *233 F-12; mail Shelbyville z 37160; rural
Pleasant Grove; RMC Place; COCKE; *233 L-16; ★ MORR; mail Newport z 37821; ● 30
Pleasant Grove; RMC Place; LINCOLN; *233 G-11; mail Fayetteville z 37334; rural
Pleasant Grove; RMC Place; MARION; mail Jasper z 37347; pop. incl. with Jasper (Inc. Place)
Pleasant Grove; MAURY; see Culleoka (RMC Place)
Pleasant Grove; RMC Place; SCOTT; *233 B-18; elev. 1,369ft./417m.; mail Winfield z 37892; rural
Pleasant Grove; RMC Place; SUMNER; *233 A-13; elev. 881ft./269m.; mail Westmoreland z 37186; rural
Pleasant Hill; RMC Place; CLAIBORNE; *233 B-20; mail Speedwell z 37870; rural
Pleasant Hill; RMC Place; CLAY; *233 B-15; elev. 937ft./286m.; mail Allons z 38541; rural
Pleasant Hill; Inc. Place; CUMBERLAND; 233 D-16; elev. 1,902ft./580m.; 🅿; z 38578; Ⓟ 494; © 544
Pleasant Hill; RMC Place; GREENE; *233 L-17; elev. 1,523ft./464m.; mail Chuckey z 37641; rural
Pleasant Hill; RMC Place; HAWKINS; *233 K-16; mail Bulls Gap z 37711; rural
Pleasant Hill; RMC Place; LAUDERDALE; 232 E-2; elev. 319ft./97m.; mail Henning z 38041; ● 60
Pleasant Hill; RMC Place; MEIGS; 233 E-17; mail Ten Mile z 37880; ● 300
Pleasant Hill; RMC Place; MOORE; *233 F-12; mail Lynchburg z 37352; pop. incl. with Lynchburg (Inc. Place)
Pleasant Hill; RMC Place; OBION; *232 B-4; mail Rives z 38253, Union City z 38261; rural
Pleasant Hill; RMC Place; POLK; *233 G-18; elev. 1,756ft./535m.; mail Copperhill z 37317; rural
Pleasant Hill; RMC Place; RUTHERFORD; *233 D-11; mail Eagleville z 37060; rural
Pleasant Hill; RMC Place; SEVIER; *233 D-20; elev. 1,000ft./305m.; ★ KNOX; mail Sevierville z 37876; rural
Pleasant Hill; RMC Place; WEAKLEY; *232 C-5; mail Martin z 38237; rural
Pleasant Point; RMC Place; CLAIBORNE; *233 B-20; elev. 1,374ft./419m.; mail New Tazewell z 37825; rural
Pleasant Point; RMC Place; LAWRENCE; *232 G-9; mail Loretto z 38469; rural
Pleasant Ridge; RMC Place; CANNON; *233 D-13; mail Woodbury z 37190; ● 30
Pleasant Ridge; RMC Place; KNOX; *233 D-19; ★ KNOX; mail Knoxville z 37921; pop. incl. with Knoxville (Inc. Place)
Pleasant Ridge; RMC Place; PUTNAM; *233 C-15; elev. 1,852ft./564m.; mail Cookeville z 38506; rural
Pleasant Shade; RMC Place; SMITH; 233 B-13; elev. 538ft./164m.; 🅿; z 37145; ● 150
Pleasant Valley; RMC Place; MACON; *233 B-13; mail Hartsville z 37074; rural
Pleasant Valley; RMC Place; SUMNER; *233 B-11; elev. 887ft./270m.; ★ NASH; mail Cottontown z 37048; rural
Pleasant Valley; RMC Place; WASHINGTON; 234 M-9; ★ JNSC-; mail Jonesborough z 37659; ● 110
Pleasant View; RMC Place; CANNON; *233 E-13; elev. 1,124ft./343m.; mail Woodbury z 37190; ● 30
Pleasant View; Inc. Place; CHEATHAM; 232 B-10; elev. 687ft./209m.; 🅿; ★ NASH; z 37146; © 2,934
Pleasant View (Sycamore Hall); RMC Place; CLAIBORNE; *233 B-20; mail Tazewell z 37879; ● 50
Pleasantville; RMC Place; HICKMAN; 232 E-8; elev. 600ft./183m.; 🅿; z 37033; ● 60
Plunketts Creek; RMC Place; SMITH; *233 C-13; elev. 500ft./152m.; mail Gordonsville z 38563; rural
Pocahontas; RMC Place; COFFEE; *233 E-13; mail Morrison z 37357; ● 30
Pocahontas; RMC Place; HARDEMAN; 232 G-5; elev. 398ft./121m.; 🅿; z 38061; ● 210
Poga; RMC Place; CARTER; *233 K-19; mail Butler z 37640; ● 30
Point Pleasant; RMC Place; COCKE; *233 L-16; ★ MORR; mail Newport z 37821; ● 50
Pointview Circle; RMC Place; WILSON; *233 C-12; elev. 500ft./152m.; ★ NASH; mail Mount Juliet z 37122; ● 50
Polk; RMC Place; OBION; 232 B-4; elev. 329ft./100m.; mail Rives z 38253; ● 100
POLK; 233 G-19; Ⓟ 13,643; © 16,050; ◆ 15,372
Pollard; RMC Place; HOUSTON; *232 C-8; elev. 513ft./156m.; mail Erin z 37061; rural
Pomona; RMC Place; CUMBERLAND; *233 D-16; elev. 1,918ft./585m.; mail Crossville z 38571; ● 150
Pomona; RMC Place; DICKSON; 233 D-16; mail Dickson z 37055; pop. incl. with Dickson (Inc. Place)
Pomona Road; RMC Place; CUMBERLAND; *233 D-16; elev. 1,800ft./549m.; mail Crossville z 38571; rural
Pond; RMC Place; DICKSON; 232 C-9; elev. 910ft./277m.; mail Dickson z 37055; ● 200
Ponderosa; RMC Place; ROANE; *233 D-18; ★ KNOX; mail Kingston z 37763; ● 100
Ponderosa Hills; RMC Place; KNOX; *233 C-19; ★ KNOX; mail Powell z 37849
Ponders Gap; RMC Place; ROANE; *233 D-17; elev. 800ft./244m.; mail Ten Mile z 37880; rural
Pond Grove; RMC Place; ROANE; *233 D-17; mail Rockwood z 37854; ● 150
Pond Hill; RMC Place; MCMINN; *233 E-17; mail Athens z 37303; rural
Pondville; RMC Place; SUMNER; *233 B-12; mail Bethpage z 37022; ● 80
Pope; RMC Place; PERRY; *232 E-7; elev. 397ft./121m.; mail Linden z 37096
Poplar (Donovan); RMC Place; ANDERSON; *233 C-18; elev. 820ft./250m.; ★ KNOX; mail Oliver Springs z 37840; rural
Poplar Corner; RMC Place; HAYWOOD; *232 E-4; elev. 387ft./118m.; mail Bells z 38006; rural
Poplar Grove; RMC Place; CLAIBORNE; *233 B-20; mail Harrogate z 37752; rural
Poplar Grove; RMC Place; HUMPHREYS; *232 D-9; mail Mc Ewen z 37101; rural
Poplar Grove; RMC Place; LAUDERDALE; *232 D-3; mail Halls z 38040; rural
Poplar Grove; RMC Place; PUTNAM; *233 C-15; elev. 966ft./294m.; mail Cookeville z 38506; rural
Poplar Grove; TIPTON; see Drummonds (RMC Place)
Poplar Hill; RMC Place; GILES; *232 G-10; elev. 735ft./224m.; mail Prospect z 38477; ● 30
Poplar Hill; RMC Place; MCMINN; *233 F-17; elev. 900ft./274m.; mail Athens z 37303, Riceville z 37370; rural
Poplar Springs; RMC Place; HENDERSON; 232 E-6; mail Lexington z 38351; ● 30
Poplar Springs; RMC Place; LOUDON; *233 E-18; ★ KNOX; mail Loudon z 37774; rural
Poplar Springs; RMC Place; ROANE; *233 D-18; mail Kingston z 37763; ● 100
Poplins Crossroads; RMC Place; BEDFORD; *233 E-12; mail Unionville z 37180; rural
Porter Court; RMC Place; HENRY; *232 B-6; mail Paris z 38242; pop. incl. with Paris (Inc. Place)
Porterfield; RMC Place; CANNON; *233 D-13; mail Milton z 37118; rural
Porter Gap; RMC Place; LAUDERDALE; *232 D-3; elev. 361ft./110m.; mail Halls z 38040; rural
Porters Chapel; RMC Place; MAURY; *232 E-10; mail Mount Pleasant z 38474; rural
Porters Creek; RMC Place; HARDEMAN; *232 G-5; elev. 440ft./134m.; mail Middleton z 38052; rural
Portland; Inc. Place; SUMNER; 233 B-12; elev. 800ft./244m.; 🅿; z 37148; Ⓟ 5,165; © 8,458
Port Royal; RMC Place; MONTGOMERY; 232 B-10; elev. 429ft./131m.; ★ CLRKV; mail Adams z 37010; ● 30
Port Serena; RMC Place; HAMILTON; *233 G-16; ★ CHTN; mail Hixson z 37343; ● 450
Postelle; RMC Place; POLK; *233 G-18; elev. 1,565ft./477m.; 🅿; z 37317; ● 240
Post Oak; RMC Place; PUTNAM; *233 C-15; elev. 1,154ft./352m.; mail Cookeville z 38506; rural
Post Oak; RMC Place; ROANE; *233 D-17; mail Rockwood z 37854; ● 250
Poteet; RMC Place; OVERTON; *233 B-16; elev. 900ft./274m.; mail Alpine z 38543; rural
Pottsville; RMC Place; MAURY; *233 E-11; elev. 649ft./198m.; mail Columbia z 38401; ● 90
Powder Springs; RMC Place; GRAINGER; 233 C-20; elev. 1,215ft./370m.; 🅿; z 37848; ● 150
Powell; RMC Place; KNOX; 233 C-19; elev. 994ft./303m.; 🅿; ★ KNOX; z 37849; Ⓟ 7,534
Powell Chapel; RMC Place; GILES; *232 F-10; mail Pulaski z 38478; rural
Powells Chapel; RMC Place; HARDEMAN; *232 G-5; mail Hornsby z 38044; rural
Powells Crossroads; Inc. Place; MARION; 233 G-15; elev. 678ft./207m.; 🅿; z 37397; Ⓟ 1,098; © 1,286
Powell Valley; RMC Place; CAMPBELL; *233 B-19; mail La Follette z 37766; summer pop. 450; ● 150
Prairie Creek; RMC Place; HAMILTON; *233 G-16; ★ CHTN; mail Soddy Daisy z 37379; pop. incl. with Lakesite (Inc. Place)
Prairie Peninsula; RMC Place; HAMILTON; *233 G-16; ★ CHTN; mail Hixson z 37343; ● 250
Prairie Plains; RMC Place; COFFEE; *233 F-13; mail Hillsboro z 37342; ● 30
Prater; RMC Place; CANNON; *233 D-13; mail Woodbury z 37190; rural
Preston Woods; RMC Place; SULLIVAN; *233 J-18; ★ JNSC-; mail Kingsport z 37660; pop. incl. with Kingsport (Inc. Place)
Price; RMC Place; LAUDERDALE; mail Henning z 38041; rural
Price's Switch; RMC Place; WHITE; *233 D-15; elev. 1,200ft./366m.; mail Sparta z 38583; rural
Pride; RMC Place; OBION; *232 B-4; mail Union City z 38261; ● 140
Primm Springs; RMC Place; HICKMAN; *232 D-10; elev. 802ft./244m.; 🅿; z 38476; ● 30
Princeton; RMC Place; WASHINGTON; *233 K-18; ★ JNSC-; mail Johnson City z 37601; pop. incl. with Johnson City (Inc. Place)
Proctor City; RMC Place; LAKE; 232 B-3; mail Tiptonville z 38079; ● 30
Prospect; RMC Place; BLOUNT; *233 D-20; ★ KNOX; mail Walland z 37886; rural
Prospect; RMC Place; BRADLEY; 233 G-16; elev. 792ft./241m.; ★ CLEV; mail Cleveland z 37312; ● 600
Prospect; RMC Place; GILES; 232 G-10; elev. 600ft./183m.; 🅿; z 38477; ● 250
Prospect; RMC Place; LINCOLN; *233 G-12; mail Fayetteville z 37334; rural
Prospect; RMC Place; LOUDON; *233 E-18; ★ KNOX; mail Loudon z 37774; rural
Prospect; RMC Place; MCMINN; *233 F-18; elev. 900ft./274m.; mail Englewood z 37329; rural
Prosperity; RMC Place; MACON; *233 B-14; mail Red Boiling Springs z 37150; rural
Prosperity; RMC Place; WILSON; *233 D-13; mail Auburntown z 37016; rural
Protemus; RMC Place; OBION; *232 B-4; elev. 340ft./104m.; mail Troy z 38260; rural
Providence; RMC Place; DAVIDSON; *233 C-11; ★ NASH; mail Nashville z 37211; pop. incl. with Nashville (Inc. Place)
Providence; RMC Place; GRUNDY; *233 F-14; mail Decherd z 37324; ● 30
Providence; RMC Place; MADISON; *232 E-4; mail Jackson z 38301; ● 50
Providence; RMC Place; SUMNER; *233 B-12; elev. 830ft./253m.; mail Westmoreland z 37186; rural
Providence; RMC Place; TROUSDALE; *233 B-13; mail Hartsville z 37074, Lebanon z 37087; rural
Pruden; RMC Place; CLAIBORNE; 233 B-19; elev. 1,248ft./380m.; 🅿; z 37851; ● 150
Pryor Ridge; RMC Place; MARION; mail Tracy City z 37387; rural
Puckett; RMC Place; RUTHERFORD; *233 E-12; mail Rockvale z 37153; rural
Pulaski; Inc. Place; ⊡ GILES; 232 F-10; elev. 709ft./216m.; 🅿 🅷 🅲 765; z 38478; Ⓟ 7,895; © 7,871
Pumpkin Center; MONROE; see East Sweetwater (RMC Place)
Pumpkintown; RMC Place; MACON; *233 B-13; mail Lafayette z 37083; ● 70
Punch; RMC Place; SMITH; *233 C-13; mail Carthage z 37030; ● 100
Puncheon Camp; RMC Place; GRAINGER; 233 B-20; elev. 1,384ft./422m.; mail Washburn z 37888; ● 30
Purdy; RMC Place; MCNAIRY; *232 F-6; mail Selmer z 38375; ● 30
Puryear; Inc. Place; HENRY; 232 B-6; elev. 608ft./185m.; 🅿; z 38251; Ⓟ 592; © 667
Push; RMC Place; OBION; *232 B-3; elev. 302ft./92m.; mail Hornbeak z 38232; rural
PUTNAM; 233 C-15; Ⓟ 51,373; © 62,315; ◆ 72,750
Pyburns; RMC Place; HARDIN; *232 G-7; elev. 5,000ft./1,524m.; mail Savannah z 38372; ● 50

Q

Quail Meador; RMC Place; WILSON; *233 C-12; mail Lebanon z 37090; ● 120
Quebeck; RMC Place; WHITE; 233 D-15; elev. 900ft./274m.; 🅿; z 38579; ● 150
Quincy; RMC Place; CROCKETT; *232 D-4; elev. 332ft./101m.; mail Alamo z 38001; rural
Quito; RMC Place; TIPTON; *232 F-2; mail Millington z 38053; rural

R

Raccoon Valley; RMC Place; UNION; mail Maynardville z 37807; pop. incl. with Maynardville (Inc. Place)
Rader; RMC Place; GREENE; *233 K-17; elev. 1,216ft./371m.; mail Greeneville z 37743; rural
Radnor; RMC Place; DAVIDSON; ★ NASH; pop. incl. with Nashville (Inc. Place)
Rafter; RMC Place; MONROE; *233 F-19; mail Tellico Plains z 37385; rural
Ragsdale; RMC Place; COFFEE; *233 E-13; mail Manchester z 37355
Raines; RMC Place; SHELBY; *232 G-1; ★ MEM; mail Memphis z 38116; pop. incl. with Memphis (Inc. Place)
Raleigh; RMC Place; SHELBY; 232 J-3; ★ MEM; mail Memphis z 38128, z 38168; pop. incl. with Memphis (Inc. Place)
Rally Hill; RMC Place; MAURY; *233 E-11; mail Columbia z 38401; rural
Ralston; RMC Place; WEAKLEY; 232 B-5; mail Martin z 38237; ● 30
Ramah; RMC Place; LAWRENCE; *232 G-9; mail Leoma z 38468; rural
Ramer; Inc. Place; MCNAIRY; 232 G-5; elev. 415ft./126m.; 🅿; z 38367; Ⓟ 337; © 354
Ramsey; RMC Place; HANCOCK; *233 J-16; elev. 1,700ft./518m.; mail Sneedville z 37869; rural
Ramsey; RMC Place; KNOX; 233 M-14; ★ KNOX; mail Knoxville z 37914; ● 700
Ramsey; RMC Place; WILSON; *233 B-12; mail Lebanon z 37087; ● 170
Randolph; RMC Place; TIPTON; *232 E-2; mail Burlison z 38015, Drummonds z 38023; ● 70
Range (Turkeytown); RMC Place; CARTER; *233 K-19; elev. 1,676ft./511m.; ★ JNSC-; mail Watauga z 37694; ● 50
Rankin; RMC Place; COCKE; *233 L-16; ★ MORR; mail Newport z 37821; ● 30
Rankin Cove; RMC Place; MARION; *233 G-14; mail Jasper z 37347; rural
Rasar; BLOUNT; see Happy Valley (RMC Place)
Rascal Town; RMC Place; LAWRENCE; *232 G-9; mail Loretto z 38469; rural
Rathburn; RMC Place; HAMILTON; *233 F-16; ★ CHTN; mail Soddy Daisy z 37379; pop. incl. with Soddy-Daisy (Inc. Place)
Raus; RMC Place; BEDFORD; *233 F-12; mail Tullahoma z 37388; rural
Raven Branch; RMC Place; COCKE; *233 M-16; elev. 1,705ft./520m.; mail Hartford z 37753; rural
Raven Hill (Raven Ridge); RMC Place; CLAIBORNE; *233 B-20; mail Tazewell z 37879; ● 30
Raven Ridge; CLAIBORNE; see Raven Hill (RMC Place)
Ravenscroft; RMC Place; WHITE; 233 D-15; 🅿; z 38583; ● 100
Rayon City; RMC Place; DAVIDSON; *233 C-11; ★ NASH; mail Old Hickory z 37138; pop. incl. with Nashville (Inc. Place)
Rays Chapel; RMC Place; BEDFORD; *233 E-11; elev. 670ft./204m.; mail Chapel Hill z 37034; ● 30
Raysville; RMC Place; MOORE; *233 F-12; mail Tullahoma z 37388; pop. incl. with Lynchburg (Inc. Place)
Readyville; RMC Place; CANNON; 233 D-13; 🅿; z 37149; ● 200
Reagan; RMC Place; HENDERSON; 232 E-6; elev. 600ft./183m.; 🅿; z 38368; ● 180
Rebel Acres; RMC Place; GILES; *232 G-10; mail Pulaski z 38478; pop. incl. with Pulaski (Inc. Place)
Rebel Meadows; RMC Place; WILLIAMSON; *233 D-11; elev. 630ft./192m.; ★ NASH; mail Franklin z 37069; pop. incl. with Franklin (Inc. Place)
Red Ash; RMC Place; CAMPBELL; *233 B-18; ★ KNOX; mail Caryville z 37714; rural
Red Bank; Inc. Place; HAMILTON; 233 I-12; elev. 721ft./220m.; 🅿; ★ CHTN; z 37415; Ⓟ 12,322; © 12,418
Red Boiling Springs; Inc. Place; MACON; 233 B-14; elev. 766ft./233m.; 🅿; z 37150; Ⓟ 905; © 1,023
Red Hill; RMC Place; BRADLEY; *233 G-17; ★ CLEV; mail Cleveland z 37323; rural
Red Hill; RMC Place; CLAIBORNE; *233 B-20; mail Harrogate z 37752; rural
Red Hill; RMC Place; COFFEE; mail Manchester z 37355; pop. incl. with Manchester (Inc. Place)
Red Hill; RMC Place; FENTRESS; *233 B-16; elev. 906ft./276m.; mail Jamestown z 38556; ● 30
Red Hill; GRAINGER; see Dotson (RMC Place)
Red Hill; RMC Place; LAWRENCE; *232 F-9; mail Ethridge z 38456, Lawrenceburg z 38464; rural
Red Hill; RMC Place; MARION; *233 F-15; mail Whitwell z 37397; rural
Red Hill; RMC Place; PICKETT; *233 A-16; elev. 956ft./291m.; mail Byrdstown z 38549; rural
Red Hill; RMC Place; WEAKLEY; *232 B-5; mail Dresden z 38225; rural
Red House; RMC Place; GRAINGER; *233 C-20; mail Blaine z 37709; rural
Red Lands; RMC Place; HAMILTON; ★ CHTN; pop. incl. with Chattanooga (Inc. Place)
Red Row; RMC Place; MAURY; *232 E-10; mail Mount Pleasant z 38474; ● 100
Redwing Farms; RMC Place; WILLIAMSON; *233 D-11; elev. 720ft./219m.; ★ NASH; mail Franklin z 37064; ● 230
Reeds Lake; RMC Place; TIPTON; *232 F-2; ★ MEM; mail Atoka z 38004; ● 150
Reed Spring; RMC Place; LOUDON; *233 E-18; ★ KNOX; mail Philadelphia z 37846; ● 50
Reedtown; COCKE; see Reidtown (RMC Place)
Reesetown; RMC Place; POLK; *233 G-18; elev. 1,720ft./524m.; mail Turtletown z 37391; rural
Rehoboth; RMC Place; DYER; *232 C-4; elev. 328ft./100m.; mail Dyersburg z 38024; rural
Reidtown (Reedtown); RMC Place; COCKE; *233 L-16; elev. 1,171ft./357m.; ★ MORR; mail Newport z 37821; ● 200
Reliance; RMC Place; POLK; 233 G-18; elev. 769ft./234m.; 🅿; z 37369; ● 350
Reubensville; RMC Place; SUMNER, ROBERTSON; *233 A-12; elev. 707ft./215m.; mail Portland z 37148; ● 30
Reverie; RMC Place; TIPTON; *232 E-1; elev. 250ft./76m.; mail Wilson z 72395; ● 15
Revilo; RMC Place; LAWRENCE; *232 G-9; elev. 909ft./277m.; mail Leoma z 38468; ● 50
RHEA; 233 E-16; Ⓟ 24,344; © 28,400; ◆ 30,579
Rheatown; RMC Place; GREENE; 233 K-17; elev. 1,560ft./475m.; mail Chuckey z 37641; ● 160
Rhyan Springs; RMC Place; OVERTON; *233 B-15; elev. 989ft./301m.; mail Monroe z 38573; rural
Rialto; RMC Place; TIPTON; *232 E-3; elev. 271ft./83m.; ★ MEM; mail Covington z 38019; ● 30
Rice Bend; RMC Place; UNICOI; 233 L-18; mail Flag Pond z 37657; ● 150
Riceville; RMC Place; MCMINN; 233 F-17; elev. 800ft./244m.; 🅿; z 37370; ● 700
Rich; RMC Place; GILES; *232 F-10; elev. 779ft./237m.; mail Lynnville z 38472; rural
Rich Acres; RMC Place; WASHINGTON; ★ JNSC-; mail Johnson City z 37601; pop. incl. with Johnson City (Inc. Place)
Richard City; RMC Place; MARION; *233 G-14; elev. 1,000ft./305m.; mail South Pittsburg z 37380; pop. incl. with South Pittsburg (Inc. Place)
Richardson; RMC Place; TIPTON; *232 E-2; elev. 278ft./85m.; mail Drummonds z 38023; rural
Richland; RMC Place; DAVIDSON; *233 C-11; ★ NASH; mail Nashville z 37209; pop. incl. with Nashville (Inc. Place)
Richland; RMC Place; GRAINGER; *233 C-20; mail Blaine z 37709; rural
Richmond; RMC Place; BEDFORD; 233 F-11; elev. 879ft./268m.; mail Petersburg z 37144; ● 80
Richview Acres; RMC Place; SEVIER; *233 D-20; ★ KNOX; mail Seymour z 37865; ● 180
Richwood; RMC Place; DYER; *232 C-3; elev. 260ft./79m.; mail Dyersburg z 38024; ● 80
Rickman; RMC Place; OVERTON; 233 C-15; elev. 1,079ft./329m.; 🅿; z 38580; ● 750
Riddleton; RMC Place; SMITH; 233 C-13; elev. 521ft./159m.; 🅿; z 37151; ● 150
Ridenour; RMC Place; UNION; *233 C-19; ★ KNOX; mail Maynardville z 37807; ● 30
Ridgedale; RMC Place; KNOX; 233 M-11; ★ KNOX; mail Knoxville z 37931; pop. incl. with Knoxville (Inc. Place)
Ridgedale; RMC Place; SULLIVAN; *233 J-19; ★ JNSC-; mail Bristol z 37620; ● 100
Ridgefield; RMC Place; SULLIVAN; *233 J-18; ★ JNSC-; mail Kingsport z 37660; pop. incl. with Kingsport (Inc. Place)
Ridge Lake North; RMC Place; HAMILTON; ★ CHTN; mail Hixson z 37343; pop. incl. with Chattanooga (Inc. Place)
Ridgely; Inc. Place; LAKE; 232 C-3; elev. 280ft./85m.; 🅿; z 38080; Ⓟ 1,775; © 1,667
Ridgeside; Inc. Place; HAMILTON; 233 G-15; ★ CHTN; mail Chattanooga z 37411; Ⓟ 400; © 389
Ridgetop; RMC Place; LEWIS; *232 E-9; elev. 900ft./274m.; mail Hampshire z 38461; ● 30
Ridgetop; Inc. Place; ROBERTSON, DAVIDSON; 233 B-11; elev. 899ft./274m.; 🅿; ★ NASH; z 37152; Ⓟ 1,132; © 1,083
Ridgeview; RMC Place; HAMBLEN; *233 K-15; elev. 1,420ft./433m.; ★ MORR; mail Morristown z 37814; pop. incl. with Morristown (Inc. Place)
Ridgeville; RMC Place; MOORE; *233 F-12; mail Lynchburg z 37352; pop. incl. with Lynchburg (Inc. Place)
Ridgewood; RMC Place; CAMPBELL; *233 C-19; elev. 960ft./293m.; mail Caryville z 37714; rural
Ridgewood Acres; RMC Place; HAMILTON; *233 G-15; ★ CHTN; pop. incl. with Chattanooga (Inc. Place)
Ridley; RMC Place; MAURY; *232 E-10; mail Columbia z 38401; pop. incl. with Mount Pleasant (Inc. Place)
Riggs Crossroads; RMC Place; WILLIAMSON; *233 E-11; elev. 800ft./244m.; mail College Grove z 37046; rural
Right; RMC Place; HARDIN; *232 F-6; elev. 472ft./144m.; mail Morris Chapel z 38361; ● 30
Rim Rock Mesa; RMC Place; WHITE; *233 D-15; mail Sparta z 38583; ● 80
Rinnie; RMC Place; CUMBERLAND; *233 C-16; elev. 1,818ft./554m.; mail Crossville z 38571; rural
Riovista; RMC Place; CARTER; *233 K-19; ★ JNSC-; mail Elizabethton z 37643; pop. incl. with Elizabethton (Inc. Place)
Ripley; Inc. Place; ⊡ LAUDERDALE; 232 D-3; elev. 459ft./140m.; 🅿 🅷; z 38063; Ⓟ 6,188; © 7,844
Ritchie; RMC Place; CLAIBORNE; *233 B-20; elev. 1,300ft./396m.; mail Tazewell z 37879; ● 30
Ritta; RMC Place; KNOX; *233 C-19; ★ KNOX; mail Knoxville z 37918; rural
Riva Lake Camp; RMC Place; FRANKLIN; *233 F-13; mail Winchester z 37398
Riverdale; RMC Place; KNOX; *233 D-20; elev. 889ft./271m.; ★ KNOX; mail Knoxville z 37914; rural
River Hill; RMC Place; UNICOI; *233 L-18; mail Erwin z 37650; ● 60
Rivermont; RMC Place; HAMILTON; ★ CHTN; pop. incl. with Chattanooga (Inc. Place)
River Oaks; RMC Place; HAMILTON; *233 G-16; ★ CHTN; mail Harrison z 37341
River Rest; RMC Place; WILLIAMSON; *233 D-11; ★ NASH; mail Franklin z 37064; ● 250
Riversburg; RMC Place; GILES; *232 F-10; mail Pulaski z 38478
Riverside; RMC Place; CLAIBORNE; *233 B-20; mail Tazewell z 37879; ● 30
Riverside; RMC Place; DAVIDSON; ★ NASH; mail Nashville z 37218; pop. incl. with Nashville (Inc. Place)
Riverside; RMC Place; SHELBY; ★ MEM; mail Memphis z 38113; pop. incl. with Memphis (Inc. Place)
Riverside; RMC Place; SULLIVAN; *233 J-19; ★ JNSC-; mail Bluff City z 37618; ● 70
Riverside Park; RMC Place; HAMILTON; *233 G-15; ★ CHTN; pop. incl. with Chattanooga (Inc. Place)
Riverton; RMC Place; FENTRESS; *233 B-16; mail Jamestown z 38556; ● 30
Riverview; RMC Place; CLAIBORNE; *233 B-20; elev. 1,109ft./338m.; mail Harrogate z 37752; ● 30
Riverview; RMC Place; SULLIVAN; *233 J-18; ★ JNSC-; mail Kingsport z 37660; pop. incl. with Kingsport (Inc. Place)
Riverview; RMC Place; UNICOI; 233 L-18; mail Erwin z 37650; ● 100
Riverview Estates; RMC Place; HICKMAN; *232 D-9; mail Centerville z 37033; pop. incl. with Centerville (Inc. Place)
Rives; Inc. Place; OBION; 232 B-4; elev. 300ft./91m.; 🅿; z 38253; Ⓟ 344; © 331
ROANE; 233 D-17; Ⓟ 47,227; © 51,910; ◆ 53,567
Roan Mountain; CDP; CARTER; 233 K-19; elev. 2,564ft./782m.; 🅿; z 37687; Ⓟ 1,220; © 1,160
Roans Creek; RMC Place; PERRY; *232 D-7; elev. 400ft./122m.; mail Lobelville z 37097; ● 30
Roaring Springs; RMC Place; GREENE; *233 K-17; mail Afton z 37616; rural
Robbins; RMC Place; PICKETT; *233 B-16; elev. 900ft./274m.; mail Byrdstown z 38549; rural
Robbins; RMC Place; SCOTT; 233 B-17; elev. 1,374ft./419m.; 🅿; z 37852; ● 500
Roberts (Herrens Chapel); RMC Place; PUTNAM; *233 C-14; elev. 1,067ft./325m.; mail Silver Point z 38582; rural
Robertson (Melwood); RMC Place; CHESTER; *232 F-5; elev. 489ft./149m.; mail Bethel Springs z 38315; rural
ROBERTSON; 233 B-11; Ⓟ 41,494; © 54,433; ◆ 66,000
Robertson Fork; RMC Place; MARSHALL; *233 F-11; mail Lynnville z 38472; rural
Robinson Crossroads; RMC Place; KNOX; *233 D-19; ★ KNOX; mail Knoxville z 37921; rural
Robinson Mill; RMC Place; LOUDON; *233 E-18; elev. 770ft./235m.; ★ KNOX; mail Loudon z 37774; rural
Roby; RMC Place; CHESTER; *232 E-6; elev. 500ft./152m.; mail Enville z 38332; rural
Rockbridge; RMC Place; SUMNER; *233 B-12; elev. 929ft./283m.; 🅿; z 37022; rural
Rock City; RMC Place; SMITH; *233 C-13; elev. 490ft./149m.; mail Carthage z 37030; ● 60
Rock City; RMC Place; SULLIVAN; *233 J-18; ★ JNSC-; mail Kingsport z 37664; ● 30
Rock Creek; RMC Place; UNICOI; *233 K-18; mail Erwin z 37650; pop. incl. with Erwin (Inc. Place)
Rockdale; RMC Place; MAURY; 232 F-10; elev. 735ft./224m.; mail Mount Pleasant z 38474; ● 100
Rockford; Inc. Place; BLOUNT; 233 D-19; elev. 900ft./274m.; 🅿; ★ KNOX; z 37853; Ⓟ 646; © 798
Rock Haven; RMC Place; GRAINGER; *233 B-20; elev. 1,086ft./331m.; ★ MORR; mail Bean Station z 37708; ● 50
Rock Hill; RMC Place; HANCOCK; *233 J-16; mail Sneedville z 37869; ● 50
Rock Hill; RMC Place; HENDERSON; *232 E-6; elev. 500ft./152m.; mail Lexington z 38351; rural
Rock Hill; RMC Place; SULLIVAN; *233 K-18; ★ JNSC-; mail Watauga z 37694; rural
Rock House; RMC Place; TROUSDALE; *233 B-13; elev. 551ft./168m.; mail Hendersonville z 37075; rural
Rock Island; RMC Place; WARREN; 233 D-14; elev. 880ft./268m.; 🅿; z 38581; ● 330
Rockland; RMC Place; SUMNER; *233 C-11; ★ NASH; mail Hendersonville z 37075; pop. incl. with Hendersonville (Inc. Place)
Rock Ledge Estates; RMC Place; HAMILTON; *233 G-16; elev. 700ft./213m.; ★ CHTN; mail Ooltewah z 37363; ● 100
Rock Springs; RMC Place; DICKSON; *232 B-10; mail Charlotte z 37036; ● 30
Rock Springs; RMC Place; DYER; *232 C-4; mail Dyersburg z 38024; rural
Rock Springs; RMC Place; HENDERSON; *232 D-6; mail Wildersville z 38388; rural
Rock Springs; RMC Place; RUTHERFORD; *233 D-11; ★ NASH; mail Christiana z 37037; pop. incl. with Smyrna (Inc. Place)
Rock Springs; RMC Place; SULLIVAN; *233 J-18; ★ JNSC-; mail Kingsport z 37663; rural
Rock Station; RMC Place; WARREN; *233 E-14; mail Rock Island z 38581; rural
Rockvale; RMC Place; RUTHERFORD; 233 E-12; elev. 750ft./229m.; 🅿; z 37153; ● 300
Rockville; RMC Place; MONROE; *233 E-18; elev. 958ft./292m.; mail Sweetwater z 37874; rural
Rockwood; Inc. Place; ROANE; 233 D-17; elev. 883ft./269m.; 🅿; z 37854; Ⓟ 5,348; © 5,774
Rockwood Hill; RMC Place; GREENE; *233 L-17; mail Greeneville z 37743; ● 580
Rocky Branch; RMC Place; BLOUNT; *233 D-20; elev. 969ft./295m.; mail Walland z 37886; rural
Rocky Creek; RMC Place; TROUSDALE; *233 B-12; mail Castalian Springs z 37031; ● 100
Rocky Fork; RMC Place; RUTHERFORD; *233 D-12; elev. 624ft./190m.; ★ NASH; mail Smyrna z 37167; rural
Rocky Fork; RMC Place; UNICOI; 233 L-18; elev. 2,155ft./657m.; mail Flag Pond z 37657; ● 60
Rocky Grove; RMC Place; SEVIER; *233 M-16; elev. 1,943ft./592m.; mail Cosby z 37722; rural
Rocky Hill; RMC Place; KNOX; *233 D-19; ★ KNOX; mail Knoxville z 37919; pop. incl. with Knoxville (Inc. Place)
Rocky Mound; RMC Place; MACON; 233 B-13; elev. 966ft./294m.; mail Westmoreland z 37186; ● 30
Rocky Point; RMC Place; HAMBLEN; *233 K-16; ★ MORR; mail Russellville z 37860; rural
Rocky Point; RMC Place; PUTNAM; *233 C-15; elev. 1,418ft./432m.; mail Cookeville z 38506; rural
Rocky Ridge; RMC Place; OVERTON; *233 B-16; elev. 932ft./284m.; mail Monroe z 38573; rural
Rocky Spring; RMC Place; MONROE; *233 E-18; mail Madisonville z 37354; rural
Rocky Springs; RMC Place; SULLIVAN; 234 L-3; ★ JNSC-; mail Piney Flats z 37686; ● 50
Rocky Valley; RMC Place; JEFFERSON; *233 C-20; ★ KNOX; mail New Market z 37820; rural
Roddy; RMC Place; RHEA; *233 D-17; mail Spring City z 37381; ● 200
Roe Junction; RMC Place; HAMBLEN; *233 K-16; ★ MORR; mail Morristown z 37813; ● 50
Ro Ellen; RMC Place; DYER; 232 C-4; elev. 298ft./91m.; mail Dyersburg z 38024; ● 280
Rogana; RMC Place; SUMNER; *233 B-12; mail Bethpage z 37022; rural
Rogers Creek; RMC Place; MCMINN; *233 E-17; mail Athens z 37303; rural
Rogers Spring; RMC Place; HARDEMAN; *232 G-4; mail Middleton z 38052; ● 100
Rogersville; Inc. Place; ⊡ HAWKINS; 233 K-16; elev. 1,294ft./394m.; 🅿 🅷; z 37857; Ⓟ 4,149; © 4,240
Rolling Acres; RMC Place; JEFFERSON; ★ MORR; mail Talbott z 37877
Rolling Acres; RMC Place; WILLIAMSON; *232 D-10; ★ NASH; mail Fairview z 37062; pop. incl. with Fairview (Inc. Place)
Rolling Hills; RMC Place; HICKMAN; *232 D-10; mail Bon Aqua z 37025; ● 100
Rolling Hills; RMC Place; MARSHALL; *233 F-11; mail Lewisburg z 37091; pop. incl. with Lewisburg (Inc. Place)
Rolling Hills; RMC Place; UNICOI; *233 K-18; mail Erwin z 37650; ● 50
Rolling Hills; RMC Place; WARREN; *233 E-14; mail Mc Minnville z 37110; ● 150
Rolling Meadows; RMC Place; WILLIAMSON; *233 D-11; ★ NASH; mail Franklin z 37064; pop. incl. with Franklin (Inc. Place)
Rollingwood; RMC Place; HAMILTON; *233 G-16; ★ CHTN; pop. incl. with Chattanooga (Inc. Place)
Rome; RMC Place; SMITH; 233 C-13; elev. 492ft./150m.; mail Carthage z 37030; ● 100
Romeo; RMC Place; GREENE; *233 K-17; elev. 1,231ft./375m.; mail Bulls Gap z 37711; ● 50
Rose Creek; RMC Place; MCNAIRY; *232 F-5; elev. 405ft./123m.; mail Selmer z 38375; ● 30
Rosedale; RMC Place; ANDERSON; *233 C-18; mail Briceville z 37710
Rose Hill; RMC Place; MADISON; *232 E-5; ★ JAC; mail Jackson z 38301; rural
Rose Hill; RMC Place; UNION; *233 B-20; ★ KNOX; mail Maynardville z 37807; rural
Rosemark; RMC Place; SHELBY; 232 F-2; elev. 337ft./103m.; ★ MEM; mail Millington z 38053; ● 140
Rose Valley; RMC Place; STEWART; *232 B-8; elev. 400ft./122m.; mail Indian Mound z 37079; rural
Roseville; RMC Place; BEDFORD; *233 F-12; mail Wartrace z 37183; rural
Roslin; RMC Place; FENTRESS; *233 C-16; elev. 1,640ft./500m.; mail Jamestown z 38556; rural
Ross Camp Ground; RMC Place; HAWKINS; *233 J-17; ★ JNSC-; mail Church Hill z 37642; rural
Rosser; RMC Place; CARROLL; 232 C-6; mail Huntingdon z 38344; ● 30
Rossview; RMC Place; MONTGOMERY; *232 B-10; elev. 554ft./169m.; ★ CLRKV; mail Clarksville z 37040; rural
Rossville; Inc. Place; FAYETTE; 232 G-3; elev. 313ft./95m.; 🅿; z 38066, z 38076; Ⓟ 291; © 380
Rotherwood (Rotherwood Heights); RMC Place; HAWKINS; *233 J-17; elev. 1,300ft./396m.; ★ JNSC-; mail Church Hill z 37642; pop. incl. with Kingsport (Inc. Place)
Rotherwood Heights; HAWKINS; see Rotherwood (RMC Place)
Round Pond; RMC Place; MONTGOMERY; *232 B-9; elev. 606ft./185m.; ★ CLRKV; mail Clarksville z 37040; ● 60
Round Rock; RMC Place; CAMPBELL; *233 C-18; mail Caryville z 37714; rural
Round Top; RMC Place; WILSON; *233 D-13; elev. 669ft./204m.; mail Alexandria z 37012; rural
Routon; RMC Place; HENRY; 232 C-6; elev. 566ft./173m.; mail Henry z 38231, Paris z 38242; ● 50
Rover; RMC Place; BEDFORD; 233 E-11; mail Eagleville z 37060, Rockvale z 37153, Unionville z 37180; ● 170
Rowark Cove; RMC Place; FRANKLIN; *233 F-13; elev. 1,020ft./311m.; mail Decherd z 37324; rural
Rowland (Rowland Station); RMC Place; WARREN; *233 E-14; mail Rock Island z 38581; ● 80
Rowland Station; WARREN; see Rowland (RMC Place)
Royal; RMC Place; BEDFORD; *233 E-12; elev. 728ft./222m.; 🅿; z 37160; rural
Royal Blue; RMC Place; CAMPBELL; 233 B-18; mail Pioneer z 37847; ● 30
Royal Oak; RMC Place; COFFEE; mail Manchester z 37355; pop. incl. with Manchester (Inc. Place)
Royal Oaks; RMC Place; WILLIAMSON; *233 D-11; elev. 700ft./213m.; ★ NASH; mail Franklin z 37068; pop. incl. with Franklin (Inc. Place)
Royal Oaks; RMC Place; WILSON; *233 C-12; ★ NASH; mail Mount Juliet z 37122; ● 500
Royer Estates; RMC Place; RUTHERFORD; *233 D-12; ★ MUR; mail Murfreesboro z 37130; pop. incl. with Murfreesboro (Inc. Place)
Rucker; RMC Place; RUTHERFORD; *233 E-12; elev. 668ft./204m.; mail Murfreesboro z 37127; ● 100
Rudderville; RMC Place; WILLIAMSON; *233 D-11; elev. 744ft./227m.; mail Franklin z 37064; rural
Rudolph; RMC Place; HAYWOOD; *232 E-4; elev. 348ft./106m.; mail Brownsville z 38012; rural
Rugby; RMC Place; MORGAN; 233 B-17; elev. 1,431ft./436m.; 🅿; z 37733; ● 30
Rugby Hills; RMC Place; SHELBY; ★ MEM; mail Memphis z 38127; pop. incl. with Memphis (Inc. Place)
Rugby Road; SCOTT; see Elgin (RMC Place)
Rural Hill; RMC Place; DAVIDSON; *233 C-11; ★ NASH; mail Nashville z 37217; pop. incl. with Nashville (Inc. Place)
Rural Hill; CDP; WILSON; *233 C-12; elev. 550ft./168m.; ★ NASH; mail Gladeville z 37071; Ⓟ 1,329; © 2,032
Rural Vale; RMC Place; MONROE; *233 F-18; mail Tellico Plains z 37385; rural
Russel Fork; RMC Place; CAMPBELL; *233 B-19; elev. 1,400ft./427m.; mail La Follette z 37766; ● 50
Russell Crossroad; RMC Place; GREENE; *233 L-17; mail Greeneville z 37743; rural
Russell Hill; RMC Place; MACON; *233 B-14; mail Pleasant Shade z 37145; rural
Russellville; RMC Place; HAMBLEN; 233 K-16; elev. 1,257ft./383m.; 🅿; ★ MORR; z 37860; ● 1,200
Rusty; RMC Place; WILLIAMSON; *232 D-10; ★ NASH; mail Fairview z 37062; pop. incl. with Fairview (Inc. Place)
Rutherford; Inc. Place; GIBSON; 232 C-5; elev. 350ft./107m.; 🅿; z 38369; Ⓟ 1,303; © 1,272
RUTHERFORD; 233 D-12; Ⓟ 118,570; © 182,023; ◆ 265,313
Rutherford Estates; RMC Place; MAURY; *232 E-10; elev. 700ft./213m.; mail Columbia z 38401; ● 200
Ruthton; RMC Place; SULLIVAN; 233 J-19; ★ JNSC-; mail Bristol z 37620; ● 900
Ruthville; RMC Place; WEAKLEY; *232 B-5; elev. 405ft./123m.; mail Martin z 38237; rural
Rutledge; Inc. Place; ⊡ GRAINGER; 233 C-20; elev. 1,015ft./309m.; 🅿; z 37861; Ⓟ 903; © 1,187
Rutledge Falls; RMC Place; COFFEE; *233 F-13; elev. 967ft./295m.; mail Manchester z 37355, Tullahoma z 37388; rural
Rutledge Hill; RMC Place; COFFEE; *233 F-13; elev. 1,000ft./305m.; mail Hillsboro z 37342; ● 50
Ryall Springs; RMC Place; HAMILTON; *233 G-16; ★ CHTN; mail Chattanooga z 37421; ● 1,150

S

Sadie; RMC Place; CARTER; *233 J-19; elev. 2,028ft./618m.; ★ JNSC-; mail Elizabethton z 37643
Sadlers; ROBERTSON; see Sadlersville (RMC Place)
Sadlersville (Sadlers); RMC Place; ROBERTSON; 232 A-10; elev. 546ft./166m.; mail Adams z 37010; ● 80
Safley; RMC Place; WARREN; *233 E-14; elev. 960ft./293m.; mail Mc Minnville z 37110; rural
Sagetown; POLK; see Antioch (RMC Place)
Sagewood Estates; RMC Place; MAURY; *232 E-10; elev. 700ft./213m.; mail Columbia z 38401; ● 650
Sailors Rest; RMC Place; MONTGOMERY; *232 B-9; elev. 387ft./118m.; mail Cumberland City z 37050; rural
Saint Andrews; RMC Place; FRANKLIN; *233 F-14; elev. 1,960ft./597m.; 🅿; z 37375; ● 50
Saint Bethlehem; RMC Place; MONTGOMERY; *232 B-9; elev. 561ft./171m.; ★ CLRKV; pop. incl. with Clarksville (Inc. Place)
Saint Clair; RMC Place; HAWKINS; 233 K-16; mail Bulls Gap z 37711; ● 250
Saint Clair; RMC Place; RHEA; *233 E-17; elev. 860ft./262m.; mail Spring City z 37381; rural
Saint Elmo; RMC Place; HAMILTON; 233 K-11; elev. 731ft./223m.; ★ CHTN; mail Chattanooga z 37409; pop. incl. with Chattanooga (Inc. Place)
Saint James; RMC Place; GREENE; *233 L-17; elev. 1,414ft./431m.; mail Greeneville z 37743; rural
Saint Joseph; Inc. Place; LAWRENCE; 232 G-9; elev. 790ft./241m.; 🅿; z 38481; Ⓟ 789; © 829
Saint Paul; RMC Place; TIPTON; mail Drummonds z 38023
Saint Peters; RMC Place; HAYWOOD; *232 E-3; mail Brownsville z 38012; rural
Sainville; RMC Place; COFFEE; *233 E-13; mail Manchester z 37355; rural
Sale Creek; RMC Place; HAMILTON; 233 F-16; elev. 727ft./222m.; 🅿; ★ CHTN; z 37304, z 37373; ● 1,200
Salem; RMC Place; COCKE; *233 L-16; elev. 1,254ft./382m.; mail Parrottsville z 37843; ● 50
Salem; RMC Place; LEWIS; *232 E-9; mail Centerville z 37033; rural
Salem; RMC Place; MONTGOMERY; *232 B-9; ★ CLRKV; mail Clarksville z 37040; rural
Salem; RMC Place; TIPTON; *232 E-2; elev. 408ft./124m.; ★ MEM; mail Atoka z 38004; rural
Salem; RMC Place; WEAKLEY; *232 C-6; elev. 5,000ft./1,524m.; mail Sharon z 38255; rural
Saltillo; Inc. Place; HARDIN; 232 F-7; elev. 414ft./126m.; 🅿; z 38370; Ⓟ 383; © 342
Samburg; Inc. Place; OBION; 232 B-3; elev. 291ft./89m.; 🅿; z 38254; Ⓟ 374; © 260
Sampson; RMC Place; BLEDSOE; *233 E-15; mail Pikeville z 37367; ● 30
Sanders; RMC Place; GRUNDY; 233 F-14; mail Tracy City z 37387; ● 90
Sandhill; RMC Place; WEAKLEY; *232 C-5; mail Gleason z 38229; rural
Sandlick; RMC Place; CLAIBORNE; *233 B-20; mail New Tazewell z 37825; rural
Sand Ridge; RMC Place; HENDERSON; *232 E-6; mail Lexington z 38351; rural
Sand Springs; RMC Place; PUTNAM; *233 C-15; elev. 1,873ft./571m.; mail Monterey z 38574; rural
Sand Switch; RMC Place; FRANKLIN; *233 F-14; mail Sewanee z 37375; rural
Sandy; RMC Place; FENTRESS; *233 C-16; mail Wilder z 38589; rural
Sandy Hook; RMC Place; MAURY; 232 E-10; elev. 696ft./212m.; mail Mount Pleasant z 38474; ● 200
Sandy Lane; RMC Place; MONROE; *233 F-18; mail Tellico Plains z 37385; rural
Sandy Point; RMC Place; BENTON; *232 C-7; mail Camden z 38320; ● 40
Sandy Ridge; RMC Place; JEFFERSON; *233 L-15; mail Dandridge z 37725; rural
Sandy Spring; RMC Place; ROBERTSON; *232 B-10; elev. 546ft./166m.; mail Cedar Hill z 37032, Pleasant View z 37146; rural
Sanford; RMC Place; MCMINN; *233 F-17; mail Riceville z 37370; ● 30
Sanford Hill; RMC Place; CHESTER; *232 F-5; mail Henderson z 38340; pop. incl. with Henderson (Inc. Place)
Sango; RMC Place; MONTGOMERY; *232 B-10; elev. 650ft./198m.; ★ CLRKV; mail Clarksville z 37040, z 37042; ● 100
Santa Fe; RMC Place; MAURY; 232 E-10; elev. 700ft./213m.; 🅿; z 38482; ● 200
Saratoga Springs; RMC Place; BLEDSOE; *233 E-15; mail Pikeville z 37367; rural
Sardis; Inc. Place; HENDERSON; 232 F-7; elev. 480ft./146m.; 🅿; z 38371; Ⓟ 305; © 445
Saulsbury; Inc. Place; HARDEMAN; 232 G-4; elev. 562ft./171m.; 🅿; z 38067; Ⓟ 106; © 99
Saundersville; RMC Place; SUMNER; *233 B-12; ★ NASH; mail Hendersonville z 37075; pop. incl. with Hendersonville (Inc. Place)
Savannah; Inc. Place; ⊡ HARDIN; 232 F-7; elev. 436ft./133m.; 🅿 🅷; z 38372; Ⓟ 6,547; © 6,917
Sawdust; RMC Place; MAURY; *232 E-10; mail Columbia z 38401; rural
Sawyers Mill; RMC Place; BENTON; 232 C-7; mail Camden z 38320; ● 60
Scandlyn; RMC Place; ROANE; *233 D-18; elev. 845ft./258m.; ★ KNOX; mail Oliver Springs z 37840; rural
Scarboro; RMC Place; ANDERSON; *233 D-18; elev. 850ft./259m.; ★ KNOX; mail Oak Ridge z 37830; pop. incl. with Oak Ridge (Inc. Place)
Scattersville; RMC Place; SUMNER; *233 B-12; elev. 785ft./239m.; mail Portland z 37148; ● 250
Scenic Point Estates; RMC Place; BLOUNT; *233 D-19; elev. 840ft./256m.; ★ KNOX; mail Louisville z 37777; ● 110
Scoot Mill; RMC Place; GREENE; *233 L-16; mail Mohawk z 37810; rural
SCOTT; 233 B-18; Ⓟ 18,358; © 21,127; ◆ 22,178
Scottsboro; RMC Place; DAVIDSON; *233 C-11; ★ NASH; mail Nashville z 37218; pop. incl. with Nashville (Inc. Place)
Scotts Hill; Inc. Place; HENDERSON, DECATUR; 232 E-7; elev. 525ft./160m.; 🅿; z 38374; Ⓟ 594; © 894
Screamer; RMC Place; MAURY; *232 F-10; elev. 863ft./263m.; mail Mount Pleasant z 38474; rural
Seeber Flats; RMC Place; ANDERSON; *233 C-18; ★ KNOX; mail Briceville z 37710; rural
Selmer; Inc. Place; ⊡ MCNAIRY; 232 G-6; elev. 442ft./135m.; 🅿 🅷; z 38375; Ⓟ 3,838; © 4,541
Sengtown; RMC Place; SUMNER; *233 A-12; elev. 851ft./259m.; mail Portland z 37148; ● 30
Sentinel Heights; RMC Place; RHEA; *233 E-16; elev. 910ft./277m.; mail Ooltewah z 37363; pop. incl. with Dayton (Inc. Place)
Sequatchie; RMC Place; MARION; 233 G-14; elev. 650ft./198m.; 🅿; z 37374; ● 600
SEQUATCHIE; 233 F-15; Ⓟ 8,863; © 11,370; ◆ 13,945
Sequoia Grove; RMC Place; BRADLEY; *233 F-17; ★ CLEV; mail Cleveland z 37312; pop. incl. with Cleveland (Inc. Place)
Sequoia Hills; RMC Place; GREENE; *233 L-17; mail Greeneville z 37743; ● 240
Sequoyah Estates; RMC Place; MONROE; mail Madisonville z 37354; pop. incl. with Madisonville (Inc. Place)
Sequoyah Hills; RMC Place; HAMILTON; *233 G-16; elev. 740ft./226m.; ★ CHTN; mail Hixson z 37343; ● 450
Sequoyah Hills; RMC Place; KNOX; *233 D-19; ★ KNOX; pop. incl. with Knoxville (Inc. Place)
Sequoyah Village; RMC Place; MONROE; mail Madisonville z 37354; pop. incl. with Madisonville (Inc. Place)
Serles; RMC Place; HARDEMAN; *232 F-5; elev. 371ft./113m.; mail Middleton z 38052; rural
Servilla (Springtown); RMC Place; POLK; *233 F-18; mail Reliance z 37369
Settlers Point; RMC Place; WILLIAMSON; *232 D-10; ★ NASH; mail Franklin z 37064; ● 30
Seven Islands; RMC Place; KNOX; *233 D-20; elev. 900ft./274m.; ★ KNOX; mail Knoxville z 37920; rural
Seven Oaks; RMC Place; KNOX; *233 D-19; ★ KNOX; mail Knoxville z 37922; ● 720
SEVIER; 233 D-20; Ⓟ 51,043; © 71,170; ◆ 87,402

Entries in **UPPERCASE** are counties.
Entries in **bold** have populations of 2,500 or more.
Names in parentheses are alternate names.
Inc. Place — Incorporated Place
RMC Place — Rand McNally Designated Place
CDP — Census Designated Place
MCD — Minor Civil Division

⊡ County Seat
▲ Minor Civil Division
elev. Elevation
🅿 Post Office

🅷 Hospital
🅲 College
■ Principal Business Center
★ Ranally Metro Area (RMA) Abbreviation
z Zip Code(s)

Ⓟ Previous Census Population
Ⓡ Revised Census Population
Ⓐ Annexation Population
● Rand McNally Population Estimate
© Final Census Population
Ⓢ Special Census Population
◆ Estimated Population

For additional definitions see Glossary, Volume 1, and Introduction, Volume 2.

Sevier Home; RMC Place; KNOX; *233 D-19; elev. 871ft./265m.; ★ KNOX; mail Knoxville z 37920; rural
Sevierville; Inc. Place; ⊡ SEVIER; 233 D-20; elev. 903ft./275m.; 🅿 🅷; ★ KNOX; z 37862-64, z 37868, z 37876; Ⓟ 7,178; © 11,757
Sewanee; FRANKLIN; see Sherwood (CDP)
Sewee; RMC Place; MEIGS; *233 E-17; mail Niota z 37826; rural
Seymour; CDP; SEVIER, BLOUNT; 233 D-20; elev. 1,059ft./323m.; 🅿; ★ KNOX; z 37865; Ⓟ 7,026; © 8,850
Shackle Island; RMC Place; SUMNER; *233 B-11; ★ NASH; mail Hendersonville z 37075; rural
Shacklett; RMC Place; CHEATHAM; 232 C-10; mail Kingston Springs z 37082; ● 180
Shades Bridge; RMC Place; WEAKLEY; *232 C-5; mail Greenfield z 38230; rural
Shadtown; UNICOI; see Marbleton (RMC Place)
Shady Grove; RMC Place; COFFEE; *233 E-13; mail Morrison z 37357; ● 30
Shady Grove; RMC Place; HAMILTON; *233 F-16; ★ CHTN; mail Soddy Daisy z 37379
Shady Grove; RMC Place; JACKSON; *233 C-14; elev. 1,038ft./316m.; mail Gainesboro z 38562; rural
Shady Grove; RMC Place; JEFFERSON; *233 D-20; elev. 1,020ft./311m.; ★ KNOX; mail Dandridge z 37725; ● 100
Shady Grove; RMC Place; KNOX; *233 D-19; elev. 900ft./274m.; ★ KNOX; mail Knoxville z 37922; rural
Shady Grove; RMC Place; LINCOLN; *233 G-12; mail Flintville z 37335; ● 50
Shady Grove; RMC Place; MONTGOMERY; *232 B-10; elev. 679ft./207m.; ★ CLRKV; mail Clarksville z 37040; rural
Shady Grove; RMC Place; MORGAN; *233 C-17; elev. 1,410ft./430m.; mail Lancing z 37770; rural
Shady Grove; RMC Place; PUTNAM; *233 C-15; elev. 1,413ft./431m.; mail Monterey z 38574; rural
Shady Grove; RMC Place; TROUSDALE; *233 B-13; mail Hartsville z 37074; rural
Shady Grove; RMC Place; WHITE; *233 D-14; mail Walling z 38587; ● 50
Shady Grove Shores; RMC Place; HAMILTON; *233 F-16; elev. 720ft./219m.; ★ CHTN; mail Soddy Daisy z 37379; rural
Shady Hill; RMC Place; HENDERSON; *232 E-6; mail Lexington z 38351
Shady Rest; RMC Place; WARREN; *233 E-14; mail Mc Minnville z 37110; rural
Shady Valley; RMC Place; JOHNSON; 233 J-19; elev. 2,840ft./866m.; 🅿; z 37688; ● 100
Shafter; RMC Place; WEAKLEY; *232 C-5; mail Greenfield z 38230; rural
Shake Rag Hill; RMC Place; WAYNE; *232 F-8; mail Waynesboro z 38485; ● 30
Shallowford; RMC Place; UNICOI; *233 L-18; elev. 1,800ft./549m.; mail Erwin z 37650; ● 100
Shandy; RMC Place; HARDEMAN; 232 F-4; elev. 363ft./111m.; mail Bolivar z 38008; ● 40
Shannondale; RMC Place; KNOX; *233 C-19; ★ KNOX; mail Knoxville z 37918; pop. incl. with Knoxville (Inc. Place)
Shannon Hills; RMC Place; HAMILTON; *233 G-16; ★ CHTN; mail Hixson z 37343; ● 300
Sharon; Inc. Place; WEAKLEY; 232 C-5; elev. 414ft./126m.; 🅿; z 38255; Ⓟ 1,047; © 988
Sharondale; RMC Place; COFFEE; mail Tullahoma z 37388; pop. incl. with Tullahoma (Inc. Place)
Sharp Place; RMC Place; FENTRESS; *233 B-17; elev. 1,703ft./519m.; mail Jamestown z 38556; rural
Sharps Chapel; RMC Place; UNION; 233 B-20; elev. 1,044ft./318m.; 🅿; z 37866; ● 30
Sharpsville; RMC Place; RUTHERFORD; *233 D-12; elev. 586ft./179m.; ★ MUR; mail Murfreesboro z 37130; rural
Shaver Town; RMC Place; SMITH; *233 C-13; elev. 700ft./213m.; mail Gordonsville z 38563; rural
Shawanee; RMC Place; CLAIBORNE; 233 B-20; elev. 1,400ft./427m.; 🅿; z 37867; ● 390
Shawnette; RMC Place; WAYNE; *232 G-8; mail Collinwood z 38450; rural
Shawtown; RMC Place; OBION; *232 B-4; elev. 466ft./142m.; mail Hornbeak z 38232; rural
Shea; CAMPBELL; see Beech Fork (RMC Place)
SHELBY; 232 G-2; Ⓟ 826,330; © 897,472; ◆ 902,495
Shelby Center (Elmore Park); RMC Place; SHELBY; *232 F-2; elev. 250ft./76m.; ★ MEM; mail Memphis z 38134; pop. incl. with Bartlett (Inc. Place)
Shelbyville; Inc. Place; ⊡ BEDFORD; 233 F-12; elev. 765ft./233m.; 🅿 🅷; z 37160-62; Ⓟ 14,049; © 16,105
Shelbyville Mills; RMC Place; BEDFORD; *233 F-12; mail Shelbyville z 37160; pop. incl. with Shelbyville (Inc. Place)
Shell Creek; RMC Place; CARTER; *233 K-19; mail Roan Mountain z 37687; ● 400
Shellmound; RMC Place; MARION; *233 G-14; mail Jasper z 37347; rural
Shellsford; RMC Place; WARREN; *233 E-14; elev. 921ft./281m.; mail Mc Minnville z 37110; rural
Shenandoah Heights; RMC Place; CARTER; ★ JNSC-; mail Johnson City z 37601
Shennendoah; RMC Place; SEVIER; *233 D-20; ★ KNOX; mail Seymour z 37865; ● 360
Shepherd; RMC Place; HAMILTON; *233 G-16; ★ CHTN; pop. incl. with Chattanooga (Inc. Place)
Shepp; RMC Place; HAYWOOD; *232 E-3; elev. 289ft./88m.; mail Stanton z 38069; rural
Sherrill Heights; RMC Place; MONROE; mail Madisonville z 37354; pop. incl. with Madisonville (Inc. Place)
Sherrilltown; RMC Place; WILSON; *233 C-13; mail Watertown z 37184; ● 30
Sherwood; RMC Place; FRANKLIN; 233 G-13; elev. 672ft./205m.; 🅿; z 37376; ● 500
Sherwood (Sewanee); CDP; FRANKLIN; 233 G-13; elev. 1,900ft./579m.; 🅷 🅲 1,611; mail Sewanee z 37375, z 37383; Ⓟ 2,128; © 2,361
Sherwood Estates; RMC Place; ANDERSON; *233 C-19; ★ KNOX; mail Clinton z 37716; ● 150
Sherwood Forest; RMC Place; HAMILTON; ★ CHTN; pop. incl. with Chattanooga (Inc. Place)
Sheybogan; RMC Place; CANNON; *233 E-13; mail Woodbury z 37190; ● 100
Shiloh; RMC Place; BEDFORD; *233 E-12; elev. 1,172ft./357m.; mail Wartrace z 37183; rural
Shiloh; RMC Place; CARROLL; *232 D-7; elev. 629ft./192m.; mail Holladay z 38341; rural
Shiloh; RMC Place; CUMBERLAND; *233 D-16; elev. 1,900ft./579m.; mail Crossville z 38555; ● 270
Shiloh; RMC Place; GRAINGER; *233 C-20; mail Rutledge z 37861; rural
Shiloh (Pittsburg Landing); RMC Place; HARDIN; 232 G-6; elev. 471ft./144m.; 🅿; z 38376; ● 120
Shiloh; RMC Place; HAWKINS; *233 J-16; mail Sneedville z 37869; rural
Shiloh; RMC Place; HUMPHREYS; mail Mc Ewen z 37101; rural
Shiloh; RMC Place; JACKSON; *233 C-14; elev. 1,008ft./307m.; mail Cookeville z 38506; rural
Shiloh; RMC Place; MONTGOMERY; *232 B-9; mail Cumberland Furnace z 37051
Shiloh; RMC Place; OVERTON; *233 B-16; mail Crawford z 38554; rural
Shiloh; RMC Place; RUTHERFORD; 233 D-12; ★ MUR; mail Murfreesboro z 37130; ● 300
Shiloh; RMC Place; SUMNER; *233 B-12; mail Gallatin z 37066; rural
Shiloh; RMC Place; WILSON; *233 C-12; ★ NASH; mail Old Hickory z 37138; ● 2,400
Shingleton; RMC Place; JOHNSON; *233 J-20; elev. 2,600ft./792m.; mail Mountain City z 37683; ● 30
Shining Rock; RMC Place; DEKALB; *233 D-14; elev. 986ft./301m.; mail Smithville z 37166; rural
Shipetown; RMC Place; KNOX; *233 C-20; ★ KNOX; mail Mascot z 37806
Shipley; RMC Place; PUTNAM; *233 C-15; elev. 1,100ft./335m.; mail Cookeville z 38506; rural
Shipps Bend; RMC Place; HICKMAN; 232 D-9; mail Centerville z 37033; pop. incl. with Centerville (Inc. Place)
Shirley; RMC Place; FENTRESS; *233 B-17; elev. 1,516ft./462m.; mail Allardt z 38504; ● 30
Shirleyton; RMC Place; MARION; *233 F-15; mail Whitwell z 37397; rural
Shooks Gap; RMC Place; KNOX; *233 D-20; elev. 881ft./269m.; ★ KNOX; mail Knoxville z 37920; ● 690
Shop Springs; RMC Place; WILSON; 233 C-13; elev. 691ft./211m.; mail Watertown z 37184; ● 170
Shore Acres; RMC Place; HAMILTON; *233 F-16; elev. 730ft./223m.; ★ CHTN; mail Soddy Daisy z 37379; ● 150
Short Creek; RMC Place; RUTHERFORD; *233 E-12; elev. 780ft./238m.; mail Christiana z 37037; rural
Short Mountain; RMC Place; CANNON; *233 D-13; mail Woodbury z 37190; ● 80
Short Tail Springs; RMC Place; HAMILTON; *233 F-16; elev. 800ft./244m.; ★ CHTN; mail Harrison z 37341; rural
Shouns; RMC Place; JOHNSON; *233 J-20; elev. 2,307ft./703m.; mail Mountain City z 37683; pop. incl. with Mountain City (Inc. Place)
Shubert; RMC Place; LEWIS; *232 E-9; mail Hohenwald z 38462; rural
Siam; RMC Place; CARTER; 234 M-5; ★ JNSC-; mail Elizabethton z 37643; ● 50
Sidonia; RMC Place; WEAKLEY; 232 C-5; elev. 374ft./114m.; mail Sharon z 38255; ● 200
Signal Hills; RMC Place; HAMILTON; ★ CHTN; mail Chattanooga z 37405; pop. incl. with Chattanooga (Inc. Place)
Signal Mountain; Inc. Place; HAMILTON; 233 G-15; elev. 1,600ft./488m.; 🅿; ★ CHTN; z 37377; Ⓟ 7,034; © 7,429
Silerton; Inc. Place; HARDEMAN, CHESTER; 232 F-5; elev. 500ft./152m.; 🅿; z 38377; Ⓟ 59; © 60
Silica; RMC Place; CAMPBELL; *233 B-18; mail Caryville z 37714; rural
Siloam; CROCKETT; see Dog Hill (RMC Place)
Siloam; RMC Place; MACON; *233 B-13; elev. 897ft./273m.; mail Westmoreland z 37186
Silvacola; RMC Place; SULLIVAN; *233 J-18; ★ JNSC-; mail Blountville z 37617; rural
Silver City; RMC Place; HAMBLEN; *233 K-16; ★ MORR; mail Russellville z 37860; rural
Silver Grove; RMC Place; SULLIVAN; 234 K-5; ★ JNSC-; mail Bluff City z 37618; ● 140
Silverhill; RMC Place; RUTHERFORD; 233 D-12; elev. 625ft./191m.; mail Lebanon z 37087, Murfreesboro z 37130; ● 80
Silver Point; RMC Place; PUTNAM; 233 C-14; elev. 1,033ft./315m.; 🅿; z 38582; ● 200
Silver Ridge; RMC Place; LOUDON; ★ KNOX; mail Lenoir City z 37771; pop. incl. with Lenoir City (Inc. Place)
Silver Springs; RMC Place; WILSON; *233 C-12; ★ NASH; mail Mount Juliet z 37122; ● 170
Silvertop; RMC Place; HOUSTON; *232 C-8; elev. 600ft./183m.; mail Mc Ewen z 37101; rural
Sims Spring; RMC Place; BEDFORD; *233 E-11; mail Shelbyville z 37160; rural
Singleton; RMC Place; BEDFORD; *233 F-12; elev. 787ft./240m.; mail Shelbyville z 37160; rural
Singleton; RMC Place; BLOUNT; *233 D-19; ★ KNOX; mail Louisville z 37777; pop. incl. with Alcoa (Inc. Place)
Sinking Cove; RMC Place; FRANKLIN; *233 G-13; mail Sherwood z 37376; rural
Sitka; RMC Place; GIBSON; 232 D-5; mail Milan z 38358; ● 50
Sixmile; RMC Place; BLOUNT; *233 E-19; ★ KNOX; mail Maryville z 37803; rural
Skaggston; RMC Place; KNOX; *233 C-20; ★ KNOX; mail Mascot z 37806; ● 80
Skinem; RMC Place; LINCOLN; 233 G-11; mail Fayetteville z 37334; ● 100
Skinner Crossroad; RMC Place; GREENE; *233 K-16; elev. 1,100ft./335m.; mail Mohawk z 37810; rural
Skullbone; RMC Place; GIBSON; *232 C-5; elev. 395ft./120m.; mail Bradford z 38316
Skyline; RMC Place; LAUDERDALE; *232 D-3; elev. 420ft./128m.; mail Ripley z 38063; pop. incl. with Ripley (Inc. Place)
Skyline Park; RMC Place; HAMILTON; *233 G-15; ★ CHTN; mail Signal Mountain z 37377; pop. incl. with Signal Mountain (Inc. Place)
Slayden; Inc. Place; DICKSON; 232 C-9; elev. 745ft./227m.; 🅿; z 37165; Ⓟ 111; © 185
Slick Rock; RMC Place; SCOTT; *233 C-18; elev. 1,218ft./371m.; mail Robbins z 37852; ● 30
Slide; RMC Place; HAWKINS; *233 K-17; mail Rogersville z 37857; rural
Smartt (Smartts); RMC Place; WARREN; 233 E-14; elev. 1,012ft./308m.; 🅿; z 37378; ● 350
Smartts; WARREN; see Smartt (RMC Place)
SMITH; 233 B-13; Ⓟ 14,143; © 17,712; ◆ 19,135
Smithfield; RMC Place; MONROE; *233 F-18; mail Tellico Plains z 37385; rural
Smith Fork; RMC Place; HARDIN; *232 F-7; elev. 500ft./152m.; mail Olivehill z 38475; rural
Smithland; RMC Place; LINCOLN; *233 G-12; elev. 798ft./243m.; mail Kelso z 37348; rural
Smith Mill; RMC Place; LINCOLN; *233 G-12; mail Fayetteville z 37334; rural
Smiths Chapel; RMC Place; MACON; *233 B-14; mail Red Boiling Springs z 37150; ● 60
Smith Springs; RMC Place; DAVIDSON; ★ NASH; mail Nashville z 37217; pop. incl. with Nashville (Inc. Place)
Smithtown; RMC Place; BLEDSOE; *233 F-16; mail Graysville z 37338; rural
Smithtown; RMC Place; MARION; *233 G-14; mail South Pittsburg z 37380; rural
Smithville; Inc. Place; ⊡ DEKALB; 233 D-14; elev. 1,032ft./315m.; 🅿 🅷; z 37166; Ⓟ 3,791; © 3,994
Smithwood; RMC Place; KNOX; *233 C-19; ★ KNOX; mail Knoxville z 37918; pop. incl. with Knoxville (Inc. Place)
Smoky Junction; RMC Place; SCOTT; 233 C-18; elev. 1,313ft./400m.; mail Huntsville z 37756; ● 100
Smoky View Estates; RMC Place; BLOUNT; *233 D-19; elev. 980ft./299m.; ★ KNOX; mail Maryville z 37804; ● 230
Smyrna; RMC Place; CARROLL; *232 D-6; mail Huntingdon z 38344; rural
Smyrna; RMC Place; PICKETT; *233 B-16; elev. 1,030ft./314m.; mail Byrdstown z 38549; rural
Smyrna; Inc. Place; RUTHERFORD; 233 D-12; elev. 543ft./166m.; 🅿; ★ NASH; z 37167; Ⓟ 13,647; © 25,569; ◆ 35,934
Smyrna; RMC Place; WARREN; *233 E-14; elev. 983ft./300m.; mail Mc Minnville z 37110; ● 180
Sneed Forest Estates; RMC Place; WILLIAMSON; *233 D-11; ★ NASH; mail Franklin z 37064; ● 100
Sneed Glen; RMC Place; WILLIAMSON; *233 D-11; ★ NASH; mail Franklin z 37064; ● 50
Sneedville; Inc. Place; ⊡ HANCOCK; 233 J-16; elev. 1,169ft./356m.; 🅿; z 37869; Ⓟ 1,446; © 1,257; Ⓡ 1,351
Snow Hill; RMC Place; HAMILTON; *233 G-16; elev. 720ft./219m.; ★ CHTN; mail Ooltewah z 37363; rural
Snows Hill (Blend); RMC Place; DEKALB; *233 D-14; elev. 1,136ft./346m.; mail Dowelltown z 37059; ● 210
Soddy-Daisy; Inc. Place; HAMILTON; 233 F-16; elev. 734ft./224m.; 🅿; ★ CHTN; z 37379, z 37384; Ⓟ 8,240; © 11,530
Solo; RMC Place; TIPTON; *232 E-3; elev. 282ft./86m.; ★ MEM; mail Covington z 38019; ● 30
Solway; RMC Place; KNOX; 233 D-19; ★ KNOX; mail Knoxville z 37931; ● 200
Somerville; Inc. Place; ⊡ FAYETTE; 232 F-3; elev. 408ft./124m.; 🅿 🅷; z 38060, z 38068, z 38075; Ⓟ 2,047; © 2,519; Ⓡ 2,534
South; RMC Place; DAVIDSON; ★ NASH; mail Nashville z 37210; pop. incl. with Nashville (Inc. Place)
South; RMC Place; HAMILTON; ★ CHTN; mail Chattanooga z 37409-10, z 37419; pop. incl. with Chattanooga (Inc. Place)
Southall; RMC Place; WILLIAMSON; *233 D-11; ★ NASH; mail Franklin z 37064; ● 50
South Berlin; RMC Place; MARSHALL; *233 E-11; elev. 800ft./244m.; mail Lewisburg z 37091; rural
South Carthage; Inc. Place; SMITH; 233 C-13; elev. 499ft./152m.; mail Carthage z 37030; Ⓟ 851; © 1,302
South Chattanooga; RMC Place; HAMILTON; ★ CHTN; pop. incl. with Chattanooga (Inc. Place)
South Cleveland; CDP; BRADLEY; *233 G-16; ★ CLEV; mail Cleveland z 37311; Ⓟ 5,372; © 6,216
South Clinton; RMC Place; ANDERSON; *233 C-19; elev. 879ft./268m.; ★ KNOX; mail Clinton z 37716; pop. incl. with Clinton (Inc. Place)
South Columbia; RMC Place; MAURY; mail Columbia z 38401; pop. incl. with Columbia (Inc. Place)
South Covington; RMC Place; TIPTON; ★ MEM; mail Covington z 38019; pop. incl. with Covington (Inc. Place)
South Daisy; RMC Place; HAMILTON; ★ CHTN; mail Soddy Daisy z 37379; pop. incl. with Soddy-Daisy (Inc. Place)
South Dyersburg; RMC Place; DYER; *232 C-3; elev. 272ft./83m.; mail Dyersburg z 38024; pop. incl. with Dyersburg (Inc. Place)
Southern Hills; RMC Place; MAURY; *232 E-10; mail Columbia z 38401; pop. incl. with Columbia (Inc. Place)
South Etowah; RMC Place; MCMINN; *233 F-18; elev. 840ft./256m.; mail Etowah z 37331; ● 30
South Fulton; Inc. Place; OBION; 232 B-5; elev. 364ft./111m.; 🅿; z 38257; Ⓟ 2,688; © 2,517
South Green; RMC Place; GREENE; *233 L-17; mail Greeneville z 37743; ● 90
South Hall; RMC Place; BLOUNT; *233 D-19; ★ KNOX; mail Alcoa z 37701; pop. incl. with Alcoa (Inc. Place)
South Harriman; RMC Place; ROANE; *233 D-17; ★ KNOX; mail Harriman z 37748; pop. incl. with Harriman (Inc. Place)
South Johnson City; RMC Place; WASHINGTON; mail Johnson City z 37601; pop. incl. with Johnson City (Inc. Place)
South Knoxville; RMC Place; KNOX; *233 D-19; elev. 889ft./271m.; ★ KNOX; mail Knoxville z 37920, z 37940; pop. incl. with Knoxville (Inc. Place)
South Liberty; RMC Place; MCMINN; *233 F-17; mail Athens z 37303; rural
South Pittsburg; Inc. Place; MARION; 233 G-14; elev. 624ft./190m.; 🅿 🅷; z 37380; Ⓟ 3,295; © 3,295
Southport; RMC Place; MAURY; *232 F-10; mail Culleoka z 38451; ● 30
Southside; RMC Place; HARDIN; *232 G-6; mail Counce z 38326; rural
Southside; RMC Place; MONTGOMERY; 232 B-9; elev. 578ft./176m.; 🅿; z 37171; ● 170
South Tunnel; RMC Place; SUMNER; 233 B-12; elev. 834ft./254m.; mail Gallatin z 37066, Portland z 37148; ● 260
Spain's Hill; RMC Place; WILSON; *233 D-12; mail Lascassas z 37085; rural
Sparkmantown; RMC Place; VAN BUREN; *233 D-15; mail Doyle z 38559; rural
Sparta; Inc. Place; ⊡ WHITE; 233 D-15; elev. 885ft./270m.; 🅿 🅷; z 38583; Ⓟ 4,681; © 4,599
Speedwell; RMC Place; CLAIBORNE; 233 B-19; elev. 1,137ft./347m.; 🅿; z 37870; ● 100
Spencer; Inc. Place; ⊡ VAN BUREN; 233 E-15; elev. 1,820ft./555m.; 🅿; z 38585; Ⓟ 1,125; © 1,713
Spencer Creek; RMC Place; WILLIAMSON; *233 D-11; ★ NASH; mail Franklin z 37064; pop. incl. with Franklin (Inc. Place)
Spencer Hill; RMC Place; MAURY; *232 F-10; mail Mount Pleasant z 38474; rural
Spencers Mill; RMC Place; DICKSON; *232 D-10; elev. 751ft./229m.; mail Burns z 37029; rural
Sportman Acres; RMC Place; WILSON; *233 C-12; ★ NASH; mail Mount Juliet z 37122; pop. incl. with Mount Juliet (Inc. Place)
Spot; RMC Place; HICKMAN; 232 D-9; mail Only z 37140; ● 60
Spout Springs; RMC Place; OBION; *232 B-4; mail Hornbeak z 38232; rural
Springbrook; RMC Place; BLOUNT; ★ KNOX; mail Alcoa z 37701; pop. incl. with Alcoa (Inc. Place)
Springbrook; RMC Place; MADISON; *232 D-5; elev. 500ft./152m.; mail Jackson z 38301; ● 150
Spring City; Inc. Place; RHEA; 233 E-17; elev. 773ft./236m.; 🅿; z 37381 & mail Grandview z 37337; Ⓟ 2,199; © 2,025
Spring Creek; RMC Place; HARDEMAN; *232 G-4; elev. 500ft./152m.; mail Saulsbury z 38067; ● 50
Spring Creek; RMC Place; MADISON; 232 D-5; elev. 477ft./145m.; 🅿; z 38378; ● 140
Spring Creek; RMC Place; MCMINN; *233 F-17; elev. 820ft./250m.; mail Athens z 37303; rural
Spring Creek; RMC Place; PERRY; *232 E-7; mail Linden z 37096; rural
Spring Creek; RMC Place; WILSON; *233 C-13; mail Lebanon z 37087; ● 120
Springdale; RMC Place; CLAIBORNE; 233 B-20; elev. 1,072ft./327m.; mail Tazewell z 37879; ● 150
Springdale; RMC Place; SULLIVAN; *233 J-18; ★ JNSC-; mail Kingsport z 37663; pop. incl. with Bristol (Inc. Place)
Springfield; Inc. Place; ⊡ ROBERTSON; 233 B-11; elev. 677ft./206m.; 🅿 🅷; z 37172; Ⓟ 11,227; © 14,329
Spring Hill; RMC Place; ANDERSON; *233 D-19; ★ KNOX; mail Clinton z 37716; rural
Spring Hill; RMC Place; HENDERSON; *232 E-6; mail Huron z 38345; rural
Spring Hill; Inc. Place; MAURY, WILLIAMSON; 232 E-10; elev. 734ft./224m.; 🅿; z 37174; Ⓟ 1,464; © 7,715; ◆ 11,283
Spring Hill; RMC Place; WHITE; *233 D-15; elev. 997ft./304m.; mail Sparta z 38583; rural
Spring Lake; RMC Place; SHELBY; *232 F-2; ★ MEM; mail Memphis z 38134; ● 220
Springmont; RMC Place; WILSON; *233 C-12; ★ NASH; mail Old Hickory z 37138; ● 1,500
Spring Place; RMC Place; KNOX; *233 C-20; ★ KNOX; mail Knoxville z 37914; ● 370
Springs Chapel; RMC Place; FENTRESS; *233 C-16; elev. 1,640ft./500m.; mail Clarkrange z 38553; rural
Springtown; POLK; see Servilla (RMC Place)
Springvale; RMC Place; HAMBLEN; *233 K-16; elev. 1,200ft./366m.; ★ MORR; mail Morristown z 37813; ● 30
Spring View; RMC Place; BLOUNT; *233 E-19; ★ KNOX; mail Maryville z 37801; rural
Springview; RMC Place; WILLIAMSON; *233 D-11; ★ NASH; mail Franklin z 37064; rural
Springville; RMC Place; HENRY; 232 C-7; elev. 414ft./126m.; 🅿; z 38256; ● 50
Spruce Pine; RMC Place; HAWKINS; *233 K-16; mail Mooresburg z 37811; rural
Spurgeon; CDP; WASHINGTON, SULLIVAN; 234 L-10; ★ JNSC-; mail Johnson City z 37615; Ⓟ 3,149; © 3,460
Squirrel Flat; RMC Place; FENTRESS; *233 B-16; elev. 1,571ft./479m.; mail Jamestown z 38556; rural
Staffords Store; RMC Place; WEAKLEY; *232 C-5; elev. 369ft./112m.; mail Greenfield z 38230; rural
Staffordtown; RMC Place; POLK; *233 G-18; mail Copperhill z 37317; pop. incl. with Copperhill (Inc. Place)
Stainville; RMC Place; ANDERSON; *233 C-18; elev. 1,331ft./406m.; mail Briceville z 37710
Stanfill; RMC Place; CAMPBELL; *233 B-18; elev. 1,160ft./354m.; mail Pioneer z 37847; ● 50
Stanley Junction; RMC Place; SCOTT; *233 B-18; mail Oneida z 37841; ● 30
Stanton; Inc. Place; HAYWOOD; 232 E-3; elev. 314ft./96m.; 🅿; z 38069; Ⓟ 487; © 615
Stantonville; Inc. Place; MCNAIRY; 232 G-6; elev. 440ft./134m.; 🅿; z 38379; Ⓟ 264; © 312
Star Point; RMC Place; PICKETT; *233 B-16; elev. 1,050ft./320m.; mail Byrdstown z 38549; summer pop. 300
State Line; RMC Place; LINCOLN; *233 G-12; mail Fayetteville z 37334; ● 200
Statesville; RMC Place; WILSON; 233 D-13; elev. 723ft./220m.; mail Watertown z 37184; ● 170
Static; RMC Place; PICKETT; 233 A-16; mail Byrdstown z 38549; ● 30
Stayton; RMC Place; DICKSON; 232 C-9; elev. 487ft./148m.; mail Cumberland Furnace z 37051; ● 100
Stella; RMC Place; GILES; 232 G-10; mail Goodspring z 38460; ● 30
Stephens; RMC Place; MORGAN; *233 C-18; ★ KNOX; mail Oliver Springs z 37840
Stephenson; RMC Place; COFFEE; *233 F-13; mail Hillsboro z 37342; ● 30
Steppsville; RMC Place; WARREN; *233 E-14; mail Mc Minnville z 37110; rural
Sterling Park; RMC Place; HAMILTON; *233 G-16; ★ CHTN; mail Hixson z 37343; ● 600
Stewart; RMC Place; HOUSTON; 232 B-8; elev. 490ft./149m.; 🅿; z 37175; ● 200
Stewart; RMC Place; WARREN; *233 D-14; mail Mc Minnville z 37110; rural
STEWART; 232 B-8; Ⓟ 9,479; © 12,370; ◆ 13,277
Stewart Chapel; RMC Place; LINCOLN; *233 G-12; mail Flintville z 37335; ● 50
Stinking Creek; RMC Place; CAMPBELL; *233 B-19; elev. 1,400ft./427m.; mail La Follette z 37766; rural
Stiversville; RMC Place; MAURY; *232 F-10; mail Culleoka z 38451; rural
Stock Creek; RMC Place; KNOX; *233 D-19; elev. 900ft./274m.; ★ KNOX; mail Knoxville z 37920; rural
Stockton; RMC Place; FENTRESS; *233 B-17; mail Jamestown z 38556; ● 30
Stockton Valley; RMC Place; LOUDON; *233 E-18; mail Loudon z 37774; rural
Stokes; RMC Place; DYER; *232 D-4; elev. 307ft./94m.; mail Friendship z 38034; rural
Stone; RMC Place; JACKSON; *233 B-14; elev. 571ft./174m.; mail Gainesboro z 38562; ● 51
Stonebrook; RMC Place; WILLIAMSON; *233 D-11; ★ NASH; mail Nolensville z 37135; pop. incl. with Nolensville (Inc. Place)
Stone River; RMC Place; DAVIDSON; ★ NASH; mail Hermitage z 37076; pop. incl. with Nashville (Inc. Place)
Stone River Estates; RMC Place; DAVIDSON; ★ NASH; mail Nashville z 37214; pop. incl. with Nashville (Inc. Place)
Stones River Homes; RMC Place; RUTHERFORD; *233 D-12; ★ NASH; mail Smyrna z 37167; pop. incl. with Smyrna (Inc. Place)
Stonewall; RMC Place; SMITH; *233 C-14; mail Elmwood z 38560, Hickman z 38567; ● 100
Stoney Fork; RMC Place; CAMPBELL; *233 C-18; elev. 1,700ft./518m.; mail Caryville z 37714; ● 50
Stoney Point; RMC Place; DICKSON; *232 C-9; mail Vanleer z 37181; rural
Stony Gap; RMC Place; HANCOCK; *233 J-16; elev. 1,771ft./540m.; mail Sneedville z 37869; rural
Stony Point; RMC Place; HAWKINS; *233 J-17; mail Surgoinsville z 37873
Strahl; RMC Place; HAWKINS; *233 K-17; mail Rogersville z 37857; ● 30
Straight Fork; RMC Place; SCOTT; *233 B-18; mail Pioneer z 37847; ● 50
Strawberry Plains; RMC Place; JEFFERSON; 233 C-20; elev. 900ft./274m.; 🅿; ★ KNOX; z 37871; ● 700
Striggersville; RMC Place; HAWKINS; 233 K-16; mail Rogersville z 37857; ● 190
Stringtown; RMC Place; GIBSON; *232 C-4; elev. 365ft./111m.; mail Kenton z 38233; rural
Stringtown; RMC Place; MONTGOMERY; *232 B-9; ★ CLRKV; mail Woodlawn z 37191; ● 30
Stroudsville; RMC Place; ROBERTSON; *232 B-10; mail Cedar Hill z 37032; rural
Stuart Heights; RMC Place; HAMILTON; ★ CHTN; pop. incl. with Chattanooga (Inc. Place)
Stump Hollow; RMC Place; RHEA; *233 E-17; elev. 800ft./244m.; mail Spring City z 37381; ● 30
Suburban Hills; RMC Place; KNOX; *233 D-19; ★ KNOX; mail Knoxville z 37901; ● 1,500
Suburban Hills; RMC Place; MCMINN; *233 F-17; elev. 880ft./268m.; mail Riceville z 37370; ● 300
Suck Creek; RMC Place; MARION; *233 G-15; mail Chattanooga z 37405; rural
Sugar Creek; RMC Place; JACKSON; *233 B-14; elev. 527ft./161m.; mail Gainesboro z 38562; rural
Sugar Creek; RMC Place; JOHNSON; *233 J-20; mail Mountain City z 37683; ● 30
Sugar Forks; RMC Place; JEFFERSON; *233 C-20; mail Dandridge z 37725; pop. incl. with Dandridge (Inc. Place)
Sugar Grove; RMC Place; BRADLEY; *233 G-17; ★ CLEV; mail Cleveland z 37323; rural
Sugar Grove; RMC Place; ROANE; *233 D-18; ★ KNOX; mail Harriman z 37748; rural
Sugar Grove; RMC Place; SUMNER; *233 A-12; mail Westmoreland z 37186; rural
Sugarlimb; RMC Place; LOUDON; *233 D-18; ★ KNOX; mail Lenoir City z 37771; ● 80
Sugar Tree; RMC Place; DECATUR; 232 D-7; elev. 416ft./127m.; 🅿; z 38380; ● 130
Suggs Creek; RMC Place; WILSON; *233 C-12; ★ NASH; mail Mount Juliet z 37122; ● 200
SULLIVAN; 233 J-19; Ⓟ 143,596; © 153,048; ◆ 153,250
Sullivan Gardens; RMC Place; SULLIVAN; 233 J-18; ★ JNSC-; mail Kingsport z 37663; ● 100
Sulphur; RMC Place; OVERTON; *233 C-15; mail Livingston z 38570; rural
Sulphura; RMC Place; SUMNER; *233 B-12; mail Portland z 37148; rural
Sulphur Creek; RMC Place; HICKMAN; *232 E-8; elev. 600ft./183m.; rural
Sulphur Springs; RMC Place; ANDERSON; mail Clinton z 37716; rural
Sulphur Springs; RMC Place; HAMBLEN; *233 L-16; elev. 1,324ft./404m.; ★ MORR; mail Morristown z 37814; ● 30
Sulphur Springs; RMC Place; LINCOLN; *233 F-11; mail Fayetteville z 37334; rural
Sulphur Springs; RMC Place; MARION; *233 G-15; mail Whitwell z 37397; pop. incl. with Powells Crossroads (Inc. Place)
Sulphur Springs; RMC Place; MCNAIRY; *232 G-5; elev. 448ft./137m.; mail Ramer z 38367, Selmer z 38375; ● 30
Sulphur Springs; RMC Place; WASHINGTON; 233 K-18; ★ JNSC-; mail Jonesborough z 37659; ● 350
Sumac; RMC Place; GILES; *232 F-10; mail Pulaski z 38478; rural
Summer City; RMC Place; BLEDSOE; 233 E-16; elev. 1,971ft./601m.; mail Pikeville z 37367; ● 100
Summerfield; RMC Place; GRUNDY; 233 F-14; mail Tracy City z 37387; pop. incl. with Monteagle (Inc. Place)
Summer Shade; RMC Place; OVERTON; *233 B-15; elev. 1,000ft./305m.; mail Allons z 38541; rural
Summertown; RMC Place; HAMILTON; *233 G-15; ★ CHTN; mail Signal Mountain z 37377; pop. incl. with Walden (Inc. Place)
Summertown; RMC Place; LAWRENCE; 232 F-9; elev. 1,019ft./311m.; 🅿; z 38483; ● 900
Summit; RMC Place; HAMILTON; *233 G-16; elev. 903ft./275m.; ★ CHTN; mail Ooltewah z 37363; pop. incl. with Chattanooga (Inc. Place)
Summit; RMC Place; HAWKINS; *233 K-16; mail Bulls Gap z 37711; rural
Summitville; RMC Place; COFFEE; 233 E-13; elev. 1,100ft./335m.; 🅿; z 37382; ● 450
SUMNER; 233 B-12; Ⓟ 103,281; © 130,449; ◆ 158,600
Sunbright; Inc. Place; MORGAN; 233 C-17; elev. 1,385ft./422m.; 🅿; z 37872; Ⓟ 568; © 577
Sunkist Beach; RMC Place; LAKE; *232 B-3; elev. 285ft./87m.; mail Tiptonville z 38079; ● 200
Sunny Brook; RMC Place; SULLIVAN; *233 J-19; ★ JNSC-; mail Bristol z 37620; pop. incl. with Bristol (Inc. Place)
Sunny Hill; RMC Place; HAYWOOD; *232 E-4; mail Brownsville z 38012; rural
Sunny Hills; RMC Place; SULLIVAN; *233 J-19; ★ JNSC-; mail Bristol z 37620
Sunnyside; RMC Place; GREENE; *233 L-17; mail Greeneville z 37743; ● 100
Sunnyside; RMC Place; HANCOCK; *233 J-15; elev. 1,350ft./411m.; mail Sneedville z 37869; rural
Sunnyside; RMC Place; SULLIVAN; *233 J-18; ★ JNSC-; mail Blountville z 37617
Sunrise; GRAINGER; see Sunset (RMC Place)
Sunrise; RMC Place; HICKMAN; *232 E-9; mail Centerville z 37033; rural
Sunrise; RMC Place; MACON; *233 B-14; mail Red Boiling Springs z 37150; rural
Sunset (Sunrise); RMC Place; GRAINGER; *233 C-20; elev. 1,000ft./305m.; mail Rutledge z 37861; ● 30
Sunset; RMC Place; PICKETT; *233 B-16; mail Byrdstown z 38549; summer pop. 100
Sunset Gap; RMC Place; COCKE, SEVIER; *233 M-16; ★ MORR; mail Cosby z 37722, Newport z 37821; rural
Sunset Hills; RMC Place; HAMBLEN; ★ MORR; mail Morristown z 37814; pop. incl. with Morristown (Inc. Place)
Sunset Hills; RMC Place; SULLIVAN; *233 J-18; ★ JNSC-; mail Kingsport z 37660; pop. incl. with Kingsport (Inc. Place)
Surgoinsville; Inc. Place; HAWKINS; 233 J-17; elev. 1,136ft./346m.; 🅿; z 37873; Ⓟ 1,499; © 1,484
Sutherland; RMC Place; JOHNSON; 233 J-20; elev. 2,082ft./635m.; mail Damascus z 24236; ● 30
Swan; RMC Place; LEWIS; *232 E-9; mail Hohenwald z 38462; pop. incl. with Hohenwald (Inc. Place)
Swan Bluff; RMC Place; HICKMAN; *232 E-9; mail Centerville z 37033; rural
Swann Chapel; RMC Place; JEFFERSON; *233 L-15; elev. 1,122ft./342m.; mail Dandridge z 37725; rural
Swannsylvania; RMC Place; JEFFERSON; *233 L-16; elev. 1,100ft./335m.; mail Dandridge z 37725; rural
Sweet Lips; RMC Place; CHESTER; *232 F-6; mail Henderson z 38340; ● 30
Sweeton Hill; RMC Place; GRUNDY; *233 F-14; mail Coalmont z 37313; pop. incl. with Coalmont (Inc. Place)
Sweetwater; RMC Place; LEWIS; *232 E-8; mail Hohenwald z 38462; rural
Sweetwater; Inc. Place; MONROE, MCMINN; 233 E-18; elev. 917ft./280m.; 🅿 🅷; z 37874; Ⓟ 5,066; © 5,586
Swift; RMC Place; HARDIN; *232 F-7; mail Savannah z 38372
Sycamore; RMC Place; CHEATHAM; *232 B-10; elev. 460ft./140m.; ★ NASH; mail Ashland City z 37015; ● 50
Sycamore; RMC Place; PUTNAM; mail Cookeville z 38501; pop. incl. with Cookeville (Inc. Place)
Sycamore Hall; CLAIBORNE; see Pleasant View (RMC Place)
Sycamore Landing; RMC Place; HUMPHREYS; *232 D-8; mail Waverly z 37185; rural
Sycamore Valley; RMC Place; CHEATHAM; *232 B-10; elev. 500ft./152m.; ★ NASH; mail Ashland City z 37015; ● 30
Sycamore Valley; RMC Place; MACON; *233 B-13; elev. 756ft./230m.; mail Lafayette z 37083; rural
Sykes; RMC Place; SMITH; *233 C-13; mail Brush Creek z 38547; ● 30
Sylvia; RMC Place; DICKSON; 232 C-9; elev. 870ft./265m.; mail Dickson z 37055; ● 100

T

Tabernacle; RMC Place; HAYWOOD; *232 E-4; elev. 358ft./109m.; mail Brownsville z 38012; rural
Tabernacle; RMC Place; TIPTON; *232 E-3; elev. 319ft./97m.; ★ MEM; mail Covington z 38019; ● 80
Tabor; RMC Place; CUMBERLAND; *233 D-16; elev. 1,835ft./559m.; mail Crossville z 38571; rural
Tackett Creek; RMC Place; CAMPBELL; *233 B-19; mail La Follette z 37766; rural
Taft; RMC Place; LINCOLN; 233 G-11; elev. 901ft./275m.; 🅿; z 38488; ● 200
Talbott; RMC Place; JEFFERSON; 233 C-20; elev. 191ft./58m.; 🅿; ★ MORR; z 37877; ● 550
Tallassee; RMC Place; BLOUNT; 233 E-19; elev. 1,200ft./366m.; 🅿; z 37878; ● 130
Talley; RMC Place; MARSHALL; *233 F-11; elev. 805ft./245m.; mail Petersburg z 37144; rural
Tampico; RMC Place; GRAINGER; *233 C-20; mail Rutledge z 37861; rural
Tanglewood; RMC Place; MONROE; *233 E-18; mail Sweetwater z 37874; pop. incl. with Aberdeen (Inc. Place)
Tanglewood; RMC Place; SMITH; *233 C-13; mail Carthage z 37030; ● 170
Tarbett; RMC Place; BLOUNT; *233 D-19; elev. 900ft./274m.; ★ KNOX; mail Rockford z 37853; ● 120
Tarlton; RMC Place; GRUNDY; *233 E-14; elev. 926ft./282m.; mail Mc Minnville z 37110; rural
Tarpley; RMC Place; GILES; *232 G-10; elev. 728ft./222m.; mail Pulaski z 38478
Tarsus; RMC Place; MONTGOMERY; *232 B-9; mail Palmyra z 37142; rural
Tasso; RMC Place; BRADLEY; 233 F-17; elev. 810ft./247m.; ★ CLEV; mail Cleveland z 37312; ● 660
Tate; RMC Place; CARROLL; *232 D-6; mail Huntingdon z 38344; ● 50
Tate Springs; RMC Place; GRAINGER; *233 K-15; elev. 1,103ft./336m.; ★ MORR; mail Bean Station z 37708; ● 120
Tatesville; RMC Place; GRUNDY; *233 F-15; mail Palmer z 37365; pop. incl. with Palmer (Inc. Place)
Tatumville; RMC Place; DYER; 232 C-4; elev. 288ft./88m.; mail Newbern z 38059; ● 50
Taylor Chapel; RMC Place; STEWART; *232 B-8; mail Dover z 37058; rural
Taylor Crossorads; RMC Place; BEDFORD; *233 E-12; mail Shelbyville z 37160; rural
Taylor Hill; RMC Place; RHEA; *233 E-16; mail Dayton z 37321; pop. incl. with Dayton (Inc. Place)
Taylor Place; RMC Place; FENTRESS; *233 B-16; mail Jamestown z 38556; ● 100
Taylors Crossroads; RMC Place; OVERTON; *233 B-15; elev. 1,000ft./305m.; mail Monroe z 38573; rural
Taylorsville; RMC Place; MAURY; *232 E-9; mail Hampshire z 38461; rural
Taylorsville; RMC Place; WILSON; *233 C-13; elev. 496ft./151m.; mail Lebanon z 37087; ● 60
Taylortown; RMC Place; LINCOLN; *233 G-11; mail Frankewing z 38459; rural
Tazewell; Inc. Place; ⊡ CLAIBORNE; 233 B-20; elev. 1,472ft./449m.; 🅿 🅷; z 37879; Ⓟ 2,150; © 2,165
Tazewell; CLAIBORNE; see New Tazewell (Inc. Place)
Teague; RMC Place; HARDEMAN; *232 F-5; elev. 384ft./117m.; mail Medon z 38356, Toone z 38381; ● 50
Tekoa; RMC Place; KNOX; 233 M-11; ★ KNOX; mail Knoxville z 37931; pop. incl. with Knoxville (Inc. Place)
Telford; RMC Place; WASHINGTON; 233 K-18; elev. 1,552ft./473m.; 🅿; ★ JNSC-; z 37690; ● 200
Tellico Hills; RMC Place; MCMINN; *233 F-17; mail Athens z 37303; pop. incl. with Athens (Inc. Place)
Tellico Plains; Inc. Place; MONROE; 233 F-18; elev. 890ft./271m.; 🅿; z 37385; Ⓟ 657; © 859
Temperance Hall; RMC Place; DEKALB; 233 C-14; elev. 595ft./181m.; mail Liberty z 37095; ● 180
Temple Hill; RMC Place; UNICOI; *233 L-18; mail Erwin z 37650; ● 200
Temple Hills Country Club Estates; RMC Place; WILLIAMSON; *232 D-10; ★ NASH; mail Franklin z 37064; ● 90
Templeton; RMC Place; DYER; *232 C-4; mail Newbern z 38059; ● 50
Templow; RMC Place; TROUSDALE; *233 B-13; mail Bethpage z 37022; rural
Tenchtown; RMC Place; FENTRESS; *233 B-16; elev. 1,638ft./499m.; mail Jamestown z 38556; rural
Ten Mile; RMC Place; MEIGS; 233 E-17; elev. 849ft./259m.; 🅿; z 37880; ● 120
Ten Mile Center; RMC Place; KNOX; ★ KNOX; mail Knoxville z 37930; pop. incl. with Knoxville (Inc. Place)
Tennemo; RMC Place; DYER; *232 C-3; ● 30
Tennessee City; RMC Place; DICKSON; *232 C-9; elev. 828ft./252m.; mail Dickson z 37055
Tennessee Hills; RMC Place; SULLIVAN; *233 J-19; ★ JNSC-; mail Bristol z 37620; pop. incl. with Bristol (Inc. Place)
Tennessee Ridge; Inc. Place; HOUSTON, STEWART; 232 C-8; elev. 742ft./226m.; 🅿; z 37178; Ⓟ 1,271; © 1,334
Terrace Hills; RMC Place; WILSON; *233 C-12; ★ NASH; mail Mount Juliet z 37122
Terrace View; RMC Place; RHEA; *233 E-17; elev. 800ft./244m.; mail Spring City z 37381; ● 30
Terrell; RMC Place; WEAKLEY; 232 B-5; elev. 337ft./103m.; mail Martin z 38237; ● 140
Terry; RMC Place; CARROLL; *232 D-6; elev. 435ft./133m.; mail Cedar Grove z 38321, Lavinia z 38348; ● 60
Terry Creek; RMC Place; CAMPBELL; 233 B-18; mail Pioneer z 37847; ● 80
Thaxton; WARREN; see Mount Zion (RMC Place)
Theodore; RMC Place; LEWIS; *232 E-9; mail Hohenwald z 38462; pop. incl. with Hohenwald (Inc. Place)
Theta; RMC Place; MAURY; 232 D-10; mail Columbia z 38401; ● 190
The Wye; RMC Place; ANDERSON; *233 C-19; ★ KNOX; mail Lake City z 37769; ● 50
Thick; RMC Place; MARSHALL; *233 E-11; mail Chapel Hill z 37034; rural
Thomas; RMC Place; PUTNAM; *233 C-14; elev. 1,075ft./328m.; mail Baxter z 38544; ● 30
Thomas Addition; RMC Place; SULLIVAN; *233 J-18; ★ JNSC-; mail Kingsport z 37665; ● 1,200
Thomas Bridge; RMC Place; SULLIVAN; *233 J-18; ★ JNSC-; mail Bluff City z 37618; pop. incl. with Bristol (Inc. Place)
Thomasville; RMC Place; CHEATHAM; *232 B-10; elev. 559ft./170m.; ★ NASH; mail Ashland City z 37015, Chapmansboro z 37035; rural
Thompsons; WILLIAMSON; see Thompson's Station (Inc. Place)
Thompson's Station (Thompsons); Inc. Place; WILLIAMSON; 233 D-11; elev. 1,052ft./321m.; 🅿; z 37179; Ⓟ 703; © 1,283
Thompsons Store; RMC Place; CLAY; *233 A-15; elev. 1,030ft./314m.; mail Celina z 38551; rural
Thorngrove; RMC Place; KNOX; *233 D-20; ★ KNOX; mail Strawberry Plains z 37871; ● 100
Thorn Hill (Idol); RMC Place; GRAINGER; 233 B-20; elev. 1,354ft./413m.; 🅿; z 37881; ● 150
Thornton; RMC Place; KNOX; ★ KNOX; mail Cosby z 37722; pop. incl. with Farragut (Inc. Place)
Three Churches; RMC Place; WAYNE; *232 F-8; elev. 606ft./185m.; mail Collinwood z 38450; rural
Three Oaks; RMC Place; LAWRENCE; *232 F-9; elev. 998ft./304m.; mail Ethridge z 38456; ● 60
Three Point; RMC Place; LAUDERDALE; *232 E-2; mail Henning z 38041
Three Points; RMC Place; KNOX; *233 C-20; ★ KNOX; mail Knoxville z 37918
Three Springs; RMC Place; HAMBLEN; *233 K-16; elev. 1,123ft./342m.; ★ MORR; mail Russellville z 37860; rural
Three Way (Fairview); Inc. Place; MADISON; 232 D-5; 🅿; ★ JAC; z 38343; © 1,375
Throckmorton; RMC Place; STEWART; *232 B-8; mail Indian Mound z 37079; rural
Thula; RMC Place; GREENE; *233 L-16; mail Mohawk z 37810; rural
Thurman Addition; RMC Place; SEVIER; mail Pigeon Forge z 37863; pop. incl. with Pigeon Forge (Inc. Place)
Tibbs; RMC Place; HAYWOOD; *232 E-3; elev. 337ft./103m.; mail Brownsville z 38012; rural
Tidwell; RMC Place; HICKMAN; *232 D-10; mail Bon Aqua z 37025; rural
Tiftona (Tiftonia); RMC Place; HAMILTON; ★ CHTN; mail Chattanooga z 37419; pop. incl. with Chattanooga (Inc. Place)
Tiftonia; HAMILTON; see Tiftona (RMC Place)
Tiger Valley; RMC Place; CARTER; *233 K-19; mail Hampton z 37658; ● 80
Tigrett; RMC Place; DYER; 232 D-4; elev. 295ft./90m.; 🅿; z 38070; ● 200
Tilghman; RMC Place; GIBSON; *232 C-4; elev. 360ft./110m.; mail Kenton z 38233; rural
Timbercrest; RMC Place; KNOX; *233 D-19; ★ KNOX; pop. incl. with Knoxville (Inc. Place)
Timberlake; RMC Place; HAWKINS; *233 K-16; elev. 1,100ft./335m.; mail Rogersville z 37857; ● 50
Timberlake; RMC Place; HENDERSON; 232 E-6; elev. 564ft./172m.; mail Lexington z 38351; pop. incl. with Lexington (Inc. Place)
Timesville; RMC Place; HAMILTON; *233 G-15; ★ CHTN; mail Signal Mountain z 37377; ● 120
Timothy; RMC Place; OVERTON; 233 B-15; mail Allons z 38541, Hilham z 38568; ● 30
Tin Cup; RMC Place; BENTON; *232 C-7; mail Camden z 38320; rural
Tinsleys Bottom; RMC Place; JACKSON; *233 B-14; elev. 600ft./183m.; mail Celina z 38551; rural
Tiprell; RMC Place; CLAIBORNE; *233 A-20; elev. 1,266ft./386m.; mail Cumberland Gap z 37724; ● 220
Tipton; RMC Place; TIPTON; 232 F-2; elev. 355ft./108m.; 🅿; ★ MEM; z 38071; pop. incl. with Atoka (Inc. Place)
TIPTON; 232 E-2; Ⓟ 37,568; © 51,271; ◆ 59,818
Tiptonville; Inc. Place; ⊡ LAKE; 232 B-3; elev. 301ft./92m.; 🅿; z 38079; Ⓟ 2,149; © 2,439
Tishamingo; RMC Place; WILSON; *233 C-12; ★ NASH; mail Mount Juliet z 37122; ● 60
Tobaccoport; RMC Place; STEWART; *232 A-8; mail Bumpus Mills z 37028; rural
Tom Murray; RMC Place; MADISON; ★ JAC; mail Jackson z 38301; pop. incl. with Jackson (Inc. Place)
Toone; Inc. Place; HARDEMAN; 232 F-4; elev. 395ft./120m.; 🅿; z 38381; Ⓟ 279; © 330
Top of the World Estates; RMC Place; BLOUNT; *233 E-19; mail Tallassee z 37878; summer pop. 400; ● 100
Topside; RMC Place; KNOX; *233 D-19; ★ KNOX; mail Knoxville z 37920; pop. incl. with Knoxville (Inc. Place)
Topsy; RMC Place; WAYNE; *232 F-8; mail Waynesboro z 38485; ● 30
Toqua; RMC Place; MONROE; *233 E-16; elev. 800ft./244m.; mail Vonore z 37885; rural
Tottys; HICKMAN; see Tottys Bend (RMC Place)
Tottys Bend (Tottys); RMC Place; HICKMAN; *232 D-9; mail Duck River z 38454; ● 50
Toulon; RMC Place; HAYWOOD; *232 D-3; mail Ripley z 38063; rural
Towee; RMC Place; POLK; *233 F-18; elev. 1,200ft./366m.; mail Reliance z 37369; rural
Towering Oaks; RMC Place; LAWRENCE; *232 F-9; elev. 980ft./299m.; mail Lawrenceburg z 38464; ● 80
Town Acres; RMC Place; GREENE; *233 K-17; mail Greeneville z 37745; pop. incl. with Greeneville (Inc. Place)
Town Creek; RMC Place; CLAIBORNE; *233 B-20; elev. 1,294ft./394m.; mail Speedwell z 37870; rural
Towne Hills; RMC Place; HAMILTON; *233 G-15; ★ CHTN; mail Hixson z 37343; pop. incl. with Chattanooga (Inc. Place)
Townsend; Inc. Place; BLOUNT; 233 E-20; elev. 1,036ft./316m.; 🅿; z 37882; Ⓟ 329; © 244
Trace End Estates; RMC Place; WILLIAMSON; *233 D-11; ★ NASH; mail Franklin z 37064; ● 50
Traceview; RMC Place; WILLIAMSON; *232 D-10; mail Franklin z 37064; ● 30
Tracy City; Inc. Place; GRUNDY; 233 F-14; elev. 1,829ft./557m.; 🅿; z 37387; Ⓟ 1,556; © 1,679
Trade; RMC Place; JOHNSON; 233 K-20; elev. 3,200ft./975m.; 🅿; z 37691; ● 180
Tradewinds; RMC Place; WILSON; *233 C-12; ★ NASH; mail Mount Juliet z 37122; ● 80
Trails End; RMC Place; WILSON; *233 C-12; ★ NASH; mail Mount Juliet z 37122; ● 250
Tranquility; RMC Place; MCMINN; *233 E-17; elev. 900ft./274m.; mail Athens z 37303, Niota z 37826; rural
Travisville; RMC Place; PICKETT; *233 B-16; mail Pall Mall z 38577; rural
Treadway; RMC Place; HANCOCK; 233 K-16; elev. 1,700ft./518m.; 🅿; z 37881; ● 100
Trenton; Inc. Place; ⊡ GIBSON; 232 D-5; elev. 338ft./103m.; 🅿 🅷; z 38382; Ⓟ 4,836; © 4,683
Trent Valley; RMC Place; HANCOCK; *233 J-16; mail Sneedville z 37869; rural
Trentville; RMC Place; KNOX; 233 C-20; ★ KNOX; mail Knoxville z 37914, Strawberry Plains z 37871; ● 420
Trezevant; Inc. Place; CARROLL; 232 C-6; elev. 464ft./141m.; 🅿; z 38258; Ⓟ 874; © 901; Ⓡ 916
Tri-Angle; RMC Place; BEDFORD; *233 E-12; mail Shelbyville z 37160; pop. incl. with Shelbyville (Inc. Place)
Trigonia; RMC Place; LOUDON; *233 E-19; mail Maryville z 37801; rural
Trimble; Inc. Place; DYER, OBION; 232 C-4; elev. 293ft./89m.; 🅿; z 38259; Ⓟ 694; © 728
Trinity; RMC Place; WILLIAMSON; *233 D-11; elev. 730ft./223m.; ★ NASH; mail Franklin z 37067; ● 30
Triune; RMC Place; WILLIAMSON; 233 D-11; ★ NASH; mail Arrington z 37014, College Grove z 37046; ● 120
Trousdale; RMC Place; WARREN; *233 E-13; elev. 1,001ft./305m.; mail Morrison z 37357; rural
TROUSDALE; 233 B-13; Ⓟ 5,920; © 7,259; ◆ 8,033
Troy; Inc. Place; OBION; 232 B-4; elev. 378ft./115m.; 🅿; z 38260; Ⓟ 1,047; © 1,273
Trundel Crossroad; RMC Place; SEVIER; 214 F-3; elev. 939ft./286m.; ★ KNOX; mail Seymour z 37865; ● 420
Tuckahoe; RMC Place; KNOX; *233 D-20; ★ KNOX; mail Strawberry Plains z 37871; rural
Tuckers Crossroads; RMC Place; WILSON; *233 C-13; elev. 633ft./193m.; mail Lebanon z 37087; ● 110
Tucker Springs; RMC Place; BRADLEY; *233 G-16; ★ CLEV; mail Mc Donald z 37353; rural
Tullahoma; Inc. Place; COFFEE, FRANKLIN; 233 F-13; elev. 1,071ft./326m.; 🅿 🅷; z 37388-89; Ⓟ 16,761; © 17,994
Tulu; RMC Place; MCNAIRY; *232 G-6; elev. 460ft./140m.; mail Michie z 38357; pop. incl. with Michie (Inc. Place)
Tumbling; RMC Place; WEAKLEY; *232 C-6; mail Mc Kenzie z 38201; rural
Tuppertown; RMC Place; ANDERSON; ★ KNOX; mail Oliver Springs z 37840; pop. incl. with Oliver Springs (Inc. Place)
Turkeytown; CARTER; see Range (RMC Place)
Turley; RMC Place; CAMPBELL; *233 B-18; mail Caryville z 37714; rural
Turners Station; RMC Place; SUMNER; *233 A-12; elev. 723ft./220m.; mail Westmoreland z 37186; rural
Turnersville; RMC Place; ROBERTSON; *232 B-10; mail Cedar Hill z 37032; rural
Turnpike; RMC Place; HAYWOOD; *232 E-3; mail Brownsville z 38012; rural
Turtletown; RMC Place; POLK; 233 G-18; elev. 1,510ft./460m.; 🅿; z 37391; ● 290
Tusculum; RMC Place; DAVIDSON; *233 C-11; ★ NASH; mail Nashville z 37211; pop. incl. with Nashville (Inc. Place)
Tusculum; Inc. Place; GREENE; 233 K-17; elev. 1,502ft./458m.; mail Greeneville z 37745; Ⓟ 1,918; © 2,004
Twin Bridges; RMC Place; MORGAN; *233 C-17; elev. 1,340ft./408m.; mail Deer Lodge z 37726; rural
Twin Cove; RMC Place; CAMPBELL; *233 C-19; ★ KNOX; mail Caryville z 37714; rural
Twin Oak; RMC Place; PUTNAM; *233 C-14; elev. 980ft./299m.; mail Baxter z 38544; rural
Twin Oaks; RMC Place; SULLIVAN; *233 J-19; ★ JNSC-; mail Bristol z 37620; rural
Twinton; RMC Place; OVERTON; 233 C-16; mail Crawford z 38554; ● 100
Twomey; RMC Place; HICKMAN; *232 D-9; mail Centerville z 37033; pop. incl. with Centerville (Inc. Place)
Tylersville; RMC Place; DYER; *232 C-3; mail Finley z 38030; rural
Tyner; RMC Place; HAMILTON; 233 J-14; ★ CHTN; pop. incl. with Chattanooga (Inc. Place)
Tyner Hills; RMC Place; HAMILTON; *233 G-16; ★ CHTN; mail Chattanooga z 37421; pop. incl. with Chattanooga (Inc. Place)
Tyson Store; RMC Place; GIBSON; *232 C-4; elev. 365ft./111m.; mail Dyer z 38330, Kenton z 38233; rural

U

Una; RMC Place; DAVIDSON; *233 C-11; elev. 663ft./202m.; ★ NASH; mail Nashville z 37217; pop. incl. with Nashville (Inc. Place)
Unaka Springs; RMC Place; UNICOI; *233 L-18; mail Erwin z 37650; ● 60
Underwood; RMC Place; MACON; *233 A-13; elev. 867ft./264m.; mail Lafayette z 37083; rural
Underwood; RMC Place; SEVIER; *233 D-20; ★ KNOX; mail Kodak z 37764; ● 30
Unicoi; RMC Place; MONROE; *233 F-18; elev. 1,000ft./305m.; mail Tellico Plains z 37385; ● 30
Unicoi; Inc. Place; UNICOI; 233 K-18; elev. 1,930ft./588m.; 🅿; z 37692; © 3,519
UNICOI; 233 L-18; Ⓟ 16,549; © 17,667; ◆ 17,716
Union; RMC Place; HARDIN; *232 F-7; mail Adamsville z 38310; pop. incl. with Union (Inc. Place)
Union; RMC Place; HAYWOOD; *232 E-4; elev. 413ft./126m.; mail Brownsville z 38012; rural
Union; RMC Place; MORGAN; *233 C-18; ★ KNOX; mail Oliver Springs z 37840; rural
Union; RMC Place; ROANE; *233 D-18; ★ KNOX; mail Kingston z 37763; pop. incl. with Oak Ridge (Inc. Place)
Union; RMC Place; UNION; *233 B-20; mail Sharps Chapel z 37866; rural
Union; RMC Place; WARREN; *233 E-14; mail Rock Island z 38581; ● 100
UNION; 233 B-19; Ⓟ 13,694; © 17,808; ◆ 18,918
Union Central; RMC Place; GIBSON; *232 D-5; elev. 400ft./122m.; mail Milan z 38358; ● 150
Union City; Inc. Place; ⊡ OBION; 232 B-4; elev. 337ft./103m.; 🅿 🅷 ■; z 38261, z 38281; Ⓟ 10,513; © 10,876; ◆ 10,760
Union Grove; RMC Place; BLOUNT; *233 E-19; mail Friendsville z 37737; ● 50
Union Grove; RMC Place; MCMINN; *233 E-17; mail Niota z 37826; rural
Union Grove; RMC Place; MEIGS; *233 E-17; mail Decatur z 37322; rural
Union Heights; RMC Place; HAMBLEN; *233 K-16; ★ MORR; mail Morristown z 37813; ● 100
Union Hill; RMC Place; CLAY; 233 B-14; elev. 895ft./273m.; mail Moss z 38575, Red Boiling Springs z 37150, Whitleyville z 38588; ● 200
Union Hill; RMC Place; DAVIDSON; *233 B-11; ★ NASH; mail Joelton z 37080; pop. incl. with Nashville (Inc. Place)
Union Hill; JACKSON; see Mount Union (RMC Place)
Union Hill; RMC Place; LAWRENCE; *232 G-9; mail Leoma z 38468; rural
Union Hill; RMC Place; SUMNER; *233 B-12; mail Gallatin z 37066; rural
Union Hill; RMC Place; TIPTON; *232 F-2; elev. 400ft./122m.; ★ MEM; mail Atoka z 38004; ● 30
Union Ridge; RMC Place; BEDFORD; *233 E-12; mail Wartrace z 37183; rural
Union Temple; RMC Place; GREENE; *233 K-17; elev. 1,522ft./464m.; mail Afton z 37616; rural
Union Valley; RMC Place; SEVIER; *233 D-20; ★ KNOX; mail Seymour z 37865; rural
Unionville; RMC Place; BEDFORD; 233 E-12; elev. 728ft./222m.; 🅿; z 37180; ● 230
Unionville; RMC Place; DYER; *232 D-3; mail Halls z 38040; rural
Unitia; RMC Place; LOUDON; *233 D-19; elev. 864ft./263m.; mail Lenoir City z 37772; ● 30
Unity; WEAKLEY; see Austin Springs (RMC Place)
University of the South; RMC Place; FRANKLIN; mail Sewanee z 37375, z 37383
Upchurch; RMC Place; GREENE; *233 K-17; mail Afton z 37616; rural
Upper Mockeson; RMC Place; LAWRENCE; *232 G-9; mail Leoma z 38468; rural
Upper Shell Creek; RMC Place; CARTER; *233 K-19; mail Roan Mountain z 37687; ● 80
Upper Sinking; RMC Place; HICKMAN; *232 E-8; rural
Uptonville; RMC Place; MADISON; *232 E-4; mail Medon z 38356, Mercer z 38392

V

Vale; RMC Place; CARROLL; 232 C-7; elev. 415ft./126m.; mail Bruceton z 38317; ● 110
Valleybrook; RMC Place; HAMILTON; *233 G-16; ★ CHTN; mail Hixson z 37343; pop. incl. with Chattanooga (Inc. Place)
Valley Brook; RMC Place; WILSON; *233 C-12; ★ NASH; mail Mount Juliet z 37122; ● 80
Valley Creek; RMC Place; CLAIBORNE; *233 B-19; elev. 1,190ft./363m.; mail Clairfield z 37715; rural
Valley Forge; RMC Place; CARTER; 234 N-5; ★ JNSC-; mail Elizabethton z 37643; ● 2,200
Valley Hills; RMC Place; SULLIVAN; *233 J-19; ★ JNSC-; mail Bristol z 37620; pop. incl. with Bristol (Inc. Place)
Valley View; RMC Place; ANDERSON; *233 C-19; elev. 815ft./248m.; ★ KNOX; mail Clinton z 37716; ● 150
Van Buren; RMC Place; HARDEMAN; *232 G-4; mail Hickory Valley z 38042; rural
VAN BUREN; 233 E-15; Ⓟ 4,846; © 5,508; ◆ 5,511
Vandever; RMC Place; CUMBERLAND; *233 D-16; mail Crossville z 38572; rural
Van Dyke; RMC Place; HENRY; *232 C-7; elev. 426ft./130m.; mail Paris z 38242; ● 30
Van Hill; RMC Place; HAWKINS; *233 K-17; mail Rogersville z 37857; rural
Vanleer; Inc. Place; DICKSON; 232 C-9; elev. 849ft./259m.; 🅿; z 37181; Ⓟ 369; © 310
Vannatta; RMC Place; BEDFORD; *233 E-12; mail Shelbyville z 37160; ● 30
Vanntown; RMC Place; LINCOLN; *233 G-12; mail Flintville z 37335; ● 50

Entries in **UPPERCASE** are counties.
Entries in **bold** have populations of 2,500 or more.
Names in parentheses are alternate names.

Inc. Place	Incorporated Place
RMC Place	Rand McNally Designated Place
CDP	Census Designated Place
MCD	Minor Civil Division
⊡	County Seat
▲	Minor Civil Division
elev.	Elevation
🅿	Post Office
🅷	Hospital
🅲	College
■	Principal Business Center
★	Ranally Metro Area (RMA) Abbreviation
z	Zip Code(s)
Ⓟ	Previous Census Population
Ⓡ	Revised Census Population
Ⓐ	Annexation Population
●	Rand McNally Population Estimate
©	Final Census Population
Ⓢ	Special Census Population
◆	Estimated Population

For additional definitions see Glossary, Volume 1, and Introduction, Volume 2.

Vardy; RMC Place; HANCOCK; ***233** J-16; elev. 1,400ft./427m.; mail Sneedville **z** 37869; rural
Vasper; RMC Place; CAMPBELL; **233** C-19; mail Caryville **z** 37714; ● 50
Vaughn's Gap; RMC Place; DAVIDSON; ★ **NASH**; mail Nashville **z** 37205; pop. incl. with Nashville (Inc. Place)
Vaughns Grove; RMC Place; GIBSON; ***232** C-5; elev. 465ft./142m.; mail Trenton **z** 38382; rural
Verdun; RMC Place; SCOTT; ***233** B-17; mail Oneida **z** 37841; rural
Vernon; RMC Place; HICKMAN; **232** D-9; mail Nunnelly **z** 37137; ● 50
Vernon Heights; RMC Place; SULLIVAN; ***233** J-18; ★ **JNSC-**; mail Kingsport **z** 37664; pop. incl. with Kingsport (Inc. Place)
Verona; RMC Place; MARSHALL; ***233** E-11; mail Lewisburg **z** 37091; ● 50
Verona Hills; RMC Place; WILSON; ***233** C-12; ★ **NASH**; mail Mount Juliet **z** 37122; ● 290
Versailles; RMC Place; RUTHERFORD; ***233** E-12; mail Rockvale **z** 37153; rural
Vesta; RMC Place; WILSON; ***233** C-12; mail Lebanon **z** 37090; rural
Vestal; RMC Place; KNOX; ***233** D-19; ★ **KNOX**; mail Knoxville **z** 37920; pop. incl. with Knoxville (Inc. Place)
Veto; RMC Place; GILES; ***232** G-10; mail Prospect **z** 38477; total pop., including Veto, AL, 60; ● 30
Viar; RMC Place; DYER; ***232** C-4; elev. 336ft./102m.; mail Dyersburg **z** 38024; rural
Victoria; RMC Place; MARION; **233** G-15; elev. 679ft./207m.; mail Whitwell **z** 37397; ● 200
Victory; RMC Place; CAMPBELL; ***233** B-19; ★ **KNOX**; mail La Follette **z** 37766; ● 50
Vildo; RMC Place; HARDEMAN; ***232** F-4; mail Whiteville **z** 38075
Villa Gardens; RMC Place; KNOX; ★ **KNOX**; mail Knoxville **z** 37918; pop. incl. with Knoxville (Inc. Place)
Village Green; RMC Place; KNOX; ***233** D-19; ★ **KNOX**; mail Knoxville **z** 37922; pop. incl. with Farragut (Inc. Place)
Vine; RMC Place; WILSON; ***233** D-12; mail Lebanon **z** 37090; ● 60
Vinegar Hill; RMC Place; SULLIVAN; ***233** J-19; ★ **JNSC-**; mail Bristol **z** 37620; rural
Vine Hill; RMC Place; DAVIDSON; pop. incl. with Nashville (Inc. Place)
Vine Ridge; RMC Place; OVERTON; **233** C-16; mail Crawford **z** 38554; ● 120
Viola; Inc. Place; WARREN; **233** E-14; elev. 995ft./303m.; 🅿; **z** 37394; Ⓟ 123; Ⓒ 129
Virtue; RMC Place; KNOX; ***233** D-19; ★ **KNOX**; mail Knoxville **z** 37922; pop. incl. with Farragut (Inc. Place)
Vise; RMC Place; DECATUR; ***232** E-7; elev. 370ft./113m.; mail Decaturville **z** 38329; rural
Vison Cross Roads; RMC Place; WARREN; ***233** E-14; mail Mc Minnville **z** 37110; rural
Volunteer; RMC Place; KNOX; pop. incl. with Knoxville (Inc. Place)
Volunteer Heights; RMC Place; CUMBERLAND; ***233** D-16; mail Crossville **z** 38555; pop. incl. with Crossville (Inc. Place)
Vonore; Inc. Place; MONROE; **233** E-18; elev. 852ft./260m.; 🅿; **z** 37885; Ⓟ 605; Ⓒ 1,162
Vose; RMC Place; BLOUNT; ***233** D-19; ★ **KNOX**; mail Alcoa **z** 37701; pop. incl. with Alcoa (Inc. Place)

W

Waco; RMC Place; GILES; **232** F-10; mail Lynnville **z** 38472; ● 80
Walden; Inc. Place; HAMILTON; **233** G-15; ★ **CHTN**; mail Signal Mountain **z** 37377; Ⓟ 1,523; Ⓒ 1,960
Walden Creek; SEVIER; see Waldens Creek (RMC Place)
Waldens Creek (Walden Creek); RMC Place; SEVIER; **214** G-4; elev. 999ft./304m.; mail Sevierville **z** 37862; pop. incl. with Pigeon Forge (Inc. Place)
Waldens Ridge; RMC Place; BLEDSOE; ***233** E-16; mail Spring City **z** 37381; rural
Waldens Ridge; RMC Place; RHEA; ***233** E-16; elev. 1,800ft./549m.; mail Dayton **z** 37321; rural
Wales; RMC Place; GILES; ***232** F-10; elev. 680ft./207m.; mail Pulaski **z** 38478
Walkertown; RMC Place; GREENE; **233** K-17; elev. 1,559ft./475m.; mail Afton **z** 37616; ● 30
Walkertown; RMC Place; HARDIN; ***232** F-7; mail Savannah **z** 38372; ● 350
Walland; RMC Place; BLOUNT; **233** E-20; elev. 929ft./283m.; 🅿; **z** 37886; ● 500
Walling; RMC Place; WHITE; **233** D-14; elev. 885ft./270m.; 🅿; **z** 38587; ● 120
Walnut Acres; RMC Place; WILLIAMSON; ***233** D-11; ★ **NASH**; mail Franklin **z** 37064
Walnut Grove; RMC Place; FRANKLIN; ***233** G-13; elev. 900ft./274m.; mail Huntland **z** 37345; rural
Walnut Grove; RMC Place; GIBSON; ***232** C-5; elev. 351ft./107m.; mail Kenton **z** 38233, Rutherford **z** 38369
Walnut Grove; RMC Place; HARDIN; ***232** G-7; mail Savannah **z** 38372; ● 100
Walnut Grove; RMC Place; LAUDERDALE; ***232** D-3; elev. 340ft./104m.; mail Ripley **z** 38063; rural
Walnut Grove; RMC Place; MEIGS; ***233** E-17; mail Decatur **z** 37322; rural
Walnut Grove; RMC Place; SEVIER; ***233** D-20; elev. 1,040ft./317m.; mail Sevierville **z** 37876; ● 60
Walnut Grove; RMC Place; SULLIVAN; **234** L-5; ★ **JNSC-**; mail Bluff City **z** 37618; ● 250
Walnut Grove; RMC Place; SUMNER; ***233** B-11; ★ **NASH**; mail Cottontown **z** 37048; disincorporated July 1, 2001; Ⓒ 677
Walnut Grove; RMC Place; TIPTON; ***232** E-2; mail Burlison **z** 38015; rural
Walnut Grove; RMC Place; TROUSDALE; ***233** B-13; mail Hartsville **z** 37074; rural
Walnut Hill; RMC Place; CROCKETT; ***232** E-4; elev. 360ft./110m.; mail Bells **z** 38006; ● 100
Walnut Hill; RMC Place; ROANE; ***233** D-18; elev. 765ft./233m.; ★ **KNOX**; mail Harriman **z** 37748; pop. incl. with Harriman (Inc. Place)
Walnut Hill; CDP; SULLIVAN; **234** J-4; ★ **JNSC-**; mail Bristol **z** 37620; Ⓟ 3,332; Ⓒ 2,756
Walnut Log; RMC Place; OBION; **232** B-4; mail Union City **z** 38261; ● 50
Walnut Shade; RMC Place; MACON; ***233** B-14; elev. 774ft./236m.; mail Red Boiling Springs **z** 37150; rural
Walter Crossroad; RMC Place; GREENE; ***233** L-17; mail Greeneville **z** 37743; rural
Walterhill; CDP; RUTHERFORD; **233** D-12; ★ **MUR**; mail Murfreesboro **z** 37129; Ⓟ 1,043; Ⓒ 1,523
Wa-Ni Village; RMC Place; GRAINGER; ***233** C-20; mail Rutledge **z** 37861; ● 150
Warcer; RMC Place; KNOX; pop. incl. with Knoxville (Inc. Place)
Ware Branch; RMC Place; HAMILTON; ***233** F-16; elev. 720ft./219m.; ★ **CHTN**; mail Harrison **z** 37341; rural
Warren; RMC Place; FAYETTE; ***232** F-3; mail Somerville **z** 38068
WARREN; **233** E-14; Ⓟ 32,992; Ⓒ 38,276; ◆ 39,931
Warrens Bluff; RMC Place; HENDERSON; ***232** E-6; mail Lexington **z** 38351; rural
Warrensburg; RMC Place; GREENE; **233** L-16; mail Mohawk **z** 37810, Mosheim **z** 37818; ● 50
Wartburg; Inc. Place; ⊡ MORGAN; **233** C-17; elev. 1,400ft./427m.; 🅿; **z** 37887; Ⓟ 932; Ⓒ 890
Wartrace; Inc. Place; BEDFORD; **233** E-12; elev. 824ft./251m.; 🅿; **z** 37183; Ⓟ 494; Ⓒ 548
Warwicktown; RMC Place; UNION; ***233** C-19; ★ **KNOX**; mail Maynardville **z** 37807; ● 30
Washburn; RMC Place; GRAINGER; **233** C-20; elev. 1,404ft./428m.; 🅿; **z** 37888; ● 340
Washington; RMC Place; RHEA; ***233** E-17; mail Dayton **z** 37321; ● 200
WASHINGTON; **233** K-18; Ⓟ 92,315; Ⓒ 107,198; ◆ 120,661
Washington Heights; RMC Place; HAMILTON; ***233** G-16; ★ **CHTN**; mail Chattanooga **z** 37406; pop. incl. with Chattanooga (Inc. Place)
Watauga; Inc. Place; CARTER, WASHINGTON; **233** K-18; elev. 1,451ft./442m.; 🅿; ★ **JNSC-**; **z** 37694; Ⓟ 389; Ⓒ 403
Watauga Flats; RMC Place; WASHINGTON; **234** M-4; elev. 1,536ft./468m.; ★ **JNSC-**; mail Johnson City **z** 37601; ● 150
Watauga Point; RMC Place; CARTER; ***233** K-19; ★ **JNSC-**; mail Elizabethton **z** 37643; pop. incl. with Elizabethton (Inc. Place)
Waterstown; RMC Place; BLOUNT; ***233** E-20; elev. 1,000ft./305m.; mail Walland **z** 37886; rural
Watertown; Inc. Place; WILSON; **233** C-13; elev. 667ft./203m.; 🅿; **z** 37184; Ⓟ 1,250; Ⓒ 1,358; Ⓡ 1,361
Water Valley; RMC Place; MAURY; ***232** E-10; mail Williamsport **z** 38487; rural
Waterville; RMC Place; BRADLEY; **233** G-17; ★ **CLEV**; mail Cleveland **z** 37323; ● 60
Watkins; RMC Place; DEKALB; ***233** D-14; elev. 1,048ft./319m.; mail Smithville **z** 37166; rural
Watkins; RMC Place; TIPTON; ***232** E-3; ★ **MEM**; mail Covington **z** 38019; pop. incl. with Covington (Inc. Place)
Watt Heights; RMC Place; MCMINN; ***233** F-17; mail Calhoun **z** 37309; pop. incl. with Calhoun (Inc. Place)
Watts Bar Dam; RMC Place; RHEA; **233** E-17; elev. 741ft./226m.; 🅿; **z** 37381; ● 60
Watts Bar Estates; RMC Place; RHEA; ***233** E-17; mail Spring City **z** 37381; ● 70
Watuaga Valley; CARTER; see Hunter (CDP)
Wauhatchie; RMC Place; HAMILTON; ***233** G-15; ★ **CHTN**; pop. incl. with Chattanooga (Inc. Place)
Waverly; Inc. Place; ⊡ HUMPHREYS; **232** C-8; elev. 546ft./166m.; 🅿 Ⓗ; **z** 37185; Ⓟ 3,925; Ⓒ 4,028
Wayland Springs; RMC Place; LAWRENCE; **232** G-9; elev. 588ft./179m.; mail Iron City **z** 38463; ● 100
WAYNE; **232** F-8; Ⓟ 13,935; Ⓒ 16,842; ◆ 16,360
Waynesboro; Inc. Place; ⊡ WAYNE; **232** F-8; elev. 800ft./244m.; 🅿 Ⓗ; **z** 38485; Ⓟ 1,824; Ⓒ 2,228
Wayside; RMC Place; WARREN; ***233** E-14; mail Mc Minnville **z** 37110; rural
WEAKLEY; **232** B-5; Ⓟ 31,972; Ⓒ 34,895; ◆ 32,771
Weakly; RMC Place; GILES; ***232** F-10; elev. 728ft./222m.; mail Lawrenceburg **z** 38464; rural
Wear Valley; RMC Place; SEVIER; **233** E-20; elev. 1,454ft./443m.; mail Sevierville **z** 37862; ● 180
Weaver; RMC Place; SULLIVAN; ***233** J-19; ★ **JNSC-**; mail Bristol **z** 37620; ● 30
Webber City; RMC Place; LAWRENCE; **232** F-9; mail Ethridge **z** 38456; ● 100
Webbtown; RMC Place; MACON; **233** B-13; mail Lafayette **z** 37083; ● 130
Webster; RMC Place; ROANE; mail Rockwood **z** 37854
Wedgewood Hills; RMC Place; KNOX; ***233** D-19; ★ **KNOX**; mail Knoxville **z** 37922
Welch Crossroad; RMC Place; UNION; ***233** B-20; mail Sharps Chapel **z** 37866; rural
Welchland; RMC Place; VAN BUREN; ***233** E-15; elev. 1,868ft./569m.; mail Spencer **z** 38585; rural
Welch's Camp; RMC Place; CAMPBELL; ***233** C-18; elev. 1,360ft./415m.; mail Caryville **z** 37714; ● 30
Well Spring; RMC Place; CAMPBELL; ***233** B-19; mail Speedwell **z** 37870; rural
Wells Station; RMC Place; SHELBY; ★ **MEM**; mail Memphis **z** 38122; pop. incl. with Memphis (Inc. Place)
Wellsville; RMC Place; BLOUNT; ***233** E-19; mail Maryville **z** 37801; rural
Wellwood; RMC Place; HAYWOOD; ***232** E-4; mail Bells **z** 38006; rural
Werner; GRUNDY; see Collins (RMC Place)
Wesleyanna; RMC Place; MCMINN; ***233** F-17; mail Athens **z** 37303, Etowah **z** 37331; rural
West; RMC Place; DAVIDSON; ★ **NASH**; mail Nashville **z** 37209; pop. incl. with Nashville (Inc. Place)
West; RMC Place; GIBSON; ***232** D-5; mail Milan **z** 38358; rural
West Cyruston; RMC Place; LINCOLN; ***233** G-11; mail Fayetteville **z** 37334; rural
Westel; RMC Place; CUMBERLAND; **233** D-17; mail Rockwood **z** 37854; ● 290
West Emory; RMC Place; KNOX; ***233** D-19; ★ **KNOX**; mail Knoxville **z** 37922; rural
Western Heights; RMC Place; HAWKINS; ***233** K-16; elev. 1,200ft./366m.; mail Rogersville **z** 37857; ● 300
Westfield Estates; RMC Place; WILLIAMSON; ***233** D-11; ★ **NASH**; mail Franklin **z** 37064; pop. incl. with Franklin (Inc. Place)
West Forest; RMC Place; KNOX; ★ **KNOX**; mail Knoxville **z** 37919; pop. incl. with Knoxville (Inc. Place)
West Fork; RMC Place; OVERTON; ***233** B-16; elev. 900ft./274m.; mail Alpine **z** 38543; rural
West Greene; RMC Place; GREENE; mail Greeneville **z** 37743
West Harpeth; RMC Place; WILLIAMSON; ***233** D-11; elev. 680ft./207m.; ★ **NASH**; mail Franklin **z** 37064; ● 30
Westhaven Village; RMC Place; KNOX; ★ **KNOX**; mail Knoxville **z** 37921; pop. incl. with Knoxville (Inc. Place)
West Hills; RMC Place; JEFFERSON; ***233** C-20; elev. 1,200ft./366m.; mail New Market **z** 37820; pop. incl. with New Market (Inc. Place)
West Hills; RMC Place; KNOX; **233** N-11; ★ **KNOX**; mail Knoxville **z** 37919; pop. incl. with Knoxville (Inc. Place)
West Hills; RMC Place; MONROE; ***233** E-19; mail Madisonville **z** 37354; ● 80
West Hills; RMC Place; ROANE; ***233** D-17; elev. 920ft./280m.; ★ **KNOX**; mail Harriman **z** 37748; pop. incl. with Harriman (Inc. Place)
West Junction; RMC Place; SHELBY; **232** L-1; ★ **MEM**; mail Memphis **z** 38101; pop. incl. with Memphis (Inc. Place)
West Knoxville; RMC Place; KNOX; ***233** D-19; elev. 880ft./268m.; ★ **KNOX**; mail Knoxville **z** 37919, **z** 37939; pop. incl. with Knoxville (Inc. Place)
West Maryville; RMC Place; BLOUNT; ***233** D-19; ★ **KNOX**; mail Maryville **z** 37801, **z** 37803; pop. incl. with Maryville (Inc. Place)
West Meade; RMC Place; DAVIDSON; ***233** C-11; elev. 507ft./155m.; ★ **NASH**; mail Nashville **z** 37205; pop. incl. with Nashville (Inc. Place)
West Miller Cove; RMC Place; BLOUNT; ***233** E-20; elev. 985ft./300m.; mail Walland **z** 37886; rural
Westmoreland; Inc. Place; SUMNER; **233** B-13; elev. 911ft./278m.; 🅿; **z** 37186; Ⓟ 1,726; Ⓒ 2,093
Westmoreland Heights; RMC Place; KNOX; **233** N-12; ★ **KNOX**; mail Knoxville **z** 37919; pop. incl. with Knoxville (Inc. Place)
West Nashville; RMC Place; DAVIDSON; ★ **NASH**; mail Nashville **z** 37209; pop. incl. with Nashville (Inc. Place)
West Oneida; RMC Place; SCOTT; ***233** B-18; mail Oneida **z** 37841; pop. incl. with Oneida (Inc. Place)
Westover; RMC Place; MADISON; **232** E-5; ★ **JAC**; mail Jackson **z** 38301; ● 600
Westpoint; RMC Place; LAWRENCE; **232** G-9; elev. 610ft./186m.; 🅿; **z** 38486; ● 300
Westport; RMC Place; CARROLL; **232** D-6; elev. 434ft./132m.; 🅿; **z** 38387; ● 160
West Ridge; RMC Place; HAWKINS; ***233** J-17; ★ **JNSC-**; pop. incl. with Mount Carmel (Inc. Place)
West Robbin; SCOTT; see West Robbins (RMC Place)
West Robbins (West Robbin); RMC Place; SCOTT; ***233** B-17; elev. 1,429ft./436m.; mail Robbins **z** 37852; ● 50
West Shiloh; RMC Place; MCNAIRY; ***232** G-6; elev. 474ft./144m.; mail Stantonville **z** 38379; ● 50
Westside Heights; RMC Place; COFFEE; mail Tullahoma **z** 37388; pop. incl. with Tullahoma (Inc. Place)
West Springbrook; RMC Place; BLOUNT; ***233** D-19; ★ **KNOX**; mail Alcoa **z** 37701; pop. incl. with Alcoa (Inc. Place)
West Union; RMC Place; WEAKLEY; ***232** B-6; mail Dresden **z** 38225; rural
West View; RMC Place; KNOX; ***233** D-19; elev. 911ft./278m.; ★ **KNOX**; mail Knoxville **z** 37921; pop. incl. with Knoxville (Inc. Place)
West View; RMC Place; WASHINGTON; ***233** K-18; elev. 500ft./152m.; mail Limestone **z** 37681; ● 50
Westview; RMC Place; WEAKLEY; ***232** B-5; mail Martin **z** 38237; pop. incl. with Martin (Inc. Place)
West View Acres; RMC Place; WILSON; ***233** C-12; mail Lebanon **z** 37090; pop. incl. with Lebanon (Inc. Place)
West View Park; RMC Place; SULLIVAN; ***233** J-18; ★ **JNSC-**; mail Kingsport **z** 37660; pop. incl. with Kingsport (Inc. Place)
Westwood; RMC Place; MAURY; **232** E-10; mail Columbia **z** 38401; pop. incl. with Columbia (Inc. Place)
Westwood Gardens; RMC Place; MADISON; ***232** E-5; ★ **JAC**; mail Jackson **z** 38301; pop. incl. with Jackson (Inc. Place)
Westwood Hills; RMC Place; BLOUNT; ***233** E-19; ★ **KNOX**; mail Maryville **z** 37803; pop. incl. with Maryville (Inc. Place)
Westwood Homes; RMC Place; COFFEE; ***233** E-13; mail Manchester **z** 37355; pop. incl. with Manchester (Inc. Place)
Wetmore; RMC Place; POLK; **233** F-18; elev. 816ft./249m.; mail Delano **z** 37325; ● 150
Wheel; RMC Place; BEDFORD; **233** E-11; mail Shelbyville **z** 37160; ● 200
Wheelerton; RMC Place; GILES; ***233** G-11; mail Dellrose **z** 38453; rural
Whispering Hills; RMC Place; OBION; ***232** B-4; elev. 490ft./149m.; mail Union City **z** 38261; ● 300
Whispering Pine; RMC Place; UNICOI; ***233** K-18; mail Unicoi **z** 37692; pop. incl. with Unicoi (Inc. Place)
Whitaker; RMC Place; BEDFORD; ***233** F-11; elev. 817ft./249m.; mail Shelbyville **z** 37160; rural
White; RMC Place; SHELBY; ***232** G-2; ★ **MEM**; mail Memphis **z** 38119-20, **z** 38187; pop. incl. with Memphis (Inc. Place)
White; RMC Place; WARREN; ***233** E-14; mail Mc Minnville **z** 37110; rural
WHITE; **233** D-14; Ⓟ 20,090; Ⓒ 23,102; ◆ 25,449
White Bluff; Inc. Place; DICKSON; **232** C-10; elev. 819ft./250m.; 🅿; **z** 37187; Ⓟ 1,988; Ⓒ 2,142
White Bluff; RMC Place; TROUSDALE; ***233** B-13; mail Hartsville **z** 37074; rural
White City; RMC Place; GRUNDY; **233** F-14; mail Tracy City **z** 37387; ● 210
White Fern; RMC Place; HENDERSON; ***232** E-6; mail Beech Bluff **z** 38313; rural
Whitehaven; RMC Place; SHELBY; ***232** G-1; ★ **MEM**; mail Memphis **z** 38116, **z** 38186; pop. incl. with Memphis (Inc. Place)
Whitehead Hills; RMC Place; CARTER; ***233** K-19; elev. 2,366ft./721m.; mail Roan Mountain **z** 37687; ● 50
White Hill; RMC Place; ROBERTSON, SUMNER; ***233** B-11; elev. 873ft./266m.; ★ **NASH**; mail Goodlettsville **z** 37072; pop. incl. with Millersville (Inc. Place)
White Hill; RMC Place; VAN BUREN; ***233** E-14; elev. 961ft./293m.; mail Rock Island **z** 38581; rural
White Horn; RMC Place; HAWKINS; ***233** K-16; mail Bulls Gap **z** 37711; rural
White House; Inc. Place; SUMNER, ROBERTSON; **233** B-11; elev. 755ft./230m.; 🅿; ★ **NASH**; **z** 37188; Ⓟ 2,987; Ⓒ 7,220; Ⓡ 7,297
White Oak; RMC Place; CAMPBELL; **233** B-19; mail La Follette **z** 37766; ● 250
White Oak; RMC Place; MORGAN; ***233** D-17; elev. 930ft./283m.; mail Oakdale **z** 37829; rural
Whiteoak Crossing; RMC Place; PERRY; ***232** E-8; mail Clifton **z** 38425; rural
White Oak Flat; RMC Place; DICKSON; ***232** C-10; elev. 755ft./230m.; mail Charlotte **z** 37036; ● 180
White Oaks; RMC Place; COFFEE; ***233** F-13; mail Manchester **z** 37355; pop. incl. with Manchester (Inc. Place)
White Pine; Inc. Place; JEFFERSON; **233** L-16; elev. 1,140ft./347m.; 🅿; ★ **MORR**; **z** 37890; Ⓟ 1,771; Ⓒ 1,997
White Rock; RMC Place; CARTER; ***233** K-19; mail Roan Mountain **z** 37687; rural
Whitesand; RMC Place; GREENE; ***233** L-17; mail Greeneville **z** 37743; rural
Whitesburg; RMC Place; HAMBLEN; **233** K-16; elev. 1,234ft./376m.; 🅿; ★ **MORR**; **z** 37891; ● 400
White Schoolhouse Corners; RMC Place; MORGAN; ***233** C-18; ★ **KNOX**; mail Oliver Springs **z** 37840; rural
Whites Creek; RMC Place; DAVIDSON; ***233** C-11; elev. 469ft./143m.; 🅿; ★ **NASH**; **z** 37189; pop. incl. with Nashville (Inc. Place)
White's Creek (Newport Camp); RMC Place; RHEA; ***233** D-17; elev. 720ft./219m.; mail Spring City **z** 37381; ● 50
Whiteside; RMC Place; MARION; **233** G-15; elev. 1,500ft./457m.; 🅿; **z** 37396; ● 600
Whiteville; Inc. Place; HARDEMAN; **232** F-4; elev. 500ft./152m.; 🅿; **z** 38075; Ⓟ 1,050; Ⓒ 3,148; Ⓡ 4,539
Whitleyville; RMC Place; JACKSON; **233** B-14; 🅿; **z** 38588; ● 60
Whitlock; RMC Place; HENRY; ***232** B-6; mail Paris **z** 38242; ● 140
Whitthorne; RMC Place; CARROLL; ***232** D-5; mail Lavinia **z** 38348; rural
Whittle Springs; RMC Place; KNOX; ***233** D-19; ★ **KNOX**; mail Knoxville **z** 37917; pop. incl. with Knoxville (Inc. Place)
Whitway; RMC Place; GIBSON; ***232** D-5; mail Milan **z** 38358; rural
Whitwell; Inc. Place; MARION; **233** F-15; elev. 675ft./206m.; 🅿; **z** 37397; Ⓟ 1,622; Ⓒ 1,660
Widow Town; RMC Place; SEVIER; ***233** D-20; elev. 1,139ft./347m.; mail Sevierville **z** 37876; ● 150
Wilder; RMC Place; FENTRESS; **233** C-16; elev. 1,539ft./469m.; 🅿; **z** 38589; ● 230
Wilder Chapel; RMC Place; FRANKLIN; ***233** F-13; elev. 1,000ft./305m.; mail Decherd **z** 37324; ● 30
Wildersville; RMC Place; HENDERSON; **232** D-6; elev. 478ft./146m.; 🅿; **z** 38388; ● 170
Wild Plum; RMC Place; CUMBERLAND; ***233** D-16; mail Crossville **z** 38572; rural
Wildwood; RMC Place; BLOUNT; **233** D-19; ★ **KNOX**; mail Maryville **z** 37804; ● 530
Wildwood Lake; CDP-Census Area Only; BRADLEY; ***233** G-17; elev. 900ft./274m.; ★ **CLEV**; mail Cleveland **z** 37311; Ⓟ 2,680; Ⓒ 3,050
Wilhite; RMC Place; PUTNAM; mail Cookeville **z** 38506; pop. incl. with Cookeville (Inc. Place)
Wilkinsville; RMC Place; TIPTON; ***232** F-2; elev. 327ft./100m.; ★ **MEM**; mail Atoka **z** 38004, Millington **z** 38053; ● 50
Willard; RMC Place; TROUSDALE; ***233** B-13; mail Hartsville **z** 37074
Willette; RMC Place; MACON; **233** B-14; elev. 992ft./302m.; mail Red Boiling Springs **z** 37150; ● 150
Williams; RMC Place; LAUDERDALE; ***232** D-3; elev. 385ft./117m.; mail Ripley **z** 38063; rural
Williams; RMC Place; MACON; ***233** B-13; elev. 947ft./289m.; mail Lafayette **z** 37083; ● 50
Williamsburg; RMC Place; MCMINN; ***233** F-18; mail Etowah **z** 37331; rural
Williams Creek; RMC Place; SCOTT; ***233** B-17; mail Oneida **z** 37841; rural
Williams Crossroads; RMC Place; DEKALB; ***233** D-14; elev. 1,015ft./309m.; mail Baxter **z** 38544; rural
WILLIAMSON; **232** D-10; Ⓟ 81,021; Ⓒ 126,638; ◆ 175,995
Williamsport; RMC Place; MAURY; **232** E-10; elev. 626ft./191m.; 🅿; **z** 38487; ● 150
Williams Springs; RMC Place; GRAINGER; ***233** B-20; elev. 1,131ft./345m.; mail Washburn **z** 37888; rural
Willis; RMC Place; HANCOCK; ***233** J-16; elev. 1,201ft./366m.; mail Kyles Ford **z** 37765; rural
Willis Spring; RMC Place; POLK; ***233** G-17; elev. 800ft./244m.; mail Old Fort **z** 37362; rural
Williston; Inc. Place; FAYETTE; **232** F-3; elev. 473ft./144m.; 🅿; **z** 38057, **z** 38066, **z** 38076; Ⓟ 427; Ⓒ 341; Ⓡ 330
Willow Grove; RMC Place; BEDFORD; ***233** F-12; mail Normandy **z** 37360; rural
Willow Grove; RMC Place; CLAY; ***233** B-15; mail Allons **z** 38541; rural
Wilmore Estates; RMC Place; JEFFERSON; ***233** L-16; ★ **MORR**; mail White Pine **z** 37890; ● 120
WILSON; **233** C-12; Ⓟ 67,675; Ⓒ 88,809; Ⓡ 88,808; ◆ 110,421
Wilson Station; RMC Place; MONROE; ***233** F-18; elev. 923ft./281m.; mail Englewood **z** 37329; rural
Wilsonville; RMC Place; COCKE; ***233** L-16; elev. 1,161ft./354m.; ★ **MORR**; mail Newport **z** 37821; pop. incl. with Newport (Inc. Place)
Winchester; Inc. Place; ⊡ FRANKLIN; **233** G-13; elev. 965ft./294m.; 🅿 Ⓗ; **z** 37398; Ⓟ 6,305; Ⓒ 7,329
Winchester Springs; RMC Place; FRANKLIN; ***233** F-13; elev. 1,011ft./308m.; mail Winchester **z** 37398; rural
Winding Ridge; RMC Place; SUMNER; ***233** B-11; elev. 896ft./273m.; ★ **NASH**; mail Goodlettsville **z** 37072; rural
Windle; RMC Place; OVERTON; ***233** B-15; mail Livingston **z** 38570; rural
Windletown; RMC Place; OVERTON; **233** C-16; mail Crawford **z** 38554; ● 30
Windrock; RMC Place; ANDERSON; ***233** C-18; ★ **KNOX**; mail Oliver Springs **z** 37840; rural
Windrow; RMC Place; RUTHERFORD; ***233** D-12; elev. 849ft./259m.; ★ **NASH**; mail Rockvale **z** 37153; rural
Windy City; RMC Place; MADISON; ***232** D-5; elev. 395ft./120m.; ★ **JAC**; mail Humboldt **z** 38343; rural
Windy Hill; RMC Place; SULLIVAN; ***233** J-19; ★ **JNSC-**; mail Bristol **z** 37620; pop. incl. with Bristol (Inc. Place)
Winfield; Inc. Place; SCOTT; **233** B-18; elev. 1,324ft./404m.; 🅿; **z** 37892; Ⓟ 564; Ⓒ 911
Wingo; RMC Place; CARROLL; ***232** C-6; elev. 372ft./113m.; mail Trezevant **z** 38258; ● 30
Winklers Crossroads; RMC Place; MACON; ***233** A-14; elev. 937ft./286m.; mail Red Boiling Springs **z** 37150; rural
Winner; RMC Place; CARTER; **233** K-19; elev. 1,752ft./534m.; ★ **JNSC-**; mail Elizabethton **z** 37643; ● 120
Winona; RMC Place; SCOTT; ***233** B-18; elev. 1,188ft./362m.; mail Huntsville **z** 37756; ● 120
Winton Town; RMC Place; COFFEE; ***233** F-13; mail Manchester **z** 37355; rural
Wirmingham; RMC Place; OVERTON; ***233** B-16; elev. 1,011ft./308m.; mail Monroe **z** 38573; rural
Withamtown; RMC Place; SUMNER; ***233** B-12; mail Bethpage **z** 37022; rural
Witt; RMC Place; HAMBLEN; **233** L-16; ★ **MORR**; mail Morristown **z** 37813; ● 150
Wixtown; RMC Place; MACON; ***233** B-13; elev. 1,020ft./311m.; mail Westmoreland **z** 37186; rural
Wolf Creek; RMC Place; COCKE; ***233** L-17; elev. 1,192ft./363m.; mail Del Rio **z** 37727; ● 50
Wolf Creek; DEKALB; see Laurel Hill (RMC Place)
Wolf Creek; RMC Place; RHEA; ***233** E-17; elev. 763ft./233m.; mail Spring City **z** 37381; ● 200
Wolf Hill; RMC Place; SUMNER; ***233** B-13; mail Bethpage **z** 37022; rural
Wolf River; RMC Place; FENTRESS; ***233** B-16; mail Pall Mall **z** 38577; rural
Womack; RMC Place; SUMNER; ***233** B-12; mail Gallatin **z** 37066; ● 30
Womack; RMC Place; WARREN; ***233** E-14; mail Mc Minnville **z** 37110; rural
Woodbine; RMC Place; DAVIDSON; ***233** C-11; ★ **NASH**; mail Nashville **z** 37211, **z** 37222; pop. incl. with Nashville (Inc. Place)
Woodbury; Inc. Place; ⊡ CANNON; **233** D-13; elev. 735ft./224m.; 🅿 Ⓗ; **z** 37190; Ⓟ 2,287; Ⓒ 2,428
Woodcliff; RMC Place; PUTNAM; ***233** C-15; elev. 1,834ft./559m.; mail Monterey **z** 38574; rural
Wooddale; RMC Place; KNOX; ***233** D-20; ★ **KNOX**; mail Knoxville **z** 37914; rural
Wooded Acres; RMC Place; KNOX; ★ **KNOX**; mail Knoxville **z** 37921; pop. incl. with Knoxville (Inc. Place)
Woodland; RMC Place; DAVIDSON; ★ **NASH**; mail Nashville **z** 37206; pop. incl. with Nashville (Inc. Place)
Woodland; RMC Place; HAYWOOD; ***232** E-4; elev. 385ft./117m.; mail Brownsville **z** 38012; rural
Woodland Acres; RMC Place; KNOX; ***233** D-19; ★ **KNOX**; mail Knoxville **z** 37919; ● 420
Woodland Acres; RMC Place; MCMINN; ***233** F-17; elev. 800ft./244m.; mail Calhoun **z** 37309, Riceville **z** 37370; ● 50
Woodland Heights; RMC Place; HAMILTON; ***233** G-15; ★ **CHTN**; pop. incl. with Chattanooga (Inc. Place)
Woodland Mills; Inc. Place; OBION; **232** B-4; elev. 368ft./112m.; 🅿; **z** 38271; Ⓟ 398; Ⓒ 296
Woodlawn; RMC Place; CUMBERLAND; ***233** D-16; elev. 1,787ft./545m.; mail Crossville **z** 38555; ● 80
Woodlawn; RMC Place; MONTGOMERY; **232** B-9; elev. 632ft./193m.; 🅿; ★ **CLRKV**; **z** 37191; ● 300
Woodlawn; RMC Place; WASHINGTON; ***233** K-18; ★ **JNSC-**; mail Jonesborough **z** 37659; ● 50
Woodlawn; RMC Place; WAYNE; **232** G-8; mail Collinwood **z** 38450; ● 400
Woodmont; RMC Place; DAVIDSON; ★ **NASH**; mail Nashville **z** 37215; pop. incl. with Nashville (Inc. Place)
Woodrow; RMC Place; SULLIVAN; ***233** J-18; ★ **JNSC-**; mail Blountville **z** 37617; rural
Woodstock; RMC Place; SHELBY; ***232** F-1; ★ **MEM**; mail Millington **z** 38053; rural
Woods Valley; RMC Place; DICKSON; ***232** C-9; mail Cumberland Furnace **z** 37051; ● 40
Woodville; RMC Place; CHESTER; ***232** F-5; elev. 462ft./141m.; mail Bethel Springs **z** 38315; rural
Woodville; RMC Place; HAYWOOD; **232** D-3; mail Ripley **z** 38063; ● 30
Woody; RMC Place; CUMBERLAND; ***233** C-16; elev. 1,900ft./579m.; mail Crossville **z** 38571; rural
Wooldridge; RMC Place; CAMPBELL; ***233** B-19; elev. 1,028ft./313m.; mail Jellico **z** 37762; ● 50
Worley; RMC Place; HAMILTON; ***233** G-16; ★ **CHTN**; pop. incl. with Chattanooga (Inc. Place)
Wright; RMC Place; KNOX; pop. incl. with Knoxville (Inc. Place)
Wrigley; RMC Place; HICKMAN; **232** D-9; elev. 800ft./244m.; 🅿; **z** 37098; ● 450
Wyatts Chapel; RMC Place; STEWART; ***232** B-8; elev. 704ft./215m.; mail Dover **z** 37058; rural
Wyatt Village; RMC Place; GRAINGER; ***233** K-16; ★ **MORR**; mail Bean Station **z** 37708; ● 300
Wynn; RMC Place; CAMPBELL; ***233** B-19; elev. 1,320ft./402m.; mail La Follette **z** 37766; ● 80
Wynnburg; RMC Place; LAKE; **232** B-3; elev. 286ft./87m.; 🅿; **z** 38077; ● 200

Y

Yager; RMC Place; WARREN; ***233** E-14; mail Mc Minnville **z** 37110; rural
Yankeetown; RMC Place; WHITE; ***233** D-15; elev. 975ft./297m.; mail Sparta **z** 38583; ● 70
Yateston (Central View); RMC Place; WHITE; ***233** D-14; elev. 301ft./92m.; mail Walling **z** 38587; ● 30
Yell; RMC Place; MARSHALL; ***233** F-11; mail Lewisburg **z** 37091; rural
Yellow Store; RMC Place; HAWKINS; ***233** J-17; mail Surgoinsville **z** 37873; rural
Yett Addition; RMC Place; SEVIER; mail Sevierville **z** 37876; pop. incl. with Sevierville (Inc. Place)
Yettland; RMC Place; SEVIER; ***233** D-20; ★ **KNOX**; mail Sevierville **z** 37876; pop. incl. with Sevierville (Inc. Place)
Yorkley; RMC Place; GILES; ***232** F-10; elev. 900ft./274m.; mail Lynnville **z** 38472; rural
Yorktown; RMC Place; WILLIAMSON; ***233** D-11; ★ **NASH**; mail Franklin **z** 37064; pop. incl. with Franklin (Inc. Place)
Yorkville; Inc. Place; GIBSON; **232** C-4; elev. 330ft./101m.; 🅿; **z** 38389; Ⓟ 347; Ⓒ 293
Young Bend; RMC Place; DEKALB; ***233** D-14; mail Smithville **z** 37166; ● 50
Youngs; MADISON; see Youngs Crossing (RMC Place)
Youngs Crossing (Youngs); RMC Place; MADISON; ***232** D-5; elev. 355ft./108m.; ★ **JAC**; mail Jackson **z** 38301; rural
Youngville; RMC Place; ROBERTSON; ***233** B-11; mail Springfield **z** 37172; rural
Y Section (Embreeville Junction); RMC Place; WASHINGTON; ***233** K-18; ★ **JNSC-**; mail Johnson City **z** 37601; pop. incl. with Johnson City (Inc. Place)
Yukon; RMC Place; LINCOLN; ***233** G-11; mail Taft **z** 38488; rural
Yuma; RMC Place; CARROLL; **232** D-6; elev. 483ft./147m.; 🅿; **z** 38390; ● 180
Yum Yum; RMC Place; FAYETTE; ***232** F-3; mail Somerville **z** 38068; rural

Z

Zack; RMC Place; BENTON; mail Camden **z** 38320
Zion Acres; MAURY; see Ashwood (RMC Place)
Zion Grove; RMC Place; SEVIER; ***233** D-20; elev. 1,600ft./488m.; mail Sevierville **z** 37862; rural
Zion Hill; RMC Place; HAWKINS; ***233** J-17; mail Rogersville **z** 37857; pop. incl. with Surgoinsville (Inc. Place)
Zion Hill; RMC Place; MCMINN; ***233** F-18; elev. 840ft./256m.; mail Englewood **z** 37329; rural

Entries in **UPPERCASE** are counties.
Entries in **bold** have populations of 2,500 or more.
Names in parentheses are alternate names.
Inc. Place — Incorporated Place
RMC Place — Rand McNally Designated Place
CDP — Census Designated Place
MCD — Minor Civil Division

⊡ County Seat
▲ Minor Civil Division
elev. Elevation
🅿 Post Office

Ⓗ Hospital
Ⓒ College
■ Principal Business Center
★ Ranally Metro Area (RMA) Abbreviation
z Zip Code(s)

Ⓟ Previous Census Population
Ⓡ Revised Census Population
Ⓐ Annexation Population
● Rand McNally Population Estimate
Ⓒ Final Census Population
Ⓢ Special Census Population
◆ Estimated Population

For additional definitions see Glossary, Volume 1, and Introduction, Volume 2.

TEXAS

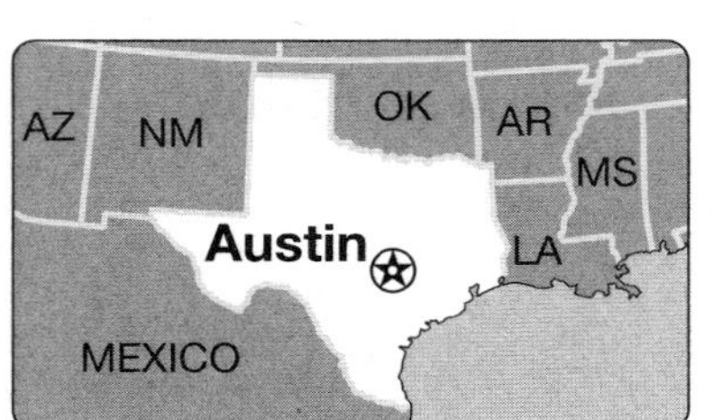

Statistics

Total area (2000) — 268,581 square miles
Land area (2000) — 261,797 square miles
Water area (2000) — 6,784 square miles
Capital — Austin
Admitted as state — December, 1845

Maps

State maps can be found on pages 142-254 in Vol. 1

Ranally Metro Areas (RMAs) and Abbreviations

Abilene, TX — ABIL
Amarillo, TX — AMA
Austin, TX — AUS
Beaumont-Port Arthur, TX — B-PA
Brownsville, TX-MEX. — BRNS
Bryan-College Station, TX — BRY-
Corpus Christi, TX — CRPX
Dallas-Fort Worth, TX — D-FW
Denton, TX — DENT
El Paso, TX-NM-MEX. — ELP
Galveston-Texas City, TX — GLV-
Houston, TX — HOU
Killeen-Temple, TX — KILL-
Lake Jackson-Freeport, TX — L.JAC-
Laredo, TX-MEX. — LAR
Longview, TX — LNGV
Lubbock, TX — LUB
Lufkin, TX — LUFK
Marshall, TX — MAR
McAllen, TX — MCAL
Midland-Odessa, TX — MIDL-
San Angelo, TX — SANG
San Antonio, TX — SANT
Sherman-Denison, TX — SHRM-
Shreveport, LA-TX — SHRE
Texarkana-Texarkana, TX-AR — TEXR-
Tyler, TX — TYL
Victoria, TX — VICT
Waco, TX — WACO
Wichita Falls, TX — WIFL

Principal Places

Place Name	Place Type	County	Population
Houston	Inc. Place	HARRIS	◆ 2,282,856
San Antonio	Inc. Place	BEXAR	◆ 1,397,606
Dallas	Inc. Place	DALLAS	◆ 1,307,392
Austin	Inc. Place	TRAVIS	◆ 859,079
Fort Worth	Inc. Place	TARRANT	◆ 738,712
El Paso	Inc. Place	EL PASO	◆ 614,182
Arlington	Inc. Place	TARRANT	◆ 403,625
Corpus Christi	Inc. Place	NUECES	◆ 281,027
Plano	Inc. Place	COLLIN	◆ 254,896
Garland	Inc. Place	DALLAS	◆ 232,052
Lubbock	Inc. Place	LUBBOCK	◆ 228,217
Laredo	Inc. Place	WEBB	◆ 211,457
Irving	Inc. Place	DALLAS	◆ 209,555
Amarillo	Inc. Place	POTTER	◆ 167,776
Pasadena	Inc. Place	HARRIS	◆ 158,911
Brownsville	Inc. Place	CAMERON	◆ 158,733
Grand Prairie	Inc. Place	DALLAS	◆ 148,394
Mesquite	Inc. Place	DALLAS	◆ 136,194
McKinney	Inc. Place	COLLIN	◆ 136,046
Abilene	Inc. Place	TAYLOR	◆ 128,599
Carrollton	Inc. Place	DALLAS	◆ 128,198
McAllen	Inc. Place	HIDALGO	◆ 127,022
Waco	Inc. Place	MCLENNAN	◆ 125,588
Killeen	Inc. Place	BELL	◆ 125,106
Denton	Inc. Place	DENTON	◆ 110,749
Wichita Falls	Inc. Place	WICHITA	◆ 108,458
Midland	Inc. Place	MIDLAND	◆ 107,795
Lewisville	Inc. Place	DENTON	◆ 107,679
Beaumont	Inc. Place	JEFFERSON	◆ 105,954
Odessa	Inc. Place	ECTOR	◆ 102,313
Richardson	Inc. Place	DALLAS	◆ 100,561
Tyler	Inc. Place	SMITH	◆ 96,120
San Angelo	Inc. Place	TOM GREEN	◆ 93,962
Round Rock	Inc. Place	WILLIAMSON	◆ 93,959
College Station	Inc. Place	BRAZOS	◆ 91,893
Bryan	Inc. Place	BRAZOS	◆ 83,439
The Woodlands	CDP-Census Area Only	MONTGOMERY	◆ 83,306
Sugar Land	Inc. Place	FORT BEND	◆ 78,783
Frisco	Inc. Place	COLLIN	◆ 78,080
Longview	Inc. Place	GREGG	◆ 75,338
Flower Mound	Inc. Place	DENTON	◆ 75,305
Baytown	Inc. Place	HARRIS	◆ 74,781
Allen	Inc. Place	COLLIN	◆ 71,527
Edinburg	Inc. Place	HIDALGO	◆ 70,849
Temple	Inc. Place	BELL	◆ 68,316
Missouri City	Inc. Place	FORT BEND	◆ 68,037
North Richland Hills	Inc. Place	TARRANT	◆ 66,542
Harlingen	Inc. Place	CAMERON	◆ 62,031
Victoria	Inc. Place	VICTORIA	◆ 61,797
Mission	Inc. Place	HIDALGO	◆ 61,732
Pharr	Inc. Place	HIDALGO	◆ 60,973
League City	Inc. Place	GALVESTON	◆ 60,805
Pearland	Inc. Place	BRAZORIA	◆ 58,929
Galveston	Inc. Place	GALVESTON	◆ 54,977
Cedar Park	Inc. Place	WILLIAMSON	◆ 54,434
Port Arthur	Inc. Place	JEFFERSON	◆ 53,652
Euless	Inc. Place	TARRANT	◆ 53,099
Rowlett	Inc. Place	DALLAS	◆ 51,939
New Braunfels	Inc. Place	COMAL	◆ 50,829
Bedford	Inc. Place	TARRANT	◆ 50,328
Conroe	Inc. Place	MONTGOMERY	◆ 50,181
Grapevine	Inc. Place	TARRANT	◆ 50,070
Mission Bend	CDP-Census Area Only	FORT BEND	◆ 47,084
San Marcos	Inc. Place	HAYS	◆ 44,841
Mansfield	Inc. Place	TARRANT	◆ 44,808
Fort Hood	CDP-Census Area Only	BELL	◆ 44,543
Haltom City	Inc. Place	TARRANT	◆ 43,252
Spring	CDP	HARRIS	◆ 43,030
Texas City	Inc. Place	GALVESTON	◆ 42,966
Georgetown	Inc. Place	WILLIAMSON	◆ 42,825
Atascocita	CDP-Census Area Only	HARRIS	◆ 42,289
DeSoto	Inc. Place	DALLAS	◆ 41,547
Coppell	Inc. Place	DALLAS	◆ 40,827
Keller	Inc. Place	TARRANT	◆ 39,507
Hurst	Inc. Place	TARRANT	◆ 39,241
Cedar Hill	Inc. Place	DALLAS	◆ 37,955
Duncanville	Inc. Place	DALLAS	◆ 37,428
Kingwood	RMC Place	HARRIS	Ⓟ 37,397
Sherman	Inc. Place	GRAYSON	◆ 37,017
The Colony	Inc. Place	DENTON	◆ 36,595
Huntsville	Inc. Place	WALKER	◆ 36,485
San Juan	Inc. Place	HIDALGO	◆ 36,197
La Porte	Inc. Place	HARRIS	◆ 35,968
Texarkana	Inc. Place	BOWIE	◆ 35,955
Rockwall	Inc. Place	ROCKWALL	◆ 35,637
Del Rio	Inc. Place	VAL VERDE	◆ 35,261
Channelview	CDP	HARRIS	◆ 35,118
Schertz	Inc. Place	GUADALUPE	◆ 33,581
Lufkin	Inc. Place	ANGELINA	◆ 32,685
Friendswood	Inc. Place	GALVESTON	◆ 32,375
Deer Park	Inc. Place	HARRIS	◆ 32,124
Weslaco	Inc. Place	HIDALGO	◆ 31,458
Socorro	Inc. Place	EL PASO	◆ 31,222
Rosenberg	Inc. Place	FORT BEND	◆ 31,027
Southlake	Inc. Place	TARRANT	◆ 30,637
Wylie	Inc. Place	COLLIN	◆ 30,315
Nacogdoches	Inc. Place	NACOGDOCHES	◆ 29,641
Lancaster	Inc. Place	DALLAS	◆ 29,562
Lake Jackson	Inc. Place	BRAZORIA	◆ 28,388
Farmers Branch	Inc. Place	DALLAS	◆ 28,311
Cleburne	Inc. Place	JOHNSON	◆ 28,043
Cloverleaf	CDP	HARRIS	◆ 27,798
Burleson	Inc. Place	JOHNSON	◆ 27,189
Big Spring	Inc. Place	HOWARD	◆ 27,034
Waxahachie	Inc. Place	ELLIS	◆ 26,640
Eagle Pass	Inc. Place	MAVERICK	◆ 25,979
Pflugerville	Inc. Place	TRAVIS	◆ 25,530
Corsicana	Inc. Place	NAVARRO	◆ 25,420
Paris	Inc. Place	LAMAR	◆ 25,286
University Park	Inc. Place	DALLAS	◆ 25,220
Greenville	Inc. Place	HUNT	◆ 25,062
Colleyville	Inc. Place	TARRANT	◆ 25,034
Kingsville	Inc. Place	KLEBERG	◆ 24,805
Weatherford	Inc. Place	PARKER	◆ 24,194
Seguin	Inc. Place	GUADALUPE	◆ 24,127
Alvin	Inc. Place	BRAZORIA	◆ 23,752
Harker Heights	Inc. Place	BELL	◆ 23,734
San Benito	Inc. Place	CAMERON	◆ 23,700
Watauga	Inc. Place	TARRANT	◆ 23,582
Copperas Cove	Inc. Place	CORYELL	◆ 23,347
Benbrook	Inc. Place	TARRANT	◆ 23,046
Marshall	Inc. Place	HARRISON	◆ 23,044
Kerrville	Inc. Place	KERR	◆ 22,357
Denison	Inc. Place	GRAYSON	◆ 22,296
Corinth	Inc. Place	DENTON	◆ 21,658
Plainview	Inc. Place	HALE	◆ 20,970
Balch Springs	Inc. Place	DALLAS	◆ 20,057
Alice	Inc. Place	JIM WELLS	© 19,010
Palestine	Inc. Place	ANDERSON	◆ 18,520
Pampa	Inc. Place	GRAY	◆ 18,433
Angleton	Inc. Place	BRAZORIA	© 18,130
Saginaw	Inc. Place	TARRANT	◆ 18,055
Brownwood	Inc. Place	BROWN	◆ 17,945
West Odessa	CDP-Census Area Only	ECTOR	© 17,799
Bay City	Inc. Place	MATAGORDA	◆ 17,468
Nederland	Inc. Place	JEFFERSON	© 17,422
Dickinson	Inc. Place	GALVESTON	© 17,093
Mineral Wells	Inc. Place	PALO PINTO	© 16,946
Canyon Lake	CDP-Census Area Only	COMAL	© 16,870
Orange	Inc. Place	ORANGE	◆ 16,507
Humble	Inc. Place	HARRIS	◆ 16,359
Ennis	Inc. Place	ELLIS	© 16,045
South Houston	Inc. Place	HARRIS	© 15,833
Jollyville	CDP	WILLIAMSON	© 15,813
Groves	Inc. Place	JEFFERSON	© 15,733
Stafford	Inc. Place	FORT BEND	© 15,681
Bellaire	Inc. Place	HARRIS	© 15,642
Gatesville	Inc. Place	CORYELL	© 15,591
Gainesville	Inc. Place	COOKE	© 15,538
Addison	Inc. Place	DALLAS	◆ 15,382
Brushy Creek	CDP-Census Area Only	WILLIAMSON	© 15,371
Uvalde	Inc. Place	UVALDE	© 14,929
Stephenville	Inc. Place	ERATH	© 14,921
Universal City	Inc. Place	BEXAR	© 14,849
White Settlement	Inc. Place	TARRANT	© 14,831
Portland	Inc. Place	SAN PATRICIO	© 14,827
Donna	Inc. Place	HIDALGO	© 14,768
Alamo	Inc. Place	HIDALGO	© 14,760
Kyle	Inc. Place	HAYS	◆ 14,662
Mount Pleasant	Inc. Place	TITUS	◆ 14,636
Belton	Inc. Place	BELL	© 14,623
Hereford	Inc. Place	DEAF SMITH	© 14,597
Sulphur Springs	Inc. Place	HOPKINS	© 14,551
Jacksonville	Inc. Place	CHEROKEE	◆ 14,316
West University Place	Inc. Place	HARRIS	© 14,211
Aldine	CDP	HARRIS	© 13,979
New Territory	CDP-Census Area Only	FORT BEND	© 13,861
Freeport	Inc. Place	BRAZORIA	◆ 13,858
Dumas	Inc. Place	MOORE	© 13,747
La Marque	Inc. Place	GALVESTON	© 13,682
Mercedes	Inc. Place	HIDALGO	© 13,649
Terrell	Inc. Place	KAUFMAN	© 13,606
Port Neches	Inc. Place	JEFFERSON	© 13,601
Leander	Inc. Place	WILLIAMSON	◆ 13,581
Taylor	Inc. Place	WILLIAMSON	© 13,575
Pecan Grove	CDP-Census Area Only	FORT BEND	© 13,551
Brenham	Inc. Place	WASHINGTON	© 13,507
Beeville	Inc. Place	BEE	© 13,129
Forest Hill	Inc. Place	TARRANT	© 12,949
Canyon	Inc. Place	RANDALL	© 12,875
Levelland	Inc. Place	HOCKLEY	© 12,866
Robstown	Inc. Place	NUECES	© 12,727
Borger	Inc. Place	HUTCHINSON	◆ 12,554
Highland Village	Inc. Place	DENTON	© 12,173
Port Lavaca	Inc. Place	CALHOUN	© 12,035
Klein	RMC Place	HARRIS	● 12,000
Rio Grande City	Inc. Place	STARR	© 11,923
Katy	Inc. Place	HARRIS	© 11,775
Vernon	Inc. Place	WILBARGER	© 11,660
Lockhart	Inc. Place	CALDWELL	© 11,615
Converse	Inc. Place	BEXAR	© 11,508
Vidor	Inc. Place	ORANGE	© 11,440
Sweetwater	Inc. Place	NOLAN	© 11,415
Kilgore	Inc. Place	GREGG	© 11,301
Athens	Inc. Place	HENDERSON	© 11,297
Henderson	Inc. Place	RUSK	© 11,273
Wells Branch	CDP-Census Area Only	TRAVIS	© 11,271
Cinco Ranch	CDP-Census Area Only	FORT BEND	© 11,196
Hewitt	Inc. Place	MCLENNAN	© 11,085
Richmond	Inc. Place	FORT BEND	© 11,081
San Elizario	CDP	EL PASO	© 11,046
El Campo	Inc. Place	WHARTON	© 10,945
Burkburnett	Inc. Place	WICHITA	© 10,927
Seagoville	Inc. Place	DALLAS	© 10,823
Snyder	Inc. Place	SCURRY	© 10,783
Galena Park	Inc. Place	HARRIS	© 10,592
La Homa	CDP-Census Area Only	HIDALGO	© 10,433
Clute	Inc. Place	BRAZORIA	© 10,424
Jacinto City	Inc. Place	HARRIS	© 10,302
Bonham	Inc. Place	FANNIN	© 9,990
Lamesa	Inc. Place	DAWSON	© 9,952
Sachse	Inc. Place	DALLAS	Ⓡ 9,884
Raymondville	Inc. Place	WILLACY	© 9,733
Andrews	Inc. Place	ANDREWS	© 9,652
Roma-Los Saenz	Inc. Place	STARR	© 9,617
Azle	Inc. Place	TARRANT	© 9,600
Santa Fe	Inc. Place	GALVESTON	© 9,548
Pecos	Inc. Place	REEVES	© 9,501
Brownfield	Inc. Place	TERRY	© 9,488
Seabrook	Inc. Place	HARRIS	© 9,443
Ingleside	Inc. Place	SAN PATRICIO	© 9,388
Eidson Road	CDP-Census Area Only	MAVERICK	© 9,348
Little Elm	Inc. Place	DENTON	◆ 9,319
Leon Valley	Inc. Place	BEXAR	© 9,239
Wharton	Inc. Place	WHARTON	© 9,237
Bellmead	Inc. Place	MCLENNAN	© 9,214
Live Oak	Inc. Place	BEXAR	© 9,156
Tomball	Inc. Place	HARRIS	© 9,089
Webster	Inc. Place	HARRIS	© 9,083
Rendon	CDP	TARRANT	© 9,022
Anderson Mill	CDP-Census Area Only	TRAVIS	© 8,953
Fredericksburg	Inc. Place	GILLESPIE	© 8,911
Highland Park	Inc. Place	DALLAS	© 8,842
Woodway	Inc. Place	MCLENNAN	© 8,733
Lumberton	Inc. Place	HARDIN	© 8,731
Graham	Inc. Place	YOUNG	© 8,716
Kirby	Inc. Place	BEXAR	© 8,673
Bridge City	Inc. Place	ORANGE	© 8,651
Pleasanton	Inc. Place	ATASCOSA	© 8,266
Fort Bliss	CDP-Census Area Only	EL PASO	© 8,264
Hillsboro	Inc. Place	HILL	© 8,232
Aransas Pass	Inc. Place	SAN PATRICIO	© 8,138
Richland Hills	Inc. Place	TARRANT	© 8,132
Fabens	CDP	EL PASO	© 8,043
Liberty	Inc. Place	LIBERTY	© 8,033
Lakeway	Inc. Place	TRAVIS	© 8,002
Beaumont Place	RMC Place	HARRIS	● 8,000
Hondo	Inc. Place	MEDINA	© 7,897
Fort Stockton	Inc. Place	PECOS	© 7,846
Robinson	Inc. Place	MCLENNAN	© 7,845
Perryton	Inc. Place	OCHILTREE	© 7,774
Commerce	Inc. Place	HUNT	© 7,669
Jasper	Inc. Place	JASPER	Ⓡ 7,657
Cleveland	Inc. Place	LIBERTY	© 7,605
Midlothian	Inc. Place	ELLIS	© 7,480
Crowley	Inc. Place	TARRANT	© 7,467
Rockport	Inc. Place	ARANSAS	© 7,385
Hidalgo	Inc. Place	HIDALGO	© 7,322
Alamo Heights	Inc. Place	BEXAR	© 7,319
Dalhart	Inc. Place	DALLAM	© 7,237
Glenn Heights	Inc. Place	DALLAS	© 7,224
Gonzales	Inc. Place	GONZALES	© 7,202
Crystal City	Inc. Place	ZAVALA	© 7,190
Pearsall	Inc. Place	FRIO	© 7,157
Crockett	Inc. Place	HOUSTON	© 7,141
Lackland AFB	CDP-Census Area Only	BEXAR	© 7,123
Highlands	CDP	HARRIS	© 7,089
Porter	RMC Place	MONTGOMERY	● 7,000
River Oaks	Inc. Place	TARRANT	© 6,985
Bacliff	CDP	GALVESTON	© 6,962
Jersey Village	Inc. Place	HARRIS	© 6,880
Windemere	CDP-Census Area Only	TRAVIS	© 6,868
Monahans	Inc. Place	WARD	© 6,821
Homestead Meadows South	CDP-Census Area Only	EL PASO	© 6,807
Navasota	Inc. Place	GRIMES	© 6,789
Lampasas	Inc. Place	LAMPASAS	© 6,786
Childress	Inc. Place	CHILDRESS	© 6,778
Carthage	Inc. Place	PANOLA	© 6,664
Greatwood	CDP-Census Area Only	FORT BEND	© 6,640
Marlin	Inc. Place	FALLS	© 6,628
West Livingston	CDP-Census Area Only	POLK	© 6,612
Fresno	CDP	FORT BEND	© 6,603
Eagle Mountain	CDP-Census Area Only	TARRANT	© 6,599
Cuero	Inc. Place	DEWITT	© 6,571
Mexia	Inc. Place	LIMESTONE	© 6,563
Littlefield	Inc. Place	LAMB	© 6,507
Kaufman	Inc. Place	KAUFMAN	© 6,490
Iowa Park	Inc. Place	WICHITA	© 6,431
Silsbee	Inc. Place	HARDIN	© 6,393
Hitchcock	Inc. Place	GALVESTON	© 6,386
Trophy Club	Inc. Place	DENTON	© 6,350
Palmview South	CDP-Census Area Only	HIDALGO	© 6,219
Boerne	Inc. Place	KENDALL	© 6,178
Lake Dallas	Inc. Place	DENTON	© 6,166
Town West	RMC Place	FORT BEND	Ⓟ 6,166
La Feria	Inc. Place	CAMERON	© 6,115
Slaton	Inc. Place	LUBBOCK	© 6,109
Gladewater	Inc. Place	GREGG	© 6,078
Cameron Park	CDP-Census Area Only	CAMERON	© 5,961
Seminole	Inc. Place	GAINES	© 5,910
Edna	Inc. Place	JACKSON	© 5,899
Timberwood Park	CDP-Census Area Only	BEXAR	© 5,889
Breckenridge	Inc. Place	STEPHENS	© 5,868
Floresville	Inc. Place	WILSON	© 5,868
Kennedale	Inc. Place	TARRANT	© 5,850
Everman	Inc. Place	TARRANT	© 5,836
Alpine	Inc. Place	BREWSTER	© 5,786
Lacy-Lakeview	Inc. Place	MCLENNAN	© 5,764
Atlanta	Inc. Place	CASS	© 5,745
Yoakum	Inc. Place	DEWITT	© 5,731
Granbury	Inc. Place	HOOD	© 5,718
Kermit	Inc. Place	WINKLER	© 5,714
Dayton	Inc. Place	LIBERTY	© 5,709
Elgin	Inc. Place	BASTROP	© 5,700
Center	Inc. Place	SHELBY	© 5,678
Sinton	Inc. Place	SAN PATRICIO	© 5,676
Carrizo Springs	Inc. Place	DIMMIT	© 5,655
Cameron	Inc. Place	MILAM	© 5,634
White Oak	Inc. Place	GREGG	© 5,624
Forney	Inc. Place	KAUFMAN	© 5,588
Rio Bravo	Inc. Place	WEBB	© 5,553
Elsa	Inc. Place	HIDALGO	© 5,549
Brady	Inc. Place	MCCULLOCH	© 5,523
Diboll	Inc. Place	ANGELINA	© 5,470
Abram-Perezville	CDP-Census Area Only	HIDALGO	© 5,444
Rockdale	Inc. Place	MILAM	© 5,439
Livingston	Inc. Place	POLK	© 5,433
Briar	CDP-Census Area Only	TARRANT	© 5,350
Whitehouse	Inc. Place	SMITH	© 5,346
Bastrop	Inc. Place	BASTROP	© 5,340
Falfurrias	Inc. Place	BROOKS	© 5,297
Sealy	Inc. Place	AUSTIN	© 5,248
Horizon City	Inc. Place	EL PASO	© 5,233
Bowie	Inc. Place	MONTAGUE	© 5,219
Decatur	Inc. Place	WISE	© 5,201
Palacios	Inc. Place	MATAGORDA	© 5,153
Gun Barrel City	Inc. Place	HENDERSON	© 5,145
Shady Hollow	CDP-Census Area Only	TRAVIS	© 5,140
Canutillo	CDP	EL PASO	© 5,129
Wake Village	Inc. Place	BOWIE	© 5,129
Coleman	Inc. Place	COLEMAN	© 5,127
Tulia	Inc. Place	SWISHER	© 5,117
Giddings	Inc. Place	LEE	© 5,105
Windcrest	Inc. Place	BEXAR	© 5,105
Rusk	Inc. Place	CHEROKEE	© 5,085
Luling	Inc. Place	CALDWELL	© 5,080
Nurillo	CDP-Census Area Only	HIDALGO	© 5,056
Alton North	CDP-Census Area Only	HIDALGO	© 5,051
Mathis	Inc. Place	SAN PATRICIO	© 5,034
Terrell Hills	Inc. Place	BEXAR	© 5,019
Keene	Inc. Place	JOHNSON	© 5,003

County Business Data

County	FIPS Code	County Seat	Land Area (Sq. Mi.)	Census Population			Wholesale Trade		Manufacturing, 2002			
				4/1/2000	4/1/1990	% Change 1990-2000	Sales, 2002 ($1,000)	% Change 1997-2002	Establish-ments	Total Employees	Value Added ($1,000)	Ranally Mfg. Units
Anderson	001	Palestine	1,071	55,109	48,024	14.8	104,770	-36.9	...	(d)	(d)	...
Andrews	003	Andrews	1,501	13,004	14,338	-9.3	(d)	(d)	...	(d)	(d)	...
Angelina	005	Lufkin	802	80,130	69,884	14.7	829,215	187.7	79	6,079	420,874	223
Aransas	007	Rockport	252	22,497	17,892	25.7	(d)	(d)	...	(d)	(d)	...
Archer	009	Archer City	910	8,854	7,973	11.0	(d)	(d)	...	(d)	(d)	...
Armstrong	011	Claude	914	2,148	2,021	6.3	(d)	(d)	...	(d)	(d)	...
Atascosa	013	Jourdanton	1,232	38,628	30,533	26.5	93,753	4.6	...	(d)	(d)	...
Austin	015	Bellville	653	23,590	19,832	18.9	(d)	(d)	39	(d)	(d)	...
Bailey	017	Muleshoe	827	6,594	7,064	-6.7	96,959	-13.5	...	(d)	(d)	...
Bandera	019	Bandera	792	17,645	10,562	67.1	(d)	(d)	...	(d)	(d)	...
Bastrop	021	Bastrop	888	57,733	38,263	50.9	(d)	(d)	55	1,055	96,422	51
Baylor	023	Seymour	871	4,093	4,385	-6.7	27,155	(d)	...	(d)	(d)	...
Bee	025	Beeville	880	32,359	25,135	28.7	(d)	(d)	...	(d)	(d)	...
Bell	027	Belton	1,060	237,974	191,088	24.5	1,806,227	(d)	140	8,236	931,638	493
Bexar	029	San Antonio	1,247	1,392,931	1,185,394	17.5	16,073,053	27.2	1,019	35,121	3,035,203	1,606
Blanco	031	Johnson City	711	8,418	5,972	41.0	(d)	(d)	...	(d)	(d)	...
Borden	033	Gail	899	729	799	-8.8	(d)	(d)	...	(d)	(d)	...
Bosque	035	Meridian	989	17,204	15,125	13.7	67,391	6.5	...	(d)	(d)	...
Bowie	037	Boston	888	89,306	81,665	9.4	(d)	(d)	70	3,264	465,661	246
Brazoria	039	Angleton	1,386	241,767	191,707	26.1	780,574	-7.1	227	13,746	4,596,289	2,432
Brazos	041	Bryan	586	152,415	121,862	25.1	519,718	21.8	112	4,897	339,367	180
Brewster	043	Alpine	6,193	8,866	8,681	2.1	23,321	27.4	...	(d)	(d)	...
Briscoe	045	Silverton	900	1,790	1,971	-9.2	6,424	(d)	...	(d)	(d)	...
Brooks	047	Falfurrias	943	7,976	8,204	-2.8	(d)	(d)	...	(d)	(d)	...
Brown	049	Brownwood	944	37,674	34,371	9.6	123,366	28.9	38	2,768	497,755	263
Burleson	051	Caldwell	666	16,470	13,625	20.9	(d)	(d)	...	(d)	(d)	...
Burnet	053	Burnet	996	34,147	22,677	50.6	65,912	88.6	48	752	58,114	31
Caldwell	055	Lockhart	546	32,194	26,392	22.0	(d)	(d)	...	(d)	(d)	...
Calhoun	057	Port Lavaca	512	20,647	19,053	8.4	(d)	(d)	22	(d)	(d)	...
Callahan	059	Baird	899	12,905	11,859	8.8	(d)	(d)	...	(d)	(d)	...
Cameron	061	Brownsville	906	335,227	260,120	28.9	(d)	(d)	242	9,678	758,186	401
Camp	063	Pittsburg	198	11,549	9,904	16.6	2,834	-78.5	...	(d)	(d)	...
Carson	065	Panhandle	923	6,516	6,576	-0.9	(d)	(d)	...	(d)	(d)	...
Cass	067	Linden	937	30,438	29,982	1.5	96,242	-9.9	24	520	27,691	15
Castro	069	Dimmitt	898	8,285	9,070	-8.7	(d)	(d)	...	(d)	(d)	...
Chambers	071	Anahuac	599	26,031	20,088	29.6	(d)	(d)	15	(d)	(d)	...
Cherokee	073	Rusk	1,052	46,659	41,049	13.7	(d)	(d)	82	2,911	198,626	105
Childress	075	Childress	710	7,688	5,953	29.1	15,533	-69.9	...	(d)	(d)	...
Clay	077	Henrietta	1,098	11,006	10,024	9.8	(d)	(d)	...	(d)	(d)	...
Cochran	079	Morton	775	3,730	4,377	-14.8	946	-88.0	...	(d)	(d)	...
Coke	081	Robert Lee	899	3,864	3,424	12.9	(d)	(d)	...	(d)	(d)	...
Coleman	083	Coleman	1,260	9,235	9,710	-4.9	29,857	-0.1	...	(d)	(d)	...
Collin	085	McKinney	848	491,675	264,036	86.2	14,503,286	102.3	404	21,271	2,001,275	1,059
Collingsworth	087	Wellington	919	3,206	3,573	-10.3	3,310	-55.2	...	(d)	(d)	...
Colorado	089	Columbus	963	20,390	18,383	10.9	77,423	-8.8	32	512	43,033	23
Comal	091	New Braunfels	561	78,021	51,832	50.5	423,694	32.4	101	3,272	336,585	178
Comanche	093	Comanche	938	14,026	13,381	4.8	66,180	-46.9	...	(d)	(d)	...
Concho	095	Paint Rock	991	3,966	3,044	30.3	(d)	(d)	...	(d)	(d)	...
Cooke	097	Gainesville	874	36,363	30,777	18.1	101,528	-0.9	67	4,399	265,807	141
Coryell	099	Gatesville	1,052	74,978	64,213	16.8	(d)	(d)	...	(d)	(d)	...
Cottle	101	Paducah	901	1,904	2,247	-15.3	(d)	(d)	...	(d)	(d)	...
Crane	103	Crane	786	3,996	4,652	-14.1	(d)	(d)	...	(d)	(d)	...
Crockett	105	Ozona	2,807	4,099	4,078	0.5	3,323	-50.2	...	(d)	(d)	...
Crosby	107	Crosbyton	900	7,072	7,304	-3.2	(d)	(d)	...	(d)	(d)	...
Culberson	109	Van Horn	3,812	2,975	3,407	-12.7	(d)	(d)	...	(d)	(d)	...
Dallam	111	Dalhart	1,505	6,222	5,461	13.9	145,600	-24.0	...	(d)	(d)	...
Dallas	113	Dallas	880	2,218,899	1,852,810	19.8	95,278,189	-5.5	2,982	137,547	16,691,677	8,831
Dawson	115	Lamesa	902	14,985	14,349	4.4	49,269	-46.1	...	(d)	(d)	...
Deaf Smith	117	Hereford	1,497	18,561	19,153	-3.1	327,290	171.0	26	701	105,696	56
Delta	119	Cooper	277	5,327	4,857	9.7	(d)	(d)	...	(d)	(d)	...
Denton	121	Denton	889	432,976	273,525	58.3	8,686,466	214.5	351	11,643	1,165,937	617
DeWitt	123	Cuero	909	20,013	18,840	6.2	87,623	1.4	27	847	71,082	38
Dickens	125	Dickens	904	2,762	2,571	7.4	(d)	(d)	...	(d)	(d)	...
Dimmit	127	Carrizo Springs	1,331	10,248	10,433	-1.8	(d)	(d)	...	(d)	(d)	...
Donley	129	Clarendon	930	3,828	3,696	3.6	(d)	(d)	...	(d)	(d)	...
Duval	131	San Diego	1,793	13,120	12,918	1.6	24,958	(d)	...	(d)	(d)	...
Eastland	133	Eastland	926	18,297	18,488	-1.0	263,535	3.1	31	848	52,172	28
Ector	135	Odessa	901	121,123	118,934	1.8	1,048,264	0.1	224	4,101	554,909	294
Edwards	137	Rocksprings	2,120	2,162	2,266	-4.6	(d)	(d)	...	(d)	(d)	...
Ellis	139	Waxahachie	940	111,360	85,167	30.8	332,266	-11.6	170	9,258	1,216,685	644
El Paso	141	El Paso	1,013	679,622	591,610	14.9	4,642,611	-23.8	643	27,796	3,165,254	1,675
Erath	143	Stephenville	1,086	33,001	27,991	17.9	141,977	19.4	41	1,636	194,646	103
Falls	145	Marlin	769	18,576	17,712	4.9	25,633	(d)	...	(d)	(d)	...
Fannin	147	Bonham	891	31,242	24,804	26.0	113,574	-39.5	35	996	85,474	45
Fayette	149	La Grange	950	21,804	20,095	8.5	152,140	-52.2	49	1,081	65,901	35
Fisher	151	Roby	901	4,344	4,842	-10.3	(d)	(d)	...	(d)	(d)	...
Floyd	153	Floydada	992	7,771	8,497	-8.5	(d)	(d)	...	(d)	(d)	...
Foard	155	Crowell	707	1,622	1,794	-9.6	5,810	(d)	...	(d)	(d)	...
Fort Bend	157	Richmond	875	354,452	225,421	57.2	7,621,754	156.4	307	10,675	1,249,654	661
Franklin	159	Mount Vernon	286	9,458	7,802	21.2	(d)	(d)	...	(d)	(d)	...
Freestone	161	Fairfield	877	17,867	15,818	13.0	33,213	25.8	...	(d)	(d)	...
Frio	163	Pearsall	1,133	16,252	13,472	20.6	42,323	(d)	...	(d)	(d)	...
Gaines	165	Seminole	1,502	14,467	14,123	2.4	57,592	-57.5	...	(d)	(d)	...
Galveston	167	Galveston	398	250,158	217,399	15.1	934,513	66.5	176	6,762	1,010,084	534
Garza	169	Post	896	4,872	5,143	-5.3	3,630	-80.6	...	(d)	(d)	...
Gillespie	171	Fredericksburg	1,061	20,814	17,204	21.0	74,447	-17.1	...	(d)	(d)	...
Glasscock	173	Garden City	901	1,406	1,447	-2.8	(d)	(d)	...	(d)	(d)	...
Goliad	175	Goliad	854	6,928	5,980	15.9	(d)	(d)	...	(d)	(d)	...
Gonzales	177	Gonzales	1,068	18,628	17,205	8.3	118,845	-22.5	20	1,131	53,755	28
Gray	179	Pampa	928	22,744	23,967	-5.1	(d)	(d)	21	942	189,828	100
Grayson	181	Sherman	934	110,595	95,021	16.4	390,048	-4.0	132	7,807	1,614,367	854
Gregg	183	Longview	274	111,379	104,948	6.1	1,007,777	-45.9	208	10,203	1,308,911	693
Grimes	185	Anderson	794	23,552	18,828	25.1	108,815	-20.6	24	1,559	188,015	99
Guadalupe	187	Seguin	711	89,023	64,873	37.2	547,148	49.4	100	5,224	685,248	363
Hale	189	Plainview	1,005	36,602	34,671	5.6	242,601	-17.6	28	(d)	(d)	...
Hall	191	Memphis	903	3,782	3,905	-3.1	6,996	-30.5	...	(d)	(d)	...
Hamilton	193	Hamilton	836	8,229	7,733	6.4	41,603	-1.2	...	(d)	(d)	...
Hansford	195	Spearman	920	5,369	5,848	-8.2	58,328	-49.8	...	(d)	(d)	...
Hardeman	197	Quanah	695	4,724	5,283	-10.6	11,888	-2.4	...	(d)	(d)	...
Hardin	199	Kountze	894	48,073	41,320	16.3	(d)	(d)	30	862	76,811	41
Harris	201	Houston	1,729	3,400,578	2,818,199	20.7	135,427,351	22.7	4,224	150,643	25,231,576	13,349
Harrison	203	Marshall	899	62,110	57,483	8.0	228,607	-28.8	75	2,778	280,812	149
Hartley	205	Channing	1,462	5,537	3,634	52.4	34,970	(d)	...	(d)	(d)	...
Haskell	207	Haskell	903	6,093	6,820	-10.7	(d)	(d)	...	(d)	(d)	...
Hays	209	San Marcos	678	97,589	65,614	48.7	240,163	37.9	125	2,908	323,715	171
Hemphill	211	Canadian	910	3,351	3,720	-9.9	15,281	44.9	...	(d)	(d)	...
Henderson	213	Athens	874	73,277	58,543	25.2	139,343	41.7	60	1,910	184,241	97
Hidalgo	215	Edinburg	1,570	569,463	383,545	48.5	3,133,619	58.1	283	7,202	746,312	395
Hill	217	Hillsboro	962	32,321	27,146	19.1	110,147	135.3	41	835	57,723	31
Hockley	219	Levelland	908	22,716	24,199	-6.1	45,098	-44.7	...	(d)	(d)	...
Hood	221	Granbury	422	41,100	28,981	41.8	(d)	(d)	42	(d)	(d)	...
Hopkins	223	Sulphur Springs	782	31,960	28,833	10.8	550,643	-9.3	43	1,550	349,591	185
Houston	225	Crockett	1,231	23,185	21,375	8.5	43,593	-11.8	22	724	66,229	35
Howard	227	Big Spring	903	33,627	32,343	4.0	(d)	(d)	26	960	144,446	76
Hudspeth	229	Sierra Blanca	4,571	3,344	2,915	14.7	(d)	(d)	...	(d)	(d)	...
Hunt	231	Greenville	841	76,596	64,343	19.0	281,413	6.8	64	(d)	(d)	...
Hutchinson	233	Stinnett	887	23,857	25,689	-7.1	48,251	-70.6	19	2,002	413,605	219
Irion	235	Mertzon	1,051	1,771	1,629	8.7	(d)	(d)	...	(d)	(d)	...
Jack	237	Jacksboro	917	8,763	6,981	25.5	37,994	191.3	...	(d)	(d)	...
Jackson	239	Edna	829	14,391	13,039	10.4	34,524	-40.9	8	(d)	(d)	...
Jasper	241	Jasper	937	35,604	31,102	14.5	193,021	86.6	25	1,903	368,353	195
Jeff Davis	243	Fort Davis	2,264	2,207	1,946	13.4	(d)	(d)	...	(d)	(d)	...
Jefferson	245	Beaumont	904	252,051	239,397	5.3	2,303,160	10.7	231	12,746	4,458,875	2,359
Jim Hogg	247	Hebbronville	1,136	5,281	5,109	3.4	7,326	-71.1	...	(d)	(d)	...
Jim Wells	249	Alice	865	39,326	37,679	4.4	166,334	19.0	...	(d)	(d)	...
Johnson	251	Cleburne	729	126,811	97,165	30.5	362,447	38.4	166	4,684	453,484	240
Jones	253	Anson	931	20,785	16,490	26.0	(d)	(d)	...	(d)	(d)	...
Karnes	255	Karnes City	750	15,446	12,455	24.0	63,092	37.6	...	(d)	(d)	...
Kaufman	257	Kaufman	786	71,313	52,220	36.6	273,453	44.5	117	4,046	317,773	168
Kendall	259	Boerne	662	23,743	14,589	62.7	96,808	-31.4	41	818	105,352	56
Kenedy	261	Sarita	1,457	414	460	-10.0	(d)	(d)	...	(d)	(d)	...
Kent	263	Jayton	902	859	1,010	-15.0	(d)	(d)	...	(d)	(d)	...
Kerr	265	Kerrville	1,106	43,653	36,304	20.2	110,850	69.0	51	686	57,865	31
Kimble	267	Junction	1,251	4,468	4,122	8.4	(d)	(d)	...	(d)	(d)	...
King	269	Guthrie	912	356	354	0.6	(d)	(d)	...	(d)	(d)	...
Kinney	271	Brackettville	1,363	3,379	3,119	8.3	(d)	(d)	...	(d)	(d)	...
Kleberg	273	Kingsville	871	31,549	30,274	4.2	(d)	(d)	...	(d)	(d)	...
Knox	275	Benjamin	849	4,253	4,837	-12.1	33,527	12.6	...	(d)	(d)	...
Lamar	277	Paris	917	48,499	43,949	10.4	152,069	-0.2	54	4,472	1,567,092	829
Lamb	279	Littlefield	1,016	14,709	15,072	-2.4	46,960	-35.3	13	693	46,152	24
Lampasas	281	Lampasas	712	17,762	13,521	31.4	(d)	(d)	...	(d)	(d)	...
La Salle	283	Cotulla	1,489	5,866	5,254	11.6	(d)	(d)	...	(d)	(d)	...
Lavaca	285	Hallettsville	970	19,210	18,690	2.8	130,794	-35.5	45	2,093	138,443	73
Lee	287	Giddings	629	15,657	12,854	21.8	47,992	-85.1	...	(d)	(d)	...
Leon	289	Centerville	1,072	15,335	12,665	21.1	74,632	32.9	...	(d)	(d)	...
Liberty	291	Liberty	1,160	70,154	52,726	33.1	(d)	(d)	35	(d)	(d)	...
Limestone	293	Groesbeck	909	22,051	20,946	5.3	55,069	(d)	22	976	72,129	38
Lipscomb	295	Lipscomb	932	3,057	3,143	-2.7	7,760	-38.1	...	(d)	(d)	...
Live Oak	297	George West	1,036	12,309	9,556	28.8	18,569	-27.0	...	(d)	(d)	...

Entries in **UPPERCASE** are counties.
Entries in **bold** have populations of 2,500 or more.
Names in parentheses are alternate names.
Inc. Place — Incorporated Place
RMC Place — Rand McNally Designated Place
CDP — Census Designated Place
MCD — Minor Civil Division

⊡ County Seat
▲ Minor Civil Division
elev. Elevation
Post Office

Hospital
College
■ Principal Business Center
★ Ranally Metro Area (RMA) Abbreviation
z Zip Code(s)

Ⓟ Previous Census Population
Ⓡ Revised Census Population
Ⓐ Annexation Population
● Rand McNally Population Estimate
Ⓒ Final Census Population
Ⓢ Special Census Population
◆ Estimated Population

For additional definitions see Glossary, Volume 1, and Introduction, Volume 2.

County	FIPS Code	County Seat	Land Area (Sq. Mi.)	Census Population			Wholesale Trade		Manufacturing, 2002			
				4/1/2000	4/1/1990	% Change 1990-2000	Sales, 2002 ($1,000)	% Change 1997-2002	Establish-ments	Total Employees	Value Added ($1,000)	Ranally Mfg. Units
Llano	299	Llano	935	17,044	11,631	46.5	87,852	2.8	...	(d)	(d)	...
Loving	301	Mentone	673	67	107	-37.4	(d)	(d)	...	(d)	(d)	...
Lubbock	303	Lubbock	899	242,628	222,636	9.0	(d)	(d)	261	6,018	546,929	289
Lynn	305	Tahoka	892	6,550	6,758	-3.1	6,935	(d)	...	(d)	(d)	...
Madison	313	Madisonville	470	12,940	10,931	18.4	(d)	(d)	...	(d)	(d)	...
Marion	315	Jefferson	381	10,941	9,984	9.6	12,154	-36.5	...	(d)	(d)	...
Martin	317	Stanton	915	4,746	4,956	-4.2	17,040	-23.1	...	(d)	(d)	...
Mason	319	Mason	932	3,738	3,423	9.2	25,925	-32.3	...	(d)	(d)	...
Matagorda	321	Bay City	1,114	37,957	36,928	2.8	(d)	(d)	...	(d)	(d)	...
Maverick	323	Eagle Pass	1,280	47,297	36,378	30.0	70,129	-17.7	...	(d)	(d)	...
McCulloch	307	Brady	1,069	8,205	8,778	-6.5	9,059	-39.1	...	(d)	(d)	...
McLennan	309	Waco	1,042	213,517	189,123	12.9	3,715,668	116.5	247	13,642	2,603,132	1,377
McMullen	311	Tilden	1,113	851	817	4.2	(d)	(d)	...	(d)	(d)	...
Medina	325	Hondo	1,328	39,304	27,312	43.9	58,186	-23.2	21	538	30,654	16
Menard	327	Menard	902	2,360	2,252	4.8	(d)	(d)	...	(d)	(d)	...
Midland	329	Midland	900	116,009	106,611	8.8	988,221	-49.0	119	1,470	115,757	61
Milam	331	Cameron	1,017	24,238	22,946	5.6	62,431	-47.9	14	1,829	294,456	156
Mills	333	Goldthwaite	748	5,151	4,531	13.7	5,614	-80.1	...	(d)	(d)	...
Mitchell	335	Colorado City	910	9,698	8,016	21.0	(d)	(d)	...	(d)	(d)	...
Montague	337	Montague	931	19,117	17,274	10.7	24,560	-54.3	...	(d)	(d)	...
Montgomery	339	Conroe	1,044	293,768	182,201	61.2	2,524,832	18.6	334	7,207	791,983	419
Moore	341	Dumas	900	20,121	17,865	12.6	(d)	(d)	17	(d)	(d)	...
Morris	343	Daingerfield	255	13,048	13,200	-1.2	(d)	(d)	17	2,240	288,793	153
Motley	345	Matador	989	1,426	1,532	-6.9	(d)	(d)	...	(d)	(d)	...
Nacogdoches	347	Nacogdoches	947	59,203	54,753	8.1	157,426	-2.6	69	4,767	470,574	249
Navarro	349	Corsicana	1,008	45,124	39,926	13.0	(d)	(d)	55	3,123	283,768	150
Newton	351	Newton	933	15,072	13,569	11.1	12,166	28.9	...	(d)	(d)	...
Nolan	353	Sweetwater	912	15,802	16,594	-4.8	(d)	(d)	13	834	116,951	62
Nueces	355	Corpus Christi	836	313,645	291,145	7.7	1,811,602	0.5	217	(d)	(d)	...
Ochiltree	357	Perryton	918	9,006	9,128	-1.3	70,167	-10.4	...	(d)	(d)	...
Oldham	359	Vega	1,501	2,185	2,278	-4.1	(d)	(d)	...	(d)	(d)	...
Orange	361	Orange	356	84,966	80,509	5.5	(d)	(d)	92	5,304	854,578	452
Palo Pinto	363	Palo Pinto	953	27,026	25,055	7.9	(d)	(d)	39	1,357	80,064	42
Panola	365	Carthage	801	22,756	22,035	3.3	52,520	-61.2	15	1,112	135,919	72
Parker	367	Weatherford	904	88,495	64,785	36.6	284,180	22.7	118	1,947	157,742	83
Parmer	369	Farwell	882	10,016	9,863	1.6	66,239	-45.7	6	(d)	(d)	...
Pecos	371	Fort Stockton	4,764	16,809	14,675	14.5	40,056	41.9	...	(d)	(d)	...
Polk	373	Livingston	1,057	41,133	30,687	34.0	78,896	-31.2	27	(d)	(d)	...
Potter	375	Amarillo	909	113,546	97,874	16.0	1,367,395	13.0	139	6,093	431,595	228
Presidio	377	Marfa	3,856	7,304	6,637	10.0	3,732	-8.2	...	(d)	(d)	...
Rains	379	Emory	232	9,139	6,715	36.1	70,818	(d)	...	(d)	(d)	...
Randall	381	Canyon	914	104,312	89,673	16.3	(d)	(d)	59	(d)	(d)	...
Reagan	383	Big Lake	1,175	3,326	4,514	-26.3	(d)	(d)	...	(d)	(d)	...
Real	385	Leakey	700	3,047	2,412	26.3	(d)	(d)	...	(d)	(d)	...
Red River	387	Clarksville	1,050	14,314	14,317	-0.0	(d)	(d)	16	655	36,754	19
Reeves	389	Pecos	2,636	13,137	15,852	-17.1	(d)	(d)	...	(d)	(d)	...
Refugio	391	Refugio	770	7,828	7,976	-1.9	9,515	-50.7	...	(d)	(d)	...
Roberts	393	Miami	924	887	1,025	-13.5	(d)	(d)	...	(d)	(d)	...
Robertson	395	Franklin	855	16,000	15,511	3.2	(d)	(d)	...	(d)	(d)	...
Rockwall	397	Rockwall	129	43,080	25,604	68.3	(d)	(d)	59	(d)	(d)	...
Runnels	399	Ballinger	1,051	11,495	11,294	1.8	26,591	-59.0	12	1,001	113,421	60
Rusk	401	Henderson	924	47,372	43,735	8.3	(d)	(d)	33	1,063	82,601	44
Sabine	403	Hemphill	490	10,469	9,586	9.2	(d)	(d)	...	(d)	(d)	...
San Augustine	405	San Augustine	528	8,946	7,999	11.8	6,244	-53.2	...	(d)	(d)	...
San Jacinto	407	Coldspring	571	22,246	16,372	35.9	(d)	(d)	...	(d)	(d)	...
San Patricio	409	Sinton	692	67,138	58,749	14.3	150,837	42.5	49	(d)	(d)	...
San Saba	411	San Saba	1,134	6,186	5,401	14.5	(d)	(d)	...	(d)	(d)	...
Schleicher	413	Eldorado	1,311	2,935	2,990	-1.8	(d)	(d)	...	(d)	(d)	...
Scurry	415	Snyder	902	16,361	18,634	-12.2	(d)	(d)	...	(d)	(d)	...
Shackelford	417	Albany	914	3,302	3,316	-0.4	3,535	31.2	...	(d)	(d)	...
Shelby	419	Center	794	25,224	22,034	14.5	105,611	6.0	29	2,217	131,325	69
Sherman	421	Stratford	923	3,186	2,858	11.5	(d)	(d)	...	(d)	(d)	...
Smith	423	Tyler	928	174,706	151,309	15.5	(d)	(d)	218	11,103	1,170,235	619
Somervell	425	Glen Rose	187	6,809	5,360	27.0	3,101	(d)	...	(d)	(d)	...
Starr	427	Rio Grande City	1,223	53,597	40,518	32.3	(d)	(d)	...	(d)	(d)	...
Stephens	429	Breckenridge	895	9,674	9,010	7.4	7,771	-29.0	...	(d)	(d)	...
Sterling	431	Sterling City	923	1,393	1,438	-3.1	(d)	(d)	...	(d)	(d)	...
Stonewall	433	Aspermont	919	1,693	2,013	-15.9	(d)	(d)	...	(d)	(d)	...
Sutton	435	Sonora	1,454	4,077	4,135	-1.4	12,054	-36.2	...	(d)	(d)	...
Swisher	437	Tulia	900	8,378	8,133	3.0	24,471	-42.1	...	(d)	(d)	...
Tarrant	439	Fort Worth	863	1,446,219	1,170,103	23.6	32,961,870	49.1	1,869	84,694	14,599,482	7,724
Taylor	441	Abilene	916	126,555	119,655	5.8	886,810	-5.0	120	2,843	263,702	140
Terrell	443	Sanderson	2,358	1,081	1,410	-23.3	(d)	(d)	...	(d)	(d)	...
Terry	445	Brownfield	890	12,761	13,218	-3.5	56,601	-47.9	...	(d)	(d)	...
Throckmorton	447	Throckmorton	912	1,850	1,880	-1.6	1,854	-11.8	...	(d)	(d)	...
Titus	449	Mount Pleasant	411	28,118	24,009	17.1	153,859	-24.3	37	4,834	925,417	490
Tom Green	451	San Angelo	1,522	104,010	98,458	5.6	(d)	(d)	102	(d)	(d)	...
Travis	453	Austin	989	812,280	576,407	40.9	(d)	(d)	747	38,015	10,910,293	5,772
Trinity	455	Groveton	693	13,779	11,445	20.4	(d)	(d)	...	(d)	(d)	...
Tyler	457	Woodville	923	20,871	16,646	25.4	20,163	(d)	...	(d)	(d)	...
Upshur	459	Gilmer	588	35,291	31,370	12.5	(d)	(d)	...	(d)	(d)	...
Upton	461	Rankin	1,242	3,404	4,447	-23.5	6,512	-73.6	...	(d)	(d)	...
Uvalde	463	Uvalde	1,557	25,926	23,340	11.1	195,053	18.0	...	(d)	(d)	...
Val Verde	465	Del Rio	3,170	44,856	38,721	15.8	(d)	(d)	...	(d)	(d)	...
Van Zandt	467	Canton	849	48,140	37,944	26.9	70,392	-0.6	42	646	50,193	27
Victoria	469	Victoria	883	84,088	74,361	13.1	623,357	47.7	75	(d)	(d)	...
Walker	471	Huntsville	787	61,758	50,917	21.3	(d)	(d)	35	778	71,779	38
Waller	473	Hempstead	514	32,663	23,390	39.6	(d)	(d)	56	1,956	226,906	120
Ward	475	Monahans	835	10,909	13,115	-16.8	28,688	-61.4	...	(d)	(d)	...
Washington	477	Brenham	609	30,373	26,154	16.1	281,835	-2.6	56	3,112	354,485	188
Webb	479	Laredo	3,357	193,117	133,239	44.9	1,216,659	10.1	95	1,418	180,648	96
Wharton	481	Wharton	1,090	41,188	39,955	3.1	323,954	-0.8	52	1,868	169,787	90
Wheeler	483	Wheeler	914	5,284	5,879	-10.1	25,445	-17.4	...	(d)	(d)	...
Wichita	485	Wichita Falls	628	131,664	122,378	7.6	(d)	(d)	147	6,903	881,250	466
Wilbarger	487	Vernon	971	14,676	15,121	-2.9	(d)	(d)	9	892	113,709	60
Willacy	489	Raymondville	597	20,082	17,705	13.4	(d)	(d)	...	(d)	(d)	...
Williamson	491	Georgetown	1,123	249,967	139,551	79.1	(d)	(d)	247	7,199	1,097,204	580
Wilson	493	Floresville	807	32,408	22,650	43.1	(d)	(d)	...	(d)	(d)	...
Winkler	495	Kermit	841	7,173	8,626	-16.8	3,742	-50.7	...	(d)	(d)	...
Wise	497	Decatur	905	48,793	34,679	40.7	205,780	4.3	64	1,119	102,534	54
Wood	499	Quitman	650	36,752	29,380	25.1	177,876	-6.1	50	726	66,160	35
Yoakum	501	Plains	800	7,322	8,786	-16.7	30,290	-58.7	...	(d)	(d)	...
Young	503	Graham	922	17,943	18,126	-1.0	55,184	-34.2	32	875	80,278	42
Zapata	505	Zapata	997	12,182	9,279	31.3	7,753	(d)	...	(d)	(d)	...
Zavala	507	Crystal City	1,298	11,600	12,162	-4.6	(d)	(d)	...	(d)	(d)	...
The State			**261,797**	**20,851,820**	**16,986,510**	**22.8**	**397,405,111**	**23.0**	**21,450**	**855,658**	**124,462,554**	**65,849**

(d) Data not available. Corresponding percentages or Ranally Manufacturing Units are estimates.
... Represents 0 or amount too minimal to be reported.

Index of Places and Counties

Entries in **UPPERCASE** are counties.
Entries in **bold** have populations of 2,500 or more.
Names in parentheses are alternate names.

Inc. Place	Incorporated Place
RMC Place	Rand McNally Designated Place
CDP	Census Designated Place
MCD	Minor Civil Division
⊡	County Seat
▲	Minor Civil Division
elev.	Elevation
[P]	Post Office
[H]	Hospital
[C]	College
■	Principal Business Center
★	Ranally Metro Area (RMA) Abbreviation
z	Zip Code(s)
Ⓟ	Previous Census Population
Ⓡ	Revised Census Population
Ⓐ	Annexation Population
●	Rand McNally Population Estimate
Ⓒ	Final Census Population
Ⓢ	Special Census Population
◆	Estimated Population

For additional definitions see Glossary, Volume 1, and Introduction, Volume 2.

Annetta North; Inc. Place; PARKER; *238 EE-6; ★ D-FW; mail Weatherford z 76087; Ⓟ 265; Ⓒ 467
Annetta South; Inc. Place; PARKER; *238 EE-6; mail Aledo z 76008; Ⓟ 413; Ⓒ 555
Annona; Inc. Place; RED RIVER; 238 EB-11; 🅿; z 75550; Ⓟ 329; Ⓒ 282
Anson; Inc. Place; ⊡ JONES; 236 WJ-14; elev. 1,731ft./528m.; 🅿 🅷; z 79501; Ⓟ 2,644; Ⓒ 2,556
Anson Jones; RMC Place; HARRIS; *239 EK-10; ★ HOU; mail Houston z 77009, z 77249; pop. incl. with Houston (Inc. Place)
Antelope; RMC Place; JACK; 238 EC-4; mail Windthorst z 76389; ● 75
Anthony; Inc. Place; EL PASO; 237 WK-1; 🅿; ★ ELP; z 79821; Ⓟ 3,328; Ⓒ 3,850
Anthony Harbor; RMC Place; SAN AUGUSTINE; *238 EG-13; mail Broaddus z 75929; ● 50
Antioch; RMC Place; CASS; *238 EC-12; elev. 454ft./138m.; mail Atlanta z 75551; rural
Antioch; RMC Place; DELTA; *238 EC-9; elev. 518ft./158m.; mail Cooper z 75432; rural
Antioch; RMC Place; HENDERSON; 238 EF-10; elev. 448ft./137m.; mail Chandler z 75758
Antioch; RMC Place; HOUSTON; *238 EH-10; mail Lovelady z 75851; rural
Antioch; RMC Place; MADISON; *238 EH-10; mail Midway z 75852; rural
Antioch; RMC Place; RUSK; *238 EE-11; mail Henderson z 75654; rural
Antioch; RMC Place; SHELBY; *238 EF-13; mail Center z 75935, Timpson z 75975; rural
Anton; Inc. Place; HOCKLEY; 236 WG-10; 🅿; z 79313; Ⓟ 1,212; Ⓒ 1,200
Apache Addition; RMC Place; GUADALUPE; mail Seguin z 78155; pop. incl. with Seguin (Inc. Place)
Apache Shores; RMC Place; TRAVIS; *238 EJ-5; ★ AUS; mail Austin z 78734; ● 550
Apolonia; RMC Place; GRIMES; *238 EI-9; elev. 415ft./126m.; mail Anderson z 77830; rural
Appelt Hill; RMC Place; LAVACA; *239 EL-7; elev. 300ft./91m.; mail Hallettsville z 77964; rural
Appleby; Inc. Place; NACOGDOCHES; 238 EG-12; mail Nacogdoches z 75961; Ⓟ 449; Ⓒ 444
Apple Springs; RMC Place; TRINITY; 238 EH-11; 🅿; z 75926; ● 225
Aquilla; Inc. Place; HILL; 238 EG-7; elev. 521ft./159m.; 🅿; z 76622; Ⓟ 136; Ⓒ 136
ARANSAS; 239 EO-7; Ⓟ 17,892; Ⓒ 22,497; ◆ 24,775
Aransas Pass; Inc. Place; SAN PATRICIO, ARANSAS, NUECES; 239 EO-7; 🅿 🅷; z 78335-36; Ⓟ 7,180; Ⓒ 8,138
Arbala; RMC Place; HOPKINS; *238 ED-9; elev. 494ft./151m.; mail Sulphur Springs z 75482; ● 100
Arbor; RMC Place; HOUSTON; *238 EH-10; mail Kennard z 75847; rural
Arbor Oaks; RMC Place; HARRIS; *239 EK-10; ★ HOU; mail Houston z 77088; pop. incl. with Houston (Inc. Place)
Arcadia; RMC Place; GALVESTON; *239 EL-11; 🅿; ★ GLV-; z 77517; pop. incl. with Santa Fe (Inc. Place)
Arcadia; RMC Place; SHELBY; *238 EF-12; elev. 353ft./108m.; mail Center z 75935
Arcadia Park; RMC Place; DALLAS; *238 ED-7; ★ D-FW; mail Dallas z 75211; pop. incl. with Dallas (Inc. Place)
ARCHER; 238 EC-4; Ⓟ 7,973; Ⓒ 8,854; ◆ 8,916
Archer City; Inc. Place; ⊡ ARCHER; 238 EC-4; elev. 1,069ft./326m.; 🅿; z 76351; Ⓟ 1,748; Ⓒ 1,848
Arcola; Inc. Place; FORT BEND; 234 H-4; 🅿; ★ HOU; z 77583; Ⓟ 666; Ⓒ 1,048
Arden; RMC Place; IRION; *237 WL-12; elev. 2,084ft./635m.; mail San Angelo z 76901; rural
Argenta; RMC Place; LIVE OAK; *239 EO-6; elev. 217ft./66m.; mail Mathis z 78368; rural
Argo; RMC Place; TITUS; 238 EC-11; mail Cookville z 75558; ● 120
Argyle; Inc. Place; DENTON; 238 ED-7; 🅿; ★ D-FW; z 76226; Ⓟ 1,575; Ⓒ 2,365
Arizona; RMC Place; WALKER; *238 EI-10; mail Riverside z 77367; rural
Arkansas Bend; RMC Place; TRAVIS; *238 EJ-5; mail Leander z 78645; ● 100
Arlam; RMC Place; RUSK; *238 EF-12; mail Garrison z 75946; rural
Arledge Ridge; RMC Place; FANNIN; *238 EC-8; mail Bonham z 75418; rural
Arlington; Inc. Place; TARRANT; 238 EE-7; 🅿 🅷 🅲 24,825 ■; ★ D-FW; z 76001-07, z 76010-19, z 76094, z 76096; Ⓟ 261,721; Ⓒ 332,969; ◆ 403,625
Arlington Heights; RMC Place; HARRIS; *239 EK-11; ★ HOU; mail Houston z 77034; pop. incl. with Houston (Inc. Place)
Arlington Heights; RMC Place; NUECES; *239 EO-6; ★ CRPX; mail Corpus Christi z 78409; pop. incl. with Corpus Christi (Inc. Place)
Arlington Heights; RMC Place; TARRANT; *238 EE-6; ★ D-FW; mail Fort Worth z 76147; pop. incl. with Fort Worth (Inc. Place)
Armstrong; RMC Place; KENEDY; 239 EQ-6; elev. 26ft./8m.; 🅿; z 78338; ● 20
ARMSTRONG; 236 WD-11; Ⓟ 2,021; Ⓒ 2,148; ◆ 2,036
Arneckeville; RMC Place; DEWITT; 239 EM-7; mail Cuero z 77954; rural
Arnett; RMC Place; CORYELL; *238 EG-5; mail Gatesville z 76528
Arnett; RMC Place; HOCKLEY; *236 WH-9; elev. 3,466ft./1,056m.; mail Levelland z 79336; rural
Arp; Inc. Place; SMITH; 238 EE-11; 🅿; z 75750; Ⓟ 812; Ⓒ 901
Arrowhead Lake; RMC Place; MONTGOMERY; *238 EI-10; mail Willis z 77378; ● 150
Arrowhead Shores; RMC Place; HOOD; *238 EE-5; mail Granbury z 76048; ● 400
Arrowhead Village; RMC Place; COMAL; *239 EK-5; mail New Braunfels z 78130
Arroyo; RMC Place; CAMERON; *239 ES-6; ★ BRNS; mail Harlingen z 78550
Arroyo Alto; CDP-Census Area Only; CAMERON; *239 ES-6; ★ BRNS; Ⓒ 320
Arroyo City; RMC Place; CAMERON; 239 ES-7; mail San Benito z 78586; ● 500
Arroyo Colorado Estates; CDP-Census Area Only; CAMERON; *239 ES-6; ★ BRNS; Ⓒ 755
Arroyo Gardens-La Tina Ranch; CDP-Census Area Only; CAMERON; *239 ES-6; Ⓒ 732
Arsenal; RMC Place; BEXAR; *239 EL-4; ★ SANT; mail San Antonio z 78283; pop. incl. with San Antonio (Inc. Place)
Art; RMC Place; MASON; 238 EI-3; 🅿; z 76820; ● 50
Artesian Forest; RMC Place; MONTGOMERY; *238 EJ-10; mail Conroe z 77304; pop. incl. with Conroe (Inc. Place)
Artesia Wells; RMC Place; LA SALLE; 239 EN-3; elev. 436ft./133m.; 🅿; z 78001; ● 50
Arthur City; RMC Place; LAMAR; 238 EB-10; elev. 429ft./131m.; 🅿; z 75411; ● 300
Arvana; RMC Place; DAWSON; *236 WI-10; elev. 3,023ft./921m.; mail Lamesa z 79331
Asa; RMC Place; MCLENNAN; *238 EG-7; mail Waco z 76706; ● 50
Asander; TITUS; see Lone Star (RMC Place)
Ash; RMC Place; HOUSTON; *238 EH-10; elev. 226ft./69m.; mail Crockett z 75835
Ashby; RMC Place; MATAGORDA; *239 EM-9; mail Palacios z 77465; rural
Asherton; Inc. Place; DIMMIT; 237 WS-14; elev. 553ft./169m.; 🅿; z 78827; Ⓟ 1,608; Ⓒ 1,342
Ashford West; RMC Place; HARRIS; *239 EK-10; ★ HOU; mail Houston z 77077, z 77244; pop. incl. with Houston (Inc. Place)
Ashland; RMC Place; UPSHUR; *238 ED-11; elev. 327ft./100m.; mail Diana z 75640; ● 50
Ashmore; RMC Place; GAINES; *236 WI-9; elev. 3,167ft./965m.; mail Loop z 79342; rural
Ashtola; RMC Place; DONLEY; *236 WE-12; elev. 2,914ft./888m.; mail Clarendon z 79226; rural
Asia; RMC Place; POLK; *238 EH-11; mail Corrigan z 75939; rural
Aspermont; Inc. Place; ⊡ STONEWALL; 236 WI-13; elev. 1,787ft./545m.; 🅿 🅷; z 79502; Ⓟ 1,214; Ⓒ 1,021
Astrodome; RMC Place; HARRIS; *239 EK-10; ★ HOU; mail Houston z 77025, z 77225; pop. incl. with Houston (Inc. Place)
Astro Hills; RMC Place; COMAL; *239 EK-5; mail New Braunfels z 78130
Atascocita; CDP-Census Area Only; HARRIS; *238 EJ-11; 🅿; ★ HOU; z 77346; Ⓒ 35,757; ◆ 42,289
Atascosa; RMC Place; BEXAR; *239 EL-4; 🅿; ★ SANT; z 78002; ● 500
ATASCOSA; 239 EM-4; Ⓟ 30,533; Ⓒ 38,628; ◆ 44,385
Atco; RMC Place; MCLENNAN; *238 EG-7; mail Waco z 76710; pop. incl. with Waco (Inc. Place)
Ater; RMC Place; CORYELL; *238 EG-5; mail Gatesville z 76528; rural
Athens; Inc. Place; ⊡ HENDERSON; 238 EF-9; elev. 492ft./150m.; 🅿 🅷; z 75751-52; Ⓟ 10,967; Ⓒ 11,297
Atlanta; Inc. Place; CASS; 238 EC-12; 🅿 🅷; z 75551; Ⓟ 6,118; Ⓒ 5,745
Atlas; RMC Place; LAMAR; *238 EC-9; elev. 520ft./158m.; mail Paris z 75460; ● 20
Atoy; RMC Place; CHEROKEE; *238 EF-11; mail Rusk z 75785; rural
Atreco; RMC Place; JEFFERSON; *238 EJ-13; ★ B-PA; mail Port Arthur z 77640
Attoyac; RMC Place; NACOGDOCHES; *238 EG-12; mail Nacogdoches z 75961
Atwell; RMC Place; CALLAHAN; *238 EF-3; mail Cisco z 76437; rural
Aubrey; Inc. Place; DENTON; 238 EC-7; elev. 691ft./211m.; 🅿; ★ DENT; z 76227; Ⓟ 1,138; Ⓒ 1,500
Auburn; RMC Place; ELLIS; *238 EE-7; elev. 602ft./183m.; mail Maypearl z 76064; rural
Audobon Park; RMC Place; HARRIS; *239 EK-11; ★ HOU; mail Humble z 77396; ● 1,200
Augusta; RMC Place; HOUSTON; 238 EG-10; mail Grapeland z 75844; ● 25
Aurora; Inc. Place; WISE; *238 ED-6; 🅿; z 76078; Ⓟ 623; Ⓒ 853; Ⓡ 875
Austin; Inc. Place; **STATE CAPITAL**; ⊡ TRAVIS, WILLIAMSON; 237 WS-9; elev. 501ft./153m.; 🅿 🅷 🅲 56,961 ■; ★ AUS; z 73301, z 73344, z 78701-05, z 78708-39, z 78741-42, z 78744-69, z 78772-74, z 78778-81, z 78783, z 78785, z 78789, z 78799; Ⓟ 465,648; Ⓒ 656,562; ◆ 859,079
AUSTIN; 239 EK-8; Ⓟ 19,832; Ⓒ 23,590; ◆ 27,317
Austin Lake Estates; RMC Place; TRAVIS; *238 EJ-6; ★ AUS; mail Austin z 78759; ● 400
Austonio; RMC Place; HOUSTON; 238 EH-10; 🅿; z 75835; ● 70
Austwell; Inc. Place; REFUGIO; 239 EN-8; 🅿; z 77950; Ⓟ 189; Ⓒ 192
Authon; RMC Place; PARKER; *238 ED-5; elev. 1,012ft./308m.; mail Weatherford z 76088; rural
Autumn Woods; RMC Place; MONTGOMERY; *238 EJ-10; ★ HOU; mail Pinehurst z 77362
Avalon; RMC Place; ELLIS; 238 EF-7; 🅿; z 76623; ● 150
Avery; Inc. Place; RED RIVER; 238 EC-11; 🅿; z 75554; Ⓟ 430; Ⓒ 462
Avinger; Inc. Place; CASS; 238 ED-12; 🅿; z 75630; Ⓟ 478; Ⓒ 464
Avoca; RMC Place; JONES; 236 WI-14; 🅿; z 79503; ● 120
Avonbell; RMC Place; POTTER; ★ AMA; mail Amarillo z 79106; pop. incl. with Amarillo (Inc. Place)
Avondale; RMC Place; CAMERON; *239 ES-6; ★ BRNS; mail Harlingen z 78550; pop. incl. with Harlingen (Inc. Place)
Avondale; RMC Place; TARRANT; *238 ED-6; mail Justin z 76247; ● 300
Axtell; RMC Place; MCLENNAN; 238 EG-7; 🅿; z 76624; ● 300
Azle; Inc. Place; TARRANT, PARKER; 238 ED-6; 🅿 🅷; ★ D-FW; z 76020, z 76098; Ⓟ 8,868; Ⓒ 9,600

B

Bacliff; CDP; GALVESTON; 234 H-10; 🅿; ★ HOU; z 77518; Ⓟ 5,549; Ⓒ 6,962
Bagby; RMC Place; FANNIN; *238 EC-9; elev. 566ft./173m.; mail Honey Grove z 75446; rural
Bagwell; RMC Place; RED RIVER; 238 EB-10; 🅿; z 75412; ● 175
Bailey; Inc. Place; FANNIN; 238 EC-8; 🅿; z 75413; Ⓟ 187; Ⓒ 213
BAILEY; 236 WF-8; Ⓟ 7,064; Ⓒ 6,594; ◆ 6,003
Baileyboro; RMC Place; BAILEY; *236 WG-8; elev. 3,821ft./1,165m.; mail Sudan z 79371; rural
Bailey Prairie (Bailey's Prairie); Inc. Place; BRAZORIA; *239 EL-10; ★ L.JAC-; mail Angleton z 77515; Ⓟ 634; Ⓒ 694
Bailey's Prairie; BRAZORIA; see Bailey Prairie (Inc. Place)
Baileyville; RMC Place; MILAM; *238 EH-7; mail Rosebud z 76570; rural
Bainer; RMC Place; LAMB; *236 WG-10; mail Littlefield z 79339; rural
Bainville; RMC Place; KARNES; *239 EM-5; mail Kenedy z 78119; rural
Baird; Inc. Place; ⊡ CALLAHAN; 238 EE-3; elev. 1,725ft./526m.; 🅿 🅷; z 79504; Ⓟ 1,658; Ⓒ 1,623
Baker; RMC Place; PARKER; *238 EE-6; mail Weatherford z 76087; rural
Bakersfield; RMC Place; PECOS; *237 WN-9; elev. 2,539ft./774m.; mail Mc Camey z 79752; rural
Balch Springs; Inc. Place; DALLAS; 238 EE-8; 🅿; ★ D-FW; z 75180-81; Ⓟ 17,406; Ⓒ 19,375; ◆ 20,057
Balcones; RMC Place; TRAVIS, WILLIAMSON; ★ AUS; mail Austin z 78717, z 78720, z 78726, z 78729-30, z 78732, z 78750, z 78759; pop. incl. with Austin (Inc. Place)
Balcones Heights; Inc. Place; BEXAR; 239 ER-11; 🅿; ★ SANT; z 78201; Ⓟ 3,022; Ⓒ 3,016
Balcones Village; RMC Place; TRAVIS; *238 EJ-6; ★ AUS; mail Austin z 78750; pop. incl. with Austin (Inc. Place)
Bald Hill; RMC Place; ANGELINA; *238 EH-12; elev. 276ft./84m.; mail Lufkin z 75901; rural
Bald Prairie; RMC Place; ROBERTSON; *238 EH-8; elev. 444ft./135m.; mail Franklin z 77856; rural
Baldwin; RMC Place; HARRISON; *238 ED-12; mail Karnack z 75661; rural
Ballinger; Inc. Place; ⊡ RUNNELS; 237 WL-14; elev. 1,628ft./496m.; 🅿 🅷; z 76821; Ⓟ 3,975; Ⓒ 4,243
Balmorhea; Inc. Place; REEVES; 237 WM-7; 🅿; z 79718; Ⓟ 765; Ⓒ 527
Balsora; RMC Place; WISE; *238 ED-5; mail Bridgeport z 76426
Bammel; RMC Place; HARRIS; 234 A-4; ★ HOU; mail Houston z 77040, z 77048, z 77090; ● 600
Bancroft; RMC Place; ORANGE; *238 EJ-13; ★ B-PA; pop. incl. with Orange (Inc. Place)
Bandera; Inc. Place; ⊡ BANDERA; 239 EK-3; elev. 1,258ft./383m.; 🅿; z 78003; Ⓟ 877; Ⓒ 957
BANDERA; 239 EK-3; Ⓟ 10,562; Ⓒ 17,645; ◆ 20,985
Bandera Falls; RMC Place; BANDERA; *239 EK-3; elev. 1,175ft./358m.; mail Pipe Creek z 78063; ● 100
Bangs; Inc. Place; BROWN; 238 EG-3; 🅿; z 76823; Ⓟ 1,555; Ⓒ 1,620
Banquete; RMC Place; NUECES; 239 EO-6; 🅿; z 78339; ● 600
Barbarosa; RMC Place; GUADALUPE; *239 EK-5; elev. 611ft./186m.; mail New Braunfels z 78130; rural
Barclay; RMC Place; FALLS; 238 EH-7; mail Lott z 76656; ● 40
Bardin Road; RMC Place; TARRANT; ★ D-FW; mail Arlington z 76001-02, z 76017-18, z 76096; pop. incl. with Arlington (Inc. Place)
Bardwell; Inc. Place; ELLIS; 238 EF-8; elev. 479ft./146m.; 🅿; z 75101; Ⓟ 387; Ⓒ 583
Barker; RMC Place; HARRIS; 234 D-1; 🅿; ★ HOU; z 77413; pop. incl. with Houston (Inc. Place)
Barksdale; RMC Place; EDWARDS; 237 WP-14; elev. 1,507ft./459m.; 🅿; z 78828; ● 300
Barnes; RMC Place; POLK; *238 EH-12; elev. 300ft./91m.; mail Moscow z 75960; rural
Barnhart; RMC Place; IRION; 237 WM-11; elev. 2,560ft./780m.; 🅿; z 76930; ● 200
Barnum; RMC Place; POLK; 238 EH-12; elev. 250ft./76m.; 🅿; z 75939; rural
Barrett; CDP; HARRIS; 234 C-8; elev. 46ft./14m.; ★ HOU; mail Crosby z 77532; Ⓟ 3,052; Ⓒ 2,872
Barrington Oaks; RMC Place; TRAVIS; *238 EJ-6; ★ AUS; mail Austin z 78759; pop. incl. with Austin (Inc. Place)
Barrington Place; RMC Place; FORT BEND; *239 EK-10; ★ HOU; mail Sugar Land z 77478; pop. incl. with Sugar Land (Inc. Place)
Barry; Inc. Place; NAVARRO; 238 EF-8; 🅿; z 75102; Ⓟ 175; Ⓒ 209
Barstow; Inc. Place; WARD; 237 WL-7; elev. 2,566ft./782m.; 🅿; z 79719; Ⓟ 535; Ⓒ 406
Bartlett; Inc. Place; WILLIAMSON, BELL; 238 EI-6; 🅿; z 76511; Ⓟ 1,439; Ⓒ 1,675
Bartley Woods; RMC Place; FANNIN; *238 EC-9; elev. 633ft./193m.; mail Windom z 75492; rural
Barton Creek; CDP-Census Area Only; TRAVIS; *238 EJ-6; ★ AUS; Ⓒ 1,589
Bartons Chapel; RMC Place; JACK; *238 ED-5; mail Jacksboro z 76458; rural
Bartonville; Inc. Place; DENTON; 238 ED-7; 🅿; ★ D-FW; z 76226; Ⓟ 849; Ⓒ 1,093
Barwise; RMC Place; FLOYD; *236 WG-11; mail Floydada z 79235
Bascom; RMC Place; SMITH; *238 EE-10; ★ TYL; mail Tyler z 75705, z 75707; ● 800
Basin; RMC Place; BREWSTER; *237 WQ-7; located in Big Bend National Park; mail Big Bend National Park z 79834; ● 40
Bassett; RMC Place; BOWIE; 238 EC-11; elev. 268ft./82m.; mail Simms z 75574; ● 100
Bastrop; Inc. Place; ⊡ BASTROP; 238 EJ-7; 🅿; z 78602; Ⓟ 4,044; Ⓒ 5,340
BASTROP; 239 EK-6; Ⓟ 38,263; Ⓒ 57,733; ◆ 73,158
Bastrop Bayou; RMC Place; BRAZORIA; *239 EL-11; ★ L.JAC-; mail Angleton z 77515; ● 30
Bastrop Beach; RMC Place; BRAZORIA; *239 EL-10; ★ L.JAC-; mail Angleton z 77515; ● 30
Bateman; RMC Place; BASTROP; *239 EK-6; mail Red Rock z 78662; rural
Batesville; RMC Place; RED RIVER; *238 EB-10; mail Clarksville z 75426; rural
Batesville; CDP; ZAVALA; 239 EM-2; elev. 713ft./217m.; 🅿; z 78829; Ⓟ 1,313; Ⓒ 1,298
Batson; RMC Place; HARDIN; 238 EJ-12; elev. 84ft./26m.; 🅿; z 77519; ● 200
Battle; RMC Place; MCLENNAN; *238 EG-7; elev. 571ft./174m.; mail Mart z 76664
Bausell and Ellis; CDP-Census Area Only; WILLACY; *239 ES-6; Ⓒ 112
Baxter; RMC Place; HENDERSON; *238 EF-9; elev. 480ft./146m.; mail Athens z 75751; rural
Bay City; Inc. Place; ⊡ MATAGORDA; 239 EM-9; elev. 56ft./17m.; 🅿 🅷 ■; z 77404, z 77414; Ⓟ 18,170; Ⓒ 18,667; ◆ 17,468
Bay Harbor; RMC Place; GALVESTON; *239 EL-11; ★ GLV-; mail Galveston z 77554; pop. incl. with Galveston (Inc. Place)
BAYLOR; 238 EB-3; Ⓟ 4,385; Ⓒ 4,093; ◆ 3,896
Bayou Vista; Inc. Place; GALVESTON; 234 A-8; 🅿; ★ GLV-; z 77563; Ⓟ 1,320; Ⓒ 1,644
Bayside; CAMERON; see Laguna Heights (CDP)
Bayside; Inc. Place; REFUGIO; 239 EO-7; 🅿; z 78340; Ⓟ 400; Ⓒ 360
Baytown; Inc. Place; HARRIS, CHAMBERS; 234 E-10; 🅿 🅷 ■; ★ HOU; z 77520-23; Ⓟ 63,850; Ⓒ 66,430; ◆ 74,781
Bayview; Inc. Place; CAMERON; 239 ES-7; elev. 27ft./8m.; 🅿; z 78566; Ⓟ 231; Ⓒ 323
Bayview Estates; RMC Place; COKE; 237 WK-13; mail Robert Lee z 76945; ● 40
Bazette; RMC Place; NAVARRO; *238 EF-8; mail Kerens z 75144; ● 60
Beach; RMC Place; MONTGOMERY; *238 EJ-10; mail Conroe z 77301; pop. incl. with Conroe (Inc. Place)
Beach City; Inc. Place; CHAMBERS; 239 EK-11; 🅿; z 77520, z 77523 & mail Baytown z 77521; Ⓟ 852; Ⓒ 1,645
Beacon Hill; RMC Place; BEXAR; ★ SANT; mail San Antonio z 78201; pop. incl. with San Antonio (Inc. Place)
Bear Creek; Inc. Place; HAYS; *238 EJ-5; ★ AUS; mail Austin z 78737; Ⓒ 360
Bear Creek Village; RMC Place; HARRIS; *239 EK-10; ★ HOU; mail Houston z 77084, z 77284; ● 1,200
Bear Grass; RMC Place; LEON; *238 EG-8; mail Jewett z 75846; rural
Beasley; Inc. Place; FORT BEND; 239 EL-9; 🅿; z 77417; Ⓟ 485; Ⓒ 590
Beattie; RMC Place; COMANCHE; 238 EF-4; mail Comanche z 76442; ● 25
Beaukiss; RMC Place; WILLIAMSON; *238 EJ-7; mail Elgin z 78621; rural
Beaumont; Inc. Place; ⊡ JEFFERSON; 238 EJ-13; 🅿 🅷 🅲 9,906 ■; ★ B-PA; z 77701-10, z 77713, z 77720, z 77725-26 & mail Lumberton z 77657; Ⓟ 114,323; Ⓒ 113,866; ◆ 105,954
Beaumont Place; RMC Place; HARRIS; 234 C-7; ★ HOU; mail Houston z 77049; ● 8,000
Beauxart Gardens; RMC Place; JEFFERSON; *238 EJ-13; ★ B-PA; mail Beaumont z 77705; ● 850
Beaver Dam; RMC Place; BOWIE; 238 EB-11; mail De Kalb z 75559; ● 85
Bebe; RMC Place; GONZALES; 239 EL-6; elev. 382ft./116m.; 🅿; z 78614; ● 30
Becker; RMC Place; KAUFMAN; *238 EE-8; mail Kaufman z 75142; rural
Beckville; Inc. Place; PANOLA; 238 EE-12; 🅿; z 75631; Ⓟ 783; Ⓒ 752
Becton; RMC Place; LUBBOCK; *236 WG-11; elev. 3,251ft./991m.; mail Lorenzo z 79343; rural
Bedford; Inc. Place; TARRANT; 235 F-6; 🅿 🅷; ★ D-FW; z 76021-22, z 76095; Ⓟ 43,762; Ⓒ 47,152; ◆ 50,328
Bedias; Inc. Place; GRIMES; 238 EI-9; 🅿; z 77831; incorporated November 20, 2003; not reported in 2000 Census; ● 400
BEE; 239 EN-6; Ⓟ 25,135; Ⓒ 32,359; ◆ 33,220
Bee Cave (Beecaves); Inc. Place; TRAVIS; *238 EJ-5; 🅿; ★ AUS; z 78733-34, z 78736, z 78738; Ⓟ 241; Ⓒ 656
Beecaves; TRAVIS; see Bee Cave (Inc. Place)
Beech Grove; RMC Place; JASPER; *238 EH-13; mail Jasper z 75951
Beechnut; RMC Place; HARRIS; ★ HOU; mail Houston z 77072, z 77272; pop. incl. with Houston (Inc. Place)
Beechwood; RMC Place; SABINE; *238 EH-13; mail Hemphill z 75948; ● 150
Bee House; RMC Place; CORYELL; 238 EG-5; 🅿; z 76525
Beeville; Inc. Place; ⊡ BEE; 239 EN-6; 🅿 🅷; z 78102, z 78104; Ⓟ 13,547; Ⓒ 13,129
Bel Air; RMC Place; HARRISON; *238 EE-12; mail Marshall z 75672; pop. incl. with Marshall (Inc. Place)
Belcherville; RMC Place; MONTAGUE; 238 EB-5; elev. 913ft./278m.; mail Nocona z 76255; ● 35
Belfalls; RMC Place; BELL; 238 EH-7; elev. 548ft./167m.; mail Troy z 76579; ● 75
Belgrade; RMC Place; NEWTON; *238 EI-14; mail Bon Wier z 75928
Belk; RMC Place; LAMAR; *238 EB-9; mail Arthur City z 75411
BELL; 238 EH-6; Ⓟ 191,088; Ⓒ 237,974; ◆ 314,420
Bellaire; Inc. Place; HARRIS; 234 E-4; elev. 57ft./17m.; 🅿; ★ HOU; z 77401-02; Ⓟ 13,842; Ⓒ 15,642
Bellaire Addition; RMC Place; SMITH; ★ TYL; mail Tyler z 75704; ● 600
Bellaire Junction; RMC Place; HARRIS; *239 EK-10; ★ HOU; pop. incl. with Houston (Inc. Place)
Bellaire West; RMC Place; HARRIS; *239 EK-10; ★ HOU; mail Houston z 77072; pop. incl. with Houston (Inc. Place)
Bell Branch; RMC Place; ELLIS; *238 EF-7; mail Italy z 76651; rural
Bellevue; Inc. Place; CLAY; 238 EC-5; elev. 1,030ft./314m.; 🅿; z 76228; Ⓟ 333; Ⓒ 386
Bellmead; Inc. Place; MCLENNAN; 238 EG-7; 🅿; ★ WACO; z 76704-05 & mail Waco z 76715; Ⓟ 8,336; Ⓒ 9,214
Bells; Inc. Place; GRAYSON; 238 EC-8; elev. 681ft./208m.; 🅿; z 75414; Ⓟ 962; Ⓒ 1,190
Bellview; RMC Place; RAINS; *238 ED-9; elev. 425ft./130m.; mail Alba z 75410, Bellville z 77418; rural
Bellville; Inc. Place; ⊡ AUSTIN; 239 EK-9; elev. 263ft./80m.; 🅿 🅷; z 77418; Ⓟ 3,378; Ⓒ 3,794
Belmar; RMC Place; POTTER; ★ AMA; mail Amarillo z 79106; pop. incl. with Amarillo (Inc. Place)
Belmena; RMC Place; MILAM; *238 EI-7; mail Cameron z 76520; rural
Belmont; RMC Place; GONZALES; 239 EL-6; elev. 363ft./111m.; 🅿; z 78604; ● 30
Belott; RMC Place; HOUSTON; *238 EG-10; elev. 367ft./112m.; mail Crockett z 75835; rural
Belt Junction; RMC Place; DALLAS; ★ D-FW; pop. incl. with Dallas (Inc. Place)
Belton; Inc. Place; ⊡ BELL; 238 EH-6; 🅿 🅲 2,713; ★ KILL-; z 76513; Ⓟ 12,476; Ⓒ 14,623
Ben; RMC Place; WOOD; *238 ED-10; mail Mineola z 75773; rural
Ben Arnold; RMC Place; MILAM; 238 EH-7; 🅿; z 76519; ● 150
Benavides; Inc. Place; DUVAL; 239 EP-5; elev. 380ft./116m.; 🅿; z 78341; Ⓟ 1,788; Ⓒ 1,686
Ben Bolt; RMC Place; JIM WELLS; 239 EP-5; 🅿; z 78342; ● 250
Benbrook; Inc. Place; TARRANT; 238 EE-6; elev. 692ft./211m.; 🅿; ★ D-FW; z 76109, z 76116, z 76126, z 76132; Ⓟ 19,564; Ⓒ 20,208; ◆ 23,046
Benchley; RMC Place; ROBERTSON; *238 EI-8; mail Bryan z 77807
Bend; RMC Place; SAN SABA; 238 EH-4; elev. 1,110ft./338m.; 🅿; z 76824; ● 100
Ben Franklin; RMC Place; DELTA; 238 EC-9; 🅿; z 75415; ● 130
Ben Hur; RMC Place; LIMESTONE; 238 EG-8; mail Mart z 76664; ● 80
Benjamin; Inc. Place; ⊡ KNOX; 236 WH-14; 🅿; z 79505; Ⓟ 225; Ⓒ 264
Bennett; RMC Place; PARKER; 238 EE-5; mail Millsap z 76066; ● 100
Bennett Estates; RMC Place; MONTGOMERY; *238 EJ-10; ★ HOU; mail Conroe z 77302; ● 650
Benoit; RMC Place; RUNNELS; *238 EG-2; mail Talpa z 76882; rural
Bentonville; RMC Place; JIM WELLS; *239 EP-5; mail Alice z 78332; ● 80
Bent Tree; RMC Place; DALLAS; *238 ED-7; ★ D-FW; mail Dallas z 75287, z 75370; pop. incl. with Dallas (Inc. Place)
Bentwater; RMC Place; MONTGOMERY; *238 EI-10; mail Montgomery z 77356; ● 900
Bentwood; RMC Place; TOM GREEN; *237 WL-13; ★ SANG; mail San Angelo z 76904; pop. incl. with San Angelo (Inc. Place)
Bentwood Acres; RMC Place; GRAYSON; *238 EB-7; mail Pottsboro z 75076; rural
Ben Wheeler; RMC Place; VAN ZANDT; 238 EE-9; 🅿; z 75754; ● 500
Berclair; RMC Place; GOLIAD; 239 EN-6; 🅿; z 78107; ● 250
Berea; RMC Place; HOUSTON; *238 EG-10; mail Crockett z 75835
Berea; RMC Place; MARION; *238 ED-12; mail Jefferson z 75657; ● 100
Bergheim; RMC Place; KENDALL; 239 EK-4; elev. 1,441ft./439m.; 🅿; z 78004; ● 20
Bergs; RMC Place; BEXAR; ★ SANT; pop. incl. with San Antonio (Inc. Place)
Berlin; RMC Place; WASHINGTON; *238 EJ-8; elev. 405ft./123m.; mail Brenham z 77833; rural
Bermuda Beach; RMC Place; GALVESTON; *239 EL-11; ★ GLV-; mail Galveston z 77554; pop. incl. with Galveston (Inc. Place)
Bernardo; RMC Place; COLORADO; 239 EK-8; mail Cat Spring z 78933; ● 35
Berry Street; RMC Place; TARRANT; ★ D-FW; mail Fort Worth z 76109-10; pop. incl. with Fort Worth (Inc. Place)
Berryville; Inc. Place; HENDERSON; *238 EF-10; mail Frankston z 75763; Ⓟ 749; Ⓒ 891
Bertram; Inc. Place; BURNET; 238 EI-5; 🅿; z 78605; Ⓟ 849; Ⓒ 1,122
Bessmay; RMC Place; JASPER; 238 EI-13; elev. 93ft./28m.; mail Buna z 77612; rural
Best; RMC Place; REAGAN; *237 WM-11; elev. 2,741ft./835m.; 🅿; z 76932; rural
Bethany; RMC Place; PANOLA; 238 EE-13; see also Bethany, LA; 🅿; z 71007; ● 50
Bethel; RMC Place; ANDERSON; *238 EF-9; mail Tennessee Colony z 75861
Bethel; RMC Place; ELLIS; *238 EE-7; mail Waxahachie z 75167; rural
Bethel; RMC Place; HENDERSON; *238 EE-9; mail Athens z 75751; rural
Bethel; RMC Place; PARKER; *238 EE-5; mail Weatherford z 76086; rural
Bethlehem; RMC Place; BOWIE; *238 EB-11; mail De Kalb z 75559; rural
Bethlehem; RMC Place; COLLIN; *238 EC-8; mail Farmersville z 75442; rural
Bethlehem; RMC Place; UPSHUR; *238 ED-11; mail Gilmer z 75644; rural
Bethsaida; RMC Place; CASS; *238 ED-12; mail Atlanta z 75551; rural
Bethsaida (Gallaway); RMC Place; PANOLA; *238 EF-13; mail Center z 75935; rural
Bettie; RMC Place; UPSHUR; 238 ED-11; mail Gilmer z 75644; ● 125
Beulah; RMC Place; ANGELINA; *238 EH-12; elev. 230ft./70m.; mail Diboll z 75941; rural
Beverly Hills; RMC Place; DALLAS; ★ D-FW; mail Dallas z 75211, z 75233, z 75236, z 75249; pop. incl. with Dallas (Inc. Place)
Beverly Hills; Inc. Place; MCLENNAN; 236 WF-6; 🅿; ★ WACO; z 76711; Ⓟ 2,048; Ⓒ 2,113
Bevil Oaks; Inc. Place; JEFFERSON; 238 EJ-12; mail Beaumont z 77708; Ⓟ 1,350; Ⓒ 1,346
Bevilport; RMC Place; JASPER; *238 EH-13; mail Jasper z 75951
BEXAR; 239 EK-4; Ⓟ 1,185,394; Ⓒ 1,392,931; ◆ 1,667,823
Beyersville; RMC Place; WILLIAMSON; *238 EI-7; mail Coupland z 78615
Biardstown; RMC Place; LAMAR; 238 EC-10; mail Paris z 75462; ● 75
Bigfoot; CDP; FRIO; 239 EM-4; elev. 645ft./197m.; 🅿; z 78005; Ⓒ 304
Big Lake; Inc. Place; ⊡ REAGAN; 237 WM-11; elev. 2,691ft./820m.; 🅿 🅷; z 76932; Ⓟ 3,672; Ⓒ 2,885
Big Oaks; RMC Place; MARION; *238 ED-11; mail Avinger z 75630; ● 50
Big Sandy; Inc. Place; UPSHUR; 238 EE-10; 🅿; z 75755, z 75797; Ⓟ 1,185; Ⓒ 1,288
Big Spring; Inc. Place; ⊡ HOWARD; 237 WK-11; elev. 2,432ft./741m.; 🅿 🅷 ■; z 79720-21; Ⓟ 23,093; Ⓒ 25,233; ◆ 27,034
Big Springs; RMC Place; RUSK; *238 EF-11; mail Henderson z 75654; rural
Big Square; RMC Place; CASTRO; *236 WF-9; mail Dimmitt z 79027; rural
Big Valley Ranchettes; RMC Place; CORYELL; *238 EH-5; ★ KILL-; mail Copperas Cove z 76522; ● 130
Big Wells; Inc. Place; DIMMIT; 239 EN-2; elev. 535ft./163m.; 🅿; z 78830; Ⓟ 756; Ⓒ 704
Billington; RMC Place; LIMESTONE; *238 EG-7; mail Axtell z 76624; rural
Billpark; RMC Place; HARRIS; ★ HOU; pop. incl. with Houston (Inc. Place)
Biloxi; RMC Place; NEWTON; *238 EI-13; mail Bon Wier z 75928; rural
Binglewood; RMC Place; HARRIS; *239 EK-10; ★ HOU; mail Houston z 77080; pop. incl. with Houston (Inc. Place)
Birch; RMC Place; BURLESON; *238 EJ-8; mail Somerville z 77879; rural
Birds; RMC Place; TARRANT; ★ D-FW; pop. incl. with Fort Worth (Inc. Place)
Birnam Wood; RMC Place; HARRIS; *238 EJ-10; ★ HOU; mail Spring z 77373; ● 1,600
Birome; RMC Place; HILL; 238 EG-7; 🅿; z 76673; ● 30
Birthright; RMC Place; HOPKINS; *238 EC-10; mail Sulphur Springs z 75482
Biry; RMC Place; MEDINA; *239 EL-3; mail Devine z 78016
Bisbee; RMC Place; TARRANT; 235 I-6; ★ D-FW; pop. incl. with Mansfield (Inc. Place)
Bishop; Inc. Place; NUECES; 239 EP-6; 🅿; z 78343; Ⓟ 3,337; Ⓒ 3,305
Bishop Hills; Inc. Place; POTTER; *236 WD-10; mail Amarillo z 79124; Ⓒ 210
Bivins; RMC Place; CASS; 238 ED-12; 🅿; z 75555; ● 200
Bixby; CDP; CAMERON; *239 ES-6; ★ BRNS; Ⓒ 356
Black; RMC Place; PARMER; 236 WE-9; 🅿; z 79035; ● 50
Black Ankle; RMC Place; SAN AUGUSTINE; *238 EG-13; mail San Augustine z 75972; rural
Blackfoot; RMC Place; ANDERSON; *238 EF-9; mail Montalba z 75853; rural
Black Hills; RMC Place; NAVARRO; *238 EF-8; mail Corsicana z 75110; rural
Blackjack; RMC Place; CHEROKEE; *238 EF-11; mail Troup z 75789; rural
Black Jack; RMC Place; ROBERTSON; *238 EI-8; mail Hearne z 77859; rural
Blackland; RMC Place; ROCKWALL; *238 ED-8; elev. 574ft./175m.; ★ D-FW; mail Royse City z 75189; rural
Black Oak; RMC Place; HOPKINS; *238 ED-10; mail Como z 75431; rural
Blackwell; Inc. Place; NOLAN, COKE; 237 WK-13; elev. 2,120ft./646m.; 🅿; z 79506; Ⓟ 339; Ⓒ 360
Blakeney; RMC Place; RED RIVER; *238 EB-10; elev. 381ft./116m.; mail Bagwell z 75412; rural
Blanchard; RMC Place; POLK; *238 EI-11; mail Livingston z 77351; ● 300
Blanco; Inc. Place; BLANCO; 238 EJ-4; elev. 1,324ft./404m.; 🅿; z 78606; Ⓟ 1,238; Ⓒ 1,505
BLANCO; 238 EI-4; Ⓟ 5,972; Ⓒ 8,418; ◆ 8,996
Blanconia; RMC Place; BEE; *239 EN-6; elev. 87ft./27m.; mail Beeville z 78102; ● 30
Bland; RMC Place; ORANGE; *238 EJ-13; ★ B-PA; mail Orange z 77630; pop. incl. with West Orange (Inc. Place)
Bland Lake; RMC Place; SAN AUGUSTINE; *238 EG-13; mail San Augustine z 75972; rural
Blanket; Inc. Place; BROWN; 238 EG-4; 🅿; z 76432; Ⓟ 381; Ⓒ 402
Bleakwood; RMC Place; NEWTON; 238 EI-13; elev. 116ft./35m.; mail Kirbyville z 75956; ● 100
Bledsoe; RMC Place; COCHRAN; 236 WH-8; elev. 3,965ft./1,209m.; 🅿; z 79314; ● 200
Bleiblerville; RMC Place; AUSTIN; 238 EJ-8; 🅿; z 78931; ● 80
Blessing; CDP; MATAGORDA; 239 EM-9; 🅿; z 77419; Ⓒ 861
Blevins; RMC Place; FALLS; *238 EH-7; elev. 546ft./166m.; mail Eddy z 76524; rural
Blewett; RMC Place; UVALDE; *239 EL-1; mail Uvalde z 78801; rural
Blodgett; RMC Place; TITUS; *238 ED-10; elev. 416ft./127m.; mail Pittsburg z 75686; ● 75
Bloomburg; Inc. Place; CASS; 238 EC-12; 🅿; z 75556; Ⓟ 376; Ⓒ 375
Bloomdale; RMC Place; COLLIN; *238 EC-8; elev. 673ft./205m.; mail Mckinney z 75069; rural
Bloomfield; RMC Place; COOKE; *238 EC-7; elev. 636ft./194m.; mail Pilot Point z 76258; rural
Blooming Grove; Inc. Place; NAVARRO; 238 EF-8; 🅿; z 76626; Ⓟ 847; Ⓒ 833
Bloomington; CDP; VICTORIA; 239 EN-8; elev. 64ft./20m.; 🅿; z 77951; Ⓟ 1,888; Ⓒ 2,562
Blossom; Inc. Place; LAMAR; 238 EB-10; 🅿; z 75416; Ⓟ 1,440; Ⓒ 1,439
Blue; RMC Place; LEE; *238 EJ-7; mail Lexington z 78947; rural
Blue Berry Hill; CDP-Census Area Only; BEE; *239 EN-6; Ⓒ 982
Bluebonnet; RMC Place; TRAVIS; ★ AUS; mail Austin z 78708, z 78727-28, z 78753, z 78758; pop. incl. with Austin (Inc. Place)
Bluegrove; RMC Place; CLAY; 238 EC-5; elev. 998ft./304m.; 🅿; z 76352; ● 110
Blue Haven Estates; RMC Place; HUNT; *238 ED-9; mail Wills Point z 75169; ● 50
Blue Lake Estates; RMC Place; LLANO; *238 EI-4; mail Marble Falls z 78654; ● 300
Blue Mound; Inc. Place; TARRANT; 235 F-4; 🅿; ★ D-FW; z 76131; Ⓟ 2,133; Ⓒ 2,388
Blue Ridge; Inc. Place; COLLIN; 238 EC-8; 🅿; z 75424; Ⓟ 521; Ⓒ 672
Blue Ridge; RMC Place; FALLS; *238 EH-8; elev. 467ft./142m.; mail Marlin z 76661; rural
Blueroan; RMC Place; COLORADO; *239 EL-9; mail Eagle Lake z 77434; rural
Blue Stem Estates; RMC Place; CORYELL; *238 EH-5; ★ KILL-; mail Copperas Cove z 76522; ● 150
Bluetown; RMC Place; CAMERON; *239 ES-6; elev. 67ft./20m.; ★ BRNS; mail Santa Maria z 78592; ● 200
Bluetown-Iglesia Antigua; CDP-Census Area Only; CAMERON; *239 ES-6; ★ BRNS; Ⓒ 692
Blue Water Key; RMC Place; HENDERSON; mail Chandler z 75758; ● 100
Bluff Dale; RMC Place; ERATH; 238 EE-5; 🅿; z 76433; ● 220
Bluff Springs; RMC Place; TRAVIS; *238 EJ-6; ★ AUS; mail Austin z 78744; rural
Bluffton; RMC Place; LLANO; 238 EI-4; elev. 1,066ft./325m.; 🅿; z 78607; ● 100
Blum; Inc. Place; HILL; 238 EF-6; 🅿; z 76627; Ⓟ 358; Ⓒ 399
Blumenthal; RMC Place; GILLESPIE; *238 EJ-4; elev. 1,504ft./458m.; mail Fredericksburg z 78624; rural
Bluntzer; RMC Place; NUECES; *239 EO-6; elev. 76ft./23m.; mail Robstown z 78380; ● 100
Bob Harris; RMC Place; HARRIS; ★ HOU; mail Pasadena z 77506; pop. incl. with Pasadena (Inc. Place)
Bob Lyons; RMC Place; GALVESTON; ★ GLV-; mail Galveston z 77552, z 77554; pop. incl. with Galveston (Inc. Place)
Bobo; RMC Place; SHELBY; *238 EF-12; mail Tenaha z 75974; rural
Boca Chica; RMC Place; CAMERON; *239 ET-6; ★ BRNS; mail Brownsville z 78520; pop. incl. with Brownsville (Inc. Place)
Boerne; Inc. Place; ⊡ KENDALL; 239 EK-4; elev. 1,405ft./428m.; 🅿; z 78006, z 78015; Ⓟ 4,274; Ⓒ 6,178
Bogata; Inc. Place; RED RIVER; 238 EC-10; elev. 417ft./127m.; 🅿; z 75417; Ⓟ 1,421; Ⓒ 1,396
Bois D'Arc; RMC Place; ANDERSON; *238 EF-9; mail Palestine z 75801; rural
Boling; RMC Place; WHARTON; 239 EL-9; elev. 81ft./25m.; 🅿; z 77420; ● 1,000
Boling-Iago; CDP-Census Area Only; WHARTON; *239 EL-9; mail Boling z 77420; Ⓟ 1,119; Ⓒ 1,271
Bolivar; RMC Place; DENTON; *238 EC-6; mail Port Bolivar z 77650, Sanger z 76266; ● 80
Bolivar Peninsula; CDP-Census Area Only; GALVESTON; *239 EK-12; Ⓒ 3,853
Bomarton; RMC Place; BAYLOR; 238 EC-2; mail Seymour z 76380; ● 15
Bon Ami; RMC Place; JASPER; *238 EI-13; elev. 148ft./45m.; 🅿; z 75956; rural
Bonanza; RMC Place; HILL; *238 EF-6; mail Whitney z 76692; summer pop. 2,000; ● 1,000
Bonanza; RMC Place; HOPKINS; 238 ED-9; mail Brashear z 75420; ● 75
Bonanza Beach; RMC Place; BURNET; *238 EI-5; mail Burnet z 78611; ● 60
Bonham; Inc. Place; ⊡ FANNIN; 238 EC-8; 🅿 🅷; z 75418; Ⓟ 6,686; Ⓒ 9,990
Bonita; RMC Place; MONTAGUE; 238 EB-6; elev. 999ft./304m.; mail Nocona z 76255; ● 30
Bonnerville; RMC Place; FREESTONE; *238 EF-9; mail Fairfield z 75840; rural
Bonney; Inc. Place; BRAZORIA; 239 EL-10; mail Angleton z 77515, Rosharon z 77583; Ⓟ 339; Ⓒ 384
Bonnie View; RMC Place; REFUGIO; *239 EO-7; elev. 29ft./9m.; mail Woodsboro z 78393; ● 100
Bono; RMC Place; JOHNSON; 238 EE-6; elev. 830ft./253m.; mail Cleburne z 76033; ● 35
Bon Wier; RMC Place; NEWTON; 238 EI-14; 🅿; z 75928; ● 500
Booker; Inc. Place; LIPSCOMB, OCHILTREE; 236 WA-13; 🅿; z 79005; Ⓟ 1,236; Ⓒ 1,315
Boonsville; RMC Place; WISE; 238 ED-5; mail Bridgeport z 76426; ● 40
Booth; RMC Place; FORT BEND; 234 G-2; elev. 77ft./23m.; 🅿; ★ HOU; z 77469; ● 120
Borden; RMC Place; COLORADO; *239 EK-8; elev. 322ft./98m.; mail Weimar z 78962; rural
BORDEN; 236 WI-11; Ⓟ 799; Ⓒ 729; ◆ 503
Borderland; RMC Place; EL PASO; 237 WK-1; ★ ELP; mail El Paso z 79932; pop. incl. with El Paso (Inc. Place)
Borger; Inc. Place; HUTCHINSON; 236 WC-11; 🅿 🅷 ■; z 79007-08; Ⓟ 15,675; Ⓒ 14,302; ◆ 12,554
Bor-ley Heights; RMC Place; JEFFERSON; *238 EJ-13; ★ B-PA; mail Beaumont z 77708; pop. incl. with Beaumont (Inc. Place)
BOSQUE; 238 EF-6; Ⓟ 15,125; Ⓒ 17,204; ◆ 17,814
Bosqueville; RMC Place; MCLENNAN; 236 WE-5; elev. 457ft./139m.; ★ WACO; mail Waco z 76708; pop. incl. with Waco (Inc. Place)
Boston; RMC Place; ⊡ BOWIE; *238 EC-12; 🅿; z 75570; pop. incl. with New Boston (Inc. Place)
Boswell; RMC Place; WALKER; mail Huntsville z 77340; rural
Botines; CDP; WEBB; *239 EP-3; mail Laredo z 78045; Ⓒ 132
Bovina; Inc. Place; PARMER; 236 WF-8; elev. 4,067ft./1,240m.; 🅿; z 79009; Ⓟ 1,549; Ⓒ 1,874
Bowie; Inc. Place; MONTAGUE; 238 EC-5; elev. 1,124ft./343m.; 🅿 🅷; z 76230; Ⓟ 4,990; Ⓒ 5,219
BOWIE; 238 EB-11; Ⓟ 81,665; Ⓒ 89,306; ◆ 91,548
Bowser; RMC Place; SAN SABA; *238 EG-3; mail Rochelle z 76872; rural
Box Canyon-Amistad; CDP-Census Area Only; VAL VERDE; *237 WQ-11; Ⓒ 76
Box Church; RMC Place; LIMESTONE; *238 EG-8; mail Groesbeck z 76642; rural
Boxelder; RMC Place; RED RIVER; 238 EC-11; mail Annona z 75550; ● 125
Boxwood; RMC Place; UPSHUR; *238 ED-11; elev. 372ft./113m.; mail Ore City z 75683; rural
Boyce; RMC Place; ELLIS; *238 EE-8; elev. 530ft./162m.; mail Waxahachie z 75165; ● 75
Boyd; RMC Place; FANNIN; *238 EB-8; mail Bonham z 75418; ● 60
Boyd; Inc. Place; WISE; 238 ED-6; 🅿; z 76023; Ⓟ 1,041; Ⓒ 1,099
Boys Ranch; RMC Place; OLDHAM; 236 WC-10; 🅿; z 79010 & mail Amarillo z 79174; ● 500
Boz; RMC Place; ELLIS; *238 EE-7; mail Waxahachie z 75167; rural
Brachfield; RMC Place; RUSK; *238 EF-11; elev. 399ft./122m.; mail Mount Enterprise z 75681; rural
Bracken; RMC Place; COMAL; 239 EP-13; ★ SANT; mail San Antonio z 78266; ● 80
Brackettville; Inc. Place; ⊡ KINNEY; 237 WQ-13; 🅿; z 78832; Ⓟ 1,740; Ⓒ 1,876
Brad; RMC Place; PALO PINTO; *238 EE-4; mail Strawn z 76475; rural
Bradfield; RMC Place; MORRIS; mail Hughes Springs z 75656; rural
Bradford; RMC Place; ANDERSON; *238 EF-9; mail Montalba z 75853; rural
Bradshaw; RMC Place; TAYLOR; 237 WK-14; mail Winters z 79567; ● 50
Brady; Inc. Place; ⊡ MCCULLOCH; 238 EH-3; elev. 1,672ft./510m.; 🅿 🅷; z 76825; Ⓟ 5,946; Ⓒ 5,523
Brady; RMC Place; SHELBY; *238 EG-12; mail Center z 75935; rural
Braeswood; RMC Place; HARRIS; *239 EK-10; ★ HOU; mail Houston z 77030; pop. incl. with Houston (Inc. Place)
Branch; RMC Place; COLLIN; 235 B-14; ★ D-FW; mail Princeton z 75407; ● 400
Branchville; RMC Place; MILAM; *238 EI-8; mail Cameron z 76520; rural
Brandon; RMC Place; HILL; 238 EF-7; 🅿; z 76628; ● 100
Bransford; RMC Place; TARRANT; *238 ED-7; ★ D-FW; mail Colleyville z 76034; pop. incl. with Colleyville (Inc. Place)
Brashear; RMC Place; HOPKINS; 238 ED-9; 🅿; z 75420; ● 280
Brazoria; Inc. Place; BRAZORIA; 239 EM-10; elev. 33ft./10m.; 🅿; ★ L.JAC-; z 77422; Ⓟ 2,717; Ⓒ 2,787
BRAZORIA; 239 EL-10; Ⓟ 191,707; Ⓒ 241,767; ◆ 306,172
Brazos; RMC Place; PALO PINTO; 238 EE-5; mail Santo z 76472; ● 50
BRAZOS; 238 EI-8; Ⓟ 121,862; Ⓒ 152,415; ◆ 194,659
Brazos Bend; Inc. Place; BRAZOS; incorporated May 24, 2004; not reported in 2000 Census; ● 50
Brazos Country; Inc. Place; AUSTIN; incorporated May 5, 2000; not reported in 2000 Census; ● 300
Brazos Point; RMC Place; BOSQUE; 238 EF-6; mail Kopperl z 76652; ● 25
Breckenridge; Inc. Place; ⊡ STEPHENS; 238 EE-3; elev. 1,202ft./366m.; 🅿 🅷; z 76424; Ⓟ 5,665; Ⓒ 5,868
Bremond; Inc. Place; ROBERTSON; 238 EH-8; 🅿; z 76629; Ⓟ 1,110; Ⓒ 876
Brenham; Inc. Place; ⊡ WASHINGTON; 238 EJ-8; 🅿 🅷; z 77833-34; Ⓟ 11,952; Ⓒ 13,507
Brentwood Manor; RMC Place; VICTORIA; *239 EM-7; mail Victoria z 77904; ● 350
Breslau; RMC Place; LAVACA; 239 EL-7; mail Hallettsville z 77964; ● 50
BREWSTER; 237 WO-8; Ⓟ 8,681; Ⓒ 8,866; ◆ 9,445
Briar; CDP-Census Area Only; TARRANT, PARKER, WISE; *238 ED-6; ★ D-FW; mail Azle z 76020, Boyd z 76023; Ⓟ 3,899; Ⓒ 5,350
Briarcliff; Inc. Place; TRAVIS; *238 EJ-5; 🅿; ★ AUS; z 78669; Ⓟ 335; Ⓒ 895
Briargrove Park; RMC Place; HARRIS; *239 EK-10; ★ HOU; mail Houston z 77042; pop. incl. with Houston (Inc. Place)
Briaroaks; Inc. Place; JOHNSON; *238 EE-6; ★ D-FW; mail Burleson z 76028; Ⓟ 535; Ⓒ 493
Briary; RMC Place; MILAM; *238 EH-7; mail Rosebud z 76570; rural
Brice; RMC Place; HALL; *236 WE-12; elev. 2,202ft./671m.; mail Clarendon z 79226; rural
Bridge City; Inc. Place; ORANGE; 238 EJ-13; 🅿; ★ B-PA; z 77611; Ⓟ 8,034; Ⓒ 8,651
Bridge Creek; RMC Place; WICHITA; ★ WIFL; mail Wichita Falls z 76308, z 76310; pop. incl. with Wichita Falls (Inc. Place)
Bridgeport; Inc. Place; WISE; 238 EC-6; 🅿; z 76426; Ⓟ 3,581; Ⓒ 4,309; Ⓡ 4,827
Bridges Chapel; RMC Place; TITUS; *238 EC-11; mail Mount Pleasant z 75455; rural
Bridle Ridge; RMC Place; VICTORIA; *239 EM-7; mail Victoria z 77904; pop. incl. with Victoria (Inc. Place)
Brierwood Bay; RMC Place; HENDERSON; *238 EF-10; mail Frankston z 75763; ● 225
Briggs; RMC Place; BURNET; 238 EI-5; 🅿; z 78608; ● 110
Briggs; RMC Place; DALLAS; ★ D-FW; pop. incl. with Dallas (Inc. Place)
Bright Star; RMC Place; RAINS; *238 ED-9; mail Alba z 75410; rural
Briscoe; RMC Place; WHEELER; 236 WC-13; elev. 2,659ft./810m.; 🅿; z 79011; ● 110
BRISCOE; 236 WE-11; Ⓟ 1,971; Ⓒ 1,790; ◆ 1,305
Bristol; RMC Place; ELLIS; 238 EE-8; elev. 506ft./154m.; mail Ennis z 75119; ● 300
Britton; RMC Place; ELLIS; 238 EE-7; ★ D-FW; mail Mansfield z 76063, Midlothian z 76065; pop. incl. with Mansfield (Inc. Place)
Broaddus; Inc. Place; SAN AUGUSTINE; 238 EG-12; elev. 261ft./80m.; 🅿; z 75929; Ⓟ 212; Ⓒ 189
Broadmoor; RMC Place; POTTER; ★ AMA; pop. incl. with Amarillo (Inc. Place)
Broadway; RMC Place; CROSBY; *236 WG-12; elev. 3,007ft./917m.; mail Crosbyton z 79322, McAdoo z 79243; rural
Broadway; RMC Place; HARRIS; ★ HOU; mail Houston z 77207; pop. incl. with Houston (Inc. Place)
Broadway; RMC Place; LAMAR; *238 EC-10; elev. 471ft./144m.; mail Paris z 75462; rural
Broadway Junction; RMC Place; LAMAR; *238 EC-10; elev. 462ft./141m.; mail Paris z 75462; rural
Brock; RMC Place; PARKER; 238 EE-5; elev. 864ft./263m.; 🅿; z 76087; ● 90
Brock Junction; RMC Place; PARKER; *238 EE-5; elev. 888ft./271m.; mail Weatherford z 76088; ● 30
Brogado; RMC Place; REEVES; *237 WM-7; mail Balmorhea z 79718
Bronco; RMC Place; YOAKUM; *236 WH-8; elev. 3,788ft./1,155m.; mail Plains z 79355; rural
Bronson; RMC Place; SABINE; 238 EG-13; 🅿; z 75930; ● 275
Bronte; Inc. Place; COKE; 237 WK-13; elev. 1,797ft./548m.; 🅿; z 76933; Ⓟ 962; Ⓒ 1,076
Brookeland; RMC Place; SABINE; 238 EH-13; elev. 174ft./53m.; 🅿; z 75931; ● 300
Brookesmith; RMC Place; BROWN; 238 EG-3; elev. 1,353ft./412m.; 🅿; z 76827; ● 100
Brook Forest; RMC Place; MONTGOMERY; *238 EJ-11; ★ HOU; mail New Caney z 77357
Brook Glen; RMC Place; HARRIS; *239 EK-11; ★ HOU; mail La Porte z 77571; pop. incl. with La Porte (Inc. Place)
Brookhaven; RMC Place; HARRIS; *239 EK-10; ★ HOU; mail Houston z 77051; pop. incl. with Houston (Inc. Place)
Brookhollow; RMC Place; DALLAS; ★ D-FW; mail Dallas z 75207, z 75212, z 75247, z 75258, z 75356; pop. incl. with Dallas (Inc. Place)
Brooks; RMC Place; JEFFERSON; *238 EJ-13; ★ B-PA; pop. incl. with Beaumont (Inc. Place)
BROOKS; 239 EQ-5; Ⓟ 8,204; Ⓒ 7,976; ◆ 7,458
Brookshier; RMC Place; RUNNELS; *238 EG-1; mail Bronte z 76933; rural
Brookshire; Inc. Place; WALLER; 239 EK-9; elev. 161ft./49m.; 🅿; z 77423; Ⓟ 2,922; Ⓒ 3,450
Brookside Village; Inc. Place; BRAZORIA; 234 G-5; 🅿; ★ HOU; z 77581; Ⓟ 1,470; Ⓒ 1,960
Brookston; RMC Place; LAMAR; 238 EB-9; 🅿; z 75421; ● 250
Broom City; RMC Place; ANDERSON; *238 EG-10; mail Elkhart z 75839; ● 20
Broome; RMC Place; STERLING; *237 WL-12; mail Sterling City z 76951; rural
Brown; RMC Place; MARTIN; *236 WJ-10; mail Ackerly z 79713; rural
BROWN; 238 EF-3; Ⓟ 34,371; Ⓒ 37,674; ◆ 37,770
Browndell; Inc. Place; JASPER; 238 EH-13; elev. 252ft./77m.; mail Brookeland z 75931; Ⓟ 192; Ⓒ 219
Brownfield; Inc. Place; ⊡ TERRY; 236 WI-9; elev. 3,308ft./1,008m.; 🅿 🅷; z 79316 & mail Tokio z 79376; Ⓟ 9,560; Ⓒ 9,488
Browning; RMC Place; SMITH; *238 EE-11; elev. 442ft./135m.; mail Tyler z 75705; ● 75
Brownlee; RMC Place; NOLAN; *236 WJ-12; mail Roscoe z 79545; rural
Brownsboro; RMC Place; CALDWELL; *239 EK-6; mail Lockhart z 78644; rural
Brownsboro; Inc. Place; HENDERSON; 238 EE-10; elev. 378ft./115m.; 🅿; z 75756; Ⓟ 545; Ⓒ 796
Brownsville; Inc. Place; ⊡ CAMERON; 239 ET-7; elev. 33ft./10m.; 🅿 🅷 🅲 23,495 ■; ★ BRNS; z 78520-23, z 78526; Ⓟ 98,962; Ⓒ 139,722; ◆ 158,733
Brownwood; Inc. Place; ⊡ BROWN; 238 EG-3; 🅿 🅷 🅲 1,328 ■; z 76801-04; Ⓟ 18,387; Ⓒ 18,813; ◆ 17,945
Brownwood; RMC Place; ORANGE; *238 EJ-13; ★ B-PA; mail Orange z 77630; pop. incl. with Orange (Inc. Place)
Broyles; RMC Place; ANDERSON; *238 EG-9; mail Palestine z 75801; rural
Bruceville; RMC Place; MCLENNAN; *238 EH-7; elev. 600ft./183m.; 🅿; z 76630; pop. incl. with Bruceville-Eddy (Inc. Place)
Bruceville-Eddy; Inc. Place; MCLENNAN, FALLS; 238 EH-7; mail Bruceville z 76630; Ⓟ 1,075; Ⓒ 1,490
Brumley; RMC Place; UPSHUR; *238 ED-11; elev. 363ft./111m.; mail Pittsburg z 75686; rural
Brundage; CDP; DIMMIT; 239 EN-2; elev. 534ft./163m.; mail Carrizo Springs z 78834; Ⓒ 31
Bruner; RMC Place; ORANGE; *238 EJ-13; ★ B-PA; mail Orange z 77630; pop. incl. with West Orange (Inc. Place)
Bruni; CDP; WEBB; 239 EP-4; 🅿; z 78344; Ⓒ 412
Brunswick; RMC Place; CHEROKEE; *238 EG-11; mail Alto z 75925; rural
Brushie Prairie; RMC Place; NAVARRO; *238 EF-8; mail Frost z 76641; rural
Brushy; RMC Place; HOOD; *238 EE-5; mail Granbury z 76048; rural
Brushy Bend Park; RMC Place; WILLIAMSON; *238 EI-6; ★ AUS; mail Round Rock z 78681; ● 200
Brushy Creek; RMC Place; ANDERSON; *238 EF-10; elev. 465ft./142m.; mail Palestine z 75801; rural
Brushy Creek; CDP-Census Area Only; WILLIAMSON; *238 EI-6; ★ AUS; mail Austin z 78717, Round Rock z 78681; Ⓟ 5,833; Ⓒ 15,371
Brushy Creek North; RMC Place; WILLIAMSON; *238 EI-6; ★ AUS; mail Round Rock z 78681; ● 600
Bryan; Inc. Place; ⊡ BRAZOS; 238 EI-8; 🅿 🅷 ■; ★ BRY-; z 77801-03, z 77805-08; Ⓟ 55,002; Ⓒ 65,660; ◆ 83,439
Bryans Mill; RMC Place; CASS; 238 EC-12; elev. 323ft./98m.; mail Naples z 75568; ● 75
Bryson; Inc. Place; JACK; 238 ED-4; 🅿; z 76427; Ⓟ 520; Ⓒ 528
Buchanan Dam; CDP; LLANO; 238 EI-4; 🅿; z 78609; Ⓟ 1,099; Ⓒ 1,688
Buchanan Lake Village; RMC Place; LLANO; *238 EI-4; mail Tow z 78672; ● 500
Buchel; RMC Place; DEWITT; *239 EL-7; mail Cuero z 77954; rural
Buckeye; RMC Place; MATAGORDA; *239 EM-9; mail Bay City z 77414; rural
Buckholts; Inc. Place; MILAM; 238 EI-7; 🅿; z 76518; Ⓟ 335; Ⓒ 387
Buckhorn; RMC Place; AUSTIN; *238 EJ-9; mail Bellville z 77418; rural
Buckhorn; RMC Place; NEWTON; *238 EI-13; elev. 130ft./40m.; mail Bon Wier z 75928; rural
Buckingham; RMC Place; DALLAS; 235 E-11; ★ D-FW; mail Richardson z 75080-81; pop. incl. with Richardson (Inc. Place)
Buckner; RMC Place; PARKER; *238 EE-5; mail Lipan z 76462; rural
Buda; Inc. Place; HAYS; 238 EJ-6; elev. 706ft./215m.; 🅿; ★ AUS; z 78610; Ⓟ 1,795; Ⓒ 2,404
Buena Vista; RMC Place; BEXAR; *239 EL-4; elev. 545ft./166m.; ★ SANT; mail Elmendorf z 78112, San Antonio z 78221; ● 160
Buena Vista; RMC Place; BURNET; *238 EI-4; mail Burnet z 78611; ● 50
Buena Vista; RMC Place; SHELBY; *238 EF-12; mail Timpson z 75975; rural
Buffalo; Inc. Place; LEON; 238 EG-9; elev. 389ft./119m.; 🅿; z 75831; Ⓟ 1,555; Ⓒ 1,804
Buffalo; MILLS; see Ebony (RMC Place)
Buffalo Gap; Inc. Place; TAYLOR; 237 WK-14; 🅿; z 79508; Ⓟ 499; Ⓒ 463
Buffalo Gap; RMC Place; TRAVIS; 238 EF-2; ★ AUS; mail Austin z 78734; ● 400
Buffalo Springs; RMC Place; CLAY; 238 EC-5; elev. 1,065ft./325m.; mail Bellevue z 76228; ● 50
Buffalo Springs; Inc. Place; LUBBOCK; *236 WH-10; Ⓒ 493
Buford; RMC Place; MITCHELL; *236 WJ-12; elev. 2,162ft./659m.; mail Colorado City z 79512
Bugbee Heights; RMC Place; HUTCHINSON; *236 WC-11; mail Sanford z 79078; ● 70
Bug Tussle; RMC Place; FANNIN; *238 EC-9; elev. 579ft./176m.; mail Ladonia z 75449; rural
Bula; RMC Place; BAILEY; 236 WG-9; 🅿; z 79320; ● 35
Bulcher; RMC Place; COOKE; 238 EB-6; elev. 813ft./248m.; mail Muenster z 76252; rural
Bullard; Inc. Place; SMITH, CHEROKEE; 238 EF-10; elev. 501ft./153m.; 🅿; ★ TYL; z 75757; Ⓟ 890; Ⓒ 1,150
Bullock; RMC Place; EASTLAND; *238 EE-4; mail Ranger z 76470; rural
Bulverde; Inc. Place; COMAL; 239 EK-4; elev. 1,096ft./334m.; 🅿; z 78163; Ⓒ 3,761
Buna; CDP; JASPER; 238 EI-13; elev. 75ft./23m.; 🅿; z 77612; Ⓟ 2,127; Ⓒ 2,269
Bunavista; RMC Place; HUTCHINSON; *236 WC-11; elev. 3,162ft./964m.; mail Borger z 79007; pop. incl. with Borger (Inc. Place)
Buncomb; RMC Place; PANOLA; *238 EF-12; mail Carthage z 75633; rural
Bunger; RMC Place; YOUNG; *238 ED-4; mail Graham z 76450
Bunker Hill; RMC Place; LAMAR; *238 EB-9; mail Sumner z 75486; rural
Bunker Hill Village; Inc. Place; HARRIS; 234 D-3; ★ HOU; mail Houston z 77024; Ⓟ 3,391; Ⓒ 3,654
Bunyan; RMC Place; ERATH; *238 EF-4; elev. 1,537ft./468m.; mail Dublin z 76446; rural
Burkburnett; Inc. Place; WICHITA; 238 EB-4; elev. 1,057ft./322m.; 🅿; ★ WIFL; z 76354; Ⓟ 10,145; Ⓒ 10,927
Burke; Inc. Place; ANGELINA; 238 EH-11; 🅿; ★ LUFK; z 75941; Ⓟ 314; Ⓒ 315
Burkett; RMC Place; COLEMAN; 238 EF-3; 🅿; z 76828; ● 100
Burkeville; RMC Place; NEWTON; *238 EH-13; 🅿; z 75932; ● 500
Burleigh; RMC Place; AUSTIN; *239 EK-9; mail Bellville z 77418; rural
Burleson; Inc. Place; JOHNSON, TARRANT; 238 EE-6; 🅿 🅷; ★ D-FW; z 76028, z 76097; Ⓟ 16,113; Ⓒ 20,976; ◆ 27,189
BURLESON; 238 EI-8; Ⓟ 13,625; Ⓒ 16,470; ◆ 16,454
Burlington; RMC Place; MILAM; 238 EH-7; elev. 432ft./132m.; 🅿; z 76519; ● 160
Burnell; RMC Place; KARNES; *239 EM-6; elev. 344ft./105m.; mail Kenedy z 78119; rural
Burnet; Inc. Place; ⊡ BURNET; 238 EI-5; elev. 1,315ft./401m.; 🅿 🅷; z 78611; Ⓟ 3,423; Ⓒ 4,735
BURNET; 238 EI-5; Ⓟ 22,677; Ⓒ 34,147; ◆ 45,957
Burns; RMC Place; BOWIE; *238 EC-12; mail Hooks z 75561; rural
Burns; COOKE; see Burns City (RMC Place)
Burns City (Burns); RMC Place; COOKE; *238 EC-7; mail Pilot Point z 76258; ● 40
Burr; RMC Place; WHARTON; 239 EL-9; mail Wharton z 77488; rural
Burrantown; RMC Place; HOUSTON; *238 EG-10; mail Grapeland z 75844; rural
Burris; RMC Place; LUBBOCK; *236 WH-10; ★ LUB; pop. incl. with Lubbock (Inc. Place)
Burris Crossing; RMC Place; EL PASO; *237 WL-2; mail Tornillo z 79853; rural
Burrow; RMC Place; HUNT; *238 ED-8; mail Royse City z 75189
Burton; Inc. Place; WASHINGTON; 238 EJ-8; 🅿; z 77835; Ⓟ 311; Ⓒ 359
Busby; RMC Place; FISHER; *236 WJ-13; elev. 2,090ft./637m.; mail Roby z 79543; rural
Busco; RMC Place; HARRIS; ★ HOU; pop. incl. with Houston (Inc. Place)
Bushland; RMC Place; POTTER; 236 WD-10; 🅿; z 79012; ● 250
Bushwhacker Peninsula; RMC Place; HENDERSON; *238 EF-9; mail Mabank z 75156; ● 120
Bushy; RMC Place; BRAZOS; *238 EI-8; mail College Station z 77845
Bustamante; RMC Place; ZAPATA; *239 EQ-3; elev. 441ft./134m.; mail Hebbronville z 78361
Busterville; RMC Place; HOCKLEY; *236 WH-10; mail Ropesville z 79358; rural
Butler; RMC Place; BASTROP; 238 EJ-7; mail Elgin z 78621; ● 150
Butler; RMC Place; FREESTONE; *238 EG-9; mail Oakwood z 75855; rural
Butterfield; CDP-Census Area Only; EL PASO; *237 WK-2; Ⓒ 61
Butter Krust; RMC Place; TRAVIS; ★ AUS; pop. incl. with Austin (Inc. Place)
Byers; Inc. Place; CLAY; 238 EB-5; 🅿; z 76357; Ⓟ 510; Ⓒ 517
Bynum; Inc. Place; HILL; 238 EF-7; 🅿; z 76631; Ⓟ 192; Ⓒ 225
Byrd; RMC Place; ELLIS; *238 EF-8; mail Ennis z 75119; rural
Byrds; RMC Place; BROWN; *238 EF-3; elev. 1,434ft./437m.; mail Brownwood z 76801; rural

C

Cabot Kingsmill; RMC Place; GRAY; *236 WD-12; mail Pampa z 79065; ● 125
Cactus; Inc. Place; MOORE; 236 WB-10; 🅿; z 79013; Ⓟ 1,529; Ⓒ 2,538
Caddo; RMC Place; STEPHENS; 238 EE-4; 🅿; z 76429; ● 200
Caddo Mills; Inc. Place; HUNT; 238 ED-8; elev. 529ft./161m.; 🅿; z 75135; Ⓟ 1,068; Ⓒ 1,149
Cadiz; RMC Place; BEE; *239 EN-5; elev. 349ft./106m.; mail Beeville z 78102; rural
Cain City; RMC Place; GILLESPIE; 238 EJ-4; elev. 1,744ft./532m.; mail Fredericksburg z 78624; ● 40
Calallen; RMC Place; NUECES; *239 EO-6; ★ CRPX; pop. incl. with Corpus Christi (Inc. Place)
Calaveras; RMC Place; WILSON; *239 EL-5; mail Floresville z 78114; rural
Calder Highlands; RMC Place; JEFFERSON; *238 EJ-13; ★ B-PA; mail Beaumont z 77706; pop. incl. with Beaumont (Inc. Place)
Calder Terrace; RMC Place; JEFFERSON; *238 EJ-13; ★ B-PA; mail Beaumont z 77706; pop. incl. with Beaumont (Inc. Place)
Caldwell; Inc. Place; ⊡ BURLESON; 238 EI-8; elev. 392ft./119m.; 🅿 🅷; z 77836; Ⓟ 3,181; Ⓒ 3,449
CALDWELL; 239 EK-6; Ⓟ 26,392; Ⓒ 32,194; ◆ 37,317
Caldwood; RMC Place; JEFFERSON; *238 EJ-13; ★ B-PA; mail Beaumont z 77707; pop. incl. with Beaumont (Inc. Place)
Caldwood Acres; RMC Place; JEFFERSON; *238 EJ-13; ★ B-PA; mail Beaumont z 77707; pop. incl. with Beaumont (Inc. Place)
Caledonia; RMC Place; RUSK; *238 EF-12; mail Garrison z 75946, Timpson z 75975; rural
Calf Creek; RMC Place; MCCULLOCH; *238 EH-2; elev. 1,849ft./564m.; mail Brady z 76825; rural
CALHOUN; 239 EN-8; Ⓟ 19,053; Ⓒ 20,647; ◆ 20,153
Call; RMC Place; NEWTON; 238 EI-13; 🅿; z 75933; ● 150

Entries in **UPPERCASE** are counties.
Entries in **bold** have populations of 2,500 or more.
Names in parentheses are alternate names.
Inc. Place — Incorporated Place
RMC Place — Rand McNally Designated Place
CDP — Census Designated Place
MCD — Minor Civil Division

⊡ County Seat
▲ Minor Civil Division
elev. Elevation
🅿 Post Office
🅷 Hospital
🅲 College
■ Principal Business Center
★ Ranally Metro Area (RMA) Abbreviation
z Zip Code(s)

Ⓟ Previous Census Population
Ⓡ Revised Census Population
Ⓐ Annexation Population
● Rand McNally Population Estimate
Ⓒ Final Census Population
Ⓢ Special Census Population
◆ Estimated Population

For additional definitions see Glossary, Volume 1, and Introduction, Volume 2.

CALLAHAN; 238 EF-2; Ⓟ 11,859; Ⓒ 12,905; ◆ 13,715
Calliham; RMC Place; MCMULLEN; 239 EN-5; elev. 230ft./70m.; 🅿; z 78007; ● 200
Callisburg; Inc. Place; COOKE; 238 EB-7; elev. 803ft./245m.; 🅿; z 76240; Ⓟ 344; Ⓒ 365
Call Junction; RMC Place; JASPER; *238 EI-13; mail Call z 75933; ● 25
Calvary; RMC Place; WOOD; *238 ED-10; mail Mineola z 75773; rural
Calvert; Inc. Place; ROBERTSON; 238 EH-8; elev. 332ft./101m.; 🅿; z 77837; Ⓟ 1,536; Ⓒ 1,426
Camden; RMC Place; POLK; 238 EH-11; elev. 282ft./86m.; 🅿; z 75934; ● 150
Camelot; RMC Place; BEXAR; 239 ER-13; ★ SANT; mail San Antonio z 78239; ● 4,000
Cameron; Inc. Place; ⊡ MILAM; 238 EI-7; 🅿 🅷; z 76520; Ⓟ 5,580; Ⓒ 5,634
CAMERON; 239 ES-7; Ⓟ 260,120; Ⓒ 335,227; ◆ 384,871
Cameron Park; CDP-Census Area Only; CAMERON; *239 ET-7; ★ BRNS; mail Brownsville z 78521; Ⓟ 3,802; Ⓒ 5,961
Camilla; RMC Place; SAN JACINTO; 238 EI-11; mail Coldspring z 77331; ● 120
CAMP; 238 ED-11; Ⓟ 9,904; Ⓒ 11,549; ◆ 12,867
Camp Air (Air); RMC Place; MASON; *238 EI-3; mail Mason z 76856; rural
Campbell; Inc. Place; HUNT; 238 EC-9; 🅿; z 75422; Ⓟ 683; Ⓒ 734
Campbellton; RMC Place; ATASCOSA; 239 EM-5; elev. 241ft./73m.; 🅿; z 78008; ● 300
Camp Dallas; RMC Place; DENTON; *238 ED-7; ★ D-FW; mail Little Elm z 75068; ● 150
Campo Alto; RMC Place; HIDALGO; *239 ES-5; ★ MCAL; mail Alamo z 78516; ● 300
Camp Ruby; RMC Place; POLK; *238 EI-11; mail Livingston z 77351; rural
Camp San Saba; RMC Place; MCCULLOCH; 238 EH-3; mail Brady z 76825; ● 30
Camp Springs; RMC Place; SCURRY; *236 WI-12; mail Hermleigh z 79526
Camp Swift; CDP-Census Area Only; BASTROP; *238 EJ-7; mail Bastrop z 78602; Ⓟ 2,681; Ⓒ 4,731
Campti; RMC Place; SHELBY; *238 EF-13; elev. 294ft./90m.; mail Center z 75935; rural
Camp Verde; RMC Place; KERR; *239 EK-3; elev. 1,615ft./492m.; 🅿; z 78010; rural
Camp Wood; Inc. Place; REAL; 237 WP-14; 🅿; z 78833; Ⓟ 595; Ⓒ 822
Cana; RMC Place; VAN ZANDT; *238 EE-9; elev. 440ft./134m.; mail Wills Point z 75169; rural
Canada Verde; RMC Place; WILSON; *239 EL-5; mail Floresville z 78114; rural
Canadian; Inc. Place; ⊡ HEMPHILL; 236 WC-13; elev. 2,424ft./739m.; 🅿 🅷; z 79014; Ⓟ 2,417; Ⓒ 2,233
Candelaria; RMC Place; PRESIDIO; 237 WO-5; mail Marfa z 79843; ● 100
Candlelight Oaks; RMC Place; HARRIS; *239 EK-10; ★ HOU; mail Houston z 77091; pop. incl. with Houston (Inc. Place)
Caney; RMC Place; MATAGORDA; *239 EM-10; mail Bay City z 77414; rural
Caney City; Inc. Place; HENDERSON; 238 EF-9; mail Malakoff z 75148; Ⓟ 170; Ⓒ 236
Caney Creek Estates; RMC Place; MONTGOMERY; *238 EJ-11; ★ HOU; mail New Caney z 77357
Cannon; RMC Place; GRAYSON; 238 EC-8; mail Van Alstyne z 75495; ● 45
Canton; Inc. Place; ⊡ VAN ZANDT; 238 EE-9; 🅿; z 75103; Ⓟ 2,949; Ⓒ 3,292
Cantu Addition; CDP-Census Area Only; BROOKS; *239 EQ-5; Ⓒ 217
Canutillo; CDP; EL PASO; 237 WK-1; 🅿; ★ ELP; z 79835; Ⓟ 4,442; Ⓒ 5,129
Canyon; RMC Place; LUBBOCK; *236 WH-10; ★ LUB; mail Lubbock z 79408; ● 50
Canyon; Inc. Place; ⊡ RANDALL; 236 WE-10; elev. 3,551ft./1,082m.; 🅿 🅷 🅲 7,412; z 79015-16; Ⓟ 11,365; Ⓒ 12,875
Canyon City; RMC Place; COMAL; *239 EK-5; mail New Braunfels z 78130
Canyon Creek Estates; RMC Place; COMAL; *239 EK-5; mail New Braunfels z 78130
Canyon Lake; CDP-Census Area Only; COMAL; *239 EK-5; 🅿; z 78130, z 78132-33; Ⓟ 9,975; Ⓒ 16,870
Canyon Lake Acres; RMC Place; COMAL; *239 EK-5; mail New Braunfels z 78130
Canyon Lake Estates; RMC Place; COMAL; *239 EK-5; mail New Braunfels z 78130
Canyon Lake Forest; RMC Place; COMAL; *239 EK-5; mail New Braunfels z 78130
Canyon Lake Hills; RMC Place; COMAL; *239 EK-5; mail New Braunfels z 78130
Canyon Lake Island; RMC Place; COMAL; *239 EK-5; mail New Braunfels z 78130
Canyon Lake Mobile Home Estates; RMC Place; COMAL; *239 EK-5; mail New Braunfels z 78130
Canyon Lake Shores; RMC Place; COMAL; *239 EK-5; mail New Braunfels z 78130
Canyon Lake Village; RMC Place; COMAL; *239 EK-5; mail New Braunfels z 78130
Canyon Lake Village West; RMC Place; COMAL; *239 EK-5; mail New Braunfels z 78130
Canyon Springs Resort; RMC Place; COMAL; *239 EK-5; mail New Braunfels z 78130
Canyon Valley; RMC Place; CROSBY; *236 WH-11; mail Post z 79356; rural
Canyon View Acres; RMC Place; COMAL; *239 EK-4; mail Bulverde z 78163; ● 300
Cape Malibu; RMC Place; MONTGOMERY; *238 EI-10; mail Willis z 77318; ● 80
Capitol; RMC Place; TRAVIS; ★ AUS; mail Austin z 78701, z 78711; pop. incl. with Austin (Inc. Place)
Caplen; RMC Place; GALVESTON; *239 EK-12; mail Gilchrist z 77617; ● 100
Capps Corner; RMC Place; MONTAGUE; *238 EB-6; elev. 963ft./294m.; mail Saint Jo z 76265
Cap Rock; RMC Place; CROSBY; *236 WH-11; elev. 3,024ft./922m.; mail Ralls z 79357; rural
Caps; RMC Place; TAYLOR; 236 WJ-14; ★ ABIL; mail Abilene z 79606; ● 80
Caradan; RMC Place; MILLS; *238 EG-4; elev. 1,562ft./476m.; mail Goldthwaite z 76844
Carancahua; RMC Place; JACKSON; *239 EM-8; mail Palacios z 77465; rural
Carbon; Inc. Place; EASTLAND; 238 EF-4; 🅿; z 76435; Ⓟ 255; Ⓒ 224
Carbondale; RMC Place; BOWIE; *238 EC-12; mail Maud z 75567; rural
Carey; RMC Place; CHILDRESS; 236 WF-13; mail Childress z 79201; ● 50
Carlisle; RMC Place; TRINITY; 238 EH-11; mail Trinity z 75862; ● 70
Carlos; RMC Place; GRIMES; *238 EI-9; elev. 245ft./75m.; mail Anderson z 77830
Carl Range; RMC Place; DALLAS; ★ D-FW; mail Irving z 75014, z 75062; pop. incl. with Irving (Inc. Place)
Carlsbad; RMC Place; TOM GREEN; 237 WL-12; 🅿; z 76934; ● 500
Carls Corner; Inc. Place; HILL; *238 EF-7; mail Hillsboro z 76645; Ⓟ 94; Ⓒ 134
Carlton; RMC Place; HAMILTON; 238 EF-5; 🅿; z 76436; ● 250
Carmine; Inc. Place; FAYETTE; 238 EJ-8; 🅿; z 78932; Ⓟ 192; Ⓒ 228
Carmona; RMC Place; POLK; *238 EH-11; mail Corrigan z 75939; rural
Caro; RMC Place; NACOGDOCHES; *238 EF-11; mail Nacogdoches z 75964; rural
Carolina Cove; RMC Place; WALKER; *238 EI-10; mail Riverside z 77367; rural
Carpenter; RMC Place; WILSON; *239 EL-5; mail Adkins z 78101; rural
Carpenters Bluff; RMC Place; GRAYSON; *238 EB-8; elev. 520ft./158m.; mail Denison z 75021; rural
Carricitos; RMC Place; CAMERON; *239 ES-6; elev. 54ft./16m.; ★ BRNS; mail San Benito z 78586; pop. incl. with Los Indios (Inc. Place)
Carrizo Hill; CDP-Census Area Only; DIMMIT; *239 EN-2; Ⓒ 548
Carrizo Springs; Inc. Place; ⊡ DIMMIT; 237 WS-14; 🅿 🅷; z 78834; Ⓟ 5,745; Ⓒ 5,655
Carroll; RMC Place; SMITH; *238 EE-10; mail Lindale z 75771; ● 60
Carroll Springs; RMC Place; ANDERSON; *238 EF-9; mail Montalba z 75853; rural
Carrollton; Inc. Place; DALLAS, COLLIN, DENTON; 238 ED-7; 🅿 🅷 ■; ★ D-FW; z 75006-07, z 75010-11; Ⓟ 82,169; Ⓒ 109,576; ◆ 128,198
Carson; RMC Place; FANNIN; *238 EB-9; mail Telephone z 75488; ● 50
CARSON; 236 WC-11; Ⓟ 6,576; Ⓒ 6,516; ◆ 6,237
Carta Valley; RMC Place; EDWARDS; *237 WP-12; elev. 1,851ft./564m.; mail Del Rio z 78840; rural
Carterville; RMC Place; CASS; *238 ED-12; elev. 284ft./87m.; mail Linden z 75563
Carthage; Inc. Place; ⊡ PANOLA; 238 EF-12; elev. 309ft./94m.; 🅿 🅷; z 75633; Ⓟ 6,496; Ⓒ 6,664
Cartwright; RMC Place; KAUFMAN; *238 EE-8; mail Kaufman z 75142; rural
Cartwright; RMC Place; WOOD; *238 ED-10; elev. 466ft./142m.; mail Winnsboro z 75494; rural
Casa Piedra; RMC Place; PRESIDIO; *237 WP-6; mail Marfa z 79843; rural
Casa View; RMC Place; DALLAS; *238 ED-8; ★ D-FW; mail Dallas z 75228; pop. incl. with Dallas (Inc. Place)
Cash; RMC Place; HUNT; 238 ED-9; mail Greenville z 75402; ● 150
Cashion Community; Inc. Place; WICHITA; incorporated February 29, 2000; not reported in 2000 Census; ● 300
Cason; RMC Place; MORRIS; 238 ED-11; elev. 335ft./102m.; 🅿; z 75636; ● 300
Cass; RMC Place; CASS; 238 EC-12; elev. 239ft./73m.; mail Bloomburg z 75556; ● 60
CASS; 238 EC-11; Ⓟ 29,982; Ⓒ 30,438; ◆ 29,137
Cassie; RMC Place; BURNET; *238 EI-4; mail Burnet z 78611; ● 150
Cassin; RMC Place; BEXAR; *239 EL-4; ★ SANT; mail San Antonio z 78221; rural
Castell; RMC Place; LLANO; 238 EI-3; elev. 1,200ft./366m.; 🅿; z 76831; ● 40
Castle Heights; RMC Place; BRAZOS; *238 EI-8; mail Bryan z 77808; pop. incl. with Bryan (Inc. Place)
Castle Hill; RMC Place; VICTORIA; *239 EM-7; ★ VICT; mail Victoria z 77904; pop. incl. with Victoria (Inc. Place)
Castle Hills; Inc. Place; BEXAR; 239 ER-11; 🅿; ★ SANT; z 78213; Ⓟ 4,198; Ⓒ 4,202
Castlewoods; RMC Place; HARRIS; *239 EK-10; ★ HOU; mail Houston z 77039; ● 800
Castolon; RMC Place; BREWSTER; 237 WQ-7; elev. 2,169ft./661m.; mail Big Bend National Park z 79834; ● 10
CASTRO; 236 WE-9; Ⓟ 9,070; Ⓒ 8,285; ◆ 6,918
Castroville; Inc. Place; MEDINA; 239 EL-4; 🅿; z 78009, z 78056; Ⓟ 2,159; Ⓒ 2,664
Catarina; CDP; DIMMIT; 239 EN-2; elev. 529ft./161m.; 🅿; z 78836; Ⓒ 135
Cat Spring; RMC Place; AUSTIN; 239 EK-9; 🅿; z 78933; ● 100
Causeway Beach; RMC Place; HENDERSON; *238 EE-9; mail Kemp z 75143; pop. incl. with Seven Points (Inc. Place)
Cave Creek; RMC Place; GILLESPIE; *238 EJ-4; mail Fredericksburg z 78624; rural
Caviness; RMC Place; LAMAR; *238 EB-9; mail Paris z 75460; ● 80
Cawthon; RMC Place; BRAZOS; 238 EJ-9; elev. 231ft./70m.; mail Navasota z 77868; ● 70
Cayote; RMC Place; BOSQUE; *238 EG-6; mail Valley Mills z 76689; rural
Cayuga; RMC Place; ANDERSON; 238 EF-9; 🅿; z 75832; ● 300
Cedar Bayou; RMC Place; GRAYSON; *238 EB-7; mail Gordonville z 76245; ● 50
Cedar Bayou; RMC Place; HARRIS; *239 EK-11; ★ HOU
Cedar Branch; RMC Place; HENDERSON; *238 EE-9; mail Mabank z 75156; ● 150
Cedar Branch; RMC Place; HOUSTON; *238 EG-10; mail Grapeland z 75844; rural
Cedar Creek; RMC Place; ANDERSON; *238 EG-10; mail Elkhart z 75839; rural
Cedar Creek; RMC Place; BASTROP; 238 EJ-6; 🅿; z 78612; ● 100
Cedar Elm; RMC Place; BEXAR; *239 EL-4; ★ SANT; mail San Antonio z 78249, z 78269; pop. incl. with San Antonio (Inc. Place)
Cedar Grove; RMC Place; CASS; *238 EC-12; mail Marietta z 75566; rural
Cedar Grove; RMC Place; CORYELL; *238 EH-5; ★ KILL-; mail Copperas Cove z 76522; pop. incl. with Copperas Cove (Inc. Place)
Cedar Grove; RMC Place; EL PASO; *237 WK-2; ★ ELP; mail El Paso z 79915; pop. incl. with El Paso (Inc. Place)
Cedar Hill; Inc. Place; DALLAS, ELLIS; 235 J-8; 🅿; ★ D-FW; z 75104, z 75106; Ⓟ 19,988; Ⓒ 32,093; ◆ 37,955
Cedar Hill; RMC Place; FLOYD; *236 WF-11; elev. 3,165ft./965m.; mail Lockney z 79241
Cedar Hills; RMC Place; BASTROP; *238 EJ-7; mail Elgin z 78621; ● 200
Cedar Lake; RMC Place; MATAGORDA; *239 EM-10; elev. 16ft./5m.; mail Bay City z 77414; rural
Cedar Lane; RMC Place; MATAGORDA; 239 EM-10; 🅿; z 77415; ● 60
Cedar Mills; RMC Place; GRAYSON; *238 EB-7; elev. 666ft./203m.; mail Gordonville z 76245; ● 20
Cedar Park; Inc. Place; WILLIAMSON, TRAVIS; 238 EI-6; elev. 910ft./277m.; 🅿; ★ AUS; z 78613, z 78630; Ⓟ 5,161; Ⓒ 26,049; ◆ 54,434
Cedar Point; RMC Place; CHAMBERS; 234 F-10; mail Baytown z 77520-21
Cedar Shores Estates; RMC Place; BOSQUE; *238 EF-6; mail Morgan z 76671; ● 200
Cedar Springs; RMC Place; FALLS; *238 EH-7; mail Rosebud z 76570
Cedar Springs; RMC Place; UPSHUR; *238 ED-11; mail Ore City z 75683; ● 125
Cedarvale; RMC Place; KAUFMAN; mail Kaufman z 75142; rural
Cedar Valley; RMC Place; TRAVIS; *238 EJ-5; elev. 1,085ft./331m.; ★ AUS; mail Austin z 78736; rural
Cedarview; RMC Place; DALLAS; *238 EE-7; elev. 800ft./244m.; ★ D-FW; mail Cedar Hill z 75104; pop. incl. with Cedar Hill (Inc. Place)
Ceder Creek; RMC Place; WALLER; *238 EJ-9; mail Hempstead z 77445; rural
Cee Vee; RMC Place; COTTLE; 236 WF-13; elev. 1,878ft./572m.; 🅿; z 79223; ● 45
Cego; RMC Place; FALLS; 238 EH-7; elev. 486ft./148m.; mail Eddy z 76524; ● 40
Cele; RMC Place; TRAVIS; *238 EJ-6; mail Manor z 78653; rural
Celeste; Inc. Place; HUNT; 238 EC-8; 🅿; z 75423; Ⓟ 733; Ⓒ 817
Celina; Inc. Place; COLLIN; 238 EC-7; 🅿; z 75009; Ⓟ 1,737; Ⓒ 1,861
Cementville; RMC Place; BEXAR; ★ SANT; pop. incl. with San Antonio (Inc. Place)
Center; RMC Place; LIMESTONE; *238 EG-8; mail Groesbeck z 76642; rural
Center; Inc. Place; ⊡ SHELBY; 238 EF-12; elev. 379ft./116m.; 🅿 🅷; z 75935; Ⓟ 4,950; Ⓒ 5,678
Center City; RMC Place; MILLS; 238 EG-4; elev. 1,393ft./425m.; mail Goldthwaite z 76844; ● 15
Center Grove; RMC Place; TITUS; *238 EC-11; elev. 421ft./128m.; mail Cookville z 75558; rural
Center Line; RMC Place; BURLESON; *238 EJ-8; mail Somerville z 77879
Center Point; RMC Place; CAMP; *238 ED-11; mail Pittsburg z 75686; ● 60
Center Point; RMC Place; ELLIS; *238 EF-7; mail Italy z 76651; rural
Center Point; RMC Place; HUNT; *238 ED-8; mail Greenville z 75402; rural
Center Point; RMC Place; KERR; 239 EK-3; elev. 1,524ft./465m.; 🅿 🅷; z 78010; ● 750
Center Point; RMC Place; PANOLA; *238 EE-12; mail Tatum z 75691; rural
Center Point; RMC Place; PARKER; *238 EE-6; mail Weatherford z 76087; rural
Center Point; RMC Place; TITUS; *238 EC-11; mail Cookville z 75558; rural
Center Point; RMC Place; UPSHUR; *238 EE-11; mail Big Sandy z 75755; rural
Centerview; RMC Place; LEON; *238 EH-9; elev. 281ft./86m.; mail Centerville z 75833; rural
Centerville; Inc. Place; ⊡ LEON; 238 EH-9; elev. 353ft./108m.; 🅿; z 75833; Ⓟ 812; Ⓒ 903
Centerville; RMC Place; TRINITY; *238 EH-11; elev. 362ft./110m.; mail Groveton z 75845; rural
Centex; RMC Place; HAYS; *239 EK-5; pop. incl. with San Marcos (Inc. Place)
Central; RMC Place; ANGELINA; 238 EG-11; mail Pollok z 75969; ● 250
Central; RMC Place; DALLAS; mail Irving z 75016, z 75038; pop. incl. with Irving (Inc. Place)
Central; RMC Place; TARRANT; ★ D-FW; mail Fort Worth z 76102; pop. incl. with Fort Worth (Inc. Place)
Central Gardens; CDP; JEFFERSON; *238 EJ-13; elev. 20ft./6m.; ★ B-PA; mail Nederland z 77627; Ⓟ 4,026; Ⓒ 4,106
Central Heights; RMC Place; JEFFERSON; ★ B-PA; mail Nederland z 77627; ● 700
Central Heights; RMC Place; NACOGDOCHES; *238 EG-11; mail Nacogdoches z 75964; ● 200
Central High; RMC Place; CHEROKEE; *238 EG-11; mail Alto z 75925; rural
Centralia; RMC Place; TRINITY; 238 EH-11; elev. 326ft./99m.; 🅿; z 75834; ● 90
Central Park; RMC Place; HARRIS; *239 EK-10; ★ HOU; mail Houston z 77011; pop. incl. with Houston (Inc. Place)
Cesar Chavez; CDP-Census Area Only; HIDALGO; *239 ES-5; ★ MCAL; Ⓒ 1,469
Cestohowa (Czestochowa); RMC Place; KARNES; *239 EM-5; mail Falls City z 78113; ● 50
Chaffee Village; RMC Place; BELL; *238 EH-6; ★ KILL-; mail Killeen z 76544
Chalk; RMC Place; COTTLE; *238 EB-1; mail Paducah z 79248; rural
Chalk Hill; RMC Place; RUSK; *238 EE-11; mail Henderson z 75652, Tatum z 75691; rural
Chalk Mountain; RMC Place; ERATH; *238 EF-5; mail Stephenville z 76401; ● 25
CHAMBERS; 239 EK-12; Ⓟ 20,088; Ⓒ 26,031; ◆ 29,519
Chambersville; RMC Place; COLLIN; *238 EC-8; mail Mckinney z 75069; pop. incl. with Weston (Inc. Place)
Chambliss; RMC Place; COLLIN; *238 EC-8; mail Anna z 75409; rural
Champion; RMC Place; NOLAN; *236 WJ-12; mail Roscoe z 79545; rural
Chances Store; RMC Place; BURLESON; *238 EI-8; elev. 221ft./67m.; mail Somerville z 77879; ● 10
Chandler; Inc. Place; HENDERSON; 238 EE-10; elev. 401ft./122m.; 🅿; z 75758; Ⓟ 1,630; Ⓒ 2,099
Channelview; CDP; HARRIS; 234 D-8; 🅿 🅷; ★ HOU; z 77530; Ⓟ 25,564; Ⓒ 29,685; ◆ 35,118
Channing; Inc. Place; ⊡ HARTLEY; 236 WC-9; elev. 3,802ft./1,159m.; 🅿; z 79018 & mail Masterson z 79058; Ⓟ 277; Ⓒ 356
Chaparral Hills; RMC Place; VAL VERDE; *237 WQ-12; mail Del Rio z 78840; ● 100
Chaparral Park; RMC Place; HAYS; *238 EJ-5; ★ AUS; mail Manchaca z 78652; ● 400
Chapel Hill; RMC Place; SMITH; *238 EE-10; ★ TYL; mail Tyler z 75707; ● 80
Chapman; RMC Place; RUSK; *238 EF-11; elev. 414ft./126m.; mail Henderson z 75652; rural
Chapman Ranch; RMC Place; NUECES; 239 EP-6; elev. 25ft./8m.; 🅿; z 78347; ● 150
Chappel; RMC Place; SAN SABA; *238 EH-4; mail San Saba z 76877; rural
Chappell Hill; RMC Place; WASHINGTON; 238 EJ-9; 🅿; z 77426; ● 600
Charco; RMC Place; GOLIAD; 239 EM-6; elev. 242ft./74m.; mail Goliad z 77963; ● 50
Charleston; RMC Place; DELTA; *238 EC-10; mail Cooper z 75432; ● 120
Charlie; RMC Place; CLAY; 238 EB-4; mail Wichita Falls z 76301; ● 90
Charlotte; Inc. Place; ATASCOSA; 239 EM-4; 🅿; z 78011; Ⓟ 1,475; Ⓒ 1,637
Chateau Forest; RMC Place; HARRIS; *239 EK-10; ★ HOU; mail Houston z 77088; pop. incl. with Houston (Inc. Place)
Chateau Woods; RMC Place; MONTGOMERY; *238 EJ-10; ★ HOU; mail Conroe z 77385; ● 800
Chatfield; RMC Place; NAVARRO; 238 EF-8; elev. 423ft./129m.; 🅿; z 75105; ● 60
Chatt; RMC Place; HILL; *238 EF-7; mail Hillsboro z 76645; rural
Cheapside; RMC Place; GONZALES; 239 EL-6; elev. 302ft./92m.; mail Cuero z 77954; ● 30
Cheek; RMC Place; JEFFERSON; *238 EJ-13; ★ B-PA; mail Beaumont z 77705; ● 50
Cherokee; RMC Place; SAN SABA; 238 EH-4; 🅿; z 76832; ● 400
CHEROKEE; 238 EF-10; Ⓟ 41,049; Ⓒ 46,659; ◆ 48,564
Cherokee Cove; RMC Place; HUNT; *238 ED-9; mail Quinlan z 75474; ● 200
Cherokee Landing; RMC Place; CHEROKEE; *238 EF-10; mail Cuney z 75759; ● 125
Cherry Spring; RMC Place; GILLESPIE; *238 EJ-3; elev. 1,788ft./545m.; mail Fredericksburg z 78624; rural
Chester; Inc. Place; TYLER; 238 EH-12; 🅿; z 75936; Ⓟ 285; Ⓒ 265
Chesterville; RMC Place; COLORADO, WHARTON; *239 EK-9; mail East Bernard z 77435; rural
Chico; Inc. Place; WISE; 238 EC-5; 🅿; z 76431; Ⓟ 800; Ⓒ 947
Chicota; RMC Place; LAMAR; 238 EB-10; 🅿; z 75425; ● 250
Chihuahua; RMC Place; HIDALGO; *239 ES-5; ★ MCAL; mail Mission z 78572; ● 300
Childress; Inc. Place; ⊡ CHILDRESS; 236 WF-13; 🅿 🅷; z 79201; Ⓟ 5,055; Ⓒ 6,778
CHILDRESS; 236 WE-13; Ⓟ 5,953; Ⓒ 7,688; ◆ 7,562
Chillicothe; Inc. Place; HARDEMAN; 238 EA-2; elev. 1,401ft./427m.; 🅿 🅷; z 79225 & mail Odell z 79247; Ⓟ 816; Ⓒ 798
Chilton; RMC Place; FALLS; 238 EH-7; elev. 428ft./130m.; 🅿; z 76632; ● 500
Chimney Corners; RMC Place; TRAVIS; ★ AUS; mail Austin z 78731, z 78755; pop. incl. with Austin (Inc. Place)
Chimney Hill; RMC Place; HARRIS; *239 EK-10; ★ HOU; mail Houston z 77041; ● 800
China; Inc. Place; JEFFERSON; 238 EJ-12; elev. 42ft./13m.; 🅿; z 77613; Ⓟ 1,144; Ⓒ 1,112
China Grove; Inc. Place; BEXAR; 239 ES-13; elev. 655ft./200m.; 🅿; ★ SANT; z 78263 & mail San Antonio z 78223; Ⓟ 872; Ⓒ 1,247
China Grove; RMC Place; SCURRY; *236 WJ-12; elev. 2,283ft./696m.; mail Hermleigh z 79526; rural
China Spring; MCLENNAN; see China Springs (RMC Place)
China Springs (China Spring); RMC Place; MCLENNAN; *238 EG-6; mail China Spring z 76633; ● 900
Chinati; RMC Place; PRESIDIO; *237 WP-5; mail Marfa z 79843; rural
Chipley; RMC Place; VICTORIA; mail Victoria z 77901; ● 15
Chireno; Inc. Place; NACOGDOCHES; 238 EG-12; elev. 324ft./99m.; 🅿; z 75937; Ⓟ 415; Ⓒ 405
Chisholm; RMC Place; ROCKWALL; *238 ED-8; elev. 503ft./153m.; mail Rockwall z 75087; pop. incl. with McLendon-Chisholm (Inc. Place)
Chita; RMC Place; TRINITY; *238 EH-11; mail Trinity z 75862
Choate; RMC Place; KARNES; 239 EM-6; elev. 299ft./91m.; mail Kenedy z 78119; ● 50
Chocolate Bayou; RMC Place; BRAZORIA; *239 EL-11; mail Alvin z 77511; rural
Choice; RMC Place; SHELBY; *238 EG-12; mail Center z 75935; rural
Chriesman; RMC Place; BURLESON; 238 EI-8; 🅿; z 77838; ● 40
Christine; Inc. Place; ATASCOSA; 239 EM-4; 🅿; z 78012; Ⓟ 368; Ⓒ 436
Christoval; CDP; TOM GREEN; 237 WM-13; elev. 2,028ft./618m.; 🅿; z 76935; Ⓒ 422
C H Rouse Estates; RMC Place; MONTGOMERY; *238 EJ-11; ★ HOU; mail Porter z 77365
Chula Vista-Orason; CDP-Census Area Only; CAMERON; *239 ES-7; Ⓒ 394
Chula Vista-River Spur; CDP-Census Area Only; ZAVALA; *239 EN-2; Ⓒ 400
Church Hill; RMC Place; CHEROKEE; *238 EF-10; elev. 550ft./168m.; mail Jacksonville z 75766; rural
Church Hill; RMC Place; RUSK; *238 EE-11; mail Henderson z 75652, z 75654; rural
Churchill (Churchill Bridge); RMC Place; BRAZORIA; *239 EM-10; mail Brazoria z 77422
Churchill Bridge; BRAZORIA; see Churchill (RMC Place)
Cibolo; Inc. Place; GUADALUPE, BEXAR; 239 EP-14; elev. 704ft./215m.; 🅿; ★ SANT; z 78108 & mail Schertz z 78154; Ⓟ 1,757; Ⓒ 3,035
Cielo Vista; RMC Place; EL PASO; *237 WK-2; ★ ELP; mail El Paso z 79925; pop. incl. with El Paso (Inc. Place)
Cienegas Terrace; CDP-Census Area Only; VAL VERDE; *237 WQ-12; mail Del Rio z 78840; Ⓒ 2,878
Cinco Ranch; CDP-Census Area Only; FORT BEND, HARRIS; *239 EK-10; ★ HOU; Ⓒ 11,196
Circle; RMC Place; LAMB; *236 WF-10; elev. 3,649ft./1,112m.; mail Olton z 79064; rural
Circle Back; RMC Place; BAILEY; *236 WG-9; elev. 3,882ft./1,183m.; mail Sudan z 79371; rural
Circle D-KC Estates; CDP-Census Area Only; BASTROP; *238 EJ-7; mail Bastrop z 78602; Ⓟ 1,247; Ⓒ 2,010
Circleville; RMC Place; TRAVIS; *238 EJ-5; ★ AUS; mail Austin z 78736; pop. incl. with Austin (Inc. Place)
Circleville; RMC Place; WILLIAMSON; *238 EI-6; elev. 548ft./167m.; mail Taylor z 76574
Cisco; Inc. Place; EASTLAND; 238 EE-3; elev. 1,629ft./497m.; 🅿; z 76437; Ⓟ 3,813; Ⓒ 3,851
Cistern; RMC Place; FAYETTE; 239 EK-7; elev. 467ft./142m.; mail Flatonia z 78941; ● 75
Citrus City; CDP; HIDALGO; *239 ES-5; ★ MCAL; mail Mission z 78572; Ⓒ 941
Citrus Grove; RMC Place; MATAGORDA; *239 EM-9; mail Palacios z 77465; rural
Civic Center; RMC Place; HARRIS; ★ HOU; mail Houston z 77208; pop. incl. with Houston (Inc. Place)
Clairemont; RMC Place; KENT; 236 WI-12; elev. 2,119ft./646m.; mail Snyder z 79549; ● 20
Clairette; RMC Place; ERATH; 238 EF-5; elev. 1,094ft./333m.; mail Hico z 76457; ● 60
Clardy; RMC Place; LAMAR; *238 EC-10; mail Pattonville z 75468; rural
Clarendon; Inc. Place; ⊡ DONLEY; 236 WE-12; elev. 2,732ft./833m.; 🅿; z 79226; Ⓟ 2,067; Ⓒ 1,974
Clareville; RMC Place; BEE; *239 EN-6; elev. 271ft./83m.; mail Beeville z 78102
Clark; DENTON; see DISH (Inc. Place)
Clark; RMC Place; LIBERTY; *238 EI-11; elev. 74ft./23m.; mail Cleveland z 77327; rural
Clarksville; Inc. Place; ⊡ RED RIVER; 238 EB-10; elev. 410ft./125m.; 🅿 🅷; z 75426; Ⓟ 4,311; Ⓒ 3,883
Clarksville City; Inc. Place; GREGG, UPSHUR; *238 EE-11; 🅿; ★ LNGV; z 75693 & mail Gladewater z 75647; Ⓟ 720; Ⓒ 806
Clarkwood; RMC Place; NUECES; *239 EO-6; ★ CRPX; mail Corpus Christi z 78406; pop. incl. with Corpus Christi (Inc. Place)
Claude; Inc. Place; ⊡ ARMSTRONG; 236 WD-11; elev. 3,407ft./1,038m.; 🅿; z 79019; Ⓟ 1,199; Ⓒ 1,313
Clauene; RMC Place; HOCKLEY; *236 WH-9; mail Levelland z 79336; rural
Clawson; RMC Place; ANGELINA; 238 EG-11; elev. 362ft./110m.; ★ LUFK; mail Lufkin z 75904; ● 175
Clay; RMC Place; BURLESON; 238 EJ-8; mail Somerville z 77879; ● 150
CLAY; 238 EC-5; Ⓟ 10,024; Ⓒ 11,006; ◆ 10,862
Clay Corner; RMC Place; PARMER; *236 WF-9; mail Muleshoe z 79347; rural
Claydesta Station; RMC Place; MIDLAND; ★ MIDL-; mail Midland z 79703, z 79705, z 79707, z 79710; pop. incl. with Midland (Inc. Place)
Clayton; RMC Place; PANOLA; 238 EF-12; 🅿; z 75637; ● 100
Claytonville; RMC Place; FISHER; *236 WJ-13; mail Sweetwater z 79556; rural
Claytonville; RMC Place; SWISHER; 236 WF-11; elev. 3,354ft./1,022m.; mail Kress z 79052; ● 50
Clear Creek; RMC Place; BELL; ★ KILL-; mail Killeen z 76544
Clear Lake City; RMC Place; HARRIS; *239 EK-11; ★ HOU; mail Houston z 77058, z 77062; pop. incl. with Houston (Inc. Place)
Clear Lake Shores; Inc. Place; GALVESTON; 234 G-9; 🅿; ★ HOU; z 77565; Ⓟ 1,096; Ⓒ 1,205
Clear Spring; RMC Place; GUADALUPE; 239 EK-5; mail New Braunfels z 78130; ● 50
Clearview; RMC Place; BASTROP; *238 EJ-7; elev. 3,891ft./1,186m.; mail Bastrop z 78602; rural
Cleburne; Inc. Place; ⊡ JOHNSON; 238 EE-6; 🅿 🅷 ■; ★ D-FW; z 76031, z 76033; Ⓟ 22,205; Ⓒ 26,005; ◆ 28,043
Clegg; RMC Place; LIVE OAK; *239 EO-5; mail George West z 78022; rural
Clemons; RMC Place; WALLER; *239 EK-9; mail Hempstead z 77445; rural
Clemville; RMC Place; MATAGORDA; 239 EM-9; 🅿; z 77414; rural
Cleveland; Inc. Place; LIBERTY; 238 EJ-11; 🅿 🅷; z 77327-28; Ⓟ 7,124; Ⓒ 7,605
Clever Creek; RMC Place; SHELBY; mail Center z 75935; rural
Cliffside; RMC Place; POTTER; *236 WD-10; ★ AMA; mail Amarillo z 79108
Clifton; Inc. Place; BOSQUE; 238 EG-6; elev. 671ft./205m.; 🅿 🅷; z 76634, z 76644; Ⓟ 3,195; Ⓒ 3,542
Clifton; RMC Place; VAN ZANDT; *238 ED-9; mail Wills Point z 75169; rural
Climax; RMC Place; COLLIN; *238 EC-8; mail Princeton z 75407; rural
Cline; RMC Place; UVALDE; *239 EL-1; elev. 996ft./304m.; mail Uvalde z 78801; rural
Clint; Inc. Place; EL PASO; 237 WL-2; 🅿; ★ ELP; z 79836; Ⓟ 1,035; Ⓒ 980
Clinton; RMC Place; HUNT; *238 ED-8; elev. 570ft./174m.; mail Caddo Mills z 75135, Cuero z 77954; ● 35
Clinton Park; RMC Place; HARRIS; *239 EK-11; ★ HOU; mail Houston z 77029; pop. incl. with Houston (Inc. Place)
Clodine; RMC Place; FORT BEND; *239 EK-10; 🅿; ★ HOU; z 77469
Close City (Ragtown); RMC Place; GARZA; *236 WH-11; elev. 2,931ft./893m.; mail Post z 79356
Cloudy; RMC Place; DALLAS; ★ D-FW; pop. incl. with Grand Prairie (Inc. Place)
Cloverleaf; CDP; HARRIS; 234 D-7; ★ HOU; mail Houston z 77015; Ⓟ 18,230; Ⓒ 23,508; ◆ 27,798
Club Lake Estates; RMC Place; SMITH; ★ TYL; mail Tyler z 75704; ● 200
Clute; Inc. Place; BRAZORIA; 239 EM-10; 🅿; ★ L.JAC-; z 77531; Ⓟ 8,910; Ⓒ 10,424
Clyde; Inc. Place; CALLAHAN; 238 EE-2; elev. 1,991ft./607m.; 🅿; z 79510; Ⓟ 3,002; Ⓒ 3,345
Coady; RMC Place; HARRIS; *239 EK-11; elev. 28ft./9m.; ★ HOU; mail Baytown z 77521; ● 150
Coahoma; Inc. Place; HOWARD; 236 WJ-11; elev. 2,427ft./740m.; 🅿; z 79511; Ⓟ 1,133; Ⓒ 932
Coal Mine; RMC Place; MEDINA; *239 EL-4; elev. 726ft./221m.; mail Lytle z 78052; pop. incl. with Lytle (Inc. Place)
Cobb; RMC Place; KAUFMAN; *238 EE-9; mail Terrell z 75161; rural
Cobb Creek; RMC Place; MADISON; *238 EH-9; mail Midway z 75852; rural
Cochran; RMC Place; AUSTIN; 238 EJ-9; mail Bellville z 77418
COCHRAN; 236 WG-8; Ⓟ 4,377; Ⓒ 3,730; ◆ 2,901
Cockrell Hill; Inc. Place; DALLAS; 235 H-9; ★ D-FW; mail Dallas z 75211; Ⓟ 3,746; Ⓒ 4,443
Coffee City; Inc. Place; HENDERSON; *238 EF-10; mail Frankston z 75763; Ⓟ 216; Ⓒ 193
Coffeeville; RMC Place; UPSHUR; *238 ED-11; elev. 373ft./114m.; mail Ore City z 75683; rural
Coit; RMC Place; COLLIN; mail Plano z 75026, z 75075, z 75093; pop. incl. with Plano (Inc. Place)
Coit; RMC Place; LIMESTONE; *238 EG-8; mail Kosse z 76653; rural
Coke; RMC Place; WOOD; *238 ED-10; elev. 486ft./148m.; mail Como z 75431; rural
COKE; 237 WK-13; Ⓟ 3,424; Ⓒ 3,864; ◆ 3,212
Coldspring; Inc. Place; ⊡ SAN JACINTO; 238 EI-11; elev. 386ft./118m.; 🅿; z 77331; Ⓟ 538; Ⓒ 691
Cole Creek Manor; RMC Place; HARRIS; *239 EK-10; ★ HOU; mail Houston z 77092; pop. incl. with Houston (Inc. Place)
Coleman; Inc. Place; ⊡ COLEMAN; 238 EG-3; elev. 1,703ft./519m.; 🅿 🅷; z 76834; Ⓟ 5,410; Ⓒ 5,127
COLEMAN; 238 EG-2; Ⓟ 9,710; Ⓒ 9,235; ◆ 8,331
Coleman Cove; RMC Place; SAN AUGUSTINE; *238 EH-12; mail Broaddus z 75929; ● 25
Coleyville; RMC Place; COTTLE; *236 WF-13; mail Childress z 79201; rural
Colfax; RMC Place; VAN ZANDT; *238 EE-9; mail Canton z 75103
College; RMC Place; BRAZOS; mail College Station z 77842, z 77844; pop. incl. with College Station (Inc. Place)
College Hill; RMC Place; BOWIE; *238 EC-11; mail De Kalb z 75559; rural
College Mound; RMC Place; KAUFMAN; *238 EE-9; mail Terrell z 75161; rural
Collegeport; RMC Place; MATAGORDA; 239 EM-9; 🅿; z 77428; ● 85
College Station; Inc. Place; BRAZOS; 238 EI-8; 🅿 🅷 🅲 45,380 ■; ★ BRY-; z 77840-45; Ⓟ 52,456; Ⓒ 67,890; ◆ 91,893
Colleyville; Inc. Place; TARRANT; 235 F-6; 🅿; ★ D-FW; z 76034; Ⓟ 12,724; Ⓒ 19,636; ◆ 25,034
COLLIN; 238 EC-7; Ⓟ 264,036; Ⓒ 491,675; Ⓡ 491,774; ◆ 791,681
COLLINGSWORTH; 236 WE-13; Ⓟ 3,573; Ⓒ 3,206; ◆ 2,992
Collinsville; Inc. Place; GRAYSON; 238 EC-7; 🅿; z 76233; Ⓟ 1,033; Ⓒ 1,235
Colmesneil; Inc. Place; TYLER; 238 EH-12; 🅿; z 75938; Ⓟ 569; Ⓒ 638
Cologne; RMC Place; GOLIAD; *239 EM-7; mail Victoria z 77901, z 77905
Colonial; RMC Place; MCLENNAN; ★ WACO; mail Waco z 76707; pop. incl. with Waco (Inc. Place)
Colony; RMC Place; FAYETTE; *239 EK-7; mail Flatonia z 78941; rural
COLORADO; 239 EK-8; Ⓟ 18,383; Ⓒ 20,390; ◆ 20,486
Colorado City; Inc. Place; ⊡ MITCHELL; 236 WJ-12; elev. 2,071ft./631m.; 🅿 🅷; z 79512; Ⓟ 4,749; Ⓒ 4,281
Colquitt; RMC Place; KAUFMAN; *238 ED-8; ★ D-FW; mail Terrell z 75160; rural
Colton; RMC Place; TRAVIS; *238 EJ-6; ★ AUS; mail Austin z 78744; rural
Columbia Lake; RMC Place; BRAZORIA; *239 EL-10; ★ L.JAC-; mail West Columbia z 77486; ● 1,250
Columbus; Inc. Place; ⊡ COLORADO; 239 EK-8; 🅿 🅷; z 78934; Ⓟ 3,367; Ⓒ 3,916
Comal; RMC Place; COMAL; *239 EK-5; ★ SANT; mail New Braunfels z 78130; rural
COMAL; 239 EK-5; Ⓟ 51,832; Ⓒ 78,021; ◆ 112,833
Comanche; Inc. Place; ⊡ COMANCHE; 238 EF-4; elev. 1,382ft./421m.; 🅿 🅷; z 76442; Ⓟ 4,087; Ⓒ 4,482
COMANCHE; 238 EF-4; Ⓟ 13,381; Ⓒ 14,026; ◆ 13,306
Comanche Cove; RMC Place; HOOD; *238 EE-6; mail Granbury z 76048; ● 400
Comanche Harbor; RMC Place; HOOD; *238 EE-6; mail Granbury z 76048; ● 350
Comanche Village; RMC Place; BELL; *238 EH-6; ★ KILL-; mail Killeen z 76544
Combes; Inc. Place; CAMERON; 239 ES-6; elev. 40ft./12m.; 🅿; ★ BRNS; z 78535; Ⓟ 2,042; Ⓒ 2,553
Combine; Inc. Place; KAUFMAN, DALLAS; *238 EE-8; 🅿; ★ D-FW; z 75159; Ⓟ 1,329; Ⓒ 1,788
Cometa; RMC Place; ZAVALA; *239 EN-1; mail Crystal City z 78839; rural
Comfort; CDP; KENDALL; 239 EK-3; elev. 1,415ft./431m.; 🅿; z 78013; Ⓟ 1,477; Ⓒ 2,358
Commerce; Inc. Place; HUNT; 238 EC-9; 🅿 🅲 8,496; z 75428-29; Ⓟ 6,825; Ⓒ 7,669
Como; Inc. Place; HOPKINS; 238 ED-10; 🅿; z 75431; Ⓟ 563; Ⓒ 621
Comstock; RMC Place; VAL VERDE; 237 WP-11; elev. 1,591ft./485m.; 🅿; z 78837, z 78851; ● 370
Comyn; RMC Place; COMANCHE; *238 EF-4; elev. 1,256ft./383m.; mail De Leon z 76444
Concan; RMC Place; UVALDE; 237 WQ-14; 🅿; z 78838; ● 100
Concepcion; CDP; DUVAL; 239 EP-5; 🅿; z 78349; Ⓒ 61
Concho; RMC Place; CONCHO; *238 EG-2; mail Paint Rock z 76866; rural
CONCHO; 238 EH-1; Ⓟ 3,044; Ⓒ 3,966; ◆ 3,620
Concord; RMC Place; CHEROKEE; 238 EF-11; mail Troup z 75789; ● 70
Concord; RMC Place; LEON; 238 EH-9; 🅿; z 77850; ● 30
Concord; RMC Place; MORRIS; *238 EC-11; mail Omaha z 75571; rural
Concord; RMC Place; RUSK; 238 EF-12; elev. 533ft./162m.; mail Mount Enterprise z 75681; rural
Concord Bridge; RMC Place; HARRIS; *239 EK-10; ★ HOU; mail Houston z 77041; ● 1,200
Concrete; RMC Place; DEWITT; 239 EL-7; mail Cuero z 77954; ● 20
Cone; RMC Place; CROSBY; 236 WG-11; 🅿; z 79357; ● 70
Conlen; RMC Place; DALLAM; *236 WB-10; mail Dalhart z 79022
Connor; RMC Place; MADISON; *238 EH-9; elev. 258ft./79m.; mail Madisonville z 77864; rural
Conroe; Inc. Place; ⊡ MONTGOMERY; 238 EJ-10; 🅿 🅷 ■; z 77301-06, z 77384-85; Ⓟ 27,610; Ⓒ 36,811; ◆ 50,181
Content (Tokeen); RMC Place; RUNNELS; *238 EF-2; mail Goldsboro z 79519, Novice z 79538; rural
Converse; Inc. Place; BEXAR; 239 EL-5; 🅿; ★ SANT; z 78109 & mail Schertz z 78154; Ⓟ 8,887; Ⓒ 11,508
Conway; RMC Place; CARSON; 236 WD-11; elev. 3,454ft./1,053m.; mail Panhandle z 79068; ● 25
COOKE; 238 EB-6; Ⓟ 30,777; Ⓒ 36,363; ◆ 38,374
Cooks Point; RMC Place; BURLESON; *238 EI-8; mail Caldwell z 77836; ● 60
Cookville; RMC Place; TITUS; 238 EC-11; 🅿; z 75558; ● 200
Cool; Inc. Place; PARKER; 238 ED-5; mail Weatherford z 76088; Ⓟ 214; Ⓒ 162
Cool Crest; RMC Place; BEXAR; 239 ES-9; ★ SANT; mail San Antonio z 78245; ● 350
Coolidge; Inc. Place; LIMESTONE; 238 EG-8; elev. 536ft./163m.; 🅿; z 76635; Ⓟ 748; Ⓒ 848
Cooper; Inc. Place; ⊡ DELTA; 238 EC-9; elev. 491ft./150m.; 🅿; z 75432; Ⓟ 2,153; Ⓒ 2,150
Copano Village; RMC Place; ARANSAS; *239 EO-7; mail Rockport z 78382; ● 200
Copeland; RMC Place; SMITH; *238 EE-10; ★ TYL; mail Tyler z 75703; ● 500
Copeville; RMC Place; COLLIN; *238 ED-8; 🅿; z 75121; ● 250
Coppell; Inc. Place; DALLAS, DENTON; 235 E-8; 🅿; ★ D-FW; z 75019, z 75099; Ⓟ 16,881; Ⓒ 35,958; ◆ 40,827
Copperas Cove; Inc. Place; CORYELL, LAMPASAS; 238 EH-5; 🅿; ★ KILL-; z 76522; Ⓟ 24,079; Ⓒ 29,592; ◆ 23,347
Copper Canyon; Inc. Place; DENTON; *238 ED-7; 🅿; ★ D-FW; z 75077 & mail Argyle z 76226; Ⓟ 978; Ⓒ 1,216
Copperfield Southcreek; RMC Place; HARRIS; *239 EK-10; ★ HOU; mail Houston z 77095; ● 1,400
Copper Mountain; RMC Place; BELL; ★ KILL-; mail Killeen z 76542, z 76547; pop. incl. with Killeen (Inc. Place)
Corbet; RMC Place; NAVARRO; *238 EF-8; elev. 399ft./122m.; mail Corsicana z 75110; ● 50
Cordele; RMC Place; JACKSON; *239 EL-8; elev. 102ft./31m.; mail Edna z 77957
Corine; RMC Place; CHEROKEE; *238 EF-10; elev. 440ft./134m.; mail Jacksonville z 75766; rural
Corinth; Inc. Place; DENTON; 238 ED-7; 🅿; ★ D-FW; z 76208, z 76210 & mail Denton z 76205; Ⓟ 3,944; Ⓒ 11,325; ◆ 21,658
Corinth; RMC Place; EASTLAND; *238 EE-3; mail Cisco z 76437; rural
Corinth; RMC Place; JONES; *238 ED-2; elev. 1,641ft./500m.; mail Stamford z 79553; rural
Corinth; RMC Place; LEON; *238 EG-9; elev. 396ft./121m.; mail Buffalo z 75831; rural
Corinth; RMC Place; VAN ZANDT; *238 EE-9; mail Grand Saline z 75140; rural
Corley; RMC Place; BOWIE; 238 EC-12; mail Maud z 75567; ● 35
Cornersville; RMC Place; HOPKINS; *238 ED-10; mail Winnsboro z 75494; rural
Cornett; RMC Place; CASS; *238 EC-11; mail Naples z 75568; rural
Cornudas; RMC Place; HUDSPETH; *237 WK-3; elev. 4,306ft./1,312m.; mail Salt Flat z 79847; rural
Coronado; RMC Place; EL PASO; ★ ELP; mail El Paso z 79912-13, z 79922, z 79932; pop. incl. with El Paso (Inc. Place)
Corpus Christi; Inc. Place; ⊡ NUECES, KLEBERG, SAN PATRICIO; 239 EO-7; 🅿 🅷 🅲 8,585 ■; ★ CRPX; z 78401-19, z 78426-27, z 78460-61, z 78463, z 78465-78, z 78480 & mail Dinero z 78350; Ⓟ 257,453; Ⓒ 277,454; ◆ 281,027
Corral City; Inc. Place; DENTON; *238 ED-7; mail Argyle z 76226; Ⓟ 46; Ⓒ 89
Corrigan; Inc. Place; POLK; 238 EH-11; elev. 233ft./71m.; 🅿; z 75939; Ⓟ 1,764; Ⓒ 1,721
Corsicana; Inc. Place; ⊡ NAVARRO; 238 EF-8; 🅿 🅷 ■; z 75109-10, z 75151; Ⓟ 22,911; Ⓒ 24,485; ◆ 25,420
Coryell; RMC Place; CORYELL; 238 EG-6; elev. 974ft./297m.; mail Valley Mills z 76689; ● 150
CORYELL; 238 EH-5; Ⓟ 64,213; Ⓒ 74,978; ◆ 71,302
Cost; RMC Place; GONZALES; 239 EL-6; elev. 372ft./113m.; 🅿; z 78614; ● 150
COTTLE; 236 WF-13; Ⓟ 2,247; Ⓒ 1,904; ◆ 1,505
Cotton Center; RMC Place; FANNIN; *238 EC-9; mail Bonham z 75418; rural
Cotton Center; RMC Place; HALE; 236 WG-10; elev. 3,471ft./1,058m.; 🅿; z 79021; ● 200
Cottondale; RMC Place; WISE; 238 ED-6; mail Paradise z 76073; ● 75
Cotton Flat; RMC Place; MIDLAND; *237 WK-10; ★ MIDL-; mail Midland z 79701; ● 250
Cotton Gin; RMC Place; FREESTONE; 238 EG-8; mail Teague z 75860; ● 50
Cottonwood; RMC Place; BRAZOS; *238 EI-8; mail Bryan z 77808; rural
Cottonwood; RMC Place; CALLAHAN; 238 EF-3; mail Baird z 79504; ● 80
Cottonwood; RMC Place; FALLS; *238 EH-7; mail Lorena z 76655; rural
Cottonwood; Inc. Place; KAUFMAN; *238 EE-8; mail Scurry z 75158; Ⓟ 156; Ⓒ 181
Cottonwood; RMC Place; MADISON; *238 EH-9; mail Madisonville z 77864, North Zulch z 77872; rural
Cottonwood; RMC Place; MCLENNAN; *238 EF-7; mail West z 76691; rural
Cottonwood Shores; Inc. Place; BURNET; *238 EI-5; 🅿; z 78657 & mail Marble Falls z 78654; Ⓟ 548; Ⓒ 877
Cotulla; Inc. Place; ⊡ LA SALLE; 239 EN-3; elev. 450ft./137m.; 🅿; z 78014 & mail Artesia Wells z 78001; Ⓟ 3,694; Ⓒ 3,614
Coughran; RMC Place; ATASCOSA; *239 EM-5; elev. 341ft./104m.; mail Pleasanton z 78064
Council Creek Village; RMC Place; BURNET; *238 EI-5; mail Burnet z 78611; ● 100
Country Campus; RMC Place; WALKER; *238 EI-10; mail Huntsville z 77320; rural
Country Club Lake Estates; RMC Place; TOM GREEN; *237 WL-13; ★ SANG; mail San Angelo z 76904; pop. incl. with San Angelo (Inc. Place)
Country Club Terrace; RMC Place; POTTER; ★ AMA; mail Amarillo z 79106; pop. incl. with Amarillo (Inc. Place)
Country Club Terrace; RMC Place; VICTORIA; *239 EM-7; ★ VICT; mail Victoria z 77904; pop. incl. with Victoria (Inc. Place)
Country Colony; RMC Place; MONTGOMERY; *238 EJ-11; ★ HOU; mail Splendora z 77372; ● 100
Country Place Acres; RMC Place; MONTGOMERY; *238 EJ-10; ★ HOU; mail Magnolia z 77355; ● 150
Country Squire Estates; RMC Place; ORANGE; *238 EJ-13; ★ B-PA; mail Orange z 77632; ● 100
County Line; RMC Place; CAMP; *238 ED-11; mail Pittsburg z 75686; rural
County Line; RMC Place; HALE; *236 WG-10; mail Shallowater z 79363; ● 30
Coupland; RMC Place; WILLIAMSON; 238 EJ-6; elev. 517ft./158m.; 🅿; z 78615; ● 500
Courtney; RMC Place; GRIMES; *238 EJ-9; mail Navasota z 77868
Cove; Inc. Place; CHAMBERS; 239 EK-11; 🅿; z 77520, z 77523 & mail Baytown z 77521; Ⓟ 402; Ⓒ 323
Cove Springs; RMC Place; CHEROKEE; *238 EF-10; mail Jacksonville z 75766; rural
Covington; Inc. Place; HILL; 238 EF-7; 🅿; z 76636; Ⓟ 238; Ⓒ 282
Covington Woods; RMC Place; FORT BEND; *239 EK-10; elev. 85ft./26m.; ★ HOU; mail Sugar Land z 77478; pop. incl. with Sugar Land (Inc. Place)
Cox; RMC Place; UPSHUR; *238 ED-11; mail Gilmer z 75644; rural
Coyanosa; CDP; PECOS; 237 WM-8; 🅿; z 79730; Ⓒ 138
Coy City; RMC Place; KARNES; *239 EM-5; mail Karnes City z 78118
Coyote Acres; CDP-Census Area Only; JIM WELLS; *239 EP-5; Ⓒ 389
Cozy Corner; RMC Place; FAYETTE; *239 EK-7; elev. 345ft./105m.; mail La Grange z 78945; rural
Crabb; RMC Place; FORT BEND; 234 G-1; elev. 83ft./25m.; ★ HOU; mail Richmond z 77469
Crabbs Prairie; RMC Place; WALKER; *238 EI-10; mail Huntsville z 77320, z 77340
Craft; RMC Place; CHEROKEE; *238 EF-10; mail Jacksonville z 75766; rural
Crafton; RMC Place; WISE; 238 EC-5; elev. 1,074ft./327m.; mail Chico z 76431
Craig; RMC Place; RUSK; *238 EE-11; mail Henderson z 75652, z 75654; rural
Crandall; Inc. Place; KAUFMAN; 238 EE-8; 🅿; ★ D-FW; z 75114; Ⓟ 1,652; Ⓒ 2,774
Crane; Inc. Place; ⊡ CRANE; 237 WL-9; elev. 2,572ft./784m.; 🅿 🅷; z 79731; Ⓟ 3,533; Ⓒ 3,191
CRANE; 237 WL-9; Ⓟ 4,652; Ⓒ 3,996; ◆ 4,127
Cranfills Gap; Inc. Place; BOSQUE; 238 EG-5; 🅿; z 76637; Ⓟ 269; Ⓒ 335
Cranz; GONZALES; see Thompsonville (RMC Place)
Crawford; Inc. Place; MCLENNAN; 238 EG-6; elev. 734ft./224m.; 🅿; z 76638; Ⓟ 631; Ⓒ 705
Creagleville; RMC Place; VAN ZANDT; *238 EE-9; mail Grand Saline z 75140; rural
Crecy; RMC Place; TRINITY; *238 EH-11; elev. 268ft./82m.; mail Groveton z 75845; rural
Creechville; RMC Place; ELLIS; *238 EE-8; elev. 430ft./131m.; mail Ennis z 75119; rural
Creedmoor; Inc. Place; TRAVIS; 238 EJ-6; elev. 633ft./193m.; 🅿; ★ AUS; z 78610 & mail Austin z 78747; Ⓟ 194; Ⓒ 211
Creekwood Addition; RMC Place; MONTGOMERY; *238 EJ-11; ★ HOU; mail Splendora z 77372; ● 200
Crescent Center; RMC Place; SAN PATRICIO; *239 EO-7; mail Portland z 78374; pop. incl. with Portland (Inc. Place)
Crescent Heights; RMC Place; HENDERSON; *238 EF-9; mail Athens z 75751; ● 250
Cresson; Inc. Place; HOOD, JOHNSON; 238 EE-6; elev. 1,054ft./321m.; 🅿; z 76035; incorporated November 6, 2001; not reported in 2000 Census; ● 250
Cresthaven; RMC Place; BEXAR; *239 EL-4; ★ SANT; mail San Antonio z 78213; pop. incl. with San Antonio (Inc. Place)
Crestwood; RMC Place; MARION; *238 ED-12; mail Avinger z 75630; ● 300
Crews; RMC Place; RUNNELS; *238 EF-2; mail Winters z 79567
Cripple Creek Farms; RMC Place; MONTGOMERY; *238 EJ-10; ★ HOU; mail Magnolia z 77355
Cripple Creek North; RMC Place; MONTGOMERY; *238 EJ-10; ★ HOU; mail Magnolia z 77355; ● 200
Crisp; RMC Place; ELLIS; *238 EE-8; mail Ennis z 75119
Crockett; Inc. Place; ⊡ HOUSTON; 238 EH-10; elev. 366ft./112m.; 🅿 🅷; z 75835; Ⓟ 7,024; Ⓒ 7,141
CROCKETT; 237 WM-11; Ⓟ 4,078; Ⓒ 4,099; ◆ 3,771
Crosby; CDP; HARRIS; 239 EK-11; elev. 47ft./14m.; 🅿; ★ HOU; z 77532; Ⓟ 1,811; Ⓒ 1,714
CROSBY; 236 WH-11; Ⓟ 7,304; Ⓒ 7,072; ◆ 5,811
Crosbyton; Inc. Place; ⊡ CROSBY; 236 WH-11; 🅿 🅷; z 79322; Ⓟ 2,026; Ⓒ 1,874
Cross; RMC Place; GRIMES; *238 EI-9; elev. 357ft./109m.; mail Iola z 77861
Cross; RMC Place; MCMULLEN; *239 EN-4; elev. 284ft./87m.; mail Jourdanton z 78026; rural
Cross Cut; RMC Place; BROWN; *238 EF-3; mail Brownwood z 76801
Cross Mountain; CDP-Census Area Only; BEXAR; *239 EK-4; ★ SANT; mail San Antonio z 78255-56; Ⓟ 1,112; Ⓒ 1,524
Cross Plains; Inc. Place; CALLAHAN; 238 EF-3; 🅿; z 76443; Ⓟ 1,063; Ⓒ 1,068
Crossroads; RMC Place; CAMP; *238 ED-11; mail Pittsburg z 75686; rural
Crossroads; RMC Place; CASS; *238 ED-11; mail Hughes Springs z 75656; rural
Crossroads; RMC Place; DELTA; *238 EC-9; elev. 510ft./155m.; mail Cooper z 75432; rural
Cross Roads; DENTON; see New Hope (Inc. Place)
Crossroads; RMC Place; HARRISON; *238 EE-12; elev. 313ft./95m.; mail Marshall z 75672; rural
Cross Roads; RMC Place; HENDERSON; 238 EF-9; elev. 374ft./114m.; mail Malakoff z 75148; ● 200
Crossroads; RMC Place; MILAM; *238 EH-8; mail Cameron z 76520; rural
Cross Roads; RMC Place; RUSK; *238 EE-11; ★ LNGV; mail Kilgore z 75662; rural
Cross Roads; RMC Place; VAN ZANDT; *238 ED-9; mail Grand Saline z 75140; rural
Cross Timber; Inc. Place; JOHNSON; *238 EE-6; ★ D-FW; mail Burleson z 76028; Ⓟ 256; Ⓒ 277
Croton; RMC Place; DICKENS; *236 WG-12; rural
Crow; RMC Place; WOOD; 238 EE-10; mail Hawkins z 75765
Crowell; Inc. Place; ⊡ FOARD; 236 WG-14; elev. 1,476ft./450m.; 🅿; z 79227; Ⓟ 1,230; Ⓒ 1,141
Crowley; Inc. Place; TARRANT, JOHNSON; 238 EE-6; 🅿; ★ D-FW; z 76036; Ⓟ 6,974; Ⓒ 7,467
Cruz Calle (Santa Cruz); RMC Place; DUVAL; *239 EP-5; mail Concepcion z 78349; rural
Cryer Creek; RMC Place; NAVARRO; *238 EF-8; mail Blooming Grove z 76626; rural
Crystal Beach; RMC Place; GALVESTON; 239 EL-12; 🅿; ★ GLV-; z 77650; ● 800
Crystal City; Inc. Place; ⊡ ZAVALA; 237 WR-14; 🅿; z 78839; Ⓟ 8,263; Ⓒ 7,190
Crystal Creek Forest; RMC Place; MONTGOMERY; *238 EJ-10; mail Conroe z 77303; ● 150
Crystal Lake; RMC Place; ANDERSON; *238 EG-10; mail Palestine z 75801; rural
Crystal Lakes Estates; RMC Place; POLK; *238 EI-11; mail Livingston z 77351; ● 200
Cuadrilla; RMC Place; EL PASO; *237 WL-2; ★ ELP; mail Clint z 79836; ● 100
Cuero; Inc. Place; ⊡ DEWITT; 239 EM-7; elev. 182ft./55m.; 🅿 🅷; z 77954; Ⓟ 6,700; Ⓒ 6,571
Cuevitas (Curvitas); CDP; HIDALGO; *239 ES-4; ★ MCAL; Ⓒ 37
CULBERSON; 237 WK-5; Ⓟ 3,407; Ⓒ 2,975; ◆ 2,345
Culleoka; RMC Place; COLLIN; 235 B-14; ★ D-FW; mail Princeton z 75407; ● 250
Cumby; Inc. Place; HOPKINS; 238 EC-9; elev. 649ft./198m.; 🅿; z 75433; Ⓟ 571; Ⓒ 616
Cumings; CDP-Census Area Only; FORT BEND; *239 EK-10; ★ HOU; Ⓒ 683
Cundiff; RMC Place; JACK; *238 EC-5; elev. 978ft./298m.; mail Jacksboro z 76458
Cuney; Inc. Place; CHEROKEE; 238 EF-10; 🅿; z 75759; Ⓟ 170; Ⓒ 145
Cunningham; RMC Place; LAMAR; 238 EC-10; 🅿; z 75434; ● 175
Curtis; RMC Place; JASPER; *238 EH-13; mail Jasper z 75951
Curvitas; HIDALGO; see Cuevitas (CDP)
Cushing; Inc. Place; NACOGDOCHES; 238 EF-11; elev. 419ft./128m.; 🅿; z 75760; Ⓟ 587; Ⓒ 637
Cusseta; RMC Place; CASS; *238 EC-12; elev. 486ft./148m.; mail Marietta z 75566; rural
Cut; RMC Place; HOUSTON; *238 EH-10; elev. 370ft./113m.; mail Crockett z 75835; rural
Cut and Shoot; Inc. Place; MONTGOMERY; 238 EJ-10; 🅿; z 77303, z 77306; Ⓟ 903; Ⓒ 1,158
Cuthand; RMC Place; RED RIVER; 238 EC-11; mail Bogata z 75417; ● 90
Cuthbert; RMC Place; MITCHELL; mail Colorado City z 79512; rural
Cyclone; RMC Place; BELL; *238 EH-7; mail Burlington z 76519
Cypress; RMC Place; FRANKLIN; *238 ED-10; mail Winnsboro z 75494; rural
Cypress; RMC Place; HARRIS; 234 B-1; 🅿; ★ HOU; z 77410, z 77429, z 77433; pop. incl. with Houston (Inc. Place)
Cypress Cove; RMC Place; COMAL; *239 EK-5; mail New Braunfels z 78130
Cypress Creek; RMC Place; KERR; *239 EK-3; elev. 1,560ft./475m.; mail Kerrville z 78028; ● 150
Cypress Creek Estates; RMC Place; HARRIS; *239 EK-10; ★ HOU; mail Cypress z 77429; ● 125
Cypress Meadow; RMC Place; HARRIS; *239 EK-10; ★ HOU; mail Katy z 77449; ● 1,500
Cypress Mill; RMC Place; BLANCO; 238 EJ-5; elev. 978ft./298m.; 🅿; z 78663 & mail Johnson City z 78636, Marble Falls z 78654, Spicewood z 78669; rural
Czestochowa; KARNES; see Cestohowa (RMC Place)

D

Dabney; RMC Place; UVALDE; *239 EL-1; mail Uvalde z 78801; rural
Dacosta; RMC Place; VICTORIA; *239 EM-8; elev. 65ft./20m.; mail Victoria z 77905; ● 80
Dacus; RMC Place; MONTGOMERY; *238 EI-9; elev. 243ft./74m.; mail Montgomery z 77316, z 77356
Daingerfield; Inc. Place; ⊡ MORRIS; 238 ED-11; 🅿; z 75638; Ⓟ 2,572; Ⓒ 2,517
Daisetta; Inc. Place; LIBERTY; 238 EJ-12; elev. 79ft./24m.; 🅿; z 77533; Ⓟ 969; Ⓒ 1,034
Dalby Springs; RMC Place; BOWIE; 238 EC-11; elev. 307ft./94m.; mail De Kalb z 75559; ● 150
Dale; RMC Place; CALDWELL; 239 EK-6; elev. 519ft./158m.; 🅿; z 78616; ● 230
Dalhart; Inc. Place; ⊡ DALLAM, HARTLEY; 236 WB-9; elev. 3,984ft./1,214m.; 🅿 🅷; z 79022; Ⓟ 6,246; Ⓒ 7,237
DALLAM; 236 WA-9; Ⓟ 5,461; Ⓒ 6,222; ◆ 6,371
Dallardsville; RMC Place; POLK; 238 EI-12; elev. 241ft./73m.; 🅿; z 77332; ● 350
Dallas; Inc. Place; ⊡ DALLAS, COLLIN, DENTON, KAUFMAN, ROCKWALL; 238 ED-7; elev. 463ft./141m.; 🅿 🅷 🅲 25,746 ■; ★ D-FW; z 75201-12, z 75214-38, z 75240-54, z 75258, z 75260-67, z 75270, z 75275, z 75277, z 75283-87, z 75301, z 75303, z 75310, z 75312-13, z 75315, z 75320, z 75323, z 75326, z 75334, z 75336, z 75339-40, z 75342-44, z 75354-60, z 75367-68, z 75370-74, z 75376, z 75378-82, z 75387, z 75389-95, z 75397-98; Ⓟ 1,006,877; Ⓒ 1,188,580; ◆ 1,307,392
DALLAS; 238 EE-8; Ⓟ 1,852,810; Ⓒ 2,218,899; Ⓡ 2,218,774; ◆ 2,400,359
Dal Nor; RMC Place; DALLAS; ★ D-FW; pop. incl. with Carrollton (Inc. Place)
Dalton; RMC Place; CASS; *238 EC-11; elev. 351ft./107m.; mail Naples z 75568; rural
Dalworthington Gardens; Inc. Place; TARRANT; 235 H-6; ★ D-FW; mail Arlington z 76015-16; Ⓟ 1,758; Ⓒ 2,186
Dalys; RMC Place; HOUSTON; *238 EG-10; mail Grapeland z 75844; rural
Dam B; RMC Place; TYLER; *238 EH-12; elev. 100ft./30m.; mail Woodville z 75979; ● 200
Damon; CDP; BRAZORIA; 239 EL-10; 🅿; z 77430; Ⓒ 535
Danbury; Inc. Place; BRAZORIA; 239 EL-10; 🅿; ★ L.JAC-; z 77534; Ⓟ 1,447; Ⓒ 1,611
Danciger; RMC Place; BRAZORIA; 239 EL-10; 🅿; z 77431; ● 30
Danevang; RMC Place; WHARTON; 239 EM-9; elev. 71ft./22m.; 🅿; z 77432; ● 75
Danville; RMC Place; GREGG; *238 EE-11; ★ LNGV; mail Kilgore z 75662; ● 200
Darco; RMC Place; HARRISON; *238 EE-12; mail Marshall z 75670, z 75672; rural
Darrouzett; Inc. Place; LIPSCOMB; 236 WA-13; 🅿; z 79024; Ⓟ 343; Ⓒ 303
Datura; RMC Place; LIMESTONE; *238 EG-8; mail Coolidge z 76635; rural
Daugherty; RAINS; see Dougherty (RMC Place)
Davenport; RMC Place; RED RIVER; *238 EB-10; elev. 393ft./120m.; mail Bagwell z 75412; rural
Davilla; RMC Place; MILAM; 238 EI-7; 🅿; z 76523; ● 250
Davis Prairie; RMC Place; LIMESTONE; *238 EG-8; mail Thornton z 76687; rural
Davisville; RMC Place; ANGELINA; *238 EG-11; ★ LUFK; mail Centerville z 75833, Lufkin z 75901; rural
Dawes; RMC Place; HARRIS; ★ HOU; pop. incl. with Houston (Inc. Place)
Dawn; RMC Place; DEAF SMITH; 236 WE-10; elev. 3,789ft./1,155m.; 🅿; z 79025; ● 60
Dawson; Inc. Place; NAVARRO; 238 EF-8; 🅿; z 76639; Ⓟ 766; Ⓒ 852
DAWSON; 236 WI-10; Ⓟ 14,349; Ⓒ 14,985; ◆ 13,443
Dayton; Inc. Place; LIBERTY; 238 EJ-11; elev. 84ft./26m.; 🅿; ★ HOU; z 77535; Ⓟ 5,151; Ⓒ 5,709
Dayton Lakes; Inc. Place; LIBERTY; 238 EJ-11; mail Dayton z 77535; Ⓟ 191; Ⓒ 101
Deadwood; RMC Place; PANOLA; *238 EF-12; mail Carthage z 75633; ● 30
DEAF SMITH; 236 WD-9; Ⓟ 19,153; Ⓒ 18,561; ◆ 18,534
Dean; Inc. Place; CLAY; 238 EB-4; elev. 963ft./294m.; mail Wichita Falls z 76301; Ⓟ 277; Ⓒ 341
Dean; RMC Place; HOCKLEY; mail Shallowater z 79363; rural
Deanville; RMC Place; BURLESON; 238 EJ-8; elev. 386ft./118m.; 🅿; z 77852; ● 130
De Berry; RMC Place; PANOLA; 238 EE-12; 🅿; z 75639; ● 200
Debora Sue Schatz; RMC Place; HARRIS; ★ HOU; mail Houston z 77042, z 77242; pop. incl. with Houston (Inc. Place)
Decatur; Inc. Place; ⊡ WISE; 238 EC-6; 🅿 🅷; z 76234; Ⓟ 4,252; Ⓒ 5,201
Decker; RMC Place; NOLAN; *238 EF-1; mail Blackwell z 79506; rural
Decker; RMC Place; TRAVIS; *238 EJ-6; ★ AUS; mail Austin z 78724, Manor z 78653; pop. incl. with Austin (Inc. Place)
Decker Prairie; RMC Place; MONTGOMERY; 238 EJ-10; 🅿; ★ HOU; z 77354-55; ● 1,000
DeCordova ; Inc. Place; HOOD; *238 EE-6; mail Granbury z 76049; incorporated January 20, 2000; not reported in 2000 Census; ● 2,800
Deep Water Point Estates; RMC Place; COLLIN; *238 ED-8; ★ D-FW; mail Copeville z 75121; ● 200
Deer Creek; RMC Place; CLAY; *238 EC-5; mail Henrietta z 76365
Deerfield Village; RMC Place; HARRIS; *239 EK-10; ★ HOU; mail Houston z 77084; pop. incl. with Houston (Inc. Place)
Deer Haven; RMC Place; LLANO; *238 EI-4; mail Marble Falls z 78654; ● 200
Deer Park; Inc. Place; HARRIS; 234 E-8; 🅿; ★ HOU; z 77536; Ⓟ 27,652; Ⓒ 28,520; ◆ 32,124
Deerwood; RMC Place; WALLER; *238 EJ-9; mail Hempstead z 77445; ● 150
De Kalb; Inc. Place; BOWIE; 238 EC-11; elev. 408ft./124m.; 🅿; z 75559; Ⓟ 1,976; Ⓒ 1,769
Delba; RMC Place; FANNIN; *238 EC-8; mail Leonard z 75452; rural
De Leon; Inc. Place; COMANCHE; 238 EF-4; 🅿 🅷; z 76444; Ⓟ 2,190; Ⓒ 2,433
Delhi; RMC Place; CALDWELL; *239 EK-6; elev. 528ft./161m.; mail Rosanky z 78953; rural
Delia; RMC Place; LIMESTONE; *238 EG-8; mail Coolidge z 76635; rural
Dell City; Inc. Place; HUDSPETH; 237 WK-4; 🅿; z 79837; Ⓟ 569; Ⓒ 413
Del Mar Heights; CDP-Census Area Only; CAMERON; *239 ES-7; Ⓒ 259
Del Mar Hills; RMC Place; WEBB; ★ LAR; mail Laredo z 78041; pop. incl. with Laredo (Inc. Place)
Delmita; RMC Place; STARR; *239 ER-5; 🅿; z 78536; ● 150
Delray; RMC Place; PANOLA; *238 EF-12; mail Carthage z 75633; rural
Del Rio; Inc. Place; ⊡ VAL VERDE; 237 WQ-12; 🅿 🅷 ■; z 78840-43, z 78847; Ⓟ 30,705; Ⓒ 33,867; ◆ 35,261
Delrose; RMC Place; UPSHUR; *238 ED-11; mail Gilmer z 75644; rural
Del Sol-Loma Linda; CDP-Census Area Only; SAN PATRICIO; *239 EO-6; Ⓒ 726
DELTA; 238 EC-9; Ⓟ 4,857; Ⓒ 5,327; ◆ 5,113
Del Valle; RMC Place; TRAVIS; 237 WT-11; 🅿; ★ AUS; z 78617; pop. incl. with Austin (Inc. Place)
Demi-John Island; RMC Place; BRAZORIA; *239 EL-11; mail Freeport z 77541; ● 100
Democrat; RMC Place; MILLS; *238 EG-4; mail Comanche z 76442; rural
De Moss; RMC Place; HARRIS; ★ HOU; mail Houston z 77074, z 77236, z 77274; pop. incl. with Houston (Inc. Place)
Denhawken; RMC Place; WILSON; *239 EL-5; mail Stockdale z 78160; rural
Denison; Inc. Place; GRAYSON; 238 EB-8; 🅿 🅷 ■; ★ SHRM-; z 75020-21; Ⓟ 21,505; Ⓒ 22,773; ◆ 22,296
Denning; RMC Place; SAN AUGUSTINE; *238 EG-12; mail San Augustine z 75972; rural
Dennis; RMC Place; PARKER; *238 EE-5; 🅿; z 76439; ● 60
Denny; RMC Place; FALLS; *238 EH-8; mail Kosse z 76653; rural
Denson Springs; RMC Place; ANDERSON; *238 EG-10; mail Grapeland z 75844; rural
Denton; RMC Place; CALLAHAN; *238 EF-2; elev. 1,981ft./604m.; mail Clyde z 79510; rural
Denton; Inc. Place; ⊡ DENTON; 238 EC-7; elev. 662ft./202m.; 🅿 🅷 🅲 45,243 ■; ★ DENT; z 76201-10; Ⓟ 66,270; Ⓒ 80,537; ◆ 110,749

Entries in **UPPERCASE** are counties.
Entries in **bold** have populations of 2,500 or more.
Names in parentheses are alternate names.

Inc. Place	Incorporated Place
RMC Place	Rand McNally Designated Place
CDP	Census Designated Place
MCD	Minor Civil Division

⊡ County Seat
▲ Minor Civil Division
elev. Elevation
🅿 Post Office
🅷 Hospital
🅲 College
■ Principal Business Center
★ Ranally Metro Area (RMA) Abbreviation
z Zip Code(s)
Ⓟ Previous Census Population
Ⓡ Revised Census Population
Ⓐ Annexation Population
● Rand McNally Population Estimate
Ⓒ Final Census Population
Ⓢ Special Census Population
◆ Estimated Population

For additional definitions see Glossary, Volume 1, and Introduction, Volume 2.

DENTON; **238** EC-7; Ⓟ 273,525; © 432,976; ◆ 666,672
Denver City; Inc. Place; YOAKUM, GAINES; **236** WI-8; 🅿 🄷; z 79323; Ⓟ 5,156; © 3,985
Denver Harbor; RMC Place; HARRIS; ***239** EK-10; ★ **HOU**; mail Houston z 77020, z 77220; pop. incl. with Houston (Inc. Place)
Deport; Inc. Place; LAMAR, RED RIVER; **238** EC-10; elev. 421ft./128m.; 🅿; z 75435; Ⓟ 746; © 718
Derby; RMC Place; FRIO; ***239** EM-3; mail Dilley z 78017
Dermott; RMC Place; SCURRY; ***236** WI-12; 🅿; z 79549; rural
Desdemona; RMC Place; EASTLAND; **238** EF-4; elev. 1,358ft./414m.; 🅿; z 76445; ● 200
Desert; RMC Place; COLLIN; ***238** EC-8; mail Blue Ridge z 75424
DeSoto; Inc. Place; DALLAS; **235** J-10; 🅿 🄷; ★ **D-FW**; z 75115, z 75123 & mail Red Oak z 75154; Ⓟ 30,544; © 37,646; ◆ 41,547
Dessau; RMC Place; TRAVIS; ***238** EJ-6; ★ **AUS**; mail Austin z 78753; ● 90
Detmold; RMC Place; MILAM; ***238** EI-7; mail Thorndale z 76577; rural
Detroit; Inc. Place; RED RIVER; **238** EB-10; 🅿; z 75436; Ⓟ 706; © 776
Devers; Inc. Place; LIBERTY; **238** EJ-12; elev. 60ft./18m.; 🅿; z 77538; Ⓟ 318; © 416
Devils Pocket (Old Laurel); RMC Place; NEWTON; ***238** EI-13; mail Buna z 77612; rural
Devine; Inc. Place; MEDINA; **239** EM-4; elev. 647ft./197m.; 🅿; z 78016; Ⓟ 3,928; © 4,140
Dew; RMC Place; FREESTONE; ***238** EG-9; elev. 464ft./141m.; mail Teague z 75860; ● 150
Dewees; RMC Place; WILSON; ***239** EM-5; elev. 430ft./131m.; mail Floresville z 78114
Deweyville; CDP; NEWTON; **238** EJ-13; 🅿; ★ **B-PA**; z 77614; Ⓟ 1,218; © 1,190
DEWITT; **239** EM-6; Ⓟ 18,840; © 20,013; ◆ 19,400
Dewville; RMC Place; GONZALES; ***239** EL-6; elev. 437ft./133m.; mail Nixon z 78140; rural
Dexter; RMC Place; COOKE; **238** EB-7; mail Gainesville z 76240; rural
D'Hanis; RMC Place; MEDINA; **239** EL-3; elev. 886ft./270m.; 🅿; z 78850; ● 600
Dial; RMC Place; FANNIN; ***238** EC-9; elev. 569ft./173m.; mail Honey Grove z 75446; ● 40
Dial; RMC Place; HUTCHINSON; ***236** WC-11; mail Borger z 79007; rural
Dialville; RMC Place; CHEROKEE; ***238** EF-10; 🅿; z 75785; ● 150
Diamondhead; RMC Place; MONTGOMERY; ***238** EJ-10; mail Montgomery z 77316; ● 75
Diana; RMC Place; UPSHUR; **238** ED-11; 🅿; z 75640; ● 500
Diboll; Inc. Place; ANGELINA; **238** EH-11; elev. 230ft./70m.; 🅿; ★ **LUFK**; z 75941; Ⓟ 4,341; © 5,470
Dicey; RMC Place; PARKER; ***238** ED-6; elev. 924ft./282m.; ★ **D-FW**; mail Weatherford z 76086; rural
Dickens; Inc. Place; ⊡ DICKENS; **236** WH-12; elev. 2,550ft./777m.; 🅿; z 79229; Ⓟ 322; © 332
DICKENS; **236** WG-12; Ⓟ 2,571; © 2,762; ◆ 2,502
Dickinson; Inc. Place; GALVESTON; **234** H-9; elev. 17ft./5m.; 🅿; ★ **GLV-**; z 77539; Ⓟ 9,497; © 17,093
Dies; TYLER; see Dies Community (RMC Place)
Dies Community (Dies); RMC Place; TYLER; ***238** EH-12; mail Woodville z 75979; rural
Dike; RMC Place; HOPKINS; **238** EC-10; 🅿; z 75437; ● 180
Dilley; Inc. Place; FRIO; **239** EN-3; 🅿; z 78017; Ⓟ 2,632; © 3,674
Dilworth; RMC Place; GONZALES; ***239** EL-7; mail Gonzales z 78629; rural
Dilworth; RMC Place; RED RIVER; ***238** EB-11; mail Clarksville z 75426; rural
Dime Box; RMC Place; LEE; **238** EJ-7; 🅿; z 77853; ● 300
DIMMIT; **239** EN-2; Ⓟ 10,433; © 10,248; ◆ 9,506
Dimmitt; Inc. Place; ⊡ CASTRO; **236** WF-9; elev. 3,877ft./1,182m.; 🅿 🄷; z 79027; Ⓟ 4,408; © 4,375
Dimple; RMC Place; RED RIVER; ***238** EB-10; elev. 448ft./137m.; mail Clarksville z 75426; ● 120
Dinero; RMC Place; LIVE OAK; **239** EO-5; 🅿; z 78350; ● 100
Ding Dong; RMC Place; BELL; ***238** EH-6; mail Killeen z 76542; rural
Dinsmore; RMC Place; WHARTON; ***239** EL-9; elev. 96ft./29m.; mail Wharton z 77488; ● 50
Direct; RMC Place; LAMAR; ***238** EB-9; mail Sumner z 75486; ● 70
Dirgin; RMC Place; RUSK; ***238** EE-12; elev. 357ft./109m.; mail Tatum z 75691; rural
DISH (Clark); Inc. Place; DENTON; incorporated May 15, 2000; not reported in 2000 Census; ● 300
Divide; RMC Place; HOPKINS; ***238** ED-9; mail Brashear z 75420; rural
Divot; RMC Place; FRIO; ***239** EM-3; mail Dilley z 78017; rural
Dixico; RMC Place; HARRIS; ★ **HOU**; pop. incl. with Houston (Inc. Place)
Dixie; RMC Place; GRAYSON; **238** EB-7; mail Whitesboro z 76273; ● 35
Dixie; RMC Place; JASPER; ***238** EH-13; mail Jasper z 75951; rural
Dixon; RMC Place; HUNT; ***238** ED-9; mail Greenville z 75402; ● 30
Doans; RMC Place; WILBARGER; ***238** EA-3; elev. 1,232ft./376m.; mail Vernon z 76384; rural
Dobbin; RMC Place; MONTGOMERY; **238** EJ-9; 🅿; z 77333; ● 475
Dobrowolski; RMC Place; ATASCOSA; ***239** EM-4; mail Jourdanton z 78026; rural
Dodd; RMC Place; CASTRO; ***236** WF-9; mail Muleshoe z 79347; rural
Dodd City; Inc. Place; FANNIN; **238** EC-9; elev. 666ft./203m.; 🅿; z 75438; Ⓟ 350; © 419
Dodge; RMC Place; WALKER; **238** EI-10; 🅿; z 77334; ● 300
Dodson (Dodsonville); Inc. Place; COLLINGSWORTH; **236** WE-14; elev. 1,789ft./545m.; 🅿; z 79230; Ⓟ 113; © 115
Dodsonville; COLLINGSWORTH; see Dodson (Inc. Place)
Doffing; CDP-Census Area Only; HIDALGO; ***239** ES-5; ★ **MCAL**; © 4,256
Dog Ridge; RMC Place; BELL; mail Belton z 76513; ● 300
Dogwood; RMC Place; TYLER; 🅿; z 75979; rural
Dogwood City; RMC Place; SMITH; ***238** EF-10; ★ **TYL**; mail Flint z 75762; ● 800
Dolen; RMC Place; LIBERTY; **238** EI-11; elev. 95ft./29m.; mail Cleveland z 77327; rural
Domino; Inc. Place; CASS; **238** EC-12; mail Queen City z 75572; Ⓟ 101; © 52
Donall Estates; RMC Place; BURNET; ***238** EI-5; mail Burnet z 78611; ● 60
Donie; RMC Place; FREESTONE; **238** EG-9; 🅿; z 75838; ● 200
DONLEY; **236** WD-12; Ⓟ 3,696; © 3,828; ◆ 4,015
Donna; Inc. Place; HIDALGO; **239** ES-5; 🅿; ★ **MCAL**; z 78537; Ⓟ 12,652; © 14,768
Doole; RMC Place; MCCULLOCH; **238** EH-2; 🅿; z 76836; ● 70
Doolittle; CDP-Census Area Only; HIDALGO; ***239** ES-5; ★ **MCAL**; © 2,358
Dorchester; Inc. Place; GRAYSON; **238** EC-8; 🅿; z 75459; Ⓟ 137; © 109
Doss; RMC Place; GILLESPIE; **238** EJ-3; elev. 1,733ft./528m.; 🅿; z 78618; ● 75
Dothan; RMC Place; EASTLAND; ***238** EE-3; mail Cisco z 76437; rural
Dotson; RMC Place; PANOLA; ***238** EF-12; mail Long Branch z 75669; rural
Dott; RMC Place; FALLS; ***238** EH-7; mail Eddy z 76524; rural
Double Bayou; RMC Place; CHAMBERS; **239** EK-12; mail Anahuac z 77514; ● 200
Double Diamond Estates; RMC Place; HUTCHINSON; mail Fritch z 79036; summer pop. 400; ● 160
Double Oak; Inc. Place; DENTON; ***238** ED-7; 🅿; ★ **D-FW**; z 75077; Ⓟ 1,664; © 2,179
Doucette; RMC Place; TYLER; **238** EI-12; elev. 320ft./98m.; 🅿; z 75942; ● 250
Doud; RMC Place; LUBBOCK; ***236** WH-10; ★ **LUB**; pop. incl. with Lubbock (Inc. Place)
Dougherty; RMC Place; FLOYD; **236** WG-12; 🅿; z 79231; ● 100
Dougherty (Daugherty); RMC Place; RAINS; ***238** ED-9; mail Emory z 75440; rural
Douglass; RMC Place; NACOGDOCHES; **238** EG-11; 🅿; z 75943; ● 125
Douglassville; Inc. Place; CASS; **238** EC-12; 🅿; z 75560; Ⓟ 192; © 175
Downing; RMC Place; COMANCHE; ***238** EF-4; elev. 1,230ft./375m.; mail Comanche z 76442
Downsville; RMC Place; MCLENNAN; ***238** EG-7; elev. 396ft./121m.; ★ **WACO**; mail Waco z 76706; ● 200
Downtown; RMC Place; BEXAR; ★ **SANT**; mail San Antonio z 78205, z 78291-99; pop. incl. with San Antonio (Inc. Place)
Downtown; RMC Place; BOWIE; ★ **TEXR-**; mail Texarkana z 75504; pop. incl. with Texarkana (Inc. Place)
Downtown; RMC Place; CAMERON; ***239** ET-6; ★ **BRNS**; mail Brownsville z 78522; pop. incl. with Brownsville (Inc. Place)
Downtown; RMC Place; DALLAS; ***238** ED-7; ★ **D-FW**; mail Irving z 75017, z 75060; pop. incl. with Irving (Inc. Place)
Downtown; RMC Place; DALLAS; ★ **D-FW**; mail Dallas z 75201-02, z 75204, z 75221, z 75250, z 75270, z 75313; pop. incl. with Dallas (Inc. Place)
Downtown; RMC Place; EL PASO; ***237** WK-2; ★ **ELP**; mail El Paso z 79901, z 79940-55; pop. incl. with El Paso (Inc. Place)
Downtown; RMC Place; GREGG; ★ **LNGV**; mail Longview z 75606; pop. incl. with Longview (Inc. Place)
Downtown; RMC Place; HIDALGO; ★ **MCAL**; mail McAllen z 78501, z 78505; pop. incl. with McAllen (Inc. Place)
Downtown; RMC Place; JEFFERSON; mail Beaumont z 77704; pop. incl. with Beaumont (Inc. Place)
Downtown; RMC Place; LUBBOCK; ★ **LUB**; mail Lubbock z 79401, z 79408; pop. incl. with Lubbock (Inc. Place)
Downtown; RMC Place; MCLENNAN; ★ **WACO**; mail Waco z 76701, z 76703, z 76706, z 76711; pop. incl. with Waco (Inc. Place)
Downtown; RMC Place; MIDLAND; mail Midland z 79701-02, z 79706; pop. incl. with Midland (Inc. Place)
Downtown; RMC Place; NUECES; ★ **CRPX**; mail Corpus Christi z 78401-03, z 78407-08; pop. incl. with Corpus Christi (Inc. Place)
Downtown; RMC Place; POTTER; ★ **AMA**; mail Amarillo z 79105; pop. incl. with Amarillo (Inc. Place)
Downtown; RMC Place; SMITH; ★ **TYL**; mail Tyler z 75710; pop. incl. with Tyler (Inc. Place)
Downtown; RMC Place; TARRANT; ★ **D-FW**; mail Fort Worth z 76101-02, z 76113; pop. incl. with Fort Worth (Inc. Place)
Downtown; RMC Place; TRAVIS; ★ **AUS**; mail Austin z 78767-68; pop. incl. with Austin (Inc. Place)
Doyle; RMC Place; LIMESTONE; ***238** EG-8; mail Groesbeck z 76642; rural
Doyle; CDP-Census Area Only; SAN PATRICIO; ***239** EO-7; © 285
Dozier; RMC Place; COLLINGSWORTH; ***236** WD-13; elev. 2,261ft./689m.; mail Shamrock z 79079
Drasco; RMC Place; RUNNELS; ***238** EF-1; elev. 2,019ft./615m.; mail Winters z 79567; rural
Draw; RMC Place; LYNN; ***236** WI-11; elev. 2,962ft./903m.; mail Tahoka z 79373
Dreka; RMC Place; SHELBY; ***238** EG-13; mail Shelbyville z 75973; rural
Dresden; RMC Place; NAVARRO; ***238** EF-8; mail Barry z 75102; rural
Dreyer; RMC Place; GONZALES; ***239** EL-7; elev. 295ft./90m.; mail Shiner z 77984
Driftwood; RMC Place; HAYS; **238** EJ-5; 🅿; z 78619; ● 100
Driftwood; RMC Place; HENDERSON; ***238** EE-9; mail Kemp z 75143; ● 200
Dripping Springs; Inc. Place; HAYS; **238** EJ-5; elev. 1,156ft./352m.; 🅿; z 78620; Ⓟ 1,033; © 1,548
Driscoll; Inc. Place; NUECES; **239** EP-6; 🅿; z 78351; Ⓟ 688; © 825
Drivers; RMC Place; NACOGDOCHES; mail Chireno z 75937; ● 50
Drop; RMC Place; DENTON; ***238** ED-6; elev. 760ft./232m.; mail Justin z 76247
Dryden; RMC Place; TERRELL; **237** WO-10; elev. 2,107ft./642m.; 🅿; z 78851; ● 30
Dubina; RMC Place; FAYETTE; ***239** EK-8; mail Schulenburg z 78956; rural
Dublin; Inc. Place; ERATH; **238** EF-5; 🅿; z 76446; Ⓟ 3,190; © 3,754
Dudley; RMC Place; CALLAHAN; ***238** EF-2; elev. 2,022ft./616m.; mail Abilene z 79602
Duffau; RMC Place; ERATH; **238** EF-5; elev. 1,126ft./343m.; mail Hico z 76457; ● 70
Dugger; RMC Place; GUADALUPE; mail Seguin z 78155; rural
Dulin; RMC Place; BROWN; mail Brookesmith z 76827; ● 35
Dumas; Inc. Place; ⊡ MOORE; **236** WC-10; elev. 3,657ft./1,115m.; 🅿 🄷; z 79029; Ⓟ 12,871; © 13,747
Dumont; RMC Place; KING; **236** WG-13; elev. 2,054ft./626m.; 🅿; z 79248; ● 50
Dunbar; RMC Place; RAINS; ***238** ED-9; mail Emory z 75440; rural
Duncanville; Inc. Place; DALLAS; **238** EE-7; 🅿 ■; ★ **D-FW**; z 75116, z 75137-38; Ⓟ 35,748; © 36,081; ◆ 37,428
Dundee; RMC Place; ARCHER; **238** EB-3; mail Holliday z 76366; ● 20
Dunlap; RMC Place; COTTLE; ***238** EA-1; elev. 1,928ft./588m.; mail Paducah z 79248; rural
Dunlay; RMC Place; MEDINA; **239** EL-3; 🅿; z 78861; ● 100
Dunn; RMC Place; SCURRY; **236** WJ-12; elev. 2,213ft./675m.; 🅿; z 79516; ● 125
Duplex; RMC Place; FANNIN; ***238** EB-8; mail Ivanhoe z 75447; rural
Duraglas; RMC Place; MCLENNAN; ★ **WACO**; pop. incl. with Waco (Inc. Place)
Durango; RMC Place; FALLS; **238** EH-7; elev. 584ft./178m.; mail Lott z 76656; ● 70
Durenville; RMC Place; MILLS; ***238** EG-4; mail Goldthwaite z 76844; ● 40
Duster; RMC Place; COMANCHE; ***238** EF-4; elev. 1,410ft./430m.; mail De Leon z 76444; rural
DUVAL; **239** EO-5; Ⓟ 12,918; © 13,120; ◆ 11,784
Dye; RMC Place; MONTAGUE; ***238** EC-6; mail Saint Jo z 76265; rural
Dyersdale; RMC Place; HARRIS; ***239** EK-11; elev. 58ft./18m.; ★ **HOU**; mail Houston z 77016, z 77050; ● 150

E

Eagle Acres; RMC Place; TARRANT; ***238** ED-6; ★ **D-FW**; mail Azle z 76020
Eagle Ford; RMC Place; DALLAS; ***238** ED-7; ★ **D-FW**; mail Dallas z 75212; pop. incl. with Dallas (Inc. Place)
Eagle Lake; Inc. Place; COLORADO; **239** EK-9; 🅿 🄷; z 77434; Ⓟ 3,551; © 3,664
Eagle Mountain; CDP-Census Area Only; TARRANT; ***238** ED-6; ★ **D-FW**; mail Fort Worth z 76135; Ⓟ 5,847; © 6,599
Eagle Pass; Inc. Place; ⊡ MAVERICK; **237** WR-13; elev. 737ft./225m.; 🅿 🄷 ■; z 78852-53; Ⓟ 20,651; © 22,413; ◆ 25,979
Earles Camp; RMC Place; HASKELL; mail Haskell z 79521; ● 20
Earles Chapel; RMC Place; CHEROKEE; ***238** EF-10; elev. 520ft./158m.; mail Jacksonville z 75766; rural
Early; Inc. Place; BROWN; **238** EG-3; 🅿; z 76802; Ⓟ 2,380; © 2,588
Earlywine; RMC Place; WASHINGTON; ***238** EJ-9; mail Brenham z 77833; rural
Earth; Inc. Place; LAMB; **236** WF-9; elev. 3,697ft./1,127m.; 🅿; z 79031; Ⓟ 1,228; © 1,109
East Afton; RMC Place; DICKENS; ***236** WG-12; elev. 2,426ft./739m.; mail Afton z 79220; rural
East Amarillo; RMC Place; POTTER; ★ **AMA**; mail Amarillo z 79104; pop. incl. with Amarillo (Inc. Place)
East Arlington; RMC Place; TARRANT; ★ **D-FW**; mail Arlington z 76007; pop. incl. with Arlington (Inc. Place)
East Austin; RMC Place; TRAVIS; ★ **AUS**; mail Austin z 78702, z 78721-22, z 78762; pop. incl. with Austin (Inc. Place)
East Bernard; Inc. Place; WHARTON; **239** EL-9; 🅿; z 77435; incorporated September 13, 2003; not reported in 2000 Census
East Bernard; CDP-Census Area Only; WHARTON; **239** EL-9; 🅿; z 77435; Ⓟ 1,544; © 1,729
East Caney; RMC Place; HOPKINS; ***238** EC-10; mail Sulphur Springs z 75482; rural
East Center; RMC Place; VAN ZANDT; ***238** EE-9; mail Grand Saline z 75140; rural
East Columbia; RMC Place; BRAZORIA; ***239** EL-10; ★ **L.JAC-**; mail West Columbia z 77486; ● 90
East Delta; RMC Place; DELTA; ***238** EC-10; mail Lake Creek z 75450; rural
East Donna; RMC Place; HIDALGO; ★ **MCAL**; mail Donna z 78537; pop. incl. with Donna (Inc. Place)
Easterly; RMC Place; ROBERTSON; **238** EH-8; mail Franklin z 77856; ● 60
Eastgate; RMC Place; LIBERTY; ***238** EJ-11; ★ **HOU**; mail Dayton z 77535; rural
East Glen; RMC Place; EL PASO; ***237** WK-2; ★ **ELP**; mail El Paso z 79936; pop. incl. with El Paso (Inc. Place)
East Grand; RMC Place; DALLAS; ★ **D-FW**; mail Dallas z 75223; pop. incl. with Dallas (Inc. Place)
East Hamilton; RMC Place; SHELBY; ***238** EG-13; mail Shelbyville z 75973; rural
Easthaven; RMC Place; HARRIS; ***239** EK-11; ★ **HOU**; mail Houston z 77075; pop. incl. with Houston (Inc. Place)
East Houston; RMC Place; HARRIS; ***239** EK-11; ★ **HOU**; mail Houston z 77028, z 77228; pop. incl. with Houston (Inc. Place)
Eastland; Inc. Place; ⊡ EASTLAND; **238** EE-4; 🅿 🄷; z 76448; Ⓟ 3,690; © 3,769
EASTLAND; **238** EE-4; Ⓟ 18,488; © 18,297; ◆ 18,427
East Liberty; RMC Place; SHELBY; ***238** EG-13; mail Center z 75935; rural
East Mountain; Inc. Place; UPSHUR; ***238** EE-11; ★ **LNGV**; mail Gilmer z 75644; Ⓟ 762; © 580
Easton; Inc. Place; GREGG, RUSK; **238** EE-12; 🅿; ★ **LNGV**; z 75641; Ⓟ 401; © 524
East Point; RMC Place; WOOD; ***238** ED-10; elev. 449ft./137m.; mail Winnsboro z 75494; rural
East Ridge; RMC Place; POTTER; ★ **AMA**; mail Amarillo z 79107; pop. incl. with Amarillo (Inc. Place)
East Tawakoni; Inc. Place; RAINS; **238** ED-9; 🅿; z 75472 & mail Lone Oak z 75453; Ⓟ 642; © 775
East Tempe; RMC Place; POLK; ***238** EI-11; mail Livingston z 77351; rural
Eastvale; RMC Place; DENTON; ***238** ED-7; ★ **D-FW**; mail The Colony z 75056; pop. incl. with The Colony (Inc. Place)
Eastview Terrace; RMC Place; BEXAR; ★ **SANT**; mail Adkins z 78101; ● 400
East Waco; RMC Place; MCLENNAN; ***238** EG-7; ★ **WACO**; pop. incl. with Waco (Inc. Place)
Eastwood; RMC Place; HARRIS; ***239** EK-10; ★ **HOU**; mail Houston z 77023, z 77223, z 77261; pop. incl. with Houston (Inc. Place)
Eastwood Heights; RMC Place; EL PASO; ***237** WK-2; ★ **ELP**; mail El Paso z 79925; pop. incl. with El Paso (Inc. Place)
Eaton; RMC Place; ROBERTSON; ***238** EH-8; mail Franklin z 77856; rural
Ebenezer; RMC Place; CAMP; ***238** ED-11; mail Pittsburg z 75686; rural
Ebenezer; RMC Place; JASPER; ***238** EH-13; mail Jasper z 75951; rural
Ebony (Buffalo); RMC Place; MILLS; ***238** EG-3; mail Mullin z 76864; rural
Echo; RMC Place; COLEMAN; ***238** EF-3; elev. 1,563ft./476m.; mail Coleman z 76834; rural
Echo; RMC Place; ORANGE; ***238** EJ-13; elev. 16ft./5m.; ★ **B-PA**; mail Orange z 77632; ● 200
Echo Hills; RMC Place; HENDERSON; mail Frankston z 75763; ● 60
Eckert; RMC Place; GILLESPIE; ***238** EJ-4; elev. 1,741ft./531m.; mail Willow City z 78675; rural
Ecleto; RMC Place; KARNES; **239** EM-6; 🅿; z 78111; ● 40
Ector; Inc. Place; FANNIN; **238** EC-8; 🅿; z 75439; Ⓟ 494; © 600
ECTOR; **237** WK-9; Ⓟ 118,934; © 121,123; ◆ 133,377
Edcouch; Inc. Place; HIDALGO; **239** ES-6; elev. 62ft./19m.; 🅿; ★ **MCAL**; z 78538; Ⓟ 2,878; © 3,342
Eddy; RMC Place; MCLENNAN; ***238** EH-7; elev. 682ft./208m.; 🅿; z 76524; pop. incl. with Bruceville-Eddy (Inc. Place)
Eden; Inc. Place; CONCHO; **237** WM-14; elev. 2,051ft./625m.; 🅿 🄷; z 76837; Ⓟ 1,567; © 2,561
Edgar; RMC Place; DEWITT; ***239** EL-7; elev. 328ft./100m.; mail Cuero z 77954; rural
Edge; RMC Place; BRAZOS; ***238** EI-8; mail Bryan z 77801, z 77808
Edgecliff; TARRANT; see Edgecliff Village (Inc. Place)
Edgecliff Village (Edgecliff); Inc. Place; TARRANT; **235** I-4; ★ **D-FW**; mail Fort Worth z 76134; Ⓟ 2,715; © 2,550
Edgewater Estates; SAN PATRICIO; see Edgewater-Paisano (CDP-Census Area Only)
Edgewater-Paisano (Edgewater Estates); CDP-Census Area Only; SAN PATRICIO; ***239** EO-6; mail Mathis z 78368; © 182
Edgewood; Inc. Place; VAN ZANDT; **238** EE-9; 🅿; z 75117; Ⓟ 1,284; © 1,348
Edgeworth; RMC Place; BELL; ***238** EH-7; elev. 429ft./131m.; mail Rogers z 76569; rural
Edhube; RMC Place; FANNIN; ***238** EC-8; mail Bonham z 75418; ● 40
Edinburg; Inc. Place; ⊡ HIDALGO; **239** ES-5; elev. 96ft./29m.; 🅿 🄷 🄲 17,337 ■; ★ **MCAL**; z 78539-42; Ⓟ 29,885; © 48,465; ◆ 70,849
Edith; RMC Place; COKE; **237** WK-12; elev. 1,954ft./596m.; mail Robert Lee z 76945; rural
Edmonson; Inc. Place; HALE; **236** WF-10; 🅿; z 79032; Ⓟ 107; © 123
Edna; Inc. Place; ⊡ JACKSON; **239** EM-8; 🅿 🄷; z 77957; Ⓟ 5,343; © 5,899
Edna Hill; RMC Place; ERATH; ***238** EF-5; mail Dublin z 76446
Edom; Inc. Place; VAN ZANDT; **238** EE-10; mail Ben Wheeler z 75754, Brownsboro z 75756; Ⓟ 300; © 322
Edroy; CDP; SAN PATRICIO; **239** EO-6; 🅿; z 78352; © 420
EDWARDS; **237** WO-13; Ⓟ 2,266; © 2,162; ◆ 2,017
Egan; RMC Place; JOHNSON; ***238** EE-6; ★ **D-FW**; mail Cleburne z 76031; ● 35
Egypt; RMC Place; LEON; ***238** EH-9; mail Centerville z 75833; rural
Egypt; RMC Place; MONTGOMERY; **239** EL-9; ★ **HOU**; mail Magnolia z 77355; ● 200
Egypt; RMC Place; WHARTON; ***239** EL-9; elev. 131ft./40m.; 🅿; z 77436; ● 120
Eidson Road; CDP-Census Area Only; MAVERICK; ***237** WR-13; © 9,348
Elam; RMC Place; DALLAS; ★ **D-FW**; pop. incl. with Dallas (Inc. Place)
Elam Springs; RMC Place; UPSHUR; ***238** ED-11; mail Big Sandy z 75755; rural
Elbert; CDP; THROCKMORTON; **238** EC-3; elev. 1,153ft./351m.; 🅿; z 76372; © 56
Elbow; RMC Place; HOWARD; ***237** WK-11; mail Big Spring z 79720; rural
El Calmino; RMC Place; SABINE; ***238** EG-13; mail Hemphill z 75948; rural
El Camino Angosto; CDP-Census Area Only; CAMERON; ***239** ES-6; ★ **BRNS**; © 254
El Campo; Inc. Place; WHARTON; **239** EL-9; 🅿 🄷; z 77437; Ⓟ 10,511; © 10,945
El Campo Club; RMC Place; CALHOUN; ***239** EM-9; mail Palacios z 77465; ● 100
El Carey Estates; RMC Place; HARRIS; ★ **HOU**; mail Seabrook z 77586; pop. incl. with Seabrook (Inc. Place)
El Cenizo; Inc. Place; WEBB; **239** EP-2; 🅿; ★ **LAR**; z 78046 & mail Laredo z 78043; Ⓟ 1,399; © 3,545
El Centro; RMC Place; WEBB; ***239** EP-2; ★ **LAR**; mail Laredo z 78042; pop. incl. with Laredo (Inc. Place)
Eldorado; Inc. Place; ⊡ SCHLEICHER; **237** WN-12; elev. 2,439ft./743m.; 🅿 🄷; z 76936; Ⓟ 2,019; © 1,951
Eldorado Center; RMC Place; NAVARRO; ***238** EF-8; mail Dawson z 76639; rural
Electra; Inc. Place; WICHITA; **238** EB-3; elev. 1,225ft./373m.; 🅿 🄷; z 76360; Ⓟ 3,113; © 3,168
Electric City; RMC Place; HUTCHINSON; **236** WC-11; elev. 2,796ft./852m.; mail Borger z 79007; ● 200
Elevation; RMC Place; MILAM; ***238** EI-7; mail Milano z 76556; rural
El Gato; RMC Place; HIDALGO; ***239** ES-5; ★ **MCAL**; mail Alamo z 78516; ● 200
Elgin; Inc. Place; BASTROP, TRAVIS; **238** EJ-6; 🅿; z 78621; Ⓟ 4,846; © 5,700
Eliasville; RMC Place; YOUNG; **238** ED-4; 🅿; z 76481; ● 150
El Indio; CDP; MAVERICK; **237** WS-13; elev. 735ft./224m.; 🅿; z 78860; © 263
Elizabeth; RMC Place; JEFFERSON; ***238** EJ-13; ★ **B-PA**; mail Beaumont z 77706; pop. incl. with Beaumont (Inc. Place)
El Jardin; RMC Place; CAMERON; ★ **BRNS**; mail Brownsville z 78520; pop. incl. with Brownsville (Inc. Place)
El Jardin Del Mar; RMC Place; HARRIS; ***239** EK-11; ★ **HOU**; mail Seabrook z 77586; pop. incl. with Pasadena (Inc. Place)
Elk; RMC Place; MCLENNAN; **238** EG-7; elev. 523ft./159m.; mail Axtell z 76624; pop. incl. with Hallsburg (Inc. Place)
Elkhart; Inc. Place; ANDERSON; **238** EG-10; 🅿; z 75839; Ⓟ 1,076; © 1,215
El Lago; Inc. Place; HARRIS; **234** G-9; 🅿; ★ **HOU**; z 77586; Ⓟ 3,269; © 3,075
Ellinger; RMC Place; FAYETTE; **239** EK-8; 🅿; z 78938; ● 250
Elliott; RMC Place; ROBERTSON; ***238** EH-8; mail Hearne z 77859; rural
Elliott; RMC Place; WILBARGER; **238** EB-3; elev. 1,193ft./364m.; mail Harrold z 76364; ● 40
Ellis; RMC Place; HOCKLEY; mail Levelland z 79338; pop. incl. with Middletown (Inc. Place)
ELLIS; **238** EE-7; Ⓟ 85,167; © 111,360; ◆ 151,330
Elmaton; RMC Place; MATAGORDA; **239** EM-9; elev. 40ft./12m.; 🅿; z 77440; ● 100
Elm Creek; CDP-Census Area Only; MAVERICK; ***237** WR-13; © 1,928
Elmdale; RMC Place; TAYLOR; ***238** EE-2; elev. 1,781ft./543m.; ★ **ABIL**; mail Abilene z 79601; pop. incl. with Abilene (Inc. Place)
Elmendorf; Inc. Place; BEXAR; **239** EL-5; 🅿; ★ **SANT**; z 78112; Ⓟ 568; © 664
Elm Flat; RMC Place; NAVARRO; ***238** EF-8; mail Kerens z 75144; rural
Elm Grove; CALDWELL; see Taylorsville (RMC Place)
Elm Grove; RMC Place; CHEROKEE; ***238** EF-11; mail Rusk z 75785; ● 50
Elm Grove; RMC Place; FAYETTE; ***239** EK-7; mail Waelder z 78959; rural
Elm Grove; RMC Place; SAN SABA; ***238** EG-3; elev. 1,467ft./447m.; mail Rochelle z 76872; rural
Elm Grove; RMC Place; WHARTON; ***239** EL-9; elev. 138ft./42m.; mail Eagle Lake z 77434
Elm Mott; RMC Place; MCLENNAN; **238** EG-7; elev. 516ft./157m.; 🅿; ★ **WACO**; z 76640; ● 950
Elmo; RMC Place; KAUFMAN; **238** EE-9; 🅿; z 75118; ● 350
Elmont; RMC Place; GRAYSON; ***238** EC-8; elev. 727ft./222m.; mail Van Alstyne z 75495; ● 25
Elm Ridge; RMC Place; MILAM; ***238** EI-7; mail Cameron z 76520; rural
Elmtown; RMC Place; ANDERSON; ***238** EF-10; mail Palestine z 75801; rural
Elmwood; RMC Place; ANDERSON; ***238** EF-10; elev. 624ft./190m.; mail Palestine z 75801; rural
Elmwood; RMC Place; GUADALUPE; mail Seguin z 78155; pop. incl. with Seguin (Inc. Place)
Eloise; RMC Place; FALLS; ***238** EH-7; elev. 314ft./96m.; mail Reagan z 76680; rural
El Oso; RMC Place; KARNES; ***239** EM-5; mail Kenedy z 78119; rural
El Paso; Inc. Place; ⊡ EL PASO; **237** WK-2; 🅿 🄷 🄲 19,842 ■; ★ **ELP**; z 79901-08, z 79910-18, z 79920, z 79922-32, z 79934-38, z 79940-55, z 79958, z 79960-61, z 79968, z 79976, z 79978, z 79980, z 79990, z 79995-99, z 88510-21, z 88523-36, z 88538-50, z 88553-63, z 88565-90, z 88595 & mail Anthony z 79821; Ⓟ 515,342; © 563,662; ◆ 614,182
EL PASO; **237** WK-2; Ⓟ 591,610; © 679,622; ◆ 729,097
El Pinon Estates; RMC Place; SAN AUGUSTINE; ***238** EH-13; mail Broaddus z 75929; ● 75
El Ranchito; RMC Place; ECTOR; ★ **MIDL-**; mail Odessa z 79766; ● 600
El Rancho Estates; RMC Place; TARRANT; ★ **D-FW**; mail Aledo z 76008; ● 200
El Refugio; CDP; STARR; ***239** ES-4; mail Rio Grande City z 78582; © 221
Elroy; RMC Place; TRAVIS; ***238** EJ-6; elev. 598ft./182m.; ★ **AUS**; mail Del Valle z 78617; ● 60
Elsa; Inc. Place; HIDALGO; **239** ES-5; elev. 66ft./20m.; 🅿; ★ **MCAL**; z 78543; Ⓟ 5,242; © 5,549
El Sauz; RMC Place; STARR; **239** ER-4; elev. 259ft./79m.; mail Rio Grande City z 78582; ● 60
El Toro; RMC Place; JACKSON; ***239** EM-8; mail Edna z 77957
Elwood; RMC Place; FANNIN; ***238** EB-9; elev. 510ft./155m.; mail Ivanhoe z 75447
Elwood; RMC Place; MADISON; ***238** EH-9; mail Midway z 75852; rural
Elwood; RMC Place; VAN ZANDT; ***238** ED-9; mail Ben Wheeler z 75754, Chandler z 75758, Wills Point z 75169; rural
Ely; RMC Place; FANNIN; ***238** EC-8; elev. 728ft./222m.; mail Ector z 75439; rural
Elysian Fields; RMC Place; HARRISON; **238** EE-12; 🅿; z 75642; ● 300
Emberson; RMC Place; LAMAR; ***238** EB-9; elev. 573ft./175m.; mail Sumner z 75486
Emblem; RMC Place; HOPKINS; ***238** EC-9; mail Sulphur Springs z 75482; rural
Emerald Valley; RMC Place; BEXAR; ★ **SANT**; mail San Antonio z 78250; ● 800
Emhouse; Inc. Place; NAVARRO; **238** EF-8; mail Corsicana z 75110; Ⓟ 195; © 159
Eminence; RMC Place; CHAMBERS; ***239** EK-12; mail South Houston z 77587; ● 100
Emmett; RMC Place; NAVARRO; ***238** EF-7; mail Frost z 76641; rural
Emory; Inc. Place; ⊡ RAINS; **238** ED-9; 🅿; z 75440; Ⓟ 963; © 1,021
Encantada; RMC Place; CAMERON; ★ **BRNS**; mail San Benito z 78586; ● 250
Encantada-Ranchito El Calaboz; CDP-Census Area Only; CAMERON; ***239** ES-6; ★ **BRNS**; mail Brownsville z 78520; Ⓟ 1,143; © 2,100
Enchanted Oaks; RMC Place; HARRIS; ★ **HOU**; mail Houston z 77288; ● 400
Enchanted Oaks; Inc. Place; HENDERSON; ***238** EE-9; 🅿; z 75156; Ⓟ 290; © 357
Encinal; Inc. Place; LA SALLE; **239** EO-3; elev. 558ft./170m.; 🅿; z 78019; Ⓟ 620; © 629
Encino; CDP; BROOKS; **239** EQ-5; elev. 127ft./39m.; 🅿; z 78353; © 177
Energy; RMC Place; COMANCHE; **238** EG-5; 🅿; z 76452; ● 70
Engle; RMC Place; FAYETTE; **239** EK-7; mail Schulenburg z 78956; ● 30
Englewood; RMC Place; HARRIS; ***239** EK-10; ★ **HOU**; pop. incl. with Houston (Inc. Place)
English; RMC Place; RED RIVER; **238** EB-11; elev. 449ft./137m.; mail Clarksville z 75426; ● 90
Enloe; RMC Place; DELTA; **238** EC-9; elev. 491ft./150m.; 🅿; z 75441; ● 150
Ennis; Inc. Place; ELLIS; **238** EE-8; 🅿; z 75119-20; Ⓟ 13,883; © 16,045
Enoch; RMC Place; UPSHUR; ***238** ED-11; elev. 438ft./134m.; mail Gilmer z 75644; rural
Enochs; RMC Place; BAILEY; **236** WG-9; 🅿; z 79324; ● 70
Ensign; RMC Place; ELLIS; ***238** EE-8; mail Ennis z 75119; rural
Enterprise; RMC Place; CHEROKEE; mail Jacksonville z 75766; rural
Enterprise; RMC Place; VAN ZANDT; ***238** ED-9; mail Wills Point z 75169; rural
Eola; RMC Place; CONCHO; **237** WM-13; elev. 1,806ft./550m.; 🅿; z 76937; ● 200
Eolian; RMC Place; STEPHENS; ***238** EE-3; elev. 1,228ft./374m.; mail Breckenridge z 76424; rural
Epsom Downs; RMC Place; HARRIS; ***239** EK-10; ★ **HOU**; mail Houston z 77093; pop. incl. with Houston (Inc. Place)
Era; RMC Place; COOKE; **238** EC-6; 🅿; z 76238; ● 275
ERATH; **238** EE-4; Ⓟ 27,991; © 33,001; ◆ 36,134
Erin; RMC Place; JASPER; ***238** EI-13; elev. 285ft./87m.; mail Jasper z 75951
Erwin; RMC Place; GRIMES; ***238** EI-9; elev. 276ft./84m.; mail Anderson z 77830
Escobares; Inc. Place; STARR, STARR; **239** ES-4; elev. 180ft./55m.; incorporated October 22, 2005; not reported in 2000 Census; ● 1,300
Escobares; CDP; STARR; **239** ES-4; elev. 180ft./55m.; mail Rio Grande City z 78582; Ⓟ 1,705; © 1,954
Escobas; RMC Place; ZAPATA; ***239** EQ-3; mail Hebbronville z 78361; rural
Eskota; RMC Place; FISHER; ***238** EE-1; elev. 1,923ft./586m.; mail Trent z 79561; rural
Esmond Estates; RMC Place; ECTOR; ★ **MIDL-**; mail Odessa z 79762; pop. incl. with Odessa (Inc. Place)
Esperanza; RMC Place; HUDSPETH; ***237** WM-3; mail Fort Hancock z 79839; rural
Esperanza; RMC Place; MONTGOMERY; ***238** EI-10; mail Willis z 77378; rural
Esquire Estates; RMC Place; HENDERSON; ***238** EF-9; mail Mabank z 75156; ● 90
Esseville; RMC Place; LIVE OAK; ***239** EN-5; elev. 349ft./106m.; mail Campbellton z 78008; rural
Estacado; RMC Place; CROSBY; ***236** WG-11; mail Lorenzo z 79343; ● 50
Estacado; RMC Place; LUBBOCK, CROSBY; ***236** WG-11; mail Lorenzo z 79343
Estacado Estates; RMC Place; RANDALL; ★ **AMA**; mail Amarillo z 79109; pop. incl. with Amarillo (Inc. Place)
Estelline; Inc. Place; HALL; **236** WF-13; elev. 839ft./256m.; 🅿; z 79233; Ⓟ 194; © 168
Estes; RMC Place; ARANSAS; **239** EO-7; mail Rockport z 78382; ● 50
Estes Addition; RMC Place; WISE; mail Newark z 76071; ● 220
Ethel; RMC Place; GRAYSON; ***238** EC-7; elev. 727ft./222m.; mail Collinsville z 76233; ● 35
Etoile; RMC Place; NACOGDOCHES; **238** EG-12; elev. 186ft./57m.; 🅿; z 75944; ● 400
Etter; RMC Place; MOORE; **236** WB-10; elev. 3,625ft./1,105m.; mail Dumas z 79029; ● 100
Eubank Acres; RMC Place; TRAVIS; ***238** EJ-6; ★ **AUS**; mail Austin z 78753; pop. incl. with Austin (Inc. Place)
Eula; RMC Place; CALLAHAN; ***238** EE-2; mail Clyde z 79510; ● 60
Eulalie; RMC Place; RUSK; ***238** EF-12; mail Timpson z 75975; rural
Euless; Inc. Place; TARRANT; **238** ED-7; 🅿; ★ **D-FW**; z 76039-40; Ⓟ 38,149; © 46,005; ◆ 53,099
Eulogy; RMC Place; BOSQUE; ***238** EF-6; elev. 773ft./236m.; mail Kopperl z 76652; rural
Eunice; RMC Place; LEON; ***238** EH-9; mail Centerville z 75833; rural
Eureka; Inc. Place; NAVARRO; **238** EF-8; elev. 396ft./121m.; mail Corsicana z 75110; Ⓟ 242; © 340
Eustace; Inc. Place; HENDERSON; **238** EE-9; elev. 428ft./130m.; 🅿; z 75124; Ⓟ 662; © 798
Evadale; CDP; JASPER; **238** EI-13; 🅿; ★ **B-PA**; z 77615; Ⓟ 1,422; © 1,430
Evant; Inc. Place; CORYELL, HAMILTON; **238** EG-5; 🅿; z 76525; Ⓟ 444; © 393
Evergreen; RMC Place; SAN JACINTO; ***238** EI-11; mail Cleveland z 77327, Coldspring z 77331; rural
Evergreen Park; RMC Place; ORANGE; ***238** EJ-13; ★ **B-PA**; mail Vidor z 77662; ● 650
Everman; Inc. Place; TARRANT; **235** I-4; 🅿; ★ **D-FW**; z 76140; Ⓟ 5,672; © 5,836
Ewell; RMC Place; UPSHUR; ***238** ED-11; elev. 420ft./128m.; mail Gilmer z 75644
Eylau; RMC Place; BOWIE; **238** EC-12; elev. 319ft./97m.; ★ **TEXR-**; mail Texarkana z 75501; ● 200
Ezzell; RMC Place; LAVACA; ***239** EL-7; mail Hallettsville z 77964; rural

F

Fabens; CDP; EL PASO; **237** WL-2; 🅿; ★ **ELP**; z 79838; Ⓟ 5,599; © 8,043
Fairbanks; RMC Place; HARRIS; ***239** EK-10; ★ **HOU**; mail Houston z 77040-41, z 77240-41; pop. incl. with Houston (Inc. Place)
Fairchilds; Inc. Place; FORT BEND; ***239** EL-10; mail Needville z 77461, Richmond z 77469; © 678
Fairfield; Inc. Place; ⊡ FREESTONE; **238** EG-9; elev. 474ft./144m.; 🅿 🄷; z 75840; Ⓟ 3,234; © 3,094
Fairgreen; RMC Place; HARRIS; ***239** EK-10; ★ **HOU**; mail Houston z 77039; ● 2,300
Fairland; RMC Place; BURNET; ***238** EI-5; mail Marble Falls z 78654; rural
Fairlie; RMC Place; HUNT; **238** EC-9; mail Commerce z 75428; ● 75
Fairmount; RMC Place; SABINE; ***238** EH-13; mail Hemphill z 75948; ● 100
Fair Oaks; BEXAR, COMAL, KENDALL; see Fair Oaks Ranch (Inc. Place)
Fair Oaks; RMC Place; LIMESTONE; ***238** EG-8; elev. 433ft./132m.; mail Donie z 75838; rural
Fair Oaks Ranch (Fair Oaks); Inc. Place; BEXAR, COMAL, KENDALL; ***239** EK-4; elev. 1,350ft./411m.; 🅿; ★ **SANT**; z 78006, z 78015; Ⓟ 1,860; © 4,695
Fair Play; RMC Place; PANOLA; ***238** EF-12; mail Beckville z 75631; ● 50
Fairview; RMC Place; BAILEY; ***236** WG-9; elev. 3,844ft./1,172m.; mail Sudan z 79371; rural
Fairview; RMC Place; BOSQUE; ***238** EG-6; mail Valley Mills z 76689; rural
Fairview; RMC Place; BRAZOS; ***238** EI-8; ★ **BRY-**; mail Bryan z 77807
Fairview; RMC Place; CASS; ***238** ED-12; mail Linden z 75563
Fairview; Inc. Place; COLLIN; ***238** ED-8; elev. 634ft./193m.; 🅿; ★ **D-FW**; z 75069 & mail Allen z 75002; Ⓟ 1,554; © 2,644
Fairview; RMC Place; GAINES; ***236** WJ-9; mail Seminole z 79360; rural
Fairview; RMC Place; HARRIS; ***239** EK-10; ★ **HOU**; mail Houston z 77006, z 77266; pop. incl. with Houston (Inc. Place)
Fairview; RMC Place; HOWARD; ***236** WJ-11; mail Big Spring z 79720; rural
Fairview; RMC Place; RUSK; ***238** EF-11; mail Reklaw z 75784; rural
Fairview; RMC Place; WILSON; ***239** EM-5; elev. 544ft./166m.; mail Floresville z 78114
Fairview; WISE; see New Fairview (Inc. Place)
Fairy; RMC Place; HAMILTON; **238** EG-5; mail Hico z 76457; ● 40
Faker; RMC Place; CAMP; **238** ED-11; mail Pittsburg z 75686; rural
Falcon; RMC Place; ZAPATA; **239** ER-3; 🅿; z 78564 & mail Roma z 78584; ● 200
Falcon Heights; CDP; STARR; **239** ER-3; 🅿; z 78545; © 335
Falcon Lake Estates; CDP-Census Area Only; ZAPATA; ***239** ER-3; © 830
Falcon Mesa; CDP; ZAPATA; ***239** ER-3; mail Zapata z 78076; © 506
Falcon Village; CDP; STARR; ***239** ER-3; mail Falcon Heights z 78545; © 78
Falfurrias; Inc. Place; ⊡ BROOKS; **239** EQ-5; 🅿; z 78355; Ⓟ 5,788; © 5,297
Fallbrook; RMC Place; HARRIS; ***239** EK-10; ★ **HOU**; mail Houston z 77038; ● 1,500
Fallon; RMC Place; LIMESTONE; ***238** EG-8; elev. 507ft./155m.; mail Mexia z 76667; rural
FALLS; **238** EH-7; Ⓟ 17,712; © 18,576; ◆ 16,161
Falls City; Inc. Place; KARNES; **239** EM-5; 🅿; z 78113; Ⓟ 478; © 591
Falman-County Acres; CDP-Census Area Only; SAN PATRICIO; ***239** EO-7; © 289
Fambrough (Pleasant View Estates); RMC Place; STEPHENS; **238** EE-3; mail Breckenridge z 76424; ● 200
Famuliner; RMC Place; COCHRAN; mail Morton z 79346; rural
Fannett; RMC Place; JEFFERSON; **238** EJ-12; elev. 18ft./5m.; mail Beaumont z 77705; ● 400
Fannin; RMC Place; GOLIAD; **239** EM-7; 🅿; z 77960; ● 160
FANNIN; **238** EB-9; Ⓟ 24,804; © 31,242; ◆ 33,176
Fargo; RMC Place; WILBARGER; ***238** EA-3; elev. 1,250ft./381m.; mail Vernon z 76384
Farmer; RMC Place; YOUNG; ***238** EC-4; elev. 1,164ft./355m.; mail Loving z 76460; rural
Farmers Branch; Inc. Place; DALLAS; **238** ED-7; 🅿; ★ **D-FW**; z 75234, z 75244 & mail Dallas z 75381; Ⓟ 24,250; © 27,508; ◆ 28,311
Farmers Valley; RMC Place; WILBARGER; ***238** EA-2; elev. 1,314ft./401m.; mail Vernon z 76384
Farmersville; Inc. Place; COLLIN; **238** EC-8; 🅿; z 75442; Ⓟ 2,640; © 3,118
Farmington; RMC Place; GRAYSON; ***238** EC-8; mail Gunter z 75058; ● 50
Farnsworth; RMC Place; OCHILTREE; **236** WB-12; elev. 2,992ft./912m.; 🅿; z 79033; ● 140
Farr Addition; RMC Place; WARD; ***237** WL-8; mail Monahans z 79756; ● 350
Farrar; RMC Place; LIMESTONE; ***238** EG-8; elev. 431ft./131m.; mail Donie z 75838; ● 30
Farrsville; RMC Place; NEWTON; ***238** EH-13; elev. 265ft./81m.; mail Wiergate z 75977; rural
Farwell; Inc. Place; ⊡ PARMER; **236** WF-8; 🅿; z 79325; Ⓟ 1,373; © 1,364
Fashing; RMC Place; ATASCOSA; **239** EM-5; elev. 438ft./134m.; mail Campbellton z 78008; rural
Fate; Inc. Place; ROCKWALL; ***238** ED-8; 🅿; ★ **D-FW**; z 75132; Ⓟ 475; © 497
Faught; RMC Place; LAMAR; ***238** EB-10; mail Paris z 75462; rural
Faulkner; RMC Place; LAMAR; ***238** EB-10; elev. 403ft./123m.; mail Detroit z 75436, Paris z 75462; rural
Fawil; RMC Place; NEWTON; ***238** EI-13; mail Bon Wier z 75928; rural
Fayburg; RMC Place; COLLIN; ***238** EC-8; elev. 596ft./182m.; mail Blue Ridge z 75424, Farmersville z 75442; rural
FAYETTE; **239** EK-7; Ⓟ 20,095; © 21,804; ◆ 22,566
Fayetteville; Inc. Place; FAYETTE; **239** EK-8; 🅿; z 78940; Ⓟ 283; © 261
Faysville; CDP; HIDALGO; **239** ES-5; ★ **MCAL**; mail Edinburg z 78539; © 348
Fedor; RMC Place; LEE; ***238** EJ-7; mail Lexington z 78947, Lincoln z 78948; rural
Fellowship; RMC Place; SHELBY; ***238** EF-13; mail Joaquin z 75954; rural
Fentress; RMC Place; CALDWELL; **239** EK-6; elev. 444ft./135m.; 🅿; z 78622; ● 300
Ferris; Inc. Place; ELLIS, DALLAS; **238** EE-8; elev. 472ft./144m.; 🅿; ★ **D-FW**; z 75125; Ⓟ 2,212; © 2,175
Fetzer; RMC Place; WALLER; ***238** EJ-9; elev. 300ft./91m.; mail Plantersville z 77363; ● 150
Fiddlers Green; RMC Place; DENTON; ★ **D-FW**; mail Frisco z 75034; rural
Field Creek; RMC Place; LLANO; ***238** EI-3; elev. 1,404ft./428m.; mail Pontotoc z 76869; rural
Fieldton; RMC Place; LAMB; **236** WG-10; 🅿; z 79326; ● 35
Fife; RMC Place; MCCULLOCH; ***238** EH-3; 🅿; z 76825; rural
Fifth Street; CDP-Census Area Only; FORT BEND; ***239** EK-10; ★ **HOU**; © 2,059
Files Valley; RMC Place; HILL; ***238** EF-7; mail Itasca z 76055
Fincastle; RMC Place; HENDERSON; ***238** EF-10; elev. 505ft./154m.; mail Frankston z 75763; rural
Fink; RMC Place; GRAYSON; ***238** EB-8; elev. 713ft./217m.; mail Pottsboro z 75076; rural
Finney; RMC Place; HALE; **236** WF-11; elev. 3,402ft./1,037m.; mail Plainview z 79072; ● 20
Finney; RMC Place; KING; ***236** WG-13; mail Paducah z 79248; rural
Fischer; RMC Place; COMAL; **239** EK-5; elev. 1,159ft./353m.; 🅿; z 78623; ● 20
FISHER; **236** WI-13; Ⓟ 4,842; © 4,344; ◆ 3,819
Fisk; RMC Place; COLEMAN; ***238** EG-2; elev. 1,665ft./507m.; mail Coleman z 76834, Gouldbusk z 76845
Fitze; RMC Place; NACOGDOCHES; ***238** EF-12; mail Garrison z 75946; rural
Fitzhugh; RMC Place; HAYS; ***238** EJ-5; elev. 1,069ft./326m.; mail Austin z 78703
Five Points; RMC Place; EL PASO; ★ **ELP**; mail El Paso z 79903, z 79923; pop. incl. with El Paso (Inc. Place)
Five Points; RMC Place; ELLIS; ***238** EE-7; elev. 609ft./186m.; mail Waxahachie z 75167; rural
Flagg; RMC Place; CASTRO; ***236** WF-9; elev. 3,794ft./1,156m.; mail Dimmitt z 79027; ● 30
Flanagan; RMC Place; RUSK; mail Tatum z 75691; rural
Flat; RMC Place; CORYELL; **238** EH-6; elev. 1,839ft./561m.; 🅿; z 76526; ● 280
Flat Fork; RMC Place; SHELBY; **238** EF-12; mail Tenaha z 75974; ● 80
Flatonia; Inc. Place; FAYETTE; **239** EK-7; elev. 455ft./139m.; 🅿; z 78941 & mail Smithville z 78957; Ⓟ 1,295; © 1,377
Flat Prairie; RMC Place; WASHINGTON; ***238** EJ-8; mail Burton z 77835; rural
Flats; RMC Place; RAINS; **238** ED-9; mail Point z 75472; ● 100
Flatwood; RMC Place; VAN ZANDT; ***238** EE-10; mail Ben Wheeler z 75754; rural
Fleetwood; RMC Place; HARRIS; ***239** EK-10; ★ **HOU**; mail Houston z 77079, z 77094; pop. incl. with Houston (Inc. Place)
Fletcher; RMC Place; HARDIN; ***238** EJ-13; ★ **B-PA**; mail Lumberton z 77657; pop. incl. with Lumberton (Inc. Place)
Flint; RMC Place; SMITH; **238** EE-10; elev. 52ft./16m.; 🅿; ★ **TYL**; z 75762; ● 700
Flint Creek; RMC Place; YOUNG; ***238** ED-4; mail Graham z 76450; rural
Flo; RMC Place; LEON; **238** EG-9; mail Buffalo z 75831; rural
Flomot; RMC Place; MOTLEY; **236** WF-12; 🅿; z 79234; ● 100
Flora; RMC Place; HOPKINS; ***238** EC-10; elev. 457ft./139m.; mail Dike z 75437; rural
Florence; Inc. Place; WILLIAMSON; **238** EI-6; elev. 997ft./304m.; 🅿; z 76527; Ⓟ 829; © 1,054
Florence Hill; RMC Place; DALLAS; ***238** EE-7; ★ **D-FW**; mail Grand Prairie z 75052; pop. incl. with Grand Prairie (Inc. Place)
Floresville; Inc. Place; ⊡ WILSON; **239** EL-5; 🅿 🄷; z 78114; Ⓟ 5,247; © 5,868
Florey; RMC Place; ANDREWS; ***236** WJ-9; elev. 3,175ft./968m.; mail Andrews z 79714; rural
Florine; RMC Place; BEXAR; ★ **SANT**; mail San Antonio z 78209; pop. incl. with San Antonio (Inc. Place)
Flour Bluff; RMC Place; NUECES; ***239** EP-7; ★ **CRPX**; mail Corpus Christi z 78418-19, z 78480; pop. incl. with Corpus Christi (Inc. Place)
Flour Bluff Junction; RMC Place; NUECES; ***239** EO-6; ★ **CRPX**; pop. incl. with Corpus Christi (Inc. Place)
Flowella; CDP; BROOKS; ***239** EQ-5; mail Falfurrias z 78355; © 134
Flower Grove; RMC Place; MARTIN; ***236** WJ-10; mail Ackerly z 79713; rural
Flower Hill; RMC Place; COLORADO; ***239** EK-8; mail Columbus z 78934; rural
Flower Mound; Inc. Place; DENTON, TARRANT; **235** D-7; 🅿; ★ **D-FW**; z 75022, z 75027-28; Ⓟ 15,527; © 50,702; ◆ 75,305
Floyd; RMC Place; HUNT; **238** ED-8; mail Greenville z 75401; ● 100
FLOYD; **236** WF-11; Ⓟ 8,497; © 7,771; ◆ 6,184
Floydada; Inc. Place; ⊡ FLOYD; **236** WG-11; 🅿; z 79235; Ⓟ 3,896; © 3,676
Fluvanna; RMC Place; SCURRY; **236** WI-11; 🅿; z 79517; ● 170
Flynn; RMC Place; LEON; **238** EH-9; 🅿; z 77855; ● 150
FOARD; **238** EB-2; Ⓟ 1,794; © 1,622; ◆ 1,294
Foard City; RMC Place; FOARD; ***238** EB-2; mail Crowell z 79227; rural
Fodice; RMC Place; HOUSTON; **238** EH-10; mail Lovelady z 75851; rural
Follett; Inc. Place; LIPSCOMB; **236** WA-13; 🅿; z 79034; Ⓟ 441; © 412
Folley; RMC Place; MOTLEY; ***236** WF-12; elev. 2,374ft./724m.; mail Quitaque z 79255; rural
Ford; RMC Place; DEAF SMITH; ***236** WD-9; mail Hereford z 79045; rural
Fords Corner; RMC Place; SAN AUGUSTINE; ***238** EG-13; elev. 346ft./105m.; mail San Augustine z 75972; rural
Fordtran; RMC Place; VICTORIA; ***239** EM-7; mail Westhoff z 77994, Yoakum z 77995; rural
Forest; RMC Place; CHEROKEE; **238** EG-11; 🅿; z 75925; ● 40
Forestburg; RMC Place; MONTAGUE; **238** EC-6; elev. 1,162ft./354m.; 🅿; z 76239; ● 125
Forest Chapel; RMC Place; LAMAR; ***238** EB-9; elev. 523ft./159m.; mail Arthur City z 75411; rural
Forest Glade; RMC Place; LIMESTONE; **238** EG-8; mail Mexia z 76667; ● 300
Forest Grove; RMC Place; COLLIN; ***238** ED-8; elev. 614ft./187m.; ★ **D-FW**; mail Mckinney z 75069
Forest Grove; RMC Place; HENDERSON; ***238** EF-10; mail Chandler z 75758; ● 300
Forest Heights; RMC Place; ORANGE; ***238** EJ-13; ★ **B-PA**; mail Orange z 77630; ● 200
Forest Hill; RMC Place; LAMAR; ***238** EB-9; mail Honey Grove z 75446; rural
Forest Hill; RMC Place; POTTER; ★ **AMA**; mail Amarillo z 79107; pop. incl. with Amarillo (Inc. Place)
Forest Hill; Inc. Place; TARRANT; **235** I-5; 🅿; ★ **D-FW**; z 76119, z 76140; Ⓟ 11,482; © 12,949
Forest Hill; RMC Place; WOOD; ***238** ED-10; mail Quitman z 75783
Forest Hill Estates; RMC Place; CORYELL; ***238** EG-6; mail Gatesville z 76528; ● 90
Forest Hills; RMC Place; MONTGOMERY; ***238** EJ-10; ★ **HOU**; mail Conroe z 77385, Fort Worth z 76140; ● 300
Forest North Estates; RMC Place; WILLIAMSON; ***238** EJ-6; ★ **AUS**; mail Austin z 78729; ● 800
Forest Spring; RMC Place; POLK; ***238** EI-11; mail Livingston z 77351; rural
Forney; Inc. Place; KAUFMAN; **238** ED-8; elev. 471ft./144m.; 🅿; ★ **D-FW**; z 75126; Ⓟ 4,070; © 5,588
Forrester; TERRY; see Foster (RMC Place)
Forreston; RMC Place; ELLIS; **238** EF-7; 🅿; z 76041; ● 200
Forsan; Inc. Place; HOWARD; **237** WK-11; elev. 2,775ft./846m.; 🅿; z 79733; Ⓟ 256; © 226
FORT BEND; **239** EL-9; Ⓟ 225,421; © 354,452; ◆ 541,323
Fort Bliss; CDP-Census Area Only; EL PASO; ***237** WK-2; 🅿; ★ **ELP**; z 79916, z 79918 & mail El Paso z 79906, z 79908; Ⓟ 13,915; © 8,264
Fort Clark Springs; RMC Place; KINNEY; ***237** WQ-13; mail Brackettville z 78832
Fort Davis; CDP; ⊡ JEFF DAVIS; **237** WN-6; elev. 4,900ft./1,494m.; 🅿; z 79734; © 1,050
Fort Gates; RMC Place; CORYELL; **238** EG-6; elev. 747ft./228m.; mail Gatesville z 76528; pop. incl. with Gatesville (Inc. Place)
Fort Hancock; CDP; HUDSPETH; **237** WL-3; elev. 3,596ft./1,096m.; 🅿; z 79839; © 1,713
Fort Hood; CDP-Census Area Only; BELL, CORYELL; ***238** EH-6; 🅿; ★ **KILL-**; z 76544; Ⓟ 35,580; © 33,711; ◆ 44,543
Fort McKavett; RMC Place; MENARD; **237** WN-13; elev. 2,171ft./662m.; 🅿; z 76841; ● 50
Fort Phantom Hill; RMC Place; JONES; ***238** EE-2; mail Abilene z 79601; rural
Fort Ringgold; RMC Place; STARR; mail Rio Grande City z 78582; pop. incl. with Rio Grande City (Inc. Place)
Fort Spunky; RMC Place; HOOD; ***238** EE-6; mail Cleburne z 76033; rural
Fort Stockton; Inc. Place; ⊡ PECOS; **237** WN-8; 🅿 🄷; z 79735; Ⓟ 8,524; © 7,846
Fort Worth; Inc. Place; ⊡ TARRANT, DENTON; **238** EE-6; 🅿 🄷 🄲 14,277 ■; ★ **D-FW**; z 76101-24, z 76126-27, z 76129-37, z 76140, z 76147-48, z 76150, z 76155, z 76161-64, z 76166, z 76177, z 76179-82, z 76185, z 76191-93, z 76195-99, z 76244 & mail Cresson z 76035; Ⓟ 447,619; © 534,694; ◆ 738,712
Foster; RMC Place; FORT BEND; ***239** EK-9; elev. 113ft./34m.; mail Richmond z 77469; rural
Foster (Forrester); RMC Place; TERRY; ***236** WI-9; elev. 3,278ft./999m.; mail Brownfield z 79316; rural
Foster Hills; RMC Place; TYLER; ***238** EH-12; elev. 200ft./61m.; mail Woodville z 75979
Foster Place; RMC Place; HARRIS; ***239** EK-10; ★ **HOU**; mail Houston z 77021, z 77221; pop. incl. with Houston (Inc. Place)
Fouke; RMC Place; WOOD; ***238** EE-10; mail Hawkins z 75765; rural
Fountain View; RMC Place; HARRIS; ***239** EK-10; ★ **HOU**; mail Houston z 77032; ● 1,300
Four Corners; RMC Place; BRAZORIA; ***239** EM-10; elev. 24ft./7m.; ★ **L.JAC-**; mail Brazoria z 77422; rural
Four Corners; CDP; FORT BEND; **234** F-1; elev. 94ft./29m.; ★ **HOU**; mail Richmond z 77469; © 2,954
Four Corners; RMC Place; MONTGOMERY; ***238** EJ-10; ★ **HOU**; mail Conroe z 77301; rural
Four Way; RMC Place; MOORE; ***236** WC-10; mail Channing z 79018; rural
Fowlerton; CDP; LA SALLE; **239** EN-4; 🅿; z 78021; © 62
Fox; RMC Place; PARKER; ***238** ED-5; elev. 1,154ft./352m.; mail Weatherford z 76088; rural
Fox Landing; RMC Place; TYLER; ***238** EH-12; elev. 95ft./29m.; mail Colmesneil z 75938; ● 50
Fox Run; RMC Place; MONTGOMERY; ***238** EJ-10; ★ **HOU**; mail Spring z 77386; ● 1,200
Foxwood; RMC Place; MONTGOMERY; ***238** EJ-10; ★ **HOU**; mail Pinehurst z 77362
Frame Switch; RMC Place; WILLIAMSON; ***238** EI-6; elev. 630ft./192m.; mail Taylor z 76574; pop. incl. with Taylor (Inc. Place)
Francitas; RMC Place; JACKSON; **239** EM-9; elev. 34ft./10m.; 🅿; z 77961; ● 120
Frankel City; RMC Place; ANDREWS; ***236** WJ-8; mail Andrews z 79714; rural
Frankell; RMC Place; STEPHENS; ***238** EE-4; elev. 1,578ft./481m.; mail Ranger z 76470; rural
Franklin; Inc. Place; ⊡ ROBERTSON; **238** EH-8; elev. 457ft./139m.; 🅿; z 77856; Ⓟ 1,336; © 1,470
FRANKLIN; **238** EC-10; Ⓟ 7,802; © 9,458; ◆ 11,347
Frank M Tajida; RMC Place; BEXAR; mail San Antonio z 78224; pop. incl. with San Antonio (Inc. Place)
Frankston; Inc. Place; ANDERSON; **238** EF-10; elev. 392ft./119m.; 🅿; z 75763; Ⓟ 1,127; © 1,209
Fratt; RMC Place; BEXAR; ***239** EL-5; elev. 753ft./230m.; ★ **SANT**; pop. incl. with San Antonio (Inc. Place)
Fred; RMC Place; TYLER; **238** EI-13; 🅿; z 77616; ● 300
Fredericksburg; Inc. Place; ⊡ GILLESPIE; **238** EJ-4; elev. 1,702ft./519m.; 🅿 🄷; z 78624; Ⓟ 6,934; © 8,911
Fredonia; RMC Place; GREGG; ***238** EE-11; ★ **LNGV**; mail Kilgore z 75662; rural
Fredonia; RMC Place; MASON; **238** EI-3; 🅿; z 76842; ● 60
Fredonia Hill; RMC Place; NACOGDOCHES; ***238** EG-11; mail Nacogdoches z 75964; pop. incl. with Nacogdoches (Inc. Place)
Freedom; RMC Place; LUBBOCK; ★ **LUB**; mail Lubbock z 79404, z 79412, z 79423, z 79452; pop. incl. with Lubbock (Inc. Place)
Freedom; RMC Place; MCLENNAN; ★ **WACO**; pop. incl. with Waco (Inc. Place)
Freedom; RMC Place; RAINS; ***238** ED-9; mail Emory z 75440; rural
Freeneytown; RMC Place; RUSK; ***238** EF-11; mail Laneville z 75667; rural
Freeport; Inc. Place; BRAZORIA; **239** EM-10; 🅿; ★ **L.JAC-**; z 77541-42; Ⓟ 11,389; © 12,708; ◆ 13,858
Freer; Inc. Place; DUVAL; **239** EO-4; elev. 528ft./161m.; 🅿; z 78357; Ⓟ 3,271; © 3,241
Freestone; RMC Place; FREESTONE; **238** EG-9; mail Donie z 75838, Teague z 75860; ● 35
FREESTONE; **238** EG-9; Ⓟ 15,818; © 17,867; ◆ 18,647
Freeway Manor; RMC Place; HARRIS; ***239** EK-11; ★ **HOU**; mail Houston z 77034; pop. incl. with Houston (Inc. Place)
Freeway Oaks Estates; RMC Place; MONTGOMERY; ***238** EJ-11; ★ **HOU**; mail Porter z 77365
Freheit; RMC Place; COMAL; ***239** EK-5; mail New Braunfels z 78130; rural
Frelsburg; RMC Place; COLORADO; **239** EK-8; mail New Ulm z 78950; ● 60
French Creek Village; RMC Place; BEXAR; ***239** EL-4; ★ **SANT**; mail San Antonio z 78240; pop. incl. with San Antonio (Inc. Place)
Frenstat; RMC Place; BURLESON; ***238** EJ-8; mail Caldwell z 77836; rural
Fresenius; RMC Place; HARDIN; ***238** EI-12; elev. 67ft./20m.; ★ **B-PA**; mail Silsbee z 77656; rural
Fresno; CDP; FORT BEND; **234** G-4; 🅿; ★ **HOU**; z 77545; Ⓟ 3,182; © 6,603
Freyburg; RMC Place; FAYETTE; ***239** EK-7; elev. 390ft./119m.; mail Schulenburg z 78956; rural
Friday; RMC Place; TRINITY; ***238** EH-10; mail Groveton z 75845
Friendship; RMC Place; JASPER; ***238** EH-13; mail Newton z 75966; rural
Friendship; RMC Place; LAMB; ***236** WG-9; elev. 3,761ft./1,146m.; mail Sudan z 79371; rural
Friendship; RMC Place; LEON; ***238** EH-9; mail Jewett z 75846; rural
Friendship; RMC Place; SMITH; ***238** EE-11; mail Gladewater z 75647; rural
Friendship; RMC Place; UPSHUR; **238** ED-11; mail Gilmer z 75644; ● 50
Friendship; RMC Place; VAN ZANDT; ***238** EE-10; mail Grand Saline z 75140; rural
Friendswood; Inc. Place; GALVESTON, HARRIS; **234** H-7; 🅿 ■; ★ **HOU**; z 77546, z 77549; Ⓟ 22,814; © 29,037; ◆ 32,375
FRIO; **239** EM-4; Ⓟ 13,472; © 16,252; ◆ 16,055
Friona; Inc. Place; PARMER; **236** WE-9; elev. 4,018ft./1,225m.; 🅿 🄷; z 79035; Ⓟ 3,688; © 3,854
Frisco; Inc. Place; COLLIN, DENTON; **238** ED-7; 🅿; ★ **D-FW**; z 75034-35; Ⓟ 6,141; © 33,714; ◆ 78,080
Fritch; Inc. Place; HUTCHINSON, MOORE; **236** WC-11; 🅿; z 79036; Ⓟ 2,335; © 2,235
Frog; RMC Place; KAUFMAN; ***238** ED-9; mail Elmo z 75118, Terrell z 75161; rural
Frognot; RMC Place; COLLIN; ***238** EC-8; elev. 612ft./187m.; mail Blue Ridge z 75424; rural
Frontier; RMC Place; WILLIAMSON; ★ **AUS**; mail Round Rock z 78664; pop. incl. with Round Rock (Inc. Place)
Frontier Lakes; RMC Place; MONTGOMERY; ***238** EI-10; mail Willis z 77378; ● 250
Fronton; CDP; STARR; **239** ES-3; mail Rio Grande City z 78582, Roma z 78584; © 599
Frosa; RMC Place; LIMESTONE; ***238** EG-8; elev. 563ft./172m.; mail Prairie Hill z 76678; rural
Frost; Inc. Place; NAVARRO; **238** EF-7; 🅿; z 76641; Ⓟ 579; © 648
Fruitland; RMC Place; MONTAGUE; **238** EC-5; mail Bowie z 76230; ● 20
Fruitvale; Inc. Place; VAN ZANDT; ***238** EE-9; 🅿; z 75127; Ⓟ 349; © 418
Frydek; RMC Place; AUSTIN; **239** EK-9; mail Sealy z 77474; ● 100
Frys Gap; RMC Place; CHEROKEE; ***238** EF-10; elev. 600ft./183m.; mail Jacksonville z 75766; rural
Fulbright; RMC Place; RED RIVER; **238** EC-10; mail Detroit z 75436; ● 100
Fuller Springs; RMC Place; ANGELINA; ***238** EG-11; ★ **LUFK**; mail Lufkin z 75901; ● 1,200
Fulshear; Inc. Place; FORT BEND; **239** EK-9; 🅿; z 77441; Ⓟ 557; © 716
Fulton; Inc. Place; ARANSAS; **239** EO-7; 🅿; z 78358; Ⓟ 763; © 1,553
Fulton Beach; RMC Place; ARANSAS; mail Fulton z 78358; pop. incl. with Fulton (Inc. Place)
Funston; RMC Place; JONES; ***238** EE-2; mail Anson z 79501
Furney Richardson; RMC Place; FREESTONE; ***238** EG-8; mail Teague z 75860; rural

G

Gail; RMC Place; ⊡ BORDEN; **236** WI-11; elev. 2,558ft./780m.; 🅿; z 79738; ● 200
GAINES; **236** WI-8; Ⓟ 14,123; © 14,467; ◆ 15,259
Gainesville; Inc. Place; ⊡ COOKE; **238** EC-7; 🅿 🄷; z 76240-41; Ⓟ 14,256; © 15,538
Galena Park; Inc. Place; HARRIS; **234** D-6; 🅿; ★ **HOU**; z 77547; Ⓟ 10,033; © 10,592
Galilee; RMC Place; SMITH; ***238** EE-10; ★ **TYL**; mail Tyler z 75709; rural
Galilee; RMC Place; WALKER; ***238** EI-10; mail Huntsville z 77320; rural
Gallatin; Inc. Place; CHEROKEE; **238** EF-11; elev. 407ft./124m.; 🅿; z 75764; Ⓟ 368; © 378
Gallaway; PANOLA; see Bethsaida (RMC Place)

Entries in **UPPERCASE** are counties.
Entries in **bold** have populations of 2,500 or more.
Names in parentheses are alternate names.
Inc. Place — Incorporated Place
RMC Place — Rand McNally Designated Place
CDP — Census Designated Place
MCD — Minor Civil Division

⊡ County Seat
▲ Minor Civil Division
elev. Elevation
🅿 Post Office

🄷 Hospital
🄲 College
■ Principal Business Center
★ Ranally Metro Area (RMA) Abbreviation
z Zip Code(s)

Ⓟ Previous Census Population
Ⓡ Revised Census Population
Ⓐ Annexation Population
● Rand McNally Population Estimate
© Final Census Population
Ⓢ Special Census Population
◆ Estimated Population

For additional definitions see Glossary, Volume 1, and Introduction, Volume 2.

Galle; RMC Place; GUADALUPE; *239 EK-5; mail Kingsbury z 78638; rural
Galloway; RMC Place; JEFFERSON; ★ B-PA
Galveston; Inc. Place; ⊡ GALVESTON; 234 B-10; 🅿 🅷 🅲 3,703 ■; ★ GLV-; z 77550-55; ℗ 59,070; © 57,247; ◆ 54,977
GALVESTON; 239 EL-12; ℗ 217,399; © 250,158; ◆ 284,037
Ganado; Inc. Place; JACKSON; 239 EM-8; elev. 63ft./19m.; 🅿; z 77962; ℗ 1,701; © 1,915
Garceno; CDP; STARR; *239 ES-4; mail Rio Grande City z 78582; © 1,438
Garciasville; RMC Place; STARR; 239 ES-4; 🅿; z 78547; ● 450
Garden Acres; RMC Place; TARRANT; *238 EE-6; ★ D-FW; mail Burleson z 76028, Euless z 76040; pop. incl. with Fort Worth (Inc. Place)
Garden City; RMC Place; ⊡ GLASSCOCK; 237 WK-11; elev. 2,635ft./803m.; 🅿; z 79739; ● 300
Garden City Park; RMC Place; HARRIS; *239 EK-10; ★ HOU; mail Houston z 77088; pop. incl. with Houston (Inc. Place)
Gardendale; CDP; ECTOR; 237 WK-9; 🅿; ★ MIDL-; z 79758; ℗ 1,103; © 1,197
Gardendale; RMC Place; LA SALLE; *239 EN-3; mail Cotulla z 78014
Gardendale; RMC Place; NUECES; *239 EP-7; ★ CRPX; mail Corpus Christi z 78404; pop. incl. with Corpus Christi (Inc. Place)
Garden Oaks; RMC Place; HARRIS; *239 EK-10; ★ HOU; mail Houston z 77018, z 77206; pop. incl. with Houston (Inc. Place)
Garden Ridge; Inc. Place; COMAL; 239 EP-14; 🅿; ★ SANT; z 78266; ℗ 1,450; © 1,882
Garden Valley; RMC Place; SMITH; 238 EE-10; 🅿; z 75771; ● 120
Garfield; RMC Place; DEWITT; *239 EM-6; mail Yorktown z 78164; rural
Garfield; CDP; TRAVIS, BASTROP; 238 EJ-6; ★ AUS; mail Del Valle z 78617, Manor z 78653; ℗ 1,336; © 1,660
Garland; RMC Place; BOWIE; *238 EC-11; mail De Kalb z 75559; rural
Garland; Inc. Place; DALLAS, COLLIN, ROCKWALL; 238 ED-8; 🅿 🅷 🅲 1,582 ■; ★ D-FW; z 75040-49; ℗ 180,650; © 215,768; ◆ 232,052
Garland; RMC Place; RED RIVER; *238 EC-11; mail Annona z 75550; rural
Garner; RMC Place; PARKER; *238 ED-5; mail Weatherford z 76088; ● 125
Garrett; Inc. Place; ELLIS; 238 EE-8; mail Ennis z 75119; ℗ 340; © 448
Garretts Bluff; RMC Place; LAMAR; *238 EB-9; mail Arthur City z 75411
Garrison; Inc. Place; NACOGDOCHES; 238 EF-12; elev. 394ft./120m.; 🅿; z 75946; ℗ 883; © 844
Garvin; RMC Place; WISE; *238 ED-6; mail Boyd z 76023; rural
Garwood; RMC Place; COLORADO; 239 EL-8; 🅿; z 77442; ● 850
Gary (Gary City); Inc. Place; PANOLA; 238 EF-12; 🅿; z 75643; ℗ 271; © 303
Gary City; PANOLA; see Gary (Inc. Place)
GARZA; 236 WH-11; ℗ 5,143; © 4,872; ◆ 4,450
Gasoline; RMC Place; BRISCOE; *236 WF-12; mail Quitaque z 79255; rural
Gastonia; RMC Place; KAUFMAN; *238 EE-8; mail Crandall z 75114; rural
Gates; RMC Place; DALLAS; ★ D-FW; pop. incl. with Dallas (Inc. Place)
Gatesville; Inc. Place; ⊡ CORYELL; 238 EG-6; 🅿 🅷; z 76528, z 76596-99; ℗ 11,492; © 15,591
Gatewood; RMC Place; HARRIS; *239 EK-10; ★ HOU; mail Houston z 77032
Gause; RMC Place; MILAM; 238 EI-8; elev. 370ft./113m.; 🅿; z 77857; ● 500
Gay Hill; RMC Place; FAYETTE; *239 EK-8; elev. 310ft./94m.; mail La Grange z 78945; rural
Gay Hill; RMC Place; WASHINGTON; 238 EJ-8; elev. 356ft./109m.; mail Brenham z 77833
Gaywood; RMC Place; HARRIS; *239 EK-10; ★ HOU; mail Houston z 77079; pop. incl. with Houston (Inc. Place)
Geneva; RMC Place; SABINE; 238 EG-13; 🅿; z 75959; ● 100
Geneva Estates; RMC Place; TRAVIS; *238 EJ-5; ★ AUS; mail Austin z 78736; ● 60
Genoa; RMC Place; HARRIS; *239 EK-11; ★ HOU; mail Houston z 77034, z 77234; pop. incl. with Houston (Inc. Place)
George; RMC Place; MADISON; *238 EH-9; elev. 364ft./111m.; mail Normangee z 77871; rural
Georges Creek; RMC Place; SOMERVELL; *238 EE-6; elev. 700ft./213m.; mail Cleburne z 76033; rural
Georgetown; Inc. Place; ⊡ WILLIAMSON; 238 EI-6; 🅿 🅷 🅲 1,277; ★ AUS; z 78626-28, z 78633; ℗ 14,842; © 28,339; ◆ 42,825
George West; Inc. Place; ⊡ LIVE OAK; 239 EN-5; 🅿; z 78022; ℗ 2,586; © 2,524
Georgia; RMC Place; LAMAR; *238 EB-9; mail Sumner z 75486; rural
Geronimo; CDP; GUADALUPE; 239 EK-5; 🅿; z 78115; © 619
Geronimo Forest; RMC Place; BEXAR; *239 EL-4; ★ SANT; mail San Antonio z 78254; ● 100
Geronimo Village; RMC Place; BEXAR; *239 EL-4; ★ SANT; mail San Antonio z 78253; ● 200
Gethsemane; RMC Place; MARION; *238 ED-12; mail Jefferson z 75657; ● 120
Gholson; Inc. Place; MCLENNAN; 238 EG-7; elev. 423ft./129m.; mail Waco z 76705; ℗ 692; © 922
Gibtown; RMC Place; JACK; *238 ED-5; mail Perrin z 76486
Giddings; Inc. Place; ⊡ LEE; 238 EJ-7; elev. 513ft./156m.; 🅿; z 78942; ℗ 4,093; © 5,105
Gilchrist; RMC Place; GALVESTON; 239 EK-12; 🅿; z 77617; summer pop. 2,000; ● 750
Gill; RMC Place; HARRISON; 238 EE-12; mail Marshall z 75670, z 75672
GILLESPIE; 238 EJ-3; ℗ 17,204; © 20,814; ◆ 23,789
Gillett; RMC Place; KARNES; 239 EL-6; elev. 354ft./108m.; 🅿; z 78111, z 78116; ● 100
Gilliland; RMC Place; KNOX; *238 EB-2; mail Crowell z 79227
Gilmer; Inc. Place; ⊡ UPSHUR; 238 ED-11; 🅿; z 75644-45; ℗ 4,822; © 4,799
Gilpin; RMC Place; DICKENS; *236 WH-12; elev. 2,139ft./652m.; mail Spur z 79370; rural
Gindale; BELL; see Leedale (RMC Place)
Ginger; RMC Place; RAINS; *238 ED-9; mail Alba z 75410; rural
Girard; CDP; KENT; 236 WH-12; 🅿; z 79518; © 62
Girvin; RMC Place; PECOS; 237 WM-9; elev. 2,328ft./710m.; 🅿; z 79740; ● 30
Givens; RMC Place; LAMAR; *238 EB-10; mail Paris z 75462; pop. incl. with Paris (Inc. Place)
Gladewater; Inc. Place; GREGG, UPSHUR; *238 EE-11; 🅿; ★ LNGV; z 75647; ℗ 6,027; © 6,078
Gladewater; RMC Place; TITUS; 238 EC-11; mail Mount Pleasant z 75455; rural
Glass; RMC Place; SOMERVELL; *238 EF-5; mail Glen Rose z 76043; rural
GLASSCOCK; 237 WK-11; ℗ 1,447; © 1,406; ◆ 1,082
Glaze City; RMC Place; GONZALES; *239 EL-7; elev. 291ft./89m.; mail Shiner z 77984
Glazier; RMC Place; HEMPHILL; 236 WB-13; 🅿; z 79014; ● 50
Glencairn; RMC Place; HARRIS; *239 EK-10; ★ HOU; mail Houston z 77084; ● 750
Glen Cove; RMC Place; COLEMAN; 238 EG-2; mail Coleman z 76834; ● 40
Glencrest; RMC Place; TARRANT; *238 EE-6; ★ D-FW; mail Fort Worth z 76119; pop. incl. with Fort Worth (Inc. Place)
Glendale; RMC Place; TRINITY; 238 EH-10; elev. 314ft./96m.; mail Trinity z 75862; ● 125
Glenfawn; RMC Place; RUSK; *238 EF-11; mail Cushing z 75760; rural
Glen Flora; RMC Place; WHARTON; 239 EL-9; elev. 119ft./36m.; 🅿; z 77443; ● 300
Glenn; RMC Place; DICKENS; 136 WG-12; elev. 2,678ft./816m.; mail Dickens z 79229; rural
Glenn Heights; Inc. Place; DALLAS, ELLIS; 235 J-10; 🅿; ★ D-FW; z 75154; ℗ 4,564; © 7,224
Glenrio; RMC Place; DEAF SMITH; 236 WD-8; mail Tucumcari z 88401; rural
Glen Rose; Inc. Place; ⊡ SOMERVELL; 238 EF-6; elev. 627ft./191m.; 🅿 🅷; z 76043; ℗ 1,949; © 2,122
Glenwood; RMC Place; POTTER; ★ AMA; mail Amarillo z 79103; pop. incl. with Amarillo (Inc. Place)
Glenwood; RMC Place; UPSHUR; 238 EE-11; mail Gilmer z 75644; ● 150
Glidden; RMC Place; COLORADO; 239 EK-8; elev. 232ft./71m.; 🅿; z 78943; ● 250
Globe; RMC Place; LAMAR; *238 EB-9; elev. 575ft./175m.; mail Sumner z 75486; rural
Glory; RMC Place; LAMAR; *238 EC-10; mail Paris z 75462; rural
Gober; RMC Place; FANNIN; *238 EC-9; 🅿; z 75443; ● 200
Godley; Inc. Place; JOHNSON; 238 EE-6; 🅿; z 76044; ℗ 569; © 879
Gold; RMC Place; GILLESPIE; *238 EJ-4; mail Fredericksburg z 78624; rural
Golden; RMC Place; WOOD; 238 ED-10; 🅿; z 75444; ● 500
Golden Acres; RMC Place; HARRIS; *239 EK-11; ★ HOU; mail Pasadena z 77503; pop. incl. with Pasadena (Inc. Place)
Golden Beach; RMC Place; LLANO; *238 EI-4; mail Llano z 78643; ● 150
Golden Oaks; RMC Place; WILLIAMSON; *238 EI-6; ★ AUS; mail Georgetown z 78628; ● 180
Golden Triangle; RMC Place; DENTON; mail Denton z 76206; pop. incl. with Denton (Inc. Place)
Goldfinch; RMC Place; FRIO; *239 EM-4; elev. 513ft./156m.; mail Bigfoot z 78005; rural
Goldsboro; RMC Place; COLEMAN; 238 EF-2; elev. 1,944ft./593m.; 🅿; z 79519; ● 40
Goldsmith; Inc. Place; ECTOR; 237 WK-9; elev. 3,141ft./957m.; 🅿; z 79741; ℗ 297; © 253
Goldthwaite; Inc. Place; ⊡ MILLS; 238 EG-4; elev. 1,581ft./482m.; 🅿; z 76844; ℗ 1,658; © 1,802
Golfcrest; RMC Place; HARRIS; *239 EK-10; ★ HOU; mail Houston z 77087; pop. incl. with Houston (Inc. Place)
Goliad; Inc. Place; ⊡ GOLIAD; 239 EN-7; elev. 171ft./52m.; 🅿; z 77963; ℗ 1,946; © 1,975
GOLIAD; 239 EM-7; ℗ 5,980; © 6,928; ◆ 7,155
Golinda; Inc. Place; FALLS, MCLENNAN; 238 EH-7; mail Lorena z 76655; ℗ 347; © 423
Gomez; RMC Place; TERRY; *236 WI-9; elev. 3,362ft./1,025m.; mail Brownfield z 79316; rural
Gonzales; Inc. Place; ⊡ GONZALES; 239 EL-6; 🅿 🅷; z 78629; ℗ 6,527; © 7,202
GONZALES; 239 EL-6; ℗ 17,205; © 18,628; ◆ 18,660
Goober Hill; RMC Place; SHELBY; *238 EG-13; mail Shelbyville z 75973; rural
Goodland; RMC Place; BAILEY; *236 WG-8; mail Sudan z 79371
Goodland; RMC Place; ROBERTSON; *238 EI-8; mail Hearne z 77859; rural
Goodlett; RMC Place; HARDEMAN; 236 WF-14; elev. 1,558ft./475m.; mail Quanah z 79252; ● 50
Goodlow; NAVARRO; see Goodlow Park (Inc. Place)
Goodlow Park (Goodlow); Inc. Place; NAVARRO; 238 EF-9; mail Kerens z 75144; ℗ 319; © 264
Goodnight; RMC Place; ARMSTRONG; *236 WE-11; elev. 3,139ft./957m.; mail Clarendon z 79226
Goodnight; RMC Place; NAVARRO; *238 EF-9; elev. 337ft./103m.; mail Kerens z 75144; ● 90
Goodrich; Inc. Place; POLK; 238 EI-11; 🅿; z 77335; ℗ 239; © 243
Good Springs; RMC Place; RUSK; *238 EF-11; mail Henderson z 75652, Laneville z 75667; rural
Goodville; RMC Place; FALLS; mail Chilton z 76632, Lott z 76656; rural
Gordon; RMC Place; LYNN; *236 WH-11; elev. 3,003ft./915m.; mail Post z 79356; rural
Gordon; Inc. Place; PALO PINTO; 238 EE-4; elev. 988ft./301m.; 🅿; z 76453; ℗ 465; © 451
Gordonville; RMC Place; GRAYSON; 238 EB-7; elev. 721ft./220m.; 🅿; z 76245; ● 150
Goree; Inc. Place; KNOX; 238 EC-2; elev. 1,457ft./444m.; 🅿; z 76363; ℗ 412; © 321
Gorman; Inc. Place; EASTLAND; 238 EF-4; elev. 1,443ft./440m.; 🅿; z 76454; ℗ 1,290; © 1,236
Gough; RMC Place; DELTA; *238 EC-9; mail Klondike z 75448; ● 25
Gould; RMC Place; CHEROKEE; *238 EF-11; mail Jacksonville z 75766; rural
Gouldbusk; RMC Place; COLEMAN; 238 EG-2; 🅿; z 76845; ● 70
Graceton; RMC Place; UPSHUR; *238 ED-11; mail Gilmer z 75644; rural
Grady; RMC Place; MARTIN; *236 WJ-10; mail Lenorah z 79749; rural
Graford; Inc. Place; PALO PINTO; 238 ED-5; 🅿; z 76449; ℗ 561; © 578
Graham (Graham Chapel); RMC Place; GARZA; *236 WI-11; mail Post z 79356; rural
Graham; RMC Place; JASPER; *238 EH-13; mail Jasper z 75951; rural
Graham; Inc. Place; ⊡ YOUNG; 238 ED-4; elev. 1,048ft./319m.; 🅿 🅷; z 76450; ℗ 8,986; © 8,716
Graham Chapel; GARZA; see Graham (RMC Place)
Granada Estates; RMC Place; TRAVIS; *238 EJ-5; ★ AUS; mail Austin z 78737; ● 750
Granbury; Inc. Place; ⊡ HOOD; 238 EE-6; elev. 722ft./220m.; 🅿 🅷; z 76048-49; ℗ 4,045; © 5,718
Grand Acres; CDP-Census Area Only; CAMERON; *239 ES-6; ★ BRNS; © 203
Grand Bluff; RMC Place; PANOLA; 238 EE-12; mail Beckville z 75631; ● 95
Grandfalls; Inc. Place; WARD; 237 WM-8; 🅿; z 79742; ℗ 583; © 391
Grand Prairie; Inc. Place; DALLAS, ELLIS, TARRANT; 238 ED-7; 🅿 🅷 ■; ★ D-FW; z 75050-54; ℗ 99,616; © 127,427; ◆ 148,394
Grand Saline; Inc. Place; VAN ZANDT; 238 EE-9; 🅿 🅷; z 75140; ℗ 2,630; © 3,028
Grandview; RMC Place; DAWSON; *236 WI-10; elev. 3,069ft./935m.; mail Odonnell z 79351; rural
Grand View; RMC Place; EL PASO; *237 WK-2; ★ ELP; mail El Paso z 79930; pop. incl. with El Paso (Inc. Place)
Grandview; RMC Place; GRAY; mail Groom z 79039; rural
Grandview; Inc. Place; JOHNSON; 238 EF-7; 🅿; z 76050; ℗ 1,245; © 1,358
Grange Hall; RMC Place; HARRISON; *238 EE-12; ★ MAR; mail Marshall z 75670, z 75672; pop. incl. with Marshall (Inc. Place)
Granger; Inc. Place; WILLIAMSON; 238 EI-6; elev. 574ft./175m.; 🅿; z 76530; ℗ 1,190; © 1,299
Grangerland; RMC Place; MONTGOMERY; 238 EJ-10; 🅿; ★ HOU; z 77302; ● 400
Granite Shoals; Inc. Place; BURNET; *238 EI-5; mail Marble Falls z 78654; ℗ 1,378; © 2,040
Granjeno; Inc. Place; HIDALGO; *239 ES-5; elev. 109ft./33m.; ★ MCAL; mail Mission z 78572; © 313
Granview Beach; RMC Place; BURNET; *238 EI-4; mail Burnet z 78611; ● 40
Grape Creek; CDP-Census Area Only; TOM GREEN; *237 WL-13; 🅿; ★ SANG; z 76901; © 3,138
Grapeland; Inc. Place; HOUSTON; 238 EG-10; elev. 481ft./147m.; 🅿; z 75844; ℗ 1,450; © 1,451
Grapetown; RMC Place; GILLESPIE; *238 EJ-4; mail Fredericksburg z 78624; rural
Grapevine; Inc. Place; TARRANT; 238 ED-7; 🅿 🅷; ★ D-FW; z 76051, z 76092, z 76099; ℗ 29,202; © 42,059; ◆ 50,070
Grapevine Town Center; RMC Place; TARRANT; *238 ED-7; ★ D-FW; mail Temple z 76501; pop. incl. with Grapevine (Inc. Place)
Grassland; RMC Place; LYNN; 236 WI-11; elev. 2,951ft./899m.; mail Post z 79356
Graves; RMC Place; MIDLAND; ★ MIDL-; mail Midland z 79708; pop. incl. with Midland (Inc. Place)
Gray; RMC Place; MARION; *238 ED-12; mail Jefferson z 75657; rural
GRAY; 236 WC-12; ℗ 23,967; © 22,744; ◆ 22,562
Grayback; RMC Place; WILBARGER; *238 EB-3; mail Electra z 76360; ● 15
Grayburg; RMC Place; HARDIN; 238 EJ-12; elev. 44ft./13m.; mail Sour Lake z 77659; ● 250
Grays Chapel; RMC Place; ANDERSON; *238 EF-9; mail Palestine z 75801; rural
GRAYSON; 238 EC-7; ℗ 95,021; © 110,595; ◆ 118,783
Grays Prairie; Inc. Place; KAUFMAN; *238 EE-8; elev. 452ft./138m.; mail Scurry z 75158; ℗ 286; © 296
Graytown; RMC Place; WILSON; *239 EL-5; mail Floresville z 78114; rural
Great Northwest; RMC Place; BEXAR; *239 EL-4; ★ SANT; mail San Antonio z 78250; pop. incl. with San Antonio (Inc. Place)
Great Oaks; RMC Place; WILLIAMSON; *238 EI-6; ★ AUS; mail Round Rock z 78681; ● 300
Great Southwest; RMC Place; TARRANT; ★ D-FW; mail Arlington z 76005, z 76011; pop. incl. with Arlington (Inc. Place)
Greatwood; CDP-Census Area Only; FORT BEND; *239 EK-10; ★ HOU; © 6,640
Green; RMC Place; KARNES; *239 EM-6; elev. 482ft./147m.; mail Kenedy z 78119; rural
Greenbriar; RMC Place; HARRIS; ★ HOU; mail Houston z 77098, z 77254; pop. incl. with Houston (Inc. Place)
Green Hill; RMC Place; TITUS; *238 EC-11; mail Mount Pleasant z 75455; rural
Green Pastures; RMC Place; HAYS; *239 EK-6; mail Kyle z 78640; ● 600
Greens Bayou; RMC Place; HARRIS; *239 EK-11; ★ HOU; mail Houston z 77015; pop. incl. with Houston (Inc. Place)
Greens Camp; RMC Place; HASKELL; mail Haskell z 79521; ● 15
Greens Creek; RMC Place; ERATH; *238 EF-5; mail Dublin z 76446; rural
Green Valley; RMC Place; DENTON; *238 EC-7; elev. 598ft./182m.; mail Aubrey z 76227; rural
Green Valley Farms; CDP-Census Area Only; CAMERON; *239 ES-6; ★ BRNS; © 720
Greenview; RMC Place; HOPKINS; *238 ED-9; elev. 518ft./158m.; mail Brashear z 75420; rural
Greenview Manor; RMC Place; HARRIS; *238 EJ-10; ★ HOU; mail Houston z 77032; pop. incl. with Houston (Inc. Place)
Greenville; Inc. Place; ⊡ HUNT; 238 ED-9; 🅿 🅷 ■; z 75401-04; ℗ 23,071; © 23,960; ◆ 25,062
Greenvine; RMC Place; WASHINGTON; 238 EJ-8; mail Burton z 77835; ● 30
Greenway; RMC Place; BEXAR; ★ SANT; mail San Antonio z 78223; ● 400
Greenwood; RMC Place; HOPKINS; *238 ED-10; mail Saltillo z 75478; ● 35
Greenwood; RMC Place; MIDLAND; *237 WK-10; mail Midland z 79701
Greenwood; RMC Place; ORANGE; *238 EJ-13; ★ B-PA; mail Mauriceville z 77626; pop. incl. with Chapel Hill (Inc. Place)
Greenwood; RMC Place; PARKER; *238 ED-5; elev. 1,106ft./337m.; mail Weatherford z 76088; rural
Greenwood; RMC Place; RED RIVER; *238 EB-11; mail Clarksville z 75426; rural
Greenwood; RMC Place; WISE; 238 EC-6; elev. 844ft./257m.; 🅿; z 76246; ● 90
Greenwood Acres; RMC Place; LLANO; *238 EI-4; mail Buchanan Dam z 78609; ● 270
Greenwood Forest; RMC Place; KERR; *238 EJ-3; mail Kerrville z 78028; ● 300
Greenwood Village; RMC Place; HARRIS; *239 EK-10; ★ HOU; mail Houston z 77093; ● 4,000
GREGG; 238 EE-11; ℗ 104,948; © 111,379; ◆ 116,854
Greggton; RMC Place; GREGG; *238 EE-11; ★ LNGV; mail Longview z 75604-05; pop. incl. with Longview (Inc. Place)
Gregory; Inc. Place; SAN PATRICIO; 239 EO-7; elev. 33ft./10m.; 🅿; ★ CRPX; z 78359; ℗ 2,458; © 2,318
Gresham; RMC Place; SMITH; *238 EE-10; ★ TYL; mail Flint z 75762, Tyler z 75703; ● 400
Grey Forest; Inc. Place; BEXAR; 239 EP-9; ★ SANT; mail Helotes z 78023, San Antonio z 78255; ℗ 425; © 418
Gribble; RMC Place; DALLAS; *238 ED-7; ★ D-FW; pop. incl. with Farmers Branch (Inc. Place)
Grice; RMC Place; UPSHUR; *238 ED-10; elev. 414ft./126m.; mail Gilmer z 75644; rural
Griffin; RMC Place; CHEROKEE; *238 EF-11; elev. 459ft./140m.; mail Troup z 75789; rural
Griffing; RMC Place; JEFFERSON; ★ B-PA; mail Port Arthur z 77640; pop. incl. with Port Arthur (Inc. Place)
Griffing Park; RMC Place; JEFFERSON; *238 EJ-13; ★ B-PA; mail Port Arthur z 77640, z 77642; pop. incl. with Port Arthur (Inc. Place)
Griffith (Oasis); RMC Place; COCHRAN; *236 WG-8; elev. 3,941ft./1,201m.; mail Morton z 79346; rural
Griffith; RMC Place; ELLIS; *238 EE-7; elev. 594ft./181m.; mail Venus z 76084; rural
Grigsby; RMC Place; SHELBY; *238 EG-12; mail Center z 75935; rural
GRIMES; 238 EI-9; ℗ 18,828; © 23,552; ◆ 26,472
Grit; RMC Place; MASON; *238 EI-3; mail Mason z 76856; rural
Grit; RMC Place; RAINS; mail Alba z 75410; rural
Groceville; RMC Place; MONTGOMERY; *238 EJ-10; mail Conroe z 77303; pop. incl. with Cut and Shoot (Inc. Place)
Groesbeck; Inc. Place; ⊡ LIMESTONE; 238 EG-8; 🅿 🅷; z 76642; ℗ 3,185; © 4,291
Groom; Inc. Place; CARSON; 236 WD-12; 🅿; z 79039; ℗ 613; © 587
Grosvenor; RMC Place; BROWN; *238 EF-3; elev. 1,514ft./461m.; mail Brownwood z 76801; rural
Groves; Inc. Place; JEFFERSON; 238 EJ-13; 🅿 🅷; ★ B-PA; z 77619; ℗ 16,513; © 15,733
Groveton; Inc. Place; ⊡ TRINITY; 238 EH-11; 🅿; z 75845; ℗ 1,071; © 1,107
Grow; RMC Place; KING; *238 EB-1; elev. 1,855ft./565m.; mail Paducah z 79248; rural
Gruenau; RMC Place; DEWITT; *239 EM-6; mail Yorktown z 78164; rural
Gruene; RMC Place; COMAL; *239 EK-5; mail New Braunfels z 78130; pop. incl. with New Braunfels (Inc. Place)
Grulla; STARR; see La Grulla (Inc. Place)
Gruver; Inc. Place; HANSFORD; 236 WB-11; elev. 177ft./54m.; 🅿; z 79040; ℗ 1,172; © 1,162
Guadalupe; RMC Place; VICTORIA; 239 EM-7; mail Victoria z 77901, z 77905; ● 90
GUADALUPE; 239 EL-5; ℗ 64,873; © 89,023; ◆ 121,123
Guadalupe Heights; RMC Place; KERR; *239 EK-3; elev. 1,626ft./496m.; mail Kerrville z 78028; ● 550
Guajillo; RMC Place; DUVAL; *239 EP-5; mail Alice z 78332; rural
Guerra; CDP; JIM HOGG; 239 EQ-4; 🅿; z 78360; © 8
Gum Springs; RMC Place; CASS; *238 EC-12; mail Douglassville z 75560; rural
Gum Springs; RMC Place; HARRISON; *238 EE-11; ★ LNGV; mail Longview z 75602; ● 600
Gum Springs; RMC Place; RUSK; *238 EF-11; mail Henderson z 75654; rural
Gun Barrel City; Inc. Place; HENDERSON; 238 EE-9; 🅿; z 75147, z 75156; ℗ 3,526; © 5,145
Gunsight; RMC Place; STEPHENS; *238 EE-4; elev. 1,420ft./433m.; mail Cisco z 76437; rural
Gunter; Inc. Place; GRAYSON; 238 EC-7; 🅿; z 75058; ℗ 898; © 1,230
Gunter; RMC Place; WOOD; *238 ED-10; elev. 415ft./126m.; mail Alba z 75410; rural
Gustine; Inc. Place; COMANCHE; 238 EG-4; 🅿; z 76455; ℗ 430; © 457
Guthrie; RMC Place; ⊡ KING; 236 WH-13; elev. 1,739ft./530m.; 🅿; z 79236; ● 160
Guy; RMC Place; FORT BEND; 239 EL-10; 🅿; z 77444; ● 75
Guys Store; RMC Place; LEON; *238 EH-9; elev. 307ft./94m.; mail Centerville z 75833; rural

H

Hacienda Heights; RMC Place; EL PASO; *237 WK-2; ★ ELP; mail El Paso z 79915; pop. incl. with El Paso (Inc. Place)
Hackberry; RMC Place; BEXAR; *239 EL-4; ★ SANT; mail San Antonio z 78210; pop. incl. with San Antonio (Inc. Place)
Hackberry (Stewart); RMC Place; COTTLE; *238 EB-1; elev. 1,691ft./515m.; mail Paducah z 79248; rural
Hackberry; Inc. Place; DENTON; 235 B-9; ★ D-FW; mail Little Elm z 75068; ℗ 200; © 544
Hackberry; RMC Place; GARZA; *236 WH-11; mail Post z 79356; rural
Hackberry; RMC Place; LAVACA; *239 EK-7; elev. 271ft./83m.; mail Schulenburg z 78956; rural
Hagansport; RMC Place; FRANKLIN; 238 EC-10; mail Talco z 75487; ● 70
Hagerville; RMC Place; HOUSTON; *238 EG-11; mail Kennard z 75847; rural
Hail; RMC Place; FANNIN; *238 EC-9; mail Windom z 75492; rural
Hainesville; RMC Place; WOOD; 238 ED-10; elev. 378ft./115m.; mail Mineola z 75773; ● 100
Halbert; RMC Place; SHELBY; *238 EG-13; mail Shelbyville z 75973; rural
Hale; RMC Place; DALLAS; pop. incl. with Dallas (Inc. Place)
HALE; 236 WF-10; ℗ 34,671; © 36,602; ◆ 35,242
Hale Center; Inc. Place; HALE; 236 WG-10; 🅿 🅷; z 79041; ℗ 2,067; © 2,263
Halesboro; RMC Place; RED RIVER; *238 EC-10; mail Bogata z 75417; rural
Halfway; RMC Place; HALE; 236 WF-10; mail Plainview z 79072; ● 60
Hall; RMC Place; MARION; *238 ED-12; mail Jefferson z 75657; rural
Hall; RMC Place; SAN SABA; *238 EH-3; elev. 1,482ft./452m.; mail Richland Springs z 76871; rural
HALL; 236 WF-12; ℗ 3,905; © 3,782; ◆ 3,152
Hallettsville; Inc. Place; ⊡ LAVACA; 239 EL-7; elev. 228ft./69m.; 🅿 🅷; z 77964; ℗ 2,718; © 2,345; ® 2,563
Halls Bluff; RMC Place; HOUSTON; *238 EG-10; mail Crockett z 75835; rural
Hallsburg; Inc. Place; MCLENNAN; 238 EG-7; mail Waco z 76705; ℗ 450; © 518
Hallsville; Inc. Place; HARRISON; 238 EE-12; elev. 369ft./112m.; 🅿; ★ LNGV; z 75650; ℗ 2,288; © 2,772
Halsell; RMC Place; CLAY; *238 EB-4; mail Henrietta z 76365; rural
Haltom City; Inc. Place; TARRANT; 238 ED-6; 🅿; ★ D-FW; z 76111, z 76117, z 76137, z 76148, z 76180; ℗ 32,856; © 39,018; ◆ 43,252
Hamby; RMC Place; TAYLOR; *238 EE-2; elev. 1,736ft./529m.; ★ ABIL; mail Abilene z 79601
Hamilton; Inc. Place; ⊡ HAMILTON; 238 EG-5; elev. 1,159ft./353m.; 🅿; z 76531; ℗ 2,937; © 2,977
HAMILTON; 238 EG-5; ℗ 7,733; © 8,229; ◆ 8,019
Hamlin; Inc. Place; JONES, FISHER; 236 WI-13; 🅿 🅷; z 79520; ℗ 2,791; © 2,248
Hamon; RMC Place; GONZALES; *239 EL-7; elev. 318ft./97m.; mail Gonzales z 78629; rural
Hampton; RMC Place; TYLER; *238 EH-12; mail Chester z 75936; pop. incl. with Chester (Inc. Place)
Hamshire; RMC Place; JEFFERSON; 239 EK-12; 🅿; z 77622; ● 600
Hancock Oak Hills; RMC Place; COMAL; *239 EK-5; mail New Braunfels z 78130
Handley; RMC Place; TARRANT; *238 EE-7; ★ D-FW; mail Fort Worth z 76112, z 76124; pop. incl. with Fort Worth (Inc. Place)
Hankamer; RMC Place; CHAMBERS; 239 EK-12; 🅿; z 77560; ● 600
Hannibal; RMC Place; ERATH; *238 EE-5; mail Stephenville z 76401; rural
Hanover; RMC Place; MILAM; *238 EI-7; mail Cameron z 76520; rural
Hansford; RMC Place; HANSFORD; *236 WB-11; mail Spearman z 79081; rural
HANSFORD; 236 WA-11; ℗ 5,848; © 5,369; ◆ 5,237
Happy; Inc. Place; SWISHER, RANDALL; 236 WE-10; 🅿; z 79042; ℗ 588; © 647
Happy Hill; RMC Place; JOHNSON; *238 EE-7; ★ D-FW; mail Alvarado z 76009; ● 80
Happy Union; RMC Place; HALE; *236 WG-11; elev. 3,322ft./1,013m.; mail Plainview z 79072
Happy Valley; RMC Place; TAYLOR; *238 EF-1; mail Wingate z 79566; rural
Harbin; RMC Place; ERATH; *238 EF-5; mail Dublin z 76446
Harbor Grove; RMC Place; DENTON; *238 ED-7; ★ D-FW; mail Lake Dallas z 75065; pop. incl. with Hickory Creek (Inc. Place)
Harborlight; RMC Place; SABINE; *238 EG-13; mail Hemphill z 75948; ● 20
Harbor Point; RMC Place; MONTGOMERY; *238 EJ-10; mail Montgomery z 77356; ● 225
HARDEMAN; 238 EA-2; ℗ 5,283; © 4,724; ◆ 3,826
Hardin; Inc. Place; LIBERTY; 238 EJ-12; elev. 81ft./25m.; 🅿; z 77561; ℗ 563; © 755
HARDIN; 238 EI-13; ℗ 41,320; © 48,073; ◆ 52,971
Hardy; RMC Place; MONTAGUE; *238 EC-6; mail Saint Jo z 76265; rural
Hare; RMC Place; WILLIAMSON; *238 EI-7; elev. 500ft./152m.; mail Taylor z 76574, Thorndale z 76577
Hargill; RMC Place; HIDALGO; 239 ER-5; 🅿; z 78549; ● 950
Harker Heights; Inc. Place; BELL; 238 EH-6; 🅿; ★ KILL-; z 76542-43, z 76548; ℗ 12,841; © 17,308; ◆ 23,734
Harkeyville; RMC Place; SAN SABA; *238 EH-4; mail San Saba z 76877; rural
Harlandale; RMC Place; BEXAR; *239 EL-4; ★ SANT; mail San Antonio z 78214; pop. incl. with San Antonio (Inc. Place)
Harleton; RMC Place; HARRISON; 238 ED-11; 🅿; z 75651; ● 300
Harlingen; Inc. Place; CAMERON; 239 ES-6; elev. 45ft./14m.; 🅿 🅷 ■; ★ BRNS; z 78550-53; ℗ 48,735; © 57,564; ◆ 62,031
Harmon; RMC Place; LAMAR; *238 EC-9; mail Honey Grove z 75446; rural
Harmony; RMC Place; ANDERSON; *238 EG-9; mail Palestine z 75801; rural
Harmony; RMC Place; PARKER; *238 EE-6; mail Weatherford z 76087; rural
Harmony; RMC Place; RUSK; *238 EE-11; ★ LNGV; mail Overton z 75684; rural
Harmony Hill; RMC Place; RUSK; *238 EE-12; mail Tatum z 75691; rural
Harper; CDP; GILLESPIE; 238 EJ-3; elev. 2,056ft./627m.; 🅿; z 78631; © 1,006
Harriet; RMC Place; TOM GREEN; *238 EG-1; mail San Angelo z 76901; rural
HARRIS; 239 EK-10; ℗ 2,818,199; © 3,400,578; ◆ 4,022,295
Harrisburg; RMC Place; HARRIS; *239 EK-11; ★ HOU; mail Houston z 77012, z 77262; pop. incl. with Houston (Inc. Place)
Harrisburg; RMC Place; JASPER; *238 EH-13; elev. 438ft./134m.; mail Jasper z 75951; rural
Harrison; RMC Place; MCLENNAN; *238 EG-7; mail Riesel z 76682; ● 75
HARRISON; 238 ED-11; ℗ 57,483; © 62,110; ◆ 63,062
Harrold; RMC Place; WILBARGER; 238 EB-3; 🅿; z 76364; ● 115
Harrys; RMC Place; DALLAS; ★ D-FW; pop. incl. with Dallas (Inc. Place)
Hart; Inc. Place; CASTRO; 236 WF-10; 🅿; z 79043; ℗ 1,221; © 1,198
Hartburg; RMC Place; NEWTON; *238 EJ-13; ★ B-PA; mail Orange z 77630
Hart Camp; RMC Place; LAMB; *236 WG-10; elev. 3,538ft./1,078m.; mail Littlefield z 79339; rural
Hartley; CDP; HARTLEY; 236 WC-9; elev. 3,904ft./1,190m.; 🅿; z 79044; © 441
HARTLEY; 236 WB-9; ℗ 3,634; © 5,537; ◆ 5,159
Harts Bluff; RMC Place; TITUS; *238 EC-11; mail Mount Pleasant z 75455; rural
Hartzo; RMC Place; MARION; mail Jefferson z 75657; rural
Harvard; RMC Place; CAMP; *238 ED-11; mail Pittsburg z 75686; rural
Harvest Acres; RMC Place; MONTGOMERY; *238 EJ-11; ★ HOU; mail Splendora z 77372; ● 100
Harvest Acres; RMC Place; TOM GREEN; *237 WL-13; ★ SANG; mail San Angelo z 76905; pop. incl. with San Angelo (Inc. Place)
Harvey; RMC Place; BRAZOS; *238 EI-9; ★ BRY-; mail College Station z 77845; pop. incl. with College Station (Inc. Place)
Harveytown; RMC Place; JASPER; *238 EH-13; mail Jasper z 75951; ● 35
Harwood; RMC Place; GONZALES; 239 EK-6; 🅿; z 78632; ● 130
Haskell; Inc. Place; ⊡ HASKELL; 236 WI-14; elev. 1,585ft./483m.; 🅿 🅷; z 79521; ℗ 3,362; © 3,106
HASKELL; 238 EC-2; ℗ 6,820; © 6,093; ◆ 5,066
Haslam; RMC Place; SHELBY; *238 EF-13; mail Joaquin z 75954; rural
Haslet; Inc. Place; TARRANT, DENTON; 238 ED-6; elev. 699ft./213m.; 🅿; ★ D-FW; z 76052; ℗ 795; © 1,134
Hasse; RMC Place; COMANCHE; 238 EF-4; elev. 1,205ft./367m.; 🅿; z 76442; ● 100
Hatchel; RMC Place; RUNNELS; *238 EG-2; mail Winters z 79567; rural
Hatchetville; RMC Place; HOPKINS; *238 EC-10; elev. 510ft./155m.; mail Dike z 75437; rural
Havana; CDP; HIDALGO; *239 ES-4; ★ MCAL; mail Mission z 78572; © 452
Hawk Cove (Whiskers Retreat); Inc. Place; HUNT; *238 ED-9; mail Quinlan z 75474; © 457
Hawkins; Inc. Place; WOOD; 238 EE-10; 🅿 🅲 675; z 75765; ℗ 1,309; © 1,331
Hawkinsville; RMC Place; MATAGORDA; *239 EM-10; mail Bay City z 77414; rural
Hawley; Inc. Place; JONES; 236 WJ-14; 🅿; z 79525; ℗ 606; © 646
Hawthorne; RMC Place; WALKER; *238 EI-10; mail New Waverly z 77358; rural
Hawthorne Place; RMC Place; HARRIS; *239 EK-10; ★ HOU; mail Houston z 77076; pop. incl. with Houston (Inc. Place)
Haynesville; RMC Place; WICHITA; 238 EB-3; elev. 1,132ft./345m.; mail Electra z 76360; ● 100
Hays; Inc. Place; HAYS; *238 EJ-6; ★ AUS; mail San Marcos z 78666; ℗ 251; © 233
HAYS; 238 EJ-5; ℗ 65,614; © 97,589; ◆ 163,599
Hazy Hollow; RMC Place; MONTGOMERY; *238 EJ-10; ★ HOU; mail Magnolia z 77354; ● 400
Heacker; RMC Place; HARRIS; ★ HOU; pop. incl. with Houston (Inc. Place)
Headlea Estates; RMC Place; ECTOR; ★ MIDL-; mail Odessa z 79762; pop. incl. with Odessa (Inc. Place)
Headsville; RMC Place; ROBERTSON; *238 EH-8; mail Kosse z 76653; rural
Heafer; RMC Place; BEXAR; *239 EL-4; ★ SANT; pop. incl. with San Antonio (Inc. Place)
Hearne; Inc. Place; ROBERTSON; 238 EI-8; 🅿; z 77859; ℗ 5,132; © 4,690
Heath; Inc. Place; ROCKWALL, KAUFMAN; *238 ED-8; elev. 502ft./153m.; 🅿; ★ D-FW; z 75032; ℗ 2,108; © 4,149
Hebbronville; CDP; ⊡ JIM HOGG; 239 EQ-4; 🅿; z 78361; ℗ 4,465; © 4,498
Hebco; RMC Place; BEXAR; ★ SANT; mail San Antonio z 78218; pop. incl. with San Antonio (Inc. Place)
Hebron; Inc. Place; DENTON; 238 ED-7; ★ D-FW; mail The Colony z 75056; ℗ 1,128; © 874
Heckville; RMC Place; LUBBOCK; *236 WG-11; elev. 3,245ft./989m.; mail Idalou z 79329; rural
Hedley; Inc. Place; DONLEY; 236 WE-12; elev. 2,627ft./801m.; 🅿; z 79237; ℗ 391; © 379
Hedwig Village; Inc. Place; HARRIS; 234 D-3; ★ HOU; mail Houston z 77024; ℗ 2,616; © 2,334
Heidelberg; CDP; HIDALGO; *239 ES-6; ★ MCAL; mail Mercedes z 78570; © 1,586
Heidenheimer; RMC Place; BELL; 238 EH-7; 🅿; ★ KILL-; z 76533; ● 300
Heights; RMC Place; GALVESTON; *239 EL-11; ★ GLV-; mail Texas City z 77590; pop. incl. with Texas City (Inc. Place)
Heights; RMC Place; HARRIS; *239 EK-10; ★ HOU; mail Houston z 77008, z 77248, z 77270; pop. incl. with Houston (Inc. Place)
Helena; RMC Place; KARNES; 239 EM-6; elev. 305ft./93m.; mail Karnes City z 78118; ● 30
Helmic; RMC Place; TRINITY; *238 EH-11; mail Groveton z 75845; rural
Helotes; Inc. Place; BEXAR; 239 EK-4; 🅿; ★ SANT; z 78023; ℗ 1,535; © 4,285
Hemphill; Inc. Place; ⊡ SABINE; 238 EG-13; 🅿 🅷; z 75948; ℗ 1,182; © 1,106
HEMPHILL; 236 WB-13; ℗ 3,720; © 3,351; ◆ 3,361
Hempstead; Inc. Place; ⊡ WALLER; 238 EJ-9; 🅿; z 77445; ℗ 3,551; © 4,691
Henderson; Inc. Place; ⊡ RUSK; 238 EF-11; 🅿 🅷; z 75652-54, z 75680; ℗ 11,139; © 11,273
HENDERSON; 238 EF-9; ℗ 58,543; © 73,277; ◆ 76,131
Henderson Chapel; RMC Place; CONCHO; *238 EH-1; mail Paint Rock z 76866; rural
Henderson Heights; RMC Place; ECTOR; *237 WK-9; ★ MIDL-; mail Odessa z 79763
Henkhaus; RMC Place; LAVACA; *239 EL-7; elev. 395ft./120m.; mail Moulton z 77975, Shiner z 77984; rural
Henly; RMC Place; HAYS; 238 EJ-5; elev. 1,333ft./406m.; mail Dripping Springs z 78620; ● 40
Hennessey; RMC Place; HARRIS; *239 EK-10; ★ HOU; pop. incl. with Houston (Inc. Place)
Henning; RMC Place; NACOGDOCHES; mail Garrison z 75946; rural
Henrietta; Inc. Place; ⊡ CLAY; 238 EB-5; elev. 912ft./278m.; 🅿 🅷; z 76365; ℗ 2,896; © 3,264
Henrys Chapel; RMC Place; CHEROKEE; *238 EF-11; elev. 405ft./123m.; mail Troup z 75789; rural
Hereford; Inc. Place; ⊡ DEAF SMITH; 236 WE-9; 🅿 🅷; z 79045; ℗ 14,745; © 14,597
Heritage Northwest; RMC Place; BEXAR; *239 EL-4; ★ SANT; mail San Antonio z 78245; pop. incl. with San Antonio (Inc. Place)
Hermits Cove; RMC Place; RAINS; *238 ED-9; mail Point z 75472; rural
Hermleigh; CDP; SCURRY; 236 WJ-12; 🅿; z 79526; © 393
Hermosa; RMC Place; REEVES; *237 WL-7; mail Pecos z 79772; rural
Herring; RMC Place; TOM GREEN; ★ SANG; mail San Angelo z 76901; pop. incl. with San Angelo (Inc. Place)
Herty; RMC Place; ANGELINA; *238 EG-11; ★ LUFK; mail Lufkin z 75901
Hewitt; Inc. Place; MCLENNAN; 238 EG-7; 🅿; ★ WACO; z 76643; ℗ 8,983; © 11,085
Hext; RMC Place; MENARD; 238 EI-2; elev. 1,849ft./564m.; 🅿; z 76848; ● 70
Hickey; RMC Place; RUSK; *238 EF-11; mail Henderson z 75654; rural
Hickory Creek; Inc. Place; DENTON; 235 B-7; 🅿; ★ D-FW; z 75065; ℗ 1,893; © 2,078
Hickory Creek; RMC Place; HUNT; *238 EC-9; elev. 663ft./202m.; mail Celeste z 75423; rural
Hickory Hill; RMC Place; CAMP; *238 ED-11; mail Pittsburg z 75686; rural
Hickory Hollow; RMC Place; SAN AUGUSTINE; *238 EG-12; mail Broaddus z 75929; ● 70
Hickston; RMC Place; GONZALES; *239 EK-7; elev. 287ft./87m.; mail Waelder z 78959; rural
Hico; Inc. Place; HAMILTON; 238 EF-5; elev. 1,021ft./311m.; 🅿; z 76457; ℗ 1,342; © 1,341
Hidalgo; Inc. Place; HIDALGO; 239 ES-5; elev. 106ft./32m.; 🅿; ★ MCAL; z 78557; ℗ 3,292; © 7,322
HIDALGO; 239 ES-5; ℗ 383,545; © 569,463; ◆ 727,772
Hidden Echo; RMC Place; HARRIS; *238 EJ-11; elev. 65ft./20m.; ★ HOU; mail Huffman z 77336; pop. incl. with Houston (Inc. Place)
Hidden Forest; RMC Place; BEXAR; ★ SANT; mail San Antonio z 78232; pop. incl. with San Antonio (Inc. Place)
Hidden Hill; RMC Place; DENTON; *238 ED-7; elev. 560ft./171m.; ★ D-FW; mail Lake Dallas z 75065; pop. incl. with Hickory Creek (Inc. Place)
Hidden Hills Harbor; RMC Place; HENDERSON; *238 EE-9; mail Mabank z 75156; ● 150
Hidden Valley; RMC Place; HARRIS; *239 EK-10; ★ HOU; mail Garrison z 75946, Houston z 77088; pop. incl. with Houston (Inc. Place)
Hideaway; Inc. Place; SMITH; *238 EE-10; 🅿; z 75771; incorporated July 20, 2001; not reported in 2000 Census; ● 2,700
Higginbotham; RMC Place; GAINES; *236 WI-8; mail Seminole z 79360
Higgins; RMC Place; JEFFERSON; *238 EJ-13; ★ B-PA; mail Beaumont z 77705; pop. incl. with Beaumont (Inc. Place)
Higgins; Inc. Place; LIPSCOMB; 236 WB-14; elev. 2,577ft./785m.; 🅿; z 79046; ℗ 464; © 425
Highbank; RMC Place; FALLS; *238 EH-7; mail Reagan z 76680
High Hill; RMC Place; FAYETTE; 239 EK-7; mail Schulenburg z 78956; ● 30
High Island; RMC Place; GALVESTON; 239 EK-12; 🅿; z 77623; summer pop. 1,500; ● 500
Highland; RMC Place; ERATH; *238 EF-4; mail Dublin z 76446; rural
Highland Acre Homes; RMC Place; HARRIS; *239 EK-10; ★ HOU; mail Houston z 77088; pop. incl. with Houston (Inc. Place)
Highland Acres; RMC Place; GRAYSON; *238 EB-8; mail Pottsboro z 75076; ● 50
Highland Acres; RMC Place; HUNT; *238 ED-9; mail Lone Oak z 75453; ● 100
Highland Addition; RMC Place; PARKER; *238 ED-6; ★ D-FW; mail Springtown z 76082; ● 50
Highland Creek Lakes; RMC Place; TRAVIS; *238 EJ-5; ★ AUS; mail Austin z 78736; ● 100
Highland Estates; RMC Place; VICTORIA; *239 EM-7; ★ VICT; mail Victoria z 77904; pop. incl. with Victoria (Inc. Place)
Highland Haven; Inc. Place; BURNET; *238 EI-4; 🅿; z 78654; © 450
Highland Heights; RMC Place; HARRIS; *239 EK-10; ★ HOU; pop. incl. with Houston (Inc. Place)
Highland Hills; RMC Place; BEXAR; *239 EL-4; ★ SANT; mail San Antonio z 78223; pop. incl. with San Antonio (Inc. Place)
Highland Hills; RMC Place; DALLAS; ★ D-FW; mail Dallas z 75241; pop. incl. with Dallas (Inc. Place)
Highland Park; Inc. Place; DALLAS; 235 F-10; ★ D-FW; mail Dallas z 75205, z 75209, z 75219; ℗ 8,739; © 8,842
Highland Range Estates; RMC Place; TOM GREEN; *237 WL-13; ★ SANG; mail San Angelo z 76901; ● 350
Highlands; CDP; HARRIS; 234 D-9; 🅿; ★ HOU; z 77562; ℗ 6,632; © 7,089
Highland Village; Inc. Place; DENTON; 235 C-7; 🅿; ★ D-FW; z 75077; ℗ 7,027; © 12,173
High Meadows; RMC Place; FORT BEND; *239 EK-10; ★ HOU; mail Sugar Land z 77478; ● 1,700
Highsaw; RMC Place; HENDERSON; *238 EF-10; mail Frankston z 75763; pop. incl. with Coffee City (Inc. Place)
Hi-Ho; RMC Place; ORANGE; *238 EJ-13; ★ B-PA; mail Orange z 77632; ● 180
Hiland Shores; RMC Place; GRAYSON; mail Pottsboro z 75076; ● 200
HILL; 238 EF-7; ℗ 27,146; © 32,321; ◆ 35,594
Hill and Dale Acres; RMC Place; MONTGOMERY; *238 EJ-11; ★ HOU; mail Splendora z 77372; ● 75
Hill City; RMC Place; HOOD; *238 EE-5; elev. 964ft./294m.; mail Tolar z 76476
Hill Country Village; Inc. Place; BEXAR; 239 EQ-12; 🅿; ★ SANT; z 78232; ℗ 1,038; © 1,028
Hillcrest (Hillcrest Village); Inc. Place; BRAZORIA; 234 I-7; ★ HOU; mail Alvin z 77511, Columbus z 78934; ℗ 695; © 722
Hillcrest Village; BRAZORIA; see Hillcrest (Inc. Place)
Hillebrandt; RMC Place; JEFFERSON; *238 EJ-13; mail Beaumont z 77705; ● 150
Hillister; RMC Place; TYLER; 238 EI-12; 🅿; z 77624; ● 300
Hillje; RMC Place; WHARTON; 239 EL-9; mail El Campo z 77437, Louise z 77455; ● 70
Hills; RMC Place; LEE; *238 EJ-7; mail Paige z 78659; rural
Hillsboro; Inc. Place; ⊡ HILL; 238 EF-7; elev. 631ft./192m.; 🅿 🅷; z 76645; ℗ 7,072; © 8,232
Hillside Estates; RMC Place; HENDERSON; *238 EF-10; mail Frankston z 75763; pop. incl. with Coffee City (Inc. Place)
Hilltop; CDP-Census Area Only; FRIO; *239 EN-3; © 300
Hilltop; RMC Place; GILLESPIE; *238 EJ-3; mail Fredericksburg z 78624; rural
Hilltop Acres; RMC Place; BEXAR; 239 ES-8; ★ SANT; mail San Antonio z 78253; ● 180
Hilltop Lakes; RMC Place; LEON; 238 EH-9; 🅿; z 77871; ● 500
Hilshire Village; Inc. Place; HARRIS; 234 D-4; ★ HOU; mail Houston z 77055; ℗ 665; © 720
Hinckley; RMC Place; LAMAR; *238 EB-10; mail Paris z 75460; pop. incl. with Paris (Inc. Place)
Hindes; RMC Place; ATASCOSA; *239 EM-4; mail Jourdanton z 78026; rural
Hinkles Ferry; RMC Place; BRAZORIA; mail Brazoria z 77422; rural
Hiram; RMC Place; KAUFMAN; *238 EE-9; elev. 448ft./137m.; mail Terrell z 75161; rural
Hitchcock; Inc. Place; GALVESTON; 239 EL-11; elev. 20ft./6m.; 🅿; ★ GLV-; z 77563; ℗ 5,868; © 6,386
Hitchland; RMC Place; HANSFORD; *236 WA-11; mail Guymon z 73942
Hix; RMC Place; BURLESON; *238 EI-8; mail Caldwell z 77836; rural
Hoard; RMC Place; WOOD; *238 EE-10; mail Mineola z 75773; ● 50
Hobbs; RMC Place; FISHER; *236 WI-13; elev. 2,068ft./630m.; mail Hermleigh z 79526, Rotan z 79546; rural
Hobson; RMC Place; KARNES; 239 EM-5; 🅿; z 78117; ● 150
Hochheim; RMC Place; DEWITT; 239 EL-7; elev. 362ft./110m.; 🅿; z 77967; ● 80
Hockley; RMC Place; HARRIS; 238 EJ-9; 🅿; ★ HOU; z 77447; pop. incl. with Houston (Inc. Place)
HOCKLEY; 236 WG-9; ℗ 24,199; © 22,716; ◆ 21,825
Hodge; RMC Place; TARRANT; ★ D-FW; pop. incl. with Fort Worth (Inc. Place)
Hodges; RMC Place; JONES; *238 EE-2; mail Hawley z 79525
Hodgson; RMC Place; BOWIE; *238 EC-11; elev. 416ft./127m.; mail De Kalb z 75559; rural
Hoen; RMC Place; MCLENNAN; *238 EG-7; elev. 517ft./158m.; mail West z 76691; rural
Hogan Acres; RMC Place; JOHNSON; ★ D-FW; mail Burleson z 76028; ● 250
Hogansville; RMC Place; RAINS; *238 ED-9; elev. 400ft./122m.; mail Alba z 75410; rural
Hogg; RMC Place; BURLESON; *238 EJ-8; mail Caldwell z 77836
Holiday Beach; RMC Place; ARANSAS; *239 EO-7; mail Rockport z 78382; ● 400
Holiday Estates; RMC Place; HUNT; *238 ED-9; mail Wills Point z 75169; ● 80
Holiday Harbor; RMC Place; MARION; mail Avinger z 75630; ● 125
Holiday Hills; RMC Place; RAINS; *238 ED-9; mail Lone Oak z 75453; ● 120
Holiday Hills Estates; RMC Place; STEPHENS; *238 ED-3; mail Breckenridge z 76424; ● 100
Holiday Lake Estates; RMC Place; POLK; *238 EI-11; mail Goodrich z 77335; ● 250
Holiday Lakes; Inc. Place; BRAZORIA; *239 EL-10; ★ LJAC-; mail Angleton z 77515; ℗ 1,039; © 1,095
Holiday Oaks; RMC Place; MONTGOMERY; *238 EJ-11; ★ HOU; mail Splendora z 77372; ● 100
Holland; Inc. Place; BELL; 238 EI-6; 🅿; z 76534; ℗ 1,118; © 1,102
Holland Quarters; RMC Place; PANOLA; *238 EF-12; mail Carthage z 75633; ● 50
Holliday; Inc. Place; ARCHER; 238 EB-4; 🅿; ★ WIFL; z 76366; ℗ 1,475; © 1,632
Hollowa Heights; RMC Place; HARRIS; *239 EK-10; ★ HOU; mail Houston z 77047
Holly; RMC Place; HOUSTON; 238 EH-10; mail Lovelady z 75851; ● 40
Holly Breach; RMC Place; CAMERON; *239 ES-7; mail Port Isabel z 78578; ● 100
Holly Grove; RMC Place; POLK; *238 EI-12; elev. 163ft./50m.; mail Livingston z 77351; rural
Holly Springs; RMC Place; CAMP; *238 ED-11; mail Pittsburg z 75686; rural
Holly Springs; RMC Place; JASPER; *238 EH-13; elev. 265ft./81m.; mail Jasper z 75951
Holly Springs; RMC Place; NACOGDOCHES; *238 EF-12; mail Garrison z 75946; ● 40
Holly Springs; RMC Place; VAN ZANDT; *238 EE-9; elev. 490ft./149m.; mail Ben Wheeler z 75754; rural
Holly Terrace; RMC Place; MONTGOMERY; *238 EJ-11; ★ HOU; mail Porter z 77365
Hollywood Park; Inc. Place; BEXAR; 239 EQ-12; 🅿; ★ SANT; z 78232; ℗ 2,841; © 2,983
Holman; RMC Place; FAYETTE; *239 EK-8; mail La Grange z 78945, Weimar z 78962; rural
Holt; RMC Place; SAN SABA; *238 EH-3; mail Rochelle z 76872; rural
Homer; RMC Place; ANGELINA; 238 EG-12; elev. 310ft./94m.; ★ LUFK; mail Lufkin z 75901; ● 350
Homer; RMC Place; JASPER; *238 EH-12; elev. 120ft./37m.; mail Jasper z 75951; rural
Homestead Meadows North; CDP-Census Area Only; EL PASO; *237 WK-2; © 4,232
Homestead Meadows South; CDP-Census Area Only; EL PASO; *237 WK-2; © 6,807
Homewood; RMC Place; JASPER; mail Jasper z 75951; ● 200
Hondo; Inc. Place; ⊡ MEDINA; 239 EL-3; elev. 895ft./273m.; 🅿 🅷; z 78861; ℗ 6,018; © 7,897
Honey Grove; Inc. Place; FANNIN; 238 EC-9; 🅿; z 75446; ℗ 1,681; © 1,746
Honey Island; RMC Place; HARDIN; 238 EI-12; elev. 104ft./32m.; mail Kountze z 77625; ● 300
Hood; RMC Place; COOKE; *238 EC-6; mail Gainesville z 76240
HOOD; 238 EE-5; ℗ 28,981; © 41,100; ◆ 50,930
Hooks; Inc. Place; BOWIE; 238 EC-12; 🅿; ★ TEXR-; z 75561; ℗ 2,684; © 2,973
Hooper; RMC Place; TRAVIS; ★ AUS; pop. incl. with Austin (Inc. Place)
Hoover; RMC Place; GRAY; *236 WC-12; mail Pampa z 79065; rural
Hoovers Valley; RMC Place; BURNET; *238 EI-5; mail Burnet z 78611; rural
Hope; RMC Place; LAVACA; *239 EL-7; mail Yoakum z 77995
Hopewell; RMC Place; FRANKLIN; *238 EC-10; elev. 482ft./147m.; mail Mount Vernon z 75457; rural
Hopewell; RMC Place; HOUSTON; *238 EH-10; mail Crockett z 75835; rural
Hopewell; RMC Place; LEON; *238 EG-9; mail Centerville z 75833; rural
HOPKINS; 238 EC-10; ℗ 28,833; © 31,960; ◆ 34,398
Horizon City; Inc. Place; EL PASO; 237 WK-2; 🅿; ★ ELP; z 79927-28; ℗ 2,308; © 5,233
Horn Hill; RMC Place; LIMESTONE; *238 EG-8; mail Groesbeck z 76642; rural
Horseshoe Bay; Inc. Place; BURNET; *238 EI-5; incorporated September 20, 2006; not reported in 2000 Census; ● 2,500
Horseshoe Bay; CDP-Census Area Only; LLANO, BURNET; *238 EI-5; 🅿; z 78657 & mail Marble Falls z 78654; ℗ 1,546; © 3,337
Horseshoe Bay South; RMC Place; BURNET; *238 EI-5; mail Marble Falls z 78654; ● 140
Horseshoe Bay West; RMC Place; LLANO; *238 EI-4; mail Marble Falls z 78654; ● 125
Horseshoe Falls; RMC Place; COMAL; *239 EK-5; mail New Braunfels z 78130
Horseshoe Lake; RMC Place; LIBERTY; *238 EI-11; mail Cleveland z 77327; ● 200
Hortense; RMC Place; POLK; *238 EH-12; elev. 350ft./107m.; mail Livingston z 77351; rural
Horton; RMC Place; DELTA; *238 EC-9; mail Commerce z 75428; rural
Horton; RMC Place; JASPER; *238 EH-13; elev. 408ft./124m.; mail Jasper z 75951; rural
Horton; RMC Place; PANOLA; *238 EE-12; mail De Berry z 75639; rural
Hostyn; RMC Place; FAYETTE; *239 EK-7; mail La Grange z 78945; rural
Houmont Park; RMC Place; HARRIS; 234 C-7; ★ HOU; mail Houston z 77044; ● 2,500
Houston; Inc. Place; ⊡ HARRIS, FORT BEND, MONTGOMERY; 234 F-5; 🅿 🅷 🅲 84,511 ■; ★ HOU; z 77001-99, z 77201-10, z 77212-13, z 77215-31, z 77233-38, z 77240-63, z 77265-80, z 77282, z 77284-94, z 77296-99, z 77598; ℗ 1,630,864; © 1,953,631; ◆ 2,282,856
HOUSTON; 238 EG-10; ℗ 21,375; © 23,185; ◆ 22,594
Howard; RMC Place; ELLIS; *238 EE-7; elev. 513ft./156m.; mail Waxahachie z 75165; rural
Howard; RMC Place; WICHITA; ★ WIFL; pop. incl. with Wichita Falls (Inc. Place)
HOWARD; 236 WJ-11; ℗ 32,343; © 33,627; ◆ 32,980
Howardwick; Inc. Place; DONLEY; 236 WE-12; elev. 2,746ft./837m.; 🅿; z 79226; ℗ 211; © 437
Howe; Inc. Place; GRAYSON; 238 EC-8; 🅿; ★ SHRM-; z 75459; ℗ 2,173; © 2,478
Howland; RMC Place; LAMAR; 238 EC-9; mail Paris z 75460; ● 50
Howth; RMC Place; WALLER; *238 EJ-9; mail Hempstead z 77445; rural
Hoxie; RMC Place; WILLIAMSON; *238 EI-6; mail Taylor z 76574; rural
Hoyte; RMC Place; MILAM; *238 EI-7; mail Cameron z 76520; rural
Hub; RMC Place; PARMER; *236 WF-9; elev. 4,040ft./1,231m.; mail Friona z 79035; ● 25
Hubbard; Inc. Place; HILL; 238 EF-7; elev. 638ft./194m.; 🅿; z 76648; ℗ 1,589; © 1,586
Huckabay; RMC Place; ERATH; 238 EE-5; mail Stephenville z 76401; ● 150
Hudson; Inc. Place; ANGELINA; 238 EH-11; ★ LUFK; mail Lufkin z 75904; ℗ 2,374; © 3,792
Hudson Bend; CDP-Census Area Only; TRAVIS; *238 EJ-5; ★ AUS; mail Austin z 78734; © 2,369
Hudson Oaks; Inc. Place; PARKER; *238 EE-6; 🅿; z 76087; ℗ 711; © 1,637
HUDSPETH; 237 WL-3; ℗ 2,915; © 3,344; ◆ 3,275
Huffhines Park; RMC Place; DALLAS; mail Richardson z 75085; pop. incl. with Richardson (Inc. Place)
Huffines; RMC Place; CASS; *238 ED-12; elev. 321ft./98m.; mail Bivins z 75555; rural
Huffman; RMC Place; HARRIS; 238 EJ-11; 🅿; ★ HOU; z 77336; ● 3,000
Hufsmith; RMC Place; HARRIS; *238 EJ-10; 🅿; ★ HOU; z 77337; ● 250
Hughes Springs; Inc. Place; CASS; 238 ED-11; elev. 367ft./112m.; 🅿; z 75656; ℗ 1,938; © 1,856
Hughey; RMC Place; GREGG; *238 EE-11; ★ LNGV; mail Kilgore z 75662; rural
Hulen Park; RMC Place; GALVESTON; *239 EL-11; ★ GLV-; mail Dickinson z 77539; pop. incl. with Texas City (Inc. Place)
Hull; RMC Place; LIBERTY; 238 EJ-12; elev. 67ft./20m.; 🅿; z 77564; ● 1,400
Hulldale; RMC Place; SCHLEICHER; *237 WM-13; mail Eldorado z 76936; rural
Humble; Inc. Place; HARRIS; 234 A-6; 🅿 🅷 ■; ★ HOU; z 77325, z 77338-39, z 77345-47, z 77396; ℗ 12,060; © 14,579; ◆ 16,359
Humble Camp; RMC Place; REFUGIO; 239 EN-7; mail Refugio z 78377; ● 100
Humble Estates; RMC Place; HARRIS; *239 EK-10; ★ HOU; mail Humble z 77396; pop. incl. with Houston (Inc. Place)
Hungerford; CDP; WHARTON; 239 EL-9; 🅿; z 77448; © 645
Hunt; RMC Place; KERR; 238 EJ-3; 🅿 🅷; z 78024; ● 650
HUNT; 238 EC-9; ℗ 64,343; © 76,596; ◆ 81,950
Hunter; RMC Place; COMAL; 239 EK-5; mail New Braunfels z 78130, z 78132; ● 40
Hunters Creek Village; Inc. Place; HARRIS; 234 D-3; ★ HOU; mail Houston z 77024; ℗ 3,954; © 4,374
Hunters Glen; RMC Place; FORT BEND; *239 EK-10; ★ HOU; mail Missouri City z 77489; pop. incl. with Missouri City (Inc. Place)
Hunters Retreat; RMC Place; MONTGOMERY; *238 EJ-10; ★ HOU; mail Magnolia z 77354; ● 300
Huntington; Inc. Place; ANGELINA; 238 EH-12; elev. 310ft./94m.; 🅿; ★ LUFK; z 75949; ℗ 1,794; © 2,068
Huntsville; Inc. Place; ⊡ WALKER; 238 EI-10; elev. 366ft./112m.; 🅿 🅷 🅲 15,935 ■; z 77320, z 77340-44, z 77348-49; ℗ 27,925; © 35,078; ◆ 36,485
Hurlwood; RMC Place; LUBBOCK; 236 WH-10; ★ LUB; mail Lubbock z 79407; ● 130
Hurnville; RMC Place; CLAY; *238 EB-5; elev. 923ft./281m.; mail Henrietta z 76365; rural
Huron; RMC Place; HILL; *238 EF-6; mail Whitney z 76692; rural
Hurst; Inc. Place; TARRANT; 238 ED-7; 🅿 ■; ★ D-FW; z 76053-54; ℗ 33,574; © 36,273; ◆ 39,241
Hurstown; RMC Place; SHELBY; *238 EF-13; mail Shelbyville z 75973; rural
Hurst Springs; RMC Place; CORYELL; mail Clifton z 76634; rural
Hutchins; Inc. Place; DALLAS; 235 I-11; 🅿; ★ D-FW; z 75141; ℗ 2,719; © 2,805
HUTCHINSON; 236 WB-11; ℗ 25,689; © 23,857; ◆ 21,353
Hutto; Inc. Place; WILLIAMSON; 238 EI-6; 🅿; z 78634; ℗ 630; © 1,250
Huxley; Inc. Place; SHELBY; 238 EF-13; mail Shelbyville z 75973; ℗ 335; © 298
Hye; RMC Place; BLANCO; 238 EJ-4; 🅿; z 78635; ● 70
Hylton; RMC Place; NOLAN; *238 EF-1; elev. 2,188ft./667m.; mail Blackwell z 79506; rural

I

Iago; RMC Place; WHARTON; 239 EL-9; elev. 86ft./26m.; mail Boling z 77420; ● 100
Ida; RMC Place; GRAYSON; 238 EC-8; mail Whitewright z 75491; ● 25
Idalou; Inc. Place; LUBBOCK; 236 WG-11; 🅿; ★ LUB; z 79329; ℗ 2,074; © 2,157
Idyle Hour Acres; RMC Place; TRAVIS; *238 EJ-6; mail Austin z 78728; ● 100
Ike; RMC Place; ELLIS; *238 EE-7; ★ D-FW; mail Waxahachie z 75165; rural
Illinois Bend; RMC Place; MONTAGUE; *238 EB-6; elev. 766ft./233m.; mail Saint Jo z 76265
Impact; Inc. Place; TAYLOR; *238 EE-2; ★ ABIL; mail Abilene z 79603; ℗ 25; © 39
Imperial; CDP; PECOS; 237 WM-9; elev. 2,393ft./729m.; 🅿; z 79743; © 428
Imperial Valley; RMC Place; HARRIS; *239 EK-10; ★ HOU; mail Houston z 77060; pop. incl. with Houston (Inc. Place)
Inadale; RMC Place; SCURRY; *236 WJ-12; elev. 2,383ft./726m.; mail Roscoe z 79545; rural
Independence; RMC Place; WASHINGTON; 238 EJ-8; mail Brenham z 77833; ● 125
India; RMC Place; ELLIS; *238 EE-8; mail Ferris z 75125; rural
Indian Creek; RMC Place; BROWN; *238 EG-3; elev. 1,321ft./403m.; mail Brownwood z 76801
Indian Gap; RMC Place; HAMILTON; *238 EG-4; elev. 1,568ft./478m.; mail Hamilton z 76531
Indian Harbor Estates; RMC Place; HOOD; *238 EE-6; mail Granbury z 76048; ● 2,000
Indian Hill; RMC Place; NEWTON; *238 EH-13; mail Wiergate z 75977; rural
Indian Hills; RMC Place; BEXAR; *239 EK-4; ★ SANT; mail Boerne z 78006; ● 100
Indian Hills; CDP-Census Area Only; HIDALGO; *239 ES-6; ★ MCAL; © 2,036
Indian Lake; Inc. Place; CAMERON; *239 ES-6; 🅿; ★ BRNS; z 78566 & mail San Benito z 78586; ℗ 390; © 541
Indian Lake; RMC Place; NEWTON; *238 EJ-13; elev. 16ft./5m.; ★ B-PA; mail Orange z 77630; ● 150
Indian Lodge; RMC Place; BOSQUE; *238 EF-6; mail Kopperl z 76652; ● 20
Indian Oaks; RMC Place; WALLER; *239 EK-9; mail Pattison z 77466; pop. incl. with Pattison (Inc. Place)
Indianola; RMC Place; CALHOUN; 239 EN-8; mail Port Lavaca z 77979; ● 50
Indian Rock; RMC Place; UPSHUR; *238 ED-11; mail Gilmer z 75644; rural
Indian Shores; RMC Place; HARRIS; *238 EJ-11; elev. 60ft./18m.; ★ HOU; mail Crosby z 77532; ● 800
Indian Springs; RMC Place; POLK; *238 EI-11; elev. 350ft./107m.; mail Livingston z 77351; ● 300
Indian Village; RMC Place; POLK; *238 EI-12; elev. 320ft./98m.; mail Livingston z 77351; ● 150
Indian Waters; RMC Place; BANDERA; *239 EK-3; mail Bandera z 78003; ● 50
Indian Woods; RMC Place; MONTGOMERY; *238 EJ-10; ★ HOU; mail Magnolia z 77355
Industry; Inc. Place; AUSTIN; 239 EK-8; 🅿; z 78944; ℗ 292; © 304
Inez; CDP; VICTORIA; 239 EM-8; elev. 63ft./19m.; 🅿; z 77968; ℗ 1,371; © 1,787
Ingleside; Inc. Place; SAN PATRICIO; 239 EO-7; elev. 16ft./5m.; 🅿; z 78362; ℗ 5,696; © 9,388

Entries in **UPPERCASE** are counties.
Entries in **bold** have populations of 2,500 or more.
Names in parentheses are alternate names.

Inc. Place	Incorporated Place
RMC Place	Rand McNally Designated Place
CDP	Census Designated Place
MCD	Minor Civil Division
⊡	County Seat
▲	Minor Civil Division
elev.	Elevation
🅿	Post Office
🅷	Hospital
🅲	College
■	Principal Business Center
★	Ranally Metro Area (RMA) Abbreviation
z	Zip Code(s)
℗	Previous Census Population
®	Revised Census Population
Ⓐ	Annexation Population
●	Rand McNally Population Estimate
©	Final Census Population
Ⓢ	Special Census Population
◆	Estimated Population

For additional definitions see Glossary, Volume 1, and Introduction, Volume 2.

Ingleside on the Bay; Inc. Place; SAN PATRICIO; ***239** EO-7; mail Ingleside z 78362; Ⓟ 529; © 659
Ingram; Inc. Place; KERR; **238** EJ-3; 🅿; z 78025; Ⓟ 1,408; © 1,740
Inks Lake Village; RMC Place; LLANO; ***238** EI-4; mail Buchanan Dam z 78609; ● 100
Inwood; RMC Place; DALLAS; ***238** ED-7; ★ **D-FW**; mail Dallas z 75209; pop. incl. with Dallas (Inc. Place)
Inwood Forest; RMC Place; HARRIS; ***239** EK-10; ★ **HOU**; mail Houston z 77088; pop. incl. with Houston (Inc. Place)
Iola; RMC Place; GRIMES; **238** EI-9; 🅿; z 77861; ● 325
Iowa Colony; Inc. Place; BRAZORIA; **234** I-4; ★ **HOU**; mail Rosharon z 77583; Ⓟ 675; © 804
Iowa Park; Inc. Place; WICHITA; **238** EB-4; elev. 1,037ft./316m.; 🅿; ★ **WIFL**; z 76367; Ⓟ 6,072; © 6,431
Ira; RMC Place; SCURRY; **236** WJ-12; elev. 2,269ft./692m.; 🅿; z 79527; ● 300
Iraan; Inc. Place; PECOS; **237** WM-10; elev. 2,227ft./679m.; 🅿 🄷; z 79744; Ⓟ 1,322; © 1,238
Irby; RMC Place; HASKELL; ***238** ED-2; mail Haskell z 79521; ● 20
Iredell; Inc. Place; BOSQUE; **238** EF-5; elev. 908ft./277m.; 🅿; z 76649; Ⓟ 339; © 360
Ireland; RMC Place; CORYELL; ***238** EG-5; elev. 1,070ft./326m.; mail Jonesboro z 76538; ● 30
Irene; RMC Place; HILL; **238** EF-7; 🅿; z 76650; ● 150
IRION; **237** WL-12; Ⓟ 1,629; © 1,771; ◆ 1,675
Ironton; RMC Place; CHEROKEE; ***238** EF-10; mail Jacksonville z 75766; rural
Irving; Inc. Place; DALLAS; **238** ED-7; 🅿 🄷 🄲 4,658 ■; ★ **D-FW**; z 75014-17, z 75037-39, z 75060-63; Ⓟ 155,037; © 191,615; ◆ 209,555
Irvington; RMC Place; HARRIS; ***239** EK-10; ★ **HOU**; mail Houston z 77009, z 77022, z 77222; pop. incl. with Houston (Inc. Place)
Isla del Sol; RMC Place; GALVESTON; ***239** EL-11; ★ **GLV-**; mail Galveston z 77554; pop. incl. with Galveston (Inc. Place)
Island; RMC Place; MADISON; ***238** EH-10; mail Galveston z 77550, Midway z 75852; rural
Italy; Inc. Place; ELLIS; **238** EF-7; elev. 571ft./174m.; 🅿; z 76651; Ⓟ 1,699; © 1,993
Itasca; Inc. Place; HILL; **238** EF-7; elev. 702ft./214m.; 🅿; z 76055; Ⓟ 1,523; © 1,503
Ivan; RMC Place; STEPHENS; ***238** ED-4; elev. 127ft./39m.; mail Breckenridge z 76424; rural
Ivanhoe; RMC Place; FANNIN; **238** EB-8; elev. 608ft./185m.; 🅿; z 75447; ● 100
Iveys Crossing; RMC Place; EL PASO; ***237** WL-2; mail Tornillo z 79853; rural
Izoro; RMC Place; LAMPASAS; **238** EH-5; elev. 1,265ft./386m.; 🅿; z 76528 & mail Copperas Cove z 76522; ● 25

J

Jacinto City; Inc. Place; HARRIS; **234** D-6; 🅿; ★ **HOU**; z 77029; Ⓟ 9,343; © 10,302
JACK; **238** EC-5; Ⓟ 6,981; © 8,763; ◆ 8,648
Jack D Watson; RMC Place; TARRANT; ★ **D-FW**; mail Fort Worth z 76161; pop. incl. with Fort Worth (Inc. Place)
Jacksboro; Inc. Place; ⊡ JACK; **238** EC-5; elev. 1,084ft./330m.; 🅿 🄷; z 76458; Ⓟ 3,350; © 4,533
Jackson; RMC Place; SHELBY; ***238** EF-13; elev. 318ft./97m.; mail Joaquin z 75954; rural
Jackson; RMC Place; VAN ZANDT; ***238** EE-9; mail Canton z 75103
JACKSON; **239** EM-8; Ⓟ 13,039; © 14,391; ◆ 13,961
Jacksonville; Inc. Place; CHEROKEE; **238** EF-10; elev. 513ft./156m.; 🅿 🄷 ■; z 75766; Ⓟ 12,765; © 13,868; ◆ 14,316
Jacobia; RMC Place; HUNT; ***238** EC-9; mail Greenville z 75401; ● 100
Jamaica Beach; Inc. Place; GALVESTON; **239** EL-11; 🅿; ★ **GLV-**; z 77554 & mail Galveston z 77550; Ⓟ 624; © 1,075
James; RMC Place; SHELBY; ***238** EF-12; elev. 292ft./89m.; mail Center z 75935; rural
James Griffith; RMC Place; HARRIS; ★ **HOU**; mail Houston z 77080, z 77243, z 77280; pop. incl. with Houston (Inc. Place)
James Moody; RMC Place; VICTORIA; ★ **VICT**; mail Victoria z 77904; pop. incl. with Victoria (Inc. Place)
Jamestown; RMC Place; NEWTON; ***238** EH-13; mail Newton z 75966, Wiergate z 75977
Jamestown; RMC Place; SMITH; ***238** EE-10; elev. 443ft./135m.; mail Mineola z 75773; ● 75
Jaques Spur; RMC Place; GRAYSON; ★ **SHRM-**; pop. incl. with Denison (Inc. Place)
Jardin; RMC Place; HUNT; ***238** EC-9; elev. 546ft./166m.; mail Commerce z 75428, Houston z 77226; rural
Jarrell; Inc. Place; WILLIAMSON; **238** EI-6; 🅿; z 76537; incorporated May 8, 2001; not reported in 2000 Census; ● 1,400
Jasper; Inc. Place; ⊡ JASPER; **238** EH-13; 🅿 🄷; z 75951; Ⓟ 6,959; © 8,247; Ⓡ 7,657
JASPER; **238** EH-13; Ⓟ 31,102; © 35,604; ◆ 34,560
Jasper Heights; RMC Place; HARRISON; ***238** EE-12; ★ **MAR**; mail Marshall z 75672; pop. incl. with Marshall (Inc. Place)
Jayton; Inc. Place; ⊡ KENT; **236** WH-13; elev. 2,009ft./612m.; 🅿; z 79528; Ⓟ 608; © 513
Jean; RMC Place; YOUNG; **238** EC-4; mail Olney z 76374; ● 100
Jeanetta; RMC Place; HARRIS; ***239** EK-10; ★ **HOU**; pop. incl. with Houston (Inc. Place)
Jeddo; RMC Place; BASTROP; ***239** EK-7; mail Rosanky z 78953; rural
JEFF DAVIS; **237** WM-5; Ⓟ 1,946; © 2,207; ◆ 2,278
Jefferson; Inc. Place; ⊡ MARION; **238** ED-12; 🅿; z 75657; Ⓟ 2,199; © 2,024
JEFFERSON; **239** EK-13; Ⓟ 239,397; © 252,051; ◆ 237,785
Jefferson Heights; RMC Place; TOM GREEN; ***237** WL-13; ★ **SANG**; mail San Angelo z 76901; pop. incl. with San Angelo (Inc. Place)
Jenkins; RMC Place; MORRIS; ***238** ED-11; elev. 300ft./91m.; mail Daingerfield z 75638; ● 150
Jennings; RMC Place; LAMAR; ***238** EC-10; mail Paris z 75462; rural
Jensen Drive; RMC Place; HARRIS; ***239** EK-10; ★ **HOU**; mail Houston z 77026, z 77226; pop. incl. with Houston (Inc. Place)
Jericho; RMC Place; DONLEY; ***236** WD-12; mail Clarendon z 79226; rural
Jericho; RMC Place; SHELBY; ***238** EG-12; mail Center z 75935; rural
Jermyn; RMC Place; JACK; **238** EC-4; 🅿; z 76459; ● 100
Jersey Village; Inc. Place; HARRIS; **234** C-3; 🅿; ★ **HOU**; z 77040-41, z 77065; Ⓟ 4,826; © 6,880
Jerusalem; RMC Place; BRAZORIA; mail Brazoria z 77422; rural
Jewett; Inc. Place; LEON; **238** EG-9; elev. 496ft./151m.; 🅿; z 75846; Ⓟ 668; © 861
Jiba; RMC Place; KAUFMAN; ***238** EE-8; elev. 413ft./126m.; mail Kaufman z 75142
JIM HOGG; **239** EQ-4; Ⓟ 5,109; © 5,281; ◆ 4,863
JIM WELLS; **239** EO-5; Ⓟ 37,679; © 39,326; ◆ 41,809
Joaquin; Inc. Place; SHELBY; **238** EF-13; elev. 223ft./68m.; 🅿; z 75954; Ⓟ 805; © 925
Joe Pool; RMC Place; DALLAS; ★ **D-FW**; mail Dallas z 75232, z 75237, z 75244, z 75376; pop. incl. with Dallas (Inc. Place)
John Dunlop; RMC Place; HARRIS; ★ **HOU**; mail Houston z 77063, z 77263; pop. incl. with Houston (Inc. Place)
John Foster; RMC Place; HARRIS; ★ **HOU**; mail Pasadena z 77502; pop. incl. with Pasadena (Inc. Place)
Johnson; RMC Place; TERRY; ***236** WH-9; elev. 3,447ft./1,051m.; mail Brownfield z 79316; rural
JOHNSON; **238** EF-6; Ⓟ 97,165; © 126,811; ◆ 150,901
Johnson City; Inc. Place; ⊡ BLANCO; **238** EJ-4; elev. 1,193ft./364m.; 🅿; z 78636; Ⓟ 932; © 1,191
Johnsville; RMC Place; ERATH; ***238** EF-5; elev. 1,234ft./376m.; mail Stephenville z 76401; rural
Johntown; RMC Place; RED RIVER; **238** EC-10; mail Bogata z 75417; ● 180
Joiner; RMC Place; FAYETTE; ***239** EK-8; elev. 260ft./79m.; mail La Grange z 78945; rural
Joinerville; RMC Place; RUSK; ***238** EF-11; 🅿; z 75658; ● 200
Joliet; RMC Place; CALDWELL; ***239** EK-6; elev. 415ft./126m.; mail Luling z 78648; rural
Jolly; Inc. Place; CLAY; **238** EB-4; mail Wichita Falls z 76301; Ⓟ 201; © 188
Jollyville; CDP; WILLIAMSON, TRAVIS; **238** EJ-6; ★ **AUS**; mail Austin z 78729; Ⓟ 15,206; © 15,813
Jonah; RMC Place; WILLIAMSON; **238** EI-6; mail Georgetown z 78626; ● 100
Jones; RMC Place; VAN ZANDT; ***238** EE-9; mail Grand Saline z 75140; rural
JONES; **238** EE-1; Ⓟ 16,490; © 20,785; ◆ 18,917
Jonesboro; RMC Place; CORYELL, HAMILTON; **238** EG-5; 🅿; z 76538; ● 150
Jones Creek; Inc. Place; BRAZORIA; **239** EM-10; 🅿; ★ **L.JAC-**; z 77541 & mail El Campo z 77437; Ⓟ 2,160; © 2,130
Jones Creek; RMC Place; WHARTON; ***239** EL-9; 🅿; z 77541 & mail El Campo z 77437; rural
Jones Prairie; RMC Place; MILAM; ***238** EH-7; mail Cameron z 76520; rural
Jonestown; Inc. Place; TRAVIS; **238** EJ-5; 🅿; ★ **AUS**; z 78645; Ⓟ 1,250; © 1,681
Jonesville; RMC Place; HARRISON; **238** EE-12; elev. 257ft./78m.; 🅿; z 75659; ● 150
Joplin; RMC Place; JACK; ***238** ED-5; mail Jacksboro z 76458
Joppa; RMC Place; BURNET; ***238** EI-5; mail Bertram z 78605; rural
Jordan; RMC Place; POTTER; ★ **AMA**; mail Amarillo z 79159; pop. incl. with Amarillo (Inc. Place)
Jordans Store; RMC Place; SHELBY; ***238** EG-13; mail Shelbyville z 75973; rural
Josephine; Inc. Place; COLLIN, HUNT; **238** ED-8; 🅿; z 75164; Ⓟ 503; © 594
Joshua; Inc. Place; JOHNSON; **238** EE-6; elev. 924ft./282m.; 🅿; ★ **D-FW**; z 76058; Ⓟ 3,828; © 4,528
Josserand; RMC Place; TRINITY; ***238** EH-11; elev. 317ft./97m.; mail Groveton z 75845; rural
Jot Em Down; RMC Place; DELTA, HUNT; ***238** EC-9; elev. 528ft./161m.; mail Pecan Gap z 75469; rural
Jourdanton; Inc. Place; ⊡ ATASCOSA; **239** EM-4; elev. 460ft./140m.; 🅿 🄷; z 78026; Ⓟ 3,220; © 3,732
Joy; RMC Place; CLAY; **238** EC-5; mail Henrietta z 76365
Jozye; RMC Place; MADISON; ***238** EH-9; mail Madisonville z 77864; rural
Juanita Craft; RMC Place; DALLAS; mail Dallas z 75315, z 75371; pop. incl. with Dallas (Inc. Place)
Jubilee Springs; RMC Place; BELL; ***238** EH-6; mail Temple z 76502; rural
Jud; RMC Place; HASKELL; ***238** EC-1; elev. 1,589ft./484m.; mail Rochester z 79544; rural
Judson; RMC Place; GREGG; **238** EE-11; elev. 424ft./129m.; 🅿; ★ **LNGV**; z 75660; ● 500
Juliff; RMC Place; FORT BEND; **234** H-4; mail Rosharon z 77583; ● 100
Julius Melcher; RMC Place; HARRIS; ***239** EK-10; ★ **HOU**; mail Houston z 77027, z 77056, z 77227, z 77256; pop. incl. with Houston (Inc. Place)
Jumbo; RMC Place; PANOLA; ***238** EF-12; mail Long Branch z 75669; rural
Junction; Inc. Place; ⊡ KIMBLE; **237** WN-14; 🅿 🄷; z 76849; Ⓟ 2,654; © 2,618
Juno; RMC Place; VAL VERDE; ***237** WO-11; mail Ozona z 76943; rural
Justiceburg; RMC Place; GARZA; **236** WI-11; elev. 2,255ft./687m.; 🅿; z 79330; ● 80
Justin; Inc. Place; DENTON; **238** ED-6; 🅿; z 76247; Ⓟ 1,234; © 1,891

K

Kadane Corner; RMC Place; WICHITA; **238** EB-4; elev. 1,018ft./310m.; mail Electra z 76360, Kamay z 76369; ● 90
Kalgary; RMC Place; CROSBY; ***236** WH-12; elev. 2,504ft./763m.; mail Spur z 79370; rural
Kamay; RMC Place; WICHITA; **238** EB-4; elev. 1,034ft./315m.; 🅿; z 76369; ● 300
Kamey; RMC Place; CALHOUN; ***239** EN-8; mail Port Lavaca z 77979
Kanawha; RMC Place; RED RIVER; **238** EB-10; elev. 474ft./144m.; mail Detroit z 75436; ● 40
Karen; RMC Place; MONTGOMERY; ***238** EJ-10; ★ **HOU**; mail Magnolia z 77354; ● 400
Karnack; RMC Place; HARRISON; **238** ED-12; 🅿; z 75661; ● 300
KARNES; **239** EM-5; Ⓟ 12,455; © 15,446; ◆ 15,078
Karnes City; Inc. Place; ⊡ KARNES; **239** EM-6; elev. 433ft./132m.; 🅿; z 78118; Ⓟ 2,916; © 3,457
Katemcy; RMC Place; MASON; **238** EI-3; mail Brady z 76825; ● 90
Katy; Inc. Place; HARRIS, FORT BEND, WALLER; **239** EK-9; elev. 142ft./43m.; 🅿 🄷; ★ **HOU**; z 77449-50, z 77491-94; Ⓟ 8,005; © 11,775
Kaufman; Inc. Place; ⊡ KAUFMAN; **238** EE-8; 🅿 🄷; z 75142; Ⓟ 5,238; © 6,490
KAUFMAN; **238** EE-8; Ⓟ 52,220; © 71,313; ◆ 102,291
Kayare; RMC Place; CAMERON; ★ **BRNS**; mail Harlingen z 78550; pop. incl. with Harlingen (Inc. Place)
K-Bar Ranch; CDP-Census Area Only; JIM WELLS; ***239** EO-6; © 350
Keechi; RMC Place; LEON; ***238** EG-9; elev. 282ft./86m.; 🅿; z 75831; rural
Keenan; RMC Place; MONTGOMERY; ***238** EJ-10; mail Montgomery z 77356; rural
Keene; Inc. Place; JOHNSON; **238** EE-6; 🅿 🄲 812; ★ **D-FW**; z 76059; Ⓟ 3,944; © 5,003
Keeter; RMC Place; WISE; ***238** ED-6; mail Boyd z 76023
Keith; RMC Place; GRIMES; ***238** EI-9; elev. 280ft./85m.; mail Iola z 77861
Keller; Inc. Place; TARRANT; **235** E-5; 🅿; ★ **D-FW**; z 76244, z 76248, z 76262; Ⓟ 13,683; © 27,345; ◆ 39,507
Kellerville; RMC Place; WHEELER; ***236** WD-13; elev. 2,520ft./768m.; mail McLean z 79057; rural
Kelly; RMC Place; COLLIN; ***238** EC-8; elev. 691ft./211m.; mail Anna z 75409; pop. incl. with Weston (Inc. Place)
Kellyville; RMC Place; MARION; **238** ED-12; elev. 256ft./78m.; mail Jefferson z 75657
Kelsey; RMC Place; UPSHUR; ***238** ED-11; mail Gilmer z 75644
Kelton; RMC Place; WHEELER; **236** WD-13; elev. 2,232ft./680m.; mail Wheeler z 79096; ● 40
Keltys; RMC Place; ANGELINA; ***238** EG-11; ★ **LUFK**; mail Lufkin z 75903; pop. incl. with Lufkin (Inc. Place)
Kemah; Inc. Place; GALVESTON; **234** G-9; elev. 12ft./4m.; 🅿; ★ **HOU**; z 77565; Ⓟ 1,094; © 2,330
Kemp; Inc. Place; KAUFMAN; **238** EE-8; elev. 383ft./117m.; 🅿; z 75143; Ⓟ 1,184; © 1,133
Kempner; Inc. Place; LAMPASAS; **238** EH-5; elev. 876ft./267m.; 🅿; ★ **KILL-**; z 76539; © 1,004
Kendalia; RMC Place; KENDALL; **239** EK-4; elev. 1,397ft./426m.; 🅿; z 78027; ● 100
KENDALL; **238** EJ-4; Ⓟ 14,589; © 23,743; ◆ 33,911
Kendleton; Inc. Place; FORT BEND; **239** EL-9; elev. 94ft./29m.; 🅿; z 77451; Ⓟ 496; © 466
Kenedy; Inc. Place; KARNES; **239** EM-6; elev. 270ft./82m.; 🅿 🄷; z 78119, z 78125; Ⓟ 3,763; © 3,487
KENEDY; **239** EQ-6; Ⓟ 460; © 414; ◆ 372
Kenefick; Inc. Place; LIBERTY; **238** EJ-11; elev. 59ft./18m.; mail Dayton z 77535; Ⓟ 435; © 667
Kennard; Inc. Place; HOUSTON; **238** EG-11; 🅿; z 75847; Ⓟ 341; © 317
Kennedale; Inc. Place; TARRANT; **235** I-5; 🅿; ★ **D-FW**; z 76060; Ⓟ 4,096; © 5,850
Kenney; RMC Place; AUSTIN; **238** EJ-8; 🅿; z 77452; ● 200
Kensing; RMC Place; DELTA; ***238** EC-10; elev. 396ft./121m.; mail Lake Creek z 75450; rural
Kent; RMC Place; CULBERSON; **237** WM-6; elev. 4,212ft./1,284m.; 🅿; z 79855; ● 50
KENT; **236** WH-12; Ⓟ 1,010; © 859; ◆ 744
Kentuckytown; RMC Place; GRAYSON; ***238** EC-8; elev. 820ft./250m.; mail Whitewright z 75491; ● 20
Kenwood Place; RMC Place; HARRIS; ***239** EK-10; ★ **HOU**; mail Houston z 77039; ● 300
Kerens; Inc. Place; NAVARRO; **238** EF-8; elev. 366ft./112m.; 🅿; z 75144; Ⓟ 1,702; © 1,681
Kermit; Inc. Place; ⊡ WINKLER; **237** WK-8; 🅿 🄷; z 79745; Ⓟ 6,875; © 5,714
Kerr; RMC Place; WILLIAMSON; ★ **AUS**; pop. incl. with Round Rock (Inc. Place)
KERR; **239** EK-2; Ⓟ 36,304; © 43,653; ◆ 48,802
Kerrick; RMC Place; DALLAM; **236** WA-10; 🅿; z 79051; ● 50
Kerrville; Inc. Place; ⊡ KERR; **238** EJ-3; elev. 1,640ft./500m.; 🅿 🄷 🄲 930 ■; z 78028-29; Ⓟ 17,384; © 20,425; ◆ 22,357
Kerrville South; RMC Place; KERR; ***239** EK-3; mail Kerrville z 78028; rural
Key; RMC Place; DAWSON; ***236** WJ-10; mail Lamesa z 79331; rural
Key Ranch Estates; RMC Place; HENDERSON; ***238** EF-9; mail Trinidad z 75163; ● 300
Kickapoo; RMC Place; ANDERSON; mail Frankston z 75763; rural
Kickapoo (TX) Reservation; Indian Reservation; MAVERICK; © 420
Kildare; RMC Place; CASS; **238** ED-12; 🅿; z 75562; ● 60
Kildare Junction; RMC Place; CASS; **238** ED-12; elev. 257ft./78m.; mail Bivins z 75555; ● 50
Kilgore; RMC Place; GOLIAD; ***239** EM-7; mail Goliad z 77963; rural
Kilgore; Inc. Place; GREGG, RUSK; **238** EE-11; 🅿 🄷; ★ **LNGV**; z 75662-63; Ⓟ 11,066; © 11,301
Killeen; Inc. Place; BELL; **238** EH-6; 🅿 🄷 ■; ★ **KILL-**; z 76540-44, z 76547-49 & mail Kempner z 76539; Ⓟ 63,535; © 86,911; ◆ 125,106
Kilowatt; RMC Place; ORANGE; ***238** EJ-13; ★ **B-PA**
Kimball; RMC Place; BOSQUE; ***238** EF-6; mail Kopperl z 76652; rural
KIMBLE; **238** EI-2; Ⓟ 4,122; © 4,468; ◆ 4,327
Kimbro; RMC Place; TRAVIS; ***238** EJ-6; mail Manor z 78653; rural
Kinard Estates; RMC Place; ORANGE; ***238** EJ-13; ★ **B-PA**; mail Orange z 77632; ● 400
King; RMC Place; CORYELL; ***238** EH-5; mail Gatesville z 76528; rural
King; RMC Place; RED RIVER; ***238** EC-11; mail Annona z 75550; rural
KING; **236** WG-13; Ⓟ 354; © 356; ◆ 302
King Ranch; RMC Place; KLEBERG; ***239** EP-6; mail Kingsville z 78363; ● 200
Kingsbury; CDP; GUADALUPE; **239** EK-6; 🅿; z 78638; © 652
Kings Cove; RMC Place; BURNET; ***238** EI-4; mail Burnet z 78611; ● 40
Kingsland; CDP; LLANO; **238** EI-4; 🅿; z 78639; Ⓟ 2,725; © 4,584
Kingsland Estates; RMC Place; LLANO; ***238** EI-4; mail Kingsland z 78639; ● 130
Kingsley; RMC Place; DALLAS; ★ **D-FW**; mail Garland z 75041, z 75047; pop. incl. with Garland (Inc. Place)
Kings Mill; RMC Place; GRAY; **236** WC-12; elev. 3,296ft./1,005m.; mail Pampa z 79065; ● 30
Kings Point; RMC Place; BEXAR; ***239** EL-4; ★ **SANT**; mail Von Ormy z 78073; ● 750
Kingston; RMC Place; HUNT; **238** EC-8; mail Greenville z 75401; ● 140
Kings Village; RMC Place; TRAVIS; ***238** EJ-6; ★ **AUS**; mail Austin z 78727, z 78734; pop. incl. with Austin (Inc. Place)
Kingsville; Inc. Place; ⊡ KLEBERG; **239** EP-6; 🅿 🄷 🄲 6,699; z 78363-64; Ⓟ 25,276; © 25,575; ◆ 24,805
Kingtown; RMC Place; NACOGDOCHES; ***238** EG-12; mail Nacogdoches z 75961
Kingwood; RMC Place; HARRIS, MONTGOMERY; **238** EJ-11; 🅿 🄷; ★ **HOU**; z 77325, z 77339, z 77345-46; pop. incl. with Houston (Inc. Place); Ⓟ 37,397
Kinkler; RMC Place; LAVACA; ***239** EL-7; mail Hallettsville z 77964; rural
KINNEY; **237** WP-13; Ⓟ 3,119; © 3,379; ◆ 3,341
Kiomatia; RMC Place; RED RIVER; ***238** EB-10; elev. 436ft./133m.; mail Detroit z 75436; rural
Kirby; Inc. Place; BEXAR; **239** EL-5; 🅿; ★ **SANT**; z 78219; Ⓟ 8,326; © 8,673
Kirbyville; Inc. Place; JASPER; **238** EI-13; elev. 104ft./32m.; 🅿; z 75956; Ⓟ 1,871; © 2,085
Kirkland; RMC Place; CHILDRESS; **236** WF-13; mail Childress z 79201; ● 80
Kirtley; RMC Place; FAYETTE; ***239** EK-7; elev. 311ft./95m.; mail Smithville z 78957; rural
Kirvin; Inc. Place; FREESTONE; **238** EG-8; elev. 462ft./141m.; 🅿; z 75848; Ⓟ 107; © 122
Kittrell; RMC Place; WALKER; ***238** EH-10; mail Trinity z 75862; rural
Kleberg; RMC Place; DALLAS; ***238** EE-8; ★ **D-FW**; mail Dallas z 75253, z 75336; pop. incl. with Dallas (Inc. Place)
KLEBERG; **239** EP-6; Ⓟ 30,274; © 31,549; ◆ 30,852
Klein; RMC Place; HARRIS; ***238** EJ-10; 🅿; ★ **HOU**; z 77379, z 77389, z 77391; ● 12,000
Klondike; RMC Place; DAWSON; ***236** WJ-10; elev. 2,883ft./879m.; mail Lamesa z 79331; ● 30
Klondike; RMC Place; DELTA; **238** EC-9; elev. 470ft./143m.; 🅿; z 75448; ● 175
Klump; RMC Place; WASHINGTON; ***238** EJ-8; mail Brenham z 77833; rural
Knapp; RMC Place; SCURRY; ***236** WJ-12; mail Ira z 79527; rural
Knickerbocker; RMC Place; TOM GREEN; **237** WM-12; elev. 2,052ft./625m.; 🅿; z 76939; ● 170
Knippa; CDP; UVALDE; **239** EL-2; elev. 982ft./299m.; 🅿; z 78870; © 739
Knob Hill; RMC Place; ERATH; ***238** EF-5; mail Stephenville z 76401; rural
Knollwood; Inc. Place; GRAYSON; ***238** EB-8; ★ **SHRM-**; mail Sherman z 75092; Ⓟ 205; © 375
Knott; RMC Place; HOWARD; **236** WJ-11; 🅿; z 79748; ● 150
KNOX; **238** EC-2; Ⓟ 4,837; © 4,253; ◆ 3,319
Knox City; Inc. Place; KNOX; **236** WH-14; 🅿; z 79529; Ⓟ 1,440; © 1,219
Koerth; RMC Place; LAVACA; ***239** EL-7; mail Hallettsville z 77964
Kohrville; RMC Place; HARRIS; **234** A-2; ★ **HOU**; mail Houston z 77040, z 77070; ● 400
Kokomo; RMC Place; EASTLAND; ***238** EF-4; elev. 1,424ft./434m.; mail Gorman z 76454; rural
Komensky; RMC Place; LAVACA; ***239** EK-7; mail Moulton z 77975; rural
Kona Kai; RMC Place; GALVESTON; ***239** EL-12; ★ **GLV-**; mail Port Bolivar z 77650; ● 200
Kopernik Shores; RMC Place; CAMERON; ***239** ES-7; mail Brownsville z 78520; ● 100
Kopperl; RMC Place; BOSQUE; **238** EF-6; elev. 575ft./175m.; 🅿; z 76652; ● 250
Kosciusko; RMC Place; WILSON; **239** EM-5; mail Stockdale z 78160; ● 100
Kosse; Inc. Place; LIMESTONE; **238** EH-8; elev. 496ft./151m.; 🅿; z 76653; Ⓟ 505; © 497
Kountze; Inc. Place; ⊡ HARDIN; **238** EI-12; elev. 81ft./25m.; 🅿; ★ **B-PA**; z 77625; Ⓟ 2,056; © 2,115
Kovar; RMC Place; BASTROP; ***239** EK-7; elev. 450ft./137m.; mail Flatonia z 78941; rural
Kress; Inc. Place; SWISHER; **236** WF-10; 🅿; z 79052; Ⓟ 739; © 826
Kreutzberg; RMC Place; KENDALL; ***239** EK-4; elev. 1,480ft./451m.; mail Boerne z 78006; rural
Krugerville; Inc. Place; DENTON; ***238** EC-7; 🅿; ★ **DENT**; z 76227; Ⓟ 735; © 903
Krum; Inc. Place; DENTON; **238** EC-7; 🅿; ★ **DENT**; z 76249; Ⓟ 1,542; © 1,979
Kurten; Inc. Place; BRAZOS; **238** EI-9; 🅿; z 77862; incorporated August 22, 2000; not reported in 2000 Census; ● 200
Kyle; Inc. Place; HAYS; **239** EK-5; 🅿; z 78640; Ⓟ 2,225; © 5,314; ◆ 14,662
Kyote; RMC Place; ATASCOSA; ***239** EM-4; elev. 596ft./182m.; mail Bigfoot z 78005; rural

L

Labatt; RMC Place; WILSON; mail Floresville z 78114; rural
La Blanca; CDP; HIDALGO; ***239** ES-5; 🅿; ★ **MCAL**; z 78558; © 2,351
La Casita; RMC Place; STARR; ***239** ES-4; elev. 154ft./47m.; mail Rio Grande City z 78582; ● 300
La Casita-Garciasville; CDP-Census Area Only; STARR; ***239** ES-4; mail Garciasville z 78547, Rio Grande City z 78582; Ⓟ 1,186; © 2,177
Laceola; RMC Place; MADISON; ***238** EH-9; elev. 291ft./89m.; mail Madisonville z 77864, Normangee z 77871; rural
Lackland AFB; CDP-Census Area Only; BEXAR; ***239** EL-4; 🅿; ★ **SANT**; z 78236; Ⓟ 9,352; © 7,123
Lackland Heights; RMC Place; BEXAR; ***239** EL-4; ★ **SANT**; mail San Antonio z 78227; pop. incl. with San Antonio (Inc. Place)
Lackland Terrace; RMC Place; BEXAR; ***239** EL-4; ★ **SANT**; mail San Antonio z 78227; pop. incl. with San Antonio (Inc. Place)
La Coste; Inc. Place; MEDINA; **239** EL-4; 🅿; z 78039; Ⓟ 1,021; © 1,255
La Cuchilla; RMC Place; HIDALGO; ★ **MCAL**; mail Mission z 78572; pop. incl. with Mission (Inc. Place)
Lacy; RMC Place; TRINITY; ***238** EH-11; mail Groveton z 75845; rural
Lacy-Lakeview; Inc. Place; MCLENNAN; **236** WD-6; elev. 487ft./148m.; 🅿; ★ **WACO**; z 76705; Ⓟ 3,617; © 5,764
Ladonia; Inc. Place; FANNIN; **238** EC-9; elev. 635ft./194m.; 🅿; z 75449; Ⓟ 658; © 667
LaFayette; RMC Place; UPSHUR; **238** ED-11; elev. 369ft./112m.; mail Pittsburg z 75686; ● 80
La Feria; Inc. Place; CAMERON; **239** ES-6; elev. 60ft./18m.; 🅿; ★ **BRNS**; z 78559; Ⓟ 4,360; © 6,115
La Feria North; CDP-Census Area Only; CAMERON; ***239** ES-6; ★ **BRNS**; © 168
Lagarto; RMC Place; LIVE OAK; ***239** EO-5; mail George West z 78022; rural
La Gloria; MAVERICK; see Seco Mines (RMC Place)
La Gloria; RMC Place; STARR; ***239** ER-4; elev. 330ft./101m.; mail Santa Elena z 78591
Lago; CDP-Census Area Only; CAMERON; ***239** ES-6; ★ **BRNS**; mail San Benito z 78586; © 246
Lago Vista; Inc. Place; TRAVIS; **238** EI-5; 🅿; ★ **AUS**; z 78645; Ⓟ 2,199; © 4,507
La Grange; Inc. Place; ⊡ FAYETTE; **239** EK-7; 🅿 🄷; z 78945; Ⓟ 3,951; © 4,478
La Grulla (Grulla); Inc. Place; STARR; **239** ES-4; mail Grulla z 78548; Ⓟ 1,335; © 1,211
Laguna Heights (Bayside); CDP; CAMERON; **239** ES-7; 🅿; z 78578; Ⓟ 1,671; © 1,990
Laguna Park; RMC Place; BOSQUE; **238** EF-6; 🅿; z 76634, z 76644; ● 550
Laguna Seca; CDP; HIDALGO; ***239** ES-6; © 251
Laguna Tres Estates; RMC Place; HOOD; ***238** EE-6; mail Granbury z 76049; ● 300
Laguna Vista; Inc. Place; CAMERON; **239** ES-7; 🅿; z 78578; Ⓟ 1,166; © 1,658
Laguna Vista Estates; RMC Place; HENDERSON; ***238** EF-9; mail Athens z 75751
La Hacienda Estates; RMC Place; TRAVIS; ***238** EJ-5; ★ **AUS**; mail Austin z 78759; ● 900
La Homa; CDP-Census Area Only; HIDALGO; ***239** ES-5; ★ **MCAL**; mail Mission z 78572; Ⓟ 1,403; © 10,433
Laird Hill; RMC Place; RUSK; **238** EE-11; 🅿; ★ **LNGV**; z 75666; ● 400
Lajitas; RMC Place; BREWSTER; **237** WQ-6; elev. 2,342ft./714m.; 🅿; z 79852; ● 80
La Joya; Inc. Place; HIDALGO; **239** ES-4; 🅿; ★ **MCAL**; z 78560; Ⓟ 2,604; © 3,303
La Junta; RMC Place; PARKER; ***238** ED-6; elev. 811ft./247m.; ★ **D-FW**; mail Azle z 76020, Springtown z 76082, Weatherford z 76086; ● 200
Lake Bonanza; RMC Place; MONTGOMERY; ***238** EJ-10; ★ **HOU**; mail Montgomery z 77316; ● 200
Lake Bridgeport; Inc. Place; WISE; ***238** EC-5; mail Bridgeport z 76426; Ⓟ 322; © 372
Lake Brownwood; CDP; BROWN; **238** EG-3; mail Brownwood z 76801; Ⓟ 1,403; © 1,694
Lake Cherokee; RMC Place; GREGG, RUSK; ***238** EE-11; ★ **LNGV**; mail Henderson z 75652, Tatum z 75691; ● 700
Lake City; Inc. Place; SAN PATRICIO; ***239** EO-6; 🅿; z 78368 & mail Sinton z 78387; Ⓟ 465; © 526
Lake Conroe Forrest; RMC Place; MONTGOMERY; ***238** EJ-10; mail Montgomery z 77316; ● 400
Lake Conroe Hills; RMC Place; MONTGOMERY; ***238** EI-10; mail Willis z 77318
Lake Creek; RMC Place; DELTA; **238** EC-10; 🅿; z 75450; ● 75
Lake Creek Estates; RMC Place; MONTGOMERY; ***238** EJ-10; mail Magnolia z 77354; ● 200
Lake Dallas; Inc. Place; DENTON; **238** ED-7; 🅿; ★ **D-FW**; z 75065; Ⓟ 3,656; © 6,166
Lake Estates; MONTGOMERY; see One Seventy Seven Lake Estates (RMC Place)
Lake Forest; RMC Place; HARRIS; ***239** EK-11; ★ **HOU**; mail Houston z 77078; pop. incl. with Houston (Inc. Place)
Lake Gardens; RMC Place; TOM GREEN; **237** WL-13; ★ **SANG**; mail San Angelo z 76901; ● 1,200
Lake Highlands; RMC Place; DALLAS; ★ **D-FW**; mail Dallas z 75238, z 75355; pop. incl. with Dallas (Inc. Place)
Lakehills (Lake Medina Highlands); CDP-Census Area Only; BANDERA; **239** EL-3; 🅿; z 78063; Ⓟ 2,147; © 4,668
Lake Jackson; Inc. Place; BRAZORIA; **239** EM-10; 🅿 🄷 🄲 4,011 ■; ★ **L.JAC-**; z 77566; the Freeport-Lake Jackson urban area is often referred to as Brazosport; Ⓟ 22,776; © 26,386; ◆ 28,388
Lake Jackson Farms; RMC Place; BRAZORIA; ***239** EL-10; ★ **L.JAC-**; mail Lake Jackson z 77566; ● 300
Lake Kiowa; CDP-Census Area Only; COOKE; ***238** EC-7; 🅿; z 76240; © 1,883
Lakeland; RMC Place; MONTGOMERY; ***238** EJ-10; ★ **HOU**; mail Conroe z 77301, z 77385; ● 200
Lakeland Heights; RMC Place; DALLAS; ***238** EE-7; ★ **D-FW**; mail Grand Prairie z 75051; pop. incl. with Grand Prairie (Inc. Place)
Lakeland Park; RMC Place; TRAVIS; ***238** EJ-5; ★ **AUS**; mail Austin z 78759; pop. incl. with Austin (Inc. Place)
Lake Livingston; RMC Place; WALKER; mail Votaw z 77376; ● 25
Lake Louise; RMC Place; MONTGOMERY; ***238** EI-10; mail Willis z 77378; ● 35
Lake Medina Highlands; BANDERA; see Lakehills (CDP-Census Area Only)
Lake Meredith Estates; RMC Place; HUTCHINSON; ***236** WC-11; mail Fritch z 79036; ● 600
Lake Merritt; RMC Place; MILLS; ***238** EG-4; mail Goldthwaite z 76844; ● 60
Lake Nocona; RMC Place; MONTAGUE; ***238** EB-6; mail Nocona z 76255; ● 200
Lake Pauline; RMC Place; HARDEMAN; ***238** EA-2; mail Quanah z 79252; rural
Lake Placid; RMC Place; GUADALUPE; ***239** EL-5; mail Seguin z 78155; ● 300
Lakeport; Inc. Place; GREGG; **238** EE-11; ★ **LNGV**; mail Longview z 75603; Ⓟ 710; © 861
Lake Ransom Canyon Village; LUBBOCK; see Ransom Canyon (Inc. Place)
Lake Rolling Wood; RMC Place; MONTGOMERY; ***238** EJ-10; mail Conroe z 77303; ● 150
Lake Shadows; RMC Place; HARRIS; ***238** EJ-11; elev. 60ft./18m.; ★ **HOU**; mail Crosby z 77532; ● 550
Lake Shore; RMC Place; BROWN; **238** EG-3; mail Brownwood z 76801; ● 300
Lake Shore Gardens; RMC Place; SAN PATRICIO; ***239** EO-6; mail Mathis z 78368; ● 300
Lakeshore Gardens-Hidden Acres; CDP-Census Area Only; SAN PATRICIO; ***239** EO-6; © 720
Lakeside; SAN PATRICIO; see Lakewood Heights (Inc. Place)
Lakeside; Inc. Place; TARRANT; **235** G-2; 🅿; ★ **D-FW**; z 76108, z 76135; Ⓟ 816; © 1,040
Lakeside Acres; RMC Place; BEXAR; ***239** EK-4; ★ **SANT**; mail Boerne z 78006; ● 100
Lakeside Beach; RMC Place; BURNET; ***238** EI-5; mail Spicewood z 78669; ● 120
Lakeside City; Inc. Place; ARCHER, WICHITA; **238** EB-4; ★ **WIFL**; mail Wichita Falls z 76308; Ⓟ 865; © 984
Lakeside Heights; RMC Place; LLANO; ***238** EI-4; mail Kingsland z 78639; ● 260
Lakeside Park Estates; RMC Place; HARRIS; ★ **HOU**; mail Channelview z 77530; ● 250
Lakeside Village; RMC Place; BOSQUE; **238** EF-6; mail Morgan z 76671; ● 600
Lakeside Village; RMC Place; POLK; ***238** EI-11; mail Livingston z 77351
Lake Splendora; RMC Place; MONTGOMERY; ***238** EJ-11; ★ **HOU**; mail Splendora z 77372; ● 200
Lake Tanglewood; Inc. Place; RANDALL; **236** WD-10; mail Amarillo z 79118; Ⓟ 637; © 825
Lake Tejas; RMC Place; SAN JACINTO; ***238** EI-11; mail Shepherd z 77371; ● 80
Lake Thomas; RMC Place; SCURRY; **236** WJ-12; mail Ira z 79527; ● 100
Laketon; RMC Place; GRAY; ***236** WC-12; elev. 3,051ft./930m.; mail Pampa z 79065; rural
Lake Victor; RMC Place; BURNET; **238** EI-5; elev. 1,381ft./421m.; mail Lampasas z 76550; ● 50
Lakeview; RMC Place; CHEROKEE; ***238** EF-10; elev. 500ft./152m.; mail Jacksonville z 75766; ● 140
Lakeview; RMC Place; DALLAS; ***238** EE-7; ★ **D-FW**; mail Grand Prairie z 75051; pop. incl. with Grand Prairie (Inc. Place)
Lakeview; RMC Place; FLOYD; ***236** WG-11; mail Floydada z 79235; rural
Lakeview; Inc. Place; HALL; **236** WE-12; 🅿; z 79239 & mail Port Arthur z 77640, Vidor z 77662; Ⓟ 202; © 152
Lakeview; RMC Place; JEFFERSON; ***238** EJ-13; ★ **B-PA**; mail Port Arthur z 77640, z 77642; pop. incl. with Port Arthur (Inc. Place)
Lakeview; RMC Place; LYNN; ***236** WH-10; elev. 3,274ft./998m.; mail Meadow z 79345; ● 35
Lakeview; RMC Place; MCLENNAN; ★ **WACO**; mail Waco z 76705; pop. incl. with Waco (Inc. Place)
Lakeview; RMC Place; ORANGE; ***238** EJ-13; ★ **B-PA**; mail Vidor z 77662; ● 150
Lakeview; RMC Place; SWISHER; ***236** WF-10; elev. 3,604ft./1,098m.; mail Tulia z 79088; ● 25
Lakeview; RMC Place; TARRANT; ***238** ED-6; ★ **D-FW**; mail Fort Worth z 76135
Lakeview; RMC Place; TOM GREEN; ***237** WL-13; ★ **SANG**; mail San Angelo z 76903; pop. incl. with San Angelo (Inc. Place)
Lake View; CDP; VAL VERDE; ***237** WQ-12; © 167
Lakeview Estates; RMC Place; JOHNSON; ★ **D-FW**; mail Cleburne z 76033; ● 40
Lakeview Estates; RMC Place; ORANGE; ***238** EJ-13; ★ **B-PA**; mail Vidor z 77662; ● 250
Lakeview Hills; RMC Place; TRAVIS; ***238** EJ-5; ★ **AUS**; mail Leander z 78645; ● 100
Lake View Park; RMC Place; COMAL; ***239** EK-5; mail New Braunfels z 78130
Lakeway; Inc. Place; TRAVIS; **238** EJ-5; 🅿; ★ **AUS**; z 78734, z 78738; Ⓟ 4,044; © 8,002
Lake Whitney Estates; RMC Place; HILL; ***238** EF-6; mail Whitney z 76692; ● 400
Lake Wildwood; RMC Place; MONTGOMERY; ***238** EJ-10; ★ **HOU**; mail Conroe z 77306; ● 150
Lakewood; RMC Place; DALLAS; ★ **D-FW**; mail Dallas z 75214, z 75359; pop. incl. with Dallas (Inc. Place)
Lakewood; RMC Place; HARRIS; ***239** EK-11; ★ **HOU**; mail Baytown z 77520; pop. incl. with Baytown (Inc. Place)
Lakewood; RMC Place; ORANGE; ***238** EJ-13; ★ **B-PA**; mail Vidor z 77662; pop. incl. with Vidor (Inc. Place)
Lakewood; RMC Place; SAN AUGUSTINE; ***238** EH-13; mail Broaddus z 75929; ● 90
Lakewood Estates; RMC Place; MONTGOMERY; ***238** EJ-10; ★ **HOU**; mail Conroe z 77304; ● 400
Lakewood Forest; RMC Place; LLANO; ***238** EI-4; mail Kingsland z 78639; ● 100
Lakewood Harbor; RMC Place; BOSQUE; **238** EF-6; mail Clifton z 76634; ● 40
Lakewood Heights; RMC Place; HARRIS; ***238** EJ-11; elev. 70ft./21m.; ★ **HOU**; mail Huffman z 77336; pop. incl. with Houston (Inc. Place)
Lakewood Heights (Lakeside); Inc. Place; SAN PATRICIO; ***239** EO-6; mail Mathis z 78368; Ⓟ 292; © 333
Lakewood Hills; RMC Place; COMAL; ***239** EK-5; mail New Braunfels z 78130
Lakewood Village; Inc. Place; DENTON; **235** B-8; 🅿; ★ **D-FW**; z 75068; Ⓟ 169; © 342
Lake Worth; Inc. Place; TARRANT; **235** G-3; 🅿; ★ **D-FW**; z 76135-36; Ⓟ 4,591; © 4,618
Lamar; RMC Place; ARANSAS; **239** EO-7; mail Rockport z 78382; ● 200
LAMAR; **238** EB-10; Ⓟ 43,949; © 48,499; ◆ 49,027
Lamar Park; RMC Place; NUECES; ***239** EP-7; ★ **CRPX**; mail Corpus Christi z 78411, z 78466; pop. incl. with Corpus Christi (Inc. Place)
La Marque; Inc. Place; GALVESTON; **234** J-9; 🅿; ★ **GLV-**; z 77568; Ⓟ 14,120; © 13,682
Lamar Terrace; RMC Place; HARRIS; ***239** EK-10; elev. 62ft./19m.; ★ **HOU**; mail Houston z 77056; pop. incl. with Houston (Inc. Place)
Lamasco; RMC Place; FANNIN; **238** EB-9; elev. 589ft./180m.; mail Telephone z 75488; ● 35
LAMB; **236** WF-9; Ⓟ 15,072; © 14,709; ◆ 13,528
Lamesa; Inc. Place; ⊡ DAWSON; **236** WI-10; 🅿 🄷; z 79331; Ⓟ 10,809; © 9,952
Lamkin; RMC Place; COMANCHE; **238** EG-5; elev. 1,056ft./322m.; mail Gustine z 76455; ● 50
Lampasas; Inc. Place; ⊡ LAMPASAS; **238** EH-5; 🅿; z 76550; Ⓟ 6,382; © 6,786
LAMPASAS; **238** EH-5; Ⓟ 13,521; © 17,762; ◆ 21,845
Lamplight Village; RMC Place; TRAVIS; ***238** EJ-6; ★ **AUS**; mail Austin z 78758; pop. incl. with Austin (Inc. Place)
Lanark; RMC Place; CASS; ***238** EC-12; elev. 339ft./103m.; mail Queen City z 75572; rural
Lancaster; Inc. Place; DALLAS; **235** J-11; 🅿 🄷; ★ **D-FW**; z 75134, z 75146; Ⓟ 22,117; © 25,894; ◆ 29,562
Lancaster; RMC Place; EL PASO; ***237** WK-2; ★ **ELP**; mail El Paso z 79907; pop. incl. with El Paso (Inc. Place)
Landa Park Highlands; RMC Place; COMAL; mail New Braunfels z 78130; pop. incl. with New Braunfels (Inc. Place)
Lane; RMC Place; HUNT; ***238** EC-8; mail Celeste z 75423, Leonard z 75452; rural
Lane City; RMC Place; WHARTON; **239** EL-9; 🅿; z 77453; ● 300
Lanely; RMC Place; FREESTONE; ***238** EG-9; elev. 459ft./140m.; mail Buffalo z 75831
Laneport; RMC Place; WILLIAMSON; ***238** EI-7; elev. 470ft./143m.; mail Taylor z 76574; rural
Lane Prairie; RMC Place; JOHNSON; ***238** EE-6; ★ **D-FW**; mail Joshua z 76058; rural
Laneville; RMC Place; RUSK; **238** EF-11; 🅿; z 75667; ● 250
Langtry; RMC Place; VAL VERDE; **237** WP-11; 🅿; z 78871; ● 30
Lanham; RMC Place; HAMILTON; ***238** EG-5; elev. 1,106ft./337m.; mail Jonesboro z 76538; rural
Lanier; RMC Place; CASS; **238** ED-12; mail Linden z 75563; rural
Lannius; RMC Place; FANNIN; **238** EC-9; elev. 620ft./189m.; mail Dodd City z 75438; ● 90
Lantana; RMC Place; CAMERON; ***239** ES-6; 🅿; ★ **BRNS**; z 76226 & mail San Benito z 78586; rural
La Paloma; CDP; CAMERON; **239** ES-6; elev. 50ft./15m.; ★ **BRNS**; mail San Benito z 78586; © 354
La Paloma-Lost Creek; CDP-Census Area Only; NUECES; ***239** EP-6; © 323
La Porte; Inc. Place; HARRIS; **234** F-8; 🅿; ★ **HOU**; z 77571-72; Ⓟ 27,910; © 31,880; ◆ 35,968
La Presa; CDP-Census Area Only; WEBB; ***239** EP-3; © 508
La Pryor; CDP; ZAVALA; **237** WR-14; elev. 746ft./227m.; 🅿; z 78872; Ⓟ 1,343; © 1,491
La Puerta; CDP; STARR; ***239** ES-4; mail Rio Grande City z 78582; © 1,636
Laredo; Inc. Place; ⊡ WEBB; **239** EO-11; elev. 414ft./126m.; 🅿 🄷 🄲 4,917 ■; ★ **LAR**; z 78040-46, z 78049; Ⓟ 122,899; © 176,576; ◆ 211,457
Laredo Ranchettes; CDP-Census Area Only; WEBB; ***239** EP-3; © 1,845
La Reforma; RMC Place; STARR; ***239** ER-5; mail Delmita z 78536
Larga Vista; CDP-Census Area Only; WEBB; ***239** EP-3; © 742
Lariat; RMC Place; PARMER; **236** WF-8; elev. 4,008ft./1,222m.; mail Farwell z 79325; ● 60
Lark; RMC Place; CARSON; **236** WD-11; elev. 3,370ft./1,027m.; mail Groom z 79039; rural
La Rosita; CDP-Census Area Only; STARR; ***239** ES-4; © 1,729
LaRue; RMC Place; HENDERSON; **238** EF-9; 🅿; z 75770; ● 160
La Salle; RMC Place; CALHOUN; ***239** EN-8; mail Port Lavaca z 77979; ● 20
La Salle; RMC Place; JACKSON; **239** EM-8; 🅿; z 77969; ● 200
LA SALLE; **239** EN-3; Ⓟ 5,254; © 5,866; ◆ 6,035
Lasana; CDP-Census Area Only; CAMERON; ***239** ES-6; ★ **BRNS**; © 135
Lasara; CDP; WILLACY; **239** ER-6; 🅿; z 78561; © 1,024
Las Colonias; CDP-Census Area Only; ZAVALA; ***239** EM-2; © 283
Las Lomas; CDP-Census Area Only; STARR; ***239** ES-4; © 2,684
Las Lomitas; CDP-Census Area Only; JIM HOGG; ***239** EQ-4; © 267
Las Milpas; RMC Place; HIDALGO; ***239** ES-5; ★ **MCAL**; mail Pharr z 78577; pop. incl. with Pharr (Inc. Place)
Las Palmas-Juarez; CDP-Census Area Only; CAMERON; ***239** ES-6; ★ **BRNS**; © 1,666
Las Quintas Fronterizas; CDP-Census Area Only; MAVERICK; ***237** WR-13; © 2,030
Las Rusias; RMC Place; CAMERON; ***239** ES-6; ★ **BRNS**; mail San Benito z 78586; pop. incl. with Los Indios (Inc. Place)
Lassater; RMC Place; MARION; **238** ED-12; mail Avinger z 75630; ● 50
Las Tiendas; RMC Place; WEBB; ***239** EO-2; mail Laredo z 78045; rural
Las Yescas (Yescas); RMC Place; CAMERON; ***239** ES-6; mail San Benito z 78586; ● 200
Latch; RMC Place; UPSHUR; ***238** ED-11; elev. 447ft./136m.; mail Gilmer z 75644; rural
Latexo; Inc. Place; HOUSTON; **238** EG-10; 🅿; z 75849; Ⓟ 289; © 272
La Tina; RMC Place; CAMERON; ***239** ES-7; mail San Benito z 78586
Latium; RMC Place; WASHINGTON; ***238** EJ-8; mail Burton z 77835; ● 20
Latonia; RMC Place; BRAZORIA; mail Brazoria z 77422; rural
Laughlin AFB; CDP-Census Area Only; VAL VERDE; ***237** WQ-12; 🅿; z 78840, z 78843; Ⓟ 2,556; © 2,225
Laureles; CDP; CAMERON; ***239** ES-6; mail San Benito z 78586; © 3,285
Laurel Heights; RMC Place; BEXAR; ***239** EL-4; ★ **SANT**; mail San Antonio z 78212; pop. incl. with San Antonio (Inc. Place)
LAVACA; **239** EL-7; Ⓟ 18,690; © 19,210; ◆ 18,687
Lavada; RMC Place; FRANKLIN; ***238** EC-10; mail Talco z 75487; rural
La Vernia; Inc. Place; WILSON; **239** EL-5; elev. 475ft./145m.; 🅿; z 78121; Ⓟ 639; © 931
La Victoria; CDP-Census Area Only; STARR; ***239** ES-4; © 1,683
La Villa; Inc. Place; HIDALGO; **239** ES-6; 🅿; ★ **MCAL**; z 78562; Ⓟ 1,388; © 1,305
Lavon; Inc. Place; COLLIN; **238** ED-8; elev. 522ft./159m.; 🅿; ★ **D-FW**; z 75166; Ⓟ 303; © 387
Lavon Beach Estates; RMC Place; COLLIN; ***238** ED-8; ★ **D-FW**; mail Farmersville z 75442; ● 250
Lavon Shores Estate; RMC Place; COLLIN; ***238** ED-8; ★ **D-FW**; mail Farmersville z 75442; ● 250
La Ward; Inc. Place; JACKSON; **239** EM-8; elev. 42ft./13m.; 🅿; z 77970; Ⓟ 162; © 200
Lawn; Inc. Place; TAYLOR; **237** WK-14; 🅿; z 79530; Ⓟ 358; © 353
Lawrence; RMC Place; KAUFMAN; **238** ED-8; mail Terrell z 75160; ● 300
Lawrence Park; RMC Place; POTTER; ★ **AMA**; mail Amarillo z 79109; pop. incl. with Amarillo (Inc. Place)
Lawrence Springs; RMC Place; VAN ZANDT; ***238** EE-9; mail Grand Saline z 75140; rural
Lazare; RMC Place; COTTLE, HARDEMAN; ***238** EA-1; mail Quanah z 79252; rural
Lazbuddie; RMC Place; PARMER; **236** WF-9; 🅿; z 79053; ● 250
Lazy Forest; RMC Place; MONTGOMERY; ***238** EJ-10; mail Conroe z 77303; ● 308
Leaday; RMC Place; COLEMAN; ***238** EG-2; elev. 1,524ft./465m.; 🅿; z 76888; rural
League City; Inc. Place; GALVESTON, HARRIS; **234** H-7; elev. 23ft./7m.; 🅿 🄷; ★ **HOU**; z 77573-74; Ⓟ 30,159; © 45,444; ◆ 60,805
Leagueville; RMC Place; HENDERSON; ***238** EE-10; mail Murchison z 75778; rural
Leakey; Inc. Place; ⊡ REAL; **237** WP-14; elev. 1,621ft./494m.; 🅿; z 78873; Ⓟ 399; © 387
Leander; Inc. Place; WILLIAMSON, TRAVIS; **238** EI-6; 🅿; ★ **AUS**; z 78641, z 78645-46; Ⓟ 3,398; © 7,596; ◆ 13,581
Leary; Inc. Place; BOWIE; ***238** EC-12; 🅿; ★ **TEXR-**; z 75561 & mail Texarkana z 75501; Ⓟ 395; © 555
Leasure Acres; RMC Place; CORYELL; ***238** EG-6; mail Gatesville z 76528; ● 30
Lebanon; RMC Place; COLLIN; ***238** ED-7; elev. 753ft./230m.; ★ **D-FW**; mail Frisco z 75035; pop. incl. with Frisco (Inc. Place)
Ledbetter; RMC Place; FAYETTE; **238** EJ-8; elev. 434ft./132m.; 🅿; z 78946; ● 80
Ledbetter Hills; RMC Place; DALLAS; ***238** EE-7; ★ **D-FW**; mail Dallas z 75236; pop. incl. with Dallas (Inc. Place)
LEE; **238** EJ-7; Ⓟ 12,854; © 15,657; ◆ 16,358
Leedale (Gindale); RMC Place; BELL; ***238** EH-7; mail Rogers z 76569; rural
Leesburg; RMC Place; CAMP; **238** ED-11; elev. 399ft./122m.; 🅿; z 75451; ● 120
Leesville; RMC Place; GONZALES; **239** EL-6; 🅿; z 78122; ● 180
Lefors; Inc. Place; GRAY; **236** WD-12; 🅿; z 79054; Ⓟ 656; © 559
Leggett; RMC Place; POLK; **238** EI-11; elev. 268ft./82m.; 🅿; z 77350; ● 350
Lehman; RMC Place; COCHRAN; ***236** WH-9; mail Morton z 79346; rural
Leigh; RMC Place; HARRISON; **238** EE-12; mail Karnack z 75661; ● 75
Lela; RMC Place; WHEELER; **236** WD-13; elev. 2,434ft./742m.; mail Shamrock z 79079; ● 80
Lelia Lake; RMC Place; DONLEY; **236** WE-12; 🅿; z 79240; ● 130
Leming; RMC Place; ATASCOSA; **239** EM-4; 🅿; z 78050; ● 600
Lena; RMC Place; FAYETTE; ***239** EK-7; elev. 333ft./101m.; mail West Point z 78963; rural
Lenorah; RMC Place; MARTIN; **236** WJ-10; 🅿; z 79749; ● 80
Lenz; RMC Place; KARNES; ***239** EM-5; elev. 324ft./99m.; mail Karnes City z 78118; rural
Leo; RMC Place; COOKE; ***238** EC-6; elev. 786ft./240m.; mail Decatur z 76234; rural
Leo; RMC Place; LEE; ***238** EJ-7; mail Lexington z 78947; rural
LEON; **238** EG-9; Ⓟ 12,665; © 15,335; ◆ 16,497
Leona; Inc. Place; LEON; **238** EH-9; 🅿; z 75850; Ⓟ 178; © 181
Leonard; Inc. Place; FANNIN; **238** EC-8; 🅿; z 75452; Ⓟ 1,744; © 1,846
Leon Junction; RMC Place; CORYELL; **238** EH-6; 🅿; z 76528; ● 50
Leon Springs; RMC Place; BEXAR; ***239** EK-4; ★ **SANT**; mail San Antonio z 78229; pop. incl. with San Antonio (Inc. Place)
Leon Valley; Inc. Place; BEXAR; **239** ER-10; elev. 826ft./252m.; 🅿; ★ **SANT**; z 78238, z 78240, z 78268 & mail San Antonio z 78250-51, z 78254; Ⓟ 9,581; © 9,239
Leroy; Inc. Place; MCLENNAN; **238** EG-7; elev. 498ft./152m.; 🅿; z 76654; Ⓟ 292; © 335
Lesley; RMC Place; HALL; **236** WE-12; mail Lakeview z 79239; ● 10
Levelland; Inc. Place; ⊡ HOCKLEY; **236** WH-9; 🅿 🄷; z 79336, z 79338; Ⓟ 13,986; © 12,866
Leveretts Chapel; RMC Place; RUSK; ***238** EE-11; ★ **LNGV**; mail Overton z 75684; ● 150
Levi; RMC Place; MCLENNAN; ***238** EG-7; elev. 471ft./144m.; mail Lorena z 76655; rural
Levita; RMC Place; CORYELL; ***238** EG-5; mail Gatesville z 76528; ● 35
Lewisville; Inc. Place; DENTON, DALLAS; **238** ED-7; 🅿 🄷; ★ **D-FW**; z 75022, z 75027-29, z 75056-57, z 75067, z 75077; Ⓟ 46,521; © 77,737; ◆ 107,679
Lewisville; RMC Place; WALLER; ***238** EJ-9; mail Hempstead z 77445; rural
Lexington; Inc. Place; LEE; **238** EJ-7; 🅿; z 78947; Ⓟ 953; © 1,178
Lexington Woods; RMC Place; HARRIS; ***238** EJ-10; ★ **HOU**; mail Spring z 77373; ● 650
Liberty; RMC Place; HAMILTON; mail Purmela z 76566; rural
Liberty; Inc. Place; ⊡ LIBERTY; **238** EJ-11; elev. 32ft./10m.; 🅿 🄷; z 77575; Ⓟ 7,733; © 8,033
Liberty; RMC Place; LUBBOCK; ***236** WG-10; elev. 3,259ft./993m.; mail Lubbock z 79401
Liberty; RMC Place; MILAM; ***238** EI-7; mail Cameron z 76520; rural
Liberty; RMC Place; NEWTON; **238** EH-13; mail Newton z 75966; ● 250
Liberty; RMC Place; RUSK; ***238** EE-12; elev. 376ft./115m.; mail Henderson z 75652, Tatum z 75691; rural
LIBERTY; **238** EJ-11; Ⓟ 52,726; © 70,154; ◆ 74,900
Liberty City; CDP; GREGG; ***238** EE-11; elev. 393ft./120m.; ★ **LNGV**; mail Gladewater z 75647, Kilgore z 75662; Ⓟ 1,607; © 1,935
Liberty Grove; RMC Place; DALLAS; ***238** ED-8; elev. 498ft./152m.; ★ **D-FW**; mail Wylie z 75098; ● 50
Liberty Grove; RMC Place; DELTA; ***238** EC-9; mail Cooper z 75432; rural
Liberty Hill; RMC Place; HOUSTON; ***238** EG-10; elev. 356ft./109m.; mail Grapeland z 75844; rural
Liberty Hill; RMC Place; MILAM; ***238** EI-7; elev. 418ft./127m.; mail Rockdale z 76567; rural
Liberty Hill; RMC Place; TITUS; ***238** EC-11; elev. 425ft./130m.; mail Mount Pleasant z 75455; rural
Liberty Hill; Inc. Place; WILLIAMSON; **238** EI-5; elev. 1,033ft./315m.; 🅿; z 78642; © 1,409
Liggett; RMC Place; DALLAS; ★ **D-FW**; pop. incl. with Irving (Inc. Place)
Lilac; RMC Place; MILAM; ***238** EI-7; mail Thorndale z 76577; rural
Lilbert; RMC Place; NACOGDOCHES; **238** EF-11; mail Cushing z 75760; ● 70
Lillian; RMC Place; JOHNSON; **238** EE-7; elev. 712ft./217m.; 🅿; ★ **D-FW**; z 76061; ● 150
Lily Grove; RMC Place; NACOGDOCHES; ***238** EG-11; mail Nacogdoches z 75964; rural
Lily Island; RMC Place; POLK; ***238** EH-11; mail Camden z 75934; ● 110
LIMESTONE; **238** EG-8; Ⓟ 20,946; © 22,051; ◆ 22,056
Lincoln; RMC Place; LEE; **238** EJ-7; 🅿; z 78948; ● 120
Lincoln City; RMC Place; HARRIS; ***239** EK-10; ★ **HOU**; mail Houston z 77088; pop. incl. with Houston (Inc. Place)
Lincoln Park; Inc. Place; DENTON; **235** A-8; ★ **D-FW**; mail Aubrey z 76227; Ⓟ 287; © 517
Lindale; Inc. Place; SMITH; **238** EE-10; elev. 547ft./167m.; 🅿; z 75771; Ⓟ 2,428; © 2,954
Linden; Inc. Place; ⊡ CASS; **238** ED-12; 🅿 🄷; z 75563; Ⓟ 2,375; © 2,256
Lindenau; RMC Place; DEWITT; **239** EL-7; mail Cuero z 77954; ● 50
Lindsay; Inc. Place; COOKE; **238** EC-7; 🅿; z 76250; Ⓟ 610; © 788
Lindsay (Lindsay Addition); CDP-Census Area Only; REEVES; ***237** WL-7; mail Pecos z 79772; © 394
Lindsay Addition; REEVES; see Lindsay (CDP-Census Area Only)
Lingleville; RMC Place; ERATH; **238** EF-4; elev. 1,558ft./475m.; 🅿; z 76401, z 76446, z 76461; ● 100
Linkwood Addition; RMC Place; TARRANT; ★ **D-FW**; mail Aledo z 76008; ● 500
Linn (San Manuel); RMC Place; HIDALGO; **239** ER-5; 🅿; z 78563; ● 100
Linn Flat; RMC Place; NACOGDOCHES; ***238** EF-11; mail Nacogdoches z 75964; rural
Linwood; RMC Place; CHEROKEE; ***238** EG-11; elev. 298ft./91m.; mail Alto z 75925; ● 40
Lipan; Inc. Place; HOOD; **238** EE-5; 🅿; z 76462; Ⓟ 354; © 425
Lipscomb; CDP; ⊡ LIPSCOMB; **236** WB-13; 🅿; z 79056; © 44
LIPSCOMB; **236** WB-13; Ⓟ 3,143; © 3,057; ◆ 3,040
Lissie; RMC Place; WHARTON; **239** EK-9; 🅿; z 77454; ● 150
Littig; RMC Place; TRAVIS; ***238** EJ-6; elev. 463ft./141m.; mail Elgin z 78621; ● 80
Little Cypress; RMC Place; ORANGE; ***238** EJ-13; ★ **B-PA**; mail Orange z 77632; ● 1,200
Little Elm; Inc. Place; DENTON; **235** B-9; 🅿; ★ **D-FW**; z 75068; Ⓟ 1,255; © 3,646; ◆ 9,319
Littlefield; Inc. Place; ⊡ LAMB; **236** WG-9; 🅿 🄷; z 79339; Ⓟ 6,489; © 6,507
Little Flock; RMC Place; BURLESON; ***238** EI-8; elev. 221ft./67m.; mail Somerville z 77879; rural
Little Hope; RMC Place; WOOD; ***238** ED-10; elev. 418ft./127m.; mail Winnsboro z 75494; rural
Little Mexico; RMC Place; PECOS; ***237** WM-8; mail Fort Stockton z 79735; ● 200
Little New York; RMC Place; GONZALES; ***239** EL-7; mail Gonzales z 78629; rural
Little Ridge; RMC Place; COLLIN; ***238** ED-8; ★ **D-FW**; mail Copeville z 75121; ● 150
Little River-Academy; Inc. Place; BELL; **238** EH-6; 🅿; ★ **KILL-**; z 76554; © 1,645
Little Rock; RMC Place; HARDIN; ***238** EJ-12; mail Kountze z 77625; rural
Lively; RMC Place; KAUFMAN; ***238** EE-8; elev. 430ft./131m.; mail Kemp z 75143; rural
Live Oak; Inc. Place; BEXAR; **239** EL-5; 🅿; ★ **SANT**; z 78233 & mail Schertz z 78154, Universal City z 78148; Ⓟ 10,023; © 9,156
Liveoak; RMC Place; PALO PINTO; ***238** EE-5; mail Santo z 76472; rural
LIVE OAK; **239** EO-5; Ⓟ 9,556; © 12,309; ◆ 11,119
Live Oak Ranchettes; RMC Place; WILLIAMSON; ***238** EI-5; mail Leander z 78641; ● 150
Live Oak Resorts; RMC Place; HILL; ***238** EF-6; mail Whitney z 76692; ● 200
Liverpool; Inc. Place; BRAZORIA; **239** EL-11; 🅿; z 77577; Ⓟ 396; © 404
Livingston; Inc. Place; ⊡ POLK; **238** EI-11; elev. 180ft./55m.; 🅿 🄷; z 77351, z 77399; Ⓟ 5,019; © 5,433
Llano; Inc. Place; ⊡ LLANO; **238** EI-4; elev. 1,040ft./317m.; 🅿 🄷; z 78643; Ⓟ 2,962; © 3,325
LLANO; **238** EI-4; Ⓟ 11,631; © 17,044; ◆ 19,005
Llano Grande; CDP-Census Area Only; HIDALGO; ***239** ES-6; ★ **MCAL**; © 3,333
Lobo; RMC Place; CULBERSON; ***237** WN-5; mail Van Horn z 79855
Locker; RMC Place; SAN SABA; ***238** EH-3; elev. 1,303ft./397m.; mail Richland Springs z 76871; rural
Lockett; RMC Place; WILBARGER; ***238** EB-3; elev. 1,289ft./393m.; mail Vernon z 76384
Lockettville; RMC Place; HOCKLEY; **236** WH-9; mail Ropesville z 79358; ● 25
Lockhart; Inc. Place; ⊡ CALDWELL; **239** EK-6; elev. 526ft./160m.; 🅿; z 78644; Ⓟ 9,205; © 11,615
Lockhill; RMC Place; BEXAR; ★ **SANT**; mail San Antonio z 78230, z 78278; pop. incl. with San Antonio (Inc. Place)
Lockney; Inc. Place; FLOYD; **236** WG-11; elev. 3,283ft./1,001m.; 🅿 🄷; z 79241; Ⓟ 2,207; © 2,056
Locust; RMC Place; GRAYSON; ***238** EB-7; mail Pottsboro z 75076; rural
Locust Grove; RMC Place; LIPSCOMB; ***236** WB-13; mail Canadian z 79014; rural
Lodi; RMC Place; MARION; **238** ED-12; elev. 253ft./77m.; 🅿; z 75564; ● 200
Loeb; RMC Place; HARDIN; **238** EJ-13; ★ **B-PA**; mail Lumberton z 77657; pop. incl. with Rose Hill Acres (Inc. Place)
Loebau; RMC Place; LEE; ***238** EJ-7; mail Lincoln z 78948; rural
Logan; RMC Place; PANOLA; ***238** EF-13; elev. 288ft./88m.; mail Center z 75935; rural
Logan Heights; RMC Place; EL PASO; ***237** WK-2; ★ **ELP**; mail El Paso z 79904; pop. incl. with El Paso (Inc. Place)
Log Cabin; Inc. Place; HENDERSON; ***238** EF-9; 🅿; z 75148; Ⓟ 487; © 733
Lohn; RMC Place; MCCULLOCH; **238** EH-3; 🅿; z 76852; ● 150
Loire; RMC Place; WILSON; ***239** EM-5; elev. 532ft./162m.; mail Pleasanton z 78064; rural
Lois; RMC Place; COOKE; ***238** EC-7; elev. 810ft./247m.; mail Valley View z 76272; rural
Lois; RMC Place; HARRIS; ***239** EK-10; ★ **HOU**; pop. incl. with Houston (Inc. Place)
Lolita; CDP; JACKSON; **239** EM-8; 🅿; z 77971; © 548
Lollipop; RMC Place; HENDERSON; ***238** EF-10; mail Frankston z 75763; pop. incl. with Berryville (Inc. Place)
Loma; RMC Place; WALKER; ***238** EI-9; mail Bedias z 77831; rural
Loma Alta; RMC Place; MCMULLEN; ***239** EO-4; mail Tilden z 78072; ● 100
Loma Alta; RMC Place; VAL VERDE; **237** WP-12; mail Del Rio z 78840; ● 25
Loma Linda East; CDP-Census Area Only; JIM WELLS; ***239** EP-5; © 214
Loma Terrace; RMC Place; EL PASO; ***237** WK-2; ★ **ELP**; mail El Paso z 79907; pop. incl. with El Paso (Inc. Place)
Loma Vista; RMC Place; ZAVALA; ***239** EM-2; elev. 675ft./206m.; mail Batesville z 78829; rural
Lomax; RMC Place; HARRIS; ***239** EK-11; ★ **HOU**; mail La Porte z 77571; pop. incl. with La Porte (Inc. Place)
Lomax; RMC Place; HOWARD; ***237** WK-11; mail Big Spring z 79720; rural
Lometa; Inc. Place; LAMPASAS; **238** EH-4; elev. 1,487ft./453m.; 🅿; z 76853; Ⓟ 625; © 782
London; RMC Place; KIMBLE; ***238** EI-2; 🅿; z 76854; ● 200
London; RMC Place; RUSK; **238** EI-2; mail New London z 75682; ● 150
Lone Camp; RMC Place; PALO PINTO; **238** EE-5; mail Palo Pinto z 76484; ● 100
Lone Cedar; RMC Place; ELLIS; ***238** EF-8; mail Blooming Grove z 76626; rural
Lone Elm; RMC Place; ELLIS; ***238** EE-7; ★ **D-FW**; mail Waxahachie z 75167; rural
Lone Grove; RMC Place; LLANO; ***238** EI-4; mail Llano z 78643; rural
Lone Oak; RMC Place; BEXAR; ***239** EL-5; ★ **SANT**; mail Adkins z 78101; rural
Lone Oak; RMC Place; COLORADO; ***239** EK-8; mail Fayetteville z 78940
Lone Oak; RMC Place; ERATH; ***238** EF-5; mail Dublin z 76446; rural
Lone Oak; Inc. Place; HUNT; **238** ED-9; 🅿; z 75453; Ⓟ 521; © 521
Lone Pine; RMC Place; ANDERSON; ***238** EF-10; mail Palestine z 75801; rural
Lone Pine; RMC Place; UPSHUR; ***238** ED-11; mail Gilmer z 75644; rural
Lone Star; RMC Place; FLOYD; ***236** WF-11; elev. 3,267ft./996m.; mail Lockney z 79241; rural
Lone Star; RMC Place; KAUFMAN; ***238** EE-8; mail Kaufman z 75142; rural
Lone Star; Inc. Place; MORRIS; **238** ED-11; 🅿; z 75668; Ⓟ 1,615; © 1,631
Lone Star (Asander); RMC Place; TITUS; ***238** EC-11; elev. 369ft./112m.; mail Cookville z 75558; rural
Long Branch; RMC Place; PANOLA; **238** EF-12; elev. 378ft./115m.; 🅿; z 75669; ● 120
Longfellow; RMC Place; PECOS; ***237** WO-9; mail Sanderson z 79848; rural
Long Hollow; RMC Place; LEON; ***238** EH-8; mail Marquez z 77865; rural
Longhorn; RMC Place; BEXAR; ***239** EL-5; ★ **SANT**; pop. incl. with San Antonio (Inc. Place)
Long Lake; RMC Place; ANDERSON; **238** EG-9; mail Palestine z 75801; ● 50
Long Lake; RMC Place; MONTGOMERY; ***238** EJ-10; ★ **HOU**; mail Magnolia z 77354; ● 75
Long Mott; RMC Place; CALHOUN; **239** EN-8; elev. 27ft./8m.; 🅿; z 77979; ● 125
Long Point; RMC Place; HARRIS; ★ **HOU**; mail Houston z 77055, z 77255; pop. incl. with Houston (Inc. Place)
Long Point; RMC Place; HARRISON; ***238** ED-12; mail Karnack z 75661; ● 100

Entries in **UPPERCASE** are counties.
Entries in **bold** have populations of 2,500 or more.
Names in parentheses are alternate names.
Inc. Place — Incorporated Place
RMC Place — Rand McNally Designated Place
CDP — Census Designated Place
MCD — Minor Civil Division

⊡ County Seat
▲ Minor Civil Division
elev. Elevation
🅿 Post Office

🄷 Hospital
🄲 College
■ Principal Business Center
★ Ranally Metro Area (RMA) Abbreviation
z Zip Code(s)

Ⓟ Previous Census Population
Ⓡ Revised Census Population
Ⓐ Annexation Population
● Rand McNally Population Estimate
© Final Census Population
Ⓢ Special Census Population
◆ Estimated Population

For additional definitions see Glossary, Volume 1, and Introduction, Volume 2.

Longpoint; RMC Place; WASHINGTON; **238** EJ-8; mail Burton z 77835; ● 25
Longview; Inc. Place; ⊡ GREGG, HARRISON; **238** EE-11; 🅿 🅷 🅲 3,983 ■; ★ **LNGV**; z 75601-08, z 75615; ℗ 70,311; © 73,344; ◆ 75,338
Longview Heights; RMC Place; HARRISON; ***238** EE-11; ★ **LNGV**; mail Longview z 75601; pop. incl. with Longview (Inc. Place)
Longworth; RMC Place; FISHER; ***238** EE-1; elev. 1,965ft./599m.; mail Roby z 79543, Sweetwater z 79556
Lon Hill; RMC Place; NUECES; ***239** EO-6; ★ **CRPX**; pop. incl. with Corpus Christi (Inc. Place)
Looneyville; RMC Place; NACOGDOCHES; ***238** EF-11; elev. 481ft./147m.; mail Cushing z 75760; rural
Loop; RMC Place; GAINES; **236** WI-9; 🅿; z 79342; ● 500
Lopeno; CDP; ZAPATA; **239** ER-3; 🅿; z 78564; © 140
Lopezville; CDP; HIDALGO; **237** WO-3; elev. 103ft./31m.; ★ **MCAL**; mail San Juan z 78589; ℗ 2,827; © 4,476
Loraine; Inc. Place; MITCHELL; **236** WJ-12; elev. 2,268ft./691m.; 🅿; z 79532; ℗ 731; © 656
Lorena; Inc. Place; MCLENNAN; **238** EH-7; 🅿; ★ **WACO**; z 76655; ℗ 1,158; © 1,433
Lorenzo; Inc. Place; CROSBY; **236** WG-11; elev. 3,167ft./965m.; 🅿; z 79343; ℗ 1,208; © 1,372
Los Alvarez; CDP-Census Area Only; STARR; ***239** ES-4; © 1,434
Los Angeles; RMC Place; LA SALLE; ***239** EN-3; mail Cotulla z 78014
Los Angeles Subdivision; CDP-Census Area Only; WILLACY; ***239** ER-6; © 86
Los Barreras; RMC Place; STARR; ***239** ES-4; mail Rio Grande City z 78582; ● 100
Los Campos; RMC Place; VAL VERDE; **237** WQ-12; mail Del Rio z 78840; ● 100
Los Ebanos; CDP; HIDALGO; **239** ES-4; 🅿; ★ **MCAL**; z 78565; © 403
Los Fresnos; Inc. Place; CAMERON; **239** ES-7; elev. 23ft./7m.; 🅿; ★ **BRNS**; z 78566; ℗ 2,473; © 4,512
Los Indios; Inc. Place; CAMERON; **239** ES-6; 🅿; ★ **BRNS**; z 78567; © 1,149
Los Jardines; RMC Place; BEXAR; ***239** EL-4; ★ **SANT**; mail San Antonio z 78237; pop. incl. with San Antonio (Inc. Place)
Losoya; RMC Place; BEXAR; ***239** EL-4; ★ **SANT**; mail San Antonio z 78221; ● 200
Los Saenz; RMC Place; STARR; mail Roma z 78584; pop. incl. with Roma-Los Saenz (Inc. Place)
Lost Creek; CDP-Census Area Only; TRAVIS; ***238** EJ-6; ★ **AUS**; mail Austin z 78746; ℗ 4,095; © 4,729
Los Velas; RMC Place; STARR; ***239** ES-4; mail Rio Grande City z 78582; ● 50
Los Villareales; CDP-Census Area Only; STARR; ***239** ES-4; © 930
Los Ybanez; Inc. Place; DAWSON; ***236** WJ-10; mail Lamesa z 79331; ℗ 83; © 32
Lott; Inc. Place; FALLS; **238** EH-7; 🅿; z 76656; ℗ 775; © 724
Louise; CDP; WHARTON; **239** EL-8; 🅿; z 77455; © 977
Love Chapel; RMC Place; CASS; ***238** ED-12; mail Hughes Springs z 75656; rural
Lovelace; RMC Place; HILL; **238** EF-7; elev. 647ft./197m.; mail Hillsboro z 76645; ● 50
Lovelady; Inc. Place; HOUSTON; **238** EH-10; 🅿; z 75851; ℗ 587; © 608
Lovell Lake; RMC Place; JEFFERSON; ***238** EJ-13; mail Beaumont z 77705; rural
Lovers Lane; RMC Place; DALLAS; mail Dallas z 75360; pop. incl. with Dallas (Inc. Place)
Loving; RMC Place; YOUNG; **238** EC-4; 🅿; z 76460; ● 250
LOVING; **237** WK-7; ℗ 107; © 67; ◆ 48
Lowake; RMC Place; CONCHO; **237** WL-13; elev. 1,750ft./533m.; 🅿; z 76855; ● 25
Lowry Crossing; Inc. Place; COLLIN; **238** ED-8; ★ **D-FW**; mail Mckinney z 75069; ℗ 865; © 1,229
Loyal Valley; RMC Place; MASON; mail Mason z 76856; rural
Loyola Beach; RMC Place; KLEBERG; **239** EP-6; mail Riviera z 78379; ● 130
Lozano; CDP; CAMERON; ***239** ES-6; 🅿; z 78568; © 324
Lubbock; Inc. Place; ⊡ LUBBOCK; **236** WH-10; 🅿 🅷 🅲 32,454 ■; ★ **LUB**; z 79401-16, z 79423-24, z 79430, z 79452-53, z 79457, z 79464, z 79490-91, z 79493, z 79499; ℗ 186,206; © 199,564; ◆ 228,217
LUBBOCK; **236** WG-10; ℗ 222,636; © 242,628; ◆ 272,430
Lucas; Inc. Place; COLLIN; **238** ED-8; elev. 571ft./174m.; 🅿; ★ **D-FW**; z 75002; ℗ 2,205; © 2,890
Luckenbach; RMC Place; GILLESPIE; ***238** EJ-3; mail Fredericksburg z 78624
Lucky Ridge; RMC Place; WISE; ***238** ED-6; mail Boyd z 76023; rural
Lueders; Inc. Place; JONES, SHACKELFORD; **236** WI-14; elev. 1,567ft./478m.; 🅿; z 79533; ℗ 365; © 300
Luella; RMC Place; GRAYSON; ***238** EC-8; ★ **SHRM-**; mail Sherman z 75090; ● 150
Lufkin; Inc. Place; ⊡ ANGELINA; **238** EG-11; elev. 316ft./96m.; 🅿 🅷 ■; ★ **LUFK**; z 75901-04, z 75915; ℗ 30,206; © 32,709; ◆ 32,685
Luling; Inc. Place; CALDWELL; **239** EK-6; 🅿 🅷; z 78648; ℗ 4,661; © 5,080
Lull; RMC Place; HIDALGO; ***239** ES-5; ★ **MCAL**; mail Edinburg z 78539; pop. incl. with Edinburg (Inc. Place)
Lumberton; Inc. Place; HARDIN; **238** EJ-13; 🅿; ★ **B-PA**; z 77657; ℗ 6,640; © 8,731
Lumkins; RMC Place; ELLIS; ***238** EF-7; mail Forreston z 76041; rural
Lums Chapel; RMC Place; LAMB; ***236** WG-9; elev. 3,491ft./1,064m.; mail Littlefield z 79339; rural
Lund; RMC Place; TRAVIS; ***238** EJ-6; mail Elgin z 78621; rural
Luther; RMC Place; HOWARD; ***236** WJ-11; elev. 2,688ft./819m.; mail Big Spring z 79720; rural
Lutie; RMC Place; COLLINGSWORTH; **236** WE-13; elev. 2,233ft./681m.; mail Shamrock z 79079; ● 30
Lydia; RMC Place; RED RIVER; **238** EC-11; mail Avery z 75554, De Kalb z 75559; ● 75
Lyford; Inc. Place; WILLACY; **239** ES-6; elev. 36ft./11m.; 🅿; z 78569; ℗ 1,674; © 1,973
Lyford South; CDP-Census Area Only; WILLACY; ***239** ES-6; © 172
LYNN; **236** WH-10; ℗ 6,758; © 6,550; ◆ 5,398
Lynn Grove; RMC Place; GRIMES; ***238** EJ-9; mail Navasota z 77868; rural
Lyons; RMC Place; BURLESON; **238** EJ-8; elev. 341ft./104m.; 🅿; z 77863; ● 300
Lytle; Inc. Place; ATASCOSA, BEXAR, MEDINA; **239** EL-4; elev. 725ft./221m.; 🅿; z 78052; ℗ 2,255; © 2,383
Lytton Springs; RMC Place; CALDWELL; ***239** EK-6; elev. 603ft./184m.; mail Dale z 78616; ● 150

M

Mabank; Inc. Place; KAUFMAN, HENDERSON; **238** EE-9; elev. 398ft./121m.; 🅿; z 75147, z 75156; ℗ 1,739; © 2,151
Mabelle; RMC Place; BAYLOR; ***238** EC-3; elev. 1,289ft./393m.; mail Seymour z 76380; rural
Mabry; RMC Place; HARRIS; ★ **HOU**; pop. incl. with Houston (Inc. Place)
Mabry; RMC Place; RED RIVER; ***238** EB-10; elev. 434ft./132m.; mail Clarksville z 75426; rural
Macdona; RMC Place; BEXAR; **239** EL-4; elev. 630ft./192m.; 🅿; ★ **SANT**; z 78054; ● 300
Macedonia; RMC Place; AUSTIN; ***239** EK-9; mail Sealy z 77474; rural
Macedonia; RMC Place; BOWIE; ***238** EC-12; ★ **TEXR-**; mail Texarkana z 75501; ● 200
Macedonia; RMC Place; BRAZORIA; mail Brazoria z 77422; rural
Macedonia; RMC Place; LIBERTY; ***238** EJ-11; mail Cleveland z 77327; rural
Macey; RMC Place; BRAZOS; ***238** EH-9; mail Hearne z 77859; rural
Mackay; RMC Place; WHARTON; ***239** EL-9; elev. 99ft./30m.; mail Wharton z 77488; pop. incl. with Wharton (Inc. Place)
Macon; RMC Place; FRANKLIN; ***238** ED-10; elev. 458ft./140m.; mail Mount Vernon z 75457; rural
Macune; RMC Place; SAN AUGUSTINE; ***238** EG-12; mail San Augustine z 75972; rural
Madero; RMC Place; HIDALGO; **237** WP-1; ★ **MCAL**; mail Mission z 78572; pop. incl. with Mission (Inc. Place)
MADISON; **238** EH-9; ℗ 10,931; © 12,940; ◆ 13,684
Madisonville; Inc. Place; ⊡ MADISON; **238** EH-9; elev. 272ft./83m.; 🅿 🅷; z 77864; ℗ 3,569; © 4,159
Madras; RMC Place; RED RIVER; ***238** EB-11; mail Clarksville z 75426; rural
Magasco; RMC Place; SABINE; **238** EG-13; elev. 300ft./91m.; mail Pineland z 75968; ● 50
Magic; RMC Place; BEXAR; ★ **SANT**; mail San Antonio z 78229, z 78280; pop. incl. with San Antonio (Inc. Place)
Maglab; RMC Place; DALLAS; ★ **D-FW**; pop. incl. with Dallas (Inc. Place)
Magnet; RMC Place; WHARTON; **239** EL-9; mail Wharton z 77488; ● 80
Magnolia; Inc. Place; MONTGOMERY; **238** EJ-10; 🅿; ★ **HOU**; z 77353-55; ℗ 940; © 1,111
Magnolia; RMC Place; SAN JACINTO; ***238** EI-11; mail Cleveland z 77327; rural
Magnolia Beach; RMC Place; CALHOUN; **239** EN-8; mail Port Lavaca z 77979; ● 200
Magnolia Bend; RMC Place; MONTGOMERY; ***238** EJ-10; ★ **HOU**; mail Conroe z 77302; ● 300
Magnolia Hills; RMC Place; MONTGOMERY; ***238** EJ-10; ★ **HOU**; mail Magnolia z 77354
Magnolia Park; RMC Place; HARRIS; ***239** EK-11; elev. 34ft./10m.; ★ **HOU**; mail Houston z 77011-12; pop. incl. with Houston (Inc. Place)
Magnolia Springs; RMC Place; JASPER; **238** EI-13; elev. 173ft./53m.; 🅿; z 75956; ● 120
Mahl; RMC Place; NACOGDOCHES; ***238** EF-11; mail Nacogdoches z 75964; rural
Mahomet; RMC Place; BURNET; ***238** EI-5; mail Bertram z 78605; rural
Mahoney; RMC Place; HOPKINS; ***238** EC-10; elev. 420ft./128m.; mail Sulphur Springs z 75482; rural
Main Place; RMC Place; DALLAS; ***238** ED-7; ★ **D-FW**; mail Dallas z 75202, z 75250; pop. incl. with Dallas (Inc. Place)
Majors; RMC Place; FRANKLIN; ***238** ED-10; elev. 477ft./145m.; mail Mount Vernon z 75457; ● 20
Malakoff; Inc. Place; HENDERSON; **238** EF-9; 🅿; z 75148; ℗ 2,038; © 2,257
Mallard; RMC Place; MONTAGUE; ***238** EC-6; elev. 987ft./301m.; mail Montague z 76251; rural
Malone; Inc. Place; HILL; **238** EF-7; elev. 481ft./147m.; 🅿; z 76660; ℗ 306; © 278
Malta; RMC Place; BOWIE; **238** EC-11; mail New Boston z 75570; ● 150
Mambrino; RMC Place; HOOD; ***238** EE-6; elev. 819ft./250m.; mail Granbury z 76048; rural
Manchaca; RMC Place; TRAVIS; **238** EJ-6; elev. 697ft./212m.; 🅿; ★ **AUS**; z 78652; ● 1,500
Manchester; RMC Place; HARRIS; ***239** EK-11; ★ **HOU**; mail Houston z 77012; pop. incl. with Houston (Inc. Place)
Manchester; RMC Place; RED RIVER; **238** EB-10; elev. 460ft./140m.; mail Bagwell z 75412; ● 100
Manda; RMC Place; TRAVIS; ***238** EJ-6; mail Manor z 78653; rural
Manheim; RMC Place; LEE; ***238** EJ-7; mail Paige z 78659; rural
Mankin; RMC Place; HENDERSON; ***238** EF-9; mail Trinidad z 75163; rural
Mankins; RMC Place; ARCHER; **238** EB-4; elev. 1,114ft./340m.; mail Holliday z 76366; ● 20
Mann's Crossing; RMC Place; BEXAR; ***239** EL-4; ★ **SANT**; mail San Antonio z 78252; rural
Manor; Inc. Place; TRAVIS; **238** EJ-6; elev. 528ft./161m.; 🅿; ★ **AUS**; z 78653; ℗ 1,041; © 1,204
Mansfield; Inc. Place; TARRANT, ELLIS, JOHNSON; **238** EE-7; 🅿 🅷; ★ **D-FW**; z 76063; ℗ 15,607; © 28,031; ◆ 44,808
Mansfield Dam; TRAVIS; see Marshall Ford (RMC Place)
Manvel; Inc. Place; BRAZORIA; **234** H-5; 🅿; ★ **HOU**; z 77578; ℗ 3,733; © 3,046
Maple; RMC Place; BAILEY; **236** WG-8; 🅿; z 79344; ● 100
Maple; RMC Place; RED RIVER; ***238** EC-11; mail Bogata z 75417; rural
Maple Crest Acres; RMC Place; ORANGE; ***238** EJ-13; ★ **B-PA**; mail Vidor z 77662; pop. incl. with Vidor (Inc. Place)
Maple Springs; RMC Place; TITUS; ***238** EC-11; mail Mount Pleasant z 75455; rural
Mapleton; RMC Place; HOUSTON; **238** EH-10; mail Crockett z 75835; ● 30
Mara; RMC Place; TARRANT; ★ **D-FW**; pop. incl. with Fort Worth (Inc. Place)
Marathon; CDP; BREWSTER; **237** WO-7; elev. 4,045ft./1,233m.; 🅿; z 79842; © 455
Marble Falls; Inc. Place; BURNET; **238** EI-5; elev. 821ft./250m.; 🅿; z 78654, z 78657 & mail Spicewood z 78669; ℗ 4,007; © 4,959
Marekville; BELL; see Zabcikville (RMC Place)
Marfa; Inc. Place; ⊡ PRESIDIO; **237** WO-6; 🅿; z 79843; ℗ 2,424; © 2,121
Margaret; RMC Place; FOARD; **238** EB-2; elev. 1,381ft./421m.; mail Crowell z 79227; ● 40
Marie; RMC Place; RUNNELS; ***238** EF-1; elev. 1,850ft./564m.; mail Bronte z 76933; rural
Marietta; Inc. Place; CASS; **238** EC-12; elev. 356ft./109m.; 🅿; z 75566; ℗ 161; © 112
Marion; Inc. Place; GUADALUPE; **239** EL-5; 🅿; ★ **SANT**; z 78124; ℗ 984; © 1,099
MARION; **238** ED-12; ℗ 9,984; © 10,941; ◆ 10,580
Market East; RMC Place; DALLAS; ***238** ED-8; ★ **D-FW**; mail Mesquite z 75150; pop. incl. with Mesquite (Inc. Place)
Markham; CDP; MATAGORDA; **239** EM-9; elev. 55ft./17m.; 🅿; z 77456; ℗ 1,206; © 1,138
Markley; RMC Place; YOUNG; ***238** EC-4; elev. 1,113ft./339m.; mail Loving z 76460; ● 30
Marlin; Inc. Place; ⊡ FALLS; **238** EH-7; 🅿 🅷; z 76661; ℗ 6,386; © 6,628
Marquez; Inc. Place; LEON; **238** EH-8; 🅿; z 77865; ℗ 270; © 220
Marshall; Inc. Place; ⊡ HARRISON; **238** EE-12; 🅿 🅷 🅲 2,208 ■; ★ **MAR**; z 75670-72; ℗ 23,682; © 23,935; ◆ 23,044
Marshall Creek; Inc. Place; DENTON; ***238** ED-7; ★ **D-FW**; mail Roanoke z 76262; ℗ 315; © 431
Marshall Ford (Mansfield Dam); RMC Place; TRAVIS; **238** EJ-5; ★ **AUS**; mail Austin z 78732; pop. incl. with Austin (Inc. Place)
Marshall Meadows; RMC Place; BEXAR; ***239** EL-4; ★ **SANT**; mail San Antonio z 78240; pop. incl. with San Antonio (Inc. Place)
Marshall Springs; RMC Place; TITUS; ***238** EC-11; mail Mount Pleasant z 75455; rural
Marston; RMC Place; POLK; ***238** EI-11; mail Livingston z 77351; ● 50
Mart; Inc. Place; MCLENNAN; **238** EG-7; elev. 533ft./162m.; 🅿; z 76664; ℗ 2,004; © 2,273
MARTIN; **236** WJ-10; ℗ 4,956; © 4,746; ◆ 4,518
Martindale; Inc. Place; CALDWELL; **239** EK-6; elev. 528ft./161m.; 🅿; z 78655; ℗ 904; © 953
Martinez; RMC Place; BEXAR; ***239** EL-5; ★ **SANT**; mail San Antonio z 78219
Martin Luther King; RMC Place; HARRIS; ***239** EK-10; ★ **HOU**; mail Houston z 77051, z 77233; pop. incl. with Houston (Inc. Place)
Martins Mills; RMC Place; VAN ZANDT; ***238** EE-9; mail Ben Wheeler z 75754; ● 125
Martin Springs; RMC Place; HOPKINS; ***238** ED-10; mail Sulphur Springs z 75482; ● 100
Martinsville; RMC Place; NACOGDOCHES; **238** EG-12; elev. 284ft./87m.; 🅿; z 75958; ● 130
Marvin; RMC Place; LAMAR; ***238** EB-10; mail Paris z 75462; rural
Maryneal; RMC Place; NOLAN; **237** WK-13; elev. 2,568ft./783m.; 🅿; z 79535; ● 120
Marysville; RMC Place; COOKE; ***238** EB-6; elev. 876ft./267m.; mail Muenster z 76252
Mason; Inc. Place; ⊡ MASON; **238** EI-3; elev. 1,538ft./469m.; 🅿; z 76856; ℗ 2,041; © 2,134
Mason; RMC Place; SABINE; ***238** EG-13; mail Hemphill z 75948; rural
MASON; **238** EI-3; ℗ 3,423; © 3,738; ◆ 3,922
Mason Lake Estates; RMC Place; LIBERTY; ***238** EI-11; mail Cleveland z 77327; ● 100
Massey Lake; RMC Place; ANDERSON; **238** EF-9; mail Tennessee Colony z 75861; ● 75
Masterson; RMC Place; MOORE; **236** WC-10; 🅿; z 79058 & mail Channing z 79018; ● 40
Matador; Inc. Place; ⊡ MOTLEY; **236** WG-12; 🅿; z 79244; ℗ 790; © 740
Matagorda; RMC Place; MATAGORDA; **239** EM-9; 🅿; z 77457; ● 850
MATAGORDA; **239** EM-10; ℗ 36,928; © 37,957; ◆ 36,481
Mathis; Inc. Place; SAN PATRICIO; **239** EO-6; 🅿; z 78368; ℗ 5,423; © 5,034
Matinburg; RMC Place; CAMP; ***238** ED-11; mail Pittsburg z 75686; rural
Matthews; RMC Place; COLORADO; ***239** EL-9; mail Eagle Lake z 77434; rural
Maud; Inc. Place; BOWIE; **238** EC-12; 🅿; ★ **TEXR-**; z 75567; ℗ 1,049; © 1,028
Mauriceville; CDP; ORANGE; **238** EJ-13; 🅿; ★ **B-PA**; z 77626; ℗ 2,046; © 2,743
Maverick; RMC Place; RUNNELS; ***238** EG-1; mail Norton z 76865
MAVERICK; **237** WQ-13; ℗ 36,378; © 47,297; ◆ 52,113
Maxdale; RMC Place; BELL; ***238** EH-6; mail Killeen z 76542; rural
Maxey; RMC Place; LAMAR; ***238** EB-9; mail Brookston z 75421; rural
Maxwell; RMC Place; CALDWELL; **239** EK-6; elev. 590ft./180m.; 🅿; z 78656; ● 350
May; RMC Place; BROWN; **238** EF-3; 🅿; z 76857; ● 300
Maydelle; RMC Place; CHEROKEE; **238** EF-10; 🅿; z 75772; ● 250
Mayfair; RMC Place; HARRIS; ***239** EK-10; ★ **HOU**; mail Houston z 77087; pop. incl. with Houston (Inc. Place)
Mayfair Terrace; RMC Place; VICTORIA; ***239** EM-7; mail Victoria z 77901; pop. incl. with Victoria (Inc. Place)
Mayfield; RMC Place; HALE; ***236** WG-10; mail Hale Center z 79041; rural
Mayfield; RMC Place; HILL; ***238** EF-7; elev. 706ft./215m.; mail Itasca z 76055; rural
Mayflower; RMC Place; NEWTON; ***238** EH-13; mail Wiergate z 75977; rural
Mayflower; RMC Place; RUSK; ***238** EE-12; mail Tatum z 75691; ● 100
Maynard; RMC Place; SAN JACINTO; ***238** EI-10; mail New Waverly z 77358; rural
Maypearl; Inc. Place; ELLIS; **238** EE-7; elev. 527ft./161m.; 🅿; z 76064; ℗ 781; © 746
Maysfield; RMC Place; MILAM; **238** EI-7; 🅿; z 76520; ● 130
McAdoo; RMC Place; DICKENS; **236** WG-12; elev. 2,984ft./910m.; 🅿; z 79243; ● 100
McAllen; Inc. Place; HIDALGO; **239** ES-5; elev. 121ft./37m.; 🅿 🅷 🅲 16,227 ■; ★ **MCAL**; z 78501-05; ℗ 84,021; © 106,414; ◆ 127,022
McBeth; RMC Place; BRAZORIA; mail Angleton z 77515; rural
McCamey; Inc. Place; UPTON; **237** WM-9; elev. 2,441ft./744m.; 🅿 🅷; z 79752; ℗ 2,493; © 1,805
McCaulley; RMC Place; FISHER; **236** WI-13; 🅿; z 79534; ● 200
McClanahan; RMC Place; FALLS; ***238** EH-7; mail Marlin z 76661; rural
McCook; RMC Place; HIDALGO; **239** ER-5; elev. 304ft./93m.; mail Edinburg z 78539; ● 90
McCoy; RMC Place; ATASCOSA; **239** EM-5; elev. 302ft./92m.; ● 20
McCoy; RMC Place; FLOYD; ***236** WG-11; mail Floydada z 79235; rural
MCCULLOCH; **238** EH-2; ℗ 8,778; © 8,205; ◆ 7,595
McDade; RMC Place; BASTROP; **238** EJ-7; 🅿; z 78650; ● 475
McDonough; RMC Place; HARRIS; ★ **HOU**; pop. incl. with Houston (Inc. Place)
McElroy; RMC Place; SABINE; ***238** EH-13; mail Pineland z 75968; rural
McFaddin; RMC Place; VICTORIA; **239** EN-7; elev. 76ft./23m.; 🅿; z 77973; ● 175
McGee Landing; RMC Place; SABINE; ***238** EG-13; mail Hemphill z 75948; ● 25
McGregor; Inc. Place; MCLENNAN, CORYELL; **238** EG-6; 🅿; z 76657; ℗ 4,683; © 4,727
McKenzie; RMC Place; MARION; ***238** ED-11; mail Avinger z 75630; ● 30
McKibben; RMC Place; HANSFORD; ***236** WB-11; mail Spearman z 79081; rural
McKinney; Inc. Place; ⊡ COLLIN; **238** EC-8; 🅿 🅷; ★ **D-FW**; z 75069-71; ℗ 21,283; © 54,369; ◆ 136,046
McKinney Acres; RMC Place; ANDREWS; ***236** WJ-9; mail Andrews z 79714; ● 200
McKnight; RMC Place; RUSK; ***238** EF-11; elev. 387ft./118m.; mail Henderson z 75652, z 75654; rural
McLean; Inc. Place; GRAY; **236** WD-13; elev. 2,860ft./872m.; 🅿; z 79057; ℗ 849; © 830
McLendon; RMC Place; ROCKWALL; ***238** ED-8; elev. 502ft./153m.; mail Rockwall z 75087; pop. incl. with McLendon-Chisholm (Inc. Place)
McLendon-Chisholm; Inc. Place; ROCKWALL; ***238** ED-8; mail Rockwall z 75087; ℗ 646; © 914
MCLENNAN; **238** EG-7; ℗ 189,123; © 213,517; ◆ 231,476
McLeod; RMC Place; CASS; **238** ED-12; 🅿; z 75565; ● 250
McMahan; RMC Place; CALDWELL; **239** EK-6; 🅿; z 78616; ● 60
McMillin; RMC Place; SAN SABA; mail San Saba z 76877; rural
MCMULLEN; **239** EN-4; ℗ 817; © 851; ◆ 919
McNair; RMC Place; HARRIS; **234** D-9; ★ **HOU**; mail Baytown z 77520-21; ● 1,400
McNair Village; RMC Place; BELL; ***238** EH-6; ★ **KILL-**; mail Killeen z 76544
McNary; RMC Place; HUDSPETH; ***237** WL-3; mail Fort Hancock z 79839; rural
McNeil; RMC Place; CALDWELL; ***239** EK-6; elev. 388ft./118m.; mail Luling z 78648; rural
McNeil; RMC Place; TRAVIS; ***238** EJ-6; 🅿; ★ **AUS**; z 78651; ● 30
McNorton; RMC Place; NUECES; ***239** EO-6; mail Corpus Christi z 78409; pop. incl. with Corpus Christi (Inc. Place)
McQueeney; CDP; GUADALUPE; **239** EK-5; 🅿; z 78123; ℗ 2,063; © 2,527
Meador Grove; RMC Place; BELL; ***238** EH-6; elev. 713ft./217m.; mail Moody z 76557; rural
Meadow; Inc. Place; TERRY; **236** WH-10; elev. 3,330ft./1,015m.; 🅿; z 79345; ℗ 547; © 658
Meadowcreek; RMC Place; FORT BEND; ***239** EK-10; ★ **HOU**; mail Missouri City z 77459; pop. incl. with Missouri City (Inc. Place)
Meadowcreek; RMC Place; TOM GREEN; ***237** WL-13; ★ **SANG**; mail San Angelo z 76904; pop. incl. with San Angelo (Inc. Place)
Meadowlakes; Inc. Place; BURNET; ***238** EI-5; 🅿; z 78654 & mail Burnet z 78611; ℗ 514; © 1,293
Meadowood Acres; RMC Place; BEXAR; **239** ET-9; ★ **SANT**; mail San Antonio z 78252; ● 500
Meadows; FORT BEND; see Meadows Place (Inc. Place)
Meadows Place (Meadows); Inc. Place; FORT BEND; **234** F-2; 🅿; ★ **HOU**; z 77477; ℗ 4,606; © 4,912
Mecca; RMC Place; MADISON; ***238** EH-9; mail Normangee z 77871; rural
Medicine Mound; RMC Place; HARDEMAN; **238** EA-2; elev. 1,486ft./453m.; mail Quanah z 79252; ● 30
Medill; RMC Place; LAMAR; ***238** EB-10; mail Paris z 75460; rural
Medina; RMC Place; BANDERA; **239** EK-3; elev. 1,445ft./440m.; 🅿; z 78055; ● 450
Medina; CDP-Census Area Only; ZAPATA; ***239** EQ-3; © 2,960
MEDINA; **239** EL-3; ℗ 27,312; © 39,304; ◆ 44,852
Medio; RMC Place; HARRIS; ★ **HOU**; pop. incl. with Houston (Inc. Place)
Meeker; RMC Place; JEFFERSON; ***238** EJ-12; ★ **B-PA**; mail Beaumont z 77706; ● 100
Meeks; RMC Place; BELL; ***238** EH-7; mail Burlington z 76519; rural
Megargel; Inc. Place; ARCHER; **238** EC-3; elev. 1,286ft./392m.; 🅿; z 76370; ℗ 244; © 248
Megaron; RMC Place; LUBBOCK; ★ **LUB**; mail Lubbock z 79423, z 79453; pop. incl. with Lubbock (Inc. Place)
Melear; RMC Place; TARRANT; ★ **D-FW**; mail Arlington z 76015-17; pop. incl. with Arlington (Inc. Place)
Melissa; Inc. Place; COLLIN; **238** EC-8; 🅿; z 75454 & mail Mckinney z 75071; ℗ 557; © 1,350
Melody Hills; RMC Place; TARRANT; ***238** ED-6; ★ **D-FW**; mail Fort Worth z 76137; pop. incl. with Fort Worth (Inc. Place)
Melrose; RMC Place; NACOGDOCHES; ***238** EG-12; elev. 365ft./111m.; mail Nacogdoches z 75961
Melrose Park; RMC Place; HARRIS; ***239** EK-10; ★ **HOU**; mail Houston z 77037; pop. incl. with Houston (Inc. Place)
Melvin; Inc. Place; MCCULLOCH; **238** EH-2; 🅿; z 76858; ℗ 184; © 155
Memorial Bend; RMC Place; HARRIS; ***239** EK-10; ★ **HOU**; mail Houston z 77042; pop. incl. with Houston (Inc. Place)
Memorial Park; RMC Place; HARRIS; ★ **HOU**; mail Houston z 77024, z 77224, z 77279; pop. incl. with Houston (Inc. Place)
Memphis; Inc. Place; ⊡ HALL; **236** WE-13; elev. 2,062ft./628m.; 🅿 🅷; z 79245; ℗ 2,465; © 2,479
Menard; Inc. Place; ⊡ MENARD; **237** WN-14; elev. 1,886ft./575m.; 🅿; z 76859; ℗ 1,606; © 1,653
MENARD; **238** EI-2; ℗ 2,252; © 2,360; ◆ 2,044
Mendiates; RMC Place; DUVAL; ***239** EO-5; mail Orange Grove z 78372; rural
Mendoza; RMC Place; CALDWELL; ***239** EK-6; elev. 618ft./188m.; mail Lockhart z 78644; rural
Menlow; RMC Place; HILL; ***238** EF-7; elev. 597ft./182m.; mail Abbott z 76621; rural
Mentone; RMC Place; ⊡ LOVING; **237** WL-7; elev. 2,685ft./818m.; 🅿; z 79754; ● 90
Mentz; RMC Place; COLORADO; ***239** EK-8; mail Alleyton z 78935; rural
Mercedes; Inc. Place; HIDALGO; **239** ES-6; 🅿; ★ **MCAL**; z 78570; ℗ 12,694; © 13,649
Mercers Gap; RMC Place; COMANCHE; ***238** EG-4; mail Comanche z 76442; rural
Mercury; RMC Place; MCCULLOCH; **238** EG-3; mail Rochelle z 76872; ● 50
Mereta; RMC Place; TOM GREEN; **237** WL-13; elev. 1,755ft./535m.; 🅿; z 76940; ● 200
Meridian; Inc. Place; ⊡ BOSQUE; **238** EF-6; 🅿; z 76665; ℗ 1,390; © 1,491
Merit; RMC Place; HUNT; ***238** EC-8; 🅿; z 75458; ● 225
Merkel; Inc. Place; TAYLOR; **236** WJ-14; elev. 1,870ft./570m.; 🅿; z 79536; ℗ 2,469; © 2,637
Merle; RMC Place; BURLESON; ***238** EI-8; mail Somerville z 77879; rural
Mertens; Inc. Place; HILL; **238** EF-7; elev. 541ft./165m.; 🅿; z 76666; ℗ 104; © 146
Mertzon; Inc. Place; ⊡ IRION; **237** WM-12; 🅿; z 76941; ℗ 778; © 839
Mesa Hills; RMC Place; EL PASO; mail El Paso z 79902, z 79912; pop. incl. with El Paso (Inc. Place)
Mesa Verde; RMC Place; POTTER; ★ **AMA**; mail Amarillo z 79107; pop. incl. with Amarillo (Inc. Place)
Mesquite; RMC Place; BORDEN; ***236** WI-11; elev. 2,962ft./903m.; mail Odonnell z 79351; rural
Mesquite; Inc. Place; DALLAS; **238** ED-8; 🅿 🅷 ■; ★ **D-FW**; z 75149-50, z 75180-82, z 75185, z 75187; ℗ 101,484; © 124,523; ◆ 136,194
Metcalf Gap; RMC Place; PALO PINTO; ***238** EE-4; mail Strawn z 76475; rural
Meusebach Creek; RMC Place; GILLESPIE; ***238** EJ-4; mail Fredericksburg z 78624; rural
Mexia; Inc. Place; LIMESTONE; **238** EG-8; 🅿 🅷; z 76667; ℗ 6,933; © 6,563
Meyerland; RMC Place; HARRIS; ***239** EK-10; ★ **HOU**; mail Houston z 77096; pop. incl. with Houston (Inc. Place)
Meyersville; RMC Place; DEWITT; **239** EM-7; elev. 232ft./71m.; 🅿; z 77974; ● 120
Miami; Inc. Place; ⊡ ROBERTS; **236** WC-12; 🅿; z 79059; ℗ 675; © 588
Mico; RMC Place; MEDINA; **239** EL-4; 🅿; z 78056; ● 100
Midcity; RMC Place; LAMAR; ***238** EB-10; elev. 518ft./158m.; mail Powderly z 75473; rural
Middlegate Village; RMC Place; HARRIS; ***239** EK-10; ★ **HOU**; mail Houston z 77095; ● 1,400
Middleton; RMC Place; LEON; ***238** EH-9; elev. 266ft./81m.; mail Centerville z 75833
Middletowne; RMC Place; GUADALUPE; mail Seguin z 78155; pop. incl. with Seguin (Inc. Place)
Middle Water; RMC Place; HARTLEY; ***236** WC-9; mail Dalhart z 79022; rural
Midfield; RMC Place; MATAGORDA; **239** EM-9; elev. 49ft./15m.; 🅿; z 77458; ● 150
Midkiff; RMC Place; UPTON; **237** WL-10; 🅿; z 79755; ● 180
Mid Lake Village; RMC Place; SABINE; ***238** EG-13; mail Hemphill z 75948; ● 200
Midland; Inc. Place; ⊡ MIDLAND, MARTIN; **237** WK-10; elev. 2,839ft./865m.; 🅿 🅷 🅲 5,801 ■; ★ **MIDL-**; z 79701-08, z 79710-12; ℗ 89,443; © 94,996; ◆ 107,795
MIDLAND; **237** WK-10; ℗ 106,611; © 116,009; ◆ 130,063
Midline; RMC Place; MONTGOMERY; ***238** EJ-11; ★ **HOU**; mail Cleveland z 77327; rural
Midlothian; Inc. Place; ELLIS; **238** EE-7; elev. 755ft./230m.; 🅿; ★ **D-FW**; z 76065 & mail Mansfield z 76063; ℗ 5,141; © 7,480
Midway; RMC Place; CASS; ***238** EC-12; mail Douglassville z 75560; rural
Midway; RMC Place; DAWSON; ***236** WJ-10; elev. 2,897ft./883m.; mail Lamesa z 79331; rural
Midway; RMC Place; FANNIN; ***238** EC-8; mail Bonham z 75418; ● 10
Midway; RMC Place; HOWARD; ***237** WK-11; mail Big Spring z 79720; ● 100
Midway; RMC Place; JIM WELLS; ***239** EO-5; mail Orange Grove z 78372; rural
Midway; RMC Place; LAVACA; ***239** EL-7; elev. 395ft./120m.; mail Shiner z 77984
Midway; RMC Place; LUBBOCK; ***236** WH-11; elev. 3,084ft./940m.; mail Slaton z 79364; rural
Midway; Inc. Place; MADISON; **238** EH-9; 🅿; z 75850, z 75852; ℗ 274; © 288
Midway; RMC Place; MONTGOMERY; ***238** EJ-10; ★ **HOU**; mail Cleveland z 77327; ● 100
Midway; RMC Place; SCURRY; ***236** WJ-12; elev. 2,250ft./686m.; mail Hermleigh z 79526; rural
Midway; RMC Place; SMITH; ***238** EE-11; mail Winona z 75792; rural
Midway; RMC Place; TITUS; ***238** EC-11; elev. 338ft./103m.; mail Mount Pleasant z 75455
Midway; RMC Place; UPSHUR; ***238** ED-11; elev. 374ft./114m.; mail Gilmer z 75644; rural
Midway; RMC Place; VAN ZANDT; ***238** EE-10; elev. 570ft./174m.; mail Ben Wheeler z 75754; rural
Midway North; CDP-Census Area Only; HIDALGO; ***239** ES-5; ★ **MCAL**; © 3,946
Midway South; CDP-Census Area Only; HIDALGO; ***239** ES-5; ★ **MCAL**; © 1,711
Midwest; RMC Place; LUBBOCK; mail Lubbock z 79407, z 79414; rural
Midyett; RMC Place; PANOLA; ***238** EE-12; mail De Berry z 75639; ● 100
Miguel; RMC Place; FRIO; ***239** EM-4; elev. 528ft./161m.; mail Bigfoot z 78005; rural
Mila Doce; CDP-Census Area Only; HIDALGO; ***239** ES-6; ★ **MCAL**; mail Elsa z 78543; ℗ 2,089; © 4,907
Milam; CDP; SABINE; **238** EG-13; 🅿; z 75959; © 1,329
MILAM; **238** EI-7; ℗ 22,946; © 24,238; ◆ 24,508
Milano; Inc. Place; MILAM; **238** EI-7; 🅿; z 76556; ℗ 408; © 400
Milburn; RMC Place; MCCULLOCH; ***238** EG-3; mail Rochelle z 76872; rural
Milby; RMC Place; TRAVIS; ★ **AUS**; pop. incl. with Austin (Inc. Place)
Mildred; Inc. Place; NAVARRO; ***238** EF-8; elev. 431ft./131m.; mail Corsicana z 75110; ℗ 173; © 405
Mile High; RMC Place; HUDSPETH; ***237** WL-3; mail Sierra Blanca z 79851; rural
Miles; Inc. Place; RUNNELS; **237** WL-13; elev. 1,805ft./550m.; 🅿; z 76861; ℗ 793; © 850
Milford; Inc. Place; ELLIS; **238** EF-7; 🅿; z 76670; ℗ 711; © 685
Mill Creek; RMC Place; WASHINGTON; ***238** EJ-8; mail Brenham z 77833; rural
Mill Creek Forest; RMC Place; MONTGOMERY; ***238** EJ-10; ★ **HOU**; mail Magnolia z 77354; ● 500
Miller; RMC Place; DALLAS; ★ **D-FW**; pop. incl. with Dallas (Inc. Place)
Miller Grove; RMC Place; CAMP; **238** ED-9; mail Pittsburg z 75686; ● 100
Miller Grove; RMC Place; HOPKINS; ***238** ED-9; elev. 529ft./161m.; mail Cumby z 75433; ● 125
Millers Cove; Inc. Place; TITUS; ***238** EC-10; mail Mount Pleasant z 75455; ℗ 75; © 120
Millersview; RMC Place; CONCHO; **237** WL-14; elev. 1,643ft./501m.; 🅿; z 76862; ● 100
Millett; RMC Place; LA SALLE; **239** EN-3; mail Cotulla z 78014; ● 40
Millheim; RMC Place; AUSTIN; ***239** EK-9; elev. 23ft./7m.; mail Sealy z 77474; rural
Millican; Inc. Place; BRAZOS; **238** EI-9; 🅿; z 77866; © 108
Mills; RMC Place; GRAYSON; ***238** EB-8; mail Denison z 75020; pop. incl. with Denison (Inc. Place)
MILLS; **238** EG-4; ℗ 4,531; © 5,151; ◆ 5,035
Millsap; Inc. Place; PARKER; **238** EE-5; elev. 826ft./252m.; 🅿; z 76066; ℗ 485; © 353
Millsville; RMC Place; SAN PATRICIO; ***239** EO-7; mail Aransas Pass z 78336; ● 100
Mill Town; RMC Place; TRINITY; ***238** EH-10; mail Trinity z 75862; pop. incl. with Trinity (Inc. Place)
Milo Center; RMC Place; DEAF SMITH; ***236** WE-9; mail Hereford z 79045; rural
Milton; RMC Place; LAMAR; ***238** EC-10; elev. 422ft./129m.; mail Deport z 75435; rural
Minden; RMC Place; RUSK; **238** EF-11; 🅿; z 75680; ● 300
Mineola; Inc. Place; WOOD; **238** EE-10; 🅿; z 75773; ℗ 4,321; © 4,550
Mineral; RMC Place; BEE; **239** EN-6; elev. 335ft./102m.; 🅿; z 78125; ● 60
Mineral Wells; Inc. Place; PALO PINTO, PARKER; **238** ED-5; elev. 911ft./278m.; 🅿 🅷; z 76067-68; ℗ 14,870; © 16,946
Minerva; RMC Place; MILAM; **238** EI-7; mail Rockdale z 76567; ● 60
Mings Chapel; RMC Place; UPSHUR; ***238** EE-11; mail Gilmer z 75644; rural
Mingus; Inc. Place; PALO PINTO; **238** EE-4; 🅿; z 76463; ℗ 215; © 246
Minter; RMC Place; LAMAR; **238** EC-10; mail Pattonville z 75468
Mirando City; CDP; WEBB; **239** EP-3; 🅿; z 78369; © 493
Mission; Inc. Place; HIDALGO; **239** ES-5; 🅿 🅷; ★ **MCAL**; z 78572-74 & mail La Joya z 78560; ℗ 28,653; © 45,408; ◆ 61,732
Mission Bend; CDP-Census Area Only; FORT BEND, HARRIS; **234** E-2; ★ **HOU**; mail Houston z 77083; ℗ 24,945; © 30,831; ◆ 47,084
Mission Valley; RMC Place; VICTORIA; ***239** EM-7; elev. 205ft./62m.; mail Victoria z 77901, z 77905; rural
Missouri City; Inc. Place; FORT BEND; **234** G-3; 🅿 🅷; ★ **HOU**; z 77459, z 77489; ℗ 36,176; © 52,913; ◆ 68,037
MITCHELL; **236** WJ-12; ℗ 8,016; © 9,698; ◆ 9,476
Mitchell Avenue; RMC Place; MCLENNAN; ★ **WACO**; mail Waco z 76708; pop. incl. with Waco (Inc. Place)
Mixon; RMC Place; CHEROKEE; ***238** EF-10; mail Troup z 75789; ● 50
Mobeetie (New Mobeetie); Inc. Place; WHEELER; **236** WC-13; elev. 2,612ft./796m.; 🅿; z 79061; ℗ 154; © 107
Mobile City; Inc. Place; ROCKWALL; ***238** ED-8; ★ **D-FW**; mail Rockwall z 75087; ℗ 161; © 196
Mockingbird; RMC Place; TRAVIS; ***238** EJ-6; ★ **AUS**; mail Austin z 78745, z 78747-48; pop. incl. with Austin (Inc. Place)
Moffat; RMC Place; BELL; **238** EH-6; mail Temple z 76502; ● 200
Moffett; RMC Place; ANGELINA; ***238** EG-12; ★ **LUFK**; mail Lufkin z 75901; rural
Monahans; Inc. Place; ⊡ WARD, WINKLER; **237** WL-8; elev. 2,624ft./800m.; 🅿 🅷; z 79756; ℗ 8,101; © 6,821
Monaville; RMC Place; WALLER; ***239** EK-9; elev. 178ft./54m.; mail Hempstead z 77445; rural
Monkstown; RMC Place; FANNIN; **238** EB-9; elev. 494ft./151m.; mail Telephone z 75488; ● 35
Monroe; LUBBOCK; see New Deal (Inc. Place)
Monroe; RMC Place; RUSK; ***238** EE-11; ★ **LNGV**; mail Kilgore z 75662; rural
Monroe City; RMC Place; CHAMBERS; **239** EK-12; 🅿; z 77514; ● 90
Mont; RMC Place; LAVACA; ***239** EL-7; mail Hallettsville z 77964; rural
Montague; RMC Place; ⊡ MONTAGUE; **238** EC-6; 🅿; z 76251; ● 300
MONTAGUE; **238** EB-5; ℗ 17,274; © 19,117; ◆ 19,550
Montague Ranch Estates; RMC Place; BANDERA; ***239** EK-3; mail Bandera z 78003; ● 30
Montalba; RMC Place; ANDERSON; **238** EF-9; 🅿; z 75853; ● 150
Mont Belvieu; Inc. Place; CHAMBERS; **234** C-10; elev. 73ft./22m.; 🅿; ★ **HOU**; z 77520, z 77523, z 77535, z 77580; ℗ 1,323; © 2,324
Monte Alto; CDP; HIDALGO; **239** ES-5; 🅿; z 78538; © 1,611
Montell; RMC Place; UVALDE; ***239** EL-1; elev. 1,290ft./393m.; mail Uvalde z 78801
Monte Oaks; RMC Place; MONTGOMERY; ***238** EJ-11; ★ **HOU**; mail New Caney z 77357
Monteola; RMC Place; BEE; ***239** EM-5; mail Kenedy z 78119; rural
Monterey; RMC Place; LUBBOCK; ★ **LUB**; mail Lubbock z 79410, z 79413, z 79493; pop. incl. with Lubbock (Inc. Place)
Montgomery; Inc. Place; MONTGOMERY; **238** EJ-10; 🅿; z 77316, z 77356; ℗ 356; © 489
MONTGOMERY; **238** EJ-10; ℗ 182,201; © 293,768; ◆ 439,793
Monthalia; RMC Place; GONZALES; ***239** EL-6; elev. 393ft./120m.; mail Cost z 78614; rural
Monticello; RMC Place; TITUS; ***238** ED-11; elev. 419ft./128m.; mail Mount Pleasant z 75455; ● 40
Montopolis; RMC Place; TRAVIS; ***238** EJ-6; ★ **AUS**; mail Austin z 78741; pop. incl. with Austin (Inc. Place)
Moody; Inc. Place; MCLENNAN; **238** EH-6; 🅿; z 76557; ℗ 1,329; © 1,400
Moore; CDP; FRIO; **239** EM-3; elev. 652ft./199m.; 🅿; z 78057; © 644
Moore; RMC Place; JASPER; mail Jasper z 75951; rural
MOORE; **236** WB-10; ℗ 17,865; © 20,121; ◆ 19,715
Moore's Chapel; RMC Place; FANNIN; ***238** EC-9; mail Bonham z 75418; rural
Moores Crossing; RMC Place; TRAVIS; ***238** EJ-6; ★ **AUS**; mail Austin z 78719, Del Valle z 78617; rural
Moore Station; Inc. Place; HENDERSON; **238** EF-10; mail LaRue z 75770; ℗ 256; © 184
Mooreville; RMC Place; FALLS; ***238** EH-7; mail Chilton z 76632; ● 90
Mooring; RMC Place; BRAZOS; ***238** EI-8; mail Bryan z 77807
Morales; RMC Place; JACKSON; ***239** EL-8; mail Edna z 77957; rural
Morales-Sanchez; CDP-Census Area Only; ZAPATA; ***239** ER-3; © 95
Moran; Inc. Place; SHACKELFORD; **238** EE-3; 🅿; z 76464; ℗ 285; © 233
Moravia; RMC Place; LAVACA; ***239** EK-7; mail Schulenburg z 78956
Morgan; Inc. Place; BOSQUE; **238** EF-6; elev. 732ft./223m.; 🅿; z 76671; ℗ 451; © 485
Morgan Creek; RMC Place; BURNET; ***238** EI-5; mail Burnet z 78611; ● 50
Morgan Farm Area; CDP-Census Area Only; SAN PATRICIO; ***239** EO-6; © 484
Morgan Mill; RMC Place; ERATH; **238** EE-5; 🅿; z 76465; ● 200
Morgans Point; Inc. Place; HARRIS; **234** F-9; elev. 30ft./9m.; ★ **HOU**; mail La Porte z 77571; ℗ 341; © 336
Morgans Point Resort; Inc. Place; BELL; ***238** EH-6; 🅿; ★ **KILL-**; z 76513; ℗ 1,766; © 2,989
Morning Glory; CDP-Census Area Only; EL PASO; ***237** WL-2; ★ **ELP**; © 627
Morningside; RMC Place; WICHITA; mail Wichita Falls z 76301-02, z 76305-06, z 76309; pop. incl. with Wichita Falls (Inc. Place)
Morningside Heights; RMC Place; EL PASO; ***237** WK-2; ★ **ELP**; mail El Paso z 79930; pop. incl. with El Paso (Inc. Place)
Morrill; RMC Place; CHEROKEE; ***238** EG-11; mail Alto z 75925; rural
MORRIS; **238** EC-11; ℗ 13,200; © 13,048; ◆ 13,230
Morris Ranch; RMC Place; GILLESPIE; ***238** EJ-3; mail Fredericksburg z 78624; rural
Morse; CDP; HANSFORD; **236** WB-11; 🅿; z 79062; © 172
Morton; Inc. Place; ⊡ COCHRAN; **236** WG-9; elev. 3,760ft./1,146m.; 🅿 🅷; z 79346; ℗ 2,597; © 2,249
Morton; RMC Place; HARRISON; ***238** ED-11; mail Diana z 75640; ● 80
Morton Valley; RMC Place; EASTLAND; ***238** EE-4; elev. 1,597ft./487m.; mail Eastland z 76448; ● 40
Moscow; RMC Place; POLK; **238** EH-11; elev. 348ft./106m.; 🅿; z 75960; ● 300
Mosheim; RMC Place; BOSQUE; **238** EG-6; mail Valley Mills z 76689; ● 100
Moss Bluff; RMC Place; LIBERTY; ***238** EJ-12; mail Liberty z 77575; ● 550
Moss Hill; RMC Place; LIBERTY; **238** EJ-12; mail Liberty z 77575; ● 150
Mostyn; RMC Place; MONTGOMERY; ***238** EJ-10; elev. 252ft./77m.; ★ **HOU**; mail Magnolia z 77354; ● 200
MOTLEY; **236** WF-12; ℗ 1,532; © 1,426; ◆ 1,280
Moulton; Inc. Place; LAVACA; **239** EK-7; 🅿; z 77975; ℗ 923; © 944
Mound; RMC Place; CORYELL; **235** F-4; 🅿; z 76558; ● 170
Mound City; RMC Place; ANDERSON; ***238** EG-10; mail Grapeland z 75844; rural
Mountain; RMC Place; CORYELL; ***238** EG-6; mail Gatesville z 76528; pop. incl. with South Mountain (Inc. Place)
Mountain City; Inc. Place; HAYS; ***238** EJ-5; 🅿; z 78610; ℗ 377; © 671
Mountain Creek; RMC Place; DALLAS; ★ **D-FW**; pop. incl. with Grand Prairie (Inc. Place)
Mountain Home; RMC Place; KERR; **238** EJ-3; elev. 1,915ft./584m.; 🅿; z 78058; ● 90
Mountain Peak; RMC Place; ELLIS; ***238** EE-7; ★ **D-FW**; mail Midlothian z 76065; ● 100
Mountain Springs; RMC Place; COOKE; ***238** EC-7; elev. 711ft./217m.; mail Pilot Point z 76258; rural
Mountain Valley Estates; RMC Place; JOHNSON; ***238** EE-6; ★ **D-FW**; mail Joshua z 76058; pop. incl. with Joshua (Inc. Place)
Mountain View; RMC Place; EL PASO; ***237** WK-2; ★ **ELP**; mail El Paso z 79904; pop. incl. with El Paso (Inc. Place)
Mount Blanco; RMC Place; CROSBY; ***236** WG-11; mail Crosbyton z 79322; rural
Mount Calm; Inc. Place; HILL; **238** EG-7; 🅿; z 76673; ℗ 303; © 310
Mount Enterprise; Inc. Place; RUSK; **238** EF-11; 🅿; z 75681; ℗ 501; © 525
Mount Enterprise; RMC Place; WOOD; ***238** ED-10; mail Mineola z 75773; rural
Mount Haven; RMC Place; CHEROKEE; ***238** EF-10; elev. 670ft./204m.; mail Jacksonville z 75766; rural
Mount Houston; RMC Place; HARRIS; ***239** EK-10; ★ **HOU**; mail Houston z 77039, z 77050; pop. incl. with Houston (Inc. Place)
Mount Joy; RMC Place; DELTA; ***238** EC-9; mail Enloe z 75441; rural
Mount Lookout; RMC Place; COMAL; ***239** EK-5; mail New Braunfels z 78130
Mount Lucas; RMC Place; LIVE OAK; ***239** EO-5; mail Dinero z 78350, George West z 78022
Mount Mitchell; RMC Place; MORRIS; ***238** EC-11; mail Omaha z 75571; rural
Mount Moriah; RMC Place; MORRIS; ***238** EC-11; mail Omaha z 75571; rural
Mount Olive; RMC Place; LAVACA; ***239** EL-7; mail Shiner z 77984, Yoakum z 77995; rural
Mount Pleasant; Inc. Place; ⊡ TITUS; **238** EC-11; 🅿 🅷 ■; z 75455-56; ℗ 12,291; © 13,935; ◆ 14,636
Mount Selman; RMC Place; CHEROKEE; **238** EF-10; 🅿; z 75757; ● 200
Mount Sylvan; RMC Place; SMITH; ***238** EE-10; mail Lindale z 75771; ● 150
Mount Union; RMC Place; JASPER; ***238** EI-13; elev. 183ft./56m.; mail Kirbyville z 75956; rural
Mount Vernon; Inc. Place; ⊡ FRANKLIN; **238** EC-10; 🅿 🅷; z 75457; ℗ 2,219; © 2,286
Mozelle; RMC Place; COLEMAN; ***238** EG-2; elev. 1,594ft./486m.; mail Coleman z 76834, Gouldbusk z 76845; rural
Muddig; RMC Place; HUNT; mail Ladonia z 75449; rural
Mudville; RMC Place; BRAZOS; ***238** EI-8; mail Bryan z 77807; rural
Muellersville; RMC Place; WASHINGTON; ***238** EJ-8; mail Brenham z 77833; rural
Muenster; Inc. Place; COOKE; **238** EC-6; elev. 1,007ft./307m.; 🅿 🅷; z 76252; ℗ 1,387; © 1,556
Mulberry; RMC Place; FANNIN; ***238** EB-8; mail Ravenna z 75476
Muldoon; RMC Place; FAYETTE; **239** EK-7; elev. 346ft./105m.; 🅿; z 78949; ● 80
Muleshoe; Inc. Place; ⊡ BAILEY; **236** WF-9; elev. 3,792ft./1,156m.; 🅿 🅷; z 79347; ℗ 4,571; © 4,530
Mulkey; RMC Place; CASTRO; ***236** WF-10; mail Dimmitt z 79027, Hart z 79043; rural
Mullin; Inc. Place; MILLS; **238** EG-4; 🅿; z 76864; ℗ 194; © 175
Mullins Prairie; RMC Place; FAYETTE; ***239** EK-8; mail La Grange z 78945; rural
Mumford; RMC Place; ROBERTSON; **238** EI-8; 🅿; z 77867; ● 200
Muncy; RMC Place; FLOYD; ***236** WG-11; mail Lockney z 79241; rural
Munday; Inc. Place; KNOX; **238** EC-2; 🅿; z 76371; ℗ 1,600; © 1,527
Muniz; CDP-Census Area Only; HIDALGO; ***239** ES-5; ★ **MCAL**; © 1,106
Munson; RMC Place; ROCKWALL; ***238** ED-8; ★ **D-FW**; mail Royse City z 75189; rural
Murchison; Inc. Place; HENDERSON; **238** EE-9; 🅿; z 75778; ℗ 510; © 592
Murphy; Inc. Place; COLLIN; **235** D-13; 🅿; ★ **D-FW**; z 75094 & mail Plano z 75074; ℗ 1,547; © 3,099
Murray; RMC Place; YOUNG; ***238** ED-3; elev. 1,214ft./370m.; mail Graham z 76450
Murryhill; RMC Place; LUBBOCK; ★ **LUB**; mail Lubbock z 79413; pop. incl. with Lubbock (Inc. Place)
Musgrove; RMC Place; WOOD; ***238** ED-10; mail Winnsboro z 75494; rural
Mustang; RMC Place; DENTON; ***238** EC-7; elev. 603ft./184m.; mail Pilot Point z 76258
Mustang; Inc. Place; NAVARRO; ***238** EF-8; mail Corsicana z 75110; ℗ 35; © 47
Mustang Mott Store; RMC Place; DEWITT; ***239** EM-6; mail Cuero z 77954; rural
Mustang Ridge; Inc. Place; TRAVIS, CALDWELL; ***238** EJ-6; ★ **AUS**; mail Buda z 78610; ℗ 576; © 785
Mykawa; RMC Place; HARRIS; ***239** EK-11; ★ **HOU**; pop. incl. with Houston (Inc. Place)
Myra; RMC Place; COOKE; **238** EC-6; 🅿; z 76253; ● 250
Myrtle Springs; RMC Place; VAN ZANDT; **238** EE-9; elev. 504ft./154m.; mail Wills Point z 75169; ● 300

N

Naaman; RMC Place; DALLAS; ***238** ED-8; ★ **D-FW**; mail Garland z 75040; pop. incl. with Garland (Inc. Place)
Nacalina (Naclina); RMC Place; NACOGDOCHES; ***238** EG-12; mail Etoile z 75944; ● 70
Naclina; NACOGDOCHES; see Nacalina (RMC Place)
Nacogdoches; Inc. Place; ⊡ NACOGDOCHES; **238** EG-11; 🅿 🅷 🅲 11,756 ■; z 75961-65; ℗ 30,872; © 29,914; ◆ 29,641
NACOGDOCHES; **238** EF-11; ℗ 54,753; © 59,203; ◆ 63,355
Nada; RMC Place; COLORADO; **239** EL-8; 🅿; z 77460; ● 170
Nadeau; RMC Place; GALVESTON; ***239** EL-11; ★ **GLV-**; mail Texas City z 77590; pop. incl. with Texas City (Inc. Place)
Nameless; RMC Place; TRAVIS; ***238** EI-5; ★ **AUS**; mail Leander z 78641; rural
Nancy; RMC Place; ANGELINA; ***238** EH-12; elev. 215ft./66m.; mail Zavalla z 75980; rural
Naples; Inc. Place; MORRIS; **238** EC-11; elev. 459ft./140m.; 🅿; z 75568; ℗ 1,508; © 1,410
Naruna; RMC Place; BURNET; ***238** EH-5; elev. 1,469ft./448m.; mail Lampasas z 76550; rural
Nash; Inc. Place; BOWIE; **238** EC-12; 🅿; ★ **TEXR-**; z 75569; ℗ 2,162; © 2,169
Nash; RMC Place; ELLIS; ***238** EF-7; elev. 521ft./159m.; mail Waxahachie z 75165; ● 60
Nassau Bay; Inc. Place; HARRIS; **234** G-8; 🅷; ★ **HOU**; mail Houston z 77058, z 77258; ℗ 4,320; © 4,170
Nassau Bay; RMC Place; HOOD; ***238** EE-6; mail Granbury z 76049; ● 300
Nasworthy Hills; RMC Place; TOM GREEN; ***237** WL-13; ★ **SANG**; mail San Angelo z 76904; pop. incl. with San Angelo (Inc. Place)
Nat; RMC Place; NACOGDOCHES; ***238** EG-11; mail Cushing z 75760, Nacogdoches z 75961; rural
Natalia; Inc. Place; MEDINA; **239** EL-4; 🅿; z 78059; ℗ 1,216; © 1,663
Navarro; Inc. Place; NAVARRO; ***238** EF-8; mail Corsicana z 75110; ℗ 193; © 191
NAVARRO; **238** EF-8; ℗ 39,926; © 45,124; ◆ 49,236
Navarro Mills; RMC Place; NAVARRO; ***238** EF-8; mail Purdon z 76679; ● 80
Navasota; Inc. Place; GRIMES; **238** EJ-9; 🅿 🅷; z 77868; ℗ 6,296; © 6,789
Navo; RMC Place; DENTON; ***238** EC-7; elev. 593ft./181m.; mail Aubrey z 76227; rural
Nazareth; Inc. Place; CASTRO; **236** WF-10; 🅿; z 79063; ℗ 293; © 356
Nebgen; RMC Place; GILLESPIE; mail Fredericksburg z 78624; rural
Necessity; RMC Place; STEPHENS; ***238** EE-4; mail Breckenridge z 76424
Nechanitz; RMC Place; FAYETTE; ***238** EJ-8; elev. 426ft./130m.; mail Ledbetter z 78946; rural
Neches; RMC Place; ANDERSON; **238** EF-10; elev. 413ft./126m.; 🅿; z 75779; ● 300
Neches Junction; RMC Place; JEFFERSON; ★ **B-PA**; mail Port Arthur z 77640; pop. incl. with Port Arthur (Inc. Place)
Nederland; Inc. Place; JEFFERSON; **238** EJ-13; 🅿 🅷; ★ **B-PA**; z 77627; ℗ 16,192; © 17,422
Needmore; RMC Place; BAILEY; ***236** WG-9; elev. 3,883ft./1,184m.; mail Sudan z 79371; ● 40
Needmore; RMC Place; DELTA; ***238** EC-9; mail Klondike z 75448; rural
Needville; Inc. Place; FORT BEND; **239** EL-9; 🅿; z 77461; ℗ 2,199; © 2,609
Negley; RMC Place; RED RIVER; ***238** EB-10; elev. 448ft./137m.; mail Clarksville z 75426
Neinda; RMC Place; JONES; ***238** ED-1; elev. 1,775ft./541m.; mail Hamlin z 79520
Nell; RMC Place; LIVE OAK; ***239** EM-5; mail Kenedy z 78119; rural
Nelson City; RMC Place; KENDALL; ***239** EK-4; mail Boerne z 78006
Nelsonville; RMC Place; AUSTIN; **239** EK-8; mail Bellville z 77418; ● 90
Nelta; RMC Place; HOPKINS; ***238** EC-10; elev. 479ft./146m.; mail Dike z 75437; rural
Nemo; RMC Place; SOMERVELL; **238** EF-6; elev. 783ft./239m.; 🅿; z 76070; ● 60
Nesbitt; Inc. Place; HARRISON; ***238** EE-12; elev. 359ft./109m.; ★ **MAR**; mail Marshall z 75670; ℗ 327; © 302
Nesbitt; RMC Place; ROBERTSON; ***238** EH-8; mail Bremond z 76629; rural
Neuville; RMC Place; SHELBY; **238** EG-12; mail Center z 75935; ● 70
Nevada; Inc. Place; COLLIN; **238** ED-8; elev. 643ft./196m.; 🅿; z 75173; ℗ 456; © 563
Newark; Inc. Place; WISE; **238** ED-6; elev. 693ft./211m.; 🅿; z 76071; ℗ 651; © 887
New Baden; RMC Place; ROBERTSON; **238** EH-8; 🅿; z 77870; ● 120
New Berlin; Inc. Place; GUADALUPE; **239** EL-5; mail La Vernia z 78121, Seguin z 78155; ℗ 188; © 467
New Bielau; RMC Place; COLORADO; ***239** EK-8; mail Weimar z 78962; rural
New Birthright; RMC Place; HOPKINS; ***238** EC-10; mail Sulphur Springs z 75482
New Boston; Inc. Place; BOWIE; **238** EC-12; 🅿; z 75570; ℗ 5,057; © 4,808
New Braunfels; Inc. Place; ⊡ COMAL, GUADALUPE; **239** EK-5; elev. 623ft./190m.; 🅿 🅷; z 78130-33, z 78135; ℗ 27,334; © 36,494; ◆ 50,829
New Bremen; RMC Place; AUSTIN; ***239** EK-8; elev. 300ft./91m.; mail New Ulm z 78950; rural
Newburg; RMC Place; COMANCHE; ***238** EG-4; mail Comanche z 76442; rural
Newby; RMC Place; LEON; **238** EG-9; mail Jewett z 75846
New Caney; RMC Place; MONTGOMERY; **238** EJ-11; elev. 95ft./29m.; 🅿; ★ **HOU**; z 77357; ● 3,000
New Caney Heights; RMC Place; MONTGOMERY; ***238** EJ-11; ★ **HOU**; mail New Caney z 77357
Newcastle; Inc. Place; YOUNG; **238** ED-4; elev. 1,147ft./350m.; 🅿; z 76372; ℗ 505; © 575
New Chapel Hill; Inc. Place; SMITH; ***238** EE-10; ★ **TYL**; mail Tyler z 75707; ℗ 439; © 553
New Clarkson; RMC Place; MILAM; ***238** EH-7; mail Rosebud z 76570; rural
New Colony; RMC Place; BELL; ***238** EH-7; mail Rogers z 76569; rural
New Colony; RMC Place; CASS; ***238** ED-12; mail Linden z 75563; rural
New Corn Hill; RMC Place; WILLIAMSON; ***238** EI-6; mail Jarrell z 76537; ● 50
New Deal (Monroe); Inc. Place; LUBBOCK; **236** WG-10; 🅿; z 79350; ℗ 521; © 708
New Fairview (Fairview); Inc. Place; WISE; **238** ED-8; mail Rhome z 76078; ℗ 206; © 877
New Falcon; CDP-Census Area Only; ZAPATA; ***239** ER-3; © 184
New Fountain; RMC Place; MEDINA; ***239** EL-3; elev. 852ft./260m.; mail Hondo z 78861; rural
Newgulf; RMC Place; WHARTON; ***239** EL-9
New Harmony; RMC Place; SHELBY; ***238** EF-13; mail Shelbyville z 75973; rural
New Harmony; RMC Place; SMITH; ***238** EE-10; mail Tyler z 75704; ● 50
Newharp; RMC Place; MONTAGUE; ***238** EC-6; mail Forestburg z 76239; rural
New Home; Inc. Place; LYNN; **236** WH-10; elev. 3,236ft./986m.; 🅿; z 79381, z 79383; ℗ 175; © 320
New Hope; RMC Place; CHEROKEE; ***238** EF-10; mail Jacksonville z 75766; ● 50
New Hope; Inc. Place; COLLIN; **235** A-13; ★ **D-FW**; mail Mckinney z 75069; ℗ 523; © 662
New Hope; RMC Place; DALLAS; ***238** ED-8; elev. 534ft./163m.; ★ **D-FW**; mail Sunnyvale z 75182; pop. incl. with Sunnyvale (Inc. Place)
New Hope (Cross Roads); Inc. Place; DENTON; ***238** EC-7; ★ **D-FW**; mail Aubrey z 76227; ℗ 361; © 603
New Hope; RMC Place; HENDERSON; ***238** EE-10; mail Brownsboro z 75756, Chandler z 75758; rural
New Hope; RMC Place; JONES; ***238** ED-2; elev. 1,572ft./479m.; mail Stamford z 79553; rural
New Hope; RMC Place; LIBERTY; ***238** EJ-12; mail Riverside z 77367; rural
New Hope; RMC Place; LIMESTONE; ***238** EG-8; mail Crockett z 75835; rural
New Hope; RMC Place; RUSK; ***238** EE-11; ★ **LNGV**; mail Kilgore z 75662; rural
New Hope; RMC Place; SMITH; ***238** EF-10; elev. 469ft./143m.; ★ **TYL**; mail Tyler z 75704; rural
New Hope; RMC Place; WOOD; ***238** EE-10; mail Mineola z 75773
New Katy; RMC Place; TRAVIS; **238** EJ-6; mail Manor z 78653; ● 60
Newlin; RMC Place; HALL; ***236** WF-13; elev. 1,799ft./548m.; mail Memphis z 79245; rural
New London; Inc. Place; RUSK; **238** EE-11; 🅿; z 75682; ℗ 926; © 987
New Lynn; RMC Place; LYNN; ***236** WH-11; mail Wilson z 79381; rural
Newman; RMC Place; EL PASO; ***237** WK-2; mail El Paso z 79924; pop. incl. with El Paso (Inc. Place)
New Mine; RMC Place; CAMP; ***238** ED-11; mail Pittsburg z 75686; rural
New Mobeetie; WHEELER; see Mobeetie (Inc. Place)
New Moore; RMC Place; LYNN; ***236** WI-10; mail Odonnell z 79351; rural
Newport; RMC Place; CLAY, JACK; **238** EC-5; mail Bowie z 76230; ● 40
Newport; RMC Place; HARRIS; ***239** EK-11; ★ **HOU**; mail Crosby z 77532; ● 4,500
New Prospect; RMC Place; RUSK; ***238** EE-11; elev. 493ft./150m.; mail Henderson z 75652; rural
New Prospect; RMC Place; SHELBY; ***238** EF-12; mail Timpson z 75975; rural
New River Lake Estates; RMC Place; LIBERTY; ***238** EI-11; mail Cleveland z 77327; ● 200
New Salem; RMC Place; FALLS; ***238** EH-7; mail Rosebud z 76570; rural
New Salem; RMC Place; PALO PINTO; ***238** EE-5; mail Santo z 76472; ● 25
New Salem; RMC Place; RUSK; **238** EF-11; mail Henderson z 75652, z 75654; ● 50
Newsome; RMC Place; CAMP; ***238** ED-10; mail Leesburg z 75451; ● 250
New Summerfield; Inc. Place; CHEROKEE; **238** EF-11; elev. 469ft./143m.; 🅿; z 75780; ℗ 521; © 998
New Sweden; RMC Place; TRAVIS; ***238** EJ-6; mail Manor z 78653; rural
New Taiton; RMC Place; WHARTON; ***239** EL-9; elev. 136ft./41m.; mail El Campo z 77437
New Territory; CDP-Census Area Only; FORT BEND; ***239** EK-10; ★ **HOU**; mail Sugar Land z 77478; © 13,861
Newton; Inc. Place; ⊡ NEWTON; **238** EH-13; elev. 182ft./55m.; 🅿; z 75966; ℗ 1,885; © 2,459
NEWTON; **238** EI-13; ℗ 13,569; © 15,072; ◆ 13,563
New Ulm; RMC Place; AUSTIN; **239** EK-8; 🅿; z 78950; ● 350
New Waverly; Inc. Place; WALKER; **238** EI-10; elev. 360ft./110m.; 🅿; z 77358; ℗ 936; © 950
New Wehdem; RMC Place; AUSTIN; ***238** EJ-8; mail Brenham z 77833; rural
New Willard; RMC Place; POLK; **238** EI-11; mail Livingston z 77351; ● 100
New York; RMC Place; HENDERSON; ***238** EF-10; elev. 488ft./149m.; mail LaRue z 75770; rural
Neylandville; Inc. Place; HUNT; **238** EC-9; mail Greenville z 75401; ℗ 94; © 56
Nickel; RMC Place; GONZALES; ***239** EL-7; elev. 438ft./134m.; mail Gonzales z 78629; rural
Nickelberry; RMC Place; CASS; ***238** EC-12; mail Marietta z 75566; rural
Nickel Creek; RMC Place; CULBERSON; ***237** WK-5; mail Carlsbad z 88220; rural
Niederwald; Inc. Place; CALDWELL, HAYS; **239** EK-6; 🅿; ★ **AUS**; z 78640; ℗ 233; © 584
Nigton; RMC Place; TRINITY; ***238** EH-11; mail Apple Springs z 75926; ● 80
Nimitz; RMC Place; BEXAR; ★ **SANT**; mail San Antonio z 78216, z 78279; pop. incl. with San Antonio (Inc. Place)
Nimrod; RMC Place; EASTLAND; ***238** EF-3; elev. 1,699ft./518m.; mail Cisco z 76437; ● 80
Nineveh; RMC Place; LEON; ***238** EG-9; mail Centerville z 75833, Oakwood z 75855; rural
Nix; RMC Place; LAMPASAS; **238** EH-5; elev. 1,384ft./422m.; mail Lampasas z 76550, Lometa z 76853; rural
Nixon; Inc. Place; GONZALES, WILSON; **239** EL-6; 🅿; z 78140; ℗ 1,995; © 2,186
Noack; RMC Place; WILLIAMSON; ***238** EI-7; mail Taylor z 76574; rural
Nobility; RMC Place; FANNIN; ***238** EC-8; mail Blue Ridge z 75424, Leonard z 75452
Noble; RMC Place; LAMAR; ***238** EC-9; mail Petty z 75470; rural
Nockenut; RMC Place; WILSON; ***239** EL-5; elev. 499ft./152m.; mail Stockdale z 78160; rural
Nocona; Inc. Place; MONTAGUE; **238** EB-6; 🅿 🅷; z 76255; ℗ 2,870; © 3,198
Nogalus; TRINITY; see Nogalus Prairie (RMC Place)
Nogalus Prairie (Nogalus); RMC Place; TRINITY; **238** EH-11; mail Groveton z 75845, Kennard z 75847; ● 100
Nolan; RMC Place; NOLAN; **237** WK-13; 🅿; z 79537; ● 100
NOLAN; **236** WJ-13; ℗ 16,594; © 15,802; ◆ 14,518
Nolanville; Inc. Place; BELL; **238** EH-6; 🅿; ★ **KILL-**; z 76559; ℗ 1,834; © 2,150
Nolte; RMC Place; GUADALUPE; ***239** EL-5; mail Seguin z 78155; ● 50
Nome; Inc. Place; JEFFERSON; **238** EJ-12; 🅿; z 77629; ℗ 448; © 515
Nona; RMC Place; HARDIN; ***238** EJ-12; elev. 67ft./20m.; mail Kountze z 77625; rural
Noodle; RMC Place; JONES; **236** WJ-13; elev. 1,827ft./557m.; mail Merkel z 79536; ● 50
Noonday; Inc. Place; SMITH; ***238** EE-10; elev. 470ft./143m.; ★ **TYL**; mail Flint z 75762; ℗ 466; © 515
Nopal; RMC Place; DEWITT; ***239** EL-6; elev. 436ft./133m.; mail Yorktown z 78164; rural
Nordheim; Inc. Place; DEWITT; **239** EM-6; elev. 417ft./127m.; 🅿; z 78141; ℗ 344; © 323

Entries in **UPPERCASE** are counties.
Entries in **bold** have populations of 2,500 or more.
Names in parentheses are alternate names.
Inc. Place — Incorporated Place
RMC Place — Rand McNally Designated Place
CDP — Census Designated Place
MCD — Minor Civil Division
⊡ County Seat
▲ Minor Civil Division
elev. Elevation
🅿 Post Office
🅷 Hospital
🅲 College
■ Principal Business Center
★ Ranally Metro Area (RMA) Abbreviation
z Zip Code(s)
℗ Previous Census Population
Ⓡ Revised Census Population
Ⓐ Annexation Population
● Rand McNally Population Estimate
© Final Census Population
Ⓢ Special Census Population
◆ Estimated Population

For additional definitions see Glossary, Volume 1, and Introduction, Volume 2.

Norias; RMC Place; KENEDY; **239** ER-6; mail Armstrong z 78338; ● 50
Norman Crossing; RMC Place; WILLIAMSON; ***238** EI-6; mail Taylor z 76574; rural
Normandy; RMC Place; MAVERICK; **237** WR-12; elev. 772ft./235m.; mail Quemado z 78877; ● 70
Normangee; Inc. Place; LEON, MADISON; **238** EH-9; elev. 388ft./118m.; 🅿; z 77871; Ⓟ 689; © 719
Normanna; CDP; BEE; **239** EN-6; 🅿; z 78142; © 121
Norse; RMC Place; BOSQUE; ***238** EG-6; mail Clifton z 76634
North; RMC Place; DALLAS; ***238** ED-8; ★ **D-FW**; mail Garland z 75044-45, Sachse z 75048; pop. incl. with Garland (Inc. Place)
North Alamo; CDP-Census Area Only; HIDALGO; ***239** ES-5; ★ **MCAL**; © 2,061
North Amarillo; RMC Place; POTTER; ★ **AMA**; mail Amarillo z 79117; pop. incl. with Amarillo (Inc. Place)
Northampton; RMC Place; HARRIS; ***238** EJ-10; ★ **HOU**; mail Spring z 77389; ● 950
North Austin; RMC Place; TRAVIS; ★ **AUS**; mail Austin z 78705, z 78751, z 78765; pop. incl. with Austin (Inc. Place)
Northaven; RMC Place; DALLAS; ★ **D-FW**; mail Dallas z 75229, z 75378; pop. incl. with Dallas (Inc. Place)
North Beach; RMC Place; NUECES; ***239** EO-7; ★ **CRPX**; mail Corpus Christi z 78402; pop. incl. with Corpus Christi (Inc. Place)
North Broadway; RMC Place; BEXAR; ★ **SANT**; mail San Antonio z 78217; pop. incl. with San Antonio (Inc. Place)
North Cedar; RMC Place; TRINITY; ***238** EH-11; mail Apple Springs z 75926; rural
North Cleveland; Inc. Place; LIBERTY; ***238** EJ-11; mail Cleveland z 77327; Ⓟ 176; © 263
Northcliff; CDP-Census Area Only; GUADALUPE, COMAL; ***239** EK-5; ★ **SANT**; mail Cibolo z 78108; © 1,819
North Concho Lake Estates; RMC Place; TOM GREEN; ***237** WL-13; ★ **SANG**; mail San Angelo z 76901; ● 125
North Cowden; RMC Place; ECTOR; ***237** WK-9; mail Gardendale z 79758; rural
Northcrest; RMC Place; MCLENNAN; ***238** EG-7; ★ **WACO**; mail Waco z 76705; pop. incl. with Lacy-Lakeview (Inc. Place); Ⓟ 1,725
Northcrest Estates; RMC Place; VICTORIA; ***239** EM-7; ★ **VICT**; mail Victoria z 77904; pop. incl. with Victoria (Inc. Place)
Northeast; RMC Place; TRAVIS; ★ **AUS**; mail Austin z 78723-25, z 78752, z 78754, z 78761; pop. incl. with Austin (Inc. Place)
Northeast Annex; RMC Place; BEXAR; mail San Antonio z 78266; pop. incl. with San Antonio (Inc. Place)
Northeast Station; RMC Place; ECTOR; ★ **MIDL-**; mail Odessa z 79764, z 79768; pop. incl. with Odessa (Inc. Place)
North Escobares; CDP-Census Area Only; STARR; ***239** ES-3; © 1,692
Northfield; RMC Place; MOTLEY; **236** WF-13; elev. 2,022ft./616m.; 🅿; z 79201; ● 25
North Fort Worth; RMC Place; TARRANT; ★ **D-FW**; pop. incl. with Fort Worth (Inc. Place)
Northgate; RMC Place; BRAZOS; mail College Station z 77841; pop. incl. with College Station (Inc. Place)
Northglen; RMC Place; HARRIS; ***239** EK-10; ★ **HOU**; mail Houston z 77084; ● 900
North Groesbeck; RMC Place; HARDEMAN; ***238** EA-2; elev. 1,536ft./468m.; mail Quanah z 79252; rural
North Heights; RMC Place; POTTER; ★ **AMA**; mail Amarillo z 79107; pop. incl. with Amarillo (Inc. Place)
North Houston; RMC Place; HARRIS; **234** C-4; elev. 114ft./35m.; 🅿; ★ **HOU**; z 77315 & mail Houston z 77086; ● 2,000
Northlake; Inc. Place; DENTON; ***238** ED-7; 🅿; z 76247 & mail Roanoke z 76262; Ⓟ 250; © 921
Northlake Estates; RMC Place; WILLIAMSON; ***238** EI-6; ★ **AUS**; mail Georgetown z 78628; ● 500
North Line Oaks; RMC Place; MONTGOMERY; ***238** EJ-10; ★ **HOU**; mail Conroe z 77385; ● 150
Northline Terrace; RMC Place; HARRIS; ***239** EK-10; ★ **HOU**; mail Houston z 77037; ● 2,700
North Loop; RMC Place; BEXAR; ***239** EL-4; ★ **SANT**; pop. incl. with San Antonio (Inc. Place)
North Oaks; RMC Place; TRAVIS; ***238** EJ-6; ★ **AUS**; mail Austin z 78753; pop. incl. with Austin (Inc. Place)
North Orange Heights; RMC Place; ORANGE; ***238** EJ-13; ★ **B-PA**; mail Orange z 77632; ● 200
North Pearsall; CDP-Census Area Only; FRIO; ***239** EM-3; © 561
North Port Arthur; RMC Place; JEFFERSON; ***238** EJ-13; ★ **B-PA**; mail Port Arthur z 77642; pop. incl. with Port Arthur (Inc. Place)
North Richland Hills; Inc. Place; TARRANT; **238** ED-7; 🅿 🅷 ■; ★ **D-FW**; z 76118, z 76180, z 76182; Ⓟ 45,895; © 55,635; ◆ 66,542
Northrup; RMC Place; LEE; **238** EJ-7; mail Giddings z 78942; ● 50
North San Antonio Hills; RMC Place; BEXAR; **239** ER-9; ★ **SANT**; mail San Antonio z 78253; ● 100
North San Pedro; CDP-Census Area Only; NUECES; ***239** EO-6; ★ **CRPX**; mail Robstown z 78380; Ⓟ 953; © 920
North Shepherd; RMC Place; HARRIS; ***238** EJ-11; ★ **HOU**; mail Houston z 77088, z 77238, z 77291; pop. incl. with Houston (Inc. Place)
North Shore Acres; RMC Place; TRAVIS; ***238** EJ-5; ★ **AUS**; mail Leander z 78645; ● 200
North Spring; RMC Place; HARRIS; ***238** EJ-10; ★ **HOU**; mail Spring z 77373; ● 900
North Uvalde; RMC Place; UVALDE; ***239** EL-2
Northwest; RMC Place; COLLIN; mail Plano z 75024-25; pop. incl. with Plano (Inc. Place)
Northwest; RMC Place; DALLAS; ★ **D-FW**; mail Dallas z 75220, z 75354; pop. incl. with Dallas (Inc. Place)
Northwest; RMC Place; TRAVIS; ★ **AUS**; mail Austin z 78756-57, z 78766; pop. incl. with Austin (Inc. Place)
Northwest Hills; RMC Place; GILLESPIE; **238** EJ-4; mail Georgetown z 78626; ● 40
Northwest Park; RMC Place; HARRIS; ***239** EK-10; elev. 105ft./32m.; ★ **HOU**; mail Houston z 77086; ● 1,800
Northwest Station; RMC Place; GREGG; ★ **LNGV**; mail Longview z 75604-05, z 75608; pop. incl. with Longview (Inc. Place)
Northwood; RMC Place; TRAVIS; ***238** EJ-6; ★ **AUS**; mail Austin z 78758; pop. incl. with Austin (Inc. Place)
North Zulch; RMC Place; MADISON; **238** EH-9; 🅿; z 77872; ● 550
Norton; RMC Place; RUNNELS; **237** WK-13; elev. 1,872ft./571m.; 🅿; z 76865; ● 75
Norwood; RMC Place; SAN AUGUSTINE; ***238** EG-12; mail San Augustine z 75972; ● 100
Notrees; RMC Place; ECTOR; **237** WK-8; 🅿; z 79759; ● 125
Nottingham; RMC Place; HARRIS; ***239** EK-10; ★ **HOU**; mail Houston z 77079; pop. incl. with Houston (Inc. Place)
Nottingham Forest; RMC Place; ORANGE; ***238** EJ-13; ★ **B-PA**; mail Orange z 77630; ● 125
Nottingham Woods; RMC Place; HOUSTON; ***238** EG-10; mail Crockett z 75835; ● 90
Novice; Inc. Place; COLEMAN; **238** EF-2; 🅿; z 79538; Ⓟ 183; © 142
Novice; RMC Place; LAMAR; ***238** EB-10; elev. 504ft./154m.; mail Paris z 75462
Novohrad; RMC Place; LAVACA; ***239** EK-7; mail Moulton z 77975; rural
Noxville; RMC Place; KIMBLE; ***238** EJ-2; elev. 2,077ft./633m.; mail Harper z 78631; rural
NUECES; **239** EP-6; Ⓟ 291,145; © 313,645; ◆ 319,581
Nugent; RMC Place; JONES; **236** WJ-14; mail Abilene z 79601; ● 50
Nurillo; CDP-Census Area Only; HIDALGO; ***239** ES-5; ★ **MCAL**; © 5,056
Nursery; RMC Place; VICTORIA; **239** EM-7; elev. 133ft./41m.; 🅿; z 77976; ● 350

O

Oakalla; RMC Place; BURNET; **238** EH-5; 🅿; z 78608 & mail Killeen z 76542; ● 80
Oak Cliff; RMC Place; DALLAS; ***238** ED-7; ★ **D-FW**; pop. incl. with Dallas (Inc. Place)
Oak Colony Estates; RMC Place; VICTORIA; ***239** EM-7; mail Victoria z 77905; ● 300
Oak Crest Estates; RMC Place; WILLIAMSON; ***238** EI-6; ★ **AUS**; mail Georgetown z 78628; ● 800
Oak Dale; RMC Place; ERATH; ***238** EF-5; mail Stephenville z 76401; rural
Oakdale; RMC Place; HOPKINS; ***238** EC-10; mail Sulphur Springs z 75482; rural
Oak Flat; RMC Place; ANGELINA; ***238** EG-12; elev. 280ft./85m.; mail Huntington z 75949; rural
Oak Flat; RMC Place; NACOGDOCHES; ***238** EF-11; mail Cushing z 75760; rural
Oak Flats; RMC Place; RUSK; ***238** EF-11; mail Mount Enterprise z 75681; rural
Oak Forest; RMC Place; GONZALES; ***239** EL-6; mail Gonzales z 78629; rural
Oak forest; RMC Place; HARRIS; ***239** EK-10; ★ **HOU**; mail Houston z 77018, z 77292; pop. incl. with Houston (Inc. Place)
Oak Forest; RMC Place; TRAVIS; ***238** EJ-6; ★ **AUS**; mail Austin z 78759; pop. incl. with Austin (Inc. Place)
Oak Grove; RMC Place; BOWIE; **238** EC-11; elev. 427ft./130m.; mail Avery z 75554; ● 90
Oak Grove; RMC Place; ELLIS; ***238** EF-8; mail Ennis z 75119; rural
Oak Grove; Inc. Place; KAUFMAN; ***238** EE-8; mail Kaufman z 75142; Ⓟ 557; © 710
Oak Grove; RMC Place; WOOD; ***238** ED-10; elev. 486ft./148m.; mail Quitman z 75783; rural
Oak Hill; RMC Place; JASPER; ***238** EH-13; mail Jasper z 75951; rural
Oak Hill; RMC Place; RUSK; ***238** EE-11; mail Henderson z 75652, Tatum z 75691; rural
Oak Hill; RMC Place; TRAVIS; **238** EJ-6; ★ **AUS**; mail Austin z 78735-36, z 78749; pop. incl. with Austin (Inc. Place)
Oak Hills Acres; RMC Place; MONTGOMERY; ***238** EJ-10; ★ **HOU**; mail Pinehurst z 77362
Oakhill Station; RMC Place; TRAVIS; ★ **AUS**; mail Austin z 78709, z 78734-39, z 78749; pop. incl. with Austin (Inc. Place)
Oakhurst; RMC Place; SAN JACINTO; **238** EI-10; 🅿; z 77359; disincorporated May 8, 2000; Ⓟ 219; © 230
Oak Island; RMC Place; CHAMBERS; ***239** EK-12; mail Anahuac z 77514; ● 250
Oak Lake Estates; RMC Place; FORT BEND; ***239** EK-10; ★ **HOU**; mail Sugar Land z 77478; ● 2,000
Oakland; RMC Place; CHEROKEE; ***238** EF-10; elev. 418ft./127m.; mail Rusk z 75785; ● 80
Oakland; RMC Place; COLORADO; **239** EK-8; 🅿; z 78951; ● 85
Oakland; RMC Place; VAN ZANDT; ***238** EE-9; elev. 491ft./150m.; mail Canton z 75103; rural
Oak Lawn; RMC Place; DALLAS; ★ **D-FW**; mail Dallas z 75219; pop. incl. with Dallas (Inc. Place)
Oak Leaf; Inc. Place; ELLIS; ***238** EE-7; 🅿; ★ **D-FW**; z 75154; Ⓟ 984; © 1,209
Oak Point; Inc. Place; DENTON; **235** A-8; 🅿; ★ **DENT**; z 75068; Ⓟ 645; © 1,747
Oak Ridge; Inc. Place; COOKE; ***238** EB-7; elev. 820ft./250m.; mail Gainesville z 76240; Ⓟ 180; © 224
Oak Ridge; Inc. Place; KAUFMAN; ***238** EE-8; mail Terrell z 75160; Ⓟ 268; © 400
Oak Ridge; RMC Place; LLANO; ***238** EI-5; mail Marble Falls z 78654; ● 130
Oak Ridge; RMC Place; NACOGDOCHES; ***238** EG-12; mail Nacogdoches z 75961; rural
Oak Ridge North; Inc. Place; MONTGOMERY; **238** EJ-10; 🅿; ★ **HOU**; z 77385-86 & mail Conroe z 77384, Spring z 77373; Ⓟ 2,454; © 2,991
Oaks; RMC Place; BEE; ***239** EN-5; mail Kenedy z 78119; rural
Oaks North; RMC Place; BEXAR; ***239** EK-4; ★ **SANT**; mail San Antonio z 78260; ● 500
Oak Terrace; RMC Place; MONTGOMERY; ***238** EJ-11; ★ **HOU**; mail Porter z 77365
Oak Trail Shores; CDP-Census Area Only; HOOD; ***238** EE-5; mail Granbury z 76048; Ⓟ 1,750; © 2,475
Oak Valley; Inc. Place; NAVARRO; ***238** EF-8; mail Corsicana z 75110; Ⓟ 388; © 401
Oak Village North; RMC Place; COMAL; ***239** EK-5; mail San Antonio z 78266; pop. incl. with Bulverde (Inc. Place)
Oakville; RMC Place; LIVE OAK; **239** EN-5; 🅿; z 78060; ● 100
Oakwilde; RMC Place; HARRIS; ***239** EK-10; ★ **HOU**; mail Houston z 77093; ● 1,200
Oakwood; Inc. Place; LEON; **238** EG-9; elev. 281ft./86m.; 🅿; z 75855; Ⓟ 527; © 471
Oakwood; RMC Place; TARRANT; ★ **D-FW**; mail Arlington z 76012; pop. incl. with Arlington (Inc. Place)
Oakwood Glen; RMC Place; HARRIS; ***238** EJ-10; ★ **HOU**; mail Spring z 77379
Oasis; COCHRAN; see Griffith (RMC Place)
Oatmeal; RMC Place; BURNET; ***238** EI-5; mail Bertram z 78605; rural
O'Brien; Inc. Place; HASKELL; **236** WH-14; elev. 1,573ft./479m.; 🅿; z 79539; Ⓟ 152; © 132
Ocee; RMC Place; MCLENNAN; ***238** EG-6; mail Crawford z 76638; rural
OCHILTREE; **236** WA-12; Ⓟ 9,128; © 9,006; ◆ 9,888
Odell; RMC Place; WILBARGER; **238** EA-2; 🅿; z 79247 & mail Chillicothe z 79225; ● 95
Odem; Inc. Place; SAN PATRICIO; **239** EO-6; elev. 75ft./23m.; 🅿; z 78370; Ⓟ 2,366; © 2,499
Odessa; Inc. Place; ⊡ ECTOR, MIDLAND; **237** WK-9; 🅿 🅷 🅲 3,462 ■; ★ **MIDL-**; z 79760-66, z 79768-69; Ⓟ 89,699; © 90,943; ◆ 102,313
Odom; RMC Place; VAN ZANDT; ***238** EE-9; mail Mabank z 75147; rural
O'Donnell; Inc. Place; LYNN, DAWSON; **236** WI-10; 🅿; z 79351; Ⓟ 1,102; © 1,011
Oenaville; RMC Place; BELL; ***238** EH-7; elev. 574ft./175m.; mail Temple z 76501
O'Farrell; RMC Place; CASS; ***238** EC-12; elev. 385ft./117m.; mail Atlanta z 75551; rural
Oglesby; Inc. Place; CORYELL; **238** EG-6; 🅿; z 76561; Ⓟ 452; © 458
Oildom; RMC Place; WICHITA; ***238** EB-4; pop. incl. with Wichita Falls (Inc. Place)
Oilton; CDP; WEBB; **239** EP-4; 🅿; z 78371; © 310
Oklahoma; RMC Place; MONTGOMERY; **238** EJ-10; ★ **HOU**; mail Magnolia z 77355; ● 700
Oklahoma Flat; RMC Place; HOCKLEY; ***236** WG-9; elev. 3,490ft./1,064m.; mail Littlefield z 79339; rural
Oklahoma Lane; RMC Place; PARMER; ***236** WF-8; elev. 4,065ft./1,239m.; mail Farwell z 79325; rural
Oklaunion; RMC Place; WILBARGER; **238** EB-3; elev. 1,240ft./378m.; 🅿; z 76373; ● 150
Okra; RMC Place; EASTLAND; ***238** EF-4; mail Carbon z 76435; rural
Ola; RMC Place; KAUFMAN; ***238** EE-9; mail Kaufman z 75142; rural
Olcott; RMC Place; HARRIS; ***239** EK-11; elev. 32ft./10m.; ★ **HOU**; pop. incl. with Houston (Inc. Place)
Old Boston; RMC Place; BOWIE; **238** EC-12; mail New Boston z 75570; ● 170
Old Bowling; RMC Place; LEON; ***238** EH-9; mail Marquez z 77865; rural
Old Brazoria; RMC Place; BRAZORIA; ***239** EM-10; ★ **L.JAC-**; mail Brazoria z 77422; pop. incl. with Brazoria (Inc. Place)
Old Dime Box; RMC Place; LEE; ***238** EJ-7; mail Dime Box z 77853
Old Downtown; RMC Place; COLLIN; mail Plano z 75074, z 75086; pop. incl. with Plano (Inc. Place)
Olden; RMC Place; EASTLAND; **238** EE-4; 🅿; z 76466; ● 500
Oldenburg; RMC Place; FAYETTE; ***239** EK-8; mail La Grange z 78945
Old Ferry; RMC Place; TRAVIS; ***238** EJ-5; ★ **AUS**; mail Spicewood z 78669; ● 250
Old Glory; RMC Place; STONEWALL; **236** WI-13; elev. 1,678ft./511m.; 🅿; z 79540; ● 70
Oldham; RMC Place; DALLAS; ***238** ED-7; ★ **D-FW**; mail Dallas z 75229; pop. incl. with Dallas (Inc. Place)
OLDHAM; **236** WC-9; Ⓟ 2,278; © 2,185; ◆ 2,011
Old Ivy; RMC Place; HOUSTON; ***238** EG-11; mail Kennard z 75847; rural
Old Kinkler; RMC Place; LAVACA; ***239** EL-7; elev. 310ft./94m.; mail Hallettsville z 77964; rural
Old Larissa; RMC Place; CHEROKEE; ***238** EF-10; mail Bullard z 75757, Jacksonville z 75766; rural
Old Laurel; NEWTON; see Devils Pocket (RMC Place)
Old Mobeetie; RMC Place; WHEELER; ***236** WD-13; mail Mobeetie z 79061
Old Moulton; RMC Place; LAVACA; ***239** EK-7; elev. 421ft./128m.; mail Moulton z 77975; rural
Old Ocean; RMC Place; BRAZORIA; **239** EL-10; 🅿; z 77463; ● 950
Old River Lake; RMC Place; LIBERTY; ***238** EJ-11; mail Cleveland z 77327; ● 225
Old River Terrace; RMC Place; HARRIS; ***239** EK-11; ★ **HOU**; mail Channelview z 77530
Old River-Winfree; Inc. Place; CHAMBERS; **238** EJ-11; ★ **HOU**; mail Baytown z 77520, z 77523, Dayton z 77535; Ⓟ 1,233; © 1,364
Old Round Rock; RMC Place; WILLIAMSON; ***238** EI-6; ★ **AUS**; mail Round Rock z 78664; pop. incl. with Round Rock (Inc. Place)
Olds; RMC Place; JASPER; ***238** EH-13; mail Jasper z 75951; rural
Old Sabinetown; RMC Place; SABINE; mail Hemphill z 75948; rural
Old Saint marys; RMC Place; REFUGIO; ***239** EO-7; mail Woodsboro z 78393; pop. incl. with Bayside (Inc. Place)
Old Salem (Salem); RMC Place; NEWTON; ***238** EI-13; mail Call z 75933; ● 85
Old Union; RMC Place; BOWIE; ***238** EC-12; elev. 324ft./99m.; mail Simms z 75574; rural
Old Union; RMC Place; LIMESTONE; ***238** EG-8; mail Thornton z 76687
Old Union; RMC Place; TITUS; ***238** EC-11; mail Mount Pleasant z 75455; rural
Old Waverly (Waverly); RMC Place; SAN JACINTO; ***238** EI-10; mail New Waverly z 77358, Willis z 77378; rural
Oletha; RMC Place; LIMESTONE; ***238** EG-8; elev. 472ft./144m.; mail Thornton z 76687
Olfen; RMC Place; RUNNELS; ***238** EG-1; mail Rowena z 76875; rural
Olin; RMC Place; HAMILTON; ***238** EF-5; elev. 1,280ft./390m.; mail Hico z 76457; rural
Olivarez; CDP-Census Area Only; HIDALGO; ***239** ES-5; ★ **MCAL**; © 2,445
Olive; RMC Place; HARDIN; ***238** EI-12; mail Kountze z 77625; rural
Olivia; RMC Place; CALHOUN; **239** EN-8; mail Port Lavaca z 77979; ● 250
Olmito; CDP; CAMERON; **239** ES-6; 🅿; ★ **BRNS**; z 78575; © 1,198
Olmos; RMC Place; BEE; ***239** EN-6; elev. 222ft./68m.; mail Skidmore z 78389; rural
Olmos; RMC Place; STARR; ***239** ES-4; mail Rio Grande City z 78582; pop. incl. with Rio Grande City (Inc. Place)
Olmos Park; Inc. Place; BEXAR; **239** ER-11; 🅿; ★ **SANT**; z 78212; Ⓟ 2,161; © 2,343
Olney; Inc. Place; YOUNG; **238** EC-4; elev. 1,184ft./361m.; 🅿 🅷; z 76374; Ⓟ 3,519; © 3,396
Olton; Inc. Place; LAMB; **236** WF-10; 🅿; z 79064; Ⓟ 2,116; © 2,288
Omaha; Inc. Place; MORRIS; **238** EC-11; 🅿; z 75571; Ⓟ 833; © 999
Omen; RMC Place; SMITH; ***238** EE-11; mail Troup z 75789, Tyler z 75705; ● 150
Onalaska; Inc. Place; POLK; **238** EI-11; 🅿; z 77360; Ⓟ 728; © 1,174
One Seventy Seven Lake Estates (Lake Estates); RMC Place; MONTGOMERY; ***238** EJ-10; mail Montgomery z 77316; ● 300
Onion Creek; CDP-Census Area Only; TRAVIS; ***238** EJ-6; ★ **AUS**; mail Austin z 78747; Ⓟ 1,544; © 2,116
Opdyke; RMC Place; HOCKLEY; **236** WH-9; mail Levelland z 79336; ● 50
Opdyke West; Inc. Place; HOCKLEY; ***236** WH-9; elev. 3,465ft./1,056m.; mail Levelland z 79336; Ⓟ 100; © 188
Opelika; RMC Place; HENDERSON; ***238** EE-10; mail Murchison z 75778; rural
Oplin; RMC Place; CALLAHAN; ***238** EF-2; mail Clyde z 79510; ● 75
O'Quinn; RMC Place; FAYETTE; ***239** EK-7; mail La Grange z 78945; rural
Ora; RMC Place; ANGELINA; ***238** EG-12; elev. 195ft./59m.; mail Huntington z 75949; rural
Oran; RMC Place; PALO PINTO; **238** ED-5; mail Graford z 76449; ● 60
Orange; Inc. Place; ⊡ ORANGE; **238** EJ-13; 🅿 🅷 ■; ★ **B-PA**; z 77630-32; Ⓟ 19,381; © 18,643; ◆ 16,507
ORANGE; **238** EJ-13; Ⓟ 80,509; © 84,966; ◆ 79,357
Orangedale; RMC Place; BEE; ***239** EN-6; mail Beeville z 78102; rural
Orangefield; RMC Place; ORANGE; **238** EJ-13; 🅿; ★ **B-PA**; z 77639; pop. incl. with Orange (Inc. Place)
Orange Grove; RMC Place; HARRIS; ***239** EK-10; ★ **HOU**; mail Houston z 77039; ● 2,000
Orange Grove; Inc. Place; JIM WELLS; **239** EO-6; 🅿; z 78372; Ⓟ 1,175; © 1,288
Orangeville; RMC Place; FANNIN; ***238** EC-8; mail Whitewright z 75491; ● 50
Orchard; Inc. Place; FORT BEND; **239** EK-9; elev. 127ft./39m.; 🅿; z 77464; Ⓟ 373; © 408
Ore City; Inc. Place; UPSHUR; **238** ED-11; 🅿; z 75683; Ⓟ 898; © 1,106
Orient; RMC Place; TOM GREEN; ***238** EG-1; mail San Angelo z 76901; rural
Orla; RMC Place; REEVES; **237** WK-6; 🅿; z 79770; ● 50
Orme; RMC Place; TARRANT; ★ **D-FW**; mail Arlington z 76010; pop. incl. with Arlington (Inc. Place)
Osage; RMC Place; CORYELL; **238** EG-6; mail Gatesville z 76528, Weimar z 78962; ● 30
Oscar; RMC Place; BELL; ***238** EH-7; ★ **KILL-**; mail Temple z 76501; rural
Osceola; RMC Place; HILL; **238** EF-7; elev. 72ft./22m.; mail Itasca z 76055; ● 100
Ottine; RMC Place; GONZALES; **239** EK-6; 🅿; z 78658; ● 130
Otto; RMC Place; FALLS; **238** EG-7; 🅿; z 76682; ● 50
Ovalo; RMC Place; TAYLOR; **237** WK-14; elev. 2,028ft./618m.; 🅿; z 79541; ● 200
Overton; Inc. Place; RUSK, SMITH; **238** EE-11; elev. 489ft./149m.; 🅿; z 75684; Ⓟ 2,105; © 2,350
Ovilla; Inc. Place; ELLIS, DALLAS; ***238** EE-7; 🅿; ★ **D-FW**; z 75154; Ⓟ 2,027; © 3,405
Owens; RMC Place; BROWN; **238** EG-3; elev. 1,474ft./449m.; mail Brownwood z 76801, May z 76857; ● 30
Owens; RMC Place; CROSBY; ***236** WH-11; mail Ralls z 79357
Owensville; RMC Place; ROBERTSON; ***238** EH-8; elev. 491ft./150m.; mail Franklin z 77856; rural
Owentown; RMC Place; SMITH; **238** EE-10; ★ **TYL**; mail Tyler z 75708; ● 120
Owl Ranch-Amargosa; CDP-Census Area Only; JIM WELLS; ***239** EO-5; © 527
Oyster Creek; Inc. Place; BRAZORIA; **239** EM-11; 🅿; ★ **L.JAC-**; z 77541; Ⓟ 912; © 1,192
Ozona; CDP; ⊡ CROCKETT; **237** WN-11; elev. 2,360ft./719m.; 🅿; z 76943; Ⓟ 3,181; © 3,436

P

Pacio; RMC Place; DELTA; ***238** EC-10; elev. 434ft./132m.; mail Lake Creek z 75450; rural
Padgett; RMC Place; YOUNG; ***238** EC-3; elev. 1,215ft./370m.; mail Olney z 76374; rural
Paducah; Inc. Place; ⊡ COTTLE; **236** WG-13; 🅿; z 79248; Ⓟ 1,788; © 1,498
Pagoda; RMC Place; TRINITY; ***238** EH-10; mail Trinity z 75862; pop. incl. with Trinity (Inc. Place)
Paige; RMC Place; BASTROP; **238** EJ-7; 🅿; z 78659; ● 200
Paint Creek; RMC Place; HASKELL; ***238** ED-2; mail Haskell z 79521; rural
Paint Rock; Inc. Place; ⊡ CONCHO; **237** WL-14; elev. 1,631ft./497m.; 🅿; z 76866; Ⓟ 227; © 320
Pakan; RMC Place; WHEELER; ***236** WD-13; elev. 2,678ft./816m.; mail Shamrock z 79079; rural
Palacios; Inc. Place; MATAGORDA; **239** EM-9; 🅿 🅷; z 77465; Ⓟ 4,418; © 5,153
Palava; RMC Place; FISHER; ***238** EE-1; mail Sweetwater z 79556; rural
Palestine; Inc. Place; ⊡ ANDERSON; **238** EG-10; 🅿 🅷 ■; z 75801-03, z 75882; Ⓟ 18,042; © 17,598; ◆ 18,520
Palestine; RMC Place; POLK; mail Chester z 75936; ● 100
Palisades; Inc. Place; RANDALL; ***236** WD-10; mail Amarillo z 79118; © 352
Palito Blanco; RMC Place; JIM WELLS; ***239** EP-5; elev. 225ft./69m.; mail Alice z 78332; ● 100
Palm Beach; RMC Place; GALVESTON; ***239** EK-11; ★ **HOU**; mail Galveston z 77554; pop. incl. with Galveston (Inc. Place)
Palmer; Inc. Place; ELLIS; **238** EE-8; 🅿; z 75152; Ⓟ 1,659; © 1,774
Palmetal; RMC Place; CAMERON; ***239** ES-6; ★ **BRNS**; pop. incl. with Harlingen (Inc. Place)
Palmetto Park; RMC Place; SAN JACINTO; mail Oakhurst z 77359; pop. incl. with Oakhurst (RMC Place)
Palm Harbor; RMC Place; ARANSAS; ***239** EO-7; mail Rockport z 78382; ● 125
Palmhurst; Inc. Place; HIDALGO; **237** WO-1; elev. 160ft./49m.; 🅿; ★ **MCAL**; z 78572-74; Ⓟ 326; © 4,872
Palm Park; RMC Place; BEXAR; **239** EL-5; ★ **SANT**; mail San Antonio z 78223; ● 250
Palm Valley; Inc. Place; CAMERON; ***239** ES-6; ★ **BRNS**; mail Harlingen z 78550; Ⓟ 1,199; © 1,298
Palmview; Inc. Place; HIDALGO; ***239** ES-5; 🅿; ★ **MCAL**; z 78572, z 78574 & mail Edinburg z 78539; Ⓟ 1,818; © 4,107
Palmview South; CDP-Census Area Only; HIDALGO; ***239** ES-5; ★ **MCAL**; © 6,219
Palo Alto; RMC Place; NUECES; ***239** EP-6; mail Bishop z 78343
Paloduro; RMC Place; ARMSTRONG; ***236** WE-11; elev. 2,829ft./862m.; mail Clarendon z 79226
Palo Pinto; RMC Place; ⊡ PALO PINTO; **238** ED-5; elev. 1,044ft./318m.; 🅿; z 76484; ● 425
PALO PINTO; **238** EE-4; Ⓟ 25,055; © 27,026; ◆ 26,703
Paluxy; RMC Place; HOOD; **238** EF-5; 🅿; z 76467; ● 55
Pamela Heights; RMC Place; HARRIS; ***239** EK-10; ★ **HOU**; mail Houston z 77045; pop. incl. with Houston (Inc. Place)
Pampa; Inc. Place; ⊡ GRAY; **236** WC-12; elev. 3,236ft./986m.; 🅿 🅷 ■; z 79065-66; Ⓟ 19,959; © 17,887; ◆ 18,433
Pancake; RMC Place; CORYELL; ***238** EG-6; elev. 1,143ft./348m.; mail Gatesville z 76528, Jonesboro z 76538; rural
Pandale; RMC Place; VAL VERDE; ***237** WO-11; elev. 1,656ft./505m.; mail Ozona z 76943; rural
Pandora; RMC Place; WILSON; **239** EL-6; elev. 451ft./137m.; 🅿; z 78143; ● 100
Panhandle; Inc. Place; ⊡ CARSON; **236** WD-11; elev. 3,456ft./1,053m.; 🅿; z 79068; Ⓟ 2,353; © 2,589
Panna Maria; RMC Place; KARNES; **239** EM-5; elev. 225ft./69m.; 🅿; z 78144; ● 110
Panola; RMC Place; PANOLA; **238** EE-12; elev. 316ft./96m.; 🅿; z 75685; ● 225
PANOLA; **238** EE-12; Ⓟ 22,035; © 22,756; ◆ 22,606
Panorama Estates; RMC Place; HUNT; ***238** ED-9; mail Wills Point z 75169; ● 250
Panorama Village; Inc. Place; MONTGOMERY; ***238** EJ-10; 🅿; z 77304; Ⓟ 1,556; © 1,965
Pantego; Inc. Place; TARRANT; **235** H-6; 🅿; ★ **D-FW**; z 76013, z 76015 & mail Arlington z 76094; Ⓟ 2,371; © 2,318
Panther Junction; RMC Place; BREWSTER; ***237** WQ-7; mail Big Bend National Park z 79834; ● 100
Papalote; RMC Place; BEE; **239** EO-6; mail Sinton z 78387; ● 70
Paradise; Inc. Place; WISE; **238** ED-6; 🅿; z 76073; © 459
Paradise Bay; RMC Place; HENDERSON; ***238** EE-9; mail Kemp z 75143; pop. incl. with Tool (Inc. Place)
Paradise Hills; RMC Place; SAN AUGUSTINE; ***238** EH-12; mail Broaddus z 75929; ● 25
Paris; Inc. Place; ⊡ LAMAR; **238** EB-10; elev. 602ft./183m.; 🅿 🅷 ■; z 75460-62; Ⓟ 24,699; © 25,898; ◆ 25,286
Park; RMC Place; FAYETTE; ***239** EK-8; mail La Grange z 78945; rural
Parkdale; RMC Place; DALLAS; ★ **D-FW**; mail Dallas z 75227; pop. incl. with Dallas (Inc. Place)
Parker; Inc. Place; COLLIN; **235** C-13; elev. 604ft./184m.; ★ **D-FW**; mail Allen z 75002, Mckinney z 75069; Ⓟ 1,235; © 1,379
Parker; RMC Place; JOHNSON; ***238** EF-7; elev. 837ft./255m.; mail Grandview z 76050; ● 35
PARKER; **238** ED-5; Ⓟ 64,785; © 88,495; ◆ 113,218
Parker Point; RMC Place; ANGELINA; ***238** EH-12; elev. 190ft./58m.; mail Zavalla z 75980; ● 60
Park Glen; RMC Place; HARRIS; ***239** EK-10; ★ **HOU**; mail Stafford z 77477; pop. incl. with Houston (Inc. Place)
Park Place; RMC Place; HARRIS; ***239** EK-11; ★ **HOU**; mail Houston z 77017, z 77217, z 77287; pop. incl. with Houston (Inc. Place)
Park Springs; RMC Place; WISE; **238** EC-5; elev. 962ft./293m.; mail Sunset z 76270; ● 80
Parkview; RMC Place; PECOS; ***237** WN-8; mail Fort Stockton z 79735; pop. incl. with Fort Stockton (Inc. Place)
Parkview Estates; RMC Place; GUADALUPE; ***239** EL-5; mail Seguin z 78155; pop. incl. with Seguin (Inc. Place)
Parkway; RMC Place; SAN AUGUSTINE; ***238** EH-13; mail Broaddus z 75929; ● 300
Parkwood; RMC Place; JASPER; ***238** EI-13; mail Buna z 77612; rural
Parkwood Estates; RMC Place; HARRIS; ***239** EK-10; ★ **HOU**; mail Houston z 77032; ● 500
PARMER; **236** WE-8; Ⓟ 9,863; © 10,016; ◆ 9,206
Parnell; RMC Place; HALL; ***236** WF-13; elev. 1,944ft./593m.; mail Childress z 79201; rural
Parvin; RMC Place; DENTON; ***238** EC-7; elev. 563ft./172m.; mail Prosper z 75078; rural
Pasadena; Inc. Place; HARRIS; **234** E-7; 🅿 🅷 🅲 350 ■; ★ **HOU**; z 77501-08; Ⓟ 119,363; © 141,674; ◆ 158,911
Paso Real; RMC Place; WILLACY; ***239** ES-6; mail Lyford z 78569; rural
Patillo; RMC Place; ERATH; **238** EE-5; mail Lipan z 76462; ● 20
Patman Switch (Turkey Creek); RMC Place; CASS; ***238** ED-11; mail Hughes Springs z 75656; ● 180
Patricia; RMC Place; DAWSON; **236** WJ-10; mail Lamesa z 79331; ● 60
Patrick; RMC Place; DALLAS; ***238** EE-8; ★ **D-FW**; mail Ferris z 75125; rural
Patrick; RMC Place; RUSK; mail Mount Enterprise z 75681; rural
Patroon; RMC Place; SHELBY; **238** EG-13; mail Shelbyville z 75973; ● 60
Pattison; Inc. Place; WALLER; ***239** EK-9; elev. 172ft./52m.; 🅿; z 77423, z 77466; Ⓟ 327; © 447
Patton; RMC Place; MCLENNAN; 🅿; z 77372 & mail Valley Mills z 76689; rural
Patton Park; RMC Place; BELL; ***238** EH-6; ★ **KILL-**; mail Killeen z 76544
Patton Village; Inc. Place; MONTGOMERY; ***238** EJ-11; elev. 105ft./32m.; ★ **HOU**; mail Splendora z 77372; Ⓟ 1,155; © 1,391
Pattonville; RMC Place; LAMAR; **238** EC-10; 🅿; z 75468; ● 220
Pauline; RMC Place; HENDERSON; ***238** EE-9; mail Eustace z 75124; rural
Pauls Store; RMC Place; SHELBY; ***238** EF-13; mail Shelbyville z 75973; rural
Pawelekville; RMC Place; KARNES; **239** EM-5; elev. 354ft./108m.; mail Falls City z 78113; ● 50
Pawnee; CDP; BEE; **239** EN-5; 🅿; z 78145; © 201
Paxton; RMC Place; SHELBY; **238** EF-12; mail Joaquin z 75954; ● 120
Paynes Corner; RMC Place; GAINES; ***236** WI-8; mail Seminole z 79360; rural
Payne Springs; Inc. Place; HENDERSON; **238** EE-9; mail Mabank z 75156; Ⓟ 606; © 683
Payton Colony; RMC Place; BLANCO; ***238** EJ-5; mail Blanco z 78606; rural
Peach Creek; BASTROP; see Salem (RMC Place)
Peach Creek; RMC Place; WHARTON; mail Wharton z 77488; rural
Peach Creek Estates; RMC Place; MONTGOMERY; ***238** EJ-11; ★ **HOU**; mail Splendora z 77372; ● 250
Peachtree; RMC Place; JASPER; ***238** EH-13; mail Jasper z 75951; rural
Peacock; RMC Place; STONEWALL; **236** WI-13; elev. 1,871ft./570m.; mail Aspermont z 79502; ● 50
Peadenville; RMC Place; PALO PINTO; **238** ED-5; elev. 1,045ft./319m.; mail Mineral Wells z 76067; ● 30
Pearl; RMC Place; CORYELL; ***238** EG-5; mail Gatesville z 76528
Pearland; Inc. Place; BRAZORIA, HARRIS; **234** G-6; elev. 54ft./16m.; 🅿; ★ **HOU**; z 77581, z 77584, z 77588; Ⓟ 18,927; © 37,640; ◆ 58,929
Pearl City; RMC Place; DEWITT; ***239** EL-7; mail Yoakum z 77995; rural
Pear Ridge; RMC Place; JEFFERSON; ***238** EJ-13; ★ **B-PA**; mail Port Arthur z 77640, z 77642; pop. incl. with Port Arthur (Inc. Place)
Pearsall; Inc. Place; ⊡ FRIO; **239** EM-3; elev. 631ft./192m.; 🅿 🅷; z 78061; Ⓟ 6,924; © 7,157
Pearsons Chapel; RMC Place; HOUSTON; ***238** EH-10; elev. 322ft./98m.; mail Lovelady z 75851; rural
Pear Valley; RMC Place; MCCULLOCH; **238** EH-2; elev. 1,582ft./482m.; 🅿; z 76852; ● 40
Peaster; RMC Place; PARKER; **238** ED-5; 🅿; z 76485; ● 80
Pebble Beach Sunset Acres; RMC Place; COLLIN; ***238** ED-8; ★ **D-FW**; mail Copeville z 75121; ● 300
Pebble Hills; RMC Place; EL PASO; ***237** WK-2; ★ **ELP**; mail El Paso z 79925, z 79935, z 79937; pop. incl. with El Paso (Inc. Place)
Pecan; RMC Place; VAL VERDE; mail Del Rio z 78841; pop. incl. with Del Rio (Inc. Place)
Pecan Acres; CDP-Census Area Only; WISE, TARRANT; ***238** ED-6; mail Newark z 76071; Ⓟ 1,587; © 2,289
Pecan Gap; Inc. Place; DELTA, FANNIN; **238** EC-9; 🅿; z 75469; Ⓟ 245; © 214
Pecangrove; RMC Place; CORYELL; mail Gatesville z 76528, Oglesby z 76561; rural
Pecan Grove; CDP-Census Area Only; FORT BEND; ***239** EK-10; ★ **HOU**; mail Richmond z 77469; Ⓟ 9,502; © 13,551
Pecan Heights; RMC Place; CAMP; ***238** ED-11; mail Pittsburg z 75686; pop. incl. with Pittsburg (Inc. Place)
Pecan Hill; Inc. Place; ELLIS; ***238** EE-7; ★ **D-FW**; mail Red Oak z 75154; Ⓟ 564; © 672
Pecan Park; RMC Place; HARRIS; ***239** EK-11; ★ **HOU**; mail Houston z 77087; pop. incl. with Houston (Inc. Place)
Pecan Plantation; CDP-Census Area Only; HOOD; ***238** EE-6; mail Granbury z 76049; © 3,544
Pecos; Inc. Place; ⊡ REEVES; **237** WL-7; elev. 2,586ft./788m.; 🅿 🅷; z 79772; Ⓟ 12,069; © 9,501
PECOS; **237** WN-9; Ⓟ 14,675; © 16,809; ◆ 16,040
Peeltown; RMC Place; KAUFMAN; ***238** EE-8; elev. 383ft./117m.; mail Scurry z 75158; rural
Peerless; RMC Place; HOPKINS; **238** EC-9; mail Sulphur Springs z 75482; ● 75
Peggy; RMC Place; ATASCOSA; **239** EM-5; elev. 386ft./118m.; 🅿; z 78062; ● 10
Pelham; RMC Place; NAVARRO; ***238** EF-7; mail Hubbard z 76648; rural
Pelican Bay; Inc. Place; TARRANT; **235** E-2; ★ **D-FW**; mail Azle z 76020; Ⓟ 1,271; © 1,505
Pendleton; RMC Place; BELL; **238** EH-6; 🅿; z 76564; ● 200
Pendleton Harbor; RMC Place; SABINE; ***238** EG-13; mail Hemphill z 75948; ● 200
Penelope; Inc. Place; HILL; **238** EF-7; 🅿; z 76676; Ⓟ 210; © 211
Peniel; RMC Place; HUNT; ***238** EC-9; elev. 1,553ft./473m.; mail Greenville z 75401; pop. incl. with Greenville (Inc. Place)
Penitas; Inc. Place; HIDALGO; **239** ES-5; 🅿; ★ **MCAL**; z 78576; Ⓟ 1,131; © 1,167
Pennington; RMC Place; TRINITY; **238** EH-10; elev. 346ft./105m.; 🅿; z 75856; ● 125
Penwell; RMC Place; ECTOR; **237** WL-9; 🅿; z 79776; ● 75
Peoria; RMC Place; HILL; **238** EF-7; mail Hillsboro z 76645; ● 100
Pep; RMC Place; HOCKLEY; **236** WG-9; 🅿; z 79353; ● 50
Percilla; RMC Place; HOUSTON; ***238** EG-10; elev. 427ft./130m.; mail Grapeland z 75844; ● 50
Perezville; RMC Place; HIDALGO; ***239** ES-5; ★ **MCAL**; mail Mission z 78572; pop. incl. with Palmview (Inc. Place)
Perico; RMC Place; DALLAM; ***236** WB-9; mail Texline z 79087; rural
Pernitas Point; Inc. Place; LIVE OAK, JIM WELLS; ***239** EO-6; mail George West z 78022, Sandia z 78383; Ⓟ 174; summer pop. 600; © 269
Perrin; RMC Place; JACK; **238** ED-5; 🅿; z 76486; ● 300
Perrin Heights; RMC Place; GRAYSON; ***238** EB-8; ★ **SHRM-**; mail Denison z 75020; pop. incl. with Denison (Inc. Place)
Perry; RMC Place; FALLS; **238** EG-7; 🅿; z 76682; ● 60
Perry Landing; RMC Place; BRAZORIA; ***239** EM-10; ★ **L.JAC-**; mail Freeport z 77541; pop. incl. with Jones Creek (Inc. Place)
Perryton; Inc. Place; ⊡ OCHILTREE; **236** WB-12; 🅿 🅷; z 79070; Ⓟ 7,607; © 7,774
Perryville; RMC Place; WOOD; ***238** ED-10; mail Gilmer z 75644, Winnsboro z 75494; rural
Pershing; RMC Place; TRAVIS; ***238** EJ-6; ★ **AUS**; mail Austin z 78702; pop. incl. with Austin (Inc. Place)
Pershing Park; RMC Place; BELL; ***238** EH-6; ★ **KILL-**; mail Killeen z 76544
Personville; RMC Place; LIMESTONE; ***238** EG-8; elev. 424ft./129m.; mail Groesbeck z 76642; rural
Pert; RMC Place; ANDERSON; ***238** EF-10; elev. 479ft./146m.; mail Palestine z 75801; rural
Peters; RMC Place; AUSTIN; **239** EK-9; mail Sealy z 77474
Petersburg; Inc. Place; HALE; **236** WG-11; 🅿; z 79250; Ⓟ 1,292; © 1,262
Peters Prairie; RMC Place; RED RIVER; ***238** EC-11; mail Clarksville z 75426; rural
Petersville; RMC Place; DEWITT; ***239** EL-7; elev. 383ft./117m.; mail Yoakum z 77995; rural
Petrolia; Inc. Place; CLAY; **238** EB-5; elev. 993ft./303m.; 🅿; z 76377; Ⓟ 762; © 782
Petronila; Inc. Place; NUECES; **239** EP-6; elev. 51ft./16m.; mail Robstown z 78380; Ⓟ 155; © 83
Petteway; RMC Place; ROBERTSON; ***238** EH-8; elev. 487ft./148m.; mail Bremond z 76629; rural
Pettibone; RMC Place; MILAM; ***238** EI-7; elev. 501ft./153m.; mail Cameron z 76520; ● 30
Pettit; RMC Place; HOCKLEY; **236** WG-9; elev. 3,633ft./1,107m.; mail Levelland z 79336; ● 80
Pettus; CDP; BEE; **239** EN-6; 🅿; z 78146; © 608
Petty; RMC Place; LAMAR; **238** EC-9; 🅿; z 75470; ● 100
Petty; RMC Place; LYNN; ***236** WH-10; elev. 3,230ft./985m.; mail Tahoka z 79373; rural
Petty's Chapel; RMC Place; NAVARRO; ***238** EF-8; mail Corsicana z 75110; ● 25
Pflugerville; Inc. Place; TRAVIS; **238** EJ-6; elev. 704ft./215m.; 🅿; ★ **AUS**; z 78660, z 78691; Ⓟ 4,444; © 16,335; ◆ 25,530
Phalba; RMC Place; VAN ZANDT; ***238** EE-9; elev. 446ft./136m.; mail Mabank z 75147
Pharr; Inc. Place; HIDALGO; **239** ES-5; elev. 115ft./35m.; 🅿 ■; ★ **MCAL**; z 78577; Ⓟ 32,921; © 46,660; ◆ 60,973
Pheasant Creek; RMC Place; FORT BEND; ***239** EK-10; ★ **HOU**; mail Sugar Land z 77478; ● 1,200
Phelan; RMC Place; BASTROP; ***238** EJ-7; mail Bastrop z 78602; rural
Phelps; RMC Place; WALKER; **238** EI-10; mail Huntsville z 77340; ● 200
Phillips; RMC Place; HUTCHINSON; **236** WC-11; 🅿; z 79007; ● 900
Phillipsburg; RMC Place; WASHINGTON; ***238** EJ-8; mail Brenham z 77833; rural
Phoenix; RMC Place; BEXAR; ***239** EL-4; ★ **SANT**; pop. incl. with San Antonio (Inc. Place)
Pickens; RMC Place; HENDERSON; ***238** EE-9; elev. 470ft./143m.; mail Athens z 75751; rural
Pickett; RMC Place; NAVARRO; ***238** EF-8; elev. 434ft./132m.; mail Corsicana z 75110; rural
Pickton; RMC Place; HOPKINS; **238** ED-10; 🅿; z 75471; ● 150
Pidcoke; RMC Place; CORYELL; ***238** EH-5; mail Gatesville z 76528
Piedmont; RMC Place; GRIMES; ***238** EI-9; mail Anderson z 77830; rural
Piedmont; RMC Place; UPSHUR; ***238** EE-11; mail Gilmer z 75644; rural
Pierce; RMC Place; WHARTON; **239** EL-9; 🅿; z 77467; ● 125
Pierce Junction; RMC Place; HARRIS; ***239** EK-10; elev. 52ft./16m.; ★ **HOU**; pop. incl. with Houston (Inc. Place)
Pierces Chapel; RMC Place; CHEROKEE; ***238** EF-10; mail Jacksonville z 75766; rural
Pike; RMC Place; COLLIN; ***238** EC-8; mail Blue Ridge z 75424; ● 70
Pilgrim; RMC Place; GONZALES; ***239** EL-6; mail Smiley z 78159; ● 25
Pilgrim Ridge; RMC Place; WALKER; ***238** EH-10; mail Riverside z 77367; rural
Pilgrims Rest; RMC Place; RAINS; ***238** ED-9; mail Alba z 75410, Emory z 75440; rural
Pilot Grove; RMC Place; GRAYSON; ***238** EC-8; mail Whitewright z 75491; ● 60
Pilot Knob; RMC Place; TRAVIS; ***238** EJ-6; elev. 569ft./173m.; ★ **AUS**; mail Austin z 78744; ● 400
Pilot Point; Inc. Place; DENTON; **238** EC-7; 🅿; z 76258; Ⓟ 2,538; © 3,538
Pine; RMC Place; CAMP; ***238** ED-11; mail Pittsburg z 75686; ● 80
Pine Acres; RMC Place; MONTGOMERY; ***238** EJ-11; ★ **HOU**; mail New Caney z 77357
Pine Branch; RMC Place; RED RIVER; ***238** EC-10; mail Bogata z 75417; rural
Pine Crest; RMC Place; JEFFERSON; ***238** EJ-13; ★ **B-PA**; mail Beaumont z 77703; pop. incl. with Beaumont (Inc. Place)
Pine Forest; RMC Place; HOPKINS; ***238** ED-10; mail Pickton z 75471; ● 50
Pine Forest; Inc. Place; ORANGE; **238** EJ-13; ★ **B-PA**; mail Vidor z 77662; Ⓟ 709; © 632
Pine Grove; RMC Place; CHEROKEE; ***238** EF-10; elev. 380ft./116m.; mail Jacksonville z 75766; rural
Pine Grove; RMC Place; NEWTON; ***238** EI-13; elev. 176ft./54m.; mail Newton z 75966; ● 160
Pine Grove; RMC Place; ORANGE; ***238** EJ-13; ★ **B-PA**; mail Orange z 77630; pop. incl. with Orange (Inc. Place)
Pine Hill; RMC Place; CHEROKEE; ***238** EF-11; mail Jacksonville z 75766; rural
Pinehill; RMC Place; RUSK; ***238** EF-12; elev. 388ft./118m.; mail Henderson z 75652; ● 40
Pinehurst; CDP; MONTGOMERY; **238** EJ-10; elev. 222ft./68m.; 🅿; ★ **HOU**; z 77362; Ⓟ 3,284; © 4,266
Pinehurst; Inc. Place; ORANGE; **238** EJ-13; ★ **B-PA**; mail Orange z 77630; Ⓟ 2,682; © 2,274
Pine Island; Inc. Place; WALLER; ***238** EJ-9; mail Hempstead z 77445; Ⓟ 571; © 849
Pine Lake; RMC Place; MONTGOMERY; ***238** EJ-10; mail Montgomery z 77316; ● 100
Pineland; Inc. Place; SABINE; **238** EG-13; elev. 250ft./76m.; 🅿; z 75968; Ⓟ 882; © 980
Pine Mills; RMC Place; WOOD; ***238** ED-10; elev. 466ft./142m.; mail Mineola z 75773; rural
Pine Park; RMC Place; SABINE; ***238** EG-13; elev. 312ft./95m.; mail Hemphill z 75948; rural
Pine Prairie; RMC Place; WALKER; ***238** EI-10; mail Huntsville z 77320
Pine Ridge; RMC Place; HARDIN; ***238** EJ-12; mail Kountze z 77625; rural
Pine Springs; RMC Place; CULBERSON; ***237** WK-5; mail Salt Flat z 79847; rural
Pine Springs; RMC Place; SMITH; ***238** EE-10; ★ **TYL**; mail Tyler z 75708
Pine Trail Estates; RMC Place; SMITH; ***238** EF-10; ★ **TYL**; mail Flint z 75762; ● 700
Pine Valley; RMC Place; ANGELINA; ***238** EH-11; ★ **LUFK**; mail Diboll z 75941; rural
Pineview; RMC Place; WOOD; ***238** ED-10; elev. 499ft./152m.; mail Winnsboro z 75494; rural
Pinewood Estates; CDP-Census Area Only; HARDIN; ***238** EJ-12; mail Beaumont z 77706; Ⓟ 1,174; © 1,633
Pinewood Estates; RMC Place; MONTGOMERY; ***238** EJ-11; ★ **HOU**; mail Splendora z 77372; ● 40
Pinewood Village; RMC Place; HARRIS; ***239** EK-10; ★ **HOU**; mail Houston z 77093; pop. incl. with Houston (Inc. Place)
Piney; RMC Place; AUSTIN; ***239** EK-9; mail Bellville z 77418; rural
Piney Grove; RMC Place; CASS; ***238** EC-12; mail Atlanta z 75551; rural
Piney Grove; RMC Place; UPSHUR; ***238** ED-10; mail Leesburg z 75451; rural
Piney Point; RMC Place; MONTGOMERY; ***238** EJ-10; ★ **HOU**; mail Conroe z 77301; ● 250
Piney Point; RMC Place; SABINE; ***238** EG-13; mail Milam z 75959; ● 40
Piney Point Village; Inc. Place; HARRIS; **234** D-3; ★ **HOU**; mail Houston z 77024; Ⓟ 3,197; © 3,380
Piney Woods; RMC Place; JASPER; ***238** EH-13; mail Jasper z 75951; rural
Pinnacle; RMC Place; UPSHUR; mail Gilmer z 75644; rural
Pioneer; RMC Place; EASTLAND; **238** EF-3; mail Rising Star z 76471; ● 40
Pioneer Trails; RMC Place; MONTGOMERY; ***238** EJ-10; ★ **HOU**; mail Conroe z 77302; ● 300
Pipe Creek; RMC Place; BANDERA; **239** EK-4; elev. 1,360ft./415m.; 🅿; z 78063; ● 100
Pirtle; RMC Place; RUSK; ***238** EE-11; ★ **LNGV**; mail Overton z 75684
Pisgah; RMC Place; SAN AUGUSTINE; ***238** EG-13; mail Broaddus z 75929
Pitner Junction; RMC Place; RUSK; ***238** EE-11; elev. 366ft./112m.; mail Overton z 75684; rural
Pittsburg; Inc. Place; ⊡ CAMP; **238** ED-11; 🅿 🅷; z 75686; Ⓟ 4,007; © 4,347
Placation Estates; RMC Place; SABINE; ***238** EG-13; mail Milam z 75959; ● 50
Place; RMC Place; CAMERON; ★ **BRNS**; pop. incl. with San Benito (Inc. Place)
Placedo; RMC Place; VICTORIA; **239** EM-8; elev. 56ft./17m.; 🅿; z 77977; ● 700
Placid; RMC Place; MCCULLOCH; **238** EH-3; elev. 1,609ft./490m.; mail Rochelle z 76872; ● 30
Plains; RMC Place; BORDEN; ***236** WI-11; mail Odonnell z 79351; rural
Plains; Inc. Place; ⊡ YOAKUM; **236** WH-8; elev. 3,645ft./1,111m.; 🅿; z 79355; Ⓟ 1,422; © 1,450
Plainview; Inc. Place; ⊡ HALE; **236** WF-11; 🅿 🅷 🅲 5,688 ■; z 79072-73; Ⓟ 21,700; © 22,336; ◆ 20,970
Plainview; RMC Place; NACOGDOCHES; ***238** EG-12; mail Nacogdoches z 75961; rural
Plainview; RMC Place; SABINE; ***238** EG-13; mail Pineland z 75968; rural
Plainview; RMC Place; WHARTON; ***239** EL-9; mail Louise z 77455; rural
Planeport; RMC Place; EL PASO; ***237** WK-2; ★ **ELP**; pop. incl. with El Paso (Inc. Place)
Plano; Inc. Place; COLLIN, DENTON; **238** ED-8; elev. 674ft./205m.; 🅿 🅷 ■; ★ **D-FW**; z 75023-26, z 75074-75, z 75086, z 75093-94; Ⓟ 128,713; © 222,030; ◆ 254,896
Plantation Place; RMC Place; FORT BEND; ***239** EK-10; ★ **HOU**; mail Sugar Land z 77478; ● 2,000
Plantersville; RMC Place; GRIMES; **238** EJ-9; 🅿; z 77363; ● 200
Plaska; RMC Place; HALL; ***236** WE-12; elev. 1,947ft./593m.; mail Memphis z 79245; rural
Plateau; RMC Place; CULBERSON; ***237** WM-5; elev. 3,942ft./1,202m.; mail Van Horn z 79855; rural
Pleak; Inc. Place; FORT BEND; **239** EL-10; elev. 85ft./26m.; mail Richmond z 77469; Ⓟ 746; © 947
Pleasant Farms; RMC Place; ECTOR; **237** WL-9; mail Odessa z 79763; ● 110
Pleasant Grove; RMC Place; BOWIE; ***238** EC-12; ★ **TEXR-**; mail Texarkana z 75503; pop. incl. with Texarkana (Inc. Place)
Pleasant Grove; RMC Place; FALLS; ***238** EH-7; elev. 438ft./134m.; mail Rosebud z 76570; rural
Pleasant Grove; RMC Place; UPSHUR; ***238** EE-11; mail Big Sandy z 75755; rural
Pleasant Grove; RMC Place; WOOD; ***238** ED-10; mail Winnsboro z 75494
Pleasant Hill; RMC Place; EASTLAND; ***238** EF-3; elev. 1,619ft./493m.; mail Cisco z 76437; rural
Pleasant Hill; RMC Place; NACOGDOCHES; ***238** EF-12; mail Garrison z 75946; rural
Pleasant Hill; RMC Place; POLK; ***238** EH-11; mail Corrigan z 75939; rural
Pleasanton; Inc. Place; ATASCOSA; **239** EM-4; 🅿; z 78064; Ⓟ 7,678; © 8,266
Pleasant Point; RMC Place; JOHNSON; ***238** EE-7; ★ **D-FW**; mail Alvarado z 76009; rural
Pleasant Ridge; RMC Place; LEON; ***238** EH-9; elev. 366ft./112m.; mail Centerville z 75833; rural
Pleasant Ridge; RMC Place; PANOLA; ***238** EF-12; mail Carthage z 75633; rural
Pleasant Springs; RMC Place; LEON; ***238** EH-9; mail Centerville z 75833; rural
Pleasant Valley; RMC Place; DALLAS; ***238** ED-8; ★ **D-FW**; mail Sachse z 75048; pop. incl. with Sachse (Inc. Place)
Pleasant Valley; RMC Place; GARZA; ***236** WH-11; elev. 2,960ft./902m.; mail Post z 79356
Pleasant Valley; RMC Place; LAMB; mail Muleshoe z 79347; rural
Pleasant Valley; RMC Place; PALO PINTO; mail Mineral Wells z 76067; rural
Pleasant Valley; RMC Place; POTTER; ***236** WD-10; elev. 3,549ft./1,082m.; ★ **AMA**; mail Amarillo z 79108; pop. incl. with Amarillo (Inc. Place)
Pleasant Valley; Inc. Place; WICHITA; **236** WA-4; ★ **WIFL**; mail Wichita Falls z 76305; Ⓟ 378; © 408
Pleasant Valley Acres; RMC Place; MONTGOMERY; ***238** EJ-10; ★ **HOU**; mail Magnolia z 77355
Pleasant View Estates; STEPHENS; see Fambrough (RMC Place)
Pledger; RMC Place; MATAGORDA; **239** EL-9; 🅿; z 77468; ● 200
Pluck; RMC Place; POLK; ***238** EH-11; elev. 210ft./64m.; mail Corrigan z 75939; rural
Plum; RMC Place; FAYETTE; **239** EK-7; 🅿; z 78952; ● 200
Plum Creek; RMC Place; FREESTONE; ***238** EG-9; mail Buffalo z 75831, Oakwood z 75855; rural
Plum Grove; Inc. Place; LIBERTY; **238** EJ-11; ★ **HOU**; mail Cleveland z 77327; Ⓟ 480; © 930
Plum Ridge; RMC Place; ANGELINA; ***238** EH-12; elev. 190ft./58m.; mail Zavalla z 75980; ● 150
Poe Prairie; RMC Place; PARKER; ***238** EE-5; mail Millsap z 76066; rural
Poetry; RMC Place; KAUFMAN; ***238** ED-8; mail Terrell z 75160; rural
Point; Inc. Place; RAINS; **238** ED-9; 🅿; z 75472; Ⓟ 645; © 792
Pointblank; Inc. Place; SAN JACINTO; **238** EI-11; 🅿; z 77364; Ⓟ 443; © 559
Point Comfort; Inc. Place; CALHOUN; **239** EM-8; 🅿; z 77978; Ⓟ 956; © 781
Point Enterprise; RMC Place; LIMESTONE; ***238** EG-8; mail Mexia z 76667
Point Loma; RMC Place; SAN PATRICIO; ***239** EO-6; mail Mathis z 78368; pop. incl. with Lakewood Heights (Inc. Place)
Point Royal; RMC Place; HENDERSON; ***238** EE-10; mail Chandler z 75758; ● 100
Point Venture; Inc. Place; TRAVIS; ***238** EJ-5; 🅿; ★ **AUS**; z 78645; incorporated August 1, 2000; not reported in 2000 Census; ● 500
Polar; RMC Place; KENT; ***236** WI-12; mail Snyder z 79549; rural
POLK; **238** EI-11; Ⓟ 30,687; © 41,133; ◆ 45,997
Pollok; RMC Place; ANGELINA; **238** EG-11; elev. 305ft./93m.; 🅿; z 75969; ● 300
Poly; RMC Place; TARRANT; ★ **D-FW**; pop. incl. with Fort Worth (Inc. Place)
Polytechnic; RMC Place; TARRANT; ★ **D-FW**; mail Fort Worth z 76105, z 76120; pop. incl. with Fort Worth (Inc. Place)
Ponder; Inc. Place; DENTON; **238** ED-6; elev. 733ft./223m.; 🅿; z 76259; Ⓟ 432; © 507
Pond Springs; RMC Place; WILLIAMSON; ***238** EJ-6; ★ **AUS**; mail Austin z 78729; ● 300
Pone; RMC Place; RUSK; ***238** EF-11; mail Henderson z 75654, Laneville z 75667; rural
Ponta; RMC Place; CHEROKEE; **238** EF-11; mail Jacksonville z 75766; ● 50
Pontotoc; RMC Place; MASON; **238** EI-3; 🅿; z 76869; ● 130
Poole; RMC Place; RAINS; ***238** ED-9; mail Emory z 75440; rural
Poolville; RMC Place; PARKER; **238** ED-5; elev. 1,134ft./346m.; 🅿; z 76487; ● 300
Porfirio; RMC Place; WILLACY; ***239** ES-6; mail Raymondville z 78580; rural
Port Acres; RMC Place; JEFFERSON; ***238** EJ-13; 🅿; ★ **B-PA**; z 77640; pop. incl. with Port Arthur (Inc. Place)
Port Alto; RMC Place; CALHOUN; **239** EM-8; elev. 10ft./3m.; mail Port Lavaca z 77979; ● 50
Port Aquarius; RMC Place; MONTGOMERY; ***238** EI-10; mail Willis z 77318; ● 390
Port Aransas; Inc. Place; NUECES; **239** EO-7; elev. 6ft./2m.; 🅿; z 78373; Ⓟ 2,233; © 3,370
Port Arthur; Inc. Place; JEFFERSON; **239** EK-13; 🅿 🅷 ■; ★ **B-PA**; z 77640-43; Ⓟ 58,724; © 57,755; ◆ 53,652
Port Bolivar; RMC Place; GALVESTON; **234** A-10; 🅿; ★ **GLV-**; z 77650; ● 1,300
Porter; RMC Place; MONTGOMERY; **238** EJ-11; elev. 102ft./31m.; 🅿; ★ **HOU**; z 77365; ● 7,000
Porter Heights; CDP-Census Area Only; MONTGOMERY; ***238** EJ-10; ★ **HOU**; mail Porter z 77365; Ⓟ 1,448; © 1,490
Porter Springs; RMC Place; HOUSTON; **238** EH-10; mail Crockett z 75835; ● 100
Porterville Timbers; RMC Place; MONTGOMERY; ***238** EJ-11; ★ **HOU**; mail Porter z 77365
Port Houston; RMC Place; HARRIS; ***239** EK-11; ★ **HOU**; mail Houston z 77029; pop. incl. with Houston (Inc. Place)
Port Isabel; Inc. Place; CAMERON; **239** ES-7; 🅿; z 78578 & mail South Padre Island z 78597; Ⓟ 4,467; © 4,865
Portland; Inc. Place; SAN PATRICIO, NUECES; **239** EO-7; 🅿; ★ **CRPX**; z 78374; Ⓟ 12,224; © 14,827
Port Lavaca; Inc. Place; ⊡ CALHOUN; **239** EN-8; 🅿 🅷; z 77979; Ⓟ 10,886; © 12,035
Port Mansfield (Redfish Bay); CDP; WILLACY; **239** ER-7; 🅿; z 78598; © 415
Port Neches; Inc. Place; JEFFERSON; **238** EJ-13; 🅿; ★ **B-PA**; z 77651; Ⓟ 12,974; © 13,601
Port O'Connor; RMC Place; CALHOUN; **239** EN-8; 🅿; z 77982; summer pop. 2,000; ● 1,200
Porvenir; RMC Place; PRESIDIO; ***237** WN-4; mail Valentine z 79854; rural
Posey; RMC Place; HOPKINS; ***238** EC-9; mail Sulphur Springs z 75482; rural
Posey; RMC Place; LUBBOCK; **236** WH-11; mail Slaton z 79364; ● 100
Post; Inc. Place; ⊡ GARZA; **236** WI-11; elev. 2,613ft./796m.; 🅿; z 79356 & mail Justiceburg z 79330; Ⓟ 3,768; © 3,708
Post Oak; RMC Place; BLANCO; ***238** EJ-4; mail Johnson City z 78636; rural
Post Oak; RMC Place; DELTA; ***238** EC-10; mail Cooper z 75432; rural
Postoak; RMC Place; FREESTONE; ***238** EG-9; mail Fairfield z 75840; rural
Postoak; RMC Place; JACK; **238** EC-5; elev. 997ft./304m.; mail Bowie z 76230; ● 50
Post Oak; RMC Place; LAMAR; ***238** EB-10; mail Blossom z 75416, Detroit z 75436
Post Oak Bend (Post Oak Bend City); Inc. Place; KAUFMAN; ***238** EE-8; mail Kaufman z 75142; Ⓟ 264; © 404
Post Oak Bend City; KAUFMAN; see Post Oak Bend (Inc. Place)
Post Oak Point; RMC Place; AUSTIN; ***239** EK-8; mail New Ulm z 78950; rural
Poteet; Inc. Place; ATASCOSA; **239** EM-4; elev. 441ft./134m.; 🅿; z 78065; Ⓟ 3,206; © 3,305
Poth; Inc. Place; WILSON; **239** EM-5; elev. 405ft./123m.; 🅿; z 78147; Ⓟ 1,642; © 1,850
Potosi; CDP; TAYLOR; **236** WJ-14; ★ **ABIL**; mail Abilene z 79601; Ⓟ 1,441; © 1,664
POTTER; **236** WC-10; Ⓟ 97,874; © 113,546; ◆ 119,336
Potters Point; RMC Place; MARION; ***238** ED-12; mail Jefferson z 75657; ● 150
Pottsboro; Inc. Place; GRAYSON; **238** EB-8; elev. 764ft./233m.; 🅿; ★ **SHRM-**; z 75076; Ⓟ 1,177; © 1,579
Pottsville; RMC Place; HAMILTON; **238** EG-5; elev. 1,309ft./399m.; 🅿; z 76565; ● 100
Pounds; RMC Place; COMANCHE; ***238** EF-4; mail De Leon z 76444; rural
Powderly; RMC Place; LAMAR; **238** EB-10; elev. 532ft./162m.; 🅿; z 75473; ● 250
Powell; Inc. Place; NAVARRO; **238** EF-8; elev. 380ft./116m.; 🅿; z 75153; Ⓟ 101; © 105
Powell Point; RMC Place; FORT BEND; ***239** EL-9; elev. 108ft./33m.; mail Kendleton z 77451; ● 100
Poynor; Inc. Place; HENDERSON; **238** EF-10; 🅿; z 75782; Ⓟ 237; © 314
Prado Verde; CDP-Census Area Only; EL PASO; ***237** WK-1; ★ **ELP**; © 200
Praesel; RMC Place; MILAM; ***238** EI-7; mail Rockdale z 76567; ● 150
Praha; RMC Place; FAYETTE; ***239** EK-7; mail Flatonia z 78941; ● 35
Prairie Dell; RMC Place; BELL; **238** EI-6; mail Salado z 76571; ● 35
Prairie Grove; RMC Place; ANGELINA; ***238** EH-11; elev. 223ft./68m.; mail Diboll z 75941; rural
Prairie Grove; RMC Place; LIMESTONE; ***238** EG-8; mail Mexia z 76667; rural
Prairie Hill; RMC Place; LIMESTONE; **238** EG-7; 🅿; z 76678; ● 200
Prairie Hill; RMC Place; WASHINGTON; ***238** EJ-8; mail Brenham z 77833; rural
Prairie Lea; RMC Place; CALDWELL; **239** EK-6; 🅿; z 78661; ● 200
Prairie Mountain; RMC Place; LLANO; ***238** EI-4; mail Llano z 78643; rural
Prairie Point; RMC Place; COOKE; **238** EC-6; mail Forestburg z 76239; ● 40
Prairie Valley; RMC Place; FAYETTE; ***239** EK-7; elev. 291ft./89m.; mail West Point z 78963; rural
Prairie Valley; RMC Place; MONTAGUE; ***238** EB-6; mail Nocona z 76255; rural
Prairie View; Inc. Place; WALLER; **238** EJ-9; 🅿 🅲 7,912; z 77445-46, z 77484; Ⓟ 4,004; © 4,410
Prairieville; RMC Place; KAUFMAN; ***238** EE-9; mail Mabank z 75147
Prattville; RMC Place; DELTA; ***238** EC-10; elev. 472ft./144m.; mail Cooper z 75432; rural
Premont; Inc. Place; JIM WELLS; **239** EP-5; 🅿; z 78375; Ⓟ 2,914; © 2,772
Presidio; Inc. Place; PRESIDIO; **237** WP-5; elev. 2,581ft./787m.; 🅿; z 79845-46; Ⓟ 3,072; © 4,167
PRESIDIO; **237** WN-5; Ⓟ 6,637; © 7,304; ◆ 7,585
Preston; RMC Place; DALLAS; ★ **D-FW**; mail Dallas z 75225; pop. incl. with Dallas (Inc. Place)
Preston (Preston Shores); RMC Place; GRAYSON; **238** EB-8; mail Pottsboro z 75076; ● 450
Preston Shores; GRAYSON; see Preston (RMC Place)
Prestonwood; RMC Place; DALLAS; ★ **D-FW**; mail Dallas z 75248, z 75252, z 75379; pop. incl. with Dallas (Inc. Place)
Prestonwood; RMC Place; TARRANT; ★ **D-FW**; mail Arlington z 76012; pop. incl. with Arlington (Inc. Place)
Price; RMC Place; JEFFERSON; ★ **B-PA**; mail Nederland z 77627; ● 200
Price; RMC Place; RUSK; **238** EF-11; 🅿; z 75687; ● 650
Priddy; RMC Place; MILLS; **238** EG-4; 🅿; z 76870; ● 180
Primera; Inc. Place; CAMERON; ***239** ES-6; elev. 41ft./12m.; ★ **BRNS**; mail Harlingen z 78550; Ⓟ 2,030; © 2,723
Primrose; RMC Place; VAN ZANDT; ***238** EE-10; mail Ben Wheeler z 75754; rural
Princeton; Inc. Place; COLLIN; **238** EC-8; elev. 580ft./177m.; 🅿; ★ **D-FW**; z 75407; Ⓟ 2,321; © 3,477

Entries in UPPERCASE are counties.
Entries in bold have populations of 2,500 or more.
Names in parentheses are alternate names.

Inc. Place	Incorporated Place
RMC Place	Rand McNally Designated Place
CDP	Census Designated Place
MCD	Minor Civil Division

⊡	County Seat
▲	Minor Civil Division
elev.	Elevation
🅿	Post Office
🅷	Hospital
🅲	College
■	Principal Business Center
★	Ranally Metro Area (RMA) Abbreviation
z	Zip Code(s)
Ⓟ	Previous Census Population
Ⓡ	Revised Census Population
Ⓐ	Annexation Population
●	Rand McNally Population Estimate
©	Final Census Population
Ⓢ	Special Census Population
◆	Estimated Population

For additional definitions see Glossary, Volume 1, and Introduction, Volume 2.

Pringle; RMC Place; HUTCHINSON; **236** WC-11; elev. 3,313ft./1,010m.; mail Stinnett **z** 79083; ● 30
Pritchett; RMC Place; UPSHUR; **238** EE-11; mail Big Sandy **z** 75755, Gilmer **z** 75644; ● 250
Proctor; RMC Place; COMANCHE; **238** EF-4; elev. 1,209ft./369m.; 🅿; **z** 76468; ● 200
Proffitt; RMC Place; YOUNG; ***238** EC-3; mail Newcastle **z** 76372; rural
Progreso; Inc. Place; HIDALGO; **239** ES-6; 🅿; ★ **MCAL**; **z** 78579; Ⓟ 3,258; © 4,851
Progreso Lakes; Inc. Place; HIDALGO; ***239** ES-6; 🅿; ★ **MCAL**; **z** 78596 & mail Progreso **z** 78579; Ⓟ 154; © 234
Progress; RMC Place; BAILEY; **236** WF-8; mail Muleshoe **z** 79347; ● 60
Progress; RMC Place; PALO PINTO; ***238** EE-5; mail Mineral Wells **z** 76067; rural
Prospect; RMC Place; MARION; ***238** ED-12; mail Jefferson **z** 75657
Prosper; Inc. Place; COLLIN; **238** EC-7; 🅿; **z** 75078; Ⓟ 1,018; © 2,097
Prosser; RMC Place; ANGELINA; ★ **LUFK**; pop. incl. with Lufkin (Inc. Place)
Providence; RMC Place; ANGELINA; ***238** EG-11; ★ **LUFK**; mail Lufkin **z** 75904; pop. incl. with Hudson (Inc. Place)
Providence; RMC Place; FLOYD; ***236** WF-11; mail Lockney **z** 79241; rural
Providence; RMC Place; POLK; ***238** EI-11; elev. 317ft./97m.; mail Livingston **z** 77351; rural
Providence; RMC Place; VAN ZANDT; mail Grand Saline **z** 75140; rural
Provident City; RMC Place; COLORADO; ***239** EL-8; mail Louise **z** 77455, Sheridan **z** 77475; rural
Pruett (Pruitt); RMC Place; CASS; ***238** ED-12; mail Jefferson **z** 75657; rural
Pruitt; CASS; see Pruett (RMC Place)
Pruitt; RMC Place; VAN ZANDT; ***238** EE-10; elev. 460ft./140m.; mail Grand Saline **z** 75140; rural
Puckett Place; RMC Place; RANDALL; ★ **AMA**; mail Amarillo **z** 79109; pop. incl. with Amarillo (Inc. Place)
Puckett West; RMC Place; POTTER; ★ **AMA**; mail Amarillo **z** 79109; pop. incl. with Amarillo (Inc. Place)
Puerto Rico; RMC Place; HIDALGO; ***239** ER-5; mail Linn **z** 78563; rural
Pullman; RMC Place; POTTER; ***236** WD-11; elev. 3,602ft./1,098m.; ★ **AMA**; pop. incl. with Amarillo (Inc. Place)
Pumphrey; RMC Place; RUNNELS; ***238** EF-1; elev. 1,981ft./604m.; mail Winters **z** 79567; rural
Pumpkin; RMC Place; SAN JACINTO; ***238** EI-10; mail New Waverly **z** 77358; rural
Pumpkin Center; RMC Place; DAWSON; ***236** WI-10; mail Lamesa **z** 79331
Pumpville; RMC Place; VAL VERDE; ***237** WP-10; elev. 1,818ft./554m.; mail Dryden **z** 78851; rural
Punkin Center; RMC Place; PARKER; ***238** ED-6; mail Weatherford **z** 76087
Purdon; RMC Place; NAVARRO; **238** EF-8; elev. 397ft./121m.; 🅿; **z** 76679; ● 130
Purley; RMC Place; FRANKLIN; **238** ED-10; mail Mount Vernon **z** 75457, Winnsboro **z** 75494; ● 120
Purmela; RMC Place; CORYELL; **238** EG-5; 🅿; **z** 76566; ● 40
Pursley; RMC Place; NAVARRO; ***238** EF-8; mail Purdon **z** 76679
Purves; RMC Place; ERATH; ***238** EF-5; elev. 1,426ft./435m.; mail Dublin **z** 76446
Putnam; Inc. Place; CALLAHAN; **238** EE-3; elev. 1,604ft./489m.; 🅿; **z** 76469; Ⓟ 103; © 88
Pyote; Inc. Place; WARD; **237** WL-8; 🅿; **z** 79777; Ⓟ 348; © 131
Pyron; RMC Place; SCURRY; ***236** WJ-12; mail Roscoe **z** 79545; rural

Q

Quail; CDP; COLLINGSWORTH; **236** WE-13; elev. 2,245ft./684m.; 🅿; **z** 79251; © 33
Quail Creek; RMC Place; VICTORIA; ***239** EM-7; ★ **VICT**; mail Victoria **z** 77905; ● 700
Quail Run; RMC Place; PECOS; ***237** WN-8; mail Fort Stockton **z** 79735; pop. incl. with Fort Stockton (Inc. Place)
Quail Valley; RMC Place; FORT BEND; ***239** EK-10; ★ **HOU**; mail Missouri City **z** 77459; pop. incl. with Missouri City (Inc. Place)
Quail Valley; RMC Place; WILLIAMSON; ***238** EI-6; ★ **AUS**; mail Georgetown **z** 78626; pop. incl. with Georgetown (Inc. Place)
Quail Valley East; RMC Place; FORT BEND; ***239** EK-10; ★ **HOU**; mail Missouri City **z** 77459; pop. incl. with Missouri City (Inc. Place)
Quanah; Inc. Place; ⊡ HARDEMAN; **236** WF-14; 🅿 🅷; **z** 79252; Ⓟ 3,413; © 3,022
Quarry; RMC Place; WASHINGTON; ***238** EJ-8; mail Brenham **z** 77833
Queen City; Inc. Place; CASS; **238** EC-12; 🅿; **z** 75572; Ⓟ 1,748; © 1,613
Quemado; CDP; MAVERICK; **237** WR-12; elev. 783ft./239m.; 🅿; **z** 78877; © 243
Quicksand; RMC Place; NEWTON; ***238** EH-13; mail Newton **z** 75966
Quihi; RMC Place; MEDINA; ***239** EL-3; mail Hondo **z** 78861; ● 100
Quinlan; Inc. Place; HUNT; **238** ED-9; 🅿; **z** 75474; Ⓟ 1,360; © 1,370
Quintana; Inc. Place; BRAZORIA; ***239** EM-11; 🅿; ★ **L.JAC-**; **z** 77541; Ⓟ 51; © 38
Quitaque; Inc. Place; BRISCOE; **236** WF-12; 🅿; **z** 79255; Ⓟ 513; © 432
Quitman; Inc. Place; ⊡ WOOD; **238** ED-10; elev. 413ft./126m.; 🅿 🅷; **z** 75783; Ⓟ 1,684; © 2,030

R

Rabb; RMC Place; NUECES; **239** EO-6; elev. 82ft./25m.; mail Robstown **z** 78380; ● 20
Rabbit Center; ERATH; see Welcome Valley (RMC Place)
Rabbs Prairie; RMC Place; FAYETTE; ***239** EK-7; elev. 266ft./81m.; mail La Grange **z** 78945; rural
Raccoon Bend; RMC Place; AUSTIN; ***238** EJ-9; mail Bellville **z** 77418; ● 150
Rachal; RMC Place; BROOKS; ***239** ER-5; elev. 121ft./37m.; mail Encino **z** 78353; ● 35
Radar Base; CDP-Census Area Only; MAVERICK; ***237** WR-13; © 162
Radium; RMC Place; JONES; ***238** ED-1; elev. 1,707ft./520m.; mail Anson **z** 79501; rural
Ragtown; GARZA; see Close City (RMC Place)
Ragtown; RMC Place; LAMAR; ***238** EB-9; elev. 494ft./151m.; mail Arthur City **z** 75411; rural
Rainbow; RMC Place; SOMERVELL; **238** EF-6; 🅿; **z** 76077; ● 80
Rainbow Hills; RMC Place; BEXAR; ***239** EL-4; ★ **SANT**; mail San Antonio **z** 78227; pop. incl. with San Antonio (Inc. Place)
RAINS; **238** ED-9; Ⓟ 6,715; © 9,139; ◆ 11,525
Raisin; RMC Place; VICTORIA; ***239** EM-7; elev. 102ft./31m.; 🅿; **z** 77905; rural
Raleigh; RMC Place; NAVARRO; ***238** EF-8; elev. 531ft./162m.; mail Frost **z** 76641; rural
Ralls; Inc. Place; CROSBY; **236** WG-11; 🅿; **z** 79357; Ⓟ 2,172; © 2,252
Ramah; RMC Place; SHELBY; ***238** EF-12; mail Tenaha **z** 75974; rural
Rambo; RMC Place; CASS; ***238** ED-12; mail Bivins **z** 75555; rural
Ramireno; RMC Place; ZAPATA; **239** EQ-3; elev. 352ft./107m.; mail San Ygnacio **z** 78067; ● 50
Ramirez; RMC Place; DUVAL; **239** EP-5; mail Realitos **z** 78376; ● 50
Ranchette Estates; CDP-Census Area Only; WILLACY; ***239** ER-6; © 133
Ranch Harbor Estates; RMC Place; HILL; ***238** EF-6; mail Whitney **z** 76692; ● 800
Ranchiti; CAMERON; see Ranchito (RMC Place)
Ranchito (Ranchiti); RMC Place; CAMERON; ***239** ES-6; elev. 49ft./15m.; ★ **BRNS**; mail San Benito **z** 78586; ● 350
Ranchitos Las Lomas; CDP-Census Area Only; WEBB; ***239** EP-3; © 334
Ranchland Acres; RMC Place; MIDLAND; ***237** WK-10; ★ **MIDL-**; mail Midland **z** 79703; ● 100
Rancho Alegre (Alice Southwest); CDP-Census Area Only; JIM WELLS; **239** EP-5; mail Alice **z** 78332; © 1,775
Rancho Banquete; CDP-Census Area Only; NUECES; ***239** EO-6; © 469
Rancho Chico; CDP-Census Area Only; SAN PATRICIO; ***239** EO-6; © 309
Rancho de la Parita; RMC Place; JIM WELLS; ***239** EO-5; mail Orange Grove **z** 78372; rural
Ranchos Penitas West; CDP-Census Area Only; WEBB; ***239** EP-2; © 520
Rancho Viejo; Inc. Place; CAMERON; **239** ES-6; 🅿; ★ **BRNS**; **z** 78575 & mail Brownsville **z** 78520; Ⓟ 885; © 1,754
Rancho Viejo; RMC Place; JIM HOGG; mail Hebbronville **z** 78361; rural
Rand; RMC Place; KAUFMAN; mail Kaufman **z** 75142; rural
Randado; RMC Place; JIM HOGG; ***239** EQ-4; mail Hebbronville **z** 78361; rural
RANDALL; **236** WE-10; Ⓟ 89,673; © 104,312; ◆ 115,829
Randolph; RMC Place; FANNIN; **238** EC-8; 🅿; **z** 75475; ● 200
Ranger; Inc. Place; EASTLAND; **238** EE-4; elev. 1,441ft./439m.; 🅿; **z** 76470; Ⓟ 2,803; © 2,584
Rangerville; RMC Place; CAMERON; ***239** ES-6; ★ **BRNS**; mail San Benito **z** 78586; former incorporated place; disincorporated January 1, 2000; Ⓟ 280; © 203
Rankin; RMC Place; ELLIS; ***238** EF-8; elev. 471ft./144m.; mail Ennis **z** 75119; rural
Rankin; Inc. Place; ⊡ UPTON; **237** WM-10; 🅿 🅷; **z** 79778; Ⓟ 1,011; © 800
Ransom Canyon (Lake Ransom Canyon Village); Inc. Place; LUBBOCK; ***236** WH-11; 🅿; ★ **LUB**; **z** 79364, **z** 79366; Ⓟ 750; © 1,011
Ratamosa; CDP-Census Area Only; CAMERON; ***239** ES-6; ★ **BRNS**; © 218
Ratcliff; RMC Place; HOUSTON; **238** EG-11; elev. 398ft./121m.; 🅿; **z** 75858; ● 200
Ratcliff; RMC Place; SAN AUGUSTINE; ***238** EG-12; mail San Augustine **z** 75972; rural
Ratcliffe; RMC Place; DEWITT; ***239** EM-7; mail Yorktown **z** 78164; rural
Ratibor; RMC Place; BELL; ***238** EH-7; mail Temple **z** 76501; rural
Rattan; RMC Place; DELTA; ***238** EC-9; elev. 513ft./156m.; mail Pecan Gap **z** 75469; rural
Ravenna; Inc. Place; FANNIN; **238** EB-8; 🅿; **z** 75476; © 215
Rayburn; RMC Place; LIBERTY; **238** EI-11; elev. 135ft./41m.; mail Cleveland **z** 77327; ● 75
Rayburn Hideaway; RMC Place; NACOGDOCHES; mail Chireno **z** 75937; ● 35
Rayland; RMC Place; FOARD; ***238** EB-2; elev. 1,300ft./396m.; mail Vernon **z** 76384
Raymondville; Inc. Place; ⊡ WILLACY; **239** ER-6; 🅿; **z** 78580, **z** 78598; Ⓟ 8,880; © 9,733
Ray Point; RMC Place; LIVE OAK; ***239** EN-5; mail Three Rivers **z** 78071
Raywood; RMC Place; LIBERTY; **238** EJ-12; 🅿; **z** 77582; ● 300
Reagan; RMC Place; FALLS; **238** EH-8; 🅿; **z** 76680; ● 220
REAGAN; **237** WL-11; Ⓟ 4,514; © 3,326; ◆ 3,157
Reagan Wells; RMC Place; UVALDE; ***239** EL-2; mail Uvalde **z** 78801
Reagor Springs; RMC Place; ELLIS; ***238** EE-7; mail Waxahachie **z** 75165; ● 50
REAL; **239** EK-2; Ⓟ 2,412; © 3,047; ◆ 2,981
Realitos; CDP; DUVAL; **239** EP-4; elev. 442ft./135m.; 🅿; **z** 78376; © 209
Reata Trails; RMC Place; WILLIAMSON; ***238** EI-6; ★ **AUS**; mail Georgetown **z** 78626; pop. incl. with Georgetown (Inc. Place)
Redbank; RMC Place; BOWIE; **238** EB-12; mail Hooks **z** 75561; ● 150
Red Bluff; RMC Place; REEVES; **237** WK-6; mail Orla **z** 79770; ● 40
Red Branch; RMC Place; LEON; ***238** EG-9; mail Oakwood **z** 75855; rural
Redfish Bay; WILLACY; see Port Mansfield (CDP)
Redford; CDP; PRESIDIO; **237** WQ-6; elev. 2,518ft./767m.; 🅿; **z** 79846; © 132
Red Gate; RMC Place; HIDALGO; **239** ER-5; mail Edinburg **z** 78539; ● 50
Red Hill; RMC Place; CASS; ***238** EC-12; elev. 303ft./92m.; mail Douglassville **z** 75560
Red Lake; RMC Place; FREESTONE; ***238** EG-9; mail Oakwood **z** 75855; ● 225
Redland; RMC Place; ANGELINA; **238** EG-11; ★ **LUFK**; mail Lufkin **z** 75901, **z** 75904; ● 700
Redland; RMC Place; LEON; ***238** EH-9; elev. 420ft./128m.; mail Centerville **z** 75833, Jewett **z** 75846; rural
Redland; RMC Place; VAN ZANDT; ***238** EE-10; mail Ben Wheeler **z** 75754; rural
Redlawn; RMC Place; CHEROKEE; ***238** EG-11; mail Alto **z** 75925
Red Lick; Inc. Place; BOWIE; ***238** EC-12; elev. 362ft./110m.; ★ **TEXR-**; mail Texarkana **z** 75503; © 853
Red Oak; Inc. Place; ELLIS; **238** EE-7; 🅿; ★ **D-FW**; **z** 75154; Ⓟ 3,124; © 4,301
Red Ranger; RMC Place; BELL; ***238** EH-7; elev. 442ft./135m.; mail Rogers **z** 76569; rural
RED RIVER; **238** EB-10; Ⓟ 14,317; © 14,314; ◆ 12,738
Red Rock; RMC Place; BASTROP; **239** EK-6; elev. 484ft./148m.; 🅿; **z** 78662; ● 80
Red Springs; RMC Place; BAYLOR; **238** EC-2; elev. 1,394ft./425m.; 🅿; **z** 76380; ● 40
Red Springs; RMC Place; BOWIE; ***238** EC-12; elev. 356ft./109m.; ★ **TEXR-**; mail Texarkana **z** 75501; rural
Red Springs; RMC Place; SMITH; ***238** EE-10; elev. 524ft./160m.; mail Lindale **z** 75771, Tyler **z** 75706; rural
Red Top; RMC Place; YOUNG; ***238** EC-4; elev. 1,183ft./361m.; mail Graham **z** 76450; rural
Redtown; RMC Place; ANDERSON; ***238** EG-10; mail Elkhart **z** 75839; rural
Redtown; RMC Place; ANGELINA; ***238** EG-11; elev. 275ft./84m.; mail Lufkin **z** 75904, Pollok **z** 75969; rural
Redwater; Inc. Place; BOWIE; **238** EC-12; 🅿; ★ **TEXR-**; **z** 75573; Ⓟ 824; © 872
Redwood; CDP; GUADALUPE; ***239** EK-5; elev. 556ft./169m.; mail San Marcos **z** 78666; © 3,586
Reedville; RMC Place; CALDWELL; ***239** EK-6; elev. 565ft./172m.; mail Maxwell **z** 78656; ● 100
Reese; RMC Place; CHEROKEE; **238** EF-10; elev. 396ft./121m.; mail Jacksonville **z** 75766; ● 80
Reese Center; CDP-Census Area Only; LUBBOCK; **236** WG-10; ★ **LUB**; © 42
Reese Village; RMC Place; LUBBOCK; mail Lubbock **z** 79416; ● 40
REEVES; **237** WL-7; Ⓟ 15,852; © 13,137; ◆ 11,271
Refugio; Inc. Place; ⊡ REFUGIO; **239** EN-7; 🅿 🅷; **z** 78377; Ⓟ 3,158; © 2,941
REFUGIO; **239** EN-7; Ⓟ 7,976; © 7,828; ◆ 7,090
Regency; RMC Place; MILLS; ***238** EG-4; elev. 1,250ft./381m.; mail Mullin **z** 76864; rural
Rehburg; RMC Place; WASHINGTON; ***238** EJ-8; mail Burton **z** 77835; rural
Rehobeth; RMC Place; PANOLA; ***238** EE-12; mail Carthage **z** 75633; rural
Reid Hope King; CDP-Census Area Only; CAMERON; ***239** ET-7; ★ **BRNS**; © 802
Reilly Springs; RMC Place; HOPKINS; **238** ED-10; elev. 476ft./145m.; mail Sulphur Springs **z** 75482; ● 75
Reinhardt; RMC Place; DALLAS; ***238** ED-8; ★ **D-FW**; pop. incl. with Dallas (Inc. Place)
Rek Hill; RMC Place; FAYETTE; **239** EK-8; mail Fayetteville **z** 78940; ● 40
Reklaw; Inc. Place; CHEROKEE, RUSK; **238** EF-11; 🅿; **z** 75784; Ⓟ 266; © 327
Relampago; CDP; HIDALGO; ***239** ES-6; ★ **MCAL**; mail Mercedes **z** 78570; © 104
Reliance; RMC Place; BRAZOS; ***238** EI-9; mail Bryan **z** 77801, **z** 77808; rural
Remolino; RMC Place; STARR; ***239** ES-4; mail Rio Grande City **z** 78582; rural
Remount; RMC Place; BEXAR; ★ **SANT**; pop. incl. with San Antonio (Inc. Place)
Rendon; CDP; TARRANT; **235** J-5; ★ **D-FW**; mail Burleson **z** 76028, Mansfield **z** 76063; Ⓟ 7,658; © 9,022
Reno; Inc. Place; LAMAR; **238** EB-10; 🅿; **z** 75462; Ⓟ 1,784; © 2,767
Reno; Inc. Place; PARKER; **238** ED-6; elev. 727ft./222m.; ★ **D-FW**; mail Azle **z** 76020; Ⓟ 2,322; © 2,441
Retreat; RMC Place; GRIMES; ***238** EJ-9; mail Navasota **z** 77868; rural
Retreat; RMC Place; HILL; ***238** EF-6; mail Blum **z** 76627
Retreat; Inc. Place; NAVARRO; **238** EF-8; elev. 471ft./144m.; mail Corsicana **z** 75110; Ⓟ 334; © 339
Retta; RMC Place; JOHNSON, TARRANT; ***238** EE-7; ★ **D-FW**; mail Burleson **z** 76028; rural
Reyes; RMC Place; DUVAL; ***239** EO-5; mail San Diego **z** 78384; rural
Rhea; RMC Place; PARMER; **236** WE-8; mail Friona **z** 79035; ● 50
Rhea Mills; RMC Place; COLLIN; ***238** EC-7; elev. 740ft./226m.; mail Mckinney **z** 75069; rural
Rhineland; RMC Place; KNOX; **236** WH-14; mail Munday **z** 76371; ● 80
Rhome; Inc. Place; WISE; **238** ED-6; 🅿; **z** 76078; Ⓟ 605; © 551
Rhonesboro; RMC Place; UPSHUR; **238** ED-10; mail Big Sandy **z** 75755, Winnsboro **z** 75494; ● 50
Ricardo; RMC Place; KLEBERG; **239** EP-6; elev. 53ft./16m.; mail Kingsville **z** 78363; ● 500
Rice; Inc. Place; NAVARRO, ELLIS; **238** EF-8; elev. 463ft./141m.; 🅿; **z** 75155; Ⓟ 564; © 798
Rices Crossing; RMC Place; WILLIAMSON; ***238** EI-6; elev. 547ft./167m.; mail Taylor **z** 76574; rural
Richards; RMC Place; GRIMES; **238** EI-9; 🅿; **z** 77873; ● 300
Richardson; Inc. Place; DALLAS, COLLIN; **238** ED-7; 🅿 🅷 🅲 14,523 ■; ★ **D-FW**; **z** 75080-83, **z** 75085; Ⓟ 74,840; © 91,802; Ⓡ 91,776; ◆ 100,561
Rich Hill; RMC Place; HARRIS; ★ **HOU**; mail Houston **z** 77057, **z** 77237, **z** 77257; pop. incl. with Houston (Inc. Place)
Richland; RMC Place; DALLAS; ★ **D-FW**; mail Dallas **z** 75243, **z** 75374; pop. incl. with Dallas (Inc. Place)
Richland; Inc. Place; NAVARRO; **238** EF-8; elev. 367ft./112m.; 🅿; **z** 76681; Ⓟ 244; © 291
Richland; RMC Place; RAINS; ***238** ED-9; mail Point **z** 75472; rural
Richland Hills; Inc. Place; TARRANT; **235** G-5; 🅿; ★ **D-FW**; **z** 76118, **z** 76180; Ⓟ 7,978; © 8,132
Richland Park; RMC Place; TARRANT; ★ **D-FW**; mail Fort Worth **z** 76118; pop. incl. with Fort Worth (Inc. Place)
Richland Springs; Inc. Place; SAN SABA; **238** EH-3; elev. 1,404ft./428m.; 🅿; **z** 76871; Ⓟ 344; © 350
Richmond; Inc. Place; ⊡ FORT BEND; **239** EK-10; 🅿 🅷; ★ **HOU**; **z** 77406-07, **z** 77469; Ⓟ 9,801; © 11,081
Richwood; Inc. Place; BRAZORIA; **239** EL-10; 🅿; ★ **L.JAC-**; **z** 77515, **z** 77531, **z** 77566; Ⓟ 2,732; © 3,012
Riderville; RMC Place; PANOLA; ***238** EE-12; mail Carthage **z** 75633; ● 80
Ridge; RMC Place; MILLS; mail Mullin **z** 76864; rural
Ridge; RMC Place; ROBERTSON; **238** EH-8; 🅿; **z** 77856
Ridgecrest; RMC Place; RANDALL; ★ **AMA**; mail Amarillo **z** 79109; pop. incl. with Amarillo (Inc. Place)
Ridgeheights; RMC Place; MIDLAND; ***237** WK-10; ★ **MIDL-**; mail Midland **z** 79701; ● 200
Ridgemere; RMC Place; POTTER; ★ **AMA**; mail Amarillo **z** 79107; pop. incl. with Amarillo (Inc. Place)
Ridgeway; RMC Place; HOPKINS; **238** EC-9; mail Sulphur Springs **z** 75482; ● 100
Ridglea; RMC Place; TARRANT; ***238** EE-6; ★ **D-FW**; mail Fort Worth **z** 76116; pop. incl. with Fort Worth (Inc. Place)
Ridings; RMC Place; FANNIN; ***238** EB-8; mail Ravenna **z** 75476; rural
Riesel; Inc. Place; MCLENNAN; **238** EG-7; 🅿; **z** 76682; Ⓟ 839; © 973
Rimwick Forrest; RMC Place; MONTGOMERY; ***238** EJ-10; ★ **HOU**; mail Magnolia **z** 77354; ● 150
Rincon; RMC Place; STARR; ***239** ER-4; mail Rio Grande City **z** 78582
Ringgold; RMC Place; MONTAGUE; **238** EB-5; 🅿; **z** 76261; ● 200
Rio Bravo; Inc. Place; WEBB; ***239** EP-2; 🅿; ★ **LAR**; **z** 78043; Ⓟ 2,987; © 5,553
Rio del Sol; RMC Place; CAMERON; ***239** ET-7; ★ **BRNS**; mail Brownsville **z** 78522; pop. incl. with Brownsville (Inc. Place)
Rio Farms; RMC Place; HIDALGO; mail Edcouch **z** 78538
Rio Frio; RMC Place; REAL; **237** WP-14; elev. 1,494ft./455m.; 🅿; **z** 78879; summer pop. 150; ● 60
Rio Grande City; Inc. Place; ⊡ STARR; **239** ES-4; 🅿 🅷; **z** 78582; Ⓟ 10,725; © 11,923
Rio Grande Village; RMC Place; BREWSTER; ***237** WQ-8; mail Big Bend National Park **z** 79834; ● 25
Rio Hondo; Inc. Place; CAMERON; **239** ES-6; elev. 29ft./9m.; 🅿; ★ **BRNS**; **z** 78583; Ⓟ 1,793; © 1,942
Rio Llano Ranch; RMC Place; LLANO; ***238** EI-4; mail Llano **z** 78643; ● 80
Riomedina; RMC Place; MEDINA; ***239** EL-4; elev. 839ft./256m.; 🅿; **z** 78066; ● 30
Rio Pecos; RMC Place; CROCKETT; ***237** WM-9; mail Girvin **z** 79740; ● 20
Rios; RMC Place; DUVAL; ***239** EP-5; mail Concepcion **z** 78349; rural
Rio Vista; Inc. Place; JOHNSON; **238** EF-6; 🅿; **z** 76093; Ⓟ 541; © 656
Rising Star; Inc. Place; EASTLAND; **238** EF-3; elev. 1,629ft./497m.; 🅿; **z** 76471; Ⓟ 859; © 835
Rita; RMC Place; BURLESON; ***238** EI-8; elev. 297ft./91m.; mail Gause **z** 77857; rural
River Bend; RMC Place; NEWTON; **238** EH-14; mail Burkeville **z** 75932; ● 30
River Bend; RMC Place; SABINE; ***238** EG-13; mail Hemphill **z** 75948; ● 70
Riverbend; RMC Place; TARRANT; ★ **D-FW**; mail Fort Worth **z** 76118; pop. incl. with Richland Hills (Inc. Place)
River Bend Estates; RMC Place; BANDERA; ***239** EK-3; mail Bandera **z** 78003; ● 30
River Brook; RMC Place; MONTGOMERY; ***238** EJ-10; ★ **HOU**; mail Conroe **z** 77385; ● 200
Riverby; RMC Place; FANNIN; ***238** EB-9; elev. 480ft./146m.; mail Telephone **z** 75488; rural
Riverdale; RMC Place; GOLIAD; ***239** EM-6; mail Goliad **z** 77963; rural
River Hill; RMC Place; PANOLA; ***238** EF-12; mail Carthage **z** 75633; ● 60
Riverland; RMC Place; CLAY; ***238** EB-5; mail Henrietta **z** 76365; rural
River Oak Lake Estates; RMC Place; TRAVIS; ***238** EJ-6; ★ **AUS**; mail Austin **z** 78758; pop. incl. with Austin (Inc. Place)
River Oaks; RMC Place; HARRIS; ***239** EK-10; ★ **HOU**; mail Houston **z** 77019, **z** 77219; pop. incl. with Houston (Inc. Place)
River Oaks; Inc. Place; TARRANT; **235** G-3; 🅿; ★ **D-FW**; **z** 76114; Ⓟ 6,580; © 6,985
River Oaks Ranch; RMC Place; BANDERA; ***239** EK-3; mail Pipe Creek **z** 78063; ● 70
River Plantation; RMC Place; MONTGOMERY; ***238** EJ-10; ★ **HOU**; mail Conroe **z** 77302; ● 700
River Ridge; RMC Place; JASPER; ***238** EH-13; mail Jasper **z** 75951; ● 40
Riverside; RMC Place; TARRANT; ***238** ED-6; ★ **D-FW**; mail Fort Worth **z** 76111; pop. incl. with Fort Worth (Inc. Place)
Riverside; Inc. Place; WALKER; **238** EI-10; 🅿; **z** 77367; Ⓟ 451; © 425
Riverside Crest; RMC Place; HARRIS; ***238** EJ-11; ★ **HOU**; mail Humble **z** 77338; pop. incl. with Houston (Inc. Place)
Riverside Terrace; RMC Place; HARRIS; ***239** EK-10; ★ **HOU**; mail Houston **z** 77021; pop. incl. with Houston (Inc. Place)
Riverwood Estates; RMC Place; HARRIS; ***239** EK-10; ★ **HOU**; mail Houston **z** 77050; pop. incl. with Houston (Inc. Place)
Riviera; RMC Place; KLEBERG; **239** EQ-6; elev. 37ft./11m.; 🅿; **z** 78379; ● 700
Riviera Beach; RMC Place; KLEBERG; ***239** EQ-6; mail Riviera **z** 78379; ● 125
Roach; RMC Place; CASS; ***238** ED-12; mail Atlanta **z** 75551; rural
Roane; RMC Place; NAVARRO; ***238** EF-8; mail Corsicana **z** 75110
Roanoke; Inc. Place; DENTON; **238** ED-7; 🅿; ★ **D-FW**; **z** 76262 & mail Keller **z** 76248; Ⓟ 1,616; © 2,810
Roans Prairie; RMC Place; GRIMES; **238** EI-9; 🅿; **z** 77875; ● 60
Roaring Springs; Inc. Place; MOTLEY; **236** WG-12; 🅿; **z** 79256; Ⓟ 264; © 265
Robards; RMC Place; BEXAR; ***239** EL-4; ★ **SANT**; pop. incl. with San Antonio (Inc. Place)
Robbins; RMC Place; LEON; **238** EH-9; mail Jewett **z** 75846; ● 20
Robert Lee; Inc. Place; ⊡ COKE; **237** WK-13; elev. 1,823ft./556m.; 🅿; **z** 76945; Ⓟ 1,276; © 1,171
ROBERTS; **236** WC-12; Ⓟ 1,025; © 887; ◆ 892
Robertson; RMC Place; CROSBY; ***236** WH-11; elev. 3,097ft./944m.; mail Lorenzo **z** 79343
ROBERTSON; **238** EH-8; Ⓟ 15,511; © 16,000; ◆ 15,490
Robinson; Inc. Place; MCLENNAN; **238** EG-7; 🅿; ★ **WACO**; **z** 76706 & mail Lorena **z** 76655; Ⓟ 7,111; © 7,845
Robstown; Inc. Place; NUECES; **239** EO-6; 🅿; ★ **CRPX**; **z** 78380; Ⓟ 12,849; © 12,727
Roby; Inc. Place; ⊡ FISHER; **236** WJ-13; elev. 1,961ft./598m.; 🅿; **z** 79543; Ⓟ 616; © 673
Rochelle; RMC Place; MCCULLOCH; **238** EH-3; 🅿; **z** 76872; ● 200
Rochester; Inc. Place; HASKELL; **236** WH-14; elev. 1,595ft./486m.; 🅿; **z** 79544; Ⓟ 458; © 378
Rock Creek; RMC Place; BRISCOE; ***236** WF-11; mail Silverton **z** 79257; rural
Rock Creek; RMC Place; MCLENNAN; ***238** EG-7; mail Waco **z** 76708; rural
Rockdale; Inc. Place; MILAM; **238** EI-7; 🅿 🅷; **z** 76567; Ⓟ 5,235; © 5,439
Rockett; RMC Place; ELLIS; ***238** EE-7; ★ **D-FW**; mail Waxahachie **z** 75165; ● 150
Rock Harbor; RMC Place; HOOD; ***238** EE-6; mail Granbury **z** 76048; ● 400
Rockhill; RMC Place; COLLIN; ***238** EC-7; elev. 734ft./224m.; ★ **D-FW**; mail Mckinney **z** 75069; pop. incl. with Frisco (Inc. Place)
Rock Hill; RMC Place; JASPER; mail Jasper **z** 75951; rural
Rock Hill; RMC Place; WOOD; ***238** ED-10; mail Quitman **z** 75783; rural
Rockhouse; RMC Place; AUSTIN; ***239** EK-8; mail New Ulm **z** 78950; rural
Rock House; RMC Place; WILLIAMSON; ***238** EI-5; mail Liberty Hill **z** 78642; rural
Rock Island; RMC Place; COLORADO; **239** EL-8; 🅿; **z** 77470; ● 200
Rock Island; RMC Place; POLK; ***238** EH-11; mail Corrigan **z** 75939; rural
Rockland; RMC Place; TYLER; **238** EH-12; elev. 127ft./39m.; 🅿; **z** 75938; ● 120
Rockne; RMC Place; BASTROP; **239** EK-6; mail Bastrop **z** 78602; ● 60
Rockport; Inc. Place; ⊡ ARANSAS; **239** EO-7; 🅿; **z** 78381-82; Ⓟ 4,753; © 7,385
Rock Prairie; RMC Place; BRAZOS; ***238** EI-9; ★ **BRY-**; mail Bryan **z** 77805; pop. incl. with College Station (Inc. Place)
Rocksprings; Inc. Place; ⊡ EDWARDS; **237** WP-13; elev. 2,410ft./735m.; 🅿; **z** 78880; Ⓟ 1,339; © 1,285
Rock Springs; RMC Place; MARION; ***238** ED-12; mail Avinger **z** 75630; rural
Rockwall; Inc. Place; ⊡ ROCKWALL; **238** ED-8; elev. 588ft./179m.; 🅿; ★ **D-FW**; **z** 75032, **z** 75087; Ⓟ 10,486; © 17,976; ◆ 35,637
ROCKWALL; **238** ED-8; Ⓟ 25,604; © 43,080; ◆ 82,864
Rockwood; RMC Place; COLEMAN; **238** EG-3; elev. 1,488ft./454m.; 🅿; **z** 76873; ● 100
Rocky Branch; RMC Place; MORRIS; ***238** EC-11; elev. 355ft./108m.; mail Daingerfield **z** 75638, Naples **z** 75568; ● 175
Rocky Creek; RMC Place; BLANCO; ***238** EJ-4; mail Hye **z** 78635; rural
Rocky Creek Park; RMC Place; WASHINGTON; ***238** EJ-8; mail Burton **z** 77835; ● 40
Rocky Hill; RMC Place; FALLS; ***238** EH-7; mail Marlin **z** 76661; rural
Rocky Mound; Inc. Place; CAMP; ***238** ED-11; elev. 427ft./130m.; mail Pittsburg **z** 75686; Ⓟ 53; © 93
Rocky Point; RMC Place; RAINS; ***238** ED-9; mail Emory **z** 75440; rural
Rocky Springs; RMC Place; ANGELINA; ***238** EG-12; elev. 332ft./101m.; mail Huntington **z** 75949; rural
Rocky Springs; RMC Place; TYLER; ***238** EH-12; mail Colmesneil **z** 75938; rural
Roddy; RMC Place; VAN ZANDT; ***238** EE-9; elev. 437ft./133m.; mail Mabank **z** 75147; rural
Rodney; RMC Place; NAVARRO; ***238** EF-8; elev. 429ft./131m.; mail Dawson **z** 76639; rural
Roganville; RMC Place; JASPER; **238** EH-13; 🅿; **z** 75956; ● 100
Rogers; Inc. Place; BELL; **238** EH-7; 🅿; **z** 76569; Ⓟ 1,131; © 1,117
Rogers Hill; RMC Place; MCLENNAN; ***238** EG-7; mail West **z** 76691; pop. incl. with Gholson (Inc. Place)
Rolling Hills; RMC Place; HUNT; ***238** ED-9; mail Lone Oak **z** 75453; ● 200
Rolling Hills; RMC Place; POTTER; **236** WA-2; ★ **AMA**; mail Amarillo **z** 79108; ● 500
Rolling Hills; RMC Place; WALLER; **238** EJ-9; mail Hempstead **z** 77445; ● 200
Rolling Hills Shores; RMC Place; HOOD; ***238** EE-5; mail Granbury **z** 76048; ● 200
Rolling Meadows; RMC Place; GREGG; ***238** EE-11; ★ **LNGV**; mail Longview **z** 75603; ● 200
Rollingwood; Inc. Place; TRAVIS; **237** WS-9; 🅿; ★ **AUS**; **z** 78746; Ⓟ 1,388; © 1,403
Roma; STARR; see Roma-Los Saenz (Inc. Place)
Roma Creek; CDP-Census Area Only; STARR; ***239** ES-3; © 610
Roma-Los Saenz (Roma); Inc. Place; STARR; **239** ES-3; mail Roma **z** 78584; Ⓟ 8,059; © 9,617
Roman Forest; Inc. Place; MONTGOMERY; ***238** EJ-11; 🅿; ★ **HOU**; **z** 77357; Ⓟ 1,033; © 1,279
Roman Hills; RMC Place; MONTGOMERY; ***238** EJ-10; mail Montgomery **z** 77316; ● 300
Romayor; RMC Place; LIBERTY; **238** EI-11; elev. 75ft./23m.; 🅿; **z** 77368; ● 150
Romero; RMC Place; HARTLEY; ***236** WC-8; elev. 4,122ft./1,256m.; mail Dalhart **z** 79022; rural
Romney; RMC Place; EASTLAND; ***238** EF-3; elev. 1,604ft./489m.; mail Rising Star **z** 76471; rural
Roosevelt; RMC Place; KIMBLE; **237** WN-13; elev. 1,934ft./589m.; 🅿; **z** 76874; ● 20
Roosevelt; RMC Place; LUBBOCK; ***236** WH-11; mail Lubbock **z** 79401
Ropes; HOCKLEY; see Ropesville (Inc. Place)
Ropesville (Ropes); Inc. Place; HOCKLEY; **236** WH-10; 🅿; **z** 79358; Ⓟ 494; © 517
Rosalie; RMC Place; RED RIVER; **238** EC-10; mail Bogata **z** 75417; ● 80
Rosanky; RMC Place; BASTROP; **239** EK-7; elev. 508ft./155m.; 🅿; **z** 78953; ● 180
Roscoe; Inc. Place; NOLAN; **236** WJ-13; elev. 2,386ft./727m.; 🅿; **z** 79545; Ⓟ 1,446; © 1,378
Rosebud; Inc. Place; FALLS; **238** EH-7; elev. 405ft./123m.; 🅿; **z** 76570; Ⓟ 1,638; © 1,493
Rose City; Inc. Place; ORANGE; **238** EA-14; ★ **B-PA**; mail Vidor **z** 77662; Ⓟ 572; © 519
Rosedale; RMC Place; FALLS; mail Marlin **z** 76661; rural
Rosedale; RMC Place; JEFFERSON; ***238** EJ-13; ★ **B-PA**; mail Beaumont **z** 77708; pop. incl. with Beaumont (Inc. Place)
Rosedale Acres; RMC Place; JEFFERSON; ***238** EJ-13; ★ **B-PA**; mail Beaumont **z** 77708; pop. incl. with Beaumont (Inc. Place)
Rose Hill; RMC Place; HARRIS; ***238** EJ-10; ★ **HOU**; mail Tomball **z** 77375; ● 250
Rose Hill; RMC Place; SAN JACINTO; ***238** EI-11; mail Coldspring **z** 77331
Rose Hill; RMC Place; WOOD; ***238** ED-10; mail Mineola **z** 75773; rural
Rose Hill Acres; Inc. Place; HARDIN; ***238** EJ-13; ★ **B-PA**; mail Lumberton **z** 77657; Ⓟ 468; © 480
Rosenberg; Inc. Place; FORT BEND; **239** EK-10; 🅿 ■; ★ **HOU**; **z** 77469, **z** 77471; Ⓟ 20,183; © 24,043; ◆ 31,027
Rosenthal; RMC Place; MCLENNAN; ***238** EG-7; mail Lorena **z** 76655; pop. incl. with Robinson (Inc. Place)
Rosevine; RMC Place; SABINE; **238** EG-13; elev. 310ft./94m.; mail Bronson **z** 75930; ● 100
Rosewood; RMC Place; UPSHUR; ***238** ED-11; elev. 473ft./144m.; mail Gilmer **z** 75644
Rosharon; RMC Place; BRAZORIA; **239** EL-10; 🅿; **z** 77583; ● 500
Rosita; RMC Place; DUVAL; ***239** EP-5; mail San Diego **z** 78384
Rosita; RMC Place; STARR; ***239** ES-4; mail Rio Grande City **z** 78582; ● 200
Rosita North; CDP-Census Area Only; MAVERICK; ***237** WR-13; © 3,400
Rosita South; CDP-Census Area Only; MAVERICK; ***237** WS-13; © 2,574
Ross; Inc. Place; MCLENNAN; ***238** EG-7; elev. 570ft./174m.; 🅿; ★ **WACO**; **z** 76684; Ⓟ 188; © 228
Ross City; RMC Place; HOWARD; ***237** WK-11; mail Big Spring **z** 79720; ● 30
Rosser; Inc. Place; KAUFMAN; **238** EE-8; elev. 368ft./112m.; 🅿; **z** 75157; Ⓟ 366; © 379
Rosslyn; RMC Place; HARRIS; ***239** EK-10; ★ **HOU**; pop. incl. with Houston (Inc. Place)
Rosston; RMC Place; COOKE; **238** EC-6; 🅿; **z** 76263; ● 60
Rossville; RMC Place; ATASCOSA; ***239** EM-4; elev. 560ft./171m.; mail Poteet **z** 78065; rural
Rotan; Inc. Place; FISHER; **236** WI-13; elev. 1,945ft./593m.; 🅿 🅷; **z** 79546; Ⓟ 1,913; © 1,611
Round Mountain; Inc. Place; BLANCO; **238** EJ-5; elev. 1,280ft./390m.; 🅿; **z** 78663; Ⓟ 59; © 111
Round Mountain; RMC Place; TRAVIS; ***238** EI-5; mail Leander **z** 78641; rural
Round Prairie; RMC Place; NAVARRO; ***238** EF-9; elev. 343ft./105m.; mail Kerens **z** 75144; rural
Round Rock; Inc. Place; WILLIAMSON, TRAVIS; **238** EI-6; 🅿 🅷; ★ **AUS**; **z** 78664-65, **z** 78680-83; Ⓟ 30,923; © 61,136; ◆ 93,959
Round Rock East; RMC Place; WILLIAMSON; ★ **AUS**; mail Round Rock **z** 78664; pop. incl. with Round Rock (Inc. Place)
Round Timber; RMC Place; BAYLOR; ***238** EC-3; elev. 1,231ft./375m.; mail Seymour **z** 76380; rural
Round Top; Inc. Place; FAYETTE; **238** EJ-8; elev. 439ft./134m.; 🅿; **z** 78954, **z** 78961; Ⓟ 81; © 77
Roundup; RMC Place; HOCKLEY; ***236** WG-10; mail Anton **z** 79313
Rowden; RMC Place; CALLAHAN; ***238** EF-3; mail Baird **z** 79504; rural
Rowena; RMC Place; RUNNELS; **237** WL-13; 🅿; **z** 76875; ● 450
Rowlett; Inc. Place; DALLAS, ROCKWALL; **235** E-13; 🅿 🅷; ★ **D-FW**; **z** 75030, **z** 75088-89; Ⓟ 23,260; © 44,503; ◆ 51,939
Roxton; Inc. Place; LAMAR; **238** EC-9; 🅿; **z** 75477; Ⓟ 639; © 694
Royal Forest; RMC Place; MONTGOMERY; ***238** EI-10; mail Conroe **z** 77303; ● 350
Royal Oaks; RMC Place; HENDERSON; ***238** EE-9; mail Kemp **z** 75143; pop. incl. with Tool (Inc. Place)
Royal Oaks; RMC Place; LLANO; ***238** EI-4; mail Kingsland **z** 78639; ● 300
Royal Oaks; RMC Place; MONTGOMERY; ***238** EJ-10; ★ **HOU**; mail Houston **z** 77254; ● 150
Royalty; RMC Place; WARD; **237** WL-8; elev. 2,467ft./752m.; mail Grandfalls **z** 79742; ● 25
Royalwood; RMC Place; HARRIS; ***239** EK-11; ★ **HOU**; mail Houston **z** 77049; ● 700
Roy Miller; RMC Place; NUECES; ★ **CRPX**; mail Corpus Christi **z** 78405, **z** 78465; pop. incl. with Corpus Christi (Inc. Place)
Roy Royall; RMC Place; HARRIS; ★ **HOU**; mail Houston **z** 77016, **z** 77293; pop. incl. with Houston (Inc. Place)
Royse City; Inc. Place; ROCKWALL, COLLIN; **238** ED-8; elev. 562ft./171m.; 🅿; ★ **D-FW**; **z** 75189; Ⓟ 2,206; © 2,957
Royston; RMC Place; FISHER; ***238** ED-1; elev. 1,928ft./588m.; mail Roby **z** 79543; rural
Rucker; RMC Place; COMANCHE; ***238** EF-4; mail De Leon **z** 76444; rural
Rugby; RMC Place; RED RIVER; **238** EC-10; mail Deport **z** 75435; ● 10
Ruidosa; RMC Place; PRESIDIO; **237** WO-5; mail Marfa **z** 79843; ● 80
Rule; Inc. Place; HASKELL; **236** WI-14; elev. 1,681ft./512m.; 🅿; **z** 79547-48; Ⓟ 783; © 698
Rumley; RMC Place; LAMPASAS; ***238** EH-5; elev. 950ft./290m.; mail Kempner **z** 76539
Run; RMC Place; HIDALGO; ***239** ES-5; ★ **MCAL**; mail Donna **z** 78537; rural
Runaway Bay; Inc. Place; WISE; **238** ED-5; 🅿; **z** 76426, **z** 76458; Ⓟ 700; © 1,104
Runge; Inc. Place; KARNES; **239** EM-6; elev. 315ft./96m.; 🅿; **z** 78151; Ⓟ 1,139; © 1,080
RUNNELS; **238** EF-1; Ⓟ 11,294; © 11,495; ◆ 10,049
Rural Shade; RMC Place; NAVARRO; ***238** EF-9; elev. 335ft./102m.; mail Kerens **z** 75144; rural
Rushwood; RMC Place; HARRIS; ***239** EK-10; ★ **HOU**; mail Houston **z** 77067; ● 3,600
Rusk; Inc. Place; ⊡ CHEROKEE; **238** EF-11; elev. 516ft./157m.; 🅿 🅷; **z** 75785; Ⓟ 4,366; © 5,085
RUSK; **238** EF-11; Ⓟ 43,735; © 47,372; ◆ 49,362
Rustling Oaks; RMC Place; HARRIS; ***239** EK-10; ★ **HOU**; mail Houston **z** 77079; pop. incl. with Houston (Inc. Place)
Rutersville; RMC Place; FAYETTE; **239** EK-8; mail La Grange **z** 78945; ● 50
Ruth Springs; RMC Place; HENDERSON; ***238** EF-9; mail Trinidad **z** 75163; ● 75
Ryanville; RMC Place; REFUGIO; ***239** EN-7; elev. 84ft./26m.; mail Refugio **z** 78377
Rye; RMC Place; LIBERTY; **238** EI-11; elev. 117ft./36m.; 🅿; **z** 77369; ● 100

S

Sabanna; RMC Place; EASTLAND; ***238** EF-3; mail Cisco **z** 76437; ● 50
Sabathany; RMC Place; PARKER; ***238** ED-6; ★ **D-FW**; mail Weatherford **z** 76086; rural
Sabinal; Inc. Place; UVALDE; **239** EL-2; elev. 955ft./291m.; 🅿; **z** 78881; Ⓟ 1,584; © 1,586
Sabine; RMC Place; JEFFERSON; ***239** EK-13; elev. 5ft./2m.; ★ **B-PA**; mail Port Arthur **z** 77640; pop. incl. with Port Arthur (Inc. Place)
SABINE; **238** EG-13; Ⓟ 9,586; © 10,469; ◆ 9,868
Sabine Pass; RMC Place; JEFFERSON; **239** EK-13; 🅿; ★ **B-PA**; **z** 77655; pop. incl. with Port Arthur (Inc. Place)
Sabine Sands; RMC Place; NEWTON; ***238** EI-14; mail Bon Wier **z** 75928; ● 60
Sabinetown; RMC Place; SABINE; ***238** EG-13; mail Hemphill **z** 75948; rural
Sachse; Inc. Place; DALLAS, COLLIN; **235** D-13; 🅿; ★ **D-FW**; **z** 75048; Ⓟ 5,346; © 9,751; Ⓡ 9,884
Sacul; RMC Place; NACOGDOCHES; **238** EF-11; elev. 310ft./94m.; 🅿; **z** 75788; ● 170
Saddle and Surrey; RMC Place; MONTGOMERY; ***238** EJ-10; mail Montgomery **z** 77316; ● 75
Sadler; Inc. Place; GRAYSON; **238** EB-7; elev. 719ft./219m.; 🅿; **z** 76264; Ⓟ 316; © 404
Sagerton; RMC Place; HASKELL; **236** WI-14; elev. 1,634ft./498m.; 🅿; **z** 79548; ● 75
Saginaw; Inc. Place; TARRANT; **235** F-3; 🅿; ★ **D-FW**; **z** 76131, **z** 76179; Ⓟ 8,551; © 12,374; ◆ 18,055
Saint Elmo; RMC Place; FREESTONE; ***238** EF-9; mail Streetman **z** 75859; ● 75
Saint Francis; RMC Place; POTTER; ***236** WD-11; ★ **AMA**; mail Amarillo **z** 79108; ● 30
Saint Francis Village; RMC Place; TARRANT; **235** I-2; ★ **D-FW**; mail Crowley **z** 76036; ● 500
Saint Hedwig; Inc. Place; BEXAR; **239** EL-5; 🅿; **z** 78152; Ⓟ 1,443; © 1,875
Saint Jo; Inc. Place; MONTAGUE; **238** EB-6; elev. 1,143ft./348m.; 🅿; **z** 76265; Ⓟ 1,048; © 977
Saint John; RMC Place; FAYETTE, LAVACA; ***239** EK-7; elev. 372ft./113m.; mail Schulenburg **z** 78956; rural
Saint John Colony; RMC Place; CALDWELL; ***239** EK-6; elev. 530ft./162m.; mail Dale **z** 78616; ● 110
Saint Lawrence; RMC Place; GLASSCOCK; ***237** WL-11; mail Garden City **z** 79739; rural
Saint Paul; Inc. Place; COLLIN; **235** C-13; ★ **D-FW**; mail Wylie **z** 75098; Ⓟ 415; © 630
Saint Paul; RMC Place; FALLS; ***238** EH-7; mail Marlin **z** 76661; rural
Saint Paul; RMC Place; LEON; ***238** EG-9; mail Oakwood **z** 75855; rural
Saint Paul; CDP; SAN PATRICIO; **239** EO-6; mail Sinton **z** 78387; © 542
Salado; Inc. Place; BELL; **238** EI-6; 🅿; ★ **KILL-**; **z** 76571; incorporated August 15, 2000; not reported in 2000 Census; ● 2,000
Salado; CDP-Census Area Only; BELL; **238** EI-6; 🅿; ★ **KILL-**; **z** 76571; Ⓟ 1,216; © 3,475
Salem (Peach Creek); RMC Place; BASTROP; ***239** EK-7; elev. 490ft./149m.; mail Rosanky **z** 78953; rural
Salem; RMC Place; MILAM; ***238** EI-7; mail Cameron **z** 76520; rural
Salem; NEWTON; see Old Salem (RMC Place)
Salem; RMC Place; SMITH; ***238** EF-11; elev. 400ft./122m.; mail Troup **z** 75789; rural
Salem; RMC Place; WOOD; ***238** ED-10; mail Alba **z** 75410; rural
Salesville; RMC Place; PALO PINTO; ***238** ED-5; mail Mineral Wells **z** 76067; ● 125
Saline; RMC Place; MENARD; ***238** EI-2; mail London **z** 76854; rural
Salineno; CDP; STARR; **239** ER-3; 🅿; **z** 78585; © 304
Salmon; RMC Place; ANDERSON; ***238** EG-10; mail Elkhart **z** 75839
Salona; RMC Place; MONTAGUE; ***238** EC-6; mail Bowie **z** 76230; rural
Salt Flat; RMC Place; HUDSPETH; **237** WK-4; 🅿; **z** 79847; ● 30
Salt Gap; RMC Place; MCCULLOCH; ***238** EH-2; elev. 1,673ft./510m.; mail Doole **z** 76836, Lohn **z** 76852; rural
Saltillo; RMC Place; HOPKINS; **238** EC-10; 🅿; **z** 75478; ● 200
Sam Houston; RMC Place; HARRIS; ★ **HOU**; mail Houston **z** 77001, **z** 77052; pop. incl. with Houston (Inc. Place)
Samnorwood; CDP; COLLINGSWORTH; **236** WD-13; elev. 2,196ft./669m.; 🅿; **z** 79077; © 39
Sam Rayburn; RMC Place; JASPER; ***238** EH-13; 🅿; **z** 75951; ● 600
Sanaloma Estates; RMC Place; WILLIAMSON; ***238** EI-6; ★ **AUS**; mail Georgetown **z** 78628; ● 130
San Angelo; Inc. Place; ⊡ TOM GREEN; **237** WL-13; elev. 1,848ft./563m.; 🅿 🅷 🅲 6,148 ■; ★ **SANG**; **z** 76901-06, **z** 76908-09; Ⓟ 84,474; © 88,439; ◆ 93,962
San Antonio; Inc. Place; ⊡ BEXAR; **239** EL-4; 🅿 🅷 🅲 46,911 ■; ★ **SANT**; **z** 78201-66, **z** 78268-70, **z** 78275, **z** 78278-80, **z** 78283-89, **z** 78291-99; Ⓟ 935,393; © 1,144,646; ◆ 1,397,606
San Augustine; Inc. Place; ⊡ SAN AUGUSTINE; **238** EG-13; 🅿 🅷; **z** 75972; Ⓟ 2,337; © 2,475
SAN AUGUSTINE; **238** EG-12; Ⓟ 7,999; © 8,946; ◆ 8,402
San Benito; Inc. Place; CAMERON; **239** ES-6; elev. 40ft./12m.; 🅿 🅷; ★ **BRNS**; **z** 78586; Ⓟ 20,125; © 23,444; ◆ 23,700
San Carlos; CDP; HIDALGO; **239** ES-5; ★ **MCAL**; mail Edinburg **z** 78539; © 2,650
Sanco; RMC Place; COKE; ***237** WK-13; mail Robert Lee **z** 76945; rural
Sanctuary; Inc. Place; PARKER; **235** E-1; ★ **D-FW**; mail Azle **z** 76020; Ⓟ 234; © 256
Sanderson; CDP; ⊡ TERRELL; **237** WO-9; elev. 2,792ft./851m.; 🅿; **z** 79848; Ⓟ 1,128; © 861
Sand Flat; RMC Place; RAINS; ***238** ED-9; mail Emory **z** 75440; rural
Sand Flat; RMC Place; SMITH; ***238** EE-10; ★ **TYL**; mail Tyler **z** 75706; ● 100
Sand Flat; RMC Place; VAN ZANDT; ***238** EE-10; elev. 464ft./141m.; mail Grand Saline **z** 75140; rural
Sand Hill; RMC Place; FLOYD; ***236** WG-11; elev. 3,221ft./982m.; mail Floydada **z** 79235; rural
Sand Hill; RMC Place; UPSHUR; ***238** ED-11; mail Gilmer **z** 75644; rural
Sandia; CDP; JIM WELLS; **239** EO-6; elev. 129ft./39m.; 🅿; **z** 78383; © 431
San Diego; Inc. Place; ⊡ DUVAL, JIM WELLS; **239** EP-5; elev. 305ft./93m.; 🅿; **z** 78384; Ⓟ 4,983; © 4,753
Sandjack; RMC Place; NEWTON; ***238** EI-13; elev. 60ft./18m.; mail Bon Wier **z** 75928; ● 60
Sandoval; RMC Place; WILLIAMSON; ***238** EI-7; mail Taylor **z** 76574; rural
Sand Ridge; RMC Place; HOUSTON; ***238** EH-10; mail Crockett **z** 75835; rural
Sand Ridge; RMC Place; WHARTON; ***239** EL-9; mail Eagle Lake **z** 77434; rural
Sand Springs; RMC Place; HOWARD; **236** WJ-11; mail Big Spring **z** 79720; ● 600
Sandusky; RMC Place; GRAYSON; **238** EB-7; elev. 744ft./227m.; mail Whitesboro **z** 76273; ● 20
Sandy; RMC Place; BLANCO; **238** EJ-4; 🅿; **z** 78636; ● 20
Sandy Acres; RMC Place; MIDLAND; ***237** WK-10; ★ **MIDL-**; mail Midland **z** 79703; ● 200
Sandy Creek; RMC Place; MILAM; ***238** EI-7; mail Milano **z** 76556; rural
Sandy Creek Arm; RMC Place; TRAVIS; ***238** EI-5; mail Leander **z** 78645; pop. incl. with Jonestown (Inc. Place)
Sandy Fork; RMC Place; GONZALES; ***239** EK-6; elev. 370ft./113m.; mail Harwood **z** 78632; rural
Sandy Harbor; RMC Place; LLANO; ***238** EI-4; mail Marble Falls **z** 78654; ● 180
Sandy Hill; RMC Place; WASHINGTON; ***238** EJ-8; mail Brenham **z** 77833; rural
Sandy Hollow-Escondidas; CDP-Census Area Only; NUECES; ***239** EO-6; © 433
Sandy Point; RMC Place; BRAZORIA; **239** EL-10; elev. 57ft./17m.; mail Rosharon **z** 77583; ● 150
Sandy Ridge; RMC Place; POLK; mail Livingston **z** 77351; ● 100
San Elizario; CDP; EL PASO; **237** WL-2; 🅿; ★ **ELP**; **z** 79849; incorporation status unclear; Ⓟ 4,385; © 11,046
San Felipe; Inc. Place; AUSTIN; **239** EK-9; 🅿; **z** 77473; Ⓟ 618; © 868
Sanford; Inc. Place; HUTCHINSON; **236** WC-11; elev. 3,028ft./923m.; 🅿; **z** 79078; Ⓟ 218; © 203
Sanford Estates; RMC Place; HUTCHINSON; ***236** WC-11; mail Fritch **z** 79036; summer pop. 150; ● 50
San Gabriel; RMC Place; MILAM; **238** EI-7; elev. 411ft./125m.; mail Thorndale **z** 76577; ● 75
San Gabriel Heights; RMC Place; WILLIAMSON; ***238** EI-6; ★ **AUS**; mail Georgetown **z** 78628; pop. incl. with Georgetown (Inc. Place)
Sanger; Inc. Place; DENTON; **238** EC-7; elev. 665ft./203m.; 🅿; ★ **DENT**; **z** 76266; Ⓟ 3,508; © 4,534
San Geromino; RMC Place; BEXAR; ***239** EK-4; mail Helotes **z** 78023; rural
San Ignacio; CDP-Census Area Only; ZAPATA; ***239** EQ-3; © 853
San Isidro; CDP; STARR; **239** ER-5; 🅿; **z** 78588; © 270
San Jacinto; RMC Place; POTTER; ★ **AMA**; mail Amarillo **z** 79106; pop. incl. with Amarillo (Inc. Place)
SAN JACINTO; **238** EI-10; Ⓟ 16,372; © 22,246; ◆ 25,499
San Jose; BEXAR; see Terrell Wells (RMC Place)
San Jose; RMC Place; DUVAL; ***239** EP-5; mail Alice **z** 78332
San Juan; Inc. Place; HIDALGO; **239** ES-5; 🅿; ★ **MCAL**; **z** 78589; Ⓟ 10,815; © 26,229; ◆ 36,197
San Juan; RMC Place; NUECES; ***239** EP-6; elev. 46ft./14m.; ★ **CRPX**; mail Corpus Christi **z** 78406; pop. incl. with Corpus Christi (Inc. Place)
San Leanna; Inc. Place; TRAVIS; ***238** EJ-6; ★ **AUS**; mail Austin **z** 78748; Ⓟ 325; © 384
San Leon; CDP; GALVESTON; **234** H-10; 🅿; ★ **GLV-**; **z** 77539; © 4,365
San Manuel; HIDALGO; see Linn (RMC Place)
San Manuel-Linn; CDP-Census Area Only; HIDALGO; ***239** ER-5; © 958
San Marcos; Inc. Place; ⊡ HAYS, CALDWELL; **239** EK-5; elev. 619ft./189m.; 🅿 🅷 🅲 27,485; **z** 78666-67; Ⓟ 28,743; © 34,733; ◆ 44,841
San Patricio; Inc. Place; SAN PATRICIO, NUECES; **239** EO-6; mail Mathis **z** 78368; Ⓟ 369; © 318
SAN PATRICIO; **239** EO-7; Ⓟ 58,749; © 67,138; ◆ 66,385
San Pedro; CDP; CAMERON; ***239** ET-6; ★ **BRNS**; mail Brownsville **z** 78520, Robstown **z** 78380; © 668
San Perlita; Inc. Place; WILLACY; **239** ER-6; 🅿; **z** 78590; Ⓟ 512; © 680
San Saba; Inc. Place; ⊡ SAN SABA; **238** EH-4; elev. 1,207ft./368m.; 🅿; **z** 76877; Ⓟ 2,626; © 2,637
SAN SABA; **238** EH-3; Ⓟ 5,401; © 6,186; ◆ 5,876
Sansom Park; Inc. Place; TARRANT; **235** G-3; ★ **D-FW**; mail Fort Worth **z** 76114; Ⓟ 3,928; © 4,181
Santa Anna; Inc. Place; COLEMAN; **238** EG-3; elev. 1,748ft./533m.; 🅿; **z** 76878; Ⓟ 1,249; © 1,081
Santa Anna; RMC Place; STARR; ***239** ER-4; mail Santa Elena **z** 78591; rural
Santa Catarina; RMC Place; STARR; ***239** ER-4; mail Rio Grande City **z** 78582
Santa Clara; Inc. Place; GUADALUPE; ***239** EK-5; ★ **SANT**; mail Marion **z** 78124; © 889
Santa Cruz; DUVAL; see Cruz Calle (RMC Place)
Santa Cruz; CDP; STARR; **239** ES-4; elev. 158ft./48m.; mail Rio Grande City **z** 78582; © 630
Santa Elena; RMC Place; STARR; **239** ER-4; 🅿; **z** 78591; ● 120
Santa Fe; Inc. Place; GALVESTON; **234** J-8; 🅿; ★ **GLV-**; **z** 77510, **z** 77517; Ⓟ 8,429; © 9,548
Santa Maria; CDP; CAMERON; **239** ES-6; 🅿; ★ **BRNS**; **z** 78592; © 846
Santa Monica; CDP; WILLACY; ***239** ES-6; mail Lyford **z** 78569, Raymondville **z** 78580; © 78
Santa Rita; RMC Place; TOM GREEN; ***237** WL-13; ★ **SANG**; mail San Angelo **z** 76901; pop. incl. with San Angelo (Inc. Place)
Santa Rosa; Inc. Place; CAMERON; **239** ES-6; elev. 53ft./16m.; 🅿; ★ **BRNS**; **z** 78593; Ⓟ 2,223; © 2,833
Santo; RMC Place; PALO PINTO; **238** EE-5; elev. 823ft./251m.; 🅿; **z** 76472; ● 450
San Ygnacio; RMC Place; ZAPATA; **239** EQ-3; elev. 327ft./100m.; 🅿; **z** 78067; ● 1,000
Saragosa; RMC Place; REEVES; **237** WM-7; 🅿; **z** 79780; ● 400
Saratoga; RMC Place; HARDIN; **238** EJ-12; elev. 67ft./20m.; 🅿; **z** 77585; ● 1,200
Sarco; RMC Place; GOLIAD; ***239** EN-7; mail Goliad **z** 77963; rural
Sardis; RMC Place; CASS; ***238** ED-12; mail Hughes Springs **z** 75656; rural
Sardis; RMC Place; ELLIS; ***238** EE-7; ★ **D-FW**; mail Midlothian **z** 76065; ● 60
Sargent; RMC Place; DALLAS; ***238** ED-7; ★ **D-FW**; pop. incl. with Dallas (Inc. Place)
Sargent; RMC Place; MATAGORDA; **239** EM-10; elev. 11ft./3m.; 🅿; **z** 77404, **z** 77414; summer pop. 2,000; ● 400
Sarita; RMC Place; ⊡ KENEDY; **239** EQ-6; 🅿; **z** 78385; ● 200
Sash; RMC Place; FANNIN; ***238** EB-9; elev. 560ft./171m.; mail Honey Grove **z** 75446; rural
Saspamco; RMC Place; WILSON; **239** EL-5; mail Elmendorf **z** 78112; ● 200
Satin; RMC Place; FALLS; ***238** EH-7; elev. 403ft./123m.; 🅿; **z** 76685; ● 100
Satsuma; RMC Place; HARRIS; ***239** EK-10; ★ **HOU**; mail Houston **z** 77040-41; pop. incl. with Jersey Village (Inc. Place)
Sattler; RMC Place; COMAL; ***239** EK-5; mail Canyon Lake **z** 78133, New Braunfels **z** 78130, **z** 78132
Saturn; RMC Place; GONZALES; ***239** EK-7; mail Gonzales **z** 78629, Harwood **z** 78632; rural
Sauney Stand; RMC Place; WASHINGTON; ***238** EJ-9; mail Chappell Hill **z** 77426; ● 120
Savage; RMC Place; CROSBY; ***236** WH-11; mail Ralls **z** 79357; rural
Savoy; Inc. Place; FANNIN; **238** EC-8; elev. 676ft./206m.; 🅿; **z** 75479; Ⓟ 877; © 850
Sayers (Sayersville); RMC Place; BASTROP; ***238** EJ-7; mail Bastrop **z** 78602; ● 30
Sayers (Adkins); RMC Place; BEXAR; ***239** EL-5; ★ **SANT**; mail Adkins **z** 78101; ● 200
Sayersville; BASTROP; see Sayers (RMC Place)
Scallorn; RMC Place; MILLS; ***238** EH-4; mail Lometa **z** 76853; rural
Scenic Heights; RMC Place; COMAL; ***239** EK-5; mail New Braunfels **z** 78130
Scenic Hills; RMC Place; GUADALUPE; ***239** EK-5; ★ **SANT**; mail Cibolo **z** 78108; ● 200
Scenic Oaks; CDP-Census Area Only; BEXAR; ***239** EK-4; ★ **SANT**; mail Helotes **z** 78023; Ⓟ 2,352; © 3,279
Scenic Terrace; RMC Place; COMAL; ***239** EK-5; mail New Braunfels **z** 78130
Scharbauer City; RMC Place; ECTOR; ***237** WK-9; ★ **MIDL-**; mail Gardendale **z** 79758; rural
Schattel; RMC Place; FRIO; ***239** EM-4; mail Bigfoot **z** 78005; rural
Schertz; Inc. Place; GUADALUPE, BEXAR, COMAL; **239** EL-5; 🅿; ★ **SANT**; **z** 78154 & mail Converse **z** 78109; Ⓟ 10,555; © 18,694; ◆ 33,581
Schicke Point; RMC Place; CALHOUN; **239** EM-9; mail Palacios **z** 77465; ● 200
SCHLEICHER; **237** WM-12; Ⓟ 2,990; © 2,935; ◆ 2,916
Schoolerville; RMC Place; HAMILTON; ***238** EG-5; mail Hamilton **z** 76531; rural
School Land; RMC Place; GONZALES; mail Nixon **z** 78140; rural
Schroeder; RMC Place; GOLIAD; ***239** EM-7; elev. 163ft./50m.; mail Goliad **z** 77963; ● 35
Schulenburg; Inc. Place; FAYETTE; **239** EK-7; 🅿; **z** 78956; Ⓟ 2,455; © 2,699
Schumannsville; RMC Place; GUADALUPE; ***239** EK-5; mail New Braunfels **z** 78130; rural
Schwab City; RMC Place; POLK; ***238** EI-11; mail Livingston **z** 77351; rural
Schwertner; RMC Place; WILLIAMSON; **238** EI-6; 🅿; **z** 76573; ● 80
Scissors; CDP; HIDALGO; ***239** ES-5; ★ **MCAL**; mail Donna **z** 78537; © 2,805
Scotland; Inc. Place; ARCHER, CLAY; **238** EC-4; 🅿; **z** 76379; Ⓟ 490; © 438
Scotsdale; RMC Place; ECTOR; ★ **MIDL-**; mail Odessa **z** 79762; pop. incl. with Odessa (Inc. Place)
Scotsdale; RMC Place; EL PASO; ★ **ELP**; mail El Paso **z** 79925; pop. incl. with El Paso (Inc. Place)
Scott; RMC Place; VAN ZANDT; ***238** EE-9; mail Wills Point **z** 75169; rural
Scottdale; RMC Place; DALLAS; ★ **D-FW**; pop. incl. with Dallas (Inc. Place)
Scottsville; Inc. Place; HARRISON; **238** EE-12; elev. 417ft./127m.; 🅿; ★ **MAR**; **z** 75688; Ⓟ 283; © 263
Scranton; RMC Place; EASTLAND; ***238** EF-3; mail Cisco **z** 76437
Scrappin Valley; RMC Place; NEWTON; ***238** EH-13; mail Wiergate **z** 75977; rural
Scroggins; RMC Place; FRANKLIN; **238** ED-10; 🅿; **z** 75480; ● 80
Scurry; Inc. Place; KAUFMAN; **238** EE-8; 🅿; **z** 75158; incorporated May 8, 2003; not reported in 2003 Census; ● 350
SCURRY; **236** WI-12; Ⓟ 18,634; © 16,361; ◆ 16,212
Seabrook; Inc. Place; HARRIS, CHAMBERS, GALVESTON; **234** G-9; elev. 14ft./4m.; 🅿; ★ **HOU**; **z** 77586; Ⓟ 6,685; © 9,443
Sea Crest Park; RMC Place; CHAMBERS; ***239** EK-11; mail Baytown **z** 77521
Seadrift; Inc. Place; CALHOUN; **239** EN-8; elev. 12ft./4m.; 🅿; **z** 77983; Ⓟ 1,277; © 1,352
Seagoville; Inc. Place; DALLAS, KAUFMAN; **238** EE-8; 🅿; ★ **D-FW**; **z** 75159; Ⓟ 8,969; © 10,823
Seagraves; Inc. Place; GAINES; **236** WI-9; elev. 3,353ft./1,022m.; 🅿; **z** 79359; Ⓟ 2,398; © 2,334
Sea Isle; RMC Place; GALVESTON; **239** EL-11; ★ **GLV-**; mail Galveston **z** 77554; pop. incl. with Galveston (Inc. Place)
Seale; RMC Place; ROBERTSON; ***238** EH-8; mail Thornton **z** 76687; rural
Sealy; Inc. Place; AUSTIN; **239** EK-9; 🅿; **z** 77474; Ⓟ 4,541; © 5,248
Seaton; RMC Place; BELL; ***238** EH-7; elev. 501ft./153m.; mail Temple **z** 76501; ● 50
Seawillow; RMC Place; CALDWELL; ***239** EK-6; mail Lockhart **z** 78644; rural
Sebastian; CDP; WILLACY; **239** ES-6; elev. 37ft./11m.; 🅿; **z** 78594; Ⓟ 1,598; © 1,864
Sebastopol; RMC Place; TRINITY; ***238** EH-10; mail Trinity **z** 75862
Seco Mines (La Gloria); RMC Place; MAVERICK; ***237** WR-13; elev. 755ft./230m.; mail Eagle Pass **z** 78852; ● 1,000
Security; RMC Place; MONTGOMERY; **238** EJ-11; ★ **HOU**; mail Cleveland **z** 77327; ● 30
Sedalia; RMC Place; COLLIN; mail Van Alstyne **z** 75495; rural
Segno; RMC Place; POLK; ***238** EI-12; elev. 207ft./63m.; 🅿; **z** 77351
Segovia; RMC Place; KIMBLE; **238** EJ-2; elev. 1,783ft./543m.; mail Junction **z** 76849; ● 15
Seguin; Inc. Place; ⊡ GUADALUPE; **239** EL-5; 🅿 🅷 🅲 1,429; **z** 78155-56; Ⓟ 18,853; © 22,011; ◆ 24,127
Sejita; RMC Place; DUVAL; ***239** EQ-5; elev. 363ft./111m.; mail Realitos **z** 78376
Selden; RMC Place; ERATH; **238** EF-5; mail Stephenville **z** 76401; ● 75
Selfs; RMC Place; FANNIN; ***238** EB-9; mail Honey Grove **z** 75446; ● 30
Selma; Inc. Place; BEXAR, COMAL, GUADALUPE; **239** EL-5; 🅿; ★ **SANT**; **z** 78154 & mail San Antonio **z** 78209; Ⓟ 520; © 788
Selman City; RUSK; see Turnertown (RMC Place)
Seminary Hill; RMC Place; TARRANT; ★ **D-FW**; mail Fort Worth **z** 76115; pop. incl. with Fort Worth (Inc. Place)
Seminole; Inc. Place; ⊡ GAINES; **236** WJ-9; elev. 3,297ft./1,005m.; 🅿 🅷; **z** 79360; Ⓟ 6,342; © 5,910
Senate; RMC Place; JACK; ***238** ED-5; mail Jacksboro **z** 76458; rural
Senior; RMC Place; BEXAR; ★ **SANT**; mail Von Ormy **z** 78073; rural
Sequoya Bend; RMC Place; HARRIS; ***239** EK-10; ★ **HOU**; mail Houston **z** 77032; ● 600
Serbin; RMC Place; LEE; **238** EJ-7; elev. 446ft./136m.; mail Giddings **z** 78942; ● 60
Serenada; CDP-Census Area Only; WILLIAMSON; ***238** EI-6; ★ **AUS**; mail Georgetown **z** 78628; Ⓟ 3,242; © 1,847
Serna; RMC Place; BEXAR; ***239** EL-4; ★ **SANT**; mail San Antonio **z** 78218, **z** 78266; pop. incl. with San Antonio (Inc. Place)
Seth Ward; CDP; HALE; **236** WF-11; elev. 3,369ft./1,027m.; mail Plainview **z** 79072; Ⓟ 1,402; © 1,926
Settlers Village; RMC Place; HARRIS; ***239** EK-10; ★ **HOU**; mail Katy **z** 77449; ● 1,000
Seven Oaks; Inc. Place; POLK; **238** EH-11; mail Leggett **z** 77350; Ⓟ 171; © 131
Seven Pines; RMC Place; UPSHUR, GREGG; ***238** EE-11; ★ **LNGV**; mail Gilmer **z** 75644, Longview **z** 75605; ● 150
Seven Points; Inc. Place; HENDERSON, KAUFMAN; ***238** EE-8; elev. 384ft./117m.; 🅿; **z** 75143; Ⓟ 723; © 1,145
Seven Sisters; RMC Place; DUVAL; ***239** EO-4; mail Freer **z** 78357; rural
Sexton; RMC Place; SABINE; ***238** EG-13; mail San Augustine **z** 75972; rural
Sexton City; RMC Place; RUSK; ***238** EE-11; mail Overton **z** 75684; rural
Seymore; RMC Place; HOPKINS; ***238** ED-10; elev. 494ft./151m.; mail Sulphur Springs **z** 75482; rural
Seymour; Inc. Place; ⊡ BAYLOR; **238** EC-3; elev. 1,292ft./394m.; 🅿 🅷; **z** 76380; Ⓟ 3,185; © 2,908
SHACKELFORD; **238** ED-2; Ⓟ 3,316; © 3,302; ◆ 3,222
Shadow Bay; RMC Place; MONTGOMERY; ***238** EI-10; mail Willis **z** 77318; ● 250
Shadow Glen; RMC Place; HARRIS; ***239** EK-11; ★ **HOU**; mail Channelview **z** 77530
Shadow Lake Estates; RMC Place; MONTGOMERY; ***238** EJ-11; ★ **HOU**; mail Porter **z** 77365
Shadowland; RMC Place; RED RIVER; ***238** EC-10; mail Deport **z** 75435; rural
Shady Acres; RMC Place; BURNET; ***238** EI-4; mail Marble Falls **z** 78654; ● 90
Shady Brook Acres; RMC Place; MONTGOMERY; ***238** EJ-10; ★ **HOU**; mail Magnolia **z** 77354; ● 250
Shady Grove; RMC Place; ANGELINA; ***238** EH-11; mail Diboll **z** 75941
Shady Grove; RMC Place; BURNET; ***238** EI-5; mail Bertram **z** 78605; rural
Shady Grove; RMC Place; CHEROKEE; ***238** EF-11; elev. 326ft./99m.; mail Rusk **z** 75785; rural
Shady Grove; RMC Place; DALLAS; ***238** ED-7; ★ **D-FW**; mail Grand Prairie **z** 75050; pop. incl. with Grand Prairie (Inc. Place)
Shady Grove; RMC Place; KERR; ***239** EK-3; elev. 1,616ft./493m.; mail Kerrville **z** 78028; rural
Shady Grove; RMC Place; NACOGDOCHES; ***238** EG-12; mail Nacogdoches **z** 75961; rural
Shady Grove; RMC Place; NAVARRO; ***238** EF-8; mail Purdon **z** 76679; rural
Shady Grove; RMC Place; PANOLA; ***238** EF-12; mail Long Branch **z** 75669; rural

Shady Grove; RMC Place; RAINS; ***238** ED-9; elev. 490ft./149m.; mail Emory **z** 75440; ● 40
Shady Grove; RMC Place; SMITH; ***238** EE-10; ★ **TYL**; mail Tyler **z** 75706; rural
Shady Grove; RMC Place; UPSHUR; ***238** ED-10; elev. 476ft./145m.; mail Big Sandy **z** 75755; ● 40
Shady Hollow; CDP-Census Area Only; TRAVIS; ***238** EJ-6; ★ **AUS**; mail Austin **z** 78739; Ⓒ 5,140
Shady Oaks; RMC Place; HENDERSON; mail Athens **z** 75751; ● 120
Shady Shores; Inc. Place; DENTON; **235** B-7; 🅿; ★ **D-FW**; **z** 76208 & mail Denton **z** 76205; Ⓟ 1,045; Ⓒ 1,461
Shafter; RMC Place; PRESIDIO; **237** WP-5; 🅿; **z** 79843; ● 30
Shallowater; Inc. Place; LUBBOCK; **236** WG-10; 🅿; **z** 79363; Ⓟ 1,708; Ⓒ 2,086
Shamrock; Inc. Place; WHEELER; **236** WD-13; elev. 2,342ft./714m.; 🅿 🅷; **z** 79079; Ⓟ 2,286; Ⓒ 2,029
Shamrock Shores; RMC Place; BROWN; ***238** EG-3; mail Brownwood **z** 76801; ● 1,000
Shankleville; RMC Place; NEWTON; ***238** EH-13; mail Burkeville **z** 75932; rural
Shannon; RMC Place; CLAY; ***238** EC-5; mail Henrietta **z** 76365
Sharp; RMC Place; MILAM; **238** EI-7; mail Buckholts **z** 76518; ● 80
Sharpstown; RMC Place; HARRIS; ***239** EK-10; ★ **HOU**; mail Houston **z** 77036; pop. incl. with Houston (Inc. Place)
Sharyland; RMC Place; HIDALGO; ***239** ES-5; ★ **MCAL**; mail Mission **z** 78572; pop. incl. with Mission (Inc. Place)
Shavano Park; Inc. Place; BEXAR; **239** EQ-11; 🅿; ★ **SANT**; **z** 78230-31, **z** 78249, **z** 78257; Ⓟ 1,708; Ⓒ 1,754
Shawnee; RMC Place; ANGELINA; ***238** EH-12; elev. 240ft./73m.; mail Huntington **z** 75949; rural
Shawnee Shores; RMC Place; HUNT; ***238** ED-9; mail Quinlan **z** 75474; ● 250
Shawnee Shores; RMC Place; SABINE; ***238** EG-13; mail Hemphill **z** 75948; ● 60
Shaws Bend; RMC Place; COLORADO; ***239** EK-8; mail Columbus **z** 78934; rural
Sheffield; RMC Place; PECOS; **237** WN-10; elev. 2,168ft./661m.; 🅿; **z** 79781; ● 450
Shelby; RMC Place; AUSTIN; **238** EJ-8; mail Fayetteville **z** 78940; ● 85
SHELBY; **238** EF-12; Ⓟ 22,034; Ⓒ 25,224; ◆ 26,783
Shelbyville; RMC Place; SHELBY; **238** EF-13; elev. 292ft./89m.; 🅿; **z** 75973; ● 300
Sheldon; CDP; HARRIS; **234** C-8; ★ **HOU**; mail Houston **z** 77028, **z** 77049; Ⓟ 1,653; Ⓒ 1,831
Shenandoah; Inc. Place; MONTGOMERY; **238** EJ-10; 🅿; ★ **HOU**; **z** 77380-81, **z** 77384-85; Ⓟ 1,718; Ⓒ 1,503
Shenandoah; RMC Place; WILLIAMSON; ***238** EJ-6; ★ **AUS**; mail Cedar Park **z** 78613; ● 950
Shep; RMC Place; TAYLOR; ***238** EF-1; elev. 2,154ft./657m.; mail Wingate **z** 79566
Shepherd; Inc. Place; SAN JACINTO; **238** EI-11; elev. 162ft./49m.; 🅿; **z** 77371; Ⓟ 1,812; Ⓒ 2,029
Shepphard; RMC Place; NEWTON; ***238** EI-13; mail Buna **z** 77612; rural
Sheridan; RMC Place; COLORADO; **239** EL-8; 🅿; **z** 77475; ● 500
Sherman; Inc. Place; ⊡ GRAYSON; **238** EC-8; 🅿 🅷 🅲 1,354 ■; ★ **SHRM-**; **z** 75090-92; Ⓟ 31,601; Ⓒ 35,082; ◆ 37,017
SHERMAN; **236** WB-10; Ⓟ 2,858; Ⓒ 3,186; ◆ 2,886
Sherry; RMC Place; RED RIVER; ***238** EC-10; elev. 371ft./113m.; mail Clarksville **z** 75426; rural
Sherwood; RMC Place; IRION; **237** WM-12; mail Mertzon **z** 76941; ● 100
Sherwood Forest; RMC Place; BEXAR; ***239** EK-4; ★ **SANT**; mail San Antonio **z** 78258; ● 100
Sherwood Place; RMC Place; HARRIS; ***239** EK-10; ★ **HOU**; mail Houston **z** 77093; ● 1,000
Sherwood Shores; RMC Place; BURNET; ***238** EI-5; mail Marble Falls **z** 78654; ● 800
Sherwood Shores; RMC Place; GRAYSON; ***238** EB-7; mail Gordonville **z** 76245; ● 450
Shields; RMC Place; COLEMAN; ***238** EG-2; elev. 1,600ft./488m.; mail Gouldbusk **z** 76845, Santa Anna **z** 76878; rural
Shiloh; RMC Place; DELTA; ***238** EC-9; mail Klondike **z** 75448; rural
Shiloh; RMC Place; LEON; ***238** EG-9; mail Oakwood **z** 75855; rural
Shiloh; RMC Place; LIBERTY; ***238** EJ-12; elev. 30ft./9m.; mail Liberty **z** 77575
Shiloh; RMC Place; LIMESTONE; ***238** EG-8; elev. 467ft./142m.; mail Mexia **z** 76667
Shiloh; RMC Place; WILLIAMSON; ***238** EI-7; mail Thrall **z** 76578; rural
Shiner; Inc. Place; LAVACA; **239** EL-7; elev. 368ft./112m.; 🅿; **z** 77984; Ⓟ 2,074; Ⓒ 2,070
Shipman Camp; RMC Place; HASKELL; mail Haskell **z** 79521; ● 60
Shirley; RMC Place; HOPKINS; ***238** ED-9; mail Sulphur Springs **z** 75482
Shirley Creek; RMC Place; NACOGDOCHES; ***238** EG-12; mail Chireno **z** 75937; ● 40
Shiro; RMC Place; GRIMES; **238** EI-9; 🅿; **z** 77876; ● 200
Shive; RMC Place; HAMILTON; ***238** EG-5; mail Hamilton **z** 76531
Shoreacres; Inc. Place; HARRIS, CHAMBERS; **234** F-9; 🅿; ★ **HOU**; **z** 77571; Ⓟ 1,316; Ⓒ 1,488
Short; RMC Place; SHELBY; ***238** EF-12; mail Center **z** 75935; rural
Sidney; RMC Place; COMANCHE; **238** EF-4; 🅿; **z** 76474; ● 200
Sienna Plantation; CDP-Census Area Only; FORT BEND; ***239** EL-10; 🅿; **z** 77459; Ⓒ 1,896
Sierra Blanca; CDP; ⊡ HUDSPETH; **237** WM-4; elev. 4,520ft./1,378m.; 🅿; **z** 79851; Ⓒ 533
Siesta Shores; RMC Place; TRAVIS; ***238** EJ-5; ★ **AUS**; mail Spicewood **z** 78669; ● 90
Siesta Shores; CDP; ZAPATA; **239** ER-3; elev. 370ft./113m.; mail Zapata **z** 78076; Ⓒ 890
Silas; RMC Place; SHELBY; ***238** EF-12; mail Timpson **z** 75975; rural
Siloam; RMC Place; BOWIE; ***238** EC-11; elev. 322ft./98m.; mail De Kalb **z** 75559, Simms **z** 75574; rural
Silsbee; Inc. Place; HARDIN; **238** EJ-13; elev. 81ft./25m.; 🅿 🅷; ★ **B-PA**; **z** 77656; Ⓟ 6,368; Ⓒ 6,393
Silver; RMC Place; COKE; ***237** WK-12; 🅿; **z** 76945, **z** 76949; ● 50
Silver City; RMC Place; MILAM; ***238** EI-7; elev. 345ft./105m.; mail Cameron **z** 76520; rural
Silver City; RMC Place; NAVARRO; ***238** EF-8; mail Purdon **z** 76679; ● 40
Silver City; RMC Place; RED RIVER; ***238** EB-10; elev. 389ft./119m.; mail Clarksville **z** 75426; rural
Silver Creek Village; RMC Place; BURNET; ***238** EI-4; mail Burnet **z** 78611; ● 200
Silver Creek Village Number 2; RMC Place; BURNET; ***238** EI-4; mail Burnet **z** 78611; ● 75
Silver Hills; RMC Place; COMAL; mail Boerne **z** 78006; ● 150
Silver Lake; RMC Place; VAN ZANDT; **238** EE-10; mail Grand Saline **z** 75140, Mineola **z** 75773; ● 45
Silverton; Inc. Place; ⊡ BRISCOE; **236** WF-11; elev. 3,278ft./999m.; 🅿; **z** 79257; Ⓟ 779; Ⓒ 771
Silver Valley; RMC Place; COLEMAN; ***238** EF-2; mail Coleman **z** 76834; rural
Simmons; RMC Place; LIVE OAK; ***239** EN-5; elev. 222ft./68m.; mail Three Rivers **z** 78071
Simmons Bottom; RMC Place; LIBERTY; ***238** EJ-11; mail Dayton **z** 77535; ● 100
Simms; RMC Place; BOWIE; **238** EC-12; 🅿; **z** 75574; ● 275
Simms; RMC Place; DEAF SMITH; ***236** WD-9; mail Hereford **z** 79045; rural
Simonton; Inc. Place; FORT BEND; **239** EK-9; 🅿; **z** 77476; Ⓟ 717; Ⓒ 718
Simpsonville; RMC Place; MATAGORDA; ***239** EM-9; mail Palacios **z** 77465; rural
Simsboro; RMC Place; FREESTONE; ***238** EG-8; mail Teague **z** 75860
Sinclair City; RMC Place; SMITH; ***238** EF-11; mail Troup **z** 75789; rural
Singer; RMC Place; LUBBOCK; ★ **LUB**; mail Lubbock **z** 79424, **z** 79464; pop. incl. with Lubbock (Inc. Place)
Singletary Sites; RMC Place; NEWTON; ***238** EI-13; mail Kirbyville **z** 75956; rural
Singleton; RMC Place; GRIMES; **238** EI-9; elev. 335ft./102m.; 🅿; **z** 77831; ● 50
Sinton; Inc. Place; ⊡ SAN PATRICIO; **239** EO-6; elev. 54ft./16m.; 🅿; **z** 78387; Ⓟ 5,549; Ⓒ 5,676
Sipe Springs; RMC Place; COMANCHE; **238** EF-4; mail Comanche **z** 76442; ● 50
Sisterdale; RMC Place; KENDALL; **239** EK-4; elev. 1,280ft./390m.; 🅿; **z** 78006; ● 40
Sivells Bend; RMC Place; COOKE; **238** EB-6; mail Gainesville **z** 76240; rural
Six Mile; RMC Place; CALHOUN; ***239** EM-8; mail Port Lavaca **z** 77979; rural
Six Points; RMC Place; NUECES; ***239** EP-7; ★ **CRPX**; mail Corpus Christi **z** 78404, **z** 78463; pop. incl. with Corpus Christi (Inc. Place)
Skellytown; Inc. Place; CARSON; **236** WC-12; elev. 3,230ft./985m.; 🅿; **z** 79080; Ⓟ 664; Ⓒ 610
Skidmore; CDP; BEE; **239** EN-6; 🅿; **z** 78389; Ⓒ 1,013
Sky Harbor; RMC Place; HOOD; ***238** EE-6; mail Granbury **z** 76049; ● 600
Skyscraper Shadows; RMC Place; HARRIS; ***239** EK-11; ★ **HOU**; mail Houston **z** 77075; pop. incl. with Houston (Inc. Place)
Slabtown; RMC Place; LAMAR; ***238** EC-10; mail Paris **z** 75462; rural
Slate Shoals; RMC Place; LAMAR; ***238** EB-10; elev. 409ft./125m.; mail Paris **z** 75462; rural
Slaton; Inc. Place; LUBBOCK; **236** WH-11; elev. 3,081ft./939m.; 🅿; **z** 79364 & mail Ransom Canyon **z** 79366; Ⓟ 6,078; Ⓒ 6,109
Slide; RMC Place; LUBBOCK; ***236** WH-10; elev. 3,251ft./991m.; mail Lubbock **z** 79424; ● 40
Slidell; RMC Place; WISE; **238** EC-6; 🅿; **z** 76267; ● 100
Sloan; RMC Place; SAN SABA; mail San Saba **z** 76877; rural
Slocum; RMC Place; ANDERSON; **238** EG-10; 🅿; **z** 75839; ● 225
Small; RMC Place; VAN ZANDT; ***238** ED-9; elev. 456ft./139m.; mail Edgewood **z** 75117; rural
Smeltertown; RMC Place; EL PASO; ***237** WK-1; ★ **ELP**; mail El Paso **z** 79927; pop. incl. with El Paso (Inc. Place)
Smetana; RMC Place; BRAZOS; ***238** EI-8; mail Bryan **z** 77807; rural
Smiley; Inc. Place; GONZALES; **239** EL-6; 🅿; **z** 78159; Ⓟ 463; Ⓒ 453
SMITH; **238** EE-11; Ⓟ 151,309; Ⓒ 174,706; ◆ 206,287
Smithfield; RMC Place; TARRANT; ***238** ED-7; ★ **D-FW**; mail North Richland Hills **z** 76180; pop. incl. with North Richland Hills (Inc. Place)
Smith Grove; RMC Place; HOUSTON; ***238** EH-10; mail Lovelady **z** 75851; rural
Smith Hill; RMC Place; BOWIE; **238** EB-12; mail Hooks **z** 75561
Smithland; RMC Place; MARION; ***238** ED-12; 🅿; **z** 75657
Smith Point; RMC Place; CHAMBERS; **239** EK-12; elev. 6ft./2m.; mail Anahuac **z** 77514; ● 300
Smiths Bend; RMC Place; BOSQUE; ***238** EG-6; mail Clifton **z** 76634; rural
Smith Springs; RMC Place; ERATH; ***238** EF-5; mail Stephenville **z** 76401; rural
Smithville; Inc. Place; BASTROP; **239** EK-7; 🅿 🅷; **z** 78957; Ⓟ 3,196; Ⓒ 3,901
Smithwick; RMC Place; BURNET; ***238** EI-5; elev. 842ft./257m.; mail Marble Falls **z** 78654; rural
Smitty; RMC Place; HENDERSON; ***238** EF-9; mail Athens **z** 75751
Smyer; Inc. Place; HOCKLEY; **236** WH-10; elev. 3,388ft./1,033m.; 🅿; **z** 79367; Ⓟ 442; Ⓒ 480
Smyrna; RMC Place; CASS; ***238** EC-12; elev. 313ft./95m.; mail Atlanta **z** 75551; rural
Smyrna; RMC Place; HARRISON; ***238** ED-11; mail Harleton **z** 75651; rural
Snook; Inc. Place; BURLESON; **238** EI-8; elev. 242ft./74m.; 🅿; **z** 77878; Ⓟ 489; Ⓒ 568
Snow Hill; RMC Place; COLLIN; ***238** EC-8; mail Farmersville **z** 75442; rural
Snow Hill; RMC Place; POLK; ***238** EH-11; mail Corrigan **z** 75939; pop. incl. with Corrigan (Inc. Place)
Snow Hill; RMC Place; UPSHUR; ***238** ED-11; mail Ore City **z** 75683; rural
Snyder; Inc. Place; ⊡ SCURRY; **236** WJ-12; 🅿 🅷; **z** 79549-50; Ⓟ 12,195; Ⓒ 10,783
Socorro; Inc. Place; EL PASO; **237** WK-2; 🅿; ★ **ELP**; **z** 79927-28 & mail El Paso **z** 79929; Ⓟ 22,995; Ⓒ 27,152; ◆ 31,222
Soda; RMC Place; POLK; ***238** EI-11; mail Livingston **z** 77351; rural
Soda Springs; RMC Place; PARKER; ***238** EE-5; mail Millsap **z** 76066; rural
Sodville; RMC Place; SAN PATRICIO; ***239** EO-6; mail Sinton **z** 78387; rural
Solis; CDP-Census Area Only; CAMERON; ***239** ES-6; ★ **BRNS**; Ⓒ 545
Solms; RMC Place; COMAL; ***239** EK-5; mail New Braunfels **z** 78130
Somerset; Inc. Place; BEXAR; **239** EL-4; 🅿; ★ **SANT**; **z** 78069; Ⓟ 1,144; Ⓒ 1,550
SOMERVELL; **238** EE-5; Ⓟ 5,360; Ⓒ 6,809; ◆ 7,975
Somerville; Inc. Place; BURLESON; **238** EJ-8; elev. 249ft./76m.; 🅿; **z** 77879; Ⓟ 1,542; Ⓒ 1,704
Sonoma; RMC Place; ELLIS; ***238** EE-8; mail Ennis **z** 75119; pop. incl. with Ennis (Inc. Place)
Sonora; Inc. Place; ⊡ SUTTON; **237** WN-12; elev. 2,133ft./650m.; 🅿 🅷; **z** 76950; Ⓟ 2,751; Ⓒ 2,924
Sour Lake; Inc. Place; HARDIN; **238** EJ-12; 🅿; **z** 77659; Ⓟ 1,547; Ⓒ 1,667
South; RMC Place; DALLAS; ★ **D-FW**; mail Garland **z** 75043, **z** 75049; pop. incl. with Garland (Inc. Place)
South Alamo; CDP-Census Area Only; HIDALGO; ***239** ES-5; Ⓒ 3,101
South Amarillo; RMC Place; POTTER; ★ **AMA**; mail Amarillo **z** 79114; pop. incl. with Amarillo (Inc. Place)
South Austin; RMC Place; TRAVIS; ★ **AUS**; mail Austin **z** 78704, **z** 78764; pop. incl. with Austin (Inc. Place)
South Bend; RMC Place; YOUNG; **238** ED-4; elev. 1,038ft./316m.; 🅿; **z** 76481; ● 125
South Bosque; RMC Place; MCLENNAN; mail Mc Gregor **z** 76657; pop. incl. with Waco (Inc. Place)
South Brice; RMC Place; HALL; ***236** WE-12; elev. 2,179ft./664m.; mail Clarendon **z** 79226; rural
Southbrook; RMC Place; HARRIS; ***239** EK-10; ★ **HOU**; mail Houston **z** 77060; ● 300
Southdown Village; RMC Place; HARRIS; ***239** EK-10; ★ **HOU**; mail Houston **z** 77095; ● 1,100
Southeast; RMC Place; TRAVIS; ★ **AUS**; mail Austin **z** 78741-42, **z** 78744, **z** 78760; pop. incl. with Austin (Inc. Place)
Southeast Crossing; RMC Place; SMITH; ★ **TYL**; mail Tyler **z** 75713; pop. incl. with Tyler (Inc. Place)
South Elm; RMC Place; MILAM; ***238** EH-7; mail Buckholts **z** 76518; rural
South End; RMC Place; JEFFERSON; ★ **B-PA**; mail Beaumont **z** 77705, **z** 77720, **z** 77725; pop. incl. with Beaumont (Inc. Place)
Southern Hills; RMC Place; TAYLOR; mail Abilene **z** 79608; pop. incl. with Abilene (Inc. Place)
South Fork Estates; CDP-Census Area Only; JIM HOGG; ***239** EQ-4; Ⓒ 47
South Gale; RMC Place; GRAYSON; ***238** EB-8; ★ **SHRM-**; mail Denison **z** 75021; rural
South Haven; RMC Place; HOWARD; **237** WK-11; mail Big Spring **z** 79720; ● 100
South Houston; Inc. Place; HARRIS; **234** F-7; 🅿; ★ **HOU**; **z** 77587; Ⓟ 14,207; Ⓒ 15,833
South Jonestown Hills; RMC Place; TRAVIS; ***238** EJ-5; ★ **AUS**; mail Leander **z** 78645; ● 100
Southlake; Inc. Place; TARRANT, DENTON; **235** E-6; 🅿; ★ **D-FW**; **z** 76092; Ⓟ 7,065; Ⓒ 21,519; ◆ 30,637
Southland; RMC Place; GARZA; **236** WH-11; 🅿; **z** 79364; ● 150
Southland Hills; RMC Place; TOM GREEN; ***237** WL-13; ★ **SANG**; mail San Angelo **z** 76904; pop. incl. with San Angelo (Inc. Place)
South Laredo; RMC Place; WEBB; ★ **LAR**; pop. incl. with Laredo (Inc. Place)
South Liberty; RMC Place; LIBERTY; ***238** EJ-11; elev. 23ft./7m.; mail Liberty **z** 77575; pop. incl. with Liberty (Inc. Place)
Southmayd; Inc. Place; GRAYSON; **238** EC-7; 🅿; ★ **SHRM-**; **z** 76268; Ⓟ 643; Ⓒ 992
Southmeadow; RMC Place; FORT BEND; ***239** EK-10; ★ **HOU**; mail Stafford **z** 77477; pop. incl. with Stafford (Inc. Place)
Southmore; RMC Place; HARRIS; ***239** EK-10; ★ **HOU**; mail Houston **z** 77004, **z** 77288; pop. incl. with Houston (Inc. Place)
South Mountain; Inc. Place; CORYELL; ***238** EG-6; mail Gatesville **z** 76528; Ⓟ 301; Ⓒ 412
South Oak Cliff; RMC Place; DALLAS; ★ **D-FW**; mail Dallas **z** 75203, **z** 75216, **z** 75339; pop. incl. with Dallas (Inc. Place)
South Padre Island; Inc. Place; CAMERON; **239** ES-7; 🅿; **z** 78597; Ⓟ 1,677; Ⓒ 2,422
South Plains; RMC Place; FLOYD; **236** WF-11; 🅿; **z** 79258; ● 100
South Point; CDP-Census Area Only; CAMERON; ***239** ET-7; ★ **BRNS**; Ⓒ 1,118
South Post Oak; RMC Place; HARRIS; ★ **HOU**; mail Houston **z** 77035, **z** 77231, **z** 77235; pop. incl. with Houston (Inc. Place)
South Purmela; RMC Place; CORYELL; ***238** EG-5; elev. 1,076ft./328m.; mail Purmela **z** 76566; rural
South San Antonio; RMC Place; BEXAR; ***239** EL-4; ★ **SANT**; mail San Antonio **z** 78211, **z** 78243; pop. incl. with San Antonio (Inc. Place)
South San Gabriel Ranches; RMC Place; WILLIAMSON; ***238** EI-6; mail Leander **z** 78641; ● 150
Southside; RMC Place; NUECES; ★ **CRPX**; mail Corpus Christi **z** 78413, **z** 78427, **z** 78472; pop. incl. with Corpus Christi (Inc. Place)
Southside Estates; RMC Place; RANDALL; ★ **AMA**; mail Amarillo **z** 79110; pop. incl. with Amarillo (Inc. Place)
Southside Place; Inc. Place; HARRIS; **234** E-4; ★ **HOU**; mail Houston **z** 77005; Ⓟ 1,392; Ⓒ 1,546
South Sulphur; RMC Place; HUNT; ***238** EC-9; elev. 553ft./169m.; mail Wolfe City **z** 75496; rural
South Temple; RMC Place; BELL; ★ **KILL-**; mail Temple **z** 76501; pop. incl. with Temple (Inc. Place)
South Texarkana; RMC Place; BOWIE; ***238** EC-12; 🅿; ★ **TEXR-**; **z** 75501; pop. incl. with Texarkana (Inc. Place)
South Toledo Bend; CDP-Census Area Only; NEWTON; ***238** EH-14; Ⓒ 576
Southton; RMC Place; BEXAR; **239** ET-12; ★ **SANT**; mail San Antonio **z** 78223; ● 100
South View Estates; RMC Place; TRAVIS; ***238** EJ-5; ★ **AUS**; mail Austin **z** 78737; ● 130
Southwest; RMC Place; TOM GREEN; ★ **SANG**; mail San Angelo **z** 76906; pop. incl. with San Angelo (Inc. Place)
Sowells Bluff; RMC Place; FANNIN; ***238** EB-8; mail Ravenna **z** 75476; rural
Sowers; RMC Place; DALLAS; ***238** ED-7; elev. 527ft./161m.; ★ **D-FW**; mail Irving **z** 75061; pop. incl. with Irving (Inc. Place)
Spade; CDP; LAMB; **236** WG-10; 🅿; **z** 79369; Ⓒ 100
Spanish Camp; RMC Place; WHARTON; **239** EL-9; mail Wharton **z** 77488
Spanish Fort; RMC Place; MONTAGUE; **238** EB-6; mail Nocona **z** 76255; ● 50
Spanish Grant; RMC Place; GALVESTON; ***239** EL-11; ★ **GLV-**; mail Galveston **z** 77554; pop. incl. with Galveston (Inc. Place)
Spanish Trail; RMC Place; HOOD; ***238** EE-6; mail Granbury **z** 76048; ● 400
Sparenberg; RMC Place; DAWSON; ***236** WJ-10; elev. 2,860ft./872m.; mail Lamesa **z** 79331; rural
Sparks; RMC Place; BELL; ***238** EH-6; elev. 470ft./143m.; mail Holland **z** 76534
Sparks; CDP-Census Area Only; EL PASO; ***237** WK-2; ★ **ELP**; mail El Paso **z** 79927; Ⓟ 1,276; Ⓒ 2,974
Speaks; RMC Place; LAVACA; **239** EL-8; elev. 146ft./45m.; 🅿; **z** 77964; ● 60
Spearman; Inc. Place; ⊡ HANSFORD; **236** WB-12; elev. 3,105ft./946m.; 🅿 🅷; **z** 79081; Ⓟ 3,197; Ⓒ 3,021
Speegleville; RMC Place; MCLENNAN; ***238** EG-7; ★ **WACO**; mail Waco **z** 76710; pop. incl. with Waco (Inc. Place)
Spence; RMC Place; HARRIS; ★ **HOU**; pop. incl. with Houston (Inc. Place)
Spicewood; RMC Place; BURNET; **238** EJ-5; elev. 779ft./237m.; 🅿; **z** 78669; ● 200
Spicewood At Balcones Village; RMC Place; TRAVIS; ***238** EJ-6; ★ **AUS**; mail Austin **z** 78750; pop. incl. with Austin (Inc. Place)
Spicewood Beach; RMC Place; BURNET; ***238** EI-5; mail Spicewood **z** 78669; ● 160
Spillers Store; RMC Place; LEON; ***238** EH-9; mail Leona **z** 75850; rural
Spillview Estates; RMC Place; HENDERSON; ***238** EE-9; mail Mabank **z** 75156; ● 125
Spindletop; RMC Place; JEFFERSON; ***238** EJ-13; ★ **B-PA**
Splawn; RMC Place; MILAM; ***238** EH-7; mail Cameron **z** 76520; rural
Splendora; Inc. Place; MONTGOMERY; **238** EJ-11; 🅿; ★ **HOU**; **z** 77372; Ⓟ 745; Ⓒ 1,275
Splendora Farms; RMC Place; MONTGOMERY; ***238** EJ-11; ★ **HOU**; mail Splendora **z** 77372; ● 300
Spofford; Inc. Place; KINNEY; **237** WQ-13; elev. 1,006ft./307m.; 🅿; **z** 78877; Ⓟ 68; Ⓒ 75
Spraberry; RMC Place; MIDLAND; ***237** WK-10; elev. 2,633ft./803m.; mail Midland **z** 79702; rural
Spring; CDP; HARRIS; **238** EJ-10; 🅿; ★ **HOU**; **z** 77373, **z** 77379-83, **z** 77386-89, **z** 77391, **z** 77393; Ⓟ 33,111; Ⓒ 36,385; ◆ 43,030
Spring Branch; RMC Place; COMAL; **239** EK-4; elev. 1,106ft./337m.; 🅿; **z** 78070 & mail Bulverde **z** 78163; ● 100
Spring Creek; RMC Place; GILLESPIE; mail Fredericksburg **z** 78624; rural
Spring Creek; RMC Place; SAN SABA; ***238** EH-4; elev. 1,395ft./425m.; mail Richland Springs **z** 76871; rural
Spring Creek Estates; RMC Place; MONTGOMERY; ***238** EJ-10; ★ **HOU**; mail Magnolia **z** 77355
Springdale; RMC Place; CASS; ***238** EC-12; mail Queen City **z** 75572
Springfield; RMC Place; ANDERSON; ***238** EF-9; elev. 391ft./119m.; mail Montalba **z** 75853, Palestine **z** 75801; rural
Springfield; RMC Place; LIMESTONE; ***238** EG-8; mail Mexia **z** 76667; pop. incl. with Mexia (Inc. Place)
Spring Forest; RMC Place; MONTGOMERY; ***238** EJ-10; ★ **HOU**; mail Spring **z** 77386; ● 300
Spring Garden-Terra Verde; CDP-Census Area Only; NUECES; ***239** EP-6; Ⓒ 693
Spring Hill; RMC Place; BOWIE; **238** EB-11; elev. 377ft./115m.; mail De Kalb **z** 75559; ● 60
Spring Hill; RMC Place; CAMP; ***238** ED-11; mail Pittsburg **z** 75686; ● 50
Spring Hill; RMC Place; GREGG; ***238** EE-11; ★ **LNGV**; mail Longview **z** 75604; pop. incl. with Longview (Inc. Place)
Spring Hill; RMC Place; GUADALUPE; ***239** EL-5; mail Seguin **z** 78155; pop. incl. with Seguin (Inc. Place)
Spring Hill; RMC Place; JASPER; ***238** EH-13; mail Jasper **z** 75951; rural
Spring Hill; RMC Place; NAVARRO; ***238** EF-8; mail Dawson **z** 76639; rural
Spring Hills; RMC Place; MONTGOMERY; ***238** EJ-10; elev. 120ft./37m.; ★ **HOU**; mail Spring **z** 77386; ● 450
Springlake; Inc. Place; LAMB; **236** WF-9; elev. 3,682ft./1,122m.; 🅿; **z** 79082; Ⓟ 132; Ⓒ 135
Spring Seat; RMC Place; LEON; ***238** EH-9; mail Jewett **z** 75846; rural
Spring Shadows; RMC Place; HARRIS; ***239** EK-10; ★ **HOU**; mail Houston **z** 77043, **z** 77080; pop. incl. with Houston (Inc. Place)
Springtown; Inc. Place; PARKER; **238** ED-6; elev. 854ft./260m.; 🅿; ★ **D-FW**; **z** 76082; Ⓟ 1,740; Ⓒ 2,062
Spring Valley; RMC Place; DALLAS; ★ **D-FW**; mail Dallas **z** 75240, **z** 75380; pop. incl. with Dallas (Inc. Place)
Spring Valley; Inc. Place; HARRIS; **234** D-3; ★ **HOU**; mail Houston **z** 77024, **z** 77055; Ⓟ 3,392; Ⓒ 3,611
Spring Valley; RMC Place; MCLENNAN; ***238** EG-7; elev. 631ft./192m.; mail Lorena **z** 76655; rural
Sprinkle; RMC Place; TRAVIS; ***238** EJ-6; ★ **AUS**; mail Austin **z** 78754; pop. incl. with Austin (Inc. Place)
Spur; Inc. Place; DICKENS; **236** WH-12; elev. 2,291ft./698m.; 🅿; **z** 79370; Ⓟ 1,300; Ⓒ 1,088
Spurger; RMC Place; TYLER; **238** EI-13; elev. 165ft./50m.; 🅿; **z** 77660; ● 600
Stacy; RMC Place; MCCULLOCH; ***238** EG-2; mail Doole **z** 76836; rural
Stafford; Inc. Place; FORT BEND, HARRIS; **234** F-3; 🅿; ★ **HOU**; **z** 77477, **z** 77497; Ⓟ 8,397; Ⓒ 15,681
Stagecoach; Inc. Place; MONTGOMERY; ***238** EJ-10; 🅿; ★ **HOU**; **z** 77355; Ⓟ 340; Ⓒ 455
Stage Coach Hills; RMC Place; BEXAR; ***239** EK-4; ★ **SANT**; mail San Antonio **z** 78255; ● 400
Stairtown; RMC Place; CALDWELL; ***239** EK-6; elev. 456ft./139m.; mail Luling **z** 78648; ● 50
Staley; RMC Place; SAN JACINTO; ***238** EI-10; mail Oakhurst **z** 77359; ● 70
Stamford; Inc. Place; JONES, HASKELL; **236** WI-14; elev. 1,614ft./492m.; 🅿 🅷; **z** 79553; Ⓟ 3,817; Ⓒ 3,636
Stamps; RMC Place; UPSHUR; ***238** ED-11; elev. 407ft./124m.; mail Gilmer **z** 75644; rural
Stanfield; RMC Place; CLAY; ***238** EB-5; mail Henrietta **z** 76365; rural
Stanger Springs; RMC Place; VAN ZANDT; ***238** EE-10; mail Ben Wheeler **z** 75754; rural
Stanton; Inc. Place; ⊡ MARTIN; **237** WK-10; elev. 2,669ft./814m.; 🅿 🅷; **z** 79782; Ⓟ 2,576; Ⓒ 2,556
Staples; RMC Place; GUADALUPE; **239** EK-6; elev. 527ft./161m.; 🅿; **z** 78670; ● 250
Star; RMC Place; MILLS; **238** EG-5; 🅿; **z** 76880; ● 100
Star Harbor; Inc. Place; HENDERSON; ***238** EF-9; mail Malakoff **z** 75148; Ⓟ 368; Ⓒ 416
STARR; **239** ER-4; Ⓟ 40,518; Ⓒ 53,597; ◆ 62,916
Star Route; RMC Place; COCHRAN; ***236** WG-8; mail Morton **z** 79346; rural
Starrville; RMC Place; SMITH; ***238** EE-11; mail Winona **z** 75792; ● 75
Startzville; RMC Place; COMAL; ***239** EK-5; mail Canyon Lake **z** 78133, New Braunfels **z** 78130, **z** 78132
Steeltown; RMC Place; JEFFERSON; ★ **B-PA**; mail Groves **z** 77619; pop. incl. with Groves (Inc. Place)
Steep Hollow; RMC Place; BRAZOS; ***238** EI-8; mail Bryan **z** 77801, **z** 77808
Steeple Chase; RMC Place; HARRIS; ***239** EK-10; ★ **HOU**; mail Houston **z** 77065; ● 1,800
Stegall; RMC Place; BAILEY; ***236** WG-8; mail Sudan **z** 79371; rural
Stella; RMC Place; HARRIS; ★ **HOU**; pop. incl. with Houston (Inc. Place)
Stellar; RMC Place; FAYETTE; ***239** EK-7; mail Muldoon **z** 78949; rural
STEPHENS; **238** ED-4; Ⓟ 9,010; Ⓒ 9,674; ◆ 9,643
Stephenville; Inc. Place; ⊡ ERATH; **238** EF-5; elev. 1,277ft./389m.; 🅿 🅷 🅲 9,464; **z** 76401-02; Ⓟ 13,502; Ⓒ 14,921
Sterley; RMC Place; FLOYD; ***236** WF-11; mail Lockney **z** 79241; rural
STERLING; **237** WK-12; Ⓟ 1,438; Ⓒ 1,393; ◆ 1,290
Sterling City; Inc. Place; ⊡ STERLING; **237** WK-12; 🅿; **z** 76951; Ⓟ 1,096; Ⓒ 1,081
Sterrett; RMC Place; ELLIS; ***238** EE-7; ★ **D-FW**; mail Waxahachie **z** 75165; pop. incl. with Waxahachie (Inc. Place)
Stewards Mill; RMC Place; FREESTONE; ***238** EF-9; mail Fairfield **z** 75840, Streetman **z** 75859; rural
Stewart; COTTLE; see Hackberry (RMC Place)
Stewart; RMC Place; RUSK; ***238** EE-11; mail Henderson **z** 75652, Tatum **z** 75691; rural
Stieren; RMC Place; GONZALES; mail Gonzales **z** 78629; rural
Stinnett; Inc. Place; ⊡ HUTCHINSON; **236** WC-11; elev. 3,219ft./981m.; 🅿; **z** 79083; Ⓟ 2,166; Ⓒ 1,936
Stith; RMC Place; JONES; ***238** EE-2; mail Merkel **z** 79536; rural
Stockard; RMC Place; HENDERSON; ***238** EE-9; elev. 435ft./133m.; mail Athens **z** 75751; rural
Stockdale; Inc. Place; WILSON; **239** EL-5; elev. 440ft./134m.; 🅿; **z** 78160; Ⓟ 1,268; Ⓒ 1,398
Stockman; RMC Place; SHELBY; **238** EF-12; mail Timpson **z** 75975; rural
Stockyards; RMC Place; TARRANT; ★ **D-FW**; mail Fort Worth **z** 76106, **z** 76164; pop. incl. with Fort Worth (Inc. Place)
Stoneburg; RMC Place; MONTAGUE; **238** EC-5; mail Bowie **z** 76230; ● 40
Stoneham; RMC Place; GRIMES; ***238** EJ-9; mail Navasota **z** 77868; rural
Stonewall; CDP; GILLESPIE; **238** EJ-4; 🅿; **z** 78671; Ⓒ 469
STONEWALL; **236** WH-13; Ⓟ 2,013; Ⓒ 1,693; ◆ 1,465
Stony; RMC Place; DENTON; ***238** EC-6; mail Ponder **z** 76259; ● 50
Stout; RMC Place; WOOD; ***238** ED-10; elev. 460ft./140m.; mail Winnsboro **z** 75494; rural
Stowell; CDP; CHAMBERS; **239** EK-12; 🅿; **z** 77661; Ⓟ 1,419; Ⓒ 1,572
Strang; RMC Place; HARRIS; ★ **HOU**; pop. incl. with La Porte (Inc. Place)
Stranger; RMC Place; FALLS; ***238** EH-8; mail Kosse **z** 76653
Stratford; Inc. Place; ⊡ SHERMAN; **236** WB-10; elev. 3,693ft./1,126m.; 🅿; **z** 79084; Ⓟ 1,781; Ⓒ 1,991
Stratton; RMC Place; DEWITT; ***239** EL-7; elev. 289ft./88m.; mail Cuero **z** 77954; rural
Strawn; Inc. Place; PALO PINTO; **238** EE-4; elev. 979ft./298m.; 🅿; **z** 76475; Ⓟ 709; Ⓒ 739
Streeter; RMC Place; MASON; elev. 1,695ft./517m.; mail Mason **z** 76856
Streetman; Inc. Place; FREESTONE, NAVARRO; **238** EF-8; elev. 368ft./112m.; 🅿; **z** 75859; Ⓟ 260; Ⓒ 203
Streets Spur; RMC Place; HARRIS; ***239** EK-10; ★ **HOU**; pop. incl. with Houston (Inc. Place)
Strickland; RMC Place; SABINE; ***238** EG-13; mail Pineland **z** 75968; rural
String Prairie; RMC Place; BASTROP; ***239** EK-7; mail Rosanky **z** 78953
Structure; RMC Place; WILLIAMSON; ***238** EI-7; mail Elgin **z** 78621; rural
Stuart Place; RMC Place; CAMERON; ***239** ES-6; elev. 49ft./15m.; ★ **BRNS**; mail Harlingen **z** 78550; rural
Stubbs; RMC Place; KAUFMAN; ***238** EE-8; mail Kemp **z** 75143; rural
Study Butte; RMC Place; BREWSTER; ***237** WQ-7; mail Terlingua **z** 79852; rural
Study Butte-Terlingua; CDP-Census Area Only; BREWSTER; ***237** WQ-7; Ⓒ 267
Stumptown; RMC Place; SABINE; ***238** EH-13; elev. 205ft./62m.; mail Brookeland **z** 75931; rural
Sturdivant; RMC Place; PALO PINTO; ***238** ED-5; mail Mineral Wells **z** 76067; ● 100
Sturgeon; RMC Place; COOKE; ***238** EB-7; mail Whitesboro **z** 76273; rural
Styx; RMC Place; KAUFMAN; ***238** EE-8; mail Kemp **z** 75143; rural
Sublime; RMC Place; LAVACA; **239** EL-8; 🅿; **z** 77986; ● 125
Sudan; Inc. Place; LAMB; **236** WG-9; elev. 3,755ft./1,145m.; 🅿; **z** 79371; Ⓟ 983; Ⓒ 1,039
Suffolk; RMC Place; UPSHUR; ***238** ED-11; mail Gilmer **z** 75644; rural
Sugar Creek; RMC Place; FORT BEND; ***239** EK-10; ★ **HOU**; mail Sugar Land **z** 77478; pop. incl. with Sugar Land (Inc. Place)
Sugar Land; Inc. Place; FORT BEND; **239** EK-10; 🅿; ★ **HOU**; **z** 77478-79, **z** 77487, **z** 77496, **z** 77498; Ⓟ 24,549; Ⓒ 63,328; ◆ 78,783
Sugar Valley; RMC Place; MATAGORDA; ***239** EL-10; mail Sweeny **z** 77480; rural
Sullivan City; Inc. Place; HIDALGO; **239** ES-4; 🅿; ★ **MCAL**; **z** 78595; Ⓟ 2,371; Ⓒ 3,998
Sulphur Bluff; RMC Place; HOPKINS; **238** EC-10; 🅿; **z** 75481; ● 280
Sulphur Springs; Inc. Place; ⊡ HOPKINS; **238** EC-10; 🅿 🅷; **z** 75482-83; Ⓟ 14,062; Ⓒ 14,551
Sulphur Springs; RMC Place; RUSK; ***238** EF-11; mail Cushing **z** 75760; rural
Summerall; RMC Place; HENDERSON; ***238** EF-9; mail Mabank **z** 75156; ● 100
Summerfield; RMC Place; CASTRO; **236** WE-9; 🅿; **z** 79085; ● 70
Summerfield; RMC Place; UPSHUR; ***238** ED-11; mail Gilmer **z** 75644; rural
Summer Hill; RMC Place; HENDERSON; ***238** EE-9; mail Athens **z** 75751; rural
Summerville; RMC Place; GONZALES; mail Gonzales **z** 78629; ● 15
Summit Heights; RMC Place; EL PASO; ***237** WK-2; ★ **ELP**; mail El Paso **z** 79904, **z** 79930-31; pop. incl. with El Paso (Inc. Place)
Sumner; RMC Place; LAMAR; **238** EB-9; 🅿; **z** 75486; ● 100
Sundown; Inc. Place; HOCKLEY; **236** WH-9; 🅿; **z** 79372; Ⓟ 1,759; Ⓒ 1,505
Sundown Glen; RMC Place; HARRIS; ***239** EK-10; ★ **HOU**; mail Katy **z** 77449; ● 1,400
Sunnylane; RMC Place; BURNET; ***238** EI-5; mail Bertram **z** 78605; rural
Sunnyside; RMC Place; CASTRO; **236** WF-9; elev. 3,731ft./1,137m.; mail Dimmitt **z** 79027; ● 70
Sunnyside; RMC Place; HARRIS; ***239** EK-10; ★ **HOU**; mail Houston **z** 77051; pop. incl. with Houston (Inc. Place)
Sunny Side; RMC Place; WALLER; ***239** EK-9; mail Brookshire **z** 77423, Hempstead **z** 77445; ● 150
Sunnyvale; Inc. Place; DALLAS; **235** G-13; 🅿; ★ **D-FW**; **z** 75182; Ⓟ 2,228; Ⓒ 2,693
Sunray; Inc. Place; MOORE; **236** WB-10; 🅿; **z** 79086; Ⓟ 1,729; Ⓒ 1,950
Sunrise; RMC Place; EL PASO; ★ **ELP**; mail El Paso **z** 79904; pop. incl. with El Paso (Inc. Place)
Sunrise; RMC Place; FALLS; ***238** EH-7; mail Marlin **z** 76661; ● 300
Sunrise; RMC Place; SAN AUGUSTINE; ***238** EG-13; mail San Augustine **z** 75972; rural
Sunrise Acres; RMC Place; EL PASO; ***237** WK-2; ★ **ELP**; mail El Paso **z** 79904; pop. incl. with El Paso (Inc. Place)
Sunrise Beach; LLANO; see Sunrise Beach Village (Inc. Place)
Sunrise Beach Village (Sunrise Beach); Inc. Place; LLANO; **238** EI-4; mail Llano **z** 78643; Ⓟ 497; Ⓒ 704
Sunset; RMC Place; LUBBOCK; ★ **LUB**; mail Lubbock **z** 79416, **z** 79490; pop. incl. with Lubbock (Inc. Place)
Sunset; RMC Place; MONTAGUE; **238** EC-6; elev. 995ft./303m.; 🅿; **z** 76270; disincorporated April 19, 2007; Ⓒ 339
Sunset Ridge; RMC Place; MONTGOMERY; ***238** EJ-10; mail Conroe **z** 77303; pop. incl. with Conroe (Inc. Place)
Sunset Valley; Inc. Place; TRAVIS; **237** WT-9; 🅿; ★ **AUS**; **z** 78735, **z** 78745; Ⓟ 327; Ⓒ 365
Sunshine Hill; RMC Place; WICHITA; ***238** EB-4; mail Electra **z** 76360; rural
Sun Valley; RMC Place; EL PASO; ***237** WK-2; ★ **ELP**; mail El Paso **z** 79924; pop. incl. with El Paso (Inc. Place)
Sun Valley; Inc. Place; LAMAR; ***238** EB-10; mail Paris **z** 75462; Ⓟ 60; Ⓒ 51
Surfside Beach; Inc. Place; BRAZORIA; **239** EM-11; 🅿; ★ **L.JAC-**; **z** 77541; Ⓟ 611; Ⓒ 763
Sutherland Springs; RMC Place; WILSON; **239** EL-5; 🅿; **z** 78161; ● 400
SUTTON; **237** WN-13; Ⓟ 4,135; Ⓒ 4,077; ◆ 4,284
Swan; RMC Place; SMITH; **238** EE-10; ★ **TYL**; mail Tyler **z** 75704, **z** 75706; ● 350
Swanson Hill; RMC Place; ANDERSON; ***238** EG-10; mail Palestine **z** 75801; rural
Swansons Landing; RMC Place; HARRISON; ***238** ED-12; mail Karnack **z** 75661; rural
Sweeny; Inc. Place; BRAZORIA; **239** EM-10; 🅿 🅷; ★ **L.JAC-**; **z** 77480; Ⓟ 3,297; Ⓒ 3,624
Sweet Home; RMC Place; GUADALUPE; ***239** EL-5; ★ **SANT**; mail Seguin **z** 78155; ● 80
Sweet Home; RMC Place; LAVACA; **239** EL-7; elev. 288ft./88m.; 🅿; **z** 77987; ● 250
Sweetwater; RMC Place; COMANCHE; mail Comanche **z** 76442; rural
Sweetwater; Inc. Place; ⊡ NOLAN; **236** WJ-13; 🅿 🅷; **z** 79556; Ⓟ 11,967; Ⓒ 11,415
Swenson; RMC Place; STONEWALL; **236** WI-13; elev. 1,772ft./540m.; mail Aspermont **z** 79502; ● 50
Swift; RMC Place; NACOGDOCHES; ***238** EG-12; elev. 516ft./157m.; mail Nacogdoches **z** 75961
SWISHER; **236** WE-11; Ⓟ 8,133; Ⓒ 8,378; ◆ 7,646
Swiss Alp; RMC Place; FAYETTE; ***239** EK-7; elev. 393ft./120m.; mail Schulenburg **z** 78956; rural
Swiss Village; RMC Place; BURNET; ***238** EI-4; mail Burnet **z** 78611; ● 50
Sycamore; RMC Place; NEWTON; ***238** EH-14; mail Burkeville **z** 75932; rural
Sylvan; RMC Place; LAMAR; ***238** EB-10; mail Paris **z** 75462; rural
Sylvester; RMC Place; FISHER; **236** WJ-13; elev. 1,855ft./565m.; 🅿; **z** 79560; ● 200

T

Tabor; RMC Place; BRAZOS; ***238** EI-8; mail Bryan **z** 77801, **z** 77808; ● 35
Tadmor; RMC Place; HOUSTON; ***238** EG-11; mail Kennard **z** 75847; rural
Taft; Inc. Place; SAN PATRICIO; **239** EO-7; 🅿; **z** 78390; Ⓟ 3,222; Ⓒ 3,396
Taft Southwest; CDP-Census Area Only; SAN PATRICIO; ***239** EO-7; mail Taft **z** 78390; Ⓟ 2,012; Ⓒ 1,721
Tahoka; Inc. Place; ⊡ LYNN; **236** WI-10; elev. 3,101ft./945m.; 🅿 🅷; **z** 79373; Ⓟ 2,868; Ⓒ 2,910
Talco; Inc. Place; TITUS; **238** EC-10; elev. 367ft./112m.; 🅿; **z** 75487; Ⓟ 592; Ⓒ 570
Talpa; RMC Place; COLEMAN; **237** WL-14; elev. 1,958ft./597m.; 🅿; **z** 76882; ● 100
Talty; Inc. Place; KAUFMAN; ***238** EE-8; elev. 445ft./136m.; ★ **D-FW**; mail Terrell **z** 75160; Ⓒ 1,028
Tanglewood; RMC Place; LEE; **238** EI-7; mail Lexington **z** 78947; ● 80
Tanglewood; RMC Place; VICTORIA; ***239** EM-7; mail Victoria **z** 77901; pop. incl. with Victoria (Inc. Place)
Tanglewood Island; RMC Place; STEPHENS; ***238** ED-3; mail Breckenridge **z** 76424; ● 200
Tanglewood Manor; RMC Place; MONTGOMERY; ***238** EJ-11; ★ **HOU**; mail New Caney **z** 77357
Tankersly; RMC Place; TOM GREEN; ***237** WM-12; mail San Angelo **z** 76901; rural
Tara; RMC Place; FORT BEND; ***239** EK-10; ★ **HOU**; mail Richmond **z** 77469; ● 1,100
Tarkington Prairie; RMC Place; LIBERTY; ***238** EJ-11; mail Cleveland **z** 77327; rural
Tarpley; RMC Place; BANDERA; **239** EK-3; elev. 1,313ft./400m.; 🅿; **z** 78883; ● 40
Tarrant; RMC Place; TARRANT; ***238** ED-7; ★ **D-FW**; mail Euless **z** 76039; pop. incl. with Fort Worth (Inc. Place)
TARRANT; **238** ED-7; Ⓟ 1,170,103; Ⓒ 1,446,219; ◆ 1,804,142
Tarzan; RMC Place; MARTIN; **236** WJ-10; elev. 2,819ft./859m.; 🅿; **z** 79783; ● 250
Tate Springs; RMC Place; TARRANT; ***238** EE-7; ★ **D-FW**; mail Arlington **z** 76003, **z** 76017; pop. incl. with Arlington (Inc. Place)
Tatum; Inc. Place; RUSK, PANOLA; **238** EE-12; 🅿; **z** 75691; Ⓟ 1,289; Ⓒ 1,175
Taylor; Inc. Place; WILLIAMSON; **238** EI-6; elev. 567ft./173m.; 🅿 🅷; **z** 76574; Ⓟ 11,472; Ⓒ 13,575
TAYLOR; **238** EF-1; Ⓟ 119,655; Ⓒ 126,555; Ⓡ 126,551; ◆ 129,722
Taylor Lake Village; Inc. Place; HARRIS; **234** G-9; 🅿; ★ **HOU**; **z** 77586; Ⓟ 3,394; Ⓒ 3,694
Taylor Landing; Inc. Place; JEFFERSON; incorporated September 19, 2005; not reported in 2000 Census; ● 200
Taylorsville (Elm Grove); RMC Place; CALDWELL; ***239** EK-6; elev. 534ft./163m.; mail Red Rock **z** 78662
Taylor Town; RMC Place; LAMAR; ***238** EC-10; elev. 403ft./123m.; mail Paris **z** 75462; ● 40
Teague; Inc. Place; FREESTONE; **238** EG-8; 🅿; **z** 75860; Ⓟ 3,268; Ⓒ 4,557
Teaselville; RMC Place; SMITH; ***238** EF-10; ★ **TYL**; mail Bullard **z** 75757; rural
Tecula; RMC Place; CHEROKEE; ***238** EF-10; elev. 415ft./126m.; mail Jacksonville **z** 75766; rural
Tehuacana; Inc. Place; LIMESTONE; **238** EG-8; 🅿; **z** 76686; Ⓟ 322; Ⓒ 307
Telegraph; RMC Place; KIMBLE; ***238** EJ-2; elev. 1,859ft./567m.; 🅿; **z** 76883; ● 15
Telephone; RMC Place; FANNIN; **238** EB-9; elev. 569ft./173m.; 🅿; **z** 75488; ● 200
Telferner; RMC Place; VICTORIA; **239** EM-7; 🅿; **z** 77988; ● 700
Telico; RMC Place; ELLIS; ***238** EE-8; elev. 395ft./120m.; mail Ennis **z** 75119; ● 95
Tell; RMC Place; CHILDRESS; **236** WF-13; elev. 1,905ft./581m.; 🅿; **z** 79259; ● 75
Temple; Inc. Place; BELL; **238** EH-6; 🅿 🅷 ■; ★ **KILL-**; **z** 76501-05, **z** 76508; Ⓟ 46,109; Ⓒ 54,514; ◆ 68,316
Temple Springs; RMC Place; JASPER; ***238** EI-13; mail Jasper **z** 75951; rural
Tenaha; Inc. Place; SHELBY; **238** EF-12; elev. 358ft./109m.; 🅿; **z** 75974; Ⓟ 1,072; Ⓒ 1,046
Tennessee; RMC Place; SHELBY; ***238** EF-12; mail Timpson **z** 75975; rural
Tennessee Colony; RMC Place; ANDERSON; **238** EF-9; elev. 375ft./114m.; 🅿; **z** 75861, **z** 75880, **z** 75884, **z** 75886; ● 300
Tennyson; RMC Place; COKE; **237** WL-13; elev. 1,885ft./575m.; 🅿; **z** 76953; ● 100
Terlingua; RMC Place; BREWSTER; **237** WQ-7; elev. 2,891ft./881m.; 🅿; **z** 79852; ● 30
Terranova; RMC Place; HARRIS; ***238** EJ-10; ★ **HOU**; mail Spring **z** 77379; ● 800
Terrell; Inc. Place; KAUFMAN; **238** ED-8; 🅿 🅷; **z** 75160-61; Ⓟ 12,490; Ⓒ 13,606
TERRELL; **237** WN-9; Ⓟ 1,410; Ⓒ 1,081; ◆ 879
Terrell Hills; Inc. Place; BEXAR; **239** ER-12; 🅿; ★ **SANT**; **z** 78209; Ⓟ 4,592; Ⓒ 5,019
Terrell Station; RMC Place; TERRELL; ***237** WO-10; elev. 2,500ft./762m.; mail Sheffield **z** 79781; ● 20
Terrell Wells (San Jose); RMC Place; BEXAR; ***239** EL-4; ★ **SANT**; mail San Antonio **z** 78221; pop. incl. with San Antonio (Inc. Place)
TERRY; **236** WH-10; Ⓟ 13,218; Ⓒ 12,761; ◆ 12,028
Terry Chapel; RMC Place; FALLS; ***238** EH-7; mail Rosebud **z** 76570; rural
Terryville; RMC Place; DEWITT; ***239** EL-7; elev. 243ft./74m.; mail Yoakum **z** 77995; rural
Texarkana; Inc. Place; BOWIE; **238** EC-12; see also Texarkana, AR; 🅿 🅷 🅲 1,670 ■; ★ **TEXR-**; **z** 75501, **z** 75503-05, **z** 75507, **z** 75599; Ⓟ 31,658; Ⓒ 34,782; ◆ 35,955
Texas City; Inc. Place; GALVESTON; **234** I-9; 🅿 🅷 ■; ★ **GLV-**; **z** 77590-92; Ⓟ 40,822; Ⓒ 41,521; ◆ 42,966
Texas City Junction; RMC Place; GALVESTON; ***239** EL-11; ★ **GLV-**; pop. incl. with Texas City (Inc. Place)
Texas Lutheran; RMC Place; GUADALUPE; ***239** EK-6; mail Seguin **z** 78155
Texas Woman's University; RMC Place; DENTON; ***238** EC-7; ★ **DENT**; mail Denton **z** 76204; pop. incl. with Denton (Inc. Place)
Texhoma; Inc. Place; SHERMAN; **236** WA-10; 🅿; **z** 73949; Ⓟ 291; Ⓒ 371
Texla; RMC Place; ORANGE; ***238** EJ-13; ★ **B-PA**; mail Mauriceville **z** 77626; ● 100
Texline; Inc. Place; DALLAM; **236** WB-8; elev. 4,693ft./1,430m.; 🅿; **z** 79087; Ⓟ 425; Ⓒ 511
Texon; RMC Place; REAGAN; **237** WM-10; elev. 2,723ft./830m.; 🅿; **z** 76932; ● 25
Thalia; RMC Place; FOARD; **238** EB-2; mail Crowell **z** 79227; ● 80
The Bluffs; RMC Place; TOM GREEN; ***237** WL-13; ★ **SANG**; mail San Angelo **z** 76901; pop. incl. with San Angelo (Inc. Place)
The Colony; Inc. Place; DENTON; **238** ED-7; 🅿; ★ **D-FW**; **z** 75034, **z** 75056; Ⓟ 22,113; Ⓒ 26,531; ◆ 36,595
Thedford; RMC Place; SMITH; ***238** EE-10; ★ **TYL**; mail Lindale **z** 75771; pop. incl. with Lindale (Inc. Place)
The Glen; RMC Place; BEXAR; ★ **SANT**
The Grove; RMC Place; CORYELL; **238** EH-6; mail Gatesville **z** 76528; ● 50
The Heights; RMC Place; BRAZORIA; ***239** EL-11; ★ **HOU**; mail Alvin **z** 77511
The Hills; Inc. Place; TRAVIS; ***238** EJ-5; 🅿; ★ **AUS**; **z** 78738; Ⓒ 1,492
The Homestead; RMC Place; TRAVIS; ***238** EJ-5; ★ **AUS**; mail Austin **z** 78736; ● 150
The Knobbs; RMC Place; LEE; ***238** EJ-7; mail Mc Dade **z** 78650; rural
Thelma; RMC Place; BEXAR; ***239** EL-4; ★ **SANT**; mail San Antonio **z** 78221; rural
Thelma; RMC Place; LIMESTONE; ***238** EG-8; elev. 526ft./160m.; mail Groesbeck **z** 76642; rural
The Oaks; RMC Place; COMAL; ***239** EK-5; mail New Braunfels **z** 78130
Theon; RMC Place; WILLIAMSON; ***238** EI-6; elev. 792ft./241m.; mail Jarrell **z** 76537; ● 25
Thermo; RMC Place; HOPKINS; ***238** ED-10; mail Sulphur Springs **z** 75482; rural
The Shores; RMC Place; RANDALL; ★ **AMA**; mail Amarillo **z** 79110; pop. incl. with Amarillo (Inc. Place)
The Woodlands; CDP-Census Area Only; MONTGOMERY; **238** EJ-10; 🅿 🅷; ★ **HOU**; **z** 77354, **z** 77380-82, **z** 77384-87, **z** 77389, **z** 77393; Ⓟ 29,205; Ⓒ 55,649; ◆ 83,306
Thicket; RMC Place; HARDIN; **238** EI-12; 🅿; **z** 77374; ● 300
Thomas; RMC Place; UPSHUR; ***238** ED-11; mail Gilmer **z** 75644, Pittsburg **z** 75686
Thomas Manor; RMC Place; EL PASO; ***237** WK-2; ★ **ELP**; mail El Paso **z** 79915; pop. incl. with El Paso (Inc. Place)
Thomaston; RMC Place; DEWITT; **239** EM-7; elev. 163ft./50m.; 🅿; **z** 77989; ● 85
Thompsons; Inc. Place; FORT BEND; **239** EL-10; 🅿; **z** 77481; Ⓟ 167; Ⓒ 236
Thompsonville (Cranz); RMC Place; GONZALES; ***239** EK-6; elev. 426ft./130m.; mail Waelder **z** 78959; rural
Thornberry; RMC Place; CLAY; ***238** EB-4; elev. 1,005ft./306m.; mail Wichita Falls **z** 76306; ● 90
Thorndale; Inc. Place; MILAM, WILLIAMSON; **238** EI-7; 🅿; **z** 76577; Ⓟ 1,092; Ⓒ 1,278
Thornton; Inc. Place; LIMESTONE; **238** EG-8; elev. 489ft./149m.; 🅿; **z** 76687; Ⓟ 540; Ⓒ 525
Thorntonville; Inc. Place; WARD; ***237** WL-8; elev. 2,604ft./794m.; mail Monahans **z** 79756; Ⓟ 693; Ⓒ 442
Thorp Spring; RMC Place; HOOD; **238** EE-5; mail Granbury **z** 76048; ● 200
Thousand Oaks; RMC Place; BEXAR; ★ **SANT**; mail San Antonio **z** 78247, **z** 78270; pop. incl. with San Antonio (Inc. Place)
Thrall; Inc. Place; WILLIAMSON; **238** EI-7; elev. 560ft./171m.; 🅿; **z** 76578; Ⓟ 550; Ⓒ 710
Three Leagues; RMC Place; MARTIN; ***236** WJ-10; mail Ackerly **z** 79713
Three Points; RMC Place; TRAVIS; ***238** EJ-6; ★ **AUS**; mail Pflugerville **z** 78660; pop. incl. with Austin (Inc. Place)
Three Rivers; Inc. Place; LIVE OAK; **239** EN-5; 🅿; **z** 78071 & mail Oakville **z** 78060; Ⓟ 1,889; Ⓒ 1,878
Three Way; RMC Place; ERATH; ***238** EF-5; mail Stephenville **z** 76401; rural
Thrifty; RMC Place; BROWN; ***238** EG-3; elev. 1,436ft./438m.; mail Brownwood **z** 76801; ● 25
Throckmorton; Inc. Place; ⊡ THROCKMORTON; **238** ED-3; elev. 1,321ft./403m.; 🅿 🅷; **z** 76483; Ⓟ 1,036; Ⓒ 905
THROCKMORTON; **238** ED-3; Ⓟ 1,880; Ⓒ 1,850; ◆ 1,583
Thurber; RMC Place; ERATH; ***238** EE-4; mail Mingus **z** 76463; ● 5
Tidewater Oaks; RMC Place; MIDLAND; ***239** EM-9; mail Palacios **z** 77465; ● 100
Tidwell; RMC Place; HUNT; ***238** EC-9; mail Greenville **z** 75401; rural
Tidwell Prairie; RMC Place; ROBERTSON; ***238** EH-8; elev. 383ft./117m.; mail Bremond **z** 76629; rural
Tierra Bonita; CDP-Census Area Only; CAMERON; ***239** ES-6; ★ **BRNS**; Ⓒ 160
Tierra Grande; CDP-Census Area Only; NUECES; ***239** EP-6; Ⓒ 362
Tierra Linda Ranch; RMC Place; GILLESPIE; ***238** EJ-3; mail Kerrville **z** 78028; ● 60
Tigertown; RMC Place; LAMAR; **238** EB-9; mail Honey Grove **z** 75446, Wolfe City **z** 75496; ● 60
Tiki Island; GALVESTON; see Village of Tiki Island (Inc. Place)
Tilden; RMC Place; ⊡ MCMULLEN; **239** EN-4; elev. 255ft./78m.; 🅿; **z** 78072; ● 450
Tilmon; RMC Place; CALDWELL; ***239** EK-6; elev. 393ft./120m.; mail Dale **z** 78616; rural
Timbercreek Canyon; Inc. Place; RANDALL; ***236** WD-10; Ⓒ 406
Timberlake Estates; RMC Place; HARRIS; ***239** EK-10; ★ **HOU**; mail Cypress **z** 77429; ● 300
Timber Lakes; RMC Place; MONTGOMERY; ***238** EJ-10; ★ **HOU**; mail Spring **z** 77380; ● 600
Timberlane Acres; RMC Place; MONTGOMERY; ***238** EJ-11; ★ **HOU**; mail Porter **z** 77365
Timber Ridge; RMC Place; BEXAR; ***239** EL-4; ★ **SANT**; mail San Antonio **z** 78251; pop. incl. with San Antonio (Inc. Place)
Timber Ridge; RMC Place; MONTGOMERY; ***238** EJ-10; ★ **HOU**; mail Spring **z** 77380; ● 500
Timberwood Park; CDP-Census Area Only; BEXAR; ***239** EK-4; ★ **SANT**; mail San Antonio **z** 78258, **z** 78260; Ⓟ 2,578; Ⓒ 5,889
Timothy; RMC Place; NAVARRO; ***238** EE-8; mail Chatfield **z** 75105; rural
Timpson; Inc. Place; SHELBY; **238** EF-12; elev. 408ft./124m.; 🅿; **z** 75975; Ⓟ 1,029; Ⓒ 1,094
Tin Top; RMC Place; PARKER; ***238** EE-5; mail Weatherford **z** 76087; rural
Tioga; Inc. Place; GRAYSON; **238** EC-7; 🅿; **z** 76271; Ⓟ 625; Ⓒ 754
Tira; Inc. Place; HOPKINS; **238** EC-10; elev. 471ft./144m.; mail Sulphur Springs **z** 75482; Ⓟ 237; Ⓒ 248
TITUS; **238** EC-11; Ⓟ 24,009; Ⓒ 28,118; ◆ 30,296
Tivoli; RMC Place; REFUGIO; **239** EN-8; elev. 36ft./11m.; 🅿; **z** 77990; ● 700
Tivydale; RMC Place; GILLESPIE; ***238** EJ-3; mail Fredericksburg **z** 78624; rural
Tobe Hahn; RMC Place; JEFFERSON; ★ **B-PA**; mail Beaumont **z** 77706, **z** 77708, **z** 77713, **z** 77726; pop. incl. with Beaumont (Inc. Place)
Toco; Inc. Place; LAMAR; **238** EB-9; mail Brookston **z** 75421; Ⓟ 127; Ⓒ 89
Todd City; RMC Place; ANDERSON; ***238** EF-10; elev. 462ft./141m.; mail Palestine **z** 75801; rural
Todd Mission; Inc. Place; GRIMES; ***238** EJ-9; mail Plantersville **z** 77363; Ⓟ 54; Ⓒ 146
Togo; RMC Place; BASTROP; ***239** EK-7; mail Smithville **z** 78957; rural
Tokeen; RUNNELS; see Content (RMC Place)
Tokio; RMC Place; TERRY; **236** WH-9; 🅿; **z** 79376; pop. incl. with Brownfield (Inc. Place)
Tolar; Inc. Place; HOOD; **238** EE-5; 🅿; **z** 76476; Ⓟ 523; Ⓒ 504
Tolbert; RMC Place; WILBARGER; ***238** EA-3; mail Vernon **z** 76384; rural
Toledo; NEWTON; see Toledo Village (RMC Place)
Toledo Village (Toledo); RMC Place; NEWTON; ***238** EH-14; elev. 113ft./34m.; mail Burkeville **z** 75932; ● 700
Toledo Village; RMC Place; SABINE; ***238** EG-13; mail Hemphill **z** 75948; ● 50
Tolosa; RMC Place; KAUFMAN; ***238** EE-8; elev. 368ft./112m.; mail Kemp **z** 75143; ● 50
Tomball; Inc. Place; HARRIS; **238** EJ-10; 🅿 🅷; ★ **HOU**; **z** 77337, **z** 77375, **z** 77377; Ⓟ 6,370; Ⓒ 9,089
Tom Bean; Inc. Place; GRAYSON; **238** EC-8; elev. 802ft./244m.; 🅿; **z** 75489; Ⓟ 827; Ⓒ 941
TOM GREEN; **237** WL-13; Ⓟ 98,458; Ⓒ 104,010; ◆ 110,908
Tomlinson Hill; RMC Place; FALLS; ***238** EH-7; mail Lott **z** 76656; rural
Tonkowon Country; RMC Place; WILLIAMSON; ***238** EI-6; ★ **AUS**; mail Georgetown **z** 78628; ● 250
Tool; Inc. Place; HENDERSON; **238** EE-9; 🅿; **z** 75143; Ⓟ 1,712; Ⓒ 2,275
Topsey; RMC Place; CORYELL; **238** EH-5; elev. 1,051ft./320m.; ★ **KILL-**; mail Copperas Cove **z** 76522; ● 35
Tornillo; CDP; EL PASO; **237** WL-2; elev. 3,582ft./1,092m.; 🅿; **z** 79853; Ⓒ 1,609
Tours; RMC Place; MCLENNAN; ***238** EG-7; mail West **z** 76691; ● 70
Tow; RMC Place; LLANO; **238** EI-4; elev. 1,038ft./316m.; 🅿; **z** 78672; ● 300
Town Bluff; RMC Place; TYLER; ***238** EI-13; elev. 221ft./67m.; mail Woodville **z** 75979
Town West; RMC Place; FORT BEND; **234** F-2; elev. 90ft./27m.; ★ **HOU**; mail Sugar Land **z** 77478; Ⓟ 6,166
Toyah; Inc. Place; REEVES; **237** WL-6; elev. 2,916ft./889m.; 🅿; **z** 79785; Ⓟ 115; Ⓒ 100
Toyahvale; RMC Place; REEVES; **237** WM-6; 🅿; **z** 79786; ● 60
Tracy; RMC Place; MILAM; ***238** EI-7; elev. 47ft./14m.; mail Rockdale **z** 76567; rural
Tradewinds; RMC Place; HENDERSON; ***238** EE-9; mail Kemp **z** 75143; pop. incl. with Tool (Inc. Place)
Tradewinds; CDP-Census Area Only; SAN PATRICIO; ***239** EO-7; Ⓒ 163
Trail Lake; RMC Place; TARRANT; ★ **D-FW**; mail Fort Worth **z** 76162; pop. incl. with Fort Worth (Inc. Place)
Travis; RMC Place; FALLS; **238** EH-7; elev. 473ft./144m.; mail Lott **z** 76656; ● 50
TRAVIS; **238** EJ-5; Ⓟ 576,407; Ⓒ 812,280; ◆ 1,077,841
Travis Peak; RMC Place; TRAVIS; mail Marble Falls **z** 78654; rural
Trawick; RMC Place; NACOGDOCHES; ***238** EF-11; mail Nacogdoches **z** 75964
Trent; Inc. Place; TAYLOR; **236** WJ-13; 🅿; **z** 79561; Ⓟ 319; Ⓒ 318
Trenton; Inc. Place; FANNIN; **238** EC-8; elev. 767ft./234m.; 🅿; **z** 75490; Ⓟ 655; Ⓒ 662
Tres Palacios Oaks; RMC Place; MIDLAND; ***239** EM-9; mail Palacios **z** 77465; ● 200
Trevat; RMC Place; TRINITY; ***238** EH-11; mail Groveton **z** 75845; rural
Triangle; RMC Place; FALLS; ***238** EH-7; mail Chilton **z** 76632; rural
Tri Cities; RMC Place; HENDERSON; ***238** EF-9; mail Athens **z** 75751; rural
Trickham; RMC Place; COLEMAN; **238** EG-3; mail Santa Anna **z** 76878; ● 30
Tri-Lake Estates; RMC Place; MONTGOMERY; ***238** EJ-10; mail Montgomery **z** 77316; ● 150
Trinidad; Inc. Place; HENDERSON; **238** EF-9; elev. 303ft./92m.; 🅿; **z** 75163; Ⓟ 1,056; Ⓒ 1,091
Trinity; Inc. Place; TRINITY; **238** EH-10; 🅿 🅷; **z** 75862; Ⓟ 2,648; Ⓒ 2,721
TRINITY; **238** EH-11; Ⓟ 11,445; Ⓒ 13,779; ◆ 14,150
Trinity Mills; RMC Place; DALLAS; ***238** ED-7; ★ **D-FW**; pop. incl. with Carrollton (Inc. Place)
Trinity River; RMC Place; TARRANT; ★ **D-FW**; mail Fort Worth **z** 76109, **z** 76185; pop. incl. with Fort Worth (Inc. Place)
Trophy Club; Inc. Place; DENTON, TARRANT; **235** D-5; 🅿; ★ **D-FW**; **z** 76262; Ⓟ 3,922; Ⓒ 6,350
Troup; Inc. Place; SMITH, CHEROKEE; **238** EF-11; 🅿; **z** 75789; Ⓟ 1,659; Ⓒ 1,949
Trout Creek; RMC Place; NEWTON; ***238** EI-13; mail Call **z** 75933, Kirbyville **z** 75956
Troy; Inc. Place; BELL; **238** EH-7; elev. 666ft./203m.; 🅿; ★ **KILL-**; **z** 76579; Ⓟ 1,395; Ⓒ 1,378
Truby; RMC Place; JONES; ***238** EE-2; mail Hawley **z** 79525
Truce; RMC Place; JACK; ***238** EC-5; mail Bowie **z** 76230; rural
Trumbull; RMC Place; ELLIS; ***238** EE-8; mail Ferris **z** 75125; ● 65
Truscott; RMC Place; KNOX; **236** WG-14; 🅿; **z** 79227; ● 60
Tucker; RMC Place; ANDERSON; **238** EG-9; elev. 292ft./89m.; mail Palestine **z** 75801; ● 150
Tuleta; CDP; BEE; **239** EN-6; 🅿; **z** 78162; Ⓒ 292
Tulia; Inc. Place; ⊡ SWISHER; **236** WF-10; 🅿 🅷; **z** 79088; Ⓟ 4,699; Ⓒ 5,117
Tulip; RMC Place; FANNIN; ***238** EB-9; elev. 489ft./149m.; mail Ivanhoe **z** 75447; rural
Tulsita; CDP; BEE; **239** EN-6; mail Kenedy **z** 78119; Ⓒ 20
Tundra; RMC Place; VAN ZANDT; ***238** EE-9; elev. 561ft./171m.; mail Canton **z** 75103; rural
Tunis; RMC Place; BURLESON; **238** EI-8; mail Caldwell **z** 77836; ● 150
Tupelo; RMC Place; NAVARRO; mail Rice **z** 75155; rural
Turkey; Inc. Place; HALL; **236** WF-12; 🅿; **z** 79261; Ⓟ 507; Ⓒ 494
Turkey Creek; CASS; see Patman Switch (RMC Place)
Turkey Creek; RMC Place; CORYELL; ***238** EH-5; ★ **KILL-**; mail Copperas Cove **z** 76522; pop. incl. with Copperas Cove (Inc. Place)
Turlington; RMC Place; FREESTONE; ***238** EG-9; elev. 475ft./145m.; mail Fairfield **z** 75840; rural
Turnbaugh Corner; RMC Place; ECTOR; ***237** WK-9; mail Notrees **z** 79759; rural
Turnersville; RMC Place; CORYELL; **238** EG-6; mail Gatesville **z** 76528; ● 100
Turnertown (Selman City); RMC Place; RUSK; **238** EF-11; 🅿; **z** 75689; ● 250
Turney; RMC Place; CHEROKEE; **238** EF-10; mail Jacksonville **z** 75766
Turtle Bayou; RMC Place; CHAMBERS; ***239** EK-12; mail Anahuac **z** 77514; ● 60
Tuscola; Inc. Place; TAYLOR; **237** WK-14; 🅿; **z** 79562; Ⓟ 620; Ⓒ 714
Tuxedo; RMC Place; JONES; ***238** ED-1; mail Stamford **z** 79553
Twin Mills; RMC Place; PRESIDIO; ***237** WP-5; rural
Twin Shores; RMC Place; MONTGOMERY; ***238** EJ-10; mail Willis **z** 77378; ● 100
Twin Valley Terrace; RMC Place; BEXAR; ***239** EL-4; ★ **SANT**; mail Von Ormy **z** 78073; ● 600
Twitty; RMC Place; WHEELER; **236** WD-13; elev. 2,252ft./686m.; 🅿; **z** 79079
Tye; Inc. Place; TAYLOR; **236** WJ-14; 🅿; ★ **ABIL**; **z** 79563; Ⓟ 1,088; Ⓒ 1,158
Tyler; Inc. Place; ⊡ SMITH; **238** EE-10; 🅿 🅷 🅲 6,733 ■; ★ **TYL**; **z** 75701-13, **z** 75798-99; Ⓟ 75,450; Ⓒ 83,650; ◆ 96,120
TYLER; **238** EI-12; Ⓟ 16,646; Ⓒ 20,871; ◆ 20,665
Tynan; CDP; BEE; **239** EO-6; 🅿; **z** 78391; Ⓒ 301
Type; RMC Place; BASTROP; mail Elgin **z** 78621; rural
Type; RMC Place; WILLIAMSON; mail Elgin **z** 78621; rural

U

Uhland; Inc. Place; HAYS, CALDWELL; **239** EK-6; 🅿; **z** 78640; Ⓟ 368; Ⓒ 386
Umbarger; RMC Place; RANDALL; **236** WE-10; 🅿; **z** 79091; ● 150
Uncertain; Inc. Place; HARRISON; **238** ED-12; mail Karnack **z** 75661; Ⓟ 194; Ⓒ 150
Union; RMC Place; BRAZOS; **236** WJ-12; mail Bryan **z** 77808; rural
Union; RMC Place; FRANKLIN; ***238** EC-10; mail Saltillo **z** 75478; rural
Union; RMC Place; LUBBOCK; ***236** WH-10; elev. 3,159ft./963m.; mail Slaton **z** 79364
Union; RMC Place; SCURRY; ***236** WJ-12; elev. 2,428ft./740m.; mail Snyder **z** 79549; ● 30
Union; RMC Place; TERRY; ***236** WI-10; elev. 3,183ft./970m.; mail Brownfield **z** 79316; rural
Union; RMC Place; WILSON; ***239** EL-6; mail Nixon **z** 78140; ● 25
Union Academy; RMC Place; ANDERSON; ***238** EF-10; mail Palestine **z** 75801; rural
Union Bluff; RMC Place; HILL; ***238** EF-7; mail Hillsboro **z** 76645; rural
Union Center; RMC Place; EASTLAND; ***238** EF-3; mail Rising Star **z** 76471; rural
Union Grove; RMC Place; BELL; ***238** EH-6; mail Belton **z** 76513; rural
Union Grove; RMC Place; CHEROKEE; ***238** EF-10; elev. 570ft./174m.; mail Jacksonville **z** 75766; rural
Union Grove; Inc. Place; UPSHUR; **238** EE-11; ★ **LNGV**; mail Gladewater **z** 75647; Ⓟ 271; Ⓒ 346
Union High; RMC Place; NAVARRO; ***238** EF-8; elev. 452ft./138m.; mail Dawson **z** 76639; rural
Union Hill; RMC Place; HENDERSON; ***238** EE-10; mail Brownsboro **z** 75756; rural
Union Hill; RMC Place; UPSHUR; ***238** ED-11; mail Gilmer **z** 75644; rural
Union Valley; Inc. Place; HUNT; ***238** ED-8; mail Royse City **z** 75189; incorporated November 6, 2007; ● 200
Unity; RMC Place; LAMAR; ***238** EB-9; elev. 548ft./167m.; mail Sumner **z** 75486; rural
Universal City; Inc. Place; BEXAR; **239** EL-5; elev. 767ft./234m.; 🅿; ★ **SANT**; **z** 78148, **z** 78150; Ⓟ 13,057; Ⓒ 14,849
University of North Texas; RMC Place; DENTON; ***238** EC-7; ★ **D-FW**; mail Denton **z** 76203; pop. incl. with Denton (Inc. Place)
University of Texas at El Paso; RMC Place; EL PASO; ***237** WK-1; ★ **ELP**; mail El Paso **z** 79902; pop. incl. with El Paso (Inc. Place)
University Park; RMC Place; BEXAR; ***239** EL-4; ★ **SANT**; mail San Antonio **z** 78228; pop. incl. with San Antonio (Inc. Place)

Entries in **UPPERCASE** are counties.
Entries in **bold** have populations of 2,500 or more.
Names in parentheses are alternate names.

Inc. Place	Incorporated Place
RMC Place	Rand McNally Designated Place
CDP	Census Designated Place
MCD	Minor Civil Division

⊡	County Seat
▲	Minor Civil Division
elev.	Elevation
🅿	Post Office
🅷	Hospital
🅲	College
■	Principal Business Center
★	Ranally Metro Area (RMA) Abbreviation
z	Zip Code(s)
Ⓟ	Previous Census Population
Ⓡ	Revised Census Population
Ⓐ	Annexation Population
●	Rand McNally Population Estimate
Ⓒ	Final Census Population
Ⓢ	Special Census Population
◆	Estimated Population

For additional definitions see Glossary, Volume 1, and Introduction, Volume 2.

University Park; Inc. Place; DALLAS; **235** F-11; ★ **D-FW**; mail Dallas **z** 75205, **z** 75225; ℗ 22,259; © 23,324; ◆ 25,220
University Place; RMC Place; NACOGDOCHES; mail Nacogdoches **z** 75961; pop. incl. with Nacogdoches (Inc. Place)
Upper Meyersville; RMC Place; DEWITT; ***239** EM-7; elev. 237ft./72m.; mail Yorktown **z** 78164; rural
Upshaw; RMC Place; NACOGDOCHES; ***238** EG-11; mail Douglass **z** 75943; rural
UPSHUR; **238** ED-11; ℗ 31,370; © 35,291; ◆ 38,391
Upton; RMC Place; BASTROP; ***239** EK-7; mail Smithville **z** 78957
UPTON; **237** WL-10; ℗ 4,447; © 3,404; ◆ 2,927
Urbana; RMC Place; SAN JACINTO; ***238** EI-11; mail Shepherd **z** 77371; rural
Utility; RMC Place; BEXAR; ★ **SANT**; mail San Antonio **z** 78219; pop. incl. with San Antonio (Inc. Place)
Utley; RMC Place; BASTROP; ***238** EJ-6; mail Bastrop **z** 78602; rural
Utopia; CDP; UVALDE; **239** EK-2; elev. 1,352ft./412m.; 🅿; **z** 78884; © 241
Uvalde; Inc. Place; ⊡ UVALDE; **237** WQ-14; elev. 907ft./276m.; 🅿 🅷; **z** 78801-02; ℗ 14,729; © 14,929
UVALDE; **239** EL-2; ℗ 23,340; © 25,926; ◆ 26,309
Uvalde Estates; CDP-Census Area Only; UVALDE; ***239** EL-2; © 1,972

V

Vacarro Manor; RMC Place; FORT BEND; ***239** EK-10; ★ **HOU**; mail Stafford **z** 77477; pop. incl. with Stafford (Inc. Place)
Valdasta; RMC Place; COLLIN; ***238** EC-8; mail Blue Ridge **z** 75424; ● 75
Valentine; Inc. Place; JEFF DAVIS; **237** WN-5; elev. 4,431ft./1,351m.; 🅿; **z** 79854; ℗ 217; © 187
Valera; RMC Place; COLEMAN; **238** EG-2; 🅿; **z** 76884 & mail Voss **z** 76888; ● 75
Valleycreek; RMC Place; FANNIN; ***238** EC-8; mail Leonard **z** 75452; rural
Valley Hi; RMC Place; BEXAR; ***239** EL-4; ★ **SANT**; mail San Antonio **z** 78227; pop. incl. with San Antonio (Inc. Place)
Valley Mills; Inc. Place; BOSQUE, MCLENNAN; **238** EG-6; elev. 635ft./194m.; 🅿; **z** 76689; ℗ 1,085; © 1,123
Valley Ranch; RMC Place; DALLAS; mail Irving **z** 75063; pop. incl. with Irving (Inc. Place)
Valley Spring; RMC Place; LLANO; **238** EI-4; 🅿; **z** 76885; ● 80
Valley View; RMC Place; COMAL; ***239** EK-5; mail New Braunfels **z** 78130; rural
Valley View; Inc. Place; COOKE; **238** EC-7; elev. 713ft./217m.; 🅿; **z** 76272; ℗ 640; © 737
Valley View; RMC Place; MCLENNAN; ***238** EG-7; ★ **WACO**; mail Waco **z** 76708; pop. incl. with Waco (Inc. Place)
Valley View; RMC Place; MITCHELL; ***236** WJ-12; elev. 2,233ft./681m.; mail Colorado City **z** 79512; rural
Valley View; RMC Place; RUNNELS; ***238** EG-1; mail Ballinger **z** 76821; rural
Valley View; RMC Place; UPSHUR; ***238** ED-11; mail Gilmer **z** 75644; ● 75
Valley View; RMC Place; WICHITA; **238** EB-4; mail Iowa Park **z** 76367; ● 100
Valley Wells; RMC Place; DIMMIT; ***239** EN-2; elev. 461ft./141m.; mail Big Wells **z** 78830; rural
Val Verde; RMC Place; MILAM; ***238** EI-7; mail Buckholts **z** 76518, Holland **z** 76534; rural
VAL VERDE; **237** WO-12; ℗ 38,721; © 44,856; ◆ 48,641
Val Verde Park; CDP-Census Area Only; VAL VERDE; ***237** WQ-12; © 1,945
Val Verde Park Estates; RMC Place; VAL VERDE; ***237** WQ-12; mail Del Rio **z** 78840; ● 160
Van; Inc. Place; VAN ZANDT; **238** EE-10; elev. 515ft./157m.; 🅿; **z** 75790; ℗ 1,854; © 2,362
Van Alstyne; Inc. Place; GRAYSON; **238** EC-8; 🅿; **z** 75495; ℗ 2,090; © 2,502
Vance; RMC Place; REAL; ***239** EK-1; mail Barksdale **z** 78828; rural
Vancourt; RMC Place; TOM GREEN; **237** WM-13; elev. 1,864ft./568m.; 🅿; **z** 76955; ● 125
Vandalia; RMC Place; RED RIVER; ***238** EB-11; mail Clarksville **z** 75426; rural
Vanderbilt; CDP; JACKSON; **239** EM-8; elev. 42ft./13m.; 🅿; **z** 77991; © 411
Vanderpool; RMC Place; BANDERA; **239** EK-2; 🅿; **z** 78885; ● 20
Vandyke; RMC Place; COMANCHE; ***238** EF-4; mail Comanche **z** 76442; rural
Vanetia; RMC Place; LEON; ***238** EH-9; mail Marquez **z** 77865; rural
Van Horn; Inc. Place; ⊡ CULBERSON; **237** WM-5; elev. 4,047ft./1,234m.; 🅿 🅷; **z** 79855; ℗ 2,930; © 2,435
Van Vleck; CDP; MATAGORDA; **239** EM-9; 🅿; **z** 77482; ℗ 1,534; © 1,411
VAN ZANDT; **238** EE-9; ℗ 37,944; © 48,140; ◆ 51,582
Varisco; RMC Place; BRAZOS; ***238** EI-8; mail Bryan **z** 77807; rural
Vasco; RMC Place; DELTA; ***238** EC-10; mail Lake Creek **z** 75450; rural
Vashti; RMC Place; CLAY; **238** EC-5; mail Bellevue **z** 76228; ● 70
Vattmannville; RMC Place; KLEBERG; ***239** EP-6; mail Riviera **z** 78379; ● 100
Vaughan; RMC Place; HILL; **238** EF-7; elev. 613ft./187m.; mail Hillsboro **z** 76645; ● 20
Vealmoor; RMC Place; HOWARD; **236** WJ-11; 🅿; **z** 79720; ● 100
Veal Station; RMC Place; PARKER; ***238** ED-6; mail Springtown **z** 76082; rural
Vedas Camp; RMC Place; HASKELL; mail Haskell **z** 79521; ● 50
Vega; Inc. Place; ⊡ OLDHAM; **236** WD-9; elev. 4,025ft./1,227m.; 🅿; **z** 79092; ℗ 840; © 936
Venable Village; RMC Place; BELL; ***238** EH-6; ★ **KILL-**; mail Killeen **z** 76544
Ventura; RMC Place; MONTGOMERY; ***238** EJ-10; elev. 192ft./59m.; ★ **HOU**; mail Magnolia **z** 77354; ● 300
Venus; Inc. Place; JOHNSON, ELLIS; **238** EE-7; elev. 673ft./205m.; 🅿; ★ **D-FW**; **z** 76084; ℗ 977; © 910; ® 1,892
Vera; RMC Place; KNOX; **238** EC-2; 🅿; **z** 76380; ● 90
Verbena; RMC Place; GARZA; ***236** WH-11; mail Post **z** 79356; rural
Verdi; RMC Place; ATASCOSA; ***239** EM-5; mail Pleasanton **z** 78064; rural
Verhalen; RMC Place; REEVES; **237** WM-7; elev. 2,803ft./854m.; 🅿; **z** 79772; ● 50
Verhelle; RMC Place; DEWITT; ***239** EM-7; elev. 165ft./50m.; mail Cuero **z** 77954, Thomaston **z** 77989; rural
Veribest; RMC Place; TOM GREEN; **237** WL-13; elev. 1,818ft./554m.; 🅿; **z** 76886; ● 40
Vernon; Inc. Place; ⊡ WILBARGER; **238** EA-3; elev. 1,216ft./371m.; 🅿 🅷; **z** 76384-85; ℗ 12,001; © 11,660
Verona; RMC Place; COLLIN; ***238** EC-8; mail Blue Ridge **z** 75424; rural
Viboras; RMC Place; STARR; **239** ER-4; mail Hebbronville **z** 78361; ● 25
Vick; RMC Place; CONCHO; **237** WM-13; elev. 1,856ft./566m.; mail Eola **z** 76937, Vancourt **z** 76955; ● 40
Vickery; RMC Place; DALLAS; ★ **D-FW**; mail Dallas **z** 75231, **z** 75382; pop. incl. with Dallas (Inc. Place)
Victoria; RMC Place; LIMESTONE; ***238** EG-7; elev. 532ft./162m.; mail Mart **z** 76664; rural
Victoria; Inc. Place; ⊡ VICTORIA; **239** EM-7; 🅿 🅷 🅲 2,652 ■; ★ **VICT**; **z** 77901-05; ℗ 55,076; © 60,603; ◆ 61,797
VICTORIA; **239** EM-7; ℗ 74,361; © 84,088; ◆ 86,236
Victory; RMC Place; MARION; ***238** ED-12; mail Avinger **z** 75630; rural
Victory City; RMC Place; BOWIE; ***238** EC-12; ★ **TEXR-**; mail Hooks **z** 75561; pop. incl. with Leary (Inc. Place)
Vidauri; RMC Place; REFUGIO; ***239** EN-7; elev. 73ft./22m.; mail Refugio **z** 78377; rural
Vidor; Inc. Place; ORANGE; **238** EJ-13; 🅿; ★ **B-PA**; **z** 77662, **z** 77670; ℗ 10,935; © 11,440
Vienna; RMC Place; LAVACA; ***239** EL-8; elev. 184ft./56m.; mail Hallettsville **z** 77964; rural
View; RMC Place; TAYLOR; **236** WJ-14; elev. 1,911ft./582m.; mail Abilene **z** 79606; ● 50
Vigo Park; RMC Place; SWISHER; **236** WE-11; elev. 3,387ft./1,032m.; 🅿; **z** 79088; ● 50
Vilas; RMC Place; BELL; ***238** EI-7; mail Holland **z** 76534; rural
Villa Cavazos; RMC Place; CAMERON; ***239** ES-6; elev. 46ft./14m.; ★ **BRNS**; mail Brownsville **z** 78520; ● 100
Villa del Sol; CDP-Census Area Only; CAMERON; ***239** ES-6; ★ **BRNS**; © 132
Village Mills; RMC Place; HARDIN; **238** EI-12; elev. 104ft./32m.; 🅿; **z** 77663; ● 300
Village of Oak Lake; RMC Place; FORT BEND; ***239** EK-10; ★ **HOU**; mail Sugar Land **z** 77478; ● 1,200
Village of Tiki Island (Tiki Island); Inc. Place; GALVESTON; **234** B-8; ★ **GLV-**; mail Galveston **z** 77554, Hitchcock **z** 77563; ℗ 537; © 1,016
Village Shores; RMC Place; COMAL; ***239** EK-5; mail New Braunfels **z** 78130
Village Station; RMC Place; MIDLAND; ★ **MIDL-**; mail Midland **z** 79704; pop. incl. with Midland (Inc. Place)
Villa Nueva; RMC Place; CAMERON; ***239** ET-6; elev. 37ft./11m.; ★ **BRNS**; mail Brownsville **z** 78520; pop. incl. with Brownsville (Inc. Place)
Villa Pancho; CDP-Census Area Only; CAMERON; ***239** ET-7; ★ **BRNS**; © 386
Villareales; RMC Place; STARR; ***239** ES-4; mail Rio Grande City **z** 78582; rural
Villa Verde; CDP-Census Area Only; HIDALGO; ***239** ES-5; © 891
Vincent; RMC Place; HOWARD; **236** WJ-11; elev. 2,333ft./711m.; mail Coahoma **z** 79511; ● 100
Vineyard; RMC Place; JACK; **238** ED-5; mail Jacksboro **z** 76458
Vinson; RMC Place; TRAVIS; ***238** EJ-6; ★ **AUS**; pop. incl. with Austin (Inc. Place)
Vinton; Inc. Place; EL PASO; ***237** WK-1; elev. 3,787ft./1,154m.; 🅿; ★ **ELP**; **z** 79821; ℗ 605; © 1,892
Violet; RMC Place; NUECES; ***239** EO-6; elev. 59ft./18m.; ★ **CRPX**; mail Robstown **z** 78380; rural
Virginia Point; RMC Place; GALVESTON; ***239** EL-11; ★ **GLV-**; mail Galveston **z** 77550; pop. incl. with Texas City (Inc. Place)
Vista del Sol; RMC Place; EL PASO; ***237** WK-2; ★ **ELP**; mail El Paso **z** 79935; pop. incl. with El Paso (Inc. Place)
Vistula; RMC Place; HOUSTON; ***238** EH-10; elev. 182ft./55m.; mail Lovelady **z** 75851; rural
Voca; RMC Place; MCCULLOCH; **238** EH-3; elev. 1,555ft./474m.; 🅿; **z** 76887; ● 60
Volente; Inc. Place; TRAVIS; ***238** EJ-5; 🅿; ★ **AUS**; **z** 78641; incorporated February 18, 2003; not reported in 2000 Census; ● 800
Von Ormy; RMC Place; BEXAR; **239** EL-4; 🅿; ★ **SANT**; **z** 78073; ● 800
Voss; RMC Place; COLEMAN; **238** EG-2; 🅿; **z** 76888; ● 20
Votaw; RMC Place; HARDIN; **238** EI-12; 🅿; **z** 77376; ● 200
Voth; RMC Place; JEFFERSON; ***238** EJ-13; ★ **B-PA**; mail Beaumont **z** 77709; pop. incl. with Beaumont (Inc. Place)
Vsetin; RMC Place; LAVACA; ***239** EL-8; elev. 250ft./76m.; mail Hallettsville **z** 77964; rural

W

Waco; Inc. Place; ⊡ MCLENNAN; **238** EG-7; 🅿 🅷 🅲 14,040 ■; ★ **WACO**; **z** 76701-08, **z** 76710-12, **z** 76714-16, **z** 76795, **z** 76797-99; ℗ 103,590; © 113,726; ◆ 125,588
Wade; RMC Place; JIM WELLS; ***239** EO-6; mail Orange Grove **z** 78372; rural
Wadsworth; RMC Place; MATAGORDA; **239** EM-9; elev. 34ft./10m.; 🅿; **z** 77483; ● 300
Waelder; Inc. Place; GONZALES; **239** EK-7; 🅿; **z** 78959; ℗ 745; © 947
Wainwright; RMC Place; BEXAR; ★ **SANT**; mail San Antonio **z** 78208; pop. incl. with San Antonio (Inc. Place)
Wainwright Heights; RMC Place; BELL; ***238** EH-6; ★ **KILL-**; mail Killeen **z** 76544
Waka; RMC Place; OCHILTREE; **236** WB-12; 🅿; **z** 79093; ● 100
Wake; RMC Place; CROSBY; ***236** WG-12; elev. 3,026ft./922m.; mail Crosbyton **z** 79322, McAdoo **z** 79243; rural
Wakefield; RMC Place; POLK; ***238** EH-11; mail Corrigan **z** 75939; rural
Wake Village; Inc. Place; BOWIE; **238** EC-12; 🅿; ★ **TEXR-**; **z** 75501; ℗ 4,757; © 5,129
Walburg; RMC Place; WILLIAMSON; **238** EI-6; elev. 849ft./259m.; 🅿; **z** 78673; ● 200
Waldeck; RMC Place; FAYETTE; ***238** EJ-8; mail Ledbetter **z** 78946; ● 30
Walden; RMC Place; JEFFERSON; ***238** EJ-13; ★ **B-PA**; pop. incl. with Beaumont (Inc. Place)
Walden; RMC Place; MONTGOMERY; ***238** EJ-10; mail Montgomery **z** 77356; ● 1,500
Walden on Lake Hourton; RMC Place; HARRIS; ***239** EK-11; ★ **HOU**; mail Humble **z** 77346; pop. incl. with League City (Inc. Place)
Waldrip; RMC Place; MCCULLOCH; ***238** EG-3; elev. 1,442ft./440m.; mail Lohn **z** 76852; rural
Walhalla; RMC Place; FAYETTE; ***238** EJ-8; mail Round Top **z** 78954; rural
WALKER; **238** EH-10; ℗ 50,917; © 61,758; ◆ 64,429
Walkers Mill; RMC Place; HARRISON; ***238** EE-12; elev. 301ft./92m.; ★ **LNGV**; mail Hallsville **z** 75650; rural
Walker Village; RMC Place; BELL; ***238** EH-6; ★ **KILL-**; mail Killeen **z** 76544
Wall; RMC Place; TOM GREEN; **237** WL-13; elev. 1,866ft./569m.; 🅿; **z** 76957; ● 200
Wallace; RMC Place; VAN ZANDT; ***238** EE-9; mail Canton **z** 75103; rural
Waller; Inc. Place; WALLER, HARRIS; **238** EJ-9; elev. 249ft./76m.; 🅿; **z** 77484; ℗ 1,493; © 2,092
WALLER; **239** EK-9; ℗ 23,390; © 32,663; ◆ 37,475
Wallis; Inc. Place; AUSTIN; **239** EK-9; elev. 131ft./40m.; 🅿; **z** 77485; ℗ 1,001; © 1,172
Wallisville; RMC Place; CHAMBERS; **239** EK-12; 🅿; **z** 77597; ● 350
Walnut Bend; RMC Place; COOKE; ***238** EB-7; mail Whitesboro **z** 76273; ● 40
Walnut Bend; RMC Place; HARRIS; ***239** EK-10; ★ **HOU**; mail Houston **z** 77042; pop. incl. with Houston (Inc. Place)
Walnut Creek; RMC Place; MONTGOMERY; ***238** EJ-10; ★ **HOU**; mail Magnolia **z** 77355
Walnut Forest; RMC Place; TRAVIS; ***238** EJ-6; ★ **AUS**; mail Austin **z** 78753; pop. incl. with Austin (Inc. Place)
Walnut Grove; RMC Place; SMITH; ***238** EF-10; ★ **TYL**; mail Troup **z** 75789, Tyler **z** 75703; rural
Walnut Hills; RMC Place; MONTGOMERY; ★ **HOU**; mail Conroe **z** 77306; pop. incl. with Dayton (Inc. Place)
Walnut Springs; Inc. Place; BOSQUE; **238** EF-6; elev. 944ft./288m.; 🅿; **z** 76690; ℗ 716; © 755
Walnut Springs; RMC Place; MONTGOMERY; ***238** EJ-10; ★ **HOU**; mail Magnolia **z** 77355; ● 200
Walston Springs; RMC Place; ANDERSON; ***238** EG-10; mail Palestine **z** 75801; rural
Walton; RMC Place; CASS; ***238** ED-12; mail Bivins **z** 75555; rural
Walton; RMC Place; VAN ZANDT; **238** EE-9; mail Athens **z** 75751; ● 90
Waltonia; RMC Place; KERR; ***238** EJ-3; rural
Wamba; RMC Place; BOWIE; ***238** EC-12; mail Texarkana **z** 75503
Waneta; RMC Place; HOUSTON; ***238** EG-10; mail Grapeland **z** 75844; rural
Waples; RMC Place; HOOD; ***238** EE-6; mail Granbury **z** 76049; rural
WARD; **237** WL-7; ℗ 13,115; © 10,909; ◆ 10,117
Warda; RMC Place; FAYETTE; **238** EJ-7; elev. 375ft./114m.; 🅿; **z** 78960; ● 100
Ward Prairie; RMC Place; FREESTONE; ***238** EG-9; mail Fairfield **z** 75840; rural
Wards Creek; RMC Place; BOWIE; ***238** EC-11; mail Simms **z** 75574; rural
Waring; RMC Place; KENDALL; **239** EK-4; 🅿; **z** 78074; ● 100
Warren; RMC Place; TYLER; ***238** EI-12; elev. 169ft./52m.; 🅿; **z** 77664; ● 700
Warren City; Inc. Place; GREGG, UPSHUR; ***238** EE-11; ★ **LNGV**; mail Gladewater **z** 75647; ℗ 250; © 343
Warrenton; RMC Place; FAYETTE; **238** EJ-8; 🅿; **z** 78961; ● 30
Warsaw; RMC Place; KAUFMAN; ***238** EE-8; mail Kaufman **z** 75142; rural
Washburn; RMC Place; ARMSTRONG; **236** WD-11; mail Claude **z** 79019; ● 160
Washington; RMC Place; WASHINGTON; **238** EJ-9; 🅿; **z** 77880; ● 300
WASHINGTON; **238** EJ-8; ℗ 26,154; © 30,373; ◆ 32,215
Washington Park; RMC Place; EL PASO; mail El Paso **z** 79905; pop. incl. with El Paso (Inc. Place)
Waskom; Inc. Place; HARRISON; **238** EE-13; 🅿; ★ **SHRE**; **z** 75692; ℗ 1,812; © 2,068
Wastella; RMC Place; NOLAN; ***236** WJ-12; mail Roscoe **z** 79545; rural
Watauga; Inc. Place; TARRANT; **235** F-5; 🅿; ★ **D-FW**; **z** 76137, **z** 76148; ℗ 20,009; © 21,908; ◆ 23,582
Water Front Park; RMC Place; COMAL; ***239** EK-5; mail New Braunfels **z** 78130
Waterloo; RMC Place; WILLIAMSON; ***238** EI-6; elev. 581ft./177m.; mail Taylor **z** 76574; rural
Waterman; RMC Place; SHELBY; ***238** EG-12; mail Center **z** 75935; rural
Waters Bluff; RMC Place; SMITH; ***238** EE-11; elev. 386ft./118m.; mail Winona **z** 75792; ● 60
Water Valley; RMC Place; TOM GREEN; **237** WL-12; elev. 2,083ft./635m.; 🅿; **z** 76958; ● 200
Waterwood; RMC Place; SAN JACINTO; ***238** EI-10; mail Huntsville **z** 77340; ● 125
Waterwood; RMC Place; WALKER; mail Huntsville **z** 77320; ● 250
Watkins; RMC Place; VAN ZANDT; ***238** EE-9; elev. 490ft./149m.; mail Canton **z** 75103; rural
Watson; RMC Place; BURNET; ***238** EI-5; elev. 1,065ft./325m.; mail Lampasas **z** 76550; rural
Watson Community; RMC Place; TARRANT; ★ **D-FW**; mail Arlington **z** 76006, **z** 76011; pop. incl. with Arlington (Inc. Place)
Watt; RMC Place; LIMESTONE; ***238** EG-7; elev. 599ft./183m.; mail Mart **z** 76664
Watterson; RMC Place; BASTROP; ***239** EK-6; mail Bastrop **z** 78602; rural
Waverly; SAN JACINTO; see Old Waverly (RMC Place)
Waxahachie; Inc. Place; ⊡ ELLIS; **238** EE-7; 🅿 🅷 🅲 1,659; ★ **D-FW**; **z** 75165, **z** 75167-68; ℗ 18,168; © 21,426; ◆ 26,640
Wayside; RMC Place; ARMSTRONG; **236** WE-11; 🅿; **z** 79094; ● 30
Wealthy; RMC Place; LEON; ***238** EH-9; mail Normangee **z** 77871; rural
Weatherford; Inc. Place; ⊡ PARKER; **238** ED-5; elev. 1,053ft./321m.; 🅿 🅷; **z** 76085-88; ℗ 14,804; © 19,000; ◆ 24,194
Weaver; RMC Place; HOPKINS; **238** EC-10; mail Saltillo **z** 75478; ● 50
WEBB; **239** EP-3; ℗ 133,239; © 193,117; ◆ 235,684
Webberville; Inc. Place; TRAVIS; ***238** EJ-6; 🅿; **z** 78621, **z** 78653; incorporated February 18, 2003; not reported in 2000 Census; ● 100
Webbville; RMC Place; COLEMAN; ***238** EF-3; elev. 1,568ft./478m.; mail Burkett **z** 76828; rural
Webster; Inc. Place; HARRIS; **234** G-8; elev. 27ft./8m.; 🅿 🅷; ★ **HOU**; **z** 77598; ℗ 4,678; © 9,083
Webster; RMC Place; WOOD; ***238** ED-10; elev. 470ft./143m.; mail Winnsboro **z** 75494; rural
Weches; RMC Place; HOUSTON; **238** EG-10; mail Grapeland **z** 75844; ● 30
Wedgewood; RMC Place; TARRANT; ***238** EE-6; ★ **D-FW**; mail Fort Worth **z** 76132-33, **z** 76162-63; pop. incl. with Fort Worth (Inc. Place)
Weedhaven; RMC Place; JACKSON; ***239** EM-8; elev. 25ft./8m.; mail Port Lavaca **z** 77979; rural
Weeping Mary; RMC Place; CHEROKEE; ***238** EG-11; mail Alto **z** 75925; ● 50
Weesatche; RMC Place; GOLIAD; **239** EM-6; elev. 239ft./73m.; 🅿; **z** 77993; ● 170
Weimar; Inc. Place; COLORADO; **239** EK-8; elev. 415ft./126m.; 🅿 🅷; **z** 78962; ℗ 2,052; © 1,981
Weinert; Inc. Place; HASKELL; **236** WH-14; 🅿; **z** 76388; ℗ 235; © 177
Weir; RMC Place; HOPKINS; ***238** EC-10; mail Sulphur Springs **z** 75482; pop. incl. with Tira (Inc. Place)
Weir; Inc. Place; WILLIAMSON; **238** EI-6; 🅿; **z** 78674; ℗ 220; © 591
Welch; RMC Place; DAWSON; **236** WI-10; 🅿; **z** 79377; ● 350
Welch Store; RMC Place; SHELBY; ***238** EG-13; mail Shelbyville **z** 75973; rural
Welcome; RMC Place; AUSTIN; ***238** EJ-8; mail Industry **z** 78944; rural
Welcome Valley (Rabbit Center); RMC Place; ERATH; ***238** EF-5; mail Stephenville **z** 76401; ● 100
Weldon; RMC Place; AUSTIN; ***238** EJ-8; mail Brenham **z** 77833; rural
Weldon; RMC Place; HOUSTON; **238** EH-10; mail Lovelady **z** 75851; ● 200
Welfare; RMC Place; KENDALL; ***239** EK-4; elev. 385ft./117m.; mail Boerne **z** 78006; rural
Wellborn; RMC Place; BRAZOS; **238** EI-8; 🅿; ★ **BRY-**; **z** 77881; ● 150
Wellington; Inc. Place; ⊡ COLLINGSWORTH; **236** WE-13; elev. 2,038ft./621m.; 🅿 🅷; **z** 79095; ℗ 2,456; © 2,275
Wellman; Inc. Place; TERRY; **236** WI-9; 🅿; **z** 79378; ℗ 239; © 203
Wells; Inc. Place; CHEROKEE; **238** EG-11; elev. 323ft./98m.; 🅿; **z** 75976; ℗ 761; © 769
Wells; RMC Place; LYNN; ***236** WI-10; elev. 3,097ft./944m.; mail Odonnell **z** 79351; rural
Wells Branch; CDP-Census Area Only; TRAVIS; ***238** EJ-6; ★ **AUS**; mail Austin **z** 78728, **z** 78753; ℗ 7,094; © 11,271
Wellswood; RMC Place; SAN AUGUSTINE; ***238** EH-12; mail Broaddus **z** 75929; ● 20
Wentworth; RMC Place; VAN ZANDT; ***238** EE-9; mail Canton **z** 75103; rural
Weser; RMC Place; GOLIAD; ***239** EM-7; elev. 220ft./67m.; mail Goliad **z** 77963; rural
Weslaco; Inc. Place; HIDALGO; **239** ES-6; elev. 81ft./25m.; 🅿 🅷; ★ **MCAL**; **z** 78596, **z** 78599; ℗ 21,877; © 26,935; ◆ 31,458
Weslaco Farm Labor Center; RMC Place; HIDALGO; pop. incl. with Weslaco (Inc. Place)
Weslayan; RMC Place; HARRIS; ★ **HOU**; mail Houston **z** 77265, **z** 77277; pop. incl. with Houston (Inc. Place)
Wesley; RMC Place; WASHINGTON; **238** EJ-8; mail Brenham **z** 77833
Wesley Grove; RMC Place; WALKER; ***238** EI-9; mail Bedias **z** 77831; rural
West; Inc. Place; MCLENNAN; **238** EG-7; elev. 646ft./197m.; 🅿 🅷; **z** 76691; ℗ 2,515; © 2,692
West Austin; RMC Place; TRAVIS; ★ **AUS**; mail Austin **z** 78763; pop. incl. with Austin (Inc. Place)
West Bluff; RMC Place; ORANGE; ***238** EJ-14; ★ **B-PA**; mail Orange **z** 77632; ● 60
Westbrae; RMC Place; HARRIS; ★ **HOU**; mail Houston **z** 77071, **z** 77271; pop. incl. with Houston (Inc. Place)
Westbrook; Inc. Place; MITCHELL; **236** WJ-12; elev. 2,158ft./658m.; 🅿; **z** 79565; ℗ 237; © 203
West Camp; RMC Place; BAILEY; ***236** WF-8; elev. 4,024ft./1,227m.; mail Farwell **z** 79325; rural
Westchase; RMC Place; HARRIS; ***239** EK-10; ★ **HOU**; mail Houston **z** 77042, **z** 77215; pop. incl. with Houston (Inc. Place)
Westchester; RMC Place; DALLAS; mail Grand Prairie **z** 75054; pop. incl. with Grand Prairie (Inc. Place)
Westcliff; RMC Place; BELL; ***238** EH-6; ★ **KILL-**; mail Belton **z** 76513; ● 320
West Cliff Park; RMC Place; POTTER; ★ **AMA**; mail Amarillo **z** 79124; pop. incl. with Amarillo (Inc. Place)
West Columbia; Inc. Place; BRAZORIA; **239** EL-10; elev. 33ft./10m.; 🅿; ★ **L.JAC-**; **z** 77486; ℗ 4,372; © 4,255
Westdale; CDP-Census Area Only; JIM WELLS; ***239** EO-5; © 295
West Delta; RMC Place; DELTA; ***238** EC-9; mail Klondike **z** 75448; rural
Western Hills; RMC Place; CORYELL; ***238** EH-5; ★ **KILL-**; mail Copperas Cove **z** 76522; pop. incl. with Copperas Cove (Inc. Place)
Westfield; RMC Place; HARRIS; **234** A-5; ★ **HOU**; mail Houston **z** 77090, **z** 77290; ● 800
Westfield Estates; RMC Place; HARRIS; ***239** EK-10; ★ **HOU**; mail Houston **z** 77093; ● 2,000
Westgate; RMC Place; HARRIS; ★ **HOU**; mail Cypress **z** 77429; ● 200
Westgate; RMC Place; TOM GREEN; ***237** WL-13; ★ **SANG**; mail San Angelo **z** 76901; pop. incl. with San Angelo (Inc. Place)
Westhaven; RMC Place; COMAL; ***239** EK-5; mail New Braunfels **z** 78130
Westhill Addition; RMC Place; WHARTON; mail El Campo **z** 77437; ● 50
Westhoff; RMC Place; DEWITT; **239** EL-6; elev. 235ft./72m.; 🅿; **z** 77994; ● 300
West Junction; RMC Place; HARRIS; ★ **HOU**; pop. incl. with Houston (Inc. Place)
Westlake; Inc. Place; DENTON, TARRANT; **235** D-6; 🅿; ★ **D-FW**; **z** 76262; ℗ 185; © 207
West Lake; RMC Place; JASPER; mail Jasper **z** 75951; rural
Westlake; RMC Place; TRAVIS; ***238** EJ-6; ★ **AUS**; mail Austin **z** 78703, **z** 78716, **z** 78733, **z** 78746; pop. incl. with West Lake Hills (Inc. Place)
West Lake Hills; Inc. Place; TRAVIS; **237** WS-9; 🅿; ★ **AUS**; **z** 78746; ℗ 2,542; © 3,116
Westlakes; RMC Place; BEXAR; ★ **SANT**; mail San Antonio **z** 78245; pop. incl. with San Antonio (Inc. Place)
Westland; RMC Place; TARRANT; ***238** EE-6; ★ **D-FW**; mail Fort Worth **z** 76116; pop. incl. with Fort Worth (Inc. Place)
Westlawn; RMC Place; ORANGE; ***238** EJ-13; ★ **B-PA**; mail Orange **z** 77632; ● 300
West Livingston; CDP-Census Area Only; POLK; ***238** EI-11; © 6,612
West Mineola; RMC Place; WOOD; ***238** EE-10; mail Mineola **z** 75773
Westminster; RMC Place; COLLIN; **238** EC-8; 🅿; **z** 75485; disincorporated May 24, 2005; ℗ 388; © 390
West Mountain; RMC Place; UPSHUR; ***238** EE-11; ★ **LNGV**; mail Gladewater **z** 75647; ● 400
West Odessa; CDP-Census Area Only; ECTOR; **236** WH-1; ★ **MIDL-**; mail Odessa **z** 79764, **z** 79769; ℗ 16,568; © 17,799
Weston; Inc. Place; COLLIN; **238** EC-7; 🅿; **z** 75097; ℗ 362; © 635
West Orange; Inc. Place; ORANGE; **238** EJ-13; 🅿; ★ **B-PA**; **z** 77630; ℗ 4,187; © 4,111
Westover; RMC Place; BAYLOR; **238** EC-3; elev. 1,293ft./394m.; mail Seymour **z** 76380; ● 20
Westover Hills; Inc. Place; TARRANT; **235** H-3; ★ **D-FW**; mail Fort Worth **z** 76107; ℗ 672; © 658
West Park; RMC Place; HARRIS; ***239** EK-10; ★ **HOU**; mail Houston **z** 77042; pop. incl. with Houston (Inc. Place)
West Pearsall; CDP-Census Area Only; FRIO; ***239** EM-3; © 349
Westphalia; RMC Place; FALLS; **238** EH-7; elev. 574ft./175m.; mail Lott **z** 76656; ● 150
West Point; RMC Place; FAYETTE; **239** EK-7; elev. 332ft./101m.; 🅿; **z** 78963; ● 200
West Point; RMC Place; LYNN; ***236** WI-10; elev. 3,216ft./980m.; mail Tahoka **z** 79373
West Port Arthur; RMC Place; JEFFERSON; ***239** EK-13; ★ **B-PA**; mail Port Arthur **z** 77640
West Saint Paul; RMC Place; SAN PATRICIO; ***239** EO-6; mail Sinton **z** 78387; rural
West Sharyland; CDP-Census Area Only; HIDALGO; ***239** ES-5; ★ **MCAL**; © 2,947
West Sinton; RMC Place; SAN PATRICIO; ***239** EO-6; mail Odem **z** 78370
West Tawakoni; Inc. Place; HUNT; **238** ED-9; 🅿; **z** 75474; ℗ 932; © 1,462
West University Place; Inc. Place; HARRIS; **234** E-4; 🅿; ★ **HOU**; **z** 77005; ℗ 12,920; © 14,211
Westview; RMC Place; MCLENNAN; ★ **WACO**; mail Waco **z** 76710, **z** 76714; pop. incl. with Waco (Inc. Place)
Westville; RMC Place; TRINITY; ***238** EH-11; mail Trinity **z** 75862; rural
West Waco; RMC Place; MCLENNAN; ★ **WACO**; mail Waco **z** 76710; pop. incl. with Waco (Inc. Place)
Westway; RMC Place; DEAF SMITH; ***236** WE-9; mail Hereford **z** 79045; ● 30
Westway; CDP-Census Area Only; EL PASO; ***237** WK-1; ★ **ELP**; mail Canutillo **z** 79835; ℗ 2,381; © 3,829
Westwood; RMC Place; JASPER; ***238** EH-13; elev. 200ft./61m.; mail Jasper **z** 75951; rural
Westwood Three; RMC Place; MONTGOMERY; ***238** EJ-10; ★ **HOU**; mail Magnolia **z** 77354; ● 200
Westworth (Westworth Village); Inc. Place; TARRANT; **235** G-3; ★ **D-FW**; mail Fort Worth **z** 76114; ℗ 2,350; © 2,124
Westworth Village; TARRANT; see Westworth (Inc. Place)
Wetmore; RMC Place; BEXAR; ***239** EL-4; 🅿; ★ **SANT**; **z** 78247; pop. incl. with San Antonio (Inc. Place)
Wetsel; RMC Place; COLLIN; ***238** ED-8; elev. 666ft./203m.; ★ **D-FW**; mail Mckinney **z** 75069; pop. incl. with Allen (Inc. Place)
Whaley; RMC Place; BOWIE; **238** EB-12; mail New Boston **z** 75570
Wharton; Inc. Place; ⊡ WHARTON; **239** EL-9; 🅿 🅷; **z** 77488; ℗ 9,011; © 9,237
WHARTON; **239** EL-9; ℗ 39,955; © 41,188; ◆ 40,315
Wheatland; RMC Place; TARRANT; ***238** EE-6; ★ **D-FW**; mail Fort Worth **z** 76116; ● 200
Wheeler; Inc. Place; ⊡ WHEELER; **236** WD-13; elev. 2,527ft./770m.; 🅿 🅷; **z** 79096; ℗ 1,393; © 1,378
WHEELER; **236** WC-13; ℗ 5,879; © 5,284; ◆ 4,767
Wheeler Springs; RMC Place; HOUSTON; ***238** EG-10; mail Crockett **z** 75835; rural
Wheelock; RMC Place; ROBERTSON; **238** EI-8; 🅿; **z** 77882; ● 150
Whiskers Retreat; HUNT; see Hawk Cove (Inc. Place)
Whispering Oaks; RMC Place; BEXAR; ***239** EL-4; ★ **SANT**; mail San Antonio **z** 78230; pop. incl. with San Antonio (Inc. Place)
Whispering Pines; RMC Place; MONTGOMERY; ***238** EJ-10; ★ **HOU**; mail Conroe **z** 77302; ● 150
Whispering Pines; RMC Place; WALKER; **238** EI-10; mail New Waverly **z** 77358; ● 75
Whispering Winds; RMC Place; BEXAR; ***239** EL-4; ★ **SANT**; mail San Antonio **z** 78264; ● 200
White; RMC Place; EL PASO; ★ **ELP**; pop. incl. with El Paso (Inc. Place)
White Bluff; RMC Place; HILL; ***238** EF-6; mail Whitney **z** 76692; ● 900
White City; RMC Place; SAN AUGUSTINE; ***238** EH-12; mail Broaddus **z** 75929; rural
White City; RMC Place; WILBARGER; ***238** EA-3; elev. 1,361ft./415m.; mail Vernon **z** 76384; rural
White Deer; Inc. Place; CARSON; **236** WD-12; 🅿; **z** 79097; ℗ 1,125; © 1,060
Whiteface; Inc. Place; COCHRAN; **236** WH-9; 🅿; **z** 79379; ℗ 512; © 465
Whiteflat; RMC Place; MOTLEY; ***236** WG-12; elev. 2,412ft./735m.; mail Flomot **z** 79234
White Hall; RMC Place; BELL; ***238** EH-6; elev. 706ft./215m.; mail Moody **z** 76557
White Hall; RMC Place; CORYELL; ***238** EG-6; elev. 1,108ft./338m.; mail Gatesville **z** 76528; rural
White Hall; RMC Place; GRIMES; ***238** EJ-9; mail Moody **z** 76557, Navasota **z** 77868; rural
Whitehall; RMC Place; KAUFMAN; ***238** EE-9; mail Mabank **z** 75147; rural
Whitehouse; Inc. Place; SMITH; **238** EE-10; 🅿; ★ **TYL**; **z** 75791; ℗ 4,032; © 5,346
Whiteland; RMC Place; MCCULLOCH; ***238** EH-2; mail Melvin **z** 76858; rural
White Mound; RMC Place; GRAYSON; ***238** EC-8; mail Sherman **z** 75090; rural
White Oak; Inc. Place; GREGG; **238** EE-11; 🅿; ★ **LNGV**; **z** 75693; ℗ 5,136; © 5,624
White Oak; RMC Place; MORRIS; ***238** EC-11; mail Omaha **z** 75571; rural
White Oak; RMC Place; TITUS; ***238** EC-11; mail Mount Pleasant **z** 75455; rural
White Oak Valley Estates; RMC Place; MONTGOMERY; ***238** EJ-10; ★ **HOU**; mail Conroe **z** 77303; ● 450
White Rock; RMC Place; DALLAS; ***238** ED-8; ★ **D-FW**; mail Dallas **z** 75218; pop. incl. with Dallas (Inc. Place)
Whiterock; RMC Place; GRAYSON; ***238** EC-8; elev. 761ft./232m.; mail Whitewright **z** 75491; rural
White Rock; RMC Place; HUNT; ***238** EC-9; mail Celeste **z** 75423; ● 40
White Rock; RMC Place; RED RIVER; **238** EB-11; mail Clarksville **z** 75426; rural
White Rock; RMC Place; ROBERTSON; ***238** EH-8; mail Bremond **z** 76629; rural
White Rock; RMC Place; SAN AUGUSTINE; ***238** EG-13; mail San Augustine **z** 75972; ● 50
Whitesboro; Inc. Place; GRAYSON; **238** EC-7; 🅿; **z** 76273 & mail Gainesville **z** 76240; ℗ 3,209; © 3,760
White Settlement; Inc. Place; TARRANT; **238** ED-6; 🅿; ★ **D-FW**; **z** 76108; ℗ 15,472; © 14,831
Whitestar; RMC Place; MOTLEY; mail Flomot **z** 79234, Matador **z** 79244; rural
White Stone; RMC Place; WILLIAMSON; ***238** EI-6; ★ **AUS**; mail Leander **z** 78641; pop. incl. with Cedar Park (Inc. Place)
Whitetail; RMC Place; WILLIAMSON; ***238** EI-6; ★ **AUS**; mail Georgetown **z** 78628; ● 350
Whiteway; RMC Place; HAMILTON; ***238** EG-5; mail Jonesboro **z** 76538; rural
Whitewright; Inc. Place; GRAYSON, FANNIN; **238** EC-8; elev. 720ft./219m.; 🅿; **z** 75491; ℗ 1,713; © 1,740
Whitharral; RMC Place; HOCKLEY; **236** WG-9; 🅿; **z** 79380; ● 200
Whitman; RMC Place; WASHINGTON; ***238** EJ-9; mail Brenham **z** 77833; rural
Whitney; Inc. Place; HILL; **238** EF-6; elev. 583ft./178m.; 🅿 🅷; **z** 76692; ℗ 1,626; © 1,833
Whitsett; RMC Place; LIVE OAK; **239** EN-5; elev. 200ft./61m.; 🅿; **z** 78075; ● 150
Whitt; RMC Place; PARKER; **238** ED-5; elev. 1,131ft./345m.; 🅿; **z** 76490; ● 150
Whitton; RMC Place; VAN ZANDT; ***238** EE-9; mail Canton **z** 75103; rural
Whon; RMC Place; COLEMAN; **238** EG-3; 🅿; **z** 76878; ● 15
WICHITA; **238** EB-4; ℗ 122,378; © 131,664; ◆ 133,695
Wichita Falls; Inc. Place; ⊡ WICHITA; **238** EB-4; elev. 954ft./291m.; 🅿 🅷 🅲 6,042 ■; ★ **WIFL**; **z** 76301-02, **z** 76305-10 & mail Sheppard AFB **z** 76311; ℗ 96,259; © 104,197; ◆ 108,458
Wickett; Inc. Place; WARD; **237** WL-8; 🅿; **z** 79788; ℗ 560; © 455
Wiedeville; RMC Place; WASHINGTON; ***238** EJ-8; mail Brenham **z** 77833; rural
Wieland; RMC Place; HUNT; ***238** ED-9; mail Greenville **z** 75402; rural
Wiergate; RMC Place; NEWTON; **238** EH-13; 🅿; **z** 75977; ● 325
Wiggins; RMC Place; MCLENNAN; ***238** EG-7; elev. 578ft./176m.; mail Bivins **z** 75555, West **z** 76691; rural
Wigginsville; RMC Place; MONTGOMERY; ***238** EJ-10; elev. 160ft./49m.; ★ **HOU**; mail Conroe **z** 77302; rural
WILBARGER; **238** EB-3; ℗ 15,121; © 14,676; ◆ 13,649
Wilcox; RMC Place; BURLESON; ***238** EI-8; mail Somerville **z** 77879; rural
Wildcat; RMC Place; COLLIN; ***238** ED-7; ★ **D-FW**; mail Plano **z** 75023, **z** 75086; pop. incl. with Plano (Inc. Place)
Wilderville; RMC Place; FALLS; ***238** EH-7; elev. 412ft./126m.; mail Rosebud **z** 76570; rural
Wild Horse; RMC Place; CULBERSON; ***237** WM-5; mail Van Horn **z** 79855; rural
Wild Hurst; RMC Place; CHEROKEE; ***238** EG-11; mail Alto **z** 75925; rural
Wildorado; RMC Place; OLDHAM; **236** WD-10; 🅿; **z** 79098; ● 200
Wild Peach Village; CDP-Census Area Only; BRAZORIA; ***239** EL-10; ★ **L.JAC-**; mail Brazoria **z** 77422; ℗ 2,440; © 2,498
Wildwood (Wildwood Resort City); RMC Place; HARDIN, TYLER; **238** EI-12; mail Village Mills **z** 77663; ● 1,000
Wildwood Resort City; HARDIN, TYLER; see Wildwood (RMC Place)
Wilkins; RMC Place; UPSHUR; ***238** EE-11; ● 70
Wilkinson; RMC Place; TITUS; ***238** EC-11; elev. 323ft./98m.; mail Mount Pleasant **z** 75455
WILLACY; **239** ER-6; ℗ 17,705; © 20,082; ◆ 20,442
Willacy County Housing Authority; RMC Place; WILLACY; ***239** ER-6; mail Raymondville **z** 78580; ● 300
Willamar; CDP; WILLACY; ***239** ES-6; mail Raymondville **z** 78580; © 15
Willchester; RMC Place; HARRIS; ***239** EK-10; ★ **HOU**; pop. incl. with Houston (Inc. Place)
William Penn; RMC Place; WASHINGTON; ***238** EJ-9; mail Brenham **z** 77833; rural
Williams; RMC Place; BROWN; ***238** EF-3; elev. 1,558ft./475m.; mail Rising Star **z** 76471; rural
Williamsburg; RMC Place; LAVACA; ***239** EL-7; mail Hallettsville **z** 77964; rural
Williamsburg Colony; RMC Place; HARRIS; ***239** EK-10; ★ **HOU**; mail Katy **z** 77449; ● 1,200
WILLIAMSON; **238** EI-6; ℗ 139,551; © 249,967; ◆ 411,010
William Spear Addition; RMC Place; SMITH; ★ **TYL**; mail Tyler **z** 75704; ● 700
Willis; Inc. Place; MONTGOMERY; **238** EI-10; elev. 380ft./116m.; 🅿; **z** 77318, **z** 77378; ℗ 2,764; © 3,985
Willow Bend; RMC Place; HARRIS; ***239** EK-10; ★ **HOU**; mail Houston **z** 77035; pop. incl. with Houston (Inc. Place)
Willow City; RMC Place; GILLESPIE; **238** EJ-4; elev. 1,711ft./522m.; 🅿; **z** 78675; ● 75
Willow Grove; RMC Place; MCLENNAN; ***238** EG-7; ★ **WACO**; mail Moody **z** 76557, Woodway **z** 76712; ● 100
Willow Grove; RMC Place; SHELBY; ***238** EF-12; mail Joaquin **z** 75954; rural
Willow Park; Inc. Place; PARKER; ***238** ED-6; 🅿; ★ **D-FW**; **z** 76008, **z** 76087; ℗ 2,328; © 2,849
Willow Place; RMC Place; HARRIS; ***238** EJ-10; ★ **HOU**; mail Houston **z** 77070, **z** 77269; pop. incl. with Houston (Inc. Place)
Willow Point; RMC Place; WISE; ***238** ED-5; mail Bridgeport **z** 76426; rural
Willow Springs; RMC Place; BELL; ***238** EH-6; ★ **KILL-**; mail Killeen **z** 76549; pop. incl. with Killeen (Inc. Place)
Willow Springs; RMC Place; FAYETTE; ***239** EK-8; mail Fayetteville **z** 78940; ● 15
Willow Springs; RMC Place; RAINS; ***238** ED-9; mail Emory **z** 75440; rural
Willow Springs; RMC Place; SAN JACINTO; ***238** EI-11; mail Coldspring **z** 77331; rural
Willowview; RMC Place; HARDEMAN; ***238** EA-2; mail Quanah **z** 79252; rural
Wills Point; Inc. Place; VAN ZANDT; **238** EE-9; 🅿; **z** 75169; ℗ 2,986; © 3,496
Wilmer; Inc. Place; DALLAS; **235** J-12; 🅿; ★ **D-FW**; **z** 75172; ℗ 2,479; © 3,393
Wilmeth; RMC Place; RUNNELS; ***238** EF-1; elev. 1,975ft./602m.; mail Winters **z** 79567; rural
Wilson; RMC Place; FALLS; ***238** EH-7; mail Burlington **z** 76519, Rosebud **z** 76570; rural
Wilson; Inc. Place; LYNN; **236** WH-10; elev. 3,117ft./950m.; 🅿; **z** 79381; ℗ 568; © 532
WILSON; **239** EL-5; ℗ 22,650; © 32,408; ◆ 41,473
Wilson Lake; RMC Place; POLK; ***238** EI-11; mail Livingston **z** 77351; ● 200
Wimberley; Inc. Place; HAYS; **239** EK-5; incorporated May 9, 2000; not reported in 2000 Census; ● 2,600
Wimberley; CDP-Census Area Only; HAYS; **239** EK-5; 🅿; **z** 78676; ℗ 2,403; © 3,797
Wimbledon Estates; RMC Place; HARRIS; ***238** EJ-10; ★ **HOU**; mail Spring **z** 77379
Winchell; RMC Place; BROWN; **238** EG-3; elev. 1,354ft./413m.; mail Brookesmith **z** 76827; ● 40
Winchester; RMC Place; FAYETTE; **239** EK-7; 🅿; **z** 78945; ● 70
Winchester Country; RMC Place; HARRIS; ***239** EK-10; ★ **HOU**; mail Houston **z** 77064; ● 2,000
Windcrest; Inc. Place; BEXAR; **239** ER-13; 🅿; ★ **SANT**; **z** 78239; ℗ 5,331; © 5,105
Windemere; RMC Place; BURNET; ***238** EJ-5; mail Spicewood **z** 78669; ● 100
Windemere; CDP-Census Area Only; TRAVIS; ***238** EJ-6; ★ **AUS**; mail Pflugerville **z** 78660; ℗ 3,207; © 6,868
Windmill; RMC Place; HARRIS; ***239** EK-11; ★ **HOU**; mail Houston **z** 77075, **z** 77275; pop. incl. with Houston (Inc. Place)
Windom; Inc. Place; FANNIN; **238** EC-9; elev. 692ft./211m.; 🅿; **z** 75492; ℗ 269; © 245
Windsong; RMC Place; HARRIS; ***239** EK-10; ★ **HOU**; mail Reserve **z** 70084; ● 900
Windsor Village; RMC Place; HARRIS; ***239** EK-10; ★ **HOU**; mail Houston **z** 77085; pop. incl. with Houston (Inc. Place)
Windthorst; Inc. Place; ARCHER, CLAY; **238** EC-4; elev. 1,079ft./329m.; 🅿; **z** 76389; ℗ 367; © 440
Winedale; RMC Place; FAYETTE; ***238** EJ-8; mail Warrenton **z** 78961
Winfield; Inc. Place; TITUS; **238** EC-10; elev. 460ft./140m.; 🅿; **z** 75493; ℗ 345; © 499
Winfree; RMC Place; CHAMBERS; ***239** EK-11; ★ **HOU**; mail Dayton **z** 77535; pop. incl. with Old River-Winfree (Inc. Place)
Winfree; RMC Place; ORANGE; ***238** EJ-13; ★ **B-PA**; mail Orange **z** 77630; rural
Wingate; RMC Place; RUNNELS; **237** WK-13; elev. 2,000ft./610m.; 🅿; **z** 79566; ● 150
Wink; Inc. Place; WINKLER; **237** WK-8; elev. 2,801ft./854m.; 🅿; **z** 79789; ℗ 1,189; © 919
Winkler; RMC Place; FREESTONE, NAVARRO; ***238** EF-9; elev. 387ft./118m.; mail Streetman **z** 75859; rural
WINKLER; **237** WK-8; ℗ 8,626; © 7,173; ◆ 6,645
Winnie; CDP; CHAMBERS; **239** EK-12; 🅿 🅷; **z** 77665; ℗ 2,238; © 2,914
Winnsboro; Inc. Place; WOOD, FRANKLIN; **238** ED-10; 🅿 🅷; **z** 75494; ℗ 2,904; © 3,584
Winona; Inc. Place; SMITH; **238** EE-10; elev. 354ft./108m.; 🅿; **z** 75792; ℗ 457; © 582
Winter Haven; RMC Place; DIMMIT; **237** WS-14; elev. 591ft./180m.; mail Crystal City **z** 78839; ● 25
Winter Hill; RMC Place; NACOGDOCHES; mail Douglass **z** 75943; rural
Winters; Inc. Place; RUNNELS; **237** WK-14; elev. 1,836ft./560m.; 🅿 🅷; **z** 79567; ℗ 2,905; © 2,880
WISE; **238** EC-6; ℗ 34,679; © 48,793; ◆ 58,857
Witting; RMC Place; LAVACA; ***239** EL-7; mail Moulton **z** 77975; rural
Wixon Valley; Inc. Place; BRAZOS; **238** EI-8; mail Bryan **z** 77808; ℗ 186; © 235
Wizard Wells; RMC Place; JACK; ***238** ED-5; mail Jacksboro **z** 76458; ● 50
Woden; RMC Place; NACOGDOCHES; **238** EG-12; 🅿; **z** 75978; ● 250
Wolf Creek; RMC Place; SAN JACINTO; ***238** EI-11; mail Coldspring **z** 77331; rural
Wolfe City; Inc. Place; HUNT; **238** EC-9; elev. 678ft./207m.; 🅿; **z** 75496; ℗ 1,505; © 1,566
Wolfforth; Inc. Place; LUBBOCK; **236** WH-10; 🅿; ★ **LUB**; **z** 79382; ℗ 1,941; © 2,554
Wolters Village; RMC Place; PALO PINTO; ***238** ED-5; mail Mineral Wells **z** 76067; pop. incl. with Mineral Wells (Inc. Place)
Womack; RMC Place; BOSQUE; ***238** EF-6; mail Clifton **z** 76634; rural
WOOD; **238** ED-10; ℗ 29,380; © 36,752; ◆ 42,433
Woodbine; RMC Place; COOKE; ***238** EC-7; elev. 766ft./233m.; mail Gainesville **z** 76240; ● 150
Woodbranch (Woodbranch Village); Inc. Place; MONTGOMERY; ***238** EJ-11; ★ **HOU**; mail New Caney **z** 77357; ℗ 1,312; © 1,305
Woodbranch Village; MONTGOMERY; see Woodbranch (Inc. Place)
Woodbury; RMC Place; HILL; **238** EF-7; elev. 644ft./196m.; mail Hillsboro **z** 76645; ● 40
Wood-Canyon Waters; RMC Place; HENDERSON; ***238** EE-9; mail Mabank **z** 75156; ● 125
Woodcreek; Inc. Place; HAYS; ***239** EK-5; 🅿; **z** 78676; ℗ 894; © 1,274
Woodcreek North; RMC Place; HAYS; ***239** EK-5; mail Wimberley **z** 78676; ● 150
Woodcrest Acres; RMC Place; HARDIN; ***238** EJ-13; ★ **B-PA**; mail Lumberton **z** 77657
Woodhaven; RMC Place; MONTGOMERY; ***238** EJ-10; mail Conroe **z** 77304; ● 150
Wood Hollow; RMC Place; MONTGOMERY; ***238** EJ-11; ★ **HOU**; mail Porter **z** 77365; ● 100
Woodlake; RMC Place; BEXAR; ***239** EL-5; ★ **SANT**; mail San Antonio **z** 78244; ● 800
Woodlake; RMC Place; TRINITY; **238** EH-11; 🅿; **z** 75865; ● 120
Woodlake Park; RMC Place; GRAYSON; ***238** EB-8; ★ **SHRM-**; mail Denison **z** 75021; rural
Woodland; RMC Place; BELL; ***238** EH-6; ★ **KILL-**; mail Belton **z** 76513; ● 300
Woodland; RMC Place; RED RIVER; **238** EB-10; elev. 525ft./160m.; mail Detroit **z** 75436; ● 60
Woodland Estates; RMC Place; SABINE; ***238** EG-13; mail Hemphill **z** 75948; ● 100
Woodland Hills; RMC Place; HENDERSON; ***238** EE-9; mail Kemp **z** 75143; ● 100
Woodland Hills; RMC Place; HILL; ***238** EF-6; mail Whitney **z** 76692; ● 800
Woodland Lakes; RMC Place; MONTGOMERY; ***238** EJ-10; ★ **HOU**; mail Magnolia **z** 77355; ● 300
Woodland Shores; RMC Place; MARION; ***238** ED-11; mail Avinger **z** 75630; ● 200
Woodlawn; RMC Place; ANGELINA; ***238** EG-11; ★ **LUFK**; mail Lufkin **z** 75904; rural
Woodlawn; RMC Place; HARRISON; **238** ED-12; 🅿; **z** 75694; ● 250
Woodley; RMC Place; HARRISON; mail Marshall **z** 75672; rural
Woodloch; Inc. Place; MONTGOMERY; ***238** EJ-10; ★ **HOU**; mail Conroe **z** 77302; ℗ 291; © 247
Woodridge Park; RMC Place; BEXAR; ***239** EL-4; ★ **SANT**; mail San Antonio **z** 78264; ● 120
Woodrow; RMC Place; LUBBOCK; **236** WH-10; elev. 3,181ft./970m.; mail Lubbock **z** 79401; ● 120
Woods; RMC Place; PANOLA; **238** EF-12; mail Tenaha **z** 75974; ● 100
Woodsboro; Inc. Place; REFUGIO; **239** EN-7; elev. 41ft./12m.; 🅿; **z** 78393; ℗ 1,731; © 1,685
Woods of Shavano; RMC Place; BEXAR; ***239** EL-4; ★ **SANT**; mail San Antonio **z** 78249; pop. incl. with San Antonio (Inc. Place)
Woodson; Inc. Place; THROCKMORTON; **238** ED-3; 🅿; **z** 76491; ℗ 262; © 296
Wood Springs; RMC Place; SMITH; ***238** EE-10; elev. 468ft./143m.; ★ **TYL**; mail Lindale **z** 75771, Tyler **z** 75706; rural
Woodville; Inc. Place; ⊡ TYLER; **238** EI-12; elev. 281ft./86m.; 🅿 🅷; **z** 75979, **z** 75990; ℗ 2,636; © 2,415
Woodway; Inc. Place; MCLENNAN; **238** EG-7; 🅿; ★ **WACO**; **z** 76712; ℗ 8,695; © 8,733
Woodway; RMC Place; VICTORIA; ***239** EM-7; ★ **VICT**; mail Victoria **z** 77904; pop. incl. with Victoria (Inc. Place)
Woody Acres; RMC Place; MONTGOMERY; ***238** EJ-11; ★ **HOU**; mail Porter **z** 77365
Woosley; RMC Place; RAINS; ***238** ED-9; mail Point **z** 75472; rural
Wooster; RMC Place; HARRIS; ***239** EK-11; ★ **HOU**; mail Baytown **z** 77520; pop. incl. with Baytown (Inc. Place)
Wortham; Inc. Place; FREESTONE; **238** EG-8; 🅿; **z** 76693; ℗ 1,020; © 1,082
Worthing; RMC Place; LAVACA; ***239** EL-7; mail Hallettsville **z** 77964
Wright City; RMC Place; RUSK, RUSK; ***238** EF-11; mail Overton **z** 75684; ● 100
Wrightsboro; RMC Place; GONZALES; **239** EL-6; elev. 302ft./92m.; 🅿; **z** 78677; ● 50
Wyldwood; CDP-Census Area Only; BASTROP; ***238** EJ-6; ★ **AUS**; mail Cedar Creek **z** 78612; ℗ 1,764; © 2,310
Wylie; Inc. Place; COLLIN, DALLAS, ROCKWALL; **238** ED-8; elev. 549ft./167m.; 🅿; ★ **D-FW**; **z** 75098; ℗ 8,716; © 15,132; ◆ 30,315
Wylie; RMC Place; TAYLOR; ***238** EE-2; elev. 1,824ft./556m.; ★ **ABIL**; mail Abilene **z** 79606; pop. incl. with Abilene (Inc. Place)
Wynnrock Estates; RMC Place; TRAVIS; ***238** EJ-5; ★ **AUS**; mail Austin **z** 78737; ● 120

Y

Yancey; RMC Place; MEDINA; **239** EM-3; 🅿; **z** 78886; ● 200
Yantis; Inc. Place; WOOD; ***238** ED-10; 🅿; **z** 75497; ℗ 210; © 321
Yarboro; RMC Place; GRIMES; ***238** EJ-9; mail Navasota **z** 77868; rural
Yard; RMC Place; ANDERSON; ***238** EF-9; mail Tennessee Colony **z** 75861; rural
Yarrelton; RMC Place; MILAM; **238** EH-7; elev. 431ft./131m.; mail Buckholts **z** 76518; ● 30
Yates; RMC Place; KIMBLE; ***238** EI-2; mail London **z** 76854; rural
Yaupon Cove; RMC Place; POLK; mail Livingston **z** 77351; ● 200
Yellowpine; RMC Place; SABINE; **238** EG-13; mail Hemphill **z** 75948; ● 60
Yescas; CAMERON; see Las Yescas (RMC Place)
Yoakum; Inc. Place; DEWITT, LAVACA; **239** EL-7; 🅿 🅷; **z** 77995; ℗ 5,611; © 5,731
YOAKUM; **236** WH-9; ℗ 8,786; © 7,322; ◆ 7,706
Yorkshire; RMC Place; HARRIS; ***239** EK-10; ★ **HOU**; mail Houston **z** 77079; pop. incl. with Houston (Inc. Place)
Yorktown; Inc. Place; DEWITT; **239** EM-6; elev. 273ft./83m.; 🅿; **z** 78164; ℗ 2,207; © 2,271
Young; RMC Place; FREESTONE; ***238** EF-9; mail Fairfield **z** 75840; rural
YOUNG; **238** ED-4; ℗ 18,126; © 17,943; ◆ 17,318
Youngsport; RMC Place; BELL; **238** EH-6; mail Killeen **z** 76542; ● 90
Yowell; RMC Place; DELTA, HUNT; ***238** EC-9; mail Commerce **z** 75428; rural
Ysleta; RMC Place; EL PASO; ***237** WK-2; ★ **ELP**; mail El Paso **z** 79907, **z** 79917; pop. incl. with El Paso (Inc. Place)
Ysleta Del Sur Pueblo; Indian Reservation; EL PASO; © 421
Yznaga; CDP-Census Area Only; CAMERON; ***239** ES-6; © 103

Z

Zabcikville (Marekville); RMC Place; BELL; ***238** EH-7; mail Temple **z** 76501; ● 35
Zacha Junction; RMC Place; DALLAS; ***238** ED-8; ★ **D-FW**; pop. incl. with Dallas (Inc. Place)
Zapata; CDP; ⊡ ZAPATA; **239** EQ-3; elev. 404ft./123m.; 🅿; **z** 78076; ℗ 7,119; © 4,856
ZAPATA; **239** EQ-3; ℗ 9,279; © 12,182; ◆ 14,182
Zapata Ranch; CDP-Census Area Only; WILLACY; ***239** ES-6; © 88
ZAVALA; **239** EM-2; ℗ 12,162; © 11,600; ◆ 11,646
Zavalla; Inc. Place; ANGELINA; **238** EH-12; elev. 222ft./68m.; 🅿; **z** 75980; ℗ 701; © 647
Zephyr; RMC Place; BROWN; **238** EG-4; 🅿; **z** 76890; ● 300
Zionsville; RMC Place; WASHINGTON; ***238** EJ-8; mail Brenham **z** 77833; rural
Zipperlandville; RMC Place; FALLS; ***238** EH-7; mail Rosebud **z** 76570; rural
Zippville; RMC Place; GUADALUPE; ***239** EL-5; mail Seguin **z** 78155; ● 150
Zorn; RMC Place; GUADALUPE; ***239** EK-5; elev. 535ft./163m.; mail San Marcos **z** 78666; rural
Zuehl; CDP; GUADALUPE; ***239** EL-5; mail Marion **z** 78124; © 346
Zummo; RMC Place; JEFFERSON; ***238** EJ-13; ★ **B-PA**; pop. incl. with Beaumont (Inc. Place)
Zunkerville; RMC Place; KARNES; ***239** EM-5; elev. 417ft./127m.; mail Kenedy **z** 78119; rural
Zybach; RMC Place; HEMPHILL, WHEELER; mail Briscoe **z** 79011; rural

Entries in **UPPERCASE** are counties.
Entries in **bold** have populations of 2,500 or more.
Names in parentheses are alternate names.
Inc. Place — Incorporated Place
RMC Place — Rand McNally Designated Place
CDP — Census Designated Place
MCD — Minor Civil Division

⊡ County Seat
▲ Minor Civil Division
elev. Elevation
🅿 Post Office

🅷 Hospital
🅲 College
■ Principal Business Center
★ Ranally Metro Area (RMA) Abbreviation
z Zip Code(s)

℗ Previous Census Population
® Revised Census Population
Ⓐ Annexation Population
● Rand McNally Population Estimate
© Final Census Population
Ⓢ Special Census Population
◆ Estimated Population

For additional definitions see Glossary, Volume 1, and Introduction, Volume 2.

UTAH

ID
WY
NV
Salt Lake City
CO
CA
AZ
NM

Statistics

Total area (2000) — 84,899 square miles
Land area (2000) — 82,144 square miles
Water area (2000) — 2,755 square miles
Capital — Salt Lake City
Admitted as state — January, 1896

Maps

State maps can be found on pages 142-254 in Vol. 1

Ranally Metro Areas (RMAs) and Abbreviations

Logan, UT — LOGN
Ogden, UT — OGD
Provo-Orem, UT — PRVO-
Salt Lake City, UT — S.L.C.

Principal Places

Place Name	Place Type	County	Population
Salt Lake City	Inc. Place	SALT LAKE	◆ 195,661
Provo	Inc. Place	UTAH	◆ 134,072
West Valley City	Inc. Place	SALT LAKE	◆ 130,870
Orem	Inc. Place	UTAH	◆ 108,097
West Jordan	Inc. Place	SALT LAKE	◆ 105,427
Sandy City	Inc. Place	SALT LAKE	◆ 96,568
Ogden	Inc. Place	WEBER	◆ 92,782
Saint George	Inc. Place	WASHINGTON	◆ 74,834
Layton	Inc. Place	DAVIS	◆ 74,452
Logan	Inc. Place	CACHE	◆ 64,415
Taylorsville	Inc. Place	SALT LAKE	◆ 60,095
Murray	Inc. Place	SALT LAKE	◆ 47,921
Bountiful	Inc. Place	DAVIS	◆ 45,365
Roy	Inc. Place	WEBER	◆ 42,230
South Jordan	Inc. Place	SALT LAKE	◆ 40,851
Kearns	CDP	SALT LAKE	◆ 40,022
Millcreek	CDP-Census Area Only	SALT LAKE	◆ 36,118
Lehi	Inc. Place	UTAH	◆ 35,653
Riverton	Inc. Place	SALT LAKE	◆ 35,602
Draper	Inc. Place	SALT LAKE	◆ 35,332
Tooele	Inc. Place	TOOELE	◆ 34,662
Pleasant Grove	Inc. Place	UTAH	◆ 33,576
Clearfield	Inc. Place	DAVIS	◆ 32,423
Spanish Fork	Inc. Place	UTAH	◆ 31,313
Midvale	Inc. Place	SALT LAKE	◆ 31,015
Cottonwood Heights	Inc. Place	SALT LAKE	◆ 30,541
Springville	Inc. Place	UTAH	◆ 27,748
Cottonwood Heights	CDP-Census Area Only	SALT LAKE	Ⓒ 27,569
Magna	CDP	SALT LAKE	◆ 27,071
Kaysville	Inc. Place	DAVIS	◆ 26,759
Cedar City	Inc. Place	IRON	◆ 25,667
East Millcreek	CDP	SALT LAKE	◆ 25,429
Eagle Mountain	Inc. Place	UTAH	◆ 25,071
South Salt Lake	Inc. Place	SALT LAKE	◆ 24,960
American Fork	Inc. Place	UTAH	◆ 22,347
Holladay	Inc. Place	SALT LAKE	◆ 20,409
Cottonwood West	CDP-Census Area Only	SALT LAKE	Ⓒ 18,727
Brigham City	Inc. Place	BOX ELDER	Ⓒ 17,411
Syracuse	Inc. Place	DAVIS	◆ 15,404
North Ogden	Inc. Place	WEBER	Ⓒ 15,026
Centerville	Inc. Place	DAVIS	Ⓒ 14,585
South Ogden	Inc. Place	WEBER	Ⓒ 14,377
Payson	Inc. Place	UTAH	Ⓒ 12,716
Clinton	Inc. Place	DAVIS	Ⓒ 12,585
Farmington	Inc. Place	DAVIS	Ⓒ 12,081
Canyon Rim	CDP-Census Area Only	SALT LAKE	Ⓒ 10,428
Oquirrh	CDP-Census Area Only	SALT LAKE	Ⓒ 10,390
North Salt Lake	Inc. Place	DAVIS	Ⓒ 8,749
Washington Terrace	Inc. Place	WEBER	Ⓒ 8,551
Price	Inc. Place	CARBON	Ⓒ 8,402
Lindon	Inc. Place	UTAH	Ⓒ 8,363
Hurricane	Inc. Place	WASHINGTON	Ⓒ 8,250
Washington	Inc. Place	WASHINGTON	Ⓒ 8,186
Highland	Inc. Place	UTAH	Ⓒ 8,172
Vernal	Inc. Place	UINTAH	Ⓒ 7,714
Riverdale	Inc. Place	WEBER	Ⓒ 7,656
Park City	Inc. Place	SUMMIT	Ⓒ 7,371
Heber City	Inc. Place	WASATCH	Ⓒ 7,291
Smithfield	Inc. Place	CACHE	Ⓒ 7,261
Little Cottonwood Creek Valley	CDP-Census Area Only	SALT LAKE	Ⓡ 7,202
Alpine	Inc. Place	UTAH	Ⓒ 7,146
Mount Olympus	CDP-Census Area Only	SALT LAKE	Ⓒ 7,103
Richfield	Inc. Place	SEVIER	Ⓒ 6,847
Summit Park	CDP	SUMMIT	Ⓒ 6,597
Woods Cross	Inc. Place	DAVIS	Ⓒ 6,419
Hyrum	Inc. Place	CACHE	Ⓒ 6,316
North Logan	Inc. Place	CACHE	Ⓒ 6,163
West Point	Inc. Place	DAVIS	Ⓒ 6,033
Grantsville	Inc. Place	TOOELE	Ⓒ 6,015
White City	CDP	SALT LAKE	Ⓡ 5,991
Mapleton	Inc. Place	UTAH	Ⓒ 5,809
Pleasant View	Inc. Place	WEBER	Ⓒ 5,632
Tremonton	Inc. Place	BOX ELDER	Ⓒ 5,592
Sunset	Inc. Place	DAVIS	Ⓒ 5,204

County Business Data

County	FIPS Code	County Seat	Land Area (Sq. Mi.)	Census Population			Wholesale Trade		Manufacturing, 2002			
				4/1/2000	4/1/1990	% Change 1990-2000	Sales, 2002 ($1,000)	% Change 1997-2002	Establish-ments	Total Employees	Value Added ($1,000)	Ranally Mfg. Units
Beaver	001	Beaver	2,590	6,005	4,765	26.0	(d)	(d)	...	(d)	(d)	...
Box Elder	003	Brigham City	5,723	42,745	36,485	17.2	(d)	(d)	60	7,807	974,430	516
Cache	005	Logan	1,165	91,391	70,183	30.2	222,149	51.8	182	9,251	654,784	346
Carbon	007	Price	1,478	20,422	20,228	1.0	230,557	31.5	...	(d)	(d)	...
Daggett	009	Manila	698	921	690	33.5	(d)	(d)	...	(d)	(d)	...
Davis	011	Farmington	304	238,994	187,941	27.2	1,625,925	37.2	276	9,611	939,417	497
Duchesne	013	Duchesne	3,238	14,371	12,645	13.6	41,168	32.5	...	(d)	(d)	...
Emery	015	Castle Dale	4,452	10,860	10,332	5.1	(d)	(d)	...	(d)	(d)	...
Garfield	017	Panguitch	5,174	4,735	3,980	19.0	(d)	(d)	...	(d)	(d)	...
Grand	019	Moab	3,682	8,485	6,620	28.2	13,537	53.2	...	(d)	(d)	...
Iron	021	Parowan	3,298	33,779	20,789	62.5	259,627	128.5	50	1,382	199,853	106
Juab	023	Nephi	3,392	8,238	5,817	41.6	16,582	54.8	...	(d)	(d)	...
Kane	025	Kanab	3,992	6,046	5,169	17.0	4,822	(d)	...	(d)	(d)	...
Millard	027	Fillmore	6,589	12,405	11,333	9.5	99,841	246.6	...	(d)	(d)	...
Morgan	029	Morgan	609	7,129	5,528	29.0	(d)	(d)	...	(d)	(d)	...
Piute	031	Junction	758	1,435	1,277	12.4	(d)	(d)	...	(d)	(d)	...
Rich	033	Randolph	1,029	1,961	1,725	13.7	(d)	(d)	...	(d)	(d)	...
Salt Lake	035	Salt Lake City	737	898,387	725,956	23.8	15,558,180	1.3	1,434	49,307	5,550,134	2,936
San Juan	037	Monticello	7,820	14,413	12,621	14.2	(d)	(d)	...	(d)	(d)	...
Sanpete	039	Manti	1,588	22,763	16,259	40.0	(d)	(d)	21	991	43,089	23
Sevier	041	Richfield	1,910	18,842	15,431	22.1	98,580	26.2	...	(d)	(d)	...
Summit	043	Coalville	1,871	29,736	15,518	91.6	(d)	(d)	40	522	48,695	26
Tooele	045	Tooele	6,930	40,735	26,601	53.1	(d)	(d)	28	1,049	132,848	70
Uintah	047	Vernal	4,477	25,224	22,211	13.6	(d)	(d)	...	(d)	(d)	...
Utah	049	Provo	1,998	368,536	263,590	39.8	1,635,839	-40.8	445	13,661	1,490,084	788
Wasatch	051	Heber City	1,177	15,215	10,089	50.8	56,017	292.5	...	(d)	(d)	...
Washington	053	St. George	2,427	90,354	48,560	86.1	(d)	(d)	122	2,192	145,283	77
Wayne	055	Loa	2,460	2,509	2,177	15.3	(d)	(d)	...	(d)	(d)	...
Weber	057	Ogden	576	196,533	158,330	24.1	2,388,039	272.8	231	12,100	1,777,081	940
The State			**82,144**	**2,233,169**	**1,722,850**	**29.6**	**22,905,100**	**7.7**	**3,061**	**109,944**	**12,158,925**	**6,433**

(d) Data not available. Corresponding percentages or Ranally Manufacturing Units are estimates.
... Represents 0 or amount too minimal to be reported.

Index of Places and Counties

A

Abraham; RMC Place; MILLARD; ***240** H-6; elev. 4,591ft./1,399m.; 🅿; z 84635
Adamsville; RMC Place; BEAVER; **240** K-6; 🅿; z 84731; ● 50
Alpine; Inc. Place; UTAH; ***240** E-8; elev. 4,957ft./1,511m.; 🅿; ★ **PRVO-**; z 84004; Ⓟ 3,492; Ⓒ 7,146
Alta; Inc. Place; SALT LAKE; **240** E-9; elev. 8,600ft./2,621m.; 🅿; z 84092; Ⓟ 397; Ⓒ 370
Altamont; Inc. Place; DUCHESNE; **241** E-11; elev. 6,375ft./1,943m.; 🅿; z 84001; Ⓟ 167; Ⓒ 178
Alton; Inc. Place; KANE; **240** M-7; elev. 7,036ft./2,145m.; 🅿; z 84710; Ⓟ 93; Ⓒ 134
Altonah; RMC Place; DUCHESNE; **241** E-11; elev. 6,681ft./2,036m.; 🅿; z 84002; ● 40
Altus; RMC Place; SUMMIT; ***240** D-9; mail Park City z 84098; ● 1,130
Amalga; Inc. Place; CACHE; **240** A-8; elev. 4,440ft./1,353m.; 🅿; ★ **LOGN**; z 84335; Ⓟ 366; Ⓒ 427
American Fork; Inc. Place; UTAH; **240** E-8; elev. 4,600ft./1,402m.; 🅿 🅷; ★ **PRVO-**; z 84003; Ⓟ 15,696; Ⓒ 21,941; ◆ 22,347
Anderson Junction; RMC Place; WASHINGTON; ***240** M-5; elev. 3,840ft./1,170m.; mail Toquerville z 84774; pop. incl. with Toquerville (Inc. Place)
Aneth; CDP; SAN JUAN; **241** M-14; elev. 4,531ft./1,381m.; 🅿; z 84510; Ⓒ 598
Angle; RMC Place; PIUTE; ***240** K-8; mail Antimony z 84712; rural
Annabella; Inc. Place; SEVIER; **240** J-8; elev. 5,301ft./1,616m.; 🅿; z 84711; Ⓟ 487; Ⓒ 603
Antimony; Inc. Place; GARFIELD; **240** K-8; elev. 6,440ft./1,963m.; 🅿; z 84712; Ⓟ 83; Ⓒ 122
Apple Valley; Inc. Place; WASHINGTON; ***240** N-5; incorporated December 15, 2004; not reported in 2000 Census; ● 550
Arcadia; RMC Place; DUCHESNE; ***241** F-11; mail Duchesne z 84021; rural
Arsenal; RMC Place; DAVIS; ***240** C-8; ★ **OGD**; mail Clearfield z 84015; pop. incl. with Sunset (Inc. Place)
Aspen Acres; RMC Place; SUMMIT; mail Oakley z 84055; summer pop. 200
Atwood; RMC Place; SALT LAKE; ***240** E-8; ★ **S.L.C.**; mail Salt Lake City z 84107; pop. incl. with Murray (Inc. Place)
Aurora; Inc. Place; SEVIER; **240** I-8; elev. 5,187ft./1,581m.; 🅿; z 84620; Ⓟ 911; Ⓒ 947
Austin; RMC Place; SEVIER; ***240** J-8; 🅿; z 84754; ● 110
Avon; CDP; CACHE; **240** B-8; elev. 5,012ft./1,528m.; mail Paradise z 84328; Ⓒ 306
Axtell; RMC Place; SANPETE; **240** I-8; elev. 5,144ft./1,568m.; 🅿; z 84621; ● 70

B

Ballard; Inc. Place; UINTAH; **241** E-12; 🅿; z 84066; Ⓟ 644; Ⓒ 566
Bauer; RMC Place; TOOELE; ***240** E-7; mail Stockton z 84071
Bear River City; Inc. Place; BOX ELDER; **240** B-8; elev. 4,255ft./1,297m.; 🅿; z 84301; Ⓟ 700; Ⓒ 750
Beaver; Inc. Place; ⊡ BEAVER; **240** K-6; elev. 5,898ft./1,798m.; 🅿 🅷; z 84713; Ⓟ 1,998; Ⓒ 2,454
BEAVER; **240** J-5; Ⓟ 4,765; Ⓒ 6,005; ◆ 5,997
Beaverdam; RMC Place; BOX ELDER; ***240** B-8; elev. 4,542ft./1,384m.; mail Collinston z 84306; ● 60
Becks; RMC Place; SALT LAKE; ***240** D-8; elev. 4,221ft./1,287m.; ★ **S.L.C.**; pop. incl. with Salt Lake City (Inc. Place)
Belmont Heights; RMC Place; SALT LAKE; ***240** E-8; ★ **S.L.C.**; mail Sandy z 84070, z 84092
Benjamin; CDP; UTAH; ***240** F-8; 🅿; ★ **PRVO-**; z 84660; Ⓒ 1,029
Ben Lomond; RMC Place; WEBER; ★ **OGD**; mail Ogden z 84404; pop. incl. with Ogden (Inc. Place)
Bennion; RMC Place; SALT LAKE; ***240** E-8; elev. 4,377ft./1,334m.; ★ **S.L.C.**; mail Salt Lake City z 84118, z 84123; pop. incl. with Taylorsville (Inc. Place)
Benson; CDP; CACHE; ***240** B-8; elev. 4,426ft./1,349m.; 🅿; ★ **LOGN**; z 84335; Ⓒ 1,451
Beryl; RMC Place; IRON; **240** L-4; elev. 5,147ft./1,569m.; 🅿; z 84714; ● 120
Beryl Junction; RMC Place; IRON; ***240** L-4; mail Beryl z 84714
Bicknell; Inc. Place; WAYNE; **240** J-9; elev. 7,128ft./2,173m.; 🅿; z 84715; Ⓟ 327; Ⓒ 353
Big Water (Glen Canyon); Inc. Place; KANE; **240** N-8; elev. 4,500ft./1,372m.; 🅿; z 84741; Ⓟ 326; Ⓒ 417
Bingham Canyon; RMC Place; SALT LAKE; ***240** E-7; 🅿; z 84006; rural
Birdseye; RMC Place; UTAH; **240** F-9; mail Fairview z 84629; ● 50
Blanding; Inc. Place; SAN JUAN; **241** L-13; elev. 6,105ft./1,861m.; 🅿; z 84511; Ⓟ 3,162; Ⓒ 3,162
Bloomington; RMC Place; WASHINGTON; ***240** N-4; mail Saint George z 84790; pop. incl. with Saint George (Inc. Place)
Bluebell; RMC Place; DUCHESNE; **241** E-11; elev. 5,203ft./1,586m.; 🅿; z 84007; ● 80
Bluff; CDP; SAN JUAN; **241** M-13; elev. 4,320ft./1,317m.; 🅿; z 84512; Ⓒ 320
Bluffdale; Inc. Place; SALT LAKE; **240** E-8; 🅿; ★ **S.L.C.**; z 84065; Ⓟ 2,152; Ⓒ 4,700
Bonanza; RMC Place; UINTAH; **241** F-13; elev. 5,456ft./1,663m.; 🅿; z 84008; ● 110
Boneta; RMC Place; DUCHESNE; ***241** E-11; elev. 6,454ft./1,967m.; mail Altamont z 84001, Mountain Home z 84051; ● 30
Bonnie; RMC Place; UTAH; ★ **PRVO-**; mail Orem z 84057-58; pop. incl. with Orem (Inc. Place)
Bothwell; RMC Place; BOX ELDER; ***240** B-7; elev. 4,329ft./1,319m.; mail Tremonton z 84337; ● 50
Boulder; GARFIELD; see Boulder Town (Inc. Place)
Boulder Town (Boulder); Inc. Place; GARFIELD; **240** L-9; elev. 6,680ft./2,036m.; mail Boulder z 84716; Ⓟ 126; Ⓒ 180
Bountiful; Inc. Place; DAVIS; **240** D-8; elev. 4,372ft./1,333m.; 🅿 🅷 ■; ★ **S.L.C.**; z 84010-11; Ⓟ 36,147; Ⓒ 41,301; ◆ 45,365
Bowery Haven; RMC Place; SEVIER; mail Richfield z 84701
BOX ELDER; **240** C-4; Ⓟ 36,485; Ⓒ 42,745; ◆ 49,819
Bradford; RMC Place; BOX ELDER; mail Tremonton z 84337; ● 155
Brendel (Crescent Junction); RMC Place; GRAND; **241** I-12; mail Thompson z 84540; rural
Brian Head; Inc. Place; IRON; ***240** L-6; elev. 11,000ft./3,353m.; 🅿; z 84719; Ⓟ 109; Ⓒ 118
Bridge Junction; RMC Place; WEBER; ★ **OGD**; pop. incl. with Ogden (Inc. Place)
Bridgeland; RMC Place; DUCHESNE; **241** F-11; elev. 5,297ft./1,615m.; 🅿; z 84021; ● 80
Brigham City; Inc. Place; ⊡ BOX ELDER; **240** B-8; elev. 4,439ft./1,353m.; 🅿 🅷; z 84302; Ⓟ 15,644; Ⓒ 17,411
Brighton (Silverlake); RMC Place; SALT LAKE; **240** E-9; 🅿; z 84121; ● 350
Brooklyn; RMC Place; SEVIER; ***240** J-7; mail Monroe z 84754; rural
Bryce; GARFIELD; see Bryce Canyon City (Inc. Place)
Bryce Canyon; RMC Place; GARFIELD; **241** A-14; elev. 7,978ft./2,432m.; 🅿; z 84764; ● 40
Bryce Canyon City (Bryce, Rubys Inn); Inc. Place; GARFIELD; **241** A-14; elev. 7,661ft./2,335m.; 🅿; z 84764; incorporated July 23, 2007; not reported in 2000 Census; ● 140
Buena Vista; RMC Place; SALT LAKE; ***240** D-8; elev. 4,230ft./1,289m.; ★ **S.L.C.**; pop. incl. with Salt Lake City (Inc. Place)
Bullfrog; RMC Place; KANE; ***240** M-10; 🅿; z 84533; summer pop. 350; ● 200
Burbank; RMC Place; MILLARD; ***240** I-4; mail Milford z 84751; rural
Burmester; RMC Place; TOOELE; ***240** D-7; elev. 4,217ft./1,285m.; mail Grantsville z 84029; ● 30
Burrville; RMC Place; SEVIER; ***240** J-8; mail Richfield z 84701; ● 40
Burton; RMC Place; SALT LAKE; ★ **S.L.C.**; pop. incl. with Salt Lake City (Inc. Place)
Bushnell (Intermountain Indian School); RMC Place; BOX ELDER; mail Brigham City z 84302; pop. incl. with Brigham City (Inc. Place)

C

Cache; CDP-Census Area Only; CACHE; ***240** A-8; Ⓒ 37
CACHE; **240** B-8; Ⓟ 70,183; Ⓒ 91,391; ◆ 129,014
Cache Junction; RMC Place; CACHE; ***240** A-8; elev. 4,448ft./1,356m.; 🅿; z 84304; ● 70
Caineville; RMC Place; WAYNE; **240** K-10; mail Torrey z 84775
Callao; RMC Place; JUAB; **240** F-4; elev. 4,334ft./1,321m.; mail Ibapah z 84034
Cannonville; Inc. Place; GARFIELD; **240** M-8; elev. 5,880ft./1,792m.; 🅿; z 84718; Ⓟ 131; Ⓒ 148
Canyon Rim; CDP-Census Area Only; SALT LAKE; ***240** D-8; ★ **S.L.C.**; mail Salt Lake City z 84106; Ⓟ 10,527; Ⓒ 10,428
Capital Reef Park; WAYNE; see Fruita (RMC Place)
CARBON; **241** G-11; Ⓟ 20,228; Ⓒ 20,422; ◆ 20,422
Carbonville; RMC Place; CARBON; ***240** G-10; mail Helper z 84526, Price z 84501; ● 600
Castle Dale; Inc. Place; ⊡ EMERY; **240** H-10; elev. 5,571ft./1,698m.; 🅿; z 84513; Ⓟ 1,704; Ⓒ 1,657
Castleton; RMC Place; GRAND; ***241** J-13; mail Moab z 84532; rural
Castle Valley; Inc. Place; GRAND; **241** J-13; 🅿; z 84532; Ⓟ 211; Ⓒ 349
Cedar City; Inc. Place; IRON; **240** L-6; elev. 5,834ft./1,778m.; 🅿 🅷 🅲 7,029; z 84720-21; Ⓟ 13,443; Ⓒ 20,527; ◆ 25,667
Cedar Fort (Cedar Valley); Inc. Place; UTAH; **240** E-8; elev. 5,100ft./1,554m.; 🅿; z 84013; Ⓟ 284; Ⓒ 341
Cedar Hills; Inc. Place; UTAH; ***240** E-8; elev. 4,666ft./1,422m.; 🅿; ★ **PRVO-**; z 84062; Ⓟ 769; Ⓒ 3,094
Cedar Valley; UTAH; see Cedar Fort (Inc. Place)
Cedarview; RMC Place; DUCHESNE; **241** E-12; mail Roosevelt z 84066; rural
Center Creek; RMC Place; WASATCH; ***240** E-9; elev. 5,927ft./1,807m.; mail Heber City z 84032; ● 480
Centerfield; Inc. Place; SANPETE; **240** H-8; elev. 5,100ft./1,554m.; 🅿; z 84622; Ⓟ 766; Ⓒ 1,048
Centerville; Inc. Place; DAVIS; **240** D-8; elev. 4,300ft./1,311m.; 🅿; ★ **S.L.C.**; z 84014; Ⓟ 11,500; Ⓒ 14,585
Central; SEVIER; see Central Valley (Inc. Place)
Central; RMC Place; WASHINGTON; **240** M-4; elev. 5,345ft./1,629m.; 🅿; z 84722; ● 100
Central Valley (Central); Inc. Place; SEVIER; ***240** J-8; elev. 5,297ft./1,615m.; 🅿; z 84754; incorporated January 28, 2005; not reported in 2000 Census; ● 280
Charleston; Inc. Place; WASATCH; **240** E-9; elev. 5,440ft./1,658m.; mail Heber City z 84032; Ⓟ 336; Ⓒ 378
Chester; RMC Place; SANPETE; ***240** H-9; elev. 5,510ft./1,679m.; 🅿; z 84623; ● 60
Circleville; Inc. Place; PIUTE; **240** K-7; elev. 6,063ft./1,848m.; 🅿; z 84723; Ⓟ 417; Ⓒ 505
Cisco; RMC Place; GRAND; **241** I-13; elev. 4,352ft./1,326m.; 🅿; z 84515
City Limits; RMC Place; SALT LAKE; ★ **S.L.C.**; pop. incl. with Salt Lake City (Inc. Place)
Clarkston; Inc. Place; CACHE; **240** A-8; elev. 4,884ft./1,489m.; 🅿; z 84305; Ⓟ 645; Ⓒ 688
Clawson; Inc. Place; EMERY; **240** H-10; elev. 5,950ft./1,814m.; 🅿; z 84516; Ⓟ 151; Ⓒ 153
Clear Creek; RMC Place; BOX ELDER; **240** A-5; mail Malta z 83342; rural
Clear Creek; RMC Place; CARBON; **240** G-9; elev. 8,303ft./2,531m.; mail Helper z 84526
Clearfield; Inc. Place; DAVIS; **240** C-8; elev. 4,484ft./1,367m.; 🅿; ★ **OGD**; z 84015-16, z 84089; Ⓟ 21,435; Ⓒ 25,974; ◆ 32,423
Cleveland; Inc. Place; EMERY; **240** H-10; elev. 5,735ft./1,748m.; 🅿; z 84518; Ⓟ 498; Ⓒ 508
Clinton; Inc. Place; DAVIS; **240** D-1; elev. 4,350ft./1,326m.; 🅿; ★ **OGD**; z 84015; Ⓟ 7,945; Ⓒ 12,585
Clover; RMC Place; TOOELE; **240** E-7; elev. 5,165ft./1,574m.; mail Rush Valley z 84069; pop. incl. with Rush Valley (Inc. Place)
Clyde; RMC Place; UTAH; ★ **PRVO-**; mail Orem z 84057-58; pop. incl. with Orem (Inc. Place)
Coalville; Inc. Place; ⊡ SUMMIT; **240** D-9; elev. 5,586ft./1,703m.; 🅿; z 84017; Ⓟ 1,065; Ⓒ 1,382
College Ward; RMC Place; CACHE; ***240** B-8; ★ **LOGN**; mail Logan z 84321, Wellsville z 84339; ● 200
Collinston; RMC Place; BOX ELDER; ***240** B-8; elev. 4,440ft./1,353m.; 🅿; z 84306; ● 60
Columbia; RMC Place; CARBON; ***241** G-11; mail East Carbon z 84520; pop. incl. with East Carbon City (Inc. Place)
Columbia Junction; RMC Place; CARBON; ***241** G-11; mail East Carbon z 84520; pop. incl. with East Carbon City (Inc. Place)
Copperton; RMC Place; SALT LAKE; **240** E-8; elev. 5,504ft./1,678m.; 🅿; ★ **S.L.C.**; z 84006; ● 800
Corinne; Inc. Place; BOX ELDER; **240** B-8; elev. 4,230ft./1,289m.; 🅿; z 84307; Ⓟ 639; Ⓒ 621
Cornish; Inc. Place; CACHE; **240** A-8; elev. 4,480ft./1,366m.; 🅿; z 84308; Ⓟ 205; Ⓒ 259
Cottonwood; RMC Place; SALT LAKE; **241** H-20; elev. 4,440ft./1,353m.; 🅿; ★ **S.L.C.**; z 84121, z 84171
Cottonwood Heights; Inc. Place; SALT LAKE; **241** I-20; incorporated January 14, 2005; not reported in 2000 Census; ● 35,200; ◆ 30,541
Cottonwood Heights; CDP-Census Area Only; SALT LAKE; **241** I-20; 🅿; ★ **S.L.C.**; z 84047, z 84093, z 84121, z 84171; Ⓟ 28,766; Ⓒ 27,569
Cottonwood Meadows; RMC Place; SALT LAKE; mail Salt Lake City z 84117; ● 850
Cottonwood West; CDP-Census Area Only; SALT LAKE; ***240** E-8; ★ **S.L.C.**; mail Salt Lake City z 84117, z 84121; Ⓟ 17,476; Ⓒ 18,727
Cove; CDP; CACHE; ***240** A-8; 🅿; z 84320; Ⓒ 443
Cove Fort; RMC Place; MILLARD; **240** J-7; mail Beaver z 84713
Crescent; RMC Place; SALT LAKE; ***240** E-8; ★ **S.L.C.**; mail Sandy z 84070, z 84092; pop. incl. with Sandy City (Inc. Place)
Crescent Junction; GRAND; see Brendel (RMC Place)
Croydon; RMC Place; MORGAN; **240** C-9; elev. 5,360ft./1,634m.; 🅿; z 84018; ● 50
Curlew Junction; RMC Place; BOX ELDER; ***240** A-6; mail Snowville z 84336
Cushing; RMC Place; SALT LAKE; ★ **S.L.C.**; mail Midvale z 84047; pop. incl. with Midvale (Inc. Place)
Cutler; BOX ELDER; see Wheelon (RMC Place)

D

DAGGETT; **241** D-12; Ⓟ 690; Ⓒ 921; ◆ 899
Dammeron Valley; RMC Place; WASHINGTON; ***240** M-4; 🅿; z 84783; ● 300
Daniel; Inc. Place; WASATCH; ***240** E-9; incorporated February 28, 2006; ● 600
Daniel; CDP-Census Area Only; WASATCH; ***240** E-9; mail Heber City z 84032; Ⓒ 770
DAVIS; **240** D-7; Ⓟ 187,941; Ⓒ 238,994; ◆ 310,982
Defas Park; RMC Place; DUCHESNE; mail Hanna z 84031; summer pop. 75
Delta; Inc. Place; MILLARD; **240** H-7; elev. 4,635ft./1,413m.; 🅿 🅷; z 84624 & mail Lynndyl z 84640; Ⓟ 2,998; Ⓒ 3,209
Deseret; RMC Place; MILLARD; **240** H-6; 🅿; z 84624; ● 300
Devils Slide; RMC Place; MORGAN; **240** C-9; elev. 5,235ft./1,596m.; mail Morgan z 84050
Dewey; BOX ELDER; see Deweyville (Inc. Place)
Deweyville (Dewey); Inc. Place; BOX ELDER; **240** B-8; elev. 4,330ft./1,320m.; 🅿; z 84309; Ⓟ 318; Ⓒ 278
Downtown; RMC Place; SALT LAKE; ★ **S.L.C.**; mail Salt Lake City z 84101; pop. incl. with Salt Lake City (Inc. Place)
Draper; Inc. Place; SALT LAKE, UTAH; **240** E-8; elev. 4,490ft./1,369m.; 🅿; ★ **S.L.C.**; z 84020; Ⓟ 7,257; Ⓒ 25,220; Ⓡ 25,216; ◆ 35,332
Dry Fork; RMC Place; UINTAH; **241** E-12; mail Vernal z 84078; ● 30
Duchesne; Inc. Place; ⊡ DUCHESNE; **241** F-11; elev. 5,514ft./1,681m.; 🅿; z 84021; Ⓟ 1,308; Ⓒ 1,408
DUCHESNE; **241** F-11; Ⓟ 12,645; Ⓒ 14,371; ◆ 17,641
Duck Creek Village; RMC Place; KANE; ***240** M-6; 🅿; z 84762; ● 400
Dugway; CDP; TOOELE; ***240** F-6; elev. 4,837ft./1,474m.; 🅿; z 84022; Ⓟ 1,761; Ⓒ 2,016
Dutch John; RMC Place; DAGGETT; **241** D-13; elev. 6,320ft./1,926m.; 🅿; z 84023; ● 200

E

Eagle Mountain; Inc. Place; UTAH; ***240** E-8; 🅿; z 84005, z 84043; Ⓒ 2,157; ◆ 25,071
East Bay; RMC Place; UTAH; ***240** F-8; ★ **PRVO-**; mail Provo z 84605; pop. incl. with Provo (Inc. Place)
East Carbon; CARBON; see East Carbon City (Inc. Place)
East Carbon City (East Carbon); Inc. Place; CARBON; **241** G-11; elev. 6,320ft./1,926m.; mail East Carbon z 84520; Ⓟ 1,270; Ⓒ 1,393
Eastland; RMC Place; SAN JUAN; **241** L-14; mail Monticello z 84535; ● 90
East Midvale; RMC Place; SALT LAKE; ★ **S.L.C.**; mail Midvale z 84047
East Millcreek; CDP; SALT LAKE; ***240** D-8; ★ **S.L.C.**; mail Salt Lake City z 84117, z 84124; Ⓟ 21,184; Ⓒ 21,385; ◆ 25,429
East Portal; RMC Place; WASATCH; ***240** F-9; mail Heber City z 84032; rural
East Roper; RMC Place; SALT LAKE; ★ **S.L.C.**; pop. incl. with Salt Lake City (Inc. Place)
Eastwood Hills; RMC Place; SALT LAKE; ***240** D-8; ★ **S.L.C.**; mail Salt Lake City z 84106
Echo; RMC Place; SUMMIT; **240** D-9; elev. 5,459ft./1,664m.; 🅿; z 84024; ● 50
Eden; RMC Place; WEBER; ***240** C-8; elev. 4,947ft./1,508m.; 🅿; z 84310; ● 350
Elberta; CDP; UTAH; **240** F-8; elev. 4,660ft./1,420m.; 🅿; z 84626; Ⓒ 278
Elgin; RMC Place; GRAND; **241** I-12; mail Green River z 84525; pop. incl. with Green River (Inc. Place)
Elk Ridge (Salem Hills); Inc. Place; UTAH; ***240** F-8; 🅿; ★ **PRVO-**; z 84651 & mail Spanish Fork z 84660; Ⓟ 771; Ⓒ 1,838
Elmo; Inc. Place; EMERY; **240** H-10; elev. 5,694ft./1,736m.; 🅿; z 84521; Ⓟ 267; Ⓒ 368
Elsimore Addition; RMC Place; SEVIER; ***240** J-7; mail Elsinore z 84724; pop. incl. with Elsinore (Inc. Place)
Elsinore; Inc. Place; SEVIER; **240** J-7; elev. 5,342ft./1,628m.; 🅿; z 84724; Ⓟ 608; Ⓒ 733
Elwood; Inc. Place; BOX ELDER; ***240** B-8; elev. 4,290ft./1,308m.; 🅿; z 84337; Ⓟ 575; Ⓒ 678
Emery; Inc. Place; EMERY; **240** I-9; elev. 6,262ft./1,909m.; 🅿; z 84522; Ⓟ 300; Ⓒ 308
EMERY; **240** I-10; Ⓟ 10,332; Ⓒ 10,860; ◆ 10,512
Emigration Canyon; RMC Place; SALT LAKE; ***240** D-8; 🅿; ★ **S.L.C.**; z 84108; pop. incl. with Salt Lake City (Inc. Place)
Emory; RMC Place; SUMMIT; **240** C-9; mail Echo z 84024; rural
Emporium; RMC Place; SUMMIT; mail Park City z 84068; pop. incl. with Park City (Inc. Place)
Enoch; Inc. Place; IRON; **240** L-6; elev. 5,550ft./1,692m.; 🅿; z 84720-21; Ⓟ 1,947; Ⓒ 3,467
Enterprise; RMC Place; MORGAN; ***240** C-8; mail Morgan z 84050; rural
Enterprise; Inc. Place; WASHINGTON; **240** L-4; elev. 5,329ft./1,624m.; 🅿; z 84725; Ⓟ 936; Ⓒ 1,285
Ephraim; Inc. Place; SANPETE; **240** H-9; elev. 5,540ft./1,689m.; 🅿; z 84627; Ⓟ 3,363; Ⓒ 4,505
Erda; CDP; TOOELE; **240** E-7; 🅿; z 84074; Ⓟ 1,113; Ⓒ 2,473
Escalante; Inc. Place; GARFIELD; **240** L-9; elev. 5,812ft./1,771m.; 🅿; z 84726; Ⓟ 818; Ⓒ 818
Esk Dale; RMC Place; MILLARD; ***240** H-4; mail Garrison z 84728; ● 100
Etna; RMC Place; BOX ELDER; **240** B-4; elev. 5,203ft./1,586m.; mail Grouse Creek z 84313; rural
Eureka; Inc. Place; JUAB; **240** F-8; elev. 6,442ft./1,964m.; 🅿; z 84628; Ⓟ 562; Ⓒ 766
Evans; RMC Place; BOX ELDER; mail Tremonton z 84337; ● 155
Evona; RMC Place; WEBER; ***240** C-8; ★ **OGD**; pop. incl. with Ogden (Inc. Place)

Entries in **UPPERCASE** are counties.
Entries in **bold** have populations of 2,500 or more.
Names in parentheses are alternate names.

Inc. Place	Incorporated Place
RMC Place	Rand McNally Designated Place
CDP	Census Designated Place
MCD	Minor Civil Division
⊡	County Seat
▲	Minor Civil Division
elev.	Elevation
🅿	Post Office
🅷	Hospital
🅲	College
■	Principal Business Center
★	Ranally Metro Area (RMA) Abbreviation
z	Zip Code(s)
Ⓟ	Previous Census Population
Ⓡ	Revised Census Population
Ⓐ	Annexation Population
●	Rand McNally Population Estimate
Ⓒ	Final Census Population
Ⓢ	Special Census Population
◆	Estimated Population

For additional definitions see Glossary, Volume 1, and Introduction, Volume 2.

F

Fairfield; Inc. Place; UTAH; **240** E-8; 🅿; z 84013; incorporated December 29, 2004; not reported in 2000 Census; ● 150

Fairview; Inc. Place; SANPETE; **240** G-9; elev. 6,033ft./1,839m.; 🅿; z 84629; Ⓟ 960; © 1,160

Farmington; Inc. Place; ⊡ DAVIS; **240** D-8; elev. 4,302ft./1,311m.; 🅿; ★ **S.L.C.**; z 84025; Ⓟ 9,028; © 12,081

Farr West; Inc. Place; WEBER; **240** A-1; elev. 4,260ft./1,298m.; 🅿; ★ **OGD**; z 84404; Ⓟ 2,178; © 3,094

Faust; RMC Place; TOOELE; **240** F-7; elev. 5,253ft./1,601m.; mail Vernon z 84080; rural

Fayette; Inc. Place; SANPETE; **240** H-8; elev. 5,050ft./1,539m.; 🅿; z 84630; Ⓟ 183; © 204

Ferron; Inc. Place; EMERY; **240** I-9; elev. 5,949ft./1,813m.; 🅿; z 84523; Ⓟ 1,606; © 1,623

Fielding; Inc. Place; BOX ELDER; **240** A-8; elev. 4,367ft./1,331m.; 🅿; z 84311; Ⓟ 422; © 448

Fillmore; Inc. Place; ⊡ MILLARD; **240** I-7; elev. 5,135ft./1,565m.; 🅿 🅷; z 84631; Ⓟ 1,956; © 2,253

Fish Lake; RMC Place; SEVIER; mail Richfield z 84701; summer pop. 100

Flowell; RMC Place; MILLARD; **240** I-7; mail Fillmore z 84631; ● 100

Foothill; RMC Place; SALT LAKE; ★ **S.L.C.**; mail Salt Lake City z 84108, z 84158; pop. incl. with Salt Lake City (Inc. Place)

Fort Duchesne; CDP; UINTAH; **241** E-12; located on Uintah and Ouray Ind. Res.; elev. 4,988ft./1,520m.; 🅿; z 84026; location of Indian Agency; Ⓟ 655; © 621

Fountain Green; Inc. Place; SANPETE; **240** G-9; elev. 6,025ft./1,836m.; 🅿; z 84632; Ⓟ 578; © 945

Francis; Inc. Place; SUMMIT; **240** E-9; elev. 6,560ft./1,999m.; 🅿; z 84036; Ⓟ 381; © 698

Freedom; RMC Place; SANPETE; ***240** G-8; mail Moroni z 84646; rural

Fremont; RMC Place; WAYNE; **240** J-9; elev. 7,240ft./2,207m.; 🅿; z 84747; ● 200

Fruita (Capital Reef Park); RMC Place; WAYNE; ***240** K-9; mail Torrey z 84775; ● 70

Fruit Heights; Inc. Place; DAVIS; **240** F-3; elev. 4,560ft./1,390m.; 🅿; ★ **S.L.C.**; z 84037; Ⓟ 3,900; © 4,701

Fruitland; RMC Place; DUCHESNE; **240** F-10; elev. 6,611ft./2,015m.; 🅿; z 84027; ● 40

G

Gadsby; RMC Place; SALT LAKE; ★ **S.L.C.**; pop. incl. with Salt Lake City (Inc. Place)

Gandy; RMC Place; MILLARD; ***240** H-4; mail Garrison z 84728; rural

Garden; CDP-Census Area Only; RICH; ***240** A-9; © 83

Garden City; Inc. Place; RICH; **240** A-9; elev. 5,960ft./1,817m.; 🅿; z 84028; Ⓟ 193; © 357

GARFIELD; **240** L-9; Ⓟ 3,980; © 4,735; ◆ 4,784

Garland; Inc. Place; BOX ELDER; **240** B-8; elev. 4,340ft./1,323m.; 🅿; z 84312; Ⓟ 1,637; © 1,943

Garrison; RMC Place; MILLARD; **240** I-4; elev. 5,273ft./1,607m.; 🅿; z 84728; ● 50

Genola; Inc. Place; UTAH; ***240** F-8; elev. 4,598ft./1,401m.; 🅿; ★ **PRVO-**; z 84655; Ⓟ 803; © 965

Glen Canyon; KANE; see Big Water (Inc. Place)

Glendale; Inc. Place; KANE; **240** M-6; elev. 5,824ft./1,775m.; 🅿; z 84729; Ⓟ 282; © 355

Glenwood; Inc. Place; SEVIER; **240** I-8; elev. 5,250ft./1,600m.; 🅿; z 84730; Ⓟ 437; © 437

Gorgosa; RMC Place; SUMMIT; mail Park City z 84098; ● 100

Goshen; Inc. Place; UTAH; **240** F-8; elev. 4,640ft./1,414m.; 🅿; ★ **PRVO-**; z 84633; Ⓟ 578; © 874

Goshute Reservation; Indian Reservation; JUAB, TOOELE; Reservation extends into NV; mail Ibapah z 84034; Ⓟ 80; © 90

Gouldings Trading Post; RMC Place; SAN JUAN; ***241** N-11; located on Navajo Nation Ind. Res.; mail Kayenta z 86033; ● 30

GRAND; **241** H-12; Ⓟ 6,620; © 8,485; ◆ 9,722

Granger; RMC Place; SALT LAKE; ***240** D-8; elev. 4,255ft./1,297m.; ★ **S.L.C.**; mail Salt Lake City z 84119; pop. incl. with West Valley City (Inc. Place)

Granite; CDP; SALT LAKE; **241** J-20; ★ **S.L.C.**; mail Sandy z 84070, z 84092; Ⓟ 3,300; © 2,018; Ⓡ 1,989

Grantsville; Inc. Place; TOOELE; **240** E-7; elev. 4,300ft./1,311m.; 🅿; z 84029; Ⓟ 4,500; © 6,015

Greendale Junction; RMC Place; DAGGETT; ***241** D-13; mail Dutch John z 84023; rural

Green River; Inc. Place; EMERY; **241** I-11; elev. 4,079ft./1,243m.; 🅿; z 84525, z 84540 & mail Cisco z 84515; Ⓟ 866; © 973

Greenville; RMC Place; BEAVER; **240** K-6; elev. 5,660ft./1,725m.; 🅿; z 84731; ● 110

Greenville; RMC Place; CACHE; ***240** B-8; ★ **LOGN**; pop. incl. with Logan (Inc. Place)

Greenwich; RMC Place; PIUTE; **240** J-8; elev. 6,850ft./2,088m.; 🅿; z 84732; ● 30

Grouse Creek; RMC Place; BOX ELDER; **240** B-4; elev. 5,325ft./1,623m.; 🅿; z 84313; ● 80

Grover; RMC Place; WAYNE; **240** K-9; mail Teasdale z 84773

Gunlock; RMC Place; WASHINGTON; **240** M-4; elev. 3,651ft./1,113m.; 🅿; z 84733; ● 150

Gunnison; Inc. Place; SANPETE; **240** H-8; elev. 5,120ft./1,561m.; 🅿 🅷; z 84634; Ⓟ 1,298; © 2,394

Gusher; RMC Place; UINTAH; **241** E-12; elev. 5,054ft./1,540m.; 🅿; z 84026; ● 160

H

Hailstone; RMC Place; WASATCH; ***240** E-9; elev. 5,962ft./1,817m.; mail Heber City z 84032; rural

Halchita; CDP; SAN JUAN; ***241** N-12; elev. 4,360ft./1,329m.; mail Mexican Hat z 84531; © 270

Halls Crossing; CDP; SAN JUAN; ***240** M-10; 🅿; z 84533; summer pop. 200; © 89

Hamilton Fort; RMC Place; IRON; ***240** L-5; mail Cedar City z 84720; ● 100

Hanksville; Inc. Place; WAYNE; **240** J-10; elev. 4,306ft./1,312m.; 🅿; z 84734; incorporated January 6, 1999; not reported in 2000 Census; Ⓡ 200

Hanna; RMC Place; DUCHESNE; **240** E-10; elev. 6,920ft./2,109m.; 🅿; z 84031; ● 70

Hardy; RMC Place; UTAH; ***240** E-8; ★ **PRVO-**; mail Pleasant Grove z 84062; pop. incl. with Lindon (Inc. Place)

Harrisburg Junction; RMC Place; WASHINGTON; ***240** M-5; mail Hurricane z 84737, Saint George z 84770; pop. incl. with Hurricane (Inc. Place)

Harrisville; Inc. Place; WEBER; **240** A-2; elev. 4,280ft./1,305m.; 🅿; ★ **OGD**; z 84404, z 84414; Ⓟ 3,004; © 3,645

Hatch; Inc. Place; GARFIELD; **240** L-7; elev. 6,917ft./2,108m.; 🅿; z 84735; Ⓟ 103; © 127

Hatton; RMC Place; MILLARD; ***240** I-7; mail Kanosh z 84637; rural

Hayden; RMC Place; UINTAH; ***241** E-12; mail Neola z 84053; ● 40

Heber; WASATCH; see Heber City (Inc. Place)

Heber City (Heber); Inc. Place; ⊡ WASATCH; **240** E-9; elev. 5,595ft./1,705m.; 🅿 🅷; z 84032; Ⓟ 4,782; © 7,291

Helper; Inc. Place; CARBON; **240** G-10; elev. 5,829ft./1,777m.; 🅿; z 84526; Ⓟ 2,148; © 2,025

Henefer; Inc. Place; SUMMIT; **240** D-9; elev. 5,336ft./1,626m.; 🅿; z 84033; Ⓟ 554; © 684

Henrieville; Inc. Place; GARFIELD; **240** L-8; elev. 6,000ft./1,829m.; 🅿; z 84736; Ⓟ 163; © 159

Hermitage; RMC Place; WEBER; mail Ogden z 84401; ● 70

Herriman; Inc. Place; SALT LAKE; **241** K-17; elev. 4,941ft./1,506m.; 🅿; z 84065, z 84096; © 1,523

Hiawatha; RMC Place; CARBON, EMERY; **240** H-10; elev. 7,200ft./2,195m.; ● 50

Hidden Lake; RMC Place; SUMMIT; mail Oakley z 84055; summer pop. 250

Highland; Inc. Place; UTAH; ***240** E-8; 🅿; ★ **PRVO-**; z 84003; Ⓟ 5,002; © 8,172

Hildale; Inc. Place; WASHINGTON; **240** N-6; elev. 5,040ft./1,536m.; 🅿; z 84784; Ⓟ 1,325; © 1,895

Hinckley; Inc. Place; MILLARD; **240** H-6; elev. 4,587ft./1,398m.; 🅿; z 84635; Ⓟ 658; © 698

Hite; RMC Place; SAN JUAN; ***241** L-11; 🅿; z 84533; rural

Holden; Inc. Place; MILLARD; **240** H-7; elev. 5,100ft./1,554m.; 🅿; z 84636; Ⓟ 402; © 400

Holiday Park; RMC Place; SUMMIT; mail Oakley z 84055

Holladay; Inc. Place; SALT LAKE; **240** D-8; 🅿; ★ **S.L.C.**; z 84117, z 84121, z 84124; © 14,561; Ⓡ 13,559; ◆ 20,409

Honeyville; Inc. Place; BOX ELDER; **240** B-8; elev. 4,280ft./1,305m.; 🅿; z 84314; Ⓟ 1,112; © 1,214

Hooper; Inc. Place; WEBER; **240** C-1; elev. 4,240ft./1,292m.; ★ **OGD**; incorporated November 30, 2000; not reported in 2000 Census; ● 4,000

Hooper; CDP-Census Area Only; WEBER; **240** C-1; 🅿; ★ **OGD**; z 84315, z 84401; Ⓟ 3,468; © 3,926

Hoovers; RMC Place; PIUTE; ***240** J-7; elev. 5,810ft./1,771m.; mail Marysvale z 84750; rural

Howell; Inc. Place; BOX ELDER; **240** B-7; elev. 4,556ft./1,389m.; 🅿; z 84316; Ⓟ 237; © 221

Hoytsville; RMC Place; SUMMIT; ***240** D-9; elev. 5,761ft./1,756m.; mail Coalville z 84017; ● 50

Hunter; RMC Place; SALT LAKE; ***240** D-8; elev. 4,291ft./1,308m.; ★ **S.L.C.**; mail Salt Lake City z 84120; pop. incl. with West Valley City (Inc. Place)

Huntington; Inc. Place; EMERY; **240** H-10; elev. 5,791ft./1,765m.; 🅿; z 84528; Ⓟ 1,875; © 2,131

Huntsville; Inc. Place; WEBER; **240** C-8; elev. 4,929ft./1,502m.; 🅿; z 84317; Ⓟ 561; © 649

Hurricane; Inc. Place; WASHINGTON; **240** M-5; elev. 3,266ft./995m.; 🅿; z 84737; Ⓟ 3,915; © 8,250

Hyde Park; Inc. Place; CACHE; **241** L-17; elev. 4,560ft./1,390m.; 🅿; ★ **LOGN**; z 84318; Ⓟ 2,190; © 2,955

Hyrum; Inc. Place; CACHE; **240** B-8; elev. 4,706ft./1,434m.; 🅿; ★ **LOGN**; z 84319; Ⓟ 4,829; © 6,316

I

Ibapah; RMC Place; TOOELE; **240** F-4; elev. 5,288ft./1,612m.; 🅿; z 84034; ● 60

Indianola; RMC Place; SANPETE; ***240** G-9; elev. 5,957ft./1,816m.; mail Fairview z 84629; ● 30

Intermountain Indian School; BOX ELDER; see Bushnell (RMC Place)

Ioka; RMC Place; DUCHESNE; ***241** F-12; elev. 5,356ft./1,633m.; mail Roosevelt z 84066; ● 50

IRON; **240** K-5; Ⓟ 20,789; © 33,779; ◆ 46,776

Ivins; Inc. Place; WASHINGTON; **240** M-4; elev. 3,080ft./939m.; 🅿; z 84738; Ⓟ 1,630; © 4,450

J

Jensen; RMC Place; UINTAH; **241** E-13; elev. 4,739ft./1,444m.; 🅿; z 84035; ● 500

Jerusalem; RMC Place; SANPETE; ***240** G-8; mail Moroni z 84646; rural

Joseph; Inc. Place; SEVIER; **240** J-7; elev. 5,435ft./1,657m.; 🅿; z 84739; Ⓟ 198; © 269

JUAB; **240** G-6; Ⓟ 5,817; © 8,238; ◆ 10,447

Junction; Inc. Place; ⊡ PIUTE; **240** K-7; elev. 6,002ft./1,829m.; 🅿; z 84740; Ⓟ 132; © 177

K

Kamas; Inc. Place; SUMMIT; **240** E-9; elev. 6,480ft./1,975m.; 🅿; z 84036; Ⓟ 1,061; © 1,274

Kanab; Inc. Place; ⊡ KANE; **240** N-7; elev. 4,909ft./1,496m.; 🅿 🅷; z 84741; Ⓟ 3,289; © 3,564

Kanarraville; Inc. Place; IRON; **240** M-5; elev. 5,541ft./1,689m.; 🅿; z 84742; Ⓟ 228; © 311

KANE; **240** M-8; Ⓟ 5,169; © 6,046; ◆ 6,707

Kanosh; Inc. Place; MILLARD; **240** I-7; elev. 5,015ft./1,529m.; 🅿; z 84637; Ⓟ 386; © 485

Kaysville; Inc. Place; DAVIS; **240** C-8; elev. 4,349ft./1,326m.; 🅿; ★ **S.L.C.**; z 84037; Ⓟ 13,961; © 20,351; ◆ 26,759

Kearns; CDP; SALT LAKE; **241** H-17; elev. 4,570ft./1,393m.; 🅿; ★ **S.L.C.**; z 84118; Ⓟ 28,374; © 33,659; ◆ 40,022

Keetley; RMC Place; WASATCH; ***240** E-9; elev. 6,069ft./1,850m.; mail Heber City z 84032; rural

Kelton; RMC Place; BOX ELDER; ***240** B-6; mail Snowville z 84336; rural

Kenilworth; RMC Place; CARBON; **240** G-10; elev. 6,520ft./1,987m.; 🅿; z 84529; ● 230

Kimball Junction; RMC Place; SUMMIT; ***240** D-9; mail Park City z 84098; ● 30

Kingston; Inc. Place; PIUTE; **240** K-7; elev. 6,012ft./1,832m.; 🅿; z 84743; Ⓟ 134; © 142

Koosharem; Inc. Place; SEVIER; **240** J-8; elev. 6,914ft./2,107m.; 🅿; z 84744; Ⓟ 266; © 276

L

Lake Point; RMC Place; TOOELE; ***240** D-7; elev. 4,243ft./1,293m.; 🅿; z 84074; ● 50

Lake Powell; RMC Place; SAN JUAN; 🅿; z 84533; ● 30

Lake Shore; CDP; UTAH; ***240** F-8; ★ **PRVO-**; mail Provo z 84601, Spanish Fork z 84660; © 755

Lakeside Resort; RMC Place; SEVIER; ***240** J-8; mail Richfield z 84701; summer pop. 100

Laketown; Inc. Place; RICH; **240** A-9; elev. 5,988ft./1,825m.; 🅿; z 84038; Ⓟ 261; © 188

Lakeview; RMC Place; UTAH; **240** H-1; ★ **PRVO-**; mail Orem z 84058, Provo z 84604; ● 100

Lapoint; RMC Place; UINTAH; **241** E-12; elev. 5,562ft./1,695m.; 🅿; z 84039; ● 350

La Sal; CDP; SAN JUAN; **241** K-13; elev. 6,960ft./2,121m.; 🅿; z 84530; © 339

La Sal Junction; RMC Place; SAN JUAN; **241** K-13; mail La Sal z 84530

La Verkin; Inc. Place; WASHINGTON; **240** M-5; elev. 3,202ft./976m.; 🅿; z 84745; Ⓟ 1,771; © 3,392

Lawrence; RMC Place; EMERY; ***240** H-10; mail Castle Dale z 84513, Huntington z 84528; ● 50

Layton; Inc. Place; DAVIS; **240** C-8; elev. 4,360ft./1,329m.; 🅿 🅷 ■; ★ **OGD**; z 84040-41; Ⓟ 41,784; © 58,474; ◆ 74,452

Leamington; Inc. Place; MILLARD; **240** G-7; elev. 4,720ft./1,439m.; 🅿; z 84638; Ⓟ 253; © 217

Leeds; Inc. Place; WASHINGTON; **240** M-5; elev. 3,460ft./1,055m.; 🅿; z 84746; Ⓟ 254; © 547

Leeton; RMC Place; UINTAH; ***241** E-12; mail Roosevelt z 84066; rural

Lehi; Inc. Place; UTAH; **240** E-8; elev. 4,562ft./1,390m.; 🅿; ★ **PRVO-**; z 84005, z 84043, z 84045; Ⓟ 8,475; © 19,028; ◆ 35,653

Leland; RMC Place; UTAH; ***240** F-8; elev. 4,560ft./1,390m.; ★ **PRVO-**; mail Spanish Fork z 84660; ● 150

Leota; RMC Place; UINTAH; ***241** F-12; elev. 4,900ft./1,494m.; mail Randlett z 84063; rural

Levan; Inc. Place; JUAB; **240** G-8; elev. 5,314ft./1,620m.; 🅿; z 84639; Ⓟ 416; © 688

Lewiston (Presto); Inc. Place; CACHE; **240** A-8; elev. 4,506ft./1,373m.; 🅿; z 84320; Ⓟ 1,532; © 1,877

Liberty; RMC Place; WEBER; ***240** C-8; elev. 5,119ft./1,560m.; 🅿; z 84310; ● 50

Lincoln; RMC Place; TOOELE; ***240** E-7; mail Tooele z 84074; ● 150

Lindon; Inc. Place; UTAH; **240** F-1; elev. 4,640ft./1,414m.; 🅿; ★ **PRVO-**; z 84042; Ⓟ 3,818; © 8,363

Little Bonanza; RMC Place; UINTAH; ***241** F-13; mail Vernal z 84078

Little Cottonwood Creek Valley; CDP-Census Area Only; SALT LAKE; ***240** E-8; ★ **S.L.C.**; mail Salt Lake City z 84121, Sandy z 84092; Ⓟ 5,042; © 7,221; Ⓡ 7,202

Little Pinto Creek; RMC Place; IRON; ***240** L-5; mail Newcastle z 84756; rural

Littleton; RMC Place; MORGAN; ***240** D-8; mail Morgan z 84050; rural

Loa; Inc. Place; ⊡ WAYNE; **240** J-8; elev. 7,060ft./2,152m.; 🅿; z 84747; Ⓟ 444; © 525

Logan; Inc. Place; ⊡ CACHE; **240** B-8; elev. 4,535ft./1,382m.; 🅿 🅷 🅲 23,623 ■; ★ **LOGN**; z 84321-23, z 84341; Ⓟ 32,762; © 42,670; ◆ 64,415

Long Valley Junction; RMC Place; KANE; **240** M-7; elev. 7,454ft./2,272m.; mail Orderville z 84758

Lund; RMC Place; IRON; **240** K-5; elev. 5,081ft./1,549m.; mail Cedar City z 84720

Lyman; Inc. Place; WAYNE; **240** J-9; elev. 7,177ft./2,188m.; 🅿; z 84749; Ⓟ 198; © 234

Lynn; RMC Place; BOX ELDER; **240** A-4; mail Oakley z 83346; rural

Lynndyl; Inc. Place; MILLARD; **240** G-7; elev. 4,780ft./1,457m.; 🅿; z 84640; Ⓟ 120; © 134

M

Macomb Junction; RMC Place; SALT LAKE; ★ **S.L.C.**; pop. incl. with Salt Lake City (Inc. Place)

Madsen; RMC Place; BOX ELDER; ***240** B-8; elev. 4,297ft./1,310m.; mail Honeyville z 84314; pop. incl. with Honeyville (Inc. Place)

Maeser; CDP; UINTAH; **241** E-13; elev. 5,599ft./1,707m.; mail Vernal z 84078; Ⓟ 2,598; © 2,855

Magna; CDP; SALT LAKE; **241** G-16; elev. 4,300ft./1,311m.; 🅿; ★ **S.L.C.**; z 84044; Ⓟ 17,829; © 22,770; ◆ 27,071

Mammoth; RMC Place; JUAB; ***240** F-8; elev. 6,384ft./1,946m.; 🅿; z 84628 & mail Provo z 84601; ● 70

Manderfield; RMC Place; BEAVER; **240** J-6; mail Beaver z 84713

Manila; Inc. Place; ⊡ DAGGETT; **241** D-12; elev. 6,360ft./1,939m.; 🅿; z 84046; Ⓟ 207; © 308

Manti; Inc. Place; ⊡ SANPETE; **240** H-8; elev. 5,620ft./1,713m.; 🅿; z 84642; Ⓟ 2,268; © 3,040

Mantua; Inc. Place; BOX ELDER; **240** B-8; elev. 5,180ft./1,579m.; 🅿; z 84324; Ⓟ 665; © 791

Mapleton; Inc. Place; UTAH; **240** F-9; elev. 4,720ft./1,439m.; 🅿; ★ **PRVO-**; z 84664; Ⓟ 3,572; © 5,809

Marion; RMC Place; SUMMIT; ***240** D-9; mail Kamas z 84036; ● 100

Marriott; RMC Place; WEBER; **240** B-2; elev. 4,263ft./1,299m.; ★ **OGD**; mail Ogden z 84404; pop. incl. with Ogden (Inc. Place)

Marriott-Slaterville; Inc. Place; WEBER; ***240** C-8; ★ **OGD**; mail Ogden z 84401, z 84404; © 1,425

Martin; RMC Place; CARBON; ***240** G-10; mail Helper z 84526; pop. incl. with Helper (Inc. Place)

Marysvale; Inc. Place; PIUTE; **240** J-7; elev. 5,950ft./1,814m.; 🅿; z 84750; Ⓟ 364; © 381

Maxwell; RMC Place; CARBON; ***240** G-10; mail Price z 84501; ● 100

Mayfield; Inc. Place; SANPETE; **240** H-8; elev. 5,550ft./1,692m.; 🅿; z 84643; Ⓟ 438; © 420

Meadow; Inc. Place; MILLARD; **240** I-7; elev. 4,840ft./1,475m.; 🅿; z 84644; Ⓟ 250; © 254

Meadowville; RMC Place; RICH; ***240** A-9; elev. 6,006ft./1,831m.; mail Laketown z 84038

Mendon; Inc. Place; CACHE; **240** B-8; elev. 4,520ft./1,378m.; 🅿; z 84325; Ⓟ 684; © 898

Mexican Hat; CDP; SAN JUAN; **241** M-12; 🅿; z 84531; Ⓟ 259; © 88

Middleton; RMC Place; WASHINGTON; ***240** N-5; mail Saint George z 84770; pop. incl. with Saint George (Inc. Place)

Midvale; Inc. Place; SALT LAKE; **241** I-19; elev. 4,375ft./1,334m.; 🅿; ★ **S.L.C.**; z 84047; Ⓟ 11,886; © 27,029; Ⓡ 26,971; ◆ 31,015

Midway; Inc. Place; WASATCH; **240** E-9; elev. 5,569ft./1,697m.; 🅿; z 84049; Ⓟ 1,554; © 2,121

Milburn; RMC Place; SANPETE; ***240** G-9; elev. 6,367ft./1,941m.; mail Fairview z 84629; rural

Milford; Inc. Place; BEAVER; **240** J-6; elev. 4,957ft./1,511m.; 🅿 🅷; z 84751; Ⓟ 1,107; © 1,451

MILLARD; **240** I-6; Ⓟ 11,333; © 12,405; ◆ 11,873

Millcreek; CDP-Census Area Only; SALT LAKE; ***240** D-8; elev. 4,692ft./1,430m.; ★ **S.L.C.**; mail Salt Lake City z 84109; Ⓟ 32,230; © 30,377; ◆ 36,118

Mills; RMC Place; JUAB; ***240** H-8; elev. 4,934ft./1,504m.; mail Levan z 84639; rural

Mills Junction; RMC Place; TOOELE; mail Tooele z 84074; ● 155

Millville; Inc. Place; CACHE; ***240** B-8; elev. 4,600ft./1,402m.; 🅿; ★ **LOGN**; z 84326; Ⓟ 1,202; © 1,507

Milton; RMC Place; MORGAN; ***240** C-8; elev. 5,015ft./1,529m.; mail Morgan z 84050; ● 130

Minersville; Inc. Place; BEAVER; **240** K-6; elev. 5,275ft./1,608m.; 🅿; z 84752; Ⓟ 608; © 817

Moab; Inc. Place; ⊡ GRAND; **241** J-13; elev. 4,025ft./1,227m.; 🅿 🅷; z 84532; Ⓟ 3,971; © 4,779

Modena; RMC Place; IRON; **240** L-4; elev. 5,475ft./1,669m.; 🅿; z 84753; ● 100

Molen; RMC Place; EMERY; ***240** I-10; mail Ferron z 84523; rural

Mona; Inc. Place; JUAB; **240** G-8; elev. 4,916ft./1,498m.; 🅿; z 84645; Ⓟ 584; © 850

Monarch; RMC Place; DUCHESNE; ***241** E-12; elev. 5,925ft./1,806m.; mail Roosevelt z 84066; rural

Monroe; Inc. Place; SEVIER; **240** J-7; elev. 5,382ft./1,640m.; 🅿; z 84754 & mail Sevier z 84766; Ⓟ 1,472; © 1,845

Montezuma Creek; CDP; SAN JUAN; **241** M-13; located on Navajo Nation Ind. Res.; elev. 4,420ft./1,347m.; 🅿; z 84534; Ⓟ 345; © 507

Monticello; Inc. Place; ⊡ SAN JUAN; **241** L-13; elev. 7,066ft./2,154m.; 🅿 🅷; z 84535; Ⓟ 1,806; © 1,958

Moore; RMC Place; EMERY; **240** I-9; elev. 6,269ft./1,911m.; mail Ferron z 84523

Morgan; Inc. Place; ⊡ MORGAN; **240** D-8; elev. 5,064ft./1,544m.; 🅿; z 84050; Ⓟ 2,023; © 2,635

MORGAN; **240** C-8; Ⓟ 5,528; © 7,129; ◆ 8,934

Moroni; Inc. Place; SANPETE; **240** G-9; elev. 5,520ft./1,682m.; 🅿; z 84646; Ⓟ 1,115; © 1,280

Motoque; RMC Place; WASHINGTON; ***240** M-4; elev. 4,350ft./1,326m.; mail Santa Clara z 84765; ● 30

Mound City; RMC Place; WASATCH; mail Midway z 84049; ● 100

Mountain Green; RMC Place; MORGAN; ***240** C-8; 🅿; z 84050; ● 50

Mountain Home; RMC Place; DUCHESNE; **241** E-11; elev. 6,994ft./2,132m.; 🅿; z 84051; ● 120

Mount Carmel; RMC Place; KANE; ***240** M-6; elev. 5,920ft./1,804m.; 🅿; z 84755; pop. incl. with Orderville (Inc. Place)

Mount Carmel Junction; RMC Place; KANE; **240** M-6; mail Mount Carmel z 84755; pop. incl. with Orderville (Inc. Place)

Mount Emmons; RMC Place; DUCHESNE; ***241** E-11; mail Altamont z 84001; ● 100

Mount Ogden; RMC Place; WEBER; ★ **OGD**; mail Ogden z 84415; pop. incl. with Ogden (Inc. Place)

Mount Olympus; CDP-Census Area Only; SALT LAKE; ***240** D-8; ★ **S.L.C.**; mail Salt Lake City z 84117; Ⓟ 7,413; © 7,103

Mount Pleasant; Inc. Place; SANPETE; **240** G-9; elev. 5,924ft./1,806m.; 🅿 🅷; z 84647; Ⓟ 2,092; © 2,707

Murray; Inc. Place; SALT LAKE; **240** D-8; elev. 4,300ft./1,311m.; 🅿 🅷 🅲 520 ■; ★ **S.L.C.**; z 84107, z 84117, z 84121, z 84123-24, z 84157; Ⓟ 31,282; © 34,024; ◆ 47,921

Myton; Inc. Place; DUCHESNE; **241** F-12; elev. 5,084ft./1,550m.; 🅿; z 84052; Ⓟ 468; © 539

N

Naples; Inc. Place; UINTAH; **241** E-13; 🅿; z 84078; Ⓟ 1,334; © 1,300

Navajo Mountain; CDP; SAN JUAN; ***240** N-10; © 379

Navajo Nation Reservation; Indian Reservation; SAN JUAN; Reservation extends into AZ and NM; mail Window Rock z 86515; Ⓟ 4,787; © 6,046

Neola; CDP; DUCHESNE; **241** E-12; elev. 6,017ft./1,834m.; 🅿; z 84053; Ⓟ 511; © 533

Nephi; Inc. Place; ⊡ JUAB; **240** G-8; elev. 5,133ft./1,565m.; 🅿 🅷; z 84648; Ⓟ 3,515; © 4,733

Nerva; RMC Place; BOX ELDER; mail Willard z 84340; ● 440

Newcastle; RMC Place; IRON; **240** L-5; elev. 5,814ft./1,772m.; 🅿; z 84756; ● 300

New Harmony; Inc. Place; WASHINGTON; **240** M-5; elev. 5,306ft./1,617m.; 🅿; z 84757; Ⓟ 101; © 190

Newton; Inc. Place; CACHE; **240** A-8; elev. 4,525ft./1,379m.; 🅿; z 84327; Ⓟ 659; © 699

Nibley; Inc. Place; CACHE; ***240** B-8; elev. 4,553ft./1,388m.; 🅿; ★ **LOGN**; z 84321; Ⓟ 1,167; © 2,045

North Creek; RMC Place; BEAVER; ***240** J-7; mail Beaver z 84713; rural

North Logan; Inc. Place; CACHE; **241** M-18; elev. 4,680ft./1,426m.; 🅿; ★ **LOGN**; z 84341; Ⓟ 3,768; © 6,163

North Ogden; Inc. Place; WEBER; **240** C-8; elev. 4,480ft./1,366m.; 🅿; ★ **OGD**; z 84404, z 84414; Ⓟ 11,668; © 15,026

North Salt Lake; Inc. Place; DAVIS; **241** E-19; elev. 4,300ft./1,311m.; 🅿; ★ **S.L.C.**; z 84054; Ⓟ 6,474; © 8,749

North Snyderville Basin; CDP-Census Area Only; SUMMIT; ***240** D-9; © 1,821

Northwest; RMC Place; SALT LAKE; ★ **S.L.C.**; mail Salt Lake City z 84116; pop. incl. with Salt Lake City (Inc. Place)

Northwestern Shoshoni Reservation; Indian Reservation; BOX ELDER; © 0

O

Oak City; Inc. Place; MILLARD; **240** H-7; elev. 5,105ft./1,556m.; 🅿; z 84649; Ⓟ 587; © 650

Oak Creek; RMC Place; SANPETE; ***240** G-9; mail Fairview z 84629

Oakley; Inc. Place; SUMMIT; **240** D-9; elev. 6,440ft./1,963m.; 🅿; z 84055; Ⓟ 522; © 948

Oasis; RMC Place; MILLARD; ***240** H-7; elev. 4,597ft./1,401m.; 🅿; z 84624; ● 100

Officer; RMC Place; SALT LAKE; ★ **S.L.C.**; pop. incl. with Salt Lake City (Inc. Place)

Ogden; Inc. Place; ⊡ WEBER; **240** C-8; elev. 4,300ft./1,311m.; 🅿 🅷 🅲 18,718 ■; ★ **OGD**; z 84201, z 84244, z 84401-05, z 84407-09, z 84412, z 84414-15; Ⓟ 63,909; © 77,226; ◆ 92,782

Oljato; RMC Place; SAN JUAN; ***241** N-11; located on Navajo Nation Ind. Res.; mail Kayenta z 86033

Oljato-Monument Valley; CDP-Census Area Only; SAN JUAN; ***241** N-11; © 864

Olmstead; RMC Place; UTAH; ***240** E-8; elev. 4,828ft./1,472m.; ★ **PRVO-**; mail Provo z 84604; pop. incl. with Orem (Inc. Place)

Onaqui; TOOELE; see Rush Valley (Inc. Place)

One Hundred and One Rancho (101 Rancho); RMC Place; WASHINGTON; ***240** M-5; elev. 3,564ft./1,086m.; mail Virgin z 84779; pop. incl. with Virgin (Inc. Place)

101 Rancho; WASHINGTON; see One Hundred and One Rancho (RMC Place)

Ophir; Inc. Place; TOOELE; **240** E-7; elev. 6,500ft./1,981m.; 🅿; z 84071; Ⓟ 25; © 23

Oquirrh; CDP-Census Area Only; SALT LAKE; ***240** E-8; ★ **S.L.C.**; mail West Jordan z 84084; Ⓟ 7,593; © 10,390

Orangeville; Inc. Place; EMERY; **240** H-10; elev. 5,772ft./1,759m.; 🅿; z 84537; Ⓟ 1,459; © 1,398

Orderville; Inc. Place; KANE; **240** M-6; elev. 5,440ft./1,658m.; 🅿; z 84758; Ⓟ 422; © 596

Orem; Inc. Place; UTAH; **240** E-8; elev. 4,770ft./1,454m.; 🅿 🅷 🅲 23,305 ■; ★ **PRVO-**; z 84057-59, z 84097; Ⓟ 67,561; © 84,324; Ⓡ 84,108; ◆ 108,097

Ouray; RMC Place; UINTAH; **241** F-12; 🅿; z 84026 & mail Randlett z 84063; ● 40

P

Paiute (UT) Reservation; Indian Reservation; WASHINGTON, IRON, MILLARD, SEVIER; © 270

Pallas; RMC Place; SALT LAKE; ★ **S.L.C.**; mail Salt Lake City z 84107; pop. incl. with Murray (Inc. Place)

Palmyra; CDP; UTAH; ***240** F-8; elev. 4,522ft./1,378m.; ★ **PRVO-**; mail Spanish Fork z 84660; © 485

Panguitch; Inc. Place; ⊡ GARFIELD; **240** L-7; elev. 6,624ft./2,019m.; 🅿 🅷; z 84759; Ⓟ 1,444; © 1,623

Paradise; Inc. Place; CACHE; **240** B-8; elev. 4,880ft./1,487m.; 🅿; z 84328; Ⓟ 561; © 759

Paragonah; Inc. Place; IRON; **240** L-6; elev. 5,897ft./1,797m.; 🅿; z 84760; Ⓟ 307; © 470

Park City; Inc. Place; SUMMIT, WASATCH; **240** D-9; elev. 7,080ft./2,158m.; 🅿; z 84060, z 84068, z 84098; Ⓟ 4,468; © 7,371

Park Terrace; RMC Place; SALT LAKE; ***240** D-8; ★ **S.L.C.**; mail Salt Lake City z 84106

Park Valley; RMC Place; BOX ELDER; **240** A-5; elev. 5,543ft./1,690m.; 🅿; z 84329; ● 60

Parowan; Inc. Place; ⊡ IRON; **240** L-6; elev. 5,990ft./1,826m.; 🅿; z 84761; Ⓟ 1,873; © 2,565

Partoun; RMC Place; JUAB; ***240** G-4; elev. 4,818ft./1,469m.; 🅿; z 84083; rural

Payson; Inc. Place; UTAH; **240** F-8; elev. 4,648ft./1,417m.; 🅿 🅷; ★ **PRVO-**; z 84651, z 84655; Ⓟ 9,510; © 12,716

Penrose; RMC Place; BOX ELDER; ***240** B-7; 🅿; z 84337

Peoa; RMC Place; SUMMIT; **240** D-9; elev. 6,192ft./1,887m.; 🅿; z 84061; ● 150

Perry; Inc. Place; BOX ELDER; **240** B-8; elev. 4,460ft./1,359m.; 🅿; z 84302; Ⓟ 1,211; © 2,383

Peruvian Park; RMC Place; SALT LAKE; ***240** E-8; ★ **S.L.C.**; mail Sandy z 84093

Peter; CDP-Census Area Only; CACHE; ***240** B-8; © 230

Peterson; RMC Place; MORGAN; **240** C-8; mail Morgan z 84050; ● 150

Pickelville (Pickleville); RMC Place; RICH; ***240** A-9; elev. 5,940ft./1,811m.; mail Garden City z 84028; pop. incl. with Garden City (Inc. Place)

Pickleville; RICH; see Pickelville (RMC Place)

Pinecrest; RMC Place; SALT LAKE; ***240** D-8; elev. 6,600ft./2,012m.; ★ **S.L.C.**; mail Salt Lake City z 84108; ● 50

Pine Mountain; RMC Place; SUMMIT; mail Oakley z 84055; summer pop. 250

Pine Valley; RMC Place; WASHINGTON; **240** M-5; 🅿; z 84781; ● 200

Pinto; RMC Place; WASHINGTON; ***240** M-5; elev. 6,052ft./1,845m.; mail Cedar City z 84720, Newcastle z 84756; rural

Pintura; RMC Place; WASHINGTON; **240** M-5; elev. 4,100ft./1,250m.; 🅿; z 84720; ● 50

Pioneer; RMC Place; SALT LAKE; ★ **S.L.C.**; mail Salt Lake City z 84147; pop. incl. with Salt Lake City (Inc. Place)

PIUTE; **240** J-8; Ⓟ 1,277; © 1,435; ◆ 1,328

Plain City; Inc. Place; WEBER; **240** C-8; elev. 4,240ft./1,292m.; 🅿; ★ **OGD**; z 84404; Ⓟ 2,722; © 3,489

Pleasant Grove; Inc. Place; UTAH; **240** E-8; elev. 4,623ft./1,409m.; 🅿; ★ **PRVO-**; z 84062; Ⓟ 13,476; © 23,468; ◆ 33,576

Pleasant View; Inc. Place; WEBER; ***240** C-8; elev. 4,398ft./1,341m.; 🅿; ★ **OGD**; z 84404, z 84414; Ⓟ 3,603; © 5,632

Plymouth; Inc. Place; BOX ELDER; **240** A-8; elev. 4,480ft./1,366m.; 🅿; z 84330; Ⓟ 267; © 328

Pollard Junction; RMC Place; SALT LAKE; ★ **S.L.C.**; pop. incl. with Salt Lake City (Inc. Place)

Portage; Inc. Place; BOX ELDER; **240** A-7; elev. 4,441ft./1,354m.; 🅿; z 84331; Ⓟ 218; © 257

Portersville; MORGAN; see Porterville (RMC Place)

Porterville (Portersville); RMC Place; MORGAN; **240** D-8; mail Morgan z 84050; ● 90

Presto; CACHE; see Lewiston (Inc. Place)

Price; Inc. Place; ⊡ CARBON; **240** G-10; elev. 5,567ft./1,697m.; 🅿 🅷; z 84501; Ⓟ 8,712; © 8,402

Promontory; RMC Place; BOX ELDER; **240** B-7; mail Corinne z 84307; rural

Providence; Inc. Place; CACHE; **240** B-8; elev. 4,600ft./1,402m.; 🅿; ★ **LOGN**; z 84332; Ⓟ 3,344; © 4,377

Provo; Inc. Place; ⊡ UTAH; **240** F-8; elev. 4,549ft./1,387m.; 🅿 🅷 🅲 32,989 ■; ★ **PRVO-**; z 84601-06; Ⓟ 86,835; © 105,166; Ⓡ 105,439; ◆ 134,072

R

Randlett; CDP; UINTAH; **241** F-12; elev. 4,810ft./1,466m.; 🅿; z 84063; Ⓟ 283; © 224

Randolph; Inc. Place; ⊡ RICH; **240** B-9; elev. 6,289ft./1,917m.; 🅿; z 84064; Ⓟ 488; © 483

Redmond; Inc. Place; SEVIER; **240** I-8; elev. 5,104ft./1,556m.; 🅿; z 84652; Ⓟ 648; © 788

Red Rock; RMC Place; WASHINGTON; mail Saint George z 84790-91; pop. incl. with Saint George (Inc. Place)

Red Wash; RMC Place; UINTAH; ***241** F-13; mail Vernal z 84078; ● 30

Redwood; RMC Place; SALT LAKE; **241** G-18; ★ **S.L.C.**; mail Salt Lake City z 84119; pop. incl. with West Valley City (Inc. Place)

Relico; RMC Place; WEBER; mail Ogden z 84401; pop. incl. with Ogden (Inc. Place)

RICH; **240** B-9; Ⓟ 1,725; © 1,961; ◆ 2,247

Richfield; Inc. Place; ⊡ SEVIER; **240** I-8; elev. 5,330ft./1,625m.; 🅿 🅷; z 84701; Ⓟ 5,593; © 6,847

Richmond; Inc. Place; CACHE; **240** A-8; elev. 4,607ft./1,404m.; 🅿; z 84333; Ⓟ 1,955; © 2,051

Richville; RMC Place; MORGAN; ***240** D-8; elev. 5,118ft./1,560m.; mail Morgan z 84050

Riverdale; Inc. Place; WEBER; **240** C-2; elev. 4,377ft./1,334m.; 🅿; ★ **OGD**; z 84405; Ⓟ 6,419; © 7,656

River Heights; Inc. Place; CACHE; **241** N-17; elev. 4,560ft./1,390m.; 🅿; ★ **LOGN**; z 84321; Ⓟ 1,274; © 1,496

Riverside; CDP; BOX ELDER; **240** B-8; elev. 4,360ft./1,329m.; 🅿; z 84334; © 678

Riverside; RMC Place; CACHE; ***240** B-8; elev. 4,425ft./1,349m.; mail Smithfield z 84335; rural

Riverton; Inc. Place; SALT LAKE; **240** E-8; elev. 4,435ft./1,352m.; 🅿; ★ **S.L.C.**; z 84065, z 84095-96; Ⓟ 11,261; © 25,011; ◆ 35,602

Rockville; Inc. Place; WASHINGTON; **240** M-6; elev. 3,746ft./1,142m.; 🅿; z 84763; Ⓟ 182; © 247

Rocky Ridge; Inc. Place; JUAB; ***240** F-8; mail Mona z 84645; © 403

Roosevelt; Inc. Place; DUCHESNE; **241** E-12; elev. 5,100ft./1,554m.; 🅿 🅷; z 84066; Ⓟ 3,915; © 4,299

Roper; RMC Place; SALT LAKE; ***240** D-8; ★ **S.L.C.**; mail Salt Lake City z 84115; pop. incl. with South Salt Lake (Inc. Place)

Rosette; RMC Place; BOX ELDER; **240** A-5; elev. 5,679ft./1,731m.; mail Park Valley z 84329

Round Valley; RMC Place; RICH; **240** B-9; mail Laketown z 84038; rural

Roy; Inc. Place; WEBER; **240** C-8; elev. 4,525ft./1,379m.; 🅿; ★ **OGD**; z 84067, z 84401; Ⓟ 24,603; © 32,885; ◆ 42,230

Rubys Inn; GARFIELD; see Bryce Canyon City (Inc. Place)

Rush Valley (Onaqui); Inc. Place; TOOELE; **240** E-7; 🅿; z 84069; Ⓟ 339; © 453

S

Sage Creek Junction; RMC Place; RICH; ***240** B-9; elev. 6,260ft./1,908m.; mail Randolph z 84064; ● 50

Saint George; Inc. Place; ⊡ WASHINGTON; **240** N-4; elev. 2,761ft./842m.; 🅿 🅷 🅲 8,976 ■; z 84770-71, z 84790-91 & mail Dammeron Valley z 84783, Veyo z 84782; Ⓟ 28,502; © 49,663; ◆ 74,834

Salem; Inc. Place; UTAH; **240** F-8; elev. 4,600ft./1,402m.; 🅿; ★ **PRVO-**; z 84653; Ⓟ 2,284; © 4,372

Salem Hills; UTAH; see Elk Ridge (Inc. Place)

Salina; Inc. Place; SEVIER; **240** I-8; elev. 5,150ft./1,570m.; 🅿; z 84654; Ⓟ 1,943; © 2,393

SALT LAKE; **240** D-7; Ⓟ 725,956; © 898,387; Ⓡ 898,412; ◆ 1,068,197

Salt Lake City; Inc. Place; **STATE CAPITAL**; ⊡ SALT LAKE; **240** D-8; elev. 4,260ft./1,298m.; 🅿 🅷 🅲 41,198 ■; ★ **S.L.C.**; z 84101-28, z 84130-34, z 84136, z 84138-39, z 84141, z 84143-45, z 84147-48, z 84150-52, z 84157-58, z 84165, z 84170-71, z 84180, z 84184, z 84189-90, z 84199; Ⓟ 159,936; © 181,743; ◆ 195,661

Samak; CDP; SUMMIT; ***240** E-9; mail Kamas z 84036; © 161

Sandy; SALT LAKE; see Sandy City (Inc. Place)

Sandy City (Sandy); Inc. Place; SALT LAKE; **240** E-8; elev. 4,475ft./1,364m.; 🅷; ★ **S.L.C.**; mail Sandy z 84070, z 84090-94; Ⓟ 75,058; © 88,418; Ⓡ 88,551; ◆ 96,568

SAN JUAN; **241** L-12; Ⓟ 12,621; © 14,413; ◆ 15,335

SANPETE; **240** H-9; Ⓟ 16,259; © 22,763; ◆ 25,865

Santa Clara; Inc. Place; WASHINGTON; **240** N-4; elev. 2,800ft./853m.; 🅿; z 84765; Ⓟ 2,322; © 4,630

Santaquin; Inc. Place; UTAH; **240** F-8; elev. 4,960ft./1,512m.; 🅿; ★ **PRVO-**; z 84655; Ⓟ 2,386; © 4,834

Saratoga Springs; Inc. Place; UTAH; ***240** E-8; 🅿; z 84045 & mail Lehi z 84043; © 1,003

Scipio; Inc. Place; MILLARD; **240** H-8; elev. 5,305ft./1,617m.; 🅿; z 84656; Ⓟ 291; © 290

Scofield; Inc. Place; CARBON; **240** G-9; elev. 7,702ft./2,348m.; 🅿; z 84526; Ⓟ 43; © 28

Sevier; RMC Place; SEVIER; **240** J-7; elev. 5,540ft./1,689m.; 🅿; z 84766

SEVIER; **240** I-9; Ⓟ 15,431; © 18,842; ◆ 20,308

Sherwood Park; RMC Place; SALT LAKE; ***240** E-8; ★ **S.L.C.**; mail Sandy z 84070, z 84092-93; pop. incl. with Sandy City (Inc. Place)

Shivwits; RMC Place; WASHINGTON; **240** M-4; mail Santa Clara z 84765; ● 30

Sigurd; Inc. Place; SEVIER; **240** I-8; elev. 5,220ft./1,591m.; 🅿; z 84657; Ⓟ 385; © 430

Silver Creek Junction; RMC Place; SUMMIT; ***240** D-9; elev. 6,432ft./1,960m.; mail Park City z 84098; ● 100

Silver Fork; RMC Place; SALT LAKE; ***240** E-9; mail Salt Lake City z 84121; ● 230

Silverlake; SALT LAKE; see Brighton (RMC Place)

Silver Reef; RMC Place; WASHINGTON; ***240** M-5; mail Leeds z 84746; ● 110

Skull Valley Reservation; Indian Reservation; TOOELE; mail Grantsville z 84029; Ⓟ 13; © 31

Slaterville; RMC Place; WEBER; ***240** C-8; elev. 4,241ft./1,293m.; ★ **OGD**; mail Ogden z 84404; pop. incl. with Marriott-Slaterville (Inc. Place)

Smithfield; Inc. Place; CACHE; **240** A-8; elev. 4,595ft./1,401m.; 🅿; ★ **LOGN**; z 84335; Ⓟ 5,566; © 7,261

Snowbird; RMC Place; SALT LAKE; ***240** E-8; elev. 8,200ft./2,499m.; 🅿; z 84092; winter pop. 1,500; ● 100

Snowville; Inc. Place; BOX ELDER; **240** A-7; elev. 4,551ft./1,387m.; 🅿; z 84336 & mail Grouse Creek z 84313; Ⓟ 251; © 177

Snyderville; RMC Place; SUMMIT; ***240** D-9; 🅿; z 84098; ● 260

Soldier Summit; RMC Place; WASATCH, UTAH; **240** F-10; elev. 7,443ft./2,269m.; mail Provo z 84601

South Jordan; Inc. Place; SALT LAKE; **241** J-18; elev. 4,450ft./1,356m.; 🅿; ★ **S.L.C.**; z 84095 & mail Riverton z 84065; Ⓟ 12,220; © 29,437; ◆ 40,851

South Ogden; Inc. Place; WEBER; **240** C-8; elev. 4,440ft./1,353m.; 🅿; ★ **OGD**; z 84403, z 84405; Ⓟ 12,105; © 14,377

South Salt Lake; Inc. Place; SALT LAKE; **241** G-19; elev. 4,250ft./1,295m.; 🅿; ★ **S.L.C.**; z 84115, z 84119, z 84165 & mail Salt Lake City z 84105-07, z 84123, z 84190; Ⓟ 10,129; © 22,038; ◆ 24,960

South Snyderville Basin; CDP-Census Area Only; SUMMIT; ***240** D-9; © 3,636

South Weber; Inc. Place; DAVIS; **240** D-3; elev. 4,510ft./1,375m.; 🅿; ★ **OGD**; z 84403, z 84405; Ⓟ 2,863; © 4,260

South Willard; CDP-Census Area Only; BOX ELDER; ***240** C-8; © 586

Spanish Fork (Spanish Fork City); Inc. Place; UTAH; **240** F-9; elev. 4,600ft./1,402m.; 🅿; ★ **PRVO-**; z 84660; Ⓟ 11,272; © 20,246; ◆ 31,313

Spanish Fork City; UTAH; see Spanish Fork (Inc. Place)

Spanish Valley; CDP-Census Area Only; SAN JUAN; ***241** J-13; © 181

Spring City; Inc. Place; SANPETE; **240** H-9; elev. 5,826ft./1,776m.; 🅿; z 84662; Ⓟ 715; © 956

Springdale; Inc. Place; WASHINGTON; **240** M-6; elev. 3,800ft./1,158m.; 🅿; z 84767, z 84779; Ⓟ 275; © 457

Springdell; RMC Place; UTAH; ***240** E-9; ★ **PRVO-**; mail Provo z 84604; ● 120

Spring Glen; RMC Place; CARBON; **240** G-10; mail Helper z 84526; ● 900

Spring Lake; CDP; UTAH; ***240** F-8; ★ **PRVO-**; mail Payson z 84651; © 469

Springville; Inc. Place; UTAH; **240** F-9; elev. 4,573ft./1,394m.; 🅿; ★ **PRVO-**; z 84663-64; Ⓟ 13,950; © 20,424; ◆ 27,748

Standrod; RMC Place; BOX ELDER; **240** A-5; mail Malta z 83342; rural

Stansbury Park; CDP; TOOELE; **240** D-7; 🅿; z 84074; Ⓟ 1,049; © 2,385

Starr; RMC Place; JUAB; ***240** G-8; elev. 4,906ft./1,495m.; mail Mona z 84645; rural

Sterling; Inc. Place; SANPETE; **240** H-8; elev. 5,560ft./1,695m.; 🅿; z 84665; Ⓟ 191; © 235

Stockton; Inc. Place; TOOELE; **240** E-7; elev. 5,100ft./1,554m.; 🅿; z 84071; Ⓟ 426; © 443

Stoddard; RMC Place; MORGAN; ***240** C-8; elev. 5,003ft./1,525m.; mail Morgan z 84050; rural

Sugar House; RMC Place; SALT LAKE; ***240** D-8; ★ **S.L.C.**; mail Salt Lake City z 84106, z 84152; pop. incl. with Salt Lake City (Inc. Place)

Sugarville; RMC Place; MILLARD; **240** H-6; elev. 4,587ft./1,398m.; 🅿; z 84624; ● 30

Summit; RMC Place; IRON; **240** L-6; elev. 6,000ft./1,829m.; 🅿; z 84772; ● 200

SUMMIT; **240** D-9; Ⓟ 15,518; © 29,736; ◆ 36,253

Summit Park; CDP; SUMMIT; ***240** D-9; mail Park City z 84098; © 6,597

Summit Point; RMC Place; SAN JUAN; **241** K-14; mail Monticello z 84535; rural

Sunnyside; Inc. Place; CARBON; **241** G-11; elev. 6,520ft./1,987m.; 🅿; z 84539; Ⓟ 339; © 404

Sunset; Inc. Place; DAVIS; **240** C-8; elev. 4,567ft./1,392m.; 🅿; ★ **OGD**; z 84015; Ⓟ 5,128; © 5,204

Sutherland; RMC Place; MILLARD; **240** H-6; elev. 4,639ft./1,414m.; 🅿; z 84624; ● 120

Sutro; RMC Place; UTAH; mail Spanish Fork z 84660; ● 150

Swan Creek; RMC Place; RICH; ***240** A-9; mail Garden City z 84028; summer pop. 100

Syracuse; Inc. Place; DAVIS; **240** C-8; elev. 4,280ft./1,305m.; 🅿; ★ **OGD**; z 84075; Ⓟ 4,658; © 9,398; ◆ 15,404

T

Tabiona; Inc. Place; DUCHESNE; **240** E-10; elev. 6,517ft./1,986m.; 🅿; z 84072; Ⓟ 120; © 149

Talmage; RMC Place; DUCHESNE; ***241** E-11; elev. 6,830ft./2,082m.; 🅿; z 84073; ● 30

Taylor; RMC Place; WEBER; **240** B-1; 🅿; ★ **OGD**; z 84401; ● 50

Taylorsville; Inc. Place; SALT LAKE; **241** H-18; elev. 4,295ft./1,309m.; 🅿; ★ **S.L.C.**; z 84084, z 84118-19, z 84123; Ⓟ 51,500; © 57,439; ◆ 60,095

Teasdale; RMC Place; WAYNE; **240** K-9; elev. 7,120ft./2,170m.; 🅿; z 84773; ● 250

Terra; RMC Place; TOOELE; ***240** E-7; 🅿; z 84022; ● 50

Thatcher; RMC Place; BOX ELDER; ***240** B-7; 🅿; z 84337; ● 30

Thompson; GRAND; see Thompson Springs (RMC Place)

Thompson Springs (Thompson); RMC Place; GRAND; **241** I-12; elev. 5,145ft./1,568m.; mail Thompson z 84540; ● 60

Thompsonville; RMC Place; PIUTE; ***240** J-7; mail Marysvale z 84750; rural

Ticaboo; RMC Place; GARFIELD; **240** L-10; 🅿; z 84533; ● 50

Timber Lakes; CDP-Census Area Only; WASATCH; ***240** E-9; © 289

Tooele; Inc. Place; ⊡ TOOELE; **240** E-7; elev. 5,020ft./1,530m.; 🅿 🅷; z 84074; Ⓟ 13,887; © 22,502; ◆ 34,662

TOOELE; **240** E-6; Ⓟ 26,601; © 40,735; ◆ 59,395

Toquerville; Inc. Place; WASHINGTON; **240** M-5; elev. 3,360ft./1,024m.; 🅿; z 84774; Ⓟ 488; © 910

Torrey; Inc. Place; WAYNE; **240** K-9; elev. 6,843ft./2,086m.; 🅿; z 84775; Ⓟ 122; © 171

Town; RMC Place; WEBER; ★ **OGD**; mail Ogden z 84402; pop. incl. with Ogden (Inc. Place)

Tremonton; Inc. Place; BOX ELDER; **240** B-7; elev. 4,290ft./1,308m.; 🅿 🅷; z 84337; Ⓟ 4,264; © 5,592

Trenton; Inc. Place; CACHE; ***240** A-8; elev. 4,460ft./1,359m.; 🅿; z 84338; Ⓟ 464; © 449

Tridell; RMC Place; UINTAH; **241** E-12; elev. 5,630ft./1,716m.; 🅿; z 84076; ● 110

Tropic; Inc. Place; GARFIELD; **240** L-8; elev. 6,295ft./1,919m.; 🅿; z 84776; Ⓟ 374; © 508

Trout Creek; RMC Place; JUAB; **240** G-4; elev. 4,709ft./1,435m.; 🅿; z 84083; rural

Tselakai Dezza; CDP-Census Area Only; SAN JUAN; ***241** M-13; © 103

U

Ucolo; RMC Place; SAN JUAN; **241** L-14; mail Monticello z 84535

Uintah; Inc. Place; WEBER; **240** C-8; elev. 4,536ft./1,383m.; 🅿; ★ **OGD**; z 84403, z 84405; Ⓟ 760; © 1,127

UINTAH; **241** F-12; Ⓟ 22,211; © 25,224; ◆ 31,194

Uintah and Ouray Reservation; Indian Reservation; UINTAH, CARBON, DUCHESNE, GRAND, UTAH, WASATCH; mail Fort Duchesne z 84026; also location of Indian Agency; Ⓟ 16,909; © 19,182

Union; RMC Place; SALT LAKE; **241** I-19; ★ **S.L.C.**; mail Midvale z 84047; pop. incl. with Midvale (Inc. Place)

Unitah Highlands; RMC Place; WEBER; mail Ogden z 84403; ● 570

Upalco; RMC Place; DUCHESNE; **241** E-11; mail Bluebell z 84007; ● 70

Upton; RMC Place; SUMMIT; **240** D-9; elev. 6,182ft./1,884m.; mail Coalville z 84017

UTAH; **240** F-9; Ⓟ 263,590; © 368,536; Ⓡ 368,540; ◆ 520,596

Utah State University; RMC Place; CACHE; ★ **LOGN**; mail Logan z 84322; pop. incl. with Logan (Inc. Place)

Ute Mountain Reservation; Indian Reservation; SAN JUAN; Reservation extends into CO and NM; © 277

Utida; RMC Place; CACHE; ***240** A-8; elev. 4,571ft./1,393m.; mail Cornish z 84308

Uvada; RMC Place; IRON; ***240** L-4; elev. 5,658ft./1,725m.; mail Modena z 84753; rural

V

Val Verda; RMC Place; DAVIS; ***240** D-8; ★ **S.L.C.**; mail Bountiful z 84010; pop. incl. with Bountiful (Inc. Place); Ⓟ 3,712

Venice; RMC Place; SEVIER; ***240** I-8; 🅿; z 84701; ● 280

Vermillion; RMC Place; SEVIER; ***240** I-8; mail Sigurd z 84657; pop. incl. with Sigurd (Inc. Place)

Vernal; Inc. Place; ⊡ UINTAH; **241** E-13; elev. 5,336ft./1,626m.; 🅿 🅷; z 84078-79; Ⓟ 6,644; © 7,714

Vernon; Inc. Place; TOOELE; **240** F-7; elev. 5,500ft./1,676m.; 🅿; z 84080; Ⓟ 181; © 236

Veyo; RMC Place; WASHINGTON; **240** M-4; elev. 4,471ft./1,363m.; 🅿; z 84782; ● 150

Vineyard; Inc. Place; UTAH; **240** H-1; elev. 4,543ft./1,385m.; 🅿; ★ **PRVO-**; z 84057-58; Ⓟ 151; © 150

Virgin; Inc. Place; WASHINGTON; **240** M-5; elev. 3,550ft./1,082m.; 🅿; z 84779; Ⓟ 229; © 394

Vivian Park; RMC Place; UTAH; ***240** E-9; mail Provo z 84604; ● 80

W

Wales; Inc. Place; SANPETE; **240** H-8; elev. 5,630ft./1,716m.; 🅿; z 84667; Ⓟ 189; © 219

Wallsburg; Inc. Place; WASATCH; **240** E-9; elev. 5,640ft./1,719m.; 🅿; z 84082; Ⓟ 252; © 274

Wanship; RMC Place; SUMMIT; **240** D-9; 🅿; z 84017; ● 200

Warren; RMC Place; WEBER; **240** A-1; elev. 4,219ft./1,286m.; ★ **OGD**; mail Ogden z 84404; ● 50

WASATCH; **240** E-10; Ⓟ 10,089; © 15,215; ◆ 21,527

Washington; Inc. Place; WASHINGTON; **240** N-5; elev. 2,761ft./842m.; 🅿; z 84780; Ⓟ 4,198; © 8,186

WASHINGTON; **240** M-5; Ⓟ 48,560; © 90,354; ◆ 148,274

Washington Terrace; Inc. Place; WEBER; **240** C-2; elev. 4,600ft./1,402m.; 🅿; ★ **OGD**; z 84405 & mail Ogden z 84403; Ⓟ 8,189; © 8,551

WAYNE; **240** K-10; Ⓟ 2,177; © 2,509; ◆ 2,581

WEBER; **240** C-8; Ⓟ 158,330; © 196,533; ◆ 238,235

Wellington; Inc. Place; CARBON; **240** G-10; elev. 5,413ft./1,650m.; 🅿; z 84542; Ⓟ 1,632; © 1,666

Wellsville; Inc. Place; CACHE; **240** B-8; elev. 4,535ft./1,382m.; 🅿; z 84339; Ⓟ 2,206; © 2,728

Wendover; Inc. Place; TOOELE; **240** D-4; elev. 4,300ft./1,311m.; 🅿; z 84083; Ⓟ 1,127; © 1,537

West Bountiful; Inc. Place; DAVIS; **241** D-19; elev. 4,260ft./1,298m.; 🅿; ★ **S.L.C.**; z 84010, z 84087; Ⓟ 4,477; © 4,484

West Haven; Inc. Place; WEBER; **240** B-1; 🅿; ★ **OGD**; z 84401 & mail Hooper z 84315, Roy z 84067; Ⓟ 2,172; © 3,976

West Jordan; Inc. Place; SALT LAKE; **240** E-8; elev. 4,370ft./1,332m.; 🅿 🅷; ★ **S.L.C.**; z 84081, z 84084, z 84088; Ⓟ 42,892; © 68,336; ◆ 105,427

West Mountain; CDP-Census Area Only; UTAH; ***240** F-8; ★ **PRVO-**; © 838

West Point; Inc. Place; DAVIS; **240** D-1; elev. 4,311ft./1,314m.; 🅿; ★ **OGD**; z 84015; Ⓟ 4,258; © 6,033

West Valley; SALT LAKE; see West Valley City (Inc. Place)

West Valley City (West Valley); Inc. Place; SALT LAKE; **240** D-8; 🅿 🅷 ■; ★ **S.L.C.**; z 84118-20, z 84128 & mail Salt Lake City z 84170; Ⓟ 86,976; © 108,896; ◆ 130,870

West Warren; RMC Place; WEBER; ***240** C-7; mail Ogden z 84404; ● 50

West Weber; RMC Place; WEBER; **240** B-1; mail Ogden z 84401, z 84404; ● 50

Wheelon (Cutler); RMC Place; BOX ELDER; ***240** A-8; mail Collinston z 84306; ● 30

White City; CDP; SALT LAKE; ***240** E-8; ★ **S.L.C.**; mail Sandy z 84070; Ⓟ 6,506; © 5,988; Ⓡ 5,991

White Mesa; CDP-Census Area Only; SAN JUAN; ***241** M-13; 🅿; z 84511; © 277

Whiterocks; CDP; UINTAH; **241** E-12; elev. 6,025ft./1,836m.; 🅿; z 84085; Ⓟ 312; © 341

Wilcken Siding; RMC Place; SALT LAKE; ★ **S.L.C.**; pop. incl. with Salt Lake City (Inc. Place)

Wildwood; RMC Place; UTAH; ***240** E-9; mail Provo z 84604; ● 60

Wildwood; RMC Place; WEBER; mail Ogden z 84401; ● 40

Willard; Inc. Place; BOX ELDER; **240** C-8; elev. 4,340ft./1,323m.; 🅿; z 84340; Ⓟ 1,298; © 1,630

Wilson; RMC Place; WEBER; ***240** C-8; ★ **OGD**; mail Ogden z 84401; pop. incl. with West Haven (Inc. Place)

Woodland; CDP; SUMMIT; ***240** E-9; mail Kamas z 84036; © 335

Woodland Hills; Inc. Place; UTAH; ***240** F-8; elev. 5,357ft./1,633m.; 🅿; ★ **PRVO-**; z 84653; Ⓟ 301; © 941

Woodruff; Inc. Place; RICH; **240** B-9; elev. 6,340ft./1,932m.; 🅿; z 84086; Ⓟ 135; © 194

Woods Cross; Inc. Place; DAVIS; **240** D-8; elev. 4,325ft./1,318m.; 🅿 🅷; ★ **S.L.C.**; z 84010, z 84087; Ⓟ 5,384; © 6,419

Woodside; RMC Place; EMERY; ***241** H-11; elev. 4,633ft./1,412m.; mail Green River z 84525; rural

Y

Yost; RMC Place; BOX ELDER; **240** A-5; elev. 5,980ft./1,823m.; mail Malta z 83342

Entries in **UPPERCASE** are counties.
Entries in **bold** have populations of 2,500 or more.
Names in parentheses are alternate names.

Inc. Place	Incorporated Place
RMC Place	Rand McNally Designated Place
CDP	Census Designated Place
MCD	Minor Civil Division

⊡	County Seat
▲	Minor Civil Division
elev.	Elevation
🅿	Post Office
🅷	Hospital
🅲	College
■	Principal Business Center
★	Ranally Metro Area (RMA) Abbreviation
z	Zip Code(s)
Ⓟ	Previous Census Population
Ⓡ	Revised Census Population
Ⓐ	Annexation Population
●	Rand McNally Population Estimate
©	Final Census Population
Ⓢ	Special Census Population
◆	Estimated Population

For additional definitions see Glossary, Volume 1, and Introduction, Volume 2.

VERMONT

CANADA ME Montpelier NY NH MA

Statistics

Total area (2000) — 9,614 square miles
Land area (2000) — 9,250 square miles
Water area (2000) — 364 square miles
Capital — Montpelier
Admitted as state — March, 1791

Maps

State maps can be found on pages 142-254 in Vol. 1
County Subdivision maps can be found on pages 255-271 in Vol. 1

Ranally Metro Areas (RMAs) and Abbreviations

Burlington, VT - BUR

Principal Places

Place Name	Place Type	County	Population
Burlington	Inc. Place	CHITTENDEN	◆ 38,966
Essex	MCD-Town	CHITTENDEN	◆ 20,417
Colchester	MCD-Town	CHITTENDEN	◆ 17,971
South Burlington	Inc. Place	CHITTENDEN	◆ 17,335
Rutland	Inc. Place	RUTLAND	◆ 17,178
Bennington	MCD-Town	BENNINGTON	◆ 15,000
Brattleboro	MCD-Town	WINDHAM	Ⓒ 12,005
Hartford	MCD-Town	WINDSOR	Ⓡ 10,385
Milton	MCD-Town	CHITTENDEN	◆ 10,318
Bennington	CDP	BENNINGTON	Ⓒ 9,168
Springfield	MCD-Town	WINDSOR	Ⓒ 9,078
Barre	Inc. Place	WASHINGTON	◆ 8,716

Place Name	Place Type	County	Population
Essex Junction	Inc. Place	CHITTENDEN	Ⓒ 8,591
Williston	MCD-Town	CHITTENDEN	◆ 8,454
Brattleboro	CDP	WINDHAM	Ⓒ 8,289
Middlebury	MCD-Town	ADDISON	Ⓒ 8,183
Montpelier	Inc. Place	WASHINGTON	Ⓒ 8,035
Barre	MCD-Town	WASHINGTON	Ⓒ 7,602
St. Johnsbury	MCD-Town	CALEDONIA	Ⓒ 7,571
Shelburne	MCD-Town	CHITTENDEN	◆ 7,430
Saint Albans	Inc. Place	FRANKLIN	◆ 7,179
Swanton	MCD-Town	FRANKLIN	◆ 6,704
Winooski	Inc. Place	CHITTENDEN	◆ 6,503
Saint Johnsbury	CDP	CALEDONIA	Ⓒ 6,319

Place Name	Place Type	County	Population
Middlebury	CDP	ADDISON	Ⓒ 6,252
Northfield	MCD-Town	WASHINGTON	Ⓒ 5,791
Lyndon	MCD-Town	CALEDONIA	Ⓒ 5,448
Jericho	MCD-Town	CHITTENDEN	◆ 5,414
Rockingham	MCD-Town	WINDHAM	Ⓒ 5,309
St. Albans	MCD-Town	FRANKLIN	◆ 5,217
Morristown	MCD-Town	LAMOILLE	Ⓒ 5,139
Newport	Inc. Place	ORLEANS	Ⓒ 5,005

County Business Data

County	FIPS Code	County Seat	Land Area (Sq. Mi.)	Census Population			Wholesale Trade		Manufacturing, 2002			
				4/1/2000	4/1/1990	% Change 1990-2000	Sales, 2002 ($1,000)	% Change 1997-2002	Establish-ments	Total Employees	Value Added ($1,000)	Ranally Mfg. Units
Addison	001	Middlebury	770	35,974	32,953	9.2	129,106	43.2	61	2,104	220,047	116
Bennington	003	Bennington, Manchester	676	36,994	35,845	3.2	(d)	(d)	82	2,654	233,551	124
Caledonia	005	St. Johnsbury	651	29,702	27,846	6.7	88,781	-50.5	58	1,765	139,399	74
Chittenden	007	Burlington	539	146,571	131,761	11.2	1,761,299	-4.0	221	18,105	2,608,551	1,380
Essex	009	Guildhall	665	6,459	6,405	0.8	(d)	(d)	16	791	40,768	22
Franklin	011	St. Albans	637	45,417	39,980	13.6	484,751	27.0	56	2,657	237,238	126
Grand Isle	013	North Hero	83	6,901	5,318	29.8	4,703	(d)	...	(d)	(d)	...
Lamoille	015	Hyde Park	461	23,233	19,735	17.7	48,825	-15.4	60	665	60,466	32
Orange	017	Chelsea	689	28,226	26,149	7.9	92,391	(d)	57	1,417	162,289	86
Orleans	019	Newport	698	26,277	24,053	9.2	65,379	(d)	45	1,445	153,797	81
Rutland	021	Rutland	933	63,400	62,142	2.0	303,703	39.1	117	4,046	299,899	159
Washington	023	Montpelier	689	58,039	54,928	5.7	533,604	(d)	149	3,150	571,364	302
Windham	025	Newfane	789	44,216	41,588	6.3	1,230,384	-1.1	105	2,520	243,415	129
Windsor	027	Woodstock	971	57,418	54,055	6.2	263,393	8.4	143	2,485	191,263	101
The State			**9,250**	**608,827**	**562,758**	**8.2**	**5,094,373**	**7.7**	**1,176**	**43,827**	**5,163,905**	**2,732**

(d) Data not available. Corresponding percentages or Ranally Manufacturing Units are estimates.
... Represents 0 or amount too minimal to be reported.

Administrative Divisions

Towns: Although all Vermont counties have towns, they may not cover the entire area of each county. Although legally incorporated, towns are not treated as incorporated places by the U.S. Census because the population often is scattered among several localities and rural areas rather than being concentrated in a single place.

Unincorporated County Subdivisions: Gores, Grants and Unorganized Towns do not possess governmental and taxing powers, and they are not listed in this index.

Cities and Villages: Incorporated cities do not form part of the townships which adjoin or surround them. Each of the incorporated villages, in contrast, legally forms part of one or more townships.

Index of Places and Counties

A

Adamant; RMC Place; WASHINGTON; ▲ East Montpelier, Calais; **242** E-5; elev. 1,044ft./318m.; 🅿; z 05640 & mail Newport z 05855; ● 60
Addison; RMC Place; ADDISON; ▲ Addison; **242** F-2; elev. 289ft./88m.; 🅿; z 05491; ● 110
Addison; MCD-Town; ADDISON; ***242** F-2; 🅿; z 05491; Ⓟ 1,023; Ⓒ 1,393
ADDISON; **242** F-3; Ⓟ 32,953; Ⓒ 35,974; ◆ 36,403
Albany; Inc. Place; ORLEANS; ▲ Albany; **242** C-6; elev. 956ft./291m.; 🅿; z 05820; Ⓟ 180; Ⓒ 165
Albany; MCD-Town; ORLEANS; ***242** C-6; 🅿; z 05820; Ⓟ 782; Ⓒ 840
Albany Center; RMC Place; ORLEANS; ▲ Albany; ***242** C-6; mail Irasburg z 05845; rural
Alburg (Alburgh); Inc. Place; GRAND ISLE; ▲ Alburg; **242** A-2; elev. 124ft./38m.; 🅿; z 05440; Ⓟ 436; Ⓒ 488
Alburg; MCD-Town; GRAND ISLE; ***242** A-2; 🅿; z 05440; Ⓟ 1,362; Ⓒ 1,952
Alburg Center; RMC Place; GRAND ISLE; ▲ Alburg; **242** B-2; mail Alburgh z 05440; ● 120
Alburgh; GRAND ISLE; see Alburg (Inc. Place)
Alburg Springs; RMC Place; GRAND ISLE; ▲ Alburg; **242** A-3; mail Alburgh z 05440; ● 110
Alfrecha; RMC Place; RUTLAND; ▲ Clarendon; ***242** I-3; elev. 556ft./169m.; mail North Clarendon z 05759; ● 50
Alpine Village; RMC Place; WASHINGTON; ▲ Warren; **242** F-4; mail Warren z 05674; ● 70
Ames Hill; RMC Place; WINDHAM; ▲ Marlboro; ***242** L-4; elev. 1,747ft./532m.; mail Marlboro z 05344; rural
Amsden; RMC Place; WINDSOR; ▲ Weathersfield; **242** I-5; elev. 597ft./182m.; mail Perkinsville z 05151; ● 60
Andover (Peaseville); RMC Place; WINDSOR; ▲ Andover; ***242** J-4; mail Chester z 05143; ● 125
Andover; MCD-Town; WINDSOR; ***242** J-4; 🅿; z 05143; Ⓟ 373; Ⓒ 496
Arlington; CDP; BENNINGTON; ▲ Sunderland, Arlington; **242** K-3; 🅿; z 05250; Ⓟ 1,311; Ⓒ 1,199
Arlington; MCD-Town; BENNINGTON; ***242** K-3; 🅿; z 05250; Ⓟ 2,299; Ⓒ 2,397
Arnold Bay; RMC Place; ADDISON; ▲ Panton; ***242** F-2; mail Vergennes z 05491; rural
Ascutney; RMC Place; WINDSOR; ▲ Weathersfield; **242** I-5; elev. 412ft./126m.; 🅿; z 05030; ● 260
Athens; RMC Place; WINDHAM; ▲ Athens; **242** K-5; 🅿; z 05143; ● 120
Athens; MCD-Town; WINDHAM; ***242** K-5; 🅿; z 05143; Ⓟ 313; Ⓒ 340
Avalon Beach; RMC Place; RUTLAND; ▲ Castleton; ***242** H-3; mail Hydeville z 05750
Averill; RMC Place; ESSEX; ▲ Norton, Averill; ***242** A-8; elev. 1,700ft./518m.; 🅿; z 05901; summer pop. 400; ● 20

B

Baileys Mills; RMC Place; WINDSOR; ▲ Reading; ***242** J-5; mail Reading z 05062; rural
Bakersfield; RMC Place; FRANKLIN; ▲ Bakersfield; **242** B-4; elev. 736ft./224m.; 🅿; z 05441; ● 370
Bakersfield; MCD-Town; FRANKLIN; ***242** B-4; 🅿; z 05441; Ⓟ 977; Ⓒ 1,215
Baltimore; MCD-Town; WINDSOR; ***242** J-5; 🅿; z 05143; Ⓟ 190; Ⓒ 250
Barnard; RMC Place; WINDSOR; ▲ Barnard; **242** H-5; elev. 1,335ft./407m.; 🅿; z 05031; ● 220
Barnard; MCD-Town; WINDSOR; ***242** H-5; 🅿; z 05031; Ⓟ 872; Ⓒ 958
Barnet; RMC Place; CALEDONIA; ▲ Barnet; **242** E-7; 🅿; z 05821; ● 150
Barnet; MCD-Town; CALEDONIA; ***242** E-7; 🅿; z 05821; Ⓟ 1,415; Ⓒ 1,690
Barnet Center; RMC Place; CALEDONIA; ▲ Barnet; ***242** E-7; mail Barnet z 05821; rural
Barnumtown; RMC Place; ADDISON; ▲ Monkton; ***242** E-3; mail New Haven z 05472; rural
Barnumville; RMC Place; BENNINGTON; ▲ Manchester; ***242** J-3; mail Manchester Center z 05255; rural
Barre; Inc. Place; WASHINGTON; **242** E-5; elev. 609ft./186m.; 🅿 🅷 ■; z 05641 & mail Williamstown z 05679; Ⓟ 9,482; Ⓒ 9,291; ◆ 8,716
Barre; MCD-Town; WASHINGTON; ***242** E-5; 🅿; z 05641 & mail Websterville z 05678, Williamstown z 05679; Ⓟ 7,411; Ⓒ 7,602
Barre Transfer; RMC Place; WASHINGTON; mail Montpelier z 05602; pop. incl. with Montpelier (Inc. Place)
Barton; Inc. Place; ORLEANS; ▲ Barton; **242** C-6; elev. 952ft./290m.; 🅿; z 05822, z 05839, z 05875; Ⓟ 908; Ⓒ 742
Barton; MCD-Town; ORLEANS; ***242** C-6; 🅿; z 05822, z 05839, z 05875; Ⓟ 2,967; Ⓒ 2,780
Bartonsville; RMC Place; WINDHAM; ▲ Rockingham; **242** J-5; mail Chester z 05143; ● 200
Basin Harbor; RMC Place; ADDISON; ▲ Ferrisburg; **242** E-2; mail Vergennes z 05491; ● 50
Bayside; RMC Place; CHITTENDEN; ▲ Colchester; ***242** D-3; ★ **BUR**; mail Winooski z 05404
Beanville; RMC Place; ORANGE; ▲ Randolph; **242** G-5; mail Randolph z 05060; ● 30
Beartown; RMC Place; BENNINGTON; ▲ Sandgate; ***242** J-3; mail Arlington z 05250; ● 40
Beaulieus Corner; RMC Place; FRANKLIN; ▲ Highgate; ***242** B-3; elev. 320ft./98m.; mail Highgate Center z 05459
Beebe Plain; RMC Place; ORLEANS; ▲ Derby; **242** A-7; 🅿; z 05823; ● 200
Beecher Falls; RMC Place; ESSEX; ▲ Canaan; **242** A-9; 🅿; z 05902; ● 350
Bellows Falls; Inc. Place; WINDHAM; ▲ Rockingham; **242** K-5; elev. 299ft./91m.; 🅿; z 05101; Ⓟ 3,313; Ⓒ 3,165
Belmont; RMC Place; RUTLAND; ▲ Mount Holly; **242** I-4; 🅿; z 05730; ● 300
Belvidere; LAMOILLE; see Belvidere Center (RMC Place)
Belvidere; MCD-Town; LAMOILLE; ***242** C-5; mail Belvidere Center z 05442, Waterville z 05492; Ⓟ 228; Ⓒ 294
Belvidere Center (Belvidere); RMC Place; LAMOILLE; ▲ Belvidere; **242** C-5; elev. 924ft./282m.; 🅿; z 05442 & mail Waterville z 05492; ● 60
Belvidere Corners; RMC Place; LAMOILLE; ▲ Belvidere; ***242** B-5; mail Belvidere Center z 05442, Waterville z 05492; rural
Belvidere Junction; RMC Place; LAMOILLE; ▲ Belvidere; ***242** C-4; mail Waterville z 05492
Bennington; CDP; ⊡ BENNINGTON; ▲ Bennington; **242** L-3; elev. 681ft./208m.; 🅿 🅷 🅲 1,079; z 05201; Ⓟ 9,532; Ⓒ 9,168
Bennington; MCD-Town; BENNINGTON; ***242** L-3; 🅿 🅲 1,079 ■; z 05201; Ⓟ 16,451; Ⓒ 15,737; ◆ 15,000
BENNINGTON; **242** K-3; Ⓟ 35,845; Ⓒ 36,994; ◆ 35,736
Bennington Center; BENNINGTON; see Old Bennington (Inc. Place)
Bennington College; RMC Place; BENNINGTON; mail Bennington z 05201; pop. incl. with North Bennington (Inc. Place)
Bennington Falls; BENNINGTON; see Paper Mill Village (RMC Place)
Benson; RMC Place; RUTLAND; ▲ Benson; **242** H-2; elev. 390ft./119m.; 🅿; z 05731, z 05743; ● 80
Benson; MCD-Town; RUTLAND; ***242** H-2; 🅿; z 05731, z 05743; Ⓟ 847; Ⓒ 1,039
Benson Landing; RMC Place; RUTLAND; ▲ Benson; ***242** H-2; mail Benson z 05731, Fair Haven z 05743; summer pop. 125
Berkshire; RMC Place; FRANKLIN; ▲ Berkshire; **242** A-4; mail East Berkshire z 05447; ● 125
Berkshire; MCD-Town; FRANKLIN; ***242** A-4; mail East Berkshire z 05447, Enosburg Falls z 05450; Ⓟ 1,190; Ⓒ 1,388
Berlin; WASHINGTON; see Berlin Corners (RMC Place)
Berlin; MCD-Town; WASHINGTON; ***242** E-5; 🅿; z 05602 & mail Barre z 05641; Ⓟ 2,561; Ⓒ 2,864
Berlin Corners (Berlin); RMC Place; WASHINGTON; ▲ Berlin; **242** E-5; elev. 1,016ft./310m.; mail Barre z 05641, Montpelier z 05602, Northfield z 05663; ● 360
Bethel; RMC Place; WINDSOR; ▲ Bethel; **242** G-5; elev. 543ft./166m.; 🅿; z 05032; ● 970
Bethel; MCD-Town; WINDSOR; ***242** G-5; 🅿; z 05032; Ⓟ 1,866; Ⓒ 1,968
Bethel Gilead; RMC Place; WINDSOR; ▲ Bethel; ***242** G-4; elev. 907ft./276m.; mail Randolph z 05060; ● 100
Binghamville; RMC Place; FRANKLIN; ▲ Fletcher; ***242** C-4; mail Cambridge z 05444; ● 100
Birdport (Bridport); RMC Place; ADDISON; ▲ Bridport; **242** F-2; mail Bridport z 05734; ● 180
Bliss Pond; RMC Place; WASHINGTON; ▲ Calais; ***242** E-5; mail Adamant z 05640; ● 70
Blissville; RMC Place; RUTLAND; ▲ Castleton; **242** H-2; elev. 433ft./132m.; mail Poultney z 05764; ● 110
Bloomfield; RMC Place; ESSEX; ▲ Bloomfield; **242** C-8; elev. 912ft./278m.; 🅿; z 05905 & mail North Stratford z 03590; ● 120
Bloomfield; MCD-Town; ESSEX; ***242** B-8; 🅿; z 05905 & mail North Stratford z 03590; Ⓟ 253; Ⓒ 261
Blossoms Corners; RMC Place; RUTLAND; ▲ Pawlet; ***242** I-3; elev. 428ft./130m.; mail West Pawlet z 05775
Bolton; RMC Place; CHITTENDEN; ▲ Bolton; **242** D-4; elev. 346ft./105m.; mail Waterbury z 05676; ● 100
Bolton; MCD-Town; CHITTENDEN; ***242** D-4; mail Waterbury z 05676; Ⓟ 971; Ⓒ 971
Boltonville; RMC Place; ORANGE; ▲ Newbury; ***242** E-7; mail Wells River z 05081
Bomoseen (Lake Bomoseen); RMC Place; RUTLAND; ▲ Castleton; **242** H-3; elev. 427ft./130m.; 🅿; z 05732; ● 250
Bondville; RMC Place; BENNINGTON; ▲ Winhall; **242** K-4; 🅿; z 05340; ● 150
Bordoville; RMC Place; FRANKLIN; ▲ Enosburg; **242** B-4; mail Enosburg Falls z 05450; ● 20
Bowlsville; RMC Place; RUTLAND; ▲ Mount Holly; **242** I-4; mail East Wallingford z 05742; ● 50
Bradford; RMC Place; ORANGE; ▲ Bradford; **242** F-7; 🅿; z 05033; former incorporated place; merged into Bradford December 1, 2004; Ⓟ 672; ● 970; Ⓒ 815
Bradford; MCD-Town; ORANGE; ***242** F-6; 🅿; z 05033; Ⓟ 2,522; Ⓒ 2,619
Bradford Center; RMC Place; ORANGE; ▲ Bradford; ***242** F-6; mail Bradford z 05033; rural
Bragg; RMC Place; WINDSOR; ▲ Norwich; ***242** H-6; elev. 954ft./291m.; mail Norwich z 05055; rural
Braintree; ORANGE; see West Braintree (RMC Place)
Braintree; MCD-Town; ORANGE; ***242** G-4; 🅿; z 05060; Ⓟ 1,174; Ⓒ 1,194
Braintree Hill; RMC Place; ORANGE; ▲ Braintree; ***242** G-4; mail Randolph z 05060
Brandon; CDP; RUTLAND; ▲ Brandon; **242** G-3; elev. 431ft./131m.; 🅿; z 05733; Ⓟ 1,902; Ⓒ 1,684
Brandon; MCD-Town; RUTLAND; ***242** G-3; 🅿; z 05733; Ⓟ 4,223; Ⓒ 3,917
Brattleboro; CDP; WINDHAM; ▲ Brattleboro; **242** L-5; elev. 240ft./73m.; 🅿 🅷 🅲 1,575; z 05301-04; Ⓟ 8,612; Ⓒ 8,289
Brattleboro; MCD-Town; WINDHAM; ***242** L-5; 🅿 🅲 1,575; z 05301-04; Ⓟ 12,241; Ⓒ 12,005
Brattleboro Center; RMC Place; WINDHAM; ▲ Brattleboro; mail Brattleboro z 05301
Bread Loaf; RMC Place; ADDISON; ▲ Ripton; ***242** G-3; 🅿; z 05753
Bridgewater; RMC Place; WINDSOR; ▲ Bridgewater; **242** H-5; 🅿; z 05034; ● 300
Bridgewater; MCD-Town; WINDSOR; ***242** H-5; 🅿; z 05034; Ⓟ 895; Ⓒ 980
Bridgewater Center; RMC Place; WINDSOR; ▲ Bridgewater; **242** H-5; elev. 957ft./292m.; mail Bridgewater Corners z 05035; ● 60
Bridgewater Corners; RMC Place; WINDSOR; ▲ Bridgewater; **242** H-5; elev. 854ft./260m.; 🅿; z 05035; ● 150
Bridport; ADDISON; see Birdport (RMC Place)
Bridport; MCD-Town; ADDISON; ***242** F-2; 🅿; z 05734; Ⓟ 1,137; Ⓒ 1,235
Brighton; MCD-Town; ESSEX; ***242** B-7; mail Island Pond z 05846; Ⓟ 1,562; Ⓒ 1,260
Brimstone Corner; RMC Place; ORANGE; ▲ West Fairlee, Vershire; ***242** G-6; elev. 777ft./237m.; mail West Fairlee z 05083
Brimstone Corners; RMC Place; RUTLAND; ▲ Pawlet; ***242** I-3; elev. 1,020ft./311m.; mail Pawlet z 05761; rural
Bristol; RMC Place; ADDISON; ▲ Bristol; **242** F-3; elev. 571ft./174m.; 🅿; z 05443; Ⓟ 1,801
Bristol; MCD-Town; ADDISON; ***242** F-3; 🅿; z 05443; Ⓟ 3,762; Ⓒ 3,788
Brockways Mills; RMC Place; WINDHAM; ▲ Rockingham; ***242** J-5; elev. 463ft./141m.; mail Chester z 05143, Springfield z 05156; ● 230
Brookfield; RMC Place; ORANGE; ▲ Brookfield; **242** F-5; elev. 1,276ft./389m.; 🅿; z 05036; ● 130
Brookfield; MCD-Town; ORANGE; ***242** F-5; 🅿; z 05036; Ⓟ 1,089; Ⓒ 1,222
Brookfield Center; RMC Place; ORANGE; ▲ Brookfield; ***242** F-5; mail Brookfield z 05036
Brookline; RMC Place; WINDHAM; ▲ Brookline; ***242** K-5; 🅿; z 05345; ● 30
Brookline; MCD-Town; WINDHAM; ***242** K-5; 🅿; z 05345; Ⓟ 403; Ⓒ 467
Brookside; RMC Place; CHITTENDEN; ▲ Westford; ***242** C-3; mail Essex Junction z 05452, Westford z 05494
Brookside; RMC Place; WINDHAM; ▲ Newfane; **242** L-4; mail South Newfane z 05351; ● 70
Brooksville; RMC Place; ADDISON; ▲ New Haven; ***242** F-3; mail Middlebury z 05753
Brownington; ORLEANS; see Brownington Village (RMC Place)
Brownington; MCD-Town; ORLEANS; ***242** B-7; 🅿; z 05860; Ⓟ 705; Ⓒ 885
Brownington Center; RMC Place; ORLEANS; ▲ Brownington; **242** B-6; elev. 1,014ft./309m.; mail Orleans z 05860; ● 60
Brownington Village (Brownington); RMC Place; ORLEANS; ▲ Brownington; **242** B-6; mail Orleans z 05860; ● 60
Brownsville; RMC Place; WINDSOR; ▲ West Windsor; **242** I-5; elev. 679ft./207m.; 🅿; z 05037; ● 100
Brunswick; MCD-Town; ESSEX; ***242** C-8; 🅿; z 05905 & mail North Stratford z 03590; Ⓟ 92; Ⓒ 107
Buck Hollow; RMC Place; FRANKLIN; ▲ Fairfax; ***242** C-3; ★ **BUR**; mail Fairfax z 05454; rural
Burke; CALEDONIA; see Burke Hollow (RMC Place)
Burke; MCD-Town; CALEDONIA; ***242** C-7; mail West Burke z 05871; Ⓟ 1,406; Ⓒ 1,571
Burke Hollow (Burke); RMC Place; CALEDONIA; ▲ Burke; **242** C-7; mail West Burke z 05871; ● 140
Burke Mountain; RMC Place; CALEDONIA; ▲ Burke; ***242** C-7; mail East Burke z 05832; ● 200
Burlington; Inc. Place; ⊡ CHITTENDEN; **242** D-3; elev. 113ft./34m.; 🅿 🅷 🅲 13,576 ■; ★ **BUR**; z 05401-03, z 05405-08; Ⓟ 39,127; Ⓒ 38,889; Ⓡ 39,824; ◆ 38,966
Burnham Hill; RMC Place; WASHINGTON; ▲ Woodbury; mail Hardwick z 05843; rural
Butlers Corners; RMC Place; CHITTENDEN; mail Essex Junction z 05452; ● 70
Butternut Bend; RMC Place; RUTLAND; ▲ Pawlet; ***242** J-3; mail Pawlet z 05761; rural
Button Bay; RMC Place; ADDISON; ▲ Ferrisburg; ***242** E-2; mail Vergennes z 05491; rural

C

Cabot; Inc. Place; WASHINGTON; ▲ Cabot; **242** D-6; elev. 1,064ft./324m.; 🅿; z 05647; Ⓟ 220; Ⓒ 239
Cabot; MCD-Town; WASHINGTON; ***242** D-6; 🅿; z 05647; Ⓟ 1,043; Ⓒ 1,213
Cadys Falls; RMC Place; LAMOILLE; ▲ Morristown; **242** C-5; elev. 555ft./169m.; mail Morrisville z 05661; ● 200
Calais; WASHINGTON; see Maple Corner (RMC Place)
Calais; MCD-Town; WASHINGTON; ***242** E-5; 🅿; z 05648; Ⓟ 1,521; Ⓒ 1,529
CALEDONIA; **242** D-6; Ⓟ 27,846; Ⓒ 29,702; ◆ 30,061
Cambridge; Inc. Place; LAMOILLE; ▲ Cambridge; **242** C-4; elev. 455ft./139m.; 🅿; z 05444; Ⓟ 292; Ⓒ 235
Cambridge; MCD-Town; LAMOILLE; ***242** C-4; 🅿; z 05444; Ⓟ 2,667; Ⓒ 3,186
Cambridge Junction; RMC Place; LAMOILLE; ▲ Cambridge; ***242** C-4; elev. 462ft./141m.; mail Jeffersonville z 05464; ● 35
Cambridgeport; RMC Place; WINDHAM; ▲ Rockingham, Grafton; **242** K-5; 🅿; z 05141; ● 100
Campbell Corner; RMC Place; ORANGE; ▲ Thetford; ***242** G-6; mail Thetford Center z 05075; rural
Canaan; RMC Place; ESSEX; ▲ Canaan; **242** A-9; 🅿; z 05901, z 05903; ● 360
Canaan; MCD-Town; ESSEX; ***242** A-9; 🅿; z 05901, z 05903; Ⓟ 1,121; Ⓒ 1,078
Castleton; RMC Place; RUTLAND; ▲ Castleton; **242** H-3; elev. 439ft./134m.; 🅿 🅲 2,130; z 05735; ● 650
Castleton; MCD-Town; RUTLAND; ***242** H-3; 🅿 🅲 2,130; z 05735; Ⓟ 4,278; Ⓒ 4,367
Castleton Corners; RMC Place; RUTLAND; ▲ Castleton; ***242** H-3; mail Bomoseen z 05732; ● 350
Cavendish; RMC Place; WINDSOR; ▲ Cavendish; ***242** I-5; elev. 929ft./283m.; 🅿; z 05142; ● 350
Cavendish; MCD-Town; WINDSOR; ***242** I-5; 🅿; z 05142; Ⓟ 1,323; Ⓒ 1,470
Cavendish Center; RMC Place; WINDSOR; ▲ Cavendish; ***242** I-5; mail Cavendish z 05142; rural
Cedar Beach; RMC Place; CHITTENDEN; ▲ Charlotte; ***242** E-2; ★ **BUR**; mail Charlotte z 05445; summer pop. 80
Center Rutland; RMC Place; RUTLAND; ▲ Rutland; **242** H-3; elev. 533ft./162m.; 🅿; z 05736; ● 500
Centervale; CALEDONIA; see Saint Johnsbury Center (RMC Place)
Centerville; RMC Place; LAMOILLE; ▲ Hyde Park; ***242** C-5; mail Hyde Park z 05655
Centerville; RMC Place; WINDSOR; ▲ Hartford; ***242** H-6; mail Hartford z 05047; rural
Centre; ORLEANS; see Newport Center (RMC Place)
Charleston; MCD-Town; ORLEANS; ***242** B-7; mail West Charleston z 05872; Ⓟ 844; Ⓒ 895
Charlotte; RMC Place; CHITTENDEN; ▲ Charlotte; **242** E-2; elev. 169ft./52m.; 🅿; ★ **BUR**; z 05445; ● 350
Charlotte; MCD-Town; CHITTENDEN; ***242** E-3; 🅿; ★ **BUR**; z 05445; Ⓟ 3,148; Ⓒ 3,569; ◆ 3,841
Checkerberry; RMC Place; CHITTENDEN; ▲ Milton; **242** C-3; ★ **BUR**; mail Milton z 05468; ● 120
Chelsea; RMC Place; ⊡ ORANGE; ▲ Chelsea; **242** F-5; 🅿; z 05038; ● 500
Chelsea; MCD-Town; ORANGE; ***242** F-5; 🅿; z 05038; Ⓟ 1,166; Ⓒ 1,250; Ⓡ 1,240
Chelsea West Hill; RMC Place; ORANGE; ▲ Chelsea; ***242** F-5; elev. 1,455ft./443m.; mail East Randolph z 05041
Chester; RMC Place; WINDSOR; ▲ Chester; **242** J-5; elev. 623ft./190m.; 🅿; z 05143-44; ● 550
Chester; MCD-Town; WINDSOR; ***242** J-5; 🅿; z 05143-44; Ⓟ 2,832; Ⓒ 3,044
Chester-Chester Depot; CDP-Census Area Only; WINDSOR; ▲ Chester; ***242** J-5; mail Chester z 05143, Chester Depot z 05144; Ⓟ 1,057; Ⓒ 999
Chester Depot; RMC Place; WINDSOR; ▲ Chester; **242** J-5; 🅿; z 05144; ● 500
Chimney Corner; RMC Place; CHITTENDEN; ▲ Colchester; ***242** C-3; ★ **BUR**; mail Colchester z 05446; rural
Chimney Point; RMC Place; ADDISON; ▲ Addison; ***242** F-2; mail Vergennes z 05491; rural
Chipman Lake; RMC Place; RUTLAND; ▲ Tinmouth; ***242** I-3; mail Danby z 05739; ● 70
Chipmans Point; RMC Place; ADDISON; ▲ Orwell; ***242** G-2; mail Orwell z 05760
Chippenhook; RMC Place; RUTLAND; ▲ Clarendon; **242** I-3; mail West Rutland z 05777; ● 190
Chiselville; RMC Place; BENNINGTON; ▲ Sunderland; **242** K-3; mail Arlington z 05250, East Arlington z 05252; ● 140
Chittenden; RMC Place; RUTLAND; ▲ Chittenden; **242** H-4; 🅿; z 05737; ● 270
Chittenden; MCD-Town; RUTLAND; ***242** H-4; 🅿; z 05737; Ⓟ 1,102; Ⓒ 1,182
CHITTENDEN; **242** D-3; Ⓟ 131,761; Ⓒ 146,571; ◆ 153,259
Clarendon; RMC Place; RUTLAND; ▲ Clarendon; **242** I-3; mail North Clarendon z 05759; ● 270
Clarendon; MCD-Town; RUTLAND; ***242** I-3; mail North Clarendon z 05759; Ⓟ 2,835; Ⓒ 2,811
Clarendon Springs; RMC Place; RUTLAND; ▲ Clarendon; **242** I-3; 🅿; z 05777; ● 200
Cleveland Corner; RMC Place; LAMOILLE; ▲ Hyde Park; ***242** C-5; mail Morrisville z 05661; rural
Cloverdale; RMC Place; CHITTENDEN; ▲ Westford; ***242** C-4; elev. 640ft./195m.; mail Cambridge z 05444, Underhill z 05489; rural
Colbyville; RMC Place; WASHINGTON; ▲ Waterbury; **242** E-4; mail Waterbury z 05676
Colchester; RMC Place; CHITTENDEN; ▲ Colchester; **242** D-3; 🅿 🅲 2,438; ★ **BUR**; z 05439, z 05446, z 05449; ● 450
Colchester; MCD-Town; CHITTENDEN; ***242** D-3; 🅿 🅲 2,438; ★ **BUR**; z 05439, z 05446, z 05449; Ⓟ 14,731; Ⓒ 16,986; ◆ 17,971
Cold River; RMC Place; RUTLAND; ▲ Shrewsbury; ***242** I-4; elev. 1,368ft./417m.; mail Cuttingsville z 05738; ● 100
Concord; RMC Place; ESSEX; ▲ Concord; **242** D-7; elev. 859ft./262m.; 🅿; z 05824; ● 350
Concord; MCD-Town; ESSEX; ***242** D-8; 🅿; z 05824; Ⓟ 1,093; Ⓒ 1,196; Ⓡ 1,209
Concord Corner; RMC Place; ESSEX; ▲ Concord; ***242** D-7; mail Concord z 05824; ● 40
Cookville (Corinth); RMC Place; ORANGE; ▲ Corinth; **242** F-6; mail Corinth z 05039; ● 140
Copperfield; RMC Place; ORANGE; ▲ Vershire; ***242** G-6; mail Vershire z 05079; rural
Copper Flat; RMC Place; ORANGE; ▲ Strafford; ***242** G-6; mail South Strafford z 05070; rural
Corinth; ORANGE; see Cookville (RMC Place)
Corinth; MCD-Town; ORANGE; ***242** F-6; 🅿; z 05039; Ⓟ 1,244; Ⓒ 1,461
Corinth Center; RMC Place; ORANGE; ▲ Corinth; ***242** F-6; mail Corinth z 05039; rural
Corinth Corners; RMC Place; ORANGE; ▲ Corinth; ***242** F-6; elev. 1,507ft./459m.; mail Corinth z 05039; rural
Cornwall; RMC Place; ADDISON; ▲ Cornwall; **242** G-3; elev. 375ft./114m.; 🅿; z 05753; ● 100
Cornwall; MCD-Town; ADDISON; ***242** G-3; 🅿; z 05753; Ⓟ 1,101; Ⓒ 1,136
Coventry; RMC Place; ORLEANS; ▲ Coventry; **242** B-6; elev. 718ft./219m.; 🅿; z 05825; ● 200
Coventry; MCD-Town; ORLEANS; ***242** B-6; 🅿; z 05825; Ⓟ 806; Ⓒ 1,014
Craftsbury; RMC Place; ORLEANS; ▲ Craftsbury; **242** C-6; 🅿; z 05826; ● 160
Craftsbury; MCD-Town; ORLEANS; ***242** C-6; 🅿; z 05826; Ⓟ 994; Ⓒ 1,136
Craftsbury Common; RMC Place; ORLEANS; ▲ Craftsbury; **242** C-6; 🅿; z 05827; ● 180
Cream Hill; RMC Place; ADDISON; ▲ Shoreham; ***242** G-2; mail Shoreham z 05770; rural
Crystal Beach; RMC Place; RUTLAND; ▲ Castleton; ***242** H-3; mail Bomoseen z 05732
Cuttingsville; RMC Place; RUTLAND; ▲ Shrewsbury; **242** I-4; elev. 997ft./304m.; 🅿; z 05738; ● 120

D

Danby; RMC Place; RUTLAND; ▲ Mount Tabor, Danby; **242** J-3; 🅿; z 05739; ● 350
Danby; MCD-Town; RUTLAND; ***242** J-3; 🅿; z 05739; Ⓟ 1,193; Ⓒ 1,292
Danby Corners; RUTLAND; see Danby Four Corners (RMC Place)
Danby Four Corners (Danby Corners); RMC Place; RUTLAND; ▲ Danby; **242** J-3; mail Danby z 05739; ● 80
Danville; RMC Place; CALEDONIA; ▲ Danville; **242** D-6; 🅿; z 05828; ● 360
Danville; MCD-Town; CALEDONIA; ***242** D-7; 🅿; z 05828; Ⓟ 1,917; Ⓒ 2,211
Danville Center; RMC Place; CALEDONIA; ▲ Danville; ***242** D-7; mail Danville z 05828
Derby; ORLEANS; see Derby Center (Inc. Place)
Derby; MCD-Town; ORLEANS; ***242** B-7; 🅿; z 05829; Ⓟ 4,479; Ⓒ 4,604
Derby Center (Derby); Inc. Place; ORLEANS; ▲ Derby; **242** B-7; mail Derby z 05829; Ⓟ 684; Ⓒ 670
Derby Line; Inc. Place; ORLEANS; ▲ Derby; **242** A-7; elev. 1,029ft./314m.; 🅿; z 05830; Ⓟ 855; Ⓒ 776
Deweys Mills; RMC Place; WINDSOR; ▲ Hartford; ***242** H-6; mail Quechee z 05059; rural
Dorset; RMC Place; BENNINGTON; ▲ Dorset; **242** J-3; elev. 962ft./293m.; 🅿; z 05251; ● 600
Dorset; MCD-Town; BENNINGTON; ***242** J-3; 🅿; z 05251; Ⓟ 1,918; Ⓒ 2,036
Dover; RMC Place; WINDHAM; ▲ Dover; **242** L-4; mail East Dover z 05341; ● 100
Dover; MCD-Town; WINDHAM; ***242** L-4; mail East Dover z 05341; Ⓟ 994; Ⓒ 1,410
Downers; RMC Place; WINDSOR; ▲ Weathersfield; ***242** I-5; elev. 613ft./187m.; mail Perkinsville z 05151
Downingville; RMC Place; ADDISON; ▲ Lincoln; ***242** F-3; mail Bristol z 05443
Dows Crossing; RMC Place; CALEDONIA; ▲ Walden; ***242** D-6; mail East Hardwick z 05836
Dowsville; RMC Place; WASHINGTON; ▲ Duxbury; ***242** E-4; mail Moretown z 05660; rural
Dummerston; WINDHAM; see Dummerston Center (RMC Place)
Dummerston; MCD-Town; WINDHAM; ***242** L-5; 🅿; z 05301 & mail Putney z 05346; Ⓟ 1,863; Ⓒ 1,915
Dummerston Center (Dummerston); RMC Place; WINDHAM; ▲ Dummerston; ***242** L-5; mail Brattleboro z 05301, Putney z 05346; ● 60
Duxbury; RMC Place; WASHINGTON; ▲ Duxbury; **242** E-4; mail Waterbury z 05676; ● 190
Duxbury; MCD-Town; WASHINGTON; ***242** E-4; mail Waterbury z 05676; Ⓟ 976; Ⓒ 1,289

Entries in **UPPERCASE** are counties.
Entries in **bold** have populations of 2,500 or more.
Names in parentheses are alternate names.

Inc. Place	Incorporated Place
RMC Place	Rand McNally Designated Place
CDP	Census Designated Place
MCD	Minor Civil Division
⊡	County Seat
▲	Minor Civil Division
elev.	Elevation
🅿	Post Office
🅷	Hospital
🅲	College
■	Principal Business Center
★	Ranally Metro Area (RMA) Abbreviation
z	Zip Code(s)
Ⓟ	Previous Census Population
Ⓡ	Revised Census Population
Ⓐ	Annexation Population
●	Rand McNally Population Estimate
Ⓒ	Final Census Population
Ⓢ	Special Census Population
◆	Estimated Population

For additional definitions see Glossary, Volume 1, and Introduction, Volume 2.

E

Eagle Point; RMC Place; ORLEANS; ▲ Derby; mail Newport z 05855; summer pop. 100
East Albany; RMC Place; ORLEANS; ▲ Albany; ***242** C-6; elev. 1,177ft./359m.; mail Irasburg z 05845
East Alburg (East Alburgh); RMC Place; GRAND ISLE; ▲ Alburg; **242** A-3; mail Alburgh z 05440; ● 70
East Alburgh; GRAND ISLE; see East Alburg (RMC Place)
East Arlington; RMC Place; BENNINGTON; ▲ Arlington; **242** K-3; elev. 723ft./220m.; 🅿; z 05252; ● 620
East Barnard; RMC Place; WINDSOR; ▲ Barnard; **242** H-5; mail South Royalton z 05068; ● 30
East Barnet; CALEDONIA; see Inwood (RMC Place)
East Barre; RMC Place; WASHINGTON; ▲ Barre; **242** F-5; 🅿; z 05649; ● 700
East Berkshire; RMC Place; FRANKLIN; ▲ Berkshire; **242** B-4; elev. 440ft./134m.; 🅿; z 05447 & mail Enosburg Falls z 05450; ● 100
East Bethel; RMC Place; WINDSOR; ▲ Bethel; **242** G-5; mail Bethel z 05032; ● 200
East Braintree; RMC Place; ORANGE; ▲ Braintree; **242** F-5; mail Randolph z 05060; ● 50
East Brighton; RMC Place; ESSEX; ▲ Brighton; ***242** B-8; elev. 1,171ft./357m.; mail Island Pond z 05846; rural
East Brookfield; RMC Place; ORANGE; ▲ Brookfield; **242** F-5; mail Brookfield z 05036, East Randolph z 05041; ● 50
East Burke; RMC Place; CALEDONIA; ▲ Burke; **242** C-7; 🅿; z 05832; ● 250
East Cabot; RMC Place; WASHINGTON; ▲ Cabot; ***242** D-6; elev. 1,599ft./487m.; mail Cabot z 05647; rural
East Calais; RMC Place; WASHINGTON; ▲ Calais; **242** E-5; 🅿; z 05650 & mail Adamant z 05640; ● 230
East Cambridge; RMC Place; LAMOILLE; ▲ Cambridge; ***242** C-4; mail Jeffersonville z 05464; rural
East Charleston; RMC Place; ORLEANS; ▲ Charleston; **242** B-7; 🅿; z 05833; ● 140
East Charlotte; RMC Place; CHITTENDEN; ▲ Charlotte; ***242** E-3; ★ **BUR**; mail Charlotte z 05445
East Clarendon; RMC Place; RUTLAND; ▲ Clarendon; ***242** I-4; mail North Clarendon z 05759; ● 250
East Concord (Mayo); RMC Place; ESSEX; ▲ Concord; **242** D-8; elev. 877ft./267m.; 🅿; z 05906; ● 150
East Corinth; RMC Place; ORANGE; ▲ Corinth; **242** F-6; 🅿; z 05040, z 05076; ● 150
East Craftsbury; RMC Place; ORLEANS; ▲ Craftsbury; ***242** C-6; mail Craftsbury z 05826
East Dorset; RMC Place; BENNINGTON; ▲ Dorset; **242** J-3; elev. 790ft./241m.; 🅿; z 05253; ● 350
East Dover; RMC Place; WINDHAM; ▲ Dover; **242** L-4; 🅿; z 05341; ● 250
East Dummerston; RMC Place; WINDHAM; ▲ Dummerston; **242** L-5; mail Putney z 05346; ● 200
East Enosburg; RMC Place; FRANKLIN; ▲ Enosburg; ***242** B-4; mail Enosburg Falls z 05450; rural
East Fairfield; RMC Place; FRANKLIN; ▲ Fairfield; **242** B-4; elev. 420ft./128m.; 🅿; z 05448; ● 160
East Fletcher; RMC Place; FRANKLIN; ▲ Fletcher; **242** C-4; mail Jeffersonville z 05464; ● 25
East Franklin; RMC Place; FRANKLIN; ▲ Franklin, Berkshire; **242** A-4; mail Franklin z 05457; ● 80
East Granville; RMC Place; ADDISON; ▲ Granville; **242** F-4; elev. 848ft./258m.; mail Roxbury z 05669; ● 70
East Hardwick; RMC Place; CALEDONIA; ▲ Hardwick; **242** D-6; 🅿; z 05836; ● 170
East Haven; RMC Place; ESSEX; ▲ East Haven; **242** C-7; 🅿; z 05837; ● 75
East Haven; MCD-Town; ESSEX; ***242** C-8; 🅿; z 05837; Ⓟ 269; © 301
East Highgate; RMC Place; FRANKLIN; ▲ Highgate; **242** B-3; mail Highgate Center z 05459; ● 130
East Hubbardton; RMC Place; RUTLAND; ▲ Hubbardton; **242** H-3; elev. 950ft./290m.; mail Castleton z 05735; ● 70
East Jamaica; RMC Place; WINDHAM; ▲ Jamaica; **242** K-4; elev. 562ft./171m.; mail Jamaica z 05343; ● 150
East Johnson; RMC Place; LAMOILLE; ▲ Johnson; **242** C-5; elev. 584ft./178m.; mail Johnson z 05656; ● 55
East Kansas; RMC Place; BENNINGTON; ▲ Sunderland; ***242** K-3; mail East Arlington z 05252; ● 50
East Lyndon; RMC Place; CALEDONIA; ▲ Lyndon; ***242** D-7; mail Lyndonville z 05851; ● 120
East Middlebury; RMC Place; ADDISON; ▲ Middlebury; **242** G-3; elev. 425ft./130m.; 🅿; z 05740 & mail Ripton z 05766; ● 500
East Monkton; RMC Place; ADDISON; ▲ Monkton; ***242** E-3; elev. 523ft./159m.; mail Bristol z 05443
East Montpelier; RMC Place; WASHINGTON; ▲ East Montpelier; **242** E-5; elev. 728ft./222m.; 🅿; z 05651 & mail Plainfield z 05667; ● 600
East Montpelier; MCD-Town; WASHINGTON; ***242** E-5; 🅿; z 05651 & mail Plainfield z 05667; Ⓟ 2,239; © 2,578
East Montpelier Center; RMC Place; WASHINGTON; ▲ East Montpelier; ***242** E-5; mail Montpelier z 05602; ● 120
East Orange; RMC Place; ORANGE; ▲ Orange; **242** F-6; elev. 1,219ft./372m.; 🅿; z 05086; ● 70
East Peacham; RMC Place; CALEDONIA; ▲ Peacham; **242** E-6; elev. 984ft./300m.; mail Peacham z 05862; ● 60
East Pittsford; RMC Place; RUTLAND; ▲ Rutland, Pittsford; ***242** H-4; elev. 1,008ft./307m.; mail Rutland z 05701; ● 50
East Poultney; RMC Place; RUTLAND; ▲ Poultney; **242** I-3; elev. 514ft./157m.; 🅿; z 05741; ● 500
East Putney; RMC Place; WINDHAM; ▲ Putney; ***242** K-5; mail Putney z 05346
East Randolph; RMC Place; ORANGE; ▲ Randolph; **242** G-5; elev. 606ft./185m.; 🅿; z 05041; ● 140
East Richford; RMC Place; FRANKLIN; **242** A-5; mail Richford z 05476; ● 100
East Roxbury; RMC Place; WASHINGTON; ▲ Roxbury; ***242** F-5; elev. 1,202ft./366m.; mail Northfield z 05663, Randolph z 05060; rural
East Rupert; RMC Place; BENNINGTON; ▲ Rupert; **242** J-3; mail Pawlet z 05761; ● 35
East Ryegate; RMC Place; CALEDONIA; ▲ Ryegate; **242** E-7; 🅿; z 05042; ● 120
East Saint Johnsbury; RMC Place; CALEDONIA; ▲ St. Johnsbury; **242** D-7; 🅿; z 05838; ● 180
East Sheldon; RMC Place; FRANKLIN; ▲ Sheldon; ***242** B-4; elev. 578ft./176m.; mail Enosburg Falls z 05450; rural
East Shoreham; RMC Place; ADDISON; ▲ Shoreham; ***242** G-2; elev. 270ft./82m.; mail Shoreham z 05770; rural
East Sutton Ridge; RMC Place; CALEDONIA; ▲ Sutton; ***242** C-7; mail Sutton z 05867; rural
East Thetford (Thetford); RMC Place; ORANGE; ▲ Thetford; **242** G-6; elev. 408ft./124m.; 🅿; z 05043 & mail Thetford z 05074; ● 150
East Topsham (Topsham); RMC Place; ORANGE; ▲ Topsham; **242** F-6; mail Topsham z 05076; ● 190
East Wallingford; RMC Place; RUTLAND; ▲ Wallingford; **242** I-4; elev. 1,193ft./364m.; 🅿; z 05742; ● 280
East Warren; RMC Place; WASHINGTON; ▲ Warren; ***242** F-4; mail Warren z 05674; rural
Eden; RMC Place; LAMOILLE; ▲ Eden; **242** C-5; elev. 1,112ft./339m.; 🅿; z 05652-53; ● 100
Eden; MCD-Town; LAMOILLE; ***242** C-5; 🅿; z 05652-53; Ⓟ 840; © 1,152
Eden Mills; RMC Place; LAMOILLE; ▲ Eden; **242** C-5; elev. 1,189ft./362m.; 🅿; z 05653; ● 130
Egypt; RMC Place; CALEDONIA; ▲ Lyndon; ***242** C-7; mail Lyndonville z 05851; ● 60
Egypt; RMC Place; FRANKLIN; ▲ Bakersfield, Fairfield; ***242** B-4; mail East Fairfield z 05448; rural
Elmore; MCD-Town; LAMOILLE; ***242** D-5; 🅿; z 05661 & mail Lake Elmore z 05657; Ⓟ 573; © 849
Ely (South Fairlee); RMC Place; ORANGE; ▲ Fairlee; **242** G-6; 🅿; z 05045; ● 50
Enosburg; MCD-Town; FRANKLIN; ***242** B-4; mail Enosburg Falls z 05450; Ⓟ 2,535; © 2,788
Enosburg Center; RMC Place; FRANKLIN; ▲ Enosburg; ***242** B-4; elev. 875ft./267m.; mail Enosburg Falls z 05450; ● 20
Enosburg Falls; Inc. Place; FRANKLIN; ▲ Enosburg; **242** B-4; elev. 422ft./129m.; 🅿; z 05450 & mail Sheldon z 05483; Ⓟ 1,350; © 1,473
Essex; CHITTENDEN; see Essex Center (RMC Place)
Essex; MCD-Town; CHITTENDEN; ***242** D-3; 🅿; ★ **BUR**; z 05451 & mail Essex Junction z 05452; Ⓟ 16,498; © 18,626; ◆ 20,417
ESSEX; **242** C-8; Ⓟ 6,405; © 6,459; ◆ 6,609
Essex Center (Essex); RMC Place; CHITTENDEN; ▲ Essex; **242** D-3; ★ **BUR**; mail Essex z 05451, Essex Junction z 05452-53; ● 850
Essex Junction; Inc. Place; CHITTENDEN; ▲ Essex; **242** D-3; elev. 347ft./106m.; 🅿; ★ **BUR**; z 05452-53 & mail Essex z 05451; Ⓟ 8,396; © 8,591
Evansville; RMC Place; ORLEANS; ▲ Brownington; **242** B-7; mail Orleans z 05860; ● 80
Evarts; WINDSOR; see North Hartland (RMC Place)

F

Fairfax; RMC Place; FRANKLIN; ▲ Fairfax; **242** C-3; 🅿; ★ **BUR**; z 05454; ● 350
Fairfax; MCD-Town; FRANKLIN; ***242** C-3; 🅿; ★ **BUR**; z 05454; Ⓟ 2,486; © 3,765; Ⓡ 3,527; ◆ 4,422
Fairfax Falls; RMC Place; FRANKLIN; ▲ Fairfax; ***242** C-3; elev. 437ft./133m.; ★ **BUR**; mail Fairfax z 05454; rural
Fairfield; RMC Place; FRANKLIN; ▲ Fairfield; **242** B-4; 🅿; z 05455; ● 130
Fairfield; MCD-Town; FRANKLIN; ***242** B-4; 🅿; z 05455; Ⓟ 1,680; © 1,800
Fairfield Station; RMC Place; FRANKLIN; ▲ Fairfield; ***242** B-4; mail Fairfield z 05455; ● 25
Fair Haven; CDP; RUTLAND; ▲ Fair Haven; **242** H-2; 🅿; z 05731, z 05743; Ⓟ 2,432; © 2,435
Fair Haven; MCD-Town; RUTLAND; ***242** H-2; 🅿; z 05731, z 05743; Ⓟ 2,887; © 2,928
Fairlee; RMC Place; ORANGE; ▲ Fairlee; **242** G-6; 🅿; z 05045; ● 400
Fairlee; MCD-Town; ORANGE; ***242** G-6; 🅿; z 05045; Ⓟ 883; © 967
Fays Corner; RMC Place; CHITTENDEN; ▲ Richmond; ***242** D-3; elev. 568ft./173m.; ★ **BUR**; mail Richmond z 05477
Fayston; MCD-Town; WASHINGTON; ***242** E-4; 🅿; z 05673 & mail Moretown z 05660; Ⓟ 846; © 1,141
Felchville (Reading); RMC Place; WINDSOR; ▲ Reading; **242** I-5; mail Reading z 05062; ● 180
Fernville; RMC Place; ADDISON; ▲ Leicester; ***242** G-3; mail Brandon z 05733
Ferrisburg; ADDISON; see Ferrisburgh (RMC Place)
Ferrisburgh (Ferrisburg); RMC Place; ADDISON; ▲ Ferrisburg; **242** E-2; elev. 218ft./66m.; 🅿; z 05456; ● 200
Fletcher; RMC Place; FRANKLIN; ▲ Fletcher; **242** C-4; mail Cambridge z 05444; ● 60
Fletcher; MCD-Town; FRANKLIN; ***242** C-4; mail Cambridge z 05444; Ⓟ 941; © 1,179
Florence; RMC Place; RUTLAND; ▲ Pittsford; **242** H-3; 🅿; z 05744; ● 120
Folsom; RMC Place; CALEDONIA; ▲ Lyndon; ***242** C-7; mail Lyndonville z 05851; rural
Fonda (Fonda Junction); RMC Place; FRANKLIN; ▲ Swanton; **242** B-3; elev. 237ft./72m.; ★ **BUR**; mail Swanton z 05488; ● 80
Fonda Junction; FRANKLIN; see Fonda (RMC Place)
Forest Dale; RMC Place; RUTLAND; ▲ Brandon; **242** G-3; 🅿; z 05745; ● 350
Foxville; RMC Place; ORANGE; ▲ Williamstown; **242** F-5; mail Graniteville z 05654; ● 250
Franklin; RMC Place; FRANKLIN; ▲ Franklin; **242** A-4; elev. 453ft./138m.; 🅿; z 05457; ● 220
Franklin; MCD-Town; FRANKLIN; ***242** A-4; 🅿; z 05457; Ⓟ 1,068; © 1,268
FRANKLIN; **242** C-4; Ⓟ 39,980; © 45,417; ◆ 47,538
Freedleyville; RMC Place; BENNINGTON; ▲ Dorset; ***242** J-3; elev. 799ft./244m.; mail East Dorset z 05253; rural

G

Gallup Mills; RMC Place; ESSEX; ▲ Victory; **242** C-8; elev. 1,311ft./400m.; mail North Concord z 05858; ● 25
Garfield; RMC Place; LAMOILLE; ▲ Hyde Park; ***242** C-5; mail Morrisville z 05661
Gassetts; RMC Place; WINDSOR; ▲ Chester; **242** J-5; elev. 716ft./218m.; mail Chester z 05143, Chester Depot z 05144; ● 60
Gaysville; RMC Place; WINDSOR; ▲ Stockbridge; **242** G-4; 🅿; z 05746; ● 250
Georgia; FRANKLIN; see Georgia Center (RMC Place)
Georgia; MCD-Town; FRANKLIN; ***242** C-3; ★ **BUR**; mail Saint Albans z 05478; Ⓟ 3,753; © 4,375; ◆ 4,418
Georgia Center (Georgia); RMC Place; FRANKLIN; ▲ Georgia; **242** C-3; elev. 394ft./120m.; ★ **BUR**; mail Saint Albans z 05478; ● 150
Georgia Plains; RMC Place; FRANKLIN; ▲ Georgia; **242** C-3; ★ **BUR**; mail Milton z 05468; ● 100
Gilman; RMC Place; ESSEX; ▲ Lunenburg; **242** D-8; elev. 877ft./267m.; 🅿; z 05904; ● 500
Glover; RMC Place; ORLEANS; ▲ Glover; **242** C-6; elev. 945ft./288m.; 🅿; z 05839; ● 250
Glover; MCD-Town; ORLEANS; ***242** C-6; 🅿; z 05839; Ⓟ 820; © 966
Goodrich Four Corners; RMC Place; WINDSOR; ▲ Norwich; ***242** H-6; elev. 622ft./190m.; mail Norwich z 05055; rural
Goose City; RMC Place; WINDHAM; ▲ Dover; ***242** L-4; mail East Dover z 05341; ● 100
Goose Green; RMC Place; ORANGE; ▲ Corinth; ***242** F-6; elev. 823ft./251m.; mail Corinth z 05039; rural
Gordon Landing; RMC Place; GRAND ISLE; ▲ Grand Isle; ***242** C-2; ★ **BUR**; mail Grand Isle z 05458; rural
Goshen; RMC Place; ADDISON; ▲ Goshen; **242** G-3; elev. 1,136ft./346m.; 🅿; z 05733; ● 50
Goshen; MCD-Town; ADDISON; ***242** G-3; 🅿; z 05733; Ⓟ 226; © 227
Goulds Mill; RMC Place; WINDSOR; ▲ Springfield; ***242** J-5; mail Springfield z 05156
Grafton; RMC Place; WINDHAM; ▲ Grafton; **242** K-5; elev. 841ft./256m.; 🅿; z 05146; ● 300
Grafton; MCD-Town; WINDHAM; ***242** J-5; 🅿; z 05146; Ⓟ 602; © 649
Grahamville; RMC Place; WINDSOR; ▲ Ludlow; ***242** I-4; elev. 1,035ft./315m.; mail Ludlow z 05149
Granby; RMC Place; ESSEX; ▲ Granby; **242** C-8; elev. 1,456ft./444m.; 🅿; z 05840; ● 35
Granby; MCD-Town; ESSEX; ***242** C-8; 🅿; z 05840; Ⓟ 85; © 86
Grand Isle; RMC Place; GRAND ISLE; ▲ Grand Isle; **242** C-2; elev. 169ft./52m.; 🅿; ★ **BUR**; z 05458; ● 250
Grand Isle; MCD-Town; GRAND ISLE; ***242** C-2; 🅿; ★ **BUR**; z 05458; Ⓟ 1,642; © 1,955; ◆ 2,000
GRAND ISLE; **242** B-2; Ⓟ 5,318; © 6,901; ◆ 7,593
Graniteville; RMC Place; WASHINGTON; ▲ Barre; **242** F-5; 🅿; z 05654; ● 500
Graniteville-East Barre; CDP-Census Area Only; WASHINGTON; ▲ Barre; ***242** F-5; mail Graniteville z 05654; Ⓟ 2,189; © 2,136
Granville; RMC Place; ADDISON; ▲ Granville; **242** F-4; elev. 1,013ft./309m.; 🅿; z 05747; ● 200
Granville; MCD-Town; ADDISON; ***242** F-4; 🅿; z 05747; Ⓟ 309; © 303
Green Acres; RMC Place; CHITTENDEN; ▲ Richmond; ★ **BUR**; mail Richmond z 05477; ● 200
Greenbank Hollow (South Danville); RMC Place; CALEDONIA; ▲ Danville; ***242** D-7; mail Danville z 05828; rural
Green Bay; RMC Place; CALEDONIA; ▲ Peacham; ***242** E-6; mail Groton z 05046; ● 30
Greenbush; RMC Place; WINDSOR; ▲ Weathersfield; ***242** I-5; elev. 606ft./185m.; mail Perkinsville z 05151; ● 40
Green River; RMC Place; WINDHAM; ▲ Guilford; ***242** M-5; elev. 719ft./219m.; mail Brattleboro z 05301
Greensboro; RMC Place; ORLEANS; ▲ Greensboro; ***242** C-6; 🅿; z 05841; ● 170
Greensboro; ORLEANS; see Greensboro Bend (RMC Place)
Greensboro; MCD-Town; ORLEANS; ***242** C-6; 🅿; z 05841; Ⓟ 717; © 770
Greensboro Bend (Greensboro); RMC Place; ORLEANS; ▲ Greensboro; **242** C-6; 🅿; z 05842 & mail Greensboro z 05841; ● 150
Greens Corners; RMC Place; FRANKLIN; ▲ Swanton; ***242** B-3; elev. 408ft./124m.; ★ **BUR**; mail Saint Albans z 05478
Groton; RMC Place; CALEDONIA; ▲ Groton; **242** E-6; 🅿; z 05046; ● 400
Groton; MCD-Town; CALEDONIA; ***242** E-6; 🅿; z 05046; Ⓟ 862; © 876
Grove; RMC Place; WINDHAM; ▲ Halifax; ***242** M-4; mail West Halifax z 05358; rural
Guildhall; RMC Place; ⊡ ESSEX; ▲ Guildhall; **242** C-9; elev. 368ft./112m.; 🅿; z 05905; ● 100
Guildhall; MCD-Town; ESSEX; ***242** D-8; 🅿; z 05905; Ⓟ 270; © 268
Guilford; RMC Place; WINDHAM; ▲ Guilford; **242** L-5; 🅿; z 05301; ● 200
Guilford; MCD-Town; WINDHAM; ***242** L-5; 🅿; z 05301; Ⓟ 1,941; © 2,046
Guilford Center; RMC Place; WINDHAM; ▲ Guilford; ***242** L-5; mail Brattleboro z 05301

H

Halifax (Halifax Center); RMC Place; WINDHAM; ▲ Halifax; **242** M-4; mail West Halifax z 05358; ● 110
Halifax; MCD-Town; WINDHAM; ***242** M-4; mail West Halifax z 05358; Ⓟ 588; © 782
Halifax Center; WINDHAM; see Halifax (RMC Place)
Halls Lake; RMC Place; ORANGE; ▲ Newbury; ***242** F-7; mail Wells River z 05081; summer pop. 300
Hammondsville; RMC Place; WINDSOR; ▲ Reading; ***242** I-5; elev. 969ft./295m.; mail Reading z 05062
Hancock; RMC Place; ADDISON; ▲ Hancock; **242** G-4; 🅿; z 05748; ● 150
Hancock; MCD-Town; ADDISON; ***242** G-4; 🅿; z 05748; Ⓟ 340; © 382
Hanksville; RMC Place; CHITTENDEN; ▲ Huntington; ***242** E-4; elev. 892ft./272m.; mail Huntington z 05462
Hardwick; RMC Place; CALEDONIA; ▲ Hardwick; **242** D-6; elev. 841ft./256m.; 🅿; z 05843; ● 1,400
Hardwick; MCD-Town; CALEDONIA; ***242** D-6; 🅿; z 05843; Ⓟ 2,964; © 3,174
Hardwick Center; RMC Place; CALEDONIA; ▲ Hardwick; ***242** D-6; elev. 1,166ft./355m.; mail Hardwick z 05843
Hardwick Street; RMC Place; CALEDONIA; ▲ Hardwick; ***242** D-6; mail East Hardwick z 05836; rural
Harmonyville; RMC Place; WINDHAM; ▲ Townshend; ***242** K-5; elev. 461ft./141m.; mail Townshend z 05353; ● 120
Harrisville; RMC Place; WINDHAM; ▲ Halifax; ***242** L-4; elev. 1,375ft./419m.; mail Brattleboro z 05301
Hartford; RMC Place; WINDSOR; ▲ Hartford; **242** H-6; 🅿; z 05047; ● 500
Hartford; MCD-Town; WINDSOR; ***242** H-6; 🅿; z 05047; Ⓟ 9,404; © 10,367; Ⓡ 10,385
Hartland; RMC Place; WINDSOR; ▲ Hartland; **242** I-5; elev. 587ft./179m.; 🅿; z 05048; ● 500
Hartland; MCD-Town; WINDSOR; ***242** I-5; 🅿; z 05048; Ⓟ 2,988; © 3,223
Hartland Four Corners; RMC Place; WINDSOR; ▲ Hartland; **242** I-5; elev. 638ft./194m.; 🅿; z 05049; ● 200
Hartwellville; RMC Place; ESSEX; ▲ East Haven; ***242** C-7; mail East Haven z 05837; ● 100
Harvey; CALEDONIA; see Harvey Hollow (RMC Place)
Harvey Hollow (Harvey); RMC Place; CALEDONIA; ▲ Danville; ***242** D-6; mail Danville z 05828
Healdville; RMC Place; RUTLAND; ▲ Mount Holly; ***242** I-4; mail Mount Holly z 05758
Heartwellville; RMC Place; BENNINGTON; ▲ Readsboro; ***242** L-3; elev. 1,785ft./544m.; mail Readsboro z 05350; ● 60
Hectorville; RMC Place; FRANKLIN; ▲ Montgomery; ***242** B-5; mail Montgomery Center z 05471
Hewitts Corners; RMC Place; WINDSOR; ▲ Pomfret; ***242** H-5; elev. 1,060ft./323m.; mail North Pomfret z 05053
Highgate; FRANKLIN; see Highgate Center (RMC Place)
Highgate; MCD-Town; FRANKLIN; ***242** B-3; mail Highgate Center z 05459; Ⓟ 3,020; © 3,397
Highgate Center (Highgate); RMC Place; FRANKLIN; ▲ Highgate; **242** B-3; elev. 308ft./94m.; 🅿; z 05459; ● 350
Highgate Falls; RMC Place; FRANKLIN; ▲ Highgate; ***242** B-3; elev. 239ft./73m.; mail Highgate Center z 05459; ● 220
Highgate Springs; RMC Place; FRANKLIN; ▲ Highgate; **242** A-3; elev. 119ft./36m.; 🅿; z 05460; ● 200
Hinesburg; RMC Place; CHITTENDEN; ▲ Hinesburg; **242** E-3; 🅿; ★ **BUR**; z 05461; ● 400
Hinesburg; MCD-Town; CHITTENDEN; ***242** E-3; 🅿; ★ **BUR**; z 05461; Ⓟ 3,780; © 4,340; ◆ 4,575
Holden; RUTLAND; see North Chittenden (RMC Place)
Holland; RMC Place; ORLEANS; ▲ Holland; **242** A-7; mail Derby z 05829, Derby Line z 05830; ● 100
Holland; MCD-Town; ORLEANS; ***242** A-7; mail Derby Line z 05830; Ⓟ 423; © 588
Hortonia; RMC Place; RUTLAND; ▲ Hubbardton; **242** H-3; elev. 492ft./150m.; mail Orwell z 05760; ● 40
Hortonville; RMC Place; RUTLAND; ▲ Mount Holly; ***242** I-4; mail Mount Holly z 05758
Houghtonville; RMC Place; WINDHAM; ▲ Grafton; **242** J-5; elev. 1,114ft./340m.; mail Grafton z 05146; ● 40
Hubbard Corner; RMC Place; FRANKLIN; ▲ Georgia; ***242** C-3; elev. 398ft./121m.; ★ **BUR**; mail Saint Albans z 05478; rural
Hubbardton; RMC Place; RUTLAND; ▲ Hubbardton; **242** H-3; elev. 422ft./129m.; mail Bomoseen z 05732, Castleton z 05735; ● 60
Hubbardton; MCD-Town; RUTLAND; ***242** H-3; mail Bomoseen z 05732, Castleton z 05735; Ⓟ 576; © 752
Huntington; RMC Place; CHITTENDEN; ▲ Huntington; **242** E-3; 🅿; z 05462; ● 280
Huntington; MCD-Town; CHITTENDEN; ***242** E-4; 🅿; z 05462; Ⓟ 1,609; © 1,861
Huntington Center; RMC Place; CHITTENDEN; ▲ Huntington; **242** E-3; mail Huntington z 05462; ● 150
Huntsville (Huntville); RMC Place; FRANKLIN; ▲ Fairfax; ***242** C-3; ★ **BUR**; mail Fairfax z 05454; rural
Huntville; FRANKLIN; see Huntsville (RMC Place)
Hutchins; RMC Place; FRANKLIN; ▲ Montgomery; ***242** B-5; mail Montgomery Center z 05471
Hyde Park; Inc. Place; ⊡ LAMOILLE; ▲ Hyde Park; **242** C-5; 🅿; z 05655; Ⓟ 457; © 415
Hyde Park; MCD-Town; LAMOILLE; ***242** C-5; 🅿; z 05655; Ⓟ 2,344; © 2,847
Hydeville; RMC Place; RUTLAND; ▲ Castleton; **242** H-2; elev. 411ft./125m.; 🅿; z 05750; ● 450

I

Indian Point; RMC Place; ORLEANS; mail Newport z 05855; pop. incl. with Newport (Inc. Place)
Inwood (East Barnet); RMC Place; CALEDONIA; ▲ Barnet; **242** E-7; mail Barnet z 05821
Ira; RMC Place; RUTLAND; ▲ Ira; **242** I-3; elev. 859ft./262m.; mail West Rutland z 05777; ● 100
Ira; MCD-Town; RUTLAND; ***242** I-3; mail West Rutland z 05777; Ⓟ 426; © 455
Irasburg; RMC Place; ORLEANS; ▲ Irasburg; **242** B-6; elev. 814ft./248m.; 🅿; z 05845; ● 230
Irasburg; MCD-Town; ORLEANS; ***242** B-6; 🅿; z 05845; Ⓟ 907; © 1,077
Irasville; RMC Place; WASHINGTON; ▲ Waitsfield; **242** E-4; elev. 773ft./236m.; mail Waitsfield z 05673; ● 135
Island Pond; CDP; ESSEX; ▲ Brighton; **242** B-7; elev. 1,191ft./363m.; 🅿; z 05846; Ⓟ 1,222; © 849
Isle La Motte; RMC Place; GRAND ISLE; ▲ Isle La Motte; **242** B-2; elev. 188ft./57m.; 🅿; z 05463; ● 130
Isle La Motte; MCD-Town; GRAND ISLE; ***242** B-2; 🅿; z 05463; Ⓟ 408; © 488

J

Jacksonville; Inc. Place; WINDHAM; ▲ Whitingham; **242** L-4; elev. 1,334ft./407m.; 🅿; z 05342; Ⓟ 244; © 237
Jamaica; RMC Place; WINDHAM; ▲ Jamaica; **242** K-4; elev. 732ft./223m.; 🅿; z 05343; ● 230
Jamaica; MCD-Town; WINDHAM; ***242** K-4; 🅿; z 05343; Ⓟ 754; © 946
Jay; RMC Place; ORLEANS; ▲ Jay; **242** B-5; 🅿; z 05859; ● 100
Jay; MCD-Town; ORLEANS; ***242** A-5; 🅿; z 05859; Ⓟ 381; © 426
Jeffersonville; Inc. Place; LAMOILLE; ▲ Cambridge; **242** C-4; elev. 459ft./140m.; 🅿; z 05464; Ⓟ 462; © 568
Jenneville; RMC Place; WINDSOR; ▲ Hartland; ***242** I-5; mail Windsor z 05089; rural
Jericho; RMC Place; CHITTENDEN; ▲ Jericho; **242** D-3; elev. 550ft./168m.; 🅿; ★ **BUR**; z 05465; disincorporated since 2000 Census; Ⓟ 1,405; © 1,457
Jericho; MCD-Town; CHITTENDEN; ***242** D-4; 🅿; ★ **BUR**; z 05465; Ⓟ 4,302; © 5,015; ◆ 5,414
Jericho Center; RMC Place; CHITTENDEN; ▲ Jericho; **242** D-3; elev. 765ft./233m.; 🅿; ★ **BUR**; z 05465; ● 120
Jerusalem; RMC Place; ADDISON; ▲ Starksboro; ***242** E-3; elev. 1,474ft./449m.; mail Bristol z 05443; ● 50
Joes Pond; RMC Place; CALEDONIA, WASHINGTON; ▲ Cabot, Danville; **242** D-6; mail West Danville z 05873; ● 100
Johnson; Inc. Place; LAMOILLE; ▲ Johnson; **242** C-5; elev. 516ft./157m.; 🅿 🅲 1,928; z 05656; Ⓟ 1,470; © 1,420
Johnson; MCD-Town; LAMOILLE; ***242** C-5; 🅿 🅲 1,928; z 05656; Ⓟ 3,156; © 3,274
Jonesville; RMC Place; CHITTENDEN; ▲ Richmond; **242** D-4; elev. 326ft./99m.; 🅿; ★ **BUR**; z 05466; ● 330

K

Kansas; RMC Place; BENNINGTON; ▲ Sunderland; ***242** K-3; elev. 833ft./254m.; mail East Arlington z 05252
Keeler Bay; RMC Place; GRAND ISLE; ▲ South Hero; ***242** C-2; ★ **BUR**; mail South Hero z 05486
Kelley Stand; RMC Place; BENNINGTON; ▲ Sunderland; ***242** K-3; mail East Arlington z 05252; rural
Kendall; WINDSOR; see Pompanoosuc (RMC Place)
Kendricks Corner; RMC Place; WINDSOR; ▲ Weathersfield, Springfield; ***242** J-5; mail North Springfield z 05150; ● 50
Killington (Sherburne Center); RMC Place; RUTLAND; ▲ Killington; ***242** H-4; 🅿; z 05751; ● 100
Killington (Sherburne); MCD-Town; RUTLAND; ***242** H-4; 🅿; z 05751; Ⓟ 738; © 1,095
Kimball; ORLEANS; see Willoughby (RMC Place)
Kirby; MCD-Town; CALEDONIA; ***242** D-7; mail Concord z 05824; Ⓟ 347; © 456
Kirby Corner; RMC Place; CHITTENDEN; ▲ Essex; ***242** D-3; ★ **BUR**; mail Williston z 05495; ● 50

L

Lake; RMC Place; ESSEX; ▲ Norton; ***242** B-8; elev. 1,349ft./411m.; mail Norton z 05907; rural
Lake Bomoseen; RUTLAND; see Bomoseen (RMC Place)
Lake Dunmore; RMC Place; ADDISON; ▲ Salisbury, Leicester; **242** G-3; mail Salisbury z 05769; ● 50
Lake Elmore; RMC Place; LAMOILLE; ▲ Elmore; **242** D-5; 🅿; z 05657; ● 140
Lake Fairlee; RMC Place; ORANGE; ▲ Fairlee, Thetford, West Fairlee; ***242** G-6; mail Fairlee z 05045; rural
Lake Hortonia; RMC Place; RUTLAND; ▲ Sudbury; ***242** H-3; mail Fair Haven z 05743, Orwell z 05760; ● 110
Lake Morey; RMC Place; ORANGE; ▲ Fairlee; mail Fairlee z 05045; summer pop. 600
Lake Park; RMC Place; ORLEANS; ▲ Derby; ***242** A-6; mail Newport z 05855; summer pop. 80
Lake Raponda; RMC Place; WINDHAM; ▲ Wilmington; mail Wilmington z 05363
Lake Rescue; RMC Place; WINDSOR; ▲ Ludlow; ***242** I-4; mail Ludlow z 05149; rural
Lake Saint Catherine; RMC Place; RUTLAND; ▲ Wells, Poultney; ***242** I-3; mail Poultney z 05764; summer pop. 3000
Lake Salem; RMC Place; ORLEANS; ▲ Derby; ***242** B-7; mail Newport z 05855; rural
Lakewood; RMC Place; FRANKLIN; ▲ Swanton; ★ **BUR**; mail Swanton z 05488; rural
LAMOILLE; **242** C-5; Ⓟ 19,735; © 23,233; ◆ 24,524
Landgrove; BENNINGTON; see North Landgrove (RMC Place)
Landgrove; MCD-Town; BENNINGTON; ***242** J-4; 🅿; z 05148; Ⓟ 134; © 144
Lapham Bay; RMC Place; ADDISON; ▲ Shoreham; ***242** G-2; mail Bridport z 05734
Larrabees Point Station; RMC Place; ADDISON; ▲ Shoreham; ***242** G-2; mail Shoreham z 05770; rural
Leicester; RMC Place; ADDISON; ▲ Leicester; **242** G-3; 🅿; z 05733; ● 50
Leicester; ADDISON; see Leicester Junction (RMC Place)
Leicester; MCD-Town; ADDISON; ***242** G-3; 🅿; z 05733; Ⓟ 871; © 974
Leicester Junction (Leicester); RMC Place; ADDISON; ▲ Leicester; **242** G-3; elev. 352ft./107m.; mail Whiting z 05778; ● 50
Lemington; RMC Place; ESSEX; ▲ Lemington; **242** B-9; 🅿; z 05903 & mail Guildhall z 05905; rural
Lemington; MCD-Town; ESSEX; ***242** B-8; 🅿; z 05903 & mail Guildhall z 05905; Ⓟ 102; © 107
Lewiston; RMC Place; WINDSOR; ▲ Norwich; ***242** H-6; elev. 387ft./118m.; mail Norwich z 05055
Lilliesville (Lillieville); RMC Place; WINDSOR; ▲ Bethel; ***242** G-4; elev. 937ft./286m.; mail Bethel z 05032
Lillieville; WINDSOR; see Lilliesville (RMC Place)
Lincoln; RMC Place; ADDISON; ▲ Lincoln; **242** F-3; elev. 971ft./296m.; 🅿; z 05443; ● 150
Lincoln; MCD-Town; ADDISON; ***242** F-3; 🅿; z 05443; Ⓟ 974; © 1,214
Lindsay Beach; RMC Place; ORLEANS; ▲ Derby; ***242** A-6; mail Newport z 05855; rural
Londonderry; RMC Place; WINDHAM; ▲ Londonderry; **242** J-4; 🅿; z 05148; ● 250
Londonderry; MCD-Town; WINDHAM; ***242** J-4; 🅿; z 05148; Ⓟ 1,506; © 1,709
Long Point; RMC Place; ADDISON; ▲ Ferrisburg; ***242** E-2; mail North Ferrisburgh z 05473; ● 30
Lowell; RMC Place; ORLEANS; ▲ Lowell; **242** B-5; elev. 996ft./304m.; 🅿; z 05847; ● 200
Lowell; MCD-Town; ORLEANS; ***242** B-5; 🅿; z 05847; Ⓟ 594; © 738
Lower Branch; RMC Place; ORANGE; ▲ Braintree; ***242** G-4; elev. 760ft./232m.; mail Randolph z 05060; rural
Lower Cabot; RMC Place; WASHINGTON; ▲ Cabot; **242** D-6; elev. 947ft./289m.; mail Marshfield z 05658; ● 60
Lower Granville; RMC Place; ADDISON; ▲ Granville; ***242** G-4; mail Granville z 05747
Lower Plain; RMC Place; ORANGE; ▲ Bradford; ***242** F-7; mail Bradford z 05033
Lower Village; RMC Place; LAMOILLE; ▲ Stowe; **242** D-4; elev. 670ft./204m.; mail Stowe z 05672; ● 300
Lower Waterford; RMC Place; CALEDONIA; ▲ Waterford; ***242** E-7; 🅿; z 05848; ● 70
Lower Websterville; RMC Place; WASHINGTON; ▲ Barre; ***242** F-5; mail Barre z 05641; ● 250
Ludlow; Inc. Place; WINDSOR; ▲ Ludlow; **242** I-4; elev. 1,067ft./325m.; 🅿; z 05149; Ⓟ 1,123; © 958
Ludlow; MCD-Town; WINDSOR; ***242** I-4; 🅿; z 05149; Ⓟ 2,302; © 2,449
Lunenburg; RMC Place; ESSEX; ▲ Lunenburg; **242** D-8; elev. 1,202ft./366m.; 🅿; z 05906; ● 260
Lunenburg; MCD-Town; ESSEX; ***242** D-8; 🅿; z 05906; Ⓟ 1,176; © 1,328; Ⓡ 1,315
Lyman; RMC Place; WINDSOR; ▲ Hartford; mail White River Junction z 05001
Lympus (Olympus); RMC Place; WINDSOR; ▲ Bethel; ***242** G-4; elev. 1,236ft./377m.; mail Bethel z 05032; rural
Lyndon (Lyndon Corners); RMC Place; CALEDONIA; ▲ Lyndon; **242** D-7; elev. 1,706ft./520m.; 🅿; z 05849; ● 450
Lyndon; MCD-Town; CALEDONIA; ***242** D-7; 🅿 🅲 1,364; z 05849; Ⓟ 5,371; © 5,448
Lyndon Center; RMC Place; CALEDONIA; ▲ Lyndon; **242** D-7; 🅿; z 05850; ● 300
Lyndon Corners; CALEDONIA; see Lyndon (RMC Place)
Lyndonville; Inc. Place; CALEDONIA; ▲ Lyndon; **242** D-7; elev. 714ft./218m.; 🅿 🅲 1,364; z 05851; Ⓟ 1,255; © 1,227

M

Mackville; RMC Place; CALEDONIA; ▲ Hardwick; ***242** D-6; elev. 933ft./284m.; mail Hardwick z 05843; ● 100
Madonna; LAMOILLE; see Smugglers Notch (RMC Place)
Maidstone; MCD-Town; ESSEX; ***242** C-8; 🅿; z 05905; Ⓟ 131; © 105
Maidstone Lake; RMC Place; ESSEX; ▲ Maidstone; mail North Stratford z 03590; summer pop. 150
Mallets Bay; RMC Place; CHITTENDEN; ▲ Colchester; ***242** D-3; ★ **BUR**; mail Colchester z 05446; summer pop. 750
Manchester; Inc. Place; ⊡ BENNINGTON; ▲ Manchester; **242** K-3; elev. 899ft./274m.; 🅿; z 05254; Ⓟ 561; © 602
Manchester; BENNINGTON; see Manchester Depot (RMC Place)
Manchester; MCD-Town; BENNINGTON; ***242** K-3; 🅿; z 05254; Ⓟ 3,622; © 4,180; Ⓡ 4,184
Manchester Center; CDP; BENNINGTON; ▲ Manchester; **242** K-3; elev. 753ft./230m.; 🅿; z 05255; Ⓟ 1,574; © 2,065; Ⓡ 2,069
Manchester Depot (Manchester); RMC Place; BENNINGTON; ▲ Manchester; ***242** K-3; mail Manchester z 05254, Manchester Center z 05255; pop. incl. with Manchester (Inc. Place)
Maple Corner (Calais); RMC Place; WASHINGTON; ▲ Calais; **242** D-5; mail Calais z 05648; ● 40
Maple Dell; RMC Place; WINDSOR; ▲ Springfield; mail Springfield z 05156; ● 30
Maquam; RMC Place; FRANKLIN; ▲ Swanton; **242** B-3; ★ **BUR**; mail Swanton z 05488; ● 200
Marlboro; RMC Place; WINDHAM; ▲ Marlboro; **242** L-4; 🅿 🅲 337; z 05344; ● 230
Marlboro; MCD-Town; WINDHAM; ***242** L-4; 🅿 🅲 337; z 05344; Ⓟ 924; © 978
Marshfield; Inc. Place; WASHINGTON; ▲ Marshfield; **242** E-6; elev. 857ft./261m.; 🅿; z 05658; Ⓟ 257; © 262
Marshfield; MCD-Town; WASHINGTON; ***242** E-6; 🅿; z 05658; Ⓟ 1,331; © 1,496
Mary Meyer; RMC Place; WINDHAM; ▲ Townshend; mail Townshend z 05353
Mayo; ESSEX; see East Concord (RMC Place)
McIndoe Falls (McIndoes); RMC Place; CALEDONIA; ▲ Barnet; **242** E-7; 🅿; z 05050; ● 200
McIndoes; CALEDONIA; see McIndoe Falls (RMC Place)
Mechanicsville; RMC Place; CHITTENDEN; ▲ Hinesburg; ***242** E-3; elev. 429ft./131m.; ★ **BUR**; mail Hinesburg z 05461; ● 150
Medburyville; RMC Place; WINDHAM; ▲ Wilmington; ***242** L-4; mail Wilmington z 05363; rural
Melville; RMC Place; FRANKLIN; ▲ Georgia; ***242** B-3; ★ **BUR**; mail Saint Albans z 05478; rural
Mendon; RMC Place; RUTLAND; ▲ Mendon; **242** H-4; elev. 1,040ft./317m.; 🅿; z 05701; ● 60
Mendon; MCD-Town; RUTLAND; ***242** H-4; 🅿; z 05701; Ⓟ 1,049; © 1,028
Merrill Corner; RMC Place; ORLEANS; ▲ Albany; ***242** C-6; mail Irasburg z 05845; rural
Middlebury; CDP; ⊡ ADDISON; ▲ Middlebury; **242** F-3; elev. 366ft./112m.; 🅿 🅷 🅲 2,350; z 05753 & mail Ripton z 05766; Ⓟ 6,007; © 6,252
Middlebury; MCD-Town; ADDISON; ***242** F-3; 🅿 🅲 2,350; z 05753; Ⓟ 8,034; © 8,183
Middlesex; RMC Place; WASHINGTON; ▲ Middlesex; **242** E-5; elev. 537ft./164m.; 🅿; z 05602; ● 200
Middlesex; MCD-Town; WASHINGTON; ***242** E-5; 🅿; z 05602; Ⓟ 1,514; © 1,729
Middlesex Center; RMC Place; WASHINGTON; ▲ Middlesex; ***242** E-5; 🅿; z 05602
Middletown; RMC Place; WINDSOR; ▲ Andover; ***242** J-4; elev. 1,562ft./476m.; mail Chester z 05143; rural
Middletown Springs; RMC Place; RUTLAND; ▲ Middletown Springs; **242** I-3; elev. 893ft./272m.; 🅿; z 05757; ● 200
Middletown Springs; MCD-Town; RUTLAND; ***242** I-3; 🅿; z 05757; Ⓟ 686; © 823
Mile Point; RMC Place; ADDISON; ▲ Ferrisburg; ***242** E-2; mail Vergennes z 05491
Miles Pond; RMC Place; ESSEX; ▲ Concord; **242** D-8; mail North Concord z 05858; summer pop. 100; ● 30
Millbrook; RMC Place; WINDSOR; ▲ Pomfret; ***242** H-5; mail North Pomfret z 05053; rural
Mill Village; RMC Place; ORANGE; ▲ Vershire; ***242** G-6; elev. 1,014ft./309m.; mail Vershire z 05079
Mill Village; RMC Place; ORLEANS; ▲ Craftsbury; ***242** C-6; mail Craftsbury Common z 05827, Rutland z 05701
Milton; RMC Place; CHITTENDEN; ▲ Milton; **242** C-3; 🅿; ★ **BUR**; z 05468; former incorporated place; merged into Milton April 22, 2003; pop. incl. with Essex Junction (Inc. Place); Ⓟ 1,578; © 1,537
Milton; MCD-Town; CHITTENDEN; ***242** C-3; 🅿; ★ **BUR**; z 05468; Ⓟ 8,404; © 9,479; ◆ 10,318
Miltonboro; RMC Place; CHITTENDEN; ▲ Milton; ***242** C-3; ★ **BUR**; mail Milton z 05468; rural
Monkton; ADDISON; see Monkton Boro (RMC Place)
Monkton; MCD-Town; ADDISON; ***242** E-3; 🅿; z 05469; Ⓟ 1,482; © 1,759
Monkton Boro (Monkton); RMC Place; ADDISON; ▲ Monkton; **242** E-3; elev. 533ft./162m.; mail Monkton z 05469; ● 180
Monkton Ridge; RMC Place; ADDISON; ▲ Monkton; ***242** E-3; mail North Ferrisburgh z 05473; ● 50
Montgomery; RMC Place; FRANKLIN; ▲ Montgomery; **242** B-5; elev. 493ft./150m.; 🅿; z 05470; ● 220
Montgomery; MCD-Town; FRANKLIN; ***242** B-5; 🅿; z 05470; Ⓟ 823; © 992
Montgomery Center; RMC Place; FRANKLIN; ▲ Montgomery; **242** B-5; 🅿; z 05471; ● 380
Montpelier; Inc. Place; **STATE CAPITAL**; ⊡ WASHINGTON; **242** E-5; elev. 525ft./160m.; 🅿 🅲 453; z 05601-04, z 05609, z 05620, z 05633; Ⓟ 8,247; © 8,035
Moretown; RMC Place; WASHINGTON; ▲ Moretown; **242** E-4; elev. 602ft./183m.; 🅿; z 05660; ● 220
Moretown; MCD-Town; WASHINGTON; ***242** E-4; 🅿; z 05660; Ⓟ 1,415; © 1,653
Moretown Common; RMC Place; WASHINGTON; ▲ Moretown; ***242** E-4; elev. 1,082ft./330m.; mail Moretown z 05660; rural
Morgan; RMC Place; ORLEANS; ▲ Morgan; **242** B-7; 🅿; z 05853; ● 80
Morgan; MCD-Town; ORLEANS; ***242** B-7; 🅿; z 05853; Ⓟ 497; © 669
Morgan Center; RMC Place; ORLEANS; ▲ Morgan; **242** B-7; mail Morgan z 05853; ● 150
Morgan Corner; RMC Place; WINDSOR; ▲ Barnard; ***242** H-5; mail Barnard z 05031; rural
Morristown (Morristown Corners); RMC Place; LAMOILLE; ▲ Morristown; ***242** D-5; elev. 759ft./231m.; 🅿; z 05661; ● 80
Morristown; MCD-Town; LAMOILLE; ***242** D-5; 🅿; z 05661; Ⓟ 4,733; © 5,139
Morristown Corners; LAMOILLE; see Morristown (RMC Place)
Morrisville; Inc. Place; LAMOILLE; ▲ Morristown; **242** D-5; elev. 682ft./208m.; 🅿 🅷; z 05657, z 05661; Ⓟ 1,984; © 2,009
Moscow; RMC Place; LAMOILLE; ▲ Stowe; **242** D-4; elev. 653ft./199m.; 🅿; z 05662; ● 260
Mosquitoville; RMC Place; CALEDONIA; ▲ Ryegate, Barnet; ***242** E-6; elev. 1,004ft./306m.; mail East Ryegate z 05042; rural
Mount Holly; RMC Place; RUTLAND; ▲ Mount Holly; **242** I-4; elev. 1,558ft./475m.; 🅿; z 05758; ● 200
Mount Holly; MCD-Town; RUTLAND; ***242** I-4; 🅿; z 05758; Ⓟ 1,093; © 1,241
Mount Snow; RMC Place; WINDHAM; ▲ Dover; ***242** L-5; 🅿; z 05356; rural
Mount Tabor; RMC Place; RUTLAND; ▲ Mount Tabor; **242** J-3; 🅿; z 05739; ● 100
Mount Tabor; MCD-Town; RUTLAND; ***242** J-4; 🅿; z 05739; Ⓟ 214; © 203

N

Nashville; RMC Place; CHITTENDEN; ▲ Jericho; ***242** D-4; ★ **BUR**; mail Jericho z 05465; rural
Neshobe Beach; RMC Place; RUTLAND; ▲ Castleton; ***242** H-3; elev. 422ft./129m.; mail Bomoseen z 05732
Newark (Newark Street); RMC Place; CALEDONIA; ▲ Newark; **242** C-7; mail West Burke z 05871; ● 70
Newark; MCD-Town; CALEDONIA; ***242** C-7; mail West Burke z 05871; Ⓟ 354; © 470
Newark Hollow; RMC Place; CALEDONIA; ▲ Newark; ***242** C-7; mail West Burke z 05871; rural
Newark Street; CALEDONIA; see Newark (RMC Place)
New Boston; RMC Place; WINDSOR; ▲ Stockbridge; ***242** G-4; mail Norwich z 05055; rural
Newbury; Inc. Place; ORANGE; ▲ Newbury; **242** F-7; 🅿; z 05051; Ⓟ 412; © 396; Ⓡ 406
Newbury; MCD-Town; ORANGE; ***242** F-7; 🅿; z 05051; Ⓟ 1,985; © 1,955; Ⓡ 1,965
Newbury Center; RMC Place; ORANGE; ▲ Newbury; ***242** F-6; mail South Ryegate z 05069, Wells River z 05081; rural
Newfane; Inc. Place; ⊡ WINDHAM; ▲ Newfane; **242** K-5; elev. 536ft./163m.; 🅿; z 05345; Ⓟ 164; © 116
Newfane; MCD-Town; WINDHAM; ***242** L-4; 🅿; z 05345; Ⓟ 1,555; © 1,680
New Haven; RMC Place; ADDISON; ▲ New Haven; **242** F-3; elev. 455ft./139m.; 🅿; z 05472; ● 140
New Haven; MCD-Town; ADDISON; ***242** F-3; 🅿; z 05472; Ⓟ 1,375; © 1,666
New Haven Mills; RMC Place; ADDISON; ▲ New Haven; **242** F-3; elev. 3,271ft./997m.; mail Bristol z 05443, New Haven z 05472; ● 100
Newport; Inc. Place; ⊡ ORLEANS; **242** B-6; elev. 723ft./220m.; 🅿 🅷; z 05855; Ⓟ 4,434; © 5,005
Newport; MCD-Town; ORLEANS; ***242** B-6; 🅿; z 05855 & mail Newport Center z 05857; does not include the City of Newport; Ⓟ 1,367; © 1,511
Newport Center (Centre); RMC Place; ORLEANS; ▲ Newport; **242** B-6; elev. 792ft./241m.; 🅿; z 05857; ● 300
North Bennington; Inc. Place; BENNINGTON; ▲ Bennington; **242** L-2; 🅿; z 05257; Ⓟ 1,520; © 1,428
Northboro; ORANGE; see North Thetford (RMC Place)
North Brattleboro; RMC Place; WINDHAM; ▲ Brattleboro; mail Brattleboro z 05304
North Burlington; RMC Place; CHITTENDEN; ★ **BUR**; mail Burlington z 05401; pop. incl. with Burlington (Inc. Place)
North Calais; RMC Place; WASHINGTON; ▲ Calais; **242** D-5; mail East Calais z 05650; ● 80
North Cambridge; RMC Place; LAMOILLE; ▲ Cambridge; ***242** C-4; mail Jeffersonville z 05464
North Chester; RMC Place; WINDSOR; ▲ Chester; ***242** J-5; mail Chester z 05143; ● 90
North Chittenden (Holden); RMC Place; RUTLAND; ▲ Chittenden; ***242** H-3; 🅿; z 05763
North Clarendon; RMC Place; RUTLAND; ▲ Clarendon; **242** I-3; elev. 588ft./179m.; 🅿; z 05759; ● 550
North Concord; RMC Place; ESSEX; ▲ Concord; **242** D-7; elev. 1,082ft./330m.; 🅿; z 05858; ● 140
North Danville; RMC Place; CALEDONIA; ▲ Danville; **242** D-7; mail Danville z 05828; ● 110
North Derby; RMC Place; ORLEANS; ▲ Derby; ***242** A-6; mail Newport z 05855
North Dorset; RMC Place; BENNINGTON; ▲ Dorset; ***242** J-3; mail East Dorset z 05253
North Duxbury; RMC Place; WASHINGTON; ▲ Duxbury; ***242** E-4; elev. 380ft./116m.; mail Waterbury z 05676
North Fairfax; RMC Place; FRANKLIN; ▲ Fairfax; ***242** C-3; elev. 723ft./220m.; ★ **BUR**; mail Fairfax z 05454
North Fayston; RMC Place; WASHINGTON; ▲ Fayston; ***242** E-4; mail Moretown z 05660
North Ferrisburg; ADDISON; see North Ferrisburgh (RMC Place)
North Ferrisburgh (North Ferrisburg); RMC Place; ADDISON; ▲ Ferrisburg; **242** E-3; 🅿; z 05473; ● 150
Northfield; Inc. Place; WASHINGTON; ▲ Northfield; **242** F-5; 🅿 🅲 1,987; z 05663; Ⓟ 1,889; © 3,208
Northfield; MCD-Town; WASHINGTON; ***242** F-4; 🅿 🅲 1,987; z 05663; Ⓟ 5,610; © 5,791
Northfield Center; RMC Place; WASHINGTON; ▲ Northfield; ***242** F-5; mail Northfield z 05663; ● 150
Northfield Falls; RMC Place; WASHINGTON; ▲ Northfield; ***242** E-5; elev. 669ft./204m.; 🅿; z 05664; ● 600
North Hartland (Evarts); RMC Place; WINDSOR; ▲ Hartland; **242** H-6; elev. 365ft./111m.; 🅿; z 05052; ● 230
North Hero; RMC Place; ⊡ GRAND ISLE; ▲ North Hero; **242** B-2; 🅿; z 05474; ● 190
North Hero; MCD-Town; GRAND ISLE; ***242** B-2; 🅿; z 05474; Ⓟ 502; © 810
North Hyde Park; RMC Place; LAMOILLE; ▲ Hyde Park; **242** C-5; elev. 854ft./260m.; 🅿; z 05665; ● 380
North Kirby; RMC Place; CALEDONIA; ▲ Kirby; ***242** D-7; mail Lyndonville z 05851; rural
North Landgrove (Landgrove); RMC Place; BENNINGTON; ▲ Landgrove; ***242** J-4; mail Londonderry z 05148; ● 50
North Montpelier; RMC Place; WASHINGTON; ▲ East Montpelier; **242** E-5; elev. 712ft./217m.; 🅿; z 05666; ● 150
North Orwell; RMC Place; ADDISON; ▲ Orwell; ***242** G-2; elev. 268ft./82m.; mail Orwell z 05760; rural
North Pawlet; RMC Place; RUTLAND; ▲ Pawlet; ***242** I-3; mail Pawlet z 05761, Wells z 05774; ● 40
North Pomfret; RMC Place; WINDSOR; ▲ Pomfret; **242** H-5; 🅿; z 05053 & mail North Thetford z 05054; ● 60
North Pownal; RMC Place; BENNINGTON; ▲ Pownal; **242** L-2; elev. 522ft./159m.; 🅿; z 05260; ● 350
North Randolph; RMC Place; ORANGE; ▲ Randolph; **242** F-5; mail East Randolph z 05041; ● 50
North Royalton; RMC Place; WINDSOR; ▲ Royalton; ***242** G-5; mail South Royalton z 05068
North Rupert; RMC Place; BENNINGTON; ▲ Rupert; ***242** J-3; elev. 754ft./230m.; mail Pawlet z 05761
North Sheldon; RMC Place; FRANKLIN; ▲ Sheldon; ***242** B-4; mail Sheldon z 05483; rural
North Sherburne; RMC Place; RUTLAND; ▲ Killington; ***242** H-4; mail Killington z 05751
North Shrewsbury; RMC Place; RUTLAND; ▲ Shrewsbury; **242** I-4; elev. 1,758ft./536m.; mail Cuttingsville z 05738; ● 80
North Springfield; RMC Place; WINDSOR; ▲ Springfield; **242** J-5; 🅿; z 05150; ● 750
North Thetford (Northboro); RMC Place; ORANGE; ▲ Thetford; **242** G-6; 🅿; z 05054; ● 110
North Troy; Inc. Place; ORLEANS; ▲ Troy; **242** A-6; 🅿; z 05859; Ⓟ 723; © 593
North Tunbridge; RMC Place; ORANGE; ▲ Tunbridge; **242** G-5; mail Tunbridge z 05077; ● 75
North Walden; RMC Place; CALEDONIA; ***242** D-6; mail East Hardwick z 05836; rural
North Wardsboro; WINDHAM; see Wardsboro (RMC Place)
North Westminster; Inc. Place; WINDHAM; ▲ Westminster; ***242** K-5; mail Bellows Falls z 05101; Ⓟ 268; © 271
North Windham; RMC Place; WINDHAM; ▲ Londonderry; ***242** J-4; elev. 1,497ft./456m.; mail Chester z 05143, West Townshend z 05359
North Wolcott; RMC Place; LAMOILLE; ▲ Wolcott; **242** C-5; elev. 863ft./263m.; mail Wolcott z 05680; ● 140
Norton; RMC Place; ESSEX; ▲ Norton; **242** A-8; 🅿; z 05907; ● 80
Norton; MCD-Town; ESSEX; ***242** A-8; 🅿; z 05907; Ⓟ 169; © 214
Norwich; RMC Place; WINDSOR; ▲ Norwich; **242** H-6; elev. 537ft./164m.; 🅿; z 05055; ● 1,000
Norwich; MCD-Town; WINDSOR; ***242** H-6; 🅿; z 05055; Ⓟ 3,093; © 3,544
Norwich University; RMC Place; WASHINGTON; mail Northfield z 05663; pop. incl. with Northfield (Inc. Place)

O

Oakland; RMC Place; FRANKLIN; ▲ Georgia; ***242** C-3; elev. 457ft./139m.; ★ **BUR**; mail Saint Albans z 05478; rural
Old Bennington (Bennington Center); Inc. Place; BENNINGTON; ▲ Bennington; ***242** L-3; mail Bennington z 05201; Ⓟ 279; © 232
Old Church; RMC Place; WINDSOR; ▲ Bethel; mail Randolph z 05060; rural
Old City; RMC Place; ORANGE; ▲ Strafford; ***242** G-6; mail Strafford z 05072; rural
Olympus; WINDSOR; see Lympus (RMC Place)
Orange; RMC Place; ORANGE; ▲ Orange; **242** F-6; 🅿; z 05641; ● 70
Orange; MCD-Town; ORANGE; ***242** F-6; 🅿; z 05641; Ⓟ 915; © 965
ORANGE; **242** F-6; Ⓟ 26,149; © 28,226; ◆ 28,411
Orchard Lane; RMC Place; WINDSOR; ▲ Springfield; mail Springfield z 05156; ● 80
Orleans; Inc. Place; ORLEANS; ▲ Barton; **242** B-6; elev. 740ft./226m.; 🅿; z 05860; Ⓟ 806; © 826
ORLEANS; **242** B-6; Ⓟ 24,053; © 26,277; ◆ 27,078
Orwell; RMC Place; ADDISON; ▲ Orwell; **242** G-2; elev. 379ft./116m.; 🅿; z 05760; ● 170
Orwell; MCD-Town; ADDISON; ***242** G-2; 🅿; z 05760; Ⓟ 1,114; © 1,185

P

Panton; RMC Place; ADDISON; ▲ Panton; **242** F-2; 🅿; z 05491; ● 45
Panton; MCD-Town; ADDISON; ***242** F-2; 🅿; z 05491; Ⓟ 606; © 682
Paper Mill Village (Bennington Falls); RMC Place; BENNINGTON; ▲ Bennington; ***242** L-2; mail North Bennington z 05257; ● 200
Passumpsic; RMC Place; CALEDONIA; ▲ Barnet; **242** E-7; elev. 526ft./160m.; 🅿; z 05861; ● 200
Pawlet; RMC Place; RUTLAND; ▲ Pawlet; **242** J-3; elev. 681ft./208m.; 🅿; z 05761; ● 230
Pawlet; MCD-Town; RUTLAND; ***242** J-3; 🅿; z 05761; Ⓟ 1,314; © 1,394
Peacham; RMC Place; CALEDONIA; ▲ Peacham; **242** E-6; elev. 1,310ft./399m.; 🅿; z 05862; ● 220
Peacham; MCD-Town; CALEDONIA; ***242** E-6; 🅿; z 05862; Ⓟ 627; © 665
Pearl; RMC Place; GRAND ISLE; ▲ Grand Isle; **242** C-2; ★ **BUR**; mail Grand Isle z 05458; ● 60
Peaseville; WINDSOR; see Andover (RMC Place)
Pedden Acres; RMC Place; WINDSOR; ▲ Springfield; ***242** J-5; mail Springfield z 05156; ● 200
Perkinsville; Inc. Place; WINDSOR; ▲ Weathersfield; **242** J-5; 🅿; z 05151; Ⓟ 148; © 142
Peru; RMC Place; BENNINGTON; ▲ Peru; **242** J-4; 🅿; z 05152; ● 150
Peru; MCD-Town; BENNINGTON; ***242** J-4; 🅿; z 05152; Ⓟ 324; © 416
Peth; RMC Place; ORANGE; ▲ Braintree; ***242** G-5; elev. 846ft./258m.; mail Randolph z 05060; rural
Pierces Corner; RMC Place; RUTLAND; ▲ Clarendon; ***242** I-4; elev. 721ft./220m.; mail North Clarendon z 05759; rural
Pikes Falls; RMC Place; WINDHAM; ▲ Jamaica; ***242** K-4; mail Jamaica z 05343; ● 50
Pittsfield; RMC Place; RUTLAND; ▲ Pittsfield; **242** H-4; 🅿; z 05762; ● 135
Pittsfield; MCD-Town; RUTLAND; ***242** G-4; 🅿; z 05762; Ⓟ 389; © 427
Pittsford; RMC Place; RUTLAND; ▲ Pittsford; **242** H-3; elev. 530ft./162m.; 🅿; z 05763; ● 650
Pittsford; MCD-Town; RUTLAND; ***242** H-3; 🅿; z 05763; Ⓟ 2,919; © 3,140
Pittsford Mills; RMC Place; RUTLAND; ▲ Pittsford; ***242** H-3; mail Pittsford z 05763; rural
Plainfield; RMC Place; WASHINGTON; ▲ Marshfield, Plainfield; **242** E-5; elev. 803ft./245m.; 🅿 🅲 548; z 05650, z 05667; ● 600
Plainfield; MCD-Town; WASHINGTON; ***242** E-6; 🅿 🅲 548; z 05650, z 05667; Ⓟ 1,302; © 1,286
Pleasant Valley; RMC Place; LAMOILLE; ▲ Cambridge; ***242** C-4; mail Cambridge z 05444
Plymouth; RMC Place; WINDSOR; ▲ Plymouth; **242** I-4; 🅿; z 05056; ● 100
Plymouth; MCD-Town; WINDSOR; ***242** I-4; 🅿; z 05056; Ⓟ 440; © 555
Plymouth Kingdom; RMC Place; WINDSOR; ▲ Plymouth; ***242** I-5; elev. 1,611ft./491m.; mail Ludlow z 05149, Plymouth z 05056; ● 25
Plymouth Union; RMC Place; WINDSOR; ▲ Plymouth; ***242** I-4; elev. 1,217ft./371m.; mail Plymouth z 05056
Pomfret; RMC Place; WINDSOR; ▲ Pomfret; **242** H-5; mail North Pomfret z 05053; ● 50
Pomfret; MCD-Town; WINDSOR; ***242** H-5; mail North Pomfret z 05053; Ⓟ 874; © 997; Ⓡ 979
Pompanoosuc (Kendall); RMC Place; WINDSOR; ▲ Norwich; ***242** H-6; mail East Thetford z 05043; rural
Post Mills; RMC Place; ORANGE; ▲ Thetford; **242** G-6; elev. 707ft./215m.; 🅿; z 05058; ● 220
Potash Bay; RMC Place; ADDISON; ▲ Addison; ***242** F-2; mail Vergennes z 05491
Potash Point; RMC Place; ADDISON; ▲ Panton; ***242** F-2; mail Vergennes z 05491; rural
Pottersville; RMC Place; LAMOILLE; ▲ Wolcott; ***242** D-5; mail Wolcott z 05680; rural
Poultney; Inc. Place; RUTLAND; ▲ Poultney; **242** I-2; elev. 432ft./132m.; 🅿 🅲 759; z 05741, z 05764; Ⓟ 1,731; © 1,575
Poultney; MCD-Town; RUTLAND; ***242** I-3; 🅿 🅲 759; z 05741, z 05764; Ⓟ 3,498; © 3,633
Pownal; RMC Place; BENNINGTON; ▲ Pownal; **242** M-2; elev. 553ft./169m.; 🅿; z 05261; ● 320
Pownal; MCD-Town; BENNINGTON; ***242** L-3; 🅿; z 05261; Ⓟ 3,485; © 3,560
Pownal Center; RMC Place; BENNINGTON; ▲ Pownal; **242** L-2; elev. 985ft./300m.; mail Pownal z 05261; ● 280

Entries in **UPPERCASE** are counties.
Entries in **bold** have populations of 2,500 or more.
Names in parentheses are alternate names.

Inc. Place	Incorporated Place
RMC Place	Rand McNally Designated Place
CDP	Census Designated Place
MCD	Minor Civil Division

⊡	County Seat
▲	Minor Civil Division
elev.	Elevation
🅿	Post Office
🅷	Hospital
🅲	College
■	Principal Business Center
★	Ranally Metro Area (RMA) Abbreviation
z	Zip Code(s)
Ⓟ	Previous Census Population
Ⓡ	Revised Census Population
Ⓐ	Annexation Population
●	Rand McNally Population Estimate
©	Final Census Population
Ⓢ	Special Census Population
◆	Estimated Population

For additional definitions see Glossary, Volume 1, and Introduction, Volume 2.

Prindle Corners; RMC Place; CHITTENDEN; ▲ Charlotte; *242 E-3; ★ BUR; mail Charlotte z 05445
Proctor; RMC Place; RUTLAND; ▲ Proctor; 242 H-3; elev. 484ft./148m.; 🄿; z 05765; ● 1,979
Proctor; MCD-Town; RUTLAND; *242 H-3; 🄿; z 05765; Ⓟ 1,979; © 1,877
Proctorsville; RMC Place; WINDSOR; ▲ Cavendish; 242 I-5; 🄿; z 05153; ● 480
Prospect Hill; RMC Place; RUTLAND; ▲ Rutland; *242 H-3; mail Rutland z 05701; rural
Prosper; RMC Place; WINDSOR; ▲ Woodstock; *242 H-5; elev. 851ft./259m.; mail Woodstock z 05091; rural
Putnamville; RMC Place; WASHINGTON; ▲ Middlesex; 242 E-5; mail Montpelier z 05602; ● 40
Putney; RMC Place; WINDHAM; ▲ Putney; 242 L-5; 🄿; z 05346; ● 1,150
Putney; MCD-Town; WINDHAM; *242 K-5; 🄿; z 05346; Ⓟ 2,352; © 2,634

Q

Quechee; RMC Place; WINDSOR; ▲ Hartford; 242 H-5; 🄿; z 05059; ● 600

R

Ralston Corner; RMC Place; ESSEX; ▲ Concord; *242 D-8; elev. 1,362ft./415m.; mail Concord z 05824; rural
Randolph; RMC Place; ORANGE; ▲ Randolph; 242 G-5; elev. 684ft./208m.; 🄿 🄷; z 05060; ● 2,200
Randolph; MCD-Town; ORANGE; *242 G-5; 🄿 🄲 1,414; z 05060; Ⓟ 4,764; © 4,853
Randolph Center; RMC Place; ORANGE; ▲ Randolph; 242 G-5; 🄿 🄲 1,414; z 05061; ● 250
Rawsonville; RMC Place; WINDHAM; ▲ Jamaica; 242 K-4; elev. 1,136ft./346m.; mail South Londonderry z 05155; ● 140
Reading; WINDSOR; see Felchville (RMC Place)
Reading; MCD-Town; WINDSOR; *242 I-5; 🄿; z 05062; Ⓟ 614; © 707
Reading Center; RMC Place; WINDSOR; ▲ Reading; *242 I-5; mail Reading z 05062; ● 30
Readsboro; RMC Place; BENNINGTON; ▲ Readsboro; 242 M-3; elev. 1,190ft./363m.; 🄿; z 05350, z 05352; ● 400
Readsboro; MCD-Town; BENNINGTON; *242 L-3; 🄿; z 05350, z 05352; Ⓟ 762; © 809; Ⓡ 805
Readsboro Falls; RMC Place; BENNINGTON; ▲ Readsboro; *242 L-3; mail Readsboro z 05350; rural
Red Village; RMC Place; CALEDONIA; ▲ Lyndon; *242 D-7; mail Lyndonville z 05851; ● 50
Reedville; RMC Place; WINDSOR; ▲ Chester; *242 J-5; elev. 822ft./251m.; mail Chester z 05143
Rhode Island Corner; RMC Place; CHITTENDEN; ▲ Hinesburg; *242 E-3; ★ BUR; mail Richmond z 05477
Rices Mills; RMC Place; ORANGE; ▲ Thetford; *242 G-6; mail Thetford Center z 05075; rural
Richford; RMC Place; FRANKLIN; ▲ Richford; 242 A-5; elev. 1,477ft./450m.; 🄿; z 05476; Ⓟ 1,425
Richford; MCD-Town; FRANKLIN; *242 A-5; 🄿; z 05476; Ⓟ 2,178; © 2,321
Richmond; RMC Place; CHITTENDEN; ▲ Richmond; 242 D-3; elev. 319ft./97m.; 🄿; ★ BUR; z 05477; ● 700
Richmond; MCD-Town; CHITTENDEN; *242 D-3; 🄿; ★ BUR; z 05477; Ⓟ 3,729; © 4,090; ◆ 4,206
Richville (Shoreham Center); RMC Place; ADDISON; ▲ Shoreham; *242 G-2; mail Shoreham z 05770
Richville; RMC Place; BENNINGTON; ▲ Manchester; *242 K-3; mail Manchester Center z 05255; rural
Ricker Mills; RMC Place; CALEDONIA; ▲ Groton; *242 E-6; elev. 1,066ft./325m.; mail Groton z 05046; rural
Ripton; RMC Place; ADDISON; ▲ Ripton; 242 G-3; 🄿; z 05766; ● 130
Ripton; MCD-Town; ADDISON; *242 F-3; 🄿; z 05766; Ⓟ 444; © 556
Riverton; WASHINGTON; see West Berlin (RMC Place)
Robinson; RMC Place; WINDSOR; ▲ Rochester; *242 G-4; mail Rochester z 05767
Rochester; RMC Place; WINDSOR; ▲ Rochester; 242 G-4; 🄿; z 05767; ● 500
Rochester; MCD-Town; WINDSOR; *242 G-4; 🄿; z 05767; Ⓟ 1,181; © 1,171
Rockingham; RMC Place; WINDHAM; ▲ Rockingham; 242 J-5; elev. 487ft./148m.; mail Bellows Falls z 05101; ● 120
Rockingham; MCD-Town; WINDHAM; *242 K-5; mail Bellows Falls z 05101; Ⓟ 5,484; © 5,309
Rockville; RMC Place; ADDISON; ▲ Starksboro; *242 E-3; mail Bristol z 05443; rural
Rocky Dale; RMC Place; ADDISON; ▲ Bristol; *242 F-3; elev. 629ft./192m.; mail Bristol z 05443; ● 60
Round Pond; RMC Place; ORANGE; ▲ Newbury; *242 F-6; mail South Ryegate z 05069; rural
Roxbury; RMC Place; WASHINGTON; ▲ Roxbury; 242 F-4; elev. 1,010ft./308m.; 🄿; z 05669; ● 300
Roxbury; MCD-Town; WASHINGTON; *242 F-4; 🄿; z 05669; Ⓟ 575; © 576
Roxbury Flat; RMC Place; WASHINGTON; ▲ Roxbury; 242 F-4; elev. 978ft./298m.; mail Roxbury z 05669; ● 40
Royalton; RMC Place; WINDSOR; ▲ Royalton; 242 G-5; elev. 516ft./157m.; mail South Royalton z 05068; ● 100
Royalton; MCD-Town; WINDSOR; *242 G-5; 🄲 613; mail South Royalton z 05068; Ⓟ 2,389; © 2,603
Rupert; RMC Place; BENNINGTON; ▲ Rupert; 242 J-2; elev. 839ft./256m.; 🄿; z 05768; ● 140
Rupert; MCD-Town; BENNINGTON; *242 J-3; 🄿; z 05768; Ⓟ 654; © 704
Russellville; RMC Place; RUTLAND; ▲ Shrewsbury; *242 I-4; mail Cuttingsville z 05738; rural
Russtown; RMC Place; WINDSOR; ▲ Hartford; *242 H-6; elev. 613ft./187m.; mail North Hartland z 05052, White River Junction z 05001; ● 120
Rutland; Inc. Place; ⊡ RUTLAND; 242 H-3; elev. 648ft./198m.; 🄿 🄷 🄲 509 ■; z 05701-02; Ⓟ 18,230; © 17,292; ◆ 17,178
Rutland; MCD-Town; RUTLAND; *242 H-3; 🄿 🄲 509; z 05701-02; does not include City of Rutland; Ⓟ 3,781; © 4,038
RUTLAND; 242 I-3; Ⓟ 62,142; © 63,400; ◆ 62,498
Ryegate; CALEDONIA; see Ryegate Corner (RMC Place)
Ryegate; MCD-Town; CALEDONIA; *242 E-7; 🄿; z 05042; Ⓟ 1,058; © 1,150
Ryegate Corner (Ryegate); RMC Place; CALEDONIA; ▲ Ryegate; 242 E-7; mail East Ryegate z 05042; ● 90

S

Saint Albans; Inc. Place; ⊡ FRANKLIN; 242 B-3; elev. 429ft./131m.; 🄿 🄷; ★ BUR; z 05478-79 & mail Saint Albans Bay z 05481; Ⓟ 7,339; © 7,650; ◆ 7,179
St. Albans; MCD-Town; FRANKLIN; *242 B-3; ★ BUR; mail Saint Albans Bay z 05481; does not include City of Saint Albans; Ⓟ 4,606; © 5,086; Ⓡ 5,324; ◆ 5,217
Saint Albans Bay; RMC Place; FRANKLIN; ▲ St. Albans; 242 B-3; elev. 109ft./33m.; 🄿; ★ BUR; z 05481 & mail Saint Albans z 05478; ● 500
St. George; MCD-Town; CHITTENDEN; *242 D-3; 🄿; ★ BUR; z 05495; Ⓟ 705; © 698; ◆ 726
Saint Johnsbury; CDP; ⊡ CALEDONIA; ▲ St. Johnsbury; 242 D-7; elev. 588ft./179m.; 🄿 🄷; z 05819; Ⓟ 6,424; © 6,319
St. Johnsbury; MCD-Town; CALEDONIA; *242 D-7; 🄿; z 05819; Ⓟ 7,608; © 7,571
Saint Johnsbury Center (Centervale); RMC Place; CALEDONIA; ▲ St. Johnsbury; 242 D-7; 🄿; z 05863; ● 450
Saint Rocks; RMC Place; FRANKLIN; ▲ Fairfield; 242 B-4; mail Sheldon z 05483; ● 25
Salisbury; RMC Place; ADDISON; ▲ Salisbury; *242 G-3; 🄿; z 05769; ● 200
Salisbury; MCD-Town; ADDISON; *242 G-3; 🄿; z 05769; Ⓟ 1,024; © 1,090
Samsonville; RMC Place; FRANKLIN; ▲ Enosburg; *242 B-4; elev. 416ft./127m.; mail Enosburg Falls z 05450
Sanderson Corner; RMC Place; FRANKLIN; ▲ Fairfax; *242 C-3; ★ BUR; mail Fairfax z 05454; rural
Sandgate; RMC Place; BENNINGTON; ▲ Sandgate; 242 K-3; 🄿; z 05250; ● 80
Sandgate; MCD-Town; BENNINGTON; *242 K-3; 🄿; z 05250; Ⓟ 278; © 353
Saxtons River; Inc. Place; WINDHAM; ▲ Rockingham; 242 K-5; elev. 528ft./161m.; 🄿; z 05154; Ⓟ 541; © 519
Scottsville; RMC Place; RUTLAND; ▲ Danby; *242 I-3; elev. 833ft./254m.; mail Danby z 05739; ● 35
Searsburg; RMC Place; BENNINGTON; ▲ Searsburg; 242 L-3; elev. 1,734ft./529m.; 🄿; z 05363; ● 50
Searsburg; MCD-Town; BENNINGTON; *242 L-3; 🄿; z 05363; Ⓟ 85; © 96
Seymour Lake; RMC Place; ORLEANS; ▲ Morgan; *242 B-7; mail Morgan z 05853; summer pop. 370
Shadow Lake; RMC Place; ORLEANS; ▲ Glover; *242 C-6; mail Glover z 05839; summer pop. 300
Shady Rill; RMC Place; WASHINGTON; ▲ Middlesex; *242 E-5; elev. 759ft./231m.; mail Montpelier z 05602
Shaftsbury; BENNINGTON; see South Shaftsbury (CDP)
Shaftsbury; MCD-Town; BENNINGTON; *242 L-3; 🄿; z 05262; Ⓟ 3,368; © 3,767
Shaftsbury Center; RMC Place; BENNINGTON; ▲ Shaftsbury; 242 L-3; elev. 1,095ft./334m.; mail Shaftsbury z 05262; ● 110
Sharon; RMC Place; WINDSOR; ▲ Sharon; 242 G-5; elev. 501ft./153m.; 🄿; z 05065; ● 250
Sharon; MCD-Town; WINDSOR; *242 G-5; 🄿; z 05065; Ⓟ 1,211; © 1,411
Shawville; RMC Place; FRANKLIN; ▲ Sheldon; *242 B-4; elev. 390ft./119m.; mail Franklin z 05457
Sheddsville; RMC Place; WINDSOR; ▲ West Windsor; *242 I-5; elev. 176ft./54m.; mail Windsor z 05089
Sheffield; RMC Place; CALEDONIA; ▲ Sheffield; 242 C-7; 🄿; z 05866; ● 230
Sheffield; MCD-Town; CALEDONIA; *242 C-7; 🄿; z 05866; Ⓟ 541; © 727
Sheffield Square; RMC Place; CALEDONIA; ▲ Sheffield; *242 C-6; elev. 1,652ft./504m.; mail Sheffield z 05866; rural
Shelburne; RMC Place; CHITTENDEN; ▲ Shelburne; 242 D-3; elev. 148ft./45m.; 🄿; ★ BUR; z 05482; ● 400
Shelburne; MCD-Town; CHITTENDEN; *242 D-2; 🄿; ★ BUR; z 05482; Ⓟ 5,871; © 6,944; ◆ 7,430
Shelburne Falls; RMC Place; CHITTENDEN; ▲ Shelburne; 242 D-3; ★ BUR; mail Shelburne z 05482; ● 120
Shelburne Road Section; RMC Place; CHITTENDEN; ★ BUR; mail South Burlington z 05403; pop. incl. with South Burlington (Inc. Place)
Sheldon; RMC Place; FRANKLIN; ▲ Sheldon; 242 B-4; elev. 373ft./114m.; 🄿; z 05455, z 05483; ● 320
Sheldon; MCD-Town; FRANKLIN; *242 B-4; 🄿; z 05455, z 05483; Ⓟ 1,748; © 1,990
Sheldon Junction; RMC Place; FRANKLIN; ▲ Sheldon; *242 B-4; elev. 347ft./106m.; mail Sheldon z 05483; ● 35
Sheldon Springs; RMC Place; FRANKLIN; ▲ Sheldon; 242 B-3; 🄿; z 05485; ● 260
Sherburne; RUTLAND; see Killington (MCD-Town)
Sherburne Center; RMC Place; RUTLAND; mail Killington z 05751; ● 25
Sherburne Center; RUTLAND; see Killington (RMC Place)
Shoreham; RMC Place; ADDISON; ▲ Shoreham; 242 G-2; elev. 333ft./101m.; 🄿; z 05770; ● 100
Shoreham; MCD-Town; ADDISON; *242 G-2; 🄿; z 05770; Ⓟ 1,115; © 1,222
Shoreham Center; ADDISON; see Richville (RMC Place)
Shrewsbury; RMC Place; RUTLAND; ▲ Shrewsbury; 242 I-4; elev. 1,633ft./498m.; 🄿; z 05738; ● 60
Shrewsbury; MCD-Town; RUTLAND; *242 I-4; 🄿; z 05738; Ⓟ 1,107; © 1,108
Simonsville; RMC Place; WINDSOR; ▲ Andover; 242 J-4; elev. 1,163ft./354m.; mail Chester z 05143; ● 80
Simpsonville; RMC Place; WINDHAM; ▲ Townshend; *242 K-5; mail Townshend z 05353; ● 50
Smithville; RMC Place; WINDSOR; ▲ Ludlow; *242 I-5; mail Ludlow z 05149
Smugglers Notch (Madonna); RMC Place; LAMOILLE; ▲ Cambridge; 🄿; z 05464
Sodom; RMC Place; BENNINGTON; ▲ Shaftsbury; *242 L-2; mail North Bennington z 05257; ● 100
South Albany; RMC Place; ORLEANS; ▲ Albany; 242 C-6; elev. 1,358ft./414m.; mail West Glover z 05875
South Alburg; RMC Place; GRAND ISLE; ▲ Alburg; 242 B-2; mail Alburgh z 05440; ● 100
South Barre; CDP; WASHINGTON; ▲ Barre; 242 E-5; 🄿; z 05670; Ⓟ 1,314; © 1,242
South Barton; ORLEANS; see Willoughby (RMC Place)
South Burlington; Inc. Place; CHITTENDEN; 242 D-3; elev. 300ft./91m.; 🄿 ■; ★ BUR; z 05403, z 05407 & mail Burlington z 05401, z 05406; Ⓟ 12,809; © 15,814; Ⓡ 14,879; ◆ 17,335
South Cabot; RMC Place; WASHINGTON; ▲ Cabot; *242 E-6; mail Marshfield z 05658
South Cambridge; RMC Place; LAMOILLE; ▲ Cambridge; *242 C-4; elev. 842ft./257m.; mail Jeffersonville z 05464
South Corinth; RMC Place; ORANGE; ▲ Corinth; *242 F-6; elev. 783ft./239m.; mail Bradford z 05033, Corinth z 05039; rural
South Danville; CALEDONIA; see Greenbank Hollow (RMC Place)
South Dorset; RMC Place; BENNINGTON; ▲ Dorset; 242 J-3; mail Dorset z 05251; ● 220
South Duxbury; RMC Place; WASHINGTON; ▲ Duxbury; *242 E-4; 🄿; z 05660
South End; RMC Place; RUTLAND; ▲ Mount Tabor; *242 J-3; mail Danby z 05739; ● 40
South Fairlee; ORANGE; see Ely (RMC Place)
South Hero; RMC Place; GRAND ISLE; ▲ South Hero; 242 C-2; elev. 152ft./46m.; 🄿; ★ BUR; z 05486; ● 350
South Hero; MCD-Town; GRAND ISLE; *242 C-2; 🄿; ★ BUR; z 05486; Ⓟ 1,404; © 1,696; ◆ 1,749
South Hinesburg; RMC Place; CHITTENDEN; ▲ Hinesburg; *242 E-3; ★ BUR; mail Hinesburg z 05461; rural
South Kirby; RMC Place; CALEDONIA; ▲ Kirby; *242 D-7; mail Concord z 05824; rural
South Lincoln; RMC Place; ADDISON; ▲ Lincoln; 242 F-3; mail Bristol z 05443; ● 70
South Londonderry; RMC Place; WINDHAM; ▲ Londonderry; 242 J-4; 🄿; z 05155; ● 400
South Lunenburg; RMC Place; ESSEX; ▲ Lunenburg; 242 D-8; mail Lunenburg z 05906; ● 100
South Newbury; RMC Place; ORANGE; ▲ Newbury; 242 F-7; mail Newbury z 05051; ● 70
South Newfane; RMC Place; WINDHAM; ▲ Newfane; 242 L-4; elev. 669ft./204m.; 🄿; z 05351; ● 150
South Northfield; RMC Place; WASHINGTON; ▲ Northfield; 242 F-5; mail Northfield z 05663; ● 80
South Peacham; RMC Place; CALEDONIA; ▲ Peacham; 242 E-6; mail Barnet z 05821; ● 90
South Pomfret; RMC Place; WINDSOR; ▲ Pomfret; 242 H-5; elev. 737ft./225m.; 🄿; z 05067; ● 160
South Poultney; RMC Place; RUTLAND; ▲ Poultney; 242 I-2; elev. 579ft./176m.; mail Poultney z 05764; ● 110
South Randolph; RMC Place; ORANGE; ▲ Randolph; *242 G-5; elev. 563ft./172m.; mail East Randolph z 05041; ● 25
South Reading; RMC Place; WINDSOR; ▲ Reading; 242 I-5; elev. 1,274ft./388m.; 🄿; z 05153; ● 130
South Richford; RMC Place; FRANKLIN; ▲ Richford; *242 B-5; mail Richford z 05476; rural
South Royalton; RMC Place; WINDSOR; ▲ Royalton; 242 G-5; elev. 502ft./153m.; 🄿 🄲 613; z 05068; ● 750
South Ryegate; RMC Place; CALEDONIA; ▲ Ryegate; 242 E-6; 🄿; z 05069; ● 450
South Shaftsbury (Shaftsbury); CDP; BENNINGTON; ▲ Shaftsbury; 242 K-3; mail Shaftsbury z 05262; © 772
South Sherburne (West Bridgewater); RMC Place; RUTLAND, WINDSOR; ▲ Bridgewater, Killington; 242 H-4; mail Bridgewater z 05034, Bridgewater Corners z 05035; ● 80
South Starksboro; RMC Place; ADDISON; ▲ Starksboro; *242 F-3; elev. 1,089ft./332m.; mail Bristol z 05443, Starksboro z 05487; rural
South Strafford; RMC Place; ORANGE; ▲ Strafford; 242 G-6; elev. 894ft./272m.; 🄿; z 05070; ● 150
South Tunbridge; RMC Place; ORANGE; ▲ Tunbridge; *242 G-5; elev. 542ft./165m.; mail South Royalton z 05068; rural
South Vershire; RMC Place; ORANGE; ▲ Vershire; *242 G-6; elev. 1,312ft./400m.; mail Vershire z 05079; rural
South Walden; RMC Place; CALEDONIA; ▲ Walden; *242 D-6; elev. 1,232ft./376m.; mail Hardwick z 05843
South Wallingford; RMC Place; RUTLAND; ▲ Wallingford; 242 I-3; mail Wallingford z 05773; ● 230
South Wardsboro; RMC Place; WINDHAM; ▲ Wardsboro; *242 K-4; elev. 1,594ft./486m.; mail Wardsboro z 05355
South Washington; RMC Place; ORANGE; ▲ Washington; *242 F-6; elev. 1,374ft./419m.; mail Washington z 05675; rural
South Wheelock; RMC Place; CALEDONIA; ▲ Wheelock; *242 D-7; mail Lyndonville z 05851
South Windham; RMC Place; WINDHAM; ▲ Windham; 242 K-4; mail West Townshend z 05359; ● 100
South Woodbury; RMC Place; WASHINGTON; ▲ Woodbury; 242 D-5; mail East Calais z 05650, Woodbury z 05681; ● 70
South Woodstock; RMC Place; WINDSOR; ▲ Woodstock; 242 H-5; elev. 1,055ft./322m.; 🄿; z 05071; ● 100
Spoonerville; RMC Place; WINDSOR; ▲ Springfield, Chester; *242 J-5; elev. 684ft./208m.; mail Chester z 05143, Chester Depot z 05144; ● 40
Springfield; CDP; WINDSOR; ▲ Springfield; 242 J-5; elev. 410ft./125m.; 🄿 🄷; z 05156; Ⓟ 4,207; © 3,938
Springfield; MCD-Town; WINDSOR; *242 J-5; 🄿; z 05156; Ⓟ 9,579; © 9,078
Stamford; RMC Place; BENNINGTON; ▲ Stamford; 242 M-3; elev. 1,130ft./344m.; 🄿; z 05352; ● 400
Stamford; MCD-Town; BENNINGTON; *242 M-3; 🄿; z 05352; Ⓟ 773; © 813
Stannard; RMC Place; CALEDONIA; ▲ Stannard; 242 D-6; mail Greensboro Bend z 05842; ● 25
Stannard; MCD-Town; CALEDONIA; *242 D-6; mail Greensboro Bend z 05842; Ⓟ 148; © 185
Starksboro; RMC Place; ADDISON; ▲ Starksboro; 242 E-3; elev. 615ft./187m.; 🄿; z 05487 & mail Bristol z 05443; ● 130
Starksboro; MCD-Town; ADDISON; *242 E-3; 🄿; z 05487 & mail Bristol z 05443; Ⓟ 1,511; © 1,898
Stevens Mills; RMC Place; FRANKLIN; ▲ Richford; 242 A-5; mail Richford z 05476; ● 30
Stevensville; RMC Place; CHITTENDEN; ▲ Underhill; *242 D-4; mail Underhill z 05489; ● 80
Stockbridge; RMC Place; WINDSOR; ▲ Stockbridge; 242 G-4; elev. 857ft./261m.; 🄿; z 05772; ● 100
Stockbridge; MCD-Town; WINDSOR; *242 H-4; 🄿; z 05772; Ⓟ 618; © 674
Stowe; RMC Place; LAMOILLE; ▲ Stowe; 242 D-5; elev. 723ft./220m.; 🄿; z 05672; Ⓟ 450
Stowe; MCD-Town; LAMOILLE; *242 D-4; 🄿; z 05672; Ⓟ 3,433; © 4,339
Strafford; RMC Place; ORANGE; ▲ Strafford; 242 G-6; 🄿; z 05072; ● 70
Strafford; MCD-Town; ORANGE; *242 G-6; 🄿; z 05072; Ⓟ 902; © 1,045
Stratton; RMC Place; WINDHAM; ▲ Stratton; *242 K-4; 🄿; z 05360; rural
Stratton; MCD-Town; WINDHAM; *242 K-4; 🄿; z 05360; Ⓟ 121; © 136
Stratton Mountain; RMC Place; BENNINGTON, WINDHAM; ▲ Stratton; *242 K-4; 🄿; z 05155; ● 50
Sudbury; RMC Place; RUTLAND; ▲ Sudbury; 242 G-3; elev. 572ft./174m.; 🄿; z 05733; ● 60
Sudbury; MCD-Town; RUTLAND; *242 G-3; 🄿; z 05733; Ⓟ 516; © 583
Sugarbush Valley; RMC Place; WASHINGTON; 🄿; z 05674
Summer Point; RMC Place; ADDISON; ▲ Ferrisburg; *242 E-2; mail Vergennes z 05491
Summit; RMC Place; RUTLAND; ▲ Mount Holly; *242 I-4; mail Mount Holly z 05758; rural
Sunderland; RMC Place; BENNINGTON; ▲ Sunderland; 242 K-3; 🄿; z 05250 & mail East Arlington z 05252; ● 220
Sunderland; MCD-Town; BENNINGTON; *242 K-3; 🄿; z 05250 & mail East Arlington z 05252; Ⓟ 872; © 850
Sutton; RMC Place; CALEDONIA; ▲ Sutton; 242 C-7; elev. 1,152ft./351m.; 🄿; z 05867; ● 130
Sutton; MCD-Town; CALEDONIA; *242 C-7; 🄿; z 05867; Ⓟ 854; © 1,001
Swanton; Inc. Place; FRANKLIN; ▲ Swanton; 242 B-3; elev. 157ft./48m.; 🄿; ★ BUR; z 05488; Ⓟ 2,360; © 2,548
Swanton; MCD-Town; FRANKLIN; *242 B-3; 🄿; ★ BUR; z 05488; Ⓟ 5,636; © 6,203; ◆ 6,704

T

Tafts Corner; RMC Place; CHITTENDEN; ▲ Williston; 242 M-10; ★ BUR; mail Williston z 05495; ● 50
Taftsville; RMC Place; WINDSOR; ▲ Woodstock; 242 H-5; elev. 669ft./204m.; 🄿; z 05073; ● 150
Talcville; RMC Place; WINDSOR; ▲ Rochester; *242 G-4; elev. 825ft./251m.; mail Rochester z 05767
Tarbellville; RMC Place; RUTLAND; ▲ Mount Holly; 242 I-4; mail East Wallingford z 05742; ● 50
The Bluffs; RMC Place; ORLEANS; mail Newport z 05855; pop. incl. with Newport (Inc. Place)
The Island; RMC Place; WINDSOR; ▲ Weston; *242 J-4; elev. 1,186ft./361m.; mail Weston z 05161
Thetford; ORANGE; see East Thetford (RMC Place)
Thetford; ORANGE; see Thetford Hill (RMC Place)
Thetford; MCD-Town; ORANGE; *242 G-6; 🄿; z 05074; Ⓟ 2,438; © 2,617
Thetford Center; RMC Place; ORANGE; ▲ Thetford; 242 G-6; 🄿; z 05075; ● 190
Thetford Hill (Thetford); RMC Place; ORANGE; ▲ Thetford; 242 G-6; 🄿; z 05074; ● 130
Thompsonburg; RMC Place; WINDHAM; ▲ Londonderry; *242 J-4; elev. 1,204ft./367m.; mail Londonderry z 05148; rural
Tinmouth; RMC Place; RUTLAND; ▲ Tinmouth; 242 I-3; elev. 1,276ft./389m.; 🄿; z 05773; ● 80
Tinmouth; MCD-Town; RUTLAND; *242 I-3; 🄿; z 05773; Ⓟ 455; © 567
Topsham; ORANGE; see East Topsham (RMC Place)
Topsham; MCD-Town; ORANGE; *242 F-6; 🄿; z 05076; Ⓟ 944; © 1,142
Topsham Four Corners; RMC Place; ORANGE; ▲ Topsham; *242 F-6; elev. 816ft./249m.; mail East Corinth z 05040, Topsham z 05076
Townshend; RMC Place; WINDHAM; ▲ Townshend; 242 K-4; elev. 574ft./175m.; 🄿 🄷; z 05353 & mail West Townshend z 05359; ● 180
Townshend; MCD-Town; WINDHAM; *242 K-5; 🄿; z 05353 & mail West Townshend z 05359; Ⓟ 1,019; © 1,149
Troy; RMC Place; ORLEANS; ▲ Troy; 242 B-6; elev. 752ft./229m.; 🄿; z 05868; ● 300
Troy; MCD-Town; ORLEANS; *242 B-6; 🄿; z 05868; Ⓟ 1,609; © 1,564
Tunbridge; RMC Place; ORANGE; ▲ Tunbridge; 242 G-5; 🄿; z 05077; ● 110
Tunbridge; MCD-Town; ORANGE; *242 G-5; 🄿; z 05077; Ⓟ 1,154; © 1,309
Tyson; RMC Place; WINDSOR; ▲ Plymouth; *242 I-4; mail Ludlow z 05149

U

Underhill (Underhill Flats); RMC Place; CHITTENDEN; ▲ Jericho, Underhill; 242 D-4; elev. 706ft./215m.; 🄿; ★ BUR; z 05489; ● 400
Underhill; MCD-Town; CHITTENDEN; *242 D-4; 🄿; z 05489; Ⓟ 2,799; © 2,980
Underhill Center; RMC Place; CHITTENDEN; ▲ Underhill; 242 D-4; elev. 804ft./245m.; 🄿; z 05490; ● 300
Underhill Flats; CHITTENDEN; see Underhill (RMC Place)
Union Village; RMC Place; ORANGE, WINDSOR; ▲ Norwich, Thetford; 242 G-6; elev. 427ft./130m.; mail East Thetford z 05043; ● 50
Upper Graniteville; RMC Place; WASHINGTON; ▲ Barre; *242 F-5; mail Graniteville z 05654; ● 250

V

Valley Lake; RMC Place; WASHINGTON; ▲ Woodbury; *242 D-5; mail Woodbury z 05681; rural
Vergennes; Inc. Place; ADDISON; 242 F-2; elev. 205ft./62m.; 🄿; z 05491; Ⓟ 2,578; © 2,741
Vernon; RMC Place; WINDHAM; ▲ Vernon; 242 M-5; elev. 301ft./92m.; 🄿; z 05354; ● 250
Vernon; MCD-Town; WINDHAM; *242 M-5; 🄿; z 05354; Ⓟ 1,850; © 2,141
Vershire; RMC Place; ORANGE; ▲ Vershire; 242 G-6; elev. 1,268ft./386m.; 🄿; z 05079; ● 120
Vershire; MCD-Town; ORANGE; *242 G-6; 🄿; z 05079; Ⓟ 560; © 629
Vershire Center; RMC Place; ORANGE; ▲ Vershire; *242 G-6; mail Vershire z 05079; rural
Vershire Heights; RMC Place; ORANGE; ▲ Vershire; *242 F-6; elev. 1,832ft./558m.; mail Vershire z 05079; ● 40
Victory; MCD-Town; ESSEX; *242 D-8; 🄿; z 05858; Ⓟ 50; © 97

W

Waitsfield; RMC Place; WASHINGTON; ▲ Waitsfield; 242 E-4; elev. 698ft./213m.; 🄿; z 05673; ● 320
Waitsfield; MCD-Town; WASHINGTON; *242 E-4; 🄿; z 05673; Ⓟ 1,422; © 1,659
Waitsfield Common; RMC Place; WASHINGTON; ▲ Waitsfield; *242 E-4; elev. 1,073ft./327m.; mail Waitsfield z 05673
Waits River; RMC Place; ORANGE; ▲ Topsham; 242 F-6; mail West Topsham z 05086; ● 70
Walden; RMC Place; CALEDONIA; ▲ Walden; 242 D-6; mail Greensboro Bend z 05842, West Danville z 05873; ● 120
Walden; MCD-Town; CALEDONIA; *242 D-6; mail West Danville z 05873; Ⓟ 703; © 782
Walden Heights (Walden Station); RMC Place; CALEDONIA; ▲ Walden; *242 D-6; elev. 1,665ft./507m.; mail West Danville z 05873; ● 50
Walden Station; CALEDONIA; see Walden Heights (RMC Place)
Wallace Pond; RMC Place; ESSEX; ▲ Canaan; *242 A-8; mail Canaan z 05903; summer pop. 200; ● 100
Wallingford; CDP; RUTLAND; ▲ Wallingford; 242 I-3; 🄿; z 05773; Ⓟ 1,148; © 948
Wallingford; MCD-Town; RUTLAND; *242 I-4; 🄿; z 05773; Ⓟ 2,184; © 2,274
Waltham; MCD-Town; ADDISON; *242 F-3; mail Vergennes z 05491; Ⓟ 454; © 479
Wardsboro (North Wardsboro); RMC Place; WINDHAM; ▲ Wardsboro; 242 K-4; elev. 995ft./303m.; 🄿; z 05355; ● 200
Wardsboro; MCD-Town; WINDHAM; *242 K-4; 🄿; z 05355; Ⓟ 654; © 854
Wardsboro Center; RMC Place; WINDHAM; ▲ Wardsboro; *242 K-4; elev. 1,111ft./339m.; mail Wardsboro z 05355
Warren; RMC Place; WASHINGTON; ▲ Warren; 242 F-4; 🄿; z 05674; ● 370
Warren; MCD-Town; WASHINGTON; *242 F-4; 🄿; z 05674; Ⓟ 1,172; © 1,681
Washington; RMC Place; ORANGE; ▲ Washington; 242 F-5; 🄿; z 05675; ● 320
Washington; MCD-Town; ORANGE; *242 F-5; 🄿; z 05675; Ⓟ 937; © 1,047
WASHINGTON; 242 E-5; Ⓟ 54,928; © 58,039; ◆ 57,956
Washington Heights; RMC Place; ORANGE; ▲ Washington; *242 F-5; mail Washington z 05675; rural
Waterbury; Inc. Place; WASHINGTON; ▲ Waterbury; 242 E-4; elev. 428ft./130m.; 🄿 🄷; z 05671, z 05676; Ⓟ 1,702; © 1,706
Waterbury; MCD-Town; WASHINGTON; *242 D-4; 🄿; z 05671, z 05676; Ⓟ 4,589; © 4,915
Waterbury Center; RMC Place; WASHINGTON; ▲ Waterbury; 242 D-4; 🄿; z 05677; ● 500
Waterford; MCD-Town; CALEDONIA; *242 D-7; 🄿; z 05819 & mail Lower Waterford z 05848; Ⓟ 1,190; © 1,104
Waterville; RMC Place; LAMOILLE; ▲ Waterville; 242 C-4; elev. 556ft./169m.; 🄿; z 05492; ● 110
Waterville; MCD-Town; LAMOILLE; *242 C-4; 🄿; z 05492; Ⓟ 532; © 697
Weathersfield; MCD-Town; WINDSOR; *242 I-5; mail Perkinsville z 05151, Springfield z 05156; Ⓟ 2,674; © 2,788
Weathersfield Bow; RMC Place; WINDSOR; ▲ Weathersfield; 242 J-5; mail Springfield z 05156; ● 150
Weathersfield Center; RMC Place; WINDSOR; ▲ Weathersfield; *242 I-5; elev. 1,194ft./364m.; mail Perkinsville z 05151, Springfield z 05156; ● 80
Websterville; RMC Place; WASHINGTON; ▲ Barre; 242 F-5; 🄿; z 05678; ● 450
Wells; RMC Place; RUTLAND; ▲ Wells; 242 I-3; 🄿; z 05774; ● 400
Wells; MCD-Town; RUTLAND; *242 I-3; 🄿; z 05774; Ⓟ 902; © 1,121
Wells River; Inc. Place; ORANGE; ▲ Newbury; 242 F-7; 🄿; z 05081; Ⓟ 424; © 325
West Addison; RMC Place; ADDISON; ▲ Addison; *242 F-2; elev. 191ft./58m.; mail Vergennes z 05491
West Arlington; RMC Place; BENNINGTON; ▲ Arlington; 242 K-3; elev. 570ft./174m.; 🄿; z 05250; ● 50
West Barnet; RMC Place; CALEDONIA; ▲ Barnet; 242 E-6; elev. 887ft./270m.; mail Barnet z 05821; ● 85
West Berkshire; RMC Place; FRANKLIN; ▲ Berkshire; *242 A-4; elev. 547ft./167m.; mail Enosburg Falls z 05450; ● 90
West Berlin (Riverton); RMC Place; WASHINGTON; ▲ Berlin; 242 E-5; elev. 589ft./180m.; 🄿; z 05663; ● 150
West Bethel; RMC Place; WINDSOR; ▲ Bethel; *242 G-4; mail Bethel z 05032; rural
West Bolton; RMC Place; CHITTENDEN; ▲ Bolton; *242 D-4; elev. 991ft./302m.; mail Jericho z 05465
West Braintree (Braintree); RMC Place; ORANGE; ▲ Braintree; 242 G-4; elev. 779ft./237m.; 🄿; z 05669 & mail Randolph z 05060; ● 110
West Branch; RMC Place; LAMOILLE; ▲ Stowe; 242 D-4; mail Stowe z 05672; ● 250
West Brattleboro; CDP; WINDHAM; ▲ Brattleboro; *242 L-5; 🄿; z 05301; Ⓟ 3,135; © 3,222
West Bridgewater; RUTLAND, WINDSOR; see South Sherburne (RMC Place)
West Bridport; RMC Place; ADDISON; ▲ Bridport; *242 G-2; mail Bridport z 05734; rural
West Brookfield; RMC Place; ORANGE; ▲ Brookfield; 242 F-5; 🄿; z 05060
West Burke; Inc. Place; CALEDONIA; ▲ Burke; 242 C-7; 🄿; z 05871; Ⓟ 353; © 364
West Castleton; RMC Place; RUTLAND; ▲ Castleton; 242 H-2; elev. 475ft./145m.; mail Fair Haven z 05743
West Charleston; RMC Place; ORLEANS; ▲ Charleston; 242 B-7; elev. 991ft./302m.; 🄿; z 05872; ● 220
West Corinth; RMC Place; ORANGE; ▲ Corinth; *242 F-6; mail Corinth z 05039
West Cornwall; RMC Place; ADDISON; ▲ Cornwall; *242 G-2; elev. 479ft./146m.; 🄿; z 05778 & mail Middlebury z 05753
West Danville; RMC Place; CALEDONIA; ▲ Danville; 242 D-6; elev. 1,559ft./475m.; 🄿; z 05873; ● 200
West Dover; RMC Place; WINDHAM; ▲ Dover; 242 L-4; elev. 1,674ft./510m.; 🄿; z 05356 & mail South Newfane z 05351; ● 350
West Dummerston; RMC Place; WINDHAM; ▲ Dummerston; 242 L-5; 🄿; z 05357; ● 160
West Enosburg; RMC Place; FRANKLIN; ▲ Enosburg; 242 B-4; elev. 440ft./134m.; mail Enosburg Falls z 05450; ● 60
West Fairlee; RMC Place; ORANGE; ▲ West Fairlee; 242 G-6; elev. 741ft./226m.; 🄿; z 05083; ● 165
West Fairlee; MCD-Town; ORANGE; *242 G-6; 🄿; z 05083; Ⓟ 633; © 726
West Fairlee Center; RMC Place; ORANGE; ▲ West Fairlee; *242 G-6; elev. 752ft./229m.; mail Fairlee z 05045; rural
Westfield; RMC Place; ORLEANS; ▲ Westfield; 242 B-5; elev. 825ft./251m.; 🄿; z 05874; ● 100
Westfield; MCD-Town; ORLEANS; *242 B-5; 🄿; z 05874; Ⓟ 422; © 503
Westford; RMC Place; CHITTENDEN; ▲ Westford; 242 C-3; elev. 467ft./142m.; 🄿; z 05494; ● 150
Westford; MCD-Town; CHITTENDEN; *242 C-3; 🄿; z 05494; Ⓟ 1,740; © 2,086
West Georgia; RMC Place; FRANKLIN; ▲ Georgia; *242 C-3; ★ BUR; mail Saint Albans z 05478
West Glover; RMC Place; ORLEANS; ▲ Glover; 242 C-6; 🄿; z 05822, z 05875; ● 50
West Groton; RMC Place; CALEDONIA; ▲ Groton; *242 E-6; mail Groton z 05046
West Guilford; RMC Place; WINDHAM; ▲ Guilford; *242 L-5; mail Brattleboro z 05301; ● 50
West Halifax; RMC Place; WINDHAM; ▲ Halifax; 242 L-4; elev. 1,154ft./352m.; 🄿; z 05358; ● 160
West Hartford; RMC Place; WINDSOR; ▲ Hartford; 242 H-5; elev. 421ft./128m.; 🄿; z 05084; ● 340
West Haven; RMC Place; RUTLAND; ▲ West Haven; 242 H-2; 🄿; z 05743; ● 40
West Haven; MCD-Town; RUTLAND; *242 H-2; 🄿; z 05743; Ⓟ 273; © 278
West Hill; RMC Place; FRANKLIN; ▲ Montgomery; *242 B-5; elev. 1,036ft./316m.; mail Enosburg Falls z 05450; ● 35
West Lincoln; RMC Place; ADDISON; ▲ Lincoln; 242 F-3; mail Bristol z 05443; ● 80
West Milton; RMC Place; CHITTENDEN; ▲ Milton; *242 C-3; elev. 115ft./35m.; ★ BUR; mail Milton z 05468
Westminster; Inc. Place; WINDHAM; ▲ Westminster; 242 K-5; 🄿; z 05158; Ⓟ 399; © 276
Westminster; MCD-Town; WINDHAM; *242 K-5; 🄿; z 05158; Ⓟ 3,026; © 3,210
Westminster Station; RMC Place; WINDHAM; *242 K-5; elev. 259ft./79m.; 🄿; z 05159
Westminster West; RMC Place; WINDHAM; ▲ Westminster; 242 K-5; elev. 806ft./246m.; 🄿; z 05346; ● 80
Westmore; RMC Place; ORLEANS; ▲ Westmore; 242 B-7; mail Barton z 05822, Orleans z 05860; ● 100
Westmore; MCD-Town; ORLEANS; *242 C-7; mail Barton z 05822, Orleans z 05860; Ⓟ 305; © 306
West Newbury; RMC Place; ORANGE; ▲ Newbury; 242 F-7; elev. 940ft./287m.; 🄿; z 05085; ● 160
West Norwich; RMC Place; WINDSOR; ▲ Norwich; *242 H-6; mail Norwich z 05055; rural
Weston; RMC Place; WINDSOR; ▲ Weston; 242 J-4; elev. 1,295ft./395m.; 🄿; z 05161; ● 300
Weston; MCD-Town; WINDSOR; *242 J-4; 🄿; z 05161; Ⓟ 488; © 630
Weston Priory; RMC Place; WINDSOR; ▲ Weston; *242 J-4; mail Weston z 05161; rural
West Pawlet; RMC Place; RUTLAND; ▲ Pawlet; 242 J-2; 🄿; z 05775; ● 300
West Rupert; RMC Place; BENNINGTON; ▲ Rupert; 242 J-2; 🄿; z 05776; ● 180
West Rutland; CDP; RUTLAND; ▲ Rutland; 242 H-3; 🄿; z 05777; Ⓟ 2,246; © 2,263
West Rutland; MCD-Town; RUTLAND; *242 H-3; 🄿; z 05777; Ⓟ 2,448; © 2,535
West Salisbury; RMC Place; ADDISON; ▲ Salisbury; *242 G-3; elev. 421ft./128m.; mail Salisbury z 05769; rural
West Sandgate; RMC Place; BENNINGTON; ▲ Sandgate; *242 K-2; mail Arlington z 05250; ● 50
West Springfield; RMC Place; WINDSOR; ▲ Springfield; *242 J-5; mail Springfield z 05156; ● 40
West Swanton; RMC Place; FRANKLIN; ▲ Swanton; *242 A-3; ★ BUR; mail Swanton z 05488; rural
West Topsham; RMC Place; ORANGE; ▲ Topsham; 242 F-6; elev. 1,248ft./380m.; 🄿; z 05086; ● 120
West Townshend; RMC Place; WINDHAM; ▲ Townshend; 242 K-4; 🄿; z 05359; ● 200
West Wardsboro; RMC Place; WINDHAM; ▲ Wardsboro; 242 K-4; elev. 1,460ft./445m.; 🄿; z 05360; ● 150
West Waterford; RMC Place; CALEDONIA; ▲ Waterford; *242 E-7; mail Saint Johnsbury z 05819; rural
West Windsor; MCD-Town; WINDSOR; *242 I-5; 🄿; z 05089 & mail Brownsville z 05037; Ⓟ 923; © 1,067
West Woodstock; RMC Place; WINDSOR; ▲ Woodstock; 242 H-5; elev. 716ft./218m.; mail Woodstock z 05091; ● 150
Weybridge; RMC Place; ADDISON; ▲ Weybridge; 242 F-3; elev. 202ft./62m.; 🄿; z 05753; ● 140
Weybridge; MCD-Town; ADDISON; *242 F-3; 🄿; z 05753; Ⓟ 749; © 824
Weybridge Hill; RMC Place; ADDISON; ▲ Weybridge; *242 F-3; elev. 415ft./126m.; mail Middlebury z 05753
Wheelock; RMC Place; CALEDONIA; ▲ Wheelock; 242 C-7; elev. 818ft./249m.; 🄿; z 05851; ● 100
Wheelock; MCD-Town; CALEDONIA; *242 C-6; 🄿; z 05851; Ⓟ 481; © 621
White River Junction; CDP; WINDSOR; ▲ Hartford; 242 H-6; elev. 368ft./112m.; 🄿 🄷; z 05001, z 05009; Ⓟ 2,521; © 2,569
Whitesville; RMC Place; WINDSOR; ▲ Cavendish; 242 I-5; elev. 773ft./236m.; mail Cavendish z 05142; ● 50
Whiting; RMC Place; ADDISON; ▲ Whiting; 242 G-3; elev. 395ft./120m.; 🄿; z 05778; ● 100
Whiting; MCD-Town; ADDISON; *242 G-3; 🄿; z 05778; Ⓟ 407; © 380
Whitingham; RMC Place; WINDHAM; ▲ Whitingham; 242 L-4; elev. 1,689ft./515m.; 🄿; z 05361; ● 330
Whitingham; MCD-Town; WINDHAM; *242 K-4; 🄿; z 05361; Ⓟ 1,177; © 1,298
Whitneyville; RMC Place; WINDHAM; ▲ Halifax; *242 L-4; mail West Halifax z 05358; rural
Wilder; CDP; WINDSOR; ▲ Hartford; 242 H-6; elev. 430ft./131m.; 🄿; z 05088; Ⓟ 1,576; © 1,636
Williamstown; RMC Place; ORANGE; ▲ Williamstown; 242 F-5; 🄿; z 05679; ● 700
Williamstown; MCD-Town; ORANGE; *242 F-5; 🄿; z 05679; Ⓟ 2,839; © 3,225
Williamsville; RMC Place; WINDHAM; ▲ Newfane; *242 L-5; elev. 521ft./159m.; 🄿; z 05362 & mail South Newfane z 05351; ● 150
Williston; RMC Place; CHITTENDEN; ▲ Williston; 242 D-3; 🄿; ★ BUR; z 05495; ● 450
Williston; MCD-Town; CHITTENDEN; *242 D-3; 🄿; ★ BUR; z 05495; Ⓟ 4,887; © 7,650; ◆ 8,454
Williston Road Section; RMC Place; CHITTENDEN; ★ BUR; mail South Burlington z 05403; pop. incl. with South Burlington (Inc. Place)
Willoughby (Kimball, South Barton); RMC Place; ORLEANS; ▲ Barton; *242 C-7; mail Barton z 05822; rural
Wilmington; RMC Place; WINDHAM; ▲ Wilmington; 242 L-4; 🄿; z 05363; ● 600
Wilmington; MCD-Town; WINDHAM; *242 L-4; 🄿; z 05363; Ⓟ 1,968; © 2,225
Windham; RMC Place; WINDHAM; ▲ Windham; 242 J-4; elev. 1,966ft./599m.; 🄿; z 05359; ● 70
Windham; MCD-Town; WINDHAM; *242 K-4; 🄿; z 05359; Ⓟ 251; © 328
WINDHAM; 242 K-4; Ⓟ 41,588; © 44,216; ◆ 42,605
Windsor; RMC Place; WINDSOR; ▲ Windsor; 242 I-6; elev. 354ft./108m.; 🄿 🄷; z 05089; ● 3,714
Windsor; MCD-Town; WINDSOR; *242 I-5; 🄿; z 05089; Ⓟ 3,714; © 3,756
WINDSOR; 242 I-5; Ⓟ 54,055; © 57,418; ◆ 55,710
Winhall; MCD-Town; BENNINGTON; *242 K-4; 🄿; z 05340; Ⓟ 482; © 702
Winooski; Inc. Place; CHITTENDEN; 242 D-3; elev. 200ft./61m.; 🄿; ★ BUR; z 05404; Ⓟ 6,649; © 6,561; ◆ 6,503
Winooski Park; RMC Place; CHITTENDEN; ▲ Colchester; 242 L-9; ★ BUR; mail Winooski z 05404; ● 400
Wolcott; RMC Place; LAMOILLE; ▲ Wolcott; 242 D-5; 🄿; z 05680; ● 180
Wolcott; MCD-Town; LAMOILLE; *242 C-5; 🄿; z 05680; Ⓟ 1,229; © 1,456
Woodbury; RMC Place; WASHINGTON; ▲ Woodbury; 242 D-5; elev. 1,164ft./355m.; 🄿; z 05681; ● 160
Woodbury; MCD-Town; WASHINGTON; *242 D-6; 🄿; z 05681; Ⓟ 766; © 809
Woodford; RMC Place; BENNINGTON; ▲ Woodford; 242 L-3; elev. 2,215ft./675m.; 🄿; z 05201; ● 60
Woodford; MCD-Town; BENNINGTON; *242 L-3; 🄿; z 05201; Ⓟ 331; © 414
Woodford Hollow; RMC Place; BENNINGTON; ▲ Woodford; 242 L-3; mail Bennington z 05201; ● 60
Woodstock; Inc. Place; ⊡ WINDSOR; ▲ Woodstock; 242 H-5; elev. 705ft./215m.; 🄿; z 05091; Ⓟ 1,037; © 977
Woodstock; MCD-Town; WINDSOR; *242 H-5; 🄿; z 05091; Ⓟ 3,212; © 3,232
Worcester; RMC Place; WASHINGTON; ▲ Worcester; 242 D-5; elev. 779ft./237m.; 🄿; z 05682; ● 220
Worcester; MCD-Town; WASHINGTON; *242 D-5; 🄿; z 05682; Ⓟ 906; © 902
Wrightsville; RMC Place; WASHINGTON; *242 E-5; elev. 725ft./221m.; mail Montpelier z 05602

Entries in **UPPERCASE** are counties.
Entries in **bold** have populations of 2,500 or more.
Names in parentheses are alternate names.
Inc. Place — Incorporated Place
RMC Place — Rand McNally Designated Place
CDP — Census Designated Place
MCD — Minor Civil Division

⊡ County Seat
▲ Minor Civil Division
elev. Elevation
🄿 Post Office

🄷 Hospital
🄲 College
■ Principal Business Center
★ Ranally Metro Area (RMA) Abbreviation
z Zip Code(s)

Ⓟ Previous Census Population
Ⓡ Revised Census Population
Ⓐ Annexation Population
● Rand McNally Population Estimate
© Final Census Population
Ⓢ Special Census Population
◆ Estimated Population

For additional definitions see Glossary, Volume 1, and Introduction, Volume 2.

VIRGINIA

OH
PA
MD
WV
KY
Richmond
TN
NC

Statistics

Total area (2000) — 42,774 square miles
Land area (2000) — 39,594 square miles
Water area (2000) — 3,180 square miles
Capital — Richmond
One of Thirteen Original States

Ranally Metro Areas (RMAs) and Abbreviations

Charlottesville, VA — CHRLTV
Danville, VA-NC — DANV
Fredericksburg, VA — FRED
Johnson City-Kingsport-Bristol, TN-VA — JNSC-
Lynchburg, VA — LYNCH
Martinsville, VA-NC — MRTNV
Newport News-Hampton, VA — NN-H
Norfolk-Virginia Beach-Chesapeake, VA — NORF-
Richmond, VA — RICH
Roanoke, VA — ROAN
Washington, DC-MD-VA — WASH

Maps

State maps can be found on pages 142-254 in Vol. 1

Principal Places

Place Name	Place Type	County	Population
Virginia Beach	Independent City		◆ 433,228
Norfolk	Independent City		◆ 250,740
Chesapeake	Independent City		◆ 216,184
Richmond	Independent City		◆ 215,053
Arlington	CDP	ARLINGTON	◆ 213,796
Newport News	Independent City		◆ 181,167
Hampton	Independent City		◆ 149,409
Alexandria	Independent City		◆ 145,772
Portsmouth	Independent City		◆ 103,198
Roanoke	Independent City		◆ 94,603
Suffolk	Independent City		◆ 81,737
Dale City	CDP	PRINCE WILLIAM	◆ 72,850
Lynchburg	Independent City		◆ 72,417
Burke	CDP	FAIRFAX	◆ 59,994
Reston	CDP	FAIRFAX	◆ 58,615
Annandale	CDP	FAIRFAX	◆ 56,926
Blacksburg	Inc. Place	MONTGOMERY	◆ 50,719
Centreville	CDP	FAIRFAX	◆ 50,571
Tuckahoe	CDP	HENRICO	◆ 49,564
Harrisonburg	Independent City		◆ 45,115
Danville	Independent City		◆ 44,437
Chantilly	CDP	FAIRFAX	◆ 42,653
Charlottesville	Independent City		◆ 41,757
Woodbridge	CDP	PRINCE WILLIAM	◆ 41,568
McLean	CDP	FAIRFAX	◆ 40,460
Lake Ridge	CDP-Census Area Only	PRINCE WILLIAM	◆ 39,571
Leesburg	Inc. Place	LOUDOUN	◆ 37,066
Mechanicsville	CDP	HANOVER	◆ 34,830
Manassas	Independent City		◆ 34,062
Petersburg	Independent City		◆ 33,332
Franconia	CDP	FAIRFAX	◆ 33,152
Springfield	CDP	FAIRFAX	◆ 31,608
Oakton	CDP	FAIRFAX	◆ 30,503
Mount Vernon	CDP	FAIRFAX	◆ 29,705
West Springfield	CDP	FAIRFAX	◆ 29,494
Jefferson	CDP-Census Area Only	FAIRFAX	◆ 28,499
Cave Spring	CDP	ROANOKE	◆ 25,986
Winchester	Independent City		◆ 25,572
Salem	Independent City		◆ 25,404
Staunton	Independent City		◆ 24,776
Fairfax	Independent City		◆ 24,135
Bailey's Crossroads	CDP-Census Area Only	FAIRFAX	◆ 24,070
Hopewell	Independent City		◆ 23,701
Fredericksburg	Independent City		◆ 23,401
Herndon	Inc. Place	FAIRFAX	◆ 22,475
Groveton	CDP	FAIRFAX	◆ 22,130
Waynesboro	Independent City		◆ 21,937
Newington	CDP	FAIRFAX	© 19,784
Tysons Corner	CDP	FAIRFAX	© 18,540
Chester	CDP	CHESTERFIELD	© 17,890
Lorton	CDP	FAIRFAX	© 17,786
Colonial Heights	Independent City		◆ 17,674
Bristol	Independent City		◆ 17,083
Christiansburg	Inc. Place	MONTGOMERY	© 16,947
Radford	Independent City		◆ 16,727
Hybla Valley	CDP	FAIRFAX	© 16,721
Bon Air	CDP	CHESTERFIELD	© 16,213
Idylwood	CDP	FAIRFAX	© 16,005
Lincolnia	CDP	FAIRFAX	© 15,788
Montclair	CDP-Census Area Only	PRINCE WILLIAM	© 15,728
Highland Springs	CDP	HENRICO	© 15,137
Rose Hill	CDP-Census Area Only	FAIRFAX	© 15,058
Laurel	CDP	HENRICO	© 14,875
Vienna	Inc. Place	FAIRFAX	© 14,453
Hollins	CDP	ROANOKE	© 14,309
Martinsville	Independent City		◆ 14,306
Wolf Trap	CDP-Census Area Only	FAIRFAX	© 14,001
Front Royal	Inc. Place	WARREN	© 13,589
Williamsburg	Independent City		◆ 13,353
Fort Hunt	CDP-Census Area Only	FAIRFAX	© 12,923
Glen Allen	CDP	HENRICO	© 12,562
East Highland Park	CDP	HENRICO	© 12,488
Poquoson	Independent City		◆ 11,958
Madison Heights	CDP	AMHERST	© 11,584
Bull Run	CDP-Census Area Only	PRINCE WILLIAM	© 11,337
Manassas Park	Independent City		◆ 11,337
Merrifield	CDP	FAIRFAX	© 11,170
Lakeside	CDP	HENRICO	© 11,157
Falls Church	Independent City		◆ 11,070
Timberlake	CDP	CAMPBELL	© 10,683
Culpeper	Inc. Place	CULPEPER	© 9,664
Pulaski	Inc. Place	PULASKI	© 9,473
Gloucester Point	CDP	GLOUCESTER	© 9,429
Sugarland Run	RMC Place	LOUDOUN	℗ 9,357
Franklin	Independent City		◆ 9,287
North Springfield	CDP	FAIRFAX	© 9,173
Lake Barcroft	CDP	FAIRFAX	© 8,906
Seven Corners	CDP	FAIRFAX	© 8,701
Linton Hall	CDP-Census Area Only	PRINCE WILLIAM	© 8,620
Great Falls	CDP	FAIRFAX	© 8,549
South Boston	Inc. Place	HALIFAX	© 8,491
Stuarts Draft	CDP	AUGUSTA	© 8,367
Countryside	RMC Place	LOUDOUN	℗ 8,349
Huntington	CDP	FAIRFAX	© 8,325
Forest	CDP	BEDFORD	© 8,006
Sterling	RMC Place	LOUDOUN	● 8,000
Dunn Loring	CDP	FAIRFAX	© 7,861
Aquia Harbour	CDP	STAFFORD	© 7,856
Wytheville	Inc. Place	WYTHE	© 7,804
Baileys Crossroads	RMC Place	FAIRFAX	● 7,800
Vinton	Inc. Place	ROANOKE	© 7,782
Abingdon	Inc. Place	WASHINGTON	© 7,780
Collinsville	CDP	HENRY	© 7,777
Sudley	CDP	PRINCE WILLIAM	© 7,719
West Gate	CDP-Census Area Only	PRINCE WILLIAM	© 7,493
Mantua	CDP	FAIRFAX	© 7,485
Lexington	Independent City		◆ 7,348
Fort Lee	CDP-Census Area Only	PRINCE GEORGE	© 7,269
Fort Belvoir	CDP-Census Area Only	FAIRFAX	© 7,176
Montrose	CDP-Census Area Only	HENRICO	© 7,018
Lake Monticello	CDP-Census Area Only	FLUVANNA	© 6,852
Farmville	Inc. Place	PRINCE EDWARD	© 6,845
Galax	Independent City		◆ 6,811
Yorkshire	CDP	PRINCE WILLIAM	© 6,732
Dumbarton	CDP	HENRICO	© 6,674
Warrenton	Inc. Place	FAUQUIER	© 6,670
Ashland	Inc. Place	HANOVER	© 6,619
Quantico Station	CDP-Census Area Only	PRINCE WILLIAM	© 6,571
Buena Vista	Independent City		◆ 6,527
Kings Park	RMC Place	FAIRFAX	● 6,500
Bedford	Independent City		◆ 6,467
Marion	Inc. Place	SMYTH	© 6,349
Smithfield	Inc. Place	ISLE OF WIGHT	© 6,324
Covington	Independent City		◆ 6,311
Kings Park West	RMC Place	FAIRFAX	● 6,300
Belle Haven	CDP	FAIRFAX	© 6,269
Wyndham	CDP-Census Area Only	HENRICO	© 6,176
Pimmit Hills	CDP	FAIRFAX	© 6,152
Bellwood	CDP	CHESTERFIELD	© 5,974
Big Stone Gap	Inc. Place	WISE	® 5,906
Ettrick	CDP	CHESTERFIELD	© 5,627
Emporia	Independent City		◆ 5,569
Commonwealth	RMC Place	ALBEMARLE	℗ 5,538
Triangle	CDP	PRINCE WILLIAM	© 5,500
Bensley	CDP-Census Area Only	CHESTERFIELD	© 5,435
Bridgewater	Inc. Place	ROCKINGHAM	© 5,203
Culmore	RMC Place	FAIRFAX	● 5,200
Bluefield	Inc. Place	TAZEWELL	© 5,078
West Gate of Lomond	RMC Place	PRINCE WILLIAM	● 5,000

County and Independent City Business Data

County	FIPS Code	County Seat[1]	Land Area (Sq. Mi.)	Census Population			Wholesale Trade		Manufacturing, 2002			
				4/1/2000	4/1/1990	% Change 1990-2000	Sales, 2002 ($1,000)	% Change 1997-2002	Establish-ments	Total Employees	Value Added ($1,000)	Ranally Mfg. Units
Accomack	001	Accomac	455	38,305	31,703	20.8	43,713	-7.2	36	3,187	426,183	225
Albemarle	003	(Charlottesville)	723	79,236	68,040	16.5	213,470	17.5	46	1,399	106,304	56
Alleghany	005	(Covington)	445	12,926	13,176	-1.9	(d)	(d)	13	791	63,158	33
Amelia	007	Amelia Court House	357	11,400	8,787	29.7	(d)	(d)	...	(d)	(d)	...
Amherst	009	Amherst	475	31,894	28,578	11.6	129,840	(d)	41	1,689	272,244	144
Appomattox	011	Appomattox	334	13,705	12,298	11.4	(d)	(d)	18	678	39,374	21
Arlington	013	Arlington	26	189,453	170,936	10.8	487,759	-40.5	54	585	35,868	19
Augusta	015	(Staunton)	970	65,615	54,677	20.0	195,179	26.9	52	4,631	765,880	405
Bath	017	Warm Springs	532	5,048	4,799	5.2	(d)	(d)	...	(d)	(d)	...
Bedford	019	(Bedford)	755	60,371	45,656	32.2	360,338	27.8	68	1,677	275,241	146
Bland	021	Bland	359	6,871	6,514	5.5	(d)	(d)	...	(d)	(d)	...
Botetourt	023	Fincastle	543	30,496	24,992	22.0	173,426	-18.9	28	1,878	143,746	76
Brunswick	025	Lawrenceville	566	18,419	15,987	15.2	44,808	62.2	19	527	39,913	21
Buchanan	027	Grundy	504	26,978	31,333	-13.9	115,559	-17.7	...	(d)	(d)	...
Buckingham	029	Buckingham	581	15,623	12,873	21.4	8,925	35.3	...	(d)	(d)	...
Campbell	031	Rustburg	504	51,078	47,572	7.4	708,217	(d)	57	3,618	578,642	306
Caroline	033	Bowling Green	533	22,121	19,217	15.1	11,901	-57.3	...	(d)	(d)	...
Carroll	035	Hillsville	476	29,245	26,594	10.0	33,289	-22.4	27	1,429	110,008	58
Charles City	036	Charles City	183	6,926	6,282	10.3	(d)	(d)	...	(d)	(d)	...
Charlotte	037	Charlotte Court House	475	12,472	11,688	6.7	6,969	-62.0	15	999	51,920	27
Chesterfield	041	Chesterfield	426	259,903	209,274	24.2	3,840,880	165.3	176	9,674	1,484,825	786
Clarke	043	Berryville	177	12,652	12,101	4.6	(d)	(d)	16	1,201	158,250	84
Craig	045	New Castle	331	5,091	4,372	16.4	(d)	(d)	...	(d)	(d)	...
Culpeper	047	Culpeper	381	34,262	27,791	23.3	(d)	(d)	33	1,406	176,829	94
Cumberland	049	Cumberland	298	9,017	7,825	15.2	1,683	-19.7	...	(d)	(d)	...
Dickenson	051	Clintwood	332	16,395	17,620	-7.0	9,725	107.1	...	(d)	(d)	...
Dinwiddie	053	Dinwiddie	504	24,533	20,960	17.0	21,174	(d)	10	(d)	(d)	...
Essex	057	Tappahannock	258	9,989	8,689	15.0	(d)	(d)	15	727	26,086	14
Fairfax	059	(Fairfax)	395	969,749	818,584	18.5	15,732,349	0.5	437	10,525	1,017,563	538
Fauquier	061	Warrenton	650	55,139	48,741	13.1	174,011	1.4	47	871	56,358	30
Floyd	063	Floyd	381	13,874	12,005	15.6	(d)	(d)	...	(d)	(d)	...
Fluvanna	065	Palmyra	287	20,047	12,429	61.3	(d)	(d)	...	(d)	(d)	...
Franklin	067	Rocky Mount	692	47,286	39,549	19.6	(d)	(d)	55	3,099	198,894	105
Frederick	069	(Winchester)	415	59,209	45,723	29.5	(d)	(d)	76	(d)	(d)	...
Giles	071	Pearisburg	357	16,657	16,366	1.8	20,432	(d)	13	1,443	228,391	121
Gloucester	073	Gloucester	217	34,780	30,131	15.4	40,158	-5.5	...	(d)	(d)	...
Goochland	075	Goochland	284	16,863	14,163	19.1	126,294	73.5	...	(d)	(d)	...
Grayson	077	Independence	443	17,917	16,278	10.1	4,144	347.0	17	737	135,184	72
Greene	079	Stanardsville	157	15,244	10,297	48.0	(d)	(d)	10	(d)	(d)	...
Greensville	081	(Emporia)	295	11,560	8,853	30.6	4,574	-75.1	7	1,506	173,251	92
Halifax	083	Halifax	819	37,355	36,030	28.7	(d)	(d)	42	3,254	320,981	170
Hanover	085	Hanover	473	86,320	63,306	36.4	2,872,325	-5.7	143	3,107	353,736	187
Henrico	087	(Richmond)	238	262,300	217,881	20.4	6,656,241	12.8	209	9,800	1,713,776	907
Henry	089	(Martinsville)	382	57,930	56,942	1.7	108,142	-20.7	72	6,484	474,391	251
Highland	091	Monterey	416	2,536	2,635	-3.8	(d)	(d)	...	(d)	(d)	...
Isle of Wight	093	Isle of Wight	316	29,728	25,053	18.7	54,174	(d)	21	(d)	(d)	...
James City	095	(Williamsburg)	143	48,102	34,859	38.0	54,779	102.7	37	2,325	996,692	527
King and Queen	097	King and Queen Court House	316	6,630	6,289	5.4	(d)	(d)	...	(d)	(d)	...
King George	099	King George	180	16,803	13,527	24.2	9,670	33.1	...	(d)	(d)	...
King William	101	King William	275	13,146	10,913	20.5	37,586	(d)	16	981	313,596	166
Lancaster	103	Lancaster	133	11,567	10,896	6.2	52,989	37.8	...	(d)	(d)	...
Lee	105	Jonesville	437	23,589	24,496	-3.7	18,855	-59.9	...	(d)	(d)	...
Loudoun	107	Leesburg	520	169,599	86,129	96.9	1,392,581	7.0	161	5,523	524,480	277
Louisa	109	Louisa	497	25,627	20,325	26.1	57,664	98.1	23	612	51,918	27
Lunenburg	111	Lunenburg	432	13,146	11,419	15.1	(d)	(d)	8	(d)	(d)	...
Madison	113	Madison	321	12,520	11,949	4.8	4,656	-38.5	...	(d)	(d)	...
Mathews	115	Mathews	86	9,207	8,348	10.3	18,419	(d)	...	(d)	(d)	...
Mecklenburg	117	Boydton	624	32,380	29,241	10.7	81,183	14.1	38	2,538	135,812	72
Middlesex	119	Saluda	130	9,932	8,653	14.8	48,725	86.2	...	(d)	(d)	...
Montgomery	121	Christiansburg	388	83,629	73,913	13.1	233,242	37.4	65	3,568	369,607	196
Nelson	125	Lovingston	472	14,445	12,778	13.0	(d)	(d)	...	(d)	(d)	...
New Kent	127	New Kent	210	13,462	10,445	28.9	(d)	(d)	...	(d)	(d)	...
Northampton	131	Eastville	207	13,093	13,061	0.2	24,949	(d)	...	(d)	(d)	...
Northumberland	133	Heathsville	192	12,259	10,524	16.5	30,144	(d)	...	(d)	(d)	...
Nottoway	135	Nottoway	315	15,725	14,993	4.9	(d)	(d)	20	675	67,586	36
Orange	137	Orange	342	25,881	21,421	20.8	147,450	115.5	24	1,891	332,653	176
Page	139	Luray	311	23,177	21,690	6.9	3,743	-16.5	22	2,442	459,182	243
Patrick	141	Stuart	483	19,407	17,473	11.1	31,676	29.3	30	1,537	71,843	38
Pittsylvania	143	Chatham	971	61,745	55,655	10.9	131,951	(d)	57	3,142	254,315	135
Powhatan	145	Powhatan	261	22,377	15,328	46.0	43,790	(d)	...	(d)	(d)	...

Entries in **UPPERCASE** are counties.
Entries in **bold** have populations of 2,500 or more.
Inc. Place — Incorporated Place
RMC Place — Rand McNally Designated Place
CDP — Census Designated Place
MCD — Minor Civil Division

⊡ County Seat
▲ Minor Civil Division
elev. Elevation
🅿 Post Office

H Hospital
C College
■ Principal Business Center
★ Ranally Metro Area (RMA) Abbreviation
z Zip Code(s)

℗ Previous Census Population
® Revised Census Population
Ⓐ Annexation Population
● Rand McNally Population Estimate
© Final Census Population
Ⓢ Special Census Population
◆ Estimated Population

For additional definitions see Glossary, Volume 1, and Introduction, Volume 2.

County	FIPS Code	County Seat[1]	Land Area (Sq. Mi.)	Census Population			Wholesale Trade		Maunfacturing, 2002			
				4/1/2000	4/1/1990	% Change 1990-2000	Sales, 2002 ($1,000)	% Change 1997-2002	Establish-ments	Total Employees	Value Added ($1,000)	Ranally Mfg. Units
Prince Edward	147	Farmville	353	19,720	17,320	13.9	37,024	19.8	22	559	41,606	22
Prince George	149	Prince George	266	33,047	27,394	20.6	569,914	813.3	23	2,095	216,015	114
Prince William	153	(Manassas)	338	280,813	215,686	30.2	1,541,149	29.4	98	2,329	181,760	96
Pulaski	155	Pulaski	321	35,127	34,496	1.8	70,058	-53.9	49	6,014	489,190	259
Rappahannock	157	Washington	267	6,983	6,622	5.5	49,312	(d)	...	(d)	(d)	...
Richmond	159	Warsaw	191	8,809	7,273	21.1	22,965	22.6	...	(d)	(d)	...
Roanoke	161	(Salem)	251	85,778	79,332	8.1	738,012	84.8	62	3,251	287,453	152
Rockbridge	163	(Lexington)	600	20,808	18,350	13.4	(d)	(d)	23	1,887	123,908	66
Rockingham	165	(Harrisonburg)	851	67,725	57,482	17.8	(d)	(d)	78	8,799	2,641,962	1,398
Russell	167	Lebanon	475	30,308	28,667	5.7	39,388	-58.1	20	1,575	90,809	48
Scott	169	Gate City	537	23,403	23,204	0.9	(d)	(d)	9	(d)	(d)	...
Shenandoah	171	Woodstock	512	35,075	31,636	10.9	177,903	107.0	40	4,599	316,633	168
Smyth	173	Marion	452	33,081	32,370	2.2	52,187	-20.5	48	4,568	267,171	141
Southampton	175	Courtland	600	17,482	17,550	-0.4	30,480	(d)	18	2,526	551,472	292
Spotsylvania	177	Spotsylvania	401	90,395	57,403	57.5	725,290	5.7	42	1,753	163,292	86
Stafford	179	Stafford	270	92,446	61,236	51.0	1,865,391	(d)	40	674	58,615	31
Surry	181	Surry	279	6,829	6,145	11.1	(d)	(d)	...	(d)	(d)	...
Sussex	183	Sussex	491	12,504	10,248	22.0	(d)	(d)	...	(d)	(d)	...
Tazewell	185	Tazewell	520	44,598	45,960	-3.0	(d)	(d)	62	1,412	105,766	56
Warren	187	Front Royal	214	31,584	26,142	20.8	(d)	(d)	27	892	368,078	195
Washington	191	Abingdon	563	51,103	45,887	11.4	946,958	11.7	62	2,212	212,007	112
Westmoreland	193	Montross	229	16,718	15,480	8.0	(d)	(d)	...	(d)	(d)	...
Wise	195	Wise	404	40,123	39,573	1.4	163,199	-8.1	...	(d)	(d)	...
Wythe	197	Wytheville	463	27,599	25,466	8.4	122,976	68.5	41	1,577	156,068	83
York	199	Yorktown	106	56,297	42,422	32.7	106,270	-23.0	39	(d)	(d)	...
Independent Cities												
Alexandria	510		15	128,283	111,183	15.4	902,076	0.3	98	1,504	161,756	86
Bedford	515		7	6,299	6,073	3.7	(d)	(d)	21	1,304	65,193	34
Bristol	520		13	17,367	18,426	-5.7	(d)	(d)	40	5,463	257,487	136
Buena Vista	530		7	6,349	6,406	-0.9	(d)	(d)	15	1,325	153,027	81
Charlottesville	540		10	45,049	40,341	11.7	232,767	-12.5	68	3,630	377,564	200
Chesapeake	550		341	199,184	151,976	31.1	2,145,325	21.3	145	4,651	460,428	244
Clifton Forge†	560		3	4,289	4,679	-8.3	(d)	(d)	...	(d)	(d)	...
Colonial Heights	570		7	16,897	16,064	5.2	87,232	(d)	11	1,156	145,606	77
Covington	580		6	6,303	6,991	-9.8	17,705	15.6	9	(d)	(d)	...
Danville	590		43	48,411	53,056	-8.8	203,462	-3.9	46	9,024	640,066	339
Emporia	595		7	5,665	5,306	6.8	49,589	(d)	13	1,145	87,130	46
Fairfax	600		6	21,498	19,622	9.6	533,014	3.5	...	(d)	(d)	...
Falls Church	610		2	10,377	9,578	8.3	(d)	(d)	...	(d)	(d)	...
Franklin	620		8	8,346	7,864	6.1	17,624	-64.0	...	(d)	(d)	...
Fredericksburg	630		11	19,279	19,027	1.3	138,260	-67.6	46	943	73,302	39
Galax	640		8	6,837	6,670	2.5	(d)	(d)	21	3,573	143,523	76
Hampton	650		52	146,437	133,793	9.5	342,117	-7.7	85	4,133	581,677	308
Harrisonburg	660		18	40,468	30,707	31.8	(d)	(d)	59	4,774	406,886	215
Hopewell	670		10	22,354	23,101	-3.2	36,937	-60.1	17	1,892	569,553	301
Lexington	678		2	6,867	6,959	-1.3	30,705	81.6	...	(d)	(d)	...
Lynchburg	680		49	65,269	66,049	-1.2	585,091	16.0	118	9,567	1,186,198	628
Manassas	683		10	35,135	27,957	25.7	381,954	-39.0	43	2,790	558,690	296
Manassas Park	685		2	10,290	6,734	52.8	67,285	83.4	...	(d)	(d)	...
Martinsville	690		11	15,416	16,162	-4.6	(d)	(d)	33	3,311	167,523	89
Newport News	700		68	180,150	170,045	5.9	621,318	2.8	121	22,213	2,730,794	1,445
Norfolk	710		54	234,403	261,229	-10.3	2,862,171	-1.8	194	9,752	1,564,248	828
Norton	720		8	3,904	4,247	-8.1	130,729	-25.3	...	(d)	(d)	...
Petersburg	730		23	33,740	38,386	-12.1	314,138	125.7	41	2,416	328,090	174
Poquoson	735		16	11,566	11,005	5.1	(d)	(d)	...	(d)	(d)	...
Portsmouth	740		33	100,565	103,907	-3.2	143,949	-14.0	66	1,864	263,282	139
Radford	750		10	15,859	15,940	-0.5	22,317	-56.8	21	2,065	189,258	100
Richmond	760		60	197,790	203,056	-2.6	7,174,020	20.0	297	15,417	11,347,830	6,004
Roanoke	770		43	94,911	96,397	-1.5	999,799	-22.7	126	4,579	556,855	295
Salem	775		15	24,747	23,756	4.2	706,433	11.1	76	4,671	769,741	407
Staunton	790		20	23,853	24,461	-2.5	109,530	-17.0	...	(d)	(d)	...
Suffolk	800		400	63,677	52,141	22.1	737,393	-10.3	55	2,229	573,164	303
Virginia Beach	810		248	425,257	393,069	8.2	2,251,068	17.1	225	5,067	605,058	320
Waynesboro	820		15	19,520	18,549	5.2	88,377	(d)	39	3,149	451,836	239
Williamsburg	830		9	11,998	11,530	4.1	19,253	(d)	...	(d)	(d)	...
Winchester	840		9	23,585	21,947	7.5	664,042	120.6	45	(d)	(d)	...
The State			**39,594**	**7,078,515**	**6,187,358**	**14.4**	**69,267,796**	**13.5**	**5,909**	**311,787**	**48,261,833**	**25,534**

(d) Data not available. Corresponding percentages or Ranally Manufacturing Units are estimates.
... Represents 0 or amount too minimal to be reported.
[1] Names in parentheses are Independent Cities that serve as county seats but are administratively independent of the county.
† Clifton Forge independent city merged with Alleghany county on July 1, 2001.

Administrative Divisions

The 39 Independent Cities of Virginia are legally separate from the counties. Some of the Independent Cities serve as county seats for adjoining counties.

For ease of comparison with other states that do not have Independent Cities, some users prefer to combine each of the Independent Cities with the county from which, originally, it was primarily separated. The combinations usually made are as follows: Alexandria city with Arlington County; Bedford city with Bedford County; Bristol city with Washington County; Buena Vista city with Rockbridge County; Charlottesville city with Albemarle County; Colonial Heights city with Dinwiddie County; Covington city with Alleghany County; Danville city with Pittsylvania County; Emporia city with Greensville County; Fairfax city with Fairfax County; Falls Church city with Fairfax County; Franklin city with Southampton County; Fredericksburg city with Spotsylvania County; Galax city with Carroll County; Harrisonburg city with Rockingham County; Hopewell city with Prince George County; Lexington city with Rockbridge County; Lynchburg city with Campbell County; Manassas city with Prince William County; Manassas Park city with Prince William County; Martinsville city with Henry County; Norton city with Wise County; Petersburg city with Dinwiddie County; Poquoson city with York County; Radford city with Montgomery County; Richmond city with Henrico County; Roanoke city with Roanoke County; Salem city with Roanoke County; Staunton city with Augusta County; Waynesboro city with Augusta County; Williamsburg city with James City County; Winchester city with Frederick County.

The Independent Cities that have annexed their parent counties are usually treated as separate city-county combinations, as follows: Chesapeake, Norfolk, and Portsmouth cities, combined under Norfolk; and Hampton, Newport News, Suffolk and Virginia Beach cities, each treated individually.

Index of Places and Counties

A

Aarons Creek; RMC Place; HALIFAX; ***244** M-10; mail Virgilina **z** 24598; ● 100
Abbey Oaks; RMC Place; FAIRFAX; ***245** D-14; ★ **WASH**; mail Vienna **z** 22182
Abbott; RMC Place; CRAIG; ***244** J-5; mail New Castle **z** 24127
Aberdeen Gardens; RMC Place; HAMPTON (Independent City); ***245** L-17; ★ **NN-H**; mail Hampton **z** 23666; pop. incl. with Hampton (Independent City)
Abert; RMC Place; BEDFORD; ***244** J-8; elev. 800ft./244m.; ★ **LYNCH**; mail Lynchburg **z** 24503; ● 50
Abilene; RMC Place; CHARLOTTE; ***244** K-10; mail Charlotte Court House **z** 23923; ● 50
Abingdon; Inc. Place; ⊡ WASHINGTON; **244** D-6; elev. 2,069ft./631m.; 🅿 🅷; **z** 24210-12; Ⓟ 7,003; Ⓒ 7,780
Accomac; Inc. Place; ⊡ ACCOMACK; **245** I-19; 🅿; **z** 23301; Ⓟ 466; Ⓒ 547
ACCOMACK; **245** I-20; Ⓟ 31,703; Ⓒ 38,305; ◆ 38,041
Accotink; RMC Place; FAIRFAX; ***245** E-15; ★ **WASH**; mail Fort Belvoir **z** 22060; ● 300
Accotink Heights; RMC Place; FAIRFAX; ***245** E-14; mail Annandale **z** 22003
Achilles; RMC Place; GLOUCESTER; **245** K-17; 🅿; ★ **NN-H**; **z** 23001; ● 650
Achsah; RMC Place; MADISON; ***245** G-11; mail Madison **z** 22727; rural
Acorn; RMC Place; WESTMORELAND; ***245** H-16; elev. 131ft./40m.; mail Hague **z** 22469; rural
Acredale; RMC Place; VIRGINIA BEACH (Independent City); ***245** M-18; elev. 23ft./7m.; ★ **NORF-**; mail Virginia Beach **z** 23464, **z** 23467; pop. incl. with Virginia Beach (Independent City)
Acree Acres; RMC Place; YORK; ***245** K-17; ★ **NN-H**; mail Yorktown **z** 23692; ● 230
Ada; RMC Place; FAUQUIER; ***245** E-12; mail Marshall **z** 20115
Adams Grove; RMC Place; SOUTHAMPTON; ***245** M-14; elev. 88ft./27m.; mail Drewryville **z** 23844; ● 50
Addison Heights; RMC Place; ARLINGTON; ***245** D-15; ★ **WASH**; mail Arlington **z** 22202
Aden; RMC Place; PRINCE WILLIAM; ***245** E-13; ★ **WASH**; mail Nokesville **z** 20181; ● 70
Adial; RMC Place; NELSON; ***244** H-9; mail Faber **z** 22938; ● 30
Adkins Store; RMC Place; CHARLES CITY; ***245** J-15; elev. 137ft./42m.; mail Providence Forge **z** 23140
Adner; RMC Place; GLOUCESTER; ***245** J-16; mail Saluda **z** 23149
Adria; RMC Place; TAZEWELL; **244** K-1; elev. 2,473ft./754m.; mail North Tazewell **z** 24630; ● 260
Adsit; RMC Place; BRUNSWICK; ***245** M-13; mail Freeman **z** 23856
Advance Mills; RMC Place; ALBEMARLE; ***245** G-11; 🅿; ★ **CHRLTV**; **z** 22968
Adwolf; CDP; SMYTH; **244** M-1; mail Marion **z** 24354; Ⓟ 1,292; Ⓒ 1,457
Afton; RMC Place; NELSON; **244** H-9; 🅿; **z** 22920; ● 120
Agricola; RMC Place; AMHERST; ***244** J-8; mail Monroe **z** 24574; rural
Ahoy Acres; RMC Place; CHESAPEAKE (Independent City); ***245** M-17; ★ **NORF-**; mail Chesapeake **z** 23321; pop. incl. with Chesapeake (Independent City)
Aiken Summit; RMC Place; HENRY; **244** N-7; mail Axton **z** 24054; ● 60
Aily; RMC Place; DICKENSON; ***244** C-5; mail Dante **z** 24237; rural
Airmont; RMC Place; LOUDOUN; ***245** D-13; elev. 493ft./150m.; mail Round Hill **z** 20141; ● 30
Ajax; RMC Place; PITTSYLVANIA; ***244** L-7; elev. 920ft./280m.; mail Sandy Level **z** 24161; rural
Alanthus; RMC Place; CULPEPER; ***245** F-12; elev. 450ft./137m.; mail Brandy Station **z** 22714; rural
Alanton; RMC Place; VIRGINIA BEACH (Independent City); ***245** L-18; elev. 15ft./5m.; ★ **NORF-**; mail Virginia Beach **z** 23450; pop. incl. with Virginia Beach (Independent City)
Albemarle; RMC Place; NORFOLK (Independent City); ★ **NORF-**; mail Norfolk **z** 23503; pop. incl. with Norfolk (Independent City)
ALBEMARLE; **244** G-10; Ⓟ 68,040; Ⓒ 79,236; Ⓡ 84,186; ◆ 95,811
Alberene; RMC Place; ALBEMARLE; ***244** H-10; mail North Garden **z** 22959
Albert; SCOTT; see Daniel Boone (RMC Place)
Alberta; Inc. Place; BRUNSWICK; **245** L-12; 🅿; **z** 23821; Ⓟ 337; Ⓒ 306
Albin; RMC Place; FREDERICK; **245** C-11; mail Winchester **z** 22603; ● 300
Alcoma; RMC Place; BUCKINGHAM; ***244** J-10; mail Buckingham **z** 23921; rural
Aldie; RMC Place; LOUDOUN; **245** D-13; 🅿; **z** 20105; ● 330
Alexander Park; RMC Place; PORTSMOUTH (Independent City); ★ **NORF-**; pop. incl. with Portsmouth (Independent City)
Alexandria; Independent City; **245** E-15; 🅿 🅷 ■; ★ **WASH**; **z** 20598, **z** 22301-15, **z** 22320, **z** 22331-34; Ⓟ 111,183; Ⓒ 128,283; ◆ 145,772
Alfonso; RMC Place; LANCASTER; ***245** I-17; elev. 99ft./30m.; 🅿; **z** 22503; rural
Algonquin Park; RMC Place; NORFOLK (Independent City); ***245** L-18; ★ **NORF-**; mail Norfolk **z** 23505; pop. incl. with Norfolk (Independent City)
Algren; RMC Place; CHESAPEAKE (Independent City); ***245** M-17; ★ **NORF-**; mail Chesapeake **z** 23321; pop. incl. with Chesapeake (Independent City)
Alhambra; RMC Place; AMHERST; ***244** I-9; elev. 1,308ft./399m.; mail Roseland **z** 22967; rural
Alice Heights; RMC Place; CHESTERFIELD; ***245** J-14; elev. 200ft./61m.; ★ **RICH**; mail Richmond **z** 23234; ● 950
Alleghany; RMC Place; ALLEGHANY; **244** I-5; 🅿; **z** 24426; ● 110
ALLEGHANY; **244** I-6; the independent city of Clifton Forge merged with Alleghany county on July 1, 2001; Ⓟ 13,176; Ⓒ 12,926; adjusted 2000 Census population is 17,215; ◆ 16,201
Alleghany Spring; RMC Place; MONTGOMERY; **244** K-5; ★ **ROAN**; mail Shawsville **z** 24162; ● 140
Allen; DICKENSON; see Stratton (RMC Place)
Allencrest; RMC Place; ARLINGTON; ***245** D-15; ★ **WASH**; mail Arlington **z** 22207
Allens Creek; RMC Place; NELSON; ***244** J-9; mail Gladstone **z** 24553; ● 30
Allenslevel; RMC Place; BUCKINGHAM; ***244** J-10; mail Dillwyn **z** 23936; rural
Allentown; RMC Place; ACCOMACK; ***245** I-19; mail Accomac **z** 23301; rural
Allison Gap; RMC Place; SMYTH; **244** D-7; elev. 1,850ft./564m.; mail Saltville **z** 24370; ● 700
Allisonia; RMC Place; PULASKI; **244** L-3; 🅿; **z** 24347; ● 100
Allmondsville (Allmonds Wharf); RMC Place; GLOUCESTER; ***245** J-16; elev. 11ft./3m.; mail Gloucester **z** 23061; ● 120
Allmonds Wharf; GLOUCESTER; see Allmondsville (RMC Place)
Allnutt; KING GEORGE; see Chestnut Hill (RMC Place)
Allwood; RMC Place; AMHERST; ***244** I-8; elev. 1,002ft./305m.; mail Amherst **z** 24521; rural
Alma; RMC Place; PAGE; **244** F-10; mail Stanley **z** 22851; ● 130
Almagro; RMC Place; DANVILLE (Independent City); ***244** N-8; ★ **DANV**; mail Danville **z** 24541; pop. incl. with Danville (Independent City)
Almira; RMC Place; WISE; ***244** B-4; mail Pound **z** 24279; pop. incl. with Pound (Inc. Place)
Alonzaville; RMC Place; SHENANDOAH; ***244** D-10; elev. 1,087ft./331m.; mail Maurertown **z** 22644; ● 30
Alpha; RMC Place; BUCKINGHAM; ***245** J-11; mail Dillwyn **z** 23936; rural
Alpine; RMC Place; FAIRFAX; ***245** E-14; ★ **WASH**; mail Annandale **z** 22003, New Market **z** 22844
Alps; RMC Place; CAROLINE; ***245** H-15; mail Milford **z** 22514; rural
Alsop; RMC Place; SPOTSYLVANIA; ***245** G-13; elev. 310ft./94m.; mail Spotsylvania **z** 22553; rural
Altavista; Inc. Place; CAMPBELL; **244** L-8; elev. 596ft./182m.; 🅿; **z** 24517; Ⓟ 3,686; Ⓒ 3,425
Alto; RMC Place; AMHERST; ***244** I-8; mail Vesuvius **z** 24483; rural
Alton; RMC Place; HALIFAX; ***244** N-9; 🅿; **z** 24520; ● 120
Alum Ridge; RMC Place; FLOYD; **244** L-4; 🅿; **z** 24091; ● 80
Alvarado; RMC Place; WASHINGTON; ***244** D-6; elev. 1,745ft./532m.; mail Abingdon **z** 24211; rural
Amburg; RMC Place; MIDDLESEX; **245** J-17; elev. 28ft./9m.; mail Deltaville **z** 23043; ● 280
Amelia; AMELIA; see Amelia Court House (RMC Place)
AMELIA; **245** K-12; Ⓟ 8,787; Ⓒ 11,400; ◆ 13,113
Amelia Court House (Amelia); RMC Place; ⊡ AMELIA; **245** K-12; 🅿; **z** 23002; ● 900
Americana Park; RMC Place; CHESTERFIELD; ★ **RICH**; mail Chester **z** 23831
Amherst; Inc. Place; ⊡ AMHERST; **244** J-9; 🅿; ★ **LYNCH**; **z** 24521; Ⓟ 1,060; Ⓒ 2,251
Amherst; RMC Place; FAIRFAX; ★ **WASH**; mail Burke **z** 22015
AMHERST; **244** J-8; Ⓟ 28,578; Ⓒ 31,894; ◆ 32,682
Amissville; RMC Place; RAPPAHANNOCK; **245** E-12; 🅿; **z** 20106; ● 200
Ammon; RMC Place; AMELIA; ***245** K-13; elev. 315ft./96m.; 🅿; **z** 23822; ● 30
Amoco; RMC Place; NEWPORT NEWS (Independent City); ★ **NN-H**; pop. incl. with Newport News (Independent City)
Amonate; RMC Place; TAZEWELL; **244** K-1; 🅿; **z** 24601; ● 400
Ampt Hill; RMC Place; CHESTERFIELD; ***245** J-14; 🅿; ★ **RICH**; **z** 23234 & mail Richmond **z** 23237
Ampthill Heights; RMC Place; RICHMOND (Independent City); ***245** J-14; ★ **RICH**; mail Richmond **z** 23234; pop. incl. with Richmond (Independent City)
Amsterdam; RMC Place; BOTETOURT; ***244** J-6; ★ **ROAN**; mail Troutville **z** 24175; ● 100
Andersonville; RMC Place; BUCKINGHAM; **244** J-10; elev. 657ft./200m.; mail Dillwyn **z** 23936; ● 70
Andover; RMC Place; WISE; ***244** C-3; elev. 1,690ft./515m.; 🅿; **z** 24215; ● 250
Andrew Lewis Place; RMC Place; ROANOKE; ***244** K-5; ★ **ROAN**; mail Salem **z** 24153; ● 300
Angola; RMC Place; CUMBERLAND; ***245** J-11; elev. 411ft./125m.; mail Farmville **z** 23901; rural
Ankum; RMC Place; BRUNSWICK; ***245** M-12; mail Lawrenceville **z** 23868
Annalee Heights; RMC Place; FAIRFAX; **249** G-4; ★ **WASH**; mail Falls Church **z** 22042; ● 1,800
Annandale; CDP; FAIRFAX; **249** H-3; 🅿; ★ **WASH**; **z** 22003 & mail Fairfax **z** 22030, Springfield **z** 22151; Ⓟ 50,975; Ⓒ 54,994; ◆ 56,926
Annandale Acres; RMC Place; FAIRFAX; ***245** E-14; ★ **WASH**; mail Annandale **z** 22003
Annandale Gardens; RMC Place; FAIRFAX; mail Annandale **z** 22003
Annandale Terrace; RMC Place; FAIRFAX; ***245** E-14; ★ **WASH**; mail Annandale **z** 22003
Annex; RMC Place; AUGUSTA; ***244** G-9; mail Staunton **z** 24401; rural
Ante; RMC Place; BRUNSWICK; ***245** M-13; elev. 296ft./90m.; mail Emporia **z** 23847; rural
Antioch; RMC Place; FLUVANNA; ***245** I-11; elev. 509ft./155m.; mail Scottsville **z** 24590; rural
Antioch Fork; RMC Place; CAROLINE; ***245** H-14; elev. 213ft./65m.; mail Milford **z** 22514; rural
Appalachia; Inc. Place; WISE; **244** C-3; elev. 1,651ft./503m.; 🅿; **z** 24216; Ⓟ 1,994; Ⓒ 1,839
Apple Grove; RMC Place; LOUISA; ***245** H-12; mail Mineral **z** 23117
Appomattox; Inc. Place; ⊡ APPOMATTOX; **244** K-9; 🅿; **z** 24522; Ⓟ 1,707; Ⓒ 1,761
APPOMATTOX; **244** J-9; Ⓟ 12,298; Ⓒ 13,705; ◆ 14,589
Aqua; ROCKBRIDGE; see Decatur (RMC Place)
Aquia Harbor; STAFFORD; see Aquia Harbour (CDP)
Aquia Harbour (Aquia Harbor); CDP; STAFFORD; ***245** F-14; ★ **WASH**; mail Stafford **z** 22554; Ⓟ 6,308; Ⓒ 7,856
Aragona Village; RMC Place; VIRGINIA BEACH (Independent City); ***245** L-18; ★ **NORF-**; mail Virginia Beach **z** 23462; pop. incl. with Virginia Beach (Independent City)
Ararat; RMC Place; PATRICK; **244** N-4; elev. 1,471ft./448m.; 🅿; **z** 24053; ● 350
Arbor Estates; RMC Place; SUFFOLK (Independent City); ★ **NORF-**; mail Suffolk **z** 23434; pop. incl. with Suffolk (Independent City)
Arbor Hill; RMC Place; AUGUSTA; ***244** H-8; mail Staunton **z** 24401
Arcadia; RMC Place; BOTETOURT; ***244** J-7; mail Buchanan **z** 24066; ● 50
Arcola; RMC Place; LOUDOUN; **245** D-13; 🅿; **z** 20148; ● 240
Arcturus; RMC Place; FAIRFAX; ***245** E-15; ★ **WASH**; mail Alexandria **z** 22308
Ardmore; RMC Place; FAIRFAX (Independent City); ***245** E-14; ★ **WASH**; mail Fairfax **z** 22030; pop. incl. with Fairfax (Independent City)
Argyle Heights; RMC Place; STAFFORD; ***245** G-14; ★ **FRED**; mail Fredericksburg **z** 22401; ● 400
Ark; RMC Place; GLOUCESTER; **245** J-17; 🅿; **z** 23003; ● 200
Arlington; CDP; ⊡ ARLINGTON; **245** D-15; 🅿 🅷 🅲 9,404 ■; ★ **WASH**; **z** 20598, **z** 22201-07, **z** 22209-10, **z** 22212-17, **z** 22219, **z** 22222, **z** 22225-27, **z** 22230, **z** 22240-46 & mail Fort Myer **z** 22211; Ⓟ 170,936; Ⓒ 189,453; ◆ 213,796
Arlington; RMC Place; HOPEWELL (Independent City); ***245** K-14; ★ **RICH**; mail Hopewell **z** 23860; pop. incl. with Hopewell (Independent City)
ARLINGTON; **245** D-14; Ⓟ 170,936; Ⓒ 189,453; ◆ 213,796
Arlington Forest; RMC Place; ARLINGTON; ***245** D-15; ★ **WASH**; mail Arlington **z** 22203
Arlington Heights; RMC Place; ARLINGTON; ***245** D-15; ★ **WASH**; mail Arlington **z** 22204
Arlington Heights; RMC Place; LYNCHBURG (Independent City); ★ **LYNCH**; pop. incl. with Lynchburg (Independent City)
Arlington Village; RMC Place; ARLINGTON; ***245** D-15; ★ **WASH**; mail Arlington **z** 22204
Arlingwood; RMC Place; ARLINGTON; ***245** D-15; ★ **WASH**; mail Arlington **z** 22207
Armel; RMC Place; FREDERICK; **245** D-11; mail Winchester **z** 22603; ● 130
Armistead Forest; RMC Place; PORTSMOUTH (Independent City); ***245** L-17; ★ **NORF-**; mail Portsmouth **z** 23703; pop. incl. with Portsmouth (Independent City)
Armstrong; RMC Place; BATH; ***244** H-7; mail Millboro **z** 24460; rural
Armstrong Gardens; RMC Place; HAMPTON (Independent City); ***245** L-17; ★ **NN-H**; mail Hampton **z** 23669; pop. incl. with Hampton (Independent City)
Aroda; RMC Place; MADISON; **245** G-11; 🅿; **z** 22709; ● 100
Arrington; RMC Place; NELSON; **244** I-9; 🅿; **z** 22922; ● 250
Arrowhead; RMC Place; VIRGINIA BEACH (Independent City); ***245** L-18; ★ **NORF-**; mail Virginia Beach **z** 23462; pop. incl. with Virginia Beach (Independent City)
Arthur; RMC Place; MONTGOMERY; ***244** K-5; ★ **ROAN**; mail Shawsville **z** 24162; ● 70
Artillery Ridge; RMC Place; SPOTSYLVANIA; ***245** G-14; ★ **FRED**; mail Fredericksburg **z** 22401; ● 140
Artrip; RMC Place; RUSSELL; ***244** C-5; elev. 1,570ft./479m.; mail Cleveland **z** 24225; rural
Arvonia; RMC Place; BUCKINGHAM; **245** I-11; elev. 415ft./126m.; 🅿; **z** 23004; ● 750
Asberrys; RMC Place; TAZEWELL; ***244** L-1; mail Tannersville **z** 24377; rural
Ashburn; RMC Place; LOUDOUN; **245** D-14; 🅿; ★ **WASH**; **z** 20146-49; Ⓟ 3,393; ● 1,300
Ashby; RMC Place; CUMBERLAND; ***245** J-11; elev. 408ft./124m.; mail Cumberland **z** 23040; rural
Ashland; Inc. Place; HANOVER; **245** I-14; 🅿 🅲 1,146; ★ **RICH**; **z** 23005; Ⓟ 5,864; Ⓒ 6,619
Ashton Heights; RMC Place; ARLINGTON; ***245** D-15; ★ **WASH**; mail Arlington **z** 22201
Ashville; RMC Place; FAUQUIER; ***245** D-12; mail Marshall **z** 20115; rural
Ashwood; RMC Place; BATH; **244** H-6; mail Hot Springs **z** 24445; ● 200
Aspen; RMC Place; CHARLOTTE; ***244** L-9; elev. 456ft./139m.; mail Phenix **z** 23959; ● 30
Aspenwall; RMC Place; CHARLOTTE; ***244** L-9; elev. 535ft./163m.; mail Brookneal **z** 24528; rural
Assawoman; RMC Place; ACCOMACK; ***245** H-20; 🅿; **z** 23302; ● 170
Atkins; CDP; SMYTH; **244** L-1; elev. 2,291ft./698m.; 🅿; **z** 24311; Ⓟ 1,130; Ⓒ 1,138
Atlantic; RMC Place; ACCOMACK; **245** H-20; 🅿; **z** 23303; ● 400
Atlantic; RMC Place; VIRGINIA BEACH (Independent City); ★ **NORF-**; mail Virginia Beach **z** 23458; pop. incl. with Virginia Beach (Independent City)
Atlantic Park; RMC Place; VIRGINIA BEACH (Independent City); ***245** L-18; ★ **NORF-**; mail Virginia Beach **z** 23451; pop. incl. with Virginia Beach (Independent City)
Atlee; RMC Place; HANOVER; **243** A-8; ★ **RICH**; mail Mechanicsville **z** 23111; ● 40
Atoka; RMC Place; FAUQUIER; ***245** D-13; mail Marshall **z** 20115; rural
Attoway; RMC Place; SMYTH; **244** M-1; mail Marion **z** 24354; ● 250
Auburn; RMC Place; FAUQUIER; ***245** E-13; mail Catlett **z** 20119; ● 100
Auburn Farm; RMC Place; LOUDOUN; ★ **WASH**; mail Ashburn **z** 20147
AUGUSTA; **244** G-8; Ⓟ 54,677; Ⓒ 65,615; ◆ 65,568
Augusta Springs; RMC Place; AUGUSTA; **244** H-8; 🅿; **z** 24411; ● 250
Aurora Hills; RMC Place; ARLINGTON; ***245** D-15; ★ **WASH**; mail Arlington **z** 22202
Austinville; RMC Place; WYTHE; **244** M-3; elev. 2,126ft./648m.; 🅿; **z** 24312; ● 850
Avalon; RMC Place; CHESAPEAKE (Independent City); ***245** L-18; ★ **NORF-**; mail Chesapeake **z** 23324; pop. incl. with Chesapeake (Independent City)
Avalon; RMC Place; NORTHUMBERLAND; ***245** H-17; elev. 102ft./31m.; mail Heathsville **z** 22473; rural
Avalon Terrace; RMC Place; VIRGINIA BEACH (Independent City); ***245** L-18; ★ **NORF-**; mail Virginia Beach **z** 23464; pop. incl. with Virginia Beach (Independent City)
Averett; RMC Place; MECKLENBURG; ***244** N-10; elev. 486ft./148m.; mail Nelson **z** 24580; ● 60
Avon; RMC Place; NELSON; **244** H-9; mail Afton **z** 22920; ● 80
Avondale; RMC Place; HANOVER; ***245** I-14; elev. 188ft./57m.; ★ **RICH**; mail Mechanicsville **z** 23116; ● 600
Avon Forest; RMC Place; FAIRFAX; ***245** E-14; ★ **WASH**; mail Fairfax Station **z** 22039; ● 60
Axtel; RMC Place; BUCKINGHAM; ***244** I-10; elev. 568ft./173m.; mail Howardsville **z** 24562; rural
Axton; RMC Place; HENRY; **244** M-7; 🅿; **z** 24054; ● 300
Aylett; RMC Place; KING WILLIAM; **245** I-15; elev. 25ft./8m.; 🅿; **z** 23009; ● 200
Aylor; RMC Place; MADISON; ***245** F-11; 🅿; **z** 22727; rural
Azalea Acres; RMC Place; NORFOLK (Independent City); ***245** L-18; ★ **NORF-**; mail Norfolk **z** 23518; pop. incl. with Norfolk (Independent City)
Azalea Court; RMC Place; HENRICO; ***245** I-14; ★ **RICH**; mail Richmond **z** 23227; ● 800
Azalea Gardens; RMC Place; HAMPTON (Independent City); ***245** L-17; ★ **NN-H**; mail Hampton **z** 23669; pop. incl. with Hampton (Independent City)

B

Bachelors Hall; RMC Place; PITTSYLVANIA; ***244** M-7; ★ **DANV**; mail Danville **z** 24541; ● 200
Backbay; RMC Place; VIRGINIA BEACH (Independent City); ***245** M-18; ★ **NORF-**; mail Virginia Beach **z** 23457; pop. incl. with Virginia Beach (Independent City)
Bacon Hollow; RMC Place; GREENE; ***244** G-10; elev. 1,026ft./313m.; mail Dyke **z** 22935; rural
Bacons Castle; RMC Place; SURRY; **243** I-1; mail Surry **z** 23883; ● 70
Bacons Fork; RMC Place; LUNENBURG; ***245** L-12; elev. 399ft./122m.; mail La Crosse **z** 23950; rural
Bacova; RMC Place; BATH; **244** H-6; 🅿; **z** 24412; ● 70
Bacova Junction; RMC Place; BATH; ***244** H-6; mail Hot Springs **z** 24445; ● 200
Baden; RMC Place; DICKENSON; ***244** C-4; mail Clintwood **z** 24228; rural
Bagby; RMC Place; CAROLINE; ***245** H-14; elev. 186ft./57m.; mail Milford **z** 22514; rural
Bagleys Mills; RMC Place; LUNENBURG; ***245** M-11; mail South Hill **z** 23970; rural
Bailey; RMC Place; TAZEWELL; ***244** K-1; mail Bluefield **z** 24605; rural
Baileys Crossroads; RMC Place; FAIRFAX; ***245** D-15; 🅿; ★ **WASH**; **z** 22041; ● 7,800
Bailey's Crossroads; CDP-Census Area Only; FAIRFAX; **249** G-5; 🅿; ★ **WASH**; **z** 22041; Ⓟ 19,507; Ⓒ 23,166; ◆ 24,070
Balcony Falls; RMC Place; ROCKBRIDGE; ***244** I-7; mail Glasgow **z** 24555; pop. incl. with Glasgow (Inc. Place)
Ballards Crossroads; RMC Place; ISLE OF WIGHT; ***245** M-16; elev. 81ft./25m.; mail Carrsville **z** 23315; rural
Ballentine Place; RMC Place; NORFOLK (Independent City); ***245** L-18; ★ **NORF-**; mail Norfolk **z** 23509; pop. incl. with Norfolk (Independent City)
Balls Hills; RMC Place; FAIRFAX; ★ **WASH**; mail Mc Lean **z** 22101
Ballston; RMC Place; ARLINGTON; ***245** D-15; ★ **WASH**; mail Arlington **z** 22203

Entries in **UPPERCASE** are counties.
Entries in **bold** have populations of 2,500 or more.
Names in parentheses are alternate names.

Inc. Place	Incorporated Place
RMC Place	Rand McNally Designated Place
CDP	Census Designated Place
MCD	Minor Civil Division
⊡	County Seat
▲	Minor Civil Division
elev.	Elevation
🅿	Post Office
🅷	Hospital
🅲	College
■	Principal Business Center
★	Ranally Metro Area (RMA) Abbreviation
z	Zip Code(s)
Ⓟ	Previous Census Population
Ⓡ	Revised Census Population
Ⓐ	Annexation Population
●	Rand McNally Population Estimate
Ⓒ	Final Census Population
Ⓢ	Special Census Population
◆	Estimated Population

For additional definitions see Glossary, Volume 1, and Introduction, Volume 2.

Ballsville; RMC Place; POWHATAN; 245 J-12; elev. 376ft./115m.; mail Powhatan Z 23139; ● 60
Baltimore Corner; RMC Place; DINWIDDIE; *245 K-13; mail Ford Z 23850; rural
Balty; RMC Place; CAROLINE; *245 H-14; elev. 228ft./69m.; mail Ruther Glen Z 22546; rural
Banco; RMC Place; MADISON; *245 F-11; 🅿; Z 22711, Z 22727; ● 30
Bandy; RMC Place; TAZEWELL; 244 K-1; 🅿; Z 24602; ● 100
Bane; RMC Place; GILES; *244 K-3; mail Pearisburg Z 24134; rural
Banner; RMC Place; WISE; 244 C-4; elev. 2,028ft./618m.; mail Coeburn Z 24230; ● 250
Banners Corner; RMC Place; RUSSELL; 244 D-5; mail Castlewood Z 24224; ● 300
Barbours Creek; RMC Place; CRAIG; *244 J-6; mail New Castle Z 24127
Barboursville; RMC Place; ORANGE; 245 G-11; 🅿; Z 22923; ● 150
Barcroft; RMC Place; ARLINGTON; *245 D-15; ★ WASH; mail Arlington Z 22204
Barfoot; RMC Place; FRANKLIN; *244 L-6; mail Rocky Mount Z 24151; rural
Barham; RMC Place; SURRY; *245 K-15; elev. 126ft./38m.; mail Spring Grove Z 23881; rural
Barhamsville; RMC Place; NEW KENT; 245 J-16; 🅿; Z 23011; ● 150
Barley; RMC Place; GREENSVILLE; 245 N-13; elev. 286ft./87m.; mail Emporia Z 23847; ● 30
Barnes Junction (Barnesville); RMC Place; CHARLOTTE; *244 M-10; mail Red Oak Z 23964
Barnesville; CHARLOTTE; see Barnes Junction (RMC Place)
Barnett; RMC Place; RUSSELL; *244 C-6; mail Lebanon Z 24266; rural
Barnetts; RMC Place; CHARLES CITY; *245 J-15; elev. 58ft./18m.; mail Charles City Z 23030; rural
Barren Ridge; RMC Place; AUGUSTA; 244 G-9; mail Staunton Z 24401; ● 110
Barren Springs; RMC Place; WYTHE; 244 L-3; 🅿; Z 24313; ● 100
Barrett Acres; RMC Place; SUFFOLK (Independent City); ★ NORF-; mail Suffolk Z 23434; pop. incl. with Suffolk (Independent City)
Bartlett; RMC Place; ISLE OF WIGHT; *245 L-17; elev. 23ft./7m.; ★ NN-H; mail Carrollton Z 23314; rural
Bartlick; RMC Place; DICKENSON; *244 B-5; mail Haysi Z 24256; ● 30
Bartons Crossroad; RMC Place; GRAYSON; *244 M-1; mail Troutdale Z 24378; rural
Bartonsville (Bartonville); RMC Place; FREDERICK; *245 D-11; mail Winchester Z 22602
Bartonville; FREDERICK; see Bartonsville (RMC Place)
Barytes; RMC Place; BRISTOL (Independent City); *244 E-5; ★ JNSC-; mail Bristol Z 24201; pop. incl. with Bristol (Independent City)
Basham; RMC Place; MONTGOMERY; *244 L-5; mail Pilot Z 24138; ● 50
Basic; RMC Place; WAYNESBORO (Independent City); mail Waynesboro Z 22980; pop. incl. with Waynesboro (Independent City)
Baskerville; RMC Place; MECKLENBURG; *245 M-11; 🅿; Z 23915; ● 100
Bassett; CDP; HENRY; 244 M-6; elev. 760ft./232m.; 🅿; ★ MRTNV; Z 24055; Ⓟ 1,579; Ⓒ 1,338
Bassett Forks; RMC Place; HENRY; *244 M-6; ★ MRTNV; mail Bassett Z 24055; ● 180
Bastian; RMC Place; BLAND; 244 K-2; 🅿; Z 24314; ● 420
Basye; RMC Place; SHENANDOAH; 244 E-9; 🅿; Z 22810; ● 150
Basye-Bryce Mountain; CDP-Census Area Only; SHENANDOAH; *244 E-10; Ⓒ 986
Batesville; RMC Place; ALBEMARLE; 244 H-10; 🅿; Z 22924; ● 200
BATH; 244 H-7; Ⓟ 4,799; Ⓒ 5,048; ◆ 4,550
Bath Alum; RMC Place; BATH; *244 H-7; mail Millboro Z 24460; rural
Battersea; RMC Place; PETERSBURG (Independent City); *245 K-14; elev. 80ft./24m.; ★ RICH; mail Petersburg Z 23803; pop. incl. with Petersburg (Independent City)
Battery; RMC Place; ESSEX; *245 H-15; elev. 160ft./49m.; mail Tappahannock Z 22560; ● 50
Battery Park; RMC Place; HENRICO; ★ RICH; mail Henrico Z 23228
Battery Park; RMC Place; ISLE OF WIGHT; *245 L-17; 🅿; ★ NN-H; Z 23304; ● 250
Battle Beach; RMC Place; SOUTHAMPTON; *245 N-16; elev. 25ft./8m.; mail Franklin Z 23851; ● 50
Battle Creek; RMC Place; PAGE; *244 F-10; mail Stanley Z 22851; ● 30
Battlefield Green; RMC Place; SPOTSYLVANIA; *245 G-13; ★ FRED; mail Fredericksburg Z 22401; ● 280
Battlefield Park; RMC Place; PETERSBURG (Independent City); ★ RICH; mail Petersburg Z 23805; pop. incl. with Petersburg (Independent City)
Bavon; RMC Place; MATHEWS; 245 J-17; elev. 5ft./2m.; 🅿; ★ NN-H; Z 23138; ● 150
Baxton; RMC Place; CHESTERFIELD; ★ RICH; mail Chester Z 23831
Bayberry Estates; RMC Place; KING GEORGE; *245 F-15; mail King George Z 22485; ● 240
Bay Colony; RMC Place; VIRGINIA BEACH (Independent City); *245 L-18; ★ NORF-; mail Virginia Beach Z 23451; pop. incl. with Virginia Beach (Independent City)
Bayford; RMC Place; NORTHAMPTON; *245 J-19; mail Franktown Z 23354; rural
Bay Island; RMC Place; VIRGINIA BEACH (Independent City); *245 L-18; elev. 15ft./5m.; ★ NORF-; mail Virginia Beach Z 23451; pop. incl. with Virginia Beach (Independent City)
Baylake Beach; RMC Place; VIRGINIA BEACH (Independent City); *245 L-18; ★ NORF-; mail Virginia Beach Z 23455; pop. incl. with Virginia Beach (Independent City)
Baylake Pines; RMC Place; VIRGINIA BEACH (Independent City); *245 L-18; ★ NORF-; mail Virginia Beach Z 23455; pop. incl. with Virginia Beach (Independent City)
Baynesville; RMC Place; WESTMORELAND; *245 G-15; mail Montross Z 22520
Bayport; RMC Place; MIDDLESEX; *245 I-16; mail Jamaica Z 23079; summer pop. 100; ● 30
Bayside; RMC Place; ACCOMACK; *245 I-19; elev. 15ft./5m.; mail Onancock Z 23417; rural
Bayside; RMC Place; VIRGINIA BEACH (Independent City); ★ NORF-; mail Virginia Beach Z 23455, Z 23471; pop. incl. with Virginia Beach (Independent City)
Bay View; RMC Place; NORTHAMPTON; 245 K-19; elev. 29ft./9m.; mail Cape Charles Z 23310; ● 180
Bayville Park; RMC Place; VIRGINIA BEACH (Independent City); *245 L-18; ★ NORF-; mail Virginia Beach Z 23455; pop. incl. with Virginia Beach (Independent City)
Baywood; RMC Place; GRAYSON; *244 M-2; mail Galax Z 24333
Beach; RMC Place; CHESTERFIELD; *245 J-13; elev. 276ft./84m.; ★ RICH; mail Chesterfield Z 23832, Z 23838
Beach Grove; RMC Place; NELSON; *244 H-9; elev. 950ft./290m.; mail Roseland Z 22967; ● 130
Beaconsdale; RMC Place; NEWPORT NEWS (Independent City); *245 K-17; ★ NN-H; mail Newport News Z 23607; pop. incl. with Newport News (Independent City)
Bealeton; RMC Place; FAUQUIER; 245 F-13; 🅿; Z 22712; ● 120
Beamantown; RMC Place; WISE; *244 D-3; mail Big Stone Gap Z 24219
Beamon; RMC Place; SUFFOLK (Independent City); *245 M-17; ★ NORF-; mail Suffolk Z 23434; pop. incl. with Suffolk (Independent City)
Bear Spring; GILES; see Berton (RMC Place)
Bear Wallow; RMC Place; BUCHANAN; *244 K-1; elev. 3,045ft./928m.; mail Jewell Ridge Z 24622; ● 30
Beaufont Hills; RMC Place; RICHMOND (Independent City); ★ RICH; mail Richmond Z 23225; pop. incl. with Richmond (Independent City)
Beaumont (Beaumont Learning Center); RMC Place; POWHATAN; *245 I-12; 🅿; Z 23014; ● 40
Beaumont Learning Center; POWHATAN; see Beaumont (RMC Place)
Beaverdam; RMC Place; HANOVER; 245 H-13; 🅿; Z 23015; ● 170
Beaverlett; RMC Place; MATHEWS; *245 J-17; elev. 7ft./2m.; 🅿; ★ NN-H; Z 23109; ● 200
Beazley; RMC Place; CAROLINE, ESSEX, KING AND QUEEN; *245 H-15; mail Tappahannock Z 22560; ● 30
Beckham; RMC Place; APPOMATTOX; *244 J-9; elev. 748ft./228m.; mail Concord Z 24538; rural
Bedford; Independent City; serves as county seat of Bedford; 244 K-7; 🅿 🅷; Z 24523; Ⓟ 6,073; Ⓒ 6,299; ◆ 6,467
BEDFORD; 244 K-7; Ⓟ 45,656; Ⓒ 60,371; ◆ 64,816
Bedford Springs; CAMPBELL; see New London (RMC Place)
Bee; RMC Place; DICKENSON; *244 C-5; 🅿; Z 24217; ● 130
Beech Fork; RMC Place; LUNENBURG; *245 L-11; elev. 550ft./168m.; mail Victoria Z 23974; ● 100
Beech Springs; RMC Place; LEE; *244 D-2; mail Jonesville Z 24263; rural
Beechwood; RMC Place; MECKLENBURG; *245 M-11; elev. 219ft./67m.; mail Bracey Z 23919; rural
Beechwood Hills; RMC Place; ARLINGTON; *245 D-15; ★ WASH; mail Arlington Z 22207
Beechwood Hills; RMC Place; CAMPBELL; *244 K-8; ★ LYNCH; mail Lynchburg Z 24502; ● 300
Beechwood Manor; RMC Place; PRINCE GEORGE; *245 K-15; ★ RICH; mail Hopewell Z 23860; ● 350
Bel Air; RMC Place; FAIRFAX; 249 G-4; ★ WASH; mail Falls Church Z 22042; ● 1,500
Belaire; RMC Place; NORFOLK (Independent City); *245 L-18; ★ NORF-; mail Norfolk Z 23518; pop. incl. with Norfolk (Independent City)
Beldor; RMC Place; ROCKINGHAM; *244 G-10; mail Elkton Z 22827; rural
Belfast Mills; RMC Place; RUSSELL; *244 C-6; mail Cedar Bluff Z 24609; rural
Bellair; RMC Place; ALBEMARLE; 243 B-2; ★ CHRLTV; mail Charlottesville Z 22903; ● 1,400
Bell Air; RMC Place; STAFFORD; *245 G-14; ★ FRED; mail Fredericksburg Z 22401; ● 260
Bellamy (Belroi); RMC Place; GLOUCESTER; *245 J-17; elev. 79ft./24m.; 🅿; ★ NN-H; Z 23061; ● 300
Bellamy; RMC Place; SCOTT; *244 D-4; 🅿; ★ JNSC-; Z 23061 & mail Gate City Z 24251; rural
Bellamy Manor; RMC Place; VIRGINIA BEACH (Independent City); *245 L-18; ★ NORF-; mail Virginia Beach Z 23464; pop. incl. with Virginia Beach (Independent City)
Bellbluff; RMC Place; CHESTERFIELD; *245 J-14; elev. 196ft./60m.; ★ RICH; mail Richmond Z 23234; ● 1,300
Belle Haven; Inc. Place; ACCOMACK, NORTHAMPTON; 245 I-19; elev. 36ft./11m.; 🅿; Z 23306; Ⓟ 526; Ⓒ 480
Belle Haven; CDP; FAIRFAX; 249 I-6; ★ WASH; mail Alexandria Z 22307; Ⓟ 6,427; Ⓒ 6,269
Belle Meade; RMC Place; FAUQUIER; *245 D-12; mail Linden Z 22642; ● 30
Bellemeade; RMC Place; RICHMOND (Independent City); ★ RICH; mail Richmond Z 23224; pop. incl. with Richmond (Independent City)
Belle Meadows; RMC Place; BRISTOL (Independent City); ★ JNSC-; mail Bristol Z 24201; pop. incl. with Bristol (Independent City)
Belle Rive; RMC Place; FAIRFAX; ★ WASH; mail Alexandria Z 22309
Belleview; RMC Place; FAIRFAX; 249 E-3; 🅿; ★ WASH; Z 22307; ● 2,300
Belleville; RMC Place; SUFFOLK (Independent City); ★ NORF-; mail Suffolk Z 23435; pop. incl. with Suffolk (Independent City)
Bellevue; RMC Place; BEDFORD; *244 J-8; elev. 903ft./275m.; mail Forest Z 24551; rural
Bellevue; RMC Place; HENRICO; 🅿; ★ RICH; Z 23227; pop. incl. with Richmond (Independent City)
Bellevue Forest; RMC Place; ARLINGTON; *245 D-15; ★ WASH; mail Arlington Z 22207
Bellmeade; RMC Place; CHESTERFIELD; ★ RICH; mail Richmond Z 23234
Bells Crossroad; RMC Place; SPOTSYLVANIA; *245 G-13; mail Spotsylvania Z 22553; rural
Bells Cross Roads; RMC Place; LOUISA; *245 H-12; mail Louisa Z 23093; ● 30
Bells Mill; RMC Place; CHESAPEAKE (Independent City); *245 M-18; ★ NORF-; mail Chesapeake Z 23320; pop. incl. with Chesapeake (Independent City)
Bell Spur; RMC Place; CARROLL; *244 M-4; mail Meadows of Dan Z 24120; rural
Bell Spur; RMC Place; PATRICK; *244 M-4; elev. 2,695ft./821m.; mail Meadows of Dan Z 24120; rural
Bells Valley; RMC Place; ROCKBRIDGE; 244 H-7; mail Goshen Z 24439; ● 40
Bellwood; CDP; CHESTERFIELD; *245 J-14; ★ RICH; mail Richmond Z 23234; Ⓟ 6,178; Ⓒ 5,974
Bellwood Estates; RMC Place; CHESTERFIELD; ★ RICH; mail Richmond Z 23237
Bellwood Manor; RMC Place; CHESTERFIELD; *245 J-14; ★ RICH; mail Richmond Z 23234; ● 300
Bellwood Terrace; RMC Place; CHESTERFIELD; ★ RICH; mail Richmond Z 23237
Belmont; RMC Place; CHARLOTTESVILLE (Independent City); ★ CHRLTV; pop. incl. with Charlottesville (Independent City)
Belmont; RMC Place; LOUDOUN; *245 D-13; ★ WASH; mail Ashburn Z 20147
Belmont; RMC Place; PRINCE WILLIAM; ★ WASH; mail Woodbridge Z 22191
Belmont; RMC Place; SPOTSYLVANIA; *245 G-12; mail Spotsylvania Z 22553; rural
Belmont Acres; RMC Place; CHESTERFIELD; *245 J-14; elev. 200ft./61m.; ★ RICH; mail Richmond Z 23234; ● 400
Belmont Circle; RMC Place; PRINCE EDWARD; *245 K-11; elev. 421ft./128m.; mail Farmville Z 23901; pop. incl. with Farmville (Inc. Place)
Belmont Farms; RMC Place; MONTGOMERY; mail Christiansburg Z 24073; pop. incl. with Christiansburg (Inc. Place)
Belmont Park Estates; RMC Place; FAIRFAX; *245 E-14; ★ WASH; mail Lorton Z 22079; ● 170
Belona; RMC Place; POWHATAN; *245 J-12; elev. 333ft./101m.; mail Powhatan Z 23139
Belroi; GLOUCESTER; see Bellamy (RMC Place)
Belspring; RMC Place; PULASKI; 244 K-4; elev. 1,774ft./541m.; 🅿; Z 24058; ● 390
Belvedere; RMC Place; FAIRFAX; 249 H-4; ★ WASH; mail Falls Church Z 22041; ● 2,200
Belvedere; RMC Place; NORFOLK (Independent City); ★ NORF-; mail Norfolk Z 23504; pop. incl. with Norfolk (Independent City)
Belvidere Beach; RMC Place; KING GEORGE; *245 G-14; mail Fredericksburg Z 22405
Belvoir; RMC Place; FAUQUIER; *245 E-13; mail Marshall Z 20115
Bena; RMC Place; GLOUCESTER; *245 K-17; elev. 9ft./3m.; 🅿; ★ NN-H; Z 23018; ● 200
Benefit; RMC Place; CHESAPEAKE (Independent City); *245 M-18; ★ NORF-; mail Chesapeake Z 23322; pop. incl. with Chesapeake (Independent City)
Benhams; RMC Place; WASHINGTON; *244 D-5; ★ JNSC-; mail Bristol Z 24202
Ben Hur; RMC Place; LEE; 244 D-2; 🅿; Z 24218; ● 390
Benmoreel; RMC Place; NORFOLK (Independent City); *245 L-17; ★ NORF-; mail Norfolk Z 23505; pop. incl. with Norfolk (Independent City)
Bennetts Creek; RMC Place; SUFFOLK (Independent City); ★ NORF-; mail Suffolk Z 23435; pop. incl. with Suffolk (Independent City)
Bennetts Harbor; RMC Place; SUFFOLK (Independent City); ★ NORF-; mail Suffolk Z 23434; pop. incl. with Suffolk (Independent City)
Bennett Springs; RMC Place; ROANOKE; *244 J-6; mail Salem Z 24153
Benns Church; RMC Place; ISLE OF WIGHT; 245 L-17; elev. 44ft./13m.; ★ NN-H; mail Carrollton Z 23314, Smithfield Z 23430; ● 100
Bensley; CDP-Census Area Only; CHESTERFIELD; 243 E-8; ★ RICH; mail Richmond Z 23234; Ⓟ 5,093; Ⓒ 5,435
Bent Creek; RMC Place; APPOMATTOX; 244 J-9; mail Gladstone Z 24553; ● 50
Bent Mountain; RMC Place; ROANOKE; 244 K-5; elev. 2,617ft./798m.; 🅿; ★ ROAN; Z 24059; ● 40
Bentonville; RMC Place; WARREN; 245 E-11; 🅿; Z 22610; ● 380
Bergton; RMC Place; ROCKINGHAM; 244 E-9; 🅿; Z 22811; ● 100
Berkeley; RMC Place; ALBEMARLE; *244 H-10; ★ CHRLTV; mail Charlottesville Z 22901
Berkley; RMC Place; NORFOLK (Independent City); *245 L-18; ★ NORF-; mail Norfolk Z 23523; pop. incl. with Norfolk (Independent City)
Berkshire; RMC Place; ARLINGTON; *245 D-15; ★ WASH; mail Arlington Z 22207
Berlin; RMC Place; SOUTHAMPTON; *245 L-15; elev. 88ft./27m.; mail Ivor Z 23866; ● 30
Berryville; Inc. Place; ⊡ CLARKE; 245 C-12; elev. 575ft./175m.; 🅿; Z 22611; Ⓟ 3,097; Ⓒ 2,963
Berton (Bear Spring); RMC Place; GILES; *244 K-4; mail Pearisburg Z 24134; rural
Bestland; RMC Place; ESSEX; *245 I-16; elev. 159ft./48m.; mail Dunnsville Z 22454; rural
Betana Park; RMC Place; FAIRFAX; *245 D-14; ★ WASH; mail Reston Z 20190
Bethany; RMC Place; WYTHE; *244 L-3; mail Austinville Z 24312; ● 100
Bethel; RMC Place; FAUQUIER; 245 E-13; ★ WASH; mail Warrenton Z 20187; ● 250
Bethel; RMC Place; HALIFAX; *244 M-9; elev. 504ft./154m.; mail Scottsburg Z 24589; ● 90
Bethel; RMC Place; PRINCE WILLIAM; *245 E-14; ★ WASH; mail Woodbridge Z 22191; rural
Bethel; RMC Place; WARREN; *245 D-11; mail Front Royal Z 22630; ● 30
Beulah Church; RMC Place; ESSEX; mail Tappahannock Z 22560; rural
Beulah Village; RMC Place; CHESTERFIELD; ★ RICH; mail Richmond Z 23234
Beulahville; RMC Place; KING WILLIAM; *245 H-15; mail Aylett Z 23009; rural
Beverley Hills; RMC Place; ALEXANDRIA (Independent City); *245 E-15; ★ WASH; mail Alexandria Z 22305; pop. incl. with Alexandria (Independent City)
Beverly Forest; RMC Place; FAIRFAX; *245 E-14; ★ WASH; mail Springfield Z 22150
Beverly Heights; RMC Place; SALEM (Independent City); *244 K-5; ★ ROAN; mail Salem Z 24153; pop. incl. with Salem (Independent City)
Beverly Hills; RMC Place; HENRICO; *245 J-13; ★ RICH; mail Henrico Z 23229; ● 2,550
Beverly Manor; RMC Place; FAIRFAX; *245 D-14; ★ WASH; mail Mc Lean Z 22101
Beverly Town; RMC Place; AMHERST; *244 I-8; elev. 1,400ft./427m.; mail Monroe Z 24574; rural
Beverlyville; RMC Place; NORTHUMBERLAND; *245 H-17; mail Reedville Z 22539; ● 40
Big Bethel; RMC Place; HAMPTON (Independent City); *245 K-17; elev. 20ft./6m.; ★ NN-H; mail Hampton Z 23666; pop. incl. with Hampton (Independent City)
Big Fork; RMC Place; MECKLENBURG; *245 M-11; elev. 323ft./98m.; mail South Hill Z 23970; rural
Big Island; RMC Place; BEDFORD; 244 J-8; 🅿; Z 24526; ● 400
Big Laurel; RMC Place; WISE; *244 C-4; mail Wise Z 24293; ● 50
Big Otter Mill; RMC Place; BEDFORD; *244 J-7; elev. 770ft./235m.; mail Bedford Z 24523; rural
Big Rock (Stric); RMC Place; BUCHANAN; 244 B-5; 🅿; Z 24603; ● 650
Big Spring; RMC Place; PAGE; *245 E-11; mail Rileyville Z 22650; rural
Big Stone Gap; Inc. Place; WISE; 244 D-3; 🅿 🅷; Z 24219; Ⓟ 4,748; Ⓒ 4,856; Ⓡ 5,906
Big Vein; RMC Place; TAZEWELL; *244 K-1; mail Pocahontas Z 24635; ● 200
Biltmore; RMC Place; HENRICO; *245 I-14; ★ RICH; mail Glen Allen Z 23060; ● 975
Binns Hall; RMC Place; CHARLES CITY; *245 J-15; elev. 120ft./37m.; mail Charles City Z 23030; rural
Birch; RMC Place; HALIFAX; *244 M-8; elev. 640ft./195m.; mail South Boston Z 24592; rural
Birchett Estates; RMC Place; PRINCE GEORGE; *245 K-14; ★ RICH; mail Prince George Z 23875; ● 500
Birchland Park; RMC Place; HALIFAX; *244 M-8; elev. 636ft./194m.; mail South Boston Z 24592; ● 40
Birchleaf; RMC Place; DICKENSON; 244 B-5; 🅿; Z 24220; ● 260
Birch Town; RMC Place; ACCOMACK; *245 H-20; mail Chincoteague Island Z 23336; pop. incl. with Chincoteague (Inc. Place)
Birchwood Gardens; RMC Place; VIRGINIA BEACH (Independent City); *245 L-18; ★ NORF-; mail Virginia Beach Z 23452; pop. incl. with Virginia Beach (Independent City)
Birchwood Park; RMC Place; JAMES CITY; *245 K-16; elev. 70ft./21m.; ★ NN-H; mail Williamsburg Z 23185; ● 150
Birdneck Acres; RMC Place; VIRGINIA BEACH (Independent City); *245 L-18; ★ NORF-; mail Virginia Beach Z 23451; pop. incl. with Virginia Beach (Independent City)
Birdsnest; RMC Place; NORTHAMPTON; 245 J-19; elev. 36ft./11m.; 🅿; Z 23307; ● 80
Birmingham; RMC Place; TAZEWELL; *244 C-6; elev. 2,030ft./619m.; mail Cedar Bluff Z 24609; ● 90
Biscoe; RMC Place; KING AND QUEEN; *245 I-15; elev. 172ft./52m.; mail Saint Stephens Church Z 23148; rural
Bishop; RMC Place; TAZEWELL; 244 K-1; 🅿; Z 24604; ● 250
Blackberry; RMC Place; HENRY; *244 M-6; ★ MRTNV; mail Bassett Z 24055; rural
Black Branch; RMC Place; MECKLENBURG; *245 M-11; elev. 500ft./152m.; mail Chase City Z 23924; rural
Black Creek; RMC Place; SOUTHAMPTON; *245 M-16; elev. 60ft./18m.; mail Franklin Z 23851; ● 70
Blackey; RMC Place; BUCHANAN; *244 B-6; elev. 1,086ft./331m.; mail Hurley Z 24620, Wolford Z 24658; ● 50
Blackford; RMC Place; RUSSELL; *244 C-6; mail Honaker Z 24260; ● 30
Blacklick; RMC Place; WYTHE; *244 L-2; mail Rural Retreat Z 24368; rural
Blackridge; RMC Place; MECKLENBURG; *245 M-12; 🅿; Z 23950; ● 60
Blacksburg; Inc. Place; MONTGOMERY; 244 K-4; elev. 2,080ft./634m.; 🅿 🅷 🅲 28,470; Z 24060-63; Ⓟ 34,590; Ⓒ 39,573; ◆ 50,719
Blacksburg; RMC Place; ROCKBRIDGE; *244 I-8; elev. 1,419ft./433m.; mail Buena Vista Z 24416; rural
Blacksburg; RMC Place; WASHINGTON; *244 D-6; mail Glade Spring Z 24340; ● 70
Blackstone; Inc. Place; NOTTOWAY; 245 L-12; elev. 427ft./130m.; 🅿; Z 23824; Ⓟ 3,497; Ⓒ 3,675
Blackwater; RMC Place; LEE; 244 E-2; 🅿; Z 24221; ● 90
Blackwater; RMC Place; VIRGINIA BEACH (Independent City); *245 M-18; ★ NORF-; mail Virginia Beach Z 23457; pop. incl. with Virginia Beach (Independent City)
Blackwater Bridge; RMC Place; VIRGINIA BEACH (Independent City); ★ NORF-; mail Virginia Beach Z 23457; pop. incl. with Virginia Beach (Independent City)
Blackwells; RMC Place; WASHINGTON; *244 D-6; mail Meadowview Z 24361; ● 30
Blackwood; RMC Place; WISE; *244 C-4; mail Norton Z 24273; ● 30
Blainesville; RMC Place; PAGE; *245 F-11; mail Luray Z 22835; ● 110
Blairs; RMC Place; PITTSYLVANIA; 244 M-8; 🅿; ★ DANV; Z 24527; ● 300
Blakes; RMC Place; MATHEWS; 245 J-17; elev. 21ft./6m.; 🅿; ★ NN-H; Z 23035; ● 100
Bland; RMC Place; ⊡ BLAND; 244 L-2; 🅿; Z 24315; ● 600
BLAND; 244 K-2; Ⓟ 6,514; Ⓒ 6,871; ◆ 7,192
Blandford; RMC Place; PETERSBURG (Independent City); *245 K-14; elev. 50ft./15m.; ★ RICH; mail Petersburg Z 23803; pop. incl. with Petersburg (Independent City)
Blanks Store; RMC Place; CHARLES CITY; *245 K-15; elev. 36ft./11m.; mail Charles City Z 23030; ● 30
Blanks Tavern; RMC Place; CHARLES CITY; *245 J-15; elev. 110ft./34m.; mail Charles City Z 23030; rural
Blevinstown; RMC Place; FAIRFAX; *245 E-14; ★ WASH; mail Fairfax Z 22030; ● 800
Bloomfield; RMC Place; LOUDOUN; *245 D-12; mail Bluemont Z 20135; ● 80
Bloomingdale; RMC Place; HENRICO; ★ RICH; mail Henrico Z 23228
Blowing Rock; RMC Place; DICKENSON; *244 B-4; mail Clintwood Z 24228; rural
Bloxom; Inc. Place; ACCOMACK; 245 H-19; 🅿; Z 23308; Ⓟ 357; Ⓒ 395; Ⓡ 403
Bluefield; Inc. Place; TAZEWELL; 244 K-2; elev. 2,389ft./728m.; 🅿 🅲 841; Z 24605; Ⓟ 5,363; Ⓒ 5,078
Blue Grass; RMC Place; HIGHLAND; 244 F-7; elev. 2,502ft./763m.; 🅿; Z 24413; ● 120
Bluemont; RMC Place; LOUDOUN; 245 D-12; 🅿; Z 20135; ● 200
Blue Mountain; RMC Place; WARREN; *245 D-12; mail Front Royal Z 22630; ● 200
Blue Ridge; CDP; BOTETOURT; 244 J-6; 🅿; ★ ROAN; Z 24064; Ⓟ 2,840; Ⓒ 3,188
Blue Ridge Farms; RMC Place; LYNCHBURG (Independent City); *244 J-8; ★ LYNCH; pop. incl. with Lynchburg (Independent City)
Blue Ridge Mountain Estates; RMC Place; WARREN; *245 E-11; mail Front Royal Z 22630, Linden Z 22642; ● 150
Blue Ridge Shores; RMC Place; LOUISA; *245 G-12; mail Louisa Z 23093; summer pop. 800; ● 560
Bluestone; RMC Place; MECKLENBURG; *244 M-10; elev. 435ft./133m.; mail Clarksville Z 23927; rural
Bluff City (Pearisburg); RMC Place; GILES; *244 K-3; mail Pearisburg Z 24134; pop. incl. with Pearisburg (Inc. Place)
Blundon Corner; RMC Place; NORTHUMBERLAND; *245 H-17; elev. 95ft./29m.; mail Edwardsville Z 22456; rural
Bocock; RMC Place; CAMPBELL; *244 J-9; ★ LYNCH; mail Lynchburg Z 24501; ● 80
Body Camp; RMC Place; BEDFORD; *244 K-7; elev. 961ft./293m.; mail Bedford Z 24523; rural
Bohannon; RMC Place; MATHEWS; *245 J-17; 🅿; ★ NN-H; Z 23021; ● 150
Boiling Spring; RMC Place; ALLEGHANY; *244 I-5; mail Covington Z 24426; rural
Boissevain; RMC Place; TAZEWELL; 244 K-1; 🅿; Z 24606; ● 900
Bolar; RMC Place; BATH; *244 G-7; 🅿; Z 24484; ● 30
Bolsters Store; RMC Place; DINWIDDIE; *245 L-13; elev. 290ft./88m.; mail Stony Creek Z 23882; rural
Bolton; RMC Place; RUSSELL; *244 D-5; mail Lebanon Z 24266; rural
Bon Air; RMC Place; ARLINGTON; *245 D-15; ★ WASH; mail Arlington Z 22205
Bon Air; CDP; CHESTERFIELD; 243 C-6; 🅿; ★ RICH; Z 23235 & mail Richmond Z 23236; Ⓟ 16,413; Ⓒ 16,213
Bonbrook; RMC Place; FRANKLIN; *244 L-6; mail Boones Mill Z 24065; rural
Bondtown; RMC Place; WISE; *244 C-4; mail Coeburn Z 24230; pop. incl. with Coeburn (Inc. Place)
Bonny Blue; RMC Place; LEE; 244 D-2; mail Saint Charles Z 24282; ● 100
Bonsack; RMC Place; ROANOKE; *244 K-6; elev. 995ft./303m.; ★ ROAN; mail Roanoke Z 24012; ● 300
Boone; RMC Place; CHESAPEAKE (Independent City); *245 L-17; ★ NORF-; pop. incl. with Chesapeake (Independent City)
Boone Mill; FRANKLIN; see Boones Mill (Inc. Place)
Boones Mill (Boone Mill); Inc. Place; FRANKLIN; 244 L-6; 🅿; ★ ROAN; Z 24065; Ⓟ 239; Ⓒ 285
Boonesville; RMC Place; ALBEMARLE; *244 G-10; elev. 762ft./232m.; 🅿; Z 22935 & mail Free Union Z 22940; rural
Boonsboro; RMC Place; BEDFORD; 245 A-18; ★ LYNCH; mail Lynchburg Z 24503; pop. incl. with Lynchburg (Independent City)
Bordeaux; RMC Place; FAIRFAX; mail Reston Z 20190
Boston; RMC Place; ACCOMACK; 245 F-12; mail Painter Z 23420; ● 50
Boston; RMC Place; CULPEPER; *245 F-12; elev. 549ft./167m.; 🅿; Z 22713; ● 60
Boston; RMC Place; SUFFOLK (Independent City); ★ NORF-; mail Suffolk Z 23434; pop. incl. with Suffolk (Independent City)
Boswells Tavern; RMC Place; LOUISA; 245 H-11; elev. 492ft./150m.; mail Gordonsville Z 22942; ● 70
BOTETOURT; 244 J-6; Ⓟ 24,992; Ⓒ 30,496; ◆ 32,199
Botha; RMC Place; FAUQUIER; *245 F-12; elev. 443ft./135m.; ★ WASH; mail Warrenton Z 20186; ● 30
Bottoms Bridge; RMC Place; NEW KENT; *245 J-15; elev. 128ft./39m.; mail Sandston Z 23150; ● 50
Boudar Gardens; RMC Place; HENRICO; *245 I-14; elev. 220ft./67m.; ★ RICH; mail Henrico Z 23228; ● 200
Boulevard Estates; RMC Place; FAIRFAX; *245 D-14; ★ WASH; mail Fairfax Z 22031
Bowers Corner; RMC Place; BRUNSWICK; *245 M-12; elev. 387ft./118m.; mail White Plains Z 23893; rural
Bowers Hill; RMC Place; CHESAPEAKE (Independent City); *245 M-17; ★ NORF-; mail Chesapeake Z 23321; pop. incl. with Chesapeake (Independent City)
Bowlers Wharf; RMC Place; ESSEX; *245 I-16; elev. 12ft./4m.; mail Tappahannock Z 22560; ● 120
Bowling; RMC Place; LEE; *244 D-2; mail Jonesville Z 24263; rural
Bowling Green; Inc. Place; ⊡ CAROLINE; 245 H-14; 🅿; Z 22427-28; Ⓟ 727; Ⓒ 936
Bowling Park; RMC Place; NORFOLK (Independent City); ★ NORF-; mail Norfolk Z 23504; pop. incl. with Norfolk (Independent City)
Bowmans Crossing; RMC Place; SHENANDOAH; *244 E-10; mail Edinburg Z 22824; ● 100
Boxley Hills; RMC Place; ROANOKE; ★ ROAN; mail Roanoke Z 24012
Boxwood; RMC Place; HENRY; *244 M-7; elev. 968ft./295m.; mail Axton Z 24054
Boyce; Inc. Place; CLARKE; 245 D-12; 🅿; Z 22620; Ⓟ 520; Ⓒ 426
Boyd Tavern; RMC Place; ALBEMARLE; *245 H-11; 🅿; ★ CHRLTV; Z 22947; ● 30
Boydton; Inc. Place; ⊡ MECKLENBURG; 245 M-11; 🅿; Z 23917; Ⓟ 453; Ⓒ 454; Ⓡ 477
Boykins; Inc. Place; SOUTHAMPTON; 245 M-15; 🅿; Z 23827; Ⓟ 658; Ⓒ 620
Bracey; RMC Place; MECKLENBURG; 245 N-12; elev. 337ft./103m.; 🅿; Z 23919; ● 100
Braddock; RMC Place; ALEXANDRIA (Independent City); *245 E-15; ★ WASH; mail Alexandria Z 22302; pop. incl. with Alexandria (Independent City)
Braddock Heights; RMC Place; ALEXANDRIA (Independent City); *245 E-15; ★ WASH; mail Alexandria Z 22302; pop. incl. with Alexandria (Independent City)
Braddock Hills; RMC Place; FAIRFAX; *245 E-14; ★ WASH; mail Annandale Z 22003
Bradford Acres; RMC Place; VIRGINIA BEACH (Independent City); ★ NORF-; mail Virginia Beach Z 23455; pop. incl. with Virginia Beach (Independent City)
Bradley Acres; RMC Place; HENRICO; *245 J-14; ★ RICH; mail Sandston Z 23150; ● 750
Bradley Forest; RMC Place; PRINCE WILLIAM; *245 E-14; ★ WASH; mail Manassas Z 20112; ● 300
Bradshaw (Bradshaw Creek); RMC Place; ROANOKE; *244 K-5; ★ ROAN; mail Elliston Z 24087; rural
Bradshaw Creek; ROANOKE; see Bradshaw (RMC Place)
Brambleton; RMC Place; NORFOLK (Independent City); *245 L-18; 🅿; ★ NORF-; Z 20148 & mail Norfolk Z 23504; pop. incl. with Norfolk (Independent City)
Branchville; Inc. Place; SOUTHAMPTON; 245 N-15; elev. 46ft./14m.; 🅿; Z 23828; Ⓟ 55; Ⓒ 123
Brand; RMC Place; AUGUSTA; *244 G-9; mail Staunton Z 24401; rural
Brand; PAGE; see Vaughn (RMC Place)
Brandon; RMC Place; PRINCE GEORGE; *245 K-15; elev. 17ft./5m.; mail Spring Grove Z 23881
Brandon Heights; RMC Place; NEWPORT NEWS (Independent City); ★ NN-H; mail Newport News Z 23601; pop. incl. with Newport News (Independent City)
Brandon Place; RMC Place; NORFOLK (Independent City); *245 L-18; ★ NORF-; mail Norfolk Z 23513; pop. incl. with Norfolk (Independent City)
Brandons Store; RMC Place; BRUNSWICK; *245 L-12; elev. 436ft./133m.; mail Blackstone Z 23824; rural
Brandon Village; RMC Place; ARLINGTON; *245 D-15; ★ WASH; mail Arlington Z 22203
Brandy Creek Estates; RMC Place; HANOVER; *245 I-14; ★ RICH; mail Mechanicsville Z 23111
Brandy Station; RMC Place; CULPEPER; 245 F-12; 🅿; Z 22714; ● 360
Brattons Bridge; RMC Place; BATH; *244 H-7; mail Millboro Z 24460; rural
Brays (Brays Fork); RMC Place; ESSEX; *245 H-16; mail Tappahannock Z 22560; ● 80
Brays Fork; ESSEX; see Brays (RMC Place)
Brayshore Park; RMC Place; GLOUCESTER; *245 J-17; ★ NN-H; mail Hayes Z 23072; ● 80
Breaks; RMC Place; DICKENSON; 244 B-5; 🅿; Z 24607; ● 150
Brecon Ridge; RMC Place; FAIRFAX; *245 E-14; ★ WASH; mail Fairfax Z 22030; ● 400
Bremo; FLUVANNA; see Bremo Bluff (RMC Place)
Bremo Bluff (Bremo); RMC Place; FLUVANNA; 245 I-11; 🅿; Z 23022; ● 190
Bren Mar Park; RMC Place; FAIRFAX; *245 E-15; ★ WASH; mail Alexandria Z 22312; ● 2,100
Brentsville; RMC Place; PRINCE WILLIAM; *245 E-14; ★ WASH; mail Bristow Z 20136; ● 240
Brentwood; RMC Place; CHESAPEAKE (Independent City); *245 M-17; ★ NORF-; mail Chesapeake Z 23323; pop. incl. with Chesapeake (Independent City)
Brentwood; RMC Place; CHESTERFIELD; *245 J-14; elev. 170ft./52m.; ★ RICH; mail Richmond Z 23234; ● 270
Brentwood Forest; RMC Place; NORFOLK (Independent City); *245 L-18; ★ NORF-; mail Norfolk Z 23518; pop. incl. with Norfolk (Independent City)
Briarcliff; RMC Place; ROANOKE; ★ ROAN; mail Vinton Z 24179; pop. incl. with Vinton (Inc. Place)
Briarwood; RMC Place; BRISTOL (Independent City); ★ JNSC-; mail Bristol Z 24201; pop. incl. with Bristol (Independent City)
Briarwood; RMC Place; PORTSMOUTH (Independent City); *245 L-17; ★ NORF-; mail Portsmouth Z 23703; pop. incl. with Portsmouth (Independent City)
Brico; RMC Place; SUFFOLK (Independent City); pop. incl. with Suffolk (Independent City)
Bridgetown; RMC Place; NORTHAMPTON; *245 J-19; mail Machipongo Z 23405; rural
Bridgewater; Inc. Place; ROCKINGHAM; 244 F-9; 🅿 🅲 1,514; Z 22812; Ⓟ 3,918; Ⓒ 5,203
Bridie Creek; GRAYSON; see Bridle Creek (RMC Place)
Bridle Creek (Bridie Creek); RMC Place; GRAYSON; *244 M-2; elev. 2,631ft./802m.; mail Independence Z 24348; ● 30
Bridlewood; RMC Place; PRINCE WILLIAM; *245 E-13; elev. 300ft./91m.; ★ WASH; mail Gainesville Z 20155; ● 400
Briery; RMC Place; PRINCE EDWARD; *245 L-11; mail Keysville Z 23947; ● 30
Briery Branch; RMC Place; ROCKINGHAM; 244 F-9; mail Dayton Z 22821; ● 160
Briggs (Old Chapel); RMC Place; CLARKE; *245 D-12; mail Berryville Z 22611
Brights; RMC Place; PITTSYLVANIA; *244 L-8; elev. 878ft./268m.; mail Gretna Z 24557; ● 100
Brightwood; RMC Place; MADISON; 245 F-11; 🅿; Z 22715; ● 250
Brilyn Park; RMC Place; FAIRFAX; *245 D-15; ★ WASH; mail Falls Church Z 22046; ● 800
Brink; RMC Place; GREENSVILLE; *245 M-13; mail Emporia Z 23847; rural
Bristol; Independent City; 244 E-5; 🅿 🅲 800 ■; ★ JNSC-; Z 24201-03, Z 24205, Z 24209; Ⓟ 18,426; Ⓒ 17,367; ◆ 17,083
Bristow; RMC Place; FAIRFAX; *245 E-14; ★ WASH; mail Annandale Z 22003
Bristow; RMC Place; PRINCE WILLIAM; 245 E-13; 🅿; ★ WASH; Z 20136; ● 200
Britain; RMC Place; LOUDOUN; *245 C-13; mail Lovettsville Z 20180; rural
Britton Hills Farms; RMC Place; HENRICO; *245 I-14; ★ RICH; mail Richmond Z 23230; ● 180
Brittonwood; RMC Place; CHESTERFIELD; *245 J-14; elev. 150ft./46m.; ★ RICH; mail Richmond Z 23234; ● 300
Broad Bay Colony; RMC Place; VIRGINIA BEACH (Independent City); *245 L-18; elev. 10ft./3m.; ★ NORF-; mail Virginia Beach Z 23451; pop. incl. with Virginia Beach (Independent City)
Broadford; RMC Place; SMYTH; 244 L-1; 🅿; Z 24316; ● 300
Broadland; RMC Place; LOUDOUN; ★ WASH; mail Ashburn Z 20148
Broad Meadows; RMC Place; HENRICO; *245 I-13; ★ RICH; mail Glen Allen Z 23060; ● 850
Broadmoor; RMC Place; CHESAPEAKE (Independent City); *245 M-17; ★ NORF-; mail Chesapeake Z 23323; pop. incl. with Chesapeake (Independent City)
Broad Rock; RMC Place; RICHMOND (Independent City); *245 J-14; ★ RICH; mail Richmond Z 23224; pop. incl. with Richmond (Independent City)
Broad Run; RMC Place; FAUQUIER, PRINCE WILLIAM; *245 E-13; 🅿; ★ WASH; Z 20137; ● 60
Broad Run Farms; RMC Place; LOUDOUN; *245 D-14; ★ WASH; mail Sterling Z 20165
Broadway; Inc. Place; ROCKINGHAM; 244 F-9; 🅿; Z 22815; Ⓟ 1,209; Ⓒ 2,192; Ⓡ 2,219
Brockroad; RMC Place; SPOTSYLVANIA; *245 G-13; ★ FRED; mail Spotsylvania Z 22553; rural
Brocks Gap; RMC Place; ROCKINGHAM; *244 E-9; elev. 1,175ft./358m.; mail Broadway Z 22815; ● 50
Brodnax; Inc. Place; BRUNSWICK, MECKLENBURG; 245 M-12; elev. 388ft./118m.; 🅿; Z 23920; Ⓟ 388; Ⓒ 317
Brokenburg; RMC Place; SPOTSYLVANIA; *245 G-13; elev. 399ft./122m.; mail Spotsylvania Z 22553
Broken Hill; RMC Place; FAUQUIER; *245 E-13; ★ WASH; mail Gainesville Z 20155; ● 150
Brookbury; RMC Place; RICHMOND (Independent City); ★ RICH; mail Richmond Z 23234; pop. incl. with Richmond (Independent City)
Brooke; RMC Place; STAFFORD; 245 F-14; 🅿; ★ WASH; Z 22430; ● 170
Brookeshire; RMC Place; KING AND QUEEN; *245 J-16; mail West Point Z 23181; ● 100
Brookfield; RMC Place; FAIRFAX; *245 D-14; ★ WASH; mail Chantilly Z 20151
Brookfield; RMC Place; STAFFORD; *245 G-14; ★ FRED; mail Fredericksburg Z 22401; ● 260
Brookfield Park; RMC Place; NORFOLK (Independent City); *245 L-18; ★ NORF-; mail Norfolk Z 23503; pop. incl. with Norfolk (Independent City)
Brookhaven; RMC Place; FAIRFAX; *245 D-15; ★ WASH; mail Mc Lean Z 22101
Brook Hill; RMC Place; HENRICO; *245 I-14; elev. 200ft./61m.; ★ RICH; mail Richmond Z 23227
Brookland Estates; RMC Place; FAIRFAX; *245 E-15; ★ WASH; mail Alexandria Z 22310
Brookland Gardens; RMC Place; HENRICO; *245 I-14; elev. 200ft./61m.; ★ RICH; mail Henrico Z 23228; ● 350
Brookledge; RMC Place; BEDFORD; *244 K-6; elev. 1,200ft./366m.; ★ ROAN; mail Vinton Z 24179; ● 100
Brooklyn; RMC Place; HALIFAX; *244 M-8; elev. 562ft./171m.; mail Sutherlin Z 24594; ● 30
Brookneal; Inc. Place; CAMPBELL; 244 L-9; elev. 560ft./171m.; 🅿; Z 24528; Ⓟ 1,344; Ⓒ 1,259
Brook Vale; RMC Place; LANCASTER; *245 I-17; mail Lancaster Z 22503; rural
Brookville; RMC Place; ALEXANDRIA (Independent City); *245 E-15; ★ WASH; mail Alexandria Z 22304; pop. incl. with Alexandria (Independent City)
Brookville; RMC Place; LYNCHBURG (Independent City); ★ LYNCH; mail Lynchburg Z 24502; pop. incl. with Lynchburg (Independent City)
Brookwood Manor; RMC Place; NEW KENT; *245 J-15; elev. 100ft./30m.; mail Quinton Z 23141; ● 180
Brosville; RMC Place; PITTSYLVANIA; *244 M-7; ★ DANV; mail Danville Z 24541; ● 200
Brown Field; RMC Place; PRINCE WILLIAM; ★ WASH; mail Quantico Z 22134; pop. incl. with Quantico (Inc. Place)
Brown Grove; RMC Place; HANOVER; *245 I-14; elev. 207ft./63m.; ★ RICH; mail Ashland Z 23005; rural
Brownsburg; RMC Place; ROCKBRIDGE; 244 H-8; 🅿; Z 24415; ● 130
Browns Corner; RMC Place; NEW KENT; *245 J-15; mail Quinton Z 23141; ● 90
Browns Cove; RMC Place; ALBEMARLE; *244 G-10; mail Crozet Z 22932
Browns Store; RMC Place; LANCASTER, NORTHUMBERLAND; *245 H-17; mail Heathsville Z 22473; rural
Brownsville; RMC Place; ALBEMARLE; *244 H-10; elev. 669ft./204m.; ★ CHRLTV; mail Charlottesville Z 22903; ● 30
Brown Town; RMC Place; AMHERST; *244 I-8; elev. 955ft./291m.; mail Amherst Z 24521; rural
Browntown; RMC Place; CAMPBELL; *244 K-8; elev. 800ft./244m.; mail Lynch Station Z 24571; ● 150
Browntown; RMC Place; WARREN; 245 E-11; 🅿; Z 22610; ● 200
Broyhill Crest; RMC Place; FAIRFAX; *245 E-14; ★ WASH; mail Annandale Z 22003
Broyhill Forest; RMC Place; ARLINGTON; *245 D-15; ★ WASH; mail Arlington Z 22207
Broyhill Park; RMC Place; FAIRFAX; 249 G-3; ★ WASH; mail Falls Church Z 22042; ● 3,700
Bruce; RMC Place; CHESAPEAKE (Independent City); *245 L-17; ★ NORF-; mail Chesapeake Z 23321; pop. incl. with Chesapeake (Independent City)
Brucetown; RMC Place; FREDERICK; *245 C-12; 🅿; Z 22622; ● 100
Bruington; RMC Place; KING AND QUEEN; 245 I-15; 🅿; Z 23023; ● 70
Brumley Gap; RMC Place; WASHINGTON; *244 D-6; mail Abingdon Z 24210
Bruno; RMC Place; SCOTT; *244 D-4; mail Hiltons Z 24258; rural
Brunswick; RMC Place; BRUNSWICK; *245 M-13; elev. 374ft./114m.; mail Lawrenceville Z 23868; rural
BRUNSWICK; 245 M-13; Ⓟ 15,987; Ⓒ 18,419; ◆ 17,455
Brush Tavern; RMC Place; CAMPBELL; *244 K-8; ★ LYNCH; mail Lynchburg Z 24502
Bryan Park; RMC Place; HENRICO; ★ RICH; mail Henrico Z 23228
Bryan Parkway; RMC Place; HENRICO; ★ RICH; mail Henrico Z 23228
Bryant; RMC Place; NELSON; *244 I-9; elev. 794ft./242m.; mail Roseland Z 22967; rural
Bryants Corner; RMC Place; GREENSVILLE; *245 M-14; elev. 81ft./25m.; mail Emporia Z 23847; rural
Bryn Mawr; RMC Place; FAIRFAX; *245 D-14; ★ WASH; mail Mc Lean Z 22101
Buchanan; Inc. Place; BOTETOURT; 244 J-7; 🅿; ★ ROAN; Z 24066; Ⓟ 1,222; Ⓒ 1,233
BUCHANAN; 244 C-6; Ⓟ 31,333; Ⓒ 26,978; ◆ 23,334
Buckhall; RMC Place; PRINCE WILLIAM; *245 E-14; ★ WASH; mail Manassas Z 20111; ● 200
Buckhorn; SUFFOLK (Independent City); see Purvis (RMC Place)
Buckingham; RMC Place; ARLINGTON; *245 D-15; ★ WASH; mail Arlington Z 22203
Buckingham; RMC Place; ⊡ BUCKINGHAM; 244 J-10; elev. 458ft./140m.; 🅿; Z 23921; ● 350
Buckingham; RMC Place; CHESTERFIELD; *245 J-13; elev. 350ft./107m.; ★ RICH; mail Midlothian Z 23112; ● 50
BUCKINGHAM; 244 I-10; Ⓟ 12,873; Ⓒ 15,623; ◆ 16,416
Buckingham Circle; RMC Place; ALBEMARLE; 243 C-2; ★ CHRLTV; mail Charlottesville Z 22903; ● 900
Buckland; RMC Place; PRINCE WILLIAM; *245 E-13; ★ WASH; mail Gainesville Z 20155; ● 70
Bucknell Heights; RMC Place; FAIRFAX; *245 E-15; ★ WASH; mail Alexandria Z 22307; ● 1,300
Bucknell Manor; RMC Place; FAIRFAX; 249 I-6; ★ WASH; mail Alexandria Z 22307; ● 2,350
Buckner; RMC Place; LOUISA; *245 H-13; mail Bumpass Z 23024; ● 50
Buckroe Beach; RMC Place; HAMPTON (Independent City); *245 L-17; ★ NN-H; mail Hampton Z 23664; pop. incl. with Hampton (Independent City)
Buckton; RMC Place; WARREN; *245 D-11; mail Strasburg Z 22657; ● 100
Buell (Money Point); RMC Place; CHESAPEAKE (Independent City); *245 M-18; ★ NORF-; mail Chesapeake Z 23324; pop. incl. with Chesapeake (Independent City)
Buena; RMC Place; CULPEPER; *245 G-12; mail Rapidan Z 22733; ● 30
Buena Vista; Independent City; 244 I-8; 🅿 🅲 737; Z 24416; Ⓟ 6,406; Ⓒ 6,349; ◆ 6,527
Buffalo Forge; RMC Place; ROCKBRIDGE; *244 I-8; mail Glasgow Z 24555; rural
Buffalo Gap; RMC Place; AUGUSTA; 244 G-8; mail Swoope Z 24479; ● 100
Buffalo Hill; RMC Place; AMHERST; *244 I-9; mail Amherst Z 24521; ● 80
Buffalo Hills; RMC Place; FAIRFAX; *245 E-14; ★ WASH; mail Falls Church Z 22044
Buffalo Junction; RMC Place; MECKLENBURG; *244 M-10; 🅿; Z 24529; ● 100
Buffalo Ridge; RMC Place; PATRICK; *244 M-5; mail Stuart Z 24171
Buffalo Springs; RMC Place; MECKLENBURG; 244 M-10; mail Buffalo Junction Z 24529; ● 50
Bufford Cross Roads; RMC Place; GREENSVILLE; *245 M-13; elev. 164ft./50m.; mail Emporia Z 23847; ● 30
Bull Run; CDP-Census Area Only; PRINCE WILLIAM; *245 E-13; ★ WASH; mail Manassas Z 20109; Ⓟ 5,525; Ⓒ 11,337
Bull Run Mountain Estates; RMC Place; PRINCE WILLIAM; *245 D-13; ★ WASH; mail Haymarket Z 20169; ● 1,600
Bumpass; RMC Place; LOUISA; 245 H-13; elev. 337ft./103m.; 🅿; Z 23024; ● 80
Buncher; RMC Place; LYNCHBURG (Independent City); ★ LYNCH; pop. incl. with Lynchburg (Independent City)
Bundy (Johnsons Mill); RMC Place; LEE; *244 D-3; mail Keokee Z 24265; rural
Bunker Hill; RMC Place; BEDFORD; *244 K-7; elev. 1,058ft./322m.; mail Bedford Z 24523; ● 30
Burdette; RMC Place; SOUTHAMPTON; *245 M-16; mail Franklin Z 23851
Burgess (Burgess Store); RMC Place; NORTHUMBERLAND; 245 H-17; 🅿; Z 22432; ● 80
Burgess Store; NORTHUMBERLAND; see Burgess (RMC Place)
Burgundy Village; RMC Place; FAIRFAX; *245 E-15; ★ WASH; mail Alexandria Z 22303; ● 1,300
Burke; CDP; FAIRFAX; 249 I-2; 🅿; ★ WASH; Z 22009, Z 22015 & mail Fairfax Z 22030, Springfield Z 22150; Ⓟ 57,734; Ⓒ 57,737; ◆ 59,994
Burke Heights; RMC Place; FAIRFAX; *245 E-14; ★ WASH; mail Burke Z 22015
Burke Hills; RMC Place; FAIRFAX; ★ WASH; mail Burke Z 22015
Burkes Garden; RMC Place; TAZEWELL; 244 L-1; elev. 3,079ft./938m.; 🅿; Z 24608; ● 50
Burkes Shop; RMC Place; CAROLINE; *245 H-14; elev. 227ft./69m.; mail Woodford Z 22580; rural
Burketown; RMC Place; AUGUSTA; *244 G-9; mail Weyers Cave Z 24486; ● 60
Burkeville; Inc. Place; NOTTOWAY; 245 K-11; elev. 522ft./159m.; 🅿 🅷; Z 23922; Ⓟ 535; Ⓒ 489
Burks Garden; RMC Place; TAZEWELL; mail Tazewell Z 24651; pop. incl. with Tazewell (Inc. Place)
Burnam Woods; RMC Place; JAMES CITY; *245 J-16; elev. 109ft./33m.; ★ NN-H; mail Toano Z 23168; ● 270
Burnleys; RMC Place; ALBEMARLE; *245 G-11; 🅿; ★ CHRLTV; Z 22923; rural
Burnside Farms; RMC Place; HANOVER; *245 I-14; ★ RICH; mail Mechanicsville Z 23116
Burnsville; RMC Place; BATH; 244 G-7; 🅿; Z 24487; ● 50
Burnt Chimney; RMC Place; FRANKLIN; 244 L-6; elev. 1,127ft./344m.; 🅿; Z 24184; ● 100
Burnt Store; RMC Place; MECKLENBURG; *245 M-12; elev. 411ft./125m.; mail La Crosse Z 23950; rural
Burnt Tree; RMC Place; MADISON; *245 G-11; mail Orange Z 22960; ● 50
Burr Hill; RMC Place; ORANGE; 245 G-12; 🅿; Z 22433; ● 90
Burrowsville; RMC Place; PRINCE GEORGE; 245 K-15; mail Disputanta Z 23842; ● 70
Burson Place; RMC Place; WASHINGTON; *244 D-5; ★ JNSC-; mail Bristol Z 24201; ● 30
Burtons; RMC Place; VIRGINIA BEACH (Independent City); *245 L-18; ★ NORF-; mail Virginia Beach Z 23455; pop. incl. with Virginia Beach (Independent City)
Burtons Creek; RMC Place; LYNCHBURG (Independent City); ★ LYNCH; pop. incl. with Lynchburg (Independent City)
Burtons Shop; RMC Place; TAZEWELL; *244 K-1; mail Tazewell Z 24651; ● 30
Bush Hill; RMC Place; FAIRFAX; ★ WASH; mail Alexandria Z 22310
Bush Hill Woods; RMC Place; FAIRFAX; *245 E-15; ★ WASH; mail Alexandria Z 22310
Bush Mill; RMC Place; SCOTT; *244 D-4; mail Nickelsville Z 24271; rural
Busthead; RMC Place; TAZEWELL; *244 K-1; mail Cedar Bluff Z 24609; rural
Bustleburg; RMC Place; ROCKBRIDGE; *244 H-8; mail Lexington Z 24450; rural
Butlers Fork; RMC Place; CAROLINE; *245 H-14; elev. 96ft./29m.; mail Milford Z 22514; rural
Butterworth; RMC Place; DINWIDDIE; *245 L-13; elev. 249ft./76m.; mail DeWitt Z 23840; rural
Butts; RMC Place; CHESAPEAKE (Independent City); *245 M-18; elev. 22ft./7m.; ★ NORF-; mail Chesapeake Z 23320; pop. incl. with Chesapeake (Independent City)
Butts Corner; RMC Place; FAIRFAX; *245 E-14; ★ WASH; mail Fairfax Station Z 22039
Butylo; RMC Place; MIDDLESEX; *245 I-16; mail Laneview Z 22504; ● 50
Bybee; RMC Place; FLUVANNA; *245 H-11; 🅿; Z 22963; ● 40
Byllesby; RMC Place; CARROLL; *244 M-3; mail Ivanhoe Z 24350; rural
Bynum Store; RMC Place; MECKLENBURG; *245 M-11; elev. 540ft./165m.; mail Chase City Z 23924; rural
Byrdton; RMC Place; NORTHUMBERLAND; *245 I-17; mail Kilmarnock Z 22482; rural

C

Cabin Point; RMC Place; SURRY; 245 K-15; elev. 67ft./20m.; mail Spring Grove Z 23881; ● 40
Cadet; RMC Place; WISE; *244 D-3; mail Big Stone Gap Z 24219; pop. incl. with Big Stone Gap (Inc. Place)
Cady; RMC Place; HANOVER; *245 I-14; elev. 100ft./30m.; ★ RICH; mail Hanover Z 23069; rural
Caira; RMC Place; CUMBERLAND; *245 J-11; mail Cumberland Z 23040; rural
Caledonia; RMC Place; GOOCHLAND; *245 I-12; elev. 468ft./143m.; mail Columbia Z 23038
Callaghan; RMC Place; ALLEGHANY; 244 I-5; mail Covington Z 24426; ● 120
Callands; RMC Place; PITTSYLVANIA; 244 M-7; elev. 1,007ft./307m.; 🅿; Z 24530; ● 150
Callao; RMC Place; NORTHUMBERLAND; 245 H-16; elev. 110ft./34m.; 🅿; Z 22435; ● 550
Callaville; RMC Place; BRUNSWICK; *245 M-13; elev. 259ft./79m.; mail Freeman Z 23856; rural
Callaway; RMC Place; FRANKLIN; 244 L-6; 🅿; Z 24067; ● 130
Callison; RMC Place; BATH; *244 H-6; mail Hot Springs Z 24445; rural
Calno; RMC Place; KING WILLIAM; *245 I-14; mail Hanover Z 23069; rural
Calvary; RMC Place; SHENANDOAH; *244 D-10; mail Woodstock Z 22664; ● 70
Calverton; RMC Place; FAUQUIER; 245 E-13; 🅿; Z 20138 & mail Broad Run Z 20137; ● 190
Calvin; RMC Place; LEE; *244 D-3; mail Keokee Z 24265; rural
Cambria; RMC Place; MONTGOMERY; *244 K-4; mail Christiansburg Z 24073; pop. incl. with Christiansburg (Inc. Place)
Cambridge; RMC Place; CHESTERFIELD; *245 J-13; ★ RICH; mail Richmond Z 23235
Camden Heights; RMC Place; NORFOLK (Independent City); *245 L-18; ★ NORF-; mail Norfolk Z 23502; pop. incl. with Norfolk (Independent City)
Camellia Shores; RMC Place; NORFOLK (Independent City); *245 L-18; ★ NORF-; mail Norfolk Z 23518; pop. incl. with Norfolk (Independent City)
Camelot; RMC Place; FAIRFAX; *245 E-14; ★ WASH; mail Annandale Z 22003; ● 2,500
Cameron; RMC Place; ALEXANDRIA (Independent City); *245 E-15; ★ WASH; mail Alexandria Z 22304; pop. incl. with Alexandria (Independent City)
Cameron Valley; RMC Place; ALEXANDRIA (Independent City); *245 E-15; ★ WASH; mail Alexandria Z 22314; pop. incl. with Alexandria (Independent City)
Camp; RMC Place; SMYTH; *244 M-2; mail Sugar Grove Z 24375; ● 60
Camp Barrett; RMC Place; STAFFORD; *245 F-14; ★ WASH; mail Quantico Z 22134
Campbell; RMC Place; ALBEMARLE; *245 H-11; 🅿; Z 22947; rural
CAMPBELL; 244 K-9; Ⓟ 47,572; Ⓒ 51,078; ◆ 52,938
Camp Creek; RMC Place; FLOYD; *244 L-5; mail Floyd Z 24091; ● 30
Campostella Heights; RMC Place; NORFOLK (Independent City); *245 L-18; ★ NORF-; mail Norfolk Z 23523; pop. incl. with Norfolk (Independent City)
Camps Mill; RMC Place; SUFFOLK (Independent City); ★ NORF-; mail Suffolk Z 23434; pop. incl. with Suffolk (Independent City)
Camptown; RMC Place; CHARLOTTE; *244 L-9; elev. 646ft./197m.; mail Brookneal Z 24528; rural
Cana; CDP; CARROLL; 244 N-4; 🅿; Z 24317; Ⓒ 1,228
Candlewax; RMC Place; RUSSELL; *244 C-6; mail Honaker Z 24260
Cannady; RMC Place; BUCHANAN; *244 B-5; elev. 1,342ft./409m.; mail Vansant Z 24656; rural
Canova; RMC Place; PRINCE WILLIAM; *245 E-14; ★ WASH; mail Manassas Z 20112; ● 150
Canterbury; RMC Place; HENRICO; *245 I-13; ★ RICH; mail Henrico Z 23229; ● 1,650
Canterbury Hills; RMC Place; ALBEMARLE; 243 B-2; ★ CHRLTV; mail Charlottesville Z 22901; ● 300
Canterbury Woods; RMC Place; FAIRFAX; *245 E-14; ★ WASH; mail Annandale Z 22003; ● 140
Canton; RMC Place; SCOTT; *244 D-3; mail Duffield Z 24244; rural
Capahosic; RMC Place; GLOUCESTER; *245 J-16; elev. 27ft./8m.; mail Gloucester Z 23061; ● 160
Cape Charles; Inc. Place; NORTHAMPTON; 245 K-18; 🅿; Z 23310; Ⓟ 1,398; Ⓒ 1,134
Cape Henry; RMC Place; VIRGINIA BEACH (Independent City); ★ NORF-; mail Virginia Beach Z 23454; pop. incl. with Virginia Beach (Independent City)
Cape Henry Shores; RMC Place; VIRGINIA BEACH (Independent City); ★ NORF-; mail Virginia Beach Z 23451; pop. incl. with Virginia Beach (Independent City)
Cape Story by the Sea; RMC Place; VIRGINIA BEACH (Independent City); *245 L-18; ★ NORF-; mail Virginia Beach Z 23451; pop. incl. with Virginia Beach (Independent City)
Capeville; RMC Place; NORTHAMPTON; *245 K-19; elev. 34ft./10m.; 🅿; Z 23313; ● 120
Capitol; RMC Place; RICHMOND (Independent City); ★ RICH; mail Richmond Z 23218-19; pop. incl. with Richmond (Independent City)
Capon Road; RMC Place; SHENANDOAH; *245 D-11; mail Strasburg Z 22657; ● 50
Capron; Inc. Place; SOUTHAMPTON; 245 M-15; 🅿; Z 23829; Ⓟ 144; Ⓒ 167; Ⓡ 173
Captain's Cove; RMC Place; ACCOMACK; *245 H-20; mail Greenbackville Z 23356; ● 150
Carbo; RMC Place; RUSSELL; *244 C-5; mail Cleveland Z 24225; ● 80
Cardinal; RMC Place; MATHEWS; *245 J-17; 🅿; ★ NN-H; Z 23025; ● 150
Cardinal Forest; RMC Place; FAIRFAX; ★ WASH; mail Springfield Z 22152
Cardova; RMC Place; CULPEPER; *245 F-12; mail Culpeper Z 22701
Cardwell; RMC Place; GOOCHLAND; *245 I-13; elev. 339ft./103m.; mail Crozier Z 23039; rural
Cardwell Town; RMC Place; SMYTH; *244 L-1; mail Saltville Z 24370
Caret; RMC Place; ESSEX; 245 H-15; elev. 145ft./44m.; 🅿; Z 22436; ● 60
Carfax; RMC Place; WISE; *244 C-5; mail Coeburn Z 24230; rural
Carlisle; RMC Place; HENRY; *244 M-6; elev. 780ft./238m.; ★ MRTNV; mail Axton Z 24054; ● 30
Carloover; RMC Place; BATH; 244 H-6; mail Hot Springs Z 24445; ● 70
Carolanne Farms; RMC Place; VIRGINIA BEACH (Independent City); *245 L-18; ★ NORF-; mail Virginia Beach Z 23462; pop. incl. with Virginia Beach (Independent City)
CAROLINE; 245 H-14; Ⓟ 19,217; Ⓒ 22,121; ◆ 28,806
Caroline Pines; RMC Place; CAROLINE; *245 H-14; mail Ruther Glen Z 22546; ● 170
Carriage Hill; RMC Place; FAIRFAX; *245 D-14; ★ WASH; mail Vienna Z 22181
Carrie; RMC Place; DICKENSON; *244 C-5; mail Cleveland Z 24225; rural
CARROLL; 244 M-3; Ⓟ 26,594; Ⓒ 29,245; ◆ 29,017
Carrollton; RMC Place; ISLE OF WIGHT; 243 K-3; 🅿; ★ NN-H; Z 23314; ● 100
Carrsbrook; RMC Place; ALBEMARLE; 245 H-11; ★ CHRLTV; mail Charlottesville Z 22901; ● 950
Carrsville; RMC Place; ISLE OF WIGHT; 245 M-16; 🅿; Z 23315; ● 300
Carsley; RMC Place; SURRY; *245 K-15; elev. 122ft./37m.; mail Waverly Z 23890; rural
Carson; RMC Place; DINWIDDIE, PRINCE GEORGE; 245 L-14; elev. 152ft./46m.; 🅿; Z 23830; ● 200
Carsonville; RMC Place; GRAYSON; *244 M-2; elev. 2,655ft./809m.; mail Independence Z 24348; ● 50
Carters Mill (Carters Mills); RMC Place; PATRICK; *244 M-4; mail Ararat Z 24053
Carters Mills; PATRICK; see Carters Mill (RMC Place)
Cartersville; RMC Place; CUMBERLAND; 245 I-12; 🅿; Z 23027; ● 380
Carterton; RMC Place; RUSSELL; *244 C-5; elev. 1,502ft./458m.; mail Lebanon Z 24266; ● 50
Carver Court; RMC Place; HAMPTON (Independent City); *245 L-17; ★ NN-H; mail Hampton Z 23669; pop. incl. with Hampton (Independent City)
Carver Gardens; RMC Place; YORK; 243 F-3; ★ NN-H; mail Williamsburg Z 23185; ● 500
Carysbrook; RMC Place; FLUVANNA; 245 I-11; mail Fork Union Z 23055; ● 30
Casanova; RMC Place; FAUQUIER; 245 E-13; 🅿; Z 20139; ● 190
Cascade; RMC Place; PITTSYLVANIA; 244 N-7; elev. 660ft./201m.; 🅿; Z 24069; ● 170
Cash; RMC Place; GLOUCESTER; *245 J-17; elev. 97ft./30m.; mail Gloucester Z 23061; rural
Cash Corner; RMC Place; ALBEMARLE; *245 H-11; elev. 527ft./161m.; mail Gordonsville Z 22942; rural
Cashville; RMC Place; ACCOMACK; *245 I-19; elev. 9ft./3m.; mail Onancock Z 23417; ● 100
Caskie; RMC Place; NELSON; *244 J-9; mail Gladstone Z 24553; rural
Castlebury Hills; RMC Place; CHESTERFIELD; ★ RICH; mail Chester Z 23831
Castle Craig; RMC Place; CAMPBELL; *244 K-8; ★ LYNCH; mail Evington Z 24550; ● 50
Castle Heights; RMC Place; MECKLENBURG; *245 M-11; mail Boydton Z 23917; ● 50
Castleton; RMC Place; RAPPAHANNOCK; *245 F-12; 🅿; Z 22716; ● 70
Castlewood; CDP; RUSSELL; 244 D-5; elev. 1,614ft./492m.; 🅿; Z 24224; Ⓒ 2,036
Catalpa; RMC Place; CULPEPER; 245 F-12; mail Culpeper Z 22701; ● 120
Catawba; RMC Place; HALIFAX; *244 L-9; elev. 584ft./178m.; mail Nathalie Z 24577; rural
Catawba; RMC Place; ROANOKE; 244 J-5; 🅿 🅷; Z 24070; ● 100
Catharpin; RMC Place; PRINCE WILLIAM; 245 E-13; 🅿; ★ WASH; Z 20143; ● 670
Catherton; RMC Place; MANASSAS (Independent City); ★ WASH; mail Manassas Z 20110; pop. incl. with Manassas (Independent City)
Catlett; RMC Place; FAUQUIER; 245 E-13; 🅿; Z 20119; ● 450
Cats Bridge; RMC Place; ACCOMACK; *245 I-19; elev. 16ft./5m.; mail Painter Z 23420; rural
Cauthornville; RMC Place; KING AND QUEEN; *245 H-15; 🅿; Z 23148; ● 70
Cavalcade; RMC Place; FAIRFAX; *245 E-14; ★ WASH; mail Annandale Z 22003
Cavalier Park; RMC Place; VIRGINIA BEACH (Independent City); *245 L-18; ★ NORF-; mail Virginia Beach Z 23451; pop. incl. with Virginia Beach (Independent City)

Entries in **UPPERCASE** are counties.
Entries in **bold** have populations of 2,500 or more.
Names in parentheses are alternate names.
Inc. Place — Incorporated Place
RMC Place — Rand McNally Designated Place
CDP — Census Designated Place
MCD — Minor Civil Division

⊡ County Seat
▲ Minor Civil Division
elev. Elevation
🅿 Post Office

🅷 Hospital
🅲 College
■ Principal Business Center
★ Ranally Metro Area (RMA) Abbreviation
Z Zip Code(s)

Ⓟ Previous Census Population
Ⓡ Revised Census Population
Ⓐ Annexation Population
● Rand McNally Population Estimate
Ⓒ Final Census Population
Ⓢ Special Census Population
◆ Estimated Population

For additional definitions see Glossary, Volume 1, and Introduction, Volume 2.

Cave Mountain; RMC Place; ROCKBRIDGE; *244 J-7; mail Natural Bridge Station z 24579; ● 150
Cave Spring; CDP; ROANOKE; 244 H-1; 🅿; ★ ROAN; z 24018; Ⓟ 24,053; Ⓒ 24,941; ◆ 25,986
Cavetown; RMC Place; PAGE; *245 E-11; mail Luray z 22835; ● 120
Caylor; RMC Place; LEE; *244 D-1; mail Ewing z 24248; ● 30
Cedar Bluff; Inc. Place; TAZEWELL; 244 L-1; 🅿; z 24609; Ⓟ 1,290; Ⓒ 1,085
Cedar Bluff; RMC Place; WASHINGTON; *244 E-6; mail Damascus z 24236; rural
Cedar Branch; RMC Place; SMYTH; *244 L-1; mail Saltville z 24370
Cedar Creek; RMC Place; FREDERICK; *245 C-11; elev. 771ft./235m.; mail Winchester z 22603; ● 30
Cedar Forest; RMC Place; PITTSYLVANIA; *244 L-9; elev. 538ft./164m.; mail Long Island z 24569; rural
Cedar Fork; RMC Place; CAROLINE; *245 H-13; elev. 275ft./84m.; mail Ruther Glen z 22546
Cedar Green; RMC Place; AUGUSTA; *244 G-8; mail Staunton z 24401; ● 110
Cedar Grove; RMC Place; HALIFAX; *244 M-9; elev. 529ft./161m.; mail Alton z 24520; rural
Cedar Grove; RMC Place; MECKLENBURG; *245 M-11; elev. 299ft./91m.; mail South Hill z 23970; rural
Cedar Grove; RMC Place; NORTHAMPTON; *245 K-19; mail Cape Charles z 23310
Cedar Grove Acres; RMC Place; CHESAPEAKE (Independent City); *245 M-17; elev. 15ft./5m.; ★ NORF-; mail Chesapeake z 23321; pop. incl. with Chesapeake (Independent City)
Cedarhill; RMC Place; PITTSYLVANIA; *244 M-8; elev. 626ft./191m.; mail Java z 24565; rural
Cedar Lawn; RMC Place; HENRICO; ★ RICH; mail Henrico z 23231
Cedar Level; RMC Place; HOPEWELL (Independent City); *245 K-14; ★ RICH; mail Hopewell z 23860; pop. incl. with Hopewell (Independent City)
Cedar Point; RMC Place; GOOCHLAND; *245 I-12; elev. 163ft./50m.; mail Goochland z 23063; rural
Cedar Springs; RMC Place; SMYTH; *244 M-2; mail Rural Retreat z 24368; ● 180
Cedar View Beach; RMC Place; ACCOMACK; *245 I-19; mail Painter z 23420; ● 30
Cedarville; RMC Place; WARREN; 245 D-11; mail Front Royal z 22630; ● 450
Cedarville; RMC Place; WASHINGTON; *244 D-6; mail Meadowview z 24361; ● 100
Cedon; RMC Place; CAROLINE; 245 H-13; elev. 237ft./72m.; mail Woodford z 22580; ● 150
Celt; RMC Place; GREENE; *245 G-11; mail Stanardsville z 22973; rural
Centenary; RMC Place; BUCKINGHAM; 244 I-10; elev. 520ft./158m.; mail Scottsville z 24590; ● 30
Center Cross; RMC Place; ESSEX; 245 I-16; elev. 126ft./38m.; 🅿; z 22437; ● 150
Center Star; RMC Place; DINWIDDIE; *245 K-13; elev. 281ft./86m.; mail Dinwiddie z 23841; rural
Centerville; RMC Place; ACCOMACK; *245 I-19; mail Modest Town z 23412; rural
Centerville; RMC Place; AUGUSTA; *244 G-9; mail Bridgewater z 22812; ● 50
Centerville; RMC Place; BEDFORD; *244 J-7; elev. 925ft./282m.; mail Bedford z 24523; ● 50
Centerville; RMC Place; GOOCHLAND; *245 I-13; ★ RICH; mail Manakin Sabot z 23103; ● 100
Centerville; RMC Place; HALIFAX; 244 M-9; elev. 500ft./152m.; mail South Boston z 24592; pop. incl. with South Boston (Inc. Place)
Centerville; RMC Place; JAMES CITY; 243 F-1; elev. 103ft./31m.; ★ NN-H; mail Williamsburg z 23188; ● 550
Centerville; KING AND QUEEN; see Shacklefords (RMC Place)
Centerville; RMC Place; LOUISA; *245 H-13; elev. 360ft./110m.; mail Mineral z 23117; rural
Central; RMC Place; RICHMOND (Independent City); ★ RICH; mail Richmond z 23241; pop. incl. with Richmond (Independent City)
Central Garage; RMC Place; KING WILLIAM; *245 I-15; mail King William z 23086
Central Gardens; RMC Place; HENRICO; *245 J-14; ★ RICH; mail Richmond z 23223; ● 1,650
Central Hill; RMC Place; ISLE OF WIGHT; 243 L-1; elev. 93ft./28m.; mail Windsor z 23487; ● 180
Centralia; RMC Place; CHESTERFIELD; 243 F-8; ★ RICH; mail Chester z 23831; ● 200
Centralia Gardens; RMC Place; CHESTERFIELD; *245 J-14; elev. 173ft./53m.; ★ RICH; mail Richmond z 23234; ● 300
Central Martinsville; RMC Place; MARTINSVILLE (Independent City); ★ MRTNV; mail Martinsville z 24112; pop. incl. with Martinsville (Independent City)
Central Plains; RMC Place; FLUVANNA; *245 I-11; elev. 461ft./141m.; mail Palmyra z 22963; rural
Central Point; RMC Place; CAROLINE; *245 H-15; elev. 184ft./56m.; mail Milford z 22514; rural
Centre Heights; RMC Place; FAIRFAX; *245 E-14; ★ WASH; mail Centreville z 20121
Centreville; CDP; FAIRFAX; 245 E-14; 🅿; ★ WASH; z 20120-22; Ⓟ 26,585; Ⓒ 48,661; ◆ 50,571
Centreville Farms; RMC Place; FAIRFAX; *245 E-14; ★ WASH; mail Centreville z 20120
Ceres; RMC Place; BLAND; 244 L-1; 🅿; z 24318; ● 50
Chadswyck; RMC Place; CHESAPEAKE (Independent City); *245 L-17; ★ NORF-; mail Chesapeake z 23321; pop. incl. with Chesapeake (Independent City)
Chalet Woods; RMC Place; FAIRFAX; *245 E-14; ★ WASH; mail Centreville z 20120
Chalk Level; RMC Place; PITTSYLVANIA; *244 L-8; mail Gretna z 24557; ● 50
Chamberlain Village; RMC Place; PRINCE WILLIAM; *245 F-14; ★ WASH; mail Quantico z 22134
Chamberlayne; CDP-Census Area Only; HENRICO; *245 I-14; ★ RICH; mail Richmond z 23227; Ⓟ 4,577; Ⓒ 4,380
Chamberlayne Farms; RMC Place; HENRICO; *245 I-14; ★ RICH; mail Richmond z 23227; ● 2,550
Chamberlayne Heights; RMC Place; HENRICO; *245 I-14; ★ RICH; mail Richmond z 23227; ● 750
Chamberlayne North; RMC Place; HENRICO; *245 I-14; ★ RICH; mail Richmond z 23227; ● 900
Chamblissburg; RMC Place; BEDFORD; 244 K-7; ★ ROAN; mail Vinton z 24179; ● 80
Champlain; RMC Place; ESSEX; 245 H-15; 🅿; z 22438; ● 150
Chance; RMC Place; ESSEX; *245 H-15; 🅿; z 22438; rural
Chancellor; RMC Place; SPOTSYLVANIA; *245 G-13; ★ FRED; mail Fredericksburg z 22401; ● 140
Chancellors Green; RMC Place; SPOTSYLVANIA; *245 G-13; ★ FRED; mail Fredericksburg z 22401; ● 350
Chancellorsville; RMC Place; SPOTSYLVANIA; *245 G-13; ★ FRED; mail Spotsylvania z 22553; rural
Chandler Forks; RMC Place; CHARLOTTE; *244 L-10; elev. 537ft./164m.; mail Charlotte Court House z 23923; rural
Chaneys; RMC Place; PITTSYLVANIA; *244 M-8; mail Java z 24565; rural
Chantilly; CDP; FAIRFAX; 245 D-14; 🅿; ★ WASH; z 20151-53; Ⓟ 29,337; Ⓒ 41,041; ◆ 42,653
Chantilly Estates; RMC Place; FAIRFAX; mail Chantilly z 20151
Chapel; RMC Place; GILES; *244 K-3; mail Narrows z 24124
Chapel Acres; RMC Place; FAIRFAX; 249 J-3; ★ WASH; mail Springfield z 22153; ● 1,200
Chapel Hill; RMC Place; ALEXANDRIA (Independent City); *245 E-15; ★ WASH; mail Alexandria z 22302; pop. incl. with Alexandria (Independent City)
Chapel Park; RMC Place; NEWPORT NEWS (Independent City); ★ NN-H; mail Newport News z 23606; pop. incl. with Newport News (Independent City)
Chapel Square; RMC Place; FAIRFAX; *245 E-14; ★ WASH; mail Annandale z 22003; ● 2,500
Charity; RMC Place; PATRICK; *244 M-5; mail Woolwine z 24185; ● 50
Charlemont; RMC Place; BEDFORD; *244 J-8; elev. 998ft./304m.; mail Big Island z 24526; rural
Charles City; RMC Place; ⊡ CHARLES CITY; 245 J-15; 🅿; z 23030; ● 50
CHARLES CITY; 245 J-15; Ⓟ 6,282; Ⓒ 6,926; ◆ 7,136
Charlie Hope; RMC Place; BRUNSWICK; *245 M-12; mail Brodnax z 23920; rural
CHARLOTTE; 244 L-10; Ⓟ 11,688; Ⓒ 12,472; Ⓡ 12,471; ◆ 12,078
Charlotte Court House; Inc. Place; ⊡ CHARLOTTE; 244 L-10; 🅿; z 23923; Ⓟ 531; Ⓒ 404; Ⓡ 463
Charlottesville; Independent City; serves as county seat of Albemarle; 244 H-10; 🅿 🅷 🅲 24,068 ■; ★ CHRLTV; z 22901-11; Ⓟ 40,341; Ⓒ 45,049; Ⓡ 40,099; ◆ 41,757
Chase City; Inc. Place; MECKLENBURG; 245 M-11; elev. 546ft./166m.; 🅿; z 23924; Ⓟ 2,442; Ⓒ 2,457
Chatham; Inc. Place; ⊡ PITTSYLVANIA; 244 M-8; 🅿; z 24531; Ⓟ 1,354; Ⓒ 1,338
Chatham Heights; RMC Place; STAFFORD; *245 G-14; ★ FRED; mail Fredericksburg z 22401; ● 700
Chatham Hill; RMC Place; SMYTH; *244 L-1; elev. 2,047ft./624m.; mail Saltville z 24370; ● 30
Chatmoss; CDP; HENRY; *244 M-6; ★ MRTNV; mail Martinsville z 24112; Ⓒ 1,742
Cheapside; RMC Place; NORTHAMPTON; *245 K-18; mail Cape Charles z 23310; ● 200
Check; RMC Place; FLOYD; 244 L-5; 🅿; z 24072; ● 80
Cheriton; Inc. Place; NORTHAMPTON; 245 K-19; 🅿; z 23316; Ⓟ 515; Ⓒ 499
Cherokee Heights; RMC Place; NORFOLK (Independent City); *245 L-18; ★ NORF-; mail Norfolk z 23518; pop. incl. with Norfolk (Independent City)
Cherry Acres; RMC Place; HAMPTON (Independent City); *245 L-17; ★ NN-H; mail Hampton z 23669; pop. incl. with Hampton (Independent City)
Cherrydale; RMC Place; ARLINGTON; *245 D-15; ★ WASH; mail Arlington z 22207
Cherry Hill; RMC Place; CHARLES CITY; *245 K-15; elev. 33ft./10m.; mail Charles City z 23030; rural
Cherry Hill; RMC Place; DINWIDDIE; *245 L-13; elev. 340ft./104m.; mail Mc Kenney z 23872; rural
Cherry Hill; RMC Place; PRINCE WILLIAM; *245 F-14; ★ WASH; mail Dumfries z 22026; ● 240
Chesapeake; Independent City; 245 M-18; 🅿 🅷 ■; ★ NORF-; z 23320-28; Ⓟ 151,976; Ⓒ 199,184; ◆ 216,184
Chesapeake; RMC Place; NORTHAMPTON; *245 J-19; mail Cape Charles z 23310; ● 30
Chesapeake Beach; RMC Place; NORTHUMBERLAND; *245 H-18; mail Reedville z 22539; ● 1,000
Chesapeake Beach; RMC Place; VIRGINIA BEACH (Independent City); *245 L-18; ★ NORF-; mail Virginia Beach z 23455; pop. incl. with Virginia Beach (Independent City)
Chesapeake Heights; RMC Place; HAMPTON (Independent City); *245 L-17; ★ NN-H; mail Hampton z 23664; pop. incl. with Hampton (Independent City)
Chesconessex; RMC Place; ACCOMACK; *245 I-19; mail Onancock z 23417; ● 100
Chesdin Manor; RMC Place; DINWIDDIE; *245 K-14; elev. 200ft./61m.; ★ RICH; mail Sutherland z 23885; ● 90
Cheshire; RMC Place; CHESTERFIELD; ★ RICH; mail Chester z 23831
Chesopeian Colony; RMC Place; VIRGINIA BEACH (Independent City); *245 L-18; ★ NORF-; mail Virginia Beach z 23452; pop. incl. with Virginia Beach (Independent City)
Chesswood; RMC Place; CHESTERFIELD; *245 J-14; elev. 173ft./53m.; ★ RICH; mail Richmond z 23234; ● 450
Chester; CDP; CHESTERFIELD; 245 J-14; 🅿; ★ RICH; z 23831, z 23836; Ⓟ 14,986; Ⓒ 17,890
Chesterbrook; RMC Place; FAIRFAX; 249 F-4; ★ WASH; mail Mc Lean z 22101; ● 1,600
Chesterbrook Gardens; RMC Place; FAIRFAX; *245 D-15; ★ WASH; mail Mc Lean z 22101
Chesterbrook Woods; RMC Place; FAIRFAX; *245 D-15; ★ WASH; mail Mc Lean z 22101; ● 2,200
Chester Estates; RMC Place; BRISTOL (Independent City); ★ JNSC-; mail Bristol z 24201; pop. incl. with Bristol (Independent City)
Chesterfield; RMC Place; ⊡ CHESTERFIELD, CHESTERFIELD; 245 J-14; ★ RICH; ● 2,200
CHESTERFIELD; 245 K-13; Ⓟ 209,274; Ⓒ 259,903; ◆ 305,237
Chesterfield Court House; CDP-Census Area Only; CHESTERFIELD; 245 J-14; ★ RICH; mail Chesterfield z 23832, z 23838; Ⓒ 3,558
Chesterfield Heights; RMC Place; NORFOLK (Independent City); *245 L-18; ★ NORF-; mail Norfolk z 23504; pop. incl. with Norfolk (Independent City)
Chester Gap; RMC Place; RAPPAHANNOCK; 245 E-11; 🅿; z 22623; ● 400
Chestnut Hill; RMC Place; FAIRFAX; *245 E-14; ★ WASH; mail Annandale z 22003
Chestnut Hill (Allnutt); RMC Place; KING GEORGE; *245 G-15; mail King George z 22485; ● 50
Chestnut Knob; RMC Place; HENRY; *244 M-6; elev. 1,098ft./335m.; ★ MRTNV; mail Martinsville z 24112; rural
Chestnut Level; RMC Place; PITTSYLVANIA; *244 M-8; mail Blairs z 24527; ● 30
Chestnut Yard; RMC Place; CARROLL; *244 M-3; mail Woodlawn z 24381; rural
Chewings Corner; RMC Place; SPOTSYLVANIA; *245 H-13; mail Partlow z 22534; rural
Chickahominy Haven; RMC Place; JAMES CITY; *245 J-16; ★ NN-H; mail Lanexa z 23089; ● 950
Chickahominy Shores; RMC Place; NEW KENT; *245 J-15; mail Lanexa z 23089; ● 350
Childress; RMC Place; MONTGOMERY; *244 L-4; elev. 1,954ft./596m.; mail Christiansburg z 24073; rural
Childry; RMC Place; HALIFAX; *244 L-9; elev. 443ft./135m.; mail Nathalie z 24577; rural
Chilesburg; RMC Place; CAROLINE; *245 H-13; elev. 325ft./99m.; mail Ruther Glen z 22546
Chilhowie; Inc. Place; SMYTH; 244 M-1; elev. 1,950ft./594m.; 🅿; z 24319; Ⓟ 1,971; Ⓒ 1,827
Chiltons; RMC Place; WESTMORELAND; *245 G-16; mail Montross z 22520; rural
Chimney Corner; RMC Place; CHESTERFIELD; ★ RICH; mail Richmond z 23234
Chimney Run; RMC Place; BATH; *244 H-6; mail Warm Springs z 24484; rural
Chincoteague (Chincoteague Island); Inc. Place; ACCOMACK; 245 H-20; 🅿; z 23336-37; Ⓟ 3,572; Ⓒ 4,317
Chincoteague Island; ACCOMACK; see Chincoteague (Inc. Place)
Chinquapin Village; RMC Place; ALEXANDRIA (Independent City); *245 E-15; ★ WASH; mail Alexandria z 22302; pop. incl. with Alexandria (Independent City)
Chippenham; RMC Place; CHESTERFIELD; ★ RICH; mail Richmond z 23234
Chisford; RMC Place; WESTMORELAND; *245 G-16; elev. 153ft./47m.; mail Montross z 22520; rural
Christ Church; RMC Place; LANCASTER; *245 I-17; elev. 48ft./15m.; mail Irvington z 22480; summer pop. 900; ● 30
Christchurch; RMC Place; MIDDLESEX; *245 I-17; elev. 89ft./27m.; 🅿; z 23031; ● 150
Christensons Corner; RMC Place; JAMES CITY; *245 J-16; elev. 112ft./34m.; ★ NN-H; mail Williamsburg z 23188; ● 100
Christians; RMC Place; AUGUSTA; *244 G-8; mail Swoope z 24479; rural
Christiansburg; Inc. Place; ⊡ MONTGOMERY; 244 K-4; 🅿; z 24068, z 24073; Ⓟ 15,004; Ⓒ 16,947
Christie; RMC Place; HALIFAX; *244 N-9; mail Virgilina z 24598; rural
Christopher Fork; RMC Place; CAROLINE; *245 H-14; elev. 230ft./70m.; mail Bowling Green z 22427; rural
Chuckatuck; RMC Place; SUFFOLK (Independent City); *245 L-17; ★ NORF-; mail Suffolk z 23432; pop. incl. with Suffolk (Independent City)
Chula; RMC Place; AMELIA; 245 J-12; mail Amelia Court House z 23002; ● 130
Church Hill; RMC Place; RICHMOND (Independent City); *245 J-14; elev. 150ft./46m.; ★ RICH; mail Richmond z 23223; pop. incl. with Richmond (Independent City)
Churchill; RMC Place; FAIRFAX; *245 D-15; ★ WASH; mail Falls Church z 22042, Richmond z 23223; ● 1,200
Churchland; RMC Place; PORTSMOUTH (Independent City); *245 L-17; ★ NORF-; mail Portsmouth z 23703; pop. incl. with Portsmouth (Independent City)
Church Road; RMC Place; DINWIDDIE; *245 K-13; 🅿; z 23833; ● 100
Church View; RMC Place; MIDDLESEX; 245 I-16; elev. 103ft./31m.; 🅿; z 23032; ● 70
Churchville; RMC Place; AUGUSTA; 244 G-8; 🅿; z 24421; ● 400
Cifax; RMC Place; BEDFORD; *244 J-8; mail Goode z 24556; rural
Circlewoods; RMC Place; FAIRFAX; *245 D-14; ★ WASH; mail Fairfax z 22031
Cismont; RMC Place; ALBEMARLE; *245 H-11; 🅿; z 22947; ● 90
Civic Center; RMC Place; RICHMOND (Independent City); ★ RICH; mail Richmond z 23240; pop. incl. with Richmond (Independent City)
Clam; RMC Place; ACCOMACK; *245 H-19; mail Bloxom z 23308; ● 30
Clancie; RMC Place; KING AND QUEEN; *245 I-16; mail Shacklefords z 23156; rural
Claraville; RMC Place; NORTHUMBERLAND; *245 H-17; elev. 103ft./31m.; mail Heathsville z 22473; rural
Claremont; RMC Place; ARLINGTON; *245 E-15; ★ WASH; mail Arlington z 22206
Claremont; Inc. Place; SURRY; 245 K-15; 🅿; z 23899; Ⓟ 358; Ⓒ 343
Clarendon; RMC Place; ARLINGTON; *245 D-15; ★ WASH; mail Arlington z 22201
Claresville; RMC Place; GREENSVILLE; *245 M-14; elev. 91ft./28m.; mail Emporia z 23847; ● 30
Clarion; CAMPBELL; see Lynch Station (RMC Place)
CLARKE; 245 D-12; Ⓟ 12,101; Ⓒ 12,652; ◆ 14,534
Clarkes Gap; RMC Place; LOUDOUN; *245 C-13; ★ WASH; mail Paeonian Springs z 20129, Waterford z 20197; rural
Clarksville; Inc. Place; MECKLENBURG; 244 M-10; 🅿; z 23927; Ⓟ 1,243; Ⓒ 1,329
Clarksville; RMC Place; WASHINGTON; *244 M-1; mail Glade Spring z 24340; pop. incl. with Glade Spring (Inc. Place)
Clarkton; RMC Place; HALIFAX; *244 L-9; mail Nathalie z 24577; rural
Clary; RMC Place; SHENANDOAH; *245 D-11; mail Strasburg z 22657; ● 30
Claudville; RMC Place; PATRICK; 244 N-4; elev. 1,459ft./445m.; 🅿; z 24076; ● 150
Clay; RMC Place; LYNCHBURG (Independent City); ★ LYNCH; pop. incl. with Lynchburg (Independent City)
Clay Bank; RMC Place; GLOUCESTER; 243 E-3; mail Gloucester z 23061; ● 200
Claypool Hill; CDP; TAZEWELL; 244 L-1; elev. 2,351ft./717m.; mail Cedar Bluff z 24609, Pounding Mill z 24637; Ⓟ 1,468; Ⓒ 1,719
Clays Mill; RMC Place; HALIFAX; *244 M-9; elev. 533ft./162m.; mail Scottsburg z 24589; ● 30
Clayville; RMC Place; POWHATAN; 245 J-13; elev. 331ft./101m.; mail Powhatan z 23139; ● 80
Clear Brook; RMC Place; FREDERICK; 245 C-12; 🅿; z 22624; ● 190
Clearbrook; RMC Place; ROANOKE; 244 K-6; ★ ROAN; mail Roanoke z 24014; ● 550
Clearfield Forest; RMC Place; FAIRFAX; ★ WASH; mail Springfield z 22151
Clearfork; RMC Place; BLAND; *244 K-2; mail Bastian z 24314; ● 50
Clearview Manor; RMC Place; FAIRFAX; *245 D-15; ★ WASH; mail Mc Lean z 22101
Clearwater Park; RMC Place; ALLEGHANY; 244 I-6; mail Covington z 24426; ● 140
Clell; RMC Place; BUCHANAN; *244 C-6; mail Oakwood z 24631; rural
Clermont Woods; RMC Place; FAIRFAX; *245 E-15; ★ WASH; mail Alexandria z 22310; ● 1,050
Cleveland; Inc. Place; RUSSELL; 244 C-5; elev. 1,534ft./468m.; 🅿; z 24225; Ⓟ 214; Ⓒ 148
Cliffield; RMC Place; TAZEWELL; 244 L-1; mail Pounding Mill z 24637; ● 150
Clifford; RMC Place; AMHERST; 244 I-9; elev. 770ft./235m.; 🅿; z 24533; ● 180
Cliffview; RMC Place; CARROLL; *244 M-3; mail Galax z 24333; pop. incl. with Galax (Independent City)
Clifton; Inc. Place; FAIRFAX; *245 E-14; 🅿; ★ WASH; z 20124; Ⓟ 176; Ⓒ 185
Clifton; RMC Place; ORANGE; *245 G-12; mail Rapidan z 22733; rural
Cliftondale; ALLEGHANY; see Cliftondale Park (RMC Place)
Cliftondale Park (Cliftondale); RMC Place; ALLEGHANY; *244 I-6; mail Clifton Forge z 24422; ● 500
Clifton Forge; Inc. Place; ALLEGHANY; 244 I-6; 🅿; z 24422; former independent city; became part of Alleghany county on July 1, 2001; Ⓟ 4,679; Ⓒ 4,289
Clifton Forge; Independent City; former independent city; became part of Alleghany county on July 1, 2001; Ⓟ 4,679; Ⓒ 4,289
Climax; RMC Place; PITTSYLVANIA; *244 L-7; mail Chatham z 24531; rural
Clinchburg; RMC Place; WASHINGTON; *244 D-6; 🅿; z 24361; ● 120
Clinchco; Inc. Place; DICKENSON; 244 C-5; 🅿; z 24226; Ⓟ 534; Ⓒ 424
Clinchport; Inc. Place; SCOTT; 244 D-3; 🅿; z 24244; Ⓟ 67; Ⓒ 77
Clintwood; Inc. Place; ⊡ DICKENSON; 244 C-4; 🅿 🅷; z 24228; Ⓟ 1,542; Ⓒ 1,549
Clito; RMC Place; GRAYSON; *244 M-2; mail Fries z 24330; rural
Clover; RMC Place; ALEXANDRIA (Independent City); *245 E-15; ★ WASH; mail Alexandria z 22314; pop. incl. with Alexandria (Independent City)
Clover; RMC Place; HALIFAX; 244 M-10; elev. 502ft./153m.; 🅿; z 24534; Ⓟ 198
Cloverdale; CDP; BOTETOURT; 244 J-6; 🅿; ★ ROAN; z 24077; Ⓟ 1,689; Ⓒ 2,986
Cloverdale; RMC Place; FLUVANNA; *245 I-11; mail Bremo Bluff z 23022; ● 30
Cloverdale Branch Junction; RMC Place; BOTETOURT; *244 J-6; ★ ROAN
Clover Hill; RMC Place; ROCKINGHAM; 244 F-9; mail Dayton z 22821; ● 100
Club Court; RMC Place; HENRICO; *245 I-14; elev. 184ft./56m.; ★ RICH; mail Richmond z 23227; ● 1,600
Cluster Springs; RMC Place; HALIFAX; 244 M-9; 🅿; z 24535; ● 260
Coaldan (Lark); RMC Place; TAZEWELL; *244 K-1; mail Richlands z 24641; ● 50
Coal Kiln; RMC Place; ACCOMACK; *245 I-19; mail Painter z 23420; ● 30
Coal Mine; RMC Place; SHENANDOAH; mail Strasburg z 22657; rural
Coan; RMC Place; NORTHUMBERLAND; *245 H-17; elev. 101ft./31m.; mail Heathsville z 22473; rural
Coatesville; RMC Place; HANOVER; *245 H-13; elev. 276ft./84m.; mail Beaverdam z 23015; rural
Cobbdale; RMC Place; FAIRFAX (Independent City); *245 D-14; ★ WASH; mail Fairfax z 22030; pop. incl. with Fairfax (Independent City)
Cobbs Creek; RMC Place; MATHEWS; *245 J-17; 🅿; ★ NN-H; z 23035; ● 250
Cobham; RMC Place; ALBEMARLE; *245 H-11; 🅿; z 22947; ● 30
Cobham Park; RMC Place; RICHMOND; *245 H-16; elev. 130ft./40m.; mail Warsaw z 22572; rural
Cobham Wharf; RMC Place; SURRY; 243 H-1; elev. 45ft./14m.; mail Surry z 23883; ● 80
Cochran; RMC Place; BRUNSWICK; *245 L-12; elev. 359ft./109m.; mail Alberta z 23821; ● 30
Cody; RMC Place; HALIFAX; *244 L-9; elev. 638ft./194m.; mail Nathalie z 24577; rural
Coeburn; Inc. Place; WISE; 244 C-4; elev. 1,992ft./607m.; 🅿; z 24230; Ⓟ 2,165; Ⓒ 1,996
Coffee; RMC Place; BEDFORD; *244 J-8; ★ LYNCH; mail Forest z 24551; rural
Cohasset; RMC Place; FLUVANNA; *245 I-11; mail Fork Union z 23055; ● 30
Cohoke; RMC Place; KING WILLIAM; *245 J-15; mail West Point z 23181; rural
Coke; RMC Place; GLOUCESTER; *245 J-17; elev. 27ft./8m.; ★ NN-H; mail Hayes z 23072; ● 200
Colchester; RMC Place; FAIRFAX; *245 E-14; ★ WASH; mail Lorton z 22079
Cold Harbor Farms; RMC Place; HANOVER; *245 I-14; ★ RICH; mail Mechanicsville z 23111; ● 220
Coldwater; RMC Place; KING AND QUEEN; *245 I-16; elev. 104ft./32m.; mail Mascot z 23108; rural
Coleman Falls; RMC Place; BEDFORD; 244 J-8; 🅿; ★ LYNCH; z 24536; ● 100
Coleman Place; RMC Place; NORFOLK (Independent City); *245 L-18; ★ NORF-; mail Norfolk z 23513; pop. incl. with Norfolk (Independent City)
Coles Creek; RMC Place; FRANKLIN; *244 L-6; mail Rocky Mount z 24151; ● 60
Coles Point; RMC Place; WESTMORELAND; 245 G-16; 🅿; z 22442; summer pop. 400; ● 300
Colleen; RMC Place; NELSON; 244 I-9; mail Arrington z 22922; ● 180
College Park; RMC Place; ALEXANDRIA (Independent City); *245 E-15; ★ WASH; mail Alexandria z 22314; pop. incl. with Alexandria (Independent City)
College Park; RMC Place; STAUNTON (Independent City); *244 G-9; mail Staunton z 24401; pop. incl. with Staunton (Independent City)
College Park; RMC Place; SUFFOLK (Independent City); ★ NORF-; mail Portsmouth z 23703; pop. incl. with Suffolk (Independent City)
Colley; RMC Place; DICKENSON; *244 B-5; mail Birchleaf z 24220; rural
Collierstown; RMC Place; ROCKBRIDGE; 244 I-7; mail Lexington z 24450; ● 70
Collingwood; RMC Place; FAIRFAX; *245 E-15; ★ WASH; mail Alexandria z 22308
Collins Crossing; RMC Place; CAROLINE; *245 G-14; mail Woodford z 22580; rural
Collinsville; CDP; HENRY; 244 M-6; 🅿; ★ MRTNV; z 24078; Ⓟ 7,280; Ⓒ 7,777
Collinwood; RMC Place; RUSSELL; *244 D-5; elev. 1,851ft./564m.; mail Lebanon z 24266
Cologne; RMC Place; KING AND QUEEN; *245 J-16; 🅿; z 23181 & mail Shacklefords z 23156; ● 30
Colonial Beach; Inc. Place; WESTMORELAND; 245 G-15; 🅿; z 22443; Ⓟ 3,132; Ⓒ 3,228
Colonial Forest; RMC Place; HANOVER; *245 I-14; ★ RICH; mail Mechanicsville z 23116; ● 300
Colonial Heights; Independent City; 245 K-14; 🅿; ★ RICH; z 23834; Ⓟ 16,064; Ⓒ 16,897; ◆ 17,674
Colonial Heights; RMC Place; NORFOLK (Independent City); *245 L-18; ★ NORF-; mail Norfolk z 23518; pop. incl. with Norfolk (Independent City)
Colonial Place; RMC Place; NORFOLK (Independent City); *245 L-18; ★ NORF-; mail Norfolk z 23508; pop. incl. with Norfolk (Independent City)
Colonial Village; RMC Place; ARLINGTON; *245 D-15; ★ WASH; mail Arlington z 22201
Colonial Williamsburg; RMC Place; WILLIAMSBURG (Independent City); mail Williamsburg z 23185; pop. incl. with Williamsburg (Independent City)
Colosse; RMC Place; ISLE OF WIGHT; *245 M-16; mail Carrsville z 23315; ● 100
Colthurst; RMC Place; ALBEMARLE; 243 B-2; ★ CHRLTV; mail Charlottesville z 22901; ● 470
Coltons Mill; RMC Place; BEDFORD; *244 J-7; elev. 949ft./289m.; mail Bedford z 24523; rural
Columbia; Inc. Place; FLUVANNA; 245 I-11; 🅿; z 23038; Ⓟ 58; Ⓒ 49
Columbia Forest; RMC Place; ARLINGTON; *245 D-15; ★ WASH; mail Arlington z 22204
Columbia Furnace; RMC Place; SHENANDOAH; *244 D-10; mail Edinburg z 22824; ● 50
Columbia Heights; RMC Place; ARLINGTON; *245 D-15; ★ WASH; mail Arlington z 22204
Columbia Park; RMC Place; HOPEWELL (Independent City); ★ RICH; mail Hopewell z 23860; pop. incl. with Hopewell (Independent City)
Columbia Pines; RMC Place; FAIRFAX; *245 E-14; ★ WASH; mail Annandale z 22003
Colvin Run (Leighs Corner); RMC Place; FAIRFAX; *245 D-14; ★ WASH; mail Great Falls z 22066
Comers Rock; RMC Place; GRAYSON; 244 M-2; elev. 2,759ft./841m.; mail Elk Creek z 24326; ● 50
Comet; RMC Place; ISLE OF WIGHT; *245 L-16; elev. 77ft./23m.; mail Smithfield z 23430; rural
Commodore Park; RMC Place; NORFOLK (Independent City); *245 L-18; ★ NORF-; mail Norfolk z 23503; pop. incl. with Norfolk (Independent City)
Commonwealth; RMC Place; ALBEMARLE; *244 H-10; ★ CHRLTV; mail Charlottesville z 22901; Ⓟ 5,538
Commonwealth Acres; RMC Place; PRINCE GEORGE; *245 K-14; elev. 150ft./46m.; ★ RICH; mail Prince George z 23875; ● 250
Comorn; RMC Place; KING GEORGE; *245 G-14; mail Fredericksburg z 22405; ● 50
Compton; RMC Place; PAGE; *245 E-11; mail Rileyville z 22650
Conaway (Conoway); RMC Place; BUCHANAN; *244 B-5; 🅿; z 24603; ● 200
Concord; RMC Place; BRUNSWICK; *245 L-13; elev. 321ft./98m.; mail Rawlings z 23876; rural
Concord; RMC Place; CAMPBELL, APPOMATTOX; 244 K-9; elev. 884ft./269m.; 🅿; ★ LYNCH; z 24538; ● 500
Concord Heights; RMC Place; SPOTSYLVANIA; *245 G-14; ★ FRED; mail Stafford z 22554; ● 420
Conde; RMC Place; FAUQUIER; *245 E-12; mail Marshall z 20115; rural
Confederate Heights; RMC Place; HENRICO; *245 I-14; ★ RICH; mail Richmond z 23222; ● 650
Conicville; RMC Place; SHENANDOAH; *244 E-10; mail Mount Jackson z 22842; ● 70
Conners Grove; RMC Place; FLOYD; *244 M-4; mail Willis z 24380; rural
Conoway; BUCHANAN; see Conaway (RMC Place)
Contra; RMC Place; KING AND QUEEN; *245 I-16; elev. 122ft./37m.; mail Center Cross z 22437; rural
Cookstown; RMC Place; SPOTSYLVANIA; *245 G-13; ★ FRED; mail Spotsylvania z 22553; rural
Coolwell; RMC Place; AMHERST; *244 J-9; ★ LYNCH; mail Amherst z 24521; rural
Cooper; RMC Place; MIDDLESEX; *245 I-17; elev. 30ft./9m.; mail Locust Hill z 23092; rural
Cootes Store; RMC Place; ROCKINGHAM; *244 E-9; mail Broadway z 22815
Copper Hill; RMC Place; FLOYD; 244 L-5; elev. 2,856ft./871m.; 🅿; z 24079; ● 100
Copper Valley; RMC Place; FLOYD; *244 L-4; mail Radford z 24141; ● 30
Corbin; RMC Place; CAROLINE; *245 G-14; 🅿; z 22446; ● 250
Corinth; RMC Place; SOUTHAMPTON; *245 L-15; elev. 87ft./27m.; mail Ivor z 23866; rural
Cornland; RMC Place; CHESAPEAKE (Independent City); *245 M-17; elev. 18ft./5m.; ★ NORF-; mail Chesapeake z 23322; pop. incl. with Chesapeake (Independent City)
Corn Valley; RMC Place; RUSSELL; *244 C-6; mail Honaker z 24260; rural
Cornwall; RMC Place; ROCKBRIDGE; *244 I-8; mail Buena Vista z 24416; ● 50
Coronado; RMC Place; NORFOLK (Independent City); *245 L-18; ★ NORF-; mail Norfolk z 23513; pop. incl. with Norfolk (Independent City)
Cottage Heights; RMC Place; NORFOLK (Independent City); *245 L-18; ★ NORF-; mail Norfolk z 23504; pop. incl. with Norfolk (Independent City)
Cottage Park; RMC Place; NORFOLK (Independent City); *245 L-18; ★ NORF-; mail Norfolk z 23503; pop. incl. with Norfolk (Independent City)
Cottage Road Park; RMC Place; NORFOLK (Independent City); *245 L-18; ★ NORF-; mail Norfolk z 23505; pop. incl. with Norfolk (Independent City)
Coulwood (Finney); RMC Place; RUSSELL; *244 C-6; elev. 1,595ft./486m.; mail Honaker z 24260; ● 80
Council; RMC Place; BUCHANAN; *244 C-6; 🅿; z 24260; ● 50
Countis Corner; WASHINGTON; see Fleenor Spring (RMC Place)
Country Club Hills; RMC Place; ARLINGTON; *245 D-15; ★ WASH; mail Arlington z 22207
Country Club Hills; RMC Place; FAIRFAX (Independent City); *245 D-14; ★ WASH; mail Fairfax z 22030; pop. incl. with Fairfax (Independent City)
Country Club Manor; RMC Place; ARLINGTON; *245 D-15; ★ WASH; mail Arlington z 22207
Country Club View; RMC Place; FAIRFAX; *245 E-14; ★ WASH; mail Fairfax z 22032; ● 1,450
Country Creek; RMC Place; FAIRFAX; *245 D-11; mail Vienna z 22181
Countryside; RMC Place; LOUDOUN; *245 D-14; ★ WASH; mail Sterling z 20165; Ⓟ 8,349
Counts; RMC Place; DICKENSON; *244 C-5; mail Dante z 24237; rural
County Line Cross Roads; RMC Place; CHARLOTTE, PRINCE EDWARD; *244 K-10; elev. 623ft./190m.; mail Charlotte Court House z 23923; rural
Court House; RMC Place; ARLINGTON; 245 I-16; ★ WASH; mail Arlington z 22216; ● 300
Courtland; Inc. Place; ⊡ SOUTHAMPTON; 245 M-15; elev. 32ft./10m.; 🅿; z 23837; Ⓟ 819; Ⓒ 1,270
Courtland Park; RMC Place; FAIRFAX; *245 D-15; ★ WASH; mail Falls Church z 22041
Courtney; RMC Place; HENRICO; *245 I-14; elev. 250ft./76m.; ★ RICH; mail Glen Allen z 23060; ● 300
Cove Colony; RMC Place; LANCASTER; *245 I-17; mail Lancaster z 22503; ● 60
Cove Creek; RMC Place; BLAND; *244 K-2; mail Bastian z 24314; ● 50
Cove Creek; RMC Place; TAZEWELL; *244 K-2; mail Tazewell z 24651
Covesville; RMC Place; ALBEMARLE; 244 H-10; 🅿; z 22931; ● 240
Covingston Corner; RMC Place; CAROLINE; *245 H-14; elev. 211ft./64m.; mail Doswell z 23047; rural
Covington; Independent City; serves as county seat of Alleghany; 244 I-6; 🅿; z 24426; Ⓟ 6,991; Ⓒ 6,303; ◆ 6,311
Cox's Chapel; RMC Place; GRAYSON; *244 N-2; mail Mouth of Wilson z 24363; ● 30
Crab Orchard; RMC Place; WISE; *244 C-4; mail Coeburn z 24230; rural
Crackers Neck; RMC Place; SCOTT; *244 D-4; mail Nickelsville z 24271; rural
Crackers Neck; RMC Place; WISE; *244 D-4; mail Big Stone Gap z 24219; rural
Craddockville; RMC Place; ACCOMACK; *245 I-19; elev. 23ft./7m.; 🅿; z 23341; ● 180
Cradock; RMC Place; PORTSMOUTH (Independent City); *245 M-17; ★ NORF-; mail Portsmouth z 23702; pop. incl. with Portsmouth (Independent City)
CRAIG; 244 J-5; Ⓟ 4,372; Ⓒ 5,091; ◆ 5,209
Craigs Mills; RMC Place; WASHINGTON; *244 D-5; mail Bristol z 24202; rural
Craig Springs; RMC Place; CRAIG; *244 J-5; mail New Castle z 24127; rural
Craigsville; Inc. Place; AUGUSTA; 244 H-8; 🅿; z 24430; Ⓟ 812; Ⓒ 979
Crandon; RMC Place; BLAND; 244 K-3; mail Bland z 24315; ● 80
Cranes Nest; RMC Place; WISE; 244 C-4; mail Coeburn z 24230; ● 200
Craney Island Estates; RMC Place; HANOVER; *245 I-14; ★ RICH; mail Mechanicsville z 23111; ● 360
Creeds; RMC Place; VIRGINIA BEACH (Independent City); *245 M-18; ★ NORF-; mail Virginia Beach z 23457; pop. incl. with Virginia Beach (Independent City)
Crescent Hill; RMC Place; HOPEWELL (Independent City); ★ RICH; mail Hopewell z 23860; pop. incl. with Hopewell (Independent City)
Crescent Hills; RMC Place; ARLINGTON; *245 D-15; ★ WASH; mail Arlington z 22207
Cresthill; RMC Place; FAUQUIER; *245 E-12; mail Hume z 22639
Crestview; RMC Place; HENRICO; *245 I-14; elev. 265ft./81m.; ★ RICH; mail Richmond z 23226; ● 2,000
Crestview; RMC Place; PRINCE EDWARD; *245 K-11; elev. 450ft./137m.; mail Farmville z 23901; pop. incl. with Farmville (Inc. Place)
Crestwood; RMC Place; CHESAPEAKE (Independent City); *245 M-18; ★ NORF-; mail Chesapeake z 23320; pop. incl. with Chesapeake (Independent City)
Crestwood Manor; RMC Place; FAIRFAX; *245 E-14; ★ WASH; mail Annandale z 22003
Crewe; Inc. Place; NOTTOWAY; 245 K-12; 🅿; z 23930; Ⓟ 2,276; Ⓒ 2,378
Criders; RMC Place; ROCKINGHAM; *244 E-9; 🅿; z 22820; ● 50
Criglersville; RMC Place; MADISON; *245 F-11; elev. 547ft./167m.; 🅿; z 22727; ● 50
Crimora; CDP; AUGUSTA; 244 G-9; 🅿; z 24431; Ⓟ 1,752; Ⓒ 1,796
Cripple Creek; RMC Place; WYTHE; *244 M-2; 🅿; z 24322; ● 230
Crittenden; RMC Place; SUFFOLK (Independent City); *245 L-17; ★ NORF-; mail Suffolk z 23433; pop. incl. with Suffolk (Independent City)
Critz; RMC Place; PATRICK; 244 M-5; elev. 1,144ft./349m.; 🅿; z 24082; ● 160
Croaker; RMC Place; JAMES CITY; *245 J-16; ★ NN-H; mail Williamsburg z 23188; ● 90
Croatan Beach; RMC Place; VIRGINIA BEACH (Independent City); *245 L-19; elev. 10ft./3m.; ★ NORF-; mail Virginia Beach z 23451; pop. incl. with Virginia Beach (Independent City)
Crockett; RMC Place; WYTHE; 244 L-2; elev. 2,344ft./714m.; 🅿; z 24323; ● 330
Crockett Springs; RMC Place; MONTGOMERY; *244 L-5; ★ ROAN; mail Shawsville z 24162; rural
Crofton; RMC Place; ROANOKE; *244 K-6; ★ ROAN; mail Vinton z 24179; ● 650
Cromwell; RMC Place; NORFOLK (Independent City); ★ NORF-; mail Norfolk z 23509; pop. incl. with Norfolk (Independent City)
Crooked Oak; RMC Place; CARROLL; *244 M-4; mail Hillsville z 24343; rural
Crossbrook; RMC Place; WISE; mail Andover z 24215; rural
Crosses Corner; RMC Place; HANOVER; *245 I-14; elev. 189ft./58m.; ★ RICH; mail Hanover z 23069; rural
Cross Junction; RMC Place; FREDERICK; 245 C-11; 🅿; z 22625; ● 50
Crosskeys; RMC Place; ROCKINGHAM; *244 G-9; mail Mount Crawford z 22841; rural
Crossroads; RMC Place; ALBEMARLE; *244 H-10; mail North Garden z 22959; ● 30
Crossroads; RMC Place; HALIFAX; *244 L-9; elev. 545ft./166m.; mail Nathalie z 24577; rural
Crouch; RMC Place; KING AND QUEEN; *245 I-15; mail Center Cross z 22437; rural
Crows; RMC Place; ALLEGHANY; *244 I-5; elev. 1,653ft./504m.; mail Covington z 24426
Crozet; CDP; ALBEMARLE; 244 H-10; 🅿; ★ CHRLTV; z 22932; Ⓟ 2,256; Ⓒ 2,820
Crozier; RMC Place; GOOCHLAND; 245 I-13; elev. 332ft./101m.; 🅿; z 23039; ● 140
Crymes Store; RMC Place; LUNENBURG; *245 L-11; elev. 543ft./166m.; mail Victoria z 23974; ● 30
Crystal City; RMC Place; ARLINGTON; ★ WASH; mail Arlington z 22202, z 22215
Crystal Hill; RMC Place; HALIFAX; 244 L-9; 🅿; z 24539; ● 220
Crystal Spring Knolls; RMC Place; ARLINGTON; *245 D-15; ★ WASH; mail Arlington z 22207
Cuckoo; RMC Place; LOUISA; 245 H-12; mail Mineral z 23117; ● 30
Cullen; RMC Place; CHARLOTTE; 244 K-10; elev. 531ft./162m.; 🅿; z 23934; ● 100
Culmore; RMC Place; FAIRFAX; 249 G-4; ★ WASH; mail Falls Church z 22041; ● 5,200
Culpeper; Inc. Place; ⊡ CULPEPER; 245 F-12; elev. 430ft./131m.; 🅿 🅷; z 22701 & mail Reva z 22735; Ⓟ 8,581; Ⓒ 9,664
CULPEPER; 245 F-12; Ⓟ 27,791; Ⓒ 34,262; ◆ 48,648
Cumberland; RMC Place; ⊡ CUMBERLAND; 245 J-11; 🅿; z 23040; ● 350
CUMBERLAND; 245 J-11; Ⓟ 7,825; Ⓒ 9,017; ◆ 9,861
Cummings Heights; RMC Place; WASHINGTON; *244 D-6; mail Abingdon z 24210; ● 250
Cumnor; RMC Place; KING AND QUEEN; *245 I-16; mail King and Queen Court House z 23085; rural
Cunningham; RMC Place; FLUVANNA; 245 H-11; 🅿; z 22963; ● 100
Curdsville; RMC Place; BUCKINGHAM; *245 J-11; elev. 474ft./144m.; mail Dillwyn z 23936; rural
Currioman Landing; RMC Place; WESTMORELAND; *245 G-16; mail Montross z 22520; rural
Currituck Farms; RMC Place; HENRICO; *245 J-14; ★ RICH; mail Sandston z 23150; ● 60
Curtis; RMC Place; BEDFORD; *244 J-7; elev. 1,200ft./366m.; mail Bedford z 24523; rural
Cuscowilla; RMC Place; MECKLENBURG; *245 M-11; elev. 36ft./11m.; mail Boydton z 23917; ● 50
Customhouse; RMC Place; NORFOLK (Independent City); ★ NORF-; mail Norfolk z 23514; pop. incl. with Norfolk (Independent City)
Cypress Chapel; RMC Place; SUFFOLK (Independent City); ★ NORF-; mail Suffolk z 23434; pop. incl. with Suffolk (Independent City)
Cypress Manor; RMC Place; SOUTHAMPTON; *245 M-15; mail Franklin z 23851; ● 250
Cypress Point; RMC Place; JAMES CITY; *245 J-16; elev. 18ft./5m.; ★ NN-H; mail Lanexa z 23089; ● 250
Cypress Point; RMC Place; SURRY; *245 K-15; elev. 50ft./15m.; mail Claremont z 23899

D

Dabney Estates; RMC Place; DINWIDDIE; *245 K-13; elev. 250ft./76m.; ★ RICH; mail Sutherland z 23885; ● 150
Dabneys; RMC Place; LOUISA; *245 I-13; 🅿; z 23102; ● 30
Dahlgren; CDP; KING GEORGE; 245 G-15; 🅿; z 22448; Ⓒ 997
Dahlia; RMC Place; GREENSVILLE; *245 N-14; mail Pleasant Hill z 27866; rural
Daileys Store; SUFFOLK (Independent City); see Sandy Bottom (RMC Place)
Dalbys; RMC Place; NORTHAMPTON; *245 K-18; mail Cape Charles z 23310
Dale City; CDP; PRINCE WILLIAM; 245 E-14; 🅿; ★ WASH; z 22193; Ⓟ 47,170; Ⓒ 55,971; ◆ 72,850
Dalecrest; RMC Place; ALEXANDRIA (Independent City); *245 E-15; ★ WASH; mail Alexandria z 22304; pop. incl. with Alexandria (Independent City)
Dale Enterprise; RMC Place; ROCKINGHAM; *244 F-9; mail Harrisonburg z 22801; ● 80
Daleville; CDP; BOTETOURT; 244 J-6; 🅿; ★ ROAN; z 24083; Ⓟ 1,163; Ⓒ 1,454
Damascus; Inc. Place; WASHINGTON; 244 E-6; elev. 1,928ft./588m.; 🅿; z 24236; Ⓟ 918; Ⓒ 981
Dam Neck; RMC Place; VIRGINIA BEACH (Independent City); ★ NORF-; mail Virginia Beach z 23461; pop. incl. with Virginia Beach (Independent City)
Dam Neck Corner; RMC Place; VIRGINIA BEACH (Independent City); *245 M-18; elev. 17ft./5m.; ★ NORF-; mail Virginia Beach z 23454; pop. incl. with Virginia Beach (Independent City)
Danbury Forest; RMC Place; FAIRFAX; *245 E-14; ★ WASH; mail Springfield z 22151
Dandy; RMC Place; YORK; *245 K-17; elev. 5ft./2m.; ★ NN-H; mail Lackey z 23694; ● 350
Daniel; RMC Place; ORANGE; *245 G-12; mail Orange z 22960
Daniel Boone (Albert); RMC Place; SCOTT; *244 D-4; ★ JNSC-; mail Gate City z 24251; ● 30
Danieltown; RMC Place; BRUNSWICK; 245 L-12; mail Alberta z 23821; ● 50
Danripple; RMC Place; HALIFAX; *244 M-9; mail South Boston z 24592
Dante; RMC Place; RUSSELL; 244 C-5; elev. 1,765ft./538m.; 🅿; z 24237; ● 700
Danville; Independent City; 244 N-8; 🅿 🅷 🅲 2,467 ■; ★ DANV; z 24540-41, z 24543-44; Ⓟ 53,056; Ⓒ 48,411; ◆ 44,437
Daphna; RMC Place; ROCKINGHAM; *244 F-9; elev. 1,110ft./338m.; mail Broadway z 22815; ● 30
Darbyville; RMC Place; LEE; *244 D-2; elev. 1,800ft./549m.; mail Saint Charles z 24282; ● 200
Dare; RMC Place; YORK; *245 K-17; ★ NN-H; mail Yorktown z 23692; ● 400
Darlington Heights; RMC Place; PRINCE EDWARD; 244 K-10; elev. 599ft./183m.; 🅿; z 23958; ● 30
Darnell Town; RMC Place; LEE; *244 D-3; mail Keokee z 24265; ● 150
Darvills; RMC Place; DINWIDDIE; 245 L-13; elev. 377ft./115m.; mail Blackstone z 23824; ● 80
Darwin; RMC Place; DICKENSON; *244 C-4; mail Clintwood z 24228; ● 120
Daugherty; RMC Place; ACCOMACK; *245 I-19; mail Accomac z 23301; ● 100
Davenport; RMC Place; BUCHANAN; 244 C-5; 🅿; z 24239; ● 100
Davis; RMC Place; ROCKBRIDGE; *244 H-8; elev. 1,929ft./588m.; mail Raphine z 24472; rural
Davis Wharf; RMC Place; ACCOMACK; *245 I-19; 🅿; z 23345; ● 60
Dawley Corner; RMC Place; VIRGINIA BEACH (Independent City); ★ NORF-; mail Virginia Beach z 23457; pop. incl. with Virginia Beach (Independent City)
Dawn; RMC Place; CAROLINE; *245 I-14; mail Doswell z 23047; rural
Dayton; Inc. Place; ROCKINGHAM; 244 F-9; 🅿; z 22821; Ⓟ 921; Ⓒ 1,344
Deans; RMC Place; SUFFOLK (Independent City); *245 L-17; ★ NORF-; mail Suffolk z 23435; pop. incl. with Suffolk (Independent City)
Deatonville; RMC Place; AMELIA; 245 K-11; elev. 455ft./139m.; mail Jetersville z 23083; ● 50
De Bree; RMC Place; NORFOLK (Independent City); ★ NORF-; mail Norfolk z 23517; pop. incl. with Norfolk (Independent City)
De Busk Mill; RMC Place; WASHINGTON; *244 M-1; mail Glade Spring z 24340; rural
Decatur (Aqua); RMC Place; ROCKBRIDGE; *244 H-8; mail Fairfield z 24435; rural
Deel; RMC Place; BUCHANAN; 244 B-6; mail Vansant z 24656; ● 200
Deep Bottom; RMC Place; HENRICO; *245 J-14; elev. 50ft./15m.; ★ RICH; mail Henrico z 23075; rural
Deep Creek; RMC Place; ACCOMACK; 243 N-5; mail Onancock z 23417; ● 150
Deep Creek; RMC Place; CHESAPEAKE (Independent City); *245 M-17; ★ NORF-; mail Chesapeake z 23323; pop. incl. with Chesapeake (Independent City)
Deep Creek; RMC Place; NEWPORT NEWS (Independent City); *245 K-17; ★ NN-H; mail Newport News z 23606; pop. incl. with Newport News (Independent City)
Deep Hole; RMC Place; ACCOMACK; *245 H-20; mail Chincoteague Island z 23336; pop. incl. with Chincoteague (Inc. Place)
Deerborne; RMC Place; RICHMOND (Independent City); ★ RICH; mail Richmond z 23234; pop. incl. with Richmond (Independent City)
Deerfield; RMC Place; AUGUSTA; 244 G-8; 🅿; z 24432; ● 270
Deerfield Estates; RMC Place; CHESTERFIELD; *245 J-14; ★ RICH; mail Chesterfield z 23832; ● 850
Deer Park; RMC Place; MANASSAS (Independent City); ★ WASH; mail Manassas z 20110; pop. incl. with Manassas (Independent City)
Deer Park Groove; RMC Place; NEWPORT NEWS (Independent City); ★ NN-H; mail Newport News z 23607; pop. incl. with Newport News (Independent City)
Deerrock; RMC Place; NELSON; mail Faber z 22938; rural
Defense General Supply Center; RMC Place; CHESTERFIELD; *245 J-14; ★ RICH; mail Richmond z 23297
De Jarnett; RMC Place; CAROLINE; *245 H-14; mail Milford z 22514; rural
Delaplane; RMC Place; FAUQUIER; 245 D-12; 🅿; z 20144; ● 200
Delaware; RMC Place; SOUTHAMPTON; *245 M-15; mail Franklin z 23851; rural
Delmar; RMC Place; WASHINGTON; *244 E-6; mail Damascus z 24236; rural
Del Ray; RMC Place; ALEXANDRIA (Independent City); *245 E-15; ★ WASH; mail Alexandria z 22301; pop. incl. with Alexandria (Independent City)
Delta; RMC Place; ALEXANDRIA (Independent City); *245 E-15; ★ WASH; mail Alexandria z 22304; pop. incl. with Alexandria (Independent City)
Deltaville; RMC Place; MIDDLESEX; 245 J-17; 🅿; z 23043; summer pop. 1,500; ● 1,000
Delton; RMC Place; PULASKI; mail Draper z 24324; rural
Denaro; RMC Place; AMELIA; *245 K-12; mail Amelia Court House z 23002; ● 30
Denbigh; RMC Place; NEWPORT NEWS (Independent City); *245 K-17; ★ NN-H; mail Newport News z 23602, z 23608-09; pop. incl. with Newport News (Independent City)
Denby Park; RMC Place; NORFOLK (Independent City); *245 L-18; ★ NORF-; mail Norfolk z 23505; pop. incl. with Norfolk (Independent City)
Dendron; Inc. Place; SURRY; 245 L-15; 🅿; z 23839; Ⓟ 305; Ⓒ 297
Denmark; RMC Place; ROCKBRIDGE; *244 H-7; mail Lexington z 24450; rural
Denniston; RMC Place; HALIFAX; *244 N-9; elev. 438ft./134m.; mail Alton z 24520; rural
Dentons Corner; RMC Place; BUCKINGHAM; *244 J-10; elev. 480ft./146m.; mail Buckingham z 23921; rural
Derby; RMC Place; WISE; *244 C-3; mail Appalachia z 24216; ● 350
Desha; RMC Place; ESSEX; *245 H-15; elev. 138ft./42m.; mail Tappahannock z 22560; ● 50
Detrick; RMC Place; SHENANDOAH; 245 E-11; mail Fort Valley z 22652; ● 40
Devon Manor; RMC Place; NORFOLK (Independent City); *245 L-18; ★ NORF-; mail Norfolk z 23503; pop. incl. with Norfolk (Independent City)
Devonshire Gardens; RMC Place; FAIRFAX; *245 D-14; ★ WASH; mail Falls Church z 22042
Dewey; RMC Place; WISE; *244 C-4; mail Pound z 24279; ● 50
DeWitt; RMC Place; DINWIDDIE; 245 L-13; elev. 301ft./92m.; 🅿; z 23840; ● 100
Diamond Grove; RMC Place; BRUNSWICK; *245 M-12; elev. 250ft./76m.; mail Brodnax z 23920; rural
Diamond Springs; RMC Place; VIRGINIA BEACH (Independent City); *245 L-18; ★ NORF-; mail Virginia Beach z 23455; pop. incl. with Virginia Beach (Independent City)
Diascund; RMC Place; JAMES CITY; *245 J-16; elev. 40ft./12m.; ★ NN-H; mail Lanexa z 23089; rural
Dickensdale; RMC Place; HENRICO; *245 I-14; ★ RICH; mail Richmond z 23230; ● 600
DICKENSON; 244 C-5; Ⓟ 17,620; Ⓒ 16,395; ◆ 16,344
Dickensonville; RMC Place; RUSSELL; *244 D-5; mail Castlewood z 24224; ● 30
Diggs; RMC Place; MATHEWS; 245 J-17; elev. 5ft./2m.; 🅿; ★ NN-H; z 23045; ● 80
Diggs Park; RMC Place; NORFOLK (Independent City); *245 L-18; ★ NORF-; mail Norfolk z 23523; pop. incl. with Norfolk (Independent City)
Dillard's Landing (Trails End); RMC Place; NEW KENT; *245 J-15; elev. 20ft./6m.; mail Providence Forge z 23140; ● 90
Dillwyn; Inc. Place; BUCKINGHAM; 245 J-11; 🅿; z 23936; Ⓟ 458; Ⓒ 447
Dinwiddie; RMC Place; ⊡ DINWIDDIE; 245 L-13; 🅿; z 23841; ● 200
DINWIDDIE; 245 L-14; Ⓟ 20,960; Ⓒ 24,533; ◆ 26,314
Dinwiddie Gardens; RMC Place; DINWIDDIE; *245 K-14; ★ RICH; mail Petersburg z 23803; ● 280
Disputanta; RMC Place; PRINCE GEORGE; 245 K-15; 🅿; z 23842; ● 550
Ditchley; RMC Place; NORTHUMBERLAND; *245 I-17; mail Kilmarnock z 22482; rural
Dixie; RMC Place; FLUVANNA; 245 I-11; mail Fork Union z 23055; ● 30
Dixie; RMC Place; MATHEWS; *245 J-17; ★ NN-H; mail Dutton z 23050; ● 30
Dixie Hill; RMC Place; FAIRFAX; *245 E-14; ★ WASH; mail Fairfax z 22030; ● 300
Dockery; RMC Place; MECKLENBURG; *245 M-12; elev. 367ft./112m.; mail South Hill z 23970; rural
Doe Hill; RMC Place; HIGHLAND; 244 F-8; 🅿; z 24433; ● 50
Dogtown; RMC Place; GOOCHLAND; *245 I-12; elev. 295ft./90m.; mail Goochland z 23063; ● 60
Dogue; RMC Place; KING GEORGE; *245 G-14; elev. 107ft./33m.; 🅿; z 22451; ● 70
Dogue Creek Village; RMC Place; FAIRFAX; ★ WASH; mail Fort Belvoir z 22060
Dogwood Hill; RMC Place; STAUNTON (Independent City); *244 G-9; mail Staunton z 24401; pop. incl. with Staunton (Independent City)
Dogwood Knoll; RMC Place; HANOVER; *245 I-14; ★ RICH; mail Mechanicsville z 23111
Dolphin; RMC Place; BRUNSWICK; 245 M-13; elev. 322ft./98m.; 🅿; z 23843; ● 80
Dominion Heights; RMC Place; ARLINGTON; *245 D-15; ★ WASH; mail Arlington z 22207
Dominion Hills; RMC Place; ARLINGTON; *245 D-15; ★ WASH; mail Arlington z 22205
Dona; RMC Place; LEE; *244 E-3; elev. 1,172ft./357m.; mail Blackwater z 24221; rural
Donna Lee Gardens; RMC Place; FAIRFAX; *245 D-14; ★ WASH; mail Falls Church z 22046
Dooms; CDP; AUGUSTA; 244 H-9; mail Waynesboro z 22980; Ⓟ 1,307; Ⓒ 1,282
Doran; RMC Place; TAZEWELL; *244 C-6; 🅿; z 24612; ● 400
Dorchester; RMC Place; RICHMOND (Independent City); ★ RICH; mail Richmond z 23234; pop. incl. with Richmond (Independent City)
Dorchester; RMC Place; WISE; *244 C-4; mail Norton z 24273; ● 100
Dorchester Junction; RMC Place; WISE; *244 C-4; mail Norton z 24273; pop. incl. with Norton (Independent City)
Dorset Woods; RMC Place; HENRICO; *245 J-13; elev. 210ft./64m.; ★ RICH; mail Henrico z 23075; ● 450
Doswell; RMC Place; HANOVER; 245 H-14; 🅿; z 23047; ● 200
Dot; RMC Place; LEE; *244 D-3; elev. 1,486ft./453m.; mail Pennington Gap z 24277; ● 30
Double Tollgate; RMC Place; CLARKE; *245 D-12; mail White Post z 22663
Douglas Park; RMC Place; PORTSMOUTH (Independent City); *245 L-17; ★ NORF-; mail Portsmouth z 23702; pop. incl. with Portsmouth (Independent City)
Douglass Park; RMC Place; ARLINGTON; *245 D-15; ★ WASH; mail Arlington z 22204
Doveville; RMC Place; FAIRFAX; *245 E-14; ★ WASH; mail Fairfax z 22032; ● 420
Dowden Terrace; RMC Place; FAIRFAX; *245 E-15; ★ WASH; mail Alexandria z 22311; ● 2,500
Downings; RMC Place; RICHMOND; *245 H-16; elev. 127ft./39m.; mail Farnham z 22460
Downtown; RMC Place; CHARLOTTESVILLE (Independent City); ★ CHRLTV; mail Charlottesville z 22902; pop. incl. with Charlottesville (Independent City)
Downtown; RMC Place; LOUDOUN; ★ WASH; mail Leesburg z 20175, z 20178; pop. incl. with Leesburg (Inc. Place)
Downtown; RMC Place; LYNCHBURG (Independent City); ★ LYNCH; mail Lynchburg z 24505; pop. incl. with Lynchburg (Independent City)
Downtown; RMC Place; MANASSAS (Independent City); ★ WASH; mail Manassas z 20110; pop. incl. with Manassas (Independent City)
Downtown; RMC Place; MONTGOMERY; mail Blacksburg z 24063; pop. incl. with Blacksburg (Inc. Place)
Doylesville; RMC Place; ALBEMARLE; *244 G-10; elev. 666ft./203m.; mail Crozet z 22932
Drakes Branch; Inc. Place; CHARLOTTE; 244 L-10; elev. 383ft./117m.; 🅿; z 23937; Ⓟ 565; Ⓒ 504
Dranesville; RMC Place; FAIRFAX; 249 D-1; ★ WASH; mail Herndon z 20170; ● 430
Draper; RMC Place; PULASKI; 244 L-3; elev. 2,144ft./653m.; 🅿; z 24324; ● 280
Drewryville; RMC Place; SOUTHAMPTON; 245 M-14; 🅿; z 23844; ● 310
Drill; RMC Place; RUSSELL; *244 C-6; mail Honaker z 24260
Driver; RMC Place; SUFFOLK (Independent City); *245 L-17; ★ NORF-; mail Suffolk z 23435; pop. incl. with Suffolk (Independent City)
Drouin Hill; RMC Place; HENRICO; *245 J-13; elev. 200ft./61m.; ★ RICH; mail Henrico z 23075; ● 250
Drum Bay; RMC Place; WESTMORELAND; *245 G-16; mail Hague z 22469; ● 80
Dry Branch; RMC Place; PULASKI; *244 K-4; elev. 1,726ft./526m.; mail Parrott z 24132; ● 50
Dryburg; RMC Place; HALIFAX; *244 M-10; elev. 409ft./125m.; mail Scottsburg z 24589; ● 50
Dryden; CDP; LEE; 244 D-3; elev. 1,440ft./439m.; 🅿; z 24243; Ⓒ 1,253
Dry Fork; RMC Place; PITTSYLVANIA; 244 M-8; elev. 631ft./192m.; 🅿; z 24549; ● 150
Dry Fork; RMC Place; WISE; *244 C-5; mail Coeburn z 24230; rural
Drytown; RMC Place; TAZEWELL; *244 K-1; mail North Tazewell z 24630; rural
Duane; RMC Place; KING WILLIAM; *245 H-14; elev. 184ft./56m.; mail Aylett z 23009; rural
Dublin; Inc. Place; PULASKI; 244 L-4; 🅿; z 24084; Ⓟ 2,012; Ⓒ 2,288
Dudley; RMC Place; HALIFAX; *244 M-9; elev. 496ft./151m.; mail Halifax z 24558; ● 30
Duffield; Inc. Place; SCOTT; 244 D-3; elev. 1,365ft./416m.; 🅿; z 24244; Ⓟ 54; Ⓒ 62
Dugspur; RMC Place; CARROLL; 244 M-4; 🅿; z 24325; ● 70
Dugwell; RMC Place; FRANKLIN; *244 L-6; mail Rocky Mount z 24151; ● 40
Duke; RMC Place; ALEXANDRIA (Independent City); *245 E-15; ★ WASH; mail Alexandria z 22304; pop. incl. with Alexandria (Independent City)
Dumbarton; CDP; HENRICO; *245 I-14; ★ RICH; mail Henrico z 23228; Ⓟ 8,526; Ⓒ 6,674
Dumfries; Inc. Place; PRINCE WILLIAM; 245 F-14; 🅿; ★ WASH; z 22025-26; Ⓟ 4,282; Ⓒ 4,937
Dunavant; RMC Place; SPOTSYLVANIA; *245 F-13; ★ FRED; mail Fredericksburg z 22401; rural
Dunbar; RMC Place; WISE; 244 C-3; mail Appalachia z 24216; ● 130
Dunbar Gardens; RMC Place; HAMPTON (Independent City); ★ NN-H; mail Hampton z 23666; pop. incl. with Hampton (Independent City)
Dunbrooke; RMC Place; ESSEX; *245 H-15; mail Tappahannock z 22560; ● 50
Duncan Gap; RMC Place; WISE; *244 C-4; mail Wise z 24293; ● 140
Duncans Mills; RMC Place; SCOTT; *244 D-4; mail Duffield z 24244; rural
Duncanville; RMC Place; WASHINGTON; *244 D-6; mail Abingdon z 24210; rural
Dundalow; RMC Place; SUFFOLK (Independent City); ★ NORF-; mail Suffolk z 23434; pop. incl. with Suffolk (Independent City)
Dundas; RMC Place; LUNENBURG; 245 L-12; elev. 456ft./139m.; 🅿; z 23938; ● 150
Dundee; RMC Place; ROANOKE; *244 K-6; elev. 1,000ft./305m.; ★ ROAN; mail Roanoke z 24014; ● 100
Dunford Town; RMC Place; TAZEWELL; *244 K-1; mail Bandy z 24602; rural
Dungadin Heights; RMC Place; WARREN; *245 D-11; mail Front Royal z 22630; ● 100
Dungannon; Inc. Place; SCOTT; 244 D-4; elev. 1,311ft./400m.; 🅿; z 24245; Ⓟ 250; Ⓒ 317
Dunlop; RMC Place; COLONIAL HEIGHTS (Independent City); *245 K-14; ★ RICH; mail Colonial Heights z 23834; pop. incl. with Colonial Heights (Independent City)
Dunn Loring; CDP; FAIRFAX; 249 F-3; 🅿; ★ WASH; z 22027 & mail Vienna z 22180, z 22182; Ⓟ 6,509; Ⓒ 7,861
Dunn Loring Woods; RMC Place; FAIRFAX; *245 D-14; ★ WASH; mail Vienna z 22180; ● 2,900
Dunnsville; RMC Place; ESSEX; 245 H-16; 🅿; z 22454; ● 150
Durmid; RMC Place; LYNCHBURG (Independent City); ★ LYNCH; pop. incl. with Lynchburg (Independent City)
Durrett Town; RMC Place; NELSON; *244 H-9; elev. 900ft./274m.; mail Afton z 22920; ● 40
Dutton; RMC Place; GLOUCESTER; 245 J-17; elev. 66ft./20m.; 🅿; z 23050; ● 270
Duty; RMC Place; BUCHANAN, DICKENSON; *244 C-5; mail Bee z 24217; ● 30
Dwale; RMC Place; DICKENSON; *244 B-5; mail Clintwood z 24228; rural
Dwina; RMC Place; WISE; *244 C-5; mail Coeburn z 24230; rural
Dye; RMC Place; RUSSELL; *244 C-6; mail Swords Creek z 24649
Dyers; RMC Place; HENRY; *244 M-6; ★ MRTNV; mail Martinsville z 24112; rural
Dyke; RMC Place; GREENE; 244 G-10; 🅿; z 22935; ● 50

E

Eads; RMC Place; ARLINGTON; ***245** D-15; ★ **WASH**; mail Arlington z 22202
Eagle Rock; RMC Place; BOTETOURT; **244** I-6; 🅿; z 24085; ● 350
Earlhurst; RMC Place; ALLEGHANY; ***244** I-5; mail Covington z 24426; rural
Earls; RMC Place; AMELIA; **245** K-12; mail Amelia Court House z 23002; ● 30
Earlysville; RMC Place; ALBEMARLE; ***244** G-10; 🅿; ★ **CHRLTV**; z 22936 & mail Barboursville z 22923; ● 200
East Brook; RMC Place; CAMPBELL; ***244** J-9; ★ **LYNCH**; mail Lynchburg z 24501; ● 280
East End; RMC Place; RICHMOND (Independent City); ★ **RICH**; mail Richmond z 23223; pop. incl. with Richmond (Independent City)
East Falls Church; RMC Place; ARLINGTON; ***245** D-15; ★ **WASH**; mail Arlington z 22205
Eastham; RMC Place; ALBEMARLE; ***245** H-11; ★ **CHRLTV**; mail Charlottesville z 22911; rural
East Hampton; RMC Place; HAMPTON (Independent City); ***245** L-17; ★ **NN-H**; mail Hampton z 23669; pop. incl. with Hampton (Independent City)
East Highland Park; CDP; HENRICO; ***245** J-14; ★ **RICH**; mail Richmond z 23222; ℗ 11,850; © 12,488
East Lexington; RMC Place; ROCKBRIDGE; **244** I-7; mail Lexington z 24450; ● 350
Eastmoreland; RMC Place; HENRICO; ★ **RICH**; mail Henrico z 23231
East Norton; RMC Place; NORTON (Independent City); mail Norton z 24273; pop. incl. with Norton (Independent City)
East Norview; RMC Place; NORFOLK (Independent City); ***245** L-18; ★ **NORF-**; mail Norfolk z 23513; pop. incl. with Norfolk (Independent City)
East Ocean View; RMC Place; NORFOLK (Independent City); ***245** L-18; ★ **NORF-**; mail Norfolk z 23503; pop. incl. with Norfolk (Independent City)
Easton Place; RMC Place; NORFOLK (Independent City); ***245** L-18; ★ **NORF-**; mail Norfolk z 23502; pop. incl. with Norfolk (Independent City)
Eastover; RMC Place; SUFFOLK (Independent City); ★ **NORF-**; mail Suffolk z 23434; pop. incl. with Suffolk (Independent City)
Eastover Gardens; RMC Place; HENRICO; ***245** J-14; ★ **RICH**; mail Henrico z 23231; ● 1,200
East Point; RMC Place; ACCOMACK; ***245** I-19; mail Onancock z 23417; ● 80
East Point; RMC Place; ROCKINGHAM; ***244** F-10; elev. 996ft./304m.; mail Elkton z 22827; rural
East Radford; RMC Place; RADFORD (Independent City); mail Radford z 24141; pop. incl. with Radford (Independent City)
East Stone Gap; RMC Place; WISE; **244** D-3; 🅿; z 24246; ● 500
East Suffolk Gardens; RMC Place; SUFFOLK (Independent City); ★ **NORF-**; mail Suffolk z 23434; pop. incl. with Suffolk (Independent City)
Eastville; Inc. Place; ⊡ NORTHAMPTON; **245** J-19; 🅿; z 23347; ℗ 185; © 203
Eastville Station; RMC Place; NORTHAMPTON; ***245** J-19; mail Eastville z 23347
Ebenezer; RMC Place; PITTSYLVANIA; ***244** M-8; mail Java z 24565; rural
Ebony; RMC Place; BRUNSWICK; **245** N-12; elev. 341ft./104m.; 🅿; z 23845; ● 100
Eclipse; RMC Place; SUFFOLK (Independent City); ★ **NORF-**; mail Suffolk z 23433; pop. incl. with Suffolk (Independent City)
Edgehill; RMC Place; KING GEORGE; **245** G-15; mail King George z 22485; ● 240
Edgehill; RMC Place; SOUTHAMPTON; ***245** M-15; elev. 33ft./10m.; mail Franklin z 23851; ● 250
Edgehill Park; RMC Place; DINWIDDIE; ***245** K-14; elev. 150ft./46m.; ★ **RICH**; mail Petersburg z 23803; ● 160
Edgemont; RMC Place; COVINGTON (Independent City); ***244** I-6; mail Covington z 24426; pop. incl. with Covington (Independent City)
Edgerton; RMC Place; BRUNSWICK; ***245** M-13; elev. 318ft./97m.; mail Lawrenceville z 23868
Edgewater; RMC Place; NORFOLK (Independent City); ***245** L-17; ★ **NORF-**; mail Norfolk z 23508; pop. incl. with Norfolk (Independent City)
Edgewood; RMC Place; PETERSBURG (Independent City); ★ **RICH**; mail Petersburg z 23805; pop. incl. with Petersburg (Independent City)
Edgewood; RMC Place; ROANOKE (Independent City); ***244** K-6; ★ **ROAN**; pop. incl. with Roanoke (Independent City)
Edinburg; Inc. Place; SHENANDOAH; **244** E-10; 🅿; z 22824; ℗ 860; © 813
Edmonds Corner; RMC Place; CHESAPEAKE (Independent City); ***245** M-18; ★ **NORF-**; mail Chesapeake z 23324; pop. incl. with Chesapeake (Independent City)
Ednam Forest; RMC Place; ALBEMARLE; **243** B-1; ★ **CHRLTV**; mail Charlottesville z 22903; ● 700
Edom; RMC Place; ROCKINGHAM; ***244** F-9; mail Linville z 22834
Edsall Park; RMC Place; FAIRFAX; ***245** E-15; ★ **WASH**; mail Springfield z 22151; ● 2,000
Edwards Shop; RMC Place; CULPEPER; ***245** F-13; mail Elkwood z 22718; ● 30
Edwardsville; RMC Place; NORTHUMBERLAND; ***245** H-17; elev. 82ft./25m.; 🅿; z 22456; ● 110
Effinger; RMC Place; ROCKBRIDGE; ***244** I-7; mail Lexington z 24450; rural
Eggleston; RMC Place; GILES; **244** K-4; 🅿; z 24086; ● 270
Eheart; RMC Place; ORANGE; **245** G-11; 🅿; z 22923; ● 90
Elam; RMC Place; PRINCE EDWARD; ***244** K-10; elev. 698ft./213m.; mail Prospect z 23960; rural
Elberon; RMC Place; SURRY; **245** L-16; elev. 116ft./35m.; 🅿; z 23846; ● 50
Elephant Fork; RMC Place; SUFFOLK (Independent City); ★ **NORF-**; mail Suffolk z 23434; pop. incl. with Suffolk (Independent City)
Elevon; RMC Place; CAROLINE, ESSEX; ***245** H-15; elev. 188ft./57m.; mail Champlain z 22438; rural
Elizabeth Park; RMC Place; NORFOLK (Independent City); ***245** L-18; ★ **NORF-**; mail Norfolk z 23502; pop. incl. with Norfolk (Independent City)
Elizabeth River Shores; RMC Place; VIRGINIA BEACH (Independent City); ***245** L-18; ★ **NORF-**; mail Virginia Beach z 23464; pop. incl. with Virginia Beach (Independent City)
Elk Creek; RMC Place; GRAYSON; **244** M-2; elev. 2,617ft./798m.; 🅿; z 24326; ● 150
Elk Garden; RMC Place; RUSSELL; ***244** C-6; elev. 2,132ft./650m.; 🅿; z 24260 & mail Lebanon z 24266; ● 50
Elk Hill; RMC Place; GOOCHLAND; ***245** I-12; mail Goochland z 23063; rural
Elko; RMC Place; HENRICO; ***245** J-15; elev. 78ft./24m.; ★ **RICH**; mail Sandston z 23150; rural
Elk Run; RMC Place; FAUQUIER; ***245** F-13; mail Midland z 22728; ● 50
Elkton; Inc. Place; ROCKINGHAM; **244** F-10; 🅿; z 22827; ℗ 1,935; © 2,042
Elkwood; RMC Place; CULPEPER; ***245** F-12; elev. 321ft./98m.; 🅿; z 22718; ● 140
Ellett; RMC Place; MONTGOMERY; ***244** K-5; mail Blacksburg z 24060, Christiansburg z 24073; ● 120
Elliston; RMC Place; MONTGOMERY; **244** K-5; 🅿; ★ **ROAN**; z 24087; ● 950
Elliston-Lafayette; CDP-Census Area Only; MONTGOMERY; ***244** K-5; ★ **ROAN**; mail Elliston z 24087; ℗ 1,243; © 1,241
Ellisville; RMC Place; LOUISA; ***245** H-12; elev. 410ft./125m.; mail Louisa z 23093; ● 30
Ellsworth; RMC Place; NORFOLK (Independent City); ***245** L-18; ★ **NORF-**; mail Norfolk z 23505; pop. incl. with Norfolk (Independent City)
Elma; RMC Place; NELSON; ***244** I-10; elev. 664ft./202m.; mail Shipman z 22971; rural
Elmhurst; RMC Place; NORFOLK (Independent City); ***245** L-18; ★ **NORF-**; mail Norfolk z 23513; pop. incl. with Norfolk (Independent City)
Elmo; RMC Place; HALIFAX; **244** M-9; elev. 560ft./171m.; mail South Boston z 24592; ● 30
Elmont; RMC Place; HANOVER; **245** I-14; elev. 219ft./67m.; ★ **RICH**; mail Ashland z 23005; ● 300
Elmwood Estates; RMC Place; FAIRFAX; ***245** D-14; ★ **WASH**; mail Mc Lean z 22101
El-Nido; RMC Place; FAIRFAX; ***245** D-15; ★ **WASH**; mail Mc Lean z 22101
Elon; RMC Place; AMHERST; **244** J-8; mail Madison Heights z 24572; ● 200
Elsom; RMC Place; KING AND QUEEN; ***245** J-16; mail West Point z 23181; rural
Eltham; RMC Place; NEW KENT; ***245** J-16; mail West Point z 23181; ● 300
Elysian Woods; RMC Place; PRINCE WILLIAM; ***245** E-14; ★ **WASH**; mail Woodbridge z 22192; ● 400
Emerald Hills; RMC Place; AUGUSTA; ***244** G-9; elev. 1,300ft./396m.; mail Fishersville z 22939; ● 50
Emmerton; RMC Place; RICHMOND; ***245** H-16; mail Warsaw z 22572; ● 100
Emory; RMC Place; WASHINGTON; **244** D-6; elev. 2,135ft./651m.; 🅿 🅲 996; z 24327; ● 1,300
Emory-Meadow View; CDP-Census Area Only; WASHINGTON; ***244** D-6; mail Emory z 24327, Meadowview z 24361; ℗ 2,248; © 2,266
Emporia; Independent City; serves as county seat of Greensville; **245** M-14; 🅿 🅷; z 23847; ℗ 5,306; © 5,665; ◆ 5,569
Endicott; RMC Place; FRANKLIN; ***244** L-5; elev. 1,162ft./354m.; mail Ferrum z 24088; rural
Enfield; RMC Place; KING WILLIAM; ***245** I-14; elev. 166ft./51m.; mail Manquin z 23106
Engleside; FAIRFAX; see Mount Vernon (CDP)
English Hills; RMC Place; HENRICO; ***245** I-13; ★ **RICH**; mail Henrico z 23228; ● 2,100
Enonville; RMC Place; BUCKINGHAM; ***244** J-10; elev. 666ft./203m.; mail Dillwyn z 23936; rural
Eppes Fork; RMC Place; MECKLENBURG; ***245** N-11; mail Townsville z 27584; rural
Epworth; RMC Place; KING WILLIAM; ***245** I-14; elev. 187ft./57m.; mail Aylett z 23009; rural
Erica; RMC Place; WESTMORELAND; ***245** G-16; elev. 16ft./5m.; mail Montross z 22520; rural
Esmont; RMC Place; ALBEMARLE; **244** I-10; 🅿; z 22937; ● 180
Esnon; RMC Place; MECKLENBURG; ***245** M-11; elev. 508ft./155m.; mail Chase City z 23924; rural
Esserville; RMC Place; WISE; **244** C-4; elev. 2,109ft./643m.; mail Norton z 24273
ESSEX; **245** H-15; ℗ 8,689; © 9,989; ◆ 11,225
Estabrook; RMC Place; NORFOLK (Independent City); ***245** L-18; ★ **NORF-**; mail Norfolk z 23513; pop. incl. with Norfolk (Independent City)
Estabrook Park; RMC Place; NORFOLK (Independent City); ***245** L-18; ★ **NORF-**; mail Norfolk z 23513; pop. incl. with Norfolk (Independent City)
Estaline; RMC Place; AUGUSTA; ***244** H-8; mail Craigsville z 24430; rural
Estes; RMC Place; RAPPAHANNOCK; ***245** E-12; mail Castleton z 22716
Ethel; RMC Place; RICHMOND; ***245** H-16; mail Warsaw z 22572; rural
Ethridge Estates; RMC Place; PRINCE GEORGE; ***245** K-14; elev. 150ft./46m.; ★ **RICH**; mail Petersburg z 23805; ● 150
Etlan; RMC Place; MADISON; **245** F-11; 🅿; z 22719; ● 100
Ettrick; CDP; CHESTERFIELD; **245** K-14; 🅿; ★ **RICH**; z 23803; ℗ 5,290; © 5,627
Euclid; RMC Place; VIRGINIA BEACH (Independent City); ***245** L-18; ★ **NORF-**; mail Virginia Beach z 23462; pop. incl. with Virginia Beach (Independent City)
Euclid Terrace; RMC Place; VIRGINIA BEACH (Independent City); ***245** L-18; elev. 20ft./6m.; ★ **NORF-**; mail Virginia Beach z 23462; pop. incl. with Virginia Beach (Independent City)
Eureka; RMC Place; CHARLOTTE; ***244** L-10; elev. 519ft./158m.; mail Keysville z 23947; ● 30
Eureka Park; RMC Place; VIRGINIA BEACH (Independent City); ***245** L-18; ★ **NORF-**; mail Virginia Beach z 23452; pop. incl. with Virginia Beach (Independent City)
Eustaces Corner; RMC Place; FAUQUIER; ***245** E-13; mail Midland z 22728; rural
Euwanee Park; RMC Place; NORFOLK (Independent City); ***245** L-18; ★ **NORF-**; mail Norfolk z 23503; pop. incl. with Norfolk (Independent City)
Evans Wharf; RMC Place; ACCOMACK; ***245** I-19; elev. 5ft./2m.; mail Onancock z 23417; rural
Everets; RMC Place; SUFFOLK (Independent City); ***245** L-17; ★ **NORF-**; mail Suffolk z 23434; pop. incl. with Suffolk (Independent City)
Evergreen; RMC Place; APPOMATTOX; **244** K-10; elev. 732ft./223m.; 🅿; z 23939; ● 170
Evergreen Hills; RMC Place; WASHINGTON; ***244** D-6; ★ **JNSC-**; mail Bristol z 24202; ● 170
Evergreen Shores; RMC Place; YORK; ***245** K-17; ★ **NN-H**; mail Seaford z 23696
Evington; RMC Place; CAMPBELL; **244** K-8; 🅿; ★ **LYNCH**; z 24550; ● 200
Ewell; RMC Place; JAMES CITY; **243** F-2; ★ **NN-H**; mail Williamsburg z 23185; ● 40
Ewing; CDP; LEE; **244** D-1; elev. 1,393ft./425m.; 🅿; z 24248; © 436
Exeter; RMC Place; WISE; ***244** C-3; 🅿; z 24216; ● 500
Exmore; Inc. Place; NORTHAMPTON; **245** J-19; 🅿; z 23350; ℗ 1,115; © 1,136

F

Faber; RMC Place; NELSON; **244** I-10; 🅿; z 22938; ● 150
Fagg; RMC Place; MONTGOMERY; ***244** K-5; mail Elliston z 24087; rural
Fairchester; RMC Place; FAIRFAX (Independent City); ***245** D-14; ★ **WASH**; mail Fairfax z 22030; pop. incl. with Fairfax (Independent City)
Fairfax; FAIRFAX; see Fairfax Station (RMC Place)
Fairfax; Independent City; serves as county seat of Fairfax; **245** E-14; elev. 447ft./136m.; 🅿 🅷 🅲 29,889 ■; ★ **WASH**; z 20151-53, z 20598, z 22030-38 & mail Fairfax Station z 22039; ℗ 19,622; © 21,498; ◆ 24,135
FAIRFAX; **245** E-14; ℗ 818,584; © 969,749; ◆ 1,007,756
Fairfax Acres; RMC Place; FAIRFAX; ***245** D-14; ★ **WASH**; mail Fairfax z 22030; ● 740
Fairfax Circle; RMC Place; FAIRFAX (Independent City); ***245** D-14; ★ **WASH**; mail Fairfax z 22031; pop. incl. with Fairfax (Independent City)
Fairfax Forest; RMC Place; FAIRFAX; ***245** D-14; ★ **WASH**; mail Fairfax z 22031; ● 760
Fairfax Station (Fairfax); RMC Place; FAIRFAX; **249** H-1; 🅿; ★ **WASH**; z 20151-53, z 22030-39; ● 210
Fairfax Villa; RMC Place; FAIRFAX; ***245** E-14; ★ **WASH**; mail Fairfax z 22030; ● 2,400
Fairfax Woods; RMC Place; FAIRFAX (Independent City); ***245** D-14; ★ **WASH**; mail Fairfax z 22030; pop. incl. with Fairfax (Independent City)
Fairfield; RMC Place; ESSEX; mail Dunnsville z 22454; ● 30
Fairfield; RMC Place; ROCKBRIDGE; **244** H-8; 🅿; z 24435; ● 600
Fairfield Park; RMC Place; PITTSYLVANIA; ***244** M-8; elev. 667ft./203m.; ★ **DANV**; mail Danville z 24540; ● 300
Fairhaven; RMC Place; FAIRFAX; ***245** E-15; ★ **WASH**; mail Alexandria z 22303; ● 1,800
Fair Hill; RMC Place; FAIRFAX; ***245** D-14; ★ **WASH**; mail Fairfax z 22031
Fairland; RMC Place; FAIRFAX; ***245** E-15; ★ **WASH**; mail Alexandria z 22312; ● 610
Fairlawn; RMC Place; COVINGTON (Independent City); ***244** I-6; mail Covington z 24426; pop. incl. with Covington (Independent City)
Fairlawn; CDP; PULASKI; **244** K-4; 🅿; z 24141; ℗ 2,399; © 2,211
Fairlawn Estates; RMC Place; NORFOLK (Independent City); ***245** L-18; ★ **NORF-**; mail Norfolk z 23502; pop. incl. with Norfolk (Independent City)
Fairlawn Heights; RMC Place; HENRICO; ***245** J-14; ★ **RICH**; mail Henrico z 23075; ● 3,080
Fairlee; RMC Place; FAIRFAX; ***245** D-14; ★ **WASH**; mail Fairfax z 22031
Fair Meadows; RMC Place; VIRGINIA BEACH (Independent City); ***245** L-18; ★ **NORF-**; mail Virginia Beach z 23462; pop. incl. with Virginia Beach (Independent City)
Fairmount Park; RMC Place; NORFOLK (Independent City); ***245** L-18; ★ **NORF-**; mail Norfolk z 23509; pop. incl. with Norfolk (Independent City)
Fair Oaks; RMC Place; FAIRFAX (Independent City); ***245** E-14; ★ **WASH**; mail Fairfax z 22032; pop. incl. with Fairfax (Independent City)
Fair Oaks; RMC Place; HENRICO; **243** C-10; ★ **RICH**; mail Henrico z 23075; ● 200
Fair Port; RMC Place; NORTHUMBERLAND; **245** H-17; mail Reedville z 22539; ● 450
Fairview; RMC Place; FAIRFAX; ***245** D-14; ★ **WASH**; mail Alexandria z 22306; pop. incl. with Fairfax (Independent City)
Fairview; RMC Place; MECKLENBURG; ***245** M-11; mail Chase City z 23924; pop. incl. with Chase City (Inc. Place)
Fairview; RMC Place; MONTGOMERY; ***244** L-4; mail Christiansburg z 24073, Riner z 24149; rural
Fairview; RMC Place; NORTHAMPTON; ***245** K-18; elev. 29ft./9m.; mail Cape Charles z 23310; ● 150
Fairview; RMC Place; PAGE; ***245** E-11; mail Luray z 22835; pop. incl. with Luray (Inc. Place)
Fairview; RMC Place; SCOTT; ***244** D-3; elev. 1,208ft./368m.; mail Duffield z 24244
Fairview Beach; CDP; KING GEORGE; **245** G-14; mail Fredericksburg z 22405; © 230
Fairview Farms; RMC Place; HAMPTON (Independent City); ***245** L-17; ★ **NN-H**; mail Hampton z 23669; pop. incl. with Hampton (Independent City)
Fairview Heights; RMC Place; ALLEGHANY; mail Clifton Forge z 24422; pop. incl. with Clifton Forge (Inc. Place)
Fairview Heights; RMC Place; LEXINGTON (Independent City); mail Lexington z 24450; pop. incl. with Lexington (Independent City)
Fairview Heights; RMC Place; LYNCHBURG (Independent City); ★ **LYNCH**; mail Lynchburg z 24501; pop. incl. with Lynchburg (Independent City)
Fairwood; RMC Place; GRAYSON; ***244** M-1; mail Troutdale z 24378; rural
Fairwood Acres; RMC Place; FAIRFAX; ***245** E-14; ★ **WASH**; mail Fairfax Station z 22039; ● 80
Falconbridge; RMC Place; CHESTERFIELD; ***245** J-14; elev. 150ft./46m.; ★ **RICH**; mail Richmond z 23234; ● 400
Falconerville; RMC Place; AMHERST; ***244** J-9; ★ **LYNCH**; mail Amherst z 24521; ● 100
Falling Creek; RMC Place; CHESTERFIELD; ★ **RICH**; mail Richmond z 23234
Falling Creek Court; RMC Place; CHESTERFIELD; ★ **RICH**; mail Richmond z 23234
Falling Creek Hills; RMC Place; CHESTERFIELD; ★ **RICH**; mail Richmond z 23234
Falling Spring; RMC Place; ALLEGHANY; **244** H-6; elev. 1,397ft./426m.; mail Hot Springs z 24445; ● 150
Falls Church; Independent City; **245** D-14; 🅿 🅷 🅲 793 ■; ★ **WASH**; z 20598, z 22040-44, z 22046; ℗ 9,578; © 10,377; ◆ 11,070
Falls Hill; RMC Place; FAIRFAX; ***245** D-14; ★ **WASH**; mail Falls Church z 22043; ● 2,680
Falls Mills; RMC Place; TAZEWELL; **244** K-2; 🅿; z 24613; ● 450
Fallville; RMC Place; GRAYSON; ***244** M-2; elev. 2,695ft./821m.; mail Elk Creek z 24326; rural
Falmouth; CDP; STAFFORD; **245** G-14; 🅿; ★ **FRED**; z 22403, z 22405-06, z 22412; ℗ 3,541; © 3,624
Falwell; RMC Place; LYNCHBURG (Independent City); ★ **LYNCH**; pop. incl. with Lynchburg (Independent City)
Fancy Gap; CDP; CARROLL; **244** M-3; 🅿; z 24328; © 260
Fancy Hill; RMC Place; AMHERST; ***244** I-8; mail Amherst z 24521; rural
Fancy Hill; RMC Place; ROCKBRIDGE; ***244** I-7; elev. 1,250ft./381m.; mail Glasgow z 24555; ● 30
Farmers; RMC Place; CAROLINE; ***245** H-14; mail Woodford z 22580; ● 70
Farmers Fork; RMC Place; ESSEX; ***245** H-15; mail Loretto z 22509; rural
Farmers Fork; RMC Place; RICHMOND; ***245** H-16; mail Warsaw z 22572; ● 30
Farmers Store; RMC Place; WYTHE; ***244** L-3; elev. 2,163ft./659m.; mail Max Meadows z 24360; rural
Farmingdale; RMC Place; HOPEWELL (Independent City); ★ **RICH**; mail Hopewell z 23860; pop. incl. with Hopewell (Independent City)
Farmington; RMC Place; ALBEMARLE; **243** B-1; ★ **CHRLTV**; mail Charlottesville z 22901; ● 250
Farmington; RMC Place; HENRICO; ***245** I-13; elev. 240ft./73m.; ★ **RICH**; mail Henrico z 23229; ● 3,600
Farmville; Inc. Place; ⊡ PRINCE EDWARD, CUMBERLAND; **245** K-11; 🅿 🅷 🅲 4,380; z 23901, z 23909, z 23943; ℗ 6,046; © 6,845
Farnham; RMC Place; RICHMOND; **245** H-16; 🅿; z 22460; ● 320
Faulconerville; RMC Place; AMHERST; ***244** J-9; elev. 886ft./270m.; ★ **LYNCH**; mail Amherst z 24521; ● 30
FAUQUIER; **245** E-12; ℗ 48,741; © 55,139; ◆ 64,341
Fauquier White Sulphur Springs; RMC Place; FAUQUIER; ***245** E-12; mail Warrenton z 20186
Favonia; RMC Place; WYTHE; **244** L-2; elev. 2,259ft./689m.; mail Wytheville z 24382; ● 130
Fawcett Gap; RMC Place; FREDERICK; ***245** C-11; mail Winchester z 22602; rural
Fayette Park; RMC Place; HENRICO; ***245** I-14; ★ **RICH**; mail Richmond z 23222; ● 350
Featherstone; RMC Place; PRINCE WILLIAM; ***245** E-14; ★ **WASH**; mail Woodbridge z 22191
Featherstone Shores; RMC Place; PRINCE WILLIAM; ***245** E-14; ★ **WASH**; mail Woodbridge z 22191
Felipos Mobile Court; RMC Place; CHESTERFIELD; ★ **RICH**; mail Richmond z 23234
Fentress; RMC Place; CHESAPEAKE (Independent City); ***245** M-18; ★ **NORF-**; mail Chesapeake z 23322; pop. incl. with Chesapeake (Independent City)
Fentress; RMC Place; VIRGINIA BEACH (Independent City); ***245** L-18; ★ **NORF-**; mail Virginia Beach z 23451; pop. incl. with Virginia Beach (Independent City)
Fenwick Park; RMC Place; FAIRFAX; ***245** D-14; ★ **WASH**; mail Falls Church z 22042
Fergusonville; RMC Place; NOTTOWAY; ***245** K-12; elev. 400ft./122m.; mail Crewe z 23930; rural
Ferncliff; RMC Place; LOUISA; ***245** H-12; mail Kents Store z 23084, Louisa z 23093; ● 50
Ferndale Gardens; RMC Place; DINWIDDIE; ***245** K-14; elev. 120ft./37m.; ★ **RICH**; mail Petersburg z 23803; ● 140
Ferndale Park; RMC Place; DINWIDDIE; ***245** K-14; elev. 130ft./40m.; ★ **RICH**; mail Petersburg z 23803; ● 90
Ferrum; CDP; FRANKLIN; **244** L-6; elev. 1,300ft./396m.; 🅿 🅲 1,039; z 24088; ℗ 1,514; © 1,313
Ferry Farms; RMC Place; STAFFORD; **245** G-14; ★ **FRED**; mail Fredericksburg z 22401; ● 4,000
Fieldale; CDP; HENRY; **244** M-6; 🅿; ★ **MRTNV**; z 24089; ℗ 1,018; © 929
Fife; RMC Place; GOOCHLAND; **245** I-12; 🅿; z 23063; ● 60
Figsboro; RMC Place; HENRY; ***244** M-6; elev. 1,103ft./336m.; ★ **MRTNV**; mail Martinsville z 24112
File; RMC Place; CAROLINE; ***245** H-14; elev. 192ft./59m.; mail Bowling Green z 22427; rural
Fincastle; Inc. Place; ⊡ BOTETOURT; **244** J-6; 🅿; ★ **ROAN**; z 24090 & mail Troutville z 24175; ℗ 236; © 359
Finchley; RMC Place; MECKLENBURG; **245** M-11; mail Clarksville z 23927; ● 80
Fine Creek Mills; RMC Place; POWHATAN; ***245** I-13; elev. 175ft./53m.; mail Powhatan z 23139; rural
Finney; RUSSELL; see Coulwood (RMC Place)
Finneywood; RMC Place; MECKLENBURG; ***245** L-11; elev. 499ft./152m.; mail Chase City z 23924; rural
First Colony; RMC Place; JAMES CITY; ***245** K-16; elev. 20ft./6m.; ★ **NN-H**; mail Williamsburg z 23188; ● 900
First Street; RMC Place; RADFORD (Independent City); mail Radford z 24141; pop. incl. with Radford (Independent City)
Fishers Hill; RMC Place; SHENANDOAH; **245** D-11; 🅿; z 22626; ● 200
Fishersville; CDP; AUGUSTA; **244** H-9; 🅿 🅷; z 22939 & mail Waynesboro z 22980; ℗ 3,230; © 4,998
Five Forks; RMC Place; AMHERST; **244** J-8; elev. 817ft./249m.; ★ **LYNCH**; mail Amherst z 24521; ● 150
Five Forks; RMC Place; BEDFORD; **245** K-13; elev. 979ft./298m.; mail Bedford z 24523; ● 30
Five Forks; RMC Place; CARROLL; ***244** M-3; mail Hillsville z 24343; ● 50
Five Forks; RMC Place; DINWIDDIE; ***245** K-13; elev. 302ft./92m.; mail Church Road z 23833; rural
Five Forks; RMC Place; HALIFAX; ***244** M-9; elev. 452ft./138m.; mail South Boston z 24592; rural
Five Forks; RMC Place; HOPEWELL (Independent City); ***245** K-14; ★ **RICH**; mail Hopewell z 23860; pop. incl. with Hopewell (Independent City)
Five Forks; RMC Place; JAMES CITY; ***245** K-16; elev. 85ft./26m.; ★ **NN-H**; mail Williamsburg z 23185; ● 200
Five Forks; RMC Place; MADISON; ***245** G-12; mail Orange z 22960; rural
Five Forks; RMC Place; NELSON; ***244** J-9; elev. 604ft./184m.; mail Gladstone z 24553; rural
Five Forks; RMC Place; PRINCE EDWARD; ***244** K-10; elev. 551ft./168m.; mail Pamplin z 23958; rural
Five Lakes; RMC Place; NEW KENT; ***245** J-15; elev. 100ft./30m.; mail Quinton z 23141; ● 300
Five Mile Fork; RMC Place; SPOTSYLVANIA; **245** G-13; ★ **FRED**; mail Fredericksburg z 22401; ● 700
Five Oaks; RMC Place; TAZEWELL; ***244** K-1; mail North Tazewell z 24630; rural
Flactem Manor; RMC Place; PRINCE GEORGE; ***245** K-14; elev. 130ft./40m.; ★ **RICH**; mail Petersburg z 23805; ● 100
Flagpond; RMC Place; SCOTT; ***244** D-3; mail Blackwater z 24221; ● 30
Flat Gap; RMC Place; WISE; ***244** C-4; mail Pound z 24279
Flat Iron; RMC Place; WESTMORELAND; ***245** G-15; elev. 172ft./52m.; mail Montross z 22520; rural
Flatridge; RMC Place; GRAYSON; ***244** M-1; mail Troutdale z 24378; ● 30
Flat Rock; RMC Place; POWHATAN; ***245** J-13; ★ **RICH**; mail Powhatan z 23139
Flatrock; RMC Place; RUSSELL; ***244** C-6; mail Honaker z 24260; ● 30
Flat Run; RMC Place; ORANGE; **245** F-13; mail Locust Grove z 22508; ● 30
Flat Spur; RMC Place; DICKENSON; ***244** C-5; mail Dante z 24237; rural
Flat Top; RMC Place; DICKENSON; ***244** C-5; mail Coeburn z 24230; ● 30
Flat Top; TAZEWELL; see Yards (RMC Place)
Flatwood; RMC Place; WYTHE; ***244** L-3; elev. 2,146ft./654m.; mail Austinville z 24312; ● 30
Flatwoods; RMC Place; BOTETOURT; ***244** J-6; mail Fincastle z 24090; rural
Fleeburg; RMC Place; PAGE; ***244** F-10; mail Shenandoah z 22849; rural
Fleenors; RMC Place; WASHINGTON; ***244** D-5; mail Bristol z 24202; rural
Fleenor Spring (Countis Corner); RMC Place; WASHINGTON; ***244** D-5; ★ **JNSC-**; mail Bristol z 24202; rural
Fleenortown; RMC Place; LEE; ***244** D-2; mail Jonesville z 24263; rural
Fleet; RMC Place; NORFOLK (Independent City); 🅿; ★ **NORF-**; z 23511; pop. incl. with Norfolk (Independent City)
Fleet (Snapp); RMC Place; WASHINGTON; ***244** M-1; mail Glade Spring z 24340; rural
Fleeton; RMC Place; NORTHUMBERLAND; ***245** I-17; mail Reedville z 22539; ● 200
Flemington; RMC Place; DICKENSON; ***244** B-4; mail Clintwood z 24228; rural
Fletcher; RMC Place; GREENE; ***245** F-11; mail Stanardsville z 22973; rural
Fletcherville; RMC Place; FAUQUIER; ***245** E-13; ★ **WASH**; mail Warrenton z 20186; ● 100
Flint Hill; RMC Place; BEDFORD; ***244** K-7; mail Moneta z 24121; rural
Flint Hill; RMC Place; RAPPAHANNOCK; **245** E-12; 🅿; z 22627; ● 400
Floris; RMC Place; FAIRFAX; ***245** D-14; ★ **WASH**; mail Herndon z 20171; ● 350
Floyd; Inc. Place; ⊡ FLOYD; **244** L-5; elev. 2,496ft./761m.; 🅿; z 24091; ℗ 396; © 432
FLOYD; **244** L-4; ℗ 12,005; © 13,874; ◆ 14,567
FLUVANNA; **245** I-11; ℗ 12,429; © 20,047; ◆ 26,252
Foneswood; RMC Place; RICHMOND, WESTMORELAND; ***245** G-15; 🅿; z 22572; ● 30
Fontaine; RMC Place; HENRY; ***244** M-6; ★ **MRTNV**; mail Ridgeway z 24148; ● 50
Ford; RMC Place; DINWIDDIE; **245** K-13; 🅿; z 23850; ● 80
Fordham; RMC Place; HAMPTON (Independent City); ***245** L-17; ★ **NN-H**; mail Hampton z 23663; pop. incl. with Hampton (Independent City)
Ford Park; RMC Place; CHESAPEAKE (Independent City); ***245** L-18; ★ **NORF-**; mail Chesapeake z 23325; pop. incl. with Chesapeake (Independent City)
Forest; CDP; BEDFORD; **244** K-8; 🅿; ★ **LYNCH**; z 24551; ℗ 5,624; © 8,006
Forest Acres; RMC Place; PRINCE GEORGE; ***245** K-14; elev. 150ft./46m.; ★ **RICH**; mail Petersburg z 23805; ● 90
Forest Hill; RMC Place; LYNCHBURG (Independent City); ***244** J-8; ★ **LYNCH**; pop. incl. with Lynchburg (Independent City)
Forest Hill; RMC Place; RICHMOND (Independent City); ★ **RICH**; mail Richmond z 23225; pop. incl. with Richmond (Independent City)
Forest Hills; RMC Place; VIRGINIA BEACH (Independent City); ***245** L-18; ★ **NORF-**; mail Virginia Beach z 23450; pop. incl. with Virginia Beach (Independent City)
Forest Lake Hills; RMC Place; HANOVER; ***245** I-14; ★ **RICH**; mail Mechanicsville z 23116; ● 300
Forest Park; RMC Place; NORFOLK (Independent City); ***245** L-18; ★ **NORF-**; mail Norfolk z 23518; pop. incl. with Norfolk (Independent City)
Forestville; RMC Place; FAIRFAX; ★ **WASH**; mail Great Falls z 22066
Forestville; RMC Place; SHENANDOAH; **244** E-10; mail Quicksburg z 22847; ● 160
Fork Mountain; RMC Place; FRANKLIN; ***244** M-6; elev. 1,101ft./336m.; mail Rocky Mount z 24151; rural
Fork Ridge; RMC Place; TAZEWELL; ***244** C-6; mail Raven z 24639; rural
Forks of Buffalo; RMC Place; AMHERST; ***244** I-8; elev. 946ft./288m.; mail Amherst z 24521; rural
Forks Of Water; RMC Place; HIGHLAND; ***244** F-7; mail Blue Grass z 24413, Monterey z 24465; rural
Forksville; RMC Place; MECKLENBURG; ***245** M-12; 🅿; z 23950; ● 1,000
Fork Union; RMC Place; FLUVANNA; **245** I-11; 🅿; z 23055; ● 400
Formosa; RMC Place; CHARLOTTE; ***244** L-10; elev. 463ft./141m.; mail Randolph z 23962; ● 30
Fort Belvoir; CDP-Census Area Only; FAIRFAX; ***245** E-15; 🅿; ★ **WASH**; z 22060; ℗ 8,590; © 7,176
Fort Blackmore; RMC Place; SCOTT; **244** D-4; elev. 1,268ft./386m.; 🅿; z 24250; ● 250
Fort Chiswell; CDP; WYTHE; ***244** L-3; 🅿; z 24360; © 911
Fort Defiance; RMC Place; AUGUSTA; **244** G-9; 🅿; z 24437; ● 120
Fortener Addition; RMC Place; SMYTH; ***244** M-1; mail Marion z 24354; ● 80
Fort Hill; RMC Place; HENRICO; ***245** I-14; elev. 298ft./91m.; ★ **RICH**; mail Richmond z 23226; ● 2,000
Fort Hill; RMC Place; LYNCHBURG (Independent City); ***244** J-8; ★ **LYNCH**; mail Lynchburg z 24502; pop. incl. with Lynchburg (Independent City)
Fort Hunt; CDP-Census Area Only; FAIRFAX; ***245** E-15; ★ **WASH**; mail Alexandria z 22306-08; ℗ 12,989; © 12,923
Fort Lee; RMC Place; HENRICO; ***245** J-14; elev. 165ft./50m.; ★ **RICH**; mail Henrico z 23075; rural
Fort Lee; CDP-Census Area Only; PRINCE GEORGE; ***245** K-14; elev. 100ft./30m.; 🅿; ★ **RICH**; z 23801; ℗ 6,895; © 7,269
Fort Lewis; RMC Place; BATH; ***244** G-7; elev. 1,527ft./465m.; mail Millboro z 24460, Salem z 24153; rural
Fort Lewis Terrace; RMC Place; SALEM (Independent City); ★ **ROAN**; mail Salem z 24153; pop. incl. with Salem (Independent City)
Fort Mitchell; RMC Place; LUNENBURG, CHARLOTTE; **245** L-11; 🅿; z 23941; ● 100
Fort Myer Heights; RMC Place; ARLINGTON; ***245** D-15; ★ **WASH**; mail Arlington z 22209
Foster; RMC Place; MATHEWS; ***245** J-17; 🅿; ★ **NN-H**; z 23056; ● 150
Fosters Falls; RMC Place; WYTHE; ***244** L-3; mail Max Meadows z 24360; ● 80
Foundation Park; RMC Place; CHESAPEAKE (Independent City); ***245** L-18; ★ **NORF-**; mail Chesapeake z 23324; pop. incl. with Chesapeake (Independent City)
Four Corners; RMC Place; FAIRFAX; ***245** D-14; ★ **WASH**; mail Vienna z 22182
Four Mile Fork; RMC Place; SPOTSYLVANIA; **245** G-14; ★ **FRED**; mail Fredericksburg z 22401; ● 420
Fourway; RMC Place; TAZEWELL; ***244** K-1; mail North Tazewell z 24630; pop. incl. with Tazewell (Inc. Place)
Fox; RMC Place; GRAYSON; ***244** M-2; elev. 2,576ft./785m.; mail Independence z 24348; ● 30
Fox Hall Park; RMC Place; NORFOLK (Independent City); ***245** L-18; ★ **NORF-**; mail Norfolk z 23502; pop. incl. with Norfolk (Independent City)
Fox Hill; RMC Place; HAMPTON (Independent City); ***245** K-17; ★ **NN-H**; mail Hampton z 23664; pop. incl. with Hampton (Independent City)
Fox Mill Estates; RMC Place; FAIRFAX; ★ **WASH**; mail Herndon z 20170
Foxwells; RMC Place; LANCASTER; ***245** I-17; mail White Stone z 22578; ● 160
Fractionville; RMC Place; WASHINGTON; ***244** D-6; mail Abingdon z 24210; pop. incl. with Abingdon (Inc. Place)
Fraleytown; RMC Place; SCOTT; ***244** D-3; mail Duffield z 24244; rural
Franconia; CDP; FAIRFAX; **249** I-4; 🅿; ★ **WASH**; z 22310 & mail Alexandria z 22315; ℗ 19,882; © 31,907; ◆ 33,152
Franconia Commons; RMC Place; FAIRFAX; ***245** E-15; ★ **WASH**; mail Alexandria z 22310
Franklin; Independent City; **245** M-16; 🅿 🅷; z 23851; ℗ 7,864; © 8,346; ◆ 9,287
FRANKLIN; **244** L-5; ℗ 39,549; © 47,286; ◆ 53,143
Franklin Farms; RMC Place; PRINCE GEORGE; ***245** K-14; elev. 168ft./51m.; ★ **RICH**; mail Petersburg z 23805; ● 150
Franklin Forest; RMC Place; FAIRFAX; ***245** D-15; ★ **WASH**; mail Mc Lean z 22101
Franklin Heights; RMC Place; FRANKLIN; ***244** L-6; mail Rocky Mount z 24151; pop. incl. with Rocky Mount (Inc. Place)
Franklin Junction; RMC Place; SUFFOLK (Independent City); ***245** M-16; ★ **NORF-**; mail Suffolk z 23438; pop. incl. with Suffolk (Independent City)
Franklin Park; RMC Place; FAIRFAX; **249** F-4; ★ **WASH**; mail Mc Lean z 22101; ● 1,800
Franks Mill; RMC Place; AUGUSTA; ***244** G-9; mail Staunton z 24401; rural
Franktown; RMC Place; NORTHAMPTON; **245** J-19; 🅿; z 23354; ● 100
FREDERICK; **245** C-11; ℗ 45,723; © 59,209; ◆ 76,080
Frederick Hall; RMC Place; LOUISA; ***245** H-13; mail Mineral z 23117; ● 50
Frederick Heights; RMC Place; FREDERICK; ***245** C-12; mail Winchester z 22602; ● 750
Fredericksburg; Independent City; **245** G-14; 🅿 🅷 🅲 4,679 ■; ★ **FRED**; z 22401-08, z 22412; ℗ 19,027; © 19,279; ◆ 23,401
Fredericksburg; RMC Place; ROCKBRIDGE; ***244** H-8; elev. 1,240ft./378m.; mail Rockbridge Baths z 24473; rural
Frederick Towne; RMC Place; FREDERICK; ***245** D-11; elev. 750ft./229m.; mail Stephens City z 22655; ● 400
Freeman; RMC Place; BRUNSWICK; ***245** M-13; 🅿; z 23856; ● 100
Freeport; RMC Place; GLOUCESTER; ***245** J-17; mail Gloucester z 23061; ● 130
Freeshade Corner; RMC Place; MIDDLESEX; ***245** J-17; elev. 72ft./22m.; mail Topping z 23169; rural
Free Union; RMC Place; ALBEMARLE; **244** G-10; 🅿; ★ **CHRLTV**; z 22940; ● 100
Friendship; RMC Place; WASHINGTON; ***244** M-1; mail Glade Spring z 24340; ● 60
Fries; Inc. Place; GRAYSON; **244** M-3; elev. 2,180ft./664m.; 🅿; z 24330; ℗ 690; © 614
Fringer; BOTETOURT; see Spec (RMC Place)
Frogtown; RMC Place; CLARKE; ***245** D-12; mail Bluemont z 20135; ● 50
Front Royal; Inc. Place; ⊡ WARREN; **245** D-11; 🅿 🅷 🅲 397; z 22630; ℗ 11,880; © 13,589
Frytown; RMC Place; FAUQUIER; ***245** E-13; ★ **WASH**; mail Warrenton z 20187; rural
Fugua Farms; RMC Place; CHESTERFIELD; ★ **RICH**; mail Richmond z 23234
Fulks Run; RMC Place; ROCKINGHAM; **244** E-9; 🅿; z 22830; ● 150
Fulton; RMC Place; RICHMOND (Independent City); ★ **RICH**; mail Henrico z 23231; pop. incl. with Richmond (Independent City)
Furnace; RMC Place; PAGE, ROCKINGHAM; ***244** F-10; mail Elkton z 22827; ● 100
Furnace Hill; RMC Place; SMYTH; ***244** M-1; mail Marion z 24354; ● 150
Furnace Mountain; RMC Place; LOUDOUN; ***245** C-13; mail Lovettsville z 20180; rural

G

Gainesboro (Gainsboro); RMC Place; FREDERICK; **245** C-11; mail Winchester z 22603; ● 80
Gaines Mill Estates; RMC Place; HANOVER; ***245** J-14; elev. 150ft./46m.; ★ **RICH**; mail Mechanicsville z 23111; ● 650
Gainesville; CDP; PRINCE WILLIAM; **245** E-13; 🅿; ★ **WASH**; z 20155-56; © 4,382
Gainsboro; FREDERICK; see Gainesboro (RMC Place)
Gala; RMC Place; BOTETOURT; **244** I-6; elev. 964ft./294m.; mail Eagle Rock z 24085; ● 30
Galax; Independent City; **244** M-3; elev. 2,382ft./726m.; 🅿 🅷; z 24333; ℗ 6,670; © 6,837; ◆ 6,811
Gallops Corner; RMC Place; VIRGINIA BEACH (Independent City); ***245** M-18; elev. 14ft./4m.; ★ **NORF-**; mail Virginia Beach z 23456; pop. incl. with Virginia Beach (Independent City)
Galts Mill; RMC Place; AMHERST; ***244** J-9; ★ **LYNCH**; mail Madison Heights z 24572; ● 50
Gammons Store; RMC Place; GOOCHLAND; ***245** I-13; elev. 298ft./91m.; mail Maidens z 23102; rural
Garden City; RMC Place; ARLINGTON; ***245** D-15; ★ **WASH**; mail Arlington z 22207
Garden City; RMC Place; HAMPTON (Independent City); ★ **NN-H**; mail Hampton z 23661; pop. incl. with Hampton (Independent City)
Garden Wood Park; RMC Place; VIRGINIA BEACH (Independent City); ***245** L-18; ★ **NORF-**; mail Virginia Beach z 23455; pop. incl. with Virginia Beach (Independent City)
Gardner; RMC Place; RUSSELL; ***244** C-6; mail Honaker z 24260; ● 50
Gardners Crossroads; RMC Place; LOUISA; ***245** H-12; mail Mineral z 23117; rural
Garfield Estates; RMC Place; PRINCE WILLIAM; ***245** E-14; ★ **WASH**; mail Woodbridge z 22191; ● 300
Gargatha; RMC Place; ACCOMACK; ***245** H-20; elev. 49ft./15m.; mail Parksley z 23421; ● 30
Garland Heights; RMC Place; CHESTERFIELD; ***245** J-14; elev. 200ft./61m.; ★ **RICH**; mail Richmond z 23234; ● 400
Garrisonville; RMC Place; STAFFORD; **245** F-14; 🅿; ★ **WASH**; z 22463; ● 300
Garrisonville Estates; RMC Place; STAFFORD; ***245** F-14; ★ **WASH**; mail Stafford z 22554; ● 550
Garysville; RMC Place; PRINCE GEORGE; **245** K-15; elev. 47ft./14m.; mail Hopewell z 23860; ● 60
Gasburg; RMC Place; BRUNSWICK; **245** N-12; elev. 300ft./91m.; 🅿; z 23857; ● 200
Gate City; Inc. Place; ⊡ SCOTT; **244** E-4; elev. 1,304ft./397m.; 🅿; ★ **JNSC-**; z 24251; ℗ 2,214; © 2,159
Gatewood; RMC Place; SPOTSYLVANIA; ***245** H-13; mail Partlow z 22534; rural
Gatewood Park; RMC Place; VIRGINIA BEACH (Independent City); ***245** L-18; elev. 15ft./5m.; ★ **NORF-**; mail Virginia Beach z 23454; pop. incl. with Virginia Beach (Independent City)
Gaylord; RMC Place; CLARKE; ***245** C-12; mail Berryville z 22611; rural
Gaynor Heights; RMC Place; HENRY; ★ **MRTNV**; mail Martinsville z 24112; ● 200
Gayton; RMC Place; HENRICO; ***245** I-13; elev. 170ft./52m.; ★ **RICH**; mail Henrico z 23075; ● 1,500
Geer; RMC Place; GREENE; ***244** G-10; mail Stanardsville z 22973; rural
Geneva Park; RMC Place; CHESAPEAKE (Independent City); ***245** M-17; ★ **NORF-**; mail Chesapeake z 23323; pop. incl. with Chesapeake (Independent City)
Genito; RMC Place; POWHATAN; ***245** J-12; elev. 303ft./92m.; mail Powhatan z 23139; rural
Genoa; RMC Place; ROCKINGHAM; ***244** E-9; mail Fulks Run z 22830; rural
Georges Fork; RMC Place; DICKENSON; ***244** B-4; mail Clintwood z 24228
Georges Mill; RMC Place; LOUDOUN; ***245** C-13; mail Lovettsville z 20180; rural
Georges Tavern; RMC Place; GOOCHLAND; **245** I-12; mail Goochland z 23063; ● 50
Georgetown; RMC Place; CHARLOTTESVILLE (Independent City); ★ **CHRLTV**; pop. incl. with Charlottesville (Independent City)
Georgetown; RMC Place; SHENANDOAH; ***244** E-10; mail Mount Jackson z 22842; rural
Georgetown East; RMC Place; CHESAPEAKE (Independent City); ***245** M-18; ★ **NORF-**; mail Chesapeake z 23325; pop. incl. with Chesapeake (Independent City)
Georgetown South; RMC Place; MANASSAS (Independent City); ★ **WASH**; mail Manassas z 20110; pop. incl. with Manassas (Independent City)
Georgetown Village; RMC Place; PRINCE WILLIAM; ***245** F-14; ★ **WASH**; mail Woodbridge z 22191; ● 2,000
George Washington Village; RMC Place; FAIRFAX; ★ **WASH**; mail Fort Belvoir z 22060
Georgian Hamlet; RMC Place; PRINCE WILLIAM; ***245** E-14; ★ **WASH**; mail Manassas z 20110
Gether; RMC Place; CAROLINE; ***245** H-14; elev. 172ft./52m.; mail Milford z 22514; rural
Getz; SHENANDOAH; see Getz Corner (RMC Place)
Getz Corner (Getz); RMC Place; SHENANDOAH; ***244** E-10; mail Mount Jackson z 22842; rural
Ghent; RMC Place; NORFOLK (Independent City); ***245** L-17; ★ **NORF-**; mail Norfolk z 23507; pop. incl. with Norfolk (Independent City)
Gholsonville; RMC Place; BRUNSWICK; ***245** M-12; elev. 360ft./110m.; mail White Plains z 23893
Gibson Station; RMC Place; LEE; ***244** D-1; mail Ewing z 24248; ● 200
Gidsville; RMC Place; AMHERST; ***244** I-9; elev. 878ft./268m.; mail Amherst z 24521; rural
Gilbert Gardens; RMC Place; HENRICO; ***245** J-14; ★ **RICH**; mail Henrico z 23231
GILES; **244** K-3; ℗ 16,366; © 16,657; ◆ 17,210
Gilmerton; RMC Place; CHESAPEAKE (Independent City); ***245** M-17; ★ **NORF-**; mail Chesapeake z 23323; pop. incl. with Chesapeake (Independent City)
Gilmore Mills; RMC Place; ROCKBRIDGE; ***244** I-7; mail Natural Bridge Station z 24579; rural
Ginter Park; RMC Place; RICHMOND (Independent City); ***245** J-14; ★ **RICH**; mail Richmond z 23227; pop. incl. with Richmond (Independent City)
Gladehill; RMC Place; FRANKLIN; **244** L-6; 🅿; z 24092; ● 80
Gladesboro; RMC Place; CARROLL; ***244** M-4; elev. 2,655ft./809m.; mail Hillsville z 24343; rural
Glade Spring; Inc. Place; WASHINGTON; **244** M-1; elev. 2,084ft./635m.; 🅿; z 24340; ℗ 1,435; © 1,374
Gladeville; WISE; see Wise (Inc. Place)
Gladstone; RMC Place; NELSON; **244** J-9; 🅿; z 24553; ● 50
Gladys; RMC Place; CAMPBELL; **244** K-9; elev. 777ft./237m.; 🅿; z 24554; ● 250
Glamorgan; RMC Place; WISE; ***244** C-4; mail Wise z 24293
Glasgow; Inc. Place; ROCKBRIDGE; **244** I-8; 🅿; z 24555; ℗ 1,140; © 1,046
Glass; RMC Place; GLOUCESTER; ***245** K-17; ★ **NN-H**; mail Hayes z 23072; ● 270
Glebe Point; RMC Place; NORTHUMBERLAND; ***245** H-17; mail Burgess z 22432; ● 190
Gleedsville; RMC Place; LOUDOUN; ***245** D-13; ★ **WASH**; mail Leesburg z 20175; rural
Glen Alden; RMC Place; FAIRFAX; ***245** E-14; ★ **WASH**; mail Fairfax z 22030; ● 370
Glen Allen; CDP; HENRICO; **243** A-7; 🅿 🅲 375; ★ **RICH**; z 23058-60; ℗ 9,010; © 12,562
Glenbrook Hills; RMC Place; HENRICO; ***245** J-13; elev. 200ft./61m.; ★ **RICH**; mail Henrico z 23075; ● 750
Glencarlyn; RMC Place; ARLINGTON; ***245** D-15; ★ **WASH**; mail Arlington z 22204
Glen Corner; RMC Place; CHESTERFIELD; ★ **RICH**; mail Richmond z 23234
Glendale; RMC Place; NEWPORT NEWS (Independent City); ***245** K-17; ★ **NN-H**; mail Newport News z 23606; pop. incl. with Newport News (Independent City)
Glendale Acres; RMC Place; CHARLES CITY; ***245** J-15; elev. 138ft./42m.; mail Charles City z 23030; ● 100
Glen Echo; RMC Place; HENRICO; ***245** J-14; ★ **RICH**; mail Richmond z 23223; ● 120
Glenford; RMC Place; WASHINGTON; ***244** D-6; mail Abingdon z 24210; rural
Glen Forest; RMC Place; FAIRFAX; ***245** D-15; ★ **WASH**; mail Falls Church z 22041; ● 2,100
Glenita (Natural Tunnel); RMC Place; SCOTT; ***244** D-3; mail Duffield z 24244; rural
Glen Lyn; Inc. Place; GILES; **244** J-3; 🅿; z 24093; ℗ 170; © 151
Glenmore; RMC Place; BUCKINGHAM; ***244** I-10; elev. 593ft./181m.; mail Howardsville z 24562; rural
Glenns; RMC Place; GLOUCESTER; ***245** J-16; elev. 89ft./27m.; mail Saluda z 23149
Glen Oaks; RMC Place; CHESTERFIELD; ★ **RICH**; mail Chester z 23831
Glen Oaks; RMC Place; FAIRFAX; ★ **WASH**; mail Burke z 22015
Glenrochie; RMC Place; WASHINGTON; mail Abingdon z 24211; ● 100
Glen Rock; RMC Place; NORFOLK (Independent City); ***245** L-18; ★ **NORF-**; mail Norfolk z 23502; pop. incl. with Norfolk (Independent City)
Glen Roy Estates; RMC Place; GLOUCESTER; ***245** J-17; elev. 10ft./3m.; ★ **NN-H**; mail Gloucester z 23061; ● 200
Glenvar; RMC Place; ROANOKE; **244** K-5; ★ **ROAN**; mail Salem z 24153; ● 200
Glen Wilton; RMC Place; BOTETOURT; **244** I-6; 🅿; z 24438; ● 200
Glenwood; RMC Place; DANVILLE (Independent City); **244** N-8; ★ **DANV**; mail Danville z 24541; pop. incl. with Danville (Independent City)
Glenwood Farms; RMC Place; HENRICO; ***245** J-14; ★ **RICH**; mail Richmond z 23223; ● 3,500
Glenwood Park; RMC Place; NORFOLK (Independent City); ***245** L-17; ★ **NORF-**; mail Norfolk z 23505; pop. incl. with Norfolk (Independent City)
Globe; RMC Place; KING WILLIAM; ***245** I-15; elev. 193ft./59m.; mail Aylett z 23009; rural
Gloucester; RMC Place; ⊡ GLOUCESTER; **245** J-17; 🅿 🅷; ★ **NN-H**; z 23061; ● 150
GLOUCESTER; **245** J-16; ℗ 30,131; © 34,780; ◆ 39,223
Gloucester Banks; RMC Place; GLOUCESTER; ***245** K-17; ★ **NN-H**; mail Gloucester Point z 23062
Gloucester Courthouse; CDP-Census Area Only; GLOUCESTER; ***245** J-17; ★ **NN-H**; mail Gloucester z 23061; ℗ 2,118; © 2,269
Gloucester Point; CDP; GLOUCESTER; **245** K-17; 🅿; ★ **NN-H**; z 23062 & mail Hayes z 23072, Ordinary z 23131, Wicomico z 23184; ℗ 8,509; © 9,429
Goddin Hill; RMC Place; HANOVER; ***245** I-14; elev. 150ft./46m.; ★ **RICH**; mail Ashland z 23005; rural
Gogginsville; RMC Place; FRANKLIN; ***244** L-6; mail Rocky Mount z 24151; ● 50
Goldbond; RMC Place; GILES; **244** J-4; elev. 1,862ft./568m.; 🅿; z 24150; ● 160
Golddale; RMC Place; ORANGE; ***245** G-13; mail Locust Grove z 22508; rural
Gold Hill; RMC Place; BUCKINGHAM; ***245** I-11; elev. 529ft./161m.; mail New Canton z 23123; ● 50
Goldvein; RMC Place; FAUQUIER; **245** F-13; 🅿; z 22720; ● 200
Gonyon; RMC Place; NORTHUMBERLAND; ***245** H-17; mail Heathsville z 22473; rural
Goochland; RMC Place; ⊡ GOOCHLAND; **245** I-12; elev. 258ft./79m.; 🅿; z 23063; ● 600
GOOCHLAND; **245** I-12; ℗ 14,163; © 16,863; ◆ 21,841
Goodall; RMC Place; HANOVER; ***245** I-13; elev. 280ft./85m.; mail Montpelier z 23192
Goode; RMC Place; BEDFORD; **244** K-8; 🅿; z 24556; ● 170
Goods Mills; RMC Place; ROCKINGHAM; ***244** G-9; mail Port Republic z 24471; rural
Goodview; RMC Place; BEDFORD; **244** K-7; elev. 986ft./301m.; 🅿; ★ **ROAN**; z 24095; ● 70
Goodwins Ferry; RMC Place; GILES; ***244** K-4; elev. 1,662ft./507m.; mail Newport z 24128; ● 30
Goose Pimple Junction; RMC Place; WASHINGTON; ***244** E-5; ★ **JNSC-**; mail Bristol z 24202; ● 50
Gordonsville; Inc. Place; ORANGE, LOUISA; **245** G-11; elev. 493ft./150m.; 🅿; z 22942; ℗ 1,351; © 1,498
Gore; RMC Place; FREDERICK; **245** C-11; 🅿; z 22637; ● 160
Goshen; Inc. Place; ROCKBRIDGE; **244** H-7; 🅿; z 24439; ℗ 366; © 406
Goshen Cross Road; RMC Place; HANOVER; ***245** H-13; elev. 270ft./82m.; mail Beaverdam z 23015; rural
Gosport; RMC Place; PORTSMOUTH (Independent City); ***245** L-17; ★ **NORF-**; mail Portsmouth z 23702; pop. incl. with Portsmouth (Independent City)
Gossan Mines; RMC Place; CARROLL; mail Galax z 24333; ● 60
Gouldin; RMC Place; HANOVER; ***245** I-13; elev. 280ft./85m.; mail Montpelier z 23192; rural
Gowrie Park; RMC Place; NORFOLK (Independent City); ***245** L-18; ★ **NORF-**; mail Norfolk z 23509; pop. incl. with Norfolk (Independent City)
Grady; RMC Place; PITTSYLVANIA; ***244** M-7; elev. 920ft./280m.; mail Callands z 24530; rural
Grafton; RMC Place; YORK; **243** H-4; elev. 57ft./17m.; 🅿; ★ **NN-H**; z 23692; ● 1,050
Grafton Village; RMC Place; STAFFORD; ***245** G-14; ★ **FRED**; mail Fredericksburg z 22401; ● 2,500
Grahams Forge; RMC Place; WYTHE; ***244** L-3; mail Max Meadows z 24360; ● 50
Grandin Road; RMC Place; ROANOKE (Independent City); ★ **ROAN**; mail Roanoke z 24015; pop. incl. with Roanoke (Independent City)
Grand View; RMC Place; HAMPTON (Independent City); ***245** K-18; ★ **NN-H**; mail Hampton z 23664; pop. incl. with Hampton (Independent City)
Grangeville; RMC Place; ACCOMACK; ***245** I-19; elev. 27ft./8m.; mail Melfa z 23410; rural
Granite Hills; RMC Place; RICHMOND (Independent City); ★ **RICH**; mail Richmond z 23225; pop. incl. with Richmond (Independent City)
Granite Springs; RMC Place; SPOTSYLVANIA; ***245** G-12; mail Spotsylvania z 22553; rural
Grant; RMC Place; GRAYSON; ***244** M-1; mail Troutdale z 24378; ● 30
Grant's Field; RMC Place; DINWIDDIE; ***245** K-14; elev. 150ft./46m.; ★ **RICH**; mail Petersburg z 23803; ● 200
Granville; RMC Place; CHARLES CITY; ***245** J-14; elev. 51ft./16m.; mail Charles City z 23030; rural
Grapefield; RMC Place; BLAND; ***244** K-2; mail Bastian z 24314; ● 50
Grassfield; RMC Place; CHESAPEAKE (Independent City); ***245** M-17; ★ **NORF-**; mail Chesapeake z 23323; pop. incl. with Chesapeake (Independent City)
Grassland; RMC Place; ORANGE; ***245** G-12; mail Rapidan z 22733; rural
Grass Ridge; RMC Place; FAIRFAX; ***245** D-15; ★ **WASH**; mail Mc Lean z 22101
Grassy Creek; RMC Place; HENRY; ***244** M-6; ★ **MRTNV**; mail Martinsville z 24112; rural
Grassy Creek; RMC Place; RUSSELL; ***244** D-5; mail Castlewood z 24224; ● 50
Gratton; RMC Place; TAZEWELL; ***244** K-1; elev. 2,777ft./846m.; mail Tazewell z 24651; ● 50
Gravel Hill; RMC Place; RICHMOND (Independent City); ★ **RICH**; mail Richmond z 23225; pop. incl. with Richmond (Independent City)
Graves Mill; RMC Place; MADISON; ***245** F-11; 🅿; z 22721, z 22727; ● 40
Graves Store; RMC Place; BEDFORD; ***244** L-7; mail Huddleston z 24104; rural
Gray; RMC Place; SUSSEX; ***245** M-14; elev. 129ft./39m.; mail Yale z 23897; rural
GRAYSON; **244** M-1; ℗ 16,278; © 17,917; Ⓡ 16,881; ◆ 16,023
Graysontown; RMC Place; MONTGOMERY; **244** L-4; mail Radford z 24141; ● 100
Graysville; RMC Place; ACCOMACK; ***245** I-19; mail Accomac z 23301; rural
Great Bridge; RMC Place; CHESAPEAKE (Independent City); ***245** M-18; ★ **NORF-**; mail Chesapeake z 23322, z 23328; pop. incl. with Chesapeake (Independent City)
Great Falls; CDP; FAIRFAX; **249** D-2; 🅿; ★ **WASH**; z 22066; ℗ 6,945; © 8,549
Great Neck Manor; RMC Place; VIRGINIA BEACH (Independent City); ***245** L-18; ★ **NORF-**; mail Virginia Beach z 23450; pop. incl. with Virginia Beach (Independent City)
Green Acres; RMC Place; FAIRFAX (Independent City); ***245** E-14; ★ **WASH**; mail Fairfax z 22030; pop. incl. with Fairfax (Independent City)
Greenbackville; RMC Place; ACCOMACK; **245** H-20; 🅿; z 23356; ● 300
Green Bay; RMC Place; PRINCE EDWARD; **245** K-11; 🅿; z 23942; ● 140
Greenbriar; RMC Place; CHARLOTTESVILLE (Independent City); ★ **CHRLTV**; pop. incl. with Charlottesville (Independent City)
Greenbriar; RMC Place; CHESTERFIELD; ***245** K-14; elev. 150ft./46m.; ★ **RICH**; mail Chester z 23831; ● 650
Greenbriar; RMC Place; FAIRFAX; ***245** D-14; ★ **WASH**; mail Fairfax z 22033
Greenbush; RMC Place; ACCOMACK; ***245** I-19; 🅿; z 23357; ● 250
Green Cove; RMC Place; WASHINGTON; ***244** M-1; mail Damascus z 24236; ● 30
Greendale; RMC Place; HENRICO; ***245** I-14; ★ **RICH**; mail Henrico z 23228
Greendale; RMC Place; WASHINGTON; **244** D-6; mail Abingdon z 24210; ● 100
Greendale Manor; RMC Place; HENRICO; ***245** I-14; ★ **RICH**; mail Richmond z 23230; ● 1,500
GREENE; **245** G-11; ℗ 10,297; © 15,244; ◆ 18,355
Greenes Corner; RMC Place; LOUISA; ***245** H-13; elev. 300ft./91m.; mail Beaverdam z 23015, Bumpass z 23024; ● 40
Greenfield; RMC Place; NELSON; ***244** H-9; elev. 690ft./210m.; mail Afton z 22920; ● 60
Greenfield; RMC Place; PITTSYLVANIA; **244** H-9; mail Gretna z 24557; ● 50
Greenfield Farms; RMC Place; PORTSMOUTH (Independent City); ***245** L-17; ★ **NORF-**; mail Portsmouth z 23703; pop. incl. with Portsmouth (Independent City)
Greenlee; RMC Place; ROCKBRIDGE; ***244** I-7; mail Natural Bridge Station z 24579
Green Oaks; RMC Place; NEWPORT NEWS (Independent City); ★ **NN-H**; mail Newport News z 23601; pop. incl. with Newport News (Independent City)
Green Pond; RMC Place; PITTSYLVANIA; ***244** L-7; elev. 948ft./289m.; mail Chatham z 24531; rural
Greens Folly Apartments; RMC Place; HALIFAX; ***244** M-9; elev. 450ft./137m.; mail South Boston z 24592; pop. incl. with South Boston (Inc. Place)
Green Spring; RMC Place; FREDERICK; ***245** C-11; mail Winchester z 22603; rural
Green Springs; RMC Place; LOUISA; ***245** H-12; elev. 530ft./162m.; mail Gordonsville z 22942
Green Springs; RMC Place; WASHINGTON; ***244** E-6; mail Abingdon z 24211; rural
GREENSVILLE; **245** M-13; ℗ 8,853; © 11,560; ◆ 12,474
Green Valley; RMC Place; BATH; ***244** H-7; elev. 1,621ft./494m.; mail Millboro z 24460; rural
Green Valley; RMC Place; BRISTOL (Independent City); ***244** D-5; ★ **JNSC-**; mail Bristol z 24202
Greenville; CDP; AUGUSTA; **244** H-8; 🅿; z 24440; © 886
Greenville; RMC Place; FAUQUIER; ***245** E-13; ★ **WASH**; mail Nokesville z 20181; ● 30
Greenway Downs; RMC Place; FAIRFAX; ***245** D-14; ★ **WASH**; mail Falls Church z 22042; ● 1,800
Greenway Hills; RMC Place; FAIRFAX (Independent City); ***245** D-14; ★ **WASH**; mail Fairfax z 22030; pop. incl. with Fairfax (Independent City)
Greenwich; RMC Place; PRINCE WILLIAM; ***245** E-13; ★ **WASH**; mail Nokesville z 20181; ● 150
Greenwich; RMC Place; VIRGINIA BEACH (Independent City); ***245** L-18; ★ **NORF-**; mail Virginia Beach z 23462; pop. incl. with Virginia Beach (Independent City)
Greenwood; RMC Place; ALBEMARLE; ***244** H-10; 🅿; ★ **CHRLTV**; z 22943; ● 200
Greenwood; RMC Place; HENRICO; ***245** I-14; ★ **RICH**; mail Glen Allen z 23060; ● 300
Greenwood; RMC Place; NORFOLK (Independent City); ***245** L-18; ★ **NORF-**; mail Norfolk z 23513; pop. incl. with Norfolk (Independent City)
Greenwood; RMC Place; ROCKINGHAM; ***244** F-10; mail Elkton z 22827; rural
Greenwood Farms; RMC Place; HAMPTON (Independent City); ***245** L-17; ★ **NN-H**; mail Hampton z 23666; pop. incl. with Hampton (Independent City)
Gregory Corner; RMC Place; MECKLENBURG; ***245** M-11; elev. 490ft./149m.; mail Skipwith z 23968; rural
Gressitt; RMC Place; KING AND QUEEN; ***245** J-16; mail Shacklefords z 23156
Gretna; Inc. Place; PITTSYLVANIA; **244** L-8; elev. 844ft./257m.; 🅿; z 24557; ℗ 1,339; © 1,257
Griffinsburg; RMC Place; CULPEPER; ***245** F-12; mail Culpeper z 22701; ● 40
Griffith; RMC Place; ALLEGHANY; ***244** H-7; mail Clifton Forge z 24422; ● 30
Grimes; RMC Place; FREDERICK; ***245** C-12; mail Winchester z 22603
Grimsleyville; RMC Place; BUCHANAN; ***244** B-6; elev. 1,886ft./575m.; mail Raven z 24639; rural
Grimstead; RMC Place; MATHEWS; ***245** J-17; 🅿; ★ **NN-H**; z 23064; ● 220
Grindall Creek; RMC Place; CHESTERFIELD; ***245** J-14; elev. 50ft./15m.; ★ **RICH**; mail Richmond z 23234; ● 1,650
Grit; RMC Place; PITTSYLVANIA; ***244** L-8; elev. 781ft./238m.; mail Hurt z 24563; ● 500
Grizzard; RMC Place; SUSSEX; ***245** M-14; elev. 123ft./37m.; mail Skippers z 23879
Groseclose; RMC Place; SMYTH; ***244** L-1; elev. 2,451ft./747m.; mail Rural Retreat z 24368; ● 120
Grotons; RMC Place; ACCOMACK; ***245** H-19; mail Jenkins Bridge z 23399; rural
Groton Town; RMC Place; ACCOMACK; ***245** H-20; elev. 30ft./9m.; mail Hallwood z 23359; rural
Grottoes; Inc. Place; ROCKINGHAM, AUGUSTA; **244** G-9; 🅿; z 24441; ℗ 1,455; © 2,114
Grove; RMC Place; JAMES CITY, YORK; **243** G-3; ★ **NN-H**; mail Williamsburg z 23188; ● 680
Grove Hill; RMC Place; PAGE; ***244** F-10; mail Shenandoah z 22849
Grove Park; RMC Place; PORTSMOUTH (Independent City); ***245** L-17; ★ **NORF-**; mail Portsmouth z 23707; pop. incl. with Portsmouth (Independent City)
Groveton; CDP; FAIRFAX; **249** I-5; ★ **WASH**; mail Alexandria z 22303, z 22306-07, z 22310; ℗ 19,997; © 21,296; ◆ 22,130
Groveton Heights; RMC Place; FAIRFAX; ***245** E-15; ★ **WASH**; mail Alexandria z 22306; ● 2,450

Entries in **UPPERCASE** are counties.
Entries in **bold** have populations of 2,500 or more.
Names in parentheses are alternate names.
Inc. Place — Incorporated Place
RMC Place — Rand McNally Designated Place
CDP — Census Designated Place
MCD — Minor Civil Division

⊡ County Seat
▲ Minor Civil Division
elev. Elevation
🅿 Post Office
🅷 Hospital
🅲 College
■ Principal Business Center
★ Ranally Metro Area (RMA) Abbreviation
z Zip Code(s)

℗ Previous Census Population
© Final Census Population
Ⓡ Revised Census Population
Ⓢ Special Census Population
Ⓐ Annexation Population
● Rand McNally Population Estimate
◆ Estimated Population

For additional definitions see Glossary, Volume 1, and Introduction, Volume 2.

Grundy; Inc. Place; ⊡ BUCHANAN; 244 B-5; elev. 1,050ft./320m.; 🄿 🄷 🄲 368; z 24614; Ⓟ 1,305; © 1,105
Guilford; RMC Place; ACCOMACK; *245 H-19; mail Bloxom z 23308; ● 150
Guilford; RMC Place; FAIRFAX; *245 E-15; ★ WASH; mail Alexandria z 22310
Guilford Heights; RMC Place; SURRY; *245 K-15; elev. 50ft./15m.; mail Claremont z 23899; ● 130
Guinea; RMC Place; CAROLINE; 245 G-14; mail Woodford z 22580; ● 80
Guinea Mills; RMC Place; CUMBERLAND; *245 J-11; mail Cumberland z 23040
Gum Spring; RMC Place; LOUISA; 245 I-12; elev. 376ft./115m.; 🄿; z 23065; ● 100
Gum Tree; RMC Place; HANOVER; *245 I-14; ★ RICH; mail Ashland z 23005; ● 40
Gunn Hall Manor; RMC Place; VIRGINIA BEACH (Independent City); *245 M-18; elev. 15ft./5m.; ★ NORF-; mail Virginia Beach z 23454; pop. incl. with Virginia Beach (Independent City)
Gunston Heights; RMC Place; FAIRFAX; *245 E-14; elev. 100ft./30m.; ★ WASH; mail Lorton z 22079; ● 100
Gunston Manor; RMC Place; FAIRFAX; *245 E-15; elev. 30ft./9m.; ★ WASH; mail Lorton z 22079; ● 400
Gunton Park; RMC Place; WYTHE; *244 L-3; mail Max Meadows z 24360; ● 30
Gwathmey; RMC Place; HANOVER; *245 I-14; ★ RICH; mail Ashland z 23005; ● 40
Gwynn; RMC Place; MATHEWS; 245 J-17; elev. 6ft./2m.; 🄿; ★ NN-H; z 23066; ● 450

H

Hacklers Store; RMC Place; GRAYSON; *244 M-2; elev. 2,817ft./859m.; mail Independence z 24348; rural
Hacksneck; RMC Place; ACCOMACK; *245 I-19; 🄿; z 23358; ● 140
Haddonfield; RMC Place; WISE; *244 B-4; elev. 1,881ft./573m.; mail Pound z 24279; rural
Hadensville; RMC Place; GOOCHLAND; 245 I-12; elev. 395ft./120m.; 🄿; z 23067; ● 80
Hagan (Hagans); RMC Place; LEE; *244 D-2; mail Jonesville z 24263; ● 40
Hagans; LEE; see Hagan (RMC Place)
Hague; RMC Place; WESTMORELAND; 245 H-16; 🄿; z 22469; ● 80
Hale Creek; RMC Place; BUCHANAN; *244 B-6; mail Pilgrims Knob z 24634; ● 30
Halemhurst; RMC Place; FAIRFAX (Independent City); *245 E-14; ★ WASH; mail Fairfax z 22032; pop. incl. with Fairfax (Independent City)
Hales Bottom; RMC Place; TAZEWELL; *244 K-2; mail Bluefield z 24605; ● 50
Halfway; RMC Place; FAUQUIER; 245 D-13; mail The Plains z 20198; ● 60
Halifax; Inc. Place; ⊡ HALIFAX; 244 M-9; 🄿; z 24558; Ⓟ 688; © 1,389
HALIFAX; 244 M-9; Ⓟ 36,030; © 37,355; Ⓡ 37,350; ◆ 35,134
Hall Addition; RMC Place; SMYTH; *244 M-1; mail Marion z 24354; ● 170
Hallieford; RMC Place; MATHEWS; *245 J-17; elev. 15ft./5m.; 🄿; ★ NN-H; z 23068; ● 220
Hallowing Point River Estates; RMC Place; FAIRFAX; *245 E-15; ★ WASH; mail Lorton z 22079; ● 500
Hallsboro; RMC Place; CHESTERFIELD; *245 J-13; elev. 265ft./81m.; ★ RICH; mail Midlothian z 23113; rural
Halls Hill; RMC Place; ARLINGTON; *245 D-15; ★ WASH; mail Arlington z 22207
Hallwood; Inc. Place; ACCOMACK; 245 H-20; 🄿; z 23359; Ⓟ 228; © 290
Hallwood; RMC Place; HAMPTON (Independent City); *245 K-17; ★ NN-H; mail Hampton z 23664; pop. incl. with Hampton (Independent City)
Hamburg; RMC Place; PAGE; 244 E-10; mail Luray z 22835; ● 30
Hamburg; RMC Place; SHENANDOAH; *244 E-10; mail Edinburg z 22824; ● 30
Hamilton; Inc. Place; LOUDOUN; 245 C-13; 🄿 🄲 672; ★ WASH; z 20158-59; Ⓟ 700; © 562
Hamiltontown; RMC Place; WISE; *244 C-4; mail Norton z 24273; rural
Hamlin; RMC Place; RUSSELL; 244 C-5; mail Castlewood z 24224; ● 300
Hamlin Estates; RMC Place; CHESTERFIELD; ★ RICH; mail Chester z 23831
Hampden Sydney; CDP; PRINCE EDWARD; 245 K-11; 🄿 🄲 1,050; z 23943; Ⓟ 1,240; © 1,264
Hampton; Independent City; 245 L-17; 🄿 🄷 🄲 6,148 ■; ★ NN-H; z 23605, z 23630, z 23651, z 23661-70, z 23681; Ⓟ 133,793; © 146,437; ◆ 149,409
Hanckel; RMC Place; WASHINGTON; *244 D-6; mail Meadowview z 24361; ● 60
Handsom; RMC Place; SOUTHAMPTON; *245 M-15; elev. 35ft./11m.; mail Franklin z 23851; ● 100
Hanging Rock; RMC Place; ROANOKE; *244 K-6; ★ ROAN; mail Salem z 24153
Hanover; RMC Place; ⊡ HANOVER; 245 I-14; 🄿; ★ RICH; z 23069; ● 500
HANOVER; 245 I-13; Ⓟ 63,306; © 86,320; ◆ 98,693
Hanover Heights; RMC Place; HANOVER; *245 I-14; elev. 190ft./58m.; ★ RICH; mail Mechanicsville z 23111; ● 300
Hansonville; RMC Place; RUSSELL; 244 D-5; mail Lebanon z 24266; ● 200
Happy Creek; RMC Place; WARREN; *245 D-11; mail Front Royal z 22630; ● 300
Harborton; RMC Place; ACCOMACK; 245 I-19; 🄿; z 23389; ● 170
Harbor View; RMC Place; FAIRFAX; *245 E-14; ★ WASH; mail Lorton z 22079; ● 550
Hardesty; WARREN; see Howellsville (RMC Place)
Hardings; RMC Place; NORTHUMBERLAND; *245 I-17; mail Kilmarnock z 22482; rural
Hardware; RMC Place; FLUVANNA; *245 I-11; elev. 257ft./78m.; mail Scottsville z 24590; rural
Hardwood; RMC Place; SCOTT; *244 E-4; mail Dungannon z 24245; rural
Hardy; RMC Place; BEDFORD; *244 K-6; elev. 1,046ft./319m.; 🄿; ★ ROAN; z 24101; ● 450
Hardyville; RMC Place; MIDDLESEX; *245 J-17; elev. 38ft./12m.; 🄿; z 23070; ● 140
Hare Valley; RMC Place; NORTHAMPTON; *245 J-19; mail Exmore z 23350; ● 50
Harman; RMC Place; BUCHANAN; 244 B-5; ● 600
Harman; RMC Place; TAZEWELL; *244 K-1; elev. 2,188ft./667m.; mail Bandy z 24602; rural
Harman Junction; RMC Place; BUCHANAN; *244 B-5; mail Grundy z 24614; ● 100
Harmony; RMC Place; HALIFAX; 244 N-9; mail Alton z 24520; ● 60
Harmony; RMC Place; SHENANDOAH; *244 D-10; mail Edinburg z 22824; rural
Harpersville; RMC Place; NEWPORT NEWS (Independent City); *245 K-17; ★ NN-H; mail Newport News z 23607; pop. incl. with Newport News (Independent City)
Harrell Siding; RMC Place; SUFFOLK (Independent City); ★ NORF-; mail Suffolk z 23434; pop. incl. with Suffolk (Independent City)
Harrisburg; RMC Place; CHARLOTTE; *244 L-10; elev. 548ft./167m.; mail Randolph z 23962; rural
Harris Grove; RMC Place; YORK; 243 G-5; ★ NN-H; mail Yorktown z 23692; ● 170
Harrisonburg; Independent City; serves as county seat of Rockingham; 244 F-9; elev. 1,352ft./412m.; 🄿 🄷 🄲 18,563 ■; z 22801-03, z 22807; Ⓟ 30,707; © 40,468; Ⓡ 40,453; ◆ 45,115
Harriston; RMC Place; AUGUSTA; 244 G-9; mail Grottoes z 24441; ● 80
Harrisville; RMC Place; SHENANDOAH; *245 D-11; mail Toms Brook z 22660; ● 60
Harrowgate; RMC Place; CHESTERFIELD; ★ RICH; mail Chester z 23831
Harryhogan; RMC Place; NORTHUMBERLAND; *245 H-17; mail Callao z 22435; ● 60
Hartfield; RMC Place; MIDDLESEX; 245 J-17; 🄿; z 23071; ● 150
Harts Shop; RMC Place; LOUISA; *245 H-13; elev. 364ft./111m.; mail Mineral z 23117; rural
Hartwood; RMC Place; STAFFORD; 245 F-13; 🄿; z 22471; ● 50
Harvey; RMC Place; LEE; *244 D-3; mail Big Stone Gap z 24219
Hassen Heights; RMC Place; BRISTOL (Independent City); ★ JNSC-; mail Bristol z 24201; pop. incl. with Bristol (Independent City)
Hatchers; RMC Place; POWHATAN; *245 J-12; mail Powhatan z 23139; rural
Hat Creek; RMC Place; CAMPBELL; *244 K-9; mail Brookneal z 24528; rural
Hatton; RMC Place; ALBEMARLE; *244 I-10; mail Scottsville z 24590; ● 30
Haven Heights; RMC Place; VIRGINIA BEACH (Independent City); *245 L-18; elev. 25ft./8m.; ★ NORF-; mail Virginia Beach z 23462; pop. incl. with Virginia Beach (Independent City)
Hawkinstown; RMC Place; SHENANDOAH; *244 E-10; mail Mount Jackson z 22842; ● 50
Hawthorne; RMC Place; NORTON (Independent City); mail Norton z 24273; pop. incl. with Norton (Independent City)
Haycock; RMC Place; FLOYD; *244 L-5; elev. 2,600ft./792m.; mail Floyd z 24091; rural
Hayes; RMC Place; GLOUCESTER; 243 F-5; 🄿; ★ NN-H; z 23072; ● 1,000
Hayfield; RMC Place; FAIRFAX; 249 J-4; ★ WASH; mail Alexandria z 22315; ● 2,350
Hayfield; RMC Place; FREDERICK; 245 C-11; 🄿; z 22601; ● 130
Haymarket; Inc. Place; PRINCE WILLIAM; 245 E-13; 🄿; ★ WASH; z 20168-69; Ⓟ 483; © 879
Haynesville; RMC Place; RICHMOND; 245 H-16; elev. 119ft./36m.; 🄿; z 22472; ● 210
Haysi; Inc. Place; DICKENSON; 244 B-5; elev. 1,266ft./386m.; 🄿; z 24256; Ⓟ 222; © 186
Hayters Gap; RMC Place; WASHINGTON; *244 D-6; mail Abingdon z 24210
Haywood; RMC Place; MADISON; 245 F-11; 🄿; z 22722 & mail Culpeper z 22701; ● 100
Hazel; RMC Place; DICKENSON; *244 C-5; mail Dante z 24237; ● 50
Hazel Heights; RMC Place; BRISTOL (Independent City); ★ JNSC-; mail Bristol z 24201; pop. incl. with Bristol (Independent City)
Head Waters; RMC Place; HIGHLAND; 244 G-8; 🄿; z 24442; ● 30
Healing Springs; RMC Place; BATH; 244 H-6; mail Hot Springs z 24445; ● 100
Healys; RMC Place; MIDDLESEX; *245 I-17; elev. 79ft./24m.; mail Hartfield z 23071; rural
Heards; RMC Place; ALBEMARLE; *244 H-10; mail Afton z 22920
Heathsville; RMC Place; ⊡ NORTHUMBERLAND; 245 H-17; elev. 101ft./31m.; 🄿; z 22473; ● 300
Hebron; RMC Place; AUGUSTA; *244 G-8; mail Staunton z 24401; rural
Hebron; RMC Place; CARROLL; *244 M-3; elev. 2,607ft./795m.; mail Galax z 24333; rural
Hebron; RMC Place; DINWIDDIE; *245 K-13; mail Wilsons z 23894; rural
Hechler Village; RMC Place; HENRICO; *245 J-14; elev. 150ft./46m.; ★ RICH; mail Richmond z 23223; ● 1,850
Heightburg; HALIFAX; see Hitesburg (RMC Place)
Heights; RMC Place; PETERSBURG (Independent City); *245 K-14; elev. 150ft./46m.; ★ RICH; mail Petersburg z 23803; pop. incl. with Petersburg (Independent City)
Helmet; RMC Place; KING AND QUEEN; *245 H-15; elev. 186ft./57m.; mail Saint Stephens Church z 23148; rural
Hematite; RMC Place; ALLEGHANY; *244 I-5; elev. 1,584ft./483m.; mail Covington z 24426
Hendricks Store; RMC Place; BEDFORD; *244 K-7; elev. 989ft./301m.; mail Moneta z 24121; rural
HENRICO; 245 J-14; 🄿; z 23075, z 23228-29, z 23231, z 23233, z 23238, z 23242, z 23250, z 23255, z 23273, z 23288, z 23294; Ⓟ 217,881; © 262,300; ◆ 300,641
Henry; RMC Place; FRANKLIN, HENRY; 244 M-6; 🄿; ★ MRTNV; z 24102; ● 220
HENRY; 244 M-6; Ⓟ 56,942; © 57,930; ◆ 55,107
Henry Clay Heights; RMC Place; HANOVER; *245 I-14; ★ RICH; mail Mechanicsville z 23111; ● 280
Henry Fork; RMC Place; FRANKLIN; *244 L-6; mail Rocky Mount z 24151; rural
Henrytown; RMC Place; SMYTH; *244 D-6; mail Saltville z 24370
Hepners; RMC Place; SHENANDOAH; *244 E-9; mail Mount Jackson z 22842; rural
Herald; RMC Place; DICKENSON, WISE; *244 C-5; mail Coeburn z 24230; rural
Heritage Court; RMC Place; HENRICO; ★ RICH; mail Henrico z 23228
Heritage Square; RMC Place; FAIRFAX; mail Annandale z 22003
Heritage Village; RMC Place; FAIRFAX; *245 E-14; ★ WASH; mail Annandale z 22003
Herman; RMC Place; CHARLOTTE; *244 L-10; elev. 513ft./156m.; mail Saxe z 23967; rural
Hermitage; RMC Place; AUGUSTA; *244 G-9; elev. 1,329ft./405m.; mail Waynesboro z 22980
Hermitage Farms; RMC Place; HENRICO; ★ RICH; mail Henrico z 23228
Hermitage Park; RMC Place; HENRICO; ★ RICH; mail Henrico z 23228
Hermosa; RMC Place; HALIFAX, PITTSYLVANIA; *244 L-9; elev. 628ft./191m.; mail Nathalie z 24577; rural
Herndon; Inc. Place; FAIRFAX; 245 D-14; 🄿; ★ WASH; z 20170-72, z 20190-92, z 20194-96, z 20598, z 22095-96; Ⓟ 16,139; © 21,655; ◆ 22,475
Hessian Hills (The Meadows); RMC Place; ALBEMARLE; *244 H-10; ★ CHRLTV; mail Charlottesville z 22901; ● 900
Hewlett; RMC Place; HANOVER; *245 H-13; elev. 282ft./86m.; mail Ruther Glen z 22546; rural
Hickory; RMC Place; CHESAPEAKE (Independent City); *245 M-18; ★ NORF-; mail Chesapeake z 23322; pop. incl. with Chesapeake (Independent City)
Hickory Flat; RMC Place; CARROLL; *244 M-3; mail Galax z 24333; rural
Hickory Ground; RMC Place; CHESAPEAKE (Independent City); *245 M-18; elev. 19ft./6m.; ★ NORF-; mail Chesapeake z 23322; pop. incl. with Chesapeake (Independent City)
Hickory Grove Acres; RMC Place; PRINCE WILLIAM; *245 D-13; ★ WASH; mail Haymarket z 20169; ● 980
Hickory Haven; RMC Place; GOOCHLAND; *245 I-13; ★ RICH; mail Manakin Sabot z 23103; ● 150
Hickory Hill; RMC Place; ALBEMARLE; *244 H-10; ★ CHRLTV; mail Charlottesville z 22903; rural
Hickory Junction; RMC Place; RUSSELL; *244 C-6; mail Honaker z 24260; ● 30
Hicks Island; RMC Place; JAMES CITY; *245 J-16; elev. 20ft./6m.; ★ NN-H; mail Lanexa z 23089; ● 80
Hicksville; RMC Place; BLAND; *244 K-2; mail Bastian z 24314; ● 30
Hiddenbrook; RMC Place; FAIRFAX; *245 D-14; ★ WASH; mail Herndon z 20170; ● 900
Hidden Valley Estates; RMC Place; CHESTERFIELD; ★ RICH; mail Chester z 23831
Hideaway Park; RMC Place; FAIRFAX; *245 D-14; ★ WASH; mail Fairfax z 22031
Hidenwood; RMC Place; NEWPORT NEWS (Independent City); *245 K-17; ★ NN-H; mail Newport News z 23606, z 23612; pop. incl. with Newport News (Independent City)
High Hill; RMC Place; HALIFAX; *244 M-10; elev. 428ft./130m.; mail Virgilina z 24598; rural
High Knob; RMC Place; WARREN; *245 D-12; mail Front Royal z 22630; ● 200
Highland; RMC Place; PULASKI; *244 K-4; mail Dublin z 24084; rural
HIGHLAND; 244 G-7; Ⓟ 2,635; © 2,536; ◆ 2,366
Highland Gardens; RMC Place; HENRICO; *245 J-14; ★ RICH; mail Richmond z 23222; ● 550
Highland Homes; RMC Place; STAFFORD; *245 G-14; ★ FRED; mail Fredericksburg z 22405; ● 600
Highland Park; RMC Place; ARLINGTON; mail Arlington z 22205
Highland Park; RMC Place; HOPEWELL (Independent City); *245 K-14; ★ RICH; mail Hopewell z 23860; pop. incl. with Hopewell (Independent City)
Highland Park; RMC Place; PORTSMOUTH (Independent City); ★ NORF-; mail Portsmouth z 23707; pop. incl. with Portsmouth (Independent City)
Highland Park; RMC Place; PRINCE WILLIAM; *245 E-14; ★ WASH; mail Manassas z 20110
Highland Park; RMC Place; RICHMOND (Independent City); *245 J-14; ★ RICH; mail Richmond z 23222; pop. incl. with Richmond (Independent City)
Highlands; RMC Place; ARLINGTON; *245 D-15; ★ WASH; mail Arlington z 22201
Highland Springs; CDP; HENRICO; 243 C-9; 🄿; ★ RICH; z 23075; Ⓟ 13,823; © 15,137
High Meadows; RMC Place; WASHINGTON; *244 E-5; ★ JNSC-; mail Bristol z 24202; ● 250
High Point; RMC Place; HOPEWELL (Independent City); ★ RICH; mail Hopewell z 23860; pop. incl. with Hopewell (Independent City)
Hightown; RMC Place; HIGHLAND; 244 F-7; 🄿; z 24465; ● 50
Highview Park; RMC Place; ARLINGTON; *245 D-15; mail Arlington z 22207
Hilander Park; RMC Place; WASHINGTON; 244 D-5; ★ JNSC-; mail Bristol z 24202; ● 400
Hill; RMC Place; SCOTT; *244 D-4; mail Gate City z 24251
Hillbrook; RMC Place; FAIRFAX; *245 E-14; ★ WASH; mail Annandale z 22003
Hillcrest; RMC Place; CUMBERLAND; *245 J-11; mail Cumberland z 23040; ● 200
Hillcrest Estates; RMC Place; PRINCE WILLIAM; *245 E-14; ★ WASH; mail Manassas z 20111; ● 200
Hillsboro; Inc. Place; LOUDOUN; 245 C-13; 🄿; z 20132, z 20134; Ⓟ 72; © 96
Hillsdale; RMC Place; SUFFOLK (Independent City); ★ NORF-; mail Suffolk z 23434; pop. incl. with Suffolk (Independent City)
Hillsman Corner; RMC Place; CAMPBELL; *244 K-8; elev. 936ft./285m.; ★ LYNCH; mail Lynchburg z 24502
Hillsville; Inc. Place; ⊡ CARROLL; 244 M-3; 🄿; z 24343; Ⓟ 2,008; © 2,607
Hill Top; RMC Place; MARTINSVILLE (Independent City); ★ MRTNV; mail Martinsville z 24112; pop. incl. with Martinsville (Independent City)
Hilltop Farms; RMC Place; CHESTERFIELD; ★ RICH; mail Chester z 23831
Hilltop Manor; RMC Place; VIRGINIA BEACH (Independent City); *245 L-18; elev. 20ft./6m.; ★ NORF-; mail Virginia Beach z 23454; pop. incl. with Virginia Beach (Independent City)
Hilltop-Oceana; VIRGINIA BEACH (Independent City); see London Bridge (RMC Place)
Hilltown; RMC Place; GRAYSON, CARROLL; *244 M-3; mail Fries z 24330; ● 250
Hillwood; RMC Place; FAIRFAX; 249 G-4; ★ WASH; mail Falls Church z 22042; ● 1,650
Hilton; SCOTT; see Hiltons (RMC Place)
Hiltons (Hilton); RMC Place; SCOTT; 244 E-4; 🄿; z 24258; ● 100
Hilton Village; RMC Place; NEWPORT NEWS (Independent City); *245 L-17; ★ NN-H; mail Newport News z 23601; pop. incl. with Newport News (Independent City)
Hinesville; RMC Place; PITTSYLVANIA; *244 M-7; elev. 842ft./257m.; ★ DANV; mail Dry Fork z 24549; rural
Hinnom; RMC Place; WESTMORELAND; *245 G-16; elev. 49ft./15m.; mail Montross z 22520; rural
Hinton; RMC Place; ROCKINGHAM; 244 F-9; 🄿; z 22831; ● 250
Hitesburg (Heightburg); RMC Place; HALIFAX; *244 M-10; mail Virgilina z 24598; rural
Hiwassee; RMC Place; PULASKI; 244 L-3; 🄿; z 24347; ● 200
Hixburg; RMC Place; APPOMATTOX; *244 K-10; elev. 647ft./197m.; mail Pamplin z 23958
Hoadly; RMC Place; PRINCE WILLIAM; *245 E-14; ★ WASH; mail Woodbridge z 22191
Hobson; RMC Place; SUFFOLK (Independent City); *245 L-17; ★ NORF-; mail Suffolk z 23436; pop. incl. with Suffolk (Independent City)
Hockley; RMC Place; KING AND QUEEN; *245 J-16; elev. 57ft./17m.; mail Shacklefords z 23156; rural
Hockman; RMC Place; TAZEWELL; mail Bluefield z 24605; pop. incl. with Bluefield (Inc. Place)
Hodges; RMC Place; CAMPBELL; 244 K-8; elev. 763ft./233m.; mail Gladys z 24554; ● 100
Hodges Ferry; RMC Place; CHESAPEAKE (Independent City); *245 L-17; ★ NORF-; mail Chesapeake z 23321; pop. incl. with Chesapeake (Independent City)
Hodges Manor; RMC Place; PORTSMOUTH (Independent City); *245 L-17; ★ NORF-; mail Portsmouth z 23701; pop. incl. with Portsmouth (Independent City)
Hodgesville; RMC Place; FRANKLIN; *244 M-7; mail Rocky Mount z 24151; ● 30
Hoges Chapel; RMC Place; GILES; *244 K-4; mail Pembroke z 24136; ● 70
Holcomb Rock; RMC Place; BEDFORD; *244 J-8; elev. 584ft./178m.; ★ LYNCH; mail Lynchburg z 24503; rural
Holdcroft; RMC Place; CHARLES CITY; *245 J-15; elev. 104ft./32m.; mail Charles City z 23030; rural
Holiday Hills; RMC Place; RICHMOND (Independent City); *245 J-13; elev. 250ft./76m.; ★ RICH; mail Richmond z 23235; pop. incl. with Richmond (Independent City)
Holiday Park; RMC Place; CHESTERFIELD; ★ RICH; mail Richmond z 23237
Holiday Point Estates; RMC Place; SUFFOLK (Independent City); ★ NORF-; mail Suffolk z 23434; pop. incl. with Suffolk (Independent City)
Holland; RMC Place; SUFFOLK (Independent City); *245 M-16; ★ NORF-; mail Suffolk z 23437; pop. incl. with Suffolk (Independent City)
Hollindale; RMC Place; FAIRFAX; *245 E-15; ★ WASH; mail Alexandria z 22306; ● 2,140
Hollin Hall; RMC Place; FAIRFAX; 249 J-6; ★ WASH; mail Alexandria z 22308; ● 3,200
Hollin Hills; RMC Place; FAIRFAX; *245 E-15; ★ WASH; mail Alexandria z 22307; ● 2,700
Hollins; CDP; ROANOKE, BOTETOURT; 244 F-3; 🄿; ★ ROAN; z 24019; Ⓟ 13,305; © 14,309
Holly Brook; RMC Place; BLAND; *244 K-3; mail Bland z 24315
Holly Grove (Inez); RMC Place; LOUISA; *245 I-13; elev. 306ft./93m.; mail Bumpass z 23024; ● 50
Holly Hills; RMC Place; POWHATAN; *245 J-13; ★ RICH; mail Powhatan z 23139; ● 600
Hollymead; RMC Place; ALBEMARLE; *245 G-11; ★ CHRLTV; mail Charlottesville z 22911; ● 980
Holly Park; RMC Place; FAIRFAX; *245 E-14; ★ WASH; mail Fairfax z 22032; ● 1,200
Holly Point; RMC Place; ISLE OF WIGHT; *245 K-16; mail Smithfield z 23430
Hollywood; RMC Place; SUFFOLK (Independent City); *245 M-17; ★ NORF-; mail Suffolk z 23434; pop. incl. with Suffolk (Independent City)
Holmes Run Acres; RMC Place; FAIRFAX; 249 G-3; ★ WASH; mail Falls Church z 22042; ● 1,400
Holmes Run Heights; RMC Place; FAIRFAX; *245 E-14; ★ WASH; mail Annandale z 22003
Holmes Run Park; RMC Place; FAIRFAX; *245 E-15; ★ WASH; mail Falls Church z 22042; ● 800
Holston; RMC Place; WASHINGTON; 244 D-6; mail Abingdon z 24210; ● 50
Holston Mill; RMC Place; SMYTH; *244 M-1; elev. 2,203ft./671m.; mail Marion z 24354; rural
Holts Crossing; RMC Place; CAMPBELL; *244 L-9; mail Gladys z 24554; rural
Home Creek; RMC Place; BUCHANAN; *244 B-6; mail Grundy z 24614; rural
Homeville; RMC Place; SUSSEX; *245 L-15; mail Waverly z 23890
Homewood; RMC Place; FAIRFAX; *245 E-14; ★ WASH; mail Burke z 22015
Honaker; Inc. Place; RUSSELL; 244 C-6; elev. 1,860ft./567m.; 🄿; z 24260; Ⓟ 950; © 945
Honey Branch; RMC Place; WISE; mail Saint Paul z 24283; rural
Honeyville; RMC Place; PAGE; *244 F-10; mail Stanley z 22851; ● 50
Hood; RMC Place; MADISON; 245 G-11; 🄿; z 22723; ● 90
Hopeton; RMC Place; ACCOMACK; *245 H-19; elev. 31ft./9m.; mail Parksley z 23421; ● 30
Hopewell; Independent City; 245 K-14; 🄿 🄷 ■; ★ RICH; z 23860; Ⓟ 23,101; © 22,354; Ⓡ 22,277; ◆ 23,701
Hopewell; RMC Place; PITTSYLVANIA; *244 M-7; mail Dry Fork z 24549; rural
Hopkins; RMC Place; ACCOMACK; *245 I-19; mail Parksley z 23421; ● 100
Horizon Hills; RMC Place; BRISTOL (Independent City); ★ JNSC-; mail Bristol z 24201; pop. incl. with Bristol (Independent City)
Horners; RMC Place; WESTMORELAND; *245 G-15; mail Montross z 22520; rural
Hornsbyville (Tampico); RMC Place; YORK; *245 K-17; ★ NN-H; mail Yorktown z 23692; ● 230
Horntown; RMC Place; ACCOMACK; *245 H-20; 🄿; z 23395; ● 300
Horse Gap; RMC Place; WISE; *244 C-4; elev. 1,688ft./515m.; mail Pound z 24279; pop. incl. with Pound (Inc. Place)
Horse Head; RMC Place; NORTHUMBERLAND; *245 H-17; mail Heathsville z 22473; rural
Horse Pasture; CDP; HENRY; 244 M-6; ★ MRTNV; mail Martinsville z 24112; Ⓟ 2,224; © 2,255
Horsepen; RMC Place; TAZEWELL; 244 K-1; 🄿; z 24619; ● 230
Horsey; RMC Place; ACCOMACK; *245 H-20; elev. 22ft./7m.; mail Oak Hall z 23396; ● 50
Hotchkiss; RMC Place; BATH; *244 H-7; mail Millboro z 24460; rural
Hot Springs; RMC Place; BATH; 244 H-6; 🄿 🄷; z 24445; ● 300
Howardsville; RMC Place; ALBEMARLE; 244 I-10; 🄿; z 24562; ● 120
Howardsville; RMC Place; LOUDOUN; *245 D-12; elev. 542ft./165m.; mail Bluemont z 20135; ● 40
Howellsville (Hardesty); RMC Place; WARREN; *245 D-12; elev. 480ft./146m.; mail Front Royal z 22630; ● 50
Howertons; RMC Place; ESSEX; *245 I-16; elev. 158ft./48m.; 🄿; z 22454
Howland; RMC Place; NORTHUMBERLAND; *245 H-17; elev. 89ft./27m.; mail Heathsville z 22473; rural
Howlett Park; RMC Place; CHESTERFIELD; ★ RICH; mail Richmond z 23234
Hubbard Springs; RMC Place; LEE; *244 D-2; elev. 1,566ft./477m.; mail Jonesville z 24263; ● 40
Huckleberry Hills; RMC Place; PRINCE GEORGE; *245 K-14; elev. 150ft./46m.; ★ RICH; mail Petersburg z 23805; ● 200
Huddle; RMC Place; WYTHE; *244 L-2; mail Wytheville z 24382; rural
Huddleston; RMC Place; BEDFORD; 244 K-7; elev. 604ft./184m.; 🄿; z 24104; ● 100
Hudgins; RMC Place; MATHEWS; 245 J-17; elev. 14ft./4m.; 🄿; ★ NN-H; z 23076; ● 230
Hudson Crossroads; RMC Place; SHENANDOAH; *244 E-10; mail Mount Jackson z 22842; rural
Hudson Terrace; RMC Place; NEWPORT NEWS (Independent City); ★ NN-H; mail Newport News z 23607; pop. incl. with Newport News (Independent City)
Huffman; RMC Place; CRAIG; *244 K-4; mail Newport z 24128
Huffville; RMC Place; FLOYD; *244 L-5; elev. 2,479ft./756m.; mail Pilot z 24138; rural
Hughes Store; RMC Place; CHARLES CITY; *245 J-15; elev. 147ft./45m.; mail Charles City z 23030; rural
Hughesville; RMC Place; LOUDOUN; *245 D-13; elev. 465ft./142m.; ★ WASH; mail Leesburg z 20175; rural
Hume; RMC Place; FAUQUIER; 245 E-12; 🄿; z 22639; ● 160
Hunterdale; RMC Place; SOUTHAMPTON; 245 M-15; mail Franklin z 23851; pop. incl. with Franklin (Independent City)
Hunter Estates; RMC Place; FAIRFAX; *245 E-15; ★ WASH; mail Lorton z 22079
Hunters Valley; RMC Place; FAIRFAX; *245 D-14; ★ WASH; mail Vienna z 22181; ● 990
Huntersville; RMC Place; NORFOLK (Independent City); *245 L-18; elev. 15ft./5m.; ★ NORF-; mail Norfolk z 23504; pop. incl. with Norfolk (Independent City)
Huntersville; RMC Place; SUFFOLK (Independent City); ★ NORF-; mail Suffolk z 23435; pop. incl. with Suffolk (Independent City)
Huntingcreek Hills; RMC Place; CHESTERFIELD; *245 J-14; elev. 190ft./58m.; ★ RICH; mail Richmond z 23234; ● 1,400
Huntington; CDP; FAIRFAX; 249 I-6; ★ WASH; mail Alexandria z 22303; Ⓟ 7,489; © 8,325
Huntington; RMC Place; HENRICO; *245 I-13; elev. 268ft./82m.; ★ RICH; mail Henrico z 23229; ● 950
Huntington; RMC Place; NEWPORT NEWS (Independent City); *245 L-17; ★ NN-H; mail Newport News z 23607; pop. incl. with Newport News (Independent City)
Huntly; RMC Place; RAPPAHANNOCK; *245 E-12; 🄿; z 22627, z 22640; ● 50
Hunton; RMC Place; HENRICO; *245 I-14; elev. 216ft./66m.; ★ RICH; mail Glen Allen z 23060; ● 150
Hunts Village; RMC Place; FAIRFAX; *245 E-14; ★ WASH; mail Fairfax z 22032
Hupp; RMC Place; ROCKINGHAM; *244 E-10; mail Timberville z 22853; rural
Hurley; RMC Place; BUCHANAN; 244 B-6; 🄿; z 24620; ● 600
Hurricane; RMC Place; WISE; *244 C-4; mail Wise z 24293; ● 70
Hurt; Inc. Place; PITTSYLVANIA; 244 L-8; elev. 736ft./224m.; 🄿; z 24563; Ⓟ 1,294; © 1,276
Huske; RMC Place; SUSSEX; *245 L-14; elev. 87ft./27m.; mail Stony Creek z 23882; rural
Hustle; RMC Place; ESSEX; 245 H-15; elev. 162ft./49m.; 🄿; z 22476; ● 100
Hyacinth; RMC Place; NORTHUMBERLAND; *245 H-16; mail Callao z 22435; ● 50
Hybla Valley; CDP; FAIRFAX; 249 J-5; ★ WASH; mail Alexandria z 22306; Ⓟ 15,491; © 16,721
Hybla Valley Farms; RMC Place; FAIRFAX; *245 E-15; ★ WASH; mail Alexandria z 22306
Hyco; RMC Place; HALIFAX; *244 M-9; mail South Boston z 24592; ● 50
Hylas; RMC Place; HANOVER; *245 I-13; elev. 269ft./82m.; mail Rockville z 23146
Hylton Park; RMC Place; CHESTERFIELD; *245 J-13; elev. 320ft./98m.; ★ RICH; mail Richmond z 23235; ● 350

I

Iberis; RMC Place; LANCASTER; *245 I-17; elev. 39ft./12m.; mail Lancaster z 22503; rural
Ida; RMC Place; PAGE; 245 F-11; mail Luray z 22835; ● 220
Idlewilde; RMC Place; COVINGTON (Independent City); *244 I-6; mail Covington z 24426; pop. incl. with Covington (Independent City)
Idylwood; CDP; FAIRFAX; *245 D-14; ★ WASH; mail Falls Church z 22043; Ⓟ 14,710; © 16,005
Igo; RMC Place; KING GEORGE; *245 G-14; mail Fredericksburg z 22405; rural
Ilda (Little River Pines); RMC Place; FAIRFAX; *245 E-14; ★ WASH; mail Fairfax z 22031; ● 300
Imboden; RMC Place; WISE; *244 C-3; elev. 1,699ft./518m.; mail Appalachia z 24216; ● 100
Independence; Inc. Place; ⊡ GRAYSON; 244 M-2; elev. 2,698ft./822m.; 🄿; z 24348; Ⓟ 988; © 971
Independent Hill; RMC Place; PRINCE WILLIAM; 245 E-14; ★ WASH; mail Manassas z 20112; ● 100
Index; RMC Place; KING GEORGE; *245 G-15; elev. 182ft./55m.; mail King George z 22485; ● 50
Indian Field; RMC Place; RICHMOND; *245 H-16; mail Warsaw z 22572; ● 110
Indian Gap; RMC Place; BUCHANAN; *244 B-6; mail Vansant z 24656; rural
Indian Hollow; RMC Place; FREDERICK; *245 C-11; elev. 651ft./198m.; mail Winchester z 22603; rural
Indian Neck; RMC Place; KING AND QUEEN; *245 H-15; elev. 175ft./53m.; 🄿; z 23148; rural
Indian River; RMC Place; CHESAPEAKE (Independent City); ★ NORF-; mail Chesapeake z 23325; pop. incl. with Chesapeake (Independent City)
Indian River Park; RMC Place; CHESAPEAKE (Independent City); *245 L-18; ★ NORF-; mail Chesapeake z 23325; pop. incl. with Chesapeake (Independent City)
Indian Rock; RMC Place; BOTETOURT; *244 J-7; mail Buchanan z 24066; rural
Indian Run Park; RMC Place; FAIRFAX; *245 E-15; ★ WASH; mail Alexandria z 22312; ● 1,200
Indian Springs; RMC Place; CHESTERFIELD; *245 J-14; elev. 150ft./46m.; ★ RICH; mail Richmond z 23234; ● 350
Indian Springs; RMC Place; FAIRFAX; ★ WASH; mail Alexandria z 22312
Indian Valley; RMC Place; FLOYD; 244 L-4; elev. 2,709ft./826m.; 🄿; z 24105; ● 120
Indika; RMC Place; ISLE OF WIGHT; *245 L-16; elev. 77ft./23m.; mail Windsor z 23487; rural
Inez; LOUISA; see Holly Grove (RMC Place)
Ingham; RMC Place; PAGE; *244 F-10; mail Shenandoah z 22849; rural
Ingleside; RMC Place; NORFOLK (Independent City); *245 L-18; ★ NORF-; mail Norfolk z 23502; pop. incl. with Norfolk (Independent City)
Ingram; RMC Place; HALIFAX; 244 M-8; elev. 711ft./217m.; 🄿; z 24597; ● 40
Inlet; RMC Place; CULPEPER; *245 F-12; mail Culpeper z 22701; ● 90
Inman; RMC Place; WISE; 244 C-3; elev. 1,704ft./519m.; mail Appalachia z 24216; pop. incl. with Appalachia (Inc. Place)
Ino; RMC Place; KING AND QUEEN; *245 I-16; elev. 136ft./41m.; mail Center Cross z 22437; rural
Interior; RMC Place; GILES; *244 J-4; elev. 2,454ft./748m.; mail Ripplemead z 24150
Intervale; RMC Place; ALLEGHANY; *244 I-6; mail Covington z 24426; ● 180
Ira; RMC Place; BUCHANAN; mail Hurley z 24620; ● 50
Irisburg; RMC Place; HENRY; *244 M-6; ★ MRTNV; mail Axton z 24054; rural
Irondale; RMC Place; WISE; *244 D-3; mail Big Stone Gap z 24219; rural
Iron Gate; Inc. Place; ALLEGHANY; 244 I-6; 🄿; z 24448; Ⓟ 417; © 404
Irongate; RMC Place; PRINCE WILLIAM; *245 E-14; ★ WASH; mail Manassas z 20109; ● 1,500
Ironto; RMC Place; MONTGOMERY; 244 K-5; elev. 1,298ft./396m.; 🄿; z 24087; ● 90
Irving; RMC Place; BEDFORD; *244 J-7; mail Thaxton z 24174; ● 30
Irvington; Inc. Place; LANCASTER; 245 I-17; elev. 31ft./9m.; 🄿; z 22480; Ⓟ 496; © 673
Irwin; RMC Place; GOOCHLAND; *245 I-12; elev. 161ft./49m.; mail Goochland z 23063; rural
Isaac; RMC Place; SOUTHAMPTON; *245 M-15; elev. 67ft./20m.; mail Franklin z 23851; rural
Island Creek; CARROLL; see Star (RMC Place)
Island Farm; RMC Place; ESSEX; *245 H-16; elev. 5ft./2m.; mail Champlain z 22438
Island Ford; RMC Place; ROCKINGHAM; *244 G-10; mail Elkton z 22827; rural
Isle of Wight; RMC Place; ⊡ ISLE OF WIGHT; 245 L-16; 🄿; z 23397; ● 70
ISLE OF WIGHT; 245 L-16; Ⓟ 25,053; © 29,728; ◆ 36,724
Isom; RMC Place; DICKENSON; *244 B-4; elev. 1,458ft./444m.; mail Clintwood z 24228; rural
Ivanhoe; RMC Place; WYTHE; 244 M-3; elev. 2,059ft./628m.; 🄿; z 24350; ● 550
Ivondale; RMC Place; RICHMOND; *245 H-16; elev. 36ft./11m.; mail Warsaw z 22572; rural
Ivor; Inc. Place; SOUTHAMPTON; 245 L-16; 🄿; z 23866; Ⓟ 324; © 320
Ivy; RMC Place; ALBEMARLE; *244 H-10; 🄿; ★ CHRLTV; z 22945; ● 300

J

Jackson Heights; RMC Place; LYNCHBURG (Independent City); ★ LYNCH; mail Lynchburg z 24501; pop. incl. with Lynchburg (Independent City)
Jacksons Ferry; RMC Place; WYTHE; *244 L-3; mail Austinville z 24312; rural
Jamaica; RMC Place; MIDDLESEX; *245 I-16; elev. 107ft./33m.; 🄿; z 23079; ● 60
JAMES CITY; 245 K-16; Ⓟ 34,859; © 48,102; ◆ 64,266
James River Estates; RMC Place; GOOCHLAND; *245 J-13; ★ RICH; mail Henrico z 23238; ● 300
James Store; RMC Place; GLOUCESTER; *245 J-17; elev. 39ft./12m.; 🄿; ★ NN-H; z 23128; ● 130
Jamesville; RMC Place; NORTHAMPTON; 245 J-19; 🄿; z 23398; ● 80
Janey; RMC Place; BUCHANAN; *244 B-6; elev. 1,224ft./373m.; mail Oakwood z 24631; ● 100
Jarratt; Inc. Place; GREENSVILLE, SUSSEX; 245 M-14; 🄿; z 23867, z 23870; Ⓟ 556; © 589
Jasper; RMC Place; LEE; 244 D-3; mail Duffield z 24244; ● 50
Java; RMC Place; PITTSYLVANIA; 244 M-8; 🄿; z 24565; ● 30
Jefferson; CDP-Census Area Only; FAIRFAX; *245 D-14; ★ WASH; mail Falls Church z 22042; Ⓟ 25,782; © 27,422; ◆ 28,499
Jefferson; RMC Place; POWHATAN; *245 I-12; elev. 343ft./105m.; mail Powhatan z 23139
Jefferson Manor; RMC Place; FAIRFAX; *245 E-15; 🄿; ★ WASH; z 22303; ● 2,400
Jefferson Mews; RMC Place; FAIRFAX; *245 D-14; ★ WASH; mail Herndon z 20170; pop. incl. with Herndon (Inc. Place)
Jefferson Park; RMC Place; PRINCE GEORGE; *245 K-14; ★ RICH; mail Hopewell z 23860; ● 450
Jeffersonton; RMC Place; CULPEPER; 245 E-12; 🄿; z 22724; ● 180
Jefferson Village; RMC Place; FAIRFAX; 249 G-4; ★ WASH; mail Falls Church z 22042; ● 2,500
Jeffress; RMC Place; MECKLENBURG; *244 M-10; elev. 325ft./99m.; mail Clarksville z 23927; ● 30
Jenkins Bridge; RMC Place; ACCOMACK; *245 H-20; elev. 6ft./2m.; 🄿; z 23399; ● 100
Jenkins Neck; RMC Place; GLOUCESTER; *245 K-17; ★ NN-H; mail Hayes z 23072; ● 350
Jennings; NOTTOWAY; see Jennings Ordinary (RMC Place)
Jennings Gap; RMC Place; AUGUSTA; *244 G-8; mail Churchville z 24421; ● 30
Jennings Ordinary (Jennings); RMC Place; NOTTOWAY; *245 K-12; mail Crewe z 23930; ● 50
Jericho; RMC Place; SUFFOLK (Independent City); ★ NORF-; mail Suffolk z 23434; pop. incl. with Suffolk (Independent City)
Jerome; RMC Place; SHENANDOAH; *244 E-10; mail Edinburg z 22824; ● 30
Jersey; RMC Place; KING GEORGE; *245 G-15; elev. 158ft./48m.; 🄿; z 22481; ● 70
Jessup Farms; RMC Place; CHESTERFIELD; *245 J-14; elev. 206ft./63m.; ★ RICH; mail Richmond z 23234; ● 400
Jester Gardens; RMC Place; CHESAPEAKE (Independent City); *245 L-17; elev. 25ft./8m.; ★ NORF-; mail Chesapeake z 23321; pop. incl. with Chesapeake (Independent City)
Jetersville; RMC Place; AMELIA; 245 K-12; 🄿; z 23083; ● 200
Jewell; TAZEWELL; see Jewell Ridge (RMC Place)
Jewell Hollow; RMC Place; PAGE; *245 E-11; mail Luray z 22835; rural
Jewell Ridge (Jewell); RMC Place; TAZEWELL; 244 B-6; 🄿; z 24622; ● 350
Jewell Valley; RMC Place; BUCHANAN; *244 B-6; 🄿; z 24622; ● 120
Johnsons Center; RMC Place; KING GEORGE; *245 G-14; elev. 187ft./57m.; mail King George z 22485; rural
Johnsons Mill; LEE; see Bundy (RMC Place)
Johnsontown; RMC Place; NORTHAMPTON; *245 J-19; mail Machipongo z 23405
Joliff; RMC Place; CHESAPEAKE (Independent City); *245 L-17; ★ NORF-; mail Chesapeake z 23321; pop. incl. with Chesapeake (Independent City)
Jolivue; CDP; AUGUSTA; 244 H-9; mail Staunton z 24401; Ⓟ 1,092; © 1,037
Jollett; RMC Place; PAGE; *244 F-10; mail Elkton z 22827; ● 120
Jones; RMC Place; SPOTSYLVANIA; *245 G-13; mail Spotsylvania z 22553; rural
Jonesboro; RMC Place; BRUNSWICK; *245 L-12; elev. 436ft./133m.; mail Blackstone z 23824; rural
Jones Corner; RMC Place; CAROLINE; *245 H-15; elev. 180ft./55m.; mail Bowling Green z 22427; rural
Jones Creek; RMC Place; MARTINSVILLE (Independent City); *244 M-6; ★ MRTNV; mail Martinsville z 24112; pop. incl. with Martinsville (Independent City)
Jones Store; CHARLOTTE; see Kings Crossroads (RMC Place)
Jonesville; Inc. Place; ⊡ LEE; 244 D-2; elev. 1,530ft./466m.; 🄿; z 24263; Ⓟ 927; © 995
Joppa Mill; RMC Place; BEDFORD; *244 K-7; elev. 734ft./224m.; mail Bedford z 24523; rural
Jordan Mines; RMC Place; ALLEGHANY; 244 I-5; 🄿; z 24426; ● 30
Josephine; RMC Place; WISE; *244 C-4; mail Norton z 24273; ● 200
Joyce Heights; RMC Place; FAIRFAX (Independent City); *245 E-14; ★ WASH; mail Fairfax z 22030; pop. incl. with Fairfax (Independent City)
Joyner; RMC Place; SOUTHAMPTON; *245 M-14; elev. 109ft./33m.; mail Capron z 23829; ● 30
Justisville; RMC Place; ACCOMACK; *245 I-19; elev. 4ft./1m.; mail Parksley z 23421; ● 50

K

Ka; RMC Place; SCOTT; *244 D-4; mail Dungannon z 24245
Karo; RMC Place; WARREN; *245 D-11; mail Front Royal z 22630; rural
Kathmoor; RMC Place; FAIRFAX; *245 E-15; ★ WASH; mail Alexandria z 22310
Keats; RMC Place; MECKLENBURG; *245 N-11; mail Manson z 27553; rural
Keeling; RMC Place; PITTSYLVANIA; 244 M-8; 🄿; z 24566; ● 50
Keene; RMC Place; ALBEMARLE; 244 H-10; elev. 545ft./166m.; 🄿; z 22946; ● 200
Keene Mill Manor; RMC Place; FAIRFAX; *245 E-14; ★ WASH; mail Springfield z 22152
Keen Mill Heights; FAIRFAX; see Orange Hunt (RMC Place)
Keen Mountain; RMC Place; BUCHANAN; *244 B-6; 🄿; z 24624; ● 250
Keezletown; RMC Place; ROCKINGHAM; 244 F-10; elev. 1,332ft./406m.; 🄿; z 22832; ● 400
Keith; RMC Place; KING WILLIAM; *245 H-14; elev. 184ft./56m.; mail Aylett z 23009
Keller; Inc. Place; ACCOMACK; 245 I-19; 🄿; z 23401; Ⓟ 235; © 173
Kells Corner; RMC Place; LUNENBURG; *245 L-11; elev. 497ft./151m.; mail Chase City z 23924; rural
Kelly; RMC Place; CAMPBELL; *244 J-9; elev. 524ft./160m.; ★ LYNCH; mail Lynchburg z 24504; rural
Kelsa; RMC Place; BUCHANAN; *244 A-6; mail Hurley z 24620
Kelso Mill; RMC Place; BEDFORD; *244 J-7; elev. 956ft./291m.; mail Bedford z 24523; rural
Kemmerer Gem Number 2; RMC Place; LEE; mail Saint Charles z 24282; ● 100
Kemp's Place; RMC Place; HENRICO; ★ RICH; mail Henrico z 23231
Kempsville; RMC Place; VIRGINIA BEACH (Independent City); *245 L-18; ★ NORF-; mail Virginia Beach z 23462; pop. incl. with Virginia Beach (Independent City)
Kempsville Colony; RMC Place; VIRGINIA BEACH (Independent City); *245 L-18; elev. 15ft./5m.; ★ NORF-; mail Virginia Beach z 23464; pop. incl. with Virginia Beach (Independent City)
Kempsville Gardens; RMC Place; VIRGINIA BEACH (Independent City); *245 L-18; elev. 10ft./3m.; ★ NORF-; mail Virginia Beach z 23462; pop. incl. with Virginia Beach (Independent City)
Kempsville Heights; RMC Place; VIRGINIA BEACH (Independent City); *245 L-18; elev. 10ft./3m.; ★ NORF-; mail Virginia Beach z 23462; pop. incl. with Virginia Beach (Independent City)
Kenbridge; Inc. Place; LUNENBURG; 245 L-12; 🄿; z 23944; Ⓟ 1,264; © 1,253
Kendall Acres; RMC Place; CHESTERFIELD; *245 J-14; elev. 150ft./46m.; ★ RICH; mail Richmond z 23234; ● 600
Kendall Grove; RMC Place; NORTHAMPTON; *245 J-19; mail Eastville z 23347; ● 30
Kenilworth; RMC Place; NORFOLK (Independent City); *245 L-18; ★ NORF-; mail Norfolk z 23503; pop. incl. with Norfolk (Independent City)
Kennard; RMC Place; RICHMOND; *245 H-16; elev. 118ft./36m.; mail Warsaw z 22572; rural
Kennelworth; RMC Place; PETERSBURG (Independent City); *245 K-14; elev. 110ft./34m.; ★ RICH; mail Petersburg z 23803; pop. incl. with Petersburg (Independent City)
Kent; RMC Place; WYTHE; *244 L-2; mail Wytheville z 24382; rural
Kent Gardens; RMC Place; FAIRFAX; *245 D-15; ★ WASH; mail Mc Lean z 22101
Kent Park; RMC Place; NORFOLK (Independent City); ★ NORF-; mail Norfolk z 23509; pop. incl. with Norfolk (Independent City)
Kents Store; RMC Place; FLUVANNA; 245 H-12; 🄿; z 23084; ● 50
Kentuck; RMC Place; PITTSYLVANIA; *244 M-8; ★ DANV; mail Ringgold z 24586; ● 50
Kenwood; RMC Place; HANOVER; *245 I-14; ★ RICH; mail Ashland z 23005
Kenwood; RMC Place; HOPEWELL (Independent City); *245 K-14; ★ RICH; mail Hopewell z 23860; pop. incl. with Hopewell (Independent City)
Keokee; CDP; LEE; 244 D-3; 🄿; z 24265; © 316
Kerfoot; RMC Place; FAUQUIER; *245 D-12; mail Delaplane z 20144; rural
Kermit; RMC Place; SCOTT; *244 E-3; mail Gate City z 24251; ● 30
Kerns; RMC Place; SCOTT; *244 D-4; mail Fort Blackmore z 24250; rural
Kernstown; RMC Place; WINCHESTER (Independent City); *245 C-11; mail Winchester z 22602; pop. incl. with Winchester (Independent City)
Kerrs Creek; RMC Place; ROCKBRIDGE; *244 I-7; elev. 1,158ft./353m.; mail Lexington z 24450; rural
Keswick; RMC Place; ALBEMARLE; 245 H-11; 🄿; ★ CHRLTV; z 22947; ● 200
Keysville; Inc. Place; CHARLOTTE; 245 L-11; elev. 642ft./196m.; 🄿; z 23947; Ⓟ 606; © 817
Key West; RMC Place; ALBEMARLE; 243 B-4; ★ CHRLTV; mail Charlottesville z 22911; ● 300
Kibler; RMC Place; PATRICK; *244 M-4; mail Ararat z 24053
Kidds Fork; RMC Place; CAROLINE; *245 H-14; elev. 200ft./61m.; mail Milford z 22514; rural
Kidd's Store; RMC Place; FLUVANNA; *245 I-11; mail Scottsville z 24590; rural
Kidville; RMC Place; AUGUSTA; *244 H-9; mail Fishersville z 22939; rural
Kiels Gardens; RMC Place; FAIRFAX; *245 E-14; ★ WASH; mail Fairfax z 22030; ● 210
Kiger Hill; RMC Place; ROCKBRIDGE; *244 I-7; mail Lexington z 24450; rural
Kilby; RMC Place; SUFFOLK (Independent City); *245 M-16; ★ NORF-; mail Suffolk z 23434; pop. incl. with Suffolk (Independent City)
Kilby Shores; RMC Place; SUFFOLK (Independent City); ★ NORF-; mail Suffolk z 23434; pop. incl. with Suffolk (Independent City)
Kildare Annex; RMC Place; HENRICO; *245 I-14; ★ RICH; mail Richmond z 23230; ● 400
Kilmarnock; Inc. Place; LANCASTER, NORTHUMBERLAND; 245 I-17; 🄿 🄷; z 22482; Ⓟ 1,109; © 1,244
Kilmarnock Wharf; RMC Place; LANCASTER; *245 I-17; mail Kilmarnock z 22482; rural
Kimages; RMC Place; CHARLES CITY; *245 J-15; elev. 74ft./23m.; mail Charles City z 23030; ● 40
Kimballton; RMC Place; GILES; *244 J-4; mail Ripplemead z 24150
Kimberley Hills; RMC Place; CUMBERLAND; *245 K-11; elev. 447ft./136m.; mail Farmville z 23901; ● 200
Kimberling; RMC Place; BLAND; *244 K-2; mail Bland z 24315; rural
Kimberly Acres; RMC Place; CHESTERFIELD; *245 J-14; elev. 186ft./57m.; ★ RICH; mail Richmond z 23234; ● 300
Kinderhook; RMC Place; GREENE; mail Stanardsville z 22973; rural
Kindrick (Stringtown); RMC Place; WYTHE; *244 L-2; mail Wytheville z 24382; ● 130
KING AND QUEEN; 245 I-15; Ⓟ 6,289; © 6,630; ◆ 6,909
King and Queen Court House; RMC Place; ⊡ KING AND QUEEN; *245 I-16; elev. 127ft./39m.; 🄿; z 23085; ● 100
King George; RMC Place; ⊡ KING GEORGE; 245 G-15; 🄿; z 22485; ● 550
KING GEORGE; 245 G-15; Ⓟ 13,527; © 16,803; ◆ 24,348
Kingsbury Manor; RMC Place; AUGUSTA; *244 H-9; elev. 1,458ft./444m.; mail Waynesboro z 22980; ● 330
Kings Corner; RMC Place; JAMES CITY; *245 J-16; elev. 62ft./19m.; ★ NN-H; mail Lanexa z 23089; rural
Kings Crossroads (Jones Store); RMC Place; CHARLOTTE; *244 M-10; elev. 471ft./144m.; mail Red Oak z 23964; rural
Kingsdale; RMC Place; SOUTHAMPTON; *245 M-16; elev. 14ft./4m.; mail Franklin z 23851; ● 300
Kings Fork; RMC Place; SUFFOLK (Independent City); ★ NORF-; mail Suffolk z 23434; pop. incl. with Suffolk (Independent City)
Kings Grant; RMC Place; VIRGINIA BEACH (Independent City); *245 L-18; elev. 10ft./3m.; ★ NORF-; mail Virginia Beach z 23452; pop. incl. with Virginia Beach (Independent City)
Kings Hill; RMC Place; HENRICO; ★ RICH; mail Henrico z 23231
Kingsland; RMC Place; CHESTERFIELD; 243 F-8; ★ RICH; mail Richmond z 23234; ● 400
Kings Park; RMC Place; FAIRFAX; 249 H-3; ★ WASH; mail Springfield z 22151; ● 6,500
Kings Park West; RMC Place; FAIRFAX; 249 H-2; ★ WASH; mail Fairfax z 22032; ● 6,300
Kings Point; RMC Place; JAMES CITY; 243 F-2; elev. 80ft./24m.; ★ NN-H; mail Williamsburg z 23185; ● 500
Kings Store; RMC Place; FLOYD; *244 L-5; elev. 2,514ft./766m.; mail Copper Hill z 24079, Floyd z 24091; rural
Kingston; RMC Place; CAMPBELL; *244 K-8; ★ LYNCH; mail Evington z 24550; ● 50
Kingston Chase; RMC Place; FAIRFAX; *245 D-14; ★ WASH; mail Herndon z 20170; ● 950
Kingstown; RMC Place; ROANOKE; 244 F-2; ★ ROAN; mail Roanoke z 24019; ● 120
Kingsville; RMC Place; PRINCE EDWARD; 245 K-11; elev. 492ft./150m.; mail Farmville z 23901; ● 50
Kingswood; RMC Place; JAMES CITY; *245 K-16; elev. 50ft./15m.; ★ NN-H; mail Williamsburg z 23185; ● 250
Kingswood Court; RMC Place; HANOVER; *245 I-14; ★ RICH; mail Mechanicsville z 23116; ● 150
Kingtown; RMC Place; BRISTOL (Independent City); *244 E-5; ★ JNSC-; mail Bristol z 24201; pop. incl. with Bristol (Independent City)
King William; RMC Place; ⊡ KING WILLIAM; 245 I-15; elev. 142ft./43m.; 🄿; z 23086; ● 90
KING WILLIAM; 245 I-15; Ⓟ 10,913; © 13,146; ◆ 16,682
Kino; RMC Place; ESSEX; *245 H-15; elev. 140ft./43m.; mail Tappahannock z 22560; ● 30
Kinsale; RMC Place; WESTMORELAND; 245 H-16; 🄿; z 22488; ● 300
Kiptopeke; RMC Place; NORTHAMPTON; *245 K-19; mail Cape Charles z 23310; rural
Kire; RMC Place; GILES; *244 J-4; mail Ripplemead z 24150; rural
Kirkside; RMC Place; FAIRFAX; *245 E-15; ★ WASH; mail Alexandria z 22306; ● 950
Klotz; RMC Place; GILES; *244 K-4; mail Ripplemead z 24150; rural
Knightly; RMC Place; AUGUSTA; *244 G-9; mail Fort Defiance z 24437; rural
Knob Hill; RMC Place; VIRGINIA BEACH (Independent City); *245 L-18; elev. 10ft./3m.; ★ NORF-; mail Virginia Beach z 23464; pop. incl. with Virginia Beach (Independent City)
Knoll; RMC Place; AMHERST; *244 J-8; elev. 772ft./235m.; mail Monroe z 24574; rural
Koehler; RMC Place; HENRY; *244 M-6; ★ MRTNV; mail Martinsville z 24112; ● 230
Koger Executive Center; RMC Place; NORFOLK (Independent City); ★ NORF-; mail Norfolk z 23506; pop. incl. with Norfolk (Independent City)
Konnarock; RMC Place; WASHINGTON; 244 M-1; mail Damascus z 24236; ● 200
Korah; RMC Place; RICHMOND (Independent City); ★ RICH; pop. incl. with Richmond (Independent City)

L

Laburnum Manor; RMC Place; HENRICO; *245 J-14; ★ RICH; mail Richmond z 23222; ● 1,600
Lacey Forest; RMC Place; ARLINGTON; *245 D-15; ★ WASH; mail Arlington z 22205
Lacey Spring; RMC Place; ROCKINGHAM; 244 F-10; 🄿; z 22833; ● 150
Lackey; RMC Place; YORK; 243 G-4; 🄿; ★ NN-H; z 23694; ● 500
La Crosse; Inc. Place; MECKLENBURG; 245 M-12; 🄿; z 23950; Ⓟ 549; © 618
Ladd; RMC Place; AUGUSTA; 244 H-9; mail Waynesboro z 22980; ● 410
Ladysmith; RMC Place; CAROLINE; 245 H-13; elev. 221ft./67m.; 🄿; z 22501; ● 200
Lafayette; RMC Place; MONTGOMERY; 244 K-5; 🄿; ★ ROAN; z 24087; ● 300
Lafayette Annex; RMC Place; NORFOLK (Independent City); *245 L-18; ★ NORF-; mail Norfolk z 23509; pop. incl. with Norfolk (Independent City)
Lafayette Boulevard; RMC Place; NORFOLK (Independent City); ★ NORF-; mail Norfolk z 23509; pop. incl. with Norfolk (Independent City)
Lafayette Shores; RMC Place; NORFOLK (Independent City); *245 L-18; ★ NORF-; mail Norfolk z 23509; pop. incl. with Norfolk (Independent City)
Lahore; RMC Place; ORANGE; 245 G-12; elev. 374ft./114m.; mail Unionville z 22567
Lake; RMC Place; NORTHUMBERLAND; *245 H-17; mail Lottsburg z 22511; rural
Lake Barcroft; CDP; FAIRFAX; *245 E-15; ★ WASH; mail Falls Church z 22041, z 22044; Ⓟ 8,686; © 8,906
Lake Caroline; RMC Place; CAROLINE; *245 H-13; mail Ruther Glen z 22546; ● 450
Lake Crystal Farms; RMC Place; CHESTERFIELD; *245 J-13; elev. 250ft./76m.; ★ RICH; mail Richmond z 23235; ● 350
Lake Hill; RMC Place; CHESTERFIELD; ★ RICH; mail Richmond z 23234
Lake Jackson; RMC Place; PRINCE WILLIAM; *245 E-14; ★ WASH; mail Manassas z 20112; ● 850
Lake Monticello; CDP-Census Area Only; FLUVANNA; *245 H-11; mail Palmyra z 22963; Ⓟ 2,331; © 6,852
Lake of the Woods; RMC Place; ORANGE; *245 G-13; 🄿; z 22508; ● 800
Lake Ridge; CDP-Census Area Only; PRINCE WILLIAM; *245 E-14; 🄿; ★ WASH; z 22192; Ⓟ 23,862; © 30,404; ◆ 39,571
Lakeside; CDP; HENRICO; 243 B-7; 🄿; ★ RICH; z 23228; Ⓟ 12,081; © 11,157
Lakeside; RMC Place; NEWPORT NEWS (Independent City); ★ NN-H; mail Newport News z 23606; pop. incl. with Newport News (Independent City)
Lakeside; RMC Place; SALEM (Independent City); ★ ROAN; mail Salem z 24153; pop. incl. with Salem (Independent City)
Lakeside Heights; RMC Place; YORK; *245 K-17; elev. 17ft./5m.; ★ NN-H; mail Yorktown z 23692; ● 300
Lakeside Hills; RMC Place; HENRICO; ★ RICH; mail Henrico z 23228
Lakeside Village; RMC Place; CUMBERLAND; 245 I-11; mail Columbia z 23038; summer pop. 200; ● 80
Lakeview; RMC Place; FREDERICK; *245 D-11; elev. 730ft./223m.; mail Stephens City z 22655; ● 30
Lakeview Acres; RMC Place; PRINCE EDWARD; *245 K-11; elev. 438ft./134m.; mail Farmville z 23901; ● 90
Lakeville Estates; RMC Place; VIRGINIA BEACH (Independent City); *245 L-18; elev. 15ft./5m.; ★ NORF-; mail Virginia Beach z 23464; pop. incl. with Virginia Beach (Independent City)
Lakewood; RMC Place; FAIRFAX; *245 E-15; ★ WASH; mail Falls Church z 22041
Lakewood; RMC Place; JAMES CITY; *245 K-16; elev. 70ft./21m.; ★ NN-H; mail Williamsburg z 23185; ● 200
Lakewood; RMC Place; NORFOLK (Independent City); *245 L-18; ★ NORF-; mail Norfolk z 23509; pop. incl. with Norfolk (Independent City)
Lakewood; RMC Place; PITTSYLVANIA; *244 N-8; elev. 544ft./166m.; ★ DANV; mail Danville z 24541; pop. incl. with Danville (Independent City)
Lamberts Point; RMC Place; NORFOLK (Independent City); *245 L-17; ★ NORF-; mail Norfolk z 23508; pop. incl. with Norfolk (Independent City)
Lambsburg; RMC Place; CARROLL; *244 N-3; 🄿; z 24351; ● 190
Lanahan; FRANKLIN; see Waidsboro (RMC Place)
Lancaster; RMC Place; ⊡ LANCASTER; 245 I-17; 🄿; z 22503; ● 80
LANCASTER; 245 I-17; Ⓟ 10,896; © 11,567; ◆ 11,551
Landmark Square; RMC Place; MANASSAS (Independent City); ★ WASH; mail Manassas z 20110; pop. incl. with Manassas (Independent City)
Land of Promise; RMC Place; VIRGINIA BEACH (Independent City); *245 M-18; elev. 12ft./4m.; ★ NORF-; mail Virginia Beach z 23457; pop. incl. with Virginia Beach (Independent City)
Land O'Pines; RMC Place; CHESTERFIELD; *245 J-14; ★ RICH; mail Chesterfield z 23832; ● 120
Landtown; RMC Place; VIRGINIA BEACH (Independent City); *245 M-18; elev. 13ft./4m.; ★ NORF-; mail Virginia Beach z 23456; pop. incl. with Virginia Beach (Independent City)
Lanes Corner; RMC Place; HANOVER; *245 I-13; elev. 274ft./84m.; ★ RICH; mail Ashland z 23005; ● 60
Lanes Corner; RMC Place; SPOTSYLVANIA; *245 G-13; elev. 395ft./120m.; mail Spotsylvania z 22553; rural
Lanesville; RMC Place; KING WILLIAM; *245 I-15; elev. 107ft./33m.; mail King William z 23086; rural
Laneview; RMC Place; ESSEX; 245 I-16; 🄿; z 22504; ● 30
Lanexa; RMC Place; NEW KENT; 245 J-15; 🄿; z 23089; ● 250
Langhorne Acres; RMC Place; FAIRFAX; *245 E-14; ★ WASH; mail Fairfax z 22031; ● 700
Langley; RMC Place; FAIRFAX; 249 E-4; ★ WASH; mail Hampton z 23665, Mc Lean z 22101; ● 1,450
Langley Forest; RMC Place; FAIRFAX; *245 D-14; ★ WASH; mail Mc Lean z 22101
Langley View; RMC Place; HAMPTON (Independent City); *245 K-17; ★ NN-H; mail Hampton z 23669; pop. incl. with Hampton (Independent City)
Lankford Corner; RMC Place; LANCASTER, NORTHUMBERLAND; *245 I-17; elev. 113ft./34m.; mail Heathsville z 22473; rural
Lantz Mills; RMC Place; SHENANDOAH; *244 E-10; mail Edinburg z 22824; ● 30
Lara; RMC Place; NORTHUMBERLAND, RICHMOND; *245 H-17; mail Lancaster z 22503; rural
Larchmont; RMC Place; ARLINGTON; *245 D-15; elev. 5ft./2m.; ★ WASH; mail Arlington z 22201
Larchmont; RMC Place; NORFOLK (Independent City); *245 L-17; elev. 5ft./2m.; ★ NORF-; mail Norfolk z 23508; pop. incl. with Norfolk (Independent City)
Lark; TAZEWELL; see Coaldan (RMC Place)
Larkspur; RMC Place; VIRGINIA BEACH (Independent City); *245 L-18; ★ NORF-; mail Virginia Beach z 23462; pop. incl. with Virginia Beach (Independent City)
Larrys Store; RMC Place; HALIFAX; *244 M-10; elev. 429ft./131m.; mail Virgilina z 24598; ● 50

Entries in **UPPERCASE** are counties.
Entries in **bold** have populations of 2,500 or more.
Names in parentheses are alternate names.
Inc. Place — Incorporated Place
RMC Place — Rand McNally Designated Place
CDP — Census Designated Place
MCD — Minor Civil Division

⊡ County Seat
▲ Minor Civil Division
elev. Elevation
🄿 Post Office
🄷 Hospital
🄲 College
■ Principal Business Center
★ Ranally Metro Area (RMA) Abbreviation
z Zip Code(s)
Ⓟ Previous Census Population
Ⓡ Revised Census Population
Ⓐ Annexation Population
● Rand McNally Population Estimate
© Final Census Population
Ⓢ Special Census Population
◆ Estimated Population

For additional definitions see Glossary, Volume 1, and Introduction, Volume 2.

Larwood Acres; RMC Place; WASHINGTON; ★ JNSC-; mail Bristol z 24202; ● 200
Lassiter Courts; RMC Place; NEWPORT NEWS (Independent City); ★ NN-H; mail Newport News z 23607; pop. incl. with Newport News (Independent City)
Laswell; RMC Place; WYTHE; *244 L-3; elev. 2,052ft./625m.; mail Max Meadows z 24360; ● 30
Latanes; RMC Place; WESTMORELAND; *245 G-15; elev. 60ft./18m.; mail Colonial Beach z 22443; rural
Lauraville; RMC Place; CAROLINE; *245 H-15; elev. 187ft./57m.; mail Milford z 22514; rural
Laurel; CDP; HENRICO; 243 A-7; ★ RICH; mail Glen Allen z 23060; Ⓟ 13,011; Ⓒ 14,875
Laurel; RMC Place; RUSSELL; *244 C-6; mail Honaker z 24260; rural
Laurel Branch; RMC Place; FLOYD; *244 L-4; mail Floyd z 24091; rural
Laureldale; RMC Place; WASHINGTON; *244 M-1; mail Damascus z 24236; rural
Laurel Dell; RMC Place; HENRICO; *245 I-14; elev. 200ft./61m.; ★ RICH; mail Henrico z 23228; ● 500
Laurel Fork; RMC Place; CARROLL; 244 M-4; elev. 1,277ft./389m.; 🅿; z 24352; ● 80
Laurel Grove; RMC Place; PITTSYLVANIA; *244 M-8; elev. 640ft./195m.; mail Sutherlin z 24594; ● 30
Laurel Grove; RMC Place; WISE; *244 C-4; elev. 2,400ft./732m.; mail Norton z 24273; ● 30
Laurel Grove Estates; RMC Place; HANOVER; *245 I-14; ★ RICH; mail Mechanicsville z 23116; ● 300
Laurel Hill; RMC Place; AUGUSTA; *244 G-9; mail Verona z 24482; ● 180
Laurel Hill; RMC Place; SHENANDOAH; mail Strasburg z 22641; rural
Laurel Manor; RMC Place; VIRGINIA BEACH (Independent City); *245 L-18; elev. 25ft./8m.; ★ NORF-; mail Virginia Beach z 23451; pop. incl. with Virginia Beach (Independent City)
Laurel Mills; RMC Place; RAPPAHANNOCK; *245 E-12; mail Castleton z 22716; ● 30
Laurel Oak; RMC Place; CHESTERFIELD; ★ RICH; mail Richmond z 23234
Laurel Park; RMC Place; HENRICO; *245 I-14; ★ RICH; mail Henrico z 23228
Laurel Park; CDP; HENRY; *244 M-6; ★ MRTNV; mail Martinsville z 24112; Ⓒ 781
Laurianne Woods; RMC Place; PRINCE WILLIAM; *245 E-13; elev. 337ft./103m.; ★ WASH; mail Gainesville z 20155; ● 130
Lawndale Farms; RMC Place; HENRICO; *245 J-14; ★ RICH; mail Henrico z 23231; ● 1,200
Lawrenceville; Inc. Place; ⊡ BRUNSWICK; 245 M-13; 🅿 🅲 681; z 23868; Ⓟ 1,486; Ⓒ 1,275
Lawrenceville Hills; RMC Place; BRUNSWICK; *245 M-13; mail Lawrenceville z 23868; ● 150
Lawson; RMC Place; ISLE OF WIGHT; 245 L-16; mail Smithfield z 23430; ● 150
Lawson Forest; RMC Place; VIRGINIA BEACH (Independent City); *245 L-18; elev. 20ft./6m.; ★ NORF-; mail Virginia Beach z 23455; pop. incl. with Virginia Beach (Independent City)
Lawson's Store; MECKLENBURG; see Spanish Grove (RMC Place)
Lawsons Store; RMC Place; RUSSELL; *244 D-5; mail Castlewood z 24224; ● 30
Lawyers; RMC Place; CAMPBELL; *244 K-8; ★ LYNCH; mail Lynchburg z 24501; ● 80
Laymantown; CDP-Census Area Only; BOTETOURT; *244 J-6; ★ ROAN; mail Blue Ridge z 24064; Ⓟ 1,942; Ⓒ 2,034
L C Page; RMC Place; NORFOLK (Independent City); *245 L-18; ★ NORF-; mail Norfolk z 23518; pop. incl. with Norfolk (Independent City)
Leaksville; RMC Place; PAGE; *244 E-10; mail Luray z 22835; ● 90
Leatherwood; RMC Place; HENRY; *244 M-7; ★ MRTNV; mail Martinsville z 24112; rural
Lebanon; Inc. Place; ⊡ RUSSELL; 244 D-5; 🅿 🅷; z 24266; Ⓟ 3,386; Ⓒ 3,273
Lebanon Church; RMC Place; SHENANDOAH; 245 D-11; 🅿; z 22641 & mail Strasburg z 22657; ● 150
Leck; RMC Place; DICKENSON; *244 C-5; mail Coeburn z 24230; rural
Leda; RMC Place; HALIFAX; *244 L-9; elev. 561ft./171m.; mail Nathalie z 24577; rural
Lee; RMC Place; GOOCHLAND; *245 I-13; mail Crozier z 23039; rural
LEE; 244 D-2; Ⓟ 24,496; Ⓒ 23,589; ◆ 23,462
Lee Acres; RMC Place; PRINCE GEORGE; *245 K-14; elev. 140ft./43m.; ★ RICH; mail Prince George z 23875; ● 100
Lee Boulevard Heights; RMC Place; FAIRFAX; *245 D-15; ★ WASH; mail Falls Church z 22044; ● 2,600
Leedstown; RMC Place; WESTMORELAND; *245 G-15; mail Colonial Beach z 22443; ● 50
Lee Forest; RMC Place; FAIRFAX; *245 E-14; ★ WASH; mail Fairfax z 22030; ● 1,000
Lee Hall; RMC Place; NEWPORT NEWS (Independent City); *245 K-17; ★ NN-H; mail Newport News z 23603; pop. incl. with Newport News (Independent City)
Lee Heights; RMC Place; ARLINGTON; *245 D-15; ★ WASH; mail Arlington z 22207
Leehigh Village; RMC Place; FAIRFAX; *245 E-14; ★ WASH; mail Fairfax z 22030; ● 300
Leemaster; RMC Place; BUCHANAN; *244 B-5; elev. 1,452ft./443m.; mail Vansant z 24656; ● 100
Lee Meadows; RMC Place; FAIRFAX; *245 E-14; ★ WASH; mail Fairfax z 22032; ● 210
Lee Mont; RMC Place; ACCOMACK; *245 I-19; 🅿; z 23421; ● 100
Lee Park; RMC Place; HENRICO; ★ RICH; mail Sandston z 23150
Leesburg; Inc. Place; ⊡ LOUDOUN; 245 D-13; elev. 352ft./107m.; 🅿 🅷; ★ WASH; z 20175-78; Ⓟ 16,202; Ⓒ 28,311; ◆ 37,066
Leesville; RMC Place; CAMPBELL; 244 K-8; mail Lynch Station z 24571; ● 50
Lee Town; RMC Place; BUCHANAN; mail Grundy z 24614; rural
Leewood Forest; RMC Place; FAIRFAX; *245 E-14; ★ WASH; mail Springfield z 22151
Leighs Corner; FAIRFAX; see Colvin Run (RMC Place)
Lenah; RMC Place; LOUDOUN; *245 D-13; mail Aldie z 20105; ● 70
Lennig; RMC Place; HALIFAX; *244 L-9; 🅿; z 24577; ● 60
Lenox; RMC Place; NORFOLK (Independent City); *245 L-18; elev. 10ft./3m.; ★ NORF-; mail Norfolk z 23503; pop. incl. with Norfolk (Independent City)
Leon; RMC Place; MADISON; 245 F-12; 🅿; z 22725; ● 40
Lerty; RMC Place; WESTMORELAND; *245 G-16; elev. 169ft./52m.; mail Montross z 22520
Leslie; RMC Place; ROANOKE; *244 K-6; elev. 1,058ft./322m.; ★ ROAN; mail Roanoke z 24014; ● 200
Lester Manor; RMC Place; KING WILLIAM; *245 I-15; mail King William z 23086; rural
Level Run; RMC Place; PITTSYLVANIA; *244 L-8; elev. 715ft./218m.; mail Hurt z 24563; ● 50
Lewinsville; RMC Place; FAIRFAX; *245 D-14; ★ WASH; mail Mc Lean z 22101
Lewinsville Heights; RMC Place; FAIRFAX; *245 D-14; ★ WASH; mail Mc Lean z 22101
Lewisetta; RMC Place; NORTHUMBERLAND; 245 H-17; 🅿; z 22511; ● 250
Lewis Park; RMC Place; FAIRFAX; *245 E-14; ★ WASH; mail Fairfax z 22030
Lewiston; RMC Place; HANOVER; *245 I-14; elev. 293ft./89m.; ★ RICH; mail Ashland z 23005; ● 40
Lewisville; RMC Place; CLARKE; *245 C-12; mail Berryville z 22611; ● 50
Lexington; Independent City; serves as county seat of Rockbridge; 244 I-7; 🅿 🅷 🅲 3,525; z 24450; Ⓟ 6,959; Ⓒ 6,867; ◆ 7,348
Liberia Woods; RMC Place; MANASSAS (Independent City); ★ WASH; mail Manassas z 20110; pop. incl. with Manassas (Independent City)
Liberty; RMC Place; HALIFAX; *244 L-9; mail Nathalie z 24577; ● 30
Liberty; RMC Place; TAZEWELL; *244 L-1; mail Tazewell z 24651; rural
Liberty Fork; RMC Place; CAROLINE; *245 H-15; elev. 185ft./56m.; mail Bowling Green z 22427; rural
Liberty Furnace; RMC Place; SHENANDOAH; *244 D-10; elev. 1,227ft./374m.; mail Edinburg z 22824; ● 30
Lick Fork; RMC Place; DICKENSON; mail Coeburn z 24230; rural
Lick Run; RMC Place; BOTETOURT; *244 I-6; mail Eagle Rock z 24085
Lick Skillet; RMC Place; SMYTH; *244 D-6; elev. 1,926ft./587m.; mail Saltville z 24370; ● 50
Lightfoot; RMC Place; JAMES CITY; 245 J-16; 🅿; ★ NN-H; z 23090; ● 400
Lignum; RMC Place; CULPEPER; 245 F-13; 🅿; z 22726; ● 180
Lilian; RMC Place; NORTHUMBERLAND; 245 H-17; mail Reedville z 22539; ● 100
Lilly; RMC Place; ROCKINGHAM; *244 F-9; mail Dayton z 22821; ● 200
Lime Hill; RMC Place; WASHINGTON; *244 D-5; elev. 1,892ft./577m.; ★ JNSC-; mail Bristol z 24202; rural
Limeton; RMC Place; WARREN; *245 E-11; mail Bentonville z 22610; ● 150
Lincoln; RMC Place; LOUDOUN; *245 C-13; 🅿; ★ WASH; z 20160; ● 300
Lincolnia; RMC Place; ALEXANDRIA (Independent City); *245 E-15; ★ WASH; mail Alexandria z 22312; pop. incl. with Alexandria (Independent City)
Lincolnia; CDP; FAIRFAX; 249 H-4; ★ WASH; mail Alexandria z 22311-12; Ⓟ 13,041; Ⓒ 15,788
Lincolnia Heights; RMC Place; FAIRFAX; 249 H-4; ★ WASH; mail Alexandria z 22312; ● 1,800
Lincolnia Park; RMC Place; FAIRFAX; *245 E-15; ★ WASH; mail Alexandria z 22312; ● 2,450
Lincoln Park; RMC Place; FAIRFAX; *245 E-14; ★ WASH; mail Fairfax z 22030
Lincoln Park; RMC Place; NORFOLK (Independent City); *245 L-18; ★ NORF-; mail Norfolk z 23513; pop. incl. with Norfolk (Independent City)
Lindell; RMC Place; WASHINGTON; *244 D-6; mail Abingdon z 24210
Linden; RMC Place; WARREN, FAUQUIER; 245 D-12; 🅿; z 22642; ● 200
Lindenwood; RMC Place; ROANOKE; *244 K-6; ★ ROAN; mail Vinton z 24179; ● 1,000
Lindsay; RMC Place; ALBEMARLE; *245 H-11; mail Gordonsville z 22942; rural
Linkhorn; RMC Place; VIRGINIA BEACH (Independent City); *245 L-18; elev. 25ft./8m.; ★ NORF-; mail Virginia Beach z 23454; pop. incl. with Virginia Beach (Independent City)
Linkhorn Estates; RMC Place; VIRGINIA BEACH (Independent City); *245 L-18; elev. 25ft./8m.; ★ NORF-; mail Virginia Beach z 23454; pop. incl. with Virginia Beach (Independent City)
Linkhorn Shores; RMC Place; VIRGINIA BEACH (Independent City); *245 L-18; elev. 10ft./3m.; ★ NORF-; mail Virginia Beach z 23451; pop. incl. with Virginia Beach (Independent City)
Linlier; RMC Place; VIRGINIA BEACH (Independent City); *245 L-18; elev. 15ft./5m.; ★ NORF-; mail Virginia Beach z 23451; pop. incl. with Virginia Beach (Independent City)
Linton Hall; CDP-Census Area Only; PRINCE WILLIAM; *245 E-13; ★ WASH; Ⓒ 8,620
Linville; RMC Place; ROCKINGHAM; *244 F-9; 🅿; z 22834; ● 180
Lipps; RMC Place; WISE; *244 C-4; elev. 2,231ft./680m.; mail Coeburn z 24230; ● 70
Lithia; RMC Place; BOTETOURT; *244 J-7; 🅿; ★ ROAN; z 24066; ● 150
Little Haven; RMC Place; VIRGINIA BEACH (Independent City); *245 L-18; elev. 15ft./5m.; ★ NORF-; mail Virginia Beach z 23452; pop. incl. with Virginia Beach (Independent City)
Little Plymouth; RMC Place; KING AND QUEEN; 245 I-16; elev. 109ft./33m.; 🅿; z 23091; ● 50
Little River Hills; RMC Place; FAIRFAX (Independent City); *245 E-14; ★ WASH; mail Fairfax z 22031; pop. incl. with Fairfax (Independent City)
Little River Pines; FAIRFAX; see Ilda (RMC Place)
Little Rocky Run; RMC Place; FAIRFAX; *245 E-14; ★ WASH; mail Clifton z 20124; ● 950
Littleton; RMC Place; SUSSEX; *245 L-15; elev. 102ft./31m.; mail Waverly z 23890; rural
Little Vienna Estates; RMC Place; FAIRFAX; *245 D-14; ★ WASH; mail Vienna z 22181; ● 1,500
Litwalton; RMC Place; LANCASTER; *245 I-17; elev. 103ft./31m.; mail Lancaster z 22503
Litz; RMC Place; WASHINGTON; *244 D-6; mail Glade Spring z 24340; rural
Lively; RMC Place; LANCASTER; 245 I-17; 🅿; z 22507; ● 300
Lloyd Place; RMC Place; SUFFOLK (Independent City); ★ NORF-; mail Suffolk z 23434; pop. incl. with Suffolk (Independent City)
Loch Laird; RMC Place; BUENA VISTA (Independent City); mail Buena Vista z 24416; pop. incl. with Buena Vista (Independent City)
Loch Lomond; CDP; PRINCE WILLIAM; *245 E-14; ★ WASH; mail Manassas z 20111; Ⓟ 3,292; Ⓒ 3,411
Lockhart Flats; RMC Place; DICKENSON; *244 B-4; mail Clintwood z 24228; rural
Locust Creek; RMC Place; LOUISA; 245 H-13; mail Bumpass z 23024; ● 50
Locust Dale; RMC Place; MADISON; 245 G-12; 🅿; z 22948; ● 40
Locust Grove; RMC Place; ORANGE; 245 G-13; 🅿; z 22508; ● 60
Locust Hill; RMC Place; MIDDLESEX; 245 I-17; 🅿; z 23092; ● 150
Locust Hill; RMC Place; WYTHE; *244 L-3; mail Max Meadows z 24360; ● 50
Locustville; RMC Place; ACCOMACK; 245 I-19; elev. 10ft./3m.; 🅿; z 23404; ● 100
Lodge; RMC Place; NORTHUMBERLAND; *245 H-17; mail Callao z 22435; rural
Lodi; RMC Place; WASHINGTON; *244 M-1; elev. 2,068ft./630m.; mail Glade Spring z 24340
Lodore; RMC Place; AMELIA; *245 J-12; elev. 367ft./112m.; mail Amelia Court House z 23002; rural
Lofton; RMC Place; AUGUSTA; *244 H-8; mail Raphine z 24472; ● 30
Logan; RMC Place; SPOTSYLVANIA; *245 G-13; mail Spotsylvania z 22553
Loisdale Estates; RMC Place; FAIRFAX; *245 E-14; ★ WASH; mail Springfield z 22150; ● 920
Lombardy Grove; RMC Place; MECKLENBURG; *245 M-11; mail South Hill z 23970; rural
London Bridge (Hilltop-Oceana); RMC Place; VIRGINIA BEACH (Independent City); *245 L-18; ★ NORF-; mail Virginia Beach z 23454; pop. incl. with Virginia Beach (Independent City)
London Towne; RMC Place; FAIRFAX; ★ WASH; mail Centreville z 20120
Lone Fountain; RMC Place; AUGUSTA; *244 G-8; elev. 1,499ft./457m.; mail Churchville z 24421; ● 50
Lone Gum; RMC Place; BEDFORD; *244 K-8; mail Huddleston z 24104; rural
Lone Pine; RMC Place; BEDFORD; *244 J-8; elev. 800ft./244m.; mail Forest z 24551; rural
Longbottom; RMC Place; BUCHANAN; *244 B-6; mail Grundy z 24614; pop. incl. with Grundy (Inc. Place)
Long Branch; RMC Place; DICKENSON; mail Dante z 24237; rural
Long Dale; RMC Place; ALLEGHANY; *244 I-6; mail Clifton Forge z 24422; rural
Longdale; RMC Place; HENRICO; *245 I-14; ★ RICH; mail Glen Allen z 23060; ● 500
Longdale Furnace; RMC Place; ALLEGHANY; 244 I-7; mail Clifton Forge z 24422; ● 150
Long Island; RMC Place; CAMPBELL; 244 L-9; 🅿; z 24569; ● 70
Long Ridge; RMC Place; CHESAPEAKE (Independent City); *245 M-18; ★ NORF-; mail Chesapeake z 23322; pop. incl. with Chesapeake (Independent City)
Longs Gap; RMC Place; GRAYSON; *244 M-2; elev. 3,200ft./975m.; mail Independence z 24348; rural
Longshop; RMC Place; MONTGOMERY; *244 K-4; mail Blacksburg z 24060; ● 70
Long Spur; RMC Place; BLAND; *244 K-3; mail Dublin z 24084; rural
Longs Store; PAGE; see Spitler (RMC Place)
Longview; RMC Place; ISLE OF WIGHT; 243 L-3; elev. 77ft./23m.; mail Smithfield z 23430; ● 50
Looneys Creek; RMC Place; BUCHANAN; *244 B-5; mail Grundy z 24614; rural
Lora Lynn Heights; RMC Place; CHESTERFIELD; ★ RICH; mail Chester z 23831
Loretto; RMC Place; ESSEX; 245 H-15; 🅿; z 22509; ● 30
Lorfax Heights; RMC Place; FAIRFAX; *245 E-14; ★ WASH; mail Lorton z 22079
Lorne; RMC Place; CAROLINE; *245 H-14; mail Ruther Glen z 22546; rural
Lorraine; RMC Place; HENRICO; *245 J-13; elev. 142ft./43m.; ★ RICH; mail Henrico z 23075; ● 150
Lorton; CDP; FAIRFAX; 245 E-14; 🅿; ★ WASH; z 20598, z 22079, z 22199; Ⓟ 15,385; Ⓒ 17,786
Lost Corner; RMC Place; CLARKE; *245 D-12; mail White Post z 22663; rural
Lost Forest; RMC Place; CHESTERFIELD; *245 J-14; elev. 150ft./46m.; ★ RICH; mail Richmond z 23234; ● 450
Lottsburg; RMC Place; NORTHUMBERLAND; 245 H-17; elev. 105ft./32m.; 🅿; z 22511; ● 450
LOUDOUN; 245 D-13; Ⓟ 86,129; Ⓒ 169,599; ◆ 297,864
Loudoun Heights; RMC Place; LOUDOUN; *245 C-13; mail Harpers Ferry z 25425; ● 400
Louisa; Inc. Place; ⊡ LOUISA; 245 H-12; elev. 468ft./143m.; 🅿; z 23093; Ⓟ 1,088; Ⓒ 1,401
LOUISA; 245 H-12; Ⓟ 20,325; Ⓒ 25,627; ◆ 33,547
Love; RMC Place; AUGUSTA; *244 H-9; mail Lyndhurst z 22952; rural
Loves Mill; RMC Place; WASHINGTON; *244 M-1; elev. 2,067ft./630m.; mail Chilhowie z 24319; ● 50
Loves Shop; RMC Place; HALIFAX; *244 M-9; mail Halifax z 24558; ● 300
Lovettsville; Inc. Place; LOUDOUN; 245 C-13; 🅿; z 20180; Ⓟ 749; Ⓒ 853
Lovingston; RMC Place; ⊡ NELSON; 244 I-9; 🅿; z 22949; ● 600
Lower Brandon; RMC Place; PRINCE GEORGE; *245 K-15; elev. 17ft./5m.; mail Spring Grove z 23881; rural
Lower Elk Creek; RMC Place; GRAYSON; *244 M-2; elev. 2,540ft./774m.; mail Elk Creek z 24326; rural
Lower Exeter; RMC Place; WISE; *244 C-3; mail Appalachia z 24216; ● 50
Lowery Hills; RMC Place; WASHINGTON; ★ JNSC-; mail Bristol z 24202; ● 350
Lowesville; RMC Place; NELSON, AMHERST; 244 I-9; 🅿; z 22967; ● 120
Low Moor; CDP; ALLEGHANY; 244 I-6; 🅿 🅷; z 24457; Ⓒ 367
Lowry; RMC Place; BEDFORD; *244 K-8; 🅿; z 24570; ● 50
Loxley Place; RMC Place; PORTSMOUTH (Independent City); *245 M-17; elev. 10ft./3m.; ★ NORF-; mail Portsmouth z 23702; pop. incl. with Portsmouth (Independent City)
Luck; RMC Place; PITTSYLVANIA; *244 M-8; mail Java z 24565; rural
Lucketts; RMC Place; LOUDOUN; 245 C-13; mail Leesburg z 20176; ● 50
Lumberton; RMC Place; SUSSEX; *245 L-15; elev. 81ft./25m.; mail Waverly z 23890; rural
Lummis; RMC Place; SUFFOLK (Independent City); ★ NORF-; mail Suffolk z 23434; pop. incl. with Suffolk (Independent City)
Lumpkin Forest; RMC Place; PITTSYLVANIA; *244 M-8; elev. 600ft./183m.; ★ DANV; mail Danville z 24540; ● 150
Lunenburg; RMC Place; ⊡ LUNENBURG; 245 L-11; elev. 512ft./156m.; 🅿; z 23952; ● 80
LUNENBURG; 245 L-11; Ⓟ 11,419; Ⓒ 13,146; ◆ 13,007
Luray; Inc. Place; ⊡ PAGE; 245 E-11; elev. 789ft./240m.; 🅿 🅷; z 22835; Ⓟ 4,587; Ⓒ 4,871
Lurich; RMC Place; GILES; *244 J-3; mail Narrows z 24124; ● 40
Lusters Gate; RMC Place; MONTGOMERY; *244 K-5; elev. 1,594ft./486m.; mail Blacksburg z 24060; ● 60
Luttrellville; RMC Place; RICHMOND, NORTHUMBERLAND; *245 H-16; mail Callao z 22435; rural
Lydia; RMC Place; GREENE; *244 G-10; mail Stanardsville z 22973; rural
Lyells; RMC Place; RICHMOND; *245 H-16; elev. 148ft./45m.; mail Warsaw z 22572
Lynchburg; Independent City; 244 J-8; 🅿 🅷 🅲 20,909 ■; ★ LYNCH; z 24501-06, z 24512-15; Ⓟ 66,049; Ⓒ 65,269; ◆ 72,417
Lynch Station (Clarion); RMC Place; CAMPBELL; 244 K-8; elev. 728ft./222m.; 🅿; z 24571; ● 500
Lyndhurst; CDP; AUGUSTA; 244 H-9; 🅿; z 22952; Ⓒ 1,527
Lynhaven; RMC Place; ALEXANDRIA (Independent City); *245 E-15; ★ WASH; mail Alexandria z 22305; pop. incl. with Alexandria (Independent City)
Lynn Grove; RMC Place; HENRICO; *245 J-14; ★ RICH; mail Richmond z 23222
Lynnhaven; RMC Place; HAMPTON (Independent City); *245 L-17; ★ NN-H; mail Hampton z 23666; pop. incl. with Hampton (Independent City)
Lynnhaven; RMC Place; VIRGINIA BEACH (Independent City); *245 L-18; ★ NORF-; mail Virginia Beach z 23450; pop. incl. with Virginia Beach (Independent City)
Lynnhaven Acres; RMC Place; VIRGINIA BEACH (Independent City); *245 L-18; elev. 10ft./3m.; ★ NORF-; mail Virginia Beach z 23452; pop. incl. with Virginia Beach (Independent City)
Lynnhaven Colony; RMC Place; VIRGINIA BEACH (Independent City); *245 L-18; elev. 10ft./3m.; ★ NORF-; mail Virginia Beach z 23451; pop. incl. with Virginia Beach (Independent City)
Lynn Shores; RMC Place; VIRGINIA BEACH (Independent City); *245 L-18; elev. 10ft./3m.; ★ NORF-; mail Virginia Beach z 23452; pop. incl. with Virginia Beach (Independent City)
Lynn Spring; RMC Place; RUSSELL; *244 C-6; mail Swords Creek z 24649
Lynnwood; RMC Place; ROCKINGHAM; *244 G-10; mail Port Republic z 24471; ● 50
Lynnwood; RMC Place; VIRGINIA BEACH (Independent City); *245 L-18; elev. 20ft./6m.; ★ NORF-; mail Virginia Beach z 23452; pop. incl. with Virginia Beach (Independent City)
Lynwood; RMC Place; PRINCE WILLIAM; ★ WASH; mail Woodbridge z 22191
Lyon Park; RMC Place; ARLINGTON; *245 D-15; mail Arlington z 22201
Lyon Village; RMC Place; ARLINGTON; *245 D-15; ★ WASH; mail Arlington z 22201

M

Mabe; RMC Place; SCOTT; *244 D-3; mail Duffield z 24244
Macanie; RMC Place; SHENANDOAH; *244 E-10; mail Mount Jackson z 22842; ● 30
Macedonia; RMC Place; ACCOMACK; *245 H-20; mail Bloxom z 23308; ● 50
Maces Springs; RMC Place; SCOTT; *244 D-4; mail Hiltons z 24258; ● 60
Machipongo; RMC Place; NORTHAMPTON; *245 J-19; 🅿; z 23405; ● 130
Macon; RMC Place; POWHATAN; 245 J-12; 🅿; z 23101; ● 40
Madison; Inc. Place; ⊡ MADISON; 245 F-11; 🅿; z 22719, z 22727; Ⓟ 307; Ⓒ 210
MADISON; 245 F-11; Ⓟ 11,949; Ⓒ 12,520; ◆ 14,051
Madison Heights; CDP; AMHERST; 244 J-8; 🅿 🅷; ★ LYNCH; z 24572; Ⓟ 11,700; Ⓒ 11,584
Madison Manor; RMC Place; ARLINGTON; *245 D-15; ★ WASH; mail Arlington z 22205
Madison Mills; RMC Place; MADISON; 245 G-12; 🅿; z 22960; ● 70
Madison Run; RMC Place; ORANGE; *245 G-12; mail Gordonsville z 22942; ● 70
Madisonville; RMC Place; CHARLOTTE; 244 K-10; elev. 692ft./211m.; mail Pamplin z 23958; ● 50
Madrid; RMC Place; AUGUSTA; *244 G-9; elev. 1,335ft./407m.; mail Waynesboro z 22980; rural
Madrillon; FAIRFAX; see Madrillon Farms (RMC Place)
Madrillon Farms (Madrillon); RMC Place; FAIRFAX; *245 D-14; ★ WASH; mail Vienna z 22182
Maggie; RMC Place; CRAIG; *244 J-5; elev. 1,809ft./551m.; mail New Castle z 24127; rural
Magnolia; RMC Place; SUFFOLK (Independent City); *245 M-17; ★ NORF-; mail Suffolk z 23434; pop. incl. with Suffolk (Independent City)
Magnolia Gardens; RMC Place; SUFFOLK (Independent City); ★ NORF-; mail Suffolk z 23434; pop. incl. with Suffolk (Independent City)
Maidens; RMC Place; GOOCHLAND; *245 I-12; elev. 222ft./68m.; 🅿; z 23102; ● 80
Major; RMC Place; BEDFORD; *244 J-8; elev. 622ft./190m.; mail Big Island z 24526; rural
Makemie Park; RMC Place; ACCOMACK; *245 H-20; elev. 19ft./6m.; mail Temperanceville z 23442; ● 130
Malbrook; RMC Place; FAIRFAX; *245 E-15; ★ WASH; mail Falls Church z 22044
Malcolm; RMC Place; WASHINGTON; *244 E-5; ★ JNSC-; mail Bristol z 24202; ● 30
Malibu; RMC Place; VIRGINIA BEACH (Independent City); *245 L-18; elev. 12ft./4m.; ★ NORF-; mail Virginia Beach z 23452; pop. incl. with Virginia Beach (Independent City)
Mallow; RMC Place; ALLEGHANY; *244 I-6; mail Covington z 24426; ● 230
Malmaison; RMC Place; PITTSYLVANIA; *244 M-8; mail Blairs z 24527; ● 50
Manakin (Manakin Sabot); RMC Place; GOOCHLAND; 245 J-13; ★ RICH; mail Manakin Sabot z 23103; ● 300
Manakin Farms; RMC Place; GOOCHLAND; *245 I-13; ★ RICH; mail Manakin Sabot z 23103; ● 370
Manakin Sabot; GOOCHLAND; see Manakin (RMC Place)
Manassas; Independent City; serves as county seat of Prince William; 245 E-14; 🅿 🅷 🅲 4,400 ■; ★ WASH; z 20108-13; Ⓟ 27,957; Ⓒ 35,135; ◆ 34,062
Manassas Park; Independent City; 245 E-14; 🅿; ★ WASH; z 20111 & mail Manassas z 20112-13; Ⓟ 6,734; Ⓒ 10,290; ◆ 11,337
Manbur; RMC Place; HENRICO; *245 J-14; elev. 146ft./45m.; ★ RICH; mail Sandston z 23150; ● 280
Manchester Mills; RMC Place; PRINCE GEORGE; *245 K-14; elev. 100ft./30m.; ★ RICH; mail Prince George z 23875; ● 200
Maness; RMC Place; LEE; *244 D-2; mail Saint Charles z 24282; ● 90
Mangohick; RMC Place; KING WILLIAM; 245 I-14; elev. 194ft./59m.; 🅿; z 23069; ● 90
Mannboro; RMC Place; AMELIA; 245 K-13; 🅿; z 23105; ● 50
Manquin; RMC Place; KING WILLIAM; 245 I-15; elev. 76ft./23m.; 🅿; z 23106; ● 100
Manry; RMC Place; SOUTHAMPTON; *245 L-15; elev. 117ft./36m.; mail Ivor z 23866; rural
Mantua; CDP; FAIRFAX; *245 D-14; ★ WASH; mail Fairfax z 22031; Ⓟ 6,804; Ⓒ 7,485
Mantua Hills; RMC Place; FAIRFAX; *245 D-14; ★ WASH; mail Fairfax z 22031; ● 1,650
Manville; RMC Place; SCOTT; *244 D-4; mail Gate City z 24251; rural
Maple Grove; RMC Place; ROCKBRIDGE; *244 I-7; mail Lexington z 24450; rural
Maple Grove; RMC Place; SPOTSYLVANIA; *245 G-13; ★ FRED; mail Fredericksburg z 22407; ● 350
Maple Grove; RMC Place; WESTMORELAND; *245 G-15; mail Colonial Beach z 22443
Maplewood; RMC Place; AMELIA; *245 K-12; elev. 398ft./121m.; mail Amelia Court House z 23002; ● 30
Mappsburg; RMC Place; ACCOMACK; *245 I-19; elev. 25ft./8m.; mail Painter z 23420; ● 30
Mappsville; RMC Place; ACCOMACK; 245 H-20; 🅿; z 23407; ● 400
Marble Valley; RMC Place; AUGUSTA; *244 G-8; elev. 1,640ft./500m.; mail Deerfield z 24432, Goshen z 24439; ● 150
Marcem; RMC Place; SCOTT; *244 D-4; ★ JNSC-; mail Gate City z 24251
Marengo; RMC Place; MECKLENBURG; *245 M-12; elev. 385ft./117m.; mail La Crosse z 23950; rural
Margo; RMC Place; SPOTSYLVANIA; *245 G-13; elev. 405ft./123m.; mail Spotsylvania z 22553
Marion; Inc. Place; ⊡ SMYTH; 244 M-1; elev. 2,178ft./664m.; 🅿 🅷; z 24354; Ⓟ 6,630; Ⓒ 6,349
Marion Hill; RMC Place; HENRICO; *245 J-14; ★ RICH; mail Henrico z 23231; ● 600
Marionville; RMC Place; NORTHAMPTON; *245 J-19; 🅿; z 23408; ● 80
Markham; RMC Place; FAUQUIER; 245 D-12; 🅿; z 22643; ● 190
Markham; RMC Place; PITTSYLVANIA; *244 L-8; elev. 507ft./155m.; mail Gretna z 24557; ● 30
Mark Haven Beach; RMC Place; ESSEX; *245 I-16; mail Tappahannock z 22560; ● 30
Marksville; RMC Place; PAGE; *244 F-10; mail Stanley z 22851; ● 30
Marlan Forest; RMC Place; FAIRFAX; *245 E-15; ★ WASH; mail Alexandria z 22307; ● 800
Marlbank; RMC Place; YORK; *245 K-17; ★ NN-H; mail Yorktown z 23692; ● 600
Marlbrook; RMC Place; ROCKBRIDGE; *244 H-8; mail Vesuvius z 24483; rural
Marrowbone Heights; RMC Place; HENRY; *244 M-6; ★ MRTNV; mail Ridgeway z 24148; ● 250
Marshall; RMC Place; FAUQUIER; 245 E-12; 🅿; z 20115-16; ● 900
Marshall Heights; RMC Place; GLOUCESTER; *245 K-17; ★ NN-H; mail Hayes z 23072; ● 650
Marsh Run; RMC Place; FAUQUIER; *245 F-13; mail Bealeton z 22712; ● 950
Marstella Estates; RMC Place; FAUQUIER; *245 E-13; ★ WASH; mail Warrenton z 20187; ● 320
Martha Gap; RMC Place; DICKENSON; *244 B-5; mail Haysi z 24256; rural
Martin Siding; RMC Place; NORTHAMPTON; *245 J-19; mail Machipongo z 23405; ● 50
Martins Store; RMC Place; NELSON; *244 H-9; mail Afton z 22920; rural
Martinsville; Independent City; serves as county seat of Henry; 244 M-6; 🅿 🅷 ■; ★ MRTNV; z 24112-15; Ⓟ 16,162; Ⓒ 15,416; ◆ 14,306
Marumsco Acres; RMC Place; PRINCE WILLIAM; *245 E-14; ★ WASH; mail Woodbridge z 22191
Marumsco Hills; RMC Place; PRINCE WILLIAM; *245 E-14; ★ WASH; mail Woodbridge z 22191
Marumsco Village; RMC Place; PRINCE WILLIAM; *245 E-14; ★ WASH; mail Woodbridge z 22191
Marumsco Woods; RMC Place; PRINCE WILLIAM; *245 E-14; ★ WASH; mail Woodbridge z 22191
Marvin; RMC Place; BUCHANAN; 244 B-6; mail Raven z 24639; ● 130
Marye; RMC Place; SPOTSYLVANIA; *245 H-13; mail Spotsylvania z 22553; rural
Marysville; RMC Place; CAMPBELL; *244 K-9; mail Gladys z 24554; rural
Maryus; RMC Place; GLOUCESTER; *245 K-17; 🅿; ★ NN-H; z 23107; ● 300
Mascot; RMC Place; KING AND QUEEN; *245 I-16; elev. 94ft./29m.; 🅿; z 23108; ● 30
Mason Cove; RMC Place; ROANOKE; *244 J-6; mail Salem z 24153; ● 50
Masonville; RMC Place; FAIRFAX; *245 E-14; ★ WASH; mail Annandale z 22003
Massanetta Springs; RMC Place; ROCKINGHAM; *244 F-9; mail Harrisonburg z 22801; ● 220
Massanutten; CDP-Census Area Only; ROCKINGHAM; *244 F-10; 🅿; z 22840; Ⓟ 990; Ⓒ 1,945
Massaponax; RMC Place; SPOTSYLVANIA; 245 G-13; ★ FRED; mail Fredericksburg z 22401, Spotsylvania z 22553; ● 210
Massies Mill; RMC Place; NELSON; 244 I-9; 🅿; z 22967; ● 120
Mathews; RMC Place; ⊡ MATHEWS; 245 J-17; 🅿; ★ NN-H; z 23109; ● 700
MATHEWS; 245 J-17; Ⓟ 8,348; Ⓒ 9,207; ◆ 9,083
Matoaca; CDP; CHESTERFIELD; 243 H-7; ★ RICH; mail Petersburg z 23803; Ⓒ 2,273
Mattaponi; RMC Place; KING AND QUEEN; 245 J-16; 🅿; z 23110; ● 350
Mattaponi Reservation; Indian Reservation; KING WILLIAM; State Reservation; Ⓒ 58
Maurertown; RMC Place; SHENANDOAH; 245 D-11; 🅿; z 22644; ● 260
Mauzy; RMC Place; ROCKINGHAM; *244 F-10; elev. 1,100ft./335m.; mail Broadway z 22815; ● 30
Mavisdale; RMC Place; BUCHANAN; 244 B-6; 🅿; z 24627; ● 450
Max Creek; RMC Place; PULASKI; *244 L-4; mail Hiwassee z 24347; ● 100
Maxie; RMC Place; BUCHANAN; 244 B-5; 🅿; z 24628; ● 400
Max Meadows; CDP; WYTHE; 244 L-3; elev. 2,028ft./618m.; 🅿; z 24360; Ⓒ 512
Maxwell; RMC Place; TAZEWELL; *244 K-1; mail Tazewell z 24651; rural
Maybrook; RMC Place; GILES; *244 K-4; elev. 1,794ft./547m.; mail Pembroke z 24136; ● 50
Mayfair Place; RMC Place; HENRICO; *245 J-14; ★ RICH; mail Richmond z 23223
Mayfield; RMC Place; HENRICO; *245 J-14; ★ RICH; mail Richmond z 23230; ● 350
Mayfield Farms; RMC Place; HANOVER; *245 I-14; ★ RICH; mail Mechanicsville z 23111
Mayflower; AMHERST; see Sardis (RMC Place)
Mayo; RMC Place; HALIFAX; 244 N-9; mail Virgilina z 24598; ● 30
Mayo; RMC Place; HENRY; *244 N-6; ★ MRTNV; mail Spencer z 24165; ● 50
Maytown; RMC Place; WISE; *244 C-4; mail Coeburn z 24230; pop. incl. with Coeburn (Inc. Place)
McAdam; RMC Place; PULASKI; *244 L-3; mail Pulaski z 24301; rural
McCall Gap; RMC Place; WASHINGTON; *244 M-1; mail Glade Spring z 24340; ● 100
McChesney Heights; RMC Place; BRISTOL (Independent City); ★ JNSC-; mail Bristol z 24201; pop. incl. with Bristol (Independent City)
McClung; RMC Place; BATH; *244 H-7; elev. 572ft./174m.; mail Millboro z 24460; rural
McClure; RMC Place; DICKENSON; 244 C-5; 🅿; z 24269; ● 350
McCoy; RMC Place; MONTGOMERY; 244 K-4; 🅿; z 24111; ● 250
McCrady; RMC Place; SMYTH; *244 L-1; mail Saltville z 24370; ● 230
McDonalds Mill; RMC Place; MONTGOMERY; *244 K-5; mail Blacksburg z 24060
McDonald's Small Farms; RMC Place; HENRICO; *245 I-13; elev. 281ft./86m.; ★ RICH; mail Glen Allen z 23060; ● 150
McDowell; RMC Place; HIGHLAND; 244 G-7; elev. 2,107ft./642m.; 🅿; z 24458; ● 170
McGaheysville; RMC Place; ROCKINGHAM; 244 G-10; 🅿; z 22840; ● 550
McHenry; RMC Place; SPOTSYLVANIA; *245 G-13; mail Spotsylvania z 22553
McKendree; RMC Place; HALIFAX; *244 M-9; elev. 589ft./180m.; mail Halifax z 24558; ● 30
McKenney; Inc. Place; DINWIDDIE; 245 L-13; 🅿; z 23872; Ⓟ 386; Ⓒ 441; Ⓡ 482
McKinley; RMC Place; AUGUSTA; *244 H-8; mail Middlebrook z 24459; ● 70
McLean; CDP; FAIRFAX; 249 F-4; 🅿; ★ WASH; z 20598, z 22067, z 22101-03, z 22106-09 & mail Falls Church z 22043, z 22046; Ⓟ 38,163; Ⓒ 38,929; ◆ 40,460
McLean Estates; RMC Place; FAIRFAX; ★ WASH; mail Mc Lean z 22101
McLean Hamlet; RMC Place; FAIRFAX; *245 D-14; ★ WASH; mail Mc Lean z 22102; ● 2,000
McLean Manor; RMC Place; FAIRFAX; *245 D-14; ★ WASH; mail Mc Lean z 22101
McMullen; RMC Place; GREENE; *245 G-11; mail Stanardsville z 22973; rural
McNeals Corner; RMC Place; LANCASTER; *245 I-17; elev. 104ft./32m.; mail Lancaster z 22503; rural
Meade; RMC Place; ESSEX; *245 H-15; elev. 128ft./39m.; mail Tappahannock z 22560; rural
Meadowbrook; RMC Place; CHESTERFIELD; *245 J-14; elev. 150ft./46m.; ★ RICH; mail Richmond z 23234; ● 1,500
Meadowbrook; RMC Place; NORFOLK (Independent City); *245 L-17; elev. 10ft./3m.; ★ NORF-; mail Norfolk z 23505; pop. incl. with Norfolk (Independent City)
Meadowbrook Forest; RMC Place; NORFOLK (Independent City); *245 L-18; ★ NORF-; mail Norfolk z 23518; pop. incl. with Norfolk (Independent City)
Meadowbrook Heights; RMC Place; CHARLOTTESVILLE (Independent City); ★ CHRLTV; pop. incl. with Charlottesville (Independent City)
Meadowcrest; RMC Place; BRISTOL (Independent City); ★ JNSC-; mail Bristol z 24201; pop. incl. with Bristol (Independent City)
Meadowood; RMC Place; HENRICO; *245 I-14; ★ RICH; mail Richmond z 23227; ● 450
Meadows of Dan; RMC Place; PATRICK; 244 M-4; 🅿; z 24120; rural
Meadows of Newgate; RMC Place; FAIRFAX; ★ WASH; mail Centreville z 20121
Meadowview; RMC Place; WASHINGTON; 244 D-6; 🅿; z 24361; ● 900
Meadville; RMC Place; HALIFAX; *244 M-9; elev. 49ft./15m.; mail Halifax z 24558; ● 30
Mears; ACCOMACK; see Mears Station (RMC Place)
Mears Station (Mears); RMC Place; ACCOMACK; *245 H-20; mail Mears z 23409; ● 100
Mearsville; RMC Place; ACCOMACK; *245 H-19; elev. 8ft./2m.; mail Mears z 23409
Mechanicsburg; RMC Place; BLAND; 244 K-3; mail Bland z 24315; ● 170
Mechanicsville; CDP; HANOVER; 243 B-9; 🅿; ★ RICH; z 23111, z 23116; Ⓟ 22,027; Ⓒ 30,464; ◆ 34,830
Mechanicsville; RMC Place; ROCKINGHAM; *244 E-10; mail Timberville z 22853; ● 30
Mechums River; RMC Place; ALBEMARLE; *244 H-10; ★ CHRLTV; mail Charlottesville z 22901; rural
MECKLENBURG; 245 M-11; Ⓟ 29,241; Ⓒ 32,380; ◆ 32,318
Media Park; RMC Place; HENRICO; ★ RICH; mail Henrico z 23231
Meetze; RMC Place; FAUQUIER; *245 E-13; ★ WASH; mail Warrenton z 20187; rural
Meherrin; RMC Place; PRINCE EDWARD, LUNENBURG; 245 K-11; 🅿; z 23954; ● 190
Melfa; Inc. Place; ACCOMACK; 245 I-19; 🅿; z 23410; Ⓟ 428; Ⓒ 450
Melrose; RMC Place; CAMPBELL; *244 L-9; mail Gladys z 24554; rural
Melrose; RMC Place; ROANOKE (Independent City); ★ ROAN; mail Roanoke z 24017; pop. incl. with Roanoke (Independent City)
Melrose Gardens; RMC Place; PRINCE WILLIAM; ★ WASH; mail Triangle z 22172
Melton; RMC Place; LOUISA; *245 G-12; mail Gordonsville z 22942; ● 30
Memorial Heights; RMC Place; FAIRFAX; *245 E-15; ★ WASH; mail Alexandria z 22306
Menchville; RMC Place; NEWPORT NEWS (Independent City); *245 K-17; elev. 37ft./11m.; ★ NN-H; mail Fort Eustis z 23604; pop. incl. with Newport News (Independent City)
Mendota; RMC Place; WASHINGTON; 244 D-5; 🅿; z 24270; ● 160
Mentow; RMC Place; BEDFORD; *244 K-8; elev. 947ft./289m.; mail Huddleston z 24104; rural
Meredithville; RMC Place; BRUNSWICK; *245 M-12; elev. 366ft./112m.; 🅿; z 23873; ● 70
Meridian Park; RMC Place; FAIRFAX; *245 D-15; ★ WASH; mail Falls Church z 22046
Merrifield; CDP; FAIRFAX; 249 G-3; 🅿; ★ WASH; z 22081-82, z 22116, z 22118-19 & mail Fairfax z 22031; Ⓟ 8,399; Ⓒ 11,170
Merrimac; CDP; MONTGOMERY; *244 K-4; mail Blacksburg z 24060; Ⓟ 1,713; Ⓒ 1,751
Merrimack Park; RMC Place; NORFOLK (Independent City); *245 L-18; ★ NORF-; mail Norfolk z 23503; pop. incl. with Norfolk (Independent City)
Merrimac Shores; RMC Place; HAMPTON (Independent City); *245 L-17; ★ NN-H; mail Hampton z 23669; pop. incl. with Hampton (Independent City)
Merry Point; RMC Place; LANCASTER; *245 I-17; elev. 83ft./25m.; 🅿; z 22513; ● 60
Messongo; RMC Place; ACCOMACK; *245 H-19; mail Jenkins Bridge z 23399; rural
Metompkin; RMC Place; ACCOMACK; *245 I-20; mail Parksley z 23421; ● 50
Mew; RMC Place; RUSSELL; *244 D-5; mail Castlewood z 24224; ● 50
Michaux; RMC Place; POWHATAN; *245 I-12; elev. 316ft./96m.; mail Powhatan z 23139; rural
Middlebrook; RMC Place; AUGUSTA; 244 H-8; elev. 1,845ft./562m.; 🅿; z 24459; ● 280
Middleburg; Inc. Place; LOUDOUN; 245 D-13; elev. 492ft./150m.; 🅿; z 20117-18; Ⓟ 549; Ⓒ 632
Middleridge; RMC Place; FAIRFAX; *245 E-14; ★ WASH; mail Fairfax z 22032; ● 850
MIDDLESEX; 245 I-17; Ⓟ 8,653; Ⓒ 9,932; ◆ 10,615
Middleton; RMC Place; HENRICO; *245 I-14; elev. 290ft./88m.; ★ RICH; mail Henrico z 23228; ● 500
Middleton Gardens; RMC Place; SALEM (Independent City); ★ ROAN; mail Salem z 24153; pop. incl. with Salem (Independent City)
Middletown; Inc. Place; FREDERICK; 245 D-11; 🅿; z 22645, z 22649; Ⓟ 1,061; Ⓒ 1,015
Middletown; RMC Place; NORTHAMPTON; *245 J-19; mail Nassawadox z 23413; rural
Middletowne Farms; RMC Place; YORK; *245 K-16; ★ NN-H; mail Williamsburg z 23185; ● 400
Midland; RMC Place; FAUQUIER; 245 F-13; 🅿; z 22728; ● 160
Midlothian; RMC Place; CHESTERFIELD; 245 J-13; 🅿; ★ RICH; z 23112-14; ● 450
Midway; RMC Place; ALBEMARLE; *244 H-10; elev. 704ft./215m.; ★ CHRLTV; mail Charlottesville z 22903; ● 50
Midway; RMC Place; HALIFAX; *244 M-10; elev. 409ft./125m.; mail Virgilina z 24598; ● 30
Midway; RMC Place; MECKLENBURG; *245 M-11; mail Baskerville z 23915; rural
Midway; RUSSELL; see Sun (RMC Place)
Midway; RMC Place; TAZEWELL; *244 L-1; mail Cedar Bluff z 24609; rural
Mike; RMC Place; CAMPBELL; *244 K-9; elev. 671ft./205m.; mail Concord z 24538
Mila; RMC Place; NORTHUMBERLAND; *245 H-17; mail Heathsville z 22473; rural
Milan; RMC Place; NORFOLK (Independent City); *245 L-18; ★ NORF-; mail Norfolk z 23508; pop. incl. with Norfolk (Independent City)
Miles; RMC Place; MATHEWS; *245 J-17; 🅿; ★ NN-H; z 23025; ● 80
Milford; RMC Place; CAROLINE; 245 H-14; 🅿; z 22514; ● 500
Millboro; RMC Place; BATH; 244 H-7; 🅿; z 24460; ● 450
Millboro Spring; BATH; see Millboro Springs (RMC Place)
Millboro Springs (Millboro Spring); RMC Place; BATH; *244 H-7; elev. 1,344ft./410m.; mail Millboro z 24460; ● 80
Mill Creek Park; RMC Place; FAIRFAX; *245 E-14; ★ WASH; mail Annandale z 22003; ● 550
Millenbeck; RMC Place; LANCASTER; *245 I-17; elev. 31ft./9m.; mail Lancaster z 22503
Miller Park; RMC Place; LYNCHBURG (Independent City); *244 J-8; ★ LYNCH; mail Lynchburg z 24501; pop. incl. with Lynchburg (Independent City)
Millers Tavern; RMC Place; ESSEX, KING AND QUEEN; 245 I-15; elev. 176ft./54m.; 🅿; z 23115; ● 50
Mill Gap; RMC Place; HIGHLAND; *244 G-7; mail Monterey z 24465; ● 30
Mill Garden; RMC Place; SPOTSYLVANIA; *245 G-13; ★ FRED; mail Spotsylvania z 22553; ● 210
Milltown; RMC Place; LOUDOUN; *245 C-13; mail Lovettsville z 20180; rural
Millwood; RMC Place; CLARKE; 245 D-12; 🅿; z 22646; ● 250
Milteer Acres; RMC Place; SUFFOLK (Independent City); ★ NORF-; mail Suffolk z 23434; pop. incl. with Suffolk (Independent City)
Mineola; RMC Place; CHESTERFIELD; ★ RICH; mail Chester z 23831
Mineral; Inc. Place; LOUISA; 245 H-12; 🅿; z 23117; Ⓟ 471; Ⓒ 424
Mine Run; RMC Place; ORANGE; 245 G-12; 🅿; z 22508; ● 30
Minnieville Estates; RMC Place; PRINCE WILLIAM; *245 E-14; ★ WASH; mail Woodbridge z 22193
Minor; RMC Place; ESSEX, KING AND QUEEN; *245 I-15; mail Tappahannock z 22560; ● 30
Mint Spring; RMC Place; AUGUSTA; 244 H-8; 🅿; z 24463; ● 150
Miona; RMC Place; ACCOMACK; *245 H-20; mail New Church z 23415; rural
Miskimon; RMC Place; LANCASTER, NORTHUMBERLAND; *245 H-17; mail Heathsville z 22473; rural
Mission Home; RMC Place; GREENE; *244 G-10; 🅿; z 22940; ● 50
Mistwood Forest; RMC Place; CHESTERFIELD; ★ RICH; mail Chester z 23831
Mitchell; CULPEPER; see Mitchells (RMC Place)
Mitchells (Mitchell); RMC Place; CULPEPER; *245 F-12; 🅿; z 22729; ● 140
Mitchelltown; RMC Place; BATH; 244 H-6; mail Hot Springs z 24445; ● 200
Mobjack; RMC Place; MATHEWS; 245 J-17; 🅿; ★ NN-H; z 23056; ● 250
Modest Town; RMC Place; ACCOMACK; 245 H-20; elev. 35ft./11m.; 🅿; z 23412; ● 100
Moffats Creek; AUGUSTA; see Newport (RMC Place)
Moffett; RMC Place; HALIFAX; *244 M-10; elev. 548ft./167m.; mail Virgilina z 24598; rural
Mogarts Beach; RMC Place; ISLE OF WIGHT; 243 J-3; elev. 25ft./8m.; mail Smithfield z 23430; ● 60
Mohemenco; POWHATAN; see Provost (RMC Place)
Mollusk; RMC Place; LANCASTER; 245 I-17; 🅿; z 22517; ● 120
Monaskon; RMC Place; LANCASTER; *245 I-17; elev. 22ft./7m.; mail Lancaster z 22503; ● 70
Moneta; RMC Place; BEDFORD; 244 K-7; elev. 851ft./259m.; 🅿; z 24121; ● 220
Money Point; CHESAPEAKE (Independent City); see Buell (RMC Place)
Moneys Corner; RMC Place; FAIRFAX; *245 D-14; ★ WASH; mail Herndon z 20170
Monroe; RMC Place; AMHERST; 244 J-8; 🅿; ★ LYNCH; z 24574; ● 400
Monroe Gardens; RMC Place; HAMPTON (Independent City); *245 L-17; ★ NN-H; mail Hampton z 23669; pop. incl. with Hampton (Independent City)
Monroe Hall; RMC Place; WESTMORELAND; *245 G-15; mail Colonial Beach z 22443; rural
Monrovia; RMC Place; ORANGE; *245 G-12; elev. 404ft./123m.; mail Orange z 22960; rural
Montague; RMC Place; ESSEX; *245 I-16; elev. 112ft./34m.; mail Laneview z 22504; ● 30
Montclair; CDP-Census Area Only; PRINCE WILLIAM; *245 E-14; 🅿; ★ WASH; z 22025 & mail Dumfries z 22026; Ⓟ 11,399; Ⓒ 15,728
Montebello; RMC Place; NELSON; 244 I-8; elev. 2,752ft./839m.; 🅿; z 24464; ● 130
Monterey; Inc. Place; ⊡ HIGHLAND; 244 F-7; elev. 2,881ft./878m.; 🅿; z 24465; Ⓟ 222; Ⓒ 158
Montevideo; RMC Place; ROCKINGHAM; *244 F-10; mail Mc Gaheysville z 22840; ● 50
Montezuma; RMC Place; ROCKINGHAM; *244 F-9; 🅿; z 22821; ● 170
Montezuma Gardens; RMC Place; HENRICO; *245 J-14; ★ RICH; mail Richmond z 23223; ● 1,750
Montford; RMC Place; ORANGE; *245 G-11; 🅿; z 22960; ● 70
Montgomery; RMC Place; MONTGOMERY; *244 K-5; ★ ROAN; mail Christiansburg z 24073; rural
MONTGOMERY; 244 L-4; Ⓟ 73,913; Ⓒ 83,629; ◆ 99,505
Monticello Park; RMC Place; ALEXANDRIA (Independent City); *245 E-15; ★ WASH; mail Alexandria z 22305; pop. incl. with Alexandria (Independent City)
Monticello Village; RMC Place; NORFOLK (Independent City); *245 L-18; elev. 15ft./5m.; ★ NORF-; mail Norfolk z 23505; pop. incl. with Norfolk (Independent City)
Monticello Woods; RMC Place; FAIRFAX; *245 E-15; ★ WASH; mail Springfield z 22150; ● 1,650
Montpelier; RMC Place; CHARLES CITY; *245 J-15; elev. 107ft./33m.; mail Charles City z 23030; rural
Montpelier; RMC Place; HANOVER; 245 I-13; 🅿; z 23192; ● 150
Montpelier; ORANGE; see Montpelier Station (RMC Place)
Montpelier Station (Montpelier); RMC Place; ORANGE; 245 G-11; 🅿; z 22957; ● 120
Montrose; CDP-Census Area Only; HENRICO; 243 D-9; ★ RICH; mail Henrico z 23231; Ⓟ 6,405; Ⓒ 7,018
Montrose Heights; RMC Place; RICHMOND (Independent City); *245 J-14; ★ RICH; mail Henrico z 23231; pop. incl. with Richmond (Independent City)
Montrose Terrace; RMC Place; HENRICO; ★ RICH; mail Henrico z 23231
Montross; Inc. Place; ⊡ WESTMORELAND; 245 G-16; 🅿; z 22520; Ⓟ 359; Ⓒ 315
Montvale; RMC Place; BEDFORD; 244 J-7; 🅿; ★ ROAN; z 24122; ● 550
Montvue; RMC Place; ALBEMARLE; 243 A-2; ★ CHRLTV; mail Charlottesville z 22901; ● 150
Monument Heights; RMC Place; HENRICO; *245 J-14; elev. 250ft./76m.; ★ RICH; mail Richmond z 23226; ● 2,500
Moon; RMC Place; MATHEWS; *245 J-17; elev. 10ft./3m.; 🅿; ★ NN-H; z 23119; ● 150
Mooreland; RMC Place; HENRICO; *245 J-13; elev. 230ft./70m.; ★ RICH; mail Henrico z 23075
Mooreland Farms; RMC Place; HENRICO; *245 J-13; ★ RICH; mail Henrico z 23229; ● 450
Moores Corner; RMC Place; STAFFORD; *245 F-14; ★ WASH; mail Stafford z 22554; rural
Moorings; RMC Place; SURRY; *245 K-16; mail Dendron z 23839; rural
Moran; RMC Place; PRINCE EDWARD; *245 K-11; mail Rice z 23966
Morattico; RMC Place; LANCASTER; 245 I-16; elev. 6ft./2m.; 🅿; z 22523; ● 270
Morefield; RMC Place; RUSSELL; *244 C-5; mail Saint Paul z 24283; ● 120
Morningside Hills; RMC Place; WASHINGTON; *244 D-6; mail Abingdon z 24210; pop. incl. with Abingdon (Inc. Place)
Morning Star; RMC Place; PAGE; *245 E-11; mail Luray z 22835; ● 130
Morris Church; RMC Place; CAMPBELL; *244 K-9; elev. 672ft./205m.; mail Brookneal z 24528; ● 30
Morrisdale; RMC Place; CHESTERFIELD; *245 K-14; elev. 80ft./24m.; ★ RICH; mail Chester z 23831; ● 1,700
Morrison; RMC Place; NEWPORT NEWS (Independent City); *245 L-17; ★ NN-H; mail Newport News z 23601; pop. incl. with Newport News (Independent City)
Morrisonville; RMC Place; LOUDOUN; *245 C-13; mail Lovettsville z 20180; rural
Morrisville; RMC Place; FAUQUIER; 245 F-13; 🅿; z 22712; ● 190
Morven; RMC Place; AMELIA; *245 J-12; elev. 403ft./123m.; mail Amelia Court House z 23002; rural
Mosby; RMC Place; FAIRFAX; 🅿; ★ WASH; z 22042
Mosby Woods; RMC Place; FAIRFAX (Independent City); *245 D-14; ★ WASH; mail Fairfax z 22030; pop. incl. with Fairfax (Independent City)
Moscow; RMC Place; AUGUSTA; *244 G-9; elev. 1,410ft./430m.; mail Mount Solon z 22843
Moseley; RMC Place; POWHATAN; 245 J-13; elev. 317ft./97m.; 🅿; z 23120; ● 120
Moss Run; RMC Place; ALLEGHANY; *244 I-5; mail Covington z 24426; rural
Mossy Creek; RMC Place; AUGUSTA; *244 G-9; mail Bridgewater z 22812, Mount Solon z 22843; rural
Motley; RMC Place; PITTSYLVANIA; 244 L-8; mail Hurt z 24563; ● 400
Motleys Mill; RMC Place; PITTSYLVANIA; *244 M-8; elev. 570ft./174m.; mail Chatham z 24531; rural
Motorun; RMC Place; MATHEWS; *245 J-17; elev. 6ft./2m.; ★ NN-H; mail Susan z 23163; rural
Mountain Falls; RMC Place; FREDERICK; *245 D-11; mail Winchester z 22602; ● 100
Mountain Gap; RMC Place; LOUDOUN; *245 D-13; ★ WASH; mail Leesburg z 20175; rural
Mountain Grove; RMC Place; BATH; *244 H-6; mail Warm Springs z 24484
Mountain Hill; RMC Place; PITTSYLVANIA; *244 N-8; elev. 656ft./200m.; ★ DANV; mail Ringgold z 24586; ● 50
Mountain Lake; RMC Place; GILES; 244 K-4; mail Pembroke z 24136; ● 30
Mountain Meadows; RMC Place; BEDFORD; *244 K-6; elev. 1,095ft./334m.; ★ ROAN; mail Vinton z 24179; ● 100
Mountain Valley; RMC Place; HENRY; *244 M-7; elev. 1,037ft./316m.; mail Martinsville z 24112
Mountain View; RMC Place; GILES; *244 K-4; mail Pearisburg z 24134; rural
Mountain View; RMC Place; KING GEORGE; mail Fredericksburg z 22406; rural
Mountain View; RMC Place; PULASKI; *244 L-4; elev. 2,027ft./618m.; mail Dublin z 24084; ● 100
Mountain View; RMC Place; ROCKBRIDGE; *244 H-8; mail Buena Vista z 24416; rural
Mountain View; STAFFORD; see Ramoth (RMC Place)
Mountain View; RMC Place; WASHINGTON; *244 D-6; mail Abingdon z 24211; ● 80
Mount Airy; RMC Place; PITTSYLVANIA; *244 L-8; elev. 648ft./198m.; mail Gretna z 24557; ● 30
Mount Alto; RMC Place; ALBEMARLE; *244 I-10; elev. 647ft./197m.; mail Esmont z 22937; rural
Mount Ararat; RMC Place; MECKLENBURG; *244 N-10; elev. 409ft./125m.; mail Clarksville z 23927; ● 150
Mount Carmel; RMC Place; HALIFAX; *244 N-9; elev. 537ft./164m.; mail Alton z 24520; rural
Mount Carmel; RMC Place; SMYTH; *244 L-1; elev. 2,210ft./674m.; mail Marion z 24354; ● 150
Mountcastle; RMC Place; NEW KENT; *245 J-15; elev. 42ft./13m.; mail Providence Forge z 23140; rural
Mount Clifton; RMC Place; SHENANDOAH; 244 E-10; mail Mount Jackson z 22842; ● 70
Mount Clinton; RMC Place; ROCKINGHAM; 244 F-9; mail Harrisonburg z 22802; ● 80
Mount Crawford; Inc. Place; ROCKINGHAM; 244 G-9; 🅿; z 22841; Ⓟ 228; Ⓒ 254; Ⓡ 286
Mount Cross; RMC Place; PITTSYLVANIA; *244 M-7; ★ DANV; mail Danville z 24540; ● 300
Mountfair; RMC Place; ALBEMARLE; *244 G-10; mail Crozet z 22932
Mount Garland; RMC Place; LOUISA; *245 H-13; elev. 324ft./99m.; mail Mineral z 23117; rural
Mount Gilead; RMC Place; LOUDOUN; *245 D-13; elev. 602ft./183m.; ★ WASH; mail Leesburg z 20175; rural
Mount Hermon; RMC Place; PITTSYLVANIA; *244 M-8; elev. 690ft./210m.; ★ DANV; mail Danville z 24540; ● 250
Mount Heron; RMC Place; BUCHANAN; 244 B-6; mail Oakwood z 24631; ● 180
Mount Holly; RMC Place; WESTMORELAND; *245 G-16; elev. 44ft./13m.; 🅿; z 22524; ● 50
Mount Jackson; Inc. Place; SHENANDOAH; 244 E-10; 🅿; z 22842; Ⓟ 1,583; Ⓒ 1,664
Mount Landing; RMC Place; ESSEX; *245 H-15; mail Tappahannock z 22560
Mount Laurel; RMC Place; HALIFAX; 244 L-10; mail Clover z 24534; ● 50
Mount Meridian; RMC Place; AUGUSTA; *244 G-9; mail Grottoes z 24441; rural
Mount Nebo; RMC Place; CHESTERFIELD; *245 J-13; elev. 350ft./107m.; ★ RICH; mail Richmond z 23235
Mount Olive; RMC Place; SHENANDOAH; 244 D-10; mail Toms Brook z 22660; ● 90
Mount Pisgah; RMC Place; AUGUSTA; *244 G-9; mail Mount Sidney z 24467; rural
Mount Pleasant; RMC Place; AMHERST; mail Amherst z 24521; rural
Mount Pleasant Estates; RMC Place; STAFFORD; *245 G-14; ★ FRED; mail Fredericksburg z 22401; ● 650
Mount Sidney; RMC Place; AUGUSTA; 244 G-9; 🅿; z 24467; ● 500
Mount Solon; RMC Place; AUGUSTA; 244 G-9; 🅿; z 22843; ● 200
Mount Vernon (Engleside); CDP; FAIRFAX; 249 J-5; 🅿; ★ WASH; z 22121 & mail Alexandria z 22309; Ⓟ 27,485; Ⓒ 28,582; ◆ 29,705
Mount Vernon Forest; RMC Place; FAIRFAX; *245 E-15; ★ WASH; mail Alexandria z 22309
Mount Vernon on the Potomac; RMC Place; FAIRFAX; ★ WASH; mail Alexandria z 22309
Mount Vernon Park; RMC Place; FAIRFAX; *245 E-15; ★ WASH; mail Alexandria z 22309
Mount Vernon Square; RMC Place; FAIRFAX; *245 E-15; ★ WASH; mail Alexandria z 22306
Mount Vernon Terrace; RMC Place; FAIRFAX; *245 E-15; ★ WASH; mail Alexandria z 22309
Mount Vernon Valley; RMC Place; FAIRFAX; ★ WASH; mail Alexandria z 22309
Mount Vernon Woods; RMC Place; FAIRFAX; *245 E-15; ★ WASH; mail Alexandria z 22309
Mount View; RMC Place; SMYTH; *244 M-1; mail Marion z 24354; ● 30
Mountville; RMC Place; LOUDOUN; *245 D-13; mail Middleburg z 20117
Mount Vinco; RMC Place; BUCKINGHAM; *244 J-10; mail Buckingham z 23921; rural
Mount Williams; RMC Place; FREDERICK; *245 C-11; mail Winchester z 22602
Mount Zephyr; RMC Place; FAIRFAX; *245 E-15; ★ WASH; mail Alexandria z 22309
Mount Zion; RMC Place; CAMPBELL; *244 K-9; elev. 764ft./233m.; mail Gladys z 24554; rural
Mouth of Laurel; RMC Place; TAZEWELL; *244 K-1; mail Cedar Bluff z 24609; rural
Mouth of Wilson; RMC Place; GRAYSON; 244 N-1; 🅿; z 24363; ● 150
Mud Fork; RMC Place; TAZEWELL; *244 K-1; mail North Tazewell z 24630; ● 30
Mudtown; RMC Place; LEXINGTON (Independent City); pop. incl. with Lexington (Independent City)
Mulch; RMC Place; RICHMOND; *245 H-16; elev. 120ft./37m.; mail Farnham z 22460; rural
Munden; RMC Place; VIRGINIA BEACH (Independent City); *245 M-18; ★ NORF-; mail Virginia Beach z 23457; pop. incl. with Virginia Beach (Independent City)
Mundy Point; RMC Place; NORTHUMBERLAND; *245 H-17; mail Callao z 22435
Munson Hill; RMC Place; FAIRFAX; *245 D-15; ★ WASH; mail Falls Church z 22041; ● 2,250
Murat; RMC Place; ROCKBRIDGE; *244 I-7; mail Lexington z 24450; rural
Murpheyville; RMC Place; WYTHE; *244 L-2; mail Rural Retreat z 24368; pop. incl. with Rural Retreat (Inc. Place)
Murphy; RMC Place; BUCHANAN; *244 C-5; elev. 1,429ft./436m.; mail Vansant z 24656; rural
Murrayfield; RMC Place; WASHINGTON; *244 M-1; mail Chilhowie z 24319; rural
Museville; RMC Place; PITTSYLVANIA; *244 L-7; elev. 940ft./287m.; mail Chatham z 24531; rural
Mustoe; RMC Place; HIGHLAND; 244 G-7; 🅿; z 24468 & mail Monterey z 24465; ● 30
Mustoe; RMC Place; KING GEORGE; *245 G-14; elev. 168ft./51m.; mail King George z 22485; rural
Mutton Hunk; RMC Place; ACCOMACK; *245 I-20; elev. 45ft./14m.; mail Parksley z 23421; rural
Myndus; RMC Place; NELSON; *244 I-9; mail Lovingston z 22949; ● 50
Myrtle; RMC Place; SUFFOLK (Independent City); *245 M-16; ★ NORF-; mail Suffolk z 23434; pop. incl. with Suffolk (Independent City)

N

Nace; RMC Place; BOTETOURT; *244 J-6; ★ ROAN; mail Troutville z 24175
Naffs; RMC Place; FRANKLIN; *244 K-6; mail Boones Mill z 24065; ● 50
Nahor; RMC Place; FLUVANNA; *245 H-11; elev. 484ft./148m.; mail Palmyra z 22963
Nain; RMC Place; FREDERICK; *245 C-11; mail Winchester z 22603
Namozine Store; RMC Place; AMELIA; *245 K-13; elev. 296ft./90m.; mail Church Road z 23833; rural
Nancy Wrights Corner; RMC Place; CAROLINE; *245 H-14; mail Woodford z 22580; ● 30
Nandua; RMC Place; ACCOMACK; *245 I-19; mail Painter z 23420; ● 30
Nansemond; RMC Place; SUFFOLK (Independent City); ★ NORF-; mail Suffolk z 23434; pop. incl. with Suffolk (Independent City)
Nansemond Shores; RMC Place; SUFFOLK (Independent City); *245 L-17; ★ NORF-; mail Suffolk z 23434; pop. incl. with Suffolk (Independent City)
Naola; RMC Place; AMHERST; *244 J-8; mail Monroe z 24574
Narrows; Inc. Place; GILES; 244 K-3; 🅿; z 24124; Ⓟ 2,082; Ⓒ 2,111
Naruna; RMC Place; CAMPBELL; 244 L-9; elev. 622ft./190m.; 🅿; z 24576; ● 200
Nash Ford; RMC Place; RUSSELL; *244 C-6; mail Cleveland z 24225; rural
Nasons; RMC Place; ORANGE; 245 G-12; 🅿; z 22960 & mail Rapidan z 22733; ● 30
Nassawadox; Inc. Place; NORTHAMPTON; 245 J-19; elev. 38ft./12m.; 🅿 🅷; z 23413; Ⓟ 564; Ⓒ 572
Nathalie; RMC Place; HALIFAX; 244 L-9; 🅿; z 24577; ● 150
National Airport; RMC Place; ARLINGTON; ★ WASH; mail Washington z 20001
National Heights; RMC Place; HENRICO; *245 J-14; ★ RICH; mail Henrico z 23231; ● 1,300

Entries in **UPPERCASE** are counties.
Entries in **bold** have populations of 2,500 or more.
Names in parentheses are alternate names.
Inc. Place — Incorporated Place
RMC Place — Rand McNally Designated Place
CDP — Census Designated Place
MCD — Minor Civil Division
⊡ County Seat
▲ Minor Civil Division
elev. Elevation
🅿 Post Office
🅷 Hospital
🅲 College
■ Principal Business Center
★ Ranally Metro Area (RMA) Abbreviation
z Zip Code(s)
Ⓟ Previous Census Population
Ⓡ Revised Census Population
Ⓐ Annexation Population
● Rand McNally Population Estimate
Ⓒ Final Census Population
Ⓢ Special Census Population
◆ Estimated Population

For additional definitions see Glossary, Volume 1, and Introduction, Volume 2.

Natural Bridge (Natural Bridge Station); RMC Place; ROCKBRIDGE; *244 I-7; 🅿; z 24578 & mail Natural Bridge Station z 24579; ● 1,500
Natural Bridge Station; ROCKBRIDGE; see Natural Bridge (RMC Place)
Natural Tunnel; SCOTT; see Glenita (RMC Place)
Natural Well; RMC Place; ALLEGHANY; 244 H-6; mail Hot Springs z 24445; ● 30
Naxera; RMC Place; GLOUCESTER; 245 J-17; elev. 10ft./3m.; 🅿; ★ NN-H; z 23061; ● 400
Naylors Beach; RMC Place; RICHMOND; *245 H-16; mail Warsaw z 22572; ● 30
Neals Corner; RMC Place; HALIFAX; *244 L-10; elev. 569ft./173m.; mail Clover z 24534; rural
Nealy Ridge; RMC Place; DICKENSON; *244 C-5; mail Clinchco z 24226; ● 50
Nebo; RMC Place; SMYTH; *244 L-1; mail Ceres z 24318; ● 30
Needmore; RMC Place; SMYTH; *244 M-1; mail Chilhowie z 24319; ● 50
Needmore; RMC Place; WISE; *244 C-4; mail Norton z 24273; ● 80
Neenah; RMC Place; WESTMORELAND; *245 H-16; elev. 131ft./40m.; mail Montross z 22520; rural
Neersville; RMC Place; LOUDOUN; *245 C-13; mail Purcellville z 20132; rural
Negro Foot; RMC Place; HANOVER; *245 I-13; elev. 296ft./90m.; ★ RICH; mail Montpelier z 23192; rural
Nellysford; RMC Place; NELSON; 244 H-9; elev. 673ft./205m.; 🅿; z 22958; ● 180
Nelson; RMC Place; MECKLENBURG; *244 N-10; 🅿; z 24580; ● 150
NELSON; 244 I-9; Ⓟ 12,778; © 14,445; ◆ 15,646
Nelson Estates; RMC Place; HENRICO; ★ RICH; mail Henrico z 23231
Nelsonia; RMC Place; ACCOMACK; 245 H-20; elev. 49ft./15m.; 🅿; z 23414; ● 150
Nelson Park; RMC Place; YORK; *245 K-16; ★ NN-H; mail Williamsburg z 23185; ● 800
Nesting; RMC Place; MIDDLESEX; *245 I-16; elev. 96ft./29m.; mail Jamaica z 23079; rural
Nethers; RMC Place; MADISON; *245 F-11; elev. 806ft./246m.; mail Sperryville z 22740; ● 30
Nettleridge; RMC Place; PATRICK; *244 N-5; elev. 1,116ft./340m.; mail Stuart z 24171; rural
New Alexandria; RMC Place; FAIRFAX; 249 I-6; ★ WASH; mail Alexandria z 22307; ● 950
New Baltimore; RMC Place; FAUQUIER; 245 E-13; 🅿; ★ WASH; z 20187; ● 550
Newbern; RMC Place; PULASKI; 244 L-4; 🅿; z 24126; ● 300
Newberry; RMC Place; LOUDOUN; *245 D-14; ★ WASH; mail Sterling z 20165
New Birchett Estates; RMC Place; PRINCE GEORGE; *245 K-14; elev. 100ft./30m.; ★ RICH; mail Prince George z 23875; ● 300
New Bohemia; RMC Place; PRINCE GEORGE; 243 I-10; ★ RICH; mail Disputanta z 23842; ● 40
New Canton; RMC Place; BUCKINGHAM; 245 I-11; 🅿; z 23123; ● 70
New Castle; Inc. Place; ⊡ CRAIG; 244 J-5; 🅿; z 24127; Ⓟ 152; © 179
New Church; RMC Place; ACCOMACK; 245 H-20; 🅿; z 23415; ● 400
Newcomb Hall; RMC Place; CHARLOTTESVILLE (Independent City); 🅿; ★ CHRLTV; z 22904; pop. incl. with Charlottesville (Independent City)
New Design; RMC Place; DANVILLE (Independent City); *244 M-8; ★ DANV; mail Danville z 24541; pop. incl. with Danville (Independent City)
New Ellett; RMC Place; MONTGOMERY; *244 K-5; mail Blacksburg z 24060; rural
New Glasgow; RMC Place; AMHERST; 244 I-9; elev. 769ft./234m.; mail Amherst z 24521; ● 50
New Hampden; RMC Place; HIGHLAND; *244 F-7; mail Blue Grass z 24413; ● 30
New Hope; RMC Place; AUGUSTA; 244 G-9; 🅿; z 24469; ● 180
New Hope; RMC Place; CHARLES CITY; *245 J-15; mail Charles City z 23030; rural
Newington; CDP; FAIRFAX; 249 J-4; 🅿; ★ WASH; z 22122; Ⓟ 17,965; © 19,784
Newington Station; RMC Place; FAIRFAX; *245 E-14; ★ WASH; mail Springfield z 22153
Newington Woods; RMC Place; FAIRFAX; *245 E-14; ★ WASH; mail Springfield z 22153
New Kent; RMC Place; ⊡ NEW KENT; 245 J-15; elev. 139ft./42m.; 🅿 🄷; z 23124; ● 100
NEW KENT; 245 J-15; Ⓟ 10,445; © 13,462; ◆ 18,459
Newland; RMC Place; RICHMOND; *245 H-16; mail Warsaw z 22572
New London (Bedford Springs); RMC Place; CAMPBELL; *244 K-8; elev. 872ft./266m.; ★ LYNCH; mail Forest z 24551
New Market; Inc. Place; SHENANDOAH; 244 E-10; 🅿; z 22844; Ⓟ 1,435; © 1,637; ® 1,732
New Market South; RMC Place; NEWPORT NEWS (Independent City); *245 L-17; ★ NN-H; pop. incl. with Newport News (Independent City)
New Point; RMC Place; MATHEWS; 245 J-17; elev. 4ft./1m.; 🅿; ★ NN-H; z 23125; ● 300
Newport (Moffats Creek); RMC Place; AUGUSTA; 244 H-8; mail Middlebrook z 24459; ● 100
Newport; RMC Place; GILES; 244 K-4; 🅿; z 24128; ● 200
Newport; RMC Place; PAGE; *244 F-10; mail Shenandoah z 22849; ● 40
Newport News; Independent City; 245 L-17; 🅿 🄷 🄲 4,730 ■; ★ NN-H; z 23601-09, z 23612, z 23628 & mail Hampton z 23630; Ⓟ 170,045; © 180,150; ® 180,697; ◆ 181,167
New Post; RMC Place; SPOTSYLVANIA; *245 G-14; ★ FRED; mail Fredericksburg z 22401; ● 140
New River; RMC Place; PULASKI; *244 K-4; 🅿; z 24129; ● 460
News Ferry; RMC Place; HALIFAX; *244 M-9; mail South Boston z 24592; rural
Newsoms; Inc. Place; SOUTHAMPTON; 245 M-15; 🅿; z 23874; Ⓟ 337; © 282; ® 288
Newstead Farm; RMC Place; PRINCE GEORGE; *245 K-14; elev. 100ft./30m.; ★ RICH; mail Prince George z 23875; ● 120
New Store; RMC Place; BUCKINGHAM; *244 J-10; elev. 664ft./202m.; mail Farmville z 23901
Newton Park; RMC Place; NORFOLK (Independent City); *245 L-18; ★ NORF-; mail Norfolk z 23523; pop. incl. with Norfolk (Independent City)
Newtown; RMC Place; ALBEMARLE; *244 H-10; elev. 1,000ft./305m.; ★ CHRLTV; mail Greenwood z 22943; rural
Newtown; RMC Place; KING AND QUEEN; 245 H-15; elev. 183ft./56m.; 🅿; z 23126; ● 100
Newtown; RMC Place; LANCASTER; *245 I-17; elev. 110ft./34m.; mail Lancaster z 22503; rural
Newtown; RMC Place; ROCKBRIDGE; *244 I-7; mail Lexington z 24450; rural
Newtown; RMC Place; ROCKINGHAM; 244 F-10; mail Elkton z 22827; ● 200
New Towne South; RMC Place; NORFOLK (Independent City); ★ NORF-; pop. incl. with Norfolk (Independent City)
Newville; RMC Place; PRINCE GEORGE; *245 K-15; elev. 128ft./39m.; mail Disputanta z 23842; rural
Newville; RMC Place; SUSSEX; *245 L-15; elev. 115ft./35m.; mail Waverly z 23890; rural
Nicelytown; RMC Place; ALLEGHANY; 244 I-7; mail Clifton Forge z 24422; ● 160
Nickelsville; Inc. Place; SCOTT; 244 D-4; 🅿; z 24271; Ⓟ 411; © 448
Niday; RMC Place; BLAND; *244 K-2; mail Narrows z 24124; rural
Nimrod Hall; RMC Place; BATH; *244 H-7; mail Millboro z 24460; rural
Ninde; RMC Place; KING GEORGE; *245 G-15; 🅿; z 22526; ● 50
Nineveh; RMC Place; WARREN; *245 D-11; mail Front Royal z 22630
Nokesville; CDP; PRINCE WILLIAM; 245 E-13; 🅿; ★ WASH; z 20181-82; © 1,236
No Mans Corner; RMC Place; CAROLINE; *245 H-14; elev. 180ft./55m.; mail Milford z 22514; rural
Nomini Grove; RMC Place; WESTMORELAND; *245 H-16; elev. 144ft./44m.; mail Warsaw z 22572; ● 40
Nora; RMC Place; DICKENSON; 244 C-5; 🅿; z 24272; ● 150
Norfolk; Independent City; 245 L-18; 🅿 🄷 🄲 29,719 ■; ★ NORF-; z 23501-15, z 23517-21, z 23523, z 23529, z 23541, z 23551; Ⓟ 261,229; © 234,403; ◆ 250,740
Norfolk Highlands; RMC Place; CHESAPEAKE (Independent City); *245 L-18; ★ NORF-; mail Chesapeake z 23325; pop. incl. with Chesapeake (Independent City)
Norge; RMC Place; JAMES CITY; 245 J-16; 🅿; ★ NN-H; z 23127; ● 1,000
Norland; RMC Place; DICKENSON; *244 B-4; mail Clintwood z 24228; rural
Norman; RMC Place; CULPEPER; 245 F-12; mail Culpeper z 22701; ● 70
North (North Arlington); RMC Place; ARLINGTON; *245 D-15; ★ WASH; mail Arlington z 22207, z 22213
North; RMC Place; MATHEWS; 245 J-17; elev. 10ft./3m.; 🅿; ★ NN-H; z 23128; ● 200
NORTHAMPTON; 245 J-19; Ⓟ 13,061; © 13,093; ◆ 13,361
North Arlington; ARLINGTON; see North (RMC Place)
North Bristol; RMC Place; BRISTOL (Independent City); ★ JNSC-; mail Bristol z 24201; pop. incl. with Bristol (Independent City)
North Fairlington; RMC Place; ARLINGTON; *245 E-15; ★ WASH; mail Arlington z 22206
Northfields; RMC Place; ALBEMARLE; 243 A-3; ★ CHRLTV; mail Charlottesville z 22901; ● 1,400
North Fork; RMC Place; LOUDOUN; *245 D-13; mail Purcellville z 20132
North Gap; RMC Place; BLAND; *244 K-2; elev. 2,088ft./636m.; mail Rocky Gap z 24366; rural
North Garden; RMC Place; ALBEMARLE; 244 H-10; 🅿; z 22959; ● 900
North Halifax; RMC Place; HALIFAX; *244 L-9; mail Nathalie z 24577; rural
North Holston; RMC Place; SMYTH; *244 L-1; elev. 1,757ft./536m.; mail Saltville z 24370; ● 200
North Jericho; RMC Place; SUFFOLK (Independent City); ★ NORF-; mail Suffolk z 23434; pop. incl. with Suffolk (Independent City)
North Linkhorn Park; RMC Place; VIRGINIA BEACH (Independent City); *245 L-18; ★ NORF-; mail Virginia Beach z 23451; pop. incl. with Virginia Beach (Independent City)
North Mountain; RMC Place; AUGUSTA; *244 G-8; elev. 2,125ft./648m.; mail Swoope z 24479; rural
North Rolleston; RMC Place; NORFOLK (Independent City); *245 L-18; ★ NORF-; mail Norfolk z 23502; pop. incl. with Norfolk (Independent City)
North Run Hills; RMC Place; HENRICO; *245 I-14; elev. 188ft./57m.; ★ RICH; mail Henrico z 23228; ● 350
North Shore; CDP-Census Area Only; FRANKLIN; *244 L-7; © 2,112
Northside; RMC Place; RICHMOND (Independent City); ★ RICH; mail Richmond z 23222; pop. incl. with Richmond (Independent City)
North Springfield; CDP; FAIRFAX; 249 H-3; 🅿; ★ WASH; z 22151; Ⓟ 8,996; © 9,173
North Stanton; RMC Place; HALIFAX; *244 L-9; mail Nathalie z 24577; ● 30
North Tazewell; RMC Place; TAZEWELL; *244 K-1; 🅿; z 24630; pop. incl. with Tazewell (Inc. Place)
NORTHUMBERLAND; 245 H-17; Ⓟ 10,524; © 12,259; ◆ 12,986
North View; RMC Place; MECKLENBURG; *245 M-11; elev. 490ft./149m.; mail South Hill z 23970
North Virginia Beach; RMC Place; VIRGINIA BEACH (Independent City); *245 L-18; ★ NORF-; mail Virginia Beach z 23451; pop. incl. with Virginia Beach (Independent City)
North Weems; RMC Place; LANCASTER; *245 I-17; mail Weems z 22576; ● 270
North Wellville; RMC Place; NOTTOWAY; *245 K-12; elev. 408ft./124m.; mail Blackstone z 23824; rural
Northwest; RMC Place; CHESAPEAKE (Independent City); *245 M-18; ★ NORF-; pop. incl. with Chesapeake (Independent City)
North Woodley; RMC Place; FAIRFAX; *245 D-14; ★ WASH; mail Falls Church z 22042; ● 2,950
Norton; Independent City; 244 C-4; elev. 2,141ft./653m.; 🅿 🄷; z 24273; Ⓟ 4,247; © 3,904; ◆ 3,762
Norton Junction; RMC Place; NORTON (Independent City); pop. incl. with Norton (Independent City)
Nortonsville; RMC Place; ALBEMARLE; *244 G-10; 🅿; ★ CHRLTV; z 22935
Norvello; RMC Place; MECKLENBURG; *245 M-11; elev. 298ft./91m.; mail Boydton z 23917; rural
Norview; RMC Place; NORFOLK (Independent City); *245 L-18; ★ NORF-; mail Norfolk z 23513; pop. incl. with Norfolk (Independent City)
Norwood; RMC Place; BEDFORD; *244 J-8; elev. 919ft./280m.; mail Forest z 24551; rural
Norwood; RMC Place; NELSON; 244 I-9; 🅿; z 24581; ● 60
Nottingham; RMC Place; RICHMOND (Independent City); ★ RICH; mail Richmond z 23235; pop. incl. with Richmond (Independent City)
Nottingham; RMC Place; SCOTT; *244 D-4; ★ JNSC-; mail Gate City z 24251; rural
Nottoway; RMC Place; ⊡ NOTTOWAY; 245 K-12; 🅿; z 23955; ● 100
NOTTOWAY; 245 K-12; Ⓟ 14,993; © 15,725; ◆ 16,009
Novelty; RMC Place; FRANKLIN; *244 L-7; mail Penhook z 24137; ● 30
Novum; RMC Place; MADISON; *245 F-11; mail Reva z 22735; rural
Nurney; RMC Place; SUFFOLK (Independent City); *245 M-16; ★ NORF-; mail Suffolk z 23434; pop. incl. with Suffolk (Independent City)
Nurneysville; RMC Place; SUFFOLK (Independent City); ★ NORF-; mail Suffolk z 23434; pop. incl. with Suffolk (Independent City)
Nutbush; RMC Place; LUNENBURG; *245 L-11; mail Green Bay z 23942
Nuttall; RMC Place; GLOUCESTER; *245 J-17; ★ NN-H; mail Gloucester z 23061; rural
Nuttsville; RMC Place; LANCASTER; *245 I-17; elev. 116ft./35m.; 🅿; z 22528; ● 30

O

Oak Corner; RMC Place; CAROLINE; *245 H-14; elev. 204ft./62m.; mail Milford z 22514; rural
Oakcrest; RMC Place; ALEXANDRIA (Independent City); *245 E-15; ★ WASH; mail Alexandria z 22302; pop. incl. with Alexandria (Independent City)
Oakcrest; RMC Place; ARLINGTON; *245 E-15; mail Arlington z 22202
Oakdale; RMC Place; CHESTERFIELD; ★ RICH; mail Richmond z 23234
Oakdale; RMC Place; ROCKBRIDGE; *244 I-7; mail Lexington z 24450; rural
Oakdale Farms; RMC Place; NORFOLK (Independent City); *245 L-18; elev. 10ft./3m.; ★ NORF-; mail Norfolk z 23505; pop. incl. with Norfolk (Independent City)
Oak Forest; RMC Place; CUMBERLAND; *245 J-11; elev. 426ft./130m.; mail Cumberland z 23040; rural
Oak Grove; RMC Place; CARROLL; *244 M-3; mail Woodlawn z 24381; rural
Oak Grove; RMC Place; CHESAPEAKE (Independent City); *245 M-18; ★ NORF-; pop. incl. with Chesapeake (Independent City)
Oak Grove; RMC Place; LOUDOUN; *245 D-14; ★ WASH; mail Sterling z 20166; ● 200
Oak Grove; RMC Place; SPOTSYLVANIA; *245 G-13; ★ FRED; mail Fredericksburg z 22401; ● 550
Oak Grove; RMC Place; WASHINGTON; *244 D-5; ★ JNSC-; mail Bristol z 24202; rural
Oak Grove; RMC Place; WESTMORELAND; 245 G-15; elev. 69ft./21m.; 🅿; z 22443; ● 150
Oak Hall; RMC Place; ACCOMACK; 245 H-20; 🅿; z 23396, z 23416; ● 250
Oak Hill; RMC Place; AUGUSTA; *244 H-9; mail Waynesboro z 22980; pop. incl. with Waynesboro (Independent City)
Oak Hill; RMC Place; GRAYSON; *244 M-1; mail Mouth of Wilson z 24363; ● 80
Oak Hill; RMC Place; HENRICO; *245 J-14; ★ RICH; mail Richmond z 23223; ● 1,100
Oak Hill; RMC Place; PAGE; *245 E-11; mail Rileyville z 22650
Oak Hill Estates; RMC Place; HANOVER; *245 I-14; elev. 242ft./74m.; ★ RICH; mail Ashland z 23005; ● 400
Oakhurst; RMC Place; PETERSBURG (Independent City); ★ RICH; mail Petersburg z 23805; pop. incl. with Petersburg (Independent City)
Oakland; RMC Place; CHESTERFIELD; ★ RICH; mail Chester z 23831
Oakland; RMC Place; SUFFOLK (Independent City); ★ NORF-; mail Suffolk z 23432; pop. incl. with Suffolk (Independent City)
Oakland Park; RMC Place; NORTHAMPTON; *245 J-19; mail Exmore z 23350; ● 100
Oak Level; RMC Place; HALIFAX; *244 M-9; mail Halifax z 24558; ● 50
Oak Level; CDP; HENRY; *244 M-6; elev. 1,258ft./383m.; ★ MRTNV; mail Bassett z 24055; © 885
Oakley; RMC Place; ESSEX; *245 I-16; elev. 123ft./37m.; mail Center Cross z 22437; rural
Oakpark; RMC Place; MADISON; *245 F-11; 🅿; z 22730; ● 50
Oak Ridge; RMC Place; FAIRFAX; *245 D-14; ★ WASH; mail Vienna z 22180
Oakridge; RMC Place; SUFFOLK (Independent City); *245 M-16; ★ NORF-; mail Suffolk z 23434; pop. incl. with Suffolk (Independent City)
Oak Ridge Estates; RMC Place; PRINCE WILLIAM; *245 E-14; ★ WASH; mail Manassas z 20112; ● 200
Oakridge Estates; RMC Place; SUFFOLK (Independent City); ★ NORF-; mail Suffolk z 23434; pop. incl. with Suffolk (Independent City)
Oakton; CDP; FAIRFAX; 249 G-2; 🅿; ★ WASH; z 22124, z 22185 & mail Vienna z 22180; Ⓟ 24,610; © 29,348; ◆ 30,503
Oak Valley Estates; RMC Place; FAIRFAX; *245 D-14; ★ WASH; mail Vienna z 22181; ● 1,350
Oakville; RMC Place; APPOMATTOX; 244 J-9; elev. 748ft./228m.; mail Appomattox z 24522; ● 50
Oakwood; RMC Place; ARLINGTON; *245 D-15; ★ WASH; mail Arlington z 22213
Oakwood; RMC Place; BUCHANAN; 244 B-6; 🅿; z 24631; ● 500
Oakwood; RMC Place; CHESTERFIELD; ★ RICH; mail Chester z 23831
Oakwood; RMC Place; FAIRFAX; *245 E-15; ★ WASH; mail Alexandria z 22310
Oakwood Forest; RMC Place; ALLEGHANY; *244 I-6; mail Covington z 24426; ● 90
Oakwood Terrace; RMC Place; NORFOLK (Independent City); *245 L-18; ★ NORF-; mail Norfolk z 23513; pop. incl. with Norfolk (Independent City)
Oatlands; RMC Place; LOUDOUN; *245 D-13; ★ WASH; mail Leesburg z 20175
Occoquan; Inc. Place; PRINCE WILLIAM, FAIRFAX; 245 E-14; 🅿; ★ WASH; z 22125; Ⓟ 361; © 759
Occupacia; RMC Place; ESSEX; *245 H-15; mail Hustle z 22476; rural
Oceana; RMC Place; VIRGINIA BEACH (Independent City); *245 L-18; ★ NORF-; mail Virginia Beach z 23454; pop. incl. with Virginia Beach (Independent City)
Ocean Park; RMC Place; VIRGINIA BEACH (Independent City); *245 L-18; ★ NORF-; mail Virginia Beach z 23455; pop. incl. with Virginia Beach (Independent City)
Ocean View; RMC Place; NORFOLK (Independent City); *245 L-18; ★ NORF-; mail Norfolk z 23503; pop. incl. with Norfolk (Independent City)
Ocoonita; RMC Place; LEE; *244 D-2; mail Jonesville z 24263
Ocran; RMC Place; LANCASTER; *245 I-17; mail White Stone z 22578; ● 150
Offutt Village; RMC Place; FALLS CHURCH (Independent City); *245 D-14; ★ WASH; pop. incl. with Falls Church (Independent City)
Oilville; RMC Place; GOOCHLAND; 245 I-13; 🅿; z 23129; ● 100
Old Chapel; CLARKE; see Briggs (RMC Place)
Old Courthouse; RMC Place; FAIRFAX; *245 D-14; ★ WASH; mail Vienna z 22182
Old Creek Estates; RMC Place; FAIRFAX; *245 E-14; ★ WASH; mail Fairfax z 22032; ● 850
Old Dominion; RMC Place; ALBEMARLE; *244 I-10; mail Schuyler z 22969; ● 30
Old Dominion Gardens; RMC Place; FAIRFAX; *245 D-14; ★ WASH; mail Mc Lean z 22101
Olde Forge; RMC Place; FAIRFAX; *245 E-14; ★ WASH; mail Fairfax z 22032; ● 1,900
Olde Hunting Hills; RMC Place; PITTSYLVANIA; *244 M-7; elev. 600ft./183m.; ★ DANV; mail Danville z 24540; ● 200
Oldewood; RMC Place; FAIRFAX; *245 D-14; ★ WASH; mail Falls Church z 22043
Oldfield; RMC Place; VIRGINIA BEACH (Independent City); ★ NORF-; pop. incl. with Virginia Beach (Independent City)
Old Glade Spring; RMC Place; WASHINGTON; *244 M-1; mail Glade Spring z 24340; rural
Old Hampton; RMC Place; HAMPTON (Independent City); ★ NN-H; mail Hampton z 23669; pop. incl. with Hampton (Independent City)
Oldhams; RMC Place; WESTMORELAND; 245 H-16; elev. 132ft./40m.; 🅿; z 22529; ● 100
Old Somerset; RMC Place; ORANGE; *245 G-11; mail Somerset z 22972; rural
Old Tavern; RMC Place; FAUQUIER; 245 E-13; mail The Plains z 20198; ● 60
Oldtown; RMC Place; GRAYSON; 244 M-3; elev. 2,547ft./776m.; mail Galax z 24333; ● 50
Old Well; RMC Place; CHARLOTTE; *244 K-9; elev. 687ft./209m.; mail Phenix z 23959; rural
Olinger; RMC Place; LEE; *244 D-3; mail Big Stone Gap z 24219
Olive; RMC Place; PORTSMOUTH (Independent City); ★ NORF-; mail Portsmouth z 23701; pop. incl. with Portsmouth (Independent City)
Omaha; RMC Place; DICKENSON; *244 C-4; mail Clintwood z 24228; rural
Omega; RMC Place; HALIFAX; *244 M-10; mail South Boston z 24592
Onancock; Inc. Place; ACCOMACK; 245 I-19; 🅿; z 23417; Ⓟ 1,434; © 1,525
O'Neal; MADISON; see Pratts (RMC Place)
Onemo; RMC Place; MATHEWS; *245 J-17; elev. 3ft./1m.; 🅿; ★ NN-H; z 23130; ● 80
Onley; Inc. Place; ACCOMACK; 245 I-19; 🅿; z 23418; Ⓟ 532; © 496
Ontario; RMC Place; CHARLOTTE; *245 L-11; mail Drakes Branch z 23937; ● 30
Opal; RMC Place; FAUQUIER; *245 E-13; ★ WASH; mail Warrenton z 20186; ● 50
Opequon; RMC Place; FREDERICK; *245 C-11; mail Winchester z 22602; ● 50
Ophelia; RMC Place; NORTHUMBERLAND; *245 H-17; 🅿; z 22530; ● 150
Oranda; RMC Place; SHENANDOAH; *245 D-11; mail Strasburg z 22657; rural
Orange; Inc. Place; ⊡ ORANGE; 245 G-12; elev. 521ft./159m.; 🅿; z 22960; Ⓟ 2,582; © 4,123
ORANGE; 245 G-12; Ⓟ 21,421; © 25,881; ◆ 34,057
Orange Hunt (Keen Mill Heights); RMC Place; FAIRFAX; *245 E-14; ★ WASH; mail Springfield z 22152-53; ● 3,400
Orapax Farms; RMC Place; NEW KENT; *245 J-15; elev. 118ft./36m.; mail Quinton z 23141; ● 110
Orbit; RMC Place; ISLE OF WIGHT; *245 L-16; elev. 80ft./24m.; mail Windsor z 23487; ● 30
Orchard Hill; RMC Place; CHESTERFIELD; *245 J-14; elev. 190ft./58m.; ★ RICH; mail Richmond z 23234; ● 600
Orchid; RMC Place; LOUISA; *245 I-12; elev. 337ft./103m.; mail Mineral z 23117
Orchid Lake; RMC Place; LOUISA; *245 I-12; elev. 350ft./107m.; mail Gum Spring z 23065; ● 70
Ordinary; RMC Place; GLOUCESTER; 243 F-4; 🅿; ★ NN-H; z 23131; ● 1,000
Ore Bank; RMC Place; BUCKINGHAM
Oregon Acres; RMC Place; PORTSMOUTH (Independent City); *245 L-17; ★ NORF-; mail Portsmouth z 23701; pop. incl. with Portsmouth (Independent City)
Oreton; RMC Place; WISE; *244 D-3; elev. 1,881ft./573m.; mail Big Stone Gap z 24219; rural
Oriana; RMC Place; NEWPORT NEWS (Independent City); *245 K-17; ★ NN-H; mail Newport News z 23602; pop. incl. with Newport News (Independent City)
Oriskany; RMC Place; BOTETOURT; 244 I-6; 🅿; z 24130; ● 80
Orkney Springs; RMC Place; SHENANDOAH; *244 E-9; 🅿; z 22845; summer pop. 300; ● 80
Orlando; RMC Place; SUFFOLK (Independent City); ★ NORF-; mail Suffolk z 23434; pop. incl. with Suffolk (Independent City)
Orlean; RMC Place; FAUQUIER; 245 E-12; 🅿; z 20128; ● 60
Orleans Village; RMC Place; FAIRFAX; *245 E-15; ★ WASH; mail Alexandria z 22312
Oronoco; RMC Place; AMHERST; *244 I-8; mail Vesuvius z 24483
Osaka; RMC Place; WISE; *244 C-3; mail Appalachia z 24216; ● 300
Osbornes Chapel; RMC Place; LEE; *244 D-3; mail Blackwater z 24221; ● 30
Osborns Gap; RMC Place; DICKENSON; *244 B-4; elev. 1,842ft./561m.; mail Clintwood z 24228; rural
Osceola; RMC Place; WASHINGTON; *244 D-6; elev. 1,891ft./576m.; mail Abingdon z 24210-11; rural
Osso; RMC Place; KING GEORGE; *245 G-14; mail Fredericksburg z 22405; rural
Othma; RMC Place; GOOCHLAND; *245 I-12; elev. 342ft./104m.; mail Sandy Hook z 23153; rural
Otter Hill; RMC Place; BEDFORD; *244 K-7; mail Bedford z 24523; rural
Otter River; RMC Place; CAMPBELL; *244 K-8; mail Lynch Station z 24571; rural
Otterville; RMC Place; BEDFORD; *244 J-7; elev. 956ft./291m.; mail Bedford z 24523; rural
Ottobine; RMC Place; ROCKINGHAM; *244 F-9; mail Dayton z 22821; rural
Ottoman; RMC Place; LANCASTER; *245 I-17; mail Lancaster z 22503
Overall; RMC Place; WARREN, PAGE; *245 E-11; mail Bentonville z 22610
Overlee Knolls; RMC Place; ARLINGTON; *245 D-15; elev. 220ft./67m.; ★ WASH; mail Arlington z 22205
Owens; RMC Place; KING GEORGE; 245 G-15; mail King George z 22485; ● 60
Owens Brooke; RMC Place; MANASSAS (Independent City); *245 E-14; ★ WASH; mail Manassas z 20110; pop. incl. with Manassas (Independent City)
Owensville; RMC Place; ALBEMARLE; *244 H-10; elev. 639ft./195m.; ★ CHRLTV; mail Charlottesville z 22901; rural
Owenton; RMC Place; KING AND QUEEN; *245 H-15; elev. 171ft./52m.; mail Saint Stephens Church z 23148; rural
Oxford; RMC Place; RICHMOND (Independent City); ★ RICH; mail Richmond z 23235; pop. incl. with Richmond (Independent City)
Oxford Furnace; RMC Place; CAMPBELL; *244 J-9; elev. 535ft./163m.; ★ LYNCH; mail Lynchburg z 24504; rural
Oyster; RMC Place; NORTHAMPTON; *245 K-19; elev. 6ft./2m.; 🅿; z 23419; ● 130
Oyster Point; RMC Place; NEWPORT NEWS (Independent City); *245 K-17; elev. 32ft./10m.; ★ NN-H; mail Newport News z 23606; pop. incl. with Newport News (Independent City)
Ozeana; RMC Place; ESSEX; *245 I-16; mail Dunnsville z 22454; rural

P

Paces; RMC Place; HALIFAX; 244 M-9; elev. 355ft./108m.; mail South Boston z 24592; ● 70
Paeonian Springs; RMC Place; LOUDOUN; *245 C-13; 🅿; ★ WASH; z 20129; ● 600
Page; RMC Place; BUCHANAN; *244 B-6; mail Oakwood z 24631; rural
PAGE; 244 F-10; Ⓟ 21,690; © 23,177; ◆ 24,378
Page Hollow; RMC Place; SMYTH; *244 L-1; mail Saltville z 24370; ● 50
Paige; RMC Place; CAROLINE; *245 H-14; mail Woodford z 22580; rural
Paineville; RMC Place; AMELIA; *245 J-12; elev. 456ft./139m.; mail Jetersville z 23083; ● 50
Paint Bank; RMC Place; CRAIG; 244 J-5; elev. 1,866ft./569m.; 🅿; z 24131; ● 80
Painter; Inc. Place; ACCOMACK; 245 I-19; elev. 37ft./11m.; 🅿; z 23420; Ⓟ 259; © 246
Paint Lick; RMC Place; TAZEWELL; *244 L-1; mail Pounding Mill z 24637; ● 50
Palls; RMC Place; KING WILLIAM; *245 I-15; mail King William z 23086; rural
Palmer; RMC Place; LANCASTER; *245 I-17; mail White Stone z 22578; ● 50
Palmer Crossroads; RMC Place; MECKLENBURG; *245 N-11; elev. 313ft./95m.; mail Norlina z 27563; rural
Palmer Springs; RMC Place; MECKLENBURG; 245 N-11; elev. 384ft./117m.; mail Boydton z 23917; ● 100
Palmyra; RMC Place; ⊡ FLUVANNA; 245 I-11; 🅿; z 22963; ● 400
Palmyra; RMC Place; SUFFOLK (Independent City); ★ NORF-; mail Suffolk z 23434; pop. incl. with Suffolk (Independent City)
Pamlico; RMC Place; NORFOLK (Independent City); *245 L-18; ★ NORF-; mail Norfolk z 23503; pop. incl. with Norfolk (Independent City)
Pamplin (Pamplin City); Inc. Place; APPOMATTOX, PRINCE EDWARD; 244 K-10; 🅿; z 23958; Ⓟ 208; © 199
Pamplin City; APPOMATTOX, PRINCE EDWARD; see Pamplin (Inc. Place)
Pamunkey Reservation; Indian Reservation; KING WILLIAM; State Reservation; © 58
Panoramic Hills; RMC Place; FAIRFAX; mail Annandale z 22003
Pardee; RMC Place; WISE; 244 C-3; mail Appalachia z 24216; ● 150
Paris; RMC Place; FAUQUIER; 245 D-12; 🅿; z 20130; ● 150
Park; RMC Place; WAYNESBORO (Independent City); mail Waynesboro z 22980; pop. incl. with Waynesboro (Independent City)
Parker; RMC Place; SPOTSYLVANIA; *245 G-13; mail Ladysmith z 22501; rural
Parkers Shores; RMC Place; WESTMORELAND; mail Sandy Point z 22577; ● 50
Parkfairfax; RMC Place; ALEXANDRIA (Independent City); *245 E-15; ★ WASH; mail Alexandria z 22302; pop. incl. with Alexandria (Independent City)
Parkglen; RMC Place; ARLINGTON; *245 D-15; ★ WASH; mail Arlington z 22204
Parklawn; RMC Place; FAIRFAX; 249 H-4; ★ WASH; mail Alexandria z 22312; ● 2,400
Park Lee Place; RMC Place; CHESTERFIELD; *245 J-14; ★ RICH; mail Richmond z 23234; ● 800
Park Place; RMC Place; NORFOLK (Independent City); *245 L-18; elev. 10ft./3m.; ★ NORF-; mail Norfolk z 23517; pop. incl. with Norfolk (Independent City)
Parksley; Inc. Place; ACCOMACK; 245 I-19; 🅿; z 23421; Ⓟ 779; © 837
Parkview; RMC Place; NEWPORT NEWS (Independent City); *245 L-17; ★ NN-H; mail Newport News z 23605; pop. incl. with Newport News (Independent City)
Park View; RMC Place; PORTSMOUTH (Independent City); *245 L-17; ★ NORF-; mail Portsmouth z 23707; pop. incl. with Portsmouth (Independent City)
Park View; RMC Place; ROCKINGHAM; *244 F-9; mail Harrisonburg z 22802; pop. incl. with Harrisonburg (Independent City)
Parkview Hills; RMC Place; FAIRFAX; *245 D-14; ★ WASH; mail Mc Lean z 22101
Parkwood; RMC Place; SPOTSYLVANIA; *245 G-14; ★ FRED; mail Fredericksburg z 22401; ● 350
Parnassus; RMC Place; AUGUSTA; *244 G-9; mail Churchville z 24421; ● 80
Parrott; RMC Place; PULASKI; 244 K-4; elev. 1,786ft./544m.; 🅿; z 24132; ● 590
Parsonage; RMC Place; RUSSELL; *244 D-5; mail Castlewood z 24224; rural
Partlow; RMC Place; SPOTSYLVANIA; 245 H-13; elev. 384ft./117m.; 🅿; z 22534; ● 100
Passapatanzy; RMC Place; KING GEORGE; *245 G-14; mail Fredericksburg z 22405; rural
Passing; RMC Place; CAROLINE; *245 H-15; mail Bowling Green z 22427; rural
Pastoria; RMC Place; ACCOMACK; *245 I-19; mail Parksley z 23421; ● 100
Patrician Manor; RMC Place; HAMPTON (Independent City); *245 L-17; ★ NN-H; mail Hampton z 23666; pop. incl. with Hampton (Independent City)
PATRICK; 244 M-4; Ⓟ 17,473; © 19,407; ◆ 18,954
Patrick Henry Heights; RMC Place; HANOVER; *245 I-14; ★ RICH; mail Mechanicsville z 23116; ● 100
Patrick Springs; CDP; PATRICK; 244 M-5; 🅿; z 24133; © 2,068
Patterson; RMC Place; BUCHANAN; 244 B-6; 🅿; z 24631; ● 200
Patterson; RMC Place; WYTHE; *244 L-3; mail Hillsville z 24343; rural
Pattonsville; RMC Place; SCOTT; 244 D-3; elev. 1,326ft./404m.; mail Duffield z 24244; ● 100
Pauls Crossroads; RMC Place; ESSEX; *245 H-15; mail Tappahannock z 22560; ● 30
Paynes Store; RMC Place; SPOTSYLVANIA; *245 G-13; ★ FRED; mail Spotsylvania z 22553; ● 100
Paytes; RMC Place; SPOTSYLVANIA; 245 G-13; mail Spotsylvania z 22553; ● 170
Peach Bottom; RMC Place; GRAYSON; *244 M-2; mail Galax z 24333; rural
Peaks; RMC Place; HANOVER; *245 I-14; elev. 195ft./59m.; ★ RICH; mail Hanover z 23069; rural
Peaksville; RMC Place; BEDFORD; *244 J-7; elev. 1,018ft./310m.; mail Bedford z 24523; rural
Peapatch; RMC Place; BUCHANAN; *244 K-1; mail Jewell Ridge z 24622; ● 30
Pearisburg; GILES; see Bluff City (RMC Place)
Pearisburg; Inc. Place; ⊡ GILES; 244 K-3; elev. 1,804ft./550m.; 🅿 🄷; z 24134; Ⓟ 2,064; © 2,729
Pearly; RMC Place; BUCHANAN; *244 B-5; mail Grundy z 24614; ● 130
Peary; RMC Place; MATHEWS; *245 J-17; elev. 6ft./2m.; 🅿; ★ NN-H; z 23138; ● 30
Pedlar Mills; RMC Place; AMHERST; *244 J-8; elev. 688ft./210m.; mail Monroe z 24574
Pedro; RMC Place; ESSEX; *245 H-15; mail Caret z 22436; ● 30
Pemberton; RMC Place; GOOCHLAND; *245 I-12; mail Goochland z 23063; rural
Pembroke; Inc. Place; GILES; 244 K-4; 🅿; z 24136; Ⓟ 1,064; © 1,134
Pembroke Manor; RMC Place; VIRGINIA BEACH (Independent City); *245 L-18; ★ NORF-; mail Virginia Beach z 23462; pop. incl. with Virginia Beach (Independent City)
Pender; RMC Place; FAIRFAX; 249 G-1; ★ WASH; mail Fairfax z 22033; ● 500
Penderbrook; RMC Place; FAIRFAX; *245 D-14; ★ WASH; mail Fairfax z 22033
Pendleton (Pendletons); RMC Place; LOUISA; 245 H-12; mail Mineral z 23117; ● 60
Pendletons; LOUISA; see Pendleton (RMC Place)
Penhook; CDP; FRANKLIN; 244 L-7; 🅿; z 24137; © 726
Penicks Mill; RMC Place; BEDFORD; *244 J-7; elev. 958ft./292m.; mail Bedford z 24523; rural
Penlan; RMC Place; BUCKINGHAM; *245 I-11; elev. 350ft./107m.; mail New Canton z 23123; rural
Penn Acres; RMC Place; CHESTERFIELD; *245 J-13; elev. 300ft./91m.; ★ RICH; mail Richmond z 23235; ● 750
Penn Daw; RMC Place; FAIRFAX; *245 E-15; ★ WASH; mail Alexandria z 22306; ● 500
Penn Daw Terrace; RMC Place; FAIRFAX; *245 E-15; ★ WASH; mail Alexandria z 22307
Pennington; LEE; see Pennington Gap (Inc. Place)
Pennington Gap (Pennington); Inc. Place; LEE; 244 D-3; 🅿 🄷; z 24277; Ⓟ 1,922; © 1,781
Penn Laird; RMC Place; ROCKINGHAM; 244 F-9; 🅿; z 22846; ● 200
Penn Lee; RMC Place; LEE; *244 D-2; mail Saint Charles z 24282; rural
Penns Store; RMC Place; PATRICK; *244 M-6; mail Spencer z 24165; rural
Pennsytown; RMC Place; NORFOLK (Independent City); *245 L-18; ★ NORF-; mail Norfolk z 23513; pop. incl. with Norfolk (Independent City)
Penola; RMC Place; CAROLINE; *245 H-14; mail Ruther Glen z 22546
Penvir; RMC Place; GILES; *244 K-3; mail Narrows z 24124; rural
Peola Mills; RMC Place; MADISON, RAPPAHANNOCK; mail Sperryville z 22740; rural
Perkin Park; RMC Place; LYNCHBURG (Independent City); ★ LYNCH; mail Lynchburg z 24501; pop. incl. with Lynchburg (Independent City)
Perrin; RMC Place; GLOUCESTER; *245 K-17; ★ NN-H; mail Hayes z 23072; ● 200
Perrowville; RMC Place; BEDFORD; *244 J-8; ★ LYNCH; mail Forest z 24551; rural
Perryville; RMC Place; SMYTH; mail Saltville z 24370; pop. incl. with Saltville (Inc. Place)
Perth; RMC Place; HALIFAX; *244 L-9; mail Nathalie z 24577; rural
Petersburg; Independent City; 245 K-14; 🅿 🄷 🄲 5,140 ■; ★ RICH; z 23801, z 23803-06; Ⓟ 38,386; © 33,740; ◆ 33,332
Peterson Chapel; RMC Place; SCOTT; *244 D-3; mail Duffield z 24244; pop. incl. with Duffield (Inc. Place)
Petunia; RMC Place; WYTHE; *244 L-2; elev. 2,336ft./712m.; mail Wytheville z 24382; pop. incl. with Wytheville (Inc. Place)
Peytonsburg; RMC Place; PITTSYLVANIA; *244 M-8; mail Java z 24565; rural
Phenix; Inc. Place; CHARLOTTE; 244 L-10; 🅿; z 23959; Ⓟ 260; © 200
Philadelphia; RMC Place; SUFFOLK (Independent City); ★ NORF-; mail Suffolk z 23434; pop. incl. with Suffolk (Independent City)
Philbeck Crossroads; RMC Place; MECKLENBURG; *244 M-10; elev. 495ft./151m.; mail Skipwith z 23968; rural
Phillip; RMC Place; WASHINGTON; *244 D-5; mail Bristol z 24202; rural
Phillis; RMC Place; MECKLENBURG; *245 M-11; elev. 328ft./100m.; mail Boydton z 23917
Philomont; RMC Place; LOUDOUN; 245 D-13; 🅿; z 20131; ● 270
Philpott; RMC Place; HENRY; *244 M-6; ★ MRTNV; mail Bassett z 24055; ● 60
Phoebus; RMC Place; HAMPTON (Independent City); *245 L-17; ★ NN-H; mail Hampton z 23663; pop. incl. with Hampton (Independent City)
Piankatank Shores; RMC Place; MIDDLESEX; *245 J-17; mail Hartfield z 23071; ● 300
Pickaway; RMC Place; PITTSYLVANIA; *244 M-8; mail Vernon Hill z 24597; rural
Pico; RMC Place; BOTETOURT; *244 J-7; elev. 1,048ft./319m.; ★ ROAN; mail Buchanan z 24066; ● 120
Piedmont; RMC Place; AUGUSTA; *244 G-9; mail Grottoes z 24441; rural
Pierces Corner; RMC Place; LANCASTER; *245 I-17; mail Lancaster z 22503; rural
Pierces Shop; RMC Place; ORANGE; *245 G-12; elev. 490ft./149m.; mail Orange z 22960; ● 30
Pigeon Hill; RMC Place; CLARKE; *245 C-12; mail Berryville z 22611; ● 80
Pilgrams Knob; BUCHANAN; see Pilgrims Knob (RMC Place)
Pilgrims Knob (Pilgrams Knob); RMC Place; BUCHANAN; *244 B-6; 🅿; z 24634; ● 200
Pilot; RMC Place; MONTGOMERY; 244 L-5; elev. 2,268ft./691m.; 🅿; z 24138; ● 120
Pimmit; RMC Place; FAIRFAX; *245 D-14; 🅿; ★ WASH; z 22043
Pimmit Hills; CDP; FAIRFAX; 249 F-3; ★ WASH; mail Falls Church z 22043; Ⓟ 6,019; © 6,152
Pine; RMC Place; PULASKI; *244 L-3; mail Draper z 24324; rural
Pineaire; RMC Place; SUFFOLK (Independent City); ★ NORF-; mail Suffolk z 23434; pop. incl. with Suffolk (Independent City)
Pine Chapel Village; RMC Place; HAMPTON (Independent City); *245 L-17; ★ NN-H; mail Hampton z 23666; pop. incl. with Hampton (Independent City)
Pinecrest; RMC Place; FAIRFAX; *245 D-14; ★ WASH; mail Alexandria z 22312; ● 810
Pinecrest Heights; RMC Place; FAIRFAX; mail Annandale z 22003
Pinedale; RMC Place; HENRICO; *245 I-13; elev. 228ft./69m.; ★ RICH; mail Henrico z 23229; ● 600
Pine Grove; RMC Place; CLARKE; *245 C-12; mail Bluemont z 20135; ● 120
Pine Grove; RMC Place; PAGE; *244 F-10; mail Stanley z 22851; ● 220
Pine Grove; RMC Place; WASHINGTON; *244 D-5; mail Mendota z 24270; rural
Pine Grove Court; RMC Place; HAMPTON (Independent City); *245 L-17; ★ NN-H; mail Hampton z 23669; pop. incl. with Hampton (Independent City)
Pine Grove Terrace; RMC Place; HAMPTON (Independent City); *245 L-17; ★ NN-H; mail Hampton z 23669; pop. incl. with Hampton (Independent City)
Pine Hill; RMC Place; HANOVER; *245 I-14; ★ RICH; mail Mechanicsville z 23116; ● 40
Pinehurst; RMC Place; PORTSMOUTH (Independent City); *245 L-17; elev. 14ft./4m.; ★ NORF-; mail Portsmouth z 23703; pop. incl. with Portsmouth (Independent City)
Pine Ridge; RMC Place; FAIRFAX; *245 D-14; ★ WASH; mail Fairfax z 22031; ● 550
Pinero; RMC Place; GLOUCESTER; *245 J-17; elev. 109ft./33m.; 🅿; z 23061; rural
Pine Springs; RMC Place; FAIRFAX; *245 D-14; ★ WASH; mail Falls Church z 22042; ● 1,700
Pine Tree; RMC Place; POWHATAN; *245 I-12; elev. 344ft./105m.; mail Cartersville z 23027; rural
Pinetta; RMC Place; CHESAPEAKE (Independent City); *245 I-18; mail Chesapeake z 23325; pop. incl. with Chesapeake (Independent City)
Pinetta; RMC Place; GLOUCESTER; *245 J-16; elev. 70ft./21m.; mail Gloucester z 23061; rural
Pineville; RMC Place; ROCKINGHAM; *244 G-10; mail Mc Gaheysville z 22840; ● 70
Pinewood Lake; RMC Place; FAIRFAX; *245 E-15; ★ WASH; mail Alexandria z 22309
Pinewood Lawns; RMC Place; FAIRFAX; *245 E-15; ★ WASH; mail Alexandria z 22309
Pinewood Park; RMC Place; MANASSAS PARK (Independent City); ★ WASH; mail Manassas z 20111; pop. incl. with Manassas Park (Independent City)
Pinewood South; RMC Place; FAIRFAX; *245 E-15; ★ WASH; mail Alexandria z 22309
Piney Grove; RMC Place; HALIFAX; *244 M-9; elev. 543ft./166m.; mail Scottsburg z 24589; rural
Piney River; RMC Place; NELSON; 244 I-9; 🅿; z 22964; ● 250
Pinners Point; RMC Place; PORTSMOUTH (Independent City); ★ NORF-; pop. incl. with Portsmouth (Independent City)
Pipers Gap; RMC Place; CARROLL; *244 M-3; elev. 2,760ft./841m.; mail Galax z 24333
Pisgah; RMC Place; TAZEWELL; *244 K-1; mail Tazewell z 24651; ● 30
Pitmans Corner; RMC Place; LANCASTER; *245 I-17; elev. 38ft./12m.; mail Weems z 22576; rural
Pittmantown; RMC Place; SUFFOLK (Independent City); ★ NORF-; mail Suffolk z 23438; pop. incl. with Suffolk (Independent City)
Pittsville; RMC Place; PITTSYLVANIA; 244 L-7; 🅿; z 24139; ● 100
PITTSYLVANIA; 244 L-8; Ⓟ 55,655; © 61,745; ◆ 61,122
Pizarro; RMC Place; FLOYD; *244 L-5; mail Floyd z 24091
Plain View; RMC Place; KING AND QUEEN; *245 J-16; elev. 100ft./30m.; 🅿; z 23156; ● 50
Plantersville; RMC Place; LUNENBURG; *245 L-11; elev. 563ft./172m.; mail Drakes Branch z 23937; rural
Plasterco; RMC Place; WASHINGTON; 244 D-6; mail Saltville z 24370; ● 300
Pleasant Gap; RMC Place; PITTSYLVANIA; *244 M-7; ★ DANV; mail Dry Fork z 24549
Pleasant Grove; RMC Place; HENRY; *244 M-6; elev. 1,066ft./325m.; ★ MRTNV; mail Martinsville z 24112; ● 140
Pleasant Grove; RMC Place; LUNENBURG; *245 L-11; elev. 492ft./150m.; mail Keysville z 23947; ● 30
Pleasant Grove; RMC Place; MECKLENBURG; *245 M-12; mail South Hill z 23970; rural
Pleasant Grove Estates; RMC Place; BRUNSWICK; *245 M-12; elev. 300ft./91m.; mail Brodnax z 23920; ● 80
Pleasant Heights; RMC Place; SMYTH; *244 L-1; mail Saltville z 24370; ● 250
Pleasant Hill; RMC Place; HARRISONBURG (Independent City); *244 F-9; mail Harrisonburg z 22801; pop. incl. with Harrisonburg (Independent City)
Pleasant Hill; RMC Place; SUFFOLK (Independent City); ★ NORF-; mail Suffolk z 23434; pop. incl. with Suffolk (Independent City)
Pleasant Ridge; RMC Place; FAIRFAX; *245 E-14; ★ WASH; mail Annandale z 22003
Pleasant Ridge; RMC Place; VIRGINIA BEACH (Independent City); *245 M-18; ★ NORF-; mail Virginia Beach z 23451; pop. incl. with Virginia Beach (Independent City)
Pleasant Shade; RMC Place; GREENSVILLE; *245 M-13; elev. 280ft./85m.; mail Emporia z 23847; rural
Pleasant Valley; RMC Place; BUCKINGHAM; *245 J-11; elev. 550ft./168m.; mail Dillwyn z 23936; rural
Pleasant Valley; RMC Place; FAIRFAX; *245 D-14; ★ WASH; mail Chantilly z 20151; ● 2,000
Pleasant Valley; RMC Place; ROCKINGHAM; *244 F-9; 🅿; z 22848; ● 80
Pleasantview; RMC Place; AMHERST; *244 J-8; mail Monroe z 24574; ● 60
Plum Creek; RMC Place; WASHINGTON; *244 M-1; mail Glade Spring z 24340; rural
Plum Point; RMC Place; NEW KENT; 245 J-16; elev. 10ft./3m.; mail West Point z 23181; ● 150
Plum Tree; RMC Place; LOUISA; *245 H-13; elev. 317ft./97m.; mail Bumpass z 23024; rural
Plymouth; RMC Place; LUNENBURG; *245 L-12; elev. 478ft./146m.; mail Kenbridge z 23944, Victoria z 23974; ● 80
Plymouth Park; RMC Place; CHESAPEAKE (Independent City); *245 L-18; ★ NORF-; mail Chesapeake z 23325; pop. incl. with Chesapeake (Independent City)
Poages Mill; RMC Place; ROANOKE; *244 K-6; ★ ROAN; mail Roanoke z 24018; ● 200
Pocahontas; RMC Place; PETERSBURG (Independent City); *245 K-14; ★ RICH; mail Petersburg z 23803; pop. incl. with Petersburg (Independent City)
Pocahontas; Inc. Place; TAZEWELL; 244 K-2; 🅿; z 24635; Ⓟ 513; © 441
Pocket (Pockett); RMC Place; LEE; *244 D-2; mail Keokee z 24265, Saint Charles z 24282; ● 30
Pockett; LEE; see Pocket (RMC Place)
Poetown; RMC Place; BUCHANAN; *244 B-5; mail Grundy z 24614; pop. incl. with Grundy (Inc. Place)
Poff; RMC Place; FLOYD; *244 L-5; elev. 2,474ft./754m.; mail Floyd z 24091; rural
Pohick Estates; RMC Place; FAIRFAX; *245 E-14; ★ WASH; mail Lorton z 22079
Point Breeze; RMC Place; ESSEX; mail Dunnsville z 22454; ● 30
Point Eastern; RMC Place; CAROLINE; *245 H-14; elev. 194ft./59m.; mail Ruther Glen z 22546
Point Pleasant; RMC Place; BLAND; *244 K-3; elev. 2,259ft./689m.; mail Bland z 24315; rural
Pons; RMC Place; ISLE OF WIGHT; *245 L-16; elev. 89ft./27m.; mail Ivor z 23866; rural
Pooch Store; RMC Place; BRUNSWICK; *245 L-13; elev. 311ft./95m.; mail Lawrenceville z 23868; rural
Poole Siding; RMC Place; DINWIDDIE; *245 K-13; mail Church Road z 23833; ● 40
Pope; RMC Place; SOUTHAMPTON; *245 M-15; elev. 68ft./21m.; mail Capron z 23829
Poplar Camp; RMC Place; WYTHE; 244 L-3; mail Max Meadows z 24360; ● 100
Poplar Cove; RMC Place; ACCOMACK; *245 I-19; mail Onancock z 23417; ● 30
Poplar Forest; RMC Place; BEDFORD; *244 K-8; elev. 800ft./244m.; ★ LYNCH; mail Forest z 24551; ● 200
Poplar Heights; RMC Place; FAIRFAX; *245 D-14; ★ WASH; mail Falls Church z 22046; ● 2,650
Poplar Hill; RMC Place; FAIRFAX; ★ WASH; mail Annandale z 22003
Poplar Hill; RMC Place; GILES; *244 K-3; elev. 1,808ft./551m.; mail Pearisburg z 24134; rural
Poplar Inn; RMC Place; CAROLINE; mail Ruther Glen z 22546; rural
Poplar Springs; RMC Place; HENRICO; *245 J-14; elev. 120ft./37m.; ★ RICH; mail Henrico z 23075; rural
Poquoson; Independent City; 245 K-17; 🅿; ★ NN-H; z 23662; Ⓟ 11,005; © 11,566; ◆ 11,958
Porter; RMC Place; ALBEMARLE; *244 I-10; mail Esmont z 22937; ● 50
Porters Cross Roads; RMC Place; WYTHE; *244 L-3; elev. 2,061ft./628m.; mail Wytheville z 24382; ● 30
Port Haywood; RMC Place; MATHEWS; *245 J-17; elev. 10ft./3m.; 🅿; ★ NN-H; z 23138; ● 300
Portlock; RMC Place; CHESAPEAKE (Independent City); *245 M-18; ★ NORF-; pop. incl. with Chesapeake (Independent City)
Port Norfolk; RMC Place; PORTSMOUTH (Independent City); *245 L-17; elev. 10ft./3m.; ★ NORF-; mail Portsmouth z 23707; pop. incl. with Portsmouth (Independent City)
Port-O-Dumfries; RMC Place; PRINCE WILLIAM; ★ WASH; mail Triangle z 22172; pop. incl. with Dumfries (Inc. Place)
Port Republic; RMC Place; ROCKINGHAM; 244 G-9; 🅿; z 24471; ● 250
Port Royal; Inc. Place; CAROLINE; 245 G-15; 🅿; z 22535; Ⓟ 204; © 170
Portside; RMC Place; PORTSMOUTH (Independent City); *245 L-17; ★ NORF-; mail Portsmouth z 23705; pop. incl. with Portsmouth (Independent City)
Portsmouth; Independent City; 245 L-17; 🅿 🄷 ■; ★ NORF-; z 23701-05, z 23707-09; Ⓟ 103,907; © 100,565; ◆ 103,198
Portsmouth Heights; RMC Place; PORTSMOUTH (Independent City); *245 L-17; ★ NORF-; mail Portsmouth z 23707; pop. incl. with Portsmouth (Independent City)
Post Oak; RMC Place; SPOTSYLVANIA; *245 G-13; elev. 336ft./102m.; mail Spotsylvania z 22553
Potato Creek; RMC Place; GRAYSON; mail Mouth of Wilson z 24363; rural
Potomac; RMC Place; ALEXANDRIA (Independent City); 🅿; z 22301 & mail Alexandria z 22305; pop. incl. with Alexandria (Independent City)
Potomac Beach; RMC Place; WESTMORELAND; *245 G-15; mail Colonial Beach z 22443; pop. incl. with Colonial Beach (Inc. Place)
Potomac Farms; RMC Place; LOUDOUN; *245 D-14; elev. 250ft./76m.; ★ WASH; mail Ashburn z 20147; ● 150
Potomac Hills; RMC Place; FAIRFAX; *245 D-15; ★ WASH; mail Mc Lean z 22101
Potomac Mills; RMC Place; WESTMORELAND; *245 G-15; mail Montross z 22520; rural
Potomac Yard; RMC Place; ALEXANDRIA (Independent City); pop. incl. with Alexandria (Independent City)
Pound; Inc. Place; WISE; 244 C-4; 🅿; z 24279; Ⓟ 995; © 1,089
Pounding Mill; RMC Place; TAZEWELL; *244 L-1; 🅿; z 24637; ● 200
Powcan; RMC Place; KING AND QUEEN; *245 I-15; mail Bruington z 23023; rural
Powell Corner (Powells Store); RMC Place; ALBEMARLE; *244 H-10; mail Esmont z 22937; rural
Powells Store; ALBEMARLE; see Powell Corner (RMC Place)
Powells Store; RMC Place; BEDFORD; *244 J-8; mail Big Island z 24526; rural
Powhatan; RMC Place; ⊡ POWHATAN; 245 J-12; 🅿; z 23139; ● 700
POWHATAN; 245 J-12; Ⓟ 15,328; © 22,377; ◆ 28,423
Prater; RMC Place; BUCHANAN; 244 B-5; mail Vansant z 24656; ● 100
Pratts (O'Neal); RMC Place; MADISON; 245 G-11; 🅿; z 22731; ● 120
Premier; RMC Place; TAZEWELL; *244 C-6; mail Red Ash z 24640; rural
Prentiss Place; RMC Place; PORTSMOUTH (Independent City); *245 L-17; ★ NORF-; mail Portsmouth z 23707; pop. incl. with Portsmouth (Independent City)
Preston; RMC Place; HENRY; *244 M-6; ★ MRTNV; mail Martinsville z 24112
Preston Hills; RMC Place; WASHINGTON; *244 D-5; ★ JNSC-; mail Bristol z 24202; ● 250
Preston King; RMC Place; ARLINGTON; *245 D-15; ★ WASH; mail Arlington z 22205
Prices Fork; RMC Place; MONTGOMERY; 244 K-4; mail Blacksburg z 24060, Christiansburg z 24073; ● 280
Prices Store; RMC Place; AMHERST; *244 J-9; ★ LYNCH; mail Madison Heights z 24572; rural
Prilliman; RMC Place; FRANKLIN; *244 L-6; mail Ferrum z 24088; rural
PRINCE EDWARD; 244 K-10; Ⓟ 17,320; © 19,720; ◆ 22,957
Prince George; RMC Place; ⊡ PRINCE GEORGE; 245 K-14; 🅿; ★ RICH; z 23875; ● 200
PRINCE GEORGE; 245 K-15; Ⓟ 27,394; © 33,047; ® 33,124; ◆ 36,416
Prince George Woods Estates; RMC Place; PRINCE GEORGE; *245 K-14; elev. 150ft./46m.; ★ RICH; mail Prince George z 23875; ● 200
Princess Anne; RMC Place; VIRGINIA BEACH (Independent City); *245 M-18; ★ NORF-; mail Virginia Beach z 23456; pop. incl. with Virginia Beach (Independent City)
PRINCE WILLIAM; 245 E-14; 🅿; z 22192; Ⓟ 215,686; © 280,813; ◆ 365,501
Proffit; RMC Place; ALBEMARLE; *245 H-11; ★ CHRLTV; mail Charlottesville z 22911; ● 220
Prospect; RMC Place; PRINCE EDWARD; 244 K-10; 🅿; z 23960; ● 400
Prospectdale; RMC Place; GILES; *244 K-3; mail Pearisburg z 24134
Providence; RMC Place; CHESAPEAKE (Independent City); ★ NORF-; pop. incl. with Chesapeake (Independent City)
Providence; RMC Place; GRAYSON; *244 M-2; elev. 2,382ft./726m.; mail Fries z 24330; ● 50
Providence; RMC Place; HALIFAX; *244 L-9; elev. 490ft./149m.; mail Nathalie z 24577
Providence Church; RMC Place; SUFFOLK (Independent City); ★ NORF-; mail Suffolk z 23434; pop. incl. with Suffolk (Independent City)
Providence Forge; RMC Place; NEW KENT; 245 J-15; 🅿; z 23140; ● 450
Providence Park; RMC Place; HENRICO; *245 J-14; ★ RICH; mail Richmond z 23222; ● 700
Provost (Mohemenco); RMC Place; POWHATAN; *245 I-12; elev. 280ft./85m.; mail Powhatan z 23139; rural
Public Fork; RMC Place; CHARLOTTE; *244 M-10; elev. 478ft./146m.; mail Saxe z 23967; rural
Pughsville; RMC Place; SUFFOLK (Independent City); ★ NORF-; mail Suffolk z 23435; pop. incl. with Suffolk (Independent City)
Pulaski; Inc. Place; ⊡ PULASKI; 244 L-3; 🅿 🄷; z 24301; Ⓟ 9,985; © 9,473
PULASKI; 244 L-3; Ⓟ 34,496; © 35,127; ◆ 35,469
Pumpkin Center; RMC Place; BLAND; *244 K-3; elev. 2,273ft./693m.; mail Bland z 24315; rural
Pungo; RMC Place; VIRGINIA BEACH (Independent City); *245 M-18; ★ NORF-; mail Virginia Beach z 23456; pop. incl. with Virginia Beach (Independent City)
Pungoteague; RMC Place; ACCOMACK; 245 I-19; elev. 30ft./9m.; 🅿; z 23422; ● 200
Purcell; RMC Place; RUSSELL; *244 C-5; mail Cleveland z 24225; rural
Purcellville; Inc. Place; LOUDOUN; 245 C-13; elev. 576ft./176m.; 🅿 🄲 325; ★ WASH; z 20132, z 20134, z 20160; Ⓟ 1,744; © 3,584
Purchase; RMC Place; SCOTT; *244 D-3; mail Duffield z 24244; rural
Purdy; RMC Place; GREENSVILLE; 245 M-13; elev. 233ft./71m.; mail Emporia z 23847; ● 50
Purvis (Buckhorn); RMC Place; SUFFOLK (Independent City); *245 M-16; ★ NORF-; mail Suffolk z 23437; pop. incl. with Suffolk (Independent City)
Puryear Corner; RMC Place; MECKLENBURG; *244 M-10; elev. 424ft./129m.; mail Clarksville z 23927; rural
Putnam; RMC Place; RUSSELL; *244 C-6; elev. 1,876ft./572m.; mail Honaker z 24260; ● 50

Q

Quail Oaks; RMC Place; CHESTERFIELD; *245 J-14; ★ RICH; mail Richmond z 23234; ● 1,400
Quantico; Inc. Place; PRINCE WILLIAM; 245 F-14; 🅿 🄲 470; ★ WASH; z 22134-35; Ⓟ 670; © 561
Quantico Station; CDP-Census Area Only; PRINCE WILLIAM, STAFFORD; *245 F-14; ★ WASH; mail Quantico z 22134; Ⓟ 7,425; © 6,571
Quarry; RMC Place; SMYTH; 244 L-1; mail Saltville z 24370; pop. incl. with Saltville (Inc. Place)
Queens Lake; RMC Place; YORK; 243 E-3; elev. 75ft./23m.; ★ NN-H; mail Williamsburg z 23185; ● 1,400
Quicksburg; RMC Place; SHENANDOAH; 244 E-10; 🅿; z 22847; ● 200
Quicks Mill; RMC Place; AUGUSTA; *244 G-9; mail Staunton z 24401; rural
Quinby; RMC Place; ACCOMACK; 245 I-19; 🅿; z 23423; ● 350
Quinque; RMC Place; GREENE; 245 G-11; 🅿; ★ CHRLTV; z 22965; ● 60
Quinton; RMC Place; NEW KENT; *245 J-15; elev. 151ft./46m.; 🅿; z 23141; ● 300

R

Rabat; RMC Place; HALIFAX; *244 L-9; elev. 610ft./186m.; mail Nathalie z 24577; rural
Raccoon Ford; RMC Place; CULPEPER; *245 F-12; 🅿; z 22701; ● 30
Racefield; RMC Place; JAMES CITY; *245 J-16; elev. 129ft./39m.; ★ NN-H; mail Toano z 23168; ● 100
Racume; RMC Place; BRUNSWICK; *245 M-13; elev. 255ft./78m.; mail Freeman z 23856; rural
Radcliffe; MECKLENBURG; see Smiths Cross Roads (RMC Place)
Radford; Independent City; 244 K-4; 🅿 🄷 🄲 9,220; z 24141-43; Ⓟ 15,940; © 15,859; ◆ 16,727
Radford University; RMC Place; RADFORD (Independent City); mail Radford z 24142; pop. incl. with Radford (Independent City)
Radiant; RMC Place; MADISON; 245 G-11; 🅿; z 22732; ● 100
Radnor Heights; RMC Place; ARLINGTON; *245 D-15; ★ WASH; mail Arlington z 22209
Ragged Point Beach; RMC Place; WESTMORELAND; *245 G-16; mail Coles Point z 22442
Raines Tavern; RMC Place; CUMBERLAND; *245 J-11; elev. 500ft./152m.; mail Farmville z 23901; ● 50
Rainswood; RMC Place; NORTHUMBERLAND; *245 H-17; elev. 148ft./45m.; mail Heathsville z 22473; rural
Raketown; RMC Place; CARROLL; *244 M-3; elev. 2,115ft./645m.; mail Ivanhoe z 24350; ● 150
Raleigh Place; RMC Place; CHESAPEAKE (Independent City); *245 L-17; elev. 15ft./5m.; ★ NORF-; mail Chesapeake z 23321; pop. incl. with Chesapeake (Independent City)
Raleigh Terrace; RMC Place; HAMPTON (Independent City); *245 L-17; ★ NN-H; mail Hampton z 23661; pop. incl. with Hampton (Independent City)
Ramoth (Mountain View); RMC Place; STAFFORD; *245 F-14; ★ WASH; mail Stafford z 22554; rural
Ramsey; RMC Place; NORTON (Independent City); mail Norton z 24273; pop. incl. with Norton (Independent City)
Ranch Acres; RMC Place; CHESTERFIELD; ★ RICH; mail Richmond z 23237
Randolph; RMC Place; CHARLOTTE; 244 L-10; elev. 335ft./102m.; 🅿; z 23962; ● 60
Random Hills; RMC Place; FAIRFAX; *245 D-14; ★ WASH; mail Fairfax z 22030; ● 160
Rangeley; RMC Place; HENRY; *244 M-6; ★ MRTNV; mail Fieldale z 24089; ● 50
Ransons; RMC Place; BUCKINGHAM; *244 I-10; elev. 482ft./147m.; mail Dillwyn z 23936; rural
Raphine; RMC Place; ROCKBRIDGE; 244 H-8; elev. 1,855ft./565m.; 🅿; z 24472; ● 250
Rapidan; RMC Place; CULPEPER; 245 G-12; 🅿; z 22733; ● 140
RAPPAHANNOCK; 245 E-11; Ⓟ 6,622; © 6,983; ◆ 7,225
Rappahannock Academy; RMC Place; CAROLINE; *245 G-14; 🅿; z 22538; rural
Rappahannock Estates; RMC Place; ESSEX; mail Dunnsville z 22454; ● 100
Rappahannock Shores; RMC Place; ESSEX; mail Dunnsville z 22454; ● 80
Rapps Mill; RMC Place; ROCKBRIDGE; *244 I-7; mail Lexington z 24450; rural
Raven; CDP; TAZEWELL, RUSSELL; 244 C-6; elev. 1,913ft./583m.; 🅿; z 24639; Ⓟ 2,640; © 2,593
Ravensworth; RMC Place; FAIRFAX; 249 H-3; ★ WASH; mail Springfield z 22151; ● 3,000
Ravensworth Grove; RMC Place; FAIRFAX; *245 E-14; ★ WASH; mail Annandale z 22003

Entries in **UPPERCASE** are counties.
Entries in **bold** have populations of 2,500 or more.
Names in parentheses are alternate names.

Inc. Place	Incorporated Place
RMC Place	Rand McNally Designated Place
CDP	Census Designated Place
MCD	Minor Civil Division
⊡	County Seat
▲	Minor Civil Division
elev.	Elevation
🅿	Post Office
🄷	Hospital
🄲	College
■	Principal Business Center
★	Ranally Metro Area (RMA) Abbreviation
z	Zip Code(s)
Ⓟ	Previous Census Population
®	Revised Census Population
Ⓐ	Annexation Population
●	Rand McNally Population Estimate
©	Final Census Population
Ⓢ	Special Census Population
◆	Estimated Population

For additional definitions see Glossary, Volume 1, and Introduction, Volume 2.

Ravensworth Park; RMC Place; FAIRFAX; ***245** E-14; ★ **WASH**; mail Annandale z 22003
Ravenwood; RMC Place; FAIRFAX; **249** G-4; ★ **WASH**; mail Falls Church z 22044; ● 2,550
Ravenwood; RMC Place; PRINCE WILLIAM; ***245** E-14; elev. 180ft./55m.; ★ **WASH**; mail Manassas z 20111; rural
Ravenwood Park; RMC Place; FAIRFAX; ***245** D-15; ★ **WASH**; mail Falls Church z 22044
Rawhide; RMC Place; LEE; ***244** D-3; mail Keokee z 24265; ● 150
Rawley Springs; RMC Place; ROCKINGHAM; **244** F-9; mail Hinton z 22831; ● 150
Rawlings; RMC Place; BRUNSWICK; ***245** L-13; elev. 299ft./91m.; 🅿; z 23876; ● 50
Raymondale; RMC Place; FAIRFAX; ***245** D-14; ★ **WASH**; mail Falls Church z 22042; ● 1,020
Raynor; RMC Place; ISLE OF WIGHT; ***245** L-16; elev. 62ft./19m.; mail Ivor z 23866; rural
Rayon Park; RMC Place; CHESTERFIELD; ★ **RICH**
Rayon Terrace; RMC Place; COVINGTON (Independent City); ***244** I-6; mail Covington z 24426; pop. incl. with Covington (Independent City)
Readus; RMC Place; SHENANDOAH; ***244** E-10; mail Edinburg z 22824; rural
Reams; RMC Place; DINWIDDIE; ***245** K-14; mail Petersburg z 23803
Reba; RMC Place; BEDFORD; ***244** J-7; elev. 1,113ft./339m.; mail Bedford z 24523; rural
Rectortown; RMC Place; FAUQUIER; **245** D-12; 🅿; z 20140; ● 300
Red Apple Orchard; RMC Place; NELSON; ***244** I-10; mail Shipman z 22971; rural
Redart; RMC Place; MATHEWS; ***245** J-17; 🅿; ★ **NN-H**; z 23076; ● 110
Red Ash; RMC Place; TAZEWELL; **244** C-6; 🅿; z 24640 & mail Shortt Gap z 24647; ● 250
Red Bank; RMC Place; HALIFAX; ***244** N-10; elev. 530ft./162m.; mail Virgilina z 24598; ● 50
Red Bank; RMC Place; NORTHAMPTON; ***245** J-19; elev. 5ft./2m.; mail Marionville z 23408; rural
Redd Shop; RMC Place; PRINCE EDWARD; ***245** K-11; elev. 513ft./156m.; mail Farmville z 23901; rural
Red Eye; RMC Place; PITTSYLVANIA; ***244** L-7; elev. 910ft./277m.; mail Chatham z 24531; rural
Red Fox Forest; RMC Place; FAIRFAX; ***245** E-14; ★ **WASH**; mail Annandale z 22003; ● 2,000
Red Hill; RMC Place; ALBEMARLE; ***244** H-10; ★ **CHRLTV**; mail North Garden z 22959; rural
Red Hill; RMC Place; CHARLOTTE; ***244** L-9; elev. 530ft./162m.; mail Brookneal z 24528; rural
Red House; RMC Place; CHARLOTTE; **244** K-9; 🅿; z 23963; ● 80
Red Lane; RMC Place; POWHATAN; ***245** J-13; mail Powhatan z 23139; ● 900
Redlawn; RMC Place; MECKLENBURG; ***245** M-11; mail Bracey z 23919
Red Mills; RMC Place; AUGUSTA; ***244** G-9; mail Crimora z 24431; rural
Red Oak; RMC Place; CHARLOTTE; **244** M-10; elev. 452ft./138m.; 🅿; z 23964; ● 50
Red Top; RMC Place; SUFFOLK (Independent City); ***245** M-17; elev. 55ft./17m.; ★ **NORF-**; mail Suffolk z 23434; pop. incl. with Suffolk (Independent City)
Red Valley; RMC Place; FRANKLIN; ***244** K-6; elev. 1,211ft./369m.; mail Boones Mill z 24065; rural
Redwood; RMC Place; FRANKLIN; **244** L-6; elev. 1,163ft./354m.; 🅿; z 24146; ● 220
Reedville; RMC Place; NORTHUMBERLAND; **245** H-17; 🅿; z 22539; ● 400
Reesedale; RMC Place; MONTGOMERY; ***244** K-5; ★ **ROAN**; mail Elliston z 24087; rural
Reese Shop; RMC Place; CHARLOTTE; ***244** L-10; elev. 564ft./172m.; mail Saxe z 23967; rural
Regina; RMC Place; LANCASTER, NORTHUMBERLAND; ***245** I-17; elev. 96ft./29m.; 🅿; z 22503; ● 30
Rehoboth; RMC Place; LUNENBURG; **245** L-11; elev. 1,507ft./459m.; mail Keysville z 23947, Victoria z 23974; ● 60
Rehoboth Church; RMC Place; LANCASTER, NORTHUMBERLAND; ***245** I-17; elev. 87ft./27m.; mail Kilmarnock z 22482; rural
Reids Ferry; RMC Place; SUFFOLK (Independent City); ***245** M-17; ★ **NORF-**; mail Suffolk z 23434; pop. incl. with Suffolk (Independent City)
Reids Grove; RMC Place; FAIRFAX; ***245** D-14; ★ **WASH**; mail Mc Lean z 22101
Relee; RMC Place; ARLINGTON
Reliance; RMC Place; WARREN; ***245** D-11; 🅿; z 22649; ● 60
Remington; Inc. Place; FAUQUIER; **245** F-13; 🅿; z 22734; Ⓟ 460; Ⓒ 624
Remlik; RMC Place; MIDDLESEX; ***245** I-16; elev. 66ft./20m.; mail Urbanna z 23175; ● 120
Remo; RMC Place; NORTHUMBERLAND; ***245** I-17; elev. 90ft./27m.; mail Wicomico Church z 22579; ● 100
Renan; RMC Place; PITTSYLVANIA; ***244** L-8; mail Gretna z 24557; ● 50
Republican Grove; RMC Place; HALIFAX; ***244** L-9; elev. 646ft./197m.; 🅿; z 24577; ● 100
Rescue; RMC Place; ISLE OF WIGHT; **245** L-17; 🅿; ★ **NN-H**; z 23424; ● 400
Reservoir Hill; RMC Place; COVINGTON (Independent City); mail Covington z 24426; pop. incl. with Covington (Independent City)
Rest; RMC Place; FREDERICK; ***245** C-12; mail Clear Brook z 22624
Reston; CDP; FAIRFAX; **245** D-14; 🅿 🅷; ★ **WASH**; z 20190-92, z 20194-96, z 20598, z 22095-96; Ⓟ 48,556; Ⓒ 56,407; ◆ 58,615
Retreat; RMC Place; FRANKLIN; ***244** L-6; elev. 1,404ft./428m.; mail Rocky Mount z 24151; rural
Reusens; RMC Place; LYNCHBURG (Independent City); ***244** J-8; ★ **LYNCH**; pop. incl. with Lynchburg (Independent City)
Reva; RMC Place; CULPEPER; ***245** F-12; 🅿; z 22735 & mail Culpeper z 22701; ● 60
Revis; RMC Place; MIDDLESEX; ***245** I-16; elev. 95ft./29m.; mail Urbanna z 23175; rural
Rexburg; RMC Place; ESSEX; ***245** H-15; elev. 168ft./51m.; mail Tappahannock z 22560; rural
Reynolds Store; RMC Place; FREDERICK; ***245** B-11; elev. 1,114ft./340m.; mail Cross Junction z 22625; rural
Rhoadesville; RMC Place; ORANGE; ***245** G-12; 🅿; z 22542; ● 160
Rice; RMC Place; PRINCE EDWARD; **245** K-11; elev. 439ft./134m.; 🅿; z 23966; ● 230
Riceville; RMC Place; PITTSYLVANIA; ***244** L-8; elev. 644ft./196m.; mail Java z 24565; ● 30
Richardson; RMC Place; CARROLL; ***244** M-3; mail Hillsville z 24343; rural
Richardsville; RMC Place; CULPEPER; **245** F-13; 🅿; z 22736; ● 120
Rich Creek; Inc. Place; GILES; **244** J-3; 🅿; z 24147; Ⓟ 670; Ⓒ 665
Richlands; Inc. Place; TAZEWELL; **244** C-6; elev. 1,967ft./600m.; 🅿 🅷; z 24641; Ⓟ 4,456; Ⓒ 4,144
Richmond; Independent City; **STATE CAPITAL** serves as county seat of Henrico; **245** J-14; 🅿 🅷 🅲 37,589 ■; ★ **RICH**; z 23173, z 23218-38, z 23240-42, z 23249-50, z 23255, z 23260-61, z 23269, z 23273-74, z 23276, z 23278-79, z 23282, z 23284-86, z 23288-95, z 23297-98; Ⓟ 203,056; Ⓒ 197,790; ◆ 215,053
RICHMOND; **245** H-16; Ⓟ 7,273; Ⓒ 8,809; ◆ 9,477
Richmond Beach; RMC Place; ESSEX; ***245** H-16; mail Tappahannock z 22560; ● 30
Richmond Heights; RMC Place; HENRICO; ***245** J-14; ★ **RICH**; mail Henrico z 23231
Richpatch; RMC Place; ALLEGHANY; ***244** I-6; mail Covington z 24426; rural
Rich Valley; RMC Place; SMYTH; mail Saltville z 24370; rural
Ridge; RMC Place; HENRICO; ***245** I-13; 🅿; ★ **RICH**; z 23233 & mail Henrico z 23242
Ridgecrest; RMC Place; FAIRFAX; ***245** D-14; ★ **WASH**; mail Oakton z 22124
Ridgefield; RMC Place; FREDERICK; ***245** D-11; elev. 766ft./233m.; mail Stephens City z 22655; ● 150
Ridgelea Estates; RMC Place; FAIRFAX; ***245** E-14; ★ **WASH**; mail Fairfax z 22031; ● 600
Ridge View (Ridgeview Estates); RMC Place; FAIRFAX; ***245** E-15; ★ **WASH**; mail Alexandria z 22310; ● 1,050
Ridgeview Estates; FAIRFAX; see Ridge View (RMC Place)
Ridgeway; RMC Place; HALIFAX; ***244** M-8; elev. 638ft./194m.; mail Vernon Hill z 24597; rural
Ridgeway; Inc. Place; HENRY; **244** N-6; elev. 941ft./287m.; 🅿; ★ **MRTNV**; z 24148; Ⓟ 752; Ⓒ 775; Ⓡ 825
Ridgeway; RMC Place; PITTSYLVANIA; ***244** L-7; mail Pittsville z 24139; rural
Rileyville; RMC Place; PAGE; **245** E-11; 🅿; z 22650; ● 150
Riner; RMC Place; MONTGOMERY; **244** L-4; elev. 2,037ft./621m.; 🅿; z 24149; ● 250
Ringgold; RMC Place; PITTSYLVANIA; **244** M-8; 🅿; ★ **DANV**; z 24586; ● 350
Rio; RMC Place; ALBEMARLE; ***245** H-11; ★ **CHRLTV**; mail Charlottesville z 22901; ● 500
Ripplemead; RMC Place; GILES; **244** K-4; 🅿; z 24150; ● 550
Rip Rap; RMC Place; HALIFAX; ***244** N-10; elev. 450ft./137m.; mail Virgilina z 24598; ● 30
Rivanna; RMC Place; ALBEMARLE; ***245** G-11; ★ **CHRLTV**; mail Earlysville z 22936; ● 750
Riverbend Estates; RMC Place; PRINCE WILLIAM; ***245** E-14; ★ **WASH**; mail Waterford z 20197
Riverdale; RMC Place; HALIFAX; **244** M-9; mail South Boston z 24592; pop. incl. with South Boston (Inc. Place)
Riverdale; RMC Place; HAMPTON (Independent City); ***245** L-17; ★ **NN-H**; mail Hampton z 23666; pop. incl. with Hampton (Independent City)
Riverdale; RMC Place; SOUTHAMPTON; ***245** N-15; elev. 39ft./12m.; mail Franklin z 23851
Riverhill; RMC Place; CARROLL; ***244** M-3; mail Galax z 24333; rural
River Hills; RMC Place; HENRICO; ***245** J-13; elev. 200ft./61m.; ★ **RICH**; mail Henrico z 23075; ● 600
Rivermont; RMC Place; AUGUSTA; ***244** H-9; mail Stuarts Draft z 24477; ● 200
Rivermont; RMC Place; CHESTERFIELD; ***245** K-14; ★ **RICH**; mail Chester z 23836; ● 500
Rivermont; RMC Place; COVINGTON (Independent City); ***244** I-6; mail Covington z 24426; pop. incl. with Covington (Independent City)
Rivermont; RMC Place; LYNCHBURG (Independent City); ***244** J-8; elev. 759ft./231m.; ★ **LYNCH**; mail Lynchburg z 24503; pop. incl. with Lynchburg (Independent City)
River Oaks; RMC Place; FAIRFAX; ***245** D-14; ★ **WASH**; mail Mc Lean z 22101
River Park; RMC Place; PORTSMOUTH (Independent City); ***245** L-17; elev. 10ft./3m.; ★ **NORF-**; mail Portsmouth z 23707; pop. incl. with Portsmouth (Independent City)
Rivers Edge; RMC Place; PRINCE GEORGE; ***245** K-15; elev. 114ft./35m.; mail Hopewell z 23860; ● 400
Riverside; RMC Place; NEWPORT NEWS (Independent City); ***245** L-17; ★ **NN-H**; mail Newport News z 23606; pop. incl. with Newport News (Independent City)
Riverside; RMC Place; ROCKBRIDGE; ***244** I-8; mail Buena Vista z 24416
Riverside Estates; RMC Place; FAIRFAX; ***245** E-15; ★ **WASH**; mail Alexandria z 22309
Riverside Gardens; RMC Place; FAIRFAX; ***245** E-15; ★ **WASH**; mail Alexandria z 22308; ● 1,100
Riverton; RMC Place; WARREN; ***245** D-11; 🅿; z 22630
Riverview; RMC Place; NORFOLK (Independent City); ***245** L-18; elev. 10ft./3m.; ★ **NORF-**; mail Norfolk z 23504; pop. incl. with Norfolk (Independent City)
Riverview; RMC Place; WISE; ***244** C-4; mail Coeburn z 24230; ● 500
Riverville; RMC Place; AMHERST; ***244** J-9; mail Gladstone z 24553; rural
Riverwood; RMC Place; ARLINGTON; ***245** D-15; ★ **WASH**; mail Arlington z 22207
Rixeyville; RMC Place; CULPEPER; **245** F-12; 🅿; z 22737; ● 120
Roanes; RMC Place; GLOUCESTER; ***245** J-17; elev. 31ft./9m.; ★ **NN-H**; mail Gloucester z 23061; rural
Roanoke; Independent City; **244** K-6; 🅿 🅷 🅲 2,298 ■; ★ **ROAN**; z 24001-20, z 24022-38, z 24040, z 24042-45, z 24048, z 24050, z 24155, z 24157; Ⓟ 96,397; Ⓒ 94,911; ◆ 94,603
ROANOKE; **244** K-5; Ⓟ 79,332; Ⓒ 85,778; ◆ 90,463
Roaring Fork; RMC Place; WISE; ***244** C-3; mail Appalachia z 24216; ● 30
Roberts Mill; RMC Place; SMYTH; ***244** M-1; mail Sugar Grove z 24375; rural
Robertsons; RMC Place; BEDFORD; ***244** K-7; mail Bedford z 24523; rural
Robin Ridge; RMC Place; HANOVER; ***245** I-14; elev. 190ft./58m.; ★ **RICH**; mail Mechanicsville z 23116; ● 400
Robinwood; RMC Place; HENRICO; ***245** J-14; ★ **RICH**; mail Henrico z 23231; ● 500
Robley; RMC Place; RICHMOND; ***245** H-16; elev. 100ft./30m.; mail Farnham z 22460
Robnel; RMC Place; MANASSAS (Independent City); ★ **WASH**; mail Manassas z 20110; pop. incl. with Manassas (Independent City)
Rochelle; RMC Place; MADISON; **245** G-11; 🅿; z 22738; ● 130
ROCKBRIDGE; **244** H-7; Ⓟ 18,350; Ⓒ 20,808; ◆ 21,927
Rockbridge Baths; RMC Place; ROCKBRIDGE; **244** H-8; 🅿; z 24473; ● 150
Rock Castle; RMC Place; GOOCHLAND; ***245** I-12; mail Goochland z 23063; rural
Rockfish; RMC Place; NELSON; ***244** I-10; 🅿; z 22971; ● 100
ROCKINGHAM; **244** E-9; Ⓟ 57,482; Ⓒ 67,725; Ⓡ 67,714; ◆ 75,495
Rock Island; RMC Place; BUCKINGHAM; ***244** I-10; elev. 453ft./138m.; mail Scottsville z 24590; rural
Rockland; RMC Place; WARREN; ***245** D-12; mail Front Royal z 22630
Rockland Village; RMC Place; FAIRFAX; mail Chantilly z 20151
Rock Mills; RMC Place; RAPPAHANNOCK; ***245** E-12; mail Castleton z 22716; rural
Rock Springs; RMC Place; CHESTERFIELD; ***245** J-14; elev. 193ft./59m.; ★ **RICH**; mail Richmond z 23234; ● 1,000
Rock Springs; RMC Place; FAUQUIER; mail Warrenton z 20187; ● 250
Rocktown; RMC Place; WASHINGTON; ***244** D-5; mail Bristol z 24202; rural
Rockville; RMC Place; HANOVER; **245** I-13; 🅿; z 23146; ● 200
Rocky Bar; RMC Place; ROCKINGHAM; ***244** G-10; mail Elkton z 22827; ● 180
Rocky Gap; RMC Place; BLAND; **244** K-2; 🅿; z 24366; ● 250
Rocky Mount; Inc. Place; ⊡ FRANKLIN; **244** L-6; 🅿 🅷; z 24151; Ⓟ 4,098; Ⓒ 4,066
Roda; RMC Place; WISE; ***244** C-3; mail Appalachia z 24216; ● 200
Rodden; RMC Place; HALIFAX; ***244** M-9; elev. 581ft./177m.; mail Nathalie z 24577; rural
Rodophil; RMC Place; AMELIA; ***245** J-12; elev. 460ft./140m.; mail Jetersville z 23083; rural
Roebuck; RMC Place; WASHINGTON; ***244** D-5; mail Abingdon z 24210; rural
Roetown; RMC Place; WASHINGTON; ***244** E-6; mail Damascus z 24236; ● 50
Rogers; RMC Place; MONTGOMERY; ***244** L-4; elev. 1,825ft./556m.; mail Christiansburg z 24073; ● 40
Roland Park; RMC Place; NORFOLK (Independent City); ***245** L-18; elev. 10ft./3m.; ★ **NORF-**; mail Norfolk z 23509; pop. incl. with Norfolk (Independent City)
Rolling Brook; RMC Place; PRINCE WILLIAM; ***245** E-14; ★ **WASH**; mail Woodbridge z 22192; ● 650
Rolling Hills; RMC Place; FAIRFAX; ***245** E-15; ★ **WASH**; mail Alexandria z 22309
Rolling Meadows; RMC Place; PRINCE GEORGE; ***245** K-14; elev. 148ft./45m.; ★ **RICH**; mail Prince George z 23875; ● 100
Rolling Valley; RMC Place; FAIRFAX; ***245** E-14; ★ **WASH**; mail Burke z 22015; ● 2,500
Rollins Fork; RMC Place; KING GEORGE; ***245** G-15; elev. 178ft./54m.; 🅿; z 22544; ● 30
Rondo; RMC Place; PITTSYLVANIA; ***244** M-7; elev. 930ft./283m.; mail Chatham z 24531; rural
Roosevelt Gardens; RMC Place; NORFOLK (Independent City); ***245** L-18; ★ **NORF-**; mail Norfolk z 23518; pop. incl. with Norfolk (Independent City)
Roseann; RMC Place; BUCHANAN; **244** B-6; mail Grundy z 24614; ● 50
Rose Bower; RMC Place; APPOMATTOX; ***244** J-10; elev. 794ft./242m.; mail Appomattox z 24522; rural
Rosedale; RMC Place; RUSSELL; **244** C-6; 🅿; z 24280; ● 100
Rose Garden; RMC Place; KING WILLIAM; ***245** I-15; elev. 122ft./37m.; mail West Point z 23181; rural
Rose Hill; CDP-Census Area Only; FAIRFAX; **249** I-5; ★ **WASH**; mail Alexandria z 22310; Ⓟ 12,675; Ⓒ 15,058
Rose Hill; CDP; LEE; **244** D-1; 🅿; z 24281; Ⓒ 714
Rose Hill Farms; RMC Place; FAIRFAX; ***245** E-15; ★ **WASH**; mail Alexandria z 22310
Roseland; RMC Place; NELSON; **244** I-9; elev. 632ft./193m.; 🅿; z 22967, z 22976; ● 100
Rosemont; RMC Place; ALEXANDRIA (Independent City); ***245** E-15; ★ **WASH**; mail Alexandria z 22301; pop. incl. with Alexandria (Independent City)
Rosemont; RMC Place; FAIRFAX; ***245** D-14; ★ **WASH**; mail Mc Lean z 22101
Rosemont; RMC Place; SUFFOLK (Independent City); ★ **NORF-**; mail Suffolk z 23434; pop. incl. with Suffolk (Independent City)
Rosemont; RMC Place; VIRGINIA BEACH (Independent City); ***245** L-18; ★ **NORF-**; mail Virginia Beach z 23452; pop. incl. with Virginia Beach (Independent City)
Roseville; RMC Place; STAFFORD; **245** F-14; ★ **WASH**; mail Stafford z 22554; ● 260
Roslyn Hills; RMC Place; HENRICO; ***245** J-13; ★ **RICH**; mail Henrico z 23229; ● 600
Rosslyn; RMC Place; ARLINGTON; ***245** D-15; 🅿; ★ **WASH**; z 22209 & mail Arlington z 22219
Roth; RMC Place; BUCHANAN; ***244** B-6; mail Oakwood z 24631
Rough Creek; RMC Place; CHARLOTTE; ***244** K-10; elev. 492ft./150m.; mail Phenix z 23959; rural
Round Bottom; RMC Place; BLAND; ***244** K-2; mail Narrows z 24124; rural
Round Hill; RMC Place; FREDERICK; ***245** C-11; elev. 897ft./273m.; mail Winchester z 22603; ● 50
Round Hill; Inc. Place; LOUDOUN; **245** C-13; 🅿; ★ **WASH**; z 20141-42; Ⓟ 514; Ⓒ 500
Round Top; RMC Place; WISE; mail Wise z 24293
Roundtree; RMC Place; FAIRFAX; ***245** D-14; ★ **WASH**; mail Falls Church z 22042
Rowe; RMC Place; BUCHANAN; **244** C-6; 🅿; z 24646; ● 250
Roxbury; RMC Place; CHARLES CITY; **245** J-15; elev. 38ft./12m.; mail Providence Forge z 23140; rural
Roxbury; RMC Place; HENRICO; ***245** I-13; elev. 250ft./76m.; ★ **RICH**; mail Henrico z 23229; ● 750
Royal City; RMC Place; BUCHANAN; ***244** B-6; elev. 1,078ft./329m.; mail Grundy z 24614; pop. incl. with Grundy (Inc. Place)
Royal Court; RMC Place; FAIRFAX; mail Annandale z 22003
Ruark; RMC Place; MIDDLESEX; ***245** J-17; mail Deltaville z 23043; ● 60
Rubermont; RMC Place; LUNENBURG; ***245** L-11; elev. 506ft./154m.; mail Victoria z 23974; ● 60
Ruby; RMC Place; STAFFORD; ***245** F-13; 🅿; ★ **WASH**; z 22545; ● 40
Ruckersville; RMC Place; GREENE; **245** G-11; 🅿; ★ **CHRLTV**; z 22968; ● 400
Rudee Heights; RMC Place; VIRGINIA BEACH (Independent City); ***245** L-19; ★ **NORF-**; mail Virginia Beach z 23451; pop. incl. with Virginia Beach (Independent City)
Rue; RMC Place; ACCOMACK; ***245** I-20; mail Parksley z 23421; ● 30
Ruff; RMC Place; MATHEWS; ***245** J-17; elev. 9ft./3m.; ★ **NN-H**; mail Mathews z 23109
Rugby; RMC Place; GRAYSON; ***244** M-1; mail Mouth of Wilson z 24363; rural
Rural Retreat; Inc. Place; WYTHE; **244** L-2; elev. 2,510ft./765m.; 🅿; z 24368; Ⓟ 972; Ⓒ 1,350
Rushmere; CDP; ISLE OF WIGHT; **243** J-2; elev. 77ft./23m.; mail Smithfield z 23430; Ⓟ 1,067; Ⓒ 1,083
Rushmere Shores; RMC Place; ISLE OF WIGHT; ***245** K-16; mail Smithfield z 23430
Russell; RMC Place; RUSSELL; ***244** C-6; mail Honaker z 24260; rural
RUSSELL; **244** C-6; Ⓟ 28,667; Ⓒ 30,308; Ⓡ 29,258; ◆ 29,287
Russell Creek; RMC Place; WISE; mail Saint Paul z 24283; rural
Rustburg; CDP; ⊡ CAMPBELL; **244** K-9; 🅿; ★ **LYNCH**; z 24588; Ⓒ 1,271
Rustic; RMC Place; CHARLES CITY; ***245** K-15; elev. 37ft./11m.; mail Charles City z 23030; rural
Rutherford; RMC Place; FAIRFAX; ***245** E-14; ★ **WASH**; mail Fairfax z 22032; ● 1,850
Ruther Glen; RMC Place; CAROLINE; ***245** H-14; 🅿; z 22546; ● 170
Ruthland; RMC Place; HENRICO; ★ **RICH**; mail Henrico z 23228
Ruthville; RMC Place; CHARLES CITY; **245** J-15; 🅿; z 23147; ● 100
Ryan; RMC Place; LOUDOUN; ***245** D-14; ★ **WASH**; mail Ashburn z 20147
Rye Cove; RMC Place; SCOTT; ***244** D-4; elev. 1,446ft./441m.; mail Duffield z 24244; rural

S

Sabot; RMC Place; GOOCHLAND; ***245** I-13; mail Manakin Sabot z 23103; rural
Sadler Heights; RMC Place; SUFFOLK (Independent City); ★ **NORF-**; mail Suffolk z 23434; pop. incl. with Suffolk (Independent City)
Sago; RMC Place; FRANKLIN; ***244** L-7; elev. 885ft./270m.; mail Penhook z 24137; ● 30
Saint Brides; RMC Place; CHESAPEAKE (Independent City); ***245** M-18; elev. 15ft./5m.; ★ **NORF-**; mail Chesapeake z 23322; pop. incl. with Chesapeake (Independent City)
Saint Charles; Inc. Place; LEE; **244** D-2; 🅿; z 24282; Ⓟ 206; Ⓒ 159
Saint Clair; RMC Place; TAZEWELL; ***244** K-2; mail Bluefield z 24605; ● 30
Saint Clair Bottom; RMC Place; SMYTH; ***244** M-1; mail Chilhowie z 24319
Saint Davids Church; RMC Place; SHENANDOAH; ***245** E-11; 🅿; z 22652; rural
Saint Elmo; RMC Place; ALEXANDRIA (Independent City); mail Alexandria z 22305; pop. incl. with Alexandria (Independent City)
Saint George; RMC Place; GREENE; ***244** G-10; elev. 769ft./234m.; mail Dyke z 22935; rural
Saint Joe; RMC Place; CHESAPEAKE (Independent City); pop. incl. with Chesapeake (Independent City)
Saint Joy; RMC Place; BUCKINGHAM; ***244** J-10; elev. 562ft./171m.; mail Buckingham z 23921; rural
Saint Just; RMC Place; ORANGE; ***245** G-12; mail Unionville z 22567
Saint Louis; RMC Place; LOUDOUN; ***245** D-13; mail Middleburg z 20117; ● 200
Saint Luke; RMC Place; SHENANDOAH; ***244** D-10; mail Woodstock z 22664
Saint Paul; Inc. Place; WISE, RUSSELL; **244** D-5; elev. 1,492ft./455m.; 🅿; z 24283; Ⓟ 1,007; Ⓒ 1,000
Saint Stephens; RMC Place; FAUQUIER; ***245** E-13; mail Catlett z 20119; rural
Saint Stephens Church; RMC Place; KING AND QUEEN; **245** I-15; 🅿; z 23148; ● 120
Salem; RMC Place; CULPEPER; ***245** F-12; mail Culpeper z 22701; ● 100
Salem; Independent City; serves as county seat of Roanoke; **244** K-6; elev. 1,060ft./323m.; 🅿 🅷 🅲 2,700 ■; ★ **ROAN**; z 24153 & mail Roanoke z 24155, z 24157; Ⓟ 23,756; Ⓒ 24,747; ◆ 25,404
Salem Woods; RMC Place; CHESTERFIELD; ***245** J-14; elev. 150ft./46m.; ★ **RICH**; mail Richmond z 23234; ● 450
Salisbury; RMC Place; CHESTERFIELD; ***245** J-13; elev. 350ft./107m.; ★ **RICH**; mail Midlothian z 23113; ● 2,300
Salona Village; RMC Place; FAIRFAX; ***245** D-15; elev. 293ft./89m.; ★ **WASH**; mail Mc Lean z 22101
Saltpetre; BOTETOURT; see Saltpetre Cave (RMC Place)
Saltpetre Cave (Saltpetre); RMC Place; BOTETOURT; ***244** I-7; mail Eagle Rock z 24085
Saltville; Inc. Place; SMYTH, WASHINGTON; **244** L-1; elev. 1,718ft./524m.; 🅿; z 24370; Ⓟ 2,300; Ⓒ 2,204
Saluda; RMC Place; ⊡ MIDDLESEX; **245** I-16; elev. 101ft./31m.; 🅿; z 23149; ● 350
Salvia; RMC Place; KING AND QUEEN; ***245** H-15; elev. 191ft./58m.; mail Saint Stephens Church z 23148; rural
Samos; RMC Place; MIDDLESEX; ***245** I-16; elev. 83ft./25m.; mail Water View z 23180; rural
Sanburne Park; RMC Place; HENRICO; ***245** J-14; ★ **RICH**; mail Sandston z 23150; ● 550
Sand Bridge; RMC Place; VIRGINIA BEACH (Independent City); ***245** M-19; ★ **NORF-**; mail Virginia Beach z 23456; pop. incl. with Virginia Beach (Independent City)
Sandidges; RMC Place; AMHERST; ***244** I-8; elev. 672ft./205m.; mail Amherst z 24521; rural
Sands; RMC Place; SOUTHAMPTON; ***245** M-15; elev. 95ft./29m.; mail Newsoms z 23874; rural
Sandston; RMC Place; HENRICO; **243** C-10; 🅿; ★ **RICH**; z 23150; ● 4,200
Sandy Bottom (Daileys Store); RMC Place; SUFFOLK (Independent City); ★ **NORF-**; mail Suffolk z 23432; pop. incl. with Suffolk (Independent City)
Sandy Fork; RMC Place; MECKLENBURG; ***244** M-10; elev. 442ft./135m.; mail Clarksville z 23927; rural
Sandy Hook; RMC Place; GOOCHLAND; **245** I-12; 🅿; z 23153; ● 100
Sandy Level; CDP; HENRY; ***244** N-7; elev. 727ft./222m.; ★ **MRTNV**; mail Axton z 24054; Ⓒ 689
Sandy Level; RMC Place; PITTSYLVANIA; **244** L-7; elev. 792ft./241m.; 🅿; z 24161; ● 150
Sandy Point; RMC Place; NORTHUMBERLAND; ***245** H-17; mail Wicomico Church z 22579; ● 200
Sandy Point (Westmoreland); RMC Place; WESTMORELAND; **245** H-16; 🅿; z 22577; ● 130
Sandy River; RMC Place; PITTSYLVANIA; ***244** M-7; elev. 908ft./277m.; mail Axton z 24054; rural
Sanford; RMC Place; ACCOMACK; ***245** H-19; 🅿; z 23426; ● 350
Sangerville; RMC Place; AUGUSTA; ***244** F-9; mail Bridgewater z 22812, Mount Solon z 22843; ● 80
Sanville; RMC Place; HENRY; ***244** M-6; elev. 1,194ft./364m.; ★ **MRTNV**; mail Bassett z 24055
Sarah; RMC Place; MATHEWS; ***245** J-17; elev. 4ft./1m.; ★ **NN-H**; mail Onemo z 23130; rural
Saratoga; RMC Place; FAIRFAX; ***245** E-14; ★ **WASH**; mail Springfield z 22153
Saratoga Place; RMC Place; SUFFOLK (Independent City); ★ **NORF-**; mail Suffolk z 23434; pop. incl. with Suffolk (Independent City)
Sardis (Mayflower); RMC Place; AMHERST; ***244** I-9; mail Amherst z 24521; rural
Saumsville; RMC Place; SHENANDOAH; ***244** D-10; mail Maurertown z 22644; ● 30
Saunders; RMC Place; RICHMOND (Independent City); ★ **RICH**; mail Richmond z 23220; pop. incl. with Richmond (Independent City)
Savage Crossing; RMC Place; SUFFOLK (Independent City); ★ **NORF-**; mail Suffolk z 23434; pop. incl. with Suffolk (Independent City)
Savageville; RMC Place; ACCOMACK; ***245** I-19; mail Onancock z 23417; ● 130
Savedge; RMC Place; SURRY; ***245** K-15; elev. 126ft./38m.; mail Spring Grove z 23881, Waverly z 23890; rural
Saxe; RMC Place; CHARLOTTE; **244** L-10; elev. 341ft./104m.; 🅿; z 23967; ● 100
Saxis; Inc. Place; ACCOMACK; **245** H-19; 🅿; z 23427; Ⓟ 367; Ⓒ 337
Sayersville; RMC Place; TAZEWELL; ***244** K-1; mail Bandy z 24602; rural
Scarborough Neck; RMC Place; ACCOMACK; ***245** I-19; mail Belle Haven z 23306; ● 30
Scenic Park; RMC Place; BRISTOL (Independent City); ***244** E-5; ★ **JNSC-**; mail Bristol z 24201
Schley; RMC Place; GLOUCESTER; ***245** J-17; 🅿; ★ **NN-H**; z 23154; ● 200
Schoolfield; RMC Place; DANVILLE (Independent City); ***244** N-8; ★ **DANV**; mail Danville z 24541; pop. incl. with Danville (Independent City)
Schuyler; RMC Place; NELSON; **244** I-10; 🅿; z 22969; ● 400
Scotland; RMC Place; SURRY; **245** K-16; mail Surry z 23883; ● 120
SCOTT; **244** D-4; Ⓟ 23,204; Ⓒ 23,403; ◆ 22,872
Scott Addition; RMC Place; WASHINGTON; ***244** D-6; mail Abingdon z 24210; pop. incl. with Abingdon (Inc. Place)
Scottie Farms; RMC Place; HENRICO; ***245** J-14; elev. 146ft./45m.; ★ **RICH**; mail Henrico z 23075; ● 350
Scottsburg; Inc. Place; HALIFAX; **244** M-10; elev. 380ft./116m.; 🅿; z 24589; Ⓟ 152; Ⓒ 145; Ⓡ 155
Scotts Crossroads; RMC Place; MECKLENBURG; ***245** M-11; elev. 498ft./152m.; mail Chase City z 23924; rural
Scotts Fork; RMC Place; AMELIA; ***245** K-12; mail Amelia Court House z 23002
Scottsville; Inc. Place; ALBEMARLE, FLUVANNA; **244** I-10; 🅿; z 24562, z 24590; Ⓟ 239; Ⓒ 555
Scottswood; RMC Place; SOUTHAMPTON; ***245** M-15; mail Franklin z 23851; ● 300
Scrabble; RMC Place; RAPPAHANNOCK; ***245** F-11; mail Woodville z 22749; rural
Scruggs; RMC Place; FRANKLIN; ***244** L-7; mail Moneta z 24121; rural
Seaboard; RMC Place; TAZEWELL; ***244** K-1; mail Richlands z 24641; ● 80
Seaford; RMC Place; YORK; **245** K-17; elev. 9ft./3m.; 🅿; ★ **NN-H**; z 23696; ● 2,700
Seaford Shores; RMC Place; YORK; ***245** K-17; ★ **NN-H**; mail Seaford z 23696
Sealston; RMC Place; KING GEORGE; ***245** G-14; 🅿; z 22547; ● 100
Seapines; RMC Place; VIRGINIA BEACH (Independent City); ★ **NORF-**; mail Virginia Beach z 23451; pop. incl. with Virginia Beach (Independent City)
Searcy; RMC Place; CHESTERFIELD; ***245** K-14; elev. 100ft./30m.; ★ **RICH**; mail Chester z 23831; ● 800
Seatack; RMC Place; VIRGINIA BEACH (Independent City); ***245** L-18; elev. 19ft./6m.; ★ **NORF-**; mail Virginia Beach z 23451; pop. incl. with Virginia Beach (Independent City)
Seaview; RMC Place; NORTHAMPTON; ***245** K-19; elev. 34ft./10m.; 🅿; z 23429; ● 50
Sebrell; RMC Place; SOUTHAMPTON; **245** M-15; mail Courtland z 23837; ● 150
Sedalia; RMC Place; BEDFORD; ***244** J-7; mail Big Island z 24526
Sedgefield; RMC Place; NEWPORT NEWS (Independent City); ***245** L-17; ★ **NN-H**; mail Newport News z 23605; pop. incl. with Newport News (Independent City)
Sedgefield Manor; RMC Place; HENRICO; ***245** I-14; elev. 200ft./61m.; ★ **RICH**; mail Henrico z 23228; ● 350
Sedley; RMC Place; SOUTHAMPTON; **245** M-15; 🅿; z 23878; ● 560
Selden; RMC Place; GLOUCESTER; ***245** J-17; ★ **NN-H**; mail Gloucester z 23061; ● 40
Selma; CDP; ALLEGHANY; **244** I-6; 🅿; z 24474; Ⓒ 485
Selma; RMC Place; STAUNTON (Independent City); ***244** G-9; pop. incl. with Staunton (Independent City)
Seminary; RMC Place; LEE; ***244** D-3; mail Big Stone Gap z 24219; rural
Seminary Valley; RMC Place; ALEXANDRIA (Independent City); ***245** E-15; ★ **WASH**; mail Alexandria z 22304; pop. incl. with Alexandria (Independent City)
Senora; RMC Place; LANCASTER; ***245** I-17; mail Lancaster z 22503; rural
Seven Corners; CDP; FAIRFAX; ***245** D-15; 🅿; ★ **WASH**; z 22044; Ⓟ 7,280; Ⓒ 8,701
Seven Fountains; RMC Place; SHENANDOAH; ***245** E-11; 🅿; z 22652; ● 30
Seven Mile Ford; RMC Place; SMYTH; **244** M-1; elev. 1,986ft./605m.; 🅿; z 24354; ● 180
Seven Pines; RMC Place; HENRICO; ***245** J-14; ★ **RICH**; mail Sandston z 23150
Seven Pines Villa; RMC Place; HENRICO; ★ **RICH**; mail Sandston z 23150
Severn; RMC Place; GLOUCESTER; **245** K-17; elev. 8ft./2m.; 🅿; ★ **NN-H**; z 23155 & mail Hayes z 23072; ● 170
Severn Manor; RMC Place; GLOUCESTER; ***245** K-17; ★ **NN-H**; mail Hayes z 23072; ● 100
Shacklefords (Centerville); RMC Place; KING AND QUEEN; **245** J-16; 🅿; z 23156; ● 250
Shacklefords Fork; RMC Place; KING AND QUEEN; ***245** J-16; elev. 95ft./29m.; mail Shacklefords z 23156; ● 40
Shadow; RMC Place; MATHEWS; ***245** J-17; elev. 10ft./3m.; 🅿; ★ **NN-H**; z 23163; ● 50
Shadow Valley; RMC Place; BRISTOL (Independent City); ★ **JNSC-**; mail Bristol z 24201; pop. incl. with Bristol (Independent City)
Shadwell; RMC Place; ALBEMARLE; ***245** H-11; 🅿; ★ **CHRLTV**; z 22947 & mail Charlottesville z 22902; rural
Shady Creek; RMC Place; CHESTERFIELD; ★ **RICH**; mail Richmond z 23234
Shady Grove; RMC Place; BEDFORD; ***244** K-7; elev. 1,040ft./317m.; mail Thaxton z 24174; ● 30
Shady Grove; RMC Place; GREENE; ***244** G-10; mail Dyke z 22935; rural
Shady Grove; RMC Place; HALIFAX; ***244** M-9; mail Virgilina z 24598; ● 30
Shady Grove; RMC Place; WASHINGTON; ***244** D-6; mail Abingdon z 24210; pop. incl. with Abingdon (Inc. Place)
Shady Oak; RMC Place; FAIRFAX; **249** D-2; ★ **WASH**; mail Great Falls z 22066; ● 180
Shadyside; RMC Place; NORTHAMPTON; ***245** J-19; elev. 37ft./11m.; mail Machipongo z 23405; rural
Shakerag; BATH; see West Warm Springs (RMC Place)
Shanghai; RMC Place; KING AND QUEEN; ***245** I-16; mail Mattaponi z 23110; rural
Shannon Hills; RMC Place; HENRY; ***244** M-6; ★ **MRTNV**; mail Ridgeway z 24148; ● 350
Shannon Park; RMC Place; WESTMORELAND; ***245** H-17; mail Sandy Point z 22577; ● 50
Sharps; RMC Place; RICHMOND; **245** I-16; elev. 14ft./4m.; 🅿; z 22548; ● 210
Shawnee Land; RMC Place; FREDERICK; ***245** C-11; mail Winchester z 22602; ● 440
Shawsville; CDP; MONTGOMERY; **244** K-5; 🅿; ★ **ROAN**; z 24162; Ⓟ 1,260; Ⓒ 1,029
Shawver Mill; RMC Place; TAZEWELL; ***244** K-1; mail Tazewell z 24651; ● 30
Shea Terrace; RMC Place; PORTSMOUTH (Independent City); ***245** L-17; elev. 10ft./3m.; ★ **NORF-**; mail Portsmouth z 23707; pop. incl. with Portsmouth (Independent City)
Sheep Town; RMC Place; CARROLL; ***244** M-3; mail Austinville z 24312; ● 50
Sheffield Court; RMC Place; CHESTERFIELD; ***245** J-13; ★ **RICH**; mail Richmond z 23235
Sheffield Terrace; RMC Place; HENRY; ***244** M-6; ★ **MRTNV**; mail Ridgeway z 24148; ● 250
Shelby; RMC Place; MADISON; ***245** G-11; 🅿; z 22727
Shelfar; RMC Place; LOUISA; ***245** I-12; mail Mineral z 23117
Shelors Mill; RMC Place; FLOYD; ***244** L-5; mail Floyd z 24091; ● 30
Shenandoah; RMC Place; HOPEWELL (Independent City); ★ **RICH**; mail Hopewell z 23860; pop. incl. with Hopewell (Independent City)
Shenandoah; Inc. Place; PAGE; **244** F-10; 🅿; z 22849; Ⓟ 2,213; Ⓒ 1,878
SHENANDOAH; **244** E-10; Ⓟ 31,636; Ⓒ 35,075; ◆ 41,168
Shenandoah Farms; RMC Place; WARREN; ***245** D-12; mail Front Royal z 22630; ● 350
Shenandoah Place; RMC Place; HENRICO; ***245** J-14; ★ **RICH**; mail Richmond z 23226; ● 700
Shenandoah Retreat; RMC Place; CLARKE; ***245** C-12; mail Bluemont z 20135; ● 300
Shenandoah Shores; RMC Place; WARREN; ***245** D-12; mail Front Royal z 22630; ● 500
Shepherds Hill; RMC Place; LEE; ***244** D-3; mail Keokee z 24265; rural
Shepherds Store; RMC Place; FLUVANNA; ***245** I-11; mail Columbia z 23038; rural
Sheppards; RMC Place; BUCKINGHAM; ***245** J-11; elev. 568ft./173m.; mail Farmville z 23901; rural
Sherando; CDP; AUGUSTA; **244** H-9; 🅿; z 22952; Ⓒ 665
Sherwill; RMC Place; CAMPBELL; ***244** K-9; elev. 824ft./251m.; mail Concord z 24538
Sherwood Forest; RMC Place; AUGUSTA; mail Staunton z 24401; ● 220
Sheva; RMC Place; PITTSYLVANIA; ***244** L-8; elev. 735ft./224m.; mail Chatham z 24531; rural
Shields; RMC Place; ACCOMACK; ***245** I-19; elev. 29ft./9m.; mail Belle Haven z 23306; ● 30
Shiloh; RMC Place; KING GEORGE; ***245** G-15; 🅿; z 22485; ● 50
Shiloh; RMC Place; SOUTHAMPTON; ***245** M-15; mail Boykins z 23827; ● 30
Shiny Rock; RMC Place; MECKLENBURG; ***244** N-10; mail Clarksville z 23927; rural
Shipman; RMC Place; NELSON; **244** I-9; 🅿; z 22971; ● 250
Shirley; RMC Place; CHARLES CITY; ***245** J-14; elev. 10ft./3m.; mail Charles City z 23030; rural
Shirley Duke; RMC Place; ALEXANDRIA (Independent City); ***245** E-15; ★ **WASH**; mail Alexandria z 22304; pop. incl. with Alexandria (Independent City)
Shirley Gate Park; RMC Place; FAIRFAX; ***245** E-14; ★ **WASH**; mail Fairfax z 22030; ● 2,150
Shockoe; RMC Place; PITTSYLVANIA; ***244** M-8; mail Chatham z 24531; rural
Shores; RMC Place; FLUVANNA; ***245** I-11; mail Palmyra z 22963
Shorewood; RMC Place; CHESAPEAKE (Independent City); ***245** L-17; ★ **NORF-**; mail Chesapeake z 23321; pop. incl. with Chesapeake (Independent City)
Short Lane; RMC Place; GLOUCESTER; ***245** J-17; elev. 79ft./24m.; ★ **NN-H**; mail Gloucester z 23061; rural
Short Pump; CDP; HENRICO; ***245** I-13; ★ **RICH**; mail Glen Allen z 23060; Ⓒ 182
Shorts Creek; RMC Place; CARROLL; ***244** M-3; elev. 2,105ft./642m.; mail Austinville z 24312; ● 30
Shortt Gap; RMC Place; BUCHANAN, TAZEWELL; **244** C-6; 🅿; z 24647; ● 50
Shoulders Hill; RMC Place; SUFFOLK (Independent City); ★ **NORF-**; mail Suffolk z 23435; pop. incl. with Suffolk (Independent City)
Shrevewood; RMC Place; FAIRFAX; ***245** D-14; ★ **WASH**; mail Falls Church z 22043; ● 2,600
Shumansville; RMC Place; CAROLINE; ***245** H-14; mail Milford z 22514
Shumate; RMC Place; GILES; ***244** K-3; mail Narrows z 24124; rural
Siddon; RMC Place; MECKLENBURG; ***244** N-10; mail Nelson z 24580; rural
Sigma; RMC Place; VIRGINIA BEACH (Independent City); ***245** M-19; ★ **NORF-**; mail Virginia Beach z 23456; pop. incl. with Virginia Beach (Independent City)
Signpine; RMC Place; GLOUCESTER; ***245** J-16; elev. 98ft./30m.; mail Gloucester z 23061; rural
Sign Post (Silva); RMC Place; ACCOMACK; ***245** H-20; elev. 36ft./11m.; mail New Church z 23415
Siler; RMC Place; FREDERICK; ***245** C-11; elev. 651ft./198m.; mail Winchester z 22603; ● 50
Silva; ACCOMACK; see Sign Post (RMC Place)
Silver Beach; RMC Place; NORTHAMPTON; **245** J-18; mail Jamesville z 23398; summer pop. 500; ● 200
Silver Springs; RMC Place; FAIRFAX; ***245** E-15; ★ **WASH**; mail Alexandria z 22310
Silverwood; RMC Place; CHESAPEAKE (Independent City); ***245** L-17; elev. 15ft./5m.; ★ **NORF-**; mail Chesapeake z 23321; pop. incl. with Chesapeake (Independent City)
Simeon; RMC Place; ALBEMARLE; ***245** H-11; elev. 538ft./164m.; ★ **CHRLTV**; mail Charlottesville z 22902; rural
Simmonsville; RMC Place; CRAIG; ***244** J-5; elev. 2,278ft./694m.; mail New Castle z 24127, Newport z 24128
Simons Corner; RMC Place; RICHMOND; ***245** H-16; elev. 33ft./10m.; mail Warsaw z 22572; rural
Simonsdale; RMC Place; PORTSMOUTH (Independent City); ***245** L-17; ★ **NORF-**; mail Portsmouth z 23701; pop. incl. with Portsmouth (Independent City)
Simonson; RMC Place; RICHMOND; ***245** I-16; mail Farnham z 22460; ● 80
Simpkins; RMC Place; NORTHAMPTON; ***245** J-19; mail Cape Charles z 23310; rural
Simpsons; RMC Place; FLOYD; ***244** L-5; elev. 2,608ft./795m.; 🅿; z 24072
Sinai; RMC Place; HALIFAX; ***244** M-9; mail South Boston z 24592; pop. incl. with South Boston (Inc. Place)
Sinclair Farms; RMC Place; HAMPTON (Independent City); ***245** L-17; ★ **NN-H**; mail Hampton z 23669; pop. incl. with Hampton (Independent City)
Singers Glen; RMC Place; ROCKINGHAM; **244** F-9; 🅿; z 22850; ● 250
Sinking Creek; RMC Place; CRAIG; ***244** J-5; mail New Castle z 24127; rural
Sinnickson; RMC Place; ACCOMACK; ***245** H-20; mail Horntown z 23395; rural
Sissons Corner; RMC Place; NORTHUMBERLAND; ***245** H-17; elev. 111ft./34m.; mail Heathsville z 22473; rural
Six Mile; RMC Place; CAMPBELL; ***244** J-9; elev. 524ft./160m.; ★ **LYNCH**; mail Lynchburg z 24504; rural
Sixmile Post; RMC Place; FRANKLIN; ***244** L-6; mail Rocky Mount z 24151; ● 50
Skeetrock; RMC Place; DICKENSON; ***244** B-5; elev. 1,879ft./573m.; mail Clintwood z 24228; rural
Skeggs; RMC Place; BUCHANAN; ***244** B-6; mail Rowe z 24646; rural
Skinquarter; RMC Place; CHESTERFIELD; ***245** J-13; mail Moseley z 23120; ● 60
Skippers; RMC Place; GREENSVILLE; **245** M-14; 🅿; z 23879; ● 300
Skipwith; RMC Place; MECKLENBURG; ***245** M-11; 🅿; z 23968; ● 200
Skipwith Farms; RMC Place; HENRICO; ***245** I-13; elev. 250ft./76m.; ★ **RICH**; mail Henrico z 23229; ● 2,200
Skipwith Farms; RMC Place; WILLIAMSBURG (Independent City); mail Williamsburg z 23185; pop. incl. with Williamsburg (Independent City)
Skyland; RMC Place; PAGE; ***245** F-11; mail Luray z 22835; summer pop. 300
Skyland Estates; RMC Place; WARREN; ***245** D-12; mail Linden z 22642; ● 350
Skymont; RMC Place; STAUNTON (Independent City); ***244** G-9; mail Staunton z 24401; pop. incl. with Staunton (Independent City)
Slabtown; RMC Place; SCOTT; ***244** D-4; elev. 1,288ft./393m.; ★ **JNSC-**; mail Gate City z 24251; rural
Slant; SCOTT; see Starnes (RMC Place)
Slate; RMC Place; BUCHANAN; ***244** B-6; mail Grundy z 24614
Slate Mills; RMC Place; RAPPAHANNOCK; ***245** F-11; elev. 576ft./176m.; mail Boston z 22713, Sperryville z 22740; ● 30
Sleepy Hole; RMC Place; SUFFOLK (Independent City); ***245** L-17; elev. 25ft./8m.; ★ **NORF-**; mail Suffolk z 23435; pop. incl. with Suffolk (Independent City)
Sleepy Hollow; RMC Place; FAIRFAX; **249** G-4; ★ **WASH**; mail Falls Church z 22042; ● 640
Sleepy Hollow Estates; RMC Place; FAIRFAX; ***245** D-15; ★ **WASH**; mail Falls Church z 22044
Sleepy Hollow Estates; RMC Place; HENRICO; ***245** J-13; elev. 250ft./76m.; ★ **RICH**; mail Henrico z 23229; ● 1,800
Sleepy Hollow Manor; RMC Place; FAIRFAX; ***245** D-15; ★ **WASH**; mail Falls Church z 22044
Sleepy Hollow Run; RMC Place; FAIRFAX; ***245** E-15; ★ **WASH**; mail Annandale z 22003
Sleepy Hollow Woods; RMC Place; FAIRFAX; ***245** E-14; ★ **WASH**; mail Annandale z 22003
Sliders; RMC Place; BUCKINGHAM; ***244** J-10; elev. 745ft./227m.; mail Dillwyn z 23936; rural
Sloantown; RMC Place; SCOTT; ***244** D-3; mail Duffield z 24244; rural
Smithfield; Inc. Place; ISLE OF WIGHT; **245** L-16; 🅿; ★ **NN-H**; z 23430-31; Ⓟ 4,686; Ⓒ 6,324
Smiths Cross Roads (Radcliffe); RMC Place; MECKLENBURG; ***245** M-12; elev. 370ft./113m.; mail South Hill z 23970; rural
Smith Store; RMC Place; BUCKINGHAM; ***244** I-10; elev. 533ft./162m.; mail Scottsville z 24590; rural
Smoky; BRUNSWICK; see Smoky Ordinary (RMC Place)
Smoky Ordinary (Smoky); RMC Place; BRUNSWICK; ***245** M-13; elev. 327ft./100m.; mail Lawrenceville z 23868
Smoots; RMC Place; CAROLINE; ***245** H-14; elev. 121ft./37m.; mail Bowling Green z 22427; rural
SMYTH; **244** L-1; Ⓟ 32,370; Ⓒ 33,081; ◆ 31,578
Snapp; WASHINGTON; see Fleet (RMC Place)
Snell; RMC Place; SPOTSYLVANIA; **245** G-13; 🅿; z 22553; ● 250
Snowden; RMC Place; AMHERST; ***244** J-8; elev. 671ft./205m.; mail Big Island z 24526; rural
Snowflake; RMC Place; SCOTT; **244** D-4; elev. 1,579ft./481m.; mail Gate City z 24251; ● 70
Snow Hill; RMC Place; KING AND QUEEN; ***245** J-16; mail Shacklefords z 23156; ● 50
Snowville; RMC Place; PULASKI; ***244** L-4; mail Hiwassee z 24347, Pulaski z 24301; ● 150
Soles; RMC Place; MATHEWS; ***245** J-17; elev. 42ft./13m.; ★ **NN-H**; mail Dutton z 23050; ● 50
Solomons Store; RMC Place; HENRICO; **245** H-11; ★ **RICH**; mail Glen Allen z 23060; ● 100
Solsburg; RMC Place; ROCKINGHAM; ***244** F-10; mail Elkton z 22827; ● 120
Somers; RMC Place; LANCASTER; ***245** I-17; elev. 41ft./12m.; mail Lancaster z 22503; rural
Somerset; RMC Place; ORANGE; **245** G-11; 🅿; z 22972; ● 210
Somerton; RMC Place; SUFFOLK (Independent City); ***245** M-16; ★ **NORF-**; mail Suffolk z 23438; pop. incl. with Suffolk (Independent City)
Somerville; RMC Place; FAUQUIER; **245** F-13; elev. 414ft./126m.; 🅿; z 22739; ● 80
Sonans; RMC Place; PITTSYLVANIA; ***244** L-8; elev. 677ft./206m.; mail Chatham z 24531; rural
Sontag; RMC Place; FRANKLIN; ***244** L-6; elev. 1,135ft./346m.; mail Rocky Mount z 24151; rural
Sorocco; RMC Place; SUFFOLK (Independent City); ★ **NORF-**; mail Suffolk z 23434; pop. incl. with Suffolk (Independent City)
Sorrell; RMC Place; CAROLINE; ***245** H-15; elev. 180ft./55m.; mail Milford z 22514; rural
Soudan; RMC Place; MECKLENBURG; ***244** N-10; elev. 312ft./95m.; mail Clarksville z 23927; ● 30
South (South Arlington); RMC Place; ARLINGTON; ***245** D-15; ★ **WASH**; mail Arlington z 22204
Southampton; RMC Place; HAMPTON (Independent City); ***245** L-17; ★ **NN-H**; mail Hampton z 23669; pop. incl. with Hampton (Independent City)
SOUTHAMPTON; **245** M-15; Ⓟ 17,550; Ⓒ 17,482; ◆ 19,965
South Anna; RMC Place; LOUISA; ***245** H-12; elev. 315ft./96m.; mail Mineral z 23117; rural
South Arlington; ARLINGTON; see South (RMC Place)
South Boston; Inc. Place; HALIFAX; **244** M-9; 🅿 🅷; z 24592; Ⓟ 6,997; Ⓒ 8,491
South Chesconessex; RMC Place; ACCOMACK; ***245** I-19; elev. 4ft./1m.; mail Onancock z 23417; ● 100
South Chester; RMC Place; CHESTERFIELD; ★ **RICH**; mail Chester z 23831
South Clinchfield; RMC Place; RUSSELL; **244** C-5; mail Cleveland z 24225; ● 150
Southern Estates; RMC Place; PRINCE GEORGE; ***245** K-14; elev. 145ft./44m.; ★ **RICH**; mail Petersburg z 23805; ● 130
Southern Pine; RMC Place; DINWIDDIE; ***245** K-14; elev. 130ft./40m.; ★ **RICH**; mail Petersburg z 23803; ● 180
South Fairlington; RMC Place; ARLINGTON; ***245** E-15; ★ **WASH**; mail Arlington z 22206
South Fairview; RMC Place; CHESAPEAKE (Independent City); ***245** L-18; ★ **NORF-**; mail Chesapeake z 23325; pop. incl. with Chesapeake (Independent City)
South Garden; RMC Place; ALBEMARLE; ***244** H-10; mail North Garden z 22959; rural
South Hill; Inc. Place; MECKLENBURG; **245** M-12; 🅿 🅷; z 23970; Ⓟ 4,217; Ⓒ 4,403
South Jackson; RMC Place; SHENANDOAH; ***244** E-10; mail Mount Jackson z 22842; ● 230
Southland Acres; RMC Place; LYNCHBURG (Independent City); ***244** K-8; ★ **LYNCH**; mail Lynchburg z 24502; pop. incl. with Lynchburg (Independent City)
South Martinsville; RMC Place; MARTINSVILLE (Independent City); ★ **MRTNV**; mail Martinsville z 24112; pop. incl. with Martinsville (Independent City)
South Norfolk; RMC Place; CHESAPEAKE (Independent City); 🅿; ★ **NORF-**; z 23324; pop. incl. with Chesapeake (Independent City)
South Plains; RMC Place; PETERSBURG (Independent City); ★ **RICH**; mail Petersburg z 23805; pop. incl. with Petersburg (Independent City)
Southport; RMC Place; PRINCE WILLIAM; ★ **WASH**; mail Woodbridge z 22191
South Richmond; RMC Place; RICHMOND (Independent City); ★ **RICH**; pop. incl. with Richmond (Independent City)
Southridge; RMC Place; FAIRFAX; ***245** D-14; ★ **WASH**; mail Mc Lean z 22101
South Roanoke; RMC Place; ROANOKE (Independent City); ★ **ROAN**; mail Roanoke z 24014; pop. incl. with Roanoke (Independent City)
Southside; RMC Place; RICHMOND (Independent City); ★ **RICH**; mail Richmond z 23224; pop. incl. with Richmond (Independent City)
South Suffolk; RMC Place; SUFFOLK (Independent City); ***245** M-17; ★ **NORF-**; mail Suffolk z 23434; pop. incl. with Suffolk (Independent City)
South Washington; RMC Place; ARLINGTON
Southwood; RMC Place; FAIRFAX; ★ **WASH**; mail Alexandria z 22309
South Woodley; RMC Place; FAIRFAX; ***245** D-14; ★ **WASH**; mail Falls Church z 22046; ● 1,100
Spainville; RMC Place; NOTTOWAY; ***245** K-12; elev. 393ft./120m.; mail Blackstone z 23824; rural
Spanish Grove (Lawson's Store); RMC Place; MECKLENBURG; ***244** M-10; elev. 564ft./172m.; mail Chase City z 23924; rural
Sparkling Springs; RMC Place; ROCKINGHAM; ***244** F-9; mail Linville z 22834; ● 50
Sparta; RMC Place; CAROLINE; **245** H-14; elev. 174ft./53m.; 🅿; z 22552; ● 30
Spec (Fringer); RMC Place; BOTETOURT; ***244** J-6; ★ **ROAN**; mail Buchanan z 24066; rural
Speedwell; RMC Place; WYTHE; **244** M-2; 🅿; z 24374; ● 300
Speegleville; RMC Place; HAMPTON (Independent City); ★ **NN-H**; mail Hampton z 23666; pop. incl. with Hampton (Independent City)
Spencer; RMC Place; HENRY; **244** M-6; elev. 883ft./269m.; 🅿; ★ **MRTNV**; z 24165; ● 180
Sperryville; RMC Place; RAPPAHANNOCK; **245** E-11; 🅿; z 22740; ● 400
Spitler (Longs Store); RMC Place; PAGE; ***244** E-10; mail Luray z 22835; rural
Spivey Store; RMC Place; SCOTT; ***244** D-4; mail Gate City z 24251; rural
Splash Dam; RMC Place; DICKENSON; ***244** B-5; elev. 1,260ft./384m.; mail Haysi z 24256; rural
Spotsylvania; RMC Place; ⊡ SPOTSYLVANIA; **245** G-13; 🅿; ★ **FRED**; z 22551, z 22553; ● 600
SPOTSYLVANIA; **245** H-13; Ⓟ 57,403; Ⓒ 90,395; ◆ 118,166
Spotsylvania Courthouse; CDP-Census Area Only; SPOTSYLVANIA; ***245** G-13; ★ **FRED**; mail Spotsylvania z 22553; Ⓟ 2,694; Ⓒ 3,833
Spottswood; RMC Place; AUGUSTA; ***244** H-8; 🅿; z 24476; ● 100
Spout Spring; RMC Place; APPOMATTOX; **244** K-9; 🅿; z 24593; ● 240
Springbrook Forest; RMC Place; FAIRFAX; ***245** E-14; ★ **WASH**; mail Annandale z 22003; ● 3,700
Spring City; RMC Place; RUSSELL; ***244** C-5; mail Cleveland z 24225; ● 50
Springcreek; RMC Place; ROCKINGHAM; ***244** F-9; mail Bridgewater z 22812; ● 100
Springdale; RMC Place; BRISTOL (Independent City); ★ **JNSC-**; mail Bristol z 24201; pop. incl. with Bristol (Independent City)
Springdale; RMC Place; HENRICO; ***245** J-14; ★ **RICH**; mail Richmond z 23222
Springfield; CDP; FAIRFAX; **249** I-4; 🅿; ★ **WASH**; z 20598, z 22009, z 22015, z 22150-53, z 22156, z 22158-61 & mail Alexandria z 22312; Ⓟ 23,706; Ⓒ 30,417; ◆ 31,608
Springfield; RMC Place; PAGE; ***245** E-11; mail Luray z 22835; ● 50
Springfield; RMC Place; ROCKBRIDGE; ***244** I-7; mail Buchanan z 24066; rural
Springfield Estates; RMC Place; FAIRFAX; ***245** E-15; ★ **WASH**; mail Springfield z 22150; ● 1,850
Springfield Forest; RMC Place; FAIRFAX; ***245** E-15; ★ **WASH**; mail Springfield z 22150; ● 1,000
Spring Garden; RMC Place; BRISTOL (Independent City); ***244** E-5; ★ **JNSC-**; mail Bristol z 24201; pop. incl. with Bristol (Independent City)
Spring Garden; RMC Place; PITTSYLVANIA; ***244** M-8; mail Chatham z 24531; ● 30
Spring Grove; RMC Place; SURRY; **245** K-15; elev. 107ft./33m.; 🅿; z 23881; ● 80
Springhaven Estates; RMC Place; FAIRFAX; ***245** D-14; ★ **WASH**; mail Mc Lean z 22102; ● 300
Spring Hill; RMC Place; AUGUSTA; ***244** G-9; mail Staunton z 24401; ● 80
Spring Meadows; RMC Place; HANOVER; ***245** I-14; ★ **RICH**; mail Mechanicsville z 23111
Spring Mills; RMC Place; APPOMATTOX, CAMPBELL; ***244** K-9; mail Concord z 24538; rural
Springvale; RMC Place; FAIRFAX; ***245** D-14; ★ **WASH**; mail Great Falls z 22066
Spring Valley; RMC Place; GRAYSON; ***244** M-2; mail Fries z 24330; ● 50
Spring Valley; RMC Place; STAFFORD; ***245** G-14; ★ **FRED**; mail Fredericksburg z 22401; ● 900
Springville; RMC Place; TAZEWELL; ***244** K-1; mail North Tazewell z 24630; ● 50
Springwood; RMC Place; BOTETOURT; **244** J-7; elev. 876ft./267m.; mail Buchanan z 24066; ● 170
Sprouses Corner; RMC Place; BUCKINGHAM; **245** J-11; 🅿; z 23936; ● 100
Stacy; RMC Place; BUCHANAN; **244** B-6; mail Grundy z 24614; ● 100
Stafford; RMC Place; ⊡ STAFFORD; **245** F-14; elev. 183ft./56m.; 🅿; ★ **WASH**; z 22554-56; ● 1,600
STAFFORD; **245** F-13; Ⓟ 61,236; Ⓒ 92,446; ◆ 121,585
Staffordshire; RMC Place; RICHMOND (Independent City); ★ **RICH**; mail Richmond z 23235; pop. incl. with Richmond (Independent City)
Staffordsville; RMC Place; GILES; ***244** K-3; 🅿; z 24167; ● 100
Stage Junction; RMC Place; FLUVANNA; ***245** I-12; mail Columbia z 23038; rural
Staleys Cross Roads; RMC Place; WYTHE; ***244** L-2; mail Rural Retreat z 24368; pop. incl. with Rural Retreat (Inc. Place)
Stanardsville; Inc. Place; ⊡ GREENE; **245** G-11; 🅿; z 22973; Ⓟ 257; Ⓒ 476
Stanley; Inc. Place; PAGE; **244** F-10; elev. 1,072ft./327m.; 🅿; z 22851; Ⓟ 1,186; Ⓒ 1,326
Stanleytown; CDP; HENRY; **244** M-6; 🅿; ★ **MRTNV**; z 24168; Ⓟ 1,563; Ⓒ 1,515
Stanleytown; RMC Place; SCOTT; ***244** D-4; mail Duffield z 24244; ● 50
Stapleton; RMC Place; AMHERST; ***244** J-9; elev. 457ft./139m.; ★ **LYNCH**; mail Madison Heights z 24572
Star (Island Creek); RMC Place; CARROLL; ***244** M-3; mail Hillsville z 24343; rural
Starkey; RMC Place; ROANOKE; ***244** K-6; ★ **ROAN**; mail Roanoke z 24018; ● 300
Starnes (Slant); RMC Place; SCOTT; ***244** D-4; mail Fort Blackmore z 24250
Star Tannery; RMC Place; FREDERICK; ***245** D-11; 🅿; z 22654; seasonal pop. 500; ● 50
State Farm; RMC Place; GOOCHLAND; ***245** I-13; 🅿; z 23160; ● 30
Statesville; RMC Place; SOUTHAMPTON; ***245** N-15; elev. 80ft./24m.; mail Newsoms z 23874; ● 50
Station Hills; RMC Place; FAIRFAX; ***245** E-14; ★ **WASH**; mail Fairfax Station z 22039; ● 110
Staunton; Independent City; serves as county seat of Augusta; **244** G-9; 🅿 🅷 🅲 2,195 ■; z 24401-02; Ⓟ 24,461; Ⓒ 23,853; ◆ 24,776
Staunton Park; RMC Place; STAUNTON (Independent City); ***244** G-9; mail Staunton z 24401; pop. incl. with Staunton (Independent City)
Steeleburg; RMC Place; TAZEWELL; ***244** L-1; mail Cedar Bluff z 24609; ● 110
Steeles Tavern; RMC Place; AUGUSTA, ROCKBRIDGE; **244** H-8; 🅿; z 24476; ● 150
Steinman; RMC Place; DICKENSON; ***244** B-5; mail Clinchco z 24226; ● 30
Stella; RMC Place; PATRICK; ***244** M-5; elev. 1,019ft./311m.; mail Patrick Springs z 24133
Stemphleytown; RMC Place; ROCKINGHAM; ***244** F-9; mail Dayton z 22821; rural
Stephens; RMC Place; WISE; **244** C-4; mail Wise z 24293; ● 400
Stephens City; Inc. Place; FREDERICK; **245** D-11; 🅿; z 22655; Ⓟ 1,186; Ⓒ 1,146
Stephenson; RMC Place; FREDERICK; **245** C-12; 🅿; z 22656; ● 560
Sterling (Sterling Park); RMC Place; LOUDOUN; **245** D-14; 🅿; ★ **WASH**; z 20163-67, z 20598; Ⓟ 20,512; ● 8,000
Sterling Park; LOUDOUN; see Sterling (RMC Place)
Sterling Point; RMC Place; PORTSMOUTH (Independent City); ***245** L-17; ★ **NORF-**; mail Portsmouth z 23703; pop. incl. with Portsmouth (Independent City)
Stevensburg; RMC Place; CULPEPER; **245** F-12; 🅿; z 22741; ● 140
Stevens Creek; RMC Place; GRAYSON; **244** M-3; mail Fries z 24330; ● 300
Stevensville; RMC Place; KING AND QUEEN; **245** I-15; 🅿; z 23161; ● 140
Stewart; RMC Place; RICHMOND (Independent City); ★ **RICH**; mail Richmond z 23221; pop. incl. with Richmond (Independent City)
Stewartsburg; RMC Place; ROCKBRIDGE; ***244** I-8; mail Buena Vista z 24416; rural
Stewartsville; RMC Place; BEDFORD; **244** K-6; ★ **ROAN**; mail Vinton z 24179; ● 100
Stickleyville; RMC Place; LEE; ***244** D-3; elev. 1,627ft./496m.; mail Duffield z 24244
Stingray Point; RMC Place; MIDDLESEX; ***245** J-17; elev. 5ft./2m.; mail Deltaville z 23043; ● 30
Stith; RMC Place; HALIFAX; ***244** M-10; elev. 504ft./154m.; mail Clover z 24534; rural
Stockton; RMC Place; HENRY; ***244** M-7; ★ **MRTNV**; mail Axton z 24054
Stoddert; RMC Place; CUMBERLAND; ***245** J-11; elev. 440ft./134m.; mail Farmville z 23901; rural
Stokesland; RMC Place; DANVILLE (Independent City); ★ **DANV**; mail Danville z 24541; pop. incl. with Danville (Independent City)
Stokesville; RMC Place; AUGUSTA; ***244** G-8; elev. 1,514ft./461m.; mail Mount Solon z 22843; rural
Stone Bridge; RMC Place; CLARKE; ***245** D-12; mail White Post z 22663; rural
Stone Creek; RMC Place; LEE; ***244** D-2; mail Pennington Gap z 24277; ● 200
Stonega; RMC Place; WISE; **244** C-3; elev. 1,827ft./557m.; 🅿; z 24216; ● 300
Stone Mountain; RMC Place; BEDFORD; ***244** K-7; mail Bedford z 24523; ● 80
Stones Mill; RMC Place; WYTHE; ***244** L-2; mail Wytheville z 24382; pop. incl. with Wytheville (Inc. Place)
Stone Springs; RMC Place; HARRISONBURG (Independent City); mail Harrisonburg z 22801; pop. incl. with Harrisonburg (Independent City)
Stonewall; RMC Place; APPOMATTOX; ***244** J-9; elev. 746ft./227m.; mail Concord z 24538; ● 30
Stonewall Acres; RMC Place; PRINCE WILLIAM; ***245** E-14; ★ **WASH**; mail Manassas z 20110
Stonewall Manor; RMC Place; FAIRFAX; ***245** D-14; elev. 388ft./118m.; ★ **WASH**; mail Vienna z 22180; ● 1,900
Stoneybrook; RMC Place; SPOTSYLVANIA; ***245** G-13; ★ **FRED**; mail Spotsylvania z 22553; ● 550
Stony; RMC Place; SCOTT; ***244** D-4; mail Dungannon z 24245; ● 30
Stony Battery; RMC Place; SMYTH; ***244** M-1; mail Marion z 24354; ● 50
Stony Creek; Inc. Place; SUSSEX; **245** L-14; 🅿; z 23882; Ⓟ 271; Ⓒ 202
Stony Man; RMC Place; PAGE; ***245** E-11; mail Luray z 22835; ● 30
Stony Point; RMC Place; ALBEMARLE; ***245** G-11; ★ **CHRLTV**; mail Charlottesville z 22911; ● 50
Stony Point Mills; RMC Place; CUMBERLAND; ***245** J-11; elev. 354ft./108m.; mail Cumberland z 23040; rural
Stony Ridge; RMC Place; TAZEWELL; ***244** K-1; mail North Tazewell z 24630; ● 90

Entries in **UPPERCASE** are counties.
Entries in **bold** have populations of 2,500 or more.
Names in parentheses are alternate names.

Inc. Place	Incorporated Place
RMC Place	Rand McNally Designated Place
CDP	Census Designated Place
MCD	Minor Civil Division

⊡ County Seat
▲ Minor Civil Division
elev. Elevation
🅿 Post Office
🅷 Hospital
🅲 College
■ Principal Business Center
★ Ranally Metro Area (RMA) Abbreviation
z Zip Code(s)
Ⓟ Previous Census Population
Ⓡ Revised Census Population
Ⓐ Annexation Population
● Rand McNally Population Estimate
Ⓒ Final Census Population
Ⓢ Special Census Population
◆ Estimated Population

For additional definitions see Glossary, Volume 1, and Introduction, Volume 2.

Stormont; RMC Place; MIDDLESEX; ***245** I-17; elev. 93ft./28m.; mail Saluda **z** 23149; rural
Story; RMC Place; SOUTHAMPTON; ***245** M-15; elev. 69ft./21m.; mail Courtland **z** 23837; rural
Stott; ISLE OF WIGHT; see Stotts Crossroads (RMC Place)
Stotts Crossroads (Stott); RMC Place; ISLE OF WIGHT; ***245** L-16; elev. 83ft./25m.; mail Zuni **z** 23898; rural
Stovall; RMC Place; HALIFAX; ***244** L-9; mail Nathalie **z** 24577; rural
Stover; RMC Place; AUGUSTA; ***244** G-8; elev. 1,512ft./461m.; mail Churchville **z** 24421; rural
Straightstone; RMC Place; PITTSYLVANIA; ***244** L-8; mail Long Island **z** 24569; rural
Strasburg; Inc. Place; SHENANDOAH; **245** D-11; elev. 578ft./176m.; 🅿; **z** 22641, **z** 22657; ℗ 3,762; © 4,017
Strasburg Junction; RMC Place; SHENANDOAH; ***245** D-11; mail Strasburg **z** 22657; ● 50
Stratford; RMC Place; WESTMORELAND; ***245** G-16; 🅿; **z** 22558; rural
Stratford Hills; RMC Place; ARLINGTON; ***245** D-15; ★ **WASH**; mail Arlington **z** 22207
Stratford Hills; RMC Place; RICHMOND (Independent City); ***245** J-14; ★ **RICH**; mail Richmond **z** 23225; pop. incl. with Richmond (Independent City)
Stratford Landing; RMC Place; FAIRFAX; ***245** E-15; ★ **WASH**; mail Alexandria **z** 22308; ● 2,900
Stratford-on-the-Potomac; RMC Place; FAIRFAX; ***245** E-15; ★ **WASH**; mail Alexandria **z** 22308; ● 1,400
Stratford Village; RMC Place; HENRICO; ***245** J-14; ★ **RICH**; mail Richmond **z** 23222; ● 300
Strathmeade Springs; RMC Place; FAIRFAX; ***245** D-14; ★ **WASH**; mail Annandale **z** 22003; ● 1,800
Strathmore; RMC Place; FLUVANNA; ***245** I-11; mail Bremo Bluff **z** 23022; rural
Stratton (Allen); RMC Place; DICKENSON; ***244** C-5; mail Clinchco **z** 24226; rural
Stric; BUCHANAN; see Big Rock (RMC Place)
Stringtown; RMC Place; CLARKE; ***245** C-12; mail Berryville **z** 22611; rural
Stringtown; WYTHE; see Kindrick (RMC Place)
Stroupes Store; RMC Place; WYTHE; ***244** L-2; mail Wytheville **z** 24382; rural
Stuart; Inc. Place; ⊡ PATRICK; **244** M-5; 🅿 🅷; **z** 24171; ℗ 965; © 961
Stuarts Draft; CDP; AUGUSTA; **244** H-9; 🅿; **z** 24477; ℗ 5,087; © 8,367
Stubbs; RMC Place; SPOTSYLVANIA; ***245** G-13; mail Spotsylvania **z** 22553; rural
Studley; RMC Place; HANOVER; **245** I-14; elev. 177ft./54m.; 🅿; ★ **RICH**; **z** 23162; ● 200
Stukeley Hall Farms; RMC Place; HENRICO; ***245** I-14; ★ **RICH**; mail Richmond **z** 23227; ● 140
Stumptown; RMC Place; LOUDOUN; ***245** C-13; mail Leesburg **z** 20176; rural
Stumptown; RMC Place; NORTHAMPTON; ***245** J-19; mail Eastville **z** 23347; rural
Suburban Apartments; RMC Place; HENRICO; ***245** I-14; ★ **RICH**; mail Richmond **z** 23230; ● 1,400
Sudley; CDP; PRINCE WILLIAM; ***245** E-14; ★ **WASH**; mail Manassas **z** 20109; ℗ 7,321; © 7,719
Sudley Manor; RMC Place; PRINCE WILLIAM; ***245** E-13; ★ **WASH**; mail Manassas **z** 20109
Suffolk; Independent City; **245** M-17; 🅿 🅷 ■; ★ **NORF-**; **z** 23432-39; ℗ 52,141; © 63,677; ◆ 81,737
Sugar Grove; CDP; SMYTH; **244** M-1; elev. 2,588ft./789m.; 🅿; **z** 24375; © 741
Sugar Hill; RMC Place; CAMPBELL; ***244** L-9; mail Brookneal **z** 24528; rural
Sugarland Run; RMC Place; LOUDOUN; ***245** D-14; ★ **WASH**; mail Sterling **z** 20164; ℗ 9,357
Sugar Loaf; RMC Place; ROANOKE; **244** H-1; ★ **ROAN**; mail Roanoke **z** 24018; ● 2,500
Suiter; RMC Place; BLAND; ***244** K-2; mail Bastian **z** 24314; ● 30
Sulgrave Manor; RMC Place; FAIRFAX; ***245** E-15; ★ **WASH**; mail Alexandria **z** 22309
Sumerduck; RMC Place; FAUQUIER; ***245** F-13; 🅿; **z** 22742; ● 100
Summerdeon; RMC Place; AUGUSTA; ***244** H-8; mail Swoope **z** 24479; rural
Summit; RMC Place; SMYTH; ***244** M-1; elev. 2,605ft./794m.; mail Sugar Grove **z** 24375; rural
Summit; RMC Place; SPOTSYLVANIA; ***245** G-14; elev. 220ft./67m.; ★ **FRED**; mail Fredericksburg **z** 22401; rural
Sun (Midway); RMC Place; RUSSELL; ***244** C-5; mail Castlewood **z** 24224; ● 150
Sunbeam; RMC Place; SOUTHAMPTON; ***245** M-15; elev. 83ft./25m.; mail Franklin **z** 23851; ● 100
Sunnybank; RMC Place; NORTHUMBERLAND; ***245** H-17; mail Reedville **z** 22539; ● 200
Sunnybrook; RMC Place; FAIRFAX; ***245** D-14; ★ **WASH**; mail Vienna **z** 22182; ● 1,500
Sunnybrook Estates; RMC Place; PRINCE WILLIAM; ***245** E-14; ★ **WASH**; mail Manassas **z** 20110
Sunny Side; RMC Place; CUMBERLAND; ***245** J-12; elev. 370ft./113m.; mail Cumberland **z** 23040
Sunnyside; RMC Place; FREDERICK; ***245** C-11; mail Winchester **z** 22603; ● 300
Sunny View; RMC Place; FAIRFAX; ***245** E-15; ★ **WASH**; mail Alexandria **z** 22309
Sunray; RMC Place; CHESAPEAKE (Independent City); ***245** M-17; ★ **NORF-**; mail Chesapeake **z** 23321; pop. incl. with Chesapeake (Independent City)
Sunset Heights; RMC Place; HENRICO; ★ **RICH**; mail Henrico **z** 23231
Sunset Hills; RMC Place; FAIRFAX; ***245** D-14; ★ **WASH**; mail Reston **z** 20190
Sunset Manor; RMC Place; FAIRFAX; ***245** E-15; ★ **WASH**; mail Alexandria **z** 22312
Sunset Village; RMC Place; SALEM (Independent City); ***244** K-6; ★ **ROAN**; mail Salem **z** 24153; pop. incl. with Salem (Independent City)
Supply; RMC Place; ESSEX; **245** H-15; elev. 185ft./56m.; 🅿; **z** 22436; ● 60
Surrey Square; RMC Place; FAIRFAX; ***245** E-14; ★ **WASH**; mail Fairfax **z** 22032; ● 300
Surry; Inc. Place; ⊡ SURRY; **245** K-16; 🅿; **z** 23883; ℗ 192; © 262
SURRY; **245** K-15; ℗ 6,145; © 6,829; ◆ 7,230
Susan; RMC Place; MATHEWS; ***245** J-17; elev. 10ft./3m.; 🅿; ★ **NN-H**; **z** 23163; ● 200
Sussex; RMC Place; ⊡ SUSSEX; **245** L-14; elev. 110ft./34m.; 🅿; **z** 23884; ● 40
SUSSEX; **245** L-14; ℗ 10,248; © 12,504; ◆ 12,468
Sussex Hilton; RMC Place; NEWPORT NEWS (Independent City); ★ **NN-H**; mail Newport News **z** 23605; pop. incl. with Newport News (Independent City)
Sutherland; RMC Place; DINWIDDIE; **245** K-13; 🅿; **z** 23885; ● 100
Sutherland; RMC Place; WISE; ***244** C-4; mail Haysi **z** 24256; rural
Sutherland Manor; RMC Place; DINWIDDIE; ***245** K-13; elev. 250ft./76m.; ★ **RICH**; mail Sutherland **z** 23885; ● 250
Sutherlin; RMC Place; HALIFAX, PITTSYLVANIA; ***244** M-8; 🅿; **z** 24594; ● 70
Sutton Place; RMC Place; FAIRFAX; ***245** D-14; ★ **WASH**; mail Fairfax **z** 22031; ● 360
Sutton Woods; RMC Place; FAIRFAX; ***245** D-14; ★ **WASH**; mail Vienna **z** 22181
Swansea Manor; RMC Place; NEWPORT NEWS (Independent City); ★ **NN-H**; mail Newport News **z** 23601; pop. incl. with Newport News (Independent City)
Swansonville; RMC Place; PITTSYLVANIA; ***244** M-7; mail Dry Fork **z** 24549
Sweet Briar; RMC Place; AMHERST; ***244** J-9; 🅿 🅲 751; ★ **LYNCH**; **z** 24595; ● 250
Sweet Briar Park; RMC Place; HENRICO; ***245** I-14; elev. 250ft./76m.; ★ **RICH**; mail Henrico **z** 23075; ● 180
Sweet Chalybeate; RMC Place; ALLEGHANY; ***244** I-5; mail Covington **z** 24426
Sweet Hall; RMC Place; KING WILLIAM; ***245** J-15; mail West Point **z** 23181; rural
Swift Creek; RMC Place; COLONIAL HEIGHTS (Independent City); ★ **RICH**; mail Colonial Heights **z** 23834; pop. incl. with Colonial Heights (Independent City)
Swift Run; RMC Place; ROCKINGHAM; ***244** F-10; mail Elkton **z** 22827; rural
Switch Back; RMC Place; BATH; ***244** H-6; mail Hot Springs **z** 24445; ● 100
Swoope; RMC Place; AUGUSTA; ***244** G-8; 🅿; **z** 24479; ● 60
Swords Creek; RMC Place; RUSSELL; **244** C-6; 🅿; **z** 24649; ● 400
Sycamore; RMC Place; PITTSYLVANIA; ***244** L-8; mail Gretna **z** 24557; ● 50
Sydnorsville; RMC Place; FRANKLIN; ***244** L-6; elev. 1,166ft./355m.; mail Rocky Mount **z** 24151
Sylvania Heights; RMC Place; SPOTSYLVANIA; ***245** G-14; ★ **FRED**; mail Fredericksburg **z** 22401; ● 700
Sylvatus; RMC Place; CARROLL; **244** M-3; mail Hillsville **z** 24343; ● 80
Syria; RMC Place; MADISON; ***245** F-11; 🅿; **z** 22743; ● 120
Syringa; RMC Place; MIDDLESEX; ***245** I-17; elev. 60ft./18m.; 🅿; **z** 23169; ● 50

T

Tabb; RMC Place; YORK; **245** K-17; 🅿; ★ **NN-H**; **z** 23693; ● 950
Tabscott; RMC Place; GOOCHLAND; ***245** H-12; elev. 496ft./151m.; mail Columbia **z** 23038; rural
Tacoma; RMC Place; WISE; **244** C-4; elev. 2,000ft./610m.; mail Coeburn **z** 24230; ● 170
Taft; RMC Place; LANCASTER; ***245** I-17; mail White Stone **z** 22578; ● 80
Talbot Park; RMC Place; NORFOLK (Independent City); ***245** L-18; elev. 10ft./3m.; ★ **NORF-**; mail Norfolk **z** 23505; pop. incl. with Norfolk (Independent City)
Tall Oaks; RMC Place; FAIRFAX; ***245** E-14; ★ **WASH**; mail Annandale **z** 22003
Tallysville; RMC Place; NEW KENT; ***245** J-15; elev. 144ft./44m.; mail New Kent **z** 23124; rural
Tampico; YORK; see Hornsbyville (RMC Place)
Tamworth; RMC Place; CUMBERLAND; ***245** I-12; 🅿; **z** 23027; rural
Tangier; Inc. Place; ACCOMACK; **245** H-18; 🅿; **z** 23440; ℗ 659; © 604; ® 691
Tanglewood; RMC Place; CHESAPEAKE (Independent City); ***245** L-18; ★ **NORF-**; mail Chesapeake **z** 23325; pop. incl. with Chesapeake (Independent City)
Tannersville; RMC Place; TAZEWELL; **244** L-1; 🅿; **z** 24377; ● 100
Tappahannock; Inc. Place; ⊡ ESSEX; **245** H-16; elev. 22ft./7m.; 🅿 🅷; **z** 22560; ℗ 1,550; © 2,068; ® 2,138
Tara; RMC Place; ARLINGTON; ***245** D-15; ★ **WASH**; mail Arlington **z** 22205
Taro; RMC Place; CHARLOTTE; ***244** K-10; elev. 612ft./187m.; mail Cullen **z** 23934; ● 40
Tarpon; RMC Place; DICKENSON; ***244** B-5; elev. 2,022ft./616m.; mail Clintwood **z** 24228; ● 30
Tasley; RMC Place; ACCOMACK; **245** I-19; 🅿; **z** 23441; ● 300
Tatum; RMC Place; ORANGE; ***245** G-12; mail Unionville **z** 22567; rural
Tauxemont; RMC Place; FAIRFAX; ***245** E-15; ★ **WASH**; mail Alexandria **z** 22308
Taylors Store; RMC Place; FRANKLIN; ***244** K-6; mail Wirtz **z** 24184; rural
Taylorstown; RMC Place; LOUDOUN; ***245** C-13; mail Leesburg **z** 20176
Taylors Valley; RMC Place; WASHINGTON; ***244** M-1; mail Damascus **z** 24236; ● 230
Taylorsville; RMC Place; HANOVER; ***245** I-14; mail Doswell **z** 23047
Taylorwood Estates; RMC Place; CHESAPEAKE (Independent City); ***245** L-17; ★ **NORF-**; mail Chesapeake **z** 23321; pop. incl. with Chesapeake (Independent City)
Tazewell; Inc. Place; ⊡ TAZEWELL; **244** K-1; elev. 2,519ft./768m.; 🅿 🅷; **z** 24608, **z** 24651; ℗ 4,176; © 4,206
TAZEWELL; **244** L-1; ℗ 45,960; © 44,598; ◆ 43,458
Teas; RMC Place; SMYTH; ***244** M-1; mail Sugar Grove **z** 24375
Teaverton; RMC Place; AUGUSTA; ***244** H-9; elev. 1,359ft./414m.; mail Fishersville **z** 22939; ● 100
Temperanceville; RMC Place; ACCOMACK; **245** H-20; 🅿; **z** 23442; ● 750
Temple Hall Estates; RMC Place; JAMES CITY; ***245** J-16; elev. 50ft./15m.; ★ **NN-H**; mail Toano **z** 23168; ● 140
Temple Hill; RMC Place; RUSSELL; ***244** D-5; mail Castlewood **z** 24224
Templeman; RMC Place; WESTMORELAND; **245** H-16; mail Montross **z** 22520; ● 40
Tenso; RMC Place; DICKENSON; ***244** B-5; mail Clinchco **z** 24226; pop. incl. with Clinchco (Inc. Place)
Tenth Legion; RMC Place; ROCKINGHAM; **244** F-10; mail Broadway **z** 22815; ● 80
Terrys Fork; RMC Place; FLOYD; ***244** L-5; elev. 2,660ft./811m.; mail Pilot **z** 24138
Tetotum; RMC Place; KING GEORGE; ***245** G-15; mail King George **z** 22485; ● 30
Thaxton; RMC Place; BEDFORD; **244** K-7; 🅿; **z** 24174; ● 250
The English Hills; RMC Place; FAIRFAX; ***245** E-14; ★ **WASH**; mail Fairfax Station **z** 22039; ● 150
The Harbors of Newport; RMC Place; PRINCE WILLIAM; ***245** E-14; ★ **WASH**; mail Woodbridge **z** 22191; ● 500
The Hollow; RMC Place; PATRICK; ***244** N-4; mail Ararat **z** 24053
The Knolls; RMC Place; PRINCE WILLIAM; ★ **WASH**; mail Woodbridge **z** 22191
Thelma; RMC Place; LOUISA; ***245** H-11; elev. 513ft./156m.; mail Gordonsville **z** 22942; rural
The Manors; RMC Place; PRINCE WILLIAM; ***245** E-14; ★ **WASH**; mail Woodbridge **z** 22192
The Meadows; ALBEMARLE; see Hessian Hills (RMC Place)
The Plains; Inc. Place; FAUQUIER; **245** E-13; 🅿; **z** 20198; ℗ 219; © 266
The Ridge; RMC Place; MECKLENBURG; ***245** M-11; elev. 378ft./115m.; mail Boydton **z** 23917; ● 50
Thessalia; RMC Place; GILES; ***244** K-3; mail Pearisburg **z** 24134; rural
The Timbers; RMC Place; FAIRFAX; ***245** E-14; ★ **WASH**; mail Springfield **z** 22152
The Villas; RMC Place; PRINCE WILLIAM; ★ **WASH**; mail Woodbridge **z** 22191
Thomas Bridge; RMC Place; SMYTH; ***244** M-1; mail Marion **z** 24354; ● 200
Thomas Corner; RMC Place; NORFOLK (Independent City); ***245** L-18; ★ **NORF-**; mail Norfolk **z** 23502, **z** 23506, **z** 23541; pop. incl. with Norfolk (Independent City)
Thomas Terrace; RMC Place; CAMPBELL; ***244** J-9; ★ **LYNCH**; mail Lynchburg **z** 24504; ● 350
Thomastown; RMC Place; BATH; ***244** H-6; mail Hot Springs **z** 24445; ● 100
Thompson Valley; RMC Place; TAZEWELL; ***244** L-1; elev. 2,743ft./836m.; mail Tazewell **z** 24651; ● 50
Thornburg; RMC Place; SPOTSYLVANIA; **245** G-13; 🅿; ★ **FRED**; **z** 22565; ● 420
Thornhill; RMC Place; ORANGE; ***245** G-12; 🅿; **z** 22960; rural
Thorn Valley; RMC Place; WYTHE; ***244** L-3; elev. 1,962ft./598m.; mail Austinville **z** 24312; ● 50
Thoroughfare; RMC Place; PRINCE WILLIAM; ***245** E-13; ★ **WASH**; mail Broad Run **z** 20137; ● 50
Thoroughgood; RMC Place; VIRGINIA BEACH (Independent City); ***245** L-18; elev. 15ft./5m.; ★ **NORF-**; mail Virginia Beach **z** 23455; pop. incl. with Virginia Beach (Independent City)
Three Forks; RMC Place; CAMPBELL; ***244** K-9; elev. 849ft./259m.; mail Rustburg **z** 24588; rural
Threemile Corner; RMC Place; LOUISA; ***245** H-12; elev. 378ft./115m.; mail Mineral **z** 23117; rural
Three Springs; RMC Place; WASHINGTON; **234** I-5; ★ **JNSC-**; mail Bristol **z** 24202; ● 120
Three Square; RMC Place; GOOCHLAND; ***245** I-12; elev. 303ft./92m.; mail Goochland **z** 23063; rural
Three Square; RMC Place; LOUISA; ***245** I-13; elev. 360ft./110m.; mail Bumpass **z** 23024; ● 30
Threeway; RMC Place; WESTMORELAND; ***245** H-16; elev. 133ft./41m.; mail Hague **z** 22469; rural
Tibbstown; RMC Place; ORANGE; ***245** G-11; mail Gordonsville **z** 22942; ● 70
Tibitha; RMC Place; NORTHUMBERLAND; ***245** H-17; elev. 14ft./4m.; mail Reedville **z** 22539; ● 80
Ticktown; RMC Place; ACCOMACK; ***245** I-19; mail Accomac **z** 23301; rural
Tidemill; RMC Place; GLOUCESTER; ***245** K-17; ★ **NN-H**; mail Hayes **z** 23072; ● 160
Tidewater; RMC Place; RICHMOND; ***245** H-16; elev. 30ft./9m.; mail Warsaw **z** 22572
Tidewater Junction; RMC Place; NORFOLK (Independent City); ★ **NORF-**; pop. incl. with Norfolk (Independent City)
Tidwells; RMC Place; WESTMORELAND; ***245** G-16; elev. 15ft./5m.; mail Montross **z** 22520; rural
Tight Squeeze; RMC Place; PITTSYLVANIA; ***244** M-8; elev. 720ft./219m.; mail Chatham **z** 24531; rural
Tignor; RMC Place; CAROLINE; ***245** H-15; elev. 177ft./54m.; mail Milford **z** 22514; rural
Timberlake; CDP; CAMPBELL; **244** K-8; 🅿; ★ **LYNCH**; **z** 24502 & mail Forest **z** 24551; ℗ 10,314; © 10,683
Timberly Heights; RMC Place; PETERSBURG (Independent City); ★ **RICH**; mail Petersburg **z** 23803; pop. incl. with Petersburg (Independent City)
Timber Ridge; RMC Place; ROCKBRIDGE; ***244** I-8; elev. 1,419ft./433m.; mail Lexington **z** 24450; ● 50
Timberville; Inc. Place; ROCKINGHAM; **244** E-10; 🅿; **z** 22853; ℗ 1,596; © 1,739
Timothy Park; RMC Place; FAIRFAX; ***245** E-15; ★ **WASH**; mail Alexandria **z** 22309
Tiny; RMC Place; DICKENSON; ***244** C-5; mail Birchleaf **z** 24220; rural
Tiptop; RMC Place; TAZEWELL; **244** K-1; 🅿; **z** 24630; ● 200
Tito; RMC Place; SCOTT; ***244** D-3; mail Duffield **z** 24244; rural
Tivis; RMC Place; DICKENSON; ***244** B-5; elev. 1,894ft./577m.; mail Haysi **z** 24256; rural
Toano; RMC Place; JAMES CITY; **245** J-16; 🅿; ★ **NN-H**; **z** 23168; ● 1,200
Tobaccoville; RMC Place; POWHATAN; ***245** J-12; elev. 396ft./121m.; mail Powhatan **z** 23139
Todds Tavern; RMC Place; SPOTSYLVANIA; ***245** G-13; ★ **FRED**; mail Spotsylvania **z** 22553; rural
Toga; RMC Place; BUCKINGHAM; ***244** J-10; elev. 568ft./173m.; mail Dillwyn **z** 23936; rural
Tola; RMC Place; CHARLOTTE; ***244** L-10; elev. 500ft./152m.; mail Phenix **z** 23959; rural
Toms Bottom; RMC Place; DICKENSON; mail Haysi **z** 24256; rural
Toms Brook; Inc. Place; SHENANDOAH; **245** D-11; 🅿; **z** 22660; ℗ 227; © 255
Toms Creek; RMC Place; WISE; ***244** C-4; mail Coeburn **z** 24230; ● 100
Tookland; RMC Place; BUCHANAN; **244** B-5; mail Grundy **z** 24614; ● 500
Topping; RMC Place; MIDDLESEX; ***245** I-17; elev. 46ft./14m.; 🅿; **z** 23169; ● 100
Toshes; RMC Place; PITTSYLVANIA; ***244** L-7; mail Pittsville **z** 24139
Totaro; RMC Place; BRUNSWICK; ***245** M-13; elev. 233ft./71m.; mail Freeman **z** 23856; rural
Town and Country Estates; RMC Place; FAIRFAX; ***245** D-14; ★ **WASH**; mail Vienna **z** 22180; ● 950
Townsend; RMC Place; NORTHAMPTON; ***245** K-19; elev. 33ft./10m.; 🅿; **z** 23443; ● 250
Trade Center; RMC Place; ALEXANDRIA (Independent City); mail Alexandria **z** 22304; pop. incl. with Alexandria (Independent City)
Trails End; NEW KENT; see Dillard's Landing (RMC Place)
Trammel; RMC Place; DICKENSON; **244** C-5; 🅿; **z** 24237; ● 400
Trapp; RMC Place; LOUDOUN; ***245** D-12; mail Upperville **z** 20184; rural
Treemont; RMC Place; CHESTERFIELD; ★ **RICH**; mail Richmond **z** 23234
Treherneville; RMC Place; NORTHAMPTON; ***245** J-19; mail Birdsnest **z** 23307; ● 250
Tremont; FAIRFAX; see Tremont Gardens (RMC Place)
Tremont Gardens (Tremont); RMC Place; FAIRFAX; ***245** D-14; ★ **WASH**; mail Falls Church **z** 22042; ● 1,550
Trenholm; RMC Place; POWHATAN; ***245** J-12; mail Powhatan **z** 23139; rural
Trents Mill; RMC Place; CUMBERLAND; ***245** J-11; elev. 251ft./77m.; mail Cumberland **z** 23040; rural
Trevilian; LOUISA; see Trevilians (RMC Place)
Trevilians (Trevilian); RMC Place; LOUISA; ***245** H-12; 🅿; **z** 23170; ● 50
Triangle; CDP; PRINCE WILLIAM; **245** F-14; 🅿; ★ **WASH**; **z** 22172; ℗ 4,740; © 5,500
Trigg; RMC Place; GILES; ***244** K-4; mail Pearisburg **z** 24134; rural
Trinity; RMC Place; BOTETOURT; ***244** J-6; ★ **ROAN**; mail Troutville **z** 24175; rural
Triplet; RMC Place; BRUNSWICK; **245** M-13; elev. 295ft./90m.; 🅿; **z** 23868; ● 40
Trout Dale; Inc. Place; GRAYSON; **244** M-1; 🅿; **z** 24378; ℗ 196; © 1,230; ® 194
Troutville; Inc. Place; BOTETOURT; **244** J-6; 🅿; ★ **ROAN**; **z** 24175 & mail Fincastle **z** 24090; ℗ 455; © 432
Trower; RMC Place; ACCOMACK; ***245** I-19; mail Wachapreague **z** 23480; ● 150
Troy; RMC Place; FLUVANNA; **245** H-11; 🅿; **z** 22974; ● 70
Trueblue; RMC Place; ORANGE; ***245** G-12; mail Culpeper **z** 22701; rural
Truxillo; RMC Place; AMELIA; ***245** J-12; elev. 383ft./117m.; mail Amelia Court House **z** 23002; rural
Tuckahoe; CDP; HENRICO; **243** B-6; ★ **RICH**; mail Henrico **z** 23229; ℗ 42,629; © 43,242; ◆ 49,564
Tuckahoe Park; RMC Place; HENRICO; ***245** I-13; elev. 300ft./91m.; ★ **RICH**; mail Henrico **z** 23229; ● 1,150
Tuckahoe Village; RMC Place; HENRICO; ***245** I-13; ★ **RICH**; mail Henrico **z** 23229; ● 4,200
Tucker Hill; RMC Place; WESTMORELAND; ***245** H-16; mail Kinsale **z** 22488; rural
Tuggle; RMC Place; PRINCE EDWARD; ***245** K-11; mail Farmville **z** 23901, Prospect **z** 23960; ● 30
Tunstall; RMC Place; NEW KENT; ***245** I-15; mail New Kent **z** 23124
Turbeville; RMC Place; HALIFAX; **244** M-9; 🅿; **z** 24592; ● 80
Turnbull; RMC Place; FAUQUIER; ***245** E-12; mail Warrenton **z** 20186; ● 30
Turners Crossroads; RMC Place; GREENSVILLE; ***245** N-13; elev. 126ft./38m.; mail Skippers **z** 23879; rural
Turner Store; RMC Place; BRUNSWICK; ***245** M-12; elev. 394ft./120m.; mail Meredithville **z** 23873; ● 30
Turnpike; RMC Place; FAIRFAX (Independent City); ★ **WASH**; mail Fairfax **z** 22031; pop. incl. with Fairfax (Independent City)
Tuscarora; RMC Place; ESSEX; mail Dunnsville **z** 22454; rural
Twin Pines; RMC Place; PORTSMOUTH (Independent City); ***245** L-17; ★ **NORF-**; mail Portsmouth **z** 23703; pop. incl. with Portsmouth (Independent City)
Twin Poplars; RMC Place; NELSON; ***244** H-9; elev. 700ft./213m.; mail Faber **z** 22938; rural
Twin Springs; RMC Place; SCOTT; ***244** D-4; mail Nickelsville **z** 24271; rural
Twymans Mill; RMC Place; MADISON; ***245** G-11; 🅿; **z** 22727; rural
Tye River; RMC Place; NELSON; ***244** I-9; 🅿; **z** 22922; ● 70
Tyler Gardens; RMC Place; FALLS CHURCH (Independent City); ***245** D-14; ★ **WASH**; mail Falls Church **z** 22046; pop. incl. with Falls Church (Independent City)
Tyler Park; RMC Place; FAIRFAX; **249** G-4; ★ **WASH**; mail Falls Church **z** 22042; ● 1,250
Tylerton; RMC Place; STAFFORD; ***245** G-14; ★ **FRED**; mail Fredericksburg **z** 22401; ● 400
Tyree; RMC Place; LYNCHBURG (Independent City); ★ **LYNCH**; pop. incl. with Lynchburg (Independent City)
Tyro; RMC Place; NELSON; ***244** I-9; 🅿; **z** 22976; ● 50
Tysons Corner; CDP; FAIRFAX; **249** F-3; ★ **WASH**; mail Vienna **z** 22182, West Mclean **z** 22103; ℗ 13,124; © 18,540
Tysons Green; RMC Place; FAIRFAX; ***245** D-14; ★ **WASH**; mail Vienna **z** 22182; ● 3,000

U

Union; RMC Place; BEDFORD; ***244** K-7; mail Thaxton **z** 24174; ● 30
Union; RMC Place; FLOYD; ***244** M-4; mail Willis **z** 24380; rural
Union Hall; CDP-Census Area Only; FRANKLIN; **244** L-7; 🅿; **z** 24176; © 957
Union Level; RMC Place; MECKLENBURG; ***245** M-11; elev. 419ft./128m.; mail South Hill **z** 23970; ● 100
Unionville; RMC Place; ORANGE; **245** G-12; 🅿; **z** 22567; ● 90
Unison; RMC Place; LOUDOUN; ***245** D-13; mail Round Hill **z** 20141; ● 50
Unity; RMC Place; SOUTHAMPTON; ***245** M-16; elev. 50ft./15m.; mail Zuni **z** 23898; rural
University Gardens Apartments; RMC Place; CHARLOTTESVILLE (Independent City); ★ **CHRLTV**; pop. incl. with Charlottesville (Independent City)
University Heights; RMC Place; HENRICO; ***245** J-13; elev. 264ft./80m.; ★ **RICH**; mail Henrico **z** 23229; ● 1,350
University of Richmond; RMC Place; RICHMOND (Independent City); ***245** J-14; 🅿; ★ **RICH**; **z** 23173
Uno; RMC Place; MADISON; ***245** G-11; 🅿; **z** 22738; rural
Upper Brandon; RMC Place; PRINCE GEORGE; ***245** K-15; elev. 23ft./7m.; mail Spring Grove **z** 23881; rural
Upperville; RMC Place; FAUQUIER; **245** D-12; 🅿; **z** 20184-85; ● 400
Upright; RMC Place; ESSEX; ***245** I-16; elev. 138ft./42m.; mail Dunnsville **z** 22454
Upshaw; RMC Place; KING WILLIAM; ***245** I-15; elev. 163ft./50m.; mail Aylett **z** 23009; rural
Urbanna; Inc. Place; MIDDLESEX; **245** I-16; 🅿; **z** 23175; ℗ 529; © 543

V

Vale; RMC Place; FAIRFAX; ***245** D-14; ★ **WASH**; mail Oakton **z** 22124
Valentine Hills; RMC Place; HENRICO; ***245** I-14; elev. 150ft./46m.; ★ **RICH**; mail Henrico **z** 23228; ● 500
Valentines; RMC Place; BRUNSWICK; **245** N-13; elev. 329ft./100m.; 🅿; **z** 23887; ● 60
Valley Brook; RMC Place; FAIRFAX; ***245** D-14; ★ **WASH**; mail Falls Church **z** 22042
Valley Creek; RMC Place; SCOTT; ***244** D-4; mail Nickelsville **z** 24271; rural
Valley Mills; RMC Place; AUGUSTA; mail Swoope **z** 24479; rural
Valley Ridge; RMC Place; ALLEGHANY; ***244** I-5; mail Covington **z** 24426; ● 270
Valley View; RMC Place; FAIRFAX; ***245** E-15; ★ **WASH**; mail Alexandria **z** 22306
Valleywood; RMC Place; PRINCE WILLIAM; ★ **WASH**; mail Woodbridge **z** 22191
Van Buren Furnace; RMC Place; SHENANDOAH; ***244** D-10; mail Maurertown **z** 22644; rural
Vanderpool; RMC Place; HIGHLAND; ***244** F-7; mail Monterey **z** 24465; rural
Vandola; RMC Place; PITTSYLVANIA; ***244** N-7; elev. 636ft./194m.; ★ **DANV**; mail Danville **z** 24541; ● 200
Vandyke; RMC Place; BUCHANAN; ***244** C-6; mail Raven **z** 24639; rural
Van Dyke; RMC Place; TAZEWELL; ***244** K-1; mail Cedar Bluff **z** 24609; rural
Vannoy Acres; RMC Place; FAIRFAX; ***245** E-14; ★ **WASH**; mail Fairfax **z** 22030
Vannoy Park; RMC Place; FAIRFAX; ***245** E-14; ★ **WASH**; mail Clifton **z** 20124; ● 50
Vansant; CDP; BUCHANAN; **244** B-5; 🅿; **z** 24656; ℗ 1,187; © 989
Varina; RMC Place; HENRICO; **243** E-9; ★ **RICH**; mail Henrico **z** 23231; ● 3,000
Varina Grove; RMC Place; HENRICO; ***245** J-14; elev. 140ft./43m.; ★ **RICH**; mail Henrico **z** 23075; ● 100
Vaucluse; RMC Place; FREDERICK; ***245** D-11; mail Stephens City **z** 22655; rural
Vaughn (Brand); RMC Place; PAGE; ***245** E-11; mail Luray **z** 22835; ● 30
Vawter Corner; RMC Place; LOUISA; ***245** G-12; elev. 371ft./113m.; mail Louisa **z** 23093; rural
Velma; RMC Place; KING AND QUEEN; ***245** I-16; elev. 80ft./24m.; mail Mascot **z** 23108; rural
Venia; RMC Place; BUCHANAN; ***244** C-6; 🅿; **z** 24260; ● 30
Vera; RMC Place; APPOMATTOX; **244** J-10; mail Appomattox **z** 24522; ● 60
Verbena; RMC Place; PAGE; ***244** F-10; mail Elkton **z** 22827; ● 80
Verdi; RMC Place; SCOTT; ***244** D-4; mail Duffield **z** 24244; rural
Vernon Hill; RMC Place; HALIFAX; **244** M-9; 🅿; **z** 24597; ● 60
Verona; CDP; AUGUSTA; **244** G-9; 🅿; **z** 24482; ℗ 3,479; © 3,638
Vertain Park; RMC Place; FAIRFAX; ***245** E-14; ★ **WASH**; mail Fairfax **z** 22032; ● 210
Vesta; RMC Place; PATRICK; **244** M-5; elev. 2,846ft./867m.; 🅿; **z** 24177; ● 150
Vests Store; RMC Place; POWHATAN; ***245** J-13; elev. 220ft./67m.; ★ **RICH**; mail Powhatan **z** 23139; rural
Vesuvius; RMC Place; ROCKBRIDGE; **244** H-8; elev. 1,429ft./436m.; 🅿; **z** 24483; ● 230
Vicey; RMC Place; BUCHANAN; ***244** B-5; elev. 1,424ft./434m.; mail Haysi **z** 24256; rural
Vicker; RMC Place; MONTGOMERY; ***244** K-4; mail Christiansburg **z** 24073; ● 150
Vicker Heights; RMC Place; MONTGOMERY; ***244** K-4; mail Christiansburg **z** 24073; ● 60
Vicksville; RMC Place; SOUTHAMPTON; ***245** M-15; mail Sedley **z** 23878; rural
Victoria; Inc. Place; LUNENBURG; **245** L-11; 🅿; **z** 23974; ℗ 1,830; © 1,821
Vienna; Inc. Place; FAIRFAX; **245** D-14; 🅿 🅲 530; ★ **WASH**; **z** 22027, **z** 22124, **z** 22180-83, **z** 22185; ℗ 14,852; © 14,453
Viers; RMC Place; DICKENSON; ***244** B-5; elev. 1,316ft./401m.; mail Haysi **z** 24256; rural
Viewtown; RMC Place; RAPPAHANNOCK; **245** E-12; 🅿; **z** 20106, **z** 22746; ● 50
Village; RMC Place; RICHMOND, NORTHUMBERLAND; **245** H-16; elev. 145ft./44m.; 🅿; **z** 22570; ● 130
Villa Heights; CDP-Census Area Only; HENRY; ***244** M-6; ★ **MRTNV**; mail Martinsville **z** 24112; ℗ 1,021; © 845
Villamay; RMC Place; FAIRFAX; ***245** E-15; ★ **WASH**; mail Alexandria **z** 22307; ● 1,250
Villamont; RMC Place; BEDFORD; **244** J-6; 🅿; ★ **ROAN**; **z** 24178; ● 200
Villboro; RMC Place; CAROLINE; ***245** G-14; mail Woodford **z** 22580
Vinegar Hill; RMC Place; CHARLOTTESVILLE (Independent City); ★ **CHRLTV**; pop. incl. with Charlottesville (Independent City)
Vinton; Inc. Place; ROANOKE; **244** K-6; 🅿; ★ **ROAN**; **z** 24179; ℗ 7,665; © 7,782
Virgilina; Inc. Place; HALIFAX; **244** N-10; 🅿; **z** 24598; ℗ 161; © 159
Virginia Beach; Independent City; **245** L-18; 🅿 🅷 🅲 9,846 ■; ★ **NORF-**; **z** 23450-67, **z** 23471, **z** 23479; ℗ 393,069; © 425,257; ◆ 433,228
Virginia City; RMC Place; WISE; ***244** C-5; mail Saint Paul **z** 24283; rural
Virginia Forest; RMC Place; FALLS CHURCH (Independent City); ***245** D-14; ★ **WASH**; mail Falls Church **z** 22046; pop. incl. with Falls Church (Independent City)
Virginia Heights; RMC Place; ARLINGTON; ***245** D-15; ★ **WASH**; mail Arlington **z** 22204
Virginia Heights; RMC Place; HENRICO; ***245** J-14; ★ **RICH**; mail Henrico **z** 23231; ● 550
Virginia Highlands; RMC Place; ARLINGTON; ***245** D-15; ★ **WASH**; mail Arlington **z** 22202
Virginia Hills; RMC Place; BRISTOL (Independent City); ★ **JNSC-**; mail Bristol **z** 24201; pop. incl. with Bristol (Independent City)
Virginia Hills; RMC Place; FAIRFAX; **249** I-5; ★ **WASH**; mail Alexandria **z** 22310; ● 2,840
Virginia Inland Port; RMC Place; WARREN; pop. incl. with Front Royal (Inc. Place)
Virginia Union University; RMC Place; RICHMOND (Independent City); ★ **RICH**; mail Richmond **z** 23220; pop. incl. with Richmond (Independent City)
Vir-Mar Beach; RMC Place; NORTHUMBERLAND; ***245** H-17; mail Heathsville **z** 22473; summer pop. 500; ● 10
Volens; RMC Place; HALIFAX; **244** L-9; elev. 679ft./207m.; mail Nathalie **z** 24577; ● 40
Volney; RMC Place; GRAYSON; **244** M-1; 🅿; **z** 24363; ● 30
Vulcan; RMC Place; ORANGE; ***245** G-12; mail Unionville **z** 22567; rural

W

Wabun; RMC Place; ROANOKE; ***244** K-5; elev. 1,116ft./340m.; ★ **ROAN**; mail Salem **z** 24153; ● 70
Wachapreague; Inc. Place; ACCOMACK; **245** I-19; 🅿; **z** 23480; ℗ 291; © 236
Wadesville; RMC Place; CLARKE; ***245** C-12; mail Berryville **z** 22611; ● 50
Waidsboro (Lanahan); RMC Place; FRANKLIN; ***244** L-6; mail Ferrum **z** 24088
Wake; RMC Place; MIDDLESEX; ***245** I-17; 🅿; **z** 23176; ● 80
Wakefield; RMC Place; ALEXANDRIA (Independent City); ***245** E-15; ★ **WASH**; mail Alexandria **z** 22304; pop. incl. with Alexandria (Independent City)
Wakefield; Inc. Place; SUSSEX; **245** L-15; 🅿; **z** 23888; ℗ 1,070; © 1,038
Wakefield Chapel; RMC Place; FAIRFAX; ***245** E-14; ★ **WASH**; mail Annandale **z** 22003; ● 220
Wakefield Forest; RMC Place; FAIRFAX; ***245** E-14; ★ **WASH**; mail Annandale **z** 22003
Wake Forest; RMC Place; MONTGOMERY; ***244** K-4; mail Blacksburg **z** 24060; ● 30
Wakeland Manor; RMC Place; FREDERICK; ***245** D-11; elev. 779ft./237m.; mail Stephens City **z** 22655; ● 300
Wakenva; RMC Place; DICKENSON; **244** C-5; mail Dante **z** 24237; ● 70
Waldrop; RMC Place; LOUISA; **245** H-11; elev. 508ft./155m.; mail Gordonsville **z** 22942; ● 60
Walhaven; RMC Place; FAIRFAX; ★ **WASH**; mail Alexandria **z** 22310
Walkers; RMC Place; NEW KENT; ***245** J-15; elev. 40ft./12m.; mail Lanexa **z** 23089; ● 50
Walker Store; RMC Place; MECKLENBURG; ***245** M-11; elev. 476ft./145m.; mail Chase City **z** 23924; rural
Walkers Well; RMC Place; PITTSYLVANIA; ***244** L-7; mail Chatham **z** 24531; rural
Walkerton; RMC Place; KING AND QUEEN; **245** I-15; 🅿; **z** 23177; ● 200
Wallace; RMC Place; WASHINGTON; ***244** D-5; ★ **JNSC-**; mail Bristol **z** 24202; ● 170
Wallaces Store; RMC Place; CHARLOTTE; ***244** L-10; mail Drakes Branch **z** 23937; rural
Wallaceton; RMC Place; CHESAPEAKE (Independent City); ***245** M-17; elev. 17ft./5m.; ★ **NORF-**; mail Chesapeake **z** 23323; pop. incl. with Chesapeake (Independent City)
Walnut Grove; RMC Place; WASHINGTON; ***244** D-5; mail Mendota **z** 24270; rural
Walnut Hill; RMC Place; PETERSBURG (Independent City); ***245** K-14; ★ **RICH**; mail Petersburg **z** 23805; pop. incl. with Petersburg (Independent City)
Walters; RMC Place; ISLE OF WIGHT; **245** M-16; 🅿; **z** 23315; ● 180
Walters Woods; RMC Place; FAIRFAX; ***245** D-15; ★ **WASH**; mail Falls Church **z** 22044
Walton; RMC Place; MONTGOMERY; ***244** K-4; mail Christiansburg **z** 24073; ● 50
Walton Furnace; RMC Place; WYTHE; ***244** L-3; mail Max Meadows **z** 24360; ● 30
Walton Park; RMC Place; CHESTERFIELD; ***245** J-13; elev. 300ft./91m.; ★ **RICH**; mail Midlothian **z** 23112; ● 500
Waltons Store; RMC Place; BEDFORD; ***244** K-8; mail Huddleston **z** 24104; rural
Wan; RMC Place; GLOUCESTER; ***245** J-17; elev. 86ft./26m.; ★ **NN-H**; mail Gloucester **z** 23061; rural
Ward; RMC Place; BUCHANAN; mail Hurley **z** 24620; rural
Wardell; RMC Place; TAZEWELL; ***244** C-6; mail Cedar Bluff **z** 24609; rural
Wards Corner; RMC Place; NORFOLK (Independent City); ***245** L-18; elev. 15ft./5m.; ★ **NORF-**; mail Norfolk **z** 23505; pop. incl. with Norfolk (Independent City)
Wards Mill; RMC Place; CARROLL; ***244** M-3; mail Galax **z** 24333; rural
Wardtown; RMC Place; NORTHAMPTON; ***245** J-19; elev. 25ft./8m.; 🅿; **z** 23482; ● 90
Ware Neck; RMC Place; GLOUCESTER; **245** J-17; 🅿; ★ **NN-H**; **z** 23178; ● 270
Wares Crossroads; RMC Place; LOUISA; ***245** H-12; elev. 428ft./130m.; mail Mineral **z** 23117; rural
Wares Wharf; RMC Place; ESSEX; ***245** H-16; mail Dunnsville **z** 22454; ● 30
Warfield; RMC Place; BRUNSWICK; **245** L-13; elev. 318ft./97m.; 🅿; **z** 23889; ● 100
Warminster; RMC Place; NELSON; ***244** I-10; mail Wingina **z** 24599; rural
Warm Springs; RMC Place; ⊡ BATH; **244** H-6; 🅿; **z** 24484; ● 280
Warner; RMC Place; MIDDLESEX; **245** I-16; elev. 103ft./31m.; 🅿; **z** 23175; ● 40
Warren; RMC Place; ALBEMARLE; ***244** I-10; mail Scottsville **z** 24590; ● 30
WARREN; **245** D-12; ℗ 26,142; © 31,584; ◆ 37,205
Warrenton; Inc. Place; ⊡ FAUQUIER; **245** E-13; 🅿 🅷; ★ **WASH**; **z** 20186-88; ℗ 4,830; © 6,670
Warren Woods; RMC Place; FAIRFAX (Independent City); ***245** E-14; ★ **WASH**; mail Fairfax **z** 22030
Warsaw; Inc. Place; ⊡ RICHMOND; **245** H-16; 🅿; **z** 22572; ℗ 961; © 1,375
Warwick; RMC Place; NEWPORT NEWS (Independent City); ***245** L-17; ★ **NN-H**; mail Newport News **z** 23601
Warwick on the James; RMC Place; NEWPORT NEWS (Independent City); ★ **NN-H**; mail Newport News **z** 23601; pop. incl. with Newport News (Independent City)
Warwick Village; RMC Place; ALEXANDRIA (Independent City); ***245** E-15; ★ **WASH**; mail Alexandria **z** 22305; pop. incl. with Alexandria (Independent City)
Washington; Inc. Place; ⊡ RAPPAHANNOCK; **245** E-11; 🅿; **z** 22747; ℗ 198; © 183
WASHINGTON; **244** D-6; ℗ 45,887; © 51,103; ◆ 54,138
Washington Corner; RMC Place; CAROLINE; ***245** G-14; elev. 167ft./51m.; mail Woodford **z** 22580; rural
Washington Gardens; RMC Place; HAMPTON (Independent City); ***245** L-17; ★ **NN-H**; mail Hampton **z** 23669; pop. incl. with Hampton (Independent City)
Washington National Airport; RMC Place; ARLINGTON; ***245** D-15; ★ **WASH**; mail Arlington **z** 22201
Washington Park; RMC Place; GREENSVILLE; ***245** M-13; elev. 150ft./46m.; mail Emporia **z** 23847; ● 400
Washington Square; RMC Place; FAIRFAX; ★ **WASH**; mail Alexandria **z** 22309
Watauga; RMC Place; WASHINGTON; ***244** D-6; elev. 1,936ft./590m.; mail Abingdon **z** 24211; rural
Waterford; RMC Place; LOUDOUN; **245** C-13; 🅿; **z** 20197; ● 400
Waterlick; RMC Place; WARREN; ***245** D-11; mail Strasburg **z** 22657; ● 100
Waterloo; RMC Place; ARLINGTON
Waterloo; RMC Place; CLARKE; ***245** D-12; mail White Post **z** 22663; ● 30
Water View; RMC Place; MIDDLESEX; **245** I-16; 🅿; **z** 23180; ● 180
Waterview; RMC Place; PORTSMOUTH (Independent City); ***245** L-17; ★ **NORF-**; mail Portsmouth **z** 23707; pop. incl. with Portsmouth (Independent City)
Watson; RMC Place; LOUDOUN; ***245** D-13; mail Leesburg **z** 20175; ● 30
Wattsville; RMC Place; ACCOMACK; ***245** H-20; 🅿; **z** 23483; ● 300
Waugh; RMC Place; BEDFORD; ***244** J-8; mail Big Island **z** 24526
Waverly; Inc. Place; SUSSEX; **245** L-15; 🅿; **z** 23890-91; ℗ 2,223; © 2,309
Waverly Hills; RMC Place; ARLINGTON; ***245** D-15; ★ **WASH**; mail Arlington **z** 22207
Waverly Village; RMC Place; SPOTSYLVANIA; ***245** G-13; ★ **FRED**; mail Fredericksburg **z** 22401; ● 700
Waxpool; RMC Place; LOUDOUN; ***245** D-13; ★ **WASH**; ● 50
Wayland; RMC Place; RICHMOND (Independent City); ***245** J-13; ★ **RICH**; mail Richmond **z** 23235; pop. incl. with Richmond (Independent City)
Waynesboro; Independent City; **244** H-9; 🅿 ■; **z** 22980; ℗ 18,549; © 19,520; ◆ 21,937
Waynewood; RMC Place; FAIRFAX; **249** J-6; ★ **WASH**; mail Alexandria **z** 22308; ● 3,450
Wayside; RMC Place; CHARLES CITY; ***245** J-15; elev. 88ft./27m.; mail Charles City **z** 23030; ● 40
Weal; RMC Place; PITTSYLVANIA; ***244** M-7; elev. 848ft./258m.; mail Chatham **z** 24531; rural
Webbtown; RMC Place; CLARKE; ***245** C-12; mail Berryville **z** 22611; rural
Weber City; RMC Place; FLUVANNA; ***245** I-11; elev. 471ft./144m.; mail Bremo Bluff **z** 23022; ● 30
Weber City; Inc. Place; SCOTT; **244** E-4; elev. 1,303ft./397m.; 🅿; ★ **JNSC-**; **z** 24290; ℗ 1,377; © 1,333
Wedgewood; RMC Place; HENRICO; ***245** I-13; elev. 300ft./91m.; ★ **RICH**; mail Henrico **z** 23229; ● 900
Weedonville; RMC Place; KING GEORGE; **245** G-15; mail King George **z** 22485; ● 180
Weems; RMC Place; LANCASTER; **245** I-17; 🅿; **z** 22576; ● 220
Weirwood; RMC Place; NORTHAMPTON; ***245** J-19; elev. 37ft./11m.; 🅿; **z** 23413; ● 100
Welchs; RMC Place; CAROLINE; ***245** H-14; mail Woodford **z** 22580; rural
Welcome; RMC Place; KING GEORGE; ***245** G-15; elev. 124ft./38m.; mail King George **z** 22485; rural
Wellford; RMC Place; RICHMOND; ***245** H-16; mail Warsaw **z** 22572
Wellington; RMC Place; FAIRFAX; **249** J-6; ★ **WASH**; mail Alexandria **z** 22308; ● 1,750
Wellington; RMC Place; PRINCE WILLIAM; ***245** E-13; ★ **WASH**; mail Manassas **z** 20109; ● 120
Wellington Heights; RMC Place; FAIRFAX; ***245** E-15; ★ **WASH**; mail Alexandria **z** 22308
Well Water; RMC Place; BUCKINGHAM; ***245** I-11; elev. 497ft./151m.; mail Scottsville **z** 24590; rural
West Arlington; RMC Place; ARLINGTON; ***245** D-15; ★ **WASH**; mail Arlington **z** 22213
West Augusta; RMC Place; AUGUSTA; **244** G-8; 🅿; **z** 24485; ● 200
West Bottom; RMC Place; FLUVANNA; ***245** I-11; mail Bremo Bluff **z** 23022; ● 30
Westbourne; RMC Place; HENRICO; ***245** I-14; ★ **RICH**; mail Richmond **z** 23230; ● 700
Westbriar; RMC Place; HENRICO; ***245** I-13; elev. 300ft./91m.; ★ **RICH**; mail Henrico **z** 23075; ● 300
Westchester; RMC Place; FAIRFAX; ***245** E-14; ★ **WASH**; mail Fairfax **z** 22031; ● 900
Westchester; RMC Place; RICHMOND (Independent City); ***245** J-13; ★ **RICH**; mail Richmond **z** 23235; pop. incl. with Richmond (Independent City)
Westdale; RMC Place; HENRICO; ***245** I-13; elev. 302ft./92m.; ★ **RICH**; mail Henrico **z** 23229; ● 900
West Dante; RMC Place; DICKENSON; ***244** C-5; mail Dante **z** 24237; ● 120
West End Manor; RMC Place; HENRICO; ***245** I-13; ★ **RICH**; mail Henrico **z** 23229; ● 2,100
Western; RMC Place; PETERSBURG (Independent City); ★ **RICH**; mail Petersburg **z** 23803; pop. incl. with Petersburg (Independent City)
West Falls Church; RMC Place; FALLS CHURCH (Independent City); ***245** D-14; ★ **WASH**; mail Falls Church **z** 22046; pop. incl. with Falls Church (Independent City)
Westfield; RMC Place; BRISTOL (Independent City); ★ **JNSC-**; mail Bristol **z** 24201; pop. incl. with Bristol (Independent City)
West Fork; RMC Place; PITTSYLVANIA; ***244** M-7; ★ **DANV**; mail Cascade **z** 24069; ● 250
West Fredericksburg; RMC Place; FREDERICKSBURG (Independent City); ★ **FRED**; mail Fredericksburg **z** 22401; pop. incl. with Fredericksburg (Independent City)
West Galax; RMC Place; GALAX (Independent City); ***244** M-3; mail Galax **z** 24333; pop. incl. with Galax (Independent City)
West Gate; CDP-Census Area Only; PRINCE WILLIAM; ***245** E-14; ★ **WASH**; mail Manassas **z** 20109; ℗ 6,565; © 7,493
West Gate of Lomond; RMC Place; PRINCE WILLIAM; ***245** E-14; ★ **WASH**; mail Manassas **z** 20109; ● 5,000
West Ghent; RMC Place; NORFOLK (Independent City); ***245** L-17; elev. 10ft./3m.; ★ **NORF-**; mail Norfolk **z** 23507; pop. incl. with Norfolk (Independent City)
Westgrove; RMC Place; FAIRFAX; ***245** E-15; ★ **WASH**; mail Alexandria **z** 22307
Westham; RMC Place; HENRICO; ***245** J-13; ★ **RICH**; mail Henrico **z** 23229; ● 4,800
Westhampton; RMC Place; FAIRFAX; ***245** D-14; ★ **WASH**; mail Falls Church **z** 22046; ● 900
Westhampton; RMC Place; HENRICO; ***245** J-14; ★ **RICH**; mail Richmond **z** 23226; ● 1,800
Westhaven; RMC Place; PORTSMOUTH (Independent City); ***245** L-17; ★ **NORF-**; mail Portsmouth **z** 23707; pop. incl. with Portsmouth (Independent City)
West Hope; RMC Place; SUSSEX; ***245** L-14; elev. 123ft./37m.; mail Stony Creek **z** 23882; ● 30
Westlake Corner; CDP-Census Area Only; FRANKLIN; ***244** K-7; © 899
Westland; RMC Place; LANCASTER; ***245** I-17; mail White Stone **z** 22578; ● 80
West Langley; RMC Place; FAIRFAX; ***245** D-14; ★ **WASH**; mail Mc Lean **z** 22101
Westlawn; RMC Place; FAIRFAX; ***245** D-14; ★ **WASH**; mail Falls Church **z** 22042; ● 2,550
West Leigh; RMC Place; ALBEMARLE; ***244** H-10; ★ **CHRLTV**; mail Charlottesville **z** 22901; ● 150
West Lexington; RMC Place; COVINGTON (Independent City); mail Lexington **z** 24450; pop. incl. with Covington (Independent City)
West Mclean; RMC Place; FAIRFAX; 🅿; **z** 22102-03
Westmoreland; RMC Place; ALBEMARLE; ***245** H-11; ★ **CHRLTV**; mail Charlottesville **z** 22901; ● 900
Westmoreland; WESTMORELAND; see Sandy Point (RMC Place)
WESTMORELAND; **245** G-15; ℗ 15,480; © 16,718; ◆ 17,709
Westmoreland Heights; RMC Place; FAIRFAX; ***245** D-15; ★ **WASH**; mail Falls Church **z** 22043; ● 800
Westmoreland Park; RMC Place; FAIRFAX; ***245** D-14; ★ **WASH**; mail Falls Church **z** 22046; ● 1,200
West Munden; RMC Place; CHESAPEAKE (Independent City); ***245** L-18; ★ **NORF-**; mail Chesapeake **z** 23324; pop. incl. with Chesapeake (Independent City)
West Norfolk; RMC Place; PORTSMOUTH (Independent City); ***245** L-17; ★ **NORF-**; mail Portsmouth **z** 23703; pop. incl. with Portsmouth (Independent City)
Westover; RMC Place; ARLINGTON; ***245** D-15; ★ **WASH**; mail Arlington **z** 22205
Westover; RMC Place; CHARLES CITY; ***245** K-15; mail Charles City **z** 23030; ● 40
Westover Hills; RMC Place; AUGUSTA; ***244** H-9; mail Waynesboro **z** 22980; ● 280
Westover Hills; RMC Place; DANVILLE (Independent City); ***244** M-7; ★ **DANV**; mail Danville **z** 24541; pop. incl. with Danville (Independent City)
Westover Hills; RMC Place; GREENSVILLE; ***245** M-13; elev. 150ft./46m.; mail Emporia **z** 23847; ● 650
Westover Hills; RMC Place; RICHMOND (Independent City); ***245** J-14; ★ **RICH**; mail Richmond **z** 23225; pop. incl. with Richmond (Independent City)
West Petersburg; RMC Place; DINWIDDIE; ***245** K-14; elev. 150ft./46m.; ★ **RICH**; mail Petersburg **z** 23803; ● 650
West Piney; RMC Place; WYTHE; ***244** L-3; mail Wytheville **z** 24382; ● 50
West Point; Inc. Place; KING WILLIAM; **245** J-16; 🅿; **z** 23181; ℗ 2,938; © 2,866
West Raven; RMC Place; TAZEWELL, RUSSELL; ***244** C-6; mail Raven **z** 24639; ● 100
West Springfield; CDP; FAIRFAX; **249** I-3; 🅿; ★ **WASH**; **z** 22152; ℗ 28,126; © 28,378; ◆ 29,494
Wests Store; RMC Place; HALIFAX; ***244** L-9; elev. 559ft./170m.; mail Nathalie **z** 24577; rural
Westview; RMC Place; AUGUSTA; ***244** G-8; mail Swoope **z** 24479; ● 60
West View; RMC Place; GOOCHLAND; ***245** I-12; elev. 186ft./57m.; mail Goochland **z** 23063; rural
Westview Hills; RMC Place; FAIRFAX; ***245** E-14; ★ **WASH**; mail Springfield **z** 22152
West Warm Springs (Shakerag); RMC Place; BATH; ***244** H-6; mail Warm Springs **z** 24484; ● 130
Westwood; RMC Place; HENRICO; 5 mi. NW of Richmond; elev. 250ft./76m.; ★ **RICH**; mail Richmond **z** 23226; ● 1,150
Westwood Estates; RMC Place; WASHINGTON; mail Abingdon **z** 24211; ● 600
Westwood Forest; RMC Place; FAIRFAX; ***245** D-14; ★ **WASH**; mail Vienna **z** 22182; ● 850
Westwood Park; RMC Place; FAIRFAX; ***245** D-14; ★ **WASH**; mail Falls Church **z** 22046; ● 3,600
Westwood Place; RMC Place; ALLEGHANY; ***244** I-6; elev. 1,440ft./439m.; mail Covington **z** 24426; ● 90
Weyanoke; RMC Place; FAIRFAX; **249** H-4; ★ **WASH**; mail Alexandria **z** 22312; ● 1,500
Weyers Cave; CDP; AUGUSTA; **244** G-9; 🅿; **z** 24486; © 1,225
Whaley; RMC Place; SUFFOLK (Independent City); ***245** M-16; ★ **NORF-**; mail Suffolk **z** 23438; pop. incl. with Suffolk (Independent City)
Whaleyville; RMC Place; SUFFOLK (Independent City); ***245** M-16; ★ **NORF-**; mail Suffolk **z** 23438; pop. incl. with Suffolk (Independent City)
Wheatfield; RMC Place; SHENANDOAH; ***245** D-11; mail Strasburg **z** 22641; rural
Wheatland; RMC Place; LOUDOUN; ***245** C-13; mail Purcellville **z** 20132; rural
Wheeler; RMC Place; LEE; ***244** D-1; mail Ewing **z** 24248; rural
Whitacre; RMC Place; FREDERICK; ***245** C-11; 🅿; **z** 22625; ● 70
White City; RMC Place; GREENSVILLE; ***245** M-14; elev. 130ft./40m.; mail Emporia **z** 23847; pop. incl. with Emporia (Independent City)
White Gate; RMC Place; GILES; ***244** K-3; elev. 1,926ft./587m.; mail Pearisburg **z** 24134; rural
White Hall; RMC Place; ALBEMARLE; ***244** G-10; elev. 722ft./220m.; 🅿; ★ **CHRLTV**; **z** 22987; ● 90
White Hall; RMC Place; FREDERICK; **244** H-10; mail Winchester **z** 22603
White Head Hall; RMC Place; SOUTHAMPTON; ***245** M-14; mail Branchville **z** 23828; rural
White Hill; RMC Place; AUGUSTA; ***244** H-9; mail Stuarts Draft **z** 24477; ● 200
White House; RMC Place; MECKLENBURG; ***244** M-10; elev. 395ft./120m.; mail Nelson **z** 24580; ● 50
White Marsh; RMC Place; GLOUCESTER; **244** E-4; elev. 55ft./17m.; 🅿; ★ **NN-H**; **z** 23183; ● 400
White Mill; RMC Place; WASHINGTON; ***244** D-6; mail Abingdon **z** 24210; rural
White Oak; RMC Place; HALIFAX; ***244** M-9; elev. 570ft./174m.; mail Halifax **z** 24558; ● 50
White Oak; RMC Place; STAFFORD; ***245** G-14; ★ **FRED**; mail Fredericksburg **z** 22401; ● 250
White Oaks; RMC Place; FAIRFAX; ***245** E-15; ★ **WASH**; mail Alexandria **z** 22307
White Oak Swamp; RMC Place; HENRICO; ***245** J-14; ★ **RICH**; mail Sandston **z** 23150; ● 160
White Plains; RMC Place; BRUNSWICK; **245** M-12; 🅿; **z** 23893; ● 80
White Post; RMC Place; CLARKE; **245** D-12; 🅿; **z** 22663; ● 200
Whites Shop; RMC Place; KING WILLIAM; ***245** I-15; mail King William **z** 23086; rural
White Stone; Inc. Place; LANCASTER; **245** I-17; elev. 51ft./16m.; 🅿; **z** 22578; ℗ 372; © 358
Whitesville; RMC Place; ACCOMACK; ***245** I-19; mail Parksley **z** 23421; ● 300
Whitethorne; RMC Place; MONTGOMERY; ***244** K-4; mail Blacksburg **z** 24060; rural
Whitetop; RMC Place; GRAYSON; **244** E-7; 🅿; **z** 24292; ● 150
Whiteville; RMC Place; CUMBERLAND; ***245** I-12; mail Cumberland **z** 23040; rural
Whitewood; RMC Place; BUCHANAN; **244** B-6; 🅿; **z** 24657; ● 150
Whitley; RMC Place; ISLE OF WIGHT; ***245** L-16; elev. 86ft./26m.; mail Windsor **z** 23487; rural
Whitlock; RMC Place; LOUISA; ***245** H-11; elev. 537ft./164m.; mail Gordonsville **z** 22942; ● 30
Whitmell; RMC Place; PITTSYLVANIA; ***244** M-7; elev. 854ft./260m.; ★ **DANV**; mail Dry Fork **z** 24549; ● 100
Whittle; RMC Place; PITTSYLVANIA; ***244** L-8; mail Chatham **z** 24531; rural
Wickford; RMC Place; FAIRFAX; ***245** E-15; ★ **WASH**; mail Alexandria **z** 22310
Wicomico; RMC Place; GLOUCESTER; **245** K-17; elev. 36ft./11m.; 🅿; ★ **NN-H**; **z** 23184; ● 1,350
Wicomico Church; RMC Place; NORTHUMBERLAND; **245** I-17; elev. 105ft./32m.; 🅿; **z** 22579; ● 450
Widewater; RMC Place; STAFFORD; ***245** F-14; ★ **WASH**; mail Stafford **z** 22554; ● 200
Widewater Beach; RMC Place; STAFFORD; ***245** F-14; ★ **WASH**; mail Stafford **z** 22554; ● 160
Wightman; RMC Place; MECKLENBURG; ***245** M-11; elev. 423ft./129m.; mail Chase City **z** 23924; rural
Wilburdale; RMC Place; FAIRFAX; ***245** E-14; ★ **WASH**; mail Annandale **z** 22003
Wilda; RMC Place; AUGUSTA; ***244** H-9; mail Greenville **z** 24440, Stuarts Draft **z** 24477; rural
Wilde Acres; RMC Place; FREDERICK; ***245** C-11; mail Winchester **z** 22602; ● 130
Wilderness; RMC Place; ORANGE; **245** G-13; mail Spotsylvania **z** 22553; ● 30
Wilderness Corner; RMC Place; SPOTSYLVANIA; ***245** G-13; ★ **FRED**; mail Spotsylvania **z** 22553; rural
Wildwood; RMC Place; FLUVANNA; ***245** H-11; 🅿; **z** 22963
Wildwood; RMC Place; HENRICO; ***245** I-14; ★ **RICH**; mail Richmond **z** 23227; ● 1,250
Wildwood Farms; RMC Place; PRINCE GEORGE; ***245** K-14; elev. 150ft./46m.; ★ **RICH**; mail Disputanta **z** 23842; ● 200
Wilkinsons Store; RMC Place; DINWIDDIE; ***245** K-13; mail Church Road **z** 23833; rural
Wilkinson Terrace; RMC Place; CHESTERFIELD; ***245** J-14; ★ **RICH**; mail Richmond **z** 23234; ● 900
Willard Park; RMC Place; NORFOLK (Independent City); ***245** L-18; elev. 10ft./3m.; ★ **NORF-**; mail Norfolk **z** 23509; pop. incl. with Norfolk (Independent City)
Williamsburg; Independent City; serves as county seat of James City; **245** K-16; elev. 86ft./26m.; 🅿 🅷 🅲 7,709 ■; ★ **NN-H**; **z** 23081, **z** 23185-88; ℗ 11,530; © 11,998; ◆ 13,353
Williamsburg Manor; RMC Place; FAIRFAX; ***245** E-15; ★ **WASH**; mail Alexandria **z** 22308
Williams Mill; RMC Place; SCOTT; ***244** D-4; ★ **JNSC-**; mail Gate City **z** 24251; rural
Williamson Road; RMC Place; ROANOKE (Independent City); ★ **ROAN**; mail Roanoke **z** 24012; pop. incl. with Roanoke (Independent City)
Williamsville; RMC Place; BATH; **244** G-7; 🅿; **z** 24487; ● 40
Willis; RMC Place; FLOYD; **244** M-4; 🅿; **z** 24380; ● 130
Willisville; RMC Place; LOUDOUN; ***245** D-12; mail Upperville **z** 20184; ● 40
Willis Wharf; RMC Place; NORTHAMPTON; **245** J-19; 🅿; **z** 23486; ● 250
Willoughby Terrace; RMC Place; NORFOLK (Independent City); ***245** L-18; elev. 15ft./5m.; ★ **NORF-**; mail Norfolk **z** 23503; pop. incl. with Norfolk (Independent City)
Willow; RMC Place; AMHERST; ***244** I-8; elev. 1,101ft./336m.; mail Amherst **z** 24521; rural
Willowbrook; RMC Place; LOUISA; ***245** I-13; elev. 300ft./91m.; mail Bumpass **z** 23024; rural
Willow Grove; RMC Place; SHENANDOAH; ***244** E-10; elev. 821ft./250m.; mail Edinburg **z** 22824; ● 30
Willow Hill; RMC Place; PRINCE GEORGE; ***245** K-15; elev. 54ft./16m.; mail Spring Grove **z** 23881; rural
Willow Lakes; RMC Place; CHESAPEAKE (Independent City); ***245** M-17; elev. 20ft./6m.; ★ **NORF-**; mail Chesapeake **z** 23321; pop. incl. with Chesapeake (Independent City)
Willow Lawn; RMC Place; HENRICO; ***245** J-14; ★ **RICH**; mail Richmond **z** 23230; ● 100
Willow Run; RMC Place; FAIRFAX; ***245** E-15; ★ **WASH**; mail Annandale **z** 22003
Willow Spring; RMC Place; RUSSELL; ***244** D-5; mail Lebanon **z** 24266; rural
Willow Woods; RMC Place; FAIRFAX; ***245** E-14; ★ **WASH**; mail Annandale **z** 22003
Wills Corner; RMC Place; ISLE OF WIGHT; **243** L-3; elev. 40ft./12m.; mail Smithfield **z** 23430; ● 50
Willston; RMC Place; FAIRFAX; ***245** D-15; ★ **WASH**; mail Falls Church **z** 22044; ● 2,400
Wilmington; RMC Place; FLUVANNA; ***245** I-11; elev. 404ft./123m.; 🅿; **z** 22963
Wilroy; RMC Place; SUFFOLK (Independent City); ***245** M-17; ★ **NORF-**; mail Suffolk **z** 23434; pop. incl. with Suffolk (Independent City)
Wilson; DINWIDDIE; see Wilsons (RMC Place)
Wilsons (Wilson); RMC Place; DINWIDDIE; **245** K-13; elev. 376ft./115m.; 🅿; **z** 23894; ● 100
Wilson Springs; RMC Place; ROCKBRIDGE; ***244** H-8; elev. 1,180ft./360m.; mail Rockbridge Baths **z** 24473; rural
Wilton Woods; RMC Place; FAIRFAX; **249** I-5; ★ **WASH**; mail Alexandria **z** 22310; ● 1,400
Winchester; Independent City; serves as county seat of Frederick; **245** C-11; 🅿 🅷 🅲 3,107 ■; **z** 22601-04; ℗ 21,947; © 23,585; ◆ 25,572
Windermere; RMC Place; PITTSYLVANIA; ***244** M-7; elev. 690ft./210m.; ★ **DANV**; mail Danville **z** 24540; ● 200
Windmill Point; RMC Place; LANCASTER; mail White Stone **z** 22578; summer pop. 100
Windsor; Inc. Place; ISLE OF WIGHT; **245** M-16; 🅿; **z** 23487; ℗ 1,025; © 916
Windsordale; RMC Place; HENRICO; ***245** I-13; elev. 250ft./76m.; ★ **RICH**; mail Henrico **z** 23229; ● 1,050
Windsor Estates; RMC Place; FAIRFAX; ***245** E-15; ★ **WASH**; mail Alexandria **z** 22310
Windsor Farms; RMC Place; RICHMOND (Independent City); ***245** J-14; ★ **RICH**; mail Richmond **z** 23221; pop. incl. with Richmond (Independent City)
Windsor Park; RMC Place; FAIRFAX; ***245** E-15; ★ **WASH**; mail Alexandria **z** 22310
Windsor Place; RMC Place; HENRICO; ***245** J-14; elev. 150ft./46m.; ★ **RICH**; mail Henrico **z** 23075; ● 300
Windsor Shades; RMC Place; NEW KENT; ***245** J-15; elev. 38ft./12m.; mail Providence Forge **z** 23140; ● 80
Windy Hill Estates; RMC Place; HANOVER; ***245** I-14; ★ **RICH**; mail Mechanicsville **z** 23111
Winesap; RMC Place; AMHERST; ***244** J-8; elev. 774ft./236m.; ★ **LYNCH**; mail Madison Heights **z** 24572; ● 150
Winfall; RMC Place; CAMPBELL; **244** K-9; elev. 860ft./262m.; mail Gladys **z** 24554; ● 60
Wingina; RMC Place; NELSON; **244** I-10; elev. 355ft./108m.; 🅿; **z** 24599; ● 80
Winona; RMC Place; NORFOLK (Independent City); ***245** L-18; elev. 10ft./3m.; ★ **NORF-**; mail Norfolk **z** 23509; pop. incl. with Norfolk (Independent City)
Winslow Hills; RMC Place; FAIRFAX; ***245** E-15; ★ **WASH**; mail Alexandria **z** 22310; ● 1,300
Winston; RMC Place; CULPEPER; ***245** F-12; 🅿; **z** 22701
Wintergreen; RMC Place; NELSON; ***244** H-9; elev. 734ft./224m.; 🅿; **z** 22958; rural
Winterham; RMC Place; AMELIA; **245** J-12; elev. 335ft./102m.; mail Amelia Court House **z** 23002; ● 40
Winterpock; RMC Place; CHESTERFIELD; **245** K-13; ★ **RICH**; mail Chesterfield **z** 23832; ● 40
Wirtz; RMC Place; FRANKLIN; **244** L-6; elev. 1,128ft./344m.; 🅿; **z** 24184; ● 150
Wise (Gladeville); Inc. Place; ⊡ WISE; **244** C-4; elev. 2,454ft./748m.; 🅿 🅷 🅲 1,911; **z** 24293; ℗ 3,193; © 3,255
WISE; **244** C-4; ℗ 39,573; © 40,123; ® 42,209; ◆ 42,042
Wistar Farms; RMC Place; HENRICO; ***245** I-14; elev. 250ft./76m.; ★ **RICH**; mail Henrico **z** 23228; ● 450
Witch Duck; RMC Place; SUFFOLK (Independent City); ★ **NORF-**; mail Virginia Beach **z** 23462, **z** 23466; pop. incl. with Suffolk (Independent City)
Withams; RMC Place; ACCOMACK; ***245** H-20; 🅿; **z** 23488; ● 120
Wittens Mills; RMC Place; TAZEWELL; ***244** K-1; elev. 2,542ft./775m.; mail North Tazewell **z** 24630; ● 30
Wolfglade; RMC Place; CARROLL; ***244** M-3; elev. 2,491ft./759m.; mail Galax **z** 24333; rural
Wolford; RMC Place; BUCHANAN; ***244** B-6; 🅿; **z** 24658; ● 250
Wolftown; RMC Place; MADISON; **245** G-11; 🅿; **z** 22748; ● 200

Wolf Trap; CDP-Census Area Only; FAIRFAX; ***245** D-14; ★ **WASH**; mail Vienna **z** 22182; ℗ 13,133; © 14,001
Wolf Trap; RMC Place; HALIFAX; ***244** M-9; mail South Boston **z** 24592; ● 50
Womacks; RMC Place; CHARLOTTE; ***244** L-10; elev. 566ft./173m.; mail Charlotte Court House **z** 23923; rural
Wood; RMC Place; SCOTT; ***244** D-4; elev. 1,290ft./393m.; mail Fort Blackmore **z** 24250; rural
Woodberry Hills; RMC Place; DANVILLE (Independent City); ★ **DANV**; mail Danville **z** 24541; pop. incl. with Danville (Independent City)
Woodbridge; CDP; PRINCE WILLIAM; **245** E-14; 🅿 🅷; ★ **WASH**; **z** 22191-95; ℗ 26,401; © 31,941; ◆ 41,568
Woodbrook; RMC Place; ALBEMARLE; ***245** H-11; ★ **CHRLTV**; mail Charlottesville **z** 22901; ● 950
Woodburn; RMC Place; LOUDOUN; ***245** D-13; elev. 472ft./144m.; ★ **WASH**; mail Leesburg **z** 20175; rural
Wood Dale; RMC Place; CHESTERFIELD; ★ **RICH**; mail Chester **z** 23831
Woodford; RMC Place; CAROLINE; **245** G-14; 🅿; **z** 22580; ● 100
Woodhaven Shores; RMC Place; NEW KENT; ***245** J-15; mail Quinton **z** 23141; ● 1,150
Woodlake Park; RMC Place; PITTSYLVANIA; ***244** M-8; elev. 600ft./183m.; ★ **DANV**; mail Danville **z** 24540; ● 100
Woodlawn; CDP; CARROLL; **244** M-3; elev. 2,521ft./768m.; 🅿; **z** 24381; © 2,249
Woodlawn; RMC Place; HOPEWELL (Independent City); ★ **RICH**; mail Hopewell **z** 23860; pop. incl. with Hopewell (Independent City)
Woodlawn Manor; RMC Place; FAIRFAX; ***245** E-15; ★ **WASH**; mail Alexandria **z** 22309
Woodlawn Park; RMC Place; FAIRFAX; ***245** E-15; ★ **WASH**; mail Alexandria **z** 22309
Woodlawn Terrace; RMC Place; FAIRFAX; ***245** E-15; ★ **WASH**; mail Alexandria **z** 22309
Woodlawn Terrace; RMC Place; HENRICO; ★ **RICH**; mail Sandston **z** 23150
Woodlawn Village; RMC Place; FAIRFAX; ★ **WASH**; mail Fort Belvoir **z** 22060
Woodlee; RMC Place; STAUNTON (Independent City); ***244** G-9; mail Staunton **z** 24401; pop. incl. with Staunton (Independent City)
Woodley Hills; RMC Place; FAIRFAX; ***245** E-15; ★ **WASH**; mail Alexandria **z** 22309; ● 2,000
Woodman Terrace; RMC Place; HENRICO; ***245** I-14; ★ **RICH**; mail Henrico **z** 23228; ● 300
Woodmill Estates; RMC Place; FAIRFAX; ★ **WASH**; mail Alexandria **z** 22309
Woodmont; RMC Place; ARLINGTON; ***245** D-15; ★ **WASH**; mail Arlington **z** 22207
Woodmont; RMC Place; CHESTERFIELD; ***245** J-13; ★ **RICH**; mail Richmond **z** 23235
Woodridge; RMC Place; ALBEMARLE; ***245** H-11; mail Scottsville **z** 24590; ● 30
Woodrum; RMC Place; STAUNTON (Independent City); mail Staunton **z** 24401; pop. incl. with Staunton (Independent City)
Woods Crossroads; RMC Place; GLOUCESTER; ***245** J-16; elev. 108ft./33m.; 🅿; **z** 23190; ● 80
Woodside Estates; RMC Place; FAIRFAX; ***245** D-14; ★ **WASH**; mail Mc Lean **z** 22102; ● 400
Woods Mill; RMC Place; NELSON; ***244** I-9; elev. 540ft./165m.; mail Faber **z** 22938; rural
Woodson; RMC Place; AMHERST; ***244** I-9; mail Roseland **z** 22967; ● 30
Woods Store; RMC Place; FLOYD; ***244** L-5; mail Floyd **z** 24091; rural
Woodstock; Inc. Place; ⊡ SHENANDOAH; **244** E-10; 🅿 🅷; **z** 22664; ℗ 3,182; © 3,952; ® 4,003
Woodville; RMC Place; RAPPAHANNOCK; **245** F-11; 🅿; **z** 22749; ● 100
Woodway; RMC Place; LEE; **244** D-3; elev. 1,459ft./445m.; mail Pennington Gap **z** 24277; ● 200
Woolwine; RMC Place; PATRICK; **244** M-5; 🅿; **z** 24185; ● 350
Worlds; RMC Place; PITTSYLVANIA; ***244** L-7; elev. 1,015ft./309m.; mail Callands **z** 24530
Worsham; RMC Place; PRINCE EDWARD; ***245** K-11; elev. 472ft./144m.; mail Farmville **z** 23901; ● 50
Worshams; RMC Place; POWHATAN; ***245** J-12; elev. 398ft./121m.; mail Powhatan **z** 23139; rural
Wren; RMC Place; CHARLOTTE; ***244** K-9; elev. 602ft./183m.; mail Phenix **z** 23959; rural
Wright; RMC Place; NORFOLK (Independent City); ★ **NORF-**; mail Norfolk **z** 23505; pop. incl. with Norfolk (Independent City)
Wright Fork; RMC Place; CAROLINE; ***245** H-14; elev. 195ft./59m.; mail Milford **z** 22514; rural
Wrights Shop; RMC Place; AMHERST; ★ **LYNCH**; mail Madison Heights **z** 24572
Wrightsville; RMC Place; CAROLINE; ***245** H-14; mail Bowling Green **z** 22427; rural
Wurno; RMC Place; PULASKI; ***244** L-3; mail Pulaski **z** 24301; rural
Wylliesburg; RMC Place; CHARLOTTE; **244** L-10; elev. 532ft./162m.; 🅿; **z** 23976; ● 280
Wyndale; RMC Place; WASHINGTON; ***244** D-6; ★ **JNSC-**; mail Abingdon **z** 24210; ● 150
Wyndham; CDP-Census Area Only; HENRICO; ***245** I-13; ★ **RICH**; © 6,176
Wythe; RMC Place; HAMPTON (Independent City); ***245** L-17; ★ **NN-H**; mail Hampton **z** 23661; pop. incl. with Hampton (Independent City)
WYTHE; **244** L-2; ℗ 25,466; © 27,599; ◆ 28,922
Wytheville; Inc. Place; ⊡ WYTHE; **244** L-2; elev. 2,284ft./696m.; 🅿 🅷; **z** 24382; ℗ 8,038; © 7,804

Y

Yacht Haven Estates; RMC Place; FAIRFAX; ***245** E-15; ★ **WASH**; mail Alexandria **z** 22309
Yadkin; RMC Place; CHESAPEAKE (Independent City); ***245** M-17; ★ **NORF-**; mail Chesapeake **z** 23323; pop. incl. with Chesapeake (Independent City)
Yale; RMC Place; SUSSEX; **245** L-14; elev. 111ft./34m.; 🅿; **z** 23897; ● 50
Yancey Mills; RMC Place; ALBEMARLE; **244** H-10; 🅿; ★ **CHRLTV**; **z** 22932; ● 200
Yanceyville; RMC Place; LOUISA; ***245** H-12; elev. 284ft./87m.; mail Louisa **z** 23093; rural
Yards (Flat Top); RMC Place; TAZEWELL; ***244** K-2; 🅿; **z** 24605; ● 200
Yellow Branch; RMC Place; CAMPBELL; ***244** K-8; elev. 942ft./287m.; ★ **LYNCH**; mail Evington **z** 24550; ● 80
Yellow Springs; RMC Place; WASHINGTON; ***244** D-6; mail Meadowview **z** 24361; ● 30
Yellow Sulphur Springs; RMC Place; MONTGOMERY; ***244** K-4; mail Christiansburg **z** 24073; ● 30
Yellow Tavern; RMC Place; HENRICO; ***245** I-14; ★ **RICH**; mail Glen Allen **z** 23060; ● 300
YORK; **245** K-16; ℗ 42,422; © 56,297; ◆ 61,412
York Manor; RMC Place; HENRICO; ***245** J-14; elev. 146ft./45m.; ★ **RICH**; mail Henrico **z** 23075; ● 700
Yorkshire; CDP; PRINCE WILLIAM; ***245** E-14; ★ **WASH**; mail Manassas **z** 20111; ℗ 5,699; © 6,732
Yorkshire Acres; RMC Place; PRINCE WILLIAM; ***245** E-14; ★ **WASH**; mail Manassas **z** 20111
Yorkshire Park; RMC Place; PRINCE WILLIAM; ***245** E-14; ★ **WASH**; mail Manassas **z** 20111; ● 2,500
York Terrace; RMC Place; YORK; **243** F-2; ★ **NN-H**; mail Williamsburg **z** 23185; ● 800
Yorktown; CDP; ⊡ YORK; **245** K-17; 🅿; ★ **NN-H**; **z** 23690-93; © 203
Yost; RMC Place; BATH; ***244** H-7; mail Millboro **z** 24460; rural
Youngers Store; RMC Place; HALIFAX; ***244** M-9; elev. 498ft./152m.; mail Halifax **z** 24558; rural
Yuma; RMC Place; SCOTT; **244** E-4; elev. 1,295ft./395m.; ★ **JNSC-**; mail Gate City **z** 24251; ● 100

Z

Zacata; RMC Place; WESTMORELAND; ***245** G-16; elev. 144ft./44m.; 🅿; **z** 22581; ● 40
Zack; RMC Place; ROCKBRIDGE; ***244** H-8; mail Middlebrook **z** 24459; rural
Zanoni; RMC Place; GLOUCESTER; ***245** J-17; 🅿; ★ **NN-H**; **z** 23061; ● 130
Zenda; RMC Place; ROCKINGHAM; ***244** F-10; mail Harrisonburg **z** 22802; rural
Zepp; RMC Place; SHENANDOAH; ***244** D-10; elev. 1,024ft./312m.; mail Maurertown **z** 22644; rural
Zion; RMC Place; LOUISA; ***245** H-11; mail Gordonsville **z** 22942; rural
Zion Crossroads; RMC Place; FLUVANNA, LOUISA; ***245** H-11; elev. 541ft./165m.; mail Gordonsville **z** 22942; ● 50
Ziontown; RMC Place; HENRICO; ***245** J-13; elev. 300ft./91m.; ★ **RICH**; mail Henrico **z** 23075; ● 550
Zuni; RMC Place; ISLE OF WIGHT; **245** L-16; elev. 40ft./12m.; 🅿; **z** 23898; ● 300

Entries in **UPPERCASE** are counties.
Entries in **bold** have populations of 2,500 or more.
Names in parentheses are alternate names.
Inc. Place — Incorporated Place
RMC Place — Rand McNally Designated Place
CDP — Census Designated Place
MCD — Minor Civil Division

⊡ County Seat
▲ Minor Civil Division
elev. Elevation
🅿 Post Office

🅷 Hospital
🅲 College
■ Principal Business Center
★ Ranally Metro Area (RMA) Abbreviation
z Zip Code(s)

℗ Previous Census Population
® Revised Census Population
Ⓐ Annexation Population
● Rand McNally Population Estimate
© Final Census Population
Ⓢ Special Census Population
◆ Estimated Population

For additional definitions see Glossary, Volume 1, and Introduction, Volume 2.

WASHINGTON

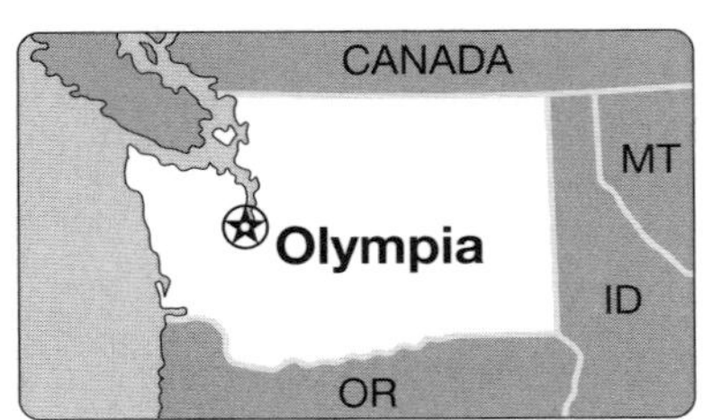

Statistics

Total area (2000) — 71,300 square miles
Land area (2000) — 66,544 square miles
Water area (2000) — 4,756 square miles
Capital — Olympia
Admitted as state — November, 1889

Maps

State maps can be found on pages 142-254 in Vol. 1

Ranally Metro Areas (RMAs) and Abbreviations

Bellingham, WA — BELNG
Bremerton, WA — BREM
Lewiston, ID-WA — LEW
Longview, WA-OR — LNGV
Olympia, WA — OLYM
Portland, OR-WA — POR
Richland-Kennewick-Pasco, WA — RICH-
Seattle, WA — SEAT
Spokane, WA-ID — SPOK
Walla Walla, WA-OR — WALL
Yakima, WA — YAK

Principal Places

Place Name	Place Type	County	Population
Seattle	Inc. Place	KING	◆ 620,567
Spokane	Inc. Place	SPOKANE	◆ 217,898
Tacoma	Inc. Place	PIERCE	◆ 217,643
Vancouver	Inc. Place	CLARK	◆ 187,888
Bellevue	Inc. Place	KING	◆ 122,870
Everett	Inc. Place	SNOHOMISH	◆ 101,837
Federal Way	Inc. Place	KING	◆ 90,845
Spokane Valley	Inc. Place	SPOKANE	◆ 89,780
Kent	Inc. Place	KING	◆ 88,762
Bellingham	Inc. Place	WHATCOM	◆ 86,430
Yakima	Inc. Place	YAKIMA	◆ 80,888
Kennewick	Inc. Place	BENTON	◆ 63,930
Renton	Inc. Place	KING	◆ 61,127
Lakewood	Inc. Place	PIERCE	◆ 60,300
Pasco	Inc. Place	FRANKLIN	◆ 58,806
Shoreline	Inc. Place	KING	◆ 55,701
Olympia	Inc. Place	THURSTON	◆ 48,985
Redmond	Inc. Place	KING	◆ 48,906
Auburn	Inc. Place	KING	◆ 47,506
Kirkland	Inc. Place	KING	◆ 47,099
Richland	Inc. Place	BENTON	◆ 44,812
Seattle Hill-Silver Firs	CDP-Census Area Only	SNOHOMISH	◆ 40,228
Edmonds	Inc. Place	SNOHOMISH	◆ 40,179
Lacey	Inc. Place	THURSTON	◆ 39,162
Cascade-Fairwood	CDP-Census Area Only	KING	◆ 38,281
Puyallup	Inc. Place	PIERCE	◆ 38,048
Sammamish	Inc. Place	KING	◆ 37,184
Longview	Inc. Place	COWLITZ	◆ 37,125
South Hill	CDP-Census Area Only	PIERCE	◆ 35,417
Burien	Inc. Place	KING	◆ 35,377
Lynnwood	Inc. Place	SNOHOMISH	◆ 35,226
University Place	Inc. Place	PIERCE	◆ 34,652
Bothell	Inc. Place	KING	◆ 32,945
Bremerton	Inc. Place	KITSAP	◆ 32,783
East Hill-Meridian	CDP-Census Area Only	KING	◆ 32,443
Marysville	Inc. Place	SNOHOMISH	◆ 32,277
Mount Vernon	Inc. Place	SKAGIT	◆ 31,805
Des Moines	Inc. Place	KING	◆ 30,975
Walla Walla	Inc. Place	WALLA WALLA	◆ 30,764
Wenatchee	Inc. Place	CHELAN	◆ 30,597
North Creek	CDP-Census Area Only	SNOHOMISH	◆ 29,326
SeaTac	Inc. Place	KING	◆ 27,857
Paine Field-Lake Stickney	CDP-Census Area Only	SNOHOMISH	◆ 27,768
Parkland	CDP	PIERCE	◆ 26,940
Cottage Lake	CDP-Census Area Only	KING	◆ 26,933
Picnic Point-North Lynnwood	CDP-Census Area Only	SNOHOMISH	◆ 26,146
Inglewood-Finn Hill	CDP-Census Area Only	KING	◆ 25,086
Mercer Island	Inc. Place	KING	◆ 24,448
Spanaway	CDP	PIERCE	◆ 24,180
North Marysville	CDP-Census Area Only	SNOHOMISH	◆ 24,105
Pullman	Inc. Place	WHITMAN	◆ 23,911
White Center	CDP	KING	◆ 23,216
Mukilteo	Inc. Place	SNOHOMISH	◆ 22,445
Oak Harbor	Inc. Place	ISLAND	◆ 21,732
Winslow	Inc. Place	KITSAP	◆ 21,423
Issaquah	Inc. Place	KING	◆ 20,964
Mountlake Terrace	Inc. Place	SNOHOMISH	◆ 20,493
Kenmore	Inc. Place	KING	◆ 19,585
Fort Lewis	CDP-Census Area Only	PIERCE	© 19,089
Tukwila	Inc. Place	KING	◆ 18,256
West Lake Stevens	CDP-Census Area Only	SNOHOMISH	© 18,071
Port Angeles	Inc. Place	CLALLAM	◆ 17,860
Orchards	CDP	CLARK	© 17,852
Salmon Creek	CDP	CLARK	© 16,767
Aberdeen	Inc. Place	GRAYS HARBOR	◆ 16,106
Silverdale	CDP	KITSAP	© 15,816
Centralia	Inc. Place	LEWIS	◆ 15,789
Elk Plain	CDP	PIERCE	© 15,697
Ellensburg	Inc. Place	KITTITAS	© 15,414
Alderwood Manor	CDP	SNOHOMISH	© 15,329
Lakeland North	CDP-Census Area Only	KING	© 15,085
Moses Lake	Inc. Place	GRANT	© 14,953
Anacortes	Inc. Place	SKAGIT	© 14,557
Maple Valley	Inc. Place	KING	© 14,209
Bryn Mawr-Skyway	CDP-Census Area Only	KING	© 13,977
Sunnyside	Inc. Place	YAKIMA	© 13,905
Monroe	Inc. Place	SNOHOMISH	© 13,795
Covington	Inc. Place	KING	© 13,783
East Wenatchee Bench	CDP-Census Area Only	DOUGLAS	© 13,658
Camano	CDP	ISLAND	© 13,347
East Renton Highlands	CDP-Census Area Only	KING	© 13,264
Lake Forest Park	Inc. Place	KING	® 12,871
Tumwater	Inc. Place	THURSTON	© 12,698
Martha Lake	CDP-Census Area Only	SNOHOMISH	© 12,633
Camas	Inc. Place	CLARK	© 12,534
Kingsgate	CDP	KING	© 12,222
Five Corners	CDP-Census Area Only	CLARK	© 12,207
Kelso	Inc. Place	COWLITZ	© 11,895
Arlington	Inc. Place	SNOHOMISH	© 11,713
Prairie Ridge	CDP-Census Area Only	PIERCE	© 11,688
Mill Creek	Inc. Place	SNOHOMISH	© 11,525
Lakeland South	CDP-Census Area Only	KING	© 11,436
Union Hill-Novelty Hill	CDP-Census Area Only	KING	© 11,265
Riverton-Boulevard Park	CDP-Census Area Only	KING	© 11,188
Enumclaw	Inc. Place	KING	© 11,116
Lea Hill	CDP-Census Area Only	KING	© 10,871
West Valley	CDP-Census Area Only	YAKIMA	© 10,433
Vashon	CDP	KING	© 10,123
Dishman	CDP	SPOKANE	© 10,031
Woodinville	Inc. Place	KING	® 9,809
Bonney Lake	Inc. Place	PIERCE	© 9,687
Lake Morton-Berrydale	CDP-Census Area Only	KING	© 9,659
Veradale	CDP	SPOKANE	© 9,387
Battle Ground	Inc. Place	CLARK	© 9,296
Hazel Dell North	CDP-Census Area Only	CLARK	© 9,261
Waller	CDP-Census Area Only	PIERCE	© 9,200
Hoquiam	Inc. Place	GRAYS HARBOR	© 9,097
Edgewood	Inc. Place	PIERCE	© 9,089
Lynden	Inc. Place	WHATCOM	© 9,020
Toppenish	Inc. Place	YAKIMA	© 8,946
Cheney	Inc. Place	SPOKANE	© 8,832
Ferndale	Inc. Place	WHATCOM	© 8,758
Graham	CDP	PIERCE	© 8,739
Sedro-Woolley	Inc. Place	SKAGIT	© 8,658
Artondale	CDP	PIERCE	© 8,630
Washougal	Inc. Place	CLARK	© 8,595
Sumner	Inc. Place	PIERCE	© 8,504
Skyway	RMC Place	KING	● 8,500
Snohomish	Inc. Place	SNOHOMISH	© 8,494
Shelton	Inc. Place	MASON	© 8,442
West Richland	Inc. Place	BENTON	© 8,385
Grandview	Inc. Place	YAKIMA	© 8,377
Port Townsend	Inc. Place	JEFFERSON	© 8,334
Maltby	CDP	SNOHOMISH	© 8,267
Summit	CDP	PIERCE	© 8,041
College Place	Inc. Place	WALLA WALLA	© 7,818
Cascade Vista	RMC Place	KING	● 7,800
Newcastle	Inc. Place	KING	© 7,737
Port Orchard	Inc. Place	KITSAP	© 7,693
Minnehaha	CDP	CLARK	© 7,689
Midland	CDP	PIERCE	© 7,414
Mill Plain	CDP-Census Area Only	CLARK	© 7,400
Clarkston	Inc. Place	ASOTIN	© 7,337
Bangor Trident Base	CDP-Census Area Only	KITSAP	© 7,253
Parkwood	CDP	KITSAP	© 7,213
Walnut Grove	CDP	CLARK	© 7,164
Chehalis	Inc. Place	LEWIS	© 7,057
Poulsbo	Inc. Place	KITSAP	© 6,813
Ephrata	Inc. Place	GRANT	© 6,808
Fairwood	CDP-Census Area Only	SPOKANE	© 6,764
Burlington	Inc. Place	SKAGIT	© 6,757
Lake Shore	CDP-Census Area Only	CLARK	© 6,670
Hazel Dell South	CDP-Census Area Only	CLARK	© 6,605
Sheridan Beach	RMC Place	KING	℗ 6,518
Gig Harbor	Inc. Place	PIERCE	© 6,465
Terrace Heights	CDP	YAKIMA	© 6,447
Normandy Park	Inc. Place	KING	© 6,392
Brier	Inc. Place	SNOHOMISH	© 6,383
Lake Stevens	Inc. Place	SNOHOMISH	© 6,361
Otis Orchards-East Farms	CDP-Census Area Only	SPOKANE	© 6,318
Selah	Inc. Place	YAKIMA	© 6,310
Hobart	CDP	KING	© 6,251
Clarkston Heights-Vineland	CDP-Census Area Only	ASOTIN	© 6,117
Steilacoom	Inc. Place	PIERCE	© 6,049
West Lake Sammamish	CDP-Census Area Only	KING	© 5,937
Fircrest	Inc. Place	PIERCE	© 5,868
Othello	Inc. Place	ADAMS	© 5,847
Milton	Inc. Place	PIERCE	© 5,795
Finley	CDP	BENTON	© 5,770
Mount Vista	CDP-Census Area Only	CLARK	© 5,770
Frederickson	CDP	PIERCE	© 5,758
East Wenatchee	Inc. Place	DOUGLAS	© 5,757
Felida	CDP	CLARK	© 5,683
Tanglewilde-Thompson Place	CDP-Census Area Only	THURSTON	© 5,670
Union Gap	Inc. Place	YAKIMA	© 5,621
Pacific	Inc. Place	KING	© 5,527
Country Homes	CDP	SPOKANE	© 5,203
Green Acres	CDP	SPOKANE	© 5,158
Hockinson	CDP	CLARK	© 5,136
East Port Orchard	CDP	KITSAP	© 5,116
Quincy	Inc. Place	GRANT	© 5,044

County Business Data

County	FIPS Code	County Seat	Land Area (Sq. Mi.)	Census Population			Wholesale Trade		Manufacturing, 2002			
				4/1/2000	4/1/1990	% Change 1990-2000	Sales, 2002 ($1,000)	% Change 1997-2002	Establish-ments	Total Employees	Value Added ($1,000)	Ranally Mfg. Units
Adams	001	Ritzville	1,925	16,428	13,603	20.8	138,380	-12.7	14	(d)	(d)	...
Asotin	003	Asotin	635	20,551	17,605	16.7	(d)	(d)	...	(d)	(d)	...
Benton	005	Prosser	1,703	142,475	112,560	26.6	410,961	34.6	116	3,714	442,756	234
Chelan	007	Wenatchee	2,921	66,616	52,250	27.5	763,533	-2.4	77	1,912	168,667	89
Clallam	009	Port Angeles	1,739	64,525	56,464	14.3	(d)	(d)	76	1,159	126,291	67
Clark	011	Vancouver	628	345,238	238,053	45.0	(d)	(d)	444	14,471	1,670,288	884
Columbia	013	Dayton	869	4,064	4,024	1.0	(d)	(d)	...	(d)	(d)	...
Cowlitz	015	Kelso	1,139	92,948	82,119	13.2	(d)	(d)	132	6,547	721,675	382
Douglas	017	Waterville	1,821	32,603	26,205	24.4	139,435	70.4	...	(d)	(d)	...
Ferry	019	Republic	2,204	7,260	6,295	15.3	(d)	(d)	...	(d)	(d)	...
Franklin	021	Pasco	1,242	49,347	37,473	31.7	458,783	-16.7	51	3,605	257,546	136
Garfield	023	Pomeroy	711	2,397	2,248	6.6	67,086	(d)	...	(d)	(d)	...
Grant	025	Ephrata	2,681	74,698	54,758	36.4	305,279	-16.5	64	3,541	330,155	175
Grays Harbor	027	Montesano	1,917	67,194	64,175	4.7	124,273	-10.6	94	3,078	326,410	173
Island	029	Coupeville	208	71,558	60,195	18.9	61,552	50.6	50	(d)	(d)	...
Jefferson	031	Port Townsend	1,814	25,953	20,146	28.8	18,328	(d)	75	731	85,633	45
King	033	Seattle	2,126	1,737,034	1,507,319	15.2	54,547,037	8.6	2,583	97,733	14,265,827	7,548
Kitsap	035	Port Orchard	396	231,969	189,731	22.3	499,919	51.1	171	2,321	168,239	89
Kittitas	037	Ellensburg	2,297	33,362	26,725	24.8	139,823	7.7	31	662	51,881	27
Klickitat	039	Goldendale	1,872	19,161	16,616	15.3	25,039	-26.2	25	547	103,679	55
Lewis	041	Chehalis	2,408	68,600	59,358	15.6	186,575	(d)	119	2,810	288,770	153
Lincoln	043	Davenport	2,311	10,184	8,864	14.9	117,163	-10.9	...	(d)	(d)	...
Mason	045	Shelton	961	49,405	38,341	28.9	112,000	6.6	50	1,466	118,047	62
Okanogan	047	Okanogan	5,268	39,564	33,350	18.6	166,732	-54.8	...	(d)	(d)	...
Pacific	049	South Bend	933	20,984	18,882	11.1	8,296	(d)	37	783	44,825	24
Pend Oreille	051	Newport	1,400	11,732	8,915	31.6	(d)	(d)	...	(d)	(d)	...
Pierce	053	Tacoma	1,679	700,820	586,203	19.6	4,492,879	-2.7	664	19,462	1,777,490	940
San Juan	055	Friday Harbor	175	14,077	10,035	40.3	12,156	(d)	...	(d)	(d)	...
Skagit	057	Mount Vernon	1,735	102,979	79,555	29.4	423,657	23.0	191	5,145	764,942	405
Skamania	059	Stevenson	1,656	9,872	8,289	19.1	(d)	(d)	...	(d)	(d)	...
Snohomish	061	Everett	2,089	606,024	465,642	30.1	4,913,065	37.9	838	49,622	8,467,858	4,480
Spokane	063	Spokane	1,764	417,939	361,364	15.7	6,102,615	25.1	583	16,442	1,505,042	796
Stevens	065	Colville	2,478	40,066	30,948	29.5	39,991	0.6	48	1,612	102,762	54
Thurston	067	Olympia	727	207,355	161,238	28.6	688,191	18.6	174	3,121	300,144	159
Wahkiakum	069	Cathlamet	264	3,824	3,327	14.9	(d)	(d)	...	(d)	(d)	...
Walla Walla	071	Walla Walla	1,271	55,180	48,439	13.9	(d)	(d)	88	1,661	236,007	125
Whatcom	073	Bellingham	2,120	166,814	127,780	30.5	905,766	-13.1	314	8,365	1,751,804	927
Whitman	075	Colfax	2,159	40,740	38,775	5.1	317,246	(d)	26	736	101,259	54
Yakima	077	Yakima	4,296	222,581	188,823	17.9	2,886,741	55.7	244	9,781	726,948	385
The State			**66,544**	**5,894,121**	**4,866,692**	**21.1**	**84,634,499**	**12.3**	**7,535**	**265,010**	**35,398,551**	**18,728**

(d) Data not available. Corresponding percentages or Ranally Manufacturing Units are estimates.
... Represents 0 or amount too minimal to be reported.

Index of Places and Counties

Entries in **UPPERCASE** are counties.
Entries in **bold** have populations of 2,500 or more.
Names in parentheses are alternate names.

Inc. Place	Incorporated Place
RMC Place	Rand McNally Designated Place
CDP	Census Designated Place
MCD	Minor Civil Division
⊡	County Seat
▲	Minor Civil Division
elev.	Elevation
▣	Post Office
🅷	Hospital
🅲	College
■	Principal Business Center
★	Ranally Metro Area (RMA) Abbreviation
z	Zip Code(s)
℗	Previous Census Population
®	Revised Census Population
Ⓐ	Annexation Population
●	Rand McNally Population Estimate
©	Final Census Population
Ⓢ	Special Census Population
◆	Estimated Population

For additional definitions see Glossary, Volume 1, and Introduction, Volume 2.

Algona; Inc. Place; KING; **248** K-9; 🅿; ★ **SEAT**; z 98001; Ⓟ 1,694; Ⓒ 2,460
Allen; RMC Place; SKAGIT; **246** C-7; mail Bow z 98232; ● 180
Allentown; RMC Place; KING; ***246** F-7; ★ **SEAT**; mail Seattle z 98178; pop. incl. with Tukwila (Inc. Place)
Allyn; RMC Place; MASON; **246** G-6; 🅿; ★ **BREM**; z 98524; ● 850
Allyn-Grapeview; CDP-Census Area Only; MASON; ***246** G-6; ★ **BREM**; mail Allyn z 98524, Grapeview z 98546; Ⓟ 1,526; Ⓒ 2,004
Almira; Inc. Place; LINCOLN; **247** F-15; elev. 1,915ft./584m.; 🅿; z 99103; Ⓟ 310; Ⓒ 302
Aloha; RMC Place; GRAYS HARBOR; **246** G-3; mail Pacific Beach z 98571; ● 50
Alpental; RMC Place; KING; ***246** G-9; elev. 3,000ft./914m.; mail Snoqualmie Pass z 98068; seasonal pop. 600; ● 50
Alpha; RMC Place; LEWIS; ***246** J-6; mail Onalaska z 98570
Altoona; RMC Place; WAHKIAKUM; **246** K-4; elev. 18ft./5m.; mail Rosburg z 98643; ● 30
Amanda Park; RMC Place; GRAYS HARBOR; **246** F-3; located on Quinault Ind. Res.; 🅿; z 98526; ● 800
Amber; RMC Place; SPOKANE; ***247** G-18; mail Cheney z 99004; rural
Amboy; CDP; CLARK; **246** L-7; elev. 400ft./122m.; 🅿; z 98601; Ⓒ 2,085
Ames Lake; CDP-Census Area Only; KING; ***246** F-8; ★ **SEAT**; mail Redmond z 98052; Ⓒ 1,435
Anacortes; Inc. Place; SKAGIT; **246** C-6; 🅿 🅷; z 98221-22; Ⓟ 11,451; Ⓒ 14,557
Anatone; RMC Place; ASOTIN; **247** K-20; elev. 3,570ft./1,088m.; 🅿; z 99401; ● 100
Anderson Island; RMC Place; PIERCE; ***246** H-6; elev. 100ft./30m.; 🅿; ★ **SEAT**; z 98303; ● 400
Angle Lake; RMC Place; KING; ★ **SEAT**; mail Seattle z 98188; pop. incl. with SeaTac (Inc. Place)
Annapolis; RMC Place; KITSAP; ***246** F-6; ★ **BREM**; mail Port Orchard z 98366; pop. incl. with Port Orchard (Inc. Place)
Appleton; RMC Place; KLICKITAT; ***246** L-10; elev. 2,308ft./703m.; 🅿; z 98602; ● 40
Appleyard; RMC Place; CHELAN; ***247** G-12; ● 1,400
Arbor Heights; RMC Place; KING; ***246** F-7; ★ **SEAT**; mail Seattle z 98146; pop. incl. with Seattle (Inc. Place)
Arcadia; RMC Place; MASON; ***246** G-6; elev. 68ft./21m.; ★ **OMA**; mail Shelton z 98584; ● 60
Arden; RMC Place; STEVENS; **247** C-18; mail Colville z 99114; ● 60
Ardenvoir; RMC Place; CHELAN; **247** F-12; 🅿; z 98811; ● 130
Argo; RMC Place; KING; ★ **SEAT**; pop. incl. with Seattle (Inc. Place)
Argyle; RMC Place; SAN JUAN; ***246** C-6; elev. 19ft./6m.; mail Friday Harbor z 98250; rural
Ariel; RMC Place; COWLITZ; **246** L-6; 🅿; z 98603; ● 100
Arletta; RMC Place; PIERCE; ***246** G-6; ★ **SEAT**; mail Gig Harbor z 98335; ● 500
Arlington; Inc. Place; SNOHOMISH; **246** D-8; 🅿 🅷; ★ **SEAT**; z 98223; Ⓟ 4,037; Ⓒ 11,713
Arlington Heights; CDP; SNOHOMISH; ***246** D-8; elev. 305ft./93m.; ★ **SEAT**; mail Arlington z 98223; Ⓒ 2,510
Armar; RMC Place; SNOHOMISH; ***246** D-8; ★ **SEAT**; mail Marysville z 98270; ● 850
Arrowhead; RMC Place; KING; ***246** F-7; elev. 82ft./25m.; ★ **SEAT**; mail Kenmore z 98028; pop. incl. with Kenmore (Inc. Place)
Arrowhead; RMC Place; PIERCE; ★ **SEAT**; mail Lakewood z 98498; pop. incl. with Lakewood (Inc. Place)
Arrowhead Beach; RMC Place; ISLAND; ***246** D-7; elev. 50ft./15m.; ★ **SEAT**; mail Camano Island z 98282; ● 50
Artic; RMC Place; GRAYS HARBOR; ***246** H-4; elev. 105ft./32m.; mail Cosmopolis z 98537; rural
Artondale; CDP; PIERCE; ***246** G-6; ★ **SEAT**; mail Gig Harbor z 98335; Ⓟ 7,141; Ⓒ 8,630
Ashford; CDP; PIERCE; **246** I-8; 🅿; z 98304; Ⓒ 267
Asotin; Inc. Place; ⊡ ASOTIN; **247** J-20; elev. 770ft./235m.; 🅿; ★ **LEW**; z 99402; Ⓟ 981; Ⓒ 1,095
ASOTIN; **247** K-20; Ⓟ 17,605; Ⓒ 20,551; ◆ 21,135
Auburn; Inc. Place; KING; **246** G-7; 🅿 🅷 ■; ★ **SEAT**; z 98001-03, z 98023, z 98047, z 98063, z 98071, z 98092-93; Ⓟ 33,102; Ⓒ 40,314; ◆ 47,506
Auburn Twin Lakes; RMC Place; KING; ***246** G-7; ★ **SEAT**; mail Federal Way z 98023; pop. incl. with Federal Way (Inc. Place)
Ault Field; CDP-Census Area Only; ISLAND; ***246** C-6; mail Oak Harbor z 98277; Ⓟ 3,795; Ⓒ 2,064
Avery; RMC Place; KLICKITAT; ***246** M-10; elev. 246ft./75m.; mail Wishram z 98673; rural
Avon; RMC Place; SKAGIT; ***246** C-7; elev. 25ft./8m.; mail Mount Vernon z 98273; ● 120
Ayer; RMC Place; WALLA WALLA; **247** J-17; elev. 486ft./148m.; mail Prescott z 99348; ● 50
Ayock Beach; RMC Place; MASON; ***246** F-5; mail Lilliwaup z 98555; ● 60
Azwell; RMC Place; CHELAN; ***247** E-13; elev. 708ft./216m.; mail Pateros z 98846; ● 50

B

Baby Island Heights; RMC Place; ISLAND; ***246** D-7; ★ **SEAT**; mail Langley z 98260; ● 150
Baileysburg; RMC Place; COLUMBIA; ***247** K-18; elev. 1,700ft./518m.; mail Dayton z 99328
Bainbridge Island; KITSAP; see Winslow (Inc. Place)
Baker Heights; RMC Place; SKAGIT; ***246** C-7; elev. 118ft./36m.; mail Mount Vernon z 98273; ● 50
Ballard; RMC Place; KING; ***246** F-7; ★ **SEAT**; mail Seattle z 98107; pop. incl. with Seattle (Inc. Place)
B and G; RMC Place; SNOHOMISH; ***246** E-7; ★ **SEAT**; mail Everett z 98201; pop. incl. with Everett (Inc. Place)
Bangor Trident Base; CDP-Census Area Only; KITSAP; ***246** F-6; ★ **BREM**; mail Silverdale z 98315; Ⓟ 3,702; Ⓒ 7,253
Banks Lake South; CDP-Census Area Only; GRANT; ***247** F-14; Ⓒ 160
Barberton; CDP; CLARK; ***246** M-6; elev. 247ft./75m.; ★ **POR**; mail Vancouver z 98665; Ⓒ 4,617
Baring; CDP; KING; **246** E-9; 🅿; z 98224; Ⓒ 233
Barstow; RMC Place; FERRY; ***247** B-17; mail Kettle Falls z 99141; ● 25
Basin City; CDP; FRANKLIN; **247** J-15; mail Mesa z 99343; Ⓒ 968
Battle Ground; Inc. Place; CLARK; **246** L-7; 🅿; ★ **POR**; z 98604; Ⓟ 3,758; Ⓒ 9,296
Battle Point; RMC Place; KITSAP; ***246** F-7; ★ **SEAT**; mail Bainbridge Island z 98110; pop. incl. with Winslow (Inc. Place)
Batum; RMC Place; ADAMS; ***247** G-16; mail Ritzville z 99169; rural
Bay Center; CDP; PACIFIC; **246** I-3; 🅿; z 98527; Ⓒ 174
Bay City; RMC Place; GRAYS HARBOR; ***246** I-3; elev. 36ft./11m.; mail Aberdeen z 98520; ● 120
Bay Shore; RMC Place; MASON; ***246** G-5; elev. 13ft./4m.; ★ **OLYM**; mail Shelton z 98584
Bay View; RMC Place; ISLAND; **246** E-7; elev. 50ft./15m.; ★ **SEAT**; mail Langley z 98260; ● 150
Bay View; CDP; SKAGIT; **246** C-7; mail Mount Vernon z 98273; Ⓒ 334
Bazinet Eddition; RMC Place; LEWIS; ***246** I-5; elev. 400ft./122m.; mail Chehalis z 98532; ● 150
Beachcombers Hidden Beach; RMC Place; ISLAND; ***246** D-7; elev. 200ft./61m.; ★ **SEAT**; mail Greenbank z 98253; ● 150
Beachcrest; RMC Place; THURSTON; ***246** H-6; elev. 100ft./30m.; ★ **OLYM**; mail Olympia z 98501; ● 80
Beach Haven; RMC Place; SAN JUAN; ***246** B-6; mail Eastsound z 98245; rural
Beacon Hill; RMC Place; COWLITZ; ***246** K-6; ★ **LNGV**; mail Longview z 98632, Seattle z 98144; ● 1,500
Beaux Arts; KING; see Beaux Arts Village (Inc. Place)
Beaux Arts Village (Beaux Arts); Inc. Place; KING; **248** E-9; ★ **SEAT**; mail Bellevue z 98004; Ⓟ 303; Ⓒ 307
Beaver (Tyee); RMC Place; CLALLAM; **246** D-2; 🅿; z 98305; ● 600
Beaver Valley; RMC Place; JEFFERSON; ***246** E-6; mail Port Ludlow z 98365
Beckett Point; RMC Place; JEFFERSON; ***246** D-6; mail Port Townsend z 98368; summer pop. 150; ● 50
Beebe; RMC Place; DOUGLAS; ***247** E-13; mail Orondo z 98843; rural
Belfair; RMC Place; MASON; **246** G-6; elev. 43ft./13m.; 🅿; ★ **BREM**; z 98528; ● 800
Bellevue; Inc. Place; KING; **246** F-7; 🅿 🅷 🅲 6,435 ■; ★ **SEAT**; z 98004-09, z 98015; Ⓟ 86,874; Ⓒ 109,569; ◆ 122,870
Bell Hill; CDP-Census Area Only; CLALLAM; ***246** D-5; Ⓒ 731
Bellingham; Inc. Place; ⊡ WHATCOM; **246** B-7; 🅿 🅷 🅲 12,797 ■; ★ **BELNG**; z 98225-29; Ⓟ 52,179; Ⓒ 67,171; ◆ 86,430
Belmont; RMC Place; WHITMAN; **247** H-20; 🅿; z 99104; ● 20
Belvidere; RMC Place; OKANOGAN; **247** D-15; mail Coulee Dam z 99116; ● 60
Bench Drive; RMC Place; GRAYS HARBOR; mail Aberdeen z 98520; pop. incl. with Aberdeen (Inc. Place)
Benge; RMC Place; ADAMS; **247** H-17; 🅿; z 99105; ● 50
Benson Hill; RMC Place; KING; ***246** G-7; elev. 400ft./122m.; ★ **SEAT**; mail Renton z 98055, z 98058; ● 1,500
BENTON; **247** J-13; Ⓟ 112,560; Ⓒ 142,475; ◆ 159,189
Benton City; Inc. Place; BENTON; **247** K-14; elev. 494ft./151m.; 🅿; ★ **RICH-**; z 99320; Ⓟ 1,806; Ⓒ 2,624
Bethel; RMC Place; KITSAP; ***246** F-6; 🅿; ★ **BREM**; z 98387 & mail Port Orchard z 98366-67; ● 500
Beverly; RMC Place; GRANT; **247** I-13; elev. 547ft./167m.; 🅿; z 99321; ● 300
Beverly Beach; RMC Place; ISLAND; ***246** D-7; ★ **SEAT**; mail Freeland z 98249; ● 100
Beverly Park; RMC Place; SNOHOMISH; ★ **SEAT**; mail Everett z 98203; pop. incl. with Everett (Inc. Place)
Bickleton; CDP; KLICKITAT; **247** L-12; 🅿; z 99322; Ⓒ 113
Big Lake; CDP; SKAGIT; **246** C-7; mail Mount Vernon z 98274; Ⓒ 1,153
Bingen; Inc. Place; KLICKITAT; **246** M-9; elev. 1,131ft./345m.; 🅿; z 98605; Ⓟ 645; Ⓒ 672
Birch Bay; CDP; WHATCOM; **246** A-6; ★ **BELNG**; mail Blaine z 98230; Ⓟ 2,656; Ⓒ 4,961
Birchfield; RMC Place; YAKIMA; ***247** J-12; elev. 994ft./303m.; ★ **YAK**; mail Yakima z 98901; rural
Birdsview; RMC Place; SKAGIT; ***246** C-8; mail Concrete z 98237; ● 400
Bissell; RMC Place; STEVENS; ***247** D-17; elev. 2,000ft./610m.; mail Hunters z 99137; rural
Bitter Lake; RMC Place; KING; ★ **SEAT**; mail Seattle z 98133, z 98177; pop. incl. with Seattle (Inc. Place)
Biz Point; RMC Place; SKAGIT; ***246** C-6; elev. 100ft./30m.; mail Anacortes z 98221; ● 70
Black Diamond; Inc. Place; KING; **246** G-8; 🅿; ★ **SEAT**; z 98010; Ⓟ 1,422; Ⓒ 3,970
Black Lake; RMC Place; STEVENS; ***247** C-18; elev. 3,702ft./1,128m.; mail Colville z 99114; rural
Black River; RMC Place; KING; ★ **SEAT**; mail Seattle z 98178
Black River Junction; RMC Place; KING; ★ **SEAT**; mail Renton z 98055; pop. incl. with Renton (Inc. Place)
Blaine; Inc. Place; WHATCOM; **246** A-6; 🅿; ★ **BELNG**; z 98230-31; Ⓟ 2,489; Ⓒ 3,770
Blakely Island; RMC Place; SAN JUAN; ***246** C-6; 🅿; z 98222; summer pop. 150; rural
Blanchard; RMC Place; SKAGIT; **246** B-7; mail Bow z 98232; ● 180
Blewett; RMC Place; CHELAN; ***247** G-11; mail Leavenworth z 98826; rural
Blockhouse; RMC Place; KLICKITAT; ***246** L-10; elev. 1,586ft./483m.; mail Goldendale z 98620
Bluecreek; RMC Place; STEVENS; **247** C-18; mail Chewelah z 99109; ● 70
Blue Lake; RMC Place; GRANT; ***247** F-14; elev. 1,100ft./335m.; mail Coulee City z 99115; ● 130
Bluelight; RMC Place; KLICKITAT; ***247** L-12; mail Bickleton z 99322; rural
Blueslide; RMC Place; PEND OREILLE; ***247** C-19; mail Cusick z 99119
Blyn; CDP; CLALLAM; **246** E-6; mail Sequim z 98382; Ⓒ 162
Boise; RMC Place; KING; ***246** H-8; elev. 72ft./22m.; ★ **SEAT**; mail Enumclaw z 98022; ● 30
Boisfort; RMC Place; LEWIS; ***246** J-5; mail Curtis z 98538; rural
Bonney Lake; Inc. Place; PIERCE; **248** N-10; 🅿; ★ **SEAT**; z 98391 & mail Sumner z 98390; Ⓟ 7,494; Ⓒ 9,687
Bordeaux; RMC Place; THURSTON; ***246** I-5; elev. 400ft./122m.; mail Littlerock z 98556; rural
Bossburg; RMC Place; STEVENS; ***247** B-17; mail Evans z 99126
Boston Harbor; RMC Place; THURSTON; ***246** H-6; ★ **OLYM**; mail Olympia z 98501, z 98506; ● 300
Bothell; Inc. Place; KING, SNOHOMISH; **246** F-7; 🅿; ★ **SEAT**; z 98011-12, z 98021, z 98028, z 98041, z 98082; Ⓟ 12,345; Ⓒ 30,150; Ⓡ 30,084; ◆ 32,945
Boulevard Park; RMC Place; KING; ***246** F-7; ★ **SEAT**; mail Seattle z 98188
Bow; RMC Place; SKAGIT; **246** C-7; 🅿; z 98232; ● 180
Boyds; RMC Place; FERRY; **247** B-17; 🅿; z 99107; ● 50
Brady; CDP; GRAYS HARBOR; ***246** H-4; mail Montesano z 98563; Ⓒ 645
Breidablick; RMC Place; KITSAP; ***246** E-6; mail Poulsbo z 98370
Bremerton; Inc. Place; KITSAP; **246** F-6; 🅿 🅷 ■; ★ **BREM**; z 98310-12, z 98314, z 98337; Ⓟ 38,142; Ⓒ 37,259; ◆ 32,783
Brewster; Inc. Place; OKANOGAN; **247** D-13; 🅿 🅷; z 98812; Ⓟ 1,633; Ⓒ 2,189
Briarwood; RMC Place; KING; ***246** F-8; elev. 500ft./152m.; ★ **SEAT**; mail Kent z 98031; ● 4,800
Bridgeport; Inc. Place; DOUGLAS; **247** E-13; elev. 829ft./253m.; 🅿; z 98813; Ⓟ 1,498; Ⓒ 2,059
Brief; RMC Place; CHELAN; ***247** E-12; elev. 1,720ft./524m.; mail Entiat z 98822; ● 30
Brier; Inc. Place; SNOHOMISH; **248** A-8; 🅿; ★ **SEAT**; z 98036; Ⓟ 5,633; Ⓒ 6,383
Briercrest; RMC Place; KING; ***246** F-7; ★ **SEAT**; pop. incl. with Seattle (Inc. Place)
Brighton; RMC Place; KING; ***246** F-7; ★ **SEAT**; pop. incl. with Seattle (Inc. Place)
Brinnon; CDP; JEFFERSON; **246** F-6; elev. 77ft./23m.; 🅿; z 98320; Ⓒ 803
Broadmoor; RMC Place; KING; ***246** F-7; ★ **SEAT**; mail Seattle z 98112; pop. incl. with Seattle (Inc. Place)
Broadway; RMC Place; KING; ***246** F-7; ★ **SEAT**; mail Seattle z 98102; pop. incl. with Seattle (Inc. Place)
Brookdale; RMC Place; PIERCE; ***246** H-7; ★ **SEAT**; mail Tacoma z 98444
Brooklane Village; RMC Place; KITTITAS; ***247** H-11; elev. 1,681ft./512m.; mail Ellensburg z 98926; pop. incl. with Ellensburg (Inc. Place)
Brooklyn; RMC Place; PACIFIC; ***246** I-4; elev. 188ft./57m.; mail Cosmopolis z 98537; rural
Browns Point; RMC Place; PIERCE; **248** K-6; ★ **SEAT**; mail Tacoma z 98422; ● 1,950
Brownstown; RMC Place; YAKIMA; **247** J-11; 🅿; z 98920; ● 50
Brownsville; RMC Place; KITSAP; ***246** F-6; ★ **BREM**; mail Bremerton z 98310, Poulsbo z 98370; ● 250
Brush Prairie; CDP; CLARK; ***246** M-6; 🅿; ★ **POR**; z 98606; Ⓟ 2,650; Ⓒ 2,384
Bryant; RMC Place; SNOHOMISH; **246** D-8; ★ **SEAT**; mail Arlington z 98223; ● 100
Bryn Mawr; RMC Place; KING; **248** G-9; ★ **SEAT**; mail Seattle z 98178; ● 1,500
Bryn Mawr-Skyway; CDP-Census Area Only; KING; ***246** F-7; ★ **SEAT**; mail Seattle z 98178; Ⓟ 12,514; Ⓒ 13,977
Buckeye; RMC Place; SPOKANE; ***247** E-19; elev. 1,700ft./518m.; mail Colbert z 99005; rural
Buckhorn; RMC Place; SAN JUAN; ***246** B-6; elev. 26ft./8m.; mail Eastsound z 98245; ● 50
Buckley; Inc. Place; PIERCE; **246** H-8; elev. 726ft./221m.; 🅿; ★ **SEAT**; z 98321; Ⓟ 3,516; Ⓒ 4,145
Bucoda; Inc. Place; THURSTON; **246** I-6; 🅿; z 98530; Ⓟ 536; Ⓒ 628
Buena; RMC Place; YAKIMA; **247** J-12; 🅿; z 98921; ● 800
Buena Vista; RMC Place; ISLAND; ***246** D-7; elev. 100ft./30m.; ★ **SEAT**; mail Stanwood z 98292; rural
Bunker; RMC Place; LEWIS; ***246** I-5; mail Chehalis z 98532
Bunker Hill; RMC Place; COWLITZ; ***246** K-5; mail Longview z 98632; rural
Burbank; CDP; WALLA WALLA; **247** K-15; 🅿; ★ **RICH-**; z 99323; Ⓟ 1,745; Ⓒ 3,303
Burbank Heights; RMC Place; WALLA WALLA; ***247** K-15; ★ **RICH-**; mail Burbank z 99323; ● 500
Burien; Inc. Place; KING; **246** G-7; 🅿 🅷; ★ **SEAT**; z 98146, z 98148, z 98166, z 98168; Ⓒ 31,881; ◆ 35,377
Burley; RMC Place; KITSAP; ***246** G-6; 🅿; ★ **BREM**; z 98322; ● 300
Burlington; Inc. Place; SKAGIT; **246** C-7; 🅿; z 98233; Ⓟ 4,349; Ⓒ 6,757
Burnett; RMC Place; PIERCE; ***246** H-8; ★ **SEAT**; mail Buckley z 98321; ● 100
Burton; RMC Place; KING; **246** G-7; 🅿; ★ **SEAT**; z 98013; summer pop. 500; ● 280
Bush Point; RMC Place; ISLAND; ***246** D-7; ★ **SEAT**; mail Freeland z 98249; ● 250
Butler Acres; RMC Place; COWLITZ; ***246** K-6; elev. 401ft./122m.; ★ **LNGV**; mail Kelso z 98626; ● 180
BZ Corner; RMC Place; KLICKITAT; **246** L-9; elev. 717ft./219m.; mail White Salmon z 98672; ● 80

C

Cabin Creek; RMC Place; KITTITAS; ***246** G-10; mail Easton z 98925; ● 60
Camaloch; RMC Place; ISLAND; ***246** D-7; elev. 200ft./61m.; ★ **SEAT**; mail Stanwood z 98292; ● 250
Camano; CDP; ISLAND; ***246** D-7; ★ **SEAT**; mail Camano Island z 98282; Ⓒ 13,347
Camano City; RMC Place; ISLAND; ***246** D-7; elev. 100ft./30m.; ★ **SEAT**; mail Camano Island z 98282, Stanwood z 98292; ● 120
Camano Country Club; RMC Place; ISLAND; ***246** D-7; ★ **SEAT**; mail Stanwood z 98292; ● 500
Camas; Inc. Place; CLARK; **223** K-20; 🅿; ★ **POR**; z 98607; Ⓟ 6,762; Ⓒ 12,534
Camas; RMC Place; STEVENS; ***247** D-18; mail Springdale z 99173; rural
Camden; RMC Place; PEND OREILLE; ***247** D-19; mail Elk z 99009; rural
Camelot; RMC Place; KING; ***246** G-7; elev. 460ft./140m.; ★ **SEAT**; mail Auburn z 98001; ● 4,900
Campbell's Glen; RMC Place; ISLAND; ***246** E-7; elev. 378ft./115m.; ★ **SEAT**; mail Clinton z 98236; ● 75
Camp Draper; KLICKITAT; see Draper Springs Camp (RMC Place)
Camp Murray; RMC Place; PIERCE; 🅿; ★ **SEAT**; z 98430
Camp Union; RMC Place; KITSAP; ***246** F-6; elev. 433ft./132m.; ★ **BREM**; mail Bremerton z 98312; ● 90
Canal Tract; RMC Place; JEFFERSON; ***246** F-6; elev. 200ft./61m.; mail Brinnon z 98320; ● 200
Canyon Park; RMC Place; KING; ★ **SEAT**; mail Bothell z 98021; pop. incl. with Bothell (Inc. Place)
Cape George; RMC Place; JEFFERSON; ***246** D-6; elev. 300ft./91m.; mail Port Townsend z 98368; ● 250
Capitol City Country Club; RMC Place; THURSTON; ***246** H-6; elev. 222ft./68m.; ★ **OLYM**; mail Olympia z 98501; pop. incl. with Lacey (Inc. Place)
Capitol Hill; RMC Place; KING; ***246** F-7; ★ **SEAT**; mail Seattle z 98102; pop. incl. with Seattle (Inc. Place)
Cap Sante; RMC Place; SKAGIT; mail Anacortes z 98221; pop. incl. with Anacortes (Inc. Place)
Carbonado; Inc. Place; PIERCE; **246** H-8; 🅿; ★ **SEAT**; z 98323; Ⓟ 495; Ⓒ 621
Care Free Loop; RMC Place; CLALLAM; ***246** E-2; elev. 360ft./110m.; mail Forks z 98331; ● 50
Carlisle; RMC Place; GRAYS HARBOR; **246** G-3; mail Copalis Crossing z 98536; ● 60
Carlsborg; CDP; CLALLAM; **246** D-5; elev. 168ft./51m.; 🅿; z 98324; Ⓒ 855
Carlton; RMC Place; OKANOGAN; **247** D-12; 🅿; z 98814; ● 70
Carnation (Tolt); Inc. Place; KING; **246** F-8; 🅿; ★ **SEAT**; z 98014; Ⓟ 1,243; Ⓒ 1,893
Carrier Annex; RMC Place; SNOHOMISH; ★ **SEAT**; mail Everett z 98204; pop. incl. with Everett (Inc. Place)
Carrolls; RMC Place; COWLITZ; **246** K-6; 🅿; ★ **LNGV**; z 98609; ● 100
Carson; RMC Place; SKAMANIA; **246** M-8; 🅿; z 98610; ● 1,000
Carson River Valley; CDP-Census Area Only; SKAMANIA; ***246** M-8; mail Carson z 98610; Ⓟ 1,678; Ⓒ 2,116
Carylon Beach; RMC Place; THURSTON; ***246** G-6; elev. 100ft./30m.; ★ **OLYM**; mail Olympia z 98501; ● 500
Cascade-Fairwood; CDP-Census Area Only; KING; ***246** G-8; ★ **SEAT**; mail Renton z 98055, z 98058; Ⓟ 30,107; Ⓒ 34,580; ◆ 38,281
Cascade Park; RMC Place; CLARK; ***246** M-6; ★ **POR**; mail Vancouver z 98683-84; pop. incl. with Vancouver (Inc. Place)
Cascade Terrace; RMC Place; PIERCE; ***246** H-7; elev. 500ft./152m.; ★ **SEAT**; mail Puyallup z 98371; ● 100
Cascade Valley; CDP-Census Area Only; GRANT; ***247** H-14; mail Moses Lake z 98837; Ⓟ 1,288; Ⓒ 1,811
Cascade Vista; RMC Place; KING; ***246** G-7; elev. 415ft./126m.; ★ **SEAT**; mail Renton z 98055, z 98058; ● 7,800
Cashmere; Inc. Place; CHELAN; **247** F-12; elev. 795ft./242m.; 🅿; z 98815; Ⓟ 2,544; Ⓒ 2,965
Castle Rock; Inc. Place; COWLITZ; **246** K-6; 🅿; ★ **LNGV**; z 98611; Ⓟ 2,067; Ⓒ 2,130
Cathan; CDP-Census Area Only; SNOHOMISH; ***246** D-7; ★ **SEAT**; mail Marysville z 98270; Ⓟ 428; Ⓒ 526
Cathcart; CDP; SNOHOMISH; **246** E-8; ★ **SEAT**; mail Snohomish z 98296; Ⓒ 3,015
Cathlamet; Inc. Place; ⊡ WAHKIAKUM; **246** K-4; elev. 53ft./16m.; 🅿; z 98612; Ⓟ 508; Ⓒ 565
Cavelero Beach; RMC Place; ISLAND; ***246** D-7; ★ **SEAT**; mail Camano Island z 98282; ● 30
Cedardale; RMC Place; SKAGIT; ***246** C-7; elev. 6ft./2m.; mail Mount Vernon z 98274; ● 30
Cedar Falls; RMC Place; KING; ***246** G-8; ★ **SEAT**; mail North Bend z 98045
Cedar Grove; RMC Place; KING; ***246** G-8; ★ **SEAT**; mail Maple Valley z 98038; ● 150
Cedarhome; RMC Place; SNOHOMISH; ***246** D-7; ★ **SEAT**; mail Stanwood z 98292; ● 200
Cedar Mountain; RMC Place; KING; ***246** G-8; ★ **SEAT**; mail Renton z 98058
Cedarview; RMC Place; PIERCE; ***246** H-8; ★ **SEAT**; mail Sumner z 98390; pop. incl. with Bonney Lake (Inc. Place)
Cedarville; RMC Place; GRAYS HARBOR; ***246** I-5; elev. 78ft./24m.; mail Oakville z 98568
Cedonia; RMC Place; STEVENS; ***247** D-17; elev. 1,708ft./521m.; mail Hunters z 99137
Center; RMC Place; JEFFERSON; ***246** E-6; mail Quilcene z 98376
Centerville; CDP; KLICKITAT; **247** M-11; elev. 1,605ft./489m.; 🅿; z 98613; Ⓒ 120
Central; RMC Place; YAKIMA; ★ **YAK**; mail Yakima z 98901; pop. incl. with Yakima (Inc. Place)
Centralia; Inc. Place; LEWIS; **246** I-6; elev. 189ft./58m.; 🅿 🅷 ■; z 98531; Ⓟ 12,101; Ⓒ 14,742; ◆ 15,789
Central Park; CDP; GRAYS HARBOR; **246** H-4; mail Aberdeen z 98520; Ⓟ 2,669; Ⓒ 2,558
Central Valley; RMC Place; KITSAP; ***246** F-6; ★ **BREM**; mail Poulsbo z 98370; ● 200
Ceres; RMC Place; LEWIS; ***246** J-5; elev. 232ft./71m.; mail Chehalis z 98532; rural
Charleston; RMC Place; KITSAP; ***246** F-6; elev. 100ft./30m.; ★ **BREM**; mail Bremerton z 98312; pop. incl. with Bremerton (Inc. Place)
Charleston Beach; RMC Place; KITSAP; ***246** F-6; elev. 100ft./30m.; ★ **BREM**; mail Bremerton z 98312; ● 300
Charter Oak; RMC Place; CLARK; ***246** L-6; elev. 332ft./101m.; ★ **POR**; mail Battle Ground z 98604; rural
Chattaroy; RMC Place; SPOKANE; **247** E-19; 🅿; z 99003; ● 450
Chehalis; Inc. Place; ⊡ LEWIS; **246** I-6; elev. 226ft./69m.; 🅿; z 98532; Ⓟ 6,527; Ⓒ 7,057
Chehalis Reservation; Indian Reservation; GRAYS HARBOR, THURSTON; mail Oakville z 98568; Ⓟ 405; Ⓒ 691
Chehalis Village; CDP-Census Area Only; GRAYS HARBOR; ***246** I-5; located on Chehalis Indian Reservation; mail Oakville z 98568; Ⓟ 282; Ⓒ 346
Chelan; Inc. Place; CHELAN; **247** E-13; 🅿 🅷; z 98816; Ⓟ 2,969; Ⓒ 3,522
CHELAN; **247** E-11; Ⓟ 52,250; Ⓒ 66,616; ◆ 70,860
Chelan Falls; RMC Place; CHELAN; **247** E-13; elev. 732ft./223m.; 🅿; z 98817; ● 300
Chelatchie (Chelatchie Prairie); RMC Place; CLARK; ***246** L-7; elev. 505ft./154m.; mail Amboy z 98601; ● 100
Chelatchie Prairie; CLARK; see Chelatchie (RMC Place)
Cheney; Inc. Place; SPOKANE; **247** F-19; 🅿 🅲 11,161; z 99004; Ⓟ 7,723; Ⓒ 8,832
Cherokee; RMC Place; OKANOGAN; ***247** C-14; mail Omak z 98841; rural
Cherokee Bay Park; RMC Place; KING; ***246** G-8; ★ **SEAT**; mail Maple Valley z 98038; pop. incl. with Maple Valley (Inc. Place)
Cherry Crest; RMC Place; KING; ★ **SEAT**; mail Bellevue z 98004; pop. incl. with Bellevue (Inc. Place)
Cherry Gardens; RMC Place; KING; ***246** F-8; elev. 100ft./30m.; ★ **SEAT**; mail Duvall z 98019; pop. incl. with Duvall (Inc. Place)
Cherry Grove; CDP; CLARK; ***246** L-6; ★ **POR**; mail Battle Ground z 98604; Ⓒ 663
Cherry Point; RMC Place; WHATCOM; ***246** B-6; elev. 60ft./18m.; ★ **BELNG**; mail Blaine z 98230; ● 700
Chesaw; RMC Place; OKANOGAN; **247** A-15; mail Oroville z 98844; ● 50
Chewelah; Inc. Place; STEVENS; **247** D-18; elev. 1,671ft./509m.; 🅿 🅷; z 99109; Ⓟ 1,945; Ⓒ 2,186
Chico; RMC Place; KITSAP; **246** F-6; ★ **BREM**; mail Bremerton z 98312; ● 450
Chimacum; RMC Place; JEFFERSON; **246** E-6; 🅿; z 98325; ● 800
Chinook; CDP; PACIFIC; **246** K-3; 🅿; z 98614; Ⓒ 457
Christopher; RMC Place; KING; ***246** G-7; ★ **SEAT**; mail Auburn z 98002; pop. incl. with Auburn (Inc. Place)
Chuckanut Village; RMC Place; WHATCOM; ***246** B-7; ★ **BELNG**; mail Bellingham z 98225; pop. incl. with Bellingham (Inc. Place)
Chumstick; RMC Place; CHELAN; ***247** F-11; mail Leavenworth z 98826; rural
Churchlake; RMC Place; PIERCE; ***246** G-8; elev. 559ft./170m.; ★ **SEAT**; mail Sumner z 98390; pop. incl. with Bonney Lake (Inc. Place)
Cicero; RMC Place; SNOHOMISH; ***246** D-8; ★ **SEAT**; mail Arlington z 98223; rural
Cinebar; RMC Place; LEWIS; **246** J-7; elev. 911ft./278m.; 🅿; z 98533; ● 80
Cispus; RMC Place; LEWIS; ***246** J-8; elev. 1,200ft./366m.; mail Randle z 98377; rural
City Center; RMC Place; WHATCOM; ★ **BELNG**; mail Bellingham z 98225; pop. incl. with Bellingham (Inc. Place)
CLALLAM; **246** E-4; Ⓟ 56,464; Ⓒ 64,525; Ⓡ 64,179; ◆ 70,563
Clallam Bay; RMC Place; CLALLAM; **246** D-3; 🅿; z 98326; summer pop. 1,500; ● 900
Claquato; RMC Place; LEWIS; ***246** I-5; elev. 197ft./60m.; mail Chehalis z 98532
Claremont; RMC Place; SNOHOMISH; ★ **SEAT**; mail Everett z 98201; pop. incl. with Everett (Inc. Place)
CLARK; **246** M-7; Ⓟ 238,053; Ⓒ 345,238; ◆ 428,020
Clarkston; Inc. Place; ASOTIN; **247** J-20; 🅿 🅷; ★ **LEW**; z 99403; Ⓟ 6,753; Ⓒ 7,337
Clarkston Heights; RMC Place; ASOTIN; ***247** J-20; ★ **LEW**; mail Clarkston z 99403; ● 1,150
Clarkston Heights-Vineland; CDP-Census Area Only; ASOTIN; ***247** J-20; ★ **LEW**; mail Clarkston z 99403; Ⓟ 2,832; Ⓒ 6,117
Clay City; RMC Place; PIERCE; ***246** H-7; elev. 600ft./183m.; mail Eatonville z 98328; ● 30
Clayton; RMC Place; STEVENS; **247** D-19; 🅿; z 99110; ● 200
Clearbrook; RMC Place; WHATCOM; ***246** A-7; elev. 67ft./20m.; mail Everson z 98247, Lynden z 98264, Sumas z 98295; rural
Clear Lake; RMC Place; PIERCE; ***246** H-7; elev. 800ft./244m.; ★ **SEAT**; mail Eatonville z 98328; ● 200
Clear Lake; CDP; SKAGIT; **246** C-7; 🅿; z 98235; Ⓒ 942
Clear Lake; RMC Place; SPOKANE; ***247** F-18; elev. 2,400ft./732m.; mail Medical Lake z 99022; ● 90
Clearview; RMC Place; SNOHOMISH; **246** E-8; ★ **SEAT**; mail Snohomish z 98290; ● 250
Clearwater; RMC Place; JEFFERSON; **246** F-2; mail Forks z 98331; ● 200
Cle Elum; Inc. Place; KITTITAS; **247** H-11; elev. 1,905ft./581m.; 🅿; z 98922; Ⓟ 1,778; Ⓒ 1,755
Cleveland; RMC Place; KLICKITAT; ***247** L-12; mail Roosevelt z 99356
Cliffdell; RMC Place; YAKIMA; **246** H-10; mail Naches z 98937; ● 50
Cline; RMC Place; STEVENS; ***247** D-18; mail Springdale z 99173; pop. incl. with Springdale (Inc. Place)
Clinton; CDP; ISLAND; **246** E-7; 🅿; ★ **SEAT**; z 98236; Ⓟ 1,564; Ⓒ 868
Clipper; RMC Place; WHATCOM; ***246** B-7; mail Deming z 98244
Cloverland; RMC Place; ASOTIN; ***247** K-20; elev. 2,919ft./890m.; mail Asotin z 99402; rural
Clover Park; RMC Place; PIERCE; ***246** H-7; ★ **SEAT**; mail Lakewood z 98499; pop. incl. with Lakewood (Inc. Place)
Clyde Hill; Inc. Place; KING; **248** D-9; 🅿; ★ **SEAT**; z 98004; Ⓟ 2,972; Ⓒ 2,890
Coal Creek; RMC Place; COWLITZ; ***246** K-5; ★ **LNGV**; mail Issaquah z 98027, Longview z 98632; ● 50
Coalfield; RMC Place; KING; **248** G-10; ★ **SEAT**; mail Renton z 98059; ● 400
Cohassett Beach; CDP-Census Area Only; GRAYS HARBOR; ***246** I-3; Ⓒ 618
Cokedale; RMC Place; SKAGIT; ***246** C-8; mail Sedro Woolley z 98284; rural
Colbert (Dean); RMC Place; SPOKANE; **247** E-19; 🅿; ★ **SPOK**; z 99005; ● 130
Colby; RMC Place; KITSAP; **248** F-5; ★ **BREM**; mail Port Orchard z 98366; ● 200
Colchester; RMC Place; KITSAP; **248** F-5; ★ **BREM**; mail Port Orchard z 98366; ● 200
Coles Corner; RMC Place; CHELAN; **247** F-11; mail Leavenworth z 98826; ● 40
Colfax; Inc. Place; ⊡ WHITMAN; **247** H-19; elev. 1,962ft./598m.; 🅿 🅷; z 99111; Ⓟ 2,713; Ⓒ 2,844
College Place; Inc. Place; WALLA WALLA; **247** L-17; 🅿 🅲 1,876; ★ **WALL**; z 99324; Ⓟ 6,308; Ⓒ 7,818
Colton; Inc. Place; WHITMAN; **247** J-20; 🅿; z 99113; Ⓟ 325; Ⓒ 386
Columbia; RMC Place; KING; ***246** F-7; ★ **SEAT**; mail Seattle z 98118; pop. incl. with Seattle (Inc. Place)
COLUMBIA; **247** K-18; Ⓟ 4,024; Ⓒ 4,064; ◆ 3,989
Columbia Beach; RMC Place; ISLAND; ***246** E-7; ★ **SEAT**; mail Clinton z 98236
Columbia Heights; RMC Place; COWLITZ; ***246** K-6; ★ **LNGV**; mail Longview z 98632; ● 2,300
Columbia Valley Gardens; RMC Place; COWLITZ; ***246** K-5; elev. 4ft./1m.; ★ **LNGV**; mail Longview z 98632; pop. incl. with Longview (Inc. Place)
Colville; Inc. Place; ⊡ STEVENS; **247** C-18; 🅿 🅷; z 99114; Ⓟ 4,360; Ⓒ 4,988
Colville Indian Agency; RMC Place; OKANOGAN; **247** D-15; located on Colville Ind. Res.; elev. 1,782ft./543m.; mail Nespelem z 99155; ● 200
Colville Reservation; Indian Reservation; FERRY, OKANOGAN; mail Nespelem z 99155; also location of Indian Agency; Ⓟ 7,047; Ⓒ 7,582
Conconully; Inc. Place; OKANOGAN; **247** C-13; 🅿; z 98819; Ⓟ 153; Ⓒ 185
Concora; RMC Place; KING; ★ **SEAT**; mail Seattle z 98188; pop. incl. with Tukwila (Inc. Place)
Concrete; Inc. Place; SKAGIT; **246** C-9; 🅿; z 98237; Ⓟ 735; Ⓒ 790
Conifer View; RMC Place; KING; ★ **SEAT**; mail Bothell z 98011; pop. incl. with Bothell (Inc. Place)
Connell; Inc. Place; FRANKLIN; **247** I-16; elev. 840ft./256m.; 🅿; z 99326; Ⓟ 2,005; Ⓒ 2,956
Conway (Fir); CDP; SKAGIT; **246** C-7; 🅿; z 98238; Ⓒ 84
Cook (Cooks); RMC Place; SKAMANIA; **246** M-9; 🅿; z 98605; ● 70
Cooks; SKAMANIA; see Cook (RMC Place)
Cooper Point; RMC Place; THURSTON; ***246** H-6; elev. 40ft./12m.; ★ **OLYM**; mail Olympia z 98501; ● 50
Copalis; GRAYS HARBOR; see Copalis Crossing (RMC Place)
Copalis Beach; CDP; GRAYS HARBOR; **246** H-3; 🅿; z 98535; summer pop. 1,200; Ⓒ 489
Copalis Crossing (Copalis); RMC Place; GRAYS HARBOR; **246** H-3; 🅿; z 98536; ● 200
Cornwall; RMC Place; WHATCOM; ★ **BELNG**; mail Bellingham z 98225; pop. incl. with Bellingham (Inc. Place)
Cosmopolis; Inc. Place; GRAYS HARBOR; **246** H-4; elev. 12ft./4m.; 🅿; z 98537; Ⓟ 1,372; Ⓒ 1,595
Cottage Lake; CDP-Census Area Only; KING; ***246** F-8; ★ **SEAT**; mail Woodinville z 98072; Ⓒ 24,330; Ⓡ 23,789; ◆ 26,933
Cottage Lake Bridle Trail; RMC Place; KING; ***246** E-8; elev. 400ft./122m.; ★ **SEAT**; mail Kirkland z 98033; ● 600
Cottonwood Beach; RMC Place; WHATCOM; ***246** A-6; ★ **BELNG**; mail Blaine z 98230
Cougar; RMC Place; COWLITZ; **246** K-7; 🅿; z 98616; ● 100
Coulee City; Inc. Place; GRANT; **247** F-14; 🅿; z 99115; Ⓟ 568; Ⓒ 600
Coulee Dam; Inc. Place; OKANOGAN, DOUGLAS, GRANT; **247** E-15; elev. 1,145ft./349m.; 🅿; z 99116; Ⓟ 1,087; Ⓒ 1,044
Country Homes; CDP; SPOKANE; **248** A-2; ★ **SPOK**; mail Spokane z 99218; Ⓟ 5,126; Ⓒ 5,203
Countryside Beach; RMC Place; THURSTON; ***246** H-6; elev. 100ft./30m.; ★ **OLYM**; mail Olympia z 98501; ● 60
Coupeville; Inc. Place; ⊡ ISLAND; **246** D-6; 🅿 🅷; z 98239; Ⓟ 1,377; Ⓒ 1,723
Cove; RMC Place; KING; ***246** G-7; ★ **SEAT**; mail Vashon z 98070; ● 125
Covington; Inc. Place; KING; **246** G-8; elev. 352ft./107m.; 🅿; ★ **SEAT**; z 98042; Ⓒ 13,783
Cowiche; RMC Place; YAKIMA; **247** I-11; 🅿; ★ **YAK**; z 98923; ● 400
COWLITZ; **246** K-6; Ⓟ 82,119; Ⓒ 92,948; ◆ 101,486
Cozy Nook; RMC Place; STEVENS; ***247** C-18; elev. 2,270ft./692m.; mail Chewelah z 99109; rural
Creosote; RMC Place; KITSAP; **248** D-5; elev. 100ft./30m.; ★ **SEAT**; mail Bainbridge Island z 98110; pop. incl. with Winslow (Inc. Place)
Crescent Bar; RMC Place; GRANT; **247** G-13; elev. 578ft./176m.; mail Quincy z 98848; ● 140
Creston; Inc. Place; LINCOLN; **247** E-16; elev. 2,436ft./742m.; 🅿; z 99117, z 99147; Ⓟ 230; Ⓒ 232
Crocker; RMC Place; PIERCE; ***246** H-8; elev. 293ft./89m.; ★ **SEAT**; mail Orting z 98360; rural
Crockett Lake Estates; RMC Place; ISLAND; ***246** D-6; elev. 100ft./30m.; mail Coupeville z 98239; ● 80
Cromwell; RMC Place; PIERCE; ***246** G-6; ★ **SEAT**; mail Gig Harbor z 98335
Crown Hill; RMC Place; KING; ***246** F-7; ★ **SEAT**; mail Seattle z 98117; pop. incl. with Seattle (Inc. Place)
Crystal Mountain; RMC Place; PIERCE; **246** H-9; mail Enumclaw z 98022; seasonal pop. 150; ● 30
Crystal Spring; RMC Place; KITSAP; **248** E-4; elev. 100ft./30m.; ★ **SEAT**; mail Bainbridge Island z 98110; pop. incl. with Winslow (Inc. Place)
Crystal Springs; RMC Place; PIERCE; ★ **SEAT**; mail Tacoma z 98466; pop. incl. with University Place (Inc. Place)
Crystal Village; RMC Place; PIERCE; ***246** H-9; elev. 2,000ft./610m.; ★ **SEAT**; mail Enumclaw z 98022; ● 200
Cumberland; RMC Place; KING; ***246** G-8; mail Enumclaw z 98022; ● 150
Cunningham; RMC Place; ADAMS; **247** I-16; ● 25
Curlew; RMC Place; FERRY; **247** A-16; 🅿; z 99118; ● 200
Curtis; RMC Place; LEWIS; **246** J-5; 🅿; z 98538; ● 50
Cushman Dam; RMC Place; MASON; ***246** G-5; elev. 865ft./264m.; mail Hoodsport z 98548; ● 120
Cusick; Inc. Place; PEND OREILLE; **247** C-19; 🅿; z 99119; Ⓟ 195; Ⓒ 212
Custer; RMC Place; PIERCE; ***246** H-7; elev. 260ft./79m.; ★ **SEAT**; mail Tacoma z 98413; pop. incl. with Lakewood (Inc. Place)
Custer; CDP; WHATCOM; **246** A-6; 🅿; z 98240; Ⓒ 299

D

Dabob; RMC Place; JEFFERSON; ***246** E-6; mail Quilcene z 98376; rural
Daisy; RMC Place; STEVENS; ***247** C-17; mail Rice z 99167; ● 30
Dalkena; RMC Place; PEND OREILLE; ***247** D-19; elev. 2,061ft./628m.; mail Newport z 99156; ● 90
Dallesport (North Dallas); CDP; KLICKITAT; **246** M-10; 🅿; z 98617; Ⓒ 1,185
Danville; RMC Place; FERRY; **247** A-16; 🅿; z 99121; ● 200
Darlington; RMC Place; SNOHOMISH; ***246** E-7; ★ **SEAT**; mail Everett z 98203; pop. incl. with Everett (Inc. Place)
Darrington; Inc. Place; SNOHOMISH; **246** D-9; elev. 549ft./167m.; 🅿; z 98241; Ⓟ 1,042; Ⓒ 1,136
Dash Point; RMC Place; PIERCE; ***246** G-7; ★ **SEAT**; mail Tacoma z 98422
Davenport; Inc. Place; ⊡ LINCOLN; **247** F-17; elev. 2,369ft./722m.; 🅿 🅷; z 99122; Ⓟ 1,502; Ⓒ 1,730
Day Creek; RMC Place; SKAGIT; ***246** C-8; mail Sedro Woolley z 98284; ● 150
Day Island; RMC Place; PIERCE; ***246** G-7; elev. 100ft./30m.; ★ **SEAT**; mail Tacoma z 98466; pop. incl. with University Place (Inc. Place)
Dayton; Inc. Place; ⊡ COLUMBIA; **247** J-18; elev. 1,613ft./492m.; 🅿 🅷; z 99328; Ⓟ 2,468; Ⓒ 2,655
Dayton; RMC Place; MASON; ***246** G-5; elev. 249ft./76m.; mail Shelton z 98584
Dean; SPOKANE; see Colbert (RMC Place)
Decatur; RMC Place; SAN JUAN; ***246** C-6; mail Anacortes z 98221; summer pop. 100; ● 30
Deep Creek; RMC Place; SPOKANE; **247** F-18; mail Medical Lake z 99022; ● 40
Deep River; RMC Place; WAHKIAKUM; ***246** J-4; mail Naselle z 98638; ● 40
Deer Harbor; RMC Place; SAN JUAN; **246** B-6; 🅿; z 98243; summer pop. 500; ● 100
Deer Island; RMC Place; PIERCE; ***246** G-7; elev. 575ft./175m.; ★ **SEAT**; mail Sumner z 98390; ● 250
Deer Lake; RMC Place; STEVENS; ***247** D-18; elev. 2,520ft./768m.; mail Loon Lake z 99148; summer pop. 2,000; ● 400
Deer Park; Inc. Place; SPOKANE; **247** E-19; 🅿 🅷; z 99006; Ⓟ 2,278; Ⓒ 3,017
Delano; RMC Place; GRANT; ***247** E-15; elev. 1,593ft./486m.; mail Grand Coulee z 99133; pop. incl. with Grand Coulee (Inc. Place)
Delano Beach; RMC Place; PIERCE; ***246** G-6; elev. 100ft./30m.; ★ **SEAT**; mail Lakebay z 98349; ● 40
Delphi; RMC Place; THURSTON; ***246** H-5; elev. 200ft./61m.; ★ **OLYM**; mail Olympia z 98501; ● 50
Delphi Country Club; RMC Place; THURSTON; ***246** H-5; elev. 400ft./122m.; ★ **OLYM**; mail Olympia z 98512; ● 200
Delridge; RMC Place; KING; ***246** F-7; ★ **SEAT**; pop. incl. with Seattle (Inc. Place)
Deming; CDP; WHATCOM; **246** B-7; 🅿; z 98244; Ⓒ 210
Denison; RMC Place; SPOKANE; ***247** E-19; elev. 1,958ft./597m.; mail Deer Park z 99006
Denny Park; RMC Place; KING; ***246** F-7; elev. 9,000ft./2,743m.; ★ **SEAT**; mail Bothell z 98011; ● 2,500
Desert Aire; CDP; GRANT; **247** I-13; elev. 560ft./171m.; 🅿; z 99349 & mail Othello z 99344; Ⓒ 1,124
Des Moines; Inc. Place; KING; **246** G-7; 🅿; ★ **SEAT**; z 98148, z 98198; Ⓟ 17,283; Ⓒ 29,267; ◆ 30,975
Devereaux Lake; RMC Place; MASON; ***246** G-6; elev. 208ft./63m.; ★ **BREM**; mail Belfair z 98528; ● 100
Dewatto; RMC Place; MASON; ***246** G-5; mail Tahuya z 98588; ● 70
Dewey; RMC Place; SKAGIT; ***246** C-7; mail Anacortes z 98221; ● 550
Dexter by the Sea; RMC Place; PACIFIC; ***246** I-3; elev. 11ft./3m.; mail Tokeland z 98590; ● 150
Diablo; RMC Place; WHATCOM; **246** B-10; mail Rockport z 98283; ● 50
Diamond; RMC Place; WHITMAN; **247** H-19; 🅿; z 99111; ● 50
Diamond Lake; RMC Place; PEND OREILLE; ***247** D-19; elev. 2,361ft./720m.; mail Newport z 99156; summer pop. 600; ● 220
Dieringer; RMC Place; PIERCE; **248** L-9; ★ **SEAT**; mail Sumner z 98390; pop. incl. with Sumner (Inc. Place)
Dines Point; RMC Place; ISLAND; ***246** D-7; elev. 100ft./30m.; ★ **SEAT**; mail Greenbank z 98253; ● 80
Disautel; RMC Place; OKANOGAN; **247** C-15; mail Omak z 98841
Discovery Bay; RMC Place; JEFFERSON; ***246** E-6; elev. 12ft./4m.; mail Port Townsend z 98368, Sequim z 98382; ● 100
Dishman; CDP; SPOKANE; **247** F-19; ★ **SPOK**; mail Spokane z 99213; Ⓟ 9,671; Ⓒ 10,031
Dixie; CDP; WALLA WALLA; **247** K-17; elev. 1,547ft./472m.; 🅿; ★ **WALL**; z 99329; Ⓒ 220
Dockton; RMC Place; KING; **248** I-6; ★ **SEAT**; mail Vashon z 98070; ● 300
Dodge; RMC Place; GARFIELD; ***247** J-18; elev. 1,252ft./382m.; mail Pomeroy z 99347; rural
Doe Bay; RMC Place; SAN JUAN; **246** B-6; mail Olga z 98279; summer pop. 100; ● 40
Dole; RMC Place; CLARK; ***246** L-7; mail Yacolt z 98675; rural
Dollar Corner (Dollar's Corner); CDP; CLARK; **246** L-6; ★ **POR**; mail Battle Ground z 98604; Ⓒ 1,039
Dollar's Corner; CLARK; see Dollar Corner (CDP)
Donald; RMC Place; YAKIMA; **247** J-12; mail Wapato z 98951; ● 50
Doty; RMC Place; LEWIS; **246** I-5; 🅿; z 98539; ● 300
Douglas; RMC Place; DOUGLAS; **247** F-13; mail Waterville z 98858; ● 40
DOUGLAS; **247** F-14; Ⓟ 26,205; Ⓒ 32,603; ◆ 37,794
Downing; RMC Place; DOUGLAS; ***247** D-13; elev. 908ft./277m.; mail Brewster z 98812, Bridgeport z 98813; ● 120
Downtown; RMC Place; CLARK; ★ **POR**; mail Vancouver z 98660; pop. incl. with Vancouver (Inc. Place)
Downtown; RMC Place; KING; ★ **SEAT**; mail Kent z 98032; pop. incl. with Kent (Inc. Place)
Downtown; RMC Place; PIERCE; ★ **SEAT**; mail Tacoma z 98401-02; pop. incl. with Tacoma (Inc. Place)
Draper Springs Camp (Camp Draper); RMC Place; KLICKITAT; ***246** L-9; elev. 2,000ft./610m.; mail Glenwood z 98619; rural
Driftwood Acres; RMC Place; KITTITAS; ***246** G-10; elev. 2,240ft./683m.; mail Ronald z 98940; ● 250
Driftwood Point; RMC Place; PIERCE; ***246** G-7; elev. 600ft./183m.; ★ **SEAT**; mail Sumner z 98390; ● 900
Driftwood Shores; RMC Place; ISLAND; ***246** D-7; ★ **SEAT**; mail Camano Island z 98282; ● 100
Dryad; RMC Place; LEWIS; ***246** I-5; elev. 301ft./92m.; mail Chehalis z 98532; ● 100
Dryden; RMC Place; CHELAN; **247** F-11; elev. 977ft./298m.; 🅿; z 98821; ● 500
Duluth; RMC Place; CLARK; ***246** L-6; elev. 283ft./86m.; ★ **POR**; mail Ridgefield z 98642; rural
Dumas; RMC Place; COLUMBIA; ***247** K-18; mail Dayton z 99328; rural
Dumas Bay-Twin Lakes; RMC Place; KING; ***246** G-7; ★ **SEAT**; mail Federal Way z 98023; pop. incl. with Federal Way (Inc. Place)
Dungeness; RMC Place; CLALLAM; **246** D-5; mail Sequim z 98382; ● 250
Dupont; Inc. Place; PIERCE; **246** H-6; 🅿; ★ **SEAT**; z 98327; Ⓟ 592; Ⓒ 2,452
Dusty; RMC Place; WHITMAN; **247** I-18; mail Lacrosse z 99143; ● 30
Duvall; Inc. Place; KING; **246** F-8; 🅿; ★ **SEAT**; z 98019; Ⓟ 2,770; Ⓒ 4,616
Duwamish; RMC Place; KING; ***246** F-7; elev. 25ft./8m.; ★ **SEAT**; mail Seattle z 98188; pop. incl. with Tukwila (Inc. Place)

E

Eagledale; RMC Place; KITSAP; **248** D-5; ★ **SEAT**; mail Bainbridge Island z 98110; pop. incl. with Winslow (Inc. Place)
Eaglemount; RMC Place; JEFFERSON; ***246** E-6; elev. 518ft./158m.; mail Port Townsend z 98368; rural
Earlington; RMC Place; KING; ★ **SEAT**; mail Renton z 98055; pop. incl. with Renton (Inc. Place)
Earlmount; RMC Place; KING; ★ **SEAT**; mail Redmond z 98052; pop. incl. with Redmond (Inc. Place)
East Aberdeen; RMC Place; GRAYS HARBOR; mail Aberdeen z 98520; pop. incl. with Aberdeen (Inc. Place)
East Cathlamet; CDP-Census Area Only; WAHKIAKUM; ***246** K-4; Ⓒ 491
East Coulee Dam; RMC Place; OKANOGAN; mail Coulee Dam z 99116; pop. incl. with Coulee Dam (Inc. Place)
East Everett; RMC Place; SNOHOMISH; ***246** E-8; elev. 128ft./39m.; ★ **SEAT**; mail Everett z 98205; ● 350
East Farms; RMC Place; SPOKANE; ***247** F-20; ★ **SPOK**; mail Newman Lake z 99025; ● 1,400
Eastgate; CDP; KING; **248** E-10; ★ **SEAT**; mail Bellevue z 98006-07; Ⓟ 4,434; Ⓒ 4,558
Eastgate; RMC Place; WALLA WALLA; ★ **WALL**; mail Walla Walla z 99362; pop. incl. with Walla Walla (Inc. Place)
East Heights; RMC Place; GRANT; ***247** E-15; elev. 1,693ft./516m.; mail Grand Coulee z 99133; ● 50
East Hill-Meridian; CDP-Census Area Only; KING; ***246** G-7; ★ **SEAT**; mail Kent z 98031, z 98042; Ⓟ 42,696; Ⓒ 29,308; ◆ 32,443
East Hoquiam; RMC Place; GRAYS HARBOR; ***246** E-3; elev. 10ft./3m.; mail Hoquiam z 98550; pop. incl. with Hoquiam (Inc. Place)
East Kittitas; RMC Place; KITTITAS; ***247** H-12; elev. 1,850ft./564m.; mail Ellensburg z 98926; rural
Eastmont; RMC Place; SNOHOMISH; ***246** E-7; elev. 500ft./152m.; ★ **SEAT**; mail Everett z 98204-05; ● 1,450
East Olympia; RMC Place; THURSTON; ***246** H-6; elev. 221ft./67m.; 🅿; ★ **OLYM**; z 98540; ● 850
Easton; CDP; KITTITAS; **246** G-10; 🅿; z 98925; summer pop. 500; Ⓒ 383
East Port Orchard; CDP; KITSAP; ***246** F-6; ★ **BREM**; mail Port Orchard z 98366; Ⓟ 5,409; Ⓒ 5,116
East Quilcene; RMC Place; JEFFERSON; ***246** E-6; mail Quilcene z 98376; ● 70
East Raymond; RMC Place; PACIFIC; ***246** I-4; elev. 200ft./61m.; mail Raymond z 98577; ● 150
East Renton Highlands; CDP-Census Area Only; KING; ***246** F-8; ★ **SEAT**; mail Fall City z 98024, Renton z 98055; Ⓟ 13,218; Ⓒ 13,264
East Seattle; RMC Place; KING; ★ **SEAT**; mail Mercer Island z 98040; pop. incl. with Mercer Island (Inc. Place)
East Selah; RMC Place; YAKIMA; ***247** I-12; ★ **YAK**; mail Yakima z 98901; ● 50
Eastsound; RMC Place; SAN JUAN; **246** B-6; 🅿; z 98245; ● 1,100
East Spokane; RMC Place; SPOKANE; ***247** F-19; ★ **SPOK**; mail Spokane z 99212; ● 2,200
East Stanwood; RMC Place; SNOHOMISH; ***246** D-7; ★ **SEAT**; mail Stanwood z 98292; pop. incl. with Stanwood (Inc. Place)
East Union; RMC Place; KING; ★ **SEAT**; mail Seattle z 98112, z 98122; pop. incl. with Seattle (Inc. Place)
Eastview Hills; RMC Place; SNOHOMISH; ***246** E-7; elev. 407ft./124m.; ★ **SEAT**; mail Everett z 98204; ● 750
East Wenatchee; Inc. Place; DOUGLAS; **247** G-12; 🅿; z 98802; Ⓟ 2,701; Ⓒ 5,757
East Wenatchee Bench; CDP-Census Area Only; DOUGLAS; ***247** G-12; mail Wenatchee z 98801; Ⓟ 12,539; Ⓒ 13,658
Eatonville; Inc. Place; PIERCE; **246** I-7; 🅿; z 98328; Ⓟ 1,374; Ⓒ 2,012
Echo; RMC Place; STEVENS; ***247** B-18; elev. 1,889ft./576m.; mail Colville z 99114; rural
Echo Lake; RMC Place; KING; ★ **SEAT**; mail Seattle z 98133; pop. incl. with Shoreline (Inc. Place)
Echo Lake; CDP-Census Area Only; SNOHOMISH; ***246** E-8; ★ **SEAT**; Ⓒ 849
Eden; RMC Place; WAHKIAKUM; ***246** K-4; mail Rosburg z 98643; rural
Edgecomb; RMC Place; SNOHOMISH; ***246** D-8; ★ **SEAT**; mail Arlington z 98223; ● 40
Edgemoor; RMC Place; WHATCOM; ★ **BELNG**; mail Bellingham z 98225; pop. incl. with Bellingham (Inc. Place)
Edgewater; RMC Place; SNOHOMISH; ***246** E-7; ★ **SEAT**; mail Everett z 98203; pop. incl. with Everett (Inc. Place)
Edgewood; Inc. Place; PIERCE; **248** L-8; 🅿; ★ **SEAT**; z 98371-72 & mail Sumner z 98390; Ⓟ 8,702; Ⓒ 9,089
Edison; CDP; SKAGIT; **246** C-7; mail Bow z 98232; Ⓒ 133
Edmonds; Inc. Place; SNOHOMISH; **246** E-7; 🅿 🅷; ★ **SEAT**; z 98020, z 98026; Ⓟ 30,744; Ⓒ 39,515; ◆ 40,179
Edwall; RMC Place; LINCOLN; **247** F-18; 🅿; z 99008; ● 100
Eglon; RMC Place; KITSAP; ***246** E-7; mail Kingston z 98346; ● 300
Elbe; CDP; PIERCE; **246** I-7; elev. 1,211ft./369m.; 🅿; z 98330; Ⓒ 21
Elberton; RMC Place; WHITMAN; ***247** H-19; mail Garfield z 99130; ● 25
Eldon; RMC Place; MASON; ***246** F-5; mail Lilliwaup z 98555; ● 60
Eldorado Hills; RMC Place; KITSAP; ***246** F-6; elev. 300ft./91m.; ★ **BREM**; mail Bremerton z 98312; ● 200
Electric City; Inc. Place; GRANT; **247** E-15; elev. 1,655ft./504m.; 🅿; z 99123; Ⓟ 910; Ⓒ 922
Elk; RMC Place; SPOKANE; **247** D-19; 🅿; z 99009; ● 70
Elk Plain; CDP; PIERCE; ***246** H-7; ★ **SEAT**; mail Spanaway z 98387; Ⓟ 12,197; Ⓒ 15,697
Ellensburg; Inc. Place; ⊡ KITTITAS; **247** H-11; 🅿 🅷 🅲 10,688; z 98926, z 98950; Ⓟ 12,361; Ⓒ 15,414
Ellisford; OKANOGAN; see Ellisforde (RMC Place)
Ellisforde (Ellisford); RMC Place; OKANOGAN; **247** B-14; mail Tonasket z 98855; ● 30
Ellisport; RMC Place; KING; **248** H-6; ★ **SEAT**; mail Vashon z 98070; ● 150
Ellsworth; RMC Place; CLARK; ***246** M-6; ★ **POR**; mail Vancouver z 98664; pop. incl. with Vancouver (Inc. Place)
Elma; Inc. Place; GRAYS HARBOR; **246** H-4; 🅿; z 98541; Ⓟ 3,011; Ⓒ 3,049
Elmer City; Inc. Place; OKANOGAN; **247** E-15; 🅿; z 99124; Ⓟ 290; Ⓒ 267
Eltopia; RMC Place; FRANKLIN; **247** J-15; 🅿; z 99330; ● 250
Elwha; RMC Place; CLALLAM; ***246** D-4; mail Port Angeles z 98363; rural
Endicott; Inc. Place; WHITMAN; **247** H-18; elev. 1,706ft./520m.; 🅿; z 99125; Ⓟ 320; Ⓒ 621; Ⓡ 348
Enetai; RMC Place; KITSAP; ***246** F-6; ★ **BREM**; mail Bremerton z 98310, z 98312; ● 200
English; SNOHOMISH; see Lakewood (RMC Place)
Enterprise; BENTON; see West Richland (Inc. Place)
Enterprise; RMC Place; STEVENS; ***247** E-17; elev. 1,959ft./597m.; mail Fruitland z 99129; rural
Entiat; Inc. Place; CHELAN; **247** F-12; 🅿; z 98822; Ⓟ 449; Ⓒ 957
Enumclaw; Inc. Place; KING; **246** G-8; 🅿 🅷; ★ **SEAT**; z 98022; Ⓟ 7,227; Ⓒ 11,116
Ephrata; Inc. Place; ⊡ GRANT; **247** G-14; 🅿 🅷; z 98823; Ⓟ 5,349; Ⓒ 6,808
Erlands Point; RMC Place; KITSAP; ***246** F-6; ★ **BREM**; mail Bremerton z 98312; ● 1,300
Erlands Point-Kitsap Lake; CDP-Census Area Only; KITSAP; ***246** F-6; ★ **BREM**; mail Bremerton z 98312; Ⓟ 2,764; Ⓒ 2,723
Eschbach; CDP; YAKIMA; ***247** I-11; ★ **YAK**; Ⓒ 400
Espanola; RMC Place; SPOKANE; ***247** F-18; 🅿; z 99022; ● 30
Esperance; CDP-Census Area Only; SNOHOMISH; ***246** E-7; ★ **SEAT**; mail Mountlake Terrace z 98043; Ⓟ 11,236; Ⓒ 3,503
Esperance; RMC Place; SPOKANE; ★ **SPOK**; pop. incl. with Spokane (Inc. Place)
Ethel; RMC Place; LEWIS; **246** J-6; 🅿; z 98542; ● 200
Etna; RMC Place; CLARK; ***246** L-6; ★ **POR**; mail Woodland z 98674; rural
Eufaula Heights; RMC Place; COWLITZ; ***246** K-5; ★ **LNGV**; mail Longview z 98632; ● 90
Eureka; RMC Place; WALLA WALLA; **247** K-16; elev. 1,061ft./323m.; mail Prescott z 99348; ● 50
Eureka; RMC Place; WHATCOM; ★ **BELNG**; mail Bellingham z 98225; pop. incl. with Bellingham (Inc. Place)
Evaline; RMC Place; LEWIS; ***246** J-6; elev. 424ft./129m.; mail Winlock z 98596; rural
Evans; RMC Place; STEVENS; **247** B-17; 🅿; z 99126; ● 70
Everett; Inc. Place; ⊡ SNOHOMISH; **246** E-7; 🅿 🅷 ■; ★ **SEAT**; z 98201, z 98203-08, z 98213; location of Puget Sound Indian Agency; Ⓟ 69,974; Ⓒ 91,488; ◆ 101,837
Evergreen; RMC Place; PIERCE; ★ **SEAT**; mail Tacoma z 98411; pop. incl. with Tacoma (Inc. Place)
Evergreen Estates; RMC Place; THURSTON; ***246** H-6; elev. 250ft./76m.; ★ **OLYM**; mail Olympia z 98513; ● 150
Evergreen Shores; RMC Place; THURSTON; ***246** H-6; elev. 140ft./43m.; ★ **OLYM**; mail Olympia z 98501; ● 120
Everson; Inc. Place; WHATCOM; **246** A-7; elev. 90ft./27m.; 🅿; ★ **BELNG**; z 98247, z 98276; Ⓟ 1,490; Ⓒ 2,035
Ewan; RMC Place; WHITMAN; **247** H-18; ● 50

F

Factoria; RMC Place; KING; ★ **SEAT**; mail Bellevue z 98006; pop. incl. with Bellevue (Inc. Place)
Fairbanks; RMC Place; WHITMAN; ***247** G-19; mail Oakesdale z 99158; rural
Fairchild AFB; CDP-Census Area Only; SPOKANE; ***247** F-18; 🅿; z 99011; Ⓟ 4,854; Ⓒ 4,357; Ⓡ 4,300
Fairfax; RMC Place; PIERCE; ***246** H-8; ★ **SEAT**; mail Carbonado z 98323; ● 40
Fairfield; Inc. Place; SPOKANE; **247** G-20; elev. 2,559ft./780m.; 🅿; z 99012; Ⓟ 446; Ⓒ 494
Fair Harbor; RMC Place; MASON; ***246** G-6; elev. 47ft./14m.; ★ **BREM**; mail Allyn z 98524; ● 40
Fairhaven; RMC Place; WHATCOM; ★ **BELNG**; mail Bellingham z 98225; pop. incl. with Bellingham (Inc. Place)
Fairholm; RMC Place; CLALLAM; ***246** D-3; mail Port Angeles z 98362-63; rural
Fairmont; RMC Place; SNOHOMISH; ***246** E-7; ★ **SEAT**; mail Everett z 98204; ● 1,800
Fairview; RMC Place; KITSAP; ***246** F-6; elev. 80ft./24m.; ★ **BREM**; mail Bremerton z 98310; ● 160
Fairview; RMC Place; YAKIMA; ***247** J-12; elev. 1,040ft./317m.; ★ **YAK**; mail Yakima z 98903; pop. incl. with Yakima (Inc. Place)
Fairwood (Fairwood Greens); RMC Place; KING; **248** H-10; elev. 492ft./150m.; ★ **SEAT**; mail Renton z 98058; ● 2,000
Fairwood; CDP-Census Area Only; SPOKANE; ***247** E-19; ★ **SPOK**; mail Spokane z 99218; Ⓟ 5,807; Ⓒ 6,764
Fairwood Greens; KING; see Fairwood (RMC Place)
Fall City; CDP; KING; **246** F-8; 🅿; ★ **SEAT**; z 98024; Ⓟ 1,582; Ⓒ 1,638
Fargher Lake; RMC Place; CLARK; ***246** L-7; elev. 682ft./208m.; ★ **POR**; mail Yacolt z 98675; ● 100
Farmington; Inc. Place; WHITMAN; **247** H-20; elev. 2,626ft./800m.; 🅿; z 99104, z 99128; Ⓟ 126; Ⓒ 153
Fawn Lake; RMC Place; MASON; ***246** H-5; elev. 50ft./15m.; mail Shelton z 98584; ● 200
Federal; RMC Place; KING; ★ **SEAT**; mail Seattle z 98104; pop. incl. with Seattle (Inc. Place)
Federal Way; Inc. Place; KING; **246** G-7; 🅿 🅷 🅲 812; ★ **SEAT**; z 98001, z 98003, z 98023, z 98063, z 98093; Ⓒ 83,259; ◆ 90,845
Felida; CDP; CLARK; ***246** M-6; elev. 206ft./63m.; ★ **POR**; mail Vancouver z 98685; Ⓟ 3,109; Ⓒ 5,683
Ferndale; Inc. Place; WHATCOM; **246** B-7; 🅿; ★ **BELNG**; z 98248; Ⓟ 5,398; Ⓒ 8,758
Fern Hill; RMC Place; PIERCE; ***246** H-7; ★ **SEAT**; mail Tacoma z 98412; pop. incl. with Tacoma (Inc. Place)
Fern Prairie; RMC Place; CLARK; ***246** M-7; elev. 459ft./140m.; ★ **POR**; mail Camas z 98607
Fernwood; RMC Place; KITSAP; ***246** F-6; ★ **BREM**; mail Port Orchard z 98366

Entries in **UPPERCASE** are counties.
Entries in **bold** have populations of 2,500 or more.
Names in parentheses are alternate names.
Inc. Place — Incorporated Place
RMC Place — Rand McNally Designated Place
CDP — Census Designated Place
MCD — Minor Civil Division

⊡ County Seat
▲ Minor Civil Division
elev. Elevation
🅿 Post Office

🅷 Hospital
🅲 College
■ Principal Business Center
★ Ranally Metro Area (RMA) Abbreviation
z Zip Code(s)

Ⓟ Previous Census Population
Ⓡ Revised Census Population
Ⓐ Annexation Population
● Rand McNally Population Estimate
Ⓒ Final Census Population
Ⓢ Special Census Population
◆ Estimated Population

For additional definitions see Glossary, Volume 1, and Introduction, Volume 2.

FERRY; 247 C-16; Ⓟ 6,295; Ⓒ 7,260; ◆ 7,084
Fife; Inc. Place; PIERCE; 248 L-7; 🅿; ★ SEAT; z 98424; Ⓟ 3,864; Ⓒ 4,784
Fife Heights; RMC Place; PIERCE; *246 G-7; ★ SEAT; mail Tacoma z 98424; ● 1,050
Finley; CDP; BENTON; *247 K-15; ★ RICH-; mail Kennewick z 99336-37; Ⓟ 4,897; Ⓒ 5,770
Finn Hall; RMC Place; COWLITZ; *246 L-6; ★ POR; mail Woodland z 98674; rural
Fir; SKAGIT; see Conway (CDP)
Fircrest; Inc. Place; PIERCE; 248 L-5; 🅿; ★ SEAT; z 98466; Ⓟ 5,258; Ⓒ 5,868
Fircrest Eddition; RMC Place; LEWIS; *246 J-6; elev. 400ft./122m.; mail Chehalis z 98532; ● 50
Firdale; RMC Place; PACIFIC; *246 I-4; elev. 168ft./51m.; mail Raymond z 98577; rural
Firdale; RMC Place; SNOHOMISH; *246 E-7; ★ SEAT; mail Edmonds z 98020; pop. incl. with Cresson (Inc. Place)
Firgrove; RMC Place; SNOHOMISH; *246 E-7; elev. 460ft./140m.; ★ SEAT; mail Everett z 98204; ● 1,300
Firwood; RMC Place; PIERCE; *246 G-7; elev. 30ft./9m.; ★ SEAT; mail Puyallup z 98371; rural
Fisher; RMC Place; CLARK; 246 M-7; ★ POR; mail Camas z 98607, Vancouver z 98683; pop. incl. with Vancouver (Inc. Place)
Five Corners; CDP-Census Area Only; CLARK; *246 M-6; ★ POR; mail Vancouver z 98662; Ⓟ 6,776; Ⓒ 12,207
Five Corners; RMC Place; FRANKLIN; *247 J-16; mail Connell z 99326; rural
Fletcher Bay; RMC Place; KITSAP; 248 D-4; ★ SEAT; mail Bainbridge Island z 98110; pop. incl. with Winslow (Inc. Place)
Florence; RMC Place; SNOHOMISH; *246 D-7; ★ SEAT; mail Stanwood z 98292; ● 60
Fobes Hill; RMC Place; SNOHOMISH; *246 E-8; elev. 195ft./59m.; ★ SEAT; mail Everett z 98205, Sumner z 98390; ● 170
Foothill; RMC Place; SPOKANE; *247 E-19; elev. 2,375ft./724m.; mail Spokane z 99217
Ford; RMC Place; STEVENS; 247 E-18; 🅿; z 99013; ● 50
Fordair; RMC Place; GRANT; *247 F-14; mail Coulee City z 99115; ● 80
Ford Park; RMC Place; CLALLAM; *246 E-2; elev. 360ft./110m.; mail Forks z 98331; pop. incl. with Forks (Inc. Place)
Fords Prairie; CDP; LEWIS; 246 I-5; elev. 175ft./53m.; mail Centralia z 98531; Ⓟ 2,480; Ⓒ 1,961
Forest; RMC Place; LEWIS; *246 J-6; elev. 298ft./91m.; mail Chehalis z 98532
Forest Beach; RMC Place; PIERCE; *246 G-6; ★ SEAT; mail Gig Harbor z 98335; ● 250
Forest Glen; RMC Place; THURSTON; *246 H-6; elev. 200ft./61m.; ★ OLYM; mail Olympia z 98501; ● 100
Forest Hills Addition; RMC Place; SPOKANE; *247 E-19; elev. 1,931ft./589m.; ★ SPOK; mail Spokane z 99208; ● 800
Forest Park; RMC Place; KING; *246 E-7; ★ SEAT; mail Seattle z 98155; pop. incl. with Lake Forest Park (Inc. Place)
Forks; Inc. Place; CLALLAM; 246 E-2; 🅿 🅷; z 98331; Ⓟ 2,715; Ⓒ 3,120
Fort Lewis; CDP-Census Area Only; PIERCE; *246 H-7; 🅿; ★ SEAT; z 98433; Ⓟ 22,224; Ⓒ 19,089
Foster; RMC Place; KING; *246 F-7; ★ SEAT; mail Seattle z 98188; pop. incl. with Tukwila (Inc. Place)
Four Corners; RMC Place; JEFFERSON; *246 D-6; mail Port Townsend z 98368; rural
Four Corners; RMC Place; THURSTON; *246 H-7; mail Yelm z 98597; rural
Four Lakes (Meadow Lake); RMC Place; SPOKANE; 247 F-19; 🅿; z 99014; ● 400
Fox Island; CDP-Census Area Only; PIERCE; *246 G-6; 🅿; ★ SEAT; z 98333; Ⓟ 2,017; Ⓒ 2,803
Fragaria; RMC Place; KITSAP; 248 H-5; ★ BREM; mail Olalla z 98359; ● 100
Frances; RMC Place; PACIFIC; 246 J-4; mail Raymond z 98577
Frankfort; RMC Place; PACIFIC; *246 K-4; elev. 250ft./76m.; mail Naselle z 98638; rural
FRANKLIN; 247 J-15; Ⓟ 37,473; Ⓒ 49,347; ◆ 75,532
Frederickson; CDP; PIERCE; *246 H-7; ★ SEAT; mail Puyallup z 98371, Tacoma z 98446; Ⓟ 3,502; Ⓒ 5,758
Freeland; CDP; ISLAND; 246 E-7; elev. 110ft./34m.; 🅿; ★ SEAT; z 98249; Ⓟ 1,278; Ⓒ 1,313
Freeman; RMC Place; SPOKANE; 247 F-20; ● 70
Fremont; RMC Place; KING; *246 F-7; ★ SEAT; mail Seattle z 98103; pop. incl. with Seattle (Inc. Place)
Friday Harbor; Inc. Place; ⊡ SAN JUAN; 246 C-6; elev. 91ft./28m.; 🅿; z 98250; Ⓟ 1,492; Ⓒ 1,989
Frisken Wye; RMC Place; MASON; *246 G-4; elev. 380ft./116m.; mail Elma z 98541; rural
Fruitland; RMC Place; STEVENS; 247 D-17; elev. 1,831ft./558m.; 🅿; z 99129; ● 50
Fruitvale; RMC Place; YAKIMA; *247 J-11; ★ YAK; mail Yakima z 98902; pop. incl. with Yakima (Inc. Place); Ⓟ 4,125
Fryelands; RMC Place; SNOHOMISH; *246 E-8; ★ SEAT; mail Monroe z 98272; pop. incl. with Monroe (Inc. Place)
Furport; RMC Place; PEND OREILLE; *247 D-19; elev. 2,090ft./637m.; mail Newport z 99156; ● 30

G

Gales Addition; RMC Place; CLALLAM; *246 D-5; mail Port Angeles z 98362; pop. incl. with Port Angeles (Inc. Place)
Galvin; RMC Place; LEWIS; *246 I-5; elev. 159ft./48m.; 🅿; z 98544; ● 200
Gamblewood; RMC Place; KITSAP; *246 E-7; elev. 100ft./30m.; mail Kingston z 98346; ● 200
Gardena; RMC Place; WALLA WALLA; *247 L-16; mail Touchet z 99360; rural
Garden City; RMC Place; GRAYS HARBOR; *246 H-5; mail McCleary z 98557
Gardiner; RMC Place; JEFFERSON; 246 D-6; mail Sequim z 98382; ● 300
Garfield; Inc. Place; WHITMAN; 247 H-20; elev. 2,467ft./752m.; 🅿; z 99130; Ⓟ 544; Ⓒ 641
GARFIELD; 247 J-19; Ⓟ 2,248; Ⓒ 2,397; ◆ 1,903
Garland; RMC Place; SPOKANE; ★ SPOK; mail Spokane z 99205; pop. incl. with Spokane (Inc. Place)
Garrett; CDP; WALLA WALLA; *247 K-17; ★ WALL; mail Walla Walla z 99362; Ⓟ 1,004; Ⓒ 1,022
Gate; RMC Place; THURSTON; *246 I-5; mail Rochester z 98579
Geneva; CDP; WHATCOM; *246 B-7; ★ BELNG; mail Bellingham z 98226; Ⓒ 2,257
George; Inc. Place; GRANT; 247 H-13; elev. 222ft./68m.; 🅿; z 98824, z 98848; Ⓟ 253; Ⓒ 528
Georgetown; RMC Place; KING; ★ SEAT; mail Ravensdale z 98051; pop. incl. with Seattle (Inc. Place)
Georgetown; RMC Place; KING; *246 G-8; ★ SEAT; mail Seattle z 98108
Getchell; RMC Place; SNOHOMISH; *246 D-8; elev. 376ft./115m.; ★ SEAT; mail Arlington z 98223, Granite Falls z 98252, Lake Stevens z 98258; ● 100
Gibraltar; RMC Place; SKAGIT; *246 C-7; elev. 118ft./36m.; mail Anacortes z 98221; ● 150
Gifford; RMC Place; STEVENS; 247 C-17; 🅿; z 99131; ● 100
Gig Harbor; Inc. Place; PIERCE; 246 G-7; 🅿; ★ SEAT; z 98329, z 98332, z 98335; Ⓟ 3,236; Ⓒ 6,465
Gilberton; RMC Place; KITSAP; *246 F-6; ★ BREM; mail Bremerton z 98310-11; ● 300
Gilmer; RMC Place; KLICKITAT; *246 L-9; mail Husum z 98623; ● 100
Glacier; CDP; WHATCOM; 246 A-8; mail Deming z 98244; Ⓒ 90
Gleed; CDP; YAKIMA; 247 I-11; 🅿; ★ YAK; z 98904; Ⓒ 2,947
Glen Acres; RMC Place; KING; *246 F-7; ★ SEAT; mail Vashon z 98070; ● 100
Glen Cove; RMC Place; JEFFERSON; *246 D-6; mail Port Townsend z 98368; ● 80
Glencove; RMC Place; PIERCE; *246 G-6; ★ SEAT; mail Gig Harbor z 98329, z 98335; ● 30
Glendale; RMC Place; ISLAND; *246 E-7; ★ SEAT; mail Clinton z 98236; ● 100
Glenoma; RMC Place; LEWIS; 246 J-8; elev. 821ft./250m.; 🅿; z 98336; ● 340
Glenrose; RMC Place; SPOKANE; 248 D-4; ★ SPOK; mail Spokane z 99203; ● 100
Glenwood; RMC Place; KITSAP; *246 G-6; elev. 349ft./106m.; ★ BREM; mail Port Orchard z 98367; ● 150
Glenwood; RMC Place; KLICKITAT; 246 L-10; elev. 1,895ft./578m.; 🅿; z 98619; ● 320
Gold Bar; Inc. Place; SNOHOMISH; 246 E-9; 🅿; z 98251; Ⓟ 1,078; Ⓒ 2,014
Goldendale; Inc. Place; ⊡ KLICKITAT; 247 L-11; elev. 1,633ft./498m.; 🅿 🅷; z 98620; Ⓟ 3,319; Ⓒ 3,760
Gooseberry Point; RMC Place; WHATCOM; *246 B-6; elev. 20ft./6m.; ★ BELNG; mail Bellingham z 98226; ● 200
Goose Prairie; RMC Place; YAKIMA; 246 I-10; elev. 3,266ft./995m.; 🅿; z 98929, z 98937; summer pop. 300; ● 40
Gorst; RMC Place; KITSAP; *246 F-6; 🅿; ★ BREM; z 98337; ● 450
Goss Lake; RMC Place; ISLAND; *246 D-7; elev. 200ft./61m.; ★ SEAT; mail Langley z 98260; rural
Govan; RMC Place; LINCOLN; *247 F-16; mail Wilbur z 99185; rural
Graham; CDP; PIERCE; 246 H-7; elev. 603ft./184m.; 🅿; ★ SEAT; z 98338; Ⓒ 8,739
Graham Point; RMC Place; MASON; *246 G-6; elev. 20ft./6m.; mail Shelton z 98584; ● 50
Grand Coulee; Inc. Place; GRANT; 247 E-15; 🅿 🅷; z 99133; Ⓟ 984; Ⓒ 897
Grand Mound; CDP; THURSTON; 246 I-5; mail Centralia z 98531, Rochester z 98579, Tenino z 98589; Ⓟ 1,394; Ⓒ 1,948
Grandview; Inc. Place; YAKIMA; 247 K-13; 🅿; z 98930; Ⓟ 7,169; Ⓒ 8,377
Granger; Inc. Place; YAKIMA; 247 K-12; elev. 731ft./223m.; 🅿; z 98932; Ⓟ 2,053; Ⓒ 2,530
Granite Falls; Inc. Place; SNOHOMISH; 246 D-8; elev. 391ft./119m.; 🅿; ★ SEAT; z 98252; Ⓟ 1,060; Ⓒ 2,347
GRANT; 247 G-14; Ⓟ 54,758; Ⓒ 74,698; ◆ 83,849
Grant Road Addition; RMC Place; DOUGLAS; *247 G-12; elev. 974ft./297m.; mail East Wenatchee z 98802; ● 1,450
Granville Grange; RMC Place; SNOHOMISH; *246 D-8; elev. 293ft./89m.; ★ SEAT; mail Granite Falls z 98252; rural
Grapeview; RMC Place; MASON; *246 G-6; 🅿; ★ BREM; z 98546; ● 500
Grassmere; RMC Place; SKAGIT; *246 C-8; mail Concrete z 98237; ● 200
Gravelly Lake; RMC Place; PIERCE; ★ SEAT; mail Lakewood z 98499; pop. incl. with Lakewood (Inc. Place)
Grayland; CDP; GRAYS HARBOR; 246 I-3; elev. 15ft./5m.; 🅿; z 98547; Ⓒ 1,002
GRAYS HARBOR; 246 G-4; Ⓟ 64,175; Ⓒ 67,194; ◆ 70,762
Grays Harbor City; RMC Place; GRAYS HARBOR; *246 H-3; mail Hoquiam z 98550; ● 300
Grays Landing; RMC Place; SPOKANE; *247 D-19; elev. 1,920ft./585m.; mail Elk z 99009; ● 35
Grays River; RMC Place; WAHKIAKUM; 246 J-4; elev. 27ft./8m.; 🅿; z 98621; ● 250
Green Acres; CDP; SPOKANE; 247 F-20; 🅿; ★ SPOK; z 99016; Ⓟ 4,625; Ⓒ 5,158
Greenbank; RMC Place; ISLAND; 246 D-7; elev. 158ft./48m.; 🅿; ★ SEAT; z 98253; ● 800
Greenbank Estates; RMC Place; ISLAND; *246 D-7; elev. 301ft./92m.; ★ SEAT; mail Greenbank z 98253; ● 50
Green Bluff; RMC Place; SPOKANE; *247 E-19; mail Chattaroy z 99003, Colbert z 99005, Mead z 99021
Green River Gorge; RMC Place; KING; *246 G-8; elev. 608ft./185m.; mail Enumclaw z 98022; rural
Greens Landing; RMC Place; CHELAN; *247 E-12; elev. 1,200ft./366m.; mail Chelan z 98816; ● 30
Greenwater; CDP; KING, PIERCE; 246 H-9; mail Enumclaw z 98022; Ⓒ 91
Greenwood; RMC Place; GRAYS HARBOR; *246 H-5; mail Aberdeen z 98520; rural
Greenwood; RMC Place; KING; *246 F-7; ★ SEAT; mail Seattle z 98103; pop. incl. with Seattle (Inc. Place)
Greenwood; RMC Place; STEVENS; *247 B-17; elev. 1,615ft./492m.; mail Kettle Falls z 99141; rural
Greenwood; RMC Place; WHATCOM; *246 A-7; elev. 92ft./28m.; ★ BELNG; mail Lynden z 98264; ● 50
Grisdale; RMC Place; GRAYS HARBOR; 246 G-4; mail Montesano z 98563; ● 50
Gromore; RMC Place; YAKIMA; *247 J-11; elev. 1,500ft./457m.; ★ YAK; mail Yakima z 98903; ● 110
Grotto; RMC Place; KING; *246 F-9; mail Skykomish z 98288; ● 50
Guemes (Guemes Island); RMC Place; SKAGIT; *246 C-6; mail Anacortes z 98221; ● 400
Guemes Island; SKAGIT; see Guemes (RMC Place)

H

Haller Lake; RMC Place; KING; *246 F-7; ★ SEAT; mail Seattle z 98133; pop. incl. with Seattle (Inc. Place)
Hamilton; Inc. Place; SKAGIT; 246 C-8; 🅿; z 98255; Ⓟ 228; Ⓒ 309
Hansville; RMC Place; KITSAP; 246 E-7; 🅿; z 98340; summer pop. 2,200; ● 1,700
Happy Valley; RMC Place; WHATCOM; *246 B-7; ★ BELNG; mail Bellingham z 98225; pop. incl. with Bellingham (Inc. Place)
Harbor Center; RMC Place; ISLAND; ★ SEAT; mail Freeland z 98249
Harbor Heights; RMC Place; PIERCE; *246 G-6; ★ SEAT; mail Graham z 98338; pop. incl. with Gig Harbor (Inc. Place)
Harmon Heights; RMC Place; KING; *246 F-8; ★ SEAT; mail North Bend z 98045; ● 120
Harper; RMC Place; KITSAP; 246 F-7; ★ BREM; mail Port Orchard z 98366; ● 150
Harrah; Inc. Place; YAKIMA; 247 J-11; 🅿; z 98933; Ⓟ 341; Ⓒ 542
Harrington; Inc. Place; LINCOLN; 247 F-17; elev. 2,140ft./652m.; 🅿; z 99134, z 99154; Ⓟ 449; Ⓒ 426
Hartford; RMC Place; SNOHOMISH; ★ SEAT; mail Lake Stevens z 98258; pop. incl. with Lake Stevens (Inc. Place)
Hartland; RMC Place; KLICKITAT; *246 M-10; elev. 1,935ft./590m.; mail Lyle z 98635; rural
Hartline; Inc. Place; GRANT; 247 F-15; 🅿; z 99135; Ⓟ 176; Ⓒ 134
Hartstene; RMC Place; MASON; *246 G-6; mail Shelton z 98584; ● 100
Harwood; RMC Place; YAKIMA; *247 J-11; ★ YAK; mail Yakima z 98902; ● 50
Hatton; Inc. Place; ADAMS; 247 I-16; 🅿; z 99344; Ⓟ 71; Ⓒ 98
Havillah; RMC Place; OKANOGAN; *247 B-15; mail Tonasket z 98855; ● 30
Hawk Acres; RMC Place; THURSTON; *246 H-6; elev. 259ft./79m.; ★ OLYM; mail Olympia z 98501; ● 80
Hay; RMC Place; WHITMAN; 247 I-18; 🅿; z 99136; ● 50
Hayford; RMC Place; SPOKANE; *247 F-19; ★ SPOK; mail Spokane z 99224; ● 160
Hays Park; RMC Place; SPOKANE; ★ SPOK; mail Spokane z 99207; pop. incl. with Spokane (Inc. Place)
Hazel; RMC Place; SNOHOMISH; *246 D-8; mail Arlington z 98223; rural
Hazel Dell; RMC Place; CLARK; *246 M-6; ★ POR; ● 4,900
Hazel Dell North; CDP-Census Area Only; CLARK; *246 M-6; ★ POR; mail Vancouver z 98665; Ⓟ 6,924; Ⓒ 9,261
Hazel Dell South; CDP-Census Area Only; CLARK; 223 J-19; ★ POR; mail Vancouver z 98665; Ⓟ 5,796; Ⓒ 6,605
Hazelwood; RMC Place; KING; 248 F-10; ★ SEAT; mail Renton z 98055-56; pop. incl. with Bellevue (Inc. Place)
Heather Downs; RMC Place; KING; ★ SEAT; mail Renton z 98055; pop. incl. with Renton (Inc. Place)
Heison; CLARK; see Heisson (RMC Place)
Heisson (Heison); RMC Place; CLARK; *246 L-7; 🅿; z 98622; ● 80
Herron Island; RMC Place; PIERCE; *246 G-6; elev. 100ft./30m.; ★ SEAT; mail Lakebay z 98349; summer pop. 500; ● 180
Hidden Valley; RMC Place; LEWIS; *246 I-8; elev. 1,800ft./549m.; mail Ashford z 98304; ● 60
Highland; RMC Place; ASOTIN; ★ LEW; mail Clarkston z 99403
Highland; CDP-Census Area Only; BENTON; *247 K-15; ★ RICH-; mail Kennewick z 99337; Ⓟ 3,656; Ⓒ 3,388
Highland Estates; RMC Place; MASON; *246 H-5; elev. 60ft./18m.; mail Shelton z 98584; ● 150
Highland Heights; RMC Place; GRAYS HARBOR; *246 G-3; mail Moclips z 98562, Pacific Beach z 98571
Highland Park; RMC Place; KING; *246 F-7; ★ SEAT; mail Seattle z 98106; pop. incl. with Seattle (Inc. Place)
Highlands; RMC Place; KING; ★ SEAT; mail Renton z 98056; pop. incl. with Renton (Inc. Place)
High Point; RMC Place; KING; ★ SEAT; mail Seattle z 98126; pop. incl. with Seattle (Inc. Place)
High Point; RMC Place; KING; *246 F-8; ★ SEAT; mail Issaquah z 98027; ● 280
High Valley; RMC Place; KING; *246 F-8; elev. 600ft./183m.; ★ SEAT; mail Issaquah z 98027; ● 200
Hillsdale; RMC Place; PIERCE; *246 G-7; ★ SEAT; pop. incl. with Tacoma (Inc. Place)
Hilltop; RMC Place; KING; *246 F-8; ★ SEAT; mail Bellevue z 98004
Hillyard; RMC Place; SPOKANE; *247 F-19; ★ SPOK; mail Spokane z 99207, z 99217; pop. incl. with Spokane (Inc. Place)
Hintzville; RMC Place; KITSAP; *246 F-6; ★ BREM; mail Bremerton z 98312; rural
Hobart; CDP; KING; *246 G-8; 🅿; ★ SEAT; z 98025; Ⓒ 6,251
Hockinson; CDP; CLARK; *246 M-7; ★ POR; mail Brush Prairie z 98606; Ⓒ 5,136
Hogans Corner; RMC Place; GRAYS HARBOR; *246 H-3; elev. 60ft./18m.; mail Hoquiam z 98550; ● 60
Hoh Reservation; Indian Reservation; JEFFERSON; mail Forks z 98331; Ⓟ 67; Ⓒ 102
Hoko; RMC Place; CLALLAM; *246 D-2; mail Clallam Bay z 98326, Sekiu z 98381; rural
Holcomb; RMC Place; PACIFIC; *246 J-4; elev. 116ft./35m.; mail Raymond z 98577; rural
Holden Village; RMC Place; CHELAN; *247 D-11; mail Chelan z 98816; summer pop. 150; ● 50
Holly; RMC Place; KITSAP; 246 F-6; mail Bremerton z 98312; seasonal pop. 100
Hollywood; RMC Place; KING; 248 B-10; ★ SEAT; mail Woodinville z 98072; ● 800
Hollywood Beach; RMC Place; CHELAN; *247 E-12; elev. 1,261ft./384m.; mail Chelan z 98816; ● 100
Holman; RMC Place; PACIFIC; *246 J-3; mail Seaview z 98644
Holmes Harbor Estates; RMC Place; ISLAND; *246 D-7; elev. 200ft./61m.; ★ SEAT; mail Greenbank z 98253; ● 100
Home; RMC Place; PIERCE; *246 G-6; 🅿; ★ SEAT; z 98349; ● 950
Home Acres; RMC Place; SNOHOMISH; *246 E-8; elev. 2ft./1m.; ★ SEAT; mail Everett z 98205; rural
Home Valley; RMC Place; SKAMANIA; 246 M-8; mail Stevenson z 98648; ● 80
Honeymoon Vista Bay; RMC Place; ISLAND; *246 D-7; elev. 100ft./30m.; ★ SEAT; mail Greenbank z 98253; ● 30
Hood; RMC Place; SKAMANIA; *246 M-9; mail Underwood z 98651; ● 25
Hoodsport; RMC Place; MASON; 246 G-5; 🅿; z 98548; ● 1,200
Hoogdal; RMC Place; SKAGIT; *246 C-7; mail Sedro Woolley z 98284; ● 50
Hooper; RMC Place; WHITMAN; 247 I-17; elev. 1,112ft./339m.; 🅿; z 99333; ● 75
Hope; RMC Place; PIERCE; *246 G-6; elev. 20ft./6m.; ★ SEAT; mail Fox Island z 98333
Hoquiam; Inc. Place; GRAYS HARBOR; 246 H-3; 🅿; z 98550; location of Olympic Peninsula Indian Agency; Ⓟ 8,972; Ⓒ 9,097
Horseshoe Lake; RMC Place; KITSAP; *246 G-6; ★ BREM; mail Port Orchard z 98366; ● 40
Houghton; RMC Place; KING; *246 F-7; ★ SEAT; mail Kirkland z 98033; pop. incl. with Kirkland (Inc. Place)
Humptulips; CDP; GRAYS HARBOR; 246 G-3; elev. 131ft./40m.; 🅿; z 98552; Ⓒ 216
Hunters; RMC Place; STEVENS; 247 D-17; 🅿; z 99129, z 99137; ● 180
Hunts Point; Inc. Place; KING; 248 D-9; 🅿; ★ SEAT; z 98004; Ⓟ 513; Ⓒ 443
Huntsville; RMC Place; COLUMBIA; *247 K-17; mail Dayton z 99328; rural
Husum; RMC Place; KLICKITAT; 246 L-9; 🅿; z 98623; ● 130
Hyak; RMC Place; KITTITAS; 246 G-9; mail Snoqualmie Pass z 98068; seasonal pop. 300; ● 50

I

Illahee; RMC Place; GRAYS HARBOR; mail Ocean Shores z 98569; pop. incl. with Ocean Shores (Inc. Place)
Illahee; RMC Place; KITSAP; 248 D-4; ★ BREM; mail Bremerton z 98311; ● 400
Ilwaco; Inc. Place; PACIFIC; 246 J-3; 🅿 🅷; z 98624; Ⓟ 815; Ⓒ 950
Image; RMC Place; CLARK; *246 M-6; elev. 100ft./30m.; ★ POR; mail Vancouver z 98682; pop. incl. with Vancouver (Inc. Place)
Impach; RMC Place; FERRY; *247 D-17; mail Inchelium z 99138; rural
Inchelium; CDP; FERRY; 247 C-17; 🅿; z 99138; Ⓟ 393; Ⓒ 389
Index; Inc. Place; SNOHOMISH; 246 E-9; elev. 532ft./162m.; 🅿; z 98256; Ⓟ 139; Ⓒ 157
Indian Beach; RMC Place; ISLAND; *246 D-7; ★ SEAT; mail Stanwood z 98292; ● 60
Indianola (Kitsap); CDP; KITSAP; *246 F-7; 🅿; ★ SEAT; z 98342; Ⓟ 1,729; Ⓒ 3,026
Indian Village; RMC Place; SKAGIT; *246 C-6; elev. 100ft./30m.; mail Anacortes z 98221; summer pop. 150; ● 30
Inglewood (Inglewood Hills); RMC Place; KING; 246 F-8; ★ SEAT; mail Bothell z 98011, Kenmore z 98028; pop. incl. with Sammamish (Inc. Place)
Inglewood-Finn Hill; CDP-Census Area Only; KING; *246 F-7; ★ SEAT; mail Bothell z 98011, Kirkland z 98033; Ⓟ 29,132; Ⓒ 22,661; ◆ 25,086
Inglewood Hills; KING; see Inglewood (RMC Place)
Inlet Island; RMC Place; PIERCE; *246 G-8; elev. 580ft./177m.; ★ SEAT; mail Sumner z 98390; pop. incl. with Bonney Lake (Inc. Place)
Innis Arden; RMC Place; KING; *246 E-7; elev. 294ft./90m.; ★ SEAT; mail Seattle z 98160; pop. incl. with Shoreline (Inc. Place)
Interbay; RMC Place; KING; *246 F-7; ★ SEAT; mail Seattle z 98119, z 98199; pop. incl. with Seattle (Inc. Place)
Intercity; RMC Place; SNOHOMISH; *246 E-7; ★ SEAT; mail Everett z 98203; pop. incl. with Everett (Inc. Place)
Interlaken; RMC Place; PIERCE; *246 H-7; elev. 260ft./79m.; ★ SEAT; mail McChord AFB z 98438; pop. incl. with Lakewood (Inc. Place)
International; RMC Place; KING; ★ SEAT; mail Seattle z 98104, z 98114, z 98144; pop. incl. with Seattle (Inc. Place)
Ione; Inc. Place; PEND OREILLE; 247 B-19; 🅿; z 99139; Ⓟ 507; Ⓒ 479
Irby; RMC Place; LINCOLN; 247 G-16; mail Odessa z 99159; ● 30
Ireland; RMC Place; CLARK; *246 M-7; elev. 800ft./244m.; ★ POR; mail Camas z 98607; rural
Irondale; RMC Place; JEFFERSON; *246 D-6; mail Port Hadlock z 98339
Iron Springs; RMC Place; GRAYS HARBOR; *246 G-3; elev. 100ft./30m.; mail Copalis Beach z 98535; ● 100
Isabella Lake; RMC Place; MASON; *246 H-5; elev. 60ft./18m.; mail Shelton z 98584; ● 80
ISLAND; 246 C-7; Ⓟ 60,195; Ⓒ 71,558; ◆ 80,900
Island Center; RMC Place; KITSAP; *246 F-7; elev. 97ft./30m.; ★ SEAT; mail Bainbridge Island z 98110; pop. incl. with Winslow (Inc. Place)
Island Lake; RMC Place; KITSAP; *246 F-6; elev. 227ft./69m.; ★ BREM; mail Poulsbo z 98370; ● 100
Issaquah; Inc. Place; KING; 246 F-8; 🅿; ★ SEAT; z 98006, z 98027, z 98029, z 98075; Ⓟ 7,786; Ⓒ 11,212; ◆ 20,964
Iverson; CLALLAM; see Shuwah (RMC Place)

J

Jamestown S'Klallam Reservation; Indian Reservation; CLALLAM; Ⓒ 9
Jared; RMC Place; PEND OREILLE; *247 C-19; mail Usk z 99180; rural
JEFFERSON; 246 F-4; Ⓟ 20,146; Ⓒ 25,953; Ⓡ 26,299; ◆ 29,449
John Sam Lake; CDP-Census Area Only; SNOHOMISH; *246 D-7; ★ SEAT; mail Marysville z 98270; Ⓟ 432; Ⓒ 753
Johnson; RMC Place; WHITMAN; *247 I-20; mail Colton z 99113; ● 100
Jordan; RMC Place; SNOHOMISH; *246 D-8; elev. 155ft./47m.; ★ SEAT; mail Arlington z 98223; rural
Jordan Road-Canyon Creek; CDP-Census Area Only; SNOHOMISH; *246 D-8; ★ SEAT; Ⓒ 2,326
Jovita; RMC Place; PIERCE, KING; *246 G-7; elev. 300ft./91m.; ★ SEAT; mail Puyallup z 98371-72; pop. incl. with Edgewood (Inc. Place)
Joyce; RMC Place; CLALLAM; 246 D-4; 🅿; z 98343; ● 150
Juanita; RMC Place; KING; *246 F-7; ★ SEAT; mail Kirkland z 98033-34; pop. incl. with Kirkland (Inc. Place)
Junction City; CDP; GRAYS HARBOR; *246 H-4; mail Aberdeen z 98520; Ⓒ 80
Juniper Beach; RMC Place; ISLAND; *246 D-7; ★ SEAT; mail Stanwood z 98292; ● 150

K

Kachees Ridge; RMC Place; KITTITAS; *246 G-10; elev. 2,261ft./689m.; mail Easton z 98925; ● 50
Kahlotus; Inc. Place; FRANKLIN; 247 I-16; elev. 901ft./275m.; 🅿; z 99335; Ⓟ 167; Ⓒ 214
Kalaloch; RMC Place; JEFFERSON; *246 F-2; mail Forks z 98331; ● 25
Kalama; Inc. Place; COWLITZ; 246 L-6; 🅿; z 98625; Ⓟ 1,210; Ⓒ 1,783
Kala Point; RMC Place; JEFFERSON; *246 D-6; elev. 200ft./61m.; mail Port Townsend z 98368; ● 200
Kalispel Reservation; Indian Reservation; PEND OREILLE, SPOKANE; mail Usk z 99180; Ⓟ 106; Ⓒ 206
Kamilche; RMC Place; MASON; *246 H-5; mail Shelton z 98584; ● 120
Kanaskat; RMC Place; KING; *246 G-8; mail Ravensdale z 98051
Kangley; RMC Place; KING; *246 G-8; mail Ravensdale z 98051; ● 100
Kapowsin; RMC Place; PIERCE; 246 H-7; elev. 629ft./192m.; 🅿; ★ SEAT; z 98344; ● 350
Keller; RMC Place; FERRY; 247 D-16; 🅿; z 99140; ● 250
Kellogg Marsh; RMC Place; SNOHOMISH; *246 D-8; elev. 112ft./34m.; ★ SEAT; mail Anacortes z 98221, Marysville z 98270; ● 1,250
Kellys Korner; RMC Place; THURSTON; *246 H-6; ★ OLYM; mail East Olympia z 98540, Olympia z 98513
Kelso; Inc. Place; ⊡ COWLITZ; 246 K-6; 🅿; ★ LNGV; z 98626; Ⓟ 11,820; Ⓒ 11,895
Kemes Beach; JEFFERSON; see Adelma Beach (RMC Place)
Kendall; CDP; WHATCOM; 246 A-8; elev. 441ft./134m.; mail Deming z 98244, Sumas z 98295; Ⓒ 158
Kenmore; Inc. Place; KING; 248 A-9; 🅿 🅲 1,001; ★ SEAT; z 98028; Ⓟ 8,917; Ⓒ 18,678; ◆ 19,585
Kennard Corner; RMC Place; SNOHOMISH; *246 E-7; ★ SEAT; mail Bothell z 98012, z 98021; ● 450
Kennedys Lagoon; RMC Place; ISLAND; *246 D-6; elev. 14ft./4m.; mail Coupeville z 98239; rural
Kennewick; Inc. Place; BENTON; 247 K-15; 🅿 🅷 ■; ★ RICH-; z 99336-38; Ⓟ 42,155; Ⓒ 54,693; ◆ 63,930
Kennydale; RMC Place; KING; *246 F-7; ★ SEAT; mail Renton z 98056; pop. incl. with Renton (Inc. Place)
Kenroy; RMC Place; DOUGLAS; *247 G-12; elev. 1,000ft./305m.; mail East Wenatchee z 98802, Wenatchee z 98801; ● 2,900
Kent; Inc. Place; KING; 246 G-7; 🅿 ■; ★ SEAT; z 98030-32, z 98035, z 98042, z 98064, z 98089; Ⓟ 37,960; Ⓒ 79,524; ◆ 88,762
Kettle Falls; Inc. Place; STEVENS; 247 B-17; elev. 1,625ft./495m.; 🅿; z 99107, z 99126, z 99141, z 99160; Ⓟ 1,272; Ⓒ 1,527
Kewa; RMC Place; FERRY; *247 D-17; mail Inchelium z 99138; rural
Key Center; RMC Place; PIERCE; *246 G-6; ★ SEAT; mail Gig Harbor z 98329, z 98335, Lakebay z 98349; ● 110
Keyport; RMC Place; KITSAP; 246 F-6; elev. 43ft./13m.; 🅿; ★ BREM; z 98345; ● 350
Keystone; RMC Place; ISLAND; *246 D-6; ★ SEAT; mail Coupeville z 98239; ● 30
Keystone; RMC Place; OKANOGAN; *247 C-14; elev. 860ft./262m.; mail Riverside z 98849; rural
Kid Valley; RMC Place; COWLITZ; *246 J-6; mail Toutle z 98649; rural
KING; 246 F-9; Ⓟ 1,507,319; Ⓒ 1,737,034; Ⓡ 1,737,044; ◆ 1,922,712
King Corner; RMC Place; CLARK; *246 L-6; ★ POR; mail Battle Ground z 98604; rural
Kingsgate; CDP; KING; *246 F-7; ★ SEAT; mail Bothell z 98011, Kirkland z 98033-34; Ⓟ 14,259; Ⓒ 12,222
Kings Lakeside; RMC Place; COWLITZ; *246 L-7; elev. 400ft./122m.; mail Ariel z 98603; ● 60
Kingston; CDP; KITSAP; 246 E-7; 🅿; z 98346; Ⓟ 1,270; Ⓒ 1,611
Kiona; RMC Place; BENTON; 247 K-14; mail Benton City z 99320; ● 60
Kirkland; Inc. Place; KING; 246 F-7; 🅿 🅷 🅲 1,281 ■; ★ SEAT; z 98033-34, z 98083; Ⓟ 40,052; Ⓒ 45,054; ◆ 47,099
Kitsap; KITSAP; see Indianola (CDP)
KITSAP; 246 F-6; Ⓟ 189,731; Ⓒ 231,969; ◆ 228,989
Kitsap Lake; RMC Place; KITSAP; *246 F-6; ★ BREM; mail Bremerton z 98312; ● 1,300
Kittitas; Inc. Place; KITTITAS; 247 H-12; elev. 1,647ft./502m.; 🅿; z 98934; Ⓟ 843; Ⓒ 1,105
KITTITAS; 247 H-11; Ⓟ 26,725; Ⓒ 33,362; ◆ 38,739
Klaber; RMC Place; LEWIS; *246 J-5; mail Curtis z 98538; rural
Klaus; RMC Place; LEWIS; *246 J-6; elev. 400ft./122m.; mail Chehalis z 98532; rural
Klickitat; CDP; KLICKITAT; 246 L-10; elev. 447ft./136m.; 🅿; z 98628, z 98670; Ⓒ 417
KLICKITAT; 247 L-11; Ⓟ 16,616; Ⓒ 19,161; ◆ 20,587
Klipsan Beach; RMC Place; PACIFIC; *246 J-3; mail Ocean Park z 98640; ● 120
Knappton; RMC Place; PACIFIC; *246 K-3; elev. 250ft./76m.; mail Naselle z 98638; rural
Koontzville; RMC Place; OKANOGAN; *247 E-15; elev. 1,000ft./305m.; mail Coulee Dam z 99116; rural
Kooskooskie; RMC Place; WALLA WALLA; 247 L-17; elev. 2,000ft./610m.; mail Walla Walla z 99362; ● 80
Kozy Kamp; RMC Place; CLARK; *246 M-6; elev. 250ft./76m.; ★ POR; mail Ridgefield z 98642; rural
Krain; RMC Place; KING; *246 G-8; ★ SEAT; mail Enumclaw z 98022; rural
Krupp; GRANT; see Marlin (Inc. Place)
Kruse; RMC Place; SNOHOMISH; *246 D-8; elev. 69ft./21m.; ★ SEAT; mail Marysville z 98271; pop. incl. with Marysville (Inc. Place)
Kruse Junction; RMC Place; SNOHOMISH; *246 D-8; ★ SEAT; mail Marysville z 98271; pop. incl. with Marysville (Inc. Place)
K Street; RMC Place; PIERCE; ★ SEAT; mail Tacoma z 98405, z 98415; pop. incl. with Tacoma (Inc. Place)
Kummer; RMC Place; KING; *246 G-8; ★ SEAT; mail Black Diamond z 98010; rural

L

Lacamas; RMC Place; LEWIS; *246 J-6; mail Onalaska z 98570; rural
La Center; Inc. Place; CLARK; 246 L-6; 🅿; ★ POR; z 98629; Ⓟ 451; Ⓒ 1,654
Lacey; Inc. Place; THURSTON; 246 H-6; 🅿 🅲 1,541; ★ OLYM; z 98503, z 98506, z 98509, z 98513, z 98516; Ⓟ 19,279; Ⓒ 31,226; ◆ 39,162
La Conner; Inc. Place; SKAGIT; 246 C-7; 🅿; z 98257; Ⓟ 656; Ⓒ 761
La Crosse; Inc. Place; WHITMAN; 247 I-18; 🅿; z 99143 & mail Hay z 99136; Ⓟ 336; Ⓒ 380
Lagoon Point; RMC Place; ISLAND; *246 D-6; elev. 208ft./63m.; ★ SEAT; mail Greenbank z 98253; ● 300
La Grande; RMC Place; PIERCE; *246 I-7; 🅿; ★ SEAT; z 98348; ● 40
Lake Alice; RMC Place; KING; *246 F-8; elev. 897ft./273m.; ★ SEAT; mail Fall City z 98024; ● 50
Lakebay; RMC Place; PIERCE; 246 G-6; 🅿; ★ SEAT; z 98349, z 98351; summer pop. 2,000; ● 600
Lake Bosworth; CDP-Census Area Only; SNOHOMISH; *246 D-8; ★ SEAT; Ⓒ 204
Lake Cavanaugh; CDP-Census Area Only; SKAGIT; *246 C-8; Ⓒ 122
Lake City; RMC Place; KING; *246 F-7; ★ SEAT; mail Seattle z 98125; pop. incl. with Seattle (Inc. Place)
Lake City; RMC Place; PIERCE; *246 H-7; ★ SEAT; pop. incl. with Lakewood (Inc. Place)
Lake Crescent; RMC Place; CLALLAM; *246 D-4; elev. 675ft./206m.; mail Port Angeles z 98362-63; summer pop. 200; ● 100
Lakedale; RMC Place; KITTITAS; *246 G-10; elev. 2,240ft./683m.; mail Ronald z 98940; ● 500
Lake Dolloff; RMC Place; KING; *246 G-7; elev. 400ft./122m.; ★ SEAT; mail Auburn z 98001; ● 750
Lake Forest Park; Inc. Place; KING; 248 B-8; 🅿; ★ SEAT; z 98155; Ⓟ 4,031; Ⓒ 13,142; Ⓡ 12,871
Lake Goodwin; CDP-Census Area Only; SNOHOMISH; *246 D-7; ★ SEAT; mail Stanwood z 98292; Ⓟ 2,437; Ⓒ 3,354
Lake Heights; RMC Place; KING; *246 F-7; ★ SEAT; mail Bellevue z 98006; pop. incl. with Bellevue (Inc. Place)
Lake Hills; RMC Place; KING; *246 F-8; ★ SEAT; mail Bellevue z 98007; pop. incl. with Bellevue (Inc. Place)
Lake Howard; RMC Place; SNOHOMISH; *246 D-7; elev. 238ft./73m.; ★ SEAT; mail Stanwood z 98292; ● 60
Lake Joy; RMC Place; KING; *246 F-8; elev. 555ft./169m.; ★ SEAT; mail Carnation z 98014; ● 200
Lake Kachees; RMC Place; KITTITAS; *246 G-10; elev. 2,400ft./732m.; mail Easton z 98925; ● 100
Lake Kathleen; RMC Place; KING; *246 F-8; elev. 550ft./168m.; ★ SEAT; mail Renton z 98059; ● 1,000
Lake Ketchum; CDP-Census Area Only; SNOHOMISH; *246 D-7; ★ SEAT; Ⓒ 1,173
Lake Ki; RMC Place; SNOHOMISH; *246 D-7; elev. 418ft./127m.; ★ SEAT; mail Arlington z 98223; ● 100
Lakeland North; CDP-Census Area Only; KING; *246 G-7; ★ SEAT; mail Auburn z 98001, Kent z 98031; Ⓟ 14,402; Ⓒ 15,085
Lakeland South; CDP-Census Area Only; KING; *246 G-7; ★ SEAT; mail Auburn z 98002; Ⓟ 9,027; Ⓒ 11,436
Lakeland Village; RMC Place; SPOKANE; *247 F-18; mail Medical Lake z 99022; pop. incl. with Medical Lake (Inc. Place)
Lake Leota; RMC Place; KING; *246 E-8; elev. 369ft./112m.; ★ SEAT; mail Woodinville z 98072; pop. incl. with Woodinville (Inc. Place)
Lake Loma; RMC Place; SNOHOMISH; *246 D-7; elev. 574ft./175m.; ★ SEAT; mail Marysville z 98271; ● 100
Lake Louise; RMC Place; PIERCE; ★ SEAT; mail Lakewood z 98498; pop. incl. with Lakewood (Inc. Place)
Lake Lucerne; RMC Place; KING; *246 G-8; elev. 175ft./53m.; ★ SEAT; mail Maple Valley z 98038; pop. incl. with Maple Valley (Inc. Place)
Lake Marcel-Stillwater; CDP-Census Area Only; KING; *246 F-8; ★ SEAT; Ⓒ 1,381
Lake Martha; RMC Place; SNOHOMISH; *246 D-7; elev. 237ft./72m.; ★ SEAT; mail Lynnwood z 98037; ● 150
Lake McDonald; RMC Place; KING; *246 G-8; elev. 600ft./183m.; ★ SEAT; mail Renton z 98059; ● 320
Lake McMurray; CDP-Census Area Only; SKAGIT; *246 D-7; Ⓒ 200
Lake Meridian; RMC Place; KING; *246 G-8; elev. 125ft./38m.; ★ SEAT; mail Kent z 98042; pop. incl. with Kent (Inc. Place)
Lake Meridian; KING; see Meridian Heights (RMC Place)
Lake Morton-Berrydale; CDP-Census Area Only; KING; *246 G-8; ★ SEAT; Ⓒ 9,659
Lake Park; PIERCE; see Spanaway (CDP)
Lake Pattison; RMC Place; THURSTON; *246 H-6; elev. 210ft./64m.; ★ OLYM; mail Olympia z 98513; ● 250
Lake Retreat; RMC Place; KING; *246 G-8; elev. 730ft./223m.; mail Ravensdale z 98051; ● 150
Lakeridge; RMC Place; KING; *246 F-7; elev. 57ft./17m.; ★ SEAT; mail Seattle z 98178; ● 1,700
Lake Roesiger; CDP-Census Area Only; SNOHOMISH; *246 E-8; ★ SEAT; Ⓒ 652
Lake Sawyer; RMC Place; KING; *246 G-8; elev. 156ft./48m.; ★ SEAT; mail Kent z 98042; pop. incl. with Black Diamond (Inc. Place)
Lakes District; PIERCE; see Lakewood (Inc. Place)
Lake Shore; CDP-Census Area Only; CLARK; *246 M-6; ★ POR; mail Vancouver z 98665, z 98685; Ⓟ 6,268; Ⓒ 6,670
Lake Stevens; Inc. Place; SNOHOMISH; 246 E-8; 🅿; ★ SEAT; z 98258; Ⓟ 3,380; Ⓒ 6,361
Lakeview; CDP-Census Area Only; GRANT; *247 G-14; Ⓒ 797
Lakeview; RMC Place; PIERCE; *246 H-7; ★ SEAT; mail Lakewood z 98499; pop. incl. with Lakewood (Inc. Place)
Lakeview Park; RMC Place; GRANT; 247 G-14; mail Soap Lake z 98851; ● 300
Lakeview Terrace; RMC Place; LINCOLN; *247 E-15; elev. 1,689ft./515m.; mail Grand Coulee z 99133; ● 50
Lake Wilderness; RMC Place; KING; *246 G-8; elev. 150ft./46m.; ★ SEAT; mail Maple Valley z 98038; pop. incl. with Maple Valley (Inc. Place)
Lakewood (Lakes District, Lakewood Center); Inc. Place; PIERCE; 246 D-7; 🅿 🅷; ★ SEAT; z 98409, z 98439, z 98492, z 98496-99; Ⓟ 55,937; Ⓒ 58,211; Ⓡ 58,293; ◆ 60,300
Lakewood (English, North Lakewood); RMC Place; SNOHOMISH; 246 D-7; ★ SEAT; mail North Lakewood z 98259; ● 500
Lakewood Center; PIERCE; see Lakewood (Inc. Place)
Lakota; RMC Place; KING; *246 G-7; ★ SEAT; mail Federal Way z 98003; pop. incl. with Federal Way (Inc. Place)
Lamoine; RMC Place; DOUGLAS; *247 F-13; elev. 2,664ft./812m.; mail Waterville z 98858; rural
Lamona; RMC Place; LINCOLN; 247 G-16; elev. 1,797ft./548m.; 🅿; z 99144; ● 40
Lamont; Inc. Place; WHITMAN; 247 G-18; elev. 1,949ft./594m.; 🅿; z 99017; Ⓟ 91; Ⓒ 106
Lancaster (Willada); RMC Place; WHITMAN; *247 H-18; mail Saint John z 99171
Langley; Inc. Place; ISLAND; 246 D-7; 🅿; ★ SEAT; z 98260; Ⓟ 845; Ⓒ 959
La Push; RMC Place; CLALLAM; 246 E-2; 🅿; z 98350; summer pop. 5,000; ● 500
Larchmont; RMC Place; PIERCE; *246 H-7; elev. 400ft./122m.; ★ SEAT; mail Tacoma z 98409
Larimers Corner; RMC Place; SNOHOMISH; *246 E-8; ★ SEAT; mail Snohomish z 98290, z 98296
Latah; Inc. Place; SPOKANE; 247 G-20; 🅿; z 99018; Ⓟ 175; Ⓒ 151
Laurel; RMC Place; KLICKITAT; *246 L-9; elev. 1,884ft./574m.; mail Glenwood z 98619; rural
Laurel; RMC Place; WHATCOM; *246 B-7; ★ BELNG; mail Bellingham z 98226; ● 200
Laurel Heights; RMC Place; SNOHOMISH; *246 E-7; ★ SEAT; mail Everett z 98203; pop. incl. with Everett (Inc. Place)
Laurelhurst; RMC Place; KING; *246 F-7; ★ SEAT; mail Seattle z 98105; pop. incl. with Seattle (Inc. Place)
Laurier; RMC Place; FERRY; 247 A-17; 🅿; z 99146; ● 50
Lawrence; RMC Place; PIERCE; ★ SEAT; mail Tacoma z 98409; pop. incl. with Tacoma (Inc. Place)
Lawrence; RMC Place; WHATCOM; 246 B-7; mail Everson z 98247; ● 30
Laws Corner; RMC Place; KLICKITAT; *246 M-9; elev. 1,953ft./595m.; mail White Salmon z 98672; rural
Lazy C; RMC Place; JEFFERSON; *246 F-6; elev. 80ft./24m.; mail Brinnon z 98320; ● 150
Leadpoint; RMC Place; STEVENS; *247 A-18; elev. 2,135ft./651m.; mail Colville z 99114; ● 40
Lea Hill; CDP-Census Area Only; KING; *246 G-7; ★ SEAT; mail Auburn z 98092; Ⓟ 6,876; Ⓒ 10,871
Leavenworth; Inc. Place; CHELAN; 247 F-11; 🅿; z 98826; Ⓟ 1,692; Ⓒ 2,074
Lebam; CDP; PACIFIC; 246 J-4; 🅿; z 98554; Ⓒ 176
Ledgewood Beach; RMC Place; ISLAND; *246 D-7; elev. 285ft./87m.; ★ SEAT; mail Coupeville z 98239; ● 150
Leland; RMC Place; JEFFERSON; 246 E-6; mail Port Townsend z 98368, Quilcene z 98376; ● 50
Lemolo; RMC Place; KITSAP; *246 F-6; ★ SEAT; mail Poulsbo z 98370; ● 120
Levey; RMC Place; FRANKLIN; *247 K-16; mail Pasco z 99301; rural
LEWIS; 246 I-6; Ⓟ 59,358; Ⓒ 68,600; ◆ 73,714
Lewisville; CDP-Census Area Only; CLARK; *246 L-7; ★ POR; Ⓒ 1,688
Lexington; RMC Place; COWLITZ; 246 K-6; ★ LNGV; mail Kelso z 98626; ● 800
Liberty; RMC Place; KITTITAS; 247 G-11; mail Cle Elum z 98922; ● 100
Liberty Lake; Inc. Place; SPOKANE; *247 F-20; 🅿; ★ SPOK; z 99019; incorporated August 31, 2001; not reported in 2000 Census; ● 3,900
Liberty Lake; CDP; SPOKANE; *247 F-20; 🅿; ★ SPOK; z 99016, z 99019; Ⓟ 2,015; Ⓒ 4,660
Liberty Park; RMC Place; SPOKANE; ★ SPOK; mail Spokane z 99202, z 99220; pop. incl. with Spokane (Inc. Place)
Lilliwaup; RMC Place; MASON; 246 F-5; 🅿; z 98555; ● 150
Lincoln; RMC Place; KITSAP; *246 F-6; elev. 360ft./110m.; mail Poulsbo z 98370; pop. incl. with Poulsbo (Inc. Place)
Lincoln; RMC Place; LINCOLN; 247 E-17; 🅿; z 99147; ● 150
LINCOLN; 247 F-16; Ⓟ 8,864; Ⓒ 10,184; ◆ 10,320
Lincoln Station; RMC Place; PIERCE; mail Tacoma z 98408, z 98418; pop. incl. with Tacoma (Inc. Place)
Lind; Inc. Place; ADAMS; 247 H-16; 🅿; z 99341; Ⓟ 472; Ⓒ 582
Linwood; SPOKANE; see Town and Country (CDP-Census Area Only)
Lisabuela; RMC Place; KING; *246 G-7; ★ SEAT; mail Vashon z 98070; rural
Littell; RMC Place; LEWIS; *246 I-5; elev. 190ft./58m.; mail Chehalis z 98532; rural
Little Boston; RMC Place; KITSAP; *246 E-7; mail Kingston z 98346, Port Gamble z 98364; ● 200
Little Falls; RMC Place; LINCOLN; *247 E-18; mail Ford z 99013
Littlerock; RMC Place; THURSTON; 246 H-5; 🅿; ★ OLYM; z 98556; ● 420
Lochsloy; CDP; SNOHOMISH; *246 D-8; elev. 239ft./73m.; ★ SEAT; mail Lake Stevens z 98258; Ⓒ 2,135
Lockamas Heights; RMC Place; CLARK; *246 M-7; elev. 250ft./76m.; ★ POR; mail Camas z 98607; ● 400
Locke; RMC Place; PEND OREILLE; *247 C-19; mail Cusick z 99119; rural
Lofall; RMC Place; KITSAP; 246 E-6; elev. 68ft./21m.; mail Poulsbo z 98370; ● 220
Lone Lake Shores; RMC Place; ISLAND; *246 E-7; elev. 40ft./12m.; ★ SEAT; mail Langley z 98260; ● 100
Lone Pine; RMC Place; OKANOGAN; *247 E-15; mail Coulee Dam z 99116; ● 60
Long Beach; Inc. Place; PACIFIC; 246 J-3; 🅿; z 98631; Ⓟ 1,236; Ⓒ 1,283
Longbranch; RMC Place; PIERCE; 246 G-6; 🅿; ★ SEAT; z 98351; ● 900
Long Lake; RMC Place; KITSAP; *246 F-6; elev. 136ft./41m.; ★ BREM; mail Port Orchard z 98366; ● 800
Long Lake; RMC Place; LINCOLN; *247 E-18; mail Ford z 99013; ● 25
Longmire; RMC Place; PIERCE; 246 I-8; elev. 2,757ft./840m.; 🅿; z 98397; ● 50
Long Point Manor; RMC Place; ISLAND; *246 D-6; elev. 52ft./16m.; mail Coupeville z 98239; ● 70
Longview; Inc. Place; COWLITZ; 246 K-6; elev. 21ft./6m.; 🅿 🅷 ■; ★ LNGV; z 98632; Ⓟ 31,499; Ⓒ 34,660; ◆ 37,125
Longview Heights; CDP-Census Area Only; COWLITZ; *246 K-5; ★ LNGV; mail Longview z 98632; Ⓟ 3,310; Ⓒ 3,513
Longview Junction; RMC Place; COWLITZ; *246 K-6; ★ LNGV; mail Kelso z 98626; pop. incl. with Kelso (Inc. Place)
Loomis; RMC Place; OKANOGAN; 247 B-14; 🅿; z 98827; ● 250
Loon Lake; RMC Place; STEVENS; 247 D-18; elev. 241ft./73m.; 🅿; z 99148; summer pop. 3,000; ● 1,000
Lopez (Lopez Island); RMC Place; SAN JUAN; 246 C-6; mail Lopez Island z 98261; ● 600
Lopez Island; SAN JUAN; see Lopez (RMC Place)
Lost Creek; RMC Place; PEND OREILLE; *247 B-19; mail Usk z 99180; rural
Lost Lake; RMC Place; ISLAND; *246 D-7; elev. 300ft./91m.; ★ SEAT; mail Stanwood z 98292; ● 50
Loveland; RMC Place; PIERCE; *246 H-7; ★ SEAT; mail Spanaway z 98387; ● 200
Lowden; RMC Place; WALLA WALLA; 247 K-16; 🅿; z 99360; ● 60
Lowell; RMC Place; SNOHOMISH; *246 E-7; ★ SEAT; mail Everett z 98203; pop. incl. with Everett (Inc. Place)
Lower Elwha Reservation; Indian Reservation; CLALLAM; mail Port Angeles z 98363; Ⓟ 67; Ⓒ 260
Loyal Heights; RMC Place; KING; *246 F-7; ★ SEAT; mail Seattle z 98117; pop. incl. with Seattle (Inc. Place)
Lucerne; RMC Place; CHELAN; 247 D-11; mail Chelan z 98816; ● 20
Lummi Island; RMC Place; WHATCOM; *246 B-6; 🅿; ★ BELNG; z 98262; summer pop. 1,500; ● 450
Lummi Reservation; Indian Reservation; WHATCOM; ★ BELNG; mail Bellingham z 98226; Ⓟ 2,274; Ⓒ 4,193
Lyle; CDP; KLICKITAT; 246 M-10; 🅿; z 98635; Ⓒ 530
Lyman; Inc. Place; SKAGIT; 246 C-8; 🅿; z 98263; Ⓟ 275; Ⓒ 409
Lynden; Inc. Place; WHATCOM; 246 A-7; elev. 103ft./31m.; 🅿; z 98264; Ⓟ 5,709; Ⓒ 9,020
Lynnwood; Inc. Place; SNOHOMISH; 246 E-7; 🅿 ■; ★ SEAT; z 98036-37, z 98046, z 98087; Ⓟ 28,695; Ⓒ 33,847; ◆ 35,226
Lynwood Center; RMC Place; KITSAP; 248 E-5; ★ SEAT; mail Bainbridge Island z 98110; pop. incl. with Winslow (Inc. Place)

M

Mabana; RMC Place; ISLAND; 246 D-7; ★ SEAT; mail Camano Island z 98282; ● 50
Mabton; Inc. Place; YAKIMA; 247 K-13; 🅿; z 98935; Ⓟ 1,482; Ⓒ 1,891
Machias; CDP; SNOHOMISH; *246 E-8; ★ SEAT; mail Snohomish z 98290; Ⓒ 1,015
Madison Park; RMC Place; KING; *246 F-7; ★ SEAT; mail Seattle z 98112; pop. incl. with Seattle (Inc. Place)
Madrona Beach; RMC Place; ISLAND; *246 D-7; ★ SEAT; mail Stanwood z 98292; summer pop. 500; ● 150
Madrona Point; RMC Place; KITSAP; *246 F-6; elev. 50ft./15m.; ★ BREM; mail Bremerton z 98312; pop. incl. with Bremerton (Inc. Place)
Mae; RMC Place; GRANT; *247 H-14; mail Moses Lake z 98837; rural
Magnolia; RMC Place; KING; ★ SEAT; mail Seattle z 98199; pop. incl. with Seattle (Inc. Place)
Makah Reservation; Indian Reservation; CLALLAM; mail Neah Bay z 98357; also location of Indian Agency; Ⓟ 1,245; Ⓒ 1,356
Malaga; RMC Place; CHELAN; 247 G-12; 🅿; z 98828; ● 450
Malden; Inc. Place; WHITMAN; 247 G-19; 🅿; z 99149; Ⓟ 189; Ⓒ 215
Malo; RMC Place; FERRY; 247 B-16; 🅿; z 99150; ● 200
Malone; RMC Place; GRAYS HARBOR; 246 H-5; 🅿; z 98559; ● 250
Malone-Porter; CDP-Census Area Only; GRAYS HARBOR; *246 H-5; Ⓒ 473
Malott; RMC Place; OKANOGAN; 247 D-13; 🅿; z 98829; ● 400
Maltby; CDP; SNOHOMISH; 246 E-8; ★ SEAT; mail Snohomish z 98290, z 98296; Ⓒ 8,267
Manchester; CDP; KITSAP; 248 F-5; 🅿; ★ BREM; z 98353 & mail Port Orchard z 98366; Ⓟ 4,031; Ⓒ 4,958
Manette; RMC Place; KITSAP; *246 F-6; ★ BREM; mail Bremerton z 98310; pop. incl. with Bremerton (Inc. Place)
Manito; RMC Place; SPOKANE; *247 F-19; ★ SPOK; mail Spokane z 99203, z 99223
Manito Club Estates; RMC Place; SPOKANE; *247 F-19; elev. 2,356ft./718m.; ★ SPOK; mail Spokane z 99203; ● 1,600
Manitou; RMC Place; PIERCE; *246 G-7; ★ SEAT; mail Tacoma z 98409; pop. incl. with Tacoma (Inc. Place)
Manitou Beach; RMC Place; KITSAP; *246 F-7; ★ SEAT; mail Rollingbay z 98061
Manor; RMC Place; CLARK; *246 M-6; elev. 222ft./68m.; ★ POR; mail Battle Ground z 98604; rural
Mansfield; Inc. Place; DOUGLAS; 247 E-14; elev. 2,262ft./689m.; 🅿; z 98830; Ⓟ 311; Ⓒ 319
Manson; RMC Place; CHELAN; 247 E-12; 🅿; z 98831; ● 800
Manzanita; RMC Place; KITSAP; *246 F-7; ★ SEAT; mail Bainbridge Island z 98110; pop. incl. with Winslow (Inc. Place)
Maple Beach; RMC Place; WHATCOM; *246 A-6; mail Point Roberts z 98281, Seabeck z 98380; summer pop. 1,500; ● 200
Maple Falls; CDP; WHATCOM; 246 A-8; elev. 643ft./196m.; 🅿; z 98266; Ⓒ 277
Maple Grove; RMC Place; CLALLAM; *246 D-4; mail Port Angeles z 98362-63; ● 50
Maple Heights-Lake Desire; CDP-Census Area Only; KING; *246 G-8; ★ SEAT; Ⓒ 2,569
Maple Hills; RMC Place; KING; *246 G-8; elev. 700ft./213m.; ★ SEAT; mail Kent z 98031; ● 1,000
Maple Leaf; RMC Place; KING; *246 F-7; ★ SEAT; pop. incl. with Seattle (Inc. Place)
Maple Valley; Inc. Place; KING; 246 G-8; 🅿; ★ SEAT; z 98038; Ⓟ 1,211; Ⓒ 14,209
Maple Valley Heights; RMC Place; KING; *246 G-8; elev. 343ft./105m.; ★ SEAT; mail Renton z 98058; ● 900
Maplewood; RMC Place; KING; *246 G-8; ★ SEAT; mail Puyallup z 98371, Renton z 98055
Maplewood Heights; RMC Place; KING; 246 G-8; elev. 376ft./115m.; ★ SEAT; mail Renton z 98059; ● 3,300
Marble; RMC Place; STEVENS; *247 B-18; mail Northport z 99157; rural
Marblemount; CDP; SKAGIT; 246 C-9; 🅿; z 98267; Ⓒ 251
Marcus; Inc. Place; STEVENS; 247 B-17; 🅿; z 99151; Ⓟ 135; Ⓒ 117
Marengo; RMC Place; ADAMS; *247 H-17; mail Ritzville z 99169; rural
Marietta; RMC Place; WHATCOM; 246 B-7; ★ BELNG; mail Bellingham z 98225-26; ● 550
Marietta-Alderwood; CDP-Census Area Only; WHATCOM; *246 B-7; ★ BELNG; mail Bellingham z 98225; Ⓟ 2,766; Ⓒ 3,594
Marine Drive; RMC Place; KITSAP; *246 F-6; ★ BREM; mail Bremerton z 98312; pop. incl. with Bremerton (Inc. Place)
Marine View Estates; RMC Place; KING; *246 G-7; elev. 300ft./91m.; ★ SEAT; mail Federal Way z 98003; pop. incl. with Federal Way (Inc. Place)
Marketown; RMC Place; ISLAND; *246 C-6; elev. 150ft./46m.; mail Oak Harbor z 98277; ● 230
Markham; CDP; GRAYS HARBOR; 246 H-3; mail Aberdeen z 98520; Ⓒ 95
Marlin (Krupp); Inc. Place; GRANT; 247 G-15; 🅿; z 98832; Ⓟ 53; Ⓒ 60
Marrowstone; CDP-Census Area Only; JEFFERSON; *246 D-6; Ⓒ 837
Marshall; RMC Place; SPOKANE; 247 F-19; 🅿; z 99020; ● 100
Martha Lake; CDP-Census Area Only; SNOHOMISH; *246 E-7; ★ SEAT; mail Bothell z 98012; Ⓟ 10,155; Ⓒ 12,633
Martin Luther King Jr Way; RMC Place; PIERCE; ★ SEAT; mail Tacoma z 98405, z 98415; pop. incl. with Tacoma (Inc. Place)
Maryhill; CDP; KLICKITAT; *247 M-11; elev. 180ft./55m.; mail Goldendale z 98620; Ⓒ 98
Marys Corner; RMC Place; LEWIS; *246 J-6; elev. 532ft./162m.; mail Chehalis z 98532; rural
Marysville; Inc. Place; SNOHOMISH; 246 D-8; 🅿; ★ SEAT; z 98270-71; Ⓟ 10,328; Ⓒ 25,315; ◆ 32,277
MASON; 246 G-5; Ⓟ 38,341; Ⓒ 49,405; ◆ 59,972
Matlock; RMC Place; MASON; 246 G-4; 🅿; z 98560; ● 130
Matneys Spur; RMC Place; FERRY; *247 B-17; mail Kettle Falls z 99141; rural
Mattawa; Inc. Place; GRANT; 247 I-13; elev. 778ft./237m.; 🅿; z 99349; Ⓟ 941; Ⓒ 2,609
Maud; RMC Place; STEVENS; *247 C-17; mail Gifford z 99131; ● 40
Maxwelton; RMC Place; ISLAND; *246 E-7; ★ SEAT; mail Clinton z 98236; summer pop. 300; ● 200
May Creek; CDP-Census Area Only; SNOHOMISH; 246 E-7; elev. 235ft./72m.; mail Gold Bar z 98251; Ⓒ 1,004
Mays Pond; RMC Place; SNOHOMISH; *246 E-7; elev. 300ft./91m.; ★ SEAT; mail Bothell z 98012; ● 2,400
Maytown; RMC Place; THURSTON; 246 I-6; mail Olympia z 98501-02; ● 70
Mazama; RMC Place; OKANOGAN; 247 C-12; 🅿; z 98833; ● 90
McChord AFB; CDP-Census Area Only; PIERCE; *246 H-7; 🅿; ★ SEAT; z 98438-39, z 98499; Ⓟ 4,538; Ⓒ 4,096
McCleary; Inc. Place; GRAYS HARBOR; 246 H-5; elev. 257ft./78m.; 🅿 🅷; z 98557; Ⓟ 1,235; Ⓒ 1,454; Ⓡ 1,484
McDonald; RMC Place; GRANT; *247 H-15; mail Moses Lake z 98837; rural
McGinnis Lake; RMC Place; OKANOGAN; *247 D-15; elev. 2,400ft./732m.; mail Coulee Dam z 99116; ● 60
McKees Beach; RMC Place; SNOHOMISH; *246 D-7; ★ SEAT; mail Stanwood z 98292; ● 100
Mckenna; RMC Place; PIERCE; 246 H-7; 🅿; ★ SEAT; z 98558; ● 350
McLoughlin Heights; RMC Place; CLARK; *246 M-6; ★ POR; pop. incl. with Vancouver (Inc. Place)
McMicken Heights; RMC Place; KING; ★ SEAT; mail Seattle z 98188; pop. incl. with SeaTac (Inc. Place)
McMillin; RMC Place; PIERCE; 246 H-7; ★ SEAT; mail Orting z 98360; ● 220
McMurray; RMC Place; SKAGIT; *246 C-7; mail Mount Vernon z 98274; ● 200
Mead; RMC Place; SPOKANE; 247 E-19; 🅿; ★ SPOK; z 99021; ● 2,150
Meadow Brook; RMC Place; KING; *246 F-8; ★ SEAT; mail Snoqualmie z 98065; pop. incl. with Snoqualmie (Inc. Place)
Meadowbrook; RMC Place; YAKIMA; *247 J-11; elev. 1,167ft./356m.; ★ YAK; mail Yakima z 98903; ● 250
Meadowdale; RMC Place; KITSAP; *246 F-6; ★ BREM; mail Bremerton z 98310; ● 150
Meadowdale; RMC Place; SNOHOMISH; *246 E-7; ★ SEAT; mail Edmonds z 98020; pop. incl. with Edmonds (Inc. Place)
Meadow Glade; CDP; CLARK; *246 M-6; ★ POR; mail Battle Ground z 98604; Ⓟ 1,584; Ⓒ 2,225
Meadow Lake; SPOKANE; see Four Lakes (RMC Place)
Medical Lake; Inc. Place; SPOKANE; 247 F-18; 🅿 🅷; z 99022; Ⓟ 3,664; Ⓒ 3,758; Ⓡ 3,815
Medina; Inc. Place; KING; 248 D-9; 🅿; ★ SEAT; z 98039; Ⓟ 2,981; Ⓒ 3,011
Meeker; RMC Place; PIERCE; *246 H-7; ★ SEAT; mail Puyallup z 98371; pop. incl. with Puyallup (Inc. Place)
Melbourne; RMC Place; GRAYS HARBOR; 246 H-4; elev. 54ft./16m.; mail Montesano z 98563; ● 50
Menlo; RMC Place; PACIFIC; 246 I-4; 🅿; z 98561; ● 250
Mercer Island; Inc. Place; KING; 248 E-9; 🅿; ★ SEAT; z 98040; Ⓟ 20,816; Ⓒ 22,036; ◆ 24,448
Meredith; RMC Place; KING; *246 G-7; ★ SEAT; mail Auburn z 98001; pop. incl. with Auburn (Inc. Place)
Meridian Heights (Lake Meridian); RMC Place; KING; 248 I-10; elev. 125ft./38m.; ★ SEAT; mail Kent z 98042; pop. incl. with Covington (Inc. Place)
Merritt; RMC Place; CHELAN; *247 E-11; elev. 2,180ft./664m.; mail Leavenworth z 98826
Mesa; Inc. Place; FRANKLIN; 247 J-15; 🅿; z 99343; Ⓟ 252; Ⓒ 425
Metaline; Inc. Place; PEND OREILLE; 247 A-19; 🅿; z 99152; Ⓟ 198; Ⓒ 162
Metaline Falls; Inc. Place; PEND OREILLE; 247 A-19; 🅿; z 99153; Ⓟ 210; Ⓒ 223
Methow; RMC Place; OKANOGAN; 247 D-13; elev. 1,153ft./351m.; 🅿; z 98834; ● 60
Miami Beach; RMC Place; KITSAP; *246 F-6; elev. 20ft./6m.; ★ BREM; mail Seabeck z 98380; summer pop. 80; rural
Mica; RMC Place; SPOKANE; 247 F-19; 🅿; z 99023; ● 130

Entries in **UPPERCASE** are counties.
Entries in **bold** have populations of 2,500 or more.
Names in parentheses are alternate names.
Inc. Place — Incorporated Place
RMC Place — Rand McNally Designated Place
CDP — Census Designated Place
MCD — Minor Civil Division

⊡ County Seat
▲ Minor Civil Division
elev. Elevation
🅿 Post Office

🅷 Hospital
🅲 College
■ Principal Business Center
★ Ranally Metro Area (RMA) Abbreviation
z Zip Code(s)

Ⓟ Previous Census Population
Ⓡ Revised Census Population
Ⓐ Annexation Population
● Rand McNally Population Estimate
Ⓒ Final Census Population
Ⓢ Special Census Population
◆ Estimated Population

For additional definitions see Glossary, Volume 1, and Introduction, Volume 2.

Midlakes; RMC Place; KING; mail Bellevue z 98015; pop. incl. with Bellevue (Inc. Place)

Midland; CDP; PIERCE; 248 N-7; ★ SEAT; mail Tacoma z 98404, z 98444-45; Ⓟ 5,587; Ⓒ 7,414

Midland Acres; RMC Place; CLARK; ★ POR; mail Camas z 98607; pop. incl. with Camas (Inc. Place)

Midvale Corner; RMC Place; ISLAND; *246 E-7; ★ SEAT; mail Clinton z 98236; ● 30

Midway; RMC Place; KING; *246 G-7; ★ SEAT; mail Kent z 98032, z 98035

Midway; RMC Place; PIERCE; 248 K-4; ★ SEAT; mail Gig Harbor z 98335; pop. incl. with Gig Harbor (Inc. Place)

Milan; RMC Place; SPOKANE; 247 E-19; mail Chattaroy z 99003; ● 80

Milco; RMC Place; COWLITZ; ★ LNGV; mail Kelso z 98626; pop. incl. with Kelso (Inc. Place)

Miles; RMC Place; LINCOLN; 247 E-17; mail Davenport z 99122; ● 30

Mill A; RMC Place; SKAMANIA; *246 M-9; mail Bingen z 98605; ● 110

Mill Creek; Inc. Place; SNOHOMISH; 246 E-7; 🅿; ★ SEAT; z 98012, z 98082; Ⓟ 7,172; Ⓒ 11,525

Miller River; RMC Place; KING; *246 F-9; mail Skykomish z 98288; rural

Mill Plain; CDP-Census Area Only; CLARK; *246 M-7; ★ POR; Ⓒ 7,400

Millwood; Inc. Place; SPOKANE; 248 B-4; 🅿; ★ SPOK; z 99212; Ⓟ 1,559; Ⓒ 1,649

Milton; Inc. Place; PIERCE, KING; 248 L-8; 🅿; ★ SEAT; z 98354; Ⓟ 4,995; Ⓒ 5,795

Mima; RMC Place; THURSTON; *246 I-5; elev. 140ft./43m.; mail Olympia z 98501; rural

Mineral; RMC Place; LEWIS; 246 I-7; 🅿; z 98355; ● 500

Mineral Springs; RMC Place; KITTITAS; *247 G-11; mail Cle Elum z 98922; rural

Minnehaha; CDP; CLARK; 223 J-19; ★ POR; mail Vancouver z 98665; Ⓟ 9,661; Ⓒ 7,689

Mirror Lake; RMC Place; KING; ★ SEAT; mail Federal Way z 98003; pop. incl. with Federal Way (Inc. Place)

Mirrormont; CDP-Census Area Only; KING; *246 G-8; elev. 797ft./243m.; ★ SEAT; mail Issaquah z 98027; Ⓟ 2,360; Ⓒ 3,804

Mission Beach; RMC Place; SNOHOMISH; *246 D-7; ★ SEAT; mail Marysville z 98271; ● 250

Misty Meadows; RMC Place; SNOHOMISH; *246 E-7; elev. 400ft./122m.; ★ SEAT; mail Bothell z 98012; ● 800

Moclips; CDP; GRAYS HARBOR; 246 G-3; 🅿; z 98562; Ⓒ 615

Mohler; RMC Place; LINCOLN; 247 G-17; 🅿; z 99154; ● 25

Molson; RMC Place; OKANOGAN; 247 A-15; mail Oroville z 98844

Mondovi; RMC Place; LINCOLN; *247 F-17; elev. 2,506ft./764m.; mail Davenport z 99122

Monitor; RMC Place; CHELAN; 247 F-12; 🅿; z 98836; ● 120

Monohon; RMC Place; KING; *246 F-8; ★ SEAT; mail Issaquah z 98029; pop. incl. with Sammamish (Inc. Place)

Monroe; Inc. Place; SNOHOMISH; 246 E-8; 🅿 🄷; ★ SEAT; z 98272; Ⓟ 4,278; Ⓒ 13,795

Monse; RMC Place; OKANOGAN; *247 D-13; mail Brewster z 98812

Monta Vista; RMC Place; PIERCE; *246 H-7; ★ SEAT; mail Lakewood z 98499; pop. incl. with Lakewood (Inc. Place)

Montborne; RMC Place; SKAGIT; *246 C-7; mail Mount Vernon z 98274; ● 250

Montesano; Inc. Place; ⊡ GRAYS HARBOR; 246 H-4; elev. 66ft./20m.; 🅿; z 98563; Ⓟ 3,064; Ⓒ 3,312

Moore; RMC Place; CHELAN; *247 D-11; elev. 1,500ft./457m.; mail Chelan z 98816; rural

Moorlands; RMC Place; KING; *246 F-7; elev. 100ft./30m.; ★ SEAT; mail Bothell z 98011; pop. incl. with Kenmore (Inc. Place)

Moran; SPOKANE; see Moran Prairie (RMC Place)

Moran Prairie (Moran); RMC Place; SPOKANE; *247 F-19; ★ SPOK; mail Spokane z 99203; ● 500

Morgan Acres; RMC Place; SPOKANE; 248 B-3; ★ SPOK; mail Spokane z 99217; ● 1,500

Morganville; RMC Place; KING; *246 G-8; ★ SEAT; mail Black Diamond z 98010; pop. incl. with Black Diamond (Inc. Place)

Morningside; RMC Place; KING; *246 F-7; ★ SEAT; pop. incl. with Seattle (Inc. Place)

Morton; Inc. Place; LEWIS; 246 J-7; 🅿 🄷; z 98356; Ⓟ 1,130; Ⓒ 1,045

Moses Lake; Inc. Place; GRANT; 247 H-14; 🅿 🄷; z 98837; Ⓟ 11,235; Ⓒ 14,953

Moses Lake North; CDP-Census Area Only; GRANT; *247 G-14; elev. 1,100ft./335m.; mail Moses Lake z 98837; Ⓟ 3,677; Ⓒ 4,232

Mossyrock; Inc. Place; LEWIS; 246 J-7; elev. 698ft./213m.; 🅿; z 98564; Ⓟ 452; Ⓒ 486

Mountain Home Park; RMC Place; COLUMBIA; *247 K-18; elev. 2,151ft./656m.; mail Dayton z 99328; rural

Mountain View; RMC Place; SKAGIT; *246 C-7; elev. 512ft./156m.; mail Mount Vernon z 98274; rural

Mountain View Beach; RMC Place; ISLAND; *246 D-7; ★ SEAT; mail Camano Island z 98282; ● 70

Mount Baker; RMC Place; WHATCOM; ★ BELNG; mail Bellingham z 98226, z 98228; pop. incl. with Bellingham (Inc. Place)

Mount Brook; RMC Place; KLICKITAT; *246 L-9; elev. 1,889ft./576m.; mail White Salmon z 98672; rural

Mount Hope; RMC Place; SPOKANE; *247 F-19; mail Fairfield z 99012; rural

Mountlake Terrace; Inc. Place; SNOHOMISH; 246 E-7; 🅿; ★ SEAT; z 98043; Ⓟ 19,320; Ⓒ 20,362; ◆ 20,493

Mount Pleasant; RMC Place; CLALLAM; *246 D-5; mail Port Angeles z 98362; ● 1,200

Mount Tahoma Estate; RMC Place; THURSTON; *246 H-6; elev. 196ft./60m.; ★ OLYM; mail Olympia z 98501; pop. incl. with Lacey (Inc. Place)

Mount Vernon; Inc. Place; ⊡ SKAGIT; 246 C-7; 🅿 🄷 ■; z 98273-74; Ⓟ 17,647; Ⓒ 26,232; ◆ 31,805

Mount Vista; CDP-Census Area Only; CLARK; *246 M-6; ★ POR; Ⓒ 5,770

Moxee; YAKIMA; see Moxee City (Inc. Place)

Moxee City (Moxee); Inc. Place; YAKIMA; 247 J-12; ★ YAK; mail Moxee z 98936; Ⓟ 814; Ⓒ 821

Muckleshoot Reservation; Indian Reservation; KING, PIERCE; ★ SEAT; mail Auburn z 98092; Ⓟ 2,991; Ⓒ 3,597

Mukilteo; Inc. Place; SNOHOMISH; 246 E-7; 🅿; ★ SEAT; z 98275; Ⓟ 6,982; Ⓒ 18,019; ◆ 22,445

Munson Point; RMC Place; MASON; *246 G-5; elev. 50ft./15m.; ★ OLYM; mail Shelton z 98584; ● 450

Murdock; RMC Place; KLICKITAT; *246 M-10; elev. 332ft./101m.; mail Lyle z 98635; ● 170

Murphy's Corner; RMC Place; SNOHOMISH; *246 E-7; elev. 455ft./139m.; ★ SEAT; mail Bothell z 98012, Everett z 98201; pop. incl. with Mill Creek (Inc. Place)

Mushroom Corner; RMC Place; THURSTON; *246 H-6; elev. 230ft./70m.; ★ OLYM; mail Olympia z 98513; ● 50

N

Naches; Inc. Place; YAKIMA; 247 I-11; 🅿; ★ YAK; z 98929, z 98937; Ⓟ 596; Ⓒ 643

Nahcotta; RMC Place; PACIFIC; 246 J-3; elev. 19ft./6m.; 🅿; z 98637; ● 200

Nahwatzel Lake; RMC Place; MASON; *246 G-5; elev. 142ft./43m.; mail Shelton z 98584; ● 200

Napavine; Inc. Place; LEWIS; 246 J-6; elev. 444ft./135m.; 🅿; z 98532, z 98565; Ⓟ 745; Ⓒ 1,361

Naselle; CDP; PACIFIC; 246 J-3; 🅿; z 98638; Ⓒ 377

National; RMC Place; PIERCE; *246 I-8; elev. 1,605ft./489m.; mail Ashford z 98304; ● 50

Navy Yard City; CDP; KITSAP; *246 F-6; ★ BREM; mail Bremerton z 98312; Ⓟ 2,905; Ⓒ 2,638

Neah Bay; CDP; CLALLAM; 246 C-2; located on Makah Ind. Res.; 🅿; z 98357; location of Indian Agency; Ⓟ 916; summer pop. 3,000; Ⓒ 794

Neilton; CDP; GRAYS HARBOR; 246 G-3; elev. 483ft./147m.; 🅿; z 98566; Ⓒ 345

Nemah; RMC Place; PACIFIC; *246 J-3; mail South Bend z 98586; ● 35

Nespelem; Inc. Place; OKANOGAN; 247 D-15; located on Colville Ind. Res.; 🅿; z 99155; Ⓟ 187; Ⓒ 212

Nespelem Community; CDP-Census Area Only; OKANOGAN; *247 D-15; located on Colville Ind. Res.; mail Nespelem z 99155; Ⓟ 291; Ⓒ 290

Newaukum; RMC Place; KING; *246 G-8; elev. 151ft./46m.; ★ SEAT; mail Auburn z 98092, Chehalis z 98532

Newcastle (Newport Hills); Inc. Place; KING; 248 F-10; 🅿; ★ SEAT; z 98056, z 98059 & mail Bellevue z 98006; Ⓟ 7,751; Ⓒ 7,737

Newhalem; RMC Place; WHATCOM; 246 B-10; mail Rockport z 98283; ● 350

New London; RMC Place; GRAYS HARBOR; *246 H-3; elev. 20ft./6m.; mail Hoquiam z 98550; ● 90

Newman Lake; RMC Place; SPOKANE; 247 E-20; 🅿; ★ SPOK; z 99025; ● 650

Newport; RMC Place; KING; *246 F-7; ★ SEAT; mail Bellevue z 98006; pop. incl. with Bellevue (Inc. Place)

Newport; Inc. Place; ⊡ PEND OREILLE; 247 D-20; 🅿 🄷; z 99156; Ⓟ 1,691; Ⓒ 1,921

Newport Hills; KING; see Newcastle (Inc. Place)

Newport Shores; RMC Place; KING; *246 F-7; ★ SEAT; mail Bellevue z 98004; pop. incl. with Bellevue (Inc. Place)

Newton; RMC Place; GRAYS HARBOR; *246 H-3; mail Hoquiam z 98550

Nighthawk; RMC Place; OKANOGAN; 247 A-14; mail Loomis z 98827, Tonasket z 98855; ● 25

Nile; RMC Place; YAKIMA; *246 I-10; mail Naches z 98937; rural

Nine Mile Falls; RMC Place; SPOKANE; *247 E-19; 🅿; ★ SPOK; z 99026; ● 330

Nisqually; THURSTON; see Nisqually Indian Community (CDP-Census Area Only)

Nisqually Indian Community (Nisqually); CDP-Census Area Only; THURSTON; *246 H-6; ★ OLYM; mail Olympia z 98501, z 98513; Ⓟ 558; Ⓒ 588

Nisqually Reservation; Indian Reservation; PIERCE, THURSTON; ★ SEAT; mail Yelm z 98597; Ⓟ 254; Ⓒ 588

Nisson; RMC Place; GRAYS HARBOR; *246 H-4; mail Hoquiam z 98550; rural

Nooksack; Inc. Place; WHATCOM; 246 A-7; elev. 84ft./26m.; 🅿; ★ BELNG; z 98247, z 98276; Ⓟ 584; Ⓒ 851; Ⓡ 863

Nooksack Reservation; Indian Reservation; WHATCOM; Ⓒ 0

Nordland; RMC Place; JEFFERSON; *246 D-6; 🅿; z 98358; ● 600

Norma Beach; RMC Place; SNOHOMISH; *246 E-7; elev. 20ft./6m.; ★ SEAT; mail Edmonds z 98026; ● 200

Norman; RMC Place; SNOHOMISH; *246 D-7; ★ SEAT; mail Stanwood z 98292; rural

Normandy Park; Inc. Place; KING; 248 H-8; 🅿; ★ SEAT; z 98148, z 98166, z 98198; Ⓟ 6,709; Ⓒ 6,392

North Beach; RMC Place; SAN JUAN; *246 B-6; elev. 31ft./9m.; mail Eastsound z 98245; ● 100

North Bend; Inc. Place; KING; 246 F-8; elev. 442ft./135m.; 🅿; ★ SEAT; z 98045; Ⓟ 2,578; Ⓒ 4,746

North Bonneville; Inc. Place; SKAMANIA; 246 M-8; 🅿; z 98639; Ⓟ 411; Ⓒ 593

North City; RMC Place; KING; *246 E-7; ★ SEAT; mail Seattle z 98155; pop. incl. with Shoreline (Inc. Place)

North Cove; RMC Place; PACIFIC; 246 I-3; mail Grayland z 98547, Tokeland z 98590; ● 70

North Creek; CDP-Census Area Only; SNOHOMISH; *246 E-8; ★ SEAT; Ⓒ 25,742; ◆ 29,326

North Dallas; KLICKITAT; see Dallesport (CDP)

Northeast Tacoma; RMC Place; PIERCE; *246 G-7; ★ SEAT; mail Tacoma z 98422; pop. incl. with Tacoma (Inc. Place)

Northgate; RMC Place; KING; ★ SEAT; mail Seattle z 98125; pop. incl. with Seattle (Inc. Place)

North Lake; RMC Place; KING; *246 G-7; elev. 4,000ft./1,219m.; ★ SEAT; mail Auburn z 98001; ● 550

North Lakewood; SNOHOMISH; see Lakewood (RMC Place)

North Lynnwood; RMC Place; SNOHOMISH; *246 E-7; ★ SEAT; mail Lynnwood z 98036; ● 1,250

North Marysville; CDP-Census Area Only; SNOHOMISH; *246 D-8; ★ SEAT; mail Arlington z 98223, Everett z 98201, Marysville z 98270-71; Ⓟ 18,711; Ⓒ 21,161; ◆ 24,105

North Omak; CDP-Census Area Only; OKANOGAN; *247 C-14; mail Omak z 98841; Ⓟ 515; Ⓒ 688

North Park; RMC Place; KING; *246 F-7; ★ SEAT; pop. incl. with Seattle (Inc. Place)

Northport; Inc. Place; STEVENS; 247 A-18; 🅿; z 99157; Ⓟ 308; Ⓒ 336

North Prosser; RMC Place; BENTON; *247 K-13; elev. 750ft./229m.; mail Prosser z 99350

North Puyallup; RMC Place; PIERCE; 248 M-8; ★ SEAT; mail Puyallup z 98372; Ⓟ 2,886

Northrup; RMC Place; KING; *246 F-7; ★ SEAT; mail Bellevue z 98008; pop. incl. with Bellevue (Inc. Place)

North Stanwood; CDP-Census Area Only; SNOHOMISH; *246 D-7; ★ SEAT; Ⓒ 468

North Sultan; CDP-Census Area Only; SNOHOMISH; *246 E-8; ★ SEAT; Ⓒ 381

Northwest Snohomish; CDP-Census Area Only; SNOHOMISH; *246 E-8; ★ SEAT; Ⓒ 2,061

Northwood; RMC Place; WHATCOM; *246 A-7; elev. 127ft./39m.; mail Lynden z 98264; ● 50

Northwoods; RMC Place; SKAMANIA; *246 L-8; elev. 1,000ft./305m.; mail Cougar z 98616; summer pop. 300; ● 20

North Yelm; CDP-Census Area Only; THURSTON; *246 H-6; ★ OLYM; mail Yelm z 98597; Ⓟ 2,075; Ⓒ 2,793

Norwood Village; RMC Place; KING; *246 F-8; ★ SEAT; mail Bellevue z 98004; pop. incl. with Bellevue (Inc. Place)

Nugents Corner; RMC Place; WHATCOM; *246 B-7; elev. 157ft./48m.; mail Everson z 98247; ● 30

O

Oakbrook; RMC Place; PIERCE; 🅿; ★ SEAT; z 98497; pop. incl. with Lakewood (Inc. Place)

Oakesdale; Inc. Place; WHITMAN; 247 H-19; elev. 2,461ft./750m.; 🅿; z 99158; Ⓟ 346; Ⓒ 420

Oak Harbor; Inc. Place; ISLAND; 246 D-6; 🅿 🄷; z 98277-78; Ⓟ 17,176; Ⓒ 19,795; ◆ 21,732

Oakland; RMC Place; PIERCE; *246 G-7; elev. 310ft./94m.; ★ SEAT; mail Tacoma z 98409; pop. incl. with Tacoma (Inc. Place)

Oak Park; RMC Place; CLARK; *246 M-7; ★ POR; mail Camas z 98607; pop. incl. with Camas (Inc. Place)

Oak Point; RMC Place; COWLITZ; *246 K-5; mail Longview z 98632; rural

Oakville; Inc. Place; GRAYS HARBOR; 246 I-5; elev. 90ft./27m.; 🅿; z 98568; Ⓟ 493; Ⓒ 675

O'Brien; RMC Place; KING; *246 G-7; ★ SEAT; mail Kent z 98032; pop. incl. with Kent (Inc. Place)

Obstruction Pass; RMC Place; SAN JUAN; *246 B-6; elev. 100ft./30m.; mail Olga z 98279; ● 50

Ocean City; CDP; GRAYS HARBOR; 246 H-3; 🅿; z 98569; summer pop. 5,000; Ⓒ 217

Ocean Grove; RMC Place; GRAYS HARBOR; *246 G-3; elev. 100ft./30m.; mail Pacific Beach z 98571; summer pop. 100

Ocean Park; CDP; PACIFIC; 246 J-3; 🅿; z 98640; Ⓟ 1,409; Ⓒ 1,459

Ocean Shores; Inc. Place; GRAYS HARBOR; 246 H-3; 🅿; z 98569; Ⓟ 2,301; Ⓒ 3,836

Ocosta; RMC Place; GRAYS HARBOR; *246 H-3; elev. 46ft./14m.; mail Aberdeen z 98520; ● 60

Odessa; Inc. Place; LINCOLN; 247 G-16; elev. 1,544ft./471m.; 🅿 🄷; z 99144, z 99159; Ⓟ 935; Ⓒ 957

Offutt Lake; RMC Place; THURSTON; *246 H-6; ★ OLYM; mail Olympia z 98501; ● 130

Ohanapecosh; RMC Place; LEWIS; *246 I-9; mail Packwood z 98361; ● 50

Okanogan; Inc. Place; ⊡ OKANOGAN; 247 C-14; elev. 860ft./262m.; 🅿; z 98840; Ⓟ 2,370; Ⓒ 2,484

OKANOGAN; 247 B-13; Ⓟ 33,350; Ⓒ 39,564; ◆ 40,214

Olalla; RMC Place; KITSAP; 248 H-5; 🅿; ★ BREM; z 98359; ● 600

Oldport; RMC Place; THURSTON; *246 H-6; elev. 100ft./30m.; ★ OLYM; mail Olympia z 98501; ● 50

Old Tacoma; RMC Place; PIERCE; *246 G-7; elev. 200ft./61m.; ★ SEAT; mail Tacoma z 98466; pop. incl. with Tacoma (Inc. Place)

Old Willapa; RMC Place; PACIFIC; *246 I-4; mail Raymond z 98577; ● 100

Olga; RMC Place; SAN JUAN; 246 B-6; 🅿; z 98279; summer pop. 500; ● 150

Olympia; Inc. Place; STATE CAPITAL; ⊡ THURSTON; 246 H-6; 🅿 🄷 🄲 4,416 ■; ★ OLYM; z 98501-09, z 98511-13, z 98516, z 98599; Ⓟ 33,840; Ⓒ 42,514; ◆ 48,985

Olympic View; RMC Place; KITSAP; *246 F-6; ★ BREM; mail Silverdale z 98383; ● 200

Olympus Ocean Estates; RMC Place; GRAYS HARBOR; *246 G-3; elev. 100ft./30m.; mail Pacific Beach z 98571; ● 100

Omak; Inc. Place; OKANOGAN; 247 C-14; elev. 837ft./255m.; 🅿 🄷; z 98841; Ⓟ 4,117; Ⓒ 4,721

Onalaska; RMC Place; LEWIS; 246 J-6; 🅿; z 98570; ● 650

Oneida; RMC Place; WAHKIAKUM; *246 K-4; elev. 25ft./8m.; mail Naselle z 98638; rural

Onion Creek; RMC Place; STEVENS; *247 B-18; elev. 2,451ft./747m.; mail Colville z 99114; rural

Opportunity; CDP; SPOKANE; 247 F-19; ★ SPOK; mail Spokane z 99206; former CDP; became part of Spokane Valley March 31, 2003; Ⓟ 22,326; Ⓒ 25,065; ◆ 0

Orcas; RMC Place; SAN JUAN; 246 B-6; 🅿; z 98280; ● 300

Orchard Avenue; RMC Place; SPOKANE; *247 F-19; ★ SPOK; mail Spokane z 99211

Orchard Heights; KITSAP; see Parkwood (CDP)

Orchard Prairie; RMC Place; SPOKANE; *247 E-19; elev. 2,380ft./725m.; ★ SPOK; mail Spokane z 99217; ● 150

Orchards ; CDP; CLARK; 246 M-6; ★ POR; mail Vancouver z 98662; Ⓟ 12,956; Ⓒ 17,852

Orient; RMC Place; FERRY; 247 A-17; 🅿; z 99160; ● 100

Orillia; RMC Place; KING; *246 G-7; ★ SEAT; mail Kent z 98032; pop. incl. with Kent (Inc. Place)

Orin; RMC Place; STEVENS; 247 C-18; elev. 1,568ft./478m.; mail Colville z 99114; ● 35

Orondo; RMC Place; DOUGLAS; 247 F-12; 🅿; z 98843; ● 400

Oroville; Inc. Place; OKANOGAN; 247 A-14; 🅿; z 98844; Ⓟ 1,505; Ⓒ 1,653

Orting; Inc. Place; PIERCE; 246 H-7; 🅿; ★ SEAT; z 98360; Ⓟ 2,106; Ⓒ 3,760; Ⓡ 3,931

Osceola; RMC Place; KING; *246 G-8; ★ SEAT; mail Enumclaw z 98022

Oso; CDP; SNOHOMISH; 246 D-8; ★ SEAT; mail Arlington z 98223; Ⓒ 246

Ostrander; RMC Place; COWLITZ; 246 K-6; ★ LNGV; mail Kelso z 98626; ● 120

Othello; Inc. Place; ADAMS; 247 I-15; elev. 1,038ft./316m.; 🅿 🄷; z 99344; Ⓟ 4,638; Ⓒ 5,847

Otis Orchards; RMC Place; SPOKANE; 247 F-20; 🅿; ★ SPOK; z 99027; ● 3,200

Otis Orchards-East Farms; CDP-Census Area Only; SPOKANE; *247 F-20; ★ SPOK; mail Newman Lake z 99025, Otis Orchards z 99027; Ⓟ 5,811; Ⓒ 6,318

Outlook; RMC Place; YAKIMA; 247 K-13; 🅿; z 98938; ● 340

Overlake; RMC Place; KING; ★ SEAT; mail Bellevue z 98007; pop. incl. with Bellevue (Inc. Place)

Oyehut-Hogans Corner; CDP-Census Area Only; GRAYS HARBOR; *246 H-3; Ⓒ 188

Oyhut; RMC Place; GRAYS HARBOR; *246 H-3; mail Hoquiam z 98550; pop. incl. with Ocean Shores (Inc. Place)

Oysterville; RMC Place; PACIFIC; 246 J-3; 🅿; z 98641; ● 50

Ozette; RMC Place; CLALLAM; 246 D-2; mail Clallam Bay z 98326; ● 50

P

Pacific; Inc. Place; KING, PIERCE; 248 L-9; 🅿; ★ SEAT; z 98047; Ⓟ 4,622; Ⓒ 5,527

PACIFIC; 246 J-4; Ⓟ 18,882; Ⓒ 20,984; ◆ 21,552

Pacific Beach; RMC Place; GRAYS HARBOR; 246 G-3; 🅿; z 98571; ● 1,200

Packwood; RMC Place; LEWIS; 246 J-9; elev. 1,051ft./320m.; 🅿; z 98361; ● 1,050

Paine Field-Lake Stickney; CDP-Census Area Only; SNOHOMISH; *246 E-7; ★ SEAT; mail Everett z 98204; Ⓟ 18,670; Ⓒ 24,383; ◆ 27,768

Painted Hills; RMC Place; SPOKANE; *247 F-19; elev. 2,200ft./671m.; ★ SPOK; mail Spokane z 99206; ● 100

Palisades; RMC Place; DOUGLAS; 247 G-13; elev. 976ft./297m.; 🅿; z 98845; ● 180

Palmer; RMC Place; KING; 246 G-8; mail Ravensdale z 98051; ● 300

Palouse; Inc. Place; WHITMAN; 247 H-20; elev. 2,426ft./739m.; 🅿; z 99161; Ⓟ 915; Ⓒ 1,011

Panhandle Lake; RMC Place; MASON; *246 H-5; elev. 150ft./46m.; mail Shelton z 98584; ● 50

Paradise Estates; RMC Place; LEWIS; *246 I-8; elev. 1,800ft./549m.; mail Ashford z 98304; ● 250

Park; RMC Place; WHATCOM; *246 B-7; elev. 319ft./97m.; ★ BELNG; mail Sedro Woolley z 98284; rural

Parker; RMC Place; YAKIMA; 247 J-12; 🅿; z 98939; ● 360

Parkland; CDP; PIERCE; 246 H-7; 🅿; ★ SEAT; z 98444-46, z 98448; Ⓟ 20,882; Ⓒ 24,053; ◆ 26,940

Park Orchard; RMC Place; KING; *246 G-7; elev. 400ft./122m.; ★ SEAT; mail Kent z 98031; ● 3,800

Park Rapids; RMC Place; STEVENS; *247 C-18; elev. 2,905ft./885m.; mail Colville z 99114; rural

Parkwater; RMC Place; SPOKANE; 248 B-4; ★ SPOK; mail Spokane z 99211; pop. incl. with Spokane (Inc. Place)

Parkwood (Orchard Heights); CDP; KITSAP; *246 F-6; ★ BREM; mail Port Orchard z 98366, Retsil z 98378; Ⓟ 6,853; Ⓒ 7,213

Pasadena Park; RMC Place; SPOKANE; 248 B-4; ★ SPOK; mail Spokane z 99206; ● 1,700

Pasco; Inc. Place; ⊡ FRANKLIN; 247 K-15; 🅿 🄷 ■; ★ RICH-; z 99301-02; Ⓟ 20,337; Ⓒ 32,066; ◆ 58,806

Pataha City; RMC Place; GARFIELD; 247 J-19; mail Pomeroy z 99347; ● 70

Pateros; Inc. Place; OKANOGAN; 247 D-13; elev. 776ft./237m.; 🅿; z 98846; Ⓟ 570; Ⓒ 643

Paterson; RMC Place; BENTON; 247 L-14; elev. 377ft./115m.; 🅿; z 99345; ● 150

Peaceful Valley; CDP-Census Area Only; WHATCOM; *246 A-8; Ⓒ 2,448

Peach Acres; RMC Place; PIERCE; *246 G-7; elev. 230ft./70m.; ★ SEAT; mail Tacoma z 98465; pop. incl. with University Place (Inc. Place)

Pearcot; RMC Place; DOUGLAS; *247 G-12; elev. 900ft./274m.; mail Wenatchee z 98801; ● 1,750

Pearson; RMC Place; KITSAP; *246 F-6; ★ BREM; mail Poulsbo z 98370; ● 130

Pe Ell; Inc. Place; LEWIS; 246 J-5; elev. 412ft./126m.; 🅿; z 98572; Ⓟ 547; Ⓒ 657

PEND OREILLE; 247 B-19; Ⓟ 8,915; Ⓒ 11,732; ◆ 12,903

Pend Orielle Village; RMC Place; PEND OREILLE; *247 A-19; elev. 2,062ft./628m.; mail Metaline Falls z 99153; ● 30

Penn Cove Park; RMC Place; ISLAND; *246 D-6; mail Oak Harbor z 98277; ● 600

Peone; RMC Place; SPOKANE; *247 E-19; ★ SPOK; mail Mead z 99021, Spokane z 99210

Perrinville; RMC Place; SNOHOMISH; *246 E-7; ★ SEAT; mail Edmonds z 98026; pop. incl. with Edmonds (Inc. Place)

Peshastin; RMC Place; CHELAN; 247 F-11; 🅿; z 98847; ● 900

Picnic Point; RMC Place; PIERCE; *246 G-6; ★ SEAT; mail Gig Harbor z 98335; ● 60

Picnic Point-North Lynnwood; CDP-Census Area Only; SNOHOMISH; *246 E-7; ★ SEAT; Ⓒ 22,953; ◆ 26,146

Piemont; RMC Place; CLALLAM; *246 D-4; mail Port Angeles z 98363; rural

PIERCE; 246 H-8; Ⓟ 586,203; Ⓒ 700,820; Ⓡ 700,818; ◆ 784,982

Pillar Rock; RMC Place; WAHKIAKUM; 246 K-4; mail Rosburg z 98643; rural

Pine City; RMC Place; WHITMAN; 247 G-19; mail Rosalia z 99170; ● 50

Pinecliff; RMC Place; YAKIMA; *246 I-10; elev. 2,190ft./668m.; mail Naches z 98937; ● 75

Pinecroft; RMC Place; SPOKANE; ★ SPOK; mail Spokane z 99214

Pine Glen; RMC Place; KITTITAS; *246 G-10; elev. 2,115ft./645m.; mail Easton z 98925; ● 60

Pinehurst; RMC Place; SNOHOMISH; *246 E-7; ★ SEAT; mail Everett z 98203; pop. incl. with Everett (Inc. Place)

Pine Lake; RMC Place; KING; *246 F-8; elev. 125ft./38m.; ★ SEAT; mail Issaquah z 98027, z 98029; pop. incl. with Sammamish (Inc. Place)

Ping; RMC Place; GARFIELD; *247 I-18; elev. 1,394ft./425m.; mail Pomeroy z 99347; rural

Pioneer; RMC Place; CLARK; *246 L-6; elev. 297ft./91m.; ★ POR; mail Ridgefield z 98642

Pioneer Square; RMC Place; KING; ★ SEAT; mail Seattle z 98104; pop. incl. with Seattle (Inc. Place)

Pipe Lake; RMC Place; KING; *246 G-8; elev. 175ft./53m.; ★ SEAT; mail Maple Valley z 98038; pop. incl. with Covington (Inc. Place)

Pitt; RMC Place; KLICKITAT; *246 L-10; mail Lyle z 98635; rural

Plain; RMC Place; CHELAN; 247 E-11; mail Leavenworth z 98826

Plaza; RMC Place; SPOKANE; 247 G-19; mail Rosalia z 99170; ● 20

Pleasant Harbor; RMC Place; JEFFERSON; *246 F-6; elev. 200ft./61m.; mail Brinnon z 98320; ● 60

Pleasant Hill; RMC Place; COWLITZ; *246 K-6; elev. 100ft./30m.; ★ LNGV; mail Kelso z 98626; ● 150

Pleasant Prairie; RMC Place; SPOKANE; *247 E-19; elev. 2,433ft./742m.; ★ SPOK; mail Spokane z 99217; rural

Pleasant Valley; RMC Place; CLARK; *246 M-6; elev. 200ft./61m.; ★ POR; mail Ferndale z 98248, Vancouver z 98686; rural

Plymouth; RMC Place; BENTON; 247 L-14; elev. 289ft./88m.; 🅿; z 99346; ● 200

Pocahontas Bay; RMC Place; SPOKANE; *247 D-19; elev. 1,920ft./585m.; mail Elk z 99009; ● 90

Point Roberts; RMC Place; WHATCOM; 246 A-5; 🅿; z 98281; summer pop. 4,000; ● 800

Point White; RMC Place; KITSAP; *246 F-7; ★ SEAT; mail Bainbridge Island z 98110; pop. incl. with Winslow (Inc. Place)

Pomeroy; Inc. Place; ⊡ GARFIELD; 247 J-19; 🅿 🄷; z 99347; Ⓟ 1,393; Ⓒ 1,517

Pomona; RMC Place; YAKIMA; *247 I-12; ★ YAK; mail Yakima z 98902; rural

Pomona Heights; RMC Place; YAKIMA; *247 I-12; elev. 1,138ft./347m.; ★ YAK; mail Yakima z 98903; ● 60

Ponder; RMC Place; PIERCE; ★ SEAT; mail Lakewood z 98499; pop. incl. with Lakewood (Inc. Place)

Ponderosa Estates; RMC Place; PIERCE; *246 H-8; ★ SEAT; mail Sumner z 98390; ● 600

Pontius Park; RMC Place; SNOHOMISH; *246 E-7; elev. 278ft./85m.; ★ SEAT; mail Bothell z 98021; pop. incl. with Bothell (Inc. Place)

Portage; RMC Place; KING; 248 I-6; ★ SEAT; mail Vashon z 98070; ● 60

Port Angeles; Inc. Place; ⊡ CLALLAM; 246 D-5; elev. 32ft./10m.; 🅿 🄷 ■; z 98362-63; Ⓟ 17,710; Ⓒ 18,397; ◆ 17,860

Port Angeles East; CDP-Census Area Only; CLALLAM; *246 D-5; elev. 175ft./53m.; mail Port Angeles z 98362; Ⓟ 2,672; Ⓒ 3,053

Port Blakely; RMC Place; KITSAP; 248 E-5; ★ SEAT; mail Bainbridge Island z 98110; pop. incl. with Winslow (Inc. Place)

Port Discovery; RMC Place; JEFFERSON; *246 E-6; elev. 100ft./30m.; mail Port Townsend z 98368; rural

Porter; RMC Place; GRAYS HARBOR; 246 H-5; elev. 54ft./16m.; mail Elma z 98541; ● 120

Port Gamble; RMC Place; KITSAP; 246 E-7; 🅿; z 98364; ● 400

Port Gamble Reservation; Indian Reservation; KITSAP; mail Kingston z 98346; Ⓟ 302; Ⓒ 699

Port Hadlock; RMC Place; JEFFERSON; ● 350

Port Hadlock-Irondale; CDP-Census Area Only; JEFFERSON; 246 D-6; mail Port Hadlock z 98339, Port Ludlow z 98365; Ⓟ 2,742; Ⓒ 3,476

Port Ludlow; CDP; JEFFERSON; *246 E-6; 🅿; z 98365; Ⓒ 1,968

Port Madison; RMC Place; KITSAP; *246 F-7; ★ SEAT; mail Bainbridge Island z 98110; pop. incl. with Winslow (Inc. Place)

Port Madison Reservation; Indian Reservation; KITSAP; mail Bremerton z 98310; Ⓟ 3,415; Ⓒ 6,536

Port Orchard; Inc. Place; ⊡ KITSAP; 246 F-6; 🅿; ★ BREM; z 98366-67; Ⓟ 4,984; Ⓒ 7,693

Port Stanley; RMC Place; SAN JUAN; *246 C-6; mail Lopez Island z 98261

Port Townsend; Inc. Place; ⊡ JEFFERSON; 246 D-6; 🅿 🄷; z 98368; Ⓟ 7,001; Ⓒ 8,334

Port Williams; RMC Place; CLALLAM; *246 D-5; mail Sequim z 98382; rural

Possession (Possession Point); RMC Place; ISLAND; *246 E-7; ★ SEAT; mail Clinton z 98236; ● 100

Possession Point; ISLAND; see Possession (RMC Place)

Possession Shores; RMC Place; ISLAND; *246 E-7; elev. 100ft./30m.; ★ SEAT; mail Clinton z 98236; ● 200

Potlatch; RMC Place; MASON; *246 G-5; located on Skokomish Ind. Res.; elev. 18ft./5m.; mail Hoodsport z 98548; ● 70

Poulsbo; Inc. Place; KITSAP; 246 F-6; elev. 15ft./5m.; 🅿; ★ BREM; z 98370; Ⓟ 4,848; Ⓒ 6,813

Poverty Bay; RMC Place; KING; *246 G-7; ★ SEAT; mail Federal Way z 98003, Kent z 98031, Redondo z 98054

Prairie; RMC Place; SKAGIT; *246 B-7; mail Sedro Woolley z 98284; ● 50

Prairie Center; RMC Place; ISLAND; *246 D-6; elev. 93ft./28m.; mail Coupeville z 98239; pop. incl. with Coupeville (Inc. Place)

Prairie Ridge; CDP-Census Area Only; PIERCE; *246 H-8; ★ SEAT; mail Sumner z 98390; Ⓟ 8,278; Ⓒ 11,688

Prescott; Inc. Place; WALLA WALLA; 247 K-17; elev. 1,055ft./322m.; 🅿; z 99348; Ⓟ 267; Ⓒ 314

Preston; RMC Place; KING; 246 F-8; elev. 508ft./155m.; 🅿; ★ SEAT; z 98050; ● 500

Priest Point; CDP-Census Area Only; SNOHOMISH; *246 D-7; ★ SEAT; mail Marysville z 98271; Ⓟ 703; Ⓒ 779

Prindle; RMC Place; SKAMANIA; *246 M-7; mail Washougal z 98671

Proctor; RMC Place; PIERCE; ★ SEAT; mail Tacoma z 98407; pop. incl. with Tacoma (Inc. Place)

Proebstel; RMC Place; CLARK; *246 M-7; ★ POR; mail Vancouver z 98662; ● 90

Prosser; Inc. Place; ⊡ BENTON; 247 K-14; 🅿 🄷; z 99350; Ⓟ 4,476; Ⓒ 4,838

Prune Hill; RMC Place; CLARK; *246 M-7; elev. 525ft./160m.; ★ POR; mail Camas z 98607; pop. incl. with Camas (Inc. Place)

Puget Island; RMC Place; WAHKIAKUM; *246 K-4; elev. 10ft./3m.; mail Cathlamet z 98612; ● 60

Pullman; Inc. Place; WHITMAN; 247 I-20; 🅿 🄷 🄲 23,655; z 98662, z 99163-64; Ⓟ 23,478; Ⓒ 24,675; Ⓡ 24,948; ◆ 23,911

Pullman Junction; RMC Place; WHITMAN; *247 I-20; pop. incl. with Pullman (Inc. Place)

Purdy; RMC Place; PIERCE; 246 G-6; ★ SEAT; mail Gig Harbor z 98332, z 98335; ● 600

Puyallup; Inc. Place; PIERCE; 246 H-7; 🅿 🄷 ■; ★ SEAT; z 98371-75; Ⓟ 23,875; Ⓒ 33,011; ◆ 38,048

Puyallup Reservation; Indian Reservation; PIERCE, KING; Ⓒ 41,335

Q

Queen Anne; RMC Place; KING; *246 F-7; ★ SEAT; mail Seattle z 98109; pop. incl. with Seattle (Inc. Place)

Queensborough; RMC Place; SNOHOMISH; *246 E-7; elev. 427ft./130m.; ★ SEAT; mail Bothell z 98021; pop. incl. with Bothell (Inc. Place)

Queets; RMC Place; JEFFERSON; 246 F-2; mail Forks z 98331; ● 200

Quendall; RMC Place; KING; ★ SEAT; mail Renton z 98055; pop. incl. with Renton (Inc. Place)

Quilcene; CDP; JEFFERSON; 246 E-6; 🅿; z 98376; Ⓒ 591

Quileute Reservation; Indian Reservation; CLALLAM; mail La Push z 98350; Ⓟ 327; Ⓒ 371

Quinault; RMC Place; GRAYS HARBOR; 246 F-3; elev. 221ft./67m.; 🅿; z 98575; ● 250

Quinault Reservation; Indian Reservation; GRAYS HARBOR, JEFFERSON; mail Taholah z 98587; Ⓟ 1,501; Ⓒ 1,370

Quincy; Inc. Place; GRANT; 247 G-13; 🅿 🄷; z 98848 & mail George z 98824; Ⓟ 3,738; Ⓒ 5,044

R

Rainer Valley; RMC Place; KING; ★ SEAT; mail Seattle z 98118; pop. incl. with Seattle (Inc. Place)

Rainier; Inc. Place; THURSTON; 246 I-6; elev. 428ft./130m.; 🅿; ★ OLYM; z 98576; Ⓟ 991; Ⓒ 1,492

Rainier Beach; RMC Place; KING; ★ SEAT; mail Seattle z 98102; pop. incl. with Seattle (Inc. Place)

Rainier Terrace; RMC Place; PIERCE; *246 H-7; elev. 460ft./140m.; ★ SEAT; mail Puyallup z 98373; ● 600

Ralston; RMC Place; ADAMS; 247 H-17; elev. 1,657ft./505m.; mail Ritzville z 99169

Rambler Park; RMC Place; YAKIMA; *247 I-11; elev. 1,181ft./360m.; ★ YAK; mail Yakima z 98908; ● 100

Randle; RMC Place; LEWIS; 246 J-8; 🅿; z 98377; ● 850

Raugust; RMC Place; GRANT; *247 H-15; elev. 1,250ft./381m.; mail Moses Lake z 98837; rural

Ravensdale; CDP; KING; 246 G-8; 🅿; ★ SEAT; z 98051; Ⓒ 816

Raymond; Inc. Place; PACIFIC; 246 I-4; elev. 14ft./4m.; 🅿; z 98577; Ⓟ 2,901; Ⓒ 2,975

Reardan; Inc. Place; LINCOLN; 247 F-18; elev. 2,496ft./761m.; 🅿; z 99029; Ⓟ 482; Ⓒ 608

Redmond; Inc. Place; KING; 246 F-8; 🅿 🄷 🄲 780 ■; ★ SEAT; z 98052-53, z 98073-74; Ⓟ 35,800; Ⓒ 45,256; ◆ 48,906

Redmond Station; RMC Place; KING; ★ SEAT; mail Redmond z 98052; pop. incl. with Redmond (Inc. Place)

Redondo; RMC Place; KING; 🅿; ★ SEAT; z 98054; pop. incl. with Des Moines (Inc. Place)

Rees Corner; RMC Place; SNOHOMISH; *246 E-8; ★ SEAT; mail Snohomish z 98296

Regal; RMC Place; SPOKANE; ★ SPOK; mail Spokane z 99223; pop. incl. with Spokane (Inc. Place)

Reintree; RMC Place; KING; *246 E-8; elev. 500ft./152m.; ★ SEAT; mail Woodinville z 98072; ● 500

Renton; Inc. Place; KING; 246 F-7; 🅿 🄷 ■; ★ SEAT; z 98055-59; Ⓟ 41,688; Ⓒ 50,052; ◆ 61,127

Republic; Inc. Place; ⊡ FERRY; 247 B-16; 🅿 🄷; z 99166; Ⓟ 940; Ⓒ 954

Reservation; RMC Place; PIERCE; ★ SEAT; pop. incl. with Tacoma (Inc. Place)

Retsil; RMC Place; KITSAP; *246 F-6; 🅿; ★ BREM; z 98378

Rhodes; RMC Place; KING; ★ SEAT; pop. incl. with Seattle (Inc. Place)

Rhodesia Beach; RMC Place; PACIFIC; *246 I-3; elev. 20ft./6m.; mail South Bend z 98586; ● 35

Rhododendron Park; RMC Place; PIERCE; *246 H-8; elev. 640ft./195m.; ★ SEAT; mail Sumner z 98390; ● 1,200

Rice; RMC Place; STEVENS; 247 C-17; elev. 1,724ft./525m.; 🅿; z 99167; ● 40

Richland; Inc. Place; BENTON; 247 K-15; 🅿 🄷 ■; ★ RICH-; z 99352-54; Ⓟ 32,315; Ⓒ 38,708; ◆ 44,812

Richmond Beach; RMC Place; KING; *246 E-7; ★ SEAT; mail Seattle z 98160, z 98177; pop. incl. with Shoreline (Inc. Place)

Richmond Highlands; RMC Place; KING; *246 E-7; ★ SEAT; mail Seattle z 98133; pop. incl. with Shoreline (Inc. Place)

Ridgecrest; RMC Place; KING; *246 F-7; elev. 119ft./36m.; ★ SEAT; mail Seattle z 98155; pop. incl. with Shoreline (Inc. Place)

Ridgefield; Inc. Place; CLARK; 246 L-6; 🅿; ★ POR; z 98642; Ⓟ 1,297; Ⓒ 2,147

Rimrock; RMC Place; YAKIMA; *246 I-10; mail Naches z 98937; summer pop. 400; ● 50

Ritzville; Inc. Place; ⊡ ADAMS; 247 H-17; 🅿 🄷; z 99169; Ⓟ 1,725; Ⓒ 1,736

Riverbend; RMC Place; CHELAN; *247 F-11; elev. 924ft./282m.; mail Cashmere z 98815, Dryden z 98821; ● 70

Riverbend; CDP-Census Area Only; KING; *246 G-9; ★ SEAT; Ⓒ 2,230

Rivercrest; RMC Place; SNOHOMISH; *246 E-7; elev. 400ft./122m.; ★ SEAT; mail Everett z 98204; ● 650

River Road; CDP-Census Area Only; CLALLAM; *246 D-5; Ⓒ 450

Riverside; Inc. Place; OKANOGAN; 247 C-14; 🅿; z 98849; Ⓟ 223; Ⓒ 348

Riverside; RMC Place; SPOKANE; ★ SPOK; mail Spokane z 99201; pop. incl. with Spokane (Inc. Place)

Riverton; RMC Place; KING; *246 F-7; elev. 365ft./111m.; mail Seattle z 98188; pop. incl. with Tukwila (Inc. Place)

Riverton-Boulevard Park; CDP-Census Area Only; KING; 248 G-8; ★ SEAT; mail Seattle z 98168, z 98188; Ⓟ 15,337; Ⓒ 11,188

Riverview; FRANKLIN; see West Pasco (CDP-Census Area Only)

Riverview Hills; RMC Place; SPOKANE; *247 E-19; elev. 1,782ft./543m.; ★ SPOK; mail Colbert z 99005; ● 400

Roanoke; RMC Place; KING; *246 F-7; ★ SEAT; mail Mercer Island z 98040; pop. incl. with Mercer Island (Inc. Place)

Robe; RMC Place; SNOHOMISH; 246 D-8; mail Granite Falls z 98252; ● 230

Robinswood; RMC Place; KING; ★ SEAT; mail Bellevue z 98008; pop. incl. with Bellevue (Inc. Place)

Roche Harbor; RMC Place; SAN JUAN; 246 B-5; 🅿; z 98250; summer pop. 1,500; ● 350

Rochester; CDP; THURSTON; 246 I-5; 🅿; z 98579; Ⓟ 1,250; Ⓒ 1,829

Rockford; Inc. Place; SPOKANE; 247 F-20; elev. 2,361ft./720m.; 🅿; z 99030; Ⓟ 481; Ⓒ 413

Rock Island; Inc. Place; DOUGLAS; 247 G-12; 🅿; z 98850; Ⓟ 524; Ⓒ 863

Rockport; CDP; SKAGIT; 246 C-9; 🅿; z 98283; Ⓒ 102

Rocky Butte; RMC Place; DOUGLAS; *247 D-13; elev. 806ft./246m.; mail Brewster z 98812; rural

Rocky Point; RMC Place; COWLITZ; *246 K-6; ★ LNGV; mail Kelso z 98626

Rocky Point; RMC Place; ISLAND; *246 D-7; elev. 91ft./28m.; ★ SEAT; mail Camano Island z 98282; ● 50

Rocky Point; RMC Place; KITSAP; *246 F-6; elev. 81ft./25m.; ★ BREM; mail Bremerton z 98312; ● 1,500

Rocky Woods; RMC Place; PIERCE; *246 H-7; elev. 484ft./148m.; ★ SEAT; mail Spanaway z 98387; ● 500

Rodena Beach; RMC Place; ISLAND; *246 D-6; elev. 100ft./30m.; ★ SEAT; mail Coupeville z 98239; ● 100

Rollingbay; RMC Place; KITSAP; *246 F-7; elev. 178ft./54m.; 🅿; ★ SEAT; z 98061; ● 750

Rolling Hills; RMC Place; ISLAND; *246 D-6; elev. 140ft./43m.; mail Oak Harbor z 98277; ● 220

Ronald; CDP; KITTITAS; 246 G-10; 🅿; z 98940; Ⓒ 265

Roosevelt; CDP; KLICKITAT; 247 M-12; elev. 354ft./108m.; 🅿; z 99356; Ⓒ 79

Roosevelt; RMC Place; SNOHOMISH; *246 E-8; ★ SEAT; mail Snohomish z 98290; ● 60

Roosevelt Beach; RMC Place; GRAYS HARBOR; *246 G-3; elev. 100ft./30m.; mail Pacific Beach z 98571

Rosalia; Inc. Place; WHITMAN; 247 G-19; elev. 2,232ft./680m.; 🅿; z 99170; Ⓟ 552; Ⓒ 648

Rosario; RMC Place; SAN JUAN; *246 B-6; mail Eastsound z 98245; ● 140

Rosario Beach; RMC Place; SKAGIT; *246 C-6; elev. 100ft./30m.; mail Anacortes z 98221; ● 100

Rosburg; RMC Place; WAHKIAKUM; 246 K-4; 🅿; z 98643 & mail Grays River z 98621; ● 90

Rosedale; RMC Place; PIERCE; *246 G-6; ★ SEAT; mail Gig Harbor z 98335; ● 350

Rose Hill; RMC Place; KING; *246 F-8; ★ SEAT; mail Kirkland z 98033; pop. incl. with Kirkland (Inc. Place)

Rosemont Beach; RMC Place; KING; *246 F-8; ★ SEAT; mail Bellevue z 98008; pop. incl. with Bellevue (Inc. Place)

Rose Valley; RMC Place; COWLITZ; *246 K-6; elev. 332ft./101m.; mail Kelso z 98626; ● 1,400

Rosewood; RMC Place; SPOKANE; *247 F-19; ★ SPOK; mail Spokane z 99208

Roslyn; Inc. Place; KITTITAS; 246 G-10; 🅿; z 98941; Ⓟ 869; Ⓒ 1,017

Roy; Inc. Place; PIERCE; 246 H-7; 🅿; ★ SEAT; z 98580; Ⓟ 258; Ⓒ 260

Royal Camp; RMC Place; GRANT; *247 H-14; mail Othello z 99344; ● 100

Royal City; Inc. Place; GRANT; 247 I-14; 🅿; z 99357; Ⓟ 1,104; Ⓒ 1,823

Ruby; RMC Place; PEND OREILLE; *247 C-19; mail Cusick z 99119; rural

Ruff; RMC Place; GRANT; 247 H-15; mail Marlin z 98832

Ruston; Inc. Place; PIERCE; 246 G-7; 🅿; ★ SEAT; z 98407; Ⓟ 693; Ⓒ 738

Ryderwood; RMC Place; COWLITZ; 246 J-5; 🅿; z 98581; ● 400

S

Saint Andrews; RMC Place; DOUGLAS; *247 F-14; elev. 2,223ft./678m.; mail Coulee City z 99115; rural

Saint John; Inc. Place; WHITMAN; 247 H-19; 🅿; z 99171; Ⓟ 499; Ⓒ 548

Saint Urbans; RMC Place; LEWIS; *246 J-6; elev. 463ft./141m.; mail Winlock z 98596; rural

Salishan; RMC Place; PIERCE; *246 G-7; ★ SEAT; mail Tacoma z 98404; pop. incl. with Tacoma (Inc. Place)

Salkum; RMC Place; LEWIS; 246 J-6; elev. 562ft./171m.; 🅿; z 98582; ● 350

Salmon Beach; RMC Place; PIERCE; *246 G-7; elev. 20ft./6m.; ★ SEAT; mail Tacoma z 98424; pop. incl. with Tacoma (Inc. Place)

Salmon Creek; CDP; CLARK; 246 M-6; ★ POR; mail Vancouver z 98686; Ⓟ 11,989; Ⓒ 16,767

Saltwater; RMC Place; KING; *246 G-7; ★ SEAT; mail Seattle z 98188; pop. incl. with Kent (Inc. Place)

Samish Island; RMC Place; SKAGIT; *246 C-7; mail Bow z 98232; ● 700

Samish Lake; RMC Place; WHATCOM; *246 B-7; elev. 300ft./91m.; ★ BELNG; mail Bellingham z 98225-26; ● 800

Sammamish; Inc. Place; KING; 246 F-8; 🅿; ★ SEAT; z 98074-75; Ⓒ 34,104; ◆ 37,184

San de Fuca; RMC Place; ISLAND; 246 D-6; elev. 20ft./6m.; mail Coupeville z 98239; ● 200

Sandy Hook; RMC Place; ISLAND; *246 E-7; elev. 100ft./30m.; ★ SEAT; mail Clinton z 98236; ● 250

Sandy Hook Park; RMC Place; KITSAP; *246 F-7; elev. 28ft./9m.; ★ SEAT; mail Poulsbo z 98370; ● 200

Sandy Point; RMC Place; ISLAND; *246 D-7; elev. 51ft./16m.; ★ SEAT; mail Langley z 98260; ● 150

SAN JUAN; 246 C-5; Ⓟ 10,035; Ⓒ 14,077; ◆ 15,303

Santiago Beach; RMC Place; GRAYS HARBOR; *246 G-2; elev. 141ft./43m.; mail Taholah z 98587; ● 80

Sappho; RMC Place; CLALLAM; *246 D-3; mail Beaver z 98305

Sara; RMC Place; CLARK; *246 M-6; ★ POR; mail Ridgefield z 98642

Saratoga Beach; RMC Place; ISLAND; *246 D-7; elev. 100ft./30m.; ★ SEAT; mail Langley z 98260; ● 50

Saratoga Heights; RMC Place; ISLAND; *246 D-7; elev. 200ft./61m.; ★ SEAT; mail Langley z 98260; ● 50

Saratoga Shores; RMC Place; ISLAND; *246 D-7; elev. 100ft./30m.; ★ SEAT; mail Camano Island z 98282; ● 30

Satsop; CDP; GRAYS HARBOR; 246 H-4; 🅿; z 98583; Ⓒ 619

Satus; CDP; YAKIMA; *247 K-12; mail Toppenish z 98948; Ⓟ 1,343; Ⓒ 746

Sauk River Estates; RMC Place; SKAGIT; *246 C-9; elev. 279ft./85m.; mail Concrete z 98237; ● 50

Sauk-Suiattle Reservation; Indian Reservation; SKAGIT, SNOHOMISH; Ⓒ 45

Sawyer; RMC Place; YAKIMA; *247 J-12; elev. 831ft./253m.; mail Wapato z 98951

Scandia; RMC Place; KITSAP; *246 F-6; ★ BREM; mail Poulsbo z 98370; ● 220

Scatchet Head; RMC Place; ISLAND; *246 E-7; elev. 200ft./61m.; ★ SEAT; mail Clinton z 98236; ● 3,500

Schawana; RMC Place; GRANT; 247 I-13; elev. 549ft./167m.; mail Beverly z 99321; ● 200

Schneiders Prairie; RMC Place; THURSTON; *246 H-5; elev. 53ft./16m.; ★ OLYM; mail Olympia z 98501; ● 320

Schwarder; RMC Place; YAKIMA; *247 J-12; elev. 1,038ft./316m.; ★ YAK; mail Yakima z 98908; pop. incl. with Union Gap (Inc. Place)

Scopa; RMC Place; KING; ★ SEAT; mail Renton z 98055; pop. incl. with Renton (Inc. Place)

Scott Lake; RMC Place; THURSTON; *246 H-6; elev. 200ft./61m.; ★ OLYM; mail Olympia z 98501; ● 300

Sea Acres; RMC Place; SAN JUAN; *246 B-6; elev. 76ft./23m.; mail Olga z 98279; ● 35

Seabeck; RMC Place; KITSAP; 246 F-6; elev. 14ft./4m.; 🅿; ★ BREM; z 98380; summer pop. 1,000; ● 500

Seabold; RMC Place; KITSAP; *246 F-7; elev. 195ft./59m.; ★ SEAT; mail Bainbridge Island z 98110; pop. incl. with Winslow (Inc. Place)

Sea First; RMC Place; KING; ★ SEAT; mail Seattle z 98104; pop. incl. with Seattle (Inc. Place)

Seahurst; RMC Place; KING; *246 F-7; 🅿; ★ SEAT; z 98062; pop. incl. with Burien (Inc. Place)

Seal Rock; RMC Place; JEFFERSON; *246 F-6; elev. 17ft./5m.; mail Brinnon z 98320; ● 50

Seamount Estates; RMC Place; JEFFERSON; *246 F-6; elev. 300ft./91m.; mail Brinnon z 98320; ● 120

SeaTac; Inc. Place; KING; 248 H-8; elev. 125ft./38m.; 🅿; ★ SEAT; z 98148, z 98158, z 98168, z 98188, z 98198; Ⓒ 25,496; ◆ 27,857

Seatons Grove; RMC Place; OKANOGAN; *247 E-15; mail Coulee Dam z 99116; ● 70

Seattle; Inc. Place; ⊡ KING; 246 F-7; 🅿 🄷 🄲 58,952 ■; ★ SEAT; z 98101-19, z 98121-22, z 98124-27, z 98129, z 98131-34, z 98136, z 98138-39, z 98141, z 98144-46, z 98148, z 98154-55, z 98158, z 98160-61, z 98164-66, z 98168, z 98170-71, z 98174-75, z 98177-78, z 98181, z 98184-85, z 98188, z 98190-91, z 98194-95, z 98198-99, z 98662; Ⓟ 516,259; Ⓒ 563,374; Ⓡ 563,376; ◆ 620,567

Seattle Heights; RMC Place; SNOHOMISH; *246 E-7; ★ SEAT; mail Lynnwood z 98036; pop. incl. with Edmonds (Inc. Place)

Seattle Hill-Silver Firs; CDP-Census Area Only; SNOHOMISH; *246 E-7; ★ SEAT; Ⓒ 35,311; ◆ 40,228

Seaview; RMC Place; PACIFIC; 246 K-3; 🅿; z 98644; summer pop. 1,000; ● 650

Sedro-Woolley; Inc. Place; SKAGIT; 246 C-7; 🅿; z 98284; Ⓟ 6,031; Ⓒ 8,658

Sekiu; RMC Place; CLALLAM; 246 D-2; 🅿; z 98381; summer pop. 2,000; ● 500

Selah; Inc. Place; YAKIMA; 247 I-11; 🅿; ★ YAK; z 98942; Ⓟ 5,113; Ⓒ 6,310

Selleck; RMC Place; KING; 246 G-8; elev. 113ft./34m.; mail Ravensdale z 98051; ● 200

Sequim; Inc. Place; CLALLAM; 246 D-5; elev. 183ft./56m.; 🅿; z 98382; Ⓟ 3,616; Ⓒ 4,334

Sequioa; RMC Place; KING; *246 G-7; elev. 129ft./39m.; ★ SEAT; mail Kent z 98031; pop. incl. with Kent (Inc. Place)

Seven Bays; RMC Place; LINCOLN; *247 E-17; 🅿; z 99122; ● 270

Seven Mile; RMC Place; SPOKANE; 248 A-1; ★ SPOK; mail Nine Mile Falls z 99026; ● 170

Shaker Church; CDP-Census Area Only; SNOHOMISH; *246 D-7; ★ SEAT; mail Marysville z 98271; Ⓟ 670; Ⓒ 787

Shana Park; RMC Place; THURSTON; *246 H-6; elev. 180ft./55m.; ★ OLYM; mail Olympia z 98501; ● 250

Shangri-La Shores; RMC Place; ISLAND; *246 D-7; elev. 100ft./30m.; ★ SEAT; mail Coupeville z 98239; ● 60

Shaw Island; RMC Place; SAN JUAN; 246 C-6; 🅿; z 98286; ● 200

Shawnee; RMC Place; WHITMAN; *247 I-19; mail Colfax z 99111; rural

Shelton; Inc. Place; ⊡ MASON; 246 G-5; 🅿 🄷; ★ OLYM; z 98584; Ⓟ 7,241; Ⓒ 8,442

Sheridan Beach; RMC Place; KING; 248 B-8; ★ SEAT; mail Seattle z 98155; pop. incl. with Lake Forest Park (Inc. Place); Ⓟ 6,518

Sheridan Park; RMC Place; KITSAP; *246 F-6; ★ BREM; mail Bremerton z 98310-11; pop. incl. with Bremerton (Inc. Place)

Sherwood Forest; RMC Place; KING; *246 F-8; ★ SEAT; mail Bellevue z 98008; pop. incl. with Bellevue (Inc. Place)

Shine; RMC Place; JEFFERSON; *246 E-6; mail Chimacum z 98325, Port Ludlow z 98365; ● 100

Shoalwater Bay Reservation; Indian Reservation; PACIFIC; mail Tokeland z 98590; Ⓟ 33; Ⓒ 69

Shore Acres; RMC Place; PIERCE; 248 K-4; ★ SEAT; mail Gig Harbor z 98335; ● 250

Shoreline; Inc. Place; KING; 246 F-7; 🅿; ★ SEAT; z 98133, z 98155, z 98177; Ⓟ 46,979; Ⓒ 53,025; Ⓡ 53,296; ◆ 55,701

Shorewood; RMC Place; KING; *246 F-7; ★ SEAT; mail Seattle z 98106, z 98146; pop. incl. with Burien (Inc. Place)

Shorewood Beach; RMC Place; PIERCE; *246 G-6; ★ SEAT; mail Fox Island z 98333

Shrine Beach; RMC Place; CHELAN; *247 E-12; elev. 1,261ft./384m.; mail Chelan z 98816; ● 200

Shuwah (Iverson); RMC Place; CLALLAM; *246 D-2; mail Forks z 98331; ● 50

Sierra Division; RMC Place; ISLAND; *246 D-6; elev. 100ft./30m.; mail Coupeville z 98239; ● 120

Sifton; RMC Place; CLARK; *246 M-7; elev. 220ft./67m.; ★ POR; mail Vancouver z 98682; ● 800

Silcott; RMC Place; ASOTIN; *247 J-20; elev. 724ft./221m.; mail Clarkston z 99403; rural

Silvana; CDP; SNOHOMISH; 246 D-7; 🅿; ★ SEAT; z 98287; Ⓒ 97

Silvana Terraces; RMC Place; SNOHOMISH; *246 D-7; ★ SEAT; mail Stanwood z 98292; rural

Silver Beach; RMC Place; WHATCOM; *246 B-7; ★ BELNG; mail Bellingham z 98225-26; pop. incl. with Bellingham (Inc. Place)

Silver Brook; RMC Place; LEWIS; *246 J-8; elev. 921ft./281m.; mail Randle z 98377; ● 520

Silver Creek; RMC Place; LEWIS; *246 J-6; elev. 679ft./207m.; 🅿; z 98585; ● 100

Silverdale; CDP; KITSAP; 246 F-6; 🅿; ★ BREM; z 98315, z 98383; Ⓟ 7,660; Ⓒ 15,816

Silver Lake; RMC Place; COWLITZ; *246 K-6; elev. 520ft./158m.; 🅿; z 98645; ● 200

Silver Lake; RMC Place; SNOHOMISH; *246 E-7; ★ SEAT; mail Everett z 98204, z 98208; ● 1,550

Silver Lake; RMC Place; SPOKANE; 246 K-6; elev. 2,400ft./732m.; mail Medical Lake z 99022; ● 100

Silverton; RMC Place; SNOHOMISH; *246 D-9; mail Granite Falls z 98252; ● 40

Similk Beach; RMC Place; SKAGIT; 246 C-7; mail Anacortes z 98221; ● 270

Sisco Heights; RMC Place; SNOHOMISH; *246 D-8; elev. 453ft./138m.; ★ SEAT; mail Arlington z 98223; ● 100

SKAGIT; 246 C-8; Ⓟ 79,555; Ⓒ 102,979; ◆ 117,689

Skagit City; RMC Place; SKAGIT; *246 C-7; elev. 22ft./7m.; mail Mount Vernon z 98273; rural

Skagit Country Club; RMC Place; SKAGIT; *246 C-7; elev. 68ft./21m.; mail Burlington z 98233; ● 500

Skamania; RMC Place; SKAMANIA; 246 M-8; elev. 55ft./17m.; mail Stevenson z 98648; ● 180

SKAMANIA; 246 L-8; Ⓟ 8,289; Ⓒ 9,872; ◆ 11,072

Skamokawa; RMC Place; WAHKIAKUM; 246 K-4; elev. 26ft./8m.; 🅿; z 98647; ● 250

Skokomish; CDP-Census Area Only; MASON; *246 G-5; located on Skokomish Ind. Res.; mail Shelton z 98584; Ⓟ 532; Ⓒ 616

Skokomish Reservation; Indian Reservation; MASON; mail Shelton z 98584; Ⓟ 483; Ⓒ 730

Skykomish; Inc. Place; KING; 246 F-9; elev. 931ft./284m.; 🅿; z 98288; Ⓟ 273; Ⓒ 214

Skyway; RMC Place; KING; 248 G-9; ★ SEAT; mail Seattle z 98178; ● 8,500

Sleepy Hollow; RMC Place; WAHKIAKUM; *246 K-4; mail Skamokawa z 98647; rural

Smithville; RMC Place; KLICKITAT; *246 M-10; elev. 400ft./122m.; mail Lyle z 98635; rural

Smokey Point; CDP; SNOHOMISH; *246 D-7; ★ SEAT; mail Arlington z 98223, North Lakewood z 98259; Ⓟ 2,620; Ⓒ 1,556

Smyrna; RMC Place; GRANT; *247 I-14; mail Royal City z 99357

Snee Oosh (Snee-oosh-Beach); RMC Place; SKAGIT; *246 C-7; located on Swinomish Ind. Res.; elev. 30ft./9m.; mail La Conner z 98257; Ⓟ 302

Snee-oosh-Beach; SKAGIT; see Snee Oosh (RMC Place)

Snohomish; Inc. Place; SNOHOMISH; 246 E-8; 🅿; ★ SEAT; z 98290-91, z 98296; Ⓟ 6,499; Ⓒ 8,494

SNOHOMISH; 246 E-9; Ⓟ 465,642; Ⓒ 606,024; ◆ 690,360

Snoqualmie; Inc. Place; KING; 246 F-8; 🅿 🄷; ★ SEAT; z 98065, z 98068; Ⓟ 1,546; Ⓒ 1,631

Snoqualmie Pass; RMC Place; KITTITAS, KING; *246 G-9; 🅿; z 98068; ● 205

Snoqualmie Pass; CDP-Census Area Only; KITTITAS; *246 G-9; 🅿; z 98068; Ⓒ 201

Soap Lake; Inc. Place; GRANT; 247 G-14; 🅿; z 98851; Ⓟ 1,149; Ⓒ 1,733

South Aberdeen; RMC Place; GRAYS HARBOR; *246 H-4; mail Aberdeen z 98520; pop. incl. with Aberdeen (Inc. Place)

South Bay; RMC Place; THURSTON; *246 H-6; ★ OLYM; mail Olympia z 98501; ● 80

South Beach; RMC Place; KITSAP; 248 E-5; elev. 100ft./30m.; ★ SEAT; mail Bainbridge Island z 98110

South Beach; RMC Place; WHATCOM; *246 A-6; elev. 20ft./6m.; mail Point Roberts z 98281; summer pop. 500; ● 60

South Bellingham; RMC Place; WHATCOM; *246 B-7; ★ BELNG; mail Bellingham z 98225; pop. incl. with Bellingham (Inc. Place)

South Bend; Inc. Place; ⊡ PACIFIC; 246 I-3; 🅿 🄷; z 98586; Ⓟ 1,551; Ⓒ 1,807

South Broadway; RMC Place; YAKIMA; *247 J-11; ★ YAK; mail Yakima z 98902-03; pop. incl. with Union Gap (Inc. Place); Ⓟ 2,735

South Cle Elum; Inc. Place; KITTITAS; 246 H-10; 🅿; z 98943; Ⓟ 457; Ⓒ 457

South Colby; RMC Place; KITSAP; 248 F-5; 🅿; ★ BREM; z 98384; ● 300

South Elma; RMC Place; GRAYS HARBOR; *246 H-4; elev. 55ft./17m.; mail Elma z 98541

Southgate; RMC Place; PIERCE; ★ SEAT; mail Lakewood z 98499; pop. incl. with Lakewood (Inc. Place)

South Hill; CDP-Census Area Only; PIERCE; 248 N-8; 🅿; ★ SEAT; z 98373-75; Ⓟ 12,963; Ⓒ 31,623; ◆ 35,417

South Montesano; RMC Place; GRAYS HARBOR; *246 H-4; mail Montesano z 98563; rural

South Park; RMC Place; KING; *246 F-7; ★ SEAT; mail Seattle z 98108; pop. incl. with Seattle (Inc. Place)

South Point; RMC Place; JEFFERSON; 246 E-6; mail Port Ludlow z 98365; ● 130

South Prairie; Inc. Place; PIERCE; 246 H-8; 🅿; ★ SEAT; z 98385; Ⓟ 180; Ⓒ 382

South Seattle; RMC Place; KING; ★ SEAT; mail Seattle z 98102; pop. incl. with Seattle (Inc. Place)

South Snohomish; RMC Place; SNOHOMISH; *246 E-8; ★ SEAT; mail Snohomish z 98296; ● 200

South Tacoma; RMC Place; PIERCE; *246 G-7; ★ SEAT; mail Tacoma z 98409; pop. incl. with Tacoma (Inc. Place)

South Union; RMC Place; THURSTON; *246 H-6; elev. 197ft./60m.; ★ OLYM; mail Lacey z 98503; ● 100

South Wenatchee; CDP; CHELAN; 247 G-12; mail Wenatchee z 98801; Ⓟ 1,207; Ⓒ 1,991

Southworth; RMC Place; KITSAP; 248 G-5; 🅿; ★ BREM; z 98386; ● 350

Entries in **UPPERCASE** are counties.
Entries in **bold** have populations of 2,500 or more.
Names in parentheses are alternate names.

Inc. Place	Incorporated Place
RMC Place	Rand McNally Designated Place
CDP	Census Designated Place
MCD	Minor Civil Division
⊡	County Seat
▲	Minor Civil Division
elev.	Elevation
🅿	Post Office
🄷	Hospital
🄲	College
■	Principal Business Center
★	Ranally Metro Area (RMA) Abbreviation
z	Zip Code(s)
Ⓟ	Previous Census Population
Ⓡ	Revised Census Population
Ⓐ	Annexation Population
●	Rand McNally Population Estimate
Ⓒ	Final Census Population
Ⓢ	Special Census Population
◆	Estimated Population

For additional definitions see Glossary, Volume 1, and Introduction, Volume 2.

Spanaway (Lake Park); CDP; PIERCE; **246** H-7; 🅿; ★ **SEAT**; **z** 98387; Ⓟ 15,001; Ⓒ 21,588; ◆ 24,180
Spangle; Inc. Place; SPOKANE; **247** G-19; 🅿; **z** 99031; Ⓟ 229; Ⓒ 240
Spokane; Inc. Place; ⊡ SPOKANE; **247** F-19; 🅿 🅷 🅲 9,240 ■; ★ **SPOK**; **z** 99201-20, **z** 99223-24, **z** 99228, **z** 99251-52, **z** 99256, **z** 99258, **z** 99260, **z** 99299; Ⓟ 177,196; Ⓒ 195,629; ◆ 217,898
SPOKANE; **247** F-19; Ⓟ 361,364; Ⓒ 417,939; ◆ 474,624
Spokane Reservation; Indian Reservation; STEVENS, LINCOLN; mail Fruitland **z** 99129; also location of Indian Agency; Ⓟ 1,475; Ⓒ 2,004
Spokane Valley; Inc. Place; SPOKANE; **247** F-19; 🅿; **z** 99016, **z** 99027, **z** 99037, **z** 99206, **z** 99211-16, **z** 99223; incorporated March 3, 2003; not reported in 2000 Census; includes Opportunity CDP; ● 81,100; ◆ 89,780
Sprague; Inc. Place; LINCOLN; **247** G-18; elev. 1,899ft./579m.; 🅿; **z** 99017, **z** 99032; Ⓟ 410; Ⓒ 490
Spring Creek; RMC Place; KITTITAS; ***246** G-10; elev. 2,240ft./683m.; mail Ronald **z** 98940; ● 50
Springdale; Inc. Place; STEVENS; **247** D-18; elev. 2,070ft./631m.; 🅿; **z** 99173; Ⓟ 260; Ⓒ 283
Spring Glen; RMC Place; KING; ***246** F-8; ★ **SEAT**; mail Fall City **z** 98024; ● 100
Squaxin Island Reservation; Indian Reservation; MASON; mail Shelton **z** 98584; Ⓒ 0
Stabler; RMC Place; SKAMANIA; ***246** L-8; elev. 1,200ft./366m.; mail Carson **z** 98610; ● 100
Stanwood; Inc. Place; SNOHOMISH; **246** D-7; 🅿; ★ **SEAT**; **z** 98282, **z** 98292; Ⓟ 1,961; Ⓒ 3,923
Starbuck; Inc. Place; COLUMBIA; **247** J-17; elev. 645ft./197m.; 🅿; **z** 99359; Ⓟ 170; Ⓒ 130
Star Lake; RMC Place; KING; ***246** G-7; ★ **SEAT**; mail Auburn **z** 98001, Kent **z** 98031; pop. incl. with Kent (Inc. Place)
Startup; CDP; SNOHOMISH; **246** E-9; 🅿; **z** 98293; Ⓒ 817
Stehekin; RMC Place; CHELAN; **247** D-11; 🅿; **z** 98852; ● 80
Steilacoom; Inc. Place; PIERCE; **246** H-6; elev. 51ft./16m.; 🅿; ★ **SEAT**; **z** 98388; Ⓟ 5,728; Ⓒ 6,049
Stella; RMC Place; COWLITZ; ***246** K-5; mail Longview **z** 98632; rural
Steptoe; RMC Place; WHITMAN; **247** H-19; elev. 2,311ft./704m.; 🅿; **z** 99174; ● 200
Sterling; RMC Place; SKAGIT; ***246** C-7; mail Sedro Woolley **z** 98284; ● 70
STEVENS; **247** D-18; Ⓟ 30,948; Ⓒ 40,066; ◆ 42,724
Stevenson; Inc. Place; ⊡ SKAMANIA; **246** M-8; 🅿; **z** 98648; Ⓟ 1,147; Ⓒ 1,200
Stiebels Corner; RMC Place; KITSAP; ***246** E-7; elev. 168ft./51m.; mail Kingston **z** 98346; rural
Stillaguamish Reservation; Indian Reservation; SNOHOMISH; Ⓒ 102
Stillwater; RMC Place; KING; ***246** F-8; ★ **SEAT**; mail Carnation **z** 98014; rural
Stimson Crossing; CDP; SNOHOMISH; ***246** D-7; ★ **SEAT**; mail Marysville **z** 98271; Ⓟ 591; Ⓒ 773
Strandell; RMC Place; WHATCOM; ***246** A-7; ★ **BELNG**; mail Everson **z** 98247; pop. incl. with Everson (Inc. Place)
Stratford; RMC Place; GRANT; **247** G-14; 🅿; **z** 98853; ● 160
Streeters; RMC Place; COWLITZ; ***246** K-6; elev. 500ft./152m.; mail Castle Rock **z** 98611; ● 600
Stringtown; RMC Place; PACIFIC; ***246** K-3; mail Ilwaco **z** 98624; ● 40
Sudden Valley; CDP; WHATCOM; ***246** B-7; ★ **BELNG**; mail Bellingham **z** 98226; Ⓟ 2,615; Ⓒ 4,165
Sultan; Inc. Place; SNOHOMISH; **246** E-8; elev. 114ft./35m.; 🅿; ★ **SEAT**; **z** 98294; Ⓟ 2,236; Ⓒ 3,344
Sumach; RMC Place; YAKIMA; ***247** J-12; elev. 1,040ft./317m.; ★ **YAK**; mail Yakima **z** 98901, **z** 98903; pop. incl. with Yakima (Inc. Place)
Sumas; Inc. Place; WHATCOM; **246** A-7; 🅿; **z** 98295; Ⓟ 744; Ⓒ 960
Summerwood; RMC Place; SPOKANE; ***247** E-19; elev. 1,800ft./549m.; ★ **SPOK**; mail Colbert **z** 99005; ● 100
Summit; CDP; PIERCE; **248** N-7; ★ **SEAT**; mail Puyallup **z** 98371, **z** 98373, Tacoma **z** 98446; Ⓟ 6,312; Ⓒ 8,041
Summit Lake; RMC Place; THURSTON; ***246** H-5; elev. 150ft./46m.; ★ **OLYM**; mail Olympia **z** 98502; summer pop. 800; ● 250
Summit Park; RMC Place; SKAGIT; ***246** C-7; mail Anacortes **z** 98221; ● 150
Summitview; CDP-Census Area Only; YAKIMA; ***247** J-11; ★ **YAK**; Ⓒ 900
Sumner; Inc. Place; PIERCE; **246** G-7; 🅿; ★ **SEAT**; **z** 98352, **z** 98390-91; Ⓟ 6,459; Ⓒ 8,504
Suncrest; RMC Place; STEVENS; ***247** E-19; elev. 1,800ft./549m.; mail Nine Mile Falls **z** 99026; ● 1,500
Sundale; RMC Place; KLICKITAT; ***247** M-12; elev. 334ft./102m.; mail Roosevelt **z** 99356
Sundins Beach; RMC Place; ISLAND; ***246** D-7; ★ **SEAT**; mail Stanwood **z** 98292; summer pop. 300; ● 100
Sun Island; RMC Place; KITTITAS; ***246** G-10; elev. 2,115ft./645m.; mail Easton **z** 98925; ● 100
Sunland Estates; RMC Place; GRANT; ***247** H-13; elev. 615ft./187m.; mail Quincy **z** 98848; ● 50
Sunlight Beach; RMC Place; ISLAND; ***246** E-7; ★ **SEAT**; mail Clinton **z** 98236; ● 180
Sunlight Shores; RMC Place; ISLAND; ***246** E-7; elev. 8ft./2m.; ★ **SEAT**; mail Clinton **z** 98236; ● 200
Sunny Bay; RMC Place; PIERCE; ***246** G-6; ★ **SEAT**; mail Gig Harbor **z** 98335; ● 50
Sunnydale; RMC Place; KING; ***246** G-7; ★ **SEAT**; mail Seattle **z** 98155; pop. incl. with Burien (Inc. Place)
Sunnyside; RMC Place; SNOHOMISH; ***246** E-8; elev. 100ft./30m.; ★ **SEAT**; mail Everett **z** 98205, Marysville **z** 98270; ● 2,150
Sunnyside; Inc. Place; YAKIMA; **247** K-13; 🅿 🅷; **z** 98944; Ⓟ 11,238; Ⓒ 13,905
Sunnyside Beach; RMC Place; PIERCE; ***246** H-6; elev. 220ft./67m.; ★ **SEAT**; mail Steilacoom **z** 98388
Sunnyslope; CDP; CHELAN; ***247** G-12; elev. 901ft./275m.; mail Wenatchee **z** 98801; Ⓟ 1,907; Ⓒ 2,521
Sunnyslope; RMC Place; KITSAP; ***246** F-6; ★ **BREM**; mail Port Orchard **z** 98366; ● 500
Sunrise; RMC Place; PIERCE; ***246** H-9; ★ **SEAT**; mail Gig Harbor **z** 98335; ● 50
Sunrise Point; RMC Place; ISLAND; ***246** D-7; ★ **SEAT**; mail Camano Island **z** 98282; ● 100
Sunset; RMC Place; WHITMAN; ***247** H-19; mail Saint John **z** 99171; ● 40
Sunset Bay; RMC Place; STEVENS; ***247** E-18; elev. 1,554ft./474m.; mail Nine Mile Falls **z** 99026; summer pop. 400; ● 50
Sunset Beach; RMC Place; GRAYS HARBOR; **248** M-4; mail Moclips **z** 98562; ● 100
Sunset Beach; RMC Place; ISLAND; ***246** D-7; ★ **SEAT**; mail Camano Island **z** 98282; ● 140
Sunset Beach; RMC Place; MASON; ***246** G-6; mail Belfair **z** 98528; summer pop. 200; ● 70
Sunset Beach; RMC Place; PIERCE; ***246** G-7; elev. 40ft./12m.; ★ **SEAT**; mail Tacoma **z** 98466
Sunset Hill; RMC Place; KING; ***246** F-7; ★ **SEAT**; pop. incl. with Seattle (Inc. Place)
Sunset Hill; RMC Place; SPOKANE; 🅿; ★ **SPOK**; **z** 99219 & mail Spokane **z** 99224
Sunset West; RMC Place; LEWIS; ***246** I-5; elev. 400ft./122m.; mail Chehalis **z** 98532; ● 100
Sunset West; RMC Place; YAKIMA; ***247** J-11; elev. 1,160ft./354m.; ★ **YAK**; mail Yakima **z** 98903; ● 260
Sunwood Lakes; RMC Place; THURSTON; ***246** H-6; elev. 270ft./82m.; ★ **OLYM**; mail Olympia **z** 98501; ● 260
Suquamish; CDP; KITSAP; ***246** F-7; elev. 202ft./62m.; 🅿; ★ **SEAT**; **z** 98392; Ⓟ 3,105; Ⓒ 3,510
Swan Trail; RMC Place; SNOHOMISH; ***246** E-8; elev. 152ft./46m.; ★ **SEAT**; mail Everett **z** 98205; ● 450
Swede Hill; RMC Place; PIERCE; ***246** G-6; elev. 200ft./61m.; ★ **SEAT**; mail Gig Harbor **z** 98332; rural
Swinomish Reservation; Indian Reservation; SKAGIT; mail La Conner **z** 98257; Ⓟ 1,390; Ⓒ 2,664
Swofford; RMC Place; LEWIS; ***246** J-7; mail Mossyrock **z** 98564; rural
Sylvan; RMC Place; PIERCE; ★ **SEAT**; mail Fox Island **z** 98333
Synarep; RMC Place; OKANOGAN; ***247** C-14; mail Riverside **z** 98849; rural

T

Tacoma; Inc. Place; ⊡ PIERCE; **246** G-7; 🅿 🅷 🅲 6,915 ■; ★ **SEAT**; **z** 98401-09, **z** 98411-13, **z** 98415-19, **z** 98421-22, **z** 98424, **z** 98430-31, **z** 98433, **z** 98438-39, **z** 98442-48, **z** 98464-67, **z** 98471, **z** 98481, **z** 98490, **z** 98492-93, **z** 98496-99; Ⓟ 176,664; Ⓒ 193,556; ◆ 217,643
Tacoma Junction; RMC Place; PIERCE; ***246** G-7; ★ **SEAT**; mail Tacoma **z** 98424; pop. incl. with Fife (Inc. Place)
Tacoma Point; RMC Place; PIERCE; ***246** G-7; elev. 549ft./167m.; ★ **SEAT**; mail Sumner **z** 98390; ● 500
Tahlequah; RMC Place; KING; **248** J-5; ★ **SEAT**; mail Vashon **z** 98070; ● 100
Taholah; CDP; GRAYS HARBOR; **246** G-2; located on Quinault Ind. Res.; elev. 17ft./5m.; 🅿; **z** 98587; Ⓟ 788; Ⓒ 824
Tahuya; RMC Place; MASON; **246** G-5; 🅿; **z** 98588; ● 450
Tampico; RMC Place; YAKIMA; **247** J-11; elev. 2,118ft./646m.; mail Yakima **z** 98902-03; ● 80
Tanglewilde; RMC Place; THURSTON; ***246** H-6; elev. 200ft./61m.; ★ **OLYM**; mail Lacey **z** 98503; ● 3,280
Tanglewilde East; RMC Place; THURSTON; ***246** H-6; elev. 220ft./67m.; ★ **OLYM**; mail Olympia **z** 98516; ● 300
Tanglewilde-Thompson Place; CDP-Census Area Only; THURSTON; ***246** H-6; elev. 200ft./61m.; ★ **OLYM**; mail Olympia **z** 98506; Ⓟ 6,061; Ⓒ 5,670
Tanner; CDP; KING; ***246** F-9; ★ **SEAT**; mail North Bend **z** 98045; Ⓒ 2,966
Teanaway; RMC Place; KITTITAS; ***247** H-11; mail Cle Elum **z** 98922
Tekoa; Inc. Place; WHITMAN; **247** G-20; elev. 2,494ft./760m.; 🅿; **z** 99033; Ⓟ 750; Ⓒ 826
Telma; RMC Place; CHELAN; **247** E-11; mail Leavenworth **z** 98826; summer pop. 350; ● 50
Tenino; Inc. Place; THURSTON; **246** I-6; 🅿; **z** 98589; Ⓟ 1,292; Ⓒ 1,447
Terminal Finance; RMC Place; KING; ★ **SEAT**; mail Seattle **z** 98134; pop. incl. with Seattle (Inc. Place)
Teronda West; RMC Place; ISLAND; ***246** D-7; elev. 100ft./30m.; ★ **SEAT**; mail Coupeville **z** 98239; ● 50
Terrace Heights; CDP; YAKIMA; ***247** J-12; ★ **YAK**; mail Yakima **z** 98901; Ⓟ 4,223; Ⓒ 6,447
Terrill Beach; RMC Place; SAN JUAN; ***246** B-6; elev. 35ft./11m.; mail Eastsound **z** 98245; ● 30
Terrys Corner; RMC Place; ISLAND; ***246** D-7; ★ **SEAT**; mail Camano Island **z** 98282; rural
Thomas; RMC Place; KING; **248** J-9; ★ **SEAT**; mail Kent **z** 98032; pop. incl. with Auburn (Inc. Place)
Thompson Place; RMC Place; THURSTON; ***246** H-6; ★ **OLYM**; mail Olympia **z** 98501, **z** 98516; ● 2,500
Thornton; RMC Place; WHITMAN; **247** H-19; elev. 2,293ft./699m.; 🅿; **z** 99176; ● 120
Thorp; CDP; KITTITAS; **247** H-11; elev. 1,635ft./498m.; 🅿; **z** 98946; Ⓒ 273
Thrashers Corner; RMC Place; SNOHOMISH; ***246** E-7; ★ **SEAT**; mail Bothell **z** 98021; pop. incl. with Bothell (Inc. Place)
Three Lakes; CDP; SNOHOMISH; ***246** E-8; ★ **SEAT**; mail Snohomish **z** 98290; Ⓒ 2,492
Thrift; RMC Place; PIERCE; ***246** H-7; elev. 747ft./228m.; ★ **SEAT**; mail Graham **z** 98338; ● 35
THURSTON; **246** I-7; Ⓟ 161,238; Ⓒ 207,355; ◆ 246,111
Tieton; Inc. Place; YAKIMA; **247** I-11; 🅿; ★ **YAK**; **z** 98947; Ⓟ 693; Ⓒ 1,154
Tiger; RMC Place; PEND OREILLE; ***247** B-19; mail Cusick **z** 99119; rural
Tillicum; RMC Place; PIERCE; ***246** H-7; 🅿; ★ **SEAT**; **z** 98492; pop. incl. with Lakewood (Inc. Place)
Tillicum Beach; RMC Place; ISLAND; ***246** D-7; ★ **SEAT**; mail Camano Island **z** 98282; ● 90
Tillicum Siding; RMC Place; PIERCE; ***246** H-7; elev. 260ft./79m.; ★ **SEAT**; mail Lakewood **z** 98492; pop. incl. with Lakewood (Inc. Place)
Timber Lakes; RMC Place; MASON; ***246** G-6; elev. 200ft./61m.; mail Shelton **z** 98584; ● 600
Timberlane; RMC Place; KING; ***246** G-8; elev. 125ft./38m.; ★ **SEAT**; mail Kent **z** 98042; pop. incl. with Covington (Inc. Place)
Titlow; RMC Place; PIERCE; ***246** G-7; ★ **SEAT**; pop. incl. with Tacoma (Inc. Place)
Tokeland; CDP; PACIFIC; **246** I-3; 🅿; **z** 98590; Ⓒ 194
Tokul; RMC Place; KING; ***246** F-8; mail Snoqualmie **z** 98065; rural
Toledo; Inc. Place; LEWIS; **246** J-6; 🅿; **z** 98591 & mail Winlock **z** 98596; Ⓟ 586; Ⓒ 653
Tolt; KING; see Carnation (Inc. Place)
Tonasket; Inc. Place; OKANOGAN; **247** B-14; 🅿 🅷; **z** 98855; Ⓟ 847; Ⓒ 994
Toppenish; Inc. Place; YAKIMA; **247** J-12; located on Yakama Ind. Res.; 🅿 🅷 🅲 1,336; **z** 98948; location of Indian Agency; Ⓟ 7,419; Ⓒ 8,946
Toroda; RMC Place; FERRY; ***247** A-16; mail Curlew **z** 99118; rural
Touchet; CDP; WALLA WALLA; **247** L-16; elev. 443ft./135m.; 🅿; **z** 99360; Ⓒ 396
Toutle; RMC Place; COWLITZ; **246** K-6; 🅿; **z** 98649 & mail Silverlake **z** 98645; ● 350
Town and Country (Linwood); CDP-Census Area Only; SPOKANE; ***247** E-19; ★ **SPOK**; mail Spokane **z** 99210; Ⓟ 4,921; Ⓒ 4,452
Tracyton; CDP; KITSAP; ***246** F-6; 🅿; ★ **BREM**; **z** 98393; Ⓟ 2,621; Ⓒ 3,267
Trafton; RMC Place; SNOHOMISH; ***246** D-8; elev. 195ft./59m.; ★ **SEAT**; mail Arlington **z** 98223; ● 100
Treasure Island; RMC Place; MASON; ***246** G-6; elev. 33ft./10m.; ★ **BREM**; mail Allyn **z** 98524; ● 230
Trentwood; CDP; SPOKANE; **248** B-5; ★ **SPOK**; mail Spokane **z** 99215; Ⓟ 4,060; Ⓒ 4,388
Tri-Cities; RMC Place; FRANKLIN; 🅿; ★ **RICH-**; **z** 99302; pop. incl. with Pasco (Inc. Place)
Trinidad; RMC Place; GRANT; ***247** G-13; mail Quincy **z** 98848; rural
Triton; RMC Place; MASON, JEFFERSON; ***246** F-6; elev. 60ft./18m.; mail Brinnon **z** 98320, Lilliwaup **z** 98555; ● 50
Trout Lake; CDP; KLICKITAT; **246** L-9; 🅿; **z** 98650; Ⓒ 494
Tucannon; RMC Place; COLUMBIA; ***247** J-18; mail Starbuck **z** 99359; rural
Tukwila; Inc. Place; KING; **248** G-9; elev. 134ft./41m.; 🅿 ■; ★ **SEAT**; **z** 98108, **z** 98138, **z** 98168, **z** 98178, **z** 98188; Ⓟ 11,874; Ⓒ 17,181; ◆ 18,256
Tulalip; RMC Place; SNOHOMISH; **246** D-7; 🅿; ★ **SEAT**; **z** 98271; ● 350
Tulalip Bay; CDP-Census Area Only; SNOHOMISH; ***246** D-7; ★ **SEAT**; mail Marysville **z** 98270-71; Ⓟ 1,395; Ⓒ 1,561
Tulalip Reservation; Indian Reservation; SNOHOMISH; ★ **SEAT**; mail Marysville **z** 98271; Ⓟ 5,046; Ⓒ 9,246
Tumtum; RMC Place; STEVENS; **247** E-18; 🅿; **z** 99034; ● 400
Tumwater; Inc. Place; THURSTON; **246** H-6; 🅿; ★ **OLYM**; **z** 98501, **z** 98511-12; Ⓟ 9,976; Ⓒ 12,698
Turner; RMC Place; COLUMBIA; ***247** J-18; elev. 2,175ft./663m.; mail Dayton **z** 99328
Turner Corner; RMC Place; SNOHOMISH; ***246** E-8; ★ **SEAT**; mail Woodinville **z** 98072; ● 30
Twisp; Inc. Place; OKANOGAN; **247** C-12; elev. 1,614ft./492m.; 🅿; **z** 98856; Ⓟ 872; Ⓒ 938
Tyee; CLALLAM; see Beaver (RMC Place)
Tyler; RMC Place; SPOKANE; **247** G-18; mail Cheney **z** 99004; ● 50

U

Umptanum; KITTITAS; see Umtanum (RMC Place)
Umtanum (Umptanum); RMC Place; KITTITAS; ***247** I-12; mail Ellensburg **z** 98926; rural
Underwood; RMC Place; SKAMANIA; **246** M-9; 🅿; **z** 98651; ● 500
Union; RMC Place; MASON; **246** G-5; 🅿; **z** 98592; summer pop. 1,500; ● 700
Union Gap; Inc. Place; YAKIMA; **247** J-12; 🅿; ★ **YAK**; **z** 98901, **z** 98903; Ⓟ 3,120; Ⓒ 5,621
Union Hill-Novelty Hill; CDP-Census Area Only; KING; ***246** F-8; ★ **SEAT**; Ⓒ 11,265
Union Mill; RMC Place; THURSTON; ***246** H-6; ★ **OLYM**; mail Olympia **z** 98501; ● 1,200
Uniontown; Inc. Place; WHITMAN; **247** J-20; elev. 2,572ft./784m.; 🅿; **z** 99179; Ⓟ 277; Ⓒ 345
University; RMC Place; KING; ***246** F-7; ★ **SEAT**; mail Seattle **z** 98105, **z** 98145; pop. incl. with Seattle (Inc. Place)
University Place; Inc. Place; PIERCE; **248** L-5; 🅿; ★ **SEAT**; **z** 98464, **z** 98466-67 & mail Tacoma **z** 98465; Ⓟ 27,701; Ⓒ 29,933; ◆ 34,652
University Village; RMC Place; KING; ★ **SEAT**; mail Seattle **z** 98105; pop. incl. with Seattle (Inc. Place)
Upper Columbia Academy; SPOKANE; see Academy (RMC Place)
Upper Preston; RMC Place; KING; ***246** F-8; ★ **SEAT**; mail Issaquah **z** 98027; ● 300
Upper Skagit Reservation; Indian Reservation; SKAGIT; Ⓒ 238
Useless Bay Country Club; RMC Place; ISLAND; ***246** E-7; elev. 72ft./22m.; ★ **SEAT**; mail Langley **z** 98260; ● 100
Usk; RMC Place; PEND OREILLE; **247** C-19; elev. 2,052ft./625m.; 🅿; **z** 99180; ● 200
Utsalady; RMC Place; ISLAND; **246** D-7; ★ **SEAT**; mail Stanwood **z** 98292; ● 230

V

Vader; Inc. Place; LEWIS; **246** J-6; 🅿; **z** 98593; Ⓟ 414; Ⓒ 590
Valley; RMC Place; STEVENS; **247** D-18; 🅿; **z** 99181; ● 300
Valleyford; RMC Place; SPOKANE; **247** F-19; 🅿; **z** 99023, **z** 99036; ● 200
Valley View; RMC Place; CLALLAM; ***246** E-2; elev. 240ft./73m.; mail Forks **z** 98331; ● 60
Van Asselt; RMC Place; KING; ★ **SEAT**; mail Seattle **z** 98108; pop. incl. with Seattle (Inc. Place)
Van Buren; RMC Place; WHATCOM; ***246** A-7; elev. 64ft./20m.; mail Everson **z** 98247; rural
Vancouver; Inc. Place; ⊡ CLARK; **223** J-19; 🅿 🅷 ■; ★ **POR**; **z** 98660-66, **z** 98668, **z** 98682-87; Ⓟ 46,380; Ⓒ 143,560; ◆ 187,888
Van Horn; RMC Place; SKAGIT; ***246** C-9; mail Concrete **z** 98237; ● 50
Vantage; CDP; KITTITAS; **247** H-13; 🅿; **z** 98950; Ⓒ 70
Van Zandt; RMC Place; WHATCOM; **246** B-8; mail Deming **z** 98244; ● 30
Vashon; CDP; KING; **246** G-7; 🅿; ★ **SEAT**; **z** 98013, **z** 98070; Ⓒ 10,123
Vashon Center; RMC Place; KING; **248** H-6; ★ **SEAT**; mail Vashon **z** 98070; ● 80
Vashon Heights; RMC Place; KING; **248** G-6; ★ **SEAT**; mail Vashon **z** 98070; ● 700
Vaughn; RMC Place; PIERCE; **246** G-6; 🅿; ★ **SEAT**; **z** 98394; ● 750
Veazey; KING; see Veazie (RMC Place)
Veazie (Veazey); RMC Place; KING; ***246** G-8; ★ **SEAT**; mail Enumclaw **z** 98022; rural
Vega; RMC Place; PIERCE; ***246** H-6; ★ **SEAT**; mail Anderson Island **z** 98303; rural
Venersborg; CDP; CLARK; ***246** L-7; elev. 504ft./154m.; mail Battle Ground **z** 98604; Ⓒ 3,274
Venice; RMC Place; KITSAP; ***246** F-7; ★ **SEAT**; mail Bainbridge Island **z** 98110; pop. incl. with Winslow (Inc. Place)
Vera; SPOKANE; see Veradale (CDP)
Veradale (Vera); CDP; SPOKANE; **248** C-5; 🅿; ★ **SPOK**; **z** 99037; Ⓟ 7,836; Ⓒ 9,387
Verlot; CDP; SNOHOMISH; **246** D-8; mail Granite Falls **z** 98252; Ⓒ 170
Vesta; RMC Place; GRAYS HARBOR; ***246** I-4; mail Cosmopolis **z** 98537; rural
View; RMC Place; CLARK; ***246** L-6; elev. 819ft./250m.; ★ **POR**; mail La Center **z** 98629; rural
View Park; RMC Place; KITSAP; ***246** F-7; ★ **BREM**; mail Port Orchard **z** 98366
View Ridge; RMC Place; KING; ***246** F-7; ★ **SEAT**; mail Seattle **z** 98115; pop. incl. with Seattle (Inc. Place)
Villa Beach; RMC Place; PIERCE; ***246** H-6; ★ **SEAT**; mail Anderson Island **z** 98303
Vinland; RMC Place; KITSAP; ***246** E-6; elev. 100ft./30m.; ★ **BREM**; mail Poulsbo **z** 98370; ● 70
Virginia; RMC Place; KITSAP; ***246** F-6; ★ **BREM**; mail Poulsbo **z** 98370; ● 130
Vision Acres; RMC Place; COWLITZ; ***246** K-6; ★ **LNGV**; mail Kelso **z** 98626; ● 60

W

Wabash; RMC Place; KING; ***246** G-8; elev. 574ft./175m.; ★ **SEAT**; mail Auburn **z** 98092, Enumclaw **z** 98022; rural
Wahkiacus (Wahkiakus); RMC Place; KLICKITAT; **246** L-10; 🅿; **z** 98670; ● 60
WAHKIAKUM; **246** J-5; Ⓟ 3,327; Ⓒ 3,824; ◆ 4,228
Wahkiakus; KLICKITAT; see Wahkiacus (RMC Place)
Waitsburg; Inc. Place; WALLA WALLA; **247** K-17; 🅿; **z** 99361; Ⓟ 990; Ⓒ 1,212
Waitts Lake; RMC Place; STEVENS; ***247** D-18; elev. 1,963ft./598m.; mail Valley **z** 99181; summer pop. 500; ● 250
Wakefield; RMC Place; OKANOGAN; ***247** D-13; mail Brewster **z** 98812; rural
Waldron; RMC Place; SAN JUAN; **246** B-6; 🅿; **z** 98297; summer pop. 300; ● 100
Walla Walla; Inc. Place; ⊡ WALLA WALLA; **247** K-17; 🅿 🅷 🅲 1,450 ■; ★ **WALL**; **z** 99362; Ⓟ 26,478; Ⓒ 29,686; ◆ 30,764
WALLA WALLA; **247** J-17; Ⓟ 48,439; Ⓒ 55,180; ◆ 57,440
Walla Walla East; CDP-Census Area Only; WALLA WALLA; ***247** K-17; ★ **WALL**; mail Walla Walla **z** 99362; Ⓟ 2,959; Ⓒ 2,479
Waller; CDP-Census Area Only; PIERCE; ***246** G-7; ★ **SEAT**; mail Puyallup **z** 98371, Tacoma **z** 98404, **z** 98443; Ⓟ 6,415; Ⓒ 9,200
Wallingford; RMC Place; KING; ***246** F-7; ★ **SEAT**; mail Seattle **z** 98103; pop. incl. with Seattle (Inc. Place)
Wallula; CDP; WALLA WALLA; **247** K-16; 🅿; **z** 99363; Ⓒ 197
Wallula Junction; RMC Place; WALLA WALLA; ***247** K-15; mail Wallula **z** 99363
Walnut Grove; CDP; CLARK; ***246** M-6; ★ **POR**; mail Vancouver **z** 98662; Ⓟ 3,906; Ⓒ 7,164
Wanapum Village; RMC Place; GRANT; ***247** I-13; elev. 535ft./163m.; mail Beverly **z** 99321; ● 80
Wapato; Inc. Place; YAKIMA; **247** J-12; 🅿; **z** 98951; Ⓟ 3,795; Ⓒ 4,582
Warden; Inc. Place; GRANT; **247** H-15; 🅿; **z** 98857; Ⓟ 1,639; Ⓒ 2,544
Warm Beach; CDP; SNOHOMISH; **246** D-7; ★ **SEAT**; mail Stanwood **z** 98292; Ⓒ 2,040
Warren; RMC Place; PIERCE; ***246** G-6; ★ **SEAT**; mail Gig Harbor **z** 98335; ● 200
Warwick; RMC Place; KLICKITAT; ***246** M-10; mail Centerville **z** 98613; rural
Washougal; Inc. Place; CLARK; **246** M-7; 🅿; ★ **POR**; **z** 98671; Ⓟ 4,764; Ⓒ 8,595
Washtucna; Inc. Place; ADAMS; **247** I-17; elev. 1,024ft./312m.; 🅿; **z** 99371; Ⓟ 231; Ⓒ 260
Waterman; RMC Place; KITSAP; **248** E-4; ★ **BREM**; mail Port Orchard **z** 98366
Waterville; Inc. Place; ⊡ DOUGLAS; **247** F-13; elev. 2,622ft./799m.; 🅿; **z** 98858; Ⓟ 995; Ⓒ 1,163
Wauconda; RMC Place; OKANOGAN; **247** B-15; 🅿; **z** 98859; ● 35
Waukon; RMC Place; LINCOLN; ***247** F-18; mail Edwall **z** 99008
Wauna; RMC Place; PIERCE; ***246** G-6; elev. 15ft./5m.; 🅿; ★ **SEAT**; **z** 98395; ● 350
Waunch Prairie; RMC Place; LEWIS; mail Centralia **z** 98531; pop. incl. with Centralia (Inc. Place)
Wautauga Beach; RMC Place; KITSAP; ***246** F-7; ★ **SEAT**; mail Port Orchard **z** 98366; ● 150
Waverly; Inc. Place; SPOKANE; **247** G-19; 🅿; **z** 99039; Ⓟ 37; Ⓒ 121
Wawawai; RMC Place; WHITMAN; ***247** I-19; mail Colton **z** 99113; rural
Weallup Lake; CDP-Census Area Only; SNOHOMISH; ***246** D-7; ★ **SEAT**; mail Marysville **z** 98270; Ⓟ 681; Ⓒ 882
Wedgwood; RMC Place; KING; ★ **SEAT**; mail Seattle **z** 98115; pop. incl. with Seattle (Inc. Place)
Weikel; RMC Place; YAKIMA; ***247** J-11; ★ **YAK**; mail Yakima **z** 98902; rural
Welcome; RMC Place; WHATCOM; ***246** B-8; elev. 376ft./115m.; mail Deming **z** 98244; ● 30
Wellpinit; RMC Place; STEVENS; **247** E-18; located on Spokane Ind. Res.; 🅿; **z** 99040; location of Indian Agency; ● 500
Wenatchee; Inc. Place; ⊡ CHELAN; **247** G-12; 🅿 🅷 ■; **z** 98801-02, **z** 98807; Ⓟ 21,756; Ⓒ 27,856; ◆ 30,597
Wenatchee Heights; RMC Place; CHELAN; ***247** G-12; mail East Wenatchee **z** 98802, Wenatchee **z** 98801; ● 100
West Beach; RMC Place; SAN JUAN; ***246** B-6; elev. 48ft./15m.; mail Eastsound **z** 98245; summer pop. 100; ● 40
West Blakely; RMC Place; KITSAP; ***246** F-7; ★ **SEAT**; mail Bainbridge Island **z** 98110; pop. incl. with Winslow (Inc. Place)
West Clarkston; RMC Place; ASOTIN; ***247** J-20; elev. 808ft./246m.; ★ **LEW**; mail Clarkston **z** 99403; ● 2,600
West Clarkston-Highland; CDP-Census Area Only; ASOTIN; ***247** J-20; ★ **LEW**; mail Clarkston **z** 99403; Ⓟ 3,913; Ⓒ 4,707
West Coulee; RMC Place; DOUGLAS; mail Coulee Dam **z** 99116; pop. incl. with Coulee Dam (Inc. Place)
Westfair; RMC Place; KING; ★ **SEAT**; mail Federal Way **z** 98023; pop. incl. with Federal Way (Inc. Place)
Westhaven; RMC Place; GRAYS HARBOR; mail Westport **z** 98595; pop. incl. with Westport (Inc. Place)
West Hills; RMC Place; KITSAP; ★ **BREM**; mail Bremerton **z** 98312; pop. incl. with Bremerton (Inc. Place)
Westlake; RMC Place; GRANT; ***247** H-14; pop. incl. with Moses Lake (Inc. Place)
West Lake Sammamish; CDP-Census Area Only; KING; ***246** F-8; ★ **SEAT**; mail Bellevue **z** 98008, Issaquah **z** 98027; Ⓟ 6,087; Ⓒ 5,937
West Lake Stevens; CDP-Census Area Only; SNOHOMISH; ***246** E-8; ★ **SEAT**; mail Lake Stevens **z** 98258; Ⓟ 12,453; Ⓒ 18,071
West Longview; CDP-Census Area Only; COWLITZ; ***246** K-5; ★ **LNGV**; mail Longview **z** 98632; Ⓟ 3,163; Ⓒ 2,882
Westmont Acres; RMC Place; GRANT; ***247** G-14; elev. 1,337ft./408m.; mail Soap Lake **z** 98851; ● 120
Weston; RMC Place; PIERCE; ★ **SEAT**; pop. incl. with Tacoma (Inc. Place)
West Park; RMC Place; KITSAP; ***246** F-6; ★ **BREM**; mail Bremerton **z** 98312; pop. incl. with Bremerton (Inc. Place)
West Pasco (Riverview); CDP-Census Area Only; FRANKLIN; ***247** K-15; ★ **RICH-**; mail Pasco **z** 99301; Ⓟ 7,312; Ⓒ 4,629
Westport; Inc. Place; GRAYS HARBOR; **246** H-3; elev. 12ft./4m.; 🅿; **z** 98595; Ⓟ 1,892; Ⓒ 2,137
West Port Madison; RMC Place; KITSAP; ***246** F-7; elev. 20ft./6m.; ★ **SEAT**; mail Bainbridge Island **z** 98110; pop. incl. with Winslow (Inc. Place)
West Richland (Enterprise); Inc. Place; BENTON; **247** K-14; 🅿; ★ **RICH-**; **z** 99353 & mail Richland **z** 99352; Ⓟ 3,962; Ⓒ 8,385
West Seattle; RMC Place; KING; ***246** F-7; ★ **SEAT**; mail Seattle **z** 98116; pop. incl. with Seattle (Inc. Place)
Westside; RMC Place; THURSTON; ★ **OLYM**; mail Olympia **z** 98502, **z** 98512; pop. incl. with Olympia (Inc. Place)
West Side Highway; CDP-Census Area Only; COWLITZ; ***246** K-6; ★ **LNGV**; mail Kelso **z** 98626, Longview **z** 98632; Ⓟ 3,641; Ⓒ 4,565
West Sound; RMC Place; SAN JUAN; **246** B-6; mail Eastsound **z** 98245; ● 100
West Tapps; RMC Place; PIERCE; ***246** G-7; elev. 543ft./166m.; ★ **SEAT**; mail Sumner **z** 98390; ● 2,200
West Valley; CDP-Census Area Only; YAKIMA; ***247** J-11; ★ **YAK**; mail Yakima **z** 98903, **z** 98908; Ⓟ 6,594; Ⓒ 10,433
Westward Siding; RMC Place; PIERCE; ***246** G-7; elev. 20ft./6m.; ★ **SEAT**; mail Tacoma **z** 98406; pop. incl. with Tacoma (Inc. Place)
West Wenatchee; CDP-Census Area Only; CHELAN; ***247** G-12; mail East Wenatchee **z** 98802, Wenatchee **z** 98801; Ⓟ 2,220; Ⓒ 1,681
Westwood; RMC Place; KING; ★ **SEAT**; mail Seattle **z** 98106, **z** 98126, **z** 98136; pop. incl. with Seattle (Inc. Place)
Westwood; RMC Place; KITSAP; ***246** F-7; ★ **SEAT**; mail Bainbridge Island **z** 98110; pop. incl. with Winslow (Inc. Place)
WHATCOM; **246** B-8; Ⓟ 127,780; Ⓒ 166,814; Ⓡ 166,826; ◆ 206,900
Wheeler; RMC Place; GRANT; **247** H-15; mail Moses Lake **z** 98837; ● 220
White Center; CDP; KING; **248** F-7; ★ **SEAT**; mail Seattle **z** 98106, **z** 98146; Ⓒ 20,975; ◆ 23,216
White Pass; RMC Place; YAKIMA; ***246** I-9; mail Naches **z** 98937; ● 40
Whites; RMC Place; GRAYS HARBOR; **246** H-5; mail Elma **z** 98541; ● 50
White Salmon; Inc. Place; KLICKITAT; **246** M-9; 🅿 🅷; **z** 98672; Ⓟ 1,861; Ⓒ 2,193
White Swan; CDP; YAKIMA; **247** J-11; located on Yakama Ind. Res.; 🅿; **z** 98952; Ⓟ 2,669; Ⓒ 3,033
WHITMAN; **247** H-18; Ⓟ 38,775; Ⓒ 40,740; ◆ 39,786
Whitney Esttes; RMC Place; LEWIS; ***246** I-5; elev. 400ft./122m.; mail Chehalis **z** 98532; ● 100
Whitstran; RMC Place; BENTON; ***247** K-13; mail Prosser **z** 99350; ● 100
Whittier Heights; RMC Place; KING; ***246** F-7; ★ **SEAT**; pop. incl. with Seattle (Inc. Place)
Wickersham; RMC Place; WHATCOM; **246** B-7; ★ **BELNG**; mail Acme **z** 98220; ● 150
Wilbur; Inc. Place; LINCOLN; **247** E-16; elev. 2,163ft./659m.; 🅿; **z** 99185; Ⓟ 863; Ⓒ 914
Wilburton; RMC Place; KING; ***246** F-7; ★ **SEAT**; mail Bellevue **z** 98004; pop. incl. with Bellevue (Inc. Place)
Wildcat Lake; RMC Place; KITSAP; ***246** F-6; ★ **BREM**; mail Bremerton **z** 98312; summer pop. 400; ● 200
Wilderness; RMC Place; THURSTON; ***246** H-6; elev. 250ft./76m.; ★ **OLYM**; mail Olympia **z** 98501; ● 300
Wiley; YAKIMA; see Wiley City (RMC Place)
Wiley City (Wiley); RMC Place; YAKIMA; **247** J-11; ★ **YAK**; mail Yakima **z** 98908; ● 300
Wilkeson; Inc. Place; PIERCE; **246** H-8; 🅿; ★ **SEAT**; **z** 98396; Ⓟ 366; Ⓒ 395
Willada; WHITMAN; see Lancaster (RMC Place)
Willapa; RMC Place; PACIFIC; **246** I-4; elev. 27ft./8m.; mail Raymond **z** 98577; ● 370
Willard; RMC Place; SKAMANIA; **246** L-9; mail Bingen **z** 98605; ● 100
Willow Grove; RMC Place; COWLITZ; ***246** K-5; ★ **LNGV**; mail Longview **z** 98632; ● 60
Wilson Creek; Inc. Place; GRANT; **247** G-15; 🅿; **z** 98860; Ⓟ 148; Ⓒ 227
Winchester; RMC Place; GRANT; **247** G-13; mail Quincy **z** 98848; ● 30
Windust; RMC Place; FRANKLIN; ***247** J-16; mail Kahlotus **z** 99335; rural
Winlock; Inc. Place; LEWIS; **246** J-6; elev. 309ft./94m.; 🅿; **z** 98596 & mail Toledo **z** 98591; Ⓟ 1,027; Ⓒ 1,166
Winona; RMC Place; WHITMAN; **247** H-18; elev. 1,487ft./453m.; mail Endicott **z** 99125; ● 50
Winslow (Bainbridge Island); Inc. Place; KITSAP; **246** F-7; ★ **SEAT**; mail Bainbridge Island **z** 98110; Ⓟ 3,081; Ⓒ 20,308; ◆ 21,423
Winthrop; Inc. Place; OKANOGAN; **247** C-12; elev. 1,760ft./536m.; 🅿; **z** 98862 & mail Mazama **z** 98833; Ⓟ 302; Ⓒ 349
Winton; RMC Place; CHELAN; ***247** F-11; mail Leavenworth **z** 98826; rural
Wishkah; RMC Place; GRAYS HARBOR; ***246** H-4; mail Aberdeen **z** 98520; ● 50
Wishram; CDP; KLICKITAT; **246** M-10; 🅿; **z** 98673; Ⓒ 324
Wishram Heights; RMC Place; KLICKITAT; ***246** M-10; elev. 600ft./183m.; mail Wishram **z** 98673; ● 100
Withrow; RMC Place; DOUGLAS; **247** F-13; mail Waterville **z** 98858; ● 60
Wollochet; RMC Place; PIERCE; **248** L-4; ★ **SEAT**; mail Gig Harbor **z** 98335; ● 300
Woodinville; Inc. Place; KING; **248** B-10; 🅿; ★ **SEAT**; **z** 98072, **z** 98077; Ⓒ 9,194; Ⓡ 9,809
Woodland; Inc. Place; COWLITZ, CLARK; **246** L-6; 🅿; ★ **POR**; **z** 98674; Ⓟ 2,500; Ⓒ 3,780
Woodland Beach; RMC Place; ISLAND; ***246** D-7; ★ **SEAT**; mail Camano Island **z** 98282; ● 100
Woodland Creek; RMC Place; THURSTON; ***246** H-6; elev. 100ft./30m.; ★ **OLYM**; mail Olympia **z** 98501; ● 100
Woodland Park; RMC Place; COWLITZ; ***246** L-7; elev. 300ft./91m.; mail Ariel **z** 98603; ● 25
Woodlawn; RMC Place; GRAYS HARBOR; ***246** H-3; mail Hoquiam **z** 98550; pop. incl. with Hoquiam (Inc. Place)
Woodmont Beach; RMC Place; KING; **248** J-8; ★ **SEAT**; mail Kent **z** 98032; pop. incl. with Des Moines (Inc. Place)
Woods Creek; CDP-Census Area Only; SNOHOMISH; ***246** E-8; ★ **SEAT**; Ⓒ 4,502
Woodsmuir; RMC Place; THURSTON; ***246** H-6; elev. 200ft./61m.; ★ **OLYM**; mail Olympia **z** 98501; ● 200
Woodway; Inc. Place; SNOHOMISH; **248** A-7; 🅿; ★ **SEAT**; **z** 98020; Ⓟ 914; Ⓒ 936
Wye Lake; RMC Place; KITSAP; ***246** G-6; elev. 340ft./104m.; ★ **BREM**; mail Port Orchard **z** 98366; ● 200

Y

Yacht Haven; RMC Place; SAN JUAN; ***246** B-5; elev. 10ft./3m.; mail Friday Harbor **z** 98250; rural
Yacolt; Inc. Place; CLARK; **246** L-7; 🅿; **z** 98675; Ⓟ 600; Ⓒ 1,055
Yakama Reservation; Indian Reservation; YAKIMA, KLICKITAT, LEWIS; mail Toppenish **z** 98948; also location of Indian Agency; Ⓟ 25,363; Ⓒ 31,646
Yakima; Inc. Place; ⊡ YAKIMA; **247** J-12; elev. 1,066ft./325m.; 🅿 🅷 ■; ★ **YAK**; **z** 98901-04, **z** 98907-09; Ⓟ 54,843; Ⓒ 71,845; ◆ 80,888
YAKIMA; **247** J-11; Ⓟ 188,823; Ⓒ 222,581; ◆ 232,770
Yale; RMC Place; COWLITZ; ***246** L-7; mail Ariel **z** 98603
Yardley; RMC Place; SPOKANE; ***247** F-19; ★ **SPOK**; mail Spokane **z** 99202; ● 200
Yarrow Point; Inc. Place; KING; **248** D-9; 🅿; ★ **SEAT**; **z** 98004; Ⓟ 962; Ⓒ 1,008
Yelm; Inc. Place; THURSTON; **246** H-6; 🅿; ★ **OLYM**; **z** 98597; Ⓟ 1,337; Ⓒ 3,289
Yeomalt; RMC Place; KITSAP; **248** D-5; elev. 100ft./30m.; ★ **SEAT**; mail Bainbridge Island **z** 98110; pop. incl. with Winslow (Inc. Place)
Yesler Terrace; RMC Place; KING; ***246** F-7; ★ **SEAT**; mail Seattle **z** 98104; pop. incl. with Seattle (Inc. Place)
Yokeko Point; RMC Place; SKAGIT; ***246** C-6; elev. 100ft./30m.; mail Anacortes **z** 98221; ● 110
Yoman Ferry; RMC Place; PIERCE; ★ **SEAT**; mail Anderson Island **z** 98303

Z

Zenith; RMC Place; KING; ★ **SEAT**; mail Seattle **z** 98188; pop. incl. with Des Moines (Inc. Place)
Zillah; Inc. Place; YAKIMA; **247** J-12; 🅿; **z** 98953; Ⓟ 1,911; Ⓒ 2,198

Entries in are counties.
Entries in **bold** have populations of 2,500 or more.
Names in parentheses are alternate names.
Inc. Place — Incorporated Place
RMC Place — Rand McNally Designated Place
CDP — Census Designated Place
MCD — Minor Civil Division

⊡ County Seat
▲ Minor Civil Division
elev. Elevation
🅿 Post Office

🅷 Hospital
🅲 College
■ Principal Business Center
★ Ranally Metro Area (RMA) Abbreviation
z Zip Code(s)

Ⓟ Previous Census Population
Ⓡ Revised Census Population
Ⓐ Annexation Population
● Rand McNally Population Estimate
Ⓒ Final Census Population
Ⓢ Special Census Population
◆ Estimated Population

For additional definitions see Glossary, Volume 1, and Introduction, Volume 2.

WEST VIRGINIA

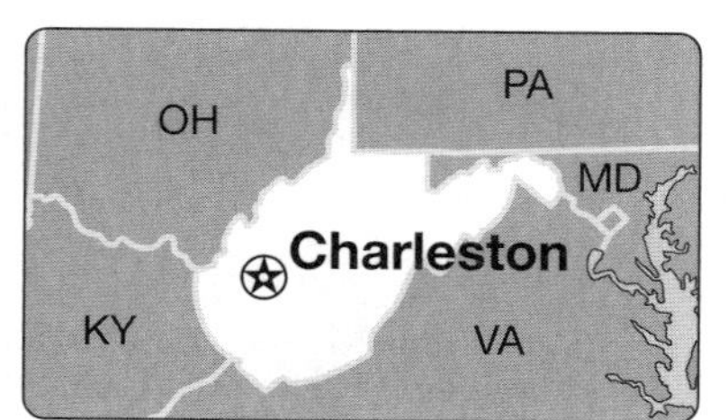

Statistics

Total area (2000) — 24,230 square miles
Land area (2000) — 24,078 square miles
Water area (2000) — 152 square miles
Capital — Charleston
Admitted as state — June, 1863

Maps

State maps can be found on pages 142-254 in Vol. 1

Ranally Metro Areas (RMAs) and Abbreviations

Beckley, WV — BECK
Charleston, WV — CHAS
Clarksburg, WV — CLRKB
Cumberland, MD-WV — CUMB
Fairmont, WV — FAIRM
Hagerstown, MD-PA-WV — HAG
Huntington, WV-KY-OH — HNTG
Morgantown, WV-PA — MORG
Parkersburg, WV-OH — PRKB
Steubenville-Weirton, OH-WV — STU-
Wheeling, WV-OH — WHL

Principal Places

Place Name	Place Type	County	Population
Charleston	Inc. Place	KANAWHA	◆ 47,848
Huntington	Inc. Place	CABELL	◆ 47,245
Parkersburg	Inc. Place	WOOD	◆ 30,929
Morgantown	Inc. Place	MONONGALIA	◆ 30,121
Wheeling	Inc. Place	OHIO	◆ 27,766
Fairmont	Inc. Place	MARION	◆ 18,578
Weirton	Inc. Place	HANCOCK	◆ 18,271
Beckley	Inc. Place	RALEIGH	◆ 16,198
Clarksburg	Inc. Place	HARRISON	◆ 15,753
Martinsburg	Inc. Place	BERKELEY	◆ 15,489
South Charleston	Inc. Place	KANAWHA	© 13,390
Teays Valley	CDP-Census Area Only	PUTNAM	© 12,704
Saint Albans	Inc. Place	KANAWHA	© 11,567
Bluefield	Inc. Place	MERCER	◆ 10,545
Cross Lanes	CDP	KANAWHA	© 10,353
Moundsville	Inc. Place	MARSHALL	© 9,998
Vienna	Inc. Place	WOOD	◆ 9,837
Dunbar	Inc. Place	KANAWHA	© 8,154
Oak Hill	Inc. Place	FAYETTE	© 7,589
Bridgeport	Inc. Place	HARRISON	© 7,306
Elkins	Inc. Place	RANDOLPH	◆ 6,832
Nitro	Inc. Place	KANAWHA	© 6,824
Cheat Lake	CDP-Census Area Only	MONONGALIA	© 6,396
Pea Ridge	CDP-Census Area Only	CABELL	© 6,363
Princeton	Inc. Place	MERCER	© 6,347
New Martinsville	Inc. Place	WETZEL	© 5,984
Buckhannon	Inc. Place	UPSHUR	© 5,725
Grafton	Inc. Place	TAYLOR	© 5,489
Keyser	Inc. Place	MINERAL	© 5,303
Hurricane	Inc. Place	PUTNAM	© 5,222

County Business Data

County	FIPS Code	County Seat	Land Area (Sq. Mi.)	Census Population			Wholesale Trade		Manufacturing, 2002			
				4/1/2000	4/1/1990	% Change 1990-2000	Sales, 2002 ($1,000)	% Change 1997-2002	Establish-ments	Total Employees	Value Added ($1,000)	Ranally Mfg. Units
Barbour	001	Philippi	341	15,557	15,699	-0.9	(d)	(d)	...	(d)	(d)	...
Berkeley	003	Martinsburg	321	75,905	59,253	28.1	(d)	(d)	40	(d)	(d)	...
Boone	005	Madison	503	25,535	25,870	-1.3	(d)	(d)	...	(d)	(d)	...
Braxton	007	Sutton	513	14,702	12,998	13.1	54,223	39.6	...	(d)	(d)	...
Brooke	009	Wellsburg	89	25,447	26,992	-5.7	35,168	(d)	27	5,644	688,372	364
Cabell	011	Huntington	282	96,784	96,827	-0.0	690,878	(d)	113	5,288	559,834	296
Calhoun	013	Grantsville	281	7,582	7,885	-3.8	(d)	(d)	...	(d)	(d)	...
Clay	015	Clay	342	10,330	9,983	3.5	(d)	(d)	...	(d)	(d)	...
Doddridge	017	West Union	320	7,403	6,994	5.8	(d)	(d)	...	(d)	(d)	...
Fayette	019	Fayetteville	664	47,579	47,952	-0.8	(d)	(d)	36	812	92,905	49
Gilmer	021	Glenville	340	7,160	7,669	-6.6	4,214	-26.6	...	(d)	(d)	...
Grant	023	Petersburg	477	11,299	10,428	8.4	(d)	(d)	13	641	54,083	29
Greenbrier	025	Lewisburg	1,021	34,453	34,693	-0.7	78,974	67.9	32	851	62,284	33
Hampshire	027	Romney	642	20,203	16,498	22.5	(d)	(d)	...	(d)	(d)	...
Hancock	029	New Cumberland	83	32,667	35,233	-7.3	381,970	795.7	30	2,571	229,172	121
Hardy	031	Moorefield	583	12,669	10,977	15.4	(d)	(d)	16	3,968	164,894	87
Harrison	033	Clarksburg	416	68,652	69,371	-1.0	(d)	(d)	63	1,778	153,416	81
Jackson	035	Ripley	466	28,000	25,938	7.9	94,807	-34.9	19	2,632	279,363	148
Jefferson	037	Charles Town	210	42,190	35,926	17.4	(d)	(d)	24	1,733	150,121	79
Kanawha	039	Charleston	903	200,073	207,619	-3.6	2,883,675	33.4	144	5,767	892,878	472
Lewis	041	Weston	382	16,919	17,223	-1.8	34,876	30.3	...	(d)	(d)	...
Lincoln	043	Hamlin	437	22,108	21,382	3.4	(d)	(d)	...	(d)	(d)	...
Logan	045	Logan	454	37,710	43,032	-12.4	143,786	-9.4	37	689	37,544	20
Marion	049	Fairmont	310	56,598	57,249	-1.1	159,575	3.1	56	1,299	139,414	74
Marshall	051	Moundsville	307	35,519	37,356	-4.9	(d)	(d)	...	(d)	(d)	...
Mason	053	Point Pleasant	432	25,957	25,178	3.1	(d)	(d)	16	(d)	(d)	...
McDowell	047	Welch	535	27,329	35,233	-22.4	(d)	(d)	...	(d)	(d)	...
Mercer	055	Princeton	420	62,980	64,980	-3.1	(d)	(d)	61	1,773	126,570	67
Mineral	057	Keyser	328	27,078	26,697	1.4	(d)	(d)	17	1,272	158,377	84
Mingo	059	Williamson	423	28,253	33,739	-16.3	46,429	-14.1	...	(d)	(d)	...
Monongalia	061	Morgantown	361	81,866	75,509	8.4	343,855	-21.7	55	2,538	275,426	146
Monroe	063	Union	473	14,583	12,406	17.5	3,630	-74.2	...	(d)	(d)	...
Morgan	065	Berkeley Springs	229	14,943	12,128	23.2	(d)	(d)	...	(d)	(d)	...
Nicholas	067	Summersville	649	26,562	26,775	-0.8	56,121	-12.5	30	829	73,247	39
Ohio	069	Wheeling	106	47,427	50,871	-6.8	(d)	(d)	53	1,173	144,975	77
Pendleton	071	Franklin	698	8,196	8,054	1.8	(d)	(d)	...	(d)	(d)	...
Pleasants	073	St. Marys	131	7,514	7,546	-0.4	(d)	(d)	6	(d)	(d)	...
Pocahontas	075	Marlinton	940	9,131	9,008	1.4	(d)	(d)	...	(d)	(d)	...
Preston	077	Kingwood	648	29,334	29,037	1.0	37,384	-61.6	27	881	52,361	28
Putnam	079	Winfield	346	51,589	42,835	20.4	(d)	(d)	41	1,879	423,398	224
Raleigh	081	Beckley	607	79,220	76,819	3.1	(d)	(d)	58	910	66,027	35
Randolph	083	Elkins	1,040	28,262	27,803	1.7	136,290	-10.6	34	1,723	129,111	68
Ritchie	085	Harrisville	454	10,343	10,233	1.1	(d)	(d)	22	1,598	122,035	65
Roane	087	Spencer	484	15,446	15,120	2.2	1,761	(d)	...	(d)	(d)	...
Summers	089	Hinton	361	12,999	14,204	-8.5	7,080	-76.0	...	(d)	(d)	...
Taylor	091	Grafton	173	16,089	15,144	6.2	(d)	(d)	...	(d)	(d)	...
Tucker	093	Parsons	419	7,321	7,728	-5.3	(d)	(d)	...	(d)	(d)	...
Tyler	095	Middlebourne	258	9,592	9,796	-2.1	(d)	(d)	12	(d)	(d)	...
Upshur	097	Buckhannon	355	23,404	22,867	2.3	95,742	26.4	26	883	113,784	60
Wayne	099	Wayne	506	42,903	41,636	3.0	128,372	(d)	36	852	117,585	62
Webster	101	Webster Springs	556	9,719	10,729	-9.4	(d)	(d)	...	(d)	(d)	...
Wetzel	103	New Martinsville	359	17,693	19,258	-8.1	11,489	-64.9	18	1,654	284,358	150
Wirt	105	Elizabeth	233	5,873	5,192	13.1	(d)	(d)	...	(d)	(d)	...
Wood	107	Parkersburg	367	87,986	86,915	1.2	320,449	-34.6	75	(d)	(d)	...
Wyoming	109	Pineville	501	25,708	28,990	-11.3	(d)	(d)	...	(d)	(d)	...
The State			**24,078**	**1,808,344**	**1,793,477**	**0.8**	**10,924,279**	**6.2**	**1,480**	**67,319**	**7,983,845**	**4,224**

(d) Data not available. Corresponding percentages or Ranally Manufacturing Units are estimates.
... Represents 0 or amount too minimal to be reported.

Index of Places and Counties

A

Aarrons Fork; RMC Place; KANAWHA; *250 F-4; ★ CHAS; mail Elkview z 25071; rural
Abbott; RMC Place; UPSHUR; *250 D-7; mail Buckhannon z 26201; ● 50
Abney; RMC Place; RALEIGH; *250 I-5; ★ BECK; mail Beaver z 25813; ● 60
Abraham; RMC Place; RALEIGH; *250 H-6; 🄿; z 25918; rural
Accoville; RMC Place; LOGAN; *250 H-3; elev. 838ft./255m.; 🄿; z 25606; ● 400
Acme; RMC Place; KANAWHA; *250 G-4; mail Eskdale z 25075
Ada; RMC Place; MERCER; *250 J-5; mail Bluefield z 24701; ● 200
Adaline; RMC Place; MARSHALL; *250 B-6; mail Cameron z 26033; rural
Adamston; RMC Place; HARRISON; *250 C-7; ★ CLRKB; mail Clarksburg z 26301; pop. incl. with Clarksburg (Inc. Place)
Adamsville; RMC Place; HARRISON; *250 C-7; elev. 1,059ft./323m.; 🄿; z 26431; rural
Addison; WEBSTER; see Webster Springs (Inc. Place)
Adlai; RMC Place; PLEASANTS; *250 C-5; mail Saint Marys z 26170; rural
Adolph; RMC Place; RANDOLPH; *250 E-8; mail Mill Creek z 26280
Adrian; RMC Place; UPSHUR; 250 E-7; elev. 1,429ft./436m.; 🄿; z 26210; ● 300
Advent; RMC Place; JACKSON; *250 E-4; elev. 800ft./244m.; 🄿; z 25231; ● 20
Afton; RMC Place; PRESTON; *250 B-9; elev. 2,663ft./812m.; mail Terra Alta z 26764; rural
Aggregates; RMC Place; RANDOLPH; *250 D-8; mail Elkins z 26241; rural
Ajax; RMC Place; MINGO; *250 H-2; mail Lenore z 25676; ● 60
Albert; TUCKER; see Douglas (RMC Place)
Albright; Inc. Place; PRESTON; 250 B-9; elev. 1,291ft./393m.; 🄿; z 26519; Ⓟ 195; © 247
Alderson; Inc. Place; GREENBRIER, MONROE; 250 I-6; elev. 1,555ft./474m.; 🄿; z 24910; Ⓟ 1,152; © 1,091
Alexander; RMC Place; UPSHUR; *250 E-7; elev. 1,849ft./564m.; 🄿; z 26218
Algoma; RMC Place; MCDOWELL; *250 J-4; elev. 1,747ft./532m.; 🄿; z 24868; pop. incl. with Northfork (Inc. Place)
Alice; RMC Place; GILMER; *250 D-6; elev. 736ft./224m.; mail Coxs Mills z 26342
Alkol; RMC Place; LINCOLN; 250 G-3; elev. 750ft./229m.; 🄿; z 25501, z 25572; ● 200
Allendale; RMC Place; MARSHALL; 250 J-10; ★ WHL; mail Wheeling z 26003; ● 150
Allen Junction; RMC Place; WYOMING; *250 I-4; elev. 1,475ft./450m.; 🄿; z 25810; ● 75
Allensville; RMC Place; BERKELEY; *250 B-13; mail Hedgesville z 25427; rural
Alloy; RMC Place; FAYETTE; *250 G-5; elev. 676ft./206m.; 🄿; z 25002; ● 25
Alma; TYLER; see Centerville (RMC Place)
Alpena; RMC Place; RANDOLPH; *250 D-9; mail Bowden z 26254
Alpheus; RMC Place; MCDOWELL; *250 J-4
Alpoca; RMC Place; WYOMING; *250 I-4; elev. 1,521ft./464m.; mail Bud z 24716; ● 50
Alta; RMC Place; FAYETTE; *250 G-5; mail Belva z 26656; ● 90
Alta; RMC Place; GREENBRIER; *250 H-7; 🄿; z 24916 & mail Lewisburg z 24901; rural
Alton; RMC Place; UPSHUR; 250 E-7; mail Adrian z 26210; ● 50
Alum Bridge; RMC Place; LEWIS; 250 D-6; elev. 807ft./246m.; 🄿; z 26321; ● 100
Alum Creek; CDP; LINCOLN; 250 G-3; 🄿; ★ CHAS; z 25003; Ⓟ 1,602; © 1,839
Alvon; RMC Place; GREENBRIER; 250 H-7; elev. 2,023ft./617m.; mail White Sulphur Springs z 24986; ● 80
Alvy; TYLER; see Stringtown (RMC Place)
Amandaville; RMC Place; KANAWHA; *250 F-3; elev. 605ft./184m.; ★ CHAS; mail Saint Albans z 25177; ● 500
Amboy; RMC Place; PRESTON; *250 C-9; elev. 2,552ft./778m.; 🄿; z 26705
Ambrosia; RMC Place; MASON; *250 E-3; mail Point Pleasant z 25550
Ameagle; RMC Place; RALEIGH; 250 H-4; elev. 1,092ft./333m.; 🄿; z 25060; ● 80
Amelia; RMC Place; KANAWHA; *250 G-5; elev. 1,170ft./357m.; mail Pond Gap z 25160; ● 50
Ames Heights; RMC Place; FAYETTE; *250 G-5; mail Fayetteville z 25840; ● 90
Amherstdale; RMC Place; LOGAN; 250 H-3; elev. 899ft./274m.; 🄿; z 25607; ● 1,100
Amherstdale-Robinette; CDP-Census Area Only; LOGAN; *250 H-3; mail Amherstdale z 25607; Ⓟ 2,435; © 1,785
Amigo; RMC Place; RALEIGH, WYOMING; *250 I-5; elev. 1,578ft./481m.; 🄿; z 25811; ● 200
Amma; RMC Place; ROANE; 250 F-5; elev. 714ft./218m.; 🄿; z 25005; ● 125
Anawalt; Inc. Place; MCDOWELL; 250 J-4; elev. 1,687ft./514m.; 🄿; z 24808; Ⓟ 329; © 272
Andersonville; RMC Place; MARSHALL; *250 B-7; mail Cameron z 26033; rural
Andrew; RMC Place; BOONE; *250 G-3; elev. 865ft./264m.; mail Peytona z 25154
Angel Terrace; RMC Place; KANAWHA; *250 F-4; ★ CHAS; mail Charleston z 25303; pop. incl. with Charleston (Inc. Place)
Angerona; RMC Place; JACKSON; *250 E-3; mail Evans z 25241; rural
Anjean; RMC Place; GREENBRIER; *250 G-6; mail Rupert z 25984; ● 20
Anmoore; Inc. Place; HARRISON; *250 C-7; elev. 1,010ft./308m.; 🄿; ★ CLRKB; z 26323; Ⓟ 686; © 685
Annamoriah; RMC Place; CALHOUN; 250 D-5; elev. 1,001ft./305m.; 🄿; z 26141; ● 40
Ansted; Inc. Place; FAYETTE; 250 G-5; elev. 1,312ft./400m.; 🄿; z 25812; Ⓟ 1,643; © 1,576
Anthony; RMC Place; GREENBRIER; 250 H-7; elev. 1,820ft./555m.; 🄿; z 24938; ● 60
Antioch; RMC Place; DODDRIDGE; mail West Union z 26456; rural
Antioch; RMC Place; MINERAL; *250 C-11; elev. 1,078ft./329m.; mail New Creek z 26743; ● 75
Aplin; RMC Place; JACKSON; *250 E-4; mail Gay z 25244; rural
Apple Farm; RMC Place; CALHOUN; *250 E-5; mail Arnoldsburg z 25234; rural
Apple Grove; RMC Place; MASON; *250 E-2; elev. 583ft./178m.; 🄿; z 25502; ● 300
Apple Grove; RMC Place; MCDOWELL; *250 I-3; elev. 1,003ft./306m.; mail Iaeger z 24844; rural
Aracoma; RMC Place; LOGAN; *250 H-3; mail Logan z 25601; ● 325
Arborland Acres; RMC Place; KANAWHA; *250 F-3; ★ CHAS; mail Saint Albans z 25177; ● 300
Arbovale; RMC Place; POCAHONTAS; *250 F-9; elev. 2,727ft./831m.; 🄿; z 24915; ● 150
Arbuckle; RMC Place; MASON; *250 E-3; elev. 577ft./176m.; 🄿; z 25123
Arbutus Park; RMC Place; HARRISON; *250 C-7; ★ CLRKB; mail Clarksburg z 26301; pop. incl. with Clarksburg (Inc. Place)
Archer Heights; RMC Place; BROOKE; *250 B-2; ★ STU-; mail Colliers z 26035; ● 50
Arcola; RMC Place; WEBSTER; *250 F-7; elev. 1,873ft./571m.; mail Cowen z 26206; rural
Ardel; RMC Place; WAYNE; *250 G-2; ★ HNTG; mail Wayne z 25570; ● 120
Arden; RMC Place; BARBOUR; 250 C-8; elev. 1,275ft./389m.; mail Moatsville z 26405; ● 75
Arden; RMC Place; BERKELEY; *250 C-13; mail Martinsburg z 25401; ● 200
Argyle; RMC Place; LOGAN; *250 H-3; elev. 935ft./285m.; mail Yolyn z 25654; ● 80
Arkansas; RMC Place; HARDY; 250 D-11; elev. 1,512ft./461m.; mail Baker z 26801; ● 100
Arlee; RMC Place; MASON; *250 E-3; elev. 654ft./199m.; mail Henderson z 25106
Arlington; RMC Place; HARRISON; *250 C-7; ★ CLRKB; mail Clarksburg z 26301; ● 200
Arlington; RMC Place; UPSHUR; 250 E-7; elev. 1,503ft./458m.; mail Rock Cave z 26234; ● 140
Arnett; RMC Place; BRAXTON; *250 E-6; mail Exchange z 26619; rural
Arnett; RMC Place; RALEIGH; 250 H-4; elev. 1,560ft./475m.; 🄿; z 25007; ● 400
Arnettsville; RMC Place; MONONGALIA; *250 B-8; ★ MORG; mail Morgantown z 26501; rural
Arnoldsburg; RMC Place; CALHOUN; 250 E-5; elev. 760ft./232m.; 🄿; z 25234; ● 140
Arthur; RMC Place; GRANT; 250 D-10; elev. 1,109ft./338m.; 🄿; z 26847; ● 25
Arthurdale; RMC Place; PRESTON; 250 C-9; elev. 1,760ft./536m.; 🄿; ★ MORG; z 26520; ● 1,500
Artie; RMC Place; RALEIGH; *250 H-4; elev. 1,331ft./406m.; 🄿; z 25008 & mail Whitesville z 25209; ● 175
Arvilla; RMC Place; PLEASANTS; *250 C-5; elev. 636ft./194m.
Asbury; RMC Place; GREENBRIER; 250 H-7; elev. 2,108ft./643m.; 🄿; z 24916; ● 30
Asco; RMC Place; MCDOWELL; *250 I-4; elev. 1,480ft./451m.; 🄿; z 24828
Ashford; RMC Place; BOONE; *250 G-4; elev. 649ft./198m.; 🄿; z 25009; ● 175
Ashland; RMC Place; MCDOWELL; *250 J-4; elev. 2,089ft./637m.; 🄿; z 24868; ● 100
Ashley; RMC Place; DODDRIDGE; 250 C-6; mail West Union z 26456; ● 30
Ashton; RMC Place; MASON; 250 E-2; elev. 561ft./171m.; 🄿; z 25503; ● 30
Aspinall; RMC Place; LEWIS; *250 D-6; elev. 851ft./259m.; mail Orlando z 26412; rural
Astor; RMC Place; TAYLOR; *250 C-8; 🄿; z 26347; ● 60
Atenville; RMC Place; LINCOLN; *250 G-2; elev. 614ft./187m.; mail Harts z 25524; ● 40
Athens; Inc. Place; MERCER; 250 J-5; elev. 2,597ft./792m.; 🄿 🄲 2,928; z 24712; Ⓟ 741; © 1,102
Atwell; RMC Place; MCDOWELL; *250 J-3; mail Bartley z 24813, Raysal z 24879; ● 100
Atwood; RMC Place; TYLER; *250 B-6; mail Reader z 26167; rural
Auburn; Inc. Place; RITCHIE; 250 D-6; elev. 827ft./252m.; 🄿; z 26325; Ⓟ 89; © 103
Augusta; RMC Place; HAMPSHIRE; 250 C-12; elev. 1,300ft./396m.; 🄿; z 26704; ● 400
Aurora; RMC Place; PRESTON; 250 C-9; elev. 2,641ft./805m.; 🄿; z 26705; ● 250
Austen; RMC Place; PRESTON; *250 C-9; mail Newburg z 26410; ● 25
Auto; RMC Place; GREENBRIER; 250 H-7; elev. 2,341ft./714m.; 🄿; z 24966; ● 10
Auvil; RMC Place; TUCKER; *250 D-9; mail Parsons z 26287; rural
Auville; RMC Place; MCDOWELL; pop. incl. with Iaeger (Inc. Place)
Avis; RMC Place; SUMMERS; *250 I-6; mail Hinton z 25951; pop. incl. with Hinton (Inc. Place)
Avon; RMC Place; DODDRIDGE; *250 D-6; elev. 891ft./272m.; mail New Milton z 26411; rural
Avondale; RMC Place; DODDRIDGE; *250 C-6; mail West Union z 26456; rural
Avondale; RMC Place; MCDOWELL; 250 J-3; elev. 1,039ft./317m.; 🄿; z 24811; ● 200
Ayers; RMC Place; CALHOUN; *250 D-5; mail Big Bend z 26136; rural

B

Bablin; RMC Place; LEWIS; *250 E-7; elev. 998ft./304m.; mail Ireland z 26376; rural
Bachman; RMC Place; FAYETTE; *250 G-5; mail Fayetteville z 25840; ● 10
Backus; RMC Place; FAYETTE; *250 H-5; mail Meadow Bridge z 25976; rural
Baden; RMC Place; MASON; *250 E-3; elev. 968ft./295m.; mail Leon z 25123; rural
Baisden; RMC Place; LOGAN; *250 H-3; 🄿; z 25608 & mail Whitman z 25652; ● 125
Baker; RMC Place; HARDY; 250 D-11; elev. 1,306ft./398m.; 🄿; z 26801; ● 80
Baker Heights; RMC Place; BERKELEY; *250 C-14; elev. 478ft./146m.; mail Martinsburg z 25401; ● 300
Baker Ridge; RMC Place; MONONGALIA; *250 B-8; elev. 1,167ft./356m.; ★ MORG; mail Morgantown z 26505, z 26508; ● 450
Bakerton; RMC Place; JEFFERSON; *250 C-14; elev. 440ft./134m.; 🄿; z 25410; ● 250
Bald Knob; RMC Place; BOONE; 250 H-4; elev. 1,094ft./333m.; 🄿; z 25208; ● 150
Baldwin; RMC Place; GILMER; *250 D-6; elev. 800ft./244m.; 🄿; z 26351
Ballard; RMC Place; MONROE; 250 I-6; elev. 2,127ft./648m.; 🄿; z 24918; ● 180
Ballengee; RMC Place; SUMMERS; *250 I-6; elev. 1,860ft./567m.; 🄿; z 24981; ● 50
Balls Gap; RMC Place; CABELL; *250 F-2; elev. 640ft./195m.; ★ HNTG; mail Milton z 25541; rural
Bancroft; Inc. Place; PUTNAM; 250 F-3; elev. 587ft./179m.; 🄿; ★ CHAS; z 25011; Ⓟ 381; © 367
Bandytown; RMC Place; BOONE; *250 H-4; elev. 999ft./304m.; 🄿; z 25204; ● 120
BARBOUR; 250 D-8; Ⓟ 15,699; © 15,557; ◆ 15,411
Barboursville; Inc. Place; CABELL; 250 F-2; elev. 583ft./178m.; 🄿 ■; ★ HNTG; z 25504; Ⓟ 2,774; © 3,183; ◆ 2,939
Bardane; RMC Place; JEFFERSON; *250 C-14; mail Kearneysville z 25430; ● 40
Bargers Springs; RMC Place; SUMMERS; *250 I-6; elev. 1,495ft./456m.; mail Forest Hill z 24935; ● 50
Barker; RMC Place; WETZEL; *250 B-6; elev. 739ft./225m.; mail Pine Grove z 26419; ● 40
Barksdale; RMC Place; SUMMERS; *250 I-6; elev. 1,350ft./411m.; mail Hinton z 25951; ● 50
Barn; RMC Place; MERCER; *250 I-5; mail Flat Top z 25841; rural
Barnabus; RMC Place; LOGAN; *250 H-3; elev. 877ft./267m.; 🄿; z 25638; ● 300
Barrackville; Inc. Place; MARION; 250 B-8; elev. 900ft./274m.; 🄿; ★ FAIRM; z 26559; Ⓟ 1,443; © 1,288
Barren Creek; RMC Place; KANAWHA; *250 F-5; mail Clendenin z 25045; rural
Barrett; RMC Place; BOONE; 250 H-4; elev. 1,003ft./306m.; 🄿; z 25208; ● 200
Barrs; RMC Place; ROANE; *250 E-4; elev. 910ft./277m.; mail Spencer z 25276
Bartley; RMC Place; MCDOWELL; 250 J-3; elev. 1,261ft./384m.; 🄿; z 24813; ● 350
Bartow; RMC Place; POCAHONTAS; 250 F-9; elev. 2,784ft./849m.; 🄿; z 24920; ● 150
Basin; RMC Place; WYOMING; *250 I-5; elev. 2,400ft./732m.; mail Herndon z 24726; rural
Basnettsville; RMC Place; MARION; *250 B-7; ★ FAIRM; mail Fairview z 26570; ● 40
Basore; RMC Place; HARDY; *250 E-11; mail Mathias z 26812; rural
Bass; RMC Place; HARDY; *250 D-11; elev. 980ft./299m.; mail Moorefield z 26836
Bath; MORGAN; see Berkeley Springs (Inc. Place)
Baxter; RMC Place; MARION; *250 B-8; elev. 891ft./272m.; 🄿; ★ FAIRM; z 26560; ● 425
Bayard; Inc. Place; GRANT; 250 C-10; elev. 2,343ft./714m.; 🄿; z 26707; Ⓟ 414; © 299
Bays Heights; RMC Place; FAYETTE; *250 H-5; ★ BECK; ● 50
Beard Heights; RMC Place; POCAHONTAS; *250 G-8; mail Marlinton z 24954; pop. incl. with Marlinton (Inc. Place)
Beards Fork; RMC Place; FAYETTE; *250 G-5; elev. 1,200ft./366m.; 🄿; z 25173; ● 200
Bear Mountain; RMC Place; BARBOUR; *250 C-8; ● 40
Bearsville; RMC Place; TYLER; *250 C-6; elev. 787ft./240m.; mail Middlebourne z 26149; rural
Beartown; RMC Place; MCDOWELL; *250 J-3; mail Iaeger z 24844; rural
Beatrice; RMC Place; RITCHIE; *250 D-5; elev. 676ft./206m.; mail Smithville z 26178
Beatysville; RMC Place; JACKSON; *250 D-4; mail Belleville z 26133; rural
Beaver; CDP; RALEIGH; 250 H-5; elev. 2,114ft./644m.; 🄿; ★ BECK; z 25813; Ⓟ 1,244; © 1,378
Bebee; RMC Place; WETZEL; *250 B-6; elev. 1,256ft./383m.; mail New Martinsville z 26155; rural
Becco; RMC Place; LOGAN; *250 H-3; mail Amherstdale z 25607
Beckley; Inc. Place; ⊡ RALEIGH; 250 H-5; elev. 2,416ft./736m.; 🄿 🄷 🄲 4,826 ■; ★ BECK; z 25801-02, z 25926; Ⓟ 18,296; © 17,254; ◆ 16,198
Beckley Junction; RMC Place; RALEIGH; *250 H-5; ★ BECK; pop. incl. with Beckley (Inc. Place)
Beckwith; RMC Place; FAYETTE; 250 G-5; elev. 1,175ft./358m.; 🄿; z 25840; ● 175
Bedington; RMC Place; BERKELEY; *250 B-14; elev. 392ft./119m.; ★ HAG; mail Martinsburg z 25401; ● 120
Beebe; RMC Place; LOGAN; *250 H-3; mail Holden z 25625; ● 120
Beech Bottom; Inc. Place; BROOKE; 250 B-2; elev. 689ft./210m.; 🄿; ★ WHL; z 26030; Ⓟ 415; © 606
Beech Creek; RMC Place; MINGO; mail Matewan z 25678; rural
Beech Glen; RMC Place; NICHOLAS; *250 G-5; elev. 709ft./216m.; mail Belva z 26656; ● 90
Beechgrove; RMC Place; RITCHIE; *250 C-5; mail Pennsboro z 26415; rural
Beech Hill; RMC Place; MASON; *250 E-3; elev. 578ft./176m.; mail Southside z 25187
Beechwood; RMC Place; WOOD; *250 C-4; ★ PRKB; mail Parkersburg z 26104; pop. incl. with Parkersburg (Inc. Place)
Beechwood; RMC Place; WYOMING; *250 I-4; mail Allen Junction z 25810; ● 100
Beelick Knob; RMC Place; FAYETTE; *250 H-6; elev. 2,440ft./744m.; mail Meadow Bridge z 25976; ● 100
Beeson; RMC Place; MERCER; *250 I-5; elev. 2,332ft./711m.; 🄿; z 24714; ● 60
Belgrove; RMC Place; JACKSON; *250 E-4; elev. 676ft./206m.; mail Kenna z 25248; rural
Belington; Inc. Place; BARBOUR; 250 D-8; elev. 1,704ft./519m.; 🄿; z 26250; Ⓟ 1,850; © 1,788
Bellburn; RMC Place; GREENBRIER; *250 G-6; 🄿; z 25972 & mail Charmco z 25958; ● 50
Belle; Inc. Place; KANAWHA; 250 G-4; elev. 617ft./188m.; 🄿; ★ CHAS; z 25015; Ⓟ 1,421; © 1,259
Bellepoint; RMC Place; SUMMERS; *250 I-6; mail Hinton z 25951; pop. incl. with Hinton (Inc. Place)
Belleville; RMC Place; WOOD; 250 D-4; elev. 593ft./181m.; 🄿; z 26133; ● 35
Bellmeade; RMC Place; MASON; *250 E-2; mail Point Pleasant z 25550; ● 300
Bellton (Denver); RMC Place; MARSHALL; *250 B-7; mail Cameron z 26033; rural

Entries in **UPPERCASE** are counties.
Entries in **bold** have populations of 2,500 or more.
Names in parentheses are alternate names.

Inc. Place	Incorporated Place
RMC Place	Rand McNally Designated Place
CDP	Census Designated Place
MCD	Minor Civil Division
⊡	County Seat
▲	Minor Civil Division
elev.	Elevation
🄿	Post Office
🄷	Hospital
🄲	College
■	Principal Business Center
★	Ranally Metro Area (RMA) Abbreviation
z	Zip Code(s)
Ⓟ	Previous Census Population
Ⓡ	Revised Census Population
Ⓐ	Annexation Population
●	Rand McNally Population Estimate
©	Final Census Population
Ⓢ	Special Census Population
◆	Estimated Population

For additional definitions see Glossary, Volume 1, and Introduction, Volume 2.

Bellview; RMC Place; MARION; *250 B-8; ★ FAIRM; mail Fairmont z 26554; pop. incl. with Fairmont (Inc. Place)
Bellwood; RMC Place; FAYETTE; *250 H-6; elev. 2,464ft./751m.; 🅿; z 25962; ● 75
Belmont; Inc. Place; PLEASANTS; 250 C-5; elev. 619ft./189m.; 🅿; z 26134; Ⓟ 912; Ⓒ 1,036
Belo; RMC Place; MINGO; *250 H-2; mail Delbarton z 25670; rural
Belva; RMC Place; NICHOLAS, FAYETTE; 250 G-5; elev. 709ft./216m.; 🅿; z 26656; ● 200
Belvedere Heights; RMC Place; JEFFERSON; *250 C-14; mail Charles Town z 25414; pop. incl. with Charles Town (Inc. Place)
Bemis; RMC Place; RANDOLPH; 250 E-9; mail Glady z 26268; ● 30
Benbush; RMC Place; TUCKER; *250 D-9; mail Thomas z 26292; ● 40
Ben Dale; RMC Place; LEWIS; *250 D-7; mail Weston z 26452; ● 200
Benson; RMC Place; HARRISON; *250 D-7; mail Jane Lew z 26378; rural
Benson Park; KANAWHA; see Wilson (RMC Place)
Bens Run; RMC Place; TYLER; 250 C-5; elev. 622ft./190m.; 🅿; z 26146; ● 150
Benton Ferry; MARION; see Bentons Ferry (RMC Place)
Bentons Ferry (Benton Ferry); RMC Place; MARION; *250 C-8; ★ FAIRM; mail Fairmont z 26554; pop. incl. with Pleasant Valley (Inc. Place)
Bentree; RMC Place; NICHOLAS, CLAY; 250 G-5; elev. 900ft./274m.; 🅿; z 25125; ● 300
Benwood; Inc. Place; MARSHALL; 250 A-6; elev. 660ft./201m.; 🅿; ★ WHL; z 26031; Ⓟ 1,669; Ⓒ 1,585
Benwood Junction; RMC Place; MARSHALL; *250 A-6; elev. 677ft./206m.; ★ WHL; mail Benwood z 26031; pop. incl. with Benwood (Inc. Place)
Berea; RMC Place; RITCHIE; 250 D-6; elev. 760ft./232m.; 🅿; z 26327; ● 30
Bergoo; RMC Place; WEBSTER; 250 F-7; elev. 2,000ft./610m.; 🅿; z 26298; ● 160
Berkeley; RMC Place; BERKELEY; *250 B-14; mail Martinsburg z 25401; ● 200
BERKELEY; 250 B-13; Ⓟ 59,253; Ⓒ 75,905; ◆ 103,022
Berkeley Springs (Bath); Inc. Place; ⊡ MORGAN; 250 B-13; elev. 612ft./187m.; 🅿 🅷; z 25411; Ⓟ 735; Ⓒ 663
Berlin; RMC Place; LEWIS; 250 D-7; elev. 1,059ft./323m.; mail Weston z 26452; ● 125
Berryburg; RMC Place; BARBOUR; *250 D-8; elev. 1,354ft./413m.; mail Flemington z 26347; rural
Berry Siding; RMC Place; BRAXTON; *250 E-6; mail Flatwoods z 26621; rural
Berryville; RMC Place; MORGAN; *250 B-13; mail Berkeley Springs z 25411; ● 300
Bertha Hill; RMC Place; MONONGALIA; *250 B-8; ★ MORG; mail Maidsville z 26541; ● 300
Berwind; RMC Place; MCDOWELL; 250 J-4; elev. 1,481ft./451m.; 🅿; z 24815; ● 550
Beryl; RMC Place; MINERAL; *250 C-11; mail Keyser z 26726; rural
Besoco; RMC Place; RALEIGH; *250 I-5; elev. 1,815ft./553m.; mail Josephine z 25857; ● 90
Bessemer; RMC Place; BERKELEY; *250 B-13; mail Martinsburg z 25401; ● 120
Bethany; Inc. Place; BROOKE; 250 B-2; elev. 818ft./249m.; 🅿 🅲 833; ★ STU-; z 26032; Ⓟ 1,139; Ⓒ 985
Bethlehem; RMC Place; HARRISON; *250 C-7; elev. 918ft./280m.; ★ CLRKB; mail Shinnston z 26431; ● 100
Bethlehem; Inc. Place; OHIO; 250 A-6; elev. 1,243ft./379m.; 🅿; ★ WHL; z 26003; Ⓟ 2,694; Ⓒ 2,651
Betty Zane; RMC Place; OHIO; *250 C-2; ★ WHL; mail Wheeling z 26003; ● 120
Beverly; Inc. Place; RANDOLPH; 250 E-8; elev. 1,946ft./593m.; 🅿; z 26253; Ⓟ 696; Ⓒ 651
Beverly Hills; RMC Place; CABELL; *250 F-2; ★ HNTG; mail Huntington z 25705; pop. incl. with Huntington (Inc. Place)
Beverly Hills; RMC Place; MARION; *250 C-8; ★ FAIRM; mail Fairmont z 26554; pop. incl. with Fairmont (Inc. Place)
Bias; RMC Place; MINGO; *250 H-2; mail Delbarton z 25670; ● 100
Bickmore; RMC Place; CLAY; 250 F-5; elev. 947ft./289m.; 🅿; z 25019; ● 80
Big Battle; RMC Place; DODDRIDGE; *250 C-6; mail Salem z 26426; rural
Bigbend; RMC Place; CALHOUN; 250 D-5; elev. 674ft./205m.; 🅿; z 26136; ● 150
Big Chimney; RMC Place; KANAWHA; 250 F-4; elev. 700ft./213m.; 🅿; ★ CHAS; z 25302; ● 650
Big Creek; RMC Place; LOGAN; *250 H-3; elev. 635ft./194m.; 🅿; z 25505; ● 140
Big Four; RMC Place; MCDOWELL; *250 J-4; mail Kimball z 24853; ● 200
Big Isaac; RMC Place; DODDRIDGE; 250 D-7; elev. 985ft./300m.; mail Salem z 26426; ● 40
Big Moses; RMC Place; TYLER; *250 C-6; mail Alma z 26320
Big Mountain; RMC Place; KANAWHA; mail Cedar Grove z 25039; pop. incl. with Cedar Grove (Inc. Place)
Big Otter; RMC Place; CLAY; *250 F-5; elev. 862ft./263m.; 🅿; z 25113; rural
Big Run; RMC Place; MARION; *250 C-7; elev. 1,054ft./321m.; mail Mannington z 26582; rural
Big Run; RMC Place; MARSHALL; *250 A-7; elev. 1,462ft./446m.; mail Cameron z 26033; rural
Big Run; RMC Place; WEBSTER; *250 F-7; elev. 1,158ft./353m.; mail Diana z 26217; ● 35
Big Run; RMC Place; WETZEL; 250 B-7; elev. 818ft./249m.; 🅿; z 26561; ● 15
Big Sandy; RMC Place; MCDOWELL; *250 I-4; elev. 1,123ft./342m.; 🅿; z 24816; ● 300
Bigson; RMC Place; BOONE; *250 H-3; elev. 813ft./248m.; mail Van z 25206; ● 125
Big Springs; RMC Place; CALHOUN; 250 D-5; elev. 775ft./236m.; 🅿; z 26137; ● 40
Big Sycamore; RMC Place; CLAY; *250 F-5; mail Indore z 25111; rural
Billings; RMC Place; ROANE; 250 E-4; mail Reedy z 25270; ● 40
Bim; RMC Place; BOONE; 250 H-4; elev. 939ft./286m.; 🅿; z 25021; ● 400
Bingamon; RMC Place; MARION; *250 C-7; elev. 1,007ft./307m.; mail Worthington z 26591; rural
Bingamon Junction; RMC Place; MARION; ★ FAIRM; mail Worthington z 26591; rural
Bingham; RMC Place; GREENBRIER; *250 G-6; 🅿; z 25958; rural
Birch River; RMC Place; NICHOLAS; 250 F-6; elev. 1,113ft./339m.; 🅿; z 26610; ● 400
Birchton; RMC Place; RALEIGH; *250 H-4; mail Whitesville z 25209; rural
Birds Creek; RMC Place; PRESTON; *250 C-9; ★ MORG; mail Newburg z 26410; rural
Bishop; RMC Place; MCDOWELL; 250 J-4; 🅿; z 24604; ● 200
Bismarck; RMC Place; GRANT; *250 C-10; elev. 3,046ft./928m.; mail Mount Storm z 26739; ● 50
Blackberry City; RMC Place; MINGO; *250 I-2; elev. 700ft./213m.; 🅿; z 25678; ● 250
Black Betsy; RMC Place; PUTNAM; *250 F-3; ★ CHAS; mail Poca z 25159; ● 150
Black Bottom; RMC Place; LOGAN; *250 H-3; mail Logan z 25601; ● 200
Blackeagle; RMC Place; WYOMING; *250 I-4; mail Mullens z 25882; ● 100
Blackhawk; RMC Place; KANAWHA; 250 J-14; ★ CHAS; mail Charleston z 25306; pop. incl. with Charleston (Inc. Place)
Blacksville; Inc. Place; MONONGALIA; 250 B-7; elev. 1,000ft./305m.; 🅿; z 26521; Ⓟ 168; Ⓒ 175
Black Wolf; RMC Place; MCDOWELL; *250 J-4; mail Pageton z 24871; rural
Blaine; RMC Place; MINERAL; *250 C-10; mail Elk Garden z 26717; ● 30
Blair; RMC Place; JEFFERSON; *250 C-14; mail Millville z 25432; ● 75
Blair; RMC Place; LOGAN; 250 H-3; elev. 990ft./302m.; 🅿; z 25022; ● 500
Blairton; RMC Place; BERKELEY; *250 C-14; mail Martinsburg z 25401; ● 100
Blakeley; RMC Place; KANAWHA; *250 G-5; mail Pond Gap z 25160
Blandville; RMC Place; DODDRIDGE; 250 C-6; elev. 818ft./249m.; 🅿; z 26456; ● 25
Blaser; RMC Place; PRESTON; *250 C-9; mail Tunnelton z 26444; rural
Blennerhassett (Blennerhassett Heights); CDP; WOOD; 250 C-4; elev. 775ft./236m.; ★ PRKB; mail Parkersburg z 26101; Ⓟ 2,924; Ⓒ 3,225
Blennerhassett Heights; WOOD; see Blennerhassett (CDP)
Blocton; RMC Place; MINGO; *250 H-2; mail Naugatuck z 25685; ● 100
Bloomery; RMC Place; HAMPSHIRE; *250 C-12; elev. 1,010ft./308m.; 🅿; z 26817; ● 50
Bloomery; RMC Place; JEFFERSON; *250 C-14; mail Charles Town z 25414; rural
Bloomingrose; RMC Place; BOONE; 250 G-4; elev. 680ft./207m.; 🅿; z 25024; ● 400
Blount; RMC Place; KANAWHA; 250 F-4; elev. 793ft./242m.; 🅿; z 25025; ● 260
Blue; RMC Place; TYLER; *250 C-6; elev. 707ft./215m.; mail Middlebourne z 26149; rural
Blue Creek; RMC Place; KANAWHA; *250 F-4; elev. 616ft./188m.; 🅿; z 25026; ● 600
Bluefield; Inc. Place; MERCER; 250 J-5; elev. 2,611ft./796m.; 🅿 🅷 🅲 1,788 ■; z 24701; Ⓟ 12,756; Ⓒ 11,451; ◆ 10,545
Blue Jay; RMC Place; RALEIGH; *250 H-5; elev. 2,360ft./719m.; 🅿; ★ BECK; z 25813
Blue Ridge Acres; RMC Place; JEFFERSON; *250 C-14; mail Harpers Ferry z 25425; ● 1,200
Blue Rock; RMC Place; RANDOLPH; *250 E-8; mail Mill Creek z 26280; rural
Bluestone; RMC Place; MERCER; *250 J-5; mail Bluefield z 24701; rural
Blue Sulphur; RMC Place; CABELL; *250 F-2; ★ HNTG; mail Ona z 25545; rural
Blue Sulphur Springs; RMC Place; GREENBRIER; *250 H-6; elev. 1,648ft./502m.; mail Alderson z 24910; rural
Blueville; RMC Place; TAYLOR; *250 C-8; elev. 1,185ft./361m.; mail Grafton z 26354; pop. incl. with Grafton (Inc. Place)
Bluewell; RMC Place; MERCER; *250 J-5; elev. 2,600ft./792m.; 🅿; z 24701; ● 2,000
Blundon; RMC Place; KANAWHA; *250 F-4; elev. 730ft./223m.; ★ CHAS; mail Elkview z 25071; rural
Boaz; CDP; WOOD; 250 C-4; ★ PRKB; mail Williamstown z 26187; Ⓟ 1,137; Ⓒ 1,345
Bob White; RMC Place; BOONE; 250 H-3; elev. 846ft./258m.; 🅿; z 25028; ● 400
Boggs; RMC Place; WEBSTER; *250 F-6; elev. 1,578ft./481m.; 🅿; z 26206
Bolair; RMC Place; WEBSTER; 250 F-7; elev. 2,271ft./692m.; mail Webster Springs z 26288; ● 150
Bolivar; Inc. Place; JEFFERSON; 250 C-14; elev. 400ft./122m.; mail Harpers Ferry z 25425; Ⓟ 1,013; Ⓒ 1,045
Bolt; RMC Place; RALEIGH; 250 H-4; elev. 1,982ft./604m.; 🅿; ★ BECK; z 25817; ● 400
Bomont; RMC Place; CLAY; 250 F-5; elev. 834ft./254m.; 🅿; z 25030; ● 90
Bonnie; RMC Place; BRAXTON; *250 E-6; elev. 947ft./289m.; mail Exchange z 26619; rural
Bonnivale; RMC Place; WOOD; 250 D-4; elev. 633ft./193m.; ★ PRKB; mail Mineral Wells z 26150; ● 150
Booher; RMC Place; TYLER; *250 C-6; mail Alma z 26320; rural
Boomer; RMC Place; FAYETTE; 250 G-5; elev. 642ft./196m.; 🅿; z 25031; ● 600
BOONE; 250 H-4; Ⓟ 25,870; Ⓒ 25,535; ◆ 24,998
Boonesborough; RMC Place; FAYETTE; *250 G-5; mail Deep Water z 25057; ● 25
Booth; RMC Place; MONONGALIA; 250 B-8; elev. 1,100ft./335m.; 🅿; ★ MORG; z 26505; ● 220
Boothsville; RMC Place; MARION; *250 C-8; ★ FAIRM; mail Fairmont z 26554; ● 150
Borderland; RMC Place; MINGO; 250 H-2; elev. 649ft./198m.; 🅿; z 25665; ● 300
Borgman; RMC Place; PRESTON; 250 C-9; mail Tunnelton z 26444; ● 40
Bottom Creek; RMC Place; MCDOWELL; *250 J-4; mail Kimball z 24853; ● 50
Boulder (Rangoon); RMC Place; BARBOUR; *250 D-8; elev. 1,375ft./419m.; mail Buckhannon z 26201; ● 50
Bowan Ridge; RMC Place; CABELL; ★ HNTG; mail Huntington z 25701; ● 400
Bowden; RMC Place; RANDOLPH; 250 E-9; elev. 2,218ft./676m.; 🅿; z 26254; ● 60
Bowlby; RMC Place; MONONGALIA; *250 B-8; elev. 1,007ft./307m.; ★ MORG; mail Maidsville z 26541; ● 80
Bowles; RMC Place; LINCOLN; *250 F-3; elev. 630ft./192m.; mail Hamlin z 25523; rural
Boyer; RMC Place; POCAHONTAS; *250 F-9; mail Arbovale z 24915; ● 45
Bozoo; RMC Place; MONROE; 250 I-6; elev. 2,214ft./675m.; 🅿; z 24963; ● 40
Braden (Lima); RMC Place; TYLER; 250 C-6; elev. 763ft./233m.; mail Jacksonburg z 26377; ● 60
Bradley; RMC Place; BOONE; *250 G-3; mail Costa z 25051
Bradley; CDP; RALEIGH; 250 H-5; elev. 2,200ft./671m.; 🅿 🅲 320; ★ BECK; z 25818; Ⓟ 2,144; Ⓒ 2,371
Bradshaw; RMC Place; LOGAN; *250 H-3; mail Whitman z 25652; ● 200
Bradshaw; Inc. Place; MCDOWELL; 250 J-3; elev. 1,188ft./362m.; 🅿; z 24817; Ⓟ 394; Ⓒ 289
Bragg; RMC Place; RALEIGH; 250 H-5; elev. 2,778ft./847m.; mail Shady Spring z 25918
Bramwell; Inc. Place; MERCER; 250 J-5; elev. 2,253ft./687m.; 🅿; z 24715; Ⓟ 620; Ⓒ 426
Branchland; RMC Place; LINCOLN; 250 G-2; elev. 592ft./180m.; 🅿; z 25506; ● 400
Brandonville; Inc. Place; PRESTON; 250 B-9; elev. 1,801ft./549m.; 🅿; z 26525; Ⓟ 73; Ⓒ 102
Brandywine; RMC Place; PENDLETON; 250 E-10; elev. 1,587ft./484m.; 🅿; z 26802; ● 200
Braxton; RMC Place; BRAXTON; *250 E-6; elev. 982ft./299m.; mail Exchange z 26619; rural
BRAXTON; 250 E-6; Ⓟ 12,998; Ⓒ 14,702; ◆ 14,617
Bream; RMC Place; KANAWHA; *250 F-4; ★ CHAS; mail Elkview z 25071; ● 30
Breeden; RMC Place; MINGO; 250 H-2; elev. 817ft./249m.; 🅿; z 25666; ● 150
Brenton; RMC Place; WYOMING; 250 I-4; elev. 1,174ft./358m.; 🅿; z 24818 & mail Fanrock z 24834; ● 700
Bretz; RMC Place; PRESTON; *250 B-9; elev. 1,800ft./549m.; 🅿; ★ MORG; z 26524; ● 300
Bretz; RMC Place; TUCKER; *250 D-9; mail Parsons z 26287; ● 100
Brick Church; RMC Place; WAYNE; *250 G-1; elev. 573ft./175m.; mail Fort Gay z 25514
Bridgeport; Inc. Place; HARRISON; 250 C-7; elev. 987ft./301m.; 🅿; ★ CLRKB; z 26330; Ⓟ 6,695; Ⓒ 7,306
Bridgeway; RMC Place; TYLER; *250 C-6; mail Middlebourne z 26149; ● 70
Brierwood; RMC Place; WOOD; *250 C-4; ★ PRKB; mail Parkersburg z 26101; ● 250
Brink; RMC Place; WETZEL; *250 B-7; mail Mannington z 26582; rural
Bristol; RMC Place; HARRISON; *250 C-7; elev. 1,040ft./317m.; 🅿; z 26426; ● 80
Broaddus; RMC Place; BARBOUR; *250 D-8; elev. 1,580ft./482m.; mail Philippi z 26416; pop. incl. with Philippi (Inc. Place)
Broad Oaks; RMC Place; HARRISON; *250 C-7; ★ CLRKB; mail Clarksburg z 26301; pop. incl. with Clarksburg (Inc. Place)
Brohard; RMC Place; WIRT, RITCHIE; 250 D-5; elev. 941ft./287m.; 🅿; z 26138; ● 50
BROOKE; 250 B-2; Ⓟ 26,992; Ⓒ 25,447; ◆ 22,952
Brookhaven; CDP; MONONGALIA; *250 B-8; ★ MORG; mail Morgantown z 26508; Ⓟ 3,836; Ⓒ 4,734
Brooklyn; RMC Place; FAYETTE; *250 H-5; mail Fayetteville z 25840; ● 85
Brooklyn (Brooklyn Junction); RMC Place; WETZEL; *250 B-6; mail New Martinsville z 26155; pop. incl. with New Martinsville (Inc. Place)
Brooklyn Junction; WETZEL; see Brooklyn (RMC Place)
Brooks; RMC Place; SUMMERS; *250 H-6; elev. 1,342ft./409m.; 🅿; z 25951
Brookside; RMC Place; PRESTON; *250 C-9; elev. 2,507ft./764m.; mail Aurora z 26705
Brounland; RMC Place; KANAWHA; *250 G-3; elev. 629ft./192m.; ★ CHAS; mail Charleston z 25314; rural
Brown; RMC Place; HARRISON; *250 C-7; mail Wallace z 26448; ● 50
Brownlow; RMC Place; TAYLOR; *250 C-8; mail Grafton z 26354; pop. incl. with Grafton (Inc. Place)
Brownsburg; RMC Place; POCAHONTAS; *250 G-8; mail Marlinton z 24954; rural
Browns Mills; RMC Place; PRESTON; *250 C-9; ★ MORG; mail Reedsville z 26547; rural
Brownsville; RMC Place; FAYETTE; *250 G-5; 🅿; z 25085; ● 60
Brownton; RMC Place; BARBOUR; 250 C-8; elev. 1,123ft./342m.; 🅿; z 26347; ● 350
Bruceton Mills; Inc. Place; PRESTON; 250 B-9; elev. 1,527ft./465m.; 🅿; z 26525; Ⓟ 132; Ⓒ 74
Bruno; RMC Place; LOGAN; *250 I-3; elev. 758ft./231m.; 🅿; z 25611; ● 500
Brush Creek; BOONE; see Ridgeview (RMC Place)
Brush Fork; RMC Place; MERCER; *250 J-5; mail Bluefield z 24701; ● 600
Brushton (Costa); RMC Place; BOONE; *250 G-4; elev. 661ft./201m.; mail Costa z 25051; ● 225
Brushy Run; RMC Place; PENDLETON; *250 E-10; elev. 1,263ft./385m.; mail Upper Tract z 26866; rural
Brydon; RMC Place; TAYLOR; *250 C-8; elev. 1,092ft./333m.; mail Simpson z 26435; rural
Bryson; RMC Place; RALEIGH; ★ BECK; mail Lester z 25865; rural
Bubbling Spring; RMC Place; HAMPSHIRE; *250 C-12; mail Yellow Spring z 26865
Buck; RMC Place; SUMMERS; *250 I-6; elev. 1,634ft./498m.; mail Hinton z 25951; rural
Buckeye; RMC Place; POCAHONTAS; 250 G-8; elev. 2,106ft./642m.; 🅿 🅷; z 24924; ● 200
Buckhannon; Inc. Place; ⊡ UPSHUR; 250 D-7; elev. 1,433ft./437m.; 🅿 🅷 🅲 1,224; z 26201; Ⓟ 5,909; Ⓒ 5,725
Bud; RMC Place; WYOMING; 250 I-4; elev. 1,594ft./486m.; 🅿; z 24716; ● 500
Buffalo; Inc. Place; PUTNAM; 250 E-3; elev. 580ft./177m.; 🅿; ★ CHAS; z 25033; Ⓟ 969; Ⓒ 1,171
Buffalo Creek; RMC Place; WAYNE; 250 H-12; elev. 564ft./172m.; ★ HNTG; mail Huntington z 25704, Kenova z 25530; ● 900
Buff Lick; RMC Place; KANAWHA; mail Cedar Grove z 25039; rural
Bula; RMC Place; MONONGALIA; *250 B-7; elev. 977ft./298m.; mail Wana z 26590; ● 30
Bulger; RMC Place; LINCOLN; *250 G-3; elev. 811ft./247m.; mail Alkol z 25501
Bull Run; RMC Place; PRESTON; *250 B-9; elev. 1,331ft./406m.; mail Reedsville z 26547
Bulltown; RMC Place; BRAXTON; *250 E-7; mail Napier z 26631; rural
Bunker Hill; RMC Place; BERKELEY; 250 C-13; elev. 550ft./168m.; 🅿; z 25413; ● 700
Bunker Hill; RMC Place; KANAWHA; *250 F-3; ★ CHAS; mail Charleston z 25309; pop. incl. with South Charleston (Inc. Place)
Bunners Ridge; RMC Place; MARION; *250 C-8; ★ FAIRM; mail Fairmont z 26554; ● 200
Burchfield; RMC Place; WETZEL; *250 B-7; elev. 870ft./265m.; mail Burton z 26562; rural
Burlington; RMC Place; MINERAL; 250 C-11; elev. 740ft./226m.; 🅿; z 26710; ● 120
Burning Springs; RMC Place; WIRT; *250 D-5; elev. 635ft./194m.; mail Creston z 26141; rural
Burnsville; Inc. Place; BRAXTON; 250 E-6; elev. 763ft./233m.; 🅿; z 26335; Ⓟ 495; Ⓒ 481
Burnsville Junction; RMC Place; BRAXTON; pop. incl. with Burnsville (Inc. Place)
Burnt House; RMC Place; RITCHIE; 250 D-5; elev. 799ft./244m.; 🅿; z 26178; ● 60
Burnwell; RMC Place; KANAWHA; *250 G-4; elev. 895ft./273m.; 🅿; z 25083; ● 150
Burton; RMC Place; WETZEL; 250 B-7; elev. 1,067ft./325m.; 🅿; z 26562; ● 100
Butchersville; RMC Place; LEWIS; *250 D-7; mail Weston z 26452; ● 75

C

Cabell; RMC Place; RALEIGH; *250 H-5; ★ BECK; mail Mabscott z 25871; ● 250
CABELL; 250 F-2; Ⓟ 96,827; Ⓒ 96,784; ◆ 94,544
Cabin Creek (Cabin Creek Junction); RMC Place; KANAWHA; *250 G-4; elev. 607ft./185m.; 🅿; z 25035; ● 800
Cabin Creek Junction; KANAWHA; see Cabin Creek (RMC Place)
Cabins; RMC Place; GRANT; 250 D-10; elev. 1,051ft./320m.; 🅿; z 26855; ● 225
Cabot; RMC Place; BOONE; *250 G-4; mail Seth z 25181; rural
Cabot Station; RMC Place; CALHOUN; *250 D-5; elev. 680ft./207m.; mail Grantsville z 26147; rural
Cairo; Inc. Place; RITCHIE; 250 C-5; elev. 678ft./207m.; 🅿; z 26337; Ⓟ 290; Ⓒ 263
Caldwell; RMC Place; GREENBRIER; 250 H-7; elev. 1,693ft./516m.; 🅿; z 24925; ● 400
Calhoun; RMC Place; BARBOUR; *250 D-8; elev. 1,924ft./586m.; mail Belington z 26250; rural
CALHOUN; 250 E-5; Ⓟ 7,885; Ⓒ 7,582; ◆ 7,044
Calis; RMC Place; MARSHALL; *250 A-7; ★ WHL; mail Cameron z 26033
Calvert; RMC Place; KANAWHA; ★ CHAS; mail Saint Albans z 25177; pop. incl. with Saint Albans (Inc. Place)
Calvin; RMC Place; NICHOLAS; 250 F-6; elev. 2,229ft./679m.; 🅿; z 26660; ● 40
Cambria; RMC Place; HARRISON; *250 C-7; ★ CLRKB; mail Lumberport z 26386; rural
Cambria; RMC Place; NICHOLAS; *250 G-5; mail Lizemores z 25125; ● 100
Camden; RMC Place; LEWIS; 250 D-7; elev. 1,096ft./334m.; 🅿; z 26338; ● 80
Camden on Gauley; Inc. Place; WEBSTER; 250 F-6; elev. 2,029ft./618m.; 🅿; z 26208; Ⓟ 171; Ⓒ 157
Cameo; RMC Place; BOONE; *250 G-3; elev. 892ft./272m.; mail Spurlockville z 25565; rural
Cameron; Inc. Place; MARSHALL; 250 A-7; elev. 1,060ft./323m.; 🅿; z 26033; Ⓟ 1,177; Ⓒ 1,212
Campbelltown; RMC Place; POCAHONTAS; 250 G-8; mail Marlinton z 24954; pop. incl. with Marlinton (Inc. Place)
Camp Creek; RMC Place; MERCER; 250 I-5; elev. 2,040ft./622m.; 🅿; z 25820; ● 60
Camp Ground; RMC Place; PRESTON; *250 C-9; mail Tunnelton z 26444; ● 50
Campus; RMC Place; WYOMING; *250 H-3; elev. 1,073ft./327m.; mail Cyclone z 24827
Canaan; RMC Place; UPSHUR; *250 E-7; mail Rock Cave z 26234; rural
Canaan Heights; RMC Place; TUCKER; *250 D-10; elev. 3,700ft./1,128m.; mail Davis z 26260; ● 30
Canaan Valley; RMC Place; TUCKER; *250 D-10; 🅿; z 26260; ● 100
Canebrake; RMC Place; MCDOWELL; *250 J-4; elev. 1,545ft./471m.; 🅿; z 24815; ● 125
Canfield; RMC Place; BRAXTON; *250 F-6; mail Sutton z 26601; rural
Canfield; RMC Place; RANDOLPH; *250 D-9; elev. 2,094ft./638m.; mail Elkins z 26241; ● 45
Cannelton; RMC Place; FAYETTE; *250 G-5; elev. 686ft./209m.; 🅿; z 25036; ● 400
Canterbury; RMC Place; MINGO; *250 H-2; mail Lenore z 25676; rural
Canton; RMC Place; DODDRIDGE; *250 C-6; mail West Union z 26456; rural
Cantwell; RMC Place; RITCHIE; *250 D-5; elev. 1,103ft./336m.; mail Harrisville z 26362; rural
Canvas; RMC Place; NICHOLAS; *250 G-6; elev. 2,137ft./651m.; 🅿; z 26662; ● 50
Canyon; RMC Place; MONONGALIA; *250 B-8; ★ MORG; mail Morgantown z 26508; ● 200
Capehart; RMC Place; MASON; *250 E-3; mail Leon z 25123; rural
Capels (Caples); RMC Place; MCDOWELL; *250 I-4; elev. 1,276ft./389m.; 🅿; z 24801; ● 150
Capitol; RMC Place; KANAWHA; ★ CHAS; mail Charleston z 25311, z 25361; pop. incl. with Charleston (Inc. Place)
Caples; MCDOWELL; see Capels (RMC Place)
Capon Bridge; Inc. Place; HAMPSHIRE; 250 C-12; elev. 819ft./250m.; 🅿; z 26711; Ⓟ 192; Ⓒ 200
Capon Springs; RMC Place; HAMPSHIRE; 250 D-12; elev. 1,136ft./346m.; 🅿; z 26823; ● 165
Carbon; RMC Place; KANAWHA; *250 G-4; elev. 1,200ft./366m.; 🅿; z 25075; rural
Carbondale; RMC Place; FAYETTE; *250 G-5; elev. 650ft./198m.; mail Cannelton z 25036; pop. incl. with Smithers (Inc. Place)
Caretta (Juno); RMC Place; MCDOWELL; 250 J-4; elev. 1,510ft./460m.; 🅿; z 24892; ● 600
Carl; RMC Place; NICHOLAS; *250 G-6; mail Leivasy z 26676
Carlisle; RMC Place; FAYETTE; *250 H-5; ★ BECK; mail Scarbro z 25917; ● 250
Carlos; RMC Place; MCDOWELL; *250 J-3; mail Iaeger z 24844; ● 75
Carolina; RMC Place; MARION; *250 C-7; elev. 1,200ft./366m.; 🅿; ★ FAIRM; z 26563; ● 650
Carpendale; MINERAL; see Maryland Junction (Inc. Place)
Carrollton; RMC Place; BARBOUR; *250 D-8; elev. 1,360ft./415m.; mail Volga z 26238; rural
Carswell; RMC Place; MCDOWELL; 250 I-4; mail Kimball z 24853; ● 450
Carter; RMC Place; UPSHUR; *250 E-7; elev. 1,866ft./569m.; mail French Creek z 26218; rural
Cascade; RMC Place; PRESTON; *250 B-9; elev. 1,700ft./518m.; 🅿; ★ MORG; z 26542 & mail Reedsville z 26547
Cashmere; RMC Place; MONROE; *250 I-6; elev. 1,974ft./602m.; mail Ballard z 24918
Cass; RMC Place; POCAHONTAS; 250 F-8; elev. 2,452ft./747m.; 🅿; z 24927; ● 150
Cassity; RMC Place; RANDOLPH; 250 E-8; mail Mabie z 26278; ● 75
Cassville; CDP; MONONGALIA; *250 B-8; 🅿; ★ MORG; z 26527 & mail Pursglove z 26546; Ⓟ 1,458; Ⓒ 1,586
Catawba; RMC Place; MARION; *250 B-8; elev. 900ft./274m.; ★ FAIRM; mail Fairmont z 26554; ● 150
Cave; RMC Place; PENDLETON; *250 F-10; elev. 2,087ft./636m.; mail Franklin z 26807; rural
Cazy; RMC Place; BOONE; *250 H-4; mail Bob White z 25028; ● 150
Cedar Grove; Inc. Place; KANAWHA; 250 G-4; elev. 618ft./188m.; 🅿; z 25039; Ⓟ 1,213; Ⓒ 862
Cedar Grove; RMC Place; WOOD; 250 C-4; ★ PRKB; mail Parkersburg z 26101; ● 350
Cedarville; RMC Place; GILMER; 250 E-6; elev. 790ft./241m.; 🅿; z 26611; ● 100
Center Hill; RMC Place; WIRT; *250 D-4; mail Elizabeth z 26143; rural
Center Point; RMC Place; DODDRIDGE; 250 C-6; elev. 790ft./241m.; 🅿; z 26339; ● 50
Centerville (Alma); RMC Place; TYLER; 250 C-6; elev. 718ft./219m.; mail Alma z 26320; ● 130
Centerville; RMC Place; WAYNE; *250 G-1; mail Prichard z 25555
Central; RMC Place; WOOD; *250 C-4; ★ PRKB; mail Parkersburg z 26101; ● 250
Centralia; RMC Place; BRAXTON; *250 E-7; elev. 1,012ft./308m.; 🅿; z 26601; ● 85
Central Station; RMC Place; DODDRIDGE; 250 C-6; elev. 816ft./249m.; mail West Union z 26456; ● 60
Century; RMC Place; BARBOUR; 250 D-8; elev. 1,500ft./457m.; 🅿; z 26201; ● 120
Century Number 2; RMC Place; BARBOUR; *250 D-8; mail Volga z 26238; ● 40
Ceredo; Inc. Place; WAYNE; 250 G-12; elev. 552ft./168m.; 🅿; ★ HNTG; z 25507; Ⓟ 1,916; Ⓒ 1,675
Ceres; RMC Place; MERCER; *250 J-5; mail Bluefield z 24701; ● 300
Chambers; RMC Place; LOGAN; *250 H-3; mail Yolyn z 25654; rural
Chapel; RMC Place; BRAXTON; *250 E-6; elev. 916ft./279m.; 🅿; z 26624; rural
Chapman; RMC Place; BRAXTON, LEWIS; *250 E-7; mail Orlando z 26412; rural
Chapman; RMC Place; WEBSTER; *250 F-7; mail Webster Springs z 26288
Chapmanville; Inc. Place; LOGAN; 250 H-3; elev. 650ft./198m.; 🅿; z 25508; Ⓟ 1,110; Ⓒ 1,211
Charleston; Inc. Place; STATE CAPITAL; ⊡ KANAWHA; 250 F-4; elev. 620ft./189m.; 🅿 🅷 🅲 1,164 ■; ★ CHAS; z 25301-06, z 25309, z 25311-15, z 25317, z 25320-39, z 25350, z 25356-58, z 25360-62, z 25364-65, z 25375, z 25387, z 25389, z 25392, z 25396; Ⓟ 57,287; Ⓒ 53,421; ◆ 47,848
Charles Town; Inc. Place; ⊡ JEFFERSON; 250 C-14; elev. 517ft./158m.; 🅿 🅲 16,571; z 25414; Ⓟ 3,122; Ⓒ 2,907
Charlton Heights; RMC Place; FAYETTE; *250 G-5; elev. 665ft./203m.; 🅿; z 25040; ● 600
Charmco; RMC Place; GREENBRIER; 250 H-6; elev. 2,400ft./732m.; 🅿; z 25958; ● 150
Chatham Hill; RMC Place; MARION; *250 B-7; ★ FAIRM; mail Farmington z 26571; ● 200
Chattaroy; CDP; MINGO; 250 I-2; elev. 705ft./215m.; 🅿; z 25667; Ⓟ 1,182; Ⓒ 1,136
Chauncey; RMC Place; LOGAN; *250 H-3; elev. 800ft./244m.; 🅿; z 25612; ● 200
Cheat Lake; CDP-Census Area Only; MONONGALIA; *250 B-8; ★ MORG; mail Morgantown z 26507-08; Ⓟ 3,992; Ⓒ 6,396
Cheat Neck; RMC Place; MONONGALIA; 250 B-8; ★ MORG; mail Morgantown z 26508; ● 500
Chelyan; RMC Place; KANAWHA; *250 G-4; elev. 619ft./189m.; mail Cabin Creek z 25035; ● 950
Cherokee; RMC Place; MCDOWELL; *250 J-4; mail Rock z 24747; rural
Cherry Falls; RMC Place; WEBSTER; 250 F-7; mail Webster Springs z 26288; ● 200
Cherry Grove; RMC Place; PENDLETON; 250 E-9; elev. 2,207ft./673m.; mail Circleville z 26804; ● 40
Cherry Run; RMC Place; MORGAN; 250 B-13; elev. 460ft./140m.; 🅿; z 25427; ● 25
Chesapeake; Inc. Place; KANAWHA; 250 G-4; elev. 600ft./183m.; 🅿; ★ CHAS; z 25315; Ⓟ 1,896; Ⓒ 1,643
Chesapeake; RMC Place; MARION; *250 B-8; ★ FAIRM; mail Fairmont z 26554; ● 150
Chester; Inc. Place; HANCOCK; 250 A-2; elev. 703ft./214m.; 🅿; z 26034; Ⓟ 2,905; Ⓒ 2,592
Chesterville; RMC Place; WOOD; *250 D-4; elev. 643ft./196m.; ★ PRKB; mail Mineral Wells z 26150; rural
Chestnut Heights; BROOKE; see Rabbit Hill (RMC Place)
Chestnut Hill; RMC Place; HANCOCK; *250 B-2; ★ STU-; mail Weirton z 26062; pop. incl. with Weirton (Inc. Place)
Chestnut Ridge; RMC Place; MONONGALIA; 250 A-4; ★ MORG; mail Morgantown z 26505; ● 800
Chiefton; RMC Place; HARRISON; *250 C-7; ★ CLRKB; mail Clarksburg z 26301; ● 120
Childs; RMC Place; WETZEL; *250 B-6; mail New Martinsville z 26155; rural
Chimney Corner; RMC Place; FAYETTE; *250 G-5; mail Gauley Bridge z 25085; rural
Chloe; RMC Place; CALHOUN; 250 E-5; elev. 793ft./242m.; 🅿; z 25235; ● 75
Christian; RMC Place; LOGAN; 250 I-3; elev. 758ft./231m.; mail Verner z 25650; ● 100
Christy Heights; RMC Place; PUTNAM; *250 F-3; ★ CHAS; mail Hurricane z 25526; ● 75
Churchville; RMC Place; LEWIS; 250 D-6; elev. 934ft./285m.; mail Camden z 26338; ● 40
Cicerone; RMC Place; ROANE; *250 E-4; mail Gandeeville z 25243
Cinco; RMC Place; KANAWHA; *250 F-4; mail Tad z 25201; ● 125
Cinderella; RMC Place; MINGO; *250 I-2; mail Williamson z 25661; ● 75
Circle View; RMC Place; RALEIGH; *250 H-5; ★ BECK; mail Beckley z 25801; ● 125
Circleville; RMC Place; PENDLETON; 250 E-9; elev. 2,047ft./624m.; 🅿; z 26804; ● 125
Cirtsville; RMC Place; RALEIGH; *250 H-5; elev. 1,662ft./507m.; ★ BECK; mail Beckley z 25801; rural
Cisco; RMC Place; RITCHIE; *250 D-5; elev. 646ft./197m.; mail Big Springs z 26137; rural
Claren; MCDOWELL; see Hensley (RMC Place)
Clarence; RMC Place; ROANE; *250 E-4; elev. 850ft./259m.; mail Gay z 25244; rural
Clarksburg; Inc. Place; ⊡ HARRISON; 250 C-7; elev. 1,011ft./308m.; 🅿 🅷 ■; ★ CLRKB; z 26301-02, z 26306, z 26461; Ⓟ 18,059; Ⓒ 16,743; ◆ 15,753
Clay; Inc. Place; ⊡ CLAY; 250 F-5; elev. 708ft./216m.; 🅿; z 25043; Ⓟ 592; Ⓒ 593
CLAY; 250 F-5; Ⓟ 9,983; Ⓒ 10,330; ◆ 10,106
Clay Junction; RMC Place; CLAY; *250 F-5; mail Clay z 25043; pop. incl. with Clay (Inc. Place)
Claypool; RMC Place; LOGAN; *250 H-3; mail Davin z 25617; ● 175
Claypool; RMC Place; SUMMERS; *250 H-6; mail Meadow Bridge z 25976; rural
Claysville; RMC Place; MINERAL; *250 C-11; elev. 1,083ft./330m.; mail New Creek z 26743; ● 80
Clayton; RMC Place; SUMMERS; *250 I-6; elev. 2,035ft./620m.; mail Alderson z 24910; rural
Clear Creek; RMC Place; RALEIGH; 250 H-4; elev. 1,464ft./446m.; 🅿; z 25044; ● 350
Clear Fork; RMC Place; WYOMING; 250 I-4; elev. 1,192ft./363m.; 🅿; z 24822; ● 150
Clearview; Inc. Place; OHIO; 250 C-2; elev. 1,109ft./338m.; ★ WHL; mail Wheeling z 26003; Ⓟ 622; Ⓒ 590
Clem; RMC Place; BRAXTON; *250 E-6; elev. 979ft./298m.; 🅿; z 26623; rural
Clemtown; RMC Place; BARBOUR; *250 C-8; mail Moatsville z 26405; rural
Clendenenville; RMC Place; GREENBRIER; *250 H-7; mail Maxwelton z 24957; rural
Clendenin; Inc. Place; KANAWHA; 250 F-4; elev. 629ft./192m.; 🅿; z 25045; Ⓟ 1,203; Ⓒ 1,116
Cleveland; RMC Place; WEBSTER; 250 E-7; elev. 1,284ft./391m.; 🅿; z 26215; ● 50
Clifftop; RMC Place; FAYETTE; 250 H-6; elev. 2,291ft./698m.; 🅿; z 25831; ● 60
Clifton; RMC Place; MASON; *250 D-3; elev. 567ft./173m.; 🅿; z 25260; ● 350
Clifton Mills; RMC Place; PRESTON; 250 B-9; elev. 1,563ft./476m.; mail Bruceton Mills z 26525; ● 30
Clinton; RMC Place; BOONE; *250 H-4; elev. 1,044ft./318m.; mail Wharton z 25208; ● 400
Clinton; RMC Place; OHIO; *250 C-2; elev. 965ft./294m.; ★ WHL; mail Triadelphia z 26059; ● 200
Clintonville; RMC Place; GREENBRIER; *250 H-6; elev. 2,648ft./807m.; 🅿; z 24931; ● 50
Clio; RMC Place; ROANE; *250 F-5; elev. 726ft./221m.; 🅿; z 25045
Clothier; RMC Place; BOONE, LOGAN; 250 H-3; elev. 806ft./246m.; 🅿; z 25047; ● 270
Clouston; RMC Place; MARSHALL; *250 A-7; mail Cameron z 26033
Clover; RMC Place; CABELL; *250 F-2; mail Glenwood z 25520; rural
Clover; RMC Place; ROANE; *250 E-5; mail Spencer z 25276
Cloverdale; RMC Place; MONROE; *250 I-6; mail Peterstown z 24963; ● 100
Clover Lick; RMC Place; POCAHONTAS; *250 F-8; elev. 2,293ft./699m.; mail Cass z 24927; rural
Coalbottom; BOONE; see Powell Creek (RMC Place)
Coalburg; RMC Place; KANAWHA; *250 G-4; mail Cabin Creek z 25035; ● 80
Coal City; CDP; RALEIGH; *250 I-5; elev. 2,599ft./792m.; 🅿; ★ BECK; z 25823; Ⓟ 1,876; Ⓒ 1,905
Coaldale; RMC Place; MERCER; *250 J-4; elev. 2,497ft./761m.; 🅿; z 24724; ● 125
Coal Fork; CDP; KANAWHA; *250 F-4; elev. 624ft./190m.; ★ CHAS; mail Charleston z 25306; Ⓟ 2,100; Ⓒ 1,350
Coal Mountain; RMC Place; WYOMING; *250 I-3; elev. 1,320ft./402m.; 🅿; z 24823; ● 200
Coalton (Womelsdorf); Inc. Place; RANDOLPH; 250 E-8; elev. 2,157ft./657m.; 🅿; z 26257; Ⓟ 277; Ⓒ 247
Coal Valley; RMC Place; LOGAN; *250 H-3; elev. 811ft./247m.; mail Clothier z 25047; ● 40
Coalwood; RMC Place; MCDOWELL; 250 J-4; elev. 1,520ft./463m.; 🅿; z 24801; ● 700
Coburn; RMC Place; WETZEL; *250 B-7; 🅿; z 26562; rural
Coco; RMC Place; KANAWHA; 250 F-4; elev. 652ft./199m.; mail Elkview z 25071; ● 50
Coger; BRAXTON; see Gem (RMC Place)
Coketon; RMC Place; TUCKER; *250 D-9; mail Thomas z 26292; ● 60
Colcord; RMC Place; RALEIGH; *250 H-4; elev. 1,079ft./329m.; 🅿; z 25048; ● 300
Cold Stream; RMC Place; HAMPSHIRE; *250 C-12; mail Capon Bridge z 26711; rural
Coldwater; RMC Place; DODDRIDGE; *250 D-6; mail New Milton z 26411; rural
Colebank; RMC Place; BARBOUR, PRESTON; *250 C-8; mail Moatsville z 26405; rural
Coleman; RMC Place; WAYNE; *250 G-1; mail Genoa z 25517, Wayne z 25570
Colfax; RMC Place; MARION; *250 C-8; elev. 893ft./272m.; 🅿; ★ FAIRM; z 26566; ● 175
Colliers; RMC Place; BROOKE; 250 B-2; elev. 796ft./243m.; 🅿; ★ STU-; z 26035; ● 600
Collinsdale; RMC Place; FAYETTE; *250 G-4; mail Gallagher z 25083; rural
Colonel; MINGO; see Thacker Mines (RMC Place)
Columbia; RMC Place; FAYETTE; *250 G-5; elev. 725ft./221m.; mail Kimberly z 25118; ● 70
Combs Addition; RMC Place; LOGAN; *250 H-3; elev. 868ft./265m.; mail Davin z 25617; ● 120
Comfort (Joe Creek); RMC Place; BOONE; *250 G-4; elev. 693ft./211m.; 🅿; z 25049; ● 300
Conaway; RMC Place; TYLER; *250 B-6; elev. 841ft./256m.; mail Middlebourne z 26149; rural
Concord; RMC Place; PRESTON; *250 C-9; elev. 1,711ft./522m.; mail Newburg z 26410; rural
Condit; RMC Place; MARION; *250 B-7; ★ FAIRM; mail Metz z 26585; rural
Confidence; RMC Place; PUTNAM; *250 F-3; ★ CHAS; mail Red House z 25168
Conings; RMC Place; GILMER; *250 D-6; elev. 896ft./273m.; mail Troy z 26443; rural
Consol Number 9; RMC Place; MARION; *250 B-7; ★ FAIRM; mail Farmington z 26571; ● 200
Cool Ridge; RMC Place; RALEIGH; 250 I-5; elev. 2,934ft./894m.; 🅿; ★ BECK; z 25825; ● 300
Coopertown; RMC Place; BOONE; *250 G-4; mail Orgas z 25148; rural
Copen; RMC Place; BRAXTON; 250 E-6; elev. 847ft./258m.; 🅿; z 26615; ● 45
Copley; RMC Place; LEWIS; *250 D-6; elev. 792ft./241m.; mail Weston z 26452; ● 90
Cora; RMC Place; LOGAN; *250 H-3; elev. 686ft./209m.; 🅿; z 25614; ● 400
Cordova; RMC Place; GREENBRIER; *250 G-7; elev. 2,448ft./746m.; mail Renick z 24966; rural
Core; RMC Place; MONONGALIA; 250 B-8; elev. 987ft./301m.; 🅿; ★ MORG; z 26541; ● 200
Corinne; RMC Place; WYOMING; 250 I-4; elev. 1,465ft./447m.; 🅿; z 25826; ● 350
Corinth; RMC Place; PRESTON; 250 C-9; elev. 2,484ft./757m.; 🅿; z 26764; ● 150
Corley; RMC Place; BARBOUR; *250 D-8; mail Belington z 26250; rural
Corley; RMC Place; BRAXTON; *250 E-6; elev. 850ft./259m.; 🅿; z 26621
Corliss; RMC Place; FAYETTE; *250 G-6; 🅿; z 25962; rural
Cornstalk; RMC Place; GREENBRIER; *250 H-7; elev. 2,161ft./659m.; mail Lewisburg z 24901; rural
Cornwallis; RMC Place; RITCHIE; *250 C-5; mail Cairo z 26337; rural
Corporation of Ranson; JEFFERSON; see Ranson (Inc. Place)
Cortland; RMC Place; TUCKER; *250 D-10; elev. 3,163ft./964m.; mail Davis z 26260; rural
Corton; RMC Place; KANAWHA; *250 F-5; elev. 700ft./213m.; 🅿; z 25045; rural
Costa; BOONE; see Brushton (RMC Place)
Cottageville; RMC Place; JACKSON; 250 E-3; elev. 580ft./177m.; 🅿; z 25239; ● 500
Cottle; RMC Place; NICHOLAS; *250 F-6; elev. 2,200ft./671m.; 🅿; z 26205; ● 600
Cotton; RMC Place; ROANE; *250 F-4; elev. 636ft./194m.; mail Clendenin z 25045
Cottontown; RMC Place; WETZEL; *250 B-7; mail Burton z 26562; rural
Countsville; RMC Place; ROANE; *250 E-4; mail Gandeeville z 25243; rural
Cove (Holidays Cove); RMC Place; HANCOCK; *250 B-2; ★ STU-; mail Weirton z 26062; pop. incl. with Weirton (Inc. Place)
Cove Creek; WAYNE; see Kiahsville (RMC Place)
Cove Gap; RMC Place; WAYNE; 250 G-2; elev. 885ft./270m.; 🅿; z 25534; ● 100
Covel; RMC Place; WYOMING; *250 I-5; elev. 2,000ft./610m.; 🅿; z 24719; ● 275
Cowen; Inc. Place; WEBSTER; 250 F-7; elev. 2,322ft./708m.; 🅿; z 26206; Ⓟ 549; Ⓒ 513
Cox Landing; RMC Place; CABELL; *250 F-2; ★ HNTG
Coxs Mills; RMC Place; GILMER; 250 D-6; elev. 789ft./240m.; 🅿; z 26342; ● 50
Coxtown; RMC Place; LEWIS; *250 D-7; mail Weston z 26452; pop. incl. with Weston (Inc. Place)
Crab Orchard; CDP; RALEIGH; 250 H-5; elev. 2,292ft./699m.; 🅿; ★ BECK; z 25827; Ⓟ 2,919; Ⓒ 2,761
Craig; RMC Place; GREENBRIER; *250 H-6; mail Rainelle z 25962; rural
Craigmoor; RMC Place; HARRISON; *250 D-7; mail Mount Clare z 26408; ● 30
Craigsville; CDP; NICHOLAS; 250 F-6; elev. 2,312ft./705m.; 🅿; z 26205; Ⓟ 1,955; Ⓒ 2,204
Cranberry; RMC Place; RALEIGH; *250 H-5; elev. 2,400ft./732m.; 🅿; ★ BECK; z 25801; ● 300
Craneco; RMC Place; LOGAN; *250 H-3; mail Lorado z 25630; ● 150
Cranesville; RMC Place; PRESTON; 250 B-9; elev. 2,615ft./797m.; mail Terra Alta z 26764; ● 30
Crany; RMC Place; WYOMING; *250 H-4; elev. 1,546ft./471m.; mail Oceana z 24870; rural
Crawford; RMC Place; LEWIS; *250 E-7; elev. 1,100ft./335m.; 🅿; z 26343; ● 60
Crawley; RMC Place; GREENBRIER; 250 H-6; elev. 2,416ft./736m.; 🅿; z 24931; ● 150
Creamery; RMC Place; MONROE; *250 I-6; elev. 1,673ft./510m.; mail Alderson z 24910; rural
Crede; KANAWHA; see Creed (RMC Place)
Creed (Crede); RMC Place; KANAWHA; *250 F-4; ★ CHAS; mail Charleston z 25302; ● 200
Cremo; RMC Place; CALHOUN; *250 E-5; mail Creston z 26141; rural
Crescent; RMC Place; FAYETTE; *250 G-5; mail Montgomery z 25136; rural
Cressmont; RMC Place; CLAY; *250 F-5; elev. 842ft./257m.; mail Clay z 25043; rural
Creston; RMC Place; WIRT; 250 D-5; elev. 648ft./198m.; 🅿; z 26141; ● 100
Crichton; RMC Place; GREENBRIER; *250 G-6; elev. 3,000ft./914m.; 🅿; z 25981; ● 150
Crickmer; RMC Place; FAYETTE; *250 H-6; elev. 2,976ft./907m.; mail Danese z 25831; rural
Crooked Creek; RMC Place; LOGAN; *250 H-3; mail Peach Creek z 25639; ● 650
Crosby; RMC Place; CLAY; *250 F-5; elev. 1,131ft./345m.; mail Lizemores z 25125; rural
Cross Lanes; CDP; KANAWHA; 250 F-3; 🅿; ★ CHAS; z 25313 & mail Charleston z 25312, z 25356; Ⓟ 10,878; Ⓒ 10,353
Crossroads; RMC Place; MONONGALIA; 250 B-7; ● 50
Crow; RMC Place; RALEIGH; *250 H-5; elev. 2,507ft./764m.; ★ BECK; mail Beaver z 25813
Crown; RMC Place; LOGAN; *250 H-3; elev. 799ft./244m.; mail Accoville z 25606; ● 600
Crown; RMC Place; MONONGALIA; *250 B-8; ★ MORG; mail Morgantown z 26501; ● 200
Crown Hill; RMC Place; KANAWHA; *250 G-4; elev. 620ft./189m.; 🅿; z 25067; ● 180
Crow Summit; RMC Place; JACKSON; *250 D-4; elev. 634ft./193m.; mail Ravenswood z 26164; rural
Crum; RMC Place; WAYNE; 250 H-2; elev. 629ft./192m.; 🅿; z 25669; ● 400
Crumpler; RMC Place; MCDOWELL; *250 I-4; elev. 2,407ft./734m.; 🅿; z 24868; ● 325
Crystal; RMC Place; MERCER; *250 J-5; mail Rock z 24747; rural
Crystal Block; RMC Place; LOGAN; *250 I-3; mail Sarah Ann z 25644
Crystal Lake; RMC Place; DODDRIDGE; *250 C-6; mail West Union z 26456; ● 100
Crystal Springs; RMC Place; RANDOLPH; *250 D-8; elev. 1,912ft./583m.; mail Elkins z 26241; ● 300
Cubana; RMC Place; RANDOLPH; *250 E-8; mail Tallmansville z 26237; rural
Cucumber; RMC Place; MCDOWELL; 250 J-4; elev. 1,560ft./475m.; 🅿; z 24826; ● 175
Culloden; CDP; CABELL, PUTNAM; 250 F-3; elev. 700ft./213m.; 🅿; ★ CHAS; z 25510; Ⓟ 2,907; Ⓒ 2,940
Cumberland Heights; RMC Place; MERCER; *250 J-5; mail Bluefield z 24701; pop. incl. with Bluefield (Inc. Place)
Cunard; RMC Place; FAYETTE; 250 H-5; elev. 1,664ft./507m.; 🅿; z 25840; ● 400
Curtin; RMC Place; WEBSTER; 250 F-7; elev. 1,800ft./549m.; 🅿; z 26288; ● 75
Curtisville; RMC Place; MARION; *250 B-7; elev. 1,019ft./311m.; mail Mannington z 26582
Cusicks Crossing; RMC Place; WETZEL; *250 B-7; mail Burton z 26562; rural
Custer Addition; RMC Place; HARRISON; *250 C-7; ★ CLRKB; mail Clarksburg z 26301; ● 250
Cutlips; RMC Place; BRAXTON; *250 E-6; elev. 852ft./260m.; mail Exchange z 26619
Cuzzart; RMC Place; PRESTON; *250 B-9; elev. 2,096ft./639m.; 🅿; z 26525
Cyclone; RMC Place; WYOMING; 250 H-4; elev. 1,149ft./350m.; 🅿; z 24827; ● 250
Cyrus; RMC Place; WAYNE; *250 F-1; mail Kenova z 25530
Czar; RMC Place; RANDOLPH; 250 E-8; mail Helvetia z 26224; ● 20

D

Dabney; RMC Place; LOGAN; *250 H-3; elev. 729ft./222m.; mail Yolyn z 25654; rural
Dahmer; RMC Place; PENDLETON; *250 F-10; elev. 2,636ft./803m.; mail Franklin z 26807; rural
Dailey; RMC Place; RANDOLPH; 250 E-8; elev. 1,970ft./600m.; 🅿; z 26259; ● 250
Daisy; RMC Place; LOGAN; *250 G-3; mail Big Creek z 25505; rural
Dakota; RMC Place; MARION; *250 B-8; ★ FAIRM; mail Fairmont z 26554; ● 150
Dale; RMC Place; TYLER; *250 C-6; elev. 900ft./274m.; mail Jacksonburg z 26377; rural
Dallas; RMC Place; MARSHALL; 250 A-7; elev. 1,400ft./427m.; 🅿; ★ WHL; z 26036; ● 350
Dallison; RMC Place; WOOD; *250 C-4; elev. 692ft./211m.; ★ PRKB; mail Walker z 26180; ● 60
Dameron; RMC Place; RALEIGH; *250 H-4; mail Glen Daniel z 25844; rural
Danese; RMC Place; FAYETTE; 250 H-6; elev. 2,628ft./801m.; 🅿; z 25831; ● 250
Daniels; CDP; RALEIGH; 250 I-5; elev. 2,374ft./724m.; 🅿; ★ BECK; z 25832; Ⓟ 1,714; Ⓒ 1,846
Dans Run; RMC Place; MINERAL; *250 B-11; ★ CUMB; mail Springfield z 26763; rural
Danville; Inc. Place; BOONE; 250 G-3; elev. 692ft./211m.; 🅿; z 25053; Ⓟ 595; Ⓒ 550
Darkesville; RMC Place; BERKELEY; *250 C-13; mail Inwood z 25428, Martinsburg z 25401; ● 400
Dartmont; RMC Place; BOONE; *250 G-3; mail Ashford z 25009; rural
Dartmoor; RMC Place; BARBOUR; *250 D-8; mail Belington z 26250; ● 30
Davenport; RMC Place; TYLER; mail Sistersville z 26175; ● 150
Davin; RMC Place; LOGAN; *250 H-3; elev. 840ft./256m.; 🅿; z 25617; ● 400
Davis; RMC Place; LOGAN; *250 H-2; mail Holden z 25625; ● 210
Davis; Inc. Place; TUCKER; 250 D-9; elev. 3,099ft./945m.; 🅿; z 26260; Ⓟ 799; Ⓒ 624
Davis Creek; RMC Place; KANAWHA; 250 J-12; ★ CHAS; mail Alum Creek z 25003; ● 600
Davisville; RMC Place; WOOD; *250 C-4; elev. 611ft./186m.; 🅿; ★ PRKB; z 26142; ● 300
Davy; Inc. Place; MCDOWELL; 250 I-4; elev. 1,189ft./362m.; 🅿; z 24828; Ⓟ 403; Ⓒ 373
Dawes; RMC Place; KANAWHA; *250 G-4; elev. 691ft./211m.; 🅿; z 25054; ● 300
Dawmont; RMC Place; HARRISON; *250 C-7; elev. 1,020ft./311m.; 🅿; ★ CLRKB; z 26301; ● 125
Dawson; RMC Place; GREENBRIER; *250 H-6; elev. 2,431ft./741m.; 🅿; z 24910
Daybrook; RMC Place; MONONGALIA; 250 B-7; mail Fairview z 26570; ● 225
Daysville; RMC Place; UPSHUR; *250 D-8; mail Buckhannon z 26201; ● 90
Deanville; RMC Place; LEWIS; *250 D-7; mail Weston z 26452; ● 300
Deanville; RMC Place; UPSHUR; *250 D-8; mail Buckhannon z 26201; ● 600
Decota; RMC Place; KANAWHA; *250 G-4; elev. 1,124ft./343m.; 🅿; z 25075
Deep Valley; RMC Place; MARION; *250 B-7; ★ FAIRM; mail Mannington z 26582
Deep Valley; RMC Place; TYLER; *250 C-6; mail Pennsboro z 26415
Deep Water; RMC Place; FAYETTE; *250 G-5; elev. 684ft./208m.; 🅿; z 25057; ● 400
Deer Creek; RMC Place; POCAHONTAS; *250 F-8; elev. 2,435ft./742m.; mail Cass z 24927
Deer Run; RMC Place; PENDLETON; *250 E-10; mail Franklin z 26807
Deerwalk; RMC Place; WOOD; *250 C-5; ★ PRKB; mail Walker z 26180; ● 40
Dehue; RMC Place; LOGAN; *250 H-3; elev. 800ft./244m.; 🅿; z 25654; ● 200
Delbarton; Inc. Place; MINGO; 250 I-2; elev. 752ft./229m.; 🅿; z 25670; Ⓟ 705; Ⓒ 474
Dellslow; RMC Place; MONONGALIA; 250 B-8; elev. 1,000ft./305m.; 🅿; ★ MORG; z 26531; ● 1,000
Delong; RMC Place; PLEASANTS; *250 C-5; mail Saint Marys z 26170; rural
Delorme (Edgarton); RMC Place; MINGO; 250 I-2; elev. 731ft./223m.; mail Edgarton z 25672; ● 300
Delray; RMC Place; HAMPSHIRE; 250 C-12; elev. 953ft./290m.; 🅿; z 26714; ● 40
Dempsey; RMC Place; FAYETTE; *250 G-5; mail Fayetteville z 25840; rural
Denver; MARSHALL; see Bellton (RMC Place)
Denver; RMC Place; PRESTON; 250 C-9; mail Tunnelton z 26444; ● 100
Denver Heights; RMC Place; MARSHALL; *250 B-7; mail Cameron z 26033; rural
Derryhale; RMC Place; FAYETTE; *250 H-5; ★ BECK; mail Glen Jean z 25846; rural
Despard; CDP; HARRISON; 250 C-7; ★ CLRKB; mail Clarksburg z 26301; Ⓟ 1,018; Ⓒ 1,039
Dessie; RMC Place; BRAXTON; *250 E-6; elev. 915ft./279m.; mail Frametown z 26623; rural
Devon; RMC Place; MINGO; *250 I-3; elev. 763ft./233m.; mail Matewan z 25678; rural
Dewitt; RMC Place; FAYETTE; *250 H-5; elev. 1,505ft./459m.; ★ BECK; mail Glen Jean z 25846; rural
Diamond; RMC Place; KANAWHA; *250 G-4; elev. 643ft./196m.; 🅿; ★ CHAS; z 25015; ● 300
Diamond; RMC Place; LOGAN; *250 H-3; mail Holden z 25625; ● 90
Diana; RMC Place; WEBSTER; 250 F-7; elev. 1,241ft./378m.; 🅿; z 26217; ● 250
Dickinson (Quincy); RMC Place; KANAWHA; *250 G-4; elev. 621ft./189m.; mail Belle z 25015; ● 200
Dickson; RMC Place; WAYNE; 250 G-2; ★ HNTG; mail Lavalette z 25535; ● 150
Dille; RMC Place; CLAY; 250 F-6; elev. 1,199ft./365m.; 🅿; z 26617; ● 260
Dingess; RMC Place; MINGO; 250 H-2; elev. 1,007ft./307m.; 🅿; z 25671; ● 200
Dink; RMC Place; CLAY; *250 F-5; elev. 885ft./270m.; mail Ivydale z 25113; rural
Divide; RMC Place; FAYETTE; *250 G-5; mail Lookout z 25868
Dixie; RMC Place; NICHOLAS, FAYETTE; 250 G-5; elev. 732ft./223m.; 🅿; z 25059; ● 450
Doane; RMC Place; WAYNE; *250 H-2; elev. 727ft./222m.; mail Dunlow z 25511; rural
Dobra; RMC Place; LOGAN; *250 H-3; elev. 833ft./254m.; mail Sharples z 25183; ● 75
DODDRIDGE; 250 C-6; Ⓟ 6,994; Ⓒ 7,403; ◆ 7,220
Dog Patch; RMC Place; LOGAN; *250 H-3; mail Logan z 25601; ● 100
Dola; RMC Place; HARRISON; *250 C-7; elev. 970ft./296m.; 🅿; ★ CLRKB; z 26386; rural
Donaldson; RMC Place; WEBSTER; *250 F-7; elev. 2,187ft./667m.; mail Cowen z 26206
Donwood; RMC Place; FAYETTE; *250 G-5; mail Montgomery z 25136; ● 50
Doortown; RMC Place; WEBSTER; *250 F-7; mail Webster Springs z 26288; ● 200
Dorcas; RMC Place; GRANT; 250 D-10; elev. 1,066ft./325m.; 🅿; z 26847; ● 50
Dorothy; RMC Place; RALEIGH; *250 H-4; elev. 984ft./300m.; 🅿; z 25060 & mail Colcord z 25048; ● 500
Dothan; RMC Place; FAYETTE; *250 H-5; elev. 687ft./209m.; 🅿; ★ BECK; z 25833; ● 100
Dott (Wenonah); RMC Place; MERCER; *250 I-5; elev. 2,440ft./744m.; 🅿; z 24736; rural
Douglas; RMC Place; CALHOUN; *250 E-5; elev. 832ft./254m.; mail Chloe z 25235
Douglas (Albert); RMC Place; TUCKER; *250 D-9; mail Thomas z 26292; ● 25
Downtown; RMC Place; CABELL; ★ HNTG; mail Huntington z 25701, z 25716-22, z 25724-29; pop. incl. with Huntington (Inc. Place)
Downtown; RMC Place; OHIO; ★ WHL; mail Wheeling z 26003; pop. incl. with Wheeling (Inc. Place)
Drennen; RMC Place; NICHOLAS; 250 G-5; elev. 1,123ft./342m.; 🅿; z 26667; ● 40
Drews Creek; RMC Place; RALEIGH; *250 H-4; mail Naoma z 25140; rural
Droop; RMC Place; POCAHONTAS; 250 G-7; elev. 3,000ft./914m.; 🅿; z 24946; ● 50
Dry Branch; RMC Place; KANAWHA; *250 G-4; elev. 633ft./193m.; 🅿; z 25061; ● 600
Dry Creek; RMC Place; RALEIGH; 250 H-4; elev. 1,263ft./385m.; 🅿; z 25062; ● 100
Dryfork; RMC Place; RANDOLPH; *250 D-9; elev. 2,200ft./671m.; 🅿; z 26263; ● 60
Dry Hill; RMC Place; RALEIGH; *250 H-5; ★ BECK; mail Beckley z 25801; ● 175
Duck; RMC Place; CLAY; 250 F-6; elev. 797ft./243m.; 🅿; z 25063; ● 40
Dudeon; RMC Place; JACKSON; mail Kenna z 25248; rural
Dudley Gap; RMC Place; CABELL; *250 F-2; elev. 875ft./267m.; mail Milton z 25541
Duffields; RMC Place; JEFFERSON; *250 C-14; mail Shenandoah Junction z 25442; rural
Duffy; RMC Place; LEWIS; *250 E-7; mail Ireland z 26376
Duhring; RMC Place; MERCER; *250 J-5; elev. 2,218ft./676m.; 🅿; z 24747
Dukes; RMC Place; ROANE; *250 E-4; elev. 693ft./211m.; mail Le Roy z 25252; rural
Dunbar; Inc. Place; KANAWHA; 250 F-3; elev. 603ft./184m.; 🅿; ★ CHAS; z 25064; Ⓟ 8,697; Ⓒ 8,154
Duncan; RMC Place; JACKSON; *250 D-4; elev. 630ft./192m.; 🅿; z 25252; rural
Dundon; RMC Place; CLAY; *250 F-5; mail Clay z 25043; rural
Dunloup; RMC Place; FAYETTE; *250 H-5; ★ BECK; mail Mount Hope z 25880; rural
Dunlow; RMC Place; WAYNE; 250 G-2; elev. 690ft./210m.; 🅿; z 25511; ● 125
Dunmore; RMC Place; POCAHONTAS; 250 F-8; elev. 2,470ft./753m.; 🅿; z 24934; ● 75
Dunns; RMC Place; MERCER; *250 I-5; elev. 1,828ft./557m.; mail Flat Top z 25841; rural
Duo; RMC Place; GREENBRIER; *250 G-6; 🅿; z 25984; ● 30
Dupont City; RMC Place; KANAWHA; *250 G-4; elev. 613ft./187m.; 🅿; ★ CHAS; z 25015; ● 450
Durbin; Inc. Place; POCAHONTAS; 250 F-9; elev. 2,732ft./833m.; 🅿; z 26264; Ⓟ 278; Ⓒ 262
Durgon; RMC Place; HARDY; 250 D-11; mail Moorefield z 26836; ● 20
Dutchman; RMC Place; RITCHIE; 250 D-5; mail Macfarlan z 26148; ● 50
Dutch Ridge; RMC Place; KANAWHA; mail Clendenin z 25045; rural
Dyer; RMC Place; WEBSTER; *250 F-7; mail Cowen z 26206

E

Eagle; RMC Place; FAYETTE; *250 G-5; mail Montgomery z 25136; ● 20
Earling; RMC Place; LOGAN; *250 H-3; elev. 729ft./222m.; 🅿; z 25632; ● 250
Earnshaw; RMC Place; WETZEL; *250 B-7; elev. 1,068ft./326m.; mail Metz z 26585; ● 30
East Bank; Inc. Place; KANAWHA; 250 G-4; elev. 620ft./189m.; 🅿; z 25067; Ⓟ 892; Ⓒ 933
East Beckley; RMC Place; RALEIGH; *250 H-5; ★ BECK; mail Beckley z 25801; pop. incl. with Beckley (Inc. Place)
East Dailey; RMC Place; RANDOLPH; *250 E-8; mail Beverly z 26253, Dailey z 26259; ● 400
Eastgulf; RMC Place; RALEIGH; *250 I-5; elev. 1,667ft./508m.; 🅿; z 25915; rural
East Huntington; RMC Place; CABELL; ★ HNTG; pop. incl. with Huntington (Inc. Place)
East Kermit; RMC Place; MINGO; *250 H-2; elev. 633ft./193m.; mail Kermit z 25674; ● 180
East Kingston (Kingston); RMC Place; FAYETTE; *250 H-5; elev. 1,480ft./451m.; mail Scarbro z 25917; ● 75
East Lynn; RMC Place; WAYNE; 250 G-2; elev. 632ft./193m.; 🅿; z 25512; ● 225
East Nitro; RMC Place; KANAWHA; *250 F-3; ★ CHAS; mail Nitro z 25143; pop. incl. with Nitro (Inc. Place)
East Oak Hill; RMC Place; FAYETTE; *250 H-5; ★ BECK; mail Oak Hill z 25901; pop. incl. with Oak Hill (Inc. Place)
East Pea Ridge; RMC Place; CABELL; *250 F-2; ★ HNTG; mail Huntington z 25705; ● 4,000
East Salem; RMC Place; HARRISON; *250 C-7; mail Salem z 26426; ● 70
Eastside; RMC Place; MARION; ★ FAIRM; mail Fairmont z 26554-55; pop. incl. with Fairmont (Inc. Place)
East View; RMC Place; HARRISON; *250 C-7; ★ CLRKB; mail Clarksburg z 26301; ● 1,000
East Williamson; RMC Place; MINGO; *250 I-2; mail Williamson z 25661; pop. incl. with Williamson (Inc. Place)
Eaton; RMC Place; WOOD; *250 D-5; ★ PRKB; mail Walker z 26180; rural
Eccles; RMC Place; RALEIGH; 250 H-5; elev. 2,083ft./635m.; 🅿; ★ BECK; z 25836; ● 900
Echo; RMC Place; WAYNE; *250 G-1; elev. 617ft./188m.; mail Wayne z 25570; rural
Eckman; RMC Place; MCDOWELL; *250 J-4; elev. 1,604ft./489m.; 🅿; z 24829; ● 300
Eden; RMC Place; BOONE; *250 G-4; mail Bloomingrose z 25024, Comfort z 25049; rural
Eden; RMC Place; OHIO; *250 A-6; ★ WHL; mail Wheeling z 26003
Eden; RMC Place; UPSHUR; *250 E-7; mail Rock Cave z 26234; rural
Edgarton; MINGO; see Delorme (RMC Place)
Edgemont; RMC Place; MARION; *250 C-8; ★ FAIRM; mail Fairmont z 26554; pop. incl. with Fairmont (Inc. Place)
Edgewater Acres; RMC Place; KANAWHA; *250 F-3; ★ CHAS; mail Saint Albans z 25177; pop. incl. with Saint Albans (Inc. Place)
Edgewood; RMC Place; HARRISON; *250 C-7; ★ CLRKB; mail Clarksburg z 26301; pop. incl. with Clarksburg (Inc. Place)
Edgewood; RMC Place; KANAWHA; *250 F-4; ★ CHAS; mail Charleston z 25302; pop. incl. with Charleston (Inc. Place)
Edgewood; RMC Place; OHIO; *250 A-6; ★ WHL; mail Wheeling z 26003; pop. incl. with Wheeling (Inc. Place)
Edgewood Acres; RMC Place; KANAWHA; *250 F-4; ★ CHAS; mail Charleston z 25302; pop. incl. with Charleston (Inc. Place)
Edison; RMC Place; MERCER; *250 J-5; elev. 2,450ft./747m.; mail Bluefield z 24701; ● 100
Edmond; RMC Place; FAYETTE; *250 G-5; elev. 2,050ft./625m.; 🅿; z 25837; ● 100
Edna; RMC Place; MONONGALIA; *250 B-8; ★ MORG; mail Morgantown z 26501; ● 80
Edray; RMC Place; POCAHONTAS; *250 G-8; mail Marlinton z 24954; rural
Edwight; RMC Place; RALEIGH; *250 H-4; elev. 985ft./300m.; mail Naoma z 25140; rural
Effie; RMC Place; WAYNE; *250 G-1; mail Fort Gay z 25514; rural
Egeria; RMC Place; MERCER, RALEIGH; *250 I-5; mail Odd z 25902; rural
Eggleton; RMC Place; PUTNAM; *250 G-3; elev. 707ft./215m.; mail Hamlin z 25523; rural
Eglon; RMC Place; PRESTON; 250 C-9; elev. 2,630ft./802m.; 🅿; z 26716; ● 120
Elana; RMC Place; ROANE; *250 E-5; elev. 857ft./261m.; mail Newton z 25266; rural
Elbert; RMC Place; MCDOWELL; *250 J-4; elev. 1,578ft./481m.; 🅿; z 24830; pop. incl. with Gary (Inc. Place)
Eldora; RMC Place; MARION; *250 C-8; ★ FAIRM; mail Fairmont z 26554; ● 120
Eleanor; Inc. Place; PUTNAM; 250 F-3; elev. 574ft./175m.; 🅿; ★ CHAS; z 25070; Ⓟ 1,256; Ⓒ 1,345
Elgood; RMC Place; MERCER; *250 J-6; elev. 2,831ft./863m.; 🅿; z 24740; rural
Elizabeth; Inc. Place; ⊡ WIRT; 250 D-4; elev. 646ft./197m.; 🅿; z 26143; Ⓟ 900; Ⓒ 994
Elk; RMC Place; KANAWHA; *250 F-4; ★ CHAS; pop. incl. with Charleston (Inc. Place)
Elk; RMC Place; TUCKER; *250 D-9; elev. 2,542ft./775m.; mail Hendricks z 26271; rural
Elk City; RMC Place; BARBOUR; *250 D-8; elev. 1,090ft./332m.; mail Philippi z 26416; ● 45
Elk Forest; RMC Place; KANAWHA; 250 I-14; elev. 681ft./208m.; ★ CHAS; mail Charleston z 25311; ● 600
Elk Garden; Inc. Place; MINERAL; 250 C-10; elev. 2,288ft./697m.; 🅿; z 26717; Ⓟ 261; Ⓒ 217
Elk Hills (Mink Shoals); RMC Place; KANAWHA; 250 I-14; elev. 620ft./189m.; ★ CHAS; mail Charleston z 25302; ● 300

Entries in **UPPERCASE** are counties.
Entries in **bold** have populations of 2,500 or more.
Names in parentheses are alternate names.
Inc. Place — Incorporated Place
RMC Place — Rand McNally Designated Place
CDP — Census Designated Place
MCD — Minor Civil Division

⊡ County Seat
▲ Minor Civil Division
elev. Elevation
🅿 Post Office

🅷 Hospital
🅲 College
■ Principal Business Center
★ Ranally Metro Area (RMA) Abbreviation
z Zip Code(s)

Ⓟ Previous Census Population
Ⓡ Revised Census Population
Ⓐ Annexation Population
● Rand McNally Population Estimate
Ⓒ Final Census Population
Ⓢ Special Census Population
◆ Estimated Population

For additional definitions see Glossary, Volume 1, and Introduction, Volume 2.

Elkhorn; RMC Place; MCDOWELL; ***250** J-4; elev. 1,920ft./585m.; 🅿; **z** 24831; ● 250
Elkhurst; RMC Place; CLAY; ***250** F-5; mail Procious **z** 25164
Elkins; Inc. Place; ⊡ RANDOLPH; **250** D-8; elev. 1,930ft./588m.; 🅿 🅷 🅲 636 ■; **z** 26241; Ⓟ 7,420; Ⓒ 7,032; ◆ 6,832
Elkridge; RMC Place; FAYETTE; ***250** G-5; elev. 985ft./300m.; mail Powellton **z** 25161; ● 140
Elkridge; RMC Place; MCDOWELL; ***250** J-4; mail Northfork **z** 24868; pop. incl. with Northfork (Inc. Place)
Elk Run Junction; RMC Place; BOONE; ***250** H-4; elev. 812ft./247m.; mail Whitesville **z** 25209; pop. incl. with Whitesville (Inc. Place)
Elkview; CDP; KANAWHA; **250** F-4; elev. 700ft./213m.; 🅿; ★ **CHAS**; **z** 25071; Ⓟ 1,047; Ⓒ 1,182
Elkwater; RMC Place; RANDOLPH; ***250** E-8; elev. 2,127ft./648m.; mail Huttonsville **z** 26273
Ellamore; RMC Place; UPSHUR, RANDOLPH; **250** D-8; elev. 1,842ft./561m.; 🅿; **z** 26267; ● 125
Ellenboro; Inc. Place; RITCHIE; **250** C-5; elev. 807ft./246m.; 🅿; **z** 26346; Ⓟ 453; Ⓒ 373
Ellison; RMC Place; SUMMERS; ***250** I-5; mail Jumping Branch **z** 25969; rural
Elm Grove; RMC Place; OHIO; **250** J-11; 🅿; ★ **WHL**; **z** 26003; pop. incl. with Wheeling (Inc. Place)
Elmira; RMC Place; BRAXTON; ***250** E-5; elev. 1,000ft./305m.; 🅿; **z** 25063; ● 20
Elm Terrace; RMC Place; OHIO; ***250** A-6; ★ **WHL**; mail Wheeling **z** 26003; pop. incl. with Wheeling (Inc. Place)
Elmwood; RMC Place; MASON; ***250** E-3; elev. 628ft./191m.; mail Leon **z** 25123; rural
Elmwood; RMC Place; WAYNE; ***250** G-2; elev. 613ft./187m.; ★ **HNTG**; mail Wayne **z** 25570
Eloise; RMC Place; WAYNE; mail Dunlow **z** 25511; pop. incl. with Westland (Inc. Place)
Elton; RMC Place; SUMMERS; **250** H-6; elev. 1,757ft./536m.; 🅿; **z** 25965; ● 90
Emma; RMC Place; PUTNAM; ***250** E-4; mail Liberty **z** 25124; rural
Emmett; RMC Place; LOGAN; ***250** I-3; elev. 864ft./263m.; 🅿; **z** 25650
Emmons; RMC Place; KANAWHA, BOONE; ***250** G-3; ★ **CHAS**; mail Alum Creek **z** 25003, Ashford **z** 25009; rural
Emoryville; RMC Place; MINERAL; ***250** C-10; elev. 2,004ft./611m.; mail Elk Garden **z** 26717; rural
Endicott; RMC Place; WETZEL; ***250** B-7; elev. 1,009ft./308m.; mail Littleton **z** 26581; rural
Engle; RMC Place; JEFFERSON; ***250** C-14; mail Harpers Ferry **z** 25425; ● 80
English; RMC Place; MCDOWELL; ***250** J-3; elev. 1,320ft./402m.; 🅿; **z** 24892; ● 250
Ennis; RMC Place; MCDOWELL; ***250** J-4; mail Switchback **z** 24887
Enoch; RMC Place; CLAY; ***250** F-6; mail Clay **z** 25043; rural
Enon; RMC Place; NICHOLAS; **250** G-6; elev. 1,513ft./461m.; mail Summersville **z** 26651; ● 60
Enterprise; CDP; HARRISON; **250** C-7; elev. 940ft./287m.; 🅿; ★ **FAIRM**; **z** 26568; Ⓟ 1,058; Ⓒ 939
Enterprise; RMC Place; WIRT; ***250** D-4; elev. 628ft./191m.; mail Palestine **z** 26160; rural
Entry Mountain; RMC Place; PENDLETON; ***250** E-10; mail Franklin **z** 26807; rural
Epperly; RMC Place; RALEIGH; ***250** I-5; ★ **BECK**; mail Coal City **z** 25823; ● 70
Erbacon; RMC Place; WEBSTER; **250** F-6; elev. 1,518ft./463m.; 🅿; **z** 26203; ● 150
Erie; RMC Place; HARRISON; ***250** C-7; ★ **CLRKB**; mail Clarksburg **z** 26301; rural
Erwin; RMC Place; PRESTON; ***250** C-9; elev. 1,444ft./440m.; mail Aurora **z** 26705
Eskdale; RMC Place; KANAWHA; **250** G-4; elev. 812ft./247m.; 🅿; **z** 25075; ● 300
Esty; RMC Place; GREENBRIER; ***250** H-7; mail Renick **z** 24966; rural
Etam; RMC Place; PRESTON; ***250** C-9; mail Rowlesburg **z** 26425
Ethel; RMC Place; LOGAN; **250** H-3; elev. 815ft./248m.; 🅿; **z** 25076; ● 130
Euclid; RMC Place; CALHOUN; ***250** E-5; elev. 792ft./241m.; mail Rosedale **z** 26636; rural
Eunice; RMC Place; RALEIGH; ***250** H-4; elev. 872ft./266m.; mail Whitesville **z** 25209; ● 125
Eureka; RMC Place; PLEASANTS; **250** C-5; elev. 630ft./192m.; 🅿; **z** 26134; ● 40
Evans; RMC Place; JACKSON; **250** E-3; elev. 605ft./184m.; 🅿; **z** 25241; ● 700
Evansdale; RMC Place; MONONGALIA; ***250** B-8; ★ **MORG**; mail Morgantown **z** 26505; pop. incl. with Morgantown (Inc. Place)
Evansville; RMC Place; PRESTON; ***250** C-8; elev. 1,330ft./405m.; mail Thornton **z** 26440; ● 35
Evenwood; RMC Place; RANDOLPH; ***250** E-9; mail Bowden **z** 26254; rural
Everettville; RMC Place; MONONGALIA; **250** B-8; elev. 900ft./274m.; 🅿; ★ **MORG**; **z** 26505; ● 375
Evergreen; RMC Place; UPSHUR; ***250** E-7; elev. 1,676ft./511m.; mail French Creek **z** 26218
Evergreen Hills; RMC Place; JACKSON; ***250** E-3; elev. 712ft./217m.; mail Cottageville **z** 25239; ● 225
Everson; RMC Place; MARION; ***250** C-7; ★ **FAIRM**; mail Fairmont **z** 26554; ● 100
Excelsior; RMC Place; MCDOWELL; ***250** J-4; mail War **z** 24892; pop. incl. with War (Inc. Place)
Excelsior; RMC Place; UPSHUR; ***250** D-8; mail Buckhannon **z** 26201; ● 100
Exchange; RMC Place; BRAXTON; **250** E-6; elev. 871ft./265m.; 🅿; **z** 26619; ● 40
Extra; RMC Place; PUTNAM; ***250** E-3; mail Red House **z** 25168; rural

F

Fairdale; RMC Place; RALEIGH; ***250** H-4; elev. 1,900ft./579m.; 🅿; ★ **BECK**; **z** 25839; ● 600
Fairlea; CDP; GREENBRIER; ***250** H-7; elev. 2,144ft./653m.; 🅿; **z** 24902; Ⓟ 1,743; Ⓒ 1,706
Fairmont; Inc. Place; ⊡ MARION; **250** C-8; elev. 991ft./302m.; 🅿 🅷 🅲 7,740 ■; ★ **FAIRM**; **z** 26554-55; Ⓟ 20,210; Ⓒ 19,097; ◆ 18,578
Fairmor; RMC Place; MONONGALIA; ***250** B-8; ★ **MORG**; mail Morgantown **z** 26505; pop. incl. with Westover (Inc. Place)
Fairplain; RMC Place; JACKSON; **250** E-4; mail Ripley **z** 25271; ● 150
Fairview; Inc. Place; MARION; **250** B-7; elev. 1,000ft./305m.; 🅿; ★ **FAIRM**; **z** 26570; Ⓟ 513; Ⓒ 435
Fairview; RMC Place; MARSHALL; ***250** B-6; elev. 1,367ft./417m.; mail Proctor **z** 26055; rural
Fairview; RMC Place; MASON; ***250** D-3; elev. 688ft./210m.; mail Letart **z** 25253
Fairview; RMC Place; MINGO; ***250** I-2; mail Williamson **z** 25661; pop. incl. with Williamson (Inc. Place)
Fallen Timber; RMC Place; WETZEL; ***250** B-7; elev. 826ft./252m.; mail Smithfield **z** 26437; rural
Falling Rock; RMC Place; KANAWHA; ***250** F-4; elev. 621ft./189m.; 🅿; **z** 25079; ● 200
Falling Spring (Renick); Inc. Place; GREENBRIER; **250** H-7; elev. 1,902ft./580m.; mail Renick **z** 24966; Ⓟ 191; Ⓒ 209
Falling Waters; RMC Place; BERKELEY; **250** B-14; elev. 400ft./122m.; 🅿; ★ **HAG**; **z** 25419; ● 200
Falls; RMC Place; GRANT; ***250** D-10; elev. 1,240ft./378m.; mail Maysville **z** 26833; rural
Falls Mill; RMC Place; BRAXTON; ***250** E-7; elev. 809ft./247m.; 🅿; **z** 26631; rural
Falls Mills; RMC Place; TYLER; ***250** C-5; mail Friendly **z** 26146; rural
Falls View; RMC Place; FAYETTE; ***250** G-5; mail Alloy **z** 25002; ● 500
Fanco; RMC Place; LOGAN; ***250** H-3; mail Accoville **z** 25606; ● 75
Fanny; RMC Place; WYOMING; ***250** I-4; mail Fanrock **z** 24834
Fanrock; RMC Place; WYOMING; ***250** I-4; elev. 1,216ft./371m.; 🅿; **z** 24834; ● 150
Far; RMC Place; WETZEL; ***250** B-6; elev. 1,293ft./394m.; mail Reader **z** 26167; rural
Farmington; Inc. Place; MARION; **250** C-7; elev. 960ft./293m.; 🅿; ★ **FAIRM**; **z** 26571; Ⓟ 414; Ⓒ 387
Farnum; RMC Place; HARRISON; ***250** C-7; ★ **CLRKB**; mail Hepzibah **z** 26369; rural
Faulkner; RMC Place; RANDOLPH; ***250** D-9; mail Elkins **z** 26241; rural
FAYETTE; **250** H-5; Ⓟ 47,952; Ⓒ 47,579; ◆ 45,822
Fayette Heights; RMC Place; FAYETTE; ***250** G-5; ★ **BECK**; mail Fayetteville **z** 25840; ● 450
Fayetteville; Inc. Place; ⊡ FAYETTE; **250** G-5; elev. 1,821ft./555m.; 🅿; ★ **BECK**; **z** 25840; Ⓟ 2,182; Ⓒ 2,754
Federal; RMC Place; MERCER; mail Bluefield **z** 24701; pop. incl. with Bluefield (Inc. Place)
Federal Mine; RMC Place; MARION; ★ **FAIRM**; pop. incl. with Grant Town (Inc. Place)
Federal Ridge; RMC Place; PLEASANTS; mail Saint Marys **z** 26170; rural
Fellowsville; RMC Place; PRESTON; **250** C-8; elev. 1,370ft./418m.; mail Tunnelton **z** 26444; ● 125
Fenwick; RMC Place; NICHOLAS; **250** G-7; elev. 2,000ft./610m.; 🅿; **z** 26202; ● 400
Ferguson; RMC Place; WAYNE; ***250** G-2; elev. 675ft./206m.; mail Dunlow **z** 25511; rural
Ferrellsburg; RMC Place; LINCOLN; **250** G-2; elev. 620ft./189m.; 🅿; **z** 25524; ● 150
Fetterman; RMC Place; TAYLOR; ***250** C-8; elev. 991ft./302m.; mail Grafton **z** 26354; pop. incl. with Grafton (Inc. Place)
Filbert; RMC Place; MCDOWELL; ***250** J-4; elev. 1,692ft./516m.; 🅿; **z** 24830
Finch; RMC Place; RITCHIE; ***250** C-5; mail Ellenboro **z** 26346
Fireco; RMC Place; RALEIGH; ***250** I-5; ★ **BECK**; mail Coal City **z** 25823; ● 180
Fisher; RMC Place; HARDY; ***250** D-11; elev. 900ft./274m.; 🅿; **z** 26818; ● 50
Fitzpatrick; RMC Place; RALEIGH; ***250** H-5; elev. 2,199ft./670m.; ★ **BECK**; mail Beckley **z** 25801; rural
Five Block; RMC Place; LOGAN; ***250** H-3; mail Blair **z** 25022
Five Forks; RMC Place; CALHOUN; **250** D-5; elev. 1,188ft./362m.; 🅿; **z** 26136; ● 75
Five Forks; RMC Place; PRESTON; ***250** B-9; elev. 2,197ft./670m.; mail Bruceton Mills **z** 26525; rural
Five Forks; RMC Place; RITCHIE; ***250** D-5; mail Harrisville **z** 26362; rural
Fivemile; RMC Place; KANAWHA; ***250** F-4; elev. 673ft./205m.; ★ **CHAS**; mail Tad **z** 25201; rural
Fivemile; RMC Place; MASON; ***250** E-3; mail Henderson **z** 25106; rural
Flaggy Meadow; RMC Place; MONONGALIA; ***250** B-8; ★ **MORG**; mail Morgantown **z** 26501; rural
Flatrock; RMC Place; MASON; **250** E-3; elev. 674ft./205m.; mail Leon **z** 25123, Point Pleasant **z** 25550; ● 70
Flat Top; RMC Place; MERCER; **250** I-5; elev. 3,245ft./989m.; 🅿; **z** 25841; ● 100
Flat Top Lake; RMC Place; RALEIGH; ***250** I-5; mail Ghent **z** 25843; summer pop. 1,400; ● 900
Flatwoods; Inc. Place; BRAXTON; **250** E-6; elev. 1,071ft./326m.; 🅿; **z** 26621; Ⓟ 324; Ⓒ 348
Flatwoods; RMC Place; JACKSON; ***250** E-3; elev. 763ft./233m.; mail Ravenswood **z** 26164; rural
Flatwoods; RMC Place; KANAWHA; ★ **CHAS**; mail Charleston **z** 25312
Flemington; Inc. Place; TAYLOR; **250** C-8; elev. 1,037ft./316m.; 🅿; **z** 26347; Ⓟ 352; Ⓒ 287
Flinderation; RMC Place; HARRISON; ***250** C-7; mail Salem **z** 26426; rural
Flint; RMC Place; DODDRIDGE; ***250** C-6; elev. 838ft./255m.; mail West Union **z** 26456
Flipping; RMC Place; MERCER; ***250** J-5; mail Rock **z** 24747; rural
Floe; RMC Place; CLAY; ***250** E-5; elev. 1,080ft./329m.; 🅿; **z** 25235; rural
Flower; RMC Place; BRAXTON; ***250** E-6; elev. 848ft./258m.; 🅿; **z** 26611; rural
Fola; RMC Place; CLAY; ***250** F-5; elev. 1,097ft./334m.; 🅿; **z** 25019; rural
Follansbee; Inc. Place; BROOKE; **250** B-2; elev. 676ft./206m.; 🅿; ★ **STU-**; **z** 26037; Ⓟ 3,339; Ⓒ 3,115
Folsom; RMC Place; WETZEL; **250** C-7; elev. 964ft./294m.; 🅿; **z** 26348; ● 200
Forest Hill; RMC Place; SUMMERS; **250** I-6; elev. 1,931ft./589m.; 🅿; **z** 24935; ● 80
Forest Hill Estates; RMC Place; BERKELEY; ***250** C-13; mail Martinsburg **z** 25401; ● 250
Forest Hills; RMC Place; KANAWHA; ***250** F-4; ★ **CHAS**; mail Charleston **z** 25314; pop. incl. with Charleston (Inc. Place)
Forest Hills; RMC Place; OHIO; ***250** A-6; ★ **WHL**; mail Wheeling **z** 26003; pop. incl. with Wheeling (Inc. Place)
Forks of Cacapon; RMC Place; HAMPSHIRE; ***250** C-12; mail Bloomery **z** 26817, Paw Paw **z** 25434; rural
Forks of Coal; RMC Place; KANAWHA; ***250** G-3; ★ **CHAS**; mail Alum Creek **z** 25003; ● 75
Forks of Hurricane; RMC Place; WAYNE; ***250** G-1; elev. 581ft./177m.; mail Fort Gay **z** 25514, Prichard **z** 25555; rural
Fort Ashby; CDP; MINERAL; **250** B-11; elev. 604ft./184m.; 🅿; ★ **CUMB**; **z** 26719; Ⓟ 1,288; Ⓒ 1,354
Fort Branch; RMC Place; LOGAN; ***250** H-3; elev. 722ft./220m.; mail Ethel **z** 25076; ● 80
Fort Gay; Inc. Place; WAYNE; **250** G-1; elev. 580ft./177m.; 🅿; **z** 25514; Ⓟ 852; Ⓒ 819
Fort Grand; RMC Place; MONONGALIA; ***250** B-8; ★ **MORG**; ● 40
Fort Hill; RMC Place; KANAWHA; ***250** F-4; ★ **CHAS**; mail Charleston **z** 25303; pop. incl. with Charleston (Inc. Place)
Fort Martin; RMC Place; MONONGALIA; ***250** B-8; ★ **MORG**; mail Maidsville **z** 26541; rural
Fort Neal; RMC Place; WOOD; 🅿; ★ **PRKB**; **z** 26103; pop. incl. with Parkersburg (Inc. Place)
Fort Run; RMC Place; HARDY; ***250** D-11; mail Moorefield **z** 26836
Fort Seybert; RMC Place; PENDLETON; ***250** E-10; elev. 1,446ft./441m.; 🅿; **z** 26802
Fort Spring; RMC Place; GREENBRIER; **250** H-7; elev. 1,625ft./495m.; 🅿; **z** 24970; ● 150
Foster; RMC Place; BOONE; ***250** G-3; elev. 868ft./265m.; 🅿; **z** 25081; ● 175
Fosterville; RMC Place; BOONE; **250** G-4; elev. 710ft./216m.; mail Seth **z** 25181; ● 200
Four Mile; RMC Place; WETZEL; ***250** B-6; elev. 789ft./240m.; mail Burton **z** 26562, Pine Grove **z** 26419; rural
Four States; RMC Place; MARION; **250** C-7; elev. 1,032ft./315m.; 🅿; ★ **FAIRM**; **z** 26572; ● 400
Fowlerstown; RMC Place; BROOKE; ***250** B-2; ★ **STU-**; mail Wellsburg **z** 26070; ● 200
Frame; RMC Place; KANAWHA; **250** F-4; elev. 668ft./204m.; ★ **CHAS**; mail Elkview **z** 25071; ● 150
Frametown; RMC Place; BRAXTON; **250** E-6; elev. 825ft./251m.; 🅿; **z** 26623; ● 180
Francis; RMC Place; HARRISON; ***250** C-7; elev. 1,016ft./310m.; mail Fairmont **z** 26554; ● 50
Francis; RMC Place; RALEIGH; ***250** I-5; pop. incl. with Rhodell (Inc. Place)
Frank; RMC Place; POCAHONTAS; **250** F-9; elev. 2,750ft./838m.; mail Bartow **z** 24920; ● 120
Frankford; RMC Place; GREENBRIER; **250** H-7; elev. 2,250ft./686m.; 🅿; **z** 24938; ● 175
Franklin; RMC Place; BROOKE; ***250** B-2; ★ **STU-**; mail Wellsburg **z** 26070; ● 50
Franklin; Inc. Place; ⊡ PENDLETON; **250** E-10; elev. 1,739ft./530m.; 🅿; **z** 26807; Ⓟ 914; Ⓒ 797; Ⓡ 886
Franklintown; RMC Place; JEFFERSON; ***250** C-14; mail Rippon **z** 25441, Summit Point **z** 25446; rural
Fraziers Bottom; RMC Place; PUTNAM; **250** F-3; elev. 573ft./175m.; 🅿; **z** 25082; ● 200
Freed; RMC Place; CALHOUN; ***250** D-5; elev. 742ft./226m.; mail Big Springs **z** 26137, Brohard **z** 26138; rural
Freeman (Simmons); RMC Place; MERCER; ***250** J-5; elev. 2,249ft./685m.; 🅿; **z** 24724; pop. incl. with Bramwell (Inc. Place)
Freemansburg; RMC Place; LEWIS; ***250** D-7; mail Weston **z** 26452; rural
Freeport; RMC Place; PRESTON; ***250** C-9; elev. 2,466ft./752m.; mail Terra Alta **z** 26764; rural
Freeport; RMC Place; WIRT; ***250** D-5; elev. 630ft./192m.; 🅿; **z** 26180; ● 15
Freeze Fork; RMC Place; LOGAN; ***250** H-3; mail Ethel **z** 25076; rural
French Creek; RMC Place; UPSHUR; **250** E-7; elev. 1,500ft./457m.; 🅿; **z** 26218 & mail Frenchton **z** 26219; ● 120
Frenchton; RMC Place; UPSHUR; **250** E-7; elev. 1,496ft./456m.; 🅿; **z** 26219; ● 150
Frew; RMC Place; TYLER; ***250** C-6; elev. 720ft./219m.; mail Middlebourne **z** 26149; rural
Friars Hill; RMC Place; GREENBRIER; ***250** H-7; elev. 2,352ft./717m.; 🅿; **z** 24938
Friendly; Inc. Place; TYLER; **250** B-5; elev. 700ft./213m.; 🅿; **z** 26146; Ⓟ 146; Ⓒ 159
Friendly View; RMC Place; RALEIGH; ***250** H-4; mail Dry Creek **z** 25062; ● 50
Frogtown; RMC Place; LOGAN; ***250** H-3; mail Holden **z** 25625; ● 120
Frost; RMC Place; POCAHONTAS; ***250** G-8; mail Marlinton **z** 24954
Frozencamp; RMC Place; JACKSON; ***250** E-4; mail Le Roy **z** 25252
Fry; RMC Place; LINCOLN; ***250** G-3; mail Harts **z** 25524; rural
Fulton; RMC Place; OHIO; ***250** A-6; ★ **WHL**; mail Wheeling **z** 26003; pop. incl. with Wheeling (Inc. Place)

G

Gaines; RMC Place; UPSHUR; ***250** E-7; mail Rock Cave **z** 26234; rural
Gallagher; RMC Place; KANAWHA; ***250** G-4; elev. 649ft./198m.; 🅿; **z** 25083; ● 200
Gallipolis Ferry; RMC Place; MASON; ***250** E-2; 🅿; **z** 25515; ● 500
Galloway; RMC Place; BARBOUR; **250** C-8; elev. 1,052ft./321m.; 🅿; **z** 26349; ● 475
Galmish; RMC Place; WETZEL; ***250** B-6; elev. 701ft./214m.; mail Pine Grove **z** 26419, Reader **z** 26167; rural
Gandeeville; RMC Place; ROANE; **250** E-4; elev. 801ft./244m.; 🅿; **z** 25243; ● 300
Ganotown; RMC Place; BERKELEY; ***250** C-13; mail Hedgesville **z** 25427; rural
Gap Mills; RMC Place; MONROE; **250** I-7; elev. 2,344ft./714m.; 🅿; **z** 24941; ● 125
Gardner; RMC Place; MERCER; ***250** J-5; mail Princeton **z** 24740; rural
Garfield; RMC Place; JACKSON, WIRT; ***250** D-4; elev. 1,004ft./306m.; mail Le Roy **z** 25252; rural
Garland; RMC Place; MCDOWELL; ***250** J-3; mail Avondale **z** 24811; ● 80
Garretts Bend; RMC Place; LINCOLN; ***250** F-3; elev. 687ft./209m.; mail Sod **z** 25564
Garrison; RMC Place; BOONE; ***250** H-4; elev. 1,202ft./366m.; 🅿; **z** 25209; ● 200
Garten; RMC Place; FAYETTE; ***250** G-5; mail Fayetteville **z** 25840; ● 175
Garwood; RMC Place; WYOMING; ***250** I-5; mail Herndon **z** 24726; ● 100
Gary; Inc. Place; MCDOWELL; **250** J-4; elev. 1,402ft./427m.; 🅿; **z** 24836; Ⓟ 1,355; Ⓒ 917
Gassaway; Inc. Place; BRAXTON; **250** E-6; elev. 841ft./256m.; 🅿 🅷; **z** 26624; Ⓟ 946; Ⓒ 901
Gaston; RMC Place; LEWIS; ***250** D-7; mail Weston **z** 26452
Gaston Junction; RMC Place; MARION; ***250** C-8; elev. 891ft./272m.; ★ **FAIRM**; mail Fairmont **z** 26554; pop. incl. with Fairmont (Inc. Place)
Gates; RMC Place; MONROE; ***250** I-7; mail Union **z** 24983; rural
Gatewood; RMC Place; FAYETTE; **250** G-5; mail Fayetteville **z** 25840; ● 250
Gauley Bridge; Inc. Place; FAYETTE; **250** G-5; elev. 677ft./206m.; 🅿; **z** 25085; Ⓟ 691; Ⓒ 738
Gauley Mill; WEBSTER; see Gauley Mills (RMC Place)
Gauley Mills (Gauley Mill); RMC Place; WEBSTER; ***250** F-7; elev. 2,050ft./625m.; 🅿; **z** 26208; ● 120
Gay; RMC Place; JACKSON; **250** E-4; elev. 786ft./240m.; 🅿; **z** 25244; ● 75
Gaymont; RMC Place; FAYETTE; ***250** G-5; mail Victor **z** 25938; rural
Gem (Coger); RMC Place; BRAXTON; ***250** E-6; elev. 778ft./237m.; 🅿; **z** 26335
Genoa; RMC Place; WAYNE; **250** G-1; elev. 645ft./197m.; 🅿; **z** 25517; ● 100
Georges Run; RMC Place; TYLER; mail West Union **z** 26456; rural
Georgetown; RMC Place; LEWIS; ***250** D-7; elev. 1,084ft./330m.; mail Horner **z** 26372; rural
Georgetown; RMC Place; MARSHALL; ***250** B-7; elev. 958ft./292m.; mail Cameron **z** 26033
Georgetown; RMC Place; MONONGALIA; ***250** B-8; ★ **MORG**; mail Morgantown **z** 26501
Gerrardstown; RMC Place; BERKELEY; ***250** C-13; elev. 676ft./206m.; 🅿; **z** 25420; ● 350
Ghent; RMC Place; RALEIGH; **250** I-5; elev. 2,986ft./910m.; 🅿; **z** 25843; ● 300
Giatto; RMC Place; MERCER; ***250** J-5; mail Matoaka **z** 24736; ● 180
Gilbert; Inc. Place; MINGO; **250** I-3; elev. 829ft./253m.; 🅿; **z** 25621; Ⓟ 456; Ⓒ 417
Gilbert Creek; CDP-Census Area Only; MINGO; ***250** I-3; mail Baisden **z** 25608; Ⓟ 1,784; Ⓒ 1,582
Gilboa; RMC Place; NICHOLAS; **250** G-6; elev. 1,311ft./400m.; 🅿; **z** 26671; ● 150
Giles; RMC Place; KANAWHA; ***250** G-4; mail Dawes **z** 25054; ● 200
Gilkerson; RMC Place; WAYNE; mail East Lynn **z** 25512; ● 30
Gill; RMC Place; LINCOLN; ***250** G-2; elev. 600ft./183m.; mail Ranger **z** 25557; rural
Gilliam; RMC Place; MCDOWELL; ***250** I-4; elev. 1,800ft./549m.; 🅿; **z** 24868; ● 50
Gillman Bottom; RMC Place; LOGAN; ***250** H-3; mail Davin **z** 25617; ● 275
Gilman; RMC Place; RANDOLPH; ***250** D-8; mail Elkins **z** 26241
Gilmer; RMC Place; GILMER; **250** E-6; elev. 756ft./230m.; 🅿; **z** 26351; ● 50
GILMER; **250** D-6; Ⓟ 7,669; Ⓒ 7,160; ◆ 6,828
Gip; RMC Place; BRAXTON; ***250** E-5; elev. 926ft./282m.; rural
Given; RMC Place; JACKSON; ***250** E-3; elev. 649ft./198m.; 🅿; **z** 25245; ● 50
Glace; RMC Place; MONROE; **250** I-7; elev. 2,569ft./783m.; 🅿; **z** 24983; ● 35
Glade Farms; RMC Place; PRESTON; ***250** B-9; elev. 2,111ft./643m.; mail Bruceton Mills **z** 26525; rural
Glade Springs; RMC Place; RALEIGH; ***250** I-5; 🅿; ★ **BECK**; **z** 25832; ● 300
Gladesville; RMC Place; PRESTON; ***250** C-8; mail Independence **z** 26374; ● 100
Glade View; RMC Place; WEBSTER; ***250** F-7; mail Cowen **z** 26206; ● 250
Gladwin; RMC Place; TUCKER; ***250** D-9; elev. 1,953ft./595m.; mail Elkins **z** 26241; rural
Glady; RMC Place; RANDOLPH; **250** E-9; elev. 2,876ft./877m.; 🅿; **z** 26268; ● 60
Glasgow; Inc. Place; KANAWHA; **250** G-4; elev. 620ft./189m.; 🅿; **z** 25086; Ⓟ 906; Ⓒ 783
Glen; RMC Place; CLAY; **250** F-5; elev. 1,014ft./309m.; 🅿; **z** 25088; ● 20
Glen Alum; RMC Place; MINGO; rural
Glendale; Inc. Place; MARSHALL; **250** A-6; elev. 642ft./196m.; 🅿 🅷; ★ **WHL**; **z** 26038; Ⓟ 1,612; Ⓒ 1,552
Glendale; RMC Place; RITCHIE; ***250** C-5; mail Cairo **z** 26337; rural
Glendale Heights; RMC Place; MARSHALL; ***250** A-6; elev. 1,058ft./322m.; ★ **WHL**; mail Glen Dale **z** 26038; ● 600
Glen Daniel; RMC Place; RALEIGH; **250** H-4; elev. 1,902ft./580m.; 🅿; ★ **BECK**; **z** 25844; ● 600
Glendon; RMC Place; BRAXTON; ***250** F-6; elev. 800ft./244m.; 🅿; **z** 26623; rural
Glen Easton; RMC Place; MARSHALL; **250** A-6; elev. 947ft./289m.; 🅿; **z** 26039; ● 120
Glen Elk; RMC Place; HARRISON; ***250** C-7; elev. 1,019ft./311m.; ★ **CLRKB**; mail Clarksburg **z** 26301; pop. incl. with Clarksburg (Inc. Place)
Glen Falls; RMC Place; HARRISON; ***250** C-7; elev. 1,056ft./322m.; ★ **CLRKB**; mail Clarksburg **z** 26301; ● 100
Glen Ferris; RMC Place; FAYETTE; ***250** G-5; elev. 680ft./207m.; 🅿; **z** 25090; ● 250
Glen Fork; RMC Place; WYOMING; **250** I-4; elev. 1,421ft./433m.; 🅿; **z** 25845; ● 450
Glengary; RMC Place; BERKELEY; **250** C-13; elev. 591ft./180m.; 🅿; **z** 25421; ● 150
Glenhayes; RMC Place; WAYNE; **250** G-1; elev. 593ft./181m.; 🅿; **z** 25514; ● 40
Glen Jean; RMC Place; FAYETTE; **250** H-5; elev. 1,600ft./488m.; 🅿; ★ **BECK**; **z** 25846; ● 400
Glenmore; RMC Place; RANDOLPH; ***250** E-8; elev. 1,983ft./604m.; mail Elkins **z** 26241; ● 70
Glen Morgan; RMC Place; RALEIGH; ***250** H-5; elev. 2,094ft./638m.; 🅿; ★ **BECK**; **z** 25813; ● 600
Glenray; RMC Place; SUMMERS; ***250** H-6; mail Alderson **z** 24910; ● 50
Glen Rogers; RMC Place; WYOMING; ***250** I-4; elev. 1,832ft./558m.; 🅿; **z** 25848; ● 400
Glen View; RMC Place; RALEIGH; ***250** H-5; ★ **BECK**; mail Crab Orchard **z** 25827
Glenville; Inc. Place; ⊡ GILMER; **250** D-6; elev. 734ft./224m.; 🅿 🅲 1,381; **z** 26351; Ⓟ 1,923; Ⓒ 1,544
Glen White; RMC Place; RALEIGH; ***250** H-5; elev. 2,200ft./671m.; 🅿; ★ **BECK**; **z** 25849; ● 400
Glenwood; RMC Place; MASON; **250** F-2; elev. 544ft./166m.; 🅿; **z** 25520; ● 150
Glenwood; RMC Place; OHIO; ***250** A-6; ★ **WHL**; mail Wheeling **z** 26003; pop. incl. with Wheeling (Inc. Place)
Glenwood Park; RMC Place; MERCER; ***250** J-5; mail Bluefield **z** 24701; ● 600
Glover Gap; RMC Place; MARION; **250** B-7; elev. 1,056ft./322m.; mail Metz **z** 26585; ● 60
Gluck; MCDOWELL; see Lex (RMC Place)
Godby Heights; RMC Place; LOGAN; ***250** H-3; mail Chapmanville **z** 25508; ● 275
Godfrey; RMC Place; MERCER; ***250** J-5; mail Rock **z** 24747; ● 125
Goffs; RMC Place; RITCHIE; ***250** D-5; elev. 714ft./218m.; mail Harrisville **z** 26362; rural
Golden; RMC Place; MARSHALL; ***250** A-7; ★ **WHL**; mail Dallas **z** 26036; rural
Golden Acres; RMC Place; HAMPSHIRE; ***250** C-12; mail Augusta **z** 26704; ● 120
Goldtown; RMC Place; JACKSON; **250** F-4; elev. 658ft./201m.; mail Kenna **z** 25248; ● 100
Goodhope; RMC Place; HARRISON; **250** D-7; ★ **CLRKB**; mail Jane Lew **z** 26378; ● 170
Goodman; RMC Place; MINGO; ***250** I-2; mail Chattaroy **z** 25667; pop. incl. with Williamson (Inc. Place)
Goodwill; RMC Place; MERCER; ***250** J-5; mail Rock **z** 24747; rural
Gordon; RMC Place; BOONE; ***250** H-4; elev. 900ft./274m.; 🅿; **z** 25093; ● 250
Gore; RMC Place; HARRISON; ***250** C-7; ★ **CLRKB**; mail Clarksburg **z** 26301; ● 200
Gormania; RMC Place; GRANT; **250** C-10; elev. 2,320ft./707m.; 🅿; **z** 26720; ● 200
Gormley; RMC Place; UPSHUR; ***250** D-8; mail Ellamore **z** 26267; rural
Goshen; RMC Place; UPSHUR; ***250** E-7; elev. 2,419ft./737m.; mail Rock Cave **z** 26234; rural
Gould; RMC Place; CLAY; ***250** F-5; mail Ivydale **z** 25113; ● 40
Gould; RMC Place; UPSHUR; ***250** E-7; mail French Creek **z** 26218; rural
Grace; RMC Place; ROANE; ***250** E-5; elev. 688ft./210m.; mail Reedy **z** 25270; rural
Grafton; Inc. Place; ⊡ TAYLOR; **250** C-8; elev. 1,004ft./306m.; 🅿 🅷; **z** 26354; Ⓟ 5,524; Ⓒ 5,489
Graham Heights; RMC Place; MARION; ***250** C-8; ★ **FAIRM**; mail Fairmont **z** 26554; ● 200
Graham Station; RMC Place; MASON; ***250** D-3; mail Letart **z** 25253; rural
Grandview; RMC Place; RALEIGH; ***250** H-5; elev. 2,478ft./755m.; ★ **BECK**; mail Beaver **z** 25813; ● 150
Grangeville; RMC Place; MARION; ***250** C-7; elev. 1,000ft./305m.; mail Mannington **z** 26582; rural
GRANT; **250** D-10; Ⓟ 10,428; Ⓒ 11,299; ◆ 12,021
Grantsville; Inc. Place; ⊡ CALHOUN; **250** D-5; elev. 713ft./217m.; 🅿 🅷; **z** 26147; Ⓟ 671; Ⓒ 565
Grant Town; Inc. Place; MARION; **250** B-8; elev. 1,000ft./305m.; 🅿; ★ **FAIRM**; **z** 26574; Ⓟ 694; Ⓒ 657
Granville; Inc. Place; MONONGALIA; **250** A-3; elev. 833ft./254m.; 🅿; ★ **MORG**; **z** 26534; Ⓟ 798; Ⓒ 778
Grape Island; RMC Place; PLEASANTS; ***250** C-5; mail Saint Marys **z** 26170; pop. incl. with Saint Marys (Inc. Place)
Grassy Meadows; RMC Place; GREENBRIER; ***250** H-6; elev. 2,451ft./747m.; 🅿; **z** 24943; ● 30
Grave Creek; RMC Place; MARSHALL; ***250** A-6; mail Moundsville **z** 26041; rural
Graydon; RMC Place; FAYETTE; ***250** G-5; mail Victor **z** 25938; rural
Graysville; RMC Place; MARSHALL; ***250** A-6; elev. 697ft./212m.; mail Proctor **z** 26055; ● 130
Great Cacapon; RMC Place; MORGAN; **250** B-12; elev. 500ft./152m.; 🅿; **z** 25422; ● 500
Green Bank; RMC Place; POCAHONTAS; **250** F-8; elev. 2,645ft./806m.; 🅿; **z** 24944; ● 200
Green Bottom; RMC Place; CABELL; ***250** F-2; elev. 584ft./178m.; mail Lesage **z** 25537; rural
GREENBRIER; **250** G-7; Ⓟ 34,693; Ⓒ 34,453; ◆ 34,238
Green Castle; RMC Place; WIRT; ***250** D-4; elev. 627ft./191m.; mail Walker **z** 26180; rural
Greendale; RMC Place; NICHOLAS; ***250** G-5; elev. 937ft./286m.; mail Belva **z** 26656; rural
Green Hill; RMC Place; WETZEL; ***250** B-6; elev. 1,308ft./399m.; mail New Martinsville **z** 26155; rural
Greenland; RMC Place; GRANT; ***250** D-10; elev. 1,514ft./461m.; mail Maysville **z** 26833
Green Spring; RMC Place; HAMPSHIRE; **250** B-12; elev. 563ft./172m.; 🅿; **z** 26722; ● 350
Greenstown; RMC Place; FAYETTE; ***250** H-5; ★ **BECK**; mail Oak Hill **z** 25901; ● 60
Green Sulphur Springs; RMC Place; SUMMERS; **250** H-6; elev. 1,600ft./488m.; 🅿; **z** 25966 & mail Meadow Bridge **z** 25976; ● 75
Green Valley; RMC Place; MERCER; ***250** J-5; 🅿; **z** 24701; ● 800
Green Valley; RMC Place; NICHOLAS; ***250** G-6; elev. 2,500ft./762m.; mail Quinwood **z** 25981; rural
Greenview; RMC Place; BOONE; **250** H-3; elev. 759ft./231m.; mail Danville **z** 25053; ● 200
Greenville (Hunt); RMC Place; LOGAN; ***250** H-3; elev. 746ft./227m.; mail Man **z** 25635; ● 400
Greenville; RMC Place; MONROE; **250** I-6; elev. 1,702ft./519m.; 🅿; **z** 24945; ● 150
Greenwood; RMC Place; BOONE; ***250** H-4; mail Wharton **z** 25208; ● 125
Greenwood; RMC Place; DODDRIDGE; **250** C-6; elev. 890ft./271m.; 🅿; **z** 26415; ● 180
Greer; RMC Place; MASON; ***250** E-3; elev. 719ft./219m.; mail Point Pleasant **z** 25550
Greer; RMC Place; MONONGALIA; ***250** B-8; ★ **MORG**; mail Morgantown **z** 26508; rural
Greggsville; RMC Place; OHIO; ***250** A-6; ★ **WHL**; mail Wheeling **z** 26003; pop. incl. with Wheeling (Inc. Place)
Greyeagle; RMC Place; MINGO; ***250** H-2; mail Kermit **z** 25674; ● 150
Griffithsville; RMC Place; LINCOLN; **250** G-3; elev. 668ft./204m.; 🅿; **z** 25521; ● 350
Grimms Landing; RMC Place; MASON; **250** E-3; elev. 567ft./173m.; 🅿; **z** 25123; ● 75
Grippe; RMC Place; KANAWHA; ***250** G-3; ★ **CHAS**; mail Charleston **z** 25314; ● 25
Grove; RMC Place; DODDRIDGE; ***250** D-6; mail New Milton **z** 26411
Groves; RMC Place; CLAY; ***250** F-6; elev. 785ft./239m.; mail Duck **z** 25063; rural
Grubbs Corner; RMC Place; BERKELEY; ***250** C-13; mail Martinsburg **z** 25401; ● 200
Guardian; RMC Place; WEBSTER; ***250** E-7; elev. 1,087ft./331m.; mail Diana **z** 26217
Gum Spring; RMC Place; MONONGALIA; ***250** B-8; elev. 2,030ft./619m.; ★ **MORG**; mail Morgantown **z** 26508
Gunville; RMC Place; MASON; ***250** E-3; elev. 948ft./289m.; mail Leon **z** 25123; rural
Guthrie; RMC Place; KANAWHA; **250** H-13; elev. 612ft./187m.; ★ **CHAS**; mail Charleston **z** 25312; ● 600
Guyandotte; RMC Place; CABELL; ***250** F-2; elev. 546ft./166m.; ★ **HNTG**; mail Huntington **z** 25702; pop. incl. with Huntington (Inc. Place)
Guyan Estates; RMC Place; CABELL; ***250** F-2; ★ **HNTG**; mail Barboursville **z** 25504; ● 800
Guyan Terrace; RMC Place; LOGAN; ***250** H-3; mail Logan **z** 25601; ● 100
Gypsy; RMC Place; HARRISON; **250** C-7; elev. 960ft./293m.; 🅿; ★ **CLRKB**; **z** 26361; ● 280

H

Hacker Valley; RMC Place; WEBSTER; **250** E-7; elev. 1,515ft./462m.; 🅿; **z** 26222; ● 150
Haddleton (Washington Heights); RMC Place; BOONE; ***250** G-3; mail Madison **z** 25130; ● 60
Hagans; RMC Place; MONONGALIA; ***250** B-8; elev. 1,022ft./312m.; ★ **MORG**; mail Maidsville **z** 26541
Hager; RMC Place; LINCOLN; ***250** G-3; elev. 701ft./214m.; mail Branchland **z** 25506
Hall; RMC Place; BARBOUR; ***250** D-8; elev. 1,368ft./417m.; mail Buckhannon **z** 26201; rural
Hallburg; RMC Place; CLAY; ***250** E-5; elev. 978ft./298m.; mail Duck **z** 25063; rural
Halleck; RMC Place; MONONGALIA; ***250** C-8; ★ **MORG**; mail Morgantown **z** 26508
Halltown; RMC Place; JEFFERSON; **250** C-14; elev. 394ft./120m.; 🅿; **z** 25423; ● 350
Halo; RMC Place; WEBSTER; ***250** F-7; mail Cowen **z** 26206; rural
Hambleton; Inc. Place; TUCKER; **250** D-9; elev. 1,685ft./514m.; 🅿; **z** 26269; Ⓟ 265; Ⓒ 246
Hamlin; Inc. Place; ⊡ LINCOLN; **250** G-2; elev. 673ft./205m.; 🅿; **z** 25523; Ⓟ 1,030; Ⓒ 1,119
Hammond; RMC Place; MARION; ***250** C-8; ★ **FAIRM**; mail Colfax **z** 26566; rural
Hampden; RMC Place; MINGO; **250** I-3; elev. 1,091ft./333m.; 🅿; **z** 25621; ● 150
HAMPSHIRE; **250** C-11; Ⓟ 16,498; Ⓒ 20,203; ◆ 22,953
Hampton (Ivanhoe); RMC Place; UPSHUR; ***250** D-7; mail Buckhannon **z** 26201; ● 100
Hancock; RMC Place; MORGAN; **250** B-13; elev. 400ft./122m.; 🅿; **z** 25411; ● 35
HANCOCK; **250** A-2; Ⓟ 35,233; Ⓒ 32,667; ◆ 28,933
Handley; Inc. Place; KANAWHA; ***250** G-4; elev. 635ft./194m.; 🅿; **z** 25102; Ⓟ 334; Ⓒ 362
Hanna; RMC Place; WOOD; ***250** D-4; elev. 615ft./187m.; ★ **PRKB**; mail Walker **z** 26180; rural
Hannahsville; RMC Place; TUCKER; ***250** C-9; mail Parsons **z** 26287
Hanover; RMC Place; WYOMING; **250** I-3; elev. 1,057ft./322m.; 🅿; **z** 24839; ● 120
Hansford; RMC Place; KANAWHA; ***250** G-4; elev. 620ft./189m.; 🅿; **z** 25103; ● 350
Hany; RMC Place; WAYNE; mail Dunlow **z** 25511; rural
Harding; RMC Place; RANDOLPH; **250** D-8; mail Belington **z** 26250; ● 90
Hardy; RMC Place; MERCER; ***250** J-5; elev. 1,940ft./591m.; mail Princeton **z** 24740; rural
HARDY; **250** D-11; Ⓟ 10,977; Ⓒ 12,669; ◆ 13,851
Harlem Heights; RMC Place; FAYETTE; ***250** H-5; ★ **BECK**; mail Oak Hill **z** 25901; pop. incl. with Oak Hill (Inc. Place)
Harlin; RMC Place; DODDRIDGE; ***250** C-6; mail West Union **z** 26456
Harman; Inc. Place; RANDOLPH; **250** D-9; elev. 2,360ft./719m.; 🅿; **z** 26270; Ⓟ 128; Ⓒ 126
Harmony; RMC Place; ROANE; ***250** E-4; elev. 720ft./219m.; 🅿; **z** 25243
Harmony Grove; RMC Place; MONONGALIA; ***250** B-8; ★ **MORG**; mail Morgantown **z** 26501; ● 40
Harper; RMC Place; PENDLETON; ***250** F-9; mail Franklin **z** 26807; rural
Harper; RMC Place; RALEIGH; ***250** H-5; elev. 2,142ft./653m.; 🅿; ★ **BECK**; **z** 25851; ● 100
Harper Heights; RMC Place; RALEIGH; ***250** H-5; ★ **BECK**; mail Beckley **z** 25801; ● 700
Harpers Ferry; Inc. Place; JEFFERSON; **250** C-14; elev. 484ft./148m.; 🅿; **z** 25425; Ⓟ 308; Ⓒ 307
Harpertown; RMC Place; RANDOLPH; ***250** D-9; elev. 1,945ft./593m.; mail Elkins **z** 26241; pop. incl. with Elkins (Inc. Place)
Harrison; RMC Place; CLAY; ***250** F-6; elev. 1,072ft./327m.; 🅿; **z** 25063; ● 30
HARRISON; **250** C-7; Ⓟ 69,371; Ⓒ 68,652; ◆ 66,760
Harrisville; Inc. Place; ⊡ RITCHIE; **250** C-5; elev. 873ft./266m.; 🅿; **z** 26362; Ⓟ 1,839; Ⓒ 1,842
Harters Hill; RMC Place; MARION; ***250** C-7; ★ **FAIRM**; mail Worthington **z** 26591; rural
Hartford; MASON; see Hartford City (Inc. Place)
Hartford City (Hartford); Inc. Place; MASON; **250** D-3; elev. 575ft./175m.; mail Hartford **z** 25247; Ⓟ 487; Ⓒ 519
Hartland; RMC Place; CLAY; **250** F-5; mail Clay **z** 25043; ● 65
Hartmansville; RMC Place; MINERAL; ***250** C-10; elev. 2,699ft./823m.; mail Elk Garden **z** 26717; ● 55
Harts; CDP; LINCOLN; **250** G-2; 🅿; **z** 25524; Ⓟ 2,332; Ⓒ 2,361
Hartwell; MCDOWELL; see Vallscreek (RMC Place)
Harvey; RMC Place; FAYETTE; ***250** H-5; elev. 1,570ft./479m.; 🅿; ★ **BECK**; **z** 25901; ● 150
Harveytown; RMC Place; CABELL; ***250** F-2; elev. 550ft./168m.; ★ **HNTG**; mail Huntington **z** 25704; pop. incl. with Huntington (Inc. Place)
Hastings; RMC Place; WETZEL; **250** B-6; elev. 726ft./221m.; 🅿; **z** 26419 & mail Jacksonburg **z** 26377; ● 50
Hatcher; RMC Place; MERCER; ***250** J-5; elev. 2,041ft./622m.; mail Princeton **z** 24740; rural
Hatcher; RMC Place; WYOMING; ***250** I-4; mail Oceana **z** 24870; pop. incl. with Oceana (Inc. Place)
Havaco; RMC Place; MCDOWELL; ***250** J-4; elev. 1,337ft./408m.; 🅿; **z** 24801; ● 180
Havana (Six Mile); RMC Place; BOONE; ***250** H-3; mail Danville **z** 25053; rural
Haywood; RMC Place; HARRISON; ***250** C-7; elev. 1,000ft./305m.; 🅿; ★ **CLRKB**; **z** 26366; ● 190
Haywood Junction; RMC Place; HARRISON; ***250** C-7; ★ **CLRKB**; mail Shinnston **z** 26431; ● 150
Hazelgreen; RMC Place; RITCHIE; ***250** D-5; elev. 795ft./242m.; 🅿; **z** 26362; rural
Hazelton; RMC Place; PRESTON; **250** B-9; elev. 1,884ft./574m.; 🅿; **z** 26525; ● 50
Hazelwood; RMC Place; RANDOLPH; ***250** E-8; mail Elkins **z** 26241; pop. incl. with Beverly (Inc. Place)
Hazy; RMC Place; RALEIGH; ***250** H-4; mail Naoma **z** 25140; rural
Headsville; RMC Place; MINERAL; ***250** C-11; mail Burlington **z** 26710
Heaters; RMC Place; BRAXTON; **250** E-6; elev. 873ft./266m.; 🅿; **z** 26627; ● 65
Heatherfield; RMC Place; JEFFERSON; ***250** C-14; mail Shepherdstown **z** 25443; ● 175
Heavener Grove; RMC Place; UPSHUR; ***250** D-8; mail Buckhannon **z** 26201; rural
Hebron; RMC Place; PLEASANTS; **250** C-5; elev. 758ft./231m.; mail Ellenboro **z** 26346; ● 25
Hedgesville; Inc. Place; BERKELEY; **250** B-13; elev. 600ft./183m.; 🅿; **z** 25427; Ⓟ 227; Ⓒ 240
Hedgeview; RMC Place; LOGAN; ***250** H-3; mail Mount Gay **z** 25637; ● 200
Heights; RMC Place; MASON; ***250** E-2; mail Point Pleasant **z** 25550; pop. incl. with Point Pleasant (Inc. Place)
Heizer; RMC Place; PUTNAM; ***250** F-3; ★ **CHAS**; mail Poca **z** 25159
Helen; RMC Place; RALEIGH; **250** I-5; elev. 1,656ft./505m.; 🅿; **z** 25853; ● 125
Helens Run; RMC Place; MARION; ***250** C-7; elev. 917ft./280m.; ★ **FAIRM**; mail Worthington **z** 26591; ● 60
Helvetia; RMC Place; RANDOLPH; **250** E-8; elev. 2,239ft./682m.; 🅿; **z** 26224; ● 150
Hemlock; RMC Place; UPSHUR; ***250** E-8; mail Helvetia **z** 26224; rural
Hemphill; RMC Place; MCDOWELL; ***250** I-4; elev. 1,289ft./393m.; 🅿; **z** 24842; pop. incl. with Welch (Inc. Place)
Henderson; Inc. Place; MASON; **250** E-2; elev. 567ft./173m.; 🅿; **z** 25106; Ⓟ 549; Ⓒ 325
Hendricks; Inc. Place; TUCKER; **250** D-9; elev. 1,716ft./523m.; 🅿; **z** 26271; Ⓟ 303; Ⓒ 319
Henlawson; RMC Place; LOGAN; **250** H-3; elev. 668ft./204m.; 🅿; **z** 25624; ● 500
Henning; RMC Place; GREENBRIER; ***250** H-7; elev. 2,222ft./677m.; mail Frankford **z** 24938
Henrietta; RMC Place; CALHOUN; ***250** D-5; mail Grantsville **z** 26147
Hensley (Claren); RMC Place; MCDOWELL; ***250** I-4; elev. 1,160ft./354m.; 🅿; **z** 24843; ● 200
Hensley Heights; RMC Place; LOGAN; ***250** H-3; mail Man **z** 25635; ● 50
Hepzibah; RMC Place; HARRISON; ***250** C-7; elev. 1,000ft./305m.; 🅿; ★ **CLRKB**; **z** 26369; ● 600
Hepzibah; RMC Place; TAYLOR; ***250** C-8; elev. 1,155ft./352m.; mail Bridgeport **z** 26330
Hereford; RMC Place; JACKSON; ***250** E-4; elev. 632ft./193m.; mail Le Roy **z** 25252
Herndon; RMC Place; WYOMING; **250** I-4; elev. 1,893ft./577m.; 🅿; **z** 24726; ● 300
Herndon Heights; RMC Place; WYOMING; ***250** I-4; mail Herndon **z** 24726; ● 100
Hernshaw; RMC Place; KANAWHA; ***250** G-4; elev. 672ft./205m.; 🅿; ★ **CHAS**; **z** 25107; ● 650
Herold; RMC Place; BRAXTON; ***250** F-6; elev. 927ft./283m.; 🅿; **z** 26601; rural
Herring; RMC Place; PRESTON; ***250** B-9; elev. 2,042ft./622m.; mail Reedsville **z** 26547; rural
Hettie; RMC Place; BRAXTON; ***250** E-7; elev. 1,388ft./423m.; mail Ireland **z** 26376; rural
Hetzel; RMC Place; LOGAN; ***250** H-3; elev. 1,002ft./305m.; mail Ethel **z** 25076; rural
Hewett; RMC Place; BOONE; **250** H-3; elev. 815ft./248m.; 🅿; **z** 25108; ● 250
Hiawatha; RMC Place; MERCER; ***250** I-5; elev. 2,403ft./732m.; 🅿; **z** 24729; ● 125
Hickory Chapel; RMC Place; MASON; ***250** E-3; mail Point Pleasant **z** 25550; rural
Hico; RMC Place; FAYETTE; **250** G-5; elev. 2,056ft./627m.; 🅿; **z** 25854; ● 900
Highland; RMC Place; RITCHIE; ***250** C-5; elev. 788ft./240m.; 🅿; **z** 26346
Highland Park; RMC Place; RANDOLPH; ***250** D-8; mail Elkins **z** 26241; ● 300
Highlawn; RMC Place; KANAWHA; ***250** F-3; ★ **CHAS**; mail Saint Albans **z** 25177; pop. incl. with Saint Albans (Inc. Place)
High View; RMC Place; HAMPSHIRE; **250** C-12; elev. 1,318ft./402m.; 🅿; **z** 26808; ● 30
Hildebrand; RMC Place; MONONGALIA; ***250** B-8; ★ **MORG**; mail Morgantown **z** 26501; rural
Hillcrest; RMC Place; MARION; ***250** C-8; ★ **FAIRM**; mail Fairmont **z** 26554; pop. incl. with Fairmont (Inc. Place)
Hilldale; RMC Place; SUMMERS; ***250** I-6; mail Hinton **z** 25951; ● 150
Hillsboro; Inc. Place; POCAHONTAS; **250** G-7; elev. 2,303ft./702m.; 🅿; **z** 24946; Ⓟ 188; Ⓒ 243
Hillsdale; RMC Place; KANAWHA; ***250** F-4; ★ **CHAS**; mail Charleston **z** 25302; pop. incl. with Charleston (Inc. Place)
Hillsdale; RMC Place; MONROE; ***250** I-7; mail Sinks Grove **z** 24976; rural
Hilltop; RMC Place; FAYETTE; ***250** H-5; elev. 1,829ft./557m.; 🅿; ★ **BECK**; **z** 25855; ● 200
Hillview; RMC Place; CABELL; ***250** F-2; ★ **HNTG**; mail Huntington **z** 25702; ● 600
Hillview; RMC Place; MARION; ***250** C-8; elev. 982ft./299m.; ★ **FAIRM**; mail Fairmont **z** 26554; pop. incl. with Whitehall (Inc. Place)
Hillview Terrace; RMC Place; MARSHALL; ***250** A-6; ★ **WHL**; mail Moundsville **z** 26041; ● 175
Hilton Village; RMC Place; FAYETTE; ***250** H-6; 🅿; **z** 25962; ● 50
Hinch; RMC Place; MINGO; ***250** I-3; elev. 1,208ft./368m.; mail Matewan **z** 25678
Hines; RMC Place; GREENBRIER; **250** H-6; elev. 2,412ft./735m.; 🅿; **z** 25958; ● 300
Hinkleville; RMC Place; UPSHUR; ***250** D-7; elev. 1,578ft./481m.; mail Buckhannon **z** 26201
Hinton; Inc. Place; ⊡ SUMMERS; **250** I-6; elev. 1,449ft./442m.; 🅿 🅷; **z** 25951; Ⓟ 3,433; Ⓒ 2,880
Hiorra; RMC Place; PRESTON; ***250** C-9; mail Newburg **z** 26410; rural
Hitop; RMC Place; KANAWHA; ***250** G-5; mail Pond Gap **z** 25160; rural
Hix; RMC Place; SUMMERS; **250** I-6; elev. 2,615ft./797m.; mail Hinton **z** 25951; rural
Hodgesville; RMC Place; UPSHUR; **250** D-8; elev. 1,427ft./435m.; mail Buckhannon **z** 26201; ● 150
Hogsett; RMC Place; MASON; ***250** E-2; elev. 564ft./172m.; mail Gallipolis Ferry **z** 25515; rural
Hokes Mill; RMC Place; GREENBRIER; ***250** I-7; mail Ronceverte **z** 24970; rural
Holbrook; RMC Place; RITCHIE; ***250** D-6; elev. 798ft./243m.; mail West Union **z** 26456; rural
Holcomb; RMC Place; NICHOLAS; ***250** G-6; elev. 2,036ft./621m.; mail Richwood **z** 26261; ● 100
Holden; CDP; LOGAN; **250** H-3; elev. 737ft./225m.; 🅿; **z** 25625; Ⓟ 1,246; Ⓒ 1,105
Holidays Cove; HANCOCK; see Cove (RMC Place)
Holly; RMC Place; KANAWHA; mail Eskdale **z** 25075; ● 50
Hollygrove; RMC Place; KANAWHA; ***250** G-4; elev. 625ft./191m.; mail Hansford **z** 25103; ● 200
Hollywood; RMC Place; MONROE; ***250** I-7; elev. 2,172ft./662m.; mail Union **z** 24983; rural
Holton; RMC Place; MORGAN; ***250** B-13; mail Berkeley Springs **z** 25411; rural
Homeland; RMC Place; LEWIS; ***250** D-7; mail Jane Lew **z** 26378; rural
Hometown; RMC Place; PUTNAM; **250** F-3; elev. 600ft./183m.; 🅿; ★ **CHAS**; **z** 25109; ● 350
Homewood; RMC Place; LEWIS; ***250** D-7; mail Weston **z** 26452; ● 250
Hominy Falls; RMC Place; NICHOLAS; ***250** G-6; elev. 2,359ft./719m.; mail Mount Nebo **z** 26679
Hoodsville; RMC Place; MARION; ***250** B-8; ★ **FAIRM**; mail Rivesville **z** 26588
Hoohoo; RMC Place; RALEIGH; ***250** H-5; ★ **BECK**; mail Lester **z** 25865; rural
Hookersville; RMC Place; NICHOLAS; ***250** F-6; mail Summersville **z** 26651; rural
Hooverson Heights; CDP; BROOKE; ***250** B-2; ★ **STU-**; mail Follansbee **z** 26037; Ⓟ 3,056; Ⓒ 2,909
Hoover Town; RMC Place; UPSHUR; ***250** E-7; mail French Creek **z** 26218; rural
Hopecrest; RMC Place; MONONGALIA; ***250** B-8; ★ **MORG**; mail Morgantown **z** 26505; pop. incl. with Morgantown (Inc. Place)
Hopeville; RMC Place; GRANT; **250** D-10; mail Cabins **z** 26855; ● 20
Hopewell; RMC Place; FAYETTE; ***250** G-5; elev. 1,461ft./445m.; mail Victor **z** 25938; rural
Hopewell; RMC Place; MARION; ***250** C-8; ★ **FAIRM**; mail Fairmont **z** 26554
Hopewell; RMC Place; PRESTON; ***250** B-9; mail Bruceton Mills **z** 26525; rural
Hopkins Fork; RMC Place; BOONE; ***250** G-4; elev. 727ft./222m.; mail Seth **z** 25181
Horner; RMC Place; LEWIS; **250** D-7; elev. 1,080ft./329m.; 🅿; **z** 26372; ● 125
Horsepen; RMC Place; MCDOWELL; **250** J-4; 🅿; **z** 24619; ● 50
Horse Shoe Run; RMC Place; PRESTON; ***250** C-9; elev. 2,612ft./796m.; 🅿; **z** 26716; ● 60
Horton; RMC Place; RANDOLPH; ***250** E-9; mail Whitmer **z** 26296; rural
Hosterman; RMC Place; POCAHONTAS; ***250** F-8; mail Durbin **z** 26264; rural
Hotchkiss; RMC Place; RALEIGH; ***250** I-4; elev. 1,690ft./515m.; ★ **BECK**; mail Slab Fork **z** 25920; ● 100
Hoult; RMC Place; MARION; ***250** B-8; ★ **FAIRM**; mail Fairmont **z** 26554; rural
Howells Mill; RMC Place; CABELL; ***250** F-2; ★ **HNTG**; mail Ona **z** 25545; ● 350
Howesville; RMC Place; PRESTON; **250** C-9; elev. 2,214ft./675m.; mail Tunnelton **z** 26444; ● 125
Hoy; RMC Place; HAMPSHIRE; ***250** C-12; elev. 1,256ft./383m.; mail Augusta **z** 26704; rural
Hubball; RMC Place; LINCOLN; ***250** G-2; elev. 605ft./184m.; mail Branchland **z** 25506; ● 60
Hubbardstown; RMC Place; WAYNE; ***250** G-1; elev. 569ft./173m.; mail Prichard **z** 25555
Hudson; RMC Place; PRESTON; ***250** B-9; elev. 1,715ft./523m.; mail Albright **z** 26519; rural
Huff Junction; RMC Place; LOGAN; ***250** H-3; elev. 749ft./228m.; mail Man **z** 25635; ● 60
Hughart; RMC Place; GREENBRIER; ***250** H-7; mail Crawley **z** 24931; rural
Hughes; RMC Place; HARRISON; ★ **CLRKB**; mail Meadowbrook **z** 26404; ● 50
Hugheston; RMC Place; KANAWHA; ***250** G-4; elev. 640ft./195m.; 🅿; **z** 25110; ● 800
Hugo; RMC Place; PUTNAM; ***250** F-3; mail Red House **z** 25168; rural
Humphrey; RMC Place; WOOD; mail Belleville **z** 26133; ● 200
Hundred; Inc. Place; WETZEL; **250** B-7; elev. 1,021ft./311m.; 🅿; **z** 26575; Ⓟ 386; Ⓒ 344
Hunt; LOGAN; see Greenville (RMC Place)
Huntersville; RMC Place; POCAHONTAS; **250** G-8; elev. 2,267ft./691m.; mail Marlinton **z** 24954; ● 125
Huntington; Inc. Place; ⊡ CABELL, WAYNE; **250** F-2; elev. 569ft./173m.; 🅿 🅷 🅲 13,940 ■; ★ **HNTG**; **z** 25701-29, **z** 25755, **z** 25770-79; Ⓟ 54,844; Ⓒ 51,475; ◆ 47,245
Hur; RMC Place; CALHOUN; ***250** E-5; mail Mount Zion **z** 26151; rural
Hurricane; Inc. Place; PUTNAM; **250** F-3; elev. 687ft./209m.; 🅿 🅷; ★ **CHAS**; **z** 25526; Ⓟ 4,461; Ⓒ 5,222
Hurst; RMC Place; LEWIS; ***250** D-6; elev. 802ft./244m.; mail Alum Bridge **z** 26321; rural
Hutchinson; RMC Place; MARION; ***250** C-7; ★ **FAIRM**; mail Worthington **z** 26591; ● 225
Huttonsville; Inc. Place; RANDOLPH; **250** E-8; elev. 2,053ft./626m.; 🅿; **z** 26273; Ⓟ 211; Ⓒ 217

I

Iaeger; Inc. Place; MCDOWELL; **250** I-3; elev. 981ft./299m.; 🅿; **z** 24844; Ⓟ 551; Ⓒ 358
Idamay; RMC Place; MARION; ***250** C-7; elev. 1,160ft./354m.; 🅿; ★ **FAIRM**; **z** 26576; ● 650
Ikes Fork; RMC Place; WYOMING; **250** I-3; elev. 1,252ft./382m.; 🅿; **z** 24845; ● 300
Independence; RMC Place; CLAY; ***250** F-5; elev. 1,371ft./418m.; mail Lizemores **z** 25125
Independence; RMC Place; JACKSON; ***250** D-4; mail Sandyville **z** 25275; rural
Independence; RMC Place; PRESTON; ***250** C-8; elev. 1,170ft./357m.; 🅿; **z** 26374; ● 150
Indian; RMC Place; KANAWHA; ★ **CHAS**; mail Saint Albans **z** 25177; pop. incl. with Saint Albans (Inc. Place)
Indian Meadows; RMC Place; CABELL; ***250** F-2; ★ **HNTG**; mail Ona **z** 25545; ● 2,000
Indian Mills; RMC Place; SUMMERS; ***250** I-6; elev. 1,630ft./497m.; 🅿; **z** 24935
Indore; RMC Place; CLAY; **250** F-5; elev. 1,000ft./305m.; 🅿; **z** 25111; ● 125
Industrial; RMC Place; HARRISON, DODDRIDGE; ***250** C-7; elev. 1,100ft./335m.; 🅿; ★ **CLRKB**; **z** 26426; pop. incl. with Clarksburg (Inc. Place)
Industry; RMC Place; CALHOUN; ***250** D-5; elev. 668ft./204m.; mail Munday **z** 26152; rural
Ingleside; RMC Place; MERCER; ***250** J-5; mail Princeton **z** 24740
Ingram Branch; RMC Place; FAYETTE; ***250** G-5; elev. 1,304ft./397m.; mail Kincaid **z** 25119; ● 100
Inkerman; RMC Place; HARDY; ***250** D-11; mail Baker **z** 26801; rural
Institute; RMC Place; KANAWHA; **250** F-3; elev. 622ft./190m.; 🅿 🅲 3,502; ★ **CHAS**; **z** 25112; ● 1,800
Intermont; RMC Place; HAMPSHIRE; ***250** D-12; mail Wardensville **z** 26851; rural
Inwood; CDP; BERKELEY; **250** C-13; elev. 570ft./174m.; 🅿; **z** 25428; Ⓟ 1,360; Ⓒ 2,084
Ireland; RMC Place; LEWIS; **250** E-7; elev. 1,141ft./348m.; 🅿; **z** 26376; ● 130
Irona; RMC Place; PRESTON; ***250** C-9; mail Kingwood **z** 26537
Iroquis; RMC Place; WYOMING; ***250** I-4; mail Stephenson **z** 25928; ● 100
Isaban; RMC Place; MCDOWELL, MINGO; ***250** I-3; elev. 1,108ft./338m.; 🅿; **z** 24846; ● 125
Island Branch; RMC Place; KANAWHA; ***250** F-4; ★ **CHAS**; mail Charleston **z** 25320; rural
Isom; RMC Place; LOGAN; ***250** H-3; elev. 885ft./270m.; mail Lake **z** 25121; ● 100
Israel; RMC Place; PRESTON; ***250** C-9; mail Tunnelton **z** 26444; rural
Itmann; RMC Place; WYOMING; ***250** I-4; elev. 1,400ft./427m.; 🅿; **z** 24847; ● 400
Iuka; RMC Place; TYLER; ***250** B-6; mail Middlebourne **z** 26149
Ivanhoe; UPSHUR; see Hampton (RMC Place)
Ivy; RMC Place; UPSHUR; ***250** D-8; mail Buckhannon **z** 26201; rural
Ivydale; RMC Place; CLAY; **250** F-5; elev. 760ft./232m.; 🅿; **z** 25113; ● 250

J

JACKSON; **250** E-4; Ⓟ 25,938; Ⓒ 28,000; ◆ 27,956
Jacksonburg; RMC Place; WETZEL; **250** B-6; elev. 746ft./227m.; 🅿; **z** 26377; ● 300
Jackson Flats; RMC Place; MCDOWELL; ***250** J-3; extends into Buchanon county, Virginia; elev. 2,305ft./703m.; mail Paynesville **z** 24873; rural
Jacksons Mill; RMC Place; LEWIS; ***250** D-7; mail Weston **z** 26452; ● 300
Jacobs Fork; RMC Place; MCDOWELL; ***250** J-4; mail Squire **z** 24884
Jacox; RMC Place; POCAHONTAS; ***250** G-7; elev. 2,582ft./787m.; mail Hillsboro **z** 24946; rural
Jakes Run; RMC Place; MONONGALIA; ***250** B-8; mail Maidsville **z** 26541; ● 75
James Crest Farms; RMC Place; RALEIGH; ***250** H-5; ★ **BECK**; mail Beckley **z** 25801; ● 200
Jamestown; RMC Place; JEFFERSON; ***250** C-13; elev. 578ft./176m.; mail Summit Point **z** 25446; ● 50
Jane Lew; Inc. Place; LEWIS; **250** D-7; elev. 1,007ft./307m.; 🅿; **z** 26378; Ⓟ 439; Ⓒ 406
Janie; RMC Place; BOONE; ***250** H-4; mail Whitesville **z** 25209; pop. incl. with Whitesville (Inc. Place)
Jarrolds Valley; RMC Place; RALEIGH; ***250** H-4; mail Whitesville **z** 25209; pop. incl. with Whitesville (Inc. Place)
Jarvisville; RMC Place; HARRISON; ***250** C-7; elev. 1,058ft./322m.; ★ **CLRKB**; mail Salem **z** 26426
Jawood; RMC Place; RALEIGH; mail Amigo **z** 25811; rural
Jayenn; MARION; see Westchester (RMC Place)
Jefferson; RMC Place; KANAWHA; ***250** F-3; 🅿; ★ **CHAS**; **z** 25177; disincorporated February 21, 2007; Ⓒ 567
JEFFERSON; **250** C-14; Ⓟ 35,926; Ⓒ 42,190; ◆ 52,499
Jeffrey; RMC Place; BOONE; **250** H-3; elev. 786ft./240m.; 🅿; **z** 25114; ● 500
Jenkinjones; RMC Place; MCDOWELL; ***250** J-4; elev. 1,925ft./587m.; 🅿; **z** 24848; ● 190
Jenks; RMC Place; LINCOLN; ***250** G-2; mail Branchland **z** 25506; rural
Jenningston; RMC Place; TUCKER; ***250** D-9; mail Bowden **z** 26254; rural
Jere; RMC Place; MONONGALIA; ***250** B-8; elev. 977ft./298m.; ★ **MORG**; mail Pursglove **z** 26546; ● 250
Jerome Park; RMC Place; MONONGALIA; ***250** B-8; ★ **MORG**; mail Morgantown **z** 26505; pop. incl. with Morgantown (Inc. Place)
Jerry Run; TAYLOR; see Rosemont (RMC Place)
Jerrys Run; RMC Place; WOOD; ***250** D-4; elev. 620ft./189m.; mail Belleville **z** 26133; rural
Jesse; RMC Place; WYOMING; **250** I-4; elev. 1,370ft./418m.; 🅿; **z** 24849; ● 250
Jimtown; RMC Place; MORGAN; ***250** B-13; mail Berkeley Springs **z** 25411
Jimtown; RMC Place; RANDOLPH; ***250** D-8; mail Coalton **z** 26257, Norton **z** 26285; rural
Job; RMC Place; RANDOLPH; **250** E-9; elev. 2,582ft./787m.; 🅿; **z** 26296 & mail Harman **z** 26270; ● 40
Jockeycamp Run; RMC Place; DODDRIDGE; ***250** C-6; mail West Union **z** 26456; rural
Jodie; RMC Place; FAYETTE; **250** G-5; elev. 720ft./219m.; 🅿; **z** 26690; ● 180
Joe Creek; BOONE; see Comfort (RMC Place)
Joetown; RMC Place; MARION; ***250** C-7; elev. 1,012ft./308m.; mail Mannington **z** 26582; ● 40
Johnnycake; RMC Place; MCDOWELL; ***250** I-3; elev. 1,075ft./328m.; mail Iaeger **z** 24844; rural
Johnsontown; RMC Place; BERKELEY; ***250** B-13; elev. 445ft./136m.; mail Hedgesville **z** 25427; ● 80
Johnstown; RMC Place; HARRISON; ***250** D-7; mail Lost Creek **z** 26385; ● 90
Johnstown; RMC Place; MCDOWELL; ***250** J-4; mail Squire **z** 24884; rural
Joker; RMC Place; CALHOUN; ***250** D-5; elev. 1,093ft./333m.; mail Creston **z** 26141; rural
Jolo; RMC Place; MCDOWELL; **250** J-3; elev. 1,320ft./402m.; 🅿; **z** 24850; ● 500
Jonben; RMC Place; RALEIGH; ***250** I-5; elev. 2,400ft./732m.; 🅿; ★ **BECK**; **z** 25823; ● 200
Jones Springs; RMC Place; BERKELEY; ***250** B-13; elev. 586ft./179m.; 🅿; **z** 25427; ● 25
Jordan; RMC Place; MARION; ***250** B-8; 🅿; ★ **FAIRM**; **z** 26554; rural
Jordan Run; RMC Place; GRANT; ***250** D-10; mail Maysville **z** 26833
Josephine; RMC Place; RALEIGH; ***250** I-5; elev. 2,077ft./633m.; 🅿; **z** 25857; ● 400
Josephs Mills; RMC Place; TYLER; ***250** C-6; elev. 732ft./223m.; mail Alma **z** 26320; rural
Joy; RMC Place; DODDRIDGE; ***250** C-6; elev. 823ft./251m.; mail West Union **z** 26456
Judson; RMC Place; SUMMERS; ***250** I-6; elev. 2,709ft./826m.; mail Alderson **z** 24910; rural
Judy Gap; RMC Place; PENDLETON; ***250** E-9; elev. 1,923ft./586m.; mail Riverton **z** 26814
Julia; RMC Place; GREENBRIER; ***250** G-7; elev. 2,151ft./656m.; mail Renick **z** 24966; rural
Julian; RMC Place; BOONE; **250** G-3; elev. 663ft./202m.; 🅿; **z** 25529; ● 200
Jumping Branch; RMC Place; SUMMERS; ***250** I-5; elev. 2,274ft./693m.; 🅿; **z** 25969; ● 200
Junction; RMC Place; HAMPSHIRE; **250** C-11; elev. 774ft./236m.; 🅿; **z** 26852; ● 15
Junior; Inc. Place; BARBOUR; **250** D-8; elev. 1,760ft./536m.; 🅿; **z** 26275; Ⓟ 542; Ⓒ 450
Juno; MCDOWELL; see Caretta (RMC Place)
Justice; RMC Place; MINGO; **250** I-3; elev. 888ft./271m.; 🅿; **z** 24851; ● 500
Justice Addition; RMC Place; LOGAN; ***250** H-3; mail Logan **z** 25601; ● 575

K

Kabletown; RMC Place; JEFFERSON; ***250** C-14; elev. 404ft./123m.; mail Charles Town **z** 25414
Kalamazoo; RMC Place; BARBOUR; ***250** D-8; elev. 1,616ft./493m.; mail Philippi **z** 26416; rural
Kanawha; RMC Place; WOOD; **250** C-4; elev. 636ft./194m.; ★ **PRKB**; mail Davisville **z** 26142; ● 150
KANAWHA; **250** F-4; Ⓟ 207,619; Ⓒ 200,073; ◆ 187,095
Kanawha City; RMC Place; KANAWHA; ***250** F-4; ★ **CHAS**; mail Charleston **z** 25304, **z** 25364; pop. incl. with Charleston (Inc. Place)
Kanawha Drive; RMC Place; GILMER; ***250** D-6; elev. 727ft./222m.; mail Glenville **z** 26351

Entries in **UPPERCASE** are counties.
Entries in **bold** have populations of 2,500 or more.
Names in parentheses are alternate names.

Inc. Place	Incorporated Place
RMC Place	Rand McNally Designated Place
CDP	Census Designated Place
MCD	Minor Civil Division
⊡	County Seat
▲	Minor Civil Division
elev.	Elevation
🅿	Post Office
🅷	Hospital
🅲	College
■	Principal Business Center
★	Ranally Metro Area (RMA) Abbreviation
z	Zip Code(s)
Ⓟ	Previous Census Population
Ⓡ	Revised Census Population
Ⓐ	Annexation Population
●	Rand McNally Population Estimate
Ⓒ	Final Census Population
Ⓢ	Special Census Population
◆	Estimated Population

For additional definitions see Glossary, Volume 1, and Introduction, Volume 2.

Kanawha Estates; RMC Place; KANAWHA; ***250** G-4; ★ **CHAS**; mail Charleston z 25304; pop. incl. with Charleston (Inc. Place)
Kanawha Falls; RMC Place; FAYETTE; ***250** G-5; elev. 668ft./204m.; [P]; z 25115; ● 70
Kanawha Head; RMC Place; UPSHUR; ***250** E-7; elev. 1,725ft./526m.; [P]; z 26228; ● 80
Kansooth; MARSHALL; see Kausooth (RMC Place)
Kasson; RMC Place; BARBOUR; ***250** C-8; elev. 1,500ft./457m.; [P]; z 26405; ● 40
Katy; RMC Place; MARION; ***250** B-7; ★ **FAIRM**; mail Fairmont z 26554; ● 100
Katy Lick; RMC Place; HARRISON; ***250** C-7; ★ **CLRKB**; mail Clarksburg z 26301; rural
Kausooth (Kansooth); RMC Place; MARSHALL; ***250** B-7; mail Cameron z 26033
Kearneysville; RMC Place; JEFFERSON; **250** C-14; elev. 549ft./167m.; [P]; z 25430 & mail Martinsburg z 25429; ● 600
Kedron; RMC Place; UPSHUR; ***250** E-8; mail Buckhannon z 26201; rural
Keeler Glade; RMC Place; PRESTON; ***250** B-9; elev. 2,259ft./689m.; mail Bruceton Mills z 26525; rural
Keenan; RMC Place; MONROE; ***250** I-7; elev. 2,327ft./709m.; mail Union z 24983
Kegley; RMC Place; MERCER; **250** J-5; elev. 2,416ft./736m.; [P]; z 24731; ● 300
Keister; RMC Place; GREENBRIER; ***250** H-7; elev. 1,773ft./540m.; mail Lewisburg z 24901; rural
Keith; RMC Place; BOONE; ***250** G-4; elev. 759ft./231m.; mail Orgas z 25148; ● 150
Kellogg; RMC Place; WAYNE; ★ **HNTG**; pop. incl. with Huntington (Inc. Place)
Kelly; RMC Place; LOGAN; ***250** H-3; mail Blair z 25022
Kelly Hill; RMC Place; KANAWHA; ***250** F-4; mail Clendenin z 25045; pop. incl. with Clendenin (Inc. Place)
Kellysville; RMC Place; MERCER; ***250** J-6; elev. 1,662ft./507m.; [P]; z 24732; ● 50
Kenna; RMC Place; JACKSON; **250** E-4; elev. 795ft./242m.; [P]; z 25248; ● 150
Kenova; Inc. Place; WAYNE; **250** F-1; elev. 561ft./171m.; [P]; ★ **HNTG**; z 25530; Ⓟ 3,748; © 3,485
Kent; RMC Place; MARSHALL; **250** B-6; mail Proctor z 26055; ● 75
Kentuck; RMC Place; JACKSON; ***250** E-4; elev. 920ft./280m.; [P]; z 25248
Kera Landing; RMC Place; JACKSON; ***250** E-3; mail Millwood z 25262; ● 800
Kerens; RMC Place; RANDOLPH; **250** D-9; elev. 1,944ft./593m.; [P]; z 26276; ● 100
Kermit; Inc. Place; MINGO; **250** H-2; elev. 625ft./191m.; [P]; z 25674; Ⓟ 342; © 209
Keslers Cross Lanes; RMC Place; NICHOLAS; ***250** G-6; elev. 1,568ft./478m.; [P]; z 26675; ● 80
Kessler; RMC Place; GREENBRIER; ***250** H-6; elev. 2,432ft./741m.; [P]; z 25984; rural
Kettle; RMC Place; ROANE; ***250** F-4; mail Gandeeville z 25243; rural
Keyes Ferry Acres; RMC Place; JEFFERSON; ***250** C-14; mail Harpers Ferry z 25425
Keyrock; RMC Place; WYOMING; ***250** I-4; mail Pineville z 24874
Keyser; Inc. Place; ⊡ MINERAL; **250** C-11; elev. 810ft./247m.; [P] [H]; z 26726; Ⓟ 5,870; © 5,303
Keystone; Inc. Place; MCDOWELL; **250** J-4; elev. 1,646ft./502m.; [P]; z 24868; Ⓟ 627; © 453
Kiahsville (Cove Creek); RMC Place; WAYNE; **250** G-2; elev. 668ft./204m.; [P]; z 25534; ● 60
Kidwell; RMC Place; TYLER; ***250** B-6; mail Middlebourne z 26149; rural
Kieffer; RMC Place; GREENBRIER; ***250** H-6; elev. 2,497ft./761m.; [P]; z 24931; ● 50
Killarm; RMC Place; MARION; ***250** C-7; ★ **FAIRM**; mail Fairmont z 26554; rural
Killarney; RMC Place; RALEIGH; ***250** I-5; elev. 1,691ft./515m.; mail Rhodell z 25915; rural
Kilsyth; RMC Place; FAYETTE; ***250** H-5; elev. 1,800ft./549m.; ★ **BECK**; ● 300
Kimball; Inc. Place; MCDOWELL; **250** J-4; elev. 1,492ft./455m.; [P]; z 24853; Ⓟ 550; © 411
Kimberly; RMC Place; FAYETTE; **250** G-5; elev. 665ft./203m.; [P]; z 25118; ● 500
Kincaid; RMC Place; FAYETTE; **250** G-5; elev. 1,134ft./346m.; [P]; z 25119; ● 450
Kincheloe; RMC Place; HARRISON; ***250** D-7; elev. 1,015ft./309m.; [P]; z 26378; rural
Kingmont; RMC Place; MARION; ***250** C-8; elev. 1,000ft./305m.; [P]; ★ **FAIRM**; z 26578; pop. incl. with Pleasant Valley (Inc. Place)
Kingston; RMC Place; FAYETTE; ***250** H-5; [P]; z 25917; ● 60
Kingston; FAYETTE; see East Kingston (RMC Place)
Kingstown; RMC Place; WETZEL; ***250** B-7; elev. 806ft./246m.; mail Big Run z 26561; rural
Kingsville; RMC Place; RANDOLPH; ***250** D-8; elev. 2,350ft./716m.; mail Coalton z 26257; rural
Kingwood; Inc. Place; ⊡ PRESTON; **250** C-9; elev. 1,863ft./568m.; [P] [H]; z 26537 & mail Albright z 26519; Ⓟ 3,243; © 2,944
Kirby; RMC Place; HAMPSHIRE; **250** D-11; elev. 1,572ft./479m.; [P]; z 26755; ● 30
Kirby Addition; RMC Place; MERCER; ***250** J-5; mail Princeton z 24740; ● 60
Kirbyton; RMC Place; BOONE; ***250** G-4; mail Seth z 25181; ● 75
Kirk; RMC Place; MINGO; ***250** H-2; mail Dingess z 25671
Kirt; RMC Place; BARBOUR; ***250** D-8; elev. 1,812ft./552m.; mail Montrose z 26283; rural
Kistler; RMC Place; LOGAN; **250** H-3; elev. 770ft./235m.; [P]; z 25628; ● 700
Kitchen; RMC Place; LOGAN; ***250** H-3; elev. 641ft./195m.; mail Chapmanville z 25508; ● 250
Kitsonville; RMC Place; LEWIS; ***250** D-7; mail Weston z 26452; pop. incl. with Weston (Inc. Place)
Kline; RMC Place; PENDLETON; ***250** E-10; mail Upper Tract z 26866
Klines Gap; RMC Place; GRANT; ***250** D-10; mail Maysville z 26833; rural
Knob Fork; RMC Place; WETZEL; ***250** B-7; [P]; z 26581
Knobs; RMC Place; MONROE; ***250** I-7; elev. 2,899ft./884m.; mail Union z 24983; rural
Knollwood; RMC Place; KANAWHA; ***250** F-4; ★ **CHAS**; mail Charleston z 25302; ● 900
Knollwood Estates; RMC Place; PUTNAM; ***250** F-3; ★ **CHAS**; mail Hurricane z 25526; ● 200
Knottsville; RMC Place; TAYLOR; ***250** C-8; elev. 1,483ft./452m.; mail Grafton z 26354; ● 25
Kodol; RMC Place; WETZEL; ***250** B-7; mail Littleton z 26581; ● 25
Kopperston; RMC Place; WYOMING; **250** H-4; elev. 1,664ft./507m.; [P]; z 24854; ● 900
Kyle; RMC Place; MCDOWELL; ***250** J-4; elev. 1,760ft./536m.; [P]; z 24855; ● 150

L

Lacoma; RMC Place; WYOMING; ***250** H-4; elev. 1,203ft./367m.; mail Cyclone z 24827; ● 100
LaFrank; RMC Place; NICHOLAS; ***250** G-7; mail Richwood z 26261; pop. incl. with Richwood (Inc. Place)
Lahmansville; RMC Place; GRANT; ***250** D-10; elev. 1,138ft./347m.; [P]; z 26731; ● 40
Lake; RMC Place; LOGAN; ***250** H-3; elev. 963ft./294m.; [P]; z 25121; ● 125
Lake Floyd; RMC Place; HARRISON; ***250** C-7; mail Salem z 26426; ● 400
Lake Ridge; RMC Place; HARRISON; ***250** C-8; [P]; ★ **CLRKB**; z 26330; ● 200
Lake Washington; PUTNAM; see Lexington Estates (RMC Place)
Lamberton; RMC Place; RITCHIE; **250** C-5; elev. 793ft./242m.; mail Ellenboro z 26346; pop. incl. with Ellenboro (Inc. Place)
Lanark; RMC Place; RALEIGH; ***250** H-5; elev. 2,228ft./679m.; [P]; ★ **BECK**; z 25860; ● 500
Landes; RMC Place; GRANT; ***250** E-10; elev. 1,100ft./335m.; mail Petersburg z 26847
Landgraff; RMC Place; MCDOWELL; ***250** J-4; mail Eckman z 24829; ● 150
Landisburg; RMC Place; FAYETTE; ***250** H-6; mail Danese z 25831; ● 60
Lando Mines; RMC Place; MINGO; ***250** I-2; elev. 838ft./255m.; mail Delbarton z 25670; ● 75
Landville; RMC Place; LOGAN; ***250** I-3; elev. 756ft./230m.; [P]; z 25635; ● 200
Laneville; RMC Place; TUCKER; ***250** D-10; mail Dryfork z 26263; rural
Lanham; RMC Place; PUTNAM; ***250** F-3; elev. 591ft./180m.; [P]; ★ **CHAS**; z 25159; ● 80
Lansing; RMC Place; FAYETTE; **250** G-5; elev. 1,864ft./568m.; [P]; z 25862; ● 400
Largent; RMC Place; MORGAN; ***250** B-12; mail Great Cacapon z 25422
Larkmead; RMC Place; WOOD; ***250** C-4; ★ **PRKB**; mail Parkersburg z 26101; ● 200
Lashmeet; RMC Place; MERCER; ***250** J-5; elev. 2,513ft./766m.; [P]; z 24733; ● 600
Lauckport; RMC Place; WOOD; ***250** C-4; ★ **PRKB**; mail Parkersburg z 26101; pop. incl. with Parkersburg (Inc. Place)
Laura Lee Mine; RMC Place; HARRISON; ***250** C-7; ★ **CLRKB**; mail Lumberport z 26386; rural
Laurel Bank; POCAHONTAS; see Slaty Fork (RMC Place)
Laurel Branch; RMC Place; MONROE; ***250** I-7; elev. 2,053ft./626m.; mail Waiteville z 24984; rural
Laurel Dale; RMC Place; MINERAL; ***250** C-10; elev. 1,294ft./394m.; mail New Creek z 26743; ● 30
Laurel Point; RMC Place; MONONGALIA; **250** B-3; ★ **MORG**; mail Morgantown z 26501; ● 80
Lavalette; RMC Place; WAYNE; **250** F-2; elev. 565ft./172m.; [P]; z 25535; ● 1,100
Lawn; RMC Place; GREENBRIER; ***250** H-6; mail Meadow Bridge z 25976; rural
Lawrenceville; RMC Place; HANCOCK; ***250** A-2; mail Chester z 26034; ● 450
Lawton; RMC Place; FAYETTE; ***250** H-5; [P]; z 25864; rural
Layland; RMC Place; FAYETTE; **250** H-5; elev. 2,500ft./762m.; [P]; z 25864; ● 30
Layopolis; GILMER; see Sand Fork (Inc. Place)
Leachtown; RMC Place; WOOD; ***250** D-4; ★ **PRKB**; mail Elizabeth z 26143
Lead Mine; RMC Place; TUCKER; **250** D-9; elev. 1,766ft./538m.; mail Parsons z 26287; ● 30
Leadsville; RMC Place; RANDOLPH; ***250** D-8; mail Elkins z 26241; rural
Leander; RMC Place; FAYETTE; ***250** G-5; rural
Leatherbark; RMC Place; CALHOUN; ***250** E-5; mail Arnoldsburg z 25234; rural
Leckie; RMC Place; MCDOWELL; ***250** J-4; elev. 1,800ft./549m.; [P]; z 24808; ● 120
Lee; RMC Place; FAYETTE; ***250** H-5; elev. 1,911ft./582m.; ★ **BECK**; mail Mount Hope z 25880; rural
Leet; RMC Place; LINCOLN; ***250** G-3; elev. 621ft./189m.; [P]; z 25524; rural
Leetown; RMC Place; JEFFERSON; ***250** C-13; mail Kearneysville z 25430; ● 225
Leevale; RMC Place; RALEIGH; ***250** H-4; elev. 845ft./258m.; mail Whitesville z 25209; rural
Leewood; RMC Place; KANAWHA; ***250** G-4; elev. 885ft./270m.; [P]; z 25075; ● 80
Leewood Park; RMC Place; OHIO; ***250** C-2; elev. 1,200ft./366m.; ★ **WHL**; mail Wheeling z 26003; pop. incl. with Wheeling (Inc. Place)
Left Hand; RMC Place; ROANE; **250** E-5; elev. 739ft./225m.; [P]; z 25251; ● 50
Lego; RMC Place; RALEIGH; ***250** I-5; elev. 1,848ft./563m.; mail Josephine z 25857; ● 50
Lehew; RMC Place; HAMPSHIRE; ***250** C-12; elev. 1,395ft./425m.; [P]; z 26865; ● 65
Leivasy; RMC Place; NICHOLAS; **250** G-6; elev. 2,368ft./722m.; [P]; z 26676; ● 150
Lenore; RMC Place; MINGO; **250** H-2; elev. 642ft./196m.; [P]; z 25676; ● 300
Lenox; RMC Place; PRESTON; **250** B-9; elev. 2,122ft./647m.; mail Albright z 26519; ● 50
Leon; Inc. Place; MASON; **250** E-3; elev. 569ft./173m.; [P]; z 25123; Ⓟ 145; © 132
Leonard; RMC Place; GREENBRIER; ***250** G-7; mail Renick z 24966; rural
Leopold; RMC Place; DODDRIDGE; ***250** D-6; elev. 843ft./257m.; mail Troy z 26443
Lerona; RMC Place; MERCER; **250** I-5; elev. 2,522ft./769m.; [P]; z 25971; ● 130
LeRoy; RMC Place; JACKSON; ***250** D-4; elev. 651ft./198m.; [P]; z 25252; ● 30
Lesage; RMC Place; CABELL; **250** F-2; elev. 1,560ft./475m.; [P]; ★ **HNTG**; z 25537; ● 250
Leslie; RMC Place; GREENBRIER; **250** G-6; elev. 2,956ft./901m.; [P]; z 25972; ● 250
Lester; Inc. Place; RALEIGH; **250** H-5; elev. 2,030ft./619m.; [P]; ★ **BECK**; z 25865; Ⓟ 420; © 322
Letart; RMC Place; MASON; **250** E-3; elev. 578ft./176m.; [P]; z 25253; ● 100
Letter Gap; RMC Place; GILMER; ***250** E-6; elev. 829ft./253m.; [P]; z 25267; ● 20
Levels; RMC Place; HAMPSHIRE; **250** B-12; elev. 1,189ft./362m.; [P]; z 25431; ● 100
LEWIS; **250** E-7; Ⓟ 17,223; © 16,919; ◆ 16,921
Lewisburg; Inc. Place; ⊡ GREENBRIER; **250** H-7; elev. 2,099ft./640m.; [P] [C] 355; z 24901; Ⓟ 3,598; © 3,624
Lex (Gluck); RMC Place; MCDOWELL; ***250** J-3; elev. 1,106ft./337m.; mail Bradshaw z 24817; ● 50
Lexington Estates (Lake Washington); RMC Place; PUTNAM; ***250** F-3; ★ **CHAS**; mail Hurricane z 25526; ● 60
Liberty; RMC Place; HARRISON; ***250** C-7; ★ **CLRKB**; mail Clarksburg z 26301; ● 250
Liberty; RMC Place; PUTNAM; **250** E-3; elev. 776ft./237m.; [P]; z 25124; ● 30
Lick Creek; RMC Place; SUMMERS; ***250** I-6; elev. 1,509ft./460m.; mail Pipestem z 25979; rural
Lico; RMC Place; KANAWHA; ***250** G-3; elev. 674ft./205m.; ★ **CHAS**; mail Charleston z 25314; rural
Lightburn; RMC Place; LEWIS; ***250** D-7; mail Jane Lew z 26378
Lila; RMC Place; MCDOWELL; ***250** J-4; elev. 1,716ft./523m.; mail Anawalt z 24808; ● 100
Lilac Hills; RMC Place; MERCER; ***250** J-5; mail Princeton z 24740; ● 100
Lillybrook; RMC Place; RALEIGH; ***250** I-5; elev. 2,053ft./626m.; ★ **BECK**; mail Josephine z 25857; rural
Lillydale; RMC Place; MONROE; ***250** I-6; elev. 793ft./242m.; mail Greenville z 24945; rural
Lillydale; RMC Place; WYOMING; ***250** I-4; elev. 1,222ft./372m.; mail Clear Fork z 24822, Lynco z 24857; ● 300
Lilly Grove; RMC Place; MERCER; ***250** J-5; mail Princeton z 24740; ● 900
Lillyhaven; RMC Place; WYOMING; ***250** I-4; elev. 1,237ft./377m.; mail Lynco z 24857; ● 450
Lilly Park; RMC Place; GREENBRIER; ***250** H-6; elev. 2,415ft./736m.; [P]; z 25962; ● 225
Lima; TYLER; see Braden (RMC Place)
Limestone; RMC Place; MARSHALL; **250** A-6; elev. 1,377ft./420m.; ★ **WHL**; mail Moundsville z 26041; ● 200
Limestone; RMC Place; MINERAL; ***250** C-11; mail Keyser z 26726; ● 125
Limestone Hill; RMC Place; WIRT; ***250** D-4; elev. 1,085ft./331m.; [P]; z 26143; rural
LINCOLN; **250** G-2; Ⓟ 21,382; © 22,108; ◆ 22,073
Linden; RMC Place; ROANE; **250** E-5; elev. 766ft./233m.; [P]; z 25259; ● 50
Lindside; RMC Place; MONROE; **250** I-6; elev. 1,995ft./608m.; [P]; z 24951; ● 200
Lindytown; RMC Place; BOONE; ***250** H-4; mail Twilight z 25204; rural
Link; RMC Place; TYLER; ***250** C-6; elev. 1,203ft./367m.; mail Reader z 26167; rural
Linn; RMC Place; GILMER; **250** D-6; elev. 807ft./246m.; [P]; z 26384; ● 125
Linwood; RMC Place; POCAHONTAS; ***250** F-8; elev. 2,953ft./900m.; mail Slatyfork z 26291; rural
Little; RMC Place; TYLER; ***250** C-5; elev. 672ft./205m.; mail Friendly z 26146; ● 80
Little Birch; RMC Place; BRAXTON; ***250** F-6; elev. 1,118ft./341m.; [P]; z 26629; ● 150
Little Falls; RMC Place; MONONGALIA; ***250** B-8; elev. 849ft./259m.; [P]; ★ **MORG**; z 26508; ● 25
Little Italy; RMC Place; CLAY; ***250** F-5; mail Ivydale z 25113; ● 50
Little Otter; RMC Place; BRAXTON; ***250** E-6; mail Gassaway z 26624; ● 150
Little Pittsburg; RMC Place; TYLER; ***250** C-6; mail Shirley z 26434; rural
Littlesburg; RMC Place; MERCER; ***250** J-5; mail Bluefield z 24701; ● 125
Littleton; RMC Place; WETZEL; **250** B-7; elev. 946ft./288m.; [P]; z 26581; disincorporated August 8, 2004; Ⓟ 198; © 207
Litwar; RMC Place; MCDOWELL; ***250** I-3; mail Iaeger z 24844; ● 40
Lively; RMC Place; FAYETTE; ***250** H-5; mail Scarbro z 25917; rural
Liverpool; RMC Place; JACKSON, ROANE; **250** E-4; elev. 669ft./204m.; [P]; z 25252; ● 60
Livingston; RMC Place; KANAWHA; ***250** G-4; elev. 666ft./203m.; [P]; z 25083; ● 150
Lizemores; RMC Place; CLAY; **250** F-5; elev. 983ft./300m.; [P]; z 25125; ● 60
Lloydsville; RMC Place; BRAXTON; ***250** E-6; mail Exchange z 26619; rural
Lobata; RMC Place; MINGO; ***250** I-2; elev. 700ft./213m.; [P]; z 25678; ● 180
Lobelia; RMC Place; POCAHONTAS; ***250** G-7; elev. 2,506ft./764m.; mail Hillsboro z 24946; rural
Lochgelly; RMC Place; FAYETTE; ***250** H-5; elev. 2,000ft./610m.; [P]; ★ **BECK**; z 25866; ● 200
Lockbridge; RMC Place; SUMMERS; ***250** H-6; elev. 2,500ft./762m.; [P]; z 25976; rural
Lockhart; RMC Place; JACKSON; ***250** D-4; elev. 617ft./188m.; mail Sandyville z 25275; rural
Lockney; RMC Place; GILMER; ***250** E-6; elev. 720ft./219m.; [P]; z 25267
Lockwood; RMC Place; NICHOLAS; **250** G-5; elev. 1,063ft./324m.; mail Summersville z 26651; ● 50
Lodgeville; RMC Place; HARRISON; ***250** C-7; ★ **CLRKB**; mail Bridgeport z 26330; ● 100
Logan; Inc. Place; ⊡ LOGAN; **250** H-3; elev. 680ft./207m.; [P] [H] ■; z 25601; Ⓟ 2,206; © 1,630; ◆ 1,411
LOGAN; **250** H-2; Ⓟ 43,032; © 37,710; ◆ 35,011
Logan Heights; RMC Place; LOGAN; ***250** H-3; mail Cora z 25614; ● 150
Logansport; RMC Place; MARION; **250** B-7; elev. 1,002ft./305m.; mail Mannington z 26582; ● 30
Lomax; RMC Place; MCDOWELL; ***250** J-3; mail War z 24892
London; RMC Place; KANAWHA; ***250** G-4; elev. 633ft./193m.; [P]; z 25126; ● 500
Lone Oak Park; RMC Place; KANAWHA; ***250** F-3; ★ **CHAS**; mail Saint Albans z 25177; ● 150
Lonetree; RMC Place; TYLER; ***250** B-6; elev. 774ft./236m.; mail Middlebourne z 26149
Longacre; RMC Place; FAYETTE; ***250** G-5; elev. 676ft./206m.; [P]; z 25186; pop. incl. with Smithers (Inc. Place)
Long Branch; RMC Place; FAYETTE; ***250** H-5; elev. 1,629ft./497m.; mail Pax z 25904; ● 80
Long Branch; RMC Place; WYOMING; ***250** I-3; elev. 1,192ft./363m.; mail Simon z 24882; ● 300
Longdale; RMC Place; MASON; ***250** D-3; elev. 578ft./176m.; mail Letart z 25253; rural
Longpole; RMC Place; MCDOWELL; ***250** I-3; elev. 1,112ft./339m.; mail Iaeger z 24844; rural
Long Run; RMC Place; DODDRIDGE; ***250** C-6; mail Salem z 26426; rural
Lookout; RMC Place; FAYETTE; **250** G-5; elev. 2,200ft./671m.; [P]; z 25868; ● 250
Loom; RMC Place; HAMPSHIRE; ***250** C-12; mail Augusta z 26704; rural
Looneyville; RMC Place; ROANE; ***250** E-5; elev. 770ft./235m.; [P]; z 25259; ● 50
Lorado; RMC Place; LOGAN; **250** H-3; elev. 1,221ft./372m.; [P]; z 25630; ● 300
Lorentz; RMC Place; UPSHUR; **250** D-7; elev. 1,444ft./440m.; [P]; z 26229; ● 100
Lorton Lick; RMC Place; MERCER; ***250** J-5; mail Bluefield z 24701; ● 200
Lost City; RMC Place; HARDY; **250** D-11; elev. 1,484ft./452m.; [P]; z 26810; ● 75
Lost Creek; Inc. Place; HARRISON; **250** D-7; elev. 1,013ft./309m.; [P]; ★ **CLRKB**; z 26385; Ⓟ 413; © 467
Lost River; RMC Place; HARDY; **250** D-11; elev. 1,383ft./422m.; [P]; z 26810; ● 60
Loudendale; RMC Place; KANAWHA; ***250** G-4; elev. 666ft./203m.; ★ **CHAS**; mail Charleston z 25314; ● 300
Loudenville; RMC Place; MARSHALL; **250** A-6; elev. 1,004ft./306m.; mail Cameron z 26033; ● 50
Loudon Heights; RMC Place; KANAWHA; ***250** F-4; ★ **CHAS**; mail Charleston z 25314; pop. incl. with Charleston (Inc. Place)
Louise; RMC Place; BROOKE; ***250** B-2; ★ **STU-**; mail Wellsburg z 26070; ● 110
Lovern; RMC Place; MERCER; ***250** I-6; mail Princeton z 24740; rural
Lowdell; RMC Place; WOOD; ***250** D-4; mail Rockport z 26169
Lowell; RMC Place; SUMMERS; ***250** I-6; mail Pence Springs z 24962; rural
Lower Belle; RMC Place; KANAWHA; ***250** G-4; ★ **CHAS**; mail Belle z 25015; ● 350
Lower Falls; RMC Place; KANAWHA; ***250** F-3; ★ **CHAS**; mail Saint Albans z 25177; ● 100
Lowgap; RMC Place; BOONE; ***250** G-3; elev. 737ft./225m.; mail Madison z 25130
Lowney; RMC Place; MINGO; ***250** H-2; elev. 809ft./247m.; mail Breeden z 25666; rural
Lowsville; RMC Place; MONONGALIA; ***250** B-8; ★ **MORG**; rural
Lubeck; CDP; WOOD; **250** C-4; elev. 755ft./230m.; ★ **PRKB**; mail Parkersburg z 26101, Washington z 26181; Ⓟ 1,579; © 1,303
Lucas; RMC Place; FAYETTE; ***250** G-5; mail Victor z 25938; rural
Lucille; RMC Place; WIRT; ***250** D-4; mail Palestine z 26160; rural
Lucretia; RMC Place; TAYLOR; ***250** C-8; elev. 1,197ft./365m.; mail Grafton z 26354; pop. incl. with Grafton (Inc. Place)
Lumberport; Inc. Place; HARRISON; **250** C-7; elev. 994ft./303m.; [P]; ★ **CLRKB**; z 26386; Ⓟ 1,014; © 937
Lundale; RMC Place; LOGAN; ***250** H-3; elev. 1,140ft./347m.; [P]; z 25630; ● 350
Lyburn; RMC Place; LOGAN; ***250** H-3; elev. 720ft./219m.; [P]; z 25632; ● 125
Lynco; RMC Place; WYOMING; ***250** I-4; elev. 1,600ft./488m.; [P]; z 24857; ● 100
Lynn; RMC Place; MINGO; ***250** I-2; mail Matewan z 25678; ● 80
Lynn Camp; RMC Place; MARSHALL; **250** B-6; elev. 715ft./218m.; mail Glen Easton z 26039; ● 40
Lynwinn; RMC Place; RALEIGH; ***250** I-5; elev. 2,611ft./796m.; ★ **BECK**; mail Coal City z 25823; ● 50
Lyonsville; RMC Place; NICHOLAS; ***250** G-5; elev. 1,120ft./341m.; mail Summersville z 26651; ● 60

M

Maben; RMC Place; WYOMING; **250** I-4; elev. 1,589ft./484m.; [P]; z 25870; ● 60
Mabie; RMC Place; RANDOLPH; **250** E-8; elev. 2,226ft./678m.; [P]; z 26278; ● 120
Mabscott; Inc. Place; RALEIGH; **250** H-5; elev. 2,320ft./707m.; [P]; ★ **BECK**; z 25871; Ⓟ 1,543; © 1,403
MacAlpine; RALEIGH; see McAlpin (RMC Place)
MacArthur; CDP; RALEIGH; ***250** H-5; elev. 2,400ft./732m.; [P]; ★ **BECK**; z 25873; Ⓟ 1,595; © 1,693
Macdale; RMC Place; MONONGALIA; ***250** B-7; mail Blacksville z 26521; ● 120
Macdonald; RMC Place; FAYETTE; ***250** H-5; elev. 1,742ft./531m.; ★ **BECK**; mail Mount Hope z 25880; ● 225
MacDunn; RMC Place; FAYETTE; ***250** G-5; mail Powellton z 25161; rural
Mace; RMC Place; POCAHONTAS; ***250** F-8; mail Slatyfork z 26291; rural
Macfarlan; RMC Place; RITCHIE; **250** D-5; elev. 655ft./200m.; [P]; z 26148; ● 70
Macksville; RMC Place; PENDLETON; ***250** E-10; mail Seneca Rocks z 26884; rural
Macomber; RMC Place; PRESTON; ***250** C-9; elev. 1,419ft./433m.; mail Rowlesburg z 26425
Madam Creek; RMC Place; SUMMERS; ***250** I-6; mail Hinton z 25951; rural
Madeline; RMC Place; RALEIGH; ***250** I-5; elev. 1,704ft./519m.; mail Amigo z 25811; rural
Madison; Inc. Place; ⊡ BOONE; **250** G-3; elev. 716ft./218m.; [P] [H]; z 25130; Ⓟ 3,051; © 2,677
Magnolia; RMC Place; MORGAN; ***250** B-12; mail Great Cacapon z 25422
Mahan; RMC Place; FAYETTE; ***250** G-4; elev. 930ft./283m.; [P]; z 25083; ● 100
Maher; RMC Place; MINGO; ***250** H-2; mail Williamson z 25661; ● 100
Mahone; RMC Place; RITCHIE; ***250** D-5; elev. 1,057ft./322m.; [P]; z 26362; rural
Maidsville; RMC Place; MONONGALIA; ***250** B-8; elev. 859ft./262m.; [P]; ★ **MORG**; z 26541; ● 200
Maitland; RMC Place; MCDOWELL; ***250** I-4; mail Welch z 24801; ● 135
Majorsville; RMC Place; MARSHALL; ***250** A-7; ★ **WHL**; mail Dallas z 26036; ● 40
Malcom Spring Heights; RMC Place; CABELL; ***250** F-2; ★ **HNTG**; mail Milton z 25541; pop. incl. with Milton (Inc. Place)
Malden; RMC Place; KANAWHA; **250** G-4; elev. 600ft./183m.; [P]; ★ **CHAS**; z 25306; ● 850
Mallory; CDP; LOGAN; **250** H-3; [P]; z 25634 & mail Davin z 25617; Ⓟ 1,126; © 1,143
Mammoth; RMC Place; KANAWHA; ***250** G-4; elev. 883ft./269m.; [P]; z 25132; ● 450
Man; Inc. Place; LOGAN; **250** H-3; elev. 733ft./223m.; [P] [H]; z 25635; Ⓟ 914; © 770
M and K Junction; RMC Place; PRESTON; mail Rowlesburg z 26425; pop. incl. with Rowlesburg (Inc. Place)
Manheim; RMC Place; PRESTON; ***250** C-9; elev. 1,384ft./422m.; [P]; z 26425; pop. incl. with Rowlesburg (Inc. Place)
Manila; RMC Place; BOONE; ***250** H-3; mail Chapmanville z 25508; rural
Mannings; RMC Place; JEFFERSON; **250** C-14; elev. 593ft./181m.; mail Harpers Ferry z 25425; ● 450
Mannington; Inc. Place; MARION; **250** B-7; elev. 975ft./297m.; [P]; ★ **FAIRM**; z 26582; Ⓟ 2,184; © 2,124
Manown; RMC Place; PRESTON; ***250** C-9; elev. 2,156ft./657m.; mail Kingwood z 26537
Mansfield; RMC Place; BARBOUR; ***250** D-8; mail Philippi z 26416; pop. incl. with Philippi (Inc. Place)
Maple Acres; RMC Place; MERCER; ***250** J-5; mail Bluefield z 24701; ● 200
Maple Fork; RMC Place; RALEIGH; ***250** H-5; ★ **BECK**; mail Mount Hope z 25880; ● 300
Maple Lake; RMC Place; HARRISON; ***250** C-8; [P]; ★ **CLRKB**; z 26330; ● 300
Maple Meadow; RMC Place; RALEIGH; ***250** H-4; elev. 1,929ft./588m.; ★ **BECK**; mail Lester z 25865; rural
Maple View; RMC Place; MERCER; ***250** J-5; mail Bluefield z 24701; ● 150
Maplewood; RMC Place; FAYETTE; ***250** H-6; elev. 2,717ft./828m.; [P]; z 25831; ● 80
Marfrance; RMC Place; GREENBRIER; ***250** G-6; elev. 3,000ft./914m.; [P]; z 25981; ● 130
Margaret; RMC Place; HARRISON; ***250** C-7; elev. 1,032ft./315m.; mail Wallace z 26448; rural
Marianna; RMC Place; WYOMING; ***250** I-4; elev. 1,236ft./377m.; [P]; z 24859 & mail Brenton z 24818; ● 75
Marie; RMC Place; SUMMERS; ***250** I-6; elev. 2,065ft./629m.; mail Ballard z 24918; rural
Marine; RMC Place; MCDOWELL; ***250** I-4; mail Davy z 24828; rural
MARION; **250** B-7; Ⓟ 57,249; © 56,598; ◆ 56,552
Market; RMC Place; DODDRIDGE; ***250** C-6; elev. 844ft./257m.; mail New Milton z 26411; rural
Markwood; RMC Place; MINERAL; ***250** C-11; elev. 878ft./268m.; mail Burlington z 26710; rural
Marlaing Addition; RMC Place; KANAWHA; ***250** F-3; ★ **CHAS**; mail Saint Albans z 25177; ● 1,200
Marland Heights; RMC Place; HANCOCK, BROOKE; ***250** B-2; ★ **STU-**; mail Weirton z 26062; pop. incl. with Weirton (Inc. Place)
Marlinton; Inc. Place; ⊡ POCAHONTAS; **250** G-8; elev. 2,130ft./649m.; [P]; z 24954; Ⓟ 1,148; © 1,204
Marlowe; RMC Place; BERKELEY; **250** B-14; elev. 514ft./157m.; ★ **HAG**; mail Falling Waters z 25419; ● 700
Marmet; Inc. Place; KANAWHA; **250** G-4; elev. 604ft./184m.; [P]; ★ **CHAS**; z 25315 & mail Charleston z 25365; Ⓟ 1,879; © 1,693
Marquess; RMC Place; PRESTON; ***250** C-8; elev. 1,337ft./408m.; mail Tunnelton z 26444; rural
Marrtown; RMC Place; WOOD; ***250** C-4; ★ **PRKB**; mail Parkersburg z 26101; ● 200
Marshall; RMC Place; JACKSON; ***250** E-4; elev. 677ft./206m.; mail Le Roy z 25252; ● 45
MARSHALL; **250** A-6; Ⓟ 37,356; © 35,519; ◆ 32,072
Marshall Terrace; RMC Place; BROOKE; ***250** B-2; ★ **WHL**; mail Wellsburg z 26070; ● 200
Marshall University; RMC Place; CABELL; ***250** F-2; ★ **HNTG**; mail Huntington z 25703, z 25755; pop. incl. with Huntington (Inc. Place)
Marshville; RMC Place; HARRISON; ***250** C-7; ★ **CLRKB**; mail Salem z 26426; ● 75
Martha; RMC Place; CABELL; ***250** F-2; ★ **HNTG**; mail Barboursville z 25504; ● 150
Marthatown; RMC Place; BOONE; ***250** H-4; mail Bim z 25021; ● 28
Martin; RMC Place; GRANT; ***250** C-10; elev. 269ft./82m.; mail New Creek z 26743
Martinsburg; Inc. Place; ⊡ BERKELEY; **250** C-13; elev. 457ft./139m.; [P] [H] ■; z 25401-05, z 25429; Ⓟ 14,073; © 14,972; ◆ 15,489
Marvel; RMC Place; FAYETTE; ***250** G-5; mail Ansted z 25812; rural
Maryland Junction (Carpendale); Inc. Place; MINERAL; ***250** B-11; ★ **CUMB**; mail Ridgeley z 26753; Ⓟ 1,087; © 954
Marytown; RMC Place; MCDOWELL; ***250** I-4; rural
Mason (Mason City); Inc. Place; MASON; **250** D-3; elev. 581ft./177m.; [P]; z 25260; Ⓟ 1,053; © 1,064
MASON; **250** E-3; Ⓟ 25,178; © 25,957; ◆ 25,240
Mason City; MASON; see Mason (Inc. Place)
Masontown; Inc. Place; PRESTON; **250** B-9; elev. 1,683ft./513m.; [P]; ★ **MORG**; z 26542; Ⓟ 737; © 647
Masonville; RMC Place; GRANT; ***250** D-10; mail Petersburg z 26847; rural
Masseyville; RMC Place; RALEIGH; ***250** H-4; mail Rock Creek z 25174; ● 70
Matewan; Inc. Place; MINGO; **250** I-2; elev. 700ft./213m.; [P]; z 25678; Ⓟ 619; © 498
Matheny; RMC Place; WYOMING; ***250** I-4; elev. 1,346ft./410m.; [P]; z 24860; ● 600
Mathias; RMC Place; HARDY; **250** E-11; elev. 1,531ft./467m.; [P]; z 26812; ● 140
Matoaka; Inc. Place; MERCER; **250** J-5; elev. 2,362ft./720m.; [P]; z 24736; Ⓟ 366; © 317
Maxine; RMC Place; BOONE; ***250** G-4; mail Comfort z 25049; ● 45
Maxwell; RMC Place; PLEASANTS; ***250** C-5; mail Saint Marys z 26170; rural
Maxwell Acres; RMC Place; MARSHALL; ***250** A-6; ★ **WHL**; mail Moundsville z 26041; pop. incl. with Moundsville (Inc. Place)
Maxwelton; RMC Place; GREENBRIER; **250** H-7; elev. 2,357ft./718m.; [P]; z 24957; ● 75
Maybeury; RMC Place; MCDOWELL; **250** J-4; elev. 2,065ft./629m.; [P]; z 24861; ● 300
Maynor; RMC Place; RALEIGH; ***250** H-5; elev. 1,703ft./519m.; ★ **BECK**; mail Beckley z 25801
Maysel; RMC Place; CLAY; **250** F-5; elev. 1,032ft./315m.; [P]; z 25133; ● 300
Maysville; RMC Place; GRANT; **250** D-10; elev. 1,284ft./391m.; [P]; z 26833; ● 150
McAlpin (MacAlpine); RMC Place; RALEIGH; ***250** I-5; elev. 1,927ft./587m.; [P]; ★ **BECK**; z 25921; rural
McCauley; RMC Place; HARDY; ***250** D-11; mail Baker z 26801; rural
McClellan; RMC Place; MARION; ***250** B-7; elev. 1,055ft./322m.; ★ **FAIRM**; mail Mannington z 26582; ● 25
McComas; RMC Place; MERCER; ***250** J-5; elev. 2,348ft./716m.; [P]; z 24747; ● 800
McConnell; RMC Place; LOGAN; ***250** H-3; elev. 700ft./213m.; [P]; z 25646; ● 800
McCorkle; RMC Place; LINCOLN; ***250** G-3; elev. 651ft./198m.; ★ **CHAS**; mail Sod z 25564; ● 100
McCreery; RMC Place; RALEIGH; ***250** H-5; ★ **BECK**; mail Layland z 25864; rural
McCurdyville; RMC Place; MONONGALIA; ***250** B-8; ● 30
McDowell; RMC Place; MCDOWELL; ***250** J-4; elev. 2,000ft./610m.; [P]; z 24868; ● 125
MCDOWELL; **250** J-4; Ⓟ 35,233; © 27,329; ◆ 22,024
McGee; RMC Place; TAYLOR; ***250** C-8; elev. 1,364ft./416m.; ★ **FAIRM**; mail Grafton z 26354
McGraws; RMC Place; WYOMING; ***250** I-4; elev. 1,806ft./550m.; [P]; z 25875-76; ● 100
McGuire Park; RMC Place; LEWIS; ***250** D-7; elev. 1,046ft./319m.; mail Weston z 26452; ● 450
McIntire; RMC Place; HARRISON; ★ **CLRKB**; mail Hepzibah z 26369; rural
McKeefrey; RMC Place; MARSHALL; **250** A-6; mail Moundsville z 26041; ● 500
McKinleyville; RMC Place; BROOKE; ***250** B-2; ★ **WHL**; mail Wellsburg z 26070; ● 150
McMechen; Inc. Place; MARSHALL; **250** A-6; elev. 669ft./204m.; [P]; ★ **WHL**; z 26040; Ⓟ 2,130; © 1,937
McRoss; RMC Place; GREENBRIER; **250** H-6; mail Rainelle z 25962; ● 150
McWhorter; RMC Place; HARRISON; ***250** D-7; elev. 1,111ft./339m.; [P]; ★ **CLRKB**; z 26385; ● 100
Mead; RMC Place; RALEIGH; ***250** I-5; elev. 1,789ft./545m.; [P]; z 25915; ● 100
Meadland; RMC Place; TAYLOR; ***250** C-8; elev. 1,318ft./402m.; mail Bridgeport z 26330
Meador; RMC Place; MINGO; ***250** I-3; [P]; z 25678; ● 45
Meadow Bluff; RMC Place; GREENBRIER; ***250** H-6; elev. 2,462ft./750m.; [P]; z 24977; ● 80
Meadow Bridge; Inc. Place; FAYETTE; **250** H-6; elev. 2,427ft./740m.; [P]; z 25966, z 25976; Ⓟ 325; © 321
Meadowbrook; RMC Place; HARRISON; ***250** C-7; elev. 940ft./287m.; [P]; ★ **CLRKB**; z 26404; ● 500
Meadowbrook; RMC Place; KANAWHA; **250** I-14; ★ **CHAS**; mail Charleston z 25311; ● 350
Meadowbrook; RMC Place; MASON; ***250** E-2; elev. 606ft./185m.; mail Point Pleasant z 25550
Meadow Creek; RMC Place; SUMMERS; ***250** H-6; elev. 1,270ft./387m.; [P]; z 25977; ● 165
Meadowdale; RMC Place; MARION; ***250** C-8; elev. 918ft./280m.; ★ **FAIRM**; mail Fairmont z 26554; ● 500
Meadowville; RMC Place; BARBOUR; ***250** D-8; elev. 1,570ft./479m.; mail Belington z 26250
Meadville; RMC Place; TYLER; ***250** C-5; elev. 737ft./225m.; ● 30
Mechanicstown; RMC Place; JEFFERSON; ***250** C-14; mail Charles Town z 25414; ● 40
Mechlenberg Heights; RMC Place; JEFFERSON; ***250** C-14; mail Shepherdstown z 25443; ● 350
Medina; RMC Place; JACKSON; ***250** D-4; mail Ravenswood z 26164; rural
Medley; RMC Place; GRANT; **250** D-11; elev. 1,043ft./318m.; [P]; z 26710; ● 20
Meighen; RMC Place; MARSHALL; ***250** B-6; elev. 693ft./211m.; mail Glen Easton z 26039; rural
Melissa; RMC Place; CABELL; ***250** F-2; elev. 577ft./176m.; ★ **HNTG**; mail Barboursville z 25504; ● 125
Mellin; RMC Place; RITCHIE; ***250** D-5; mail Harrisville z 26362; rural
Melrose; RMC Place; MERCER; ***250** J-5; mail Athens z 24712; ● 200
Melville; RMC Place; LOGAN; ***250** H-3; mail Stollings z 25646; ● 60
MERCER; **250** I-5; Ⓟ 64,980; © 62,980; ◆ 61,130
Mercers Bottom; RMC Place; MASON; ***250** E-2; elev. 583ft./178m.; mail Leon z 25123
Meriden; RMC Place; BARBOUR; ***250** D-8; elev. 304ft./93m.; mail Philippi z 26416; rural
Merrimac; RMC Place; MINGO; ***250** I-2; elev. 682ft./208m.; mail Williamson z 25661; ● 100
Metz; RMC Place; MARION; **250** B-7; elev. 1,000ft./305m.; [P]; ★ **FAIRM**; z 26585; ● 120
Meyerstown; RMC Place; JEFFERSON; ***250** C-14; mail Charles Town z 25414
Miami; RMC Place; KANAWHA; **250** G-4; elev. 678ft./207m.; [P]; z 25134; ● 450
Micco; RMC Place; LOGAN; ***250** H-3; elev. 763ft./233m.; mail Switzer z 25647
Middlebourne; Inc. Place; ⊡ TYLER; **250** C-6; elev. 745ft./227m.; [P]; z 26149; Ⓟ 922; © 870
Middle Grave Creek; RMC Place; MARSHALL; ***250** A-6; mail Moundsville z 26041; rural
Middle Run; RMC Place; BRAXTON; ***250** F-6; elev. 1,236ft./377m.; mail Frametown z 26623; rural
Middleway; RMC Place; JEFFERSON; ***250** C-13; elev. 500ft./152m.; [P]; z 25430; ● 350
Midkiff; RMC Place; LINCOLN; **250** G-2; elev. 594ft./181m.; [P]; z 25540; ● 250
Midland; RMC Place; RANDOLPH; ***250** E-8; elev. 2,004ft./611m.; mail Elkins z 26241; ● 50
Midway; RMC Place; FAYETTE; ***250** H-5; ★ **BECK**; mail Oak Hill z 25901; rural
Midway; RMC Place; MERCER; ***250** J-5; mail Bluefield z 24701; ● 500
Midway; RMC Place; PUTNAM; ***250** F-3; elev. 575ft./175m.; ★ **CHAS**; mail Red House z 25168; ● 150
Midway; RMC Place; RALEIGH; ***250** I-5; elev. 2,520ft./768m.; [P]; ★ **BECK**; z 25878; ● 700
Mifflin; RMC Place; LOGAN; ***250** H-3; elev. 822ft./251m.; mail Clothier z 25047; ● 70
Milam; RMC Place; HARDY; **250** E-10; elev. 1,216ft./371m.; [P]; z 26838; ● 30
Milam; RMC Place; WYOMING; ***250** I-4; mail Mc Graws z 25875; rural
Milburn; RMC Place; FAYETTE; ***250** H-5; mail Charleston z 25304; ● 50
Mile Branch; RMC Place; MCDOWELL; ***250** I-3; mail Iaeger z 24844; ● 100
Millard; RMC Place; ROANE; ***250** E-5; mail Spencer z 25276; rural
Millbrook; RMC Place; HAMPSHIRE; ***250** C-12; elev. 1,271ft./387m.; mail Capon Bridge z 26711; rural
Mill Creek; Inc. Place; RANDOLPH; **250** E-8; elev. 2,067ft./630m.; [P]; z 26280; Ⓟ 685; © 662
Millersville; RMC Place; MARION; ***250** C-8; ★ **FAIRM**; mail Fairmont z 26554; pop. incl. with Pleasant Valley (Inc. Place)
Millertown; RMC Place; TAYLOR; ***250** C-8; elev. 1,461ft./445m.; mail Grafton z 26354
Milliken; RMC Place; KANAWHA; ***250** F-4; ★ **CHAS**; mail Elkview z 25071; ● 150
Mill Point; RMC Place; POCAHONTAS; ***250** G-8; elev. 2,208ft./673m.; [P]; z 24946
Mill Run; RMC Place; TUCKER; ***250** D-9; mail Hendricks z 26271; rural
Millstone; RMC Place; CALHOUN; **250** E-5; elev. 792ft./241m.; [P]; z 25261; ● 60
Milltown; RMC Place; BOONE; ***250** G-4; mail Seth z 25181; rural
Millville; RMC Place; JEFFERSON; ***250** C-14; elev. 400ft./122m.; [P]; z 25432; ● 400
Millwood; RMC Place; JACKSON; ***250** E-3; elev. 571ft./174m.; [P]; z 25262; ● 120
Milo; RMC Place; CALHOUN; ***250** E-5; elev. 789ft./240m.; mail Chloe z 25235; rural
Milton; Inc. Place; CABELL; **250** F-2; elev. 584ft./178m.; [P]; ★ **CHAS**; z 25541; Ⓟ 2,242; © 2,206
Minden; RMC Place; FAYETTE; **250** H-5; elev. 1,600ft./488m.; [P]; ★ **BECK**; z 25879; ● 1,000
MINERAL; **250** C-11; Ⓟ 26,697; © 27,078; ◆ 26,461
Mineral City; RMC Place; LOGAN; ***250** H-3; mail Davin z 25617; ● 200
Mineralwells; RMC Place; WOOD; **250** C-4; elev. 666ft./203m.; [P]; ★ **PRKB**; z 26120-21, z 26150; ● 200
Mineralwells; CDP-Census Area Only; WOOD; ***250** D-4; ★ **PRKB**; mail Mineral Wells z 26150; Ⓟ 1,698; © 1,860
Mingo; RMC Place; RANDOLPH; **250** F-8; elev. 2,640ft./805m.; [P]; z 26294; ● 50
MINGO; **250** H-2; Ⓟ 33,739; © 28,253; ◆ 26,454
Mink Shoals; KANAWHA; see Elk Hills (RMC Place)
Minnehaha Springs; RMC Place; POCAHONTAS; **250** G-8; elev. 2,334ft./711m.; [P]; z 24954; ● 50
Minnie; RMC Place; WETZEL; ***250** B-6; elev. 645ft./197m.; mail New Martinsville z 26155; rural
Minnora; RMC Place; CALHOUN; ***250** E-5; elev. 737ft./225m.; [P]; z 25268; ● 20
Miracle Run; RMC Place; MONONGALIA; ***250** B-7; mail Fairview z 26570; ● 20
Missouri Branch; RMC Place; WAYNE; ***250** H-2; mail Dunlow z 25511; rural
Mitchell Branch; RMC Place; MINGO; ***250** I-2; mail Red Jacket z 25692
Mitchell Heights; Inc. Place; LOGAN; **250** H-3; elev. 660ft./201m.; mail Logan z 25601; Ⓟ 265; © 301
Moatstown; RMC Place; PENDLETON; ***250** F-10; elev. 2,445ft./745m.; mail Sugar Grove z 26815; rural
Moatsville; RMC Place; BARBOUR; ***250** C-8; elev. 1,234ft./376m.; [P]; z 26405; ● 60
Mobley; RMC Place; WETZEL; ***250** B-7; elev. 885ft./270m.; mail Smithfield z 26437
Mohawk (Wyoming); RMC Place; MCDOWELL; ***250** I-3; elev. 931ft./284m.; [P]; z 24862; ● 100
Mohegan; RMC Place; MCDOWELL; ***250** I-4; ● 40
Moler Crossroads; RMC Place; JEFFERSON; ***250** C-14; mail Shepherdstown z 25443; rural
Monarch; RMC Place; KANAWHA; ***250** G-4; mail Cedar Grove z 25039; rural
Monaville; RMC Place; LOGAN; ***250** H-3; elev. 715ft./218m.; [P]; z 25601; ● 300
Monclo; RMC Place; LOGAN; ***250** H-3; mail Sharples z 25183; ● 50
Monitor; RMC Place; LOGAN; ***250** H-3; elev. 678ft./207m.; mail Wilkinson z 25653
Monitor; RMC Place; MONROE; ***250** I-7; mail Sinks Grove z 24976
Monkeytown; RMC Place; PENDLETON; mail Riverton z 26814; rural
Monongah; Inc. Place; MARION; **250** C-7; elev. 900ft./274m.; [P]; ★ **FAIRM**; z 26554-55; Ⓟ 1,018; © 939
MONONGALIA; **250** B-8; Ⓟ 75,509; © 81,866; ◆ 92,413
MONROE; **250** I-6; Ⓟ 12,406; © 14,583; Ⓡ 13,193; ◆ 13,518
Montana (Montana Mines); RMC Place; MARION; ***250** B-8; elev. 1,000ft./305m.; ★ **FAIRM**; mail Montana Mines z 26586; ● 200
Montana Mines; MARION; see Montana (RMC Place)
Montcalm; CDP; MERCER; **250** J-5; elev. 2,215ft./675m.; [P]; z 24737; Ⓟ 1,023; © 885
Montcoal; RMC Place; RALEIGH; **250** H-4; elev. 940ft./287m.; [P]; z 25140; ● 150
Monterville; RMC Place; RANDOLPH; **250** F-8; elev. 2,948ft./899m.; [P]; z 26282; ● 100
Montgomery; Inc. Place; FAYETTE, KANAWHA; **250** G-5; elev. 640ft./195m.; [P] [H] [C] 1,474; z 25136; Ⓟ 2,449; © 1,942
Montgomery Heights; RMC Place; FAYETTE; ***250** G-5; mail Deep Water z 25057; ● 125
Montpelier; RMC Place; HARRISON; ***250** C-7; ★ **CLRKB**; mail Clarksburg z 26301; pop. incl. with Clarksburg (Inc. Place)
Montrose; Inc. Place; RANDOLPH; **250** D-9; elev. 1,997ft./609m.; [P]; z 26283; Ⓟ 140; © 156
Moore; RMC Place; TUCKER; ***250** D-9; elev. 1,816ft./554m.; mail Montrose z 26283; ● 75
Moorefield; Inc. Place; ⊡ HARDY; **250** D-11; elev. 829ft./253m.; [P]; z 26836; Ⓟ 2,148; © 2,375
Mooresville; RMC Place; MONONGALIA; ***250** B-8; elev. 965ft./294m.; mail Maidsville z 26541; ● 100
MORGAN; **250** B-12; Ⓟ 12,128; © 14,943; ◆ 16,527
Morgan Heights; RMC Place; MONONGALIA; ***250** B-8; ★ **MORG**; mail Morgantown z 26501; pop. incl. with Westover (Inc. Place)
Morgan Hills; RMC Place; RALEIGH; ***250** H-5; ★ **BECK**; mail Beckley z 25801; ● 30
Morgansville; RMC Place; DODDRIDGE; ***250** C-6; elev. 812ft./247m.; mail West Union z 26456; rural
Morgantown; Inc. Place; ⊡ MONONGALIA; **250** B-8; elev. 892ft./272m.; [P] [H] [C] 27,115 ■; ★ **MORG**; z 26501-02, z 26504-08; Ⓟ 25,879; © 26,809; ◆ 30,121
Morning Star; RMC Place; ROANE; ***250** E-4; mail Spencer z 25276; rural
Morristown; RMC Place; WIRT; ***250** D-4; elev. 677ft./206m.; mail Elizabeth z 26143; rural
Morrisvale; RMC Place; BOONE; **250** G-3; elev. 753ft./230m.; [P]; z 25565; ● 100
Mossy; RMC Place; FAYETTE; ***250** H-5; elev. 1,424ft./434m.; mail Scarbro z 25917
Moundsville; Inc. Place; ⊡ MARSHALL; **250** A-6; elev. 692ft./211m.; [P]; ★ **WHL**; z 26041; Ⓟ 10,753; © 9,998
Mountain; RMC Place; RITCHIE; **250** C-6; elev. 865ft./264m.; [P]; z 26415; ● 40
Mountain Cove; RMC Place; FAYETTE; ***250** G-5; elev. 1,611ft./491m.; mail Mount Olive z 25185, Victor z 25938; rural
Mountaindale; RMC Place; PRESTON; ***250** B-9; mail Bruceton Mills z 26525; rural
Mountaineer; RMC Place; MONONGALIA; ★ **MORG**; mail Morgantown z 26506; pop. incl. with Morgantown (Inc. Place)
Mountain Mission; RMC Place; JEFFERSON; ***250** C-14; mail Harpers Ferry z 25425; ● 500
Mountain View; RMC Place; LOGAN; ***250** I-3; mail Sarah Ann z 25644; rural
Mountain View; RMC Place; PRESTON; ***250** C-9; mail Tunnelton z 26444; rural
Mount Alto; RMC Place; JACKSON; **250** E-3; elev. 700ft./213m.; [P]; z 25264; ● 100
Mount Carbon; RMC Place; FAYETTE; ***250** G-5; elev. 642ft./196m.; [P]; z 25139; ● 200
Mount Clare; RMC Place; HARRISON; ***250** C-7; elev. 1,007ft./307m.; [P]; ★ **CLRKB**; z 26408; ● 900
Mount de Chantel; RMC Place; OHIO; ***250** A-6; ★ **WHL**; mail Wheeling z 26003; pop. incl. with Wheeling (Inc. Place)
Mount Echo; RMC Place; OHIO; ***250** C-2; ★ **WHL**; mail Valley Grove z 26060; rural
Mount Gay; RMC Place; LOGAN; **250** H-3; elev. 669ft./204m.; [P]; z 25637; ● 700
Mount Gay-Shamrock; CDP-Census Area Only; LOGAN; ***250** H-3; mail Cora z 25614, Logan z 25601, Mount Gay z 25637, Verdunville z 25649, Wilkinson z 25653; Ⓟ 3,377; © 2,623
Mount Harmony; RMC Place; MARION; ***250** B-8; elev. 1,068ft./326m.; ★ **FAIRM**; mail Fairmont z 26554; ● 150
Mount Hope; Inc. Place; FAYETTE; **250** H-5; elev. 1,699ft./518m.; [P]; ★ **BECK**; z 25880; Ⓟ 1,573; © 1,487
Mount Hope; RMC Place; ROANE; ***250** E-4; mail Walton z 25286; rural
Mount Liberty; RMC Place; BARBOUR; ***250** D-8; mail Philippi z 26416
Mount Lookout; RMC Place; NICHOLAS; **250** G-6; elev. 1,960ft./597m.; [P]; z 26678; ● 400
Mount Nebo; RMC Place; NICHOLAS; **250** G-6; elev. 2,058ft./627m.; [P]; z 26679; ● 150
Mount Nebo; RMC Place; PRESTON; ***250** B-9; mail Albright z 26519; rural
Mount Olive; RMC Place; MASON; ***250** F-3; elev. 927ft./283m.; mail Ashton z 25503; rural
Mount Olive; RMC Place; ROANE; ***250** E-4; mail Spencer z 25276; rural
Mount Olivet; RMC Place; MARSHALL; **250** J-10; elev. 1,252ft./382m.; ★ **WHL**; mail Wheeling z 26003; ● 250
Mount Pleasant; RMC Place; JEFFERSON; ***250** C-13; mail Summit Point z 25446; ● 60
Mount Storm; RMC Place; GRANT; **250** C-10; elev. 2,832ft./863m.; [P]; z 26739; ● 400
Mount Tabor; RMC Place; RALEIGH; ***250** H-5; elev. 2,482ft./757m.; ★ **BECK**; mail Beckley z 25801; ● 300
Mount Vernon; RMC Place; PRESTON; ***250** B-9; ★ **MORG**; mail Reedsville z 26547
Mount Vernon; RMC Place; PUTNAM; ***250** F-3; ★ **CHAS**; mail Hurricane z 25526; pop. incl. with Cookeville (Inc. Place)
Mountview; RMC Place; SUMMERS; ***250** I-5; mail Cool Ridge z 25825; rural
Mount Welcome; RMC Place; ROANE; ***250** F-4; elev. 1,120ft./341m.; mail Walton z 25286; rural
Mount Zion; RMC Place; CALHOUN; **250** E-5; elev. 1,133ft./345m.; [P]; z 26151; ● 40
Moyers; RMC Place; PENDLETON; ***250** F-10; elev. 2,214ft./675m.; [P]; z 26815
Mozart; RMC Place; OHIO; ***250** A-6; [P]; ★ **WHL**; z 26003; pop. incl. with Wheeling (Inc. Place)
Mozer; RMC Place; PENDLETON; ***250** E-10; elev. 1,583ft./482m.; mail Upper Tract z 26866
Mud; RMC Place; LINCOLN; ***250** G-3; mail Spurlockville z 25565; rural
Muddlety; RMC Place; NICHOLAS; ***250** F-6; elev. 1,851ft./564m.; mail Summersville z 26651
Mudfork; RMC Place; CALHOUN; ***250** E-5; elev. 892ft./272m.; mail Chloe z 25235; rural
Mullenix Addition; RMC Place; WOOD; ***250** C-4; ★ **PRKB**; mail Williamstown z 26187; ● 300
Mullens; Inc. Place; WYOMING; **250** I-4; elev. 1,426ft./435m.; [P]; z 25882; Ⓟ 2,006; © 1,769
Mullensville; RMC Place; WYOMING; ***250** I-4; elev. 1,274ft./388m.; mail Pineville z 24874; ● 100
Munday; RMC Place; WIRT; **250** D-5; elev. 714ft./218m.; [P]; z 26152; ● 30
Murphy; RMC Place; BARBOUR; ***250** D-8; mail Buckhannon z 26201; rural
Murphytown; RMC Place; WOOD; **250** C-4; elev. 640ft./195m.; ★ **PRKB**; mail Davisville z 26142; ● 130
Murraysville; RMC Place; JACKSON; ***250** D-3; elev. 600ft./183m.; [P]; z 26164
Muses Bottom; RMC Place; JACKSON; ***250** D-3; mail Ravenswood z 26164; rural
Musick; RMC Place; MINGO; ***250** I-3; mail Varney z 25696; rural
Myra; RMC Place; LINCOLN; ***250** G-2; elev. 675ft./206m.; [P]; z 25544; ● 50
Myrtle; RMC Place; BOONE
Myrtle; RMC Place; MINGO; ***250** H-2; elev. 706ft./215m.; [P]; z 25670

N

Nallen; RMC Place; FAYETTE; **250** G-6; elev. 1,900ft./579m.; [P]; z 26680; ● 65
Nancy Run; RMC Place; ROANE; ***250** E-5; mail Spencer z 25276
Naoma; RMC Place; RALEIGH; ***250** H-4; elev. 1,200ft./366m.; [P]; z 25140; ● 500
Napier; RMC Place; BRAXTON; **250** E-6; elev. 820ft./250m.; [P]; z 26631; ● 40
National; RMC Place; MONONGALIA; ***250** B-8; ★ **MORG**; mail Morgantown z 26501; ● 100
Natrium; RMC Place; MARSHALL; mail Proctor z 26055; rural
Naugatuck; RMC Place; MINGO; **250** H-2; elev. 638ft./194m.; [P]; z 25685; ● 250
Neal; RMC Place; WAYNE; ***250** F-1; ★ **HNTG**; mail Kenova z 25530; rural
Nebo; RMC Place; CLAY; ***250** E-5; elev. 929ft./283m.; [P]; z 25141; ● 40
Nebo; RMC Place; UPSHUR; ***250** D-8; elev. 2,102ft./641m.; mail Buckhannon z 26201; rural
Needmore; RMC Place; HARDY; ***250** D-11; mail Baker z 26801
Neibert; RMC Place; LOGAN; ***250** H-3; elev. 720ft./219m.; mail Lyburn z 25632; ● 150
Nellis; RMC Place; BOONE; **250** G-3; elev. 800ft./244m.; [P]; z 25142; ● 300
Nelson; RMC Place; BOONE; ***250** G-4; mail Seth z 25181
Nemours; RMC Place; MERCER; ***250** J-5; elev. 2,400ft./732m.; [P]; z 24738; ● 100
Neola; RMC Place; GREENBRIER; ***250** H-8; elev. 2,034ft./620m.; [P]; z 24986
Neptune; RMC Place; JACKSON; ***250** D-3; elev. 589ft./180m.; mail Ravenswood z 26164; rural
Nestlow; RMC Place; WAYNE; ***250** G-2; elev. 792ft./241m.; mail East Lynn z 25512
Nestorville; RMC Place; BARBOUR; **250** D-8; mail Moatsville z 26405; ● 75
Nethkin; RMC Place; MINERAL; ***250** C-10; elev. 1,600ft./488m.; mail Keyser z 26726; ● 50
Nettie; RMC Place; NICHOLAS; **250** G-6; elev. 2,764ft./842m.; [P]; z 26681; ● 600
Neville; RMC Place; RALEIGH; ★ **BECK**; mail Beckley z 25801; pop. incl. with Beckley (Inc. Place)
Newark; RMC Place; WIRT; ***250** D-4; [P]; z 26143; ● 120
Newberne; RMC Place; GILMER; ***250** D-6; elev. 880ft./268m.; [P]; z 26362 & mail Coxs Mills z 26342; ● 30
Newburg; Inc. Place; PRESTON; **250** C-8; elev. 1,230ft./375m.; [P]; z 26410 & mail Independence z 26374; Ⓟ 378; © 360
New Creek; RMC Place; MINERAL; **250** C-11; elev. 1,000ft./305m.; [P]; z 26743; ● 350
New Cumberland; Inc. Place; ⊡ HANCOCK; **250** A-2; elev. 700ft./213m.; [P]; ★ **STU-**; z 26047; Ⓟ 1,363; © 1,099
Newdale; RMC Place; WETZEL; ***250** B-6; elev. 1,416ft./432m.; mail New Martinsville z 26155; rural
Newell; CDP; HANCOCK; **250** A-2; elev. 691ft./211m.; [P]; z 26050; Ⓟ 1,724; © 1,602
New England; RMC Place; WOOD; **250** C-4; elev. 720ft./219m.; [P]; z 26181; ● 100
New Era; RMC Place; JACKSON; ***250** D-4; elev. 613ft./187m.; mail Sandyville z 25275; ● 150
Newhall; RMC Place; MCDOWELL; ***250** J-4; elev. 1,576ft./480m.; [P]; z 24866; ● 300
New Hamlin; RMC Place; LINCOLN; ***250** G-2; elev. 642ft./196m.; mail Hamlin z 25523; pop. incl. with Hamlin (Inc. Place)
New Haven; Inc. Place; MASON; **250** D-3; elev. 581ft./177m.; [P]; z 25265; Ⓟ 1,632; © 1,559
New Hill; RMC Place; MARION; ***250** C-7; ★ **FAIRM**; mail Worthington z 26591; rural
New Hill; RMC Place; MONONGALIA; ***250** B-8; ★ **MORG**; mail Cassville z 26527; ● 300
New Hope; RMC Place; MERCER; ***250** J-5; mail Princeton z 24740; ● 75
Newlon; UPSHUR, RANDOLPH; see Newlonton (RMC Place)
Newlonton (Newlon); RMC Place; UPSHUR, RANDOLPH; ***250** E-7; mail Selbyville z 26236; rural
New Manchester; RMC Place; HANCOCK; **250** A-2; elev. 1,177ft./359m.; [P]; ★ **STU-**; z 26056; ● 700
New Martinsville; Inc. Place; ⊡ WETZEL; **250** B-6; elev. 628ft./191m.; [P] [H]; z 26155; Ⓟ 6,705; © 5,984
New Milton; RMC Place; DODDRIDGE; **250** C-6; elev. 830ft./253m.; [P]; z 26411; ● 30
New Richmond; RMC Place; WYOMING; ***250** I-4; elev. 1,360ft./415m.; [P]; z 24867; ● 500
Newton; RMC Place; ROANE; **250** F-5; elev. 721ft./220m.; [P]; z 25266; ● 120
Newtown; RMC Place; FAYETTE; ***250** H-5; ★ **BECK**; mail Oak Hill z 25901; rural
Newtown; RMC Place; MINGO; **250** I-2; elev. 1,000ft./305m.; [P]; z 25686; ● 350
Newville; RMC Place; BRAXTON; **250** E-6; elev. 1,138ft./347m.; [P]; z 26601; ● 60
Next; RMC Place; TYLER; ***250** B-6; mail Sistersville z 26175; rural
NICHOLAS; **250** F-6; Ⓟ 26,775; © 26,562; ◆ 25,755
Nicolette; RMC Place; WOOD; ***250** C-4; ★ **PRKB**; mail Parkersburg z 26101; ● 90
Nicut; RMC Place; CALHOUN; ***250** E-5; elev. 854ft./260m.; [P]; z 26636; ● 25
Nimitz; RMC Place; SUMMERS; **250** I-5; elev. 2,531ft./771m.; [P]; z 25978; ● 300
Nitro; Inc. Place; KANAWHA, PUTNAM; **250** F-3; elev. 604ft./184m.; [P]; ★ **CHAS**; z 25143; Ⓟ 6,851; © 6,824
Nitro Park Addition; RMC Place; KANAWHA; ★ **CHAS**; mail Nitro z 25143; ● 300
Nobe; RMC Place; CALHOUN; ***250** D-5; elev. 1,071ft./326m.; [P]; z 26137
Nolan; RMC Place; MINGO; **250** H-2; elev. 654ft./199m.; [P]; z 25661; ● 500
Nollville; RMC Place; BERKELEY; ***250** C-13; mail Martinsburg z 25401; ● 90
Normantown; RMC Place; GILMER; **250** E-6; elev. 741ft./226m.; [P]; z 25267; ● 50
North Berkeley; RMC Place; MORGAN; ***250** B-13; mail Berkeley Springs z 25411; ● 350
Northfork; Inc. Place; MCDOWELL; **250** J-4; elev. 1,708ft./521m.; [P]; z 24868; Ⓟ 656; © 519
North Hills; RMC Place; MONONGALIA; ***250** B-8; ★ **MORG**; mail Morgantown z 26505; ● 300
North Hills; Inc. Place; WOOD; **250** C-4; ★ **PRKB**; mail Parkersburg z 26101; Ⓟ 849; © 880
North Matewan; RMC Place; MINGO; ***250** I-2; elev. 721ft./220m.; [P]; z 25688; ● 550
North Mitchell Heights; RMC Place; LOGAN; ***250** H-3; mail Logan z 25601; ● 100
North Mountain; RMC Place; BERKELEY; ***250** B-13; ★ **HAG**; mail Hedgesville z 25427; ● 40
North Page; RMC Place; FAYETTE; ***250** G-5; mail Page z 25152; ● 90
North Parkersburg; RMC Place; WOOD; ***250** C-4; [P]; ★ **PRKB**; z 26104; pop. incl. with Parkersburg (Inc. Place)
North River Mills; RMC Place; HAMPSHIRE; ***250** C-12; mail Capon Bridge z 26711; rural
North Spring; RMC Place; WYOMING; ***250** I-3; elev. 1,090ft./332m.; [P]; z 24869; ● 150
North View; RMC Place; HARRISON; ***250** C-7; ★ **CLRKB**; mail Clarksburg z 26301; pop. incl. with Clarksburg (Inc. Place)
Norton; RMC Place; RANDOLPH; **250** D-8; elev. 1,971ft./601m.; [P]; z 26285; ● 400
Norwood; RMC Place; MARION; ***250** C-8; ★ **FAIRM**; mail Fairmont z 26554; pop. incl. with Fairmont (Inc. Place)
Numan; RMC Place; DODDRIDGE; ***250** C-6; mail Salem z 26426; rural
Nuriva; RMC Place; WYOMING; ***250** I-4; mail Mullens z 25882; pop. incl. with Mullens (Inc. Place)
Nursery Gap; RMC Place; WAYNE; ***250** G-2; mail Fort Gay z 25514; rural
Nutter Farm; RMC Place; RITCHIE; ***250** C-5; elev. 733ft./223m.; mail Big Springs z 26137; rural
Nutter Fort; Inc. Place; HARRISON; **250** C-7; elev. 1,004ft./306m.; [P]; ★ **CLRKB**; z 26301; Ⓟ 1,819; © 1,686
Nutter Fort Stonewood; RMC Place; HARRISON; elev. 965ft./294m.; ★ **CLRKB**; mail Clarksburg z 26301; pop. incl. with Nutter Fort (Inc. Place)
Nutterville; RMC Place; GREENBRIER; ***250** G-6; mail Quinwood z 25981; rural

O

Oakdale; RMC Place; HARRISON; ***250** C-7; elev. 988ft./301m.; mail Mannington z 26582; rural
Oak Flat; RMC Place; PENDLETON; **250** E-10; elev. 1,533ft./467m.; mail Brandywine z 26802; ● 25
Oak Hill; Inc. Place; FAYETTE; **250** H-5; elev. 1,961ft./598m.; [P] [H]; ★ **BECK**; z 25901; Ⓟ 6,812; © 7,589
Oakmont; RMC Place; MINERAL; ***250** C-10; elev. 1,808ft./551m.; mail Elk Garden z 26717; ● 30
Oakmont; RMC Place; OHIO; ***250** A-6; ★ **WHL**; mail Wheeling z 26003; pop. incl. with Wheeling (Inc. Place)
Oak Ridge; RMC Place; FAYETTE; ***250** G-5; mail Fayetteville z 25840; ● 50
Oakvale; Inc. Place; MERCER; **250** J-5; elev. 1,721ft./525m.; [P]; z 24739-40; Ⓟ 165; © 142
Oakview Heights; RMC Place; WAYNE; ***250** F-1; ★ **HNTG**; mail Kenova z 25530; ● 400
O'Brion; RMC Place; CLAY; ***250** F-6; elev. 814ft./248m.; mail Duck z 25063
Oceana; Inc. Place; WYOMING; **250** I-4; elev. 1,269ft./387m.; [P]; z 24870; Ⓟ 1,791; © 1,550
Odaville; RMC Place; JACKSON; ***250** D-4; mail Sandyville z 25275; ● 40
Odd; RMC Place; RALEIGH; **250** I-5; elev. 2,652ft./808m.; [P]; z 25902; ● 200
Ogden; RMC Place; WOOD; ***250** C-4; ★ **PRKB**; mail Waverly z 26184; rural
OHIO; **250** B-2; Ⓟ 50,871; © 47,427; Ⓡ 47,433; ◆ 43,474
Ohley; RMC Place; KANAWHA; ***250** G-4; elev. 777ft./237m.; [P]; z 25075 & mail Dawes z 25054; ● 275
Olcott; RMC Place; KANAWHA; ***250** G-3; elev. 702ft./214m.; ★ **CHAS**; mail Charleston z 25314; ● 120
Old Arthur; RMC Place; GRANT; ***250** D-10; mail Petersburg z 26847; rural
Old Fields; RMC Place; HARDY; **250** D-11; elev. 788ft./240m.; [P]; z 26845, z 26852; ● 50
Omar; RMC Place; LOGAN; **250** H-3; elev. 814ft./248m.; [P]; z 25638; ● 600
Omps; RMC Place; MORGAN; ***250** B-13; elev. 928ft./283m.; mail Berkeley Springs z 25411; rural

Entries in **UPPERCASE** are counties.
Entries in **bold** have populations of 2,500 or more.
Names in parentheses are alternate names.
Inc. Place — Incorporated Place
RMC Place — Rand McNally Designated Place
CDP — Census Designated Place
MCD — Minor Civil Division
⊡ County Seat
▲ Minor Civil Division
elev. Elevation
[P] Post Office
[H] Hospital
[C] College
■ Principal Business Center
★ Ranally Metro Area (RMA) Abbreviation
z Zip Code(s)
Ⓟ Previous Census Population
Ⓡ Revised Census Population
Ⓐ Annexation Population
● Rand McNally Population Estimate
© Final Census Population
Ⓢ Special Census Population
◆ Estimated Population
For additional definitions see Glossary, Volume 1, and Introduction, Volume 2.

Ona; RMC Place; CABELL; **250** F-2; elev. 631ft./192m.; 🅿; ★ **HNTG**; z 25545; ● 500

Onego; RMC Place; PENDLETON; **250** E-10; elev. 1,767ft./539m.; 🅿; z 26886; ● 30

O'Neil; RMC Place; HARRISON; ***250** C-7; ★ **CLRKB**; mail Clarksburg z 26301; ● 100

Oney Gap; RMC Place; MERCER; ***250** J-5; mail Princeton z 24740; rural

Onoto; RMC Place; POCAHONTAS; ***250** G-8; mail Marlinton z 24954; pop. incl. with Marlinton (Inc. Place)

Opekiska; RMC Place; MONONGALIA; ***250** B-8; ★ **MORG**; mail Morgantown z 26501; rural

Oral Lake; RMC Place; HARRISON; ***250** C-8; ★ **CLRKB**; mail Bridgeport z 26330; ● 80

Orchard; RMC Place; MONROE; ***250** I-6; mail Ballard z 24918; rural

Orchard Hills; RMC Place; JEFFERSON; ***250** C-14; mail Ranson z 25438; ● 550

Organ Cave; RMC Place; GREENBRIER; ***250** I-7; 🅿; z 24970; rural

Orgas; RMC Place; BOONE; **250** G-4; elev. 742ft./226m.; 🅿; z 25148; ● 175

Orient Hill; RMC Place; GREENBRIER; ***250** G-6; elev. 3,000ft./914m.; 🅿; z 25958; ● 75

Orlando; RMC Place; LEWIS, LEWIS; ***250** E-6; elev. 780ft./238m.; 🅿; z 26412; ● 150

Orleans Cross Roads; RMC Place; MORGAN; ***250** B-12; mail Great Cacapon z 25422; rural

Orma; RMC Place; CALHOUN; **250** E-5; elev. 767ft./234m.; 🅿; z 25268; ● 25

Orr; RMC Place; PRESTON; ***250** B-9; mail Terra Alta z 26764; rural

Ortin Heights; RMC Place; PUTNAM; ***250** F-3; ★ **CHAS**; mail Nitro z 25143; pop. incl. with Poca (Inc. Place)

Orville; RMC Place; LOGAN; ***250** H-3; elev. 830ft./253m.; mail Yolyn z 25654; ● 50

Osage; RMC Place; MONONGALIA; ***250** B-8; elev. 907ft./276m.; 🅿; ★ **MORG**; z 26543; Ⓟ 183

Osborne; RMC Place; KANAWHA; ***250** F-4; elev. 623ft./190m.; mail Clendenin z 25045; ● 170

Osbornes Mills; RMC Place; ROANE; ***250** F-5; mail Clendenin z 25045; rural

Oscar; RMC Place; GREENBRIER; ***250** G-7; mail Renick z 24966; rural

O'Toole; RMC Place; MCDOWELL; ***250** J-4; mail Anawalt z 24808; rural

Otsego; RMC Place; WYOMING; ***250** I-4; mail Mullens z 25882; ● 125

Ottawa; RMC Place; BOONE; ***250** H-3; elev. 796ft./243m.; 🅿; z 25149; ● 400

Otto; RMC Place; ROANE; ***250** E-5; mail Spencer z 25276; rural

Ovapa; RMC Place; CLAY; ***250** F-5; elev. 864ft./263m.; 🅿; z 25164; ● 80

Overfield; RMC Place; BARBOUR; ***250** D-8; elev. 1,050ft./320m.; mail Philippi z 26416

Owings; RMC Place; HARRISON; ***250** C-7; elev. 1,052ft./321m.; 🅿; z 26431; ● 175

Oxford; RMC Place; DODDRIDGE; ***250** C-6; mail West Union z 26456

P

Packs Branch; RMC Place; FAYETTE; ***250** H-5; elev. 1,721ft./525m.; mail Mount Hope z 25880; rural

Packsville; RMC Place; RALEIGH; ***250** H-4; elev. 900ft./274m.; 🅿; z 25209; ● 100

Pad; RMC Place; ROANE; ***250** E-5; mail Walton z 25286; rural

Paden City; Inc. Place; WETZEL, TYLER; **250** B-6; elev. 640ft./195m.; 🅿; z 26159; Ⓟ 2,862; © 2,860

Page; RMC Place; FAYETTE; **250** G-5; elev. 1,120ft./341m.; 🅿; z 25152; ● 500

Pageton; RMC Place; MCDOWELL; **250** J-4; elev. 1,577ft./481m.; 🅿; z 24871; ● 300

Palace Valley; RMC Place; UPSHUR; ***250** E-8; elev. 2,102ft./641m.; mail Helvetia z 26224; rural

Palermo; RMC Place; LINCOLN; ***250** G-3; 🅿; z 25506; ● 25

Palestine; RMC Place; GREENBRIER; ***250** H-6; elev. 1,585ft./483m.; mail Alderson z 24910; rural

Palestine; RMC Place; WIRT; **250** D-4; elev. 712ft./217m.; 🅿; z 26160; ● 135

Pansy; RMC Place; GRANT; ***250** D-10; elev. 1,083ft./330m.; mail Petersburg z 26847

Panther; RMC Place; MCDOWELL; **250** I-3; elev. 940ft./287m.; 🅿; z 24872; ● 200

Paradise; RMC Place; PUTNAM; ***250** F-3; elev. 1,020ft./311m.; ★ **CHAS**; mail Liberty z 25124

Parchment Valley; RMC Place; JACKSON; ***250** E-3; mail Ripley z 25271; rural

Parcoal; RMC Place; WEBSTER; ***250** F-7; elev. 1,757ft./536m.; 🅿; z 26288; ● 100

Pardee; RMC Place; LOGAN; ***250** H-4; mail Lorado z 25630; rural

Parkersburg; Inc. Place; ⊡ WOOD; **250** C-4; elev. 649ft./198m.; 🅿 🅷 🅲 3,884 ■; ★ **PRKB**; z 26101-06; Ⓟ 33,862; © 33,099; ◆ 30,929

Parkview; RMC Place; OHIO; ***250** A-6; ★ **WHL**; mail Wheeling z 26003; pop. incl. with Wheeling (Inc. Place)

Park View; RMC Place; TAYLOR; ***250** C-8; mail Grafton z 26354; ● 175

Parkway Terrace; RMC Place; KANAWHA; ***250** F-3; ★ **CHAS**; mail Saint Albans z 25177; pop. incl. with Saint Albans (Inc. Place)

Par Metta Crest; RMC Place; WOOD; ***250** C-4; ★ **PRKB**; mail Waverly z 26184; ● 125

Parsley Bottom; RMC Place; MINGO; ***250** H-2; mail Lenore z 25676; ● 140

Parsons; Inc. Place; ⊡ TUCKER; **250** D-9; elev. 1,652ft./504m.; 🅿; z 26287; Ⓟ 1,453; © 1,463

Patterson Creek; RMC Place; MINERAL; ***250** B-11; elev. 574ft./175m.; 🅿; ★ **CUMB**; z 26753; ● 150

Paw Paw; Inc. Place; MORGAN; **250** B-12; elev. 572ft./174m.; 🅿; z 25434; Ⓟ 538; © 524

Pax; Inc. Place; FAYETTE; **250** H-5; elev. 1,629ft./497m.; 🅿; z 25904; Ⓟ 167; © 174

Paynesville; RMC Place; MCDOWELL; ***250** J-3; elev. 2,348ft./716m.; 🅿; z 24873; ● 30

Peach Creek; RMC Place; LOGAN; ***250** H-3; elev. 668ft./204m.; 🅿; z 25639; ● 450

Pea Ridge; CDP-Census Area Only; CABELL; ***250** F-2; ★ **HNTG**; mail Huntington z 25705; Ⓟ 6,535; © 6,363

Pecks Mill; RMC Place; LOGAN; ***250** H-3; elev. 654ft./199m.; 🅿; z 25547; ● 350

Pecks Run; RMC Place; UPSHUR; ***250** D-8; mail Buckhannon z 26201; rural

Peeltree; RMC Place; BARBOUR; ***250** D-8; mail Volga z 26238

Peewee; RMC Place; WIRT; ***250** D-4; elev. 682ft./208m.; mail Le Roy z 25252

Pemberton; RMC Place; RALEIGH; ***250** I-5; elev. 2,284ft./696m.; 🅿; ★ **BECK**; z 25878; ● 150

Pence Springs; RMC Place; SUMMERS; **250** I-6; elev. 1,531ft./467m.; 🅿; z 24962; ● 100

PENDLETON; **250** E-10; Ⓟ 8,054; © 8,196; ◆ 7,298

Peniel; RMC Place; ROANE; ***250** E-4; elev. 735ft./224m.; mail Reedy z 25270; rural

Pennsboro; Inc. Place; RITCHIE; **250** C-6; elev. 867ft./264m.; 🅿; z 26415; Ⓟ 1,282; © 1,199

Pentress; RMC Place; MONONGALIA; **250** B-8; elev. 939ft./286m.; 🅿; ★ **MORG**; z 26544; ● 200

Peora; RMC Place; HARRISON; ***250** C-7; 🅿; z 26431; ● 100

Pepper; RMC Place; BARBOUR; ***250** D-8; mail Bridgeport z 26330

Perkins; RMC Place; GILMER; **250** E-6; elev. 800ft./244m.; 🅿; z 26636; ● 20

Perry; RMC Place; HARDY; ***250** D-12; mail Wardensville z 26851; rural

Persinger; RMC Place; NICHOLAS; ***250** F-6; elev. 1,987ft./606m.; mail Summersville z 26651; rural

Petersburg; Inc. Place; ⊡ GRANT; **250** D-10; elev. 937ft./286m.; 🅿 🅷; z 26847; Ⓟ 2,360; © 2,423

Peterson; RMC Place; LEWIS; ***250** E-7; elev. 851ft./259m.; mail Walkersville z 26447

Peterstown; Inc. Place; MONROE; **250** J-6; elev. 1,624ft./495m.; 🅿; z 24963; Ⓟ 550; © 499

Petroleum; RMC Place; RITCHIE; ***250** D-5; elev. 698ft./213m.; 🅿; z 26161; ● 50

Pettit Heights; RMC Place; BROOKE; ***250** B-2; ★ **WHL**; mail Wellsburg z 26070; ● 100

Pettry; RMC Place; MERCER; ***250** I-5; elev. 2,571ft./784m.; mail Athens z 24712; rural

Pettry Bottom; RMC Place; RALEIGH; ***250** H-4; mail Naoma z 25140; rural

Pettus; RMC Place; RALEIGH; **250** H-4; elev. 855ft./261m.; 🅿; z 25209; ● 75

Pettyville; RMC Place; WOOD; ***250** C-4; elev. 640ft./195m.; ★ **PRKB**; mail Parkersburg z 26101; ● 500

Peytona; RMC Place; BOONE; **250** G-4; elev. 676ft./206m.; 🅿; z 25154; ● 400

Pharoah; RMC Place; WAYNE; mail Prichard z 25555; rural

Phico; RMC Place; LOGAN; ***250** H-3; elev. 657ft./200m.; mail Chapmanville z 25508; ● 175

Philippi; Inc. Place; ⊡ BARBOUR; **250** D-8; elev. 1,307ft./398m.; 🅿 🅷 🅲 747; z 26416; Ⓟ 3,132; © 2,870

Pickaway; RMC Place; MONROE; **250** I-7; elev. 2,169ft./661m.; 🅿; z 24976; ● 30

Pickens; RMC Place; RANDOLPH; **250** E-7; elev. 2,701ft./823m.; 🅿; z 26230; ● 150

Pickle Street; RMC Place; LEWIS; ***250** D-6; mail Alum Bridge z 26321

Pickshin; RMC Place; RALEIGH; ***250** I-5; elev. 1,997ft./609m.; mail Josephine z 25857; rural

Pie; RMC Place; MINGO; **250** I-3; elev. 1,274ft./388m.; mail Delbarton z 25670; ● 50

Piedmont; RMC Place; MERCER; ***250** I-5; mail Matoaka z 24736; ● 65

Piedmont; Inc. Place; MINERAL; **250** C-11; elev. 935ft./285m.; 🅿; z 26750; Ⓟ 1,094; © 1,014

Pierce; RMC Place; TUCKER; ***250** D-9; mail Thomas z 26292; ● 60

Pierpont; RMC Place; MONONGALIA; ***250** B-8; elev. 1,253ft./382m.; ★ **MORG**; mail Morgantown z 26508; ● 100

Pierpont; RMC Place; WYOMING; ***250** I-4; elev. 1,632ft./497m.; mail Maben z 25870; ● 75

Pigeon; RMC Place; ROANE; ***250** F-5; elev. 868ft./265m.; 🅿; z 25164; rural

Pike; RMC Place; RITCHIE; **250** C-5; elev. 794ft./242m.; mail Ellenboro z 26346; ● 40

Pikeside; RMC Place; BERKELEY; ***250** C-13; mail Martinsburg z 25401; ● 900

Pikeview Acres; RMC Place; BERKELEY; ***250** C-13; mail Martinsburg z 25401; ● 300

Pinch; CDP; KANAWHA; **250** F-4; 🅿; ★ **CHAS**; z 25156; Ⓟ 2,695; © 2,811

Pine Bluff; RMC Place; HARRISON; ***250** C-7; 🅿; z 26431; rural

Pine Creek; RMC Place; LOGAN; ***250** H-2; elev. 1,155ft./352m.; mail Holden z 25625; rural

Pine Grove; RMC Place; MARION; ***250** B-8; elev. 918ft./280m.; ★ **FAIRM**; mail Fairmont z 26554; rural

Pine Grove; Inc. Place; WETZEL; **250** B-6; elev. 716ft./218m.; 🅿; z 26419; Ⓟ 701; © 571

Pineknob; RMC Place; RALEIGH; ***250** H-4; elev. 1,354ft./413m.; mail Naoma z 25140; rural

Pineville; Inc. Place; ⊡ WYOMING; **250** I-4; elev. 1,321ft./403m.; 🅿; z 24859, z 24874; Ⓟ 865; © 715

Piney; RMC Place; WETZEL; ***250** B-6; mail Reader z 26167; rural

Piney View; CDP; RALEIGH; ***250** H-5; elev. 2,343ft./714m.; 🅿; ★ **BECK**; z 25906; Ⓟ 1,085; © 1,046

Pinoak; RMC Place; MERCER; ***250** I-5; mail Lashmeet z 24733, Rock z 24747; rural

Pipestem; RMC Place; SUMMERS; **250** I-5; elev. 2,389ft./728m.; 🅿; z 25979; ● 15

Pisgah; RMC Place; PRESTON; ***250** B-9; elev. 2,079ft./634m.; mail Bruceton Mills z 26525; ● 90

Pleasant Creek; RMC Place; BARBOUR; ***250** C-8; mail Philippi z 26416; rural

Pleasant Dale; RMC Place; HAMPSHIRE; ***250** C-12; mail Augusta z 26704; rural

Pleasantdale; RMC Place; PRESTON; ***250** B-9; mail Kingwood z 26537; rural

Pleasant Hill; RMC Place; CALHOUN; ***250** D-5; mail Grantsville z 26147

Pleasant Home; RMC Place; WOOD; mail Belleville z 26133; rural

Pleasant Run; RMC Place; TUCKER; ***250** D-9; elev. 1,742ft./531m.; mail Kerens z 26276; rural

PLEASANTS; **250** C-5; Ⓟ 7,546; © 7,514; ◆ 7,058

Pleasant Valley; RMC Place; HANCOCK; ***250** B-2; ★ **STU-**; mail Weirton z 26062

Pleasant Valley; Inc. Place; MARION; **250** C-8; 🅿; ★ **FAIRM**; z 26554 & mail Fairmont z 26555; © 3,124

Pleasant Valley; RMC Place; MARSHALL; **250** A-6; elev. 1,302ft./397m.; ★ **WHL**; mail Cameron z 26033; ● 60

Pleasant Valley; RMC Place; OHIO; ***250** A-6; ★ **WHL**; mail Wheeling z 26003; pop. incl. with Wheeling (Inc. Place)

Pleasant View; RMC Place; JACKSON; ***250** D-3; elev. 589ft./180m.; mail Ravenswood z 26164; rural

Pleasant View; RMC Place; LINCOLN; **250** G-2; mail Branchland z 25506; ● 150

Pleasant View; RMC Place; MARION; ***250** B-8; ★ **FAIRM**; mail Rivesville z 26588; ● 120

Pleasant View; RMC Place; WOOD; ***250** C-4; ★ **PRKB**; mail Parkersburg z 26101; rural

Pleasure Valley; RMC Place; BARBOUR; ***250** D-8; mail Montrose z 26283; ● 50

Pliny; RMC Place; PUTNAM; **250** E-3; elev. 574ft./175m.; 🅿; z 25082; ● 100

Pluto; RMC Place; RALEIGH; ***250** I-5; elev. 2,502ft./763m.; mail Hinton z 25951; rural

Poca; Inc. Place; PUTNAM; **250** F-3; elev. 582ft./177m.; 🅿; ★ **CHAS**; z 25159; Ⓟ 1,124; © 1,013

POCAHONTAS; **250** F-8; Ⓟ 9,008; © 9,131; ◆ 8,268

Pocatalico; RMC Place; KANAWHA; **250** F-4; elev. 729ft./222m.; ★ **CHAS**; mail Charleston z 25320; ● 1,500

Poe; RMC Place; NICHOLAS; ***250** G-6; elev. 1,370ft./418m.; mail Keslers Cross Lanes z 26675; ● 30

Point Lick; RMC Place; KANAWHA; ***250** F-4; ★ **CHAS**; mail Charleston z 25306; ● 150

Point Mills; RMC Place; OHIO; ***250** A-7; ★ **WHL**; mail Triadelphia z 26059

Point Pleasant; Inc. Place; ⊡ MASON; **250** E-2; elev. 569ft./173m.; 🅿 🅷; z 25550; Ⓟ 4,996; © 4,637

Points; RMC Place; HAMPSHIRE; **250** C-12; elev. 1,083ft./330m.; 🅿; z 25437; ● 30

Polard; RMC Place; TYLER; ***250** B-6; elev. 739ft./225m.; mail Middlebourne z 26149; rural

Polemic; RMC Place; BRAXTON; ***250** F-6; elev. 1,206ft./368m.; mail Sutton z 26601; rural

Polk Gap; RMC Place; WYOMING; ***250** I-4; mail Maben z 25870; rural

Pondco; RMC Place; BOONE; ***250** H-4; elev. 977ft./298m.; mail Wharton z 25208

Pond Creek; RMC Place; WOOD; ***250** D-3; elev. 604ft./184m.; mail Belleville z 26133; rural

Pond Gap; RMC Place; KANAWHA; ***250** G-5; elev. 1,071ft./326m.; 🅿; z 25160; ● 80

Pool; RMC Place; NICHOLAS; ***250** G-6; elev. 2,096ft./639m.; 🅿; z 26684; ● 80

Port Amherst; RMC Place; KANAWHA; **250** J-14; elev. 613ft./187m.; ★ **CHAS**; mail Charleston z 25306; ● 350

Porters Falls; RMC Place; WETZEL; **250** B-6; elev. 678ft./207m.; 🅿; z 26162; ● 75

Porterwood; RMC Place; TUCKER; ***250** D-9; elev. 1,694ft./516m.; mail Montrose z 26283; ● 50

Porto Rico; RMC Place; DODDRIDGE; ***250** D-6; mail New Milton z 26411; rural

Posey; RMC Place; RALEIGH; ***250** H-4; mail Saxon z 25180; rural

Potomac; RMC Place; OHIO; ***250** C-2; elev. 968ft./295m.; ★ **WHL**; mail Wheeling z 26003; rural

Potomac Park; RMC Place; BERKELEY; ***250** B-14; ★ **HAG**; mail Falling Waters z 25419; ● 150

Powell; RMC Place; MARION; ***250** C-8; elev. 904ft./276m.; ★ **FAIRM**; mail Fairmont z 26554; rural

Powell Creek (Coalbottom); RMC Place; BOONE; ***250** G-3; elev. 766ft./233m.; mail Madison z 25130; ● 40

Powellton; CDP; FAYETTE; **250** G-5; elev. 834ft./254m.; 🅿; z 25161; Ⓟ 1,905; © 1,796

Power; RMC Place; BROOKE; ***250** B-2; ★ **WHL**; mail Wellsburg z 26070; ● 90

Powhatan; RMC Place; MCDOWELL; ***250** J-4; elev. 1,800ft./549m.; 🅿; z 24868; ● 225

Prairietown; RMC Place; CABELL; ***250** F-2; ★ **HNTG**; mail Salt Rock z 25559; rural

Pratt; Inc. Place; KANAWHA; **250** G-4; elev. 620ft./189m.; 🅿; z 25162; Ⓟ 640; © 551

Premier; RMC Place; MCDOWELL; **250** J-4; elev. 1,423ft./434m.; 🅿; z 24878; ● 300

Prenter; RMC Place; BOONE; **250** H-4; elev. 965ft./294m.; 🅿; z 25181; ● 300

PRESTON; **250** B-9; Ⓟ 29,037; © 29,334; ◆ 30,161

Price Hill; RMC Place; BOONE; ***250** G-3; elev. 752ft./229m.; mail Madison z 25130; pop. incl. with Madison (Inc. Place)

Price Hill; RMC Place; RALEIGH; ***250** H-5; ★ **BECK**; mail Bradley z 25818

Pricetown; RMC Place; LEWIS; ***250** D-7; mail Weston z 26452; ● 300

Pricetown; RMC Place; WETZEL; **250** B-7; elev. 895ft./273m.; mail Smithfield z 26437; ● 85

Prichard; RMC Place; WAYNE; **250** G-1; elev. 600ft./183m.; 🅿; z 25555; ● 375

Priestly; RMC Place; LINCOLN; ***250** G-3; ★ **CHAS**; mail Alum Creek z 25003; rural

Prince; RMC Place; FAYETTE; **250** H-5; elev. 1,197ft./365m.; 🅿; z 25907; ● 200

Princeton; Inc. Place; ⊡ MERCER; **250** J-5; elev. 2,446ft./746m.; 🅿 🅷; z 24740; Ⓟ 7,043; © 6,347

Princewick; RMC Place; RALEIGH; ***250** I-5; elev. 2,465ft./751m.; 🅿; ★ **BECK**; z 25908; ● 300

Procious; RMC Place; CLAY; **250** F-5; elev. 664ft./202m.; 🅿; z 25164; ● 125

Proctor; RMC Place; WETZEL; **250** B-6; elev. 635ft./194m.; 🅿; z 26055; ● 150

Propstburg; RMC Place; PENDLETON; ***250** F-10; mail Brandywine z 26802; rural

Prospect Valley; RMC Place; HARRISON; ***250** C-7; elev. 998ft./304m.; ★ **CLRKB**; mail Shinnston z 26431; rural

Prosperity; CDP; RALEIGH; **250** H-5; elev. 2,472ft./753m.; 🅿; ★ **BECK**; z 25909; Ⓟ 1,322; © 1,310

Prudence; RMC Place; FAYETTE; ***250** H-5; ★ **BECK**; mail Fayetteville z 25840; ● 100

Pruntytown; RMC Place; TAYLOR; **250** C-8; elev. 1,205ft./367m.; mail Grafton z 26354; ● 150

Pullman; Inc. Place; RITCHIE; **250** D-6; elev. 845ft./258m.; 🅿; z 26421 & mail Berea z 26327; Ⓟ 109; © 169

Pumpkintown; RMC Place; RANDOLPH; ***250** E-8; elev. 2,524ft./769m.; mail Coalton z 26257; rural

Purgitsville; RMC Place; HAMPSHIRE; **250** C-11; elev. 934ft./285m.; 🅿; z 26845, z 26852; ● 50

Puritan Mines; RMC Place; MINGO; ***250** I-2; mail Delbarton z 25670; ● 127

Pursglove; RMC Place; MONONGALIA; ***250** B-8; elev. 904ft./276m.; 🅿; ★ **MORG**; z 26546; ● 200

Pursley; RMC Place; TYLER; ***250** B-6; elev. 784ft./239m.; mail Sistersville z 26175

PUTNAM; **250** F-3; Ⓟ 42,835; © 51,589; ◆ 55,316

Putney; RMC Place; KANAWHA; ***250** G-4; mail Mammoth z 25132; rural

Q

Quaker; RMC Place; WAYNE; ***250** G-2; elev. 700ft./213m.; mail Dunlow z 25511; rural

Quarrier; RMC Place; KANAWHA; ***250** G-4; elev. 971ft./296m.; mail Eskdale z 25075; rural

Queens; RMC Place; UPSHUR; ***250** E-8; elev. 1,924ft./586m.; mail Tallmansville z 26237

Queen Shoals; RMC Place; CLAY, KANAWHA; ***250** F-5; elev. 641ft./195m.; mail Clendenin z 25045; ● 40

Quick; RMC Place; KANAWHA; **250** F-4; elev. 687ft./209m.; 🅿; z 25045; ● 100

Quiet Dell; RMC Place; HARRISON; **250** C-7; elev. 1,046ft./319m.; mail Mount Clare z 26408; ● 400

Quincy; KANAWHA; see Dickinson (RMC Place)

Quinland; RMC Place; BOONE; ***250** G-3; mail Uneeda z 25205; ● 250

Quinnimont; RMC Place; FAYETTE; ***250** H-5; elev. 1,300ft./396m.; mail Prince z 25907; ● 100

Quinwood; Inc. Place; GREENBRIER; **250** G-6; elev. 3,000ft./914m.; 🅿; z 25981; Ⓟ 559; © 435

R

Rabbit Hill (Chestnut Heights); RMC Place; BROOKE; ***250** B-2; ★ **WHL**; mail Wellsburg z 26070; ● 225

Rachel; RMC Place; MARION; ***250** B-7; elev. 966ft./294m.; 🅿; ★ **FAIRM**; z 26587; ● 300

Racine; RMC Place; BOONE; **250** G-4; elev. 692ft./211m.; 🅿; z 25165; ● 450

Racy; RMC Place; RITCHIE; ***250** D-5; mail Petroleum z 26161; rural

Rada; RMC Place; HAMPSHIRE; ***250** C-11; elev. 862ft./263m.; mail Purgitsville z 26852; rural

Radnor; RMC Place; WAYNE; **250** G-1; elev. 700ft./213m.; 🅿; z 25517; ● 60

Ragland; RMC Place; MINGO; **250** I-2; elev. 890ft./271m.; 🅿; z 25690; ● 400

Rainelle; Inc. Place; GREENBRIER; **250** H-6; elev. 2,403ft./732m.; 🅿; z 25962; Ⓟ 1,681; © 1,545

Raines Corner; RMC Place; MONROE; ***250** I-6; mail Lindside z 24951, Union z 24983; rural

Raleigh; RMC Place; RALEIGH; ***250** H-5; elev. 2,129ft./649m.; 🅿; ★ **BECK**; z 25911; ● 900

RALEIGH; **250** H-5; Ⓟ 76,819; © 79,220; ◆ 78,261

Ramage; RMC Place; BOONE; **250** H-3; elev. 763ft./233m.; 🅿; z 25114; ● 200

Ramp; RMC Place; SUMMERS; ***250** H-6; mail Sandstone z 25985

Ramsey; RMC Place; FAYETTE; ***250** G-5; elev. 1,507ft./459m.; 🅿; z 25938; ● 30

Rand; RMC Place; KANAWHA; **250** G-4; ★ **CHAS**; mail Charleston z 25306; ● 2,200

Randall; RMC Place; MONONGALIA; ***250** B-8; elev. 828ft./252m.; ★ **MORG**; mail Osage z 26543; ● 30

RANDOLPH; **250** E-8; Ⓟ 27,803; © 28,262; ◆ 27,917

Ranger; RMC Place; LINCOLN; **250** G-2; elev. 612ft./187m.; 🅿; z 25557; ● 180

Rangoon; BARBOUR; see Boulder (RMC Place)

Ranson (Corporation of Ranson); Inc. Place; JEFFERSON; **250** C-14; elev. 520ft./158m.; 🅿 🅷; z 25438; Ⓟ 2,890; © 2,951

Raven; RMC Place; NICHOLAS; mail Summersville z 26651; rural

Ravencliff; RMC Place; WYOMING; ***250** I-4; elev. 1,800ft./549m.; 🅿; z 25913; ● 200

Raven Rock; RMC Place; PLEASANTS; ***250** C-5; elev. 647ft./197m.; mail Saint Marys z 26170

Ravenswood; Inc. Place; JACKSON; **250** D-3; elev. 620ft./189m.; 🅿; z 26164; Ⓟ 4,189; © 4,031

Rawl; RMC Place; MINGO; ***250** I-2; elev. 686ft./209m.; 🅿; z 25691; ● 200

Rayburn; RMC Place; MASON; ***250** E-3; elev. 660ft./201m.; mail Point Pleasant z 25550; rural

Raymond City; RMC Place; PUTNAM; ***250** F-3; ★ **CHAS**; mail Poca z 25159; ● 240

Raysal; RMC Place; MCDOWELL; ***250** J-3; elev. 1,200ft./366m.; 🅿; z 24879; ● 500

Reader; RMC Place; WETZEL; **250** B-6; elev. 689ft./210m.; 🅿; z 26167; ● 500

Ream; RMC Place; MCDOWELL; ***250** J-4; mail Gary z 24836; pop. incl. with Gary (Inc. Place)

Reamer; RMC Place; KANAWHA; ***250** F-4; elev. 645ft./197m.; mail Clendenin z 25045; ● 200

Red Campbell; RMC Place; LOGAN; ***250** H-3; mail Ethel z 25076; rural

Red Creek; RMC Place; TUCKER; **250** D-9; elev. 2,596ft./791m.; 🅿; z 26289; ● 80

Red House; RMC Place; PUTNAM; ***250** F-3; elev. 579ft./176m.; 🅿; ★ **CHAS**; z 25168; ● 300

Red Jacket; CDP; MINGO; **250** I-2; elev. 791ft./241m.; 🅿; z 25692; Ⓟ 760; © 728

Red Run; RMC Place; TUCKER; ***250** D-9; mail Hendricks z 26271; rural

Red Spring; RMC Place; FAYETTE; ***250** H-6; mail Meadow Bridge z 25976; rural

Redstar; RMC Place; FAYETTE; ***250** H-5; elev. 1,800ft./549m.; 🅿; ★ **BECK**; z 25901; ● 50

Red Sulphur Springs; RMC Place; MONROE; ***250** I-6; mail Ballard z 24918

Reedson; RMC Place; JEFFERSON; ***250** C-14; mail Shenandoah Junction z 25442; rural

Reedsville; Inc. Place; PRESTON; **250** B-9; elev. 1,820ft./555m.; 🅿; ★ **MORG**; z 26547; Ⓟ 482; © 517

Reedy; Inc. Place; ROANE; **250** E-4; elev. 678ft./207m.; 🅿; z 25270; Ⓟ 271; © 198

Reedyville; RMC Place; ROANE; ***250** E-4; elev. 750ft./229m.; mail Spencer z 25276; rural

Reeses Mill; RMC Place; MINERAL; ***250** C-11; mail Keyser z 26726; rural

Reger; RMC Place; UPSHUR; ***250** D-8; mail Buckhannon z 26201; rural

Renick; GREENBRIER; see Falling Spring (Inc. Place)

Renicks Valley; RMC Place; GREENBRIER; ***250** G-7; mail Renick z 24966; rural

Rensford; RMC Place; KANAWHA; **250** F-4; mail Charleston z 25306; ● 200

Replete; RMC Place; WEBSTER; ***250** E-7; 🅿; z 26222

Reynoldsville; RMC Place; HARRISON; ***250** C-7; elev. 1,100ft./335m.; 🅿; ★ **CLRKB**; z 26422; ● 400

Rhodell; Inc. Place; RALEIGH; ***250** I-5; elev. 1,618ft./493m.; 🅿; z 25915; Ⓟ 221; © 234

Richard; RMC Place; MONONGALIA; ***250** B-8; ★ **MORG**; mail Morgantown z 26508; ● 200

Richardson; RMC Place; CALHOUN; ***250** E-5; mail Arnoldsburg z 25234; rural

Richlands; RMC Place; GREENBRIER; ***250** H-7; mail Lewisburg z 24901; rural

Richwood; Inc. Place; NICHOLAS; **250** G-7; elev. 2,194ft./669m.; 🅿 🅷; z 26261; Ⓟ 2,808; © 2,477

Rider; RMC Place; HARRISON; ***250** D-7; elev. 1,051ft./320m.; ★ **CLRKB**; mail Lost Creek z 26385; rural

Ridersville; RMC Place; MORGAN; ***250** B-13; mail Berkeley Springs z 25411; ● 150

Ridgedale; RMC Place; MONONGALIA; ***250** B-8; ★ **MORG**; mail Morgantown z 26508

Ridge Farms; RMC Place; MARION; ***250** B-8; ★ **FAIRM**; mail Rivesville z 26588; rural

Ridgeley; Inc. Place; MINERAL; **250** B-11; elev. 622ft./190m.; 🅿; ★ **CUMB**; z 26753; Ⓟ 779; © 762

Ridgeview (Brush Creek); RMC Place; BOONE; ***250** G-3; elev. 797ft./243m.; 🅿; z 25169; ● 300

Ridgeview; RMC Place; LOGAN; ***250** H-3; mail Mount Gay z 25637; ● 100

Ridgeville; RMC Place; MINERAL; ***250** C-11; mail Burlington z 26710

Ridgeway; RMC Place; BERKELEY; **250** C-13; elev. 589ft./180m.; 🅿; z 25440; ● 350

Riffle; RMC Place; BRAXTON; ***250** E-6; elev. 924ft./282m.; 🅿; z 26619 & mail Sutton z 26601; rural

Rift; RMC Place; MCDOWELL; ***250** J-4; mail War z 24892

Rig; RMC Place; HARDY; **250** D-11; elev. 1,000ft./305m.; 🅿; z 26836; ● 125

Rinehart; RMC Place; HARRISON; ***250** C-7; elev. 1,066ft./325m.; mail Wallace z 26448; ● 60

Ringgold; RMC Place; MONONGALIA; ***250** B-8; ★ **MORG**; mail Morgantown z 26508

Rio; RMC Place; HAMPSHIRE; **250** D-12; elev. 1,136ft./346m.; 🅿; z 26755; ● 150

Ripley; Inc. Place; ⊡ JACKSON; **250** E-4; elev. 616ft./188m.; 🅿 🅷; z 25271; Ⓟ 3,023; © 3,263

Ripley Landing; RMC Place; JACKSON; ***250** E-3; elev. 576ft./176m.; mail Millwood z 25262

Ripling Waters; RMC Place; JACKSON; mail Kenna z 25248; rural

Rippon; RMC Place; JEFFERSON; **250** C-14; elev. 534ft./163m.; 🅿; z 25441; ● 250

Rita; RMC Place; LOGAN; ***250** H-3; mail Lyburn z 25632; rural

RITCHIE; **250** D-5; Ⓟ 10,233; © 10,343; ◆ 10,139

Riverbend; RMC Place; KANAWHA; ***250** F-3; ★ **CHAS**; mail Saint Albans z 25177; ● 400

Riverdale Acres; RMC Place; KANAWHA; ***250** F-3; ★ **CHAS**; mail Nitro z 25143

Riverlake Estates; RMC Place; KANAWHA; ***250** F-3; ★ **CHAS**; mail Saint Albans z 25177; pop. incl. with Saint Albans (Inc. Place)

Riverside; RMC Place; KANAWHA; ***250** G-4; mail Glasgow z 25086; ● 150

Riverside; RMC Place; MONONGALIA; ***250** B-8; ★ **MORG**; mail Morgantown z 26501; pop. incl. with Westover (Inc. Place)

Riverton; RMC Place; PENDLETON; **250** E-10; elev. 1,809ft./551m.; 🅿; z 26814; ● 100

Rivesville; Inc. Place; MARION; ***250** B-8; elev. 874ft./266m.; 🅿; ★ **FAIRM**; z 26588; Ⓟ 1,064; © 913

Rivesville Junction; RMC Place; MARION; ★ **FAIRM**; pop. incl. with Rivesville (Inc. Place)

Roach; RMC Place; CABELL; ***250** F-2; elev. 581ft./177m.; ★ **HNTG**; mail Barboursville z 25504; rural

ROANE; **250** E-4; Ⓟ 15,120; © 15,446; ◆ 14,794

Roanoke; RMC Place; LEWIS; ***250** D-7; elev. 1,059ft./323m.; 🅿; z 26447; ● 95

Roberts; RMC Place; DODDRIDGE; ***250** C-6; mail West Union z 26456; rural

Robertsburg; RMC Place; PUTNAM; **250** E-3; elev. 563ft./172m.; 🅿; ★ **CHAS**; z 25123; ● 100

Robey; RMC Place; HARRISON; ***250** C-7; elev. 938ft./286m.; ★ **CLRKB**; mail Lumberport z 26386; rural

Robinette; RMC Place; LOGAN; **250** H-3; elev. 939ft./286m.; 🅿; z 25607; ● 150

Robin Hood; BOONE; see Twilight (RMC Place)

Robson; RMC Place; FAYETTE; **250** G-5; elev. 873ft./266m.; 🅿; z 25173; ● 250

Rock; RMC Place; MERCER; ***250** J-5; elev. 2,229ft./679m.; 🅿; z 24747; ● 150

Rock Camp; RMC Place; MONROE; ***250** I-6; mail Lindside z 24951; ● 60

Rock Castle; RMC Place; JACKSON; ***250** E-3; elev. 713ft./217m.; 🅿; z 25245; ● 20

Rock Cave; RMC Place; UPSHUR; **250** E-7; elev. 1,721ft./525m.; 🅿; z 26215, z 26234; ● 400

Rock Creek; RMC Place; RALEIGH; **250** H-4; elev. 1,330ft./405m.; 🅿; z 25174; ● 200

Rockdale; RMC Place; BROOKE; ***250** B-2; elev. 679ft./207m.; ★ **STU-**; mail Wellsburg z 26070; ● 50

Rockford; RMC Place; HARRISON; ***250** D-7; elev. 1,057ft./322m.; ★ **CLRKB**; mail Lost Creek z 26385; rural

Rock Forge; RMC Place; MONONGALIA; **250** B-5; elev. 973ft./297m.; ★ **MORG**; mail Morgantown z 26508; ● 200

Rock Gap; RMC Place; MORGAN; ***250** B-13; mail Berkeley Springs z 25411; rural

Rock Lake; RMC Place; MARION; ***250** C-8; ★ **FAIRM**; mail Fairmont z 26554; ● 400

Rock Lake Village; RMC Place; KANAWHA; ***250** F-3; ★ **CHAS**; mail Charleston z 25309; pop. incl. with South Charleston (Inc. Place)

Rocklick; RMC Place; MARSHALL; ***250** A-7; mail Cameron z 26033

Rock Oak; RMC Place; HARDY; ***250** D-11; mail Baker z 26801; rural

Rockport; RMC Place; WOOD; **250** D-4; elev. 700ft./213m.; 🅿; z 26169; ● 50

Rockridge; RMC Place; MCDOWELL; ***250** J-3; elev. 2,223ft./678m.; mail Paynesville z 24873; rural

Rock Run; RMC Place; DODDRIDGE; ***250** C-6; mail West Union z 26456; rural

Rocksdale; RMC Place; CALHOUN; ***250** E-5; mail Arnoldsburg z 25234; rural

Rockton; RMC Place; BRAXTON; ***250** E-6; mail Frametown z 26623; rural

Rock View; RMC Place; WYOMING; **250** I-4; elev. 1,636ft./499m.; 🅿; z 24880; ● 400

Rockville; RMC Place; LINCOLN; ***250** G-2; mail Midkiff z 25540; rural

Rocky Fork; RMC Place; KANAWHA; ***250** F-3; elev. 587ft./179m.; ★ **CHAS**; mail Charleston z 25312; rural

Rodemer; RMC Place; PRESTON; ***250** C-9; mail Terra Alta z 26764; rural

Roderfield; RMC Place; MCDOWELL; **250** I-3; elev. 1,090ft./332m.; 🅿; z 24881; ● 1,000

Rohr; RMC Place; PRESTON; ***250** B-9; ★ **MORG**; mail Reedsville z 26547; rural

Rolfe; RMC Place; MCDOWELL; ***250** J-4; mail Northfork z 24868; ● 70

Rollins Branch; RMC Place; WYOMING; ***250** H-4; mail Oceana z 24870; ● 200

Romance; RMC Place; JACKSON; ***250** F-4; elev. 681ft./208m.; 🅿; z 25248

Romines Mills; RMC Place; HARRISON; ***250** D-7; mail Lost Creek z 26385; rural

Romney; Inc. Place; ⊡ HAMPSHIRE; **250** C-11; elev. 830ft./253m.; 🅿 🅷; z 26757; Ⓟ 1,966; © 1,940

Romont; RMC Place; FAYETTE; ***250** G-5; elev. 1,193ft./364m.; mail Ansted z 25812; rural

Ronceverte; Inc. Place; GREENBRIER; **250** H-7; elev. 1,668ft./508m.; 🅿 🅷; z 24970; Ⓟ 1,754; © 1,557

Ronda; RMC Place; KANAWHA; ***250** G-4; elev. 656ft./200m.; mail Drybranch z 25061; ● 225

Roneys Point; RMC Place; OHIO; ***250** A-7; ★ **WHL**; mail Triadelphia z 26059; ● 80

Rosbys Rock; RMC Place; MARSHALL; ***250** A-6; mail Moundsville z 26041

Rosebud; RMC Place; HARRISON; ***250** C-7; ★ **CLRKB**; mail Lumberport z 26386; rural

Rosedale; RMC Place; BRAXTON, GILMER; **250** E-6; elev. 778ft./237m.; 🅿; z 26636; ● 175

Rosedale; RMC Place; FAYETTE; ***250** H-5; ★ **BECK**; mail Oak Hill z 25901; pop. incl. with Oak Hill (Inc. Place)

Rosedale; RMC Place; MONONGALIA; ***250** B-8; ★ **MORG**; mail Maidsville z 26541; ● 35

Rosemont (Jerry Run); RMC Place; TAYLOR; ***250** C-8; elev. 1,005ft./306m.; 🅿; z 26424; ● 300

Roseville Addition; RMC Place; KANAWHA; ***250** F-3; ★ **CHAS**; mail Saint Albans z 25177

Rossmore; RMC Place; LOGAN; ***250** H-3; elev. 720ft./219m.; 🅿; z 25601; ● 200

Rough Run; RMC Place; GRANT; ***250** E-10; mail Upper Tract z 26866; rural

Round Bottom; RMC Place; WETZEL; ***250** B-7; elev. 1,075ft./328m.; mail Hundred z 26575

Rowlesburg; Inc. Place; PRESTON; **250** C-9; elev. 1,406ft./429m.; 🅿; z 26425; Ⓟ 648; © 613

Roxalana; RMC Place; ROANE; ***250** E-5; elev. 991ft./302m.; mail Looneyville z 25259; rural

Ruddle; RMC Place; PENDLETON; ***250** E-10; elev. 1,538ft./469m.; mail Franklin z 26807

Rumble; RMC Place; BOONE; **250** G-4; mail Ashford z 25009; ● 250

Runa; RMC Place; NICHOLAS; ***250** G-6; elev. 2,200ft./671m.; 🅿; z 26679; rural

Rupert; Inc. Place; GREENBRIER; **250** H-6; elev. 2,432ft./741m.; 🅿; z 25984; Ⓟ 1,104; © 940

Rush Creek; RMC Place; ROANE; mail Spencer z 25276; rural

Rusk; RMC Place; RITCHIE; ***250** D-5; mail Petroleum z 26161; rural

Russelldale; RMC Place; MINERAL; ***250** C-11; mail Burlington z 26710; rural

Russellville; RMC Place; FAYETTE, GREENBRIER; ***250** G-6; elev. 1,900ft./579m.; mail Nallen z 26680

Russett; RMC Place; CALHOUN; ***250** E-5; mail Grantsville z 26147

Ruth; RMC Place; KANAWHA; **250** F-4; elev. 697ft./212m.; ★ **CHAS**; mail Charleston z 25314; pop. incl. with South Charleston (Inc. Place)

Ruthbelle; RMC Place; PRESTON; ***250** B-9; mail Albright z 26519; ● 40

Ruthdale; RMC Place; KANAWHA; **250** J-12; ★ **CHAS**; mail Charleston z 25314; ● 65

Rutherford; RMC Place; RITCHIE; ***250** D-5; elev. 698ft./213m.; mail Harrisville z 26362; rural

Rutledge; RMC Place; KANAWHA; ***250** F-4; ★ **CHAS**; mail Charleston z 25311

Ryanville; RMC Place; HARRISON; ***250** C-7; ★ **CLRKB**; mail Bridgeport z 26330; ● 100

Rymer; RMC Place; MARION; ***250** B-7; elev. 1,028ft./313m.; mail Mannington z 26582; ● 35

S

Sabine; RMC Place; WYOMING; **250** I-4; elev. 1,538ft./469m.; 🅿; z 25916; ● 250

Sabraton; RMC Place; MONONGALIA; ***250** B-8; ★ **MORG**; mail Morgantown z 26505, z 26508; pop. incl. with Morgantown (Inc. Place)

Sago; RMC Place; UPSHUR; ***250** D-7; mail Buckhannon z 26201; rural

Saint Albans; Inc. Place; KANAWHA; **250** F-3; elev. 600ft./183m.; 🅿; ★ **CHAS**; z 25177; Ⓟ 11,257; © 11,567

Saint Clara; RMC Place; DODDRIDGE; ***250** D-6; mail Alum Bridge z 26321; rural

Saint Cloud; RMC Place; MONONGALIA; ***250** B-7; elev. 1,499ft./457m.; rural

Saint George; RMC Place; TUCKER; **250** D-9; elev. 1,556ft./474m.; 🅿; z 26287; ● 60

Saint Joe; RMC Place; PRESTON; ***250** C-9; mail Albright z 26519; pop. incl. with Albright (Inc. Place)

Saint Joseph; RMC Place; MARSHALL; **250** B-6; elev. 1,410ft./430m.; mail Proctor z 26055; ● 60

Saint Marys; Inc. Place; ⊡ PLEASANTS; **250** C-5; elev. 628ft./191m.; 🅿; z 26170; Ⓟ 2,148; © 2,017

Salem; RMC Place; FAYETTE; ***250** H-5; ★ **BECK**; mail Oak Hill z 25901; ● 275

Salem; Inc. Place; HARRISON; **250** C-7; elev. 1,052ft./321m.; 🅿 🅲 786; z 26426; Ⓟ 2,063; © 2,006

Salt Hill; RMC Place; JACKSON; ***250** E-4; mail Ripley z 25271; rural

Saltlick Bridge; RMC Place; BRAXTON; ***250** E-6; elev. 806ft./246m.; mail Heaters z 26627; rural

Saltpetre; RMC Place; WAYNE; ***250** G-1; elev. 700ft./213m.; mail Fort Gay z 25514

Salt Rock; RMC Place; CABELL; **250** F-2; elev. 585ft./178m.; 🅿; ★ **HNTG**; z 25559; ● 450

Salt Sulphur Springs; RMC Place; MONROE; ***250** I-7; elev. 1,896ft./578m.; mail Union z 24983

Saltwell; RMC Place; HARRISON; ***250** C-7; elev. 1,001ft./305m.; 🅿; ★ **CLRKB**; z 26431 & mail Bridgeport z 26330; rural

Sam Black Church; RMC Place; GREENBRIER; ***250** H-6; mail Crawley z 24931; ● 45

Sanderson; RMC Place; KANAWHA; ***250** F-4; mail Clendenin z 25045; rural

Sand Fork (Layopolis); Inc. Place; GILMER; **250** E-6; elev. 745ft./227m.; 🅿; z 26430; Ⓟ 196; © 176

Sand Hill; RMC Place; MARSHALL; ***250** A-7; ★ **WHL**; mail Wheeling z 26003

Sand Hill; RMC Place; WOOD; ***250** C-4; ★ **PRKB**; mail Parkersburg z 26101; ● 750

Sandlick; RMC Place; MERCER; ***250** J-5; elev. 2,586ft./788m.; mail Bluefield z 24701; ● 350

Sand Ridge; RMC Place; CALHOUN; **250** E-5; elev. 1,204ft./367m.; 🅿; z 25234; ● 15

Sand Run; RMC Place; UPSHUR; ***250** D-8; mail Buckhannon z 26201

Sandstone; RMC Place; SUMMERS; **250** H-6; elev. 1,295ft./395m.; 🅿; z 25985; ● 250

Sandy; RMC Place; KANAWHA; ***250** F-4; ★ **CHAS**; mail Pinch z 25156; ● 400

Sandy Huff; RMC Place; MCDOWELL; ***250** I-3; mail Iaeger z 24844; ● 250

Sandy Summit; RMC Place; ROANE; ***250** E-4; mail Le Roy z 25252; rural

Sandyville; RMC Place; JACKSON; **250** E-4; elev. 598ft./182m.; 🅿; z 25275; ● 150

Sanford; RMC Place; MARION; ***250** B-8; ★ **FAIRM**; mail Fairmont z 26554; rural

Sanger; RMC Place; FAYETTE; ***250** H-5; ★ **BECK**; mail Oak Hill z 25901; rural

Sanoma; RMC Place; WIRT; ***250** D-5; elev. 657ft./200m.; 🅿; z 26160; rural

Sarah; RMC Place; CABELL; ***250** F-2; ★ **HNTG**; mail Salt Rock z 25559; rural

Sarah Ann; RMC Place; LOGAN; ***250** H-3; elev. 1,020ft./311m.; 🅿; z 25644; ● 250

Sardis; RMC Place; HARRISON; ***250** C-7; elev. 968ft./295m.; ★ **CLRKB**; mail Clarksburg z 26301; rural

Sarton; RMC Place; MONROE; ***250** I-6; elev. 2,500ft./762m.; 🅿; z 24983; ● 25

Sassafras; RMC Place; MASON; ***250** D-3; elev. 704ft./215m.; mail West Columbia z 25287; rural

Sattes; RMC Place; KANAWHA; ***250** F-3; elev. 601ft./183m.; ★ **CHAS**; mail Nitro z 25143; pop. incl. with Nitro (Inc. Place)

Saulsbury; RMC Place; WOOD; ***250** D-4; ★ **PRKB**; mail Mineral Wells z 26150; rural

Saulsville; RMC Place; WYOMING; ***250** I-4; elev. 1,946ft./593m.; 🅿; z 25876; ● 60

Saunders (Three Forks); RMC Place; LOGAN; ***250** H-4; mail Lorado z 25630; rural

Saxman; RMC Place; NICHOLAS; ***250** G-6; mail Fenwick z 26202; rural

Saxon; RMC Place; RALEIGH; ***250** H-4; elev. 1,800ft./549m.; 🅿; z 25180; ● 60

Scarbro; RMC Place; FAYETTE; ***250** H-5; elev. 1,800ft./549m.; 🅿; ★ **BECK**; z 25917; ● 600

Scary; RMC Place; PUTNAM; ***250** F-3; ★ **CHAS**; mail Saint Albans z 25177; ● 125

Scherr; RMC Place; GRANT; **250** D-10; elev. 1,565ft./477m.; 🅿; z 26726; ● 25

Schrader; RMC Place; KANAWHA; ***250** F-4; mail Elkview z 25071; rural

Schultz; RMC Place; PLEASANTS; **250** C-5; elev. 724ft./221m.; mail Saint Marys z 26170; ● 75

Scott; PUTNAM; see Scott Depot (RMC Place)

Scott Depot (Scott); RMC Place; PUTNAM; **250** F-3; elev. 690ft./210m.; 🅿; ★ **CHAS**; z 25560; ● 1,500

Scrabble; RMC Place; BERKELEY, JEFFERSON; ***250** B-14; elev. 367ft./112m.; mail Shepherdstown z 25443; ● 50

Seaman; RMC Place; ROANE; ***250** D-4; elev. 706ft./215m.; mail Le Roy z 25252; rural

Secondcreek; RMC Place; MONROE; ***250** I-7; elev. 1,862ft./568m.; 🅿; z 24974; ● 30

Sedalia; RMC Place; DODDRIDGE; **250** C-6; elev. 844ft./257m.; mail Salem z 26426; ● 50

Seebert; RMC Place; POCAHONTAS; **250** G-8; elev. 2,050ft./625m.; 🅿; z 24946; ● 30

Selbyville; RMC Place; UPSHUR; ***250** E-7; elev. 1,886ft./575m.; 🅿; z 26236; ● 90

Seminole; RMC Place; HARRISON; ***250** C-7; ★ **CLRKB**; mail Gypsy z 26361; ● 60

Seneca; RMC Place; MONONGALIA; ***250** B-8; ★ **MORG**; mail Morgantown z 26505; pop. incl. with Morgantown (Inc. Place)

Seneca Rocks; RMC Place; PENDLETON; **250** E-10; elev. 1,566ft./477m.; 🅿; z 26884; ● 75

Seng Creek; RMC Place; BOONE; ***250** H-4; mail Whitesville z 25209; ● 150

Servia; RMC Place; BRAXTON; ***250** E-6; elev. 899ft./274m.; mail Duck z 25063

Seth; RMC Place; BOONE; **250** G-4; elev. 698ft./213m.; 🅿; z 25181; ● 750

Seven Pines; RMC Place; MARION; ***250** B-7; elev. 1,072ft./327m.; mail Mannington z 26582; rural

Shady Brook; RMC Place; LEWIS; ***250** D-7; mail Weston z 26452; pop. incl. with Weston (Inc. Place)

Shady Spring; CDP; RALEIGH; **250** I-5; elev. 2,696ft./822m.; 🅿; ★ **BECK**; z 25918; Ⓟ 1,929; © 2,078

Shafer; RMC Place; TUCKER; ***250** C-9; elev. 1,874ft./571m.; mail Parsons z 26287; rural

Shamrock; RMC Place; LOGAN; ***250** H-3; mail Cora z 25614; ● 500

Shanghai; RMC Place; BERKELEY; ***250** C-13; elev. 529ft./161m.; mail Hedgesville z 25427

Shanks; RMC Place; HAMPSHIRE; **250** C-12; elev. 1,130ft./344m.; 🅿; z 26761; ● 100

Shannondale; RMC Place; JEFFERSON; ***250** C-14; mail Harpers Ferry z 25425; ● 900

Sharon; RMC Place; KANAWHA; **250** G-4; elev. 668ft./204m.; ● 300

Sharon Heights; RMC Place; MINGO; ***250** I-3; mail Gilbert z 25621; ● 50

Sharples; RMC Place; LOGAN; ***250** H-3; elev. 855ft./261m.; 🅿; z 25183; ● 130

Shegon; RMC Place; LOGAN; ***250** H-3; mail Verdunville z 25649; ● 200

Shenandoah Junction; RMC Place; JEFFERSON; ***250** C-14; elev. 520ft./158m.; 🅿; z 25442; ● 300

Shepherdstown; Inc. Place; JEFFERSON; **250** C-14; elev. 406ft./124m.; 🅿 🅲 3,970; z 25443; Ⓟ 1,287; © 803; Ⓡ 1,202

Sheridan; RMC Place; LINCOLN; ***250** G-2; elev. 595ft./181m.; mail Branchland z 25506

Sherman; RMC Place; JACKSON; **250** D-3; elev. 591ft./180m.; 🅿; z 26164; ● 60

Sherrard; RMC Place; MARSHALL; ***250** A-6; elev. 1,311ft./400m.; ★ **WHL**; mail Wheeling z 26003; ● 120

Sherwood; RMC Place; DODDRIDGE; ***250** C-6; elev. 831ft./253m.; mail West Union z 26456; rural

Shiloh; RMC Place; RALEIGH; ***250** H-4; ★ **BECK**; mail Glen Daniel z 25844; rural

Shiloh; RMC Place; TYLER; ***250** C-5; mail Friendly z 26146

Shinnston; Inc. Place; HARRISON; **250** C-7; elev. 1,000ft./305m.; 🅿; ★ **CLRKB**; z 26431; Ⓟ 2,543; © 2,295

Shirley; RMC Place; TYLER; **250** C-6; elev. 733ft./223m.; 🅿; z 26434; ● 135

Shively; RMC Place; LOGAN; ***250** H-2; elev. 680ft./207m.; 🅿; z 25508; rural

Shoals; RMC Place; WAYNE; **250** F-1; elev. 580ft./177m.; 🅿; ★ **HNTG**; z 25562; ● 70

Shock; RMC Place; GILMER; ***250** E-6; elev. 747ft./228m.; 🅿; z 26638; ● 10

Short Creek; RMC Place; BROOKE, OHIO; **250** B-2; elev. 662ft./202m.; 🅿; ★ **WHL**; z 26058; ● 300

Short Creek Valley; RMC Place; OHIO, BROOKE; ***250** C-2; ★ **WHL**; mail Wheeling z 26003; rural

Short Gap; RMC Place; MINERAL; **250** B-11; elev. 818ft./249m.; 🅿; ★ **CUMB**; z 26726 & mail Ridgeley z 26753; ● 500

Short Line Junction; RMC Place; HARRISON; ★ **CLRKB**; mail Clarksburg z 26301; pop. incl. with Clarksburg (Inc. Place)

Shrewsbury; RMC Place; KANAWHA; ***250** G-4; elev. 628ft./191m.; 🅿; z 25015; ● 650

Sias; RMC Place; LINCOLN; **250** G-2; elev. 690ft./210m.; 🅿; z 25506; ● 35

Sidneyville; RMC Place; JACKSON; ***250** E-3; elev. 718ft./219m.; mail Ripley z 25271

Sigman; RMC Place; PUTNAM; ***250** F-3; elev. 1,054ft./321m.; ★ **CHAS**; mail Red House z 25168; rural

Silver Grove; RMC Place; JEFFERSON; ***250** C-14; mail Harpers Ferry z 25425; ● 200

Silver Hill; RMC Place; WETZEL; ***250** B-6; elev. 1,137ft./347m.; mail New Martinsville z 26155; rural

Silver Lake; RMC Place; PRESTON; **250** C-9; mail Eglon z 26716; ● 120

Silverton; RMC Place; JACKSON; ***250** D-4; mail Ravenswood z 26164; ● 250

Simmons; MERCER; see Freeman (RMC Place)

Simoda; RMC Place; PENDLETON; ***250** E-9; elev. 2,978ft./908m.; mail Riverton z 26814; rural

Simon; RMC Place; WYOMING; ***250** I-3; elev. 1,126ft./343m.; 🅿; z 24882; ● 20

Simpson; RMC Place; TAYLOR; **250** C-8; elev. 1,093ft./333m.; 🅿; z 26435; ● 250

Sinclair; RMC Place; PRESTON; ***250** C-9; elev. 1,489ft./454m.; mail Moatsville z 26405; rural

Sinks Grove; RMC Place; MONROE; **250** I-7; elev. 2,175ft./663m.; 🅿; z 24976; ● 75

Sir Johns Run; RMC Place; MORGAN; ***250** B-13; mail Berkeley Springs z 25411; ● 30

Sissonville; CDP; KANAWHA; **250** F-4; 🅿; ★ **CHAS**; z 25320 & mail Charleston z 25312, z 25360; Ⓟ 4,290; © 4,399

Sistersville; Inc. Place; TYLER; **250** B-5; elev. 647ft./197m.; 🅿 🅷; z 26175; Ⓟ 1,797; © 1,588

Six; RMC Place; MCDOWELL; ***250** J-4; elev. 1,550ft./472m.; ● 100

Six Mile; BOONE; see Havana (RMC Place)

Skeetersville; RMC Place; JEFFERSON; ***250** C-14; mail Shenandoah Junction z 25442; rural

Skelton; RMC Place; RALEIGH; ***250** H-5; elev. 2,320ft./707m.; 🅿; ★ **BECK**; z 25919; pop. incl. with Beckley (Inc. Place)

Skygusty; RMC Place; MCDOWELL; ***250** J-4; elev. 1,600ft./488m.; 🅿; z 24801 & mail Pageton z 24871; ● 140

Slab Fork; RMC Place; RALEIGH; **250** I-4; elev. 1,867ft./569m.; 🅿; ★ **BECK**; z 25920; ● 150

Slabtown; RMC Place; MINGO; ***250** I-3; mail Gilbert z 25621; ● 100

Slagle; RMC Place; LOGAN; ***250** H-3; mail Yolyn z 25654; rural

Slanesville; RMC Place; HAMPSHIRE; **250** C-12; elev. 1,189ft./362m.; 🅿; z 25444; ● 150

Slate; RMC Place; WOOD; ***250** D-4; elev. 605ft./184m.; ★ **PRKB**; mail Elizabeth z 26143

Slaty Fork (Laurel Bank); RMC Place; POCAHONTAS; **250** F-8; elev. 2,728ft./831m.; 🅿; z 26209, z 26291; ● 100

Sleepy Creek; RMC Place; MORGAN; ***250** B-13; mail Berkeley Springs z 25411; ● 40

Smithburg; RMC Place; DODDRIDGE; **250** C-6; elev. 797ft./243m.; 🅿; z 26436; ● 120

Smith Crossroads; RMC Place; MORGAN; ***250** B-13; elev. 611ft./186m.; mail Berkeley Springs z 25411; rural

Smithers; Inc. Place; FAYETTE, KANAWHA; **250** G-5; elev. 643ft./196m.; 🅿; z 25186; Ⓟ 1,162; © 904

Smithfield; Inc. Place; WETZEL; **250** C-7; elev. 846ft./258m.; 🅿; z 26437; Ⓟ 205; © 177

Smithtown; RMC Place; MONONGALIA; ***250** B-8; ★ **MORG**; mail Morgantown z 26508; rural

Smithville; RMC Place; RITCHIE; **250** D-5; elev. 690ft./210m.; 🅿; z 26178; ● 200

Smoke Hole; RMC Place; PENDLETON; ***250** E-10; mail Upper Tract z 26866; rural

Smoot; RMC Place; GREENBRIER; **250** H-6; elev. 2,471ft./753m.; 🅿; z 24977; ● 125

Snider; RMC Place; PRESTON; ***250** C-9; mail Kingwood z 26537

Snowden; RMC Place; LINCOLN; ***250** G-3; elev. 786ft./240m.; mail Yawkey z 25573; rural

Snowflake; RMC Place; GREENBRIER; ***250** H-7; mail Ronceverte z 24970; ● 30

Snow Hill; RMC Place; KANAWHA; **250** J-14; ★ **CHAS**; mail Charleston z 25311; ● 275

Sod; RMC Place; LINCOLN; **250** G-3; elev. 789ft./240m.; 🅿; ★ **CHAS**; z 25564; ● 150

Sodom; RMC Place; LOGAN; ***250** H-3; mail Sharples z 25183; ● 40

Sophia; Inc. Place; RALEIGH; **250** I-5; elev. 2,317ft./706m.; 🅿; ★ **BECK**; z 25921; Ⓟ 1,182; © 1,301

South Charleston; Inc. Place; KANAWHA; **250** F-4; elev. 600ft./183m.; 🅿 🅷; ★ **CHAS**; z 25303, z 25309; Ⓟ 13,645; © 13,390

South Fork Junction; RMC Place; MCDOWELL; mail Paynesville z 24873; rural

South Hills; RMC Place; KANAWHA; ***250** F-4; ★ **CHAS**; mail Charleston z 25314; pop. incl. with Charleston (Inc. Place)

South Hills; RMC Place; MONONGALIA; ***250** B-8; ★ **MORG**; mail Morgantown z 26508; pop. incl. with Morgantown (Inc. Place)

South Madison; RMC Place; BOONE; ***250** G-3; mail Madison z 25130; pop. incl. with Madison (Inc. Place)

South Park; RMC Place; KANAWHA; ***250** F-4; ★ **CHAS**; mail Charleston z 25304; pop. incl. with Charleston (Inc. Place)

South Park; RMC Place; LEWIS; ***250** D-7; mail Jane Lew z 26378; ● 100

South Park; RMC Place; MONONGALIA; ***250** B-8; ★ **MORG**; mail Morgantown z 26501; pop. incl. with Morgantown (Inc. Place)

South Parkersburg; RMC Place; WOOD; ***250** C-4; elev. 638ft./194m.; ★ **PRKB**; mail Parkersburg z 26101; pop. incl. with Parkersburg (Inc. Place)

South Ruffner; RMC Place; KANAWHA; ***250** F-4; ★ **CHAS**; mail Charleston z 25304; pop. incl. with Charleston (Inc. Place)

Southside; RMC Place; MASON; **250** E-3; elev. 567ft./173m.; 🅿; z 25187; ● 50

South Side Junction; RMC Place; FAYETTE; mail Thurmond z 25936; pop. incl. with Thurmond (Inc. Place)

South Worthington; RMC Place; MARION; ***250** C-7; ★ **FAIRM**; mail Worthington z 26591; ● 100

Spangler; RMC Place; KANAWHA; ***250** G-5; elev. 1,076ft./328m.; mail Pond Gap z 25160

Spanishburg; RMC Place; MERCER; ***250** I-5; elev. 2,101ft./640m.; 🅿; z 25922; ● 150

Spaulding; RMC Place; MINGO; ***250** H-2; elev. 800ft./244m.; mail Breeden z 25666; rural

Speed; RMC Place; ROANE; ***250** E-4; mail Spencer z 25276

Speedway; RMC Place; MERCER; ***250** I-5; elev. 2,563ft./781m.; mail Athens z 24712; ● 75

Spelter; RMC Place; HARRISON; ***250** C-7; elev. 1,000ft./305m.; 🅿; ★ **CLRKB**; z 26438; ● 400

Spencer; Inc. Place; ⊡ ROANE; **250** E-4; elev. 749ft./228m.; 🅿 🅷; z 25276; Ⓟ 2,279; © 2,352

Spice; RMC Place; POCAHONTAS; ***250** G-7; elev. 1,987ft./606m.; mail Hillsboro z 24946; rural

Sprague; RMC Place; RALEIGH; ***250** H-5; elev. 2,360ft./719m.; 🅿; ★ **BECK**; z 25802, z 25926; ● 2,000

Sprattsville; RMC Place; MINGO; ***250** I-3; mail Gilbert z 25621; ● 80

Spread; RMC Place; CLAY; ***250** F-5; mail Clay z 25043; rural

Sprigg; RMC Place; MINGO; ***250** I-2; elev. 704ft./215m.; 🅿; z 25661; ● 80

Spring Creek; RMC Place; GREENBRIER; ***250** H-7; mail Renick z 24966; ● 40

Spring Dale; RMC Place; FAYETTE; **250** H-6; elev. 2,732ft./833m.; 🅿; z 25986; ● 200

Springdale; RMC Place; OHIO; **250** I-11; ★ **WHL**; mail Wheeling z 26003; ● 400

Springfield; RMC Place; HAMPSHIRE; **250** C-11; elev. 733ft./223m.; 🅿; z 26763; ● 350

Spring Hill; RMC Place; KANAWHA; ***250** F-3; elev. 600ft./183m.; 🅿; ★ **CHAS**; z 25309; pop. incl. with South Charleston (Inc. Place)

Spring Hill Chapel; RMC Place; HARRISON; ***250** C-7; ★ **CLRKB**; mail Clarksburg z 26301; rural

Springton; RMC Place; MERCER; ***250** I-5; mail Matoaka z 24736; rural

Spring Valley; RMC Place; WAYNE; **250** G-12; ★ **HNTG**; mail Huntington z 25701; ● 900

Spruce Valley; RMC Place; LOGAN; ***250** H-3; elev. 961ft./293m.; mail Blair z 25022; rural

Spurlockville; RMC Place; LINCOLN; **250** G-3; elev. 761ft./232m.; 🅿; z 25565; ● 25

Squire; RMC Place; MCDOWELL; **250** J-4; elev. 1,669ft./509m.; 🅿; z 24884; ● 450

Stanaford; CDP; RALEIGH; ***250** H-5; elev. 2,400ft./732m.; 🅿; ★ **BECK**; z 25927; Ⓟ 1,706; © 1,443

Standard; RMC Place; KANAWHA; ***250** G-4; elev. 694ft./212m.; 🅿; z 25083; ● 160

Star City; Inc. Place; MONONGALIA; **250** B-8; elev. 829ft./253m.; 🅿; ★ **MORG**; z 26504-05; Ⓟ 1,251; © 1,366

Statler Run; RMC Place; MONONGALIA; mail Fairview z 26570; rural

Statts Mills; RMC Place; JACKSON; **250** E-4; elev. 702ft./214m.; 🅿; z 25271; ● 25

Stealey; RMC Place; HARRISON; ***250** C-7; ★ **CLRKB**; mail Clarksburg z 26301; pop. incl. with Clarksburg (Inc. Place)

Steeles; RMC Place; WYOMING; ***250** I-3; mail Iaeger z 24844; ● 50

Steelton; RMC Place; WETZEL; ***250** B-6; elev. 655ft./200m.; mail New Martinsville z 26155; pop. incl. with New Martinsville (Inc. Place)

Stephenson; RMC Place; WYOMING; ***250** I-5; elev. 1,518ft./463m.; 🅿; z 25928; ● 250

Steptown; RMC Place; WAYNE; **250** H-2; mail Kermit z 25674; ● 150

Stevensburg; RMC Place; PRESTON; ***250** C-9; mail Tunnelton z 26444; rural

Stewart; RMC Place; WOOD; ***250** C-4; ★ **PRKB**; mail Parkersburg z 26101; ● 75

Stewartstown; RMC Place; MONONGALIA; ***250** B-8; elev. 1,264ft./385m.; ★ **MORG**; mail Morgantown z 26508

Stickney; RMC Place; RALEIGH; ***250** H-4; elev. 1,000ft./305m.; 🅿; z 25140; rural

Stinson; RMC Place; CALHOUN; ***250** E-5; mail Chloe z 25235; rural

Stirrat; RMC Place; LOGAN; ***250** H-3; elev. 1,000ft./305m.; 🅿; z 25670; ● 125

Stohrs Cross Roads; RMC Place; MORGAN; ***250** B-13; elev. 688ft./210m.; mail Berkeley Springs z 25411; rural

Stollings; RMC Place; LOGAN; ***250** H-3; elev. 675ft./206m.; 🅿; z 25646; ● 900

Stone Branch; RMC Place; LOGAN; ***250** H-3; elev. 644ft./196m.; mail Chapmanville z 25508; ● 250

Stonecoal (Stonecoal Yard); RMC Place; WAYNE; ***250** H-2; elev. 626ft./191m.; mail Kermit z 25674; ● 40

Stonecoal Yard; WAYNE; see Stonecoal (RMC Place)

Stoneville; RMC Place; WYOMING; ***250** I-4; mail Fanrock z 24834; ● 60

Stonewall; RMC Place; KANAWHA; ★ **CHAS**; mail Charleston z 25302, z 25362; pop. incl. with Charleston (Inc. Place)

Stonewood; Inc. Place; HARRISON; **250** C-7; elev. 1,000ft./305m.; 🅿; ★ **CLRKB**; z 26301; Ⓟ 1,996; © 1,815

Stonewood Forest; RMC Place; MONONGALIA; ***250** B-8; ★ **MORG**; mail Morgantown z 26501; pop. incl. with Morgantown (Inc. Place)

Stony Bottom; RMC Place; POCAHONTAS; ***250** F-8; elev. 2,329ft./710m.; 🅿; z 24927; ● 40

Stony River; RMC Place; GRANT; ***250** C-10; mail Mount Storm z 26739; rural

Stotesbury; RMC Place; RALEIGH; ***250** I-5; ★ **BECK**; mail Sophia z 25921; ● 40

Stotlers Crossroads; RMC Place; MORGAN; ***250** B-13; elev. 740ft./226m.; mail Berkeley Springs z 25411

Stouts Mills; RMC Place; GILMER; ***250** E-6; elev. 750ft./229m.; 🅿; z 26430

Stover; RMC Place; RALEIGH; ***250** H-4; elev. 1,732ft./528m.; ★ **BECK**; mail Glen Daniel z 25844; ● 100

Stowe; RMC Place; LOGAN; ***250** H-3; mail Amherstdale z 25607; ● 70

Strange Creek; RMC Place; BRAXTON; ***250** F-6; elev. 800ft./244m.; 🅿; z 25063; ● 60

Streby; RMC Place; GRANT; ***250** D-10; elev. 1,746ft./532m.; mail Maysville z 26833; rural

Streeter; RMC Place; SUMMERS; ***250** I-5; elev. 2,007ft./612m.; 🅿; z 25969; rural

Stringtown; RMC Place; BARBOUR; ***250** D-8; elev. 1,727ft./526m.; mail Belington z 26250

Stringtown; RMC Place; MARION; ***250** C-7; mail Mannington z 26582; rural

Stringtown; RMC Place; ROANE; ***250** E-5; elev. 732ft./223m.; mail Spencer z 25276; rural

Stringtown (Alvy); RMC Place; TYLER; **250** C-6; elev. 822ft./251m.; mail Jacksonburg z 26377; ● 120

Stumptown; RMC Place; GILMER; **250** E-5; elev. 719ft./219m.; 🅿; z 25267; ● 100

Sugar Camp; RMC Place; DODDRIDGE; ***250** C-6; mail New Milton z 26411; rural

Sugar Grove; RMC Place; PENDLETON; **250** F-10; elev. 1,881ft./573m.; 🅿; z 26815; ● 35

Sugar Valley; RMC Place; PLEASANTS; ***250** C-5

Sugar Valley; RMC Place; PRESTON; ***250** B-9; elev. 1,722ft./525m.; mail Bruceton Mills z 26525; rural

Sullivan; RMC Place; RALEIGH; ***250** I-5; elev. 2,280ft./695m.; 🅿; ★ **BECK**; z 25813; ● 100

Sullivan; RMC Place; RANDOLPH; ***250** D-8; mail Elkins z 26241; rural

Sully; RMC Place; RANDOLPH; ***250** D-9; mail Bowden z 26254; rural

Sulphur City; RMC Place; MINERAL; ***250** C-10; mail Elk Garden z 26717; ● 25

Sulphur Springs; RMC Place; LOGAN; ***250** H-2; mail Holden z 25625; ● 200

Sumerco; RMC Place; LINCOLN; **250** G-3; elev. 1,198ft./365m.; 🅿; z 25567; ● 150

Summerlee; RMC Place; FAYETTE; ***250** H-5; 🅿; ★ **BECK**; z 25901; ● 200

Summers; RMC Place; DODDRIDGE; ***250** D-6; elev. 825ft./251m.; mail West Union z 26456; rural

SUMMERS; **250** I-6; Ⓟ 14,204; © 12,999; Ⓡ 14,389; ◆ 12,865

Summersville; Inc. Place; ⊡ NICHOLAS; **250** G-6; elev. 1,894ft./577m.; 🅿 🅷; z 26651; Ⓟ 2,906; © 3,294

Summit; RMC Place; LINCOLN; ***250** G-3; ★ **CHAS**; mail Sumerco z 25567; rural

Summit; RMC Place; WOOD; ***250** C-4; ★ **PRKB**; mail Parkersburg z 26101; ● 250

Summit Park; RMC Place; HARRISON; ***250** C-7; ★ **CLRKB**; mail Clarksburg z 26301; ● 300

Summit Point; RMC Place; JEFFERSON; ***250** C-13; elev. 620ft./189m.; 🅿; z 25446; ● 300

Sun; RMC Place; FAYETTE; ***250** H-5; ★ **BECK**; mail Glen Jean z 25846; rural

Sunbeam; RMC Place; LOGAN; ***250** H-3; mail Ethel z 25076; ● 200

Suncrest; RMC Place; MONONGALIA; ***250** B-8; ★ **MORG**; mail Morgantown z 26505; pop. incl. with Morgantown (Inc. Place)

Entries in **UPPERCASE** are counties.
Entries in **bold** have populations of 2,500 or more.
Names in parentheses are alternate names.

Inc. Place	Incorporated Place
RMC Place	Rand McNally Designated Place
CDP	Census Designated Place
MCD	Minor Civil Division

⊡ County Seat
▲ Minor Civil Division
elev. Elevation
🅿 Post Office

🅷 Hospital
🅲 College
■ Principal Business Center
★ Ranally Metro Area (RMA) Abbreviation
z Zip Code(s)

Ⓟ Previous Census Population
Ⓡ Revised Census Population
Ⓐ Annexation Population
● Rand McNally Population Estimate
© Final Census Population
Ⓢ Special Census Population
◆ Estimated Population

For additional definitions see Glossary, Volume 1, and Introduction, Volume 2.

Suncrest Lake; RMC Place; MONONGALIA; ***250** B-8; ★ **MORG**; mail Morgantown **z** 26505; pop. incl. with Morgantown (Inc. Place)
Sundial; RMC Place; RALEIGH; **250** H-4; elev. 1,040ft./317m.; 🅿; **z** 25140; ● 90
Sun Flower; RMC Place; ROANE; ***250** D-4; elev. 740ft./226m.; mail Le Roy **z** 25252; rural
Sun Hill; RMC Place; WYOMING; ***250** I-4; elev. 1,178ft./359m.; mail Clear Fork **z** 24822, Simon **z** 24882; ● 140
Sunlight; RMC Place; GREENBRIER; ***250** H-7; mail Williamsburg **z** 24991; rural
Sunrise; RMC Place; WOOD; ***250** C-4; ★ **PRKB**; mail Parkersburg **z** 26101; ● 200
Sunset Acres; RMC Place; LEWIS; ***250** D-7; mail Weston **z** 26452; ● 250
Sunset Beach; RMC Place; MONONGALIA; ***250** B-8; ★ **MORG**; mail Morgantown **z** 26508; ● 250
Sunset Court; RMC Place; LOGAN; ***250** H-3; elev. 648ft./198m.; mail Chapmanville **z** 25508; ● 400
Sunshine; RMC Place; MARION; ***250** B-7; ★ **FAIRM**; mail Mannington **z** 26582; ● 90
Sun Valley; RMC Place; HANCOCK; ***250** B-2; ★ **STU-**; mail Weirton **z** 26062; ● 120
Sun Valley; RMC Place; HARRISON; ***250** C-7; ★ **CLRKB**; mail Clarksburg **z** 26301; ● 250
Sun Valley; RMC Place; KANAWHA; ***250** F-3; ★ **CHAS**; mail Saint Albans **z** 25177; ● 310
Superior; RMC Place; MCDOWELL; ***250** I-4; elev. 1,350ft./411m.; 🅿; **z** 24801; ● 120
Superior Bottom; RMC Place; LOGAN; ***250** H-3; mail Omar **z** 25638; ● 120
Surosa; RMC Place; MINGO; ***250** I-2; mail Matewan **z** 25678; ● 50
Surveyor; RMC Place; RALEIGH; ***250** H-5; elev. 1,993ft./607m.; 🅿; ★ **BECK**; **z** 25932; ● 300
Susanna; MCDOWELL; see Yukon (RMC Place)
Sutton; Inc. Place; ⊡ BRAXTON; **250** E-6; elev. 840ft./256m.; 🅿; **z** 26601; Ⓟ 939; © 1,011
Swandale; RMC Place; CLAY; ***250** F-6; mail Clay **z** 25043; rural
Sweeneysburg; RMC Place; RALEIGH; ***250** H-5; ★ **BECK**; mail Beckley **z** 25801; rural
Sweet Acres; RMC Place; KANAWHA; ***250** F-3; ★ **CHAS**; mail Saint Albans **z** 25177; pop. incl. with Saint Albans (Inc. Place)
Sweetland; RMC Place; LINCOLN; ***250** G-3; elev. 649ft./198m.; 🅿; **z** 25523
Sweet Run; RMC Place; WAYNE; ***250** F-1; ★ **HNTG**; mail Kenova **z** 25530; rural
Sweet Springs; RMC Place; MONROE; **250** I-7; elev. 2,029ft./618m.; 🅿; **z** 24941; ● 120
Swiss; RMC Place; NICHOLAS; **250** G-5; elev. 795ft./242m.; 🅿; **z** 26690; ● 250
Switchback; RMC Place; MCDOWELL; ***250** J-4; elev. 2,088ft./636m.; 🅿; **z** 24887; ● 120
Switzer; CDP; LOGAN; **250** H-3; elev. 729ft./222m.; 🅿; **z** 25647; Ⓟ 1,004; © 1,138
Sycamore; RMC Place; CALHOUN; ***250** E-5; mail Millstone **z** 25261; rural
Sycamore; RMC Place; HARRISON; ***250** C-7; ★ **CLRKB**; mail Clarksburg **z** 26301; rural
Sycamore; RMC Place; LOGAN; ***250** H-3; mail Holden **z** 25625; ● 150
Sydnor Addition; RMC Place; MINGO; ***250** I-2
Sylvester; Inc. Place; BOONE; ***250** H-4; 🅿; **z** 25193; Ⓟ 191; © 195

T

Table Rock; RMC Place; RALEIGH; ***250** H-5; mail Beaver **z** 25813; rural
Tablers; BERKELEY; see Tablers Station (RMC Place)
Tablers Station (Tablers); RMC Place; BERKELEY; **250** C-13; mail Inwood **z** 25428; ● 100
Tacy; RMC Place; BARBOUR; ***250** D-8; elev. 1,693ft./516m.; mail Philippi **z** 26416
Tad; RMC Place; KANAWHA; ***250** F-4; elev. 659ft./201m.; 🅿; ★ **CHAS**; **z** 25201; ● 300
Tague; RMC Place; BRAXTON; ***250** E-6; elev. 823ft./251m.; mail Frametown **z** 26623; rural
Talbott; RMC Place; BARBOUR; ***250** D-8; elev. 2,260ft./689m.; mail Belington **z** 26250
Talcott; RMC Place; SUMMERS; **250** I-6; elev. 1,513ft./461m.; 🅿; **z** 24981; ● 400
Tallmansville; RMC Place; UPSHUR; **250** D-8; elev. 1,687ft./514m.; 🅿; **z** 26237; ● 120
Tamcliff; RMC Place; MINGO; ***250** I-3; elev. 807ft./246m.; mail Gilbert **z** 25621; ● 70
Tams; RMC Place; RALEIGH; ***250** I-5; elev. 1,730ft./527m.; 🅿; ★ **BECK**; **z** 25921; rural
Tango; RMC Place; LINCOLN; ***250** G-3; mail Hamlin **z** 25523; rural
Tanner; RMC Place; GILMER; **250** D-6; elev. 755ft./230m.; 🅿; **z** 26137; ● 100
Tannery; RMC Place; HARDY; ***250** D-11; mail Moorefield **z** 26836; pop. incl. with Moorefield (Inc. Place)
Taplin; RMC Place; LOGAN; ***250** H-3; elev. 793ft./242m.; 🅿; **z** 25632; ● 150
Tappan; RMC Place; TAYLOR; ***250** C-8; ★ **FAIRM**; mail Grafton **z** 26354; rural
Tarico Heights; RMC Place; BERKELEY; ***250** C-13; elev. 576ft./176m.; mail Bunker Hill **z** 25413; ● 400
Tariff; RMC Place; ROANE; **250** E-5; elev. 811ft./247m.; 🅿; **z** 25259; ● 20
Tate; RMC Place; BRAXTON; ***250** E-6; elev. 982ft./299m.; mail Frametown **z** 26623; rural
Tavennersville; RMC Place; WOOD; ***250** C-4; ★ **PRKB**; mail Parkersburg **z** 26101; pop. incl. with Parkersburg (Inc. Place)
TAYLOR; **250** C-8; Ⓟ 15,144; © 16,089; ◆ 15,948
Taylorville; RMC Place; MINGO; **250** I-2; elev. 867ft./264m.; mail Delbarton **z** 25670; ● 350
Teaberry; RMC Place; GREENBRIER; ***250** H-7; mail Lewisburg **z** 24901; rural
Teays; RMC Place; PUTNAM; ***250** F-3; elev. 707ft./215m.; 🅿; ★ **CHAS**; **z** 25569; ● 1,800
Teays Valley; CDP-Census Area Only; PUTNAM; ***250** F-3; ★ **CHAS**; mail Scott Depot **z** 25560, Teays **z** 25569; Ⓟ 8,436; © 12,704
Tempa; RMC Place; SUMMERS; ***250** H-6; elev. 2,835ft./864m.; mail Alderson **z** 24910; rural
Ten Mile; RMC Place; UPSHUR; ***250** E-8; elev. 1,630ft./497m.; mail Tallmansville **z** 26237; ● 90
Tennerton; RMC Place; UPSHUR; **250** D-7; elev. 1,473ft./449m.; 🅿; **z** 26201; ● 1,800
Terra Alta; Inc. Place; PRESTON; **250** C-9; elev. 2,559ft./780m.; 🅿; **z** 26764; Ⓟ 1,713; © 1,456
Terry; RMC Place; RALEIGH; ***250** H-5; elev. 1,200ft./366m.; 🅿; ★ **BECK**; **z** 25864; ● 125
Tesla; RMC Place; BRAXTON; **250** F-6; elev. 1,200ft./366m.; 🅿; **z** 26629; ● 60
Teter; RMC Place; UPSHUR; ***250** D-8; mail Volga **z** 26238
Teterton; RMC Place; PENDLETON; ***250** E-10; elev. 2,340ft./713m.; mail Seneca Rocks **z** 26884; rural
Thacker; RMC Place; MINGO; ***250** I-2; elev. 718ft./219m.; 🅿; **z** 25672; ● 200
Thacker Mines (Colonel); RMC Place; MINGO; ***250** I-2; ● 60
Thayer; RMC Place; FAYETTE; ***250** H-5; elev. 1,111ft./339m.; mail Thurmond **z** 25936
The Mileground; RMC Place; MONONGALIA; ***250** B-8; ★ **MORG**; mail Morgantown **z** 26505; ● 200
The Y; RMC Place; JACKSON; ***250** E-4; elev. 598ft./182m.; mail Sandyville **z** 25275; ● 100
Thoburn; RMC Place; MARION; ***250** C-7; ★ **FAIRM**; mail Fairmont **z** 26554; ● 450
Thomas; Inc. Place; TUCKER; **250** D-9; elev. 3,100ft./945m.; 🅿; **z** 26292; Ⓟ 573; © 452
Thompson Heights; RMC Place; PUTNAM; ***250** F-3; ★ **CHAS**; mail Hurricane **z** 25526; ● 250
Thompson Town; RMC Place; LOGAN; ***250** H-3; mail Verdunville **z** 25649; ● 200
Thornhill; RMC Place; MERCER; ***250** J-5; mail Rock **z** 24747; rural
Thornton; RMC Place; TAYLOR; **250** C-8; elev. 1,047ft./319m.; 🅿; **z** 26440; ● 150
Thornwood; RMC Place; POCAHONTAS; **250** F-9; mail Bartow **z** 24920; ● 80
Thorpe; RMC Place; MCDOWELL; ***250** J-4; elev. 1,435ft./437m.; 🅿; **z** 24888
Three Churches; RMC Place; HAMPSHIRE; **250** C-12; elev. 1,303ft./397m.; 🅿; **z** 26757; ● 35
Threefork Bridge; RMC Place; PRESTON; ***250** C-8; mail Independence **z** 26374; rural
Three Forks; LOGAN; see Saunders (RMC Place)
Three Mile; RMC Place; KANAWHA; ***250** F-4; elev. 636ft./194m.; mail Elkview **z** 25071; rural
Thurmond; Inc. Place; FAYETTE; ***250** H-5; elev. 1,074ft./327m.; 🅿; **z** 25936; Ⓟ 39; © 7
Thursday; RMC Place; RITCHIE; ***250** D-5; mail Smithville **z** 26178; rural
Tichenal; RMC Place; HARRISON; ***250** D-7; mail Lost Creek **z** 26385; rural
Tidewater; RMC Place; MCDOWELL; mail Kimball **z** 24853; rural
Tilden; RMC Place; RALEIGH; ***250** H-5; ★ **BECK**; mail Beaver **z** 25813; rural
Tioga; RMC Place; NICHOLAS; **250** F-6; elev. 2,242ft./683m.; 🅿; **z** 26691; ● 150
Tipton; RMC Place; NICHOLAS; ***250** G-5; mail Summersville **z** 26651; rural
Tolleys; RMC Place; RALEIGH; ***250** H-5; elev. 1,982ft./604m.; ★ **BECK**; mail Beckley **z** 25801; rural
Toll Gate; RMC Place; RITCHIE; **250** C-6; elev. 800ft./244m.; 🅿; **z** 26415; ● 35
Tomahawk; RMC Place; BERKELEY; ***250** B-13; mail Hedgesville **z** 25427; ● 40
Toney; RMC Place; LINCOLN; ***250** G-3; elev. 621ft./189m.; mail Harts **z** 25524; rural
Toney Fork; RMC Place; WYOMING; ***250** I-4; elev. 1,362ft./415m.; mail Oceana **z** 24870; ● 250
Topins Grove; RMC Place; JACKSON; ***250** D-4; elev. 641ft./195m.; mail Ravenswood **z** 26164; rural
Tornado; CDP; KANAWHA; **250** F-3; 🅿; ★ **CHAS**; **z** 25202; Ⓟ 1,006; © 1,111
Trace Junction; RMC Place; LOGAN; ***250** H-3; mail Holden **z** 25625; ● 200
Trap Hill; RMC Place; RALEIGH; ***250** H-4; ★ **BECK**; mail Glen Daniel **z** 25844
Triadelphia; Inc. Place; OHIO; **250** C-2; elev. 755ft./230m.; 🅿; ★ **WHL**; **z** 26059; Ⓟ 835; © 817
Tribble; RMC Place; MASON; ***250** E-3; mail Leon **z** 25123; rural
Triplett; RMC Place; CLAY; ***250** F-5; mail Clay **z** 25043
Tripp; RMC Place; WAYNE; ***250** H-1; elev. 610ft./186m.; mail Crum **z** 25669; rural
Triune; RMC Place; MONONGALIA; ***250** C-8; ★ **MORG**; mail Morgantown **z** 26508; rural
Trout; RMC Place; GREENBRIER; ***250** H-7; elev. 2,266ft./691m.; 🅿; **z** 24991
Troy; RMC Place; GILMER; **250** D-6; elev. 762ft./232m.; 🅿; **z** 26443; ● 125
Troy Town; RMC Place; LOGAN; ***250** H-3; mail Verdunville **z** 25649; ● 60
Trubada; RMC Place; GILMER; ***250** D-6; mail Glenville **z** 26351; rural
True; RMC Place; SUMMERS; ***250** I-6; elev. 2,451ft./747m.; 🅿; **z** 25951; ● 10
Tuckahoe; RMC Place; GREENBRIER; ***250** H-7; elev. 2,028ft./618m.; mail White Sulphur Springs **z** 24986; rural
TUCKER; **250** D-9; Ⓟ 7,728; © 7,321; ◆ 6,736
Tunnelton; Inc. Place; PRESTON; **250** C-9; elev. 1,816ft./554m.; 🅿; **z** 26444; Ⓟ 331; © 336
Turkey Knob; RMC Place; FAYETTE; ***250** H-5; elev. 1,717ft./523m.; ★ **BECK**; mail Mount Hope **z** 25880; ● 75
Turkey Knob; RMC Place; MARION; ***250** C-7; ★ **FAIRM**; mail Worthington **z** 26591; rural
Turner Douglass; RMC Place; PRESTON; ***250** C-9; mail Oakland **z** 21550, Terra Alta **z** 26764; rural
Turnertown; RMC Place; LEWIS; ***250** D-7; mail Weston **z** 26452; ● 250
Turtle Creek; RMC Place; BOONE; ***250** G-3; elev. 793ft./242m.; 🅿; **z** 25203; ● 40
Twilight (Robin Hood); RMC Place; BOONE; ***250** H-4; elev. 1,071ft./326m.; 🅿; **z** 25204; ● 150
Twin Branch; RMC Place; MCDOWELL; ***250** I-4; elev. 1,178ft./359m.; 🅿; **z** 24828; ● 175
Two Lick; RMC Place; HARRISON; mail Jane Lew **z** 26378; rural
Two Mile; RMC Place; KANAWHA; ***250** F-4; elev. 600ft./183m.; ★ **CHAS**; mail Charleston **z** 25301
Two Run; RMC Place; WIRT; ***250** D-4; 🅿; **z** 26160; rural
Tyler; RMC Place; TYLER; **250** C-6; mail Alma **z** 26320; ● 70
TYLER; **250** C-6; Ⓟ 9,796; © 9,592; ◆ 8,587
Tyler Heights; RMC Place; KANAWHA; ***250** F-3; ★ **CHAS**; mail Charleston **z** 25312; ● 4,500
Tyler Mountain; RMC Place; KANAWHA; **250** I-12; elev. 650ft./198m.; ★ **CHAS**; mail Charleston **z** 25312; ● 450
Tyrone; RMC Place; MONONGALIA; ***250** B-8; ★ **MORG**; mail Morgantown **z** 26508; ● 300

U

Uffington; RMC Place; MONONGALIA; ***250** B-8; ★ **MORG**; mail Morgantown **z** 26508; rural
Uler; RMC Place; ROANE; ***250** E-5; elev. 767ft./234m.; 🅿; **z** 25266
Uneeda; RMC Place; BOONE; **250** G-3; elev. 737ft./225m.; 🅿; **z** 25205; ● 450
Unger; RMC Place; MORGAN; **250** C-13; elev. 887ft./270m.; 🅿; **z** 25411; ● 100
Union; Inc. Place; ⊡ MONROE; **250** I-7; elev. 2,071ft./631m.; 🅿; **z** 24983; Ⓟ 566; © 548
Union Addition; RMC Place; KANAWHA; mail Montgomery **z** 25136; ● 150
Union City; RMC Place; MCDOWELL; **250** J-3; mail Iaeger **z** 24844; ● 150
Union Ridge; RMC Place; CABELL; ***250** F-2; elev. 934ft./285m.; mail Ona **z** 25545
Uniontown; RMC Place; WETZEL; ***250** B-7; mail Littleton **z** 26581; ● 20
United; RMC Place; KANAWHA; ***250** H-4; mail Eskdale **z** 25075; rural
Upland; RMC Place; MASON; ***250** F-3; mail Fraziers Bottom **z** 25082
Upland; RMC Place; MCDOWELL; ***250** J-4; ● 120
Upper Addis Run; RMC Place; RITCHIE; ***250** D-5; mail Harrisville **z** 26362; rural
Upperglade; RMC Place; WEBSTER; **250** F-7; elev. 2,302ft./702m.; 🅿; **z** 26266; ● 400
Upper Leatherwood; RMC Place; CLAY; ***250** F-5; elev. 702ft./214m.; mail Bickmore **z** 25019; rural
Upper Tract; RMC Place; PENDLETON; **250** E-10; elev. 1,495ft./456m.; 🅿; **z** 26866; ● 90
Upper Whitman; RMC Place; LOGAN; ***250** H-3; mail Whitman **z** 25652; ● 350
UPSHUR; **250** E-7; Ⓟ 22,867; © 23,404; ◆ 23,397
Upton; RMC Place; MARION; ***250** B-7; ★ **FAIRM**; mail Fairview **z** 26570; rural
Upton Creek; RMC Place; KANAWHA; ***250** F-3; ★ **CHAS**; mail Saint Albans **z** 25177; ● 300
Ury; RMC Place; RALEIGH; ***250** I-5; mail Helen **z** 25853; ● 20
Utica; RMC Place; JACKSON; ***250** D-4; elev. 667ft./203m.; mail Belleville **z** 26133; rural
Uvilla; RMC Place; JEFFERSON; ***250** C-14; elev. 500ft./152m.; mail Shenandoah Junction **z** 25442; rural

V

Vadis; RMC Place; LEWIS; ***250** D-6; elev. 782ft./238m.; 🅿; **z** 26321
Vago; RMC Place; GREENBRIER; ***250** H-7; mail Frankford **z** 24938; rural
Vale; RMC Place; GREENBRIER; ***250** H-6; elev. 2,428ft./740m.; mail Meadow Bridge **z** 25976; rural
Valley Bend; RMC Place; BARBOUR; ***250** D-8; elev. 1,951ft./595m.; mail Belington **z** 26250; rural
Valley Bend; RMC Place; RANDOLPH; **250** E-8; elev. 2,010ft./613m.; 🅿; **z** 26293; ● 450
Valley Chapel; RMC Place; LEWIS; ***250** D-7; elev. 1,012ft./308m.; 🅿; **z** 26452; ● 35
Valley Falls; RMC Place; MARION; ***250** C-8; elev. 998ft./304m.; ★ **FAIRM**; mail Colfax **z** 26566; rural
Valley Fork; RMC Place; CLAY; ***250** F-5; elev. 939ft./286m.; 🅿; **z** 25285; ● 25
Valley Furnace; RMC Place; BARBOUR; ***250** D-8; mail Moatsville **z** 26405; rural
Valley Grove; Inc. Place; OHIO; **250** C-2; elev. 957ft./292m.; 🅿; ★ **WHL**; **z** 26060; Ⓟ 569; © 405; Ⓡ 430
Valley Head; RMC Place; RANDOLPH; **250** F-8; elev. 2,400ft./732m.; 🅿; **z** 26294; ● 450
Valley Mills; RMC Place; WOOD; ***250** C-4; elev. 712ft./217m.; ★ **PRKB**; mail Parkersburg **z** 26101; ● 150
Valley Point; RMC Place; PRESTON; **250** B-9; mail Albright **z** 26519; ● 160
Vallscreek (Hartwell); RMC Place; MCDOWELL; ***250** J-4; elev. 1,576ft./480m.; 🅿; **z** 24815; ● 200
Van; RMC Place; BOONE; **250** H-3; elev. 819ft./250m.; 🅿; **z** 25206; ● 600
Vanclevesville; RMC Place; BERKELEY; ***250** C-14; mail Martinsburg **z** 25401; ● 100
Vandalia; RMC Place; KANAWHA; ***250** F-4; ★ **CHAS**; mail Charleston **z** 25303; pop. incl. with Charleston (Inc. Place)
Vandalia; RMC Place; LEWIS; ***250** D-7; elev. 1,073ft./327m.; mail Walkersville **z** 26447
Van Junction; RMC Place; BOONE; mail Van **z** 25206
Vanville; RMC Place; BERKELEY; ***250** C-13; elev. 570ft./174m.; mail Martinsburg **z** 25401; ● 100
Van Voorhis; RMC Place; MONONGALIA; ***250** B-8; ★ **MORG**; mail Morgantown **z** 26508; ● 40
Varney; RMC Place; MINGO; **250** I-2; elev. 968ft./295m.; 🅿; **z** 25696; ● 250
Vaucluse; RMC Place; PLEASANTS; ***250** C-5; mail Saint Marys **z** 26170; rural
Vaughan; RMC Place; NICHOLAS; ***250** G-5; elev. 811ft./247m.; mail Belva **z** 26656; ● 95
Vegan; RMC Place; UPSHUR; ***250** D-8; mail Ellamore **z** 26267; rural
Venus; RMC Place; MCDOWELL; ***250** J-4; mail Gary **z** 24836
Verdunville; RMC Place; LOGAN; **250** H-3; elev. 748ft./228m.; 🅿; **z** 25649; ● 500
Verner; RMC Place; MINGO; ***250** I-3; elev. 765ft./233m.; 🅿; **z** 25650; ● 200
Victor; RMC Place; FAYETTE; ***250** G-5; elev. 1,385ft./422m.; 🅿; **z** 25938; ● 80
Victoria; RMC Place; PRESTON; ***250** C-8; elev. 1,296ft./395m.; mail Independence **z** 26374; rural
Vienna; Inc. Place; WOOD; **250** C-4; elev. 640ft./195m.; 🅿 🅲 545 ■; ★ **PRKB**; **z** 26105 & mail Parkersburg **z** 26101; Ⓟ 10,862; © 10,861; ◆ 9,837
Villa; RMC Place; KANAWHA; ***250** F-4; ★ **CHAS**; mail Charleston **z** 25311; rural
Viola; RMC Place; MARION; ***250** B-8; ★ **FAIRM**; mail Fairmont **z** 26554; rural
Viola; RMC Place; MARSHALL; ***250** A-7; elev. 809ft./247m.; ★ **WHL**; mail Moundsville **z** 26041, Wheeling **z** 26003; rural
Virginia; BROOKE; see Virginville (RMC Place)
Virginia Heights; RMC Place; KANAWHA; ***250** F-3; ★ **CHAS**; mail Saint Albans **z** 25177; ● 1,800
Virginia Manor; RMC Place; MONONGALIA; ***250** B-8; ★ **MORG**; mail Morgantown **z** 26505; pop. incl. with Morgantown (Inc. Place)
Virginville (Virginia); RMC Place; BROOKE; ***250** B-2; ★ **STU-**; mail Colliers **z** 26035; ● 40
Viropa; RMC Place; HARRISON; ***250** C-7; ★ **FAIRM**; mail Shinnston **z** 26431; ● 75
Vivian; RMC Place; MCDOWELL; ***250** J-4; elev. 1,533ft./467m.; 🅿; **z** 24853; ● 100
Volcano; RMC Place; WOOD; ***250** C-5; ★ **PRKB**; mail Walker **z** 26180; rural
Volga; RMC Place; BARBOUR; **250** D-8; elev. 1,437ft./438m.; 🅿; **z** 26238; ● 140
Vulcan; RMC Place; MINGO; **250** I-2; elev. 800ft./244m.; 🅿; **z** 25672; ● 100

W

Wadestown; RMC Place; MONONGALIA; **250** B-7; elev. 1,021ft./311m.; 🅿; **z** 26590; ● 150
Wadeville; RMC Place; WOOD; ***250** D-4; elev. 681ft./208m.; mail Belleville **z** 26133
Wahoo; RMC Place; MARION; ***250** C-7; ★ **FAIRM**; mail Fairmont **z** 26554; rural
Wainville; RMC Place; WEBSTER; ***250** F-7; elev. 1,572ft./479m.; mail Cowen **z** 26206
Waiteville; RMC Place; MONROE; **250** I-7; elev. 2,200ft./671m.; 🅿; **z** 24984; ● 40
Waldeck; RMC Place; LEWIS; ***250** D-7; mail Weston **z** 26452; ● 75
Walgrove; RMC Place; KANAWHA; ***250** F-4; mail Elkview **z** 25071; rural
Walker; RMC Place; WOOD; ***250** D-4; elev. 630ft./192m.; 🅿; ★ **PRKB**; **z** 26180; ● 25
Walkersville; RMC Place; LEWIS; **250** E-7; elev. 1,089ft./332m.; 🅿; **z** 26447; ● 150
Wallace; RMC Place; HARRISON; **250** C-7; elev. 1,017ft./310m.; 🅿; **z** 26448; ● 475
Wallback; RMC Place; CLAY; ***250** F-5; elev. 770ft./235m.; 🅿; **z** 25285; ● 25
Walnut; RMC Place; CALHOUN; ***250** E-5; elev. 858ft./262m.; mail Chloe **z** 25235; rural
Walnut Bottom; RMC Place; HARDY; ***250** D-11; mail Fisher **z** 26818; rural
Walnut Grove; RMC Place; JEFFERSON; ***250** C-14; mail Charles Town **z** 25414; pop. incl. with Fairfield (Inc. Place)
Walnut Hill; RMC Place; LOGAN; ***250** H-3; mail Whitman **z** 25652; ● 150
Walton; RMC Place; ROANE; **250** E-4; elev. 700ft./213m.; 🅿; **z** 25286; ● 350
Wana; RMC Place; MONONGALIA; **250** B-7; elev. 1,028ft./313m.; 🅿; **z** 26590; ● 130
Wanda; RMC Place; LOGAN; ***250** H-3; elev. 769ft./234m.; mail Ethel **z** 25076; ● 200
War; Inc. Place; MCDOWELL; **250** J-4; elev. 1,355ft./413m.; 🅿; **z** 24892; Ⓟ 1,081; © 788
Ward; RMC Place; KANAWHA; ***250** G-4; elev. 721ft./220m.; mail Cedar Grove **z** 25039; rural
Warden; RMC Place; RALEIGH; ***250** H-5; ★ **BECK**; mail Stanaford **z** 25927; ● 600
Wardensville; Inc. Place; HARDY; **250** D-12; elev. 1,011ft./308m.; 🅿; **z** 26851; Ⓟ 140; © 246
War Eagle; RMC Place; MINGO; ***250** I-3; mail Iaeger **z** 24844; rural
Warriormine; RMC Place; MCDOWELL; ***250** J-4; elev. 1,375ft./419m.; 🅿; **z** 24894; pop. incl. with War (Inc. Place)
Warwood; RMC Place; OHIO; ***250** C-2; 🅿; ★ **WHL**; **z** 26003; pop. incl. with Wheeling (Inc. Place)
Washburn; RMC Place; RITCHIE; ***250** D-5; elev. 765ft./233m.; mail Harrisville **z** 26362; rural
Washington; CDP; WOOD; **250** C-4; 🅿; ★ **PRKB**; **z** 26181; Ⓟ 1,030; © 1,170
Washington Heights; BOONE; see Haddleton (RMC Place)
Washington Lake; RMC Place; WOOD; ★ **PRKB**; mail Washington **z** 26181; ● 150
Waterloo; RMC Place; MASON; ***250** E-3; elev. 578ft./176m.; mail Leon **z** 25123; rural
Watson; RMC Place; MARION; ***250** C-8; ★ **FAIRM**; mail Fairmont **z** 26554; pop. incl. with Fairmont (Inc. Place)
Waverly; RMC Place; WOOD; ***250** C-4; elev. 621ft./189m.; 🅿; ★ **PRKB**; **z** 26184; ● 300
Wayne; Inc. Place; ⊡ WAYNE; **250** G-2; elev. 708ft./216m.; 🅿; ★ **HNTG**; **z** 25570; Ⓟ 1,128; © 1,105
WAYNE; **250** G-2; Ⓟ 41,636; © 42,903; ◆ 40,227
Wayside; RMC Place; MONROE; **250** I-6; elev. 1,984ft./605m.; 🅿; **z** 24985; ● 40
Weaver; RMC Place; RANDOLPH; ***250** D-8; mail Belington **z** 26250
Webb; RMC Place; WAYNE; ***250** H-1; elev. 603ft./184m.; mail Crum **z** 25669
Weberwood; RMC Place; KANAWHA; ***250** F-4; ★ **CHAS**; mail Charleston **z** 25303; pop. incl. with South Charleston (Inc. Place)
Webster; RMC Place; TAYLOR; ***250** C-8; elev. 1,019ft./311m.; mail Grafton **z** 26354
WEBSTER; **250** F-7; Ⓟ 10,729; © 9,719; ◆ 9,071
Webster Springs (Addison); Inc. Place; ⊡ WEBSTER; **250** F-7; elev. 1,480ft./451m.; 🅿 🅷; **z** 26288; Ⓟ 674; © 808
Weircrest; RMC Place; HANCOCK; ***250** B-2; ★ **STU-**; mail Weirton **z** 26062; pop. incl. with Weirton (Inc. Place)
Weirton; Inc. Place; HANCOCK, BROOKE; **250** B-2; elev. 760ft./232m.; 🅿 🅷 ■; ★ **STU-**; **z** 26062; Ⓟ 22,124; © 20,411; ◆ 18,271
Weirton Heights; RMC Place; HANCOCK; ***250** B-2; ★ **STU-**; mail Weirton **z** 26062; pop. incl. with Weirton (Inc. Place)
Welch; Inc. Place; ⊡ MCDOWELL; **250** J-4; elev. 1,306ft./398m.; 🅿; **z** 24801; Ⓟ 3,028; © 2,683
Wellford; RMC Place; KANAWHA; ***250** F-5; elev. 628ft./191m.; mail Clendenin **z** 25045; rural
Wellington Heights; RMC Place; BARBOUR; ***250** D-8; mail Philippi **z** 26416; ● 100
Wellsburg; Inc. Place; ⊡ BROOKE; **250** B-2; elev. 660ft./201m.; 🅿; ★ **WHL**; **z** 26070; Ⓟ 3,385; © 2,891
Wendel; RMC Place; TAYLOR; ***250** C-8; elev. 1,200ft./366m.; 🅿; **z** 26347; ● 40
Wenonah; MERCER; see Dott (RMC Place)
Werner; RMC Place; BARBOUR; ***250** D-8; elev. 2,237ft./682m.; mail Belington **z** 26250
Werth; RMC Place; NICHOLAS; ***250** F-6; elev. 1,935ft./590m.; mail Summersville **z** 26651
West Carbon; KANAWHA; see Winifrede (RMC Place)
Westchester (Jayenn); RMC Place; MARION; ***250** C-8; ★ **FAIRM**; mail Fairmont **z** 26554; ● 500
West Columbia; RMC Place; MASON; ***250** D-3; elev. 575ft./175m.; 🅿; **z** 25287; ● 300
West Dunbar; RMC Place; KANAWHA; ***250** F-3; ★ **CHAS**; mail Dunbar **z** 25064; pop. incl. with Dunbar (Inc. Place)
West End; RMC Place; PRESTON; ***250** C-9; mail Tunnelton **z** 26444; rural
West Gilbert; RMC Place; MINGO; mail Gilbert **z** 25621; pop. incl. with Gilbert (Inc. Place)
West Grafton; RMC Place; TAYLOR; ***250** C-8; mail Grafton **z** 26354; pop. incl. with Grafton (Inc. Place)
West Hamlin; Inc. Place; LINCOLN; **250** G-2; elev. 590ft./180m.; 🅿; **z** 25571; Ⓟ 423; © 696
West Huntington; RMC Place; CABELL; ***250** F-1; ★ **HNTG**; pop. incl. with Huntington (Inc. Place)
West Junction; RMC Place; BOONE; ***250** H-3; mail Van **z** 25206
West Liberty; Inc. Place; OHIO; **250** B-2; elev. 1,203ft./367m.; 🅿 🅲 2,265; ★ **WHL**; **z** 26074; Ⓟ 1,434; © 1,220
West Logan; Inc. Place; LOGAN; **250** H-3; elev. 680ft./207m.; 🅿; **z** 25601; Ⓟ 524; © 418
West Milford; Inc. Place; HARRISON; **250** D-7; elev. 980ft./299m.; 🅿; ★ **CLRKB**; **z** 26451; Ⓟ 519; © 651
Westmoreland; RMC Place; WAYNE; ***250** F-1; elev. 544ft./166m.; ★ **HNTG**; pop. incl. with Huntington (Inc. Place)
Weston; Inc. Place; ⊡ LEWIS; **250** D-7; elev. 1,017ft./310m.; 🅿 🅷; **z** 26452; Ⓟ 4,994; © 4,317
Westover; Inc. Place; MONONGALIA; **250** B-8; 🅿; ★ **MORG**; **z** 26501-02; Ⓟ 4,201; © 3,941
West Pea Ridge; RMC Place; CABELL; **250** G-14; ★ **HNTG**; mail Huntington **z** 25705; ● 2,500
West Raleigh; RMC Place; RALEIGH; ★ **BECK**
West Union; Inc. Place; ⊡ DODDRIDGE; **250** C-6; elev. 828ft./252m.; 🅿; **z** 26456; Ⓟ 830; © 806
West Van Voorhis; RMC Place; MONONGALIA; ***250** B-8; ★ **MORG**; mail Maidsville **z** 26541; rural
Westview Estates; RMC Place; PUTNAM; ***250** F-3; ★ **CHAS**; mail Hurricane **z** 25526; ● 250
West Williamson; RMC Place; MINGO; ***250** I-2; mail Williamson **z** 25661; pop. incl. with Williamson (Inc. Place)
WETZEL; **250** B-6; Ⓟ 19,258; © 17,693; ◆ 15,816
Weyanoke; RMC Place; MERCER; ***250** J-5; mail Matoaka **z** 24736; ● 100
Wharncliffe; RMC Place; MINGO; ***250** I-3; elev. 873ft./266m.; 🅿; **z** 25651; ● 250
Wharton; RMC Place; BOONE; ***250** H-4; elev. 965ft./294m.; 🅿; **z** 25208; ● 250
Wheeler; RMC Place; WEBSTER; ***250** E-7; elev. 1,384ft./422m.; mail Hacker Valley **z** 26222; rural
Wheeling; Inc. Place; ⊡ OHIO, MARSHALL; **250** A-6; elev. 672ft./205m.; 🅿 🅷 🅲 1,244 ■; ★ **WHL**; **z** 26003; Ⓟ 34,882; © 31,419; ◆ 27,766
Wheeling Island; RMC Place; OHIO; ***250** A-6; ★ **WHL**; mail Wheeling **z** 26003; pop. incl. with Wheeling (Inc. Place)
Whipple; RMC Place; FAYETTE; ***250** H-5; ★ **BECK**; mail Scarbro **z** 25917; ● 200
Whitby; RMC Place; RALEIGH; ***250** I-5; elev. 2,400ft./732m.; 🅿; ★ **BECK**; **z** 25823; ● 100
Whitehall; Inc. Place; MARION; **250** C-8; 🅿; ★ **FAIRM**; **z** 26554-55; © 595
White Oak; RMC Place; RALEIGH; ***250** I-5; elev. 2,835ft./864m.; 🅿; ★ **BECK**; **z** 25989; ● 300
White Oak Springs; RMC Place; PRESTON; ***250** C-9; elev. 2,733ft./833m.; mail Terra Alta **z** 26764; rural
White Pine; RMC Place; CALHOUN; ***250** D-5; elev. 772ft./235m.; mail Grantsville **z** 26147; rural
Whites Addition; RMC Place; LOGAN; ***250** H-3; mail Wilkinson **z** 25653; ● 150
Whites Creek; RMC Place; WAYNE; ***250** G-1; mail Prichard **z** 25555; rural
White Sulphur Springs; Inc. Place; GREENBRIER; **250** H-7; elev. 1,900ft./579m.; 🅿; **z** 24986; Ⓟ 2,779; © 2,315
Whitesville; Inc. Place; BOONE; **250** H-4; elev. 819ft./250m.; 🅿; **z** 25209; Ⓟ 486; © 520
Whitman; RMC Place; LOGAN; **250** H-3; elev. 800ft./244m.; 🅿; **z** 25652; ● 450
Whitman Junction; RMC Place; LOGAN; ***250** H-3; elev. 689ft./210m.; mail Whitman **z** 25652; ● 50
Whitmer; RMC Place; RANDOLPH; **250** E-9; elev. 2,761ft./842m.; 🅿; **z** 26296; ● 200
Whittaker; RMC Place; KANAWHA; ***250** G-4; elev. 802ft./244m.; 🅿; **z** 25083; rural
Wick; RMC Place; TYLER; **250** C-5; elev. 772ft./235m.; 🅿; **z** 26149; ● 60
Wickham; RMC Place; RALEIGH; ***250** H-5; ★ **BECK**; mail Mabscott **z** 25871; ● 200
Widen; RMC Place; CLAY; **250** F-6; elev. 1,143ft./348m.; 🅿; **z** 25211; ● 200
Wikel; RMC Place; MONROE; ***250** I-6; mail Greenville **z** 24945
Wilbur; RMC Place; TYLER; ***250** C-6; elev. 1,038ft./316m.; 🅿; **z** 26320
Wilcoe; RMC Place; MCDOWELL; ***250** J-4; elev. 1,374ft./419m.; 🅿; **z** 24895; pop. incl. with Gary (Inc. Place)
Wildcat; RMC Place; LEWIS; ***250** E-7; elev. 980ft./299m.; 🅿; **z** 26376; rural
Wilding; RMC Place; JACKSON; ***250** D-4; mail Ravenswood **z** 26164
Wiles Hill; RMC Place; MONONGALIA; ***250** B-8; ★ **MORG**; mail Morgantown **z** 26505; pop. incl. with Morgantown (Inc. Place)
Wiley Ford; CDP; MINERAL; ***250** B-11; elev. 627ft./191m.; 🅿; ★ **CUMB**; **z** 26767; © 1,095
Wileyville; RMC Place; WETZEL; **250** B-6; elev. 805ft./245m.; 🅿; **z** 26581; ● 100
Wilkinson; RMC Place; LOGAN; ***250** H-3; elev. 720ft./219m.; 🅿; **z** 25653; ● 900
Willard; RMC Place; HARRISON; ***250** C-7; elev. 993ft./303m.; ★ **CLRKB**; mail Shinnston **z** 26431; ● 30
William; RMC Place; TUCKER; ***250** D-9; elev. 2,986ft./910m.; mail Thomas **z** 26292
Williamsburg; RMC Place; GREENBRIER; **250** H-7; elev. 2,184ft./666m.; 🅿; **z** 24991; ● 225
Williamsburg Colony; RMC Place; CABELL; ***250** F-2; ★ **HNTG**; mail Barboursville **z** 25504; ● 800
Williams Mountain; RMC Place; BOONE; ***250** G-4; elev. 1,633ft./498m.; mail Seth **z** 25181; ● 100
Williamson; Inc. Place; ⊡ MINGO; **250** I-2; elev. 665ft./203m.; 🅿 🅷 ■; **z** 25661; Ⓟ 4,154; © 3,414; ◆ 3,046
Williamsport; RMC Place; GRANT; ***250** C-11; elev. 1,029ft./314m.; mail Burlington **z** 26710; ● 20
Williamstown; Inc. Place; WOOD; **250** C-4; elev. 611ft./186m.; 🅿; ★ **PRKB**; **z** 26187; Ⓟ 2,774; © 2,996
Willis Branch; RMC Place; FAYETTE; **250** H-5; mail Mount Hope **z** 25880; ● 100
Willow Bend; RMC Place; MONROE; ***250** I-7; elev. 1,915ft./584m.; 🅿; **z** 24983; rural
Willow Island; RMC Place; PLEASANTS; ***250** C-5; elev. 615ft./187m.; 🅿; **z** 26134
Willowton; RMC Place; MERCER; ***250** J-6; mail Princeton **z** 24740
Wilmore; RMC Place; MCDOWELL; ***250** I-3; elev. 1,029ft./314m.; mail Iaeger **z** 24844; rural
Wilsie; RMC Place; BRAXTON; ***250** E-6; elev. 911ft./278m.; 🅿; **z** 26623; ● 25
Wilson (Benson Park); RMC Place; KANAWHA; ***250** F-4; 🅿; ★ **CHAS**; **z** 26707 & mail Charleston **z** 25302; ● 100
Wilsonburg; RMC Place; HARRISON; ***250** C-7; elev. 1,000ft./305m.; 🅿; ★ **CLRKB**; **z** 26461 & mail Clarksburg **z** 26301; ● 200
Wilsondale; RMC Place; WAYNE; **250** H-2; elev. 766ft./233m.; 🅿; **z** 25699; ● 40
Wilsontown; RMC Place; UPSHUR; ***250** E-7; elev. 1,560ft./475m.; mail Rock Cave **z** 26234; rural
Winding Gulf; RMC Place; RALEIGH; ***250** I-5; elev. 2,400ft./732m.; 🅿; ★ **BECK**; **z** 25908 & mail Coal City **z** 25823; ● 40
Windom; RMC Place; WYOMING; ***250** I-4; mail Brenton **z** 24818; rural
Windsor Heights; Inc. Place; BROOKE; ***250** B-2; elev. 1,000ft./305m.; 🅿; ★ **WHL**; **z** 26075; Ⓟ 454; © 431
Windy; RMC Place; WIRT; ***250** D-4; mail Elizabeth **z** 26143, Palestine **z** 26160; rural
Winebrenners Crossroads; RMC Place; BERKELEY; ***250** C-14; mail Martinsburg **z** 25401; rural
Winfield; RMC Place; MARION; ***250** C-8; elev. 983ft./300m.; ★ **FAIRM**; mail Fairmont **z** 26554; ● 125
Winfield; Inc. Place; ⊡ PUTNAM; **250** F-3; elev. 600ft./183m.; 🅿; ★ **CHAS**; **z** 25213; Ⓟ 1,164; © 1,858
Wingrove; RMC Place; FAYETTE; ***250** H-5; ★ **BECK**; mail Scarbro **z** 25917; ● 100
Winifrede (West Carbon); RMC Place; KANAWHA; ***250** G-4; elev. 706ft./215m.; 🅿; ★ **CHAS**; **z** 25214; ● 700
Winona; RMC Place; FAYETTE; ***250** G-5; elev. 1,917ft./584m.; 🅿; **z** 25942; ● 200
WIRT; **250** D-4; Ⓟ 5,192; © 5,873; ◆ 5,775
Wiseburg; RMC Place; JACKSON; ***250** D-4; elev. 638ft./194m.; mail Sandyville **z** 25275; rural
Witcher; RMC Place; KANAWHA; ***250** G-4; 🅿; ★ **CHAS**; **z** 25015; ● 250
Wolfcreek; RMC Place; MONROE; **250** I-6; elev. 1,600ft./488m.; 🅿; **z** 24993; ● 30
Wolfe; RMC Place; MERCER; ***250** J-4; elev. 2,400ft./732m.; 🅿; **z** 24751; ● 120
Wolf Pen; RMC Place; WYOMING; **250** I-4; elev. 1,289ft./393m.; ● 60
Wolf Run; RMC Place; MARSHALL; ***250** A-7; elev. 972ft./296m.; ★ **WHL**; mail Cameron **z** 26033; rural
Wolf Summit; RMC Place; HARRISON; ***250** C-7; elev. 1,136ft./346m.; 🅿; ★ **CLRKB**; **z** 26426; ● 200
Womelsdorf; RANDOLPH; see Coalton (Inc. Place)
Wood; RMC Place; MASON; ***250** E-3; mail Leon **z** 25123; rural
WOOD; **250** D-4; Ⓟ 86,915; © 87,986; ◆ 84,208
Woodburn; RMC Place; MONONGALIA; ***250** B-8; ★ **MORG**; mail Morgantown **z** 26505; pop. incl. with Morgantown (Inc. Place)
Woodland Forest; RMC Place; PUTNAM; ***250** F-3; ★ **CHAS**; mail Winfield **z** 25213; ● 300
Woodland Park; RMC Place; MARION; ★ **FAIRM**; pop. incl. with Fairmont (Inc. Place)
Woodland Park; RMC Place; WOOD; ***250** C-4; ★ **PRKB**; mail Parkersburg **z** 26101; pop. incl. with Parkersburg (Inc. Place)
Woodlands; RMC Place; MARSHALL; ***250** A-6; mail Proctor **z** 26055; rural
Woodrow; RMC Place; POCAHONTAS; ***250** G-8; elev. 3,211ft./979m.; mail Marlinton **z** 24954; rural
Woodruff; RMC Place; MARSHALL; ***250** B-7; elev. 966ft./294m.; mail Cameron **z** 26033; rural
Woodsdale; RMC Place; OHIO; ***250** A-6; ★ **WHL**; mail Wheeling **z** 26003; pop. incl. with Wheeling (Inc. Place)
Woodville; RMC Place; LINCOLN, BOONE; ***250** G-3; elev. 685ft./209m.; 🅿; **z** 25572; ● 180
Woodward Woods; RMC Place; KANAWHA; ***250** F-4; ★ **CHAS**; mail Charleston **z** 25312; pop. incl. with Charleston (Inc. Place)
Woosley; RMC Place; WYOMING; ***250** I-4; mail Welch **z** 24801; rural
Worth; RMC Place; MCDOWELL; ***250** J-4; elev. 1,901ft./579m.; 🅿; **z** 24868; ● 75
Worthington; Inc. Place; MARION; **250** C-7; elev. 900ft./274m.; 🅿; ★ **FAIRM**; **z** 26591; Ⓟ 233; © 170
Wriston; RMC Place; FAYETTE; ***250** H-5; 🅿; ★ **BECK**; **z** 25840; rural
Wyatt; RMC Place; HARRISON; **250** C-7; elev. 971ft./296m.; 🅿; **z** 26463; ● 120
Wyco; RMC Place; WYOMING; ***250** I-4; elev. 1,560ft./475m.; 🅿; **z** 25943; ● 150
Wymer; RMC Place; RANDOLPH; ***250** E-9; elev. 3,182ft./970m.; 🅿; **z** 26254; rural
Wyoma; RMC Place; MASON; ***250** E-2; elev. 893ft./272m.; mail Gallipolis Ferry **z** 25515; rural
Wyoming; MCDOWELL; see Mohawk (RMC Place)
Wyoming; RMC Place; WYOMING; ***250** I-4; elev. 1,212ft./369m.; 🅿; **z** 24898; ● 275
WYOMING; **250** I-4; Ⓟ 28,990; © 25,708; ◆ 22,898

Y

Yards; RMC Place; MERCER; ***250** J-5; 🅿; **z** 24605; ● 350
Yates Crossing; RMC Place; CABELL; ***250** F-2; ★ **HNTG**; mail Ona **z** 25545; ● 300
Yawkey; RMC Place; LINCOLN; **250** G-3; elev. 693ft./211m.; 🅿; **z** 25573; ● 175
Yellow Spring; RMC Place; HAMPSHIRE; **250** D-12; elev. 901ft./275m.; 🅿; **z** 26865; ● 100
Yolyn; RMC Place; LOGAN; ***250** H-3; elev. 1,040ft./317m.; 🅿; **z** 25654; ● 50
Youngs Bottom; RMC Place; KANAWHA; ***250** F-4; mail Elkview **z** 25071
Youngstown; RMC Place; FAYETTE; ***250** G-5; mail Fayetteville **z** 25840; ● 90
Yukon (Susanna); RMC Place; MCDOWELL; ***250** J-4; elev. 1,335ft./407m.; 🅿; **z** 24892; ● 300

Z

Zela; RMC Place; NICHOLAS; ***250** G-6; elev. 1,268ft./386m.; mail Summersville **z** 26651; rural
Zenith; RMC Place; MONROE; ***250** I-7; mail Lindside **z** 24951; rural
Zigler; RMC Place; PENDLETON; ***250** E-10; elev. 2,089ft./637m.; mail Franklin **z** 26807; rural
Zinnia; RMC Place; DODDRIDGE; ***250** C-6; elev. 898ft./274m.; mail Salem **z** 26426
Zion; RMC Place; UPSHUR; ***250** E-7; mail French Creek **z** 26218; rural

WISCONSIN

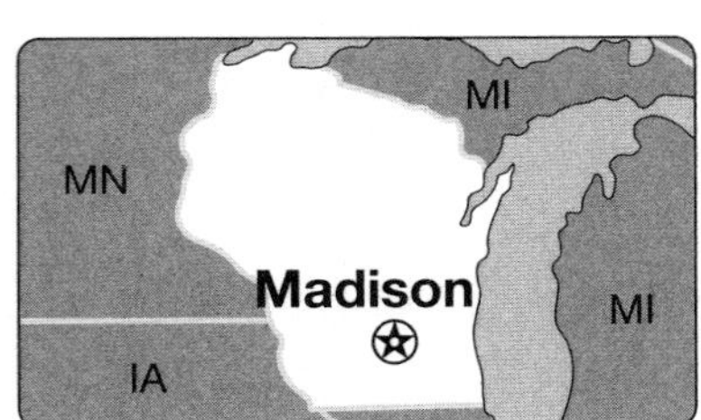

Statistics

Total area (2000) — 65,498 square miles
Land area (2000) — 54,310 square miles
Water area (2000) — 11,188 square miles
Capital — Madison
Admitted as state — May, 1848

Maps

State maps can be found on pages 142-254 in Vol. 1
County Subdivision maps can be found on pages 255-271 in Vol. 1

Ranally Metro Areas (RMAs) and Abbreviations

Appleton, WI — APP
Chicago, IL-IN-WI — CHI
Dubuque, IA-WI-IL — DUB
Duluth, MN-WI — DUL
Eau Claire WI — EAUC
Fond du Lac, WI — FDLC
Green Bay, WI — GRBY
Janesville, WI — JNSV
Kenosha, WI — KEN
La Crosse, WI-MN — LACRO
Madison, WI — MAD
Manitowoc, WI — MNTW
Milwaukee, WI — MILW
Minneapolis-St. Paul, MN-WI — MPLS-
Oshkosh, WI — OSH
Rockford, IL-WI — RKFD
Sheboygan, WI — SHEB
Wausau, WI — WAUS

Principal Places

Place Name	Place Type	County	Population
Milwaukee	Inc. Place	MILWAUKEE	◆ 663,318
Madison	Inc. Place	DANE	◆ 242,014
Green Bay	Inc. Place	BROWN	◆ 103,405
Kenosha	Inc. Place	KENOSHA	◆ 95,243
Racine	Inc. Place	RACINE	◆ 78,041
Appleton	Inc. Place	OUTAGAMIE	◆ 72,266
Eau Claire	Inc. Place	EAU CLAIRE	◆ 67,610
Oshkosh	Inc. Place	WINNEBAGO	◆ 66,764
West Allis	Inc. Place	MILWAUKEE	◆ 66,521
Waukesha	Inc. Place	WAUKESHA	◆ 66,377
Janesville	Inc. Place	ROCK	◆ 61,931
La Crosse	Inc. Place	LA CROSSE	◆ 53,873
Wauwatosa	Inc. Place	MILWAUKEE	◆ 51,340
Sheboygan	Inc. Place	SHEBOYGAN	◆ 48,783
Fond du Lac	Inc. Place	FOND DU LAC	◆ 41,442
New Berlin	Inc. Place	WAUKESHA	◆ 39,494
Greenfield	Inc. Place	MILWAUKEE	◆ 38,860
Wausau	Inc. Place	MARATHON	◆ 38,305
Brookfield	Inc. Place	WAUKESHA	◆ 38,268
Beloit	Inc. Place	ROCK	◆ 35,770
Franklin	Inc. Place	MILWAUKEE	◆ 35,373
Menomonee Falls	Inc. Place	WAUKESHA	◆ 34,465
Manitowoc	Inc. Place	MANITOWOC	◆ 32,644
Oak Creek	Inc. Place	MILWAUKEE	◆ 32,242
West Bend	Inc. Place	WASHINGTON	◆ 29,949
Superior	Inc. Place	DOUGLAS	◆ 26,767
Sun Prairie	Inc. Place	DANE	◆ 26,428
Fitchburg	Inc. Place	DANE	◆ 25,523
Stevens Point	Inc. Place	PORTAGE	◆ 25,469
Mount Pleasant	Inc. Place	RACINE	◆ 25,257
Caledonia	Inc. Place	RACINE	◆ 24,781
Caledonia	MCD-Town	RACINE	◆ 24,781
Neenah	Inc. Place	WINNEBAGO	◆ 24,640
South Milwaukee	Inc. Place	MILWAUKEE	◆ 23,535
De Pere	Inc. Place	BROWN	◆ 23,306
Muskego	Inc. Place	WAUKESHA	◆ 22,762
Watertown	Inc. Place	JEFFERSON	◆ 22,244
Grand Chute	MCD-Town	OUTAGAMIE	◆ 21,750
Mequon	Inc. Place	OZAUKEE	◆ 21,502
Cudahy	Inc. Place	MILWAUKEE	© 18,429
Germantown	Inc. Place	WASHINGTON	© 18,260
Ashwaubenon	Inc. Place	BROWN	© 17,634
Wisconsin Rapids	Inc. Place	WOOD	◆ 17,097
Marshfield	Inc. Place	WOOD	◆ 17,091
Menasha	Inc. Place	WINNEBAGO	© 16,331
Pleasant Prairie	Inc. Place	KENOSHA	© 16,136
Menasha	MCD-Town	WINNEBAGO	© 15,858
Middleton	Inc. Place	DANE	© 15,770
Allouez	Inc. Place	BROWN	© 15,443
Beaver Dam	Inc. Place	DODGE	◆ 15,175
Greendale	Inc. Place	MILWAUKEE	◆ 15,146
Menomonie	Inc. Place	DUNN	© 14,937
Onalaska	Inc. Place	LA CROSSE	© 14,839
Whitefish Bay	Inc. Place	MILWAUKEE	© 14,163
Glendale	Inc. Place	MILWAUKEE	◆ 14,111
Shorewood	Inc. Place	MILWAUKEE	© 13,763
Howard	Inc. Place	BROWN	© 13,546
Whitewater	Inc. Place	WALWORTH	© 13,437
Bellevue	Inc. Place	BROWN	● 13,300
Kaukauna	Inc. Place	OUTAGAMIE	© 12,983
Chippewa Falls	Inc. Place	CHIPPEWA	© 12,925
Two Rivers	Inc. Place	MANITOWOC	© 12,639
River Falls	Inc. Place	PIERCE	© 12,560
Oconomowoc	Inc. Place	WAUKESHA	© 12,382
Stoughton	Inc. Place	DANE	© 12,354
Brown Deer	Inc. Place	MILWAUKEE	© 12,170
Weston	Inc. Place	MARATHON	© 12,079
Bellevue Town	CDP-Census Area Only	BROWN	© 11,828
Pewaukee	Inc. Place	WAUKESHA	© 11,783
Fort Atkinson	Inc. Place	JEFFERSON	© 11,621
Cedarburg	Inc. Place	OZAUKEE	® 11,102
Hartford	Inc. Place	WASHINGTON	© 10,905
Monroe	Inc. Place	GREEN	© 10,843
Marinette	Inc. Place	MARINETTE	◆ 10,815
Waupun	Inc. Place	FOND DU LAC	© 10,718
Baraboo	Inc. Place	SAUK	© 10,711
Plover	Inc. Place	PORTAGE	© 10,520
Little Chute	Inc. Place	OUTAGAMIE	© 10,476
Port Washington	Inc. Place	OZAUKEE	© 10,467
Grafton	Inc. Place	OZAUKEE	® 10,464
Richfield	MCD-Town	WASHINGTON	© 10,373
Merrill	Inc. Place	LINCOLN	© 10,146
Suamico	Inc. Place	BROWN	● 10,000
Platteville	Inc. Place	GRANT	© 9,989
Burlington	Inc. Place	RACINE	© 9,936
Salem	MCD-Town	KENOSHA	© 9,871
Portage	Inc. Place	COLUMBIA	© 9,728
Sturgeon Bay	Inc. Place	DOOR	© 9,437
Lisbon	MCD-Town	WAUKESHA	© 9,359
Somers	MCD-Town	KENOSHA	© 9,059
Waunakee	Inc. Place	DANE	© 8,995
Sussex	Inc. Place	WAUKESHA	© 8,828
Hudson	Inc. Place	ST. CROIX	© 8,775
Saint Francis	Inc. Place	MILWAUKEE	© 8,662
Sparta	Inc. Place	MONROE	© 8,648
Ashland	Inc. Place	ASHLAND	© 8,620
Waukesha	MCD-Town	WAUKESHA	© 8,596
Tomah	Inc. Place	MONROE	© 8,419
Rice Lake	Inc. Place	BARRON	® 8,312
Shawano	Inc. Place	SHAWANO	© 8,298
Pewaukee	Inc. Place	WAUKESHA	© 8,170
Monona	Inc. Place	DANE	© 8,018
Merton	MCD-Town	WAUKESHA	© 7,988
Antigo	Inc. Place	LANGLADE	◆ 7,962
Delavan	Inc. Place	WALWORTH	© 7,956
Hartland	Inc. Place	WAUKESHA	© 7,905
Reedsburg	Inc. Place	SAUK	© 7,827
Delafield	MCD-Town	WAUKESHA	© 7,820
Grand Rapids	MCD-Town	WOOD	© 7,801
Plymouth	Inc. Place	SHEBOYGAN	© 7,781
Hales Corners	Inc. Place	MILWAUKEE	© 7,765
Norway	MCD-Town	RACINE	© 7,600
Rib Mountain	MCD-Town	MARATHON	© 7,556
Oregon	Inc. Place	DANE	© 7,514
Oconomowoc	MCD-Town	WAUKESHA	© 7,451
Ripon	Inc. Place	FOND DU LAC	® 7,450
De Forest	Inc. Place	DANE	© 7,368
Jefferson	Inc. Place	JEFFERSON	© 7,338
Elkhorn	Inc. Place	WALWORTH	© 7,305
Genesee	MCD-Town	WAUKESHA	© 7,284
Vernon	MCD-Town	WAUKESHA	© 7,227
Lake Geneva	Inc. Place	WALWORTH	© 7,148
New London	Inc. Place	WAUPACA	© 7,085
Verona	Inc. Place	DANE	© 7,052
Beloit	MCD-Town	ROCK	© 7,038
Fox Point	Inc. Place	MILWAUKEE	© 7,012
Madison	MCD-Town	DANE	© 7,005
Washington	MCD-Town	EAU CLAIRE	© 6,995
Rhinelander	Inc. Place	ONEIDA	◆ 6,950
Mukwonago	MCD-Town	WAUKESHA	© 6,868
Greenville	MCD-Town	OUTAGAMIE	© 6,844
Sheboygan Falls	Inc. Place	SHEBOYGAN	© 6,772
Altoona	Inc. Place	EAU CLAIRE	© 6,698
Delafield	Inc. Place	WAUKESHA	© 6,472
McFarland	Inc. Place	DANE	© 6,416
Brookfield	MCD-Town	WAUKESHA	© 6,390
Burlington	MCD-Town	RACINE	© 6,384
New Richmond	Inc. Place	ST. CROIX	© 6,310
Elm Grove	Inc. Place	WAUKESHA	© 6,249
Hudson	MCD-Town	ST. CROIX	© 6,213
Holmen	Inc. Place	LA CROSSE	© 6,200
Mukwonago	Inc. Place	WAUKESHA	© 6,162
Kimberly	Inc. Place	OUTAGAMIE	© 6,146
Rib Mountain	CDP-Census Area Only	MARATHON	© 6,059
Prairie du Chien	Inc. Place	CRAWFORD	© 6,018
Waterford	MCD-Town	RACINE	© 5,938
Sheboygan	MCD-Town	SHEBOYGAN	© 5,874
Mount Horeb	Inc. Place	DANE	© 5,860
Buchanan	MCD-Town	OUTAGAMIE	© 5,827
Kronenwetter	Inc. Place	MARATHON	● 5,800
Harrison	MCD-Town	CALUMET	© 5,756
Algoma	MCD-Town	WINNEBAGO	© 5,702
Waupaca	Inc. Place	WAUPACA	© 5,676
Cedarburg	MCD-Town	OZAUKEE	® 5,550
Bloomfield	MCD-Town	WALWORTH	© 5,537
Hobart	Inc. Place	BROWN	● 5,500
Hull	MCD-Town	PORTAGE	© 5,493
Saratoga	MCD-Town	WOOD	© 5,383
Berlin	Inc. Place	GREEN LAKE	© 5,305
Sturtevant	Inc. Place	RACINE	© 5,287
Windsor	MCD-Town	DANE	© 5,286
Dunn	MCD-Town	DANE	© 5,270
Freedom	MCD-Town	OUTAGAMIE	© 5,241
Onalaska	MCD-Town	LA CROSSE	© 5,210
Wind Lake	CDP	RACINE	© 5,202
Lafayette	MCD-Town	CHIPPEWA	© 5,199
Milton	Inc. Place	ROCK	© 5,132
Twin Lakes	Inc. Place	KENOSHA	© 5,124
Richland Center	Inc. Place	RICHLAND	© 5,114

County Business Data

County	FIPS Code	County Seat	Land Area (Sq. Mi.)	Census Population			Wholesale Trade		Manufacturing, 2002			
				4/1/2000	4/1/1990	% Change 1990-2000	Sales, 2002 ($1,000)	% Change 1997-2002	Establish-ments	Total Employees	Value Added ($1,000)	Ranally Mfg. Units
Adams	001	Friendship	648	18,643	15,682	18.9	(d)	(d)	...	(d)	(d)	...
Ashland	003	Ashland	1,044	16,866	16,307	3.4	55,314	36.5	31	1,274	66,933	35
Barron	005	Barron	863	44,963	40,750	10.3	114,532	-25.5	95	6,304	474,578	251
Bayfield	007	Washburn	1,476	15,013	14,008	7.2	12,690	128.2	...	(d)	(d)	...
Brown	009	Green Bay	529	226,778	194,594	16.5	4,731,078	66.1	442	24,991	4,066,544	2,151
Buffalo	011	Alma	684	13,804	13,584	1.6	24,704	-48.1	...	(d)	(d)	...
Burnett	013	Siren	822	15,674	13,084	19.8	4,306	-57.9	29	838	97,697	52
Calumet	015	Chilton	320	40,631	34,291	18.5	(d)	(d)	63	5,793	551,620	292
Chippewa	017	Chippewa Falls	1,010	55,195	52,360	5.4	(d)	(d)	131	4,846	565,428	299
Clark	019	Neillsville	1,216	33,557	31,647	6.0	106,761	49.7	88	2,998	291,863	154
Columbia	021	Portage	774	52,468	45,088	16.4	(d)	(d)	104	5,633	671,139	355
Crawford	023	Prairie du Chien	573	17,243	15,940	8.2	55,918	-74.7	28	1,767	381,701	202
Dane	025	Madison	1,202	426,526	367,085	16.2	5,607,504	28.9	584	25,172	2,997,689	1,586
Dodge	027	Juneau	882	85,897	76,559	12.2	371,318	-29.8	171	10,446	1,346,930	713
Door	029	Sturgeon Bay	483	27,961	25,690	8.8	33,185	-14.8	65	2,244	160,615	85
Douglas	031	Superior	1,309	43,287	41,758	3.7	1,029,966	(d)	61	(d)	(d)	...
Dunn	033	Menomonie	852	39,858	35,909	11.0	(d)	(d)	49	2,224	672,145	356
Eau Claire	035	Eau Claire	638	93,142	85,183	9.3	976,743	59.2	106	5,295	672,494	356
Florence	037	Florence	488	5,088	4,590	10.8	(d)	(d)	...	(d)	(d)	...
Fond du Lac	039	Fond du Lac	723	97,296	90,083	8.0	814,763	54.3	166	10,515	1,097,909	581
Forest	041	Crandon	1,014	10,024	8,776	14.2	12,709	-5.9	...	(d)	(d)	...
Grant	043	Lancaster	1,148	49,597	49,264	0.7	200,957	15.2	67	2,769	375,903	199
Green	045	Monroe	584	33,647	30,339	10.9	223,425	7.0	78	1,923	224,695	119
Green Lake	047	Green Lake	354	19,105	18,651	2.4	27,093	-17.0	52	1,758	154,475	82
Iowa	049	Dodgeville	763	22,780	20,150	13.1	(d)	(d)	37	603	45,895	24
Iron	051	Hurley	757	6,861	6,153	11.5	12,401	4.2	...	(d)	(d)	...
Jackson	053	Black River Falls	987	19,100	16,588	15.1	7,765	-11.1	22	801	59,511	31
Jefferson	055	Jefferson	557	74,021	67,783	9.2	648,688	39.1	160	11,171	1,280,233	677
Juneau	057	Mauston	768	24,316	21,650	12.3	41,974	-45.8	48	2,122	168,884	89
Kenosha	059	Kenosha	273	149,577	128,181	16.7	(d)	(d)	205	9,685	1,041,892	551
Kewaunee	061	Kewaunee	343	20,187	18,878	6.9	(d)	(d)	46	1,947	108,669	57
La Crosse	063	La Crosse	453	107,120	97,904	9.4	(d)	(d)	173	(d)	(d)	...
Lafayette	065	Darlington	634	16,137	16,076	0.4	97,590	56.9	...	(d)	(d)	...
Langlade	067	Antigo	873	20,740	19,505	6.3	208,679	-4.2	48	1,559	125,356	66
Lincoln	069	Merrill	883	29,641	26,993	9.8	(d)	(d)	59	3,458	346,066	183
Manitowoc	071	Manitowoc	592	82,887	80,421	3.1	257,683	0.2	193	12,376	1,238,392	655
Marathon	073	Wausau	1,545	125,834	115,400	9.0	(d)	(d)	233	17,140	1,569,985	831
Marinette	075	Marinette	1,402	43,384	40,548	7.0	(d)	(d)	97	5,833	711,960	377
Marquette	077	Montello	455	15,832	12,321	28.5	(d)	(d)	25	1,165	102,713	54
Menominee	078	Keshena	358	4,562	3,890	17.3	(d)	(d)	...	(d)	(d)	...
Milwaukee	079	Milwaukee	242	940,164	959,275	-2.0	15,157,730	16.5	1,293	67,611	7,983,283	4,224
Monroe	081	Sparta	901	40,899	36,633	11.6	129,510	-46.4	62	3,510	289,584	153
Oconto	083	Oconto	998	35,634	30,226	17.9	(d)	(d)	68	2,707	189,241	100
Oneida	085	Rhinelander	1,124	36,776	31,679	16.1	(d)	(d)	60	1,506	173,048	92
Outagamie	087	Appleton	640	160,971	140,510	14.6	(d)	(d)	327	18,286	1,930,172	1,021
Ozaukee	089	Port Washington	232	82,317	72,831	13.0	957,323	52.6	230	11,432	1,190,133	630
Pepin	091	Durand	232	7,213	7,107	1.5	58,187	112.5	...	(d)	(d)	...
Pierce	093	Ellsworth	576	36,804	32,765	12.3	(d)	(d)	52	1,190	97,196	51
Polk	095	Balsam Lake	917	41,319	34,773	18.8	80,009	-28.9	109	3,794	248,323	131
Portage	097	Stevens Point	806	67,182	61,405	9.4	740,987	94.5	81	4,778	542,866	287
Price	099	Phillips	1,253	15,822	15,600	1.4	16,232	-60.9	47	2,344	290,583	154
Racine	101	Racine	333	188,831	175,034	7.9	3,341,343	-12.5	341	16,405	3,836,814	2,030
Richland	103	Richland Center	586	17,924	17,521	2.3	52,542	63.0	29	1,512	134,607	71
Rock	105	Janesville	720	152,307	139,510	9.2	1,848,564	8.3	238	14,994	5,753,424	3,044
Rusk	107	Ladysmith	913	15,347	15,079	1.8	15,388	220.7	29	1,851	150,570	80
St. Croix	109	Hudson	722	63,155	50,251	25.7	(d)	(d)	155	5,692	487,562	258
Sauk	111	Baraboo	838	55,225	46,975	17.6	(d)	(d)	107	6,277	628,214	332
Sawyer	113	Hayward	1,256	16,196	14,181	14.2	36,104	51.4	47	541	39,980	21

Entries in **UPPERCASE** are counties.
Entries in **bold** have populations of 2,500 or more.
Names in parentheses are alternate names.

Inc. Place	Incorporated Place
RMC Place	Rand McNally Designated Place
CDP	Census Designated Place
MCD	Minor Civil Division

⊡ County Seat
▲ Minor Civil Division
elev. Elevation
🅿 Post Office

H Hospital
C College
■ Principal Business Center
★ Ranally Metro Area (RMA) Abbreviation
z Zip Code(s)

Ⓟ Previous Census Population
® Revised Census Population
Ⓐ Annexation Population
● Rand McNally Population Estimate
© Final Census Population
Ⓢ Special Census Population
◆ Estimated Population

For additional definitions see Glossary, Volume 1, and Introduction, Volume 2.

County	FIPS Code	County Seat	Land Area (Sq. Mi.)	Census Population 4/1/2000	Census Population 4/1/1990	Census Population % Change 1990-2000	Wholesale Trade Sales, 2002 ($1,000)	Wholesale Trade % Change 1997-2002	Manufacturing, 2002 Establish-ments	Manufacturing, 2002 Total Employees	Manufacturing, 2002 Value Added ($1,000)	Manufacturing, 2002 Ranally Mfg. Units
Shawano	115	Shawano	893	40,664	37,157	9.4	230,218	20.0	74	2,021	162,836	86
Sheboygan	117	Sheboygan	514	112,646	103,877	8.4	669,818	-43.5	242	20,115	2,212,591	1,171
Taylor	119	Medford	975	19,680	18,901	4.1	15,780	-80.5	36	3,213	198,811	105
Trempealeau	121	Whitehall	734	27,010	25,263	6.9	65,971	-47.5	58	4,332	400,227	212
Vernon	123	Viroqua	795	28,056	25,617	9.5	62,105	-17.8	32	866	81,548	43
Vilas	125	Eagle River	874	21,033	17,707	18.8	(d)	(d)	...	(d)	(d)	...
Walworth	127	Elkhorn	555	93,759	75,000	25.0	733,834	-16.9	219	10,381	1,303,832	690
Washburn	129	Shell Lake	810	16,036	13,772	16.4	15,704	-28.3	37	1,200	126,773	67
Washington	131	West Bend	431	117,493	95,328	23.3	1,493,812	34.8	337	14,829	1,359,694	719
Waukesha	133	Waukesha	556	360,767	304,715	18.4	10,293,752	-10.7	1,107	45,125	4,509,751	2,386
Waupaca	135	Waupaca	751	51,731	46,104	12.2	147,854	27.1	106	7,023	589,488	312
Waushara	137	Wautoma	626	23,154	19,385	19.4	81,066	48.6	34	658	41,921	22
Winnebago	139	Oshkosh	439	156,763	140,320	11.7	2,434,847	123.6	310	23,924	2,929,411	1,550
Wood	141	Wisconsin Rapids	793	75,555	73,605	2.6	567,747	-10.9	138	8,395	1,021,921	541
The State			**54,310**	**5,363,675**	**4,891,769**	**9.6**	**68,510,712**	**19.8**	**9,915**	**503,588**	**61,501,462**	**32,539**

(d) Data not available. Corresponding percentages or Ranally Manufacturing Units are estimates.
... Represents 0 or amount too minimal to be reported.

Administrative Divisions

Towns: All Wisconsin counties are divided into townships, except for areas within cities or villages. Townships are legally incorporated units and may levy taxes, elect certain officials, and carry on limited governmental functions. Only townships with an active government recognized by the U.S. Census of Governments are printed in this index.

Cities and Villages: The incorporated cities and villages do not form parts of towns which adjoin or surround them.

Index of Places and Counties

A

Abbotsford; Inc. Place; CLARK, MARATHON; **252** H-7; elev. 1,410ft./430m.; 🅿; z 54405; Ⓟ 1,916; Ⓒ 1,956

Abells Corners; RMC Place; WALWORTH; ▲ Sugar Creek, Lafayette; ***253** O-12; elev. 881ft./269m.; mail Elkhorn z 53121; ● 40

Abrams; RMC Place; OCONTO; ▲ Abrams; **252** I-13; 🅿; z 54101; ● 350

Abrams; MCD-Town; OCONTO; ***252** I-13; 🅿; z 54101; Ⓟ 1,347; Ⓒ 1,757

Ackerville; RMC Place; WASHINGTON; ▲ Polk; ***253** N-12; ★ **MILW**; mail Slinger z 53086; ● 25

Ackley; MCD-Town; LANGLADE; ***252** G-10; mail Antigo z 54409; Ⓟ 550; Ⓒ 510

Ada; RMC Place; SHEBOYGAN; ▲ Herman; **253** L-13; ★ **SHEB**; mail Elkhart Lake z 53020; ● 130

Adams; Inc. Place; ADAMS; **253** K-8; elev. 960ft./293m.; 🅿; z 53910; Ⓟ 1,715; Ⓒ 1,914; Ⓡ 1,831

Adams; MCD-Town; ADAMS; ***253** K-8; 🅿; z 53910 & mail Friendship z 53934; Ⓟ 1,170; Ⓒ 1,267

Adams; MCD-Town; GREEN; ***253** O-9; mail Argyle z 53504; Ⓟ 452; Ⓒ 464

Adams; MCD-Town; JACKSON; ***252** J-6; mail Black River Falls z 54615; Ⓟ 1,167; Ⓒ 1,208

Adams; RMC Place; WALWORTH; ▲ Troy; ***253** O-12; elev. 919ft./280m.; mail East Troy z 53120; rural

ADAMS; **253** L-9; Ⓟ 15,682; Ⓒ 18,643; Ⓡ 19,920; ◆ 20,287

Adams Beach; RMC Place; SHAWANO; ▲ Belle Plaine; ***252** I-11; elev. 808ft./246m.; mail Clintonville z 54929; ● 300

Addison; RMC Place; WASHINGTON; ▲ Addison; ***253** M-12; mail Allenton z 53002; ● 50

Addison; MCD-Town; WASHINGTON; ***253** M-12; mail Allenton z 53002; Ⓟ 3,051; Ⓒ 3,341

Adell; Inc. Place; SHEBOYGAN; **253** L-13; elev. 900ft./274m.; 🅿; ★ **SHEB**; z 53001; Ⓟ 510; Ⓒ 517

Adrian; MCD-Town; MONROE; ***253** K-7; mail Norwalk z 54648; Ⓟ 520; Ⓒ 682

Advance; RMC Place; SHAWANO; ▲ Green Valley; ***252** I-12; elev. 859ft./262m.; mail Cecil z 54111; ● 30

Afton; RMC Place; ROCK; ▲ Rock; **253** P-10; 🅿; ★ **JNSV**; z 53501; ● 250

Agenda; MCD-Town; ASHLAND; ***252** D-7; mail Butternut z 54514; Ⓟ 591; Ⓒ 513

Ahnapee; MCD-Town; KEWAUNEE; ***252** I-14; mail Algoma z 54201; Ⓟ 941; Ⓒ 977

Ainsworth; MCD-Town; LANGLADE; ***252** G-10; mail Pearson z 54462; Ⓟ 474; Ⓒ 571

Akan; MCD-Town; RICHLAND; ***253** M-7; mail Soldiers Grove z 54655; Ⓟ 444; Ⓒ 444

Alaska; RMC Place; KEWAUNEE; ▲ Pierce; **252** I-14; mail Kewaunee z 54216; ● 30

Alban; MCD-Town; PORTAGE; ***252** I-10; mail Rosholt z 54473; Ⓟ 860; Ⓒ 897

Albany; Inc. Place; GREEN; **253** P-9; elev. 800ft./244m.; 🅿; z 53502; Ⓟ 1,140; Ⓒ 1,191

Albany; MCD-Town; GREEN; ***253** O-9; 🅿; z 53502; does not include the Village of Albany; Ⓟ 598; Ⓒ 775

Albany; MCD-Town; PEPIN; ***252** I-4; mail Mondovi z 54755; Ⓟ 507; Ⓒ 620

Albertville; RMC Place; CHIPPEWA; ▲ Howard; ***252** H-4; mail Colfax z 54730; ● 35

Albion; RMC Place; DANE; ▲ Albion; **253** O-10; mail Edgerton z 53534; ● 240

Albion; MCD-Town; DANE; ***253** O-10; mail Edgerton z 53534; Ⓟ 1,964; Ⓒ 1,823

Albion; MCD-Town; JACKSON; ***252** J-6; mail Black River Falls z 54615; Ⓟ 904; Ⓒ 1,093

Albion; MCD-Town; TREMPEALEAU; ***252** I-5; mail Eleva z 54738; Ⓟ 696; Ⓒ 595

Alden; MCD-Town; POLK; ***252** G-2; mail New Richmond z 54017; Ⓟ 2,133; Ⓒ 2,615

Alderley; RMC Place; DODGE; ▲ Ashippun; ***253** N-12; mail Oconomowoc z 53066; ● 60

Algoma; Inc. Place; KEWAUNEE; **252** I-14; elev. 600ft./183m.; 🅿; z 54201; Ⓟ 3,353; Ⓒ 3,357

Algoma; MCD-Town; WINNEBAGO; ***253** K-11; ★ **OSH**; mail Oshkosh z 54901; Ⓟ 3,442; Ⓒ 5,702

Allen; RMC Place; EAU CLAIRE; ▲ Clear Creek; **252** I-5; elev. 974ft./297m.; mail Strum z 54770; ● 30

Allens Grove; RMC Place; WALWORTH; ▲ Darien; **253** P-11; mail Darien z 53114; ● 180

Allenton; RMC Place; WASHINGTON; ▲ Addison; **253** M-12; 🅿; z 53002; ● 850

Allenville; RMC Place; WINNEBAGO; ▲ Vinland; ***253** K-11; mail Oshkosh z 54904; ● 60

Allouez; Inc. Place; BROWN; **253** S-3; 🅿; ★ **GRBY**; z 54301; Ⓟ 14,431; Ⓒ 15,443

Allouez; RMC Place; DOUGLAS; ***252** B-3; elev. 636ft./194m.; ★ **DUL**; pop. incl. with Superior (Inc. Place)

Alma; Inc. Place; ⊡ BUFFALO; **252** J-4; elev. 687ft./209m.; 🅿; z 54610; Ⓟ 790; Ⓒ 942

Alma; MCD-Town; BUFFALO; ***252** J-4; 🅿; z 54610; does not include the City of Alma; Ⓟ 479; Ⓒ 377

Alma; MCD-Town; JACKSON; ***252** J-6; mail Alma Center z 54611; Ⓟ 831; Ⓒ 983

Alma Center; Inc. Place; JACKSON; **252** J-6; elev. 1,000ft./305m.; 🅿; z 54611; Ⓟ 416; Ⓒ 446

Almena; Inc. Place; BARRON; **252** G-3; elev. 1,187ft./362m.; 🅿; z 54805; Ⓟ 625; Ⓒ 720

Almena; MCD-Town; BARRON; ***252** F-3; 🅿; z 54805 & mail Comstock z 54826; does not include the Village of Almena; Ⓟ 773; Ⓒ 910

Almon; MCD-Town; SHAWANO; ***252** H-10; mail Bowler z 54416; Ⓟ 557; Ⓒ 591

Almond; Inc. Place; PORTAGE; **252** J-9; elev. 1,300ft./396m.; 🅿; z 54909; Ⓟ 455; Ⓒ 459

Almond; MCD-Town; PORTAGE; ***252** J-9; 🅿; z 54909; does not include the Village of Amherst; Ⓟ 590; Ⓒ 679

Alpha; RMC Place; BURNETT; ▲ Wood River; **252** E-2; mail Grantsburg z 54840; ● 50

Alto; RMC Place; FOND DU LAC; ▲ Alto; **253** L-11; mail Brandon z 53919; ● 200

Alto; MCD-Town; FOND DU LAC; ***253** L-11; mail Brandon z 53919; Ⓟ 1,145; Ⓒ 1,103

Altoona; Inc. Place; EAU CLAIRE; **252** I-5; elev. 900ft./274m.; 🅿; ★ **EAUC**; z 54720; Ⓟ 5,889; Ⓒ 6,698

Alverno; RMC Place; MANITOWOC; ***253** K-13; ★ **MNTW**; mail Manitowoc z 54220; rural

Alvin; RMC Place; FOREST; ▲ Alvin; **252** E-11; 🅿; z 54542; ● 90

Alvin; MCD-Town; FOREST; ***252** E-11; 🅿; z 54542; Ⓟ 145; Ⓒ 186

Amberg; RMC Place; MARINETTE; ▲ Amberg; **252** F-13; elev. 893ft./272m.; 🅿; z 54102; ● 450

Amberg; MCD-Town; MARINETTE; ***252** F-13; 🅿; z 54102; Ⓟ 917; Ⓒ 854

Amery; Inc. Place; POLK; **252** G-2; elev. 1,060ft./323m.; 🅿 🅷; z 54001; Ⓟ 2,657; Ⓒ 2,845

Amherst; Inc. Place; PORTAGE; **252** J-10; elev. 1,050ft./320m.; 🅿; z 54406; Ⓟ 792; Ⓒ 964

Amherst; MCD-Town; PORTAGE; ***252** J-10; 🅿; z 54406 & mail Scandinavia z 54977; does not include the Village of Amherst; Ⓟ 1,335; Ⓒ 1,435

Amherst Junction; Inc. Place; PORTAGE; **252** J-10; elev. 1,126ft./343m.; 🅿; z 54407; Ⓟ 269; Ⓒ 305

Amnicon; MCD-Town; DOUGLAS; ***252** C-4; mail South Range z 54874; Ⓟ 929; Ⓒ 1,074

Amnicon Falls; RMC Place; DOUGLAS; ▲ Amnicon; ***252** C-4; mail South Range z 54874; ● 30

Anacker; RMC Place; COLUMBIA; ▲ Fort Winnebago; ***253** L-9; mail Portage z 53901; rural

Anderson; MCD-Town; BURNETT; ***252** F-2; mail Grantsburg z 54840; Ⓟ 324; Ⓒ 372

Anderson; MCD-Town; IRON; ***252** C-7; mail Upson z 54565; Ⓟ 69; Ⓒ 61

Angelica; RMC Place; SHAWANO; ▲ Angelica; **252** I-12; mail Pulaski z 54162; ● 100

Angelica; MCD-Town; SHAWANO; ***252** I-12; mail Pulaski z 54162; Ⓟ 1,417; Ⓒ 1,635

Angelo; RMC Place; MONROE; ▲ Angelo; **253** K-6; mail Sparta z 54656; ● 110

Angelo; MCD-Town; MONROE; ***253** K-6; mail Sparta z 54656; Ⓟ 1,219; Ⓒ 1,268

Angus; RMC Place; WASHBURN; ▲ Cedar Lake; ***252** F-4; mail Birchwood z 54817

Aniwa; Inc. Place; SHAWANO; **252** H-10; elev. 1,414ft./431m.; 🅿; z 54408; Ⓟ 249; Ⓒ 272

Aniwa; MCD-Town; SHAWANO; ***252** H-10; 🅿; z 54408 & mail Birnamwood z 54414; does not include the Village of Aniwa; Ⓟ 601; Ⓒ 586

Annaton; RMC Place; GRANT; ▲ Clifton; ***253** O-7; mail Stitzer z 53825; rural

Anson; RMC Place; CHIPPEWA; ▲ Anson; ***252** H-5; elev. 946ft./288m.; mail Chippewa Falls z 54729; ● 50

Anson; MCD-Town; CHIPPEWA; ***252** H-5; mail Jim Falls z 54748; Ⓟ 1,634; Ⓒ 1,881

Anston; RMC Place; BROWN; ▲ Pittsfield; **252** I-12; elev. 747ft./228m.; ★ **GRBY**; mail Green Bay z 54301; ● 80

Anthony; RMC Place; EAU CLAIRE; ▲ Drammen; ***252** I-4; elev. 940ft./287m.; mail Mondovi z 54755; rural

Antigo; Inc. Place; ⊡ LANGLADE; **252** G-10; elev. 1,498ft./457m.; 🅿 🅷 ■; z 54409; Ⓟ 8,276; Ⓒ 8,560; ◆ 7,962

Antigo; MCD-Town; LANGLADE; ***252** G-10; 🅿; z 54409; does not include the City of Antigo; Ⓟ 1,406; Ⓒ 1,487

Apollonia; RMC Place; RUSK; ▲ Stubbs; ***252** F-5; mail Bruce z 54819; ● 35

Apple Creek; RMC Place; OUTAGAMIE; ▲ Vandenbroek; ***252** J-12; ★ **APP**; mail Appleton z 54915; ● 100

Apple River; MCD-Town; POLK; ***252** F-3; mail Balsam Lake z 54810; Ⓟ 815; Ⓒ 1,067

Appleton; Inc. Place; ⊡ OUTAGAMIE, CALUMET, WINNEBAGO; **252** J-12; elev. 780ft./238m.; 🅿 🅷 🅲 1,480 ■; ★ **APP**; z 54911-15, z 54919; Ⓟ 65,695; Ⓒ 70,087; ◆ 72,266

Applewood; RMC Place; DANE; ▲ Middleton; ***253** N-9; elev. 1,100ft./335m.; ★ **MAD**; mail Madison z 53711; ● 100

Arbor Vitae; RMC Place; VILAS; ▲ Arbor Vitae; **252** E-9; 🅿; z 54568; summer pop. 600; ● 220

Arbor Vitae; MCD-Town; VILAS; ***252** E-9; 🅿; z 54568; Ⓟ 2,531; Ⓒ 3,153

Arcade Acres; RMC Place; FOND DU LAC; ▲ Ripon; ***253** L-11; elev. 840ft./256m.; mail Ripon z 54971; ● 150

Arcadia; Inc. Place; TREMPEALEAU; **252** J-4; elev. 728ft./222m.; 🅿 🅷; z 54612; Ⓟ 2,166; Ⓒ 2,402

Arcadia; MCD-Town; TREMPEALEAU; ***252** J-5; 🅿; z 54612; does not include the City of Arcadia; Ⓟ 1,710; Ⓒ 1,555

Arena; Inc. Place; IOWA; **253** N-8; elev. 735ft./224m.; 🅿; z 53503; Ⓟ 525; Ⓒ 685

Arena; MCD-Town; IOWA; ***253** N-8; 🅿; z 53503; does not include the Village of Arena; Ⓟ 1,301; Ⓒ 1,444

Argonne; RMC Place; FOREST; ▲ Argonne; **252** F-11; elev. 641ft./195m.; 🅿; z 54511; ● 300

Argonne; MCD-Town; FOREST; ***252** E-11; 🅿; z 54511; Ⓟ 497; Ⓒ 532

Argyle; Inc. Place; LAFAYETTE; **253** P-8; elev. 810ft./247m.; 🅿; z 53504; Ⓟ 798; Ⓒ 823

Argyle; MCD-Town; LAFAYETTE; ***253** O-8; 🅿; z 53504; does not include the Village of Argyle; Ⓟ 424; Ⓒ 479

Arkansaw; RMC Place; PEPIN; ▲ Waterville; **252** I-3; 🅿; z 54721; ● 200

Arkdale; RMC Place; ADAMS; ▲ Strongs Prairie; ***253** K-8; 🅿; z 54613; ● 150

Arland; RMC Place; BARRON; ▲ Arland; **252** G-3; elev. 1,217ft./371m.; mail Clayton z 54004; ● 40

Arland; MCD-Town; BARRON; ***252** G-3; mail Clayton z 54004; Ⓟ 609; Ⓒ 670

Arlington; Inc. Place; COLUMBIA; **253** M-10; elev. 1,052ft./321m.; 🅿; z 53911; Ⓟ 440; Ⓒ 484

Arlington; MCD-Town; COLUMBIA; ***253** M-9; 🅿; z 53911 & mail Lodi z 53555; does not include the Village of Arlington; Ⓟ 748; Ⓒ 848

Armenia; MCD-Town; JUNEAU; ***253** K-8; mail Necedah z 54646; Ⓟ 592; Ⓒ 707

Armstrong; RMC Place; FOND DU LAC; ▲ Osceola; ***253** L-12; mail Saint Cloud z 53079; ● 50

Armstrong; OCONTO; see Mountain (MCD-Town)

Armstrong Creek; RMC Place; FOREST; ▲ Armstrong Creek; **252** F-12; elev. 1,516ft./462m.; 🅿; z 54103; ● 200

Armstrong Creek; MCD-Town; FOREST; ***252** F-12; 🅿; z 54103; Ⓟ 460; Ⓒ 463

Arnott; RMC Place; PORTAGE; ▲ Stockton; **252** J-9; elev. 1,135ft./346m.; mail Stevens Point z 54481; ● 50

Arpin; Inc. Place; WOOD; ▲ Arpin; **252** I-8; 🅿; z 54410; Ⓟ 312; Ⓒ 337

Arpin; MCD-Town; WOOD; ***252** I-8; 🅿; z 54410; Ⓟ 806; Ⓒ 786

Artesia Beach; RMC Place; FOND DU LAC; ▲ Calumet; ***253** K-12; elev. 750ft./229m.; mail Malone z 53049; ● 50

Arthur; MCD-Town; CHIPPEWA; ***252** H-5; mail Cadott z 54727; Ⓟ 756; Ⓒ 710

Arthur; RMC Place; GRANT; ▲ Lima; **253** O-7; mail Platteville z 53818; ● 70

Ashford; RMC Place; FOND DU LAC; ▲ Ashford; ***253** M-12; mail Campbellsport z 53010; ● 50

Ashford; MCD-Town; FOND DU LAC; ***253** M-12; mail Campbellsport z 53010; Ⓟ 1,598; Ⓒ 1,773

Ashippun; RMC Place; DODGE; ▲ Ashippun; **253** N-12; elev. 858ft./262m.; 🅿; z 53003; ● 450

Ashippun; MCD-Town; DODGE; ***253** N-12; 🅿; z 53003; Ⓟ 1,783; Ⓒ 2,308

Ashland; Inc. Place; ⊡ ASHLAND; **252** C-6; elev. 671ft./205m.; 🅿 🅷 🅲 712; z 54806; location of Great Lakes Indian Agency; Ⓟ 8,695; Ⓒ 8,620

Ashland; MCD-Town; ASHLAND; ***252** C-6; 🅿 🅲 712; z 54806 & mail High Bridge z 54846; does not include the City of Ashland; Ⓟ 567; Ⓒ 603

ASHLAND; **252** D-6; Ⓟ 16,307; Ⓒ 16,866; ◆ 15,871

Ash Ridge; RMC Place; RICHLAND; ▲ Forest, Bloom; ***253** M-7; elev. 1,284ft./391m.; mail Viola z 54664; rural

Ashton; RMC Place; DANE; ▲ Springfield; ***253** N-9; ★ **MAD**; mail Middleton z 53562; ● 60

Ashton Corners; RMC Place; DANE; ▲ Springfield; **253** R-5; elev. 974ft./297m.; ★ **MAD**; mail Middleton z 53562; ● 140

Ashwaubenon; Inc. Place; BROWN; **253** S-2; elev. 630ft./192m.; 🅿; ★ **GRBY**; z 54304, z 54313 & mail Green Bay z 54324; Ⓟ 16,376; Ⓒ 17,634

Askeaton; RMC Place; BROWN; ▲ Holland; ***252** J-13; elev. 740ft./226m.; mail Greenleaf z 54126; rural

Astico; RMC Place; DODGE; ▲ Elba; **253** M-11; mail Columbus z 53925; ● 40

Athelstane; RMC Place; MARINETTE; ▲ Athelstane; **252** F-12; elev. 933ft./284m.; 🅿; z 54104; ● 110

Athelstane; MCD-Town; MARINETTE; ***252** F-12; 🅿; z 54104; Ⓟ 437; Ⓒ 601

Athens; Inc. Place; MARATHON; **252** H-8; elev. 1,360ft./415m.; 🅿; z 54411; Ⓟ 951; Ⓒ 1,095

Atlanta; MCD-Town; RUSK; ***252** F-5; mail Bruce z 54819; Ⓟ 585; Ⓒ 627

Atlas; RMC Place; POLK; ▲ Laketown; **252** F-2; mail Luck z 54853; ● 70

Attica; RMC Place; GREEN; ▲ Brooklyn; ***253** O-9; mail Albany z 53502; ● 40

Atwater; RMC Place; DODGE; ▲ Chester; ***253** M-11; elev. 932ft./284m.; mail Burnett z 53922; rural

Atwood; RMC Place; CLARK; ▲ Green Grove; ***252** H-7; elev. 1,291ft./393m.; mail Owen z 54460

Auburn; MCD-Town; CHIPPEWA; ***252** H-4; mail New Auburn z 54757; Ⓟ 474; Ⓒ 580

Auburn; MCD-Town; FOND DU LAC; ***253** M-12; mail Kewaskum z 53040; Ⓟ 1,790; Ⓒ 2,075

Auburndale; Inc. Place; WOOD; **252** I-8; elev. 1,220ft./372m.; 🅿; z 54412; Ⓟ 665; Ⓒ 738

Auburndale; MCD-Town; WOOD; ***252** I-8; 🅿; z 54412; does not include the Village of Auburndale; Ⓟ 844; Ⓒ 829

Auburn Lake; RMC Place; FOND DU LAC; ▲ Auburn; ***253** M-12; elev. 970ft./296m.; mail Campbellsport z 53010; summer pop. 100; ● 40

Augusta; Inc. Place; EAU CLAIRE; **252** I-5; elev. 960ft./293m.; 🅿; z 54722; Ⓟ 1,510; Ⓒ 1,460

Aurora; RMC Place; FLORENCE; ▲ Aurora; **252** E-12; elev. 1,072ft./327m.; mail Niagara z 54151; ● 450

Aurora; MCD-Town; FLORENCE; ***252** E-12; mail Niagara z 54151; Ⓟ 1,036; Ⓒ 1,186

Aurora; MCD-Town; TAYLOR; ***252** G-6; mail Gilman z 54433; Ⓟ 473; Ⓒ 386

Aurora; MCD-Town; WAUSHARA; ***253** K-11; mail Berlin z 54923; Ⓟ 846; Ⓒ 971

Auroraville; RMC Place; WAUSHARA; ▲ Aurora; **253** K-10; elev. 775ft./236m.; mail Berlin z 54923; ● 100

Avalanche; RMC Place; VERNON; ▲ Webster; **253** M-6; elev. 859ft./262m.; mail Viroqua z 54665; ● 30

Avalon; RMC Place; ROCK; ▲ Bradford; **253** P-11; 🅿; z 53505; ● 200

Avoca; Inc. Place; IOWA; **253** N-7; elev. 698ft./213m.; 🅿; z 53506; Ⓟ 474; Ⓒ 608

Avon; RMC Place; LAFAYETTE; ▲ Darlington; **253** P-8; mail Darlington z 53530; pop. incl. with Darlington (Inc. Place)

Avon; RMC Place; ROCK; ▲ Avon; ***253** P-10; mail Brodhead z 53520; ● 50

Avon; MCD-Town; ROCK; ***253** P-10; mail Brodhead z 53520; Ⓟ 570; Ⓒ 586

Aztalan; MCD-Town; JEFFERSON; ***253** N-11; mail Johnson Creek z 53038; Ⓟ 1,476; Ⓒ 1,447

B

Babcock; RMC Place; WOOD; ▲ Remington; **252** J-8; elev. 975ft./297m.; 🅿; z 54413; ● 200

Bad River Reservation; Indian Reservation; ASHLAND, IRON; mail Ashland z 54806; also location of Indian Agency; Ⓟ 916; Ⓒ 1,411

Bagley; Inc. Place; GRANT; **253** O-5; elev. 625ft./191m.; 🅿; z 53801; Ⓟ 306; Ⓒ 339

Bagley; MCD-Town; OCONTO; ***252** H-12; mail Pound z 54161; Ⓟ 271; Ⓒ 333

Baileys Harbor; RMC Place; DOOR; ▲ Baileys Harbor; **252** B-13; elev. 595ft./181m.; 🅿; z 54202; ● 400

Baileys Harbor; MCD-Town; DOOR; ***252** B-13; 🅿; z 54202; Ⓟ 780; Ⓒ 1,003

Bain; RMC Place; KENOSHA; ★ **KEN**; pop. incl. with Pleasant Prairie (Inc. Place)

Bakerville; RMC Place; WOOD; ▲ Lincoln; **252** I-7; elev. 1,318ft./402m.; mail Marshfield z 54449; ● 50

Baldwin; Inc. Place; ST. CROIX; **252** H-2; elev. 1,140ft./347m.; 🅿 🅷; z 54002; Ⓟ 2,022; Ⓒ 2,667

Baldwin; MCD-Town; ST. CROIX; ***252** H-3; 🅿; z 54002 & mail Woodville z 54028; does not include the Village of Baldwin; Ⓟ 911; Ⓒ 903

Balsam Lake; Inc. Place; ⊡ POLK; **252** F-2; elev. 1,155ft./352m.; 🅿; z 54810; Ⓟ 792; Ⓒ 950

Balsam Lake; MCD-Town; POLK; ***252** F-2; 🅿; z 54810 & mail Saint Croix Falls z 54024; does not include the Village of Balsam Lake; Ⓟ 1,067; Ⓒ 1,384

Bancroft; RMC Place; PORTAGE; ▲ Pine Grove; **252** J-9; 🅿; z 54921; ● 230

Bangor; Inc. Place; LA CROSSE; **253** L-6; elev. 740ft./226m.; 🅿; z 54614; Ⓟ 1,076; Ⓒ 1,400

Bangor; MCD-Town; LA CROSSE; ***253** L-6; 🅿; z 54614 & mail Rockland z 54653; does not include the Village of Bangor; Ⓟ 598; Ⓒ 583

Baraboo; Inc. Place; ⊡ SAUK; **253** M-9; elev. 894ft./272m.; 🅿 🅷; z 53913; Ⓟ 9,203; Ⓒ 10,711

Baraboo; MCD-Town; SAUK; ***253** M-9; 🅿; z 53913 & mail North Freedom z 53951; does not include the City of Baraboo; Ⓟ 1,503; Ⓒ 1,828

Barksdale; RMC Place; BAYFIELD; ▲ Barksdale; ***252** C-6; mail Ashland z 54806; ● 25

Barksdale; MCD-Town; BAYFIELD; ***252** C-6; mail Ashland z 54806; Ⓟ 756; Ⓒ 801

Barnes; MCD-Town; BAYFIELD; ***252** D-5; 🅿; z 54873; Ⓟ 473; Ⓒ 610

Barneveld; Inc. Place; IOWA; **253** O-8; elev. 1,220ft./372m.; 🅿; z 53507; Ⓟ 660; Ⓒ 1,088

Barnum; RMC Place; CRAWFORD; ▲ Haney; **253** N-6; elev. 680ft./207m.; mail Gays Mills z 54631; ● 30

Barre; MCD-Town; LA CROSSE; ***253** L-5; mail La Crosse z 54601; Ⓟ 909; Ⓒ 1,014

Barre Mills; RMC Place; LA CROSSE; ▲ Barre; ***253** L-5; elev. 723ft./220m.; mail La Crosse z 54601; ● 50

Barron; Inc. Place; ⊡ BARRON; **252** G-4; elev. 1,115ft./340m.; 🅿 🅷; z 54812; Ⓟ 2,986; Ⓒ 3,248

Barron; MCD-Town; BARRON; ***252** F-4; 🅿; z 54812; does not include the City of Barron; Ⓟ 1,015; Ⓒ 1,014

BARRON; **252** F-4; Ⓟ 40,750; Ⓒ 44,963; ◆ 45,084

Barronett; RMC Place; BARRON; ▲ Lakeland; **252** F-3; 🅿; z 54813; ● 140

Barronett; MCD-Town; WASHBURN; ***252** F-3; mail Shell Lake z 54871; Ⓟ 373; Ⓒ 405

Barron Junction; RMC Place; BARRON; mail Barron z 54812; pop. incl. with Barron (Inc. Place)

Bartelme; MCD-Town; SHAWANO; ***252** H-11; mail Bowler z 54416; Ⓟ 618; Ⓒ 700

Barton; RMC Place; WASHINGTON; ***253** M-12; mail West Bend z 53090; pop. incl. with West Bend (Inc. Place)

Barton; MCD-Town; WASHINGTON; ***253** M-12; mail West Bend z 53090; Ⓟ 2,637; Ⓒ 2,546

Basco; RMC Place; DANE; ▲ Montrose; ***253** O-9; elev. 895ft./273m.; mail Belleville z 53508; ● 60

Bashaw; RMC Place; BURNETT; ▲ Dewey; ***252** E-3; elev. 1,061ft./323m.; mail Shell Lake z 54871, Spooner z 54801; ● 60

Bashaw; MCD-Town; WASHBURN; ***252** E-3; mail Shell Lake z 54871; Ⓟ 756; Ⓒ 921

Bass Bay; RMC Place; WAUKESHA; ★ **MILW**; mail Muskego z 53150; pop. incl. with Muskego (Inc. Place)

Bassett; RMC Place; KENOSHA; ▲ Randall; ***253** P-12; 🅿; ★ **CHI**; z 53101; ● 350

Bass Lake; MCD-Town; SAWYER; ***252** E-5; mail Hayward z 54843; Ⓟ 1,717; Ⓒ 2,244

Bass Lake; MCD-Town; WASHBURN; ***252** E-4; mail Springbrook z 54875; Ⓟ 337; Ⓒ 535

Basswood; RMC Place; RICHLAND; ▲ Eagle; ***253** N-7; elev. 732ft./223m.; mail Muscoda z 53573; rural

Batavia; RMC Place; SHEBOYGAN; ▲ Scott; ***253** M-13; mail Adell z 53001; ● 250

Bateman; RMC Place; CHIPPEWA; ▲ Lafayette; ***252** H-5; elev. 937ft./286m.; ★ **EAUC**; mail Chippewa Falls z 54729; ● 50

Bay City; Inc. Place; PIERCE; **252** I-2; elev. 692ft./211m.; 🅿; z 54723; Ⓟ 578; Ⓒ 465; Ⓡ 491

Bayfield; Inc. Place; BAYFIELD; **252** B-6; elev. 700ft./213m.; 🅿; z 54814; Ⓟ 686; Ⓒ 611

Bayfield; MCD-Town; BAYFIELD; ***252** B-6; 🅿; z 54814; does not include the City of Bayfield; Ⓟ 603; Ⓒ 625

BAYFIELD; **252** C-5; Ⓟ 14,008; Ⓒ 15,013; ◆ 15,116

Bay Settlement; RMC Place; BROWN; ▲ Scott; ***252** I-13; elev. 730ft./223m.; ★ **GRBY**; mail Green Bay z 54301; pop. incl. with Green Bay (Inc. Place)

Bayside; Inc. Place; MILWAUKEE, OZAUKEE; **251** B-6; elev. 650ft./198m.; 🅿; ★ **MILW**; z 53217; Ⓟ 4,789; Ⓒ 4,518

Bayview; MCD-Town; BAYFIELD; ***252** B-6; mail Milwaukee z 53207, z 53235, Washburn z 54891; Ⓟ 402; Ⓒ 491

Bay View; RMC Place; KEWAUNEE; ▲ Red River; ***252** I-13; 🅿; z 53207 & mail Luxemburg z 54217; rural

Bay View Saint Francis; RMC Place; MILWAUKEE; ★ **MILW**; mail Milwaukee z 53207, z 53235; pop. incl. with Milwaukee (Inc. Place)

Beachs Corners; RMC Place; TREMPEALEAU; ▲ Ettrick; ***253** K-5; mail Ettrick z 54627; ● 40

Bear Bluff; MCD-Town; JACKSON; ***253** K-7; mail Warrens z 54666; Ⓟ 149; Ⓒ 128

Bear Creek; Inc. Place; OUTAGAMIE; **252** I-11; elev. 817ft./249m.; 🅿; z 54922; Ⓟ 418; Ⓒ 415

Bear Creek; MCD-Town; SAUK; ***253** N-8; mail Plain z 53577; Ⓟ 521; Ⓒ 497

Bear Creek; MCD-Town; WAUPACA; ***252** I-11; 🅿; z 54922; Ⓟ 787; Ⓒ 838

Bear Lake; MCD-Town; BARRON; ***252** F-4; mail Rice Lake z 54868; Ⓟ 530; Ⓒ 587

Bear Lake; RMC Place; RUSK; ▲ Rusk; ***252** G-5; elev. 1,156ft./352m.; mail Chetek z 54728; rural

Bear Valley; RMC Place; RICHLAND; ▲ Ithaca; **253** N-8; mail Hillpoint z 53937; ● 25

Beaver; MCD-Town; CLARK; ***252** I-7; mail Loyal z 54446; Ⓟ 703; Ⓒ 854

Beaver; RMC Place; MARINETTE; ▲ Beaver; **252** G-13; elev. 667ft./203m.; 🅿; z 54114; ● 100

Beaver; MCD-Town; MARINETTE; ***252** G-13; 🅿; z 54114; Ⓟ 1,041; Ⓒ 1,123

Beaver; MCD-Town; POLK; ***252** F-3; mail Turtle Lake z 54889; Ⓟ 663; Ⓒ 753

Beaver Brook; RMC Place; WASHBURN; ▲ Beaver Brook; ***252** E-4; elev. 1,302ft./397m.; mail Shell Lake z 54871; rural

Beaver Brook; MCD-Town; WASHBURN; ***252** E-4; mail Shell Lake z 54871; Ⓟ 580; Ⓒ 643

Beaver Dam; Inc. Place; DODGE; **253** M-11; elev. 879ft./268m.; 🅿 🅷 ■; z 53916; Ⓟ 14,196; Ⓒ 15,169; ◆ 15,175

Beaver Dam; MCD-Town; DODGE; ***253** M-11; 🅿; z 53916; does not include the City of Beaver Dam; Ⓟ 3,097; Ⓒ 3,440

Beaver Edge; RMC Place; DODGE; ▲ Beaver Dam; ***253** M-11; elev. 889ft./271m.; mail Beaver Dam z 53916; ● 50

Beecher; RMC Place; MARINETTE; ▲ Beecher; ***252** F-13; elev. 970ft./296m.; mail Pembine z 54156; ● 35

Beecher; MCD-Town; MARINETTE; ***252** F-13; mail Pembine z 54156; Ⓟ 626; Ⓒ 783

Beecher Lake; RMC Place; MARINETTE; ▲ Beecher; ***252** F-13; mail Pembine z 54156; ● 30

Beechwood; RMC Place; SHEBOYGAN; ▲ Scott; ***253** M-13; mail Adell z 53001; ● 150

Beetown; RMC Place; GRANT; ▲ Beetown; **253** O-6; 🅿; z 53802; ● 180

Beetown; MCD-Town; GRANT; ***253** O-6; 🅿; z 53802; Ⓟ 782; Ⓒ 734

Belcrest; RMC Place; ROCK; ▲ Beloit; ***253** P-10; ★ **RKFD**; mail Beloit z 53511; ● 80

Beldenville; RMC Place; PIERCE; ▲ Trimbelle; **252** I-2; elev. 980ft./299m.; 🅿; z 54003; ● 150

Belgium; Inc. Place; OZAUKEE; **253** M-13; elev. 736ft./224m.; 🅿; z 53004; Ⓟ 928; Ⓒ 1,678

Belgium; MCD-Town; OZAUKEE; ***253** M-13; 🅿; z 53004; does not include the Village of Belgium; Ⓟ 1,405; Ⓒ 1,513

Bell; MCD-Town; BAYFIELD; ***252** B-5; mail Cornucopia z 54827; Ⓟ 237; Ⓒ 230

Bell Center; Inc. Place; CRAWFORD; **253** N-6; elev. 700ft./213m.; mail Gays Mills z 54631; Ⓟ 127; Ⓒ 116

Belle Plaine; RMC Place; SHAWANO; ▲ Belle Plaine; **252** I-11; mail Shawano z 54166; ● 50

Belle Plaine; MCD-Town; SHAWANO; ***252** I-11; mail Shawano z 54166; Ⓟ 1,792; Ⓒ 1,867

Belleville; Inc. Place; DANE, GREEN; **253** O-9; elev. 870ft./265m.; 🅿; z 53508; Ⓟ 1,456; Ⓒ 1,908

Bellevue; Inc. Place; BROWN; **252** J-13; incorporated February 14, 2003; not reported in 2000 Census; ● 13,300

Bellevue Town; CDP-Census Area Only; BROWN; ▲ Bellevue; ***252** J-13; ★ **GRBY**; mail Green Bay z 54311; Ⓟ 7,541; Ⓒ 11,828

Bell Heights; RMC Place; OUTAGAMIE; ***252** J-12; ★ **APP**; mail Appleton z 54911; pop. incl. with Appleton (Inc. Place)

Bellinger; RMC Place; TAYLOR; ▲ Roosevelt, Taft; ***252** H-6; elev. 1,292ft./394m.; mail Thorp z 54771

Belmont; Inc. Place; LAFAYETTE; **253** O-7; elev. 1,050ft./320m.; 🅿; z 53510; Ⓟ 823; Ⓒ 871

Belmont; MCD-Town; LAFAYETTE; ***253** O-7; 🅿; z 53510 & mail Platteville z 53818; does not include the Village of Belmont; Ⓟ 737; Ⓒ 676

Belmont; MCD-Town; PORTAGE; ***252** J-10; mail Almond z 54909; Ⓟ 540; Ⓒ 623

Beloit; Inc. Place; ROCK; **253** P-10; elev. 750ft./229m.; 🅿 🅷 🅲 1,329 ■; ★ **RKFD**; z 53511-12; Ⓟ 35,573; Ⓒ 35,775; ◆ 35,770

Beloit; MCD-Town; ROCK; ***253** P-10; 🅿 🅲 1,329; ★ **RKFD**; z 53511-12; does not include the City of Beloit; Ⓟ 6,778; Ⓒ 7,038

Belvidere; MCD-Town; BUFFALO; ***252** J-4; mail Alma z 54610; Ⓟ 505; Ⓒ 442

Benderville (Red Banks); RMC Place; BROWN; ▲ Scott; ***252** I-13; elev. 615ft./187m.; ★ **GRBY**; mail Green Bay z 54301; ● 100

Benet Lake; RMC Place; KENOSHA; ▲ Salem; ***253** P-13; 🅿; ★ **CHI**; z 53102; ● 30

Bennett; RMC Place; DOUGLAS; ▲ Bennett; **252** C-4; 🅿; z 54873; ● 40

Bennett; MCD-Town; DOUGLAS; ***252** C-4; 🅿; z 54873; Ⓟ 525; Ⓒ 622

Benoit; RMC Place; BAYFIELD; ▲ Mason, Keystone; **252** C-6; elev. 900ft./274m.; 🅿; z 54816; ● 30

Benton; Inc. Place; LAFAYETTE; **253** P-7; elev. 932ft./284m.; 🅿; z 53803; Ⓟ 898; Ⓒ 976

Benton; MCD-Town; LAFAYETTE; ***253** P-7; 🅿; z 53803; does not include the Village of Benton; Ⓟ 507; Ⓒ 469

Bergen; MCD-Town; MARATHON; ***252** I-9; mail Mosinee z 54455; Ⓟ 499; Ⓒ 615

Bergen; MCD-Town; VERNON; ***253** L-5; mail Stoddard z 54658; Ⓟ 1,223; Ⓒ 1,317

Berlin; Inc. Place; GREEN LAKE, WAUSHARA; **253** K-11; elev. 764ft./233m.; 🅿 🅷; z 54923; Ⓟ 5,371; Ⓒ 5,305

Berlin; MCD-Town; GREEN LAKE; ***253** K-11; 🅿; z 54923; does not include the City of Berlin; Ⓟ 996; Ⓒ 1,145

Berlin; MCD-Town; MARATHON; ***252** H-9; mail Wausau z 54401; Ⓟ 849; Ⓒ 887

Bern; MCD-Town; MARATHON; ***252** H-8; mail Athens z 54411; Ⓟ 550; Ⓒ 562

Berry; MCD-Town; DANE; ***253** N-9; mail Cross Plains z 53528; Ⓟ 1,248; Ⓒ 1,084

Bethel; RMC Place; WOOD; ▲ Richfield; **252** I-8; elev. 1,236ft./377m.; mail Arpin z 54410; ● 100

Bethesda; RMC Place; WAUKESHA; ▲ Genesee; ***253** O-12; elev. 839ft./256m.; ★ **MILW**; mail Waukesha z 53189; rural

Bevent; RMC Place; MARATHON; ▲ Bevent, Reid; **252** I-9; mail Hatley z 54440; ● 110

Bevent; MCD-Town; MARATHON; ***252** I-9; mail Hatley z 54440; Ⓟ 978; Ⓒ 1,126

Big Bend; MCD-Town; RUSK; ***252** G-5; mail Bruce z 54819; Ⓟ 386; Ⓒ 402

Big Bend; Inc. Place; WAUKESHA; **253** O-12; elev. 780ft./238m.; 🅿; ★ **MILW**; z 53103; Ⓟ 1,299; Ⓒ 1,278

Big Falls; MCD-Town; RUSK; ***252** F-6; mail Ladysmith z 54848; Ⓟ 107; Ⓒ 107

Big Falls; Inc. Place; WAUPACA; **252** I-10; elev. 900ft./274m.; 🅿; z 54926; Ⓟ 75; Ⓒ 85

Big Flats; RMC Place; ADAMS; ▲ Big Flats; ***253** K-8; elev. 1,000ft./305m.; mail Arkdale z 54613, Friendship z 53934

Big Flats; MCD-Town; ADAMS; ***253** K-8; mail Arkdale z 54613; Ⓟ 731; Ⓒ 946

Big Patch; RMC Place; GRANT; ▲ Smelser; ***253** P-7; mail Platteville z 53818; ● 90

Big Spring; RMC Place; ADAMS; ▲ New Haven; **253** L-9; mail Grand Marsh z 53936; ● 40

Big Suamico; BROWN; see Suamico (Inc. Place)

Billings Park; RMC Place; DOUGLAS; ***252** B-3; ★ **DUL**; mail Superior z 54880; pop. incl. with Superior (Inc. Place)

Binghamton; RMC Place; OUTAGAMIE; ▲ Black Creek; ***252** J-12; elev. 827ft./252m.; mail Black Creek z 54106; ● 30

Birch; RMC Place; ASHLAND; ▲ Sanborn; ***252** C-7; mail Saxon z 54559; rural

Birch; MCD-Town; LINCOLN; ***252** G-9; mail Irma z 54442; Ⓟ 675; Ⓒ 801

Birch Creek; MCD-Town; CHIPPEWA; ***252** G-5; mail Holcombe z 54745; Ⓟ 500; Ⓒ 520

Birchwood; Inc. Place; WASHBURN; **252** F-4; elev. 1,264ft./385m.; 🅿; z 54817 & mail Edgewater z 54834, Mikana z 54857; Ⓟ 443; Ⓒ 518

Birchwood; MCD-Town; WASHBURN; ***252** E-4; 🅿; z 54817 & mail Edgewater z 54834, Mikana z 54857; does not include the Village of Birchwood; Ⓟ 329; Ⓒ 453

Birchwood Lake; RMC Place; FOND DU LAC; ▲ Osceola; ***253** L-12; elev. 1,050ft./320m.; mail Campbellsport z 53010; ● 50

Birnamwood; Inc. Place; SHAWANO, MARATHON; **252** H-10; elev. 1,300ft./396m.; 🅿; z 54414; Ⓟ 693; Ⓒ 795

Birnamwood; MCD-Town; SHAWANO; ***252** H-10; 🅿; z 54414; does not include the Village of Birnamwood; Ⓟ 632; Ⓒ 711

Biron; Inc. Place; WOOD; **252** J-9; elev. 1,026ft./313m.; mail Wisconsin Rapids z 54494; Ⓟ 794; Ⓒ 915

Black Brook; MCD-Town; POLK; ***252** G-2; mail Clear Lake z 54005; Ⓟ 964; Ⓒ 1,208

Black Creek; Inc. Place; OUTAGAMIE; **252** J-12; elev. 790ft./241m.; 🅿; z 54106; Ⓟ 1,152; Ⓒ 1,192

Black Creek; MCD-Town; OUTAGAMIE; ***252** J-12; 🅿; z 54106; does not include the Village of Black Creek; Ⓟ 1,169; Ⓒ 1,268

Black Earth; Inc. Place; DANE; **253** N-9; elev. 818ft./249m.; 🅿; z 53515; Ⓟ 1,248; Ⓒ 1,320

Black Earth; MCD-Town; DANE; ***253** N-9; 🅿; z 53515 & mail Mazomanie z 53560; does not include the Village of Black Earth; Ⓟ 365; Ⓒ 449

Black Hawk; RMC Place; SAUK; ▲ Troy; **253** N-8; elev. 775ft./236m.; mail Spring Green z 53588; ● 80

Black River; RMC Place; SHEBOYGAN; ▲ Wilson; ***253** L-14; elev. 590ft./180m.; ★ **SHEB**; mail Sheboygan z 53081; ● 700

Black River Falls; Inc. Place; ⊡ JACKSON; **252** J-6; elev. 796ft./243m.; 🅿 🅷; z 54615; Ⓟ 3,490; Ⓒ 3,618

Blackwell; RMC Place; FOREST; ▲ Blackwell; **252** F-11; mail Laona z 54541; ● 90

Blackwell; MCD-Town; FOREST; ***252** F-11; mail Laona z 54541; Ⓟ 384; Ⓒ 347

Black Wolf; MCD-Town; WINNEBAGO; ***253** K-12; ★ **OSH**; mail Oshkosh z 54901; Ⓟ 2,154; Ⓒ 2,330

Blaine; MCD-Town; BURNETT; ***252** D-3; mail Danbury z 54830; Ⓟ 172; Ⓒ 224

Blaine; RMC Place; PORTAGE; ▲ Belmont; ***252** J-10; mail Almond z 54909; ● 40

Blair; Inc. Place; TREMPEALEAU; **252** J-5; elev. 859ft./262m.; 🅿; z 54616; Ⓟ 1,126; Ⓒ 1,273

Blanchard; MCD-Town; LAFAYETTE; ***253** O-8; mail Blanchardville z 53516; Ⓟ 220; Ⓒ 261

Blanchardville; Inc. Place; LAFAYETTE, IOWA; **253** O-8; elev. 833ft./254m.; 🅿; z 53516; Ⓟ 802; Ⓒ 806

Blenker; RMC Place; WOOD; ▲ Milladore; **252** I-8; 🅿; z 54415; ● 120

Bloom; MCD-Town; RICHLAND; ***253** M-7; mail La Farge z 54639; Ⓟ 540; Ⓒ 487

Bloom City; RMC Place; RICHLAND; ▲ Bloom; **253** M-7; 🅿; z 54634; ● 80

Bloomer; Inc. Place; CHIPPEWA; **252** H-5; elev. 1,011ft./308m.; 🅿 🅷; z 54724; Ⓟ 3,085; Ⓒ 3,347

Bloomer; MCD-Town; CHIPPEWA; ***252** G-5; 🅿; z 54724; does not include the City of Bloomer; Ⓟ 880; Ⓒ 926

Bloomfield; MCD-Town; WALWORTH; ***253** P-12; mail Genoa City z 53128; Ⓟ 3,723; Ⓒ 5,537

Bloomfield; MCD-Town; WAUSHARA; ***253** K-11; mail Pine River z 54965; Ⓟ 922; Ⓒ 1,018

Bloomingdale; RMC Place; VERNON; ▲ Clinton; **253** L-6; mail Westby z 54667; ● 70

Blooming Grove; MCD-Town; DANE; ***253** N-10; ★ **MAD**; mail Madison z 53701; Ⓟ 2,079; Ⓒ 1,768

Bloomington; Inc. Place; GRANT; **253** O-6; elev. 960ft./293m.; 🅿; z 53804; Ⓟ 776; Ⓒ 701

Bloomington; MCD-Town; GRANT; ***253** O-6; 🅿; z 53804 & mail Glen Haven z 53810; does not include the Village of Bloomington; Ⓟ 364; Ⓒ 399

Bloomville; RMC Place; LINCOLN; ▲ Schley, Russell; **252** G-9; elev. 1,434ft./437m.; mail Gleason z 54435; ● 35

Blueberry; RMC Place; DOUGLAS; ▲ Maple; ***252** C-4; elev. 1,137ft./347m.; mail Maple z 54854; ● 40

Blue Mounds; Inc. Place; DANE; **253** O-8; elev. 1,261ft./384m.; 🅿; z 53517; Ⓟ 446; Ⓒ 708

Blue Mounds; MCD-Town; DANE; ***253** O-9; 🅿; z 53517 & mail Mount Horeb z 53572; does not include the Village of Blue Mounds; Ⓟ 667; Ⓒ 842

Blue River; Inc. Place; GRANT; **253** N-7; elev. 676ft./206m.; 🅿; z 53518; Ⓟ 438; Ⓒ 429

Bluff Siding; RMC Place; BUFFALO; ▲ Buffalo; **253** K-4; mail Fountain City z 54629; ● 40

Bluffview; RMC Place; SAUK; ▲ Sumpter; ***253** M-9; mail Baraboo z 53913; ● 400

Boardman; RMC Place; ST. CROIX; ▲ Richmond; **252** H-2; elev. 947ft./289m.; mail Hudson z 54016, New Richmond z 54017; ● 100

Boaz; Inc. Place; RICHLAND; **253** M-7; elev. 740ft./226m.; mail Muscoda z 53573, Richland Center z 53581; Ⓟ 131; Ⓒ 137

Bohners Lake; CDP-Census Area Only; RACINE; ▲ Burlington; ***253** P-12; mail Burlington z 53105; Ⓟ 1,553; summer pop. 2,500; Ⓒ 1,952

Bolt; RMC Place; KEWAUNEE; ▲ Franklin; ***252** J-13; mail Denmark z 54208; rural

Boltonville; RMC Place; WASHINGTON; ▲ Farmington; **253** M-13; elev. 869ft./265m.; mail Kewaskum z 53040; ● 200

Bonduel; Inc. Place; SHAWANO; **252** I-12; elev. 875ft./267m.; 🅿; z 54107, z 54182; Ⓟ 1,210; Ⓒ 1,416

Bone Lake; MCD-Town; POLK; ***252** F-3; mail Frederic z 54837; Ⓟ 503; Ⓒ 710

Borth; RMC Place; WAUSHARA; ▲ Poysippi; **253** K-11; mail Berlin z 54923; ● 35

Boscobel; Inc. Place; GRANT; **253** N-6; elev. 680ft./207m.; 🅿 🅷; z 53805; Ⓟ 2,706; Ⓒ 3,047

Boscobel; MCD-Town; GRANT; ***253** N-6; 🅿; z 53805; does not include the City of Boscobel; Ⓟ 426; Ⓒ 433

Bosstown; RMC Place; RICHLAND; ▲ Sylvan; ***253** M-7; mail Richland Center z 53581; ● 20

Boulder Junction; RMC Place; VILAS; ▲ Boulder Junction; **252** D-9; 🅿; z 54512; ● 460

Boulder Junction; MCD-Town; VILAS; ***252** D-9; 🅿; z 54512; Ⓟ 884; Ⓒ 958

Bovina; MCD-Town; OUTAGAMIE; ***252** J-11; mail Shiocton z 54170; Ⓟ 957; Ⓒ 1,130

Bowers; RMC Place; WALWORTH; ▲ Lafayette; ***253** P-12; mail Elkhorn z 53121; rural

Bowler; Inc. Place; SHAWANO; **252** H-10; elev. 1,080ft./329m.; 🅿; z 54416; Ⓟ 279; Ⓒ 343

Boyceville; Inc. Place; DUNN; **252** H-3; elev. 948ft./289m.; 🅿; z 54725; Ⓟ 913; Ⓒ 1,043

Boyd; Inc. Place; CHIPPEWA; **252** H-6; elev. 1,105ft./337m.; 🅿; z 54726; Ⓟ 683; Ⓒ 680

Boydtown; RMC Place; CRAWFORD; ▲ Marietta; ***253** N-6; mail Wauzeka z 53826; ● 35

Brackett; RMC Place; EAU CLAIRE; ▲ Washington; **252** I-5; mail Fall Creek z 54742; ● 120

Bradford; MCD-Town; ROCK; ***253** P-11; mail Avalon z 53505; Ⓟ 1,030; Ⓒ 1,007

Bradley; RMC Place; LINCOLN; ▲ Bradley; **252** F-9; elev. 1,458ft./444m.; mail Tomahawk z 54487; ● 60

Bradley; MCD-Town; LINCOLN; ***252** F-9; mail Tomahawk z 54487; Ⓟ 2,231; Ⓒ 2,573

Branch; RMC Place; MANITOWOC; ▲ Manitowoc Rapids; **253** K-13; elev. 750ft./229m.; 🅿; ★ **MNTW**; z 54247; ● 160

Brandon; Inc. Place; FOND DU LAC; **253** L-11; elev. 999ft./304m.; 🅿; z 53919; Ⓟ 872; Ⓒ 912

Branstad; RMC Place; BURNETT; ▲ Grantsburg; ***252** E-2; mail Grantsburg z 54840; ● 30

Brant; RMC Place; CALUMET; ▲ Chilton; ***253** K-12; elev. 933ft./284m.; mail Chilton z 53014; rural

Brantwood; RMC Place; PRICE; ▲ Knox; **252** F-8; elev. 690ft./210m.; 🅿; z 54513; ● 50

Braund Addition; RMC Place; MONROE; ▲ Tomah; ***253** K-7; elev. 1,040ft./317m.; mail Tomah z 54660; ● 70

Brazeau; MCD-Town; OCONTO; ***252** H-12; mail Pound z 54161; Ⓟ 1,169; Ⓒ 1,408

Breed; RMC Place; OCONTO; ▲ Breed; **252** H-12; mail Suring z 54174; ● 35

Breed; MCD-Town; OCONTO; ***252** H-12; mail Suring z 54174; Ⓟ 564; Ⓒ 657

Briarcrest Estates; RMC Place; ROCK; ▲ Harmony; ***253** O-11; elev. 920ft./280m.; ★ **JNSV**; mail Janesville z 53545; pop. incl. with Janesville (Inc. Place)

Briarton; RMC Place; SHAWANO; ▲ Lessor; **252** I-12; elev. 819ft./250m.; mail Pulaski z 54162; ● 30

Briarwood; RMC Place; DANE; ***253** O-9; elev. 1,000ft./305m.; ★ **MAD**; mail Oregon z 53575; pop. incl. with Fitchburg (Inc. Place)

Brice Prairie; CDP-Census Area Only; LA CROSSE; ▲ Onalaska; ***253** K-5; ★ **LACRO**; mail Onalaska z 54650; Ⓟ 1,031; Ⓒ 1,804

Brickson Park; RMC Place; DANE; ▲ Dunn; ***253** O-10; elev. 850ft./259m.; ★ **MAD**; mail Mc Farland z 53558; summer pop. 250; ● 120

Bridge Creek; MCD-Town; EAU CLAIRE; ***252** I-5; mail Augusta z 54722; Ⓟ 1,440; Ⓒ 1,844

Bridgeport; RMC Place; CRAWFORD; ▲ Bridgeport; **253** O-5; elev. 768ft./234m.; mail Prairie du Chien z 53821; ● 60

Bridgeport; MCD-Town; CRAWFORD; ***253** N-5; mail Prairie du Chien z 53821; Ⓟ 753; Ⓒ 946

Briggsville; RMC Place; MARQUETTE; ▲ Douglas; **253** L-9; 🅿; z 53920; ● 380

Brigham; MCD-Town; IOWA; ***253** O-8; mail Barneveld z 53507; Ⓟ 692; Ⓒ 908

Brighton; RMC Place; KENOSHA; ▲ Brighton; ***253** P-13; mail Kansasville z 53139; ● 80

Brighton; MCD-Town; KENOSHA; ***253** P-13; mail Kansasville z 53139; Ⓟ 1,264; Ⓒ 1,450

Brighton; MCD-Town; MARATHON; ***252** I-7; mail Unity z 54488; Ⓟ 610; Ⓒ 611

Brill; RMC Place; BARRON; ▲ Oak Grove; **252** F-4; 🅿; z 54818; ● 130

Brillion; Inc. Place; CALUMET; **253** K-13; elev. 820ft./250m.; 🅿; z 54110; Ⓟ 2,840; Ⓒ 2,937

Brillion; MCD-Town; CALUMET; ***253** K-13; 🅿; z 54110; does not include the City of Brillion; Ⓟ 1,300; Ⓒ 1,438

Bristol; MCD-Town; DANE; ***253** N-10; mail Sun Prairie z 53590; Ⓟ 1,850; Ⓒ 2,698

Bristol; RMC Place; KENOSHA; ▲ Bristol; **253** P-13; 🅿; ★ **CHI**; z 53104; ● 680

Bristol; MCD-Town; KENOSHA; ***253** P-13; 🅿; ★ **CHI**; z 53104; Ⓟ 3,968; Ⓒ 4,538

Bristow; RMC Place; VERNON; ▲ Sterling; ***253** M-6; elev. 748ft./228m.; mail Viroqua z 54665; rural

Brockway; RMC Place; JACKSON; mail Black River Falls z 54615; ● 500

Brockway; MCD-Town; JACKSON; ***252** J-6; mail Black River Falls z 54615; Ⓟ 1,222; Ⓒ 2,580

Brodhead; Inc. Place; GREEN; **253** P-10; elev. 790ft./241m.; 🅿; z 53520; Ⓟ 3,165; Ⓒ 3,180

Brodtville; RMC Place; GRANT; ▲ Wyalusing; ***253** O-5; mail Bagley z 53801; rural

Brokaw; Inc. Place; MARATHON; **252** H-9; elev. 1,220ft./372m.; 🅿; z 54417; Ⓟ 224; Ⓒ 107

Brookfield; Inc. Place; WAUKESHA; **253** N-13; elev. 828ft./252m.; 🅿 🅷 ■; ★ **MILW**; z 53005, z 53008, z 53045, z 53072; Ⓟ 35,184; Ⓒ 38,649; ◆ 38,268

Brookfield; MCD-Town; WAUKESHA; ***253** N-12; 🅿; ★ **MILW**; z 53005, z 53008, z 53045, z 53072 & mail Waukesha z 53189; does not include the City of Brookfield; Ⓟ 4,232; Ⓒ 6,390

Brookhaven; RMC Place; WOOD; ▲ Grand Rapids; ***252** J-9; elev. 1,025ft./312m.; mail Wisconsin Rapids z 54494; ● 60

Brooklyn; Inc. Place; GREEN, DANE; **253** O-10; elev. 980ft./299m.; 🅿; z 53521; Ⓟ 789; Ⓒ 916

Brooklyn; MCD-Town; GREEN; ***253** O-9; 🅿; z 53521; does not include the Village of Brooklyn; Ⓟ 764; Ⓒ 944

Brooklyn; MCD-Town; GREEN LAKE; ***253** L-10; mail Green Lake z 54941; Ⓟ 1,798; Ⓒ 1,904

Brooklyn; MCD-Town; WASHBURN; ***252** E-4; mail Trego z 54888; Ⓟ 276; Ⓒ 281

Brooks; RMC Place; ADAMS; ▲ New Chester; **253** L-9; elev. 957ft./292m.; 🅿; z 53952; ● 150

Brookside; RMC Place; ADAMS; ▲ Easton; ***253** L-8; mail Adams z 53910; ● 80

Brookside; RMC Place; OCONTO; ▲ Pensaukee; **252** I-13; mail Abrams z 54101; ● 75

Brooks Ridge; RMC Place; DANE; ▲ Bristol; ***253** N-10; mail Sun Prairie z 53590; ● 90

Brothertown; RMC Place; CALUMET; ▲ Brothertown; **253** K-12; mail Chilton z 53014; ● 200

Brothertown; MCD-Town; CALUMET; ***253** K-12; mail Chilton z 53014; Ⓟ 1,409; Ⓒ 1,404

BROWN; **252** J-13; Ⓟ 194,594; Ⓒ 226,778; Ⓡ 226,658; ◆ 247,919

Brown Deer; Inc. Place; MILWAUKEE; **251** B-5; elev. 679ft./207m.; 🅿; ★ **MILW**; z 53209, z 53223; Ⓟ 12,236; Ⓒ 12,170

Browning; MCD-Town; TAYLOR; ***252** G-7; mail Medford z 54451; Ⓟ 740; Ⓒ 850

Browns Lake (Cedar Park); CDP-Census Area Only; RACINE; ▲ Burlington; ***253** P-12; mail Burlington z 53105; Ⓟ 1,725; Ⓒ 1,933

Brownsville; Inc. Place; DODGE; **253** M-12; elev. 1,000ft./305m.; 🅿; z 53006; Ⓟ 415; Ⓒ 570

Browntown; Inc. Place; GREEN; **253** P-9; elev. 850ft./259m.; 🅿; z 53522; Ⓟ 256; Ⓒ 252

Bruce; Inc. Place; RUSK; **252** F-5; elev. 1,106ft./337m.; 🅿; z 54819; Ⓟ 844; Ⓒ 787

Entries in **UPPERCASE** are counties.
Entries in **bold** have populations of 2,500 or more.
Names in parentheses are alternate names.

Inc. Place	Incorporated Place
RMC Place	Rand McNally Designated Place
CDP	Census Designated Place
MCD	Minor Civil Division

⊡	County Seat
▲	Minor Civil Division
elev.	Elevation
🅿	Post Office
🅷	Hospital
🅲	College
■	Principal Business Center
★	Ranally Metro Area (RMA) Abbreviation
z	Zip Code(s)
Ⓟ	Previous Census Population
Ⓡ	Revised Census Population
Ⓐ	Annexation Population
●	Rand McNally Population Estimate
Ⓒ	Final Census Population
Ⓢ	Special Census Population
◆	Estimated Population

For additional definitions see Glossary, Volume 1, and Introduction, Volume 2.

Bruemmerville; RMC Place; KEWAUNEE; ▲ Ahnapee; ***252** I-14; mail Algoma z 54201; ● 30
Brule; RMC Place; DOUGLAS; ▲ Brule; **252** C-4; 🅿; z 54820; ● 280
Brule; MCD-Town; DOUGLAS; ***252** C-4; 🅿; z 54820; Ⓟ 527; Ⓒ 591
Brunswick; MCD-Town; EAU CLAIRE; ***252** I-4; mail Eau Claire z 54701; Ⓟ 1,506; Ⓒ 1,598
Brushville; RMC Place; WAUSHARA; ▲ Bloomfield; ***253** K-10; mail Pine River z 54965; rural
Brussels; RMC Place; DOOR; ▲ Brussels; **252** I-14; elev. 754ft./230m.; 🅿; z 54204; ● 150
Brussels; MCD-Town; DOOR; ***252** I-14; 🅿; z 54204; Ⓟ 1,042; Ⓒ 1,112
Bryant; RMC Place; LANGLADE; ▲ Price; **252** G-10; elev. 1,586ft./483m.; 🅿; z 54418; ● 100
Buchanan; MCD-Town; OUTAGAMIE; ***252** J-12; ★ **APP**; mail Appleton z 54911; Ⓟ 2,484; Ⓒ 5,827
Buck Creek; RMC Place; RICHLAND; ▲ Rockbridge; ***253** M-7; mail Richland Center z 53581; rural
Buckhorn Corner; RMC Place; DODGE; ▲ Trenton; ***253** M-11; elev. 970ft./296m.; mail Beaver Dam z 53916; rural
Buckman; RMC Place; BROWN; ▲ Eaton; ***252** J-13; elev. 831ft./253m.; mail Denmark z 54208; ● 30
Budd; RMC Place; VERNON; ▲ Jefferson; ***253** M-6; mail Viroqua z 54665; ● 35
Budsin; RMC Place; MARQUETTE; ▲ Crystal Lake; ***253** L-10; elev. 822ft./251m.; mail Neshkoro z 54960; ● 40
Buena Park; RMC Place; RACINE; ▲ Waterford; ***253** O-12; ★ **MILW**; mail Waterford z 53185; ● 500
Buena Vista; MCD-Town; PORTAGE; ***252** J-9; mail Plover z 54467; Ⓟ 1,170; Ⓒ 1,187
Buena Vista; MCD-Town; RICHLAND; ***253** N-7; mail Lone Rock z 53556; Ⓟ 1,547; Ⓒ 1,575
Buena Vista; RMC Place; WAUKESHA; ▲ Delafield; ***253** N-12; ★ **MILW**; mail Pewaukee z 53072; ● 350
Buffalo; BUFFALO; see Buffalo City (Inc. Place)
Buffalo; MCD-Town; BUFFALO; ***253** K-4; mail Fountain City z 54629; does not include the City of Buffalo; Ⓟ 686; Ⓒ 667
Buffalo; MCD-Town; MARQUETTE; ***253** L-10; mail Montello z 53949; Ⓟ 792; Ⓒ 1,085
BUFFALO; **252** J-4; Ⓟ 13,584; Ⓒ 13,804; ◆ 13,794
Buffalo City (Buffalo); Inc. Place; BUFFALO; **252** J-4; elev. 672ft./205m.; 🅿; z 54622; Ⓟ 915; Ⓒ 1,040
Buffalo Estates; RMC Place; MARQUETTE; ▲ Packwaukee; ***253** L-9; mail Montello z 53949; ● 25
Bundy; RMC Place; LINCOLN; ▲ Harrison; ***252** F-9; mail Gleason z 54435
Bunker Hill; RMC Place; RICHLAND; ▲ Westford; ***253** M-7; elev. 1,257ft./383m.; mail Cazenovia z 53924; rural
Burke; RMC Place; DANE; ▲ Burke; **253** R-9; elev. 895ft./273m.; ★ **MAD**; mail Sun Prairie z 53590; ● 100
Burke; MCD-Town; DANE; ***253** N-10; ★ **MAD**; mail Sun Prairie z 53590; Ⓟ 3,004; Ⓒ 2,990
Burkhardt; RMC Place; ST. CROIX; ▲ St. Joseph; **252** H-2; ★ **MPLS-**; mail Hudson z 54016; ● 60
Burlington; Inc. Place; RACINE, WALWORTH; **253** P-12; elev. 766ft./233m.; 🅿 🅷; z 53105; Ⓟ 8,855; Ⓒ 9,936
Burlington; MCD-Town; RACINE; ***253** P-12; 🅿; z 53105; does not include the City of Burlington; Ⓟ 5,833; Ⓒ 6,384
Burnett; RMC Place; DODGE; ▲ Burnett; **253** M-11; elev. 875ft./267m.; 🅿; z 53922; ● 300
Burnett; MCD-Town; DODGE; ***253** M-11; 🅿; z 53922; Ⓟ 915; Ⓒ 919
BURNETT; **252** E-2; Ⓟ 13,084; Ⓒ 15,674; ◆ 16,285
Burnett Corners; RMC Place; DODGE; ▲ Burnett; ***253** M-11; elev. 920ft./280m.; mail Burnett z 53922; rural
Burns; RMC Place; LA CROSSE; ▲ Burns; ***253** K-6; elev. 800ft./244m.; mail Bangor z 54614
Burns; MCD-Town; LA CROSSE; ***253** K-6; mail Bangor z 54614; Ⓟ 977; Ⓒ 979
Burnside; MCD-Town; TREMPEALEAU; ***252** J-4; mail Independence z 54747; Ⓟ 653; Ⓒ 529
Burr Oak; RMC Place; LA CROSSE; ▲ Farmington; ***253** K-5; mail Mindoro z 54644
Burton; RMC Place; GRANT; ▲ Waterloo; **253** P-6; mail Potosi z 53820; ● 30
Busseyville; RMC Place; JEFFERSON; ▲ Sumner; ***253** O-10; elev. 796ft./243m.; mail Edgerton z 53534; ● 60
Butler; MCD-Town; CLARK; ***252** I-6; mail Thorp z 54771; Ⓟ 91; Ⓒ 88
Butler; Inc. Place; WAUKESHA; **251** D-4; elev. 745ft./227m.; 🅿; ★ **MILW**; z 53007; Ⓟ 2,079; Ⓒ 1,881
Butte des Morts; RMC Place; WINNEBAGO; ▲ Winneconne; **253** K-11; 🅿; ★ **OSH**; z 54927; ● 570
Butternut; Inc. Place; ASHLAND; **252** E-7; elev. 1,503ft./458m.; 🅿; z 54514; Ⓟ 416; Ⓒ 407
Butternut Island; RMC Place; DODGE; ▲ Hubbard; ***253** M-11; mail Juneau z 53039; ● 80
Byrds Creek; RMC Place; RICHLAND; ▲ Richwood; **253** N-7; mail Blue River z 53518; ● 35
Byron; RMC Place; FOND DU LAC; ▲ Byron; **253** L-12; 🅿; z 53006; ● 80
Byron; MCD-Town; FOND DU LAC; ***253** L-12; 🅿; z 53006; Ⓟ 1,634; Ⓒ 1,550
Byron; MCD-Town; MONROE; ***253** K-7; mail Camp Douglas z 54618; Ⓟ 1,250; Ⓒ 1,394

C

Cable; RMC Place; BAYFIELD; ▲ Cable; **252** D-5; elev. 1,370ft./418m.; 🅿; z 54821; ● 300
Cable; MCD-Town; BAYFIELD; ***252** D-5; 🅿; z 54821; Ⓟ 817; Ⓒ 836
Caddy Vista; RMC Place; RACINE; ▲ Caledonia; **251** J-6; elev. 700ft./213m.; ★ **MILW**; mail Caledonia z 53108; ● 900
Cadiz; MCD-Town; GREEN; ***253** P-9; mail Browntown z 53522; Ⓟ 913; Ⓒ 863
Cadott; Inc. Place; CHIPPEWA; **252** H-5; elev. 979ft./298m.; 🅿; z 54727; Ⓟ 1,328; Ⓒ 1,345
Cady; MCD-Town; ST. CROIX; ***252** H-3; mail Wilson z 54027; Ⓟ 643; Ⓒ 710
Cainville; RMC Place; ROCK; ▲ Magnolia; ***253** P-10; mail Evansville z 53536; rural
Calamine; RMC Place; LAFAYETTE; ▲ Willow Springs; **253** O-8; mail Mineral Point z 53565; ● 70
Calamus; MCD-Town; DODGE; ***253** M-11; mail Beaver Dam z 53916; Ⓟ 1,009; Ⓒ 1,005
Caldwell; RMC Place; RACINE; ▲ Waterford; ***253** O-12; elev. 845ft./258m.; ★ **MILW**; mail Mukwonago z 53149; ● 120
Caledonia; MCD-Town; COLUMBIA; ***253** M-9; mail Portage z 53901; Ⓟ 1,031; Ⓒ 1,171
Caledonia; Inc. Place; RACINE; ▲ Caledonia; ***253** O-13; elev. 730ft./223m.; 🅿; ★ **MILW**; z 53108; ● 24,400; ◆ 24,781
Caledonia; MCD-Town; RACINE; ***253** O-13; 🅿; ★ **MILW**; z 53108; incorporated as Caledonia village November 16, 2005; Ⓟ 20,999; Ⓒ 23,614; ◆ 24,781
Caledonia; MCD-Town; TREMPEALEAU; ***253** K-5; mail Galesville z 54630; Ⓟ 555; Ⓒ 759
Caledonia; MCD-Town; WAUPACA; ***252** J-11; mail Fremont z 54940; Ⓟ 1,177; Ⓒ 1,466
Calhoun; RMC Place; WAUKESHA; ***253** N-13; ★ **MILW**; mail New Berlin z 53151; pop. incl. with New Berlin (Inc. Place)
Callon; RMC Place; MARATHON; ▲ Weston; ***252** H-9; elev. 1,238ft./377m.; ★ **WAUS**; mail Schofield z 54476; pop. incl. with Weston (Inc. Place)
Calumet; MCD-Town; FOND DU LAC; ***253** K-12; mail Malone z 53049; Ⓟ 1,444; Ⓒ 1,514
CALUMET; **253** K-12; Ⓟ 34,291; Ⓒ 40,631; ◆ 44,100
Calumet Harbor; FOND DU LAC; see Pipe (RMC Place)
Calumetville; RMC Place; FOND DU LAC; ▲ Calumet; **253** K-12; elev. 802ft./244m.; mail Malone z 53049; ● 80
Calvary; RMC Place; FOND DU LAC; ▲ Marshfield; ***253** L-12; elev. 944ft./288m.; mail Mount Calvary z 53057; ● 80
Calvert; RMC Place; LA CROSSE; ▲ Shelby; ***253** L-5; ★ **LACRO**; pop. incl. with La Crosse (Inc. Place)
Cambria; Inc. Place; COLUMBIA; **253** M-10; elev. 868ft./265m.; 🅿; z 53923; Ⓟ 768; Ⓒ 792
Cambridge; Inc. Place; DANE, JEFFERSON; **253** O-10; elev. 850ft./259m.; 🅿; z 53523; Ⓟ 963; Ⓒ 1,101
Cameron; Inc. Place; BARRON; **252** G-4; elev. 1,097ft./334m.; 🅿; z 54822; Ⓟ 1,273; Ⓒ 1,546
Cameron; MCD-Town; WOOD; ***252** I-8; mail Marshfield z 54449; Ⓟ 522; Ⓒ 510
Campbell; MCD-Town; LA CROSSE; ***253** L-5; ★ **LACRO**; mail La Crosse z 54601; Ⓟ 4,478; Ⓒ 4,410
Campbellsport; Inc. Place; FOND DU LAC; **253** M-12; elev. 1,040ft./317m.; 🅿; z 53010; Ⓟ 1,732; Ⓒ 1,913
Camp Douglas; Inc. Place; JUNEAU; **253** L-7; elev. 933ft./284m.; 🅿; z 54618, z 54637; Ⓟ 512; Ⓒ 592
Campia; RMC Place; BARRON; ▲ Rice Lake, Doyle; **252** F-4; mail Rice Lake z 54868; ● 50
Camp Lake; CDP; KENOSHA; ▲ Salem; ***253** P-13; elev. 776ft./237m.; 🅿; ★ **CHI**; z 53109 & mail Trevor z 53179; Ⓟ 2,291; Ⓒ 3,255
Camp Leonard; RMC Place; DANE; ▲ Dunn; ***253** O-10; elev. 850ft./259m.; ★ **MAD**; mail Mc Farland z 53558; summer pop. 100; ● 40
Canton; RMC Place; BARRON; ▲ Sumner; **252** F-4; elev. 1,105ft./337m.; 🅿; z 54868; ● 100
Canton; MCD-Town; BUFFALO; ***252** I-4; mail Durand z 54736; Ⓟ 309; Ⓒ 304
Capitol; RMC Place; DANE; ***253** N-10; ★ **MAD**; mail Madison z 53701, z 53703; pop. incl. with Madison (Inc. Place)
Carey; MCD-Town; IRON; ***252** D-7; mail Hurley z 54534; Ⓟ 175; Ⓒ 191
Carlsville; RMC Place; DOOR; ▲ Sevastopol, Egg Harbor; **252** B-13; elev. 735ft./224m.; mail Sturgeon Bay z 54235; ● 50
Carlton; MCD-Town; KEWAUNEE; ***252** J-14; mail Kewaunee z 54216; Ⓟ 1,041; Ⓒ 1,000
Carnot; RMC Place; DOOR; ▲ Clay Banks; ***252** I-14; elev. 678ft./207m.; mail Forestville z 54213
Carol Beach; KENOSHA; see Carol Beach Estates (RMC Place)
Carol Beach Estates (Carol Beach); RMC Place; KENOSHA; ***253** M-13; elev. 607ft./185m.; mail Kenosha z 53143
Caroline; RMC Place; SHAWANO; ▲ Grant; **252** I-11; elev. 902ft./275m.; 🅿; z 54928; ● 200
Carrollville; RMC Place; MILWAUKEE; ***253** O-13; ★ **MILW**; mail Oak Creek z 53154; pop. incl. with Oak Creek (Inc. Place)
Carson; MCD-Town; PORTAGE; ***252** I-9; mail Junction City z 54443; Ⓟ 1,327; Ⓒ 1,299
Carter; RMC Place; FOREST; ▲ Wabeno; **252** G-11; mail Wabeno z 54566; ● 100
Cary; MCD-Town; WOOD; ***252** J-7; mail Pittsville z 54466; Ⓟ 385; Ⓒ 398
Caryville; RMC Place; DUNN; ▲ Rock Creek; **252** I-4; mail Eau Claire z 54701; ● 50
Cascade; Inc. Place; SHEBOYGAN; **253** L-13; elev. 883ft./269m.; 🅿; z 53011; Ⓟ 620; Ⓒ 666; Ⓡ 681
Casco; Inc. Place; KEWAUNEE; **252** I-14; elev. 740ft./226m.; 🅿; z 54205; Ⓟ 544; Ⓒ 572
Casco; MCD-Town; KEWAUNEE; ***252** I-14; 🅿; z 54205 & mail Kewaunee z 54216; does not include the Village of Casco; Ⓟ 1,010; Ⓒ 1,153
Casco Junction; RMC Place; KEWAUNEE; ▲ Luxemburg; elev. 726ft./221m.; mail Luxemburg z 54217
Casey; MCD-Town; WASHBURN; ***252** E-3; mail Spooner z 54801; Ⓟ 401; Ⓒ 466
Cashton; Inc. Place; MONROE; **253** L-6; elev. 1,360ft./415m.; 🅿; z 54619; Ⓟ 780; Ⓒ 1,005
Cassel; MCD-Town; MARATHON; ***252** H-8; mail Edgar z 54426; Ⓟ 816; Ⓒ 847
Cassian; MCD-Town; ONEIDA; ***252** F-9; mail Harshaw z 54529; Ⓟ 668; Ⓒ 962
Cassville; Inc. Place; GRANT; **253** P-6; elev. 621ft./189m.; 🅿; z 53806; Ⓟ 1,144; Ⓒ 1,085
Cassville; MCD-Town; GRANT; ***253** O-6; 🅿; z 53806; does not include the Village of Cassville; Ⓟ 554; Ⓒ 487
Castle Rock; RMC Place; GRANT; ▲ Castle Rock; ***253** N-7; elev. 900ft./274m.; mail Montfort z 53569
Castle Rock; MCD-Town; GRANT; ***253** N-7; mail Fennimore z 53809; Ⓟ 311; Ⓒ 314
Caswell; MCD-Town; FOREST; ***252** F-11; mail Argonne z 54511; Ⓟ 94; Ⓒ 102
Cataract; RMC Place; MONROE; ▲ Little Falls; **253** K-6; elev. 847ft./258m.; 🅿; z 54620; ● 170
Catawba; Inc. Place; PRICE; **252** F-7; elev. 1,495ft./456m.; 🅿; z 54515; Ⓟ 178; Ⓒ 149
Catawba; MCD-Town; PRICE; ***252** F-7; 🅿; z 54515 & mail Ogema z 54459; does not include the Village of Catawba; Ⓟ 276; Ⓒ 283
Cato; RMC Place; MANITOWOC; ▲ Cato; ***253** K-13; elev. 863ft./263m.; 🅿; z 54230; ● 100
Cato; MCD-Town; MANITOWOC; ***253** K-13; 🅿; z 54230; Ⓟ 1,503; Ⓒ 1,616
Cavour; RMC Place; FOREST; ▲ Caswell; ***252** F-11; elev. 1,479ft./451m.; 🅿; z 54511; ● 25
Cayuga; RMC Place; ASHLAND; ▲ Morse; ***252** D-6; mail Mellen z 54546; ● 30
Cazenovia; Inc. Place; RICHLAND, SAUK; **253** M-8; elev. 951ft./290m.; 🅿; z 53924; Ⓟ 288; Ⓒ 326
Cecil; Inc. Place; SHAWANO; **252** I-12; elev. 811ft./247m.; 🅿; z 54111; Ⓟ 373; Ⓒ 466
Cedar; RMC Place; IRON; ▲ Gurney; ***252** C-7; mail Saxon z 54559; ● 25
Cedarburg; Inc. Place; OZAUKEE; **253** N-13; elev. 780ft./238m.; 🅿; ★ **MILW**; z 53012; Ⓟ 9,895; Ⓒ 10,908; Ⓡ 11,102
Cedarburg; MCD-Town; OZAUKEE; ***253** M-13; 🅿; ★ **MILW**; z 53012; does not include the City of Cedarburg; Ⓟ 5,334; Ⓒ 5,744; Ⓡ 5,550
Cedar Creek; RMC Place; WASHINGTON; ▲ Polk; ***253** M-12; ★ **MILW**; mail West Bend z 53095; ● 90
Cedar Falls; RMC Place; DUNN; ▲ Red Cedar; **252** H-4; mail Menomonie z 54751; ● 100
Cedar Grove; Inc. Place; SHEBOYGAN; **253** M-13; elev. 711ft./217m.; 🅿; ★ **SHEB**; z 53013; Ⓟ 1,521; Ⓒ 1,887
Cedar Lake; MCD-Town; BARRON; ***252** F-4; mail Rice Lake z 54868; Ⓟ 741; Ⓒ 944
Cedar Park; RACINE; see Browns Lake (CDP-Census Area Only)
Cedar Point; RMC Place; WALWORTH; ▲ Linn; ***253** P-12; mail Williams Bay z 53191; pop. incl. with Williams Bay (Inc. Place)
Cedar Rapids; MCD-Town; RUSK; ***252** F-6; mail Glen Flora z 54526; Ⓟ 30; Ⓒ 37
Center; MCD-Town; OUTAGAMIE; ***252** J-12; ★ **APP**; mail Appleton z 54911; Ⓟ 2,716; Ⓒ 3,163
Center; MCD-Town; ROCK; ***253** P-10; mail Janesville z 53545; Ⓟ 861; Ⓒ 1,005
Center House; RMC Place; GREEN LAKE; ▲ Green Lake; ***253** L-11; mail Markesan z 53946; ● 30
Center Lake Woods; RMC Place; KENOSHA; ▲ Salem; ***253** P-13; elev. 750ft./229m.; ★ **CHI**; mail Trevor z 53179; ● 700
Center Valley; RMC Place; OUTAGAMIE; ▲ Center; ***252** J-12; ★ **APP**; mail Black Creek z 54106; ● 60
Centerville; MCD-Town; MANITOWOC; ***253** K-13; mail Cleveland z 53015; Ⓟ 685; Ⓒ 713
Centerville; RMC Place; TREMPEALEAU; ▲ Trempealeau; **253** K-5; elev. 737ft./225m.; mail Galesville z 54630; ● 120
Central Avenue; RMC Place; DOUGLAS; ★ **DUL**; pop. incl. with Superior (Inc. Place)
Central Park; RMC Place; DOUGLAS; ***252** B-3; ★ **DUL**; mail Superior z 54880; pop. incl. with Superior (Inc. Place)
Centuria; Inc. Place; POLK; **252** F-2; elev. 1,225ft./373m.; 🅿; z 54824; Ⓟ 790; Ⓒ 865
Chaffey; RMC Place; DOUGLAS; ▲ Summit; ***252** C-3; elev. 1,308ft./399m.; mail Foxboro z 54836; rural
Chain o' Lakes; RMC Place; WAUPACA; ▲ Farmington, Dayton; ***252** J-10; mail Waupaca z 54981; ● 600
Chain o' Lakes-King; CDP-Census Area Only; WAUPACA; ▲ Farmington, Dayton; ***252** J-10; mail King z 54946, Waupaca z 54981; Ⓟ 1,667; Ⓒ 2,215
Chambers Island; RMC Place; DOOR; ▲ Gibraltar; mail Fish Creek z 54212
Champion; RMC Place; BROWN; ▲ Green Bay; **252** C-12; elev. 772ft./235m.; mail New Franken z 54229; ● 60
Chapel Ridge Heights; RMC Place; BROWN; ▲ Scott; ***252** I-13; elev. 766ft./233m.; ★ **GRBY**; mail Green Bay z 54301; pop. incl. with Green Bay (Inc. Place)
Charlesburg; RMC Place; CALUMET; ▲ Brothertown; ***253** K-12; mail Chilton z 53014; ● 150
Charlestown; MCD-Town; CALUMET; ***253** K-13; mail Chilton z 53014; Ⓟ 875; Ⓒ 789
Charlie Bluff; RMC Place; ROCK; ▲ Milton; ***253** O-11; elev. 784ft./239m.; ★ **JNSV**; mail Milton z 53563; ● 190
Chase; RMC Place; OCONTO; ▲ Chase; ***252** I-12; elev. 768ft./234m.; mail Sobieski z 54171; ● 30
Chase; MCD-Town; OCONTO; ***252** I-12; mail Sobieski z 54171; Ⓟ 1,375; Ⓒ 2,082
Chaseburg; Inc. Place; VERNON; **253** L-5; elev. 728ft./222m.; 🅿; z 54621; Ⓟ 365; Ⓒ 306
Chelsea; RMC Place; TAYLOR; ▲ Chelsea; **252** G-7; 🅿; z 54451; ● 100
Chelsea; MCD-Town; TAYLOR; ***252** G-7; 🅿; z 54451; Ⓟ 731; Ⓒ 719
Chenequa; Inc. Place; WAUKESHA; ***253** N-12; elev. 953ft./290m.; ★ **MILW**; mail Hartland z 53029, Nashotah z 53058; Ⓟ 601; Ⓒ 583
Cherokee; RMC Place; MARATHON; ▲ Hull; ***252** H-8; elev. 1,282ft./391m.; mail Colby z 54421
Cherrywood; RMC Place; DANE; ▲ Middleton; ***253** N-9; elev. 1,100ft./335m.; ★ **MAD**; mail Verona z 53593; ● 450
Chester; MCD-Town; DODGE; ***253** M-11; mail Waupun z 53963; Ⓟ 1,393; Ⓒ 960
Chetek; Inc. Place; BARRON; **252** G-4; elev. 1,050ft./320m.; 🅿; z 54728; Ⓟ 1,953; Ⓒ 2,180
Chetek; MCD-Town; BARRON; ***252** G-4; 🅿; z 54728; does not include the City of Chetek; Ⓟ 1,446; Ⓒ 1,686
Chicago Corners; RMC Place; OUTAGAMIE; ▲ Oneida; ***252** J-12; mail De Pere z 54115; rural
Chicog; MCD-Town; WASHBURN; ***252** D-3; mail Trego z 54888; Ⓟ 182; Ⓒ 268
Chief Lake; CDP-Census Area Only; SAWYER; ▲ Hunter; ***252** E-5; mail Hayward z 54843; Ⓟ 570; Ⓒ 625
Chili; RMC Place; CLARK; ▲ Fremont; **252** I-7; elev. 1,235ft./376m.; 🅿; z 54420; ● 230
Chilton; Inc. Place; ⊡ CALUMET; **253** K-12; elev. 902ft./275m.; 🅿 🅷; z 53014; Ⓟ 3,240; Ⓒ 3,708
Chilton; MCD-Town; CALUMET; ***253** K-12; 🅿; z 53014; does not include the City of Chilton; Ⓟ 998; Ⓒ 1,130
Chimney Rock; MCD-Town; TREMPEALEAU; ***252** J-5; mail Strum z 54770; Ⓟ 267; Ⓒ 276
Chippewa; MCD-Town; ASHLAND; ***252** E-6; mail Butternut z 54514; Ⓟ 405; Ⓒ 433
CHIPPEWA; **252** H-5; Ⓟ 52,360; Ⓒ 55,195; ◆ 60,908
Chippewa Falls; Inc. Place; ⊡ CHIPPEWA; **252** H-5; elev. 902ft./275m.; 🅿 🅷; ★ **EAUC**; z 54729, z 54774; Ⓟ 12,727; Ⓒ 12,925
Christiana; MCD-Town; DANE; ***253** O-10; mail Cambridge z 53523; Ⓟ 1,182; Ⓒ 1,313
Christiana; MCD-Town; VERNON; ***253** L-6; mail Westby z 54667; Ⓟ 851; Ⓒ 871
Christie; RMC Place; CLARK; ▲ Weston; **252** I-7; elev. 1,176ft./358m.; mail Neillsville z 54456; ● 30
Christilla Heights; RMC Place; ROCK; ***253** P-10; ★ **RKFD**; mail Beloit z 53511; pop. incl. with Beloit (Inc. Place)
Cicero; RMC Place; OUTAGAMIE; ▲ Cicero; ***252** I-12; elev. 855ft./261m.; mail Seymour z 54165; rural
Cicero; MCD-Town; OUTAGAMIE; ***252** I-12; mail Seymour z 54165; Ⓟ 1,126; Ⓒ 1,092
City of Pewaukee; WAUKESHA; see Pewaukee (Inc. Place)
City Point; RMC Place; JACKSON; ▲ City Point; **252** J-7; elev. 965ft./294m.; mail Pittsville z 54466; ● 60
City Point; MCD-Town; JACKSON; ***252** J-7; elev. 965ft./294m.; mail Pittsville z 54466; Ⓟ 193; Ⓒ 189
City View Heights; RMC Place; DANE; ▲ Sun Prairie; ***253** N-10; ★ **MAD**; mail Sun Prairie z 53590; ● 80
Clam Falls; RMC Place; POLK; ▲ Clam Falls; **252** F-3; 🅿; z 54837; ● 80
Clam Falls; MCD-Town; POLK; ***252** F-3; 🅿; z 54837; Ⓟ 596; Ⓒ 547
Clam Lake; RMC Place; ASHLAND; ▲ Shanagolden, Gordon; **252** D-6; elev. 1,421ft./433m.; 🅿; z 54517; summer pop. 150; ● 50
Clark; RMC Place; CLARK; ▲ Hixon; ***252** H-6; mail Withee z 54498; rural
CLARK; **252** I-7; Ⓟ 31,647; Ⓒ 33,557; ◆ 33,116
Clark Mills; MANITOWOC; see Clarks Mills (RMC Place)
Clarks Mills (Clark Mills); RMC Place; MANITOWOC; ▲ Liberty; ***253** K-13; elev. 841ft./256m.; mail Reedsville z 54230; ● 160
Clarks Point; RMC Place; WINNEBAGO; ▲ Winneconne; ***253** K-11; ★ **OSH**; mail Winneconne z 54986; ● 120
Clarno; RMC Place; GREEN; ▲ Clarno; **253** P-9; elev. 909ft./277m.; mail Monroe z 53566; ● 50
Clarno; MCD-Town; GREEN; ***253** P-9; mail Monroe z 53566; Ⓟ 1,011; Ⓒ 1,079
Clay Banks; MCD-Town; DOOR; ***252** C-13; mail Algoma z 54201; Ⓟ 379; Ⓒ 410
Clayton; MCD-Town; CRAWFORD; ***253** M-6; mail Soldiers Grove z 54655; Ⓟ 794; Ⓒ 956
Clayton; Inc. Place; POLK; **252** G-3; elev. 1,206ft./368m.; 🅿; z 54004; Ⓟ 450; Ⓒ 507
Clayton; MCD-Town; POLK; ***252** G-3; 🅿; z 54004; does not include the Village of Clayton; Ⓟ 780; Ⓒ 912
Clayton; MCD-Town; WINNEBAGO; ***253** K-11; mail Neenah z 54956; Ⓟ 2,264; Ⓒ 2,974
Clear Creek; MCD-Town; EAU CLAIRE; ***252** I-5; mail Strum z 54770; Ⓟ 692; Ⓒ 712
Clearfield; MCD-Town; JUNEAU; ***253** K-8; mail New Lisbon z 53950; Ⓟ 502; Ⓒ 737
Clear Lake; Inc. Place; POLK; **252** G-3; elev. 1,201ft./366m.; 🅿; z 54005; Ⓟ 932; Ⓒ 1,051
Clear Lake; MCD-Town; POLK; ***252** G-3; 🅿; z 54005; does not include the Village of Clear Lake; Ⓟ 744; Ⓒ 800
Clear Lake; RMC Place; ROCK; ▲ Milton; ***253** O-10; elev. 850ft./259m.; ★ **JNSV**; mail Milton z 53563; ● 100
Clearwater Lake; RMC Place; ONEIDA; ▲ Three Lakes; **252** E-10; mail Eagle River z 54521, Three Lakes z 54562; ● 150
Cleghorn; RMC Place; EAU CLAIRE; ▲ Pleasant Valley; ***252** I-5; mail Eleva z 54738; ● 75
Cleveland; MCD-Town; CHIPPEWA; ***252** G-5; mail Cornell z 54732; Ⓟ 758; Ⓒ 900
Cleveland; MCD-Town; JACKSON; ***252** I-6; mail Fairchild z 54741; Ⓟ 452; Ⓒ 438
Cleveland; Inc. Place; MANITOWOC; **253** K-13; elev. 640ft./195m.; 🅿; z 53015; Ⓟ 1,398; Ⓒ 1,361
Cleveland; MCD-Town; MARATHON; ***252** I-8; mail Stratford z 54484; Ⓟ 982; Ⓒ 1,160
Cleveland; MCD-Town; TAYLOR; ***252** G-6; mail Gilman z 54433; Ⓟ 235; Ⓒ 262
Clifford; RMC Place; PRICE; ▲ Knox; ***252** F-8; mail Tripoli z 54564
Clifton; MCD-Town; GRANT; ***253** O-7; mail Livingston z 53554; Ⓟ 306; Ⓒ 304
Clifton; RMC Place; MONROE; ▲ Clifton; **253** L-7; mail Camp Douglas z 54618; ● 40
Clifton; MCD-Town; MONROE; ***253** L-7; mail Camp Douglas z 54618; Ⓟ 587; Ⓒ 693
Clifton; MCD-Town; PIERCE; ***252** H-2; mail River Falls z 54022; Ⓟ 1,119; Ⓒ 1,657
Clinton; MCD-Town; BARRON; ***252** F-3; mail Almena z 54805; Ⓟ 849; Ⓒ 920
Clinton (Clinton Junction); Inc. Place; ROCK; **253** P-11; elev. 949ft./289m.; 🅿; z 53525; Ⓟ 1,849; Ⓒ 2,162
Clinton; MCD-Town; ROCK; ***253** P-11; 🅿; z 53525; does not include the Village of Clinton; Ⓟ 899; Ⓒ 893
Clinton; MCD-Town; VERNON; ***253** L-6; mail Cashton z 54619; Ⓟ 1,093; Ⓒ 1,354
Clinton Junction; ROCK; see Clinton (Inc. Place)
Clintonville; Inc. Place; WAUPACA; **252** I-11; elev. 825ft./251m.; 🅿; z 54929; Ⓟ 4,351; Ⓒ 4,736
Clover; MCD-Town; BAYFIELD; ***252** B-5; mail Herbster z 54844; Ⓟ 213; Ⓒ 211
Clover; RMC Place; MANITOWOC; ▲ Manitowoc; ***253** K-14; elev. 671ft./205m.; ★ **MNTW**; mail Manitowoc z 54220; ● 90
Cloverland; MCD-Town; DOUGLAS; ***252** B-4; mail Maple z 54854; Ⓟ 246; Ⓒ 247
Cloverland; MCD-Town; VILAS; ***252** E-9; mail Eagle River z 54521; Ⓟ 768; Ⓒ 919
Clyde; RMC Place; IOWA; ▲ Clyde; ***253** N-8; elev. 752ft./229m.; mail Avoca z 53506; rural
Clyde; MCD-Town; IOWA; ***253** N-7; mail Avoca z 53506; Ⓟ 391; Ⓒ 322
Clyman; Inc. Place; DODGE; **253** N-11; elev. 900ft./274m.; 🅿; z 53016; Ⓟ 370; Ⓒ 388
Clyman; MCD-Town; DODGE; ***253** M-11; 🅿; z 53016 & mail Juneau z 53039; does not include the Village of Clyman; Ⓟ 742; Ⓒ 849
Cobb; Inc. Place; IOWA; **253** O-7; elev. 1,165ft./355m.; 🅿; z 53526; Ⓟ 440; Ⓒ 442
Cobban; RMC Place; CHIPPEWA; ▲ Anson; ***252** H-5; mail Cornell z 54732; rural
Cobb Town; RMC Place; WAUPACA; ***252** J-10; elev. 864ft./263m.; mail Waupaca z 54981; rural
Cochrane; Inc. Place; BUFFALO; **252** J-4; elev. 685ft./209m.; 🅿; z 54622; Ⓟ 475; Ⓒ 435
Coddington; RMC Place; PORTAGE; ▲ Plover; ***252** J-9; mail Plover z 54467; rural
Colburn; MCD-Town; ADAMS; ***253** K-9; mail Hancock z 54943; Ⓟ 154; Ⓒ 181
Colburn; RMC Place; CHIPPEWA; ▲ Colburn; ***252** H-6; elev. 1,128ft./344m.; mail Boyd z 54726; ● 50
Colburn; MCD-Town; CHIPPEWA; ***252** H-6; mail Boyd z 54726; Ⓟ 731; Ⓒ 727
Colby; Inc. Place; CLARK, MARATHON; **252** H-7; elev. 1,350ft./411m.; 🅿; z 54421; Ⓟ 1,532; Ⓒ 1,616
Colby; MCD-Town; CLARK; ***252** H-7; 🅿; z 54421; does not include the City of Colby; Ⓟ 846; Ⓒ 908
Cold Spring; RMC Place; JEFFERSON; ▲ Cold Spring; ***253** O-11; mail Fort Atkinson z 53538; ● 35
Cold Spring; MCD-Town; JEFFERSON; ***253** O-11; mail Fort Atkinson z 53538; Ⓟ 683; Ⓒ 766
Coleman; Inc. Place; MARINETTE; **252** H-13; elev. 715ft./218m.; 🅿; z 54112; Ⓟ 839; Ⓒ 716
Colfax; Inc. Place; DUNN; **252** H-4; elev. 940ft./287m.; 🅿; z 54730; Ⓟ 1,110; Ⓒ 1,136
Colfax; MCD-Town; DUNN; ***252** H-4; 🅿; z 54730; does not include the Village of Colfax; Ⓟ 691; Ⓒ 909
Colgate; RMC Place; WASHINGTON, WAUKESHA; ▲ Lisbon, Richfield; **251** B-1; 🅿; ★ **MILW**; z 53017; ● 90
Collins; RMC Place; MANITOWOC; ▲ Rockland; **253** K-13; 🅿; z 54207; ● 200
Coloma; Inc. Place; WAUSHARA; **253** K-9; elev. 1,044ft./318m.; 🅿; z 54930; Ⓟ 383; Ⓒ 461
Coloma; MCD-Town; WAUSHARA; ***253** K-9; 🅿; z 54930; does not include the Village of Coloma; Ⓟ 499; Ⓒ 748; Ⓡ 660
Coloma Corners; RMC Place; WAUSHARA; ▲ Coloma; ***253** K-9; mail Coloma z 54930; ● 25
Columbia; RMC Place; CLARK; ▲ Hewett; ***252** J-6; elev. 952ft./290m.; mail Neillsville z 54456; rural
COLUMBIA; **253** M-10; Ⓟ 45,088; Ⓒ 52,468; ◆ 55,539
Columbus; Inc. Place; COLUMBIA, DODGE; **253** M-10; elev. 871ft./265m.; 🅿 🅷; z 53925; Ⓟ 4,093; Ⓒ 4,479
Columbus; MCD-Town; COLUMBIA; ***253** M-10; 🅿; z 53925; does not include the City of Columbus; Ⓟ 838; Ⓒ 711
Combined Locks; Inc. Place; OUTAGAMIE; **253** O-4; elev. 690ft./210m.; 🅿; ★ **APP**; z 54113; Ⓟ 2,190; Ⓒ 2,422
Commonwealth; RMC Place; FLORENCE; ▲ Commonwealth; **252** E-12; mail Florence z 54121; ● 240
Commonwealth; MCD-Town; FLORENCE; ***252** E-12; mail Florence z 54121; Ⓟ 407; Ⓒ 419
Como (Lake Como); CDP; WALWORTH; ▲ Geneva; ***253** P-12; elev. 911ft./278m.; mail Lake Geneva z 53147; Ⓟ 1,353; Ⓒ 1,870
Comstock; RMC Place; BARRON; ▲ Crystal Lake; **252** F-3; 🅿; z 54826; ● 100
Concord; RMC Place; JEFFERSON; ▲ Concord; ***253** N-11; elev. 852ft./260m.; mail Oconomowoc z 53066; ● 75
Concord; MCD-Town; JEFFERSON; ***253** N-11; mail Oconomowoc z 53066; Ⓟ 1,896; Ⓒ 2,023
Conference Point; RMC Place; WALWORTH; ▲ Linn; mail Williams Bay z 53191; pop. incl. with Williams Bay (Inc. Place)
Connors Point; RMC Place; DOUGLAS; ★ **DUL**; pop. incl. with Superior (Inc. Place)
Connorsville; RMC Place; DUNN; ▲ New Haven; **252** G-3; elev. 996ft./304m.; mail Boyceville z 54725, Downing z 54734; ● 130
Conover; RMC Place; VILAS; **252** D-10; elev. 1,659ft./506m.; 🅿; z 54519; summer pop. 700; ● 380
Conover; MCD-Town; VILAS; ***252** D-10; 🅿; z 54519; Ⓟ 932; Ⓒ 1,137
Conrath; Inc. Place; RUSK; **252** G-6; elev. 1,136ft./346m.; 🅿; z 54731; Ⓟ 92; Ⓒ 98
Cooks Valley; MCD-Town; CHIPPEWA; ***252** H-4; mail Bloomer z 54724; Ⓟ 594; Ⓒ 632
Cooksville; RMC Place; ROCK; ▲ Porter; ***253** O-10; elev. 877ft./267m.; mail Evansville z 53536; ● 100
Coomer; RMC Place; BURNETT; ▲ La Follette; ***252** E-3; elev. 993ft./303m.; mail Frederic z 54837; rural
Coon; MCD-Town; VERNON; ***253** L-6; mail Chaseburg z 54621; Ⓟ 701; Ⓒ 683
Coon Rock; RMC Place; IOWA; ▲ Arena; ***253** N-8; elev. 724ft./221m.; mail Arena z 53503; rural
Coon Valley; Inc. Place; VERNON; **253** L-6; elev. 735ft./224m.; 🅿; z 54623; Ⓟ 817; Ⓒ 714
Cooperstown; RMC Place; MANITOWOC; ▲ Cooperstown; **252** J-13; elev. 782ft./238m.; mail Denmark z 54208; ● 50
Cooperstown; MCD-Town; MANITOWOC; ***252** J-13; mail Maribel z 54227; Ⓟ 1,320; Ⓒ 1,403; Ⓡ 1,389
Coral City; RMC Place; TREMPEALEAU; ▲ Pigeon; ***252** J-5; elev. 834ft./254m.; mail Whitehall z 54773; ● 80
Corinth; RMC Place; MARATHON; ▲ Johnson; ***252** H-8; mail Athens z 54411
Corliss; RACINE; see Sturtevant (Inc. Place)
Cormier; RMC Place; BROWN; ***252** I-13; ★ **GRBY**; mail Green Bay z 54301; pop. incl. with Howard (Inc. Place)
Cornelia; RMC Place; GRANT; ▲ Harrison; ***253** P-7; mail Platteville z 53818; ● 40
Cornell; Inc. Place; CHIPPEWA; **252** G-5; elev. 1,100ft./335m.; 🅿; z 54732; Ⓟ 1,541; Ⓒ 1,466
Corning; MCD-Town; LINCOLN; ***252** G-8; mail Merrill z 54452; Ⓟ 795; Ⓒ 826
Cornucopia; RMC Place; BAYFIELD; ▲ Bell; **252** B-5; 🅿; z 54827; ● 250
Cottage Grove; Inc. Place; DANE; ***253** N-10; elev. 888ft./271m.; 🅿; ★ **MAD**; z 53527; Ⓟ 1,131; Ⓒ 4,059
Cottage Grove; MCD-Town; DANE; ***253** N-10; 🅿; ★ **MAD**; z 53527; does not include the Village of Cottage Grove; Ⓟ 3,525; Ⓒ 3,839
Cottonville; RMC Place; ADAMS; ▲ Preston; ***253** K-8; elev. 976ft./297m.; mail Friendship z 53934; ● 120
Couderay; Inc. Place; SAWYER; **252** E-5; elev. 1,265ft./386m.; 🅿; z 54828; Ⓟ 92; Ⓒ 96
Couderay; MCD-Town; SAWYER; ***252** E-5; 🅿; z 54828 & mail Exeland z 54835; does not include the Village of Couderay; Ⓟ 386; Ⓒ 469
Country Estates; RMC Place; WALWORTH; ▲ Lyons; ***253** P-12; elev. 868ft./265m.; mail Burlington z 53105; ● 200
County Line; RMC Place; MARINETTE, OCONTO; ▲ Little River, Grover; **252** B-11; mail Oconto z 54153; ● 40
Courtland; MCD-Town; COLUMBIA; ***253** M-10; mail Fall River z 53932; Ⓟ 528; Ⓒ 463
Cranberry Lake; RMC Place; PRICE; ▲ Worcester; ***252** F-7; mail Phillips z 54555; rural
Crandon; Inc. Place; ⊡ FOREST; **252** F-11; elev. 1,629ft./497m.; 🅿; z 54520; Ⓟ 1,958; Ⓒ 1,961
Crandon; MCD-Town; FOREST; ***252** F-10; 🅿; z 54520; does not include the City of Crandon; Ⓟ 529; Ⓒ 614
Cranmoor; RMC Place; WOOD; ▲ Cranmoor; ***252** J-8; elev. 982ft./299m.; mail Wisconsin Rapids z 54495; rural
Cranmoor; MCD-Town; WOOD; ***252** J-8; mail Wisconsin Rapids z 54495; Ⓟ 185; Ⓒ 175
CRAWFORD; **253** N-6; Ⓟ 15,940; Ⓒ 17,243; ◆ 16,890
Cream; RMC Place; BUFFALO; ▲ Lincoln; **252** J-4; elev. 775ft./236m.; mail Alma z 54610; ● 30
Crescent; RMC Place; CHIPPEWA; ▲ Arthur; ***252** H-5; elev. 1,138ft./347m.; mail Cadott z 54727; ● 35
Crescent; MCD-Town; ONEIDA; ***252** F-9; mail Rhinelander z 54501; Ⓟ 1,790; Ⓒ 2,071
Crescent Park; RMC Place; DANE; ▲ Dunn; ***253** O-10; elev. 848ft./258m.; ★ **MAD**; mail Mc Farland z 53558; ● 50
Crestview; RMC Place; RACINE; ▲ Caledonia; ***253** O-13; ★ **MILW**; mail Racine z 53402; ● 3,500
Crestview; RMC Place; ROCK; ▲ Beloit; ***253** P-10; ★ **RKFD**; mail Beloit z 53511; ● 1,000
Crivitz; Inc. Place; MARINETTE; **252** G-13; elev. 681ft./208m.; 🅿; z 54114; Ⓟ 996; Ⓒ 998
Cross; MCD-Town; BUFFALO; ***253** K-4; mail Fountain City z 54629; Ⓟ 307; Ⓒ 366
Cross Lake; RMC Place; KENOSHA; ▲ Salem; ***253** P-13; elev. 800ft./244m.; ★ **CHI**; mail Trevor z 53179; ● 600
Cross Plains; Inc. Place; DANE; **253** N-9; elev. 859ft./262m.; 🅿; ★ **MAD**; z 53528; Ⓟ 2,098; Ⓒ 3,084
Cross Plains; MCD-Town; DANE; ***253** N-9; 🅿; ★ **MAD**; z 53528; Ⓟ 1,320; Ⓒ 1,419
Crystal; MCD-Town; WASHBURN; ***252** E-4; mail Spooner z 54801; Ⓟ 279; Ⓒ 323
Crystal Lake; MCD-Town; BARRON; ***252** F-3; mail Comstock z 54826; Ⓟ 700; Ⓒ 778
Crystal Lake; MCD-Town; MARQUETTE; ***253** K-10; mail Neshkoro z 54960; Ⓟ 400; Ⓒ 513
Crystal Lake Corners; RMC Place; WAUPACA; ▲ Dayton; ***252** J-10; elev. 930ft./283m.; mail Waupaca z 54981; ● 30
Cuba City; Inc. Place; GRANT, LAFAYETTE; **253** P-7; elev. 1,012ft./308m.; 🅿; z 53803, z 53807; Ⓟ 2,024; Ⓒ 2,156
Cudahy; Inc. Place; MILWAUKEE; **253** O-13; elev. 700ft./213m.; 🅿; ★ **MILW**; z 53110; Ⓟ 18,659; Ⓒ 18,429
Cumberland; Inc. Place; BARRON; **252** F-3; elev. 1,251ft./381m.; 🅿 🅷; z 54829; Ⓟ 2,163; Ⓒ 2,280
Cumberland; MCD-Town; BARRON; ***252** F-3; 🅿; z 54829; does not include the City of Cumberland; Ⓟ 884; Ⓒ 942
Curran; MCD-Town; JACKSON; ***252** J-5; mail Hixton z 54635; Ⓟ 351; Ⓒ 366
Curran; RMC Place; KEWAUNEE; ▲ Franklin; ***252** J-13; elev. 752ft./229m.; mail Denmark z 54208; ● 25
Curtiss; Inc. Place; CLARK; **252** H-7; elev. 1,370ft./418m.; 🅿; z 54422; Ⓟ 173; Ⓒ 198
Cushing; RMC Place; POLK; ▲ Sterling, Laketown; **252** F-2; elev. 982ft./299m.; 🅿; z 54006; ● 200
Custer; RMC Place; PORTAGE; ▲ Stockton; **252** J-9; elev. 1,175ft./358m.; 🅿; z 54423; ● 170
Cutler; RMC Place; JUNEAU; ▲ Cutler; ***253** K-7; elev. 925ft./282m.; 🅿; z 54618 & mail Necedah z 54646; rural
Cutler; MCD-Town; JUNEAU; ***253** K-7; 🅿; z 54618 & mail Necedah z 54646; Ⓟ 314; Ⓒ 282
Cylon; RMC Place; ST. CROIX; ▲ Cylon; ***252** G-2; elev. 1,061ft./323m.; mail New Richmond z 54017, Wilson z 54027; ● 80
Cylon; MCD-Town; ST. CROIX; ***252** G-3; mail New Richmond z 54017; Ⓟ 639; Ⓒ 629
Czechville; RMC Place; BUFFALO; ▲ Milton; ***253** K-4; elev. 682ft./208m.; mail Fountain City z 54629; rural

D

Dacada; RMC Place; OZAUKEE, SHEBOYGAN; ▲ Holland, Belgium; ***253** M-13; ★ **MILW**; mail Random Lake z 53075; ● 60
Dairyland; RMC Place; DOUGLAS; ▲ Dairyland; **252** D-3; 🅿; z 54830
Dairyland; MCD-Town; DOUGLAS; ***252** D-3; 🅿; z 54830; Ⓟ 222; Ⓒ 186
Dakota; RMC Place; WAUSHARA; ▲ Dakota; ***253** K-10; elev. 843ft./257m.; mail Wautoma z 54982; ● 100
Dakota; MCD-Town; WAUSHARA; ***253** K-10; mail Wautoma z 54982; Ⓟ 1,092; Ⓒ 1,259
Dale; RMC Place; OUTAGAMIE; ▲ Dale; ***252** J-11; elev. 806ft./246m.; 🅿; z 54931; ● 500
Dale; MCD-Town; OUTAGAMIE; ***252** J-11; 🅿; z 54931; Ⓟ 1,818; Ⓒ 2,288
Daleyville; RMC Place; DANE; ▲ Perry; **253** O-8; mail Mount Horeb z 53572; ● 80
Dallas; Inc. Place; BARRON; **252** G-4; elev. 1,054ft./321m.; 🅿; z 54733; Ⓟ 452; Ⓒ 356
Dallas; MCD-Town; BARRON; ***252** G-4; 🅿; z 54733; does not include the Village of Dallas; Ⓟ 548; Ⓒ 604
Dalton; RMC Place; GREEN LAKE; ▲ Kingston; **253** L-10; elev. 861ft./262m.; 🅿; z 53926; ● 250
Danbury; RMC Place; BURNETT; ▲ Swiss; **252** E-3; 🅿; z 54830; ● 350
Dancy; RMC Place; MARATHON; ▲ Knowlton; **252** I-9; mail Mosinee z 54455; ● 80
Dane; Inc. Place; DANE; **253** N-9; elev. 1,115ft./340m.; 🅿; z 53529; Ⓟ 621; Ⓒ 799
Dane; MCD-Town; DANE; ***253** N-9; 🅿; z 53529 & mail Lodi z 53555; does not include the Village of Dane; Ⓟ 921; Ⓒ 968
DANE; **253** N-9; Ⓟ 367,085; Ⓒ 426,526; ◆ 500,552
Daniels; MCD-Town; BURNETT; ***252** E-2; mail Siren z 54872; Ⓟ 602; Ⓒ 665
Danville; RMC Place; DODGE; ▲ Elba; **253** M-11; mail Columbus z 53925; ● 40
Darboy; RMC Place; CALUMET, OUTAGAMIE; ▲ Buchanan, Harrison; **253** O-3; elev. 750ft./229m.; ★ **APP**; mail Appleton z 54915; ● 350
Darien; Inc. Place; WALWORTH; **253** P-11; elev. 948ft./289m.; 🅿; z 53114; Ⓟ 1,158; Ⓒ 1,572
Darien; MCD-Town; WALWORTH; ***253** P-11; 🅿; z 53114 & mail Delavan z 53115; does not include the Village of Darien; Ⓟ 1,490; Ⓒ 1,747
Darlington; Inc. Place; ⊡ LAFAYETTE; **253** P-8; elev. 817ft./249m.; 🅿 🅷; z 53530; Ⓟ 2,235; Ⓒ 2,418
Darlington; MCD-Town; LAFAYETTE; ***253** P-8; 🅿; z 53530; does not include the City of Darlington; Ⓟ 867; Ⓒ 757
Davis Corners (Glen); RMC Place; ADAMS; ▲ Jackson; ***253** L-9; elev. 1,045ft./319m.; mail Grand Marsh z 53936; rural
Day; MCD-Town; MARATHON; ***252** I-8; mail Stratford z 54484; Ⓟ 1,010; Ⓒ 1,023
Dayton; RMC Place; GREEN; ▲ Exeter; **253** O-9; mail Belleville z 53508; ● 150
Dayton; MCD-Town; RICHLAND; ***253** M-7; mail Richland Center z 53581; Ⓟ 706; Ⓒ 723
Dayton; MCD-Town; WAUPACA; ***252** J-10; mail Waupaca z 54981; Ⓟ 1,992; Ⓒ 2,734
Deansville; RMC Place; DANE; ▲ Medina; ***253** N-10; elev. 884ft./269m.; ★ **MAD**; mail Marshall z 53559; ● 60
Decatur; MCD-Town; GREEN; ***253** P-9; mail Brodhead z 53520; Ⓟ 1,076; Ⓒ 1,688
Deckers Corner; RMC Place; OZAUKEE; ▲ Cedarburg; ***253** M-13; elev. 870ft./265m.; ★ **MILW**; mail Cedarburg z 53012; ● 40
Dedham; RMC Place; DOUGLAS; ▲ Superior; ***252** C-3; elev. 797ft./243m.; mail Foxboro z 54836; rural
Deerbrook; RMC Place; LANGLADE; ▲ Neva; **252** G-10; elev. 1,530ft./466m.; 🅿; z 54424 & mail Bryant z 54418; ● 200
Deer Creek; MCD-Town; OUTAGAMIE; ***252** I-11; mail Shiocton z 54170; Ⓟ 724; Ⓒ 682
Deer Creek; MCD-Town; TAYLOR; ***252** H-7; mail Stetsonville z 54480; Ⓟ 738; Ⓒ 733
Deerfield; Inc. Place; DANE; **253** N-10; elev. 950ft./290m.; 🅿; ★ **MAD**; z 53531; Ⓟ 1,617; Ⓒ 1,971
Deerfield; MCD-Town; DANE; ***253** N-10; 🅿; ★ **MAD**; z 53531; does not include the Village of Deerfield; Ⓟ 1,181; Ⓒ 1,470
Deerfield; MCD-Town; WAUSHARA; ***253** K-9; mail Hancock z 54943; Ⓟ 454; Ⓒ 629
Deer Park; RMC Place; EAU CLAIRE; ▲ Washington; ***252** I-5; elev. 912ft./278m.; mail Fall Creek z 54742; ● 230
Deer Park; Inc. Place; ST. CROIX; **252** G-2; elev. 1,058ft./322m.; 🅿; z 54007; Ⓟ 237; Ⓒ 227
De Forest; Inc. Place; DANE; **253** N-10; elev. 949ft./289m.; 🅿; ★ **MAD**; z 53532; Ⓟ 4,882; Ⓒ 7,368
Dekorra; MCD-Town; COLUMBIA; ***253** M-9; mail Poynette z 53955; Ⓟ 1,829; Ⓒ 2,350
Delafield; Inc. Place; WAUKESHA; **253** N-12; 🅿; ★ **MILW**; z 53018; Ⓟ 5,347; Ⓒ 6,472
Delafield; MCD-Town; WAUKESHA; ***253** N-12; 🅿; ★ **MILW**; z 53018 & mail Pewaukee z 53072; does not include the City of Delafield; Ⓟ 5,735; Ⓒ 7,820
Delavan; Inc. Place; WALWORTH; **253** P-11; elev. 940ft./287m.; 🅿; z 53115; Ⓟ 6,073; Ⓒ 7,956
Delavan; MCD-Town; WALWORTH; ***253** P-11; 🅿; z 53115; does not include the City of Delavan; Ⓟ 4,195; Ⓒ 4,559
Delavan Lake; CDP; WALWORTH; ▲ Walworth, Delavan; ***253** P-11; mail Delavan z 53115; Ⓟ 2,177; Ⓒ 2,352
Dell; RMC Place; VERNON; ▲ Clinton; ***253** L-6; mail Westby z 54667; rural
Dellona; MCD-Town; SAUK; ***253** M-8; mail Wisconsin Dells z 53965; Ⓟ 768; Ⓒ 1,199
Dell Prairie; MCD-Town; ADAMS; ***253** L-9; mail Dellwood z 53927, Wisconsin Dells z 53965; Ⓟ 1,063; Ⓒ 1,415
Dellwood (Holmsville); RMC Place; ADAMS; ▲ Strongs Prairie; **253** K-8; elev. 918ft./280m.; 🅿; z 53927; ● 120
Delmar; MCD-Town; CHIPPEWA; ***252** H-6; mail Boyd z 54726; Ⓟ 994; Ⓒ 941
Delta; MCD-Town; BAYFIELD; ***252** C-5; 🅿; z 54856; Ⓟ 215; Ⓒ 235
Delton; MCD-Town; SAUK; ***253** M-9; mail Reedsburg z 53959; Ⓟ 1,599; Ⓒ 2,024
Denmark; Inc. Place; BROWN; **252** J-13; elev. 880ft./268m.; 🅿; z 54208; Ⓟ 1,612; Ⓒ 1,958
Denoon; RMC Place; WAUKESHA; ***253** O-12; ★ **MILW**; mail Muskego z 53150; pop. incl. with Muskego (Inc. Place)
Denzer; RMC Place; SAUK; ▲ Honey Creek; ***253** M-8; elev. 816ft./249m.; mail North Freedom z 53951; ● 40
De Pere; Inc. Place; BROWN; **252** J-13; elev. 610ft./186m.; 🅿 🅲 2,015; ★ **GRBY**; z 54115; Ⓟ 16,569; Ⓒ 20,559; ◆ 23,306
De Pere; BROWN; see Ledgeview (MCD-Town)
Deronda; RMC Place; POLK; ▲ Lincoln, Garfield; **252** G-2; elev. 1,069ft./326m.; 🅿; z 54001; ● 90
De Soto; Inc. Place; VERNON, CRAWFORD; **253** M-5; elev. 653ft./199m.; 🅿; z 54624; Ⓟ 326; Ⓒ 366
Detroit Harbor (Washington Island); RMC Place; DOOR; ▲ Washington; **252** A-14; mail Washington Island z 54246; ● 400
Dewey; MCD-Town; BURNETT; ***252** E-3; mail Hertel z 54845, Shell Lake z 54871; Ⓟ 482; Ⓒ 565
Dewey; RMC Place; DOUGLAS; ▲ Superior; ***252** C-3; elev. 815ft./248m.; mail Superior z 54880; rural
Dewey; MCD-Town; PORTAGE; ***252** I-9; mail Stevens Point z 54481; Ⓟ 849; Ⓒ 975
Dewey; MCD-Town; RUSK; ***252** F-6; mail Tony z 54563; Ⓟ 487; Ⓒ 523
Dewhurst; MCD-Town; CLARK; ***252** J-6; mail Neillsville z 54456; Ⓟ 197; Ⓒ 321
Dexter; MCD-Town; WOOD; ***252** J-8; mail Pittsville z 54466; Ⓟ 354; Ⓒ 379
Dexterville; RMC Place; WOOD; ▲ Dexter; **252** J-8; mail Pittsville z 54466; ● 50
Diamond Bluff; RMC Place; PIERCE; ▲ Diamond Bluff; **252** I-2; mail Hager City z 54014; ● 180
Diamond Bluff; MCD-Town; PIERCE; ***252** I-2; mail Hager City z 54014; Ⓟ 492; Ⓒ 479
Dickeyville; Inc. Place; GRANT; **253** P-7; elev. 957ft./292m.; 🅿; z 53808; Ⓟ 862; Ⓒ 1,043
Diefenbach Corners; RMC Place; WASHINGTON; ▲ Polk; ***253** M-12; elev. 1,133ft./345m.; ★ **MILW**; mail Slinger z 53086; rural
Dilly; RMC Place; VERNON; ▲ Forest; ***253** L-7; mail Hillsboro z 54634; rural
Disco; RMC Place; JACKSON; ▲ Albion; ***252** J-6; elev. 969ft./295m.; mail Black River Falls z 54615
Dobie; RMC Place; BARRON; ▲ Oak Grove; ***252** F-4; elev. 1,173ft./358m.; mail Rice Lake z 54868; rural
Dodge; RMC Place; TREMPEALEAU; ▲ Dodge; **253** K-4; elev. 673ft./205m.; 🅿; z 54625; ● 160
Dodge; MCD-Town; TREMPEALEAU; ***253** K-4; 🅿; z 54625; Ⓟ 397; Ⓒ 414
DODGE; **253** M-11; Ⓟ 76,559; Ⓒ 85,897; ◆ 85,132
Dodges Corners; RMC Place; WAUKESHA; ▲ Vernon; ***253** O-12; elev. 871ft./265m.; ★ **MILW**; mail Mukwonago z 53149; rural
Dodgeville; Inc. Place; ⊡ IOWA; **253** O-8; elev. 1,222ft./372m.; 🅿 🅷; z 53533, z 53595; Ⓟ 3,882; Ⓒ 4,220
Dodgeville; MCD-Town; IOWA; ***253** O-8; 🅿; z 53533, z 53595; does not include the City of Dodgeville; Ⓟ 1,172; Ⓒ 1,407
Doering; RMC Place; LINCOLN; ▲ Schley; ***252** G-9; mail Gleason z 54435
Donald; RMC Place; TAYLOR; ▲ Pershing; ***252** G-6; mail Gilman z 54433
DOOR; **252** I-14; Ⓟ 25,690; Ⓒ 27,961; ◆ 27,132
Dorchester; Inc. Place; CLARK, MARATHON; **252** H-7; elev. 1,420ft./433m.; 🅿; z 54425; Ⓟ 697; Ⓒ 827
Dorns Twilight Beach; RMC Place; CALUMET; ▲ Stockbridge; ***253** K-12; mail Chilton z 53014; ● 40
Doty; MCD-Town; OCONTO; ***252** G-11; mail Mountain z 54149; Ⓟ 184; Ⓒ 249
Dotyville; RMC Place; FOND DU LAC; ▲ Forest; ***253** L-12; elev. 1,056ft./322m.; mail Mount Calvary z 53057; ● 100
Douglas; MCD-Town; MARQUETTE; ***253** L-9; mail Endeavor z 53930; Ⓟ 684; Ⓒ 768
DOUGLAS; **252** C-3; Ⓟ 41,758; Ⓒ 43,287; ◆ 43,388
Dousman; Inc. Place; WAUKESHA; **253** N-12; elev. 870ft./265m.; 🅿; ★ **MILW**; z 53118; Ⓟ 1,277; Ⓒ 1,584
Dover; MCD-Town; BUFFALO; ***252** J-4; mail Mondovi z 54755; Ⓟ 451; Ⓒ 484
Dover; MCD-Town; RACINE; ***253** O-13; mail Union Grove z 53182; Ⓟ 3,631; Ⓒ 3,908
Dovre; MCD-Town; BARRON; ***252** G-4; mail New Auburn z 54757; Ⓟ 561; Ⓒ 680
Downing; Inc. Place; DUNN; **252** H-3; elev. 983ft./300m.; 🅿; z 54734; Ⓟ 250; Ⓒ 257
Downing Junction; RMC Place; DUNN; mail Downing z 54734; pop. incl. with Downing (Inc. Place)
Downsville; RMC Place; DUNN; ▲ Dunn; **252** I-3; 🅿; z 54735; ● 220
Downtown; RMC Place; BROWN; ★ **GRBY**; mail Green Bay z 54305; pop. incl. with Green Bay (Inc. Place)
Downtown; RMC Place; WINNEBAGO; ★ **OSH**; mail Oshkosh z 54902; pop. incl. with Oshkosh (Inc. Place)
Doyle; MCD-Town; BARRON; ***252** F-4; mail Rice Lake z 54868; Ⓟ 460; Ⓒ 498
Doylestown; Inc. Place; COLUMBIA; **253** M-10; elev. 960ft./293m.; 🅿; z 53928; Ⓟ 316; Ⓒ 328
Drammen; MCD-Town; EAU CLAIRE; ***252** I-4; mail Elk Mound z 54739; Ⓟ 767; Ⓒ 800
Draper; RMC Place; SAWYER; ▲ Draper; ***252** E-6; elev. 1,500ft./457m.; mail Winter z 54896; ● 30
Draper; MCD-Town; SAWYER; ***252** E-6; mail Winter z 54896; Ⓟ 208; Ⓒ 171
Dresser; Inc. Place; POLK; **252** G-2; elev. 920ft./280m.; 🅿; z 54009; Ⓟ 614; Ⓒ 732
Drovers Woods; RMC Place; DANE; ▲ Sun Prairie; ***253** N-10; ★ **MAD**; mail Marshall z 53559; rural
Drummond; RMC Place; BAYFIELD; ▲ Drummond; **252** C-5; 🅿; z 54832; ● 360
Drummond; MCD-Town; BAYFIELD; ***252** D-5; 🅿; z 54832; Ⓟ 417; Ⓒ 541
Drywood; RMC Place; CHIPPEWA; ▲ Arthur; ***252** H-5; mail Cadott z 54727; ● 30
Duck Creek; RMC Place; BROWN; ***252** I-13; ★ **GRBY**; mail Green Bay z 54301; pop. incl. with Howard (Inc. Place)
Dudley; RMC Place; LINCOLN; ▲ Russell; ***252** G-9; mail Gleason z 54435; rural
Dunbar; RMC Place; MARINETTE; ▲ Dunbar; **252** F-12; 🅿 🅲 651; z 54119; ● 300
Dunbar; MCD-Town; MARINETTE; ***252** F-12; 🅿 🅲 651; z 54119 & mail Pembine z 54156; Ⓟ 838; Ⓒ 1,303
Dunbarton; RMC Place; LAFAYETTE; ▲ Shullsburg, Gratiot; ***253** P-8; elev. 992ft./302m.; mail Shullsburg z 53586
Dundas; RMC Place; CALUMET; ▲ Woodville; ***252** J-12; mail Kaukauna z 54130; ● 30
Dundee; RMC Place; FOND DU LAC; ▲ Osceola; **253** L-12; mail Campbellsport z 53010; ● 140
Dunkirk; RMC Place; DANE; ▲ Dunkirk; ***253** O-10; elev. 873ft./266m.; ★ **MAD**; mail Stoughton z 53589; ● 30
Dunkirk; MCD-Town; DANE; ***253** O-10; mail Stoughton z 53589; Ⓟ 2,121; Ⓒ 2,053
Dunn; MCD-Town; DANE; ***253** O-10; ★ **MAD**; mail Mc Farland z 53558; Ⓟ 5,274; Ⓒ 5,270
Dunn; MCD-Town; DUNN; ***252** I-3; mail Menomonie z 54751; Ⓟ 1,315; Ⓒ 1,492
DUNN; **252** H-4; Ⓟ 35,909; Ⓒ 39,858; ◆ 42,957
Duplainville; RMC Place; WAUKESHA; **251** E-2; elev. 856ft./261m.; ★ **MILW**; mail Waukesha z 53189; pop. incl. with Pewaukee (Inc. Place)
Dupont; MCD-Town; WAUPACA; ***252** I-11; mail Marion z 54950; Ⓟ 634; Ⓒ 741
Durand; Inc. Place; ⊡ PEPIN; **252** I-3; elev. 721ft./220m.; 🅿 🅷; z 54736; Ⓟ 2,003; Ⓒ 1,968
Durand; MCD-Town; PEPIN; ***252** I-3; 🅿; z 54736; does not include the City of Durand; Ⓟ 604; Ⓒ 694
Durham; RMC Place; WAUKESHA; ***253** O-13; elev. 796ft./243m.; ★ **MILW**; mail Muskego z 53150; pop. incl. with Muskego (Inc. Place)
Duvall; RMC Place; KEWAUNEE; ▲ Red River; ***252** I-13; mail Luxemburg z 54217; ● 30
Dyckesville; RMC Place; BROWN, KEWAUNEE; ▲ Red River, Green Bay; **252** I-13; mail Luxemburg z 54217; ● 400

E

Eagle; MCD-Town; RICHLAND; ***253** N-7; mail Muscoda z 53573; Ⓟ 611; Ⓒ 593
Eagle; Inc. Place; WAUKESHA; **253** O-12; elev. 949ft./289m.; 🅿; ★ **MILW**; z 53119; Ⓟ 1,182; Ⓒ 1,707
Eagle; MCD-Town; WAUKESHA; ***253** O-12; 🅿; ★ **MILW**; z 53119; does not include the Village of Eagle; Ⓟ 2,028; Ⓒ 3,117
Eagle Corners; RMC Place; RICHLAND; ▲ Eagle; ***253** N-7; elev. 740ft./226m.; mail Muscoda z 53573; rural
Eagle Lake; CDP-Census Area Only; RACINE; ▲ Dover; ***253** O-13; elev. 800ft./244m.; mail Kansasville z 53139; Ⓟ 1,196; summer pop. 1,500; Ⓒ 1,320
Eagle Lake Manor; RMC Place; RACINE; ▲ Dover; ***253** P-13; elev. 800ft./244m.; mail Kansasville z 53139
Eagle Point; MCD-Town; CHIPPEWA; ***252** H-5; mail Chippewa Falls z 54729; Ⓟ 2,542; Ⓒ 3,049
Eagle River; Inc. Place; ⊡ VILAS; **252** E-10; elev. 1,647ft./502m.; 🅿 🅷; z 54521; Ⓟ 1,374; Ⓒ 1,443
Eagleton; RMC Place; CHIPPEWA; ▲ Eagle Point; **252** H-5; elev. 989ft./301m.; mail Bloomer z 54724; ● 40
Eagleville; RMC Place; WAUKESHA; ▲ Eagle; ***253** O-12; ★ **MILW**; mail Mukwonago z 53149; ● 60
Earl; RMC Place; WASHBURN; ▲ Springbrook; **252** E-4; mail Springbrook z 54875; ● 60
East Bristol; RMC Place; DANE; ▲ Bristol; ***253** N-10; mail Columbus z 53925; ● 80
East Delavan; RMC Place; WALWORTH; ▲ Delavan; ***253** P-12; mail Delavan z 53115; ● 200
East Ellsworth; RMC Place; PIERCE; ***252** I-2; 🅿; z 54010; pop. incl. with Ellsworth (Inc. Place)
East End; RMC Place; DOUGLAS; ***252** B-3; ★ **DUL**; mail Superior z 54880; pop. incl. with Superior (Inc. Place)
East Farmington; RMC Place; POLK; ▲ Farmington; **252** G-2; elev. 1,045ft./319m.; mail Osceola z 54020; ● 100
East Friesland; RMC Place; COLUMBIA; ▲ Randolph; ***253** M-10; elev. 974ft./297m.; mail Randolph z 53956; ● 30
East Krok; RMC Place; KEWAUNEE; ▲ West Kewaunee; ***252** J-14; elev. 728ft./222m.; mail Kewaunee z 54216; ● 30
Eastman; Inc. Place; CRAWFORD; **253** N-6; elev. 1,224ft./373m.; 🅿; z 54626; Ⓟ 369; Ⓒ 437
Eastman; MCD-Town; CRAWFORD; ***253** N-6; 🅿; z 54626 & mail Wauzeka z 53826; does not include the Village of Eastman; Ⓟ 745; Ⓒ 790
Easton; RMC Place; ADAMS; ▲ Easton; **253** L-8; mail Adams z 53910; ● 170
Easton; MCD-Town; ADAMS; ***253** L-9; mail Adams z 53910; Ⓟ 824; Ⓒ 1,194
Easton; MCD-Town; MARATHON; ***252** H-9; mail Ringle z 54471; Ⓟ 1,039; Ⓒ 1,062
East Troy; Inc. Place; WALWORTH; **253** O-12; elev. 840ft./256m.; 🅿; ★ **MILW**; z 53120; Ⓟ 2,664; Ⓒ 3,564
East Troy; MCD-Town; WALWORTH; ***253** O-12; 🅿; ★ **MILW**; z 53120; does not include the Village of East Troy; Ⓟ 3,687; Ⓒ 3,830
East Waupun; RMC Place; DODGE; ▲ Chester; ***253** L-11; elev. 880ft./268m.; mail Waupun z 53963; ● 40
Eastwood; RMC Place; WOOD; ▲ Grand Rapids; ***252** J-9; elev. 1,025ft./312m.; mail Wisconsin Rapids z 54494; ● 50
Eaton; MCD-Town; BROWN; ***252** J-13; mail Luxemburg z 54217; Ⓟ 1,128; Ⓒ 1,414
Eaton; MCD-Town; CLARK; ***252** I-7; mail Greenwood z 54437; Ⓟ 640; Ⓒ 665
Eaton; MCD-Town; MANITOWOC; ***253** K-13; mail Kiel z 53042; Ⓟ 761; Ⓒ 761
Eau Claire; Inc. Place; ⊡ EAU CLAIRE, CHIPPEWA; **252** I-4; elev. 796ft./243m.; 🅿 🅷 🅲 10,505 ■; ★ **EAUC**; z 54701-03; Ⓟ 56,856; Ⓒ 61,704; ◆ 67,610
EAU CLAIRE; **252** I-5; Ⓟ 85,183; Ⓒ 93,142; ◆ 102,337
Eau Galle; RMC Place; DUNN; ▲ Eau Galle; **252** I-3; 🅿; z 54737 & mail Woodville z 54028; ● 200
Eau Galle; MCD-Town; DUNN; ***252** I-3; 🅿; z 54737 & mail Woodville z 54028; Ⓟ 854; Ⓒ 797
Eau Galle; MCD-Town; ST. CROIX; ***252** H-3; mail Woodville z 54028; Ⓟ 756; Ⓒ 882
Eau Pleine; MCD-Town; MARATHON; ***252** I-8; mail Stratford z 54484; Ⓟ 688; Ⓒ 750
Eau Pleine; MCD-Town; PORTAGE; ***252** I-9; mail Junction City z 54443; Ⓟ 944; Ⓒ 931
Eckers Lakeland; RMC Place; CALUMET; ▲ Stockbridge; ***253** K-12; mail Chilton z 53014; ● 50
Eden; Inc. Place; FOND DU LAC; **253** L-12; elev. 1,015ft./309m.; 🅿; z 53019; Ⓟ 610; Ⓒ 687
Eden; MCD-Town; FOND DU LAC; ***253** L-12; 🅿; z 53019 & mail Campbellsport z 53010; Ⓟ 1,037; Ⓒ 979
Eden; MCD-Town; IOWA; ***253** O-7; mail Cobb z 53526; Ⓟ 381; Ⓒ 397
Edgar; Inc. Place; MARATHON; **252** H-8; elev. 1,250ft./381m.; 🅿; z 54426; Ⓟ 1,318; Ⓒ 1,386
Edgerton; Inc. Place; ROCK; **253** O-10; elev. 820ft./250m.; 🅿 🅷; ★ **JNSV**; z 53534; Ⓟ 4,254; Ⓒ 4,933
Edgewater; RMC Place; SAWYER; ▲ Edgewater; **252** E-5; 🅿; z 54834; ● 100
Edgewater; MCD-Town; SAWYER; ***252** F-5; 🅿; z 54834; Ⓟ 509; Ⓒ 586
Edgewater Estates; RMC Place; ROCK; ▲ La Prairie; ***253** P-10; ★ **JNSV**; mail Beloit z 53511; ● 100
Edgewood; RMC Place; WAUKESHA; ***253** N-12; ★ **MILW**; mail Pewaukee z 53072; pop. incl. with Pewaukee (Inc. Place)
Edmund; RMC Place; IOWA; ▲ Linden; **253** O-7; elev. 1,210ft./369m.; 🅿; z 53535; ● 150
Edson (Edson Center); RMC Place; CHIPPEWA; ▲ Edson; ***252** H-6; elev. 1,082ft./330m.; mail Boyd z 54726; ● 30
Edson; MCD-Town; CHIPPEWA; ***252** H-6; mail Boyd z 54726; Ⓟ 913; Ⓒ 966
Edson Center; CHIPPEWA; see Edson (RMC Place)
Edwards; RMC Place; SHEBOYGAN; ▲ Herman; ***253** L-13; elev. 760ft./232m.; ★ **SHEB**; mail Cleveland z 53015; ● 35
Egg Harbor; Inc. Place; DOOR; **252** B-13; elev. 600ft./183m.; 🅿; z 54209; Ⓟ 183; Ⓒ 250
Egg Harbor; MCD-Town; DOOR; ***252** B-13; 🅿; z 54209; Ⓟ 1,019; Ⓒ 1,194
Eidsvold; RMC Place; CLARK; ▲ Thorp; ***252** H-6; mail Stanley z 54768; rural
Eileen; MCD-Town; BAYFIELD; ***252** C-6; mail Ashland z 54806; Ⓟ 665; Ⓒ 640
Eisenstein; MCD-Town; PRICE; ***252** E-7; mail Park Falls z 54552; Ⓟ 679; Ⓒ 669
Eland; Inc. Place; SHAWANO; **252** H-10; elev. 1,235ft./376m.; 🅿; z 54427; Ⓟ 247; Ⓒ 251
Elba; MCD-Town; DODGE; ***253** M-11; mail Columbus z 53925; Ⓟ 964; Ⓒ 1,086
Elcho; RMC Place; LANGLADE; ▲ Elcho; **252** G-10; 🅿; z 54428; ● 550
Elcho; MCD-Town; LANGLADE; ***252** G-10; 🅿; z 54428; Ⓟ 1,075; Ⓒ 1,317
Elderon; Inc. Place; MARATHON; **252** I-10; elev. 1,199ft./365m.; 🅿; z 54429; Ⓟ 175; Ⓒ 189
Elderon; MCD-Town; MARATHON; ***252** I-10; 🅿; z 54429 & mail Hatley z 54440; does not include the Village of Elderon; Ⓟ 605; Ⓒ 567
Eldorado; RMC Place; FOND DU LAC; ▲ Eldorado; **253** L-11; elev. 880ft./268m.; 🅿; z 54932; ● 250
Eldorado; MCD-Town; FOND DU LAC; ***253** L-11; 🅿; z 54932; Ⓟ 1,409; Ⓒ 1,447
Eleva; Inc. Place; TREMPEALEAU; **252** I-5; elev. 865ft./264m.; 🅿; z 54738; Ⓟ 491; Ⓒ 635
Elk; MCD-Town; PRICE; ***252** F-7; mail Phillips z 54555; Ⓟ 1,059; Ⓒ 1,183
Elk Creek; RMC Place; TREMPEALEAU; ▲ Hale; ***252** J-5; mail Independence z 54747; ● 40

Entries in **UPPERCASE** are counties.
Entries in **bold** have populations of 2,500 or more.
Names in parentheses are alternate names.
Inc. Place — Incorporated Place
RMC Place — Rand McNally Designated Place
CDP — Census Designated Place
MCD — Minor Civil Division

⊡ County Seat
▲ Minor Civil Division
elev. Elevation
🅿 Post Office
🅷 Hospital
🅲 College
■ Principal Business Center
★ Ranally Metro Area (RMA) Abbreviation
z Zip Code(s)
Ⓟ Previous Census Population
Ⓡ Revised Census Population
Ⓐ Annexation Population
● Rand McNally Population Estimate
Ⓒ Final Census Population
Ⓢ Special Census Population
◆ Estimated Population

For additional definitions see Glossary, Volume 1, and Introduction, Volume 2.

Elk Grove; RMC Place; LAFAYETTE; ▲ Elk Grove; *253 P-7; mail Cuba City z 53807; ● 30

Elk Grove; MCD-Town; LAFAYETTE; *253 P-7; mail Cuba City z 53807; Ⓟ 476; Ⓒ 463

Elkhart Lake; Inc. Place; SHEBOYGAN; 253 L-13; elev. 945ft./288m.; 🅿; ★ **SHEB**; z 53020; Ⓟ 1,019; Ⓒ 1,021

Elkhorn; Inc. Place; ⊡ WALWORTH; 253 P-12; elev. 1,033ft./315m.; 🅿 🅷; z 53121; Ⓟ 5,337; Ⓒ 7,305

Elk Mound; Inc. Place; DUNN; 252 H-4; elev. 925ft./282m.; 🅿; z 54739; Ⓟ 765; Ⓒ 785

Elk Mound; MCD-Town; DUNN; *252 H-4; 🅿; z 54739; does not include the Village of Elk Mound; Ⓟ 749; Ⓒ 1,121

Ella; RMC Place; PEPIN; ▲ Frankfort; 252 I-3; mail Arkansaw z 54721

Ellenboro; RMC Place; GRANT; ▲ Ellenboro; *253 O-7; mail Lancaster z 53813; rural

Ellenboro; MCD-Town; GRANT; *253 O-7; mail Lancaster z 53813; Ⓟ 521; Ⓒ 608

Ellington; MCD-Town; OUTAGAMIE; *252 J-11; mail Hortonville z 54944; Ⓟ 2,099; Ⓒ 2,535

Ellis; RMC Place; PORTAGE; ▲ Sharon; *252 I-9; elev. 1,171ft./357m.; mail Stevens Point z 54481; ● 30

Ellison Bay; RMC Place; DOOR; ▲ Liberty Grove; 252 A-13; 🅿; z 54210; ● 380

Ellisville; RMC Place; KEWAUNEE; ▲ Montpelier; 252 J-13; mail Luxemburg z 54217; ● 50

Ellsworth; Inc. Place; ⊡ PIERCE; 252 I-2; elev. 1,226ft./374m.; 🅿; z 54010-11 & mail Beldenville z 54003; Ⓟ 2,706; Ⓒ 2,909

Ellsworth; MCD-Town; PIERCE; *252 I-2; 🅿; z 54010-11 & mail Beldenville z 54003; does not include the Village of Ellsworth; Ⓟ 1,030; Ⓒ 1,064

Elm Grove; Inc. Place; WAUKESHA; 251 E-3; elev. 746ft./227m.; 🅿; ★ **MILW**; z 53122; Ⓟ 6,261; Ⓒ 6,249

Elmhurst; RMC Place; LANGLADE; ▲ Rolling; *252 H-10; elev. 1,476ft./450m.; mail Antigo z 54409

Elm Island; RMC Place; RACINE; ▲ Waterford; *253 O-12; ★ **MILW**; mail Waterford z 53185; ● 300

Elmore; RMC Place; FOND DU LAC; ▲ Ashford; 253 M-12; mail Campbellsport z 53010; ● 80

Elm Tree Corners; RMC Place; BROWN; *252 I-13; elev. 636ft./194m.; ★ **GRBY**; mail Green Bay z 54301; pop. incl. with Howard (Inc. Place)

Elmwood; Inc. Place; PIERCE; 252 I-3; elev. 870ft./265m.; 🅿; z 54740; Ⓟ 775; Ⓒ 841

Elmwood Park; Inc. Place; RACINE; 253 P-13; ★ **MILW**; mail Racine z 53405; Ⓟ 534; Ⓒ 474

El Paso; RMC Place; PIERCE; ▲ El Paso; 252 I-2; mail Beldenville z 54003; ● 90

El Paso; MCD-Town; PIERCE; *252 I-3; mail Beldenville z 54003; Ⓟ 641; Ⓒ 690

Elroy; Inc. Place; JUNEAU; 253 L-7; elev. 959ft./292m.; 🅿; z 53929; Ⓟ 1,533; Ⓒ 1,578

Elton; RMC Place; LANGLADE; ▲ Evergreen; 252 G-11; 🅿; z 54430; ● 130

Embarrass; Inc. Place; WAUPACA; 252 I-11; elev. 808ft./246m.; 🅿; z 54933; Ⓟ 461; Ⓒ 399; Ⓡ 487

Emerald; RMC Place; ST. CROIX; ▲ Glenwood; 252 H-3; elev. 1,155ft./352m.; 🅿; z 54013; ● 120

Emerald; MCD-Town; ST. CROIX; *252 H-3; 🅿; z 54013; Ⓟ 630; Ⓒ 691

Emerald Grove; RMC Place; ROCK; ▲ Bradford; 253 P-11; elev. 903ft./275m.; mail Janesville z 53546; ● 90

Emery; MCD-Town; PRICE; *252 F-8; mail Brantwood z 54513; Ⓟ 322; Ⓒ 325

Emmet; MCD-Town; DODGE; *253 N-11; mail Watertown z 53098; Ⓟ 1,014; Ⓒ 1,221

Emmet; MCD-Town; MARATHON; *252 I-8; mail Edgar z 54426; Ⓟ 732; Ⓒ 842

Empire; MCD-Town; FOND DU LAC; *253 L-12; ★ **FDLC**; mail Fond du Lac z 54935; Ⓟ 2,485; Ⓒ 2,620

Enchanted Valley Estates; RMC Place; DANE; ▲ Middleton, Springfield; *253 N-9; elev. 1,100ft./335m.; ★ **MAD**; mail Middleton z 53562; ● 150

Endeavor; Inc. Place; MARQUETTE; 253 L-9; elev. 785ft./239m.; 🅿; z 53930; Ⓟ 316; Ⓒ 440

Enterprise; RMC Place; ONEIDA; ▲ Enterprise; 252 F-10; elev. 1,626ft./496m.; mail Pelican Lake z 54463; ● 90

Enterprise; MCD-Town; ONEIDA; *252 F-10; mail Pelican Lake z 54463; Ⓟ 271; Ⓒ 274

Ephraim; Inc. Place; DOOR; 252 A-13; elev. 600ft./183m.; 🅿; z 54211; Ⓟ 261; Ⓒ 353

Erdman; RMC Place; SHEBOYGAN; ▲ Sheboygan; *253 L-13; elev. 676ft./206m.; ★ **SHEB**; mail Sheboygan z 53083; ● 160

Erin; MCD-Town; WASHINGTON; *253 N-12; ★ **MILW**; mail Hartford z 53027, New Richmond z 54017; Ⓟ 2,817; Ⓒ 3,664

Erin Corner; RMC Place; ST. CROIX; ▲ Erin Prairie; *252 H-2; mail New Richmond z 54017; rural

Erin Prairie; MCD-Town; ST. CROIX; *252 H-2; mail Baldwin z 54002; Ⓟ 647; Ⓒ 658

Esadore Lake; TAYLOR; see Murat (RMC Place)

Esdaile; RMC Place; PIERCE; ▲ Hartland; *252 I-2; mail Bay City z 54723; ● 70

Esofea; RMC Place; VERNON; ▲ Jefferson; *253 L-6; mail Westby z 54667; ● 30

Estella; MCD-Town; CHIPPEWA; *252 G-5; mail Cornell z 54732; Ⓟ 449; Ⓒ 469

Ettrick; Inc. Place; TREMPEALEAU; 253 K-5; elev. 771ft./235m.; 🅿; z 54627; Ⓟ 461; Ⓒ 521

Ettrick; MCD-Town; TREMPEALEAU; *253 K-5; 🅿; z 54627; does not include the Village of Ettrick; Ⓟ 1,339; Ⓒ 1,284

Eureka; MCD-Town; POLK; *252 F-2; mail Saint Croix Falls z 54024; Ⓟ 1,201; Ⓒ 1,338

Eureka; RMC Place; WINNEBAGO; ▲ Rushford; 253 K-11; 🅿; z 54934; ● 250

Eureka Center; RMC Place; POLK; ▲ Eureka; *252 F-2; elev. 1,062ft./324m.; mail Saint Croix Falls z 54024; ● 40

Euren; RMC Place; KEWAUNEE; ▲ Lincoln; 252 I-14; elev. 751ft./229m.; mail Casco z 54205; ● 40

Evansville; Inc. Place; ROCK; 253 O-10; elev. 897ft./273m.; 🅿; z 53536; Ⓟ 3,174; Ⓒ 4,039

Evergreen; MCD-Town; LANGLADE; *252 G-11; mail White Lake z 54491; Ⓟ 483; Ⓒ 468

Evergreen; CDP-Census Area Only; MARATHON; ▲ Kronenwetter; *252 H-9; elev. 1,191ft./363m.; ★ **WAUS**; mail Mosinee z 54455; Ⓟ 3,423; Ⓒ 3,611

Evergreen; MCD-Town; WASHBURN; *252 E-3; mail Spooner z 54801; Ⓟ 910; Ⓒ 1,076

Excelsior; RMC Place; RICHLAND; ▲ Richwood; 253 N-6; mail Blue River z 53518; ● 75

Excelsior; MCD-Town; SAUK; *253 M-8; mail Rock Springs z 53961; Ⓟ 1,194; Ⓒ 1,410

Exeland; Inc. Place; SAWYER; 252 F-5; elev. 1,200ft./366m.; 🅿; z 54835; Ⓟ 180; Ⓒ 212

Exeter; MCD-Town; GREEN; *253 O-9; mail Belleville z 53508; Ⓟ 756; Ⓒ 1,261

Exile; RMC Place; PIERCE; ▲ Rock Elm; *252 I-3; elev. 1,172ft./357m.; mail Plum City z 54761; rural

F

Fahey Heights; RMC Place; DANE; ▲ Oregon, Rutland; *253 O-10; elev. 982ft./299m.; mail Oregon z 53575; ● 250

Fairbanks; MCD-Town; SHAWANO; *252 I-10; mail Tigerton z 54486; Ⓟ 600; Ⓒ 687

Fairburn; RMC Place; GREEN LAKE; ▲ Seneca; *253 K-10; elev. 774ft./236m.; mail Berlin z 54923; rural

Fairchild; Inc. Place; EAU CLAIRE; 252 I-6; elev. 1,080ft./329m.; 🅿; z 54741; Ⓟ 504; Ⓒ 564

Fairchild; MCD-Town; EAU CLAIRE; *252 I-6; 🅿; z 54741; does not include the Village of Fairchild; Ⓟ 312; Ⓒ 351

Fairfield; RMC Place; ROCK, WALWORTH; ▲ Darien, Bradford; *253 P-11; elev. 920ft./280m.; mail Darien z 53114; ● 25

Fairfield; MCD-Town; SAUK; *253 M-9; mail Baraboo z 53913; Ⓟ 826; Ⓒ 1,023

Fairplay; RMC Place; GRANT; ▲ Jamestown; *253 P-7; elev. 885ft./270m.; ★ **DUB**; mail Hazel Green z 53811

Fairview; RMC Place; CRAWFORD; ▲ Utica; *253 M-6; mail Ferryville z 54628; ● 30

Fairview Beach; RMC Place; WINNEBAGO; ▲ Oshkosh; *253 K-12; ★ **OSH**; mail Oshkosh z 54901; ● 100

Fairwater; Inc. Place; FOND DU LAC; 253 L-11; elev. 940ft./287m.; 🅿; z 53931; Ⓟ 302; Ⓒ 350

Fall City; RMC Place; DUNN; ▲ Spring Brook; *252 I-4; mail Elk Mound z 54739; ● 40

Fall Creek; Inc. Place; EAU CLAIRE; 252 I-5; elev. 939ft./286m.; 🅿; z 54742; Ⓟ 1,034; Ⓒ 1,236

Fall Hall Glen; RMC Place; JACKSON; ▲ Manchester; *253 K-6; mail Black River Falls z 54615; rural

Fall River; Inc. Place; COLUMBIA; 253 M-10; elev. 858ft./262m.; 🅿; z 53932; Ⓟ 842; Ⓒ 1,097

Falun; RMC Place; BURNETT; ▲ Wood River, Daniels; 252 E-2; mail Grantsburg z 54840; ● 100

Fargo; RMC Place; VERNON; ▲ Franklin; *253 M-6; mail Viroqua z 54665; rural

Farmersville; RMC Place; DODGE; ▲ Williamstown, LeRoy; *253 M-12; mail Mayville z 53050; ● 40

Farmhill; RMC Place; PIERCE; ▲ Rock Elm; *252 I-3; elev. 1,147ft./350m.; mail Elmwood z 54740; rural

Farmington; RMC Place; JEFFERSON; ▲ Farmington; *253 N-11; mail Watertown z 53094; ● 50

Farmington; MCD-Town; JEFFERSON; *253 N-11; mail Watertown z 53094; Ⓟ 1,404; Ⓒ 1,498

Farmington; MCD-Town; LA CROSSE; *253 K-5; mail Mindoro z 54644; Ⓟ 1,576; Ⓒ 1,733

Farmington; MCD-Town; POLK; *252 G-2; mail New Richmond z 54017; Ⓟ 1,267; Ⓒ 1,625

Farmington; MCD-Town; WASHINGTON; *253 M-13; mail Kewaskum z 53040; Ⓟ 2,523; Ⓒ 3,239

Farmington; MCD-Town; WAUPACA; *252 J-10; mail Waupaca z 54981; Ⓟ 3,602; Ⓒ 4,148

Fayette; RMC Place; LAFAYETTE; ▲ Fayette; 253 O-8; mail Darlington z 53530; ● 40

Fayette; MCD-Town; LAFAYETTE; *253 O-8; mail Darlington z 53530; Ⓟ 390; Ⓒ 366

Fence; RMC Place; FLORENCE; ▲ Fence; 252 E-12; elev. 1,548ft./472m.; 🅿; z 54120; ● 100

Fence; MCD-Town; FLORENCE; *252 E-11; 🅿; z 54120; Ⓟ 222; Ⓒ 231

Fennimore; Inc. Place; GRANT; 253 O-6; elev. 1,200ft./366m.; 🅿; z 53809; Ⓟ 2,378; Ⓒ 2,387

Fennimore; MCD-Town; GRANT; *253 O-7; 🅿; z 53809; does not include the City of Fennimore; Ⓟ 556; Ⓒ 599

Fenwood; Inc. Place; MARATHON; 252 H-8; elev. 1,300ft./396m.; 🅿; z 54426; Ⓟ 214; Ⓒ 174

Fern; MCD-Town; FLORENCE; *252 E-12; mail Florence z 54121; Ⓟ 112; Ⓒ 153

Ferryville; Inc. Place; CRAWFORD; 253 M-5; elev. 634ft./193m.; 🅿; z 54628; Ⓟ 154; Ⓒ 174

Fifield; RMC Place; PRICE; ▲ Fifield; 252 E-7; elev. 1,451ft./442m.; 🅿; z 54524; ● 330

Fifield; MCD-Town; PRICE; *252 E-7; 🅿; z 54524; Ⓟ 863; Ⓒ 989

Fillmore; RMC Place; WASHINGTON; ▲ Farmington; *253 M-13; elev. 848ft./258m.; mail Fredonia z 53021; ● 110

Finley; RMC Place; JUNEAU; ▲ Finley; 253 K-8; elev. 952ft./290m.; mail Necedah z 54646; ● 30

Finley; MCD-Town; JUNEAU; *253 K-8; mail Necedah z 54646; Ⓟ 66; Ⓒ 84

Fish Creek; RMC Place; DOOR; ▲ Gibraltar; 252 A-13; elev. 583ft./178m.; 🅿; z 54212; summer pop. 2,000; ● 300

Fisk; RMC Place; WINNEBAGO; ▲ Utica; *253 K-11; elev. 838ft./255m.; mail Oshkosh z 54904; ● 30

Fitchburg; Inc. Place; DANE; 253 T-7; elev. 1,000ft./305m.; 🅿; ★ **MAD**; z 53575, z 53593, z 53711, z 53713, z 53719; Ⓟ 15,648; Ⓒ 20,501; ◆ 25,523

Fitzgerald Corners; RMC Place; WAUPACA; ▲ Weyauwega; *252 J-11; mail Manawa z 54949; rural

Five Corners; RMC Place; OUTAGAMIE; ▲ Osborn, Freedom; *252 J-12; elev. 818ft./249m.; ★ **APP**; mail Appleton z 54915; rural

Five Corners; RMC Place; OZAUKEE; ▲ Cedarburg; *253 M-13; elev. 877ft./267m.; ★ **MILW**; mail Cedarburg z 53012; ● 40

Five Points; RMC Place; RICHLAND; ▲ Akan; *253 N-7; mail Blue River z 53518; rural

Flambeau; MCD-Town; PRICE; *252 E-7; mail Phillips z 54555; Ⓟ 459; Ⓒ 535

Flambeau; RMC Place; RUSK; ▲ Washington; *252 G-5; mail Holcombe z 54745; ● 50

Flambeau; MCD-Town; RUSK; *252 F-5; mail Ladysmith z 54848; Ⓟ 1,018; Ⓒ 1,067

Flambeau Ridge; RMC Place; CHIPPEWA; ▲ Birch Creek; *252 G-5; mail Holcombe z 54745; rural

Flintville; RMC Place; BROWN; 252 I-13; ★ **GRBY**; mail Green Bay z 54301; ● 60

Florence; RMC Place; ⊡ FLORENCE; ▲ Florence; 252 E-12; elev. 1,296ft./395m.; 🅿; z 54121; ● 750

Florence; MCD-Town; FLORENCE; *252 E-12; 🅿; z 54121; Ⓟ 2,097; Ⓒ 2,319

FLORENCE; 252 E-12; Ⓟ 4,590; Ⓒ 5,088; ◆ 4,538

Folsom; RMC Place; VERNON; ▲ Franklin; *253 M-6; elev. 1,170ft./357m.; mail Soldiers Grove z 54655; rural

Fonda; RMC Place; MILWAUKEE; ★ **MILW**; pop. incl. with Milwaukee (Inc. Place)

Fond du Lac; Inc. Place; ⊡ FOND DU LAC; 253 L-12; elev. 760ft./232m.; 🅿 🅷 🅲 3,040 ■; ★ **FDLC**; z 54935-37; Ⓟ 37,757; Ⓒ 42,203; ◆ 41,442

Fond du Lac; MCD-Town; FOND DU LAC; *253 L-12; 🅿 🅲 3,040; ★ **FDLC**; z 54935-37; does not include the City of Fond du Lac; Ⓟ 2,308; Ⓒ 2,027

FOND DU LAC; 253 L-12; Ⓟ 90,083; Ⓒ 97,296; ◆ 98,467

Fontana (Fontana-on-Geneva Lake); Inc. Place; WALWORTH; 253 P-12; elev. 900ft./274m.; 🅿; z 53125; Ⓟ 1,635; Ⓒ 1,754

Fontana-on-Geneva Lake; WALWORTH; see Fontana (Inc. Place)

Fontenoy; RMC Place; BROWN; ▲ New Denmark; *252 J-13; mail Denmark z 54208; ● 30

Footville; Inc. Place; ROCK; 253 P-10; elev. 830ft./253m.; 🅿; z 53537; Ⓟ 764; Ⓒ 788

Ford; MCD-Town; TAYLOR; *252 G-6; mail Gilman z 54433; Ⓟ 254; Ⓒ 276

Forest; MCD-Town; FOND DU LAC; *253 L-12; mail Fond du Lac z 54935; Ⓟ 1,094; Ⓒ 1,108

Forest; MCD-Town; RICHLAND; *253 M-7; mail Viola z 54664; Ⓟ 339; Ⓒ 390

Forest; RMC Place; ST. CROIX; ▲ Forest; 252 G-3; mail Glenwood City z 54013; ● 50

Forest; MCD-Town; ST. CROIX; *252 G-3; mail Glenwood City z 54013; Ⓟ 614; Ⓒ 590

Forest; MCD-Town; VERNON; *253 L-7; mail La Farge z 54639; Ⓟ 543; Ⓒ 583

FOREST; 252 F-11; Ⓟ 8,776; Ⓒ 10,024; ◆ 9,643

Forest Junction; RMC Place; CALUMET; ▲ Brillion; 253 K-12; elev. 828ft./252m.; 🅿; z 54123; ● 200

Forestville; Inc. Place; DOOR; 252 I-14; elev. 633ft./193m.; 🅿; z 54213; Ⓟ 470; Ⓒ 429

Forestville; MCD-Town; DOOR; *252 I-14; 🅿; z 54213; does not include the Village of Forestville; Ⓟ 999; Ⓒ 1,086

Fort Atkinson; Inc. Place; JEFFERSON; 253 O-11; elev. 790ft./241m.; 🅿 🅷; z 53538; Ⓟ 10,227; Ⓒ 11,621

Fort Winnebago; MCD-Town; COLUMBIA; *253 M-9; mail Portage z 53901; Ⓟ 825; Ⓒ 855

Forward; RMC Place; DANE; ▲ Perry; *253 O-9; mail Mount Horeb z 53572; rural

Foster; MCD-Town; CLARK; *252 I-6; mail Willard z 54493; Ⓟ 85; Ⓒ 95

Foster; RMC Place; EAU CLAIRE; ▲ Clear Creek; 252 I-5; mail Osseo z 54758; ● 90

Fountain; MCD-Town; JUNEAU; *253 L-7; mail Elroy z 53929; Ⓟ 633; Ⓒ 582

Fountain City; Inc. Place; BUFFALO; 253 K-4; elev. 663ft./202m.; 🅿; z 54629; Ⓟ 938; Ⓒ 983

Fountain Prairie; MCD-Town; COLUMBIA; *253 M-10; mail Fall River z 53932; Ⓟ 743; Ⓒ 810

Four Corners; RMC Place; BURNETT; ▲ Trade Lake; *252 F-2; mail Frederic z 54837, Luck z 54853; rural

Four Corners; RMC Place; DOUGLAS; ▲ Superior; *252 C-3; elev. 1,056ft./322m.; mail Superior z 54880; rural

Foxboro; RMC Place; DOUGLAS; ▲ Summit; 252 C-3; 🅿; z 54836; ● 100

Fox Creek; RMC Place; POLK; ▲ Georgetown; *252 F-3; mail Balsam Lake z 54810

Fox Lake; Inc. Place; DODGE; 253 M-11; elev. 920ft./280m.; 🅿; z 53933; Ⓟ 1,269; Ⓒ 1,454

Fox Lake; MCD-Town; DODGE; *253 M-11; 🅿; z 53933; does not include the City of Fox Lake; Ⓟ 1,938; Ⓒ 2,402

Foxmoor Hills; RMC Place; DANE; ▲ Burke; *253 N-10; ★ **MAD**; mail Sun Prairie z 53590; ● 250

Fox Point; Inc. Place; MILWAUKEE; 253 N-13; elev. 672ft./205m.; 🅿; ★ **MILW**; z 53217; Ⓟ 7,238; Ⓒ 7,012

Fox River; RMC Place; KENOSHA; ▲ Salem; *253 P-12; ★ **CHI**; mail Burlington z 53105; ● 200

Francis Creek; Inc. Place; MANITOWOC; 253 K-13; 🅿; z 54214; Ⓟ 562; Ⓒ 681

Frankfort; MCD-Town; MARATHON; *252 H-8; mail Edgar z 54426; Ⓟ 606; Ⓒ 651

Frankfort; MCD-Town; PEPIN; *252 I-3; mail Arkansaw z 54721; Ⓟ 322; Ⓒ 362

Franklin; RMC Place; JACKSON; ▲ Franklin; 253 K-5; mail Taylor z 54659; ● 50

Franklin; MCD-Town; JACKSON; *253 K-5; mail Taylor z 54659; Ⓟ 431; Ⓒ 325

Franklin; MCD-Town; KEWAUNEE; *252 J-13; mail Kewaunee z 54216; Ⓟ 990; Ⓒ 997

Franklin; MCD-Town; MANITOWOC; *253 K-13; mail Reedsville z 54230; Ⓟ 1,325; Ⓒ 1,293

Franklin; Inc. Place; MILWAUKEE; 253 O-13; elev. 750ft./229m.; 🅿; ★ **MILW**; z 53132; Ⓟ 21,855; Ⓒ 29,494; ◆ 35,373

Franklin; MCD-Town; SAUK; *253 N-8; mail Loganville z 53943; Ⓟ 668; Ⓒ 696

Franklin; RMC Place; SHEBOYGAN; ▲ Herman; *253 L-13; ★ **SHEB**; mail Plymouth z 53073; ● 100

Franklin; MCD-Town; VERNON; *253 M-6; mail Viroqua z 54665; Ⓟ 926; Ⓒ 923

Franksville; CDP; RACINE; ▲ Caledonia; 253 O-13; elev. 735ft./224m.; 🅿; ★ **MILW**; z 53126; former CDP; became part of Caledonia November 16, 2005; Ⓒ 1,789

Franzen; MCD-Town; MARATHON; *252 I-10; mail Wittenberg z 54499; Ⓟ 532; Ⓒ 505

Frazer; RMC Place; SHAWANO; ▲ Maple Grove; *252 I-12; elev. 957ft./292m.; mail Pulaski z 54162; rural

Frederic; Inc. Place; POLK; 252 F-2; elev. 1,200ft./366m.; 🅿; z 54837; Ⓟ 1,124; Ⓒ 1,262

Fred John; RMC Place; MILWAUKEE; ★ **MILW**; mail Milwaukee z 53225; pop. incl. with Milwaukee (Inc. Place)

Fredonia; Inc. Place; OZAUKEE; 253 M-13; elev. 800ft./244m.; 🅿; ★ **MILW**; z 53021; Ⓟ 1,558; Ⓒ 1,934

Fredonia; MCD-Town; OZAUKEE; *253 M-13; 🅿; ★ **MILW**; z 53021 & mail Random Lake z 53075; does not include the Village of Fredonia; Ⓟ 2,043; Ⓒ 2,903; Ⓡ 2,083

Freedom; MCD-Town; FOREST; *252 G-11; mail Wabeno z 54566; Ⓟ 296; Ⓒ 376

Freedom; RMC Place; OUTAGAMIE; ▲ Freedom; 252 J-12; 🅿; ★ **APP**; z 54130-31, z 54165, z 54913; ● 400

Freedom; MCD-Town; OUTAGAMIE; *252 J-12; 🅿; ★ **APP**; z 54131; Ⓟ 4,114; Ⓒ 5,241

Freedom; MCD-Town; SAUK; *253 M-8; mail North Freedom z 53951; Ⓟ 422; Ⓒ 416

Freeman; MCD-Town; CRAWFORD; *253 M-5; mail Ferryville z 54628; Ⓟ 692; Ⓒ 719

Freistadt; RMC Place; OZAUKEE; *253 N-13; ★ **MILW**; mail Thiensville z 53092; pop. incl. with Mequon (Inc. Place)

Fremont; MCD-Town; CLARK; *252 I-7; mail Chili z 54420; Ⓟ 963; Ⓒ 1,190

Fremont; Inc. Place; WAUPACA; 252 J-11; elev. 750ft./229m.; 🅿; z 54940; Ⓟ 632; Ⓒ 666

Fremont; MCD-Town; WAUPACA; *252 J-11; 🅿; z 54940; does not include the Village of Fremont; Ⓟ 561; Ⓒ 632

French Island; CDP-Census Area Only; LA CROSSE; ▲ Campbell; 253 L-5; ★ **LACRO**; mail La Crosse z 54601; Ⓟ 4,478; Ⓒ 4,410

Frenchville; RMC Place; TREMPEALEAU; ▲ Gale; *253 K-5; mail Ettrick z 54627; ● 30

Friendship; Inc. Place; ⊡ ADAMS; 253 K-8; elev. 950ft./290m.; 🅿 🅷; z 53927, z 53934; Ⓟ 728; Ⓒ 698; Ⓡ 781

Friendship; MCD-Town; FOND DU LAC; *253 L-12; ★ **FDLC**; mail Fond du Lac z 54937; Ⓟ 2,220; Ⓒ 2,406

Friesland; Inc. Place; COLUMBIA; 253 M-10; elev. 1,000ft./305m.; 🅿; z 53923, z 53935; Ⓟ 271; Ⓒ 298

Frog Creek; MCD-Town; WASHBURN; *252 D-4; mail Minong z 54859; Ⓟ 155; Ⓒ 160

Fulton; RMC Place; ROCK; ▲ Fulton; *253 O-10; elev. 796ft./243m.; ★ **JNSV**; mail Edgerton z 53534; ● 110

Fulton; MCD-Town; ROCK; *253 O-10; ★ **JNSV**; mail Edgerton z 53534; Ⓟ 2,867; Ⓒ 3,158

Fussville; RMC Place; WAUKESHA; *253 N-13; ★ **MILW**; mail Menomonee Falls z 53051; pop. incl. with Menomonee Falls (Inc. Place)

G

Gad; RMC Place; TAYLOR; ▲ Browning; *252 H-8; mail Medford z 54451; ● 30

Gale; MCD-Town; TREMPEALEAU; *253 K-5; mail Galesville z 54630; Ⓟ 1,563; Ⓒ 1,426

Galesville; Inc. Place; TREMPEALEAU; 253 K-5; elev. 712ft./217m.; 🅿; z 54630; Ⓟ 1,278; Ⓒ 1,427

Galloway; RMC Place; MARATHON; ▲ Franzen; 252 I-10; elev. 1,174ft./358m.; 🅿; z 54432; ● 120

Garden Valley; MCD-Town; JACKSON; *252 J-6; mail Alma Center z 54611; Ⓟ 386; Ⓒ 406

Garden Village; RMC Place; ROCK; ▲ Beloit; *253 P-10; ★ **RKFD**; mail Beloit z 53511; ● 1,300

Gardner; MCD-Town; DOOR; *252 H-14; mail Brussels z 54204; Ⓟ 1,025; Ⓒ 1,197

Garfield; MCD-Town; JACKSON; *252 I-5; mail Osseo z 54758; Ⓟ 421; Ⓒ 529

Garfield; MCD-Town; POLK; *252 G-2; mail Amery z 54001; Ⓟ 1,107; Ⓒ 1,443

Garfield; RMC Place; PORTAGE; ▲ New Hope; *252 I-10; elev. 1,147ft./350m.; mail Amherst Junction z 54407; rural

Garnet; RMC Place; FOND DU LAC; ▲ Calumet; *253 K-12; elev. 943ft./287m.; mail Malone z 53049; ● 30

Gays Mills; Inc. Place; CRAWFORD; 253 M-6; elev. 700ft./213m.; 🅿; z 54631; Ⓟ 578; Ⓒ 625

Genesee; RMC Place; WAUKESHA; ▲ Genesee; 253 O-12; ★ **MILW**; mail Mukwonago z 53149; ● 450

Genesee; MCD-Town; WAUKESHA; *253 O-12; ★ **MILW**; mail Mukwonago z 53149; Ⓟ 5,986; Ⓒ 7,284

Genesee Depot; RMC Place; WAUKESHA; ▲ Genesee; *253 O-12; elev. 909ft./277m.; 🅿; ★ **MILW**; z 53127; ● 580

Geneva; MCD-Town; WALWORTH; *253 P-12; mail Elkhorn z 53121; Ⓟ 3,472; Ⓒ 4,099

Geneva Road; RMC Place; KENOSHA; ★ **KEN**; pop. incl. with Pleasant Prairie (Inc. Place)

Genevista; RMC Place; WALWORTH; ▲ Linn; *253 P-12; elev. 949ft./289m.; mail Lake Geneva z 53147; ● 160

Genoa; Inc. Place; VERNON; 253 M-5; elev. 700ft./213m.; 🅿; z 54632; Ⓟ 266; Ⓒ 263

Genoa; MCD-Town; VERNON; *253 M-5; 🅿; z 54632 & mail De Soto z 54624; does not include the Village of Genoa; Ⓟ 661; Ⓒ 705

Genoa City; Inc. Place; WALWORTH, KENOSHA; 253 P-12; elev. 824ft./251m.; 🅿; z 53128; Ⓟ 1,277; Ⓒ 1,949

Georgetown; RMC Place; GRANT; ▲ Smelser; *253 P-7; elev. 996ft./304m.; mail Cuba City z 53807; ● 60

Georgetown; MCD-Town; POLK; *252 F-3; mail Luck z 54853; Ⓟ 780; Ⓒ 1,004

Georgetown; MCD-Town; PRICE; *252 F-7; mail Kennan z 54537; Ⓟ 195; Ⓒ 164

Germania; RMC Place; IRON; *252 C-8; mail Montreal z 54550; pop. incl. with Montreal (Inc. Place)

Germania; RMC Place; MARQUETTE; ▲ Shields; 253 L-10; mail Neshkoro z 54960; ● 60

Germania; MCD-Town; SHAWANO; *252 I-10; mail Tigerton z 54486; Ⓟ 410; Ⓒ 339

Germantown; MCD-Town; JUNEAU; *253 L-8; mail Mauston z 53948; Ⓟ 615; Ⓒ 1,174

Germantown; RMC Place; RICHLAND; ▲ Westford; *253 M-7; mail Cazenovia z 53924; rural

Germantown; Inc. Place; WASHINGTON; 253 N-13; elev. 863ft./263m.; 🅿; ★ **MILW**; z 53022; Ⓟ 13,658; Ⓒ 18,260

Germantown; MCD-Town; WASHINGTON; *253 N-12; 🅿; ★ **MILW**; z 53022 & mail Richfield z 53076; Ⓟ 258; Ⓒ 278

Gibbsville; RMC Place; SHEBOYGAN; ▲ Lima; *253 L-13; elev. 722ft./220m.; ★ **SHEB**; mail Oostburg z 53070, Sheboygan Falls z 53085; ● 200

Gibraltar; MCD-Town; DOOR; *252 A-13; mail Fish Creek z 54212; Ⓟ 939; Ⓒ 1,063

Gibson; MCD-Town; MANITOWOC; *252 J-13; mail Mishicot z 54228; Ⓟ 1,445; Ⓒ 1,352

Gibson; RMC Place; MILWAUKEE; ★ **MILW**; pop. incl. with Milwaukee (Inc. Place)

Gilbert; RMC Place; LINCOLN; ▲ Bradley; *252 G-9; elev. 1,444ft./440m.; mail Tomahawk z 54487; rural

Gile; RMC Place; IRON; *252 C-7; 🅿; z 54525; pop. incl. with Montreal (Inc. Place)

Gillett; Inc. Place; OCONTO; 252 H-12; elev. 812ft./247m.; 🅿; z 54124; Ⓟ 1,303; Ⓒ 1,256; Ⓡ 1,262

Gillett; MCD-Town; OCONTO; *252 H-12; 🅿; z 54124; does not include the City of Gillett; Ⓟ 1,026; Ⓒ 1,085; Ⓡ 1,090

Gillingham; RMC Place; RICHLAND; ▲ Marshall; 253 M-7; elev. 802ft./244m.; mail Richland Center z 53581; ● 100

Gills Rock; RMC Place; DOOR; ▲ Liberty Grove; 252 A-13; mail Ellison Bay z 54210; summer pop. 200; ● 100

Gilman; MCD-Town; PIERCE; *252 H-3; mail Spring Valley z 54767; Ⓟ 762; Ⓒ 772

Gilman; Inc. Place; TAYLOR; 252 G-6; elev. 1,216ft./371m.; 🅿; z 54433-34; Ⓟ 412; Ⓒ 474

Gilmanton; RMC Place; BUFFALO; ▲ Gilmanton; 252 J-4; elev. 786ft./240m.; 🅿; z 54743; ● 150

Gilmanton; MCD-Town; BUFFALO; *252 J-4; 🅿; z 54743; Ⓟ 469; Ⓒ 470

Gingles; MCD-Town; ASHLAND; *252 C-6; mail Ashland z 54806; Ⓟ 492; Ⓒ 640

Glasgow; RMC Place; TREMPEALEAU; ▲ Gale; *253 K-5; elev. 733ft./223m.; mail Ettrick z 54627; rural

Gleason; RMC Place; LINCOLN; ▲ Russell; 252 G-9; 🅿; z 54435; ● 200

Glen; ADAMS; see Davis Corners (RMC Place)

Glenbeulah; Inc. Place; SHEBOYGAN; 253 L-13; elev. 973ft./297m.; 🅿; z 53023; Ⓟ 386; Ⓒ 378

Glencoe; MCD-Town; BUFFALO; *252 J-4; mail Fountain City z 54629; Ⓟ 502; Ⓒ 478

Glendale; Inc. Place; MILWAUKEE; 253 N-13; elev. 650ft./198m.; 🅿 ■; ★ **MILW**; z 53209, z 53211-12, z 53217; Ⓟ 14,088; Ⓒ 13,367; ◆ 14,111

Glendale; RMC Place; MONROE; ▲ Glendale; 253 L-7; elev. 1,073ft./327m.; mail Kendall z 54638; ● 30

Glendale; MCD-Town; MONROE; *253 L-7; mail Kendall z 54638; Ⓟ 564; Ⓒ 579; Ⓡ 563

Glen Flora; Inc. Place; RUSK; 252 F-6; elev. 1,276ft./389m.; 🅿; z 54526; Ⓟ 108; Ⓒ 93

Glen Haven; RMC Place; GRANT; ▲ Glen Haven; 253 O-5; 🅿; z 53810; ● 170

Glen Haven; MCD-Town; GRANT; *253 O-6; 🅿; z 53810; Ⓟ 548; Ⓒ 490

Glenmore; MCD-Town; BROWN; *252 J-13; mail Denmark z 54208; Ⓟ 1,057; Ⓒ 1,187

Glenwood; MCD-Town; ST. CROIX; *252 H-3; mail Glenwood City z 54013; Ⓟ 700; Ⓒ 755

Glenwood City; Inc. Place; ST. CROIX; 252 H-3; elev. 1,026ft./313m.; 🅿; z 54013; Ⓟ 1,026; Ⓒ 1,183

Glidden; RMC Place; ASHLAND; ▲ Jacobs; 252 D-7; 🅿; z 54527; ● 500

Globe; RMC Place; CLARK; ▲ Weston; *252 I-6; elev. 1,127ft./344m.; mail Neillsville z 54456; rural

Goetz; MCD-Town; CHIPPEWA; *252 H-5; mail Cadott z 54727; Ⓟ 640; Ⓒ 695

Goodman; RMC Place; MARINETTE; ▲ Goodman; 252 F-12; 🅿; z 54125; ● 460

Goodman; MCD-Town; MARINETTE; *252 F-12; 🅿; z 54125; Ⓟ 758; Ⓒ 820

Goodnow; RMC Place; ONEIDA; ▲ Cassian; *252 F-9; mail Harshaw z 54529; rural

Goodrich; RMC Place; TAYLOR; ▲ Goodrich; 252 G-8; elev. 1,424ft./434m.; mail Medford z 54451; ● 40

Goodrich; MCD-Town; TAYLOR; *252 G-8; mail Medford z 54451; Ⓟ 454; Ⓒ 487

Gooseville; RMC Place; SHEBOYGAN; ▲ Sherman; *253 M-13; ★ **SHEB**; mail Random Lake z 53075; rural

Gordon; MCD-Town; ASHLAND; *252 D-6; mail Glidden z 54527; Ⓟ 301; Ⓒ 357

Gordon; RMC Place; DOUGLAS; ▲ Gordon; 252 D-4; elev. 1,035ft./315m.; 🅿; z 54838; ● 450

Gordon; MCD-Town; DOUGLAS; *252 D-4; 🅿; z 54838; Ⓟ 553; Ⓒ 645

Gotham; RMC Place; RICHLAND; ▲ Buena Vista; 253 N-7; 🅿; z 53540; ● 300

Grafton; Inc. Place; OZAUKEE; 253 M-13; elev. 770ft./235m.; 🅿; ★ **MILW**; z 53024; Ⓟ 9,340; Ⓒ 10,312; Ⓡ 10,464

Grafton; MCD-Town; OZAUKEE; *253 M-13; 🅿; ★ **MILW**; z 53024; does not include the Village of Grafton; Ⓟ 3,745; Ⓒ 4,132; Ⓡ 3,980

Grand Chute; MCD-Town; OUTAGAMIE; *252 J-12; 🅿; ★ **APP**; z 54911-15; Ⓟ 14,490; Ⓒ 18,392; ◆ 21,750

Grand Marsh; RMC Place; ADAMS; ▲ New Chester; 253 L-9; elev. 1,010ft./308m.; 🅿; z 53936; ● 300

Grand Rapids; MCD-Town; WOOD; *252 J-9; mail Wisconsin Rapids z 54494; Ⓟ 7,071; Ⓒ 7,801

Grand View; RMC Place; BAYFIELD; ▲ Grandview; 252 C-5; 🅿; z 54839; ● 280

Grandview; MCD-Town; BAYFIELD; *252 D-6; 🅿; z 54839; Ⓟ 419; Ⓒ 483

Grange Hall; PIERCE; see Ono (RMC Place)

Granite Heights; RMC Place; MARATHON; ▲ Texas; *252 H-9; elev. 1,215ft./370m.; mail Wausau z 54403; rural

Grant; MCD-Town; CLARK; *252 I-7; mail Granton z 54436; Ⓟ 890; Ⓒ 920

Grant; MCD-Town; DUNN; *252 H-4; mail Colfax z 54730; Ⓟ 412; Ⓒ 426

Grant; MCD-Town; MONROE; *253 K-7; mail Warrens z 54666; Ⓟ 346; Ⓒ 483

Grant; MCD-Town; PORTAGE; *252 J-9; mail Wisconsin Rapids z 54494; Ⓟ 1,673; Ⓒ 2,020

Grant; MCD-Town; RUSK; *252 G-5; mail Ladysmith z 54848; Ⓟ 847; Ⓒ 767

Grant; MCD-Town; SHAWANO; *252 I-11; mail Marion z 54950; Ⓟ 946; Ⓒ 974

GRANT; 253 O-6; Ⓟ 49,264; Ⓒ 49,597; ◆ 49,731

Granton; Inc. Place; CLARK; 252 I-7; elev. 1,160ft./354m.; 🅿; z 54436; Ⓟ 379; Ⓒ 406

Grantsburg; Inc. Place; BURNETT; 252 E-2; elev. 950ft./290m.; 🅿 🅷; z 54840; Ⓟ 1,144; Ⓒ 1,369

Grantsburg; MCD-Town; BURNETT; *252 E-2; 🅿; z 54840; Ⓟ 860; Ⓒ 967

Granville; RMC Place; MILWAUKEE; *253 N-13; elev. 737ft./225m.; ★ **MILW**; pop. incl. with Milwaukee (Inc. Place)

Gratiot; Inc. Place; LAFAYETTE; 253 P-8; elev. 850ft./259m.; 🅿; z 53541; Ⓟ 207; Ⓒ 252

Gratiot; MCD-Town; LAFAYETTE; *253 P-8; 🅿; z 53541; does not include the Village of Gratiot; Ⓟ 709; Ⓒ 653

Gravesville; RMC Place; CALUMET; ▲ Charlestown; *253 K-12; mail Chilton z 53014; pop. incl. with Chilton (Inc. Place)

GREEN; 253 P-9; Ⓟ 30,339; Ⓒ 33,647; ◆ 36,314

Green Acres; RMC Place; WALWORTH; ▲ Geneva; *253 P-12; elev. 1,014ft./309m.; mail Elkhorn z 53121; pop. incl. with Elkhorn (Inc. Place)

Green Bay; Inc. Place; ⊡ BROWN; 252 J-13; elev. 594ft./181m.; 🅿 🅷 🅲 5,822 ■; ★ **GRBY**; z 54229, z 54301-08, z 54311, z 54313, z 54324, z 54344; Ⓟ 96,466; Ⓒ 102,313; Ⓡ 102,767; ◆ 103,405

Green Bay; MCD-Town; BROWN; *252 I-13; 🅿 🅲 5,822; ★ **GRBY**; z 54229, z 54301-08, z 54311, z 54313, z 54324, z 54344; does not include the City of Green Bay; Ⓟ 1,292; Ⓒ 1,772

Greenbush; RMC Place; SHEBOYGAN; ▲ Greenbush; 253 L-13; elev. 972ft./296m.; 🅿; z 53026; ● 200

Greenbush; MCD-Town; SHEBOYGAN; *253 L-13; 🅿; z 53026; Ⓟ 1,943; Ⓒ 2,773; Ⓡ 2,619

Greendale; Inc. Place; MILWAUKEE; 251 G-5; elev. 740ft./226m.; 🅿 ■; ★ **MILW**; z 53129; Ⓟ 15,128; Ⓒ 14,405; ◆ 15,146

Greenfield; MCD-Town; LA CROSSE; *253 L-5; mail Coon Valley z 54623; Ⓟ 1,617; Ⓒ 1,538

Greenfield; Inc. Place; MILWAUKEE; 253 O-13; elev. 820ft./250m.; 🅿 🅷 ■; ★ **MILW**; z 53219-21, z 53228 & mail Milwaukee z 53227; Ⓟ 33,403; Ⓒ 35,476; ◆ 38,860

Greenfield; MCD-Town; MONROE; *253 K-7; mail Tomah z 54660; Ⓟ 556; Ⓒ 626

Greenfield; MCD-Town; SAUK; *253 M-9; mail Baraboo z 53913; Ⓟ 758; Ⓒ 911

Greenfield Park; RMC Place; DANE; *253 O-9; ★ **MAD**; mail Madison z 53711; pop. incl. with Fitchburg (Inc. Place)

Green Grove; MCD-Town; CLARK; *252 H-7; mail Owen z 54460; Ⓟ 628; Ⓒ 902; Ⓡ 675

Green Lake; Inc. Place; ⊡ GREEN LAKE; 253 L-11; elev. 828ft./252m.; 🅿; z 54941; Ⓟ 1,064; Ⓒ 1,100

Green Lake; MCD-Town; GREEN LAKE; *253 L-11; 🅿; z 54941; does not include the Village of Green Lake; Ⓟ 1,335; Ⓒ 1,258

GREEN LAKE; 253 L-10; Ⓟ 18,651; Ⓒ 19,105; ◆ 18,412

Green Lake Terrace; RMC Place; GREEN LAKE; ▲ Princeton; *253 L-10; elev. 810ft./247m.; mail Green Lake z 54941; ● 230

Greenleaf; RMC Place; BROWN; ▲ Wrightstown; *252 J-13; 🅿; z 54126; ● 480

Greenstreet; RMC Place; MANITOWOC; ▲ Cooperstown; *252 J-13; mail Maribel z 54227; rural

Green Valley; MCD-Town; MARATHON; *252 I-8; mail Mosinee z 54455; Ⓟ 396; Ⓒ 514

Green Valley; RMC Place; SHAWANO; ▲ Green Valley; 252 I-12; elev. 813ft./248m.; 🅿; z 54127; ● 110

Green Valley; MCD-Town; SHAWANO; *252 I-12; 🅿; z 54127; Ⓟ 984; Ⓒ 1,024

Greenville; RMC Place; OUTAGAMIE; ▲ Greenville; 252 J-11; 🅿; ★ **APP**; z 54942; ● 300

Greenville; MCD-Town; OUTAGAMIE; *252 J-11; 🅿; ★ **APP**; z 54942; Ⓟ 3,806; Ⓒ 6,844

Greenwood; Inc. Place; CLARK; 252 I-7; elev. 1,168ft./356m.; 🅿; z 54437; Ⓟ 969; Ⓒ 1,079

Greenwood; MCD-Town; TAYLOR; *252 G-8; mail Medford z 54451; Ⓟ 634; Ⓒ 642

Greenwood; MCD-Town; VERNON; *253 M-7; mail Hillsboro z 54634; Ⓟ 574; Ⓒ 770

Gregorville; RMC Place; KEWAUNEE; ▲ Lincoln; *252 I-14; elev. 716ft./218m.; mail Algoma z 54201; rural

Grellton; RMC Place; JEFFERSON; ▲ Milford; *253 N-11; mail Watertown z 53094; ● 40

Gresham; Inc. Place; SHAWANO; 252 H-11; elev. 940ft./287m.; 🅿; z 54128; Ⓟ 515; Ⓒ 575

Grimms; RMC Place; MANITOWOC; ▲ Cato; *253 K-13; elev. 843ft./257m.; mail Reedsville z 54230; rural

Grover; MCD-Town; MARINETTE; *252 H-13; mail Peshtigo z 54157; Ⓟ 1,670; Ⓒ 1,729

Grover; MCD-Town; TAYLOR; *252 G-7; mail Medford z 54451; Ⓟ 214; Ⓒ 233

Grow; MCD-Town; RUSK; *252 G-6; mail Tony z 54563; Ⓟ 450; Ⓒ 473

Guenther; MCD-Town; MARATHON; *252 I-9; mail Mosinee z 54455; Ⓟ 258; Ⓒ 302

Gull Lake; MCD-Town; WASHBURN; *252 E-4; mail Springbrook z 54875; Ⓟ 148; Ⓒ 158

Gurney; RMC Place; IRON; ▲ Gurney; 252 C-7; elev. 1,094ft./333m.; 🅿; z 54559; ● 110

Gurney; MCD-Town; IRON; *252 C-7; 🅿; z 54559; Ⓟ 143; Ⓒ 158

H

Hackett; MCD-Town; PRICE; *252 F-7; mail Phillips z 54555; Ⓟ 214; Ⓒ 202

Hager; PIERCE; see Hager City (RMC Place)

Hager City (Hager); RMC Place; PIERCE; ▲ Trenton; 252 I-2; 🅿; z 54014; ● 200

Halder; RMC Place; MARATHON; ▲ Emmet; 252 I-8; mail Mosinee z 54455; ● 40

Hale; RMC Place; TREMPEALEAU; ▲ Hale; *252 J-5; mail Osseo z 54758; rural

Hale; MCD-Town; TREMPEALEAU; *252 J-5; mail Osseo z 54758; Ⓟ 971; Ⓒ 988

Hales Corners; Inc. Place; MILWAUKEE; 253 O-13; elev. 780ft./238m.; 🅿; ★ **MILW**; z 53130, z 53132; Ⓟ 7,623; Ⓒ 7,765

Hallie; RMC Place; CHIPPEWA; ▲ Hallie; *252 H-5; ★ **EAUC**; mail Chippewa Falls z 54729, Eau Claire z 54703; ● 1,300

Hallie; MCD-Town; CHIPPEWA; *252 H-5; ★ **EAUC**; mail Chippewa Falls z 54729, Eau Claire z 54703; Ⓟ 4,531; Ⓒ 4,703

Halsey; MCD-Town; MARATHON; *252 H-8; mail Athens z 54411; Ⓟ 512; Ⓒ 645

Hamburg; RMC Place; MARATHON; ▲ Hamburg; 252 H-8; 🅿; z 54411

Hamburg; MCD-Town; MARATHON; *252 H-8; 🅿; z 54411; Ⓟ 768; Ⓒ 910

Hamburg; MCD-Town; VERNON; *253 L-5; mail Chaseburg z 54621; Ⓟ 712; Ⓒ 848

Hamilton; MCD-Town; LA CROSSE; *253 L-5; ★ **LACRO**; mail West Salem z 54669; Ⓟ 1,633; Ⓒ 2,301; Ⓡ 2,103

Hammel; MCD-Town; TAYLOR; *252 G-7; mail Medford z 54451; Ⓟ 633; Ⓒ 735

Hammond; Inc. Place; ST. CROIX; 252 H-2; elev. 1,105ft./337m.; 🅿; z 54015 & mail Baldwin z 54002; Ⓟ 1,097; Ⓒ 1,153

Hammond; MCD-Town; ST. CROIX; *252 H-2; 🅿; z 54015 & mail Baldwin z 54002; does not include the Village of Hammond; Ⓟ 819; Ⓒ 947

Hampden; MCD-Town; COLUMBIA; *253 M-10; mail Rio z 53960; Ⓟ 566; Ⓒ 563

Hamples Corners; RMC Place; OUTAGAMIE; ▲ Center; *252 J-12; elev. 794ft./242m.; ★ **APP**; mail Appleton z 54915; rural

Hampton; RMC Place; MILWAUKEE; ★ **MILW**; mail Milwaukee z 53218; pop. incl. with Milwaukee (Inc. Place)

Hancock; Inc. Place; WAUSHARA; 253 K-9; elev. 1,089ft./332m.; 🅿; z 54943; Ⓟ 382; Ⓒ 463

Hancock; MCD-Town; WAUSHARA; *253 K-9; 🅿; z 54943; does not include the Village of Hancock; Ⓟ 467; Ⓒ 531

Haney; MCD-Town; CRAWFORD; *253 N-6; mail Gays Mills z 54631; Ⓟ 384; Ⓒ 330

Hannibal; RMC Place; TAYLOR; ▲ Cleveland; 252 G-6; elev. 1,267ft./386m.; 🅿; z 54439; ● 70

Hanover; RMC Place; ROCK; ▲ Plymouth; 253 P-10; 🅿; z 53542; ● 300

Hansen; MCD-Town; WOOD; *252 J-8; mail Vesper z 54489; Ⓟ 698; Ⓒ 707

Happy Corners; RMC Place; GRANT; ▲ Hazel Green; *253 P-7; mail Cuba City z 53807; rural

Harbor; RMC Place; MILWAUKEE; ★ **MILW**; mail Milwaukee z 53204; pop. incl. with Milwaukee (Inc. Place)

Harding; MCD-Town; LINCOLN; *252 G-8; mail Merrill z 54452; Ⓟ 283; Ⓒ 334

Harmony; RMC Place; MARINETTE; ▲ Grover; 252 B-11; elev. 700ft./213m.; mail Peshtigo z 54157; ● 35

Harmony; MCD-Town; PRICE; *252 F-7; mail Catawba z 54515; Ⓟ 203; Ⓒ 211

Harmony; MCD-Town; ROCK; *253 O-11; ★ **JNSV**; mail Janesville z 53545; Ⓟ 2,138; Ⓒ 2,351

Harmony; MCD-Town; VERNON; *253 M-5; mail Viroqua z 54665; Ⓟ 551; Ⓒ 739

Harmony Grove; RMC Place; COLUMBIA; ▲ Lodi; *253 M-9; elev. 800ft./244m.; mail Lodi z 53555; ● 400

Harris; MCD-Town; MARQUETTE; *253 L-9; mail Montello z 53949; Ⓟ 715; Ⓒ 729

Harrison; MCD-Town; CALUMET; *253 K-12; ★ **APP**; mail Appleton z 54911; Ⓟ 3,195; Ⓒ 5,756

Harrison; MCD-Town; GRANT; *253 O-7; mail Platteville z 53818; Ⓟ 544; Ⓒ 497

Harrison; RMC Place; LINCOLN; ▲ Harrison; 252 F-9; elev. 596ft./182m.; mail Gleason z 54435; ● 30

Harrison; MCD-Town; LINCOLN; *252 F-9; mail Gleason z 54435; Ⓟ 660; Ⓒ 793

Harrison; MCD-Town; MARATHON; *252 H-10; mail Antigo z 54409; Ⓟ 383; Ⓒ 418

Harrison; MCD-Town; WAUPACA; *252 I-10; mail Iola z 54945; Ⓟ 432; Ⓒ 509

Harrisville; RMC Place; MARQUETTE; ▲ Harris; 253 L-9; elev. 820ft./250m.; mail Montello z 53949, Westfield z 53964; ● 200

Harshaw; RMC Place; ONEIDA; ▲ Cassian; *252 F-9; 🅿; z 54529; ● 100

Hartford; Inc. Place; WASHINGTON, DODGE; 253 M-12; elev. 992ft./302m.; 🅿 🅷; z 53027; Ⓟ 8,188; Ⓒ 10,905

Hartford; MCD-Town; WASHINGTON; *253 N-12; 🅿; z 53027; does not include the City of Hartford; Ⓟ 3,243; Ⓒ 4,031

Hartland; MCD-Town; PIERCE; *252 I-2; mail Ellsworth z 54011; Ⓟ 766; Ⓒ 814

Hartland; MCD-Town; SHAWANO; *252 I-12; mail Bonduel z 54107; Ⓟ 764; Ⓒ 825

Hartland; Inc. Place; WAUKESHA; 253 N-12; elev. 930ft./283m.; 🅿; ★ **MILW**; z 53029; Ⓟ 6,906; Ⓒ 7,905

Harvey Estates; RMC Place; DANE; ▲ Pleasant Springs; *253 O-10; elev. 878ft./268m.; ★ **MAD**; mail Stoughton z 53589; ● 120

Hatchville; RMC Place; DUNN; ▲ Lucas; *252 H-3; elev. 1,202ft./366m.; mail Menomonie z 54751; rural

Hatfield; RMC Place; JACKSON; ▲ Adams; 252 J-6; elev. 886ft./270m.; mail Merrillan z 54754; summer pop. 500; ● 150

Hatley; Inc. Place; MARATHON; 252 H-10; elev. 1,280ft./390m.; 🅿; z 54440; Ⓟ 295; Ⓒ 476

Hauer; RMC Place; SAWYER; ▲ Sand Lake; *252 E-5; mail Stone Lake z 54876; rural

Haugen; Inc. Place; BARRON; 252 F-4; elev. 1,229ft./375m.; 🅿; z 54841 & mail Brill z 54818; Ⓟ 305; Ⓒ 287

Haven; RMC Place; SHEBOYGAN; ▲ Mosel; *253 L-13; 🅿; z 53083; ● 40

Hawkins; Inc. Place; RUSK; 252 F-6; elev. 1,369ft./417m.; 🅿; z 54530; Ⓟ 375; Ⓒ 317

Hawkins; MCD-Town; RUSK; *252 F-6; 🅿; z 54530; does not include the Village of Hawkins; Ⓟ 163; Ⓒ 170

Hawthorne; RMC Place; DOUGLAS; ▲ Hawthorne; 252 C-4; 🅿; z 54842; ● 120

Hawthorne; MCD-Town; DOUGLAS; *252 C-4; 🅿; z 54842; Ⓟ 1,049; Ⓒ 1,045

Hayes; RMC Place; OCONTO; ▲ How; 252 H-12; mail Suring z 54174; ● 30

Hay River; MCD-Town; DUNN; *252 H-3; mail Boyceville z 54725; Ⓟ 510; Ⓒ 546

Hayton; RMC Place; CALUMET; ▲ Charlestown; 253 K-13; elev. 833ft./254m.; mail Chilton z 53014; ● 100

Hayward; Inc. Place; ⊡ SAWYER; 252 E-5; elev. 1,198ft./365m.; 🅿 🅷; z 54843; Ⓟ 1,897; Ⓒ 2,129

Hayward; MCD-Town; SAWYER; *252 E-5; 🅿; z 54843; does not include the City of Hayward; Ⓟ 3,017; Ⓒ 3,279

Hazel Green; Inc. Place; GRANT, LAFAYETTE; 253 P-7; elev. 950ft./290m.; 🅿; z 53811; Ⓟ 1,171; Ⓒ 1,183

Hazel Green; MCD-Town; GRANT; *253 P-7; 🅿; z 53811; does not include the Village of Hazel Green; Ⓟ 1,108; Ⓒ 1,043

Hazelhurst; RMC Place; ONEIDA; ▲ Hazelhurst; 252 E-9; elev. 1,612ft./491m.; 🅿; z 54531; ● 500

Hazelhurst; MCD-Town; ONEIDA; *252 E-9; 🅿; z 54531; Ⓟ 927; Ⓒ 1,267

Heafford Junction; RMC Place; LINCOLN; ▲ Bradley; 252 F-9; elev. 1,491ft./454m.; 🅿; z 54532; ● 200

Heart Prairie; RMC Place; WALWORTH; ▲ La Grange; *253 O-11; mail Whitewater z 53190; ● 25

Hebel; RMC Place; BROWN; ▲ New Denmark, Glenmore; *252 J-13; mail Denmark z 54208; ● 30

Hebron; CDP; JEFFERSON; ▲ Hebron; 253 O-11; elev. 840ft./256m.; mail Fort Atkinson z 53538; Ⓒ 243

Hebron; MCD-Town; JEFFERSON; *253 O-11; mail Fort Atkinson z 53538; Ⓟ 975; Ⓒ 1,135

Hegg; RMC Place; TREMPEALEAU; ▲ Ettrick; *253 K-5; mail Ettrick z 54627; ● 50

Helena; RMC Place; IOWA; ▲ Arena; *253 N-8; mail Arena z 53503; rural

Helenville; CDP; JEFFERSON; ▲ Jefferson; 253 O-11; elev. 845ft./258m.; 🅿; z 53137; Ⓒ 225

Helvetia; MCD-Town; WAUPACA; *252 I-10; mail Ogdensburg z 54962; Ⓟ 587; Ⓒ 649

Hendren; MCD-Town; CLARK; *252 I-6; mail Willard z 54493; Ⓟ 542; Ⓒ 513

Henrietta; MCD-Town; RICHLAND; *253 M-7; mail Cazenovia z 53924; Ⓟ 617; Ⓒ 479

Henrysville; RMC Place; BROWN; ▲ Eaton; *252 J-13; elev. 897ft./273m.; mail Luxemburg z 54217; rural

Herbster; RMC Place; BAYFIELD; ▲ Clover; 252 B-5; elev. 614ft./187m.; 🅿; z 54844; ● 75

Herman; MCD-Town; DODGE; *253 M-12; mail Rubicon z 53078; Ⓟ 1,127; Ⓒ 1,207

Herman; MCD-Town; SHAWANO; *252 I-11; mail Shawano z 54166; Ⓟ 739; Ⓒ 741

Herman; MCD-Town; SHEBOYGAN; *253 L-13; ★ **SHEB**; mail Sheboygan Falls z 53085; Ⓟ 1,820; Ⓒ 2,044

Herman Center; RMC Place; DODGE; ▲ Herman; *253 M-12; elev. 1,118ft./341m.; mail Mayville z 53050; rural

Herold; RMC Place; BUFFALO; ▲ Belvidere; *252 J-4; elev. 1,274ft./388m.; mail Alma z 54610; rural

Hersey; RMC Place; ST. CROIX; ▲ Springfield; 252 H-3; mail Wilson z 54027; ● 85

Hertel; RMC Place; BURNETT; ▲ La Follette; 252 E-3; 🅿; z 54845; ● 50

Hewett; MCD-Town; CLARK; *252 I-6; mail Neillsville z 54456; Ⓟ 314; Ⓒ 314

Hewitt; MCD-Town; MARATHON; *252 H-9; mail Wausau z 54401; Ⓟ 508; Ⓒ 545

Hewitt; Inc. Place; WOOD; ▲ Marshfield; 252 I-8; 🅿; z 54441; Ⓟ 595; Ⓒ 670

Hiawatha Trail Estates; RMC Place; ADAMS; ▲ Quincy; *253 L-8; elev. 900ft./274m.; mail Friendship z 53934; ● 40

Hickory Corners; RMC Place; OCONTO; ▲ Maple Valley; *252 H-12; elev. 837ft./255m.; mail Suring z 54174; ● 35

Hickory Grove; MCD-Town; GRANT; *253 N-7; mail Boscobel z 53805; Ⓟ 409; Ⓒ 443

Hickory Hill; RMC Place; DANE; ▲ Middleton; *253 O-10; elev. 1,100ft./335m.; ★ **MAD**; mail Verona z 53593; ● 110

Hickory Hill Estates; RMC Place; DANE; ▲ Middleton; *253 N-9; elev. 1,050ft./320m.; ★ **MAD**; mail Verona z 53593; ● 100

Hickory Meadows; RMC Place; DANE; ▲ Vienna; *253 N-10; elev. 950ft./290m.; mail Waunakee z 53597; ● 150

High Bridge; RMC Place; ASHLAND; ▲ Ashland; 252 C-6; 🅿; z 54846; ● 100

High Cliff; RMC Place; CALUMET; ▲ Harrison; *253 K-12; ★ **APP**; mail Menasha z 54952; pop. incl. with Sherwood (Inc. Place)

Highland; MCD-Town; DOUGLAS; *252 C-4; mail Lake Nebagamon z 54849; Ⓟ 207; Ⓒ 245

Highland; Inc. Place; IOWA; 253 N-7; elev. 1,200ft./366m.; 🅿; z 53543; Ⓟ 799; Ⓒ 855

Highland; MCD-Town; IOWA; *253 N-7; 🅿; z 53543; does not include the Village of Highland; Ⓟ 756; Ⓒ 797

Highland Park; RMC Place; FOND DU LAC; ▲ Calumet; *253 L-12; elev. 763ft./233m.; mail Malone z 53049; ● 50

Highland Shore; RMC Place; WINNEBAGO; ▲ Algoma; *253 K-11; ★ **OSH**; mail Oshkosh z 54904; ● 100

Hika; RMC Place; MANITOWOC; *253 L-13; mail Cleveland z 53015

Hilbert; Inc. Place; CALUMET; 253 K-12; elev. 839ft./256m.; 🅿; z 54129; Ⓟ 1,211; Ⓒ 1,089

Hilbert Junction; RMC Place; CALUMET; *253 K-12; elev. 829ft./253m.; mail Hilbert z 54129; pop. incl. with Hilbert (Inc. Place)

Hiles; RMC Place; FOREST; ▲ Hiles; 252 F-10; 🅿; z 54511; ● 100

Hiles; MCD-Town; FOREST; *252 E-10; 🅿; z 54511; Ⓟ 312; Ⓒ 404

Hiles; MCD-Town; WOOD; *252 J-7; mail Pittsville z 54466; Ⓟ 144; Ⓒ 188

Hill; MCD-Town; PRICE; *252 G-7; mail Ogema z 54459; Ⓟ 360; Ⓒ 364

Hilldale; RMC Place; DANE; ★ **MAD**; mail Madison z 53705; pop. incl. with Madison (Inc. Place)

Hill Point; RMC Place; SAUK; ▲ Washington; 253 M-8; 🅿; z 53937; ● 100

Hillsboro; Inc. Place; VERNON; 253 L-7; elev. 1,001ft./305m.; 🅿 🅷; z 54634; Ⓟ 1,288; Ⓒ 1,302

Hillsboro; MCD-Town; VERNON; *253 L-7; 🅿; z 54634 & mail Kendall z 54638; does not include the City of Hillsboro; Ⓟ 642; Ⓒ 766

Hillsdale; RMC Place; BARRON; ▲ Maple Grove; 252 G-4; 🅿; z 54733; ● 180

Hillside; RMC Place; DANE; ▲ Christiana; *253 O-10; mail Cambridge z 53523; rural

Hilltop; RMC Place; MILWAUKEE; ★ **MILW**; mail Milwaukee z 53205, z 53233; pop. incl. with Milwaukee (Inc. Place)

Hines; RMC Place; DOUGLAS; ▲ Hawthorne, Amnicon; *252 C-4; mail South Range z 54874; rural

Hingham; RMC Place; SHEBOYGAN; ▲ Lima; 253 L-13; 🅿; ★ **SHEB**; z 53031; ● 250

Hintz; RMC Place; OCONTO; ▲ Underhill; *252 H-12; mail Gillett z 54124; rural

Hixon; MCD-Town; CLARK; *252 H-7; mail Withee z 54498; Ⓟ 673; Ⓒ 740

Hixton; Inc. Place; JACKSON; 252 J-6; elev. 925ft./282m.; 🅿; z 54635; Ⓟ 345; Ⓒ 446

Hixton; MCD-Town; JACKSON; *252 J-6; 🅿; z 54635; does not include the Village of Hixton; Ⓟ 652; Ⓒ 611

Hoard; MCD-Town; CLARK; *252 H-7; mail Curtiss z 54422; Ⓟ 805; Ⓒ 594; Ⓡ 821

Hobart; Inc. Place; BROWN; *252 I-13; 🅿; z 54313 & mail Green Bay z 54303; incorporated May 13, 2003; not reported in 2000 Census; ● 5,500

Ho-Chunk Reservation; Indian Reservation; JACKSON, DANE, JUNEAU, MONROE, SAUK, SHAWANO, WOOD; Ⓒ 638

Hofa Park; RMC Place; SHAWANO; ▲ Maple Grove; *252 I-12; elev. 904ft./276m.; mail Seymour z 54165; ● 40

Hogarty; RMC Place; MARATHON; ▲ Harrison, Plover; *252 H-10; elev. 1,465ft./447m.; mail Aniwa z 54408

Holcombe; RMC Place; CHIPPEWA; ▲ Lake Holcombe; 252 G-5; 🅿; z 54745; ● 330

Holiday Heights; RMC Place; ADAMS; ▲ Quincy; *253 L-8; elev. 900ft./274m.; mail Friendship z 53934; ● 100

Holiday Hills; RMC Place; ROCK; ▲ Beloit; *253 P-10; ★ **RKFD**; mail Beloit z 53511; ● 500

Holland; RMC Place; BROWN; ▲ Holland; 252 J-12; elev. 769ft./234m.; mail Kaukauna z 54130; ● 100

Holland; MCD-Town; BROWN; *252 J-13; mail Kaukauna z 54130; Ⓟ 1,237; Ⓒ 1,339

Holland; MCD-Town; LA CROSSE; *253 K-5; mail Holmen z 54636; Ⓟ 2,172; Ⓒ 3,042

Holland; MCD-Town; SHEBOYGAN; *253 M-13; ★ **SHEB**; mail Oostburg z 53070; Ⓟ 2,567; Ⓒ 2,360

Hollandale; Inc. Place; IOWA; 253 O-8; elev. 862ft./263m.; 🅿; z 53544; Ⓟ 256; Ⓒ 283

Hollister; RMC Place; LANGLADE; ▲ Wolf River; 252 G-11; elev. 1,378ft./420m.; mail White Lake z 54491; ● 50

Holmen; Inc. Place; LA CROSSE; 253 K-5; elev. 718ft./219m.; 🅿; ★ **LACRO**; z 54636; Ⓟ 3,236; Ⓒ 6,200

Holmsville; ADAMS; see Dellwood (RMC Place)

Holton; MCD-Town; MARATHON; *252 H-7; mail Abbotsford z 54405; Ⓟ 971; Ⓒ 907

Holway; MCD-Town; TAYLOR; *252 H-7; mail Medford z 54451; Ⓟ 779; Ⓒ 854

Holy Cross; RMC Place; OZAUKEE; ▲ Belgium; *253 M-13; elev. 782ft./238m.; mail Belgium z 53004; ● 70

Homestead; MCD-Town; FLORENCE; *252 E-12; mail Florence z 54121; Ⓟ 337; Ⓒ 378

Honey Creek; MCD-Town; SAUK; *253 M-8; mail Plain z 53577; Ⓟ 725; Ⓒ 736

Honey Creek; RMC Place; WALWORTH, RACINE; ▲ Rochester, Spring Prairie; 253 O-12; elev. 783ft./239m.; 🅿; ★ **MILW**; z 53138; ● 400

Honey Lake; RMC Place; RACINE, WALWORTH; ▲ Spring Prairie, Rochester; *253 O-12; ★ **MILW**; mail Burlington z 53105; ● 700

Hoopers Mill; RMC Place; JEFFERSON; ▲ Milford; *253 N-11; mail Lake Mills z 53551; rural

Hope; RMC Place; DANE; ▲ Cottage Grove; *253 N-10; elev. 870ft./265m.; ★ **MAD**; mail Cottage Grove z 53527; rural

Horicon; Inc. Place; DODGE; 253 M-11; elev. 884ft./269m.; 🅿; z 53032; Ⓟ 3,873; Ⓒ 3,775

Horns Corners; RMC Place; OZAUKEE; ▲ Cedarburg; *253 M-13; elev. 849ft./259m.; ★ **MILW**; mail Cedarburg z 53012; ● 50

Horse Creek; RMC Place; POLK; ▲ Alden; *252 G-2; mail Osceola z 54020, Star Prairie z 54026; ● 50

Hortonia; MCD-Town; OUTAGAMIE; *252 J-11; ★ **APP**; mail New London z 54961; Ⓟ 883; Ⓒ 1,063

Hortonville; Inc. Place; OUTAGAMIE; 252 J-11; elev. 794ft./242m.; 🅿; ★ **APP**; z 54944; Ⓟ 2,029; Ⓒ 2,357

Houlton; RMC Place; ST. CROIX; ▲ St. Joseph; 252 H-1; 🅿; ★ **MPLS-**; z 54082; ● 250

How; MCD-Town; OCONTO; *252 H-12; mail Suring z 54174; Ⓟ 564; Ⓒ 563

Howard; Inc. Place; BROWN; 252 I-13; elev. 590ft./180m.; 🅿; ★ **GRBY**; z 54303, z 54313; Ⓟ 9,874; Ⓒ 13,546

Howard; MCD-Town; CHIPPEWA; *252 H-4; mail Colfax z 54730; Ⓟ 625; Ⓒ 648

Howards Grove (Howards Grove-Millersville); Inc. Place; SHEBOYGAN; 253 L-13; 🅿; ★ **SHEB**; z 53083; Ⓟ 2,329; Ⓒ 2,792

Howards Grove-Millersville; SHEBOYGAN; see Howards Grove (Inc. Place)

Hubbard; MCD-Town; DODGE; *253 M-11; mail Horicon z 53032; Ⓟ 1,390; Ⓒ 1,643

Hubbard; MCD-Town; RUSK; *252 F-5; mail Ladysmith z 54848; Ⓟ 216; Ⓒ 168

Hubbleton; RMC Place; JEFFERSON; ▲ Milford; *253 N-11; mail Watertown z 53094; ● 80

Hub City; RMC Place; RICHLAND; ▲ Henrietta; 253 M-7; mail Richland Center z 53581; ● 100

Hubertus; RMC Place; WASHINGTON; ▲ Richfield; 251 A-1; elev. 1,014ft./309m.; 🅿; ★ **MILW**; z 53033; ● 170

Hudson; Inc. Place; ⊡ ST. CROIX; 252 H-2; elev. 780ft./238m.; 🅿 🅷; ★ **MPLS-**; z 54016 & mail Houlton z 54082; Ⓟ 6,378; Ⓒ 8,775

Hudson; MCD-Town; ST. CROIX; *252 H-2; 🅿; ★ **MPLS-**; z 54016 & mail Houlton z 54082; does not include the City of Hudson; Ⓟ 3,692; Ⓒ 6,213

Hughes; MCD-Town; BAYFIELD; *252 C-5; mail Brule z 54820; Ⓟ 334; Ⓒ 408

Huilsburg; RMC Place; DODGE; ▲ Herman; *253 M-12; elev. 1,119ft./341m.; mail Rubicon z 53078; ● 30

Hull; MCD-Town; MARATHON; *252 H-7; mail Colby z 54421; Ⓟ 836; Ⓒ 773

Hull; MCD-Town; PORTAGE; *252 I-9; mail Stevens Point z 54481; Ⓟ 5,559; Ⓒ 5,493

Humbird; RMC Place; CLARK; ▲ Mentor; 252 I-6; 🅿; z 54746; ● 250

Humboldt; RMC Place; BROWN; ▲ Humboldt; *252 J-13; elev. 800ft./244m.; mail New Franken z 54229; ● 30

Humboldt; MCD-Town; BROWN; *252 J-13; mail Luxemburg z 54217; Ⓟ 1,334; Ⓒ 1,338

Hunter; MCD-Town; SAWYER; *252 E-5; mail Hayward z 54843; Ⓟ 557; Ⓒ 765

Hunting; RMC Place; SHAWANO; ▲ Grant; *252 I-10; mail Tigerton z 54486; rural

Huntington; RMC Place; ST. CROIX; ▲ Star Prairie; *252 G-2; mail New Richmond z 54017; ● 60

Hurley; Inc. Place; ⊡ IRON; 252 C-8; elev. 1,493ft./455m.; 🅿; z 54534 & mail Upson z 54565; Ⓟ 1,782; Ⓒ 1,818

Huron; RMC Place; CHIPPEWA; ▲ Colburn; *252 H-6; mail Stanley z 54768

Hurricane; RMC Place; GRANT; ▲ South Lancaster; *253 O-6; elev. 986ft./301m.; mail Lancaster z 53813; rural

Husher; RMC Place; RACINE; ▲ Caledonia; *253 O-13; ★ **MILW**; mail Caledonia z 53108; ● 70

Hustisford; Inc. Place; DODGE; 253 M-11; elev. 860ft./262m.; 🅿; z 53034; Ⓟ 979; Ⓒ 1,135

Hustisford; MCD-Town; DODGE; *253 M-11; 🅿; z 53034 & mail Juneau z 53039; does not include the Village of Hustisford; Ⓟ 1,209; Ⓒ 1,379

Hustler; Inc. Place; JUNEAU; 253 L-7; elev. 929ft./283m.; 🅿; z 54637; Ⓟ 156; Ⓒ 113

Hutchins; MCD-Town; SHAWANO; *252 H-10; mail Birnamwood z 54414; Ⓟ 523; Ⓒ 539

Hyde; RMC Place; IOWA; ▲ Ridgeway; *253 N-8; elev. 784ft./239m.; mail Ridgeway z 53582; rural

I

Idlewild; RMC Place; DOOR; ▲ Nasewaupee; *252 H-14; mail Sturgeon Bay z 54235; summer pop. 200; ● 70

Iduna; RMC Place; TREMPEALEAU; ▲ Ettrick; *253 K-5; mail Ettrick z 54627; rural

Imalone; RMC Place; RUSK; ▲ Murry; *252 F-5; mail Bruce z 54819; rural

Independence; Inc. Place; TREMPEALEAU; 252 J-5; elev. 782ft./238m.; 🅿; z 54747; Ⓟ 1,041; Ⓒ 1,244

Indian Creek; RMC Place; POLK; ▲ Lorain; *252 F-3; mail Frederic z 54837

Indianford; RMC Place; ROCK; ▲ Fulton; 253 O-10; ★ **JNSV**; mail Edgerton z 53534; ● 250

Indian Shores; RMC Place; WINNEBAGO; ▲ Winneconne; *253 K-11; ★ **OSH**; mail Winneconne z 54986; ● 120

Ingram; Inc. Place; RUSK; 252 F-6; elev. 1,290ft./393m.; 🅿; z 54526; Ⓟ 91; Ⓒ 76

Inlet; RMC Place; WALWORTH; ▲ Delavan; *253 P-11; mail Delavan z 53115; ● 450

Ino; RMC Place; BAYFIELD; ▲ Keystone; 252 C-5; elev. 977ft./298m.; mail Mason z 54856

Institute; RMC Place; DOOR; ▲ Sevastopol; 252 B-13; mail Sturgeon Bay z 54235; ● 50

Iola; Inc. Place; WAUPACA; 252 J-10; elev. 955ft./291m.; 🅿; z 54945, z 54990; Ⓟ 1,125; Ⓒ 1,298

Iola; MCD-Town; WAUPACA; *252 I-10; 🅿; z 54945, z 54990; does not include the Village of Iola; Ⓟ 637; Ⓒ 818

IOWA; 253 N-7; Ⓟ 20,150; Ⓒ 22,780; ◆ 23,417

Irma; RMC Place; LINCOLN; ▲ Birch; 252 G-9; 🅿; z 54442; ● 100

IRON; 252 D-7; Ⓟ 6,153; Ⓒ 6,861; ◆ 6,116

Iron Belt; RMC Place; IRON; ▲ Knight; 252 C-7; 🅿; z 54536; ● 470

Iron Ridge; Inc. Place; DODGE; 253 M-12; elev. 916ft./279m.; 🅿; z 53035; Ⓟ 887; Ⓒ 998

Iron River; RMC Place; BAYFIELD; ▲ Iron River; 252 C-5; 🅿; z 54847; ● 900

Entries in **UPPERCASE** are counties.
Entries in **bold** have populations of 2,500 or more.
Names in parentheses are alternate names.

Inc. Place	Incorporated Place
RMC Place	Rand McNally Designated Place
CDP	Census Designated Place
MCD	Minor Civil Division
⊡	County Seat
▲	Minor Civil Division
elev.	Elevation
🅿	Post Office
🅷	Hospital
🅲	College
■	Principal Business Center
★	Ranally Metro Area (RMA) Abbreviation
z	Zip Code(s)
Ⓟ	Previous Census Population
Ⓡ	Revised Census Population
Ⓐ	Annexation Population
●	Rand McNally Population Estimate
Ⓒ	Final Census Population
Ⓢ	Special Census Population
◆	Estimated Population

For additional definitions see Glossary, Volume 1, and Introduction, Volume 2

Iron River; MCD-Town; BAYFIELD; *252 C-5; 🅿; z 54847; Ⓟ 901; Ⓒ 1,059
Ironton; Inc. Place; SAUK; **253** M-8; elev. 954ft./291m.; mail La Valle z 53941; Ⓟ 200; Ⓒ 250
Ironton; MCD-Town; SAUK; *253 M-8; mail Reedsburg z 53959; does not include the Village of Ironton; Ⓟ 585; Ⓒ 650
Irving; MCD-Town; JACKSON; *253 K-6; mail Black River Falls z 54615; Ⓟ 565; Ⓒ 602
Irvington; RMC Place; DUNN; ▲ Menomonie; **252** H-3; elev. 771ft./235m.; mail Menomonie z 54751; ● 120
Isaar; RMC Place; OUTAGAMIE; ▲ Seymour; *252 I-12; mail Seymour z 54165; ● 50
Isabelle; MCD-Town; PIERCE; *252 I-2; mail Bay City z 54723; Ⓟ 196; Ⓒ 315; Ⓡ 289
Island Beach; RMC Place; WINNEBAGO; ▲ Algoma; *253 K-12; ★ **OSH**; mail Oshkosh z 54901; ● 100
Island Lake; RMC Place; RUSK; ▲ Big Bend; **252** G-5; mail New Auburn z 54757; ● 30
Island Park; RMC Place; WINNEBAGO; ▲ Rushford; *253 K-11; elev. 750ft./229m.; mail Omro z 54963; seasonal pop. 55; rural
Itasca; RMC Place; DOUGLAS; *252 B-3; elev. 647ft./197m.; ★ **DUL**; mail Superior z 54880; pop. incl. with Superior (Inc. Place)
Ithaca; RMC Place; RICHLAND; ▲ Ithaca; **253** M-7; elev. 734ft./224m.; mail Richland Center z 53581; ● 100
Ithaca; MCD-Town; RICHLAND; *253 M-7; mail Richland Center z 53581; Ⓟ 632; Ⓒ 648
Ives; RMC Place; RACINE; *253 O-13; elev. 649ft./198m.; ★ **MILW**; mail Racine z 53404
Ives Grove; RMC Place; RACINE; ▲ Yorkville; **251** J-8; ★ **MILW**; mail Sturtevant z 53177, Union Grove z 53182; ● 50
Ixonia; CDP; JEFFERSON; ▲ Ixonia; **253** N-11; elev. 870ft./265m.; 🅿; ★ **MILW**; z 53036; Ⓒ 642
Ixonia; MCD-Town; JEFFERSON; *253 N-11; 🅿; ★ **MILW**; z 53036; Ⓟ 2,789; Ⓒ 2,902

J

Jackson; MCD-Town; ADAMS; *253 L-9; mail Oxford z 53952; Ⓟ 641; Ⓒ 926
Jackson; MCD-Town; BURNETT; *252 E-3; mail Webster z 54893; Ⓟ 457; Ⓒ 765
Jackson; Inc. Place; WASHINGTON; **253** M-12; elev. 896ft./273m.; 🅿; ★ **MILW**; z 53037; Ⓟ 2,486; Ⓒ 4,938
Jackson; MCD-Town; WASHINGTON; *253 M-13; 🅿; ★ **MILW**; z 53037; does not include the Village of Jackson; Ⓟ 3,172; Ⓒ 3,516
JACKSON; **252** J-7; Ⓟ 16,588; Ⓒ 19,100; ◆ 20,050
Jacksonport; RMC Place; DOOR; ▲ Jacksonport; **252** B-13; elev. 593ft./181m.; mail Sturgeon Bay z 54235; summer pop. 350; ● 60
Jacksonport; MCD-Town; DOOR; *252 B-13; mail Sturgeon Bay z 54235; Ⓟ 689; Ⓒ 738
Jacobs; MCD-Town; ASHLAND; *252 D-7; mail Glidden z 54527; Ⓟ 885; Ⓒ 835
Jamestown; MCD-Town; GRANT; *253 P-7; ★ **DUB**; mail Cuba City z 53807; Ⓟ 2,175; Ⓒ 2,077
Janesville; Inc. Place; ⊡ ROCK; **253** P-10; elev. 858ft./262m.; 🅿 🅷 ■; ★ **JNSV**; z 53545-48; Ⓟ 52,133; Ⓒ 59,498; Ⓡ 60,200; ◆ 61,931
Janesville; MCD-Town; ROCK; *253 O-10; 🅿; ★ **JNSV**; z 53545-48; does not include the City of Janesville; Ⓟ 3,198; Ⓒ 3,750; Ⓡ 3,048
Jefferson; MCD-Town; GREEN; *253 P-9; mail Juda z 53550; Ⓟ 1,130; Ⓒ 1,212
Jefferson; Inc. Place; ⊡ JEFFERSON; **253** O-11; elev. 795ft./242m.; 🅿; z 53549; Ⓟ 6,078; Ⓒ 7,338
Jefferson; MCD-Town; JEFFERSON; *253 O-11; 🅿; z 53549 & mail Helenville z 53137; does not include the City of Jefferson; Ⓟ 2,673; Ⓒ 2,265
Jefferson; MCD-Town; MONROE; *253 L-6; mail Cashton z 54619; Ⓟ 815; Ⓒ 800
Jefferson; MCD-Town; VERNON; *253 M-6; mail Westby z 54667; Ⓟ 915; Ⓒ 974
JEFFERSON; **253** N-11; Ⓟ 67,783; Ⓒ 74,021; Ⓡ 75,767; ◆ 80,262
Jefferson Junction; RMC Place; JEFFERSON; ▲ Aztalan; *253 N-11; elev. 811ft./247m.; mail Jefferson z 53549; rural
Jenkynsville; RMC Place; LAFAYETTE; ▲ Elk Grove, Benton; *253 P-7; elev. 976ft./297m.; mail Cuba City z 53807; ● 20
Jennings (Lennox); RMC Place; ONEIDA; ▲ Schoepke; **252** F-10; mail Pelican Lake z 54463; ● 40
Jericho; RMC Place; CALUMET; ▲ Brothertown; *253 K-12; mail Chilton z 53014; ● 80
Jericho; RMC Place; WAUKESHA; ▲ Mukwonago, Eagle; *253 O-12; elev. 902ft./275m.; ★ **MILW**; mail Eagle z 53119; rural
Jewett; RMC Place; ST. CROIX; ▲ Erin Prairie; *252 G-2; mail New Richmond z 54017; rural
Jim Falls; RMC Place; CHIPPEWA; ▲ Anson; **252** H-5; elev. 956ft./291m.; 🅿; z 54748; ● 300
Johannesburg; RMC Place; ST. CROIX; ▲ Star Prairie; *252 G-2; elev. 900ft./274m.; mail New Richmond z 54017; rural
Johnsburg; RMC Place; FOND DU LAC; ▲ Taycheedah; **253** L-12; ★ **FDLC**; mail Fond du Lac z 54935, Malone z 53049; ● 180
Johnson; MCD-Town; MARATHON; *252 H-8; mail Athens z 54411; Ⓟ 923; Ⓒ 993
Johnson Creek; Inc. Place; JEFFERSON; **253** N-11; elev. 812ft./247m.; 🅿; z 53038, z 53094; Ⓟ 1,259; Ⓒ 1,581
Johnsonville; RMC Place; SHEBOYGAN; ▲ Sheboygan Falls; *253 L-13; ★ **SHEB**; mail Sheboygan Falls z 53085; ● 65
Johnstown; MCD-Town; POLK; *252 F-3; mail Turtle Lake z 54889; Ⓟ 410; Ⓒ 520
Johnstown; RMC Place; ROCK; ▲ Johnstown; *253 P-11; mail Avalon z 53505; ● 50
Johnstown; MCD-Town; ROCK; *253 O-11; mail Avalon z 53505; Ⓟ 850; Ⓒ 802
Johnstown Center; RMC Place; ROCK; ▲ Johnstown; **253** P-11; mail Janesville z 53546; ● 90
Jonesdale; RMC Place; IOWA; ▲ Waldwick; *253 O-8; mail Mineral Point z 53565; ● 25
Jones Island; RMC Place; MILWAUKEE; ★ **MILW**; pop. incl. with Milwaukee (Inc. Place)
Jordan; MCD-Town; GREEN; *253 P-9; mail Argyle z 53504; Ⓟ 545; Ⓒ 577
Jordan; RMC Place; PORTAGE; ▲ Hull; *252 I-9; mail Stevens Point z 54481; rural
Jordan Center; RMC Place; GREEN; ▲ Jordan; *253 P-9; elev. 843ft./257m.; mail Argyle z 53504; ● 25
Jordan Lake; RMC Place; ADAMS; ▲ Jackson; *253 L-9; elev. 957ft./292m.; mail Oxford z 53952; ● 100
Juda; RMC Place; GREEN; ▲ Jefferson; **253** P-9; 🅿; z 53550; ● 450
Jump River; RMC Place; TAYLOR; ▲ Jump River; **252** G-6; 🅿; z 54434; ● 80
Jump River; MCD-Town; TAYLOR; *252 G-6; 🅿; z 54434; Ⓟ 330; Ⓒ 311
Junction City; Inc. Place; PORTAGE; **252** I-9; elev. 1,150ft./351m.; 🅿; z 54443; Ⓟ 502; Ⓒ 440
Juneau; Inc. Place; ⊡ DODGE; **253** M-11; elev. 920ft./280m.; 🅿; z 53039; Ⓟ 2,157; Ⓒ 2,485
Juneau; RMC Place; MILWAUKEE; ★ **MILW**; mail Milwaukee z 53202-03; pop. incl. with Milwaukee (Inc. Place)
JUNEAU; **253** K-8; Ⓟ 21,650; Ⓒ 24,316; ◆ 26,538

K

Kaiser; RMC Place; PRICE; ▲ Lake; *252 E-7; mail Park Falls z 54552; ● 30
Kansasville; RMC Place; RACINE; ▲ Dover; *253 P-13; elev. 823ft./251m.; 🅿; z 53139; ● 280
Kaukauna; Inc. Place; OUTAGAMIE; **252** J-12; elev. 710ft./216m.; 🅿; ★ **APP**; z 54130-31 & mail Wrightstown z 54180; Ⓟ 11,982; Ⓒ 12,983
Kaukauna; MCD-Town; OUTAGAMIE; *252 J-12; 🅿; z 54130-31 & mail Wrightstown z 54180; does not include the City of Kaukauna; Ⓟ 939; Ⓒ 1,142; Ⓡ 1,116
Keene; RMC Place; PORTAGE; ▲ Buena Vista; *252 J-9; mail Bancroft z 54921; rural
Keenville; RMC Place; WINNEBAGO; ▲ Oshkosh; *253 K-12; ★ **OSH**; mail Oshkosh z 54901; ● 200
Kekoskee; Inc. Place; DODGE; **253** M-11; elev. 909ft./277m.; mail Mayville z 53050; Ⓟ 188; Ⓒ 169
Kelley; MARATHON; see Kelly (RMC Place)
Kellner; RMC Place; PORTAGE, WOOD; ▲ Grand Rapids, Grant; **252** J-9; mail Wisconsin Rapids z 54494; ● 200
Kellnersville; Inc. Place; MANITOWOC; **252** J-13; elev. 827ft./252m.; 🅿; z 54215; Ⓟ 350; Ⓒ 374
Kelly; MCD-Town; BAYFIELD; *252 C-6; mail Mason z 54856; Ⓟ 383; Ⓒ 377
Kelly (Kelley); RMC Place; MARATHON; ▲ Weston; *252 H-9; elev. 1,219ft./372m.; ★ **WAUS**; mail Schofield z 54476; pop. incl. with Weston (Inc. Place)
Kempster; RMC Place; LANGLADE; ▲ Upham, Neva; **252** G-10; elev. 1,628ft./496m.; 🅿; z 54424
Kendall; MCD-Town; LAFAYETTE; *253 O-7; mail Darlington z 53530; Ⓟ 363; Ⓒ 320
Kendall; Inc. Place; MONROE; **253** L-7; elev. 1,021ft./311m.; 🅿; z 54638; Ⓟ 453; Ⓒ 469; Ⓡ 482
Kennan; Inc. Place; PRICE; **252** F-7; elev. 1,505ft./459m.; 🅿; z 54537; Ⓟ 169; Ⓒ 171
Kennan; MCD-Town; PRICE; *252 F-7; 🅿; z 54537; does not include the Village of Kennan; Ⓟ 330; Ⓒ 378
Kenosha; Inc. Place; ⊡ KENOSHA; **253** P-13; elev. 610ft./186m.; 🅿 🅷 🅲 7,764 ■; ★ **KEN**; z 53140-44, z 53158; Ⓟ 80,352; Ⓒ 90,352; ◆ 95,243
KENOSHA; **253** P-14; Ⓟ 128,181; Ⓒ 149,577; ◆ 164,148
Keshena; CDP; ⊡ MENOMINEE; ▲ Menominee; **252** H-11; elev. 829ft./253m.; 🅿; z 54135; Ⓟ 685; Ⓒ 1,394
Keshena Falls; RMC Place; MENOMINEE; ▲ Menominee; *252 H-11; mail Keshena z 54135; ● 40
Kettle Moraine Lake; RMC Place; FOND DU LAC; ▲ Osceola; *253 L-12; elev. 1,050ft./320m.; mail Campbellsport z 53010; summer pop. 150; ● 70
Kewaskum; Inc. Place; WASHINGTON, FOND DU LAC; **253** M-12; elev. 940ft./287m.; 🅿; z 53040; Ⓟ 2,515; Ⓒ 3,274; Ⓡ 3,277
Kewaskum; MCD-Town; WASHINGTON; *253 M-12; 🅿; z 53040; does not include the Village of Kewaskum; Ⓟ 1,139; Ⓒ 1,119
Kewaunee; Inc. Place; ⊡ KEWAUNEE; **252** J-14; elev. 700ft./213m.; 🅿 🅷; z 54216; Ⓟ 2,750; Ⓒ 2,806
KEWAUNEE; **252** J-14; Ⓟ 18,878; Ⓒ 20,187; ◆ 20,200
Keyeser; RMC Place; COLUMBIA; ▲ Leeds; *253 N-10; elev. 1,000ft./305m.; mail De Forest z 53532; ● 25
Keyesville; RMC Place; RICHLAND; ▲ Ithaca; *253 M-7; elev. 1,114ft./340m.; mail Hillpoint z 53937; rural
Keystone; MCD-Town; BAYFIELD; *252 C-5; mail Ashland z 54806; Ⓟ 320; Ⓒ 369
Keystone; RMC Place; CHIPPEWA; ▲ Cleveland; *252 G-5; elev. 1,167ft./356m.; mail Cornell z 54732; rural
Kickapoo; MCD-Town; VERNON; *253 M-6; mail Readstown z 54652; Ⓟ 472; Ⓒ 566
Kickapoo Center; RMC Place; VERNON; ▲ Kickapoo; *253 M-6; mail Viola z 54664; rural
Kiel; Inc. Place; MANITOWOC, CALUMET; **253** K-13; elev. 933ft./284m.; 🅿; z 53042; Ⓟ 2,910; Ⓒ 3,450
Kieler; RMC Place; GRANT; ▲ Jamestown; **253** P-7; elev. 853ft./260m.; 🅿; ★ **DUB**; z 53812; ● 480
Kildare; MCD-Town; JUNEAU; *253 L-8; mail Lyndon Station z 53944; Ⓟ 491; Ⓒ 557
Kimball; MCD-Town; IRON; *252 C-7; mail Hurley z 54534; Ⓟ 513; Ⓒ 540
Kimberly; Inc. Place; OUTAGAMIE; **252** J-12; elev. 734ft./224m.; 🅿; ★ **APP**; z 54136; Ⓟ 5,406; Ⓒ 6,146
King; MCD-Town; LINCOLN; *252 F-9; mail Tomahawk z 54487; Ⓟ 675; Ⓒ 842
King; RMC Place; WAUPACA; ▲ Farmington; **252** J-10; elev. 898ft./274m.; 🅿; z 54946; ● 750
Kingsbridge; RMC Place; MANITOWOC; ▲ Mishicot, Kossuth; *252 J-14; elev. 622ft./190m.; ★ **MNTW**; mail Two Rivers z 54241; rural
Kingston; Inc. Place; GREEN LAKE; **253** L-10; elev. 800ft./244m.; 🅿; z 53939; Ⓟ 346; Ⓒ 288
Kingston; MCD-Town; GREEN LAKE; *253 L-10; 🅿; z 53939 & mail Dalton z 53926; does not include the Village of Kingston; Ⓟ 776; Ⓒ 900
Kingston; MCD-Town; JUNEAU; *253 K-7; mail Mather z 54641; Ⓟ 57; Ⓒ 58
Kinnickinnic; MCD-Town; ST. CROIX; *252 H-2; mail River Falls z 54022; Ⓟ 1,139; Ⓒ 1,400
Kirby; RMC Place; MONROE; ▲ Lincoln; *253 K-7; mail Warrens z 54666; rural
Kirchhayn; RMC Place; WASHINGTON; ▲ Jackson; *253 N-13; elev. 885ft./270m.; ★ **MILW**; mail Cedarburg z 53012; ● 60
Klevenville; RMC Place; DANE; ▲ Springdale; *253 N-9; mail Mount Horeb z 53572; ● 30
Klondike (Timme); RMC Place; OCONTO; ▲ Brazeau; **252** H-12; elev. 792ft./241m.; mail Coleman z 54112, Pound z 54161; ● 50
Kloten; RMC Place; CALUMET; ▲ Stockbridge; *253 K-12; elev. 1,024ft./312m.; mail Chilton z 53014; rural
Knapp; Inc. Place; DUNN; **252** H-3; elev. 930ft./283m.; 🅿; z 54749; Ⓟ 419; Ⓒ 421
Knapp; MCD-Town; JACKSON; *252 J-7; mail Warrens z 54666; Ⓟ 257; Ⓒ 275
Kneeland; RMC Place; RACINE; ▲ Raymond; *253 O-13; ★ **MILW**; mail Caledonia z 53108; rural
Knellsville; RMC Place; OZAUKEE; ▲ Port Washington; *253 M-13; ★ **MILW**; mail Port Washington z 53074; ● 80
Knight; MCD-Town; IRON; *252 D-7; mail Iron Belt z 54536; Ⓟ 265; Ⓒ 284
Knowles; RMC Place; DODGE; ▲ Lomira; **253** M-12; 🅿; z 53048; ● 160
Knowlton; RMC Place; MARATHON; ▲ Knowlton; *252 I-9; mail Mosinee z 54455; ● 100
Knowlton; MCD-Town; MARATHON; *252 I-9; mail Mosinee z 54455; Ⓟ 1,414; Ⓒ 1,688
Knox; MCD-Town; PRICE; *252 F-8; mail Brantwood z 54513; Ⓟ 420; Ⓒ 399
Kodan; RMC Place; KEWAUNEE; ▲ Ahnapee; *252 I-14; elev. 656ft./200m.; mail Algoma z 54201; rural
Kohler (Little Kohler); RMC Place; OZAUKEE; ▲ Fredonia; *253 M-13; elev. 850ft./259m.; ★ **MILW**; mail Fredonia z 53021; ● 60
Kohler; Inc. Place; SHEBOYGAN; **253** L-13; elev. 676ft./206m.; 🅿; ★ **SHEB**; z 53044; Ⓟ 1,817; Ⓒ 1,926
Kohlsville; RMC Place; WASHINGTON; ▲ Wayne; *253 M-12; mail West Bend z 53090; ● 70
Kolberg; RMC Place; DOOR; ▲ Brussels; *252 I-14; elev. 705ft./215m.; mail Forestville z 54213
Komensky; MCD-Town; JACKSON; *252 J-6; mail Merrillan z 54754; Ⓟ 292; Ⓒ 462
Konsin Beach; RMC Place; CALUMET; ▲ Stockbridge; *253 K-12; mail Chilton z 53014; ● 40
Koshkonong; MCD-Town; JEFFERSON; *253 O-11; mail Fort Atkinson z 53538; Ⓟ 2,984; Ⓒ 3,395
Koshkonong; RMC Place; ROCK; ▲ Milton; *253 O-11; elev. 820ft./250m.; ★ **JNSV**; mail Fort Atkinson z 53538; rural
Kossuth; MCD-Town; MANITOWOC; *253 K-13; mail Manitowoc z 54220; Ⓟ 1,951; Ⓒ 2,033
Krakow; RMC Place; SHAWANO; ▲ Angelica; **252** I-12; 🅿; z 54137, z 54171; ● 350
Kroghville; RMC Place; JEFFERSON; ▲ Lake Mills; *253 N-10; mail Waterloo z 53594; rural
Krok; RMC Place; KEWAUNEE; ▲ West Kewaunee; *252 J-14; elev. 728ft./222m.; mail Kewaunee z 54216; rural
Kronenwetter; Inc. Place; MARATHON; *252 I-9; mail Mosinee z 54455; incorporated January 1, 2003; not reported in 2000 Census; ● 5,800
Kunesh; RMC Place; BROWN; ▲ Pittsfield; *252 I-12; elev. 754ft./230m.; ★ **GRBY**; mail Green Bay z 54301, Pulaski z 54162; ● 30

L

Lac Courte Oreilles Reservation; Indian Reservation; SAWYER; ▲ Ojibwa, Bass Lake, Couderay, Hayward, Hunter, Ojibwa, Radisson, Sand Lake; mail Stone Lake z 54876; Ⓟ 1,699; Ⓒ 2,886
Lac du Flambeau; CDP; VILAS; ▲ Lac du Flambeau; **252** E-8; elev. 1,635ft./498m.; 🅿; z 54538; Ⓟ 1,423; summer pop. 2,000; Ⓒ 1,646
Lac du Flambeau; MCD-Town; VILAS; *252 E-8; 🅿; z 54538; Ⓟ 2,433; Ⓒ 3,004
Lac du Flambeau Reservation; Indian Reservation; VILAS, IRON, ONEIDA; ▲ Lac du Flambeau, Sherman; mail Ashland z 54806, Lac du Flambeau z 54538; Ⓟ 2,211; Ⓒ 2,995
Lac La Belle; Inc. Place; WAUKESHA; **253** N-12; elev. 860ft./262m.; ★ **MILW**; mail Oconomowoc z 53066; Ⓟ 258; Ⓒ 329
La Crosse; Inc. Place; ⊡ LA CROSSE; **253** L-5; elev. 669ft./204m.; 🅿 🅷 🅲 12,417 ■; ★ **LACRO**; z 54601-03; Ⓟ 51,003; Ⓒ 51,818; ◆ 53,873
LA CROSSE; **253** L-5; Ⓟ 97,904; Ⓒ 107,120; ◆ 114,967
Ladoga; RMC Place; FOND DU LAC; ▲ Waupun, Springvale; *253 L-11; elev. 907ft./276m.; mail Waupun z 53963; rural
Ladysmith; Inc. Place; ⊡ RUSK; **252** F-5; elev. 1,144ft./349m.; 🅿 🅷; z 54848; Ⓟ 3,938; Ⓒ 3,932
La Farge; Inc. Place; VERNON; **253** M-6; elev. 797ft./243m.; 🅿; z 54639; Ⓟ 766; Ⓒ 775
Lafayette; MCD-Town; CHIPPEWA; *252 H-5; ★ **EAUC**; mail Chippewa Falls z 54729; Ⓟ 4,448; Ⓒ 5,199
Lafayette; MCD-Town; MONROE; *253 K-6; mail Sparta z 54656; Ⓟ 298; Ⓒ 318
Lafayette; MCD-Town; WALWORTH; *253 O-12; mail Elkhorn z 53121; Ⓟ 1,276; Ⓒ 2,251
LAFAYETTE; **253** P-8; Ⓟ 16,076; Ⓒ 16,137; ◆ 15,304
La Follette; MCD-Town; BURNETT; *252 E-3; mail Siren z 54872; Ⓟ 416; Ⓒ 511
La Grange; MCD-Town; MONROE; *253 K-7; mail Tomah z 54660; Ⓟ 1,507; Ⓒ 1,761
La Grange; RMC Place; WALWORTH; ▲ La Grange; *253 O-11; elev. 945ft./288m.; mail Whitewater z 53190; ● 30
La Grange; MCD-Town; WALWORTH; *253 O-11; mail Whitewater z 53190; Ⓟ 1,643; Ⓒ 2,444
Lake; MCD-Town; MARINETTE; *252 G-13; mail Porterfield z 54159; Ⓟ 989; Ⓒ 1,064
Lake; RMC Place; MILWAUKEE; *253 O-13; ★ **MILW**; pop. incl. with Milwaukee (Inc. Place)
Lake; MCD-Town; PRICE; *252 E-7; mail Park Falls z 54552; Ⓟ 1,333; Ⓒ 1,319
Lake Beulah; RMC Place; WALWORTH; ▲ East Troy; **253** O-12; elev. 832ft./254m.; ★ **MILW**; mail East Troy z 53120; ● 300
Lake Camelot; RMC Place; ADAMS; ▲ Rome; mail Rudolph z 54475
Lake Church; RMC Place; OZAUKEE; ▲ Belgium; *253 M-13; mail Belgium z 53004; ● 100
Lake Como; WALWORTH; see Como (CDP)
Lake Como Beach; RMC Place; WALWORTH; ▲ Geneva; mail Lake Geneva z 53147
Lake Delton; Inc. Place; SAUK; **253** M-9; elev. 894ft./272m.; 🅿; z 53940; Ⓟ 1,470; Ⓒ 1,982
Lake Eau Claire; RMC Place; EAU CLAIRE; ▲ Bridge Creek; *252 I-5; elev. 944ft./288m.; mail Augusta z 54722; summer pop. 500; ● 150
Lake Emily; RMC Place; PORTAGE; ▲ Amherst; *252 J-10; mail Amherst Junction z 54407; summer pop. 300; ● 150
Lakefield; RMC Place; OZAUKEE; ▲ Cedarburg; *253 N-13; elev. 702ft./214m.; ★ **MILW**; mail Grafton z 53024; ● 40
Lake Five; RMC Place; WASHINGTON, WAUKESHA; ▲ Lisbon, Richfield; *253 N-12; elev. 989ft./301m.; ★ **MILW**; mail Colgate z 53017; ● 200
Lake Geneva; Inc. Place; WALWORTH; **253** P-12; elev. 880ft./268m.; 🅿; z 53147; Ⓟ 5,979; Ⓒ 7,148
Lake George; RMC Place; KENOSHA; ▲ Bristol; *253 P-13; elev. 780ft./238m.; ★ **CHI**; mail Bristol z 53104; summer pop. 450; ● 250
Lake George; RMC Place; ONEIDA; ▲ Pelican; *252 F-10; mail Rhinelander z 54501; ● 80
Lake Hallie; Inc. Place; CHIPPEWA; ▲ Hallie; *252 H-5; ★ **EAUC**; mail Chippewa Falls z 54729; incorporated February 18, 2003; not reported in 2000 Census
Lake Holcombe; MCD-Town; CHIPPEWA; *252 G-5; mail Holcombe z 54745; Ⓟ 920; Ⓒ 1,010
Lake Ivanhoe; RMC Place; WALWORTH; ▲ Bloomfield; *253 P-12; elev. 897ft./273m.; mail Lake Geneva z 53147; ● 800
Lake Keesus; RMC Place; WAUKESHA; ▲ Merton; *253 N-12; elev. 997ft./304m.; ★ **MILW**; mail Hartland z 53029; summer pop. 700; ● 280
Lake Koshkonong; CDP-Census Area Only; JEFFERSON; *253 O-11; Ⓒ 1,219
Lake Lac La Belle; CDP-Census Area Only; JEFFERSON; *253 N-12; ★ **MILW**; Ⓒ 833
Lakeland; MCD-Town; BARRON; *252 F-3; mail Barronett z 54813; Ⓟ 789; Ⓒ 963
Lake Lorraine; RMC Place; WALWORTH; ▲ Richmond; *253 O-11; elev. 1,000ft./305m.; mail Delavan z 53115; ● 200
Lake Mills; Inc. Place; JEFFERSON; **253** N-11; elev. 831ft./253m.; 🅿; z 53551; Ⓟ 4,143; Ⓒ 4,843
Lake Mills; MCD-Town; JEFFERSON; *253 N-11; 🅿; z 53551; does not include the City of Lake Mills; Ⓟ 1,584; Ⓒ 1,936
Lake Nebagamon; Inc. Place; DOUGLAS; **252** C-4; elev. 1,149ft./350m.; 🅿; z 54849; Ⓟ 900; Ⓒ 1,015
Lake Ripley; CDP-Census Area Only; JEFFERSON; ▲ Oakland; *253 O-10; mail Cambridge z 53523; Ⓟ 1,218; Ⓒ 1,603
Lake Shangrila; CDP-Census Area Only; KENOSHA; ▲ Salem, Bristol; *253 P-13; elev. 837ft./255m.; ★ **CHI**; mail Bristol z 53104; Ⓒ 805
Lake Sherwood; RMC Place; ADAMS; ▲ Rome; *253 K-9; elev. 1,000ft./305m.; mail Nekoosa z 54457; summer pop. 2,000; ● 500
Lakeside; MCD-Town; DOUGLAS; *252 B-4; mail South Range z 54874; Ⓟ 569; Ⓒ 609
Lake Tichigan; RACINE; see Tichigan (RMC Place)
Lake Tomahawk (Tomahawk Lake); RMC Place; ONEIDA; ▲ Lake Tomahawk; **252** E-9; elev. 1,632ft./497m.; 🅿; z 54539; ● 700
Lake Tomahawk; MCD-Town; ONEIDA; *252 E-9; 🅿; z 54539; Ⓟ 851; Ⓒ 1,160
Laketown; MCD-Town; POLK; *252 F-2; mail Cushing z 54006; Ⓟ 921; Ⓒ 918
Lake Wazeecha; CDP-Census Area Only; WOOD; ▲ Grand Rapids; *252 J-9; elev. 1,032ft./315m.; mail Wisconsin Rapids z 54494; Ⓟ 2,278; Ⓒ 2,659
Lake Windsor; RMC Place; DANE; ▲ Windsor; *253 N-10; ★ **MAD**; mail Windsor z 53598
Lake Wisconsin; CDP-Census Area Only; COLUMBIA, SAUK; ▲ Caledonia, Dekorra, Lodi, Merrimac, West Point; *253 M-9; mail Lodi z 53555, Merrimac z 53561, Poynette z 53955; Ⓟ 2,268; Ⓒ 3,493
Lake Wissota; CDP; CHIPPEWA; ▲ Lafayette; *252 H-5; elev. 926ft./282m.; ★ **EAUC**; mail Chippewa Falls z 54729; Ⓟ 2,175; Ⓒ 2,458
Lakewood; RMC Place; ADAMS; ▲ Strongs Prairie; *253 K-8; mail Arkdale z 54613; ● 150
Lakewood; RMC Place; OCONTO; ▲ Lakewood; **252** G-11; elev. 1,271ft./387m.; 🅿; z 54138; ● 300
Lakewood; MCD-Town; OCONTO; *252 G-12; 🅿; z 54138; Ⓟ 607; Ⓒ 875
Lamartine; RMC Place; FOND DU LAC; ▲ Lamartine; **253** L-11; mail Fond du Lac z 54935, Oakfield z 53065; ● 150
Lamartine; MCD-Town; FOND DU LAC; *253 L-11; mail Oakfield z 53065; Ⓟ 1,607; Ⓒ 1,616
Lamont; RMC Place; LAFAYETTE; ▲ Lamont; **253** P-8; elev. 1,071ft./326m.; mail Darlington z 53530; ● 30
Lamont; MCD-Town; LAFAYETTE; *253 P-8; mail Darlington z 53530; Ⓟ 254; Ⓒ 267
Lampson; RMC Place; WASHBURN; ▲ Brooklyn; **252** E-4; elev. 1,137ft./347m.; mail Trego z 54888; ● 60
Lanark; MCD-Town; PORTAGE; *252 J-10; mail Waupaca z 54981; Ⓟ 1,154; Ⓒ 1,449
Lancaster; Inc. Place; ⊡ GRANT; **253** O-6; elev. 1,100ft./335m.; 🅿 🅷; z 53813; Ⓟ 4,192; Ⓒ 4,070
Land O' Lakes; RMC Place; VILAS; ▲ Land O'Lakes; **252** D-10; 🅿; z 54540; summer pop. 3,000; ● 700
Land O'Lakes; MCD-Town; VILAS; *252 D-9; mail Land O Lakes z 54540; Ⓟ 839; Ⓒ 882
Landstad; RMC Place; SHAWANO; ▲ Lessor; *252 I-12; elev. 838ft./255m.; mail Bonduel z 54107; ● 20
Langes Corners; RMC Place; BROWN; ▲ New Denmark; *252 J-13; elev. 860ft./262m.; mail Denmark z 54208; ● 50
Langlade; RMC Place; LANGLADE; ▲ Wolf River; **252** G-11; elev. 1,257ft./383m.; mail White Lake z 54491; ● 80
Langlade; MCD-Town; LANGLADE; *252 G-11; mail Pickerel z 54465; Ⓟ 415; Ⓒ 472
LANGLADE; **252** G-10; Ⓟ 19,505; Ⓒ 20,740; ◆ 20,102
Lannon; Inc. Place; WAUKESHA; **251** C-2; elev. 900ft./274m.; 🅿; ★ **MILW**; z 53046; Ⓟ 924; Ⓒ 1,009
Laona; RMC Place; FOREST; ▲ Laona; **252** F-11; elev. 1,580ft./482m.; 🅿; z 54541; ● 750
Laona; MCD-Town; FOREST; *252 F-11; 🅿; z 54541; Ⓟ 1,387; Ⓒ 1,367
La Pointe; RMC Place; ASHLAND; ▲ La Pointe; **252** B-6; 🅿; z 54850; summer pop. 2,000; ● 100
La Pointe; MCD-Town; ASHLAND; *252 B-7; 🅿; z 54850; Ⓟ 147; Ⓒ 246
La Prairie; MCD-Town; ROCK; *253 P-11; mail Janesville z 53545; Ⓟ 943; Ⓒ 929
Lark; RMC Place; BROWN; ▲ Morrison; *252 J-13; elev. 925ft./282m.; mail Greenleaf z 54126; ● 100
Larrabee; RMC Place; MANITOWOC; ▲ Gibson; *252 J-13; elev. 741ft./226m.; mail Two Rivers z 54241; ● 90
Larrabee; MCD-Town; WAUPACA; *252 I-11; mail Clintonville z 54929; Ⓟ 1,388; Ⓒ 1,301
Larsen; RMC Place; WINNEBAGO; ▲ Clayton; **253** K-11; 🅿; z 54947; ● 200
Lasleys Point; RMC Place; WINNEBAGO; ▲ Winneconne; *253 K-11; elev. 765ft./233m.; ★ **OSH**; mail Winneconne z 54986; ● 60
Lauderdale; RMC Place; WALWORTH; ▲ La Grange; *253 O-12; mail Elkhorn z 53121; summer pop. 2,000; ● 600
La Valle; Inc. Place; SAUK; **253** M-8; elev. 896ft./273m.; 🅿; z 53941; Ⓟ 446; Ⓒ 326
La Valle; MCD-Town; SAUK; *253 M-8; 🅿; z 53941; does not include the Village of La Valle; Ⓟ 1,005; Ⓒ 1,203
LaVerne Dilweg; RMC Place; BROWN; ★ **GRBY**; mail Green Bay z 54303; pop. incl. with Green Bay (Inc. Place)
Lawrence; MCD-Town; BROWN; *252 J-12; ★ **GRBY**; mail De Pere z 54115; Ⓟ 1,363; Ⓒ 1,548
Lawrence; RMC Place; MARQUETTE; ▲ Westfield; *253 L-9; mail Westfield z 53964; ● 100
Lawrence; MCD-Town; RUSK; *252 F-6; mail Glen Flora z 54526; Ⓟ 240; Ⓒ 240
Lawton; RMC Place; PIERCE; ▲ Martell; *252 I-2; elev. 1,096ft./334m.; mail Beldenville z 54003; rural
Lead Mine; RMC Place; LAFAYETTE; ▲ New Diggings; **253** P-7; mail Cuba City z 53807; ● 80
Lebanon; RMC Place; DODGE; ▲ Lebanon; **253** N-11; 🅿; z 53047; ● 300
Lebanon; MCD-Town; DODGE; *253 N-11; 🅿; z 53047; Ⓟ 1,630; Ⓒ 1,664
Lebanon; MCD-Town; WAUPACA; *252 J-11; mail New London z 54961; Ⓟ 1,290; Ⓒ 1,648
Ledges; RMC Place; DANE; ▲ Burke; *253 N-10; elev. 950ft./290m.; ★ **MAD**; mail De Forest z 53532; ● 230
Ledgeview (De Pere); MCD-Town; BROWN; ★ **GRBY**; mail De Pere z 54115, Green Bay z 54301; Ⓟ 1,558; Ⓒ 3,363
Leeds; RMC Place; COLUMBIA; ▲ Leeds; *253 N-10; elev. 1,059ft./323m.; mail Arlington z 53911, Morrisonville z 53571; ● 60
Leeds; MCD-Town; COLUMBIA; *253 M-10; mail Morrisonville z 53571; Ⓟ 809; Ⓒ 813
Leeds Center; RMC Place; COLUMBIA; ▲ Leeds; *253 M-10; elev. 1,060ft./323m.; mail Arlington z 53911; rural
Leeman; RMC Place; OUTAGAMIE; ▲ Maine; *252 I-11; elev. 796ft./243m.; mail Shiocton z 54170; rural
Legend Lake; CDP-Census Area Only; MENOMINEE; *252 H-11; Ⓒ 1,533
Leipsig; RMC Place; DODGE; ▲ Beaver Dam; *253 M-11; mail Beaver Dam z 53916; rural
Leland; RMC Place; SAUK; ▲ Honey Creek; **253** M-8; mail North Freedom z 53951; ● 50
Lemington; RMC Place; SAWYER; ▲ Couderay; *252 E-5; mail Exeland z 54835; rural
Lemonweir; MCD-Town; JUNEAU; *253 L-8; mail Mauston z 53948; Ⓟ 1,707; Ⓒ 1,763
Lena; Inc. Place; OCONTO; **252** H-13; elev. 714ft./218m.; 🅿; z 54139; Ⓟ 590; Ⓒ 510; Ⓡ 529
Lena; MCD-Town; OCONTO; *252 H-13; 🅿; z 54139; does not include the Village of Lena; Ⓟ 790; Ⓒ 769; Ⓡ 757
Lennox; ONEIDA; see Jennings (RMC Place)
Lenroot; MCD-Town; SAWYER; *252 D-5; mail Hayward z 54843; Ⓟ 966; Ⓒ 1,165
Leola; MCD-Town; ADAMS; *253 K-9; mail Bancroft z 54921; Ⓟ 217; Ⓒ 265
Leon; RMC Place; MONROE; ▲ Leon; **253** L-6; elev. 783ft./239m.; mail Sparta z 54656; ● 120
Leon; MCD-Town; MONROE; *253 L-6; mail Necedah z 54646; Ⓟ 746; Ⓒ 858
Leon; MCD-Town; WAUSHARA; *253 K-10; mail Pine River z 54965; Ⓟ 992; Ⓒ 1,281
Leonards Point; RMC Place; WINNEBAGO; ▲ Algoma; *253 K-11; elev. 763ft./233m.; ★ **OSH**; mail Oshkosh z 54904; ● 100
Leopolis; RMC Place; SHAWANO; ▲ Pella, Herman; **252** I-11; elev. 943ft./287m.; 🅿; z 54948; ● 150
LeRoy; RMC Place; DODGE; ▲ LeRoy; **253** M-11; elev. 1,052ft./321m.; mail Lomira z 53048; ● 100
LeRoy; MCD-Town; DODGE; *253 M-11; mail Lomira z 53048; Ⓟ 1,025; Ⓒ 1,116
Leslie; RMC Place; LAFAYETTE; ▲ Belmont; *253 O-7; elev. 1,158ft./353m.; mail Belmont z 53510
Lessor; MCD-Town; SHAWANO; *252 I-11; mail Bonduel z 54107; Ⓟ 892; Ⓒ 1,112
Levis; MCD-Town; CLARK; *252 J-7; mail Neillsville z 54456; Ⓟ 492; Ⓒ 504
Lewis; RMC Place; POLK; ▲ Clam Falls; **252** F-2; elev. 1,058ft./322m.; 🅿; z 54837; ● 230
Lewiston; RMC Place; COLUMBIA; ▲ Lewiston; *253 M-9; elev. 809ft./247m.; mail Wisconsin Dells z 53965; ● 30
Lewiston; MCD-Town; COLUMBIA; *253 M-9; mail Wisconsin Dells z 53965; Ⓟ 1,123; Ⓒ 1,187
Leyden; RMC Place; ROCK; ▲ Center, Janesville; *253 O-10; ★ **JNSV**; mail Janesville z 53545; ● 20
Liberty; MCD-Town; GRANT; *253 O-7; mail Stitzer z 53825; Ⓟ 569; Ⓒ 552
Liberty; MCD-Town; MANITOWOC; *253 K-13; mail Valders z 54245; Ⓟ 1,218; Ⓒ 1,287
Liberty; MCD-Town; OUTAGAMIE; *252 J-11; mail Shiocton z 54170; Ⓟ 702; Ⓒ 834
Liberty; MCD-Town; VERNON; *253 M-6; mail Viola z 54664; Ⓟ 189; Ⓒ 167
Liberty Grove; MCD-Town; DOOR; *252 A-13; mail Baileys Harbor z 54202; Ⓟ 1,506; Ⓒ 1,858
Liberty Pole; RMC Place; VERNON; ▲ Franklin; **253** M-6; mail Viroqua z 54665; ● 50
Liddell (Old Anson); RMC Place; CHIPPEWA; ▲ Anson; *252 H-5; elev. 1,052ft./321m.; mail Chippewa Falls z 54729; rural
Lilly Lake; RMC Place; KENOSHA; ▲ Wheatland; *253 P-12; elev. 756ft./230m.; mail Burlington z 53105; summer pop. 600; ● 400
Lily; RMC Place; LANGLADE; ▲ Langlade; **252** G-11; 🅿; z 54491
Lima; MCD-Town; GRANT; *253 O-7; mail Platteville z 53818; Ⓟ 691; Ⓒ 721
Lima; MCD-Town; PEPIN; *252 I-4; mail Durand z 54736; Ⓟ 649; Ⓒ 716
Lima; ROCK; see Lima Center (RMC Place)
Lima; MCD-Town; ROCK; *253 O-11; mail Whitewater z 53190; Ⓟ 1,285; Ⓒ 1,312
Lima; MCD-Town; SHEBOYGAN; *253 L-13; ★ **SHEB**; mail Sheboygan Falls z 53085; Ⓟ 2,715; Ⓒ 2,948
Lima Center (Lima); RMC Place; ROCK; ▲ Lima; **253** O-11; mail Whitewater z 53190; ● 200
Lime Ridge; Inc. Place; SAUK; *253 M-8; elev. 1,180ft./360m.; 🅿; z 53942; Ⓟ 152; Ⓒ 169
Lincoln; MCD-Town; ADAMS; *253 K-9; mail Westfield z 53964; Ⓟ 318; Ⓒ 311
Lincoln; MCD-Town; BAYFIELD; *252 C-6; mail Mason z 54856; Ⓟ 294; Ⓒ 293
Lincoln; MCD-Town; BUFFALO; *252 J-4; mail Alma z 54610; Ⓟ 250; Ⓒ 187
Lincoln; MCD-Town; BURNETT; *252 E-2; mail Webster z 54893; Ⓟ 228; Ⓒ 286
Lincoln; MCD-Town; EAU CLAIRE; *252 I-5; mail Augusta z 54722; Ⓟ 1,002; Ⓒ 1,080
Lincoln; MCD-Town; FOREST; *252 F-11; mail Crandon z 54520; Ⓟ 630; Ⓒ 1,005
Lincoln; RMC Place; KEWAUNEE; ▲ Lincoln; **252** I-14; elev. 842ft./257m.; mail Casco z 54205; ● 50
Lincoln; MCD-Town; KEWAUNEE; *252 I-14; mail Casco z 54205; Ⓟ 996; Ⓒ 957
Lincoln; MCD-Town; MONROE; *253 K-7; mail Warrens z 54666; Ⓟ 765; Ⓒ 827
Lincoln; MCD-Town; POLK; *252 G-2; mail Amery z 54001; Ⓟ 1,835; Ⓒ 2,304
Lincoln; MCD-Town; TREMPEALEAU; *252 J-5; mail Whitehall z 54773; Ⓟ 894; Ⓒ 829
Lincoln; MCD-Town; VILAS; *252 E-10; mail Eagle River z 54521; Ⓟ 2,310; Ⓒ 2,579
Lincoln; MCD-Town; WOOD; *252 I-7; mail Marshfield z 54449; Ⓟ 1,429; Ⓒ 1,554
LINCOLN; **252** G-8; Ⓟ 26,993; Ⓒ 29,641; ◆ 29,327
Lind; MCD-Town; WAUPACA; *252 J-10; mail Weyauwega z 54983; Ⓟ 1,157; Ⓒ 1,381
Lind Center; RMC Place; WAUPACA; ▲ Lind; *252 J-10; mail Waupaca z 54981; ● 50
Linden; Inc. Place; IOWA; **253** O-7; elev. 1,101ft./336m.; 🅿; z 53553 & mail Edmund z 53535; Ⓟ 429; Ⓒ 615
Linden; MCD-Town; IOWA; *253 O-7; 🅿; z 53553 & mail Edmund z 53535, Mineral Point z 53565; does not include the Village of Linden; Ⓟ 773; Ⓒ 873
Lindina; MCD-Town; JUNEAU; *253 L-8; mail Mauston z 53948; Ⓟ 796; Ⓒ 730
Lindsey; RMC Place; WOOD; ▲ Rock; **252** I-7; elev. 1,155ft./352m.; mail Marshfield z 54449; ● 50
Linn; MCD-Town; WALWORTH; *253 P-12; mail Hebron z 60034; Ⓟ 2,062; Ⓒ 2,194
Linton; RMC Place; WALWORTH; ▲ Linn; *253 P-12; mail Lake Geneva z 53147; ● 30
Linwood; MCD-Town; PORTAGE; *252 J-9; mail Stevens Point z 54481; Ⓟ 1,035; Ⓒ 1,111
Lisbon; MCD-Town; JUNEAU; *253 L-8; mail New Lisbon z 53950; Ⓟ 862; Ⓒ 1,020
Lisbon; MCD-Town; WAUKESHA; *253 N-12; 🅿; ★ **MILW**; z 53089; Ⓟ 8,277; Ⓒ 9,359
Little Black; RMC Place; TAYLOR; ▲ Little Black; *252 H-7; mail Medford z 54451; ● 60
Little Black; MCD-Town; TAYLOR; *252 H-7; mail Medford z 54451; Ⓟ 1,195; Ⓒ 1,148
Little Chicago; RMC Place; MARATHON; ▲ Hamburg, Berlin; **252** H-8; elev. 1,275ft./389m.; mail Marathon z 54448; ● 50
Little Chute; Inc. Place; OUTAGAMIE; **252** J-12; elev. 728ft./222m.; 🅿; ★ **APP**; z 54140, z 54911; Ⓟ 9,207; Ⓒ 10,476
Little Falls; MCD-Town; MONROE; *253 K-6; mail Sparta z 54656; Ⓟ 1,137; Ⓒ 1,334
Little Falls; RMC Place; POLK; ▲ Alden; **252** G-2; mail Amery z 54001; ● 40
Little Grant; MCD-Town; GRANT; *253 O-6; mail Lancaster z 53813; Ⓟ 375; Ⓒ 257
Little Hope; RMC Place; WAUPACA; ▲ Dayton; *252 J-10; mail Waupaca z 54981; ● 30
Little Kohler; OZAUKEE; see Kohler (RMC Place)
Little Prairie; RMC Place; WALWORTH; ▲ Troy; *253 O-12; elev. 956ft./291m.; mail Eagle z 53119, East Troy z 53120; ● 150
Little Rapids; RMC Place; BROWN; ▲ Lawrence; *252 J-12; ★ **GRBY**; mail De Pere z 54115; ● 100
Little Rice; MCD-Town; ONEIDA; *252 F-8; mail Tripoli z 54564; Ⓟ 196; Ⓒ 314
Little River; MCD-Town; OCONTO; *252 H-13; mail Oconto z 54153; Ⓟ 1,003; Ⓒ 1,065
Little Rose; RMC Place; MARATHON; ▲ Eau Pleine; *252 I-8; mail Stratford z 54484; rural
Little Round Lake; CDP-Census Area Only; SAWYER; ▲ Hunter; *252 E-5; mail Hayward z 54843; Ⓟ 871; Ⓒ 948
Little Sturgeon; RMC Place; DOOR; ▲ Gardner; *252 H-14; mail Sturgeon Bay z 54235; ● 70
Little Suamico; RMC Place; OCONTO; ▲ Little Suamico; **252** I-13; 🅿; ★ **GRBY**; z 54141; ● 180
Little Suamico; MCD-Town; OCONTO; *252 I-13; 🅿; ★ **GRBY**; z 54141; Ⓟ 2,637; Ⓒ 3,877
Little Wolf; MCD-Town; WAUPACA; *252 J-11; mail Manawa z 54949; Ⓟ 1,326; Ⓒ 1,445; Ⓡ 1,430
Livingston; Inc. Place; GRANT, IOWA; **253** O-7; elev. 1,164ft./355m.; 🅿; z 53554; Ⓟ 576; Ⓒ 597
Loddes Mill; RMC Place; SAUK; ▲ Prairie du Sac; *253 N-8; elev. 743ft./226m.; mail Sauk City z 53583; rural
Lodi; Inc. Place; COLUMBIA; **253** N-9; elev. 833ft./254m.; 🅿; z 53555; Ⓟ 2,093; Ⓒ 2,882
Lodi; MCD-Town; COLUMBIA; *253 M-9; 🅿; z 53555; does not include the City of Lodi; Ⓟ 1,913; Ⓒ 2,791
Loganville; Inc. Place; SAUK; **253** M-8; elev. 960ft./293m.; 🅿; z 53943; Ⓟ 228; Ⓒ 276
Lohrville; Inc. Place; WAUSHARA; **253** K-10; elev. 802ft./244m.; mail Redgranite z 54970; Ⓟ 368; Ⓒ 408
Lombard; RMC Place; CLARK; ▲ Withee; *252 H-6; mail Thorp z 54771; ● 25
Lomira; Inc. Place; DODGE; **253** M-12; elev. 1,039ft./317m.; 🅿; z 53048; Ⓟ 1,542; Ⓒ 2,233
Lomira; MCD-Town; DODGE; *253 M-12; 🅿; z 53048 & mail Brownsville z 53006; does not include the Village of Lomira; Ⓟ 1,280; Ⓒ 1,228
London; RMC Place; DANE, JEFFERSON; ▲ Lake Mills, Deerfield; *253 N-10; ★ **MAD**; mail Cambridge z 53523; ● 200
Lone Rock; RMC Place; JUNEAU; ▲ Orange; *253 K-8; elev. 903ft./275m.; mail Camp Douglas z 54618; rural
Lone Rock; Inc. Place; RICHLAND; **253** N-8; elev. 706ft./215m.; 🅿; z 53556; Ⓟ 641; Ⓒ 929
Long Lake; RMC Place; FLORENCE; ▲ Long Lake; **252** E-11; 🅿; z 54542; ● 200
Long Lake; MCD-Town; FLORENCE; *252 E-11; 🅿; z 54542; Ⓟ 205; Ⓒ 197
Long Lake; RMC Place; FOND DU LAC; ▲ Osceola; *253 L-12; elev. 1,026ft./313m.; mail Cascade z 53011; ● 150
Long Lake; MCD-Town; WASHBURN; *252 F-4; mail Birchwood z 54817; Ⓟ 583; Ⓒ 737
Longwood; RMC Place; CLARK; ▲ Longwood; **252** H-7; elev. 1,245ft./379m.; mail Withee z 54498; ● 40
Longwood; MCD-Town; CLARK; *252 H-7; mail Withee z 54498; Ⓟ 661; Ⓒ 698
Lookout; RMC Place; BUFFALO; ▲ Dover; *252 J-4; elev. 874ft./266m.; mail Mondovi z 54755
Loomis; RMC Place; MARINETTE; ▲ Lake; **252** G-13; mail Porterfield z 54159; ● 45
Lorain; MCD-Town; POLK; *252 F-3; mail Frederic z 54837; Ⓟ 299; Ⓒ 328
Loretta; RMC Place; SAWYER; ▲ Draper; **252** E-6; elev. 1,443ft./440m.; 🅿; z 54896; ● 100
Lost Lake; RMC Place; DODGE; ▲ Calamus; *253 M-10; elev. 929ft./283m.; mail Randolph z 53956; rural
Louisburg; RMC Place; GRANT; ▲ Jamestown; *253 P-7; elev. 896ft./273m.; ★ **DUB**; mail Cuba City z 53807; ● 60
Louis Corners; RMC Place; MANITOWOC; ▲ Schleswig; *253 K-13; elev. 912ft./278m.; mail Kiel z 53042; ● 30
Lowell; Inc. Place; DODGE; **253** M-11; elev. 800ft./244m.; 🅿; z 53557; Ⓟ 300; Ⓒ 366
Lowell; MCD-Town; DODGE; *253 M-11; 🅿; z 53557 & mail Reeseville z 53579; Ⓟ 1,146; Ⓒ 1,169
Lower Nemahbin Lake; RMC Place; WAUKESHA; ▲ Summit; *253 N-12; elev. 886ft./270m.; ★ **MILW**; mail Oconomowoc z 53066; ● 460
Lowville; MCD-Town; COLUMBIA; *253 M-10; mail Poynette z 53955; Ⓟ 938; Ⓒ 987
Loyal; Inc. Place; CLARK; **252** I-7; elev. 1,240ft./378m.; 🅿; z 54446; Ⓟ 1,244; Ⓒ 1,308
Loyal; MCD-Town; CLARK; *252 I-7; 🅿; z 54446; does not include the City of Loyal; Ⓟ 718; Ⓒ 787
Loyd; RMC Place; RICHLAND; ▲ Willow; **253** M-7; elev. 813ft./248m.; mail Cazenovia z 53924; ● 40
Lublin; Inc. Place; TAYLOR; **252** H-6; elev. 1,289ft./393m.; 🅿; z 54447; Ⓟ 129; Ⓒ 110
Lucas; MCD-Town; DUNN; *252 H-3; mail Menomonie z 54751; Ⓟ 644; Ⓒ 658
Luck; Inc. Place; POLK; **252** F-2; elev. 1,240ft./378m.; 🅿; z 54853; Ⓟ 1,022; Ⓒ 1,210
Luck; MCD-Town; POLK; *252 F-2; 🅿; z 54853 & mail Frederic z 54837; does not include the Village of Luck; Ⓟ 880; Ⓒ 881
Ludington; RMC Place; EAU CLAIRE; ▲ Ludington; **252** H-5; mail Fall Creek z 54742; ● 25
Ludington; MCD-Town; EAU CLAIRE; *252 I-5; mail Fall Creek z 54742; Ⓟ 906; Ⓒ 998
Lugerville; RMC Place; PRICE; ▲ Flambeau; *252 E-7; mail Phillips z 54555; ● 50
Lund; RMC Place; PEPIN, PIERCE; ▲ Maiden Rock, Pepin; **252** I-3; elev. 1,139ft./347m.; mail Stockholm z 54769; ● 45
Lunds; RMC Place; SHAWANO; ▲ Waukechon; *252 I-11; mail Shawano z 54166; ● 40
Luxemburg; Inc. Place; KEWAUNEE; **252** I-13; elev. 800ft./244m.; 🅿; z 54217; Ⓟ 1,151; Ⓒ 1,935
Luxemburg; MCD-Town; KEWAUNEE; *252 I-13; 🅿; z 54217; does not include the Village of Luxemburg; Ⓟ 1,387; Ⓒ 1,402
Lykens; RMC Place; POLK; ▲ Balsam Lake; *252 F-2; elev. 1,092ft./333m.; mail Balsam Lake z 54810; ● 30
Lymantown; RMC Place; PRICE; ▲ Lake; **252** E-7; mail Park Falls z 54552; pop. incl. with Park Falls (Inc. Place)
Lyndhurst; RMC Place; SHAWANO; ▲ Herman; *252 H-11; elev. 950ft./290m.; mail Gresham z 54128; ● 40
Lyndon; JUNEAU; see Lyndon Station (Inc. Place)
Lyndon; MCD-Town; JUNEAU; *253 L-8; mail Lyndon Station z 53944; Ⓟ 790; Ⓒ 1,217
Lyndon; MCD-Town; SHEBOYGAN; *253 L-13; mail Plymouth z 53073; Ⓟ 1,432; Ⓒ 1,468; Ⓡ 1,463
Lyndon Station (Lyndon); Inc. Place; JUNEAU; **253** L-8; elev. 900ft./274m.; 🅿; z 53944; Ⓟ 474; Ⓒ 458
Lynn; RMC Place; CLARK; ▲ Lynn; *252 I-7; elev. 1,150ft./351m.; mail Granton z 54436; ● 100
Lynn; MCD-Town; CLARK; *252 I-7; mail Granton z 54436; Ⓟ 703; Ⓒ 834
Lynne; MCD-Town; ONEIDA; *252 F-8; mail Tripoli z 54564; Ⓟ 157; Ⓒ 210
Lynxville; Inc. Place; CRAWFORD; ▲ Seneca; **253** N-6; elev. 638ft./194m.; 🅿; z 54626, z 54640; Ⓟ 153; Ⓒ 176
Lyons; RMC Place; WALWORTH; ▲ Lyons; **253** P-12; elev. 802ft./244m.; 🅿; z 53148; ● 600
Lyons; MCD-Town; WALWORTH; *253 P-12; 🅿; z 53148; Ⓟ 2,579; Ⓒ 3,440

M

Mackford; MCD-Town; GREEN LAKE; *253 L-11; mail Markesan z 53946; Ⓟ 616; Ⓒ 585
Mackville; RMC Place; OUTAGAMIE; ▲ Center; **252** J-12; elev. 815ft./248m.; ★ **APP**; mail Appleton z 54915; ● 200
Madge; MCD-Town; WASHBURN; *252 E-4; mail Sarona z 54870; Ⓟ 349; Ⓒ 454
Madison; Inc. Place; **STATE CAPITAL**; ⊡ DANE; **253** N-10; elev. 863ft./263m.; 🅿 🅷 🅲 43,099 ■; ★ **MAD**; z 53701-08, z 53711, z 53713-19, z 53725-26, z 53744, z 53774, z 53777-79, z 53782-86, z 53788-94 & mail Middleton z 53562, Verona z 53593; Ⓟ 191,262; Ⓒ 208,054; ◆ 242,014
Madison; MCD-Town; DANE; *253 N-9; 🅿 🅲 43,099; ★ **MAD**; z 53701-08, z 53711, z 53713-19, z 53725-26, z 53744, z 53774, z 53777-79, z 53782-86, z 53788-94 & mail Middleton z 53562, Verona z 53593; does not include the City of Madison; Ⓟ 6,442; Ⓒ 7,005
Madsen; RMC Place; MANITOWOC; ▲ Liberty; *253 K-13; elev. 813ft./248m.; mail Manitowoc z 54220; rural
Magenta; RMC Place; EAU CLAIRE; ★ **EAUC**; mail Eau Claire z 54701; pop. incl. with Eau Claire (Inc. Place)
Magnolia; RMC Place; ROCK; ▲ Magnolia; *253 P-10; elev. 943ft./287m.; mail Evansville z 53536; ● 50
Magnolia; MCD-Town; ROCK; *253 P-10; mail Evansville z 53536; Ⓟ 717; Ⓒ 854
Maiden Rock; Inc. Place; PIERCE; **252** I-3; elev. 689ft./210m.; 🅿; z 54750; Ⓟ 146; Ⓒ 121
Maiden Rock; MCD-Town; PIERCE; *252 I-3; 🅿; z 54750; does not include the Village of Maiden Rock; Ⓟ 649; Ⓒ 589
Maine; MCD-Town; MARATHON; *252 H-9; mail Wausau z 54401; Ⓟ 2,206; Ⓒ 2,407
Maine; MCD-Town; OUTAGAMIE; *252 I-11; mail Shiocton z 54170; Ⓟ 791; Ⓒ 831
Mallwood; RMC Place; ROCK; ▲ Milton; *253 O-10; elev. 830ft./253m.; ★ **JNSV**; mail Edgerton z 53534; ● 500
Malone; RMC Place; FOND DU LAC; ▲ Taycheedah, Marshfield; *253 L-12; 🅿; ★ **FDLC**; z 53049; ● 45
Manawa; Inc. Place; WAUPACA; **252** J-11; elev. 825ft./251m.; 🅿; z 54949; Ⓟ 1,169; Ⓒ 1,330
Manchester; RMC Place; GREEN LAKE; ▲ Manchester; *253 L-10; 🅿; z 53946; ● 150
Manchester; MCD-Town; GREEN LAKE; *253 L-10; 🅿; z 53946; Ⓟ 774; Ⓒ 848
Manchester; MCD-Town; JACKSON; *253 K-6; mail Black River Falls z 54615; Ⓟ 563; Ⓒ 680
Manitowish; RMC Place; IRON; ▲ Mercer; **252** D-8; elev. 1,592ft./485m.; mail Mercer z 54547; ● 80
Manitowish Waters; RMC Place; VILAS; ▲ Manitowish Waters; **252** D-8; 🅿; z 54545; summer pop. 1,500; ● 400
Manitowish Waters; MCD-Town; VILAS; *252 D-8; 🅿; z 54545; Ⓟ 651; Ⓒ 646
Manitowoc; Inc. Place; ⊡ MANITOWOC; **253** K-14; elev. 606ft./185m.; 🅿 🅷 🅲 516 ■; ★ **MNTW**; z 54220-21; Ⓟ 32,520; Ⓒ 34,053; ◆ 32,644
Manitowoc; MCD-Town; MANITOWOC; *253 K-14; 🅿 🅲 516; ★ **MNTW**; z 54220-21; does not include the City of Manitowoc; Ⓟ 937; Ⓒ 1,073
MANITOWOC; **253** K-13; Ⓟ 80,421; Ⓒ 82,887; Ⓡ 82,893; ◆ 78,654
Manitowoc Rapids; RMC Place; MANITOWOC; *253 K-14; ★ **MNTW**; mail Manitowoc z 54220; pop. incl. with Manitowoc (Inc. Place)
Manitowoc Rapids; MCD-Town; MANITOWOC; *253 K-13; ★ **MNTW**; mail Manitowoc z 54220; Ⓟ 2,579; Ⓒ 2,520
Maple; RMC Place; DOUGLAS; ▲ Maple; **252** C-4; 🅿; z 54854; ● 200
Maple; MCD-Town; DOUGLAS; *252 C-4; 🅿; z 54854; Ⓟ 667; Ⓒ 649
Maple Bluff; Inc. Place; DANE; **253** R-8; elev. 900ft./274m.; ★ **MAD**; mail Madison z 53704; Ⓟ 1,352; Ⓒ 1,358
Maple Creek; MCD-Town; OUTAGAMIE; *252 J-11; mail New London z 54961; Ⓟ 695; Ⓒ 687
Maple Grove; MCD-Town; BARRON; *252 G-4; mail Dallas z 54733; Ⓟ 926; Ⓒ 968
Maple Grove; RMC Place; MANITOWOC; ▲ Maple Grove, Franklin; *253 K-13; elev. 904ft./276m.; mail Reedsville z 54230; ● 30
Maple Grove; MCD-Town; MANITOWOC; *253 K-13; mail Brillion z 54110; Ⓟ 888; Ⓒ 852
Maple Grove; MCD-Town; SHAWANO; *252 I-12; mail Pulaski z 54162; Ⓟ 1,159; Ⓒ 1,045
Maple Heights; RMC Place; CALUMET; ▲ Brothertown; *253 K-12; elev. 750ft./229m.; mail Chilton z 53014; summer pop. 150; ● 50
Maple Hills; RMC Place; WALWORTH; ▲ Linn; *253 P-12; elev. 1,100ft./335m.; mail Fontana z 53125; ● 125
Maplehurst; MCD-Town; TAYLOR; *252 H-7; mail Withee z 54498; Ⓟ 300; Ⓒ 359
Maple Plain; MCD-Town; BARRON; *252 F-3; mail Cumberland z 54829; Ⓟ 610; Ⓒ 876
Mapleton; RMC Place; WAUKESHA; ▲ Oconomowoc; *253 N-12; ★ **MILW**; mail Oconomowoc z 53066; ● 90
Maple Valley; MCD-Town; OCONTO; *252 H-12; mail Suring z 54174; Ⓟ 690; Ⓒ 670
Maplewood; RMC Place; DOOR; ▲ Forestville; **252** I-14; elev. 703ft./214m.; 🅿; z 54226; ● 125
Marathon (Marathon City); Inc. Place; MARATHON; **252** H-8; elev. 1,245ft./379m.; 🅿; ★ **WAUS**; z 54448; Ⓟ 1,606; Ⓒ 1,640
Marathon; MCD-Town; MARATHON; *252 H-9; 🅿; ★ **WAUS**; z 54448; does not include the Village of Marathon; Ⓟ 978; Ⓒ 1,085
MARATHON; **252** H-8; Ⓟ 115,400; Ⓒ 125,834; ◆ 128,854
Marathon City; MARATHON; see Marathon (Inc. Place)
Marblehead; RMC Place; FOND DU LAC; ▲ Eden; *253 L-12; elev. 1,000ft./305m.; mail Eden z 53019; ● 60
Marcellon; RMC Place; COLUMBIA; ▲ Marcellon; *253 M-10; mail Pardeeville z 53954; ● 40
Marcellon; MCD-Town; COLUMBIA; *253 M-10; mail Portage z 53901; Ⓟ 880; Ⓒ 1,024
March Rapids; RMC Place; MARATHON; ▲ Eau Pleine; *252 H-8; elev. 1,283ft./391m.; mail Stratford z 54484; rural
Marengo; RMC Place; ASHLAND; ▲ White River; **252** C-6; 🅿; z 54846, z 54855; ● 220
Marengo; MCD-Town; ASHLAND; *252 D-6; 🅿; z 54846, z 54855; Ⓟ 284; Ⓒ 362
Maribel; Inc. Place; MANITOWOC; **252** J-13; elev. 861ft./262m.; 🅿; z 54227; Ⓟ 372; Ⓒ 264; Ⓡ 284
Marietta; MCD-Town; CRAWFORD; *253 N-6; mail Boscobel z 53805; Ⓟ 532; Ⓒ 510
Marinette; Inc. Place; ⊡ MARINETTE; **252** H-14; elev. 598ft./182m.; 🅿 🅷 ■; z 54143; Ⓟ 11,843; Ⓒ 11,749; ◆ 10,815
MARINETTE; **252** G-12; Ⓟ 40,548; Ⓒ 43,384; ◆ 42,001
Marion; MCD-Town; GRANT; *253 N-6; mail Boscobel z 53805; Ⓟ 484; Ⓒ 517
Marion; MCD-Town; JUNEAU; *253 L-8; mail Mauston z 53948; Ⓟ 351; Ⓒ 433
Marion; Inc. Place; WAUPACA, SHAWANO; **252** I-11; elev. 850ft./259m.; 🅿; z 54950; Ⓟ 1,242; Ⓒ 1,297
Marion; MCD-Town; WAUSHARA; *253 K-10; mail Neshkoro z 54960; Ⓟ 1,478; Ⓒ 2,065
Markesan; Inc. Place; GREEN LAKE; **253** L-10; elev. 847ft./258m.; 🅿; z 53946; Ⓟ 1,496; Ⓒ 1,396
Marquette; Inc. Place; GREEN LAKE; **253** L-10; 🅿; z 53947; Ⓟ 182; Ⓒ 169
Marquette; MCD-Town; GREEN LAKE; *253 L-10; 🅿; z 53947 & mail Markesan z 53946; does not include Village of Marquette; Ⓟ 400; Ⓒ 481
MARQUETTE; **253** L-9; Ⓟ 12,321; Ⓒ 15,832; Ⓡ 14,555; ◆ 14,758
Marshall; Inc. Place; DANE; **253** N-10; elev. 870ft./265m.; 🅿; ★ **MAD**; z 53559; Ⓟ 2,329; Ⓒ 3,432
Marshall; MCD-Town; RICHLAND; *253 M-7; mail Richland Center z 53581; Ⓟ 550; Ⓒ 600
Marshall; MCD-Town; RUSK; *252 G-6; mail Conrath z 54731; Ⓟ 630; Ⓒ 683
Marshfield; MCD-Town; FOND DU LAC; *253 L-12; mail Mount Calvary z 53057; Ⓟ 1,130; Ⓒ 1,118
Marshfield; Inc. Place; WOOD, MARATHON; **252** I-8; elev. 1,262ft./385m.; 🅿 🅷 ■; z 54404, z 54449, z 54472 & mail Hewitt z 54441; Ⓟ 19,291; Ⓒ 18,800; ◆ 17,091
Marshfield; MCD-Town; WOOD; *252 I-8; 🅿; z 54404, z 54449, z 54472 & mail Hewitt z 54441; does not include the City of Marshfield; Ⓟ 769; Ⓒ 811
Marshland; RMC Place; BUFFALO; ▲ Buffalo; *253 K-4; mail Fountain City z 54629
Martell; RMC Place; PIERCE; ▲ Martell; **252** H-2; mail Spring Valley z 54767; ● 100
Martell; MCD-Town; PIERCE; *252 H-2; mail Spring Valley z 54767; Ⓟ 866; Ⓒ 1,070
Martinsville; RMC Place; DANE; ▲ Springfield; **253** N-9; ★ **MAD**; mail Cross Plains z 53528; ● 150
Martintown; RMC Place; GREEN; ▲ Cadiz; *253 P-9; mail Browntown z 53522; ● 100
Marxville; RMC Place; DANE; ▲ Berry; *253 N-9; mail Mazomanie z 53560; ● 40
Mary Lake; RMC Place; DANE; ▲ Westport; *253 N-9; elev. 880ft./268m.; ★ **MAD**; mail Waunakee z 53597; ● 500
Marytown; RMC Place; FOND DU LAC; ▲ Calumet; **253** L-12; elev. 965ft./294m.; mail New Holstein z 53061; ● 200
Mason; Inc. Place; BAYFIELD; **252** C-6; elev. 940ft./287m.; 🅿; z 54816, z 54856; Ⓟ 102; Ⓒ 72
Mason; MCD-Town; BAYFIELD; *252 C-5; 🅿; z 54816, z 54856; does not include the Village of Mason; Ⓟ 296; Ⓒ 326
Mather; RMC Place; JUNEAU; ▲ Kingston; **253** K-7; 🅿; z 54641; ● 50
Matteson; MCD-Town; WAUPACA; *252 I-11; mail Clintonville z 54929; Ⓟ 889; Ⓒ 956
Mattoon; Inc. Place; SHAWANO; **252** H-10; elev. 1,275ft./389m.; 🅿; z 54450; Ⓟ 431; Ⓒ 466
Mauston; Inc. Place; ⊡ JUNEAU; **253** L-8; elev. 883ft./269m.; 🅿 🅷; z 53948; Ⓟ 3,439; Ⓒ 3,740
Maxville; RMC Place; BUFFALO; ▲ Maxville; **252** I-3; elev. 776ft./237m.; mail Durand z 54736; ● 30
Maxville; MCD-Town; BUFFALO; *252 I-3; mail Durand z 54736; Ⓟ 370; Ⓒ 325
May Corner; RMC Place; MARINETTE; ▲ Grover; *252 H-13; elev. 656ft./200m.; mail Peshtigo z 54157; rural
Mayfield; RMC Place; WASHINGTON; ▲ Polk; *253 M-12; ★ **MILW**; mail Jackson z 53037; ● 125
Mayville; MCD-Town; CLARK; *252 H-7; mail Dorchester z 54425; Ⓟ 932; Ⓒ 919
Mayville; Inc. Place; DODGE; **253** M-12; elev. 920ft./280m.; 🅿; z 53050; Ⓟ 4,374; Ⓒ 4,902
Mazomanie; Inc. Place; DANE; **253** N-8; elev. 775ft./236m.; 🅿; z 53560; Ⓟ 1,377; Ⓒ 1,485
Mazomanie; MCD-Town; DANE; *253 N-9; 🅿; z 53560; does not include the Village of Mazomanie; Ⓟ 982; Ⓒ 1,185
McAllister; RMC Place; MARINETTE; ▲ Wagner; **252** G-13; mail Wausaukee z 54177; ● 50
McCartney; RMC Place; GRANT; ▲ Waterloo; *253 P-6; mail Cassville z 53806; rural
McFarland; Inc. Place; DANE; **253** N-10; elev. 870ft./265m.; 🅿; ★ **MAD**; z 53558; Ⓟ 5,232; Ⓒ 6,416
McKinley; RMC Place; POLK; ▲ McKinley; *252 F-3; mail Cumberland z 54829
McKinley; MCD-Town; POLK; *252 F-3; mail Cumberland z 54829; Ⓟ 327; Ⓒ 328
McKinley; MCD-Town; TAYLOR; *252 G-6; mail Sheldon z 54766; Ⓟ 403; Ⓒ 418
McManus; RMC Place; CRAWFORD; ▲ Utica; *253 M-6; mail Ferryville z 54628; rural
McMillan; MCD-Town; MARATHON; *252 I-8; mail Marshfield z 54449; Ⓟ 1,697; Ⓒ 1,790
McNaughton; RMC Place; ONEIDA; ▲ Newbold; **252** F-9; 🅿; z 54543; ● 150
Mead; MCD-Town; CLARK; *252 I-6; mail Greenwood z 54437; Ⓟ 249; Ⓒ 290
Meadowbrook; MCD-Town; SAWYER; *252 F-5; mail Exeland z 54835; Ⓟ 192; Ⓒ 146
Mecan; MCD-Town; MARQUETTE; *253 L-10; mail Montello z 53949; Ⓟ 541; Ⓒ 726
Medary; MCD-Town; LA CROSSE; *253 L-5; ★ **LACRO**; mail Onalaska z 54650; Ⓟ 1,585; Ⓒ 1,463
Medford; Inc. Place; ⊡ TAYLOR; **252** G-7; elev. 1,476ft./450m.; 🅿 🅷; z 54451; Ⓟ 4,283; Ⓒ 4,350
Medford; MCD-Town; TAYLOR; *252 G-7; 🅿; z 54451; Ⓟ 1,961; Ⓒ 2,216
Medina; MCD-Town; DANE; *253 N-10; ★ **MAD**; mail Marshall z 53559; Ⓟ 1,124; Ⓒ 1,235
Medina; RMC Place; OUTAGAMIE; ▲ Dale; **252** J-11; 🅿; z 54944; ● 250
Meeker; RMC Place; WASHINGTON; *253 N-12; ★ **MILW**; mail Germantown z 53022; pop. incl. with Germantown (Inc. Place)
Meeme; RMC Place; MANITOWOC; ▲ Meeme; *253 K-13; elev. 777ft./237m.; mail Newton z 53063; rural
Meeme; MCD-Town; MANITOWOC; *253 K-13; mail Newton z 53063; Ⓟ 1,516; Ⓒ 1,538
Meenon; MCD-Town; BURNETT; *252 E-3; mail Webster z 54893; Ⓟ 956; Ⓒ 1,172
Meggers; RMC Place; MANITOWOC; ▲ Schleswig; *253 K-13; elev. 893ft./272m.; mail New Holstein z 53061; rural
Mellen; Inc. Place; ASHLAND; **252** D-6; elev. 1,250ft./381m.; 🅿; z 54546; Ⓟ 935; Ⓒ 845
Melnik; RMC Place; MANITOWOC; ▲ Kossuth, Gibson; *252 J-13; elev. 801ft./244m.; mail Whitelaw z 54247; rural
Melrose; Inc. Place; JACKSON; **253** K-6; 🅿; z 54642; Ⓟ 551; Ⓒ 529
Melrose; MCD-Town; JACKSON; *253 K-6; 🅿; z 54642; does not include the Village of Melrose; Ⓟ 357; Ⓒ 402
Melrose Park; RMC Place; WINNEBAGO; ▲ Algoma; *253 K-11; ★ **OSH**; mail Oshkosh z 54901; ● 300
Melvina; Inc. Place; MONROE; **253** L-6; elev. 876ft./267m.; mail Cashton z 54619; Ⓟ 115; Ⓒ 93
Menasha; Inc. Place; WINNEBAGO, CALUMET; **253** K-12; elev. 764ft./233m.; 🅿; ★ **APP**; z 54952; Ⓟ 14,711; Ⓒ 16,331
Menasha; MCD-Town; WINNEBAGO; *252 J-12; 🅿; ★ **APP**; z 54952; does not include the City of Menasha; Ⓟ 13,975; Ⓒ 15,858
Menchalville; RMC Place; MANITOWOC; ▲ Franklin; **252** J-13; elev. 862ft./263m.; mail Reedsville z 54230; ● 80
Mendota; RMC Place; DANE; ★ **MAD**; pop. incl. with Madison (Inc. Place)
Menekaunee; RMC Place; MARINETTE; mail Marinette z 54143; pop. incl. with Marinette (Inc. Place)
Menominee; MCD-Town; MENOMINEE; *252 H-11; mail Neopit z 54150; Ⓟ 3,890; Ⓒ 4,562
MENOMINEE; **252** H-11; Ⓟ 3,890; Ⓒ 4,562; ◆ 4,612
Menominee Reservation; Indian Reservation; MENOMINEE; ▲ Red Springs; mail Keshena z 54135, Neopit z 54150; Ⓟ 2,672; Ⓒ 3,216
Menominee/Stockbridge-Munsee joint use area; SHAWANO; Indian Reservation; Ⓒ 295
Menomonee Falls; Inc. Place; WAUKESHA; **253** N-13; elev. 840ft./256m.; 🅿 🅷 ■; ★ **MILW**; z 53051-52; Ⓟ 26,840; Ⓒ 32,647; ◆ 34,465
Menomonie; DUNN; see North Menomonie (RMC Place)
Menomonie; Inc. Place; ⊡ DUNN; **252** H-3; elev. 877ft./267m.; 🅿 🅷 🅲 8,327; z 54751; Ⓟ 13,547; Ⓒ 14,937
Menomonie; MCD-Town; DUNN; *252 H-3; 🅿 🅲 8,327; z 54751; does not include the City of Menomonie; Ⓟ 2,732; Ⓒ 3,174

Entries in **UPPERCASE** are counties.
Entries in **bold** have populations of 2,500 or more.
Names in parentheses are alternate names.

Inc. Place	Incorporated Place
RMC Place	Rand McNally Designated Place
CDP	Census Designated Place
MCD	Minor Civil Division
⊡	County Seat
▲	Minor Civil Division
elev.	Elevation
🅿	Post Office
🅷	Hospital
🅲	College
■	Principal Business Center
★	Ranally Metro Area (RMA) Abbreviation
z	Zip Code(s)
Ⓟ	Previous Census Population
Ⓡ	Revised Census Population
Ⓐ	Annexation Population
●	Rand McNally Population Estimate
Ⓒ	Final Census Population
Ⓢ	Special Census Population
◆	Estimated Population

For additional definitions see Glossary, Volume 1, and Introduction, Volume 2.

Menomonie Junction; RMC Place; DUNN; *252 H-3; mail Menomonie z 54751; pop. incl. with Menomonie (Inc. Place)
Mentor; MCD-Town; CLARK; *252 I-6; mail Humbird z 54746; Ⓟ 521; Ⓒ 570
Mequon; Inc. Place; OZAUKEE; 253 N-13; elev. 680ft./207m.; 🄿 🄷 🄲 5,574; ★ **MILW**; z 53092, z 53097; Ⓟ 18,885; Ⓒ 21,823; Ⓡ 22,643; ◆ 21,502
Mercer; RMC Place; IRON; ▲ Mercer; 252 D-8; 🄿; z 54547; summer pop. 3,000; ● 1,300
Mercer; MCD-Town; IRON; *252 D-8; 🄿; z 54547; Ⓟ 1,325; Ⓒ 1,732
Meridean; RMC Place; DUNN; ▲ Peru; 252 I-4; mail Mondovi z 54755; ● 80
Merrill; Inc. Place; ⊡ LINCOLN; 252 G-9; elev. 1,263ft./385m.; 🄿 🄷; z 54452; Ⓟ 9,860; Ⓒ 10,146
Merrill; MCD-Town; LINCOLN; *252 G-9; 🄿; z 54452; does not include the City of Merrill; Ⓟ 2,716; Ⓒ 2,979
Merrillan; Inc. Place; JACKSON; 252 J-6; elev. 937ft./286m.; 🄿; z 54754; Ⓟ 553; Ⓒ 585
Merrimac; Inc. Place; SAUK; 253 M-9; elev. 801ft./244m.; 🄿; z 53561; Ⓟ 392; Ⓒ 416
Merrimac; MCD-Town; SAUK; *253 M-9; 🄿; z 53561; does not include the Village of Merrimac; Ⓟ 737; Ⓒ 868
Merton; Inc. Place; WAUKESHA; 253 N-12; elev. 950ft./290m.; 🄿; ★ **MILW**; z 53056; Ⓟ 1,199; Ⓒ 1,926
Merton; MCD-Town; WAUKESHA; *253 N-12; 🄿; ★ **MILW**; z 53056 & mail Hartland z 53029; does not include the Village of Merton; Ⓟ 6,430; Ⓒ 7,988
Meteor; MCD-Town; SAWYER; *252 F-5; mail Exeland z 54835; Ⓟ 111; Ⓒ 170
Metomen; MCD-Town; FOND DU LAC; *253 L-11; mail Ripon z 54971; Ⓟ 685; Ⓒ 709
Metz; RMC Place; WINNEBAGO; ▲ Wolf River; *253 K-11; mail Fremont z 54940; ● 50
Mid-City; RMC Place; MILWAUKEE; ★ **MILW**; mail Milwaukee z 53208; pop. incl. with Milwaukee (Inc. Place)
Middle Inlet; RMC Place; MARINETTE; ▲ Middle Inlet; 252 G-13; elev. 710ft./216m.; 🄿; z 54114; ● 45
Middle Inlet; MCD-Town; MARINETTE; *252 G-13; 🄿; z 54114; Ⓟ 744; Ⓒ 831
Middle Ridge; RMC Place; LA CROSSE; ▲ Washington; 253 L-6; mail Bangor z 54614; ● 40
Middleton; Inc. Place; DANE; 253 N-9; elev. 940ft./287m.; 🄿; ★ **MAD**; z 53562; Ⓟ 13,289; Ⓒ 15,770
Middleton; MCD-Town; DANE; *253 N-9; 🄿; ★ **MAD**; z 53562; does not include the Village of Middleton; Ⓟ 3,628; Ⓒ 4,594
Middle Village; CDP-Census Area Only; MENOMINEE, SHAWANO; *252 H-11; Ⓒ 351
Midway; RMC Place; BROWN; *252 J-13; ★ **GRBY**; mail Green Bay z 54301; pop. incl. with Allouez (Inc. Place)
Midway; RMC Place; LA CROSSE; ▲ Onalaska; 253 L-5; elev. 657ft./200m.; ★ **LACRO**; mail Onalaska z 54650; ● 100
Mifflin; RMC Place; IOWA; ▲ Mifflin; *253 O-7; elev. 955ft./291m.; mail Rewey z 53580; ● 80
Mifflin; MCD-Town; IOWA; *253 O-7; mail Rewey z 53580; Ⓟ 564; Ⓒ 617
Mikana; RMC Place; BARRON; ▲ Cedar Lake; 252 F-4; 🄿; z 54857; ● 250
Mikesville; RMC Place; WINNEBAGO; ▲ Clayton; *253 K-11; elev. 811ft./247m.; mail Oshkosh z 54901; rural
Milan; RMC Place; MARATHON; ▲ Johnson; 252 H-8; 🄿; z 54411; ● 130
Milford; RMC Place; JEFFERSON; ▲ Milford; 253 N-11; elev. 811ft./247m.; mail Lake Mills z 53551; ● 80
Milford; MCD-Town; JEFFERSON; *253 N-11; mail Lake Mills z 53551; Ⓟ 1,007; Ⓒ 1,055
Milladore; Inc. Place; WOOD, PORTAGE; 252 I-8; elev. 1,195ft./364m.; 🄿; z 54454; Ⓟ 314; Ⓒ 268
Milladore; MCD-Town; WOOD; *252 I-8; 🄿; z 54454 & mail Auburndale z 54412; does not include the Village of Milladore; Ⓟ 719; Ⓒ 706
Millard; RMC Place; WALWORTH; ▲ Sugar Creek; *253 O-11; elev. 938ft./286m.; mail Elkhorn z 53121; ● 80
Mill Center; RMC Place; BROWN; ▲ Pittsfield; *252 I-12; elev. 760ft./232m.; ★ **GRBY**; mail Green Bay z 54301; pop. incl. with Howard (Inc. Place)
Millersville; RMC Place; SHEBOYGAN; *253 L-13; ★ **SHEB**; mail Sheboygan z 53083; pop. incl. with Howards Grove (Inc. Place)
Millhome; RMC Place; MANITOWOC; ▲ Schleswig; *253 L-13; mail Kiel z 53042; rural
Millston; RMC Place; JACKSON; ▲ Millston; 253 K-6; 🄿; z 54643; ● 80
Millston; MCD-Town; JACKSON; *252 J-7; 🄿; z 54643; Ⓟ 154; Ⓒ 136
Millstone Heights; RMC Place; DANE; ▲ Windsor; *253 N-10; elev. 950ft./290m.; ★ **MAD**; mail De Forest z 53532; ● 150
Milltown; Inc. Place; POLK; 252 F-2; elev. 1,246ft./380m.; 🄿; z 54858; Ⓟ 786; Ⓒ 888
Milltown; MCD-Town; POLK; *252 F-2; 🄿; z 54858; does not include the Village of Milltown; Ⓟ 949; Ⓒ 1,146
Millville; RMC Place; GRANT; ▲ Millville; 253 N-6; mail Mount Hope z 53816; ● 30
Millville; MCD-Town; GRANT; *253 N-6; mail Woodman z 53827; Ⓟ 169; Ⓒ 147
Milton; MCD-Town; BUFFALO; *253 K-4; mail Fountain City z 54629; Ⓟ 450; Ⓒ 517
Milton; Inc. Place; ROCK; 253 O-11; elev. 900ft./274m.; 🄿; ★ **JNSV**; z 53563; Ⓟ 4,434; Ⓒ 5,132
Milton; MCD-Town; ROCK; *253 O-11; 🄿; ★ **JNSV**; z 53563; does not include the Village of Milton; Ⓟ 2,363; Ⓒ 2,844
Milton Junction; RMC Place; ROCK; *253 O-11; elev. 889ft./271m.; ★ **JNSV**; mail Milton z 53563; pop. incl. with Milton (Inc. Place)
Milwaukee; Inc. Place; ⊡ MILWAUKEE, WASHINGTON, WAUKESHA; 253 N-13; elev. 634ft./193m.; 🄿 🄷 🄲 56,033 ■; ★ **MILW**; z 53201-28, z 53233-35, z 53237, z 53244, z 53259, z 53263, z 53267-68, z 53274, z 53278, z 53288, z 53290, z 53293, z 53295; Ⓟ 628,088; Ⓒ 596,974; ◆ 663,318
MILWAUKEE; 253 N-13; Ⓟ 959,275; Ⓒ 940,164; ◆ 1,019,231
Mindoro; RMC Place; LA CROSSE; ▲ Farmington; 253 K-5; elev. 786ft./240m.; 🄿; z 54644; ● 300
Mineral Point; Inc. Place; IOWA; 253 O-8; elev. 1,135ft./346m.; 🄿; z 53565; Ⓟ 2,428; Ⓒ 2,617
Mineral Point; MCD-Town; IOWA; *253 O-8; 🄿; z 53565; does not include the City of Mineral Point; Ⓟ 851; Ⓒ 867
Minersville; RMC Place; ASHLAND; ▲ Ashland; *252 C-6; elev. 811ft./247m.; mail Marengo z 54855; ● 30
Minnesota Junction; RMC Place; DODGE; ▲ Oak Grove; 253 M-11; elev. 923ft./281m.; mail Horicon z 53032; ● 100
Minocqua; RMC Place; ONEIDA; ▲ Minocqua; 252 E-9; elev. 1,603ft./489m.; 🄿; z 54548; summer pop. 3,000; ● 1,280
Minocqua; MCD-Town; ONEIDA; *252 E-8; 🄿; z 54548; Ⓟ 3,486; Ⓒ 4,859
Minong; Inc. Place; WASHBURN; 252 D-4; elev. 1,064ft./324m.; 🄿; z 54859; Ⓟ 521; Ⓒ 531
Minong; MCD-Town; WASHBURN; *252 D-4; 🄿; z 54859; does not include the Village of Minong; Ⓟ 730; Ⓒ 858
Mishicot; Inc. Place; MANITOWOC; 252 J-14; 🄿; ★ **MNTW**; z 54228; Ⓟ 1,296; Ⓒ 1,422
Mishicot; MCD-Town; MANITOWOC; *252 J-14; 🄿; ★ **MNTW**; z 54228; does not include the Village of Mishicot; Ⓟ 1,344; Ⓒ 1,409
Mitchell; MCD-Town; SHEBOYGAN; *253 L-13; mail Waldo z 53093; Ⓟ 944; Ⓒ 1,132; Ⓡ 1,286
Modena; RMC Place; BUFFALO; ▲ Modena; 252 J-4; 🄿; z 54755; ● 80
Modena; MCD-Town; BUFFALO; *252 J-4; 🄿; z 54755; Ⓟ 360; Ⓒ 318
Moeville; RMC Place; PIERCE; ▲ Trimbelle; *252 I-2; elev. 995ft./303m.; mail Ellsworth z 54011; rural
Mole Lake; RMC Place; FOREST; ▲ Nashville; 252 F-10; mail Crandon z 54520; ● 250
Molitor; MCD-Town; TAYLOR; *252 G-7; mail Medford z 54451; Ⓟ 183; Ⓒ 263
Monches; RMC Place; WAUKESHA; ▲ Merton; *253 N-12; ★ **MILW**; mail Hartland z 53029; ● 100
Mondovi; Inc. Place; BUFFALO; 252 I-4; elev. 800ft./244m.; 🄿; z 54755, z 54764; Ⓟ 2,491; Ⓒ 2,634
Mondovi; MCD-Town; BUFFALO; *252 I-4; 🄿; z 54755, z 54764; does not include the City of Mondovi; Ⓟ 545; Ⓒ 449
Monico; RMC Place; ONEIDA; ▲ Monico; 252 F-10; 🄿; z 54501; ● 150
Monico; MCD-Town; ONEIDA; *252 F-10; 🄿; z 54501; Ⓟ 294; Ⓒ 364
Monona; Inc. Place; DANE; 253 N-10; elev. 898ft./274m.; 🄿; ★ **MAD**; z 53713-14, z 53716; Ⓟ 8,637; Ⓒ 8,018
Monroe; ADAMS; see Monroe Center (RMC Place)
Monroe; MCD-Town; ADAMS; *253 K-8; mail Arkdale z 54613; Ⓟ 305; Ⓒ 363
Monroe; Inc. Place; ⊡ GREEN; 253 P-9; elev. 1,099ft./335m.; 🄿 🄷; z 53566; Ⓟ 10,241; Ⓒ 10,843
Monroe; MCD-Town; GREEN; *253 P-9; 🄿; z 53566; Ⓟ 1,066; Ⓒ 1,142
MONROE; 253 L-7; Ⓟ 36,633; Ⓒ 40,899; Ⓡ 40,896; ◆ 43,722
Monroe Center (Monroe); RMC Place; ADAMS; ▲ Monroe; 253 K-8; elev. 945ft./288m.; mail Arkdale z 54613; ● 100
Montana; RMC Place; BUFFALO; ▲ Montana; *252 J-4; elev. 812ft./247m.; mail Independence z 54747; ● 40
Montana; MCD-Town; BUFFALO; *252 J-4; mail Independence z 54747; Ⓟ 316; Ⓒ 306
Montello; Inc. Place; ⊡ MARQUETTE; 253 L-10; elev. 782ft./238m.; 🄿; z 53949; Ⓟ 1,329; Ⓒ 1,397
Montello; MCD-Town; MARQUETTE; *253 L-10; 🄿; z 53949; does not include the City of Montello; Ⓟ 940; Ⓒ 1,043
Monterey; RMC Place; WAUKESHA; ▲ Oconomowoc; 253 N-12; ★ **MILW**; mail Oconomowoc z 53066; ● 120
Montfort; Inc. Place; GRANT, IOWA; 253 O-7; elev. 1,150ft./351m.; 🄿; z 53569; Ⓟ 676; Ⓒ 663
Monticello; Inc. Place; GREEN; 253 O-9; elev. 847ft./258m.; 🄿; z 53570; Ⓟ 1,140; Ⓒ 1,146
Monticello; MCD-Town; LAFAYETTE; *253 P-8; mail Balsam Lake z 54810; Ⓟ 182; Ⓒ 148
Montpelier; MCD-Town; KEWAUNEE; *252 J-13; mail Luxemburg z 54217; Ⓟ 1,369; Ⓒ 1,371
Montreal; Inc. Place; IRON; 252 C-7; elev. 1,650ft./503m.; 🄿; z 54550 & mail Upson z 54565; Ⓟ 838; Ⓒ 838
Montrose; MCD-Town; DANE; *253 O-9; mail Belleville z 53508; Ⓟ 1,032; Ⓒ 1,134
Moon; RMC Place; MARATHON; ▲ Mosinee, Bergen; *252 I-9; elev. 1,256ft./383m.; ★ **WAUS**; mail Mosinee z 54455; ● 50
Moose Junction; RMC Place; DOUGLAS; ▲ Dairyland; *252 D-3; elev. 1,229ft./375m.; mail Danbury z 54830; rural
Moquah; RMC Place; BAYFIELD; ▲ Pilsen; 252 C-6; elev. 849ft./259m.; 🄿; z 54806; ● 50
Morgan; RMC Place; OCONTO; ▲ Morgan; *252 I-12; elev. 797ft./243m.; mail Oconto Falls z 54154; ● 90
Morgan; MCD-Town; OCONTO; *252 I-12; mail Oconto Falls z 54154; Ⓟ 815; Ⓒ 882
Morgan; RMC Place; SHAWANO; ▲ Red Springs; *252 H-11; elev. 1,005ft./306m.; mail Gresham z 54128; ● 60
Morris; MCD-Town; SHAWANO; *252 I-10; mail Tigerton z 54486; Ⓟ 453; Ⓒ 485
Morrison; RMC Place; BROWN; ▲ Morrison; 252 J-13; elev. 919ft./280m.; mail Greenleaf z 54126; ● 210
Morrison; MCD-Town; BROWN; *252 J-13; mail Greenleaf z 54126; Ⓟ 1,493; Ⓒ 1,651
Morrisonville; RMC Place; DANE; ▲ Windsor; 253 N-10; elev. 964ft./294m.; 🄿; ★ **MAD**; z 53571; ● 500
Morris Park; RMC Place; DANE; ▲ Dunn; *253 O-10; elev. 900ft./274m.; ★ **MAD**; mail Mc Farland z 53558; ● 150
Morse; RMC Place; ASHLAND; ▲ Gordon; *252 D-7; mail Glidden z 54527, Mellen z 54546; ● 50
Morse; MCD-Town; ASHLAND; *252 D-6; mail Mellen z 54546; Ⓟ 481; Ⓒ 515
Moscow; MCD-Town; IOWA; *253 O-8; mail Barneveld z 53507; Ⓟ 528; Ⓒ 594
Mosel; MCD-Town; SHEBOYGAN; *253 L-13; mail Cleveland z 53015; Ⓟ 918; Ⓒ 839
Mosinee; Inc. Place; MARATHON; 252 I-9; elev. 1,153ft./351m.; 🄿; ★ **WAUS**; z 54455; Ⓟ 3,820; Ⓒ 4,063
Mosinee; MCD-Town; MARATHON; *252 I-9; 🄿; ★ **WAUS**; z 54455; does not include the City of Mosinee; Ⓟ 1,638; Ⓒ 2,146
Mosling; RMC Place; OCONTO; ▲ Underhill, Gillett; *252 H-12; elev. 849ft./259m.; mail Gillett z 54124; ● 25
Moundville; MCD-Town; MARQUETTE; *253 L-9; mail Endeavor z 53930; Ⓟ 457; Ⓒ 574
Mountain; RMC Place; OCONTO; ▲ Mountain; 252 G-12; 🄿; z 54149; ● 300
Mountain (Armstrong); MCD-Town; OCONTO; *252 G-12; 🄿; z 54149; Ⓟ 730; Ⓒ 860
Mount Calvary; Inc. Place; FOND DU LAC; 253 L-12; elev. 987ft./301m.; 🄿; z 53057; Ⓟ 558; Ⓒ 956
Mount Hope; Inc. Place; GRANT; 253 O-6; elev. 1,100ft./335m.; 🄿; z 53816; Ⓟ 173; Ⓒ 186
Mount Hope; MCD-Town; GRANT; *253 O-6; 🄿; z 53816; does not include the Village of Mount Hope; Ⓟ 240; Ⓒ 225
Mount Horeb; Inc. Place; DANE; 253 O-9; elev. 1,230ft./375m.; 🄿; z 53572; Ⓟ 4,182; Ⓒ 5,860
Mount Ida; RMC Place; GRANT; ▲ Mount Ida; 253 O-6; mail Fennimore z 53809; ● 45
Mount Ida; MCD-Town; GRANT; *253 O-6; mail Fennimore z 53809; Ⓟ 510; Ⓒ 523
Mount Morris; RMC Place; WAUSHARA; ▲ Mount Morris; 253 K-10; mail Wautoma z 54982; ● 130
Mount Morris; MCD-Town; WAUSHARA; *253 K-10; mail Wautoma z 54982; Ⓟ 767; Ⓒ 1,092
Mount Pleasant; MCD-Town; GREEN; *253 O-9; mail Albany z 53502; Ⓟ 539; Ⓒ 547
Mount Pleasant; Inc. Place; RACINE; *253 O-13; mail Racine z 53401; incorporated September 16, 2003; not reported in 2000 Census; ● 25,400; ◆ 25,257
Mount Sterling; Inc. Place; CRAWFORD; 253 N-6; elev. 1,180ft./360m.; 🄿; z 54645; Ⓟ 217; Ⓒ 215
Mount Tabor; RMC Place; VERNON; ▲ Forest; *253 L-7; mail Kendall z 54638
Mount Vernon; RMC Place; DANE; ▲ Springdale; 253 O-9; mail Mount Horeb z 53572, Verona z 53593; ● 180
Mount Zion; RMC Place; CRAWFORD; ▲ Scott; 253 N-6; elev. 1,178ft./359m.; mail Boscobel z 53805
Mukwa; MCD-Town; WAUPACA; *252 J-11; mail New London z 54961; Ⓟ 2,304; Ⓒ 2,773
Mukwonago; Inc. Place; WAUKESHA, WALWORTH; 253 O-12; elev. 837ft./255m.; 🄿; ★ **MILW**; z 53149; Ⓟ 4,464; Ⓒ 6,162
Mukwonago; MCD-Town; WAUKESHA; *253 O-12; 🄿; ★ **MILW**; z 53149; does not include the Village of Mukwonago; Ⓟ 5,967; Ⓒ 6,868
Murat (Esadore Lake); RMC Place; TAYLOR; ▲ Hammel; *252 G-7; mail Medford z 54451; ● 45
Murphy Corner; RMC Place; OUTAGAMIE; ▲ Freedom; *252 J-12; ★ **APP**; mail Kaukauna z 54130; rural
Murry; MCD-Town; RUSK; *252 F-5; mail Bruce z 54819; Ⓟ 291; Ⓒ 275
Muscoda; Inc. Place; GRANT, IOWA; 253 N-7; elev. 690ft./210m.; 🄿; z 53573; Ⓟ 1,287; Ⓒ 1,453
Muscoda; MCD-Town; GRANT; *253 N-7; 🄿; z 53573; does not include the Village of Muscoda; Ⓟ 566; Ⓒ 674
Muskego; Inc. Place; WAUKESHA; 253 O-13; elev. 800ft./244m.; 🄿; ★ **MILW**; z 53150; Ⓟ 16,813; Ⓒ 21,397; ◆ 22,762
Myra; RMC Place; WASHINGTON; ▲ Trenton; *253 M-13; mail West Bend z 53095; ● 40

N

Nabob; RMC Place; WASHINGTON; ▲ West Bend; *253 M-12; mail West Bend z 53090; ● 40
Namakagon; MCD-Town; BAYFIELD; *252 D-6; mail Cable z 54821; Ⓟ 276; Ⓒ 285
Namur; RMC Place; DOOR; ▲ Union; 252 C-12; mail Brussels z 54204; ● 30
Naples; MCD-Town; BUFFALO; *252 I-4; mail Mondovi z 54755; Ⓟ 496; Ⓒ 584
Nasbro; RMC Place; DODGE; ▲ Lomira; *253 M-12; mail Brownsville z 53006
Nasewaupee; MCD-Town; DOOR; *252 H-14; mail Sturgeon Bay z 54235; Ⓟ 1,798; Ⓒ 1,873
Nashotah; Inc. Place; WAUKESHA; *253 N-12; elev. 940ft./287m.; 🄿; ★ **MILW**; z 53058; Ⓟ 567; Ⓒ 1,266
Nashville; MCD-Town; FOREST; *252 F-11; mail Crandon z 54520; Ⓟ 871; Ⓒ 1,157
Nasonville; RMC Place; WOOD; ▲ Lincoln; *252 I-7; mail Marshfield z 54449; ● 30
Navarino; RMC Place; SHAWANO; ▲ Navarino; 252 I-12; 🄿; z 54107; ● 130
Navarino; MCD-Town; SHAWANO; *252 I-11; 🄿; z 54107; Ⓟ 439; Ⓒ 422
Necedah; Inc. Place; JUNEAU; 253 K-8; elev. 925ft./282m.; 🄿; z 54646; Ⓟ 743; Ⓒ 888
Necedah; MCD-Town; JUNEAU; *253 K-8; 🄿; z 54646; does not include the Village of Necedah; Ⓟ 1,601; Ⓒ 2,156
Neda; RMC Place; DODGE; ▲ Hubbard; *253 M-12; elev. 1,000ft./305m.; mail Iron Ridge z 53035; ● 60
Neenah; Inc. Place; WINNEBAGO; 253 K-12; elev. 750ft./229m.; 🄿 🄷 ■; ★ **APP**; z 54956-57; Ⓟ 23,219; Ⓒ 24,507; ◆ 24,640
Neenah; MCD-Town; WINNEBAGO; *253 K-12; 🄿; ★ **APP**; z 54956-57; does not include the City of Neenah; Ⓟ 2,691; Ⓒ 2,657
Neillsville; Inc. Place; ⊡ CLARK; 252 I-7; elev. 1,022ft./312m.; 🄿 🄷; z 54456; Ⓟ 2,680; Ⓒ 2,731
Nekimi; MCD-Town; WINNEBAGO; *253 K-11; mail Oshkosh z 54901; Ⓟ 1,525; Ⓒ 1,419
Nekoosa; Inc. Place; WOOD; 252 J-8; elev. 950ft./290m.; 🄿; z 54457; Ⓟ 2,557; Ⓒ 2,590
Nelma; RMC Place; FOREST; ▲ Alvin; 252 E-11; 🄿; z 54542; ● 40
Nelson; Inc. Place; BUFFALO; 252 J-3; elev. 680ft./207m.; 🄿; z 54756; Ⓟ 388; Ⓒ 395
Nelson; MCD-Town; BUFFALO; *252 J-3; 🄿; z 54756; Ⓟ 571; Ⓒ 586
Nelsonville; Inc. Place; PORTAGE; 252 J-10; elev. 1,075ft./328m.; 🄿; z 54458; Ⓟ 171; Ⓒ 191
Nenno; RMC Place; WASHINGTON; ▲ Addison; *253 M-12; mail Allenton z 53002; ● 60
Neopit; CDP; MENOMINEE; ▲ Menominee; 252 H-11; 🄿; z 54150; Ⓟ 615; Ⓒ 839
Neosho; Inc. Place; DODGE; 253 N-12; elev. 883ft./269m.; 🄿; z 53059; Ⓟ 658; Ⓒ 593
Nepeuskun; MCD-Town; WINNEBAGO; *253 K-11; mail Ripon z 54971; Ⓟ 647; Ⓒ 689
Neshkoro; Inc. Place; MARQUETTE; 253 K-10; elev. 800ft./244m.; 🄿; z 54960; Ⓟ 384; Ⓒ 453
Neshkoro; MCD-Town; MARQUETTE; *253 K-10; 🄿; z 54960; does not include the Village of Neshkoro; Ⓟ 489; Ⓒ 595
Neuern; RMC Place; KEWAUNEE; ▲ Luxemburg; *252 J-13; mail Luxemburg z 54217; rural
Neva; RMC Place; LANGLADE; ▲ Neva; *252 G-10; mail Deerbrook z 54424; rural
Neva; MCD-Town; LANGLADE; *252 G-10; mail Deerbrook z 54424; Ⓟ 910; Ⓒ 994
Neva Corners; RMC Place; LANGLADE; ▲ Neva; *252 G-10; mail Deerbrook z 54424
Newald; RMC Place; FOREST; ▲ Ross; 252 E-11; elev. 1,569ft./478m.; 🄿; z 54511; ● 260
New Amsterdam; RMC Place; LA CROSSE; ▲ Holland; 253 K-5; mail Holmen z 54636; ● 150
Newark; RMC Place; ROCK; ▲ Newark; *253 P-10; elev. 817ft./249m.; mail Beloit z 53511; ● 30
Newark; MCD-Town; ROCK; *253 P-10; mail Beloit z 53511; Ⓟ 1,514; Ⓒ 1,571
New Auburn; Inc. Place; CHIPPEWA, BARRON; 252 G-4; elev. 1,108ft./338m.; 🄿; z 54757; Ⓟ 485; Ⓒ 562
New Berlin; Inc. Place; WAUKESHA; 251 F-3; elev. 900ft./274m.; 🄿; ★ **MILW**; z 53146, z 53151; Ⓟ 33,592; Ⓒ 38,220; ◆ 39,494
Newbold; MCD-Town; ONEIDA; *252 E-9; mail Rhinelander z 54501; Ⓟ 2,281; Ⓒ 2,710
Newburg; Inc. Place; WASHINGTON, OZAUKEE; 253 M-13; elev. 850ft./259m.; 🄿; z 53060; Ⓟ 875; Ⓒ 1,119
Newburg Corners; RMC Place; LA CROSSE; ▲ Washington; *253 L-6; mail Bangor z 54614; ● 35
New Centerville; RMC Place; ST. CROIX; ▲ Rush River; *252 H-2; mail Baldwin z 54002; ● 40
New Chester; MCD-Town; ADAMS; *253 L-9; mail Grand Marsh z 53936; Ⓟ 1,675; Ⓒ 864; Ⓡ 2,141
New Denmark; MCD-Town; BROWN; *252 J-13; mail Denmark z 54208; Ⓟ 1,370; Ⓒ 1,482
New Diggings; RMC Place; LAFAYETTE; ▲ New Diggings; 253 P-7; mail Shullsburg z 53586; ● 100
New Diggings; MCD-Town; LAFAYETTE; *253 P-7; mail Scales Mound z 61075; Ⓟ 485; Ⓒ 473
New Fane; RMC Place; FOND DU LAC; ▲ Auburn; *253 M-12; elev. 978ft./298m.; mail Kewaskum z 53040; ● 120
New Franken; RMC Place; BROWN; ▲ Scott, Humboldt; 252 I-13; elev. 813ft./248m.; 🄿; ★ **GRBY**; z 54229; ● 250
New Glarus; Inc. Place; GREEN; 253 O-9; elev. 900ft./274m.; 🄿; z 53574; Ⓟ 1,899; Ⓒ 2,111
New Glarus; MCD-Town; GREEN; *253 O-9; 🄿; z 53574; does not include the Village of New Glarus; Ⓟ 571; Ⓒ 943
New Haven; MCD-Town; ADAMS; *253 L-9; mail Briggsville z 53920; Ⓟ 511; Ⓒ 657
New Haven; MCD-Town; DUNN; *252 G-3; mail Clear Lake z 54005; Ⓟ 658; Ⓒ 656
New Holstein; Inc. Place; CALUMET; 253 K-13; elev. 935ft./285m.; 🄿; z 53061-62; Ⓟ 3,342; Ⓒ 3,301
New Holstein; MCD-Town; CALUMET; *253 K-13; 🄿; z 53061-62; does not include the City of New Holstein; Ⓟ 1,406; Ⓒ 1,457
New Hope; MCD-Town; PORTAGE; *252 I-10; mail Amherst Junction z 54407; Ⓟ 694; Ⓒ 736
New Lisbon; Inc. Place; JUNEAU; 253 L-8; elev. 891ft./272m.; 🄿; z 53950; Ⓟ 1,491; Ⓒ 1,436
New London; Inc. Place; WAUPACA, OUTAGAMIE; 252 J-11; elev. 789ft./240m.; 🄿 🄷; z 54961; Ⓟ 6,658; Ⓒ 7,085
New Lyme; MCD-Town; MONROE; *253 K-6; mail Sparta z 54656; Ⓟ 156; Ⓒ 141
New Miner; RMC Place; JUNEAU; ▲ Armenia; 253 K-8; mail Necedah z 54646; ● 45
New Munster; RMC Place; KENOSHA; ▲ Wheatland; *253 P-12; elev. 771ft./235m.; 🄿; z 53152; ● 370
New Odanah; RMC Place; ASHLAND; ▲ Sanborn; *252 C-7; elev. 628ft./191m.; mail Ashland z 54806, Odanah z 54861; ● 110
Newport; MCD-Town; COLUMBIA; *253 M-9; mail Wisconsin Dells z 53965; Ⓟ 536; Ⓒ 681
New Post; CDP; SAWYER; ▲ Couderay; 252 E-5; elev. 1,328ft./405m.; 🄿; z 54828; Ⓟ 243; Ⓒ 367
New Prospect; RMC Place; FOND DU LAC; ▲ Auburn; *253 L-12; elev. 978ft./298m.; mail Campbellsport z 53010; ● 30
New Richmond; Inc. Place; ST. CROIX; 252 G-2; elev. 982ft./299m.; 🄿 🄷; z 54017; Ⓟ 5,106; Ⓒ 6,310
New Rome; RMC Place; ADAMS; ▲ Rome; *253 K-8; mail Nekoosa z 54457; rural
Newry; RMC Place; VERNON; ▲ Christiana; 253 L-6; mail Cashton z 54619; ● 40
Newton; RMC Place; MANITOWOC; ▲ Newton; 253 K-13; elev. 659ft./201m.; 🄿; z 53063; ● 80
Newton; MCD-Town; MANITOWOC; *253 K-13; 🄿; z 53063; Ⓟ 2,242; Ⓒ 2,241
Newton; MCD-Town; MARQUETTE; *253 K-9; mail Westfield z 53964; Ⓟ 470; Ⓒ 550
Newton; RMC Place; VERNON; ▲ Harmony; *253 M-5; elev. 733ft./223m.; mail Viroqua z 54665; rural
Newtonburg; RMC Place; MANITOWOC; ▲ Newton; *253 K-13; elev. 810ft./247m.; mail Manitowoc z 54220; ● 25
Newville; RMC Place; ROCK; ▲ Fulton; 253 O-10; ★ **JNSV**; mail Edgerton z 53534; ● 250
Niagara; Inc. Place; MARINETTE; 252 I-13; 🄿; z 54151; Ⓟ 1,999; Ⓒ 1,880
Niagara; MCD-Town; MARINETTE; *252 F-13; 🄿; z 54151 & mail Norway z 49870; does not include the Village of Niagara; Ⓟ 891; Ⓒ 924
Nichols; Inc. Place; OUTAGAMIE; ▲ Cicero; 252 I-12; 🄿; z 54152; Ⓟ 254; Ⓒ 307
Nippersink Manor; RMC Place; WALWORTH; ▲ Bloomfield; mail Genoa City z 53128
Nokomis; MCD-Town; ONEIDA; *252 F-9; mail Tomahawk z 54487; Ⓟ 999; Ⓒ 1,363
Nora; RMC Place; DANE; ▲ Deerfield, Cottage Grove; *253 N-10; elev. 953ft./290m.; ★ **MAD**; mail Deerfield z 53531; rural
Norman; RMC Place; KEWAUNEE; ▲ Carlton; *252 J-14; mail Kewaunee z 54216; ● 25
Norrie; RMC Place; MARATHON; ▲ Norrie; 252 H-10; mail Birnamwood z 54414; ● 90
Norrie; MCD-Town; MARATHON; *252 H-10; mail Birnamwood z 54414; Ⓟ 874; Ⓒ 967
Norske; RMC Place; WAUPACA; ▲ Harrison; *252 I-10; mail Iola z 54945; rural
North Andover; RMC Place; GRANT; ▲ Glen Haven; 253 O-6; mail Glen Haven z 53810; ● 50
North Bay; RMC Place; DOOR; ▲ Liberty Grove; *252 A-13; elev. 595ft./181m.; mail Baileys Harbor z 54202; ● 80
North Bay; Inc. Place; RACINE; 253 O-13; elev. 600ft./183m.; ★ **MILW**; mail Racine z 53402; Ⓟ 246; Ⓒ 260
North Bend; RMC Place; JACKSON; ▲ North Bend; 253 K-5; mail Melrose z 54642; ● 110
North Bend; MCD-Town; JACKSON; *253 K-5; mail Melrose z 54642; Ⓟ 419; Ⓒ 397
North Bristol; RMC Place; DANE; ▲ Bristol; 253 N-10; elev. 941ft./287m.; mail Sun Prairie z 53590; ● 110
North Cape; RMC Place; RACINE; ▲ Raymond, Norway; *253 O-13; elev. 801ft./244m.; ★ **MILW**; mail Franksville z 53126; ● 200
North Clayton; RMC Place; CRAWFORD; ▲ Clayton; *253 M-6; mail Soldiers Grove z 54655; rural
Northeim; RMC Place; MANITOWOC; ▲ Newton; *253 K-14; mail Newton z 53063; ● 30
Northfield; RMC Place; JACKSON; ▲ Northfield; 252 J-5; elev. 950ft./290m.; 🄿; z 54635; ● 80
Northfield; MCD-Town; JACKSON; *252 J-5; 🄿; z 54635; Ⓟ 572; Ⓒ 586
North Fond du Lac; Inc. Place; FOND DU LAC; 253 L-12; elev. 770ft./235m.; 🄿; ★ **FDLC**; z 54935, z 54937; Ⓟ 4,292; Ⓒ 4,557
North Freedom; Inc. Place; SAUK; 253 M-8; elev. 867ft./264m.; 🄿; z 53951; Ⓟ 591; Ⓒ 649
North Grimms; RMC Place; MANITOWOC; ▲ Cato; *253 K-13; mail Reedsville z 54230; rural
North Hudson; Inc. Place; ST. CROIX; 252 H-2; ★ **MPLS-**; mail Hudson z 54016; Ⓟ 3,101; Ⓒ 3,463
North La Crosse; RMC Place; LA CROSSE; *253 L-5; elev. 654ft./199m.; ★ **LACRO**; pop. incl. with La Crosse (Inc. Place)
North Lake; RMC Place; WALWORTH; ▲ Sugar Creek; *253 O-11; elev. 950ft./290m.; mail Elkhorn z 53121; ● 100
North Lake; RMC Place; WAUKESHA; ▲ Merton; *253 N-12; 🄿; ★ **MILW**; z 53064; ● 750
North Lancaster; MCD-Town; GRANT; *253 O-6; mail Lancaster z 53813; Ⓟ 548; Ⓒ 515
Northland; RMC Place; WAUPACA; ▲ Harrison; *252 I-10; elev. 1,046ft./319m.; mail Iola z 54945; ● 50
North Leeds; RMC Place; COLUMBIA; ▲ Leeds; *253 M-10; mail Arlington z 53911; ● 50
North Lowell; RMC Place; DODGE; ▲ Lowell; *253 M-11; mail Juneau z 53039; rural
North Madison; RMC Place; DANE; ★ **MAD**; pop. incl. with Madison (Inc. Place)
North Menomonie (Menomonie); RMC Place; DUNN; *252 H-3; mail Menomonie z 54751; pop. incl. with Menomonie (Inc. Place)
North Milwaukee; RMC Place; MILWAUKEE; *253 N-13; ★ **MILW**; mail Milwaukee z 53209; pop. incl. with Milwaukee (Inc. Place)
North Park; RMC Place; RACINE; ▲ Caledonia; *253 O-13; elev. 623ft./190m.; ★ **MILW**; mail Racine z 53402; ● 1,580
Northport; RMC Place; DOOR; ▲ Liberty Grove; *252 A-14; mail Ellison Bay z 54210
Northport; RMC Place; WAUPACA; ▲ Mukwa; 252 J-11; mail New London z 54961; ● 300
North Prairie; Inc. Place; WAUKESHA; 253 O-12; elev. 944ft./288m.; 🄿; ★ **MILW**; z 53153; Ⓟ 1,322; Ⓒ 1,571
North Shore; RMC Place; MILWAUKEE; ★ **MILW**; mail Milwaukee z 53217; pop. incl. with Milwaukee (Inc. Place)
North Tomah; RMC Place; MONROE; ▲ La Grange; *253 K-7; elev. 960ft./293m.; mail Tomah z 54660; rural
Northwoods Beach; RMC Place; SAWYER; ▲ Bass Lake; 252 E-5; 🄿; z 54843; summer pop. 2,000; ● 350
Northwynde; RMC Place; DANE; ▲ Bristol; *253 N-10; mail Sun Prairie z 53590; ● 100
North York; RMC Place; ASHLAND; ▲ Ashland; *252 C-6; mail High Bridge z 54846; rural
Norton; RMC Place; DUNN; ▲ Tainter; *252 H-4; elev. 931ft./284m.; mail Colfax z 54730; ● 30
Norwalk; Inc. Place; MONROE; 253 L-7; elev. 1,030ft./314m.; 🄿; z 54648; Ⓟ 564; Ⓒ 653
Norway; MCD-Town; RACINE; *253 O-13; ★ **MILW**; mail Union Grove z 53182; Ⓟ 5,493; Ⓒ 7,600
Norway Grove; RMC Place; DANE; ▲ Vienna; *253 N-9; mail De Forest z 53532; rural
Norwegian Bay; RMC Place; WINNEBAGO; ▲ Wolf River; *253 K-11; elev. 750ft./229m.; mail Fremont z 54940; ● 100
Norwood; MCD-Town; LANGLADE; *252 H-10; mail Antigo z 54409; Ⓟ 842; Ⓒ 918
Nutterville; RMC Place; MARATHON; ▲ Easton; *252 H-9; ★ **WAUS**; mail Wausau z 54403; rural
Nye; RMC Place; POLK; ▲ Osceola; 252 G-2; elev. 967ft./295m.; mail Osceola z 54020; ● 75

O

Oak Center; RMC Place; FOND DU LAC; ▲ Oakfield; *253 L-11; elev. 899ft./274m.; mail Oakfield z 53065; ● 50
Oak Creek; Inc. Place; MILWAUKEE; 253 O-13; elev. 700ft./213m.; 🄿; ★ **MILW**; z 53154; Ⓟ 19,513; Ⓒ 28,456; ◆ 32,242
Oakdale; Inc. Place; MONROE; ▲ Oakdale; 253 K-7; elev. 956ft./291m.; 🄿; z 54649; Ⓟ 162; Ⓒ 297
Oakdale; MCD-Town; MONROE; *253 K-7; 🄿; z 54649; Ⓟ 643; Ⓒ 679
Oakfield; Inc. Place; FOND DU LAC; 253 L-12; elev. 894ft./272m.; 🄿; z 53065; Ⓟ 1,003; Ⓒ 1,012
Oakfield; MCD-Town; FOND DU LAC; *253 L-11; 🄿; z 53065; does not include the Village of Oakfield; Ⓟ 822; Ⓒ 767
Oak Grove; MCD-Town; BARRON; *252 F-4; mail Rice Lake z 54868; Ⓟ 906; Ⓒ 911
Oak Grove; RMC Place; DODGE; ▲ Oak Grove; *253 M-11; mail Juneau z 53039; ● 100
Oak Grove; MCD-Town; DODGE; *253 M-11; mail Juneau z 53039; Ⓟ 1,200; Ⓒ 1,126
Oak Grove; MCD-Town; PIERCE; *252 I-2; mail Prescott z 54021; Ⓟ 1,120; Ⓒ 1,522
Oak Hill; RMC Place; JEFFERSON; ▲ Sullivan; *253 O-11; elev. 827ft./252m.; mail Palmyra z 53156; ● 30
Oakland; MCD-Town; BURNETT; *252 E-3; mail Webster z 54893; Ⓟ 480; Ⓒ 778
Oakland; MCD-Town; DOUGLAS; *252 C-3; mail South Range z 54874; Ⓟ 993; Ⓒ 1,144
Oakland; RMC Place; JEFFERSON; ▲ Oakland; *253 O-11; elev. 887ft./270m.; mail Fort Atkinson z 53538; ● 30
Oakland; MCD-Town; JEFFERSON; *253 O-11; mail Fort Atkinson z 53538; Ⓟ 2,526; Ⓒ 3,135
Oakley; RMC Place; GREEN; ▲ Spring Grove; *253 P-9; elev. 854ft./260m.; mail Juda z 53550; ● 25
Oakridge; RMC Place; PIERCE; ▲ Maiden Rock; *252 I-2; mail Bay City z 54723; rural
Oak Shores; RMC Place; WALWORTH; ▲ Linn; *253 P-12; elev. 909ft./277m.; mail Fontana z 53125; ● 100
Oakwood; RMC Place; MILWAUKEE; *253 O-13; elev. 699ft./213m.; ★ **MILW**; mail Oak Creek z 53154; pop. incl. with Oak Creek (Inc. Place)
Oasis; MCD-Town; WAUSHARA; *253 K-9; mail Plainfield z 54966; Ⓟ 389; Ⓒ 405
Oconomowoc; Inc. Place; WAUKESHA; 253 N-12; elev. 873ft./266m.; 🄿 🄷; ★ **MILW**; z 53066; Ⓟ 10,993; Ⓒ 12,382
Oconomowoc; MCD-Town; WAUKESHA; *253 N-12; 🄿; ★ **MILW**; z 53066 & mail Okauchee z 53069; does not include the City of Oconomowoc; Ⓟ 7,323; Ⓒ 7,451
Oconomowoc Lake; Inc. Place; WAUKESHA; *253 N-12; ★ **MILW**; mail Oconomowoc z 53066; Ⓟ 493; Ⓒ 564
Oconto; Inc. Place; ⊡ OCONTO; 252 H-13; elev. 591ft./180m.; 🄿 🄷; z 54153; Ⓟ 4,474; Ⓒ 4,708
Oconto; MCD-Town; OCONTO; *252 H-13; 🄿; z 54153 & mail Lena z 54139; does not include the City of Oconto; Ⓟ 999; Ⓒ 1,251
OCONTO; 252 H-12; Ⓟ 30,226; Ⓒ 35,634; Ⓡ 35,652; ◆ 37,407
Oconto Falls; Inc. Place; OCONTO; 252 H-12; elev. 735ft./224m.; 🄿 🄷; z 54154; Ⓟ 2,584; Ⓒ 2,843
Oconto Falls; MCD-Town; OCONTO; *252 H-12; 🄿; z 54154; does not include the City of Oconto Falls; Ⓟ 1,014; Ⓒ 1,139
Odanah; CDP; ASHLAND; ▲ Sanborn; 252 C-6; elev. 610ft./186m.; 🄿; z 54861; Ⓟ 190; Ⓒ 254
Ogdensburg; Inc. Place; WAUPACA; 252 J-10; elev. 861ft./262m.; 🄿; z 54962; Ⓟ 220; Ⓒ 224
Ogema; RMC Place; PRICE; ▲ Ogema; 252 F-7; elev. 1,583ft./482m.; 🄿; z 54459; ● 300
Ogema; MCD-Town; PRICE; *252 F-7; 🄿; z 54459; Ⓟ 860; Ⓒ 882
Oil City; RMC Place; MONROE; ▲ Sheldon; *253 L-7; mail Ontario z 54651; rural
Ojibwa; RMC Place; SAWYER; ▲ Ojibwa; 252 E-5; elev. 1,254ft./382m.; 🄿; z 54862; ● 100
Ojibwa; MCD-Town; SAWYER; *252 E-5; 🄿; z 54862; Ⓟ 250; Ⓒ 267
Okauchee; RMC Place; WAUKESHA; ▲ Oconomowoc; 253 N-12; 🄿; ★ **MILW**; z 53069; ● 1,500
Okauchee Lake; CDP-Census Area Only; WAUKESHA; ▲ Summit, Merton, Oconomowoc; *253 N-12; elev. 883ft./269m.; ★ **MILW**; mail Nashotah z 53058, Oconomowoc z 53066, Okauchee z 53069; Ⓟ 3,819; Ⓒ 3,916
Okee; RMC Place; COLUMBIA; ▲ West Point, Lodi; 253 M-9; mail Lodi z 53555; ● 300
Old Albertville; RMC Place; CHIPPEWA; ▲ Wheaton; *252 H-4; mail Colfax z 54730, Elk Mound z 54739; ● 40
Old Anson; CHIPPEWA; see Liddell (RMC Place)
Old Ashippun; RMC Place; DODGE; ▲ Ashippun; *253 N-12; elev. 892ft./272m.; mail Ashippun z 53003
Old Lebanon; RMC Place; DODGE; ▲ Lebanon; *253 N-11; mail Watertown z 53098; ● 100
Oliver; Inc. Place; DOUGLAS; 252 B-3; elev. 649ft./198m.; ★ **DUL**; mail Superior z 54880; Ⓟ 265; Ⓒ 358
Olivet; RMC Place; PIERCE; ▲ Spring Lake; *252 I-3; mail Spring Valley z 54767; ● 30
Oma; MCD-Town; IRON; *252 D-8; mail Hurley z 54534; Ⓟ 260; Ⓒ 355
Omro; Inc. Place; WINNEBAGO; 253 K-11; elev. 760ft./232m.; 🄿; ★ **OSH**; z 54963; Ⓟ 2,836; Ⓒ 3,177
Omro; MCD-Town; WINNEBAGO; *253 K-11; 🄿; ★ **OSH**; z 54963 & mail Oshkosh z 54901; does not include the City of Omro; Ⓟ 1,616; Ⓒ 1,875
Onalaska; Inc. Place; LA CROSSE; 253 L-5; elev. 716ft./218m.; 🄿; ★ **LACRO**; z 54650; Ⓟ 11,284; Ⓒ 14,839
Onalaska; MCD-Town; LA CROSSE; *253 K-5; 🄿; ★ **LACRO**; z 54650; Ⓟ 5,803; Ⓒ 5,210
Oneida; CDP; OUTAGAMIE, BROWN; ▲ Oneida, Hobart; 252 J-12; 🄿; ★ **GRBY**; z 54155; Ⓟ 808; Ⓒ 1,070
Oneida; MCD-Town; OUTAGAMIE; *252 J-12; 🄿; z 54155; Ⓟ 3,858; Ⓒ 4,001; Ⓡ 4,147
ONEIDA; 252 F-10; Ⓟ 31,679; Ⓒ 36,776; ◆ 35,604
Oneida (WI) Reservation; Indian Reservation; OUTAGAMIE, BROWN; ▲ Oneida, Hobart; mail Oneida z 54155; also location of Indian Agency; Ⓟ 13,389; Ⓒ 21,319
Ono (Grange Hall); RMC Place; PIERCE; ▲ Union, Salem; *252 I-3; mail Maiden Rock z 54750; ● 30
Ontario; Inc. Place; VERNON; 253 L-7; elev. 900ft./274m.; 🄿; z 54651; Ⓟ 407; Ⓒ 476
Oostburg; Inc. Place; SHEBOYGAN; 253 L-13; elev. 680ft./207m.; 🄿; ★ **SHEB**; z 53070; Ⓟ 1,931; Ⓒ 2,660
Orange; MCD-Town; JUNEAU; *253 K-7; mail Camp Douglas z 54618; Ⓟ 581; Ⓒ 549
Orange Mill; RMC Place; JUNEAU; ▲ Orange; *253 L-7; mail Camp Douglas z 54618; rural
Oregon; Inc. Place; DANE; 253 O-9; elev. 949ft./289m.; 🄿; ★ **MAD**; z 53575; Ⓟ 4,519; Ⓒ 7,514
Oregon; MCD-Town; DANE; *253 O-9; 🄿; ★ **MAD**; z 53575; does not include the Village of Oregon; Ⓟ 2,428; Ⓒ 3,148
Orfordville; Inc. Place; ROCK; 253 P-10; elev. 915ft./279m.; 🄿; z 53576 & mail Hanover z 53542; Ⓟ 1,219; Ⓒ 1,272
Orienta; MCD-Town; BAYFIELD; *252 B-5; mail Port Wing z 54865; Ⓟ 114; Ⓒ 101
Orihula; RMC Place; WINNEBAGO; ▲ Wolf River; *253 K-11; mail Fremont z 54940; ● 50
Orion; RMC Place; RICHLAND; ▲ Orion; *253 N-7; mail Muscoda z 53573; ● 90
Orion; MCD-Town; RICHLAND; *253 N-7; mail Muscoda z 53573; Ⓟ 604; Ⓒ 628
Osborn; MCD-Town; OUTAGAMIE; *252 J-12; mail Seymour z 54165; Ⓟ 784; Ⓒ 1,029
Osceola; MCD-Town; FOND DU LAC; *253 L-12; mail Campbellsport z 53010; Ⓟ 1,588; Ⓒ 1,802
Osceola; Inc. Place; POLK; 252 G-2; elev. 820ft./250m.; 🄿 🄷; z 54020; Ⓟ 2,075; Ⓒ 2,421
Osceola; MCD-Town; POLK; *252 G-2; 🄿; z 54020; does not include the City of Osceola; Ⓟ 1,337; Ⓒ 2,085
Oshkosh; Inc. Place; ⊡ WINNEBAGO; 253 K-11; elev. 755ft./230m.; 🄿 🄷 🄲 11,080 ■; ★ **OSH**; z 54901-04, z 54906; Ⓟ 55,006; Ⓒ 62,916; ◆ 66,764
Oshkosh; MCD-Town; WINNEBAGO; *253 K-12; 🄿 🄲 11,080; ★ **OSH**; z 54901-04, z 54906; does not include the City of Oshkosh; Ⓟ 4,655; Ⓒ 3,234
Osman; RMC Place; MANITOWOC; ▲ Meeme; 253 K-13; mail Newton z 53063; ● 50
Osseo; Inc. Place; TREMPEALEAU; 252 I-5; elev. 959ft./292m.; 🄿 🄷; z 54758; Ⓟ 1,551; Ⓒ 1,669
Ostrander; RMC Place; WAUPACA; ▲ Mukwa; *252 J-11; mail New London z 54961; rural
Otis; RMC Place; LINCOLN; ▲ Merrill; *252 G-9; mail Irma z 54442; ● 60
Otsego; RMC Place; COLUMBIA; ▲ Otsego; *253 M-10; mail Columbus z 53925, Rio z 53960; ● 100
Otsego; MCD-Town; COLUMBIA; *253 M-10; mail Columbus z 53925; Ⓟ 647; Ⓒ 757
Ottawa; MCD-Town; WAUKESHA; *253 O-12; ★ **MILW**; mail Dousman z 53118; Ⓟ 2,988; Ⓒ 3,758
Otter Creek; MCD-Town; DUNN; *252 H-4; mail Wheeler z 54772; Ⓟ 339; Ⓒ 474
Otter Creek; MCD-Town; EAU CLAIRE; *252 I-5; mail Augusta z 54722; Ⓟ 459; Ⓒ 531
Oulu; MCD-Town; BAYFIELD; *252 B-5; mail Iron River z 54847; Ⓟ 513; Ⓒ 540
Ourtown; RMC Place; SHEBOYGAN; ▲ Lima; *253 L-13; ★ **SHEB**; mail Sheboygan Falls z 53085; ● 30
OUTAGAMIE; 252 J-12; Ⓟ 140,510; Ⓒ 160,971; Ⓡ 161,091; ◆ 174,897
Owen; Inc. Place; CLARK; 252 H-7; elev. 1,245ft./379m.; 🄿; z 54460; Ⓟ 895; Ⓒ 936
Oxbo; RMC Place; SAWYER; ▲ Draper; *252 E-6; mail Park Falls z 54552; ● 50
Oxford; Inc. Place; MARQUETTE; 253 L-9; elev. 857ft./261m.; 🄿; z 53952; Ⓟ 499; Ⓒ 536
Oxford; MCD-Town; MARQUETTE; *253 L-9; 🄿; z 53952; does not include the Village of Oxford; Ⓟ 637; Ⓒ 859
OZAUKEE; 253 M-13; Ⓟ 72,831; Ⓒ 82,317; ◆ 83,813

P

Pacific; MCD-Town; COLUMBIA; *253 M-9; mail Pardeeville z 53954; Ⓟ 1,944; Ⓒ 2,518
Packwaukee; RMC Place; MARQUETTE; ▲ Packwaukee; 253 L-9; 🄿; z 53953; ● 450
Packwaukee; MCD-Town; MARQUETTE; *253 L-9; 🄿; z 53953; Ⓟ 1,135; Ⓒ 2,574; Ⓡ 1,297
Paddock Lake; Inc. Place; KENOSHA; 253 P-13; elev. 800ft./244m.; ★ **CHI**; mail Salem z 53168; Ⓟ 2,662; Ⓒ 3,012
Padus; RMC Place; FOREST; ▲ Wabeno; *252 F-11; elev. 1,593ft./486m.; mail Wabeno z 54566; rural
Palmyra; Inc. Place; JEFFERSON; 253 O-11; elev. 848ft./258m.; 🄿; z 53156; Ⓟ 1,539; Ⓒ 1,766
Palmyra; MCD-Town; JEFFERSON; *253 O-11; 🄿; z 53156; does not include the Village of Palmyra; Ⓟ 1,177; Ⓒ 1,145
Paoli; RMC Place; DANE; ▲ Montrose; 253 O-9; mail Belleville z 53508; ● 100
Pardeeville; Inc. Place; COLUMBIA; 253 M-10; elev. 815ft./248m.; 🄿; z 53954; Ⓟ 1,630; Ⓒ 1,982
Parfreyville; RMC Place; WAUPACA; ▲ Dayton; *252 J-10; mail Waupaca z 54981; ● 60
Paris; MCD-Town; GRANT; *253 P-7; mail Cuba City z 53807; Ⓟ 749; Ⓒ 754
Paris; RMC Place; KENOSHA; ▲ Paris; *253 P-13; elev. 755ft./230m.; mail Union Grove z 53182; ● 60
Paris; MCD-Town; KENOSHA; *253 P-13; mail Union Grove z 53182; Ⓟ 1,482; Ⓒ 1,473
Park Falls; Inc. Place; PRICE; 252 E-7; elev. 1,490ft./454m.; 🄿 🄷; z 54552; Ⓟ 3,104; Ⓒ 2,793
Parkland; MCD-Town; DOUGLAS; *252 C-3; mail South Range z 54874; Ⓟ 1,326; Ⓒ 1,240
Parklawn; RMC Place; MILWAUKEE; ★ **MILW**; mail Milwaukee z 53216; pop. incl. with Milwaukee (Inc. Place)
Park Ridge; Inc. Place; PORTAGE; 252 J-9; elev. 1,095ft./334m.; mail Stevens Point z 54481; Ⓟ 546; Ⓒ 488
Parnell; RMC Place; SHEBOYGAN; ▲ Mitchell; *253 L-13; mail Cascade z 53011; rural
Parrish; RMC Place; LANGLADE; ▲ Parrish; 252 G-9; mail Gleason z 54435; ● 30
Parrish; MCD-Town; LANGLADE; *252 G-9; mail Gleason z 54435; Ⓟ 81; Ⓒ 108
Patch Grove; Inc. Place; GRANT; 253 O-6; elev. 1,060ft./323m.; 🄿; z 53817; Ⓟ 202; Ⓒ 166
Patch Grove; MCD-Town; GRANT; *253 O-6; 🄿; z 53817 & mail Prairie du Chien z 53821; does not include the Village of Patch Grove; Ⓟ 378; Ⓒ 390
Patzau; RMC Place; DOUGLAS; ▲ Summit; 252 C-3; mail Foxboro z 54836; ● 50
Pearson; RMC Place; LANGLADE; ▲ Ainsworth; 252 G-10; 🄿; z 54462; summer pop. 500; ● 60
Peck; MCD-Town; LANGLADE; *252 G-10; mail Deerbrook z 54424; Ⓟ 402; Ⓒ 354
Peebles; RMC Place; FOND DU LAC; ▲ Taycheedah; 253 L-12; elev. 816ft./249m.; ★ **FDLC**; mail Fond du Lac z 54935; ● 100
Peeksville; MCD-Town; ASHLAND; *252 D-7; mail Glidden z 54527; Ⓟ 167; Ⓒ 176
Pelican; MCD-Town; ONEIDA; *252 F-10; mail Rhinelander z 54501; Ⓟ 3,202; Ⓒ 2,902
Pelican Lake; RMC Place; ONEIDA; ▲ Schoepke; 252 F-10; elev. 1,604ft./489m.; 🄿; z 54463; ● 200
Pella; RMC Place; SHAWANO; ▲ Pella; 252 I-11; mail Marion z 54950; ● 100
Pella; MCD-Town; SHAWANO; *252 I-11; mail Marion z 54950; Ⓟ 885; Ⓒ 877
Pell Lake; CDP; WALWORTH; ▲ Bloomfield; 253 P-12; elev. 871ft./265m.; 🄿; z 53157; Ⓟ 2,018; Ⓒ 2,988
Pembine; RMC Place; MARINETTE; ▲ Pembine; 252 F-13; elev. 968ft./295m.; 🄿; z 54119, z 54156; ● 550
Pembine; MCD-Town; MARINETTE; *252 F-13; 🄿; z 54119, z 54156; Ⓟ 817; Ⓒ 1,036
Pence; RMC Place; IRON; ▲ Pence; 252 C-7; 🄿; z 54550; ● 70
Pence; MCD-Town; IRON; *252 C-7; 🄿; z 54550; Ⓟ 181; Ⓒ 198
Peninsula Center; RMC Place; DOOR; ▲ Baileys Harbor; *252 B-13; elev. 718ft./219m.; mail Baileys Harbor z 54202; ● 50
Pensaukee; RMC Place; OCONTO; ▲ Pensaukee; 252 H-13; elev. 591ft./180m.; mail Oconto z 54153; ● 150
Pensaukee; MCD-Town; OCONTO; *252 I-13; mail Oconto z 54153; Ⓟ 979; Ⓒ 1,214
Pepin; Inc. Place; PEPIN; 252 J-3; elev. 720ft./219m.; 🄿; z 54759; Ⓟ 873; Ⓒ 878
Pepin; MCD-Town; PEPIN; *252 J-3; 🄿; z 54759; does not include the City of Pepin; Ⓟ 696; Ⓒ 580
PEPIN; 252 I-3; Ⓟ 7,107; Ⓒ 7,213; ◆ 7,366
Peplin; RMC Place; MARATHON; ▲ Kronenwetter; *252 I-9; elev. 1,211ft./369m.; ★ **WAUS**; mail Mosinee z 54455; ● 30
Perkinstown; RMC Place; TAYLOR; ▲ Grover; 252 G-7; mail Medford z 54451; ● 100
Perry; MCD-Town; DANE; *253 O-9; mail Mount Horeb z 53572; Ⓟ 646; Ⓒ 670
Pershing; MCD-Town; TAYLOR; *252 G-6; mail Gilman z 54433; Ⓟ 217; Ⓒ 180
Peru; MCD-Town; DUNN; *252 I-4; mail Mondovi z 54755; Ⓟ 203; Ⓒ 247
Peru; RMC Place; PORTAGE; ▲ New Hope; 252 I-10; mail Amherst Junction z 54407; ● 40
Peshtigo; Inc. Place; MARINETTE; 252 H-13; elev. 600ft./183m.; 🄿; z 54157; Ⓟ 3,154; Ⓒ 3,357
Peshtigo; MCD-Town; MARINETTE; *252 H-13; 🄿; z 54157 & mail Marinette z 54143; does not include the City of Peshtigo; Ⓟ 3,564; Ⓒ 3,819
Petersburg; RMC Place; CRAWFORD; ▲ Haney; 253 N-6; mail Gays Mills z 54631; ● 35
Petty Acres; RMC Place; DANE; ▲ Pleasant Springs; *253 O-10; elev. 863ft./263m.; ★ **MAD**; mail Stoughton z 53589; ● 200
Pewaukee (Village of Pewaukee); Inc. Place; WAUKESHA; 253 N-12; elev. 859ft./262m.; 🄿; ★ **MILW**; z 53072; Ⓟ 4,941; Ⓒ 8,170
Pewaukee (City of Pewaukee); Inc. Place; WAUKESHA; *253 N-12; 🄿; ★ **MILW**; z 53072 & mail Waukesha z 53186; Ⓟ 9,621; Ⓒ 11,783
Phantom Lake; RMC Place; WAUKESHA; ▲ Mukwonago; *253 O-12; elev. 842ft./257m.; ★ **MILW**; mail Mukwonago z 53149; ● 220
Pheasant Branch; RMC Place; DANE; *253 N-9; ★ **MAD**; mail Middleton z 53562; pop. incl. with Middleton (Inc. Place)
Phelps; RMC Place; VILAS; ▲ Phelps; 252 D-10; elev. 1,770ft./539m.; 🄿 🄷; z 54554; summer pop. 2,000; ● 900
Phelps; MCD-Town; VILAS; *252 D-10; 🄿; z 54554; Ⓟ 1,187; Ⓒ 1,350
Phillips; Inc. Place; ⊡ PRICE; 252 F-7; elev. 1,480ft./451m.; 🄿; z 54555; Ⓟ 1,592; Ⓒ 1,675
Phipps; RMC Place; SAWYER; ▲ Lenroot; *252 D-5; elev. 1,233ft./376m.; mail Hayward z 54843; rural
Phlox; RMC Place; LANGLADE; ▲ Norwood; 252 H-10; 🄿; z 54464; ● 150
Piacenza; RMC Place; WINNEBAGO; ▲ Winneconne; *253 K-11; ★ **OSH**; mail Winneconne z 54986; ● 40
Pickerel; RMC Place; FOREST, LANGLADE; ▲ Langlade, Nashville; 252 G-11; 🄿; z 54465; summer pop. 700; ● 300
Pickett; RMC Place; WINNEBAGO; ▲ Utica; 253 L-11; 🄿; z 54964; ● 170
Piehl; MCD-Town; ONEIDA; *252 F-10; mail Rhinelander z 54501; Ⓟ 66; Ⓒ 93
Pierce; MCD-Town; KEWAUNEE; *252 I-14; mail Kewaunee z 54216; Ⓟ 724; Ⓒ 897
PIERCE; 252 I-3; Ⓟ 32,765; Ⓒ 36,804; ◆ 40,191
Pigeon; MCD-Town; TREMPEALEAU; *252 J-5; mail Whitehall z 54773; Ⓟ 845; Ⓒ 894
Pigeon Falls; Inc. Place; TREMPEALEAU; 252 J-5; elev. 882ft./269m.; 🄿; z 54760; Ⓟ 289; Ⓒ 388
Pike Lake; RMC Place; MARATHON; ▲ Reid, Elderon; *252 I-10; elev. 1,248ft./380m.; mail Hatley z 54440; ● 150
Pilsen; MCD-Town; BAYFIELD; *252 C-5; mail Ashland z 54806; Ⓟ 203; Ⓒ 203
Pilsen; RMC Place; KEWAUNEE; ▲ Montpelier; 252 J-13; elev. 888ft./271m.; mail Luxemburg z 54217; ● 50
Pine Bluff; RMC Place; DANE; ▲ Cross Plains; *253 N-9; elev. 993ft./303m.; ★ **MAD**; mail Cross Plains z 53528; ● 150
Pine Creek; RMC Place; TREMPEALEAU; ▲ Dodge; *253 K-4; elev. 768ft./234m.; mail Dodge z 54625; ● 60
Pine Grove; RMC Place; BROWN; ▲ Ledgeview, Eaton, Glenmore, New Denmark; *252 J-13; ★ **GRBY**; mail Denmark z 54208; rural
Pine Grove; MCD-Town; PORTAGE; *252 J-9; mail Bancroft z 54921; Ⓟ 949; Ⓒ 904
Pinehurst; RMC Place; EAU CLAIRE; ▲ Seymour; *252 H-5; ★ **EAUC**; mail Eau Claire z 54703; pop. incl. with Eau Claire (Inc. Place)
Pine Lake; RMC Place; IRON; ▲ Oma; *252 D-8; mail Hurley z 54534; summer pop. 100; ● 30
Pine Lake; MCD-Town; ONEIDA; *252 F-9; mail Rhinelander z 54501; Ⓟ 2,445; Ⓒ 2,720
Pine River; RMC Place; LINCOLN; ▲ Pine River; *252 G-9; mail Merrill z 54452; rural
Pine River; MCD-Town; LINCOLN; *252 G-9; mail Merrill z 54452; Ⓟ 1,552; Ⓒ 1,877
Pine River; RMC Place; WAUSHARA; ▲ Leon; 253 K-10; 🄿; z 54965; ● 150
Pine Valley; MCD-Town; CLARK; *252 I-7; mail Neillsville z 54456; Ⓟ 1,032; Ⓒ 1,121
Pipe (Calumet Harbor); RMC Place; FOND DU LAC; ▲ Calumet; 253 L-12; mail Malone z 53049; ● 100
Pipersville; RMC Place; JEFFERSON; ▲ Ixonia; *253 N-11; ★ **MILW**; mail Watertown z 53094; ● 80
Pittsfield; MCD-Town; BROWN; *252 I-12; ★ **GRBY**; mail Green Bay z 54301; Ⓟ 2,165; Ⓒ 2,433
Pittsville; Inc. Place; WOOD; 252 J-8; elev. 1,032ft./315m.; 🄿; z 54466; Ⓟ 838; Ⓒ 866
Plain; Inc. Place; SAUK; 253 N-8; elev. 810ft./247m.; 🄿; z 53577; Ⓟ 691; Ⓒ 792
Plainfield; Inc. Place; WAUSHARA; 253 K-9; elev. 1,110ft./338m.; 🄿; z 54966; Ⓟ 839; Ⓒ 899
Plainfield; MCD-Town; WAUSHARA; *253 K-9; 🄿; z 54966; does not include the Village of Plainfield; Ⓟ 529; Ⓒ 533
Plainville; RMC Place; ADAMS; ▲ Dell Prairie; 253 L-8; mail Wisconsin Dells z 53965; ● 50
Plat; RMC Place; WASHINGTON; ▲ Richfield; *253 N-12; ★ **MILW**; mail Colgate z 53017; ● 100
Platteville; Inc. Place; GRANT; 253 O-7; elev. 994ft./303m.; 🄿 🄷 🄲 6,813; z 53818; Ⓟ 9,708; Ⓒ 9,989
Platteville; MCD-Town; GRANT; *253 P-7; 🄿 🄲 6,813; z 53818; does not include the City of Platteville; Ⓟ 1,415; Ⓒ 1,343
Pleasant Prairie; Inc. Place; KENOSHA; 253 P-13; 🄿; ★ **KEN**; z 53158 & mail Kenosha z 53142-43; Ⓟ 11,961; Ⓒ 16,136
Pleasant Ridge; RMC Place; IOWA; ▲ Dodgeville; *253 N-8; mail Dodgeville z 53533; rural
Pleasant Springs; MCD-Town; DANE; *253 O-10; ★ **MAD**; mail Stoughton z 53589; Ⓟ 2,660; Ⓒ 3,053
Pleasant Valley; MCD-Town; EAU CLAIRE; *252 I-5; mail Eau Claire z 54701; Ⓟ 2,076; Ⓒ 2,681
Pleasant Valley; MCD-Town; ST. CROIX; *252 H-2; mail Hammond z 54015; Ⓟ 384; Ⓒ 430
Pleasant Valley; RMC Place; VERNON, LA CROSSE; ▲ Bergen, Shelby; *253 L-5; elev. 700ft./213m.; mail Stoddard z 54658; ● 120
Pleasantville; RMC Place; TREMPEALEAU; ▲ Hale; 252 J-5; mail Osseo z 54758; ● 35
Plover; MCD-Town; MARATHON; *252 H-10; mail Birnamwood z 54414; Ⓟ 568; Ⓒ 686
Plover; Inc. Place; PORTAGE; 252 J-9; elev. 1,075ft./328m.; 🄿; z 54467; Ⓟ 8,176; Ⓒ 10,520
Plover; MCD-Town; PORTAGE; *252 J-9; 🄿; z 54467; Ⓟ 2,223; Ⓒ 2,415
Plugtown; RMC Place; CRAWFORD; ▲ Scott; *253 N-6; mail Boscobel z 53805; rural
Plum City; Inc. Place; PIERCE; 252 I-3; elev. 815ft./248m.; 🄿; z 54761; Ⓟ 534; Ⓒ 574
Plum Lake; MCD-Town; VILAS; *252 D-9; mail Sayner z 54560; Ⓟ 465; Ⓒ 486
Plymouth; MCD-Town; JUNEAU; *253 L-7; mail Elroy z 53929; Ⓟ 601; Ⓒ 639
Plymouth; MCD-Town; ROCK; *253 P-10; mail Janesville z 53545; Ⓟ 1,189; Ⓒ 1,270
Plymouth; Inc. Place; SHEBOYGAN; 253 L-13; elev. 830ft./253m.; 🄿 🄷; ★ **SHEB**; z 53073; Ⓟ 6,769; Ⓒ 7,781
Plymouth; MCD-Town; SHEBOYGAN; *253 L-13; 🄿; ★ **SHEB**; z 53073; does not include the City of Plymouth; Ⓟ 2,911; Ⓒ 3,115
Poland; RMC Place; BROWN; ▲ Eaton; 252 J-13; mail Green Bay z 54301; ● 80
Polar; RMC Place; LANGLADE; ▲ Polar; 252 G-10; mail Bryant z 54418; ● 120
Polar; MCD-Town; LANGLADE; *252 G-10; mail Bryant z 54418; Ⓟ 900; Ⓒ 995
Polifka Corners; RMC Place; MANITOWOC; ▲ Kossuth; *252 J-13; elev. 800ft./244m.; mail Whitelaw z 54247; rural
Polk; MCD-Town; WASHINGTON; *253 M-12; ★ **MILW**; mail Richfield z 53076; Ⓟ 3,540; Ⓒ 3,938
POLK; 252 F-2; Ⓟ 34,773; Ⓒ 41,319; ◆ 43,997
Polley; RMC Place; TAYLOR; ▲ Ford; *252 G-6; mail Gilman z 54433; rural
Polonia; RMC Place; PORTAGE; ▲ Sharon; 252 I-9; mail Custer z 54423; ● 100
Poniatowski; RMC Place; MARATHON; ▲ Rietbrock; *252 H-8; mail Edgar z 54426; ● 100
Poplar; Inc. Place; DOUGLAS; 252 C-4; elev. 985ft./300m.; 🄿; z 54864; Ⓟ 516; Ⓒ 552
Popple Lake; RMC Place; CHIPPEWA; ▲ Eagle Point; *252 H-5; elev. 986ft./301m.; mail Chippewa Falls z 54729; ● 50
Popple River; RMC Place; FOREST; ▲ Popple River; *252 E-11; elev. 1,523ft./464m.; mail Long Lake z 54542; ● 40
Popple River; MCD-Town; FOREST; *252 E-11; mail Long Lake z 54542; Ⓟ 42; Ⓒ 79
Porcupine; RMC Place; PEPIN; ▲ Frankfort; *252 I-3; mail Arkansaw z 54721; rural
Portage; Inc. Place; ⊡ COLUMBIA; 253 M-9; elev. 800ft./244m.; 🄿 🄷; z 53901; Ⓟ 8,640; Ⓒ 9,728
PORTAGE; 252 J-9; Ⓟ 61,405; Ⓒ 67,182; ◆ 69,560
Port Andrew; RMC Place; RICHLAND; ▲ Richwood; 253 N-7; elev. 699ft./213m.; mail Blue River z 53518; ● 40
Port Edwards; Inc. Place; WOOD; 252 J-8; elev. 975ft./297m.; 🄿; z 54469; Ⓟ 1,848; Ⓒ 1,944
Port Edwards; MCD-Town; WOOD; *252 J-8; 🄿; z 54469 & mail Nekoosa z 54457; does not include the Village of Port Edwards; Ⓟ 1,351; Ⓒ 1,446
Porter; MCD-Town; ROCK; *253 O-10; mail Janesville z 53545; Ⓟ 953; Ⓒ 925
Porterfield; RMC Place; MARINETTE; ▲ Porterfield; 252 G-13; 🄿; z 54159; ● 50
Porterfield; MCD-Town; MARINETTE; *252 G-13; 🄿; z 54159; Ⓟ 1,805; Ⓒ 1,991
Portland; RMC Place; DODGE; ▲ Portland; 253 N-11; mail Waterloo z 53594; ● 200
Portland; MCD-Town; DODGE; *253 N-11; mail Waterloo z 53594; Ⓟ 994; Ⓒ 1,106
Portland; RMC Place; MONROE; ▲ Portland; 253 L-6; elev. 1,312ft./400m.; mail Cashton z 54619; ● 45
Portland; MCD-Town; MONROE; *253 L-6; mail Cashton z 54619; Ⓟ 733; Ⓒ 686
Port Washington; Inc. Place; ⊡ OZAUKEE; 253 M-13; elev. 612ft./187m.; 🄿; ★ **MILW**; z 53074; Ⓟ 9,338; Ⓒ 10,467
Port Washington; MCD-Town; OZAUKEE; *253 M-13; 🄿; ★ **MILW**; z 53074; does not include the City of Port Washington; Ⓟ 1,480; Ⓒ 1,631
Port Wing; RMC Place; BAYFIELD; ▲ Port Wing; 252 B-5; 🄿; z 54865; ● 250
Port Wing; MCD-Town; BAYFIELD; *252 B-5; 🄿; z 54865; Ⓟ 434; Ⓒ 420
Portz Siding; RMC Place; WAUKESHA; ★ **MILW**; pop. incl. with Waukesha (Inc. Place)
Poskin; RMC Place; BARRON; ▲ Clinton; 252 G-3; elev. 1,191ft./363m.; 🄿; z 54812; ● 90
Post Lake; RMC Place; LANGLADE; ▲ Elcho; 252 F-10; mail Elcho z 54428; ● 250
Postville (Stewart); RMC Place; GREEN; ▲ York; 253 O-9; mail Blanchardville z 53516; ● 30
Potosi; Inc. Place; GRANT; 253 P-6; elev. 800ft./244m.; 🄿; z 53820; Ⓟ 654; Ⓒ 711
Potosi; MCD-Town; GRANT; *253 O-6; 🄿; z 53820; does not include the Village of Potosi; Ⓟ 963; Ⓒ 831
Potter; Inc. Place; CALUMET; ▲ Rantoul; 253 K-13; 🄿; z 54160; Ⓟ 252; Ⓒ 223; Ⓡ 252
Potter Lake; CDP-Census Area Only; WALWORTH; ▲ East Troy; *253 O-12; elev. 850ft./259m.; ★ **MILW**; mail East Troy z 53120; Ⓟ 1,096; Ⓒ 1,099
Potts Corners; RMC Place; VERNON; ▲ Stark; *253 L-6; mail La Farge z 54639; rural
Pound; Inc. Place; MARINETTE; 252 H-13; elev. 725ft./221m.; 🄿; z 54161; Ⓟ 434; Ⓒ 355
Pound; MCD-Town; MARINETTE; *252 H-13; 🄿; z 54161 & mail Lena z 54139; does not include the Village of Pound; Ⓟ 1,386; Ⓒ 1,367
Powell; RMC Place; IRON; ▲ Mercer; *252 D-8; elev. 1,596ft./486m.; mail Mercer z 54547
Powers Lake; CDP; KENOSHA, WALWORTH; ▲ Bloomfield, Randall, Wheatland; *253 P-12; 🄿; ★ **CHI**; z 53159; Ⓟ 1,044; summer pop. 2,200; Ⓒ 1,500
Poygan; MCD-Town; WINNEBAGO; *253 K-11; mail Omro z 54963; Ⓟ 824; Ⓒ 1,037
Poynette; Inc. Place; COLUMBIA; 253 M-9; elev. 847ft./258m.; 🄿; z 53955; Ⓟ 1,662; Ⓒ 2,266
Poy Sippi; RMC Place; WAUSHARA; ▲ Poysippi; 253 K-10; elev. 778ft./237m.; 🄿; z 54967; ● 450
Poysippi; MCD-Town; WAUSHARA; *253 K-11; mail Poy Sippi z 54967; Ⓟ 929; Ⓒ 972
Praag; RMC Place; BUFFALO; ▲ Lincoln; *252 J-4; elev. 855ft./261m.; mail Alma z 54610
Prairie Corners; RMC Place; GRANT; ▲ Hazel Green; *253 P-7; elev. 906ft./276m.; mail Cuba City z 53807; ● 40
Prairie du Chien; Inc. Place; ⊡ CRAWFORD; 253 N-5; elev. 632ft./193m.; 🄿 🄷; z 53821; Ⓟ 5,659; Ⓒ 6,018
Prairie du Chien; MCD-Town; CRAWFORD; *253 N-5; 🄿; z 53821; does not include the City of Prairie du Chien; Ⓟ 927; Ⓒ 1,076
Prairie du Sac; Inc. Place; SAUK; 253 N-9; elev. 780ft./238m.; 🄿 🄷; z 53578; Ⓟ 2,380; Ⓒ 3,231
Prairie du Sac; MCD-Town; SAUK; *253 N-9; 🄿; z 53578 & mail Sauk City z 53583; does not include the Village of Prairie du Sac; Ⓟ 1,271; Ⓒ 1,138

Entries in **UPPERCASE** are counties.
Entries in **bold** have populations of 2,500 or more.
Names in parentheses are alternate names.
Inc. Place — Incorporated Place
RMC Place — Rand McNally Designated Place
CDP — Census Designated Place
MCD — Minor Civil Division

⊡ County Seat
▲ Minor Civil Division
elev. Elevation
🄿 Post Office
🄷 Hospital
🄲 College
■ Principal Business Center
★ Ranally Metro Area (RMA) Abbreviation
z Zip Code(s)
Ⓟ Previous Census Population
Ⓡ Revised Census Population
Ⓐ Annexation Population
● Rand McNally Population Estimate
Ⓒ Final Census Population
Ⓢ Special Census Population
◆ Estimated Population

For additional definitions see Glossary, Volume 1, and Introduction, Volume 2.

Prairie Farm; Inc. Place; BARRON; **252** G-3; elev. 1,040ft./317m.; 🄿; Z 54762; Ⓟ 494; © 508

Prairie Farm; MCD-Town; BARRON; ***252** G-3; 🄿; Z 54762; does not include the Village of Prairie Farm; Ⓟ 567; © 603

Prairie Lake; MCD-Town; BARRON; ***252** G-4; mail Chetek Z 54728; Ⓟ 1,129; © 1,369

Prairie View Heights; RMC Place; DANE; ▲ Bristol; ***253** N-10; mail Sun Prairie Z 53590; ● 350

Pray; RMC Place; JACKSON; ▲ City Point; ***252** J-7; elev. 978ft./298m.; mail Pittsville Z 54466; ● 50

Prentice; Inc. Place; PRICE; **252** F-7; elev. 1,540ft./469m.; 🄿; Z 54556; Ⓟ 571; © 626

Prentice; MCD-Town; PRICE; ***252** F-7; 🄿; Z 54556; does not include the Village of Prentice; Ⓟ 486; © 479

Prescott; Inc. Place; PIERCE; **252** I-1; elev. 780ft./238m.; 🄿; Z 54021; Ⓟ 3,243; © 3,764

Presque Isle; RMC Place; VILAS; ▲ Presque Isle; **252** D-9; 🄿; Z 54557; summer pop. 500; ● 260

Presque Isle; MCD-Town; VILAS; ***252** D-9; 🄿; Z 54557; Ⓟ 471; © 513

Preston; MCD-Town; ADAMS; ***253** K-9; mail Friendship Z 53934; Ⓟ 1,057; © 1,360

Preston; RMC Place; GRANT; ▲ Wingville, Fennimore; **253** O-7; mail Fennimore Z 53809; ● 50

Preston; MCD-Town; TREMPEALEAU; ***252** J-5; mail Blair Z 54616; Ⓟ 963; © 951

Price; RMC Place; JACKSON; ▲ Garfield; **252** I-6; elev. 1,082ft./330m.; mail Fairchild Z 54741; ● 20

Price; MCD-Town; LANGLADE; ***252** G-10; mail Bryant Z 54418; Ⓟ 248; © 243

PRICE; **252** F-7; Ⓟ 15,600; © 15,822; ◆ 13,716

Primrose; MCD-Town; DANE; ***253** O-9; mail Verona Z 53593; Ⓟ 595; © 682

Princeton; Inc. Place; GREEN LAKE; **253** L-10; elev. 775ft./236m.; 🄿; Z 54968; Ⓟ 1,458; © 1,504

Princeton; MCD-Town; GREEN LAKE; ***253** L-10; 🄿; Z 54968; does not include the City of Princeton; Ⓟ 1,363; © 1,540

Prospect; RMC Place; WAUKESHA; ***253** O-12; ★ **MILW**; mail New Berlin Z 53151; pop. incl. with New Berlin (Inc. Place)

Pukwana Beach; RMC Place; FOND DU LAC; ▲ Calumet; ***253** K-12; elev. 751ft./229m.; mail Malone Z 53049; ● 30

Pulaski; Inc. Place; BROWN, SHAWANO; **252** I-12; elev. 795ft./242m.; 🄿; Z 54162; Ⓟ 2,200; © 3,060

Pulaski; MCD-Town; IOWA; ***253** N-7; mail Avoca Z 53506; Ⓟ 392; © 381

Pulcifer; RMC Place; SHAWANO; ▲ Green Valley; **252** H-12; 🄿; Z 54124; ● 100

Purdy; RMC Place; VERNON; ▲ Sterling; ***253** M-5; elev. 704ft./215m.; mail Viroqua Z 54665; rural

Q

Quarry; RMC Place; MANITOWOC; ▲ Rockland; ***253** K-13; elev. 821ft./250m.; mail Reedsville Z 54230; rural

Quincy; MCD-Town; ADAMS; ***253** L-8; mail Adams Z 53910; Ⓟ 927; © 1,181

Quincy Details; RMC Place; ADAMS; ▲ Quincy; ***253** L-8; elev. 900ft./274m.; mail Friendship Z 53934; ● 100

Quinney; RMC Place; CALUMET; ▲ Stockbridge; ***253** K-12; mail Chilton Z 53014; ● 45

R

Racine; Inc. Place; ⊡ RACINE; **253** O-13; elev. 626ft./191m.; 🄿 🄷 ■; ★ **MILW**; Z 53401-08; Ⓟ 84,298; © 81,855; ◆ 78,041

RACINE; **253** O-13; Ⓟ 175,034; © 188,831; ◆ 192,307

Radisson; Inc. Place; SAWYER; **252** E-5; elev. 1,245ft./379m.; 🄿; Z 54867; Ⓟ 237; © 222

Radisson; MCD-Town; SAWYER; ***252** E-5; 🄿; Z 54867; does not include the Village of Radisson; Ⓟ 412; © 465

Raintree; RMC Place; DANE; ▲ Windsor; ***253** N-10; ★ **MAD**; mail Sun Prairie Z 53590; ● 200

Randall; MCD-Town; KENOSHA; ***253** P-12; ★ **CHI**; mail Richmond Z 60071; Ⓟ 2,395; © 2,929

Randolph; MCD-Town; COLUMBIA; ***253** M-10; 🄿; Z 53956-57 & mail Cambria Z 53923; does not include the Village of Randolph; Ⓟ 676; © 699

Randolph; Inc. Place; DODGE, COLUMBIA; **253** M-10; elev. 964ft./294m.; 🄿; Z 53956-57; Ⓟ 1,729; © 1,869

Random Lake; Inc. Place; SHEBOYGAN; **253** M-13; elev. 901ft./275m.; 🄿; ★ **SHEB**; Z 53075; Ⓟ 1,439; © 1,551

Range; RMC Place; POLK; ▲ Beaver, Apple River; **252** G-3; elev. 1,168ft./356m.; mail Amery Z 54001; ● 100

Rankin; RMC Place; KEWAUNEE; ▲ Pierce; ***252** I-14; mail Algoma Z 54201; rural

Rantoul; MCD-Town; CALUMET; ***253** K-13; mail Chilton Z 53014; Ⓟ 895; © 841; Ⓡ 812

Rattman Heights; RMC Place; DANE; ▲ Burke; ***253** N-10; elev. 1,000ft./305m.; ★ **MAD**; mail Madison Z 53718; ● 300

Ravenoaks; RMC Place; DANE; ▲ Oregon; ***253** O-9; elev. 1,000ft./305m.; ★ **MAD**; mail Oregon Z 53575; ● 200

Rawson; RMC Place; MILWAUKEE; ★ **MILW**; mail South Milwaukee Z 53172; pop. incl. with Oak Creek (Inc. Place)

Raymond (Raymond Center); RMC Place; RACINE; ▲ Raymond; ***253** O-13; elev. 742ft./226m.; ★ **MILW**; mail Franksville Z 53126; ● 100

Raymond; MCD-Town; RACINE; ***253** O-13; ★ **MILW**; mail Franksville Z 53126; Ⓟ 3,243; © 3,516

Raymond Center; RACINE; see Raymond (RMC Place)

Readfield; RMC Place; WAUPACA; ▲ Caledonia; ***252** J-11; 🄿; Z 54969; ● 180

Readstown; Inc. Place; VERNON; **253** M-6; elev. 760ft./232m.; 🄿; Z 54652; Ⓟ 420; © 395

Red Banks; BROWN; see Benderville (RMC Place)

Red Banks; RMC Place; WAUPACA; ▲ Fremont; ***252** J-11; mail Fremont Z 54940

Red Cedar; MCD-Town; DUNN; ***252** H-4; mail Menomonie Z 54751; Ⓟ 1,417; © 1,673

Red Cliff; RMC Place; BAYFIELD; ▲ Russell; **252** B-6; elev. 640ft./195m.; mail Bayfield Z 54814; ● 250

Red Cliff Reservation; Indian Reservation; BAYFIELD; ▲ Russell, Bayfield; mail Bayfield Z 54814; Ⓟ 686; © 1,078

Redgranite; Inc. Place; WAUSHARA; **253** K-10; elev. 789ft./240m.; 🄿; Z 54970; Ⓟ 1,009; © 1,040

Red Mound; RMC Place; VERNON; ▲ Wheatland; **253** M-5; mail De Soto Z 54624; ● 45

Red River; MCD-Town; KEWAUNEE; ***252** I-13; mail Casco Z 54205; Ⓟ 1,407; © 1,476

Red River; RMC Place; SHAWANO; ▲ Richmond; **252** I-11; mail Shawano Z 54166; ● 25

Red Rock; RMC Place; LAFAYETTE; ▲ Darlington; ***253** P-8; mail Darlington Z 53530; rural

Red Springs; MCD-Town; SHAWANO; ***252** H-11; mail Gresham Z 54128; Ⓟ 614; © 981

Redville; RMC Place; CLARK; ▲ Maplehurst; ***252** H-7; mail Withee Z 54498; rural

Reedsburg; Inc. Place; SAUK; **253** M-8; elev. 926ft./282m.; 🄿 🄷; Z 53958-59; Ⓟ 5,834; © 7,827

Reedsburg; MCD-Town; SAUK; ***253** M-8; 🄿; Z 53958-59; does not include the City of Reedsburg; Ⓟ 1,367; © 1,236

Reedsville; Inc. Place; MANITOWOC; **253** K-13; elev. 820ft./250m.; 🄿; Z 54230; Ⓟ 1,182; © 1,187

Reeseville; Inc. Place; DODGE; **253** N-11; elev. 856ft./261m.; 🄿; Z 53579; Ⓟ 673; © 703

Reeve; RMC Place; BARRON; ▲ Vance Creek; **252** G-3; mail Clayton Z 54004; ● 50

Reid; MCD-Town; MARATHON; ***252** I-9; mail Hatley Z 54440; Ⓟ 1,057; © 1,191

Reighmoor; RMC Place; WINNEBAGO; ▲ Omro; ***253** K-11; ★ **OSH**; mail Omro Z 54963; ● 120

Remington; MCD-Town; WOOD; ***252** J-8; mail Babcock Z 54413; Ⓟ 304; © 305

Reseburg; MCD-Town; CLARK; ***252** H-6; mail Greenwood Z 54437; Ⓟ 687; © 740

Reserve; CDP; SAWYER; ▲ Couderay; **252** E-5; mail Stone Lake Z 54876; Ⓟ 371; © 436

Retreat; RMC Place; VERNON; ▲ Sterling; **253** M-5; mail De Soto Z 54624; ● 80

Rewey; Inc. Place; IOWA; **253** O-7; elev. 1,140ft./347m.; 🄿; Z 53580; Ⓟ 220; © 311

Rhine (Rhine Center); RMC Place; SHEBOYGAN; ▲ Rhine; ***253** L-13; ★ **SHEB**; mail Elkhart Lake Z 53020; ● 80

Rhine; MCD-Town; SHEBOYGAN; ***253** L-13; ★ **SHEB**; mail Elkhart Lake Z 53020; Ⓟ 2,235; © 2,244

Rhine Center; SHEBOYGAN; see Rhine (RMC Place)

Rhinelander; Inc. Place; ⊡ ONEIDA; **252** F-9; elev. 1,554ft./474m.; 🄿 🄷 ■; Z 54501; Ⓟ 7,427; © 7,735; ◆ 6,950

Rib Falls; RMC Place; MARATHON; ▲ Rib Falls; ***252** H-8; mail Edgar Z 54426; ● 100

Rib Falls; MCD-Town; MARATHON; ***252** H-8; mail Edgar Z 54426; Ⓟ 860; © 907

Rib Lake; Inc. Place; TAYLOR; **252** G-8; elev. 1,565ft./477m.; 🄿; Z 54470; Ⓟ 887; © 878

Rib Lake; MCD-Town; TAYLOR; ***252** G-8; 🄿; Z 54470; does not include the Village of Rib Lake; Ⓟ 746; © 768

Rib Mountain; CDP-Census Area Only; MARATHON; ▲ Rib Mountain, Stettin; ***252** H-9; ★ **WAUS**; mail Wausau Z 54401; Ⓟ 4,634; © 6,059

Rib Mountain; MCD-Town; MARATHON; ***252** H-9; ★ **WAUS**; mail Wausau Z 54401; Ⓟ 5,605; © 7,556

Rice Lake; Inc. Place; BARRON; **252** F-4; elev. 1,140ft./347m.; 🄿 🄷; Z 54868; Ⓟ 7,998; © 8,320; Ⓡ 8,312

Rice Lake; MCD-Town; BARRON; ***252** F-4; 🄿; Z 54868; does not include the City of Rice Lake; Ⓟ 2,473; © 3,026

Richardson; RMC Place; POLK; ▲ Clayton; **252** G-3; elev. 1,194ft./364m.; mail Clayton Z 54004; ● 100

Richfield; MCD-Town; ADAMS; ***253** K-9; mail Friendship Z 53934; Ⓟ 159; © 144

Richfield; RMC Place; WASHINGTON; ▲ Richfield; **253** N-12; elev. 974ft./297m.; 🄿; ★ **MILW**; Z 53076; ● 350

Richfield; MCD-Town; WASHINGTON; ***253** N-12; 🄿; ★ **MILW**; Z 53076; Ⓟ 8,993; © 10,373

Richfield; MCD-Town; WOOD; ***252** I-8; mail Marshfield Z 54449; Ⓟ 1,344; © 1,523

Richford; RMC Place; WAUSHARA; ▲ Richford; **253** K-9; mail Coloma Z 54930; ● 50

Richford; MCD-Town; WAUSHARA; ***253** K-9; mail Coloma Z 54930; Ⓟ 455; © 588

Richland; MCD-Town; RICHLAND; ***253** M-7; mail Richland Center Z 53581; Ⓟ 1,423; © 1,364

Richland; MCD-Town; RUSK; ***252** F-6; mail Glen Flora Z 54526; Ⓟ 185; © 206

RICHLAND; **253** M-7; Ⓟ 17,521; © 17,924; ◆ 18,384

Richland Center; Inc. Place; ⊡ RICHLAND; **253** M-7; elev. 731ft./223m.; 🄿 🄷; Z 53581; Ⓟ 5,018; © 5,114

Richmond; MCD-Town; SHAWANO; ***252** I-11; mail Shawano Z 54166; Ⓟ 1,587; © 1,719

Richmond; MCD-Town; ST. CROIX; ***252** H-2; mail New Richmond Z 54017; Ⓟ 1,400; © 1,556

Richmond; RMC Place; WALWORTH; ▲ Richmond; ***253** O-11; mail Delavan Z 53115; ● 700

Richmond; MCD-Town; WALWORTH; ***253** O-11; mail Delavan Z 53115; Ⓟ 1,405; © 1,835

Richwood; RMC Place; DODGE; ▲ Shields; ***253** N-11; mail Watertown Z 53098; ● 100

Richwood; MCD-Town; RICHLAND; ***253** N-7; mail Blue River Z 53518; Ⓟ 662; © 618

Ridgeland; Inc. Place; DUNN; **252** G-4; elev. 1,079ft./329m.; 🄿; Z 54763; Ⓟ 246; © 265

Ridgeville; MCD-Town; MONROE; ***253** L-7; mail Norwalk Z 54648; Ⓟ 497; © 491

Ridgeway; Inc. Place; IOWA; **253** O-8; elev. 1,167ft./356m.; 🄿; Z 53582; Ⓟ 577; © 689

Ridgeway; MCD-Town; IOWA; ***253** O-8; 🄿; Z 53582; does not include the Village of Ridgeway; Ⓟ 557; © 581

Rief's Mills; RMC Place; MANITOWOC; ▲ Kossuth, Franklin; ***253** K-13; elev. 750ft./229m.; mail Whitelaw Z 54247; ● 100

Rietbrock; MCD-Town; MARATHON; ***252** H-8; mail Athens Z 54411; Ⓟ 888; © 927

Riley (Rileys); RMC Place; DANE; ▲ Springdale; ***253** N-9; mail Verona Z 53593; ● 35

Rileys; DANE; see Riley (RMC Place)

Rileys Point; RMC Place; DOOR; ▲ Gardner; ***252** H-14; elev. 586ft./179m.; mail Sturgeon Bay Z 54235; summer pop. 100; ● 40

Ringle; RMC Place; MARATHON; ▲ Ringle; **252** H-9; elev. 1,334ft./407m.; 🄿; Z 54471; ● 200

Ringle; MCD-Town; MARATHON; ***252** H-9; 🄿; Z 54471; Ⓟ 1,279; © 1,408

Rio; Inc. Place; COLUMBIA; **253** M-10; elev. 974ft./297m.; 🄿; Z 53960; Ⓟ 768; © 938

Rio Creek; RMC Place; KEWAUNEE; ▲ Lincoln, Casco; **252** I-14; elev. 703ft./214m.; 🄿; Z 54201; ● 100

Riplinger; RMC Place; CLARK; ▲ Unity; **252** I-7; elev. 1,294ft./394m.; mail Spencer Z 54479; ● 100

Ripon; Inc. Place; FOND DU LAC; **253** L-11; elev. 943ft./287m.; 🄿 🄷 🄲 981; Z 54971; Ⓟ 7,241; © 6,828; Ⓡ 7,450

Ripon; MCD-Town; FOND DU LAC; ***253** L-11; 🄿 🄲 981; Z 54971; does not include the City of Ripon; Ⓟ 1,419; © 2,001; Ⓡ 1,379

Rising Sun; RMC Place; CRAWFORD; ▲ Utica; **253** M-6; mail Ferryville Z 54628; ● 30

River Falls; Inc. Place; PIERCE, ST. CROIX; **252** H-2; elev. 880ft./268m.; 🄿 🄷 🄲 6,229; ★ **MPLS-**; Z 54022; Ⓟ 10,610; © 12,560

River Falls; MCD-Town; PIERCE; ***252** H-2; 🄿 🄲 6,229; Z 54022; does not include the City of River Falls; Ⓟ 1,944; © 2,304

River Hills; Inc. Place; MILWAUKEE; **251** B-5; elev. 700ft./213m.; 🄿; ★ **MILW**; Z 53209, Z 53217; Ⓟ 1,612; © 1,631

Rivermoor; RMC Place; WINNEBAGO; ▲ Winneconne; ***253** K-11; ★ **OSH**; mail Omro Z 54963; ● 150

Riverside; RMC Place; LAFAYETTE; ▲ Gratiot; ***253** P-8; mail Gratiot Z 53541; rural

Riverview; MCD-Town; OCONTO; ***252** G-12; mail Mountain Z 54149; Ⓟ 483; © 829

Riverwood; RMC Place; ADAMS; ▲ Strongs Prairie; ***253** K-8; elev. 929ft./283m.; mail Arkdale Z 54613; ● 60

River Wood Estates; RMC Place; DANE; ▲ Dunkirk; ***253** O-10; elev. 850ft./259m.; ★ **MAD**; mail Stoughton Z 53589; ● 200

Robbins; ONEIDA; see Sugar Camp (RMC Place)

Roberts; Inc. Place; ST. CROIX; **252** H-2; elev. 1,010ft./308m.; 🄿; Z 54023; Ⓟ 1,043; © 969

Robinson (Robinson Hillside); RMC Place; WALWORTH; ▲ Linn; ***253** P-12; elev. 946ft./288m.; mail Lake Geneva Z 53147; summer pop. 300; ● 200

Robinson Hillside; WALWORTH; see Robinson (RMC Place)

Rochester; Inc. Place; RACINE; **253** O-12; elev. 777ft./237m.; 🄿; ★ **MILW**; Z 53167; Ⓟ 978; © 1,149

Rochester; MCD-Town; RACINE; ***253** O-12; 🄿; ★ **MILW**; Z 53167 & mail Burlington Z 53105; does not include the City of Rochester; Ⓟ 1,844; © 2,254

Rock; MCD-Town; ROCK; ***253** P-10; ★ **JNSV**; mail Janesville Z 53545; Ⓟ 3,172; © 3,338

Rock; MCD-Town; WOOD; ***252** I-7; mail Pittsville Z 54466; Ⓟ 764; © 856

ROCK; **253** O-10; Ⓟ 139,510; © 152,307; ◆ 159,860

Rockbridge; RMC Place; RICHLAND; ▲ Rockbridge; **253** M-7; elev. 777ft./237m.; mail Richland Center Z 53581; ● 100

Rockbridge; MCD-Town; RICHLAND; ***253** M-7; mail Richland Center Z 53581; Ⓟ 662; © 721

Rock Creek; MCD-Town; DUNN; ***252** I-4; mail Mondovi Z 54755; Ⓟ 696; © 793

Rockdale; Inc. Place; DANE; **253** O-10; elev. 850ft./259m.; mail Cambridge Z 53523; Ⓟ 235; © 214

Rock Elm; RMC Place; PIERCE; ▲ Rock Elm; **252** I-3; mail Elmwood Z 54740; ● 30

Rock Elm; MCD-Town; PIERCE; ***252** I-3; mail Elmwood Z 54740; Ⓟ 519; © 504

Rock Falls; RMC Place; DUNN; ▲ Rock Creek; **252** I-4; elev. 861ft./262m.; 🄿; Z 54764; ● 130

Rock Falls; MCD-Town; LINCOLN; ***252** G-9; mail Irma Z 54442; Ⓟ 463; © 598

Rockfield; RMC Place; WASHINGTON; ▲ Germantown; **253** N-13; elev. 890ft./271m.; 🄿; ★ **MILW**; Z 53022; pop. incl. with Germantown (Inc. Place)

Rock Lake; RMC Place; KENOSHA; ★ **CHI**; mail Trevor Z 53179

Rockland; MCD-Town; BROWN; ***252** J-13; mail De Pere Z 54115; Ⓟ 974; © 1,522

Rockland; Inc. Place; LA CROSSE; **253** L-6; elev. 752ft./229m.; 🄿; Z 54653; Ⓟ 509; © 628; Ⓡ 625

Rockland; MCD-Town; MANITOWOC; ***253** K-13; mail Collins Z 54207; Ⓟ 911; © 896

Rock Springs; Inc. Place; SAUK; **253** M-8; elev. 1,000ft./305m.; 🄿; Z 53961; Ⓟ 432; © 425

Rockton; RMC Place; VERNON; ▲ Whitestown; **253** L-7; elev. 884ft./269m.; mail La Farge Z 54639; ● 35

Rockville; RMC Place; GRANT; ▲ Potosi; ***253** O-6; mail Potosi Z 53820; ● 50

Rockville; RMC Place; MANITOWOC; ▲ Schleswig; ***253** K-13; mail Kiel Z 53042; ● 100

Rockwood; RMC Place; MANITOWOC; ▲ Manitowoc Rapids; ***253** K-13; mail Manitowoc Z 54220; ● 130

Rocky Corners; RMC Place; MARATHON; ▲ Guenther; ***252** I-9; mail Mosinee Z 54455; rural

Rocky Run; RMC Place; PORTAGE; ▲ Linwood; ***252** I-9; mail Stevens Point Z 54481; rural

Rodell; RMC Place; EAU CLAIRE; ▲ Lincoln; ***252** I-5; mail Augusta Z 54722; rural

Rogersville; RMC Place; FOND DU LAC; ▲ Lamartine; ***253** L-11; elev. 915ft./279m.; mail Rosendale Z 54974; ● 35

Rolling; MCD-Town; LANGLADE; ***252** H-10; mail Antigo Z 54409; Ⓟ 1,316; © 1,452

Rolling Acres; RMC Place; DANE; ▲ Dunkirk; ***253** O-10; elev. 873ft./266m.; ★ **MAD**; mail Stoughton Z 53589; ● 100

Rolling Ground; RMC Place; CRAWFORD; ▲ Clayton; ***253** M-6; elev. 1,230ft./375m.; mail Soldiers Grove Z 54655; ● 20

Rolling Prairie; RMC Place; DODGE; ▲ Oak Grove; ***253** M-11; elev. 941ft./287m.; mail Juneau Z 53039; ● 50

Romance; RMC Place; VERNON; ▲ Harmony; ***253** M-5; mail Genoa Z 54632; ● 25

Rome; MCD-Town; ADAMS; ***253** K-8; mail Nekoosa Z 54457; Ⓟ 1,674; © 2,656

Rome; CDP; JEFFERSON; ▲ Sullivan; **253** O-11; elev. 832ft./254m.; mail Sullivan Z 53178; © 574

Roosevelt; MCD-Town; BURNETT; ***252** F-3; mail Barronett Z 54813; Ⓟ 175; © 197

Roosevelt; MCD-Town; TAYLOR; ***252** H-6; mail Lublin Z 54447; Ⓟ 429; © 444

Root River; RMC Place; MILWAUKEE; ★ **MILW**; mail Milwaukee Z 53227; pop. incl. with Milwaukee (Inc. Place)

Rose; MCD-Town; WAUSHARA; ***253** K-10; mail Wild Rose Z 54984; Ⓟ 486; © 595

Rosecrans; RMC Place; MANITOWOC; ▲ Cooperstown; ***252** J-13; elev. 872ft./266m.; mail Maribel Z 54227; ● 30

Rose Lawn; RMC Place; SHAWANO; ▲ Maple Grove; ***252** I-12; elev. 890ft./271m.; mail Seymour Z 54165; ● 25

Rosemere; RMC Place; MANITOWOC; ★ **MNTW**; mail Manitowoc Z 54220; pop. incl. with Manitowoc (Inc. Place)

Rosendale; Inc. Place; FOND DU LAC; **253** L-11; elev. 900ft./274m.; 🄿; Z 54974; Ⓟ 777; © 923

Rosendale; MCD-Town; FOND DU LAC; ***253** L-11; 🄿; Z 54974 & mail Pickett Z 54964; does not include the Village of Rosendale; Ⓟ 770; © 783

Rosholt; Inc. Place; PORTAGE; **252** I-10; elev. 1,150ft./351m.; 🄿; Z 54473; Ⓟ 512; © 518

Rosiere; RMC Place; KEWAUNEE; ▲ Lincoln; **252** I-14; mail Casco Z 54205; ● 60

Ross; MCD-Town; FOREST; ***252** E-11; mail Argonne Z 54511; Ⓟ 159; © 167

Ross; RMC Place; VERNON; ▲ Liberty; ***253** M-6; mail Viroqua Z 54665; rural

Rostok; RMC Place; KEWAUNEE; ▲ Pierce; ***252** J-14; mail Kewaunee Z 54216

Rothschild; Inc. Place; MARATHON; **252** H-9; elev. 1,200ft./366m.; 🄿; ★ **WAUS**; Z 54474; Ⓟ 3,310; © 4,970

Round Lake; MCD-Town; SAWYER; ***252** E-5; mail Hayward Z 54843; Ⓟ 727; © 962

Rowleys Bay; RMC Place; DOOR; ▲ Liberty Grove; ***252** A-13; elev. 595ft./181m.; mail Ellison Bay Z 54210; ● 70

Roxbury; RMC Place; DANE; ▲ Roxbury; **253** N-9; elev. 868ft./265m.; mail Sauk City Z 53583; ● 150

Roxbury; MCD-Town; DANE; ***253** N-9; mail Sauk City Z 53583; Ⓟ 1,536; © 1,700

Royalton; RMC Place; WAUPACA; ▲ Royalton; **252** J-11; elev. 822ft./251m.; 🄿; Z 54961; ● 250

Royalton; MCD-Town; WAUPACA; ***252** J-11; 🄿; Z 54961; Ⓟ 1,458; © 1,523; Ⓡ 1,544

Rozellville; RMC Place; MARATHON; ▲ Day; **252** I-8; elev. 1,259ft./384m.; mail Stratford Z 54484; ● 250

Rubicon; RMC Place; DODGE; ▲ Rubicon; **253** M-12; elev. 1,013ft./309m.; 🄿; Z 53078; ● 110

Rubicon; MCD-Town; DODGE; ***253** M-12; 🄿; Z 53078; Ⓟ 1,709; © 2,005

Ruby; MCD-Town; CHIPPEWA; ***252** G-6; mail Holcombe Z 54745; Ⓟ 464; © 446

Rudolph; Inc. Place; WOOD; **252** J-8; elev. 1,138ft./347m.; 🄿; Z 54475; Ⓟ 451; © 423

Rudolph; MCD-Town; WOOD; ***252** J-9; 🄿; Z 54475; Ⓟ 1,180; © 1,161

Rural; RMC Place; WAUPACA; ▲ Dayton; **252** J-10; elev. 876ft./267m.; mail Waupaca Z 54981; ● 200

Rushford; MCD-Town; WINNEBAGO; ***253** K-11; mail Omro Z 54963; Ⓟ 1,361; © 1,471

Rush Lake; RMC Place; WINNEBAGO; ▲ Nepeuskun; ***253** K-11; mail Ripon Z 54971; ● 50

Rush River; MCD-Town; ST. CROIX; ***252** H-2; mail Baldwin Z 54002; Ⓟ 419; © 498

Rusk; MCD-Town; BURNETT; ***252** E-3; mail Spooner Z 54801; Ⓟ 396; © 420

Rusk; RMC Place; DUNN; ▲ Red Cedar; **252** H-4; elev. 905ft./276m.; mail Menomonie Z 54751; ● 150

Rusk; MCD-Town; RUSK; ***252** G-5; mail Chetek Z 54728; Ⓟ 443; © 475

RUSK; **252** F-5; Ⓟ 15,079; © 15,347; ◆ 14,210

Russell; MCD-Town; BAYFIELD; ***252** A-6; mail Bayfield Z 54814; Ⓟ 978; © 1,216

Russell; MCD-Town; LINCOLN; ***252** G-9; mail Gleason Z 54435; Ⓟ 671; © 693

Russell; MCD-Town; SHEBOYGAN; ***253** L-13; mail Saint Cloud Z 53079; Ⓟ 362; © 399

Russell; RMC Place; TREMPEALEAU; ▲ Chimney Rock; ***252** J-5; mail Independence Z 54747; rural

Rutland; MCD-Town; DANE; ***253** O-10; mail Stoughton Z 53589; Ⓟ 1,584; © 1,887

S

Sabin; RMC Place; RICHLAND; ▲ Sylvan; ***253** M-7; mail Richland Center Z 53581; rural

Saint Anna; RMC Place; CALUMET, SHEBOYGAN; ▲ New Holstein; ***253** L-13; mail New Holstein Z 53061; ● 200

Saint Anthony; RMC Place; WASHINGTON; ▲ Addison; ***253** M-12; mail Allenton Z 53002; ● 70

Saint Catherines Bay; RMC Place; CALUMET; ▲ Stockbridge; ***253** K-12; mail Hilbert Z 54129; pop. incl. with Stockbridge (Inc. Place)

Saint Cloud; Inc. Place; FOND DU LAC; **253** L-12; elev. 930ft./283m.; 🄿; Z 53079; Ⓟ 494; © 497

ST. CROIX; **252** H-2; Ⓟ 50,251; © 63,155; ◆ 82,993

Saint Croix Falls; Inc. Place; POLK; **252** F-2; elev. 900ft./274m.; 🄿 🄷; Z 54024; Ⓟ 1,640; © 2,033

St. Croix Falls; MCD-Town; POLK; ***252** F-2; mail Centuria Z 54824, Saint Croix Falls Z 54024; does not include the City of Saint Croix Falls; Ⓟ 1,034; © 1,119

St. Croix Reservation; Indian Reservation; POLK, BARRON, BURNETT; ▲ Sand Lake; mail Danbury Z 54830; Ⓟ 427; © 481

Saint Francis; Inc. Place; MILWAUKEE; **253** O-13; elev. 700ft./213m.; 🄿; ★ **MILW**; Z 53235 & mail Milwaukee Z 53207; Ⓟ 9,245; © 8,662

Saint George; RMC Place; SHEBOYGAN; ▲ Wilson, Lima; ***253** L-13; elev. 712ft./217m.; ★ **SHEB**; mail Sheboygan Falls Z 53085; rural

Saint Germain; RMC Place; VILAS; ▲ St. Germain; **252** E-9; 🄿; Z 54558; summer pop. 1,500; ● 400

St. Germain; MCD-Town; VILAS; ***252** E-9; mail Saint Germain Z 54558; Ⓟ 1,319; © 1,932

Saint John; RMC Place; CALUMET; ▲ Woodville; ***253** K-12; mail Hilbert Z 54129; ● 70

Saint Joseph; RMC Place; FOND DU LAC; ▲ Marshfield; ***253** L-12; elev. 935ft./285m.; mail Saint Cloud Z 53079; rural

Saint Joseph; RMC Place; LA CROSSE; ▲ Greenfield; **253** L-6; elev. 1,301ft./397m.; mail La Crosse Z 54601; ● 200

St. Joseph; MCD-Town; ST. CROIX; ***252** H-2; ★ **MPLS-**; mail Houlton Z 54082, Hudson Z 54016; Ⓟ 2,657; © 3,436

Saint Kilian; RMC Place; FOND DU LAC, WASHINGTON; ▲ Wayne, Ashford; **253** M-12; mail Campbellsport Z 53010; ● 80

Saint Lawrence; RMC Place; WASHINGTON; ▲ Hartford, Addison; **253** M-12; elev. 1,071ft./326m.; mail Hartford Z 53027; ● 220

St. Lawrence; MCD-Town; WAUPACA; ***252** J-10; mail Ogdensburg Z 54962; Ⓟ 697; © 740

St. Marie; MCD-Town; GREEN LAKE; ***253** L-10; mail Princeton Z 54968; Ⓟ 348; © 341

Saint Martins; RMC Place; MILWAUKEE; ***253** O-13; ★ **MILW**; mail Franklin Z 53132; pop. incl. with Franklin (Inc. Place)

Saint Marys; RMC Place; MONROE; ▲ Jefferson; **253** L-6; elev. 1,379ft./420m.; mail Cashton Z 54619; ● 25

Saint Michaels; RMC Place; WASHINGTON; ▲ Farmington; **253** M-12; elev. 1,054ft./321m.; mail Kewaskum Z 53040; ● 110

Saint Nazianz; Inc. Place; MANITOWOC; **253** K-13; elev. 900ft./274m.; 🄿; Z 54232; Ⓟ 693; © 749

Saint Peter; RMC Place; FOND DU LAC; ▲ Taycheedah; ***253** L-12; elev. 1,076ft./328m.; ★ **FDLC**; mail Fond du Lac Z 54935, Malone Z 53049; ● 400

Saint Wendel; RMC Place; MANITOWOC; mail Cleveland Z 53015; pop. incl. with Cleveland (Inc. Place)

Salem; RMC Place; KENOSHA; ▲ Salem; **253** P-13; 🄿; ★ **CHI**; Z 53168; ● 1,150

Salem; MCD-Town; KENOSHA; ***253** P-13; 🄿; ★ **CHI**; Z 53168; Ⓟ 7,146; © 9,871

Salem; MCD-Town; PIERCE; ***252** I-3; mail Maiden Rock Z 54750; Ⓟ 514; © 505

Salem Oaks; RMC Place; KENOSHA; ▲ Salem; ***253** P-13; ★ **CHI**; mail Salem Z 53168

Sampson; MCD-Town; CHIPPEWA; ***252** G-5; mail New Auburn Z 54757; Ⓟ 817; © 816

Sampson; RMC Place; OCONTO; ▲ Morgan; **252** I-12; mail Sobieski Z 54171; ● 25

Sanborn; RMC Place; ASHLAND; ▲ White River; **252** C-6; 🄿; Z 54806; ● 40

Sanborn; MCD-Town; ASHLAND; ***252** C-6; 🄿; Z 54806 & mail Odanah Z 54861; Ⓟ 998; © 1,272

Sand Bay; RMC Place; BAYFIELD; ▲ Russell; ***252** A-6; mail Bayfield Z 54814

Sand Bay; RMC Place; DOOR; ▲ Nasewaupee; ***252** H-14; elev. 590ft./180m.; mail Sturgeon Bay Z 54235; summer pop. 300; ● 40

Sand Creek; RMC Place; DUNN; ▲ Sand Creek; **252** G-4; 🄿; Z 54765; ● 200

Sand Creek; MCD-Town; DUNN; ***252** G-4; 🄿; Z 54765; Ⓟ 568; © 586

Sand Lake; MCD-Town; BURNETT; ***252** E-3; mail Webster Z 54893; Ⓟ 439; © 556

Sand Lake; RMC Place; POLK; ▲ Osceola; ***252** G-2; elev. 1,145ft./349m.; mail Dresser Z 54009; ● 30

Sand Lake; MCD-Town; SAWYER; ***252** E-5; mail Stone Lake Z 54876; Ⓟ 821; © 774

Sand Prairie; RMC Place; RICHLAND; ▲ Richwood; ***253** N-7; elev. 691ft./211m.; mail Blue River Z 53518; rural

Sandusky; RMC Place; SAUK; ▲ Washington; ***253** M-8; mail Hillpoint Z 53937; ● 25

Saratoga; MCD-Town; WOOD; ***252** J-8; mail Wisconsin Rapids Z 54494; Ⓟ 4,775; © 5,383

Sarona; RMC Place; WASHBURN; ▲ Sarona; **252** F-4; elev. 1,300ft./396m.; 🄿; Z 54870; summer pop. 500; ● 100

Sarona; MCD-Town; WASHBURN; ***252** F-4; 🄿; Z 54870; Ⓟ 391; © 382

SAUK; **253** M-8; Ⓟ 46,975; © 55,225; ◆ 59,250

Sauk City; Inc. Place; SAUK; **253** N-9; elev. 757ft./231m.; 🄿; Z 53583; Ⓟ 3,019; © 3,109

Saukville; Inc. Place; OZAUKEE; **253** M-13; elev. 760ft./232m.; 🄿; ★ **MILW**; Z 53080; Ⓟ 3,695; © 4,068

Saukville; MCD-Town; OZAUKEE; ***253** M-13; 🄿; ★ **MILW**; Z 53080 & mail Port Washington Z 53074; does not include the Village of Saukville; Ⓟ 1,754; © 1,755

SAWYER; **252** E-5; Ⓟ 14,181; © 16,196; ◆ 17,300

Saxeville; RMC Place; WAUSHARA; ▲ Saxeville; **253** K-10; 🄿; Z 54976; ● 120

Saxeville; MCD-Town; WAUSHARA; ***253** K-10; 🄿; Z 54976; Ⓟ 846; © 974

Saxon; RMC Place; IRON; ▲ Saxon; **252** C-7; elev. 1,115ft./340m.; 🄿; Z 54559; ● 210

Saxon; MCD-Town; IRON; ***252** C-7; 🄿; Z 54559; Ⓟ 335; © 350

Saylesville; RMC Place; DODGE; ▲ Rubicon; ***253** N-12; elev. 924ft./282m.; mail Rubicon Z 53078; rural

Saylesville; RMC Place; WAUKESHA; ▲ Genesee; ***253** O-12; elev. 812ft./247m.; ★ **MILW**; mail Waukesha Z 53189; ● 80

Sayner; RMC Place; VILAS; ▲ Plum Lake; **252** E-9; 🄿; Z 54560 & mail Star Lake Z 54561; summer pop. 1,200; ● 300

Scandinavia; Inc. Place; WAUPACA; **252** J-10; elev. 931ft./284m.; 🄿; Z 54977; Ⓟ 298; © 349

Scandinavia; MCD-Town; WAUPACA; ***252** J-10; 🄿; Z 54977; does not include the Village of Scandinavia; Ⓟ 890; © 1,075

Scarboro; RMC Place; KEWAUNEE; ▲ Luxemburg; ***252** I-14; elev. 700ft./213m.; mail Luxemburg Z 54217; rural

Schey Acres; RMC Place; DANE; ▲ Sun Prairie; ***253** N-10; ★ **MAD**; mail Sun Prairie Z 53590; ● 80

Schiller; BROWN; see Sugar Bush (RMC Place)

Schleswig; MCD-Town; MANITOWOC; ***253** K-13; mail Kiel Z 53042; Ⓟ 1,641; © 1,900

Schley; MCD-Town; LINCOLN; ***252** G-9; mail Merrill Z 54452; Ⓟ 838; © 909

Schmidt Corner; RMC Place; WAUPACA; ***252** I-10; mail Tigerton Z 54486; rural

Schnappsville; RMC Place; MARATHON; ▲ Rietbrock; ***252** H-8; elev. 1,438ft./438m.; mail Athens Z 54411; rural

Schoepke; MCD-Town; ONEIDA; ***252** F-10; mail Pelican Lake Z 54463; Ⓟ 378; © 352

Schofield; Inc. Place; MARATHON; **252** H-9; elev. 1,198ft./365m.; 🄿; ★ **WAUS**; Z 54476; Ⓟ 2,415; © 2,117

School Hill; RMC Place; MANITOWOC; ▲ Meeme; ***253** K-13; mail Kiel Z 53042; ● 150

Schraven Circle; RMC Place; FOND DU LAC; ▲ Lamartine; ***253** L-12; elev. 832ft./254m.; mail Fond du Lac Z 54937; ● 50

Scott; MCD-Town; BROWN; ***252** I-13; ★ **GRBY**; mail Green Bay Z 54301, New Franken Z 54229; Ⓟ 2,044; © 3,712; Ⓡ 3,138

Scott; MCD-Town; BURNETT; ***252** E-3; mail Webster Z 54893; Ⓟ 419; © 590

Scott; MCD-Town; COLUMBIA; ***253** M-10; mail Cambria Z 53923; Ⓟ 639; © 791

Scott; MCD-Town; CRAWFORD; ***253** N-6; mail Blue River Z 53518; Ⓟ 453; © 503

Scott; MCD-Town; LINCOLN; ***252** G-9; mail Merrill Z 54452; Ⓟ 1,210; © 1,287

Scott; MCD-Town; MONROE; ***253** K-7; mail Warrens Z 54666; Ⓟ 120; © 117

Scott; MCD-Town; SHEBOYGAN; ***253** M-13; mail Adell Z 53001; Ⓟ 1,671; © 1,804

Scottish Highlands; RMC Place; DANE; ▲ Bristol; ***253** N-10; mail Sun Prairie Z 53590; ● 75

Sechlerville; RMC Place; JACKSON; ▲ Hixton; **252** J-6; elev. 927ft./283m.; mail Hixton Z 54635; ● 50

Seeley (Seeleys); RMC Place; SAWYER; ▲ Lenroot; **252** D-5; mail Hayward Z 54843; ● 80

Seeleys; SAWYER; see Seeley (RMC Place)

Seif; MCD-Town; CLARK; ***252** I-6; mail Neillsville Z 54456; Ⓟ 211; © 212

Seneca; RMC Place; CRAWFORD; ▲ Seneca; **253** N-6; 🄿; Z 54654; ● 220

Seneca; MCD-Town; CRAWFORD; ***253** N-6; 🄿; Z 54654; Ⓟ 873; © 893

Seneca; MCD-Town; GREEN LAKE; ***253** K-10; mail Berlin Z 54923; Ⓟ 395; © 424

Seneca; MCD-Town; SHAWANO; ***252** I-11; mail Tilleda Z 54978; Ⓟ 538; © 567

Seneca; MCD-Town; WOOD; ***252** J-8; mail Wisconsin Rapids Z 54494; Ⓟ 1,133; © 1,202

Sequoia; RMC Place; MILWAUKEE; ★ **MILW**; mail Milwaukee Z 53223-24; pop. incl. with Milwaukee (Inc. Place)

Sevastopol; MCD-Town; DOOR; ***252** H-14; mail Sturgeon Bay Z 54235; Ⓟ 2,552; © 2,667

Seven Mile Creek; MCD-Town; JUNEAU; ***253** L-8; mail Lyndon Station Z 53944; Ⓟ 383; © 369

Sextonville; RMC Place; RICHLAND; ▲ Buena Vista; **253** N-7; 🄿; Z 53584; ● 250

Seymour; CDP-Census Area Only; EAU CLAIRE; ▲ Seymour; ***252** H-5; ★ **EAUC**; mail Eau Claire Z 54703; Ⓟ 1,557; © 1,474

Seymour; MCD-Town; EAU CLAIRE; ***252** H-5; ★ **EAUC**; mail Eau Claire Z 54701; Ⓟ 2,757; © 2,978

Seymour; MCD-Town; LAFAYETTE; ***253** P-7; mail Shullsburg Z 53586; Ⓟ 401; © 363

Seymour; Inc. Place; OUTAGAMIE; **252** J-12; elev. 791ft./241m.; 🄿; Z 54165; Ⓟ 2,782; © 3,335

Seymour; MCD-Town; OUTAGAMIE; ***252** I-12; 🄿; Z 54165; Ⓟ 1,217; © 1,216

Seymour Corners; RMC Place; LAFAYETTE; ▲ Seymour; ***253** P-7; mail Shullsburg Z 53586; rural

Shamrock; RMC Place; JACKSON; ▲ Manchester; ***253** K-6; elev. 842ft./257m.; mail Black River Falls Z 54615

Shanagolden; RMC Place; ASHLAND; ▲ Shanagolden; ***252** D-7; elev. 1,529ft./466m.; mail Glidden Z 54527; ● 50

Shanagolden; MCD-Town; ASHLAND; ***252** D-6; mail Glidden Z 54527; Ⓟ 172; © 150

Shantytown; RMC Place; MARATHON; ▲ Bevent; ***252** I-9; elev. 1,175ft./358m.; mail Rosholt Z 54473; rural

Sharon; MCD-Town; PORTAGE; ***252** I-9; mail Rosholt Z 54473; Ⓟ 1,742; © 1,936

Sharon; Inc. Place; WALWORTH; **253** P-11; elev. 1,027ft./313m.; 🄿; Z 53585; Ⓟ 1,250; © 1,549

Sharon; MCD-Town; WALWORTH; ***253** P-11; 🄿; Z 53585; Ⓟ 1,016; © 912

Shawano; Inc. Place; ⊡ SHAWANO; **252** I-11; elev. 821ft./250m.; 🄿 🄷; Z 54166; Ⓟ 7,598; © 8,298

SHAWANO; **252** I-11; Ⓟ 37,157; © 40,664; ◆ 40,893

Shawano North Beach; RMC Place; SHAWANO; ▲ Wescott; ***252** H-11; elev. 812ft./247m.; mail Shawano Z 54166; ● 730

Shawtown; RMC Place; EAU CLAIRE; ▲ Union; ***252** I-4; ★ **EAUC**; mail Eau Claire Z 54703; pop. incl. with Eau Claire (Inc. Place)

Sheboygan; Inc. Place; ⊡ SHEBOYGAN; **253** L-14; elev. 633ft./193m.; 🄿 🄷 🄲 4,073 ■; ★ **SHEB**; Z 53081-83; Ⓟ 49,676; © 50,792; ◆ 48,783

Sheboygan; MCD-Town; SHEBOYGAN; ***253** L-13; 🄿 🄲 4,073; ★ **SHEB**; Z 53081-83; does not include the City of Sheboygan; Ⓟ 3,866; © 5,874

SHEBOYGAN; **253** L-13; Ⓟ 103,877; © 112,646; Ⓡ 112,656; ◆ 113,523

Sheboygan Falls; Inc. Place; SHEBOYGAN; **253** L-13; elev. 659ft./201m.; 🄿; ★ **SHEB**; Z 53085; Ⓟ 5,823; © 6,772

Sheboygan Falls; MCD-Town; SHEBOYGAN; ***253** L-13; 🄿; ★ **SHEB**; Z 53085; does not include the City of Sheboygan Falls; Ⓟ 1,908; © 1,706

Sheil; RMC Place; DANE; ▲ Oregon; ***253** O-9; elev. 1,000ft./305m.; ★ **MAD**; mail Oregon Z 53575; ● 200

Shelby; MCD-Town; LA CROSSE; ***253** L-5; ★ **LACRO**; mail La Crosse Z 54601; Ⓟ 5,151; © 4,687

Sheldon; MCD-Town; MONROE; ***253** L-7; mail Ontario Z 54651; Ⓟ 521; © 682

Sheldon; Inc. Place; RUSK; **252** G-6; elev. 1,129ft./344m.; 🄿; Z 54766; Ⓟ 268; © 256

Shell Lake; Inc. Place; ⊡ WASHBURN; **252** E-4; elev. 1,230ft./375m.; 🄿 🄷; Z 54871; Ⓟ 1,161; © 1,309

Shennington; RMC Place; MONROE; ▲ Byron; **253** K-7; elev. 911ft./278m.; mail Camp Douglas Z 54618; ● 45

Shepley; RMC Place; SHAWANO; ▲ Birnamwood, Almon; ***252** H-10; elev. 1,175ft./358m.; mail Wittenberg Z 54499

Sheridan; MCD-Town; DUNN; ***252** G-3; mail Boyceville Z 54725; Ⓟ 468; © 483

Sheridan; RMC Place; WAUPACA; ▲ Farmington; ***252** J-10; mail Waupaca Z 54981; ● 40

Sherman; MCD-Town; CLARK; ***252** I-7; mail Spencer Z 54479; Ⓟ 736; © 831

Sherman; MCD-Town; DUNN; ***252** H-3; mail Menomonie Z 54751; Ⓟ 725; © 748

Sherman; MCD-Town; IRON; ***252** D-8; mail Park Falls Z 54552; Ⓟ 267; © 336

Sherman; MCD-Town; SHEBOYGAN; ***253** M-13; ★ **SHEB**; mail Random Lake Z 53075; Ⓟ 1,461; © 1,520

Sherman Center; RMC Place; SHEBOYGAN; ▲ Sherman; ***253** M-13; elev. 934ft./285m.; ★ **SHEB**; mail Random Lake Z 53075; rural

Sherry; RMC Place; WOOD; ▲ Sherry; **252** I-8; mail Milladore Z 54454; ● 120

Sherry; MCD-Town; WOOD; ***252** I-8; mail Milladore Z 54454; Ⓟ 787; © 809

Sherwood; Inc. Place; CALUMET; ▲ Harrison; **253** K-12; 🄿; ★ **APP**; Z 54169; Ⓟ 837; © 1,550

Sherwood; MCD-Town; CLARK; ***252** J-7; mail Pittsville Z 54466; Ⓟ 195; © 252

Shields; MCD-Town; DODGE; ***253** N-11; mail Watertown Z 53098; Ⓟ 500; © 554

Shields; MCD-Town; MARQUETTE; ***253** L-10; mail Montello Z 53949; Ⓟ 408; © 456

Shiocton; Inc. Place; OUTAGAMIE; **252** J-11; elev. 765ft./233m.; 🄿; Z 54170; Ⓟ 913; © 954

Shirley; RMC Place; BROWN; ▲ Glenmore; ***252** J-13; elev. 941ft./287m.; mail De Pere Z 54115; ● 60

Shopiere; RMC Place; ROCK; ▲ Turtle; **253** P-11; ★ **RKFD**; mail Beloit Z 53511; ● 200

Shorewood; Inc. Place; MILWAUKEE; **253** N-13; elev. 679ft./207m.; 🄿; ★ **MILW**; Z 53211; Ⓟ 14,116; © 13,763

Shorewood Hills; Inc. Place; DANE; **253** S-6; elev. 950ft./290m.; ★ **MAD**; mail Madison Z 53705; Ⓟ 1,680; © 1,732

Shortville; RMC Place; CLARK; ▲ Washburn; ***252** J-7; elev. 1,007ft./307m.; mail Neillsville Z 54456

Shoto; RMC Place; MANITOWOC; ▲ Two Rivers; ***253** K-14; ★ **MNTW**; mail Two Rivers Z 54241; ● 80

Shullsburg; Inc. Place; LAFAYETTE; **253** P-7; elev. 1,021ft./311m.; 🄿; Z 53586; Ⓟ 1,236; © 1,246

Shullsburg; MCD-Town; LAFAYETTE; ***253** P-7; 🄿; Z 53586; does not include the City of Shullsburg; Ⓟ 363; © 364

Sidney; RMC Place; CLARK; ▲ Pine Valley; ***252** I-7; elev. 1,089ft./332m.; mail Neillsville Z 54456

Sigel; MCD-Town; CHIPPEWA; ***252** H-5; mail Cadott Z 54727; Ⓟ 736; © 825

Sigel; MCD-Town; WOOD; ***252** J-8; mail Wisconsin Rapids Z 54494; Ⓟ 1,192; © 1,130

Silica; RMC Place; FOND DU LAC; ▲ Taycheedah; ***253** L-12; ★ **FDLC**; mail Malone Z 53049; ● 50

Silver Cliff; MCD-Town; MARINETTE; ***252** F-12; 🄿; Z 54104; Ⓟ 259; © 529

Silver Creek; RMC Place; SHEBOYGAN; ▲ Sherman; ***253** M-13; elev. 912ft./278m.; ★ **SHEB**; mail Random Lake Z 53075; ● 100

Silver Lake; Inc. Place; KENOSHA; **253** P-12; elev. 755ft./230m.; 🄿; ★ **CHI**; Z 53170, Z 53199; Ⓟ 1,801; © 2,341

Silver Lake; RMC Place; WALWORTH; ▲ Sugar Creek; **253** K-10; elev. 920ft./280m.; mail Elkhorn Z 53121; ● 200

Silver Lake; RMC Place; WAUSHARA; ▲ Marion; ***253** K-10; mail Wautoma Z 54982; ● 300

Sinsinawa; RMC Place; GRANT; ▲ Hazel Green; ***253** P-7; 🄿; Z 53824; ● 250

Sioux; RMC Place; BAYFIELD; ▲ Bayfield; ***252** B-6; elev. 608ft./185m.; mail Washburn Z 54891; rural

Sioux Creek; MCD-Town; BARRON; ***252** G-4; mail Chetek Z 54728; Ⓟ 635; © 689

Siren; Inc. Place; ⊡ BURNETT; **252** E-2; elev. 996ft./304m.; 🄿; Z 54872; Ⓟ 863; © 988

Siren; MCD-Town; BURNETT; ***252** E-3; 🄿; Z 54872; does not include the Village of Siren; Ⓟ 910; © 873

Sister Bay; Inc. Place; DOOR; **252** A-13; elev. 587ft./179m.; 🄿; Z 54234; Ⓟ 675; © 886

Skanawan; MCD-Town; LINCOLN; ***252** G-9; mail Irma Z 54442; Ⓟ 312; © 354

Slab City; RMC Place; SHAWANO; ▲ Hartland; ***252** I-12; elev. 904ft./276m.; mail Bonduel Z 54107; ● 40

Slabtown; RMC Place; JEFFERSON; ▲ Sullivan; ***253** O-11; mail Jefferson Z 53549; rural

Slades Corner; RMC Place; KENOSHA; ▲ Wheatland; ***253** P-12; mail Burlington Z 53105; ● 100

Slinger; Inc. Place; WASHINGTON; **253** M-12; elev. 1,069ft./326m.; 🄿; ★ **MILW**; Z 53086; Ⓟ 2,340; © 3,901

Slovan; RMC Place; KEWAUNEE; ▲ Casco; ***252** I-14; mail Casco Z 54205

Smelser; MCD-Town; GRANT; ***253** P-7; mail Cuba City Z 53807; Ⓟ 763; © 756

Sobieski; RMC Place; OCONTO; ▲ Little Suamico; **252** I-13; elev. 657ft./200m.; 🄿; ★ **GRBY**; Z 54171; ● 250

Sobieski Corners; RMC Place; OCONTO; ▲ Little Suamico; ***252** I-13; elev. 642ft./196m.; ★ **GRBY**; mail Little Suamico Z 54141; rural

Sokaogon Chippewa Community; Indian Reservation; FOREST; © 298

Soldiers Grove; Inc. Place; CRAWFORD; **253** M-6; elev. 730ft./223m.; 🄿; Z 54655; Ⓟ 564; © 653

Solon Springs; Inc. Place; DOUGLAS; **252** C-4; elev. 1,100ft./335m.; 🄿; Z 54873; Ⓟ 575; © 576

Solon Springs; MCD-Town; DOUGLAS; ***252** C-4; 🄿; Z 54873; does not include the Village of Solon Springs; Ⓟ 619; © 807

Somers; RMC Place; KENOSHA; ▲ Somers; **253** P-13; 🄿; ★ **KEN**; Z 53171; ● 530

Somers; MCD-Town; KENOSHA; ***253** P-13; 🄿; ★ **KEN**; Z 53171; Ⓟ 7,861; © 9,059

Somerset; Inc. Place; ST. CROIX; **252** G-2; elev. 860ft./262m.; 🄿; ★ **MPLS-**; Z 54025; Ⓟ 1,065; © 1,556

Somerset; MCD-Town; ST. CROIX; ***252** G-2; 🄿; ★ **MPLS-**; Z 54025 & mail Stillwater Z 55082; does not include the Village of Somerset; Ⓟ 1,975; © 2,644

Somo; MCD-Town; LINCOLN; ***252** F-8; mail Tripoli Z 54564; Ⓟ 116; © 121

Soperton; RMC Place; FOREST; ▲ Wabeno; ***252** F-11; mail Wabeno Z 54566

South Beaver Dam; RMC Place; DODGE; ▲ Calamus, Beaver Dam; **253** M-11; elev. 892ft./272m.; mail Beaver Dam Z 53916; ● 60

South Byron; RMC Place; FOND DU LAC; ▲ Byron; ***253** L-12; 🄿; Z 53006; ● 50

South Chase; RMC Place; OCONTO; ▲ Chase; ***252** I-12; elev. 779ft./237m.; mail Pulaski Z 54162; ● 50

South Chippewa; RMC Place; CHIPPEWA; ★ **EAUC**; mail Chippewa Falls Z 54729; pop. incl. with Chippewa Falls (Inc. Place)

South Fork; MCD-Town; RUSK; ***252** F-6; mail Hawkins Z 54530; Ⓟ 119; © 120

South Itasca; RMC Place; DOUGLAS; ***252** B-3; ★ **DUL**; mail Superior Z 54880

South Janesville; RMC Place; ROCK; ★ **JNSV**; mail Janesville Z 53545; pop. incl. with Janesville (Inc. Place)

South Kenosha; RMC Place; KENOSHA; ***253** P-13; ★ **KEN**; mail Kenosha Z 53143; pop. incl. with Pleasant Prairie (Inc. Place)

South Lancaster; MCD-Town; GRANT; ***253** O-6; mail Lancaster Z 53813; Ⓟ 905; © 808

South Luxemburg; RMC Place; KEWAUNEE; ▲ Luxemburg; mail Luxemburg Z 54217; pop. incl. with Luxemburg (Inc. Place)

South Milwaukee; Inc. Place; MILWAUKEE; **253** O-13; elev. 664ft./202m.; 🄿; ★ **MILW**; Z 53172; Ⓟ 20,958; © 21,256; ◆ 23,535

South Necedah; RMC Place; JUNEAU; mail Necedah Z 54646; pop. incl. with Necedah (Inc. Place)

South Randolph; RMC Place; DODGE; ▲ Westford; ***253** M-10; mail Randolph Z 53956; ● 30

South Range; RMC Place; DOUGLAS; ▲ Parkland; **252** C-3; elev. 763ft./233m.; 🄿; Z 54874; ● 120

South Side; RMC Place; DANE; ★ **MAD**; mail Madison Z 53713, Z 53715, Z 53725; pop. incl. with Madison (Inc. Place)

South Superior; RMC Place; DOUGLAS; ***252** B-3; ★ **DUL**; pop. incl. with Superior (Inc. Place)

South Wayne; Inc. Place; LAFAYETTE; **253** P-8; elev. 803ft./245m.; 🄿; Z 53587; Ⓟ 478; © 484

Sparta; Inc. Place; ⊡ MONROE; **253** K-6; elev. 793ft./242m.; 🄿 🄷; Z 54656; Ⓟ 7,788; © 8,648

Sparta; MCD-Town; MONROE; ***253** K-6; 🄿; Z 54656; does not include the City of Sparta; Ⓟ 2,385; © 2,750; Ⓡ 2,753

Spaulding; RMC Place; JACKSON; ▲ City Point; ***252** J-7; elev. 965ft./294m.; mail Pittsville Z 54466; rural

Spencer; Inc. Place; MARATHON; **252** I-7; elev. 1,310ft./399m.; 🄿; Z 54479; Ⓟ 1,757; © 1,932

Spencer; MCD-Town; MARATHON; ***252** I-7; 🄿; Z 54479; does not include the Village of Spencer; Ⓟ 1,036; © 1,341

Spider Lake; MCD-Town; SAWYER; ***252** D-5; mail Hayward Z 54843; Ⓟ 362; © 391

Spirit; RMC Place; PRICE; ▲ Spirit; **252** F-8; elev. 1,685ft./514m.; mail Brantwood Z 54513; ● 35

Spirit; MCD-Town; PRICE; ***252** G-8; mail Brantwood Z 54513; Ⓟ 345; © 315

Spirit Falls; RMC Place; LINCOLN; ▲ Tomahawk; ***252** F-8; elev. 1,487ft./453m.; mail Tripoli Z 54564; rural

Split Rock; RMC Place; SHAWANO; ▲ Fairbanks; ***252** I-10; mail Tigerton Z 54486; ● 50

Spokeville; RMC Place; CLARK; ▲ Sherman, Loyal; ***252** I-7; elev. 1,273ft./388m.; mail Loyal Z 54446, Spencer Z 54479; ● 30

Spooner; Inc. Place; WASHBURN; **252** E-4; elev. 1,065ft./325m.; 🄿 🄷; Z 54801; Ⓟ 2,464; © 2,653

Spooner; MCD-Town; WASHBURN; ***252** E-4; 🄿; Z 54801; Ⓟ 644; © 677

Sprague; RMC Place; JUNEAU; ▲ Necedah; ***253** K-8; mail Necedah Z 54646

Spread Eagle; RMC Place; FLORENCE; ▲ Florence; **252** E-12; elev. 1,196ft./365m.; mail Florence Z 54121; summer pop. 800; ● 200

Spring Bluff; RMC Place; ADAMS; ▲ Richfield; ***253** L-9; mail Coloma Z 54930; rural

Spring Brook; MCD-Town; DUNN; ***252** I-4; mail Menomonie Z 54751; Ⓟ 1,293; © 1,320

Springbrook; RMC Place; WASHBURN; ▲ Springbrook; **252** E-4; 🄿; Z 54875; ● 120

Springbrook; MCD-Town; WASHBURN; ***252** E-4; 🄿; Z 54875; Ⓟ 403; © 536

Springdale; MCD-Town; DANE; ***253** O-9; mail Verona Z 53593; Ⓟ 1,258; © 1,530

Springfield; MCD-Town; DANE; ***253** N-9; ★ **MAD**; mail Cross Plains Z 53528; Ⓟ 2,650; © 2,762

Springfield; MCD-Town; JACKSON; ***252** J-5; mail Taylor Z 54659; Ⓟ 476; © 567

Springfield; MCD-Town; MARQUETTE; ***253** K-9; mail Westfield Z 53964; Ⓟ 480; © 628

Springfield; MCD-Town; ST. CROIX; ***252** H-3; mail Glenwood City Z 54013; Ⓟ 772; © 808

Springfield; RMC Place; WALWORTH; ▲ Lyons; **253** P-12; elev. 851ft./259m.; 🄿; Z 53176; ● 270

Springfield Corners; RMC Place; DANE; ▲ Springfield; ***253** N-9; ★ **MAD**; mail Dane Z 53529; ● 100

Springfield Corners; RMC Place; MARQUETTE; ▲ Springfield; ***253** K-9; mail Westfield Z 53964; rural

Spring Green; Inc. Place; SAUK; **253** N-8; elev. 729ft./222m.; 🄿; Z 53588; Ⓟ 1,283; © 1,444

Spring Green; MCD-Town; SAUK; ***253** N-8; 🄿; Z 53588; does not include the Village of Spring Green; Ⓟ 1,329; © 1,585

Spring Grove; MCD-Town; GREEN; ***253** P-9; mail Juda Z 53550; Ⓟ 745; © 861

Spring Hill Edition; RMC Place; DANE; ▲ Pleasant Springs; ***253** O-10; elev. 870ft./265m.; ★ **MAD**; mail Stoughton Z 53589; ● 130

Spring Lake; MCD-Town; PIERCE; ***252** H-3; mail Spring Valley Z 54767; Ⓟ 565; © 550

Spring Lake; RMC Place; WAUSHARA; ▲ Marion; **253** K-10; mail Neshkoro Z 54960; ● 130

Spring Prairie; RMC Place; WALWORTH; ▲ Spring Prairie; ***253** P-12; elev. 1,018ft./310m.; mail Elkhorn Z 53121; ● 90

Spring Prairie; MCD-Town; WALWORTH; ***253** O-12; mail Elkhorn Z 53121; Ⓟ 1,752; © 2,089

Springstead; RMC Place; IRON; ▲ Sherman; ***252** E-8; elev. 1,619ft./493m.; mail Park Falls Z 54552; ● 100

Springvale; MCD-Town; COLUMBIA; ***253** M-10; mail Rio Z 53960; Ⓟ 466; © 550

Springvale; MCD-Town; FOND DU LAC; ***253** L-11; mail Rosendale Z 54974; Ⓟ 750; © 727

Spring Valley; RMC Place; MANITOWOC; ▲ Meeme; **253** K-13; mail Newton Z 53063; ● 40

Spring Valley; Inc. Place; PIERCE, ST. CROIX; **252** H-3; elev. 940ft./287m.; 🄿; Z 54767; Ⓟ 1,051; © 1,189

Spring Valley; MCD-Town; ROCK; ***253** P-10; mail Orfordville Z 53576; Ⓟ 790; © 813

Springville; MCD-Town; ADAMS; ***253** L-9; mail Wisconsin Dells Z 53965; Ⓟ 785; © 1,167

Springville; RMC Place; VERNON; ▲ Jefferson; ***253** M-6; mail Viroqua Z 54665; ● 50

Springwater; MCD-Town; WAUSHARA; ***253** K-10; mail Wild Rose Z 54984; Ⓟ 1,088; © 1,389

Spruce; RMC Place; OCONTO; ▲ Spruce; ***252** H-12; mail Lena Z 54139; ● 50

Spruce; MCD-Town; OCONTO; ***252** H-12; mail Lena Z 54139; Ⓟ 776; © 871

Stanberry; RMC Place; WASHBURN; ▲ Stinnett; ***252** E-4; mail Springbrook Z 54875; ● 40

Standart; RMC Place; IOWA; ▲ Dodgeville; ***253** N-8; mail Dodgeville Z 53533; rural

Stanfold; MCD-Town; BARRON; ***252** F-4; mail Barron Z 54812; Ⓟ 644; © 669

Stangelville; RMC Place; KEWAUNEE; ▲ Franklin; **252** J-13; elev. 804ft./245m.; mail Denmark Z 54208; ● 100

Stanley; MCD-Town; BARRON; ***252** F-4; mail Cameron Z 54822; Ⓟ 2,087; © 2,229; Ⓡ 2,237

Stanley; Inc. Place; CHIPPEWA; **252** H-6; elev. 1,100ft./335m.; 🄿 🄷; Z 54768; Ⓟ 2,011; © 1,898

Stanton; MCD-Town; DUNN; ***252** H-3; mail Boyceville Z 54725; Ⓟ 637; © 715

Stanton; MCD-Town; ST. CROIX; ***252** G-2; mail New Richmond Z 54017; Ⓟ 1,042; © 1,003

Stark; MCD-Town; VERNON; ***253** M-7; mail La Farge Z 54639; Ⓟ 259; © 349

Starks; RMC Place; ONEIDA; ▲ Stella; **252** F-10; elev. 1,630ft./497m.; mail Rhinelander Z 54501; ● 50

Star Lake; RMC Place; VILAS; ▲ Plum Lake; **252** E-9; 🄿; Z 54561; summer pop. 200; ● 100

Star Prairie; Inc. Place; ST. CROIX; **252** G-2; elev. 950ft./290m.; 🄿; Z 54026; Ⓟ 507; © 574

Star Prairie; MCD-Town; ST. CROIX; ***252** G-2; mail Somerset Z 54025; does not include the Village of Star Prairie; Ⓟ 2,098; © 2,944

Star Valley; RMC Place; CRAWFORD; ▲ Utica; ***253** M-6; elev. 764ft./233m.; mail Soldiers Grove Z 54655; rural

Starview Heights; RMC Place; ROCK; ▲ Harmony; ***253** O-11; elev. 900ft./274m.; ★ **JNSV**; mail Janesville Z 53545; ● 200

State Line; RMC Place; KENOSHA; ***253** P-13; elev. 635ft./194m.; ★ **KEN**; mail Kenosha Z 53142; pop. incl. with Pleasant Prairie (Inc. Place)

State Street; RMC Place; RACINE; ★ **MILW**; mail Racine Z 53404; pop. incl. with Racine (Inc. Place)

Stebbinsville; RMC Place; ROCK; ▲ Porter; ***253** O-10; mail Edgerton Z 53534; rural

Stella; MCD-Town; ONEIDA; ***252** F-10; mail Rhinelander Z 54501; Ⓟ 525; © 633

Stephenson; MCD-Town; MARINETTE; ***252** G-12; mail Crivitz Z 54114; Ⓟ 2,288; © 3,065

Stephenson Island; RMC Place; MARINETTE; ***252** H-14; mail Marinette Z 54143; pop. incl. with Marinette (Inc. Place)

Stephensville; RMC Place; OUTAGAMIE; ▲ Ellington; ***252** J-11; mail Hortonville Z 54944; ● 250

Sterling; MCD-Town; POLK; ***252** F-2; mail Cushing Z 54006; Ⓟ 591; © 724

Sterling; MCD-Town; VERNON; ***253** M-6; mail De Soto Z 54624; Ⓟ 598; © 713

Stetsonville; Inc. Place; TAYLOR; **252** H-7; elev. 1,450ft./442m.; 🄿; Z 54480; Ⓟ 511; © 563

Stettin; MCD-Town; MARATHON; ***252** H-9; mail Wausau Z 54401; Ⓟ 2,191; © 2,191

Steuben; Inc. Place; CRAWFORD; **253** N-6; elev. 675ft./206m.; 🄿; Z 54657; Ⓟ 161; © 177

Stevens Point; Inc. Place; ⊡ PORTAGE; **252** J-9; elev. 1,093ft./333m.; 🄿 🄷 🄲 8,823 ■; Z 54481-82, Z 54492; Ⓟ 23,006; © 24,551; ◆ 25,469

Stevenstown; RMC Place; LA CROSSE; ▲ Farmington; **253** K-5; mail Gays Mills Z 54631; ● 45

Stewart; GREEN; see Postville (RMC Place)

Stiles; RMC Place; OCONTO; ▲ Stiles; **252** H-13; 🄿; Z 54139; ● 100

Stiles; MCD-Town; OCONTO; ***252** H-13; 🄿; Z 54139; Ⓟ 1,243; © 1,465

Stiles Junction; RMC Place; OCONTO; ▲ Stiles; ***252** H-13; elev. 656ft./200m.; mail Lena Z 54139; rural

Stinnett; MCD-Town; WASHBURN; ***252** D-4; mail Springbrook Z 54875; Ⓟ 202; © 263

Stitzer; RMC Place; GRANT; ▲ Liberty; **253** O-7; elev. 1,191ft./363m.; 🄿; Z 53825; ● 200

Stockbridge; Inc. Place; CALUMET; **253** K-12; elev. 820ft./250m.; 🄿; Z 53088; Ⓟ 579; © 649

Stockbridge; MCD-Town; CALUMET; ***253** K-12; 🄿; Z 53088 & mail Chilton Z 53014; does not include the Village of Stockbridge; Ⓟ 1,317; © 1,383

Stockbridge-Munsee Community; Indian Reservation; SHAWANO; ▲ Red Springs, Bartelme; mail Bowler Z 54416; Ⓟ 1,272; © 1,527

Stockholm; Inc. Place; PEPIN; **252** J-3; elev. 690ft./210m.; 🄿; Z 54769; Ⓟ 89; © 97

Stockholm; MCD-Town; PEPIN; ***252** J-3; 🄿; Z 54769; does not include the Village of Stockholm; Ⓟ 173; © 75

Stockton; RMC Place; PORTAGE; ▲ Stockton; ***252** J-9; elev. 1,133ft./345m.; mail Stevens Point Z 54481; ● 50

Stockton; MCD-Town; PORTAGE; ***252** J-9; mail Stevens Point Z 54481; Ⓟ 2,494; © 2,896

Stoddard; Inc. Place; VERNON; **253** L-5; elev. 646ft./197m.; 🄿; Z 54658; Ⓟ 775; © 815

Stonebank; RMC Place; WAUKESHA; ▲ Merton; ***253** N-12; ★ **MILW**; mail Oconomowoc Z 53066; ● 500

Stone Lake; RMC Place; SAWYER, WASHBURN; ▲ Sand Lake, Stone Lake; **252** E-4; 🄿; Z 54876; ● 300

Stone Lake; MCD-Town; WASHBURN; ***252** E-4; 🄿; Z 54876; Ⓟ 446; © 544

Stony Ridge; RMC Place; DANE; ▲ Burke; ***253** N-10; ★ **MAD**; mail Sun Prairie Z 53590; pop. incl. with Sun Prairie (Inc. Place)

Stoughton; Inc. Place; DANE; **253** O-10; elev. 850ft./259m.; 🄿 🄷; ★ **MAD**; Z 53589; Ⓟ 8,786; © 12,354

Stowell; RMC Place; MILWAUKEE; ★ **MILW**; pop. incl. with Milwaukee (Inc. Place)

Strader; RMC Place; EAU CLAIRE; ▲ Otter Creek, Bridge Creek; ***252** I-5; mail Augusta Z 54722; rural

Stratford; Inc. Place; MARATHON; **252** I-8; elev. 1,255ft./383m.; 🄿; Z 54484; Ⓟ 1,515; © 1,523

Strickland; MCD-Town; RUSK; ***252** G-5; mail Weyerhaeuser Z 54895; Ⓟ 262; © 300

Strongs Prairie; MCD-Town; ADAMS; ***253** K-8; mail Arkdale Z 54613; Ⓟ 1,028; © 1,115

Strum; Inc. Place; TREMPEALEAU; **252** I-5; elev. 915ft./279m.; 🄿; Z 54770; Ⓟ 949; © 1,001

Stubbs; MCD-Town; RUSK; ***252** G-5; mail Bruce Z 54819; Ⓟ 573; © 587

Sturgeon Bay; Inc. Place; ⊡ DOOR; **252** H-14; elev. 588ft./179m.; 🄿 🄷; Z 54235; Ⓟ 9,176; © 9,437

Sturgeon Bay; MCD-Town; DOOR; ***252** I-14; 🄿; Z 54235; does not include the City of Sturgeon Bay; Ⓟ 853; © 865

Sturtevant (Corliss); Inc. Place; RACINE; **253** O-13; elev. 727ft./222m.; 🄿; ★ **MILW**; Z 53177; Ⓟ 3,803; © 5,287

Suamico (Big Suamico); Inc. Place; BROWN; ▲ Suamico; **252** I-13; elev. 593ft./181m.; 🄿; ★ **GRBY**; Z 54173 & mail Green Bay Z 54313; incorporated September 8, 2003; not reported in 2000 Census; ● 10,000

Sugar Bush (Schiller); RMC Place; BROWN; ▲ Humboldt; ***252** J-13; mail Luxemburg Z 54217; ● 30

Sugar Bush; RMC Place; OUTAGAMIE; ▲ Maple Creek; ***252** J-11; elev. 829ft./253m.; mail New London Z 54961; ● 100

Sugar Camp (Robbins); RMC Place; ONEIDA; ▲ Sugar Camp; **252** E-10; mail Rhinelander Z 54501; ● 180

Sugar Camp; MCD-Town; ONEIDA; ***252** E-10; mail Rhinelander Z 54501; Ⓟ 1,375; © 1,781

Sugar Creek; MCD-Town; WALWORTH; ***253** O-11; mail Elkhorn Z 53121; Ⓟ 2,661; © 3,331

Sugar Grove; RMC Place; VERNON; ▲ Kickapoo; ***253** M-6; mail Soldiers Grove Z 54655; rural

Sugar Island; RMC Place; DODGE; ▲ Lebanon; ***253** N-11; mail Watertown Z 53098; ● 50

Sullivan; Inc. Place; JEFFERSON; **253** O-11; elev. 860ft./262m.; 🄿; Z 53178; Ⓟ 432; © 688

Sullivan; MCD-Town; JEFFERSON; ***253** O-11; 🄿; Z 53178 & mail Jefferson Z 53549; does not include the Village of Sullivan; Ⓟ 1,929; © 2,124

Summit; RMC Place; DANE; ★ **MAD**; pop. incl. with Madison (Inc. Place)

Summit; MCD-Town; DOUGLAS; ***252** C-3; mail Foxboro Z 54836; Ⓟ 1,009; © 1,042

Summit; MCD-Town; JUNEAU; ***253** L-8; mail Mauston Z 53948; Ⓟ 600; © 623

Summit; MCD-Town; LANGLADE; ***252** G-9; mail Gleason Z 54435; Ⓟ 190; © 168

Entries in **UPPERCASE** are counties.
Entries in **bold** have populations of 2,500 or more.
Names in parentheses are alternate names.

Inc. Place	Incorporated Place
RMC Place	Rand McNally Designated Place
CDP	Census Designated Place
MCD	Minor Civil Division

⊡	County Seat
▲	Minor Civil Division
elev.	Elevation
🄿	Post Office
🄷	Hospital
🄲	College
■	Principal Business Center
★	Ranally Metro Area (RMA) Abbreviation
Z	Zip Code(s)
Ⓟ	Previous Census Population
Ⓡ	Revised Census Population
Ⓐ	Annexation Population
●	Rand McNally Population Estimate
©	Final Census Population
Ⓢ	Special Census Population
◆	Estimated Population

For additional definitions see Glossary, Volume 1, and Introduction, Volume 2.

Summit; MCD-Town; WAUKESHA; ***253** N-12; ★ **MILW**; mail Nashotah z 53058; Ⓟ 4,003; © 4,999

Summit Corners; RMC Place; WAUKESHA; ▲ Summit; ***253** N-12; elev. 884ft./269m.; ★ **MILW**; mail Oconomowoc z 53066; ● 30

Summit Lake; RMC Place; LANGLADE; ▲ Upham; **252** G-10; elev. 1,727ft./526m.; 🅿; z 54485; ● 200

Sumner; RMC Place; BARRON; ▲ Sumner; ***252** G-4; elev. 1,089ft./332m.; mail Cameron z 54822; rural

Sumner; MCD-Town; BARRON; ***252** G-4; mail Rice Lake z 54868; Ⓟ 550; © 598

Sumner; MCD-Town; JEFFERSON; ***253** O-11; mail Fort Atkinson z 53538; Ⓟ 822; © 904

Sumner; MCD-Town; TREMPEALEAU; ***252** I-5; mail Osseo z 54758; Ⓟ 711; © 806

Sumpter; MCD-Town; SAUK; ***253** M-9; mail North Freedom z 53951; Ⓟ 747; © 1,021

Sunburst; RMC Place; DANE; ▲ Burke; ***253** N-10; elev. 1,030ft./314m.; ★ **MAD**; mail Madison z 53718; ● 250

Sun Prairie; Inc. Place; DANE; **253** N-10; elev. 951ft./290m.; 🅿; ★ **MAD**; z 53590, z 53596; Ⓟ 15,333; © 20,369; ◆ 26,428

Sun Prairie; MCD-Town; DANE; ***253** N-10; 🅿; ★ **MAD**; z 53590, z 53596 & mail Marshall z 53559; does not include the City of Sun Prairie; Ⓟ 1,839; © 2,308

Sunset; RMC Place; MARATHON; ▲ Wausau, Easton; ***252** H-9; elev. 1,399ft./426m.; ★ **WAUS**; mail Wausau z 54403; rural

Sunset Beach; RMC Place; CALUMET; ▲ Stockbridge; ***253** K-12; mail Chilton z 53014; pop. incl. with Stockbridge (Inc. Place)

Sunset Beach; RMC Place; DODGE; ▲ Beaver Dam, Trenton; ***253** M-11; elev. 880ft./268m.; mail Beaver Dam z 53916; ● 200

Sunset Ridge; RMC Place; DANE; ▲ Bristol; ***253** N-10; mail Sun Prairie z 53590; ● 120

Superior; Inc. Place; ⊡ DOUGLAS; **252** B-3; elev. 642ft./196m.; 🅿 🅲 2,924 ■; ★ **DUL**; z 54880; Ⓟ 27,134; © 27,368; ◆ 26,767

Superior; DOUGLAS; see Superior Village (Inc. Place)

Superior; MCD-Town; DOUGLAS; ***252** C-3; 🅿 🅲 2,924; z 54880 & mail Foxboro z 54836; Ⓟ 1,911; © 2,058

Superior Village (Superior); Inc. Place; DOUGLAS; ***252** B-3; elev. 675ft./206m.; 🅷; ★ **DUL**; mail Superior z 54880; Ⓟ 481; © 500

Suring; Inc. Place; OCONTO; **252** H-12; elev. 804ft./245m.; 🅿; z 54174; Ⓟ 626; © 605

Sussex; Inc. Place; WAUKESHA; **253** N-12; elev. 915ft./279m.; 🅿; ★ **MILW**; z 53089; Ⓟ 5,039; © 8,828

Swiss; MCD-Town; BURNETT; ***252** D-3; mail Danbury z 54830; Ⓟ 645; © 815

Sylvan; RMC Place; RICHLAND; ▲ Sylvan; ***253** M-7; elev. 1,257ft./383m.; mail Viola z 54664; ● 30

Sylvan; MCD-Town; RICHLAND; ***253** M-7; mail Viola z 54664; Ⓟ 507; © 547

Sylvania; RMC Place; RACINE; ▲ Yorkville, Mount Pleasant; ***253** P-13; elev. 767ft./234m.; ★ **MILW**; mail Sturtevant z 53177; rural

Sylvester; MCD-Town; GREEN; ***253** P-9; mail Juda z 53550; Ⓟ 746; © 809

Symco; RMC Place; WAUPACA; ▲ Union; **252** J-11; mail Bear Creek z 54922, Manawa z 54949; ● 100

T

Tabor; RMC Place; RACINE; ▲ Caledonia; ***253** O-13; ★ **MILW**; mail Racine z 53404; rural

Taegesville; RMC Place; MARATHON; ▲ Maine, Berlin; ***252** H-9; elev. 1,390ft./424m.; mail Wausau z 54401

Taft; MCD-Town; TAYLOR; ***252** H-6; mail Thorp z 54771; Ⓟ 367; © 361

Tainter; MCD-Town; DUNN; ***252** H-4; mail Colfax z 54730; Ⓟ 1,756; © 2,116

Tainter Lake; CDP-Census Area Only; DUNN; ▲ Tainter; ***252** H-4; mail Colfax z 54730; Ⓟ 1,716; © 2,089

Tamarack; RMC Place; TREMPEALEAU; ▲ Arcadia; ***253** K-5; elev. 815ft./248m.; mail Arcadia z 54612; rural

Tarrant; RMC Place; PEPIN; ▲ Lima; ***252** I-4; elev. 818ft./249m.; mail Durand z 54736

Taus; RMC Place; MANITOWOC; ▲ Franklin; ***253** K-13; elev. 860ft./262m.; mail Reedsville z 54230; ● 50

Taycheedah; RMC Place; FOND DU LAC; ▲ Taycheedah; **253** L-12; 🅿; ★ **FDLC**; z 54935; ● 300

Taycheedah; MCD-Town; FOND DU LAC; ***253** L-12; 🅿; ★ **FDLC**; z 54935; Ⓟ 3,383; © 3,666

Taylor; Inc. Place; JACKSON; **252** J-5; elev. 880ft./268m.; 🅿; z 54659; Ⓟ 419; © 513

TAYLOR; **252** G-7; Ⓟ 18,901; © 19,680; ◆ 19,119

Teegarden; RMC Place; DUNN; ▲ Lucas; ***252** H-3; elev. 887ft./270m.; mail Menomonie z 54751; rural

Tell; RMC Place; BUFFALO; ▲ Alma; ***252** J-4; mail Alma z 54610; rural

Tennyson; Inc. Place; GRANT; **253** P-6; elev. 930ft./283m.; mail Potosi z 53820; Ⓟ 378; © 370

Terrace Park; RMC Place; DANE; ▲ Windsor; ***253** N-10; elev. 950ft./290m.; ★ **MAD**; mail De Forest z 53532; ● 250

Tess Corners; RMC Place; WAUKESHA; ***253** O-13; ★ **MILW**; mail Muskego z 53150; pop. incl. with Muskego (Inc. Place)

Teutonia; RMC Place; MILWAUKEE; ★ **MILW**; mail Milwaukee z 53206; pop. incl. with Milwaukee (Inc. Place)

Texas; MCD-Town; MARATHON; ***252** H-9; mail Wausau z 54401; Ⓟ 1,643; © 1,703

Theresa; Inc. Place; DODGE; **253** M-12; elev. 940ft./287m.; 🅿; z 53091; Ⓟ 771; © 1,252

Theresa; MCD-Town; DODGE; ***253** M-12; 🅿; z 53091 & mail Mayville z 53050; does not include the Village of Theresa; Ⓟ 1,083; © 1,080

Thiensville; Inc. Place; OZAUKEE; **253** N-13; elev. 700ft./213m.; 🅿; ★ **MILW**; z 53092, z 53097; Ⓟ 3,301; © 3,254

Thiry Daems; RMC Place; KEWAUNEE; ▲ Red River; ***252** I-13; elev. 727ft./222m.; mail Luxemburg z 54217; rural

Thompson; RMC Place; WASHINGTON; ▲ Erin; ***253** N-12; ★ **MILW**; mail Hartford z 53027; ● 50

Thompsonville; RMC Place; RACINE; ▲ Raymond, Caledonia; ***253** O-13; ★ **MILW**; mail Franksville z 53126

Thornapple; MCD-Town; RUSK; ***252** F-5; mail Bruce z 54819; Ⓟ 757; © 811

Thornton; RMC Place; SHAWANO; ▲ Richmond; **252** I-11; elev. 860ft./262m.; mail Shawano z 54166; ● 50

Thorp; Inc. Place; CLARK; **252** H-6; elev. 1,220ft./372m.; 🅿; z 54771; Ⓟ 1,657; © 1,536

Thorp; MCD-Town; CLARK; ***252** H-6; 🅿; z 54771 & mail Stanley z 54768; does not include the City of Thorp; Ⓟ 710; © 730

Three Lakes; RMC Place; ONEIDA; ▲ Three Lakes; **252** E-10; elev. 1,666ft./508m.; 🅿; z 54562; ● 850

Three Lakes; MCD-Town; ONEIDA; ***252** E-10; 🅿; z 54562; Ⓟ 2,004; © 2,339

Tibbets; RMC Place; WALWORTH; ▲ Sugar Creek; ***253** O-11; elev. 938ft./286m.; mail Elkhorn z 53121; ● 50

Tichigan (Lake Tichigan, Tichigan Lake); RMC Place; RACINE; ▲ Waterford; ***253** O-12; elev. 796ft./243m.; ★ **MILW**; mail Waterford z 53185; ● 950

Tichigan Lake; RACINE; see Tichigan (RMC Place)

Tiffany; MCD-Town; DUNN; ***252** H-3; mail Boyceville z 54725; Ⓟ 594; © 633

Tiffany; RMC Place; ROCK; ▲ Turtle, La Prairie; ***253** P-11; ★ **RKFD**; mail Beloit z 53511; ● 100

Tigerton; Inc. Place; SHAWANO; **252** I-10; elev. 1,010ft./308m.; 🅿; z 54486; Ⓟ 815; © 764

Tilden; RMC Place; CHIPPEWA; ▲ Tilden; ***252** H-5; mail Chippewa Falls z 54729; ● 100

Tilden; MCD-Town; CHIPPEWA; ***252** H-5; mail Chippewa Falls z 54729; Ⓟ 1,079; © 1,185

Tilleda; RMC Place; SHAWANO; ▲ Seneca; **252** I-11; 🅿; z 54978; ● 130

Timme; OCONTO; see Klondike (RMC Place)

Tioga; RMC Place; CLARK; ▲ Hendren; ***252** I-6; mail Willard z 54493; rural

Tipler; RMC Place; FLORENCE; ▲ Tipler; **252** E-11; elev. 1,537ft./468m.; 🅿; z 54542; ● 50

Tipler; MCD-Town; FLORENCE; ***252** E-11; 🅿; z 54542; Ⓟ 174; © 205

Tisch Mills; RMC Place; MANITOWOC, KEWAUNEE; ▲ Mishicot, Carlton; **252** J-14; elev. 638ft./194m.; 🅿; ★ **MNTW**; z 54240; ● 200

Token Creek; RMC Place; DANE; ▲ Windsor, Burke; ***253** N-10; ★ **MAD**; mail De Forest z 53532; ● 200

Tomah; Inc. Place; MONROE; **253** K-7; elev. 960ft./293m.; 🅿 🅷; z 54660; Ⓟ 7,570; © 8,419

Tomah; MCD-Town; MONROE; ***253** K-7; 🅿; z 54660; does not include the City of Tomah; Ⓟ 1,076; © 1,194

Tomahawk; Inc. Place; LINCOLN; **252** F-9; elev. 1,450ft./442m.; 🅿; z 54487, z 54532; Ⓟ 3,328; © 3,770

Tomahawk; MCD-Town; LINCOLN; ***252** G-8; 🅿; z 54487, z 54532; does not include the City of Tomahawk; Ⓟ 370; © 439

Tomahawk Lake; ONEIDA; see Lake Tomahawk (RMC Place)

Tonet; RMC Place; KEWAUNEE; ▲ Red River, Luxemburg; ***252** I-13; elev. 717ft./219m.; mail Luxemburg z 54217; rural

Tony; Inc. Place; RUSK; **252** F-6; elev. 1,225ft./373m.; 🅿; z 54563; Ⓟ 114; © 105

Towerville; RMC Place; CRAWFORD; ▲ Utica; ***253** M-6; mail Soldiers Grove z 54655; ● 30

Townsend; RMC Place; OCONTO; ▲ Townsend; **252** G-11; elev. 1,361ft./415m.; 🅿; z 54175; ● 420

Townsend; MCD-Town; OCONTO; ***252** G-11; 🅿; z 54175; Ⓟ 715; © 963

Trade Lake; RMC Place; BURNETT; ▲ Trade Lake; **252** F-2; mail Frederic z 54837; ● 60

Trade Lake; MCD-Town; BURNETT; ***252** F-2; mail Frederic z 54837; Ⓟ 831; © 871

Trade River; RMC Place; BURNETT; ▲ Anderson; ***252** F-2; mail Grantsburg z 54840

Trego; RMC Place; WASHBURN; ▲ Trego; **252** E-4; elev. 1,086ft./331m.; 🅿; z 54888; ● 250

Trego; MCD-Town; WASHBURN; ***252** E-4; 🅿; z 54888; Ⓟ 709; © 885

Trempealeau; Inc. Place; TREMPEALEAU; **253** K-5; elev. 691ft./211m.; 🅿; z 54661; Ⓟ 1,039; © 1,319

Trempealeau; MCD-Town; TREMPEALEAU; ***253** K-5; 🅿; z 54661; does not include the Village of Trempealeau; Ⓟ 1,341; © 1,618

TREMPEALEAU; **252** J-5; Ⓟ 25,263; © 27,010; ◆ 27,864

Trenton; MCD-Town; DODGE; ***253** M-11; mail Beaver Dam z 53916; Ⓟ 1,299; © 1,301

Trenton; MCD-Town; PIERCE; ***252** I-2; mail Hager City z 54014; Ⓟ 1,583; © 1,737

Trenton; MCD-Town; WASHINGTON; ***253** M-13; mail West Bend z 53095; Ⓟ 4,028; © 4,440

Trevor; RMC Place; KENOSHA; ▲ Salem; ***253** P-13; elev. 776ft./237m.; 🅿; ★ **CHI**; z 53102, z 53179; ● 800

Trimbelle; RMC Place; PIERCE; ▲ Trimbelle; ***252** I-2; mail Ellsworth z 54011; ● 30

Trimbelle; MCD-Town; PIERCE; ***252** I-2; mail Ellsworth z 54011; Ⓟ 1,482; © 1,511

Tripoli; RMC Place; ONEIDA; ▲ Lynne; **252** F-8; 🅿; z 54564; ● 70

Tripp; MCD-Town; BAYFIELD; ***252** C-5; mail Iron River z 54847; Ⓟ 182; © 209

Troy; MCD-Town; SAUK; ***253** N-8; mail Sauk City z 53583; Ⓟ 867; © 773

Troy; MCD-Town; ST. CROIX; ***252** H-2; ★ **MPLS-**; mail River Falls z 54022; Ⓟ 2,850; © 3,661

Troy; RMC Place; WALWORTH; ▲ Troy; ***253** O-12; mail East Troy z 53120, Elkhorn z 53121; ● 120

Troy; MCD-Town; WALWORTH; ***253** O-12; ★ **MILW**; mail East Troy z 53120; Ⓟ 2,051; © 2,328

Troy Center; RMC Place; WALWORTH; ▲ Troy; ***253** O-12; mail East Troy z 53120; ● 230

True; MCD-Town; RUSK; ***252** F-6; mail Glen Flora z 54526; Ⓟ 310; © 291

Truesdell; RMC Place; KENOSHA; ***253** P-13; ★ **KEN**; mail Kenosha z 53142; pop. incl. with Pleasant Prairie (Inc. Place)

Truman; RMC Place; LAFAYETTE; ▲ Kendall; ***253** O-7; elev. 1,048ft./319m.; mail Darlington z 53530; rural

Tuckaway; RMC Place; MILWAUKEE; ★ **MILW**; mail Milwaukee z 53221; pop. incl. with Milwaukee (Inc. Place)

Tuleta Hills; RMC Place; GREEN LAKE; ▲ Green Lake; ***253** L-10; mail Markesan z 53946; summer pop. 150

Tunnel City; RMC Place; MONROE; ▲ Greenfield; **253** K-7; elev. 1,053ft./321m.; 🅿; z 54662; ● 220

Turner Estates; RMC Place; ROCK; ▲ Beloit; ***253** P-10; ★ **RKFD**; mail Beloit z 53511; ● 125

Turtle; MCD-Town; ROCK; ***253** P-11; ★ **RKFD**; mail Beloit z 53511; Ⓟ 2,456; © 2,444

Turtle Creek; RMC Place; ROCK; ▲ Turtle; ***253** P-10; ★ **RKFD**; mail Beloit z 53511; pop. incl. with Beloit (Inc. Place)

Turtle Lake; Inc. Place; BARRON, POLK; **252** G-3; elev. 1,264ft./385m.; 🅿; z 54889 & mail Clayton z 54004; Ⓟ 817; © 1,065

Turtle Lake; MCD-Town; BARRON; ***252** G-3; 🅿; z 54889 & mail Clayton z 54004; does not include the Village of Turtle Lake; Ⓟ 621; © 622

Turtle Lake; RMC Place; WALWORTH; ▲ Richmond; ***253** O-11; elev. 929ft./283m.; mail Delavan z 53115; ● 250

Tustin; RMC Place; WAUSHARA; ▲ Bloomfield; **253** K-11; mail Fremont z 54940; ● 110

Twelfth Street Junction; RMC Place; DOUGLAS; ***252** B-3; ★ **DUL**; pop. incl. with Superior (Inc. Place)

Twelve Corners; RMC Place; OUTAGAMIE; ▲ Center; ***252** J-12; ★ **APP**; mail Black Creek z 54106; rural

Twenty-Eighth Street Junction; RMC Place; DOUGLAS; ***252** B-3; ★ **DUL**; pop. incl. with Superior (Inc. Place)

Twin Bluffs; RMC Place; RICHLAND; ▲ Orion; **253** N-7; elev. 707ft./215m.; mail Richland Center z 53581; ● 80

Twin Grove; RMC Place; GREEN; ▲ Jefferson; ***253** P-9; elev. 948ft./289m.; mail Juda z 53550; ● 50

Twin Lakes; Inc. Place; KENOSHA; **253** P-12; elev. 809ft./247m.; 🅿; ★ **CHI**; z 53181; Ⓟ 3,989; © 5,124

Two Creeks; RMC Place; MANITOWOC; ▲ Two Creeks; **252** J-14; mail Two Rivers z 54241; ● 50

Two Creeks; MCD-Town; MANITOWOC; ***252** J-14; mail Two Rivers z 54241; Ⓟ 466; © 551

Two Rivers; Inc. Place; MANITOWOC; **253** K-14; elev. 595ft./181m.; 🅿 🅷; ★ **MNTW**; z 54241; Ⓟ 13,030; © 12,639

Two Rivers; MCD-Town; MANITOWOC; ***253** K-14; 🅿; ★ **MNTW**; z 54241; does not include the City of Two Rivers; Ⓟ 2,147; © 1,912

U

Ubet; RMC Place; POLK; ▲ Garfield; ***252** G-2; elev. 1,116ft./340m.; mail Dresser z 54009; rural

Underhill; RMC Place; OCONTO; ▲ Underhill; **252** H-12; 🅿; z 54124; ● 100

Underhill; MCD-Town; OCONTO; ***252** H-12; 🅿; z 54124; Ⓟ 668; © 846

Union; MCD-Town; BURNETT; ***252** E-2; mail Danbury z 54830; Ⓟ 221; © 351

Union; MCD-Town; DOOR; ***252** I-13; mail Brussels z 54204; Ⓟ 721; © 880

Union; MCD-Town; EAU CLAIRE; ***252** H-4; ★ **EAUC**; mail Eau Claire z 54701; Ⓟ 2,446; © 2,402

Union; RMC Place; GRANT; ▲ Lima; ***253** O-7; elev. 1,097ft./334m.; mail Platteville z 53818

Union; MCD-Town; PIERCE; ***252** I-3; mail Maiden Rock z 54750; Ⓟ 643; © 618

Union; RMC Place; ROCK; ▲ Union; ***253** O-10; elev. 945ft./288m.; mail Evansville z 53536; ● 40

Union; MCD-Town; ROCK; ***253** O-10; mail Evansville z 53536; Ⓟ 1,537; © 1,860

Union; MCD-Town; VERNON; ***253** M-7; mail Hillsboro z 54634; Ⓟ 420; © 531

Union; MCD-Town; WAUPACA; ***252** I-11; mail Manawa z 54949; Ⓟ 733; © 804

Union Center; Inc. Place; JUNEAU; **253** L-7; elev. 922ft./281m.; 🅿; z 53962; Ⓟ 197; © 214

Union Grove; Inc. Place; RACINE; **253** P-13; elev. 780ft./238m.; 🅿; ★ **MILW**; z 53182; Ⓟ 3,669; © 4,322

Unity; Inc. Place; CLARK, MARATHON; **252** H-7; elev. 1,338ft./408m.; 🅿; z 54488; Ⓟ 452; © 368

Unity; MCD-Town; CLARK; ***252** I-7; 🅿; z 54488; does not include the Village of Unity; Ⓟ 735; © 745

Unity; MCD-Town; TREMPEALEAU; ***252** I-5; mail Strum z 54770; Ⓟ 473; © 556

Upham; MCD-Town; LANGLADE; ***252** G-10; mail Summit Lake z 54485; Ⓟ 626; © 689

Upson; RMC Place; IRON; ▲ Anderson; **252** C-7; elev. 1,497ft./456m.; 🅿; z 54565; ● 70

Urne; RMC Place; BUFFALO; ▲ Nelson, Modena; **252** J-4; elev. 825ft./251m.; mail Durand z 54736; ● 50

Utica; MCD-Town; CRAWFORD; ***253** M-6; mail Soldiers Grove z 54655; Ⓟ 738; © 674

Utica; RMC Place; DANE; ▲ Christiana; ***253** O-10; elev. 956ft./291m.; mail Cambridge z 53523; ● 50

Utica; RMC Place; WAUKESHA; ▲ Summit; ***253** N-12; ★ **MILW**; mail Oconomowoc z 53066; rural

Utica; MCD-Town; WINNEBAGO; ***253** K-11; mail Pickett z 54964; Ⓟ 1,046; © 1,168

V

Valders; Inc. Place; MANITOWOC; **253** K-13; elev. 840ft./256m.; 🅿; z 54245; Ⓟ 905; © 948

Valley; RMC Place; VERNON; ▲ Forest; **253** L-7; mail La Farge z 54639; ● 60

Valley Junction; RMC Place; MONROE; ▲ Byron; **253** K-7; mail Tomah z 54660; ● 100

Valmy; RMC Place; DOOR; ▲ Sevastopol; **252** B-13; mail Sturgeon Bay z 54235; ● 30

Valton; RMC Place; SAUK; ▲ Woodland; ***253** M-7; elev. 1,031ft./314m.; mail Wonewoc z 53968; ● 50

Van Buskirk; RMC Place; IRON; ▲ Oma; ***252** C-8; elev. 1,513ft./461m.; mail Hurley z 54534; rural

Vance Creek; MCD-Town; BARRON; ***252** G-3; mail Rice Lake z 54868; Ⓟ 611; © 747

Vandenbroek; MCD-Town; OUTAGAMIE; ***252** J-12; ★ **APP**; mail Kaukauna z 54130; Ⓟ 1,291; © 1,351

Van Dyne; RMC Place; FOND DU LAC; ▲ Friendship; **253** L-12; 🅿; ★ **FDLC**; z 54979; ● 300

Vaudreuil; RMC Place; JACKSON; ▲ Brockway; ***252** J-6; mail Black River Falls z 54615

Veedum; RMC Place; WOOD; ▲ Dexter; ***252** J-8; mail Pittsville z 54466; ● 30

Vermont; MCD-Town; DANE; ***253** N-9; mail Black Earth z 53515; Ⓟ 678; © 839

Vernon; MCD-Town; WAUKESHA; ***253** O-12; 🅿; ★ **MILW**; z 53186, z 53188 & mail Big Bend z 53103; Ⓟ 7,549; © 7,227

VERNON; **253** M-6; Ⓟ 25,617; © 28,056; ◆ 29,087

Verona; Inc. Place; DANE; **253** O-9; elev. 970ft./296m.; 🅿; ★ **MAD**; z 53593; Ⓟ 5,374; © 7,052

Verona; MCD-Town; DANE; ***253** O-9; 🅿; ★ **MAD**; z 53593; does not include the Village of Verona; Ⓟ 2,137; © 2,153

Vesper; Inc. Place; WOOD; **252** J-8; elev. 1,110ft./338m.; 🅿; z 54489; Ⓟ 598; © 541

Victory; RMC Place; VERNON; ▲ Wheatland; **253** M-5; elev. 629ft./192m.; 🅿; z 54624; ● 120

Victory Heights; RMC Place; ROCK; ▲ Beloit; ***253** P-10; ★ **RKFD**; mail Beloit z 53511; ● 90

Vienna; MCD-Town; DANE; ***253** N-9; mail De Forest z 53532; Ⓟ 1,351; © 1,294

Vignes; RMC Place; DOOR; ▲ Clay Banks; ***252** I-14; mail Sturgeon Bay z 54235; rural

Vilas; RMC Place; DANE; ▲ Cottage Grove; ***253** N-10; ★ **MAD**; mail Cottage Grove z 53527; ● 70

Vilas; MCD-Town; LANGLADE; ***252** G-10; mail Deerbrook z 54424; Ⓟ 257; © 249

VILAS; **252** D-9; Ⓟ 17,707; © 21,033; ◆ 21,841

Village of Pewaukee; WAUKESHA; see Pewaukee (Inc. Place)

Villard; RMC Place; MILWAUKEE; ★ **MILW**; mail Milwaukee z 53209; pop. incl. with Milwaukee (Inc. Place)

Vinland; MCD-Town; WINNEBAGO; ***253** K-12; mail Oshkosh z 54901; Ⓟ 1,688; © 1,849

Viola; Inc. Place; RICHLAND, VERNON; **253** M-6; elev. 770ft./235m.; 🅿; z 54664; Ⓟ 644; © 667

Viroqua; Inc. Place; ⊡ VERNON; **253** M-6; elev. 1,160ft./354m.; 🅿 🅷; z 54665; Ⓟ 3,922; © 4,335

Viroqua; MCD-Town; VERNON; ***253** M-6; 🅿; z 54665; does not include the City of Viroqua; Ⓟ 1,499; © 1,560

Voltz Lake; RMC Place; KENOSHA; ▲ Salem; ***253** P-13; elev. 810ft./247m.; ★ **CHI**; mail Trevor z 53179; summer pop. 500; ● 110

W

Wabeno; RMC Place; FOREST; ▲ Wabeno; **252** F-11; elev. 1,540ft./469m.; 🅿; z 54566; ● 960

Wabeno; MCD-Town; FOREST; ***252** F-11; 🅿; z 54566; Ⓟ 1,012; © 1,264

Wagner; MCD-Town; MARINETTE; ***252** G-13; mail Wausaukee z 54177; Ⓟ 660; © 722

Waldo; Inc. Place; SHEBOYGAN; **253** L-13; elev. 838ft./255m.; 🅿; z 53093; Ⓟ 442; © 450

Waldwick; RMC Place; IOWA; ▲ Waldwick; **253** O-8; mail Mineral Point z 53565; ● 60

Waldwick; MCD-Town; IOWA; ***253** O-8; mail Mineral Point z 53565; Ⓟ 487; © 500

Wales; Inc. Place; WAUKESHA; **253** O-12; elev. 1,002ft./305m.; 🅿; ★ **MILW**; z 53183; Ⓟ 2,471; © 2,523

Walhain; RMC Place; KEWAUNEE; ▲ Luxemburg; ***252** I-13; elev. 784ft./239m.; mail Luxemburg z 54217; rural

Walsh; RMC Place; MARINETTE; ▲ Porterfield; **252** G-13; mail Porterfield z 54159; ● 30

Walworth; Inc. Place; WALWORTH; **253** P-11; elev. 998ft./304m.; 🅿; z 53184; Ⓟ 1,614; © 2,304

Walworth; MCD-Town; WALWORTH; ***253** P-11; 🅿; z 53184; does not include the Village of Walworth; Ⓟ 1,341; © 1,676

WALWORTH; **253** O-11; Ⓟ 75,000; © 93,759; ® 92,013; ◆ 99,984

Wandawega; RMC Place; WALWORTH; ▲ Sugar Creek; **253** O-12; mail Elkhorn z 53121; summer pop. 1,500; ● 500

Wanderoos; RMC Place; POLK; ▲ Garfield; **252** G-2; mail Amery z 54001; ● 110

Wards Corners; RMC Place; SAUK; ▲ Washington; ***253** M-8; mail Hillpoint z 53937; rural

Warner; MCD-Town; CLARK; ***252** I-7; mail Greenwood z 54437; Ⓟ 599; © 627

Warren; MONROE; see Warrens (Inc. Place)

Warren; MCD-Town; ST. CROIX; ***252** H-2; mail Roberts z 54023; Ⓟ 1,008; © 1,320

Warren; MCD-Town; WAUSHARA; ***253** K-10; mail Berlin z 54923; Ⓟ 550; © 675

Warrens (Warren); Inc. Place; MONROE; ▲ Lincoln; **253** K-7; 🅿; z 54666; Ⓟ 343; © 286

Warrentown; RMC Place; PIERCE; ▲ Maiden Rock; ***252** I-2; mail Maiden Rock z 54750; rural

Wascott; RMC Place; DOUGLAS; **252** D-4; elev. 1,090ft./332m.; 🅿; z 54838, z 54890 & mail Minong z 54859; ● 150

Wascott; MCD-Town; DOUGLAS; ***252** D-4; 🅿; z 54838, z 54890 & mail Minong z 54859; Ⓟ 535; © 714

Washburn; Inc. Place; ⊡ BAYFIELD; **252** B-6; elev. 654ft./199m.; 🅿; z 54891; Ⓟ 2,285; © 2,280

Washburn; MCD-Town; BAYFIELD; ***252** B-5; 🅿; z 54891; does not include the City of Washburn; Ⓟ 490; © 541

Washburn; MCD-Town; CLARK; ***252** J-7; mail Neillsville z 54456; Ⓟ 310; © 304

WASHBURN; **252** E-4; Ⓟ 13,772; © 16,036; ◆ 16,667

Washington; MCD-Town; DOOR; ***252** A-14; mail Washington Island z 54246; Ⓟ 623; © 660

Washington; MCD-Town; EAU CLAIRE; ***252** I-5; mail Fall Creek z 54742; Ⓟ 6,226; © 6,995

Washington; MCD-Town; GREEN; ***253** O-9; mail Monticello z 53570; Ⓟ 587; © 627

Washington; MCD-Town; LA CROSSE; ***253** L-6; mail Cashton z 54619; Ⓟ 598; © 738

Washington; MCD-Town; RUSK; ***252** G-5; mail Bruce z 54819; Ⓟ 301; © 312

Washington; MCD-Town; SAUK; ***253** M-8; mail Hillpoint z 53937; Ⓟ 798; © 904

Washington; MCD-Town; SHAWANO; ***252** I-12; mail Bonduel z 54107; Ⓟ 1,620; © 1,903

Washington; MCD-Town; VILAS; ***252** E-10; mail Eagle River z 54521; Ⓟ 1,189; © 1,577

WASHINGTON; **253** M-12; Ⓟ 95,328; © 117,493; ® 117,496; ◆ 128,894

Washington Island; DOOR; see Detroit Harbor (RMC Place)

Washington Square; RMC Place; MARATHON; ★ **WAUS**; mail Wausau z 54402; pop. incl. with Wausau (Inc. Place)

Waterford; Inc. Place; RACINE; **253** O-12; elev. 790ft./241m.; 🅿; ★ **MILW**; z 53185; Ⓟ 2,431; © 4,048

Waterford; MCD-Town; RACINE; ***253** O-12; 🅿; ★ **MILW**; z 53185; does not include the City of Waterford; Ⓟ 4,255; © 5,938

Waterford North; CDP-Census Area Only; RACINE; ▲ Waterford; ***253** O-12; ★ **MILW**; mail Waterford z 53185; Ⓟ 1,604; © 4,761

Waterford Woods; RMC Place; RACINE; ▲ Waterford; ***253** O-12; elev. 800ft./244m.; ★ **MILW**; mail Waterford z 53185; ● 600

Waterloo; MCD-Town; GRANT; ***253** O-6; mail Potosi z 53820; Ⓟ 588; © 557

Waterloo; Inc. Place; JEFFERSON; **253** N-10; elev. 819ft./250m.; 🅿; z 53594; Ⓟ 2,712; © 3,259

Waterloo; MCD-Town; JEFFERSON; ***253** N-11; 🅿; z 53594 & mail Lake Mills z 53551; does not include the Village of Waterloo; Ⓟ 694; © 832

Watertown; Inc. Place; JEFFERSON, DODGE; **253** N-11; elev. 823ft./251m.; 🅿 🅷 🅲 866 ■; z 53094, z 53098; Ⓟ 19,142; © 21,598; ◆ 22,244

Watertown; MCD-Town; JEFFERSON; ***253** N-11; 🅿 🅲 866; z 53094, z 53098; does not include the City of Watertown; Ⓟ 1,840; © 1,876

Waterville; MCD-Town; PEPIN; ***252** I-3; mail Arkansaw z 54721; Ⓟ 875; © 859

Waterville; RMC Place; WAUKESHA; ▲ Summit; ***253** N-12; ★ **MILW**; mail Oconomowoc z 53066; rural

Watterstown; MCD-Town; GRANT; ***253** N-7; mail Boscobel z 53805; Ⓟ 361; © 362

Waubeek; MCD-Town; PEPIN; ***252** I-3; mail Durand z 54736; Ⓟ 316; © 364

Waubeesee; RMC Place; RACINE; ▲ Norway; ***253** O-12; ★ **MILW**; mail Waterford z 53185

Waubeka; RMC Place; OZAUKEE; ▲ Fredonia; **253** M-13; 🅿; ★ **MILW**; z 53021; ● 350

Waubesa Heights; RMC Place; DANE; ▲ Dunn; ***253** O-10; elev. 950ft./290m.; ★ **MAD**; mail Mc Farland z 53558; ● 300

Waucousta; RMC Place; FOND DU LAC; ▲ Osceola; ***253** L-12; mail Campbellsport z 53010; ● 40

Waukau; RMC Place; WINNEBAGO; ▲ Rushford; **253** K-11; 🅿; z 54980; ● 240

Waukechon; MCD-Town; SHAWANO; ***252** I-11; mail Shawano z 54166; Ⓟ 876; © 928

Waukesha; Inc. Place; ⊡ WAUKESHA; **253** N-12; elev. 821ft./250m.; 🅿 🅷 🅲 3,292 ■; ★ **MILW**; z 53146, z 53151, z 53186-89; Ⓟ 56,958; © 64,825; ◆ 66,377

Waukesha; MCD-Town; WAUKESHA; ***253** O-12; 🅿 🅲 3,292; ★ **MILW**; z 53146, z 53151, z 53186-89; does not include the City of Waukesha; Ⓟ 7,566; © 8,596

WAUKESHA; **253** O-12; Ⓟ 304,715; © 360,767; ◆ 374,390

Waumandee; RMC Place; BUFFALO; ▲ Waumandee; **252** J-4; 🅿; z 54622; ● 100

Waumandee; MCD-Town; BUFFALO; ***252** J-4; 🅿; z 54622; Ⓟ 521; © 515

Waunakee; Inc. Place; DANE; **253** N-9; elev. 925ft./282m.; 🅿; ★ **MAD**; z 53597; Ⓟ 5,897; © 8,995

Waupaca; Inc. Place; ⊡ WAUPACA; **252** J-10; elev. 870ft./265m.; 🅿 🅷; z 54981; Ⓟ 4,957; © 5,676

Waupaca; MCD-Town; WAUPACA; ***252** J-10; 🅿; z 54981; does not include the City of Waupaca; Ⓟ 1,111; © 1,155

WAUPACA; **252** J-10; Ⓟ 46,104; © 51,731; ® 51,825; ◆ 51,729

Waupun; Inc. Place; FOND DU LAC, DODGE; **253** L-11; elev. 904ft./276m.; 🅿 🅷; z 53963; Ⓟ 8,207; © 10,718

Waupun; MCD-Town; FOND DU LAC; ***253** L-11; 🅿; z 53963; does not include the City of Waupun; Ⓟ 1,409; © 1,385

Wausau; Inc. Place; ⊡ MARATHON; **252** H-9; elev. 1,195ft./364m.; 🅿 🅷 ■; ★ **WAUS**; z 54401-03; Ⓟ 37,060; © 38,426; ◆ 38,305

Wausau; MCD-Town; MARATHON; ***252** H-9; 🅿; ★ **WAUS**; z 54401-03; does not include the City of Wausau; Ⓟ 2,133; © 2,214

Wausaukee; Inc. Place; MARINETTE; **252** G-13; elev. 744ft./227m.; 🅿; z 54177; Ⓟ 656; © 572

Wausaukee; MCD-Town; MARINETTE; ***252** G-13; 🅿; z 54177; does not include the Village of Wausaukee; Ⓟ 937; © 1,196

WAUSHARA; **253** K-10; Ⓟ 19,385; © 23,154; ® 23,066; ◆ 24,634

Wautoma; Inc. Place; ⊡ WAUSHARA; **253** K-10; elev. 867ft./264m.; 🅿; z 54982; Ⓟ 1,784; © 1,998

Wautoma; MCD-Town; WAUSHARA; ***253** K-10; 🅿; z 54982; does not include the City of Wautoma; Ⓟ 1,088; © 1,312

Wauwatosa; Inc. Place; MILWAUKEE; **251** E-4; elev. 672ft./205m.; 🅿 🅷 ■; ★ **MILW**; z 53210, z 53213, z 53222, z 53225-26; Ⓟ 49,366; © 47,271; ◆ 51,340

Wauzeka; Inc. Place; CRAWFORD; **253** N-6; elev. 657ft./200m.; 🅿; z 53826; Ⓟ 595; © 768

Wauzeka; MCD-Town; CRAWFORD; ***253** N-6; 🅿; z 53826; does not include the Village of Wauzeka; Ⓟ 399; © 369

Waverly; RMC Place; PIERCE; ▲ Rock Elm, El Paso; ***252** I-3; elev. 1,097ft./334m.; mail Elmwood z 54740

Wayne; MCD-Town; LAFAYETTE; ***253** P-8; mail South Wayne z 53587; Ⓟ 510; © 496

Wayne; RMC Place; WASHINGTON; ▲ Wayne; ***253** M-12; elev. 1,054ft./321m.; mail Campbellsport z 53010; ● 60

Wayne; MCD-Town; WASHINGTON; ***253** M-12; mail Campbellsport z 53010; Ⓟ 1,374; © 1,727

Wayside; RMC Place; BROWN; ▲ Morrison; **252** J-13; mail Greenleaf z 54126; ● 200

Webb Lake; RMC Place; BURNETT; ▲ Webb Lake; **252** E-3; 🅿; z 54830; ● 60

Webb Lake; MCD-Town; BURNETT; ***252** D-3; 🅿; z 54830; Ⓟ 200; © 381

Webster; Inc. Place; BURNETT; **252** E-3; elev. 981ft./299m.; 🅿; z 54893; Ⓟ 623; © 653

Webster; MCD-Town; VERNON; ***253** M-6; mail La Farge z 54639; Ⓟ 529; © 676

Weirgor; MCD-Town; SAWYER; ***252** F-5; mail Exeland z 54835; Ⓟ 356; © 370

Wellington; MCD-Town; MONROE; ***253** L-7; mail Ontario z 54651; Ⓟ 566; © 544

Wells; MCD-Town; MONROE; ***253** L-6; mail Sparta z 54656; Ⓟ 442; © 529

Wentworth; RMC Place; DOUGLAS; ▲ Amnicon; **252** C-4; elev. 939ft./286m.; 🅿; z 54874; ● 100

Werley; RMC Place; GRANT; ▲ Mount Ida; ***253** N-6; elev. 766ft./233m.; mail Fennimore z 53809; ● 25

Wescott; MCD-Town; SHAWANO; ***252** I-11; mail Shawano z 54166; Ⓟ 3,085; © 3,653

West Allis; Inc. Place; MILWAUKEE; **251** F-4; elev. 730ft./223m.; 🅿 🅷 ■; ★ **MILW**; z 53214, z 53219, z 53227; Ⓟ 63,221; © 61,254; ◆ 66,521

West Allis Towne Centre; RMC Place; MILWAUKEE; ***253** N-13; ★ **MILW**; mail Milwaukee z 53214; pop. incl. with West Allis (Inc. Place)

West Baraboo; Inc. Place; SAUK; **253** M-9; elev. 886ft./270m.; mail Baraboo z 53913; Ⓟ 1,021; © 1,248

West Bend; Inc. Place; ⊡ WASHINGTON; **253** M-12; elev. 893ft./272m.; 🅿 🅷 ■; z 53090, z 53095; Ⓟ 23,916; © 28,152; ◆ 29,949

West Bend; MCD-Town; WASHINGTON; ***253** M-12; 🅿; z 53090, z 53095; does not include the City of West Bend; Ⓟ 4,607; © 4,834

West Bloomfield; RMC Place; WAUSHARA; ▲ Bloomfield; **253** K-10; elev. 828ft./252m.; mail Weyauwega z 54983; ● 65

Westboro; RMC Place; TAYLOR; ▲ Westboro; **252** G-7; 🅿; z 54490; ● 200

Westboro; MCD-Town; TAYLOR; ***252** G-7; 🅿; z 54490; Ⓟ 663; © 660

Westby; Inc. Place; VERNON; **253** L-6; elev. 1,298ft./396m.; 🅿; z 54667; Ⓟ 1,866; © 2,045

West Denmark; RMC Place; POLK; ▲ Luck; ***252** F-2; mail Luck z 54853; rural

West De Pere; RMC Place; BROWN; ***252** J-13; elev. 607ft./185m.; ★ **GRBY**; mail De Pere z 54115; pop. incl. with De Pere (Inc. Place)

Western; RMC Place; MILWAUKEE; ★ **MILW**; mail Milwaukee z 53210; pop. incl. with Milwaukee (Inc. Place)

Westfield; Inc. Place; MARQUETTE; **253** L-9; elev. 865ft./264m.; 🅿; z 53964; Ⓟ 1,125; © 1,217

Westfield; MCD-Town; MARQUETTE; ***253** L-9; 🅿; z 53964; does not include the Village of Westfield; Ⓟ 520; © 689

Westfield; MCD-Town; SAUK; ***253** M-8; mail Loganville z 53943; Ⓟ 578; © 611

Westford; MCD-Town; DODGE; ***253** M-11; mail Beaver Dam z 53916; Ⓟ 1,248; © 1,400

Westford; MCD-Town; RICHLAND; ***253** M-7; mail Cazenovia z 53924; Ⓟ 513; © 594

West Jacksonport; RMC Place; DOOR; ▲ Jacksonport; ***252** B-13; elev. 725ft./221m.; mail Egg Harbor z 54209; rural

West Kewaunee; MCD-Town; KEWAUNEE; ***252** J-14; mail Kewaunee z 54216; Ⓟ 1,215; © 1,287

West La Crosse; RMC Place; LA CROSSE; ***253** L-5; elev. 643ft./196m.; ★ **LACRO**; mail La Crosse z 54601

West Lima; RMC Place; RICHLAND; ▲ Bloom; **253** M-7; elev. 1,291ft./393m.; 🅿; z 54639; ● 40

Westlyn; RMC Place; WOOD; ▲ Grand Rapids; ***252** J-9; elev. 1,025ft./312m.; mail Wisconsin Rapids z 54494; ● 150

West Marshland; MCD-Town; BURNETT; ***252** E-2; mail Grantsburg z 54840; Ⓟ 293; © 331

West Milwaukee; Inc. Place; MILWAUKEE; **251** F-5; elev. 647ft./197m.; 🅿; ★ **MILW**; z 53214-15, z 53219; Ⓟ 3,973; © 4,201

Weston; MCD-Town; CLARK; ***252** I-7; mail Neillsville z 54456; Ⓟ 662; © 638

Weston; RMC Place; DUNN; ▲ Weston; **252** H-3; mail Menomonie z 54751; ● 30

Weston; MCD-Town; DUNN; ***252** I-3; mail Menomonie z 54751; Ⓟ 560; © 630

Weston; Inc. Place; MARATHON; ▲ Weston; ***252** H-9; 🅿; ★ **WAUS**; z 54476 & mail Rothschild z 54474; Ⓟ 9,714; © 12,079

Weston; MCD-Town; MARATHON; ***252** H-9; 🅿; ★ **WAUS**; z 54476 & mail Rothschild z 54474; Ⓟ 11,450; © 514

West Oshkosh; RMC Place; WINNEBAGO; pop. incl. with Oshkosh (Inc. Place)

West Plainfield; RMC Place; WAUSHARA; ▲ Plainfield; ***253** K-9; mail Plainfield z 54966; rural

West Point; MCD-Town; COLUMBIA; ***253** M-9; mail Lodi z 53555; Ⓟ 1,285; © 1,634

Westport; MCD-Town; DANE; ***253** N-9; 🅿; ★ **MAD**; z 53597; Ⓟ 2,732; © 3,586

Westport; RMC Place; RICHLAND; ▲ Richwood; ***253** N-6; mail Blue River z 53518; rural

West Prairie; RMC Place; VERNON; ▲ Sterling; ***253** M-6; mail Viroqua z 54665; ● 40

West Racine; RMC Place; RACINE; ★ **MILW**; mail Racine z 53405, z 53408; pop. incl. with Racine (Inc. Place)

West Rosendale; RMC Place; FOND DU LAC; ▲ Rosendale; ***253** L-11; elev. 924ft./282m.; mail Rosendale z 54974; ● 50

West Salem; Inc. Place; LA CROSSE; **253** L-5; elev. 742ft./226m.; 🅿; ★ **LACRO**; z 54669; Ⓟ 3,611; © 4,540; ® 4,738

Westside; RMC Place; DANE; ★ **MAD**; mail Madison z 53711, z 53717, z 53719; pop. incl. with Madison (Inc. Place)

West Sweden; RMC Place; POLK; ▲ West Sweden; ***252** F-2; mail Frederic z 54837; rural

West Sweden; MCD-Town; POLK; ***252** F-2; mail Frederic z 54837; Ⓟ 682; © 731

Weyauwega; Inc. Place; WAUPACA; **252** J-11; elev. 800ft./244m.; 🅿; z 54983; Ⓟ 1,665; © 1,806

Weyauwega; MCD-Town; WAUPACA; ***252** J-11; 🅿; z 54983; does not include the City of Weyauwega; Ⓟ 653; © 627

Weyerhaeuser; Inc. Place; RUSK; **252** G-5; elev. 1,203ft./367m.; 🅿; z 54895; Ⓟ 283; © 353

Wheatland; RMC Place; KENOSHA; ▲ Wheatland; ***253** P-12; elev. 763ft./233m.; mail Burlington z 53105; ● 160

Wheatland; MCD-Town; KENOSHA; ***253** P-12; mail Burlington z 53105; Ⓟ 3,263; © 3,292

Wheatland; MCD-Town; VERNON; ***253** M-5; mail De Soto z 54624; Ⓟ 436; © 533

Wheaton; MCD-Town; CHIPPEWA; ***252** H-4; mail Elk Mound z 54739; Ⓟ 2,279; © 2,366

Wheeler; Inc. Place; DUNN; **252** H-4; elev. 938ft./286m.; 🅿; z 54772; Ⓟ 348; © 317

Whispering Pines; RMC Place; OUTAGAMIE; ***252** J-12; elev. 763ft./233m.; ★ **APP**; pop. incl. with Appleton (Inc. Place)

Whitcomb; RMC Place; SHAWANO; ▲ Wittenberg; ***252** I-10; mail Tigerton z 54486; rural

White Creek; RMC Place; ADAMS; ▲ Easton; **253** L-8; mail Wisconsin Dells z 53965; ● 50

Whitefish Bay; RMC Place; DOOR; ▲ Sevastopol; **252** B-13; mail Sturgeon Bay z 54235; ● 30

Whitefish Bay; Inc. Place; MILWAUKEE; **253** N-13; elev. 650ft./198m.; 🅿; ★ **MILW**; z 53211, z 53217; Ⓟ 14,272; © 14,163

Whitehall; Inc. Place; ⊡ TREMPEALEAU; **252** J-5; elev. 820ft./250m.; 🅿 🅷; z 54773; Ⓟ 1,494; © 1,651

White Lake; Inc. Place; LANGLADE; **252** G-11; elev. 1,286ft./392m.; 🅿; z 54491; Ⓟ 304; © 329

Whitelaw; Inc. Place; MANITOWOC; **253** K-13; elev. 857ft./261m.; 🅿; z 54247; Ⓟ 700; © 730

White Oak Springs; MCD-Town; LAFAYETTE; ***253** P-7; mail Shullsburg z 53586; Ⓟ 116; © 97

White River; MCD-Town; ASHLAND; ***252** C-6; mail Marengo z 54855; Ⓟ 771; © 892

Whitestown; MCD-Town; VERNON; ***253** L-7; mail La Farge z 54639; Ⓟ 471; © 509

Whitewater; Inc. Place; WALWORTH, JEFFERSON; **253** O-11; elev. 829ft./253m.; 🅿 🅲 10,502; z 53190; Ⓟ 12,636; © 13,437

Whitewater; MCD-Town; WALWORTH; ***253** O-11; 🅿 🅲 10,502; z 53190; does not include the City of Whitewater; Ⓟ 1,378; © 1,399

Whiting; Inc. Place; PORTAGE; **252** J-9; elev. 1,069ft./326m.; mail Stevens Point z 54481; Ⓟ 1,838; © 1,760

Whittlesey; RMC Place; TAYLOR; ▲ Chelsea; **252** G-7; mail Medford z 54451; ● 80

Wien; MCD-Town; MARATHON; ***252** H-8; mail Edgar z 54426; Ⓟ 705; © 712

Wild Rose; Inc. Place; WAUSHARA; **253** K-10; elev. 935ft./285m.; 🅿 🅷; z 54984; Ⓟ 676; © 765

Wilkinson; MCD-Town; RUSK; ***252** F-5; mail Weyerhaeuser z 54895; Ⓟ 51; © 66

Willard; RMC Place; CLARK; ▲ Hendren; **252** I-6; elev. 1,179ft./359m.; 🅿; z 54493; ● 60

Willard; MCD-Town; RUSK; ***252** G-5; mail Conrath z 54731; Ⓟ 448; © 539

Williams Bay; Inc. Place; WALWORTH; **253** P-12; elev. 950ft./290m.; 🅿; z 53191; Ⓟ 2,108; © 2,415

Williamstown; MCD-Town; DODGE; ***253** M-11; mail Horicon z 53032; Ⓟ 722; © 646

Willow; MCD-Town; RICHLAND; ***253** M-7; mail Cazenovia z 53924; Ⓟ 572; © 493

Willow Springs; MCD-Town; LAFAYETTE; ***253** O-8; mail Mineral Point z 53565; Ⓟ 656; © 632

Willow Springs; RMC Place; WAUKESHA; ***253** N-12; ★ **MILW**; mail Menomonee Falls z 53051; pop. incl. with Menomonee Falls (Inc. Place)

Wilmot; RMC Place; KENOSHA; ▲ Salem; **253** P-12; 🅿; ★ **CHI**; z 53192; ● 600

Wilson; MCD-Town; DUNN; ***252** G-4; mail Dallas z 54733; Ⓟ 490; © 500

Wilson; RMC Place; EAU CLAIRE; ▲ Wilson; ***252** H-6; elev. 980ft./299m.; mail Boyd z 54726; rural

Wilson; MCD-Town; EAU CLAIRE; ***252** I-6; mail Boyd z 54726; Ⓟ 477; © 420

Wilson; MCD-Town; LINCOLN; ***252** F-8; mail Tomahawk z 54487; Ⓟ 238; © 299

Wilson; MCD-Town; RUSK; ***252** F-5; mail Birchwood z 54817; Ⓟ 67; © 84

Wilson; MCD-Town; SHEBOYGAN; ***253** L-13; ★ **SHEB**; mail Sheboygan z 53081; Ⓟ 2,842; © 3,227

Wilson; Inc. Place; ST. CROIX; **252** H-3; elev. 1,155ft./352m.; 🅿; z 54027; Ⓟ 163; © 176

Wilton; Inc. Place; MONROE; **253** L-7; elev. 995ft./303m.; 🅿; z 54670; Ⓟ 478; © 519

Wilton; MCD-Town; MONROE; ***253** L-7; 🅿; z 54670; does not include the Village of Wilton; Ⓟ 777; © 925

Winchester; RMC Place; VILAS; ▲ Winchester; **252** D-8; 🅿; z 54557 & mail Larsen z 54947, Manitowish Waters z 54545; summer pop. 350; ● 150

Winchester; MCD-Town; VILAS; ***252** D-8; 🅿; z 54557 & mail Larsen z 54947, Manitowish Waters z 54545; Ⓟ 354; © 454

Winchester; RMC Place; WINNEBAGO; ▲ Winchester; ***253** K-11; mail Larsen z 54947; ● 230

Winchester; MCD-Town; WINNEBAGO; ***253** K-11; mail Larsen z 54947; Ⓟ 1,433; © 1,676

Wind Lake; CDP; RACINE; ▲ Norway; **253** O-13; elev. 797ft./243m.; 🅿; ★ **MILW**; z 53185; Ⓟ 3,748; © 5,202

Wind Point; Inc. Place; RACINE; **253** O-13; elev. 600ft./183m.; ★ **MILW**; mail Racine z 53402; Ⓟ 1,941; © 1,853

Windsor; CDP; DANE; ▲ Windsor; **253** N-10; elev. 902ft./275m.; 🅿; ★ **MAD**; z 53598; Ⓟ 2,182; © 2,533

Windsor; MCD-Town; DANE; ***253** N-10; 🅿; ★ **MAD**; z 53598; Ⓟ 4,620; © 5,286

Windsor Hills; RMC Place; DANE; ▲ Windsor; ***253** N-10; elev. 1,034ft./315m.; ★ **MAD**; mail De Forest z 53532; ● 80

Windsor Prairie; RMC Place; DANE; ▲ Vienna; ***253** N-10; elev. 900ft./274m.; mail De Forest z 53532; ● 70

Winfield; MCD-Town; SAUK; ***253** M-8; mail Reedsburg z 53959; Ⓟ 649; © 752

Wingville; MCD-Town; GRANT; ***253** O-7; mail Montfort z 53569; Ⓟ 340; © 394

Winnebago; RMC Place; WINNEBAGO; ▲ Oshkosh; **253** L-3; 🅿 🅷; ★ **OSH**; z 54985; ● 400

WINNEBAGO; **253** K-11; Ⓟ 140,320; © 156,763; ◆ 164,668

Winnebago Heights; RMC Place; FOND DU LAC; ▲ Calumet; ***253** L-12; elev. 763ft./233m.; mail Malone z 53049; ● 30

Winnebago Mission; RMC Place; JACKSON; ▲ Komensky; ***252** J-6; mail Black River Falls z 54615; ● 60

Winneboujou; RMC Place; DOUGLAS; ▲ Brule; ***252** C-4; elev. 1,036ft./316m.; mail Brule z 54820; rural

Winneconne; Inc. Place; WINNEBAGO; **253** K-11; elev. 753ft./230m.; 🅿; ★ **OSH**; z 54986; Ⓟ 2,059; © 2,401

Winneconne; MCD-Town; WINNEBAGO; ***253** K-11; 🅿; ★ **OSH**; z 54986 & mail Butte des Morts z 54927; does not include the Village of Winneconne; Ⓟ 1,761; © 2,145

Winter; Inc. Place; SAWYER; **252** E-6; elev. 1,365ft./416m.; 🅿; z 54896 & mail Ojibwa z 54862; Ⓟ 383; © 344

Winter; MCD-Town; SAWYER; ***252** E-6; 🅿; z 54896 & mail Ojibwa z 54862; does not include the Village of Winter; Ⓟ 801; © 969

Wiota; RMC Place; LAFAYETTE; ▲ Wiota; **253** P-8; mail South Wayne z 53587; ● 140

Wiota; MCD-Town; LAFAYETTE; ***253** P-8; mail South Wayne z 53587; Ⓟ 945; © 900

Wisconsin Dells; Inc. Place; COLUMBIA, ADAMS, SAUK; **253** M-9; elev. 912ft./278m.; 🅿; z 53965; Ⓟ 2,393; © 2,418

Wisconsin Rapids; Inc. Place; ⊡ WOOD; **252** J-8; elev. 1,028ft./313m.; 🅿 🅷 ■; z 54494-95; Ⓟ 18,245; © 18,435; ◆ 17,097

Withee; Inc. Place; CLARK; **252** H-7; elev. 1,272ft./388m.; 🅿; z 54498; Ⓟ 503; © 508

Withee; MCD-Town; CLARK; ***252** H-6; 🅿; z 54498 & mail Thorp z 54771; does not include the Village of Withee; Ⓟ 767; © 885

Wittenberg; Inc. Place; SHAWANO; **252** I-10; elev. 1,180ft./360m.; 🅿; z 54432, z 54499; Ⓟ 1,145; © 1,177

Wittenberg; MCD-Town; SHAWANO; ***252** I-10; 🅿; z 54432, z 54499; does not include the Village of Wittenberg; Ⓟ 877; © 894

Witwen; RMC Place; SAUK; ▲ Troy; ***253** N-8; mail Sauk City z 53583; ● 50

Wolf Creek; RMC Place; POLK; ▲ Eureka; ***252** F-2; mail Saint Croix Falls z 54024; ● 40

Wolf Lake; RMC Place; FOND DU LAC; ▲ Marshfield; ***253** L-12; elev. 935ft./285m.; mail Saint Cloud z 53079; summer pop. 300; ● 50

Wolf River; MCD-Town; LANGLADE; ***252** G-11; mail White Lake z 54491; Ⓟ 750; © 856

Wolf River; MCD-Town; WINNEBAGO; ***253** K-11; mail Fremont z 54940; Ⓟ 1,037; © 1,223

Wonewoc; Inc. Place; JUNEAU; **253** L-7; elev. 938ft./286m.; 🅿; z 53968; Ⓟ 793; © 834

Wonewoc; MCD-Town; JUNEAU; ***253** L-7; 🅿; z 53968 & mail Elroy z 53929; does not include the Village of Wonewoc; Ⓟ 770; © 783

Wood; MCD-Town; WOOD; ***252** J-8; mail Pittsville z 54466; Ⓟ 773; © 786

WOOD; **252** I-8; Ⓟ 73,605; © 75,555; ◆ 71,985

Woodboro; RMC Place; ONEIDA; ▲ Woodboro; **252** F-9; elev. 1,619ft./493m.; mail Rhinelander z 54501

Woodboro; MCD-Town; ONEIDA; ***252** F-9; mail Rhinelander z 54501; Ⓟ 703; © 685

Wooddale; RMC Place; SAWYER; ▲ Edgewater; ***252** F-5; mail Birchwood z 54817; ● 30

Woodford; RMC Place; LAFAYETTE; ▲ Wiota; **253** P-8; elev. 793ft./242m.; 🅿; z 53599; ● 100

Woodhull; RMC Place; FOND DU LAC; ▲ Lamartine; ***253** L-11; mail Eldorado z 54932; ● 40

Woodland; RMC Place; DODGE; ▲ Rubicon, Herman; **253** M-12; elev. 952ft./290m.; 🅿; z 53099; ● 120

Woodland; MCD-Town; SAUK; ***253** M-7; mail Wonewoc z 53968; Ⓟ 584; © 783

Woodman; Inc. Place; GRANT; **253** N-6; elev. 680ft./207m.; 🅿; z 53827; Ⓟ 120; © 96

Woodman; MCD-Town; GRANT; ***253** N-6; 🅿; z 53827; does not include the Village of Woodman; Ⓟ 182; © 194

Woodmohr; MCD-Town; CHIPPEWA; ***252** H-5; mail Bloomer z 54724; Ⓟ 1,086; © 883

Wood River; MCD-Town; BURNETT; ***252** E-2; mail Grantsburg z 54840; Ⓟ 948; © 974

Woodruff; RMC Place; ONEIDA; ▲ Woodruff; **252** E-9; 🅿 🅷; z 54568; summer pop. 3,000; ● 1,500

Woodruff; MCD-Town; ONEIDA; ***252** E-9; 🅿; z 54568; Ⓟ 1,634; © 1,982

Woodstock; RMC Place; RICHLAND; ▲ Henrietta; **253** M-7; mail Richland Center z 53581; ● 60

Woodville; MCD-Town; CALUMET; ***253** K-12; mail Hilbert z 54129; Ⓟ 1,071; © 993

Woodville; Inc. Place; ST. CROIX; **252** H-3; elev. 1,180ft./360m.; 🅿; z 54028; Ⓟ 942; © 1,104

Woodworth; RMC Place; KENOSHA; ▲ Bristol; ***253** P-13; elev. 752ft./229m.; 🅿; ★ **CHI**; z 53194; ● 150

Worcester; RMC Place; PRICE; ▲ Hackett; ***252** F-7; mail Phillips z 54555; ● 40

Worcester; MCD-Town; PRICE; ***252** F-7; mail Phillips z 54555; Ⓟ 1,582; © 1,711

Worden; MCD-Town; CLARK; ***252** H-6; mail Thorp z 54771; Ⓟ 575; © 657

Wrightstown; Inc. Place; BROWN; **252** J-12; elev. 656ft./200m.; 🅿; z 54180 & mail Kaukauna z 54130; Ⓟ 1,262; © 1,934

Wrightstown; MCD-Town; BROWN; ***252** J-13; 🅿; z 54180 & mail De Pere z 54115, Kaukauna z 54130; does not include the Village of Wrightstown; Ⓟ 1,750; © 2,013

Wuertsburg; RMC Place; MARATHON; ▲ Johnson; ***252** H-8; elev. 1,442ft./440m.; mail Athens z 54411; rural

Wyalusing; RMC Place; GRANT; ▲ Wyalusing; **253** O-5; mail Bagley z 53801; ● 80

Wyalusing; MCD-Town; GRANT; ***253** O-5; mail Bagley z 53801; Ⓟ 364; © 370

Wyeville; Inc. Place; MONROE; **253** K-7; elev. 925ft./282m.; 🅿; z 54660; Ⓟ 154; © 146

Wyocena; Inc. Place; COLUMBIA; **253** M-10; elev. 826ft./252m.; 🅿; z 53969; Ⓟ 620; © 668

Wyocena; MCD-Town; COLUMBIA; ***253** M-10; 🅿; z 53969 & mail Rio z 53960; does not include the Village of Wyocena; Ⓟ 1,228; © 1,543

Wyoming; MCD-Town; IOWA; ***253** N-8; mail Spring Green z 53588; Ⓟ 338; © 364

Wyoming; MCD-Town; WAUPACA; ***252** I-10; mail Iola z 54945; Ⓟ 283; © 285

Y

Yahara Heights; RMC Place; DANE; ▲ Westport; ***253** N-9; elev. 900ft./274m.; ★ **MAD**; mail Waunakee z 53597; ● 250

Yarnell; RMC Place; SAWYER; ▲ Couderay; ***252** F-5; mail Birchwood z 54817; rural

Yellow Lake; RMC Place; BURNETT; ▲ Oakland; **252** E-2; 🅿; z 54830; summer pop. 300; ● 70

Yellowstone; RMC Place; LAFAYETTE; ▲ Fayette; ***253** O-8; mail Blanchardville z 53516; rural

York; MCD-Town; CLARK; ***252** I-7; mail Granton z 54436; Ⓟ 857; © 853

York; MCD-Town; DANE; ***253** N-10; mail Columbus z 53925; Ⓟ 649; © 703

York; MCD-Town; GREEN; ***253** O-9; mail Blanchardville z 53516; Ⓟ 509; © 605

York; RMC Place; JACKSON; ▲ Northfield; **252** J-5; mail Osseo z 54758; ● 40

York Center; RMC Place; DANE; ▲ York; ***253** N-10; mail Marshall z 53559; ● 25

Yorkville; RMC Place; RACINE; ▲ Yorkville; ***253** O-13; elev. 753ft./230m.; ★ **MILW**; mail Union Grove z 53182; ● 40

Yorkville; MCD-Town; RACINE; ***253** O-13; ★ **MILW**; mail Union Grove z 53182; Ⓟ 2,901; © 3,291

Young America; RMC Place; WASHINGTON; ▲ Barton; ***253** M-12; mail West Bend z 53090; ● 90

Yuba; Inc. Place; RICHLAND; **253** M-7; elev. 1,868ft./569m.; 🅿; z 54634 & mail La Farge z 54639; Ⓟ 77; © 92

Z

Zachow; RMC Place; SHAWANO; ▲ Angelica; **252** I-12; elev. 862ft./263m.; 🅿; z 54182; ● 150

Zander; RMC Place; MANITOWOC; ▲ Gibson; ***252** J-13; elev. 733ft./223m.; mail Denmark z 54208; ● 20

Zenda; RMC Place; WALWORTH; ▲ Linn; **253** P-12; elev. 979ft./298m.; 🅿; z 53195; ● 200

Zittau; RMC Place; WINNEBAGO; ▲ Wolf River; **253** K-11; elev. 774ft./236m.; mail Fremont z 54940; ● 60

Zoar; CDP; MENOMINEE; ***252** H-11; © 124

WYOMING

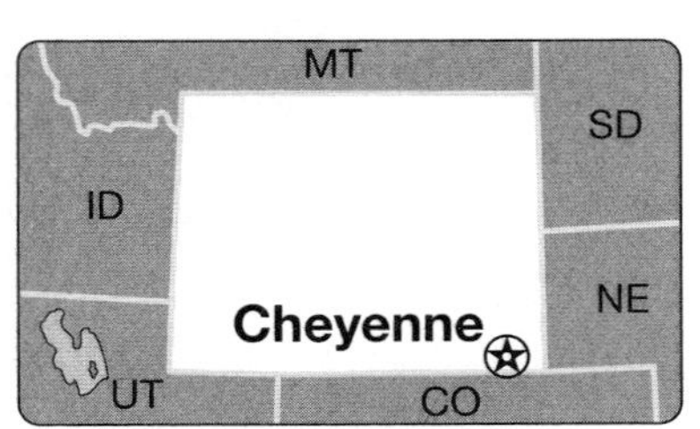

Statistics

Total area (2000) — 97,814 square miles
Land area (2000) — 97,100 square miles
Water area (2000) — 714 square miles
Capital — Cheyenne
Admitted as state — July, 1890

Maps

State maps can be found on pages 142-254 in Vol. 1

Ranally Metro Areas (RMAs) and Abbreviations

Casper, WY — CASP
Cheyenne, WY — CHEY

Principal Places

Place Name	Place Type	County	Population
Cheyenne	Inc. Place	LARAMIE	◆ 55,204
Casper	Inc. Place	NATRONA	◆ 54,218
Laramie	Inc. Place	ALBANY	◆ 26,572
Gillette	Inc. Place	CAMPBELL	◆ 26,499
Rock Springs	Inc. Place	SWEETWATER	◆ 21,975
Sheridan	Inc. Place	SHERIDAN	◆ 17,541
Green River	Inc. Place	SWEETWATER	© 11,808
Evanston	Inc. Place	UINTA	© 11,507
Riverton	Inc. Place	FREMONT	◆ 10,382
Rawlins	Inc. Place	CARBON	Ⓡ 9,006
Cody	Inc. Place	PARK	© 8,835
Jackson	Inc. Place	TETON	© 8,647
Lander	Inc. Place	FREMONT	© 6,867
Torrington	Inc. Place	GOSHEN	© 5,776
Powell	Inc. Place	PARK	© 5,373
Douglas	Inc. Place	CONVERSE	© 5,288
Worland	Inc. Place	WASHAKIE	© 5,250

County Business Data

County	FIPS Code	County Seat	Land Area (Sq. Mi.)	Census Population			Wholesale Trade		Manufacturing, 2002			
				4/1/2000	4/1/1990	% Change 1990-2000	Sales, 2002 ($1,000)	% Change 1997-2002	Establish-ments	Total Employees	Value Added ($1,000)	Ranally Mfg. Units
Albany	001	Laramie	4,273	32,014	30,797	4.0	51,054	-39.9	28	559	58,551	31
Big Horn	003	Basin	3,137	11,461	10,525	8.9	12,673	-14.9	...	(d)	(d)	...
Campbell	005	Gillette	4,797	33,698	29,370	14.7	394,934	67.8	33	578	50,445	27
Carbon	007	Rawlins	7,896	15,639	16,659	-6.1	20,171	-20.9	...	(d)	(d)	...
Converse	009	Douglas	4,255	12,052	11,128	8.3	22,381	-46.7	...	(d)	(d)	...
Crook	011	Sundance	2,859	5,887	5,294	11.2	(d)	(d)	...	(d)	(d)	...
Fremont	013	Lander	9,182	35,804	33,662	6.4	114,181	34.0	...	(d)	(d)	...
Goshen	015	Torrington	2,225	12,538	12,373	1.3	210,954	0.0	...	(d)	(d)	...
Hot Springs	017	Thermopolis	2,004	4,882	4,809	1.5	(d)	(d)	...	(d)	(d)	...
Johnson	019	Buffalo	4,166	7,075	6,145	15.1	8,526	23.3	...	(d)	(d)	...
Laramie	021	Cheyenne	2,686	81,607	73,142	11.6	537,339	100.9	53	1,660	189,548	100
Lincoln	023	Kemmerer	4,069	14,573	12,625	15.4	17,727	80.0	...	(d)	(d)	...
Natrona	025	Casper	5,340	66,533	61,226	8.7	1,102,365	12.0	95	1,767	149,240	79
Niobrara	027	Lusk	2,626	2,407	2,499	-3.7	(d)	(d)	...	(d)	(d)	...
Park	029	Cody	6,942	25,786	23,178	11.3	196,167	279.0	...	(d)	(d)	...
Platte	031	Wheatland	2,085	8,807	8,145	8.1	20,258	(d)	...	(d)	(d)	...
Sheridan	033	Sheridan	2,523	26,560	23,562	12.7	125,361	-14.2	...	(d)	(d)	...
Sublette	035	Pinedale	4,883	5,920	4,843	22.2	15,966	47.6	...	(d)	(d)	...
Sweetwater	037	Green River	10,425	37,613	38,823	-3.1	217,686	15.5	31	1,394	535,642	283
Teton	039	Jackson	4,008	18,251	11,172	63.4	57,165	16.1	...	(d)	(d)	...
Uinta	041	Evanston	2,082	19,742	18,705	5.5	86,835	18.7	...	(d)	(d)	...
Washakie	043	Worland	2,240	8,289	8,388	-1.2	101,767	219.8	...	(d)	(d)	...
Weston	045	Newcastle	2,398	6,644	6,518	1.9	3,880	-7.1	...	(d)	(d)	...
The State			**97,100**	**493,782**	**453,588**	**8.9**	**3,331,043**	**30.8**	**560**	**9,608**	**1,430,036**	**757**

(d) Data not available. Corresponding percentages or Ranally Manufacturing Units are estimates.
... Represents 0 or amount too minimal to be reported.

Index of Places and Counties

Entries in **UPPERCASE** are counties.
Entries in **bold** have populations of 2,500 or more.
Names in parentheses are alternate names.

Inc. Place	Incorporated Place
RMC Place	Rand McNally Designated Place
CDP	Census Designated Place
MCD	Minor Civil Division
⊡	County Seat
▲	Minor Civil Division
elev.	Elevation
[P]	Post Office
[H]	Hospital
[C]	College
■	Principal Business Center
★	Ranally Metro Area (RMA) Abbreviation
z	Zip Code(s)
Ⓟ	Previous Census Population
Ⓡ	Revised Census Population
Ⓐ	Annexation Population
●	Rand McNally Population Estimate
©	Final Census Population
Ⓢ	Special Census Population
◆	Estimated Population

For additional definitions see Glossary, Volume 1, and Introduction, Volume 2.

Mountain Home; RMC Place; ALBANY; **254** H-11; 🅿; **z** 82072 & mail Laramie **z** 82070; ● 40
Mountain View; CDP; NATRONA; **254** G-1; ★ **CASP**; mail Casper **z** 82604; Ⓟ 1,345; Ⓒ 103
Mountain View; Inc. Place; UINTA; **254** H-5; elev. 6,800ft./2,073m.; 🅿; **z** 82939 & mail Lonetree **z** 82936; Ⓟ 1,189; Ⓒ 1,153
Muddy Gap; RMC Place; CARBON; **254** F-9; 🅿; **z** 82301; ● 20
Mule Creek Junction; RMC Place; NIOBRARA; ***254** D-13; mail Lusk **z** 82225; rural
Museum; RMC Place; LARAMIE; ★ **CHEY**; mail Cheyenne **z** 82001; pop. incl. with Cheyenne (Inc. Place)

N

Natrona; RMC Place; NATRONA; **254** E-10; elev. 5,600ft./1,707m.; 🅿; **z** 82646; ● 10
NATRONA; **254** E-9; Ⓟ 61,226; Ⓒ 66,533; ◆ 73,475
Newcastle; Inc. Place; ⊡ WESTON; **254** C-13; elev. 4,317ft./1,316m.; 🅿 🅷; **z** 82701, **z** 82715; Ⓟ 3,028; Ⓒ 3,065; Ⓡ 3,249
New Fork; RMC Place; SUBLETTE; ***254** E-6; mail Boulder **z** 82923; rural
New Haven; RMC Place; CROOK; ***254** B-12; 🅿; **z** 82720; ● 30
New Jelm; RMC Place; ALBANY; ***254** H-11; mail Jelm **z** 82063; ● 30
NIOBRARA; **254** E-13; Ⓟ 2,499; Ⓒ 2,407; ◆ 2,544
Node; RMC Place; NIOBRARA; **254** E-13; elev. 4,937ft./1,505m.; 🅿; **z** 82225; ● 20
North Rock Springs; CDP-Census Area Only; SWEETWATER; ***254** G-7; mail Rock Springs **z** 82901; Ⓟ 2,471; Ⓒ 1,974
Number One; RMC Place; LARAMIE; ★ **CHEY**; mail Cheyenne **z** 82001; pop. incl. with Cheyenne (Inc. Place)

O

Oakley; CDP-Census Area Only; LINCOLN; ***254** G-5; Ⓒ 18
O'Donnell; RMC Place; PARK; ***254** B-7; elev. 4,480ft./1,366m.; mail Powell **z** 82435; rural
Old Faithful; RMC Place; TETON; ***254** B-5; mail Yellowstone National Park **z** 82190
Opal; Inc. Place; LINCOLN; **254** G-5; elev. 6,666ft./2,032m.; 🅿; **z** 83124; Ⓟ 95; Ⓒ 102
Orchard Valley; RMC Place; LARAMIE; **254** H-13; ★ **CHEY**; mail Cheyenne **z** 82007; ● 1,800
Orin; RMC Place; CONVERSE; ***254** E-12; elev. 4,697ft./1,432m.; 🅿; **z** 82633; ● 30
Orpha; RMC Place; CONVERSE; ***254** E-12; mail Douglas **z** 82633
Osage; CDP; WESTON; **254** C-13; elev. 4,311ft./1,314m.; 🅿; **z** 82723; Ⓒ 215
Oshoto; RMC Place; CROOK; **254** B-12; elev. 4,109ft./1,252m.; 🅿; **z** 82721; ● 30
Osmond; RMC Place; LINCOLN; ***254** E-4; elev. 6,329ft./1,929m.; mail Afton **z** 83110; ● 100
Otto; RMC Place; BIG HORN; **254** B-8; elev. 4,160ft./1,268m.; 🅿; **z** 82434; ● 50
Owl Creek; CDP-Census Area Only; HOT SPRINGS; **254** C-8; Ⓒ 11

P

Pahaska; RMC Place; PARK; **254** B-6; elev. 6,674ft./2,034m.; mail Cody **z** 82414; summer pop. 80
Paradise Valley; RMC Place; NATRONA; ***254** E-10; ★ **CASP**; mail Casper **z** 82601; pop. incl. with Casper (Inc. Place)
PARK; **254** C-7; Ⓟ 23,178; Ⓒ 25,786; ◆ 27,668
Parkerton; RMC Place; CONVERSE; 🅿; **z** 82637; rural
Parkman; CDP; SHERIDAN; **254** A-9; elev. 4,301ft./1,311m.; 🅿; **z** 82838; Ⓒ 137
Pavillion; Inc. Place; FREMONT; **254** D-7; elev. 5,460ft./1,664m.; 🅿; **z** 82523; Ⓟ 126; Ⓒ 165
Piedmont; RMC Place; UINTA; ***254** H-5; elev. 7,059ft./2,152m.; 🅿; **z** 82933; rural
Pine Bluffs; Inc. Place; LARAMIE; **254** H-14; elev. 5,040ft./1,536m.; 🅿; **z** 82082; Ⓟ 1,054; Ⓒ 1,153
Pinedale; Inc. Place; ⊡ SUBLETTE; **254** E-6; elev. 7,175ft./2,187m.; 🅿; **z** 82941; Ⓟ 1,181; Ⓒ 1,412
Pine Haven; Inc. Place; CROOK; **254** B-12; 🅿; **z** 82721; Ⓟ 141; Ⓒ 222
Pitchfork Ranch; RMC Place; PARK; ***254** C-7; mail Meeteetse **z** 82433; summer pop. 400; ● 20
PLATTE; **254** G-12; Ⓟ 8,145; Ⓒ 8,807; ◆ 8,208
Point of Rocks; CDP; SWEETWATER; **254** G-7; elev. 6,520ft./1,987m.; 🅿; **z** 82942; Ⓒ 3
Pole Creek Addition; RMC Place; SUBLETTE; ***254** E-6; mail Pinedale **z** 82941; ● 80
Powder River; CDP; NATRONA; **254** E-10; elev. 5,710ft./1,740m.; 🅿; **z** 82648; Ⓒ 51
Powell; Inc. Place; PARK; **254** B-7; elev. 4,391ft./1,338m.; 🅿 🅷; **z** 82435; Ⓟ 5,292; Ⓒ 5,373

Prospector Village; RMC Place; CAMPBELL; ***254** B-12; mail Gillette **z** 82717; ● 200
Purple Sage; CDP-Census Area Only; SWEETWATER; ***254** H-6; Ⓒ 413

Q

Quealy; RMC Place; SWEETWATER; ***254** H-7; 🅿; **z** 82901; rural

R

Rafter J Ranch; CDP-Census Area Only; TETON; ***254** D-5; mail Jackson **z** 83001; Ⓟ 1,092; Ⓒ 1,138
Ralston; CDP; PARK; **254** B-7; elev. 4,558ft./1,389m.; 🅿; **z** 82440; Ⓒ 233
Ranchester; Inc. Place; SHERIDAN; **254** A-9; elev. 3,760ft./1,146m.; 🅿; **z** 82839, **z** 82844; Ⓟ 676; Ⓒ 701
Ranchettes; CDP-Census Area Only; LARAMIE; ***254** H-13; mail Cheyenne **z** 82009; Ⓟ 4,038; Ⓒ 4,869
Rawhide Village; RMC Place; CAMPBELL; ***254** B-12; mail Gillette **z** 82717; pop. incl. with Gillette (Inc. Place)
Rawlins; Inc. Place; ⊡ CARBON; **254** G-9; elev. 6,769ft./2,063m.; 🅿 🅷; **z** 82301, **z** 82310; Ⓟ 9,380; Ⓒ 8,538; Ⓡ 9,006
Recluse; RMC Place; CAMPBELL; **254** B-11; elev. 4,100ft./1,250m.; 🅿; **z** 82725; ● 30
Redbird; RMC Place; NIOBRARA; **254** D-13; rural
Red Butte; CDP-Census Area Only; NATRONA; ***254** E-10; ★ **CASP**; Ⓒ 439
Red Buttes Village; RMC Place; NATRONA; ***254** E-10; ★ **CASP**; mail Casper **z** 82604; ● 150
Red Desert; RMC Place; SWEETWATER; ***254** G-8; 🅿; **z** 82336; ● 30
Red Lane; RMC Place; HOT SPRINGS; ***254** D-8; mail Thermopolis **z** 82443; rural
Reliance; CDP; SWEETWATER; **254** G-7; elev. 6,540ft./1,993m.; 🅿; **z** 82943; Ⓒ 665
Reno; RMC Place; CAMPBELL; ***254** D-12; mail Wright **z** 82732
Reno Junction; RMC Place; CAMPBELL; ***254** D-12; mail Wright **z** 82732
Riovista; RMC Place; SWEETWATER; ***254** H-6; elev. 6,160ft./1,878m.; mail Green River **z** 82935
Riverside; Inc. Place; CARBON; **254** H-10; elev. 7,136ft./2,175m.; 🅿; **z** 82325; Ⓟ 85; Ⓒ 59
Riverton; Inc. Place; FREMONT; **254** E-8; elev. 4,964ft./1,513m.; 🅿 🅷 ■; **z** 82501; Ⓟ 9,202; Ⓒ 9,310; ◆ 10,382
Riverview; RMC Place; NIOBRARA; ***254** D-13; mail Edgemont **z** 57735; rural
Robertson; CDP; UINTA; **254** H-5; elev. 7,288ft./2,221m.; 🅿; **z** 82944; Ⓒ 59
Rockeagle; RMC Place; GOSHEN; ***254** G-13; 🅿; **z** 82223; rural
Rock River; Inc. Place; ALBANY; **254** G-11; elev. 6,891ft./2,100m.; 🅿; **z** 82058, **z** 82083; Ⓟ 190; Ⓒ 235
Rock Springs; Inc. Place; SWEETWATER; **254** G-7; elev. 6,271ft./1,911m.; 🅿 🅷 ■; **z** 82901-02, **z** 82942; Ⓟ 19,050; Ⓒ 18,708; ◆ 21,975
Rockypoint; RMC Place; CAMPBELL; ***254** A-12; elev. 3,923ft./1,196m.; mail Moorcroft **z** 82721; rural
Rolling Hills; Inc. Place; CONVERSE; **254** E-11; 🅿; **z** 82637; Ⓟ 330; Ⓒ 449
Rozet; RMC Place; CAMPBELL; **254** B-12; elev. 4,290ft./1,308m.; 🅿; **z** 82727; ● 40
Ryan Park; RMC Place; CARBON; **254** H-10; 🅿; **z** 82331; ● 30

S

Saddlestring; RMC Place; JOHNSON; **254** B-10; elev. 5,520ft./1,682m.; 🅿; **z** 82840; ● 10
Sage; RMC Place; LINCOLN; **254** G-4; mail Cokeville **z** 83114; rural
Sand Draw; RMC Place; FREMONT; **254** E-8; 🅿; **z** 82501
Saratoga; Inc. Place; CARBON; **254** H-10; elev. 6,788ft./2,069m.; 🅿; **z** 82331; Ⓟ 1,969; Ⓒ 1,726
Savery; RMC Place; CARBON; **254** H-9; elev. 6,463ft./1,970m.; 🅿; **z** 82332; ● 50
Seminoe Dam; RMC Place; CARBON; **254** F-10; mail Sinclair **z** 82334; ● 40
Shawnee; RMC Place; CONVERSE; **254** E-12; elev. 5,059ft./1,542m.; 🅿; **z** 82229; ● 30
Shell; RMC Place; BIG HORN; **254** B-9; elev. 4,226ft./1,288m.; 🅿; **z** 82441; ● 70
Sheridan; Inc. Place; ⊡ SHERIDAN; **254** B-10; elev. 3,745ft./1,141m.; 🅿 🅷 ■; **z** 82801; Ⓟ 13,900; Ⓒ 15,804; ◆ 17,541
SHERIDAN; **254** A-10; Ⓟ 23,562; Ⓒ 26,560; ◆ 28,826
Sheridan Gardens; RMC Place; SHERIDAN; ***254** B-10; elev. 3,760ft./1,146m.; mail Sheridan **z** 82801; ● 100
Shirley Basin; RMC Place; CARBON; ***254** F-11; elev. 7,050ft./2,149m.; 🅿; **z** 82615; ● 100

Shoshoni; Inc. Place; FREMONT; **254** D-8; elev. 4,840ft./1,475m.; 🅿; **z** 82649; Ⓟ 497; Ⓒ 635
Sinclair; Inc. Place; CARBON; **254** G-10; elev. 6,593ft./2,010m.; 🅿; **z** 82334; Ⓟ 500; Ⓒ 423
Skull Creek; RMC Place; WESTON; ***254** C-13; mail Osage **z** 82723; ● 30
Slater; CDP; PLATTE; ***254** G-13; 🅿; **z** 82201; Ⓒ 82
Sleepy Hollow; CDP-Census Area Only; CAMPBELL; ***254** C-12; mail Gillette **z** 82718; Ⓟ 1,194; Ⓒ 1,177
Smoot; CDP; LINCOLN; **254** F-4; 🅿; **z** 83126; Ⓒ 182
South Flat; CDP-Census Area Only; WASHAKIE; ***254** C-8; Ⓒ 374
South Greeley; CDP-Census Area Only; LARAMIE; ***254** H-13; ★ **CHEY**; mail Cheyenne **z** 82007; Ⓟ 3,723; Ⓒ 4,201
South Jackson; RMC Place; TETON; ***254** D-5; elev. 6,035ft./1,839m.; mail Jackson **z** 83001; ● 30
South Laramie; RMC Place; ALBANY; ***254** H-12; mail Laramie **z** 82070; ● 1,560
South Park; CDP-Census Area Only; TETON; ***254** D-5; Ⓒ 864
South Pass City; RMC Place; FREMONT; **254** F-7; elev. 7,805ft./2,379m.; 🅿; **z** 82520; ● 30
South Torrington; RMC Place; GOSHEN; **254** G-13; mail Torrington **z** 82240; ● 380
Spotted Horse; RMC Place; CAMPBELL; ***254** B-11; mail Arvada **z** 82831; rural
Star Valley Ranch; Inc. Place; LINCOLN; ***254** E-4; ● 1,500
Star Valley Ranch; CDP-Census Area Only; LINCOLN; ***254** E-4; 🅿; **z** 83127; Ⓒ 776
Story; CDP; SHERIDAN; **254** B-10; elev. 5,080ft./1,548m.; 🅿; **z** 82832, **z** 82842; summer pop. 1,500; Ⓒ 887
SUBLETTE; **254** F-6; Ⓟ 4,843; Ⓒ 5,920; ◆ 9,281
Sundance; Inc. Place; ⊡ CROOK; **254** B-13; elev. 4,765ft./1,452m.; 🅿 🅷; **z** 82729; Ⓟ 1,139; Ⓒ 1,161
Sunrise; RMC Place; NATRONA; ★ **CASP**; mail Casper **z** 82604; pop. incl. with Casper (Inc. Place)
Sunrise; RMC Place; PLATTE; **254** F-13; 🅿; **z** 82215; ● 30
Sunshine; RMC Place; PARK; ***254** C-7; elev. 6,496ft./1,980m.; mail Meeteetse **z** 82433; rural
Superior; Inc. Place; SWEETWATER; **254** G-7; elev. 6,900ft./2,103m.; 🅿; **z** 82945; Ⓟ 273; Ⓒ 244
Sussex; RMC Place; JOHNSON; ***254** D-11; 🅿; **z** 82639; rural
Sweeney Ranch; CDP-Census Area Only; SWEETWATER; ***254** H-7; Ⓒ 17
SWEETWATER; **254** H-8; Ⓟ 38,823; Ⓒ 37,613; ◆ 41,698
Sweetwater Station; RMC Place; FREMONT; ***254** F-8; 🅿; **z** 82520; ● 30

T

Table Rock; CDP; SWEETWATER; ***254** G-8; Ⓒ 82
Taylor; RMC Place; CAMPBELL; ***254** D-11; elev. 5,000ft./1,524m.; mail Midwest **z** 82643; rural
Taylor; CDP-Census Area Only; LINCOLN; ***254** F-4; Ⓒ 90
Ten Sleep; Inc. Place; WASHAKIE; **254** C-9; elev. 4,436ft./1,352m.; 🅿; **z** 82442; Ⓟ 311; Ⓒ 304
TETON; **254** C-5; Ⓟ 11,172; Ⓒ 18,251; ◆ 20,508
Teton Village; CDP; TETON; **254** D-5; elev. 6,320ft./1,926m.; 🅿; **z** 83025; Ⓒ 175
Thayne; Inc. Place; LINCOLN; **254** E-4; 🅿; **z** 83127; Ⓟ 267; Ⓒ 341
The Buttes; CDP-Census Area Only; ALBANY; ***254** H-12; Ⓒ 31
Thermopolis; Inc. Place; ⊡ HOT SPRINGS; **254** D-8; elev. 4,326ft./1,319m.; 🅿 🅷; **z** 82443; Ⓟ 3,247; Ⓒ 3,172
Three Forks; RMC Place; CARBON; ***254** F-9; elev. 6,269ft./1,911m.; mail Rawlins **z** 82301; rural
Thunder Basin; RMC Place; LARAMIE; ***254** H-13; mail Burns **z** 82053; ● 100
Tie Siding (Hermosa); RMC Place; ALBANY; **254** H-12; elev. 7,830ft./2,387m.; 🅿; **z** 82084; ● 30
Torrington; Inc. Place; ⊡ GOSHEN; **254** F-13; elev. 4,106ft./1,252m.; 🅿 🅷; **z** 82240; Ⓟ 5,651; Ⓒ 5,776
Tower Junction; RMC Place; PARK; ***254** A-5; mail Yellowstone National Park **z** 82190
Turnerville; CDP-Census Area Only; LINCOLN; ***254** E-4; 🅿; **z** 83110 & mail Bedford **z** 83112; Ⓒ 155

U

Ucross; RMC Place; SHERIDAN; ***254** B-10; mail Clearmont **z** 82835; rural
UINTA; **254** H-4; Ⓟ 18,705; Ⓒ 19,742; ◆ 20,874
Ulm; RMC Place; SHERIDAN; ***254** B-10; elev. 4,449ft./1,356m.; mail Clearmont **z** 82835; rural

Upton; Inc. Place; WESTON; **254** C-13; elev. 4,235ft./1,291m.; 🅿; **z** 82730; Ⓟ 980; Ⓒ 872
Urie; RMC Place; UINTA; **254** H-5; 🅿; **z** 82937; ● 250
Uva; RMC Place; PLATTE; ***254** F-12; elev. 4,464ft./1,361m.; 🅿; **z** 82201; rural

V

Valley; RMC Place; PARK; ***254** C-6; mail Cody **z** 82414
Valley View; RMC Place; LARAMIE; mail Laramie **z** 82070; ● 300
Van Tassell; Inc. Place; NIOBRARA; **254** E-13; 🅿; **z** 82242; Ⓟ 8; Ⓒ 18
Veteran; CDP; GOSHEN; **254** G-13; elev. 4,220ft./1,286m.; 🅿; **z** 82243; Ⓒ 28
Vista West; RMC Place; CROOK; ***254** B-13; mail Sundance **z** 82729; ● 50
Vista West; CDP-Census Area Only; NATRONA; ***254** E-10; Ⓒ 1,008

W

Walcott; RMC Place; CARBON; **254** G-10; elev. 6,620ft./2,018m.; 🅿; **z** 82335; ● 30
Waltman; RMC Place; NATRONA; **254** E-9; rural
Wamsutter; Inc. Place; SWEETWATER; **254** G-8; elev. 6,740ft./2,054m.; 🅿; **z** 82336; Ⓟ 240; Ⓒ 261
Wapiti; RMC Place; PARK; **254** B-6; elev. 5,600ft./1,707m.; 🅿; **z** 82450; ● 60
Wapiti Valley; RMC Place; PARK; ***254** B-6; elev. 5,961ft./1,817m.; mail Wapiti **z** 82450; ● 60
Warren AFB; CDP-Census Area Only; LARAMIE; ***254** H-13; ★ **CHEY**; mail Cheyenne **z** 82001, Ft Warren AFB **z** 82005; Ⓟ 3,832; Ⓒ 4,440
WASHAKIE; **254** C-8; Ⓟ 8,388; Ⓒ 8,289; ◆ 8,008
Washakie Ten; CDP-Census Area Only; WASHAKIE; ***254** C-8; Ⓒ 604
Washam; CDP-Census Area Only; SWEETWATER; ***254** H-6; Ⓒ 43
Western Hills; RMC Place; LARAMIE; ★ **CHEY**; mail Cheyenne **z** 82001; pop. incl. with Cheyenne (Inc. Place)
West Lance Creek; RMC Place; NIOBRARA; ***254** E-13; elev. 4,410ft./1,344m.; mail Lance Creek **z** 82222; ● 10
West Laramie; RMC Place; ALBANY; ***254** H-12; mail Laramie **z** 82070; pop. incl. with Laramie (Inc. Place)
Weston; RMC Place; CAMPBELL; **254** B-12; elev. 3,800ft./1,158m.; 🅿; **z** 82716, **z** 82731; ● 20
WESTON; **254** C-13; Ⓟ 6,518; Ⓒ 6,644; ◆ 7,404
West River; CDP-Census Area Only; WASHAKIE; ***254** C-8; Ⓒ 321
West Thumb; RMC Place; TETON; ***254** B-5; mail Yellowstone National Park **z** 82190; rural
Westview Circle; CDP-Census Area Only; PLATTE; ***254** G-12; Ⓒ 67
Wheatland; Inc. Place; ⊡ PLATTE; **254** G-12; elev. 4,748ft./1,447m.; 🅿 🅷; **z** 82201; Ⓟ 3,271; Ⓒ 3,548
Willwood; RMC Place; PARK; **254** B-7; elev. 4,335ft./1,321m.; 🅿; **z** 82435; ● 30
Wilson; CDP; TETON; **254** D-5; elev. 6,150ft./1,875m.; 🅿; **z** 83014; Ⓒ 1,294
Winchester (Chatham); CDP; WASHAKIE; ***254** C-8; mail Worland **z** 82401; Ⓒ 60
Wind River Reservation; Indian Reservation; FREMONT, HOT SPRINGS; mail Fort Washakie **z** 82514; also location of Indian Agency; Ⓟ 23,157; Ⓒ 23,245
Wolf; RMC Place; SHERIDAN; ***254** B-9; elev. 4,600ft./1,402m.; 🅿; **z** 82844; ● 5
Wolf's Addition; RMC Place; ALBANY; ***254** H-11; mail Laramie **z** 82072; ● 30
Woods Landing; RMC Place; ALBANY; ***254** H-11; mail Jelm **z** 82063; summer pop. 100; ● 20
Woods Landing-Jelm; CDP-Census Area Only; ALBANY; ***254** H-11; Ⓒ 100
Worland; Inc. Place; ⊡ WASHAKIE; **254** C-8; elev. 4,061ft./1,238m.; 🅿 🅷; **z** 82401, **z** 82430; Ⓟ 5,742; Ⓒ 5,250
Wright; Inc. Place; CAMPBELL; **254** C-12; 🅿; **z** 82732; Ⓟ 1,236; Ⓒ 1,347
Wyarno; RMC Place; SHERIDAN; **254** B-10; elev. 3,780ft./1,152m.; 🅿; **z** 82845; ● 40
Wyodak; RMC Place; CAMPBELL; **254** B-12; mail Gillette **z** 82718; ● 80

Y

Yoder; Inc. Place; GOSHEN; **254** G-13; elev. 4,250ft./1,295m.; 🅿; **z** 82244; Ⓟ 136; Ⓒ 169
Y-O Ranch; CDP-Census Area Only; PLATTE; ***254** G-12; Ⓒ 242